Hoover's Handbook of

American Business 2016

Austin, Texas

Hoover's Handbook of American Business 2016 is intended to provide readers with accurate and authoritative information about the enterprises covered in it. Hoover's researched all companies and organizations profiled, and in many cases contacted them directly so that companies represented could provide information. The information contained herein is as accurate as we could reasonably make it. In many cases we have relied on third-party material that we believe to be trustworthy, but were unable to independently verify. We do not warrant that the book is absolutely accurate or without error. Readers should not rely on any information contained herein in instances where such reliance might cause financial loss. The publisher, the editors, and their data suppliers specifically disclaim all warranties, including the implied warranties of merchantability and fitness for a specific purpose. This book is sold with the understanding that neither the publisher, the editors, nor any content contributors are engaged in providing investment, financial, accounting, legal, or other professional advice.

The financial data (Historical Financials sections) in this book are from a variety of sources. Mergent Inc., provided selected data for the Historical Financials sections of publicly traded companies. For private companies and for historical information on public companies prior to their becoming public, we obtained information directly from the companies or from trade sources deemed to be reliable. Hoover's, Inc., is solely responsible for the presentation of all data.

Many of the names of products and services mentioned in this book are the trademarks or service marks of the companies manufacturing or selling them and are subject to protection under US law. Space has not permitted us to indicate which names are subject to such protection, and readers are advised to consult with the owners of such marks regarding their use. Hoover's is a trademark of Hoover's, Inc.

HOOVERS™
A D&B COMPANY

10 9 8 7 6 5 4 3 2 1

Publishers Cataloging-in-Publication Data

Hoover's Handbook of American Business 2016

   Includes indexes.

   ISBN: 978-1-63053-822-4

   ISSN 1055-7202

   1. Business enterprises — Directories. 2. Corporations — Directories.

HF3010 338.7

U.S. AND WORLD BOOK SALES

Mergent Inc.

580 Kingsley Park Drive
Fort Mill, SC
29715
Phone: 800-342-5647
e-mail: orders@mergent.com
Web: www.mergentbusinesspress.com

Mergent Inc.

CEO: Jonathan Worrall

Executive Managing Director: John Pedernales

Executive Vice President of Sales: Fred Jenkins

Managing Director of Relationship Management: Chris Henry

Managing Director of Print Products: Thomas Wecera

Director of Print Products: Charlot Volny

Director of Data: Mohamed Hanif

Quality Assurance Editor: Wayne Arnold

Production Research Assistant: Wayne Arnold

MERGENT CUSTOMER SERVICE
Support and Fulfillment Manager: Melanie Horvat

ABOUT MERGENT INC.

Mergent, Inc. is a leading provider of business and financial data on global publicly listed companies. Based in the U.S, the company maintains a strong global presence, with offices in New York, Charlotte, San Diego, London, Tokyo and Melbourne.

Founded in 1900, Mergent operates one of the longest continuously collected databases of: descriptive and fundamental information on domestic and international companies; pricing and terms and conditions data on fixed income and equity securities; and corporate action data.

In addition, Mergent's Indxis subsidiary develops and licenses equity and fixed income investment products based on its proprietary investment methodologies. Our licensed products have over $9 billion in assets under management and are offered by major investment management firms. The Indxis calculation platform is the chosen technology for some of the world's largest index companies. Its index calculation and pricing distribution protocols are used to administer index rules and distribute real-time pricing data.

Abbreviations

AFL-CIO – American Federation of Labor and Congress of Industrial Organizations

AMA – American Medical Association

AMEX – American Stock Exchange

ARM – adjustable-rate mortgage

ASP – application services provider

ATM – asynchronous transfer mode

ATM – automated teller machine

CAD/CAM – computer-aided design/computer-aided manufacturing

CD-ROM – compact disc – read-only memory

CD-R – CD-recordable

CEO – chief executive officer

CFO – chief financial officer

CMOS – complementary metal oxide silicon

COO – chief operating officer

DAT – digital audiotape

DOD – Department of Defense

DOE – Department of Energy

DOS – disk operating system

DOT – Department of Transportation

DRAM – dynamic random-access memory

DSL – digital subscriber line

DVD – digital versatile disc/digital video disc

DVD-R – DVD-recordable

EPA – Environmental Protection Agency

EPROM – erasable programmable read-only memory

EPS – earnings per share

ESOP – employee stock ownership plan

EU – European Union

EVP – executive vice president

FCC – Federal Communications Commission

FDA – Food and Drug Administration

FDIC – Federal Deposit Insurance Corporation

FTC – Federal Trade Commission

FTP – file transfer protocol

GATT – General Agreement on Tariffs and Trade

GDP – gross domestic product

HMO – health maintenance organization

HR – human resources

HTML – hypertext markup language

ICC – Interstate Commerce Commission

IPO – initial public offering

IRS – Internal Revenue Service

ISP – Internet service provider

kWh – kilowatt-hour

LAN – local-area network

LBO – leveraged buyout

LCD – liquid crystal display

LNG – liquefied natural gas

LP – limited partnership

Ltd. – limited

mips – millions of instructions per second

MW – megawatt

NAFTA – North American Free Trade Agreement

NASA – National Aeronautics and Space Administration

NASDAQ – National Association of Securities Dealers Automated Quotations

NATO – North Atlantic Treaty Organization

NYSE – New York Stock Exchange

OCR – optical character recognition

OECD – Organization for Economic Cooperation and Development

OEM – original equipment manufacturer

OPEC – Organization of Petroleum Exporting Countries

OS – operating system

OSHA – Occupational Safety and Health Administration

OTC – over-the-counter

PBX – private branch exchange

PCMCIA – Personal Computer Memory Card International Association

P/E – price to earnings ratio

RAID – redundant array of independent disks

RAM – random-access memory

R&D – research and development

RBOC – regional Bell operating company

RISC – reduced instruction set computer

REIT – real estate investment trust

ROA – return on assets

ROE – return on equity

ROI – return on investment

ROM – read-only memory

S&L – savings and loan

SCSI – Small Computer System Interface

SEC – Securities and Exchange Commission

SEVP – senior executive vice president

SIC – Standard Industrial Classification

SOC – system on a chip

SVP – senior vice president

USB – universal serial bus

VAR – value-added reseller

VAT – value-added tax

VC – venture capitalist

VoIP – Voice over Internet Protocol

VP – vice president

WAN – wide-area network

WWW – World Wide Web

Contents

List of Lists

Companies Profiled

Companies Profiled (continued)

Companies Profiled (continued)

Companies Profiled (continued)

About Hoover's Handbook of American Business 2016

In these tough economic times, it pays to have all the facts, whether you're making business, financial, or employment decisions. When you need information about companies, *Hoover's Handbook of American Business* is the place to turn for answers. Throughout its history, it has stood as one of America's respected sources of business information, packed with the information you need.

We at Hoover's Business Press pledge we will continue our work to add more value to this already valuable resource. So search away for the business information you need to make the important decisions facing you. Leave the fact-finding and digging and the sorting and sifting to the editors at Hoover's.

Hoover's Handbook of American Business is the first of our four-title series of handbooks that covers, literally, the world of business. The series is available as an indexed set, and also includes *Hoover's Handbook of World Business, Hoover's Handbook of Private Companies,* and *Hoover's Handbook of Emerging Companies.* This series brings you information on the biggest, fastest-growing, and most influential enterprises in the world.

HOOVER'S ONLINE FOR BUSINESS NEEDS

In addition to the 2,550 companies featured in our handbooks, comprehensive coverage of more than 40,000 business enterprises is available in electronic format on our website, Hoover's Online (www.hoovers.com). Our goal is to provide one site that offers authoritative, updated intelligence on US and global companies, industries, and the people who shape them. Hoover's has partnered with other prestigious business information and service providers to bring you all the right business information, services, and links in one place.

We welcome the recognition we have received as a provider of high-quality company information — online, electronically, and in print — and continue to look for ways to make our products more available and more useful to you.

We believe that anyone who buys from, sells to, invests in, lends to, competes with, interviews with, or works for a company should know all there is to know about that enterprise. Taken together, this book and the other Hoover's products and resources represent the most complete source of basic corporate information readily available to the general public.

This latest version of *Hoover's Handbook of American Business* contains, as always, profiles of the largest and most influential companies in the United States. Each of the companies profiled here was chosen because of its important role in American business. For more details on how these companies were selected, see the section titled "Using Hoover's Handbooks."

HOW TO USE THIS BOOK

This book has four sections:

1. "Using Hoover's Handbooks" describes the contents of our profiles and explains the ways in which we gather and compile our data.

2. "A List-Lover's Compendium" contains lists of the largest, smallest, best, most, and other superlatives related to companies involved in American business.

3. The company profiles section makes up the largest and most important part of the book — 750 profiles of major US enterprises.

4. Three indexes complete the book. The first sorts companies by industry groups, the second by headquarters location. The third index is a list of all the executives found in the Executives section of each company profile.

Using Hoover's Handbooks

SELECTION OF THE COMPANIES PROFILED

The 750 enterprises profiled in this book include the largest and most influential companies in America. Among them are:

- more than 710 publicly held companies, from 3M to Zions Bancorporation
- more than 30 large private enterprises (such as Cargill and Mars)
- several mutual and cooperative organizations (such as State Farm and Ace Hardware)
- a selection of other enterprises (such as Kaiser Foundation Health Plan, the US Postal Service, and the Tennessee Valley Authority) that we believe are sufficiently large and influential enough to warrant inclusion.

In selecting these companies, our foremost question was "What companies will our readers be most interested in?" Our goal was to answer as many questions as we could in one book — in effect, trying to anticipate your curiosity. This approach resulted in four general selection criteria for including companies in the book:

1. Size. The 500 or so largest American companies, measured by sales and by number of employees, are included in the book. In general, these companies have sales in excess of $2 billion, and they are the ones you will have heard of and the ones you will want to know about. These are the companies at the top of the *FORTUNE*, *Forbes*, and *Business Week* lists. We have made sure to include the top private companies in this number.

2. Growth. We believe that relatively few readers will be going to work for, or investing in, the railroad industry. Therefore, only a few railroads are in the book. On the other hand, we have included a number of technology firms, as well as companies that provide medical products and services — pharmaceutical and biotech companies, health care insurers, and medical device makers.

3. Visibility. Most readers will have heard of the Hilton Worldwide and Harley-Davidson companies. Their service or consumer natures make them household names, even though they are not among the corporate giants in terms of sales and employment.

4. Breadth of coverage. To show the diversity of economic activity, we've included, among others, a professional sports team, one ranch, the Big Four accounting firms, and one of the largest law firms in the US. We feel that these businesses are important enough to enjoy at least "token" representation. While we might not emphasize certain industries, the industry leaders are present.

ORGANIZATION

The profiles are presented in alphabetical order. This alphabetization is generally word by word, which means that Legg Mason precedes Leggett & Platt. You will find the commonly used name of the enterprise at the beginning of the profile; the full, legal name is found in the Locations section. If a company name is also a person's name, like Walt Disney, it will be alphabetized under the first name; if the company name starts with initials, like J. C. Penney or H.J. Heinz, look for it under the combined initials (in the above examples, JC and HJ, respectively). Basic financial data is listed under the heading Historical Financials; also included is the exchange on which the company's stock is traded if it is public, the ticker symbol used by the stock exchange, and the company's fiscal year-end.

The annual financial information contained in the profiles is current through fiscal year-ends occurring as late as May 2014. We have included certain nonfinancial developments, such as officer changes, through September 2014.

OVERVIEW

In the first section of the profile, we have tried to give a thumbnail description of the company and what it does. The description will usually include information on the company's strategy, reputation, and ownership. We recommend that you read this section first.

HISTORY

This extended section, included for almost all companies in the book, reflects our belief that every enterprise is the sum of its history and that you have to know where you came from in order to know where you are going. While some companies have limited historical awareness, we think the vast majority of the enterprises in this book have colorful backgrounds. We have tried to focus on the people who made the enterprises what they are today. We have found these histories to be full of twists and ironies; they make fascinating reading.

EXECUTIVES

Here we list the names of the people who run the company, insofar as space allows. In the case of public companies, we have shown the ages and total compensation of key officers. In some cases the published data is for the previous year although the company has announced promotions or retirements since year-end. Total compensation is the sum of salary, bonus, and the value of any other benefits, such as stock options or deferred compensation.

Although companies are free to structure their management titles any way they please, most modern corporations follow standard practices. The ultimate power in any corporation lies with the shareholders, who elect a board of directors, usually including officers or "insiders" as well as individuals from outside the company. The chief officer, the person on whose desk the buck stops, is usually called the chief executive officer (CEO). Often, he or she is also the chairman of the board.

As corporate management has become more complex, it is common for the CEO to have a "right-hand person" who oversees the day-to-day operations of the company, allowing the CEO plenty of time to focus on strategy and long-term issues. This right-hand person is usually designated the chief operating officer (COO) and is often the president of the company. In other cases one person is both chairman and president.

A multitude of other titles exists, including chief financial officer (CFO), chief administrative officer, and vice chairman. We have always tried to include the CFO, the chief legal officer, and the chief human resources or personnel officer. Our best advice is that officers' pay levels are clear indicators of who the board of directors thinks are the most important members of the management team.

The people named in the Executives section are indexed at the back of the book.

The Executives section also includes the name of the company's auditing (accounting) firm, where available.

LOCATIONS

Here we include the company's full legal name and its headquarters, street address, telephone and fax numbers, and Web site, as available. The back of the book includes an index of companies by headquarters locations.

In some cases we have also included information on the geographic distribution of the company's business, including sales and profit data. Note that these profit numbers, like those in the Products/Operations section below, are usually operating or pretax profits rather than net profits. Operating profits are generally those before financing costs (interest income and payments) and before taxes, which are considered costs attributable to the whole company rather than to one division or part of the world. For this reason the net income figures (in the Historical Financials section) are usually much lower, since they are after interest and taxes. Pretax profits are after interest but before taxes.

Headquarters for companies that are incorporated in Bermuda, but whose operational headquarters are in the US, are listed under their US address.

PRODUCTS/OPERATIONS

This section lists as many of the company's products, services, brand names, divisions, subsidiaries, and joint ventures as we could fit. We have tried to include all its major lines and all familiar brand names. The nature of this section varies by company and the amount of information available. If the company publishes sales and profit information by type of business, we have included it.

COMPETITORS

In this section we have listed companies that compete with the profiled company. This feature is included as a quick way to locate similar companies and compare them. The universe of competitors includes all public companies and all private companies with sales in excess of $500 million. In a few instances we have identified smaller private companies as key competitors.

HISTORICAL FINANCIALS

Here we have tried to present as much data about each enterprise's financial performance as we could compile in the allocated space. The information varies somewhat from industry to industry and is less complete in the case of private companies that do not release data (although we have always tried to provide annual sales and employment). There are a few industries, venture capital and investment banking, for example, for which revenue numbers are unavailable as a rule.

The following information is generally present.

A 5-year table, with relevant annualized compound growth rates, covers:
- Sales — fiscal year sales (year-end assets for most financial companies)
- Net income — fiscal year net income (before accounting changes)
- Net profit margin — fiscal year net income as a percent of sales (as a percent of assets for most financial firms)
- Employees — fiscal year-end or average number of employees
- Stock price — the fiscal year close
- P/E — high and low price/earnings ratio
- Earnings per share — fiscal year earnings per share (EPS)
- Dividends per share — fiscal year dividends per share
- Book value per share — fiscal year-end book value (common shareholders' equity per share)

The information on the number of employees is intended to aid the reader interested in knowing whether a company has a long-term trend of increasing or decreasing employment. As far as we know, we are the only company that publishes this information in print format.

The numbers on the left in each row of the Historical Financials section give the month and the year in which the company's fiscal year actually ends. Thus, a company with a March 31, 2015, year-end is shown as 3/15.

In addition, we have provided in graph form a stock price history for most public companies. The graphs, covering up to five years, show the range of trading between the high and the low price, as well as the closing price for each fiscal year. Generally, for private companies, we have graphed net income, or, if that is unavailable, sales.

Key year-end statistics in this section generally show the financial strength of the enterprise, including:

- Debt ratio (long-term debt as a percent of shareholders' equity)
- Return on equity (net income divided by the average of beginning and ending common shareholders' equity)
- Cash and cash equivalents
- Current ratio (ratio of current assets to current liabilities)
- Total long-term debt (including capital lease obligations)

- Number of shares of common stock outstanding
- Dividend yield (fiscal year dividends per share divided by the fiscal year-end closing stock price)
- Dividend payout (fiscal year dividends divided by fiscal year EPS)
- Market value at fiscal year-end (fiscal year-end closing stock price multiplied by fiscal year-end number of shares outstanding)

Per share data has been adjusted for stock splits. The data for public companies has been provided to us by Mergent Inc. Other public company information was compiled by Hoover's, which takes full responsibility for the content of this section.

In the case of private companies that do not publicly disclose financial information, we usually did not have access to such standardized data. We have gathered estimates of sales and other statistics from numerous sources.

Hoover's Handbook of

American Business

A List-Lover's Compendium

The 300 Largest Companies by Sales in
Hoover's Handbook of American Business 2016

Rank	Company	Sales ($ bil.)	Rank	Company	Sales ($ bil.)	Rank	Company	Sales ($ bil.)
1	Wal-Mart Stores, Inc.	$485651	60	Cisco Systems, Inc.	$49161	119	AutoNation, Inc.	$20862
2	Exxon Mobil Corp.	$411939	61	Dow Chemical Co.	$48778	120	ManpowerGroup	$20763
3	Apple Inc	$233715	62	Sysco Corp.	$48681	121	Duke Energy Corp	$23925
4	Chevron Corporation	$211970	63	Humana, Inc.	$48500	122	Alcoa, Inc.	$23906
5	Berkshire Hathaway Inc.	$194673	64	Enterprise Products Partners	$47951	123	Capital One Financial Corp	$23869
6	McKesson Corp.	$179045	65	FedEx Corp	$47453	124	Time Warner Cable Inc	$23697
7	Phillips 66	$164093	66	Caterpillar Inc.	$47011	125	Halliburton Company	$23633
8	UnitedHealth Group Inc	$157107	67	Ingram Micro Inc.	$46487	126	International Paper Co	$23617
9	CVS Health Corp	$153290	68	Coca-Cola Co (The)	$45998	127	Northrop Grumman Corp	$23526
10	General Motors Co.	$152356	69	Lockheed Martin Corp.	$45600	128	Arrow Electronics, Inc.	$23282
11	Ford Motor Co. (DE)	$149558	70	Plains GP Holdings, L.P	$43464	129	Raytheon Co.	$23247
12	General Electric Co	$148589	71	Plains All American Pipeline	$43464	130	AFLAC Inc.	$22728
13	AmerisourceBergen Corp.	$135962	72	World Fuel Services Corp.	$43386	131	Burlington Northern & Santa F	$22714
14	AT&T Inc	$132447	73	American Airlines Group Inc	$42650	132	Staples Inc	$22492
15	Valero Energy Corp.	$130844	74	Merck & Co., Inc	$42237	133	Emerson Electric Co.	$22304
16	Verizon Communications Inc	$127079	75	Tyson Foods, Inc.	$41373	134	Occidental Petroleum Corp	$21947
17	Fannie Mae	$116461	76	Delta Air Lines, Inc. (DE)	$40704	135	Union Pacific Corp	$21813
18	Costco Wholesale Corp	$116199	77	Tesoro Corporation	$40633	136	Amgen Inc	$21662
19	Federal Reserve System	$114299	78	Best Buy Inc	$40339	137	Fluor Corp.	$21532
20	Kroger Co (The)	$108465	79	Goldman Sachs Group, Inc.	$40085	138	National Oilwell Varco Inc	$21440
21	Amazon.com Inc.	$107006	80	United Continental Holdings	$38901	139	Freeport-McMoRan Inc	$21438
22	Walgreens Boots Alliance Inc	$103444	81	Honeywell International Inc	$38581	140	U.S. Bancorp (DE)	$21392
23	HP Inc	$103355	82	Oracle Corp.	$38226	141	Nucor Corp.	$21105
24	Cardinal Health, Inc.	$102531	83	Morgan Stanley	$37953	142	Abbott Laboratories	$20247
25	JPMorgan Chase & Co	$102102	84	Johnson Controls Inc	$37179	143	AbbVie Inc.	$19960
26	Express Scripts Holding Co	$101752	85	HCA Holdings Inc	$36918	144	Danaher Corp.	$19914
27	Marathon Petroleum Corp.	$98102	86	American Express Co.	$35999	145	PBF Energy Inc	$19828
28	Boeing Co.	$96114	87	Allstate Corp.	$35239	146	Southwest Airlines Co	$19820
29	Bank of America Corp.	$95181	88	Cigna Corp	$34914	147	HollyFrontier Corp.	$19764
30	Microsoft Corporation	$93580	89	INTL FCStone Inc.	$34676	148	Lilly (Eli) & Co.	$19616
31	International Business Machi	$92793	90	CHS Inc	$34582	149	Devon Energy Corp.	$19566
32	Citigroup Inc	$90572	91	Sprint Corp (New)	$34532	150	Xerox Corp	$19540
33	Wells Fargo & Co.	$88372	92	Mondelez International Inc	$34244	151	Progressive Corp. (OH)	$19391
34	Home Depot Inc	$83176	93	General Dynamics Corp.	$31469	152	Starbucks Corp.	$19163
35	Archer Daniels Midland Co.	$81201	94	Sears Holdings Corp	$31198	153	Icahn Enterprises LP	$19157
36	Philip Morris International	$80106	95	Publix Super Markets, Inc.	$30802	154	Paccar Inc.	$19115
37	Procter & Gamble Co	$76279	96	NIKE Inc	$30601	155	Cummins, Inc.	$19110
38	Alphabet Inc	$74989	97	3M Co	$30274	156	Kohl's Corp.	$19023
39	Comcast Corp	$74510	98	T-Mobile US Inc	$29564	157	Dollar General Corp	$18910
40	Johnson & Johnson	$74331	99	Exelon Corp.	$29447	158	Community Health Systems, In	$18639
41	Anthem Inc	$73874	100	TJX Companies, Inc.	$29078	159	Hartford Financial Services	$18614
42	MetLife Inc	$73316	101	Twenty-First Century Fox Inc	$28987	160	Kimberly-Clark Corp.	$18591
43	Target Corp	$72618	102	Deere & Co.	$28863	161	Southern Co.	$18467
44	Freddie Mac	$69367	103	Macy's Inc	$28105	162	Lear Corp.	$18211
45	Federal Reserve Bank Of New Y	$68824	104	Avnet Inc	$27925	163	Sunoco Logistics Partners L.	$18088
46	American International Group	$64406	105	Tech Data Corp.	$27671	164	EOG Resources, Inc.	$18035
47	Pepsico Inc.	$63056	106	McDonald's Corp	$27441	165	CenturyLink, Inc.	$18031
48	United Parcel Service Inc	$58232	107	Time Warner Inc	$27359	166	AECOM	$17990
49	Aetna Inc.	$58003	108	Travelers Companies Inc (The	$26800	167	Facebook, Inc.	$17928
50	Lowe's Companies Inc	$56223	109	Rite Aid Corp.	$26528	168	Jabil Circuit, Inc.	$17899
51	United Technologies Corp	$56098	110	Teachers Insurance & Annuity	$26197	169	Supervalu Inc.	$17820
52	Energy Transfer Equity L P	$55691	111	Qualcomm, Inc.	$25281	170	General Mills, Inc.	$17630
53	ConocoPhillips	$55517	112	Du Pont (E.I.) de Nemours &	$25130	171	United States Steel Corp.	$17507
54	Intel Corp	$55355	113	Gilead Sciences, Inc.	$24890	172	Exelon Generation Co LLC	$17393
55	Prudential Financial, Inc.	$54105	114	Baker Hughes Inc.	$24551	173	Colgate-Palmolive Co.	$17277
56	Disney (Walt) Co. (The)	$52465	115	Altria Group Inc	$24522	174	Global Partners LP	$17270
57	Hewlett Packard Enterprise C	$52107	116	EMC Corp. (MA)	$24440	175	Murphy USA Inc	$17210
58	Energy Transfer Partners LP	$51158	117	Chesapeake Energy Corp.	$20951	176	Penske Automotive Group Inc	$17177
59	Pfizer Inc	$49605	118	Whirlpool Corp	$20891	177	AES Corp.	$17146
						178	PG&E Corp. (Holding Co.)	$17090

SOURCE: MERGENT INC., DATABASE, AUGUST 2015

Rank	Company	Sales ($ bil.)	Rank	Company	Sales ($ bil.)	Rank	Company	Sales ($ bil.)
179	NextEra Energy Inc	$17021	220	Marriott International, Inc.	$13796	261	WestRock Co	$11381
180	American Electric Power Co.,	$17020	221	Lincoln National Corp.	$13554	262	Stanley Black & Decker Inc	$11339
181	Thermo Fisher Scientific Inc	$16890	222	Nordstrom, Inc.	$13506	263	Marathon Oil Corp.	$11258
182	NGL Energy Partners LP	$16802	223	Robinson (C.H.) Worldwide, I	$13470	264	First Data Corp (New)	$11152
183	Baxter International Inc.	$16671	224	Edison International	$13413	265	Sherwin–Williams Co.	$11130
184	Tenet Healthcare Corp.	$16615	225	Illinois Tool Works, Inc.	$13405	266	BlackRock, Inc.	$11081
185	Centene Corp	$16560	226	Southern California Edison C	$13380	267	Voya Financial Inc	$11071
186	Bristol–Myers Squibb Co.	$16560	227	Synnex Corp	$13338	268	Hertz Global Holdings Inc	$11046
187	Goodyear Tire & Rubber Co.	$16443	228	Viacom Inc	$13268	269	Ross Stores, Inc.	$11042
188	The Gap, Inc.	$16435	229	Yum! Brands, Inc.	$13105	270	Sempra Energy	$11035
189	PNC Financial Services Group	$16281	230	Texas Instruments, Inc.	$13045	271	Tennessee Valley Authority	$11003
190	Micron Technology Inc.	$16192	231	Marsh & McLennan Companies I	$12951	272	Automatic Data Processing In	$10939
191	Office Depot, Inc.	$16096	232	Consolidated Edison, Inc.	$12919	273	Reinsurance Group of America	$10904
192	Bank of New York Mellon Corp	$16046	233	DaVita HealthCare Partners I	$12795	274	Public Service Enterprise Gr	$10886
193	NRG Energy Inc	$15868	234	CST Brands Inc	$12758	275	Horton (D.R.) Inc.	$10824
194	ConAgra Foods, Inc.	$15832	235	Synchrony Financial	$12727	276	Consolidated Edison Co. of N	$10786
195	Whole Foods Market, Inc.	$15389	236	Parker Hannifin Corp.	$12712	277	Lauder (Estee) Cos., Inc. (T	$10780
196	PPG Industries, Inc.	$15360	237	Entergy Corp. (New)	$12495	278	Biogen Inc	$10764
197	Genuine Parts Co.	$15342	238	Dominion Resources Inc	$12436	279	State Street Corp.	$10687
198	Performance Food Group Co	$15270	239	VF Corp.	$12282	280	Reynolds American Inc	$10675
199	Western Refining Inc	$15154	240	Praxair, Inc.	$12273	281	Schein (Henry), Inc.	$10630
200	Omnicom Group, Inc.	$15134	241	Ameriprise Financial Inc	$12268	282	Norfolk Southern Corp.	$10511
201	FirstEnergy Corp.	$15026	242	Penney (J.C.) Co.,Inc. (Hold	$12257	283	Unum Group	$10510
202	Monsanto Co.	$15001	243	Oneok Inc.	$12195	284	Hilton Worldwide Holdings In	$10502
203	Land O' Lakes Inc	$14966	244	ONEOK Partners LP	$12192	285	Liberty Interactive Corp	$10499
204	Dish Network Corp	$14643	245	Computer Sciences Corp.	$12173	286	Reliance Steel & Aluminum Co	$10452
205	Las Vegas Sands Corp	$14584	246	L–3 Communications Holdings,	$12124	287	Univar Inc	$10374
206	Kellogg Co	$14580	247	Jacobs Engineering Group, In	$12115	288	DTE Energy Co.	$10337
207	Western Digital Corp.	$14572	248	CDW Corp	$12075	289	Assurant Inc	$10325
208	Kinder Morgan Inc.	$14403	249	Principal Financial Group, I	$11964	290	Huntsman Corp	$10299
209	Aramark	$14329	250	Santander Holdings USA Inc.	$11919	291	Becton, Dickinson & Co.	$10282
210	Loews Corp.	$14325	251	Bed, Bath & Beyond, Inc.	$11881	292	Core Mark Holding Co Inc	$10280
211	Ecolab, Inc.	$14281	252	CSX Corp	$11811	293	Cognizant Technology Solutio	$10263
212	Carmax Inc.	$14269	253	Federal Reserve Bank of San F	$11704	294	AutoZone, Inc.	$10187
213	Health Net, Inc.	$14009	254	Xcel Energy, Inc.	$11686	295	Navistar International Corp.	$10140
214	Waste Management, Inc. (DE)	$13996	255	Donnelley (R. R.) & Sons Co.	$11603	296	MGM Resorts International	$10082
215	WellCare Health Plans Inc	$13890	256	PPL Corp	$11499	297	Grainger (W.W.), Inc.	$9965
216	CBS Corp	$13886	257	Leucadia National Corp.	$11486	298	Stryker Corp.	$9946
217	Visa Inc	$13880	258	L Brands, Inc	$11454	299	Group 1 Automotive, Inc.	$9938
218	Textron Inc.	$13878	259	Hess Corp	$11439	300	BB&T Corp.	$9926
219	Apache Corp.	$13851	260	Florida Power & Light Co.	$11421			

The Most Profitable Companies in
Hoover's Handbook of American Business 2016

Rank	Company	Net Income ($ bil.)	Rank	Company	Net Income ($ bil.)	Rank	Company	Net Income ($ bil.)
1	Apple Inc	$53394	60	Federal Reserve System	$4363	119	Cigna Corp	$2102
2	Exxon Mobil Corp.	$32520	61	Walgreens Boots Alliance Inc	$4220	120	PPG Industries, Inc.	$2102
3	Wells Fargo & Co.	$23057	62	PNC Financial Services Group	$4207	121	Raytheon Co.	$2074
4	JPMorgan Chase & Co	$21762	63	Time Warner Inc	$3827	122	Aetna Inc.	$2041
5	Berkshire Hathaway Inc.	$19872	64	MasterCard Inc	$3808	123	State Street Corp.	$2037
6	Chevron Corporation	$19241	65	Facebook, Inc.	$3688	124	Franklin Resources, Inc.	$2035
7	Wal-Mart Stores, Inc.	$16363	66	Valero Energy Corp.	$3630	125	Southern Co.	$2031
8	Alphabet Inc	$16348	67	Lockheed Martin Corp.	$3614	126	Northrop Grumman Corp	$1990
9	Johnson & Johnson	$16323	68	Biogen Inc	$3547	127	CSX Corp	$1968
10	General Electric Co	$15233	69	Morgan Stanley	$3467	128	Du Pont (E.I.) de Nemours &	$1953
11	Fannie Mae	$14208	70	Travelers Companies Inc (The	$3439	129	Deere & Co.	$1940
12	Microsoft Corporation	$12193	71	BlackRock, Inc.	$3294	130	Viacom Inc	$1922
13	Gilead Sciences, Inc.	$12101	72	NIKE Inc	$3273	131	Chesapeake Energy Corp.	$1917
14	International Business Machi	$12022	73	Reynolds American Inc	$3253	132	Illinois Tool Works, Inc.	$1899
15	Merck & Co., Inc	$11920	74	Marathon Oil Corp.	$3046	133	Thermo Fisher Scientific Inc	$1894
16	Intel Corp	$11420	75	United Parcel Service Inc	$3032	134	Duke Energy Corp	$1883
17	Oracle Corp.	$9938	76	General Dynamics Corp.	$2965	135	HCA Holdings Inc	$1875
18	General Motors Co.	$9687	77	AFLAC Inc.	$2951	136	Time Warner Cable Inc	$1844
19	Verizon Communications Inc	$9625	78	EOG Resources, Inc.	$2915	137	Weyerhaeuser Co	$1826
20	Pfizer Inc	$9135	79	Micron Technology Inc.	$2899	138	AbbVie Inc.	$1774
21	Cisco Systems, Inc.	$8981	80	American Airlines Group Inc	$2882	139	Suntrust Banks, Inc.	$1774
22	Goldman Sachs Group, Inc.	$8477	81	Allstate Corp.	$2850	140	PPL Corp	$1737
23	Disney (Walt) Co. (The)	$8382	82	Las Vegas Sands Corp	$2841	141	Baxalta Inc	$1737
24	Twenty-First Century Fox Inc	$8306	83	Enterprise Products Partners	$2834	142	Publix Super Markets, Inc.	$1735
25	Comcast Corp	$8163	84	Texas Instruments, Inc.	$2821	143	Kroger Co (The)	$1728
26	Freddie Mac	$7690	85	Starbucks Corp.	$2757	144	eBay Inc.	$1725
27	Dow Chemical Co.	$7685	86	EMC Corp. (MA)	$2714	145	Baker Hughes Inc.	$1719
28	United Technologies Corp	$7608	87	Emerson Electric Co.	$2710	146	Praxair, Inc.	$1694
29	American International Group	$7529	88	Lowe's Companies Inc	$2698	147	Simon Property Group, Inc.	$1652
30	Yahoo! Inc.	$7522	89	Danaher Corp.	$2598	148	American Electric Power Co.,	$1634
31	Philip Morris International	$7493	90	Anthem Inc	$2570	149	Ameriprise Financial Inc	$1619
32	Ford Motor Co. (DE)	$7373	91	Bank of New York Mellon Corp	$2567	150	Edison International	$1612
33	Citigroup Inc	$7313	92	Priceline Group Inc. (The)	$2551	151	Devon Energy Corp.	$1607
34	Coca-Cola Co (The)	$7098	93	Marathon Petroleum Corp.	$2524	152	Paccar Inc.	$1604
35	Procter & Gamble Co	$7036	94	National Oilwell Varco Inc	$2502	153	Celgene Corp.	$1602
36	Amgen Inc	$6939	95	Baxter International Inc.	$2497	154	Blackstone Group LP	$1585
37	ConocoPhillips	$6869	96	Express Scripts Holding Co	$2476	155	Bristol-Myers Squibb Co.	$1565
38	Home Depot Inc	$6345	97	NextEra Energy Inc	$2469	156	Southern California Edison C	$1565
39	Visa Inc	$6328	98	Hewlett Packard Enterprise C	$2461	157	Johnson Controls Inc	$1563
40	MetLife Inc	$6309	99	Federal Reserve Bank Of New Y	$2398	158	Norfolk Southern Corp.	$1556
41	AT&T Inc	$6224	100	Lilly (Eli) & Co.	$2391	159	Macy's Inc	$1526
42	American Express Co.	$5885	101	Costco Wholesale Corp	$2377	160	Public Service Enterprise Gr	$1518
43	U.S. Bancorp (DE)	$5851	102	Santander Holdings USA Inc.	$2335	161	Florida Power & Light Co.	$1517
44	UnitedHealth Group Inc	$5813	103	Discover Financial Services	$2323	162	Lincoln National Corp.	$1515
45	Pepsico Inc.	$5452	104	Hess Corp	$2317	163	Macerich Co. (The)	$1499
46	Qualcomm, Inc.	$5271	105	Monsanto Co.	$2314	164	International Finance Corp.	$1483
47	CVS Health Corp	$5237	106	Voya Financial Inc	$2300	165	Fifth Third Bancorp (Cincinn	$1481
48	Boeing Co.	$5176	107	Abbott Laboratories	$2284	166	McKesson Corp.	$1476
49	Altria Group Inc	$5070	108	Exelon Corp.	$2250	167	Western Digital Corp.	$1465
50	Bank of America Corp.	$4833	109	Archer Daniels Midland Co.	$2248	168	Marsh & McLennan Companies I	$1465
51	3M Co	$4833	110	BB&T Corp.	$2226	169	Automatic Data Processing In	$1453
52	Union Pacific Corp	$4772	111	TJX Companies, Inc.	$2215	170	PG&E Corp. (Holding Co.)	$1450
53	Honeywell International Inc	$4768	112	Mondelez International Inc	$2184	171	Cognizant Technology Solutio	$1439
54	Phillips 66	$4762	113	Southwest Airlines Co	$2181	172	Stryker Corp.	$1439
55	McDonald's Corp	$4758	114	Colgate-Palmolive Co.	$2180	173	CBS Corp	$1413
56	HP Inc	$4554	115	Williams Cos Inc (The)	$2114	174	Cummins, Inc.	$1399
57	Delta Air Lines, Inc. (DE)	$4526	116	Rite Aid Corp.	$2109	175	CF Industries Holdings Inc	$1390
58	Capital One Financial Corp	$4428	117	Synchrony Financial	$2109	176	Plains All American Pipeline	$1384
59	Burlington Northern & Santa F	$4397	118	Caterpillar Inc.	$2102	177	Prudential Financial, Inc.	$1381
						178	Applied Materials, Inc.	$1377

SOURCE: MERGENT INC., DATABASE, AUGUST 2015

The Most Profitable Companies in
Hoover's Handbook of American Business 2016 (continued)

Rank	Company	Net Income ($ bil.)	Rank	Company	Net Income ($ bil.)	Rank	Company	Net Income ($ bil.)
179	Ford Motor Credit Company LL	$1363	220	Spectra Energy Corp	$1082	261	Kohl's Corp.	$867
180	Corning, Inc.	$1339	221	Duke Energy Carolinas LLC	$1072	262	Sherwin-Williams Co.	$866
181	Energy Transfer Partners LP	$1336	222	M & T Bank Corp	$1066	263	Citizens Financial Group Inc	$865
182	Southern Copper Corp	$1333	223	Dollar General Corp	$1065	264	Virginia Electric & Power Co	$858
183	Schwab (Charles) Corp.	$1321	224	Tegna Inc	$1062	265	Western Union Co.	$852
184	Dominion Resources Inc	$1310	225	Regions Financial Corp	$1062	266	Alaska Air Group, Inc.	$848
185	Motorola Solutions Inc.	$1299	226	Consolidated Edison Co. of N	$1058	267	Hershey Company (The)	$847
186	Waste Management, Inc. (DE)	$1298	227	FedEx Corp	$1050	268	CA Inc	$846
187	Graham Holdings Co.	$1294	228	VF Corp.	$1048	269	Harley-Davidson Inc	$845
188	Yum! Brands, Inc.	$1293	229	Macquarie Infrastructure Cor	$1042	270	Tesoro Corporation	$843
189	Progressive Corp. (OH)	$1281	230	L Brands, Inc	$1042	271	Magellan Midstream Partners	$840
190	Air Products & Chemicals, In	$1278	231	Mosaic Co. (The)	$1029	272	Constellation Brands Inc	$839
191	Intercontinental Exchange In	$1274	232	Xcel Energy, Inc.	$1021	273	Exelon Generation Co LLC	$835
192	The Gap, Inc.	$1262	233	Kimberly-Clark Corp.	$1013	274	Activision Blizzard, Inc.	$835
193	Sempra Energy	$1262	234	Parker Hannifin Corp.	$1013	275	Rockwell Automation, Inc.	$828
194	Georgia Power Co.	$1242	235	Spectra Energy Partners LP	$1004	276	American Tower Corp (New)	$825
195	Principal Financial Group, I	$1234	236	St. Jude Medical, Inc.	$1002	277	Eversource Energy	$820
196	Best Buy Inc	$1233	237	USG Corp	$991	278	TD Ameritrade Holding Corp	$813
197	PayPal Holdings Inc	$1228	238	Moody's Corp.	$989	279	Northern Trust Corp	$812
198	T Rowe Price Group, Inc.	$1223	239	Teachers Insurance & Annuity	$984	280	Edwards Lifesciences Corp	$811
199	General Mills, Inc.	$1221	240	Continental Resources Inc.	$977	281	Lennar Corp.	$803
200	Tyson Foods, Inc.	$1220	241	Qwest Corp	$970	282	Grainger (W.W.), Inc.	$802
201	Cardinal Health, Inc.	$1215	242	Xerox Corp	$969	283	Alabama Power Co.	$800
202	Noble Energy, Inc.	$1214	243	RiverSource Life Insurance C	$965	284	Skyworks Solutions, Inc.	$798
203	Ecolab, Inc.	$1203	244	Entergy Corp. (New)	$960	285	Hartford Financial Services	$798
204	Federal Reserve Bank of Richm	$1202	245	Radian Group, Inc.	$960	286	Spirit AeroSystems Holdings	$789
205	Toyota Motor Credit Corp.	$1197	246	Bed, Bath & Beyond, Inc.	$957	287	QEP Resources Inc	$784
206	AutoZone, Inc.	$1160	247	Dish Network Corp	$945	288	Whirlpool Corp	$783
207	McGraw Hill Financial, Inc.	$1156	248	Pioneer Natural Resources Co	$930	289	CHS Inc	$781
208	Ally Financial Inc	$1150	249	Ross Stores, Inc.	$925	290	O'Reilly Automotive, Inc.	$778
209	Navient Corp	$1149	250	Southwestern Energy Company	$924	291	CenturyLink, Inc.	$772
210	Humana, Inc.	$1147	251	Vornado Realty L.P.	$912	292	AES Corp.	$769
211	Public Storage	$1144	252	ONEOK Partners LP	$910	293	Santander Consumer USA Holdi	$766
212	Discovery Communications, In	$1139	253	Murphy Oil Corp	$906	294	Expedia Inc	$764
213	United Continental Holdings	$1132	254	KeyCorp	$900	295	Chemtura Corp	$763
214	CIT Group, Inc.	$1130	255	Newfield Exploration Co.	$900	296	Stanley Black & Decker Inc	$761
215	CME Group Inc	$1127	256	Taubman Centers, Inc.	$893	297	Vornado Realty Trust	$760
216	Tennessee Valley Authority	$1111	257	VMware Inc	$886	298	PSEG Power LLC	$760
217	Omnicom Group, Inc.	$1094	258	Symantec Corp.	$878	299	Fiserv, Inc.	$754
218	Consolidated Edison, Inc.	$1092	259	Electronic Arts	$875	300	Marriott International, Inc.	$753
219	Lauder (Estee) Cos., Inc. (T	$1089	260	Dover Corp	$870			

The 300 Largest Employers in
Hoover's Handbook of American Business 2016

Rank	Company	Employees
1	Wal-Mart Stores, Inc.	2,200,000
2	Kelly Services, Inc.	563,300
3	Yum! Brands, Inc.	505,000
4	United Parcel Service Inc	435,000
5	McDonald's Corp	420,000
6	Kroger Co (The)	400,000
7	International Business Machi	379,592
8	Home Depot Inc	371,000
9	Walgreens Boots Alliance Inc	360,000
10	Target Corp	347,000
11	Berkshire Hathaway Inc.	316,000
12	General Electric Co	305,000
13	HP Inc	287,000
14	Lowe's Companies Inc	266,000
15	Aramark	265,500
16	Wells Fargo & Co.	264,500
17	Pepsico Inc.	263,000
18	AT&T Inc	253,000
19	CVS Health Corp	243,000
20	JPMorgan Chase & Co	241,359
21	Citigroup Inc	241,000
22	Hewlett Packard Enterprise C	240,000
23	Starbucks Corp.	238,000
24	Amazon.com Inc.	230,800
25	HCA Holdings Inc	225,000
26	Robert Half International In	225,000
27	Bank of America Corp.	224,000
28	General Motors Co.	215,000
29	Cognizant Technology Solutio	211,500
30	Costco Wholesale Corp	205,000
31	UnitedHealth Group Inc	200,000
32	Ford Motor Co. (DE)	199,000
33	TJX Companies, Inc.	198,000
34	United Technologies Corp	197,200
35	Sears Holdings Corp	196,000
36	Disney (Walt) Co. (The)	185,000
37	Starwood Hotels & Resorts Wo	180,400
38	Verizon Communications Inc	177,300
39	Publix Super Markets, Inc.	175,000
40	Community Health Systems, In	167,000
41	Macy's Inc	166,900
42	FedEx Corp	166,000
43	Boeing Co.	161,400
44	Jabil Circuit, Inc.	161,000
45	Hilton Worldwide Holdings In	157,000
46	Corporate Resource Services	150,800
47	Darden Restaurants, Inc. (Un	150,000
48	Xerox Corp	147,500
49	Comcast Corp	141,000
50	The Gap, Inc.	141,000
51	Johnson Controls Inc	139,000
52	Kohl's Corp.	137,000
53	Lear Corp.	136,200
54	Oracle Corp.	132,000
55	Coca-Cola Co (The)	129,200
56	Honeywell International Inc	129,000
57	Johnson & Johnson	126,500
58	Best Buy Inc	125,000
59	Convergys Corp.	125,000
60	Marriott International, Inc.	123,500
61	ABM Industries, Inc.	120,000
62	Microsoft Corporation	118,000
63	Penney (J.C.) Co.,Inc. (Hold	114,000
64	American Airlines Group Inc	113,300
65	Tyson Foods, Inc.	113,000
66	Lockheed Martin Corp.	112,000
67	Emerson Electric Co.	110,800
68	Apple Inc	110,000
69	Procter & Gamble Co	110,000
70	Tenet Healthcare Corp.	108,989
71	Intel Corp	107,300
72	Caterpillar Inc.	105,700
73	Dollar General Corp	105,500
74	Mondelez International Inc	104,000
75	Bloomin' Brands Inc.	100,000
76	General Dynamics Corp.	99,900
77	Whirlpool Corp	97,000
78	Barrett Business Services, I	93,040
79	AECOM	92,000
80	Whole Foods Market, Inc.	90,900
81	Dollar Tree, Inc.	90,000
82	3M Co	89,446
83	Rite Aid Corp.	89,000
84	United Continental Holdings	84,000
85	Delta Air Lines, Inc. (DE)	83,000
86	Philip Morris International	82,500
87	Brookdale Senior Living Inc	81,300
88	AutoZone, Inc.	81,000
89	L Brands, Inc	80,100
90	Staples Inc	79,075
91	Pfizer Inc	78,300
92	Abbott Laboratories	77,000
93	Western Digital Corp.	76,449
94	Exxon Mobil Corp.	75,300
95	Omnicom Group, Inc.	74,900
96	Advance Auto Parts Inc	73,000
97	GameStop Corp	73,000
98	Synnex Corp	72,500
99	Cracker Barrel Old Country S	72,000
100	Cisco Systems, Inc.	71,833
101	Ross Stores, Inc.	71,400
102	Danaher Corp.	71,000
103	McKesson Corp.	70,400
104	Merck & Co., Inc	70,000
105	EMC Corp. (MA)	70,000
106	Computer Sciences Corp.	70,000
107	Universal Health Services, I	68,700
108	MGM Resorts International	68,100
109	MetLife Inc	68,000
110	Donnelley (R. R.) & Sons Co.	68,000
111	Caesars Entertainment Corp	68,000
112	O'Reilly Automotive, Inc.	67,926
113	Nordstrom, Inc.	67,000
114	U.S. Bancorp (DE)	66,750
115	Icahn Enterprises LP	66,559
116	Baxter International Inc.	66,000
117	Goodyear Tire & Rubber Co.	66,000
118	HanesBrands Inc	65,300
119	American International Group	65,000
120	Halliburton Company	65,000
121	Northrop Grumman Corp	65,000
122	Chevron Corporation	64,700
123	Brinks Co (The)	64,100
124	Jacobs Engineering Group, In	64,000
125	National Oilwell Varco Inc	63,642
126	Abercrombie & Fitch Co.	63,000
127	NIKE Inc	62,600
128	Baker Hughes Inc.	62,000
129	Alphabet Inc	61,814
130	Kindred Healthcare Inc	61,500
131	Raytheon Co.	61,000
132	Bed, Bath & Beyond, Inc.	60,000
133	Autoliv Inc.	60,000
134	Chipotle Mexican Grill Inc	59,330
135	Alcoa, Inc.	59,000
136	VF Corp.	59,000
137	Jones Lang LaSalle Inc	58,100
138	International Paper Co	58,000
139	DaVita HealthCare Partners I	57,900
140	Deere & Co.	57,200
141	Humana, Inc.	57,000
142	Marsh & McLennan Companies I	57,000
143	Fidelity National Financial	56,883
144	Time Warner Cable Inc	56,600
145	Office Depot, Inc.	56,000
146	Morgan Stanley	55,802
147	Cummins, Inc.	55,200
148	Automatic Data Processing In	55,000
149	Parker Hannifin Corp.	54,754
150	American Express Co.	54,000
151	PNC Financial Services Group	53,587
152	Brinker International, Inc.	53,000
153	Du Pont (E.I.) de Nemours &	52,000
154	CBRE Group Inc	52,000
155	Sysco Corp.	51,700
156	Anthem Inc	51,500
157	Thermo Fisher Scientific Inc	51,000
158	Michaels Companies Inc	51,000
159	Amphenol Corp.	50,700
160	Sykes Enterprises, Inc.	50,450
161	Stanley Black & Decker Inc	50,400
162	RMR Group Inc (The)	50,400
163	Bank of New York Mellon Corp	50,300
164	Southwest Airlines Co	49,583
165	Becton, Dickinson & Co.	49,517
166	Dow Chemical Co.	49,500
167	Aetna Inc.	48,800
168	Federal-Mogul Holdings Corp	48,600
169	Las Vegas Sands Corp	48,500
170	Prudential Financial, Inc.	48,331
171	Burlington Northern & Santa F	48,000
172	Illinois Tool Works, Inc.	48,000
173	Ascena Retail Group Inc	48,000
174	Union Pacific Corp	47,457
175	Ecolab, Inc.	47,430
176	Interpublic Group of Compani	47,400
177	Regis Corp.	47,000
178	Capital One Financial Corp	46,000

SOURCE: MERGENT INC., DATABASE, AUGUST 2015

Rank	Company	Employees	Rank	Company	Employees	Rank	Company	Employees
179	TeleTech Holdings, Inc.	46,000	220	Cheesecake Factory Inc. (The	35,700	261	LKQ Corp	29,500
180	Panera Bread Co.	45,400	221	Freeport-McMoRan Inc	35,000	262	CSX Corp	29,000
181	Marathon Petroleum Corp.	45,340	222	Pilgrims Pride Corp.	35,000	263	Tenneco Inc	29,000
182	T-Mobile US Inc	45,000	223	Cardinal Health, Inc.	34,500	264	Duke Energy Corp	28,344
183	CenturyLink, Inc.	45,000	224	PVH Corp	34,100	265	Sally Beauty Holdings Inc	28,330
184	L-3 Communications Holdings,	45,000	225	Goldman Sachs Group, Inc.	34,000	266	Praxair, Inc.	27,780
185	Quest Diagnostics, Inc.	45,000	226	Textron Inc.	34,000	267	Energy Transfer Equity L P	27,605
186	Hyatt Hotels Corp	45,000	227	Burlington Stores Inc	34,000	268	Red Robin Gourmet Burgers In	27,543
187	Foot Locker, Inc.	44,568	228	Apollo Education Group, Inc.	34,000	269	Volt Information Sciences, I	27,400
188	PPG Industries, Inc.	44,400	229	Archer Daniels Midland Co.	33,900	270	Genesco Inc.	27,325
189	Cedar Fair LP	44,100	230	Envision Healthcare Holdings	33,748	271	Civitas Solutions Inc	27,100
190	Lauder (Estee) Cos., Inc. (T	44,000	231	BB&T Corp.	33,400	272	Stryker Corp.	27,000
191	Sanmina Corp	43,854	232	Avon Products, Inc.	33,200	273	EMCOR Group, Inc.	27,000
192	Texas Roadhouse Inc	43,300	233	Ryder System, Inc.	33,100	274	Owens-Illinois, Inc.	27,000
193	Kimberly-Clark Corp.	43,000	234	Qualcomm, Inc.	33,000	275	Cooper-Standard Holdings, In	27,000
194	General Mills, Inc.	42,000	235	Hertz Global Holdings Inc	33,000	276	Universal Corp.	27,000
195	WestRock Co	41,400	236	Republic Services, Inc.	33,000	277	Williams Sonoma Inc	26,800
196	Barnes & Noble Inc	41,000	237	Jarden Corp	33,000	278	Progressive Corp. (OH)	26,501
197	Six Flags Entertainment Corp	40,900	238	YRC Worldwide Inc	33,000	279	Southern Co.	26,369
198	Allstate Corp.	40,200	239	ConAgra Foods, Inc.	32,900	280	Tailored Brands Inc	26,100
199	Dillard's Inc.	40,000	240	Bob Evans Farms, Inc.	32,341	281	AutoNation, Inc.	26,000
200	Fidelity National Informatio	40,000	241	Mohawk Industries, Inc.	32,300	282	ManpowerGroup	26,000
201	LifePoint Health Inc	40,000	242	Command Center, Inc.	32,210	283	AbbVie Inc.	26,000
202	Waste Management, Inc. (DE)	39,800	243	Ruby Tuesday, Inc.	32,100	284	Dover Corp	26,000
203	Sherwin-Williams Co.	39,674	244	Cintas Corp.	32,000	285	Express Scripts Holding Co	25,900
204	Lilly (Eli) & Co.	39,135	245	Micron Technology Inc.	31,800	286	Energy Transfer Partners LP	25,682
205	Genuine Parts Co.	39,000	246	Casey's General Stores, Inc.	31,766	287	Time Warner Inc	25,600
206	Supervalu Inc.	38,500	247	Select Medical Holdings Corp	31,400	288	Monsanto Co.	25,500
207	Huntington Ingalls Industrie	38,000	248	Tegna Inc	31,250	289	Visteon Corp.	25,500
208	American Eagle Outfitters, I	38,000	249	Wendy's Co (The)	31,200	290	AMERCO	25,400
209	Colgate-Palmolive Co.	37,700	250	Texas Instruments, Inc.	31,003	291	Bright Horizons Family Solut	25,400
210	Wyndham Worldwide Corp	37,700	251	Sprint Corp (New)	31,000	292	Bon-Ton Stores Inc	25,200
211	Dick's Sporting Goods, Inc	37,600	252	Mattel Inc	31,000	293	Bristol-Myers Squibb Co.	25,000
212	Fluor Corp.	37,508	253	Travelers Companies Inc (The	30,900	294	News Corp (New)	25,000
213	On Assignment, Inc.	37,500	254	Norfolk Southern Corp.	30,456	295	Ralph Lauren Corp	25,000
214	Cigna Corp	37,200	255	NCR Corp.	30,200	296	Masco Corp.	25,000
215	Buffalo Wild Wings Inc	37,200	256	Avis Budget Group Inc	30,000	297	KBR Inc	25,000
216	Quintiles Transnational Hold	36,100	257	BorgWarner Inc	30,000	298	Avery Dennison Corp.	25,000
217	Big Lots, Inc.	36,100	258	State Street Corp.	29,970	299	CH2M Hill Companies Ltd	25,000
218	Laboratory Corporation of Am	36,000	259	Kellogg Co	29,790	300	Ingles Markets, Inc.	25,000
219	Corning, Inc.	35,700	260	Exelon Corp.	29,762			

Rank	Company	Sales ($ bil.)	Rank	Company	Sales ($ bil))	Rank	Company	Sales ($ bil.)
1	Wal-Mart Stores, Inc.	$485,651	68	Coca-Cola Co (The)	$45,998	135	Union Pacific Corp	$21,813
2	Exxon Mobil Corp.	$411,939	69	Lockheed Martin Corp.	$45,600	136	Amgen Inc	$21,662
3	Apple Inc	$233,715	70	Plains GP Holdings, L.P	$43,464	137	Fluor Corp.	$21,532
4	Chevron Corporation	$211,970	71	Plains All American Pipeline	$43,464	138	National Oilwell Varco Inc	$21,440
5	Berkshire Hathaway Inc.	$194,673	72	World Fuel Services Corp.	$43,386	139	Freeport-McMoRan Inc	$21,438
6	McKesson Corp.	$179,045	73	American Airlines Group Inc	$42,650	140	U.S. Bancorp (DE)	$21,392
7	Phillips 66	$164,093	74	Merck & Co., Inc	$42,237	141	Nucor Corp.	$21,105
8	UnitedHealth Group Inc	$157,107	75	Tyson Foods, Inc.	$41,373	142	Abbott Laboratories	$20,247
9	CVS Health Corp	$153,290	76	Delta Air Lines, Inc. (DE)	$40,704	143	AbbVie Inc.	$19,960
10	General Motors Co.	$152,356	77	Tesoro Corporation	$40,633	144	Danaher Corp.	$19,914
11	Ford Motor Co. (DE)	$149,558	78	Best Buy Inc	$40,339	145	PBF Energy Inc	$19,828
12	General Electric Co	$148,589	79	Goldman Sachs Group, Inc.	$40,085	146	Southwest Airlines Co	$19,820
13	AmerisourceBergen Corp.	$135,962	80	United Continental Holdings	$38,901	147	HollyFrontier Corp.	$19,764
14	AT&T Inc	$132,447	81	Honeywell International Inc	$38,581	148	Lilly (Eli) & Co.	$19,616
15	Valero Energy Corp.	$130,844	82	Oracle Corp.	$38,226	149	Devon Energy Corp.	$19,566
16	Verizon Communications Inc	$127,079	83	Morgan Stanley	$37,953	150	Xerox Corp	$19,540
17	Fannie Mae	$116,461	84	Johnson Controls Inc	$37,179	151	Progressive Corp. (OH)	$19,391
18	Costco Wholesale Corp	$116,199	85	HCA Holdings Inc	$36,918	152	Starbucks Corp.	$19,163
19	Federal Reserve System	$114,299	86	American Express Co.	$35,999	153	Icahn Enterprises LP	$19,157
20	Kroger Co (The)	$108,465	87	Allstate Corp.	$35,239	154	Paccar Inc.	$19,115
21	Amazon.com Inc	$107,006	88	Cigna Corp	$34,914	155	Cummins, Inc.	$19,110
22	Walgreens Boots Alliance Inc	$103,444	89	INTL FCStone Inc.	$34,676	156	Kohl's Corp.	$19,023
23	HP Inc	$103,355	90	CHS Inc	$34,582	157	Dollar General Corp	$18,910
24	Cardinal Health, Inc.	$102,531	91	Sprint Corp (New)	$34,532	158	Community Health Systems, In	$18,639
25	JPMorgan Chase & Co	$102,102	92	Mondelez International Inc	$34,244	159	Hartford Financial Services	$18,614
26	Express Scripts Holding Co	$101,752	93	General Dynamics Corp.	$31,469	160	Kimberly-Clark Corp.	$18,591
27	Marathon Petroleum Corp.	$98,102	94	Sears Holdings Corp	$31,198	161	Southern Co.	$18,467
28	Boeing Co.	$96,114	95	Publix Super Markets, Inc.	$30,802	162	Lear Corp.	$18,211
29	Bank of America Corp.	$95,181	96	NIKE Inc	$30,601	163	Sunoco Logistics Partners L.	$18,088
30	Microsoft Corporation	$93,580	97	3M Co	$30,274	164	EOG Resources, Inc.	$18,035
31	International Business Machi	$92,793	98	T-Mobile US Inc	$29,564	165	CenturyLink, Inc.	$18,031
32	Citigroup Inc	$90,572	99	Exelon Corp.	$29,447	166	AECOM	$17,990
33	Wells Fargo & Co.	$88,372	100	TJX Companies, Inc.	$29,078	167	Facebook, Inc.	$17,928
34	Home Depot Inc	$83,176	101	Twenty-First Century Fox Inc	$28,987	168	Jabil Circuit, Inc.	$17,899
35	Archer Daniels Midland Co.	$81,201	102	Deere & Co.	$28,863	169	Supervalu Inc.	$17,820
36	Philip Morris International	$80,106	103	Macy's Inc	$28,105	170	General Mills, Inc.	$17,630
37	Procter & Gamble Co	$76,279	104	Avnet Inc	$27,925	171	United States Steel Corp.	$17,507
38	Alphabet Inc	$74,989	105	Tech Data Corp.	$27,671	172	Exelon Generation Co LLC	$17,393
39	Comcast Corp	$74,510	106	McDonald's Corp	$27,441	173	Colgate-Palmolive Co.	$17,277
40	Johnson & Johnson	$74,331	107	Time Warner Inc	$27,359	174	Global Partners LP	$17,270
41	Anthem Inc	$73,874	108	Travelers Companies Inc (The	$26,800	175	Murphy USA Inc	$17,210
42	MetLife Inc	$73,316	109	Rite Aid Corp.	$26,528	176	Penske Automotive Group Inc	$17,177
43	Target Corp	$72,618	110	Teachers Insurance & Annuity	$26,197	177	AES Corp.	$17,146
44	Freddie Mac	$69,367	111	Qualcomm, Inc.	$25,281	178	PG&E Corp. (Holding Co.)	$17,090
45	Federal Reserve Bank Of New Y	$68,824	112	Du Pont (E.I.) de Nemours &	$25,130	179	NextEra Energy Inc	$17,021
46	American International Group	$64,406	113	Gilead Sciences, Inc.	$24,890	180	American Electric Power Co.,	$17,020
47	Pepsico Inc.	$63,056	114	Baker Hughes Inc.	$24,551	181	Thermo Fisher Scientific Inc	$16,890
48	United Parcel Service Inc	$58,232	115	Altria Group Inc	$24,522	182	NGL Energy Partners LP	$16,802
49	Aetna Inc.	$58,003	116	EMC Corp. (MA)	$24,440	183	Baxter International Inc.	$16,671
50	Lowe's Companies Inc	$56,223	117	Chesapeake Energy Corp.	$20,951	184	Tenet Healthcare Corp.	$16,615
51	United Technologies Corp	$56,098	118	Whirlpool Corp	$20,891	185	Centene Corp	$16,560
52	Energy Transfer Equity L P	$55,691	119	AutoNation, Inc.	$20,862	186	Bristol-Myers Squibb Co.	$16,560
53	ConocoPhillips	$55,517	120	ManpowerGroup	$20,763	187	Goodyear Tire & Rubber Co.	$16,443
54	Intel Corp	$55,355	121	Duke Energy Corp	$23,925	188	The Gap, Inc.	$16,435
55	Prudential Financial, Inc.	$54,105	122	Alcoa, Inc.	$23,906	189	PNC Financial Services Group	$16,281
56	Disney (Walt) Co. (The)	$52,465	123	Capital One Financial Corp	$23,869	190	Micron Technology Inc.	$16,192
57	Hewlett Packard Enterprise C	$52,107	124	Time Warner Cable Inc	$23,697	191	Office Depot, Inc.	$16,096
58	Energy Transfer Partners LP	$51,158	125	Halliburton Company	$23,633	192	Bank of New York Mellon Corp	$16,046
59	Pfizer Inc	$49,605	126	International Paper Co	$23,617	193	NRG Energy Inc	$15,868
60	Cisco Systems, Inc.	$49,161	127	Northrop Grumman Corp	$23,526	194	ConAgra Foods, Inc.	$15,832
61	Dow Chemical Co.	$48,778	128	Arrow Electronics, Inc.	$23,282	195	Whole Foods Market, Inc.	$15,389
62	Sysco Corp.	$48,681	129	Raytheon Co.	$23,247	196	PPG Industries, Inc.	$15,360
63	Humana, Inc.	$48,500	130	AFLAC Inc.	$22,728	197	Genuine Parts Co.	$15,342
64	Enterprise Products Partners	$47,951	131	Burlington Northern & Santa F	$22,714	198	Performance Food Group Co	$15,270
65	FedEx Corp	$47,453	132	Staples Inc	$22,492	199	Western Refining Inc	$15,154
66	Caterpillar Inc.	$47,011	133	Emerson Electric Co.	$22,304	200	Omnicom Group, Inc.	$15,134
67	Ingram Micro Inc.	$46,487	134	Occidental Petroleum Corp	$21,947	201	FirstEnergy Corp.	$15,026

Rank	Company	Sales ($ bil.)	Rank	Company	Sales ($ bil.)	Rank	Company	Sales ($ bil.)
202	Monsanto Co.	$15,001	269	Ross Stores, Inc.	$11,042	336	Cameron International Corp	$8,782
203	Land O' Lakes Inc	$14,966	270	Sempra Energy	$11,035	337	Steel Dynamics Inc.	$8,756
204	Dish Network Corp	$14,643	271	Tennessee Valley Authority	$11,003	338	Suntrust Banks, Inc.	$8,707
205	Las Vegas Sands Corp	$14,584	272	Automatic Data Processing	$10,939	339	Anadarko Petroleum Corp	$8,698
206	Kellogg Co	$14,580	273	Reinsurance Group of Am	$10,904	340	News Corp (New)	$8,633
207	Western Digital Corp.	$14,572	274	Public Service Enterprise Gr	$10,886	341	Targa Resources Corp	$8,617
208	Kinder Morgan Inc.	$14,403	275	Horton (D.R.) Inc.	$10,824	342	Dollar Tree, Inc.	$8,602
209	Aramark	$14,329	276	Consolidated Edison Co.	$10,786	343	eBay Inc.	$8,592
210	Loews Corp.	$14,325	277	Lauder (Estee) Cos., Inc.	$10,780	344	Pilgrims Pride Corp.	$8,583
211	Ecolab, Inc.	$14,281	278	Biogen Inc	$10,764	345	Caesars Entertainment Corp	$8,516
212	Carmax Inc.	$14,269	279	State Street Corp.	$10,687	346	Avis Budget Group Inc	$8,485
213	Health Net, Inc.	$14,009	280	Reynolds American Inc	$10,675	347	Tenneco Inc	$8,420
214	Waste Management, Inc. (DE)	$13,996	281	Schein (Henry), Inc.	$10,630	348	Delek US Holdings Inc	$8,324
215	WellCare Health Plans Inc	$13,890	282	Norfolk Southern Corp.	$10,511	349	Jarden Corp	$8,287
216	CBS Corp	$13,886	283	Unum Group	$10,510	350	PVH Corp	$8,241
217	Visa Inc	$13,880	284	Hilton Worldwide Holdings In	$10,502	351	United Natural Foods Inc.	$8,185
218	Textron Inc.	$13,878	285	Liberty Interactive Corp	$10,499	352	Campbell Soup Co.	$8,082
219	Apache Corp.	$13,851	286	Reliance Steel & Aluminum	$10,452	353	Universal Health Services, I	$8,065
220	Marriott International, Inc.	$13,796	287	Univar Inc	$10,374	354	Fidelity National Financial	$8,024
221	Lincoln National Corp.	$13,554	288	DTE Energy Co.	$10,337	355	BorgWarner Inc	$8,023
222	Nordstrom, Inc.	$13,506	289	Assurant Inc	$10,325	356	Ball Corp	$7,997
223	Robinson (C.H.) Worldwide, I	$13,470	290	Huntsman Corp	$10,299	357	Enbridge Energy Partners, L.	$7,965
224	Edison International	$13,413	291	Becton, Dickinson & Co.	$10,282	358	Franklin Resources, Inc.	$7,949
225	Illinois Tool Works, Inc.	$13,405	292	Core Mark Holding Co Inc	$10,280	359	FMC Technologies, Inc.	$7,943
226	Southern California Edison C	$13,380	293	Cognizant Technology Solutio	$10,263	360	SpartanNash Co.	$7,916
227	Synnex Corp	$13,338	294	AutoZone, Inc.	$10,187	361	Wesco International, Inc.	$7,890
228	Viacom Inc	$13,268	295	Navistar International Corp.	$10,140	362	Quanta Services, Inc.	$7,851
229	Yum! Brands, Inc.	$13,105	296	MGM Resorts International	$10,082	363	Mohawk Industries, Inc.	$7,803
230	Texas Instruments, Inc.	$13,045	297	Grainger (W.W.), Inc.	$9,965	364	TravelCenters of America LLC	$7,779
231	Marsh & McLennan Compani	$12,951	298	Stryker Corp.	$9,946	365	Casey's General Stores, Inc.	$7,767
232	Consolidated Edison, Inc.	$12,919	299	Group 1 Automotive, Inc.	$9,938	366	Sealed Air Corp.	$7,751
233	DaVita HealthCare Partners I	$12,795	300	BB&T Corp.	$9,926	367	Eversource Energy	$7,742
234	CST Brands Inc	$12,758	301	Air Products & Chemicals, In	$9,895	368	Williams Cos Inc (The)	$7,637
235	Synchrony Financial	$12,727	302	Advance Auto Parts Inc	$9,844	369	Ralph Lauren Corp	$7,620
236	Parker Hannifin Corp.	$12,712	303	Charter Communications Inc	$9,754	370	Virginia Electric & Power Co	$7,579
237	Entergy Corp. (New)	$12,495	304	AGCO Corp.	$9,724	371	Interpublic Group of Compani	$7,537
238	Dominion Resources Inc	$12,436	305	CNA Financial Corp.	$9,692	372	Visteon Corp.	$7,509
239	VF Corp.	$12,282	306	MasterCard Inc	$9,667	373	Blackstone Group LP	$7,485
240	Praxair, Inc.	$12,273	307	Ally Financial Inc	$9,667	374	Quest Diagnostics, Inc.	$7,435
241	Ameriprise Financial Inc	$12,268	308	Molina Healthcare Inc	$9,667	375	Hershey Company (The)	$7,422
242	Penney (J.C.) Co.,Inc. (Hold	$12,257	309	Applied Materials, Inc.	$9,659	376	Veritiv Corp	$7,407
243	Oneok Inc.	$12,195	310	Discover Financial Services	$9,611	377	Weyerhaeuser Co	$7,403
244	ONEOK Partners LP	$12,192	311	Genworth Financial, Inc. (Ho	$9,565	378	Boston Scientific Corp.	$7,380
245	Computer Sciences Corp.	$12,173	312	Eastman Chemical Co.	$9,527	379	Duke Energy Carolinas LLC	$7,351
246	L-3 Communications Holdin	$12,124	313	Dean Foods Co.	$9,503	380	Federal-Mogul Holdings Corp	$7,317
247	Jacobs Engineering Group, In	$12,115	314	Lennar Corp.	$9,474	381	Terex Corp. (New)	$7,309
248	CDW Corp	$12,075	315	Owens & Minor, Inc. (New)	$9,440	382	Newmont Mining Corp. (Holdin	$7,292
249	Principal Financial Group, I	$11,964	316	GameStop Corp	$9,296	383	O'Reilly Automotive, Inc.	$7,216
250	Santander Holdings USA Inc.	$11,919	317	Hormel Foods Corp.	$9,264	384	Foot Locker, Inc.	$7,151
251	Bed, Bath & Beyond, Inc.	$11,881	318	Celgene Corp.	$9,256	385	Masco Corp.	$7,142
252	CSX Corp	$11,811	319	PayPal Holdings Inc	$9,248	386	Berkley (W. R.) Corp.	$7,129
253	Federal Reserve Bank of	$11,704	320	Autoliv Inc.	$9,241	387	Pacific Mutual Holding Coma	$7,073
254	Xcel Energy, Inc.	$11,686	321	CenterPoint Energy, Inc	$9,226	388	Coca-Cola Enterprises Inc	$7,011
255	Donnelley (R. R.) & Sons Co.	$11,603	322	Priceline Group Inc. (The)	$9,224	389	Huntington Ingalls Industrie	$6,957
256	PPL Corp	$11,499	323	Sonic Automotive, Inc.	$9,197	390	Dover Corp	$6,956
257	Leucadia National Corp.	$11,486	324	Toyota Motor Credit Corp.	$9,142	391	MetLife Insurance Company of	$6,903
258	L Brands, Inc	$11,454	325	Republic Services, Inc.	$9,115	392	Live Nation Entertainment, I	$6,867
259	Hess Corp	$11,439	326	Corning, Inc.	$9,111	393	Federal Reserve Bank Of Atlan	$6,861
260	Florida Power & Light Co.	$11,421	327	CVR Energy Inc	$9,110	394	Dick's Sporting Goods, Inc	$6,814
261	WestRock Co	$11,381	328	Crown Holdings Inc	$9,097	395	Peabody Energy Corp	$6,792
262	Stanley Black & Decker Inc	$11,339	329	Mosaic Co. (The)	$9,056	396	Dillard's Inc.	$6,780
263	Marathon Oil Corp.	$11,258	330	CBRE Group Inc	$9,050	397	Netflix Inc.	$6,780
264	First Data Corp (New)	$11,152	331	Georgia Power Co.	$8,988	398	Alon USA Energy Inc	$6,779
265	Sherwin-Williams Co.	$11,130	332	HD Supply Holdings Inc	$8,882	399	Level 3 Communications, Inc.	$6,777
266	BlackRock, Inc.	$11,081	333	Avon Products, Inc.	$8,851	400	Darden Restaurants, Inc.	$6,764
267	Voya Financial Inc	$11,071	334	Qwest Corp	$8,838	401	LKQ Corp	$6,740
268	Hertz Global Holdings Inc	$11,046	335	CVR Refining, LP	$8,830	402	UGI Corp.	$6,691

Rank	Company	Sales ($ bil.)
403	Expedia Inc	$6,672
404	Spirit AeroSystems Holdings	$6,644
405	Buckeye Partners, L.P.	$6,620
406	Dana Holding Corp	$6,617
407	NCR Corp.	$6,591
408	Ryder System, Inc.	$6,572
409	Expeditors International of	$6,565
410	Symantec Corp.	$6,508
411	AK Steel Holding Corp.	$6,506
412	Fifth Third Bancorp (Cincinn	$6,504
413	Seaboard Corp.	$6,473
414	Calpine Corp	$6,472
415	NiSource Inc. (Holding Co.)	$6,471
416	Cablevision Systems Corp.	$6,461
417	CMS Energy Corp	$6,456
418	Anixter International Inc	$6,446
419	Chemours Co (The)	$6,432
420	EMCOR Group, Inc.	$6,425
421	Fidelity National Informatio	$6,414
422	Sanmina Corp	$6,375
423	CenterPoint Energy Resources	$6,367
424	KBR Inc	$6,366
425	Avery Dennison Corp.	$6,330
426	iHeartMedia Inc	$6,319
427	Rockwell Automation, Inc.	$6,308
428	Discovery Communications, In	$6,265
429	Harley-Davidson Inc	$6,229
430	Trinity Industries, Inc.	$6,170
431	Hunt (J.B.) Transport Servic	$6,165
432	Consumers Energy Co.	$6,165
433	Owens-Illinois, Inc.	$6,156
434	Harman International Industr	$6,155
435	Federal Reserve Bank of Richm	$6,148
436	Santander Consumer USA Holdi	$6,127
437	Erie Indemnity Co.	$6,124
438	Netapp Inc	$6,123
439	Dr Pepper Snapple Group Inc	$6,121
440	Oshkosh Corp (New)	$6,098
441	A-Mark Precious Metals, Inc	$6,070
442	Barnes & Noble Inc	$6,069
443	Schwab (Charles) Corp.	$6,058
444	Ameren Corp.	$6,053
445	VMware Inc	$6,035
446	Constellation Brands Inc	$6,028
447	Mattel Inc	$6,024
448	Laboratory Corporation of Am	$6,012
449	Tegna Inc	$6,008
450	Commercial Metals Co.	$5,989
451	Starwood Hotels & Resorts Wo	$5,983
452	PulteGroup, Inc.	$5,982
453	General Cable Corp. (DE)	$5,980
454	Graybar Electric Co., Inc.	$5,979
455	Energy Future Holdings Corp	$5,978
456	Baxalta Inc	$5,952
457	Alabama Power Co.	$5,942
458	MRC Global Inc	$5,933
459	Spectra Energy Corp	$5,903
460	Midcoast Energy Partners LP	$5,894
461	Motorola Solutions Inc.	$5,881
462	Asbury Automotive Group, Inc	$5,868
463	Packaging Corp of America	$5,853
464	Windstream Holdings Inc	$5,830
465	United Rentals, Inc.	$5,817
466	JetBlue Airways Corp	$5,817
467	HRG Group Inc	$5,816
468	Calumet Specialty Product Pa	$5,791
469	Southern Copper Corp	$5,788

Rank	Company	Sales ($ bil.)
470	Quintiles Transnational Hold	$5,738
471	HanesBrands Inc	$5,732
472	Newell Rubbermaid, Inc.	$5,727
473	American Financial Group Inc	$5,713
474	Tractor Supply Co.	$5,712
475	Smucker (J.M.) Co.	$5,693
476	Celanese Corp (DE)	$5,674
477	Regions Financial Corp	$5,674
478	Ingredion Inc	$5,668
479	Clorox Co (The)	$5,655
480	Navient Corp	$5,637
481	St. Jude Medical, Inc.	$5,622
482	Western Union Co.	$5,607
483	Alaska Air Group, Inc.	$5,598
484	SanDisk Corp.	$5,565
485	Domtar Corp	$5,563
486	Kelly Services, Inc.	$5,563
487	Northern Tier Energy LP	$5,556
488	Wyndham Worldwide Corp	$5,536
489	Old Republic International C	$5,531
490	Advanced Micro Devices, Inc.	$5,506
491	Murphy Oil Corp	$5,476
492	CH2M Hill Companies Ltd	$5,468
493	PSEG Power LLC	$5,434
494	Wynn Resorts Ltd	$5,434
495	Jones Lang LaSalle Inc	$5,430
496	Gallagher (Arthur J.) & Co.	$5,392
497	Lithia Motors, Inc.	$5,390
498	Ashland Inc	$5,387
499	Salesforce.Com Inc	$5,374
500	Host Hotels & Resorts Inc	$5,354

Hoover's Handbook of

American Business

The Companies

1st Source Corp.

Need a bank? Don't give it a 2nd thought. Contact 1st Source Corporation parent of 1st Source Bank which provides commercial and consumer banking services through nearly 80 branches in northern Indiana and southwestern Michigan. The bank offers deposit accounts; business agricultural and consumer loans; residential and commercial mortgages; credit cards; and trust services. Its specialty finance group provides financing for aircraft automobile fleets trucks and construction and environmental equipment through about two-dozen offices nationwide; such loans account for nearly half of 1st Source's portfolio.

Geographic Reach

Indiana-based 1st Source serves customers across 17 counties in Michigan and its home state.

Operations

The firm operates nearly 80 banking center locations across Indiana and Michigan. 1st Source's Specialty Finance Group boasts more than 20 locations that offer specialized financing for new and used private and cargo aircraft automobiles and light trucks for leasing and rental agencies medium and heavy duty trucks and construction and environmental equipment.

Sales and Marketing

To keep its name in front of existing and potential customers 1st Source spends millions on advertising. In fiscal 2013 the firm spent about $4.9 million on ads up from 2012's $4.2 million.

Financial Performance

Fiscal 2013's revenue slipped some 2% –or $6.5 million –to $256.8 million from $263.3 million in 2012. 1st Source points to both a drop in mortgage banking income due to lower loan production volumes and a decrease in investment securities for the overall decline. During the reporting period net income increased some 11% to $54.9 million vs. 2012's $49.6 million thanks to drops in interest and non-interest expenses. Cash flow decreased to $86.9 million as compared to $93.2 million in 2012 due in part to a decline in interest receivables and asset changes.

Strategy

The company offers mutual funds through an agreement with Wasatch Advisors which has owned its 1st Source Monogram family of funds (now the Wasatch - 1st Source Funds) since 2008. Bank subsidiary 1st Source Insurance sells corporate and personal property/casualty coverage and group and individual life and health insurance.

1st Source has expanded its aircraft leasing business which accounts for the largest portion of its specialty finance activities into Brazil and Mexico and may be looking to expand into other selected markets in South America.

EXECUTIVES

President and Chief Operating Officer Specialty Finance Group 1st Source Bank, Allen R. Qualey, age 62, $263,654 total compensation
Chairman and CEO, Christopher J. (Chris) Murphy, age 68, $695,000 total compensation
EVP 1st Source Bank, Steven J. Wessell, age 65, $209,070 total compensation
EVP Administration Secretary and General Counsel, John B. Griffith, age 57, $311,000 total compensation
EVP CFO and Treasurer, Andrea G. Short, age 52, $220,000 total compensation
President, James R. Seitz, age 62
EVP and Chief Credit Officer 1st Source Bank, Jeffrey L. Buhr, $226,565 total compensation
Vice President Senior Loan Workout Officer, Richard (Dick) Rozenboom

Vice President, John Lutz
Assistant Vice President And Relationship Manager, Connie Lemler
Assistant Vice President Lease Accounting Manager, Joe Malinowski
Vice President, David (Dave) Wertz
Vice Chairman, Wellington D. (Duke) Jones, age 70
Auditors: BKD LLP

LOCATIONS

HQ: 1st Source Corp.
  100 North Michigan Street, South Bend, IN 46601
Phone: 574 235-2000
Web: www.1stsource.com

PRODUCTS/OPERATIONS

2013 Sales

	$ mil.	% of total
Interest		
Loans & leases	161	63
Investment securities taxable	14	6
Investment securities tax-exempt	4	1
Non-interest		
Trust fees	17	8
Equipment rental income	16	6
Service charges on deposits accounts	9	4
Debit card income	8	3
Mortgage banking income	5	2
Insurance commissions	5	2
Other	14	5
Total	**256**	**100**

Selected Subsidiaries

1st Source Bank
  1st Source Commercial Aircraft Leasing
  1st Source Corporation Investment Advisors Inc.
  1st Source Insurance Inc.
  1st Source Specialty Finance Inc.
  Michigan Transportation Finance Corporation
  SFG Aircraft Inc.
  SFG Equipment Leasing Corporation I
1st Source Funding LLC
1st Source Intermediate Holding LLC
1st Source Leasing Inc.
1st Source Master Trust

COMPETITORS

Bank of America	MainSource Financial
Fifth Third	Old National Bancorp
Huntington Bancshares	PNC Financial
JPMorgan Chase	U.S. Bancorp
KeyCorp	Wells Fargo

HISTORICAL FINANCIALS

Company Type: Public

Income Statement

FYE: December 31

	ASSETS ($ mil.)	NET INCOME ($ mil.)	INCOME AS % OF ASSETS	EMPLOYEES
12/14	4,829	58	1.2%	1,100
12/13	4,722	54	1.2%	1,100
12/12	4,550	49	1.1%	1,180
12/11	4,374	48	1.1%	1,160
12/10	4,445	41	0.9%	1,160
Annual Growth	**2.1%**	**8.9%**	**—**	**(1.3%)**

2014 Year-End Financials

Debt ratio: 1.58%	No. of shares (mil.): 26
Return on equity: 9.68%	Dividends
Cash ($ mil.): 66	Yield: 2.2%
Current ratio: —	Payout: 32.6%
Long-term debt ($ mil.): —	Market value ($ mil.): 901

	STOCK PRICE ($) FY Close	P/E High/Low	PER SHARE ($) Earnings	Dividends	Book Value
12/14	34.31	16 13	2.17	0.71	23.41
12/13	31.94	16 11	2.03	0.68	21.88
12/12	22.09	14 11	1.84	0.66	20.95
12/11	25.33	14 10	1.78	0.58	19.67
12/10	20.24	19 13	1.10	0.61	18.29
Annual Growth	**14.1%**	**— —**	**18.6%**	**3.9%**	**6.4%**

3M Co

Loath to be stuck on one thing 3M makes everything from tape to high-tech security gear. The diversified company makes products through five operating segments: Industrial; Safety and Graphics; Electronics and Energy; Health Care; and Consumer. Well-known brands include Post-it notes Scotch tapes Scotchgard fabric protectors Scotch-Brite scouring pads and Filtrete home air filters. 3M sells products directly to users and through numerous wholesalers retailers distributors and dealers worldwide. Industrial its largest segment accounted for about 34% of 3M's total revenues in 2014.

HISTORY

Five businessmen in Two Harbors Minnesota founded Minnesota Mining and Manufacturing (3M) in 1902 to sell corundum to grinding-wheel manufacturers. The company soon needed to raise working capital. Co-founder John Dwan offered his friend Edgar Ober 60% of 3M's stock. Ober persuaded Lucius Ordway VP of a plumbing business to help underwrite 3M. In 1905 the two took over the company and moved it to Duluth.

In 1907 future CEO William McKnight joined 3M as a bookkeeper. Three years later the plant moved to St. Paul. The board of directors declared a dividend to shareholders in the last quarter of 1916 and 3M hasn't missed a dividend since. The next two products 3M developed —Scotch-brand masking tape (1925) and Scotch-brand cellophane tape (1930) —assured its future.

McKnight introduced one of the first employee pension plans in 1931 and in the late 1940s he implemented a vertical management structure. 3M introduced the first commercially viable magnetic recording tape in 1947.

In 1950 after a decade of work and $1 million in development costs 3M employee Carl Miller completed the Thermo-Fax copying machine which was the foundation of 3M's duplicating division.

Products in the 1960s included 3M's dry-silver microfilm photographic products carbonless papers overhead projection systems and medical and dental products. The company moved into pharmaceuticals radiology energy control and office markets in the 1970s and 1980s.

A 3M scientist developed Post-it Notes (1980) because he wanted to attach page markers to his church hymnal. Recalling that a colleague had developed an adhesive that wasn't very sticky he brushed some on paper and began a product line that now generates hundreds of millions of dollars each year.

In 1990 the company bought sponge maker O-Cel-O. But not all of its inventions have brought 3M good news. In 1995 along with fellow silicone breast-implant makers Baxter International and

Bristol-Myers Squibb it agreed to settle thousands of personal-injury claims related to implants. The companies paid an average of $26000 per claim.

3M spun off its low-profit imaging and data-storage businesses in 1996 as Imation Corp. and closed its audiotape and videotape businesses. The next year 3M sold its National Advertising billboard business to Infinity Outdoor for $1 billion and its Media Network unit (a printer of advertising inserts) to Time Warner.

The company created the 3M Nexcare brand for its line of first-aid and home health products in 1998. To regain earnings growth 3M closed about 10% of its plants in the US and abroad; it also discontinued unprofitable product lines. The next year 3M sold its heart-surgery-equipment health care unit to Japan's Terumo and its Eastern Heights Bank subsidiary to Norwest Bank of Minnesota. It also bought out Hoechst AG's 46% stake in Dyneon LLC a fluorine elastomer joint venture between the two companies.

3M bought Polaroid's Technical Polarizer and Display Films business and a controlling stake in Germany-based Quante AG (telecom systems) in 2000. In addition the company decided to halt the manufacture of many of its Scotchgard-brand repellent products due to research revealing that one of the compounds (perfluorooctane sulfonate) used in the manufacturing process is "persistent and pervasive" in the environment and in people's bloodstreams. As 2000 drew to a close 3M named GE executive James McNerney to succeed L. D. DeSimone as its chairman and CEO. With the sale of Eastern Heights and several health care businesses (including its cardiovascular systems unit) 3M was rewarded with its second-best financial performance in 14 years.

3M then bought Robinson Nugent (electronic connectors) and MicroTouch Systems (touch screens) in 2001. It also announced plans to cut 6000 jobs and authorized a stock buy-back program of up to $2.5 billion.

The company changed its legal name from Minnesota Mining and Manufacturing Company to 3M Company that year. Also in 2002 3M restructured its business segments around end uses rather than products or raw materials. So the Health Care segment encompassed everything from transdermal skin patches to software for hospital coding and classification. Similarly the Consumer and Office Business unit became responsible for Post-its O-Cel-O sponges wood-finishing materials and air conditioner filters. By the end of that year the company had cut more than 8500 jobs 11% of its total workforce.

Nevertheless a strong year in 2003 emboldened the company to look to expand. 3M closed a deal to buy fellow Minnesota resident HighJump Software a maker of supply chain software for businesses in February 2004. CEO McNerney left 3M in 2005 to join Boeing in the same capacity and was replaced by George Buckley formerly of the Brunswick Corporation.

That year the company made a billion-dollar acquisition of liquid filtration producer CUNO. 3M's own filtration products business —primarily air filters —amounted to more than $1 billion in annual sales before the deal and the deal added nearly half that. (3M eventually changed CUNO's name to 3M Purification.)

The company signaled a new strategic direction in 2006 when it broke up its pharmaceutical unit along geographic lines and sold it in pieces. In total 3M got $2.1 billion for the sale of its pharmaceutical operations. The next year it sold HighJump Software. High-tech venture capital firm Battery Ventures bought HighJump to set it up as a stand-alone company.

The company then ran through another string of acquisitions in 2007 buying companies such as

Unifam Lingualcare Innovative Paper Technologies and Diamond Productions.

Its 2008 acquisition of protection products maker Aearo Technologies helped 3M's sales growth in the area of safety security and protection services. It added to the unit with the purchase (through its 3M Canada subsidiary) of Toronto-based MTI PolyFab which makes thermal and acoustic insulation for aerospace products. 3M also capitalized on its purchase of Beiersdorf subsidiary Futuro which makes medical products such as wraps elastic bandages and compression hosiery.

3M made two moves into the high-tech security field in 2010. The company acquired Cogent Inc. for $943 million. Known as Cogent Systems the firm provides finger palm face and iris biometric systems for governments law enforcement agencies and commercial enterprises. 3M also acquired Attenti Ltd. an Israeli manufacturer of people-tracking technology for $230 million. Attenti makes remote monitoring devices to track people awaiting trial or on probation as well as for elder-care facilities to monitor patient safety.

The company expanded its consumer and office business line in 2010 by acquiring a majority stake in Japanese company A-One the top office label brand in Asia and the second-largest label business worldwide. It also acquired Alpha Beta Enterprise a manufacturer of box sealing tape and masking tape headquartered in Taiwan. Both acquisitions will expand 3M's presence in the global packaging market.

Also in 2010 3M acquired J.R. Phoenix Ltd. a manufacturer of hand hygiene and skin care products for health care and professional use. The majority of J.R. Phoenix products are sold under the Laura Line brand in Canada. The deal expanded 3M's line of hand hygiene skin care products to the healthcare market in Canada. The company also acquired UK-based Dailys Ltd. a global supplier of non-woven disposable chemical protective coveralls for industrial use.

The company made several acquisitions in 2010 including Minnesota-based Arizant which manufactures forced-air warming garments designed to prevent hypothermia in surgical settings a growing international market estimated at some $1 billion per year.

3M completed nine acquisitions in 2011 that totaled $649 million including the do-it-yourself unit and professional division of France's GPI Group a manufacturer and marketer of home improvement products such as tapes hooks insulation and floor protection products. The deal boosts 3M's presence in Western Europe. It also added to its growing Industrial and Transportation segment by acquiring a majority stake in Switzerland-based Winterthur Technology Group an international supplier of precision grinding technologies that makes grinding tools used in the aircraft automotive industrial and steel industries.

Back in the US it acquired Florida-based Nida-Core a manufacturer of structural honeycomb core and fiber-reinforced foam core materials and Nida-Core's French affiliate Structiso SARL. The acquisition allows 3M's Engineered Products and Solutions department to build on its composite and engineered materials product portfolio.

In a related deal in 2012 3M acquired Maryland-based CodeRyte which provides clinical natural language processing (NLP) technology and computer-assisted coding for healthcare outpatient providers. Terms of the sale were not disclosed. 3M will apply CodeRyte's NLP technology to its new 3M 360 Encompass system used by its 3M Health Information Systems division for clinical documentation and coding workflows. More than 5000 hospitals worldwide use 3M's coding for patient data for measurement and reimbursement purposes.

The 3M system also addresses data problems resulting from health care reform requirements.

In an effort to broaden its global presence in office education and consumer products in 2012 3M acquired the Office and Consumer Products business of Avery Dennison Corp. for $550 million.

Continuing a quest for technology buys on 2012 3M acquired the Federal Signal Technologies Group (FSTech) from Federal Signal Corp. for $110 million in cash. FSTech focuses on hardware and software services for the $3 billion electronic tolling industry. The business also complements offerings from 3M's Traffic Safety Systems Division.

Growing its ceramics portfolio in 2012 it also bought advanced technical ceramics producer Ceradyne for $860 million. The deal adds Ceradyne's advanced ceramics technologies portfolio to its own diversified product line.

EXECUTIVES

Executive Vice President Health Care Business, Brad Sauer

Senior Vice President Corporate Supply Chain Operations, John (Jack) Woodworth

EVP Safety and Graphics Business Group, Frank R. Little

Chairman President and CEO, Inge G. Thulin, age 62, $1,392,560 total compensation

EVP Health Care Business Group, Joaquin Delgado, age 55, $467,016 total compensation

EVP International Operations, Hak Cheol (H. C.) Shin, age 58, $765,496 total compensation

SVP Marketing and Sales, Jesse G. Singh

EVP Electronics and Energy Business Group, Michael A. Kelly, age 59, $550,950 total compensation

SVP Business Transformation and Information Technology, Julie L. Bushman, $599,029 total compensation

SVP Business Transformation Americas, James L. (Jim) Bauman

EVP Industrial Business Group, Michael F. Roman

SVP and CFO, Nicholas C. Gangestad, age 50, $449,493 total compensation

EVP Consumer, Michael G. Vale, age 49, $559,971 total compensation

SVP Research and Development and CTO, Ashish K. Khandpur

Senior Vice President Global Research, Tom Anastasio

Vice President, Patrick (Paddy) Deconinck

National Sales Manager, John (Jack) Schiltgen

National Sales Manager, Jim Stevens

Vice President Finance International and Staff Information technology, Ippocratis Vrohidis

Vice President Research and Development 3m Infection Prevention Division, Ann Meitz

Vice President Traffic Safety Systems Division, Atul Shukla

National Account Manager, Curt Goswick

Product Devpt Engineer, Gregg Jager

Vice President New Market Development, Patrick (Paddy) Hiner

Vice President Finance and Human Resources, Philip Hanson

National Sales Manager, Max Miller

Vice President Finance and Human Resources, Jenny Boxall

Vice President Large Store Finance, Fred Richards

Vice President Human Resources, Kathleen Rossette

Vice President Procurement, Keith P Weber

Vice President Information Technology Management Information Systems, Steve Carlson

National Sales Manager, Jay Reese

Vice President Sales and Marketing North America, David (Dave) Cairns

Vice President of Quality, Dan Tenney

Vice President of Business Development, Richard (Dick) Nimer
National Account Manager, Rick Bennett
Vice President Global Marketing Critical and Chronic Care Solutions Division, Leslie McDonnell
Vice President of Sales, Paul Drews
National Accounts Manager, Mark Ritt
Vice President Digital Systems Technology, David (Dave) Frazee
Executive Vice President Corporate Marketing, Michael (Mel) Macdonald
Vice President and General Manager of Office Supplies Division, Bill Smith
Vice President and Associate General Counsel, Ann Marie Hanrahan
Senior Vice President Marketing, Douglas Michael
Division Vice President 3M Optical Systems, Ty Silberhorn
National Account Manager, Christian Rudeen
Vice President, Charles M (Chas) Byrne
Vice President Engineering, Hector Dalton
Vice President Mobile Interactive Solutions Division, Mark Colin
Vice President International, Jim Walsh
Vice President Hearing Conservation Products, Brian Myers
Vice President Sales, Tim Mcginnis
Vice President Operations, Stuart Zerneri
Vice President Of Us Sales, Dan Simenc
Vice President Investor Relations and Corporate Communications, Dan Mcintyre
Vice President Personal Care, Debra Rechtenwald
Vice President Technical Services and Information Technology, Ronen Shraga
Vice President Of Marketing, Sharon Cohen
Vice President Internal Audit, Dave Werpy
Vice President of Operations, Martin (Marti) Barila
Vice President and General Manager Corrosion Protection Products, Paiul Acito
Vice President Marketing, Peter (Pete) Fritz
National Account Manager, Brian Yetter
Vice President Customer Service, Angel Zimmerman
Market Vice President For Automotive, Steve Deb Schreiner
Vice President Research and Development, James (Jamie) Sax
National Account Manager, Adam Shaw
Vice President and General Manager of Electrical Markets Division, Steece Paul
Vice President Information Technology Operations, Don Ashton
National Sales Manager, John Angelo
National Account Manager, Oscar Johnson
Vice President Global Sustainability, Gayle Schueller
National Account Manager, Bob Moris
Vice President 3M Abrasive Systems Division, Chris Holmes
National Account Manager, Bart Rasmussen
Vice President Quality Assurance And Food Safety, David Schutt
National Sales Manager, John Sedwitz
National Sales Manager 3M Personal Safety Division, Scott Helterbrand
Finance Vice President, Tom Pepinski
Vice President Corporate Development and Marketing, Gokhan Kuruc
National Accounts Manager, Mike Savage
Vice President Implementations, George Moon
National Sales Manager, Chris Decolli
Vice President Environmental Health and Safety Operations, Jean Sweeney
Vice President, Dave Davidson
National Sales Manager, Scott McConnell
Vice President 3M Supply Chain Business Transformation, Chuck Byrne
National Sales Manager Home Environment Markets Division, Jim Schmidt

Vice President Inhalation And Conventional Drug Delivery, Marcello Napol
Senior Vice President Operations Redmond, A Dubner
Vice President Information Technology, Stefanie T Kittelson
Vice President Human Resources International Operations, Marlene McGrath
Vice President, Mare Baracco
Vice President Engineering and Manufacturing, Billy Roberts
Division Vice President 3M Electrical Markets Division, Paul D Steece
Vice President of Engineering, Terry Boczek
Senior Vice President LEGAL Affairs and General COUNSEL, Ivan Fong
Abm, Vincent Clark
Board Member, Ray Weber
Secretary Office of Sustainability, Sue Wilson
Abm, Pat Meifert
Board Member, Aaron Volkart
Board Member, Frederick (Fred) Palensky
Auditors: PricewaterhouseCoopers LLP

LOCATIONS

HQ: 3M Co
3M Center, St. Paul, MN 55144
Phone: 651 733-1110   Fax: 651 733-9973
Web: www.3M.com

2014 Sales

	% of total
US	37
Asia/Pacific	30
Europe Africa & Middle East	23
Latin America & Canada	10
Total	100

PRODUCTS/OPERATIONS

2014 Sales

	$ mil.	% of total
Industrial	10,990	34
Safety & Graphics	5,732	18
Electronics & Energy	5,604	17
Health Care	5,572	17
Consumer	4,523	14
Corporate	4	-
Adjustments	(604)	-
Total	31,821	100

Selected Segments and Products

Industrial and Transportation
  Automotive aftermarket products
  Automotive products
  Closures for disposable diapers
  Coated and nonwoven abrasives
  Films
  Filtration products
  Specialty adhesives
  Tapes
Health Care
  Dental products
  Drug delivery systems
  Health information systems
  Infection prevention
  Medical and surgical supplies
  Microbiology products
  Skin health products
Safety Security and Protection
  Commercial cleaning products
  Consumer safety products
  Corrosion protection products
  Floor matting
  Occupational health and safety products
  Safety and security products
  Track and trace products
Consumer and Office
  Carpet and fabric protectors
  Commercial cleaning products
  Fabric protectors (Scotchgard)
  High-performance cloth (Scotch-Brite)
  Home-improvement products
  Repositionable notes (Post-it)
  Scour pads (Scotch-Brite)
  Sponges (O-Cel-O)
  Tape (Scotch)
Display and Graphics
  Commercial graphics systems
  Optical films for electronic display
  Specialty film and media products
  Traffic control materials
Electro and Communications
  Insulating and splicing products for electronics telecommunications and electrical industries
  Packaging and interconnection devices

Selected Mergers and Acquisitions

COMPETITORS

ACCO Brands	Honeywell
BASF SE	International
Bayer AG	Illinois Tool Works
Beiersdorf	Johnson & Johnson
Bostik	Kimberly-Clark
Carlisle Companies	RPM International
Corning	Ricoh Company
Danaher	S.C. Johnson
DuPont	Sealed Air Corp.
GE	Sika
H.B. Fuller	Tyco
Henkel	

HISTORICAL FINANCIALS

Company Type: Public

Income Statement

FYE: December 31

	REVENUE ($ mil.)	NET INCOME ($ mil.)	NET PROFIT MARGIN	EMPLOYEES
12/15	30,274	4,833	16.0%	89,446
12/14	31,821	4,956	15.6%	89,800
12/13	30,871	4,659	15.1%	88,667
12/12	29,904	4,444	14.9%	87,677
12/11	29,611	4,283	14.5%	84,198
Annual Growth	0.6%	3.1%	—	1.5%

2015 Year-End Financials

Debt ratio: 33.14%
Return on equity: 38.95%
Cash ($ mil.): 1,798
Current ratio: 1.54
Long-term debt ($ mil.): 8,799

No. of shares (mil.): 609
Dividends
  Yield: 2.7%
  Payout: 52.9%
Market value ($ mil.): 91,789

	STOCK PRICE ($) FY Close	P/E High/Low	PER SHARE ($) Earnings	Dividends	Book Value
12/15	150.64	22 18	7.58	4.10	19.21
12/14	164.32	22 16	7.49	3.42	20.64
12/13	140.25	20 14	6.72	2.54	26.39
12/12	92.85	15 13	6.32	2.36	25.58
12/11	81.73	16 12	5.96	2.20	22.19
Annual Growth	16.5%	— —	6.2%	16.8%	(3.5%)

A-Mark Precious Metals, Inc

LOCATIONS

HQ: A-Mark Precious Metals, Inc
429 Santa Monica Blvd., Suite 230, Santa Monica, CA 90401
Phone: 310 587-1477
Web: www.amark.com

HISTORICAL FINANCIALS

Company Type: Public

Income Statement

FYE: June 30

	REVENUE ($ mil.)	NET INCOME ($ mil.)	NET PROFIT MARGIN	EMPLOYEES
06/15	6,070	7	0.1%	52
06/14	5,979	8	0.1%	55
06/13	7,247	12	0.2%	31
06/12	7,782	10	0.1%	—
06/11	6,988	12	0.2%	—
Annual Growth	(3.5%)	(13.6%)	—	—

2015 Year-End Financials

Debt ratio: 45.11%	No. of shares (mil.): 6
Return on equity: 13.38%	Dividends
Cash ($ mil.): 20	Yield: 0.9%
Current ratio: 1.16	Payout: 11.6%
Long-term debt ($ mil.): —	Market value ($ mil.): 73

	STOCK PRICE ($) FY Close	P/E High/Low		PER SHARE ($) Earnings	Dividends	Book Value
06/15	10.47	12	9	1.00	0.10	8.02
06/14	11.16	13	10	1.09	0.00	7.10
Annual Growth	(1.6%)	—	—	(2.1%)	—	3.1%

Abbott Laboratories

Filling baby bottles and treating disease... these are the habits of Abbott. Abbott Laboratories is a top health care products manufacturer. Its nutritional products division makes such well-known brands as Similac infant formula and the Ensure line of nutrition supplements while its drug division sells branded generic medicines (such as antibiotics and gastroenterology medicines) in international markets. The company also makes diagnostic instruments (including tests and assays) vascular medical devices such as its Xience drug-eluting stents and the FreeStyle diabetes care line as well as eye care products. Abbott spun off its nongeneric pharmaceutical operations into AbbVie in 2013.

Operations

After more than a year of planning Abbott separated its medical and pharmaceutical operations in January 2013 by distributing shares of the newly public AbbVie to its shareholders. Flatly put the split separated Abbott's stable business from its riskier operations: While the AbbVie pharma operations accounted for roughly 45% of Abbott's revenues its R&D work was inherently more expensive and riskier and a number of its commercial products face patent expiration over the next few years.

The Abbott name stuck with the businesses that previously made up its diversified medical products division including its nutritional branded generic pharmaceutical diagnostic and vascular businesses (the new operating units). Each unit previously accounted for about 10% to 15% of the company's revenues. The Nutritionals business is the largest operating segment (accounting for 35% of sales) following the AbbVie spinoff. Diagnostic Products comes in second representing 23% of sales while the branded generic pharmaceuticals (now called Established Pharmaceutical) and Vascular segments tie for third at 15% each.

Drug-coated stent Xience is one of the company's top products and key to its growth initia-

tives. The Vascular segment makes other devices for coronary endovascular vessel closure and structural heart procedures. Meanwhile the Diagnostic segment's products include point-of-care tests molecular diagnostic products and information management systems for diagnostic laboratories.

Abbott also makes diabetic testing products through its Abbott Diabetes Care unit and it makes equipment for cataract and vision correction procedures (including LASIK equipment) through its Abbott Medical Optics subsidiary.

Geographic Reach

Abbott's products are sold in more than 150 countries. The company earns about 30% of revenues in the domestic market 40% in emerging markets (especially Brazil China India and Russia) and 30% in non-US developed markets (including Canada Western Europe Japan and Australia).

Sales and Marketing

Abbott conducts distribution operations both from its own distribution centers and from third-party distribution partners. Established pharmaceutical and nutritional customers include health care organizations wholesalers pharmacies retailers government agencies and third-party distribution entities. Diagnostic and vascular products are sold to blood banks hospitals physicians plasma protein therapeutic companies and commercial laboratories.

Financial Performance

In the face of multiple challenges Abbott has been standing strong in the global business market in recent years. However in 2013 revenue decreased by 45% from $39 billion to $21.8 billion and decreased another 7% in 2014 to $20 billion; both years' declines were largely due to the AbbVie spinoff and the loss of the unit's income from the books. Additionally the group lowered prices in the Vascular segment as a result of pricing pressures in the US and other major markets.

Net income fell 11% to $2.3 billion in 2014 due to higher provisions for taxes as well as an expense of $18.3 million to extinguish debt related to the company's acquisition of CFR Pharmaceuticals that year.

Cash flow from operations increased 11% to $3.7 billion in 2014 as operating results improved and the company paid out lower cash contributions to pension plans. Other factors such as cash generated from income taxes and less cash used in trade accounts payable also contributed to the rise.

StrategyAcross the years Abbott has made acquisitions and strategic alliances (in fields including research and marketing) to bolster its offerings and its geographic presence. It focuses on building country-specific portfolios to best meet the needs of each nation. For example the company has more than 300 active branded generic development projects for emerging markets. In 2014 Abbott spent some $1.3 billion on research to discover and develop new products and processes or improve on existing products and processes. (That figure was down from the $1.4 billion and $1.5 billion it spent in 2013 and 2012 respectively.)

However its biggest restructuring move was spinning off its branded pharmaceutical operations as AbbVie. AbbVie took the potential rewards of discovering a blockbuster drug but also the high risk and costs of R&D.

In the R&D realm Abbott is hard at work on developing next-generation Xience products that include Xience nano a version of the product for use in small vessels and Xience PRIME a next-generation version Xience being tested in a range of sizes including small vessel and long lengths. In addition Abbott has steadily grown its medical device offerings for other therapeutic applications.

Other Vascular pipeline products include Absorb the first drug eluting bioresorbable vascular scaffold device for the treatment of coronary artery

disease; and MitraClip a device designed to treat mitral regurgitation.

Abbott is also widening its offering of clinical diagnostics tools including the introduction of laboratory software to boost diagnostic data management capabilities. To boost its point-of-care diagnostics offerings Abbott announced plans to buy Alere for $5.8 billion in early 2016. Alere makes tests for cancers cardiovascular disease and infections such as HIV and malaria among others.

Product development has also led to new nutritional product launches such as new Ensure Complete shakes and Perfectly Simple (gluten and preservative-free) ZonePerfect protein bars. To further bolster the nutritional business Abbott built a new manufacturing plant in Ohio and opened its first nutritional R&D center in India.

Other new or development products include cataract removal system TECNIS-1 Monofocal IOL and TECNIS Multifocal intraocular lenses (which restore vision to people with cataracts) the latter of which is available in the US.

In 2015 Abbott sold its non-US developed markets specialty and branded generics operations to Mylan. The sale included a portfolio of more than 100 pharmaceutical products in markets including Europe Japan Canada Australia and New Zealand; upon closing of the deal Abbott received a 21% stake in the combined company. The company also sold its animal health business to Zoetis in early 2015.

Mergers and Acquisitions

The company struck two smaller deals in 2013: Abbott purchased IDEV Technologies a developer of radiology and surgery-related peripheral devices for some $310 million to grow in the peripheral technology market. It also acquired OptiMedica for some $250 million to enter the laser cataract surgery market.

The spree continued in 2014 when the company doubled its operations in Latin America and upped its commitment to fast-growing markets by paying around $3 billion including debt for CFR Pharmaceuticals. The Chile-based branded-pharmaceutical maker has manufacturing facilities in Chile Colombia Peru and Argentina. Later that year Abbott acquired a controlling stake of Russian pharmaceutical maker Veropharm. The $315 million deal added manufacturing capabilities in Russia and broadened Abbott's presence in that country. At year-end Abbott bought private medical device company Topera ($250 million) a developer of electrophysiology technologies to detect and treat atrial fibrillation.

In 2015 Abbott bought the rest of Tendyne Holdings that it didn't already own for $225 million; it also agreed to buy Cephea Valve Technologies. Both of those medical device firm acquisitions will boost Abbott's portfolio of mitral valve replacement therapies.

HISTORY

Dr. Wallace Abbott started making his dosimetric granule (a pill that supplied uniform quantities of drugs) at his home outside Chicago in 1888. Aggressive marketing earned Abbott the American Medical Association's criticism though much of the medical profession supported him.

During WWI Abbott scientists synthesized anesthetics previously available only from Germany. Abbott improved its research capacity in 1922 by buying Dermatological Research Laboratories; in 1928 it bought John T. Milliken and its well-trained sales force. Abbott went public in 1929.

Salesman DeWitt Clough became president in 1933. International operations began in the mid-1930s with branches in Argentina Brazil Cuba Mexico and the UK.

Abbott was integral to the WWII effort; the US made only 28 pounds of penicillin in 1943 before the company began to ratchet up production. Consumer infant and nutritional products (such as Selsun Blue shampoo Murine eye drops and Similac formula) joined the roster in the 1960s. The FDA banned Abbott's artificial sweetener Sucaryl in 1970 saying it might be carcinogenic and in 1971 millions of intravenous solutions were recalled following contamination deaths.

Robert Schoellhorn became CEO in 1979; profits increased but research and development was cut. In the 1980s Abbott began selling Japanese-developed pharmaceuticals in the US.

EXECUTIVES

Vice President Internal Audit, Robert Funck
Vice President Diagnostic Commercial Operations Europe Africa and Middle East, Jaime Contreras
Chairman and CEO, Miles D. White, age 60, $1,973,077 total compensation
EVP Finance and CFO, Thomas C. (Tom) Freyman, age 61, $1,012,604 total compensation
EVP Human Resources, Stephen R. (Steve) Fussell, age 58, $454,689 total compensation
EVP Ventures, John M. Capek, age 53, $696,807 total compensation
EVP Nutritional Products, John C. Landgraf, age 63, $743,269 total compensation
EVP Global Commercial Operations Abbott Nutrition, Heather L. Mason, age 55
EVP Corporate Development, Richard W. Ashley, age 72, $629,532 total compensation
EVP Established Pharmaceuticals, Michael J. Warmuth, age 53
SVP International Nutrition, J. Scott White, age 46
EVP Medical Devices, Robert B. Ford
EVP Diagnostic Products, Brian J. Blaser, age 50, $690,000 total compensation
EVP General Counsel and Secretary, Hubert L. Allen, $650,000 total compensation
Senior Non IT Management Chief Executive Officer Chief Financial Officer Vice President Directo, Randi Pickens
Vice President Capital Sales and Marketing, Rick Green
Executive Vice President Insurance Information technology, Pamela S (Pam) Crawford
Vice President Regulatory Affairs, Evelyn Lopez
Divisional Vice President Pharma Research And Development, Leanna Walther
Vice President Government Affairs, Makoto Tamura
Regional Vice President, Martin (Marti) Eaves
Senior Vice President, Ann Long
Divisional Vice President, Mark Wheeler
Division Vice President Human Resources, Deborah (Deb) Billig
Medical Director, Julia Maurer
Vice President Of Industry Relations, Pam Norton
Senior Vice President, Tammy Berzin
National Sales Manager, Joao Norberto
Legal Secretary, Priscilla Macaldo
National Sales Manager, John (Jack) Rankin
Dvp Compensation, Mark Fanning
National Account Manager, Kim Earley
DVP Marketing, Lisa Rose
Medical Director, David Carter
Divisional Vice President Marketing, Renaud Gabay
Divisional Vice President International Marketing, Gilles Lachkar
Divisional Vice President of Marketing, Elana Gold
Vice President Marketing Therapeutic Nutrition Division, Steve Robinson
National Sales Manager, Osama Abed
National Account Manager, Riley Wilson
Vice President Global Marketing, Ann Nicholson
Divisional Vice President, Andy Brookes
DVP Global Marketing, Scott Lance

Senior Vice President Abbott Nutrition Products Division, Donald M (Don) Patton
Vice President, Gregor Eibes
Medical Director, Thomas Podsadecki
Senior Vice President Central Region, Pamela Switalski
Divisional Vice President, Brian Wentworth
Senior Management (Senior Vice President General Manager Director), Jamie Dobson
Divisional Vice President Global, Ulises Carrillo
Associate Medical Director, Ann Eldred
Vice President, Brian Ford
National Accounts Manager, Brian Fellows
Medical Director, Refaat Hegazi
Senior Vice President, Maureen Snider
Vice President Sales Training And Development, Randee Stelman
DVP International Quality, Volker Watschke
Medical Director, Lyra Xie
Vice President Compliance, Susan Slane
Medical Director, Beth McQuiston
National Sales Manager, Noel Albis
Group Vice President, Tiffany Cincotta
Senior Vice President, Curtis Michols
Vice President International Sales And Marketing, Jerry Tu
National Sales Manager EPD, Raymond Lazaro
Division Vice President Pediatric Commercial Operations, Rich Schaefer
Divisional Vice President Ww Regulatory Affairs, Brian Kersten
National Account Manager, Terry Young
Divisional Vice President Abbott Informatics Solutions, Dave Champagne
Vice President Marketing And Human Resources, Jennifer Pestikas
National Account Manager, Elizabeth Ulrich
Medical Director, Roger Trinh
Medical Director, Gwendolyn Janssen
Divisional Vice President Coronary Sales, Bill Davis
National Sales Manager EPD, Ashraf Naguib
Vice President of Marketing, Rick Kozloski
National Sales Manager AMO Division Turkey, Harun Belen
Vice President US Sales Electrophysiology Division, Shane Brown
Divisional Vice President of Operations, Anton Herbig
CVP and Chief Economist, Gene Huang
Divisional Vice President and Assistant Treasurer, Benjamin (Ben) Oosterbaan
Area Treasurer, Quintin Noble
Secretary, Meri Marijani
Secretary, Nancy Gonzalez
Secretary and Operations supervisor, Tracy Luo
Auditors: Ernst & Young LLP

LOCATIONS

HQ: Abbott Laboratories
100 Abbott Park Road, Abbott Park, IL 60064-6400
Phone: 224 667-6100
Web: www.abbott.com

2014 Sales

	$ mil.	% of total
US	6,123	30
China	1,321	7
India	1,009	5
Germany	978	5
Japan	968	5
The Netherlands	788	4
Switzerland	707	3
Russia	536	3
Brazil	508	3
France	488	2
Canada	462	2
UK	447	2
Italy	436	2
Spain	310	2
Other countries	5,166	25
Total	**20,247**	**100**

PRODUCTS/OPERATIONS

2014 Sales

	$ mil.	% of total
Nutritionals	6,953	35
Diagnostics	4,721	23
Established pharmaceuticals	3,118	15
Vascular	2,986	15
Other	2,469	12
Total	**20,247**	**100**

Selected Products

Nutritional
Alimentum (infant formula)
EAS nutritional brands
AdvantEdge (nutritional supplements)
Myoplex (nutritional supplements)
Ensure (adult nutrition)
Freego (enteral pump)
Glucerna (nutritional beverage for diabetics)
Isomil (soy-based infant formula)
Jevity (liquid food for enteral feeding)
NeoSure (infant formula)
Osmolite
Pedialyte (pediatric electrolyte solution)
PediaSure (children's nutrition)
Similac (infant formula)
Zone Perfect (nutritional bars)
Established Pharmaceuticals (branded generics)
Creon (pancreatic enzyme replacement therapy)
Duphaston (progesterone deficiency)
Klacid (macrolide antibiotic)
Diagnostic
Abbott PRISM (high-volume blood-screening system)
ARCHITECT (clinical chemistry system)
AxSYM (clinical chemistry system)
Cell-Dyn (hematology systems and reagents)
Diagnostic and screening assays
Informatics and automation solutions for lab use
i-STAT (blood analyzer)
m2000 (instrument that detects and measures infectious agents)
Vysis (genomic-based tests)
PathVysion (breast cancer diagnostic test)
UroVysion (bladder cancer)
Medical Devices (former vascular division)
Absorb (vascular scaffold)
Acculink/Accunet (carotid stent)
Asahi (coronary guidewires licensed from Asahi Intecc)
Hi-Torque Balance Middleweight (coronary guidewire licensed from Asahi Intecc)
MitraClip (valve repair)
Multi-Link 8 Multi-Link Mini Vision and Multi-Link Vision (coronary metallic stents)
Perclose (vessel closure)
StarClose (vessel closure)
Trek (balloon dilation)
Xience V Xience nano and Xience Prime (drug-eluting stents)
Voyager (balloon dilation)

Selected Acquisitions

COMPETITORS

Allergan plc	Merck
AstraZeneca	Mylan
Bard	NBTY
Baxter International	Nature's Sunshine
Bayer AG	Nestl©
Becton Dickinson	Novartis
Boston Scientific	Perrigo
Cordis	Pfizer
Danone	Ranbaxy Laboratories
Dr. Reddy's	Roche Holding
GNC	Sandoz International
GlaxoSmithKline	GmbH
Heinz	Sanofi
Herbalife Ltd.	Schiff Nutrition
Johnson & Johnson	International
LifeScan	Shionogi & Co.
Mannatech	Sun Pharmaceutical
Mead Johnson	Teva

Company Type: Public

Income Statement

FYE: December 31

	REVENUE ($ mil.)	NET INCOME ($ mil.)	NET PROFIT MARGIN	EMPLOYEES
12/14	20,247	2,284	11.3%	77,000
12/13	21,848	2,576	11.8%	69,000
12/12	39,873	5,962	15.0%	91,000
12/11	38,851	4,728	12.2%	91,000
12/10	35,166	4,626	13.2%	90,000
Annual Growth	(12.9%)	(16.2%)	—	(3.8%)

2014 Year-End Financials

Debt ratio: 19.01%	No. of shares (mil.): 1,508
Return on equity: 9.78%	Dividends
Cash ($ mil.): 4,063	Yield: 1.9%
Current ratio: 1.45	Payout: 69.2%
Long-term debt ($ mil.): 3,408	Market value ($ mil.): 67,892

	STOCK PRICE ($) FY Close	P/E High/Low	PER SHARE ($) Earnings	Dividends	Book Value
12/14	45.02	31 24	1.49	0.88	14.27
12/13	38.33	40 20	1.62	0.56	16.26
12/12	65.50	19 14	3.72	2.01	16.95
12/11	56.23	19 15	3.01	1.88	15.95
12/10	47.91	19 15	2.96	1.72	14.47
Annual Growth	(1.5%)	— —	(15.8%)	(15.4%)	(0.3%)

AbbVie Inc.

AbbVie came from Abbott but is making a life of its own. The biopharmaceutical research company was spun off from its former parent health care products maker Abbott Labs in 2013. AbbVie has seven facilities making products that are available in more than 170 countries. Its key drugs include arthritis and Crohn's disease treatment Humira; TriCor Trilipix Simcor and Niaspan for high cholesterol; HIV drugs Kaletra and Norvir; and low testosterone treatment AndroGel among others. Humira which is best known as a rheumatoid arthritis drug accounts for more than 60% of AbbVie's sales. With its main product's patent protection expiring in 2016 the R&D firm is looking for the next big thing.

IPO

Although the company filed going-public documents with the SEC it was not a standard initial public offering since it was a spinoff. AbbVie started life on its own with $4.6 billion in cash and equivalents from Abbott Labs. The market valued the company at about $54.4 billion.

Operations

AbbVie's products focus on treating conditions such as chronic autoimmune diseases (including rheumatoid arthritis psoriasis and Crohn's disease) hepatitis C HIV endometriosis thyroid disease Parkinson's disease low testosterone and complications from chronic kidney disease and cystic fibrosis. The company has a pipeline of promising new medications: It has more than 30 compounds in phase 2 or phase 3 development that cover such areas as immunology liver disease oncology renal disease neurological disease and women's health.

The company has a collaboration agreement with Ablynx NV to develop ALX-0061 for the treatment of rheumatoid arthritis and systemic lupus erythemoatosus; it has a similar agreement with Galapagos NV to discover and develop commer-

cialize cystic fibrosis therapies. With Alvine Pharmaceuticals it has an agreement to develop an oral treatment (ALV003) for patients with celiac disease.

In addition to its portfolio of existing and developmental drugs AbbVie's operations include its global R&D apparatus focused on small molecule drugs and biologics and its sales marketing and distribution network delivering its products to more than 170 countries.

Geographic Reach

AbbVie collects some 45% of sales outside the US. Key foreign markets include Brazil Canada France Germany Italy Japan the Netherlands Spain and the UK. The company also has R&D facilities in Germany and China and has a stated goal of expanding in emerging markets.

The company has four R&D facilities in the US (located in Abbott Park Illinois; Chicago; Redwood City California; and Worcester Massachusetts).

Sales and Marketing

AbbVie markets its products to managed care providers including HMOs and pharmacy benefit managers (PBMs) hospitals and government agencies (including the US Department of Veterans Affairs and the Department of Defense). Its pharmaceutical products are primarily distributed in the US through independent wholesalers; to a lesser extent it also sells them directly to pharmacies and patients. Internationally AbbVie principally markets to payors physicians and state regulatory bodies.

In 2014 three wholesale distributors — McKesson Cardinal Health and AmerisourceBergen –accounted for practically all of the company's sales in the US.

AbbVie spent $665 million on advertising in 2014 up from $626 million in 2013 and $506 million in 2012.

Financial Performance

When it was a division of Abbott Labs the company generated about $18 billion in revenue annually and reported about $5 billion in earnings. Little change in sales is expected as the company continues to sell existing products and push those in development through the FDA approval process. A drop in sales of $2.5 billion is expected as patents expire though sales leaders Humira and AndroGel should pick up the slack. The company also continues to receive approval for additional uses for Humira including US and European Commission labeling for adult and pediatric Crohn's disease. Going forward AbbVie will spend about 13%-14% of sales on R&D each year.

Over the past five year the company has seen steady growth. In 2014 revenue grew 6% to $20 billion as sales of Humira remained strong both in the US and abroad (thanks largely to its approval for new indications). Other products that have performed well include Synthroid Creon and Duodopa.

Despite the revenue growth though net income fell in both 2013 and 2014. In 2014 it slipped 57% to $1.8 billion as the company paid more interest on outstanding debt. A terminated $54 billion merger with Shire also added to AbbVie's expenses that year as it ultimately agreed to pay Shire a breakup fee of about $1.6 billion.

The failed Shire merger also contributed to a decline in operating cash flow which fell 43% to $3.5 billion.

Strategy

After spending about $12 billion and two years acquiring and assimilating European and Indian pharmaceutical manufacturers and a US drug development firm Abbott cut AbbVie loose to take greater risks and hopefully pay higher dividends to investors.

As the company faces the patent expirations of many of its top sellers between 2011 and 2016

(Aluvia TriCor Niaspan Humira) having a strong R&D focus is key to AbbVie's continued success. It has more than 30 candidates in the pipeline including treatments in immunology oncology neuroscience hepatitis C chronic kidney disease and women's health. If any one of those reaches the market the risky development process will pay off for the research pharmaceuticals company. AbbVie has said that 2015 is the target for seeing its pipeline bear fruit. The company plans to keep adding to its pipeline through strategic licensing deals and partnerships.

The company is also considering acquisitions to boost its drug development stockpile. In a major move to boost its drug pipeline AbbVie bought Pharmacyclics which markets the promising cancer medication Imbruvica for $21 billion in 2015. The purchase should help lighten AbbVie's dependence on Humira and other key treatments.

It's also willing to collaborate to develop new drugs. To that end it teamed up with Alvine Pharmaceuticals for a celiac disease cure Ablynx for inflammatory disease and Galapagos NV for cystic fibrosis. All these happened in 2013. In 2014 the company entered into an agreement with Calico Life Sciences to discover and develop therapies for age-related diseases including neurodegeneration and cancer. Also that year it teamed up with Infinity Pharmaceuticals to develop duvelisib for cancer treatment.

AbbVie is also concentrating on boosting sales of Humira by expanding its share of the market and its presence in underserved markets. In 2014 Humira was given US approval for the treatment of patients with chronic genotype 1 hepatitis C virus infection.

Mergers and Acquisitions

The company intends to invest in manufacturing operations in Asia. In 2014 AbbVie acquired a small molecule active pharmaceutical ingredient (API) manufacturing facility in Singapore its first manufacturing facility in Asia; the facility both expands its global operations and increases its capacity for compounds within its immunology and oncology pipelines.

EXECUTIVES

Chairman and CEO, Richard A. (Rick) Gonzalez, age 61, $1,595,961 total compensation

EVP Business Development External Affairs and General Counsel, Laura J. Schumacher, age 52, $957,577 total compensation

EVP Commercial Operations, Carlos Alban, age 53, $844,461 total compensation

EVP and CFO, William J. Chase, age 47, $923,711 total compensation

EVP Research and Development and Chief Scientific Officer, Michael E. Severino, $503,750 total compensation

Vice President Human Resources Operations, Leanna Walther

Vice President Gm, Michael Jones

Vice President Head Of Ventures And Early Stage Collaborations, David (Dave) Donabedian

Medical Director, Hana Florian

Divisional Vice President Clinical Operations, Gillian Hodkinson

Vice President Immunology Clinical Development, John (Jack) Medich

Vice President Talent Management, Angela Lane

National Sales Manager, Scott Moore

Associate Medical Director, Roger Trinh

Vice President Finance, Kevin Buckbee

Vice President, Toni Morrell

National Sales Manager, Teresa Stotts

Medical Director, Heikki Mansikka

National Sales Manager, Marie Glenn

Vice President Information Technology Research and Development, Michael (Mel) Carlin

Vice President Drug Device, Christopher (Chris) Kurtz
Vice President Global Medical Affairs Strategy and Execution, Dominik Hochli
Vice President Heor, Tony Hebden
Vice President Licensing and Acquisitions, Tiffany Cincotta
Vice President, Tracy Baskerville
Medical Director, Peng Lu
Medical Director, Bruce Barger
Vice President Head of Licensing and Acquisitions, John (Jack) Poolos
Vice President, Keith Hendricks
Vice President Biologics Development and Manufacturing Launch, Ralph H Lambalot
Vice President Licensing and Acquisitions, David (Dave) Fishman
National Sales Manager, Randee Stelman
Vice President Business Support, Bets Lillo
Vice President Process Research And Development, Shuhong Zhang
Associate Medical Director, Stanley Wang
Medical Director Immunology, Marc Levesque
Medical Director, Justin Ricker
Vice President of Sales and Marketing, Taymar Hartman
Vice President of Manufacturing and Quality (us and Puerto Rico) Commercial Supplier Qaops, Patrick (Paddy) Kenefick
Medical Director, Boris Renjifo
Vice President DATA and STATISTICAL SCIENCES, Frank F Shen
Vice President General Manager Global, Nadia Dac
Vice President Health And Welfare Benefits, Lois Lourie
Medical Director, Yan Luo
Medical Director, Tina Antachopoulou
Vice President Med Safety Evaluation, Linda Scarazzini
Medical Director, Elisabeth Rouffiac
Medical Director, Karen Yuen
National Sales Manager, Wesley Hughes
Area Vice President, Alberto Colzi
Associate Medical Director Latinoam??rica, Leandro Castillo
Medical Director, Damian Gruca
Associate Medical Director, Jasmina Kalabic
Vice President Intellectual Property And Strategy, Johanna Corbin
Vice President Distribution And Logistics Services, Russell (Russ) Garich
National Sales Manager, Michihiro Kimura
Medical Director, David Carter
Medical Director, Suzanne Green
Medical Director, Elisa Cerri
Medical Director, Manuel Uribe-granja
National Sales Manager, Cheryl Lawrence-tarr
Medical Director Medical Safety Evaluation, Atif Abbas
Vice President Latin America, Santiago Luque
Vice President Pharmaceutical Discovery, Jim Sullivan
Vice President Us Endocrinology, Marianne Sutcliffe
Medical Director, Sameh Anis
Vice President, Tracie Haas
National Sales Manager, Ellen Kraemer
National Sales Manager, Latonya Wright
Vice President Japan Asia Pacific, Esteban Plata
Senior Vice President and Chief Scientific Officer, Kristie Bartee
Associate Medical Director Western Europe And Canada, Mark Bondin
Vice President Discovery Neuroscience Pa, James Summers
Senior Vice President And President Operations, Azita Saleki-Gerhardt
Vice President Sales and Marketing New Launches, Saeed Motahari
Medical Director Pharmacovigilance and Patient Safety, Robert (Bob) Walsh

Vice President Global Commercial And Health Communications, Greg Miley
Associate Medical Director Global Pharmacovigilance, Nataliya Kuptsova-Clarkson
Senior Manager Talent Pro Executive Vice President, Melissa (Mel) Aufmann
Senior Vice President Biologic Prod Superintendent, Eidamarie Ruiz
Vice President Internal Audit, Michael (Mel) Higgins
Vice President Compensation, Andrew (Andy) Brown
Divisional Vice President, Wulff-Erik Von Borcke
Vice President Regional Manufacturing Operations Europe, Thomas (Thom) Scheidmeir
Board Member, Marvin Bembry
Auditors: Ernst & Young LLP

LOCATIONS

HQ: AbbVie Inc.
1 North Waukegan Road, North Chicago, IL 60064-6400
Phone: 847 932-7900
Web: www.abbvie.com

2014 Sales

	$ mil.	% of total
US	10,845	54
Germany	1,035	5
The Netherlands	969	5
UK	722	4
France	584	3
Japan	581	3
Canada	551	3
Spain	534	3
Brazil	435	2
Italy	432	2
Rest of the world	3,272	16
Total	**19,960**	**100**

PRODUCTS/OPERATIONS

2014 Sales

	$ mil.	% of total
Humira	12,543	62
Androgel	932	5
Kaletra	870	4
Synagis	835	4
Lupron	778	4
Synthroid	709	4
Sevoflurane	550	3
Creon	516	3
Dyslipidemia	328	2
Duodopa	220	1
Viekira	78	-
Other	1,629	8
Total	**19,960**	**100**

COMPETITORS

Amgen	Merck
AstraZeneca	Novartis
Baxter International	Pfizer
Bayer AG	Roche Holding
Bristol-Myers Squibb	Sanofi
Eli Lilly	Teva
GlaxoSmithKline	

HISTORICAL FINANCIALS

Company Type: Public

Income Statement

FYE: December 31

	REVENUE ($ mil.)	NET INCOME ($ mil.)	NET PROFIT MARGIN	EMPLOYEES
12/14	19,960	1,774	8.9%	26,000
12/13	18,790	4,128	22.0%	25,000
12/12	18,380	5,275	28.7%	21,500
12/11	17,443	3,433	19.7%	30,000
12/10	15,637	4,177	26.7%	—
Annual Growth	**6.3%**	**(19.3%)**	**—**	**—**

2014 Year-End Financials

Debt ratio: 54.49%	No. of shares (mil.): 1,591
Return on equity: 56.91%	Dividends
Cash ($ mil.): 8,348	Yield: 2.5%
Current ratio: 1.41	Payout: 150.9%
Long-term debt ($ mil.): 10,565	Market value ($ mil.): 104,141

	STOCK PRICE ($) FY Close	P/E High/Low		PER SHARE ($) Earnings	Dividends	Book Value
12/14	65.44	63	42	1.10	1.66	1.09
12/13	52.81	21	13	2.56	1.60	2.83
Annual Growth	**5.5%**	**—**	**—**	**(19.0%)**	**0.9%**	**(21.1%)**

Advance Auto Parts Inc

Advance Auto Parts (AAP) has taken the lead in the race to become the #1 provider of automotive aftermarket parts in North America. Serving both the do-it-yourself (DIY) and professional installer markets AAP operates nearly 5300 stores under the Advance Auto Parts Autopart International (AI) Carquest and Worldpac banners in the US and Canada. Its stores carry brand-name replacement parts batteries maintenance items and automotive chemicals for individual car owners. AAP's Carquest AI and Worldpac stores cater to commercial customers including garages service stations and auto dealers. AAP acquired General Parts International in 2014.

Operations

AAP's Parts and batteries and accessories account for more than 80% of product sales revenue while chemicals and oil each make up nearly 10%. Among the brands there are nearly 3900 stores under the Advance Auto Parts banner 1125 stores under Carquest more than 110 Worldpac stores and some 210 stores operating under the Autopart International brand. In addition the company serves some 1350 independently-owned Carquest branded stores in 49 states Puerto Rico the Virgin Islands and Canada.

Geographic Reach

The auto parts chain has stores in all 50 states as well as Puerto Rico the US Virgin Islands and Canada. Florida is the company's largest market with more than 500 stores. North Carolina New York Ohio Pennsylvania and Georgia are also major markets for Advance Auto Parts each home to more than 250 stores.

Sales & Marketing

The auto parts dealer spent $96.4 million on advertising in 2014 up from $69.1 million and $83.9 million in 2013 and 2012 respectively. Advance Auto Parts builds it marketing and advertising campaigns around radio direct marketing digital and local marketing. Its "Service is our best part" campaign targets core DIY customers and emphasizes service. The company also employs Spanish-language television radio and outdoor ads to reach Latinos.

Financial Performance

AAP has enjoyed revenue growth for the past several years as consumers continued to hold onto their cars and get them fixed more often. Stores rang up a record $9.84 billion in sales in fiscal 2014 (ended January 2015) an increase of more than 50% versus 2013 mostly thanks to $3 billion in added sales from the recent acquisition of General Parts International (GPI) which added hundreds of new stores to AAP's network. Higher revenue pushed profit higher for a third straight year with net income in 2014 jumping by 26% to a record $493.8 million despite higher costs associated with the acquisition and integration on GPI.Operations provided $709 million or 30% more cash than in 2013 thanks to higher earnings and higher non-cash expenses.The recession and its aftermath has been a driver behind AAP's earnings. High unemployment and stagnant income growth led Americans to hang on to their cars longer and rely more on mechanics for maintenance and repairs to keep vehicles in good working condition. Now with the economy improving and new car sales rising AAP's same-store growth rate is slowing.

Strategy

In a move that created the largest automotive aftermarket parts provider in North America and surpassed rival AutoZone is sales AAP acquired privately-held General Parts International (GPI) a distributor and supplier of original equipment and aftermarket replacement products for commercial markets operating under the CARQUEST and WORLDPAC brands. Following the purchase of GPI which closed in January 2014 AAP undertook a corporate reorganization in June 2014 around two store support centers in the Southeast closed an office in Minnesota and consolidated its California Bay Area e-business teams to its Newark California location which also serves as the headquarters for WORLDPAC.AAP has been looking to the commercial market for growth opportunities and recently exceeded its 50% sales target from the segment in 2014. To better serve commercial customers AAP has added more parts from key manufacturers to its inventory and expanded its workforce with parts professionals delivery drivers and sales representatives. The acquisition of both GPI and B.W.P. Distributors in 2013 and 2012 respectively helped boost commercial sales as its business is more weighted to commercial customers than the company's Advance stores. In 2014 as a result the company generated 57% of its sales from its commercial customers (up from 40.4% the year before) which helped lead to a record-breaking year for both revenue and profit.AAP continues to expand its store network in both new and existing markets to grow its commercial and DIY customer base. In 2014 it opened more than 120 AAP and AI stores while adding more than 1335 Carquest and Worldpac stores through its GPI acquisition. From fiscal 2004 through January 2015 the company has more than doubled its retail reach from 2652 stores to 5372 stores.

Mergers and Acquisitions

In January 2014 AAP acquired General Parts International (GPU) for about $2.1 billion. GPI is a privately-held distributor and supplier of original equipment and aftermarket replacement parts to commercial markets operating under the CARQUEST and WORLDPAC brands. The deal added 1233 Carquest stores 103 Worldpac branches in 45 states and Canada and the business of nearly 1400 independently-owned Carquest stores to AAP's network —creating the largest automotive aftermarket parts provider in North America with sales of more than $9.3 billion.

In late 2012 to boost its store count significantly overnight and add to its distribution capacity AAP acquired B.W.P. Distributors Inc. to take over about 125 BWP company-owned stores and a pair of BWP distribution centers in Massachusetts and New Jersey. As part of the deal AAP transferred rights to distribute to more than 90 independently owned locations to an affiliate of auto supply company General Parts International which will operate one of BWP's distribution centers in New York.

Ownership

The investment firm Ruane Cunniff & Goldfarb owns about 10% of AAP's shares.

Company Background

Founded as Advance Stores Company in 1929 AAP was a general merchandise retailer until the '80s. From there the company shifted its focus to automotive parts retailing targeting DIY customers.

EXECUTIVES

Vice President Human Resources, Chip Grubb
Executive Vice President Busn Dev, Jim Wade
SVP Information Technology, Donna Justiss
EVP and CFO, Michael A. (Mike) Norona, age 51, $560,570 total compensation
CEO and Director, Darren R. Jackson, age 51, $930,288 total compensation
EVP Merchandising Marketing and Supply Chain, Charles E. Tyson, age 52, $478,375 total compensation
President, George Sherman, $670,674 total compensation
President Autopart International, Michael Creedon
President WORLDPAC, Bob Cushing
President CARQUEST Canada, Steve Gushie
SVP Human Resources, Tammy Finley
SVP and CIO, James A. (Andy) Paisley
SVP and Chief Marketing Officer, Walter Scott
Svp-market Availability, Jon Dehne
Senior Vice President, William (Bill) Carter
Assistant Vice President Strategic Store Systems, Craig Anderman
Senior Vice President Operations, Mike Pack
Vice President Information Technology, David Jones
Vice President Internal Audit, Tom Belt
Vice President Self Service Purchasing, Kim Buskirk
Vice President Chief Information Security Officer, Joel Yonts
Vice President Information Technology, Joyce Maruniak
Regional Vice President, Scott Kear
Vice President of Marketing and Communication, Melissa (Mel) Kidwell
Senior Vice President Supply Chain, Todd Greener
Vice President Distribution Operations, Jason Howes
Vice President Of Asset Protection, Mike Cox
Vice President, Roger Crain
National Sales Manager, Chad Schnitz
RVP, Rich Flaherty
Regional Vice President, Larry Russell
Regional Vice President, Ernesto Valderrama
Vice President, Warren Shatzer
Regional Vice President, Edwin Colon
Vice President Of Human Resources, Kathy Gillis
Vice President Information Technology, John (Jack) Shurtleff
Vice President Commercial Sales, Joe Caruthers
Vice President Finance, Harry Levinson
Vice President Store Development, Jim Germann
Vice President Information Technology, Greg Springer
Vice President Design and Development Real Estate, Tom Drapac
Vice President of Operations, Bob Lingsch
Senior Vice President General Counsel, Sarah Powell
Senior Vice President DIY and Commercial Information technology Support, Bill Carter
Regional Vice President, Ralph Gonzalez
Senior Vice President Area, Joe Gonzalez
Vice President Commercial Marketing, John (Jack) Hanighen
Vice President of Design and Development, Thomas (Thom) Drapac
Treasurer and Vice President, Kevin Quinn
Chairman, John C. (Jack) Brouillard, age 66
Auditors: Deloitte & Touche LLP

LOCATIONS

HQ: Advance Auto Parts Inc
5008 Airport Road, Roanoke, VA 24012
Phone: 540 362-4911
Web: www.AdvanceAutoParts.com

2013 AAP Locations

	No.
Florida	479
North Carolina	256
Georgia	246
Ohio	227
Pennsylvania	210
New York	194
Virginia	192
Texas	179
Tennessee	141
South Carolina	137
Illinois	127
Alabama	122
Michigan	119
Indiana	110
Kentucky	104
Massachusetts	96
New Jersey	95
Maryland	90
West Virginia	73
Wisconsin	64
Louisiana	62
Connecticut	59
Colorado	58
Mississippi	57
Missouri	48
Oklahoma	31
Arkansas	28
Iowa	28
Kansas	28
Puerto Rico	25
Nebraska	24
New Hampshire	22
Rhode Island	22
Minnesota	19
Vermont	18
Maine	16
Delaware	13
South Dakota	7
Wyoming	4
New Mexico	1
Virgin Islands	1
Total	**3,832**

2013 AI Locations

	No.
Florida	40
New York	33
Massachusetts	31
Pennsylvania	22
New Jersey	18
Connecticut	16
Maryland	11
Virginia	9
New Hampshire	8
Georgia	6
North Carolina	5
Ohio	5
Maine	4
Rhode Island	4
South Carolina	2
Alabama	1
Delaware	1
District of Columbia	1
Total	**217**

PRODUCTS/OPERATIONS

2013 Sales

	% of total
Parts & batteries	65
Accessories	15
Chemicals	10
Oil	10
Other	1
Total	**100**

2013 Sales

	$ mil.	% of total
AAP	6,171	95
AI	337	5
Adjustment	(14.7)	-
Total	**6,493**	**100**

COMPETITORS

AutoZone	Sears
Fisher Auto Parts	Somerset Tire Service
Genuine Parts	U.S. Auto Parts
Keystone Automotive Operations	Uni-Select
	VIP
O' Reilly Automotive	Wal-Mart
Pep Boys	Whitney Automotive
Replacement Parts	Group

HISTORICAL FINANCIALS

Company Type: Public

Income Statement

FYE: January 3

	REVENUE ($ mil.)	NET INCOME ($ mil.)	NET PROFIT MARGIN	EMPLOYEES
01/15*	9,843	493	5.0%	73,000
12/13	6,493	391	6.0%	71,867
12/12	6,205	387	6.2%	55,000
12/11	6,170	394	6.4%	53,000
01/11	5,925	346	5.8%	51,000
Annual Growth	13.5%	9.3%	—	9.4%

*Fiscal year change

2015 Year-End Financials

Debt ratio: 20.56%
Return on equity: 27.61%
Cash ($ mil.): 104
Current ratio: 1.27
Long-term debt ($ mil.): 1,636

No. of shares (mil.): 73
Dividends
  Yield: 0.0%
  Payout: 3.5%
Market value ($ mil.): 11,587

	STOCK PRICE ($) FY Close	P/E High/Low		PER SHARE ($) Earnings	Dividends	Book Value
01/15*	158.56	24	16	6.71	0.24	27.41
12/13	109.92	21	13	5.32	0.24	20.82
12/12	71.51	17	12	5.22	0.24	16.50
12/11	69.63	14	10	5.11	0.24	11.65
01/11	66.15	17	10	3.95	0.24	12.68
Annual Growth	24.4%	—	—	14.2%	(0.0%)	21.2%

*Fiscal year change

Advanced Micro Devices, Inc.

Advanced Micro Devices (AMD) makes well-regarded processors for customers such as Hewlett-Packard Sony and Dell but it remains a distant #2 in PC and server microprocessors behind Intel. AMD in the past has at times eroded Intel's market share thanks to the popularity of its PC-powering Athlon and Opteron processor families as well as its newer A-series of processors that combine computing and graphics on a chip. In addition to its computing solutions the company generates more than 40% of sales from embedded processors and other chips for enterprise and semi-customized design. Most of AMD's sales are from

international customers with China as its single biggest market.

OperationsThe company operates through two segments: computing and graphics and enterprise embedded and semi-custom. Computing and graphics products accounting for 67% of sales include AMD's x86 series of chips for PCs and graphic processors game systems and other devices. The products from the enterprise embedded and semi-custom segment 43% of sales are used in data centers kiosks machine-to-machine applications and security and storage systems.

AMD outsources manufacturing of its products to third-party foundries including GLOBAL-FOUNDRIES (GF) and Taiwan Semiconductor Manufacturing Company while it performs assembly test and packaging of its microprocessor and embedded processors at its own facilities in China and Malaysia.

Geographic ReachChina is the company's largest market accounting for nearly 42% of sales. Japan is #2 with 24%. The US Singapore and Europe 19% 7% and 6% respectively. AMD saw double-digit declines across most geographic markets in 2013 including a nearly 40% drop in Singapore and an 8% drop in China. The US however generated 20% more sales and sales in Japan increased 89%.

The company more than 40 locations worldwide about 20 of them in the Asia-Pacific region.

Sales and MarketingThe company markets its products through a direct sales force as well as through a network of independent distributors and sales representatives. Hewlett-Packard (HP) Microsoft and Sony are its largest customers each accounting for more than 13% of sales. AMD's top five customers generate about 61% of sales.

AMD's marketing and advertising expenses have fallen in recent years dropping to about $194 million in 2014 from $210 million in 2013 and $287 million in 2012.

Financial PerformanceAMD's revenue perked up in 2014 with an increase for the first time since 2011. Revenue rose almost 4% in 2014 to $5.5 billion from $5.3 billion in 2013. Sales for the company's enterprise embedded and semi-custom segment leaped 51% in 2014 while those of the computing and graphics segment fell 16%. Better sales of its semi-custom system-on-a-chip (SoCs) helped boost revenue. Lower desktop and chipset sales cut into the sales of the computing and graphics segment.

Despite the higher revenue AMD's loss deepened in 2014 to $403 million compared to an $83 million loss in 2013. The cost of sales was higher for the company's SoCs in 2014 and it had higher restructuring charges in 2014 than the year before. A big chunk of the company's expenses was a $233 million charge taken on the value of the goodwill for the computing and graphics segment.

Cash outflow from operations was $98 million in 2014 an improvement from outflow of $148 million in 2013.

Strategy

AMD seeks to accelerate sales with its accelerated processing unit (APU) chips. The A-series of chips are designed to combine computing and graphics capabilities in a single system for high efficiency and lower power consumption. Sales of SoCs to Microsoft for its Xbox and Sony for its Playstation boosted AMD's revenue from its enterprise embedded and semi-custom segment. The company also sold Radeon chips to Apple Inc. for use in its iMac systems with Retina display.

The company reduced its headcount by 6% by the end of 2014 and was reducing its real estate holdings heading into 2015 go cut operating costs 11%. The 2014 round follows other restructurings in 2011 and 2012.

HISTORY

Early History

Silicon Valley powerhouse Fairchild Camera & Instrument axed marketing whiz Jerry Sanders reportedly for wearing a pink shirt on a sales call to IBM. In 1969 Sanders and seven friends started a semiconductor company (just as his former boss Intel co-founder Robert Noyce had done a year earlier) based on chip designs licensed from other companies.

Advanced Micro Devices (AMD) went public in 1972. Siemens eager to enter the US semiconductor market paid $30 million for nearly 20% of AMD in 1977. (Siemens had sold off its stake by 1991). In 1982 AMD inked a deal with Intel that let AMD make exact copies of Intel's iAPX86 microprocessors used in IBM and compatible PCs.

By the mid-1980s the company was developing its own chips. In 1987 AMD sued Intel for breaking the 1982 agreement that allowed AMD to second-source Intel's new 386 chips. Intel countersued for copyright infringement when AMD introduced versions of Intel's 287 math coprocessor (1990) 386 chip (1991) and 486 chip (1993).

AMD acquired Monolithic Memories in 1987 broadening its portfolio of memory devices. The company began work on its Submicron Development Center at headquarters in Sunnyvale California where crucial work on future products would be done.

EXECUTIVES

LOCATIONS

HQ: Advanced Micro Devices, Inc.
One AMD Place, Sunnyvale, CA 94088
Phone: 408 749-4000
Web: www.amd.com

2014 Sales

	$ mil.	% of total
China	2,324	48
Japan	1,324	24
US	1,030	19
Singapore	371	7
Europe	325	6
Other regions	132	2
Total	**5,506**	**100**

PRODUCTS/OPERATIONS

2014 Sales

	$ mil.	% of total
Computing solutions	3,132	57
Graphics & other	2,374	43
Total	**5,506**	**100**

Selected Products

Computing
  Accelerated processing units (APUs; Fusion combines central processing and graphics processing units on a single chip)
  Microprocessors (Athlon Opteron Phenom Sempron and Turion lines)
  Motherboard reference design kits and chipsets
Graphics
  Embedded graphics processing units
  Macintosh notebook and desktop PC graphics processors (Radeon)
  Motherboard chipsets (for AMD and Intel processors)
  Server and workstation graphics processing units
Personal connectivity
  Embedded processors
  Networking chips

COMPETITORS

ARM Holdings	NVIDIA
Analog Devices	NXP Semiconductors
Atmel	SANYO Semiconductor
Centaur Technology	STMicroelectronics
Hitachi	Samsung Electronics
IBM	Sigma Designs
Imagination	Silicon Image
Technologies	Silicon Integrated
Intel	Systems
Marvell Technology	Silicon Motion
Matrox Electronic	Texas Instruments
Systems	VIA Technologies
MediaTek	

HISTORICAL FINANCIALS

Company Type: Public

Income Statement
FYE: December 27

	REVENUE ($ mil.)	NET INCOME ($ mil.)	NET PROFIT MARGIN	EMPLOYEES
12/14	5,506	(403)	—	9,700
12/13	5,299	(83)	—	10,671
12/12	5,422	(1,183)	—	10,340
12/11	6,568	491	7.5%	11,100
12/10	6,494	471	7.3%	11,100
Annual Growth	(4.0%)	—	—	(3.3%)

2014 Year-End Financials

Debt ratio: 58.72%
Return on equity: (-110.56%)
Cash ($ mil.): 1,040
Current ratio: 1.90
Long-term debt ($ mil.): 2,035

No. of shares (mil.): 776
Dividends
  Yield: —
  Payout: —
Market value ($ mil.): 2,056

	STOCK PRICE ($) FY Close	P/E High/Low	PER SHARE ($) Earnings	Dividends	Book Value
12/14	2.65	— —	(0.53)	0.00	0.24
12/13	3.78	— —	(0.11)	0.00	0.75
12/12	2.28	— —	(1.60)	0.00	0.75
12/11	5.40	14 7	0.66	0.00	2.28
12/10	8.04	15 9	0.64	0.00	1.48
Annual Growth	(24.2%)	— —	—	—	—(36.5%)

ADVANTAGE ELECTRIC SERVICES LLC

Auditors: PLANTE & MORAN PLLC TRAVERSE

LOCATIONS

HQ: ADVANTAGE ELECTRIC SERVICES LLC
2238 TRAVERSEFIELD DR, TRAVERSE CITY, MI 496869251
Phone: 2319294900
Web: WWW.ADVANTAGEMI.COM

HISTORICAL FINANCIALS

Company Type: Private

Income Statement
FYE: December 31

	REVENUE ($ mil.)	NET INCOME ($ mil.)	NET PROFIT MARGIN	EMPLOYEES
12/12	5,240	329	6.3%	35
12/08	10	1	10.1%	—
12/06	13	1	7.9%	—
12/05	818	0	—	—
Annual Growth	—	—	—	—

2012 Year-End Financials

Debt ratio: ——
Return on equity: 6.30%
Cash ($ mil.): 1,320
Current ratio: 3.00
Long-term debt ($ mil.): —

Dividends
  Yield: —
  Payout: —
Market value ($ mil.): —

AECOM

AECOM means never having to say Architecture Engineering Consulting Operations and Maintenance. One of the world's top engineering and design groups AECOM (formerly AECOM Technology) provides planning consulting and construction management services for civil and infrastructure construction to government and private clients in 150 countries. The company also provides facilities management and maintenance logistics IT services and systems integration services. AECOM projects have included project management for the Saadiyat Island Cultural District in Abu Dhabi and master planning for the 2012 London Olympics. AECOM acquired competitor URS Corp and homebuilder Hunt Construction Group in late 2014.

Operations

AECOM operate three business segments: Design and Consulting Services (DCS) which generated 44% of the company's total revenue in fiscal 2015 (ended September 2015) and consisted of planning consulting architectural and engineering design services; Construction Services (CS) which made up 37% of AECOM's total revenue and included construction for buildings energy infrastructure and industrial facilities; and Management Services (MS) which contributed another 19% to the company's total revenue and counted AECOM's facilities management and maintenance training logistics consulting technical assistance and systems integration and IT services (mostly for US government and other national governments worldwide).

Geographic Reach

Based in California AECOM serves clients in 150 countries. The company generated 70% of its revenue from the US in FY2015 another 10% in Europe about 8% from the Asia Pacific region and another 7% from Canada.

Sales and Marketing

AECOM serves several sectors such as transportation facilities environmental energy water and government. During fiscal 2015 (ended September) about 50% of AECOM's revenue came from private-sector clients while the other 50% came from contracts with government entities including 24% coming from direct contracts with agencies of the US federal government 14% with US state and local governments and 12% from non-US governments.Financial PerformanceAECOM has struggled to meaningfully grow its revenue or profits over the past few years as its revenue costs have risen. The firm had a breakout year in fiscal 2015 (ended September 30 2015) however as its revenue more than doubled to $18 billion from company acquisitions made during the fiscal year especially with the late 2014 acquisition of URS Corporation. All segments and regions enjoyed sharp business growth with revenue from the US Canada and Europe growing by more than 120% each.Despite strong revenue growth in FY2015 AECOM suffered a net loss of $154.8 million (compared to a profit of $229.9 million in FY2014) mostly as it incurred $398.4 million worth of acquisition and integration expenses related to its URS Corporation acquisition. The firm's operating cash levels more than doubled for the year to $764.4 million mostly thanks to the timing of receipts and payments of working capital (including accounts receivables accounts payables accrued expenses and billings in excess of costs on uncompleted contracts).

Strategy

Together domestic and foreign governments accounted for nearly 50% of AECOM's business during FY2015. The lopsidedness could make the company vulnerable to government spending cuts or political unrest. However as the world's infrastructure needs grow AECOM stands to benefit from the resulting increase in project opportunities. In 2015 AECOM expanded its operations in India to capitalize on the added infrastructure spending by the government adding the $7.3 billion- Dholera New Township project in Gujarat and the $3 billion- "Seabird" naval base project in Karwar to its books. The firm also began expanding into South Australia to work on government projects later in 2015.

AECOM works to boost its customer base by deepening its relationships with clients offering a broad range of services and leveraging opportunities in core markets. In 2014 exercising a new way to expand its business the company launched its AECOM Global Fund I (AECOM Capital) which would invest in public-private partnership (P3) and private-sector real estate projects for which AECOM could provide with equity capital design engineering and construction services. Additionally the fund leverages the firm's P3 expertise to allow clients to fund projects without direct investment by AECOM.

Growth by acquisition is also a large part of its strategy as it enables the company to cement its leadership position in its existing markets. AECOM has acquired more than 35 companies during the past decade expanding geographically and filling out its operations with like-minded companies later absorbing them into its existing units. During FY2015 AECOM spent about $5.15 billion on acquisitions (mostly spent on URS Corp) up from $88.5 million and $82 million on acquisitions in fiscal years 2014 and 2013 respectively. In addition AECOM works through joint venture agreements to extend the reach of its operations. In 2013 for instance the company's Australian arm partnered with Aurecon Design. Under a multimillion-dollar contract the pair provided the design services for the $1.07-billion Moreton Bay Rail project in Australia.

Mergers and Acquisitions

In October 2014 AECOM purchased URS for some $4 billion plus the assumption of debt. The deal which created a $19 billion engineering services powerhouse with employees in some 150 countries advances AECOM's strategy of creating an integrated delivery platform for providing its services across the globe.

Looking to strengthen its construction services business AECOM in late 2014 also acquired Hunt Construction Group. The move makes AECOM one of the nation's largest builders. Purchases in 2013 included South Africa-based BKS Group and Asia-based KPK Quantity Surveyors. Company Background In 2012 the company bought Chinese environmental specialist Capital Engineering Corporation further expanding its presence in Asia.

Previous acquisitions include real estate company Tishman's construction business Spain-based INOCSA Ingenieria government national security intelligence services firm McNeil Technologies project management consultancy Davis Langdon Montreal-based RSW and India-based consulting firm Spectral Services.

EXECUTIVES

Vice President Leasing, David B Kilpatrick
SVP and CEO Metro New York, Christopher O. (Chris) Ward
Chief Executive AECOM Capital, John T. Livingston
Group President Design and Consulting Services, Frederick W. (Fred) Werner, age 62, $630,804 total compensation
Chairman and CEO, Michael S. (Mike) Burke, age 52, $950,567 total compensation
Group President Building Construction, Daniel P. McQuade
EVP and General Counsel, Carla Christofferson
President, Stephen M. (Steve) Kadenacy, age 46, $630,804 total compensation
Group President End Markets, Michael J. Donnelly, age 53
Group President Energy Infrastructure and Industrial Construction, George L. Nash, age 54
Group President Management Services, Randall A. (Randy) Wotring, age 58
EVP and Chief Strategy Officer, Kevin A. Lynch, age 50
CEO Africa, Carlos Pone
EVP and CFO, W. Troy Rudd, age 51
Vice President Director Water Treatment Technol, Yujung Chang
Executive Vice President Chief Human Resources Officer, Rick Heinick
Vice President of Information Technology, Richard (Dick) Song
Vice President, Richard (Dick) Paupst

Vice President, Lucy Pugh
Vice President Design build, Dave Herer
Vice President, John (Jack) Anderson
Vice President, Will Wright
Vice President Southern California District Operations Manager, Lewis Cornell
Vice President Strategic Development Director, Samara Barend
Associate Vice President and Operations Manager Philly and DE, David (Dave) Didier
Assistant Vice President Technical Director, Richard (Dick) Silos
Vice President Shared Services, Bill Parker
District Manager Associate Vice President, Mark Wisthuff
Senior Vice President Florida District General Manager, Bruce Koenig
Associate Vice President And Hydrogeologist, Keith Ryan
Vice President Assistant General Counsel, David (Dave) Gan
Executive Vice President Government, James M (Jamie) Jaska
Vice President Enterprise Application Planning and Strategic Initiatives, Eileen Vessella
Vice President Internal, Pete Florstedt
Senior Vice President Treasurer, Arlene Moore
Senior Vice President Chief Safety Officer, Andrew (Andy) Peters
Vice President Transit Rail, Michael (Mel) Marino
Vice Chairman, Daniel R. (Dan) Tishman, age 60
Auditors: Ernst & Young LLP

LOCATIONS

HQ: AECOM
1999 Avenue of the Stars, Suite 2600, Los Angeles, CA 90067
Phone: 213 593-8000
Web: www.aecom.com

2015 Sales

	$ mil.	% of total
US	12,599	70
Asia/Pacific	1,385	8
Canada	1,308	7
Europe	1,796	10
Other foreign countries	899	5
Total	**17,989**	**100**

Selected Subsidiaries

AECOM Global Inc. a Delaware Corporation
AECOM Inc. a Delaware Corporation
AECOM Technical Services Inc. a California Corporation
AECOM USA Inc. a New York Corporation
National Security Programs Inc. a Virginia Corporation
Tishman Construction Corporation a Delaware Corporation

PRODUCTS/OPERATIONS

2015 Sales by Segment

	% of total
Design and Consulting Services(DCS)	44
Construction Services(CS)	37
Management Services(MS)	19
Total	**100**

2015 Sales By Client

	$ mil.	% of total
Government		
US federal		
DCS	764	4
CS	291	2
MS	3,172	18
Non-US Government	2,198	12
US state & local Government	2,592	14
Private (worldwide)	8,971	50
Total	**17,989**	**100**

Selected Projects

BHP Billiton Rapid Growth Project Stage 5 Australia
Chrysler — St. Louis Regional Economic Adjustment Strategy Missouri USA

Coca-Cola Divisional Headquarters Shanghai China
Coca-Cola Water Treatment Efficiency Study
Decommissioning of firefighting equipment facility Milan Italy
GE Strategic Supplier Initiative
General Electric Commercial Finance Headquarters Norwalk Connecticut
GlaxoSmithKline SMART Working program
La Jolla Office Commons
Microsoft Building 5
Nokia Siemens Networks (NSN)
Northparkes Mines New South Wales Australia

COMPETITORS

ABB	Louis Berger
Amec Foster Wheeler	MWH Global
Bechtel	Parsons Brinckerhoff
Black & Veatch	Parsons Corporation
CH2M HILL	STV
Fluor	Skidmore Owings
Henkels & McCoy	Terracon
Jacobs Engineering	Tutor Perini
KBR	

HISTORICAL FINANCIALS

Company Type: Public

Income Statement

FYE: September 30

	REVENUE ($ mil.)	NET INCOME ($ mil.)	NET PROFIT MARGIN	EMPLOYEES
09/15	17,989	(154)	—	92,000
09/14	8,356	229	2.8%	43,300
09/13	8,153	239	2.9%	45,500
09/12	8,218	(58)	—	46,800
09/11	8,037	275	3.4%	45,000
Annual Growth	**22.3%**	**—**	**—**	**19.6%**

2015 Year-End Financials

Debt ratio: 32.87%	No. of shares (mil.): 151
Return on equity: (-5.54%)	Dividends
Cash ($ mil.): 683	Yield: —
Current ratio: 1.29	Payout: —
Long-term debt ($ mil.): 4,446	Market value ($ mil.): 4,161

	STOCK PRICE ($) FY Close	P/E High/Low		PER SHARE ($) Earnings	Dividends	Book Value
09/15	27.51	—	—	(1.04)	0.00	22.53
09/14	33.75	16	12	2.33	0.00	22.61
09/13	31.27	15	8	2.35	0.00	21.05
09/12	21.16	—	—	(0.52)	0.00	20.27
09/11	17.67	13	8	2.33	0.00	20.66
Annual Growth	**11.7%**	**—**	**—**	**—**	**—**	**2.2%**

AEROTEK INC.

Aerotek a unit of staffing powerhouse Allegis Group offers commercial and technical staffing services throughout North America. Through several divisions Aerotek staffs workers such as engineers mechanics scientists and technical professionals as well as administrative staff members general laborers and tradespeople. The company also provides training and support services. Along with aerospace auto and engineering companies Aerotek's clients include companies from the construction energy manufacturing health care and finance industries.

Geographic Reach

The company has more than 200 office locations across the US Canada Europe (including the UK Germany and the Netherlands) and Singapore.

Strategy

Aerotek has expanded its operations over the years through organic growth and acquisitions especially in niche markets such as the biotechnology health care clinical research chemical and plastics sectors. Despite the economic downturn demand within these industries has been consistent along with engineering giving Aerotek some continuity during the recession. Aerotek has also widened its client focus to include the niche market of minority and woman-owned companies.

EXECUTIVES

VP Technical and Professional Services, Mark Cooper
President, Todd M. Mohr
CFO, Thomas B. (Tom) Kelly
SVP Operations, John Flanigan
Regional VP Northeast, John Rudy
Regional VP Midwest, Marty Schager
Regional VP Central, Mike Hansen
Regional VP West, Tony Bartolucci
Regional VP Northwest, Brooks Wells
VP Canada, Bryan Toffey
Regional VP Southwest, Brad Kennedy
Regional VP Mid-Atlantic, Jeff Colvin
Regional VP Southeast, Greg Jones
Vice President of Human Resources, Tanya Axenson
Auditors: PRICEWATERHOUSECOOPERS LLP B

LOCATIONS

HQ: AEROTEK INC.
7301 PARKWAY DR, HANOVER, MD 210761159
Phone: 4106945100
Web: WWW.AEROTEK.COM

PRODUCTS/OPERATIONS

Selected Industries
Accounting and Finance
Administrative
Aerospace
Architecture
Automotive
Aviation
Call Center
Clinical Research
Construction
Energy
Engineering
Environmental
Labor
Manufacturing
Mortgage
Scientific

COMPETITORS

AMN Healthcare	MSX International
Adecco	ManpowerGroup
Bryant Bureau	On Assignment
CDI	Pinnacle Staffing
COMFORCE	Randstad Holding
Kelly Services	Robert Half
Kforce	

HISTORICAL FINANCIALS

Company Type: Private

Income Statement

FYE: December 31

	REVENUE ($ mil.)	NET INCOME ($ mil.)	NET PROFIT MARGIN	EMPLOYEES
12/13	5,268	0	—	4,200
12/12	5,119	307	6.0%	—
12/11	4,481	226	5.0%	—
12/10	3,446	0	—	—
Annual Growth	15.2%	—	—	—

2013 Year-End Financials

Debt ratio: ——
Return on equity: —
Cash ($ mil.): 8
Current ratio: 3.20
Long-term debt ($ mil.): —

Dividends
Yield: —
Payout: —
Market value ($ mil.): —

AES Corp.

AES is out to please power customers around the world. A leading independent power producer the company has interests in 137 generation facilities in 18 countries throughout the Americas Asia Africa Europe and the Middle East that gave it a net generating capacity of 35000 MW in 2014. (It also has one coal-fired project under development with a total capacity of 1320 MW). AES sells electricity to utilities and other energy marketers through wholesale contracts or on the spot market. AES also sells power directly to customers worldwide through stakes in distribution utilities mainly in Latin America and the US.

HISTORY

Applied Energy Services (AES) was founded in 1981 three years after passage of the Public Utilities Regulation Policies Act which enabled small power firms to enter electric generation markets formerly dominated by utility monopolies. Cofounders Roger Sant and Dennis Bakke who had served in President Nixon's Federal Energy Administration saw that an independent power producer (IPP) could make money by generating cheap power in large volumes to sell to large power consumers and utilities.

AES set about building massive cogeneration plants (producing both steam and electricity) in 1983. The first plant Deepwater went into operation near Houston in 1986. By 1989 AES had three plants on line and it then opened plants in Connecticut and Oklahoma. In 1991 the company formally renamed AES went public but one plant's falsified emissions reports caused AES's stock to plummet in 1992.

Facing environmental groups' opposition to new power plant construction and an overall glut in the US power market AES bought interests in two Northern Ireland plants in 1992 and began expanding into Latin America in 1993. Also in 1993 AES set up a separately traded subsidiary AES China Generating Co. to focus on Chinese development projects. AES won a plant development contract with the Puerto Rico Electric Power Authority (1994) and a bid to privatize an Argentine hydrothermal company (1995).

In 1996 AES began adding stakes in electric utility and distribution companies to its portfolio including interests in formerly state-owned Brazilian electric utilities Light-Serviços de Eletricidade (1996) and CEMIG (1997); one Brazilian and two Argentine distribution companies (1997); and a distribution company in El Salvador (1998).

AES almost doubled its revenues after buying Destec Energy's international operations from NGC (now Dynegy) in 1997. By the next year prospects in international markets were dimming so AES turned to the US market again. It bought three California plants from Edison International and arranged for The Williams Companies to supply natural gas to the facilities and market the electricity generated. AES also won a bid to buy six plants from New York State Electric & Gas (now Energy East) affiliate NGE.

Also in 1998 despite black days in many world markets AES bought 90% of Argentine electric distribution company Edelap and a 45% stake in state-owned Orissa Power Generation in India. Its moves paid off: AES posted a 70% gain in sales that year.

It bought CILCORP an Illinois utility holding company in an $886 million deal in 1999. Boosting its presence in the UK AES bought the Drax power station a 3960-MW coal-fired plant from National Power. It also bought a majority stake in Brazilian data transmission company Eletronet from Brazil's government-owned utility ELETROBRÁS. In 2000 AES increased its interests in Brazilian power distributors. It also gained a 73% stake (later expanded to 87%) in Venezuelan electric utility Grupo EDC in a $1.5 billion hostile takeover.

The next year AES bought IPALCO the parent of Indianapolis Power & Light in a $3 billion deal. Also in 2001 AES acquired the outstanding shares of Chilean generation company Gener in which it previously held a 60% stake.

That year AES moved to take control of CANTV Venezuela's #1 telecom company. Through Grupo EDC which already owned 6.9% of CANTV AES offered to buy 43.2% of the company. But AES withdrew the offer after the CANTV board rejected it. (AES sold Grupo EDC's stake in CANTV the following year.) AES also sold some generation assets in Argentina to TOTAL FINA ELF (now TOTAL) for about $370 million.

In 2002 AES sold its 24% interest in Light Serviços de Eletricidade (Light) to Electricité de France (EDF) in exchange for a 20% stake in Brazilian utility Eletropaulo (increasing its stake in Eletropaulo to 70%). In that same year the company sold its retail energy marketing unit (AES NewEnergy) to Constellation Energy Group for $240 million and its CILCORP subsidiary which holds utility Central Illinois Light to Ameren.

In 2007 the company acquired two 230 MW petroleum coke-fired power generation facilities in Tamuin Mexico for $611 million. It also bought a 51% stake in Turkish power generator IC ICTAS Energy Group.

AES has faced controversy in Brazil where an unstable power market has caused the company to default on debts incurred from its purchases of stakes in local utilities (as well as bankrupt telecom firm Eletronet) in recent years. To restructure its debt with Banco Nacional de Desenvolvimento Economico e Social (BNDES) AES completed a deal in 2007 in which the firm's interests in AES Eletropaulo AES Uruguaiana AES Tiete and AES Sul was placed into a new holding company (Brasiliana Energia). AES owns 50.1% of that company while BNDES holds 49.9%.

To raise cash in 2008 and 2009 AES sold the AES Ekibastuz power plant and Maikuben coal mine in Kazakhstan to Kazakhmys (renamed KAZ Minerals) for $1.1 billion.

In 2008 the company boosted it assets in the Philippines acquiring the 660 MW Masinloc coal-fired power plant in Barangay Bula for $930 million.

EXECUTIVES

EVP and CFO, Thomas M. (Tom) O'Flynn, age 55, $650,000 total compensation
President and CEO, Andr ©R. Gluski, age 58, $1,130,000 total compensation
EVP General Counsel and Corporate Secretary, Brian A. Miller, age 49, $568,000 total compensation
SVP Technology and Services and CIO, Elizabeth Hackenson, age 54, $420,000 total compensation
SVP Global Engineering and Construction, Michael (Mike) Chilton

SVP and COO, Bernerd Da Santos, $339,248 total compensation
Vice President, Alison Zimlich
CIO Chief Technology Officer Vice President Information Technology, Ricardo Vega
Vice President Corporate Strategy and Investment, Carla Tully
Vice President, Ruben Saavedra
Vice President, Aaron Tesnow
Vice President Financial Planning And Analysis, Ben Seto
Vice President, Robert Mill
Vice President Of Information Systems, Ramon Eulacio
Vice President (Human Resources), Paritosh Mishra
Vice President Finanzas, Rosa Alvarado
Vice President Market Operations, Bryan Robinson
Vice President Global People Strategy and Talent Management, Geoff Ryan
Chairman, Charles O. Rossotti, age 75
Board Director, Kevin Walker
Auditors: Ernst & Young LLP

LOCATIONS

HQ: AES Corp.
4300 Wilson Boulevard, Arlington, VA 22203
Phone: 703 522-1315   **Fax:** 703 528-4510
Web: www.aes.com

2014 Sales

	$ mil.	% of total
Brazil	6,009	35
US	3,828	22
Chile	1,624	9
El salvador	832	5
Dominican Republic	802	5
United Kigdom	533	3
Argentina	463	3
Colombia	552	3
Philippines	451	2
Mexico	434	3
Bulgaria	410	2
Puerto Rico	348	2
Panama	263	2
Jordan	262	1
Kazakhstan	161	1
Sri Lanka	107	1
Other countries	67	0
Total	**17,146**	**100**

2014 Sales

	% of total
Brazil SBU	35
US SBU	22
Andes SBU	16
MCAC SBU	16
Europe SBU	8
Asia SBU	3
Corporate and Other	0
Total	**100**

PRODUCTS/OPERATIONS

2014 Sales

	$ mil.	% of total
Regulated	8,874	52
Non-regulated	8,272	48
Total	**17,146**	**100**

Selected Electric Utilities and Distribution Companies

AES CLESA (electric utility El Salvador)
AES Edelap (electric utility Argentina)
AES Eden (electric utility Argentina)
AES Edes (electric utility Argentina)
AES Gener (electric generation Chile)
AES India Private Ltd.
AES SeaWest Inc.
Brasiliana Energia
   AES Sul Distribuidora Gaucha de Energia SA (AES Sul electric utility Brazil)
   AES Tiete (power generation Brazil)
   AES Uruguaiana (power generation Brazil)

Eletropaulo Metropolitana Eletricidade de São Paulo S.A. (AES Electropaulo electric distribution Brazil)
CAESS (electric utility El Salvador)
Companhia Energética de Minas Gerais (CEMIG Brazil)
DPL (electric utility US)
EEO (electric utility El Salvador)
IC ICTAS Energy Group (power generation Turkey)
IPALCO Enterprises Inc. (holding company)

COMPETITORS

Alliant Energy	Enterprise Products
Berkshire Hathaway Energy	Exelon
Bonneville Power	Huadian Power
CMS Energy	IBERDROLA
CPFL Energia	Indeck Energy
Calpine	International Power
CenterPoint Energy	NRG Energy
Duke Energy	NextEra Energy
Dynegy	Nicor Gas
E.ON UK	PG&E Corporation
Edison International	Public Service Enterprise Group
Endesa S.A.	Sempra Energy
Energias de Portugal	Siemens AG
Energy Future	Tractebel Engineering
Enersis	Xcel Energy
Entergy	

HISTORICAL FINANCIALS

Company Type: Public

Income Statement

FYE: December 31

	REVENUE ($ mil.)	NET INCOME ($ mil.)	NET PROFIT MARGIN	EMPLOYEES
12/14	17,146	769	4.5%	18,500
12/13	15,891	114	0.7%	22,000
12/12	18,141	(912)	—	25,000
12/11	17,274	58	0.3%	27,000
12/10	16,647	9	0.1%	29,000
Annual Growth	**0.7%**	**204.0%**	**—**	**(10.6%)**

2014 Year-End Financials

Debt ratio: 53.53%
Return on equity: 17.56%
Cash ($ mil.): 1,539
Current ratio: 1.12
Long-term debt ($ mil.): 18,725

No. of shares (mil.): 703
Dividends
   Yield: 1.4%
   Payout: 40.8%
Market value ($ mil.): 9,692

	STOCK PRICE ($) FY Close	P/E High/Low	PER SHARE ($) Earnings	Dividends	Book Value
12/14	13.77	15 12	1.06	0.20	6.18
12/13	14.51	102 71	0.15	0.16	6.10
12/12	10.70	— —	(1.21)	0.04	6.24
12/11	11.84	191 135	0.07	0.00	7.87
12/10	12.18	1413 890	0.01	0.00	8.29
Annual Growth	**3.1%**	**—**	**—220.9%**	**—**	**(7.1%)**

Aetna Inc.

Life death health or injury —Aetna's got an insurance policy to cover it. The company one of the largest health insurers in the US also offers life and disability insurance as well as retirement savings products. Its health care division offers HMO PPO point of service (POS) health savings account (HSA) and traditional indemnity coverage along with dental vision behavioral health and Medicare and Medicaid plans to groups and individuals. The health care segment covers some 24 million med-

ical members. Aetna's group insurance segment sells life and disability insurance nationwide and its large case pensions segment offers pensions annuities and other retirement savings products.

HISTORY

Hartford Connecticut businessman and judge Eliphalet Bulkeley started Connecticut Mutual Life Insurance in 1846. Agents gained control of the firm the following year. Undeterred Bulkeley and a group of Hartford businessmen founded Aetna Life Insurance in 1853 as a spinoff of Aetna Fire Insurance. Among its offerings was coverage for slaves a practice for which the company apologized in 2000.

A nationwide agency network fueled early growth at Aetna which expanded in the 1860s by offering a participating life policy returning dividends to policyholders based on investment earnings. (This let Aetna compete with mutual life insurers.) In 1868 Aetna became the first firm to offer renewable term life policies.

Eliphalet's son Morgan became president in 1879. Aetna moved into accident (1891) health (1899) workers' compensation (1902) and auto and other property insurance (1907) during his 43-year tenure. He served as Hartford mayor Connecticut governor and US senator all the while leading Aetna.

By 1920 the company sold marine insurance and by 1922 it was the US's largest multiline insurer. Aetna overexpanded its nonlife lines (particularly autos) during the 1920s threatening its solvency. It survived the Depression by restricting underwriting and rebuilding reserves.

After WWII the firm expanded into group life health and accident insurance. In 1967 it reorganized into holding company Aetna Life and Casualty.

The 1960s 1970s and 1980s were go-go years: The company added lines and bought and sold everything from an oil services firm to commercial real estate. The boom period led to a bust and a 1991 reorganization in which Aetna eliminated 8000 jobs withdrew from such lines as auto insurance and sold its profitable American Reinsurance.

To take advantage of the boom in retirement savings in 1995 it got permission to set up bank AE Trust to act as a pension trustee.

With its health care business accounting for some 60% of sales by 1995 the company restructured in the late 1990s. Aetna sold its property/casualty behavioral managed care (1997) and individual life insurance (1998) businesses. It then expanded overseas and bought U.S. Healthcare and New York Life's NYLCare managed health business (1998).

Controversy marred 1998. Contract terms —including a "gag" clause against discussing uncovered treatments —prompted 400 Texas doctors to leave its system; defections followed in Kentucky and West Virginia. Consumers balked over Aetna's refusal to cover some treatments including experimental procedures and advanced fertility treatments. One group sued for false advertising.

EXECUTIVES

EVP and General Counsel Law & Regulatory Affairs, William J. Casazza, age 60, $523,347 total compensation
EVP and President Healthagen Health Services, Gary W. Loveman, age 54
EVP Humana Integration and Enterprise Strategy, Rick Jelinek
EVP Corporate Affairs, Steven B. Kelmar
CEO Medicity, Nancy J. Ham, age 54
Chairman and CEO, Mark T. Bertolini, age 58, $996,169 total compensation

EVP Operations and Technology, Margaret M. (Meg) McCarthy, age 61, $627,960 total compensation

EVP CFO and Chief Enterprise Risk Officer, Shawn M. Guertin, age 51, $697,318 total compensation

President and CEO ActiveHealth Management, Richard Noffsinger

EVP Consumer Products and Enterprise Marketing, Dijuana K. Lewis, age 56

EVP and Chief Medical Officer, Harold L. Paz, age 60

EVP Aetna International, Richard di Benedetto

CEO Aetna Medicaid, Pamela Sedmak

President, Karen S. Rohan, age 52, $649,514 total compensation

EVP Government Services, Francis S. (Fran) Soistman, age 58, $597,701 total compensation

President Aetna Capital Management, Mark D. Garber

Medical Director Quality Management, Robert (Bob) Mcdonough

Vice President Enterprise Solutions Product Engineering, Loren Jenkins

Vice President Behavioral Health, Louise Murphy

Medical Director, Lori Stetz

Vice President of Sales and Service, Janice C Washeleski

Vice President of Public Policy for Government Affairs, Christina Nyquist

National Account Manager, Douglas Schoener

Vice President Of Logistics, Karen Fechko

Vice President, Lyn Stalnaker

Assistant Vice President Fleet Operations, Staci Padgett

Vice President, Stacy Patrick

Vice President And Chief Technology Of, Michael Connolly

Vice President Client Management, Sue Helke

Vice President Member Experience and Digital Innovation, Ann Zaminski

Vice President Sales, Tina Ortega

Senior Vice President Strategy and Operations, Louise McCleery

Vice President Of Business Development, Debbie Dexter

Vice President Of Network Operations, Robert Kleman

Medical Director, Calvin (Cal) Warren

Vice President Acute Hospital Finance, Susan (Sue) Tindall

Medical Director, Richard Fornadel

Vice President Sales and Marketing for National Accounts, Sheryl Burke

Medical Director Northeast Region, Robert (Bob) Willig

Vice President of Product Management, Kris Hunt

Vice President Of Business Development In New York, Miguel Centeno

Network Vice President, Brendhan Green

Medical Director Ambulatory Detoxification Program, Betty Days

Senior Vice President Legal Affairs, Robert (Bob) Kessler

Vice President, Sam Freeman

Senior Executive Vice President Chief Financial Officer And Chief Operating Officer, Lael Nelson

Fourth Vice President Communications, Gwen Burchett

Vice President Network, Lauren Jeffers

Vice President Employee Benefits, Michael Bergman

Vice President of Operations Corporate Medicaid Division, Debra Pennington

Vice President Of Information Technology Security Architecture, Mark Coederre

Vice President Integrated Marketing and eCommerce, Eric Paczewitz

Vice Presidentm Information Services, Greg Krause

Vice President, Michael (Mel) Hoss

Vice President, Michelle Gagnon

Medical Director National Medical Policy and Operations, Gregg Pane

Vice President Sales and Service, Michele Butman

Medical Director, Benjamin Alouf

Vice President Business Development, Eric Tate

Regional Vice President of Business Development, Taira A Green-Kelley

Vice President, Eleanor Menegus

Vice President Sales, Laura Snyder

Vice President, Sherry Baker

Vice President Sales And Marketing, Paul Harriat

Vice President Business Development, Christopher (Chris) Rodriguez

Senior Vice President Branch Manager, Stacey K Bennett

Vice President Business Development and Alternate Channels, Galen Kimbrue

Vice President Health Related Financia, Christine Skelly

Regional Vice President Labor Division, Joseph (Jo) Scibilia

Vice President Client Management, Patrick (Paddy) Sweeney

Vice President Sales, David K (Dave) Firestone

Regional Vice President, Janet Grant

Associate Medical Director, Dena Allchin

Regional Vice President, Tony Clark

Senior Vice President Sales and Service, Regina Hunter

Vice President, Noreen Giannini

Medical Director, Gerald Scallion

National Account Manager, Lecretia Faulcon

Vice President National Accounts Western, Michael (Mel) Robinson

Vice President Sales And Service Florida Middle Market, Todd Slawter

Vice President Of Sales And Service Dental, Kathy Dibble

Corportate Vice President Community Relations and Urban Marketing, Floyd Green

Regional Vice President Sales, Kirk Rosin

Vice President Sales and Service, Marc Neely

Medical Director, Susan (Sue) Brashear

Regional Vice President of Sales, Brett Estep

Vice President Health Services, Ron Austin

Vice President Customer Service Operations, Doug Porter

Pharmacy Manager, Alpa Patel

Medical Director, William Wood

National Accounts Manager, Linda Reid

Vice President Financial Advisor, Jim McCunney

Sales Vice President, John Russo

Vice President, Tim Meyers

Vice President Client Management, Jacqueline McCaffrey

Vice President Client Solutions, Jennifer (Jen) Boehm

Vice President Information Technology, Beverly Wilson

Senior Vice President, David Mahder

Senior Vice President Of Engineering, Daniel Johnson

Vice President and General Manager Funeral Director and Embalmer, James (Jamie) Finnegan

Vice President Sales, James E (Jamie) Ross

Vice President Communications and Marketing, Dawn M Muller

Vice President Realtor, Carrie Lanteri

Vice President Sales, John (Jack) Gialamas

Vice President Medical Operations and Chief Medical Officer Medicare, Robert (Bob) Mirsky

Sales Vice President Aetna Public and Labor, Matt Sherrill

Vice President Acute Care Division, Gerard Hamill

Director Of Pharmacy Western Region, Friedmann Yrena

Senior Vice President Strategy And Operations, Michelle Copenhaver

Sales Vice President National Accounts, Louie Heerwagen

Regional Vice President Sales, Rassi Christina

Vice President of Marketing and Business Development, Jane L (Ginny) Batchelder

Vice President Sales and Marketing, Melinda R Gallagher

Senior Vice President of Product Group, Mary Fox

Vice President Sales, Susan (Sue) Lopes

Vice President New Businesses, Andrew (Andy) Lee

Medical Director National Accounts, Chere Covin

Regional Vice President, Kurt Small

Regional Vice President Bh, Mark Hartinger

Senior Vice President, Sandra Paskiewicz

Vice President Human Resources and Employee Development, Anna Gill

Regional Vice President North Central, William (Bill) Berenson

Vice President Security Financial Advisor, Tom Nasby

Vice President Human Resources, Michelle Mathieu

Medical Director, Andrew Oliveira

Vice President Technical Operations, Debra Bernard

Vice President, Kim Thielemann

Vice President Market Development, Kimberly Sizemore

Medical Director, Dexter Campinha

Senior Vice President, Irma Owens

Network Vice President South Florida, David (Dave) Weisman

Director Of Pharmacy Network Services, Kate Perkins

Vice President Sales And Account Management, Gayle Morico

Network Vice President, Thomas (Thom) Nasby

Vice President Sales And Client Management National Accounts, Dina Segro-nogueira

Vice President Customer Servi, Kevin Lile

Vice President Sales, David (Dave) Burton

Senior Vice President West And Ma, Michael Bahr

Sales Vice President, Brian Katits

Vice President State Governmental Affairs Ne Region, Tim Meyer

National Sales Vice President Faith Based and Non Profit Segment, Paul Williams

Regional Vice President Labor Division, Matt Emm

Vice President Pharmacy Contracting, Debra Keena

Vice President Consumer Strategy and Operations, Andre Napoli

Senior Vice President Strategy and Operations, Michelle (Mitch) Copenhaver

Vice President Consumer Prod Management Vol, Robert (Bob) Brown

Vice President Consumer Bus Sales and Distr, Kerry Sain

Vice President Actuarial and Underwriting (National Accounts), Andy Hiles

Vice President, Dana Benbow

Auditors: KPMG LLP

LOCATIONS

HQ: Aetna Inc.
151 Farmington Avenue, Hartford, CT 06156
Phone: 860 273-0123
Web: www.aetna.com

PRODUCTS/OPERATIONS

2014 Sales

	$ mil.	% of total
Health care		
Commercial premiums	28,563	49
Government premium	20,999	36
Fees & other	5,114	9
Net investment income	367	1
Net realized capital gains	64	—
Group insurance	2,489	4
Large case pensions	404	1
Total	**58,003**	**100**

Selected Products and Services

Behavioral and Mental Health Plans
Dental Plans
Disability Insurance
Health Expense Funds
Life Insurance
Medicaid
Medical Plans
Medicare
Pharmacy
Student Health
Support Programs
Vision Plans
Wellness Programs and Discounts

Selected Acquisitions

COMPETITORS

AMERIGROUP	Humana
Anthem	Independence Blue
Blue Cross	Cross
CIGNA	Kaiser Foundation
Centene	Health Plan
Chubb Limited	Magellan Health
Coventry Health Care	MetLife
DeCare Dental	Molina Healthcare
Delta Dental Plans	Principal Financial
Guardian Life	Prudential
HCSC	USAA
Health Net	UnitedHealth Group
HealthSpring	WellCare Health Plans
Highmark	

HISTORICAL FINANCIALS

Company Type: Public

Income Statement

FYE: December 31

	ASSETS ($ mil.)	NET INCOME ($ mil.)	INCOME AS % OF ASSETS	EMPLOYEES
12/14	53,402	2,040	3.8%	48,800
12/13	49,871	1,913	3.8%	48,600
12/12	41,494	1,657	4.0%	35,000
12/11	38,593	1,985	5.1%	33,300
12/10	37,739	1,766	4.7%	34,000
Annual Growth	9.1%	3.7%	—	9.5%

2014 Year-End Financials

Debt ratio: 15.13%	No. of shares (mil.): 349
Return on equity: 14.32%	Dividends
Cash ($ mil.): 1,420	Yield: 1.0%
Current ratio: —	Payout: 15.0%
Long-term debt ($ mil.): —	Market value ($ mil.): 31,073

	STOCK PRICE ($) FY Close	P/E High/Low		PER SHARE ($) Earnings	Dividends	Book Value
12/14	88.83	16	11	5.68	0.90	41.40
12/13	68.59	13	8	5.33	0.80	38.72
12/12	46.31	10	7	4.81	0.70	31.76
12/11	42.19	9	6	5.22	0.45	28.94
12/10	30.51	8	6	4.18	0.04	25.73
Annual Growth	30.6%	—	—	8.0%	117.8%	12.6%

AFLAC Inc.

Would you buy insurance from a duck? Aflac counts on it! To soften the financial stresses during periods of disability or illness Aflac sells supplemental health and life insurance policies including coverage for accidents intensive care dental vision and disability as well as for specific conditions (primarily cancer) and general life policies. It is a leading supplier of supplemental insurance in the US and is an industry leader in Japan's life and cancer insurance markets. Aflac which is marketed through —and is an acronym for —American Family Life Assurance Company sells policies that pay cash benefits for hospital confinement emergency treatment and medical appliances.

Operations

Aflac acts as a management company overseeing the operations of its subsidiaries by providing management services and making capital available. Its principal business is supplemental health and life insurance which is marketed and administered through its subsidiary American Family Life Assurance Company of Columbus (Aflac) which operates in the US and as a branch in Japan (Aflac Japan). Aflac individual and group insurance products help provide protection to more than 50 million people around the world.

Geographic Reach

Despite its US roots Aflac makes more than 70% of its insurance sales in Japan where its policies fill in gaps not covered by the national health insurance system. Aflac has a presence in all 50 US states and in Puerto Rico and the Virgin Islands.

Sales and Marketing

In Japan Aflac primarily sells through an independent corporate agency system in which corporations form subsidiaries to sell Aflac insurance to their employees. Changes in regulations now allow the company to sell through banks and post offices and it has also opened retail shops where consumers can purchase directly from sales associates. In the US Aflac sells mainly at the workplace with employers deducting premiums from paychecks through sales associates of its Continental American Insurance Company subsidiary (known as Aflac Group Insurance). Building on its strong brand recognition —due largely to the company's popular TV ads featuring a valiant spokes-duck — Aflac has invested in its US business by adding more sales associates and expanding its distribution to include independent insurance brokers.

By the end of 2014 the company had agreements to sell its products with 371 banks approximately 90% of the total number of banks in Japan. Banks contributed 21.5% of Aflac Japan's new annualized premium sales in 2014.

Aflac's extensive distribution network includes more than 74000 licensed sales associates and brokers in US. In 2014 the company recruited more than 900 new sales agencies. Independent corporate and individual agencies contributed more than 45% of new annualized premium sales that year compared with 44% in 2013 and 35% in 2012.

The company's advertising costs in 2014 were $229 million down from $240 million in 2013.

Financial Performance

The company saw a steady growth in revenues over the last few years. However revenue declined 5% in both 2013 and 2014 (when Aflac reported $22.7 billion revenue). The decline was driven by reductions in net premiums (primarily for supplemental health insurance) derivatives and other gains and sales and redemptions due to the weaker yen/dollar exchange rate. Aflac Japan's overall sales declined in 2014 primarily as a result of declines in sales of the first sector WAYS product. (WAYS is a life insurance policy that allows policyholders to convert a portion of their life insurance to medical nursing care or fixed annuity benefits at a predetermined age).

Aflac's net income fell 7% to $2.9 billion in 2014 as a result of the company's lower revenue and also due to an increase in interest expenses.

Operating cash flow has followed the firm's revenue trends since 2009. In 2014 operating cash flow decreased by $4 billion to $6.5 billion due to a decline in cash generated by increase in policy liabilities and changes in income tax liabilities.

Strategy

The company is focusing on improving and expanding its distribution network and product development processes and on strengthening its low-cost model. As part of its US sales strategy Aflac continues to focus on growing and enhancing the effectiveness of its US sales team.

Aflac has formed a partnership with Daido Life Insurance Company under which Daido will sell Aflac's cancer insurance policies to members of Hojinkai a non-profit organization associated with 900000 small and mid-sized member businesses across Japan. Aflac Japan and Japan Post Holdings signed a new alliance agreement in 2013 which boosted the number of postal outlets offering Aflac's cancer products from 1000 to 10000; Japan Post intends to further expand that figure to 20000 outlets by early 2016.

The company anticipates a potential increase in demand for its products as the US adopts a more comprehensive major medical health insurance plan. Its sales target and focus in 2015 is centered around the sale of Aflac Japan's third sector products including cancer and medical.

Aflac has created new life insurance products for the Japanese market. In addition to standard life insurance it has also introduced child endowment products that pay out part of the benefit when the child enters high school and then functions like an annuity for four years during college. In 2014 Aflac Japan introduced New Cancer DAYS which provides enhanced cancer coverage including outpatient treatments and multiple cancer occurrence benefits.

In 2015 Aflac launched a new critical illness plan Critical Care Protection which provides a range of coverage options as well as new benefits for heart conditions.

HISTORY

American Family Life Assurance Company (AFLAC) was founded in Columbus Georgia in 1955 by brothers John Paul and William Amos to sell life health and accident insurance. Competition was fierce and the little company did poorly. With AFLAC nearing bankruptcy the brothers looked for a niche.

The polio scares of the 1940s and 1950s had spawned insurance coverage written especially against that disease; the Amos brothers (whose father was a cancer victim) took a cue from that concept and decided to sell cancer insurance. In 1958 they introduced the world's first cancer-expense policy. It was a hit and by 1959 the company had written nearly a million dollars in premiums and expanded across state lines.

The enterprise grew quickly during the 1960s especially after developing its cluster-selling approach in the workplace where employers were usually willing to make payroll deductions for premiums. By 1971 the company was operating in 42 states.

While visiting the World's Fair in Osaka in 1970 John Amos decided to market supplemental cancer coverage to the Japanese whose national health care plan left them exposed to considerable expense from cancer treatment. After four years the company finally won approval to sell in Japan since the policies did not threaten existing markets and because the Amoses found notable backers in the insurance and medical industries. AFLAC became one of the first US insurance companies to enter the Japanese market and it enjoyed an eight-year monopoly on the cancer market. Back in the US in 1973 AFLAC organized a holding company and began buying television stations in the South and Midwest.

The 1980s were marked by US and state government inquiries into dread disease insurance.

Critics said such policies were a poor value because they were relatively expensive and covered only one disease. However the inquiries led nowhere and demand for such insurance increased bringing new competition. In the 1980s AFLAC's scales tilted: US growth slowed while business grew in Japan which soon accounted for most of the company's sales.

EXECUTIVES

Svp-global Coo Investment Div, Joseph R (Jo) Meyer
EVP, Kenneth S. (Ken) Janke, age 57
President, Kriss Cloninger, age 67, $975,000 total compensation
Chairman and CEO, Daniel P. (Dan) Amos, age 63, $1,441,100 total compensation
EVP and CFO, Frederick J. (Fred) Crawford
President Aflac International; Chairman Aflac Japan, Charles D. Lake, age 54, $333,333 total compensation
EVP and General Counsel, Audrey Boone Tillman, age 50
President and COO Aflac Japan, Hiroshi Yamauchi, age 63
EVP; COO Aflac Group Insurance, Daniel J. (Dan) Lebish
President Aflac, Paul S. Amos, age 40, $667,900 total compensation
EVP; President Aflac U.S., Teresa L. White, age 49
SVP Business Services and President and CEO Communicorp, Eric B. Seldon
EVP and Global Chief Investment Officer, Eric M. Kirsch, $585,000 total compensation
Managing Director and Global Head of Credit Global Investments, Bradley E. Dyslin
SVP and CIO, Julia K. Davis
Managing Director and Global Chief Investment Risk Officer, Chakravarthi (Chak) Raghunathan
Managing Director and Chief Investments Technology Officer Global Investments, J. Pete Kelso
SVP and Global Chief Risk Officer, J. Todd Daniels
Managing Director and Global Head Macro Investment Strategy Portfolio Solutions and Trading Global Investments, Timothy (Chip) Stevens
Managing Director and Chief Investment Officer Global Investments, Teresa Q. McTague
Senior Vice President Worksite Marketing, John T (Jack) Harmeling
Senior Vice President Broker Sales and Aflac Benefits Solutions, Drew Niziak
Second Vice President, Ed Donahue
Second Vice President, Mary Keim
Vice President Controller Financial Reporting And Regulatory Compliance, Michael (Mel) Bruder
Senior Vice President, Kazuhiro Yamazaki
Second Vice President of Compliance, Deborah (Deb) Grantham
Vice President Information Technology Application Delivery, Tyler Bennett
Assistant Vice President Marketing, James Wardrup
Vice President Group Marketing, Jim Faile
Vice President Risk Management Development, Richard Sun
Vice President and Director Information Technology, Bryan Rogers
Vice President Product Marketing, Tom Morey
Second Vice President National Broker Marketing, Jeramy Tipton
Vice President Information Technology, John Brannen
Second Vice President Support Services, Kevin Dunlap
National Account Manager, Adam Bradshaw
Vice President Sales, Peter Crahan
Vice Presdent, Marc Lower

Second Vice President Corporate Tax, Robert (Bob) Landi
Second Vice President, Oz Roberts
Vice President Commissions, Jeff Arrington
Vice President Sales Support, Debbie Griffen
Second Vice President of Information Technology, Robert (Bob) Phibbs
Senior Vice President Federal Relations, David (Dave) Pringle
National Accounts Manager, Christine Harpster
Second Vice President, Jason Goodroe
Vice President, Michael Fisher
Senior Vice President Director Sales, Brad Jones
Vice President Salesforce Development, Lance Osborne
Assistant Vice President Trade Operations, John Nestorson
Second Vice President, Kimberly Reynolds
Second Vice President Compliance, James (Jamie) Hennessy
Market Vice President Broker Sales, Mark Hellickson
Senior Vice President and Director Sales, Mike Tomlinson
Vice President Information Technology, Jill Jacques
Vice President Information Technology, Brian Abeyta
Vice President Marketing, Tony Turner
Senior Vice President, Yuji Arai
Second Vice President, Tammy Briggs
Second Vice President Investor Relations, Robin Mullins
Vice President U.s. Risk Officer, Michel Perreault
Second Vice President, Hitoshi Oda
Vice President, Ron Agypt
Second Vice President Claims, Jefferey Engel
Vice President Information Technology, Jeff Link
Vice President Eastern Broker Div., William (Bill) Farmer
Vice President Treasury Corporate Finance, Nick Bettin
Senior Vice President Investment Strategy And Risk Management, Bill Wright
Vice President Risk Actuary, Charles (Chas) Qin
Senior Vice President Investor Relations, Robin Wilkey
Second Vice President Human Resources, Chad Melvin
Senior Vice President Investor Relations, Ken Janke
Vice President Enterprise Enrollment Operations, Eunice Holmes
Sec Tres, Danny Ivy
Board Member, Jeromy Song
Chapter Treasurer, Susan Faust
Board Member, Stephen Purdom
Auditors: KPMG LLP

LOCATIONS

HQ: AFLAC Inc.
  1932 Wynnton Road, Columbus, GA 31999
Phone: 706 323-3431   **Fax:** 706 596-3488
Web: www.aflac.com

PRODUCTS/OPERATIONS

2014 Sales

	$ mil.	% of total
Aflac Japan	16,555	72
Aflac US	5,859	26
Realized investment gains	171	1
Corporate	281	1
Other business	43	-
Adjustments	(181)	-
Total	**22,728**	**100**

COMPETITORS

American Fidelity Assurance Company	Meiji Yasuda Life
	MetLife

American National Insurance	Nippon Life Insurance
Asahi Mutual Life	Taiyo Life
CNO Financial	Torchmark
Colonial Life & Accident	Unum Group

HISTORICAL FINANCIALS

Company Type: Public

Income Statement

FYE: December 31

	ASSETS ($ mil.)	NET INCOME ($ mil.)	INCOME AS % OF ASSETS	EMPLOYEES
12/14	119,767	2,951	2.5%	9,525
12/13	121,307	3,158	2.6%	9,141
12/12	131,094	2,866	2.2%	8,965
12/11	117,102	1,964	1.7%	8,562
12/10	101,039	2,344	2.3%	8,211
Annual Growth	**4.3%**	**5.9%**	**—**	**3.8%**

2014 Year-End Financials

Debt ratio: 4.41%
Return on equity: 17.90%
Cash ($ mil.): 4,658
Current ratio: —
Long-term debt ($ mil.): —
No. of shares (mil.): 442
Dividends
  Yield: 2.4%
  Payout: 23.4%
Market value ($ mil.): 27,029

	STOCK PRICE ($) FY Close	P/E High/Low		PER SHARE ($) Earnings	Dividends	Book Value
12/14	61.09	10	9	6.50	1.50	41.47
12/13	66.80	10	7	6.76	1.42	31.82
12/12	53.12	9	6	6.11	1.34	34.16
12/11	43.26	14	7	4.18	1.23	28.96
12/10	56.43	12	8	4.95	1.14	23.54
Annual Growth	**2.0%**	**—**	**—**	**7.0%**	**7.1%**	**15.2%**

AGCO Corp.

AGCO's annual harvests may be smaller than those of major rivals John Deere and CNH but it reaps some healthy profits. AGCO makes tractors combines hay and forage tools sprayers grain storage and protein production systems seeding and tillage implements and replacement parts for agricultural end uses. It sells through a global network of some 3100 dealers and distributors spanning 140 countries. It also builds diesel engines gears and generators through its AGCO Sisu Power unit. Core brands include Massey Ferguson GSI Challenger Valtra (Finland-based) and Fendt (Germany). The company offers financing services to retail customers and dealers via a venture with Dutch company Rabobank.

HISTORY

In 1861 American Edward Allis purchased the bankrupt Reliance Works a leading Milwaukee-based manufacturer of sawmills and flour-milling equipment. Under shrewd management The Reliance Works of Edward P. Allis & Co. weathered financial troubles - bankruptcy in the Panic of 1873 —but managed to renegotiate its debt and recover. By the time Allis died in 1889 Reliance Works employed some 1500 workers.

The company branched into different areas of manufacturing in the late 19th century and by the 20th century the Edward P. Allis Co. (as it was then known) was the world leader in steam engines. In 1901 the company merged with another manufacturing giant Fraser & Chalmers to form the Allis-Chalmers Company. In the 1920s and 1930s Allis-Chalmers entered the farm equipment market.

Although overshadowed by John Deere and International Harvester (IH) Allis-Chalmers made key contributions to the industry —the first rubber-tired tractor (1932) and the All-Crop harvester. Allis-Chalmers spun off its farm equipment business in the 1950s and phased out several unrelated products. The company with its orange-colored tractors expanded and prospered from the 1940s through the early 1970s. Then the chafing farm economy of the late 1970s and early 1980s hurt Allis-Chalmers' sales.

After layoffs and a plant shutdown in 1984 the company was purchased in 1985 by German machinery maker Klockner-Humbolt-Deutz (KHD) who moved the company (renamed Deutz-Allis) to Georgia. In the mid-1980s low food prices hurt farmers and low demand hurt the equipment market. KHD was never able to bring profits up to a satisfactory level and in 1990 the German firm sold the unit to the US management in a buyout led by Robert Ratliff. Ratliff believed the company could succeed by acquiring belly-up equipment makers turning them around and competing on price.

Renamed AGCO the company launched a buying spree in 1991 that included Fiat's Hesston (1991) White Tractor (1991) the North American distribution rights for Massey Ferguson (1993) and White-New Idea (1993). The bumper crop of product growth enabled it to slice into the market share of competitors Deere and Case. AGCO went public in 1992. Its 1994 purchase of the remainder of Massey Ferguson (with 20% of the world market) vaulted AGCO to prominence among the world's leading farm equipment makers.

In 1996 AGCO launched a five-year plan for European growth. In 1997 the company acquired German farm equipment makers Fendt and Dronniberg. It also picked up Deutz Argentina a supplier of agricultural equipment engines and vehicles as part of an effort to expand into Latin and South America.

AGCO entered the agricultural sprayer market in 1998 by acquiring the Spra-Coupe line from Ingersoll-Rand and the Willmar line from Cargill. A worldwide drop in farm equipment sales caused AGCO to cut about 10% of its workforce.

To further overcome stalled sales and slumping profits in 1999 the company announced it was permanently closing an Ohio plant and would cease production at a Texas plant. The next year AGCO closed its Missouri plant and trimmed its workforce by about 5%.

In 2001 AGCO acquired fertilizer equipment manufacturer Ag-Chem Equipment and the next year it completed the purchase of certain assets relating to the design assembly and marketing of the MT 700 and MT 800 series of Caterpillar's Challenger rubber-tracked farm tractors.

AGCO added to its harvesting equipment segment in 2002 by purchasing Beloit-based Sunflower Manufacturing for an undisclosed price. That year AGCO suffered a tragic loss when president and CEO John Shumejda and SVP Ed Swingle were killed in an airplane accident in the UK.

The company added Valtra in early 2004 a global tractor and off-road engine maker to its fold for about $750 million. In 2004 chairman Robert Ratliff handed Martin Richenhagen the president and CEO titles he had taken on after the death of Shumejda.

AGCO announced late in 2006 a new growth initiative dubbed "Always Growing." The strategy makes some basic assumptions about the trends emerging in global agriculture. They include the increase in mega-farms exponential growth in cer-

tain developing countries increased demand for biofuels in developed nations and increasingly advanced technology.

In 2007 it bought Indúustria Agríacutecola Fortaleza Limitada a leading Brazilian maker of farm implements and purchased a 50% stake in Laverda an Italian harvesting equipment producer to further expand its overseas presence.

It partnered with Topcon and Sauer-Danfoss in 2008 to provide steering technology for its professional farming equipment. The company formed a joint venture with one of Russia's leading industrial equipment producers CTP to assemble engines.

AGCO has taken advantage of public funding too. In 2009 the company was selected by the US Department of Energy for a $5 million grant to determine whether a hay product can be used to supply large biomass feedstock to biofuel processors. AGCO is working with renewable fuel companies and industry experts to develop an efficient method of collecting and transporting biomass to production plants.

In an effort to reduce costs and selling and administrative expenses as well as align inventory supply with global market demand AGCO restructured during 2010 and 2009. The company cut headcount and closed and consolidated manufacturing facilities in the US UK France Germany Spain Finland and Denmark. AGCO also instituted temporary plant shutdowns in all of its factories and cut production reducing both its company and dealer inventories.

Filling a regional product niche AGCO in late 2010 purchased UK-based Sparex from Rubicon Partners Industries for £53 million (more than $75 million). Sparex is a global distributor of tractor replacement parts; it extends AGCO's portfolio of accessories as well as its reach into for the agricultural aftermarket.

In 2011 AGCO scooped up its remaining 50% stake in Laverda S.p.A. a JV that manufactures mid-range combine harvesters for sale in the Europe/Africa/Middle East region. Later that year AGCO acquired GSI Holdings from Centerbridge Partners for roughly $928 million. GSI manufactures grain conditioning and drying material handling and bulk storage equipment. The company also makes poultry and swine feeding confinement and environmental control systems.

EXECUTIVES

SVP and CFO, Andrew H. (Andy) Beck, age 51, $521,250 total compensation
SVP; General Manager Asia Pacific, Gary L. Collar, age 58, $473,750 total compensation
Chairman President and CEO, Martin H. Richenhagen, age 62, $1,329,556 total compensation
SVP; General Manager North America, Robert B. Crain, age 55, $306,667 total compensation
SVP and Chief Supply Chain Officer, Hans-Bernd Veltmaat, age 60, $571,375 total compensation
SVP Global Grain and Protein GSI, Thomas Welke
SVP; General Manager Europe Africa and Middle East, Rob Smith
Svp Global Grain & Protein, Tom Welke
Vice President Compliance Officer, Roger Batkin
Vice President General Counsel, Debra Kuper
Vice President World Wide Procurement, Paul Blackmore
Vice President Sales, Dennis Heinecke
Vice President Director Manager, Joey Goodson
Vice President Manager Director, David Curts
Vice President Finance, Brian Zydel
Vice President of Field Sales North America, Bill Hurley
Vice President Purchasing and Materials, Torsten Dehner
Vice President and Treasurer, David (Dave) Williams

Vice President Director Manager, Steve Murphy
Senior Vice President Human Resources, Lucinda Smith
Vice President President, Hans Lehmann
Vice President Product Engineering, Luiz Ghiggi
Vice President Purchasing Logistics and Materials, Gustavo Taboas
Vice President Finance, Frederic Devienne
National Sales Manager, Martin Mills
Vice President Challenger Business Development, Alistair (Al) Mclelland
Senior Vice President Engineering, Helmut Endres
Senior Vice President Engineering, Gary Ball
Vice President Managing Director China India, Andreas Weishaar
Auditors: KPMG LLP

LOCATIONS

HQ: AGCO Corp.
  4205 River Green Parkway, Duluth, GA 30096
Phone: 770 813-9200
Web: www.agcocorp.com

2014 Sales

	$ mil.	% of total
Europe		
Germany	1,240	13
France	828	9
Finland & Scandinavia	808	8
UK & Ireland	490	5
Other Europe	1,376	14
US	1,985	20
South America	1,646	17
Canada	333	4
Middle East & Africa	414	4
Asia	253	3
Australia & New Zealand	234	2
Mexico Central America & Caribbean	112	1
Total	**9,723**	**100**

PRODUCTS/OPERATIONS

2014 Sales

	$ mil.	% of total
Tractors	5,566	57
Replacement parts	1,390	14
Grain storage & protein production systems	851	9
Combines	581	9
Application equipment	459	6
Other machinery	875	5
Total	**9,723**	**100**

Selected Products

Application equipment
Combine Harvesters
Grounds care
Hay and forage
Implements attachments and material handling
Power generation
Seeding and tillage
Tractors

COMPETITORS

Buhler Industries	Komatsu
CNH Industrial	Kubota
Caterpillar	Mahindra
Deere	Toro Company

HISTORICAL FINANCIALS

Company Type: Public

Income Statement

FYE: December 31

	REVENUE ($ mil.)	NET INCOME ($ mil.)	NET PROFIT MARGIN	EMPLOYEES
12/14	9,723	404	4.2%	20,800
12/13	10,786	592	5.5%	22,100
12/12	9,962	516	5.2%	20,300
12/11	8,773	585	6.7%	17,400
12/10	6,896	220	3.2%	14,300
Annual Growth	**9.0%**	**16.4%**	**—**	**9.8%**

2014 Year-End Financials

Debt ratio: 14.76%
Return on equity: 10.84%
Cash ($ mil.): 363
Current ratio: 1.59
Long-term debt ($ mil.): 997

No. of shares (mil.): 89
Dividends
  Yield: 0.9%
  Payout: 9.0%
Market value ($ mil.): 4,029

	STOCK PRICE ($) FY Close	P/E High/Low		PER SHARE ($) Earnings	Dividends	Book Value
12/14	45.20	13	10	4.36	0.44	38.68
12/13	59.19	10	8	6.01	0.40	41.19
12/12	49.12	10	7	5.30	0.00	35.79
12/11	42.97	10	5	5.95	0.00	30.82
12/10	50.66	21	11	2.29	0.00	28.54
Annual Growth	(2.8%)	—	—	17.5%	—	7.9%

Air Products & Chemicals, Inc.

Air Products and Chemicals looks for its profits to expand like the gases it sells. The company provides gases such as argon hydrogen nitrogen and oxygen to manufacturers health care facilities and energy markets. Air Products' largest segment (through fiscal 2014) was Merchant Gases which manufactures atmospheric process and specialty gases delivered from tanker truck trailer or on-site. The company's Tonnage Gases segment serves the global refining and chemical industries while its Electronics and Performance Materials unit serves electronics and other manufacturing companies. Air Products also makes gas containers and equipment that separates air purifies hydrogen and liquefies gas.

HISTORY

In the early 1900s Leonard Pool the son of a boilermaker began selling oxygen to industrial users. By the time he was 30 he was district manager for Compressed Industrial Gases. In the late 1930s Pool hired engineer Frank Pavlis to help him design a cheaper more efficient oxygen generator. In 1940 they had the design and Pool established Air Products in Detroit (initially sharing space with the cadavers collected by his brother who was starting a mortuary science college). The company was based on a simple breakthrough concept: the provision of on-site gases. Instead of delivering oxygen in cylinders Pool proposed to build oxygen-generating facilities near large-volume gas users and then lease them reducing distribution costs.

Although industrialists encouraged Pool to pursue his ideas few orders were forthcoming and the company faced financial crisis. The outbreak of WWII got the company out of difficulty as the US military became a major customer. During the war the company moved to Chattanooga Tennessee for the available labor.

The end of the war brought with it another downturn as demand dried up. By waiting at the Weirton Steel plant until a contract was signed Pool won a contract for three on-site generators. Weirton was nearly the company's only customer. Pool relocated the company to Allentown Pennsylvania to be closer to the Northeast's industrial market where he could secure more contracts with steel companies.

The Cold War and the launching of the Sputnik satellite in 1957 propelled the company's growth. Convinced that Soviet rockets were powered by liquid hydrogen the US government asked Air Products to supply it with the volatile fuel. The company entered the overseas market that year through a joint venture with Butterley (UK) to which it licensed its cryogenic processes and equipment. The company went public in 1961 and formed a subsidiary in Belgium in 1964.

Air Products diversified into chemicals when it bought Houdry Process (chemicals and chemical-plant maintenance 1962) and Airco's chemicals and plastics operations in the 1970s. The company continued to diversify in the mid-1980s as it built large-scale plants for its environmental- and energy-systems business and added Anchor Chemical and the industrial chemicals unit of Abbott Labs.

In 1995 and 1996 Air Products expanded into China and other countries by winning 20 contracts with semiconductor makers. It bought Carburos Metálicos Spain's #1 industrial gas supplier in 1996. To focus on its core gas and chemical lines the company shed most of its environmental- and energy-systems business.

Expanding further in Europe Air Products bought the methylamines and derivatives unit of UK-based Imperial Chemical Industries (ICI) in 1997. The company sold its remaining interest in American Ref-Fuel (a waste-to-energy US operation).

In 1998 Air Products bought Solkatronic Chemicals and opened a methylamines plant in Florida to complement its ICI purchase. To further target semiconductor makers it formed Air Products Electronic Chemicals and allied with AlliedSignal Chemical (now part of Honeywell International).

The next year Air Products and France's L'Air Liquide agreed to buy and break up BOC Group. European Union regulators initially approved the deal but in 2000 the companies shelved the plan when other regulatory issues arose. Also in 2000 Air Products sold its polyvinyl alcohol business to Celanese for about $326 million. The company boosted its European presence in 2001 with the acquisition of Messer Griesheim's (Germany) respiratory home-care business and 50% of AGA's Netherlands industrial gases operations.

Air Products was hurt by the slowdown in manufacturing primarily in the electronics and steel industries which are major customers for gases. Its chemical revenues also were hurt by pressure on pricing. To improve profits the company initiated cost cuts including job cuts (about 10% of its employees) and divestitures such as its US packaged gas business.

The company broadened its health care operations in late 2002 by acquiring American Homecare Supply. It appeared briefly that Air Products wanted to devote a great deal of attention to the health care business. The company had created its Air Products Healthcare unit in 1999 and expanded it greatly three years later with the acquisition of American Homecare Supply. Air Products proceeded to add to the division through subsequent acquisitions; however the US portion of the business never performed to the company's expectations and Air Products sold the domestic operations of the health care unit in 2008 and 2009.

It also decided to divest its chemicals operations in the latter half of the decade. Those operations included the production of catalysts surfactants and intermediates derived from vinyl acetate monomer (VAM) all of which it sold in 2008. Air Products had sold its amines business to chemical company Taminco in 2006. The company's polymers operations which were run through a joint venture with Wacker-Chemie called Air Products Polymers were divested in 2008. The company

sold most of its holdings in the JV to Wacker for $265 million though two facilities that had belonged to the joint venture were sold to Ashland Performance Materials.

In 2007 Air Products made a small but strategic move into Eastern Europe. The company took advantage of Linde's selloff of some BOC assets after the German company bought BOC in 2006. Air Products acquired the Polish Gazy SP for just under $500 million with the hopes of moving into the Central and Eastern European markets to take advantage of the migration of manufacturing to the region.

In 2010 the company made a major bid to buy rival Airgas but it was rejected. The Airgas board considered the $5.1 billion offer too low. Air Products extended its tender offer to Airgas stockholders several times making its "best and final offer" of $70 a share in December 2010. Airgas also rejected that offer.

In late 2012 Air Products opened an advanced gas applications laboratory in Shanghai to support the increasing needs in high-growth markets in China across Asia.

In addition to growing organically the company has been divesting operations to focus on its higher growth operations and to pursue strategic acquisitions. By early 2012 the company began divesting units to focus on more profitable operations. It sold its homecare business in continental Europe (which supplied oxygen and infusion treatments in Belgium France Germany Portugal and Spain) to Germany's Linde for $750 million. The company also began evaluating its homecare assets in Argentina Brazil Ireland and the UK.

With more money in its coffers from divestments in 2012 the company acquired Germany-based ROVI Cosmetics International which develops delivery systems for the personal care industry in Europe. The unit is now part of the company's Performance Materials division. To extend its Latin American footprint Air Products in 2012 acquired a 67% stake in Indura S.A. an industrial gas company in Chile for $884 million.

EXECUTIVES

Chairman President and CEO, Seifi Ghasemi, age 69, $295,385 total compensation
VP Energy-from-Waste, David J. Taylor, age 60
EVP Industrial Gases, Corning F. Painter, age 52, $491,538 total compensation
President Industrial Gases-Europe Middle East and Africa, Ivo Bols
President Industrial Gases -Asia, Wilbur W. Mok
President Industrial Gases -Middle East India Egypt and Turkey, Richard Boocock
SVP and CFO, M. Scott Crocco, age 50, $529,038 total compensation
SVP General Counsel and Chief Administrative Officer, John D. Stanley, age 57, $565,577 total compensation
President Industrial Gases Americas, Marie Ffolkes
EVP Materials Technology, Guillermo Novo, age 52
VP China Industrial Gases, Choon Seong Saw
VP and CIO, Alyssa A. Budraitis
VP and General Manager Performance Materials Division, Robert W. Thomas
Vice President and General Manager Performance Materials, Patricia A (Pat) Mattimore
Vice President Human Resources, Jennifer (Jen) Woo
Vice President Finance, Kent Shaibley
Vice President and General Manager Healthcare, John W (Jack) Marsland
Regional Vice President General Manager Southeast Asia and Asia Base Gases Air Products Asia Inc., Robert (Bob) Lewis
Secretary, Mary Afflerbach

Secretary Management Information, Cyndie Kazlas
Auditors: KPMG LLP

LOCATIONS

HQ: Air Products & Chemicals, Inc.
7201 Hamilton Boulevard, Allentown, PA 18195-1501
Phone: 610 481-4911   **Fax:** 610 481-5900
Web: www.airproducts.com

2014 Sales

	$ mil.	% of total
North America		
US	4,507	43
Canada	311	3
Europe	2,628	25
Asia (Excluding China)	1,389	13
China	981	10
Latin America	621	6
Total	**10,439**	**100**

PRODUCTS/OPERATIONS

2014 Sales

	$ mil.	% of total
Merchant Gases	4,250	41
Tonnage Gases	3,288	32
Electronics & Performance Materials	2,449	23
Equipment & Energy	450	4
Total	**10,439**	**100**

Selected Products and Services

Industrial Gases
  Argon
  Carbon dioxide
  Carbon monoxide
  Helium
  Hydrogen
  Nitrogen
  Oxygen
  Synthesis gas
Equipment and Services
  Air-pollution control systems
  Air-separation equipment
  Hydrogen-purification equipment
  Natural gas-liquefaction equipment

COMPETITORS

Aceto	Messer Group
Airgas	Praxair
BASF SE	Taiyo Nippon Sanso
Bayer AG	The Linde Group
L' Air Liquide	

HISTORICAL FINANCIALS

Company Type: Public

Income Statement

FYE: September 30

	REVENUE ($ mil.)	NET INCOME ($ mil.)	NET PROFIT MARGIN	EMPLOYEES
09/15	9,894	1,277	12.9%	19,700
09/14	10,439	991	9.5%	21,200
09/13	10,180	994	9.8%	21,600
09/12	9,611	1,167	12.1%	21,300
09/11	10,082	1,224	12.1%	18,900
Annual Growth	(0.5%)	1.1%	—	1.0%

2015 Year-End Financials

Debt ratio: 33.71%
Return on equity: 17.49%
Cash ($ mil.): 206
Current ratio: 0.80
Long-term debt ($ mil.): 3,949

No. of shares (mil.): 215
Dividends
  Yield: 2.5%
  Payout: 66.9%
Market value ($ mil.): 27,476

	STOCK PRICE ($) FY Close	P/E High/Low	PER SHARE ($) Earnings	Dividends	Book Value
09/15	127.58	27 20	5.88	3.20	33.66
09/14	130.18	29 22	4.61	3.02	34.49
09/13	106.57	23 16	4.68	2.77	33.35
09/12	82.70	17 13	5.44	2.50	30.48
09/11	76.37	17 13	5.63	2.23	27.57
Annual Growth	13.7%	— —	1.1%	9.4%	5.1%

Airgas Inc.

Airgas has floated to the top of the industrial gas distribution industry. Its North American network of more than 1100 locations includes retail stores gas fill plants specialty gas labs production facilities (16 air separation plants) and distribution centers. Airgas distributes argon carbon dioxide hydrogen nitrogen oxygen and a variety of medical and specialty gases as well as dry ice and protective equipment (hard hats goggles). Its gases production unit operates air-separation plants that produce oxygen nitrogen and argon. The company also sells welding machines. In 2015 France's Air Liquide SA agreed to buy Airgas for $13.4 billion.

HISTORY

In the early 1980s Peter McCausland was a corporate attorney involved in mergers and acquisitions for Messer Griesheim a large German industrial gas producer. When the German firm declined McCausland's recommendation in 1982 to buy Connecticut Oxygen he raised money from private sources and bought it himself. He acquired other distributors and then left Messer Griesheim in 1987 to run Airgas full-time.

Airgas began buying mostly small local and regional gas distributors in the US. By 1994 strategy shifted to purchasing larger "superregional" distributors such as Jimmie Jones Co. and Post Welding Supply of Alabama which added about $70 million combined to the company's revenues.

Airgas then began "rolling up" additional similar businesses. In 1995 it bought more than 25 companies and two years later it added more than 20 gas distributors. Also in 1997 Airgas expanded its manufacturing capabilities by building five plants that could fast-fill whole pallets of gas cylinders (the old manual system rolls cylinders two at a time). By 2000 the company had about 100 cylinder fill plants.

Struggling to integrate acquisitions while dealing with softening markets Airgas began a companywide realignment in 1998. To that end it sold its calcium carbide and carbon products operations to former partner Elkem ASA later that year; the company also consolidated 34 hubs into 16 regional companies and sold its operations in Poland and Thailand to Germany-based Linde in 1999.

In 2000 Airgas acquired distributor Mallinckrodt's Puritan-Bennett division (gas products for medical uses) with 36 locations in the US and Canada. The company also acquired the majority of Air Products' US packaged gas business excluding its electronic gases and magnetic resonance imaging-related helium operations in 2002.

In 2004 and 2005 it bought units from giants like Air Products and Chemicals BOC and LaRoche Industries. In 2006 Airgas continued to build with the purchase of 10 businesses includ-

ing Union Industrial Gas which supplies Texas and much of the Southwest and then Linde's US bulk gas business for $495 million the next year. Linde in the process of integrating its 2006 acquisition of BOC then sold to Airgas a portion of its US packaged gas business for $310 million.

Rival Air Products had made a major bid to buy Airgas in 2010 but was rebuffed. Air Products extended its tender offer to Airgas stockholders several times and made a "best and final offer" of $70 a share (almost $6 billion) in December 2010. Airgas said it was holding out for $78 a share and rejected that offer too. In early 2011 a Delaware judge ruled for Airgas in a suit brought by Air Products to set aside a "poison pill" defense used by the Airgas board to fend off the takeover try. Following the verdict Air Products dropped its bid.

Airgas acquired six businesses in 2010 including Tri-Tech an independent distributor with 16 locations throughout Florida Georgia and South Carolina and annual sales of $31 million.

In 2011 Airgas reorganized its 12 regional segments into four new business support divisions — North South Central and West –to leverage a new SAP information systems platform in 2011. Each of the units is headed by a division president. The new company structure is designed to accelerate sales growth and pricing management and create operating efficiencies.

In fiscal 2012 the company added eight businesses with total annual sales of about $106 million. The largest of the businesses acquired were ABCO Gases Welding and Industrial Supply Company (ABCO); Pain Enterprises; and Industrial Welding Supplies of Hattiesburg (doing business as Nordan Smith). Connecticut-based ABCO has 12 industrial and gas welding supply locations throughout New England. Indiana-based Pain operates 20 dry ice and liquid carbon dioxide production and distribution sites. Mississippi-based Nordan Smith has 17 locations that distribute industrial medical and specialty gases and supplies thoughout Alabama Arkansas and Mississippi.

EXECUTIVES

President Airgas USA, Andrew R. (Andy) Cichocki, $296,936 total compensation
President Airgas North Division, Pamela J. (Pam) Claypool, age 61
Area Vice President, Tracy Mcdowell
SVP Sales and Marketing, Ronald J. (Ron) Stark, age 51
President and CEO, Michael L. (Mike) Molinini, age 65, $862,750 total compensation
SVP and CIO, Robert A. Dougherty, age 58, $263,779 total compensation
President Airgas South, John F. Sheehan
SVP and CFO, Robert M. (Bob) McLaughlin, age 59, $470,453 total compensation
Division President Gases Production, Thomas S. Thoman, age 52
Division President West, Douglas L. (Doug) Jones, age 59
SVP and General Counsel, Robert H. Young, age 65, $397,272 total compensation
Division President Central, Terry L. Lodge, age 58
President East Region, Jack Appolonia
Vice President Medical, Richard (Dick) Sniezek
Vice President Safety, Tom Hanus
Vice President of Information technology Airgas Mid South, George Turner
Vice President Central Division, Don Berndsen
Vice President Information Technology, Brian Rodden
Vice President of Finance, Mike Allison
Vice President Business Development, Bruce Woerner
Vice President, James Cook
National Sales Manager, Jerry Anderskow

Vice President, Cindi Brown
Vice President, Angela Cobb
Vice President Retail Sales, Andrea Zamora
Vice President Gas Supply Chain, Buddy Edwards
Vice President Of Global Operations, Josh Mosko
Vice President Area, David (Dave) Webb
Vice President Finance, Monica Garza
Assistant Vice President, Tracy Pfeffer
Vice President Of Plant Operations, Roger Weber
Vice President of Bulk Operations, Steve Scheuring
Vice President Finance, Sandra Fowler-hurt
Area Vice President, Jason Kirby
Vice President, Lennett Gensel
Vice President, Brandon Helms
Vice President Gas Operations, Ted Schulte
Vice President, Bob Collier
Vice President, Brenda Sabatino
Vice President Pkg Gas, John Harris
Vice President Of Finance, Jennifer Mihaljcic
Vice President Finance, Michael (Mel) Maley
Vice President Infrastructure Operations And
  Technical Services, Rajan Ramamoorthy
Vice President Of Finance, Randall Cornelius
Vice President Of Sales, Susan Starnes
Regional Vice President, David Burnstein
Vice President Enterprise Information Technology
  Infrastructure, Anthony Green
Vice President Strategic Accounts, Otto Gaus
Area Vice President, Jeff Mann
National Sales Manager, Sheila Boyle
Area Vice President, Brian Blackwood
Assistant Vice President Corporate Development,
  Brian Shammo
Vice President Hardgoods, David (Dave) Levin
Vice President Operations, Tony Simonetta
Division Vice President of Sales, Mark Johnston
Vice President, Wayne Wilson
Area Vice President, Kent Carter
Vice President Sales and Marketing, Gene Klein
Executive Chairman, Peter McCausland, age 64
Secretary, Jennifer (Jen) Zajac
Treasurer, Kirk Jordan
Board Member, Eric Chase
Board Member, Sal Gonzalez
Auditors: KPMG LLP

LOCATIONS

HQ: Airgas Inc.
  259 North Radnor-Chester Road, Suite 100, Radnor,
  PA 19087-5283
Phone: 610 687-5253   Fax: 610 687-1052
Web: www.airgas.com

PRODUCTS/OPERATIONS

2015 Sales

	% of total
Manufacturing & Metal Fabrication	29
Non Residential (Energy & Infrastructure) construction	14
Life Science & Healthcare	14
Food Beverage & Retail	13
Energy & Chemical Production & Distribution	12
Basic Material & Services	12
Government & Others	6
Total	**100**

2015 Sales

	$ mil.	% of total
Distribution	4,773	89
Other Operations	560	11
Adjustments	(29.2)	-
Total	**5,304**	**100**

Selected Products and Services

Products
  Carbon dioxide
  Dry ice
  Industrial gases
  Argon
  Helium
  Hydrogen
  Liquid oxygen
  Nitrogen
  Nitrous oxide
  Oxygen
  Safety equipment
  Specialty gases
Services
  Container rental
  Welding equipment rental

Selected Subsidiaries

Airgas Canada
Airgas Carbonic
Airgas East
Airgas Great Lakes
Airgas Intermountain
Airgas Medical Services
Airgas Mid America
Airgas Mid South
Airgas Nitrous Oxide
Airgas Nor Pac
Airgas North Central
Airgas Northern California & Nevada
Airgas Refrigerant
Airgas Safety
Airgas South
Airgas Southwest
Airgas Specialty Gases
Airgas Specialty Products
Airgas West
National Welders Supply Company dba Airgas National
  Welders
Nitrous Oxide Corp.
Red-D-Arc
WorldWide Welding LLC

COMPETITORS

Air Products	Matheson Tri-Gas
American Air Liquide	Praxair Distribution
L' Air Liquide	Valley National Gases
Lincoln Electric	W.W. Grainger

HISTORICAL FINANCIALS

Company Type: Public

Income Statement

FYE: March 31

	REVENUE ($ mil.)	NET INCOME ($ mil.)	NET PROFIT MARGIN	EMPLOYEES
03/15	5,304	368	6.9%	17,000
03/14	5,072	350	6.9%	16,000
03/13	4,957	340	6.9%	15,000
03/12	4,746	313	6.6%	15,000
03/11	4,251	249	5.9%	14,000
Annual Growth	5.7%	10.2%	—	5.0%

2015 Year-End Financials

Debt ratio: 38.92%
Return on equity: 18.44%
Cash ($ mil.): 50
Current ratio: 1.25
Long-term debt ($ mil.): 1,748

No. of shares (mil.): 75
Dividends
  Yield: 2.0%
  Payout: 45.0%
Market value ($ mil.): 7,996

	STOCK PRICE ($) FY Close	P/E High/Low	PER SHARE ($) Earnings	Dividends	Book Value
03/15	106.11	24 21	4.85	2.20	28.55
03/14	106.51	24 20	4.68	1.92	24.84
03/13	99.16	23 18	4.35	1.60	21.04
03/12	88.97	22 14	4.00	1.25	22.83
03/11	66.42	24 20	2.93	1.01	21.80
Annual Growth	12.4%	— —	13.4%	21.5%	7.0%

AK Steel Holding Corp.

Automobile sales help AK Steel's business keep rolling though it also has operations in the infrastructure and manufacturing industries. The company manufactures carbon stainless and electrical steel. It sells hot- and cold-rolled carbon steel to construction companies steel distributors and service centers and automotive and industrial machinery producers. AK Steel also sells cold-rolled and aluminum-coated stainless steel to automakers. The company produces electrical steels (iron-silicon alloys with unique magnetic properties) for makers of power transmission and distribution equipment.

Geographic Reach

AK Steel has eight steelmaking finishing and tubing facilities in Indiana Michigan Kentucky Ohio Pennsylvania and West Virginia. The company also operates subsidiaries in the UK the Netherlands Italy France Germany and other countries. The US accounted for 88% of AK Steel's 2014 revenues.

Operations

The steelmaker operates on a consolidated integrated basis in order to use the most appropriate equipment and facilities for the production of each product. Its major subsidiaries include AK Tube LLC AK Coal Resources Inc and Magnetation LLC. AK Tube produces carbon and stainless electric resistance welded tubular steel products for truck automotive and other markets.

It produces flat-rolled value-added carbon steels including premium-quality coated cold-rolled and hot-rolled carbon steel products and specialty stainless and electrical steels that are sold in sheet and strip form as well as carbon and stainless steel that is finished into welded steel tubing.

It also works through joint ventures to share costs. Its Magnetation LLC joint venture with Magnetation Inc. uses advanced magnetic separation technology to recover iron ore from existing stockpiles of previously-mined material. In addition AK Steel indirectly owns 50% of Vicksmetal/Armco Associates a joint venture with Sumitomo unit Vicksmetal Company. The joint venture slits electrical steel primarily for AK Steel and for third parties.

Sales and MarketingAK Steel sells a major portion of its flat-rolled carbon steel products and stainless steel products to US automotive manufacturers and to distributors service centers and converters. It sells electrical steel products (in the US and globally) to manufacturers of power transmission and distribution transformers and electrical motors and generators to the infrastructure and manufacturing customers.

The automotive industry accounted for 53% of the company's net sales in 2014; distributors and converters 29%; infrastructure and manufacturing 18%.

Financial Performance

In 2014 net revenues increased by 17% due to higher shipments thanks to the addition of shipments from Dearborn Works following the acquisition of Dearborn in September 2014 and higher shipments of carbon steel to the automotive and infrastructure and manufacturing markets.

Carbon steel was the major contributor of net revenues up 21% over the previous year. The total shipment was 6.1 million tons in 20114 (up from 5.3 million tons in 2013).The company has reported consecutive net losses over the last five years.

AK Steel's net loss attributable to AK Holding in 2014 was $96.9 million compared to $46.8 million in 2013. It included a pension corridor charge and other Post employment benefits settlement loss of $5.5 million. The net loss in 2014 also included Dearborn acquisition-related costs of $31.7 million. The company recorded an accumulated deficit of $2.5 billion in 2014.In 2014 cash from operating activities increased by 193%.

Strategy

The steel industry has been consolidating for years as troubled companies have been snapped up by market leaders. AK Steel has maintained its independence however in part because of its status as a leading supplier of some high-grade niche products such as components of stainless steel exhaust systems for carmakers.In 2015 the company announced plans to build a new world-class research and innovative center in Middletown Ohio by investing $36 million. This center will provide advanced technical support to its customers and develop new and improved products.

In a refinancing move in 2013 the company's Magnetation LLC joint venture completed a $325 million senior secured note offering and has entered into a $50 million senior secured credit facility. The proceeds will be used to fund construction of a new plant in Reynolds Indiana to produce high-quality iron ore pellets to supply AK Steel's blast furnaces in Ohio and Kentucky. Magnetation will provide the company with 50% of its annual iron ore requirements beginning in 2015.

Mergers and Acquisitions

Growing its assets in 2014 AK Steel acquired Severstal North America's integrated steelmaking plant in Dearborn Michigan for $707 million.

HISTORY

George Verity who was in the roofing business in Cincinnati around the turn of the century often had trouble getting sheet metal so in 1900 he founded his own steel company American Rolling Mill. His first plant in Middletown Ohio was followed by a second production facility 11 years later in Ashland Kentucky. Plant superintendent John Tytus whose family was in paper milling applied those rolling techniques to make American Rolling Mill's steel more uniform in thickness.

In 1926 Columbia Steel developed a process to overcome several production problems inherent in the Tytus method and in 1930 American Rolling Mill bought Columbia Steel. The company changed its name to Armco Steel in 1948.

Armco began diversifying in the 1950s and continued diversifying until the early 1980s. Subsidiaries were involved in coal oil and gas-drilling equipment and insurance and financial services among other things. In 1978 the company changed its name to Armco Inc.

Armco began shedding subsidiaries in the early 1980s. Sales and market share increased as the company approached the billion-dollar mark at the end of the decade. In 1989 Armco formed Armco Steel Company with Japan's Kawasaki Steel Corporation.

The company's sales reached $1.3 billion in 1991 though the high operating expenses in the steel industry of the 1990s kept profits low. Armco began looking outside the company for help and in 1992 it persuaded retired steel executive Tom Graham to head the company. Graham brought with him another industry veteran Richard Wardrop who would succeed Graham as CEO in 1995. After evaluating the company's holdings the two divested more than 10 subsidiaries and divisions. Armco also worked on improving quality and customer service with special emphasis placed on timely delivery.

In 1994 Armco's limited partnership with Kawasaki was altered and AK Steel Holding Corporation was formed with AK Steel Corporation as its main subsidiary and the Middletown and Ashland plants as its production base. The holding company went public the same year raising more than $650 million enabling the company to pay off its debt.

AK Steel Holding moved its headquarters to Middletown Ohio in 1995. Despite many naysayers Graham then pushed a plan to build a state-of-the-art $1.1 billion steel production facility. Many doubted the wisdom of going into long-term debt so soon after coming out of the hole —especially when a similar facility had produced lackluster results for Inland Steel. Graham stuck by his plant and in 1997 ground was broken on the facility in Spencer County near Rockport Indiana (Rockport Works). Graham retired that year and Wardrop took over as chairman.

In 1998 the company opened its Rockport Works cold-rolling mill and began operating a hot-dip galvanizing and galvannealing line. The next year AK Steel bought former parent Armco for $842 million. AK Steel acquired welded steel tubing maker Alpha Tube Corporation (renamed AK Tube LLC) in 2001. In late 2001 the company took a charge of $194 million for losses in its pension fund which had been battered by a weak stock market and lowered interest rates.

AK Steel sold its Sawhill Tubular Division to John Maneely Company (Collingswood NJ) for roughly $50 million in 2002.

AK Steel offered to purchase National Steel which was operating under Chapter 11 bankruptcy protection. However AK Steel's bid was trumped in 2003 by one from U.S. Steel that included a ratified labor agreement with the United Steelworkers of America. AK Steel also lost out in an effort to acquire Rouge Industries (later Severstal North America).

Chairman and CEO Wardrop and president John Hritz left their posts in September 2003. CFO James Wainscott was named president and CEO and Robert Jenkins became chairman. (Wainscott succeeded Jenkins as chairman in January 2006.)

In an effort to reduce its debt AK Steel in 2004 sold its Douglas Dynamics unit a maker of snow and ice removal equipment for $260 million and its Greens Port Industrial Park a 600-acre development in Houston for $75 million.

In 2007 the company moved its corporate headquarters to West Chester Ohio.

EXECUTIVES

VP Finance and CFO, Jaime Vasquez
EVP General Counsel and Secretary, David C. Horn, age 64, $692,276 total compensation
CEO, Roger K. Newport, age 50, $460,257 total compensation
VP Operations, Keith J. Howell, age 49, $340,000 total compensation
President and COO, Kirk W. Reich, age 47, $359,872 total compensation
VP Engineering Raw Materials and Energy, Maurice A. Reed, age 52
VP Research and Innovation, Eric S. Petersen, age 45
Executive Vice President Of Information Technology, Steve Boston
Senior Vice President of Human Resources, Larry Zizzo
Vice President and Controller, Gary Sussman
Vice President Human Resources, Lawrence F Zizzo
Chairman, James L. (Jim) Wainscott, age 58
Board Member, James Franzer
Auditors: Ernst & Young LLP

LOCATIONS

HQ: AK Steel Holding Corp.
9227 Centre Pointe Drive, West Chester, OH 45069
Phone: 513 425-5000 **Fax:** 513 425-5220
Web: www.aksteel.com

2014 Sales

	$ mil.	% of total
United States	5,750	88
Foreign countries	755	12
Total	**6,505**	**100**

PRODUCTS/OPERATIONS

2014 Sales (by Market)

	% of total
Automotive	53
Distributors & converters	29
Infrastructure & manufacturing	18
Total	**100**

2014 Sales (by product)

	$ mil.	% of total
Carbon steel	4,423	68
Stainless & electrical steel	1,836	28
Tubular steel	231	4
Other	14	0
Total	**6,505**	**100**

Carbon Steels
Alumized
Coil coated products
Cold rolled
Electrogalvanized
Enameling products
Hot dip galvanized
Hot dip galvannealed
Hot rolled
Ultalume®
Stainless Steels
Austentic
Duplex Alloy
Ferritic
Martensitic
Precipitation hardening
Electrical Steels
Nonoriented
Oriented
TRAN-COR® H
Antimicrobial Coated Steels

COMPETITORS

ArcelorMittal USA	Steel Dynamics
Dofasco	Union Electric Steel
Ferralloy	United States Steel
Kobe Steel USA	Worthington Industries
Nucor	

HISTORICAL FINANCIALS

Company Type: Public

Income Statement

FYE: December 31

	REVENUE ($ mil.)	NET INCOME ($ mil.)	NET PROFIT MARGIN	EMPLOYEES
12/14	6,505	(96)	—	8,000
12/13	5,570	(46)	—	6,400
12/12	5,933	(1,027)	—	6,400
12/11	6,468	(155)	—	6,600
12/10	5,968	(128)	—	6,600
Annual Growth	**2.2%**	**—**	**—**	**4.9%**

2014 Year-End Financials

Debt ratio: 50.48%	No. of shares (mil.): 177
Return on equity: —	Dividends
Cash ($ mil.): 70	Yield: —
Current ratio: 1.80	Payout: —
Long-term debt ($ mil.): 2,452	Market value ($ mil.): 1,053

	STOCK PRICE ($)	P/E	PER SHARE ($)		
	FY Close	High/Low	Earnings	Dividends	Book Value
12/14	5.94	— —	(0.65)	0.00	(2.78)
12/13	8.20	— —	(0.34)	0.00	(1.62)
12/12	4.60	— —	(9.06)	0.15	(3.72)
12/11	8.26	— —	(1.41)	0.20	3.52
12/10	16.37	— —	(1.17)	0.20	5.86
Annual Growth	(22.4%)	— —	—	—	—

Alabama Power Co.

Alabama Power powers up Southern Rockers and many others in the heart of Dixie. The Southern Company subsidiary provides electricity to 1.4 million residential and business customers in a 44500 sq. ml. service area in Alabama. The utility operates more than 83000 miles of power lines and it has nuclear hydroelectric and fossil-fueled power plant interests that give it a generating capacity of more than 12000 MW. Alabama Power sells wholesale power to more than 15 municipal and rural distribution utilities; it also provides steam transmission (used for heating and cooling buildings) in downtown Birmingham Alabama and sells electric appliances (such as thermostats ovens and washing machines).

Geographic Reach

The company sells electricity at retail in 400 Alabama cities and towns (including Anniston Birmingham Gadsden Mobile Montgomery and Tuscaloosa) as well as in rural areas and at wholesale to 14 municipally-owned electric distribution systems 11 of which are served indirectly through sales to Alabama Municipal Electric Authority and two rural distributing cooperative associations.

Operations

Alabama Power owns coal reserves near its Plant Gorgas power plant and uses the output of coal from the reserves in its generating plants. It has cogeneration contracts with 12 industrial customers and purchased 151 million KWHs from these companies in 2013.SEGCO (a public utility company jointly owned by Alabama Power and sister company Georgia Power) owns electric generating units with a capacity of 1019 MW at Plant Gaston on the Coosa River near Wilsonville Alabama. Alabama Power owns 92% ownership in Plant Miller Units 1 and 2 which have a total capacity of 1320 MW.

Financial Performance

The company reported a 2% increase in revenues in 2013 primarily due to higher retail revenues and wholesale revenues from affiliates partially offset by the wholesale revenues from non-affiliates. Retail revenues increased due to favorable weather (which pushed up demand) higher fuel revenues and increased revenues associated with a new plant; partially offset by a drop in revenues related to net investments related to the certification of one of its newer plants. That year its wholesale revenues from sales to affiliates grew due to an increase in energy sales fueled by higher energy prices partially offset by a lower capacity revenues. Wholesale revenues from sales to non-affiliates decreased as a result of a drop in capacity revenues and a decline in revenues from energy sales.The company's net income was almost flat in 2013 as the increase in revenues was offset by higher fuel expenses (an 11% increase in the average cost of KWHs generated by natural gas and a 10% increase in KWHs generated by coal). Net

cash provided from operating activities increased by $538 million in 2013 primarily due to changes in timing of fossil fuel stock purchases and payment of accounts payable and the collection of fuel cost recovery revenues.

Strategy

An active player in the larger community in 2014 Alabama Power and B.A.S.S. (a fishing association) signed an agreement to enhance and maintain sport-fishing resources on the 11 lakes managed by Alabama Power. Growing its green energy portfolio in 2013 Alabama Power partnered with City of Montgomery to set up electric vehicle charging station. In the same vein in 2012 the company received approval from the state Public Service Commission to purchase more electricity from midwestern wind projects. It agreed to buy 202 MW of power from a Oklahoma wind park being developed by TradeWind Energy and which is expected to commence operations in 2014. It also agreed to a 202 MW deal with TradeWind Energy's Buffalo Dunes Wind Project in Kansas.

Company Background

In 2011 Alabama Power completed a six-year $1.7 billion clean air project that called for the installation of scrubbers (air pollution control devices) at all seven of its largest coal fired plants in Alabama. By 2010 six scrubbers were in operation at four power plants in Jefferson Shelby Walker and Mobile counties.

In 2009 Alabama Power began exploring the possibility of generating power by burning wood and other renewable fuels at one of its coal-fired plants in response to government regulations calling for lower carbon emissions. In 2010 the company teamed up with The Westervelt Company agreeing to buy biomass-fuel (waste wood material) from the timber company.

EXECUTIVES

Vice President Corporate Relations, Nick Sellers
Vice President IT, George Kustos
Vice President of Corporate Real Estate, Myrk Harkins
Vice President Of Environmental Affairs, Matthew Bowden
Vice President It, Bob Bailey
Vice President Of Corporate Relations, Julian Smith
Vice President Production, Jim Heilbron
Vice President, Christopher (Chris) Womack
Vice President, Tony Smoke
Vice President Birmingham Division, Bobbie Knight
Vice President regulatory Services and Finance, Zeke Smith
Senior Vice President And General Counsel, Gordon Martin
Vice President, Mike Saxon
Executive Vice President External Affairs, Steven Spencer
Vice President Of Corporate Services, Bob Weaver
Vice President Of Planning and Corporate Development, Chris Bell
Vice President Power Delivery Distribution, P Danny Glover
Vice President and Assistant Treasurer, Patterson Ronald
Treasurer, Randy Derieux
Auditors: Deloitte & Touche LLP

LOCATIONS

HQ: Alabama Power Co.
  600 North 18th Street, Birmingham, AL 35203
Phone: 205 257-1000
Web: www.alapower.com

PRODUCTS/OPERATIONS

2013 Sales

	$ mil.	% of total
Retail		
Residential	2,079	37
Commercial	1,477	26
Industrial	1,369	24
Other retail	27	1
Wholesale	460	8
Other	206	4
Total	**5,618**	**100**

COMPETITORS

AEP	Entergy
AES	Ferrellgas Partners
Alagasco	NextEra Energy
Duke Energy	Sempra Energy

HISTORICAL FINANCIALS

Company Type: Public

Income Statement

FYE: December 31

	REVENUE ($ mil.)	NET INCOME ($ mil.)	NET PROFIT MARGIN	EMPLOYEES
12/14	5,942	800	13.5%	6,935
12/13	5,618	751	13.4%	6,896
12/12	5,520	743	13.5%	6,778
12/11	5,702	747	13.1%	6,632
12/10	5,976	746	12.5%	6,552
Annual Growth	**(0.1%)**	**1.8%**	**—**	**1.4%**

2014 Year-End Financials

Debt ratio: 32.26%	No. of shares (mil.): 30
Return on equity: 12.67%	Dividends
Cash ($ mil.): 273	Yield: 5.4%
Current ratio: 1.22	Payout: 72.2%
Long-term debt ($ mil.): 6,176	Market value ($ mil.): 824

	STOCK PRICE ($)	P/E	PER SHARE ($)		
	FY Close	High/Low	Earnings	Dividends	Book Value
12/14	26.97	— —	(0.00)	1.46	210.79
12/13	25.44	— —	(0.00)	1.46	202.60
12/12	28.09	— —	(0.00)	1.46	199.20
12/11	26.38	— —	(0.00)	1.46	197.36
12/10	25.05	— —	(0.00)	1.46	199.03
Annual Growth	**1.9%**	**— —**	**—**	**(0.0%)**	**1.4%**

Alaska Air Group, Inc.

Whether you want to capture a "Kodiak" moment or down a daiquiri by the Sea of Cortez an Alaska Air Group airplane can fly you there. Operating through primary subsidiary Alaska Airlines and regional carrier Horizon Air the group flies more than 29 million passengers to more than 100 destinations in the US (mainly western states including Alaska and Hawaii) Canada and Mexico. The group's primary hub is Seattle (accounting for almost two-thirds of passengers) but it also flies out of key markets such as Portland Oregon; Los Angeles; and Anchorage Alaska. Alaska Airlines has a fleet of about 140 Boeing 737 jets. Horizon Air operates more than 50 Bombardier Q400 turboprops.

Geographic Reach

Alaska Air Group serves more than 100 cities through an expansive network in Alaska the contiguous 48 states Hawaii Canada and Mexico. The company leases operations training and aircraft maintenance facilities in Portland and Spokane as well as line maintenance stations in Boise Bellingham Eugene San Jose Medford Redmond Seattle and Spokane. It also leases call center facilities in Phoenix and Boise.

Operations

Accounting for 93% of revenue the passenger segment's Alaska line is divided into Alaska Mainline (70%) which makes flights with average stage lengths that are more than 1000 miles and Alaska Regional (15%) which for shorter distances. Regional airline Horizon sells all of its capacity to Alaska under a capacity purchase agreement. In a given year Mainline operations carry 21 million revenue passengers while regional operations which includes Horizon transport more than 8 million revenue passengers mainly in Washington Oregon Idaho and California.

As its name would imply the airline transports more passengers between Alaska and the US mainland than any other airline. Besides its own flights the segment provides passenger service through contracts with SkyWest Airlines and Peninsula Airways. Carrying about 4% of all US domestic passenger traffic the segment also includes such non-ticket revenue as reservations fees ticket change fees and charges for baggage service.

Freight and mail account for 2% of revenue. The Other segment around 13% of revenue includes the Mileage Plan on-board food and beverages commissions from car and hotel vendors and travel insurance. The Mileage Plan awards miles for flights on Alaska Horizon and partner airlines and sells miles to third parties.

Sales and Marketing

The airline tickets are distributed through the airline's website and through traditional and online travel agencies who use global distribution systems to obtain their fare and inventory data from airlines and reservation call centers located in Phoenix; Kent Washington; and Boise Idaho.

The company has increased its investment in advertising year-over-year; in 2014 the company spent $49 million on advertising compared to $28 million in 2013.

Financial Performance

Alaska Air's revenue has grown steadily over the last few years. In 2014 its revenues increased by 4% due to an 8% increase in mainline passenger capacity by new routes the addition of seats to the existing fleet and along with the delivery of 10 737-900ERs. Revenues from regional passengers also rose as the result of an increase in capacity offset by lower passenger revenues per available seat mile and an increase in its Mileage Plan revenues. Net income has grown consistently. In 2014 income increased by 19% due to higher revenues and lower expenses on aircraft fuel and aircraft maintenance offset by a rise in non-fuel expenses due to increased capacity resulting in higher wages and benefits and landing fees. Alaska Air's operating cash flows have also increased steadily. In 2014 it increased by 5% due to higher income an increase in inflows from advance ticket sales air traffic liability and decrease in pension outflows. This was offset by increased outflows in accounts receivable and lower inflows from deferred revenues and a deferred tax provision.

Strategy

Besides focusing on key markets such as Seattle and Los Angeles another important component of Alaska Air's strategy includes marketing alliances with other airlines for reciprocal frequent flyer mileage credit and codesharing. Alaska has relationships with about a dozen major airlines such as AMR's American Airlines Air France Delta Air Lines and Qantas as well as two other regional airlines besides SkyWest and Peninsula Air: Era Alaska and Kenmore Air.

Like the airline industry as a whole Alaska Air has been challenged by fluctuating fuel costs which have been known to head up even higher in Alaska's operating territory of the West Coast than in the Gulf and East coasts. Alaska cushions itself against such volatility with crude oil call options jet fuel refining margin swap contracts and the acquisition of more fuel-efficient aircraft including the Boeing 737-800 and 737-900ER.

As of 2015 the company was seeking government approval to begin service from Orange County California.

Growing its Seattle hub in 2014 it launched service to six new cities: Albuquerque Baltimore Cancun Detroit New Orleans and Tampa. In 2014 the company expanded its partnership with SkyWest Airlines with the addition of three new destinations from Alaska's Northwest hubs. SkyWest has purchased seven E175 aircraft to fly on behalf of Alaska Air. The first three aircraft will arrive in 2015 and the remaining four in 2016. Through this partnership the company will offer 298 peak-day departures to 81 destinations from Seattle. From Portland starting in July 1015 Alaska Airlines plans to offer 125 peak-day departures to 44 destinations more than any other carrier.

HISTORY

Pilot Mac McGee started McGee Airways in 1932 to fly cargo between Anchorage and Bristol Bay Alaska. He joined other local operators in 1937 to form Star Air Lines which began airmail service between Fairbanks and Bethel in 1938. In 1944 a year after buying three small airlines Star adopted the name Alaska Airlines.

The company expanded to include freight service to Africa and Australia in 1950. This expansion coupled with the seasonal nature of the airline's business caused losses in the early 1970s. Developer Bruce Kennedy gained control of the board turning the firm around by the end of 1973. But the Civil Aeronautics Board forced the carrier to drop service to northwestern Alaska in 1975 and by 1978 it served only 10 Alaskan cities and Seattle.

Kennedy became CEO the next year. The 1978 Airline Deregulation Act allowed Alaska Air to move into new areas as well as regain the routes it had lost. By 1982 it was the largest airline flying between Alaska and the lower 48 states.

In 1985 the airline reorganized forming Alaska Air Group as its holding company. The next year Alaska Air Group bought Jet America Airlines (expanding its routes eastward to Chicago St. Louis and Dallas) and Seattle-based Horizon Air Industries (which served 30 Northwest cities). When competition in the East and Midwest cut profits in 1987 Kennedy shut down Jet America to focus on West Coast operations.

To counterbalance summer traffic to Alaska the airline began service to two Mexican resorts in 1988. Fuel prices and sluggish traffic hurt 1990 earnings but Alaska Air Group stayed in the black unlike many other carriers. Kennedy retired as chairman and CEO in 1991.

That year the airline began service to Canada and seasonal flights to two Russian cities. Neil Bergt's MarkAir airline declared war cutting fares and horning in on Alaska Air Group's territory. Alaska Air Group's profits were slashed and MarkAir went into bankruptcy.

Alaska Air extended Russian flights to year-round in 1994. The airline began service to Vancouver in 1996. That year it became the first major US carrier to use the GPS satellite navigation system. In 1997 it added service to more than a dozen new cities but halted service to Russia because of that country's economic woes in 1998.

Alaska Air Group and Dutch airline KLM agreed to a marketing alliance in 1998 that included reciprocal frequent-flier programs and code-sharing and in 1999 it added code-sharing agreements with several major airlines including American and Continental. Alaska Airlines developed an online check-in system a first among US carriers.

In 2000 an Alaska Airlines MD-83 crashed into the Pacific Ocean near Los Angeles killing all 88 people on board. A federal investigation of Alaska Airlines' maintenance practices found deficiencies but the FAA eventually accepted the airline's plan to tighten safety standards.

Like most carriers in the latter part of 2001 Alaska Airlines cut back its flights as a result of reduced demand after the September 11 terrorist attacks. As demand slowly returned in 2002 Alaska Airlines began to add new destinations and increase the number of flights on some established routes.

In 2005 Alaska Airlines announced plans to buy 35 Boeing 737-800s between 2006 and 2011.

EXECUTIVES

Vice President of Flight Operations for Alaska Airlines, Gary Beck

Chairman President and CEO Alaska Air Group Alaska Airlines and Horizon Air, Bradley D. (Brad) Tilden, age 54, $436,769 total compensation

President and COO Horizon Airlines, David L. (Dave) Campbell

SVP Communications and External Affairs, Joseph A. (Joe) Sprague, $275,577 total compensation

Staff VP Finance and Controller; Staff VP Finance and Controller Alaska Airlines, Brandon S. Pedersen, age 48, $327,692 total compensation

EVP and Chief Commercial Officer, Andrew R. Harrison, $282,500 total compensation

COO and EVP Operations Alaska Airlines, Benito (Ben) Minicucci, age 48, $359,231 total compensation

VP and CIO, Veresh Sita

Managing Director Loyalty, Ryan Butz

Vice President Human Resources, Tammy Young

Vice President Of Marketing, Jimmy Johnson

Assistant To The Executive Vice President Finance And Chief Financial Officer, Lorraine Hurt

Vice President of Marketing, Sangita Woerner

Board Member, Gemma Hawley

Auditors: KPMG LLP

LOCATIONS

HQ: Alaska Air Group, Inc.
   19300 International Boulevard, Seattle, WA 98188
Phone: 206 392-5040
Web: www.alaskaair.com

PRODUCTS/OPERATIONS

2014 Sales

	$ mil.	% of total
Passenger Revenue — Mainline	3,774	70
Passenger Revenue — Regional	805	15
Freight & mail	114	2
Other	675	13
Total	**5,368**	**100**

2014 Sales

	$ mil.	% of total
Alaska	5	93
Horizon	376	7
Adjustments -371 -		
Total	**5,368**	**100**

COMPETITORS

Aeromexico	Mesa Air
Air Canada	SkyWest
Allegiant Travel	Southwest Airlines

American Airlines
 Group
Delta Air Lines
Hawaiian Holdings
JetBlue

US Airways
United Continental
Virgin America
WestJet

HISTORICAL FINANCIALS
Company Type: Public

Income Statement
FYE: December 31

	REVENUE ($ mil.)	NET INCOME ($ mil.)	NET PROFIT MARGIN	EMPLOYEES
12/15	5,598	848	15.1%	15,143
12/14	5,368	605	11.3%	13,952
12/13	5,156	508	9.9%	13,177
12/12	4,657	316	6.8%	12,932
12/11	4,317	244	5.7%	12,806
Annual Growth	6.7%	36.5%	—	4.3%

2015 Year-End Financials

Debt ratio: 10.50%
Return on equity: 37.37%
Cash ($ mil.): 73
Current ratio: 0.92
Long-term debt ($ mil.): 571

No. of shares (mil.): 125
Dividends
 Yield: 0.9%
 Payout: 12.9%
Market value ($ mil.): 10,078

	STOCK PRICE ($) FY Close	P/E High/Low		PER SHARE ($) Earnings	Dividends	Book Value
12/15	80.51	13	9	6.56	0.80	19.26
12/14	59.76	22	9	4.42	0.50	16.18
12/13	73.37	22	12	3.58	0.20	14.76
12/12	43.09	35	14	2.20	0.00	10.10
12/11	75.09	45	30	1.67	0.00	8.27
Annual Growth	1.8%	—	—	40.9%	—	23.5%

ALASKA PERMANENT FUND CORPORATION

Auditors: KPMG LLP ANCHORAGE AK

LOCATIONS

HQ: ALASKA PERMANENT FUND CORPORATION
 801 W 10TH ST STE 302, JUNEAU, AK 998011878
Phone: 9077961500

HISTORICAL FINANCIALS
Company Type: Private

Income Statement
FYE: June 30

	ASSETS ($ mil.)	NET INCOME ($ mil.)	INCOME AS % OF ASSETS	EMPLOYEES
06/13	49,797	4,520	9.1%	36
06/12	45,043	192	0.4%	—
06/11	45,240	6,885	15.2%	—
06/10	37,052	0	—	—
Annual Growth	10.4%	—	—	—

Alcoa, Inc.

While many of its aluminum products may be lightweight Alcoa is anything but. It is one of the world's top producers of alumina (aluminum's principal ingredient from bauxite) and aluminum. Operations include bauxite mining alumina refining and aluminum smelting; products include alumina and alumina-based chemicals automotive components and sheet aluminum for beverage cans. Markets include the aerospace automotive and construction industries. Non-aluminum products include precision castings and aerospace and industrial fasteners. In 2015 the company announced plans to separate into two public companies —an upstream company (aluminum production) and a value-add company (aluminum products) —by mid-2016.

HISTORY

In 1886 two chemists one in France and one in the US simultaneously discovered an inexpensive process for aluminum production. The American Charles Hall pursued commercial applications. Two years later with an investor group led by Captain Alfred Hunt Hall formed the Pittsburgh Reduction Company. Its first salesman Arthur Davis secured an initial order for 2000 cooking pots.

In 1889 the Mellon Bank loaned the company $4000. In 1891 the firm recapitalized with the Mellon family holding 12% of the stock.

Davis led the business after Hunt died in 1899 and stayed on until 1957 (he died in 1962 at age 95). The company introduced aluminum foil (1910) and found applications for aluminum in new products such as airplanes and cars. It became the Aluminum Company of America in 1907.

By the end of WWI Alcoa had integrated backward into bauxite mining and forward into end-use production. By the 1920s the Mellons had raised their stake to 33%.

The government and Alcoa had debated antitrust issues in court for years since the smelting patent expired in 1912. Finally a 1946 federal ruling forced the company to sell many operations built during WWII as well as its Canadian subsidiary (Alcan).

In the competitive aluminum industry of the 1960s Alcoa's lower-cost production helped it seize market share especially in beverage cans. In the 1970s Alcoa began offering engineered products such as aerospace components and in the 1980s it invested in research acquisitions and plant modernization.

Paul O'Neill (former president of International Paper) arrived as CEO in 1987 and shifted the company's focus back to aluminum. Sales and earnings set records the next two years but plunged afterward reflecting a weak global economy and record-low aluminum prices. Then the fall of the Soviet Union in the early 1990s led to a worldwide glut as Russian exports soared.

In 1994 Alcoa cut its production as part of a two-year accord with Western and Russian producers. That year the company agreed to pool its alumina and chemical operations with Australia's Western Mining Corp.

Alcoa formed a joint venture with Shanghai Aluminum Fabrication Plant in China. The company expanded in Europe in 1996 acquiring Italy's state-run aluminum business followed by the purchase of Inespal Spain's state-run aluminum operations in 1998. Alcoa also bought #3 US aluminum producer Alumax for $3.8 billion in 1998 but only after divesting its cast-plate operations.

Known by the nickname "Alcoa" since the late 1920s the company adopted that as its official name in 1999. O'Neill retired as CEO in 1999; COO Alain Belda succeeded him. Later that year Alcoa bought the 50% of aluminum auto parts maker A-CMI that it did not already own from Hayes Lemmerz International.

In 2000 Alcoa bought aluminum extrusion maker Excel Extrusions from Noranda (now called Falconbridge) and paid $4.5 billion for Reynolds Metals after agreeing to divest some assets —including all of Reynolds' alumina refineries —to satisfy regulators. The same month Alcoa acquired Cordant Technologies. Alcoa also assumed Cordant's 85% ownership of Howmet International (castings) as a result of the transaction —and later acquired the remainder of Howmet. Late in 2000 President-elect George W. Bush named Alcoa's chairman Paul O'Neill to be treasury secretary. (O'Neill subsequently resigned the post in December 2002.)

Alcoa sold its majority stake in the Worsley alumina refinery (Australia) to BHP Billiton in 2001 for about $1.5 billion as part of its refinery divestments. Treasury Secretary O'Neill completed the sale of his more than $90 million worth of Alcoa stock and options in June. In late November Alcoa and BHP Billiton combined their North American metals distribution businesses to create Integris Metals —a joint venture with revenues of about $1.5 billion. (The two subsequently sold the JV to Ryerson in 2005.)

EXECUTIVES

Chairman and CEO, Klaus Kleinfeld, age 57, $1,440,000 total compensation
EVP and Group President Engineered Products and Solutions, Olivier M. Jarrault, age 54, $550,000 total compensation
EVP and CFO, William F. (Bill) Oplinger, age 48, $500,000 total compensation
EVP and Global President Global Rolled Products, Kay H. Meggers, age 51, $433,696 total compensation
EVP Chief Legal Officer and Secretary, Audrey Strauss, age 67, $565,000 total compensation
President International Project Development and Asset Management, Kenneth (Ken) Wisnoski, age 60
President Transportation and Construction Solutions Group, Karl Tragl, age 53
EVP and President Alcoa Global Business Services, Graeme W. Bottger
President Global Primary Products, Roy Harvey
COO Alcoa Investment Castings Forgings and Extrusions; President Alcoa Defense, Eric V. Roegner, age 46
EVP and CTO, Raymond J. (Ray) Kilmer
COO Alcoa Global Primary Products, T̃mas M̃r Sigurdsson
EVP Human Resources and Environment Health Safety and Sustainability, Vas Nair
Vice President Finance, Jim Herring
Exec V Pres, Robert (Bob) Wilt
Vice President Information Technology, Michael Mueller
Vice President and Treasurer, Peter (Pete) Hong
Auditors: PricewaterhouseCoopers LLP

LOCATIONS

HQ: Alcoa, Inc.
 390 Park Avenue, New York, NY 10022-4608
Phone: 212 836-2732
Web: www.alcoa.com

2014 Sales

	$ mil.	% of total
US	12,103	51
Spain	3,359	14
Australia	3,028	13
Brazil	1,398	6
France	915	4
Russia	642	3
Hungary	630	2
United Kigdom	464	2
China	415	2
Germany	229	0
Italy	150	1
Netherlands	36	0
Norway	31	0
Other	506	2
Total	**23,906**	**100**

2013 Sales

	$ mil.	% of total
US	11,766	52
Australia	3,240	14
Spain	2,282	10
Brazil	1,221	5
France	862	4
Russia	683	3
Hungary	555	2
United Kigdom	475	2
Netherlands	524	2
China	259	1
Germany	230	1
Italy	157	1
Norway	283	1
Other	495	2
Total	**23,032**	**100**

PRODUCTS/OPERATIONS

2014 Sales

	% of total
Flat-rolled aluminum	32
Primary aluminum	25
Alumina	14
Investment castings	7
Fastening systems	7
Architectural aluminum systems	4
Aluminum wheels	3
Other extruded aluminum and forged products	4
Others	4
Total	**100**

Selected Products

Commercial windows and doors
Engineering
Extruding
Finishing and electrostatic painting
Glass cutting
Insulating
Tempering
Flat-rolled products
Light gauge sheet products
Rigid container sheet and foil (packaging market)
Sheet and plate mill products (transportation and
  construction markets)
Primary aluminum
Smelted from alumina which is derived from bauxite
Engineered products and solutions
Aluminum wheels castings fasteners forgings
Alumina and chemicals
Alumina
Alumina-based chemicals
Bauxite
Transportation services for alumina and bauxite

COMPETITORS

BHP Billiton	Quanex Building
Chinalco	Products
Crown Holdings	RUSAL
Hydro Aluminium	Rio Tinto Alcan
National Aluminium	Superior Industries
Nippon Light Metal	

HISTORICAL FINANCIALS

Company Type: Public

Income Statement

FYE: December 31

	REVENUE ($ mil.)	NET INCOME ($ mil.)	NET PROFIT MARGIN	EMPLOYEES
12/14	23,906	268	1.1%	59,000
12/13	23,032	(2,285)	—	60,000
12/12	23,700	191	0.8%	61,000
12/11	24,951	611	2.4%	61,000
12/10	21,013	254	1.2%	59,000
Annual Growth	**3.3%**	**1.4%**	**—**	**0.0%**

2014 Year-End Financials

Debt ratio: 23.67%	No. of shares (mil.): 1,216
Return on equity: 2.34%	Dividends
Cash ($ mil.): 1,877	Yield: 0.7%
Current ratio: 1.49	Payout: 57.1%
Long-term debt ($ mil.): 8,769	Market value ($ mil.): 19,211

	STOCK PRICE ($) FY Close	P/E High/Low	PER SHARE ($) Earnings	Dividends	Book Value
12/14	15.79	84 48	0.21	0.12	10.11
12/13	10.63	— —	(2.14)	0.12	9.89
12/12	8.68	60 45	0.18	0.12	12.37
12/11	8.65	32 15	0.55	0.12	13.01
12/10	15.39	70 40	0.24	0.12	13.32
Annual Growth	**0.6%**	**— —**	**(3.3%)**	**(0.0%)**	**(6.6%)**

Alleghany Corp.

After a spell as a conglomerate with interests ranging from minerals to steel fasteners Alleghany found that it really prefers property/casualty insurance with a smattering of good old real estate. Alleghany's subsidiaries include Transatlantic Holdings (TransRe) which offers property/casualty reinsurance (risk coverage for insurers) globally through Transatlantic Reinsurance Fair American and Trans Re Zurich. The company also issues specialty property/casualty insurance policies through RSUI Group and Capitol Transamerica (CATA). Alleghany's offerings are marketed in the US and abroad.

HISTORY

Alleghany was formed in 1929 by Clevelanders Mantis and Oris Van Sweringen as a pyramid railroad holding company. It collapsed in 1934 and after passing through several hands it was bought in 1937 by speculator Robert Young with backing from Woolworth heir Allan Kirby.

Young resurrected the company's Chesapeake and Ohio railroad but another holding Missouri Pacific Railroad (Mo-Pac) failed to thrive and Young embarked on a 40-year struggle to maximize Mo-Pac's value. Young focused on railroads even as the industry declined but he also made other investments including a chunk of IDS (which became the US's largest mutual fund company) and real estate. He also trimmed company holdings from nearly 70 to about 10. By the time Young committed suicide in 1958 Alleghany was in trouble and Kirby who had always kept to the shadows took over.

In his first three years at the helm Kirby fought a takeover attempt by Abraham Sonnabend and a proxy fight with investors John and Clint Murchison. After being ousted briefly in 1961 Kirby re-emerged in control of the company. Allan suffered

a stroke in 1965 and his son Fred Morgan "F. M." Kirby II took over.

In 1966 the company sold its interest in the New York Central railroad (bought in 1945) and eight years later finally emerged from the Mo-Pac mess with about $42 million in cash and some stock. Alleghany used the cash to buy metal fabricating company MSL Industries and the rest of IDS.

Fred Kirby's mantra was flexibility and in 1984 he sold IDS to American Express for a then-flabbergasting $800 million including a pile of stock. Kirby used these proceeds to buy Chicago Title & Trust the same year. Two years later he liquidated the old Alleghany and reincorporated Alleghany Financial CT&T's parent as Alleghany Corporation.

Kirby used the cash from the American Express deal to buy and then spin off a construction company. Other purchases followed in the 1990s including more title operations a California thrift and in 1991 Celite which produced filtration materials. This line was expanded the next year with the purchase of Harborlite. After several purchases in direct insurance (quickly flipped for a profit) in 1993 Alleghany bought Underwriters Re.

In 1994 and 1995 the company bought up shares of Burlington Northern Railroad which merged with Santa Fe in 1995.

In the 1990s CT&T lost market share through industry consolidation so in 1998 Alleghany spun off CT&T's title operations (later acquired by Fidelity National Financial). The next year hit by a down market in reinsurance Alleghany agreed to sell Underwriters Re to Swiss Reinsurance keeping its hand in the market via Alleghany Underwriting Holdings Ltd. (AUL).

In 1999 the company bulked up its asset management operations through acquisitions and in 2000 its industrial fastener business Heads & Threads International bought Acktion's Reynold's Fasteners unit. In 2001 Alleghany sold Lloyd's reinsurer Alleghany Underwriting to Bermuda-based Talbot Holdings and Dutch bank ABN Amro bought the company's asset management business.

The company built up its insurance operations with the purchase of Resurgens Specialty Underwriting (RSUI Group) a subsidiary of British insurance powerhouse Royal & Sun Alliance. It also expanded insurance operations with the 2004 acquisitions of Capitol Transamerica and Darwin National Assurance Company (formerly known as U.S. AEGIS Energy Insurance Company) later renamed as Darwin Professional Underwriters. In early 2006 it took Darwin through an initial public offering and used the funds to reduce its equity interest while retaining majority ownership. (Alleghany's 55% stake in Darwin was sold to Allied World Assurance in 2008.)

While Alleghany collected insurance firms it shed other operations. The company sold Heads & Threads to a management-led investors group in 2004. In 2005 it sold its World Minerals subsidiary (diatomite production) to the US branch of Imerys in a deal valued at about $217 million.

Hurricane Katrina took a serious bite out of profits in 2005. In response Alleghany Insurance Holdings created AIHL Re a reinsurance subsidiary to provide reinsurance directly to RSUI while RSUI worked to reduce its exposure and increased its prices on property insurance. Once the reinsurance market settled down AIHL Re was allowed to go dormant in 2008.

During the quieter 2006 and 2007 hurricane seasons Alleghany found it still had an appetite for insurance providers. The company plunked down $120 million in cash to purchase 33% of monoline homeowners insurance provider Homesite Group in 2006 and spent $198 million to acquire Employers Direct in 2007.

Alleghany held 55% of Darwin Professional Underwriters a specialty property/casualty insurance writer but in 2008 sold it to Allied World Assurance for approximately $300 million.

F. M. Kirby retired as chairman at the end of 2006. His brother Allan Kirby retired from the board in 2010 leaving Jefferson Kirby F. M.'s son as the last family member on the board as directors. F. M. died at the age of 91 in early 2011.

Transatlantic Holdings caught Alleghany's eye and in early 2012 the company paid some $3.4 billion for the long-tail reinsurer. The deal's announcement in late 2011 ended a months-long buyout battle for Transatlantic.

EXECUTIVES

Chairman and CEO CapSpecialty Inc. (f/k/a Capitol Transamerica Corporation), Stephen J. Sills, age 66
President and CEO, Weston M. Hicks, age 59, $1,000,000 total compensation
President and CEO Alleghany Properties, David J. Bugatto, age 50
President and CEO Transatlantic Holdings Inc., Michael C. (Mike) Sapnar, age 48
Chairman President and CEO Pacific Compensation Corporation, Janet D. (Jan) Frank, age 64
SVP Head of Fixed Income and Treasurer, Roger B. Gorham, age 52, $600,000 total compensation
SVP General Counsel and Secretary, Christopher K. Dalrymple, age 47, $600,000 total compensation
Chairman and CEO RSUI Group Inc., David E. (Dave) Leonard
SVP and CFO, John L. (Jack) Sennott, age 49, $600,000 total compensation
EVP, Joseph P. Brandon, $800,000 total compensation
President and CEO Alleghany Capital Corporation, David Van Geyzel
Vice President Tax Director, Johnathan Carr
Vice President Finance, Kerry Jacobs
Vice President Tax Director, John (Jack) Carr
Chairman, Jefferson W. Kirby, age 53
Auditors: Ernst & Young LLP

LOCATIONS

HQ: Alleghany Corp.
7 Times Square Tower, 17th Floor, New York, NY 10036
Phone: 212 752-1356   **Fax:** 212 759-8149
Web: www.alleghany.com

PRODUCTS/OPERATIONS

2014 Revenues

	$ mil.	% of total
Reinsurance		
Casualty & Other	2,282	44
Property	1,048	20
Insurance		
RSUI Group	828	16
Capitol Transamerica Corporation (CATA)	184	4
Pacific Compensation Corporation (PCC)	67	1
Net investment income	459	8
Capital gains	247	4
Other	314	3
Total	**5,231**	**100**

2014 Sales

	% of total
Net premium earned	84
Net investment income	8
Net realized capital gains	5
Other	3
Total	**100**

Selected operating companies

Alleghany Capital Corporation
Alleghany Properties LLC
Capitol Transamerica Corporation
Pacific Compensation Corporation

Roundwood Asset Management LLC
RSUI Group Inc.
Transatlantic Holdings Inc.

COMPETITORS

AIG	PartnerRe
CNA Surety	Reinsurance Group of
California Casualty	America
Everest Re	RenaissanceRe
General Re	State Compensation
Hannover Re	Insurance Fund
Liberty Mutual Agency	State Farm
Munich Re Group	Swiss Re
Nationwide	Travelers Companies
OdysseyRe	Unico American
Ohio Casualty	

HISTORICAL FINANCIALS

Company Type: Public

Income Statement
FYE: December 31

	ASSETS ($ mil.)	NET INCOME ($ mil.)	INCOME AS % OF ASSETS	EMPLOYEES
12/14	23,489	679	2.9%	2,067
12/13	23,361	628	2.7%	1,985
12/12	22,807	702	3.1%	1,506
12/11	6,478	143	2.2%	763
12/10	6,431	198	3.1%	745
Annual Growth	**38.2%**	**36.0%**	**—**	**29.1%**

2014 Year-End Financials

Debt ratio: 7.52%	No. of shares (mil.): 16
Return on equity: 9.44%	Dividends
Cash ($ mil.): 605	Yield: —
Current ratio: —	Payout: —
Long-term debt ($ mil.): —	Market value ($ mil.): 7,441

	STOCK PRICE ($) FY Close	P/E High/Low		PER SHARE ($) Earnings	Dividends	Book Value
12/14	463.50	12	9	41.40	0.00	465.51
12/13	399.96	11	9	37.44	0.00	412.96
12/12	335.42	8	6	45.48	0.00	379.13
12/11	285.29	21	17	16.20	0.00	342.12
12/10	306.37	14	12	21.85	0.00	325.31
Annual Growth	**10.9%**	**—**	**—**	**17.3%**	**—**	**9.4%**

ALLEGIS GROUP INC.

Clients in need of highly skilled technical and other personnel might want to take the pledge of Allegis. The group is one of the world's largest staffing and recruitment firms. Among its companies are Aerotek (engineering automotive and scientific professionals) Stephen James Associates (recruitment for accounting financial and cash management positions) and TEKsystems (information technology staffing and consulting). Other Allegis units include sales support outsourcer MarketSource. Chairman Jim Davis helped found the company (originally known as Aerotek) in 1983 to provide contract engineering personnel to two clients in the aerospace industry.

Geographic Reach

The company operates through more than 300 offices worldwide including its corporate headquarters in Hanover Maryland. Outside of the US the company has operations in Canada Europe the Middle East the Pacific Rim Puerto Rico and the UK.

Operations

Allegis Group has more than 12000 internal employees including 3000 dedicated recruiters and 130000 contract employees working with customers around the world.

Strategy

The company has expanded its geographical footprint and improved its position in specialist staffing markets through the use of acquisitions.

Mergers and Acquisitions

Allegis Group acquired Talent2 during fiscal 2014. Talent2's strong presence in the Asia Pacific region combined with Allegis Group's dominant position in North America will help both organizations to better serve clients needs.

EXECUTIVES

CEO, Michael (Mike) Salandra
CFO, Paul J. Bowie
CIO, Mercedes Kelch
President - International Operations, Chris Hartman
V President-tax, Michael (Mel) Bison
Senior Vice President RPO Operations, Gil Smith
Vice President Information Technology, Chuck Masters
Vice President State Government Affairs, Cheryl Ann Stewart
Vice President Human Resources, Connie Lee
Vice President Global Accounts Director, Bob Nappi
Chairman, James C. (Jim) Davis
Auditors: PRICEWATERHOUSECOOPERS LLP BA

LOCATIONS

HQ: ALLEGIS GROUP INC.
7301 PARKWAY DR, HANOVER, MD 210761159
Phone: 4105793000
Web: WWW.ALLEGISGROUP.COM

PRODUCTS/OPERATIONS

Selected Subsidiaries

Aerotek
  Aerotek Automotive
  Aerotek Aviation LLC
  Aerotek Canada
  Aerotek CE
  Aerotek Commercial Staffing
  Aerotek E&E
  Aerotek Energy Services
  Aerotek Germany
  Aerotek Netherlands
  Aerotek Professional Services
  Aerotek Scientific LLC
  Aerotek United Kingdom
Allegis Group Canada
Allegis Group Europe
Allegis Group India
Allegis Group Services
InSearch Worldwide
  Major Lind
MarketSource Inc
Stephen James Associates
TEKsystems
  TEKsystems Canada
  TEKsystems Germany
  TEKsystems Netherlands
  TEKsystems United Kingdom

COMPETITORS

ASG Renaissance	Kelly Services
Adecco	Korn/Ferry
CDI	ManpowerGroup
Curran Partners	RDL Corporation
ExecuNet	Randstad Holding
Heidrick & Struggles	Robert Half
Horton International	Snelling Staffing
Innovative Management Solutions Group	Volt Information

HISTORICAL FINANCIALS

Company Type: Private

Income Statement

	REVENUE ($ mil.)	NET INCOME ($ mil.)	NET PROFIT MARGIN	EMPLOYEES
12/13	10,440	0	—	85,000
12/12	9,544	0	—	—
12/11	8,275	438	5.3%	—
12/10	6,405	0	—	—
Annual Growth	**17.7%**	—	—	—

FYE: December 31

2013 Year-End Financials

Debt ratio: ——
Return on equity: —
Cash ($ mil.): 511
Current ratio: 2.70
Long-term debt ($ mil.): —

Dividends
Yield: —
Payout: —
Market value ($ mil.): —

Alliance Data Systems Corp.

Hoping to forge an alliance between consumers and retailers Alliance Data Systems provides private-label credit card financing and processing and database and direct marketing services to more than 1500 companies. Its client base includes retailers like ANN J. Crew Pottery Barn and Victoria's Secret as well as banks (Bank of America) grocery and drugstore chains gas stations and hospitality media and pharmaceutical companies. Alliance Data's Epsilon unit develops customer loyalty programs and performs database marketing and strategic consulting services while LoyaltyOne operates the AIR MILES rewards and data-driven marketer BrandLoyalty. About 90% of Alliance Data's business is in North America.

OperationsAlliance Data Systems operates main business segments: Private Label Services and Credit (which made up 44% of 2014 revenues); Epsilon (29% of revenues); and LoyaltyOne (27% of revenues). The Private Label Services and Credit division provides risk management services account origination funding transaction processing collections and marketing services for its private label and co-brand retail credit card programs.Broadly speaking Alliance Data Systems generated 43% of its revenue from finance charges in 2014 while about 30% came from database marketing fees and direct marketing services 21% came from redemption charges and 6% came from transaction charges.Geographic Reach

The US accounts for more than three-quarters of Alliance's annual sales. Canada is next with about 15% while the Europe Middle East and Africa (EMEA) region and the Asia Pacific region contribute 10% and 2% respectively.

Sales and Marketing

Alliance Data's 10 largest clients accounted for 38% of its revenue in 2014. The biggest clients of Alliance Data's largest business Private Label Services and Credit (PLSC) include L Brands (owner of Victoria's Secret and Bath & Body Works) and Ascena Retail Group (Lane Bryant Dress Barn) and their affiliates. These clients accounted for 17% and 13% respectively of PLSC's 2014 sales. Alliance Data's LoyaltyOne business counts Bank of Montreal and Canada-based grocer Sobeys as its largest clients representing 25% and 10% of the segment's revenue.Alliance has been increasing

its advertising spend in recent years. It spent $239.5 million on advertising in 2014 compared to $206.6 million and $166.1 million in 2013 and 2012 respectively.

Financial Performance

Alliance Data's revenues and profits have doubled since 2010 as consumers usage of reward programs and credit/debit cards has ballooned.The company's revenue spiked by 23% to a record $5.3 billion in 2014 with double-digit growth across all of its segments. Most of this was driven by its LoyaltyOne business which grew by 53% after its acquisition of BrandLoyalty. The company's Private Label Services and Credit business swelled by 18% as average credit card and loan receivables balances increased with strong cardholder spending and new client signups. Epsilon grew by 10% as agency revenue increased with higher demand on the automotive vertical; as marketing technology demand increased with database builds and new clients; and as revenues from the company's Conversant acquisition took effect.Alliance's net income also rose by 2% to $506.3 million thanks to higher revenues and lower interest expenses on its long-term debt as more of its senior notes matured during the year. The firm's operating cash levels jumped by 34% to $1.34 billion on higher cash earnings.

Strategy

Alliance Data in 2015 continued focusing on building its customer loyalty programs and shaping its direct and digital marketing business. It's been shifting away from mass marketing to more focused transaction-based direct marketing utilizing data analysis in customer acquisition and retention campaigns. The company's 2014 acquisitions of digital marketing company Conversant and data-driven focused BrandLoyalty emphasized these strategies while also bolstering Alliance's marketing expertise broadening its service offerings and expanding its geographic reach further into Europe Asia and Latin America.With credit and debit card usage becoming increasingly popular and driving the Alliance's excellent financial performance the company has continued to seek co-branded partnerships with a variety of retailers to grow its borrower base in recent years. In 2015 and 2014 for example Alliance launched new co-branded credit card lines in partnership with media companies Univision and HSN International Diamond Distributors and Red Roof Inn.

The company's LoyaltyOne business also continues to keep its loyalty program business thriving through long-term renewals and new signups. During early 2015 and throughout 2014 it signed new multi-year agreements with major Canadian grocery and pharmacy retailers Metro Ontario Sobeys Loblow and Katz Group Canada; apparel retailers DSW Designer Shoe Warehouse Ann Inc (which owns Ann Taylor and Loft brands) and Eddie Bauer; airliner Virgin America; and Moneris Solutions Canada's largest credit and debit card processor. In 2013 it signed similar agreements with apparel chain Old Navy Eastlink Irving Oil and Staples Canada to participate as sponsors in the AIR MILES Reward Program. LoyaltyOne's AIR MILES is Canada's largest loyalty program with more than 170 brand name sponsors including Canada Safeway Shell Canada and Bank of Montreal. It is estimated that some two-thirds of the country's households participate in the AIR MILES program.

Mergers and Acquisitions

In December 2014 Alliance bought digital marketing company Conversant Inc in a deal valued at about $2.3 billion. The marketing company specialized in offering end-to-end digital marketing services to allow clients to effectively target their customers across all channels. The deal also expanded Alliance's operations in Europe and Asia

as well as in Latin America as Conversant owned a 37% stake in CBSM (Companhia Brasileira De Servicos De Marketing) the operator of the dotz coalition loyalty program in Brazil.In January 2014 Alliance Data purchased a controlling interest in BrandLoyalty Group B.V. a Netherlands-based data-driven loyalty marketer that designs custom loyalty programs for grocers worldwide. The deal expanded Alliance's reach as well as BrandLoyalty generated most of its revenues in Europe and in key markets in Asia and Latin America and had plans to expand into Russia and China. Alliance raised its interest to a 70% stake in BrandLoyalty not long after its initial investment and planned to acquire the remainder of the marketer over the following four years.

In November 2012 it bought the Hyper Marketing group of companies for nearly $452 million. In connection with the Hyper Marketing purchase Alliance Data purchased Advecor Inc. a marketing services agency for $12.2 million in December 2012.

Company Background

Handling so much client data carries a lot of risk. In 2011 Epsilon was exposed in a massive online data breach. Hackers managed to crack the system gaining access to millions of customer names and emails. More than 40 companies' email databases were impacted by the breach one of the largest in history.Alliance Data Systems was formed by the 1996 acquisition by Welsh Carson Anderson & Stowe of J.C. Penney's transaction services business and L Brands' credit card bank operation Comenity Bank (formerly World Financial Network Bank which is now a subsidiary of the company.

EXECUTIVES

EVP and CFO, Charles L. Horn, age 54, $580,000 total compensation
President and CEO, Edward J. (Ed) Heffernan, age 53, $1,081,500 total compensation
EVP; President LoyaltyOne, Bryan A. Pearson, age 52, $494,788 total compensation
EVP; President Epsilon, Bryan J. Kennedy, age 46, $565,000 total compensation
EVP; President Retail Credit Services, Melisa A. Miller, age 56, $540,000 total compensation
Senior Vice President And Chief Accounti, Laura Santillan
Vice President Client Sales, Gwen Mannarino
Senior Vice President Tax, Jeffrey Fair
Vice President Cobrand, Tom Evich
Vice President Internal Audit, Shane Hogan
Vice President Corporate Development, Jeff Chesnut
Vice President State And Local Tax, Jim Taylor
Chairman, Robert A. Minicucci, age 62
Auditors: Deloitte & Touche LLP

LOCATIONS

HQ: Alliance Data Systems Corp.
7500 Dallas Parkway, Suite 700, Plano, TX 75024
Phone: 214 494-3000
Web: www.alliancedata.com

2014 Sales

	$ mil.	% of total
US	3,867	73
Canada	851	16
Europe Middle East and Africa	463	9
Asia Pacific	101	2
Other	19	0
Total	**5,302**	**100**

PRODUCTS/OPERATIONS

2014 Sales

	$ mil.	% of total
Net finance charges	2,303	43
Database marketing fees & direct marketing services	1,438	27
Redemption	1,053	21
Transaction	337	6
Other	169	3
Total	**5,302**	**100**

2014 Sales By Segment

	$ mil.	% of total
Private-label services & credit	2,395	44
Epsilon	1,522	29
LoyaltyOne	1	27
Corporate & other	0	-
Adjustments	(22.0)	-
Total	**5,302**	**100**

Selected Products and Services

Epsilon
  Marketing Services
  Agency services
  Database design & management
  Data services
  Analytical services
  Traditional & digital communications
LoyaltyOne
  AIR MILES Reward program
  Loyalty services
  Customer analytics
  Creative services
Private Label Services & Credit
  Receivables Financing
  Underwriting & risk management
  Receivables funding
  Processing Services
  New account processing
  Bill processing
  Remittance processing
  Customer care
  Marketing Services

COMPETITORS

ATCO I-Tek	Discover
Affinion Group	Maritz
American Express	PGi
Capital One	Payment Processing
Chockstone	Total System Services

HISTORICAL FINANCIALS

Company Type: Public

Income Statement

FYE: December 31

	REVENUE ($ mil.)	NET INCOME ($ mil.)	NET PROFIT MARGIN	EMPLOYEES
12/14	5,302	506	9.5%	15,000
12/13	4,319	496	11.5%	12,000
12/12	3,641	422	11.6%	10,700
12/11	3,173	315	9.9%	8,600
12/10	2,791	193	6.9%	7,600
Annual Growth	17.4%	27.1%	—	18.5%

2014 Year-End Financials

Debt ratio: 41.17%
Return on equity: 31.14%
Cash ($ mil.): 1,077
Current ratio: 2.19
Long-term debt ($ mil.): 8,134
No. of shares (mil.): 63
Dividends
  Yield: —
  Payout: —
Market value ($ mil.): 18,253

	STOCK PRICE ($) FY Close	P/E High/Low	PER SHARE ($) Earnings	Dividends	Book Value
12/14	286.05	34 27	7.87	0.00	37.55
12/13	262.93	26 14	7.42	0.00	16.60
12/12	144.76	18 12	6.58	0.00	10.65
12/11	103.84	17 11	5.45	0.00	3.53
12/10	71.03	21 14	3.48	0.00	0.45
Annual Growth	41.7%	— —	22.6%		—202.3%

Allstate Corp.

Ya gotta hand it to Allstate. The "good hands" company has managed to work its way towards the top of the property/casualty insurance pile. The company is the second-largest personal lines insurer in the US just behind rival State Farm. Its Allstate Protection segment sells auto homeowners and other property/casualty insurance products in Canada and the US. Allstate Financial provides life insurance through subsidiaries including Allstate Life and American Heritage Life. It also provides investment products targeting affluent and middle-income consumers. Allstate Motor Club provides emergency road service.

Operations

Allstate Protection's property/casualty businesses —which cover about 16 million households —account for more than 85% of the entire company's total premiums. Most of the segment's sales come from traditional auto and homeowners policies. In addition to traditional property/casualty policies Allstate sells specialty products including coverage for motorcycle and boat owners renters and landlords and mobile home dwellers. It also provides roadside assistance as well as auto protection and service coverage sold through dealerships. Commercial products are geared towards small business owners.

Subsidiaries Esurance (auto insurance) Encompass (package policies) and Answer Financial (agency sales) operate online and have a combined customer base of close to 840000 and growing.

All of the company's life insurance annuities and banking services operate through Allstate Financial. While these sales account for approximately 10% of the company's total revenue Allstate considers them to be useful for deepening relationships with Allstate Protection customers.

Geographic Reach

Allstate's largest property/casualty markets are California Florida New York Pennsylvania and Texas. The company operates throughout the US and in Puerto Rico the US Virgin Islands Guam and Canada.

Sales and Marketing

Allstate maintains a network of about 10000 exclusive agencies which sell its Allstate-branded insurance products through approximately 23200 licensed sales professionals. It also offers these products and Encompass-branded products through some 2000 independent agencies that are primarily located in rural areas of the US. Other products are sold through financial representatives online and over the phone.

To better compete with its faster-growing direct-to-consumer competitors Progressive and GEICO Allstate has been expanding its marketing efforts to reach younger consumers who like to compare and purchase insurance online.

In 2014 Allstate spent $23.5 million on advertising.

Financial Performance

Allstate has seen steady revenue growth over the past five years primarily due to organic measures. In 2014 it posted a 2% increase in revenue to $35.2 billion due to higher property/casualty premiums earned mainly in the auto and homeowners lines. A decline in the cost of its reinsurance program also helped revenue growth that year.

Net income rose 25% in 2014 to $2.8 billion largely due to the absence of loss on extinguishment of debt which had impacted Allstate's bottom line in 2013. Although the company had increased premiums and lower contributions toward benefit plans cash flow from operations decreased 24% to

$3.2 billion due to higher claim and income tax payments.

Strategy

Allstate is focused on growing its number of insurance policies in force increasing premiums maintaining profitability in the auto segment and increasing returns in the homeowners and annuity segments. It is also focused on proactively managing its investments modernizing its operating model and building long-term growth platforms. To grow policy sales the company is enhancing its independent agency network (especially in targeted geographic areas) sales support organization and online sales platforms. It is also working to increase cross-sales of voluntary benefit products through its exclusive agents as well as to form new strategic alliances and develop new product offerings. Subsidiary Esurance is expanding both by adding new complementary products and by launching its products in new geographical locations. At the same time Allstate is working to reduce its operational costs.

The company is continuing to invest in automotive telematics or wireless device technologies that track drivers' habits through which it can provide more accurate policy pricing.

To slim down on its less-profitable operations in 2014 Allstate sold its Lincoln Benefit Life unit to Resolution Life Holdings for $600 million to reduce its exposure to spread-based operations. The company retains a majority of its US life operations. It also sold Sterling Collision Centers to Service King Collision Repair Centers. In addition in 2013 Allstate announced that it would stop direct sales of fixed annuities by the end of the year due to unattractive returns; the company will instead sell fixed annuities issued by third parties.

Catastrophe management is also a key part of the company's stability. To limit its exposure to catastrophic claims in the face of increasing severe weather events in recent years Allstate has quit writing new homeowners policies in some coastal areas including California and Florida that are vulnerable to hurricane wind storms and earthquakes. While it still renews existing homeowners policies in California the company tweaked its underwriting to reduce exposure to claims for fires following earthquakes.

HISTORY

Allstate traces its origins to a friendly game of bridge played in 1930 on a Chicago-area commuter train by Sears president Robert Wood and a friend insurance broker Carl Odell. The insurance man suggested Sears sell auto insurance through the mail. Wood liked the idea financed the company and in 1931 put Odell in charge (that hand of bridge must have shown Wood that Odell was no dummy). The company was named Allstate after one of Sears' tire brands. Allstate was born just as Sears was beginning its push into retailing and Allstate went with it selling insurance out of all the new Sears stores.

Growth was slow during the Depression and WWII but the postwar boom was a gold mine for both Sears and Allstate. Suburban development made cars a necessity; 1950s prudence necessitated car insurance; and Sears made it easy to buy the insurance at their stores and increasingly at freestanding agencies.

In the late 1950s Allstate added home and other property/casualty insurance lines. It also went into life insurance —in-force policies zoomed from zero to $1 billion in six years the industry's fastest growth ever.

Sears formed Allstate Enterprises in 1960 as an umbrella for all its noninsurance operations. In 1970 that firm bought its first savings and loan (S&L). The insurer continued to acquire other

S&Ls and to add subsidiaries throughout the 1970s and 1980s.

This strategy dovetailed with Sears' strategy which was to become a diversified financial services company. In 1985 Sears introduced the Discover Card through Allstate's Greenwood Trust Company. However by the late 1980s it was obvious Sears would never be a financial services giant. Moreover it was losing so much in retailing that by 1987 Allstate was the major contributor to corporate net income. Sears began to dismantle its financial empire in the 1990s.

Allstate also suffered from a backlash against high insurance rates. When Massachusetts instituted no-fault insurance in 1989 Allstate stopped writing new auto insurance there. Later the company had to refund $110 million to customers to settle a suit with California over rate rollbacks required by 1988's Proposition 103.

Allstate went public in 1993 when Sears sold about 20% of its stake. That year it began reducing its operations in Florida to protect itself against high losses from hurricanes. Two years later the retailer sold its remaining interest to its shareholders. Also in 1995 Allstate sold 70% of PMI its mortgage insurance unit to the public.

EXECUTIVES

Senior Vice President Marketing, Robert (Bob) Apatoff
EVP Claims and Chief Claims Officer, Michael J. Roche, age 64
Vice President, Sari Macrie
Chairman President and CEO, Thomas J. Wilson, age 57, $1,141,346 total compensation
Vice President Finance, Norma Gorman
Senior Vice President, Bryan Anderson
EVP Marketing Innovation and Corporate Relations Allstate Insurance, Sanjay Gupta, age 47
President The Allstate Corporation and CEO Allstate Life Insurance Company, Matthew E. (Matt) Winter, age 59, $766,539 total compensation
President Emerging Businesses, Don Civgin, age 54, $700,000 total compensation
EVP Allstate Brand Operations, James D. DeVries, age 51
EVP Product Integration and Management, W. Guy Hill
EVP Product Operations Allstate Insurance, Steven P. Sorenson, age 51
EVP and Chief Investment Officer Allstate Investments, Judith P. (Judy) Greffin, age 54, $664,807 total compensation
EVP Technology and Strategic Ventures, Suren Gupta, $537,404 total compensation
President West Territory Allstate Personal Lines, Thomas F. Clarkson
President East Territory, David Prendergast
President Business to Business, Katherine (Kathy) Mabe
EVP and CFO, Steven E. (Steve) Shebik, $652,500 total compensation
EVP and General Counsel Allstate Insurance, Susan L. Lees
EVP Allstate Brand Distribution, James A. Haskins
EVP Human Resources, Harriet Harty
Vice President Technology and Operations The Allstate Corpor, Butch Necastro
Senior Vice President Of Claims, Mark McGillivray
Department Head, Paul Schutt
Senior Vice President Technology and Operations Infrastructure Architecture and Innovation, Jim Ditmore
Assistant Vice President, Steve King
Vice President and Assistant General Counsel, William (Bill) Vainisi
Vice President, Brian Frank
Assistant Vice President, David Nadig
Vice President, Chad Belher

Vice President Of National Accounts, Darin Reeser
Assistant Vice President of Claims, Bill Daly
Field Vice President, John (Jack) Kane
Associate Vice President Claims, Erik Kiehn
Assistant Vice President Corporate Relations At Allstate Insurance Company, Robert (Bob) Murphy
Vice President Sales And Account Management, Lai Agemura
Vice President Management Information Systems, Darlene Calvert
Vice President Human Resources, Joseph Testor
Vice President, Scott Harris
Senior Vice President Marketing, Scott Vanderlinden
Vice President And General Manager Defense Systems Division, Elizabeth (Beth) Gutierrez
West Central Region Field Senior Vice President, Jeff Thompson
Vice President of Consumer Household Unit, Keith Rutman
Assistant Vice President Claims, James (Jamie) Murray
Vice President Director Manager, Deborah (Deb) Lawrence
Vice President Marketing And Business, Patrick (Paddy) Rogers
Assistant Vice President claims, Christine Sullivan
Executive Vice President, Steven (Steve) Lee
Vice President Director Manager, Carl Majeski
Vice President Product Technology, Daniel Necastro
Assistant Vice President, James Haidu
Vice President, Eddie Ledesma
Field Vice President, Harvey Knobloch
Vice President, David Stephens
Senior Vice President Product Service Innovation and Development, Howard Hayes
Vice President Field Claims Eastern Region, Dan Hebel
Assistant Vice President, Kerry Flack
Field Vice President, Roger Odle
Afvp, Brian Walsh
Vice President, Heather Vangrevenhof
Field Vice President, Jim Neumann
Vice President And Senior Key Account Manager, Stephen Lipker
National Account Manager, Kimberly Purdy
Vice President National Accounts, James (Jamie) Dettman
Assistant Vice President, James Jonske
VPN Engineer, John (Jack) Rivera
Assistant Vice President Risk Management, Laura Bartlett
Assistant Vice President Allstate Marketing Customer Communication Division, Richard (Dick) Heneberry
Assistant Vice President of Enterprise Infrastructure, Pete Corrigan
Vice President Of Field Operations, Gary Mellini
Vice President Emerging Businesses and Consumer Household Allstate Insurance, Julie Parsons
Vice President, Robert (Bob) Transon
Vice President And Divisional CIO, Peter (Pete) Logothetis
Vice President, Patricia Engelman
Assistant Vice President Loan Operations Officer, Joe Hancock
Vice President Business Development, Glenn Solfest
Assistant Vice President Corporate Finance Mergers and Acquisitions, Karen Duffy
Vice President Finance, Steve Petti
Vice President Operations, Nate Pualengco
Vice President, Elizabeth Smith
Vice President National Accounts, William (Bill) Prince
Assistant Vice President Finance, Kevin Corbett
Vice President of Operations Barron Insurance Group, Darryl Graham

Vice President Information Technology, John Roszkowski
Assistant Vice President Infrastructure Services, Sandy Figurski
Vice President Director Manager, Jim Jamieson
Vice President Manager Director, Bob Halter
Senior Vice President Aic (Corporate Relations And Interim Chief Marketing Officer), Joan Walker
Vice President Director Manager, Howard Gurvitz
Senior Vice President Human Resources, Joan Crockett
Vice President, Ryan Briggs
Vice President, Tony Smid
Vice President Talent Acquisition, Cathy Winn
Vice President, Shane O'Brien
Floridian Executive Vice President, George Grawe
Vice President Marketing, Lisa Coch
Executive Vice President Human Resources, Liz Oppenhuis
Field Senior Vice President, Alice Byrne
Vice President Policy Administration, Lori Rutten
Vice President Finance, Michael Kasper
Vice President Engineering, Irene Jarmulska
Management Vice President, Glen Clark
Vice President Finance, Joy Sweet
Assistant Vice President Chief Financial Officer (Technology and Operations), Michael (Mel) Scardina
Assistant Vice President Product Innovation, Roger Parker
Vice President Customer Contact Center Operations, Shayna Schulz
Assistant Vice President Assistant General Counsel And Assistant Secretary, Susie Lees
Senior Vice President AIC Allstate Protection Product Operations, Steve Sorenson
Vice President, Ralph Eureste
Senior Vice President Secretary General Counsel and Director, Michael (Mel) Velotta
Vice President Tax, Scott Harper
Vice President of Sales Emerging Businesses Affinity Solutions, Rob Gamble Rob Gamble
Vice President Sales, Dan Maloney
Vice President, Rhonda Woodard
Senior Vice President, Steven L (Steve) Groot
Vice President Sales, Craig Smith
Vice President Information Technology Group, James (Jamie) Baum
Vice President Marketing, Christian Lopez
Assistant Vice President Financial Resource Admin., Mike Scardina
Assistant Vice President Allstate Marketing Customer Experience, Jessica Rivera
Vice President Marketing, Lisad Cochrane
Vice Chair, Jeff Dunning
Treasurer, Michelle Ackerman
Board Member, David (Dave) O'Kelly
Auditors: Deloitte & Touche LLP

LOCATIONS

HQ: Allstate Corp.
2775 Sanders Road, Northbrook, IL 60062
Phone: 847 402-5000
Web: www.allstate.com

PRODUCTS/OPERATIONS

2014 Revenues

	$ mil.	% of total
Property/liability		
Auto	19,344	53
Homeowners	6,904	20
Other personal lines	1,662	5
Commercial lines	476	1
Other business lines	542	2
Others	1,851	6
Allstate Financial	4,432	13
Corporate & other	28	-
Total	35,239	100

Selected Subsidiaries

Allstate Insurance Company of Canada
Allstate Life Insurance Company
Allstate Motor Club
American Heritage Life Insurance Company
Encompass Insurance Company
Esurance Insurance Company
Kennett Capital Inc.
Northbrook Indemnity Company
Pafco Insurance Company (Canada)
Sterling Collision Centers Inc.

COMPETITORS

Farmers Group	Prudential
GEICO	State Farm
Hanover Insurance	The Hartford
Liberty Mutual	Torchmark
MetLife	Travelers Companies
Nationwide	USAA
Progressive	
Corporation	

HISTORICAL FINANCIALS

Company Type: Public

Income Statement

FYE: December 31

	ASSETS ($ mil.)	NET INCOME ($ mil.)	INCOME AS % OF ASSETS	EMPLOYEES
12/14	108,533	2,850	2.6%	40,200
12/13	123,520	2,280	1.8%	39,400
12/12	126,947	2,306	1.8%	38,600
12/11	125,563	788	0.6%	37,600
12/10	130,874	928	0.7%	35,700
Annual Growth	(4.6%)	32.4%	—	3.0%

2014 Year-End Financials

Debt ratio: 4.79%
Return on equity: 13.02%
Cash ($ mil.): 657
Current ratio: —
Long-term debt ($ mil.): —

No. of shares (mil.): 418
Dividends
  Yield: 1.5%
  Payout: 18.1%
Market value ($ mil.): 29,365

	STOCK PRICE ($) FY Close	P/E High/Low		PER SHARE ($) Earnings	Dividends	Book Value
12/14	70.25	11	8	6.27	1.12	53.36
12/13	54.54	11	8	4.81	1.00	47.84
12/12	40.17	9	6	4.68	0.88	42.96
12/11	27.41	23	15	1.51	0.84	37.27
12/10	31.88	21	16	1.71	0.80	35.68
Annual Growth	21.8%	—	—	38.4%	8.8%	10.6%

Ally Financial Inc

Ally Financial wants to be your friend in the financing business. In addition to owning the branchless Ally Bank the company provides auto financing for almost 17000 auto dealerships (mostly GM and Chrysler) and their customers. Ally Financial also provides financing services for large- and mid-market companies through Ally Corporate Finance (formerly GMAC Commercial Finance). It exited the mortgage business in 2013 when Residential Capital (ResCap) went bankrupt. Formerly known as GMAC and once majority-owned by US taxpayers following a federal bailout in 2008 Ally Financial went public in 2014.

IPO

Ally Financial went public in April 2014 raising some $2.4 billion in the largest IPO of the year at that point. All proceeds went to the U.S. government or in other words US taxpayers. The U.S.

Treasury Department held a partial stake in the company following the transaction but sold its remaining shares in December 2014.

Operations

Ally Financial carries nearly $152 billion in assets. The company operates three business segments: Automotive Finance which provides auto financing to consumers and auto dealers is the largest making up nearly 75% of sales. Ally's insurance operations provide financial and insurance products mostly through auto dealers and brings in 25%. Its now-defunct mortgage operations business managed the company's held-for-sale investments and mortgage portfolios.The firm's banking subsidiary Ally Bank is a member-FDIC bank that provides traditional checking deposit CD savings money market and IRA accounts. Ally's Corporate Finance division offers financing to middle-market business across a wide range of sectors.

Geographic Reach

Ally Financial has corporate offices in Detroit; New York City; and Charlotte North Carolina. It has additional offices in Chicago; Dallas; Philadelphia and Pittsburgh Pennsylvania; Duluth Georgia; Jacksonville Florida; and Little Rock Arkansas. While Ally Bank is headquartered in Midvale Utah the subsidiary is an online direct bank that doesn't have branches.Sales and MarketingAlly Financial and its subsidiaries serve more than 4 million consumers and 17000 auto dealers. Some of its top clients include General Motors and Chrysler. Ally's insurance operations sells its consumer financial and insurance products primarily through the automotive dealer channel while commercial insurance products are sold to dealers. As a direct bank Ally Bank raises deposit funds via its internet telephone mobile and mail channels. Its 784000-strong customer base continues to grow and its customer satisfaction score has reliably exceeded 90%.Ally Financial spent $111 million on advertising and marketing in 2014 or about 18% less than in 2013 and 23% less than it spent in 2012.

Financial Performance

Ally's revenue rebounded by 1% to $9.67 billion in 2014 mostly thanks to growth in its operating lease revenue from higher lease remarketing fee income as its clients' lease termination volume doubled. Its consumer financing revenue also grew as its GM and non-GM/Chrysler consumer originations rose by 7% and 45% respectively. Ally faced some offsetting headwinds in its revenue growth however as income from its insurance and discontinued mortgage operations declined.Despite rocky fluctuations in profit over the past few years net income rocketed by 219% to $1.15 billion in 2014. Higher revenue was partially to thank but the healthy profit growth was mostly driven by lower expenses as the company paid down its higher-cost debt and continued to streamline its operations to increase efficiency.Operations provided $3.4 billion or 36% more cash than in 2013 mostly thanks to higher earnings.

Strategy

Ally Financial is nearing the end of a reorganization that entailed selling off its international operations and exiting the mortgage business to better focus on its core automotive lending business. Management hopes the divestitures will free up cash and help the company benefit from the accelerating recovery in the auto industry and economy.In early 2015 Ally Financial sold its 40% stake in the China joint venture SAIC-GMAC Automotive Finance Company to General Motors Financial Company and GMAC UK (both subsidiaries of General Motors) which freed up resources and even netted Ally Financial a $400 million after-tax gain.

In February 2013 Ally sold its Canadian auto finance business to Royal Bank of Canada. A few months later it sold its Mexican insurance business ABA Seguros to ACE for $865 million. In October it sold its business in Europe and Latin America as well as a joint venture in China to GM Financial for $611 million. Also in 2013 it sold its business lending operations to Walter Investment Management Corp. completed the sales of agency mortgage servicing rights (MSRs) to Ocwen Financial Corp. and Quicken Loans Inc. and exited the correspondent lending channel.Shifting from its cost cutting focus into growth Ally Financial plans to diversify its product lines and build its dealer network through stronger relationships. In 2014 for example the company enjoyed great success in fostering its non-GM/Chrysler channel which has significantly boosted its leased vehicle volume — and was a key reason revenue rose during the year.

Company Background

Ally Financial was founded as a subsidiary of General Motors in 1919. It was owned by GM until 2006 when the automaker sold a 51% stake in the company to the Cerberus Capital Management investment group for some $7 billion.

EXECUTIVES

General Counsel, William B. Solomon, age 63, $500,000 total compensation
President Auto Finance, Tim M. Russi
CIO, Michael Baresich
President and CEO Dealer Financial Services, Jeffrey J. (JB) Brown, age 41, $600,000 total compensation
President and CEO Ally Commercial Finance LLC, William (Bill) Hall
President and CEO Ally Bank, Diane Morais
CFO, Christopher A. Halmy, age 46, $500,000 total compensation
President Ally Insurance, Douglas Timmerman
Assistant Vice President, Michelle Brown
Executive Vice President Organizational Effectiveness, Renee Otjen
Group Vice President, Robert Stahl
Senior Vice President eCommerce, Tanja Castor
Vice President Customer Service, Dave Vasquez
Vice President, John Williams
Senior Vice President Offshore, Joe Glick
Vice President, Brian Baranaskas
Vice President Alliance Sales, Mark Manzo
Vice President, Tom Brent
Senior Vice President Total Rewards, Richard (Dick) Strahota
Vice President, Mike Goeller
Regional Vice President, David Rowe
Regional Vice President, Michael Kimmel
Vice President Strategic Planning and Implementation GMAC Automotive Finance, John (Jack) Jones
Chairman, Franklin W. (Fritz) Hobbs, age 67
Corporate Treasurer, Bradley Brown
Auditors: Deloitte & Touche LLP

LOCATIONS

HQ: Ally Financial Inc
200 Renaissance Center, P.O. Box 200, Detroit, MI 48265-2000
Phone: 866 710-4623
Web: www.ally.com

PRODUCTS/OPERATIONS

Selected Operations

Automotive
  Commercial finance
  Consumer finance
  Dealer inventory insurance

Extended service contracts
Loan servicing
Vehicle remarketing services
Corporate
Asset-based lending
Health capital
Resort finance
Structured finance
Mortgage
Loan servicing
Residential mortage loans
Other lending

COMPETITORS

Bank of America
Citigroup
Ford Motor Credit
Mercedes-Benz Credit
Mercedes-Benz Financial Services USA
Mitsubishi Motors Credit of America
Toyota Motor Credit
Volkswagen Financial Services

HISTORICAL FINANCIALS

Company Type: Public

Income Statement

FYE: December 31

	ASSETS ($ mil.)	NET INCOME ($ mil.)	INCOME AS % OF ASSETS	EMPLOYEES
12/14	151,828	1,150	0.8%	6,900
12/13	151,167	361	0.2%	7,100
12/12	182,347	1,196	0.7%	10,600
12/11	184,059	(157)	—	14,800
12/10	172,008	1,075	0.6%	14,400
Annual Growth	(3.1%)	1.7%	—	(16.8%)

2014 Year-End Financials

Debt ratio: 43.84%
Return on equity: 7.77%
Cash ($ mil.): 5,576
Current ratio: —
Long-term debt ($ mil.): —

No. of shares (mil.): 480
Dividends
  Yield: —
  Payout: —
Market value ($ mil.): 11,340

	STOCK PRICE ($) FY Close	P/E High/Low	PER SHARE ($) Earnings	Dividends	Book Value
12/14	23.62	4727 11	1.83	0.00	32.07
Annual Growth	—	— —	—	—	—

Alon USA Energy Inc

Could anything be finer than FINA? Perhaps Alon is. Alon USA Energy is the driving force behind Alon (formerly FINA)-branded marketing and refining operations throughout the US Southwest. The Delek US Holdings unit provides fuel to 640 Alon-branded retail sites. It owns or operates about 300 convenience stores under the 7-Eleven and Alon brands. It also sub-licenses the Alon brand to distributors supplying 115 additional locations. Alon USA Energy's refineries in California (two) Louisiana (one) and Oregon (one) have a combined throughput capacity of 144000 barrels per day. It also indirectly owns a 70000 barrels-per-day refinery in Texas. The company is also a top asphalt producer.

Geographic Reach

The company operates crude oil refineries in California Louisiana and Oregon (and Texas through Alon USA Partners) and is an independent refiner and marketer of petroleum products pri-

marily in the western and south-central regions of the US.

Operations

In addition to its oil refining assets and gas station network Alon USA Energy is the largest 7-Eleven licensee in the US and a leading convenience store operator in the Texas cities of El Paso Big Spring Lubbock Midland and Odessa. In 2012 the company operated 298 owned and leased convenience stores primarily in Central and West Texas and in New Mexico.

Alon USA Energy owns 100% of the general partner and 82% of the limited partner interests in Alon USA Partners LP which owns the Big Spring refinery in Texas. The refinery produces ultra-low sulfur gasoline ultra-low sulfur diesel jet fuel petrochemical feedstocks petrochemicals asphalt and other petroleum products.

Financial Performance

Alon USA Energy's revenues grew by 12% in 2012 thanks to higher refinery throughput volumes and increased retail sales volumes coupled with stronger refined product prices. Asphalt revenues increased due to higher asphalt product pricing partially offset by lower sales volumes. Higher retail fuel sales prices and volumes and merchandise sales lifted retail revenues.The company reported an 86% increase in net income in 2012 due to higher revenues and a decreased loss from heating oil call option crack spread contracts.Except for the recession-driven revenue slump in 2009 Alon USA Energy saw a growth in revenues between 2008 to 2012.

Strategy

Leveraging its refining assets in Texas and to raise cash in 2012 the company spun off Alon USA Partners LP (in an $184 million IPO) to own and operate the 70000 barrels per day Big Spring refinery which markets petroleum products primarily in West Texas Central Texas Oklahoma New Mexico and Arizona.

A part of a brand unification push (and in anticipation of the expiration of the FINA brand license in 2012) in 2011 company introduced a new Alon design and logo to replace the FINA brand at all of the locations served by company's branded marketing segment.

In 2012 Alon USA Energy entered into a supply and offtake agreement with J. Aron & Company for its California refinery operations.

Ownership

Delek US Holdings owns about 48% of Alon USA Energy.

Company Background

Alon Israel Oil formed Alon USA Energy in 2000 to acquire FINA Inc.'s downstream assets.

Looking to ramp up its refinery capacity in 2010 Alon USA Energy acquired the 70000-barrels-per-day Bakersfield California refinery from bankrupt Pilot Flying J for $40 million. The deal enabled the company to avoid a costly planned expansion involving the building of a hydrocracker unit at its nearby Paramount California refinery.

EXECUTIVES

SVP, Claire A. Hart, age 59, $263,878 total compensation
President and CEO, W. Paul Eisman, age 60, $507,664 total compensation
SVP and CFO, Shai Even, age 47, $328,622 total compensation
SVP Refining, Jimmy C. Crosby, age 56
SVP Supply, Alan P. Moret, age 61, $347,834 total compensation
SVP Asphalt Marketing, Scott Rowe
Vice Chairman, Jeff D. Morris, age 63
Chairman, Ezra Uzi Yemin, age 47
Auditors: KPMG LLP

LOCATIONS

HQ: Alon USA Energy Inc
  12700 Park Central Dr., Suite 1600, Dallas, TX 75251
Phone: 972 367-3600
Web: www.alonusa.com

PRODUCTS/OPERATIONS

2011 Sales

	$ mil.	% of total
Refining & unbranded marketing	6,505	81
Retail & branded marketing	907	11
Asphalt	603	8
Total	**8,017**	**100**

Selected Subsidiaries

Alon Asphalt Bakersfield Inc.
Alon Assets Inc.
Alon Pipeline Logistics LLC
Alon USA Asphalt Inc.
Alon USA Capital Inc.
Alon USA Delaware LLC
Alon USA GP LLC
Alon USA Inc.
Alon USA Interests LLC
Alon USA LP
Alon USA Operating Inc.
Alon USA Partners LP (82%)
Alon USA Pipeline Inc.
Alon USA Refining Inc.
Paramount Petroleum Corporation
Skinny' s LLC
Southwest Convenience Stores LLC

COMPETITORS

BP	HollyFrontier
Chevron	Koch Industries Inc.
ConocoPhillips	Marathon Petroleum
Exxon Mobil	Shell Oil Products
Hess Corporation	Valero Energy

HISTORICAL FINANCIALS

Company Type: Public

Income Statement

FYE: December 31

	REVENUE ($ mil.)	NET INCOME ($ mil.)	NET PROFIT MARGIN	EMPLOYEES
12/14	6,779	38	0.6%	2,745
12/13	7,046	48	0.7%	2,740
12/12	8,017	90	1.1%	2,824
12/11	7,186	43	0.6%	2,824
12/10	4,030	(132)	—	2,821
Annual Growth	13.9%	—	—	(0.7%)

2014 Year-End Financials

Debt ratio: 25.61%
Return on equity: 6.23%
Cash ($ mil.): 214
Current ratio: 1.31
Long-term debt ($ mil.): 548

No. of shares (mil.): 69
Dividends
  Yield: 4.1%
  Payout: 220.8%
Market value ($ mil.): 882

	STOCK PRICE ($) FY Close	P/E High/Low	PER SHARE ($) Earnings	Dividends	Book Value
12/14	12.67	30 21	0.55	0.53	9.15
12/13	16.54	64 27	0.33	0.38	8.71
12/12	18.09	12 6	1.24	0.16	9.54
12/11	8.71	19 7	0.69	0.16	7.06
12/10	5.98	— —	(2.27)	0.16	6.31
Annual Growth	20.6%	— —	—	34.9%	9.7%

Alphabet Inc

If you don't know what the term Google means there's a leading Internet search engine you can use to find out. Taking its name from "googol" — the mathematical term for the value represented by a one followed by 100 zeros —Google offers targeted search results from billions of Web pages. Results are based on a proprietary algorithm; its technology for ranking Web pages is called PageRank. The firm generates revenue through ad sales. Advertisers deliver relevant ads targeted to search queries or Web content. The Google Network is a network of third-party customers that use Google's ad programs to deliver relevant ads to their own sites. In October 2015 Google formally became part —and by far the biggest part —of the Alphabet Inc. holding company.

Change in Company Type

The Google search and advertising business and several of the company's "side projects" comprise the Alphabet holding company. Each unit has its own CEO and reports financials. The move is aimed at increasing transparency accountability and focus. The Alphabet lineup is Google which will include search ads maps apps YouTube and Android; Calico which studies longevity; Nest which develops smart thermostats smoke alarms and other smart home devices; Fiber the high-speed Internet infrastructure venture; Google Ventures and Google Capital the company's investment entities; and incubator projects such as Google X where the company is developing a self-driving vheicle. Segment reporting of the units begins with Q4 2015. Alphabet Inc. will replace Google as the publicly-traded entity but the two classes of shares will keep trading on Nasdaq as GOOGL and GOOG.

Geographic Reach

In order to face its international rivals head on Google operates in more than 50 countries. International domains include Google.ba Google.dm Google.nr Google.co.jp and Google.ca and the Google interface is available in more than 100 languages. In keeping with its "googol" theme the company's headquarters in Mountain View California is referred to as "the Googleplex" a play on googolplex —a one followed by a googol zeros.

Operations

Because the technology industry demands constant innovation Google has been nothing short of relentless in its efforts to develop or acquire new services and products in order to stay ahead of such rivals as Yahoo! and Microsoft. Since its founding as search engine the company has branched out to provide Web portal services such as Webmail (Gmail) blogging (Blogger) photo sharing (Picasa) interactive maps (Google Maps) and Web browsing (Google Chrome).

In addition its Android operating system is a platform for mobile and tablet products; Google has also released an Android smart phone. The company sells digital content such as apps music and movies through Google Play Store (formerly called Android Market). Google subsidiaries include YouTube and DoubleClick.

Despite this plethora of diverse offerings Google's lead in Internet search is still fueled by its advertising system comprised of its AdWords and AdSense products (89% of its revenue stemmed from advertising in 2014). Customers of AdWords seek to drive traffic from Google to their sites and generate leads. Advertisers bid on keywords and have their ads appear as links on the right-hand column of Google's search results page under the sponsored links heading.

Through AdSense for Search Google powers the search capabilities of other publishers' websites and search engines product. With AdSense for Content Google delivers ads to a publisher's website that are targeted to the content on the publisher's site and the publisher shares in the revenue generated when readers click on the ads. AdSense customers are publishers of third-party websites that comprise the Google AdSense Network. The AdSense Network includes many small websites but has also attracted several big players in online publishing and e-commerce including AOL Ask.com and NYTimes.com.

Financial Performance

Google has historically reported year-over-year revenue and net income growth and fiscal 2014 was no different.revenues climbed from $59.8 billion in 2013 to peak at a record-setting $66 billion in 2014. Net income also surged 12% from $12.9 billion in 2013 to reach a milestone $14.4 billion in 2014. (Note: the company's 2013 financials were restated to reflect the divestiture of its Motorola Mobility and Motorola Home businesses.)

The historic growth for 2014 was attributed to the increase in advertising revenues generated by Google websites Google Network Members' websites and hardware product sales. The growth in advertising was fueled by a 20% spike in the number of aggregate paid clicks through its advertising programs from 2013 to 2014. Google was also helped by monetization improvements including new and richer ad formats; an increase in aggregate traffic across all platforms; the continued global expansion of its products advertisers and user base; and an increase in the number of Google Network Members.

Like its revenues and net income Google's cash flow from operations has also significantly increased year-over-year. Cash flow in 2014 increased to $22.4 billion compared to $18.7 billion in 2013 due to the higher net income and changes in working capital as a result of cash generated from prepaid revenue share expenses and other assets.

Strategy

In order to enter new markets and maintain a portfolio of innovative offerings Google is continuing its strategy of new product development. The company launched its Google + social networking service in 2011 to directly compete with market leader Facebook.

Meanwhile in a move that allows advertisers to better understand the consumer patterns and behavior of those it's attempting to reach through Google in 2012 the company unveiled a new privacy policy. To the chagrin of privacy advocates the update places all the information Google collects about users across its various products (YouTube Gmail and the rest) into one unified database. Google said it made the change to simplify its privacy policy. The update reduces 60 different privacy policies into one.

Mergers and Acquisitions

Armed with its significant pile of cash Google keeps growing through the use of specific acquisitions. In 2014 it obtained start-up Titan Aerospace a maker of high-altitude drones that can go five years without having to land or refuel. The company will join Google's Project Loon which is working to deliver Internet signals to parts of the world currently offline via high-altitude balloons.

In 2014 Google purchased Nest Labs a company that specializes in reinventing devices in the home such as thermostats and smoke alarms. Google also in 2014 picked up Skybox Imaging a satellite imaging company for $478 million in cash. The company plans for that transaction to complement Google Maps' accuracy. In addition Google in 2013 paid a little more than $1 billion for mapping service Waze. The deal kept Waze out of the hands of

Google's rivals and gave it technology that improved its navigation systems.

The company completed its biggest acquisition to date in 2012 when it bought phone hardware maker Motorola Mobility for $12.5 billion. The deal was a major indicator that the company was shifting its strategy beyond its core Internet operations to increase its penetration in the fast-growing mobile market. The purchase allowed it to better compete with smartphone rival Apple by bolstering the adoption of its Android mobile software. However in less than two years Google decided to exit the money-losing smartphone business. In early 2014 it agreed to sell Motorola Mobility to Lenovo for $2.9 billion. The Chinese PC maker will own the Motorola brand and its products (the Moto X Moto G and the DROID Ultra series) while Google will continue to own Motorola's technology patents.

HISTORY

Google is the product of two computer science grad students Sergey Brin and Larry Page who met in 1995 at Stanford University where they studied methods of searching and organizing large datasets. They discovered a formula to rank the order of random search results by relevancy and in 1997 they adopted the name Google to their findings. In 1998 the two presented their discovery at the World Wide Web Conference and by 1999 they had raised almost $30 million in funding from private investors venture capital firms and Stanford University. Later that year the Google site was launched.

Brin and Page hired tech industry veteran Eric Schmidt (former CTO at Sun Microsystems and former CEO of Novell) in 2001 as Google's CEO. Brin previously the company's chairman adopted the role of president of technology and Page previously CEO of Google became president of product. Also in 2001 Google launched AdWords its search-based advertising service. The following year the company launched another advertising service the context-based AdSense.

In 2004 the company entered the social networking sphere with the launch of its Orkut product which allows users (by invitation only) to search and connect with one another through online networks of friends. Later that year the once highly secretive company went public in one of the most anticipated IPOs ever raising $1.6 billion.

EXECUTIVES

Vice President Sales Greater China, John (Jack) Liu
SVP Display and Advertising, Neal Mohan
CEO, Sundar Pichai, age 43
SVP Android Chrome OS and Chromecast, Hiroshi Lockheimer
SVP Global Sales and Operations, Phillipp Schindler
Senior Vice President Search, Amit Singhal
Senior Vice President Business Operations, Shona Brown
Vice President, Andy Milo
Vice President Business Operations (Strategy), Matthew (Matt) Stepka
Vice President Marketing, Keith Jameson
Senior Vice President, Belvia Sharp
Vice President And Deputy General Counsel, Don Harrison
Vice President Global Search Partnerships, Patrick (Paddy) Jabal
Vice President Corporate Development Isreal, Ted Fike
Vice President Human Resources, Amy Buchen
Senior Vice President Global Operations, Dan Zhang
Vice President, Glen Anderson
Vice President and General Counsel, Joanna Flint

Vice President Engineering, Douglas (Doug) Merrill
Vice President and Chief Internet Evangelist,
 Vinton Cerf
Vice President Of Sales, Lonny Gulden
**Vice President Keepin Information Technology
 Real,** Luke Mahe
Vice President Search Engineering, Ben Gomes
**Vice President Product Management Emea And
 Latin America,** Mario Queiroz
Senior Vice President, Alex Brown
Vice President International Sales and, Amit Singh
Senior Vice President Products, Salar Kamangar
Board Member, Lauren Desmond
Assistant Treasurer, Wilson Tsai
Board Member, Marc Ellenbogen
Board Member, Jonathan Cranmer
Executive Board Member, Neil Guilbeaux
Assistant Treasurer, Tony Altobelli
Auditors: Ernst & Young LLP

LOCATIONS

HQ: Alphabet Inc
 1600 Amphitheatre Parkway, Mountain View, CA 94043
Phone: 650 253-0000
Web: www.abc.xyz

2014 Sales

	$ mil.	% of total
US	28,139	42
UK	6,483	10
Other countries	31,379	48
Total	**66,001**	**100**

PRODUCTS/OPERATIONS

2014 Sales

	$ mil.	% of total
Advertising		
Google sites	45,085	68
Google networks	13,971	21
Other revenue	6,945	11
Total	**66,001**	**100**

Selected Operations and Products

Advertising programs
 AdSense (network ad program for online publishers)
 AdWords (text-based ad placement for advertisers)
 DoubleClick (digital marketing technology and
 services)
Internet search and content
 Google Alerts (news and search e-mail alerts)
 Google Earth (3-D satellite imagery)
 Google Image Search
 Google Labs (online services research and
 development)
 Google Local (localized search)
 Google Mobile (wireless device content)
 Google News
 Google Play Store (marketplace for digital content)
 Google Video
 Google Web Search
 YouTube
Tools and applications
 Android (mobile operating system)
 Blogger (blogging tools)
 Gmail (Web-based e-mail)
 Google Analytics (Web traffic measurement)
 Google Chrome (Web browser)
 Google Desktop Search
 Google Language Tools (translation tools)
 Google Talk (instant messaging)
 Google Toolbar (browser plug-in application)
 Nexus S (smart phone)
 Picasa (digital photo organization and sharing)

COMPETITORS

AOL	MSN
Apple Inc.	Myspace
Ask.com	NetEase
Baidu	SINA
Blucora	Shopping.com
CityGrid Media	Shopzilla
Conversant	Sohu.com

Daum Communications	Twitter
Facebook	Yahoo!
LiveJournal	craigslist
LookSmart	

HISTORICAL FINANCIALS

Company Type: Public

Income Statement

FYE: December 31

	REVENUE ($ mil.)	NET INCOME ($ mil.)	NET PROFIT MARGIN	EMPLOYEES
12/15	74,989	16,348	21.8%	61,814
12/14	66,001	14,444	21.9%	53,600
12/13	59,825	12,920	21.6%	47,756
12/12	50,175	10,737	21.4%	53,861
12/11	37,905	9,737	25.7%	32,467
Annual Growth	**18.6%**	**13.8%**	**—**	**17.5%**

2015 Year-End Financials

Debt ratio: 3.54%
Return on equity: 14.54%
Cash ($ mil.): 16,549
Current ratio: 4.67
Long-term debt ($ mil.): 1,995

No. of shares (mil.): 687
Dividends
 Yield: —
 Payout: —
Market value ($ mil.): 534,764

	STOCK PRICE ($) FY Close	P/E High/Low	PER SHARE ($) Earnings	Dividends	Book Value
12/15	778.01	34 22	22.84	0.00	175.07
12/14	530.66	57 23	21.02	0.00	153.64
12/13	1,120.71	58 36	19.07	0.00	129.99
12/12	707.38	47 34	16.16	0.00	108.67
12/11	645.90	43 31	14.88	0.00	89.48
Annual Growth	**4.8%**	**— —**	**11.3%**	**—**	**18.3%**

Altria Group Inc

The house the Marlboro Man built Altria Group owns the largest cigarette company in the US. Altria operates through subsidiary Philip Morris USA which sells Marlboro —the world's #1-selling cigarette brand. Controlling about half of the US tobacco market Altria manufactures cigarettes under the Parliament Virginia Slims and Basic brands among many. Altria however has diversified from solely a cigarette maker to a purveyor of cigars and pipe tobacco through John Middleton Co. smokeless tobacco products through UST and wine through Ste. Michelle Wine Estates. Another subsidiary Philip Morris Capital Corp. holds a group of finance leases. Altria also owns a 27% stake in SABMiller.

HISTORY

Philip Morris opened his London tobacco store in 1847 and by 1854 was making his own cigarettes. Morris died in 1873 and his heirs sold the firm to William Thomson just before the turn of the century. Thomson introduced his company's cigarettes to the US in 1902. American investors bought the rights to leading Philip Morris brands in 1919 and in 1925 the new company Philip Morris & Co. introduced Marlboro which targeted women smokers and produced modest sales.

When the firm's larger competitors raised their prices in 1930 Philip Morris Companies countered by introducing inexpensive cigarettes that caught on with Depression-weary consumers. By 1936 it was the fourth-biggest cigarette maker.

The firm acquired Benson & Hedges in 1954. It signed ad agency Leo Burnett which promptly initiated the Marlboro Man campaign. Under Joseph Cullman (who became president in 1957) Philip Morris experienced tremendous growth overseas. After dipping to sixth place among US tobacco companies in 1960 it rebounded at home thanks to Marlboro's growing popularity among men (Marlboro became the #1 cigarette brand in the world in 1972).

In 1970 Philip Morris bought the nation's seventh-largest brewer Miller Brewing and with aggressive marketing it vaulted to #2 among US beer makers by 1980. To protect itself against a shrinking US tobacco market in 1985 Philip Morris paid $5.6 billion for General Foods (Kool-Aid Post Stove Top). In 1988 it bought Kraft (Miracle Whip Velveeta). The next year Philip Morris joined Kraft with General Foods.

In 1994 Australian Geoffrey Bible became CEO. By late 1998 the company and its rivals had settled tobacco litigation with most states agreeing to pay about $250 billion over 25 years to receive protection from further state suits.

In 1999 Philip Morris bought three cigarette brands (L&M Chesterfield and Lark) from the Brooke Group. The US government filed a massive lawsuit against Big Tobacco and Philip Morris admitted —no kidding —that smoking increases the risk of getting cancer and other illnesses.

In 2000 Philip Morris vowed to appeal after a state court awarded $74 billion in punitive damages to Florida smokers. The court later ruled that Philip Morris Lorillard and the Liggett Group would pay at least $709 million in the case regardless of the outcome but would not have to pay damages until after the appeals are resolved. A Los Angeles jury awarded Richard Boeken $3 billion in punitive damages. The company appealed even after Boeken later agreed to reduced damages of $100 million. (Boeken died in 2002.)

In December 2000 Philip Morris completed its purchase of Nabisco Holdings for $18.9 billion. In June 2001 Philip Morris spun off Kraft Foods in what was the second-largest IPO in US history; it retained an 84% stake in the company and 97% of the voting rights.

In April 2002 CFO Louis Camilleri succeeded Bible as CEO; in September Camilleri became chairman upon Bible's retirement. In July 2002 Philip Morris sold Miller Brewing to South African Breweries for $5.6 billion ($3.6 billion in SAB stock and the assumption of $2 billion in Miller debt) in July 2002.

In the ongoing saga of tobacco-related litigation Philip Morris said it would appeal an October 2002 verdict by a California jury that ordered the company to pay $28 billion in punitive damages the most ever in an individual tobacco liability lawsuit (later reduced to $28 million). In January 2003 Philip Morris changed its name to Altria Group in an effort to distance itself from its tobacco litigation. In April a Florida appeals court threw out the state's multibillion-dollar judgment (made in 2000) against Philip Morris USA and four other US tobacco companies stating that thousands of Florida smokers could not lump their complaints together in a single case.

In March 2003 Philip Morris USA lost an Illinois lawsuit which claimed the company's use of the word "light" was misleading and violated Illinois consumer fraud laws. The judge ordered Philip Morris USA to pay damages of $10 billion and post a $12 billion bond. The Illinois Supreme Court has lowered the bond to $7 billion and agreed to hear Philip Morris USA's appeal of the original verdict.

In 2005 Altria purchased a $4.8 billion stake in Indonesia's third-largest tobacco firm PT Hanjaya Mandala Sampoerna which makes kreteks or clove cigarettes. Also in 2005 the company formed a long-term alliance with China National Tobacco Corp.

In mid-2006 Altria unseated Roger Deromedi from Kraft's top spot and appointed Irene Rosenfeld to head the company. The executive realignment was part of Altria's plan to spin off Kraft. Deromedi a 28-year Kraft veteran had been under fire for the unit's stale sales since taking over as sole CEO in 2003. Rosenfeld spent more than 20 years at Kraft and exited the firm in mid-2003 as president of Kraft Foods North America. The former chairman and CEO of Frito-Lay Rosenfeld is known for her integration expertise as well as restructuring and turning around companies.

In March 2007 Altria completed the spinoff of Kraft Foods to Altria shareholders. Also in 2007 Altria bought US cigar maker John Middleton from privately held Bradford Holdings. Based in Pennsylvania John Middleton specializes in machine-made cigars —most notably the Black & Mild brand. The deal was valued at $2.2 billion. A year later in March 2008 Altria spun off its Philip Morris International arm also to shareholders and moved its headquarters from New York City's Park Avenue to Richmond Virginia to be closer to its bread and butter operations. (As part of the move Altria in late 2007 agreed to sell the headquarters that has housed the firm since 1982 to a unit of privately held Global Holdings for some $525 million. Altria relocated about 100 of its about 500 employees in the move from New York City to Richmond.)

In January 2009 the company purchased smokeless tobacco maker UST as well as its wine business. The $11 billion deal gave Altria a significant foothold in the US smokeless tobacco market garnering popular brands Copenhagen and Skoal into Altria's fold. Following the acquisition Altria consolidated the sales forces of UST's U.S. Smokeless Tobacco brands and Philip Morris USA and relocated U.S. Smokeless Tobacco Company to Richmond Virginia. Altria has since launched a new versions of certain brands designed to compete with value-priced brands such as Reynolds American's Grizzly and Swedish Match AB's Timber Wolf.

In June 2009 the passage of the Family Smoking and Tobacco Control Act by the US Congress gave the U.S. Food and Drug Administration unprecedented authority to regulate tobacco products including the authority to regulate marketing ban candy flavorings and reduce nicotine in tobacco products.

EXECUTIVES

EVP and CTO, John R. (Jack) Nelson, age 64, $770,000 total compensation

Chairman President and CEO, Martin J. (Marty) Barrington, age 62, $1,241,667 total compensation

President and CEO Ste. Michelle Wine Estates, Theodor P. (Ted) Baseler, age 61

President and CEO Altria Group Distribution, Craig A. Johnson, age 63, $850,833 total compensation

EVP Strategy and Business Development, Howard A. Willard, age 52, $676,833 total compensation

President and CEO U.S. Smokeless Tobacco, Brian W. Quigley

President and CEO Philip Morris Capital, John J. Mulligan

President and General Manager Nu Mark LLC, Jose Luis (Joe) Murillo

CFO, William F. (Billy) Gifford, age 45

EVP and General Counsel, Denise F. Keane, age 64, $890,500 total compensation

VP Investor Relations Altria Client Services, Clifford B. Fleet

Auditors: PricewaterhouseCoopers LLP

LOCATIONS

HQ: Altria Group Inc
6601 West Broad Street, Richmond, VA 23230
Phone: 804 274-2200
Web: www.altria.com

PRODUCTS/OPERATIONS

2014 Income

	% of total
Smokeable products	89
Smokeless products	7
Wine	3
All other	1
Total	**100**

Selected Subsidiaries

F.W. Rickard Seeds Inc.
Green Smoke Inc.
International Wine & Spirits Ltd.
John Middleton Co.
Philip Morris Capital Corp.
Philip Morris USA Inc.
Stag's Leap Wine Cellars LLC
Ste. Michelle Wine Estates Ltd.
U.S. Smokeless Tobacco Co. LLC
UST LLC

COMPETITORS

Altadis	Lorillard
Anheuser-Busch	Molson Coors
Anheuser-Busch InBev	North Atlantic Trading
British American	Ravenswood Winery
Tobacco	Reynolds American
Constellation Brands	Sebastiani Vineyards
E. & J. Gallo	Swedish Match
Heineken	Treasury Wine Estates
Japan Tobacco	Americas
Loews	Vector Group

HISTORICAL FINANCIALS

Company Type: Public

Income Statement

FYE: December 31

	REVENUE ($ mil.)	NET INCOME ($ mil.)	NET PROFIT MARGIN	EMPLOYEES
12/14	24,522	5,070	20.7%	9,000
12/13	24,466	4,535	18.5%	9,000
12/12	24,618	4,180	17.0%	9,100
12/11	23,800	3,390	14.2%	9,900
12/10	24,363	3,905	16.0%	10,000
Annual Growth	0.2%	6.7%	—	(2.6%)

2014 Year-End Financials

Debt ratio: 42.62%
Return on equity: 142.16%
Cash ($ mil.): 3,321
Current ratio: 0.90
Long-term debt ($ mil.): 13,693
No. of shares (mil.): 1,971
Dividends
  Yield: 4.0%
  Payout: 91.7%
Market value ($ mil.): 97,135

	STOCK PRICE ($) FY Close	P/E High/Low		PER SHARE ($)		
				Earnings	Dividends	Book Value
12/14	49.27	20	13	2.56	2.00	1.53
12/13	38.39	17	14	2.26	1.84	2.07
12/12	31.44	18	14	2.06	1.70	1.58
12/11	29.65	18	14	1.64	1.58	1.80
12/10	24.62	14	10	1.87	1.46	2.49
Annual Growth	18.9%	—	—	8.2%	8.2%	(11.4%)

Amazon.com Inc.

What began as Earth's biggest bookstore has become Earth's biggest everything store. Expansion has propelled Amazon.com in innumerable directions. While the website still offers millions of books movies games and music selling other items —such as electronics apparel and accessories auto parts home furnishings health and beauty aids toys and groceries —contributes some two-thirds of sales. Shoppers can also download e-books games MP3s and films to their computers or handheld devices including Amazon's own portable e-reader the Kindle. Amazon also offers products and services such as self-publishing online advertising e-commerce platform hosting and a co-branded credit card.

HISTORY

Company BackgroundJeff Bezos was researching the Internet in the early 1990s for hedge fund D.E. Shaw. He realized that book sales would be a perfect fit with e-commerce because book distributors already kept meticulous electronic lists. Bezos who as a teen had dreamed of entrepreneurship in outer space took the idea to Shaw. The company passed on the idea but Bezos ran with it trekking cross country to Seattle (close to a facility owned by major book distributor Ingram) and typing up a business plan along the way.

Bezos founded Amazon.com in 1994. After months of preparation he launched a website in July 1995 (Douglas Hofstadter's Fluid Concepts and Creative Analogies was its first sale); it had sales of $20000 a week by September. Bezos and his team kept working with the site pioneering features that now seem mundane such as one-click shopping customer reviews and e-mail order verification.

Amazon went public in 1997. Moves to cement the Amazon.com brand included becoming the sole book retailer on AOL's website and Netscape's commercial channel.

In 1998 the company launched its online music and video stores and it began to sell toys and electronics. Amazon also expanded its European reach with the purchases of online booksellers in the UK and Germany and it acquired the Internet Movie Database. Bezos also expanded the company's base of online services buying Junglee (comparison shopping) and PlanetAll (address book calendar reminders).

By midyear Amazon.com had attracted so much attention that its market capitalization equaled the combined values of profitable bricks-and-mortar rivals Barnes & Noble and Borders Group even though their combined sales were far greater than the upstart's. Late that year Amazon formed a promotional link with Hoover's publisher of this profile.

After raising $1.25 billion in a bond offering early in 1999 Amazon.com began a spending spree with deals to buy all or part of several dotcoms. However some have since been sold (HomeGrocer.com) and others have gone out of business or bankrupt —Pets.com living.com (furniture). It also bought the catalog businesses of Back to Basics and Tool Crib of the North.

Amazon.com began conducting online auctions in early 1999 and partnered with venerable auction house Sotheby's. Also that year Amazon added distribution facilities including one each in England and Germany.

In 2000 the company inked a 10-year deal with Toysrus.com to set up a co-branded toy and video game store. (The partnership came to a bitter end in 2006 after Toys "R" Us sued Amazon.com when it began selling toys from other companies.) Also that year Amazon.com added foreign-language sites for France and Japan.

In 2001 Amazon cut 15% of its workforce as part of a restructuring plan that also forced a $150 million charge. That year the company also made a deal with Borders to provide inventory fulfillment content and customer service for borders.com. As part of a deal to expand their marketing partnership AOL invested $100 million in Amazon.com in 2001. Later that year Amazon purchased some assets from Egghead.com (which filed for Chapter 11 in August) and relaunched the site.

In 2002 the firm introduced clothing sales featuring hundreds of retailers including names such as The Gap Nordstrom and Lands' End. Amazon.com received accreditation from ICANN (the Internet Corporation for Assigned Names and Numbers) as an Internet domain name registrar becoming one of about 160 entities permitted to register Internet addresses.

The company launched its Search Inside the Book feature in 2003. The tool allows customers to search the text inside books for more relevant search returns. At launch the search feature covered more than 120000 books from over 190 publishers. Amazon expanded into China in 2004 with the purchase of Joyo.com. (It renamed the unit Joyo Amazon in 2007.)

In 2005 Amazon launched Amazon Prime a two-day shipping service for an annual fee of $79.

Amazon.com began testing the online dry grocery waters in 2006. It launched the Amazon Fresh delivery service for the Seattle area a year later to include perishables.

The company acquired shopping site Shopbop.com in 2006 boosting its apparel offerings. Also that year IBM filed a pair of patent infringement lawsuits alleging that Amazon.com has been violating at least five of its patents –including technologies that govern how the online retailer handles product recommendations and displays advertising –for about four years. In 2007 the two companies settled the litigation and signed a long-term patent cross-license agreement.

The Internet bookseller in November 2007 introduced the Kindle an electronic portable book reader. The launch Amazon's first foray into the tech hardware market is aimed at kindling demand for electronic books.

Also in 2007 Amazon launched Endless.com which sells shoes and accessories; Askville.com where users can solicit answers from others on the site; and the Amazon MP3 site which offers digital music free of copyright restrictions. In addition Amazon acquired audiobook publisher Brilliance Audio.

Amazon stayed focused on entertainment in 2008. The company launched Amazon Video On Demand a service that gives customers the option to stream or download ad-free digital movies and TV shows on Macs or PCs. It also purchased Abe-Books an online retailer of more than 110 million primarily used rare and out-of-print books as well as Shelfari a social-networking site for booklovers. Additionally Amazon.com sold its UK and German online DVD rental services to Internet movie-rental company LOVEFiLM International in exchange for stock. The deal gave Amazon about a 40% stake in LOVEFiLM.

Shopping was also at the top of Amazon's list in 2008. In May the company invested in The Talk Market a user-generated TV Shopping Channel. In June Amazon launched an online office supplies store and sewed up the acquisition of the online fabrics retailer Fabrics.com.

In June 2009 Amazon agreed to pay Toys "R" Us $51 million to settle a dispute dating back to

2004. The settlement was related to a partnership that gave the toy seller exclusive rights to supply some of the toys on Amazon's site. In November Amazon completed its $888 million acquisition of shoe e-tailer Zappos –the #1 online shoe and apparel retailer. (Besides footwear and clothing Zappos also sells handbags housewares and beauty products.) The purchase allowed Amazon to boost its sales and expand its products portfolio by leveraging Zappos' widely recognized customer service expertise.

In mid-2010 Amazon acquired Woot Inc. a pioneer in the deal-of-the-day genre of online retailing. While neither Amazon or Woot would disclose the selling price reports valued the deal at about $110 million in cash.

In January 2011 Amazon completed its move to a new corporate headquarters in Seattle's South Lake Union neighborhood. Amazon also made several acquisitions that year. The company acquired the remaining shares it didn't already own in LOVEFiLM International. It purchased a pair of UK companies: online book seller The Book Depository and digital agency Pushbutton (later folding the operation into its Amazon Development Centre in London). The behemoth also picked up voice-to-text startup Yap based in Charlotte North Carolina that year.

Kiva Systems which Amazon bought in 2012 was purchased to provide the firm with a boost in automation capabilities. Amazon picked up some former talent including Amazon ex Dave Schappell when it bought online education marketplace Teachstreet and shuttered the site in 2012. Acquiring England's Evi and its namesake cloud-based Artificial Intelligence expertise in 2012 offered Amazon a leg up in answer engine technology.

To extend the reach of its Kindle range Amazon in 2013 acquired Poland's IVONA Software. Months after being bought by Amazon in 2013 social cataloging company Goodreads announced it had amassed some 20 million members. In 2013 Amazon also purchased electrowetting display panel expert Liquavista from Samsung Electronics which had held the company for fewer than three years.

Investments in 2014 include acquiring the .buy domain for nearly $4.6 million. Besides the domain purchase Amazon has been focused on games. It acquired Silent Hill: Homecoming video game developer Double Helix Games based in Irvine California. Its newest release Strider is available on five platforms. Amazon also bought cloud-based digital comics platform ComiXology in 2014. In late 2014 Amazon purchased game-streaming site Twitch which boasted 55 million monthly active users after talks with Google turned to antitrust concerns.

EXECUTIVES

Vice President Kindle Content, Russell Grandinetti
SVP Consumer Business, Jeffrey A. (Jeff) Wilke, age 49, $165,000 total compensation
Chairman President and CEO, Jeffrey P. (Jeff) Bezos, age 52, $81,840 total compensation
SVP International Consumer Business, Diego Piacentini, age 54, $175,000 total compensation
SVP Web Services, Andrew R. (Andy) Jassy, age 48, $160,000 total compensation
VP and CFO, Brian T. Olsavsky
Vice President Tba Technology, Charles Griffith
Vice President Seller Applications Technology, Paul Kotas
Vice President Home Improvements, John Witham
Vice President and Associate General Counsel, Andrew (Andy) DeVore
Safety Vpp Program Manager, Jennifer (Jen) McNeal
National Sales Manager, Kevin Sontgerath

Vice President Information Technology, Yvette Bohanan
Executive Vice President, Rich Williams, age 40
Vice President Of Legal Retail Team, Amber Beckman
Vice President Human Resources Kindle, John (Jack) Olsen
Senior Vice President Worldwide Operations, Marc Onetto
Vice President Worldwide Discovery, Kim Rachmeler
Vice President E Commerce Platform Services, Gene Pope
Vice President Information Technology, Kathryn Giorgianni
Vice President Corporate Sales Development, Robert Saltzman
Auditors: Ernst & Young LLP

LOCATIONS

HQ: Amazon.com Inc.
  410 Terry Avenue North, Seattle, WA 98109-5210
Phone: 206 266-1000   **Fax:** 206 266-1821
Web: www.amazon.com

2014 Sales

	$ mil.	% of total
North America	55,469	62
International		
Germany	11,919	14
United Kingdom	8,341	9
Japan	7,912	9
Other countries	5,347	6
Total	**88,988**	**100**

PRODUCTS/OPERATIONS

2014 Sales

	$ mil.	% of total
Electronics & other general merchandise	60,886	69
Media	22,505	25
Other	5,597	6
Total	**88,988**	**100**

2014 Sales

	$ mil.	% of total
Product	70,080	79
Services	18,908	21
Total	**88,988**	**100**

Selected Departments

Apparel shoes and jewelry
Books
  Books
  Kindle e-books
  Textbooks
  Magazines
Computers and office
  Computers and accessories
  Computer components
  Office products and supplies
  PC games
  Software
Digital downloads
  Amazon shorts
  Game downloads
  Kindle Store
  MP3 downloads
Electronics
  Audio TV and home theater
  Camera photo and video
  Car electronics and GPS
  Cell phones and service
  Home appliances
  MP3 and media players
  Musical instruments
  Video games
Grocery health and beauty
  Beauty
  Diapers
  Gourmet food
  Grocery
  Health and personal care
  Natural and organic
Home and garden

Bedding and bath
Furniture and decor
Home appliances
Home improvement
Kitchen and dining
Patio lawn and garden
Pet supplies
Sewing craft and hobby
Vacuums and storage
Kindle
  Books
  Blogs
  Magazines
  Newspapers
Movies music and games
  Blu-ray
  Movies and TV
  Music
  Musical instruments
  Video games
  Video On Demand
Sports and outdoors
  Action sports
  Camping and hiking
  Cycling
  Exercise and fitness
  Fan gear
  Golf
  Team sports
Tools auto and industrial
  Automotive
  Home improvement
  Industrial and scientific
  Lighting and electrical
  Motorcycle and ATV
  Outdoor power equipment
  Plumbing fixtures
  Power and hand tools
Toys kids and baby
  Apparel (kids and baby)
  Baby
  Books
  Movies
  Music
  Software
  Toys and games
  Video games

Selected Operations

A9.com (search technology development)
Amazon.ca (Canada)
Amazon.cn (China)
Amazon.de (Germany)
Amazon.fr (France)
Amazon.co.jp (Japan)
Amazon.co.uk (UK)
Audible (audiobooks and other recorded content)
Endless (shoes and handbags)
Internet Movie Database (IMDb)
IVONA Software
Joyo (China)
LOVEFiLM International Ltd.
Woot.com (US)
Zappos.com (US)

COMPETITORS

Alibaba Group	J. C. Penney
Apple Inc.	Kering
AutoNation	Lowe's
AutoZone	Macy's
Barnes & Noble	Netflix
Best Buy	Office Depot
Bluefly	OfficeMax
Books-A-Million	Overstock.com
Buy.com	Peapod LLC
Columbia House	Provide Gifts
Costco Wholesale	Rack Room Shoes
DSW	Sears
Finish Line	Shoe Carnival
Foot Locker	Staples
Google	TJX Companies
HSN	Target Corporation
Hastings Entertainment	The Gap
Hollywood Media	Wal-Mart
Home Depot	Yahoo!
IAC	eBay
Indigo Books & Music	shoebuy.com

HISTORICAL FINANCIALS

Company Type: Public

Income Statement

FYE: December 31

	REVENUE ($ mil.)	NET INCOME ($ mil.)	NET PROFIT MARGIN	EMPLOYEES
12/15	107,006	596	0.6%	230,800
12/14	88,988	(241)	—	154,100
12/13	74,452	274	0.4%	117,300
12/12	61,093	(39)	—	88,400
12/11	48,077	631	1.3%	56,200
Annual Growth	22.1%	(1.4%)	—	42.4%

2015 Year-End Financials

Debt ratio: 21.67%
Return on equity: 4.94%
Cash ($ mil.): 19,808
Current ratio: 1.08
Long-term debt ($ mil.): 14,183
No. of shares (mil.): 471
Dividends
  Yield: —
  Payout: —
Market value ($ mil.): 318,344

	STOCK PRICE ($) FY Close	P/E High/Low	PER SHARE ($) Earnings	Dividends	Book Value
12/15	675.89	542 224	1.25	0.00	28.42
12/14	310.35	— —	(0.52)	0.00	23.10
12/13	398.79	674 414	0.59	0.00	21.23
12/12	250.87	— —	(0.09)	0.00	18.04
12/11	173.10	177 116	1.37	0.00	17.05
Annual Growth	40.6%	— —	(2.3%)	—	13.6%

Ambac Financial Group, Inc.

Ambac Financial Group used to give an A+ to school bonds until its own ratings fell to C's. Ambac Assurance the holding company's primary subsidiary sold financial guarantee insurance and other credit enhancement products for municipal bonds in the US market. HoweverÂthe company has halted all new business and has placed its remaining business inÂ"run-off" —meaning it is only taking in premium payments and paying out claims as it is able.ÂAlready operating under "rehabilitation" by Wisconsin regulators Ambac Financial filed for Chapter 11Âbankruptcy in 2010.

Bankruptcy

In late 2010 after missing a scheduled interest payment and failing to reach an agreement for a prepackaged bankruptcy proceeding with its creditors the company voluntarily filed for Chapter 11 bankruptcy protection. Through the filing Ambac hopes to restructure more than $1.6 billion in outstanding debt. The company is also haggling with the IRS over $700 million in potentially improper tax refunds between 2003 and 2008.

The bankruptcy court approved a plan of reorganization for Ambac in 2012 but the company was unable to immediately consummate the reorganization.

Geographic Reach

Ambac's run-off operations primarily bring in revenues from the US market which accounts for three-fourths of revenues. The company also has international operations (also in runoff) in markets including Australia Austria Germany Italy and the UK.

Operations

In addition to its core financial guarantee offerings in better days Ambac also insured infrastruc-

ture and utility finance deals internationally. Its Ambac Financial Services unit offered interest rate swaps credit swaps and investment management primarily to states and municipal authorities tied to their bond financing. These operations are also in run-off through means including transaction terminations settlements and scheduled contract amortizations.

How did a once-solid municipal bond insurer fall so hard? Along with other US bond insurers including FGIC and MBIA the US subprime mortgage meltdown knocked the wind out of Ambac. Its financial guarantee business fizzled and the company began to post heavy losses. Meanwhile Ambac's portfolio bulged with collateralized debt obligations of asset-backed securities —the financial equivalent of a sack of rotten potatoes once the credit markets turned sour.

The company scrambled to restructure through multiple measures from 2007 through 2009 but was ultimately unable to stabilize its finances. Ambac's insurance ratings slid down from "AAA" in early 2007 to "CC" in 2010 putting a serious crimp on its ability to write new business.

The company stopped actively marketing insurance policies during 2008 and eventually placed its financial services business into run-off as well. Unable to resolve its debts with creditors Ambac filed for Chapter 11 bankruptcy in 2010. By 2011 the independent ratings houses of Standard and Poors and Moodys had withdrawn all formal ratings of Ambac.

Financial Performance

Ambac's run-off (existing account) insurance operations brought in some $686 million in revenues in 2012 a 131% increase over 2011 results and the first sign of improved earnings after two years of declining revenues. The growth was attributed to higher premiums earnings improved investment income and accelerated earnings from customer refinancing of Ambac-insured debt. The company posted a loss of $257 million that year an improvement over losses of nearly $2 billion in 2011 due to reduced operating interest loss and reorganization expenses.

Strategy

Ambac's strategy is focused around reorganizing its capital structure and financial obligations through the bankruptcy process. It is also working to increase the residual value of its financial guarantee business through loss mitigation efforts on poorly performing transactions as well as to maximize investment returns.

HISTORY

Mortgage Guaranty Insurance Corporation (MGIC) in 1971 founded American Municipal Bond Assurance Corporation (Ambac Indemnity) in Milwaukee. That year Ambac wrote the very first municipal bond insurance policy —Âfor a bond to fund a medical building and a sewage treatment facility in Juneau Alaska. New York City's 1975 moratorium on debt payments helped make the new product more attractive. The company wrote the first insurance policies for mutual funds (1977) and secondary market municipal bonds (1983). In 1981 Ambac moved to New York; four years later it became a Citibank subsidiary. It went public in 1991.

In 1995 Ambac and rival MBIA allied to offer bond insurance overseas. Two years later the company formed a UK subsidiary to serve Europe. In recognition of the growing market the joint venture was amended in 2000 to provide for individual operations by the two partners in Europe though they continued to reinsure each other there and to work jointly in Japan. Ambac went on a buying spree in 1996 and 1997 buying the investment advisory and broker dealer operations of Cadre

HOOVER'S HANDBOOK OF AMERICAN BUSINESS 2016

and Construction Loan Insurance (renamed Connie Lee Holdings) a guarantor of college bonds and hospital infrastructure bonds.

In 1998 as Ambac lost share in the US municipal bond market because it declined to cut premiums the company began concentrating on asset-backed securities and international bonds. Two years later Ambac entered the Japanese market through a joint venture with Yasuda Fire & Marine.

The company sold its Cadre Financial Services and Ambac Securities divisions in 2004 but kept Connie Lee for the future.

The US subprime mortgage meltdown took its toll on Ambac. Its financial guarantee business had slowed to a trickle by late 2007 when the company posted losses of $3.5 billion for the last quarter of that year.

The large rating houses took a dim view of Ambac's weakening reserves prompting the company to scramble for a plan in late 2007. It scrapped one plan to split apart its municipal bond business from its increasingly risky US mortgage securities then hit on another plan to raise $1.5 billion through stock sales.

To steady itself during 2008 the company took a few deep breaths quit underwriting certain types of structured finance business (especially asset- and mortgage-backed securities) dropped its dividends down to a penny per share promoted its Chief Risk Officer David Wallis to serve as CEO and pinned its future on its public finance business.

In 2008 Ambac went back and reactivated a somewhat dusty Connie Lee with the hopes that guaranteeing municipal construction bonds would be a stable business. To get Construction Loan Insurance Company ready for its debut Ambac tucked $850 million of capital into its pocketbook. In 2009 it changed Connie Lee's name to Everspan Financial Guarantee but was unable to raise additional capital and eventually put the whole plan back on the shelf indefinitely.

By 2010 with no new business coming in the company resigned itself to mitigating its losses and trying to coax better yields from its investment portfolio. Its stinkier holdings were sent off to auction with any proceeds earmarked to pay interest on the company's remaining debts. The company filed for Chapter 11 bankruptcy in November 2010.

David Wallis announced his resignation in mid-2011 along with the company's General Counsel. Internal executive Diana Adams was tapped to serve as president and CEO.

EXECUTIVES

Senior Managing Director Chief Accounting Officer and Controller, Robert B. Eisman, age 47, $500,000 total compensation
Senior Managing Director CFO and Treasurer, David Trick, age 44, $625,000 total compensation
Co-Chairman and Interim CEO and President, Nader Tavakoli, age 56
Senior Managing Director and General Counsel, Stephen M. Ksenak, age 49
Senior Managing Director Restructuring and Corporate Development, David Barranco, age 44
Senior Managing Director RMBS Risk Management, Iain H. Bruce, age 55
Senior Managing Director Portfolio and Credit Risk Management, Cathleen J. Matanle, age 62
Senior Managing Director CIO and Chief Administrative Office, Michael Reilly, age 58
Vice President Of Information Technology, Michael Braganca
Vice President Technology, Lee Gigante
Vice President, Emily He
Vice President, Karl Bejasa

First Vice President, Art Heffner
First Vice President, Ronaldo Contreras
Vice President, Valerie Anderson
Assistant Vice President, John (Jack) Osmanzai
Vice President, Bonnie Lim
First Vice President Structured Real Estate, Gregory Mayer
First Vice President Housing Group, Kelly Wimmer
Vice President, David (Dave) Woolley
Vice President Investment Accounting, Gary Stein
Vice President Technology, Scott Brown
Assistant Vice President Risk Operations, Pranay Nadkarni
Vice President Of Finance, Michael Klaassens
Assistant Vice President, Linda Crocitto
Vice President, Andrew Zuniga
Vice President Senior Vice President Finance Director, Thomas (Thom) Staskowski
Assistant Vice President Finance, Chris Dudonis
Vice President, Justine Kong
First Vice President, Tracy Pridgen
Vice President Financial Control, Robyn Leong
Senior Vice President, Richard White
Assistant Vice President In Technology, Venka Korsapati
Vice President Information Technology, David Murelli
First Vice President Credit Risk Management, Robert Bose
First Vice President, Yuliang LI
Auditors: KPMG LLP

LOCATIONS

HQ: Ambac Financial Group, Inc.
One State Street Plaza, New York, NY 10004
Phone: 212 658-7470

2014 Premium earned by geography

	% of total
US	80
UK	13
Other international	7
Total	**100**

PRODUCTS/OPERATIONS

2014 Net Premiums Earned

	% of total
Public finance	65
Structured finance	18
International finance	17
Total	**100**

Selected Services

Adversely Classified Credit
Amendment Waiver and Consen
Credit Risk Management (CRM)
International Finance Insured Portfolio
U.S. Public Finance Insured Portfolio
U.S. Structured Finance

COMPETITORS

Assured Guaranty	MBIA
FGIC	

HISTORICAL FINANCIALS

Company Type: Public

Income Statement

FYE: December 31

	ASSETS ($ mil.)	NET INCOME ($ mil.)	INCOME AS % OF ASSETS	EMPLOYEES
12/14	25,159	483	1.9%	188
12/13*	27,106	505	1.9%	212
04/13	0	3,349	—	—
12/12	27,007	(256)	—	226
12/11	27,113	(1,960)	—	227
Annual Growth	**(2.5%)**	**—**		**(6.1%)**

*Fiscal year change

2014 Year-End Financials

Debt ratio: 55.06%	No. of shares (mil.): 45
Return on equity: 46.02%	Dividends
Cash ($ mil.): 73	Yield: —
Current ratio: —	Payout: —
Long-term debt ($ mil.): —	Market value ($ mil.): 1,103

	STOCK PRICE ($) FY Close	P/E High/Low		PER SHARE ($) Earnings	Dividends	Book Value
12/14	24.50	3	2	10.31	0.00	31.09
12/13*	24.56	2	1	10.91	0.00	15.62
Annual Growth	(0.1%)	—	—	(1.9%)	—	25.8%

*Fiscal year change

Ameren Corp.

Ameren provides the power that makes much of the American Midwest run. The holding company distributes electricity to 2.8 million customers and natural gas to 940000 customers in Missouri and Illinois through regulated utility subsidiaries Union Electric (which does business as Ameren Missouri) and Ameren Ilinois. Ameren has a generating capacity of about 10272 MW (primarily coal-fired) most of which is controlled by Ameren Missouri). Ameren operates a nuclear power facility two hydroelectric plants and several coal-fired plants and natural gas-fired facilities. It also purchases green power including wind power and solar.

HISTORY

More than 30 St. Louis companies had built a chaotic grid of generators and power lines throughout the city by 1900. Two years later many of them merged into the Union Company which attracted national notice when it lit the St. Louis World's Fair in the first broad demonstration of electricity's power. In 1913 the company by then named Union Electric (UE) began buying electricity from an Iowa dam 150 miles away —the greatest distance power had ever been transmitted in such quantity.

UE pushed into rural Missouri and began buying and building fossil-fuel plants. Despite a slowdown during the Depression UE built Bagnell Dam on Missouri's Osage River in the early 1930s to gather power for a hydroelectric plant. At the onset of WWII construction began on new plants with larger generators and lower production costs; however demand for electricity lagged. In the late 1940s UE compensated by joining a "power pool" a system of utilities with interconnected transmission lines that shared electricity.

Growth in the 1950s came from acquisitions including Missouri Power & Light (1950) and Missouri Edison (1954). During the 1960s and 1970s UE built five new plants including the Labadie plant (2300 MW) one of the largest coal-fired plants in the US.

UE began producing nuclear energy in 1984 at its Callaway nuke. High costs and the expenses of a scrapped second plant caused UE to battle the Missouri Public Service Commission throughout the 1980s for rate increases.

Charles Mueller became president in 1993 and CEO one year later. He oversaw continued staff reductions and cost cutting through the 1990s in an increasingly competitive market. In 1997 UE expanded into Illinois through its purchase of CIP-

SCO which owned utility Central Illinois Public Service Company (CIPS).

CIPS began as a Mattoon Illinois streetcar company in the early 1900s. The firm bought Mattoon's electric power plant in 1904 and began growing its power business buying small electric companies in the 1920s and 1930s. CIPS built five generating units in the 1940s and 1950s and became part-owner (along with UE) of Electric Energy Inc. which built a power plant on the Ohio River. The company bought Illinois Electric and Gas Company in the 1960s and the state's Gas Utilities in the 1980s. To prepare for competition under deregulation CIPS created holding company CIPSCO in the 1990s to diversify.

UE's purchase of CIPSCO expanded its geographic scope and the new company was named Ameren in 1997 to reflect its American energy focus. The next year the company committed to adding generating capacity through several natural gas-fired combustion turbines. It joined nine other utilities to form the Midwest Independent System Operator to manage their transmission needs.

In 1999 Ameren bought a 245-mile railroad line between St. Louis and Kansas City to help the area's economic development. Looking for new opportunities in deregulated energy markets the company purchased Data & Metering Specialties.

In 2000 Ameren created subsidiary AmerenEnergy Generating to operate its nonregulated power plants and affiliate AmerenEnergy Marketing to sell the generating facilities' power. When deregulation took effect in Illinois in 2002 the company transferred AmerenCIPS' power plants to AmerenEnergy Generating. In 2003 Ameren acquired CILCORP the holding company for electric and gas utility Central Illinois Light (now operating as AmerenCILCO) from independent power producer AES in a $1.4 billion deal. To further expand its utility operations Ameren acquired power and gas utility Illinois Power from Dynegy in a $2.3 billion deal in 2004. As part of the agreement Ameren gained Dynegy's 20% stake in power generator Electric Energy in which Ameren already held a 60% stake.

In 2007 Ameren subsidiary AmerenUE moved into wind power operations by contracting to buy 100 MW of wind power from Horizon Wind Energy's Rail Splitter Wind Farm located near Delavan Illinois.

In 2010 the company combined AmerenIP AmerenCIPS and AmerenCILCO into one entity Ameren Illinois in order to streamline operations and reduce confusion among customers. The three Illinois utilities have operated as a single business since 2004 and deliver energy to more than 1100 communities. Ameren Illinois also operates some 21400 miles of natural gas distribution and transmission lines.

Ameren's overall revenues decreased by 9% in 2012 due to a 24% drop Merchant Generation sales caused by lower market prices and a sales contract in 2011 that was not supplied in 2012. Ameren Illinois' revenues dropped by 10% due to lower wholesale distribution revenues primarily due to lower demand and the recognition of a reserve for revenues subject to a refund which dropped revenues by $6 million. Ameren Missouri's revenues declined by only 3% due to reduced purchased power expenses as a result of a FERC-ordered refund which helped to improve margins. The company reported a net loss of $974 million in 2012 (a whopping 288% drop compared to 2011) due to lower sales and higher operating expenses as well as an increase in impairment and other charges.

Ameren opened a waste-to-energy plant in 2012. In 2012 Ameren Missouri entered into an agreement with Westinghouse Electric to exclu-

sively support Westinghouse's application for the Department of Energy's Small Modular Reactors investment funds of up to $452 million.

EXECUTIVES

Chairman President and CEO, Warner L. Baxter, age 54, $854,647 total compensation
EVP and CFO, Martin J. Lyons, age 48, $566,500 total compensation
Chairman President and CEO Ameren Services, Daniel F. Cole, age 61, $292,000 total compensation
Chairman President and CEO Ameren Illinois, Richard J. Mark, age 60
SVP Corporate Planning and Corporate Oversight, Mark C. Birk, age 47
Chairman President and CEO Ameren Missouri, Michael L. Moehn, age 46, $458,370 total compensation
Chairman President and CEO Ameren Transmission Company of Illinois, Maureen A. Borkowski, age 55
VP and CIO Information Technology and Ameren Services Center, Mary P. Heger
SVP and Chief Nuclear Officer Ameren Missouri, Fadi M. Diya, $397,358 total compensation
Senior Vice President sales and Customer Service, Mike Jacobi
Vice President of Human Resources, John (Jack) Fey
Vice President South America, Benjamin Roush
Vice President Sales and Marketing Sales and Mar, Jason Johnston
Vice President Research And Development, Rick Garpow
Vice President Corporate Development, Steve M Kidwell
Vice President And Tax Counsel Ameren Services V, Gregory Nelson
Vice President Power Operations, Chuck Naslund
Auditors: PricewaterhouseCoopers LLP

LOCATIONS

HQ: Ameren Corp.
 1901 Chouteau Avenue, St. Louis, MO 63103
Phone: 314 621-3222
Web: www.ameren.com

PRODUCTS/OPERATIONS

2014 Sales

	$ mil.	% of total
Ameren Missouri	3,526	58
Ameren Illinois	2,496	42
Intersegment Eliminations	31	-
Total	**6,053**	**100**

2014 Sales

	$ mil.	% of total
Electric	4,913	81
Gas	1,140	19
Total	**6,053**	**100**

COMPETITORS

AES	Great Plains Energy
Atmos Energy	Midwest Generation
Empire District	Nicor Gas
Electric	Southern Union
Exelon	

HISTORICAL FINANCIALS

Company Type: Public

Income Statement

FYE: December 31

	REVENUE ($ mil.)	NET INCOME ($ mil.)	NET PROFIT MARGIN	EMPLOYEES
12/14	6,053	586	9.7%	8,527
12/13	5,838	289	5.0%	8,527
12/12	6,828	(974)	—	9,097
12/11	7,531	519	6.9%	9,323
12/10	7,638	139	1.8%	9,474
Annual Growth	**(5.6%)**	**43.3%**	**—**	**(2.6%)**

2014 Year-End Financials

Debt ratio: 30.67%
Return on equity: 8.84%
Cash ($ mil.): 5
Current ratio: 0.91
Long-term debt ($ mil.): 6,120
No. of shares (mil.): 242
Dividends
 Yield: 3.4%
 Payout: 68.2%
Market value ($ mil.): 11,191

	STOCK PRICE ($) FY Close	P/E High/Low	PER SHARE ($) Earnings	Dividends	Book Value
12/14	46.13	20 15	2.40	1.61	27.67
12/13	36.16	31 26	1.18	1.60	26.97
12/12	30.72	— —	(4.01)	1.60	27.27
12/11	33.13	16 12	2.15	1.56	32.64
12/10	28.19	51 41	0.58	1.54	32.15
Annual Growth	**13.1%**	**— —**	**42.6%**	**1.1%**	**(3.7%)**

American Airlines Group Inc

American Airlines Group (AAG) knows America's spacious skies –and lots of others. After merging with US Airways in late 2013 AAG is one of the largest airlines in the world. The combined airline together with its third-party regional carriers including Air Wisconsin Chautauqua ExpressJet Mesa Republic and SkyWest operate nearly 6700 daily flights to roughly 340 destinations in more than 50 countries. American and US Airways operate 980 mainline jets and regional subsidiaries and third-party regional carriers operate nearly 565 regional jets. AAG extends its geographic reach through code-sharing arrangements and is part of the oneworld Alliance.

Change of Company Type

In late 2013 AMR merged with rival US Airways in a deal worth $11 billion. The milestone transaction created the world's largest airline. The combined entity kept the American Airlines name and is led by former US Airways CEO Doug Parker.

Geographic Reach

AAG has primary hubs in Charlotte North Carolina; Chicago Dallas/Fort Worth; Los Angeles; Miami; New York; Philadelphia; Phoenix; and Washington DC. It provides international service to Canada Mexico Europe the Middle East the Caribbean Central and South America and Asia. Revenues from foreign operations (flights serving international destinations) were approximately 33% of American's total operating revenues and approximately 24% of US Airways' total operating revenues for 2014. The US accounted for about 67% of AAG's revenue in 2014.

Operations

Following the truism that you have to spend money to make money AMR ordered 460 single-aisle jets –200 Boeing 737s and 260 Airbus A320s for delivery between 2013 and 2022; it is the largest aircraft order in history. The new aircraft are designed for fuel efficiency and should save on operating costs. (During 2014 the company took delivery of 82 mainline aircraft and retired 69 older legacy mainline aircraft.)

In 2015 AAG received the delivery of its first Boeing 787 Dreamliner. The company has placed firm orders for 42 Boeing 787 aircraft with the right to acquire an additional 58.

Financial Performance

Due primarily to its merger with US Airways AAG has achieved extraordinary growth over the last few years. Revenues soared 59% from $26.7 billion in 2013 to peak at a record-shattering $42.7 billion in 2014. After suffering six straight years of net losses (mostly due to restructuring charges associated with its US Airways merger) AAG posted $2.9 billion in profits during 2014 due to the additional revenue coupled with the absence of those extra charges.

The historic revenue growth for 2014 was driven by a 52% bump in mainline passenger revenues as the air travel industry experienced higher demand and additional revenue from the sale of frequent flyer mileage credits. AAG also experienced significant rises from its regional (102%) cargo (28%) and "other" (72%) segments. Domestic revenues skyrocketed by 86% while revenue from its Atlantic region jumped 50% during 2014.

The company's operating cash flow has fluctuated over the last five years. In 2014 cash flow increased by over 350% to $3.08 billion due to the increased profits and increased inflows from accounts payable.

Strategy

AAG is adding new aircraft and new service into markets which cater to a wide breadth of industries – entertainment banking and finance energy technology and manufacturing. This includes direct service to all of American's hubs with the most nonstop flights from LAX to New York (JFK); Dallas/Fort Worth; Miami; Philadelphia; Washington DC (DCA); Phoenix; and Charlotte North Carolina.

HISTORY

In 1929 Sherman Fairchild created a New York City holding company called the Aviation Corporation (AVCO) combining some 85 small airlines in 1930 to create American Airways. In 1934 the company had its first dose of financial trouble after the government suspended private airmail for months. Corporate raider E. L. Cord took over and named the company American Airlines.

EXECUTIVES

EVP Corporate Affairs, Stephen L. (Steve) Johnson, age 58, $566,067 total compensation
Chairman and CEO AAG American and US Airways Group, W. Douglas (Doug) Parker, age 53, $687,884 total compensation
President, J. Scott Kirby, age 47, $642,512 total compensation
EVP People and Communications, Elise R. Eberwein, age 49
EVP and CFO, Derek J. Kerr, age 50, $563,860 total compensation
EVP and COO, Robert D. Isom, age 51, $591,254 total compensation
SVP and CIO, Maya Leibman
SVP and CIO, Beverly K. Goulet, age 60
Vice President and Treasurer, Thomas (Thom) Weir
National Sales Manager, Michael (Mel) Fricke
Vice President Customer Experience, Ken Gilbert
Vice President, Brian McMenamy

Vice President And Corporate Secretary, Ken Wimberly
Auditors: KPMG LLP

LOCATIONS

HQ: American Airlines Group Inc
4333 Amon Carter Blvd., Fort Worth, TX 76155
Phone: 817 963-1234   **Fax:** 817 967-9641
Web: www.aa.com

2013 Sales

	$ mil.	% of total
DOT Domestic	15,376	57
DOT Latin America	6,288	24
DOT Atlantic	3,756	14
DOT Pacific	1,323	5
Total	**26,743**	**100**

Selected Hub Locations

Chicago (O' Hare)
Dallas/Fort Worth (DFW)
Los Angeles
Miami
New York City

PRODUCTS/OPERATIONS

2013 Sales

	$ mil.	% of total
Mainline Passenger	20,218	76
Regional passenger	3,131	12
Cargo	685	2
Other	2,709	10
Total	**26,743**	**100**

COMPETITORS

Air France-KLM	Lufthansa
AirTran Airways	Mesa Air
Alaska Air	SkyWest
China Southern Airlines	Southwest Airlines
	Spirit Airlines
Delta Air Lines	UPS
FedEx	United Air Lines
Frontier Airlines	United Continental
Greyhound	Virgin Atlantic
Hawaiian Holdings	Airways
JetBlue	

HISTORICAL FINANCIALS

Company Type: Public

Income Statement
FYE: December 31

	REVENUE ($ mil.)	NET INCOME ($ mil.)	NET PROFIT MARGIN	EMPLOYEES
12/14	42,650	2,882	6.8%	113,300
12/13	26,743	(1,834)	—	110,400
12/12	24,855	(1,876)	—	77,750
12/11	23,979	(1,979)	—	80,100
12/10	22,170	(471)	—	78,250
Annual Growth	**17.8%**	**—**	**—**	**9.7%**

2014 Year-End Financials

Debt ratio: 40.90%
Return on equity: —
Cash ($ mil.): 1,768
Current ratio: 0.90
Long-term debt ($ mil.): 16,196

No. of shares (mil.): 697
Dividends
  Yield: 0.3%
  Payout: 5.0%
Market value ($ mil.): 37,406

	STOCK PRICE ($) FY Close	P/E High/Low		PER SHARE ($) Earnings	Dividends	Book Value
12/14	53.63	13	6	3.93	0.20	2.90
12/13	25.25	—	—	(11.25)	0.00	(10.46)
12/12	0.80	—	—	(14.99)	0.00	(63.78)
12/11	0.35	—	—	(15.82)	0.00	(56.79)
12/10	7.79	—	—	(3.78)	0.00	(31.68)
Annual Growth	**62.0%**	—	—	—	—	—

American Electric Power Company, Inc.

American Electric Power (AEP) takes its slice of the US power pie out of Middle America. The holding company is one of the largest power generators and distributors in the US. AEP owns the nation's largest electricity transmission system a network of almost 40000 miles. It also has 230000 miles of distribution lines. Its electric utilities have 5.3 million customers in 11 states and have about 32000 MW of largely coal-fired generating capacity. AEP is a top wholesale energy company; it markets electricity in the US. To raise cash in 2015 the company agreed to sell its commercial barging operations that transport liquids coal and dry bulk commodities on the Ohio Illinois and lower Mississippi Rivers.

HISTORY

In 1906 Richard Breed Sidney Mitchell and Henry Doherty set up American Gas & Electric (AG&E) in New York to buy 23 utilities from Philadelphia's Electric Company of America. With properties in seven northeastern US states AG&E began acquiring and merging small electric properties creating the predecessors of Ohio Power (1911) Kentucky Power (1919) and Appalachian Power (1926). AG&E also bought the predecessor of Indiana Michigan Power (1925).

By 1926 the company was operating in Indiana Kentucky Michigan Ohio Virginia and West Virginia. In 1935 AG&E engineer Philip Sporn later known as the Henry Ford of power introduced his high-voltage high-velocity circuit breaker. AG&E picked up Kingsport Power in 1938.

Becoming president in 1947 Sporn began an ambitious building program that continued through the 1960s. Plants designed by AG&E (renamed American Electric Power in 1958) were among the world's most efficient and electric rates stayed 25%-38% below the national average.

AEP bought Michigan Power in 1967 six years after Donald Cook succeeded Sporn as president. Cook who refused to attach scrubbers to the smokestacks of coal-fired plants was criticized in the early 1970s by environmental protesters. AEP's first nuclear plant named in Cook's honor went on line in Michigan in 1975. He retired in 1976.

The firm moved from New York to Columbus Ohio in 1980 after buying what is now Columbus Southern Power (formed in 1883). It set up AEP Generating in 1982 to provide power to its electric utilities.

AEP began converting its second nuke Zimmer to coal in 1984. In 1992 AEP finally began installing scrubbers at its coal-fired Gavin plant in Ohio after being ordered to comply with the Clean Air Act. It also cleaned up its image by planting millions of trees in 1996.

The company formed AEP Communications after Congress passed the Telecommunications Act of 1996. The next year AEP jumped into the UK's deregulated electric market; AEP and New Century Energies (now Xcel Energy) bought Yorkshire Electricity (later Yorkshire Power Group) for $2.8 billion. However a $109 million UK windfall tax on the transaction —and increased wholesale competition —hurt AEP's bottom line.

As the normally staid electric industry succumbed to merger mania AEP agreed in 1997 to buy Central and South West (CSW) of Texas in a $6.6 billion deal. AEP's sales would nearly double and CSW was to bring its own UK utility SEE-BOARD and other overseas holdings.

In 1998 AEP bought a 20% stake in Pacific Hydro an Australian power producer and CitiPower an Australian electric distribution company. AEP also bought Equitable Resources' Louisiana natural gas midstream operations including an intrastate pipeline. In 1999 China's Pushan Power Plant (70%-owned by AEP) began operations. Environmental concerns resurfaced that year when the EPA sued the utility alleging its old coal-powered plants which had been grandfathered from the Clean Air Act had been quietly upgraded to extend their lives.

Regulators approved the company's acquisition of CSW in 2000 but AEP had to agree to relinquish control of its 22000 miles of transmission lines to an independent operator. The CSW deal closed later that year. (However the SEC's approval of the deal was challenged by a federal appeals court in 2002.)

AEP sold its 50% stake in Yorkshire Power Group to Innogy (now RWE npower) in 2001; it also purchased Houston Pipe Line Co. (which it later sold in early 2005) from Enron for $727 million. AEP became one of the largest US barge operators that year when it bought MEMCO Barge Line from Progress Energy. It also purchased two UK coal-fired power plants (4000 MW) from Edison Mission Energy a subsidiary of Edison International in a $960 million deal.

In 2002 AEP sold its UK utility SEEBOARD to Electricité de France in a $2.2 billion deal; it also sold its Australian utility CitiPower to a consortium led by Cheung Kong Infrastructure and Hongkong Electric for $855 million. The following year the company sold two of its competitive Texas retail electric providers (WTU Retail Energy and CPL Retail Energy) to UK utility Centrica. It also divested its power plant development subsidiary AEP Pro Serv and its stakes in telecom firms C3 Communications and AFN.

The company sold two UK power plants to Scottish and Southern Energy for $456 million in 2004 and it sold a 50% stake in a third UK plant to Scottish Power in a $210 million deal. AEP also sold four independent power plants in Florida and Colorado to Bear Stearns for $156 million that year.

In 2006 the company sold its Plaquemine cogeneration plant to Dow Chemical for $64 million. Also that year it formed a joint venture company with MidAmerican Energy Holdings to build and own new electric transmission assets within the Electric Reliability Council of Texas.

AEP settled an eight-year lawsuit with the US government in 2007 and agreed to pay more than $4.6 billion to reduce hazardous air pollution from 16 coal-burning power plants.

In 2011 the company reached a $425 million settlement covering all claims with BOA and Enron related to their purchase of Houston Pipeline Company from Enron in 2001.

Growing its retail business in the US in 2012 AEP acquired Chicago-based Blue Star Energy and its independent retail electric supplier BlueStar Energy Solutions. The company has about 23000 customer accounts. The deal also gives AEP the opportunity to hedge the output of its soon-to-be unregulated Ohio power generation.

By the end of 2012 AEP was operating 310 MW of wind power facilities and had about 180 MW of long-term purchase power agreements for wind power.

EXECUTIVES

SVP and Chief Administrative Officer, Lana L. Hillebrand, age 54, $490,680 total compensation
Vice President External Affairs, Julio Reyes

EVP and COO, Robert P. (Bob) Powers, age 60, $695,339 total compensation
President and COO Southwestern Electric Power, Venita McCellon-Allen, age 56, $410,919 total compensation
EVP and Chief External Officer, Dennis E. Welch, age 63, $465,283 total compensation
VP Corporate Communications; President American Electric Power Foundation, Dale E. Heydlauff, age 55
President and COO Appalachian Power, Charles R. Patton, age 56
EVP Energy Supply, Charles E. (Chuck) Zebula, age 55
EVP and CFO, Brian X. Tierney, age 48, $695,339 total compensation
President and COO Public Service Company of Oklahoma, J. Stuart Solomon, age 53
Chairman President and CEO, Nicholas K. (Nick) Akins, age 55, $1,240,754 total compensation
EVP General Counsel and Secretary, David M. Feinberg, age 46, $568,679 total compensation
EVP Generation, Mark C. McCullough, age 57
President and COO Indiana Michigan Power, Paul Chodak, age 51
President and COO AEP Ohio, Pablo A. Vegas, age 42
President and COO AEP Texas, A. Wade Smith, age 51
President and COO Kentucky Power, Gregory G. (Greg) Pauley, age 63
EVP AEP Transmission, Lisa M. Barton, age 49
President Transource, Antonio Smyth
Senior Vice President Corporate Planning and Budgeting, Lonni Dieck
Executive Vice President Sales and Marketing, Johnathan Powers
Vice President Energy Marketing, Scott Slisher
Vice President of Human Resources, Dorothy Coleman
Vice President of Human Resources, Pamela (Pam) Mabry
Senior Vice President Corporate Communications, Charles (Chas) Zbula
Executive Vice President Operations, Paul Vegliante
Senior Vice President and Chief Information Officer AEPSC, Joseph (Jo) Hamrock
National Account Manager, W B Mosser
Vice President Risk Maangement and Market Oversite, Stephan T Haynes
Vice President Coal and Emissions Trading AEP Service, John (Jack) Massey
Senior Vice President Strategic Policy Analysis American Electric Power Service Corporation, Bruce H Braine
Vice President Power Projects and Asset Investments Commercial Operations, Timothy (Tim) Light
Vice President Audit Services American Electric Power Service Corporation, Richard A (Dick) Mueller
Vice President, Albert M (Al) Smoak
Vice President, Thomas L (Thom) Kirkpatrick
Vice President External Affairs, Brian Bond
Senior Vice President, Lionel Nowell
Senior Vice President Commercial Operations, Barbara (Barb) Radous
Vice President, Gonzalo Sandoval
Vice President and Director, John (Jack) Keane
Vice President Business Logistics, John (Jack) Harper
Vice President Of Sales, Andrew (Andy) Cox
Senior Vice President and Chief Nuclear Officer Cook Nuclear Plant, Lawrence J Weber
Vice President, Chris Johnson
Vice President, John (Jack) Moore
Vice President, Mike Davis
Vice President Finance, Monnie Hise
Senior Vice President, Armando Pena

Senior Vice President Chief Accounting Officer and Controller, Joe Buonaiuto
Vice President Energy Marketing Asset Investments and Renewables, Kevin Brady
Vice President Soln Technical Support, Marsha Ryan
Vice President of Corporate Planning Tech, Ollie Sever
Senior Vice President Commercial Operations, Todd Busby
Vice President Business Development, Dan Rogier
Vice President Western Generation Asse, Stephen (Steve) Burge
Vice President Governmental Affairs Aepsc, Anthony Kavanagh
Vice President Of Marketing, Steve Haynes
Vice President Business Development, Paul Graf
Senior Vice President Corporate Accounting Planning And Strategy, Stephen (Steve) Smith
Vice President Andcio, Richard (Dick) Secor
Vice President Generating Assets, Mark Peifer
Vice President Human Resources Services, Mark Welch
Vice President Research and Development, Craig Rhoades
Senior Vice President, Jeffrey (Jeff) Cross
Vice President Transmission Grid Development, Robert (Bob) Bradish
Senior Vice President Governmental Affairs, Tony Kavanagh
Vice President Procurement, Jim Henry
Vice President Governmental Affairs, Gregory Clark
Senior Vice President Energy Marketing, Brian W Neville
Vice President Regulatory and Finance, Chris Potter
Vice President Information Technology Infrastructu, Michael (Mel) Hart
Vice President of Marketing, Dave Ferguson
Assistant Secretary, Thomas (Thom) Berkemeyer
Treasurer, Carolyn Gordon
Secretary, Doshia Richardson
Auditors: Deloitte & Touche LLP

LOCATIONS

HQ: American Electric Power Company, Inc.
1 Riverside Plaza, Columbus, OH 43215-2373
Phone: 614 716-1000   **Fax:** 614 223-1823
Web: www.aep.com

PRODUCTS/OPERATIONS

2014 Sales

	$ mil.	% of total
Vertically integrated utilities	9,484	50
Transmission and distribution utilities	4,814	25
Generation and marketing	3,850	20
AEP river operations	700	4
AEP transmission holdco	192	1
Corporation and others	95	0
Adjustments	(2115)	-
Total	**17,020**	**100**

Selected Subsidiaries

AEP Energy Services Inc. (energy marketing and trading)
AEP Generating Co. (electricity generator marketer)
AEP Retail Energy (retail energy marketing in deregulated territories)
AEP Texas Central Company (formerly Central Power and Light electric utility)
AEP Texas North Company (formerly West Texas Utilities electric utility)
AEP Towers (wireless communications towers)
Appalachian Power Company (electric utility)
Columbus Southern Power Company (electric utility)
Indiana Michigan Power Company (electric utility)
Kentucky Power Company (electric utility)
Kingsport Power Company (electric utility)
Ohio Power Company (electric utility)
Public Service Company of Oklahoma (electric utility)
Southwestern Electric Power Company (electric utility)

Wheeling Power Company (electric utility)
Utility Distribution/Customer Service Divisions
AEP Ohio (handles distribution customer service and
external affairs functions for Columbus Southern
Power Company Ohio Power Company and Wheeling
Power Company)
AEP Texas (handles distribution customer service and
external affairs functions for AEP Texas Central
Company and AEP Texas North Company)
Appalachian Power (handles distribution customer
service and external affairs functions for Appalachian
Power Company and Kingsport Power Company)
Indiana Michigan Power (handles distribution customer
service and external affairs functions for Indiana
Michigan Power Company)
Kentucky Power (handles distribution customer service
and external affairs functions for Kentucky Power
Company)
Public Service Company of Oklahoma (handles
distribution customer service and external affairs
functions for Public Service Company of Oklahoma)
Southwestern Electric Power Company (handles
distribution customer service and external affairs
functions for Southwestern Electric Power Company)

COMPETITORS

BP	Energy Future
CMS Energy	Entergy
Calpine	Exelon
CenterPoint Energy	FirstEnergy
Constellation Energy	NiSource
Group	PG&E Corporation
DTE	Sempra Energy
Delmarva Power	Southern Company
Dominion Resources	TVA
Duke Energy	Xcel Energy
Dynegy	

HISTORICAL FINANCIALS

Company Type: Public

Income Statement

FYE: December 31

	REVENUE ($ mil.)	NET INCOME ($ mil.)	NET PROFIT MARGIN	EMPLOYEES
12/14	17,020	1,634	9.6%	18,529
12/13	15,357	1,480	9.6%	18,521
12/12	14,945	1,259	8.4%	18,513
12/11	15,116	1,946	12.9%	18,710
12/10	14,427	1,214	8.4%	18,712
Annual Growth	4.2%	7.7%	—	(0.2%)

2014 Year-End Financials

Debt ratio: 33.59%
Return on equity: 9.93%
Cash ($ mil.): 644
Current ratio: 0.56
Long-term debt ($ mil.): 16,181

No. of shares (mil.): 489
Dividends
  Yield: 3.3%
  Payout: 55.3%
Market value ($ mil.): 29,717

	STOCK PRICE ($) FY Close	P/E High/Low		PER SHARE ($) Earnings	Dividends	Book Value
12/14	60.72	19	14	3.34	2.03	34.37
12/13	46.74	17	14	3.04	1.95	32.98
12/12	42.68	17	14	2.60	1.88	31.37
12/11	41.31	10	8	4.02	1.85	30.33
12/10	35.98	15	12	2.53	1.71	28.46
Annual Growth	14.0%	—	—	7.2%	4.4%	4.8%

American Equity Investment Life Holding Co

Eagles' nests aren't particularly downy but American Equity Investment Life Holding (American Equity Life) helps middle income investors plan for a softer retirement. The company issues and administers fixed-rate and indexed annuities through subsidiaries American Equity Investment Life Insurance Eagle Life Insurance Company and American Equity Investment Life Insurance Company of New York. Licensed in 50 states and the District of Columbia the company sells its products through about 30000 independent agents and 45 national marketing associations. American Equity Life targets individuals between the ages of 45 and 75. The company also offers a variety of whole term and universal life insurance products.

Geographic Reach

Though the company is licensed in all fifty US states five big states bring in the bulk of its business. California Florida Illinois Pennsylvania and Texas together account for some 40% of American Equity Life's premiums.

Sales and Marketing

American Equity Life sells its products through 45 national marketing associations covering about 30000 independent agents.

Financial Performance

After several years of slow steady growth in 2013 American Equity Life reported a 64% jump in revenue from %1.7 million to $2.6 million as it saw increases in annuity product sales net investment income and gains on investments. The change lead to a huge increase in net income from $118 million to $253 million. A change in collateral held for derivatives lead to a 10% increase in cash from operations from $785 to $863.

Strategy

The company is working to increase sales in core service territories by enhancing its relationships with regional independent agents and introducing new products.

EXECUTIVES

Vice Chairman President and CEO, John M. Matovina, age 60, $677,500 total compensation
EVP and Secretary, Debra J. Richardson, age 58, $492,500 total compensation
President American Equity Life Insurance Co., Ronald J. (Ron) Grensteiner, $430,000 total compensation
EVP and Chief Investment Officer, Jeffrey D. (Jeff) Lorenzen, age 49
CFO and Treasurer, Ted M. Johnson, age 45, $445,000 total compensation
EVP and COO, Bruce D. Cheek
Vice President Information Technology, Ted Hughes
Regional Vice President, Denny Southern
Assistant Vice President Andndash; Technical Services, Kevin Seuferer
Founder and Executive Chairman, David J. (D.J.) Noble, age 83
Auditors: KPMG LLP

LOCATIONS

HQ: American Equity Investment Life Holding Co
  6000 Westown Parkway, West Des Moines, IA 50266
Phone: 515 221-0002
Web: www.american-equity.com

PRODUCTS/OPERATIONS

2013 Sales

	$ mil.	% of total
Net investment income	1,383	51
Change in fair value of derivatives	1,076	41
Annuity product charges	103	4
Premiums	45	2
Net realized gains on investments	40	2
Net OTTI losses	(6.2)	-
Loss on extinguishment of debt	(32.5)	
Total	**2,610**	**100**

COMPETITORS

Allianz Life	National Western
Aviva	Nationwide
FBL Financial	Northwestern Mutual
Fidelity & Guaranty	Presidential Life
Life	Prudential
Great American Life	Sammons Financial
Integrity Life	Security Benefit Group
Midland National Life	The Hartford

HISTORICAL FINANCIALS

Company Type: Public

Income Statement

FYE: December 31

	ASSETS ($ mil.)	NET INCOME ($ mil.)	INCOME AS % OF ASSETS	EMPLOYEES
12/14	43,989	126	0.3%	418
12/13	39,621	253	0.6%	416
12/12	35,133	57	0.2%	388
12/11	30,874	86	0.3%	386
12/10	26,426	42	0.2%	360
Annual Growth	13.6%	30.9%	—	3.8%

2014 Year-End Financials

Debt ratio: 1.52%
Return on equity: 7.15%
Cash ($ mil.): 701
Current ratio: —
Long-term debt ($ mil.): —

No. of shares (mil.): 76
Dividends
  Yield: 0.6%
  Payout: 11.3%
Market value ($ mil.): 2,220

	STOCK PRICE ($) FY Close	P/E High/Low		PER SHARE ($) Earnings	Dividends	Book Value
12/14	29.19	17	12	1.58	0.20	28.13
12/13	26.38	7	3	3.38	0.18	19.63
12/12	12.21	14	11	0.89	0.15	27.86
12/11	10.40	10	6	1.37	0.12	24.36
12/10	12.55	18	9	0.68	0.10	16.47
Annual Growth	23.5%	—	—	23.5%	18.9%	14.3%

American Express Co.

American Express makes money even if you do leave home without it. Best known for its charge cards and revolving credit cards the company is also one of the world's largest providers of travel services. And yes the company still issues traveler's checks. Its travel agency operations have thousands of locations worldwide and its Travelers Cheque Group is the world's largest issuer of traveler's checks. Still the company's charge and credit cards are its bread and butter; American Express boasts $159 billion in assets $1 trillion in annual billed business and has more than 110 million cards in circulation in 130-plus countries worldwide.

HISTORY

Company BackgroundIn 1850 Henry Wells and his two main competitors combined their delivery services to form American Express. When directors refused to expand to California in 1852 Wells and executive William Fargo formed Wells Fargo while remaining at American Express.

American Express merged with Merchants Union Express in 1868 and developed a money order to compete with the government's postal money order. Fargo's difficulty in cashing letters of credit in Europe led to the offering of Travelers Cheques in 1891.

In WWI the US government nationalized and consolidated all express delivery services compensating the owners. After the war American Express incorporated as an overseas freight and financial services and exchange provider (the freight operation was sold in 1970). In 1958 the company introduced the American Express charge card. It bought Fireman's Fund American Insurance (sold gradually between 1985 and 1989) and Equitable Securities in 1968.

James Robinson CEO from 1977 to 1993 hoped to turn American Express into a financial services supermarket. The company bought brokerage Shearson Loeb Rhoades in 1981 and investment banker Lehman Brothers in 1984 among others. In 1987 it introduced Optima a revolving credit card to compete with MasterCard and Visa. It had no experience in underwriting credit cards though and was badly burned by losses.

Most of the financial units were combined as Shearson Lehman Brothers. But the financial services supermarket never came to fruition and losses in this area brought a steep drop in earnings in the early 1990s. Harvey Golub was brought in as CEO in 1993 to restore stability.

The company sold its brokerage operations as Shearson (to Travelers now Citigroup) and spun off investment banking as Lehman Brothers in 1994. In late 1996 it teamed with Advanta Corp. to allow Advanta Visa and MasterCard holders to earn points in the American Express Membership Rewards program. The move sparked a lawsuit from Visa and MasterCard which prohibit their member banks from doing business with American Express. That set off a spate of lawsuits culminating in the US Justice Department filing an antitrust suit against Visa and MasterCard. A federal judge sided with the Justice Department in 2001 but Visa and MasterCard appealed.

In 1997 Kenneth Chenault became president and COO putting him in line to succeed Golub.

Online banking service Membership B@nking was launched in 1999. That year American Express invested in Ticketmaster (the ticketing giant that merged with Live Nation Entertainment in 2010). In 2000 the company established a headquarters in Beijing to develop business in China. Also that year American Express bought more than 4500 ATMs from Electronic Data Systems (now HP Enterprise Services) making it a leading US operator of ATMs.

In 2001 Chenault replaced Golub as chairman and CEO. American Express was hit hard that year by bad investments in below-investment grade bonds by its money-management unit which shaved about $1 billion from earnings. Adding to its woes the company's employees at its New York City headquarters across the street from the World Trade Center were displaced by the 2001 terrorist attacks; its headquarters reopened in May 2002.

To grow its corporate travel management business Amex acquired Rosenbluth International a leading global travel management company with corporate travel operations in 15 countries in 2003. When Rosenbluth became fully integrated into the organization in mid-2004 American Ex-

press announced a relaunch of its corporate travel organization renamed American Express Business Travel.

American Express underwent a mild shakeup in late 2004 when it cut 2.5% of its workforce in a restructuring that included the company's business travel operations. The restructuring also included the sale of the company's banking operations in Bangladesh Egypt Luxembourg and Pakistan and the relocation of some finance operations. On a brighter note the company that year announced a milestone agreement with Industrial and Commercial Bank of China (ICBC) one of the biggest banks in China to issue the first American Express-branded credit cards in that country.To focus on its travel and credit card operations the company in 2005 spun off Ameriprise Financial (formerly American Express Financial Advisors) a provider of insurance mutual funds investment advice and brokerage and asset management services. Toward that same end American Express sold its Tax and Business Services division to H&R Block and its UK-based American Express Financial Services Europe to TD Waterhouse (now part of TD AMERITRADE). Also in 2005 the company sold its equipment leasing business to Key Equipment Finance.In 2007 the company's business travel division bought the rest of Farrington American Express Travel Services Limited it didn't already own. The travel management company had been a joint venture with Farrington Travel. The move was part of American Express's global expansion push especially in the Asia-Pacific region.The company discontinued its Travelers Cheque card that year after determining that customers preferred paper travelers checks over a stored-value card. However sales of the travelers checks continued to decline in 2007 affected by the rising use of ATMs among other factors.Also in 2007 American Express reached a $2.5 billion settlement with Visa and other defendants including JPMorgan Chase Capital One U.S. Bancorp and Wells Fargo dropping them from the lawsuit that alleged the companies conspired to block American Express from the bank-issued card business in the US. The following year it reached a $1.8 billion settlement with Mastercard the final remaining defendant in the suit.American Express sold the international operations of American Express Bank to Stanchart in 2008.American Express became a banking holding company in 2009. As a result it received some $3.4 billion from the Troubled Asset Relief Fund (TARP) early that year; it repaid the debt within months.

EXECUTIVES

EVP and Chief Marketing Officer, John D. Hayes, age 61

EVP and CIO, Marc D. Gordon, age 54

Vice President, Fred Bishop

Chairman and CEO, Kenneth I. (Ken) Chenault, age 64, $2,000,000 total compensation

EVP and CFO, Jeffrey C. (Jeff) Campbell, age 54, $1,000,000 total compensation

Group President Global Corporate Services, Stephen J. (Steve) Squeri, age 56, $1,250,000 total compensation

EVP and General Counsel, Laureen E. Seeger, age 53

Chief Risk Officer; President Risk and Information Management Group, Ashwini (Ash) Gupta, age 62

President Global Network and International Consumer Services, Douglas E. Buckminster, age 55, $600,000 total compensation

EVP World Service, James P. Bush, age 56

President U.S. Consumer Services, Joshua G. (Josh) Silverman, age 46

President Global Merchant Services, Anre Williams, age 49

President Global Corporate Payments, Susan Sobbott, age 50

President Enterprise Growth, Neal Sample

Managing Director Europe the Middle East and Africa (EMEA) American Express Global Business Travel, Elyes Mrad

President and CEO Amex Bank of Canada; President and General Manager Amex Canada Inc., Rob McClean

Vice President, Molly Faust

Senior Vice President Corporate Affairs And Communications, Michael (Mel) O'Neill

Senior Vice President U.S Small Merchants, Ed Jay

Vice President Global Social Media Strategy, Shari Forman

Vice President and General Manager, Vincent Campana

Vice President Human Resources American Express, Kent Price

Vice President Of Technology Procurment, Steven (Steve) Squadere

Vice President Membership Rewards, Andrea Zaretsky

Vice President Operations, Camlin McGowan

Corporate Officer Executive Vice President, Jim Bush

Vice President Marketing, Kathleen King

Vice President Strategic Planning And Analytics, Boriana Tchobanova

Vice President Strategic Technology Relationships, Kelley King

Vice President Marketing, Lisa Parkin

Vice President Client Services, Michael (Mel) Sahuto

Vice President Technology, Shyamala Chalakudi

Vice President Of Strategic Planning Operations, Eduardo Orozco

Vice President, Martin Muscheid

Vice President, Nigel Greenwood

Vice President Network Management, Karen Czack

Vice President Us Controller, Bryan Nazworth

Vice President Finance Global Rewards, Francois Horikawa

Senior Vice President Advice and Information, Becky Roloff

Vice President Enterprise Growth Strategy, Courtney Kelso

Vice President, Helen Salmon

Vice President Enterprise Growth Strategy, Neel Chopdekar

Vice President Systems Infrastructure and Systems Assurance, Jaime Hullinger

Vice President Marketing, Debra Price

Vice President Global Human Resources Strategy and Planning, Valerie (Val) Grillo

Vice President, Edward Corella

Vice President Network Solutions, Pat Smith

Senior Vice President Of Finance, Sharon Kensington

Vice President Security, Sharon Kerr

Vice President Digital Solutions, Karen Schmidt

Senior Vice President Human Resources Relationship Leader and Head of Talent, Gaby Giglio

Senior Vice President, Penny Frank

Vice President Public Affairs and Communications Global Customer Servicing, Chuck Wallington

Vice President B2B Solution Development, Andrew (Andy) Jamison

Vice President, Dionne Rogers

Senior Vice President Risk Management, Shen Chang

Vice President Information Management and Consumer Marketing, Lee Chau

Vice President Marketing, Colin Kennedy

Vice President, Meredith Cosgrove

Senior Vice President Investment Operations, Peter (Pete) Anderson
Vice President, Gail Wasserman
Vice President Merchant Risk Management, Ashwani Bhardwaj
Vice President Global Treasury Controller, Steven (Steve) Swanson
Vice President of Global Advertising, Deborah (Deb) Curtis
Vice President corporate Development mergers and Acquisitions, Neil Pirie
Vice President Marketing Global Network Services EMEA, Alisa Copeman
Vice President, David (Dave) Rabkin
Vice President Information Technology, Vic Verma
Vice President Marketing Development, Trang Dinh
Vice President Human Resources Asia Pacific, Chris Meyrick
Vice President Marketing, Johnathan Callahan
Vice President Information Technology, Dale Leitman
Vice President of Customer Marketing Development, Eddie Alvarez
Vice President Global Payment Options, Chuck Grahmann
Vice President Co Brand Partnership Management, Jon Gantman
Vice President Information Records Management, Lynn Molfetta
Vice President Strategic Sales, Jessica Patel
Vice President Information Technology, Amy Bloebaum
Executive Vice President Human Resources, Manu Narang
Vice President And General Manager, Debra Davies
Vice President Social Marketing Innovation, Phil Wilson
Senior Vice President, John Stack
Vice President Global Business and Market Development, David (Dave) Wolf
Vice President Product Development, Dave Pereira
Vice President Field Channel Marketing, Katya Skorik
Vice President Risk Management, Ravi Varma
Vice President Network Management, Brandy Williams
Vice President, Tina Eide
Vice President, Anne Louvigny
Vice President Finance Manda Controller, Dylan Haverty-Stacke
Vice President Reengineering, Bhagirath Gohil
Vice President Finance, Avi Beinhacker
Senior Vice President Operations, Terry Flynn
Vice President Technology American Express Bank Te, Marc Brown
Vice President Marketing, Elizabeth (Beth) Curtis
Vice President Technologies, Dave Rapsas
Vice President Network Management, Tim Williams
Vice President Technologies End to End Product Enablement, Linda Carter-Tai
Vice President of Technologies Global Resources, Jim Sharp
Vice President Consumer Card Marketing, Molly Brady
Vice President, Richard Lesman
Vice President organization Effectiveness, Elaine Mason
Vice President Strategic Technology Relationships, Janice King
Vice President Finance, Stephen Ferris
Vice President EMEA Procurement, Maggie Willis
Vice President, Doris Daif
Vice President, Eric Beck
Vice President Facilities, Samuel Brick
Vice President Technologies US Digital, Keshav Narsipur
Vice President Fraud Risk Strategy, Irfan Tareen
Vice President Delivery Transformation, Randy Brokaw

Vice President And Business Partner human Resources, Patricia (Pat) Huska
Vice President Database Marketing, Gunit Kaur
Vice President of Fee Based Services, Eric Feldstein
Vice President Regulatory Affairs, Victor Gold
Vice President Operations, John (Jack) Koslow
Vice President, Brady Fife
Vice President, Christina Selwyn
Vice President Of Co Brand Finance, Ian Woolley
Vice President and Controller, Lawrence Belmonte
Senior Vice President of Global Human Resources, Gabriella Giglio
Vice President Digital Acquisition, John (Jack) Dotto
Vice President Marketing, Thomas Wojciechowski
Vice President General Manager Marketing, Armandm Milleville
Senior Vice President Social Media Strategy, Shari FForman
Vice President of US Network Marketing Merchant Services, Cristina Scardino
Vice President Marketing, Ellen Goodman
Vice President of Global Collections Americas, Oscar Marquez
Vice President Customer Care Strategy, Jill Grafflin
Vice President Compliance, Nitish Pandey
Vice President Of Flight Operations, Jeff Lee
Vice President Call Center Management, Jeff Johnson
Vice President Card Services and Pricing, Jeff Chwast
Vice President Finance Global Real Estate, Jay Shah
Vice President Executive And Employee Communications, Ann Dykman
Senior Corporate Management Vice President General Manager, Jack Dunn
Vice President, Aiessa Moyna
Vice President American Express Travel, Ramesh Devaraj
Vice President Tax Counsel, Anne Pontrelli
Vice President General Tax Counsel, Joe Gagliano
Vice President Of Risk, Vernon Marshall
Vice President Risk Management, Lei Chen
Vice President Corporate Comptrollers Office, Elaine McDonnell
Vice President Of Legal Affairs, Todd Miller
Vice President Technologies Communications, Gerilyn Cammarato
Vice President New York City Client Management, Lisa Skiptunis
Vice President Marketing and Servicing Review, Harvey Raymundo
Senior Vice President, Patricia (Pat) Locke
Vice President Online Consumer Travel, Christopher (Chris) Besendorfer
Vice President Of Credit Operations, Todd Schemm
Vice President, Laura Fink
Auditors: PricewaterhouseCoopers LLP

LOCATIONS

HQ: American Express Co.
200 Vesey Street, New York, NY 10285
Phone: 212 640-2000   **Fax:** 212 640-0404
Web: www.americanexpress.com

2014 Sales

	% of total
United States	72
EMEA	11
Japan Asia/Pacific and Australia	9
Latin America Canada and the Caribbean	8
Others	-
Total	**100**

PRODUCTS/OPERATIONS

2014 Sales

	$ mil.	% of total
Non-interest		
Discount revenue	19,493	54
Net card fees	2,712	8
Travel commissions & fees	1,118	3
Other commissions & fees	2,508	7
Other	2,989	8
Interest income		
Loans including fees	6,929	20
Interest & dividends on investment securities	179	-
Deposits with banks & other	71	-
Total	**35,999**	**100**

2014 Revenue

	$ mil.	% of total
US Card Services	18,518	52
International Card Services	5,822	16
Global Network & Merchant Services	5,478	15
Global Commercial Services	5,188	14
Corporate & other	993	3
Total	**35,999**	**100**

COMPETITORS

BCD Travel	JPMorgan Chase
Bank of America	JTB Corp.
Barclays	MasterCard
Capital One	Ovation Travel Group
Citibank	PayPal
Discover	Visa Inc
Expedia	Western Union
HSBC	

HISTORICAL FINANCIALS

Company Type: Public

Income Statement
FYE: December 31

	REVENUE ($ mil.)	NET INCOME ($ mil.)	NET PROFIT MARGIN	EMPLOYEES
12/14	35,999	5,885	16.3%	54,000
12/13	34,932	5,359	15.3%	62,800
12/12	33,808	4,482	13.3%	63,500
12/11	32,282	4,935	15.3%	62,500
12/10	30,242	4,057	13.4%	61,000
Annual Growth	4.5%	9.7%	—	(3.0%)

2014 Year-End Financials

Debt ratio: 38.61%	No. of shares (mil.): 1,023
Return on equity: 29.30%	Dividends
Cash ($ mil.): 22,288	Yield: 1.0%
Current ratio: 1.11	Payout: 18.2%
Long-term debt ($ mil.): 57,955	Market value ($ mil.): 95,180

	STOCK PRICE ($) FY Close	P/E High/Low	PER SHARE ($) Earnings	Dividends	Book Value
12/14	93.04	17 14	5.56	0.98	20.21
12/13	90.73	18 12	4.88	0.86	18.32
12/12	57.48	16 12	3.89	0.78	17.09
12/11	47.17	13 10	4.12	0.72	16.15
12/10	42.92	14 11	3.35	0.72	13.56
Annual Growth	21.3%	— —	13.5%	8.0%	10.5%

American Financial Group Inc

American Financial Group (AFG) insures American businessmen in pursuit of the great American

Dream. Through the Great American Insurance Group of companies and its flagship Great American Insurance Company AFG offers commercial property/casualty insurance focused on specialties such as workers' compensation professional liability ocean and inland marine and multiperil crop insurance. The company also provides surety coverage for contractors and risk management services. For individuals and employers AFG provides a wide range of annuity policies sold through its Great American Financial Resources (GAFRI) subsidiary.

HISTORY

When his father became ill in the mid-1930s Carl Lindner Jr. dropped out of high school to take over his family's dairy business. He built it into a large ice-cream store chain called United Dairy Farmers. Lindner branched out in 1955 with Henthy Realty and in 1959 he bought three savings and loans. The next year Lindner changed the company's name to American Financial Corp. (AFC). He took it public in 1961 using the proceeds to buy United Liberty Life Insurance (1963) and Provident Bank (1966).

Lindner also formed the American Financial Leasing & Services Company in 1968 to lease airplanes computers and other equipment. In 1969 the company acquired Phoenix developer Rubenstein Construction and renamed it American Continental. AFC bought several life casualty and mortgage insurance firms in the 1970s including National General parent of Great American Insurance Group later the core of AFC's insurance segment. The company also moved into publishing by buying 95% of the Cincinnati Enquirer paperback publisher Bantam Books and hardback publisher Grosset & Dunlap.

But the publishing interests soon went back on the block as Lindner concentrated on insurance which was then suffering from an industry-wide slowdown. In addition to selling the Enquirer AFC spun off American Continental in 1976. American Continental's president was Charles Keating who had joined AFC in 1972 and whose brother published the Enquirer. Keating (who was later jailed released then eventually pleaded guilty in connection with the failure of Lincoln Savings) underwent an SEC investigation during part of his time at AFC for alleged improprieties at Provident Bank. The bank was spun off in 1980.

Lindner took AFC private in 1981. That year following a strategy of bottom-feeding the firm began building its interest in the non-railroad assets of Penn Central the former railroad that had emerged from bankruptcy as an industrial manufacturer. Later that decade AFC increased its ownership in United Brands (later renamed Chiquita Brands International) from 29% to 45%. Lindner installed himself as CEO and reversed that company's losses. In 1987 AFC acquired a TV company Taft Communications (renamed Great American Communications) entailing a heavy debt load. To reduce its debt AFC trimmed its holdings including Circle K Hunter S&L and an interest in Scripps Howard Broadcasting.

Great American Communications went bankrupt in 1992 and emerged the next year as Citicasters Inc. (sold 1996). In 1995 Lindner created American Financial Group to effect the merger of AFC and Premier Underwriters of which he owned 42%. The result was American Financial Group (AFG).

Lindner's bipartisan political donations gained publicity when it became known that his gifts to Republicans had brought support in a dispute with the European Union over the banana trade. The next year AFG sold some noncore units including software consultancy Millennium Dynamics and

its commercial insurance operations. In 1999 AFG bought direct-response auto insurer Worldwide Insurance Company as part of its efforts to build depth in the highly commodified auto insurance market.

In 2000 American Financial Group agreed to pay $75 million over the next 30 years to get its name on the Cincinnati Reds' new stadium known as Great American Ball Park. In 2001 AFG sold its Japanese property/casualty division to Japanese insurer Mitsui Marine & Fire (now Mitsui Sumitomo Insurance).

AFG's results in the 1990s were uneven and it typically did not make an underwriting profit. In 2003 the insurer kept operating expenses down (partly by merging two of its holding company subsidiaries into AFG) and swung to a profit even though premium revenue was down.

The company shed some commercial lines to concentrate on its property/casualty and life and annuities businesses. To refine its mix AFG transferred Atlanta Casualty Company Infinity Insurance Company Leader Insurance Company and Windsor Insurance Company into 40%-owned Infinity Property and Casualty which went public in 2003. In 2004 the business exchanged its stake in Provident Financial Group for a holding in National City Corporation.

In 2006 AFG expanded its Great American Financial Resources (GAFRI) unit through the purchase of a block of fixed annuity products from Old Standard Life Insurance. GAFRI also acquired Ceres Group and its health insurance subsidiary Continental General Insurance. To balance things out GAFRI sold its Great American Life Assurance of Puerto Rico unit to Triple-S Management that year.

In 2008 the company purchased 67% of medical malpractice insurer and Lloyd's of London member Marketform Group for $75 million; AFG stopped writing new malpractice policies through Marketform the following year. The company also acquired Louisiana-based workers' compensation provider Strategic Comp Holdings in 2008.

In 2010 AFG's majority owned National Interstate subsidiary acquired property/casualty insurer Vanliner Group which specializes in moving and storage coverage for $114 million from UniGroup.

Founder and chairman Carl Lindner retired as CEO in 2005 and died in 2011. No one was named to replace him as chairman but two of his sons Carl Lindner III and Craig Lindner carried on as co-CEOs.

EXECUTIVES

Co-President Co-CEO and Director, S. Craig Lindner, age 60, $1,150,000 total compensation
Co-President Co-CEO and Director, Carl H. Lindner, age 62, $1,150,000 total compensation
President American Money Management, John B. Berding, age 52, $800,000 total compensation
EVP and CFO, Joseph E. (Jeff) Consolino, age 48, $817,307 total compensation
SVP and Chief Administrative Officer, Michelle A. (Shelly) Gillis, $293,284 total compensation
SVP and General Counsel, Vito C. Peraino, $535,960 total compensation
Board Member, William (Bill) Verity
Auditors: Ernst & Young LLP

LOCATIONS

HQ: American Financial Group Inc
301 East Fourth Street, Cincinnati, OH 45202
Phone: 513 579-2121
Web: www.afginc.com

PRODUCTS/OPERATIONS

2014 Sales

	$ mil.	% of total
Property/casualty	4,181	73
Annuity	1,214	21
Runoff long term care & life	194	4
Realized gains on securities	52	1
Other	72	1
Total	**5,713**	**100**

Selected Subsidiaries

Property/Casualty
  American Empire Surplus Lines Insurance Company
  Great American Insurance Company
  Mid-Continent Casualty Company
  National Interstate Insurance Company
  Republic Indemnity Company of America
Annuities and Life Insurance
  Great American Financial Resources Inc. (GAFRI)
  Annuity Investors Life Insurance
  Great American Life Insurance Company
Real estate investments
  Charleston Harbor Resort and Marina
  Mountain View Grand Resort
  Sailfish Marina and Resort
  Skipjack Cove Yachting Resort and Bay Bridge Marina

COMPETITORS

AIG	Midland National Life
Allianz	Munich Re Group
Allstate	Mutual of Omaha
Arch Capital	National Western
Aviva	Pacific Life
CNA Financial	RLI
Chubb Limited	The Hartford
Cincinnati Financial	Tokio Marine
HCC Insurance	Travelers Companies
Jackson National Life	W. R. Berkley
LSW	Wells Fargo
Liberty Mutual	XL Group plc
Markel	Zenith National
MetLife	Zurich Insurance Group

HISTORICAL FINANCIALS

Company Type: Public

Income Statement

FYE: December 31

	ASSETS ($ mil.)	NET INCOME ($ mil.)	INCOME AS % OF ASSETS	EMPLOYEES
12/14	47,535	452	1.0%	7,200
12/13	42,087	471	1.1%	6,300
12/12	39,171	488	1.2%	6,100
12/11	36,042	343	1.0%	6,500
12/10	32,454	479	1.5%	6,450
Annual Growth	**10.0%**	**(1.4%)**	**—**	**2.8%**

2014 Year-End Financials

Debt ratio: 2.23%	No. of shares (mil.): 87
Return on equity: 9.54%	Dividends
Cash ($ mil.): 1,343	Yield: 3.1%
Current ratio: —	Payout: 36.1%
Long-term debt ($ mil.): —	Market value ($ mil.): 5,326

	STOCK PRICE ($) FY Close	P/E High/Low		PER SHARE ($) Earnings	Dividends	Book Value
12/14	60.72	12	10	4.97	1.91	55.63
12/13	57.72	11	7	5.16	1.81	51.38
12/12	39.52	8	7	5.09	0.97	51.45
12/11	36.89	11	9	3.33	0.66	46.45
12/10	32.29	7	6	4.33	0.58	42.50
Annual Growth	**17.1%**	**—**	**—**	**3.5%**	**35.0%**	**7.0%**

American International Group Inc

LOCATIONS

HQ: American International Group Inc
175 Water Street, New York, NY 10038
Phone: 212 770-7000
Web: www.aig.com

HISTORICAL FINANCIALS

Company Type: Public

Income Statement

FYE: December 31

	ASSETS ($ mil.)	NET INCOME ($ mil.)	INCOME AS % OF ASSETS	EMPLOYEES
12/14	515,581	7,529	1.5%	65,000
12/13	541,329	9,085	1.7%	64,000
12/12	548,633	3,438	0.6%	63,000
12/11	555,773	17,798	3.2%	57,000
12/10	683,443	7,786	1.1%	63,000
Annual Growth	(6.8%)	(0.8%)	—	0.8%

2014 Year-End Financials

Debt ratio: 6.05%
Return on equity: 7.26%
Cash ($ mil.): 1,758
Current ratio: —
Long-term debt ($ mil.): —

No. of shares (mil.): 1,375
Dividends
Yield: 0.8%
Payout: 8.2%
Market value ($ mil.): 77,066

	STOCK PRICE ($) FY Close	P/E High/Low		PER SHARE ($) Earnings	Dividends	Book Value
12/14	56.01	11	9	5.20	0.50	77.69
12/13	51.05	8	6	6.13	0.20	68.62
12/12	35.30	18	12	2.04	0.00	66.38
12/11	23.20	6	2	9.44	0.00	55.33
12/10	57.62	5	2	11.60	0.00	607.41
Annual Growth	(0.7%)	—	—	(18.2%)	—	(40.2%)

American National Insurance Co. (Galveston, TX)

True to its name American National Insurance Company (ANICO) offers agricultural commercial and personal property/casualty insurance as well as life insurance annuities supplemental health credit and other types of insurance throughout the US Puerto Rico and other territories. It subsidiaries include Garden State Life Insurance Standard Life and Accident Insurance and Farm Family Holdings. It markets its products through independent and career agents broker-dealers employee benefit advisors financial representatives and managing general underwriters. Variable products are securities products distributed through ANICO Financial Services Inc.

Geographic Reach

ANICO headquartered in Galveston Texas is licensed to conduct business in all states except New York. Business is conducted in New York by American National Life Insurance Company of New York a subsidiary of ANICO.

The company serves about 6 million customers throughout the US and in Puerto Rico Guam and American Samoa.

Operations

ANICO operates in five segments: Life (including whole term universal indexed and variable life insurance) Annuity (fixed indexed and variable annuity products) Health (Medicare Supplement stop-loss credit disability insurance) Property/Casualty (personal and commercial coverage) and Corporate and Other (income from investments not related to the insurance segments as well as non-insurance operations).

While the company considers its Life and Annuity segments to be its main focus it earns more of its premiums from property/casualty insurance. Together both groups make up more than a third of the company's total revenues; altogether premiums account for nearly 60% of revenues. Investment income accounts for about a third of sales.

Sales and Marketing

ANICO markets life insurance and annuities through Independent Marketing Group (IMG) which utilizes independent agents serving middle-income and wealthy clients. IMG markets policies through financial institutions employee benefits organizations broker-dealers marketing organizations and independent agents and brokers. It also sells life insurance using direct mail Internet and telemarketing campaigns. The company's Career Sales and Service Division primarily serves the middle-income market (life annuities and health coverage) though exclusive employee agents. The group's Health segment performs marketing through independent agents and managing general underwriters.

ANICO Direct is the direct-to-the-consumer sales and marketing division of the ANICO family of companies.

Financial Performance

ANICO's revenues have hovered around $3 billion for the past five years. The company's revenue decreased by 2% in 2014 due to a decline in net realized investment gains and net investment income partially offset by an increase in premiums. The drop in net investment income was primarily from decreased interest rates on bonds and mortgage loans of $52.8 million from decreased option income of $31.2 million (due to smaller gains on the S&P index) and decreased other invested asset income of $3.9 million due to fewer joint venture dispositions. Net realized gains decreased $76.1 million during 2014 primarily as a result a weaker market conditions compared very strong markets for the type and location of investment real estate sold in 2013. In 2014 ANICO's net income decreased by 8% as the result of higher policyholder benefits payments for annuity and lower revenues. The company's operating cash flow has been moving up over the last five years. In 2014 operating cash flow increased by 2% due to an increase in cash provided by policyholder liabilities.

Strategy

In its quest to be a leading financial products and services company ANICO aims to maintain the conservative business practices it has upheld for more than a century including controlling risk factors in its growth and investment strategies. The company looks to maintain strong finances through profitable growth primarily by investing in its distribution channels expanding into new geographic markets and enhancing marketing programs. To reach a new market ANICO launched a new product series ANICO Strategy Indexed Annuity PLUS in 2013.

The company is also committed to providing exemplary customer service and to offering innovative diversified and competitively priced products to meet the needs of its policyholders and agents. ANICO also occasionally grows by acquiring like-minded businesses. It occasionally exits businesses after reassessing its exposure.

Company Background

ANICO was founded by Galveston businessman W. L. Moody in 1905. Robert Moody Sr. a descendent of his serves as the company's chairman and CEO. His children Russell Moody and Frances Anne Moody-Dahlberg serve as directors and his son Robert Moody Jr. serves as an advisory director.

The Moody Foundation a charitable trust controlled by Robert Moody and his family and the Moody National Bank together own about 70% of the company.

Based in hurricane-prone Galveston Texas ANICO knows firsthand the importance of property/casualty insurance and how to evaluate risk. The company withdrew from writing some policies along the Atlantic and Gulf coasts in 2005 and in 2008 it moved its claims processing facilities further inland to San Antonio.

ANICO launched the American National Life Insurance Company of New York in 2010.

EXECUTIVES

EVP Independent Marketing Group; President and COO American National Life Insurance Company of New York, David A. Behrens, age 52, $470,475 total compensation
EVP Multiple Line; Chairman President and CEO American National Property And Casualty, Gregory V. Ostergren, age 59, $540,094 total compensation
Executive Vice President, George Crume
EVP, Steven H. Schouweiler, age 68
President and CEO, James E. Pozzi, age 64, $671,667 total compensation
SEVP Corporate Risk Officer and Chief Actuary, Ronald J. Welch, age 69, $408,887 total compensation
Senior Vice President Real Estate Mortgage Loan Investments, Scott Brast
EVP CFO and Treasurer, John J. Dunn, age 55, $386,325 total compensation
EVP, James W. Pangburn, age 58
EVP and CIO, Johnny D. Johnson, age 62
EVP, Hoyt J. Strickland, age 58
Assistant Vice President Health Systems Support, Ron Ostermayer
Assistant Vice President Service Support and Operations, Robert (Bob) Lindemann
AVice President Corporate Planning, Wayne Smith
Vice President Compliance, James Stelling
Vice President Of Operations, Dan Williams
Vice President Broker Dealer Marketing, Steven Dobbe
National Sales Manager, Mike Sawdey
AVice President Corporate Research, Deborah (Deb) Janson
Assistant Vice President Life Insurance, Sharon Garner
Assistant Vice President And Illustration Actuary, Joseph (Jo) Cantu
National Sales Manager, Sam Castello
National Sales Manager, Kendra Kelly
Vice President Financial Markets, Murray Klein
Regional Vice President Sales and Marketing, Linda Dennison
Vice President of Product Development, Kara Phillips
Vice President, Joe Cantu
Vice President, Sabrina Bermudez
National Sales Manager, Michael Kresl
National Sales Manager, Cliff McConville
Vice President Director of Computer Division, Mark Andrews

Vice President, Matthew Ostiguy
Vice President Life Policy Administration, Bruce Pavelka
Assistant Vice President Tax, Larry Linares
Assistant Vice President Director of Advanced Life Sales, Wayne J Cucco
Assistant Vice President And Assistant Actuary, Michael Shumate
Senior Vice President, Ronald Price
Vice President Portfolio Management, John (Jack) Maidlow
Associate Medical Director, Kim Mlcak
National Sales Manager, Ed Ferrin
National Sales Manager, J Taylor
Senior Vice President Securities Investments, Gordon Dixon
Vice President Marketing, Debie Knowles
Assistant Vice President Data Communications Messaging (Its), Jimmy Watson
National Sales Manager South Broker Dealer Marketing, Jason Weaver
Vice President, Vince Matthews
Assistant Vice President And Director Telecommunications, James McEniry
Senior Vice President And Actuary, Frank Broll
Vice President Fixed Income Investment, Anne Lemire
Assistant Vice President and Associate Medical Director, John (Jack) White
Assistant Vice President Director Life Marketing Sales Director, Clu Jon O'Neal
Senior Vice President Of Human Reources, Bruce Lepard
Chairman, Robert L. Moody, age 79
Secretary Treasurer, Bob Schefft
Auditors: KPMG LLP

LOCATIONS

HQ: American National Insurance Co. (Galveston, TX)
One Moody Plaza, Galveston, TX 77550-7999
Phone: 409 763-4661   Fax: 409 766-6502
Web: www.anico.com

PRODUCTS/OPERATIONS

2014 Revenue

	$ mil.	% of total
Premiums		
Property/casualty	1,101	36
Life	307	10
Accident and Health	216	7
Annuity	190	6
Net investment income	932	31
Other policy revenues	224	7
Realized investment gains	41	2
Other income	36	1
Total	**3,050**	**100**

Selected Subsidiaries

American National Life Insurance Company of Texas (ANTEX)
American National Life Insurance Company of New York
American National Property and Casualty Company (ANPAC)
ANICO Financial Services Inc.
Farm Family Casualty Insurance Company
Farm Family Life Insurance Company
Garden State Life Insurance Company
Pacific Property and Casualty Company
Standard Life and Accident Insurance Company
United Farm Family Insurance Company

COMPETITORS

Allstate	Nationwide
American Financial Group	New York Life
CNO Financial	Penn Mutual
Farmers Group	Prudential
Mutual of Omaha	State Farm
National Western	Torchmark
	USAA

HISTORICAL FINANCIALS

Company Type: Public

Income Statement

FYE: December 31

	ASSETS ($ mil.)	NET INCOME ($ mil.)	INCOME AS % OF ASSETS	EMPLOYEES
12/14	23,552	247	1.0%	3,138
12/13	23,324	268	1.2%	3,078
12/12	23,107	191	0.8%	3,075
12/11	22,524	192	0.9%	3,207
12/10	21,413	144	0.7%	3,251
Annual Growth	**2.4%**	**14.5%**	**—**	**(0.9%)**

2014 Year-End Financials

Debt ratio: 0.46%
Return on equity: 5.73%
Cash ($ mil.): 209
Current ratio: —
Long-term debt ($ mil.): —

No. of shares (mil.): 26
Dividends
Yield: 2.7%
Payout: 33.8%
Market value ($ mil.): 3,070

	STOCK PRICE ($) FY Close	P/E High/Low	PER SHARE ($) Earnings	Dividends	Book Value
12/14	114.26	13 11	9.18	3.08	164.94
12/13	114.54	12 7	9.97	3.08	155.81
12/12	68.29	11 9	7.11	3.08	142.63
12/11	73.03	12 9	7.20	3.08	136.35
12/10	85.62	22 14	5.40	3.08	135.44
Annual Growth	**7.5%**	**— —**	**14.2%**	**(0.0%)**	**5.0%**

Ameriprise Financial Inc

What combines the spark of American enterprise with financial advisor services? Ameriprise Financial Inc. Ameriprise provides a variety of financial products including mutual funds savings plans personal trust services retail brokerage and insurance products through its various brands and affiliates —which include Ameriprise Financial Columbia Management RiverSource and others. Ameriprise has more than $806 billion in assets under management and distributes its products primarily through a network of 10000 financial advisors. Founded in 1894 Ameriprise Financial was spun off from American Express.

OperationsAmeriprise Financial operates four main segments. Its Advice & Wealth Management segment generates more than 35% of revenue and provides distribution services for both affiliated and non-affiliated products and services. The next largest segment is Asset Management which brings in more than 25% of revenue and provides investment management services for client assets and the company's own assets.The Asset Management division charges investment and advisory management fees accordingly to the company's Annuities and Protection segments which each generate around 20% of revenue. While Columbia Management covers Ameriprise's main asset management market in the US its Threadneedle brand is quickly growing overseas. Geographic Reach

Ameriprise Financial and its affiliates have headquarters in Minneapolis New York Boston and London. About 90% of the firm's revenue is generated in the US. The majority of the firm's international operations are conducted through Threadneedle Investments.Sales and MarketingAmeriprise's 10000 financial advisors serve more than two million individual business and institutional clients nationwide.
Financial Performance

Ameriprise Financial's revenue jumped by 10% to $12.27 billion in 2014 marking the company's sixth straight year of revenue growth. The top-line boost in 2014 was mostly thanks to a spike in management and financial advice fees as the firm's assets under management (AUM) swelled with the rising stock market and new accounts. Indeed the company's average AUM balance grew by 10% to $58 billion. Higher revenue also drove profit higher for a second straight year with net income rising by 21% to $1.62 billion. Operations provided $2.4 billion or 76% more cash than in 2013 thanks to a combination of higher earnings an influx of cash from its freestanding derivatives and related collateral and because the company sold off more investment properties and purchased fewer new properties than in 2013.
Strategy

Ameriprise has been steadily growing its assets under management and expanding its client base (focusing on the affluent and mass affluent with more than $100000 in assets to invest). Indeed in 2014 new business along with a rising stock market contributed to a 10% jump in average assets under management and took the company to record-high revenue and profit. The company also is focused on geographic areas where those clients are congregated and has closed or consolidated offices in areas with less potential. The company believes its asset management services are well equipped in the US and Europe and is prepared to grow its capabilities through its Threadneedle brand and other affiliates to expand into new global and emerging markets in Asia Australia the Middle East and Africa. In 2013 the firm completed the conversion of its federal savings bank subsidiary Ameriprise Bank FSB to a limited powers national trust bank now known as Ameriprise National Trust Bank. In connection with the conversion the bank stopped taking deposits and extending credit. Ameriprise Financial continues to offer clients certain deposit and credit products via referral arrangements to third parties.Beyond expansion Ameriprise Financial continues to improve on its technology platform by introducing new products like deposit investment advisory accounts products of other companies e-commerce and brokerage capabilities for its financial advisors and their clients.

EXECUTIVES

Vice President Retirement Wealth Strategies, Craig Brimhall
Chairman and CEO, James M. (Jim) Cracchiolo, age 56, $950,000 total compensation
CEO Global Asset Management, William F. (Ted) Truscott, age 54, $650,000 total compensation
EVP and CFO, Walter S. Berman, age 73, $650,000 total compensation
EVP Human Resources, Kelli A. Hunter, age 54
President Advice and Wealth Management Products and Service Delivery, Joseph E. (Joe) Sweeney, age 54, $375,000 total compensation
Chief Strategy Officer; President Insurance and Annuities, John R. Woerner, age 46
EVP and General Counsel, John C. Junek, age 65, $375,000 total compensation
EVP Marketing Corporate Communications and Community Relations, Deirdre D. McGraw, age 45
COO; President Advice & Wealth Management Business Development, Neal Maglaque
EVP and CIO, Randy Kupper
EVP and Global Chief Investment Officer, Colin Moore, $425,000 total compensation
EVP and Head of Ameriprise Franchise Advisor Channel, Bill Williams

EVP Ameriprise Advisor Group, Pat O'Connell
Executive Vice President, Gumer C Alvero
Regional Vice President, Carey Robinson
Vice President Corporate Counsel, Mike Newman
Vice President Operations, George Tsafaridis
Vice President, William Emptage
Vice President of Marketing and Business Development, Heather Klaas Melloh
Vice President Human Resources, Karen Dekker
Senior Vice President Chief Actuary, Steve Gathje
Vice President and Chief Counsel, Karen Wilson
Vice President Interactive Marketing, Sean Kellenberger
Vice President Financial Applications Support Controllership, John (Jack) Mead
Vice President Local Marketing Client Acquisition, Jennifer (Jen) McCafferty
Vice President East Division, George Fakete
Vice President External Products Group, Tracy Anderson
Vice President Investment Research Group, Lyle Schonberger
Vice President Wholesaling operations, Mike Kirchner
Vice President Technical Advisory Group, Michael (Mel) Mattox
Vice President, Eric Paluck
Vice President Risk Mitigation, Craig Wallenta
Vice President Technology Planning And Administration, Paula Bash
Vice President, Robert Bokern
Vice President ??? Field Strategy, Stephen Ehele
Vice President Marketing Programs, Cynthia Dutcher-Flack
Senior Administrative Assistant To Senior Vice President, Barb Smith
Vice President of Sales and Marketing, Stephanie Rustad
Vice President Mortgage Loan Administration, Nancy Hughes
Vice President Business Development and National, Lynn Abbott
Regional Vice President, Phillip (Phil) Buckner
Financial Advisor Associate Vice President, Nick Pietrocola
Vice President Procurement, Steve Strauss
Vice President, Lori Arrell
Vice President Compliance, Jeff Soderstrom
Vice President=CLR Project Management Office, Mike Greene
Associate Vice President, Michael (Mel) Marchetta
Vice President Product Development and Research, Kent Bergene
Field Vice President, Brad Sabol
Vice President General Manager Managed Products, Greg Nordmeyer
Franchise Field Vice President, Timothy (Tim) Crain
Financial Advisor Vice President, Barry Craine
Franchise Field Vice President, Dean McGill
Vice President Information Technology, Clarissa Ramos
Vice President Compensation Human Resources, Jason Williams
Vice President Product Management Financial Planning and Advice, Sarah Arnold
Vice President Human Resources Program, Kristi Kooda-Chizek
Vice President Insurance Marketing, Thomas Maki
Field Vice President, Debra Bennett
Associate Vice President, Nayan Apma
Vice President Claim Operations, Tom Boogaard
Vice President Of Investments, Mark Andrews
Vice President Portfolio Manager, Nic Pifer
Regional Vice President, Peter (Pete) Mitchell
Vice President Financial Planning, Marcy Keckler
Vice President General Counsel Organization Administration and Project Management Office, Kelly Schall

Group Vice President Of The NE Market Group, Jody Johnson
Vice President Technologies, Venky Ramanan
Vice President, Gerard Smyth
Financial Advisor Senior Vice President, David (Dave) Shores
Vice President Financial Advisor, Matthew (Matt) Lane
Regional Vice President, Martin Christopher
Vice President Vendor Management, Joel Clauson
RVP Retirement Plans, Matthew (Matt) Miller
Vice President, Kathy Miller
Vice President, Peder Gustafson
Regional Vice President, John Leahy
Vice President Finance, Jennifer (Jen) Seifriz
Vice President Finance, Rob Bardot
Vice President Financial Advisor, Paul Hoghaug
Vice President Sales, Leann Thomas
Associate Vice President, Dan Shontere
Vice President Finance (Advice and Wealth Management), Deepa Roongta
Regional Vice Presidet, Matt Buschy
Vice President Training And Development, Lamont Boykins
Vice President Of Technical Department, Jacqueline Glockner
Vice President Corp Finance and Mergers and Acquisitions, Joseph (Jo) Wallace
Vice President Field Strategy and Implement, Mark Traut
Vice President, Nate Pugliese
Vice President Marketing, Linda Moriarty
Senior Regional Vice President Insurance West, Bj Seastone
Board Member And Alumni Committee Chair, Edie Haughney
Auditors: PricewaterhouseCoopers LLP

LOCATIONS

HQ: Ameriprise Financial Inc
1099 Ameriprise Financial Center, Minneapolis, MN 55474
Phone: 612 671-3131
Web: www.ameriprise.com

PRODUCTS/OPERATIONS

2014 Sales

	$ mil.	% of total
Management & financial advice fees	5,810	48
Distribution fees	1,894	15
Net investment income	1,741	14
Premiums	1,385	11
Other	1,438	12
Total	**12,268**	**100**

2014 Sales

	% of total
Advice & wealth management	36
Asset management	26
Annuities	20
Protection	18
Others	-
Total	**100**

Selected Subsidiaries and Affiliates

American Enterprise Investment Services Inc.
Ameriprise Financial Services Inc.
Ameriprise Bank FSB
Ameriprise Certificate Company
Ameriprise Trust Company
Columbia Management Investment Advisers LLC
Columbia Management Investment Distributors Inc.
IDS Property Casualty Insurance Company
J. & W. Seligman & Co. Incorporated
RiverSource Distributors Inc.
RiverSource Life Insurance Co. of New York
Threadneedle Asset Management Holdings

Selected Brands

Ameriprise Financial®
Columbia Management®
RiverSource®

COMPETITORS

AXA Financial	MassMutual
Allstate	Merrill Lynch
Bank of America	MetLife
Bank of New York	Nationwide Financial
Mellon	New York Life
Calamos Asset	Northwestern Mutual
Management	PNC Financial
Capital Group	Primerica
Charles Schwab	Principal Financial
Citigroup	Prudential
FMR	Regions Financial
First Eagle Investment	State Street
Mangement	TIAA-CREF
John Hancock Financial	U.S. Bancorp
Services	
Lincoln Financial	
Group	

HISTORICAL FINANCIALS

Company Type: Public

Income Statement

FYE: December 31

	REVENUE ($ mil.)	NET INCOME ($ mil.)	NET PROFIT MARGIN	EMPLOYEES
12/14	12,268	1,619	13.2%	12,209
12/13	11,199	1,334	11.9%	12,039
12/12	10,217	1,029	10.1%	12,235
12/11	10,192	1,076	10.6%	11,139
12/10	9,976	1,097	11.0%	10,472
Annual Growth	**5.3%**	**10.2%**	**—**	**3.9%**

2014 Year-End Financials

Debt ratio: 6.81%	No. of shares (mil.): 183
Return on equity: 19.85%	Dividends
Cash ($ mil.): 3,028	Yield: 1.7%
Current ratio: 0.86	Payout: 29.8%
Long-term debt ($ mil.): 9,929	Market value ($ mil.): 24,216

	STOCK PRICE ($) FY Close	P/E High/Low		PER SHARE ($) Earnings	Dividends	Book Value
12/14	132.25	16	12	8.30	2.26	44.37
12/13	115.05	17	10	6.44	2.01	42.64
12/12	62.63	14	10	4.62	1.43	44.58
12/11	49.64	15	8	4.37	0.87	46.21
12/10	57.55	14	8	4.18	0.71	43.47
Annual Growth	**23.1%**	**—**	**—**	**18.7%**	**33.6%**	**0.5%**

Ameris Bancorp

Ameris Bancorp enjoys the financial climate of the Deep South. It is the holding company of Ameris Bank which holds roughly $3.6 billion in assets and serves retail and consumer customers through more than 75 full-service and mortgage branches in Alabama Georgia South Carolina and northern Florida. In addition to its standard banking products and services the bank also provides treasury services mortgage and refinancing solutions and investment services through an agreement with Raymond James Financial. Loans secured by commercial real estate accounted for approximately 45% of the company's loan portfolio while 1-4 family residential and construction & land development mortgages accounted for nearly a quarter and about 10% respectively.

Operations

Like most banks Ameris earns the vast majority of its recurring revenue (71.5%) from interest income from loans. Nearly 80% of these loans are made up of commercial real estate 1-4 family residential and construction & land development loans. The remaining 20% are from a mix of commercial multi-family residential and consumer loans (home improvement home equity personal lines of credit auto loans and student loans).

Traditional banking products (deposit accounts) and services along with investment products and services (which primarily earn income from fees and commissions) made up about 28% of the bank's annual sales in fiscal 2013.

Sales and Marketing

Through an acquisition-oriented growth strategy Ameris seeks to grow its brand and presence in the markets it currently serves in Georgia Alabama Florida and South Carolina as well as in neighboring communities. In addition the bank expects its community-oriented philosophy will help strengthen existing customer relations and attract new customers.

The company spent $1.62 million on advertising and public relations in Fiscal Year 2013 just under the $1.622 million it spent in 2012 and more than double the $722000 it spent in 2011. The company increased its advertising spending by $900000 during 2012 to support its revenue and growth- strategies during the year.

Financial Performance

Ameris carried $3.67 billion in total assets as of December 31 2013. Loans made up $2.5 billion (approximately 68.9% of total assets). The bank also reported carrying $3 billion in deposits.

Ameris' net revenue dipped in fiscal 2013 declining 5% to $163 million from its high of $172 million in 2012 mostly from an $11.3 million dip in non-interest revenue. But this dip in non-interest revenue is primarily because the bank recorded a large gain of $20 million from acquisitions in 2012. When excluding this acquisition gain from 2012's revenues and thanks to $6.1 million revenue increase in mortgage banking activity management reports that total non-interest income actually increased $8.7 million in 2013 compared to 2012. A decline in interest-earning loan assets from $2.47 billion in 2013 compared to $2.5 billion in 2012 also played a role in the dip in net revenues.

Thanks to aggressive acquisitions and despite revenue decreasing net income jumped a whopping 43% to $20 million in 2013 from $14 million in 2012. This is only slightly below the bank's net income high of $21 million in 2011. It's most notable acquisition of Prosperity Bank increased Ameris' total assets by $744.9 million and added $449.7 million in loans to its interest-earning loan portfolio. Adding to the extra income from new loans Ameris collected higher net interest margins on all of its loans which increased to 4.74% in 2013 from 4.60% in 2012.

Strategy

Ameris also plans to continue using its community banking philosophy to lessen its risk and identify prime local lending markets. Management reports that by encouraging a personalized service experience and building deeper customer relationships the bank has already grown a "substantial" base of low-cost core deposits (which pad the bank's reserves and lessen financial risk). And between its bench of experienced decision makers and lenders operating in a "decentralized" structure (which differentiates Ameris from mega banks) and its deep familiarity with local markets management believes the bank can better identify prime growth markets (for lending and bank services) with managed risk in the years ahead.

Mergers and Acquisitions

Integral to the bank's growth strategy Ameris has aggressively acquired banks to broaden its reach into its primary southern markets. In addition to acquiring several troubled and failing banks with help from the FDIC Ameris merged with Prosperity Bank in 2013 which broadened its reach into

Florida through Prosperity's branches in St. Augustine Jacksonville Panama City Lynn Haven Palatka and Ormand Beach.

Company Background

Georgia's economy was one of the hardest hit in the US during the recession and Ameris has taken advantage of the plethora of banks seized by regulators in the state. Since 2009 the company has acquired about 10 failed banks in Georgia though FDIC-assisted transactions adding some 20 branches to its network. Ameris also snagged the failed First Bank of Jacksonville in Florida which had two locations.

EXECUTIVES

EVP and COO, Andrew B. (Andy) Cheney, age 65, $347,917 total compensation
SVP and Director of Credit Administration, Jon S. Edwards, age 53, $209,583 total compensation
SVP and Director of Human Resources, Cindi H. Lewis, age 61, $90,333 total compensation
President and CEO, Edwin W. (Ed) Hortman, age 61, $455,000 total compensation
EVP and CFO, Dennis J. Zember, age 45, $283,542 total compensation
EVP and Chief Risk Officer, Stephen A. Melton, $259,375 total compensation
CIO, Thomas S. (Stan) Limerick
Vice President Of Operations, Allyson Hickey
Assistant Vice President, Ann Dunn
Chairman, Daniel B. Jeter, age 63
Auditors: Crowe Horwath LLP

LOCATIONS

HQ: Ameris Bancorp
310 First Street S.E., Moultrie, GA 31768
Phone: 229 890-1111
Web: www.amerisbank.com

PRODUCTS/OPERATIONS

Selected Acquisitions
American United Bank
Central Bank of Georgia
 Darby Bank
First Bank of Jacksonville
High Trust Bank
 Montgomery
One Georgia Bank
Satilla Community Bank
Tifton Banking Company
United Security Bank

COMPETITORS

BBVA Compass Bancshares	First South Bancorp (NC)
Bank of America	Regions Financial
Capital City Bank	Southwest Georgia Financial
Colony Bankcorp	SunTrust
Community Capital Bancshares	Thomasville Bancshares

HISTORICAL FINANCIALS

Company Type: Public

Income Statement

FYE: December 31

	ASSETS ($ mil.)	NET INCOME ($ mil.)	INCOME AS % OF ASSETS	EMPLOYEES
12/14	4,037	38	1.0%	1,027
12/13	3,667	20	0.5%	984
12/12	3,019	14	0.5%	866
12/11	2,994	21	0.7%	746
12/10	2,972	(3)	—	709
Annual Growth	8.0%	—	—	9.7%

2014 Year-End Financials

Debt ratio: 2.71%	No. of shares (mil.): 26
Return on equity: 11.34%	Dividends
Cash ($ mil.): 164	Yield: 0.5%
Current ratio: —	Payout: 13.5%
Long-term debt ($ mil.): —	Market value ($ mil.): 686

	STOCK PRICE ($) FY Close	P/E High/Low		PER SHARE ($) Earnings	Dividends	Book Value
12/14	25.64	18	13	1.46	0.15	13.67
12/13	21.11	28	16	0.75	0.00	12.62
12/12	12.49	29	22	0.46	0.00	11.72
12/11	10.28	15	11	0.76	0.00	12.37
12/10	10.54	—	—	(0.35)	0.00	11.56
Annual Growth	24.9%	—	—	—	—	4.3%

AmerisourceBergen Corp.

AmerisourceBergen is the source for many of North America's pharmacies and health care providers. The distribution company serves as a go-between for drug makers and the pharmacies doctors' offices hospitals and other health care providers that dispense drugs. Operating primarily in the US and Canada it distributes generic branded and over-the-counter pharmaceuticals as well as some medical supplies and other products using its network of more than two dozen facilities. Its specialty distribution unit focuses on sensitive and complex biopharmaceuticals. Other operations include pharmaceutical packaging. AmerisourceBergen also provides commercialization and consulting services to its customers.

Operations

The company operates through an alphabet soup of subsidiaries. Its main operating segment — pharmaceutical distribution — consists of its AmerisourceBergen Drug Corporation (ABDC) and AmerisourceBergen Specialty Group (ABSG). The company's remaining revenues (classified under the "other" segment) come from the AmerisourceBergen Consulting Services (ABCS) and World Courier (specialty logistics) units. Its AmerisourceBergen Packaging Group (ABPG) was taken apart in 2012 and its American Health Packaging and AndersonBrecon businesses were moved into other divisions. (AndersonBrecon was divested in 2013.)

Its primary distribution business ABDC offers a full range of generic and brand-name pharmaceuticals over-the-counter products and home health care supplies and equipment. Meanwhile ABSG delivers specialty drugs for particular diseases (especially cancer) directly to the doctors who administer them.

The company's consulting services business helps retailers and manufacturers coordinate marketing programs to successfully launch new biotech drugs and increase sales of existing drugs. ABCS also provides sales tracking and logistics support as well as research field staffing co-pay assistance programs and risk mitigation services. In addition the division provides group purchasing merchandising and managed care services to independent and hospital-based pharmacies.

Geographic Reach

The company operates about 30 distribution centers throughout the US and has 150 offices in more than 50 countries worldwide.

Sales and Marketing

AmerisourceBergen's ABDC division serves customers including hospitals and health systems retail and mail order pharmacies medical clinics and long-term care facilities throughout North America. Pharmacy chain Express Scripts the company's biggest customer contributes about 24% of revenue.

Each of the company's segments have independent sales and marketing personnel who specialize in the unit's specific offerings. AmerisourceBergen also has a corporate marketing group for branding and broad-scale initiatives.

Financial Performance

In 2013 revenue increased 11% from $79.5 billion to $88 billion as sales picked up at Express Scripts and Walgreen and in the company's specialty group. However an increase in the cost of goods sold the loss of a group purchasing organization customer and reduced sales of oncology drugs lead to a 40% decline in net income. In 2013 AmerisourceBergen signed a 10-year agreement to supply a joint venture between Walgreen and Alliance Boots; it made additional drug purchases to service the contract which added about $90 million to its cost of goods sold for the year. Accordingly cash from operations also dropped by about 40% from $1.3 billion to $788 million due to the inventory increase associated with the Walgreen Alliance Boots deal.

Strategy

AmerisourceBergen's mission is to help its customers reduce health care expenses increase channel efficiencies and improve the quality of patient outcomes.

The company benefits from forming large supply agreements with key clients and factors such as competitive pressures and industry consolidation can occasionally hamper (or assist) the company's growth efforts in this area. In 2012 its biggest customer Medco Health Solutions (17% of revenues) merged with Express Scripts which contracted with one of AmerisourceBergen's competitors; however following the merger Express Scripts alleviated concerns when it signed a new supply agreement with AmerisourceBergen. The company expected the new Express Scripts contract to boost revenues in 2013 and it did. Increased spending to service the contract did take a bite out of net income and cash flow though. In 2013 it also signed an agreement to supply Walgreen and Alliance Boots (through their joint venture) for 10 years.

AmerisourceBergen occasionally divests noncore operations to focus on key areas of growth. In 2013 the company sold its AndersonBrecon division which provided contract packaging services to an investor group led by Frazier Healthcare for some $308 million. It also sold its AmerisourceBergen Canada Corporation (ABCC) pharma distribution business that year while retaining its Canadian specialty distribution operations.

Mergers and Acquisitions

Acquisitions have helped AmerisourceBergen expand its reach to new customer segments and geographic markets. In 2014 it purchased about 20% of Brazilian pharmaceutical wholesaler Profarma Distribuidora de Produtos Farmcêuticos; the two companies then launched a joint venture to provide pharmaceutical distribution in Brazil.

In 2015 the company boosted its presence in the animal health industry when it acquired MWI Veterinary Supply. Also that year it agreed to pay $2.6 billion for PharMEDium Healthcare in a move to expand its compounded drug distribution operations.

HISTORY

In 1977 Cleveland millionaire and horse racing enthusiast Tinkham Veale went into the drug wholesaling business. His company Alco Standard (now IKON Office Solutions) already owned chemical electrical metallurgical and mining companies but by the late 1970s the company was pursuing a strategy of zeroing in on various types of distribution businesses.

Alco's first drug wholesaler purchase was The Drug House (Delaware and Pennsylvania); the next was Duff Brothers (Tennessee). The company then bought further wholesalers in the South East and Midwest. Its modus operandi was to buy small well-run companies for cash and Alco stock and leave the incumbent management in charge.

By the early 1980s Alco was the US's third-largest wholesale drug distributor and growing quickly (28% between 1983 and 1988) at a time of mass consolidation in the industry (the number of wholesalers dropped by half between 1980 and 1992). In 1985 Alco Standard spun off its drug distribution operations as Alco Health Services retaining 60% ownership.

Alco Health boosted its sales above $1 billion mostly via acquisitions and expanded product lines. The company offered marketing and promotional help to its independent pharmacy customers (which were beleaguered by the growth of national discounters) and also targeted hospitals nursing homes and clinics.

The US was in the midst of its LBO frenzy in 1988 but an Alco management group failed in its attempt. Rival McKesson then tried to acquire Alco Health but that deal fell through for antitrust reasons. Later in 1988 management turned for backing to Citicorp Venture Capital in another buyout attempt. This time the move succeeded and a new holding company Alco Health Distribution was formed.

In 1993 Alco Health was named as a defendant in suits by independent pharmacies charging discriminatory pricing policies; a ruling the next year limited its liability. To move away from a reliance on independent drugstores Alco Health began targeting government entities and others.

Alco Health went public as AmeriSource Health in 1995. Throughout the next year AmeriSource made a series of acquisitions to move into related areas including inventory management technology drugstore pharmaceutical supplies and disease-management services for pharmacies.

In 1997 AmeriSource acquired Alabama-based Walker Drug for $140 million adding 1500 independent and chain drugstores in the Southeast to its customer list. That year McKesson once again made an offer to buy AmeriSource this time for $2.4 billion while two other major wholesale distributors Cardinal Health and Bergen Brunswig reached a similar pact. The deals were scrapped in 1998 when the Federal Trade Commission voted against both pacts and a federal judge supported that decision.

Later that year AmeriSource signed a five-year deal to become the exclusive pharmaceutical supplier to not-for-profit Sutter Health; in 1999 it renewed similar contracts with the US Department of Veterans Affairs and Pharmacy Provider Services Corporation. That year AmeriSource bought Midwest distributor C.D. Smith Healthcare.

In 2001 AmeriSource bought Bergen Brunswig and the combined company renamed itself AmerisourceBergen.

EXECUTIVES

EVP Retail Strategy; President Good Neighbor Pharmacy, David W. (Dave) Neu, age 58, $626,538 total compensation

Vice President Corporate And Investor Re, Barbara (Barb) Brungess

President and CEO, Steven H. Collis, age 54, $1,185,962 total compensation

EVP and CFO, Tim G. Guttman, age 56, $632,692 total compensation

EVP and Chief Marketing Officer, Gina K. Clark

VP Deputy General Counsel and Secretary, John G. Chou, age 59, $584,077 total compensation

EVP New Market Development and Chief Strategy Officer, Lawrence C. (Larry) Marsh

EVP; President AmerisourceBergen Specialty Group, James D. Frary, age 43, $515,000 total compensation

EVP and President Global Sourcing and Manufacturer Relations, Peyton R. Howell, age 48

EVP and Chief Information Officer, Dale Danilewitz

EVP; President AmerisourceBergen Drug Corporation, Robert P. Mauch

Vice President Gerneric RX Product Development, Brian Jones

Vice President Customer Solutions And Support, Kathie Manning

Vice President Operations, Joe Williamson

Vice President DCM Operations, Frank Dicenso

Group Vice President Retail Sales, George Rafferty

Vice President Risk Management, Woody Hope

Vice President Marketing Strategy, Matthew (Matt) Webb

Group Vice President Professional Services Health, Richard (Dick) Hudson

Vice President Enterprise Applications, Perry Sandberg

Vice President, Dustin Bateman

Vice President Information Technology Enterprise Architecture, Mike Biesanz

Vice President Strategic Accounts, Susan Bertot

GVP Business Management Retail, Anthony Caffentzis

Vice President, Michael Wondrasch

Vice President Financial Planning And Analysis, Marty Frankenfield

Vice President Of Retina Translation Medicine, Rhonda Mason

Vice President, Mike Clarke

Vice President Of Sales, Pam Miller

Vice President Sales, David Tingue

Vice President, Richard Tremonte

Vice President Human Resources, Jay Webster

Director Managed Care and PPN Operations, Chris Prieve

Vice President Contracts and Chargebacks, Mindy Stensrud

Vice President Contracts Chargebacks, Linda Ewald

Vice President of Real Estate, Michael (Mel) Kline

Vice President Global Sourcing Operations, Barbara (Barb) Miller

Vice President, Mike Gelgor

Vice President Professional Services, Christopher (Chris) Wernke

Vice President Customer Programs And Solutions, Carol Sirianni

Vice President Customer Support Services Amerisourcebergen Corporation, Tony Guarino

Vice President Information Security, Gerhard Cerny

Vice President Global Materials Management, Pam Olson

Vice President Information Services, Terry Forrest

Vice President Buying Groups, Alan (Al) Wilson

Vice President Health SYS Solutions, Rick Lang

Vice President alternate care, Dan Register

Vice President Health Systems Sales, Michael Haddad

Vice President Human Resources, Emily Lightfoot

Senior Vice President Finance, Albert Morales

Vice President Professional Services, Joel Weber Pharmd

Vice President Financial Processes, Brian Mangiaracina
Lead Vice President Sales, Scott Snyder
Senior Vice President, Gina Kootswatewa
Vice President Supply Chain Solutions, Wesley Jones
Vice President Human Resources Specialty Group, Meryl Harari
Vice President Segment Sales Csp, Deanna L Bush
Executive Assistant To Senior Vice President Chief Human Resources Officer And Chief Information Officer, Kelly Jakeman
Vice President Sales Oncology Service Line, Laurie Barton
Vice President Sales Theracom, Bob Landers
Vice President Tax, Daniel (Dan) Hirst
Vice President Strategic Accounts, Steve Iampietro
Vice President Information Technology, Jeanne Fisher
Senior Vice President And Chief Inform, Thomas (Thom) Murphy
Vice President Marketing, Michael (Mel) Clarke
Ass. Vice President Corp. Accounts, BJ Centers
Vice President Sales, J Thurmon
Vice President Information Services, Bayard Jones
Senior Vice President Finance Amerisourcebergen Drug Corporation, David (Dave) Senior
Vice President Clinical Science, Ncole Alvi
Chairman, Richard C. Gozon, age 77
Auditors: Ernst & Young LLP

LOCATIONS

HQ: AmerisourceBergen Corp.
1300 Morris Drive, Chesterbrook, PA 19087-5594
Phone: 610 727-7000   Fax: 610 647-0141
Web: www.amerisourcebergen.com

PRODUCTS/OPERATIONS

2013 Sales

	$ mil.	% of total
Pharmaceutical distribution	86,388	98
Other	1,763	2
Adjustments	(192.3)	-
Total	**87,959**	**100**

Selected Acquisitions

COMPETITORS

Allergan plc	McKesson
BioScrip	Medline Industries
Cardinal Health	Owens & Minor
Express Scripts	PSS World Medical
FFF Enterprises	Quality King
H. D. Smith Wholesale Drug	Roadnet
Henry Schein	UPS
	US Oncology

HISTORICAL FINANCIALS

Company Type: Public

Income Statement

FYE: September 30

	REVENUE ($ mil.)	NET INCOME ($ mil.)	NET PROFIT MARGIN	EMPLOYEES
09/15	135,961	(134)	—	17,500
09/14	119,569	276	0.2%	14,000
09/13	87,959	433	0.5%	13,000
09/12	79,489	718	0.9%	14,500
09/11	80,217	706	0.9%	10,300
Annual Growth	**14.1%**	**—**	**—**	**14.2%**

2015 Year-End Financials

Debt ratio: 12.59%
Return on equity: (-10.41%)
Cash ($ mil.): 2,167
Current ratio: 0.90
Long-term debt ($ mil.): 3,493
No. of shares (mil.): 206
Dividends
  Yield: 1.2%
  Payout: —
Market value ($ mil.): 19,653

	STOCK PRICE ($) FY Close	P/E High/Low	PER SHARE ($) Earnings	Dividends	Book Value
09/15	94.99	— —	(0.62)	1.16	3.06
09/14	77.30	64 50	1.17	0.94	8.82
09/13	61.10	33 21	1.84	0.84	10.09
09/12	38.71	15 13	2.80	0.52	10.44
09/11	37.27	17 12	2.54	0.43	10.98
Annual Growth	**26.4%**	**— —**	**—**	**28.2%**	**(27.3%)**

Amgen Inc

Amgen is among the biggest of the biotech big'uns and it's determined to get even bigger. The company uses cellular biology and medicinal chemistry to target cancers kidney ailments inflammatory disorders and metabolic diseases. Its top protein-based therapeutic products include Neulasta and Neupogen (both used as anti-infectives in cancer patients) Aranesp and Epogen (used to fight anemia in chronic kidney disease and cancer patients) and Enbrel for rheumatoid arthritis. In addition Amgen has extensive drug research and development programs. Its products are marketed in 75 countries to doctors hospitals pharmacies and other health care providers.

HISTORY

Amgen was formed as Applied Molecular Genetics in 1980 by a group of scientists and venture capitalists to develop health care products based on molecular biology. George Rathmann a VP at Abbott Laboratories and researcher at UCLA became the company's CEO and first employee. Rathmann decided to develop a few potentially profitable products rather than conduct research. The company initially raised $19 million.

Amgen operated close to bankruptcy until 1983 when company scientist Fu-Kuen Lin cloned the human protein erythropoietin (EPO) which stimulates the body's red blood cell production. Amgen went public that year. It formed a joint venture with Kirin Brewery in 1984 to develop and market EPO. The two firms also collaborated on recombinant human granulocyte colony stimulating factor (G-CSF later called Neupogen) a protein that stimulates the immune system.

Amgen joined Johnson & Johnson subsidiary Ortho Pharmaceutical (later Ortho-McNeil Pharmaceutical) in a marketing alliance in 1985 and created a tie with Roche in 1988. Fortunes soared in 1989 when the FDA approved Epogen (the brand name of EPO) for anemia. (It is most commonly used to counter side effects of kidney dialysis.)

In 1991 Amgen received approval to market Neupogen to chemotherapy patients. A federal court ruling also gave it a US monopoly for EPO. The following year Amgen won another dispute forcing a competitor to renounce its US patents for G-CSF.

As the company grew it needed to transform itself from startup to going concern; to do so Amgen hired MCI veteran Kevin Sharer as president in 1992. Neupogen's usage was expanded in 1993 to include treatment of severe chronic neutropenia (low white-blood-cell count).

In 1993 Amgen became the first American biotech to gain a foothold in China through an agreement with Kirin Pharmaceuticals to sell Neupogen (under the name Gran) and Epogen there. The purchase of Synergen in 1994 added another

research facility accelerating the pace of and increasing the number of products in research and clinical trials.

Although Amgen had two proven sellers in Epogen and Neupogen its growth lay in its pipeline. In 1997 Amgen and partner Regeneron Pharmaceuticals reported the failure of human trials for a drug to treat Lou Gehrig's disease. Still its new drug Stemgen for breast cancer patients undergoing chemotherapy was recommended for approval by an FDA advisory committee in 1998.

Amgen had to swallow a couple of tough legal pills in 1998. First a dispute with J&J over Amgen's 1985 licensing agreement with Ortho Pharmaceutical ended when an arbiter ordered Amgen to pay about $200 million. Later that year however Amgen won a legal battle with J&J over the rights to a promising anemia drug.

Work on its product pipeline continued in 1999: Amgen ended development of obesity and Parkinson's disease drugs after clinical trials produced discouraging results while it began human tests with partner Guilford Pharmaceuticals on a drug designed to regenerate damaged nerve cells in the brains of Parkinson's disease patients. (Guilford and Amgen ended the collaboration in 2001.)

In 2000 the firm resumed its battle to keep its stranglehold on the Epogen market: It sued Transkaryotic Therapies and Aventis (later Sanofi-Aventis) for alleged patent violations over its Epogen product in both the US and the UK. Although it initially won its case in the UK that verdict was overturned in 2002 making Amgen vulnerable to competition before Epogen's patents expire in 2004. That year it won EU and US approval for Aranesp an updated version of Epogen; Amgen in 2002 teamed with former J&J marketing partner Fresenius to sell Aranesp in Germany and take some market share away from J&J. Meanwhile an arbitration committee found J&J had breached its contract with Amgen when it sold Procrit to the dialysis market which Amgen had reserved for itself in their 1985 licensing deal.

In 2003 the company bought leukemia and rheumatoid arthritis drugs maker Immunex. As part of the FTC's blessing on the $10.3 billion union Amgen and Immunex licensed some technologies to encourage competition. Merck Serono gained access to Enbrel data and Regeneron Pharmaceuticals licensed some interleukin inhibitor rights.

The next year Amgen spent $1.3 billion to purchase the remaining 79% of cancer treatment technology maker Tularik that it did not already own.

EXECUTIVES

EVP Operations, Madhavan Balachandran, $772,961 total compensation
VP and General Manager LACAN Region, Laura Hamill
EVP Full Potential Initiatives, Brian M. McNamee, age 59
SVP Global Marketing and Commercial Development, Suzanne Blaug
EVP Global Commercial Operations, Anthony C. (Tony) Hooper, age 60, $1,005,653 total compensation
SVP Global Business Services, Michael A. Kelly, age 58, $511,757 total compensation
EVP Research and Development, Sean E. Harper, age 52, $899,948 total compensation
Chairman and CEO, Robert (Bob) Bradway, age 53, $1,505,769 total compensation
SVP Global Medical and Chief Medical Officer, Paul R. Eisenberg
SVP and Head European Region, Corinne Le Goff
SVP Manufacturing, Esteban Santos
Vice President Human Resources, Ted Bagley
Vice President Of Finance, George Helmer

Vice President Information Technology, Laura Irvin
Medical Director, Lucy Yan
Vice President, Charlotte Gabriel
Vice President Of The Commercial Division, Paul Hankey
Senior Vice President Operations Technology, Alison Moore
Medical Director, Jane (Ginny) Parnes
Vice President of Legal Compliance, Maria Mendoza
First Vice President Wealth Management, Saket Malhotra
Vice President of Heavy Construction, Lisa Myers
Vice President Research, Sasha Kamb
Vice President Drug Delivery, Sheldon Moberg
Vice President Finance, Elliot Beimel
Vice President Finance, Anton Rabushka
Vice President Marketing, Andrew (Andy) Hodgins
Vice President and General Manager Cardiovascular and Inflamation Business Units, Vanessa Broadhurst
Vice President Sales, Mike Tilton
Vice President Human Resources, Brian Sweeney
Vice President Finance, Janis Naeve
National Account Manager, Jay Lamba
Vice President And General Manager Scandinavia Classifieds, Keith Gabrielli
Vice President Global Marketing Therapeutic Area Head, Peter Sandor
Corp. Vice President Sales, Craig Burgess
Vice President, Jerry Murry
Senior Vice President Chief Financial Officer, Jennifer Swiecki
Vice President Us CV Marketing, Mark Neumann
Vice President Operations, Eduardo Cetlin
Vice President Global Regulatory Affairs, Mark Taisey
Vice President Installation Division, Judy McElwain
Vice President, Sharon Stoddard
Pharm D, Billy West
Medical Director, Hong Sun
Vice President, Thomas Hampe
Medical Director Observational Research, Scott Stryker
Medical Director, Vladimir Hanes
Senior Vice President, Rolf K Hoffmann
Vice President, Joe McConnell
Vice President Finance and Treasurer, Mary Lehmann
Vice President Manufacturing, Kimball Hall
Finance Vice President, Tonya Cheng
Medical Director, Wayne Tsuji
Vice President, Andy Clyne
National Sales Manager, Mike Ellis
Medical Director Latin America, Jorge Otero
Associate Medical Director Medical Affairs, Mark Rutstein
Vice President Of Information Technology, Ugur Yilmaz
Vice President Private Business Banker, Karen Lewis
Senior Vice President Human Resources, Michelle (Mitch) Bloxton
Vice President Sales, John Snowden
Vice President Global Line Head Pharmacokinetics And Drug Metabolism, Guy Padbury
Vice President Corporate Accounts, Aston William
Vice President and General Counsel, Robert (Bob) Sexton
Vice President Of Pre Clinical Research, David Balaban
Senior Vice President Global Development, Elliott Levy
Vice President General Manager France, Jean Monin
Vice President of Intenet Channel, John (Jack) Caldwell
Vice President Of Engineering, Carletto Pardo
Vice President General Manager Us Bone Health Bu, Ken Keller

Seniorvice President Of Manufacturing, Madhu Balachandran
Medical Director, Colleague Suijkerbuijk
Vice President of Pre Clinical Research, David (Dave) Balaban
Vice President Operations, Martin (Marti) Vantrieste
Vice President Global Safey, Paul R Eisenberg MD Mph
Executive Vice President Global Commercial Operations, Anthony CHooper
AC Assistant Secretary Credit Analysis, Lucy Kern
Board Member, Ryan Metheny
Board Member, Jeff Cottonaro
Board Member, Jonie Anderson
Chairman Emeritus, Marie Wright
Auditors: Ernst & Young LLP

LOCATIONS

HQ: Amgen Inc
One Amgen Center Drive, Thousand Oaks, CA 91320-1799
Phone: 805 447-1000   Fax: 805 447-1010
Web: www.amgen.com

2014 Sales

	$ mil.	% of total
US	15,396	77
Other countries	4,667	23
Total	20,063	100

Selected Locations

Algeria
Australia
Austria
Belgium
Brazil
Bulgaria
Canada
China
Colombia
Croatia
Czech Republic
Denmark
Egypt
Estonia Japan
Finland
France
Germany
Greece
Hong Kong
Hungary
Iceland
India
Ireland
Italy
Latvia
Lithuania
Luxembourg
Mexico
Netherlands
Norway
Poland
Portugal
Romania
Russia
Saudi Arabia
Slovakia
Slovenia
South Africa
Spain
Sweden
Switzerland
Turkey
United Arab Emirates
United Kingdom
United States

PRODUCTS/OPERATIONS

2014 Sales

	$ mil.	% of total
Product sales		
Neulasta	4,596	23
Enbrel	4,688	23
Epogen	2,031	10
Aranesp	1,930	10
Neupogen	1,159	6
XGEVA	1,221	6
Sensipar/Mimpara	1,158	6
Prolia	1,030	5
Vectibix	505	2
Nplate	469	2
Kyprolis	331	2
Other products	209	1
Other	736	4
Total	20,063	100

Top Selling Products
Neupogen/Neulasta (chemotherapy-induced neutropenia - low white blood cells and cancer-related infections)
Enbrel (rheumatoid arthritis psoriasis)
Aranesp (chemotherapy-induced anemia and chronic renal failure anemia sustained duration Epogen)
Epogen (anemia in chronic renal failure)
Sensipar/Mimpara (also known as Mimpara chronic kidney disease)
Xgeva (to prevent bone fractures)
Vectibix (monoclonal antibody for colorectal cancer)
Nplate (romiplostim for autoimmune bleeding disorder ITP or immune thrombocytopenic purpura)
Prolia (po

COMPETITORS

AbbVie	Johnson & Johnson
Abbott Labs	Merck
Affymax	Merck KGaA
Apotex	Millennium: The Takeda
AstraZeneca	Oncology Company
Bayer HealthCare	Nektar Therapeutics
Pharmaceuticals Inc.	Novartis
Bristol-Myers Squibb	Pfizer
Celgene	Roche Holding
Chugai	Sanofi
Eli Lilly	Shire
Fresenius Medical Care	Takeda Pharmaceutical
Genentech	Teva
GlaxoSmithKline	UCB
Hospira	

HISTORICAL FINANCIALS

Company Type: Public

Income Statement

	REVENUE ($ mil.)	NET INCOME ($ mil.)	NET PROFIT MARGIN	EMPLOYEES
12/15	21,662	6,939	32.0%	17,900
12/14	20,063	5,158	25.7%	17,900
12/13	18,676	5,081	27.2%	20,000
12/12	17,265	4,345	25.2%	18,000
12/11	15,582	3,683	23.6%	17,800
Annual Growth	8.6%	17.2%	—	0.1%

FYE: December 31

2015 Year-End Financials

Debt ratio: 44.09%   No. of shares (mil.): 754
Return on equity: 25.77%   Dividends
Cash ($ mil.): 4,144   Yield: 1.9%
Current ratio: 4.44   Payout: 37.7%
Long-term debt ($ mil.): 29,306   Market value ($ mil.): 122,397

	STOCK PRICE ($) FY Close	P/E High/Low		PER SHARE ($) Earnings	Dividends	Book Value
12/15	162.33	19	14	9.06	3.16	37.25
12/14	159.29	25	16	6.70	2.44	33.90
12/13	114.08	18	12	6.64	1.88	29.28
12/12	86.20	16	11	5.52	1.44	25.20
12/11	64.21	16	12	4.04	0.56	23.92
Annual Growth	26.1%	—	—	22.4%	54.1%	11.7%

Amphenol Corp.

Amphenol knows it's all about connections. A leading manufacturer of connector and interconnect products its serves the communications industrial medical and military markets. Amphenol's interconnect products are used to conduct electrical and optical signals in computers wired and wireless communications and networking equipment medical instruments office equipment aircraft and spacecraft and energy applications. Its Times Fiber Communications subsidiary is a leading maker of coaxial cable for the cable TV industry and flat-ribbon cable for computer and telecommunications products. With customers in about 70 countries more than two thirds of its sales come from outside the US led by customers in China.

Operations

Amphenol is the global leader for high-performance circular environmental connectors designed to military specifications. The company's circular environmental connectors used to connect electronic and fiber optic systems in aircraft guided missiles radar military vehicles are designed for specific environmentally-intense applications.

The company's Interconnect Products and Assemblies segment accounts for 93% of its sales with cable products accounting for the rest.

In terms of markets about 28% of sales go to mobile devices and mobile networks; 32% to automotive and industrial markets; 17% to military and commercial aerospace; and 16% to IT and data communications.

In the automotive and industrial markets the company sees growth for products designed for hybrid-electrical vehicles alternative energy generation and medical equipment.

Through its Times Fiber Communications subsidiary Amphenol is the world's #2 manufacturer of coaxial cable for the cable television market behind global leader CommScope.

Geographic Reach

The company has manufacturing and assembly operations worldwide in more than 20 countries with just-in-time plants near major customers. Specific plants are located in Australia Canada China Czech Republic Estonia France Germany India Japan Korea Malaysia Mexico Slovakia Taiwan and the UK.

Sales and Marketing

Amphenol's products are sold in more than 10000 customer locations worldwide (one customer can have components sent to multiple manufacturing locations). Its products are sold directly to original equipment manufacturers (OEMs) electronics manufacturing services (EMS) original design manufacturers (ODMs) cable system operators IT companies and through manufacturers' representatives and distributors. No single customer accounts for more than 10% of sales while sales to its distributor channels represent about 13% of revenue.

Financial Performance

Amphenol's revenue and net income grew in 2014 for the fifth straight year. For the year revenue reached $5.3 billion a 15% increase from 2013's $4.6 billion. The company posted sales increases in all of its markets but for a dip in IT and data communications. Sales to the industrial market rose about $276 million from business with energy and heavy equipment markets. Automotive sales also posted a big gain u $271 million driven primarily by the increasing use of technology in vehicles and higher production runs. Sales to mobile networks rose nearly $112 million as telecom providers built out networks around the world. The aerospace and mobile device markets saw sales rise by 449 million and $46 million respectively.

Net income rose about 11.5% to $709 million on the higher sales. Cash flow from operations was about $881 million for 2014 compared to about $770 million in 2013.

Strategy

Amphenol considers the industry to be highly fragmented so acquisitions are part of its growth strategy. It looks for high growth businesses that can augment its product portfolio customer base or geographic reach. It bought five companies in 2013 for a total of $485 million. It spent $252 million in 2012 and $300 million in 2011 for acquisitions. Besides spending to acquire differentiating products Amphenol increased spending by $11 million to $103 million in 2013 to develop new products. About 20% of its 2013 sales came from products less than two years old.

Mergers and Acquisitions

In 2015 Amphenol acquired FCI Electronics a marker of interconnect products for $1.275 million. The addition of FCI gives Amphenol a wider selection of technologies and a broader market of customers.

HISTORY

Amphenol was founded in 1932 as The American Phenolic Corporation by Arthur J. Schmitt who wanted to mass produce vacuum tube sockets used in making radios. He discovered that insulating plastic could produce tube sockets in a faster and easier method that using Bakelite or ceramic. The company's first customer was RCA.

During World War II Amphenol's 5015 AN series connector becomes known as the "Amphenol Connector" by military maintenance crews. (The B-29 Super Fortress contains more than 1600 Amphenol connectors.) The company's Sidney NY facility was designated a site of national importance and was defended from air strikes.

As telephone networks expanded Amphenol invented the Amphenol blue ribbon cable which became the standard for Bell.

Amphenol has grown its business with select acquisitions including the industrial/avionics connector business of PCD and the custom connector assembly business of Insilco Holding. In 2005 it purchased Teradyne's Connection Systems division for about $390 million; the unit makes printed circuit board interconnect products.

Amphenol's plant in Sidney New York was damaged in sudden and severe flooding in mid-2006. Flood-related losses beyond insurance coverage reached almost $21 million. Amphenol's management and employees worked 12-hour shifts for three weeks to clean up and restore the manufacturing facility which serves the aerospace and industrial markets.

EXECUTIVES

SVP and Group General Manager IT and Communications Products Division, Richard E. (Rick) Schneider, age 57, $475,000 total compensation

SVP and Group General Manager Aerospace and Industrial Operations, Gary A. Anderson, age 64, $486,000 total compensation

President CEO and Director, Richard A. (Adam) Norwitt, age 46, $1,000,000 total compensation

SVP and Group General Manager International Military and Aerospace Operations, Luc Walter, age 56, $513,845 total compensation

SVP and CFO, Craig A. Lampo, age 45

SVP and Group General Manager Worldwide RF and Microwave Products, Zachary W. Raley, age 46, $471,000 total compensation

VP and Group General Manager Automotive and Sensor Products division, John Treanor, age 57

VP and Group General Manager Mobile Consumer Products, Di Yang, age 47

Vice President Sales Industrial Operations, Martin (Marti) Booker

Vice President and Group General Manager Mobile Consumer Products, Alessandro Perrotta

Vice President Operations, Frank Holcombe

Vice President Purchasing, Jay Oldenburg

Vice President Human Resources, Jerome Monteith

Vice President and Group General Manager Global Interconnect Systems Group, Frank Carroccia

Vice President of Information Technology, Craig Southard

Vice President Secretary and General Counsel, Edward (Ed) Wetmore

Auditors: Deloitte & Touche LLP

LOCATIONS

HQ: Amphenol Corp.
358 Hall Avenue, Wallingford, CT 06492
Phone: 203 265-8900   **Fax:** 203 265-8746
Web: www.amphenol.com

2014 Sales

	$ mil.	% of total
US	1,673	31
China	1,440	27
Other countries	2,231	42
Total	**5,345**	**100**

PRODUCTS/OPERATIONS

2014 Sales

	$ mil.	% of total
Interconnect products & assemblies	4,992	93
Cable products	352	7
Total	**5,345**	**100**

Selected Brands

Amphenol
Kai Jack
Matrix
Pyle-National
Sine
Socapex
Spectra-Strip
Times Fiber
Tuchel

Selected Products

Interconnect products
  Automotive interconnect systems
  CATV interconnects
  Data/telecom connectors
  Fiber-optic connectors and systems
  Filter connectors
  Flexible circuit interconnects
  High-performance connectors
  Industrial power connectors
  Radio-frequency coaxial connectors
  Smart card connectors
Cable products
  Electronic cable
  Engineered cable assemblies
  Times Fiber coaxial cable
  Wireless cable products
Other
  Mobile and portable antennas

COMPETITORS

3M	Molex
ARRIS	Northrop Grumman
AVX	Panduit
Alcatel-Lucent	Radiall
CommScope	Smiths Group
Corning	Spirent
FCI	Sumitomo Electric
Hirose Electric	TE Connectivity
Hon Hai	TT electronics
Huber + Suhner Inc.	Telect
Japan Aviation	Thomas & Betts
Electronics Industry	Tri-Star Electronics
Methode Electronics	International

HISTORICAL FINANCIALS

Company Type: Public

Income Statement

FYE: December 31

	REVENUE ($ mil.)	NET INCOME ($ mil.)	NET PROFIT MARGIN	EMPLOYEES
12/14	5,345	709	13.3%	50,700
12/13	4,614	635	13.8%	44,500
12/12	4,292	555	12.9%	41,600
12/11	3,939	524	13.3%	39,100
12/10	3,554	496	14.0%	39,100
Annual Growth	10.7%	9.3%	—	6.7%

2014 Year-End Financials

Debt ratio: 38.05%
Return on equity: 24.59%
Cash ($ mil.): 968
Current ratio: 3.35
Long-term debt ($ mil.): 2,672

No. of shares (mil.): 309
Dividends
  Yield: 0.8%
  Payout: 42.0%
Market value ($ mil.): 16,675

	STOCK PRICE ($) FY Close	P/E High/Low	PER SHARE ($) Earnings	Dividends	Book Value
12/14	53.81	47 20	2.21	0.45	9.38
12/13	89.18	44 32	1.96	0.61	9.04
12/12	64.70	38 27	1.70	0.42	7.60
12/11	45.39	38 26	1.53	0.03	6.66
12/10	52.78	37 27	1.41	0.06	6.61
Annual Growth	0.5%	— —	11.9%	65.5%	9.1%

AmTrust Financial Services Inc

Insurance holding company AmTrust Financial Services likes a mix of businesses on its plate. Its subsidiaries offer a range of commercial property/casualty insurance products for small and midsized customers including workers' compensation products auto and general liability workplace and agricultural coverage and extended service and warranty coverage of consumer and commercial goods. It also provides a small amount of personal auto reinsurance. It operates in Bermuda Ireland the UK and the US and distributes its products through brokers agents and claims administrators. The firm's customers include restaurants retailers physicians' offices auto and electronics manufacturers and trucking operations.

OperationsAmTrust's revenue comes primarily from premium income from its largest three segments: Specialty Risk and Extended Warranty which coverage for consumer products and specialty coverage (about 35% of revenue in 2014); Small Commercial Business which provides workers' compensation to small businesses (46%); and Specialty Program operations which includes workers' comp general and corporate auto liability and other insurance products (19%). The remainder of revenue comes primarily from the smaller Personal Lines Reinsurance segment and from investment income.

Geographic Reach

AmTrust sells insurance products in all 50 US states the District of Columbia and Puerto Rico as well as parts of Europe and the Caribbean. Bermuda where one of its reinsurers is located accounts for 35% of revenue while the US brings in 34%. In total the company operates in 50 countries worldwide.

Amtrust also provides third-party adminstrator services (claims handling and call center services) for the consumer products and automotive industries in the US Canada Europe and Asia.

Sales and Marketing

The company distributes its products via a network of more than 9400 retail and wholesale agents. Unaffiliated third parties sell its small commercial business and specialty risk and extended warranty products.

Financial PerformanceAs a result of an aggressive acquisition strategy AmTrust has seen steadily increasing revenue and profits over the last five years. Revenue increased 52% to $4 billion from $2.7 billion in 2014 due primarily to growth in the small commercial business and specialty risk and extended warranty businesses. Small business commercial premiums nearly doubled (to $1.6 billion); retention also continued to improve. Specialty risk and extended warranty premiums increased 52% to $1.2 billion that year.

Net income rose 58% to $447 million in 2014 driven by higher sales and assisted by foreign currency gains. However this was partially offset by increased losses and loss adjustment expenses. Cash flow from operations increased 26% to $1.1 billion.

StrategyKey to AmTrust's overall business strategy is keeping its portfolio diversified by both business line and geography. Acquisitions are a key aspect of growth; it targets the small to midsized customer markets in the US which have higher volumes and lower risk. In 2013 it purchased six insurance and warranty companies picked up another three in 2014 and continued its buying spree with even larger purchases in 2015.

The company also expands by forming new distribution partnerships hiring new specialty lines underwriters and developing new client relationships.Mergers and AcquisitionsThe company has been able to expand its product offerings and geographic reach through acquisitions of smaller competitors though it approaches its purchases with a conservative eye avoiding huge financial investments.

AmTrust bought Wells Fargo's Warranty Solutions business in 2015 for $152 million. Warranty Solutions underwrites vehicle service contracts and auto-related finance and insurance products to dealerships around the nation; the purchase expands AmTrust's existing vehicle warranty operations and adds new fees and service revenue. Also that year the company's North America segment acquired the crop insurance operations of The Climate Corporation a division of Monsanto. Next it struck a deal to acquire Texas-based property/casualty insurer Republic Companies for $233 million. It also agreed to buy the European mortgage insurance business of Genworth Financial. Other deals that year included the acquisitions of CorePointe a Michigan-based property/casualty firm serving car dealers and auto repair shops; TMI Solutions a warranty and consumer protection coverage provider; and Oryx Insurance Brokerage which serves the construction industry in upstate New York.

In 2014 AmTrust bought The Insco Dico Group to improve its position in domestic surety bonds and new insurance products. The deal which included subsidiary Builders Insurance Services was worth $89 million. Later in the year the company purchased Blue Cross Blue Shield affiliate Comp Options Insurance Company a Florida-based workers' compensation provider.

Deals in 2013 included the acquisitions of Sequoia Insurance (a provider of commercial property/casualty products in the Western US) for some $60 million as well as Mutual Insurers Holding parent of First Nonprofit Insurance (property and liability coverage for not-for-profit entities) for an undisclosed price.AmTrust also expanded in the warranty market through the purchase of UK-based Car Car Plan from Ally Financial for $70 million in 2013. Other purchases that year included Sagicor Europe Limited for $92 million Mutual Insurers Holding for $49 million and CPPNA Holdings for $40 million.

EXECUTIVES

President CEO and Director, Barry D. Zyskind, age 44, $975,000 total compensation

EVP and COO, Michael J. Saxon, age 57, $700,000 total compensation

EVP and CFO, Ronald E. Pipoly, age 49, $600,000 total compensation

EVP and CIO, Christopher M. Longo, age 42, $600,000 total compensation

CEO AmTrust Europe; President AmTrust International Insurance, Max G. Caviet, age 62, $856,735 total compensation

EVP and Chief Legal Officer, David H. Saks, age 48

Assistant Vice President Of Loss Control, Gordon Celliers

Assistant Vice President, Rick McKenna

Executive Vice President, Kathleen Murphy

Vice President Of Underwriting, Christopher Coons

National Sales Manager, Matthew Craven

Vice President Finance, Grace Pan

Assistant Vice President Of Finance, Lindsay Santos

Vice President of Sales, Bruce Caldwell

Vice President, Hilly Gross

Assistant Vice President Insurance Business Consultant (Financial Systems), Thomas Harding

Senior Vice President Human Resources, Kevin Oxley

Vice President Finance, Stephen Brandt

Vice President Sales, Dennis Tebon

Assistant Vice President, Tony Weddle

Vice President Surety, Michael (Mel) Doyle

Vice President Corporate Counsel, Henry Hsu

Vice President Underwriting, Jerry Fort

Vice President, Julie Nielsen

Senior Vice President, Ariel Gorelik

Assistant Vice President Finance, Cindy Warren

Vice President Business Applications, Michael Frampton

Assistant Vice President Of Operations, Gina Bilak

Vice President Strategic Development, Zachary Wolf

Vice President Mobile Products, Don Cunningham

Associate Vice President Sales and Marketing, Lauren Dunnigan

Vice President Of Underwriting, Henry Sibley

Vice President Partnership Marketing Retail, David (Dave) Gandrud

Vice President Media Acquisition, Eli Toron

Vice President and Chief Actuary CPD Division, Bill Fisanick

Executive Vice President Systems Innovation, Brian Fullerton

Vice President Securities and Corporate Counsel, Catherine (Cathy) Miller

Vice President Claims, Tom Brashear

Vice President Of Ceded Reinsurance, David Tenhoor

Vice President Specialty Risk Associate General Counsel, Jason Thompson

Executive Vice President Amtrust Title Division, Barry Flavin

Vice President of Strategic Development for Mergers and Acquisitions, Adam Karkowsky

Senior Vice President Marketing, Scott Roe

Chairman, Michael Karfunkel, age 73

Assistant Treasurer, Chaim Halberstam

Treasurer, Harry Schlachter

Auditors: BDO USA, LLP

HQ: AmTrust Financial Services Inc
 59 Maiden Lane, 43rd Floor, New York, NY 10038
Phone: 212 220-7120
Web: www.amtrustgroup.com

2014 Sales

	$ mil.	% of total
Bermuda	1,417	35
US	1,394	34
Other countries	1,272	31
Total	**4,084**	**100**

PRODUCTS/OPERATIONS

2014 Sales

	$ mil.	% of total
Small commercial business	1,606	39
Specialty risk & extended warranty	1,232	30
Specialty program	678	17
Service & fee income	409	10
Net investment income	131	3
Personal lines reinsurance & net gain on investments	25	1
Total	**4,084**	**100**

Selected Acquisitions

COMPETITORS

AIG	Liberty Mutual
Allianz Insurance	National Indemnity
Amica Mutual	Company
Bankers Financial	The Hartford
Berkshire Hathaway	Travelers Companies
FCCI	

HISTORICAL FINANCIALS

Company Type: Public

Income Statement

FYE: December 31

	ASSETS ($ mil.)	NET INCOME ($ mil.)	INCOME AS % OF ASSETS	EMPLOYEES
12/14	13,847	447	3.2%	5,100
12/13	11,257	290	2.6%	3,238
12/12	7,417	177	2.4%	2,100
12/11	5,682	170	3.0%	1,900
12/10	4,182	142	3.4%	1,400
Annual Growth	**34.9%**	**33.1%**	**—**	**38.2%**

2014 Year-End Financials

Debt ratio: 6.69%	No. of shares (mil.): 155
Return on equity: 25.64%	Dividends
Cash ($ mil.): 902	Yield: 3.0%
Current ratio: —	Payout: 31.1%
Long-term debt ($ mil.): —	Market value ($ mil.): 8,746

	STOCK PRICE ($) FY Close	P/E High/Low	PER SHARE ($) Earnings	Dividends	Book Value
12/14	56.25	20 11	2.73	0.85	13.10
12/13	32.69	23 15	1.84	0.53	9.69
12/12	28.69	25 18	1.17	0.34	7.74
12/11	23.75	23 15	1.14	0.28	6.12
12/10	17.50	18 12	0.98	0.24	4.97
Annual Growth	**33.9%**	**— —**	**29.3%**	**37.2%**	**27.4%**

Anadarko Petroleum Corp

Anadarko Petroleum has ventured beyond its original area of operation –the Anadarko Basin — to explore for develop produce and market oil natural gas natural gas liquids and related products worldwide. In 2014 the large independent company reported proved reserves (92% of which is located in the US) of 2.9 billion barrels of oil equivalent. Additional assets include coal trona (natural soda ash) and other minerals. Anadarko operates a handful of gas-gathering systems in the Mid-Continent. Internationally the company has substantial oil and gas interests in Algeria. It also has holdings in Brazil China Indonesia Mozambique and West Africa.

Geographic Reach

Anadarko's assets include US onshore resource plays in the Rocky Mountains area the southern US and the Appalachian basin. It is one the largest independent producers in the deepwater Gulf of Mexico and has production and exploration activities worldwide including high-potential basins located in Alaska Algeria Brazil China Côte d'Ivoire Ghana Kenya Liberia Mozambique New Zealand Sierra Leone and other countries.

In 2014 the US accounted for 80% of Anadarko's total revenues.

Operations

The company is engaged in oil and gas exploration and production (including gas crude oil condensate and NGLs); the midstream activities of gathering processing treating and transporting oil natural gas and NGLs production; and the marketing of oil natural gas and NGLs in the US and oil from Algeria China and Ghana. NGLs sales represent revenues from the sale of products derived from the processing of Anadarko's natural-gas production.

Sales and Marketing

Anadarko sells crude oil and natural gas via a range of contractual agreements. At the end of 2014 Anadarko was contractually committed to deliver 874 billion cu. ft. of natural gas to various US customers through 2031. That year Anadarko also was contractually committed to deliver 9 million barrels of oil to ports in Algeria and Ghana through 2015.

Financial Performance

In 2014 revenues increased by 27% due to increased sales from Oil and Gas Exploration & Production and Midstream. The average natural-gas price Anadarko received increased primarily due to low industry natural gas storage levels as a result of colder than average winter temperatures and the associated high residential heating demand in early 2014. In addition natural gas prices increased as a result of higher industrial natural gas demand reduced natural gas imports from Canada and continued strength in exports to Mexico.Anadarko's oil and condensate sales volumes increased by 44000 barrels a day; however the company's natural gas sales volumes decreased by 63 million cu. ft. per day. Gathering processing and marketing sales increased by $6 million due to higher gathering and processing revenue associated with higher volumes increased natural gas prices and improved infrastructure partially offset by higher processing and transportation expenses due to the higher volumes.In 2014 the company incurred a loss of $2.5 billion compared to 2013. The primary reason was due to Tronox-related contingent loss and income tax expenses partially offset by higher revenues. In 2014 Anadarko and Kerr-McGee en-

tered into a settlement agreement for $5.15 billion resolving all claims asserted in the Tronox Adversary Proceeding. (Kerr-McGee spun off its chemicals unit into Tronox just before being acquired by Anadarko. In 2014 a federal judge found that this move unfairly saddled Tronox with liabilities that ultimately bankrupted it in 2009). Anadarko recognized Tronox-related contingent losses of $4.3 billion in 2014 associated with the Tronox-related contingent loss recognized in 2011.In 2014 Anadarko's net cash provided by operating activities decreased by $422 million due to Tronox-related costs and a change in Algeria exceptional profits tax settlement and accounts receivable.

Strategy

Anadarko explores in high-potential proven and emerging basins worldwide. Developing a portfolio of primarily unconventional resources provides the company with a stable base of capital-efficient predictable and repeatable development opportunities.Activities in the Rockies primarily focus on expanding existing fields to increase production and adding proved reserves through horizontal drilling infill drilling and down-spacing operations. The Company drilled 569 wells and completed 487 wells in the Rockies during 2014. The Company plans to continue its drilling program in 2015 focusing on the Wattenberg field. In 2015 the Company expects to focus its exploration and appraisal activity in East Africa Côte d'Ivoire and Colombia.To raise cash to pay down debt and help it exploit its US shale assets (a growth segmentAnadarko sold its interest in the non-operated Vito deepwater development along with several surrounding exploration blocks in the Gulf of Mexico for $500 million; and sold its interest in the Pinedale/Jonah assets in Wyoming for $581 million. That year it also agreed to sell its Chinese assets for $1.1 billion.In 2014 Anadarko entered into an agreement with the plaintiffs (in the Tronox Adversary Proceeding to resolve all claims against Kerr-McGee which stemmed from alleged actions by Kerr-McGee prior to its acquisition by Anadarko in 2006. That year the company agreed to pay the federal government $5.15 billion (the largest ever settlement for environmental contamination) to settle claims related to the cleanup of thousands of sites tainted with hazardous chemicals.

In 2013 Anadarko agreed to sell 10% of its property off the shores of Mozambique to Oil and Natural Gas Corp. Ltd. for $2.64 billion.

Mergers and Acquisitions

In 2015 Anadarko made a bid to acquire Apache which was rebuffed.

In 2013 Anadarko acquired a number of US oil and gas assets for about $500 million.

HISTORY

In 1959 the Panhandle Eastern Pipe Line Company set up Anadarko (named after the Anadarko Basin) to carry out its gas exploration and production activities. The new company was also formed to take advantage of a ruling by the Federal Power Commission (now the Federal Energy Regulatory Commission) to set lower price ceilings for producing properties owned by pipeline companies.

The company grew rapidly during the early 1960s largely because of its gas-rich namesake. It bought Ambassador Oil of Fort Worth Texas in 1965 –adding interests in 19 states in the US and Canada. The firm also relocated from Kansas to Fort Worth.

Anadarko began offshore exploration in the Gulf of Mexico in 1970 and focused there early in the decade. After moving to Houston in 1974 Anadarko increased its oil exploration activities when the energy crisis led to higher gas prices. A deal with Amoco (now part of BP) led to major finds on Matagorda Island off the Texas coast in the early 1980s.

To realize shareholder value Panhandle spun off Anadarko in 1986 —separating transmission from production. At the time more than 90% of Anadarko's reserves were natural gas. The next year Anadarko made new discoveries in Canada.

Low domestic natural gas prices led Anadarko overseas. It signed a production-sharing agreement with Algeria's national oil and gas firm SONATRACH in 1989. The deal covered 5.1 million acres in the Sahara. Two years later Anadarko began operating in the South China Sea and in Alaska's North Slope.

Back home the company spent $190 million in 1992 for properties in West Texas and in 1993 Anadarko began divesting noncore assets. Along with some of its partners the company also discovered oil in the Mahogany Field offshore Louisiana. Production from Mahogany began in 1996.

In 1997 Anadarko added exploration acreage in the North Atlantic and Tunisia.

Anadarko expanded its presence in western Canada in 2001 by buying Berkley Petroleum for more than $1 billion in cash and assumed debt.

Expanding its presence and asset base in the lucrative resource plays in the Rocky Mountains and the deepwater Gulf of Mexico in 2006 Anadarko acquired midstream operator Western Gas and fellow explorer Kerr-McGee for about $26 billion.

EXECUTIVES

SVP Information Technology Services and CIO, Mario M. Coll, age 55

EVP General Counsel and Chief Administrative Officer, Robert K. (Bobby) Reeves, age 57, $700,000 total compensation

Chairman President and CEO, R. A. (Al) Walker, age 58, $1,300,000 total compensation

EVP International and Deepwater Exploration, Robert P. (Bob) Daniels, age 57, $700,000 total compensation

EVP U.S. Onshore Exploration and Production, Darrell E. Hollek

EVP International and Deepwater Operations, James J. (Jim) Kleckner, age 58

VP Worldwide Marketing, A. Scott Moore

EVP U.S. Onshore Exploration and Production, Charles A. (Chuck) Meloy, age 56, $700,000 total compensation

EVP Finance and Chief Financial Officer, Robert G. (Bob) Gwin, age 52, $750,000 total compensation

VP Exploration (West Africa), Gregory A. (Greg) Jewell

VP Operations (Mozambique), Donald H. MacLiver

SVP International Exploration, Ernest A. Leyendecker

VP Operations (Algeria), L. Allen Sanders

VP Operations (Africa/Asia), John A. Broman

VP Operations (Southern and Appalachia), Daniel E. (Danny) Brown

SVP Operations (Rockies), Bradley J. (Brad) Holly

VP Worldwide Drilling, Stephen J. (Steve) Bosworth

VP Operations (West Texas), Chad R. McAllaster

VP Operations (Maverick Basin), Tommy Thompson

VP Operations (Wattenberg), Craig R. Walters

VP Land (U.S. Onshore), Edward L. Wood

Vice President Transactions, Joseph (Jo) Carroll

Vice President In Charge of Drain Information Technology, Larry Hutson

Vice President Ehs, David McBride

Vice President, Joseph Jacobs

Finance Vice President, Dustin David

Vice President Operations, Sofia Norman

Vice President Safety and Training, Steve Olson

Vice President Marketing, John (Jack) Bretz

Vice President International Commercial Dev, Dave Anderson

Vice President Information Technology, Bob Almonte

Vice President EandP Services and Minerals, Robert (Bob) Abendschein

Assistant Treasurer Western Gas Partners, Nick Matovich

Auditors: KPMG LLP

LOCATIONS

HQ: Anadarko Petroleum Corp
1201 Lake Robbins Drive, The Woodlands, TX 77380-1046
Phone: 832 636-1000
Web: www.anadarko.com

2014 Sales

	% of total
US	80
Algeria	15
Other countries	5
Total	**100**

PRODUCTS/OPERATIONS

2014 Sales

	$ mil.	% of total
Oil & Gas Exploration & Production	16,721	88
Midstream	1,819	9
Marketing	517	3
Adjustments	(587)	-
Total	**18,470**	**100**

COMPETITORS

Adams Resources	Exxon Mobil
Apache	Hunt Consolidated
BP	Jones Energy
Cabot Oil & Gas	Key Energy
Chesapeake Energy	National Fuel Gas
Chevron	Noble Energy
Cimarex	Pioneer Natural
ConocoPhillips	Resources
Devon Energy	Royal Dutch Shell
EOG	

HISTORICAL FINANCIALS

Company Type: Public

Income Statement

FYE: December 31

	REVENUE ($ mil.)	NET INCOME ($ mil.)	NET PROFIT MARGIN	EMPLOYEES
12/15	8,698	(6,692)	—	5,800
12/14	18,470	(1,750)	—	6,100
12/13	14,581	801	5.5%	5,700
12/12	13,411	2,391	17.8%	5,200
12/11	13,967	(2,649)	—	4,800
Annual Growth	**(11.2%)**	**—**	**—**	**4.8%**

2015 Year-End Financials

Debt ratio: 33.94%	No. of shares (mil.): 508
Return on equity: (-41.13%)	Dividends
Cash ($ mil.): 939	Yield: 2.2%
Current ratio: 0.95	Payout: —
Long-term debt ($ mil.): 15,718	Market value ($ mil.): 24,693

	STOCK PRICE ($) FY Close	P/E High/Low		PER SHARE ($) Earnings	Dividends	Book Value
12/15	48.58	—	—	(13.18)	1.08	25.22
12/14	82.50	—	—	(3.47)	0.99	38.94
12/13	79.32	62	47	1.58	0.54	43.39
12/12	74.31	18	12	4.74	0.36	41.22
12/11	76.33	—	—	(5.32)	0.36	36.33
Annual Growth	**(10.7%)**	—	—	—	**31.6%**	**(8.7%)**

Anixter International Inc

When it comes to getting wired Anixter International's got the connections. The company is a distributor of communication products used to connect voice video data and security systems. It sells 400000-plus products including electrical and electronic wire cable and security system components to some 125000 customers in a host of industries. Anixter operates primarily through special sales forces —Electric and Electronic Wire and Cable and Enterprise Cabling and Security Solutions —operating from about 250 warehouses and sales centers in 50 countries. Although Anixter gets its products from thousands of suppliers almost one-third come from just five companies.

Geographic Reach

Anixter operates through a network of warehouses and sales offices consisting of 200 locations in the US more than 25 in Canada 30 in the UK and 37 throughout the rest of Europe 36 in Latin America almost 15 in Asia and six spanning Australia and New Zealand. North America accounted for about 70% of its revenue in 2015.

Operations

Anixter's massive distribution capacity is central to delivering goods whenever and wherever its customers demand. In addition to turn-on-a-dime delivery the company's reach has cultivated a broad customer base; no one customer accounts for more than 3% of sales. Not content however to rest on its distribution might Anixter moves beyond solely aggregating and marketing products to offering a slate of inventory management services for customers as well as testing facilities for its suppliers.

In 2015 the company sold its fasteners segment and now operates through two segments: Enterprise Cabling and Security Solutions which supplies products to a diverse range of industries including finance transportation education government health care and retail; and Electrical and Electronic Wire and Cable which caters to the industrial and original equipment manufacturer (OEM) markets.

Sales and Marketing

More than two dozen industries are represented among Anixter customers —markets such as education government health care manufacturing retail and transportation. Anixter also serves contractors and integrators who install and maintain communications networks and data centers. International national regional and local OEMs number among Anixter's customers as well procuring wire cable fasteners and other small components to help finish the manufacturing of their own products typically with short lead times.

Financial Performance

From 2014 to 2015 Anixter's revenues increased 4% from $6.23 billion to peak at a record-setting $6.45 billion. Profits however fell 3% from $201 million in 2014 to $195 million in 2015 due to increased expenses associated with acquisitions. Anixter's operating cash flow in 2015 also decreased 69% to $104 million primarily due to the erosion of profits.

The historic revenue growth for 2015 was fueled by a 7% spike in sales from Enterprise Cabling and Security Solutions segment due to a previous acquisition and improvement in its core communications and datacenter business. The segment also posted a 3% organic sales increase. This growth was offset by a decline in Electrical and Electronic Wire and Cable segment sales which was affected by lower foreign exchange and lower copper prices.

Strategy

The company's operations are driven organically through both product and service expansions. At the same time Anixter doesn't hesitate to go after niche acquisition opportunities that promise to expand its technical expertise and geographic reach. For example in 2014 it picked up Tri-Ed an independent distributor of security and low-voltage technology products based in Woodbury New York.

In 2015 Anixter agreed to acquire the Power Solutions business belonging to HD Supply Holdings for $825 million in cash. The business distributes electrical transmission and distribution products power plant MRO supplies and smart-grid products and also arranges materials management and procurement outsourcing for the power generation and distribution industries.

In 2015 the company sold its fasteners segment to American Industrial Partners a middle-market private equity firm for $380 million in cash. The proceeds of the sale will be utilized for paying down debt and extending its acquisition strategy. The sale enhanced the company's focus on its other core segments.

HISTORY

Anixter International was founded in 1957 by two brothers Alan and Bill Anixter along with a small group of employees in Evanston Illinois. The company was known as Anixter Brothers at the time and it supplied distributors and wholesalers looking for an alternative to buying wire and cable in bulk quantities directly from manufacturers. The company went public on the American Stock Exchange in 1967. Anixter became an international company when Anixter United Kingdom was formed in 1972.

EXECUTIVES

EVP and CFO, Theodore A. (Ted) Dosch, $520,000 total compensation

EVP Human Resources, Rodney A. Smith, $300,000 total compensation

Vice President Utilities, Steven (Steve) Dean

EVP General Counsel and Corporate Secretary, Justin C. Choi

President and CEO, Robert J. (Bob) Eck, $930,000 total compensation

EVP Global Enterprise Cabling and Security Solutions, William A. (Bill) Galvin, $464,500 total compensation

EVP Operations, William A. (Bill) Standish, $430,000 total compensation

Vice President Strategic Sales Programs, Steve Keller

Vice President contrl, Terry Faber

Vice President Sales, Mike Eccleston

Vice President Marketing, Felice Tinelli

Area Sales Vice President, Jim Richter

EMEA Operations Vice President, Frederic Bernard

Vice President Marketing, Scott Quinton

Vice President Information Services, Pat Kelliher

Vice President Mining, Sam Pino

Regional Vice President, Terry Bender

Vice President Sales Anixter Security Solutions, Lee Mehler

Vice President National Accounts Business Development, Severin Mulligan

Vice President Internal Audit, Ania Ross

Vice President Channel Sales, Larry Spatz

Vice President, Kevin Newell

Vice President Sales Global Accounts, Mike Larkin

Vice President Of Purchasing, Dawn Galluzzi

Vice President Of Marketing, David Crossland

Area Vice President, Ron Hendry

Vice President Of Information Technology, Josh Gauci

Assistant Vice President Sales, Denny Stanton

Regional Vice President Region 3, Robert (Bob) Catney

Vice President Finance, Ken Maurer

Vice President Sales, Robert Nemecek

Vice President Marketing, Kimberly Thomas

Vice President Sales Global Accounts, Karen Delattre

Senior Vice President N.A. Operations, Jay Zwart

Senior Vice President Global Finance Anixter International Inc., Ted Dosch

Chairman, Samuel Zell, age 73

Auditors: Ernst & Young LLP

LOCATIONS

HQ: Anixter International Inc
2301 Patriot Blvd., Glenview, IL 60026
Phone: 224 521-8000
Web: www.anixter.com

PRODUCTS/OPERATIONS

2015 Sales

	% of total
Enterprise cabling & security	53
Electrical & electronic wire/cable	32
Original equipment manufacturing	15
Total	**100**

2015 Sales

	% of total
North America	69
Europe	17
Rest of world	14
Total	**100**

Selected Products and Services

Products
  Electrical wire and cable (power cable)
  Electronic wire and cable (coax)
  Fasteners and connectors ("C" class)
  Industrial networking communications
  Network cabling (copper and fiber)
  Networking wireless and voice electronics
  Security (video surveillance access control)
Supply chain services
  Database tracking
  Deployment
  Inventory management
  Logistics
  Product enhancement and packaging
  Sourcing

COMPETITORS

Acuity Brands	Ingram Micro
Agilysys	Kirby Risk
Air Products	Lawson Products
Airgas	MSC Industrial Direct
Arrow Electronics	Park-Ohio Holdings
Avnet	Patterson Companies
Border States Electric	Precision Industries
Consolidated	Premier Farnell
Electrical	Rexel
Crescent Electric	Richardson Electronics
Supply	Sonepar
Essendant	TESSCO
Fastenal	Tech Data
Genuine Parts	W.W. Grainger
Gexpro	WESCO International
Graybar Electric	Watsco
Henry Schein	

HISTORICAL FINANCIALS

Company Type: Public

Income Statement

FYE: January 2

	REVENUE ($ mil.)	NET INCOME ($ mil.)	NET PROFIT MARGIN	EMPLOYEES
01/15	6,445	194	3.0%	9,100
01/14*	6,226	200	3.2%	8,200
12/12	6,253	124	2.0%	8,300
12/11	6,146	188	3.1%	8,200
12/10	5,472	108	2.0%	7,989
Annual Growth	**4.2%**	**15.8%**	**—**	**3.3%**

*Fiscal year change

2015 Year-End Financials

Debt ratio: 33.67%
Return on equity: 18.08%
Cash ($ mil.): 92
Current ratio: 2.51
Long-term debt ($ mil.): 1,207

No. of shares (mil.): 33
Dividends
  Yield: —
  Payout: —
Market value ($ mil.): 2,922

	STOCK PRICE ($) FY Close	P/E High/Low		PER SHARE ($)		
				Earnings	Dividends	Book Value
01/15	88.18	18	13	5.84	0.00	34.19
01/14*	89.61	15	11	6.04	5.00	31.27
12/12	62.64	19	13	3.69	4.50	29.81
12/11	59.64	14	8	5.36	0.00	30.13
12/10	59.73	19	12	3.05	3.25	29.45
Annual Growth	**10.2%**	**—**	**—**	**17.6%**	**—**	**3.8%**

*Fiscal year change

Annaly Capital Management Inc

Annaly cannily invests its capital. A real estate investment trust (REIT) Annaly Capital Management invests in and manages a portfolio of mortgage-backed securities including mortgage pass-through certificates collateralized mortgage obligations and agency callable debentures. Commencing operations in 1997 the firm primarily invests in high-quality securities issued or guaranteed by the likes of Freddie Mac Fannie Mae and Ginnie Mae and backed by single-family residential mortgages. More than 95% of Annaly's assets are agency mortgage-backed securities which carry an implied AAA rating. The firm is externally managed by Annaly Management Company LLC.

Operations

As part of its business Annaly Capital boasts nearly 10 subsidiaries. Its Fixed Income Discount Advisory Company (FIDAC) subsidiary provides investment advisory and asset management services. RCap Securities operates as a broker/dealer. Shannon Funding provides warehouse financing to residential mortgage originators and corporate middle market lending specialist Charlesfort Capital Management. Annaly Capital's European advisory arm is FIDAC Europe while its security investment unit is FIDAC FSI. Annaly Commercial Real Estate Group acquires multi-family and commercial properties. All subsidiaries are also structured as REITs.

Geographic Reach

Based in New York Annaly Capital is a self-advised and self-managed REIT that operates globally.

Financial Performance

Annaly Capital's revenues and profits had been trending higher over the past few years thanks to unrealized and realized gains on investments as interest rates have declined and as investment markets have been favorable. In 2014 however both Annaly's revenues and profits sharply reversed course with the firm suffering a net loss of $842.1 million mostly as its unrealized gains on interest rates swaps turned into a $948.8 million loss (compared to a $2 billion gain in 2013) for the year. The REIT also collected less interest income on most of its investments as margins continued to be squeezed in the low-interest environment and incurred realized losses upon the termination of interest rate swaps and the selling of some of its investments and trading assets.Annaly's operating cash climbed sharply to $6.1 billion in 2014 after adjusting its earnings for non-cash items mostly related to net proceeds from repurchase agreements of RCap investments.

Strategy

Unlike many mortgage REITs Annaly doesn't focus on owning actual real estate. The company makes its money based on the interest rate spread: When interest rates go down Annaly's returns tend to go up. It does this by borrowing short-term loans which typically carry lower interest rates and using that money to invest in mortgage-backed securities which typically carry higher rates. As such the troubled economy actually benefited the REIT as lowered short-term interest rates widened the interest rate spread which translates into higher interest income.

Also part of Annaly's strategy the firm works to finance purchases of mortgage-backed securities with the proceeds from equity and debt offerings and repurchase agreements. It also seeks to minimize prepayment risk by structuring a diversified portfolio with a variety of prepayment characteristics and through other means as well as issues new equity or debt and increase the size of its balance sheet when opportunities in the market for mortgage-backed securities are likely to allow growth in earnings per share. The REIT has also been expanding its commercial real estate platform acquiring "quality commercial and multi-family properties with stable cash flows at attractive yields." In late 2014 subsidiary Annaly Commercial Real Estate Group acquired a portfolio of 11 grocery-anchored shopping centers spanning some 1.48 million square feet which would be overseen by New York-based commercial real estate company JADD Management. At the time Annaly had roughly $1.6 billion invested in commercial real estate loans and properties.Mergers and AcquisitionsIn April 2013 as part of kicking off Annaly's commercial real estate expansion strategy subsidiary CXS Acquisition Corporation purchased commercial real estate asset owner CreXus Investment Corporation and its full portfolio of its commercial properties. CreXus was renamed and became Annaly Commercial Real Estate Group.

EXECUTIVES

CFO, Glenn A. Votek, age 56, $91,346 total compensation
President CEO and Director, Kevin G. Keyes, age 47, $375,000 total compensation
CTO, Michael Maffattone
Chief Investment Officer Agency and RMBS, David L. Finkelstein
Chief Credit Officer, Timothy P. Coffey
Managing Director and Head of Agency and Non-Agency MBS Risk, Johanna Griffin
Managing Director Syndications, John Montesi
Vice President, Nathalie Uribe
Vice President, Gary Gordon
Executive Vice President, Laura Demare
Executive Vice President, Matthew (Matt) Higgins
Vice President, Jason Kump
Vice President, Sam Rodman
Chairman, Wellington J. Denahan, age 51
Auditors: Ernst & Young LLP

LOCATIONS

HQ: Annaly Capital Management Inc
1211 Avenue of the Americas, New York, NY 10036
Phone: 212 696-0100 **Fax:** 212 696-9809
Web: www.annaly.com

PRODUCTS/OPERATIONS

2014 Sales

	$ mil.	% of total
Interest income	2,632	100
Other income(loss)	(2747.6)	-
Total	**0**	**100**

Selected Subsidiaries

Fixed Income Discount Advisory Company Delaware corporation
RCap Securities Inc. Maryland corporation
FIDAC Housing Cycle Fund LLC Delaware limited liability company
FHC Master Fund Ltd. a Cayman Islands exempted company (wholly owned subsidiary of FIDAC Housing Cycle Fund LLC)
Shannon Funding LLC Delaware limited liability company
Charlesfort Capital Management LLC Delaware limited liability company
FIDAC FSI LLC Delaware limited liability company
CXS Acquisition Corporation a Maryland corporation

COMPETITORS

AG Mortgage Investment Trust	JAVELIN Mortgage
	MFA Financial
Capstead Mortgage	Newcastle Investment
Impac Mortgage Holdings	Redwood Trust
Institutional	iStar Financial Inc
Financial Markets	

HISTORICAL FINANCIALS

Company Type: Public

Income Statement

FYE: December 31

	ASSETS ($ mil.)	NET INCOME ($ mil.)	INCOME AS % OF ASSETS	EMPLOYEES
12/14	88,355	(842)	—	25
12/13	81,922	3,729	4.6%	48
12/12	133,452	1,735	1.3%	147
12/11	109,630	344	0.3%	147
12/10	83,026	1,267	1.5%	114
Annual Growth	**1.6%**	**—**	**—**	**(31.6%)**

2014 Year-End Financials

Debt ratio: 1.42%	No. of shares (mil.): 947
Return on equity: (-6.54%)	Dividends
Cash ($ mil.): 1,741	Yield: 11.1%
Current ratio: —	Payout: 150.0%
Long-term debt ($ mil.): —	Market value ($ mil.): 10,244

	STOCK PRICE ($) FY Close	P/E High/Low		PER SHARE ($) Earnings	Dividends	Book Value
12/14	10.81	—	—	(0.96)	1.20	14.06
12/13	9.97	4	3	3.74	1.50	13.09
12/12	14.04	10	8	1.71	2.05	16.81
12/11	15.96	51	42	0.37	1.97	16.28
12/10	17.92	9	7	2.04	2.65	15.68
Annual Growth	**(11.9%)**	**—**	**—**	**—**	**(18.0%)**	**(2.7%)**

Anthem Inc

Health benefits provider Anthem (formerly WellPoint) is the king of the Blues. Through its subsidiaries the firm provides health coverage to nearly 40 million members. One of the largest health insurers in the US it is a Blue Cross and Blue Shield Association (BCBSA) licensee in more than a dozen states (where it operates under the Anthem Empire and BCBS monikers) and provides plans under the Unicare Amerigroup and CareMore names in other parts of the country. Plans include PPO HMO indemnity and hybrid plans offered to employers individuals and Medicare and Medicaid recipients. It also provides administrative services to self-insured groups as well as specialty insurance products. In mid-2015 Anthem agreed to acquire rival Cigna.

HISTORY

Anthem's earliest predecessor prepaid hospital plan Blue Cross of Indiana was founded in 1944. Unlike other Blues Blue Cross of Indiana never received tax advantages or mandated discounts so it competed as a private insurer. Within two years it had 100000 members; by 1970 there were nearly 2 million.

Blue Shield of Indiana another Anthem precursor also grew rapidly after its 1946 formation as a mutual insurance company to cover doctors' services. The two organizations shared expenses and jointly managed the state's Medicare and Medicaid programs.

The 1970s and early 1980s were difficult as Indiana's economy stagnated and health insurance competition increased. In 1982 the joint operation restructured adding new management and service policies to improve its performance.

Following the 1982 merger of the national Blue Cross and Blue Shield organizations the Indiana Blues merged in 1985 as Associated Insurance Companies. The next year the company moved outside Indiana began diversifying to help insulate itself from such industry changes as the shift to managed care and renamed itself Associated Group to reflect a broader focus.

By 1990 Associated Group had more than 25 operating units with nationwide offerings including health insurance HMO services life insurance insurance brokerage financial services and software and services for the insurance industry.

The group grew throughout the mid-1990s buying health insurer Southeastern Mutual Insurance (including Kentucky Blue Cross and Blue Shield) in 1992 diversified insurer Federal Kemper (a Kemper Corporation subsidiary) in 1993 and Seattle-based property/casualty brokerage Pettit-Morry in 1994. That year it entered the health care delivery market with the creation of American Health Network.

In 1995 the company merged with Ohio Blues licensee Community Mutual and took the Anthem name. Merger-related charges caused a loss that year.

Anthem bounced back the next year thanks to cost-cutting and customers switching to its more profitable managed care plans. Anthem divested its individual life insurance and annuity business and its Anthem Financial subsidiaries. Its 1996 deal to buy Blue Cross and Blue Shield of New Jersey fell apart in 1997 because of New Jersey Blue's charitable status. Anthem did manage to buy Blue Cross and Blue Shield of Connecticut that year.

Anthem in 1997 sold four property/casualty insurance subsidiaries to Vesta Insurance Group. It bought the remainder of its Acordia property/casualty unit (workers' compensation) then sold Acordia's brokerage operations. That year Anthem was involved in court battles regarding the Blue mergers in Kentucky as well as in Connecticut where litigants feared a rise in their premiums. Expenses related to merging Blues organizations contributed to a loss that year.

Anthem shed the rest of its noncore operations in 1998 selling subsidiary Anthem Health and Life Insurance Company to Canadian insurer Great-West Life Assurance. Its proposed purchase of Blue Cross and Blue Shield of Maine (which it acquired in 2000) and merger with the Blues in Rhode Island were met with outcries similar to those that dogged earlier pairings.

Larry Glasscock was appointed president and CEO of the company in 1999. Under Glasscock's leadership Anthem aggressively expanded through mergers and acquisitions. It bought Blues plans in Colorado Nevada and New Hampshire in 1999 and finalized the acquisition of Maine's Blue plan in 2000.

In 2001 it became a publicly traded company and sold its military insurance business to Humana. In the next couple of years it snapped up Virginia-based Trigon Healthcare and a Wisconsin Blue plan.

And in 2004 Anthem made its biggest leap yet deciding to merge with WellPoint Health Networks in a deal that would make it the nation's largest health insurer. After the merger —which added Blue plans in California Georgia Missouri and Wisconsin —Anthem changed its name to WellPoint.

EXECUTIVES

EVP and Chief Administrative Officer, Gloria M. McCarthy, age 62, $666,926 total compensation
EVP Clinical Health Policy and Chief Medical Officer, Samuel R. Nussbaum, age 66
Chairman President and CEO, Joseph R. Swedish, age 63, $1,250,000 total compensation
EVP and President and CEO Commercial and Specialty Business, Ken R. Goulet, age 55, $750,022 total compensation
EVP and CFO, Wayne S. DeVeydt, age 45, $750,002 total compensation
President Specialty Business and West Region, Pam Kehaly
EVP and Chief Human Resources Officer, Jose D. Tomas, age 47
SVP and CIO, Thomas Miller
EVP and Chief Strategy Officer, Martin Silverstein, age 60
EVP and President Government Business, Peter D. Haytaian, age 45, $547,569 total compensation
EVP and General Counsel, Thomas C. Zielinski
President Dental, Michael Malouf
EVP and President Commercial and Specialty Business, Brian Griffin
President National Accounts, Morgan Kendrick
Vice President Business Information Technology, Laura Hancock
Regional Vice President, Tim Masheck
Assistant Vice President Information Technology Project Management Office, Sheri Coyner
Regional Vice President Of Sales And Account Mana, Paul Nobile
Regional Vice President and Medical Director, Tony Linares
Medical Director, Pete Bowers
Medical Director, Ravinder Mohini
Vice President, Melisa Hinders
Vice President, Renee Hunter
Vice President, Keith Heckel
Vice President, Ryan Judy

Vice President Provider Engagement And Contracting, Andrew (Andy) Ellis
Vice President Real Estate, Jim Ardell
Vice President of Customer Support, John M (Jack) Murphy
Vice President Medicare Rev Management, Eric Cahow
Assistant Vice President Network Development, Christina Pike
Vice President Investor Relations, Doug Simpson
National Staff Vice President Medical Director Medicare Advantage, Richard (Dick) Frank
Vice President Enterprise Technology Operations, Tom Place
RVP Finance, Sabine D'Amico
General Vice President Manager, Steve Scott
Associate Vice President HPS Operations, Janie Leo
RVP Product Management, Michele Manowitz
Vice President Application Devpmt, Darren Ghanayem
Treasurer, David (Dave) Kretchmer
Auditors: Ernst & Young LLP

LOCATIONS

HQ: Anthem Inc
120 Monument Circle, Indianapolis, IN 46204-4903
Phone: 317 488-6000
Web: www.antheminc.com

PRODUCTS/OPERATIONS

2014 Premiums

	% of total
Commercial and specialty business	54
Government business	46
Total	**100**

2014 Sales

	% of total
Premiums	93
Administrative fee	6
Other revenue	-
Net investment income	1
Net realized gains on investments	-
Other	-
Total	**100**

Selected Operations

Blue-licensed subsidiaries
  Anthem Blue Cross (California)
  Anthem Blue Cross and Blue Shield (Colorado Connecticut Kentucky Indiana Maine Missouri Nevada New Hampshire Ohio Virginia Wisconsin)
  Blue Cross Blue Shield of Georgia
  Empire Blue Cross Blue Shield (New York)
Non-Blue Cross Subsidiaries and Affiliates
  AIM Specialty Health (benefits management)
  American Imaging Management (Diagnostic imaging)
  Anthem Life Insurance (life and accident)
  Anthem Workers' Compensation
  CareMore (Medicare Advantage and special needs plans)
  DeCare Dental (Dental benefit management)
  HealthCore (Clinical research)
  HealthLink (Administrative services)
  Golden West Dental & Vision (Dental/vision California)
  Meridian Resource Company (Cost containment)
  National Government Services (Administration of government contracts)
  Resolution Health (Cost containment)
  TrustSolutions (Fraud prevention)
  UniCare (Health care plans)

COMPETITORS

Aetna
Assurant
CIGNA
ConnectiCare
Coventry Health Care
Delta Dental Plans
HCSC

Harvard Pilgrim
Health Net
Humana
Kaiser Foundation Health Plan
Medical Mutual
MetLife
Molina Healthcare
Southern California Permanente Medical Group
UnitedHealth Group
WellCare Health Plans

HISTORICAL FINANCIALS

Company Type: Public

Income Statement

FYE: December 31

	REVENUE ($ mil.)	NET INCOME ($ mil.)	NET PROFIT MARGIN	EMPLOYEES
12/14	73,874	2,569	3.5%	51,500
12/13	71,023	2,489	3.5%	48,200
12/12	61,711	2,655	4.3%	43,500
12/11	60,710	2,646	4.4%	37,700
12/10	58,801	2,887	4.9%	37,500
Annual Growth	**5.9%**	**(2.9%)**	**—**	**8.3%**

2014 Year-End Financials

Debt ratio: 24.41%	No. of shares (mil.): 268
Return on equity: 10.49%	Dividends
Cash ($ mil.): 2,151	Yield: 1.3%
Current ratio: 1.72	Payout: 22.7%
Long-term debt ($ mil.): 14,127	Market value ($ mil.): 33,693

	STOCK PRICE ($) FY Close	P/E High/Low		PER SHARE ($) Earnings	Dividends	Book Value
12/14	125.67	14	9	8.99	1.75	90.45
12/13	92.39	11	7	8.20	1.50	84.44
12/12	60.92	9	6	8.18	1.15	78.11
12/11	66.25	11	8	7.25	1.00	68.62
12/10	56.86	10	7	6.94	0.00	63.04
Annual Growth	**21.9%**	**—**	**—**	**6.7%**	**—**	**9.4%**

Anworth Mortgage Asset Corp.

What's an Anworth? Depends on the mortgage market. An externally managed real estate investment trust (REIT) Anworth Mortgage invests in mortgage-related assets primarily mortgage-backed securities (MBS) guaranteed by the US government or federally sponsored entities Fannie Mae Freddie Mac and Ginnie Mae. As a REIT the trust is exempt from paying federal income tax so long as it distributes dividends back to shareholders. Anworth Mortgage funds its investment activities mainly through short-term loans.

EXECUTIVES

EVP and Chief Investment Officer, Joseph E. McAdams, age 46, $700,000 total compensation
EVP, Heather U. Baines, age 73, $50,495 total compensation
Chairman President and CEO, Joseph Lloyd McAdams, age 69, $925,000 total compensation
SVP and Portfolio Manager, Bistra Pashamova, age 44, $275,000 total compensation
CFO Treasurer and Secretary, Charles J. Siegel, age 65, $250,000 total compensation
Auditors: McGladrey LLP

LOCATIONS

HQ: Anworth Mortgage Asset Corp.
1299 Ocean Avenue, Second Floor, Santa Monica, CA 90401
Phone: 310 255-4493   **Fax:** 310 434-0070
Web: www.anworth.com

PRODUCTS/OPERATIONS

2013 Sales

	% of total
Interest income	
Interest on Agency MBS	95
Gain on sales of Agency MBS	5
Recovery on Non-Agency MBS	-
Total	**100**

COMPETITORS

AG Mortgage Investment Trust	Huntington Preferred Capital
ARMOUR Residential REIT	Impac Mortgage Holdings
American Capital Agency Corp.	Institutional Financial Markets
American Capital Mortgage	MFA Financial
Annaly Capital Management	Newcastle Investment
Capstead Mortgage	Redwood Trust
DVL	Two Harbors
Hatteras Financial	Webster Preferred Capital

HISTORICAL FINANCIALS

Company Type: Public

Income Statement

FYE: December 31

	ASSETS ($ mil.)	NET INCOME ($ mil.)	INCOME AS % OF ASSETS	EMPLOYEES
12/14	7,298	28	0.4%	—
12/13	8,619	75	0.9%	—
12/12	9,285	100	1.1%	—
12/11	8,813	122	1.4%	—
12/10	7,790	110	1.4%	12
Annual Growth	(1.6%)	(28.7%)	—	—

2014 Year-End Financials

Debt ratio: 0.51%	No. of shares (mil.): 109
Return on equity: —	Dividends
Cash ($ mil.): 14	Yield: 10.6%
Current ratio: —	Payout: 311.1%
Long-term debt ($ mil.): —	Market value ($ mil.): 573

	STOCK PRICE ($) FY Close	P/E High/Low	PER SHARE ($) Earnings	Dividends	Book Value
12/14	5.25	31 23	0.18	0.56	7.15
12/13	4.21	13 8	0.49	0.50	6.50
12/12	5.78	10 8	0.67	0.69	7.66
12/11	6.28	8 7	0.90	0.94	7.53
12/10	7.00	8 7	0.87	0.97	7.39
Annual Growth	(6.9%)	— —	(32.6%)	(12.8%)	(0.8%)

Apache Corp.

There's more than only a patch of oil for Apache. The oil and gas exploration and production company has onshore and offshore operations in major oil patches around the world including in North America as well as in Australia Egypt and the UK North Sea. In North America it is active in the Gulf of Mexico the Gulf Coast of Texas and Louisiana the Permian Basin in West Texas the Anadarko Basin in Oklahoma and Canada's Western Sedimentary Basin. In 2014 the company reported worldwide estimated proved reserves of 2.4 billion barrels of oil equivalent. In 2015 Anadarko Petroleum made a bid to acquire Apache which was rebuffed.

HISTORY

Originally Raymond Plank wanted to start a magazine. Then it was an accounting and tax-assistance service. Plank and his co-founding partner Truman Anderson had no experience in any of these occupations but their accounting business succeeded. In the early 1950s Plank and Anderson branched out again founding APA a partnership to invest in new ventures including oil and gas exploration. The partnership founded Apache Oil in Minnesota in 1954. Investors put up the money and Apache managed the drilling spreading the risk over several projects.

As problems with government regulations in the oil industry mounted during the 1960s Apache diversified into real estate. The real estate operations were pivotal in driving a wedge between Plank and Anderson. In 1963 Anderson called a board meeting to ask the directors to fire Plank. Instead Anderson resigned and Plank took over.

Apache's holdings soon encompassed 24 firms including engineering electronics farming and water-supply subsidiaries. Understanding that its fortunes were tied to varying oil and gas prices the company reassessed its diversified structure in the 1970s. When the energy crisis rocketed oil prices skyward Apache sold its non-energy operations which would have been hurt by the price increases.

Apache formed Apache Petroleum in 1981 as an investment vehicle to take advantage of tax laws favoring limited partnerships. Initially the strategy was a success but it fell victim in the mid-1980s to a one-two punch: Oil prices sank like a rock and Congress put an end to the tax advantage. After suffering its first loss in 1986 Apache reorganized into a conventional exploration and production company.

Still under Plank's leadership the company began steadily buying oil and gas properties and companies in 1991. That year it purchased oil and gas sites with more than 100 million barrels of reserves from Amoco and put the wells back into production. By buying Hadson Energy Resources which operated fields in western Australia Apache gained entry into the relatively unexplored region in 1993.

In 1995 Apache merged with Calgary Canada-based DEKALB Energy (later renamed DEK Energy) and continued picking up properties. It bought $600 million worth of US reserves from Texaco (acquired by Chevron in 2001) that year. In 1996 it expanded its Chinese operations and bought Phoenix Resource Companies which operated solely in Egypt. A 1998 agreement with Texaco expanded its Chinese acreage thirtyfold. Apache also bought oil and gas properties and production facilities in waters off western Australia from a Mobil unit.

Apache joined with FX Energy and Polish Oil & Gas in 1998 to begin exploratory drilling in Poland. It also worked with XCL and China National Oil & Gas Exploration & Development in Bohai Bay though the project was slowed by a dispute between Apache and XCL over costs. In 1999 Apache bought Gulf of Mexico assets from a unit of Royal Dutch Shell and acquired oil and gas properties in western Canada from Shell Canada. That year Apache sold its Ivory Coast oil and gas holdings for $46 million.

Still shopping however Apache agreed in 2000 to buy assets in western Canada and Argentina with proved reserves of more than 700 billion cu. ft. of natural gas equivalent from New Zealand's Fletcher Challenge Energy. To help pay for the $600 million acquisition which closed in 2001 Apache sold $100 million in stock to Shell which acquired other Fletcher Challenge Energy assets. Apache bought the Canadian assets of Phillips Petroleum (later ConocoPhillips) for $490 million in 2000 and acquired the Egyptian assets of Repsol YPF for $410 million in 2001.

Late in 2002 in a move aimed at boosting its natural gas production by more than 10% Apache acquired 234000 net acres of land in southern Louisiana for $260 million. That year the company also announced three oil discoveries in the Carnarvon Basin offshore Western Australia.

Apache acquired UK and US oil and gas assets in 2003 from BP for $1.3 billion. The main prize was the Forties field one of the North Sea's oldest discoveries (dating back to the early 1970s) and its largest.

In 2004 it acquired more than two dozen mature US and Canadian fields from Exxon Mobil for $347 million and Gulf of Mexico properties from Anadarko Petroleum for $525 million. In 2005 Hurricane Katrina destroyed eight of its 241 Gulf rigs.

In 2009 Apache founder Raymond Plank retired as chairman of the company. He had been its chief executive from Apache's founding in 1954 until his retirement in 2002 when he remained as chairman. CEO Steven Farris took up the additional title of chairman when Plank stepped down completely.

The company bounced back from a sup-par 2009 when the global recession low commodities prices and a slump in demand suppressed its revenues.

In 2010 it bought Gulf of Mexico shelf assets from Devon Energy (which is shedding assets to raise cash) for $1 billion. The acquisition added some 41 million barrels of proved reserves and some 477200 acres to Apache's asset base.

It also acquired Mariner Energy for $2.7 billion (including Mariner Energy's debt of $1.6 billion) giving the company an entry into the deepwater Gulf of Mexico. Mariner's deepwater portfolio includes 125 blocks seven discoveries under development and more than 50 prospects. The deal is a natural extension of Apache's commitment to develop the Gulf of Mexico as a primary area of production and anticipates a rebounding economy and an increasing demand for oil.

With BP looking to raise cash to defray the cost of its rig disaster in the Gulf of Mexico in 2010 Apache took the opportunity to buy BP assets in Canada Egypt and the US (Permian Basin) for about $7 billion. The deal boosted Apache's estimated proved reserves by 385 million barrels of oil equivalent.

In Canada the company moved in 2010 to expand its supply base buying 51% of a proposed liquefied natural gas (LNG) export terminal in British Columbia operated by Kitimat LNG Inc.

The company grew its North Sea assets in 2012 buying Exxon Mobil's Beryl Field and related properties for about $1.75 billion.

Growing its unconventional assets in the US that year the company acquired Cordillera Energy Partners for $2.85 billion. The privately held company owned 254000 net acres of tight sand plays in Oklahoma and Texas. In 2012 Apache also bought 49% of Burrup Holdings an ammonia fertilizer plant in Western Australia for $439 million. The deal with one of the world's largest ammonia plants secures a long-term market for Apache's natural gas production in the region.

In 2012 Apache and Chevron agreed to build and operate the Kitimat LNG project and develop natural gas resources at the Liard and Horn River basins in British Columbia Canada. Chevron Canada will assume operatorship of the LNG plant and related pipeline.

EXECUTIVES

EVP and CTO, Michael S. (Mike) Bahorich, age 58, $700,000 total compensation
VP Information Technology, Aaron S. G. Merrick, age 53
Vice President Expl and Product Gulf R, Jon Jeppesen
Vice President Tax, Jon Sauer
EVP and General Counsel, P. Anthony Lannie, age 61, $665,625 total compensation
Senior Region Vice President Houston Region, James L. (Jim) House, age 54
EVP Human Resources, Margery M. (Margie) Harris, age 54
President and CEO, John J. Christmann, age 48, $725,000 total compensation
EVP Corporate Reservoir Engineering, W. Kregg Olson, age 61
EVP International and Offshore Exploration and Production Technology, Thomas E. Voytovich, age 58, $725,000 total compensation
Regional VP Egypt and General Manager Apache Egypt, Thomas M. (Tom) Maher, age 57
Region VP UK Region and Managing Director Apache North Sea, Cory L. Loegering, age 60
Senior Region Vice President Permian Region, Faron J. Thibodeaux, age 55
Staff VP North America Oil and Gas Marketing, Mark J. Bright, age 53
Region VP Canada Region and President Apache Canada, Grady L. Ables, age 54
Senior Region Vice President Delaware Basin Region, Steven J. Keenan, age 59
VP North American Land Government Affairs and Real Estate, Timothy R. Custer, age 54
EVP and CFO, Stephen J. Riney, age 55
Vice President Investor Relations, Gary T Clark
Executive Vice President & Region Vice President Central Region, Robert V Johnston
Regional Vice President Australia Region, Brett Darley
Regional Vice President Gulf Coast Region, Mark Bauer
Vice President Environmental Health and Safety Organization, Jon Graham
Executive Vice President and General Counsel, P A Lannie
Vice President Gulf Coast Onshore Region, Paul McKinney
RVP Australia, Tim Wall
Chairman, John E. Lowe, age 57
Secretary Admin Ii, Jan Ostendorf
Auditors: Ernst & Young LLP

LOCATIONS

HQ: Apache Corp.
One Post Oak Central, 2000 Post Oak Boulevard, Suite 100, Houston, TX 77056-4400
Phone: 713 296-6000
Web: www.apachecorp.com

2014 Sales

	$ mil.	% of total
US	5,744	41
Egypt	3,539	26
UK (North Sea)	2,316	17
Australia	1,058	8
Canada	1,092	8
Total	13,749	100

COMPETITORS

Abraxas Petroleum	Hess Corporation
Adams Resources	Jones Energy
Anadarko Petroleum	Pioneer Natural
BP	Resources
Chesapeake Energy	Qatargas
Chevron	Range Resources
Devon Energy	Royal Dutch Shell
EOG	Santos Ltd
Exxon Mobil	XTO Energy
Helmerich & Payne	

HISTORICAL FINANCIALS
Company Type: Public

Income Statement

FYE: December 31

	REVENUE ($ mil.)	NET INCOME ($ mil.)	NET PROFIT MARGIN	EMPLOYEES
12/14	13,851	(5,060)	—	4,950
12/13	16,054	2,288	14.3%	5,342
12/12	17,078	2,001	11.7%	5,976
12/11	16,888	4,584	27.1%	5,299
12/10	12,092	3,032	25.1%	4,449
Annual Growth	3.5%	—	—	2.7%

2014 Year-End Financials

Debt ratio: 20.10%
Return on equity: (-17.06%)
Cash ($ mil.): 769
Current ratio: 1.75
Long-term debt ($ mil.): 11,245
No. of shares (mil.): 376
Dividends
  Yield: 1.5%
  Payout: —
Market value ($ mil.): 23,596

	STOCK PRICE ($) FY Close	P/E High/Low	PER SHARE ($) Earnings	Dividends	Book Value
12/14	62.67	— —	(14.06)	0.95	68.89
12/13	85.94	17 12	5.50	0.77	84.38
12/12	78.50	23 15	4.92	0.66	80.00
12/11	90.58	11 7	11.47	0.60	75.48
12/10	119.23	14 10	8.46	0.60	63.75
Annual Growth	(14.9%)	— —	—	12.2%	2.0%

APPLE HOSPITALITY REIT INC

Auditors: ERNST & YOUNG LLP RICHMOND V

LOCATIONS

HQ: APPLE HOSPITALITY REIT INC
814 E MAIN ST, RICHMOND, VA 232193306
Phone: 8043448121
Web: WWW.APPLEREITNINE.COM

HISTORICAL FINANCIALS
Company Type: Private

Income Statement

FYE: December 31

	ASSETS ($ mil.)	NET INCOME ($ mil.)	INCOME AS % OF ASSETS	EMPLOYEES
12/14	3,779	6	0.2%	6
12/13	1,491	115	7.7%	—
12/12	1,526	75	4.9%	—
12/11	1,700	0	—	—
Annual Growth	30.5%	—	—	—

Apple Inc

Apple has an "i" for revolutionary technology. Since release the company's iPhone —which accounts for the largest portion of its sales —has spurred a revolution in cell phones and mobile computing. Apple also continues to innovate its core Mac desktop and laptop computers all of which feature its OS X operating system including the iMac all-in-one desktop for the consumer and education markets the MacBook Air ultra-portable laptop and the high-end Mac Pro and MacBook Pro for consumers and professionals. The company's popular iPad tablet computer has become another game-changer in the consumer market. It generates nearly two-thirds of sales outside the US.

HISTORY

College dropouts Steve Jobs (1955-2011) and Steve Wozniak founded Apple in 1976 in California's Santa Clara Valley. After Jobs' first sales call brought an order for 50 units the duo built the Apple I in his garage and sold it without a monitor keyboard or casing. Demand convinced Jobs there was a distinct market for small computers and the company's name (a reference to Jobs' stint on an Oregon farm) and the computer's user-friendly look and feel set it apart from others.

By 1977 Wozniak added a keyboard color monitor and eight peripheral device slots (which gave the machine considerable versatility and inspired numerous third-party add-on devices and software). Sales jumped from $7.8 million in 1978 to $117 million in 1980 the year Apple went public. In 1983 Wozniak left the firm and Jobs hired PepsiCo's John Sculley as president. Apple rebounded from failed product introductions that year by unveiling the Macintosh in 1984. After tumultuous struggles with Sculley Jobs left in 1985 and founded NeXT a designer of applications for developing software. That year Sculley ignored Microsoft founder Bill Gates' appeal for Apple to license its products and make the Microsoft platform an industry standard.

Apple blazed the desktop publishing trail in 1986 with its Mac Plus and LaserWriter printers. The following year it formed the software firm that later became Claris (and ultimately FileMaker). The late 1980s brought new competition from Microsoft whose Windows operating system (OS) featured a graphical interface akin to Apple's. Apple sued but lost its claim to copyright protection in 1992.

In 1993 Apple unveiled the Newton handheld computer but sales were slow. Earnings fell drastically so the company trimmed its workforce. (Sculley was among the departed.) In 1994 Apple cried "uncle" and began licensing clones of its OS hoping a flurry of cheaper Mac-alikes would encourage software developers. By 1996 struggling Apple realized Mac clones were stealing sales. That year it hired Gilbert Amelio formerly of National Semiconductor as CEO.

The company bought NeXT in 1997 but sales kept dropping and it subsequently cut about 30% of its workforce canceled projects and trimmed research costs. Meanwhile Apple's board ousted Amelio and Jobs took the position back on an interim basis. The CEO forged a surprising alliance with Microsoft which included releasing a Mac version of Microsoft's popular office software. To protect market share Jobs also stripped the cloning license from chief imitator Power Computing and put it out of business.

In 1998 Apple jumped back into the race with its colorful cocktail of iMacs and its first server software the Mac OS X. That year the company also revamped its profitable Claris unit (by cutting 300 employees shifting most operations to Apple and renaming it FileMaker) and stopped making its Newton handheld device and printer products.

Apple in 1999 opened a new chapter in portable computing with the introduction of its iBook laptop and (taking a cue from Dell) began selling built-to-order systems online. In 2000 after two and a half years as the semipermanent executive in charge Jobs took the "interim" out of his title and revamped the company's Web site around a suite of consumer Internet services. Jobs unveiled overhauled desktop lines later that year including an eight-inch cube-shaped G4. The company ended 2000 on a sour note as an industrywide slowdown and poor response to the G4 cube resulted in Apple's first unprofitable quarter in years.

Apple opened 2001 with another round of product upgrades including faster processors components such as CD and DVD burners and an ultraslim version of its PowerBook called Titanium. The company also made a move to reclaim some of its slipping share in the education market purchasing software maker PowerSchool. Soon Apple confirmed a long-rumored plan to open a chain of retail stores in the US. The company then acquired DVD authoring software maker Spruce Technologies. In line with its strategy to market Macs as "digital hubs" for devices such as cameras and other peripherals Apple closed the year with the introduction of a digital music player called the iPod.

In 2002 Apple introduced a new look for its iMac line; featuring a half-dome base and a flat-panel display supported by a pivoting arm the redesign was the first departure from the original (and at the time radical) all-in-one design since iMac's debut in 1998. Looking to reclaim market share in the education sector Apple then introduced the eMac —a computer similar to the iMac to be sold only to students and educators (Apple later introduced a retail version). It continued its product push that year with the announcement that it would begin offering a rack-mount server called Xserve. In 2004 Apple debuted a streamlined iMac design powered by its G5 processor.

Apple announced it would begin incorporating Intel processors into its PC lines in 2005 ending more than a decade of using PowerPC microprocessors; the transition was completed the following year. Also that year Apple Motorola and Cingular Wireless (now AT&T Mobility) announced the debut of a mobile phone with iTunes functionality. Apple also unveiled the iPod nano an updated (and even smaller) version of its miniature iPod model as well as an iPod capable of playing video. In 2006 Apple reached a settlement in a dispute with Creative Technology over technology used in digital music players; Apple agreed to pay the company $100 million in exchange for a license to use Creative's patent related to navigation and organization.

The company also launched an online movie service in 2006 and previewed a device called iTV for watching downloaded content on televisions. (Apple announced availability of its television device redubbed Apple TV early the following year.)

Apple unveiled a mobile phone offering called the iPhone in 2007. To reflect the growing breadth of its product portfolio the company announced it would change its name from Apple Computer to simply Apple. The company kicked off 2008 with the release of an updated Apple TV device in conjunction with an iTunes movie rental service.

Looking toward the continued development of its mobile devices Apple purchased P.A. Semi a developer of low-power processors in 2008. In an-

other move intended to bring more of its chip design in-house Apple bought Intrinsity a provider of chip design software in 2010.

After beginning 2011 with a leave of absence and then stepping down as CEO Steve Jobs died on October 5 2011. COO Tim Cook had been named CEO after Jobs' resignation though Jobs retained the chairman title until his death.

EXECUTIVES

CEO, Timothy D. (Tim) Cook, age 54, $1,748,462 total compensation
SVP Worldwide Marketing, Philip W. Schiller, age 55, $494,942 total compensation
SVP Software Engineering, Craig Federighi, age 46
SVP Retail and Online Stores, Angela Ahrendts, age 54, $411,538 total compensation
SVP Internet Software and Services, Eduardo H. (Eddy) Cue, age 51, $947,596 total compensation
Chief Design Officer, Jonathan Ive
VP Marketing Communications, Tor Myhren, age 43
SVP and CFO, Luca Maestri, age 52, $717,211 total compensation
COO, Jeffrey E. (Jeff) Williams, age 51, $947,596 total compensation
SVP Hardware Engineering, Daniel (Dan) Riccio, age 53, $866,061 total compensation
SVP Hardware Technologies, Johny Srouji
Vice President Product Design, Dan Riccio
Vice President Procurement Vice President World Wide Procurement, Jeff Williams
National Sales Manager, Todd Conneely
Senior Vice President, Dan Whisenhunt
Vice President, Jennifer Henard
Vice President Engineering, Lucy Chen
Senior Vice President General Counsel And Secretary, John (Jack) Phillips
Vice President, Eric Herm
Vice President Of It, Oconnor Niall
First Vice President Of Human Resources, Ann Bowers
Vice President Legal Marketing, Kevin Saul
Vice President Business Development, Mark Thompson
Vice President Of Product Design, Doug Field
Director, Arthur D. (Art) Levinson, age 65
Auditors: Ernst & Young LLP

LOCATIONS

HQ: Apple Inc
 1 Infinite Loop, Cupertino, CA 95014
Phone: 408 996-1010   **Fax:** 408 974-2483
Web: www.apple.com

2014 Sales

	$ mil.	% of total
Americas	65,232	36
Asia/Pacific		
China	29,846	16
Japan	14,982	8
Other countries	10,344	6
Europe	40,927	22
Retail	21,462	12
Total	**182,795**	**100**

PRODUCTS/OPERATIONS

2014 Sales

	% of total
iPhone	56
iPad	17
Mac	13
iTunes software and services	10
Accessories	3
iPod	1
Total	**100**

Selected Products

Hardware
 Desktop computers (iMac Mac mini Mac Pro)
 Displays (Cinema Thunderbolt)
 External hard drives (Time Capsule)
 Keyboards
 Media devices (Apple TV)
 Mice (Mighty Mouse)
 Mobile phones (iPhone)
 Portable computers (MacBook MacBook Air MacBook Pro)
 Portable digital music player (iPod iPod nano iPod shuffle iPod touch)
 Rack-mount servers (Xserve)
 Stereo systems (iPod Hi-Fi)
 Storage systems (Xserve RAID)
 Tablet computers (iPad)
 Wearable technology (Apple Watch)
 Webcams (iSight)
 Wireless networking systems (AirPort)
Software
 MultimediaDVD Studio Pro FinalCut GarageBand iDVD iLife suite iMovie iPhoto iTunes Quicktime Soundtrack)
 Networking (Apple Remote Desktop AppleShare IP)
 Operating system (OS X)
 Personal productivity (AppleWorks FileMaker iWork Keynote Pages)
 Server (Mac OS X Server)
 Storage area network (SAN) file system (Xsan)
 Web browser (Safari)
Online Services
 Applications for iPad iPhone iPod touch (App Store)
 Applications for Mac (Mac App Store)
 Cloud service (iCloud)
 E-books (iBooks)
 Electronic greeting cards (iCard)
 E-mail (Webmail)
 Online multimedia store (iTunes)
 Personal Web page creation (HomePage)
 Remote network storage (iDisk)
 Software (antivirus backup)
 Technical support (AppleCare)

COMPETITORS

AT&T	MTV Networks
Acer	MediaNet Digital
Adobe Systems	Microsoft
Amazon.com	NEC
Best Buy	Netflix
BlackBerry	Nokia
Bose	Oracle
Cisco Systems	Panasonic Corp
Comcast	Philips Electronics
Creative Technology	RealNetworks
D-Link	Red Hat
Dell	Samsung Electronics
Ericsson	SanDisk
Fujitsu Technology Solutions	Seagate Technology
Google	Sharp Electronics
HP	Sony
HTC Corporation	Sony Mobile
IBM	Target Corporation
Intel	Time Warner Cable
Iriver	Toshiba
Kyocera	Wal-Mart
LG Electronics	Yahoo!
Lenovo	eMusic.com

HISTORICAL FINANCIALS

Company Type: Public

Income Statement

FYE: September 26

	REVENUE ($ mil.)	NET INCOME ($ mil.)	NET PROFIT MARGIN	EMPLOYEES
09/15	233,715	53,394	22.8%	110,000
09/14	182,795	39,510	21.6%	97,000
09/13	170,910	37,037	21.7%	84,400
09/12	156,508	41,733	26.7%	76,100
09/11	108,249	25,922	23.9%	63,300
Annual Growth	**21.2%**	**19.8%**	**—**	**14.8%**

2015 Year-End Financials

Debt ratio: 22.19%—
Return on equity: 46.38%
Cash ($ mil.): 21,120
Current ratio: 1.11
Long-term debt ($ mil.): 53,463

Dividends
Yield: 0.0%
Payout: 21.4%
Market value ($ mil.): —

	STOCK PRICE ($) FY Close	P/E High/Low	PER SHARE ($) Earnings	Dividends	Book Value
09/15	114.71	14 10	9.22	1.98	21.39
09/14	100.75	100 14	6.45	1.81	19.02
09/13	482.75	117 68	5.68	1.63	19.63
09/12	667.11	110 57	6.31	0.38	17.98
09/11	404.30	103 70	3.95	0.00	11.78
Annual Growth	(27.0%)	— —	23.6%	—	16.1%

Applied Materials, Inc.

Applied Materials makes the machines that make computer chips flat panel TVs and solar energy devices. The company's equipment vies for supremacy in many segments of the chip-making process including deposition (layering film on wafers) etching (removing portions of chip material to allow precise construction of circuits) and semiconductor metrology and inspection equipment. The company's plan to acquire its rival Tokyo Electron the second biggest equipment maker died in 2015 due to antitrust concern from US regulators.

Operations

Applied operates in four reportable segments: Silicon Systems Group Applied Global Services Display and Energy and Environmental Solutions.

The Silicon Systems Group 64% of revenue segment develops manufactures and sells a wide range of manufacturing equipment used to fabricate semiconductor chips also referred to as integrated circuits (ICs). The Applied Global Services segment 26% of revenue encompasses products and services designed to improve the performance and productivity and reduce the environmental impact of the fab operations of semiconductor LCD and solar PV manufacturers.

The Display Segment 8% includes Applied's products for manufacturing thin film transistor liquid crystal displays (TFT- LCDs) for televisions personal computers (PCs) tablet PCs smartphones and other consumer-oriented electronic applications. The Energy and Environmental Solutions segment 2% includes manufacturing systems to produce products for the generation and conservation of energy.

Geographic Reach

Applied has operations in the US Asia/Pacific and Europe. Customers in the Asia/Pacific region (where Taiwan accounts for 27% of total revenue) represented more than three quarters of total sales in 2015 (ended October). Customers in the US accounted for 17% and customers from Europe contributed the remaining 7%.

Sales and Marketing

Due to the highly technical nature of its products Applied's direct sales force does most of the company's marketing and selling worldwide. Leading customers for Applied's chip making equipment include Taiwan Semiconductor Manufacturing Company (18% of sales) Samsung Electronics (15% of sales).

Financial Performance

Applied posted its second straight year of revenue growth and third consecutive year of profit

growth in 2015 (ended October). The company might be climbing back to its all-time high revenue and profit marks reached in 2011 when it reported $10.5 billion in revenue and turned a profit of $1.9 billion.

The company's revenue was $9.6 billion in 2015. The increases in the Applied Global Services and Display segments outpaced the Silicon Systems segment's increase. Applied Global Services sales were up $331 million a 15% increase and Display revenue rose $154 million a 27% increase. Silicon Systems showed a 4% increase for the year up $157 million. Revenue from the Energy and Environmental Solutions segment fell 24% (following a 60% increase in 2014).

Increased sales helped propel net income to a 28% increase to $1.4 billion n 2015. The company also set aside less for income taxes.

Applied's cash flow from operations moderated to $1.16 billion in 2015 from $1.8 billion om 2014 due to changes in inventories and deferred revenue.

Strategy

Applied spends about 15% of its revenue on research and development each year to stay ahead of the requirements of semiconductor companies for equipment to make smaller denser and cheaper computer chips. The chip industry is volatile usually rising or falling with economic conditions. Applied also must contend with fewer chip makers. More chips companies rely on third parties such as Taiwan Semiconductor Manufacturing Corp. to make their products. Giant chip companies such as Intel and Samsung still do most of their own manufacturing.

In 2015 Applied restructured its Energy and Environmental segment to reduce costs to reach a lower break-even level.

To keep up with the chip industry's constant drive toward smaller circuits larger wafers and new technologies such as copper interconnects Applied relies heavily R&D efforts. The company spends more than 15% of sales on R&D each year.

In order to be closer to its customers Applied has established R&D support and manufacturing facilities outside the US with primary offices in China Germany India Israel Italy Singapore South Korea Switzerland and Taiwan. The company also outsources certain of its manufacturing and supply chain functions to third parties that are located in the US India China South Korea and Malaysia among other countries.

To keep up with the chip industry's constant drive toward smaller circuits larger wafers and new technologies such as copper interconnects Applied relies heavily R&D efforts. The company spends more than 15% of sales on R&D each year.

Applied uses a combination of acquisitions and internal development to bolster its moves into the few areas of chip manufacturing —such as atomic layer deposition and ion implantation —where it is not already a major player.

Applied's strategic priorities include increasing its presence in wafer fab and display equipment and services and improving profitability of its solar operations. Applied intends to continue investment in 300mm 450mm and other semiconductor technologies to strengthen the product pipeline and to invest in the enhancement of technical relationships with customers.

Mergers and Acquisitions

Applied Materials and Tokyo Electron halted their proposed merger in April 2015 because they decided they couldn't clear antitrust concerns of regulators. The deal would have combined the two biggest companies in their industry but allowed them to cut costs and increase efficiencies. Now Applied will have to find other ways to deal with the rising costs of equipping a semiconductor fab with increasingly sophisticated instruments.

HISTORY

Early History

Applied Materials was founded in 1967 in Mountain View California as a maker of chemical vapor deposition systems for fabricating semiconductors. After years of rapid growth the company went public in 1972. Two years later it purchased wafer maker Galamar Industries.

In 1975 Applied Materials suffered a 45% drop in sales as the semiconductor industry (and the US economy) contracted. Financial and managerial problems plagued the company following the recession so in 1976 James Morgan a former division manager for conglomerate Textron was chosen to replace founder Michael McNeilly as CEO. Two years later Morgan also became chairman.

After selling Galamar (1977) and other non-core units and extending the company's line of credit Morgan announced a plan to move into Japan. The company's first joint venture Applied Materials Japan was set up in 1979.

Applied got into the ion implanter market in 1980 through its acquisition of the UK's Lintott Engineering.

EXECUTIVES

Executive Vice President and General Manager Silicon Systems Group, Randhir Thakur
Vice President and General Manager Etch and Cleans Business, Ellie Yieh
Group VP and General Manager Transistor and Interconnect Group, Steve Ghanayem
Group VP and General Manager Imaging and Process Control Group, Robert J. Perlmutter, age 58
SVP CTO and President Applied Ventures LLC, Omkaram (Om) Nalamasu, age 56, $426,154 total compensation
Group VP and CIO, Jay Kerley
President CEO and Director, Gary E. Dickerson, age 57, $980,000 total compensation
SVP and CFO, Robert J. (Bob) Halliday, age 60, $575,000 total compensation
SVP and General Manager New Markets and Service Group, Ali Salehpour, age 53, $485,385 total compensation
Group VP and General Manager Patterning and Packaging Group, Prabu G. Raja
Vice President Investor Relations, Michael (Mel) Sullivan
Vice President Marketing, Dana Tribula
Vice President Communications And Public Affairs, Joe Pon
Regional President, Russell Tham
Vice President Worldwide Operations and Supply Chain, Marc Haugen
Vice President Human Resources, Blake Wolfe
Segment Chief Financial Officer Vice President Finance, Larry Sparks
Vice President, Om Nalamasu
Vice President, Shelly Zeigler
Vice President and General Manager Applied Global Services, Charlie Pappis
Vice President, Joe Nolan
Executive Vice President of Structured Finance, Sameer Deshpande
Vice President, Aninda Moitra
Vice President Marketing, Shayne Bennett
Senior Vice President Gc And Corp Secretary, Thomas (Thom) Larkins
Corporate Vice President Global Rewards, Greg Lawler
Vice President Corporate Strategic Marketing, Jc Moran
Chairman, Willem P. (Wim) Roelandts, age 71
Assistant Treasurer, Avi Cohen-hillel
Corporate Vice President Treasurer, Robert (Bob) Friess
Auditors: KPMG LLP

LOCATIONS

HQ: Applied Materials, Inc.
 3050 Bowers Avenue, P.O. Box 58039, Santa Clara, CA 95052-8039
Phone: 408 727-5555
Web: www.appliedmaterials.com

2015 Sales

	$ mil.	% of total
Asia/Pacific		
Taiwan	2,600	27
Korea	1,654	17
China	1,623	17
Japan	1,078	11
Southeast Asia	432	4
US	1,630	17
Europe	642	7
Total	**9,659**	**100**

PRODUCTS/OPERATIONS

2015 Sales

	$ mil.	% of total
Silicon Systems	6,135	64
Applied Global Services	2,531	26
Display	780	8
Energy & Environmental Solutions	213	2
Total	**9,659**	**100**

Products and Technologies
Semiconductor
Display
Solar
Roll to Roll WEB Coating
Emerging Technologies and Products
Automation Software
Product Library

Selected Products

Chemical mechanical polishing/planarization systems (wafer polishing)
Deposition systems (deposit layers of conducting and insulating material on wafers)
 Dielectric deposition (chemical vapor deposition or CVD)
 Metal (CVD electroplating or physical vapor deposition)
 Silicon and thermal deposition
 Sputtering (physical vapor deposition) for solar cells
 Thin-film silicon solar cells
 Web coating for flexible solar cells
Etch systems (remove portions of a wafer surface for circuit construction)
Inspection systems (defect review for reticles — patterned plates which hold precise images of chip circuit patterns —and wafers)
Ion implant systems (implant ions into wafer surface to change conductive properties)
Manufacturing process optimization software
Metrology systems
 CD-SEM (scanning electron microscope system)
Optical monitoring systems (for glass or web coating systems)
Rapid thermal processing systems (heat wafers to change electrical characteristics)

COMPETITORS

AIXTRON	Mattson Technology
ASM International	Micronic Laser Systems
Axcelis Technologies	Nanometrics
CollabRx	Nikon
EG Systems	Rudolph Technologies
Ebara	SCREEN Holdings
FEI	Spire Corp.
GT Advanced Technologies	Sumitomo Heavy Industries
Hitachi	TEL FSI
Hitachi Kokusai Electric	Tokyo Electron
	ULVAC
Intevac	Veeco Instruments
KLA-Tencor	Zygo
Lam Research	

HISTORICAL FINANCIALS

Company Type: Public

Income Statement

FYE: October 25

	REVENUE ($ mil.)	NET INCOME ($ mil.)	NET PROFIT MARGIN	EMPLOYEES
10/15	9,659	1,377	14.3%	15,500
10/14	9,072	1,072	11.8%	14,950
10/13	7,509	256	3.4%	14,500
10/12	8,719	109	1.3%	15,000
10/11	10,517	1,926	18.3%	13,900
Annual Growth	**(2.1%)**	**(8.0%)**	**—**	**2.8%**

2015 Year-End Financials

Debt ratio: 29.67%
Return on equity: 17.84%
Cash ($ mil.): 4,797
Current ratio: 2.44
Long-term debt ($ mil.): 3,342

No. of shares (mil.): 1,160
Dividends
 Yield: 0.0%
 Payout: 35.7%
Market value ($ mil.): 19,070

	STOCK PRICE ($) FY Close	P/E High/Low		PER SHARE ($)		
				Earnings	Dividends	Book Value
10/15	16.44	23	13	1.12	0.40	6.56
10/14	20.99	26	19	0.87	0.40	6.44
10/13	17.71	86	48	0.21	0.38	5.89
10/12	10.65	147	111	0.09	0.34	6.04
10/11	12.62	12	7	1.45	0.30	6.74
Annual Growth	**6.8%**	—	—	**(6.3%)**	**7.5%**	**(0.7%)**

Aramark

Keeping employees fed and clothed is one mark of this company. ARAMARK is the world's #3 contract foodservice provider (behind Compass Group and Sodexo) and the #2 uniform supplier (behind Cintas) in the US. It offers corporate dining services and operates concessions at many sports arenas and other entertainment venues while its ARAMARK Refreshment Services unit is a leading provider of vending and beverage services. The firm also provides facilities management services. Through ARAMARK Uniform and Career Apparel the company supplies uniforms for healthcare public safety and technology workers. Founded in 1959 ARAMARK became a public company again in 2013.

HISTORY

Davre Davidson began his career in foodservice by selling peanuts from the backseat of his car in the 1930s. He landed his first vending contract with Douglas Aircraft (later McDonnell Douglas now part of Boeing) in 1935. Through that relationship Davidson met William Fishman of Chicago who had vending operations in the Midwest. Davidson and Fishman merged their companies in 1959 to form Automatic Retailers of America (ARA). Davidson became chairman and CEO of the new company; Fishman served as president.

Focusing on candy beverage and cigarette machines ARA became the leading vending machine company in the US by 1961 with operations in 38 states. Despite slimmer profit margins ARA moved into food vending in the early 1960s. It acquired 150 foodservice businesses between 1959 and 1963 quickly becoming a leader in the operation of cafeterias at colleges hospitals and work sites. The company (which changed its name to ARA Services in 1966) grew so rapidly that the FTC

stepped in; ARA agreed to restrict future food vending acquisitions.

ARA provided foodservices at the 1968 Summer Olympics in Mexico City beginning a long-term relationship with the amateur sports event. The company also diversified into publication distribution that year and in 1970 it expanded into janitorial and maintenance services. A foray into residential care for the elderly began in 1973 (and ended in 1993 with the sale of the subsidiary). ARA also entered into emergency room staffing services (sold 1997). The company expanded into child care (National Child Care Centers) in 1980.

CFO Joseph Neubauer became CEO in 1983 and was named chairman in 1984. To avoid a hostile takeover shortly thereafter he led a $1.2 billion leveraged buyout. After the buyout ARA began refining its core operations. It acquired Szabo (correctional foodservices) in 1986 Children's World Learning Centers in 1987 and Coordinated Health Services (medical billing services) in 1993.

ARA changed its name to ARAMARK in 1994 as part of an effort to raise its profile with its ultimate customers the public. The company's concession operations suffered from long work stoppages in baseball (1994) and hockey (1995). ARAMARK acquired Galls (North America's #1 supplier of public safety equipment) in 1996 and in 1997 announced plans to become 100% employee-owned.

The following year ARAMARK entered into a joint venture with privately held Anderson News Company exchanging its magazine distribution operations for a minority stake in the new business. In 2000 the company was on hand to supply foodservices to the Olympic Games in Sydney.

With the new millennium the company was focused on expansion buying the food and beverage concessions business of conglomerate Ogden Corp. for $236 million. The company penned a 10-year deal with Boeing in 2000 to supply foodservices to about 100 locations one of the biggest foodservice contracts ever. It also bought the Correctional Foodservice Management division of G4S Secure Solutions (USA) then named The Wackenhut Corporation.

ARAMARK continued its expansion with the purchase of ServiceMaster's management services division in 2001 for about $800 million —opening doors in nonfood management groundskeeping and custodial services. However the company lost a bid to cater the 2002 Olympic Games in Salt Lake City to rival Compass Group. In late 2001 ARAMARK went public.

The company bought Hilton's 14 Harrison Conference Centers and university lodgings for about $49 million in 2002. Also it paid $100 million for Premier Inc.'s Clinical Technology Services which maintains and repairs clinical equipment in about 170 hospitals and healthcare facilities in the US. ARAMARK also completed its acquisition of Fine Host Corporation which added approximately 900 client locations for about $100 million.

In 2003 ARAMARK exited the child care business when it sold its Educational Resources unit (operator of Children's World Learning Centers) to Michael Milken's Knowledge Learning Corporation for $225 million. ARAMARK later bought Restauración Colectiva and Rescot a foodservice company based in Zaragoza Spain. Longtime executive Bill Leonard was named president and CEO that year with Neubauer taking on the title of executive chairman.

Expanding its Canadian presence in cleanroom services in 2004 ARAMARK acquired Toronto-based Cleanroom Garments a supplier of apparel and accessories for Canadian manufacturers in pharmaceutical aerospace and automotive industries. The company's Healthcare Management Services group meanwhile signed a 10-year agreement with Evanston Northwestern Healthcare to provide managed services to three Chicago-area hospitals. That year ARAMARK made its first foray into China by acquiring a 90% stake in Bright China Service Industries a facilities services firm. After a brief reign Leonard resigned that year and Neubauer returned to being CEO of the company.

In 2007 Neubauer with the backing of such investment firms as CCMP Capital Thomas H. Lee Partners and Warburg Pincus took ARAMARK private for $8.3 billion including the assumption of $2 billion in debt.

The company provided catering and other foodservices for the 2008 Olympic Games in Beijing. That year ARAMARK also acquired The Patman Group expanding its reach into India.

In 2011 ARAMARK sold its ownership stake in SeamlessWeb to Spectrum Equity Investors for $50 million. SeamlessWeb provides online and mobile food ordering.

EXECUTIVES

Chairman President and CEO, Eric J. Foss, age 57, $1,417,240 total compensation
Executive Vice President Human Resources, Lynn B. McKee, age 59, $666,034 total compensation
COO Uniform and Refreshment Services, Brad C. Drummond
COO Education, Brent J. Franks
EVP and CFO, Stephen P. (Steve) Bramlage, age 44
COO Europe, Harrald F. Kroeker, age 57
COO Healthcare and Business and Industry Facilities, Victor L. Crawford, age 54
COO Sports Leisure Corrections and Business Dining, Marc Bruno
Executive Vice President General Counsel Secretary, Stephen R. (Steve) Reynolds, age 57, $515,307 total compensation
COO Emerging Markets, Marty Welch
Vice President Of Technology, Lesa Bradford
Senior Vice Presiden, John (Jack) Ryan
Senior Vice President Finance, Christina Morrison
Assistant Vice President Integration Clinical Technology Services, Todd Wells
Associate Vice President, Brian Drew
Vice President Finance, Barbara Ratliff
Regional Vice President, Trevor Ferguson
Multi service Management.Facilities.Vice President, David A (Dave) Kimball
Associate Vice President of Marketing, Karen Parker
Vice President Strategic Partnerships, Ed Snowden
Regional Vice President Sales Aramark Uniform Services, Ryan Flaherty
Strategic Development Vice President, Sanjeev Midha
Vice President, David Heidenberg
Vice President Audit and Controls, Mike Murphy
Associate Vice President, Larry Weger
Associate Vice President, Alan (Al) Leo
Executive Vice President Customer Support, Terrance Ransfer
Vice President Global Operational Excellence, Autumn Bayles
Vice President, Tracy Tomkiewicz
Vice President Operations, Ayman Assanassios
Regional Vice President, Keith Roe
Vice President Investor Relations, Ian Bailey
Vice President of Marketing, Mark S Mendes
Senior Vice President Global Supply Chain, Scott Barnhart
Vice President Compliance, Julianne Duss
Vice President Diagnostic Imaging Technic, John Frasik
Region Vice President, Jim Hinds
Vice President Director of Network Infrastructure, Bill Keefe
Senior Vice President Legal Affairs (2004), James Lee

Senior Vice President Sales and Marketing (Aramark Healthcare), Russell (Russ) Procopio
Regional Vice President, Peter J (Pete) Evola
Associate Vice President, Eric Brown
Vice President Of Marketing, Mark Roberts
Senior Vice President Global Human Resou, Silvana Battaglia
Regional Vice President, Brad Nielsen
Vice President Of Sales, Betsy Kline
Assistant Vice President Leadership And Organizational Deve, Ash Hanson
Vice President Operations, Daniel Natterman
Vice President Supply Chain Fleet Manage, Art Wake
Vice President Of Global Business Servic, Brian Gabbard
Vice President Of Market Development, Alan (Al) Cobb
Assistant Vice President, Paul Sizer
Regional Vice President ARAMARK Business Dining, Prentiss Hall
Associate Vice President, Emanuel Maxwell
Auditors: KPMG LLP

LOCATIONS

HQ: Aramark
Aramark Tower, 1101 Market Street, Philadelphia, PA 19107
Phone: 215 238-3000
Web: www.aramark.com

2015 Sales

	$ mil.	% of total
The US	10,727	75
Other countries	3,601	25
Total	**14,329**	**100**

PRODUCTS/OPERATIONS

2015 Sales

	$ mil.	% of total
FSS North America	9,950	69
FSS International	2,858	20
Uniform	1,520	11
Total	**14,329**	**100**

Brands
WearGuard
Crest
Aramark
Services
Food hospitality and facilities
Rental sale and maintenance of uniform apparel and other items

Selected Operations
Food and support services
ARAMARK Colleges and Universities
ARAMARK Conference Centers
ARAMARK Convention Centers
ARAMARK Correctional Services
ARAMARK Cultural Attractions
ARAMARK Facility Services
ARAMARK Food Services
ARAMARK Healthcare
ARAMARK Higher Education
ARAMARK Innovative Dining Solutions
ARAMARK Parks and Resorts
ARAMARK Refreshment Services (vending services)
ARAMARK Senior Living
ARAMARK Sports and Entertainment
Uniform and career apparel
ARAMARK Cleanroom Services
ARAMARK Uniform & Career Apparel
Galls (tactical equipment and apparel)

COMPETITORS

ABM Industries	G&K Services
Autogrill	Healthcare Services
Centerplate	ISS A/S
Cintas	SSP
Compass Group	Serco
Delaware North	Sodexo
Elior	UniFirst

HISTORICAL FINANCIALS

Company Type: Public

Income Statement

FYE: October 2

	REVENUE ($ mil.)	NET INCOME ($ mil.)	NET PROFIT MARGIN	EMPLOYEES
10/15	14,329	235	1.6%	265,500
10/14*	14,832	148	1.0%	269,500
09/13	13,945	69	0.5%	272,000
09/12	13,505	103	0.8%	—
09/11	13,082	83	0.6%	—
Annual Growth	2.3%	29.5%	—	—

*Fiscal year change

2015 Year-End Financials

Debt ratio: 51.78%	No. of shares (mil.): 239
Return on equity: 13.14%	Dividends
Cash ($ mil.): 122	Yield: 1.1%
Current ratio: 1.09	Payout: 37.9%
Long-term debt ($ mil.): 5,212	Market value ($ mil.): 7,397

	STOCK PRICE ($) FY Close	P/E High/Low		PER SHARE ($) Earnings	Dividends	Book Value
10/15	30.83	34	26	0.96	0.35	7.85
10/14*	26.44	45	34	0.63	0.23	7.34
Annual Growth	3.9%	—	—	11.1%	11.3%	1.7%

*Fiscal year change

Archer Daniels Midland Co.

Archer-Daniels-Midland's (ADM) forges every link the food chain from field to processing to store. One of the world's largest processors of agricultural commodities the company converts corn oilseeds and wheat into products for food animal feed industrial and energy uses at some 300 processing plants worldwide. The company is also a leading manufacturer of protein meal vegetable oil corn sweeteners flour biodiesel ethanol and other value-added food and feed ingredients. ADM operates an extensive US grain elevator and global transportation network that buys stores transports and resells feed commodities for the ag processing industry connecting crops with markets on six continents.

Operations
ADM's businesses —agricultural services (the largest accounting for about 47% of sales) oilseeds (soybeans cottonseed canola and flaxseed) processing (about 39%) and corn processing (about 13%) —can be best understood in the light of changing agricultural commodity prices. Commodity prices impact sales and the cost of products sold. And in ADM's corn and other food and feed processing operations commodity prices raise (or lower) the cost of raw materials. Energy prices weather events crop health as well as government programs and shifts in population can also influence ADM's performance.

A big part of ADM's business is getting products from one place to another. It has developed a comprehensive transportation network that moves commodities and processed products around the world. It owns or leases trucks trailers railroad tank and hopper cars river barges towboats and ocean-going vessels.

Geographic Reach

The US is ADM's largest market accounting for about 49% of total sales. Switzerland and Germany each represent about 10% with more than 140 other countries contributing the rest. ADM currently owns or leases about 300 processing plants and more than 460 procurement facilities nearly 35% of which operate on international soil.

Financial Performance

In 2014 ADM's sales fell about 10% to $81.2 billion. Sales of ag services and corn processing were off as lower prices offset a higher volumes of sales while oilseeds processing contended with lower volume and lower prices.All three segments posted 10% decreases in revenue.

ADM's net income on the other hand leaped 67% higher in 2015 to $2.25 billion.The profit came from an 11% lower cost of products because of large harvests in the US and South America.

Cash flow from operations was $4.9 billion for 2014 compared to $5.2 billion in 2013. The decrease was attributed to a change in segregated cash and investments and accrued expenses.

Strategy

ADM's acquisitions of two companies that supply natural ingredients and foods give it a foothold in a fast growing facet of the food business as consumers seek more natural healthier fare and shying away from processed products. The company created a division based on those acquisitions to supply natural flavor ingredients flavor systems proteins emulsifiers soluble fiber polyols hydrocolloids sorbitol xanthan gum natural health and nutrition products and other specialty food and feed ingredients.

The company continued its international expansion with activities in Central America and China. ADM opened distribution and merchandising offices in El Salvador and Guatemala in 2015. In China the company is building a feed-premix plant in Zhangzhou bringing the number of Chinese feed plants to four. Back in the US ADM opened a feed plant in Minnesota for the growing Midwest market.

As the company adds new products to its portfolio it is keeps an eye on operations that fail to meet expectations. To that end in 2015 ADM sold its chocolate business to Cargill for about $440 million and its cocoa business including equipment and facilities to Singaporean ingredients company Olam International for about $1.2 billion.

Mergers and Acquisitions

ADM made two deals in 2015 that boost its transportation capacity South American and Europe. Agri Port Services ADM's joint steamship agency with North Lilly International acquired Blue Ocean Agencia Maritima Ltd. which services vessels at ports in Brazil. In Europe AMD acquired complete ownership of North Star Shipping and Minmetal. The acquisition adds export facilities on the Black Sea from the port of Constanta Romania.

HISTORY

Early History

John Daniels began crushing flaxseed to make linseed oil in 1878 and in 1902 he formed Daniels Linseed Company in Minneapolis. George Archer another flaxseed crusher joined the company the following year. In 1923 the company bought Midland Linseed Products and became Archer Daniels Midland (ADM). ADM kept buying oil processing companies in the Midwest during the 1920s. It also started to research the chemical composition of linseed oil.

ADM entered the flour milling business in 1930 when it bought Commander-Larabee (then the #3 flour miller in the US). In the 1930s the company discovered a method for extracting lecithin (an emulsifier food additive used in candy and other products) from soybean oil significantly lowering its price.

The enterprise grew rapidly following WWII. By 1949 it was the leading processor of linseed oil and soybeans in the US and was fourth in flour milling. During the early 1950s ADM began foreign expansion in earnest.

In 1966 the company's leadership passed to Dwayne Andreas a former Cargill executive who had purchased a block of Archer family stock. Andreas focused ADM on soybeans including the production of textured vegetable protein a cheap soybean by-product used in foodstuffs.

EXECUTIVES

SVP and Chief Risk Officer and President North America, Mark A. Bemis, age 54
VP and President Risk Management Corn Processing, Gary L. Towne, age 60
SVP Agricultural Services Business Unit; President Europe, Joseph D. (Joe) Taets, age 49, $650,004 total compensation
EVP and CFO, Ray G. Young, age 54, $795,837 total compensation
SVP General Counsel and Secretary, D. Cameron Findlay, age 56, $700,000 total compensation
VP and President Asia-Pacific, Ismael Roig, age 48
VP and President Milling, Mark L. Kolkhorst, age 50
SVP and President Corn Processing, Christopher M. (Chris) Cuddy
President Sweeteners and Starches, Kris Lutt
VP and Managing Director Agricultural Services International, Domingo A. Lastra, age 47
Chairman President and CEO, Juan R. Luciano, age 53, $990,840 total compensation
SVP Research and Development and CTO, Todd Werpy
VP and CIO, Martin (Marty) Schoenthaler
President North American Oilseeds, John McGowan
President North American Oils, Ray Bradbury
President Ethanol, Craig Willis
President Golden Peanut and Tree Nuts, Greg Mills
SVP and President Oilseeds Processing Business Unit, Gregory A. (Greg) Morris, age 43
SVP and President Wild Flavors and Specialty Ingredients, Vince F. Macciocchi
President Wild Flavors, Kenneth Campbell
President Specialty Commodities, Manda Tweten
Vice President and Treasurer, Douglas (Doug) Ostermann
Vice President Global Procurement, Marty Wendt
Vice President Of Research And Development, Leif Solheim
Vice President, Todd Saathoff
Vice President Bio Products, John Hansen
Vice President Human Resources Canada And Cost Management, Crocifissa Mandraccia
Vice President Agronomy, Steve Bolen
Vice President Oilseeds Portfolio Optimization, Scott WalkerWalker
Vice President Operations and General Manager, Barry Jacobs
Vice President Government Relations, Shannon S Herzfeld
Vice President Manufacturing ADM MILLI, John (Jack) Little
Vice President Government Relations, Shannon Herzfield
Vice President and Chief Accountant, Jack Rioux
Vice President Manufacturing Operations North American Oilseed, Bruno Ejankowski
National Sales Manager Dextrose, Robert (Bob) Geraty
Vice President State Government Relations, Greg Webb
Vice President and Chief Accountant, Kenny Steward
Vice President and Chief Human Resource Officer, Scott Bergstreser
Vice President Manager Director, Jennifer (Jen) Cook
Vice President Specialty Food Ingredients, Kevin Burgau
Vice President Investor Services, Chris Damilatis
Senior Vice President and Chief Risk Officer, Craig E Huss
Vice President Global Tax, Marc Hinch
Vice President Corn Processing, Randall Kampfe
Vice President Human Resources, Randy Moon
Vice President Customer Excellence, Ruth Wisener
Vice President And Director of Operations, Nicholas Lauer
Auditors: Ernst & Young LLP

LOCATIONS

HQ: Archer Daniels Midland Co.
77 West Wacker Drive, Suite 4600, Chicago, IL 60601
Phone: 312 634-8100
Web: www.adm.com

2014 Sales

	$ mil.	% of total
US	39,609	49
Switzerland	10,118	12
Germany	7,174	9
Other countries	24,300	30
Total	**81,201**	**100**

PRODUCTS/OPERATIONS

2014 Sales

	$ mil.	% of total
Agricultural services	41,150	47
Oilseeds processing	34,196	39
Corn processing	11,814	13
Other	885	1
Intersegment Elimination	(6844)	-
Total	**81,201**	**100**

Selected Commodities

Barley
Corn
Milo (sorghum)
Oats
Oilseeds
Rice
Rye
Wheat

Selected Brands

Consumer food
  Casa (canned refried beans)
  Commander (wheat flour)
  Five Roses (wheat flour)
  Gigantic (wheat flour)
  Midland Harvest (rice)
  Novasoy (soy supplement)
  Top King (wheat flour)
  VegeFull (cooked ground beans)
Industrial food
  Ambrosia (chocolate)
  CardioAid (plant sterol)
  EnviroStrip (dry-stripping)
  Evolution Chemicals (sustainable alternative chemical)
  NovaLipid (fats and oils)
  NovaSoy (isoflavones)
  VegeFull (dried bean-based food ingredient)

Selected Products

Agricultural
  Fertilizer
Feed ingredients
  Animal nutrition
  Corn co-products
  Milling products
  Oils/energy products
  Premixes
  Specialty feed ingredients
Food
  Acidulants
  Beverage alcohol

Edible beans and bean ingredients
Fiber
Flour and whole grains
Lecithin
Natural-source vitamin E
Oils
Plant sterols
Polyols and gums
Proteins
Rice
Soy isoflavones
Starches
Sweeteners
Fuel
　Biodiesel
　Ethanol
Industrials
　Acidulants
　De-icers
　Dispersants
　Dust control products
　Emulsifiers and thickeners
　Fermentation nutrients
　Fertilizers
　Industrial oils
　Polyols
　Propylene glycol
　Solvents
　Starches
　Superabsorbents

Selected Services

Agriculture
　Grain merchandising
　Grain milling
　Grain processing
Information
　Billing and invoicing
　Inventory
　Logistics
　Payment
　Product search
Transportation
　Land
　Rail
　Truck
　Water
　Ocean
　River

Selected Subsidiaries Joint Ventures and Other Holdings

Almidones Mexicanos S.A. (50% wet corn milling plant Mexico)
Alfred C. Toepfer International (80% agricultural commodities trading and processed products Germany)
Compagnie Industrielle et Financiere des Produits Amylaces SA (Luxembourg) (42% joint venture investments in food feed ingredients and bioenergy)
Eaststarch C.V. (50% wet corn milling plants Netherlands)
Edible Oils Limited (50% procure package sell edible oils UK)
Golden Peanut LLC (100% peanut hulls oil meal and seed)
Gruma S.A.B. de C.V (23% corn flour and corn tortilla manufacturer Mexico)
Kalama Export Company (45% grain export elevator)
Red Star Yeast LLC (40% joint venture fresh and dry yeast manufacturer US and Canada)
Stratas Foods LLC (50% procure package sell edible oils North America)
Telles LLC (50% market sell corn-based bioplastic)

COMPETITORS

AGRI Industries	Liberty Vegetable Oil
Abengoa Bioenergy	LifeLine
Ag Processing Inc.	Little Sioux Corn
Agrium	Processors
Ajinomoto	Louis Dreyfus
Andersons	Commodities
Barry Callebaut	Louis Dreyfus Group
Bartlett and Company	MGP Ingredients
Bayer CropScience	Malt Products
Brenntag North America	Corporation
Bunge Limited	Monsanto Company
CHS	Nestl©

CP Kelco	Nisshin Oillio
Cargill	Northern Growers
Cosun	Omega Protein
Danisco A/S	Pacific Ethanol
Dow AgroSciences	Pioneer Hi-Bred
DuPont Agriculture	Renewable Energy Group
General Mills	Riceland Foods
Green Brick Partners	Scoular
Green Plains	Syngenta
Hain Celestial	Sdzucker
Hershey	Tate & Lyle
Ingredion	Viterra Inc.

HISTORICAL FINANCIALS

Company Type: Public

Income Statement

FYE: December 31

	REVENUE ($ mil.)	NET INCOME ($ mil.)	NET PROFIT MARGIN	EMPLOYEES
12/14	81,201	2,248	2.8%	33,900
12/13	89,804	1,342	1.5%	31,100
12/12*	46,729	692	1.5%	30,600
06/12	89,038	1,223	1.4%	30,000
06/11	80,676	2,036	2.5%	30,700
Annual Growth	0.2%	2.5%	—	2.5%

*Fiscal year change

2014 Year-End Financials

Debt ratio: 12.92%　　　　　No. of shares (mil.): 637
Return on equity: 11.32%　　Dividends
Cash ($ mil.): 1,099　　　　　Yield: 1.8%
Current ratio: 1.67　　　　　Payout: 32.9%
Long-term debt ($ mil.): 5,558　Market value ($ mil.): 33,124

	STOCK PRICE ($) FY Close	P/E High/Low	PER SHARE ($) Earnings	Dividends	Book Value
12/14	52.00	16　11	3.43	0.96	30.73
12/13	43.40	22　13	2.02	0.76	30.59
12/12*	27.39	32　23	1.05	0.70	28.71
06/12	29.52	18　13	1.84	0.69	27.27
06/11	30.15	12　8	3.13	0.62	27.82
Annual Growth	14.6%	—　—	2.3%	11.6%	2.5%

*Fiscal year change

Arrow Electronics, Inc.

Arrow Electronics knows its target market. The company is a leading global distributor of electronic components and computer products alongside rival Avnet. It sells semiconductors passive components interconnect products and computer peripherals to more than 100000 equipment manufacturers and commercial customers. Arrow also provides value-added services such as materials planning design and engineering inventory management and contract manufacturing. It distributes products made by such manufacturers as IBM Panasonic Microsoft and Intel. The company operates from some 460 locations across the globe (serving some 56 countries); half of its sales comes from the Americas.

Operations

Arrow operates in two segments —global components and Enterprise Computing Solutions (ECS). The larger division global components accounts for about two-thirds of sales. Its product offerings consist of semiconductors; passive electromechanical and interconnect products such as capacitors resistors potentiometers power supplies relays switches and connectors; and computing and memory products. Most of its customers' or-

ders are too large or too frequent to be available via a direct purchase from the manufacturer.

Its Enterprise Computing Solutions (ECS) business —which sells hardware software storage and security products to value-added resellers —makes up about a third of sales. ECS has added professional consulting cloud computing managed services and technical training as the business unit expands its support for resellers and systems integrators beyond hardware sales.

Geographic ReachThe company generates 50% of sales from the Americas (mostly the US) with Europe the Middle East and Africa (EMEA) and the Asia-Pacific region contributing 30% and 20% respectively.

Altogether Arrow has 300 sales offices and 40 distribution centers in 56 countries worldwide.

Sales and MarketingArrow serves more than 100000 OEMs and contract manufacturers through its components business segment and value-added resellers through its ECS business segment. Most of its sales are made on an order-by-order basis rather than through long-term sales contracts.

Industries served include aerospace and defense computers gaming industrial equipment instrumentation medical and scientific devices networking optoelectronics and telecommunications equipment.

Financial Performance

Sales grew 7% in 2014 to $21 billion as both segments posted similar rates of sales increases. Sales were up around the world but the Asia-Pacific region and Europe grew at rates of 11% and 10% while the Americas grew at 3%. Profits jumped 25% to $498 million in 2014. The big change besides higher revenue was that Arrow spent about $41 million less on restructuring in 2014 than it did in 2013. The company has more than $92 million of expenses for restructuring in 2014 related to the elimination of almost 1200 positions and vacating about 40 facilities in an effort to streamline operations and reduce real estate costs. Cash flow from operations was $673 million in 2014 compared to $450 million in 2013.

Strategy

Along with rival Avnet Arrow is highly acquisitive in order to consolidate competition grow its footprint and increase product offerings. The company maintains its competitive edge by offering more value-added services to diversify its revenue stream. It also keeps its supplier base large so that customers can procure from a one-stop shop rather than purchase from several different vendors.

Arrow added to its ECS offerings through partnerships and alliances. Arrow added SoftLayer an IBM company to its partners through which it offers cloud services. It made similar arrangements with Splunk to resell its enterprise software and with Nutanix for its IT services.

Mergers & Acquisitions

Arrow continues to expand its service capabilities and global presence primarily through acquisitions. In the first half of 2014 it bought five companies the largest of which is Data Mogul AG for about $105 million. The acquisition further extends Arrow's reach in Europe. Another acquisition United Technical Publishing a division of Hearst Business Media adds to Arrow's lineup a producer of directories e-newsletters engineering websites inventory access tools and databases.

HISTORY

Early History

Arrow Radio began in 1935 in New York City as an outlet for used radio equipment. In the mid-1960s the company was selling various home entertainment products and wholesaling electronic parts. In 1968 three Harvard Business School graduates got Arrow in their sights. Duke Glenn Roger Green and John Waddell led a group of investors that acquired the company for $1 million in borrowed money. The three also bought a company that reclaimed lead from used car batteries.

With the money they made in the lead reclamation business the trio enlarged Arrow's wholesale electronics distribution inventory. The company expanded rapidly during the 1970s primarily through internal growth and by 1977 it had become the US's fourth-largest electronics distributor. In 1979 Arrow bought the #2 US distributor Cramer Electronics. Although the purchase of West Coast-based Cramer was financed with junk bonds and left Arrow deeply in debt revenues doubled. Arrow went public in 1979.

One year later a hotel fire killed 13 members of Arrow's senior management including Glenn and Green. Waddell who had remained at company headquarters to answer questions about a stock split announced that day was named acting CEO. Company stock fell 19% the first day it traded after the fire and another 14% before the end of the month. Adding to the company's woes a slump hit the electronics industry in 1981. That year Arrow's board lured Alfred Stein to leave Motorola Inc. and lead the company's new management team as president and CEO; Waddell remained chairman.

EXECUTIVES

EVP Finance and Operations and CFO, Paul J. Reilly, age 58, $700,000 total compensation
Chairman President and CEO, Michael J. (Mike) Long, age 57, $1,150,000 total compensation
COO Global Components and Global Enterprise Computing Solutions, Andrew S. (Andy) Bryant, age 60, $559,526 total compensation
VP and CIO, Vincent P. (Vin) Melvin, age 51
President Global Components, Eric J. Schuck, $500,000 total compensation
President Global Enterprise Computing Solutions, Sean J. Kerins, $481,511 total compensation
National Account Manager, Maureen van Hoek
Vice President Corporate Communications, Rich Kylberg
Vice President, Donna Tikkanen-davis
Vice President Of Sales Northwest Region, Kent Smith
National Account Manager, Tom Baker
Vice President, Daniel (Dan) Shea
National Account Manager, Dundee Dempsey
National Account Manager, Nancy Perez
Vice President Of Global Logistics, Bill Foster
National Account Manager, Jack Olson
Vice President Marketing East Division, Deborah (Deb) Philbrick
National Account Manager, Kevin Giordano
National Account Manager, Ann Russett
Vice President Regional Sales, Mark Hagan
Operations Vice President, Vickie Wilson
Vice President Global Operations, Ernest Keith
Senior Vice President General Counsel Secretary Arrow S3, Kelleye Chube
Vice President Finance, Chris Stansbury
Vice President And Treasurer, Michael Taunton
Senior Vice President Human Resources, John McMahon
National Account Manager, Jeffrey (Jeff) Wolfe
Vice President Business Process Excellence, Leonie Tipton
Vice President Security Ecs Esvn, Russell Zientek
Board Member, Sharad Kulkarni
Secretary, Mil Cheung
Auditors: Ernst & Young LLP

LOCATIONS

HQ: Arrow Electronics, Inc.
9201 East Dry Creek Road, Centennial, CO 80112
Phone: 303 824-4000
Web: www.arrow.com

2014 Sales

	$ mil.	% of total
Americas	11,340	50
Europe Middle East & Africa	6,864	30
Asia/Pacific	4,564	20
Total	**22,768**	**100**

Selected Acquisitions

FY 2013
ComputerLinks
FY 2012
ALTIMATE Group
Asset Recovery Corporation
Global Link Technology
Redemtech
Seed International
TechTurn

PRODUCTS/OPERATIONS

2014 Sales

	$ mil.	% of total
Global Components	14,313	63
Global Enterprise computing solutions (ECS)	8,455	37
Total	**22,768**	**100**

Selected Products and Services

Computer Products
  Communication control equipment
  Controllers
  Design systems
  Desktop computers
  Flat-panel displays
  Microcomputer boards and systems
  Monitors
  Printers
  Servers
  Software
  Storage products
  System chassis and enclosures
  Workstations
Electronic Components
  Capacitors
  Connectors
  Potentiometers
  Power supplies
  Relays
  Resistors
  Switches
Services
  Analysis implementation and support
  Component design
  Contract manufacturing
  Forecast and order management
  Inventory management

COMPETITORS

Avnet	Richardson Electronics
Digi-Key	SYNNEX
Future Electronics	TTI Inc.
Heilind Electronics	Tech Data
Ingram Micro	WPG Holdings
N.F. Smith	Yosun
Newark Corporation	ePlus

HISTORICAL FINANCIALS

Company Type: Public

Income Statement

FYE: December 31

	REVENUE ($ mil.)	NET INCOME ($ mil.)	NET PROFIT MARGIN	EMPLOYEES
12/15	23,282	497	2.1%	18,500
12/14	22,768	498	2.2%	17,000
12/13	21,357	399	1.9%	16,500
12/12	20,405	506	2.5%	16,500
12/11	21,390	598	2.8%	15,700
Annual Growth	**2.1%**	**(4.5%)**	**—**	**4.2%**

2015 Year-End Financials

Debt ratio: 18.62%   No. of shares (mil.): 90
Return on equity: 12.00%   Dividends
Cash ($ mil.): 273   Yield: —
Current ratio: 1.52   Payout: —
Long-term debt ($ mil.): 2,380   Market value ($ mil.): 4,926

	STOCK PRICE ($) FY Close	P/E High/Low		PER SHARE ($) Earnings	Dividends	Book Value
12/15	54.18	12	10	5.20	0.00	45.56
12/14	57.89	12	9	4.98	0.00	43.32
12/13	54.25	14	9	3.85	0.00	41.83
12/12	38.08	9	7	4.56	0.00	37.58
12/11	37.41	9	5	5.17	0.00	32.81
Annual Growth	**9.7%**	**—**	**—**	**0.1%**	**—**	**8.6%**

Asbury Automotive Group, Inc

Asbury Automotive Group has made a living out of being large. The company oversees more than 85 dealerships which operate around 105 auto franchises in about a dozen states including the Carolinas Florida Texas and Virginia. The dealerships sell some 30 different brands of US and foreign new and used vehicles. Asbury also offer parts service and collision repair from about 30 repair centers as well as financing insurance and warranty and service contracts. The auto dealer has grown by acquiring large locally branded dealership groups as well as smaller groups and individually owned dealerships throughout the US. Customers include individual buyers and fleet operators.

Operations
In 2014 the company sold 95564 new vehicles (representing 55% of its total revenues).

Some 85% of Asbury Automotive's sales come from import brands. Honda represented 18% of new vehicle revenue while Nissan and Toyota each accounted for 12%.

Geographic Reach
Asbury Automotive operates dealerships in 18 metropolitan markets throughout the US. Aside from the Carolinas Florida Texas and Virginia Asbury has dealerships in Arkansas Georgia Mississippi Missouri and New Jersey.

Sales and Marketing
Asbury advertises on TV radio and newspaper as well as through Internet-based campaigns including search engine marketing website optimization and through third-party websites.

The company advertising expenses totaled approximately $34 million in 2014 compared with $33 million in 2013.

Financial Performance
More than five years of increasing revenue continued in 2014 when Asbury Automotive reported a 10% increase in revenue to $5.8 billion. The increase was driven by a 9% uptick in new car sales and an 11% increase in used car sales. Even parts and service and financing got in on the act.

Net income has also been growing with 2014 bringing a 2% upswing to $111.6 million due to the higher sales volume. This was partially offset by an increase in operating expenses. Cash flow from operations rose 66% to $84.2 million that year.

Strategy
The historically acquisitive Asbury Automotive has resumed its acquisitive ways in recent years

after a temporary slowdown during the aftermath of the recession. The company is also expanding by opening stand-alone used vehicle stores under the Q Auto brand name. It opened its second such store in Jacksonville in 2014.

Mergers and Acquisitions

In 2014 Asbury Automotive purchased the assets of one franchise in South Carolina after buying three franchises in 2013. It bought dealerships in Florida Georgia and Texas in 2015.

EXECUTIVES

President CEO and Director, Craig T. Monaghan, age 58, $950,000 total compensation

EVP and COO, David W. Hult, age 49, $116,667 total compensation

VP Operations, Keith R. Style, age 42, $391,250 total compensation

VP General Counsel and Secretary, George A. Villasana, age 47, $368,750 total compensation

VP and CIO, Barry Cohen

Vice President Manufacturer Relations, Matthew (Matt) Mees

Vice President, Matt Mees

Vice President, John Rooks

Vice President North Region, Daniel Clara

Vice President Manufacturer Relations, Matthew Mees

Senior Vice President Chief Operating Officer, Michael (Mel) Kearney

Vice President Corporate Development, George Karolis

Vice President Operations, Stuart (Stu) Bailey

Chairman, Thomas C. DeLoach, age 68

Auditors: Ernst & Young LLP

LOCATIONS

HQ: Asbury Automotive Group, Inc
2905 Premiere Parkway N.W., Suite 300, Duluth, GA 30097
Phone: 770 418-8200
Web: www.asburyauto.com

PRODUCTS/OPERATIONS

2014 Sales

	$ mil.	% of total
New vehicles	3,230	55
Used vehicles	1,741	30
Parts & service	666	11
Finance & insurance	229	4
Total	**5,867**	**100**

2014 New Vehicle Sales

	% of total
Luxury	39
Mid-line import	47
Mid-line domestic	14
Total	**100**

Selected Brands

Coggin Automotive Group
Courtesy Autogroup
David McDavid Auto Group
Gray-Daniels Auto Family
Nalley Automotive Group
North Point Auto Group
Plaza Motor Company

COMPETITORS

AutoNation	Penske Automotive
Buchanan Automotive	Group
CarMax	Ron Tonkin Family of
Ferman Automotive	Dealerships
Group 1 Automotive	Scott-McRae
Hendrick Automotive	Sonic Automotive
Island Lincoln-Mercury	

HISTORICAL FINANCIALS

Company Type: Public

Income Statement

FYE: December 31

	REVENUE ($ mil.)	NET INCOME ($ mil.)	NET PROFIT MARGIN	EMPLOYEES
12/14	5,867	111	1.9%	8,300
12/13	5,334	109	2.0%	7,600
12/12	4,640	82	1.8%	7,000
12/11	4,276	67	1.6%	6,800
12/10	3,936	38	1.0%	7,100
Annual Growth	**10.5%**	**30.8%**	**—**	**4.0%**

2014 Year-End Financials

Debt ratio: 67.25%
Return on equity: 23.86%
Cash ($ mil.): 2
Current ratio: 1.23
Long-term debt ($ mil.): 678

No. of shares (mil.): 28
Dividends
  Yield: —
  Payout: —
Market value ($ mil.): 2,166

	STOCK PRICE ($) FY Close	P/E High/Low		PER SHARE ($) Earnings	Dividends	Book Value
12/14	75.92	21	12	3.71	0.00	15.60
12/13	53.74	16	9	3.51	0.00	15.95
12/12	32.03	12	8	2.61	0.00	12.86
12/11	21.56	10	7	2.08	0.00	10.43
12/10	18.48	16	8	1.14	0.00	8.75
Annual Growth	**42.4%**	**—**	**—**	**34.3%**	**—**	**15.5%**

Ashland Inc

Ashland's three business units are built on chemicals and cars. Ashland Performance Materials makes specialty resins polymers and adhesives. Specialty Ingredients makes cellulose ethers vinyl pyrrolidones and biofunctionals. It offers industry-leading products technologies and resources for solving formulation and product-performance challenges. Consumer Markets led by subsidiary Valvoline runs an oil-change chain in the US and sells Valvoline oil and Zerex antifreeze. The company's Ashland Specialty Ingredients unit produces polymers and additives for the food personal care pharmaceutical and other industries. In 2015 Ashland announced plans to spin off Valvoline.

HISTORY

After moving to Kentucky in 1917 Fred Miles formed the Swiss Oil Company. In 1924 Swiss Oil bought a refinery in Catlettsburg a rough town near sedate Ashland and created a unit called Ashland Refining. Miles battled Swiss Oil directors for control lost and resigned in 1927.

Swiss Oil bought Tri-State Refining in 1930 and Cumberland Pipeline's eastern Kentucky pipe network in 1931. Swiss Oil changed its name to Ashland Oil and Refining in 1936. After WWII it bought small independent oil firms acquiring the Valvoline name in 1950 by buying Freedom-Valvoline.

The firm formed Ashland Chemical in 1967 after buying Anderson-Prichard Oil (1958) United Carbon (1963) and ADM Chemical (1967). Ashland Chemical changed its name to Ashland Oil. It added the SuperAmerica convenience store chain (1970) and started exploring for oil in Nigeria after OPEC nations raised oil prices.

Scandal hit in 1975 the year Ashland Coal was formed. CEO Orin Atkins admitted to ordering Ashland executives to make illegal contributions to

the 1972 Nixon presidential campaign. Atkins was deposed in 1981 after the company made questionable payments to highly placed "consultants" with connections to oil-rich Middle Eastern governments. In 1988 Atkins was arrested for trying to fence purloined documents regarding litigation between Ashland and the National Iranian Oil Company (NIOC). Ashland which launched the federal investigation that led to Atkins' arrest settled with NIOC in 1989. Atkins pleaded guilty and received probation.

Ashland went on a shopping spree in the 1990s. The company bought Permian (crude oil gathering and marketing) in 1991 and merged it into Scurlock Oil. In 1992 Ashland Chemical bought most of Unocal's chemical distribution business and two years later it bought two companies that produce chemicals for the semiconductor industry. Also in 1994 Ashland made a promising oil discovery in Nigeria.

The company by then named Ashland Inc. spent $368 million on 14 acquisitions to expand its energy and chemical divisions in 1995. It received a $75 million settlement with Columbia Gas System (now Columbia Energy Group) for abrogated natural gas contracts resulting from Columbia's bankruptcy.

In 1996 president Paul Chellgren became CEO and with the company under shareholder fire began a major reorganization. The next year Arch Mineral and Ashland Coal combined to form Arch Coal with Ashland owning 58%. Also that year Ashland made more than a dozen acquisitions to bolster its chemical and construction businesses. Its exploration unit renamed Blazer Energy was sold to Norway's Statoil for $566 million.

Ashland joined USX-Marathon (now Marathon Oil) in 1998 to create Marathon Ashland Petroleum (now called Marathon Petroleum). It bought 20 companies including Eagle One Industries a maker of car-care products and Masters-Jackson a group of highway construction companies. Ashland reduced its holdings in Arch Coal from 58% to 12% in 2000; it sold the remainder in early 2001.

In 2002 the company was jolted when Chellgren was forced to retire after violating a company policy prohibiting romantic office relationships. James O'Brien replaced Chellgren.

Ashland had a record year in 2001 but was hampered in 2002 by smaller profits from MAP which was hurt by reduced demand for petroleum products and tighter margins. Ashland Distribution also hurt the bottom line which led Ashland to reorganize that unit's management and sales teams.

After that record year Ashland came back to earth with much smaller profits in 2002 and the next year; APAC particularly was hit hard in 2003. The construction division swung from $120 million in profits in 2002 to a loss of more than $40 million in 2003; the company attributes the decline to unusual weather conditions which can greatly affect the construction business more than others. (The pendulum swung back into the black in 2004 with more than $100 million in operating income.)

The company commenced a grand reorganization of its business soon after that. Beginning in 2005 it sold its former petroleum refining joint venture (with Marathon Oil) re-named Marathon Petroleum Company; acquired car cleaning products maker Car Brite for Valvoline; purchased Degussa's water treatment business (operating as Stockhausen); and bought adhesives and coatings company Northwest Coatings. Another big deal though provided a complementary book end to the sale of Marathon Petroleum. In 2006 Ashland sold construction unit APAC (which supplied highway materials built bridges and paved streets) to Oldcastle Materials for $1.3 billion. The move coming as it did on the heels of the divestiture of MAP transformed Ashland into solely a chemicals company.

In 2008 Ashland paid $3.3 billion to buy specialty chemicals company Hercules which added greatly to its water treatment and resins businesses. That move was just the latest in a series of transactions in the latter half of the decade that transformed Ashland from a multi-industry conglomerate into strictly a chemicals operations. Among other moves the company sold its half of a refining joint venture with Marathon Oil and construction unit APAC. The deal provided Ashland already with a healthy international business with even more of a global presence.

Ashland formed a 50-50 joint venture with Süd-Chemie AG in 2010 to produce foundry chemicals. Süd-Chemie manages the operation called ASK Chemicals GmbH which is headquartered in Germany.

That year Ashland through a subsidiary sold its pentaerythritol business to Perstorp Polyols a subsidiary of Perstorp AB. The sale also fit into Ashland's strategy to focus on its core specialty chemicals business.

In a major move in 2011 Ashland acquired ISP and combined it with Ashland Aqualon Functional Ingredients as Ashland Specialty Ingredients. The $3.2 billion deal for New Jersey-based ISP which produced specialty chemicals and performance-enhancing products for consumer and industrial markets helped Ashland expand into markets with higher margin and higher growth. Adding ISP also stretched Ashland's global reach.

Another key transaction that helped complete the company's transformation was the 2011 sale of its Ashland Distribution segment which represented more than a third of its overall business to an affiliate of private equity giant TPG Capital for $979 million. The move allowed Ashland to grow its high-margin specialty chemicals sector and focus on its remaining four business segments.

The company continued its streamlining in 2012. It sold some of its emulsion polymers assets including its Vinac and Flexbond product lines to Celanese Corp. a major producer of emulsion polymers for industrial customers. Subsidiary Hercules Incorporated now integrated within the Water Technologies unit sold its aviation and refrigerant lubricants business known as synlubes to Calumet Missouri.

Ashland's busines model includes strategic partnerships. In 2013 it signed a deal to develop and commercialize products containing UPM's Biofibrils technology (nanofibrillated cellulose products that can be used for shaping materials). technology. That year it signed distribution agreements with Cathay Composites (to distribute Ashland's resin chemistries and technology solutions for composite manufacturing in Europe) and Dorf Ketal Chemicals LLC (to distribute Ashland's process and water treatment offerings for oil and gas companies in North America and the Caribbean.

EXECUTIVES

VP Chief Information and Administrative Services Officer, Anne T. Schumann, age 54
SVP and President Valvoline, Samuel J. Mitchell, age 52, $388,522 total compensation
SVP and President Ashland Chemicals Group, Luis Fernandez-Moreno, age 53, $456,457 total compensation
SVP and CFO, J. Kevin Willis, age 48, $421,154 total compensation
SVP General Counsel Secretary and Chief Compliance Officer, Peter J. Ganz, age 51, $481,672 total compensation
Chairman and CEO, William A. (Bill) Wulfsohn, age 53

Vice President Operations and Environmental Health and Safety, Steven (Steve) Post
Vice President Sales, Phyllis Mattmiller
Global Vice President Operations Wilmington DE, Rick Pekarski
Vice President Tax, Scott Gregg
Vice President Household Care, Kevin O'Brien
Vice President of Tax Tax Attorney, Fred Greenwood
Vice President, Blair Boggs
Vice President Manager Director, Jennifer (Jen) Burke
GM and Vice President of Environamental and Process Solutions, Siegfried Menk
Vice President of Operations, Stephen G (Steve) Cronin
Vp And Chief Human Resources And Communications Officer, Susan B Esler, age 55
National Account Manager, Todd Mullins
Vice President Operations And Supply Chain (The Valvoline Company), Mitchell Skaggs
Vice President Information Technology, Larry Cassity
Vice President Information Technology Detail, Peter Collette
National Account Manager, Debbie King
Vice President Controller, J William Heitman
Group Vice President Technology Growth Strategy, May Shana'a
Vice President of Human Resources, Aletha Mcalister
Board Member, Lori Palmer
Auditors: Ernst & Young LLP

LOCATIONS

HQ: Ashland Inc
50 E. RiverCenter Boulevard, P.O. Box 391, Covington, KY 41012-0391
Phone: 859 815-3333
Web: www.ashland.com

2015 Sales

	% of total
North America	53
Europe	24
Asia/Pacific	16
Latin America & Other	7
Total	**100**

PRODUCTS/OPERATIONS

2015 Sales

	% of total
Specialty Ingredients	42
Valvoline	37
Performance Materials	21
Total	**100**

COMPETITORS

Aceto	Chemtura
Arkema	DuPont
BASF SE	HELM U.S.
BP Lubricants USA	Hexion
Brenntag	

HISTORICAL FINANCIALS

Company Type: Public

Income Statement

FYE: September 30

	REVENUE ($ mil.)	NET INCOME ($ mil.)	NET PROFIT MARGIN	EMPLOYEES
09/15	5,387	309	5.7%	10,500
09/14	6,121	233	3.8%	11,000
09/13	7,813	683	8.7%	15,000
09/12	8,206	26	0.3%	15,000
09/11	6,502	414	6.4%	15,000
Annual Growth	**(4.6%)**	**(7.1%)**	**—**	**(8.5%)**

2015 Year-End Financials

Debt ratio: 37.05%
Return on equity: 9.34%
Cash ($ mil.): 1,257
Current ratio: 2.24
Long-term debt ($ mil.): 3,348

No. of shares (mil.): 67
Dividends
Yield: 1.4%
Payout: 23.5%
Market value ($ mil.): 6,742

	STOCK PRICE ($) FY Close	P/E High/Low		PER SHARE ($) Earnings	Dividends	Book Value
09/15	100.62	29	21	4.48	1.46	45.33
09/14	104.10	36	28	3.00	1.36	51.19
09/13	92.48	11	8	8.57	1.13	59.13
09/12	71.60	233	130	0.33	0.80	51.00
09/11	44.14	13	8	5.17	0.65	53.01
Annual Growth	**22.9%**	**—**	**—**	**(3.5%)**	**22.4%**	**(3.8%)**

Associated Banc-Corp

A lot of Midwesterners are associated with Associated Banc-Corp the holding company for Associated Bank. One of the largest banks based in Wisconsin the bank operates about 200 branches in that state as well as in Illinois and Minnesota. Catering to consumers and local businesses it offers deposit accounts loans mortgage banking credit and debit cards and leasing. The bank's wealth management division offers investments trust services brokerage insurance and employee group benefits plans. Commercial loans including agricultural construction and real estate loans make up more than 60% of bank's loan portfolio. The bank also writes residential mortgages consumer loans and home equity loans.

Operations

Associated Banc-Corp boasts total assets of more than $27 billion making it one of the 50 largest publicly traded US bank holding companies. More than 70% of revenue comes from interest income mostly from loans. Roughly 60% of Associated Banc-Corp's $18 billion loan portfolio consists of commercial and industrial real estate construction commercial real estate loans and lease financing.Nearly 30% of the company's income is from non-interest sources including: trust service fees service charges insurance commissions brokerage and annuity commissions and mortgage banking income among others. It also offers benefits consulting services through its Associated Financial Group subsidiary.

Geographic Reach

The company offers a full range of financial products and services in more than 200 banking locations serving more than 100 communities throughout Wisconsin Illinois and Minnesota and commercial financial services in Indiana Michigan Missouri Ohio and Texas.

Sales and Marketing

Associated Banc-Corp spent $26.1 million on business development and advertising in 2014 compared to $23.3 million in 2013 and $21.3 million in 2012.

Financial Performance

Associated Banc-Corp's revenue has remained flat for the past several years at just above $1 billion. Revenue in 2014 inched up by less than 1% to $1.03 billion mostly thanks to higher interest income as loan assets grew by 11% and as interest and dividends on investment securities also grew by double digits. Offsetting much of this growth the company's net mortgage banking income shrunk by $28 million (56%) driven by lower gains on sales and related income as secondary mortgage production declined.Profit levels have been steadily rising over the past several years since losses in 2009 and 2010 with net income in 2014 rising by 1% to $190.51 million. Higher revenue combined with lower interest expenses on deposits and lower personnel costs all helped to boost the company's bottom line.Despite higher earnings cash from operations fell 56% to $212.74 million primarily as the company made fewer net proceeds from the sale of its mortgage loans held for sale. The company's total loans grew by 11% to $17.6 billion in 2014 while total deposits rose by 9% to $18.77 billion.

Strategy

The company intends to continue pursuing a profitable growth strategy by carefully screening its prospective customers in light of the risks expenses and difficulties frequently encountered by companies in significant growth stages of development. Associated Banc-Corp hopes to keep its momentum going via organic growth including increasing its fee income and commercial deposits among other measures. It is also remodeling or relocating many of its branches.Associated Banc-Corp also plans to continue strong loan business growth. For 2015 the company expects high single-digit annual average loan growth after posting loan double-digit loan growth across most categories in 2014.Mergers and AcquisitionsIn early 2015 subsidiary Associated Financial Group agreed to buy Minnesota-based Ahmann & Martin Co a risk and benefits consulting firm to gain new clients and expand its financial risk and insurance product and service lines.

Company Background

Hampered by one of the worst economic environments in recent history the bank saw an increase in nonperforming loans (particularly business- and housing-related loans) and more than tripled its provision for loan losses from 2008 to 2009. The company cut its losses in 2010 and nearly turned a profit as it concentrated on improving its credit quality. It moved away from construction lending and its nonperforming loans and its provisions for loan losses decreased. Even though 2011 revenues were down Associated Banc-Corp returned to profitability as credit quality continued to improve.

EXECUTIVES

EVP and Chief Risk Officer, Arthur G. (Art) Heise, age 57

President and CEO, Philip B. (Phil) Flynn, age 57, $1,250,000 total compensation

EVP General Counsel and Corporate Secretary, Randall J. Erickson, age 56, $406,667 total compensation

EVP and Head Retail Banking, David L. Stein, age 51, $545,849 total compensation

EVP and Chief Human Resources Officer, Judith M. Docter, age 54

EVP and Chief Credit Officer, Scott S. Hickey, age 59, $644,531 total compensation

EVP and Chief Strategy Officer, Oliver Buechse, age 46

EVP and Head Commercial Real Estate, Breck F. Hanson

EVP and Head Corporate Banking, Donna N. Smith

EVP and Head Specialized Industries and Commercial Financial Services, John A. Utz, $348,417 total compensation

EVP and Head Community Markets, Timothy J. Lau

EVP and CFO, Christopher J. Del Moral-Niles, $477,500 total compensation

EVP and Chief Audit Executive, Patrick J. Derpinghaus

EVP CIO and COO, James Yee, $458,333 total compensation

EVP and Head Private Client and Institutional Services, William M. Bohn

President Southern Illinois, Phillip Hickman

Vice President Residential Construction Division, Robert (Bob) Burda

Assistant Vice President Insured Risk Manager, Jean Ehren

Vice President Customer Care Program And Operations Manager, Wendy Kumm

Vice President And Investment Officer, Mark Tumpach

Assistant Vice President Loss Mitigation Charge Off and Recovery, Jerry Ferkey

Vice President Commercial Banking, Keith Prusko

Vice President Of Call Centre, Michael Fumelle

Assistant Vice President Business System Analyst, Mark Molski

Senior Vice President, Ron Murphy

Bank Manager Assistant Vice President, Randall Hellesen

Vice President Atm Channel Manager, Deanna Helminiak

Assistant Vice President Collections Supervisor II, Brandon Brown

Vice President Mortgage Underwriting Supervisor, Tammy Kurey

Senior Vice President Specialized Financial Services, Chris O'Brien

Assistant Vice President Senior Bank Manager, Kim Klinkner

Senior Vice President Senior Credit Of, Phillip Mattix

Vice President Controller, Teresa Gutierrez

Vice President Commercial Real Estate Division, Rosemary Kehr

Senior Vice President, Joseph Gehrke

Senior Vice President, Anthony Bohaty

Vice President Treasury Management, Herbert Abrahamson

Executive Vice President, Diana Paltz

Vice President Private Banking, Kristine Burke

Vice President, Brett Stone

Vice President, Angela O'Neill

Executive Vice President and Treasurer, Christopher Del Moral (Chris) Nile

Assistant Vice President, Terri Grider

Assistant Vice President Residential Loan Officer, Kim Anders

Executive Vice President and Director Human Resources, Judy Docter

Vice President, Anne Dix

Vice President Facilities Services Manager, Michael (Mel) Teska

Vice President, Greg Conner

Vice President, Jodi Sowinski

Vice President, Gina Frease

Vice President, Leslie Olma

Vice President, Guy Ringle

Vice President, Jamie Mesa

Vice President, Charles Garcia

Vice President, Jenny Plebanski

Vice President Field Exams, Jeff Kohr

Vice President Residential Appraisal Compliance Of, Thomas Kneesel

Executive Vice President Specialized Financial Services Group Leader, Johnathan Utz

Vice President International Banking, Paul Eversman

Vice President Regional Credit Manager, Daniel Thompson (Dan) Crc

Assistant Vice President and Senior Credit Analyst, Erik Swan Crc

Senior Vice President Regional Manager, Gregory T Warsek

Vice President Commercial Banking At Associated Bank, Adam Lutostanski

Vice President Commercial Banking, Joshua (Josh) Neeb

Vice President Project Manager Information Technology Business Solutions, Jason Makowski

Vice President Project Manager Information Technology Business Solutions, Rob Whitemore

Vice President, Brad Amundsen

Vice President Senior Residential Lending Manager, Rich Christensen

Chairman, William R. Hutchinson, age 72

Board Member, John (Jack) Williams

Treasurer, Tim Watson

Treasurer, Matthew Wolf

Auditors: KPMG LLP

LOCATIONS

HQ: Associated Banc-Corp
433 Main Street, Green Bay, WI 54301
Phone: 920 491-7500
Web: www.associatedbank.com

PRODUCTS/OPERATIONS

2014 Sales

	$ mil.	% of total
Interest		
Loans including fees	598	58
Investment securities including dividends	131	13
Other	6	1
Noninterest		
Service charges on deposit accounts	68	6
Card-based & other nondeposit fees	49	5
Trust Service fees	48	5
Insurance Commissions	44	4
Other	79	8
Total	1	100

COMPETITORS

Anchor BanCorp	Northern Trust
Bank Mutual	TCF Financial
Harris	U.S. Bancorp
KeyCorp	

HISTORICAL FINANCIALS

Company Type: Public

Income Statement

FYE: December 31

	ASSETS ($ mil.)	NET INCOME ($ mil.)	INCOME AS % OF ASSETS	EMPLOYEES
12/15	27,715	188	0.7%	4,383
12/14	26,821	190	0.7%	4,300
12/13	24,226	188	0.8%	4,600
12/12	23,487	178	0.8%	4,900
12/11	21,924	139	0.6%	5,100
Annual Growth	6.0%	7.7%	—	(3.7%)

2015 Year-End Financials

Debt ratio: 3.35%	No. of shares (mil.): 151
Return on equity: 6.56%	Dividends
Cash ($ mil.): 454	Yield: 2.1%
Current ratio: —	Payout: 33.3%
Long-term debt ($ mil.): —	Market value ($ mil.): 2,836

	STOCK PRICE ($) FY Close	P/E High/Low		PER SHARE ($) Earnings	Dividends	Book Value
12/15	18.75	17	14	1.19	0.41	19.42
12/14	18.63	17	13	1.16	0.37	18.48
12/13	17.40	16	12	1.10	0.33	17.61
12/12	13.12	15	11	1.00	0.23	17.25
12/11	11.17	23	14	0.66	0.04	16.41
Annual Growth	13.8%	—	—	15.9%	78.9%	4.3%

ASSOCIATED WHOLESALE GROCERS INC.

Associated Wholesale Grocers (AWG) knows its customers can't live on bread and milk alone. The second-largest retailer-owned cooperative in the US (behind Wakefern Food Corporation) AWG supplies more than 2900 retail outlets in more than 30 states from nine distribution centers. In addition to its wholesale grocery operation AWG offers a variety of business services to its members including marketing and merchandising programs shelf management insurance and store design. AWG was founded by a group of independent grocers in 1924.

HISTORY

About 20 Kansas City Kansas-area grocers met in a local grocery in 1924 and organized the Associated Grocers Company to get better deals on purchases and advertising. They elected J. C. Harline president and each chipped in a few hundred dollars to make their first purchases. It took a while to find a manufacturer who would sell directly to them; a local soap maker was finally convinced and others gradually followed.

In 1926 the group was incorporated as Associated Wholesale Grocers (AWG). It outgrew two warehouses in four years finally moving to a 16000-sq.-ft. facility big enough to add new lines and more products. Membership doubled between 1930 and 1932 as grocers moved from ordering products a year ahead to the new wholesale concept and members took seriously the slogan: "Buy Sell Buy Some More." They met every week to plan how to sell their products and buyer and advertising manager Harry Small gave sales presentations and advertising ideas (his trade-in plan for old brooms sold more than two train-carloads of brooms in two weeks). Heavy newspaper advertising also paid off; AWG topped $1 million in sales in 1933.

The cooperative made its first acquisition in 1936 buying Progressive Grocers a warehouse in Joplin Missouri; a second warehouse named Associated Grocers was acquired the next year in Springfield Missouri. AWG continued building and expanding warehouses and annual sales were at $11 million by 1951.

Louis Fox became CEO in 1956. Fox maximized year-end rebates for members led several acquisitions and formed a new subsidiary for financing stores and small shopping centers where AWG members had a presence (Supermarket Developers). Sales increased nearly 15-fold to over $200 million in his first 15 years.

James Basha who succeeded Fox when he retired in 1984 saw sales reach $2.4 billion by the time of his own retirement in 1992.

Basha was followed by former COO Mike DeFabis once a deputy mayor of Indianapolis. DeFabis orchestrated several acquisitions including 41 Kansas City-area stores —most of which were quickly bought by members —from bankrupt Food Barn Stores in 1994 and 29 Oklahoma stores and a warehouse from Safeway spinoff Homeland Stores in 1995 (members bought all the stores).

AWG's non-food subsidiary Valu Merchandisers was established in 1995; its new Kansas warehouse began shipping health and beauty aids and housewares the following year to help members

battle big discounters. Members narrowly defeated a proposal in late 1996 to convert the cooperative into a public company. Proponents promptly petitioned for a second vote which was defeated early the next year.

AWG veteran Doug Carolan succeeded DeFabis in 1998 becoming only the fifth CEO in the cooperative's history. The company bought five Falley's and 33 Food 4 Less stores in Kansas and Missouri from Fred Meyer in 1998 for $300 million. In a break with tradition AWG began operating the stores rather than selling them to members.

In 2000 after a months-long labor dispute with the Teamsters was resolved Carolan left AWG. The company's CFO Gary Phillips was named president and CEO later that year. In 2001 the company debuted a new format ALPS (Always Low Price Stores) —small stores that carry a limited selection of grocery top-sellers. Also that year AWG's Kansas City division began distributing to more than 10 new stores that had formerly been served by Fleming at the time the #1 US wholesale food distributor.

In 2002 supermarket operator Homeland Stores which operates stores in Oklahoma emerged from bankruptcy as a fully owned subsidiary of AWG. AWG formed a new subsidiary Associated Retail Grocers to oversee Homeland and its Falley's chain.

As a result of the 2003 sale of Fleming Companies' wholesale distribution business AWG picked up food distribution centers in Nebraska (two) Oklahoma (one) and Tennessee (two) and general-merchandise distribution centers in Tennessee and Kansas.

Introducing a "dollar" section in its stores in 2004 proved successful leading AWG to expand the category to more than 1000 food and non-food items. The following year it merged the corporate offices of its Homeland and Food 4 Less chains.

AWG took steps to expand its capacity and its territory in 2007 when it acquired a distribution center in Fort Worth from Albertsons. The cooperative also took on supply operations for Albertsons locations in Arkansas Louisiana and Texas.

In 2009 AWG acquired the assets of Little Rock Arkansas-based Affiliated Foods Southwest in 2009 adding about a dozen new stores.

During 2010 the firm introduced a paperless coupon program.

In December 2011 AWG sold its corporate supermarkets to a group of employees. The corporate stores included 76 retail locations operating under the Homeland United of Oklahoma and Country mart banners in Oklahoma and the Super Saver banner in northern Texas.

In late 2012 AWG completed a 35000-square-foot addition to its corporate headquarters in Kansas City. The location is also home to AWG's Kansas City distribution centers and its Valu Merchandisers division.

EXECUTIVES

Vice President Corporate Controller, Gary Koch
EVP Division Operations, David Smith
Senior Vice President Grocery Products, Dan Funk
Vice President Of Sales, Joe Busch
Senior Vice President Distribution, Richard (Dick) Kearns
Svp And Division Manager Fort Worth, Linda Lawson
Vice President Store Engineering, John (Jack) Crumley
Vice President Corporate Human Resources, Susan (Sue) Ott
Vice President Investor, Lisa Fox
Senior Vice President Springfield, Tim Bellanti
Vice President, Don Ketter
Vice President, Gary Jennings

Senior Vice President Gen Concl, Frances Puhl
Senior Vice President Finance, David (Dave) Carl
Senior Vice President and Division Manager Kansas City, Bill Quade
Senior Vice President and Division Manager Kansas City, Bob Pickerill
Senior Vice President Perishables, Jerry Edney
Senior Vice President and Division Manager Gulf Coast, Bob Durand
Auditors: GRANT THORNTON LLP KANSAS CIT

LOCATIONS

HQ: ASSOCIATED WHOLESALE GROCERS INC.
5000 KANSAS AVE, KANSAS CITY, KS 661061135
Phone: 9132881000
Web: WWW.AWGINC.COM

Selected States Served
Alabama
Arizona
Arkansas
Colorado
Florida
Georgia
Idaho
Illinois
Indiana
Iowa
Kansas
Kentucky
Louisiana
Michigan
Minnesota
Mississippi
Missouri
Montana
Nebraska
New Mexico
North Carolina
North Dakota
Ohio
Oklahoma
South Carolina
South Dakota
Tennessee
Texas
Utah
Virginia
West Virginia
Wisconsin
Wyoming

COMPETITORS

Affiliated Foods	GSC Enterprises
Affiliated Foods Midwest	H. T. Hackney
Alex Lee	McLane
Associated Grocers Inc.	SUPERVALU
C&S Wholesale	SpartanNash
Central Grocers	Wakefern Food
Dearborn Wholesale Grocers	Wal-Mart

HISTORICAL FINANCIALS

Company Type: Private

Income Statement

FYE: December 28

	REVENUE ($ mil.)	NET INCOME ($ mil.)	NET PROFIT MARGIN	EMPLOYEES
12/13	8,380	192	2.3%	5,500
12/12	7,852	175	2.2%	—
12/11	7,766	169	2.2%	—
12/10	7,251	0	—	—
Annual Growth	4.9%	—	—	—

2013 Year-End Financials

Debt ratio: —
Return on equity: 2.30%
Cash ($ mil.): 59
Current ratio: 0.40
Long-term debt ($ mil.): —

Dividends
Yield: —
Payout: —
Market value ($ mil.): —

Assurant Inc

From credit cards to trailer parks Assurant provides a range of specialty insurance products. Through Assurant Solutions and Assurant Specialty Property the company offers such products as credit protection insurance manufactured home coverage creditor-placed homeowners insurance pre-need funeral policies and extended warranties for electronics appliances and vehicles. Individuals and small employer groups can choose from several types of health coverage offered by Assurant Health while group life dental and disability products are available through the Assurant Employee Benefits segment. Assurant's products are distributed through sales offices and independent agents across the US and abroad.

Operations

Assurant Solutions Assurant Specialty Property Assurant Health and Assurant Employee Benefits comprise Assurant's four operating segments. The Solutions unit which accounts for about 40% of revenues provides products such as debt-protection administration mobile device protection credit-related policies warranties and funeral insurance. Specialty Property lines include lender-placed homeowners insurance renters insurance and manufactured housing insurance; that segment brings in about 30% of Assurant's revenues. Assurant Health (19% of sales) offers individual and small employer health coverage while Assurant Employee Benefits (12%) focuses primarily on group life disability and dental policies.

Corporate & Other rounds out the company's business and accounts for about 1% of revenues.

Geographic Reach

Some 85% of Assurant's sales are in the US but the company also operates in Canada and Mexico as well as in Puerto Rico and about a dozen Latin American European and Asian countries. International sales are focused on extended-service contracts and credit insurance (debt protection coverage for unemployment death or other events) through partnering retail and institutional distributors. The company also offers funeral policies (used to fund funeral expenses) in Canada.

Sales and Marketing

Insurance products and services are distributed through a group sales force located in 32 offices. The company also sells its products through independent brokers agents employee benefit specialists financial institution representatives and third-party marketing organizations as well as through retail outlets including mortgage loan offices funeral homes and retailers.

Financial Performance

After experiencing slight declines early in the decade Assurant saw 3% growth in revenues in 2012 followed by 6% growth to $9.1 billion in 2013 and 15% growth to $10.4 billion in 2014. Growth in 2014 was largely driven by a 17% increase in the Solutions segment which did well domestically due to rising vehicle service contract sales and price increases. Specialty Property rose 11% on the acquisitions of Field Asset Services and StreetLinks as well as growth in net earned premiums for lender-placed homeowners coverage. The smaller segments Health and Employee Benefits also saw increases of 23% and 3% respectively; this followed a decline for both units in fiscal 2013.

Net income which was flat the prior couple of years declined to $471 million in 2014 (versus $489 million in 2013) despite the revenue growth. That decline was primarily due to higher operating expenses related to acquisitions benefit payouts and general administrative costs. Overall profits

have risen dramatically due to reduced impairment charges following sagging profits between 2008 and 2010 (caused by a variety of factors including a decline in the credit insurance market and the settlement of an SEC investigation).

Cash flow from operations fell 62% to $394 million in 2014 due to changes in the timing of payments a change in commissions payable and cash used in premium stabilization programs.

Strategy

The company typically expands by pursuing a conservative acquisition strategy investing in small purchases that neatly complement its existing offerings. In addition Assurant partners with other companies to expand its reach. For example the company in 2014 boosted its presence in Latin America with the $115 million investment in services assistant business Ike Asistencia. With that partnership the company will enjoy cross-selling opportunities of complementary products in several countries including Mexico.

In light of the rapid growth of the Internet of Things in 2014 Assurant launched the Connected Living division of its Solutions segment. The launch will blend its mobile and extended warranty programs businesses to deliver a comprehensive suite of products (mobile device coverage extended protection plans for consumer electronics and home appliances data security solutions) for customers with connected devices.

The company has been focused on growing its presence in the mortgage and multifamily housing industries. In 2014 Assurant expanded bought risk management firm eMortgage Logic which provides residential valuation products and services. In addition to property appraisals eMortgage's services include regulatory and compliance services and local market analytics. Other related deals include the recent purchases of StreetLinks and SureDeposit.

With its sights set on growth in the mortgage and multifamily markets Assurant sold its general agency business and carrier American Reliable Insurance Company (personal lines and agricultural property/casualty coverage) to a US subsidiary of Global Indemnity for $114 million. The sale allows the Specialty Property segment to better organize its business structure and to have more funding towards market growth.

With a wary eye on US health care reform the company has begun to streamline its group and individual health insurance operations in the hopes that it can cash in on industry opportunities that might arise. It started offering more low-cost insurance products such as high-deductable low-premium health plans with limited benefits to meet current market needs. In 2015 the company announced exit plans for Assurant Health which as an insurer focused on serving small employers and individuals has been struggling under the Affordable Care Act. Assurant plans to sell certain Assurant Health assets to National General Holdings and shutter the rest of the business by 2017. It will continue with its primary focus on niche products such as extended-service contracts and manufactured home coverage.

In another divestiture the company has agreed to sell Assurant Employee Benefits to Sun Life Financial in a deal valued at some $975 million. This will further allow Assurant to focus on such products as property credit renters funeral and flood policies.

Mergers and Acquisitions

In 2013 Assurant acquired UK-based mobile phone insurance provider Lifestyle Services Group (LSG) expanding its presence in Europe. The company also acquired Field Asset Services (property preservation restoration and inspection services) from FirstService Corporation for $55 million. The following year it bought CWI Group which pro-

vides mobile insurance administration in France for $71 million. Additionally Assurant invested $115 million in Iké Asistencia which provides roadside assistance home assistance travel protection and other products in Latin America (primarily Mexico).

Also in 2014 Assurant bought eMortgage Logic provider of residential valuation products and technology for $28 million. It also acquired appraisal management outfit StreetLinks from Novation Companies for $66 million.

Company Background

Assurant traces its roots to the LaCrosse Mutual Aid Association which was founded in 1892 to provide disability insurance in Wisconsin. The company formerly known as Fortis Inc. was spun off by the Fortis group (now known as Ageas) in 2004 and became publicly traded.

In 2010 the company resolved a nearly three-year-long SEC investigation into the company's finances. The investigation was part of a more widespread SEC investigation into the use by several companies (including Assurant) of finite reinsurance contracts which if manipulated can fraudulently lead investors into misunderstanding a company's bottom line. Assurant was never charged with fraud; but the company paid $3.5 million to settle non-fraud-related violations and settle the investigation without admitting or denying wrongdoing.

EXECUTIVES

EVP Chief Legal Officer and Secretary, Bart R. Schwartz, age 62, $520,000 total compensation
EVP Chief Communication and Marketing Officer, Francesca Luthi
President CEO and Director, Alan B. Colberg, age 53, $598,750 total compensation
EVP Chief Risk Officer CFO and Treasurer, Christopher J. Pagano, age 51
President and CEO Assurant Solutions, S. Craig Lemasters, age 54, $565,000 total compensation
President and CEO Assurant Specialty Property, Gene E. Mergelmeyer, age 56, $596,250 total compensation
EVP and Chief Strategy Officer, Peter Walker, age 42
EVP and Chief Human Resources Officer, Robyn Price Stonehill
Assistant Vice President, Drew Kovalsky
Svp Finance (Taxation), Melissa J T Hall, age 48
Vice President And general Manager, Gerald (Jerry) Daly
Vice President Hazard Product Business Manager, Shawn Kelly
Senior Vice President, Lynn Gelsomin
Senior Vice President Global Sales And Business Development, Allen Tuthill
Senior Vice President Global Sales and Business Development, Allen (Al) Tuthill
Non-Executive Chair of the Board, Elaine D. Rosen, age 62
Auditors: PricewaterhouseCoopers LLP

LOCATIONS

HQ: Assurant Inc
  28 Liberty Street, 41st Floor, New York, NY 10005
Phone: 212 859-7000
Web: www.assurant.com

2014 Sales

	$ mil.	% of total
US	8,874	85
Other countries	1,506	15
Total	**10,381**	**100**

PRODUCTS/OPERATIONS

2014 Sales

	$ mil.	% of total
Solutions	4,179	40
Specialty Property	2,909	28
Health	2,020	19
Employee Benefits	1,193	12
Corporate & other	79	1
Total	**10,381**	**100**

Business S

Assurant Solutions
  Credit insurance (domestic and international)
  Debt protection/deferment
  Preneed life insurance (pre-funded funeral insurance)
  Warranties and Extended Service Contracts (ESCs domestic and international)
Assurant Specialty Property
  Homeowners insurance (creditor-placed and voluntary)
  Manufactured housing insurance (creditor-placed and voluntary)
  Other specialty property personal lines (primarily flood and renters insurance)
Assurant Health
  Health Savings Accounts and Health Reimbursement Accounts (HSAs and HRAs)
  Individual health insurance
  Short-term health and student insurance
  Small employer group health insurance
Assurant Employee Benefits
  Group disability
  Group dental
  Group life

COMPETITORS

Allstate	Home Buyers Warranty
AmTrust Financial	Homesteaders Life
American Home Shield	Humana
Americo	Maiden Holdings
Asurion	Monumental Life
Bankers Financial	Mutual of Omaha
CIGNA	NGL Insurance
Delta Dental Plans	Nationwide
Fidelity National	QBE First
Financial	State Farm
First American	The Warranty Group
Great American	United Concordia
Insurance Company	Warrantech

HISTORICAL FINANCIALS

Company Type: Public

Income Statement

FYE: December 31

	ASSETS ($ mil.)	NET INCOME ($ mil.)	INCOME AS % OF ASSETS	EMPLOYEES
12/15	30,043	141	0.5%	16,700
12/14	31,562	470	1.5%	17,600
12/13	29,714	488	1.6%	16,600
12/12	28,946	483	1.7%	14,600
12/11	27,115	545	2.0%	14,100
Annual Growth	**2.6%**	**(28.6%)**	**—**	**4.3%**

2015 Year-End Financials

Debt ratio: 3.90%	No. of shares (mil.): 65
Return on equity: 2.92%	Dividends
Cash ($ mil.): 1,288	Yield: 1.7%
Current ratio: —	Payout: 76.9%
Long-term debt ($ mil.): —	Market value ($ mil.): 5,304

	STOCK PRICE ($) FY Close	P/E High/Low		PER SHARE ($) Earnings	Dividends	Book Value
12/15	80.54	42	29	2.05	1.37	68.70
12/14	68.43	11	9	6.44	1.06	74.77
12/13	66.37	10	5	6.30	0.96	67.29
12/12	34.70	8	6	5.67	0.81	65.92
12/11	41.06	7	6	5.58	0.70	56.79
Annual Growth	**18.3%**	**—**	**—**	**(22.1%)**	**18.3%**	**4.9%**

Astoria Financial Corp.

Astoria Financial is the holding company for Astoria Bank (formerly Astoria Federal) one of the largest thrifts in New York with deposits totaling $9.7 billion. The bank has more than 85 branches in and around New York City and on Long Island in addition to a network of third-party mortgage brokers spanning more than a dozen states and Washington DC. It offers standard deposit products such as CDs and checking savings and retirement accounts. With these funds Astoria Bank primarily writes loans and invests in mortgage-backed securities. Subsidiary AF Insurance Agency sells life and property/casualty coverage to bank customers. New York Community Bancorp agreed to acquire Astoria in late 2015.

OperationsAstoria Bank's $11.85 billion loan portfolio is made up of mostly of mortgage loans. Nearly 60% of its total loan portfolio is secured by residential properties while 40% is secured by multi-family properties and commercial real estate. Revenue-wise the bank makes nearly 45% of its revenue from residential mortgage loans and more than 30% of total revenue from its multi-family and commercial real estate loans. Around 10% of its revenue comes from mortgage-backed and other securities.Geographic ReachThe company's 87 banking and loan production offices serve the greater New York City metropolitan area encompassing Brooklyn Queens and Nassau Suffolk and Westchester counties. It also has a broker network in four states mostly along the East Coast.Sales and MarketingThe company spent $12.5 million on advertising in 2014 or nearly double the $6.4 million it spent in 2013 mostly as it spent more toward growing its banking business during the year which includes opening of its Manhattan and Melville branches in New York. In 2014 its boost in advertising was designed to increase brand awareness in the busy commuter travel hub of Pennsylvania Station in New York City for the month of September 2014.Astoria spent $6.39 million on advertising in 2012.Financial Performance

Astoria Financial's revenue has been declining in recent years from a shrinking loan business. Indeed in 2014 the bank's loan assets shrank by 3% to $11.96 billion while deposits shrank by more than 3% to $9.5 billion.Revenue in 2014 fell by nearly 7% to $547.2 million mostly because of a 17% decline in residential mortgage loan interest income as repayments outpaced originations and as interest margins shrank during the year due to the low-interest environment. Mortgage banking income also plummeted by 75% but this is because the bank in 2013 was able to collect a nonrecurring $5.4 million recovery on some of its serviced loans previously thought to be bad. Despite falling revenue profit grew for a second straight year jumping by 44% to $95.92 million in 2014. The boost in net income was mostly thanks to a $9.5 million credit to loan loss provisions (compared to a $19.6 million charge in 2013) as its loan portfolio's credit quality improved coupled with a $15.7 million reduction in income tax expense thanks to the NYS income tax legislation passed that year. Astoria also paid lower interest expense as it continued to restructure its borrowings and pay down its debt and because it paid lower interest on its deposit accounts. Operations provided $134.08 million or 42% less cash than in 2013 primarily as the bank collected less cash from proceeds for sales of its loans held-for-sale.

Strategy

To turn around its financial situation and grow its loan business Astoria Bank has set its sights on growing its branch network particularly in Manhat-

tan. Indeed the community bank opened a branch in Midtown in March 2014 and has plans to open seven more branches in Manhattan and on Long Island by the end of 2016.

While the bank's residential mortgage loan business has been shrinking in recent years its multifamily and commercial real estate mortgage business has been growing. In 2014 the bank collected 9% more in interest income from its multi-family and commercial real estate mortgages as those loan assets grew by $720.9 million over the year. As a result the loan portfolio share of these multi-family and commercial real estate loans grew from 58% in 2013 to to 65% of the bank's overall loan portfolio in 2013.

Company Background

Established in 1888 Astoria Federal Savings changed its name to Astoria Bank in June 2014 to better reflect its broadened scope of financial services and products.

EXECUTIVES

Vice Chairman; SEVP and COO, Gerard C. Keegan, age 68, $600,000 total compensation
President and CEO, Monte N. Redman, age 64, $930,000 total compensation
EVP and Chief Support Services Officer, Josie Callari
EVP and CIO, Robert J. DeStefano
EVP and Managing Director Retail Banking Group, Brian T. Edwards
SEVP and Chief Lending Officer, Hugh J. Donlon
EVP and Managing Director Business Banking Group, Stephen J. Sipola, $400,000 total compensation
SEVP Secretary and Chief Risk Officer, Alan P. Eggleston, $515,000 total compensation
SEVP and CFO, Frank E. Fusco, $515,000 total compensation
Vice President Consumer Loans, Walter Krzyminski
Vice President Of Information Security, Rise Jacobs
Vice President, Marsha Marangiello
First Vice President, Marty McAleer
Vice President And Director Enterprise Risk Modeling, Tom Villella
Vice President, Janet Kovacs
First Assistant Vice President Marketing Manager, Bryan Kuhl
Vice President Business Banking, Michael Devoe
First Vice President, Michael Lechleider
Senior Vice President Treasurer, Daniel Dougherty
First Vice President, Michael (Mel) Lechleider
Chairman, Ralph F. Palleschi, age 68
Auditors: KPMG LLP

LOCATIONS

HQ: Astoria Financial Corp.
  One Astoria Bank Plaza, Lake Success, NY 11042-1085
Phone: 516 327-3000   **Fax:** 516 327-7860
Web: www.astoriabank.com

PRODUCTS/OPERATIONS

2014 Sales

	$ mil.	% of total
Interest		
Residential mortgage loans	241	44
Multifamily commercial real estate & construction mortgage loans	178	33
Mortgage-backed and other securities	57	10
Consumer & other loans	8	2
Other	6	1
Noninterest		
Customer service fees	35	6
Income from bank owned life insurance	8	2
Mortgage banking income	3	1
Others	7	1
Total	**547**	**100**

COMPETITORS

Apple Bank for Savings	Flushing Financial
Bank of America	HSBC USA
Capital One	JPMorgan Chase
Citibank	New York Community
Dime Community	Bancorp
Bancshares	TD Bank USA

HISTORICAL FINANCIALS

Company Type: Public

Income Statement

FYE: December 31

	ASSETS ($ mil.)	NET INCOME ($ mil.)	INCOME AS % OF ASSETS	EMPLOYEES
12/14	15,640	95	0.6%	1,649
12/13	15,793	66	0.4%	1,603
12/12	16,496	53	0.3%	1,614
12/11	17,022	67	0.4%	1,730
12/10	18,089	73	0.4%	1,662
Annual Growth	(3.6%)	6.8%	—	(0.2%)

2014 Year-End Financials

Debt ratio: 8.62%	No. of shares (mil.): 99
Return on equity: 6.19%	Dividends
Cash ($ mil.): 143	Yield: 1.2%
Current ratio: —	Payout: 18.8%
Long-term debt ($ mil.): —	Market value ($ mil.): 1,335

	STOCK PRICE ($) FY Close	P/E High/Low	PER SHARE ($) Earnings	Dividends	Book Value
12/14	13.36	16 14	0.88	0.16	15.81
12/13	13.83	23 15	0.60	0.16	15.37
12/12	9.36	20 15	0.55	0.25	13.15
12/11	8.49	22 9	0.70	0.52	12.70
12/10	13.91	22 15	0.78	0.52	12.69
Annual Growth	(1.0%)	— —	3.1%	(25.5%)	5.7%

AT&T Inc

Through its subsidiaries affiliates and operating companies holding company AT&T is the industry-leading provider of wireline voice communications services in the US. Customers use AT&T-branded telephone Internet and VoIP services; it also sells digital TV under the U-verse brand. Key markets include California Illinois and Texas. The company's corporate government and public sector clients use its conferencing managed network and wholesale communications services. Subsidiary AT&T Mobility is the second-largest US mobile carrier by both sales and subscriptions (after Verizon Wireless). It provides mobile services to more than 126 million subscribers.

Operations

AT&T's wireless segment outpaced the company's wireline business in 2014 accounting for 56% of the company's revenue. The wireless business grew at a 6% rate for the year while wireline declined 1%. The wireline segment is composed of switched and dedicated network transport dial-up and broadband Internet access network integration data equipment sales and converged video communications.

Geographic Reach

The company has spectrum licenses in all 50 US states Puerto Rico and Washington DC. Its wireless services and mobile broadband services are available in about 200 countries.

Sales and Marketing

AT&T has pushed its mobile services through increased advertising and marketing efforts that tout the benefits of the mobile Internet. A key component of this was an exclusive agreement with Apple to carry the iPhone in the US from the time of its debut in the summer of 2007 until early 2011 when top rival Verizon also began to offer the device. AT&T reaped significant rewards from this partnership which helped drive the growth and profits of its wireless business. It spends about $3 billion a year on advertising.

Financial Performance

AT&T's revenue increased nearly 3% to $132.4 billion in 2014 from 2013. The overall rise was helped by a 47% jumped in equipment revenue as postpaid customers bought devices on installment instead of the device subsidy model. The company's U-verse offerings were strong sellers but legacy wireline continued to decline.

At $6.2 billion the company's 2014 net income was just a third of what it reported in 2013. The 2013 profit included a gain related to pension and post-employment benefit plans. In 2014 AT&T had higher cost of sales and general expenses compared to 2013.

Cash flow from operations fell to about $31.3 million in 2014 from $35 million in 2013.

Strategy

AT&T is building its fiber-to- the-home technology to provide residences and business with higher Internet speeds which will enable other technologies. The $4 billion program called Project VIP is aimed at bringing more customers to IP-based services as well as to subscribe to higher value entertainment services. The company ended 2104 with 12.2 million Internet subscribers and about 6 million video subscribers. AT&T has stepped up expansion and adjusted rates of its high-speed Internet service in areas where it competes with services such as Google Fiber.

The company bid more than $18 billion for spectrum auctioned by the Federal Communications Commission (FCC). AT&T wants to maintain its high-speed network to carry large amounts of video which accounted for more than 50% of its network traffic in 2014.

AT&T is seeking to diversify its revenue streams through acquisitions. By the end of 2015 the company expects that wireless and wired business services will be its biggest source of revenue followed by US TV and Internet service US consumer mobile and Latin American TV and mobile.

As wireline services decline AT&T is divesting some those assets. In October 2014 it completed the sale of its Connecticut wireline operations to Frontier Communications for $2 billion.

Mergers and Acquisitions

AT&T has been using acquisitions to build its mobile data capabilities and expand its service area and subscriber numbers. In one of its biggest acquisitions the company bought satellite pay-TV provider DIRECTV for $48.5 billion in mid-2015. The combination enables AT&T to offer new packaged services and deliver content on mobile devices TVs laptops cars and airplanes.

Two other significant acquisitions will make AT&T one of the biggest mobile carriers in Mexico almost overnight (as corporate dealings go). The company closed its purchase of Iusacell in early 2015 and should close on its Nextel Mexico purchase by the middle of the year. With the transactions AT&T's nearly nationwide service area in Mexico will cover 100 million people.

In 2014 it purchased Leap Wireless (which operates under the Cricket brand) for some $1.2 billion in an effort to build its profile in the prepaid market and expand its LTE network.

A move that could affect AT&T and other carriers came in early 2015 when the FCC proposed regulating the Internet under the Telecommunica-

tions Acts of 1934. The proposed regulation is to ensure net neutrality. AT&T has filed suit against the proposed regulation. The company is challenging is challenging the FCC's reclassification of the Internet as a telecommunications network.

Previously a deal to buy smaller rival T-Mobile USA from Deutsche Telekom fell apart amid strong government opposition in 2012. AT&T had to pay Deutsche Telekom a break-up fee valued at about $6 billion including $3 billion in cash along with wireless spectrum licenses and a national roaming agreement worth another $3 billion.

HISTORY

Early History

In 1878 a dozen customers signed up for the first telephone exchange in St. Louis (later Bell Telephone Company of Missouri). That exchange and the Missouri and Kansas Telephone Company later merged into Southwestern Bell which became a regional arm of the AT&T monopoly in 1917.

The old AT&T was broken up in 1984 and Southwestern Bell emerged as a regional Bell operating company (RBOC) with local phone service rights in five states a cellular company a directory business and a stake in R&D arm Bellcore (now Telcordia). In 1987 the company bought paging and cellular franchises from Metromedia.

Edward Whitacre a Texan who worked his way from measuring phone wire to an executive spot at Southwestern Bell became CEO in 1990. That year the RBOC joined with France Telecom and Mexican conglomerate Grupo Carso to purchase 20% of Teléfonos de México (Telmex) the former state monopoly.

Renamed SBC Communications in 1994 the company hired lobbyists the next year to coax the Texas Legislature to pass a bill that would deter local phone competitors. It worked: New entrants had to build a phone network to serve every house in a 27-mile square.

The federal Telecommunications Act passed in 1996 and the following year SBC acquired Pacific Telesis the parent of Pacific Bell and Nevada Bell. That year the FCC denied SBC's request to enter Oklahoma's long-distance market saying the company had not done enough to encourage competition. Undeterred SBC launched a legal assault on the Telecom Act itself which proved to be unsuccessful.

SBC bought Southern New England Telecommunications (SNET) in 1998 gaining a foothold on the East Coast. The next year the company bought Comcast's cellular operations and took a minority stake in Williams Communications Group (now WilTel Communications) —the first significant investment in a long-distance carrier by a Baby Bell.

SBC completed the $62 billion purchase of Ameritech in 1999 after weathering a year-long regulatory review. The acquisition extended SBC's local access dominance into five Midwestern states but about half of Ameritech's wireless business was sold as a condition of the deal. SBC agreed to provide competitive local phone service in 30 cities outside its home territory by 2002 to win regulatory approval. Also in 1999 the company announced plans to spend $6 billion over three years to make its networks capable of delivering high-speed DSL Internet access to 80% of its customers.

EXECUTIVES

SEVP External and Legislative Affairs, James W. (Jim) Cicconi, age 63, $800,000 total compensation

CEO AT&T Mexico and Iusacell, F. Thaddeus Arroyo, age 51

SEVP Human Resources, William A. (Bill) Blase, age 60

SEVP and CFO, John J. Stephens, age 56, $765,833 total compensation
Chairman and CEO, Randall L. Stephenson, age 55, $1,691,667 total compensation
CEO AT&T Business Solutions, Andrew M. (Andy) Geisse, age 58
CEO AT&T Entertainment and Internet Services AT&T Services Inc., John T. Stankey, age 53, $920,000 total compensation
SEVP and Global Marketing Officer, Lori Lee
SEVP AT&T Technology and Network Operations, John M. Donovan
President AT&T Oklahoma, Steve Hahn
President AT&T Kansas, Mike Scott
President AT&T Georgia and AT&T Southeast, Bill Leahy
Senior Associate General Counsel, David R. McAtee
Senior Vice President Federal Regulatory, Robert (Bob) Quinn
Vice President Segment Marketing Enablement, Ellyce Brenner
Assistant Vice President Growth Platforms, Marcus Owenby
Vice President, Judy Phillips
Vice President Tax, Lawrence J Ruzicka
Vice President General Manager Sales, Wanda Simmons
Senior Vice President Of Emerging Devices, Chris Penrose
Sales Vice President, Laurine Eidson
Sales Vice President Premier Client Group, Sean Murphy
Senior Vice President Finance, David Muro
Sales Center Vice President, Rick A Zambrano
Vice President Of Sales, Michael Eisenhardt
Assistant Vice President C And E Osp, James Keown
Vice President Of Workforce Development And Diversity, Belinda Grant-anderson
Vice President, Dennis Whiteside
Assistant Vice President Wholesale, Kathy Wilkinson
Regional Vice President, Craig Warbinton
Vice President Customer Service, Steve Schoonmaker
Assistant Vice President, Josh Goodell
Vice President Wholesale Wireline Sales, Joan Jambor
Senior Vice President U Verse Field Oprations, Randy Tomlin
National Sales Manager, Laurie Perryman
Information Technology Vice President, Hulsey R David
Assistant Vice President Sales Operations, Sandra Galst
Assistant Vice President Ran Engineering, Rajive Beri
Regional Vice President Business Integrated Solutions At At And T Mobility, Maurice Styles
Vice President Wholesale Strategy and Business Development, Adrienne P Scott
Assistant Vice President Emerging Devices Organization, Ken Diprima
Vice President Business Development Emerging Devices, Joseph Mosele
Sales Center Vice President, Craig Dieckhoner
Assistant Vice President Mobility Service Operations Global Network Operations, Mike Hargrove
Sales Vice President, Patrick Reay
Vice President Financial Planning, George Goeke
Senior Vice President Corporate Strategy, Steve McGaw
Vice President Sales, Connie Boyle
Vice President Of Acquisitions, James Bielar
Rvp, Meredith Caram
Vice President Specialty Solutions, Christopher Poli
Assistant Vice President Information Technology, Joe Greer
Associate Vice President, Tara Colon

Assistant Vice President Network Services, Raymond Perkins
Vice President Fleet Operations, Jerome Webber
Vice President Gm, Joey Schultz
Vice President Audit Services, Gerard R Chicoine
Vice President Product Marketing Management, Ebrahim Keshavarz
Vice President Communication S, Monte Cely
Vice President Product Marketing, Jason Porter
Assistant Vice President Network Contracting, Roland Tunez
Assistant Vice President Business Advertising, Kelly Thengvall
Vice President And General Manager, Gary Lackhouse
Vice President, Philip Johnson
Sales Vice President, Steve Williams
Vice President Pricing Coe, Brian K Anderson
Evp International External Aff, Antonio Amendola
Assistant Vice President Home Solutions, Amy McCracken
Dvp Impl Center Ma, Cheri Brookshire
Senior Vice President And Assistant General Counsel, William (Bill) Drexel
Assistant Vice President Sales Operations, Suzanne Galvanek
Regional Vice President Global Access Management, Bob Flappan
Vice President Brand Identity And Design, Gregg Heard
Vice President Att Com, Philip Bienert
Senior Vice President BCS, Vicki Jones
Assistant Vice President Service Management, Bob Peters
Assistant Vice President Product Marketing Management, Danielle M Lee
Vice President, Michele Smith
Assistant Vice President Information Technology Operations, Bawcum Ross
Vice President And General Manager New York New Jersey, Thomas Devito
Vice President Of Vod Programming, Richard (Dick) Wellerstein
Regional Vice President Sales, Russ Porter
Vice President Investor Relations, John Palmer
Vice President Supply Chain, Keith Connolly
Regional Vice President External Affairs, Brooke Thomson
Regional Vice President West Global Markets, Michael (Mel) Stice
Vice President Of Chemical Development, Damon Holzer
Vice President Corporate Communications, Kathy Van Buskirk
Vice President U Verse Product Managemetn, G W Shaw
Vice President Long Distance Compliance Relief, Michael Gilliam
National Account Manager, Erik Fonbon
Vice President Technology and Product Management, Ronald (Ron) Kalin
Assistant Vice President Financial Analysis, Matthew Davis
Vice President Customer Service, Susan (Sue) Prince
Att Ravpn Contact, Sam Tuffaha
Vice President, John (Jack) Hyland
Senior Vice President, Bruce Goemaat
Area Vice President, Suzette Dolter
Assistant Vice President Ran Engineering West Region, Ignacio Angulo
Director Evpn, Gregory Feenstra
Assistant Vice President Enterprise Managed Services, Bill Kramer
Vice President Bus Solutions Digital Experience, Laura Merling
Vice President Finance, Phil Schmidt
Vice President Of Voice Technologies, Marian Croak

Area Vice President At And T Mobility Smb, Jeff Goldstein
RVP Business Integrated Solutions, Martha K Wells
Vice President, Michael Flanagan
Vice President Small Business Product Management, Tom Hughes
Regional Vice President, Stephen Vergine
Sales Center Vice President, Vicky Santangelo
Executive Vice President Wholesale And Gem Solutio, Sherry Morse
Assistant Vice President Global Media Relations, Fletcher Cook
Assistant Vice President Project Program Management, William Schutts
Sales Vice President, Kerry Rogers
Assistant Vice President (Assistant Vice President) Accounting, Lonnie Shirey
RVP Business Integrated Solutions, Kim Whitworth
Vice President Of Project Development, Jeff Lewis
Regional Vice President West Region, Randy Chepenik
Vice President Signature Client Group Northeast Regional, Stephen Leggett
Vice President, Polly Bessel
National Account Manager, Kevin Moore
Regional Vice President, Dan Masters
Sales Center Vice President Mobility, William (Bill) Stovall
National Account Manager, Dean Ramsey
Regional Vice President Sales, Jennifer (Jen) Ball
Sales Center Vice President, Steve D'Lugos
Assistant Vice President Financial Analysis, Shareron Willis
Vice President Gbs Business Oprs Quality and Compliance, John (Jack) Potter
At And T Home Solutions Assistant Vice President, Valerie Scheder
Senior Vice President, Andy Morgan
Assistant Vice President, Stephen Waken
Vice President, Dan Lafond
Vice President, Tim O'Brien
Vice President, Kuruvilla Cherian
Vice President, Duff Armstrong
Assistant Vice President Accounting, James Lacy
Regional Vice President, Bill Walsh
Sales Vice President, Dan Roche
National Sales Manager, Steve Mitchell
Vice President Network Technology And Engineering, Patricia Harris
Mse And Vpn Engineering, Glenn Williman
Customer Network Operations Vice President, Marvonia Walker
Vice President, Gary Greiner
Regional Vice President, Marianne Benton
Assistant Vice President of Marketing Strategy and Analysis, Mitch Farber
Sales Vice President, Fred Monacelli
Vice President Audit Services, Gerry Chicoine
Assistant Vice President U verse and Video Product Marketing, John (Jack) Blinkiewicz
Vice President Application And Service Management, Jerrie Kertz
Assistant Vice President Finance Global Client Group, Matt Monahan
Senior Vice President External Affairs, Holly Reed
Auditors: Ernst & Young LLP

LOCATIONS

HQ: AT&T Inc
208 S. Akard St., Dallas, TX 75202
Phone: 210 821-4105
Web: www.att.com

PRODUCTS/OPERATIONS

2014 Sales

	$ mil.	% of total
Wireless service	73,992	56
Data	58,425	44
Others	30	-
Total	**132,447**	**100**

2014 Sales

	% of total
Service	89
Equipment	11
Total	**100**

Selected Services

Voice
  Local
  Long-distance
  Wholesale
Data
  Application management
  Data equipment sales
  Data storage
  Database management
  Dedicated Internet service
  Digital television
  Directory and operator assistance
  Disaster recovery
  Enterprise networking
  Hardware and operating system management
  Internet access and network integration
  Managed Web hosting
  Network design
  Network implementation
  Network installation
  Network integration
  Network management
  Outsourcing
  Packet services
  Private lines
  Satellite video
  Switched and dedicated transport
  Voice-over-IP networks
  Wholesale networking
  WiFi

COMPETITORS

Cablevision Systems	Level 3 Communications
CenturyLink	SAVVIS
Charter Communications	Sprint Communications
Comcast	T-Mobile USA
Consolidated Communications	TDS Metrocom
Cox Communications	Telephone & Data Systems
DIRECTV	Time Warner Cable
DISH Network	U.S. Cellular
EarthLink	Verizon
Equinix	XO Holdings
Frontier Communications	

HISTORICAL FINANCIALS

Company Type: Public

Income Statement

FYE: December 31

	REVENUE ($ mil.)	NET INCOME ($ mil.)	NET PROFIT MARGIN	EMPLOYEES
12/14	132,447	6,224	4.7%	253,000
12/13	128,752	18,249	14.2%	243,000
12/12	127,434	7,264	5.7%	242,000
12/11	126,723	3,944	3.1%	256,420
12/10	124,280	19,864	16.0%	266,590
Annual Growth	**1.6%**	**(25.2%)**	**—**	**(1.3%)**

2014 Year-End Financials

Debt ratio: 28.03%—
Return on equity: 7.02%
Cash ($ mil.): 8,603
Current ratio: 0.86
Long-term debt ($ mil.): 76,011

Dividends
  Yield: 5.4%
  Payout: 154.6%
Market value ($ mil.): —

STOCK PRICE ($) FY Close	P/E High/Low		PER SHARE ($) Earnings	Dividends	Book Value
12/14	33.59	31 27	1.19	1.84	16.65
12/13	35.16	12 10	3.39	1.80	17.41
12/12	33.71	31 23	1.25	1.76	16.55
12/11	30.24	48 41	0.66	1.72	17.81
12/10	29.38	9 7	3.35	1.68	18.89
Annual Growth	**3.4%**	**— —**	**(22.8%)**	**2.3%**	**(3.1%)**

Autoliv Inc.

Autoliv puts some drive behind the Bee Gees' jive about stayin' alive. The world's #1 manufacturer of car safety equipment aims to save lives by increasing the survivability statistics of traffic accidents. It makes components such as seat belts airbags anti-whiplash systems and safety electronics. Other products include rollover protection systems steering wheels (with airbags) night vision systems radar systems and child seats. The company caters to about every car maker in the industry and has more than 100 locations around the globe.

Geographic Reach

Autoliv has 21 crash test tracks 18 technical centers and 80 production facilities in 28 countries. Its US operations are overseen by Autoliv ASP Inc. Its largest markets are the Americas (34% of total sales) Europe (33%) and Asia (33%).

Operations

Autoliv operates through three primary segments: airbags and associated products (65% of total sales) seat belts and associated products (30%) and active safety products (5%).

Beginning in 2015 the company launched a new internal structure consisting of two business segments: passive safety (including airbags and seatbelts) and electronics (including passive safety electronics and active safety) to manage its business operations.

Sales and Marketing

General Motors is Autoliv's largest customer accounting for 14% of sales in 2014 while Ford and Renault/Nissan each accounted for 11% of sales.

Financial Performance

Autoliv has enjoyed four straight years of unprecedented growth with revenues jumping 9% from $8.8 billion in 2013 to $9.2 billion in 2014 — a historic milestone for the company. Its profits declined slightly dropping 4% from $486 million in 2013 to $468 million in 2014 due to a rise in research and development expenses.

The historic growth for 2014 was fueled by a 42% spike in active safety products sales and an 8% jump in sales from China. The growth in China was fueled by additional sales from the models Ford VW Baojun Great Wall and Haima. Operations in Europe and the Americas also reported growth for 2014.

Autoliv's operating cash flow has fluctuated over the last five years. It decreased by 15% from $838 million in 2013 to $713 million in 2014.

Strategy

The company is focused on growing by increasing its organic sales overseas. In 2014 the company began production on two of its largest investments a propellant plant and a textile center in China. A major advantage to expansion outside of its traditional market of North America is that cars built in developing economies have tended to lightly adopt safety features —so there is room for further penetration.

HISTORY

Autoliv traces its origins back to 1956 when Autoliv AB a Swedish corporation pioneered automotive seat belt technology. By 1967 the company had invented the retractor belt. Granges Weda AB another maker of seat belt retractors acquired the company in 1975. Electrolux bought the Granges Group (later renamed SAPA) in 1989 and changed its name to Electrolux Autoliv. Throughout the 1980s and 1990s the company continued to grow through acquisitions buying seat belt manufacturing operations primarily in Europe but also in Australia and New Zealand. In 1994 the company changed its name to Autoliv AB and went public with Electrolux selling all its shares during the offering.

EXECUTIVES

Group VP Quality, Svante Mogefors, age 61
Chairman President and CEO, Jan Carlson, age 55, $1,202,299 total compensation
Group VP Sales and Engineering, Steven (Steve) Fredin, age 53, $526,000 total compensation
Group VP Finance and CFO, Mats Wallin, age 50, $508,297 total compensation
President Passive Safety, George Chang, $595,541 total compensation
Group VP Purchasing, Henrik Arrland
President Electronics, Steven Rod Cage 53
Group VP Product and Process Development and CTO, Johan L Tvenholm, age 45
President Autoliv Europe, Jonas Nilsson, age 43, $387,240 total compensation
Vice President Global Business Unit, Walter Guertler
Vice President Human Resources, Kim Kovac
Vice President, Erin Patrick
Vice President For Ford Business, Stefan Kroenung
Vice President Corporate Communications, Thomas (Thom) Jonsson
Treasurer, Craig Briggs
Auditors: Ernst & Young AB

LOCATIONS

HQ: Autoliv Inc.
Vasagatan 11, 7th Floor, SE-111 20, Box 70381, Stockholm SE-107 24
Phone: (46) 8 587 20 600
Web: www.autoliv.com

2014 Sales

	% of total
Americas	34
Europe	33
Asia	
China	16
Japan	7
Rest of Asia	10
Total	**100**

PRODUCTS/OPERATIONS

2014 Sales

	% of total
Airbags & associated products	65
Seatbelts & associated products	30
Active safety products	5
Total	**100**

Selected Products

Anti-whiplash seats
Child restraints
Electronics
Frontal airbags
Inflators
Leg airbags
Seat belts
Side-impact airbags
Steering wheels

Selected Subsidiaries and Affiliates

Airbags International Ltd (UK)
Autoflator AB
Autoliv AB
Autoliv Argentina SA
Autoliv ASP BV (The Netherlands)
Autoliv ASP Inc. (US)
Autoliv Australia Proprietary Ltd
Autoliv Autosicherheitstechnik GmbH (Germany)
Autoliv BKI SA (Spain)
Autoliv BV (The Netherlands)
Autoliv Canada Inc
Autoliv Cankor Otomotiv Emniyet Sistemleri Sanayi Ve
   (Turkey)
Autoliv China Electronics Co. Ltd
Autoliv do Brasil Ltda.
Autoliv East Europe AB
Autoliv Electronics AB
Autoliv Electronics SAS (France)
Autoliv France SNC
Autoliv Holding BV (The Netherlands)
Autoliv Holding Inc. (US)
Autoliv Holding Ltd. (UK)
Autoliv Italia S.P.A.
Autoliv Japan Ltd
Autoliv KFT (Hungary)
Autoliv KLE SAU (Spain)
Autoliv Ltd (UK)
Autoliv Nichiyo Co. (Japan)
Autoliv Overseas BV (The Netherlands)
Autoliv Poland Sp zoo
Autoliv Romania SA
Autoliv Safety Technology Inc. (US)
Autoliv Sicherheitstechnik GmbH (Germany)
Autoliv Southern Africa Pty Ltd
Autoliv Stakupress GmbH (Germany)
Autoliv Sverige AB
Autoliv Thailand Ltd
Autoliv UK Holding Ltd
Marling BV (The Netherlands)
Mei-An Autoliv Co. (59% Taiwan)
Nanjing Hongguang Autoliv Vehicle Safety Co. Ltd. (50%
   China)
NSK Safety Technology (Thailand) Co. Ltd.
OEA Inc. (US)
Svensk Airbag AB
Van Oerle Alberton BV (The Netherlands)
Van Oerle Alberton Holding BV (The Netherlands)
Van Oerle Webco Pty Ltd (Australia)

COMPETITORS

AISIN World Corp.	Key Safety Systems
ASHIMORI INDUSTRY CO. LTD.	Kongsberg Automotive
	Magna International
Autocam	Mitsubishi Electric
Bosch Corp.	NFA
CASCO Products	Neaton Auto Products
DENSO	Nihon Plast
Delphi Automotive Systems	Nippon Kayaku
	Sequa
Ensign-Bickford	Special Devices
Gentex	Takata
Hella	Toyoda Gosei
Honeywell International	Toyoda Boshoku
	Valeo
International Textile Group	ZF TRW Automotive

HISTORICAL FINANCIALS

Company Type: Public

Income Statement

FYE: December 31

	REVENUE ($ mil.)	NET INCOME ($ mil.)	NET PROFIT MARGIN	EMPLOYEES
12/14	9,240	467	5.1%	60,000
12/13	8,803	485	5.5%	56,500
12/12	8,266	483	5.8%	50,900
12/11	8,232	623	7.6%	47,900
12/10	7,170	590	8.2%	43,300
Annual Growth	6.5%	(5.7%)	—	8.5%

2014 Year-End Financials

Debt ratio: 21.51%	No. of shares (mil.): 88
Return on equity: 12.63%	Dividends
Cash ($ mil.): 1,529	Yield: 2.0%
Current ratio: 1.93	Payout: 47.3%
Long-term debt ($ mil.): 1,521	Market value ($ mil.): 9,416

	STOCK PRICE ($) FY Close	P/E High/Low		PER SHARE ($) Earnings	Dividends	Book Value
12/14	106.12	21	17	5.06	2.12	38.63
12/13	91.80	19	13	5.07	2.00	42.18
12/12	67.39	13	10	5.08	1.89	39.36
12/11	53.49	12	7	6.65	1.73	37.33
12/10	78.94	12	6	6.39	0.65	32.90
Annual Growth	7.7%	—	—	(5.7%)	34.4%	4.1%

Automatic Data Processing Inc.

The original outsourcer Automatic Data Processing (ADP) has still got it. ADP is one of the largest payroll and tax filing processors in the world serving about 625000 clients. Employer services (payroll processing tax and benefits administration services) account for the majority of the company's sales and its PEO (professional employer organization) services are provided through ADP TotalSource. Other offerings include accounting auto collision estimates for insurers employment background checks desktop support and business development training services. The company in 2014 spun off its former dealer services segment.

Geographic Reach

The company provides services in more than 100 countries spread across the Americas Europe the Middle East Africa and the Asia Pacific region.

OperationsIn 2014 the company spun off its former dealer services segment (contributed 15% of 2014 revenue). It now operates across two segments.The employer services segment (67%) offers a range of business outsourcing and HCM services throughout 35 countries. Its Professional Employer Organization (PEO) services segment (18%; aka ADP TotalSource) provides employment administration outsourcing services through a co-employment relationship in which employees who work at a client's location are co-employed by ADP and its client.

Sales and Marketing

The company targets businesses of four types: Small Businesses with 1-49 employees; Midsized Business with 50-999 employees; Large Business with 1000+ employees; and Multinational Business with any number of employees.

Financial Performance

ADP has achieved unprecedented growth over the last several years with revenues climbing 8% from $11.3 billion in 2013 to peak at a record-setting $12.2 billion in 2014. Profits also jumped 8% from $1.4 billion to $1.5 billion over that same time period. Net cash inflow increased 16% in 2014 due to additional cash inflows.

The historic growth for ADP was fueled by increases in all its segments. Employer services sales spiked due to new business started during the year from new business bookings growth an increase in the number of employees on the company's clients' payrolls and the impact of price increases. PEO services revenue increased due to a rise in the average number of worksite employees resulting in a surge in the number of new clients and growth in the company's existing clients.

The rise in profits for ADP in 2014 was driven by the increased revenues coupled with the absence of goodwill impairment losses it incurred the previous year.

Strategy

Over the years the data processing giant has been fortifying its core employer services and PEO operations while restructuring and working to cut costs in its dealer services division. Across all segments ADP has been expanding internationally and extending its services through acquisitions. It also continues to boost its Web-based software offerings and small-business services. In late 2014 it spun off its ADP Dealer Services operations to form CDK Global in order to focus on its core operations.

Mergers and Acquisitions

The company acquired two businesses during fiscal 2013 for approximately $40.4 million while it acquired seven businesses in fiscal 2012 for an aggregate purchase price of approximately $292.3 million.

HISTORY

In 1949 22-year-old Henry Taub started Automatic Payrolls a manual payroll preparation service in Paterson New Jersey. Taub's eight accounts created gross revenue of around $2000 that year. In 1952 his brother Joe joined the company and a childhood friend Frank Lautenberg took a pay cut to become its first salesman. Automatic Payrolls grew steadily during the 1950s. In 1961 the company went public and changed its name to Automatic Data Processing (ADP).

EXECUTIVES

President and CEO, Carlos A. Rodriguez, age 51, $900,000 total compensation

Corporate VP and Chief Human Resources Officer, Dermot J. O'Brien, age 48, $488,001 total compensation

VP and CFO, Jan Siegmund, age 51, $550,001 total compensation

VP Product Development and CIO, Michael L. (Mike) Capone, age 48

EVP Worldwide Sales and Marketing, Edward B. (Ed) Flynn, age 55

President Major Account Services and ADP Canada, Anish D. Rajparia, age 44

President Global Enterprise Solutions, Mark D. Benjamin, age 43

President Small Business Services Retirement Services and Insurance Services, John C. Ayala, age 47

President Added Value Services, Douglas W. (Doug) Politi, age 52

President Employer Services - TotalSource, Maria Black, age 40

VP Global Product and Technology, Stuart Sackman

Vice President, Gordon Hourihan

Vice President Product Development, Lawrence Niech

Gvp Ivr Contact, Tong Lin

Division Vice President, Art Baumann

Vice President Human Resources, Deb Hughes

Vice President Imp Operations, Chris Pollock

Medical Director Vice President, Daniela Weinberger

Vice President Operations, James (Jamie) Blake

Vice President Of Sales Minneapolis, Randy Nixon

Vice President Majors, Anthony Horton

Vice President, Randy Terbush

Senior Vice President Development, Max Li

Vice President Comprehensive Services Payroll, Mary Reppermund

Vice President Sales, Jeffrey Schilling
Vice President Inside Sales, Mike Keim
Vice President And Assistant General Counsel, Barry Eisler
Vice President Of Sales, Jason Rayvis
Vice President Corporate, Michael Lindemann
Division Vice President Sales And Operations, Bill Crawford
Vice President Of Information Technology, Bill Washkau
Division Vice President Sales, Peter (Pete) Lynch
Vice President Telesales, Bill Graff
Vice President Offshore, Craig Spendiff
Vice President Sales Operations, Jenna Booth
Vice President Product Management, Anna Carsen
Vice President Client Servcies, Laurie Machado
Vice President Sales, Robert Sprague
National Account Manager, Susan Peebles
Vice President Sales, Peter Allison
Vice President, Huyen Tran
Vice President Telesales, Christina Badawy
Vice President Sales, Bryan Colteaux
Division Vice President Sales, Anthony Maggio
Vice President Project Management Office, Helen Vesce
National Sales Manager, William (Bill) Cordes
Division Vice President, Darrell Nickerson
NAS Senior Vice President, Sharon Cox
Vice President Sales, Nicholas Pirrung
Vice President Product Management, Lisa Lane
Vice President Technical Services, Jennifer (Jen) Marasovich
Vice President Small Business Services, Laci Buzzelli
Vice President Software Asset Management, Vito Vito Giuliani Giuliani
Vice President Of Operations, Mike Searles
Vice President, Mitch Kleiman
Senior Vice President Corporate Development, Amy Martorello
Vice President Implementation Mas Core, Mark L Brahmstadt
Staff Vice President Corporate Development, David Garfinkel
Vice President Sales Sbs, Anthony D Miskowiec
Vice President Information Technology Business Security, Josh Sowers
Vice President Finance And Division Controller, Jeff Burns
Vice President Business Development, Jason Rusnak
Senior Vice President National Accounts, Christine Wood
Vice President Chief Security Officer, Roland Cloutier
Vice President Of Global Network Services, Vincent Patrizio
Vice President Information Technology, Kathy Ferro
Division Vice President Sales, Scott Halperin
Vice President Hosting and Release Management, Jeff DiNome
Division Vice President Strategy and Business Development, Amit Jain
Vice President Implementation, Robert (Bob) Hecker
Divisional Vice President Service Delivery, Cathy Backman
Vice President Of Sales, Jim Warner
Vice President Financial and Compliance Services, Ava Fanelli
Vice President Of Sales Operations, Bob Larosa
Vice President Product Management, Jennifer Cambern
Vice President Sales and Marketing, Mike Bell
Division Vice President Nas, Rick Evarts
Vice President Product Management, William (Bill) Giaconia
Vice President Financial, Johnathan Coleman

Vice President Workers Compensation, Carla Ferreira
Vice President, Mark Pfleger
Vice President Implementation, Skip Gilbert
Vice President Of Business Development, Marc Horn
Vice President Strategy and Business Development, Margaret (Peg) Woodard
Vice President Sales, Paul Smith
Vice President Market Insights and Analytics, Ahu Yildirmaz
Vice President Of Sales, Scott Tithof
Vice President Service Centers, Rob Longshore
Dvp Rgm National Accounts, Jay Little
Vice President Corporate Finance, Mike Burns
Vice President Public Relations, Ravi Marrapu
Dvp Sales Operations, Matthew Bolson
Vice President Sales, Venkatachalam Subramaniam
Vice President Of Client Services, Frank Burgos
Vice President Tolalsource Northeast, Cathleen Brown
Vice President, Jaclyn Schweiger
Vice President National Accounts Implementation Services, Greg Flach
Vice President Spending Accounts and COBRA Service, Jane (Ginny) Smith
Vice President Sales Strategy, Sean Wood
Vice President Information Technology, Greg Rowe
Senior Vice President of Corproate Procurement, Dee Dacosta
Senior Vice President Real Estate, Paula Bothwell
Vice President Administration, Kristine Fisher
National Sales Manager Private Equity, Dave Ciccone
Vice President Of Customer Service Department Adp, John Gutierrez
Vice President of Strategic Advisory Services, Christopher (Chris) Ryan
Vice President Of Government Affairs, Tricia Russo
Vice President Corporate Purchasing, Marti Marti Daniels Daniels
Vice President, Heather Milhime-simpson
Vice President Benefits Outsrcng Cnsltnt, Linda Mott
Vice President Sales, Gus Perez
Vice President Inbound Service Specl Prod, Joseph (Jo) Mullany
Regional Vice President of Sales, Javier Hernan
Vice President Eastern Midwest Region, Marie Fladung
Vice President Converged Security Servic, Kit Menches
Vice President Client Services, Alisa Ross
Vice President Marketing and Strategy, Rick Ayala
Senior Vice President ES Marketing, Sandy Angevine
Vice President Of Sales, Shaun Scott
Vice President Client Services, Julie Farraj
National Sales Manager, Jerry Scholl
Vice President of Sales, Anna Santolucito
National Sales Manager, C J Donnelly
Vice President Benefits Outsrcng Cnsltnt, Mary Schafer
Vice President Of Sales, John Goglia
Division Vice President, Dave Piromalli
Vice President of Sales, Stephanie Karasiak
Vice President Tax Accounting, Sharon Gaglione
Vice President Benefits Outsrcng Cnsltnt, Bernadette Nace
Vice President Technical Services, Randy Byrne
Senior Vice President, Jessica McIlwain
Vice President Implementation MA, Terence Crowe
Vice President Property Services, Stephen (Steve) Bonsall
Vice President Sales, Vanessa Calderon
Vice President Implementation, Jeff Ciupak
Vice President Sales Europe, Tim Johnson
Vice President Of Sales, Jeff Phelps
Vice President Impl Project Management MA, Sallie Workman

Vice President Technical Services, Don Speer
Vice President, Ed Hurley-wales
NAS TLM Assistant Vice President, Debbie Strayer
Area Vice Presidentmajor Accounts Sales, Dave Witucki
Vice President of Client Base Acquisitions, Wendy Hellman
Sbs Central Dvp, Michele Tomassetti
Vice President Group Client Services, Sterling Sterling Norcross Norcross
Vice President of Sales Indiana Region, Keith Campanelli
Vice President Assistant General Counsel, Jonathan Gluck
Vice President Of Sales, Nick Lenoble
Vice President, Steve Nolan
Vice President Compensation, Val Stubbins
Vice President Account Management, Johnathan Keegan
Auditors: Deloitte & Touche LLP

LOCATIONS

HQ: Automatic Data Processing Inc.
  One ADP Boulevard, Roseland, NJ 07068
Phone: 973 974-5000   Fax: 973 974-5390
Web: www.adp.com

2013 Sales

	$ mil.	% of total
US	9,114	81
Europe	1,279	11
Canada	464	4
Other	451	4
Total	**11,310**	**100**

PRODUCTS/OPERATIONS

2013 Sales

	$ mil.	% of total
Employer services	7,914	70
PEO services	1,973	18
Dealer services	1,813	16
Other	41	-
Client fund interest (212.9) (4)		
Total	**11,310**	**100**

Selected Services

Dealer Services
  Business management
  Computer systems sales
  Employee productivity training
  Hardware maintenance
  Manufacturer and dealer data communications networks
  Software licensing and support
  Vehicle registration services
Employer Services
  401(k) record keeping and reporting
  Benefits administration and outsourcing
  Employment screening and background checks
  Human resource record keeping and reporting
  Payroll processing
  Tax filing
  Unemployment compensation management

Selected Mergers & Acquisitions

COMPETITORS

Avatar Systems	Insperity
CBIZ	Intuit
Ceridian	Oasis Outsourcing
Computer Sciences	Paychex
Corp.	Reynolds and Reynolds
Enertia Software	Total System Services
Global Payments	TriNet Group
HP Enterprise Services	Ultimate Software

HISTORICAL FINANCIALS

Company Type: Public

Income Statement

FYE: June 30

	REVENUE ($ mil.)	NET INCOME ($ mil.)	NET PROFIT MARGIN	EMPLOYEES
06/15	10,938	1,452	13.3%	55,000
06/14	12,206	1,515	12.4%	61,000
06/13	11,310	1,405	12.4%	60,000
06/12	10,665	1,388	13.0%	57,000
06/11	9,879	1,254	12.7%	51,000
Annual Growth	2.6%	3.7%	—	1.9%

2015 Year-End Financials

Debt ratio: 0.03%
Return on equity: 25.31%
Cash ($ mil.): 1,639
Current ratio: 1.06
Long-term debt ($ mil.): 9

No. of shares (mil.): 466
Dividends
Yield: 2.4%
Payout: 66.5%
Market value ($ mil.): 37,419

	STOCK PRICE ($) FY Close	P/E High/Low	PER SHARE ($) Earnings	Dividends	Book Value
06/15	80.23	29 23	3.05	1.95	10.31
06/14	79.28	26 22	3.14	1.88	13.89
06/13	68.86	25 19	2.89	1.70	12.83
06/12	55.66	20 16	2.82	1.55	12.63
06/11	52.68	22 15	2.52	1.42	12.25
Annual Growth	11.1%	— —	4.9%	8.3%	(4.2%)

AutoNation, Inc.

AutoNation wants to instill patriotic fervor in the fickle car-buying public. The brainchild of entrepreneur Wayne Huizenga (Waste Management Blockbuster) AutoNation is the #1 auto dealer in the US (ahead of Penske Automotive Group and Sonic Automotive). The firm owns some 280 new-vehicle franchises (down from 300 in 2008) in 15 states and it conducts online sales through Auto-Nation.com and individual dealer websites. It sells 34 new brands of new vehicles. An active acquirer of local retail brands the company is in the midst of transitioning them to the AutoNation name. In addition to auto sales AutoNation provides maintenance and repair services sells auto parts and finances and insures vehicles.

Geographic Reach

AutoNation has 232 dealership locations in 15 states. Florida Texas and California are its largest markets accounting for 26% 22% and 18% of sales respectively.

Operations

AutoNation divides the vehicle market into three segments: Domestic Import and Premium Luxury. Imports account for more than 35% of sales while Domestic brands represent about a third. Its core brands of new vehicles include Toyota Ford Honda Nissan and General Motors.

The Premium Luxury Segment which sells new vehicles manufactured primarily by Mercedes-Benz BMW and Lexus contributes about 30% of Auto-Nation's sales.

Sales and Marketing

AutoNation reported advertising expenses of $164.9 million in 2014 down from $166.4 million in 2013.

Financial Performance

The company has reported an upward trend in revenues since 2010.In 2014 its net sales increased by 9% due to increased sales from all of its segments.Domestic revenues grew due to an increase

in new and used vehicle unit volume and higher revenues per new and used vehicle retailed.Import revenues rose as a result of an increase in new vehicle unit volume.Premium Luxury sales increased during 2014 due to an increase in volume and higher revenue per new and used vehicle retailed.AutoNation's 2014 net income increased by 12% as the result of increased sales partially offset by higher selling general and administrative expenses (primarily due to a performance-driven increase in compensation expense an rise in store and corporate overhead expenses and an increase in gross advertising expenditures excluding the impact of expenses incurred in 2013 related to its re-branding initiative).

Net cash provided by the operating activities increased by $1 million in 2014.

Strategy

The auto dealer is banking on the caché of the AutoNation name to win sales and market share.

The company has invested and will continue to invest significantly in the AutoNation retail brand with the goals of enhancing its strong customer satisfaction and expanding its market share. In 2015 AutoNation launched an AutoNation branded vehicle service contract the "AutoNation Vehicle Protection Plan" to be sold in all Domestic and Import AutoNation stores. That year the company divested two Import stores. In 2014 it divested its customer lead distribution business.

The company also focuses on geographic penetration with the opening of stores in the region. In 2014 AutoNation opened stores in the Mobile Alabama market and the Seattle-Bellevue Washington market.

In 2013 the company began marketing its domestic and import stores under the AutoNation retail brand in local markets. The re-branding of the stores which previously operated under various local market retail brands (including Mike Shad in Jacksonville Florida and GO in Colorado) was completed that year. (The exception is the company's luxury dealership business which will continue to operate under their existing retail brands.) Using its website store signage and media presence the car dealer is working to increase consumer awareness of the AutoNation brand.

A key element of the firm's business strategy is its diversified portfolio of 30-plus brands spanning imports premium luxury vehicles and domestic autos. Over the past decade AutoNation has increased the percentage of import and luxury cars it sells. It clusters dealerships within markets so that they can share inventory cross-sell to customers and reduce marketing costs –basically cutting and combining costs in an attempt to become the auto industry's Wal-Mart. As the economy improves AutoNation has been looking for acquisition and new store opportunities.

Mergers and Acquisitions

Historically AutoNation has been a driving force in the consolidation of the US car sales business. After an hiatus during the recession and credit crunch which put the brakes on acquisitions by mega dealers such as AutoNation the company is back in acquisition mode.

The company purchased five stores in the first six months of 2015 including a Mercedes-Benz store in San Jose California a Chrysler Dodge Jeep Ram store in Valencia California and a Jaguar Land Rover and Volvo store in Spokane Washington.

In 2014 AutoNation acquired Audi Mercedes-Benz Porsche and Volvo stores in the Seattle-Bellevue market from Barrier Motors. As a result AutoNation owned and operated 22 franchises in Washington including 13 franchises in the Seattle-Bellevue market. In 2013 the company acquired 12 franchises.

HISTORY

AutoNation started in 1980 as Republic Resources which brokered petroleum leases did exploration and production and blended lubricants. In 1989 after oil prices crashed and a stockholder group tried to force Republic into liquidation Browning-Ferris Industries (BFI) founder Thomas Fatjo gained control of the company and refocused it on a field he knew well –solid waste. He renamed the firm Republic Waste.

Michael DeGroote founder of BFI rival Laidlaw bought into Republic in 1990. (Fatjo left the next year.) DeGroote's investment funded more acquisitions. Republic moved into hazardous waste in 1992 just before the industry nosedived due to stringent new environmental rules. In 1994 Republic spun off its hazardous-waste operations as Republic Environmental Systems and Republic's stock began rising immediately.

That attracted the attention of Wayne Huizenga who had founded Waste Management and Blockbuster Video. To him Republic was not merely a midsized solid-waste firm. No Huizenga saw Republic as a publicly traded vehicle that could allow him to tap into the stock market to fund his latest project: an integrated nationwide auto dealer –a first for the highly fragmented and localized industry.

In 1995 Republic bought Hudson Management a trash business owned by Huizenga's brother-in-law and Huizenga bought a large interest in Republic. As a result Huizenga took control of Republic's board. The firm became Republic Industries and DeGroote stepped back from active management.

Huizenga's investment helped Republic acquire more waste businesses and his name brought a flood of new investors. The firm diversified with electronic security acquisitions but growth in this field faltered with a failed bid to buy market leader ADT in 1996. (Republic sold its security division to Ameritech in 1997.)

By 1996 Huizenga's still-separate auto concept AutoNation was operational with 55 automobile franchises and seven used-car stores. Republic bought Alamo Rent A Car and National Car Rental System and in 1997 AutoNation was bought by Republic. The combined company continued buying dealerships and car rental firms at a sizzling rate.

Republic spun off its solid-waste operations to the public in 1998 as Republic Services. That year Republic bought or agreed to buy 181 new-car franchises opened nine AutoNation USA dealerships and opened 62 CarTemps USA insurance-replacement locations.

Republic became AutoNation in 1999.

EXECUTIVES

Chairman President and CEO, Michael J. (Mike) Jackson, age 67, $1,250,000 total compensation
EVP Secretary and General Counsel, Jonathan P. Ferrando, age 50, $700,000 total compensation
SVP Information Technology, Allan Stejskal, age 57
SVP Corporate Communications and Public Policy and Chief Marketing Officer, Marc Cannon
EVP and CFO, Cheryl Miller, age 43, $446,552 total compensation
EVP and COO, William R. (Bill) Berman, age 49
SVP Customer Care, Alan J. McLaren, age 49, $572,663 total compensation
President Eastern Region, Jim Bender
President Western Region, Lance Iserman
President Central Region, Ron Ardisonne
Senior Vice President, Alex Muxo
Vice President Information Technology, Avril O'Brien
Vice President, Phil Dupree

Vice President Corporate Development, Raul
  Rodriguez
Vice President Media Services, Ed Cicale
Regional Vice President of Finance, Mitch McGuire
Vice President Information Technology
  Infrastructure and Architecture, Bill Bellas
Executive Vice President, Robert Henninger
Vice President Assistant General Counsel, Jill
  Bilanchone
Vice President Sales, Mike Rossman
Litigation Head Deputy General Counsel And Vice
  President, Kenneth Rollin
Vice President Online and Direct Marketing, Jenny
  Watson
Vice President Corporate Real Estate Services, Jeff
  Shupert
Vice President of Audit Services, Tom Samartino
Vice President, Scott May
Senior Vice President Legal, Coleman Edmunds
Vice President Corporate Development, Raul
  Rodriguez Jr
Vice President eCommerce, Famous Rhodes
Assistant Treasurer, David Schoenborn
Board Member, Jim Drews
Auditors: KPMG LLP

LOCATIONS

HQ: AutoNation, Inc.
  200 S.W. 1st Avenue, Fort Lauderdale, FL 33301
Phone: 954 769-6000
Web: www.autonation.com

2014 Stores

	Owned	Franchised
Florida	57	66
Texas	40	49
California	39	44
Colorado	17	24
Arizona	15	17
Nevada	10	11
Georgia	10	11
Washington	16	22
Illinois	7	7
Tennessee	7	8
Ohio	4	4
Minnesota	1	1
Virginia	2	2
Maryland	4	5
Alabama	3	5
Total	**232**	**276**

PRODUCTS/OPERATIONS

2014 Sales

	$ mil.	% of total
New vehicle	10,972	57
Used vehicle	4,385	23
Parts & service	2,822	15
Finance & insurance	750	4
Other	177	1
Total	**19,108**	**100**

2014 Sales

	$ mil.	% of total
Import	6,717	35
Domestic	6,359	33
Luxury	5,889	31
Corporate & other	142	1
Total	**19,108**	**100**

COMPETITORS

Asbury Automotive   JM Family Enterprises
Brown Automotive   Lithia Motors
CarMax   Penske Automotive
Ed Morse Auto   Group
Group 1 Automotive   Potamkin Automotive
Hendrick Automotive   Sonic Automotive
Holman Enterprises

HISTORICAL FINANCIALS
Company Type: Public

Income Statement

	REVENUE ($ mil.)	NET INCOME ($ mil.)	NET PROFIT MARGIN	EMPLOYEES
12/15	20,862	442	2.1%	26,000
12/14	19,108	418	2.2%	24,000
12/13	17,517	374	2.1%	22,000
12/12	15,668	316	2.0%	21,000
12/11	13,832	281	2.0%	19,400
Annual Growth	**10.8%**	**12.0%**	**—**	**7.6%**

FYE: December 31

2015 Year-End Financials

Debt ratio: 24.76%
Return on equity: 20.02%
Cash ($ mil.): 74
Current ratio: 0.91
Long-term debt ($ mil.): 1,753

No. of shares (mil.): 110
Dividends
  Yield: —
  Payout: —
Market value ($ mil.): 6,611

	STOCK PRICE ($) FY Close	P/E High/Low	PER SHARE ($) Earnings	Dividends	Book Value
12/15	59.66	17 14	3.89	0.00	21.20
12/14	60.41	17 13	3.52	0.00	18.29
12/13	49.69	18 13	3.04	0.00	17.05
12/12	39.70	19 13	2.52	0.00	13.97
12/11	36.87	21 14	1.91	0.00	13.95
Annual Growth	**12.8%**	**— —**	**19.5%**	**—**	**11.0%**

AutoZone, Inc.

Imagine that you are in your garage making
some weekend car repairs. The wheel cylinders
are leaking ... the brake shoe adjuster nut is rusted
solid ... you're about to enter ... the AutoZone.
With more than 5100 stores in the US and Puerto
Rico it's the nation's #1 auto parts chain. It also
operates some 440 stores in Mexico and seven in
Brazil. AutoZone stores sell hard parts (alternators
engines batteries) maintenance items (oil antifreeze) accessories (car stereos floor mats) and
non-automotive merchandise under brand names
as well as under private labels. AutoZone's commercial sales program distributes parts and other
products to garages dealerships and other businesses.

Operations

As part of its business AutoZone operates
through one reportable segment: Auto Parts
Stores. Besides being a retailer and distributor of
auto parts and accessories AutoZone produces
sells and maintains diagnostic and repair information software used in the auto repair industry
through its ALLDATA business and sells directly
to customers through its e-commerce site auto-
zone.com.

Geographic Reach

Based in Tennessee AutoZone sells auto and
light truck parts chemicals and accessories through
more than 5100 AutoZone stores in 49 US states
the District of Columbia and Puerto Rico. Texas
California Florida Ohio and Illinois represent the
company's largest markets and together account
for more than a third of locations. The company's
fast-growing subsidiary in Mexico AutoZone de
México operates more than 440 stores.
AutoZone also has stores in Brazil.

AutoZone has distribution centers in more than
half a dozen US states and Mexico and has store

support centers in California and Tennessee as
well as Mexico and Brazil.

Sales and Marketing

AutoZone relies on targeted advertising and promotions to build its brand offer advice about the
overall importance of vehicle maintenance and position its business as a great value. To drive traffic
to its stores the retailer advertises on broadcast and
Internet media. It works to educate consumers
about which products they need through use of in-
store signage and circulars as well as creative product placement and promotions.

Leveraging a consistent store format each AutoZone store boasts between 85% and 90% of selling space –up to 45% of which is dedicated to hard
parts inventory. Stores are outfitted with Z-net AutoZone's proprietary electronic catalog that gives
employees advice and information for customers'
vehicles down to the year make model and engine
type.

Financial Performance

AutoZone has achieved extraordinary growth
over the last few years with revenues climbing 8%
from $9.5 billion in 2014 to peak at a record-set-
ting $10.2 billion in fiscal 2015 (ended August).
Profits also jumped 8% to $1.2 billion in 2015 an-
other company milestone.

The historic growth for 2015 was fueled by a 4%
boost in domestic same store sales and $185 mil-
lion in sales from new stores. Improvements in domestic same store sales were driven by a higher average transaction value partially offset by a drop
in the number of transactions. During the past five
years AutoZone has grown its stores network by
more than 20% (from 4627 stores in 2010 to 5609
stores in 2015). During the same time period annual revenues have surged from $7.4 billion to
$10.2 billion.

Cash from operations has also followed the upward trend established by revenue and net income.
In 2015 the company reported operating cash flow
of $1.5 billion up 14%.

Strategy

The company's core strategy includes expanding its stores network. It added about 200 stores
in fiscal 2015 and is focusing on new-store development while also enhancing its existing stores
and infrastructure. Among its focus are "hub"
stores which offer a larger product selection and
deliver items to local satellite stores. In fiscal 2015
AutoZone opened 10 hub stores bringing the total
to about 175.

AutoZone has grown quickly through a series of
acquisitions over the past several years but now is
focused on internal growth and development.
Among the factors AutoZone considers when
opening new stores is how many cars in an area
are OKVs or "our kind of vehicles" that is cars
older than seven years and no longer under their
manufacturers' warranty.

The company is growing quickly in Mexico
where cars are even older –and in need of more
repairs –than in the US. The auto parts retailer also
loans tools and sells merchandise and diagnostic
and repair advice online. In addition to parts the
stores also offer diagnostic testing for starters alternators and batteries. (The shops do not sell tires
or perform general auto repairs.) In fiscal 2015 AutoZone continued expanding in the emerging market of Brazil opening a handful of new stores.

Mergers and Acquisitions

In 2014 the company purchased Interamerican
Motor Corporation (IMC) a large distributor of OE
quality import replacement parts in the US for approximately $80 million which operates 17 loca-
tions. To build its online presence AutoZone in
2013 acquired AutoAnything an online retailer of
specialized automotive products.

HISTORY

Joseph "Pitt" Hyde took over the family grocery wholesale business Malone & Hyde (established 1907) in 1968. He expanded into specialty retailing opening drugstores sporting goods stores and supermarkets but his fortunes began to race on Independence Day 1979 when he opened his first Auto Shack auto parts store in Forrest City Arkansas.

Using retailing behemoth Wal-Mart as a model Hyde concentrated on smaller markets in the South and Southeast emphasizing everyday low prices and centralized distribution operations. He stressed customer service to provide his do-it-yourself customers with expert advice on choosing parts. While a number of retailers have tried to copy Wal-Mart's successful model Hyde had an inside track: Before starting Auto Shack he served on Wal-Mart's board for seven years.

Auto Shack had expanded into seven states by 1980 and by 1983 it had 129 stores in 10 states. The next year Malone & Hyde's senior management with investment firm Kohlberg Kravis Roberts (KKR) took the company private in an LBO. Auto Shack continued to expand reaching 192 stores in 1984. The company was spun off to Malone & Hyde's shareholders in 1987 and Malone & Hyde's other operations were sold. The company changed its name to AutoZone in 1987 in part to settle a lawsuit with RadioShack.

EXECUTIVES

Senior Vice President Secretary And General Counse, Harry L Goldsmith

EVP Finance Information Technology and ALLDATA and CFO, William T. (Bill) Giles, age 56, $544,385 total compensation

Chairman President and CEO, William C. (Bill) Rhodes, age 50, $1,000,000 total compensation

SVP Merchandising and Store Development, Mark A. Finestone, age 54, $418,154 total compensation

SVP Supply Chain and International, William W. Graves, age 55, $418,154 total compensation

SVP Store Operations and Store Development, Thomas B. Newbern, age 53

SVP and CIO, Ronald B. (Ron) Griffin, $407,692 total compensation

SVP Marketing, Albert (Al) Saltiel

Vice President Supply Chain, Rodney Halsell

Vice President Purchasing, Billy Edwards

Vice President Transportation and Logistics, Solomon Woldeslassie

National Account Manager, Dave Yunker

Assistant Treasurer, Steve Beussink

Auditors: Ernst & Young LLP

LOCATIONS

HQ: AutoZone, Inc.
123 South Front Street, Memphis, TN 38103
Phone: 901 495-6500
Web: www.autozone.com

2015 Stores

	No
US	5,141
Mexico	441
Brazil	7
IMC branches	20
Total	0 5,609

PRODUCTS/OPERATIONS

2015 Sales

	$ mil.	% of total
Auto parts stores	9,824	96
Other	362	4
Total	**10,187**	**100**

Selected Merchandise

Accessories
  Car stereos
  Floor mats
  Lights
  Mirrors
Hard Parts
  Alternators
  Batteries
  Brake shoes and pads
  Carburetors
  Clutches
  Engines
  Spark plugs
  Starters
  Struts
  Water pumps
Maintenance Items
  Antifreeze
  Brake fluid
  Engine additives
  Oil
  Power steering fluid
  Transmission fluid
  Waxes
  Windshield wipers
Other
  Air fresheners
  Dent filler
  Hand cleaner
  Paint
  Repair manuals
  Tools

Selected Brands

ALLDATA
AutoZone
Duralast
Duralast Gold
Valucraft

COMPETITORS

Advance Auto Parts	Kmart
CARQUEST	O' Reilly Automotive
Costco Wholesale	Pep Boys
Fisher Auto Parts	Sears
Genuine Parts	Target Corporation
Goodyear Tire & Rubber	Wal-Mart

HISTORICAL FINANCIALS

Company Type: Public

Income Statement

FYE: August 29

	REVENUE ($ mil.)	NET INCOME ($ mil.)	NET PROFIT MARGIN	EMPLOYEES
08/15	10,187	1,160	11.4%	81,000
08/14	9,475	1,069	11.3%	76,000
08/13	9,147	1,016	11.1%	71,000
08/12	8,603	930	10.8%	70,000
08/11	8,072	848	10.5%	65,000
Annual Growth	**6.0%**	**8.1%**	**—**	**5.7%**

2015 Year-End Financials

Debt ratio: 57.58%
Return on equity: —
Cash ($ mil.): 175
Current ratio: 0.84
Long-term debt ($ mil.): 4,624

No. of shares (mil.): 30
Dividends
  Yield: —
  Payout: —
Market value ($ mil.): 22,270

	STOCK PRICE ($) FY Close	P/E High/Low	PER SHARE ($) Earnings	Dividends	Book Value
08/15	726.39	20 14	36.03	0.00	(55.49)
08/14	538.84	17 13	31.57	0.00	(50.21)
08/13	419.94	16 12	27.79	0.00	(49.20)
08/12	365.08	17 12	23.48	0.00	(41.81)
08/11	301.30	15 11	19.47	0.00	(31.27)
Annual Growth	**24.6%**	**— —**	**16.6%**	**—**	**—**

Avery Dennison Corp.

Avery Dennison is easy to label: It's a global leader in the making of adhesive labels used on packaging mailers and other items. Pressure-sensitive adhesives and materials account for more than half of its sales. Its Pressure-sensitive Materials (PSM) unit is split into two other units: Label and Packaging Materials (LPM) and Graphics and Reflective Solutions (GRS). Under the Avery Dennison and Fasson brands it makes papers films and foils coated with adhesive and sold in rolls to printers. Its most widely used products are the self-adhesive stamps used by the US Postal Service. It also makes retail branding and security tags printer systems and fasteners as well as medical adhesive products.

HISTORY

Avery Dennison was created in 1990 by the merger of Avery International and Dennison Manufacturing. In 1935 Stanton Avery founded Kum-Kleen Products which would become Avery International. After a fire destroyed the plant's equipment in 1938 Avery who had renamed the company Avery Adhesives improved the machinery used in making the labels.

During and after WWII Avery Adhesives shifted toward the industrial market for self-adhesives. The company incorporated in 1946. At that time Avery Adhesives sold 80% of its production consisting of industrial labels to manufacturers that labeled their own products.

The company lost its patent rights for self-adhesive labels in 1952 transforming the firm and the entire industry. As a result a new division was created —the Avery Paper Company (later renamed Fasson) —to produce and market self-adhesive base materials.

Avery Adhesives went public in 1961. Three years later it had four divisions: label products base materials Rotex (hand-operated embossing machines) and Metal-Cal (anodized and etched aluminum foil for nameplates). Renamed Avery International in 1976 the company closed some manufacturing facilities and cut 8% of its workforce in the late 1980s.

In 1990 Avery International merged with Dennison Manufacturing. Dennison was started in 1844 by the father-and-son team of Andrew and Aaron Dennison to produce jewelry boxes. By 1849 Aaron's younger brother Eliphalet Whorf (E.W.) was running the business and expanding it into tags labels and tissue paper. Dennison was incorporated in 1878 with $150000 in capital.

By 1911 Dennison sold tags gummed labels paper boxes greeting cards sealing wax and tissue paper and it had stores in Boston Chicago New York City Philadelphia St. Louis and London. Henry Dennison E.W.'s grandson was president from 1917 to 1952.

From the 1960s to the 1980s Dennison spent heavily on research and development and helped to develop such products as electronic printers and pregnancy test supplies. In the mid-1980s the firm reorganized its operations selling seven businesses closing four others and focusing on stationery systems and packaging.

In addition to office products and product identification and control systems the 1990 merger combined Dennison's office products operations in France (Doret and Cheval Ordex) with Avery International's sizable self-adhesive base materials business.

Avery Dennison sold its 50% interest in a Japanese label converting company Toppan in 1996 clearing the way to develop its own businesses in Asia. In 1997 an alliance with Taiwanese rival Four Pillars turned sour when Avery Dennison accused the company of stealing trade secrets. (Two executives at Four Pillars were convicted of corporate espionage in 1999.)

President and COO Philip Neal was promoted to CEO in 1998. (He became chairman in 2000.) In 1999 adhering to its goal of global expansion Avery Dennison formed office products joint ventures in Germany with Zweckform Buro-Produkte and in Japan with Hitachi Maxell. Record 1998 sales and earnings were dampened by the news of slowing growth and in 1999 Avery Dennison closed five plants and began laying off workers. Later that year the company bought Stimsonite a maker of reflective highway safety products.

In early 2000 Avery Dennison began a $40 million expansion of its Chinese manufacturing operations while eliminating 1500 jobs worldwide. Later in the year the company agreed to jointly package instant imaging and labeling products with Polaroid. Several acquisitions in 2001 included CD Stomper (CD and DVD labels and software). Avery Dennison continued its acquisitive ways in 2002 acquiring Jackstadt (German maker of pressure-sensitive adhesive materials) RVL Packaging (maker of woven and printed labels and other tags for the apparel and retail industries) and L&E Packaging (key supplier and printer for RVL).

In 2003 the company sold its European package label converting business (including plants in Denmark and France) to label and packaging company CCL Industries. As part of the deal Avery Dennison began to supply pressure-sensitive base materials to CCL Industries. The divestiture was part of the company's strategy to concentrate its efforts in adhesive materials office products and retail information services.

Phillip Neal retired as chairman and CEO in 2005 and was replaced by director Kent Kresa as chairman and by Dean Scarborough as president and CEO.The company completed a restructuring program in 2010 it began in 2008 that generated a total of $180 million in cost savings. It also paid down some $300 million in debt during that same period.In 2011 Avery also decided to divest its Metalure pigments business which it sold to the Eckart Effect Pigments division of ALTANA. Eckart had been the distributor of the PVD-type aluminum pigments for more than 20 years.

EXECUTIVES

Chairman and CEO, Dean A. Scarborough, age 60, $1,095,000 total compensation
Vp And General Manager Roll Materials Europe Central Region, Martin Rapp, age 56
President Retail Branding and Information Solutions, R. Shawn Neville, age 52, $575,031 total compensation
SVP and CIO, Richard W. (Rich) Hoffman
SVP and Chief Human Resources Officer, Anne Hill, age 56, $488,090 total compensation
President Materials Group, Georges Gravanis
President and COO, Mitchell R. Butier, age 44, $620,029 total compensation
SVP and CFO, Anne L. Bramman, age 48
SVP General Counsel and Secretary, Susan C. Miller
Vice President Information Technology, Ed Lee
Vice President Marketing Materials, Shelley Whiting
Vice President, Vikas Arora
Auditors: PricewaterhouseCoopers LLP

LOCATIONS

HQ: Avery Dennison Corp.
207 Goode Avenue, Glendale, CA 91203
Phone: 626 304-2000
Web: www.averydennison.com

2014 Sales

	$ mil.	% of total
Europe	2,074	33
Asia	1,914	30
US	1,529	24
Latin America	522	8
Other regions	289	5
Total	**6,330**	**100**

PRODUCTS/OPERATIONS

2014 Sales

	$ mil.	% of total
Pressure-Sensitive Materials	4,658	74
Retail Branding & Information Services	1,591	25
Vancive Medical Technologies	80	1
Total	**6,330**	**100**

Selected Brands

Avery
Avery Dennison
Avery Graphics
Fasson

COMPETITORS

3M	Checkpoint Systems
ACCO Brands	Esselte
Beam Suntory	H.B. Fuller
Bemis	Newell Rubbermaid
Bostik	UPM-Kymmene
Brady Corporation	

HISTORICAL FINANCIALS

Company Type: Public

Income Statement

FYE: January 3

	REVENUE ($ mil.)	NET INCOME ($ mil.)	NET PROFIT MARGIN	EMPLOYEES
01/15*	6,330	248	3.9%	25,000
12/13	6,140	215	3.5%	26,000
12/12	6,035	215	3.6%	29,800
12/11	6,026	190	3.2%	30,400
01/11	6,512	316	4.9%	32,100
Annual Growth	(0.7%)	(5.9%)	—	(6.1%)

*Fiscal year change

2015 Year-End Financials

Debt ratio: 26.37%	No. of shares (mil.): 90
Return on equity: 19.14%	Dividends
Cash ($ mil.): 227	Yield: 0.0%
Current ratio: 1.20	Payout: 51.5%
Long-term debt ($ mil.): 945	Market value ($ mil.): 4,685

	STOCK PRICE ($) FY Close	P/E High/Low	PER SHARE ($) Earnings	Dividends	Book Value
01/15*	51.79	20 16	2.60	1.34	11.79
12/13	50.48	23 16	2.16	1.14	15.51
12/12	34.40	17 13	2.08	1.08	15.82
12/11	28.68	24 13	1.78	1.00	15.61
01/11	42.34	14 10	2.97	0.80	15.62
Annual Growth	5.2%	— —	(3.3%)	13.8%	(6.8%)

*Fiscal year change

Avis Budget Group Inc

Whether you're a business traveler on an expense account or a family on vacation counting every penny Avis Budget Group (ABG) has a car rental brand for you. The company's core brands include: Avis Rent A Car which targets corporate and leisure travelers at the high end of the market; Budget Rent A Car and Payless Car Rental both marketed to those on a budget; and Zipcar a car-sharing service. The rental car operator boasts nearly 5500 Avis and 3500 Budget branches across some 175 countries in North America Europe Australia and New Zealand and generates nearly 70% of its revenue from its on-airport locations. Avis's Budget Truck is one of the leading truck rental businesses in the US.

HISTORY

Company BackgroundCendant began life through the 1997 merger of CUC International and HFS. A giant in hospitality HFS was cobbled together as Hospitality Franchise Systems by LBO specialist Blackstone Group in 1992. With brands including Days Inn Ramada and Howard Johnson HFS went public that year. In 1995 HFS bought real estate firm Century 21. The next year it added Electronic Realty Associates (ERA) and Coldwell Banker. Also in 1996 HFS acquired the Super 8 Motels brand as well as car-rental firm Avis (founded by Warren Avis in 1946 it went through a succession of owners until acquired by HFS). The next year HFS sold 75% of Avis' #1 franchisee to the public and later bought relocation service firm PHH.

In an attempt to leverage the power of his brands HFS CEO Henry Silverman began looking at direct marketing giant CUC International. CUC was founded in 1973 as Comp-U-Card America by Walter Forbes and other investors envisioning a computer-based home shopping network. During the 1980s CUC developed as a discount direct marketer and catalog-based shopping club. It went public in 1983 with 100000 members. CUC saw explosive growth as it signed up 7.6 million members between 1989 and 1993. In 1996 CUC acquired Rent Net an online apartment rental service and later bought entertainment software publishers Davidson & Associates and Sierra On-Line. In 1997 CUC bought software maker Knowledge Adventure and launched online shopping site NetMarket.

CUC and HFS completed their $14.1 billion merger in December 1997 with Silverman as CEO and Forbes as chairman. While the name Cendant was derived from "ascendant" the marriage quickly headed in the opposite direction. Accounting irregularities from before the merger that had inflated CUC's revenue and pretax profit by about $500 million were revealed in 1998. Cendant's stock price tumbled taking a $14 billion hit in one day. Forbes resigned that summer. Silverman quickly took action and began to sell off operations. Cendant Software National Leisure Group (now World Travel Holdings) National Library of Poetry and Match.com all were sold that year for a total of about $1.4 billion. The company also acquired Jackson Hewitt the US's #2 tax-preparation firm and UK-based National Parking.

Through 1999 the company continued to sell assets. Cendant sold its fleet business —including PHH Vehicle Management Services —to Avis Rent A Car for $5 billion and sold its Entertainment Publications unit the world's largest coupon book marketer and publisher to The Carlyle Group. Cendant later paid $2.8 billion in one of the largest shareholder class action lawsuit settlements. (Accounting firm Ernst & Young also settled with Cendant shareholders for $335 million.)

In 2000 Cendant introduced Move.com a relocation and real estate Internet portal. Also that year the company launched Cendant Internet Group to help cement its presence on the Web and bought the brand name and franchising rights of AmeriHost Inns from AmeriHost Properties. Later in 2000 cable programming company Liberty Media (now Liberty Interactive) invested $400 million in Cendant. The next year the company began licensing and outsourcing its Incentives and Marketing Services business (practically all of the businesses that made up the former CUC International) to Trilegiant a new company formed by the units' management.

In 2001 after selling Move.com to Homestore (later called Move) for $761 million Cendant sought to expand its travel holdings with a slew of acquisitions. Its purchases included timeshare resort firm Fairfield Communities ($690 million); travel services firm Galileo International ($2.4 billion); online travel reservation service Cheap Tickets ($425 million); and vacation timeshare marketer Equivest Finance ($100 million). In late 2001 Cendant cut some 6000 jobs to improve its bottom line and announced that during the next year or so it would cut an additional 10000 jobs and eliminate about 7% of its franchised hotels.

In 2002 the company sold its UK-based National Car Park unit which accounted for 3% of sales as part of its strategy to sell off noncore businesses. In June Cendant bought TRUST International from Bertelsmann and later that year purchased car-rental company Budget Rent A Car for about $110 million then slashed costs by closing facilities and laying off more than 450 employees. The company also purchased Novasol AS which rented out private vacation homes in Northern Europe.

Cendant terminated its licensing and services agreements with Trilegiant in January 2004 and in February Sotheby's Holdings sold its 15 Sotheby's International Realty offices (along with the brand's licensing rights) to the company for about $100 million. In March Cendant's Jackson Hewitt subsidiary filed for its IPO. In May the company purchased Dutch vacation rental company Landal Green Parks (LGP) for about $150 million. Also that month former chairman Walter Forbes and former vice chairman E. Kirk Shelton went on trial for federal fraud and conspiracy stemming from the pre-merger accounting irregularities. (Shelton was found guilty of multiple counts of fraud in early 2005.) In October CFO Ronald Nelson was named president taking over for Henry Silverman who remained chairman and CEO.

In 2004 Cendant acquired online travel firm Orbitz in a deal valued at about $1.25 billion. Quick on the heels of the Orbitz deal the company Cendant also purchased ebookers (a European online travel site now called Flightbookers) in a deal worth about $400 million and acquired two travel groups collectively known as Gullivers for about $1.1 billion.

As 2004 wound to a close Cendant completed the acquisition of the Ramada International Hotels & Resorts brand and franchising operations from Marriott International. Cendant already owned the rights to the brand and franchising operations in the US and Canada which included some 820 US properties and about 70 Canadian properties. In 2005 Cendant acquired the Wyndham hotel brand from Wyndham International Inc. for $101 million. The deal included the franchise agreements for 82 hotels and the management contracts for another 29 hotels but not the actual properties which were located in the US Mexico and the Caribbean. The next year Cendant acquired the Baymont Inn & Suites brand of limited-service midscale lodging

from Blackstone's La Quinta Corporation (now LQ Management). The Baymont Inn & Suites brand covered 115 franchised properties; the properties themselves were not included in the deal.

Cendant in 2005 spun off its mortgage operations PHH Mortgage (formerly Cendant Mortgage) and fleet management (PHH Arval) businesses under the PHH Corporation umbrella. Also that year Cendant spun off Wright Express (payment processing and information services for fleet management) in an IPO and sold its marketing services division to Apollo Management for about $1.8 billion.

The divestitures that began in 2005 culminated in the unwinding of the Cendant conglomerate the next year. The company spun off its hotel and real estate operations and sold its travel services division in 2006 reconfiguring itself around its rental car businesses and renaming itself Avis Budget Group. Silverman became chairman and CEO of the company's real estate business Realogy and Nelson took over as chairman and CEO of the slimmed-down Avis Budget Group which took on its new name in September 2006.

Warren Avis the founder of Avis Rent A Car died in April 2007 at the age of 92. In October the company acquired a 48% stake in chauffeured transportation company Carey International for $60 million. (In 2009 due to losses at Carey it wrote down its investment in the company to zero.)

Avis Budget Group acquired Avis Europe plc in October 2011. In March 2013 it purchased Zipcar Inc. the world's leading car sharing network.

EXECUTIVES

Executive Vice President Of Sales And Marketing, Thomas (Thom) Gartland
Regional Sales Vice President, Peter (Pete) Vereb
President and CFO, David B. Wyshner, age 48, $700,000 total compensation
President International, Mark J. Servodidio, age 50, $372,549 total compensation
EVP Chief Strategy and Development Officer, W. Scott Deaver, age 64
CEO, Larry De Shon, age 56, $700,000 total compensation
EVP and CIO, Gerard Insall
EVP and General Counsel, Michael K. Tucker, age 57
Managing Director Western Region Avis Budget EMEA, Massimo Marsili
President Americas, Joseph A. (Joe) Ferraro, age 58
EVP and Chief Human Resources Officer (CHRO), Edward P. (Ned) Linnen, age 45
President Zipcar International, Nicholas Cole
Vice President It, John Turato
Vice President, David (Dave) Calabria
Vice President International Controller, Gerard Monusky
Vice President Technical Operations Real Estate In, Jennifer (Jen) Smith
Vice President Counsel and Government Affairs, Robert (Bob) Muhs
Senior Vice President Strategic Customer Leadersh, Gina Bruzzichesi
Vice President Human Resources, April Scavone
Vice President Tax, Izzy Martins
Vice President Of Information Technology, Joe Kirrane
Vice President Fleet Administration, Joseph (Jo) Biondo
Vice President Information Technology, John Page
Senior Vice President, Robert Bouta
Vice President Finance, Bill Thomas
Vice President, Joe Biondo
Vice President Area, Jeff Eisenbarth
Vice President Quality and Customer Care, Diane Karl

Vice President Sales Southern Region, Malcolm McNett
Senior Vice President Benefits, Edward Pictroski
Senior Vice President Corporate Accounts, Robert Chaps
Vice President, Tom Hocker
Vice President Vehicle MandD, Jerry Bernacki
Vice President, Jacob Stepan
Vice President Sales And Marketing, John Barrows
Senior Vice President Marketing Avis Budget Group Inc, Becky Alseth
Vice President Business Marketing, Glenn Burke
Vice President of Engineering, Jennifer (Jen) Rodean
Senior Vice President Information Technology, Jeff Edwards
Vice President Human Resources, Roger Deverman
Senior Vice President {Sv}, Neil Rook
Vice President Sales At Budget Truck R, Clive Burton
Vice President Global Account Sales, Matthew Tolan
Senior Vice President Fleet Services, Michael Schmidt
Vice President Global Travel and Partnerships, Tom Villani
Vice President eCommerce, Joseph (Jo) Kirrane
Vice President Investor Relations, David (Dave) Crowther
Vice President Pricing And Revenue Management, ED Sorensen
Vice President Marketing, Jack Dailey
Chairman, Ronald L. (Ron) Nelson, age 63
Vice Chairman, F. Robert (Bob) Salerno, age 62
Board Member, Keith Domingo
Board Member, Connie Crawley
Vice President and Treasurer, Rochelle Tarlowe
Advisory Board Member, Mike Perruzzi
Board Member, John Hardy
Senior Vice President and Secretary, Jean Sera
Treasurer, Diane Matthews
Auditors: Deloitte & Touche LLP

LOCATIONS

HQ: Avis Budget Group Inc
6 Sylvan Way, Parsippany, NJ 07054
Phone: 973 496-4700
Web: www.avisbudgetgroup.com

2014 Locations

	Avis	Budget
North America		
Company-operated	1,400	1,100
Licensees	300	400
International		
Company-operated	1,150	600
Licensees	2,600	1,400
Total	**5,450**	**3,500**

2014 Sales

	$ mil.	% of total
North America car rental	5,533	65
International car rental	2,588	31
Truck rental	364	4
Total	**8,485**	**100**

2014 Car Rental Sales

	% of total
On-Airport	67
Off-airport	33
Total	**100**

PRODUCTS/OPERATIONS

2014 Sales

	$ mil.	% of total
Vehicle rental	6,026	71
Others	2,459	29
Total	**8,485**	**100**

HISTORICAL FINANCIALS

Company Type: Public

Income Statement
FYE: December 31

	REVENUE ($ mil.)	NET INCOME ($ mil.)	NET PROFIT MARGIN	EMPLOYEES
12/14	8,485	245	2.9%	30,000
12/13	7,937	16	0.2%	29,000
12/12	7,357	290	3.9%	28,000
12/11	5,900	(29)	—	28,000
12/10	5,185	54	1.0%	21,000
Annual Growth	13.1%	45.9%	—	9.3%

2014 Year-End Financials

Debt ratio: 67.98%	No. of shares (mil.): 105
Return on equity: 34.12%	Dividends
Cash ($ mil.): 624	Yield: —
Current ratio: 1.21	Payout: —
Long-term debt ($ mil.): 11,508	Market value ($ mil.): 7,012

	STOCK PRICE ($) FY Close	P/E High/Low		PER SHARE ($) Earnings	Dividends	Book Value
12/14	66.33	30	15	2.22	0.00	6.29
12/13	40.42	263	132	0.15	0.00	7.24
12/12	19.82	7	4	2.42	0.00	7.07
12/11	10.72	—	—	(0.28)	0.00	3.91
12/10	15.56	31	16	0.49	0.00	3.95
Annual Growth	43.7%	—	—	45.9%	—	12.3%

Avnet Inc

If you need an electronic component Avnet probably has it. The company is the world's top distributor of electronic components (including connectors and semiconductors) enterprise computing and storage products and embedded subsystems ahead of Arrow Electronics and Ingram Micro. Avnet's suppliers include more than 700 component and systems makers; its largest supplier of parts for distribution is IBM. Avnet distributes these products to some 100000 manufacturers and resellers worldwide. Avnet distributes products from around 300 locations in more than 80 countries. It also offers a host of value-added design supply chain and aftermarket services.

HISTORY

In 1921 before the advent of commercial battery-operated radios Charles Avnet started a small ham radio replacement parts distributorship in Manhattan selling parts to designers inventors and ship-to-shore radio users on docked ships. The stock market crash in 1929 left the business strapped; it went bankrupt in 1931. A few years later Avnet founded another company making car radio kits and antennas. But competition got the best of him and that company also went bankrupt.

During WWII Charles joined his sons Lester and Robert founded Avnet Electronic Supply to sell parts to government and military contractors. After the war the company bought and sold surplus electrical and electronic parts. A contract from Bendix Aviation spurred company growth and Avnet

opened a West Coast warehouse. In 1955 it incorporated as Avnet Electronics Supply with Robert as chairman and CEO and Lester as president. Sales reached $1 million that year although the company lost $17000. It changed its name to Avnet Electronics in 1959.

In 1960 Avnet made its first acquisition British Industries and went public. Acquisitions continued throughout the 1960s with Hamilton Electro (1962) Fairmount Motor Products (1963) Carol Wire & Cable (1968) and Time Electronic Sales (1968).

To acknowledge its diversification into motors and other products the company again changed its name to Avnet Inc. in 1964. Robert Avnet died the next year and Lester took over as chairman; Lester died in 1970.

In 1973 Intel which introduced the microprocessor signed Avnet as a distributor and by 1979 Avnet's sales topped $1 billion. A soft 1982 market caused price declines that led Avnet to sell its wire and cable business. The company consolidated many of its operations to its Arizona headquarters in 1987.

During 1991 and 1992 Avnet spent more than $100 million for acquisitions strategic to the European market. In 1993 it bought the US's third-largest distributor Hall-Mark Electronics and acquired Penstock the top US distributor of microwave radio-frequency products in 1994. Avnet was Europe's #2 electronics distributor by 1994 despite having had almost no European operations prior to 1990. The company continued to expand globally acquiring Hong Kong-based distributor WKK Semiconductor in 1995 among others. Also that year Avnet began selling off its nonelectronics operations.

In 1998 it reorganized around separate global computer and electronics businesses. Also that year president and COO Roy Vallee became chairman and CEO. As part of its restructuring the company sold its Allied Electronics subsidiary to UK-based components distributor Electrocomponents in 1999 for $380 million. That year Avnet acquired rival Marshall Industries in a deal valued at about $760 million.

In 2000 Avnet acquired IBM midrange server distributor Savoir Technology Group in a $140 million deal making Avnet the leading distributor of IBM midrange products. Later that year it acquired a part of Germany-based EBV Group (semiconductor distribution) and RKE (computer products and services) both from German utility giant E.ON in a cash deal worth about $740 million. In 2001 Avnet acquired smaller rival Kent Electronics for about $600 million.

In 2003 it combined its Computer Marketing Group and its Applied Computing Group to form Avnet Technology Solutions. The next year it launched Avnet Logistics as a separate business unit to provide assembly asset management distribution programming and warehousing services to its customers.

In 2005 it established Avnet Managed Technologies (AMT) to offer IT services to small and midsized businesses. Operating directly and with other providers of products and services AMT was set up to provide data center managed services help desk support and Microsoft Exchange mailbox hosting.

Avnet acquired semiconductor distributor Memec Group Holdings for $663 million in 2005. Later that year the company sold the assets of its radio-frequency and microwave components business to Teledyne Technologies. To focus the operations of Avnet Technology Solutions on distribution Avnet sold its Hewlett-Packard end-user business to Logicalis and its Avnet Enterprise Solutions business to networking firm Calence. Both transactions closed in 2006.

In 2007 Avnet acquired Access Distribution the computer products distribution business of General Electric for about $410 million in cash. Access Distribution which specialized in computer hardware made by Sun Microsystems was integrated into Avnet Technology Solutions. Also that year the company acquired the European Enterprise Infrastructure division of Magirus Group and integrated it into the European operations of Avnet Technology Solutions.

Later in 2007 Avnet bought the IT Solutions division of Acal for about $83 million in cash and integrated into the European operations of Avnet Technology Solutions. Horizon Technology Group bought in 2008 for about €98.5 million ($150 million) in cash also became part of Technology Solutions in Europe. And Mumbai-based Ontrack Solutions became part of Avnet Technology Solutions Asia/Pacific.

In 2008 Avnet acquired Nippon Denso Industry Co. Ltd.which doubled Electronics Marketing's business in Japan. The purchase of Source Electronics boosted the geographic reach of Avnet Electronics Marketing in South America through operations in Brazil.

In 2009 which saw sales drop almost 10% for the first time in years Avnet continued acquisitions in international markets. It bought Abacus Group a European component distributor based in the UK for $61 million in cash. Avnet made Abacus part of Electronics Marketing EMEA forming Avnet Abacus.

The company's business in Asia was relatively strong during 2009 with sales there nearly doubling for the year. Avnet acquired certain assets of Vietnam-based IT distributor Sunshine Joint Stock Company and integrated it into its Technology Solutions Asia business. Additionally the company bought a controlling interest in Vanda Group a systems integrator and software applications developer based in China from Hutchison Whampoa. Vanda complemented Avnet Technology Solutions' recently launched distribution business in China adding a vertically integrated service offering and extensive base of customers in the banking financial services telecommunications and government markets. It also let Avnet expand its reach across China Hong Kong and Macau where Vanda had a strong local brand.

Teaming with Sanko Holding Group Avnet picked up a more than 50% interest in a joint venture in Turkey in 2009. The operation Avnet Technology Solutions Sanayi ve Ticaret A.S. is one of the largest IT distributors in Turkey.

In 2010 it bought a handful of companies the largest being rival Bell Microproducts for about $630 million in assumed debt and cash. Avnet was attracted to Bell Micro's strong presence in fast-growing Latin America as well as its position in data center products and embedded systems. Avnet combined Bell Micro's Latin American and European businesses and its North American data center business into Avnet Technology Solutions. Bell Micro's North American embedded components business was integrated into Avnet Electronics Marketing. (Acquired in the Bell Micro deal VAR and IT infrastructure solutions provider New ProSys was sold in early 2011.)

In another 2010 acquisition Avnet bought a majority stake in Asian distributor Unidux continuing a run of acquisitions in the region from the previous year and tripling the business of Avnet Electronics Marketing in Japan. China-based Eurotone Electric Limited added a line of components for solar and wind power applications for the fast-growing alternative energy market in the region.

Continuing its shopping spree Avnet also bought Broadband Integrated Resources that year. The company is a small provider of technical repair and logistics services to US cable companies including Time Warner Comcast and Charter Communications. The purchase was part of Avnet's strategy to expand into adjacent value-added service areas through acquisitions of companies with an established North American customer base. Broadband became part of Avnet Logistics Services.

In 2011 Avnet president and COO Rick Hamada succeeded long-time CEO Roy Vallee who remained chairman.

EXECUTIVES

VP and President Avnet Technology Solutions EMEA, Graeme A. Watt, age 54
Vice President Business Development Avnet Cilico, Alex Iuorio
CEO, Richard P. (Rick) Hamada, age 56, $900,000 total compensation
SVP and Chief Human Resources Officer, MaryAnn G. Miller, age 57, $425,000 total compensation
VP; SVP European Finance and Strategic Planning Electronics Marketing Europe Middle East and Africa, Patrick Zammit
VP and President Avnet Technology Solutions Americas, Jeff Bawol
SVP and CIO, Stephen R. (Steve) Phillips, age 51
SVP Global Business Development Avnet Electronics Marketing and President Avnet EM Holdings Japan, Tom McCartney
President Electronics Marketing Asia, Stephen Wong
VP Corporate Marketing and Communications, R. Kevin Sellers
SVP and President Avnet Electronics Marketing, Gerald W. (Gerry) Fay, age 55, $418,750 total compensation
SVP CFO Controller and Assistant Secretary, Kevin Moriarty, age 50, $525,000 total compensation
SVP and Chief Global Logistics and Operations Officer, Mike Buseman
VP and President Avnet Technology Solutions Asia Pacific, William Chu
VP and President Avnet Electronics Marketing Americas, Ed Smith
President SILICA, Mario Orlandi
VP and President Avnet Electronics Marketing EMEA, Miguel Fernandez
Svp-logistics Warehousing & Di, Robert (Bob) Brenner
Senior Vice President Global Supply Chain and Strategic Accounts, Lynn Torrel
Senior Vice President Avent Commercial Americas, Pablo Suarez
Call Center customer Service Director Vice President, Paul Love
Vice President Human Resources Ats Emea, Jan Hermans
Vice President Sales, Kassia Lathrop
Vice President Sales, Bradley Fehling
Vice President Sales HP Solutions, Jessica Yeck
Vice President, Susan (Sue) Engle
Vice President Global Contracts, Steven Larson
Vice President Marketing, Brian Gosling
Vice President Strategy Services, Patrick (Paddy) Jewett
Vice President Standard Product, Simon McLean
Vice President Director Of Sales, Chuck Delphsenior
Vice President Sales, David Butkiewicz
Senior Vice President Information Technology, Dave Bent
Vice President Of Sales, Ronald Brinckerhoff
Vice President Sales, John Fijak
Senior Vice President Director Corporate Accounts, Steve Boysen
Vice President Sales, Donna McGurk
Vice President Of Emerging Markets, Mike Kenney
Vice President, Doug Adams

Vice President Logistics Warehouse And Distribution, Alan Harper
Vice President, Rusty Murdaugh
Vice President of Global Operations Systems, Doug Halbert
Vice President, Brian Chan
Vice President, Glenn Bassett
Vice President Finance and Accounting, Kenneth (Ken) Jacobson
Vice President Of Sales Ibm Solutions, Trisha Cooke
Vice President Services, Timothy (Tim) Harper
Vice President, Eric Berry
Vice President, Dave Ward
Vice President Finance and Global Audit Executive, David (Dave) Schintzius
Senior Vice President, Dennis Losik
Vice President Director Material Mgmnt, John Bartels
Vice President Strategic Operations, Scott Stanton
Vice President Human Resources, Joanne Toh
Vice President Sales, Michele Blazier
Vice President Global Security, Anthony Ventriere
Vice President Sales, Phil Brinkley
Vice President andndash; Leasing, Jack Camarda
Vice President Sales, Brad Johnson
Vice President Sales, Valerie Suchomel
Vice President Sales, Peter Rzonca
Vice President For IBM Software Sales, Brad Wilson
Vice President Global Operations, Derinda Ehrlich
PA to Matthew Gower Vice President of Sales UK Technology Solutions, Claire Sheppard
Vice President, Diane Woodburn
Vice President, Ray Ramey
National Account Manager, Will Plantillas
Vice President Human Resources, C Chan
Vice President Sales and Marketing, Tal Segman
Senior Vice President Materials, Frank Hardin
Vice President Global and Strategic Accounts, Peter (Pete) Stenseth
Chairman, William H. (Bill) Schumann, age 64
Board Member, Phillip Carabillas
Auditors: KPMG LLP

LOCATIONS

HQ: Avnet Inc
   2211 South 47th Street, Phoenix, AZ 85034
Phone: 480 643-2000
Web: www.avnet.com

2014 Sales

	% of total
Americas	40
Europe Middle East & Africa	30
Asia/Pacific	30
Total	**100**

PRODUCTS/OPERATIONS

2014 Sales by Operating Group

	$ mil.	% of total
Electronics Marketing (EM)		
Asia	6,604	24
Europe Middle East & Africa	5,094	19
Americas	4,844	18
Technology Solutions (TS)		
Americas	6,084	22
Europe Middle East & Africa	3,151	11
Asia	1,719	6
Total	**27,499**	**100**

2014 Sales by Product Category

	$ mil.	% of total
Semiconductors	13,160	48
Computer products	10,527	38
Passives electromechanical & other	2,972	11
Connectors	794	3
Total	**27,499**	**100**

COMPETITORS

Allied Electronics	N.F. Smith
Arrow Electronics	Premier Farnell
Digi-Key	SYNNEX
Future Electronics	TTI Inc.
Heilind Electronics	Tech Data
Ingram Micro	WPG Holdings

HISTORICAL FINANCIALS

Company Type: Public

Income Statement

FYE: June 27

	REVENUE ($ mil.)	NET INCOME ($ mil.)	NET PROFIT MARGIN	EMPLOYEES
06/15	27,924	571	2.0%	18,800
06/14	27,499	545	2.0%	19,000
06/13	25,458	450	1.8%	18,500
06/12*	25,707	567	2.2%	19,100
07/11	26,534	669	2.5%	17,600
Annual Growth	1.3%	(3.8%)	—	1.7%

*Fiscal year change

2015 Year-End Financials

Debt ratio: 18.31%	No. of shares (mil.): 135
Return on equity: 11.98%	Dividends
Cash ($ mil.): 932	Yield: 0.0%
Current ratio: 2.02	Payout: 15.5%
Long-term debt ($ mil.): 1,646	Market value ($ mil.): 5,702

	STOCK PRICE ($) FY Close	P/E High/Low		Earnings	Dividends	Book Value
06/15	42.09	11	9	4.12	0.64	34.58
06/14	43.71	12	9	3.89	0.60	35.37
06/13	33.60	11	8	3.21	0.00	31.29
06/12*	30.86	10	6	3.79	0.00	27.40
07/11	32.55	9	5	4.34	0.00	26.55
Annual Growth	6.6%	—	—	(1.3%)	—	6.8%

*Fiscal year change

Avon Products, Inc.

Avon calling —calling for a younger crowd overseas reps and improved global operational efficiencies. Avon Products the world's top direct seller of cosmetics and beauty-related items is busy building a global brand and enticing more consumers to buy its products. Direct selling remains its modus operandi; sales also come from catalogs and a website. Its lineup includes cosmetics fragrances toiletries apparel home furnishings and more. Avon boasts more than 6 million independent representatives worldwide. With sales and distribution operations in more than 100 countries nearly 90% of sales come from outside the US. Avon is working to transform its business amid falling sales and profits.

Operations

Avon sells beauty fashion and home goods accounting for 71% 16% and 10% of sales respectively. The company's core beauty business consists of color cosmetics fragrances skin care and personal care. Fashion consists of fashion jewelry watches apparel footwear accessories and children's products. Home consists of gift and decorative products housewares entertainment and leisure products children's products and nutritional products. It exited direct jewelry sales in mid-2013 with the sale of Silpada Designs.

Geographic Reach

Avon calls on households in some 60 countries worldwide. In addition to these countries and territories its products were distributed in 41 other countries and territories. Indeed Avon Products rings up just 11% of its sales in the US. Latin America is a major market for the cosmetics company accounting for nearly 50% of sales. (Brazil alone contributes 22%.) It also operates in Russia China the UK and Germany among other countries.

Sales and Marketing

Avon recruits sales reps and customers largely through personal contact including recommendation from current representatives and customers and local market advertising. Sales promotions and sales development activities are directed at assisting reps. The company also relies on television and print advertising to sell its cosmetics and other products. The company reported advertising expenses of some $177 million in 2014 $202 million in 2013 and $251 million in 2012.

Financial Performance

Avon has struggled to consistently grow sales in recent years while dealing with a steep decline in net income. Its sales decreased by 11% in 2014 due to a drop in the number of active independent sales reps partially offset by the higher average order size. Sales of beauty and fashion and home products declined. The was driven by lower sales in North America the Asia/Pacific region Latin America and Europe the Middle East and Africa as a result of the unfavorable impact from foreign exchange and the drop in active independent sales reps. The company's net loss increased by 589% in 2014 due to lower revenues and an increase in income taxes. The effective tax rate in 2014 was negatively impacted by a non-cash income tax charge of $405 million largely due to a valuation allowance against deferred tax assets of $384 million primarily due to strong US dollar. Operating cash flow decreased by 33% in 2014 due to the higher net loss and a change in inventories.

Strategy

In late 2015 the company agreed to sell its North American operations to investor Cerberus Capital Management. A group of activist Avon shareholders is trying to block the deal.

CEO Sheri McCoy who joined Avon in 2012 is working to stabilize the business and return it to sustainable growth. To the end the company has set a cost-savings target of $400 million by the end of 2015. To get there Avon reduced global headcount including 15% of total jobs in 2014 and exited the South Korea and Vietnam markets as well as noncore businesses.

For a company known for its personal touch Avon in recent years appears to have lost touch with its customers. The company's plans to use money freed up by its recent reorganization to fund investment in consumer research product innovation and advertising (for selling products and recruiting sales reps). In 2014 the company launched a redesigned website which is a critical component of its digital strategy to enhance the social selling experience for Avon representatives and their customers.

Building on its growing business in Latin America in 2014 the company and Greek skincare brand KORRES entered into a partnership there to develop manufacture and market KORRES products. Also in 2014 Avon stuck a deal with fragrance giant (and former hostile suitor) Coty under which Avon Brazil's 1.5 million independent sales reps sell select Coty fragrances in Brazil.

Avon in 2013 sold its Silpada Designs (acquired in 2010) direct sales sterling silver jewelry business for $85 million in cash (plus an earn-out of up to $15 million if Silpada achieves specific earnings targets over two years.) The sale to Rhinestone Holdings a newly-formed company created by Sil-

pada's founders allowed Avon to focus on reviving its core business.

HISTORY

In the 1880s book salesman David McConnell gave small bottles of perfume to New York housewives who listened to his sales pitch. The perfume was more popular than the books so in 1886 McConnell created the California Perfume Company and hired women to sell door-to-door. (He renamed the company Avon Products in 1939 after being impressed by the beauty of Stratford-upon-Avon in England.) Through the 1950s these women mostly housewives seeking extra income made Avon a major force in the cosmetics industry.

From the 1960s until the mid-1980s Avon was the world's largest cosmetics company known for its appeal to middle-class homemakers. But the company hit hard times in 1974 –a recession made many of its products too pricey for blue-collar customers and women were leaving home for the workforce. Discovering that Avon's traditional products had little appeal for younger women Avon began an overhaul of its product line introducing the Colorworks line for teenagers with the slogan "It's not your mother's makeup."

Avon acquired prestigious jeweler Tiffany & Co. in 1979 (sold 1984) to help improve the company's image. To boost profits it entered the retail prestige fragrance business by launching a joint venture with Liz Claiborne (1985) and buying Giorgio Armani (1987 the Giorgio Beverly Hills retail operations were sold in 1994). But Liz Claiborne dissolved the joint venture when Avon bought competitor Parfums Stern in 1987 (sold 1990). It sold 40% of Avon Japan (begun 1969) to the Japanese public that year.

Avon Color cosmetics were introduced in 1988 and sleepwear preschool toys and videos followed in 1989. The company introduced apparel in 1994 and the next year worked with designer Diane Von Furstenberg to launch a line of clothing.

Mattel and Avon joined forces in 1996 to sell toys –Winter Velvet Barbie became Avon's most successful product introduction ever. In 1997 the company launched a new home furnishings catalog and bought direct seller Discovery Toys (sold 1999). Late in 1997 it began a $400 million restructuring program.

Passing over several high-ranking female executives (the company felt they weren't ready) Avon made Charles Perrin its CEO in mid-1998. Andrea Jung the brain behind the makeover became president. Avon also began selling makeup in 1998 at mall kiosks and through a catalog. Late that year The Avon Centre day spa opened in Manhattan.

In 1999 Jung became Avon's first female CEO by replacing the retiring Perrin. Former Goodyear and Rubbermaid CEO Stanley Gault was elected chairman of the board. In March 2000 Avon announced an alliance with Swiss pharmaceutical group Roche to develop a line of women's vitamins and nutritional products (its first) launched in 2001.

In June 2001 the company relaunched its Web site; the site allows Avon representatives to transact business through their own personal Web pages. In September Jung was elected chairman of the board. That year Avon also ceased marketing its beComing line in Penney's stores and added the brand to its direct-selling line of products.

In 2002 as part of a move to improve operating efficiencies Avon closed its jewelry manufacturing plant in San Sebastián Puerto Rico. The closure marked Avon's exit from jewelry manufacturing. It now outsources its full jewelry line by purchasing finished goods from Asia. In another cost-cutting move Avon laid off 3500 employees or 8%

of its workforce that March saying that the economic recession in Argentina which accounts for about 5% of Avon's sales made the layoffs necessary. The next month Avon announced the closing of production operations in Northampton UK and a shift of these operations to its facility in Garwolin Poland reflecting what the company called a continuation of its plan to improve efficiency and integration.

As part of its focus on the younger market in 2003 Avon launched a new cosmetics line called "mark." –targeted to the 16-24 age group. Named for young women making their mark on the world the line includes 300 products such as cosmetics skin care fragrance accessories jewelry and handbags.

In 2004 Avon agreed to pay some $50 million for a 20% stake in its two Chinese joint ventures with Masson Group.

In 2010 Avon bought Silpada Designs a Kansas-based direct seller of sterling silver jewelry with operations in the US Canada and the UK for $650 million. The acquisition was the company's largest in more than a decade. Three years later in July 2013 Avon sold Silpada to Rhinestone Holdings a newly-formed company created by Silpada's founders for $85 million in an all-cash transaction.

The struggling company became a takeover target in 2012 when its smaller rival Coty made an unsolicited $10.7 billion offer for the business which Avon rejected.

EXECUTIVES

SVP and President Europe Middle East and Africa; Head Global Field Operations, John P. Higson, age 56, $589,744 total compensation
CEO, Sherilyn S. (Sheri) McCoy, age 57, $1,200,000 total compensation
SVP and President Asia Pacific, Nilesh Patel
SVP and President Latin America and Andean Cluster; Head Global Brand Marketing, Fernando J. Acosta, $733,904 total compensation
SVP and President North America, Pablo M Mu ±oz, $327,055 total compensation
SVP and President Avon Brazil and South Market Group, David Legher, $487,339 total compensation
EVP and CFO, James S. Scully
SVP Business Transformation and Global Supply Chain, David Powell
SVP Global Strategy, Brian Salsberg
Vice President Us Sales, Eddie Silcock
Senior Vice President Global Supply Chain, John (Jack) Owen
Chairman, Douglas R. (Doug) Conant, age 65
Auditors: PricewaterhouseCoopers LLP

LOCATIONS

HQ: Avon Products, Inc.
  777 Third Avenue, New York, NY 10017-1307
Phone: 212 282-5000   **Fax:** 212 282-6035
Web: www.avon.com

2014 Sales

	$ mil.	% of total
Brazil	1,909	22
United States	1,008	11
Rest of the world	5,933	67
Total	**8,851**	**100**

PRODUCTS/OPERATIONS

2014 Sales

	$ mil.	% of total
Beauty	6,269	71
Fashion	1,407	16
Home	939	10
Other	252	3
Total	**8,851**	**100**

COMPETITORS

Alticor	Johnson & Johnson
Amway China	Kracie
Bath & Body Works	L' Or©al
BeautiControl	LVMH
Beiersdorf	Macy' s
Body Shop	Mary Kay
Chanel	Murad Inc.
Clarins	Nu Skin
Colgate-Palmolive	Perrigo
Coty Inc.	Prestige Cosmetics
Dana Classic	Procter & Gamble
Fragrances	Revlon
Dillard' s	Shaklee
Elizabeth Arden Inc	Shiseido
Est©e Lauder	Target Corporation
Forever Living	Tupperware Brands
Hanover Direct	Unilever
J. C. Penney	Wal-Mart
Jafra	

HISTORICAL FINANCIALS

Company Type: Public

Income Statement

FYE: December 31

	REVENUE ($ mil.)	NET INCOME ($ mil.)	NET PROFIT MARGIN	EMPLOYEES
12/14	8,851	(388)	—	33,200
12/13	9,955	(56)	—	36,700
12/12	10,717	(42)	—	39,100
12/11	11,291	513	4.5%	40,600
12/10	10,862	606	5.6%	42,000
Annual Growth	(5.0%)	—	—	(5.7%)

2014 Year-End Financials

Debt ratio: 47.32%
Return on equity: (-55.52%)
Cash ($ mil.): 960
Current ratio: 1.45
Long-term debt ($ mil.): 2,463

No. of shares (mil.): 434
Dividends
  Yield: 2.5%
  Payout: —
Market value ($ mil.): 4,082

	STOCK PRICE ($) FY Close	P/E High/Low	PER SHARE ($) Earnings	Dividends	Book Value
12/14	9.39	— —	(0.88)	0.24	0.67
12/13	17.22	— —	(0.13)	0.24	2.56
12/12	14.36	— —	(0.10)	0.75	2.82
12/11	17.47	26 14	1.18	0.92	3.65
12/10	29.06	25 18	1.39	0.88	3.86
Annual Growth	(24.6%)	— —	—	(27.7%)	(35.5%)

Baker Hughes Inc.

Baker Hughes cooks up dozens of products and services for the global petroleum market. Through its Drilling and Evaluation segment Baker Hughes makes products and services used to drill oil and natural gas wells. It also makes bits and drilling fluids and submersible pumps. Through its Completion and Production segment the company provides equipment and services used from the completion phase through the productive life of oil and natural gas wells. Its Industrial Service segment provides equipment and services for the refining process and pipeline industries. In 2014 the company agreed to acquired by Halliburton for about $35 billion.

Geographic ReachBaker Hughes operates in more than 80 countries. It divides its business into four regions: North America Latin America Europe/Africa/Russia Caspian (EARC) and Middle East/Asia Pacific (MEAP). North America generates more than 50% of sales with both EARC and the fast-growing MEAP segments accounting for about 20% and Latin America 10%.

Its Industrial Services segment included locations in Houston Texas Barnsdall Oklahoma and in the UK.

Operations
Baker Hughes is a supplier of oilfield services products technology and systems to the worldwide oil and natural gas business. It also provide services and products to the downstream chemicals and process and pipeline services referred to as Industrial Services.The company's oilfield operations include Drilling and Evaluation and Completion and Production.Drilling and Evaluation products and services consist of Drill Bits Drilling Services Wireline Services and Drilling and Completion Fluids.Completion and Production consists of Completion Systems Wellbore Intervention Intelligent Production Systems Artificial Lift Upstream Chemicals Pressure Pumping.Industrial Services consists of downstream chemicals (which provides products and services that help to increase refinery production and improve plant safety and equipment reliability) and process and pipeline services (which if engaged in the inspection pre-commissioning and commissioning of new and existing pipeline systems and process plants).

Sales and MarketingThe company markets its products and services through its own sales organizations. Customers include integrated major and super-major oil and natural gas firms and independent oil and natural gas companies as well as national or state-owned oil companies.

Baker Hughes' revenues are generated from the sale of products and services to major national and independent oil and natural gas companies worldwide.

Financial PerformanceBaker Hughes has reported rising revenues over the last five years.In 2014 revenues increased by 10% due to sales increase across all product lines in particular drilling services artificial lift and pressure pumping.North America's sales increased due to revenue growth in pressure pumping operations and by reversing the oversupply of hydraulic fracturing equipment.Latin America revenues decreased due to reductions in Brazil and Venezuela partially offset by increased revenue throughout the rest of the region. Revenues declined across most product lines in Brazil due to lower activity levels.In the EARC segment the company delivered strong revenue growth in Africa Continental Europe and Russia Caspian driven by increased result of activity growth and share gains across most of the region in west Africa. In Continental Europe revenue growth was driven by increased demand for completion and production product lines. In the North Sea drilling and evaluation activity increases in the UK were entirely offset by reduced activity in Norway. In the Russia Caspian region revenue growth was driven by increased activity in completion and production.MEAP revenue posted strong revenue growth in virtually all geographies most notably in Saudi Arabia Iraq the Arabian Gulf Southeast Asia and China. In Saudi Arabia revenue increases were primarily related to activity growth in integrated operations contracts.Industrial Services revenue increased primarily driven by the acquisition of a complementary pipeline services business.In 2014 Baker Hughes' net income jumped by 57% due to an increase in revenues from services and a decrease in marketing general and administrative expenses driven by acquisition and deconsolidation activities.That year the company's cash from operating activities decreased by 7% due to an increase in depreciation and amortization changes in accounts receivable inventories accounts payable accrued employee compensation and other accrued liabilities.

StrategyThe company has grown through product innovation (it developed the first oil well drill bit for rock in 1909) strategic alliances and acquisitions.

However faced by slumping oil prices that were dragging down demand for its services in 2015 the company announced plans to adapt to changing market conditions and align its cost structure with near-term activity levels. This included the decision to close several facilities across the world and to reduce the global workforce by 7000.

In a major industry consolidation move in 2014 the company agreed to be acquired by rival oil service giant Halliburton for about $35 billion.

In 2014 Baker Hughes increased its R&D spend to $613 million (from $556 million and $497 million in 2013 and 2012 respectively) and introduced more than 100 products or product enhancements including the SureTrak steerable drilling liner service and the SHADOW series of frac plugs with disintegrating frac balls. In early 2014 it opened the $60 million Artificial Lift Research and Technology Center in Claremore Oklahoma.

Growing its portfolio in 2014 Baker Hughes signed an agreement with CGG for RoqSCAN technology offered by CGG. RoqSCAN is a real-time fully portable quantitative and automated rock properties and mineralogical analyzer.

The company routinely evaluates potential acquisitions of businesses that enhance their current operations or expand their operations into new markets or product lines and would sell business operations that are not considered part of their core business. In 2014 it paid $314 million for acquisitions.

Mergers and Acquisitions
In 2014 Baker Hughes purchased (for about $250 million) the pipeline and specialty services business of Weatherford which added subsea pipeline commissioning services and ultrasonic inline inspection technologies to Baker's portfolio. Earlier that year it acquired Texas-based oilfield software company Perfomix.

HISTORY

Howard Hughes Sr. and partner Walter Sharp opened a plant in Houston and their company Sharp & Hughes soon had a near monopoly on rock bits. When Sharp died in 1912 Hughes bought his partner's half of the company incorporating as Hughes Tool. Hughes held 73 patents when he died in 1924; the company passed to Howard Hughes Jr.

It is estimated that between 1924 and 1972 Hughes Tool provided Hughes Jr. with $745 million in pretax profits which he used to diversify into movies (RKO) airlines (TWA) and Las Vegas casinos. In 1972 he sold the company to the public for $150 million. After 1972 the company expanded into tools for aboveground oil production. In 1974 under the new leadership of chairman James Leach Hughes bought the oil field equipment business of Borg-Warner.

In 1913 drilling contractor Carl Baker organized the Baker Casing Shoe Company in California to collect royalties on his three oil tool inventions. The firm began to make its own products in 1918 and during the 1920s it expanded nationally opened global trade and formed Baker Oil Tools (1928). The company grew in the late 1940s and the 1950s as oil drilling boomed.

One of Baker Hughes' major acquisitions came in 2010 when in a major industry consolidation it acquired oil field services titan BJ Services for $6.9 billion. The acquisition expanded Baker Hughes' portfolio adding pressure pumping to its product offering giving it a stronger platform for international growth and the ability to better compete for large integrated project contracts in the unconventional gas and deepwater markets. In particular the purchase strengthened the company's integrated services and expanded its reservoir capabilities.

EXECUTIVES

SVP; Chief Legal and Governance Officer, Alan R. Crain, age 64, $742,192 total compensation
SVP and CFO, Kimberly A. Ross, age 50, $132,308 total compensation
Chairman and CEO, Martin S. Craighead, age 56, $1,236,538 total compensation
President North America, Richard L. Williams, age 60
VP and CIO, Archana (Archie) Deskus
VP and Chief Integration Officer, Belgacem Chariag, age 52, $691,923 total compensation
VP and Chief Strategy Officer, Derek Mathieson, age 44, $634,615 total compensation
President Europe Africa and Russia Caspian, Arthur L. (Art) Soucy, age 52
President Middle East and Asia Pacific, Khaled Nouh
President Global Products and Services, Richard Ward
VP and CTO, Mario Ruscev
President Latin America, Julio Lera
Vice President For Drilling Services, Mathias Schlecht
Vice President, Mikhail Gladkikh
Area Vice President, Ruben Develasco
Vice President Procurement, Daniel Richardson
Vice President North America, Keith Gill
Vice President Investor Relations, Gary Flaharty
Vice President, Derek Allan
Vice President, Ronald Martz
Vice President Finance, Dennis Eubanks
Vice President Human Resources, Murali Kuppuswamy
Vice President, Ralph Crabtree
Board Member, James Stewart
Board Member, Becky Tice
Auditors: DELOITTE & TOUCHE LLP

LOCATIONS

HQ: Baker Hughes Inc.
2929 Allen Parkway, Suite 2100, Houston, TX 77019-2118
Phone: 713 439-8600   **Fax:** 713 439-8699
Web: www.bakerhughes.com

2014 Sales

	$ mil.	% of total
North America	12,078	49
Middle East & Asia/Pacific	4,456	18
Europe Africa Russia & the Caspian	4,417	18
Latin America	2,236	9
Industrial service	1,364	6
Total	**24,551**	**100**

PRODUCTS/OPERATIONS

2014 Sales

	$ mil.	% of total
Completion & Production	14,572	59
Drilling & Evaluation	8,615	35
Industrial Services	1,364	6
Total	**24,551**	**100**

Selected Operations

Drilling and Evaluation
   Drill bits
   Drilling and completion fluids
   Drilling services
   Wireline services
Completion and Production
   Artificial lift
   Completion systems
   Intelligent production systems
   Pressure pumping
   Upstream chemicals
   Wellbore intervention
Industrial Services and Other

COMPETITORS

Aker Solutions	Petroleum Geo-Services
CE Franklin	Precision Drilling
CGG	Schlumberger
FMC	TETRA Technologies
Halliburton	Technip
John Wood Group	Weatherford
Nabors Well Services	International
Nalco	Wenzel Downhole Tools
National Oilwell Varco	

HISTORICAL FINANCIALS
Company Type: Public

Income Statement
FYE: December 31

	REVENUE ($ mil.)	NET INCOME ($ mil.)	NET PROFIT MARGIN	EMPLOYEES
12/14	24,551	1,719	7.0%	62,000
12/13	22,364	1,096	4.9%	59,400
12/12	21,361	1,311	6.1%	58,800
12/11	19,831	1,739	8.8%	57,700
12/10	14,414	812	5.6%	53,100
Annual Growth	**14.2%**	**20.6%**	**—**	**4.0%**

2014 Year-End Financials

Debt ratio: 14.34%
Return on equity: 9.46%
Cash ($ mil.): 1,740
Current ratio: 2.60
Long-term debt ($ mil.): 3,913

No. of shares (mil.): 434
Dividends
   Yield: 1.1%
   Payout: 21.6%
Market value ($ mil.): 24,334

	STOCK PRICE ($) FY Close	P/E High/Low		PER SHARE ($) Earnings	Dividends	Book Value
12/14	56.07	19	13	3.92	0.64	42.91
12/13	55.26	24	17	2.47	0.60	40.44
12/12	40.85	18	13	2.97	0.60	38.71
12/11	48.64	20	11	3.97	0.60	36.03
12/10	57.17	28	17	2.60	0.60	32.64
Annual Growth	**(0.5%)**	**—**	**—**	**17.5%**	**1.6%**	**7.1%**

Ball Corp

The well-rounded Ball Corporation perpetually pitches packaging to companies producing food beverage and household goods. Food and beverage packaging includes steel cans and aluminum slugs. Ball's packaging revenue derives primarily from a relatively few beverage making customers owning brands spanning Argentina Brazil China Europe and North America. Ball Aerospace & Technologies manufactures an array of aerospace systems from satellites to tactical antennas as well as providing systems engineering services. Ball Corporation operates through 90 locations around the world.

Geographic Reach

Ball Corporation operates 90 locations spanning Asia Europe North America and South America. The US accounts for 60% of its net sales.

Operations

Ball divides its operations between four business segments. The largest metal beverage packaging Americas and Asia accounts for 49% of sales. This segment's operations are located in the US Canada Brazil and China; it distributes containers mainly to companies that make carbonated soft drinks beer energy drinks and other beverages.

The metal beverage packaging Europe segment representing 22% of sales includes the manufacturing of metal beverage containers extruded aluminum aerosol containers and aluminum slugs in the Czech Republic France Germany the Netherlands Poland Serbia and the UK.

Metal food and household products packaging Americas 18% of sales caters to the US Canada and Argentina. The company's smallest segment aerospace and technologies 11% of sales makes and sells aerospace and related products for the defense civil space and commercial space markets.

Sales and Marketing

Ball's packaging revenue derives primarily from long-term contracts with a relatively few customers: Coca-Cola MillerCoors and the US government accounted for 11% 10% and 10% of total 2014 sales respectively.

Financial Performance

After experiencing a revenue decline in 2013 Ball saw its revenues climb 1% to nearly $8.6 billion in 2014. The growth was fueled by a 4% spike in both aerospace and technologies and metal beverage packaging Europe sales. Aerospace and technologies' growth was attributed to higher sales for civil space contracts and US national defense contracts.

Ball's profits surged 16% to peak at a record-setting $470 million in 2014. This was fueled by the revenue increase coupled with reduced amortization depreciation and interest expenses. The company's operating cash flow increased by 20% in 2014 due to changes in receivables inventories and accrued employee costs.

Mergers and Acquisitions

Ball's blueprint has been pretty simple over the years: it acquires similar companies around the world to widen its customer base and extend its geographical reach. Ball in 2015 completed its acquisition of Sonoco's metal end and closure facilities in Canton Ohio. The Canton plants which produce multiple-sized closures for the food can market will become part of Ball's global metal food and household products packaging division.

In a sweeping move for the industry the company announced in early 2015 it was acquiring Rexam one of its biggest rivals for around $6.8 billion. If approved by regulators the deal would create the world's largest maker of food and beverage cans. The combined company is projected to generate $15 billion in sales and create $300 million in annual cost savings.

HISTORY

The Ball Corporation began in 1880 when Frank Ball and his four brothers started making wood-jacket tin cans to store and transport kerosene and other materials. In 1884 the company switched to tin-jacketed glass containers for kerosene lamps. The lamps however were soon displaced by Thomas Edison's electric light bulb.

The Ball brothers then learned that the patent to the original sealed-glass storage container (the Mason jar) had expired. By 1886 the brothers had entered the sealed-jar business and imprinted their jars with the Ball name. In their first year they made 12500 jars and sparked a patent war with the two reigning jar producers who asserted that they controlled the correct patents and threatened to sue. The Ball lawyers proved that the patents had expired and the jar remained Ball's mainstay for many years.

The company began diversifying but a 1947 antitrust ruling prohibited it from buying additional glass subsidiaries. Ball decided to take advantage of the space race by buying Control Cells (aerospace science research) in 1957; that operation became Ball Brothers Research Corporation (later Ball Aerospace Systems Division). The Soviets launched Sputnik that year igniting a massive US scientific effort in 1958 and Ball won federal contracts to make equipment for the US space program.

Ball established its metal beverage-container business in 1969 when it bought Jeffco Manufacturing of Colorado. The operation soon won contracts to supply two-piece cans to Budweiser Coca-Cola Dr Pepper Pepsi and Stroh's Beer.

EXECUTIVES

SVP and CFO, Scott C. Morrison, age 53, $1,149,327 total compensation
Chairman President and CEO, John A. Hayes, age 50, $1,149,327 total compensation
SVP Human Resources and Administration, Lisa A. Pauley, age 53, $439,475 total compensation
President North American Metal Beverage Packaging Division, Daniel W. Fisher
VP General Counsel and Corporate Secretary, Charles E. Baker, age 58, $460,156 total compensation
VP Information Technology and Services, Leroy J. Williams, age 51
President Ball Packaging Europe, Colin Gillis, age 61
SVP; President Ball Aerospace and Technologies, Robert D. (Rob) Strain, age 58
President Ball Asia Pacific Limited, Gihan Atapattu, age 50
SVP and COO Metal Food and Household Products Packaging, James N. Peterson, age 46
President Latapack-Ball Embalagens Ltda., Anthony (Tony) Barnett, age 50
SVP; COO Global Metal Beverage Packaging, Erik Bouts, age 53
VP; General Manager Ball Aerocan Americas, Daniel J. Rabbit
Vice President Engineering, Joe Atwell
Vice President Operational Planning and Administra, Jim Curtin
Vice President Operations, Mike Shuster
Vice President Global Sourcing, Robert (Bob) Lauterbach
Executive Vice President Administration and Corporate Secretary, David A (Dave) Westerlund
Vp Diversity & Inclusion, Manette Snow
Vice President Human Resources, John (Jack) Olson

Vice President Corporate Development, Tom Wiley
Vice President Of Operations, Rachel Peled
Vice President Human Resources, Karine Finck
Vice President Information Technology, Bob Smith
Vice President Of Human Resources, Randy Chastian
Purchasing Vice President, John Martin
Vice President and General Manager, Stan Platek
Vice President Of Innovation, Mike Vaughan
Vice President Human Resources, James Stevens
Vice President Of Marketing, Drew Couch
Vice President Of Marketing, Bill Braun
Vice President Plastic Container Operations, Larry Green
Vice President and Treasurer, Jeff A Knobel
Vice President and Controller, Shawn Barker
Senior Vice President Sales and Marketing Metal Food Containers, Tom Hale
Vice President Marketing and Corporate Affairs, Jim Peterson
Board Member, Chris Barkley
Auditors: PricewaterhouseCoopers LLP

LOCATIONS

HQ: Ball Corp
10 Longs Peak Drive, P.O. Box 5000, Broomfield, CO 80021-2510
Phone: 303 469-3131
Web: www.ball.com

2014

	$ mil.	% of total
US	5,091	59
Foreign	3,479	41
Total	**8,570**	**100**

PRODUCTS/OPERATIONS

2014 Sales

	$ mil.	% of total
Metal beverage packaging Americas & Asia	4,247	49
Metal beverage packaging Europe	1,896	22
Metal food & household products packaging	1,504	18
Aerospace & technologies	935	11
Corporate & intercompany eliminations	(12)	-
Total	**8,570**	**100**

Selected Products

Aerospace and technologies
 Aerospace technology and components
 Antennas and microwave systems
 Satellites and spacecraft
 Space-based instruments and sensors
 Tactical instruments and sensors
 Technical services
Packaging
 Aerosol cans
 Beverage cans
 Food cans
 Paint and general line cans

COMPETITORS

Alcoa	Rexam
Amcor	Rio Tinto Alcan
Anchor Glass	Rockwell Collins
BWAY	Saint-Gobain
Boeing	Containers
CLARCOR	Sequa
Consolidated Container	Silgan
Crown Holdings	Teledyne Technologies
Owens-Illinois	Tetra Laval

HISTORICAL FINANCIALS

Company Type: Public

Income Statement

FYE: December 31

	REVENUE ($ mil.)	NET INCOME ($ mil.)	NET PROFIT MARGIN	EMPLOYEES
12/15	7,997	280	3.5%	15,200
12/14	8,570	470	5.5%	14,500
12/13	8,468	406	4.8%	14,600
12/12	8,735	403	4.6%	15,000
12/11	8,630	444	5.1%	15,000
Annual Growth	**(1.9%)**	**(10.8%)**	**—**	**0.3%**

2015 Year-End Financials

Debt ratio: 52.49%
Return on equity: 24.59%
Cash ($ mil.): 224
Current ratio: 1.02
Long-term debt ($ mil.): 5,054
No. of shares (mil.): 142
Dividends
 Yield: 0.7%
 Payout: 24.3%
Market value ($ mil.): 10,349

	STOCK PRICE ($) FY Close	P/E High/Low	PER SHARE ($) Earnings	Dividends	Book Value
12/15	72.73	38 30	1.99	0.52	8.79
12/14	68.17	21 14	3.30	0.52	7.54
12/13	51.66	19 15	2.73	0.52	8.44
12/12	44.75	17 14	2.55	0.40	7.44
12/11	35.71	28 11	2.63	0.28	7.60
Annual Growth	**19.5%**	**— —**	**(6.7%)**	**16.7%**	**3.7%**

Banc of California Inc

Banc of California (formerly PacTrust Bank) offers deposit and loan services at 15 branches in Southern California's Los Angeles Orange County and San Diego. Customers enjoy checking savings and money market accounts as well as mobile online and card payment services telephone banking automated bill payment safe deposit boxes direct deposit and wire transfers. Customers can also access their accounts through a nationwide network of 30000 surcharge-free ATMs. In addition Banc of California operates more than 65 mortgage loan production offices in California Arizona Oregon Montana Virginia and Washington.

Mergers and Acquisitions
Banc of California has grown through acquisitions. In 2012 it paid $15.5 million for Gateway Business Bank and $37 million for Beach Business Bank. The next year it took over The Private Bank of California for $25 million and bought The Palisades Group a residential mortgage investment advisory firm and specialty finance company CS Financial. In 2014 it announced plans to buy 20 branches of Banco Popular North America to reach California's Hispanic community.

Strategy
Banc of California also streamlines it business through divestitures. In 2013 it sold eight branches to AmericanWest Bank in order to reshape its retail branch network to focus on servicing small – to midsized businesses and high net worth families.

EXECUTIVES

Senior Vice President Branch Operations, Rachel Carrillo
EVP and CFO, Ronald J. Nicolas, age 56, $346,354 total compensation
Chairman President and CEO, Steven A. Sugarman, age 40, $599,039 total compensation

Treasurer and Chief Investment Officer, Craig S. Naselow, age 51

Chief Lending Officer, Jeffrey T. Seabold, age 48, $237,949 total compensation

Chief Risk Officer, Hugh F. Boyle, age 55, $67,417 total compensation

President Warehouse Lending, Zoila Price

CIO, Matthew A. March

Head Central Operations, Thedora Nickel

President The Palisades Group, Stephen M. Kirch

President Banc Home Loans, Ted Ray

CFO, James McKinney

Senior Vice President, Tina Van der Zee

Executive Vice President And Chief Administrative Officer, Richard (Dick) Herrin

Group Vice President, John (Jack) Grosvenor

Vice President Information Systems, Chris Giglio

Vice President Information Technology Operations, Ken Plummer

Vice President Information Security and Privacy Officer, Joe Jaramillo

Evp Finance, Fred Mahintorabi

Regional Vice President, Mike Falce

Assistant Vice President Information Technology Service Delivery Manager, Robert (Bob) Skau

Vice President Physical Security, Gary Dersarkissian

Vice President Commercial Servicing Manager, Sylvia Jaques

Assistant Vice President Secondary Marketing, Jennifer (Jen) McGaw

Assistant Vice President Business Continuity Analyst, Rebecca Christy

Vice President Change Management, Raquel Gillett

Vice President Director of Sales, Steve Preimesberger

Assistant Vice President Servicing, Julian Tioseco

Vice President And Business Development Officer, Jason Fischer

Assistant Vice President, Maribel Flores

Senior Vice President Corporate Client, Jesse Martin

Assistant Vice President Underwriter, Erin Stuart

Vice President Credit Administration, Edward (Ed) Massey

Assistant Vice President Branch Manager, Jason Sparks

Vice President Treasury Manager, AL Sondag

Assistant Vice President Senior Marketing Director Creative, Jason Marcos

Senior Vice President Loan Group Manager Private Bank, Gary Seferian

Vice President Director of Sales and Service, Todd Reinheimer

Assistant Vice President Accounting, Courtney Smith

Assistant Vice President Corporate Facilities, Karen Koepsell

Vice President Human Resources Pacific Trust Bank, Lisa Moss

Executive Vice President And Chief Lending Officer, Chang Liu

Senior Vice President, David (Dave) Cobb

Vice President Deposit Operations Manager, Xuan Wu

Assistant Vice President Central Operations, Robert (Bob) Faucett

Assistant Vice President Operations Manager Deposit Operations, Sharon Murray

Vice Chairman, Chad T. Brownstein

Auditors: KPMG LLP

LOCATIONS

HQ: Banc of California Inc
18500 Von Karman Ave., Suite 1100, Irvine, CA 92612
Phone: 855 361-2262
Web: www.bancofcal.com

PRODUCTS/OPERATIONS

2013 Sales

	% of total
Interest and dividend income	
Loans including fees	53
Securities and others	2
Noninterest income	
Net gain on mortgage banking activities	31
Gain on sale of branches	6
Net gain on sale of loans	4
Loan servicing income	1
Customer service fees	1
Others	2
Total	**100**

COMPETITORS

American Business Bank	East West Bancorp
Bank of America	JPMorgan Chase
Bank of the West	MUFG Americas Holdings
BofI	PacWest Bancorp
California Bank & Trust	Pacific Mercantile
	Pacific Premier
City National	Simplicity Bancorp
Comerica	U.S. Bancorp

HISTORICAL FINANCIALS

Company Type: Public

Income Statement

FYE: December 31

	ASSETS ($ mil.)	NET INCOME ($ mil.)	INCOME AS % OF ASSETS	EMPLOYEES
12/14	5,971	30	0.5%	1,470
12/13	3,628	0	0.0%	1,384
12/12	1,682	6	0.4%	614
12/11	999	(2)	—	147
12/10	861	2	0.3%	107
Annual Growth	62.3%	81.0%	—	92.5%

2014 Year-End Financials

Debt ratio: 1.57%
Return on equity: 7.32%
Cash ($ mil.): 233
Current ratio: —
Long-term debt ($ mil.): —

No. of shares (mil.): 34
Dividends
Yield: 4.1%
Payout: 64.0%
Market value ($ mil.): 399

	STOCK PRICE ($) FY Close	P/E High/Low	PER SHARE ($) Earnings	Dividends	Book Value
12/14	11.47	15 11	0.91	0.48	14.47
12/13	13.41	— —	(0.14)	0.48	16.13
12/12	12.27	33 26	0.40	0.48	15.87
12/11	10.25	— —	(0.31)	0.45	15.85
12/10	13.27	35 14	0.37	0.25	13.98
Annual Growth	(3.6%)	— —	25.2%	17.7%	0.9%

BancFirst Corp. (Oklahoma City, Okla)

This Oklahoma bank wants to be more than OK. It wants to be super. BancFirst Corporation is the holding company for BancFirst a super-community bank that emphasizes decentralized management and centralized support. BancFirst operates about 95 locations in some 52 Oklahoma communities. It serves individuals and small to midsized businesses offering traditional deposit products such as checking and savings accounts CDs and IRAs. Commercial real estate lending (including farmland and multifamily residential loans) makes up more than a third of the bank's loan portfolio while one-to-four family residential mortgages represent about 20%. The bank also issues business construction and consumer loans.Geographic ReachBancFirst has 95 banking locations serving more than 52 communities across Oklahoma.OperationsThe company has four principal business units: metropolitan banks community banks other financial services and executive operations and support. Metropolitan and community banks offer traditional banking products such as commercial and retail lending and a full line of deposit accounts. Metropolitan banks consist of banking locations in the metropolitan Oklahoma City and Tulsa areas. Community banks consist of banking locations in communities throughout Oklahoma. Other financial services are specialty product business units including guaranteed small business lending residential mortgage lending trust services securities brokerage electronic banking and insurance. The executive operations and support groups represent executive management operational support and corporate functions that are not allocated to the other business units.The company's BancFirst Insurance Services arm sells property/casualty coverage while the bank's trust and investment management division oversees some $1.5 billion of assets on behalf of clients. Bank subsidiaries Council Oak Investment Corporation and Council Oak Real Estate focus on small business and property investments respectively. Sales and MarketingThe bank customers are generally small to medium-sized businesses engaged in light manufacturing local wholesale and retail trade commercial and residential real estate development and construction services agriculture and the energy industry. In 2013 BancFirst spent about $6.6 million for advertising and promotion (compared to $7.3 million a year earlier).Financial PerformanceIn 2013 BancFirst's revenues decreased by 1% due to lower interest income as a result of a decline in loan rates partially offset by lower deposit rates and increased loan volume and by a rise in noninterest income (thanks to higher in service charge revenue as a result of increases in deposits trust revenues and insurance commissions).That year the company's net income increased by 5% primarily due to a decrease in interest paid on deposits and borrowings and a lower provision for loan losses due to reductions in adversely graded loans.The company's operating cash inflow increased to $78.1 million in 2013 (from $60.3 million in 2012) primarily due to increased net income and change in working capital.StrategyBancFirst's strategy focuses on providing a full range of commercial banking services to retail customers and small to medium-sized businesses in both the nonmetropolitan trade centers and cities in the metropolitan statistical areas of Oklahoma. It operates as a “super community bank” managing its community banking offices on a decentralized basis which permits them to be responsive to local customer needs. Underwriting funding customer service and pricing decisions are made by presidents in each market within the company's strategic parameters.Company BackgroundThe company has been buying smaller banks to expand in Oklahoma. In 2011 it acquired FBC Financial Corporation and its subsidiary bank 1st Bank Oklahoma with about five branches throughout the state. In 2010 BancFirst acquired Union Bank of Chandler Okemah National Bank and Exchange National Bank of Moore adding about another five branches. It acquired First State Bank Jones in 2009 to expand in eastern Oklahoma.President and CEO David Rainbolt owns some 40% of BancFirst .

EXECUTIVES

Senior Human Resources Vice President, Mike Rogers

Executive Vice President Marketing, Barrie Higginbotham

EVP Asset Quality BancFirst, Dale E. Petersen, age 64

EVP Financial Services BancFirst, D. Jay Hannah, age 59

Executive Vice President Investments of BancFirst, Robert (Bob) Neville

EVP Interim CFO and Chief Risk Officer, Randy P. Foraker, age 59, $200,000 total compensation

President and CEO, David E. Rainbolt, age 59, $390,000 total compensation

Regional Executive BancFirst, E. Wayne Cardwell, age 74

EVP and CIO BancFirst, Scott Copeland, age 50

SEVP; President and CEO BancFirst, Dennis L. Brand, age 67, $490,000 total compensation

Vice Chairman BancFirst Corp. and BancFirst; CEO Council Oak Partners, William O. Johnstone, age 67, $200,000 total compensation

Regional Executive BancFirst, Karen James, age 59

Executive Vice President; Director - Community Banking, Darryl Schmidt, age 53, $315,000 total compensation

Regional Executive BancFirst, David M. Seat, age 64

Executive Vice President and Chief Technology Officer of BancFirst, David Westman, age 59

Regional Executive BancFirst, David R. Harlow, age 52

CFO, Kevin Lawrence

Executive Vice President, Jay Hannah

Senior Vice President, Gail Norman

Vice President, Steve Winkler

Senior Vice President, Patrick Lippmann

Senior Vice President General Manager, Michael (Mel) Kernan

Senior Vice President Business Development, Casey Bell

Senior Vice President, Dave Brubaker

Assistant Vice President, Neisha Kelley

Assistant Vice President, Shelley Beene

Senior Vice President, Stephanie Mercer

Senior Vice President Compliance, Kelly Foster

Senior Vice President, Blane Allen

Senior Vice President, John (Jack) Huff

Senior Vice President Stratford, Wes Westbrooks

Senior Vice President Controller, Jennifer Weast

Executive Vice President Prague, Dale Bugg

Vice President, Bill Sanford

Vice President Treasury Management Sales, Ashlea Briggs

Vice President Commercial Lending, Tanner Eckler

Vice President, Pat Hackler

Senior Vice President, Brian Renz

Senior Vice President, Betsy Blue

Vice President Chief Sales Officer, Steven Ackerman

Senior Vice President, Gerald (Jerry) Snyder

Vice President, James (Jamie) Dickson

Senior Vice President Of Marketing, Jay Hana

Vice President Project Manager, Jennifer (Jen) Seargent

Vice President Marketing Merchant Services, Debbie Barnhill

Vice President, Gina Lambillotte

Vice President Of Marketing, Ben Herrington

Senior Vice President, Jamie Stephenson

Senior Vice President, Charles K (Chas) Holland

Vice President, Paul D Fleming

Vice President, Linda Cumpton

Vice President Mortgage Lending, Shelly Matthews

Senior Vice President, Brian Davis

Vice President Of Treasury Management Sales, Leslie Wilkerson

Senior Vice President, Allen Scroggins

Vice President International Trade Services, Fran Straughn

Executive Vice President Bartlesville, Justin Krebbs

Vice President Corporate Finance Controller, Brian Morris

Executive Vice President, Ron Ludwick

Customer service Officer Senior Vice President, Alice Beine Alice Beine

Senior Vice President, Diane Sisemore

Assistant Vice President Network Services, Dian Joysizemore

Senior Vice President, Cheryl Borelli

Senior Vice President and General Counsel, Brian Pierson

Executive Vice President Chief Credit Officer, Darryl Scmidt

Senior Vice President The Student Lending Department At The Branch, Tina Seawright

Vice Chairman, James R. Daniel, age 75

Vice Chairman BancFirst Corp. and BancFirst, K. Gordon Greer, age 78

Chairman, H. E. (Gene) Rainbolt, age 86

Abm, Debbie White

Treasurer Executive Vice President Operations, Randy Forake

Auditors: BKD, LLP

LOCATIONS

HQ: BancFirst Corp. (Oklahoma City, Okla)
101 North Broadway, Oklahoma City, OK 73102-8405
Phone: 405 270-1086   **Fax:** 405 270-1089
Web: www.bancfirst.com

PRODUCTS/OPERATIONS

2013 Sales

	$ mil.	% of total
Interest		
Loans including fees	167	62
Securities	6	2
Other	4	2
Noninterest		
Service charges on deposits	52	21
Insurance commissions	14	5
Trust revenue	8	3
Cash management	6	2
Other	9	3
Total	**267**	**100**

Selected Subsidiaries

BancFirst
  BancFirst Agency Inc. (credit life insurance)
  BancFirst Community Development Corporation
  Council Oak Investment Corporation (small business investments)
  Council Oak Real Estate Inc. (real estate investments)
Council Oak Partners LLC
BancFirst Insurance Services Inc.

COMPETITORS

Arvest Bank	Midland Financial
BOK Financial	Southwest Bancorp
Bank of America	UMB Financial
International Bancshares	Wells Fargo

HISTORICAL FINANCIALS

Company Type: Public

Income Statement

FYE: December 31

	ASSETS ($ mil.)	NET INCOME ($ mil.)	INCOME AS % OF ASSETS	EMPLOYEES
12/14	6,574	63	1.0%	1,688
12/13	6,038	54	0.9%	1,653
12/12	6,022	51	0.9%	1,635
12/11	5,608	45	0.8%	1,641
12/10	5,060	42	0.8%	1,533
Annual Growth	**6.8%**	**10.9%**	**—**	**2.4%**

2014 Year-End Financials

Debt ratio: 0.41%
Return on equity: 10.96%
Cash ($ mil.): 1,913
Current ratio: —
Long-term debt ($ mil.): —
No. of shares (mil.): 15
Dividends
  Yield: 2.0%
  Payout: 33.0%
Market value ($ mil.): 983

	STOCK PRICE ($) FY Close	P/E High/Low	PER SHARE ($) Earnings	Dividends	Book Value
12/14	63.39	17 12	4.04	1.30	39.30
12/13	56.06	16 11	3.49	1.20	36.33
12/12	42.36	13 11	3.36	1.12	34.09
12/11	37.54	15 10	2.93	1.04	31.95
12/10	41.19	17 13	2.70	0.96	29.84
Annual Growth	**11.4%**	**— —**	**10.6%**	**7.9%**	**7.1%**

BancorpSouth Inc.

Like Elvis Presley BancorpSouth has grown beyond its Tupelo roots. It's the holding company for BancorpSouth Bank which operates some 290 branches in nine southern and midwestern states. Catering to consumers and small and midszed businesses the bank offers checking and savings accounts loans credit cards and commercial banking services. BancorpSouth also sells insurance and provides brokerage investment advisory and asset management services throughout most of its market area. Real estate loans including consumer and commercial mortgages and home equity construction and agricultural loans comprise approximately three-quarters of its loan portfolio. BancorpSouth has assets of $13 billion.

Geographic Reach

Mississippi-based BancorpSouth Bank operates in Alabama Arkansas Florida Illinois Louisiana Mississippi Missouri Tennessee and Texas. BancorpSouth's insurance and financial advisory businesses also operate in Illinois and Florida respectively.

Financial Performance

BancorpSouth reported net income of $94.1 million in 2013 an increase of 12% versus 2012. The decreased provision for credit losses was the primary factor contributing to the rise. Net interest revenue —the bank's primary source of revenue — fell 4% year over year to $$398.9 million the fourth consecutive year of decline. Net interest revenue declined because the decrease in interest expense was more than offset by the decrease in interest revenue as the yield on earning assets declined by a greater amount than that of interest-bearing liabilities. Noninterest income also declined on lower mortgage origination revenue in 2013 versus 2012.

Strategy

The regional bank has grown via the acquisition of other banks and insurance agencies and by opening new branches most recently in Texas and Louisiana. To reduce its reliance on interest-related revenue BancorpSouth hopes to diversify its revenue stream by increasing the amount it generates from mortgage lending insurance brokerage and securities activities. To this end subsidiary BancorpSouth Insurance Services has acquired small insurance agencies in Arkansas Missouri and Texas.

Mergers and Acquisitions

In 2014 BancorpSouth agreed to acquire Central Community Corp. the holding company for First State Bank Central Texas headquartered in Austin Texas. First State Bank operates 31 branches in Austin Round Rock Killeen and several other Central Texas communities. Bancorp-South has also agreed to purchase Ouachita Bancshares Corp. with a dozen branches in Louisiana. Both deals were announced in January 2014 and were expected to close promptly. However they've been delayed because BancorpSouth needs more time to get regulatory approvals and to meet "closing conditions necessary to complete" the mergers. The merger agreements valued at a combined $325 million in stock and cash have been extended to mid-2015.

EXECUTIVES

EVP BancorpSouth Inc. and Vice Chairman BancorpSouth Bank, Gordon R. Lewis, age 66, $386,238 total compensation

EVP BancorpSouth Inc. and Vice Chairman BancorpSouth Bank, William James Threadgill, age 61, $322,393 total compensation

EVP and Corporate Secretary BancorpSouth and BancorpSouth Bank, Cathy S. Freeman, age 50

Chairman and CEO BancorpSouth Inc. and BancorpSouth Bank, James D. (Dan) Rollins, age 56, $700,000 total compensation

CFO and Treasurer BancorpSouth Inc.; EVP CFO and Cashier BancorpSouth Bank, William L. (Bill) Prater, age 55, $360,000 total compensation

EVP BancorpSouth Inc. and Vice Chairman and Chief Lending Officer BancorpSouth Bank, James R. Hodges

President and COO, Chris A. Bagley

Executive Vice President, Ron Hodges

Executive Vice President Of Operations, Roy Snook

Senior Vice President Recovecy Administrations, Julie Clemmer

Vice President Retail Sales and Operations Coordinator, Angela (Angie) Lavalais

Senior Vice President, William (Bill) Sutton

Senior Vice President, Bob Aycock

Executive Vice President, Ron Hendrix

Vice President Finance, David Poole

First Vice President, Jason Walker

Executive Vice President, Cathy Robertson

Vice President Of Mortgage Finance, Roger Sanderson

Senior Vice President, David Ferrell

Senior Vice President Commercial Real Estate, David Williamson

Vice President, Brent Waldrop

Vice President Accounting, Patti Hammack

Vice President Management Information Systems Database Administrator, Audrey Thomas

First Vice President, Demario Hilliard

Vice President Marketing, Carla Flemon

Vice President Security, Cathy Talbot

Vice President Data Management, Jo Phillips

Executive Vice President, John Lotz

Vice President Of Loans, Gary Harder

Executive Vice President, Clyde Guyse

Vice President, Paula Bradford

Vice Chairman, James (Jamie) Threadgill

Auditors: KPMG LLP

LOCATIONS

HQ: BancorpSouth Inc.
One Mississippi Plaza, 201 South Spring Street,
Tupelo, MS 38804
Phone: 662 680-2000
Web: www.bancorpsouth.com

PRODUCTS/OPERATIONS

2013 Sales

	$ mil.	% of total
Interest		
Loans & leases	396	55
Securities	48	7
Other	4	
Noninterest		
Insurance commissions	97	13
Deposit service charges	52	7
Mortgage lending	45	6
Credit card debit card and merchant fees	33	5
Trust income	13	2
Other	33	5
Total	**724**	**100**

Selected Subsidiaries

BancorpSouth Bank
  BancorpSouth Insurance Services Inc.
  BancorpSouth Investment Services Inc.
  BancorpSouth Municipal Development Corporation
  Century Credit Life Insurance Company
  Personal Finance Corporation

COMPETITORS

BBVA Compass Bancshares	Hancock Holding
	Regions Financial
Capital One	Renasant
First Horizon	SunTrust
Great Southern Bancorp	Trustmark

HISTORICAL FINANCIALS

Company Type: Public

Income Statement

FYE: December 31

	ASSETS ($ mil.)	NET INCOME ($ mil.)	INCOME AS % OF ASSETS	EMPLOYEES
12/14	13,326	116	0.9%	3,820
12/13	13,029	94	0.7%	4,005
12/12	13,397	84	0.6%	4,231
12/11	12,995	37	0.3%	4,244
12/10	13,615	22	0.2%	4,311
Annual Growth	**(0.5%)**	**50.2%**	**—**	**(3.0%)**

2014 Year-End Financials

Debt ratio: 0.76%
Return on equity: 7.49%
Cash ($ mil.): 357
Current ratio: —
Long-term debt ($ mil.): —

No. of shares (mil.): 96
Dividends
  Yield: 1.1%
  Payout: 20.6%
Market value ($ mil.): 2,167

	STOCK PRICE ($) FY Close	P/E High/Low		PER SHARE ($) Earnings	Dividends	Book Value
12/14	22.51	21	16	1.21	0.25	16.69
12/13	25.42	26	14	0.99	0.12	15.89
12/12	14.54	17	12	0.90	0.04	15.34
12/11	11.02	37	19	0.45	0.14	15.13
12/10	15.95	87	45	0.27	0.88	14.64
Annual Growth	**9.0%**	**—**	**—**	**45.5%**	**(27.0%)**	**3.3%**

Bank of America Corp.

Among the nation's largest banks by assets (alongside JPMorgan Chase and Citigroup) ubiquitous Bank of America operates one of the country's most extensive branch networks with some 4800 locations and more than 15800 ATMs. The bank's core services include consumer and small business banking corporate banking credit cards mortgage lending and asset management. Its online banking operation counts 31 million active users and 17 million-plus mobile users. Thanks largely to its acquisition of Merrill Lynch known as "The Bull" Bank of America is also one of the world's leading wealth managers –with more than $2 trillion under management —and boasts a beefed up trading and international businesses.

HISTORY

Bank of America predecessor NationsBank was formed as the Commercial National Bank in 1874 by citizens of Charlotte North Carolina. In 1901 George Stephens and Word Wood formed what became American Trust Co. The banks merged in 1957 to become American Commercial Bank which in 1960 merged with Security National to form North Carolina National Bank.

In 1968 the bank formed holding company NCNB which by 1980 was the largest bank in North Carolina. Under the leadership of Hugh McColl who became chairman in 1983 NCNB became the first southern bank to span six states.

NCNB profited from the savings and loan crisis of the late 1980s by managing assets and buying defunct thrifts at fire-sale prices. The company nearly doubled its assets in 1988 when the FDIC chose it to manage the shuttered First Republicbank then Texas' largest bank. The company renamed itself NationsBank in 1991.

In 1993 the company bought Chicago Research & Trading a government securities dealer and provider of oil and gas financing. A 1993 joint venture with Dean Witter and Discover to open securities brokerages in banks led to complaints that customers were not fully informed of the risks of some investments and that brokers were paying rebates to banking personnel for customer referrals. Dean Witter withdrew from the arrangement in 1994 and SEC investigations and a class-action lawsuit ensued. NationsBank settled the lawsuit for about $30 million the next year. (The company agreed to pay nearly $7 million to settle similar charges in 1998.)

NationsBank scooped up St. Louis-based Boatmen's Bancshares and Montgomery Securities (now Banc of America Securities) in 1997. The next year it bought Barnett Banks Florida's #1 bank.

Enter BankAmerica. Founded in 1904 as Bank of Italy BankAmerica had once been the US's largest bank but had fallen behind as competitors consolidated. The company's board of directors was pondering ways to become more competitive and in 1998 decided a merger was the best way. With the ink barely dry on its Barnett Banks deal NationsBank obliged.

After the merger the combined firm announced it would write down a billion-dollar bad loan to D.E. Shaw & Co. which followed the same Russian-investment-paved path of descent as Long-Term Capital Management. David Coulter (head of the old BankAmerica which made the loan) took the fall for the loss resigning as president; the balance of power shifted to the NationsBank side in 1999 when Kenneth Lewis took the post.

The Russian debacle and merger hiccups led the firm in early 1999 to reorganize and reduce overseas operations; it sold its private banking operations in Europe and Asia to UBS. Also that year it bought the recreational-vehicle financing unit of Associates First Capital (now part of Citigroup) 50% of Denver-based mutual fund firm Marsico Capital Management (it bought the rest in 2001) and BA Merchant Services. The bank also changed its name to Bank of America and began offering online banking through America Online. To avoid a court battle the bank settled charges that it retained proceeds from unclaimed bonds in California.

In 1999 the company earned the ire of labor officials for a program in which employees were recruited to maintain ATMs without being paid or provided supplies. EVP Frank Gentry who crafted the NationsBank/BankAmerica deal retired in 2000 signaling an end to the company's buying spree. Its focus turned inward as it set about the difficult integration of the two firms.

McColl retired as chairman in 2001. Later that year the company announced it would cease its subprime lending and car leasing operations.

In 2003 Bank of America's mutual fund chief Robert Gordon was among several employees who left the firm amidst a New York attorney general's investigation into hedge fund client Canary Capital Partners which allegedly had access to Bank of America's trading platform to make illegal after-hours trades of the company's erstwhile Nations Funds. Bank of America also paid $10 million for failing to provide documents to the SEC during its investigation of the scandal the largest-ever fine levied by the regulatory body for such an infraction.

The company sold its securities clearing and broker/dealer services units to ADP in 2004. In early 2005 the company struck a deal with regulators to implement tighter controls cut fees charged to investors exit the mutual fund clearing business and pay more than $500 million in fines including $140 million to settle complaints against FleetBoston. Also that year Bank of America remitted about another $460 million to settle investor claims that it did not adequately conduct due diligence when underwriting bonds of doomed telecom firm WorldCom in 2001 and 2002. (The claim involved 17 other investment banks as well; Citigroup paid more than $2.2 billion to clear itself of similar charges in late 2004).

Bank of America previously fattened up by purchasing northeastern banking behemoth Fleet-Boston for some $50 billion in 2004 and credit card giant MBNA for approximately $35 billion in cash and stock in early 2006. The latter deal roughly doubled the bank's credit card customer base (as well as its income from credit card fees) and gave the bank access to some 5000 organizations and institutions with which MBNA had affinity marketing relationships.

In early 2007 the company shed its venture capital arm BA Venture Partners (now Scale Venture Partners) to focus on middle-market private equity investments carried out by its BA Capital Investors unit.

In 2007 Bank of America bought U.S. Trust from Charles Schwab for more than $3 billion and acquired Chicago-based LaSalle Bank from Netherlands-based ABN AMRO for some $21 billion. Following the acquisition of U.S. Trust Bank of America merged the asset manager with its private banking and wealth management business to form U.S. Trust Bank of America Private Wealth Management. Prior acquisitions include credit card giant MBNA in 2006 a deal that doubled the bank's credit card customer base and its income from credit card fees.

In an effort to boost the economy and stimulate lending the US government in 2008 bought some $250 billion worth of preferred shares in the country's top banks. Approximately $45 billion of that was slated for Bank of America ($20 billion more than the original investment total). As a result of the government intervention US Treasury official (and so-called "pay czar") ordered then-CEO Lewis to receive no salary in 2009 and slashed compensation for other highly paid employees. Bank of America finished paying back the debt in late 2009.

As the global economy reeled from a credit freeze and subsequent recession in 2008 Bank of America added to its coffers by buying up troubled mortgage lender Countrywide Financial and investment bank Merrill Lynch. Countrywide had fallen on hard times as one of the hardest-hit victims of the subprime mortgage crisis. The deal was initially for $4 billion in stock but was finalized at around $2.5 billion as the economic climate sunk.

The Countrywide purchase made Bank of America the largest residential mortgage lender and ser-

vicer in the US. The company also settled a lawsuit contending that Countrywide engaged in deceptive lending practices. Bank of America agreed to pay more than $8 billion toward reductions on interest rates and principals of some 400000 troubled mortgage accounts. To avoid the stigma of the subprime loan crisis Countrywide was renamed Bank of America Home Loans in 2009.

Bank of America paid some $50 billion in stock to buy Merrill Lynch which had been crippled by the global credit crisis. Hoping to increase its upfront account fee revenues Bank of America began making a concerted push to cross-promote Merrill Lynch's wealth management business to the bank's affluent clients.

However the Merrill Lynch deal also brought its fair share of headaches. With the approval of Bank of America leadership the failed investment bank gave early bonuses worth billions to its executives prompting angry Bank of America shareholders and lawmakers to cry foul. The Securities and Exchange Commission slapped Bank of America with a $33 million fine for misleading shareholders about the bonuses. That fine was rejected by a federal judge in 2009 and the matter was ordered to go to trial. Bank of America ultimately agreed to pay $150 million in a settlement. In another Merrill Lynch-related settlement Bank of America agreed to pay $315 million in 2011 for claims that Merrill Lynch made false and misleading statements about its mortgage-backed securities sold to investors.

Then-CEO Ken Lewis in particular came under fire for not disclosing how bleak Merrill Lynch's financial condition was prior to the purchase; Lewis in turn said he had been implicitly pressured by the government to keep the troubles under wraps to prevent the deal from collapsing. A push to oust Lewis at the company's annual meeting in 2009 didn't pass but shareholders split the chairman and CEO positions to provide more accountability to the public. Director Walter Massey was named chairman and Lewis stepped down at the end of the year. Brian Moynihan the head of consumer and small business banking succeeded Lewis as CEO. Longtime Dupont CEO Charles Holliday took over as chairman in 2010 replacing the retiring Massey.

EXECUTIVES

Executive Vice Chairman Global Investment Bank, Jeffrey M. (Jeff) Peek, age 68
Chairman and CEO, Brian T. Moynihan, age 56, $1,500,000 total compensation
Chief Operations and Technology Officer, Catherine P. (Cathy) Bessant
COO, Thomas K. (Tom) Montag, age 59, $1,000,000 total compensation
President Preferred and Small Business Banking, Dean Athanasia
Vice Chairman Global Energy Investment Banking, Scott Van Bergh
CEO Brazil, Rodrigo Xavier
Chairman Global Infrastructure and Vice Chairman Global Corporate and Investment Banking Europe, David Azema
President Retail Banking, Thong M. Nguyen
President Strategic Initiatives, Terry Laughlin
CEO Bank of America Merchant Services, Tim Tynan
President New Mexico, Michael Rodriguez
Chairman China Investment Banking, Alex To
Market President Central Florida, Steven Alch
Chief Risk Officer, Geoffrey S. Greener
CFO, Paul Donofrio
Vice Chairman Global Corporate and Investment Banking, John Utendahl
Market President Kansas City, Gary C. Jankowitz
Vice President Corporate Recruiter, Irma Ramirez

Senior Vice President Senior Technology Manager, Danny McCoy
Senior Vice President Data Access Management, Brian Metzner
Information Technology Team Manager Assistant Vice President, Leo Kaplin
Vice President Portfolio Manager, Bill Collins
Assistant Vice President Operations Analyst, Karen Dartt
Vice President Operations Project Consultant, Carol Rogers
Assistant Vice President Senior Finance Analyst, Reagan Newcomer
Vice President Human Resources Manager, Michelle (Mitch) John
Senior Vice President, Michael Crawford
Senior Vice President Leadership Development Executive, Stephanie Asbury
Senior Vice President Process Design, George Freebersyser
Senior Vice President Planning, Jessica Dunn
Vice President Operations Manager, Candice S Lee
Senior Vice President, Dianne Douglas
Senior Vice President Security, Phil Rogan
Senior Vice President Card Marketing Product Manager, Stephen (Steve) Powers
Vice President, Lynn Wallace
Senior Vice President, Marc Mathies
Vice President Small Business Banking, Marco Sarmiento
Senior Vice President Operations Risk, William Kelly
Senior Vice President, Robert (Bob) Maloney
Vice President, Kevin Kleinhomer
Senior Vice President, Darrell Minott
Senior Vice President Senior Credit Products Officer, Bill Franey
Vice President, Maria Morales
Senior Vice President Business Support, Steven Duis
Vice President Process Manager, Diana Johnston
Vice President, Adam Walsh
Senior Vice President RISK Home Equity Loss Forecasting, Steven (Steve) Lindsey
Senior Vice President Portfolio Manager, Craig Murlless
Vice President Environmental Services, John Schovanec
Senior Vice President Information Architecture, Michelle (Mitch) Boston
Vice President Senior Operations Project Manager, John Leber
Vice President, Sanjay Dhulia
Vice President Senior Operations Consultant, Sylvia Coats
Vice President, Jessica Sherbert
Vice President Application Development, Chris Schrader
Vice President, Michael Kamenca
Assistant Vice President BA, Rosemary Kluge
Assistant Vice President Process Design Consultant, Jennifer Montgomery
Senior Vice President Finance Manager, Caroline Green
Vice President Senior Financial Analyst, Noreen Brennan
Vice President, Prashant Bidkar
Senior Vice President Of Organizational Development, Cynthia Bowman
Vice President Senior Operations Project Consultant, Rochelle Herman
Vice President Of Operations, Sethu Iyer
Assistant Vice President, Paul Barzellato
Senior Vice President, Debbie Kirby
Senior Vice President, Todd Chitester
Vice President, Rajesh Narayanan
Senior Vice President Director Corporate Audit Global Risk Management, Daniel (Dan) Varghese
Senior Vice President Cdfi Lending And Investing, Susan (Sue) Harper

Vice President Senior CREDIT REVIEW Officer, Charles A Chuck (Chas) Windell
Vice President Cyber Forensics, Mark Brock
Vice President, Richard Weindel
Assistant Vice President Financial Analyst, Ryan McKay
Senior Vice President, Jennifer Ehresman
Senior Vice President Finance Manager, Paul Claiborne
Vice President, Aram Andonian
Assistant Vice President; Senior Auditor, David (Dave) Kamensky
Executive Vice President Mortgage Banking, Joe Loevner
Assistant Vice President Banking Center Manager Ii, Tasha Bondurant
Senior Vice President Of Project Management Office, Marjan Mohtashami
Senior Vice President Mortgage, Kevin Lopresto
First Vice President Portfolio, Cindy Denney
Assistant Vice President, Payal Shah
Assistant Vice President Branch Manager, David Cintron
Assistant Vice President Senior Business Control Specialist, Ellen Guevel
Vice President Technology Manager, Param Subramanian
Vice President Technology Manager, Prashanth Kolar
Associate Vice President, Junaid Dadabhoy
Assistant Vice President Senior Auditor, Anna Gudapati
Assistant Vice President Technology, Amy Bundgus
Vice President Risk Management, Sean Sides
Senior Vice President, Nevila Nace
Vice President Manager Business Support, Ajumon Zacharia
Vice President Market Risk Management, Vikramaditya Penna
Senior Vice President Fulfillment, Seetal Charotari
Assistant Vice President Operations, Danielle Ruffins
Assistant Vice President Consumer, Nick Trosper
Vice President Applications Programming Capital Markets, Suhail Naqvi
Assistant Vice President, Charles Everhart
Assistant Vice President Operations, Oriana Sulstarova
Vice President Global Banking, Murdock Buffkin
Assistant Vice President Quantitative, Kaloyan Todorov
Vice President Manager Finance Business Support, Marie Hakim
Assistant Vice President Senior Analyst, Silva Nasr
Vice President Team Manager, Yosvany Baez
Assistant Vice President Senior, Bhavna Battu
Senior Vice President Senior Credit, Don Bressoud
Senior Vice President, Colleen Beierwaltes
Vice President Service Delivery, Andrew Harman
Assistant Vice President Banking Center, David (Dave) Garfias
Assistant Vice President Quantitative Operations Associate, Smita Biswas
Vice President, George Harcar
Vice President Operational Risk, Kevin Stump
Assistant Vice President Business, Aaron Drayer
Assistant Vice President Human Resources Advisor, Suzanne Middleton
Senior Vice President Operations, Scott Thabet
Vice President Consultant, Robert Rexroat
Vice President Business Control Manager, Cameron Tennyson
Vice President Senior Business Control Specialist, Tracy Hawley
Vice President Market Information, Raymond Bem
Vice President Banking Center Manager, Roxana Kouchekali
Assistant Vice President Banking Center, Alina Diner

Banking Center Manager Assistant Vice President, Spencer Cron
Assistant Vice President Compliance, Kate Cibotti
Banking Center Manager Vice President, Sharon Surujballi
Assistant Vice President Service, Natalia Saba
Senior Vice President Operational Risk Manager, Stephen Corrado
Senior Vice President Business Support, Kimberly Kole
Assistant Vice President Personal, Seth Williams
Senior Vice President Consumer Market Manager, David Lang
Assistant Vice President Risk, Lulu Calbazana
Vice President Consumer Market Manager, Nila Yousufi
Vice President Predictive Analytics, Tom Braden
Vice President Senior Operations, Donna Dallago
Vice President Business Control Manager, Moses Sulukyan
Senior Vice President Risk Management, Garrett Walter
Vice President, Dakun Xu
Assistant Vice President Banking Center Manager, Chad Potts
Vice President Representative, Esther Carrier
Vice President Business Control Manager, Daniel Chamblee
Assistant Vice President Global, Kim Calicdan
Assistant Vice President Mortgage, Heather Pollock
Vice President Business Controls, Jayson Citron
Assistant Vice President Banking Center, Alma Prout
Assistant Vice President Senior Credit, Kim Weaver
Senior Vice President Risk Management, Kathleen Stiebris
Vice President Program Management, Carolyn Gambuti
Auditors: PricewaterhouseCoopers LLP

LOCATIONS

HQ: Bank of America Corp.
Bank of America Corporate Center, 100 N. Tryon Street, Charlotte, NC 28255
Phone: 704 386-5681
Web: www.bankofamerica.com

PRODUCTS/OPERATIONS

2014 Sales

	$ mil.	% of total
Interest income	50,886	53
Non-interest income	44,295	47
Total	95,181	100

2014 Net Revenue

	% of total
Consumer & Business Banking	35
Global Wealth & Investment Management	21
Global Banking	19
Global Markets	19
Consumer Real Estate Services	6
Other	-
Total	100

Selected Products & Services

Capital raising and advisory
Card solutions
Equipment finance/leasing
Fraud prevention
Interest rate currency and commodity risk management
Investment solutions and management
Lending and financing
Liquidity management
Merchant services
Mergers and acquisitions
Payments/receivables management
Philanthropic management
Retirement and benefit plan services
Trade services

COMPETITORS

BB&T	JPMorgan Chase
Bank of New York Mellon	KeyCorp
Capital One	MUFG Americas Holdings
Citigroup	Morgan Stanley
Citizens Financial Group	PNC Financial
Goldman Sachs	RBC Financial Group
HSBC	State Street
HSBC USA	SunTrust
	U.S. Bancorp
	Wells Fargo

HISTORICAL FINANCIALS

Company Type: Public

Income Statement

FYE: December 31

	ASSETS ($ mil.)	NET INCOME ($ mil.)	INCOME AS % OF ASSETS	EMPLOYEES
12/14	2,104,534	4,833	0.2%	224,000
12/13	2,102,273	11,431	0.5%	242,000
12/12	2,209,974	4,188	0.2%	267,000
12/11	2,129,046	1,446	0.1%	282,000
12/10	2,264,909	(2,238)	—	288,000
Annual Growth	(1.8%)	—	—	(6.1%)

2014 Year-End Financials

Debt ratio: 11.05%—
Return on equity: 2.03%
Cash ($ mil.): 138,589
Current ratio: —
Long-term debt ($ mil.): —
Dividends
Yield: 0.6%
Payout: 33.3%
Market value ($ mil.): —

	STOCK PRICE ($) FY Close	P/E High/Low		PER SHARE ($) Earnings	Dividends	Book Value
12/14	17.89	50	40	0.36	0.12	23.15
12/13	15.57	17	12	0.90	0.04	21.97
12/12	11.61	44	22	0.25	0.04	21.98
12/11	5.56	1525	499	0.01	0.04	21.84
12/10	13.34	—	—	(0.37)	0.04	22.63
Annual Growth	7.6%	—	—	—	31.6%	0.6%

Bank of Hawaii Corp

Bank of Hawaii knows there's no place like home. The firm is the holding company for Bank of Hawaii (familiarly known as Bankoh) which has about 75 branches and 460-plus ATMs in its home state plus an additional dozen in American Samoa Guam Palau and Saipan. Founded in 1897 the bank operates through four business segments: retail banking for consumers and small businesses in Hawaii; commercial banking including property/casualty insurance for middle-market and large corporations (this segment also includes the bank's activities beyond the state); investment services such as trust asset management and private banking; and treasury which performs corporate asset and liability management services.

Geographic Reach

Despite its name Bank of Hawaii provides a broad range of financial services and products to customers in not only Hawaii but in Guam and other Pacific islands.

Operations

Bank of Hawaii operates through several segments including retail banking commercial banking investment services and treasury. In fiscal 2013 consumer loans accounted for 59% of its total loan portfolio; commercial loans made up the rest.

Sales and Marketing

Bank of Hawaii spends about $5 million each year on advertising.

Financial Performance

The bank network in fiscal 2013 logged $584.7 million in revenue representing a $36 million drop from 2012's $620.7 million. Bank of Hawaii points to lower margins from reinvesting investment securities and the origination of new loans at lower yields for the declines. Additionally its mortgage banking income dropped by $16.5 million (or 46%) in 2013 vs. 2012 as rising interest rates slowed refinancing activity and its related loan sales margins. Net income dropped $15.6 million from 2012 to 2013's $150.5 million. Meanwhile cash flow from operations rose $241.9 million –by some $19.5 million –during the reporting period from $222.5 million.

Strategy

Banking in paradise isn't always easy: Hawaii is known for its high cost of living and its reliance on the tourism industry. As the second-largest bank on the archipelago Bank of Hawaii's performance often mirrors that of the state since loans secured by homes and new home construction represent the largest portion of the company's lending. Due to the recent economic environment in the state the bank has curtailed its lending activities which cut into its bottom line. Its 2011 results were also negatively impacted by a federal law that went into effect the previous year that puts caps on overdraft fees.

The company's growth –limited by geography –comes methodically. Bank of Hawaii continuously looks for ways to expand. It has installed some 60 ATMs inside McDonald's restaurants throughout Hawaii and it introduced ATMs inside McDonald's restaurants in Guam. In addition to growing its ATM network Bank of Hawaii has also introduced a special mobile banking fleet which includes shuttle-sized vehicles that offer ATMs and wireless technology inside.

HISTORY

Bank of Hawaii was chartered in 1897 and initially capitalized at $400000. The company opened its first branch in 1903 on neighboring island Kauai and over the next 20 years branches were added on the other islands. It had branches on every major island in the archipelago by 1930 the same year it bought Bank of Maui.

During WWII Bank of Hawaii provided banking services to soldiers and sailors on their way to the Pacific theater. In 1959 Hawaii became a state and Bank of Hawaii became a member of the FDIC. In its first forays out of state it opened branches on Midway Island and Kwajalein Atoll followed by branches in American Samoa Guam the Marshall Islands Ponape Saipan and Yap. The company also established alliances with Crédit Lyonnais and the Bank of New Zealand setting up outposts in New Caledonia Tahiti Tonga and Western Samoa (now simply Samoa). In 1968 the company formed its Bank of Hawaii International subsidiary to hold its foreign operations.

Bank of Hawaii reorganized as a bank holding company Hawaii Bancorporation in 1971. It continued its westward expansion acquiring substantial stakes in Banque de Nouvelle Calédonie and Bank of Tonga. The company moved into leasing operations in 1973 and changed its name to Bancorp Hawaii in 1979.

During the 1980s the company began to grow via acquisitions. It established a Tokyo branch in 1981 merged with the Hawaiian Trust Company (1985) and made its first appearance on the US mainland by buying First National Bank of Arizona (1989). In 1990 the company acquired FirstFed America a holding company for banks in Hawaii and Guam.

Coinciding with the state's economic slump Bancorp Hawaii began fiddling with its subsidiaries in a search for the right mix of businesses. It consolidated units (such as American Trust and Bishop Trust with Hawaiian Trust Company) and branches and dissolved certain operations (Pacific Century Asset Management; founded 1994 closed 1997). It also reactivated some other operations such as its Bankoh Corporation in 1994 dormant since 1984 when it was established as Hawaiian Hong Kong Holdings. The company entered insurance brokerage with Pacific Century Insurance Agency formerly Pan-Ocean Insurance in 1995.

In 1997 Bancorp Hawaii bought CU Bancorp holding company for California United Bank (renamed Pacific Century Bank) giving it access to the manic California banking market. That year the company also changed its name to Pacific Century Financial Corporation to better reflect its geographic diversity.

In 1998 Pacific Century in response to the Asian economic crisis announced that it was cutting jobs and writing off around $17 million in bad loans which resulted in slumping earnings that year. The company remained eager to grow however purchasing two South Seas banks from Paribas and expanding its insurance offerings through the purchase of broker Triad/AIG Insurance Agency. The bank also increased its stake in Australia's Bank of Queensland. But the next year the bank cut more than 1000 jobs.

In 2000 Bank of Hawaii unveiled televised tellers that allowed bank workers to serve two customers at once. In other cost-saving moves Pacific Century sold its credit card portfolio to American Express and sold its stakes in Bank of Tonga Samoa-based Pacific Commercial Bank Banque de Tahiti Bank of Hawaii-Nouvelle Calédonie (New Caledonia) and Australia's Bank of Queensland in 2001.

The company then unloaded its Pacific Century Bank franchise selling its Arizona branches to Zions Bancorporation and its Southern California offices to U.S. Bancorp. It also sold its branches in Fiji Papua New Guinea and Vanuatu to Australia and New Zealand Banking Group. France's La Caisse Nationale des Caisses d'Epargne et de Prévoyance (CNCE) bought Bank of Hawaii Corporation's operations in Tahiti and New Caledonia. The company closed offices in Hong Kong Seoul Singapore and Taipei as well.

After divesting most of its South Pacific business Pacific Century Financial reverted to the Bank of Hawaii moniker in 2002.

EXECUTIVES

Vice Chairman and CFO, Kent T. Lucien, age 61, $423,500 total compensation

SEVP Controller and Principal Accounting Officer, Dean Y. Shigemura

Chairman President and CEO, Peter S. Ho, age 51, $754,847 total compensation

Vice Chairman and Chief Risk Officer, Mary E. Sellers, age 59, $392,730 total compensation

Vice Chairman Operations and Technology, Sharon M. Crofts

Vice Chairman and Chief Administrative Officer, Mark A. Rossi, age 66, $423,769 total compensation

Vice Chairman; Chief Commercial Officer, Wayne Y. Hamano, $310,097 total compensation

Vice Chairman and Residential and Consumer Lending Group Manager, Derek J. Norris, age 65, $224,615 total compensation

SEVP and CIO, Sheh Bertram

Senior Vice President and Private Banking Manager, Todd Nohara

Executive Vice President, Galen Nakamura

Senior Vice President, Erlinda D Alegre

Assistant Vice President and Operations Manager, Chris Onzuka

Executive Vice President, James Polk

Senior Vice President, Kevin Baptist

Assistant Vice President, Gregory Biegen

Vice President International Banking Division, Chris Whang

Vice President and Senior Trust Officer, Kevin Malmud

Vice President Training and Support, Nancy Murayama

Vice President Information Management Systems Group, Scott Higashino

Assistant Vice President Dealer Marketing Relationship Officer, Craig Ito

Vice President, Maryellen Ing

Assistant Vice President, Sherie Char

Senior Vice President And Senior Audit Manager, James P (Jamie) Garcia

Assistant Vice President, Dora Rivera

Vice President Senior Credit Compliance Officer, Mary Cutler

Senior Vice President Private Client Services, Bonnie Fong

Vice President, Raylette Dacosin

Assistant Vice President, Gil Farias

Vice President, Toshiya Matsumoto

Vice President Community Engagement And Events Manager, Momi Akimseu

Vice President, Dean Uyeda

Vice President and West Oahu Isb Area Manager Of Bank Of Hawaii, Charleen Deuprey

Vice President Risk Manager, Marc Adelberger

Senior Vice President Corporate Banking, John (Jack) McKenna

Vice President Corporate Banking, Steven (Steve) Nakahara

Vice President SFL Estate Settlement And Relationship Manager, Okawa Iris

Assistant Vice President, Mark Martinez

Senior Vice President And Manager, Coleen Shoji

Vice President, Aiwah Ng

Executive Vice President, Edward (Ed) Kim

Vice President, Carolyn Yoshihara

Senior Vice President, Bo Wheeler

Vice President Senior Trust Officer, Wanda Ching

Vice President, George Sumner

Senior Vice President, Brent Flygar

Vice President, Glen Aoki

Vice President Consumer Recovery, Rose Grace

Vice President, Anthony Goo

Senior Vice President, Nick Ondrejka

Vice President Fiduciary Wealth Advisor, Clayton Kauhane

Executive Vice President, Cindy Wyrick

Vice President Distributed Systems Man, Vance Jones

Financial Consultant And Vice President, Christopher Otto

Vice President Mortgage, Shanae A Souza

Vice President, Gareth Kaneshiro

Treasury Department Vice President, Michael (Mel) Ching

Senior Vice President, Kevin Sakamoo

Assistant Vice President And Compliance Officer, Sheila Honzaki

Senior Vice President Director of Corporate Security, Brian Ishikawa

Senior Operations Coordinator and Assistant Vice President, Melissa (Mel) Poblete

Vice President Electronic Delivery Systems Man, Jordan Ige

Vice President Private Client Services, Annalena Zanolini

Senior Vice President, Stephen (Steve) Rodgers

Vice President, Helen Chang

Senior Executive Vice President, Tom Koide

Vice President, Helen Kim

Vice Chairman, Donna A. Tanoue, age 61

Vice Chairman and Chief Retail Officer, Peter M. Biggs

Secretary, Fran Sur

LOCATIONS

HQ: Bank of Hawaii Corp
130 Merchant Street, Honolulu, HI 96813
Phone: 888 643-3888
Web: www.boh.com

PRODUCTS/OPERATIONS

2013 Sales

	% of total
Interest	
Loans & leases including fees	43
Investment securities	25
Other	-
Non-interest	
Fees exchange & other service charges	9
Trust & asset management	8
Service charges on deposit accounts	6
Mortgage banking	3
Insurance	2
Bank-owned life insurance	1
Other	3
Total	**100**

Selected Subsidiaries

Bank of Hawaii
Bank of Hawaii Leasing Inc.
BNE Airfleets Corporation (Barbados)
Pacific Century Leasing International Inc.
Bank of Hawaii Insurance Services Inc.
Bank of Hawaii International Inc.
Bankoh Investment Partners LLC
Bankoh Investment Services Inc.
BOH Wholesale Insurance Agency Inc.
Pacific Century Advisory Services Inc.
Pacific Century Insurance Services Inc.
Pacific Century Life Insurance Corporation

COMPETITORS

American Savings Bank	First Hawaiian Bank
Australia and New Zealand Banking	HSBC
Bank of America	Territorial Bancorp
Central Pacific Financial	Westpac Banking

HISTORICAL FINANCIALS

Company Type: Public

Income Statement

FYE: December 31

	ASSETS ($ mil.)	NET INCOME ($ mil.)	INCOME AS % OF ASSETS	EMPLOYEES
12/14	14,787	163	1.1%	2,200
12/13	14,084	150	1.1%	2,200
12/12	13,728	166	1.2%	2,300
12/11	13,846	160	1.2%	2,400
12/10	13,126	183	1.4%	2,400
Annual Growth	3.0%	(3.0%)	—	(2.2%)

2014 Year-End Financials

Debt ratio: 0.16%
Return on equity: 15.78%
Cash ($ mil.): 175
Current ratio: —
Long-term debt ($ mil.): —

No. of shares (mil.): 43
Dividends
  Yield: 3.0%
  Payout: 49.4%
Market value ($ mil.): 2,593

	STOCK PRICE ($) FY Close	P/E High/Low	PER SHARE ($) Earnings	Dividends	Book Value
12/14	59.31	17 14	3.69	1.80	24.13
12/13	59.14	18 13	3.38	1.80	22.75
12/12	44.05	13 11	3.67	1.80	22.83
12/11	44.49	14 10	3.39	1.80	21.82
12/10	47.21	14 11	3.80	1.80	21.02
Annual Growth	5.9%	— —	(0.7%)	(0.0%)	3.5%

Bank of New York Mellon Corp

Big Apple meet Iron City. The Bank of New York Mellon (BNY Mellon) is the result of the marriage of Bank of New York and Pittsburgh's Mellon Financial. BNY Mellon is one of the largest securities servicing companies in the world and a leader in asset management and corporate trust and treasury services. The firm boasts more than $28.5 trillion in assets under custody and administration and some $1.7 trillion of assets under management. BNY Mellon's state-chartered bank subsidiary Bank of New York Mellon offers asset issuer treasury broker-dealer and asset management services while BNY Mellon N.A. offers wealth management services.

HISTORY

In 1784 Alexander Hamilton (at 27 already a Revolutionary War hero and economic theorist) and a group of New York merchants and lawyers founded New York City's first bank The Bank of New York (BNY). Hamilton saw a need for a credit system to finance the nation's growth and to establish credibility for the new nation's chaotic monetary system.

Hamilton became US secretary of the treasury in 1789 and soon negotiated the new US government's first loan —for $200000 —from BNY. The bank later helped finance the War of 1812 by raising $16 million and the Civil War by loaning the government $150 million. In 1878 BNY became a US Treasury depository for the sale of government bonds.

The bank's conservative fiscal policies and emphasis on commercial banking enabled it to weather economic turbulence in the 19th century. In 1922 it merged with New York Life Insurance and Trust (formed in 1830 by many of BNY's directors) to form Bank of New York and Trust. The bank survived the crash of 1929 and remained profitable paying dividends throughout the Depression. In 1938 it reclaimed its Bank of New York name.

During the mid-20th century BNY expanded its operations and its reach through acquisitions including Fifth Avenue Bank (trust services 1948) and Empire Trust (serving developing industries 1966). In 1968 the bank created holding company The Bank of New York Company to expand statewide through purchases such as Empire National Bank (1980).

BNY relaxed its lending policies in the 1980s and began to build its fee-for-service side boosting its American Depositary Receipts business by directly soliciting European companies and seeking government securities business. The bank bought New York rival Irving Trust in a 1989 hostile takeover and in 1990 began buying other banks' credit card portfolios.

As the economy cooled in the early 1990s BNY's book of highly leveraged transactions and nonperforming loans suffered so the company sold many of those loans.

In the mid-1990s BNY bought processing and trust businesses and continued to build its retail business in the suburbs. It pared noncore operations selling its mortgage banking unit (and in 1998 moved its remaining mortgage operations into a joint venture with Alliance Mortgage); credit card business (1998); and factoring and asset-based lending operations (1999). In late 1997 and again in 1998 the bank tried to woo Mellon Bank

(now Mellon Financial) into a merger but was rejected; it had better luck in 2006.

The growth of the firm's custody services accelerated in the late 1990s. In 1997 BNY bought operations from Wells Fargo Signet Bank (later part of First Union) and NationsBank (now Bank of America). By 1998 BNY had bought some two dozen corporate trust businesses. Two years later it acquired the trust operations of Royal Bank of Scotland and Barclays Bank.

During this period BNY also built its other operations largely through purchases. It bought the Bank of Montreal's UK-based fiscal agency business (1998) and Eastbrook Capital Management which manages assets for businesses and wealthy individuals (1999).

Scandal rocked the firm in 1999 when the US began investigating the possible flow of money related to Russian organized crime; the following year a former bank executive admitted to having laundered about $7 billion through BNY. The bank reached a non-prosecution agreement in the US in 2005 and four years later agreed to a $14 million settlement with Russia.

In 2000 BNY bought the corporate trust business of Dai-Ichi Kangyo Bank (now part of Mizuho Financial) and Harris Trust and Savings Bank. It also purchased a trio of securities clearing and processing firms in addition to hedge fund manager Ivy Asset Management. The next year BNY bought the corporate trust operations of U.S. Trust.

Purchases in 2002 included equity research firm Jaywalk institutional trader Francis P. Maglio & Co. and a pair of Boston-area asset managers for high-net-worth individuals Gannet Welsh & Kotler and Beacon Fiduciary Advisors. BNY bought Pershing from Credit Suisse First Boston in 2003.

Fallout from the money laundering scandal lingered. In 2006 the Federal Reserve accused the bank of not tightening its own controls to prevent a recurrence of illegal activity. But there were apparently no hard feelings between BNY and the federal government who tapped the company in 2008 to act as custodian for the US Treasury's $700 million Troubled Asset Relief Program (TARP) meant to provide liquidity to banks.

The Bank of New York jettisoned much of its traditional banking services for more lucrative fee-based securities and financial services swapping virtually all its retail branches in metropolitan New York for JPMorgan Chase's corporate trust business in 2006. Both units were valued at more than $2 billion each and JPMorgan Chase paid an additional $150 million in cash to make up the difference.

In 2007 Bank of New York merged with Mellon Financial to create BNY Mellon). It was the New York company's third attempt to acquire the Pittsburgh-based firm. The deal cemented the company's status as one of the largest securities servicing companies in the world and augmented its other other areas of focus including asset management and corporate trust and treasury services.

The company followed that transaction with the sale of Mellon 1st Business Bank to U.S. Bancorp in 2008.

In 2009 the company acquired Insight Investment Management which specializes in liability-driven investment services fixed income products and alternative investments from Lloyds Bank for some $387 million. Also that year BNY Mellon bought analytics firm Portsmouth Financial Systems. The acquisition offered customers more transparency in structured credit portfolios.

In 2010 BNY Mellon sold one of the last remnants of Mellon Financial's banking operations the Florida-based Mellon United National Bank to Banco de Sabadell. Mellon had previously sold most of its retail business to Royal Bank of Scotland's US banking arm Citizens Financial Group in 2001.

EXECUTIVES

Chairman and CEO, Gerald L. Hassell, age 63, $1,000,000 total compensation
Vice President Information Technology, Anna Reis
Vice Chairman and CFO, Thomas P. (Todd) Gibbons, age 58, $650,000 total compensation
Chief of Staff, Richard F. (Rich) Brueckner, age 65
President, Karen B. Peetz, age 59, $650,000 total compensation
Vice Chairman and CEO Investment Services, Brian T. Shea
President Investment Management, Mitchell E. Harris
Vice Chairman and CEO Investment Management and BNY Mellon Markets Group, Curtis Y. Arledge, age 50, $650,000 total compensation
Chairman Asia Pacific, Stephen D. (Steve) Lackey
EVP and Chairman EMEA, Michael Cole-Fontayn
SEVP and CIO, Suresh Kumar
SEVP and Chief Human Resources Officer, Monique R. Herena
SEVP and Head Client Service Delivery, Doug Shulman
SEVP and Chief Risk Officer, James S. (Jim) Wiener
CEO BNY Mellon Wealth Management, Larry Hughes
President BNY Mellon Markets Group, Michelle Neal, age 41
Vice President Information Technology, Joe Gerbino
Vice President, James (Jamie) Aibel
Vice President Business Development, Anthony Moro
Vice President Securities Reference Data Project Management, Edward (Ed) Perlmutter
Vice President Information Security Bank of New York Mellon, Michelle (Mitch) Wraight
Assistant Vice President Information S, Ray Dickenson
Senior Vice President, John Weisenhorn
Executive Vice President, R J Bryant
Vice President Of Sales and Marketing, Trent Witthoeft
Assistant Vice President Systems And Technology, Rebecca Stalker
Vice President Business Development Channels, Harry Jin
Vice President Structured Trade, Robert (Bob) Martin
Vice President Retirement and Subadvisory Sales Director at BNY Mellon, Will Blackall
Vice President Relationship Manager, Mary Snyder
Vice President, Richard (Dick) Miller
Vice President Program Management, Franklin Howard
Executive Vice President, James (Jamie) Vallone
Vice President Sales Director, Kevin Worsh
Assistant Vice President, Curtis Jeremiah
Vice President Information Technology Service Man, Steve Capilitan
Vice President Operations, John (Jack) Profeta
Assistant Vice President Corporate actions, Nadya Benjamin
Vice President, Frank Austin
Senior Relationship Manager And Vice President, Mahmoud Salem
Vice President, Charles (Chas) Austin
Vice President Of Quality Assurance For New Products, Patricia Murray
Vice President Mutual Fund Accounting, Rosemary Seppe
Vice President Sales and Marketing, Chris Evans
Vice President of Compliance, David (Dave) Cullmann
Vice President Data Architecture, Renjay Yin
Vice President, Patricia (Pat) Aquaro

Vice President Financial Markets And Treasury Services Division, Priya Nagrani
Vice President, Peter (Pete) Gesell
Vice President Investment Advisor, Grace Allen
Vice President and Portfolio Management Fixed Income, Jason Vaitukaitis
Vice President Operations, Lori Cimino
Assistant Vice President Systems, Kenneth Kenneth Newman (Ken) Newman
Vice President Information Technology, James (Jamie) Milella
Vice President and Senior Sales Director for A, Gary Rzucidlo
Senior Vice President, John (Jack) Cetorelli
Vice President, Samuel (Sam) Savitt
Vice President Information Technology, Joseph (Jo) Aboulafia
Vice President, Keith Koble
Vice President For Storage Infrastructure, Mohan Arumugam
Vice President, Jose Matamoros
Vice President Operations Management, Kim Macey
Vice President, Anthony Lalima
Senior Vice President and Director of, Robert (Bob) Perego
Vice President, Stephen (Steve) Donovan
Vice President, Patricia Gallagher
Vice President Community Development Group, Jon Gamby
Vice President, Mary George
Vice President, Louann Weidman
Ast. Vice President, Vijay Bhojwani
Assistant Vice President, Bryan Chan
Vice President, David (Dave) Friedman
Assistant Vice President, Tammy Dong
Assistant Vice President Global Securities Lending Systems, Chris Sieradzki
Vice President Client Management, Mark Wrigley
Vice President, Nancy Schulkind
Vice President;Project Manager, Rob Snyder
Vice President Wire Systems Department Manager, Lloyd Hart
Senior Vice President, Mario Molina
Vice President Technology, Niels Lauritzen
Vice President Securities Lending Department, Janice Colombo
Vice President Corporate Trust Administration, Stephen (Steve) Giurlando
Vice President Global Trade Finance Servs Div, Andrea Ratay
Vice President Data Security Administration, Monroe Davis
Senior Vice President Emerging Technology Bank Of New York Mellon, Susan Vismor
Vice President, Thomas (Thom) Powderly
Assistant Vice President Information Security Bank, Steve Dekay
Vice President, Randolph Medrano
Vice President, Cary Jones
Vice President Finance, Liya Wang
Vice President, Ellie Whalen
Vice President, Raymond Connery
Assistant Vice President Information Solutions Analyst, Brian Kitograd
Assistant Vice President, Matthew Brock
Vice President Infrastructure, Glenn Hett
Vice President And Regional Manager Latin America Division, Angelo Francica
Assistant Vice President, Jeffrey Roe
Vice President, Lynda Amari
Vice President, Richard (Dick) Fronapfel
Vice President, Joseph Schnorr
Assistant Vice President, Victor Francis
Senior Vice President Legal Affairs, Bill Robinson
Assistant Vice President Investments, Remy Quito
Vice President Finance, Daniel McCarron
Vice President Technology Risk Management, Steven Henne
Vice President Human Resource, Rose Bodnar

Assistant Vice President Of Enterprise Portal Architecture, Jerome Wong
Vice President, Edward Dougherty
Assistant Vice President, John Rushmore
Vice President, David Sunderwirth
Assistant Vice President, Ann Lynch
Vice President, Gordon Wong
Senior Vice President Chief Administrative Officer Asset Servicing, George Gilmer
Vice President, Mary Milner
Vice President Global Markets, Melanie Wong
Vice President Customer Technology Solutions Delivery, Carl Hagelin
Vice President, Charles Baker
Vice President Client Management, Gregg Scheuing
Executive Vice President And Chief Operating Officer Dual Officer, Linda Lillard
Vice President, Justin Verdesca
Vice President, Brian Stern
Assistant Vice President Information Security, Sam Dekay
Assistant Vice President, Panagiota Bouboulis
Vice President And Relationship Manager, Mark Hochgesang
Vice President Marketing Operation, Michelle Nulty
Vice President Global Trade Financial Services Division, Toula Tavlarides
Vice President And Client Executive, Maurice Campbell
Vice President, Brian Weddington
Vice President, Melinda Valentine
Vice President Information Technology, Joseph Hole
Vice President Foreign Exchange, John Bundy
Vice President Alternative Investments Accounting, Ronald Caskran
Assistant Vice President Business Services Group, Danny Wong
Vice President, Paul Angotta
Vice President, Elizabeth Wagner
Vice President, Claudia Leslie
Vice President, Brenda Stone
Vice President Investor Services, Paula Litrell
Vice President North American Banks Division, Joseph Barnes
Vice President Business Solutions Group, Bradley Jones
Vice President, Reyne Macadaeg
Vice President Application Development, Brian Burton
Assistant Vice President, Glenn Obando
Assistant Vice President Systems, Kenneth Newman
Vice President, Peter Helt
Vice President Mutual Funds Division, Linda Pizzuti
Assistant Vice President, Kerri Shenkin
Vice President Information Technology, Dmitriy Malamud
Vice President, Paul Meskiewicz
Vice President, Rebecca Newman
Vice President, Derrick Cornelious
Auditors: KPMG LLP

LOCATIONS

HQ: Bank of New York Mellon Corp
225 Liberty Street, New York, NY 10286
Phone: 212 495-1784
Web: www.bnymellon.com

PRODUCTS/OPERATIONS

2013 Revenue

	$ mil.	% of total
Investment servicing fees		
Asset servicing	3,905	26
Clearing services	1,264	8
Issuer services	1,090	7
Treasury services	554	4
Interest	3,352	22

Investment management & performance fees	3,395	22
Foreign exchange & other trading revenue	674	4
Investment & other income	416	3
Distribution & servicing	180	1
Income from consolidated investmentmanagement funds	183	1
Financing-related fees	172	1
Net securities gains	141	1
Total	**15,326**	**100**

Selected Subsidiaries and Business Lines

Alcentra Investments Limited (sub-investment-grade debt asset management Bermuda)
BNY Capital Markets Holdings Inc.
BNY Mellon Asset Management International Holdings Limited (institutional asset management UK)
The Dreyfus Corporation (mutual funds)
HedgeMark International LLC
Insight Investment Management (global) Limited (UK)
Mellon Capital Management Corporation
Newton Investment Management Limited (active investment management UK)
Pershing Group LLC (securities clearing)
Walter Scott & Partners Limited (global equity investment management Scotland)
WestLB Mellon Asset Management KAG (European and global fixed income UK 50%)

COMPETITORS

Bank of America	JPMorgan Chase
Barclays	Liquid Holdings
BlackRock	Northern Trust
Citigroup	PNC Financial
Credit Suisse (USA)	State Street
Deutsche Bank	TriState Capital
HSBC	UBS

HISTORICAL FINANCIALS

Company Type: Public

Income Statement

FYE: December 31

	ASSETS ($ mil.)	NET INCOME ($ mil.)	INCOME AS % OF ASSETS	EMPLOYEES
12/14	385,303	2,567	0.7%	50,300
12/13	374,310	2,111	0.6%	51,100
12/12	358,990	2,445	0.7%	49,500
12/11	325,266	2,569	0.8%	48,700
12/10	247,259	2,581	1.0%	48,000
Annual Growth	**11.7%**	**(0.1%)**	**—**	**1.2%**

2014 Year-End Financials

Debt ratio: 5.26%
Return on equity: 6.85%
Cash ($ mil.): 123,147
Current ratio: —
Long-term debt ($ mil.): —

No. of shares (mil.): 1,118
Dividends
  Yield: 1.6%
  Payout: 27.2%
Market value ($ mil.): 45,366

	STOCK PRICE ($) FY Close	P/E High/Low		PER SHARE ($) Earnings	Dividends	Book Value
12/14	40.57	19	14	2.15	0.66	33.48
12/13	34.94	20	15	1.74	0.58	32.85
12/12	25.70	13	10	2.03	0.52	31.31
12/11	19.91	16	9	2.03	0.48	27.62
12/10	30.20	16	12	2.05	0.36	26.06
Annual Growth	**7.7%**	**—**	**—**	**1.2%**	**16.4%**	**6.5%**

Bank of North Dakota (Bismarck, N.D.)

EXECUTIVES

Pres-ceo, Eric Hardmeyer
Auditors: Eide Bailly LLP

LOCATIONS

HQ: Bank of North Dakota (Bismarck, N.D.)
1200 Memorial Hwy, PO Box 5509, Bismarck, ND 58506-5509
Phone: 701 328-5600
Web: www.banknd.nd.gov

HISTORICAL FINANCIALS

Company Type: Public

Income Statement

FYE: December 31

	ASSETS ($ mil.)	NET INCOME ($ mil.)	INCOME AS % OF ASSETS	EMPLOYEES
12/14	7,215	110	1.5%	—
12/13	6,873	94	1.4%	—
12/12	6,155	81	1.3%	—
12/11	5,375	70	1.3%	—
12/10	4,029	61	1.5%	168
Annual Growth	**15.7%**	**15.7%**	**—**	**—**

2014 Year-End Financials

Debt ratio: 7.55%—
Return on equity: 18.43%
Cash ($ mil.): 362
Current ratio: —
Long-term debt ($ mil.): —

Dividends
  Yield: —
  Payout: —
Market value ($ mil.): —

Bank of the Ozarks, Inc.

Bank of the Ozarks is the holding company for the bank of the same name which has about 175 branches in Alabama Arkansas California the Carolinas Florida Georgia New York and Texas. Focusing on individuals and small to midsized businesses the $9-billion bank offers traditional deposit and loan services in addition to personal and commercial trust services retirement and financial planning and investment management. Commercial real estate and construction and land development loans make up the largest portion of Bank of the Ozarks' loan portfolio followed by residential mortgage business and agricultural loans. Bank of the Ozarks grows its loan and deposit business by acquiring smaller banks and opening branches across the US.

OperationsThe bank makes three-fourths of its total revenue from interest income while the rest comes from fee-based sources. About 43% of Bank of the Ozark's total revenue came from non-purchased loan interest in 2014 while another 26% came from interest on purchased loans and a further 8% came from interest on its investment securities. The rest of its revenue came from service charges on deposit accounts (8% of revenue) mortgage lending income (1%) trust income (1%) and other non-recurring sources.Geographic Reach

Bank of the Ozarks had 174 branches in eight states at the end of 2014 with 81 of them in Alabama and another 75 branches split among Georgia North Carolina and Texas. It has two loan offices in Houston and Manhattan that serve as an extension of the bank's Dallas-based Real Estate Specialties Group.Sales and MarketingThe bank spent $3.03 million on advertising and public relations expenses in 2014 compared to $2.2 million and $4.09 million in 2013 and 2012 respectively.

Financial Performance

Bank of the Ozarks' annual revenues and profits have doubled since 2010 mostly as its loan assets have doubled from recent bank acquisitions spawning higher interest income. The bank's revenue jumped 31% to $376 million during 2014

mostly thanks to strong purchased and non-purchased loan asset growth during the year from recent bank acquisitions. Its non-interest income grew 12% thanks to a 20% increase in deposit account service charges stemming from newly acquired deposit customers.Strong revenue growth in 2014 boosted Bank of the Ozarks' net income by 30% to $119 million for the year. Its operating cash levels jumped 22% to $61 million during the year mostly thanks to higher cash earnings.

Strategy

Bank of the Ozarks continues its strategy of loan and deposit volume growth by acquiring smaller banks in new and existing geographic markets. It has also opened new branches and loan offices sparingly. During 2014 for example the bank opened retail branches in Bradenton Florida; Cornelius North Carolina; and Hilton Head Island South Carolina along with a new loan production office in Asheville North Carolina.

Mergers and Acquisitions

In November 2015 the bank purchased C1 Financial along with its 32 CI Bank branches on the west coast of Florida and in Miami-Dade and Orange Counties. The deal added $1.7 billion in total assets $1.4 billion in loans and $1.3 billion in deposits.In August 2015 the bank purchased Bank of the Carolinas Corporation (BCAR) –and its eight Bank of the Carolinas branches in North Carolina $345 million in total assets $277 million in loans and $296 million in deposits –for a total price of $65.4 million.In February 2015 Bank of the Ozarks bought Intervest Bancshares Corporation and its seven Intervest National Bank branches in (five in Clearwater Florida and two more in New York City and Pasadena Florida) for $238.5 million. The deal added $1.5 billion in assets including $1.1 billion in loans and $1.2 billion in deposits.In May 2014 it bought Arkansas-based Summit Bancorp Inc. and its 23 Summit Bank branches across Arkansas for $42.5 million though it closed more than a handful of them later in the year.In March 2014 the company acquired Houston-based Bancshares Inc. and its subsidiary Omnibank N.A. for $21.5 million adding three branches in Houston Texas and a branch each in Austin Cedar Park Lockhart and San Antonio.

Company Background

The expansion strategy of Bank of the Ozarks - which had a mere five branches in Arkansas 20 years ago –centered on opening new locations in smaller communities in Arkansas. But with the financial crash the bank was able to expand to more states through a series of FDIC-assisted transactions to take over failed banks. It bought Chestatee State Bank First Choice Community Bank Horizon Bank Oglethorpe Bank Park Avenue Bank Unity National and Woodlands Bank.

Chairman and CEO George Gleason initially bought the bank more than three decades ago at age 25.

EXECUTIVES

Chief Credit Officer Bank of the Ozarks, Darrel Russell, age 61, $252,308 total compensation
Chairman; Chief Executive Officer of the Company and the Bank, George G. Gleason, age 61, $1,730,769 total compensation
President Leasing Division Bank of the Ozarks, Scott Hastings, age 57, $181,925 total compensation
President Mortgage Division Bank of the Ozarks, Gene Holman, age 67, $150,042 total compensation
President Trust and Wealth Management Division Bank of the Ozarks, Rex Kyle, age 58, $241,674 total compensation
President Real Estate Specialties Group Bank of the Ozarks, Dan Thomas, age 52, $1,242,308 total compensation

CFO and Chief Accounting Officer Bank of the Ozarks Inc. and Bank of the Ozarks, Greg McKinney, age 47, $368,077 total compensation
Chief Operating Officer and Chief Banking Officer of the Company and the Bank, Tyler Vance, age 40, $366,923 total compensation
President Western Division, Don Keesee
Vice President Leasing, Rick Robertson
Executive Vice President Real Estate Specialties Group, Jock Naponic
Senior Vice President, Patrick Brown
Vice President, Jeremy McAlister
Senior Vice President Training, Lorie Smith
Vice President Special Assets, Michelle Petersen
Vice President Relationship Manager, Ray Dunavant
Vice President, Jo Langston
Vice President Information Technology Webloyalty, Steve Due
Vice President, Ann Holder
Vice President Accounting, Tina Chandler
Vice President, Steve Poston
Vice President Leasing, Ronnie DeMarco
Vice President, Wes Anderson
Vice President, Barry Steele
Vice President, Jeffery Martin
Executive Vice President, Stewart Griggs
Senior Vice President And Regional Operations Manager, Janet Paulette
Assistant Vice President, Corum Webb
Vice President Branch Manager, Laura Wyne
Vice President, Kevin Gross
Vice President Of Leasing, Todd Parsley
Vice President Technology Services Manager, Jeff Starke
Vice President Commercial Lending, Jason Wallis
Assistant Vice President, Robbie Strange
Vice President Commercial Lender, Denise McKenzie
Vice President Commercial Lending, Adam Carter
Senior Vice President Market Leader, Russell Hewatt
Vice President and Branch Manager, Olivia Howard
Vice President Commercial Lending, Jeff Cooper
Vice President Deposit Operations, Libby Buck
Vice President Commercial Lender, Steven (Steve) Reynolds
Senior Vice President Market Leader, Torrie Sunstrom
Vice President, Brad Webb
Vice President, Kris Knowlton
Assistant Vice President Branch Manager Consumer Lending Business Lending, Joey Parker
Assistant Vice President Special Assets Division, Nikki Kundrat
Executive Vice President Market Leader, Kenny Maguire
Executive Vice President, Samuel McHard
Vice President Originations, Carrie Nichols
Vice President Real Estate Specialties Group, Beverly Houston
Vice President Mortgage Market Manager, Tammy Whitley
Vice President Commercial Banking, Rick Kollhoff
Vice President Marketing, Duane Bickings
Assistant Vice President Credit Analyst, Chris Henderson
Senior Vice President Real Estate Acquisitions And Development, Phil Byers
Assistant Vice President Branch Manager, Danielle Childers
Senior Vice President, Sheila Mayden
Auditors: Crowe Horwath LLP

LOCATIONS

HQ: Bank of the Ozarks, Inc.
17901 Chenal Parkway, Little Rock, AR 72223
Phone: 501 978-2265   **Fax:** 501 978-2224
Web: www.bankozarks.com

PRODUCTS/OPERATIONS

2014 Sales

	$ mil.	% of total
Interest income		
Non-purchased loans and leases	162	43
Purchased loans	98	26
Investment securities	30	8
Non-interest income		
Service charges on deposit accounts	26	8
Other income from purchased loans net	14	4
Others	43	11
Total	**376**	**100**

Selected Services

Personal Banking
Apple PayChecking AccountsCredit CardsFree Bill PayFREE Debit CardsCustom Debit CardsEMV Chip CardsMobile BankingMortgage LoansMy Change KeeperOnline BankingOverdraft ProtectionPersonal LoansReloadable Spending CardsRetirement PlanningReorder ChecksSafe
Business Banking
Business ProductsApple Pay for BusinessDebit CardEMV Chip CardsBusiness Credit CardsChecking & Money MarketCommercial LoansExpress DepositMerchant ProcessingOnline BankingOverdraft ProtectionReorder ChecksTreasury Management Services
Online & Mobile Banking
Online BankingMobile BankingMobile DepositOnline Bill Pay
Wealth Management Services
Investment ProgramsFinancial PlanningCustomer Service

COMPETITORS

Arvest Bank	IBERIABANK
BOK Financial	JPMorgan Chase
BancorpSouth	Regions Financial
Bank of America	Simmons First
Bear State Financial	SunTrust
Cullen/Frost Bankers	Wells Fargo
Home BancShares	

HISTORICAL FINANCIALS

Company Type: Public

Income Statement

FYE: December 31

	ASSETS ($ mil.)	NET INCOME ($ mil.)	INCOME AS % OF ASSETS	EMPLOYEES
12/14	6,766	118	1.8%	1,479
12/13	4,787	87	1.8%	1,223
12/12	4,040	77	1.9%	1,120
12/11	3,839	101	2.6%	1,084
12/10	3,273	63	2.0%	881
Annual Growth	19.9%	16.7%	—	13.8%

2014 Year-End Financials

Debt ratio: 3.78%
Return on equity: 15.47%
Cash ($ mil.): 150
Current ratio: —
Long-term debt ($ mil.): —
No. of shares (mil.): 79
Dividends
  Yield: 1.2%
  Payout: 30.9%
Market value ($ mil.): 3,031

	STOCK PRICE ($) FY Close	P/E High/Low	PER SHARE ($) Earnings	Dividends	Book Value
12/14	37.92	46 20	1.52	0.47	11.37
12/13	56.59	48 28	1.21	0.36	8.48
12/12	33.47	31 25	1.11	0.25	7.20
12/11	29.63	36 13	1.47	0.19	6.16
12/10	43.35	47 30	0.94	0.15	4.69
Annual Growth	(3.3%)	— —	12.8%	33.0%	24.7%

BankUnited Inc.

BankUnited is uniting the north and south again. It's the bank holding company for BankUnited N.A. which provides standard banking services to individuals and businesses through about 100 branches in 15 Florida counties and six banking centers in the New York metro area (following the purchase of the New York private bank Herald National). BankUnited was formed in 2009 following the demise of the former BankUnited FSB which collapsed under the weight of bad mortgages. A team of private investors bought BankUnited from the FDIC injected $900 million in fresh capital and in 2011 took the company public via an initial public offering (IPO); it was the first IPO of a rescued bank during the economic crisis.

Financial Performance
BankUnited reported net income of $208.9 million in 2013 a decline of 1% versus 2012. Net interest income increased by $48.6 million over the same period to $646.2 million. Total deposits grew by $2 billion to $10.5 billion while demand deposits increased to 27% of total deposits.

Strategy
BankUnited has placed its bets on two large and growing markets: the Miami metro area; and the Tri-State area where its has four branches in Manhattan one in Long Island and another in Brooklyn. With Florida showing signs of economic recovery and growth potential in New York the bank hopes to use its capital strength and expertise to grow its loan portfolio both through originations and acquisitions with a primary focus on commercial and commercial real estate lending. (It also invests in residential real estate but does not acquire or write subprime residential loans.)

The company offers national equipment financing services through United Capital Business Lending and municipal leasing via Pinnacle Public Finance. BankUnited also provides wealth management through insurance agency BankUnited Investment Services.

Mergers and Acquisitions
In February 2012 BankUnited acquired Herald National Bank for $65 million in cash and stock. At the time of the purchase BankUnited converted to a bank holding company. It also converted the charter of subsidiary BankUnited from a thrift to a national commercial bank. Herald National was merged into BankUnited in mid-2012.

In 2010 BankUnited expanded its offerings and diversified its loan portfolio when it acquired a small business lending platform from Butler Capital Corporation. It also bought a municipal leasing business from Koch Financial Corp.

IPO
BankUnited raised some $783 million in its IPO nearly 20% more than it sought in its pricing. The funds are helping the bank expand both in Florida (where it operates in about a dozen counties) and into select new markets (such as New York). CEO Kanasthe former head of North Fork Bank led a similar expansion for North Fork in the first half of the decade and will likely use his experience to repeat the strategy with BankUnited.

Financier Wilbur Ross who serves on BankUnited's board of directors owns 15% of the company through WL Ross & Co.

EXECUTIVES

Svp Real Estate Lending Dept, Scott Lublin
Vice President Hub Manager, Amy Ouellette
Vice President, Kenneth Lipke
Senior Vice President, Sandra Mayor

Vice President, Cynthia Lash
Vice President, Laura Lowy
Vice President Commercial Real Estate, Kitty Yen
Vice President, Bill Williams
Vice President, Peter Dumelle
Assistant Vice President Network Engineering, Pedro Garcia
Senior Vice President Associate General Counsel, Alina Pastiu
Vice President Of Benefits Compensation And Payroll, Candace Angulo
Senior Vice President, Arnold Altman
Vice President Credit Officer, Patrick Rigney
Vice President Branch Manager Iv, Carmen Garcia
Assistant Vice President Application System Support, Andrea Hamilton
Vice President Cash Management Officer, Christina M Siconolfi
Vice President Operations, Claire Angelozzi
Assistant Vice President Credit Analyst, Maria Caicedo
Senior Executive Vice President, Vincent Post
Vice President And Branch Manager, Alden Bing
Vice President, Lee Elmslie
Vice President Portfolio Manager For Commercial Real Estate, Sabine S%2E Bouchereau
Svp Corp Banking Exec, Roger Harbeson
Senior Vice President Retail Banking, Ken Delisle
Vice President Information Technology, Carl Wallace
Vice President, Dale Mather
Vice President, Frank Puccio
Assistant Vice President Commercial Real Estate, Andrew Bonomo
Vice President Community Development And Outreach, Katrina Wright
Vice President Banking Center Assistant Manager, Theresa Schuman
Vice President Private Banker, Rebecca Lozano
Vice President Electronic Banking, Juliana Tancrati
Vice President Commercial Banker, Jaime Fimiani
Vice President Accounting Department, Dorrett Boothe
Vice President Portfolio Analytics Manager, Matthew (Matt) Crawford
Vice President, Ellie Rodriguez
Executive Vice President Market President For The West Coast Of Florida, Debbie Layer
Senior Vice President Business Improvement And Loss Share, Doreen Pleffner
Senior Vice President Bsa Officer, Scott Nathan
Vice President Commercial Portfolio Mana, Anthony Martinez
Senior Vice President NYC Business Banking Team Leader, Gene Sullivan
Vice President Busines Banker, Nicholas Marrone
Assistant Vice President Default Call Ce, Thomas Rousseau
Senior Vice President Enterprise Stress Testing, Filippo Ghia
Senior Vice President Marketing And Public Relations, Mary Harris
Senior Vice President associate General Counsel, Anabel Nemrow
Senior Vice President Commercial Private, Kelly Sheehan
Auditors: KPMG LLP

LOCATIONS

HQ: BankUnited Inc.
14817 Oak Lane, Miami Lakes, FL 33016
Phone: 305 569-2000
Web: www.bankunited.com

PRODUCTS/OPERATIONS

2013 Sales

	$ mil.	% of total
Interest		
Loans including fees	618	71
Interest & dividends on investments available for sale	114	13
Other	5	1
Noninterest		
Income from resolution of covered assets	78	9
Service charges and fees	14	2
FDIC reimburesement of cost of resolution of covered assets	9	1
Gain on investment sercurities	8	1
Other income	23	2
Adjustment	(103.1)	-
Total	769	100

COMPETITORS

BB&T
BBX Capital
Bank of America
Capital One
Citibank
Great Florida Bank
Interamerican Bank
JPMorgan Chase
M&T Bank
New York Community Bancorp

Ocean Bankshares
Regions Financial
Seacoast Banking
Signature Bank
SunTrust
TD Bank USA
Valley National Bancorp
Wells Fargo

HISTORICAL FINANCIALS

Company Type: Public

Income Statement
FYE: December 31

	ASSETS ($ mil.)	NET INCOME ($ mil.)	INCOME AS % OF ASSETS	EMPLOYEES
12/14	19,210	204	1.1%	1,647
12/13	15,046	208	1.4%	1,623
12/12	12,375	211	1.7%	1,429
12/11	11,322	63	0.6%	1,365
12/10	10,869	184	1.7%	1,263
Annual Growth	15.3%	2.5%	—	6.9%

2014 Year-End Financials

Debt ratio: 0.06%
Return on equity: 10.26%
Cash ($ mil.): 180
Current ratio: —
Long-term debt ($ mil.): —

No. of shares (mil.): 101
Dividends
  Yield: 2.9%
  Payout: 41.7%
Market value ($ mil.): 2,945

	STOCK PRICE ($) FY Close	P/E High/Low	PER SHARE ($) Earnings	Dividends	Book Value
12/14	28.97	18 14	1.95	0.84	20.19
12/13	32.92	16 12	2.01	0.84	19.09
12/12	24.44	13 11	2.05	0.72	19.02
12/11	21.99	47 31	0.62	0.56	15.71
Annual Growth	7.1%	— —	33.2%	10.7%	6.5%

Banner Corp.

Flagging bank accounts? See Banner Corporation. Banner is the holding company for Banner Bank which serves the Pacific Northwest through about 100 branches and 10 loan production offices in Washington Oregon and Idaho. The company also owns Islanders Bank which operates three branches in Washington's San Juan Islands. The banks offer standard products such as deposit accounts credit cards and business and consumer loans. Commercial loans including business agriculture construction and multifamily mortgage loans account for about 90% of the company's portfolio. Bank subsidiary Community Financial writes residential mortgage and construction loans.

Geographic Reach

Washington-based Banner Bank is focused on five primary markets in the Northwest: the Puget Sound region of Washington; the greater Portland Oregon market; Boise Idaho; and Spokane Washington. The fifth is the bank's historical base in the agricultural communities in the Columbia Basin region of Washington and Oregon.

Sales and Marketing

Banner Corp. reported advertising and marketing expenses of $6.9 million in 2013 versus $7.2 million in 2012. Banner Bank launched a redesigned website and new ad campaign in Boise Seattle and Portland and on social media in fall 2014.

Financial Performance

The regional bank holding company reported revenue of $223 million in 2013 an increase of 4% versus 2012. The rise in revenue was due to increased operating income as a result of gains on the sale of securities and a fee received from the termination of the bank's proposed acquisition of Home Federal Bancorp. The bank's growing customer base led to increased income from deposit fees and other service charges of $1.3 billion (5%) in 2013 versus the prior year. Net income declined 28% in 2013 versus 2012 to $46.6 million primarily due to higher provision for income tax expenses. After three consecutive years of losses (2008 thru 2010) the bank returned to profitability in 2011 and has remained profitable.

Banner Corp. has total consolidated assets of about $4.5 billion.

Strategy

Historically Banner Corp. has grown by acquisition. Since going public (in 1995) Banner has acquired about 10 commercial banks. Islanders Bank was acquired in 2007 the same year Banner acquired F&M Bank and NCW Community Bank of Wenatchee both also based in Washington. After the spate of acquisitions the company focused on opening branches. The company continues to look for acquisition opportunities with an eye on banks shut down by regulators.

In 2013 however a plan to merge with Home Federal Bancorp was terminated when that bank received a better offer from Cascade Bancorp. Also the company abandoned plans to buy Idaho Banking Company out of bankruptcy after being outbid.

Mergers and Acquisitions

In August 2014 Banner Bank acquired Siuslaw Financial Group the holding company for Siuslaw Bank the operator of 10 branches along the coast of Oregon. In June 2014 Banner Bank purchased six branches in Oregon from Sterling Savings Bank.

EXECUTIVES

EVP and CFO, Lloyd W. Baker, age 66, $253,542 total compensation
EVP Retail Banking and Administration, Cynthia D. Purcell, age 57, $289,038 total compensation
EVP and Chief Lending Officer, Richard B. Barton, age 71, $257,598 total compensation
President and CEO, Mark J. Grescovich, age 50, $715,000 total compensation
EVP and Real Estate Lending Manager Banner Bank, Douglas M. Bennett, age 62, $236,174 total compensation
EVP Risk Management and Compliance Officer, Tyrone J. Bliss, age 57
EVP and CIO, Steven W. (Steve) Rust, age 67
EVP Retail Products and Services, Gary W. Wagers, age 54

Quillin SVP Commercial Executive East Region,
M. Kirk Quillin
SVP Commercial Executive West Region, James T.
(Jim) Reed
Senior Vice President SBA Manager, Walter
Mclaughlin
Assistant Vice President Training Specialist, Tris
Bendickson-kellogg
Vice President, Jamie Albertini
Assistant Vice President Customer Service
Manager, Nicki Buchanan
Vice Chairman Banner Corporation and Banner
Bank, Jesse G. Foster, age 77
Chairman Banner Corporation and Banner Bank,
Gary L. Sirmon, age 72
Auditors: Moss Adams LLP

LOCATIONS

HQ: Banner Corp.
10 South First Avenue, Walla Walla, WA 99362
Phone: 509 527-3636
Web: www.bannerbank.com

PRODUCTS/OPERATIONS

2013 Sales

	$ mil.	% of total
Interest		
Loans receivable	167	75
Securities & cash equivalents	7	3
Mortgage-backed securities	5	2
Noninterest		
Deposit fees & other service charges	26	12
Mortgage banking	11	5
Other	5	3
Total	**223**	**100**

Selected Subsidiaries

Banner Bank
Islanders Bank

COMPETITORS

BancWest	KeyCorp
Bank of America	Sound Financial
Cascade Bancorp	U.S. Bancorp
Columbia Banking	Umpqua Holdings
FCA	Washington Federal
Glacier Bancorp	Wells Fargo

HISTORICAL FINANCIALS

Company Type: Public

Income Statement

FYE: December 31

	ASSETS ($ mil.)	NET INCOME ($ mil.)	INCOME AS % OF ASSETS	EMPLOYEES
12/14	4,723	54	1.1%	1,193
12/13	4,388	46	1.1%	1,131
12/12	4,265	64	1.5%	1,173
12/11	4,257	5	0.1%	1,111
12/10	4,406	(61)	—	1,092
Annual Growth	1.8%	—	—	2.2%

2014 Year-End Financials

Debt ratio: 3.29%
Return on equity: 9.65%
Cash ($ mil.): 126
Current ratio: —
Long-term debt ($ mil.): —

No. of shares (mil.): 19
Dividends
  Yield: 1.6%
  Payout: 25.9%
Market value ($ mil.): 842

	STOCK PRICE ($) FY Close	P/E High/Low		PER SHARE ($) Earnings	Dividends	Book Value
12/14	43.02	16	13	2.79	0.72	29.82
12/13	44.82	19	12	2.40	0.54	27.63
12/12	30.73	10	6	3.16	0.04	26.10
12/11	17.15	—	—	(0.15)	0.02	30.39
12/10	2.32	—	—	(7.21)	0.28	31.71
Annual Growth	107.5%	—	—	—	26.6%	(1.5%)

BANNER HEALTH

Hoist this Banner high! Banner Health is one of the largest secular not-for-profit health systems in the US. The organization operates 28 acute-care hospitals (with roughly 4000 beds). It also operates clinics nursing homes clinical laboratories ambulatory surgery centers home health agencies and other healthcare-related organizations including physician practices and a captive insurance company. Banner Health participates in medical research in areas such as Alzheimer's disease and spinal cord injuries through its Banner Sun Health Research division. The company which has almost 300000 members provides services in seven states in the western US; its largest concentration of facilities is in Arizona.

Operations

Banner Health is one of the first not-for-profit hospital operators to reinsure its employees through its captive insurance company Samaritan Insurance Funding. By offering this service Banner Health is able to diversify its risk improve cash flow and lower life insurance costs by about half a million dollars a year.

The multi-specialty system also operates a health plan in Arizona for Medicare-eligible patients. Its MediSunONE plan includes Medicare and Medicare Part D. The company has joined forces with Aetna in what is called an accountable care collaboration (ACO). An ACO uses technology and a team-based approach to care for the hospital's patients. Doctors and hospitals assume accountability for patient outcomes and are rewarded financially for achieving higher quality greater efficiency and overall better patient outcomes. The partnership also includes a new product called Aetna Whole Health that allows Banner's patients access to a line of Aetna services including their own electronic patient record.

The system's specialty centers include Banner Alzheimer's Institute Banner Concussion Center Banner Heart Hospital and the Western States Burn Center. In addition Banner Health trains 270 doctors per year at Banner Good Samaritan and Northern Colorado Medical Center.

Banner Health also partners with M.D. Anderson Cancer Center to operate a comprehensive cancer center in Phoenix. Services include medical oncology radiation oncology surgical oncology pathology laboratory diagnostic imaging as well as other supportive clinical services. M.D. Anderson has clinical oversight for all aspects of care delivery.

Education looms large on Banner Health's list of priorities –the hospital operates one of the country's largest simulation education centers at its Banner Corporate Center-Mesa. Simulation education is an expanding field in which medical students use computerized mannequins to improve their surgical and medical skills. The school's research has paid off and with Scottsdale Healthcare Osborn Medical Center Banner Health invented the Sapien Transcatheter Heart Valve an artificial heart valve that can replace a diseased aortic heart valve without the open heart surgery that previously was required.In 2013 Banner Health provided $520 million for community benefit.

Geographic Reach

Banner Health operates in Alaska Arizona California Colorado Nebraska Nevada and Wyoming.

Financial Performance

Banner Health's income is generally derived through three channels: third-party payers such as commercial insurance managed care agreements Medicare and Medicaid and a small portion of self-pay patients as well as by borrowing funds and receiving philanthropic donations.

Its revenues grew by 5% in 2013 from $4.9 million to $5.1 million. Prudent investing boosted net income by 39% from $615 to $855.

Strategy

The health system has grown through construction. Banner Health is nearly always engaged in some sort of construction renovation or upgrade at its numerous facilities. The organization has more than $1 billion in construction projects in progress or completed in recent years. The system has expanded its facilities at Banner Baywood Medical Center Banner Del E. Webb Medical Center Banner Desert Medical Center Banner Thunderbird Medical Center Cardon Children's Medical Center and McKee Medical Center.

Banner Health is constructing a Fort Collins facility on a 28-acre campus which is scheduled to open in 2015 with a two-story hospital featuring an emergency department a 24-bed inpatient unit labor and delivery rooms medical imaging women's services surgical services and lab services.

In 2014 Arizona Banner Health completed a $62.6 million 111000-sq. ft. expansion project of the outpatient cancer facility adding three linear accelerators 30 clinic exam rooms and 13 infusion bays. It also allowed for the expansion of the Laboratory Intake Center and the Welcome Center and includes the Cox Center for Integrative Oncology and Cancer Prevention; and completed a $161 million expansion project which includes the addition of a new tower an expanded emergency department and expanded surgical obstetrical and medical imaging capabilities.

In 2014 Banner Network Colorado and Humana announced a new Accountable Care agreement covering individuals and families purchasing insurance in Weld and Larimer counties through Connect for Health Colorado and through Humana commercial health maintenance organization health plans for small employers.In 2013 Banner Health opened Banner Goldfield Medical Center to provide patient-centered care to the communities of Apache Junction and Gold Canyon.

Mergers and Acquisitions

Banner Health does occasionally pick up a new hospital through acquisition. For instance in 2015 the company acquired The University of Arizona Health Network (now Banner - University Medicine). As a result University Medicine is the new academic medicine division of Banner Health which includes three academic medical centers: Banner - University Medical Center Tucson Banner - University Medical Center Phoenix and Banner - University Medical Center South.

In 2014 Banner Health acquired Casa Grande Regional Medical Center and renamed it as the Banner Casa Grande Medical Center.

Company BackgroundBanner Good Samaritan Medical Center first opened its doors as a 20-bed hospital in 1911. The medical center which is four months older than the state of Arizona marked its 100th anniversary in October 2011.

EXECUTIVES

EVP and Chief Administrative Officer, Ronald R. (Ron) Bunnell
SVP and Chief Marketing Officer, Alexandra Morehouse-Reynolds
President CEO and Director, Peter S. Fine, age 63
EVP and Chief Medical Officer, John Hensing
EVP University Medicine, Kathy Bollinger
CEO Northern Colorado Service Area (Banner Fort Collins Medical Center McKee Medical Center North Colorado Medical Center), Richard O. (Rick) Sutton
EVP Community Delivery, Rebecca (Becky) Kuhn

Interim CEO Fairbanks Memorial Hospital/Denali Center, Sheldon G. Stadnyk
CEO Banner University Medical Center South and Banner University Medical Center Tucson, Tom Dickson
CEO Banner Baywood Medical Center; CEO Banner Heart Hospital, Julie Nunley
President Western Region, Jim Ferando
CEO East Morgan County Hospital, Linda Thorpe
President Arizona East Division, Todd S. Werner, age 47
SVP and CFO, Dennis Dahlen
CEO Banner Boswell Medical Center, Dave Cheney
President Arizona West Division, Rob Gould
CEO Pharmacy Services, Pam Nenaber
CEO Banner Baywood Medical Center and Banner Heart Hospital, Laura Robertson
CEO Banner Medical Group, Jim Brannon
CEO Platte County Memorial Hospital, Shelby Nelson
CEO Cardon Children's Medical Center, Rhonda Anderson
CEO Banner Thunderbird Medical Center, Deb Krmpotic
CEO Banner Research, Eric (Bill) Reiman
EVP Strategic Growth; CEO Banner Health Network, Chuck Lehn
CEO Banner Del E. Webb Medical Center, Debbie Flores
CEO University Medical Center Phoenix, Steve Narang
CEO Banner Ironwood Medical Center and Banner Goldfield Medical Center, Sharon Lind
President and CEO Banner Health Foundation; President and CEO Banner Alzheimer's Foundation, Andy Kramer Petersen
President and CEO University Medical Group, Jason Krupp
SVP Information Technology and CIO, Ryan Smith
CEO Banner Casa Grande Medical Center, Rona Curphy
CEO Banner Estrella Medical Center, Courtney Ophaug
CEO Banner Gateway Medical Center and Banner MD Anderson Cancer Center, Lamont Yoder
CEO Banner Home Care/Hospice, Lynn Rosenbach
CEO Banner Surgery Centers, Robert Thunberg
CEO Banner Lassen Medical Center, Catherine Harshbarger
CEO Banner Churchill Community Hospital, Hoyt Skabelund
CEO Washakie Medical Center, Jay Stallings
CEO Ogallala Community Hospital, Drew Dostal
CEO Banner Behavioral Health Hospital, Brian Beutin
VP and CEO Banner Health Network, Lisa Stevens Anderson
Chief Medical Officer Banner Health Network, Nishant (Shaun) Anand
CEO Page Hospital, Brian Kellar
CEO Sterling Regional MedCenter, Jeff Shelton
Vice President Human Resources Banner Me, Diane Ekstrand
Vice President Ethics and Compliance, David (Dave) Ledbetter
Vice President Of Materials Management, Doug Bowen
Director Of Infection Control, Marti Reich
Vice President Of Information Services, Steve Eiss
Director Of Nursing, Jennifer Kramer
Vice President Information Services, Frank Wallace
Vice President Brand Services, Julie Sherman
Assistant Vice President Information Technology, Michael Cherry
Vice President Of Marketing, Steven Kisiel
Vice President Of Clinical Operations, Maggie Row
Vice President, Therese Valadez
Vice President Management, Laura Brunner
Medical Director, Clinton Clarke

Vice President Of Information Technology, Mary Hubenthal
Vice President, Tricia Barger
Vice President, Samantha Endsley
Vice President, Diahann Groves
Medical Librarian, Bryan Nugent
Director Of Hospice Services, Amberly Molosky
Director Of Nursing, Angela Bonkowski
Vice President Organizational Performance, Twila Burdick
Vice President, Brian Smit
Medical Director Of Minimally Invasive Gynecology, Patrick (Paddy) Wilson
Director Of Clinical Services, Kristina Day
Director Of Nursing Medical Specialty Services, Susan Eubanks
Vice President Operations, Lillian Ruedrich
Vice President Business Health, Rebecca Havlisch
Medical Director, Carol Williams
Vice President Technology and Materials, Deb Dahl
Medical Records Director, Carol Robinson
Senior Vice President General Counsel, David (Dave) Bixby
Executive Vice President and Chief Administrative Officer, Ron Bunnell
Director, Christopher H. (Chris) Volk
Chairman, Larry S. Lazarus
Secretary, Krista Finlayson
Secretary, William (Bill) Shumway
Secretary, Laura Snow
Treasurer, Brenda Schaefer
Treasurer, Paul Nolde-morrissey
Auditors: ERNST & YOUNG LLP PHOENIX AZ

LOCATIONS

HQ: BANNER HEALTH
1441 N 12TH ST, PHOENIX, AZ 850062887
Phone: 6027474000
Web: WWW.BANNERHEALTH.COM

Selected Facilities
Alaska
 Fairbanks Memorial Hospital
 Tanana Valley Clinic
Arizona
 Banner Baywood
 Banner Boswell
 Banner Del E. Webb
 Banner Desert
 Banner Estrella
 Banner Gateway
 Banner Good
 Samaritan
 Banner Heart
 Banner Ironwood
 Banner MD Anderson Cancer Center
 Banner Thunderbird
 Banner University Medical Center
 Cardon Children's
 Page Hospital
California
 Banner Lassen Community Hospital
Colorado
 East Morgan County Hospital
 North Colorado Medical Center
 McKee Medical Center
 Sterling Regional MedCenter
Nebraska
 Ogallala Community Hospital
Nevada
 Banner Churchill Community Hospital
Wyoming
 Community Hospital
 Platte County Memorial Hospital
 Washakie Medical Center

PRODUCTS/OPERATIONS

2013 Sales

	$ mil.	% of total
Patient service revenues	4,412	87
Medical insurance premiums	439	8
Other	233	5
Total	**5,085**	**100**

COMPETITORS

Community Health Systems
Dignity Health
HCA
Iasis Healthcare
Inova
John C. Lincoln Health Network
Memorial Health System of East Texas
Northern Arizona Healthcare
Phoenix Children's Hospital
Poudre Valley Health System
Providence Health & Services
Scottsdale Healthcare
St. Joseph Health System
Tenet Healthcare
Texas Health Resources
Wyoming Medical Center
Yuma Regional Medical Center

HISTORICAL FINANCIALS
Company Type: Private

Income Statement
FYE: December 31

	REVENUE ($ mil.)	NET INCOME ($ mil.)	NET PROFIT MARGIN	EMPLOYEES
12/13	5,085	854	16.8%	35,000
12/12	4,878	614	12.6%	—
12/11	4,741	0	0.0%	—
12/10	4,863	0	—	—
Annual Growth	**1.5%**	—	—	—

2013 Year-End Financials

Debt ratio: ——
Return on equity: 16.80%
Cash ($ mil.): 133
Current ratio: 0.70
Long-term debt ($ mil.): —
Dividends
 Yield: —
 Payout: —
Market value ($ mil.): —

Barnes & Noble Inc

Barnes & Noble does business by the book and the NOOK. As the #1 bookstore chain in the US it operates 650 Barnes & Noble superstores in all 50 states and Washington DC. Stores range in size from 3000 sq. ft. to 60000 sq. ft. and stock between 22000 and 163000 book titles. It also sells books and other media online. The company's digital subsidiary NOOK Media develops supports and creates digital content and products for the digital reading and digital education markets. Heavy losses have led the company to restructure its operations. In 2015 it spun off its education division (which oversees the college bookstores unit Barnes & Noble College Booksellers) as Barnes & Noble Education.

HISTORY

Barnes & Noble dates back to 1873 when Charles Barnes went into the used-book business in Wheaton Illinois. By the turn of the century he was operating a thriving bookselling operation in Chicago. His son William took over as president in 1902. William sold his share in the firm in 1917 (to C. W. Follett who built Follett Corp.) and moved to New York City where he bought an interest in established textbook wholesalers Noble & Noble. The company was soon renamed Barnes & Noble. It first sold mainly to colleges and libraries providing textbooks and opening a large Fifth Avenue shop. Over the next three decades Barnes & Noble became one of the leading booksellers in the New York region.

Enter Leonard Riggio who worked at a New York University bookstore to help pay for night school. He studied engineering but got the itch for bookselling. In 1965 at age 24 he borrowed $5000 and opened Student Book Exchange NYC a college bookstore. Beginning in the late 1960s he expanded by buying other college bookstores.

In 1971 Riggio paid $1.2 million for the Barnes & Noble store on Fifth Avenue. He soon expanded the store and in 1974 he began offering jaw-dropping competitor-maddening discounts of up to 40% for best-sellers. Acquiring Marlboro Books five years later the company entered the mail-order and publishing business.

By 1986 Barnes & Noble had grown to about 180 outlets (including 142 college bookstores). Along with Dutch retailer Vendex that year it bought Dayton Hudson's B. Dalton mall bookstore chain (about 800 stores) forming BDB Holding Corp. (Vendex had sold its shares by 1997.) In 1989 the company acquired the Scribner's Bookstores trade name and the Bookstop/Bookstar superstore chain. BDB began its shift to superstore format and streamlined its operations to integrate Bookstop and Doubleday (acquired in 1990) into its business.

BDB changed its name to Barnes & Noble in 1991. With superstore sales booming the retailer went public in 1993 (the college stores remained private). It bought 20% of Canadian bookseller Chapters (now Indigo Books) in 1996 (sold in 1999).

The bookseller went online in 1997 and in 1998 sold a 50% stake in its Web operation subsidiary to Bertelsmann (which it re-purchased in 2003) in an attempt to strengthen both companies in the battle against online rival Amazon.com.

Also in 1998 Barnes & Noble agreed to buy #1 US book distributor Ingram Book Group but the deal was called off in 1999 because of antitrust concerns. Also in 1999 barnesandnoble.com went public and Barnes & Noble bought small book publisher J.B. Fairfax International USA which included coffee-table book publisher Michael Friedman Publishing Group. Later that year the company bought a 49% stake in book publishing portal iUniverse.com (later reduced to 22%). It also bought Riggio's financially struggling Babbage's Etc. a chain of about 500 Babbage's Software Etc. and GameStop stores for $215 million.

Subsidiary Babbage's Etc. (renamed GameStop Inc.) acquired video game retailer Funco for $161.5 million in 2000. In 2001 Barnes & Noble joined barnesandnoble.com in acquiring a majority stake in magazine subscription seller enews.com.

The company completed an IPO of its GameStop unit in 2003 reducing its ownership interest to about 63%. Leonard also handed over the CEO title to his brother Steve Riggio. Another development during that busy year included shutting down enews.com due to repeated quarterly losses.

In 2003 the company beefed up its self-publishing efforts with the purchase of Sterling Publishing a specialist in how-to and craft books. In addition Barnes & Noble's half-owned BOOK magazine shut down. The next year saw Barnes & Noble exit the video game retailing business when it spun off its remaining shares in GameStop.

In 2009 the firm sold its majority interest in Calendar Club for $7 million.

CEO Steve Riggio was replaced by William Lynch president of Barnes&Noble.com in 2010. Riggio remained chairman of the company. Barnes & Noble closed the last of its small-format B. Dalton bookstores in early 2010. (B. Dalton which once numbered more than 900 stores had been closing stores since 1989.) Later in the year hedge fund manager William Ackman offered to finance a $960 million merger of Barnes & Noble and its smaller rival Borders but nothing came of it.

CEO Lynch resigned in mid-2013 following an earnings report that underscored Barnes & Noble's failed attempt at building up its Nook division. CFO Michael Huseby was appointed chief executive of the Nook division and president of Barnes & Noble.

EXECUTIVES

President NOOK Consumer Business, Mahesh Veerina, age 51
CFO, Allen W. Lindstrom, age 48, $489,615 total compensation
CEO, Ronald D. (Ron) Boire, age 54
EVP Digital Content NOOK Media and Chief Marketing Officer, Doug Carlson
COO, Jaime Carey, age 54, $493,846 total compensation
EVP Sterling Publishing, Theresa Thompson
CIO, William E. (Bill) Wood, age 44
VP and Chief Digital Officer, Frederic D. (Fred) Argir
Regional Vice President East Coast, Daniel (Dan) Gerber
Executive Vice President Distribution And Logistics, William F Duffy
Executive Vice President, William (Bill) Maloney
Vice President Internet Marketing, Mark Vottini
Vice President Of Marketing, Janine Juergensonn
Vice President Ecommerce Search, Yufan Hu
Vice President Controller Int Chief Financial Officer, Allen (Al) Lindstorm
Vice President Tax, Philip O'Reilly
Executive Chairman, Leonard S. (Len) Riggio, age 74
Auditors: Ernst & Young LLP

LOCATIONS

HQ: Barnes & Noble Inc
    122 Fifth Avenue, New York, NY 10011
Phone: 212 633-3300
Web: www.barnesandnoble.com

2015 US Retail Stores

	No.
Alabama	7
Alaska	2
Arizona	15
Arkansas	5
California	72
Colorado	16
Connecticut	12
Delaware	2
District of Columbia	1
Florida	41
Georgia	19
Hawaii	2
Idaho	3
Illinois	28
Indiana	12
Iowa	7
Kansas	4
Kentucky	7
Louisiana	7
Maine	1
Maryland	13
Massachusetts	17
Michigan	20
Minnesota	17
Mississippi	3
Missouri	12
Montana	4
Nebraska	4
Nevada	4
New Hampshire	4
New Jersey	24
New Mexico	3
New York	41
North Carolina	21
North Dakota	3
Ohio	18
Oklahoma	5
Oregon	7
Pennsylvania	26
Rhode Island	3
South Carolina	10
South Dakota	1
Tennessee	8
Texas	51
Utah	10
Vermont	1
Virginia	24
Washington	18
West Virginia	1
Wisconsin	11
Wyoming	1
Total	**648**

PRODUCTS/OPERATIONS

2015 Stores

	No.
B&N Retail	648
B&N College	688
Total	**1,336**

2015 Sales

	$ mil.	% of total
B&N Retail	4,108	67
B&N College	1,772	29
NOOK	263	4
Adjustment	(75.0)	-
Total	**6,069**	**100**

COMPETITORS

Amazon.com	Half Price Books
Apple Inc.	Hastings Entertainment
Best Buy	Sony
Books-A-Million	Target Corporation
Buy.com	Wal-Mart
Costco Wholesale	

HISTORICAL FINANCIALS

Company Type: Public

Income Statement

FYE: May 2

	REVENUE ($ mil.)	NET INCOME ($ mil.)	NET PROFIT MARGIN	EMPLOYEES
05/15	6,069	36	0.6%	41,000
05/14*	6,381	(47)	—	41,000
04/13	6,839	(157)	—	33,850
04/12	7,129	(68)	—	30,000
04/11	6,998	(73)	—	35,000
Annual Growth	**(3.5%)**	**—**	**—**	**4.0%**

*Fiscal year change

2015 Year-End Financials

Debt ratio: —	No. of shares (mil.): 63
Return on equity: 3.97%	Dividends
Cash ($ mil.): 74	Yield: —
Current ratio: 1.19	Payout: —
Long-term debt ($ mil.): —	Market value ($ mil.): 1,436

	STOCK PRICE ($) FY Close	P/E High/Low		PER SHARE ($) Earnings	Dividends	Book Value
05/15	22.70	123	75	0.21	0.00	18.80
05/14*	16.68	—	—	(1.12)	0.00	11.13
04/13	18.15	—	—	(3.02)	0.00	12.16
04/12	13.68	—	—	(1.41)	0.00	12.97
04/11	10.99	—	—	(1.31)	0.75	14.37
Annual Growth	**19.9%**	—	—	—	—	**6.9%**

*Fiscal year change

Baxalta Inc

LOCATIONS

HQ: Baxalta Inc
1200 Lakeside Drive, Bannockburn, IL 60015
Phone: 224 940-2000
Web: www.baxalta.com

HISTORICAL FINANCIALS

Company Type: Public

Income Statement

FYE: December 31

	REVENUE ($ mil.)	NET INCOME ($ mil.)	NET PROFIT MARGIN	EMPLOYEES
12/14	5,952	1,737	29.2%	16,000
12/13	5,555	1,288	23.2%	—
12/12	5,310	1,248	23.5%	—
Annual Growth	5.9%	18.0%	—	—

Baxter International Inc.

Baxter International makes a wide variety of medical products. The company is a leading manufacturer of intravenous (IV) fluids and systems; it also makes infusion pumps pre-filled syringes biological sealants and inhaled anesthetics as well as dialyzers and other products for the treatment of end-stage renal disease (ESRD). Baxter's former BioScience division makes protein and plasma therapies to treat hemophilia and immune disorders. In 2015 Baxter split its operations into two companies —one focused on biopharmaceuticals (Baxalta) and the other on medical products (Baxter).

HISTORY

Idaho surgeon Ralph Falk his brother Harry and California physician Donald Baxter formed Don Baxter Intravenous Products in 1931 to distribute the IV solutions Baxter made in Los Angeles. Two years later the company opened its first plant located outside Chicago. Ralph Falk bought Baxter's interest in 1935 and began R&D efforts leading to the first sterilized vacuum-type blood collection device (1939) which could store blood for weeks instead of hours. Product demand during WWII spurred sales above $1.5 million by 1945.

In 1949 the company created Travenol Laboratories to make and sell drugs. Baxter went public in 1951 and began an acquisition program the next year. In 1953 failing health caused both Falks to give control to William Graham a manager since 1945. Under Graham's leadership Baxter absorbed Wallerstein (1957); Fenwal Labs (1959); Flint Eaton (1959); and Dayton Flexible Products (1967).

In 1975 Baxter's headquarters moved to Deerfield Illinois. In 1978 the company debuted the first portable dialysis machine and had $1 billion in sales. Vernon Loucks Jr. became CEO two years later. Baxter claimed the title of the world's leading hospital supplier in 1985 when it bought American Hospital Supply (a Baxter distributor from 1932 to 1962). Offering more than 120000 products and an electronic system that connected customers with some 1500 vendors Baxter captured nearly 25% of the US hospital supply market in 1988. That year it became Baxter International.

In 1992 Baxter spun off Caremark (home infusion therapy and mail-order drugs) but kept a division that controlled 75% of the world's dialysis machine market.

In 1993 Baxter pleaded guilty (and was temporarily suspended from selling to the Veterans Administration) to bribing Syria to remove Baxter from a blacklist for trading in Israel.

The company entered the US cardiovascular perfusion services market in 1995 with the purchases of PSICOR and SETA. Baxter along with two other silicone breast-implant makers agreed to settle thousands of claims (at an average of $26000 each) from women suffering side-effects from the implants. The next year Baxter spun off its cost management and hospital supply business as Allegiance (sold to Cardinal Health in 1999).

Buys in 1997 boosted Baxter's presence in Europe and its share of the open-heart-surgery devices market. That year it agreed to pay about 20% of a $670 million legal settlement in a suit relating to hemophiliacs infected with HIV from blood products.

In response to concerns posed by shareholders Baxter in 1999 said it would phase out the use of PVC (polyvinyl chloride) in some products by 2010. In 2000 the firm spun off its underperforming cardiovascular unit as Edwards Lifesciences. To strengthen core operations it lined up a number of purchases including North American Vaccine.

Purchases in 2001 included the cancer treatment unit of chemicals firm Degussa. Also that year Baxter withdrew dialysis equipment from Spain and Croatia after patients who used its products died. It also ended production of two types of dialyzers that were sold there. As the number of deaths mounted to more than 50 in seven countries Baxter began facing lawsuits; it later settled with the families of many of the patients. In September 2002 the FDA issued a warning when several patients died after using Baxter's Meridian dialysis machines. The same year Baxter bought Fusion Medical to expand its BioScience unit.

Robert L. Parkinson Jr. took over as chairman and CEO in April 2004. Parkinson succeeded Harry M. Jansen Kraemer Jr. William Graham who remained on the Baxter board of directors as honorary chairman emeritus after his official retirement in 1996 died in 2006.

In 2005 the FDA seized Baxter's existing inventories of previously recalled 6000 Colleague Volumetric Infusion Pumps and nearly 1000 Syndeo PCA Syringe Pumps; the federal agency resorted to these measures after the company did not fix production and design problems with the pumps in a suitable amount of time after batches of the product had been recalled earlier that year.

Baxter's product troubles didn't end there. In 2008 Baxter halted production of heparin after hundreds of bad reactions (including several deaths) occurred in patients using the drug. Subsequent investigations focused on raw heparin supplied to Baxter by a Chinese factory which apparently added a cheaper ingredient into the drug which contaminated it. Heparin-related litigation continued for Baxter in following years.

In 2009 the company acquired the hemofiltration (renal replacement therapy) product line of Edwards Lifesciences in a $65 million deal.

To meet increasing demand Baxter also expanded its infusion systems portfolio that year by entering an agreement to distribute medical device maker SIGMA's Spectrum large volume infusion pumps domestically and internationally. The deal also gave Baxter a 40% stake in the company (with the option to buy the rest) as well as access to future products under development. In 2012 Baxter exercised its right to buy and paid $90 million in cash for the remaining 60% of the company.

The addition of the Spectrum system was especially helpful when the FDA ordered the company to recall all of its Colleague infusion pumps in the US market in 2010. Patients were given the option of receiving Spectrum pumps to replace the Colleague systems.

As part of restructuring efforts in 2010 the company sold its noncore US generic injectables business to Hikma Pharmaceuticals for about $112 million. Baxter divested the business to focus on its proprietary injectable formulation and packaging operations. The sale also included Baxter's manufacturing facility in New Jersey and a warehouse and distribution center in Tennessee.

The company grew its BioScience operations in 2010 by acquiring all of the hemophilia-related assets from privately-held Archemix in a deal worth up to $315 million. Archemix has products under development including a synthetic hemophilia treatment to improve the body's blood clotting capabilities. Then to jump into the bone grafting market the company spent some $330 million to acquire UK-based ApaTech which sells bone grafting materials in the US and Europe; the deal gave Baxter manufacturing and research facilities in Germany the UK and the US.

EXECUTIVES

Corporate VP and CIO, Paul E. Martin
Chairman and CEO, Jos Œ. (Joe) Almeida, age 53
Corporate VP Human Resources, Jeanne K. Mason, age 60, $525,308 total compensation
Corporate VP General Counsel and Corporate Secretary, David P. Scharf, age 47, $651,000 total compensation
Corporate VP and CFO, James K. Saccaro, age 42
Corporate VP; President Hospital Products, Brik V. Eyre
Corporate VP; President Renal, Jill M. Schaaf
Corporate VP Operations, Timothy P. Lawrence
Corporate VP and Chief Scientific Officer, Marcus Schabacker
Corporate VP and President International, Paul Vibert
Vice President, Kathy Azuara
Medical Director, Guenter Zuelow
Vice President Sales, Eric Walker
Corporate Vice President; President International, Jean-Luc J Butel
National Account Manager, Chris Dozer
Vice President Of Global Medical Affairs, Sarah Prichard
Vice President Marketing, Paul Grozier
Vice President Sales And Marketing, Marc Lopresti
Vice President of Research and Development Medical Products, DrMarcus Schabacker
Senior Vice President Finance, Thierry Dillard
Vice President Of Finance, Scott Bohaboy
Vice President Discovery And Scientific Support, Clifford (Cliff) Holmes
Vice President Human Resources Global Functions, Darin Buser
Medical Director, Bruce Culleton
Vice President Information Technology Renal Divisi, Cathy Skala
Vice President of Environment Health and Safety, Arthur (Art) Gibson
Medical Director, Mahmoud Loghman-Adham
Associate Medical Director, Carol Schermer
National Account Manager, Theresa Anderson
Vice President Sales for National Accounts, Gregg Boyer
Vice President Manufacturing Latin America Canada, Edwin Betancourt

Senior Vice President of Quality, Joe Tsiakals
Medical Director, Steve Abrams
Medical Director Global Research and Development In BioScience Business, David (Dave) Gelmont
Vice President and Senior Executive Assistant Global Information Technology, Barbara (Barb) Laakso
Vice President International Business Operations, Lou Amendola
Vice President Human Resources, Mike Edicola
Vice President Talent Management, Irina Konstantinovsky
Regional Vice President Western Canada, Catherine (Cathy) Von Der Ahe
Vice President Corporate Communications, Laureen Cassidy
Vice President Hospital Sales, Mike Canzoneri
Medical Director, Borut Cizman
Corporate Vice President and Chief Scientific Officer, Norbert Riedel
Vice President of Global Research and Development, Noel Barrett
Vice President Sales, Joe Pudlo
Vice President Business Planning and Development, Kurt Johnson
Vice President Facilities Engineering, Ron Trudeau
Vice President Operations Bioscience Division, Allen (Al) Harmon
Corporate Vice President And Cio, Karenann Terrell
Vice President Finance, Patrick Marschall
Human Resources Vice President Latin America, Paulo Bolgar
Vice President Business Development, Frank Parilla
Vice President Clinical Affairs, Anita Stephens
Vice President Global Business Development, Joe Novicki
Vice President Employee Services, Faye Katt
Vice President Biosurgery Research And Development, Russ Holscher
Vice President Global Technical Operations, Lien-lung Sheu
Vice President Of Global Pre clinical, Hans-Peter Schwarz
Vice President Of Quality Control, Deborah Brown
Vice President Hospital International Marketing, Stephen (Steve) Merrick
Vice President Strategic Planning, Mike Martin
Vice President Supply Chain Planning, Prabir Sen-Gupta
Vice President Information Technology, Kristie Zinselmeier
Vice President Human Resources, Paulohenrique Bolgar
Vice President US BioScience Market Access, Peter (Pete) O'Malley
Assistant Treasurer, Todd S Young
Treasurer, Anthony Krombach
Board Member, Henry (Hal) Doyle
Board Member, Bret Corrick
Auditors: PricewaterhouseCoopers LLP

LOCATIONS

HQ: Baxter International Inc.
One Baxter Parkway, Deerfield, IL 60015-4625
Phone: 224 948-2000   **Fax:** 847 948-2964
Web: www.baxter.com

2014 Sales

	$ mil.	% of total
US	7,015	42
International	9,656	58
Total	**16,671**	**100**

PRODUCTS/OPERATIONS

2014 Sales

	$ mil.	% of total
Medical Products		
Renal	4,172	25
Fluid systems	3,222	19
Specialty pharmaceuticals	1,574	9
BioPharma solutions	1,004	6
BioScience		
Hemophilia	3,718	22
BioTherapeutics	2,224	13
BioSurgery	747	6
Total	**16,671**	**100**

Selected Acquisitions

COMPETITORS

Amgen	Grifols
Bayer HealthCare	Hospira
Becton Dickinson	Kimberly-Clark Health
Biogen	Novartis
CSL	Novo Nordisk
CSL Behring	Sanofi Pasteur
CareFusion	Terumo
Fresenius Medical Care	ZymoGenetics
Genzyme	

HISTORICAL FINANCIALS

Company Type: Public

Income Statement

FYE: December 31

	REVENUE ($ mil.)	NET INCOME ($ mil.)	NET PROFIT MARGIN	EMPLOYEES
12/14	16,671	2,497	15.0%	66,000
12/13	15,259	2,012	13.2%	61,000
12/12	14,190	2,326	16.4%	51,000
12/11	13,893	2,224	16.0%	48,500
12/10	12,843	1,420	11.1%	48,000
Annual Growth	6.7%	15.2%	—	8.3%

2014 Year-End Financials

Debt ratio: 35.90%
Return on equity: 30.12%
Cash ($ mil.): 2,925
Current ratio: 1.71
Long-term debt ($ mil.): 7,606
No. of shares (mil.): 542
Dividends
  Yield: 5.1%
  Payout: 82.7%
Market value ($ mil.): 39,751

	STOCK PRICE ($) FY Close	P/E High/Low	PER SHARE ($) Earnings	Dividends	Book Value
12/14	73.29	17 14	4.56	2.05	14.97
12/13	69.55	20 17	3.66	1.92	15.58
12/12	66.66	16 12	4.18	1.57	12.70
12/11	49.48	16 12	3.88	1.27	11.74
12/10	50.62	26 17	2.39	1.18	11.31
Annual Growth	9.7%	— —	17.5%	14.8%	7.3%

BB&T Corp.

BB&T Corporation provides traditional banking insurance investment banking and wealth management services through more than 1800 bank branches across the South and Southeastern US. The holding company's flagship subsidiary Branch Banking and Trust (BB&T) is one of North Carolina's oldest banks and a leading originator of residential mortgages in the Southeast. The company also operates investment bank Scott & Stringfellow. Boasting assets of nearly $190 billion BB&T is one of the largest financial services holding companies in the US.

HISTORY

Company BackgroundIn 1872 Alpheus Branch son of a wealthy planter founded Branch and Company a mercantile business in Wilson North Carolina. He and Thomas Jefferson Hadley who was organizing a public school system created the Branch and Hadley bank later that same year. The private bank helped rebuild farms and small businesses after the Civil War.

In 1887 Branch bought out Hadley and changed the bank's name to Branch and Company Bankers. Two years later Branch secured a state trust charter for the Wilson Banking and Trust Company. He never got the business running however and died in 1893. The trust charter was amended to change the name to Branch Banking and Company and Branch and Company Bankers was folded into it in 1900.

In 1907 the bank finally got its trust operations running and began calling itself Branch Banking and Trust Company. In 1922 it opened its first insurance department; the next year it started its mortgage loan activities.

BB&T survived the 1929 stock market crash with the help of the Post Office. Nervous customers withdrew their funds from BB&T and other banks and deposited them in postal savings accounts unaware that BB&T was the local Post Office's bank and the withdrawn funds went right back to the bank. BB&T opened six more branches between 1929 and 1933.

After WWII consumerism skyrocketed resulting in more car loans and mortgages. During the 1960s and 1970s the bank embarked on a series of mergers and acquisitions forming the thin end of a buying wedge that would widen significantly in the coming decades.

By 1994 BB&T was the fourth-largest bank in North Carolina. In 1995 it merged with North Carolina's fifth-largest bank Southern National Corp. founded in 1897.

With banking regulations loosening to allow different types of operations BB&T in 1997 made several acquisitions including banks thrifts and securities brokerage Craigie.

BB&T's 1998 activities included three bank acquisitions that pushed it into metro Washington DC. The company also increased holdings in fields such as insurance sales venture capital for Southern businesses and investment banking (through its acquisition of Scott & Stringfellow Financial the South's oldest NYSE member).

In 1999 Craigie was melded into Scott & Stringfellow. That year BB&T bought several insurance companies and small banks. The company continued its march through the South the following year buying several Georgia banks and Tennessee's BankFirst. In 2001 BB&T purchased South Carolina's FirstSpartan Financial multibank holding company Century South Banks Maryland-based FCNB Corporation and western Georgia's Community First Banking Company. To bolster its presence in the Washington DC market it bought Virginia Capital Bancshares and F&M National.

BB&T purchased Alabama-based Cooney Rikard & Curtin a wholesale insurance broker active in 45 states in 2002. Also that year it added about 100 branches in Kentucky after buying MidAmerica Bancorp and AREA Bancshares and entered the coveted Florida market following its purchase of Regional Financial the privately held parent of First South Bank.

Acquisitions continued the following three years as the bank swallowed First Virginia Banks among other targets. It took a break in 2005 to assimilate its holdings before joining the acquisition hunt in 2006 with deals for banks in Georgia (Main Street

Banks) and Tennessee (First Citizens Bancorp) and in South Carolina (Coastal Financial) in 2007.

EXECUTIVES

Senior Vice President, Michael (Mel) Smith
Senior Executive Vice President Manager Of Administrative Services, Robert Greene
Chairman and CEO, Kelly S. King, age 67, $1,000,000 total compensation
President and President Community Banking, Ricky K. Brown, age 59, $665,000 total compensation
Piedmont Regional President (North Carolina), Steven B. (Steve) Wiggs, age 57
COO, Christopher L. (Chris) Henson, age 54, $665,000 total compensation
SEVP and Manager Risk Management, Barbara F. Duck, age 49
SEVP and Deposit Services Manager, Donna C. Goodrich, age 53
SEVP and Chief Risk Officer, Clarke R. Starnes, age 56, $560,000 total compensation
SEVP and CFO, Daryl N. Bible, age 54, $560,000 total compensation
SEVP and Chief Communications Officer, Cynthia A. Williams
SEVP General Counsel Secretary and Chief Corporate Governance Officer, Robert J. Johnson
SEVP and President & CEO Scott & Stringfellow LLC, W. Rufus Yates
President Greater Birmingham, Josh Petty, age 37
Executive Vice President Marketing, Debbie Kerr
Vice President, Cindy Powell
Senior Vice President and Manager Credit Risk Review, Jimmy Godwin
Vice President, Stuart Hamilton
Senior Vice President, James Lamm
Senior Vice President, Mieke Deboer
Senior Vice President Wealth Management Team Direc, Craig Frye
Vice President, Chris Furner
Vice President Business Deposits Officer, Laurie Zapletal
Senior Vice President, Cindy McGoldrick
Senior Vice President Simulation Manager, Tammy Jarrell
Vice President, Ann Hardison
Vice President Information Technology Section, Greg Stone
Assistant Vice President, Ghezal Gobar
Vice President Senior Team Leader Acquired Asset Group SFL, John (Jack) Breitfelder
Vice President Family Risk Manager, Kimberly Smith
Vice President And Manager Is Section Bbandt Corporation, Bill Colon
Vice President Information Technology Strategy, Craig Moss
Vice President, Debrah More
Vice President Wealth Management Team, John Ware
Commercial Banker Assistant Vice President, Bridget Nodianos
Vice President, Jonathan (Jon) Schneider
Senior Vice President, Brad Pollock
Vice President Asset Resolution Group, Jay Tucker
Senior Vice President, Jim Sherrick
Assistant Vice President Product Group Marketing M, Cathy Powell
Senior Vice President, Steve Gray
Senior Vice President, Samuel Scott
Sales And Service Leader Vice President, Obi Chukwumah
Assistant Vice President at Market Risk, Jingnong Chen
Vice President, Stephen Lewis
Regional Retail Banking Manager Senior Vice President a, Debbie Hance
Vice President Assistant General Counsel, Kevin Brekka

Senior Vice President Information Technology Risk Management Systems, James (Jamie) Kerby
Assistant Vice President Commercial Real Estate Portfolio Manager, Seth Einstein
Vice President, Pam Goracke
Vice President of Operations and Partner, Benjamin (Ben) Mears
Vice President Energy Group, James Giordano
Vice President, Sandra Abraham
Assistant Vice President, Sharna Pearson
Senior Vice President, Steve Sprecher
Vice President Sales Support Product Development, Connie Reeves
Senior Vice President, Howard Brooks
Financial Center Leader Ii Assistant Vice President, Tanya Dobbins
Vice President, Jay Hall
Assistant Vice President Compliance Risk Officer T, Katherine (Kate) Cox
Vice President, Nicole Irby
Senior Vice President Payment Solutions Risk Manager, Joe Potuzak
Vice President, Terri Miller
Senior Vice President, Kevin Meeks
Vice President Business Development, Aimee Creamer
Vice President Information Technology Enterprise Architecture, Fred Phillippi
Vice President Business Development, Claudy Gardner
Senior Vice President, Carletha Ward
Senior Vice President Erm Credit Risk Review Team Manager, Bob Nail
Vice President Human Resources, Betty Putney
Senior Vice President, David Wellborn
First Vice President Information Technology, Dave McMillan
Vice President Family Risk Management, Gina Jurch
Senior Vice President Syndicated Finance, Mike Skorich
Certified Employment Consultant III Assistant Vice President, Lucinda Austin
Executive Vice President Marketing, Brenda Lean
Area President, Ryan Kennedy
Vice President Financial Data Reporting Manager, Vallie Martin
Senior Vice President, Charles Gebbert
Assistant Vice President, Zach Thornton
Assistant Vice President, Jeff Laws
Senior Vice President abl, Jennifer (Jen) Cummins
Senior Attorney Vice President, Anna Pray
Vice President, Carl Dillon
Assistant Vice President Area Operations Officer, Eric Ortiz
Executive Vice President Marketing, Barbara (Barb) Crane
Vice President Mortgage Loan Officer, Kym Childress
Manager Information Technology Solutions Architecture Vice President, Derek Efird
Senior Vice President, David (Dave) Stroud
Assistant Vice President Financial Center Leader Hablo Espaiiol, Gil Rolon
Senior Vice President, Brian Strout
Senior Vice President Credit Risk, Nancy Williams
Vice President Institutional Sales, Angela Dreelin
Mortgage Loan Off And Assistant Vice President, Ann Adams
Vice President Sales And Service Leader, Kim Allen
Assistant Vice President, Marie Murrain
Assistant Vice President Insurance Accounting Operations Manager, Bonnie Edwards
Vice President And Product Manager Corporate Deposits, Christine Figueredo
Vice President Private Advisor Wealth Management, Alan (Al) Majak
Vice President Portfolio Risk Officer, Matt Wagner
Vice President And Consultant, Andrew (Andy) Zevola

Vice President, Duncan Moseley
Assistant Vice President, Cassie Pruitt
Vice President, Michael Walter
Assistant Vice President Healthcare Investment Banking, Michelle (Mitch) LE
Vice President Commercial Lending Cre Group, Wright Perkins
Senior Vice President, Sam Fisher
Assistant Vice President Area Operations Officer II Hub Team Leader, Ann Hicks
Vice President Business Services Officer, Mark Spivey
Assistant Vice President, Patty Garcia
Vice President, Paul McBroom
Assistant Vice President, Jason Matthews
Assistant Vice President, Scott Parks
Assistant Vice President Operations Team Leader, Lucinda Beard
Vice President, Jane Phillips
Vice President, Mark Holmes
Vice President, Karen Starnes
Assistant Vice President, Dan Owens
Enterprise Management Systems Assistant Vice President, Ajit Khanna
Client Sever Engineer IV Vice President BBandt, Dan Phelan
Assistant Vice President Appraisal Review Officer II, Dave Outland
Senior Vice President, Stanley Gunter
Vice President, Susan Holt
Vice President, Sarah Rodriguez
Vice President, Nanci Campbell
Market Leader IV Vice President, Michael (Mel) Benetto
Vice President Commercial Lender, Bradley Curelop
Vice President Of District Operations, Wilborn Roberson
Vice President Credit Risk Review Officer, Kevin Yarbrough
Vice President Employee Benefits, Kimbra Fossen
Senior Vice President Corporate Bankin, Troy Weaver
Assistant Vice President Risk and Information Of, Chevol Davis
Vice President. New Business Development Officer, Katrina Morelock
Senior Vice President Credit Risk Review Team Leader, Nancy Ortkiese
Senior Vice President, Siddharth Patel
Assistant Vice President, Janice Smith
Senior Vice President Senior Credit Officer, Thomas Findlay
Credit Officer Vice President, Jerry Morrison
Vice President Financial Center Leader, Elizabeth Dominguez-martinez
Senior Vice President, Clark Wilson
Asset Manager Vice President, Jared Williams
Senior Vice President, Warren Takacs
Vice President Information Technology Solutions Architect, Pete Savastano
Vice President Mortgage Loan Officer, Scott Umberger
Vice President Information Technology, Jeff Anders
Information Technology Distinguished Technologist Vice President, Craig Gerber
Vice President, Spencer Jones
Assistant Vice President Financial Center Leader Iii, Connie Morales
Vice President, Jim Murray
Assistant Vice President Large, Cathy Lyons
Senior Vice President, Benjamin Sharpe
Auditors: PricewaterhouseCoopers LLP

LOCATIONS

HQ: BB&T Corp.
200 West Second Street, Winston-Salem, NC 27101
Phone: 336 733-2000   **Fax:** 336 671-2399
Web: www.bbt.com

2014 Branches

	No.
Virginia	361
North Carolina	358
Florida	325
Georgia	161
Maryland	125
South Carolina	113
Alabama	88
Kentucky	82
Texas	82
West Virginia	77
Tennessee	52
Washington DC	13
Total	**1,837**

PRODUCTS/OPERATIONS

2014 Sales

	$ mil.	% of total
Interest income	6,142	60
Non-interest income	3,784	40
Total	**9,926**	**100**

Selected Services

Commercial
  Asset management
  Association services
  Capital markets services
  Commercial deposit services
  Commercial finance
  Commercial middle market lending
  Commercial mortgage lending
  Institutional trust services
  Insurance
  Insurance premium finance
  International banking services
  Leasing
  Merchant services
  Payment solutions
  Private equity investments
  Real estate lending
  Supply chain management
Retail
  Asset management
  Automobile lending
  Bankcard lending
  Consumer finance
  Home equity lending
  Insurance
  Investment brokerage services
  Mobile/online banking
  Payment solutions
  Retail deposit services
  Sales finance
  Small business lending
  Wealth management/private banking

Selected Subsidiaries & Affiliates

American Coastal Insurance Company
BB&T Equipment Finance Corporation
BB&T Financial FSB
  Sheffield Financial
BB&T Insurance Services Inc.
BB&T Investment Services Inc.
BB&T Securities LLC
Branch Banking and Trust Company
Clearview Correspondent Services
CRC Insurance Services
Grandbridge Real Estate Capital LLC
Lendmark Financial Services Inc.
McGriff Seibels & Williams Inc.
MidAmerica Gift Certificate Company
Prime Rate Premium Finance Corporation Inc.
  AFCO Credit Corporation
Regional Acceptance Corporation
Stanley Hunt DuPree & Rhine Inc.
Sterling Capital Management LLC

COMPETITORS

Bank of America	PNC Financial
Capital One	Regions Financial
Fifth Third	SunTrust
First Citizens	Synovus
BancShares	United Bankshares
First Horizon	Wells Fargo
JPMorgan Chase	

HISTORICAL FINANCIALS

Company Type: Public

Income Statement

FYE: December 31

	ASSETS ($ mil.)	NET INCOME ($ mil.)	INCOME AS % OF ASSETS	EMPLOYEES
12/14	186,814	2,226	1.2%	33,400
12/13	183,010	1,729	0.9%	33,700
12/12	183,872	2,028	1.1%	34,000
12/11	174,579	1,332	0.8%	31,800
12/10	157,081	854	0.5%	31,400
Annual Growth	**4.4%**	**27.1%**	**—**	**1.6%**

2014 Year-End Financials

Debt ratio: 9.00%
Return on equity: 9.45%
Cash ($ mil.): 2,542
Current ratio: —
Long-term debt ($ mil.): —

No. of shares (mil.): 720
Dividends
  Yield: 2.4%
  Payout: 34.5%
Market value ($ mil.): 28,028

	STOCK PRICE ($) FY Close	P/E High/Low	PER SHARE ($) Earnings	Dividends	Book Value
12/14	38.89	15 13	2.75	0.95	33.77
12/13	37.32	17 13	2.19	1.12	32.21
12/12	29.11	12 9	2.70	0.76	30.24
12/11	25.17	16 10	1.83	0.64	24.98
12/10	26.29	30 19	1.16	0.60	23.67
Annual Growth	**10.3%**	**— —**	**24.1%**	**12.2%**	**9.3%**

BBCN Bancorp Inc.

National commercial banks nsk

EXECUTIVES

Evp And Chief Credit Officer, Mark Lee
Chairman President & Chief Executive Officer, Kevin S Kim
Evp And Chief Lending Officer Bbcn Bank, Jason K Kim, age 49
Vice President And Systems Support Manager, Joshua Chu
Senior Vice President And Manager, Andrew Park
First Vice President Olympic Branch Southern California, Anthony Kim
Vice President Compliance Officer, Robin West
Assistant Vice President and Senior Human Resources Analyst, Soon Bae
Auditors: BDO USA, LLP

LOCATIONS

HQ: BBCN Bancorp Inc.
  3731 Wilshire Boulevard, Suite 1000, Los Angeles, CA 90010
Phone: 213 639-1700   **Fax:** 213 235-3033
Web: www.bbcnbank.com

HISTORICAL FINANCIALS

Company Type: Public

Income Statement

FYE: December 31

	ASSETS ($ mil.)	NET INCOME ($ mil.)	INCOME AS % OF ASSETS	EMPLOYEES
12/14	7,140	88	1.2%	915
12/13	6,475	81	1.3%	835
12/12	5,640	83	1.5%	704
12/11	5,166	27	0.5%	678
12/10	2,963	(7)	—	376
Annual Growth	**24.6%**	**—**	**—**	**24.9%**

2014 Year-End Financials

Debt ratio: 0.59%
Return on equity: 10.47%
Cash ($ mil.): 462
Current ratio: —
Long-term debt ($ mil.): —

No. of shares (mil.): 79
Dividends
  Yield: 2.4%
  Payout: 33.0%
Market value ($ mil.): 1,143

	STOCK PRICE ($) FY Close	P/E High/Low	PER SHARE ($) Earnings	Dividends	Book Value
12/14	14.38	16 12	1.11	0.35	11.10
12/13	16.59	16 11	1.03	0.25	10.19
12/12	11.57	13 10	0.99	0.05	9.62
12/11	9.45	20 11	0.53	0.00	10.21
12/10	9.86	— —	(0.30)	0.00	9.44
Annual Growth	**9.9%**	**— —**	**—**	**—**	**4.1%**

Becton, Dickinson and Co.

Don't worry you'll only feel a slight prick if Becton Dickinson (BD) is at work. The company's BD Medical segment is one of the top global manufacturers of syringes and other injection and infusion devices. BD Medical also makes IV catheters and syringes prefillable drug delivery systems self-injection devices for diabetes patients and related supplies such as anesthesia trays and sharps disposal systems. The BD Diagnostics segment offers tools for collecting specimens and the equipment and reagents to detect diseases in them. Finally BD caters to researchers through its BD Biosciences unit which makes reagents antibodies and cell imaging systems used in basic and clinical research.

Operations

The company's largest operating segment is the BD Medical division which accounts for more than half of annual revenues. The BD Diagnostics division accounts for about a third of sales while the Biosciences division brings in about 15% of annual earnings.

Sales of safety devices have experienced positive growth in recent years especially in international markets. Other areas contributing to BD Medical's operations include sales of prefilled syringes and diabetic pen needles. Key products in the BD Diagnostics segment include safety-engineered blood collection equipment and automated diagnostic platforms. The BD Biosciences segment offers cell analysis equipment and supplies including flow cytometry (cell sorting) systems monoclonal antibodies (single-source proteins) and kits for cellular analysis and cell culture media.

Geographic Reach

BD has manufacturing marketing and warehousing operations in about 50 countries in the Americas Europe and Asia.

Though the company is working to increase international sales (especially in emerging markets) the US remains its largest segment accounting for more than 40% of sales. The European segment which includes operations in Africa and the Middle East is BD's second-largest operating region accounting for about 30% of revenues.

Sales and Marketing

BD's customers include entities in health care (including hospitals and pharmacies) drug development medical research (including academic and government labs) clinical research (such as reference labs and blood banks) and agricultural or food analysis. It uses a direct sales force and independent representatives to market and distribute its products in the US and abroad. In the US products are sold primarily to distributors who then resell to end-users.

Financial Performance

Revenues in fiscal 2013 (ended September) rose about 4% to $8.1 billion. Sales in the US grew a modest 2% across all segments with sales internationally growing 6% across all segments. New products acquisitions and safety-engineered products led the growth for the Medical and Diagnostics segments; the growth of Biosciences was driven primarily by instrument and reagent sales in emerging markets.

Net income was up more than 10% that year (to some $1.3 billion) as income from discontinued operations (Discovery Labware) was $364 million compared to $60 million the prior year. Cash flow from operations —$1.7 billion in 2013 —has remained quite consistent over the past several years.

Strategy

BD is focused on expanding by investing in R&D with a focus on its core medical technology segments (it spent $494 million on R&D in 2013 compared to $472 million in 2012). Through the BD Medical unit BD has been cashing in on the increased emphasis on safety in health care delivery by introducing a number of safety-engineered devices that prevent accidental needlesticks and thus exposure to infected blood. BD Diagnostics is doing the same growing through sales of its safety-engineered blood collection equipment including the BD Vacutainer system.

In addition to improving safety BD is working to improve drug delivery methods increasing the speed of disease diagnosis and advancing pharmaceutical research techniques. The company supplements its internal R&D programs by forming partnerships and conducting acquisitions. BD expanded its capabilities to meet customer needs by opening a new distribution center in North Carolina in 2012. In 2014 it purchased a biotech company to provide next generation sequencing (NGS); the move gives BD access to the NGS market and expands its genomics offerings.

BD has also divested non-core operations in recent years to focus its resources its faster growing operations. The company sold its Discovery Labware unit (excluding its advanced bioprocessing platform) to Corning for $720 million in cash in November 2012. The unit made pipettes tubes and other basic equipment used in labs. In early 2015 it sold prescription unit BD Rx (which included a pharmaceutical manufacturing plant in North Carolina) to a division of Fresenius for an undisclosed amount. The two companies also signed a 10-year agreement through which Fresenius Kabi USA will provide BD with a portfolio of intravenous fluids.

Mergers and Acquisitions

In 2013 BD purchased Austria's Cato Software Solutions which makes a suite of comprehensive medication safety software. The following year it acquired Alverix an optoelectronics-focused diagnostic instruments company for about $40 million to enhance its point-of-care testing offerings.

In 2014 the company acquired GenCell Biosystems an Irish biotech firm with proprietary technologies for next generation genomic sequencing.

As a way to address hospitals' need for an end-to-end medication management system BD in 2015 purchased smart medical device maker CareFusion. The move faced tough scrutiny from shareholders since the $12.2 billion price wasn't much of a premium over the stock price and from government officials since CareFusion recently paid $40.1 to settle charges that it promoted off-label prescriptions of its products and paid off physicians to push its wares.

Subsidiary BD Life Sciences acquired Cellular Research a biotechnology R&D startup specializing in single-cell genomic analysis. The deal aligns with BD's broader genomics strategy which includes plans to launch such products as an automated next-generation sequencing library prep system.

HISTORY

Maxwell Becton and Fairleigh Dickinson established a medical supply firm in New York in 1897. In 1907 the company moved to New Jersey and became one of the first US firms to make hypodermic needles.

During WWI Becton Dickinson (BD) made all-glass syringes and introduced the cotton elastic bandage. After the war its researchers designed an improved stethoscope and created specialized hypodermic needles. The company supplied medical equipment to the armed forces during WWII. Becton and Dickinson helped establish Fairleigh Dickinson Junior College (now Fairleigh Dickinson University) in 1942. The company continued to develop products such as the Vacutainer blood-collection apparatus its first medical laboratory aid.

After the deaths of Dickinson (1948) and Becton (1951) their respective sons Fairleigh Jr. and Henry took over. The company introduced disposable hypodermic syringes in 1961. BD went public in 1963 to raise money for new expansion. In the 1960s the company opened plants in Brazil Canada France and Ireland and climbed aboard the conglomeration bandwagon by diversifying into such businesses as industrial gloves (Edmont 1966) and computer systems (Spear 1968). BD also went on a major acquisition spree in its core fields during the 1960s and 1970s buying more than 25 medical supply testing and lab companies by 1980.

Wesley Howe successor to Fairleigh Dickinson Jr. expanded the company's foreign sales in the 1970s. Howe thwarted a takeover by the diversifying oil giant Sun Company (now Sunoco) in 1978 and began to sell BD's non-medical businesses in 1983 ending with the 1989 sale of Edmont. Acquisitions including Deseret Medical (IV catheters surgical gloves and masks; 1986) sharpened BD's focus on medical and surgical supplies.

In the 1990s BD formed a number of alliances and ventures including a 1991 agreement to make and market Baxter International's InterLink needleless injection system which reduces the risk of accidental needle sticks and a 1993 joint venture with NeXagen (now part of Gilead Sciences) to make and market in vitro diagnostics. As tuberculosis reemerged in the US as a serious health threat the firm improved its TB-detection and drug-resistance test systems which cut testing time from as much as seven weeks to less than two.

In 1996 BD introduced GlucoWatch (a glucose monitoring device developed by Cygnus) and acquired the diagnostic business and brand name of MicroProbe (now Epoch Pharmaceuticals).

Previously known on Wall Street as a homely company that focused on cutting costs BD changed its image with a string of acquisitions beginning in 1997. The firm acquired PharMingen (biomedical research reagents) and Difco Laboratories (microbiology media) which broadened its product lines. BD also collaborated with Nanogen on diagnosis products for infectious disease.

EXECUTIVES

EVP and COO, William A. Kozy, age 64, $721,000 total compensation

Chairman President and CEO, Vincent A. (Vince) Forlenza, age 62, $985,000 total compensation

EVP and President Global Health, Gary M. Cohen, age 57, $605,700 total compensation

SVP and General Counsel, Jeffrey S. Sherman, age 60, $540,750 total compensation

CIO, Stephen (Steve) Sichak, age 57

EVP Administration and CFO, Christopher R. (Chris) Reidy, age 58, $690,188 total compensation

SVP and Chief Marketing Officer, Nabil Shabshab, age 49

EVP and President Life Sciences, Linda M. Tharby, age 47

EVP and President Medical Segment, Thomas E. Polen, age 42

President Greater Asia, James Lim, age 50

President Europe EMA and the Americas, Alexandre Conroy, age 51

EVP and Chief Quality Officer, Pierre Boisier

SVP Research and Development and Chief Medical Officer, Ellen R. Strahlman, age 57, $615,750 total compensation

EVP and Chief Human Resources Officer, Jerome V. Hurwitz, age 61

EVP and Chief Regulatory Officer, Richard J. Naples

WW Vice President Research and Development BD Rapid Diagnostics, John (Jack) Carrino

Vice President Global Sustainability, Glenn Barbi

Vice President Human Resources, Jerry Hurwitz

Auditors: Ernst & Young LLP

LOCATIONS

HQ: Becton, Dickinson and Co.
1 Becton Drive, Franklin Lakes, NJ 07417-1880
Phone: 201 847-6800
Web: www.bd.com

2013 Sales

	$ mil.	% of total
US	3,353	42
Europe	2,512	31
Asia/Pacific	1,006	12
Other	1,183	15
Total	**8,054**	**100**

PRODUCTS/OPERATIONS

2013 Sales

	$ mil.	% of total
Medical	4,306	53
Diagnostics	2,646	33
Biosciences	1,102	14
Total	**8,054**	**100**

Selected Acquisitions

COMPETITORS

Abbott Labs	Life Technologies
Affymetrix	Corporation
Agilent Technologies	Meridian Bioscience
Alere	Novo Nordisk
B. Braun Melsungen	Retractable
Bard	Technologies
Baxter International	Roche Diagnostics
Beckman Coulter	Safety Syringes
Bio-Rad Labs	Sekisui Diagnostics

Boston Scientific
Dako
Fresenius
Gen-Probe
Harvard Bioscience
Hologic
Hospira
Johnson & Johnson
Kimberly-Clark Health

Siemens Healthcare
 Diagnostics
Terumo
Thermo Fisher
 Scientific
Trinity Biotech
Unilife
bioM©rieux

HISTORICAL FINANCIALS

Company Type: Public

Income Statement

FYE: September 30

	REVENUE ($ mil.)	NET INCOME ($ mil.)	NET PROFIT MARGIN	EMPLOYEES
09/15	10,282	695	6.8%	49,517
09/14	8,446	1,185	14.0%	30,619
09/13	8,054	1,293	16.1%	29,979
09/12	7,708	1,169	15.2%	29,555
09/11	7,828	1,270	16.2%	29,369
Annual Growth	7.1%	(14.0%)	—	14.0%

2015 Year-End Financials

Debt ratio: 47.81%
Return on equity: 11.38%
Cash ($ mil.): 1,424
Current ratio: 1.38
Long-term debt ($ mil.): 11,370

No. of shares (mil.): 210
Dividends
 Yield: 1.8%
 Payout: 58.5%
Market value ($ mil.): 27,951

	STOCK PRICE ($) FY Close	P/E High/Low	PER SHARE ($) Earnings	Dividends	Book Value
09/15	132.66	45 33	3.35	2.40	34.00
09/14	113.81	20 16	5.99	2.18	26.32
09/13	100.02	16 11	6.49	1.98	25.99
09/12	78.56	14 12	5.59	1.80	21.00
09/11	73.32	16 13	5.62	1.64	22.48
Annual Growth	16.0%	— —	(12.1%)	10.0%	10.9%

Bed, Bath & Beyond, Inc.

Bed Bath & Beyond (BBB) has everything you need to play "house" for real. It's the nation's #1 superstore domestics retailer with more than 1000 BBB stores throughout the US Puerto Rico and Canada. The stores' floor-to-ceiling shelves stock better-quality (brand-name and private-label) goods in two main categories: domestics (bed linens bathroom and kitchen items) and home furnishings (cookware and cutlery small household appliances picture frames and more). BBB also operates 270 Cost Plus and World Market stores and three smaller specialty chains: about 80 Christmas Tree Shops; almost 100 buybuy BABY stores; and 50 Harmon discount health and beauty shops.

Operations

Beyond its main BBB chain of about 1020 stores the retailer operates 270 stores under the names World Market Cost Plus World Market and World Market Stores banners. It also operates more than 95 buybuy BABY shops almost 80 Christmas Tree Shops and 50 stores under the names Harmon and Harmon Face Values. In Mexico BBB also has a joint venture with Mexican retailer Home & More where it currently operates five stores under the BBB banner.Sales of home furnishings generated 64% of the retailer's total revenue in fiscal 2014 (ended February 2015) while domestic merchandise made up 36% of total revenue during the year.

Geographic Reach

Nearly all of the New Jersey-based retailer's 1500 stores are in the US though 44 of its stores are located across six Canadian provinces while three inhabit Puerto Rico. Roughly one-third of the company's stores are in five US states: California Texas Florida New York and New Jersey.

Sales and Marketing

BBB likes to locate its stores in strip malls and power strip shopping centers in suburban areas of medium and large-sized cities. It also places its stores near major off-price and conventional malls.The chain relies exclusively on circulars mailings and word-of-mouth for advertising. BBB spent $308.4 million on advertising in fiscal 2014 (ended February 2015) a sizable jump compared with $280.5 million the prior year and $250 million the year before that.

Financial Performance

BBB's sales have been steadily growing for each of the past few years thanks to a strengthening US economy and increased business stemming from its 2012 acquisitions of Cost Plus and Linen Holdings. BBB's sales grew by 3% to a record $11.88 billion in fiscal 2014 (ended February 2015) with approximately 71% of the sales increase being driven by an increase in comparable store sales and the rest coming from the company's new store sales. Comparable store sales grew by 2.4% for the year (the same percentage as in FY2013) thanks to higher transaction spending and transaction volumes. Comparable sales through the company's customer website and mobile applications grew by more than 50% for the year.The retailer's profit declined for a second year despite higher sales in FY2014 with net income falling by 6% to $957.47 million. Most of the decline resulted from higher selling general and administrative expenses related to technology costs (and related depreciation) and increased advertising spending. BBB also incurred roughly $49 million more in interest expenses as it issued more long-term debt Notes in July 2014. Cash from operations also shrank by 15% to $1.19 billion in FY2014 as the retailer generated less in earnings and slowed its short-term borrowing cash inflows during the year from accounts payable and merchandise credit and gift card liabilities.

Strategy

BBB reiterated in 2015 that its strategy is to expand its market reach either through strategic acquisitions or organically by adding stores in both new and existing markets. To this end the retailer added 22 new stores in fiscal 2015 after opening 33 stores the year before. BBB also reiterated in 2015 that it wants to further enhance its omnichannel capabilities through such initiatives as adding new functionality to its e-commerce and mobile sites and by opening new distribution centers for both direct to consumer and store fulfillment. Additionally it planned to expand specialty departments in its stores in areas such as health and beauty care baby specialty food and specialty beverage sections.

The retailer's decentralized structure allows store managers to have more control than their peers at other retailers (and the company has less manager turnover). BBB cuts costs by locating its stores in strip shopping centers freestanding buildings and off-price malls rather than in pricier regional malls. To cut costs further its vendors ship merchandise directly to the stores eliminating the expense of a central distribution center and reducing warehousing costs.

Mergers and Acquisitions

In June 2012 the company bought Cost Plus which operates nearly 260 stores in 30 states under the World Market Cost Plus World Market and Cost Plus Imports banners via a successful tender offer. The acquisition followed an 18-month partnership between the two chains during which

specialty food departments were added to some BBB stores. BBB sought to boost foot traffic and fend off online and discount retail competitors by adding food and drink to its merchandise menu. (About 40% of Cost Plus sales come from food and drink.)

Also in June 2012 the retailer acquired New Jersey-based Linen Holdings a privately-held distributor of bath bed and table linens for about $105 million. Linen Holdings' customers included hotels cruise lines food service establishments and health care operators.

HISTORY

Company BackgroundWarren Eisenberg and Leonard Feinstein both employed by a discounter called Arlan's brainstormed an idea in 1971 for a chain of stores offering only home goods. They were betting that customers were in Feinstein's words interested in a "designer approach to linens and housewares." The two men started two small linens stores (about 2000 sq. ft) named bed n bath one in New York and one in New Jersey.

Expansion came at a fairly slow pace as the company moved only into California and Connecticut by 1985. By then the time was right for such a specialty retailer: Department stores were cutting back on their houseware lines to focus on the more profitable apparel segment and baby boomers were spending more leisure time at their homes (and more money on spiffing them up). Eisenberg and Feinstein opened a 20000-sq.-ft. superstore in 1985 that offered a full line of home furnishings. The firm changed its name to Bed Bath & Beyond (BBB) two years later in order to reflect its new offerings.

With the successful superstore format the company built all new stores in the larger design. BBB grew rapidly; square footage quadrupled between 1992 and 1996. The company went public in 1992. That year it eclipsed the size of its previous stores when it opened a 50000-sq.-ft. store in Manhattan. (It later enlarged this store to 80000 sq. ft.; the company's stores now average 42000 sq. ft.)

BBB's management has attributed its success in part to the leeway it gives its store managers who monitor inventory and have the freedom to try new products and layouts. One example often cited by the company is the case of a manager who decided to sell glasses by the piece instead of in sets. Sales increased 30% and the whole chain incorporated the practice.

The retailer opened 28 new stores in 1996 33 in 1997 (its first-ever billion-dollar sales year) and 45 in 1998.

In 1999 the company dipped a toe into the waters of e-commerce by agreeing to buy a stake in Internet Gift Registries which operates the WeddingNetwork website. The company later began offering online sales and bridal registry services. Keeping up its rapid expansion pace the company opened 70 stores in 1999 85 in 2000 and 95 in 2001.

In 2002 BBB acquired Harmon Stores a health and beauty aid retailer with 29 stores in three states. It acquired Christmas Tree Shops a giftware and household items retailer with 23 stores in six states for $200 million in 2003.

In March 2007 BBB acquired buybuy BABY which operates eight stores on the East Coast for $67 million. The retailer opened its first Canadian location in Ontario north of Toronto in December. In 2008 BBB added three more stores in Canada and its first locations in Mexico via a joint venture there under the Home & More banner.

In June 2012 the company bought Cost Plus which operates nearly 260 stores in 30 states under the World Market Cost Plus World Market and Cost Plus Imports banners for $495 million in cash.

EXECUTIVES

VP CFO and Treasurer, Eugene A. (Gene) Castagna, age 49, $1,670,769 total compensation
Vice President - Corporate Development; President Harmon Stores, G. William Waltzinger
Senior Vice President, Ronald (Ron) Curwin
Vice President Supply Chain, Nancy Katz
Vice President Construction Store Development, Jim Brendle
Vice President Safety Loss Prevention, William (Bill) Plate
Vice President Real Estate, Seth Geldzahler
Vice President Store Operations, Ed Kopil
Vice President Application Development, Robert (Bob) Claybrook
Vice President, Ross Richman
President and Chief Merchandising Officer, Arthur (Art) Stark, age 60, $1,670,769 total compensation
SVP Stores, Matthew Fiorilli, age 58, $1,555,769 total compensation
CEO and Director, Steven H. (Steve) Temares, age 56, $3,967,500 total compensation
CEO Cost Plus Inc., Barry J. Feld, age 58
CFO, Susan E. Lattmann, age 47, $730,769 total compensation
Vice President Information Technology Finance, Tim Kirchner
Vice President Controller, Robyn D'Elia
Vice President, Jordan Heller
Vice President Tax, Steve Taplits
Vice President Omni Channel Solutions And Supply Chain Technology, Alex Zelikovsky
Vice President Of Transportation, Doug Hanley
Vice President Information Technology, Guy Miller
Vice President Customer Service, Hank Rinehardt
Vice President, Lynda Pak
Vice President Of Information Technology, Louis Sepe
Vice President Safety Loss Prevention, Jim O'Connor
Vice President Sustainability, Kenneth (Ken) Frankel
Vice President Customer Service And Bridal, Hank Reinhart
Vice President Merchandise Planning And Allocation, Nika Markus
Vice President Corporate Counsel, Michael (Mel) Callahan
Vice President Northeast Region, Martin (Marti) Eisenberg
Vice President, Lisa Cavanagh
Vice President Store Operations, Christine Pirog
Auditors: KPMG LLP

LOCATIONS

HQ: Bed, Bath & Beyond, Inc.
650 Liberty Avenue, Union, NJ 07083
Phone: 908 688-0888   **Fax:** 908 810-8813
Web: www.bedbathandbeyond.com

2015 Stores

	No.
California	186
Texas	115
Florida	97
New York	96
New Jersey	89
Illinois	57
Ohio	51
Virginia	47
North Carolina	45
Michigan	44
Massachusetts	43
Pennsylvania	43
Arizona	42
Georgia	37
Washington	37
Colorado	34
Tennessee	27
Connecticut	24
Indiana	24
Missouri	24
South Carolina	24
Maryland	23
Alabama	22
Louisiana	20
Canada	20
Oregon	17
Wisconsin	16
Minnesota	15
Utah	15
New Hampshire	14
Nevada	13
Kansas	11
Kentucky	11
Iowa	10
Albert Canada	10
Idaho	9
Oklahoma	9
Montana	9
New Mexico	9
Maine	8
Arkansas	7
Mississippi	7
British Columbia Canada	7
Nebraska	6
Rhode Island	5
Delaware	4
South Dakota	3
Puerto Rico	3
Vermont	3
West Virginia	3
District of Columbia	3
Alaska	2
Hawaii	2
North Dakota	2
Wyoming	2
New Brunswick Canada	2
Manitoba Canada	1
Newfoundland Canada	1
Novia Scotia Canada	1
Prince Edward Island Canada	1
Saskatchewan Canada	1
Total	**1,513**

PRODUCTS/OPERATIONS

Selected Merchandise

Domestics
Bath accessories
Hampers
Shower curtains
Towels
Bed linens
Bedspreads
Pillows
Sheets
Kitchen textiles
Cloth napkins
Dish towels
Placemats
Tablecloths
Window treatments
Home Furnishings
Basic housewares
Accessories (lamps chairs accent rugs)
General housewares (brooms ironing boards)
Small appliances (blenders coffeemakers vacuums)
Storage items (hangers organizers shoe racks)
General home furnishings
Artificial plants and flowers
Candles
Gift wrap
Picture frames
Seasonal merchandise
Wall art
Kitchen and tabletop items
Cookware
Cutlery
Flatware
Gadgets
Glassware
Serveware

2015 Stores

	No.
Bed Bath & Beyond	1,019
World Market	270
buybuy BABY	96
Christmas Tree Shops	78
Harmon Face Values	50
Total	**1,513**

COMPETITORS

Amazon.com	Kmart
Art.com	Macy's
Babies "R" Us	Pier 1 Imports
Burlington Coat	Ross Stores
Factory	Sears
Children's Place	Sensational Beginnings
Container Store	TJX Companies
Dillard's	Target Corporation
Euromarket Designs	Tuesday Morning
Garden Ridge	Corporation
Gymboree	Wal-Mart
IKEA	Wayfair
J. C. Penney	Williams-Sonoma

HISTORICAL FINANCIALS

Company Type: Public

Income Statement

FYE: February 28

	REVENUE ($ mil.)	NET INCOME ($ mil.)	NET PROFIT MARGIN	EMPLOYEES
02/15*	11,881	957	8.1%	60,000
03/14	11,503	1,022	8.9%	58,000
03/13	10,914	1,037	9.5%	57,000
02/12	9,499	989	10.4%	48,000
02/11	8,758	791	9.0%	45,000
Annual Growth	7.9%	4.9%	—	7.5%

*Fiscal year change

2015 Year-End Financials

Debt ratio: 22.19%
Return on equity: 28.73%
Cash ($ mil.): 875
Current ratio: 2.10
Long-term debt ($ mil.): 1,500
No. of shares (mil.): 174
Dividends
  Yield: —
  Payout: —
Market value ($ mil.): 13,004

	STOCK PRICE ($) FY Close	P/E High/Low		PER SHARE ($) Earnings	Dividends	Book Value
02/15*	74.66	15	11	5.07	0.00	15.75
03/14	67.82	17	12	4.79	0.00	19.19
03/13	56.93	16	12	4.56	0.00	18.42
02/12	60.35	15	11	4.06	0.00	16.66
02/11	47.85	16	12	3.07	0.00	15.62
Annual Growth	11.8%	—	—	13.4%	—	0.2%

*Fiscal year change

Beneficial Bancorp Inc

LOCATIONS

HQ: Beneficial Bancorp Inc
1818 Market Street, Philadelphia, PA 19103
Phone: 215 864-6000
Web: www.thebeneficial.com

HISTORICAL FINANCIALS

Company Type: Public

Income Statement

FYE: December 31

	ASSETS ($ mil.)	NET INCOME ($ mil.)	INCOME AS % OF ASSETS	EMPLOYEES
12/14	4,751	18	0.4%	830
12/13	4,583	12	0.3%	842
12/12	5,006	14	0.3%	—
12/11	0	11	—	—
Annual Growth	—	17.8%	—	—

Debt ratio: 0.53%
Return on equity: 2.94%
Cash ($ mil.): 534
Current ratio: —
Long-term debt ($ mil.): —

No. of shares (mil.): 75
Dividends
Yield: —
Payout: —
Market value ($ mil.): —

	STOCK PRICE ($) FY Close	P/E High/Low	PER SHARE ($) Earnings	Dividends	Book Value
12/14	0.00	— —	0.24	0.00	8.12
Annual Growth	—	— —	—	—	—

Berkley (W. R.) Corp.

W. R. Berkley is a holding company with a full basket. The firm offers an assortment of commercial property/casualty insurance across three segments. Its domestic insurance segment underwrites complex third-party liability risks professional liability and commercial transportation insurance for small to midsized business customers and state and local governments. It also develops self-insuring programs aimed at employers and employer groups. International insurance offers the same services to customers in 60 countries in Europe the Americas Scandinavia and Australia. Its reinsurance unit allows insurance companies in the US Europe and Asia/Pacific region to pool their risks in order to reduce their liability.

Operations

After years of dividing its US business into several units with additional groups for international and reinsurance Berkley in 2013 rearranged into Insurance - Domestic (67% of revenue in 2014) Insurance - International (12%) and Reinsurance - Global (11%). The company had been working to grow its international operations and had reached the point where it was ready to give the unit its own operating segment.Geographic ReachBerkley offers insurance and reinsurance through more than 50 operating units in 60 nations in North America South America Europe and the Asia/Pacific region.Sales and MarketingThe specialty insurance business sells its high-risk coverage products directly and through brokers to a wide variety of clients. The regional products business' offerings are sold through a network of non-exclusive commission-based independent agents.Financial PerformanceContinuing a multi-year trend of steady growth in 2014 Berkley reported an 11% increase in revenue from $6.4 billion to $7.1 billion. A combination of rate increases and expansion into new markets led to the uptick. More than three-quarters of policies that expire each year are renewed. Net realized gains on investment sales also rose in 2014 doubling to $254 million due to the sale of real estate (including an $86 million gain from the sale of a London office building) investment funds and securities.Higher revenues helped lead to an increase in net income which rose 29% to $650 million in 2014; this was partially offset by an increase in operating expenses and income tax costs. Cash flow from operations slipped 10% to $735 million both due to lower reinsurance and other underwriting activity volume as well as an increase in income taxes paid.StrategyStrategically Berkley's decentralized structure promotes the development of specialized expertise in a range of areas and enables the company to adapt to cyclical market conditions and insulate itself from great risk. While the company has made a handful of acquisitions through the years

(for example it bought a specialty property/casualty distribution firm in 2014) it prefers to expand by forming new operating units after identifying needs in specific areas. In 2013 it added Berkley Design Professional Underwriters and Berkley Southeast Insurance Group.The company also focuses on growing world markets including South America Australia and the Asia/Pacific region. Additionally Berkley exercises insightful discretion in exiting insurance lines as demand diminishes. In 2014 it sold an aviation-related business for $16 million.

EXECUTIVES

President Berkley Design Professional Underwriters, Stephen L. (Steve) Porcelli
SVP Investments; President Berkley Dean & Company, James G. Shiel, age 55, $625,000 total compensation
Senior Vice President Admitted Specialty Lines, Peter (Pete) Kamford
Vice President, Joan E Kapfer
Assistant Vice President and Actuarial, Thomas P (Thom) Boyle
Vice President Internal Audit, Michele Fleckenstein
President Verus Underwriting Managers LLC, Dale H. Pilkington
SVP and CFO, Eugene G. Ballard, age 62, $625,000 total compensation
CEO, W. Robert (Rob) Berkley, age 42, $850,000 total compensation
President Admiral Insurance, Steven S. Zeitman
President and CEO Berkley Custom Insurance Managers, Michael P. Fujii, age 61
President Berkley Mid-Atlantic Group, Susan N. Grady
President and CEO Berkley Regional Specialty LLC, Paul S. McAuliffe
President Berkley Public Entity Managers, Richard B. (Rich) Vincelette
President and CEO Nautilus Insurance Group LLC, Thomas M. (Tom) Kuzma
President and CEO W. R. Berkley Insurance (Europe) Limited, Stuart Wright
President Continental Western Group, Michael G. Connor
President and CEO Berkley Latin America and Caribbean, Eduardo I. Llobet
President and CEO Berkley Net Underwriters LLC, John K. Goldwater
SVP Information Technology, Kevin H. Ebers, age 57
President Berkley Life Sciences, Jill E. Wadlund
President Key Risk Insurance, Robert W. (Rob) Standen
President Clermont Specialty Managers Ltd., William J. (Bill) Johnston
Chairman Berkley Risk Administrators Company LLC, J. Michael Foley
President and CEO Berkley North Pacific Group LLC, Jeffrey R. (Jeff) Dehn
President Vela Insurance Services LLC, David A. Jordan
President and CEO Berkley Select; President Monitor Liability Managers, Joseph G. (Joe) Shores
President and CEO American Mining Insurance Group LLC, Chandler F. Cox
President Berkley Asset Protection Underwriting Managers LLC, Joseph P. Dowd
President Berkley Aviation LLC, Jason R. Niemela
President Berkley Offshore Underwriting Managers LLC, Frank A. Costa
President Berkley Professional Liability LLC, John R. Benedetto
President Gemini Transportation Underwriters LLC, Rocco P. Modafferi
President Berkley RE America, Jon A. Schriber
President Berkley Canada, Andrew Steen

President and CEO Berkley Re Asia Pacific, K. Grant Robson
General Manager Berkley Re Hong Kong, Eric Chan
President and CEO Berkley Accident and Health LLC, Christopher C. Brown
President Berkley FinSecure, Michael Dandini
President Berkley Specialty Underwriting Managers LLC, Kenneth J. Berger
President Berkley Medical Excess Underwriters, Collin J. Suttie
President Berkley Southeast Insurance Group, Dennis L. Barger
President Preferred Employers Group LLC, Steven A. (Steve) Gallacher
President Acadia Insurance Group LLC, Douglas M. Nelson
President Berkley Oil and Gas Specialty Services LLC, Carol A. Randall
President Berkley Technology Underwriters LLC, Matthew A. (Matt) Mueller
President Riverport Insurance Company, James B. Ketterson
CEO Berkley RE UK Limited, Richard Fothergill
VP and Chief Marketing Officer, Jonathan M. Levine
VP and CIO, Kanchana Sarathy
President Berkley Program Specialists, Wayne H. Carter
President Union Standard Insurance Group, Keith Mitchell
President Carolina Casualty Insurance Group, Gerald B. (Gerry) Bushey
President Berkley Surety Group, Andrew M. Tuma
President Midwest Employers Casualty Company, Timothy F. (Tim) Galvin
CEO Berkley Insurance Australia, Tony Wheatley
CEO W. R. Berkley Syndicate 1967, Alastair Blades
CEO Berkley Re Australia and New Zealand, Anthony (Tony) Piper
CEO Berkley Re Singapore, Ross Dalgleish
President Berkley Re Direct, Gregory A. Douglas
President Facultative ReSources, Joseph L. Sullivan
Vice President, Steven Samoskevich
Vice President, Michael Harris
Senior Vice President, Robert Berkley
Assistant Vice President Corporate Actuary, Laura Stevens
Senior Vice President at Berkley Technology Services, Mike Sciole
Vp-corporate Actuary, Dana Frantz
Assistant Vice President And Corporate Actuary, Gene Zhang
Vice President, Nicholas Lang
Senior Vice President, Gordon Olver
Assistant Vice President Of Application Development, Jim Leonardis
Vice President, Marie Gwin
Assistant Vice President Catastrophe Risk Manager, Robert (Bob) Sabio
Regional Vice President Western Canada, Steven (Steve) Cade
Senior Vice President Underwriting, Belinda Mattucci
Group Vice President, Steven Walsh
Vice President, Josephine Raimondi
Vice President, Andrea Trimble
Vice President Core Systems, Frank Vedder
Vice President Corporate Actuary, Jessica Somerfeld
Assistant Vice President, Nicholas Bayliss
Vice President External Financial Communications, Karen Horvath
Senior Vice President Underwriting, Joseph (Jo) Walsh
Vice President and Controller, Clement Patafio
Senior Vice President and Chief Corporate Actuary, Paul Hancock
Vice President, Carol La Punzina
Senior Vice President Reinsurance Operations, C Madsen

Assistant Vice President and Actuary, Bryan V Spero
Senior Vice President International Operations, Steven W (Steve) Taylor
Vice President, Stephen (Steve) Samoskevich
Assistant Vice President Human Resources, Jan Whiting
Vice President Claims, Brian Yoshikuni
Assistant Vice President, Jason R Lewis
Vice President Chief Compliance Officer, Scott Mansolillo
Senior Vice President, William (Bill) Rohde
Vice President, John (Jack) Littzi
Vice President, Joyce Krech
Senior Vice President Alternative Markets, Robert (Bob) Stone
Chairman, William R. (Bill) Berkley, age 69
Assistant Treasurer, George Richardson
Vice Chairman, Tom Kellogg
Auditors: KPMG LLP

LOCATIONS

HQ: Berkley (W. R.) Corp.
475 Steamboat Road, Greenwich, CT 06830
Phone: 203 629-3000   **Fax:** 203 629-3492
Web: www.wrberkley.com

PRODUCTS/OPERATIONS

2014 Sales

	% of total
Net premium earned	81
Net investment income	8
Net investment gains	3
Insurance service fee	2
Revenues from wholly-owned investees	6
Other income	-
Total	**100**

2014 Sales

% of total	$ mil
Insurance domestic	67
Insurance international	12
Reinsurance global	11
Other	10
Total	**100**

Selected Property/Casualty Segments
Specialty (includes excess and surplus lines and admitted specialty lines)
Regional (commercial lines property/casualty)
Alternative markets (includes excess workers' compensation monoline workers' compensation accident and health and insurance services)
Reinsurance (facultative or treaty basis; participates in business written through Lloyd' s of London)
International business (global underwriting)

COMPETITORS

AIG	Munich Re America
Allied Group	Munich Re Group
Allied World Assurance	Nationwide
American Financial	Ohio Casualty
Group	Old Republic
Arch Capital	PartnerRe
Berkshire Hathaway	Selective Insurance
CNA Financial	Swiss Re
Chubb Limited	Transatlantic
Everest Re	Reinsurance
Farmers Group	Travelers Companies
General Re	White Mountains
HCC Insurance	Insurance Group
Liberty Mutual	

HISTORICAL FINANCIALS
Company Type: Public

Income Statement

FYE: December 31

	ASSETS ($ mil.)	NET INCOME ($ mil.)	INCOME AS % OF ASSETS	EMPLOYEES
12/14	21,716	649	3.0%	7,521
12/13	20,551	505	2.5%	7,247
12/12	20,155	510	2.5%	7,412
12/11	18,487	394	2.1%	6,642
12/10	17,528	449	2.6%	6,253
Annual Growth	5.5%	9.6%	—	4.7%

2014 Year-End Financials

Debt ratio: 11.31%	No. of shares (mil.): 126
Return on equity: 14.56%	Dividends
Cash ($ mil.): 674	Yield: 2.7%
Current ratio: —	Payout: 28.8%
Long-term debt ($ mil.): —	Market value ($ mil.): 6,497

	STOCK PRICE ($) FY Close	P/E High/Low	PER SHARE ($) Earnings	Dividends	Book Value
12/14	51.26	11 7	4.86	1.43	36.21
12/13	43.39	12 10	3.55	0.39	32.79
12/12	37.74	11 9	3.56	1.35	31.66
12/11	34.39	13 9	2.71	0.31	29.15
12/10	27.38	9 8	2.90	0.27	26.26
Annual Growth	17.0%	— —	13.8%	51.7%	8.4%

Berkshire Hathaway Inc.

Berkshire Hathaway is the holding company where Warren Buffett one of the world's richest men (along with his good friend Bill Gates) spreads his risk by investing in a variety of industries from insurance and utilities to apparel and food and building materials to jewelry and furniture retailers. Its core insurance subsidiaries include GEICO National Indemnity and reinsurance giant General Re. The company's other large holdings include Marmon Group McLane Company MidAmerican Energy and Shaw Industries. Buffett holds more than 20% of Berkshire Hathaway which owns a majority of more than 50 firms in all and has equity stakes in about a dozen others.

Operations
Berkshire Hathaway operates as a holding company with a highly decentralized structure without integrated business functions (such as sales marketing purchasing legal or human resources). Practicing a minimal day-to-day management leadership style (only setting a tone from the top) the firm owns a diverse group of companies from a variety of industries with its core subsidiaries being insurance re-insurance freight rail transportation utilities and energy generation companies. Berkshire Hathaway's largest non-insurance holdings include Burlington Northern Santa Fe (BNSF) McLane Marmon MidAmerican Energy and Lubrizol. Other subsidiaries include commercial property casualty insurance group Berkshire Hathaway Specialty Insurance Berkshire Hathaway Energy and its real estate arm Berkshire Hathaway Property Advisors. Berkshire also holds significant equity stakes in about a dozen companies including Coca-Cola and Wells Fargo. In August 2015 the firm agreed to ac-

quire the US areospace components giant Precision Castparts.
Financial Performance
Buffett's famed investment vehicle has been enjoying several straight years of revenue and profit growth highlighting the legendary investors' knack for choosing financially successful companies over the long term. Berkshire's revenue jumped by 7% to a record-setting $194.67 billion in 2014 mostly thanks to 17% growth in its Railroad Utilities and Energy businesses and 6% growth in its insurance businesses. Much of the growth was driven by Berkshire Hathaway Energy GEICO and the firm's manufacturing subsidiaries. The firm's Finance and Financial Products businesses declined by 20% for the year however offsetting some of Berkshire's top-line growth. With the exception of 2008 Berkshire's revenue has grown every year and has more than doubled over the past decade.Higher revenue and lower income tax expenses drove Berkshire Hathaway's net income up 2% to a record $19.87 billion during the same period. Meanwhile cash from operations surged by 16% to $32.01 billion.
Strategy
Berkshire Hathaway seeks out large companies with consistent earnings easy-to-understand business models and like-minded leadership. Most acquisitions are made with cash and most firms retain their management after the transaction. Buffett and longtime business partner Charlie Munger attempt to run the company like a small business albeit on a much larger scale. It operates as a collection of individual enterprises; Buffett and Munger largely keep their hands off portfolio companies' day-to-day operations but allocate capital and control risk.
In a letter to shareholders Buffett once declared "Our elephant gun has been reloaded and my trigger finger is itchy." Hunting big game (i.e. acquiring big companies) has become somewhat of a necessity for Berkshire Hathaway to continue on its growth trajectory but the company benefits from not being married to any particular industry as it seeks out its quarry. Toward its "big game" investment strategy in early 2016 Berkshire entered new markets after acquiring aerospace components giant Precision Castparts for $32.3 billion (in Berkshire's largest ever deal) and its 2015 acquisition of the Van Tuyl Group the largest privately-held automotive dealership group in the US. After the largest buyout in retail automotive history was complete Buffett's firm renamed the Dallas-based dealership group Berkshire Hathaway Automotive. Also in 2015 Berkshire Hathaway completed its acquisition of Procter & Gamble's Duracell battery unit for some $1.7 billion in a transaction that helped investors avoid a big tax bill. In 2014 Berkshire bought Charter Brokerage a non-asset based third-party logistics provider for the petroleum and chemical Industries from Arsenal Capital Partners. It also boosted its energy holdings by buying SNC-Lavalin Group's AltaLink which allowed it to expand its electricity transmission in western Canada. Additionally that year it bought a wholly-owned subsidiary of Graham Holdings including WPLG a Miami television station.
Berkshire Hathaway's $28-billion purchase of ketchup giant H.J. Heinz in 2013 is also a textbook example of the firm's investment strategy as the firm and its investment partner Brazil's 3G Capital took the ketchup maker private to speed its transformation into a global food business. In late 2012 the firm also acquired Omaha-based online party supplier Oriental Trading Company.
Ownership
Chairman and CEO Buffett is the company's controlling shareholder. He owns about 21% of Berkshire Hathaway's shares.

HISTORY

Warren Buffett bought his first stock —three shares of Cities Service —at age 11. In the 1950s he studied at Columbia University under famed investor Benjamin Graham. Graham's axioms: Use quantitative analysis to discover companies whose intrinsic worth exceeds their stock prices; popularity is irrelevant; the market will vindicate the patient investor.

In 1956 Buffett then 25 founded Buffett Partnership. Its $105000 in initial assets multiplied as the company bought Berkshire Hathaway (textiles 1965) and National Indemnity (insurance 1967). When Buffett nixed the partnership in 1969 because he believed stocks were overvalued value per share had risen 30-fold.

EXECUTIVES

SVP and CFO, Marc D. Hamburg, age 65, $1,225,000 total compensation
Chairman and CEO, Warren E. Buffett, age 85, $100,000 total compensation
President Berkshire Hathaway Travel Protection, Dean Silvey
Vice President, Sharon Heck
Vice President, Mark Millard
Vice President, Daniel (Dan) Jaksich
Vice President Information Technology Security, Mark Hamberg
Vice Chairman, Charles T. (Charlie) Munger, age 91
Board Member, Thomas Murphy
Auditors: Deloitte & Touche LLP

LOCATIONS

HQ: Berkshire Hathaway Inc.
3555 Farnam Street, Omaha, NE 68131
Phone: 402 346-1400
Web: www.berkshirehathaway.com

PRODUCTS/OPERATIONS

2014 Sales

	$ mil.	% of total
Insurance & other		
Sales & service revenues	97	50
Insurance premiums earned	41,253	20
Other investment income	8,529	5
Railroad utilities & energy	40,690	21
Finance & financial products	7,104	4
Total	**194,673**	**100**

Subsidiaries and Selected Holdings
Acme Brick
Acme Building Brands (face brick and other building materials)
Albecca (custom framing products)
Applied Un
Ben Bridge
Benjamin Moore (architectural and industrial paint)
Berkshire Hathaway Assurance Corporation
Berkshire Hathaway Credit Corporation
Berkshire
Berkshire Hathaway Life Insurance Company of Nebraska
BH Finance (proprietary investment strategies)
Boat Ameri
Borsheim J
The Buffal
Burlington
Business W
California Insurance Company
Central States Indemnity Co. of Omaha (credit and disability insurance)
Clayton Homes (manufactured housing and financing)
CORT Business Services Corp. (provider of rental furniture accessories and related services)
CTB International (manufacturer of equipment and systems for poultry hog and egg production)
Cypress Insurance Company
Delta Wholesale Liquors
The Fechheimer Brothers (uniforms and accessories)
FlightSafety International (high technology training to operators of aircraft and ships)

Forest Riv
Fruit of t
Garan Inc.
GEICO (pro
General Re
H.H. Brown Shoe Company
Helzberg's
International Dairy Queen Inc. (licensing and servicing Dairy Queen Stores)
Iscar (cutting tools Israel)
Johns Manville (building and equipment insulation)
Jordan's Furniture (retailing home furnishings)
Justin Brands (western footwear and apparel)
Kansas Bankers Surety Company
Lubrizol (
Marmon Holdings (manufacturing and service)
McLane Company (wholesale distribution of groceries and non-food items)
Medical Protective Company (Med Pro; professional liability insurer)
MidAmerican Energy Holdings Company
HomeServices of America Inc. (residential real estate brokerage)
Kern River Gas Transmission Company
Northern Electric
Northern Natural Gas
Pacific Power
Rocky Mountain Power
Yorkshire Electricity
MiTek (bui
National I
Nebraska Furniture Mart (retailing home furnishings)
NetJets Inc. (fractional ownership programs for general aviation aircraft)
Oriental T
The Pampered Chef Ltd. (kitchenware and housewares)
Precision Steel Warehouse (steel service center)
R.C. Willey Home Furnishings (home furnishings retailer)
Richline G
Russell Br
Scott Fetzer Company (manufacture and distribution of diversified products)
See's Candies (boxed chocolates and other confectionery products)
Shaw Industries (carpets and rugs)
Sofft Shoe
Star Furniture Co. (home furnishings retailer)
TTI Inc. (
Wesco Fina
Wells Lamo
World Book
XTRA Corpo

COMPETITORS

AEA Investors	KKR
Allstate	Lincoln Financial
Apollo Global	Group
Management	Loews
Bain Capital	Progressive
BlackRock	Corporation
Blackstone Group	State Farm
CIGNA	TPG
CNA Financial	The Carlyle Group
HM Capital Partners	The Hartford

HISTORICAL FINANCIALS

Company Type: Public

Income Statement

FYE: December 31

	ASSETS ($ mil.)	NET INCOME ($ mil.)	INCOME AS % OF ASSETS	EMPLOYEES
12/14	526,186	19,872	3.8%	316,000
12/13	484,931	19,476	4.0%	32,000
12/12	427,452	14,824	3.5%	288,500
12/11	392,647	10,254	2.6%	271,000
12/10	372,229	12,967	3.5%	260,000
Annual Growth	**9.0%**	**11.3%**	**—**	**5.0%**

2014 Year-End Financials

Debt ratio: 15.24%
Return on equity: 8.60%
Cash ($ mil.): 63,269
Current ratio: —
Long-term debt ($ mil.): —
No. of shares (mil.): 1
Dividends
Yield: —
Payout: —
Market value ($ mil.): 247

	STOCK PRICE ($) FY Close	P/E High/Low	PER SHARE ($) Earnings	Dividends	Book Value
12/14	150.15	0	012,092.0	0.0	146185
12/13	118.56	0	011,850.0	0.00	134973
12/12	89.70	0	08,977.00	0.00	114213
12/11	76.30	0	06,215.00	0.00	99860
12/10	80.11	0	07,928.00	0.00	95453
Annual Growth	**17.0%**	**— —**	**11.1%**	**—**	**11.2%**

Berkshire Hills Bancorp, Inc.

Berkshire Hills Bancorp is the holding company for Berkshire Bank which serves individuals and small businesses through some 60 branches in Massachusetts New York Connecticut and Vermont. Established in 1846 the bank provides standard deposit products such as savings checking and money market accounts CDs and IRAs in addition to credit cards investments private banking wealth management and lending services. Real estate mortgages make up nearly three-quarters of Berkshire Hills Bancorp's loan portfolio which also includes business and consumer loans. In addition to its banking activities the company also owns insurance agency Berkshire Insurance Group.

Geographic Reach

Berkshire Hills Bancorp also is eyeing further expansion into Connecticut and other parts of New England and New York by opening new branches and through acquisitions.

Financial Performance

Berkshire Hills Bancorp's revenue increased in fiscal 2013 compared to the prior year. It reported $262 million in revenue for fiscal 2013 up from $230 million in fiscal 2012. Net income also went up to $58 million in fiscal 2013 compared to the $47 million Berkshire Hills Bancorp reported for net income in fiscal 2012.

The company's cash on hand increased by more than $100 million in fiscal 2013 compared to fiscal 2012 levels.

Strategy

Berkshire Hills Bancorp which was established in 1846 believes one of its competitive advantages is the regional niche it serves which has been relatively unscathed by the recession compared to other parts of the country.

The bank's performance has been boosted by an increase in business development in the company's market area in addition to growth in its asset-based lending and private banking businesses. The bank also has grown its loans and deposits and has plans to grow its insurance and wealth management operations as well.

EXECUTIVES

President and CEO, Michael P. Daly, age 53, $575,000 total compensation
SEVP Human Resources, Linda A. Johnston
COO Berkshire Bank, Sean A. Gray, $350,000 total compensation
SEVP Commercial Banking, George F. Bacigalupo, $229,554 total compensation
President Berkshire Bank, Richard M. Marotta, $350,000 total compensation
EVP, Glenn S. Welch, age 53

SEVP and CFO, Josephine Iannelli, age 43, $177,404 total compensation
Svp Comm'l Regional Leader, Sheryl L McQuade
Senior Vice President, Mark Foster
Vice President Information Technology Infrastructure, John White
Senior Vice President Information Technology, Gary Urkevich
Vice President Od, Lauren Harvey
Senior Vice President Asset Based Lending, Jim Hickson
Auditors: PricewaterhouseCoopers LLP

LOCATIONS

HQ: Berkshire Hills Bancorp, Inc.
24 North Street, Pittsfield, MA 01201
Phone: 413 443-5601
Web: www.berkshirebank.com

COMPETITORS

Bank of America	KeyCorp
Citizens Financial	Pathfinder Bancorp
Group	Sovereign Bank
Hudson City Bancorp	TD Bank USA

HISTORICAL FINANCIALS

Company Type: Public

Income Statement
FYE: December 31

	ASSETS ($ mil.)	NET INCOME ($ mil.)	INCOME AS % OF ASSETS	EMPLOYEES
12/14	6,502	33	0.5%	1,091
12/13	5,672	41	0.7%	939
12/12	5,296	33	0.6%	1,012
12/11	3,991	17	0.4%	760
12/10	2,880	13	0.5%	599
Annual Growth	22.6%	25.2%	—	16.2%

2014 Year-End Financials

Debt ratio: 1.57%
Return on equity: 4.86%
Cash ($ mil.): 71
Current ratio: —
Long-term debt ($ mil.): —

No. of shares (mil.): 25
Dividends
  Yield: 2.7%
  Payout: 52.9%
Market value ($ mil.): 671

	STOCK PRICE ($) FY Close	P/E High/Low	PER SHARE ($) Earnings	Dividends	Book Value
12/14	26.66	20 16	1.36	0.72	28.17
12/13	27.27	18 14	1.65	0.72	27.08
12/12	23.86	16 14	1.49	0.69	26.53
12/11	22.19	24 18	0.98	0.65	26.17
12/10	22.11	23 17	0.99	0.64	27.56
Annual Growth	4.8%	— —	8.3%	3.0%	0.5%

Best Buy Inc

Best Buy wants to be the best consumer electronics outlet in the US and beyond. The multinational retailer sells both products and services through three primary channels: about 1700 retail stores online and call centers. Its branded store banners include Best Buy Best Buy Express Best Buy Mobile Five Star Future Shop Geek Squad Magnolia Audio Video and Pacific Sales. Its stores sell a variety of electronic gadgets movies music computers mobile phones and appliances. On the services side it offers installation and maintenance technical support and subscriptions for mobile phone and Internet services.

HISTORY

Company BackgroundTired of working for a father who ignored his ideas on how to improve the business (electronics distribution) Dick Schulze quit. In 1966 with a partner he founded Sound of Music a Minnesota home/car stereo store. Schulze bought out his partner in 1971 and began to expand the chain. While chairing a school board Schulze saw declining enrollment and realized his target customer group 15- to 18-year-old males was shrinking. In the early 1980s he broadened his product line and targeted older more affluent customers by offering appliances and VCRs.

After a 1981 tornado destroyed his best store (but not its inventory) Schulze spent his entire marketing budget to advertise a huge parking-lot sale. The successful sale taught him the benefits of strong advertising and wide selection combined with low prices. In 1983 Schulze changed the company's name to Best Buy and began to open larger superstores. The firm went public two years later.

Buoyed by the format change and the fast-rising popularity of the VCR Best Buy grew rapidly. Between 1984 and 1987 it expanded from eight stores to 24 and sales jumped from $29 million to $240 million. In 1988 another 16 stores opened and sales jumped by 84%. But Best Buy began to butt heads with many expanding consumer electronics retailers and profits took a beating.

To set Best Buy apart from its competitors in 1989 Schulze introduced the Concept II warehouse-like store format. Thinking that customers could buy products without much help Schulze cut payroll by taking sales staff off commission and reducing the number of employees per store by about a third. The concept proved to be such a hit in the company's home territory Minneapolis/St. Paul that it drove major competitor Highland Appliance to bankruptcy. Customers were happy but many of Best Buy's suppliers believing sales help was needed to sell products pulled their products from Best Buy stores. The losses didn't seem to hurt Best Buy; it took on Sears and Montgomery Ward in the Chicago market in 1989 and continued expanding.

In 1994 the company debuted Concept III an even larger store format. Best Buy opened 47 new stores in 1995 but found itself swimming in debt. Earnings plummeted in fiscal 1997 partly due to a huge PC inventory made obsolete by Intel's newer product. Best Buy started selling CDs on its website in 1997. That year it realized it had overextended itself with its expansion super-sized stores and financing promotions. Best Buy underwent a speedy massive makeover by scaling back expansion and doing away with its policy of "no money down no monthly payments no interest" (and next-to-no profits).

In 1999 Best Buy began to enter new markets (including New England) and introduced its Concept IV stores which highlighted digital products and featured stations for computer software and DVD demonstrations. Also in 1999 Best Buy formed a separate subsidiary for its online operations (BestBuy.com Inc.) and invested $10 million in consumer electronics information website etown.com (etown.com closed down in February 2001).

In 2000 Best Buy agreed to pay $88 million for Seattle-based Magnolia Hi-Fi a privately held chain of 13 high-end audio and video stores. In early 2001 Best Buy bought The Musicland Group (at the time operator of more than 1300 Sam Goody Suncoast On Cue and Media Play music stores) for about $425 million. The company began its international expansion in November 2002 with its $377 million acquisition of Future Shop Canada's leading consumer electronics retailer. Over the next year Best Buy opened eight of its own Best Buy stores in Ontario Canada.

In June 2002 Schulze turned over his responsibilities as CEO to vice chairman Brad Anderson; Schulze remained as chairman of the board. Best Buy acquired Geek Squad a computer support provider for $3 million the same year.

Best Buy shut down more than 100 Musicland stores (90 Sam Goody music stores and 20 Suncoast video stores) and laid off about 700 employees in January 2003; in June it sold the entire Musicland subsidiary (then about 1100 stores) to an affiliate of investment firm Sun Capital Partners. Three years later Best Buy purchased Pacific Sales Kitchen and Bath Centers which sells appliances and offers assistance on residential remodeling for $410 million.

Philip Schoonover a top executive in charge of customer segments defected to rival Circuit City in 2004. The company also dismissed Ernst & Young as its independent auditor after a former board member disclosed personal business dealings with the firm.

In 2006 the chain acquired home appliance and remodeling retailer Pacific Sales Kitchen and Bath Centers for about $410 million.

To facilitate its expansion in China Best Buy purchased a 75% stake in Jiangsu Five Star Appliance Co. in May 2006 and later opened the first Best Buy store in China in Shanghai.

To enhance its technology product offering for small businesses Best Buy in fiscal 2008 acquired Seattle-based Speakeasy a provider of broadband voice data and IT services. The deal valued at some $97 million made Speakeasy a wholly owned subsidiary that operates through the Best Buy for Business unit. Speakeasy CEO Bruce Chatterley as well as his management team was retained to run the Speakeasy operation once the deal closed. In a bid to add digital music downloads to its playlist Best Buy acquired a majority stake in Napster for about $127 million. The retailer's 2008 purchase of the music-swapping service included Napster's approximately 700000 digital entertainment subscribers.

In June 2008 Best Buy acquired a 50% stake in Carphone Warehouse's European and US retail interests for about $2.2 billion. In late October the company acquired digital music pioneer Napster for about $127 million via a tender offer for the firm's shares.

In early 2009 the retailer acquired the 25% of China's Jiangsu Five Star Appliance that it didn't already own. It also entered the Mexican market with its first store there.

CEO Brad Anderson retired in mid-2009 and COO and longtime employee Brian Dunn took over as CEO. Dunn's stint as chief executive lasted about three years. The 28-year company veteran stepped down in April 2012 handing his CEO title in the interim to board director Mike Mikan. In September 2012 the company named turnaround expert and Frenchman Hubert Joly to the position of CEO. Previously Joly served as head of T.G.I. Friday's and Radisson parent Carlson.

EXECUTIVES

EVP Chief Administrative Officer and Chief Financial Officer, Sharon L. McCollam, age 53, $925,000 total compensation
Chairman and CEO, Hubert Joly, age 56, $1,175,000 total compensation
Chief Merchandising Officer, R. Michael (Mike) Mohan, age 47, $650,000 total compensation
President E-commerce, Mary Lou Kelley
President U.S. Retail and Chief Human Resources Officer, Shari L. Ballard, age 48, $700,000 total compensation

EVP and General Counsel, Keith J. Nelsen, age 51, $550,000 total compensation
Vice President Retail Operations, Christopher (Chris) Schmidt
Vice President Enterprise Architecture, Bala Subramanian
Vice President Customer Experience and Strategy, Beau Gray
Senior Vice President And Chief Design, Aura Oslapas
Vice President Global Talent Acquisition, Jim Floyd
Auditors: Deloitte & Touche LLP

LOCATIONS

HQ: Best Buy Inc
7601 Penn Avenue South, Richfield, MN 55423
Phone: 612 291-1000
Web: www.bestbuy.com

PRODUCTS/OPERATIONS

2015 Sales by Geography

	% of total
United States	89
Canada	10
Other	1
Total	**100**

2015 US Stores by Brand

	No.
Best Buy	1,050
Best Buy Mobile	367
Pacific Sales	29
Magnolia Audio Video	2
Total	**1,448**

2015 International Stores by Brand

	No.
Canada	
Future Shop	133
Best Buy	71
Best Buy Mobile stand-Alone Stores	56
Mexico	
Best Buy	18
Best Buy Express	5
Total	**283**

2015 Sales by Domestic Category

	% of total
Products	
Computing & mobile phones	47
Consumer electronics	31
Entertainment	9
Appliances	7
Services	5
Other	1
Total	**100**

2015 Sales Segment

	in million
	% of total
Domestic	89
International	11
Total	**100**

2015 Sales by International Category

	% of total
Products	
Computing & mobile phones	49
Consumer electronics	30
Entertainment	9
Appliance	5
Services	6
Other	1
Total	**100**

Selected Brands

Domestic
  Best Buy
  Best Buy Mobile
  Geek Squad
  Magnolia Audio Video
  Pacific Sales
International
  Canada

Best Buy
Best Buy Mobile
Cell Shop
Connect Pro
Future Shop
Geek Squad
China
Five Star
Europe
The Carphone Warehouse
The Phone House
Geek Squad
Mexico
Best Buy
Geek Squad

Selected Products

Consumer Electronics
  Audio
  Car stereos
  Home theater audio systems
  MP3 players
  Satellite radio systems
  Video
  Digital cameras and camcorders
  DVD players
  Televisions
Computing and mobile phones
  Computers
  Networking equipment
  Office furniture
  Printers
  Scanners
  Supplies
  Telephones
Entertainment
  CDs
  Computer software
  DVDs
  Subscription plans
  Video game hardware and software
Appliances
  Dishwashers
  Microwave ovens
  Refrigerators
  Stoves and ranges
  Vacuum cleaners
  Washers and dryers

COMPETITORS

ARTISTdirect	METRO AG
Amazon.com	MSN
Apple Inc.	MediaNet Digital
Audible Inc.	Myspace
Barnes & Noble	Office Depot
Brilliant Digital	OfficeMax
Entertainment	RadioShack
Brookstone	RealNetworks
Buy.com	Sears Holdings
Buzz Media	Sony Music
Conn's	Staples
Costco Wholesale	Systemax
Darty	Target Corporation
Dell	Trans World
Fry's Electronics	Entertainment
Gateway Inc.	Virgin Group
HMV Retail	Wal-Mart
Hastings Entertainment	Yahoo!
Home Depot	eMusic.com
Lowe's	

HISTORICAL FINANCIALS

Company Type: Public

Income Statement

FYE: January 31

	REVENUE ($ mil.)	NET INCOME ($ mil.)	NET PROFIT MARGIN	EMPLOYEES
01/15*	40,339	1,233	3.1%	125,000
02/14	42,410	532	1.3%	140,000
02/13	45,085	(441)	—	165,000
03/12	50,705	(1,231)	—	167,000
02/11	50,272	1,277	2.5%	180,000
Annual Growth	**(5.4%)**	**(0.9%)**	**—**	**(8.7%)**

*Fiscal year change

2015 Year-End Financials

Debt ratio: 10.63%
Return on equity: 27.53%
Cash ($ mil.): 2,432
Current ratio: 1.51
Long-term debt ($ mil.): 1,580
No. of shares (mil.): 351
Dividends
  Yield: 0.0%
  Payout: 20.6%
Market value ($ mil.): 12,372

	STOCK PRICE ($) FY Close	P/E High/Low		PER SHARE ($) Earnings	Dividends	Book Value
01/15*	35.20	11	6	3.49	0.72	14.21
02/14	23.54	28	10	1.53	0.68	11.50
02/13	16.11	—	—	(1.30)	0.66	9.05
03/12	24.31	—	—	(3.36)	0.62	10.97
02/11	32.37	15	10	3.08	0.58	16.82
Annual Growth	**2.1%**	**—**	**—**	**3.2%**	**5.6%**	**(4.1%)**

*Fiscal year change

Big Lots, Inc.

Big Lots believes that a product's shelf life depends solely on which shelf it's on. The company is North America's #1 broadline closeout retailer with about 1570 Big Lots stores in 48 US states and seven provinces in Canada. It sells a variety of brand-name products including food and other consumables furniture housewares seasonal items and toys that have been overproduced returned discontinued or result from liquidations typically at 20%-40% below discounters' prices. Its wholesale division sells its discounted merchandise to a variety of retailers manufacturers distributors and other wholesalers.

Geographic Reach

Big Lots rings up 97% of its sales in the US. The company's largest markets are California Texas Florida and Ohio home to about a third of its stores and representing 35% of fiscal 2014 sales. Big Lots entered the Canadian market in 2011 with its acquisition of the Liquidation World chain there for about $1.8 million plus debt. The purchase formed the foundation of the retailer's new Canadian subsidiary Big Lots Canada. The addition of the Canadian stores contributed an additional $177 million to Big Lots coffers in fiscal 2014.

Operations

Big Lots boasts seven regional distribution centers one each in Alabama California Oklahoma Ohio and Pennsylvania and two in Canada to receive process and distribute the majority of its merchandise to its retail locations across North America. (The retailer acquires a quarter of its merchandise from overseas vendors including about 25% from vendors in China.)

Sales and Marketing

The centerpiece of the chain's US marketing efforts is its television campaign which combines elements of strategic branding and promotion. Big Lots also distributes printed advertising circulars through a combination of newspaper inserts and mailings in all of its US markets. In Canada its marketing efforts have been limited to in-store promotional materials.

Strategy

Big Lots has been working hard to rebound from declining growth in the US. The company has lost business to dollar store rivals such as Dollar Tree and Dollar General as well as other discount stores. To compensate it has focused on getting the most bang for its buck from its real estate and store locations.

HISTORY

As a kid growing up in Columbus Ohio Russian-born Sol Shenk (pronounced "Shank") couldn't stand to pay full price for anything. His frugality blossomed into a knack for buying low and wholesaling. After a failed effort to make auto parts Shenk began the precursor to Consolidated Stores in 1967 backed by brothers Alvin Saul and Jerome Schottenstein.

The company started by wholesaling closeout auto parts and buying retailers' closeout items to sell to other retailers. By 1971 Shenk had branched into retailing selling closeout auto parts through a small chain of Corvair Auto Stores.

One of Shenk's sons suggested they devote space in the Corvair stores to closeout merchandise other than car parts. Sales surged and Shenk decided to sell the Corvair outlets and focus on closeout stores. The first Odd Lots opened in 1982. Consolidated grew more than 100% annually for the next three years. By 1986 the year after it went public the company was opening two stores a week in midsized markets around the Midwest.

Shenk found that people would buy anything as long as the price was right. Two years after the mania for Rubik's Cubes ended Odd Lots bought 6 million of the puzzles (once priced at $8) at 8 cents apiece marked them up 500% and sold them all.

By 1987 the company had nearly 300 Odd Lots/Big Lots stores. But runaway growth had created massive inventory shortages and losses as disappointed customers stopped browsing the company's sparsely stocked shelves. The woes coincided with a falling-out with the Schottensteins. Shenk retired in 1989.

Apparel and electronics retail executive William Kelley was named chairman and CEO the next year. Kelley returned Consolidated to its closeout roots and increased sales through acquisitions and creating new discount chains.

Consolidated doubled its size in 1996 with the $315 million purchase of more than 1000 struggling Kay-Bee Toys (now KB Toys) stores from Melville Corp. The expansion continued with the 1998 purchase of top closeout competitor Mac Frugal's Bargains - Closeouts. (Mac Frugal's had nearly bought Consolidated in 1989 before Consolidated board members vetoed the deal.) The $1 billion acquisition of Mac Frugal's gave Consolidated another 326 western stores under the Pic 'N' Save and Mac Frugal's names.

In 1999 Consolidated combined its online toy sales operations with those of BrainPlay.com to form KBkids.com. In mid-2000 Kelley was ousted as CEO handing the title over to CFO Michael Potter.

In December 2000 the company sold KB Toys (including KBkids.com) to a group led by KB management and global private equity firm Bain Capital for about $300 million. In mid-2001 the company changed its name to Big Lots and began converting all stores to that name to establish a national brand. Big Lots bought the inventory of bankrupt Internet home furnishings giant Living.com in June.

In 2002 the company completed converting 434 stores to the Big Lots banner including 380 stores previously operating under the names of Odd Lots Mac Frugal's and Pic 'N' Save. The name changes were part of a larger initiative to broaden the appeal of closeout retailing and to establish a unified national brand. During the year Big Lots opened 87 new stores and closed 42 others.

In 2003 Big Lots continued to remodel stores opened 86 new locations and closed 36 others. In 2004 the company opened about 100 new stores and continued to add furniture departments to its existing stores. The company shuttered 174 stores in 2005 including 43 Big Lots Furniture stores and exited the frozen food business. Store closures continued in 2006 with a net loss of 25 locations.

In 2011 Big Lots acquired the Ontario Canada-based Liquidation World chain of 89 stores marking its entry into Canada.

EXECUTIVES

EVP Chief Merchandising and Operating Officer, Lisa M. Bachmann, age 53, $646,154 total compensation

EVP Human Resources and Store Operations, Michael A. (Mike) Schlonsky, age 48, $404,615 total compensation

VP Strategic Planning and Investor Relations, Timothy A. (Tim) Johnson, age 47, $503,846 total compensation

President CEO and Director, David J. (Dave) Campisi, age 59, $942,308 total compensation

VP Merchandise Support, Stewart Wenerstrom, age 48

SVP Distribution and Transportation Services, Carlos V. Rodriguez, $337,692 total compensation

EVP and Chief Merchandising Officer, Richard R. Chene, age 52, $500,000 total compensation

Executive Legal Secretary, Shelly Duncan

Svp Gen Msde Mngr Food/consuma, Trey Johnson

Vice President Talent Management, Stella Keane

Vice President Global Transportation, Michael Burns

Regional Vice President Marketing, Mike Jasinowski

Regional Vice President, William (Bill) Boas

Vice President Real Estate, Tom Thomas

Vice President Food, Michael Morales

Vice President Of Loss Prevention, Deanna Bonachea

Vice President Asset Protection, Steve McClain

Senior Vice President General CounselandCorporate Secretary, Ronald (Ron) Robins

Vice President Sourcing, Carlos Samper

Vice President Home Texiles, Kevin Kuehl

Vice President Merchandise Planning, Craig Hart

Vice President, Joshua (Josh) Nanberg

Vice President and Manager Technical Support, Chinthaka Liyanapathirana

Vice President eCommerce and Omnichannel, Oscar Castro

Chairman, Philip E. Mallott, age 57

Treasurer, Jeremy Yeomans

Auditors: Deloitte & Touche LLP

LOCATIONS

HQ: Big Lots, Inc.
300 Phillipi Road, P.O. Box 28512, Columbus, OH 43228-5311
Phone: 614 278-6800   **Fax:** 614 278-6666
Web: www.biglots.com

2015 US Stores

	No.
California	159
Texas	116
Florida	105
Ohio	99
North Carolina	74
Pennsylvania	69
New York	63
Georgia	55
Michigan	46
Tennessee	47
Indiana	46
Virginia	41
Arizona	39
Illinois	35
Kentucky	40
South Carolina	34
Alabama	30
Missouri	25
Maryland	26
Washington	28
New Jersey	28
Louisiana	24
Massachusetts	19
Colorado	19
Oklahoma	18
West Virginia	17
Connecticut	13
Mississippi	14
Oregon	15
Wisconsin	12
Nevada	13
Arkansas	12
New Mexico	12
Minnesota	7
Utah	9
Kansas	8
Idaho	6
Maine	6
New Hampshire	7
Delaware	5
Vermont	4
Iowa	3
Nebraska	3
Montana	3
Wyoming	2
North Dakota	1
Rhode Island	1
South Dakota	1
District of Columbia	1
Total	**1,460**

PRODUCTS/OPERATIONS

2015 US Sales

	$ mil.	% of total
Furniture	1,160	22
Seasonal	888	17
Consumables	953	18
Food	822	16
Home	499	10
Electronics & other	394	8
Soft home	460	9
Total	**5,177**	**100**

COMPETITORS

99 Cents Only	Michaels Companies
Amazon.com	Quality King
BJ's Wholesale Club	Ross Stores
Costco Wholesale	Salvation Army
Dollar General	Sears
Dollar Tree	Simply Amazing
Family Dollar Stores	TJX Companies
Fred's	Target Corporation
Goodwill Industries	Tuesday Morning
Gordon Brothers Group	Corporation
J. C. Penney	Variety Wholesalers
Jo-Ann Stores	Wal-Mart
Kmart	Walgreen

HISTORICAL FINANCIALS

Company Type: Public

Income Statement

	REVENUE ($ mil.)	NET INCOME ($ mil.)	NET PROFIT MARGIN	EMPLOYEES
01/15*	5,177	114	2.2%	36,100
02/14	5,301	125	2.4%	38,100
02/13	5,400	177	3.3%	37,300
01/12	5,202	207	4.0%	37,400
01/11	4,952	222	4.5%	35,600
Annual Growth	1.1%	(15.3%)	—	0.3%

*Fiscal year change

FYE: January 31

2015 Year-End Financials

Debt ratio: 3.80%	No. of shares (mil.): 52
Return on equity: 13.55%	Dividends
Cash ($ mil.): 52	Yield: 0.0%
Current ratio: 1.77	Payout: 24.7%
Long-term debt ($ mil.): 62	Market value ($ mil.): 2,429

Biogen Inc

With its pipeline full of biotech drugs Biogen (formerly Biogen Idec) aims to meet the unmet needs of patients around the world. The biotech giant is focused on developing treatments in the areas of immunology and neurology. Its product roster includes best-selling Avonex a popular drug for the treatment of relapsing multiple sclerosis (MS); Tysabri a drug treatment for MS and Crohn's disease; Rituxan a monoclonal antibody developed jointly with Genentech that treats non-Hodgkin's lymphoma and rheumatoid arthritis; and Fumaderm a psoriasis drug marketed in Germany. Other products include Plegridy for MS and Alprolix for hemophilia B. Founded in 1978 Biogen serves customers in more than 90 countries.

Operations

Among Biogen's top selling drugs Avonex is sold in markets around the globe and accounts for 30% of annual revenues. The firm's Avonex pen is a single-use autoinjector version of the drug for once-weekly dosing.

Tecfidera (which accounts for another 30% of revenue) is an oral therapy marketed in the US for the treatment of patients with relapsing forms of MS. It is sold in Europe for patients with relapsing-remitting MS (RRMS).

Another top-selling global drug is Tysabri bringing in about 20% of revenues. Tysabri was co-marketed with Elan until 2013 when Biogen purchased full rights. Despite the drug's troubled regulatory history –the drug can only be prescribed under a strict risk management plan due to the possible side effect of a rare brain condition –the company continues to pursue additional uses for the drug.

Rituxan sales conducted through the Genentech partnership account for another 20% of sales and are classified as "unconsolidated joint business" revenues. In addition to non-Hodgkin's lymphoma and rheumatoid arthritis Rituxan is approved to treat leukemia follicular lymphoma and vasculitis. Another drug MS treatment Fampyra (also known as Ampyra) is sold in partnership with Acorda Therapeutics.

In addition to gaining revenue from the development and sales of its products (both directly and through partnerships) Biogen receives royalties on some patents it has licensed to other companies. For instance The Medicines Company pays royalties on sales of anticoagulant Angiomax.

Products in Biogen's pipeline include the anti-LINGO program for MS BIIB037 and (in collaboration with Eisai) BAN2401 for Alzheimer's disease and STX-100 for idiopathic pulmonary fibrosis. The company is partnering with AbbVie Biotherapeutics to develop and commercialize Zinbryta another MS treatment; it also has a collaboration agreement with Acorda to develop and market MS treatment products containing fampri-

dine outside the US. In addition Biogen has three separate agreements with Isis to develop and commercialize antisense therapeutics for the treatment of myotonic dystrophy type 1.

Geographic Reach

Biogen has offices in the US Australia Canada Japan the US and several European countries. It has direct sales operations in about 30 countries and operates through distribution partners in another 60 countries. The US accounted for about 70% of revenue.

Sales and Marketing

The company primarily distributes its products in the US through wholesale pharmaceutical distributors mail-order specialty distributors and shipping service providers. Two wholesale distributors AmerisourceBergen and McKesson each account for more than 10% of the firm's total revenues. Outside of the US distribution varies but includes wholesale pharmaceutical distributors and third-party distribution partners.

Avonex is marketed through Biogen's direct sales force to specialist physicians and hospitals in North America Europe and select other countries around the globe. The company also handles global marketing efforts for Tysabri. Genentech handles sales and marketing duties for Rituxan while marketing duties for Fampyra are split with Acorda (Biogen sells the drug in Europe and Canada while Acorda sells it in the US).

Financial Performance

Biogen's revenues and profits have steadily risen over the years as sales of its products have increased including a 40% increase in revenues to some $9.7 billion in 2014 due to significant growth in Tecfidera sales. Revenues related to Tysabri sales also grew that year primarily due to price increases.

Net income spiked 58% from $1.8 billion to $2.9 billion due to revenue growth and the absence of collaboration expenses after Biogen bought Tysabri from Elan (now owned by Perrigo) and launched Tecfidera. Cash from operations has also shown steady growth over the last five years including in 2014 when the company reported a 25% increase to $2.9 billion due to higher profits and a decline in cash used in inventory.

Strategy

The company pursues growth through a combination of internal R&D efforts and through partnerships alliances and acquisitions. R&D expenses totaled $1.9 billion in 2014 up from $1.4 billion in 2013 and $1.3 billion in 2012.

Biogen's pipeline of drug candidates is focused on treatments for central nervous system ailments including Alzheimer's MS amyotrophic lateral sclerosis (ALS) hemophilia neuropathic pain and lupus. In addition to proprietary candidates the company has collaborative development candidates with Genentech Portola Pharmaceuticals (lupus and rheumatoid arthritis) Isis Pharmaceuticals (spinal muscular atrophy) and other drugmakers and it continuously looks to expand its pipeline through acquisitions and partnerships.

The company's newest treatments include those for hemophilia (Eloctate and Alprolix) and MS (Tecfidera).

Biogen continues to initiate agreements with other firms to develop new products. In 2014 it entered into an agreement with Eisai to jointly develop E2609 and BAN2401 two Eisai candidates for the treatment of Alzheimer's disease. It also entered into an R&D and commercialization agreement with Sangamo BioSciences through which the partners will develop candidates for the treatment of sickle-cell disease and beta-thalassemia. The following year Biogen entered into a collaboration with Fondazione Telethon and Ospedale San Raffaele to develop gene therapies for the treatment of hemophilia A and B.

Although Biogen's annual revenues were up for 2014 sales of Tecfidera slowed down during 2015 the same year that Tysabri failed in a late-stage clinical trial for secondary progressive MS. The company responded to these setbacks by initiating certain restructuring efforts including stopping tests for Tysabri's effectiveness against secondary progressive MS as well as stopping test for pipeline drug anti-TWEAK's effectiveness against lupus nephritis. Biogen also cut some 880 employees (about 11% of its workforce) that year.

Mergers and Acquisitions

Biogen has expanded its operations through purchases of drug development firms as well as by purchasing commercialized and development-stage drugs. In 2013 Biogen purchased full rights to Tysabri from partner Elan for some $3.3 billion. Following the transaction the companies no longer split profits from the sales of the drug.

In 2015 the company agreed to buy UK-based Convergence Pharmaceuticals a clinical-stage biopharmaceutical to gain access to that firm's CNV1014802 candidate for the treatment of trigeminal neuralgia and sciatica.

HISTORY

Biogen Idec was formed out of the 2003 merger of IDEC Pharmaceuticals and Biogen.

The company began experiencing troubles with its lead product –Tysabri developed with partner Elan –soon after its formation. Sales were temporarily halted in 2005 after several patients died from a rare neurological condition. The companies were allowed to reintroduce Tysabri in 2006 (when it was also launched in Europe) under a strict risk management plan that insures sufficient doctor and patient education about risks and proper usage.

Activist investor Carl Icahn held a minority stake in the company for several years and kept a watchful eye over his investment. In 2007 he bullied the company to put itself up for sale but no buyer came through. Then he began a series of proxy battles in an attempt to stack the board with his own nominees to gain further control. By 2010 he had secured three seats on the board filled with his own representatives and resumed talks of seeing Biogen Idec broken into parts and/or sold to a larger pharmaceutical company.

Ichan's persistence might have contributed to the retirement of Biogen Idec's long-time CEO James Mullen in mid-2010 with George Scangos (former CEO of Exelixis) stepping in as Mullen's replacement. Scangos implemented sharp changes in late 2010 launching a reorganization plan aimed at reducing operational costs and increasing efficiencies. The plan included a 13% workforce reduction and a streamlining of R&D programs to focus primarily on neurological disease. Biogen Idec halted or licensed out its oncology and cardiovascular development programs and consolidated a number of US sites. As a sign that he was pleased with Mullen's work in early 2011 Icahn reduced his ownership stake and did not seek to gain control of more board seats; he sold his remaining interests in the firm in mid-2011.

EXECUTIVES

CEO, George A. Scangos, age 67, $1,375,000 total compensation
EVP Research and Development, Douglas E. (Doug) Williams, age 56, $766,831 total compensation
EVP Corporate Development, Steven H. Holtzman, age 60, $576,923 total compensation
EVP Chief Legal Officer and Corporate Secretary, Susan H. Alexander, age 59, $533,000 total compensation

EVP Human Resources, Kenneth A. (Ken) DiPietro, age 57
EVP Finance and CFO, Paul J. Clancy, age 54, $698,389 total compensation
EVP Global Commercial Operations, Stuart A. (Tony) Kingsley, age 51, $675,129 total compensation
EVP Pharmaceutical Operations and Technology, John G. Cox, age 52, $625,648 total compensation
EVP Technology and Business Solutions, Adriana (Andi) Karaboutis, $133,846 total compensation
Group SVP and Chief Medical Officer, Alfred W. Sandrock, $564,596 total compensation
SVP and Chief Scientific Officer, Spyros Artavanis-Tsakonas, age 68
SVP and CIO, Matt Griffiths
SVP and Chief Strategy Officer, Adam M. Koppel, $306,923 total compensation
Vice President Global Public Affairs, Katja Buller
V Pres Fin-cao, Gregory F Covino
Vice President Research, Michael Gilman
Vice President Customer Support, Janis Meyer
Vice President, Howard Horn
Medical Director, Lahar Mehta
Vice President Patient Services, Mike Krzan
Vice President, Adam Adamson
Associate Medical Director, Monica Mann
Vice President Safety, Gary Bloomgren
Medical Director, Wildon Farwell
Vice President Business Development, John (Jack) McDonald
Medical Director, Martha Fournier
Vice President Of Marketing, Scott Dreyer
Vice President Chemical and Molecular Therapeutics, Alan (Al) Buckler
Vice President Corporate Strategy And Portfolio Management, Samantha Singer
Senior Vice President, Samantha Calvert
Vice President People and Organization Capability, James (Jamie) Shillaber
Medical Director, Sarah Sheikh
Senior Vice President Translational Medicine And Technology, Timothy Harris
Vice President, Todd Nichols
Medical Director Clinical Development, Mark Beatty
Medical Director Safety And Benefit Risk Management, Lynda Cristiano
Vice President Of Quality, Sid Senroy
Senior Vice President Program Management, Johnathan Palmer
Vice President Global Commercial Strategy, Adrian Gottschalk
Vice President Immunology Research, Joanne Viney
Vice President Treasurer, Michael Dambach
Executive Vice President Human Resources, Scott Handren
Executive Vice President Of Human Resources, Kenneth Dipetrio
Vice President Of Global Medical Affairs Biogen Idec's Avonex, Thorsten Eickenhorst
Vice President Managing Director, Simon Jordan
Vice President Research And Development Technology, Andrew Allen
Vice President Market Access, Brian McGinty
Vice President Executive Director Biogen Idec Innovation Incubator, Rainer Fuchs
Vice President Medical Research, Bradley Maroni
Vice President Market Access and Reimbursement, Robyn Peters
Associate Medical Director, Brendon Boot
Vice President Head of Research and Development Japan Biogen Idec Japan, Shinichi Torii
Executive Vice President, Tony Kingsley
medical director Italy, Andrea Paolillo
Chairman, Stelios Papadopoulos, age 67
Abm, Karmon Warren
Board Member, Joseph Florio

Senior Vice President Marketing Relations and Treasurer, Jon Vanderplas
Abm, Don Benson
ABM, Jim Pehanick
ABM, Linde Smith
Auditors: PricewaterhouseCoopers LLP

LOCATIONS

HQ: Biogen Inc
225 Binney Street, Cambridge, MA 02142
Phone: 617 679-2000
Web: www.biogenidec.com

2014 Sales

	$ mil.	% of total
US	5,566	57
Europe		
Germany	811	8
Other European countries	1,383	14
Asia	112	3
Other regions & countries	328	3
Unconsolidated joint business revenue and other	1,499	15
Total	**9,703**	**100**

PRODUCTS/OPERATIONS

2014 Sales

	$ mil.	% of total
Products		
Avonex	3,013	31
Tecfidera	2,909	30
Tysabri	1,959	20
Other products	321	4
Unconsolidated joint business (Genentech collaboration) & other	1,499	15
Total	**9,703**	**100**

Selected Products
Approved
Avonex (multiple sclerosis)
Fampyra (multiple sclerosis with Acorda Therapeutics)
Fumaderm (severe psoriasis in Germany only)
Rituxan (non-Hodgkin's lymphoma chronic lymphocytic leukemia follicular lymphoma rheumatoid arthritis vasculitis)
Tecfidera (multiple sclerosis)
Tysabri (multiple sclerosis Crohn's disease; with Elan Pharmaceuticals)
In development
BG-12 (relapsing multiple sclerosis)
Daclizumab (relapsing forms of multiple sclerosis)
GA101 (chronic lymphocytic leukemia non-Hodgkin's lymphoma)
Factor V111 Fc (hemophilia A)
Factor IX Fc (hemophilia B)
Plegridy (PEGylated interferon beta 1a relapsing forms of multipler sclerosis)
Tysabri (secondary-progressive MS)

COMPETITORS

AbbVie	Johnson & Johnson
Abbott Labs	Millennium: The Takeda
Amgen	Oncology Company
Bayer HealthCare Pharmaceuticals	Novartis
	Pfizer
Bristol-Myers Squibb	Roche Holding
Cephalon	Sanofi
Genmab	Teva
GlaxoSmithKline	UCB

HISTORICAL FINANCIALS
Company Type: Public

Income Statement
FYE: December 31

	REVENUE ($ mil.)	NET INCOME ($ mil.)	NET PROFIT MARGIN	EMPLOYEES
12/15	10,763	3,547	33.0%	7,350
12/14	9,703	2,934	30.2%	7,550
12/13	6,932	1,862	26.9%	6,850
12/12	5,516	1,380	25.0%	5,950
12/11	5,048	1,234	24.5%	5,000
Annual Growth	**20.8%**	**30.2%**	**—**	**10.1%**

2015 Year-End Financials

Debt ratio: 33.46%	No. of shares (mil.): 218
Return on equity: 35.15%	Dividends
Cash ($ mil.): 1,308	Yield: —
Current ratio: 2.60	Payout: —
Long-term debt ($ mil.): 6,521	Market value ($ mil.): 66,968

	STOCK PRICE ($) FY Close	P/E High/Low	PER SHARE ($) Earnings	Dividends	Book Value
12/15	306.35	31 17	15.34	0.00	42.88
12/14	339.45	29 22	12.37	0.00	46.08
12/13	279.57	38 18	7.81	0.00	36.48
12/12	146.37	27 20	5.76	0.00	29.43
12/11	110.05	23 13	5.04	0.00	26.54
Annual Growth	**29.2%**	**— —**	**32.1%**	**—**	**12.7%**

BlackRock, Inc.

Now this is the kind of rock you want in your stocking. With some $4.65 trillion in assets under management BlackRock is the world's largest public investment management firm. It specializes in equity and fixed income products as well as alternative and multi-class instruments which it invests in on behalf of institutional and retail investors worldwide; it does not engage in proprietary trading. Clients include pension plans governments insurance companies mutual funds endowments foundations and charities. BlackRock also provides risk management services through BlackRock Solutions and is a leading provider of exchange-traded funds (ETFs) through iShares. The firm has offices in 30 countries.

OperationsBlackRock manages some $4.65 trillion in assets with its more than 135 investment teams. The BlackRock Solutions division provides risk management advisory and enterprise investment system services. iShares one of BlackRock's brands is a leading provider of exchange-traded funds (ETFs).Geographic Reach

New York-based BlackRock has more than 70 offices in 30 countries with three-fourths of these offices in North America and Europe. About two-thirds of its revenue is generated in the Americas primarily in the US Canada Brazil and Mexico. Europe is the firm's second largest market contributing nearly 30% of revenue. The Asia-Pacific region accounts for about 5%. BlackRock has clients and investments in more than 100 countries.Sales and MarketingBlackRock serves 21 out of the 25 largest endowments and foundation organizations in the US. It also serves around 90 of the Fortune 100 companies and more than 90% of the largest US retirement plans. BlackRock focuses on establishing and maintaining its investment management relationships by marketing its services through financial professionals pension consultants third-party distribution relationships or directly to investors themselves. The company spent $413 million toward marketing and promotional expenses in 2014 up from $409 million in 2013 and up 8% from the $384 million spent in 2012.

Financial Performance

Thanks to a rising stock market and a growing investor base BlackRock has more than tripled its assets under management since 2007 –from $1.3 trillion to $4.65 trillion at the end of 2014 –which has led strong fee and advisory income growth over the past few years.Revenue jumped by 9% to $11.08 billion in 2014 marking the firm's fifth consecutive year of strong growth as the firm collected more in investment advisory and administration fees and securities lending income. Its BlackRock Solutions (risk management) division income also grew by 10% furthering the firm's top-line growth. BlackRock also saw its sixth year of consecutive profit growth with net income rising 12% to $3.29 billion in 2014. Operations provided $3.08 billion or 15% less cash than in 2013 mostly because the company spent more toward its trading investments and paying down its payables and accrued liabilities.

Strategy

The global investment firm has amassed quite an impressive portfolio of holdings and is often the largest shareholder of entities it invests in (including General Electric and Exxon Mobil). BlackRock traditionally focuses investments on developed economies but the company has broadened its sights to include emerging markets in Asia the Middle East and Latin America. The firm plans to expand its client base further to the point where it does more than half of its business outside the US. (Approximately 48% of its client assets under management come from outside the US.) To this end in early 2015 the firm expanded its Open Trading alliance with MarketAxess Holdings into Europe with the goal of improving liquidity and cutting transaction costs for fixed-income institutions and investors in Europe —much as the strategic alliance has successfully done in the US.

BlackRock also continues to introduce new investment products to meet changing client needs as part of its overall retail growth strategy. In 2014 the firm's iShares Exchange Traded Funds business launched four new core funds to meet the needs of long-term investors seeking exposure to international equities and US fixed income products. The new products offer investors efficient access to a diversified pool of investment grade corporate credit securities with a defined maturity date daily liquidity and price transparency. Along with these and more bond offerings the firm also introduced in 2014 the BlackRock Multi-Manager Alternative Strategies Fund (BMMAX) to give individual investors a way to access multiple alternative investment strategies via one open-end mutual fund. Additionally in 2014 BlackRock partnered with Tradeweb Markets to create electronic trading services in the rates and derivatives markets.

Mergers and Acquisitions

In November 2015 BlackRock agreed to buy Bank of America's $87 billion-money market fund business boosting its global cash-management business up 30% to $372 billion in assets under management. The deal comes as Bank of America and other large banks have faced regulatory pressure to simplify their businesses in the years following the global financial crisis. In 2013 the firm acquired private-equity real estate investment advisory firm MGPA to expand its real estate business in the Asia-Pacific region and Europe. MGPA managed about $12 billion focusing on real estate funds management co-investments and separate-account mandates for institutional investors. It had about a dozen offices in the Asia-Pacific region and Europe in cities such as Shanghai Kuala Lumpur and Warsaw.

The deal followed BlackRock's 2013 acquisition of Credit Suisse's ETFs business which included 58 ETFs. The ISIN codes and identifiers remained unchanged as part of the purchase.

In 2012 the firm expanded in Canada through the acquisition of fund manager Claymore Investments. In September of that year BlackRock acquired Swiss Re Private Equity Partners the European private equity and infrastructure fund of funds business of Swiss Re expands its own private equity fund of funds group into infrastructure investing as well as broadening its presence in Europe and Asia.

Company Background

BlackRock is led by CEO Laurence Fink who has overseen a string of major acquisitions in recent years expanding into private equity real estate energy and hedge funds as investors look to diversify beyond stock and bond funds. Fink engineered a blockbuster merger with Barclays Global Investors (BGI) in 2009. In the deal which was several years in the making BlackRock bought Barclays Global Investors from UK banking giant Barclays for some $15 billion. The deal resulted in a new company operating under the BlackRock name. Barclays Bank retained a 20% stake in the combined firm but Fink remained in charge of the enterprise. The merger nearly tripled BlackRock's assets under management and propelled the company to the top of the international money management industry by enhancing its investment and risk management capabilities. The deal also gave BlackRock a much larger footprint outside the US and added more than 3500 new employees.

EXECUTIVES

President, Robert S. (Rob) Kapito, age 57, $750,000 total compensation

Chairman and CEO, Laurence D. (Larry) Fink, age 62, $900,000 total compensation

Chairman and Country Head Japan, Yoshiyuki Izawa, age 67

Senior Managing Director and Head of Retail and iShares, Robert W. (Rob) Fairbairn, age 49, $350,000 total compensation

Senior Managing Director and Chief Risk Officer, Bennett W. Golub, age 57

Senior Managing Director and Chief Product Officer, J. Richard (Rich) Kushel, age 48

Senior Managing Director; Global Head Alpha Strategies, Quintin R. Price

Chairman and Senior Adviser BlackRock France Belgium and Luxembourg, Jean-Fran $ois Cirelli, age 57

Senior Managing Director; Head Asia/Pacific, Ryan D. Stork

Senior Managing Director; Global Head iShares, Mark K. Wiedman

Senior Managing Director; Global Head Marketing and Communications, Linda G. Robinson, age 62

Senior Managing Director; Global Head of Human Resources, Jeffrey A. Smith, age 44

Senior Managing Director; Global Head Institutional Client Business; Chairman BlackRock Alternative Advisors, Mark S. McCombe, age 48

Senior Managing Director and General Counsel, Matthew J. Mallow, age 71

Senior Managing Director and Head of Europe Middle East & Africa, David Blumer

Senior Managing Director and CFO, Gary S. Shedlin, $500,000 total compensation

Senior Managing Director and COO; Global Head BlackRock Solutions, Rob L. Goldstein, $500,000 total compensation

Senior Managing Director and Global Head of Multi-Asset Strategies; Head and Chief Investment Officer Scientific Active Equity, Kenneth F. (Ken) Kroner

Senior Managing Director and Global Head Beta Strategies, Amy L. Schioldager

Senior Managing Director; Global Head Business Operations and Technology, Derek K. Stein

Senior Managing Director; Global Head Corporate Strategy, Salim Ramji

Vice President Human Resources, Katie Nedl

Vice President Technology, Karl Wieman

Vice President, Paul L Audet

Regional Vice President, Robb Falaguerra

Executive Vice President, Stephanie Clarke

Vice President Institutional Sales Benelux, Norbert Van Veldhuizen

Executive Vice President, Nick Hutton

Vice President, Andrew (Andy) Berg

Vice President PMG GT Glbl Trading Research, Abhijit Chandra

Vice President Finance, Jennifer Shoup

Vice President of IP Services Product Management, Darren Focareta

Vice President CRM Database Marketing Manager, Sorin Tudor

Vice President Global Infrastructure and Network Management, Karen Chan

Vice President Director Account Management, Neil Blundell

Vice President, Paul Horowitz

Vice President Treasury Americas, Aga Linnell Aga Linnell

Vice President, Marques Johnson

Senior Compliance Manager Vice President, Beth Moore

Executive Vice President, Alastair McCarmick

Vice President, Brian Thackray

Vice President Investment Knowledge Strategist, Brooke Juniper

Vice President, Peter Falkowski

Vice President E Business Operations, Wendy Guthrie Harris

Vice President, Victor Glazer

Executive Vice President, Clinton Soose

Vice President, Nigel Benson

Vice President Channel Strategy and Marketing, Kathleen Mariboe

Vice President Of Broker Dealer Services, Mark Persiani

Vice President, Chad Dziedzic

Vice President, Lisa Sanner

Vice President, John Prins

Vice President Finance, Micheal Graci

Vice President, Kathy Aubin

Vice President Business Development, Joe Ernst

Vice President, Matt Miller

Vice President Finance, Roger Castoral

Vice President Infrastructure Investment Group, Tyler Mcconnell

Vice President, Scott Wert

Vice President, Simone Gartmond

Vice President, Michael (Mel) Diaz

Vice President, John Mills

Vice President Operations, Bryan White

Vice President, Sharda Lekhraj

Vice President Information Technology, Richard Bravery

Assistant Vice President, Richard (Dick) Steel

Vice President, Gregor Streyzowsky

Vice President, Jeff Nickell

Vice President, Bridget Dean-hammel

Vice President Program Management, Jennifer Galler

Vice President Marketing, Kimberly Beck

Vice President, Susie Shrem

Vice President Of Marketing, Richard Li

Vice President, Karen Goldman

Vice President Information Technology Audit, Mark Goodwin

Vice President, Simon Rafferty

Vice President Sourcing, Michael Schnalzer

Vice President, Andrew Chaiken

Executive Vice President And Fund Manager, Apoorva Shah

Vice President, Phil Green

Vice President Fixed Income Portfolio Management Group, Sriram Reddy

Vice President, Douglas Pheeney

Vice President, Richard (Dick) Mejzak

Vice President Trader portfolio Manager Cash Managment, Gene Meshechek

Vice President User Experience And Design, Devjit Basu

Vice President, Sanjay Narayan

Vice President, Diane Parish

Vice President, Jeff Puntney

Vice President, Jason Devlin
Vice President Compliance, John (Jack) Longhurst
Vice President, Kate Bruestle
Vice President Lateral Recruiting, Laura Young
Executive Vice President, Dhawal Dalal
Vice President Event Management, Wendy Dooley
Vice President, Benjamin Cunningham
Vice President, Kelly Sanderson
Vice President Information Technology, Tom Tucker
Vice President Critical Infrastructure, Ed Cannon
Vice President Business Operations, David Birnbaum
Vice President, Ned Rosenman
Vice President Development, Anoop Kaushik
Vice President, Francine Perrone
Vice President, Lauren Giametta
Vice President, Kiran Vuppala
Vice President, Benjamin Friedlander
Vice President Market Research, Katie Herzog
Vice President Legal and Compliance, Lee Adkins
Vice President, Amanda Huckle
Vice President, Brian Fitzpatrick
Vice President Business Finance, Rajiv Khurana
Vice President Portfolio Manager, Edward Ingold
Vice President, Susan Lapczynski
Vice President, Loryn Sperber
Vice President, Ashish Sharma
Vice President, Sam Eisenberg
Vice President Legal and Compliance, Nicole Rosser
Vice President, Anirban Mitra
Assistant Vice President, Kumar Duvvuri
Vice President, Jeremy Jones
Vice President, David Edson
Vice President, Miranda Harrison
Vice President, Ying Li
Vice President Product Management, Jeff Lambert
Vice President, Patricia Belcher
Vice President, Radha Subramanian
Vice President Legal and Compliance, Danny Riemer
Vice President, Mufaddal Karachiwala
Vice President, David Curtin
Vice President, Ryan Shriber
Vice President, John Buck
Vice President, Sukhbir Gill
Vice President, Thomas Dara
Vice President Of Human Resources, Toretha McGuire
Vice President, Kenny Ma
Vice President, Charles Harrington
Vice President, Jorge Diaz
Vice President Portfolio Manager, Brett Buchness
Vice President, Amy Goldfarb
Vice President Digital, Sareena Dalla
Vice President, Stephanie Lupo
Vice President, Christine Brooks
Vicepresident, Rodrigo Castaneda
Vice President Access And Identity Management, Nikhil Mathur
Vice President, Jeff Brown
Vice President, Chen Ai
Vice President, Vidy Vairavamurthy
Vice President Aladdin And Technology, Paul Dearman
Vice President, Madhavi Chugh
Vice President Media Services, Lisa Sturdivant
Vice President Us Board Governing Services, Danielle Costantino
Vice President Social Media Strategist, Erin Meijer
Auditors: Deloitte & Touche LLP

LOCATIONS

HQ: BlackRock, Inc.
 55 East 52nd Street, New York, NY 10055
Phone: 212 810-5300
Web: www.blackrock.com

2014 Sales

	$ mil.	% of total
Americas	7,286	66
Europe	3,246	29
Asia/Pacific	549	5
Total	**11,081**	**100**

PRODUCTS/OPERATIONS

2014 Sales

	$ mil.	% of total
Investment advisory administration fees & securities lending		
Equity	5,337	47
Fixed income	2,171	20
Multi-asset class	1,236	11
Alternative investments	1,103	10
Cash management	292	3
BlackRock Solutions & advisory	635	6
Distribution fees	70	1
Other revenue	237	2
Total	**11,081**	**100**

COMPETITORS

Allianz Global Investors	Federated Investors
Bank of New York Mellon	Legg Mason
	Morgan Stanley
Charles Schwab	Principal Global
Dimensional Fund Advisors	State Street
	UBS
	Waddell & Reed

HISTORICAL FINANCIALS

Company Type: Public

Income Statement

FYE: December 31

	REVENUE ($ mil.)	NET INCOME ($ mil.)	NET PROFIT MARGIN	EMPLOYEES
12/14	11,081	3,294	29.7%	12,200
12/13	10,180	2,932	28.8%	11,400
12/12	9,337	2,458	26.3%	10,500
12/11	9,081	2,337	25.7%	10,100
12/10	8,612	2,063	24.0%	9,127
Annual Growth	6.5%	12.4%	—	7.5%

2014 Year-End Financials

Debt ratio: 2.06%
Return on equity: 12.24%
Cash ($ mil.): 5,723
Current ratio: 2.70
Long-term debt ($ mil.): 4,938

No. of shares (mil.): 164
Dividends
 Yield: 2.1%
 Payout: 39.9%
Market value ($ mil.): 58,921

	STOCK PRICE ($) FY Close	P/E High/Low	PER SHARE ($) Earnings	Dividends	Book Value
12/14	357.56	19 15	19.25	7.72	166.07
12/13	316.47	18 12	16.87	6.72	158.83
12/12	206.71	15 12	13.79	6.00	150.42
12/11	178.24	16 11	12.37	5.50	180.90
12/10	190.58	23 13	10.55	4.00	198.86
Annual Growth	17.0%	— —	16.2%	17.9%	(4.4%)

Blackstone Group LP (The)

Throw a rock and you're bound to hit a Blackstone investment. The Blackstone Group is one of the world's largest real estate private equity and alternative asset managers in the world with over $330 billion in assets under management and such notable holdings as Michaels Stores SeaWorld and Crocs. The firm manages investment vehicles including private equity funds funds of hedge funds and real estate funds. It also provides advisory services on mergers and acquisitions restructuring and other transactions for corporations. Clients include public and corporate pensions financial institutions and individuals. About 60% of its revenue comes from performance fees while one-third comes from management and advisory fees.

Operations

The Blackstone Group is organized into five business segments. Its Real Estate segment (which generated 39% of Blackstone's total revenue during 2014) manages numerous funds that invest in commercial properties around the world primarily in the US and Europe. The Private Equity segment (36% of revenue) boasts more than $90 billion in assets under management (about 75% of which are in the US) and has traditionally been involved in leveraged buyouts of developed companies though it has evolved to invest in younger ventures as well. All cases are in friendly transactions.Blackstone's Hedge Fund Solutions business (10% of revenue) Blackstone Alternative Asset Management (BAAM) has more than $64 billion in assets under management. The company's Credit business (9% of revenue) GSO Capital Partners focuses on credit-oriented alternative asset management. Finally its financial advisory unit (6% of revenue) provides global corporate advisory services including fund placement services for alternative investment funds.

Blackstone in late 2014 announced plans to spin off its financial and strategic advisory services its restructuring and reorganization advisory services and its Park Hill fund placement business into a new company that will be strategically combined with PJT Partners an independent financial advisory firm founded by Paul J. Taubman. As part of the plan current Blackstone unitholders will initially own some 65% of the new entity with Taubman (who will serve as chairman) and his partners owning the remaining 35%.

Geographic Reach

New York-based Blackstone Group has two dozen offices worldwide. In the US the firm has branches in Atlanta Boston Chicago Houston and California (in Los Angeles Menlo Park Santa Monica and San Francisco). Its overseas offices are in Beijing Dubai Dublin Dusseldorf Hong Kong London Madrid Montecito Mumbai Paris Seoul Shanghai Singapore Sydney and Tokyo.

Financial PerformanceBlackstone Group's revenues and profits have skyrocketed over the past few years mostly thanks to strong performance fee growth and modest management and advisory fee growth; all of which have been buoyed by appreciating financial markets real estate property and portfolio company valuations.The firm's revenue jumped 13% to $7.5 billion in 2014 mostly driven by a 23% rise in performance fee income that stemmed from strong performance in its Private Equity division's BCP V and BCP VI funds which generated net returns of 24% and 18% respectively. Blackstone's revenues were also helped by a 14% boost in management and advisory fee income from across its Hedge Fund Solutions Private Equity Real Estate and Credit segments.Higher revenue and strong cost controls in 2014 drove Blackstone's net income up 35% to $1.6 billion. The firm's operating cash levels fell 53% to $1.7 billion mostly after adjusting its earnings for non-cash gains on investments.

Strategy

Blackstone's Real Estate division has been growing at an even faster clip than its Private Equity business over the past few years thanks to a slew of prudent property investments that have seen healthy valuation gains in the hot real estate market. In early 2016 the firm bought BioMed Realty Trust to broaden its exposure to the fast-growing healthcare sector. In 2015 Blackstone purchased some $3.3 billion worth of office properties located in the hot markets of Southern California Seattle and Chicago from General Electric as it wound down its GE Capital business. Also that year it purchased three shopping malls in Portugal and Spain (to be managed by its European retail platform Multi Corporation which managed 25 shopping centers in the two countries) by acquiring shares of the CG Malls Europe Fund.In late 2014 as part of its strategy to exit its office holdings acquired in 2007 near the market's peak Blackstone sold 26 Northern California office locations to Hudson Pacific Properties for a staggering $3.5 billion. Also in 2014 Blackstone made a series of strategic shopping center retail property trades buying more than 70 shopping centers in a $1.9 billion transaction through a joint venture it formed with DDR Corp. and selling its majority stake in 39 U.S. shopping centers to joint-venture partner Kimco Realty Corp. for $512.3 million ($925 million when including debt).In 2013 the firm purchased the Hughes Center complex in Las Vegas for $347 million to eventually benefit from the region's rebound. Blackstone was also part of an investor group that bought Extended Stay Hotels owner HVM which was in bankruptcy. All of the hospitality investment activity helped bring in a dramatic rise in revenues in 2013.

Not to be forgotten Blackstone's legacy Private Equity division is known as a hands-on investor that builds up its portfolio companies' values before selling them off for large profits. Some of its pending and completed acquisitions in 2015 included: US Charlotte-based independent jewelry retailer Diamonds Direct; private mortgage insurance provider PMI Group; Stearns Holdings and national mortgage lender subsidiary Stearns Lending; and Center Parcs UK which operated five short break destinations across the UK that attracted some two million guests annually. During 2014 it agreed to buy the European wealth-management business of Friends Life Group for $609 million through its tactical fund and acquired industrial products maker Gates Global from Onex Corp. and Canada Pension Plan Investment Board for $5.4 billion marking Blackstone's biggest private-equity transaction since taking over hotel operator Hilton Worldwide in 2007. Also in 2014 Blackstone bought industrial and automotive parts maker Gates Corporation and took a stake in body repair chain Service King Collision Repair. The private equity division's 2013 acquisitions included Strategic Partners from Credit Suisse ThoughtFocus Technologies Multi Corporation BV Asclepius Group and a 40% stake in Eletson Gas LLC.The Private Equity division has also made some profitable exits in recent years. In 2015 Blackstone generated $1.67 billion after selling US-based security services provider AlliedBarton to Wendel SE. In late 2013 the firm took Hilton Worldwide public generating a gain of nearly $10 billion on its original investment made back in 2007. Some of its other big deals made during the year included the successful IPOs of hospitality giant Extended Stay America and retail REIT Brixmor. Additionally Blackstone's Private Equity division has been investing in companies in new markets overseas including in emerging and developing markets such as China India and Brazil. In 2014 it bought Spanish bank Catalunya Banc's more than $8 billion loan portfolio and made its first Australian investment after agreeing to buy Orica's chemicals business which operated in Australia New Zealand and Latin America. In India Blackstone made its largest acquisition to date in September 2015 when it bought the majority of Serco

Group's Business Process Outsourcing (BPO) operations for £250 million ($386 million). In Brazil Blackstone owns about 40% of Pátria a large investment management and corporate advisory firm there. In China following its strategy to invest in high-growth Chinese companies through its partnership with the Shanghai-Pudong district government a consortium led by Blackstone agreed in late 2013 to acquire China-based global consulting and technology services company Pactera Technology International Ltd. for about $600 million. The move marked Blackstone's foray into China's technology outsourcing industry a sector traditionally dominated by Indian firms.

Company Background

Founded in 1985 by industry veterans Peter Peterson and CEO Stephen Schwarzman the once-reclusive Blackstone went public in June 2007. The public offering which was a first among major US private equity firms valued Blackstone at upwards of $4 billion.In 2012 in capitalizing on the boom in energy markets Blackstone completed fundraising for its first energy-focused private equity fund Blackstone Energy Partners L.P. with total fund commitments of $2.4 billion. The firm also raised $13.3 billion for its seventh global real estate fund BREP VII making it the biggest real estate fund in the world. In 2013 Blackstone acquired secondary private fund of funds unit Strategic Partners Fund Solutions in a deal that added some $9.4 billion in assets under management.

EXECUTIVES

President and COO, Hamilton E. (Tony) James, age 64, $350,000 total compensation
Chairman and CEO, Stephen A. Schwarzman, age 68, $350,000 total compensation
Senior Managing Director; Head Private Equity Portfolio Operations, David L. (Dave) Calhoun, age 58
Senior Managing Director and CFO, Michael S. Chae, age 46
Senior Managing Director GSO Capital Partners, Bennett J. Goodman, age 57
Senior Managing Director; Head Tactical Opportunities, David S. Blitzer, age 45
Global Head Real Estate, Jonathan D. Gray, age 45
Senior Managing Director; Head Multi-Asset Investing and External Relations, Joan Solotar, age 50, $350,000 total compensation
Vice Chairman; President and CEO Blackstone Alternative Asset Management, J. Tomilson Hill, age 66, $350,000 total compensation
Senior Managing Director Private Equity London, Joseph P. Baratta, age 44
Senior Managing Director and Chief Legal Officer, John G. Finley, age 58, $350,000 total compensation
CTO, William Murphy
Senior Managing Director and Chairman Greater China, Liping Zhang
Vice President, Anthony Riccio
Senior Vice President Human Resources, Padraic McGovern
Vice President, Ken Allen
Assistant Vice President, Michael Degen
Vice President, Killian Maher
Assistant Vice President, Sukie Xu
Assistant Vice President, Rebecca Bower
Vice President, Stanley Go
Senior Vice President, Amy Blake
Assistant Vice President, Samuel Victor
Vice President, Melanie Endo
Vice President Information Technology, John Fitzpatrick
Vice President, Martin Makowiecki
Vice President Information Technology, Robert Kalik

Vice President, David Vanvlack
Vice President, Christine Cangir
Vice President, Rita Mangalick
Vice President Esourcing, Blake Vogt
Senior Vice President Credit Business, Leanne Gonzalez
Vice President Human Resources, Scott Rivas
Assistant Vice President, Madhuri Sanapathi
Vice President, John Wander
Senior Vice President, Daniel Lee
Vice President Information Technology, Michael Scaturo
Vice President, Stephane Aubry
Vice President Information Technology, Daniel (Dan) Moy
Vice President, Ronald Lintag
Assistant Vice President, Becky Stoehr
Senior Vice President, Komal Dadlaney
Vice President Engineering, Jeffrey (Jeff) Kobos
Vice President Credit Business, Jimmy Wang
Divisional Vice President, Byung U Choi
Assistant Vice President, Eric Akil
Vice President, Brij Kalaria
Assistant Vice President, Chad Whipple
Vice President, Nentcho Nentchev
Vice President Information Technology, Allan Barja
Assistant Vice President, Vincent Barberesi
Vice President, Raphael Kiam
Assistant Vice President, Anna Fields
Assistant Vice President, Shakeel Amir
Assistant Vice President, Satie Prashaud
Vice President, Michael Schlappig
Assistant Vice President, Rageim Walker
Assistant Vice President, Mariya Laforestrie
Senior Vice President, Jonathan Davies
Vice President Finance New York, Ryan Smith
Vice President, Adam Schlesinger
Assistant Vice President, Urian Yap
Vice President, Ilan Halal
Vice President, Kelli Kahn
Assistant Vice President, Kelly Yan
Assistant Vice President, Graeme Humphreys
Vice President, Justin Smith
Vice President, John Miller
Vice President, Thomas Kali
Assistant Vice President, Seth Rosenblatt
Vice President, Victor Waingort
Vice President, Stephen O'Connor
Vice President, Michael Distefano
Assistant Vice President, Megan McCann
Vice President, James Hannigan
Assistant Vice President, Veronica Colon
Assistant Vice President, Jason Drum
Vice President, Ivan Brockman
Vice President Of Information Technology, Bryan Shelby
Assistant Vice President, Katie Brackenbury
Assistant Vice President, Anna Ryvkov
Vice President Business Analyst, Cindy Hwang
Vice President, Jamie Baird
Assistant Vice President, Jeffrey Nirenberg
Vice President, David (Dave) Britman
Vice President, Taylor Carvajal
Vice President, Jason Umlah
Assistant Vice President, Shannon Farley
Assistant Vice President, Joshua Wallin
Vice President, Brett Crandall
Assistant Vice President, Daniel Fromm
Vice President, Christian Vardeleon
Vice President, Jack Pitts
Vice President, Katherine Daco
Assistant Vice President Telecommunications, William Petilli
Vice President, Sebastian Grasso
Vice President, Steve Long
Vice President, Gregory Bilse
Assistant Vice President, Sofia Koo
Senior Vice President, Bryan Sullivan
Vice President, Kevin Gee
Vice President, Paul Sheaffer

Vice President, Mike Wilcox
Senior Vice President, Wendy Lai
Vice President, Daniel Aron
Vice President, John Wrafter
Vice President, Swapna Kanekar
Vice President, Libby Barrett
Vice President, Christopher Marich
Vice President, Louise Somers
Assistant Vice President, Sheenam Chadha
Vice President Information Technology Innovations and Infrastructure Group, Colleen Coda
Vice President, Matthew Pedley
Vice President, Andreas Mang
Vice President, Catherine Brackenbury
Vice President, Yelena Bluvshteyn
Vice President, Mark Tornga
Vice President, Michelle Harika
Assistant Vice President, Jane Lvovskiy
Vice President, Roberta Osborne
Senior Vice President Culinary Strateg, Brian Williams
Vice President, Brett Newman
Assistant Vice President, Kristina Lam
Assistant Vice President Asset, Christopher McGrath
Vice President, Michael O'Hara
Vice President Finance, Peter (Pete) Moeller
Vice President Information Technology Innovations and Infrastructure Group, Young Cha
Vice President Finance, Christopher Duff
Vice President, Paul Tuffin
Vice President Software Development, David Tanzer
Vice President Corporate Services, Carolyn Milea
Senior Vice President, Frank Machado
Assistant Vice President, Amanda Hewitson
Vice President Internal Audit, Esther Friedman
Vice President, Adam Hermida
Senior Vice President, Chaim Miller
Vice President, Matthew Howell
Vice President, Sal Aloia
Assistant Vice President, Vinny Scutro
Assistant Vice President, Michael Pavone
Vice President, Daniel Chang
Vice President, Sobin Mathew
Vice President, Robin Wynn
Vice President, Thomas Procida
Assistant Vice President, Nina Bojanova
Vice President, Gordon McKemie
Assistant Vice President, Michael Amoroso
Vice President, Jared Becker
Auditors: Deloitte & Touche LLP

LOCATIONS

HQ: Blackstone Group LP (The)
345 Park Avenue, New York, NY 10154
Phone: 212 583-5000
Web: www.blackstone.com

PRODUCTS/OPERATIONS

2014 Sales

	$ mil.	% of total
Performance fees	4,374	59
Management and advisory fees	2,497	33
Investment income	534	7
Interest & dividends &Other	79	1
Total	**7,484**	**100**

2014 Sales

	% of total
Real Estate	39
Private Equity	36
Hedge fund solutions	10
Credit	9
Financial advisory	6
Others	-
Total	**100**

Selected Investments

Allcargo
Alliant Insurance Services
AlliedBarton Security Services
Antares Restaurant Group
Apria Healthcare
Axis Capital
BankUnited
Bayview Asset Management
Biomet
Caesars Entertainment (formerly Harrah's Entertainment)
Catalent Pharma Solutions
Celanese
Center Parcs
Charter Communications
China Animal Healthcare Ltd.
China National Bluestar Group
CMS Computers Ltd.
Crestwood Midstream Partners
CTI Holdings
Cumulus Media Partners
DJO
Dili Group
eAccess
Emcure
Equity Office Properties
Extended Stay America
Freescale Semiconductor Group
Gates Corporation
Gateway Rail Freight Ltd.
Gerresheimer Group
Gokaldas Exports Limited
Gold Toe-Moretz
Houghton Mifflin
Imperial Home Décor
Independent Clinical Services
Intelenet Global Services
Intertrust
Klöckner Pentaplast
Leica Camera
Maldivian Air
Michaels Stores
Mivisa Envases S.A.U.
Monnet
Montecito
Moser Baer Energy
MTAR Technologies Private
Nuziveedu Seeds
Osum Oil Sands Corp.
PBF Energy
People's Choice TV
Performance Food Group
Pinnacle Foods Corporation
Polymer Group Inc.
RGIS Inventory Specialists
Sonalike International Tractors
SeaWorld Parks & Entertainment
Summit Materials
Stiefel Laboratories
SunGard
Team Health
Texas Genco
Tragus
TRW Automotive
UCAR
United Biscuits
Vivint Inc.
The Weather Channel
Western Integrated Networks

COMPETITORS

AEA Investors	Heico Companies
American Financial Group	Hellman & Friedman
Apollo Global Management	Investcorp
	Jordan Company
Bain Capital	KKR
Berkshire Hathaway	Leonard Green
Clayton Dubilier & Rice	MacAndrews & Forbes
	Silver Lake
Goldman Sachs	TPG
HM Capital Partners	The Carlyle Group
Haas Wheat	Thomas H. Lee Partners

HISTORICAL FINANCIALS

Company Type: Public

Income Statement

FYE: December 31

	REVENUE ($ mil.)	NET INCOME ($ mil.)	NET PROFIT MARGIN	EMPLOYEES
12/14	7,484	1,584	21.2%	2,190
12/13	6,613	1,171	17.7%	2,010
12/12	4,019	218	5.4%	1,780
12/11	3,252	(168)	—	1,585
12/10	3,119	(370)	—	1,440
Annual Growth	24.5%	—	—	11.1%

2014 Year-End Financials

Debt ratio: 28.36%	No. of shares (mil.): 595
Return on equity: —	Dividends
Cash ($ mil.): 3,220	Yield: 5.7%
Current ratio: 0.96	Payout: 75.8%
Long-term debt ($ mil.): 8,937	Market value ($ mil.): 20,150

	STOCK PRICE ($) FY Close	P/E High/Low		PER SHARE ($) Earnings	Dividends	Book Value
12/14	33.83	14	11	2.58	1.92	11.85
12/13	31.50	16	8	1.98	1.18	11.01
12/12	15.59	41	28	0.41	0.52	9.83
12/11	14.01	—	—	(0.35)	0.62	9.54
12/10	14.15	—	—	(1.02)	0.60	10.49
Annual Growth	24.3%	—	—	—	33.7%	3.1%

BNC Bancorp

BNC Bancorp knows the ABCs of the financial world. The firm is the holding company for Bank of North Carolina which boasts more than 55 branches mostly across North and South Carolina but also in Virginia. In addition to offering traditional loan and deposit products (including checking savings and money market accounts credit cards and certificates of deposits) for local business and retail customers BNC also offers wealth management retirement planning and brokerage services and insurance products. Nearly 40% of its loans are commercial real estate loans while residential mortgages make up another 15%. Founded in 1991 the bank now has more than $5 billion in total assets.

OperationsBNC Bancorp generated 76% of its revenue from loan interest in 2014 and another 10% from interest on its tax-exempt and taxable securities. About 4% of revenue came from mortgage fees while another 4% came from service charges on accounts. The bank staffed 823 full-time employees at the end of 2014.Geographic ReachAbout 60% of Thomasville-based BNC Bancorp's 57 branches are located in North Carolina while more than 20% are in South Carolina. The rest of its branches are located in Virginia.Sales and MarketingThe bank serves individuals and small to medium-sized local businesses.Financial PerformanceBNC Bancorp's revenues and profits have been growing at a healthy clip thanks mostly to new loan business from acquisitions and declining loan loss provisions as its loan portfolio's credit quality has improved with the strengthened economy. The company's revenue jumped by 13% to a record $183.2 million in 2014 as it boosted its loan assets by one-third after its three bank acquisitions made during the year. Its non-interest income also grew by nearly double digits thanks to higher fee income on newly acquired deposit accounts. Higher revenue lower interest expense on deposits and a continued decline in loan loss provisions in 2014 drove BNC Bancorp's net income higher by 70% to $29.4 million. The company's operating cash levels fell by 75% to $40.5 million for the year after adjusting its earnings for non-cash income sources.StrategyBNC Bancorp has made a string of acquisitions in recent years to grow its loan business and branch network. Its 2014 acquisitions added nearly $770 million in new loan business (boosting BNC's total loan assets by 33% in one year) while its 2015 acquisitions of Valley Financial Corporation and seven branches of CertusBank alone added almost $840 million in new loan assets. Additionally its Valley Financial acquisition extended the bank's reach into Virginia for the first time.Mergers and AcquisitionsIn July 2015 BNC Bancorp entered Virginia for the first time after acquiring Valley Financial Corporation which added $854 million in assets $628 million in new loan business and nine branches in Roanoke and Salem Virginia. In June 2015 the company agreed to buy seven branch offices in South Carolina from CertusBank which also included $284 million in deposits and $210 million in loans. In December 2014 BNC Bancorp furthered its reach into South Carolina after purchasing Harbor National Bank including the commercial bank's four branches in the Charleston and Mt. Pleasant. The deal also added some $325 million in total assets and $281 million worth of new loan business. In June 2014 the company bought Community First Financial Group along with its $165.4 million in loan assets and three Harrington Bank branches based in the Raleigh-Durham-Chapel Hill area of North Carolina. In April 2014 BNC acquired South Street Financial and its four Home Savings Bank branches in Charlotte North Carolina. The deal added $278 million in total assets and $195 million in new loan business.In November 2012 BNC Bancorp purchased First Trust Bank and its three branches in the Charlotte area for some $35 million. Its 2012 acquisitions of Regent Bank and single-branch KeySource Financial further extended the bank's reach in the state.

Company Background

In 2010 the company acquired the failed Beach First National Bank in an FDIC-facilitated transaction expanding Bank of North Carolina's branch network into South Carolina. BNC Bancorp acquired another failed bank in 2011 with assistance from the FDIC Blue Ridge Savings Bank in North Carolina.

EXECUTIVES

President CEO and Director; President and CEO Bank of North Carolina, W. Swope Montgomery, age 66, $345,200 total compensation
EVP COO and Director; EVP and COO Bank of North Carolina, Richard D. Callicutt, age 56, $268,650 total compensation
EVP and CFO BNC and Bank of North Carolina, David B. Spencer, age 52, $251,200 total compensation
Vice President Special Assets, Danny Broach
Assistant Vice President Branch Manager, Lucy Ortiz
Vp Sba Underwriter, Nisha Desai
Vice President, Ann Walker
Vice President, Daren Fuller
Assistant Vice President Business Services Support Team Leader, Kristen Curtis
Senior Vice President City Executive, John Bencini
Vice President Commercial Lending, Ray Singleton
Chairman Emeritus, W. Groome Fulton, age 76
Chairman of the Board, Thomas R. Sloan, age 70
Auditors: Cherry Bekaert LLP

LOCATIONS

HQ: BNC Bancorp
3980 Premier Drive, Suite 210, High Point, NC 27265
Phone: 336 476-9200
Web: www.bankofnc.com

PRODUCTS/OPERATIONS

2014 Sales

	$ mil.	% of total
Interest		
Loans including fees	140	76
Debt securities	17	10
Other	0	-
Noninterest		
Mortgage fees	7	4
Service charges	6	4
Other	11	6
Total	**183**	**100**

COMPETITORS

BB&T
Bank of America
Carolina Bank
CommunityOne Bancorp
First Bancorp (NC)
First Citizens
  BancShares

NewBridge Bancorp
Piedmont Federal
Southern Community
  Financial
Wells Fargo

HISTORICAL FINANCIALS

Company Type: Public

Income Statement

FYE: December 31

	ASSETS ($ mil.)	NET INCOME ($ mil.)	INCOME AS % OF ASSETS	EMPLOYEES
12/14	4,072	29	0.7%	823
12/13	3,229	17	0.5%	620
12/12	3,083	10	0.3%	564
12/11	2,454	6	0.3%	455
12/10	2,149	7	0.4%	372
Annual Growth	**17.3%**	**39.7%**	**—**	**22.0%**

2014 Year-End Financials

Debt ratio: 2.01%
Return on equity: 8.88%
Cash ($ mil.): 85
Current ratio: —
Long-term debt ($ mil.): —
No. of shares (mil.): 32
Dividends
  Yield: 1.1%
  Payout: 19.8%
Market value ($ mil.): 561

	STOCK PRICE ($) FY Close	P/E High/Low	PER SHARE ($) Earnings	Dividends	Book Value
12/14	17.21	19 15	1.01	0.20	11.98
12/13	17.14	28 13	0.61	0.20	9.94
12/12	8.01	18 14	0.48	0.20	11.45
12/11	7.25	20 14	0.45	0.20	18.00
12/10	9.00	17 11	0.61	0.20	16.81
Annual Growth	**17.6%**	**— —**	**13.4%**	**(0.0%)**	**(8.1%)**

Boeing Co. (The)

Boeing has built a big name for itself as one of the world's largest aerospace companies. In addition to commercial jet aircraft like the much anticipated 787 Dreamliner the company manufactures military aircraft including the Apache the Chinook and the Osprey. It also produces satellites missile defense systems and launch systems. These products are rounded out by a portfolio of services. Major customers include the US Department of Defense and NASA. Additionally Boeing provides airplane financing and leasing services to both commercial and military customers.

Geographic Reach

Boeing's principal operations are in the US Canada and Australia with some key suppliers and subcontractors located in Europe and Japan. Boeing makes about 40% of its total revenues in the US and about 60% from international markets (primarily Europe Asia/Pacific and the Middle East).

Operations

Boeing operates through several segments. Boeing Commercial Airplanes designs manufactures and services commercial jet aircraft for both passengers and cargo. Models include the 737 narrow body the fuel efficient 737 MAX and the 747 767 and 777 wide bodies. Commercial Airplanes continues to develop the 787 Dreamliner more than 800 of which are on order by some 55 airlines around the world.

Three more segments - Boeing Military Aircraft Network & Space Systems (N&SS) and Global Services & Support - are collectively organized under Boeing Defense Space & Security (BDS). BDS provides design modification and support services for large-scale systems including missiles munitions aerial refuelers transporters and space-craft. BDS acts as a systems integrator on several programs including NASA's International Space Station and Missile Defense Agency's Ground-based Midcourse Defense.

Finally fifth segment Boeing Capital Corporation (BCC) is a financing arm that generates support revenues for the company.

Financial Performance

Despite the slow economy and the late launching of its Dreamliner jet Boeing's revenue levels reached historic heights in 2014 capping out at almost $81 billion. This represents a 5% increase when compared to 2013. Its profits jumped 19% from $4.6 billion in 2013 to roughly $5.5 billion in 2014 due to lower expenses for the year. (Both these 2014 totals represented company milestones.)

The historic growth for 2014 was mainly due to a 13% increase in Commercial Airplanes revenues thanks to higher new airplane deliveries across all programs. Sales from Africa skyrocketed by more than 300% from 2013 to 2014. Other markets with rising sales included Europe (12%) Canada (28%) Oceania (6%) and China (4%). These increases were offset by a 12% drop in Military Aircraft sales during 2014.

Being's operating cash flow has also exploded over the last four years climbing from $2.95 billion in 2010 to nearly $8.7 billion in 2014.

Strategy

The key component for Boeing's growth involves the much anticipated launching of its fleet of 787 Dreamliner jets. Throughout 2012 and early 2013 the jets were plagued with problems regarding the plane's battery system. The Dreamliner is the first plane in the world to use lithium-ion batteries which are lighter hold more power and are able to recharge more quickly. Throughout 2013 Boeing tested out the new battery system's design in hopes of the fleet restarting commercial flights within the year.

Flight testing of the 787-9 Dreamliner variant occurred in 2014 and its first delivery was in mid-2014. The 787-10 is on plan for first delivery in 2018 and will incorporate a high degree of shared design elements and parts commonality with the 787-9 to likewise minimize risk and lower development and fleet maintenance costs. The 777X (Boeing's newest twin-engine jet with 12% lower fuel consumption and 10% lower operating costs than its competitors) is slated for firm configuration in 2015 and first delivery in 2020.

Another essential part of Boeing's strategy is winning US government contracts which typically accounts for nearly 35% of the company's revenues each year. Boeing in 2011 was awarded a $35 billion contract for aerial refueling tankers from the US Air Force. The contract could be the largest awarded for some time as the Department of Defense faces budgetary constraints over the next 10 years.

Because of cutbacks the DoD is shifting course by shrinking ground forces and putting more emphasis on C4ISR (Command Control Communications Computers Intelligence Surveillance and Reconnaissance) cyber and space technologies special operations and unmanned airborne systems (UAS). Boeing is aligning with this shift by making investments and acquisitions that enhance its capabilities in these areas.

Mergers and Acquisitions

In 2014 the company acquired Ventura Solutions a hardware and software engineering company that provides custom products and services for government customers. Ventura will operate as part of Boeing Network & Space Systems. Also in 2014 Boeing picked up AerData Group B.V. a Netherlands-based provider of integrated software products for lease management engine fleet planning and records management. AerData's products will become part of Boeing Edge an integrated suite of aviation services.

Boeing in 2013 acquired CPU Technology's Acalis business in a deal that helped Boeing address its global customers' need to protect warfighters from information-assurance attacks. Acalis microprocessors contain hardware and software that can guard mission-critical onboard systems in Boeing platforms. The acquisition was part of Boeing's strategy of increasing its vertical depth to differentiate its offerings and provide value for its global aerospace and defense customers.

HISTORY

Bill Boeing who had already made his fortune in Washington real estate built his first airplane in 1916 with naval officer Conrad Westervelt. His Seattle company Pacific Aero Products changed its name to Boeing Airplane Company the next year. During WWI Boeing built training planes for the US Navy and began the first international airmail service (between Seattle and Victoria British Columbia). The company added a Chicago-San Francisco route in 1927 and established an airline subsidiary Boeing Air Transport. The airline's success was aided by Boeing's Model 40A the first plane to use Frederick Rentschler's new air-cooled engine.

Rentschler and Boeing combined their companies as United Aircraft and Transport in 1929 and introduced the all-metal airliner in 1933. The next year new antitrust rules forced United Aircraft and Transportation to sell portions of its operations as United Air Lines and United Aircraft (later United Technologies). This left Boeing Airplane (as it was known until 1961) with the manufacturing concerns.

EXECUTIVES

Vice President Supplier Management, Stanley (Stan) Deal

Senior Vice President Government Operations, Timothy J (Tim) Keating

Vice President Of Business Development, Jeff Trauberman

President Shared Services Group, Robert J. (Rob) Pasterick, age 59

SVP Engineering Operations and Technology and CTO, John J. Tracy, age 60, $623,089 total compensation

EVP and General Counsel, J. Michael (Mike) Luttig, age 60, $877,480 total compensation

Vice Chairman and President and CEO Commercial Airplanes, Raymond L. (Ray) Conner, age 59, $1,002,500 total compensation

President CEO and Director, Dennis A. Muilenburg, age 51, $1,135,389 total compensation

President Boeing Military Aircraft Boeing Defense Space & Security, Christopher M. (Chris) Chadwick, age 54

President Phantom Works Boeing Defense Space and Security, Darryl W. Davis

President Network and Space Systems Boeing Defense Space & Security, Craig R. Cooning

SVP Global Sales and Marketing, John Wojick

EVP Business Development and Strategy and CFO, Gregory D. (Greg) Smith, age 48, $809,231 total compensation

President BDS DevelopmentBoeing Defense Space & Security, James (Jim) O'Neill

President Boeing Military Aircraft Boeing Defense Space and Security, Shelley K. Lavender, age 51

SVP and President Boeing International, Bertrand-Marc (Marc) Allen, age 41

CIO, Ted Colbert

President Boeing Capital Corporation, Timothy Myers

President Global Services and Support (GS&S) Boeing Defense Space and Security, Leanne Caret

President Spectrolab Inc., Tony Mueller

V Pres, Todd Fleming

Vice President Brand Management and Advertising, Anne Toulouse

Vice President Sales Latin America and Africa, Ihssane Mounir

Executive Vice President, Gary Fitzmire

Vice President Engineering and Technology, Daryl Pelc

Vice President IT Product Systems Boeing Company, Nancy Bailey

Executive Vice President, Michael Caimona

Vice President Information Systems, Terry Samford

Vice President Business Development, Pam Carter

Senior Vice President Of Software Technology, Norman Cole

Vice President Global Trade Services, Haynes Arnett

Boeing Vice President of Leasing Sales, Bill Collins

Vice President 787 Derivatives, Mark Jenks

Vice President Of Information Solutions, Dewey Houck

Vice President, Ronald (Ron) Hinderberger

Vice President, Karen Tang

Vice President Of International Finance, Darcel Stewart

Vice President Of Boeing, Richard (Dick) Milford

Vice President Marketing and Finance, Jose Hernandez

Vice President Financial Planning and Analysis, Diana Sands

Regional Vice President, David Cazer

Vice President Of Strategic Development, Bill Bonadio

Vice President Human Resources, Grace Miller

Senior Vice President, Marilyn R Gamblin

Vice President Of Business Development, Pat Schondel

Executive Vice President, Pete Desalvo

Vice President, Darcel Wesen

Vice President, Bonnie Christianson

Executive Vice President Marketing, Seddik Belyamani

Vice President Investor Relations, Stephanie Pope

Vice President Of Site Services, Larry Edwards

Vice President Finance, Ming Zhou

Vice President general Manager Supplier Management Commercial Airplanes, Kent Fisher

Vice President Of Corporate Strategy, Rik Geiersbach

Vice President Fleet Management Commercial Aviation Services, Jay Maloney

Vice President And General Manager, Debra Rub-Zenko

Vice President Strategy and Business Development, Winslow Farrell

Vice President Sales, Mitzy Gough

Vice President, Jeff Geear

Vice President Customer Support, Kausar Talat

Executive Vice President, George Ward

National Account Manager, Jacqueline Stephenson

Senior Vice President, George Smith

Vice President, Phyllis Ditocco

Vice President, Paula Nosca-lay

Vice President Sales, Brent Bogar

Vice President Air Traffic Management, Kevin Brown

Vice President Administration And Corporate Secretary, Kevin Pilgrim

Vice President Of Business Development, Jeffrey Kohler

Vice President of Finance for Airplane Programs, Rick Gross

Vice President Product Development, Elizabeth Lund

Vice President, James Hoskinson

Vice President of Sales for Digital Division, Keith P White

Vice President Customer Support Americas, Larry Slate

Vice President Business Development, Doug Miller

Vice President Business Systems and Administration, Renee L Stober

Vice President Communications Government Operations, Gordon Johndroe

Vice President, Darrel Roby

Vice President and Program Manager Commercial Programs, John (Jack) Mulholland

Vice President And Managing Director, Mike Kurth

Vice President, Barbara Disser

Vice President Sales, Van Gallard

Vice President Engineering Structures Integrated Defense Systems, William (Bill) Carrier

Vice President Environmental Health and Safety Affairs, Lisa F Lockett

Vice President Customer Support Europe Russia and Central Asia, Todd Nelp

Vice President Chief Project Engineer and Deputy Program Manager, Michael (Mel) Teal

Vice President, Jay Byunn

Vice President Of Supplier Management, Jim Wigfall

Vice President, Garth S Williams

Vice President, Robert Noel

Vice President Business Development, Christopher Raymond

Vice President Information Technology Strategic Capture and Campaigns, John (Jack) Bruns

Vice President, Brett Fischer

Vice President, Tim Sele

Vice President Accounting And Financial Reporting, Michael (Mel) Cleary

Vice President, Randy Woolard

Vice President, Bruce Dennis

Vice President, Tobias Bright

Vice President Of Compliance, Frederick Shaheen

Vice President Engineering, Bruce Deshetler

Executive Vice President Global Franchise Development, Rich Hoffman

Vice President And General Manager, Kim Pastega

Vice President Information Services, Per Noren

Vice President And Chief Project Engineer, Bruce Dickinson

Executive Vice President, Sudhakar Shetty

Vice President Technical Director, Thomas Schultz

Machined Parts Finisher Vice President Ecf 2009., Geri Marquardt

Senior Vice President of International Relations, Thomas (Thom) Pickering

Vice President Supply Chain, Ken Shaw

Vice President General Manager Mobility Division, Jean Chamberlin
Vice President of Sales and Marketing, Harry W Gray
Vice President Of Business Development, Dawn Harms
Vice President Airplane Development Finance, Jon Emery
Vice President Government Affairs, Arthur McEntire
Capital Vice President For Asia And, Foster Arata
Vice President of Commercial Airplane Sales, Ken Schultz
Vice President, Alex Lopez
Vice President P 8 Program, Rick Heerdt
Vice President Commu, James Schlueter
Vice President Communications Washington D.C. Operations, Maureen P Cragin
Executive Vice President, James (Jamie) Bell
Senior Vice President Communications, Tom Downey
Vice President Business Development ARMY Systems, Leo Brooks
Senior Vice President Public Policy, Tim Keating
Vice President Senior Technical Analyst, David (Dave) Gigrich
Vice President Air Force Precision En, Jack Catton
Vice President, Stan Deal
Vice President Global Corporate Citizenship, Lianne Stein
Vice President Operations 737 Program, Lindblad Eric
Vice President, Shelly Huff
Vice President Boeing Military Aircraft Saudi Arabia, Gene Cunningham
Vice President General Manager Airplane Development Commercial Airplanes, Scott Fancher
Ipsec VPN Product Manager, Stephen (Steve) Hatch
Chairman, W. James (Jim) McNerney, age 65
Board Member, Mary Dowell
Board Member, Jack Commerford
Board Member, Bill Crawford
Secretary, Mark Little
Assistant Treasurer, Ruud Roggekamp
Secretary, Kandice Taylor
Treasurer, Renee Jarvi
Secretary, Bruce Cadiz
Board Member, James Powers
Board Member, Daniel Anderson
Assistant Treasurer, Verett Mims
Assistant Treasurer Risk Management and Insurance, Michael (Mel) Tarling
Board Member, Guy Johnson
Board Member, Nancy Kaatman
Board Member, Thi Tran
Board Member, Scott Bovard
Board Member, Gina Breukelman
Auditors: DELOITTE & TOUCHE LLP

LOCATIONS

HQ: Boeing Co. (The)
  100 North Riverside Plaza, Chicago, IL 60606-1596
Phone: 312 544-2000
Web: www.boeing.com

2013 Sales

	$ mil.	% of total
US	37,592	43
Asia		
China	10,555	14
Other Asia	12,200	12
Europe	10,622	12
Middle East	9,165	11
Oceania	1	2
Canada	1,486	2
Latin American Caribbean & other	2,725	3
Africa	621	1
Total	**86,623**	**100**

PRODUCTS/OPERATIONS

2013 Sales

	$ mil.	% of total
Commercial Airplanes	52,981	61
Defense Space & Security		
Military Aircraft	15,936	18
Global Services & Support	8,749	10
Network & Space Systems	8,512	10
Boeing Capital	408	1
Other	102	-
Adjustments	(65)	-
Total	**86,623**	**100**

Selected Products and Services

Commercial Airplanes
Products
  737 Next Generation (short-to-medium-range two-engine jet)
  747 (long-range four-engine jet)
  767 (medium-to-long-range two-engine jet)
  777 (long-range two-engine jet)
  Boeing Business Jet
  787 Dreamliner (in development; long-range super-efficient 200-250 passenger capacity)
  747-8 (in development;
Services
  Engineering modification and logistics
  Maintenance repair and overhaul
  Boeing Training & Flight Services
Defense Space & Security
  Military Aircraft
  AH-64 Apache
  B-1B Lancer
  B-2 Spirit
  F/A-18 Hornet
  F-15E Strike Eagle
  F-22 Raptor
  T-45 Flight Training System
  A160 Hummingbird
  Harpoon
  Insitu
  C-17 Globemaster III
  CH-47D/F Chinook
  V-22 Osprey
  Global Services & Support
  Integrated logistics
  Maintenance modifications and upgrades
  Training systems
  Government services
  Network & Space Systems
  Electronic and mission
  Cyber security
  Infrastructure
  Intelligence
  Logistics command and control
  Satellite and ground operations
  Space exploration

COMPETITORS

AgustaWestland	General Dynamics
Airbus	Kaman
Airbus Group	Lockheed Martin
BAE SYSTEMS	Northrop Grumman
Bombardier	Raytheon
COMAC	Rockwell Collins
Dassault Aviation	Textron
Embraer	Thales
Finmeccanica	United Technologies
GE Aviation	

HISTORICAL FINANCIALS

Company Type: Public

Income Statement

FYE: December 31

	REVENUE ($ mil.)	NET INCOME ($ mil.)	NET PROFIT MARGIN	EMPLOYEES
12/15	96,114	5,176	5.4%	161,400
12/14	90,762	5,446	6.0%	165,500
12/13	86,623	4,585	5.3%	168,400
12/12	81,698	3,900	4.8%	174,400
12/11	68,735	4,018	5.8%	171,700
Annual Growth	**8.7%**	**6.5%**	**—**	**(1.5%)**

2015 Year-End Financials

Debt ratio: 10.55%
Return on equity: 69.01%
Cash ($ mil.): 11,302
Current ratio: 1.35
Long-term debt ($ mil.): 8,730
No. of shares (mil.): 666
Dividends
  Yield: 2.5%
  Payout: 45.7%
Market value ($ mil.): 96,387

	STOCK PRICE ($) FY Close	P/E High/Low	PER SHARE ($) Earnings	Dividends	Book Value
12/15	144.59	21 17	7.44	3.64	9.50
12/14	129.98	19 16	7.38	2.92	12.26
12/13	136.49	23 12	5.96	1.94	19.90
12/12	75.36	15 13	5.11	1.76	7.76
12/11	73.35	15 11	5.34	1.68	4.72
Annual Growth	**18.5%**	**— —**	**8.6%**	**21.3%**	**19.1%**

BofI Holding, Inc.

BofI Holding owns Bank of Internet USA a savings bank that operates online in all 50 states. The bank offers checking savings and money market accounts CDs and ATM and check cards. Multifamily real estate loans account for nearly two-thirds of the company's loan portfolio althoughÂ the bankÂonly offers them in selected states; it also acquires them on the secondary market. Offered nationwide single-family residential mortgages make up nearly 30% of its loan portfolio. Bank of Internet USA also issues homeÂequity automobileÂand recreational vehicle loans. Officers and directors own more than 30% of BofI Holding's stock.

EXECUTIVES

EVP and CFO, Andrew J. Micheletti, age 56, $220,000 total compensation
President and CEO, Gregory Garrabrants, age 44, $375,000 total compensation
EVP Specialty Finance and Chief Legal Officer, Eshel Bar-Adon, $205,000 total compensation
EVP and Chief Credit Officer, Thomas Constantine, $205,000 total compensation
EVP and Chief Lending Officer, Brian Swanson, age 35, $185,000 total compensation
Senior Vice President, Jason Kenoyer
Vice President CONTROLLER, Pete Bauer
Chairman, Theodore C. (Ted) Allrich, age 69
Vice Chairman, Nicholas A. Mosich
Auditors: BDO USA, LLP

LOCATIONS

HQ: BofI Holding, Inc.
  4350 La Jolla Village Drive, Suite 140, San Diego, CA 92122
Phone: 858 350-6200
Web: www.bofiholding.com

COMPETITORS

Bank of America	ISN Bank
Citigroup	MUFG Americas Holdings
E*TRADE Bank	Steel Partners
First IB	Holdings

HISTORICAL FINANCIALS
Company Type: Public

Income Statement
FYE: June 30

	ASSETS ($ mil.)	NET INCOME ($ mil.)	INCOME AS % OF ASSETS	EMPLOYEES
06/15	5,823	82	1.4%	467
06/14	4,403	55	1.3%	366
06/13	3,090	40	1.3%	312
06/12	2,386	29	1.2%	230
06/11	1,940	20	1.1%	173
Annual Growth	31.6%	41.6%	—	28.2%

2015 Year-End Financials

Debt ratio: 0.09%	No. of shares (mil.): 62
Return on equity: 18.29%	Dividends
Cash ($ mil.): 222	Yield: —
Current ratio: —	Payout: —
Long-term debt ($ mil.): —	Market value ($ mil.): 6,562

	STOCK PRICE ($) FY Close	P/E High/Low	PER SHARE ($) Earnings	Dividends	Book Value
06/15	105.71	79 49	1.34	0.00	8.59
06/14	73.47	109 48	0.96	0.00	6.41
06/13	45.82	65 26	0.72	0.00	4.88
06/12	19.76	32 20	0.58	0.00	4.49
06/11	14.41	36 24	0.47	0.00	3.54
Annual Growth	64.6%	— —	30.2%	—	24.8%

BOK Financial Corp.

Will your money BOK? Multibank holding company BOK Financial tries to make sure it is. With seven principal banking divisions in eight midwestern and southwestern states BOK offers a range of financial services to consumers and regional businesses. In addition to traditional deposit lending and trust services the banks provide investment management wealth advisory and mineral and real estate management services through a network of about 200 branches in Arizona Arkansas Colorado Kansas Missouri New Mexico Oklahoma and Texas. Brokerage subsidiary BOSC underwrites public private and municipal securities. BOK also owns electronic funds network TransFund and institutional asset manager Cavanal Hill.

Geographic Reach

Tulsa-based BOK Financial offers full service banking in Arizona northwest Arkansas Colorado Kansas Missouri New Mexico Oklahoma and Texas. Oklahoma is the company's largest market. Indeed BOK is the largest financial institution in Oklahoma with 14% of the state's total deposits. Bank of Oklahoma has 31% and 11% of the market share in the Tulsa and Oklahoma City areas respectively.

Financial Performance

BOK's revenue declined by nearly 7% in 2013 versus 2012 to $1.36 billion on a continuing slide in interest revenue and lower fees and commissions on mortgages. Trust fees and commissions were up $16 million (20%) and transaction card revenue was up $8.8 million over the prior year. Net income declined by 10% over the same period to $316.6 million on higher operating expenses for personnel and data processing and communications. Loan volume increased for the third consecutive year while nonperforming assets continued their steady decline.

Strategy

BOK emphasizes local decision-making at its flagship subsidiary Bank of Oklahoma and its operating divisions Bank of Texas Bank of Albuquerque Bank of Arkansas Colorado State Bank Bank of Kansas City and Bank of Arizona. Commercial loans primarily to the energy services health care and wholesale and retail industries make up the majority of the company's loan portfolio. Commercial real estate residential mortgage car and consumer loans round out its lending activities.

With nearly half of its business in its home state of Oklahoma BOK is looking to metropolitans areas such as Dallas/Fort Worth Houston Denver Kansas City and Phoenix for expansion either through acquisitions or by opening new branches. In 2013 Bank of Kansas City continued to grow in the Kansas City market with a new full-service banking center there as well as a wealth management and mortgage office.

The company is also focused on diversifying its revenue stream by growing its mortgage banking brokerage and wealth management operations. (In 2012 it acquired Denver-based The Milestone Group which oversees some $1.3 billion for wealthy investors.)

Mergers and Acquisitions

In March 2014 BOK acquired GTRUST Financial Corp. an independent trust and asset management company in Topeka Kansas. The acquisition added $600 million in assets to BOK's wealth management business and extended its product offering and client base in the Kansas market. In April 2014 the firm bought MBM Advisors a Houston-based independent full service retirement and pension plan investment firm and SEC registered investment adviser. The purchase increased BOK's retirement and assets under management by $1.25 billion while expanding its wealth management capabilities and presence in Houston.

EXECUTIVES

Senior Executive Vice President of Bank of Oklahoma, Steven (Steve) Bradshaw
Senior Vice President, Charlie Anderson
Vice President of Operations, Miriam Bywater
Executive Vice President Consumer Banking, Patrick (Paddy) Piper
Vice President Senior Petroleum Engineer, Sterling Kirk Condry
Assistant Vice President Project Manager II Operations, Michael (Mel) Vegher
Vice President Corporate Sourcing Services, James Leblanc
Vice President, Jim Summers
Vice President, Marcia Estes
Assistant Vice President Appraisal Rev, Mary Engleman
Senior Vice President, Pam Schloeder
Senior Vice President, Guy Evangelista
Vice President Help Desk, Blu Bean
Vice President Production, Kathy Davis
Vice President of Community Development Group, Paula Bryant-Ellis
Senior Vice President, Michael Bickel
Vice President Risk Management And Compliance Officer, Matthew (Matt) Ruth
Senior Vice President Information Technology, Jane (Ginny) Romine
Senior Vice President Of Information Security, Brian Foster
Vice President, Alice Worthington
Senior Vice President Credit Administration, Carol Cable
Senior Vice President, Lee Allen
Vice President And Fraud Investigator, Danial Warma
Vice President Business Performance Measurement, Richard (Dick) Hubbard

Senior Vice President Institutional Investments BOSC, Michael (Mel) Brown
Vice President, Debi Briscoe
Vice President Consumer Compliance, Dean Miller
Vice President of Corporate Recruiting Banking and Finance, Roxanna Maciel
Auditors: Ernst & Young LLP

LOCATIONS

HQ: BOK Financial Corp.
Bank of Oklahoma Tower, Boston Avenue at Second Street, Tulsa, OK 74172
Phone: 918 588-6000
Web: www.bokf.com

PRODUCTS/OPERATIONS

2013 Sales

	$ mil.	% of total
Interest		
Loans	498	38
Available-for-sale securities	207	15
Other	39	2
Noninterest		
Brokerage & trading	125	9
Mortgage banking	121	9
Transaction card revenue	116	8
Trust fees and commissions	96	6
Deposit service charges and fees	95	6
Bank-owned life insurance	10	3
Other	48	4
Total	1,359	100

Selected Banking Subsidiaries

Bank of Albuquerque National Association
Bank of Arizona National Association
Bank of Arkansas National Association
Bank of Kansas City National Association
Bank of Oklahoma National Association
Bank of Texas National Association
Colorado State Bank & Trust

COMPETITORS

BBVA Compass Bancshares	First National of Nebraska
Bank of America	JPMorgan Chase
Bank of the West	Regions Financial
CoBiz Financial	UMB Financial
Comerica	Wells Fargo
Commerce Bancshares	Zions Bancorporation

HISTORICAL FINANCIALS
Company Type: Public

Income Statement
FYE: December 31

	ASSETS ($ mil.)	NET INCOME ($ mil.)	INCOME AS % OF ASSETS	EMPLOYEES
12/14	29,089	292	1.0%	4,743
12/13	27,015	316	1.2%	4,632
12/12	28,148	351	1.2%	4,704
12/11	25,493	285	1.1%	4,511
12/10	23,941	246	1.0%	4,432
Annual Growth	5.0%	4.3%	—	1.7%

2014 Year-End Financials

Debt ratio: 1.30%	No. of shares (mil.): 69
Return on equity: 9.25%	Dividends
Cash ($ mil.): 2,475	Yield: 2.7%
Current ratio: —	Payout: 37.2%
Long-term debt ($ mil.): —	Market value ($ mil.): 4,150

	STOCK PRICE ($)	P/E	PER SHARE ($)		
	FY Close	High/Low	Earnings	Dividends	Book Value
12/14	60.04	17 14	4.22	1.62	47.78
12/13	66.32	15 12	4.59	1.54	43.86
12/12	54.46	12 10	5.13	2.47	43.29
12/11	54.93	13 11	4.17	1.13	40.36
12/10	53.40	15 12	3.61	0.99	36.97
Annual Growth	3.0%	— —	4.0%	13.1%	6.6%

Booz Allen Hamilton Holding Corp.

For almost a century consultants at Booz Allen Hamilton have been helping US government agencies operate more efficiently at home and abroad. The firm provides a wide range of management consulting and technology integration services; its specialties include information technology operations organization and change program management strategy training programs and systems engineering. Booz Allen has long-established relationships with such agencies as the Department of Defense the Federal Aviation Administration and the Internal Revenue Service. Investment firm The Carlyle Group owns a majority interest in the consulting firm which was founded in 1914.

Geographic Reach

Booz Allen Hamilton's headquarters are located in McLean Virginia. The firm also has offices in Annapolis Junction Maryland; Rockville Maryland; San Diego California; Herndon Virginia and Washington D.C. It opened an office in Singapore during 2015 that will serve as the firm's base for operations in Southeast Asia.

Sales and Marketing

Besides the US defense industry and its other major government clients the firm serves customers in the financial services healthcare energy retail and automotive markets.

Financial Performance

The firm's revenue has been decreasing in the last three fiscal years. Its revenue decreased by 4% to $5.48 billion during fiscal 2014 compared to $5.48 billion in fiscal 2013. The drop was primarily due to lower demand primarily driven by challenges in the federal government spending environment.

Booz Allen Hamilton's net income has been fluctuating in recent fiscal years. Its net income was $232.19 million in fiscal 2014. That was an increase compared to the prior fiscal period.

Strategy

The consulting firm plans to continue to grow its client base (about 1200 in the US operating under more than 5800 contracts) across a wide spectrum of government agencies and departments. Though almost entirely focused on US government clients (98% of revenue) Booz Allen undertakes a variety of engagements. Key markets include civil government agencies responsible for energy finance health and transportation as well as defense and national security agencies.

Booz Allen is also focused on enhancing its cyber-security products and services in the commercial market.

Mergers and Acquisitions

During fiscal 2014 the firm acquired Boston-based Epidemico. Epidemico is an informatics company providing early insights continuous monitoring and consumer engagement for varied aspects of population health. Also that year Booz Allen Hamilton acquired a Baltimore-based healthcare unit of Genova Technologies.

HISTORY

Edwin Booz graduated from Northwestern University in 1914 with degrees in economics and psychology and started a statistical analysis firm in Chicago. After serving in the army during WWI he returned to his firm renamed Edwin Booz Surveys. In 1925 Booz hired his first full-time assistant George Fry and in 1929 he hired a second James Allen. By then the company had a long list of clients including U.S. Gypsum the Chicago Tribune and Montgomery Ward which was losing a retail battle with Sears Roebuck and Co.

In 1935 Carl Hamilton joined the partnership and a year later it was renamed Booz Fry Allen & Hamilton. The firm prospered well into the next decade by providing advice based on "independence that enables us to say plainly from the outside what cannot always be said safely from within" according to a company brochure.

During WWII the firm worked increasingly on government and military contracts. Fry opposed the pursuit of such work for consultants and left in 1942. The firm was renamed Booz Allen & Hamilton. Hamilton died in 1946 and the following year Booz retired (he died in 1951) leaving Allen as chairman. He successfully steered the firm into lucrative postwar work for clients such as Johnson Wax RCA and the US Air Force.

A separate company Booz Allen Applied Research Inc. (BAARINC) was formed in 1955 for technical and government consulting including missile and weaponry work as well as consulting with NASA. By the end of the decade Time had dubbed Booz Allen "the world's largest most prestigious management consultant firm." The partnership was incorporated as a private company in 1962 and in 1967 commissioner Pete Rozelle requested its services for the merger of the National Football League and American Football League.

When Allen retired in 1970 Charlie Bowen became the new chairman and the company went public. However as the economy stalled during the energy crisis spending for consultants plunged. Jim Farley replaced Bowen in 1975 and the company was taken private again in 1976. A turnaround was engineered and the firm was soon helping Chrysler through its 1979 bailout and developing strategies for the breakup of AT&T in 1984.

Booz Allen again experienced trouble in the 1980s after Farley instituted a competition to select his successor. Michael McCullough was eventually chosen in 1984 but the 10-month election process turned into a dogfight that pitted partner against partner taking an enormous toll on morale. McCullough began restructuring the firm along industry lines creating a department store of services in an industry characterized by boutique houses. The turmoil was too much and by 1988 nearly a third of the partners had quit.

William Stasior became chairman in 1991 and reorganized Booz Allen yet again splitting it down public and private sector lines. Allen died in 1992 the same year the firm moved to McLean Virginia. The company began privatization work in the former Soviet Union and in Eastern Europe in 1992 and continued to emphasize government business including contracts with the IRS (1995) for technology modernization and with the General Services Administration (1996) to provide technical and management support for all federal telecommunications users.

In 1998 the company won a 10-year $200 million contract with the US Defense Department to establish a scientific and technical data warehouse. Ralph Shrader was appointed CEO in early 1999; Stasior retired as chairman later that year. Booz Allen acquired Scandinavian consulting firm Carta in 1999 and formed a venture capital firm for startups with Lehman Brothers in 2000. The company announced in late 2000 that it would spin off Aestix its e-commerce business but reconsidered amid a general economic slowdown and hostile IPO market. (The unit was integrated back into Booz Allen in 2002.)

Booz Allen saw an increase in work related to defense and national security after the terrorist attacks of September 11 2001. Engagements included work related to the reconstruction of Iraq (as a subcontractor on telecommunications projects managed by Lucent) and in 2003 Booz Allen was awarded a contract from the US Health Resources and Services Administration to help establish and operate a bioterrorism technical support center.

In 2008 Booz Allen spun off its commercial consulting business as an independent firm Booz & Company. The spinoff was part of a transaction in which investment firm The Carlyle Group acquired a controlling interest in the Booz Allen's government-related consulting business which retained the Booz Allen name.

Striving to alleviate debt Booz Allen launched an initial public offering on the New York Stock Exchange in November 2010.

EXECUTIVES

Executive Vice President, David Aldrich
Senior Vice President, Gary Rahl
EVP Middle East and North Africa (MENA), Nabih Maroun
EVP Systems Delivery Business, Gary D. Labovich
SVP, Reggie Van Lee
President and CEO, Horacio D. Rozanski, age 47, $1,050,000 total compensation
EVP Operations Defense Group, Ronald T. (Ron) Kadish, age 66
EVP Justice and Homeland Security Business, Thad W. Allen
EVP Air Force Materiel Command Air Force Space Command and Missile Defense, Henry A. (Trey) Obering
EVP Civil Health Business, Nancy Hardwick
SVP, Gary D. Mather
EVP Civil and Commercial Group, Lloyd W. Howell, age 53
EVP Chief Administrative Officer (CAO) and Chief Information Security Officer (CISO) and, Joseph W. (Joe) Mahaffee, age 58
EVP International Business, John D. (Jack) Mayer, age 69, $825,000 total compensation
EVP and Client Service Officer Justice and Homeland Security and Transportation (JHT), Michael M. (Mike) Thomas
EVP Justice and Homeland Security Business, Patrick F. Peck, age 57
VP, Fred K. Blackburn
EVP Defense and Intelligence Group Systems Delivery, Gary C. Cubbage
VP, Karen Dahut
VP, Maria Darby
EVP Environment Energy Installations and Facilities and Military Health Business, Judith H. (Judi) Dotson
EVP Strategic Innovation Group, Michael A. Farber
VP, Laurene (Laurie) Gallo
VP, Patricia Goforth
EVP Defense Business, Tom Greenspon
EVP and Client Service Officer (CSO) Air Force Business, Gregory Harrison
EVP International Business, Michael W. (Mike) Jones
EVP Strategic Innovation Group, David Kletter

EVP Military Intelligence and Cybersecurity
  Business, Christopher Ling
EVP Defense and Intelligence Group, Joseph (Joe)
  Logue, age 50, $1,050,000 total compensation
EVP Emerging Technologies and Mission
  Solutions, Angela M. (Angie) Messer
EVP Navy and Marine Corp, Anthony (Tony) Mitchell
EVP Health Business, Susan L. Penfield
VP, Robin L. Portman
EVP Engineering, Joseph F. (Joe) Sifer
EVP Unified Combatant Commands, Ted Sniffin
VP, William Stewart
EVP Advanced Engineering and Rapid
  Prototyping, Bill A. Thoet
EVP and Chief Personnel Officer, Betty Thompson
EVP Commercial Business, Emile Trombetti
VP Advanced Enterprise Integration, Gregory G.
  (Greg) Wenzel
VP, Christopher Pierce
EVP Signals Intelligence (SIGINT) Technical
  Analysis, James Allen
EVP National Agencies Account Defense
  Business, Joan A. Dempsey
EVP Booz Allen Engineering Services (BES) and
  Foreign Military Sales (FMS), Lee Wilbur
EVP Civil Health Business, Kristine Martin
  Anderson
SVP CFO and Treasurer, Kevin Cook
EVP and General Counsel, Nancy Laben
EVP System Delivery Business, Jim Summers
VP and CIO, Kevin Winter
EVP Energy Chemicals and Utilities, Walid Fayad
EVP Middle East and North Africa, Ramez Shehadi
EVP Command Control Communications
  Computers Intelligence Surveillance and
  Reconnaissance (C4ISR), Steve Soules
Vice President, Sarah St Clair
Vice President Human Resources, Marianne Malizia
Vice President, Laplante Larry
Senior Management (Senior Vice President
  General Manager Director), Jonathan (Jon) Allen
Vice President, Jeff Fossum
Vice President, Bill Ott
Vice President, Kevin Vigilante
Vice President, Theodore (Theo) Kraemer
Vice President, Tom Moorman
Vice President, Michael Orozco
Vice President, Ralph Lawrence
Vice President, Souheil Moukaddem
Vice President, Lucy Stribley
Vice President, Lutfi Zakhour
Vice President, Danny Karam
Vice President, Adham Sleiman
Vice President, Donald Busson
Vice President, Fady Kassatly
Vice President, Josh Sullivan
Admin Vice President Information Technology,
  Lori Jones
Vice President, Timothy Andrews
Second Vice President, Chris Galanty
Senior Vice President, Corrine Kosar
Vice President, J Neely
Vice President, Chris Pierce
Vice President Sales And Marketing, Scott Barr
Vice President Based, Robert Ramseur
Vice President, Stephen Moore
Vice President, Ken Wiegand
Senior Vice President, Leslie Difonzo
Senior Vice President, Susan Lawrence
Vice President Technical Services, Felix Yao
Senior Vice President, George Schu
Vice President, Terry Thompson
Vice President, Kristine Rohls
Vice President, Michael Isman
Executive Vice President and the Chief
  Information Security Officer, Joe Mahaffee
Vice President, Dov S Zakheim
Vice President of Information Technology, Joe
  Sifer
Senior Vice President, Elizabeth (Beth) Thompson

Vice President, Scott Welles
Vice President, Rob Silverman
Vice President, Ken Mills
Senior Vice President, Stephen (Steve) Soules
Chairman, Ralph W. Shrader, age 71
Chapter Treasurer, Michelle (Mitch) Boucher
Board Member, Dennis Gibson
Auditors: Ernst & Young LLP

LOCATIONS

HQ: Booz Allen Hamilton Holding Corp.
  8283 Greensboro Drive, McLean, VA 22102
Phone: 703 902-5000
Web: www.boozallen.com

PRODUCTS/OPERATIONS

Selected Markets Served
Civil government
  Benefits and entitlements
  Federal finance
  International development and diplomacy
Defense
  Air Force
  Army
  Joint staff and combatant commands
  Navy and Marine Corps
  Office of the Secretary of Defense and defense agencies
  Space
Energy
Environment
Health
  Health informatics
  Health not-for-profit/nongovernmental organizations
  International public health
  US public health
Homeland security
Intelligence
Law enforcement
Not-for-profit/nongovernmental organizations
Transportation
  Aviation infrastructure
  Highways and automotive technology
  Passenger rail and mass transit

Selected Practice Areas
Assurance and resilience
Economic and business analysis
Information technology
Modeling and simulation
Organization and strategy
Supply chain and logistics
Systems engineering and integration

COMPETITORS

A.T. Kearney	IBM
Accenture	L-3 Communications
BAE SYSTEMS	Leidos
Bain & Company	Lockheed Martin
Boeing	MAXIMUS
Boston Consulting	ManTech
CACI International	McKinsey & Company
Capgemini	Northrop Grumman
Computer Sciences	PA Consulting
Corp.	PRTM Management
Deloitte Consulting	Raytheon
General Dynamics	Unisys
HP Enterprise Services	

HISTORICAL FINANCIALS

Company Type: Public

Income Statement

FYE: March 31

	REVENUE ($ mil.)	NET INCOME ($ mil.)	NET PROFIT MARGIN	EMPLOYEES
03/15	5,274	232	4.4%	22,500
03/14	5,478	232	4.2%	22,700
03/13	5,758	219	3.8%	24,500
03/12	5,859	239	4.1%	25,000
03/11	5,591	84	1.5%	25,000
Annual Growth	(1.4%)	28.7%	—	(2.6%)

2015 Year-End Financials

Debt ratio: 56.52%
Return on equity: 129.88%
Cash ($ mil.): 207
Current ratio: 1.37
Long-term debt ($ mil.): 1,569
No. of shares (mil.): 149
Dividends
  Yield: 5.0%
  Payout: 94.8%
Market value ($ mil.): 4,315

	STOCK PRICE ($) FY Close	P/E High/Low	PER SHARE ($) Earnings	Dividends	Book Value
03/15	28.94	19 13	1.52	1.46	1.25
03/14	22.00	14 8	1.54	2.40	1.15
03/13	13.44	12 8	1.45	8.36	1.55
03/12	17.03	11 7	1.70	0.09	8.31
03/11	18.01	27 24	0.66	0.00	6.47
Annual Growth	12.6%	— —	23.2%	—(33.7%)	

BorgWarner Inc

If suburbanites need four-wheel-drive vehicles to turbocharge their urban drive that's OK with Borg-Warner. The company is a leading maker of engine and drivetrain products for the world's major automotive manufacturers. Products include turbochargers air pumps timing chain systems four-wheel-drive and all-wheel-drive transfer cases (primarily for light trucks and SUVs) and transmission components. Its largest customers include Volkswagen Ford and Daimler. The company nets around 75% of sales from outside the US; more than half come from its European operations.

Geographic Reach

BorgWarner operates nearly 60 manufacturing and technical facilities in some 20 countries (including more than a dozen in the US and about half a dozen each in Germany China and South Korea). Europe is by far BorgWarner's largest market; Germany accounts for roughly 25% of total sales and Hungary and France collectively account for 11%. The US generates around 25% of its sales with South Korea and China combined representing almost 20%.

Operations

BorgWarner divides its operations into the two segments of engine products (about 70% of total sales) and drivetrain products (about 30%). The engine group optimizes engines for fuel efficiency reduced emissions and enhanced performance and includes engine timing systems boosting systems ignition systems air and noise management and cooling and controls. The drivetrain group provides automotive transmission components. Turbochargers for light vehicles is the company's largest product line representing 30% of sales.

Key divisions and units include BorgWarner TorqTransfer Systems BorgWarner Transmission Systems BorgWarner Morse TEC and BorgWarner BERU Systems. BorgWarner also operates nine joint ventures located in China India and South Korea.

Sales and Marketing

The company markets its products to OEMs of light vehicles (passenger cars sport-utility vehicles vans and light trucks) through separate sales teams for its two product divisions. In 2014 Volkswagen and Ford generated 17% and 13% of the company's overall sales respectively. Other key customers include Chrysler Nissan and General Motors.

Financial Performance

BorgWarner has seen its net revenues reach historic levels as the global economy bounces back and the demand for automobiles increases. The company's revenue increased 8% from $7.44 billion in 2013 to peak at $8.3 billion in 2014 a milestone amount for the company. Profits also surged 5% from $624 million in 2013 to peak at a record-setting $656 million in 2014.

The historic growth for 2014 was due to a 7% spike in drivetrain sales and a 14% jump in engine sales as a result of higher sales of turbochargers EGR components and engine timing systems including variable cam timing devices. BorgWarner also experienced high growth in the the important Asia/Pacific region with sales jumping 11% in South Korea and 39% in China during the year.

BorgWarner experienced three straight years of increased operating cash flow until 2013 when it experienced a $160 million decline. However in 2014 operating cash flow recovered by 12% to reach $802 million.

Strategy

The engine maker's strategy is to follow market share as it shifts away from Detroit and toward Asia and Europe. Manufacturing operations are situated close to demand enabling the company to ship products directly from its plant to the customer. Western automotive companies are scrambling to grab a piece of the market in Asia particularly in China which is signaling to overtake the US as the largest automotive market in the world. In 2014 BorgWarner opened its newest production facility in Taicang China.

In addition BorgWarner like many of its peers has steadily increased its presence in South Korea (where Hyundai and Kia reside) and is investing in India Brazil and Eastern Europe. In 2013 it opened a new production facility in Itatiba City Brazil and a new facility in Manesar India.

Mergers and Acquisitions

BorgWarner has been generating additional revenue over the years through the use of acquisitions. In a milestone transaction in late 2015 the company acquired Remy International for $1.2 billion. Remy is a global producer of rotating electrical components with key technologies and operations spanning 10 countries. The deal enhanced BorgWarner's rapidly developing powertrain electrification technology line.

In 2014 it acquired Gustav Wahler GmbH & Co. KG a producer of exhaust gas recirculation (EGR) valves and tubes as well as engine thermostats for both on- and off-road applications for $111 million. The acquisition strengthened BorgWarner's strategic position as a producer of complete EGR systems and created additional market opportunities in both passenger and commercial vehicle applications. Gustav has locations in Germany Brazil China Slovakia and the US.

HISTORY

BorgWarner traces its roots to the 1928 merger of major Chicago auto parts companies Borg & Beck (clutches) Warner Gear (transmissions) Mechanics Universal Joint and Marvel Carburetor. The newly named Borg-Warner Corporation quickly began buying other companies including Ingersoll Steel & Disc (agricultural blades and discs) and Norge (refrigerators).

EXECUTIVES

VP General Counsel and Secretary, John J. Gasparovic, age 57, $441,250 total compensation

VP; President and General Manager BorgWarner Transmissions Systems, Robin Kendrick, age 50, $406,250 total compensation

VP and CIO, Jamal M. Farhat

VP; President BorgWarner China, Tom Tan

VP Marketing Public Relations Communications and Government Affairs, Scott D. Gallett, age 49

VP and CFO, Ronald T. (Ron) Hundzinski, age 56, $526,250 total compensation

President and CEO, James R. Verrier, age 52, $967,500 total compensation

VP; President and General Manager BorgWarner Emissions Systems, Brady D. Ericson, age 43

VP; President and General Manager BorgWarner Morse TEC, Joseph F. Fadool, age 48

VP; President and General Manager BorgWarner Turbo Systems, Fr © © ic B. Lissalde, age 47, $657,188 total compensation

VP and CTO, Chris Thomas

VP; President and General Manager BorgWarner Thermal Systems, Daniel Paterra, age 60

VP; President and General Manager BorgWarner TorqTransfer Systems, Stefan Demmerle, age 50

Vice President And Treasurer, Jan Bertsch

Vice President Of Information Technology, Sandra Short

Vice President Engineering, Olaf Toedter

Vice President, David (Dave) Hasson

Vice President Human Resources, Monica Rottman

Torque Transfer Vice President Of Engi, Mark Perlick

Vice President Global Supply Chain Turbo Systems, Radhika Batra

Vice President Manufacturing Strategi, Steve Snyder

Vice President Finance (Transmissions Systems), Chris Gropp

Vice President Global Supply Chain Management, Thomas Babineau

Director, Alexis P. Michas, age 57

Auditors: PricewaterhouseCoopers LLP

LOCATIONS

HQ: BorgWarner Inc
3850 Hamlin Road, Auburn Hills, MI 48326
Phone: 248 754-9200
Web: www.borgwarner.com

2014 Sales

	$ mil.	% of total
Europe		
Germany	2,145	26
Hungary	518	6
France	405	5
Other countries	1,097	13
US	2,008	24
China	885	11
South Korea	623	8
Other regions	622	7
Total	**8,305**	**100**

PRODUCTS/OPERATIONS

2014 Sales

	$ mil.	% of total
Engine	5,673	68
Drivetrain	2,631	32
Total	**80,305**	**100**

Selected Mergers and Acquisitions

FY2014
Gustav Wahler GmbH & Co. KG ($110 million; Germany; producer of exhaust gas recirculation valves and tubes)

FY2011
Haldex Traction Systems ($205 million; Sweden; all-wheel drive systems)

FY2010
BERU Eichenauer GmbH (Germany; maker of electric cabin heaters)
Dytech ENSA SL (Spain; emissions equipment maker)

Selected Products

Engine Group
Air-control valves
Chain tensioners and snubbers
Complete engine induction systems
Complex solenoids and multi-function modules
Crankshaft and camshaft sprockets
Diesel cabin heaters

Diesel cold starting systems (glow plugs and instant starting systems)
Electric air pumps
Engine hydraulic pumps
Exhaust gas-recirculation (EGR) coolers modules tubes and valves
Fan clutches
Fans and fan drives
Front-wheel and four-wheel-drive chain and timing-chain systems
High-temperature sensors (for exhaust gas aftertreatment systems)
Ignition coils
Intake manifolds
On-off fan drives
Single-function solenoids
Throttle bodies
Throttle position sensors
Tire pressure sensors
Transfer cases
Turbochargers
Drivetrain Group
Four-wheel-drive and all-wheel-drive transfer cases
Friction plates
One-way clutches
Torque converter lock-up clutches
Transmission bands

Selected Joint Ventures

BERU Korea Co. Ltd. (51% South Korea ignition coils and pumps)
Borg-Warner Shenglong (Ningbo) Co. Ltd. (70% China fans and fan drives)
BorgWarner TorqTransfer Systems Beijing Co. Ltd. (80% China transfer cases)
BorgWarner Transmission Systems Korea Inc. (60% South Korea transmission components)
BorgWarner United Transmission Systems Co. Ltd. (66% China transmission components)
BorgWarner-Vikas Emissions Systems India Private Limited (60% India EGR coolers)
Divgi-Warner Limited (60% India transfer cases and automatic locking hubs)
SeohanWarner Turbo Systems Ltd. (71% South Korea turbochargers)

COMPETITORS

American Axle & Manufacturing	Meritor
DENSO	Mitsubishi Heavy Industries
Dana Holding	Modine Manufacturing
Delphi Automotive Systems	NGK SPARK PLUG
GKN	Renold
Honeywell International	Robert Bosch
IHI Corp.	Schaeffler Technologies
JTEKT	Tsubaki Nakashima
Kolbenschmidt Pierburg	Valeo
Magna Powertrain	Visteon

HISTORICAL FINANCIALS

Company Type: Public

Income Statement

FYE: December 31

	REVENUE ($ mil.)	NET INCOME ($ mil.)	NET PROFIT MARGIN	EMPLOYEES
12/15	8,023	609	7.6%	30,000
12/14	8,305	655	7.9%	22,000
12/13	7,436	624	8.4%	19,700
12/12	7,183	500	7.0%	19,100
12/11	7,114	550	7.7%	19,250
Annual Growth	**3.0%**	**2.6%**	**—**	**11.7%**

2015 Year-End Financials

Debt ratio: 29.02%	No. of shares (mil.): 219
Return on equity: 17.01%	Dividends
Cash ($ mil.): 577	Yield: 1.2%
Current ratio: 1.33	Payout: 18.9%
Long-term debt ($ mil.): 2,124	Market value ($ mil.): 9,481

	STOCK PRICE ($) FY Close	P/E High/Low	PER SHARE ($) Earnings	Dividends	Book Value
12/15	43.23	23 14	2.70	0.52	16.20
12/14	54.95	23 17	2.86	0.51	15.97
12/13	55.91	40 20	2.70	0.25	15.62
12/12	71.62	39 27	2.09	0.00	13.34
12/11	63.74	32 22	2.23	0.00	11.00
Annual Growth	(9.3%)	— —	5.0%	—	10.2%

Boston Private Financial Holdings, Inc.

Boston Private Financial Holdings (BPFH) is a holding company for firms engaged in wealth management and private banking including Boston Private Bank & Trust which operates branches in New England New York Los Angeles and the San Francisco Bay Area. (The bank sold its branches in the Pacific Northwest in 2013.) BPFH also owns four other wealth advisory and investment management firms. The company offers private banking wealth advisory investment management deposits and lending and trust services to wealthy individuals corporations and institutional clients. All told BPFH and its affiliates have more than $30 billion in managed or advised assets.

Operations

In addition to Boston Private Bank & Trust Co. BPFH's other affiliates include: investment advisory firms Anchor Capital Advisors and Dalton Greiner Hartman Maher & Co.; wealth managers Bingham Osborn & Scarborough and KLS Professional Advisors Group; as well as newly-acquired Banyan Partners a registered investment advisor. BPFH sold its majority-owned affiliate Davidson Trust Co. (DTC) in 2012. DTC was part of the holding company's wealth advisory business.

Financial Performance

Boston Private Financial Holdings (BPFH) reported revenue of $339.5 million in 2013 an increase of less than 1% versus 2012. The modest uptick was due to increased recurring fees from its investment management wealth advisory and private banking wealth management and trust businesses as well as other income and a gain on the sale of loans. Assets under management and advisory (AUM) increased 19% during 2013 due to $3.7 billion of market appreciation and $0.2 billion of net inflows. All three of the BPFH's segments experienced gains in AUM.

Net income grew 32% in 2013 compared with 2012 to $70.5 million on a decline in interest expense on deposits partially offset by a 2% increase in average balance. The lower interest rate environment in the US has allowed the company's banking arm to lower interest rates on money markets accounts and certificates of deposit.

Strategy

Since its founding in 1987 Boston Private has had a voracious appetite for acquiring smaller trust companies private banks and wealth managers. While the firm put the brakes on its expansion and shifted strategies amid the economic recession. Indeed it divested about a half-dozen money management subsidiaries as way to raise capital and reduce risk. Also in 2011 the company consolidated its four banking charters into Boston Private Bank & Trust to simplify its structure and cut costs.

However with the economy and financial markets on the mend the company has resumed making acquisitions most recently to build its wealth management business.

Mergers Acquisitions and Divestments

In October 2014 Boston Private Bank & Trust Co. acquired Banyan Partners LLC an independent registered investment advisory firm based in Palm Beach Florida. With more than $4.5 billion in client assets Banyan has offices in Boston Miami Naples Atlanta Wisconsin Texas and California. The purchase furthered the bank's aim of expanding the reach and accelerating the development of its wealth management business.

In May 2013 Boston Private Bank & Trust sold three offices in the Pacific Northwest to focus on its banking business in California and New England. The bank recorded a $10.6 million pretax gain on the sale.

EXECUTIVES

EVP and General Counsel, Margaret W. (Megan) Chambers, age 56, $360,000 total compensation
President Boston Private Financial Holdings Inc. and CEO Boston Private Bank and Trust Company, Mark D. Thompson, age 58, $730,000 total compensation
President Boston Private Bank & Trust Company, George G. Schwartz
EVP CFO and Chief Administrative Officer, David J. Kaye, age 51, $425,000 total compensation
CEO, Clayton G. (Clay) Deutsch, $675,000 total compensation
EVP and Chief Risk Officer, Timothy MacDonald, $275,000 total compensation
SVP; Director Corporate Strategic Initiatives, Richard C. Byron
CEO Boston Private Wealth LLC, Corey A. Griffin
EVP; Director Human Capital Resources, Martha T. Higgins
CEO Boston Private Wealth LLC, Peter J. Raimondi
Assistant Vice President, Kelly Stewart
Assistant Vice President, Joe Lavigne
Assistant Vice President Senior Marketing, Jill Amato
Senior Vice President, Robert (Bob) Buffum
Vice President Investment Management and Trust, Rawson Hubbell
Vice President Deposit Operations wire Services, Cathy Squillacioti
Auditors: KPMG LLP

LOCATIONS

HQ: Boston Private Financial Holdings, Inc.
Ten Post Office Square, Boston, MA 02109
Phone: 617 912-1900
Web: www.bostonprivate.com

PRODUCTS/OPERATIONS

2013 Sales

	$ mil.	% of total
Interest and dividend income		
Loans	191	56
Mortgage-backed securities	5	2
Investment securities	5	2
Federal funds sold and other	1	-
Fees and other income		
Investment management & trust fees	43	13
Wealth advisory fees	42	12
Other	50	15
Total	**339**	**100**

Selected Subsidiaries & Affiliates

Anchor Capital Advisors LLC
Bingham Osborn & Scarborough LLC
Boston Private Bank & Trust Company
Dalton Greiner Hartman Maher & Co. LLC
KLS Professional Advisors Group LLC

COMPETITORS

Bank of America	FMR
Brown Brothers Harriman	JPMorgan Chase
Central Bancorp	Morgan Stanley
Century Bancorp (MA)	Sovereign Bank
Citigroup	TD Bank USA
Citizens Financial Group	TriState Capital
	Wells Fargo

HISTORICAL FINANCIALS

Company Type: Public

Income Statement

FYE: December 31

	ASSETS ($ mil.)	NET INCOME ($ mil.)	INCOME AS % OF ASSETS	EMPLOYEES
12/14	6,797	68	1.0%	875
12/13	6,437	70	1.1%	781
12/12	6,465	53	0.8%	827
12/11	6,048	39	0.6%	878
12/10	6,152	(10)	—	890
Annual Growth	2.5%	—	—	(0.4%)

2014 Year-End Financials

Debt ratio: 1.56%
Return on equity: 10.29%
Cash ($ mil.): 172
Current ratio: —
Long-term debt ($ mil.): —
No. of shares (mil.): 82
Dividends
　Yield: 2.3%
　Payout: 36.7%
Market value ($ mil.): 1,117

	STOCK PRICE ($) FY Close	P/E High/Low	PER SHARE ($) Earnings	Dividends	Book Value
12/14	13.47	18 14	0.79	0.32	8.48
12/13	12.62	18 13	0.68	0.24	7.94
12/12	9.01	17 13	0.61	0.04	7.66
12/11	7.94	16 10	0.46	0.04	7.26
12/10	6.55	— —	(0.29)	0.04	6.80
Annual Growth	19.8%	— —	—	68.2%	5.7%

Boston Scientific Corp.

Boston Scientific knows that nothing is simple in matters of the heart. The company makes medical supplies and devices used to diagnose and treat conditions in a variety of medical fields with an emphasis on cardiovascular products and cardiac rhythm management (CRM). It also makes devices used for electrophysiology endoscopy pain management (neuromodulation) urology and women's health. Its 13000 products —made in about a dozen factories worldwide –include biopsy forceps catheters coronary and urethral stents defibrillators needles and pacemakers. Boston Scientific markets its products in more than 100 countries.

Operations

Boston Scientific's largest segments make cardiovascular and cardiac rhythm products: The interventional cardiology products (coronary stents catheters guidewires) segment generates about 30% of annual revenues while peripheral intervention products (non-coronary vascular stents) bring in 10% of sales. The CRM business (pacemakers and implanted coronary defibrillators or ICDs) accounts for more than 25% of the company's sales.

Boston Scientific's other product segments account for about 30% of sales with endoscopy bringing in some 20% followed by the urology/women's health neuromodulation and electrophysiology divisions.

Geographic Reach

While the US is still Boston Scientific's largest single market international sales have grown to make up more than half of total sales. Boston Scientific has six manufacturing plants outside the US (three in Ireland two in Costa Rica and one in Puerto Rico). Other international facilities include physician training centers in France China and Japan and research operations in Ireland in China.

Sales and Marketing

Hospitals clinics outpatient facilities and medical offices are the company's key customers and in the US large group purchasing organizations (GPOs) hospital networks and other buying groups acting on behalf of their customers make up a significant portion of its sales. During 2014 the company marketed its products to some 25000 hospitals clinics outpatient facilities and medical offices around the world.

Boston Scientific markets products through direct disease-focused sales forces in the US and about 40 other major international markets; it also uses dealers and distributors in certain countries. Some products are marketed through partnerships; for instance Boston Scientific distributes urology laser systems made by Lumenis through a development and commercialization agreement.

Financial Performance

Market challenges including economic conditions competitive pressures and product safety issues took a toll on Boston Scientific's revenues in recent years. Sales were also impacted by asset divestitures and the company saw revenue declines until 2013. However in 2014 Boston Scientific reported 3% growth due primarily to constant currency increases in net sales and higher volumes from its interventional cardiology ($97 million) electrophysiology ($74 million) endoscopy ($66 million) and peripheral interventions ($56 million) businesses. These gains were partially offset by losses related to the sale of its neurovascular business.

Profits have fluctuated over the past few years as Boston Scientific has worked to offset declining sales with restructuring measures. The company reported a net loss of a whopping $4 billion in 2012 due to increased expenses —primarily caused by a $3.6 billion goodwill impairment charge on the decreased value of its operations in the EMEA (Europe Middle East and Africa) markets —as well as due to lower revenues. The company also revised the value of its US CRM business by some $748 million that year. In 2013 it recovered slightly as goodwill impairment charges eased. It reported a net loss of $121 million. The company reported another modest recovery in 2014 when it lost $119 million.

Cash flow from operations increased 14% to $1.2 billion that year due to reductions in its accounts receivable and lower interest and debt extinguishment payments. However higher inventory levels and contingent consideration payments partially offset those gains.

Strategy

The company is focused on growth measures that drive innovation in core markets expansion of its global commercial presence and diversification into additional areas of disease. Its strategies include acquisitions research and development partnerships and internal development efforts. Boston Scientific spends about 11% of its net sales (about $817 million in 2014) on R&D each year and strives to lead the market for minimally invasive medical devices that address unmet patient needs. Product launches in 2013 included a stint an imaging catheter a valve and an ablation catheter. Boston Scientific also looks to expand geographically and is working to build an infrastructure to support growth in such emerging markets as China India and Brazil. It opened an innovation

center in China in 2013. Two years later it entered a partnership with Frankenman Medical Equipment to develop manufacture and market products in China.

Faced with a number of challenges including historic recalls safety issues and fierce competition in certain product categories Boston Scientific is keen on implementing restructuring measures to improve efficiencies to give it a competitive edge. These include asset sales process streamlining revamping cost structures (for manufacturing and R&D organizations) leveraging preferred vendors and improving productivity. As part of its reorganization efforts Boston Scientific has consolidated its global headquarters operations to its campus in Marlborough Massachusetts. The company has also conducted several rounds of layoffs.

In Japan in 2014 the company launched its Promus PREMIER Everolimus-Eluting Platinum Chromium Coronary Stent System. Also that year Boston Scientific initiated the full commercial launch of its POLARIS Imaging System which supports products including intravascular ultrasound catheters.

In mid-2015 Boston Scientific acquired Endo International subsidiary American Medical Systems' urology portfolio which includes its men's health and prostate health businesses for $1.6 billion. The acquired businesses which generated some $400 million in sales in 2014 became part of Boston Scientific's urology/women's health division strengthening its position in the urology device market.

In a separate deal the company is buying medical device company Xlumena which makes minimally invasive devices for endoscopic ultrasound procedures. That purchase will boost Boston Scientific's portfolio of treatments for pancreatic pseudocysts. Boston Scientific has also agreed to buy the interventional radiology portfolio of Texas-based CeloNova Biosciences for $70 million plus additional milestone payments. The deal will includes CeloNova's Embozene and Oncozene drug-eluting microspheres (small particles that slow or stop the blood supply to growths or tumors).

Mergers and Acquisitions

The company has purchased a number of smaller businesses in the past few years expanding product offerings in areas including electrophysiology mapping and ablation systems as well as coronary occlusion catheter systems. In 2014 it bought the Interventional Division of Bayer for $414 million expanding its portfolio of treatments for challenging vascular conditions. That year it also bought the remaining 72% stake in pre-commercial stage company IoGyn it didn't already own.

In 2015 Boston Scientific agreed to buy Endo International's American Medical Systems urology portfolio for $1.6 billion plus an additional funds based on 2016 sales. That deal brings in a portfolio of products for treating conditions including benign prostatic hyperplasia male stress urinary incontinence and erectile disfunction.

HISTORY

Many medical companies start near a hospital but Boston Scientific's roots sprouted at a children's soccer game where two dads found common ground. John Abele and Peter Nicholas had complementary interests: Wharton MBA Nichols wanted to run his own company; philosophy and physics graduate Abele wanted a job that would help people.

In 1979 the two men founded Boston Scientific to buy medical device maker Medi-Tech. Abele and Nicholas had to borrow half a million dollars from a bank and raise an additional $300000. Medi-Tech's primary product was a steerable catheter a soft-tipped device that could be maneuvered within

the body. The catheter revolutionized gallstone operations in the early 1970s and Boston Scientific expanded on the success of the product. The company adapted it for a slew of new procedures for the heart lungs intestines and other organs.

Boston Scientific's sales were healthy in 1983 but the firm still lacked funds. It eagerly accepted $21 million from Abbott Laboratories in exchange for a 20% stake. New FDA regulations slowed product introduction and put a crimp in the company's growth. Boston Scientific found a legal loophole in the late 1980s to avoid lengthy delays: The company described its products in the vaguest possible terms so upgraded devices were considered similar enough to predecessors to escape the in-depth scrutiny of the new approval process. Still Abele and Nicholas had to mortgage their personal properties to stay afloat before this linguistic legerdemain helped to clear government red tape. Boston Scientific returned to profitability in 1991 and went public the next year buying back Abbott Laboratories' interest in the company as well.

Boston Scientific acquired a bevy of medical device companies throughout the late 1990's which expanded its range of cardiology products and doubled sales. Among them were SCIMED Life Systems Heart Technology Meadox Medicals EP Technologies and Symbiosis Target Therapeutics and Pfizer's catheter stent and angioplasty equipment business.

EXECUTIVES

President and CEO, Michael F. (Mike) Mahoney, age 50, $921,302 total compensation

EVP Rhythm Management, Joseph M. (Joe) Fitzgerald, age 51, $454,082 total compensation

EVP and CFO, Daniel J. (Dan) Brennan, age 49, $450,000 total compensation

SVP; President Neuromodulation, Maulik Nanavaty, age 53

President Endoscopy, Michael P. (Mike) Phalen, age 56

EVP Chief Administrative Officer Secretary and General Counsel, Timothy A. (Tim) Pratt, age 65, $627,337 total compensation

EVP and Global Chief Medical Officer, Keith D. Dawkins, age 64

EVP; President Asia-Pacific Middle East and Africa, Supratim Bose, age 62, $537,326 total compensation

SVP; President Endoscopy, David A. (Dave) Pierce, age 51

SVP; President Interventional Cardiology, Kevin J. Ballinger, age 42, $392,781 total compensation

SVP; President Urology and Women's Health, Karen Prange, age 51

SVP; President Peripheral Interventions, Jeffrey B. (Jeff) Mirviss, age 49

EVP Operations, Edward F. Mackey, age 52

SVP Manufacturing and Supply Chain, John B. (Brad) Sorenson, age 47

SVP: President Europe, Eric Th Paut, age 53

Vice President Sales, Lee Sullivan

Vice President Mg And Galway Operations, Aaron Milton

Vice President Government Affairs, Steve LaPierre

Vice President Research And Development, Tim Girton

Vice President Marketing Peripheral Interventions, John (Jack) Crowley

Vice President General Counsel, Jean F Lance

Medical Director Global Medical Safety, Olaf Hedrich

Vice President Corporate Tax, Douglas J Cronin

Vice President Senior Strategic Alliance Counselor, Vance Brown

Vice President International Quality, Rosaleen Burke

Vice President Corporate Sales, Randall Renners
Vice President Regulatory Affairs, Angie Raun
Senior Vice President Global Sales and Marketing, Maria Williams
Vice President Communications and Progra, Marilee Grant
Vice President Sales Information technology and Training, Reaz Ali
Vice President Human Resources Business, Mat Johnson
National Account Manager, Benjamin Bottcher
Sr V Pres Hr, Wendy Carruthers
Area Vice President, Scott Berens
Vice President Cardiology Litigation, Peter (Pete) Gafner
Director International Tax, Douglas (Doug) Cronin
Vice President of Sales, Allen (Al) Meacham
Medical Director, Thomas (Thom) Christen
Vice President Quality Assurance Cardiovascular, John (Jack) Donohue
Vice President Corporate Accounting, Jon Monson
Vice President Quality Assurance, Thomas (Thom) Fleming
Vice President Of Operations And Gener, Jorge Perera
Vice President Manager Director, Ru Zheng
Vice President Marketing, Mona Patel
Area Vice President, Mike Blastick
Senior Vice President Chief Accounting Officer a, Capello Jeffrey
Vice President Senior Counsel CRM, Kelly Phillips
Vice President of Sales and Strategic Accounts, Samuel (Sam) Conaway
Medical Director, Paul Underwood
Senior V President Of Finance, Richard (Dick) Warren
Vice President Health Economics and Reimbursement, Parashar Patel
Vice President Sales And Marketing, Richard (Dick) Sanders
Vptreasurer, Robert (Bob) Castagna
Vice President, Prabodh Mathur
Vice President Of Operations, Sean Aherne
Vice President Finance And Japan, David (Dave) Morris
National Sales Manager, Vanina Becchi
Vice President, Akira Kitamura
Vice President And General Manager, Masaru Yokomaku
Vice President And General Manager, Yasuhiro Oishi
Vice President, Rodamni Peppa
National Sales Manager Germany, Raphael Ujlaky
National Sales Manager, Juan Ferrer
Vice President, Francisco Ascencion
Medical Director Peripheral Interventions, Juan Diaz-Cartelle
Vice President, Julie Zeiler
Vice President Global Marketing Endoscopy, Meghan Scanlon
Vice President of Research and Development Electrophysiology Division, Michael (Mel) Wallace
Vice President Of Information Technology And General Superintendent, Neha Khera
National Sales Manager, Rahul Garg
Senior Vice President; President Peripheral Interventions, Jeff Mirviss
Vice President Quality Assurance, John (Jack) Daley
Vice President Development Systems Corporate Technology and Development, David (Dave) Bee
Vice President Global Regulatory Affairs, Tamima Itani
Vice President QA Neuromodulation, Patrick (Paddy) Crotteau
Chairman, Peter M. (Pete) Nicholas, age 73
Board Member, Steve Naylor
Board Member, Richard (Dick) Clark
Board Member, Charles Dockendorff
Auditors: Ernst & Young LLP

LOCATIONS

HQ: Boston Scientific Corp.
300 Boston Scientific Way, Marlborough, MA 01752-1234
Phone: 508 683-4000
Web: www.bostonscientific.com

2014 Sales

	$ mil.	% of total
US	3,885	53
Japan	678	9
Other countries	2,813	38
Sales generated from divested businesses	4	-
Total	**7,380**	**100**

PRODUCTS/OPERATIONS

2014 Sales

	$ mil.	% of total
Interventional cardiology	2,057	28
Cardiac rhythm management	1,912	26
Endoscopy	1,323	18
Peripheral interventions	850	12
Urology/Women's Health	535	7
Neuromodulation	472	6
Electrophysiology	227	3
Sales generated from divested businesses	4	-
Total	**7,380**	**100**

Selected Products

Cardiovascular
  Interventional Cardiology
  PolarCath peripheral dilation system
  PROMUS drug-eluting stents
  TAXUS drug-eluting stents
  VeriFLEX bare-metal stents
  WALLSTENT carotid artery stents
  Cardiac Rhythm Management (CRM)
  ACUITY steerable ventricular leads
  COGNIS cardiac resynchronization defibrillator
  LATITUDE remote patient monitoring system
  TELIGEN implantable cardiac defibrillator
  Other cardiovascular
  Cutting Balloon dilation device
  FilterWire EZ embolic protection system
  iLab ultrasound imaging catheter system
  Maverick balloon catheters
Endoscopy
  Radial Jaw 4 single-use biopsy forceps (gastrointestinal)
  RX Biliary System (bile duct surgeries)
  SpyGlass direct visualization system (pancreatic system)
Urology/Women's Health
  Genesys Hydro ThermAblator (endometrial ablation system)
Neuromodulation
  Precision Spinal Cord Stimulation system (chronic pain)
Electrophysiology
  Blazer Prime temperature ablation catheters

Selected Acquisitions

COMPETITORS

Abbott Labs	Hologic
American Medical Systems	Johnson & Johnson
	LeMaitre Vascular
Bard	Medtronic
Cook Group	St. Jude Medical
Edwards Lifesciences	ZOLL

HISTORICAL FINANCIALS

Company Type: Public

Income Statement

FYE: December 31

	REVENUE ($ mil.)	NET INCOME ($ mil.)	NET PROFIT MARGIN	EMPLOYEES
12/14	7,380	(119)	—	24,000
12/13	7,143	(121)	—	23,000
12/12	7,249	(4,068)	—	24,000
12/11	7,622	441	5.8%	24,000
12/10	7,806	(1,065)	—	25,000
Annual Growth	(1.4%)	—	—	(1.0%)

2014 Year-End Financials

Debt ratio: 25.01%
Return on equity: (-1.83%)
Cash ($ mil.): 587
Current ratio: 1.27
Long-term debt ($ mil.): 3,859
No. of shares (mil.): 1,327
Dividends
  Yield: —
  Payout: —
Market value ($ mil.): 17,589

	STOCK PRICE ($) FY Close	P/E High/Low	PER SHARE ($) Earnings	Dividends	Book Value
12/14	13.25	— —	(0.09)	0.00	4.86
12/13	12.02	— —	(0.09)	0.00	4.95
12/12	5.73	— —	(2.89)	0.00	5.07
12/11	5.34	27 18	0.29	0.00	7.83
12/10	7.57	— —	(0.70)	0.00	7.43
Annual Growth	15.0%	— —	—	—	(10.0%)

Bristol-Myers Squibb Co.

Bristol-Myers Squibb (BMS) makes drugs for the brain heart and other body parts. The biopharmaceutical's blockbuster cardiovascular lineup includes heart disease drug Plavix and Avapro for hypertension. BMS also makes antipsychotic medication Abilify and HIV treatments Reyataz and Sustiva. Most of its sales come from products in the therapeutic areas of cardiovascular care hepatitis B immunology metabolics neuroscience oncology and virology. BMS has global research facilities and manufacturing plants mainly in the US and Europe and its products are marketed to health care practitioners hospitals and managed care providers in 100 countries.

HISTORY

Bristol-Myers Squibb is the product of a merger of rivals.

Squibb was founded by Dr. Edward Squibb in New York City in 1858. He developed techniques for making pure ether and chloroform; he turned the business over to his sons in 1891.

Sales of $414000 in 1904 grew to $13 million by 1928. The company supplied penicillin and morphine during WWII. In 1952 it was bought by Mathieson Chemical which in turn was bought by Olin Industries in 1953 forming Olin Mathieson Chemical. Squibb maintained its separate identity.

From 1968 to 1971 Olin Mathieson went through repeated reorganizations and adopted the Squibb name. Capoten and Corgard two major cardiovascular drugs were introduced in the late 1970s. Capoten was the first drug engineered to attack a specific disease-causing mechanism.

Squibb formed a joint venture with Denmark's Novo (now Novo Nordisk) in 1982 to sell insulin.

William Bristol and John Myers founded Clinton Pharmaceutical in Clinton New York in 1887 (renamed Bristol-Myers in 1900) to sell bulk pharmaceuticals. The firm made antibiotics after the 1943 purchase of Cheplin Biological Labs. It began expanding overseas in the 1950s and eventually bought Clairol (1959); Mead Johnson (drugs infant and nutritional formula; 1967); and Zimmer (orthopedic implants 1972). Bristol-Myers launched new drugs to treat cancer (Platinol 1978) and anxiety (BuSpar 1986). That year it acquired biotech companies Oncogen and Genetic Systems.

The firm bought Squibb in 1989. In 1990 the new company bought arthroscopy products and implant business lines and joined Eastman Kodak and Elf Aquitaine to develop new heart drugs in 1993. Despite these initiatives earnings slipped. In 1994 company veteran Charles Heimbold became CEO and moved to increase profits. BMS in 1995 bought wound and skin care products firm Calgon Vestal Laboratories. Also that year the company along with fellow silicone breast implant makers 3M and Baxter International agreed to settle thousands of personal injury claims at an average of $26000 per claim.

Facing an antitrust suit filed by independent drugstores BMS and other major drugmakers agreed in 1996 to charge pharmacies the same prices as managed care groups for medications. That year the company formed a generic drug unit and launched Pravachol.

Over the next two years BMS tweaked its product line buying drug cosmetics and consumer products companies and brands. Having refined its product line the firm began a series of officer reassignments that were widely interpreted as an effort to find a successor for Heimbold who retired in 2001.

In 1999 the firm pulled its backing for EntreMed after the biotech had problems duplicating results for a cancer drug candidate. BMS helped market promising diabetes drug Avandia (from Glaxo-SmithKline which ended the deal in 2002) and teamed with Millennium Pharmaceuticals to study the genetic makeup of tumors.

As the company entered the 21st century it began streamlining. It sold its Sea Breeze skin care brand (1999); Matrix Essentials hair care products unit (2000); and Clairol hair and personal care products business (2001). BMS also spun off its Zimmer orthopedic implant unit in 2001. More changes came in 2004: The firm sold its Mead Johnson Adult Nutritional business.

In 2002 BMS was dealt a blow when a judge ruled that the company had illegally blocked Mylan Labs and Watson Pharmaceuticals from selling generic versions of BuSpar.

The firm bought a 20% stake in ImClone to collaborate on the development of cancer drug Erbitux and to stay on top of the cancer drug market. Instead BMS found itself embroiled in the controversy over insider information and stock deals surrounding the biotech. Persistence paid off however; Erbitux was approved by the FDA in 2004.

During 2005 the company cleaned out parts of its medicine cabinet. Analgesics Excedrin and Bufferin had made the company a household name but in 2005 the company sold its US and Canadian consumer products operations to Novartis. The deal also meant saying goodbye to such brands as Comtrex (cold medications) Choice (blood sugar monitoring supplies) and Keri (lotions skin care). Sales for the its US and Canadian consumer products operations reached about $270 million in 2004.

That same year BMS sold Oncology Therapeutics Network which distributes cancer drugs to oncology doctors to private equity firm One Equity Partners. The unit had accounted for about 13% of sales in 2004.

As part of an agreement with the New Jersey US Attorney's office in 2005 to settle an investigation into inventory control and accounting practices the company split the role of chairman and CEO into two separate offices. Long-time BMS director James Robinson III was elected the company's new chairman with Peter Dolan in the CEO role. James Cornelius took over as CEO in 2006 and became chairman in 2008 bring the two roles back together.

While the patent expiration on blockbuster Plavix was still five years off in mid-2006 Canadian generics maker Apotex managed to flood the market with a generic version of Plavix for several weeks. The release of the drug followed bungled attempts by BMS to negotiate a deal with Apotex that would have kept it off the market. The debacle led to federal investigations into whether that deal violated anti-trust laws (among other things) and also resulted in the ouster of CEO Peter Dolan (replaced by James Cornelius). Though a judge put a halt to the manufacturing of the generic until the courts could straighten the whole thing out the short-term generic competition hurt Plavix sales to the tune of more than $1 billion. BMS ultimately wound up paying more than $150 million to settle lawsuits and agreed that it would report any future deals struck with generics makers.

The company announced a reorganizational plan in 2007 named the string-of-pearls strategy. As part of its efforts to remake itself into a purely biopharmaceutical player BMS began jettisoning its non-pharmaceutical businesses. During 2008 the company sold its Medical Imaging unit to private equity firm Avista Capital Partners for $525 million and Avista Capital Partners and Nordic Capital paid $4.1 billion to acquire BMS' Conva-Tec ostomy and wound-care subsidiary. Then in 2009 the company divested its Mead Johnson subsidiary which sold Enfamil infant formula and other nutritional products for children.

EXECUTIVES

EVP General Counsel and Corporate Secretary, Sandra Leung, age 54, $849,750 total compensation
CEO, Giovanni Caforio, age 51, $915,962 total compensation
EVP and CFO, Charles A. Bancroft, age 56, $910,520 total compensation
EVP and Chief Scientific Officer, Francis Cuss, age 60, $875,000 total compensation
SVP Enterprise Services and CIO, Paul von Autenried, age 53
President Global Manufacturing and Supply, Louis S. (Lou) Schmukler, age 59
Vice President, Tom Gibbs
Vice President USP Strategy and Operations, Jeff Conklin
Vice President, Albert (Al) DiEnna
Medical Director, William Petkun
Vice President Finance, Charles (Chas) McClafferty
Vice President Development Lead Full Development, Elisabeth (Betsy) Svanberg
Vice President And Deputy General Counsel, Louis Wille
Vice President Global Medical Information, Patrick (Paddy) Reilly
Vice President Information Management Permfail, Michael (Mel) Kauffman
Vice President and General Manager China GMS, Robin Edwards
Vice President Global Regulatory Sciences Oncology, Mark Moyer
Associate Medical Director Global Pharmacovigilance, Hewei LI

Vice President Global Pharmacovigilance and Epidemiology, Debra Feldman
Vice President Headquarters Medical Oncology Nivolumab, Denise Williams
Vice President Clinical Pharmacology and Pharmacometrics, Rick Bertz
Vice President Applied Biotechnology and Discovery, John (Jack) Houston
Vice Presiden Information Management, Kathleen Natriello
Vice President Global Biometric Sciences, Dominic Labriola
Senior Vice President Policy and Government Affairs, Richard L (Dick) Thompson
National Accounts Manager, Brad Sheppard
Vice President Chief Sales Officer, Mark Wagner
Medical Director, Simon Portsmouth
Executive Chairman, Lamberto Andreotti, age 64
Assistant Treasurer, Scott R Massengill
Auditors: DELOITTE & TOUCHE LLP

LOCATIONS

HQ: Bristol-Myers Squibb Co.
345 Park Avenue, New York, NY 10154
Phone: 212 546-4000   **Fax:** 212 546-4020
Web: www.bms.com

2014 Sales

	$ mil.	% of total
US	7,716	49
Europe	3,592	22
Other countries & regions	3,459	22
Other	1,112	7
Total	**15,879**	**100**

PRODUCTS/OPERATIONS

2014 Sales

	$ mil.	% of total
Abilify	2,020	12
Orencia	1,652	10
Sustiva	1,444	9
Reyataz	1,362	9
Baraclude	1,441	9
Sprycel	1,493	9
Yervoy	1,308	8
Eliquis	774	5
Erbitux	723	5
Hepatitis C Franchise	256	2
Opdivo	6	-
Diabetes Alliance	295	2
Mature products & other	3,105	20
Total	**15,879**	**100**

Selected Pharmaceuticals

Cardiovascular
  Eliquis (atrial fibrillation with Pfizer)
Immunology
  Nulojix (kidney rejection)
  Orencia (rheumatoid arthritis)
Metabolism
  Bydureon (type 2 diabetes)
  Byetta (type 2 diabetes)
Neuroscience
  Abilify (schizophrenia bipolar disorder major depressive disorder; with Otsuka)
  Emsam (major depressive disorder)
Oncology
  Erbitux (colorectal head and neck cancer with Lilly)
  Ixempra (ixabepilone)
  Sprycel (chronic myeloid leukemia with Otsuka)
  Yervoy (metastatic melanoma)
Virology
  Baraclude (chronic hepatitis B)
  Reyataz (HIV)
  Sustiva Franchise (includes Atripla and Sustiva for HIV with Gilead)

COMPETITORS

AbbVie	Johnson & Johnson
Abbott Labs	Merck
Allergan plc	Mylan
Amgen	Novartis

Apotex
AstraZeneca
Biogen
Boehringer Ingelheim
Eli Lilly
Genentech
GlaxoSmithKline

Pfizer
Ranbaxy Laboratories
Roche Holding
Sandoz International
GmbH
Sanofi
Teva

HISTORICAL FINANCIALS

Company Type: Public

Income Statement

FYE: December 31

	REVENUE ($ mil.)	NET INCOME ($ mil.)	NET PROFIT MARGIN	EMPLOYEES
12/15	16,560	1,565	9.5%	25,000
12/14	15,879	2,004	12.6%	25,000
12/13	16,385	2,563	15.6%	28,000
12/12	17,621	1,960	11.1%	28,000
12/11	21,244	3,709	17.5%	27,000
Annual Growth	(6.0%)	(19.4%)	—	(1.9%)

2015 Year-End Financials

Debt ratio: 21.07%
Return on equity: 10.75%
Cash ($ mil.): 2,385
Current ratio: 1.30
Long-term debt ($ mil.): 6,550

No. of shares (mil.): 1,669
Dividends
Yield: 2.1%
Payout: 160.2%
Market value ($ mil.): 114,811

	STOCK PRICE ($) FY Close	P/E High/Low	PER SHARE ($) Earnings	Dividends	Book Value
12/15	68.79	75 61	0.93	1.49	8.55
12/14	59.03	51 39	1.20	1.45	8.94
12/13	53.15	35 21	1.54	1.41	9.19
12/12	32.59	31 26	1.16	1.36	8.36
12/11	35.24	16 11	2.16	1.32	9.44
Annual Growth	18.2%	— —	(19.0%)	3.1%	(2.5%)

Brookdale Senior Living Inc

Over the brook and through the dale to grandmother's house we go! Brookdale Senior Living operates assisted and independent living centers and retirement communities for middle- and upper-income elderly clients. Brookdale has approximately 1000 facilities offering more than 331000 studio one-bedroom and two-bedroom units in 46 states. Services for its residents include meals 24-hour emergency response housekeeping concierge services transportation and recreational activities. Brookdale's continuing care retirement centers include skilled nursing units that serve Alzheimer's patients and others who require ongoing care. The company also owns eldercare company Emeritus Corporation.

Operations

While some of Brookdale's facilities provide intensive nursing services that are reimbursed by third-parties including Medicare and Medicaid most of the company's facilities are independent or assisted-living centers that targets higher-end clients with minimal medical needs.

Brookdale's largest operating segment is its assisted living division which provides daily living services to residents and accounted for 44% of revenues in 2014. The company's retirement centers segment operates upscale independent living facilities for middle and upper-income seniors and accounts for 15% of sales. Brookdale's continuing care retirement communities (CCRC) segment provides a mix of independent assisted and nursing care services within one location. The CCRC operations are divided into rental (13% of annual revenues) and entry fee (5%) divisions based on whether residents pay an upfront fee or monthly rental fees.

The remainder of revenue comes from its management services segment and its Brookdale Ancillary Services (formerly known as innovative senior care) segment. The management services division receives fees for facilities that Brookdale operates on behalf of third parties. The Brookdale Ancillary Services division provides outpatient therapy home health and hospice services to residents of Brookdale and non-Brookdale facilities as well as seniors living in their own homes.

At the end of 2014 the company owned or leased 982 communities with more than 83000 units and managed 161 third-party owned or partially owned communities with more than 27600 units.

Geographic Reach

Brookdale has more than 1100 communities in 46 states. Its largest markets Florida and Texas are home to almost 30% of its communities. Other key states include North Carolina Ohio and Michigan. About half of the company's sales come from its leased communities and more than 40% are generated from owned communities.

Sales and Marketing

Due to its focus on high-income customers more than 80% of its revenues come from private pay customers. By keeping its exposure to federal programs (Medicare and Medicaid) to a minimum the company is less vulnerable (though not immune) to changes in reimbursement levels.

The company uses direct marketing teams to target potential residents and family members as well as referral sources including hospital discharge agents social workers home health agents and clergy members. It also seeks to promote its brand through event sponsoring and online print signage and direct mail advertising programs.

Financial Performance

Brookdale's revenues peaked in 2014 rising 32% to $3.8 billion thanks to growth seen across nearly all of its segments. The company saw 60% growth in its assisted living division (led by increases in average monthly revenue per unit). Management fees and reimbursement costs also increased primarily due to the 2014 acquisition of Emeritus Corporation. Meanwhile Brookdale Ancillary Services revenue rose 49% to $95.7 million (again largely due to the Emeritus acquisition). Finally the retirement centers segment rose 11% that year.

However the company has reported losses over a period of several years despite the growth in revenue. Its net income plummeted from a loss of $3.6 million in 2013 to a loss of $149.4 million in 2014 due to factors such as increasing operating expenses and administrative expenses facilities leasing expenses and depreciation and amortization related to the Emeritus acquisition. The higher losses contributed to a decline in operating cash flow that year which fell to $243 million (versus $366 million in 2013).

Strategy

Though the company continues to grow through acquisitions Brookdale's main strategic focus is on maximizing profits and increasing occupancy rates at existing facilities. Brookdale expects to benefit from an uptick in demand as the US population of seniors (people age 75 and older) steadily increases. It aims to attract and retain residents through sales and marketing initiatives including brand recognition programs. The company has also launched an initiative to expand or redevelop existing facilities to increase capacity or to add new services. Brookdale is also interested in meeting the demand for rehabilitation and long-term skilled nursing care as well as partnering with local doctors to help minimize hospital readmissions.

Brookdale is also looking to grow its income by widening its offering of ancillary services by extending its Brookdale Ancillary Services program to new facilities as well as by introducing new services such as wellness and physical fitness programs.

In 2014 Brookdale Senior Living and HCP created a $1.2 billion joint venture owning an initial portfolio of 14 entry fee CCRCs. The companies also agreed to amend the triple-net leases on 202 HCP-owned senior housing communities formerly operated by Emeritus Corporation which was acquired by Brookdale that year. In 2015 HCP and Brookdale acquired 35 private pay senior housing communities from Chartwell Retirement Residences for $847 million. The portfolio which Brookdale manages is 90% owned by HCP and 10% owned by Brookdale.

To raise cash in 2013 the company sold four communities for a total of $35.2 million

Mergers and Acquisitions

In 2014 Brookdale purchased fellow senior living firm Emeritus for nearly $3 billion. The move gave Brookdale a nationwide network of senior care facilities adding 10 states and bringing its total number of communities to 1100.

Brookdale previously expanded its network in 2013 through the purchase of a dozen communities with 871 units for a total of some $162 million; these facilities were also previously operated under lease contracts. It acquired an additional seven senior living centers with 613 units (six of which it already operated) from Chartwell later that year for some $81 million. That year the company also purchased two home health agencies and one hospice agency for $2.6 million.

HISTORY

Brookdale Senior Living was formed through the 2005 merger of Brookdale Living Communities and Alterra Healthcare. The combined organization expanded through additional acquisitions in the following years.

Difficult economic conditions caused Brookdale to cut back on its spending during 2009 and 2010. During that time it turned its attention inward and worked to improve occupancy rates at existing facilities. The senior housing industry as a whole was affected by the downturn in the housing market causing a precipitous drop in occupancy rates industry-wide.

Sensing improved economic conditions in 2011 Brookdale acquired private facility operator Horizon Bay adding 90 residential facilities in the southern and midwestern US. Horizon Bay's independent and assisted living facilities complement Brookdale's existing properties as they cater to high-end customers. The acquisition also reinforced the company's existing presence in several markets and opened a few new markets. As part of the deal Brookdale entered restructured lease arrangements on certain facilities with Horizon Bay's former shareholders Chartwell Seniors Housing REIT and HCP.

In 2012 it partnered with online services firm Connected Living to increase Internet training and social networking capabilities at several Brookdale communities in California. In early 2012 the company paid $121 million for nine communities it had formerly operated through lease agreements. The facilities included a total of some 1300 living units.

EXECUTIVES

President, Mark W. Ohlendorf, age 55, $499,538 total compensation
EVP Corporate Development, H. Todd Kaestner, age 60
EVP Finance, George T. Hicks, age 58
EVP and Chief Administrative Officer, Bryan D. Richardson, age 57, $367,631 total compensation
EVP Chief Accounting Officer and Treasurer, Kristin A. Ferge, age 42, $254,769 total compensation
CFO, Lucinda M. (Cindy) Baier, age 51
CEO, T. Andrew (Andy) Smith, age 55, $841,216 total compensation
EVP and Chief People Officer, Glenn O. Maul, $250,000 total compensation
COO, Labeed Diab, age 45
Director Of Nursing, Bernadita Balderian
Vice President Of Administration, Gelynna Shaw
Division President, Mary Patchett
Vice President, Linda May
Vice President Legal Employment Affairs, Jack Leebron
Senior Vice President Of Dining, Joska Hajdu
Vice President Of Procurement, Jeff Patton
Senior Vice President, Don Ross
Vice President, Glen Kiger
Regional Vice President Operations, Patty Luessenhop
Vice President, Marla Sovereign
Physical Therapy Director, Becky Lemery
Senior Vice President Acquisitions, Christian Maingot
Vice President Brand Marketing, Jonathan (Jon) Ruchman
Senior Vice President Strategic Planning And Investor Relations, Ross Roadman
Regional Vice President Region 5, Steve Flynt
Chairman, Daniel A. Decker, age 62
Auditors: Ernst & Young LLP

LOCATIONS

HQ: Brookdale Senior Living Inc
   111 Westwood Place, Suite 400, Brentwood, TN 37027
Phone: 615 221-2250
Web: www.brookdale.com

2014 Community Locations

	No.
Florida	138
Texas	131
California	94
Ohio	60
Washington	55
Colorado	39
Arizona	37
Illinois	21
North Carolina	63
Oregon	45
Michigan	37
Virginia	19
New York	35
Tennessee	35
Indiana	24
South Carolina	25
Georgia	27
Oklahoma	33
Kansas	24
Other states	201
Total	**1,143**

PRODUCTS/OPERATIONS

2014 Revenues

	$ mil.	% of total
Resident fees		
Assisted living	1,685	44
Retirement centers	582	15
Continuing care retirement communities (CCRCs) - rental	493	13
Continuing care retirement communities (CCRCs) - entry fee	202	5
Management services	530	14
Brookdale Ancillary Services	337	9
Total	**3,831**	**100**

2014 Units

	% of total
Managed communities	25
Assisted living	19
Home health service	17
Therapy services	16
Retirement centers	8
Third parties	8
CCRCS	7
Total	**100**

COMPETITORS

ACTS Retirement-Life Communities
Amedisys
American Baptist Homes of the West
Apria Healthcare
Atria Senior Living
BPM Senior Living
Capital Senior Living
Colson & Colson
Consulate Health Care
Enlivant
Evangelical Lutheran Good Samaritan Society
Five Star Quality Care
Golden Horizons
HCP
HCR ManorCare
Horizon Bay
Life Care Centers
Life Care Services
SavaSeniorCare
Sunrise Senior Living
Ventas
Welltower

HISTORICAL FINANCIALS

Company Type: Public

Income Statement

FYE: December 31

	REVENUE ($ mil.)	NET INCOME ($ mil.)	NET PROFIT MARGIN	EMPLOYEES
12/15	4,960	(458)	—	81,300
12/14	3,831	(149)	—	82,000
12/13	2,891	(3)	—	49,000
12/12	2,770	(65)	—	47,900
12/11	2,457	(68)	—	46,400
Annual Growth	19.2%	—	—	15.1%

2015 Year-End Financials

Debt ratio: 64.01%
Return on equity: (-17.16%)
Cash ($ mil.): 88
Current ratio: 0.59
Long-term debt ($ mil.): 6,196
No. of shares (mil.): 188
Dividends
  Yield: —
  Payout: —
Market value ($ mil.): 3,477

	STOCK PRICE ($) FY Close	P/E High/Low		Earnings	Dividends	Book Value
12/15	18.46	—	—	(2.48)	0.00	13.06
12/14	36.67	—	—	(1.01)	0.00	15.41
12/13	27.18	—	—	(0.03)	0.00	7.99
12/12	25.32	—	—	(0.54)	0.00	7.91
12/11	17.39	—	—	(0.56)	0.00	8.30
Annual Growth	1.5%	—	—	—	—	12.0%

Brookline Bancorp Inc (DE)

Brookline Bancorp is the holding company for Brookline Bank Bank Rhode Island (BankRI) and First Ipswich Bank (formerly The First National Bank of Ipswich) which together operate more than 45 full-service branches in eastern Massachusetts and Rhode Island. Commercial and multifamily mortgages backed by real estate such as apartments condominiums and office buildings account for the largest portion of the company's loan portfolio followed by indirect auto loans commercial loans and consumer loans. Established in 1997 as Brookline Savings Bank the bank went public five years later and changed its name to Brookline Bank in 2003. Brookline Bancorp. has expanded by acquiring other regional banks.

Geographic Reach

Boston-based Brookline Bancorp operates 47 full-service branches in greater Boston and greater Providence Rhode Island.

Operations

The holding company also provides indirect automobile loans through Brookline Bank and equipment financing through its Eastern Funding and Macrolease Corp. subsidiaries. Eastern Funding LLC a majority-owned firm with more than $1 billion in in direct loans that specializes in financing coin-operated laundry dry cleaning and convenience store equipment in the New York City metropolitan area.

Financial Performance

The multi-bank holding company has $5.3 billion in assets. In 2013 Brookline Bancorp reported net income of $35.4 million compared with $37.1 million in 2012. Net earnings from operations were $36 million in 2013 compared to $41.1 million for 2012.

Strategy

Brookline has grown from a sleepy suburban community savings bank to a publicly-traded commercial lender with loan volumes that put it among Massachusetts' top banks. As it transitions to a commercial bank Brookline has also been growing geographically through acquisitions.

Mergers and Acquisitions

In January 2012 Brookline acquired Providence-headquartered Bancorp Rhode Island for $234 million in cash and stock adding 18 BankRI branches in that state. BankRI retained its brand and operates as a subsidiary of Brookline Bancorp.

In February 2011 it acquired The First National Bank of Ipswich a six-branch bank serving Massachusetts' North Shore. The $19.7 million transaction gave First National Bank of Ipswich a much-needed boost as that bank had been struggling with loan losses during the recession. It also expanded Brookline Bancorp's market area as there was no overlap between the two banks.

Brookline Bancorp's board rejected a takeover offer by an unnamed suitor in early 2010. Two directors had voted to accept the bid however including former longtime chairman Richard Chapman. Both resigned in the aftermath of the vote.

EXECUTIVES

President and CEO, Paul A. Perrault, age 64, $675,000 total compensation
COO, James M. Cosman, $250,000 total compensation
President and CEO Bank Rhode Island, Mark J. Meiklejohn, $310,000 total compensation
Chief Risk Officer General Counsel and Secretary, Michael W. McCurdy
Chief Credit Officer, M. Robert Rose, $272,000 total compensation
President and CEO The First National Bank of Ipswich, Russell G. Cole
CFO, Carl M. Carlson
Vice President Project Management, Esther Pinto
Senior Vice President, Bill Mackenzie
Vice President Regional Manager, Cathy Pierce
Vice President, Tony Glazier
Vice President Of Commercial Lending, Tim Steiner

Vice President Underwriting And Operations,
Gretchen Annese
Chairman, Joseph J. Slotnik, age 79
Treasurer, Reed H Whitman
Auditors: KPMG LLP

LOCATIONS

HQ: Brookline Bancorp Inc (DE)
131 Clarendon Street, Boston, MA 02116
Phone: 617 425-4600
Web: www.brooklinebancorp.com

COMPETITORS

Bank of America	Eastern Bank
Boston Private	Sovereign Bank
Central Bancorp	TD Bank USA
Century Bancorp (MA)	
Citizens Financial	
Group	

HISTORICAL FINANCIALS

Company Type: Public

Income Statement

FYE: December 31

	ASSETS ($ mil.)	NET INCOME ($ mil.)	INCOME AS % OF ASSETS	EMPLOYEES
12/14	5,799	42	0.7%	725
12/13	5,325	35	0.7%	720
12/12	5,147	37	0.7%	662
12/11	3,299	27	0.8%	358
12/10	2,720	26	1.0%	266
Annual Growth	20.8%	12.3%	—	28.5%

2014 Year-End Financials

Debt ratio: 1.43%	No. of shares (mil.): 70
Return on equity: 6.82%	Dividends
Cash ($ mil.): 62	Yield: 3.3%
Current ratio: —	Payout: 59.6%
Long-term debt ($ mil.): —	Market value ($ mil.): 709

	STOCK PRICE ($) FY Close	P/E High/Low	PER SHARE ($) Earnings	Dividends	Book Value
12/14	10.03	17 14	0.61	0.34	9.06
12/13	9.55	20 16	0.51	0.34	8.70
12/12	8.50	18 14	0.53	0.34	8.70
12/11	8.44	24 15	0.47	0.34	8.50
12/10	10.85	25 19	0.46	0.34	8.39
Annual Growth	(1.9%)	— —	7.3%	(0.0%)	2.0%

Buckeye Partners, L.P.

Buckeye Partners serves the Buckeye State and then some. Its main subsidiary Buckeye Pipe Line stretches about 1800 miles from Massachusetts to Illinois. Other pipelines include Laurel Pipe Line (Pennsylvania) Everglades Pipe Line (Florida) and Wood River Pipe Lines (Illinois Indiana Missouri and Ohio). It markets refined petroleum products in a number of the geographic areas served by its pipeline and terminal operations. In the US Buckeye Partners operates about 6000 miles of pipeline and more than 120 storage terminals capable of holding more than 110 million barrels of refined petroleum. It also has storage assets in the Bahamas.

Geographic Reach

The company's operations are conducted and are located in the continental US St. Lucia and The Bahamas. The company has commercial offices in Breinigsville Pennsylvania and in Houston Texas.

Operations

The company operates in four business segments: Pipelines and Terminals; Global Marine Terminals; Merchant Services; and Development & Logistics.

The Merchant Services segment (81% of 2014 revenues) is a wholesale distributor of petroleum products in the US and in the Caribbean. The segment owns five terminals which are operated by the Pipelines and Terminals segment. Its products include gasoline propane ethanol biodiesel and petroleum distillates such as heating oil diesel fuel kerosene and fuel oil.

Buckeye Partners' Pipelines and Terminals (13% of sales) transports refined petroleum products including gasoline jet fuel diesel fuel heating oil and kerosene from major supply sources to terminals and airports primarily in the US Northeast and Upper Midwest.The Global Marine Terminals segment provides marine bulk storage and marine terminal throughput services along the US East Coast and the Caribbean. The segment has liquid petroleum product terminals with a capacity of more than 59 million barrels.

The Development and Logistics segment provides turn-key operations and maintenance asset development and construction services for third-party pipeline and energy assets including ownership and operation of two underground propane storage caverns in Huntington Indiana and Tuscola Illinois with 800000 barrels of throughput and storage capability.

Sales and Marketing

Merchant Services customers consist of product wholesalers and major commercial users.The Pipelines and Terminals segment's terminals derive most of their revenues from various fees paid by customers. A throughput fee is charged for receiving products into the terminal and delivering them to trucks barges ships or pipelines and it distribute its products to third parties.

Financial Performance

Buckeye Partners' revenues increased by 31% in 2014 due to higher product sales volumes in Merchant Services segment as well as the benefit of new terminals (acquired from Hess in 2013) in both the Pipelines and Terminals and Global Marine Terminals segments. These increases were partially offset by the litigation contingency reserve associated with ongoing FERC proceedings in its Pipelines and Terminals segment.Revenues from Pipelines and Terminals increased due to capital investments in internal growth and diversification initiatives and pipeline tariff rates.Global Marine Terminals's sales grew as the result of growth in storage and terminalling revenues stemming from the Hess assets and ancillary services.Merchant Services revenues increased due to higher volumes sold partially offset by a decrease in refined petroleum product sales.In 2014 Buckeye Partners' net income increased by 70% due to changes in bad debt and income tax (expense) benefit and loss from discontinued operations.Cash from operating activities grew by 56% due to a decrease in impairment of assets of discontinued operations of natural gas changes in net changes in fair value of derivatives changes in inventories and changes in accrued and other current liabilities.

Strategy

The company intends to optimize expand and diversify its portfolio of energy assets through acquisitions and organic growth projects.

In 2015 Buckeye Partners expected to complete the construction of 3.8 million barrels of additional storage capacity in its Corpus Christi facilities. It also planned additional investments in projects including potential pipeline extensions and expansions for transportation and/or storage of crude oil refined products and natural gas liquids both in the Midwest and on the East Coast.The company will continue to evaluate opportunities throughout 2015 to acquire or construct assets that are complementary to its businesses and support its long-term growth strategy.>

To refocus on its core businesses Buckeye Partners divested its natural gas non-core operations in 2014. This segment was led by Buckeye Gas Storage LLC which owns a natural gas facility in Northern California that is connected to Pacific Gas and Electric's intrastate gas pipeline system. In 2014 the company sold this Natural Gas Storage disposal group for $103.4 million.

In late 2013 the company realigned its business segments to support its business in light of recent growth through acquisitions. It eliminated its previously reported International Operations and Energy Services segments and created the Global Marine Terminals and Merchant Services segments.

Mergers and Acquisitions

Expanding its geographic and product diversity with a premier position on the US Gulf Coast and in the prolific Eagle Ford shale in 2014 Buckeye Partners bought an 80% interest in Buckeye Texas Partners LLC for $860 million.

In 2013 the company acquired 20 liquid petroleum products terminals along the US East Coast with total storage capacity of 39 million barrels from Hess for $850 million.

Company Background

Continuing to grow its Northeast assets in 2012 Buckeye Partners acquired a liquid petroleum products marine terminal facility in New York Harbor from Chevron for $260 million.

Buckeye Partners traces its roots to 1886 when The Buckeye Pipe Line Company was incorporated as a subsidiary of the Standard Oil.

EXECUTIVES

SVP Buckeye GP and President Domestic Pipelines and Terminals, Robert A. Malecky, age 51, $412,019 total compensation
SVP Buckeye GP and President Global Marine Terminals, Khalid A. Muslih, age 43, $412,019 total compensation
Chairman President and CEO Buckeye GP, Clark C. Smith, age 60, $756,730 total compensation
CIO, Kathleen J. (Kathy) Sinatore
EVP and CFO, Keith E. St.Clair, age 58, $482,693 total compensation
SVP Buckeye GP and President Buckeye Services, William J. Hollis
SVP General Counsel and Secretary, Todd J. Russo
Vice President Human Resources, Mark Esselman
Vice President Business Development, Ismael Hernandez
Member Board Of Directors, Barbara (Barb) Duganier
Auditors: Deloitte & Touche LLP

LOCATIONS

HQ: Buckeye Partners, L.P.
One Greenway Plaza, Suite 600, Houston, TX 77046
Phone: 832 615-8600
Web: www.buckeye.com

2014 Sales

	$ mil.	% of total
US	6,279	95
International	341	5
Total	**6,620**	**100**

PRODUCTS/OPERATIONS

2014 Sales

	$ mil.	% of total
Merchant services	5,358	81
Pipeline & terminals	858	13
Global marine terminals	395	6
Development & logistics	81	1
Adjustments (73.5) (1)		
Total	**6,620**	**100**

COMPETITORS

AmeriGas Partners	Ferrellgas Partners
CMS Energy	Plains All American
Duke Energy	Pipeline
Enbridge	Sunoco Logistics
Enbridge Energy	Williams Companies

HISTORICAL FINANCIALS

Company Type: Public

Income Statement

FYE: December 31

	REVENUE ($ mil.)	NET INCOME ($ mil.)	NET PROFIT MARGIN	EMPLOYEES
12/14	6,620	272	4.1%	1,430
12/13	5,054	160	3.2%	1,270
12/12	4,357	226	5.2%	1,020
12/11	4,759	108	2.3%	1,029
12/10	3,151	43	1.4%	859
Annual Growth	20.4%	58.7%	—	13.6%

2014 Year-End Financials

Debt ratio: 43.96%
Return on equity: —
Cash ($ mil.): 8
Current ratio: 1.02
Long-term debt ($ mil.): 3,388

No. of shares (mil.): 127
Dividends
  Yield: 5.8%
  Payout: 429.6%
Market value ($ mil.): 9,612

	STOCK PRICE ($) FY Close	P/E High/Low		PER SHARE ($) Earnings	Dividends	Book Value
12/14	75.66	37	29	2.28	4.43	29.14
12/13	71.01	49	30	1.49	4.23	26.64
12/12	45.41	28	19	2.32	4.15	24.12
12/11	63.98	57	48	1.20	4.03	24.69
12/10	66.83	42	32	1.65	3.83	19.49
Annual Growth	3.2%	—	—	8.4%	3.7%	10.6%

Burlington Northern & Santa Fe Railway Co. (The)

BNSF Railway operates one of the largest railroad networks in North America. A wholly-owned subsidiary of Burlington Northern Santa Fe itself a unit of Berkshire Hathaway the company provides freight transportation over a network of about 32500 route miles of track across two-thirds of the western US and two provinces in Canada. BNSF Railway owns or leases a fleet of about 8000 locomotives. It also has some 30 intermodal facilities that help to transport agricultural consumer and industrial products as well as coal. In addition to major cities and ports BNSF Railway serves smaller markets in alliance with short-line partners.

Geographic Reach

The company's network is spread across 28 US states and three Canadian provinces.

Operations

BNSF Railway serves more than 40 ports and 30 intermodal facilities and operates 1600 trains per day.

In 2014 it hauled nearly 1 million carloads of agricultural commodities; more than 5 million intermodal shipments (truck trailers or containers); nearly 2 million carloads of industrial products; and almost 2.3 million coal shipments. All told the company hauled more than 10 million carloads in 2014.

Sales and Marketing

BNSF Railway serves smaller markets by working closely with 200 shortline partners. It has also forms marketing agreements with other rail carriers expanding the marketing reach for each railroad and their customers.

Financial Performance

In 2014 the company's revenues rose by 5.6% due to increased capacity offset by the negative effects of severe winter weather conditions early in the year which dampened transportation activities. BNSF Railway generated 31% of its revenues in 2014 from consumer products; 28% from industrial products; 22% from coal; and 19% from agricultural products.It also reported a 1.8% increase in cars/units handled and a 3.5% increase in average revenue per car/unit for the year.The company accounted for more than 56% of Burlington Northern Santa Fe's net revenues for 2014.

Strategy

As part of its capital plan of $6 billion for 2015 the company has planned some major capital projects to maintain and grow its rail network.In its northern region the company has plans to invest $1.5 billion across eight states for engineering maintenance and line expansion projects of which $700 million is planned for projects to expand the rail lines and Positive Train Control (PTC advanced technologies designed to automatically stop or slow a train before accidents occur) in that region. In the southern region it plans to spend $800 million in nine states for engineering maintenance and line expansion projects of which $175 million is planned for line expansion initiatives and continued implementation of PTC.The overall $6 billion investment for 2015 includes $2.9 billion to replace and maintain core network and related assets nearly $1.5 billion on expansion and efficiency projects $200 million for continued implementation of PTC and $1.4 billion for locomotives freight cars and other equipment acquisitions.

In 2014 the company made capital investments for line expansion system improvement projects additional equipment and new employee hires. BNSF Railway had a 2013 capital program (to strengthen its infrastructure) valued at $4.1 billion.

EXECUTIVES

President and CEO, Carl R. Ice, age 58
EVP Law and Corporate Affairs, Roger Nober, age 50
EVP and CFO, Julie A. Piggott
EVP and Chief Marketing Officer, Stevan B. Bobb
EVP Operations, Gregory C. Fox
Vice President and General Counsel, Charles (Chas) Shewmake
Chairman President and CEO, Matthew K. Rose, age 56
Auditors: Deloitte & Touche LLP

LOCATIONS

HQ: Burlington Northern & Santa Fe Railway Co. (The) 2650 Lou Menk Drive, Fort Worth, TX 76131-2830
Phone: 800 795-2673
Web: www.bnsf.com

COMPETITORS

American Commercial Lines	Kansas City Southern Railway
Canadian National Railway	Kirby Corporation
Canadian Pacific Railway	Landstar System
Ingram Industries	Norfolk Southern
J.B. Hunt	Schneider National
	Union Pacific Railroad
	Werner Enterprises

HISTORICAL FINANCIALS

Company Type: Public

Income Statement

FYE: December 31

	REVENUE ($ mil.)	NET INCOME ($ mil.)	NET PROFIT MARGIN	EMPLOYEES
12/14	22,714	4,397	19.4%	48,000
12/13	21,552	4,271	19.8%	43,000
12/12	20,478	3,720	18.2%	41,000
12/11	19,229	3,273	17.0%	39,000
12/10	14,835	2,382	16.1%	38,000
Annual Growth	11.2%	16.6%	—	6.0%

2014 Year-End Financials

Debt ratio: 1.89%
Return on equity: 8.85%
Cash ($ mil.): 585
Current ratio: 1.05
Long-term debt ($ mil.): 1,326

No. of shares (mil.): 0
Dividends
  Yield: —
  Payout: —
Market value ($ mil.): —

Cablevision Systems Corp.

Cablevision Systems is a leading provider of digital television phone and Internet services in the New York City metropolitan area. Through its Optimum brand the company serves nearly 3 million subscribers who receive at least one of the services. It also provides voice data and managed technology services to commercial customers through Cablevision Lightpath. Other operations include newspaper publishing (NYC's Newsday and community papers) regional news and sports networks and cable television advertising. Cablevision agreed to be bought by Altice a telecommunications company based in France. The $17.7 billion deal reached in 2015 was expected to face regulatory scrutiny.

Operations

Cablevision generates about 89% of its revenue from the Optimum cable services with Lightpath providing 5% and other segments accounting for about 6%.

Financial PerformanceThe company's revenue rose 3.6% to $6.46 billion in 2014 from $6.2 billion in 2013. The company instituted higher rates for its services in 2013 and 2014 which bumped up revenue.has been falling or stagnant for the past four years. Net income dropped by a third in 2014 to $311.4 billion due to discontinued operations. Cash flow from operations grew however to nearly $1.4 billion in 2014 from $1.1 billion in 2014 on a change in working capital that resulted from a change in prepaid expenses.

StrategyAfter several years of divestments —including Optimum West movie theaters cable channels and Madison Square Garden operations Cablevision has slimmed down to focus on its New York City telecommunications operations. In 2015 Cablevision launched Freewheel a low-cost WiFi phone service over Wi-Fi that carries unlimited data talk and text. The first WiFi service phone from a cable provider FreeWheel is offered with a Motorola Moto G smartphone.

The proposed acquisition by Altice would make Cablevision the French company's second holding in the US after St. Louis-based Suddenlink. It appears that Altice has more acquisitions planned for North America and Cablevision provides a strong urban base while Suddenlink reaches smaller markets throughout the country.

HISTORY

Early History

In 1954 Charles Dolan helped form Sterling Manhattan Cable which won the cable-TV franchise for lower Manhattan in 1965. It began broadcasting pro basketball and hockey courtesy of Madison Square Garden (MSG) in 1967. In 1970 Dolan started Home Box Office (HBO) the first nationwide pay-TV channel and hired Gerald Levin to run it.

Dolan took the company public as Sterling Communications; its partner media giant Time (now part of Time Warner) came to own 80% of Sterling. Costs mounted however and in 1973 Time liquidated Sterling (but kept HBO).

Dolan bought back the New York franchises and formed Long Island Cable Communications Development. He changed its name to Cablevision and expanded around New York and Chicago. In 1980 Cablevision formed Rainbow Programming which soon included the American Movie Classics and Bravo channels; in 1983 it launched the popular SportsChannel (now Fox Sports New York). Cablevision went public in 1986 and bought two Connecticut cable systems that year and one in Massachusetts the next.

EXECUTIVES

Senior Vice President Treasurer, Kevin Watson
CEO, James L. Dolan, age 59, $2,000,000 total compensation
EVP Media and Community Relations, Charles (Charlie) Schueler
CTO, David E. Dibble, age 55
EVP and General Counsel, David G. Ellen, age 50, $1,200,000 total compensation
Vice Chairman EVP and CFO, Gregg G. Seibert, age 59, $1,875,000 total compensation
President, Brian G. Sweeney, age 50, $1,300,000 total compensation
EVP Government and Public Affairs, Lisa Rosenblum, age 59
COO, Kristin A. Dolan, age 48, $1,346,154 total compensation
EVP Human Resources and Administration, Sandra P. Kapell
SVP and CIO, Keith Sherwell
EVP Sales and Marketing, Robert Sullivan
EVP Programming, Tom Montemagno
Vice President Network Infrastructure and Operations, John (Jack) Cavallaro
Senior Vice President Technology Integration, Al Azralon
Vice President Facilities And Operations, Dave Schnurman
Senior Vice President Human Resources Business Partner, Colleen Schmidt
Vice President Regulatory And Government Affairs, Evlyn Tsimis
Vp-investor Relations, Cindi Buckwalter
Senior Vice President Executive Director Creative Services, Mickey Paxton
Vice President Wireless Product Development, Timothy Farrell
Vice President Pricing And Planning, Kevan Jackson

Vice President Product Management, Keith Agabob
Vice President of Sales, Mike Zangrillo
Senior Vice President New Business Development, Benjamin Ben Tatta
Vice President Advanced Streaming Technology Corporate Technology, Peter (Pete) Caramanica
Vice President Engineering, Paul Hess
Senior Vice President Business Planning Intercarrier And Admin, Joseph Caruso
Vice President Benefits, Chris Clarke
Vice President Of Business Aviation, Phil Stang
Vice President Ad Sales Research, William Chambers
Senior Vice President Network Management And Operations, Pragash Pillai
Vice President Video Product Strategy and Operations, Paul Strickland
Vice President Professional Services, Joel Dougherty
Vice President, Kevin Battles
Vice President Product Integration and Management, Michael (Mel) Valentin
Vice President Financial Planning And Analysis, Kenneth Gallagher
Vice President Broadband Technology Integration, Joseph Godas
Vice President Regional Sales, Michael Felicetti
Vice President Management Information Systems, James Keane
Senior Vice President Application Development, Kevin Brosnan
Vice President Collections, Frank Naples
Vice President Customer Service, Robert Cruickshank
Vice President National Sales, Steve Mirabile
Director Media Relations, Lindsey Calabrese
Vice President Internal Communications, Laura Gorham
Vice President National Sales, Gerald Healy
Vice President Inventory Management, Kim Snyder
Senior Vice President Human Resources Business Partner, James Maloney
Vice President Government And Regulatory Strategy, Lee Schroeder
Vice President Software Development, Rich Neil
Vice President Regional Sales, Michael (Mel) Felicetti
Vice President Financial Planning And Analysis, Kenneth (Ken) Gallagher
Vice President Human Resources and Administration, Patty Fitzpatrick
Senior Vice President Technology Local Media, Tom Donohue
Treasury Vice President, Amy Schall
Senior Vice President And Controller, Wm Harper
Senior Vice President Sales, Denis Coleman
Vice President Sales, Phil Decabia
Vice President Finance and Administration, Victor Curreri
Chairman, Charles F. Dolan, age 89
Vice Chairman, Hank J. Ratner, age 56
Secretary, Barbara (Barb) Bowden
Auditors: KPMG LLP

LOCATIONS

HQ: Cablevision Systems Corp.
1111 Stewart Avenue, Bethpage, NY 11714
Phone: 516 803-2300
Web: www.cablevision.com

PRODUCTS/OPERATIONS

2014 Sales

	$ mil.	% of total
Cable	5,784	89
Light path	353	5
Others	361	6
Inter-segment eliminations	(38.3)	-
Total	**6,460**	**100**

COMPETITORS

AT&T	DISH Network
CenturyLink	EchoStar
Charter Communications	RCN Corporation
Comcast	Time Warner Cable
Cox Communications	Verizon
DIRECTV	Vonage

HISTORICAL FINANCIALS
Company Type: Public

Income Statement
FYE: December 31

	REVENUE ($ mil.)	NET INCOME ($ mil.)	NET PROFIT MARGIN	EMPLOYEES
12/14	6,460	311	4.8%	14,968
12/13	6,232	465	7.5%	15,369
12/12	6,705	233	3.5%	18,889
12/11	6,700	291	4.4%	17,815
12/10	7,231	360	5.0%	19,065
Annual Growth	(2.8%)	(3.6%)	—	(5.9%)

2014 Year-End Financials

Debt ratio: 143.28%	No. of shares (mil.): 274
Return on equity: —	Dividends
Cash ($ mil.): 850	Yield: 2.9%
Current ratio: 1.10	Payout: 53.1%
Long-term debt ($ mil.): 9,134	Market value ($ mil.): 5,663

	STOCK PRICE ($) FY Close	P/E High/Low	PER SHARE ($) Earnings	Dividends	Book Value
12/14	20.64	18 13	1.15	0.60	(18.38)
12/13	17.93	11 8	1.75	0.60	(19.74)
12/12	14.94	21 12	0.87	0.60	(21.30)
12/11	14.22	36 12	1.02	0.58	(20.33)
12/10	33.84	28 18	1.20	0.48	(21.33)
Annual Growth	(11.6%)	— —	(1.1%)	6.0%	—

Caesars Entertainment Corp

Caesars Entertainment Corporation (formerly Harrah's Entertainment) likes to spread its bets. The firm owns and/or operates more than 50 casinos (under such names as Harrah's Horseshoe and Rio) in 14 US states and five countries. Altogether its facilities —including hotels dockside and riverboat casinos and Native American gaming establishments —boast more than 3 million sq. ft. of casino space and some 43000 hotel rooms. Among its many locations on the Vegas Strip are Caesars Palace Paris Las Vegas and Planet Hollywood. The company went public in 2012 more than a year after it cancelled a previous IPO.

HISTORY

William Harrah and his father founded their first bingo parlor in Reno Nevada in 1937. Using the income from that business Harrah opened his first casino Harrah's Club in downtown Reno in 1946. In 1955 and 1956 he bought several clubs in Stateline Nevada (near Lake Tahoe). Harrah built the company by using promotions to draw middle-class Californians to his clubs.

During the 1960s the entrepreneur expanded his operations in Lake Tahoe and in 1968 he built a 400-room hotel tower in Reno. Harrah's went public in 1971. After Harrah's death in 1978 the company expanded outside Nevada by building a hotel and casino in Atlantic City New Jersey.

Holiday Inns bought Harrah's in 1980 for about $300 million. The hotelier already owned a 40% interest in River Boat Casino which operated a casino next to a Holiday Inn in Las Vegas. When Holiday Inns acquired the other 60% of the casino/hotel in 1983 Harrah's took over its management. Holiday Inns became Holiday Corporation in 1985. The following year UK brewer Bass PLC put up $100 million for 10% of Holiday Corporation.

In 1990 Bass acquired the Holiday Inn hotel chain for $2.2 billion. The rest of Holiday Corporation including Harrah's was renamed Promus under chairman Michael Rose.

In the early 1990s Harrah's built a casino on Ak-Chin Indian land near Phoenix and opened riverboat casinos in Joliet Illinois; Shreveport Louisiana; and North Kansas City Missouri. In 1995 Promus spun off its hotel operations as Promus Hotel Corporation and changed the name of its casino business to Harrah's Entertainment. (Promus was acquired by Hilton Hotels later called Hilton Worldwide in 1999.)

Also in 1995 Harrah's gambled and lost. Big. Its New Orleans casino was shelved even before it was finished —a victim of Louisiana's Byzantine politics. Eager for the right to build what would be a $395 million 200000-sq.-ft. casino in the heart of the city Harrah's had made a number of ill-advised concessions to state and municipal officials. It agreed not to offer hotel rooms or food at the casino (forgoing about 20% of anticipated revenues) and promised to make an annual $100 million minimum payment to the state in addition to 19% of the casino's revenues. In the end the fiasco's price tag reached $900 million (only half of which went to casino construction costs) and Harrah's put the project into bankruptcy to stop the bleeding. (It resumed construction in 1999 and finally opened the casino at the end of the year.)

In 1997 Rose retired as chairman and was replaced by CEO Philip Satre. In 1998 Harrah's bought competitor Showboat with properties in Las Vegas and Atlantic City and management of a New South Wales Australia casino. A Louisiana Supreme Court ruling that year allowed the company to resume work on the New Orleans casino (albeit a stake of less than 45% which was later increased to 63%). Harrah's also invested in Las Vegas-based National Airlines that year.

In early 1999 Harrah's bought Rio Hotel & Casino (also a partner in National Airlines) which operates one upscale casino on the Las Vegas Strip for about $525 million. In 2000 the company bought riverboat casino operator Players International for $425 million. Also that year Harrah's had to write off about $39 million in investments and loans to National Airlines which filed for bankruptcy. The company had a 48% stake in the airline.

Harrah's continued its acquisition streak in 2001 with the purchase of Harveys Casino Resorts with four locations in Colorado Iowa and Nevada for $675 million. (It sold the Colorado location in 2002.) The 452-room Harrah's Atlantic City hotel tower was opened in 2002. Also that year the company began construction of a second 800-room tower at its Atlantic City Showboat casino. Later in 2002 Harrah's acquired the shares of JCC Holding company it didn't already own for $54.1 million. It also acquired Louisiana Downs a Thoroughbred racetrack in Bossier City for $157 million. Harrah's subsequently turned Louisiana Downs into a full-blown casino.

In 2004 Harrah's acquired casino operator Horseshoe Gaming for $1.45 billion. The purchase added several properties to Harrah's portfolio (in Hammond Indiana; Bossier City Louisiana; and

Tunica Mississippi). In order to gain regulatory approval for the purchase Harrah's later sold its Harrah's Shreveport casino to Boyd Gaming for $190 million. The sale was intended to limit Harrah's exposure in the Louisiana market.

The following year Harrah's completed a monster-sized deal the $9.4 billion acquisition of rival Caesars Entertainment Inc. which rocketed the company to the top of the gaming world. To appease regulators the company sold its Harrah's Tunica and East Chicago casinos to Colony Capital. In 2005 Harrah's bought the Imperial Palace one of the last few independent casinos on the Las Vegas Strip for $370 million.

The effects of Hurricane Katrina were felt at the company's Biloxi and Gulfport Mississippi locations which suffered extensive damage. Harrah's sold the Gulfport location such as it was and rebuilt the Biloxi site which re-opened in 2006. Also that year Harrah's acquired the remaining assets of Casino Magic Biloxi from Pinnacle Entertainment; Harrah's sold two subsidiaries that own businesses in Lake Charles Louisiana. In addition to the Casino Magic assets Pinnacle paid Harrah's some $25 million in the deal.

In 2006 Harrah's sold its Flamingo Laughlin hotel-casino and an undeveloped land parcel in Atlantic City to American Real Estate Partners. It also purchased casino operator London Clubs International for $586 million. London Clubs operates seven UK casinos as well as two in Egypt and one in South Africa.

The company acquired Macau Orient Golf one of only two golf courses in Macau China in 2007 for some $577 million. It subsequently re-branded the property Caesars Macau Golf. Caesars made the deal to enter the popular Chinese market joining rivals Las Vegas Sands Wynn Resorts and MGM Resorts International which already own casinos in Macau. In 2008 the company ceased to be a publicly traded company after being bought out by two private equity firms.

In 2010 Harrah's purchased the beleaguered Planet Hollywood Resort & Casino in Las Vegas. (The property is separate from Planet Hollywood International). Harrah's was attracted to Planet Hollywood proximity to its other resorts on the Strip as well as its strong brand name. The deal — the company's first new Vegas property since it bought Caesars Palace in 2005 —gave the firm its eighth connected property on the Strip's east side.

Also in 2010 the company filed to go public. However later that year it cancelled the IPO due to unfavorable market conditions and weak investor demand. In addition to its massive debt Harrah's lacked interest from investors due to the fact that its holdings are focused on domestic markets and the company has no plans to expand in the fast-growing Chinese market of Macau where its competitors have had much success.

After cancelling the IPO the company changed its name from Harrah's Entertainment to Caesars Entertainment Corporation. Though it continues to use the Harrah's brand at one of its bigger properties the company made the identity change to capitalize on the Caesar's name which it sees as 'the world's preeminent and most respected casino brand."

The company went public in 2012 raising little more than $16 million in a small IPO.

EXECUTIVES

EVP Communications and Government Relations, Janis L. (Jan) Jones Blackhurst, age 67
President and CEO, Mark P. Frissora, age 59
Vice President, Gene Stark
EVP General Counsel and Chief Regulatory and Compliance Officer, Timothy R. (Tim) Donovan, age 59, $700,000 total compensation

Global President Destination Markets, Thomas M. (Tom) Jenkin, age 60, $1,200,000 total compensation
EVP Domestic Development, Gregory (Greg) Miller, age 54
President Hospitality, Robert J. (Bob) Morse
CTO, Charly Paelinck
EVP Human Resources, Mary H. Thomas, age 48
CEO Caesars Entertainment Operating Company (CEOC), John W. R. Payne, age 46, $1,125,000 total compensation
CFO, Eric Hession, age 41
President International Development, Steven M. Tight, age 59
EVP and Chief Commercial Officer, Tariq M. Shaukat, age 42, $700,000 total compensation
Entertainment Vice President, John (Jack) Maddox
Vice President Of Finance, Jill Barrett
National Sales Manager, Krissy Lee
Vice President Information Technology, Scott Campbell
National Sales Manager In Market, Katie Curran
Vice President of Non Gaming Operations, Joseph (Jo) Giunta
Vice President Casino Operations, Ryan Hammer
National Sales Manager, Christina Gibbons
Vice President Of Finance, Jerry Fox
Vice President Of Marketing, Joe Schatz
Vice President of Marketing Caesars Entertainment Atlantic City, Jocelyn Allison
Vice President Human Resources, Leisha Hammer
Vice President Of Casino Marketing, Napoleon Chio
Divisional Vice President of Finance, Holly Gagnon
Vice President Public Relations Lv Regio, Debbie Munch
Vice President of Distribution Leisure Sales, Annette Weishaar
Vice President Compensation and Leadership, Mike McLellan
Vice President Government Relations, Karlos Lasane
Vice President Strategic Sourcing, Diana Caballero
Vice President Human Resources, Norris Hamilton
Vice President Credit and Collections, Joe Flippen
Vice President Of Operations, Dan Real
Vice President Marketing Portfolio, Jana Rygiel
Vice President Of Global Infrastructure, Shawn McGovern
National Sales Manager, Helen Tsang
Regional Vice President Direct Marketing, Pete Graziano
Vice President Of Operations, Julie Sola
Regional Vice President Human Resources, Matt Krystofiak
Vice President Of Csa, Terry Byrnes
Vice President, Nora West
Vice President Of Slot Operations, Stephen Bimson
Vice President Of Tax, Carol Tabrizi
Vice President LV Regional Tele Services, Mary Dennis
Vice President Marketing, Luann Pappas
Regional Vice President and Vice President Marketing, Mike Stratton
National Sales Manager, Jon Clinton
Vice President Catering Conventions and Events, Don Ross
Vice President and Chief Counsel Regional Operations, Tim Lambert
Vice President Enterprise Analytics, Blake Segal
Vice President Email Marketing, Christopher Jenner
National Sales Manager, Robin Eissinger
National Sales Manager, Jason Gaudet
Vice President Of Business Strategy And Revenue Management, Ruben Sigala
Senior Vice President Government Relations And Development, David (Dave) Satz
Vice President and Chief Counsel Enterprise Shared Services, Lisa Mathis
Vice President Information Technology Development, Charley Paelinck
Vice President of Strategic Data, Dave Kowal

Vice President Of Hospitality Operations, Scott Lokke

Vice President Of Player Development, Kathy Garrison

National Sales Manager, Kurt Dietz

Senior Vice President General Manager, Michael Rich

Vice President And General Manager, Karie L Hall

Vice President and Associate Chief Counsel Employment Law, Jeffrey D (Jeff) Winchester

National Sales Manager, Teresa Hemphill

Vice President Finance And Capital Analytics, Robert (Bob) Brimmer

Vice President Of Player Development, Mark Mitchell

National Sales Manager, Kristie Stevens

Vice President Of Marketing, Joshua Kanter

Executive Vice President, Steven (Steve) Bell

Vice President Of Asia Development, William Shen

National Sales Manager, Justin Siegel

Vice President Of Player Development, Steve Moy

Vice President International Marketing, Bruce Bommarito

Vice President Hotel Operations, Steve Opdyke

Vice President Human Resources, Laura Wilson

Regional Vice President of Nightlife Operations Eastern Division, Howard Weiss

Vice President Casino Operations, Mark Kelly

National Sales Manager, Misty Sparks

National Sales Manager, Dave Goldstein

Vice President Agm, Gerry Tuthill

Vice President Marketing Los Angeles Branch, Lynda Thipavong

Vice President Ess Travel Management, Steven Markhoff

National Sales Manager Labor, Judy Sereni

National Sales Manager, Jennifer Veselko

Vice President Human Resources, Colleen Moore

Vice President Of Marketing, Jennifer Nocco

Vice President Of Human Resources, Melinda Mackey

Vice President, Vickilynn Guveiyian

Vice President Casino Operations, William Kelly

Vice President Luxury Hotel Operations, Gigi Vega

National Sales Manager, Peter Cancila

Vice President Finance, Janae Sternberg

National Sales Manager, Krissy Jasperson

Vice President Of Customer Loyalty, Michael Marino

Regional Vice President Of Marketing, Holly Campano

Regional Vice President Government Relations, Joseph (Jo) Tyrrell

Vice President Gaming Analytics, Nathan Armogan

Vice President, Antonios Clapsis

National Sales Manager, Grant Kehler

Vice President Of Human Resources, Ricky Busey

Vice President Marketing On Site, Kristin J Westberg

Vice President Digital Marketing, Greg Cannon

Vice President and Chief Counsel Intellectual Property, John C (Jack) Wilson

Vice President of Surveillance, Conrad Hamel

Senior Vice President and Chief Counsel Operations, Elizabeth (Beth) Nelson

Executive Vice President General Counsel and Chief Regulatory and Compliance Officer, Tim Donovan

Vice President of Food and Beverage, Dave Monroe

Vice President Casino Marketing, Eric Zilewicz

Regional Vice President Government Relations, A Baker

Senior Vice President Government and Communications, Jan Blackhurst

Vice President Chief Accounting Officer Caesars Entertainment Operating Company, Ken Kuick

Senior Vice President Retail, Terri Monsour

Vice President Assistant Controller, Kenneth (Ken) Kuick

Vice President International Marketing, Jose Lopez

National Sales Manager, Matthew (Matt) Waltersdorf

Vice President Information Technology Project Management Office and Shared Services at Caesars Entertainment Corporation, Mary Lynn Palenik

Vice President of Casino Operations Casino Marketing and Retail, Xenia Wunderlich

Chairman, Gary W. Loveman, age 54

Pac Treasurer, Lindsay Garcia

Secretary, Michael (Mel) Cohen

Auditors: Deloitte & Touche LLP

LOCATIONS

HQ: Caesars Entertainment Corp
One Caesars Palace Drive, Las Vegas, NV 89109
Phone: 702 407-6000
Web: www.caesars.com

PRODUCTS/OPERATIONS

2014 Sales

	$ mil.	% of total
Casino	5,418	55
Food & beverage	1,522	16
Rooms	1,207	13
Reimbursed management costs	252	3
Management fees	58	1
Other	1,197	12
Promotional allowances	(1138)	-
Total	**8,516**	**100**

COMPETITORS

Boyd Gaming	Pinnacle Entertainment
Isle of Capri Casinos	Station Casinos
Kerzner International	Tropicana
Las Vegas Sands	Entertainment
MGM Resorts	Trump Resorts
Mashantucket Pequot	Wynn Resorts

HISTORICAL FINANCIALS

Company Type: Public

Income Statement

FYE: December 31

	REVENUE ($ mil.)	NET INCOME ($ mil.)	NET PROFIT MARGIN	EMPLOYEES
12/14	8,516	(2,783)	—	68,000
12/13	8,559	(2,948)	—	68,000
12/12	8,586	(1,497)	—	68,000
12/11	8,834	(687)	—	70,000
12/10	8,818	(831)	—	69,000
Annual Growth	(0.9%)	—	—	(0.4%)

2014 Year-End Financials

Debt ratio: 98.63%
Return on equity: —
Cash ($ mil.): 2,806
Current ratio: 0.20
Long-term debt ($ mil.): 7,434

No. of shares (mil.): 145
Dividends
  Yield: —
  Payout: —
Market value ($ mil.): 2,275

	STOCK PRICE ($) FY Close	P/E High/Low	PER SHARE ($) Earnings	Dividends	Book Value
12/14	15.69	— —	(19.53)	0.00	(34.46)
12/13	21.54	— —	(22.93)	0.00	(22.82)
12/12	6.92	— —	(11.95)	0.00	(3.28)
Annual Growth	22.7%	— —	—	—	—

Calpine Corp

Calpine may get hot but it also knows how to blow off some steam. In 2014 the independent power producer and marketer controlled 27000 MW of generating capacity (and 309 MW under construction) through interests in 88 primarily natural gas-fired power plants in 18 US states and Canada. This fleet also includes 15 geothermal power plants in California. Calpine the leading geothermal power producer in North America owns 725 MW of capacity at the largest geothermal facility in the US (the Geysers in northern California) and which accounts for 40% of the country's geothermal energy. The company has major presence in the wholesale power markets in California the Mid-Atlantic and Texas.

Geographic Reach

Serving customers in 18 US states and Canada Calpine's operating segments are West (including geothermal) Texas and East (including Canada). The company has regional office in Dublin (California) Wilmington (Delaware) Pasadena (Texas) Washington DC Sacramento and Austin (Texas).

California Texas and the Northeast region are the largest wholesale power markets in the US.

Operations

The company's segments are West (including geothermal) Texas and East (including Canada). Texas accounted for 40% of Calpine's revenues in 2014; East 31%; and West 29%.

Other Calpine operations include construction consulting and management services; turbine component manufacturing; and critical power provision for high-tech companies.

Its indirect subsidiaries include Calpine Construction Finance Company L.P. (and its units Hermiston Power LLC and Brazos Valley Energy LLC) and Calpine Development Holdings Inc.

Sales and Marketing

The company sells wholesale power steam capacity renewable energy credits and ancillary services to their customers which include utilities independent electric system operators industrial and agricultural companies retail power providers municipalities power marketers and others. Calpine's utility electricity is distributed via its distribution network underground lines and transmission system.

Calpine sells electricity to wholesalers and end-users primarily through long-term contracts; the firm also trades power on the wholesale market. In 2014 grid operator PJM accounted for more than 10% of Calpine's total revenues.

Financial Performance

The company has recorded strong revenue growth over the last five years. In 2014 its net revenues increased by 27%. The West segment reported an increase due to the positive impact from Russell City and Los Esteros power plants reporting an increase in MW in operation partially offset by the expiration of a tolling contract associated with Calpine's Delta Energy Center. Texas saw a 38% increase in revenues due to the acquisition of the Guadalupe Energy Center and expansions of its Deer Park and Channel Energy Centers. An increase in average total MW in operation and in generation and a higher commodity margin also contributed to the strong growth. East segment revenues rose as the result of the sale of six power plants. The increase in commodity margin was due to colder than normal weather resulting in higher margins lower natural gas price. This rise was partially offset by lower contribution from hedges lower regulatory capacity revenues from PJM and the expiration of a power purchase agreement (PPA) associated with the Osprey Energy Center partially offset by a new PPA associated with Osprey Energy Center. In 2014 Calpine's net income increased by almost 6600% due to higher sales and the gain from the sale of six power plants in the East segment.

Cash from operating activities increased by 56% in 2014.

Strategy

The company's goal is to continue to grow its generation presence in core markets with an emphasis on acquisitions expansions or modernizations of existing power plants. Calpine is also actively seeking divestiture opportunities of non-core assets in order to pay down debt. Calpine also plans to focus on competitive wholesale power markets and advocate for market-driven solutions that result in nondiscriminatory forward price signals for investors.

The company has disposed of most of its natural gas reserves and gathering and transportation assets in order to focus on power generation. It is seeking to grow organically and through negotiating supply contracts and by making selected acquisitions supported by asset sales to ensure financial stability.

To raise cash to pay down debt in 2014 Calpine sold six of its power plants (with 3500 MW) to privately-held LS Power Equity Advisors for $1.6 billion.

In 2014 Calpine had two power plants under construction.

That year the company agreed to supply electric generation capacity and power to American Electric Power Service Corporation as agent for Public Service Company of Oklahoma from Calpine's Oneta Energy Center (a natural gas fired power plant).

In 2013 to raise cash Calpine sold its Riverside Energy Center (a 600 MW natural gas plant in Beloit Wisconsin to Wisconsin Power and Light for $400 million.

Mergers and Acquisitions

In 2015 Calpine acquired retail electric provider Champion Energy Marketing for $240 million plus working capital adjustments.

Growing its generating capacity in Texas in 2014 Calpine bought a power plant owned by MinnTex Power Holdings LLC with a nameplate capacity of 1050 MW for $625 million. It also purchased a 1050 MW combined-cycle power plant from a unit of Wayzata Investment Partners for $625 million. The natural gas-fired plant is 30 miles northeast of San Antonio.

That year the company also bought a 809 MW combined-cycle power plant from Exelon for $530 million. The natural gas-fired plant in North Weymouth Massachusetts expands Calpine's footprint in the New England competitive wholesale power market.

Company Background

In 2012 the company acquired an 800-MW natural gas-fired combined-cycle power plant in Central Texas from Bosque Power Co. for $432 million. That year it sold the Broad River Energy Center to Broad River Power LLC an affiliate of Energy Capital Partners LLC for $427 million.

In 2010 Calpine purchased 4490 MW of power plants from Pepco Holdings for about $1.7 billion. The acquisition added Conectiv Energy's power plants (18 operating and one under construction) to Calpine's fleet helping to strengthen its market position in the Eastern US.

EXECUTIVES

Senior Vice President CAO, Jim Deidiker
EVP Chief Legal Officer and Secretary, W. Thaddeus Miller, age 64, $816,493 total compensation
President and CEO, John B. (Thad) Hill, age 48, $895,903 total compensation
EVP and CFO, Zamir Rauf, age 55, $594,647 total compensation
SVP West Region, Alex Makler
EVP Power Operations, Tom Webb
EVP and Chief Commercial Officer, W.G. (Trey) Griggs
Vice President And Assistant General Counsel, Rosemary Antonopoulos
Vice President Technical Services, Bill Valagura
Vice President Sales, Heather Hazen
Vice President Engineering And Constr, Darron Granger
Vice President Physical Trading And Operations, Bob Hayes
Vice President Development and Optimization Engineering, Tom Long
Senior Vice President and Chief Administrative Officer, Hether Benjamin-Brown
Vice President, James (Jamie) Sandt
Vice President Corporate Asset Management, Andre Walker
Executive Vice President Chief Legal Off, W Miller
Chairman, Jack A. Fusco, age 52
Vice President Finance and Treasurer, Stacey Peterson
Vice Chairman, Keith Young
Treasurer and Vice President Finance, Todd A Thornton
Auditors: PricewaterhouseCoopers LLP

LOCATIONS

HQ: Calpine Corp
717 Texas Avenue, Suite 1000, Houston, TX 77002
Phone: 713 830-2000
Web: www.calpine.com

2014 Sales

	$ mil.	% of total
Texas	3,229	40
East	2,449	31
West	2,352	29
Total	**8,030**	**100**

COMPETITORS

AEP	Duke Energy
AES	Edison International
Berkshire Hathaway Energy	Enel North America
	PG&E Corporation
CMS Energy	PSEG Power
Covanta	Sempra Energy

HISTORICAL FINANCIALS

Company Type: Public

Income Statement

FYE: December 31

	REVENUE ($ mil.)	NET INCOME ($ mil.)	NET PROFIT MARGIN	EMPLOYEES
12/15	6,472	235	3.6%	2,209
12/14	8,030	946	11.8%	2,052
12/13	6,301	14	0.2%	2,157
12/12	5,478	199	3.6%	2,151
12/11	6,800	(190)	—	2,101
Annual Growth	(1.2%)	—	—	1.3%

2015 Year-End Financials

Debt ratio: 64.19%
Return on equity: 7.25%
Cash ($ mil.): 906
Current ratio: 1.34
Long-term debt ($ mil.): 11,868
No. of shares (mil.): 356
Dividends
  Yield: —
  Payout: —
Market value ($ mil.): 5,161

	STOCK PRICE ($) FY Close	P/E High/Low	PER SHARE ($) Earnings	Dividends	Book Value
12/15	14.47	36 18	0.64	0.00	8.72
12/14	22.13	10 8	2.31	0.00	8.84
12/13	19.51	734602	0.03	0.00	8.19
12/12	18.13	44 34	0.42	0.00	8.74
12/11	16.33	— —	(0.39)	0.00	8.93
Annual Growth	(3.0%)	— —	—	—	(0.6%)

Calumet Specialty Product Partners LP

Specialty hydrocarbon producer Calumet Specialty Products Partners operates in three business segments: specialty products fuel products and oilfield services. The specialty products unit the company's largest processes crude oil into lubricating oils solvents waxes and other petroleum products. It sells these items to industrial customers who use them in the manufacture of basic automotive consumer and industrial goods. The fuel products unit processes oil into unleaded gasoline diesel fuel and jet fuel. Calumet also produces asphalt. In terms of its customer base in 2014 the company had 5400 specialty products accounts and 700 fuel products accounts.

Geographic Reach

The company has 18 plants in northwest Louisiana northwest Wisconsin northern Montana western Pennsylvania southeastern Texas Illinois New Jersey Minnesota eastern Missouri and North Dakota. Calumet operates three refineries in Louisiana: Shreveport (with a throughput capacity of about 60000 barrels per day) Cotton Valley (13500 barrels per day) and Princeton (10000 barrels per day).

It has a refinery in Wisconsin (45000 barrels per day) Montana refinery (10000 barrels per day) and San Antonio refinery in Texas (17500 barrels per day). The company also has two white mineral oil processing facilities (in Pennsylvania and Texas) with a total capacity of 6800 barrels per day). It also owns and operates product terminals in Burnham Illinois; Rhinelander Wisconsin; Crookston Minnesota; and Proctor Minnesota with storage capacities of 150000 166000 156000 and 200000 barrels of oil equivalent respectively.

Operations

Fuel products accounted for 64% of Calumet's 2014 revenues; specialty products 30% and oilfield services 6%.

Sales and Marketing

Fuel products produced at the San Antonio refinery are sold locally in Texas. Shreveport refinery can be sold locally or to the Midwest region of the U.S. through the TEPPCO pipeline. Local sales are made from the TEPPCO terminal in Bossier City Louisiana Finished fuel products produced at the Superior refinery are sold through the Superior refinery truck rack several Magellan pipeline terminals in Minnesota Wisconsin Iowa North Dakota South Dakota Nevada Utah Wyoming Washington Idaho and Montana and through its Duluth terminal. The Superior wholesale fuel business also sells gasoline wholesale to Calumet branded gas stations located throughout the Upper Midwest (including Minnesota Wisconsin and Michigan) which are owned and operated by independent franchisees. The Superior refinery ships finished fuel products by railcar truck and pipeline service. Asphalt products produced at the Superior refinery are shipped by railcar and truck service and are sold through terminals in Rhinelander and Crookston and through other leased terminals in the U.S.Finished fuel products sales are primarily made through spot agreements and short-term contracts. Asphalt is primarily sold through spot agreements and short-term contracts with customers primarily located in and around the Upper Midwest North Dakota South Dakota Utah and New York.

Calumet's specialty products are sold to domestic and international customers who purchase them primarily as raw material components for basic industrial consumer and automotive goods. It also blends and markets specialty products through its Royal Purple Bel-Ray TruFuel and Quantum brands. Specialty products are distributed via railcars trucks and barges. Oilfield services markets products to the oil and gas exploration industry throughout the US.

Financial Performance

Calumet has enjoyed unprecedented revenue growth over the last few years. In 2014 net revenues increased by 7% was due to the revenue from the oilfield services segmentFuel products sales rose due primarily to increased volume partially offset by a decrease in the average selling price per barrel and a $5.9 million increase in realized derivative losses recorded in sales on their fuel products cash flow hedges. Sales volumes increased primarily due to increased sales volume of gasoline jet fuel and asphalt primarily as a result of increased production at the Superior and Montana refineries due to turnaround activity in 2013 and increased production at the San Antonio refinery as a result of the crude oil unit expansion partially offset by extended turnaround activity in 2014 at the Shreveport refinery. Specialty products segment sales decreased primarily as a result of incremental sales from the Bel-Ray and United Petroleum Acquisitions and an increase in the average selling price per barrel partially offset by lower sales volume. Legacy operations' sales increased due to increase in the average selling price per barrel primarily as a result of higher lubricating oil sales prices and improved product mix. Legacy operations' sales volumes decreased due primarily to lower sales volumes of lubricating oils and solvents due to market conditions partially offset by increased sales volumes of packaged and synthetic specialty products.Revenue from oilfield services segment sales increased as a result of the Anchor Drilling Fluids and Specialty Oilfield Solutions (SOS) acquisitions in 2014.The company recorded a net loss in 2014 of $112.2 million (compared to net gain in 2013) due to an increase in selling transportation Debt extinguishment costs and higher interest expense.Selling expenses increased due to incremental selling expenses related to the Anchor Bel-Ray and SOS acquisitions an increase in advertising expense and increase in professional fees expense.

Transportation expenses increased due primarily to expenses related to the Anchor Bel-Ray and SOS Acquisitions and increased crude oil sales to third parties partially offset by decreased lubricating oil sales.

Debt extinguishment costs of $89.9 million in 2014 were due primarily to the redemption of the remaining 2019 Notes with a portion of the net proceeds from the issuance of the 2021 Notes.In 2014 Calumet's cash from operating activities increased by 480% due to a decline in inventory accounts receivable and turnaround costs $44.8 million related to the early settlement of certain crack spread derivative instruments and a gain on sales of Renewable Identification Numbers (RINs) to

track renewable transportation fuels of $18.2 million.

Strategy

Calumet is focusing on growing assets and businesses that generate stable cash flows. The company has built up a stable base of clients through offering them a range of services and a long-term commitment that few of its rivals can match. It works with customers from product design stage to delivery. It also helps clients expand their product offerings and market these items to new customers. Buoyed by robust oil prices Calumet is relying heavily on acquisitions to expand its asset base.

Effective 2014 the company added oilfield services segment that manufactures and markets products and provides oilfield services including drilling fluids completion fluids production chemicals and solids control services to the oil and gas exploration industry throughout the US.

In the future Calumet intends to continue to consider strategic acquisitions of assets or agreements with third parties that offer the opportunity for operational efficiencies the potential for increased utilization and expansion of facilities or the expansion of product offerings in each of their specialty products fuel products and oilfield services segments. In addition it may pursue selected acquisitions in new geographic or product areas to the extent we perceive similar opportunities.In 2014 the company invested $440 million in an organic growth campaign. That year Calumet launched a 50/50 joint venture in a 20000-barrel-per-day refinery in Dickinson North Dakota to sell diesel among other finished products into the local market.

Mergers and Acquisitions

To augment its specialty products unit Calumet in 2014 obtained ADF Holdings an owner of a provider and marketer of drilling fluids completion fluids and production chemicals for $237 million. Also in 2014 the company swallowed up Bel-Ray Company a maker of high-performance lubricants for $54 million and specialty oil field products provider SOS for $30 million.

In 2014 Calumet also acquired United Petroleum Company a wholesale supplier and distributor of premium motor oils coolants and greases.

The company in 2013 acquired the San Antonio Texas refinery and associated crude oil pipeline terminal and related assets of NuStar Energy units NuStar Refining LLC and NuStar Logistics L.P. for $115.7 million.

Company Background

In 2012 Calumet acquired an aviation and refrigerant lubricants business from Ashland subsidiary Hercules (for $20 million) and Louisiana-based specialty petroleum packaging and distribution company TruSouth Oil for $27 million. That year it also picked up Texas-based Royal Purple a manufacturer of high-performance lubicants for the automotive industrial marine and motorcycle and racing industries. The $333 million purchase added to the company's specialty products segment. Growing its refinery assets that year Calumet also bought Montana Refining Company for $201 million.

EXECUTIVES

EVP CFO and Secretary, R. Patrick Murray, age 43, $329,600 total compensation
EVP Sales, William A. Anderson, age 46, $279,130 total compensation
EVP Operations, Ed Juno, age 62
CEO, Timothy Go, age 48
Vice President Of Human Resources, David Burford

Vice President Information Technology Operations and Program Management Office, Michael (Mel) Rhoades
Vice President investor and Media Relations, Noel Ryan
Vice President Physical Trading And Information Technology, Phillip (Phil) Hays
Vice President Planning and Economics Calumet Gp, Jeffrey D (Jeff) Smith
Vice President Finance, Pat Murray
Vice President Lubricant Sales, Shane Terry
Chairman Calumet GP, Fred M. Fehsenfeld, age 64
Executive Vice Chairman Calumet GP, F. William Grube, age 67
Treasurer, Dee Winchester
Board Member, Daniel J (Dan) Sajkowski
Auditors: Ernst & Young LLP

LOCATIONS

HQ: Calumet Specialty Product Partners LP
2780 Waterfront Parkway East Drive, Suite 200, Indianapolis, IN 46214
Phone: 317 328-5660
Web: www.calumetspecialty.com

PRODUCTS/OPERATIONS

2014 Sales

	$ mil.	% of total
Fuel products		
Gasoline	1,443	25
Diesel	1,197	21
Jet fuel	199	3
Asphalt heavy fuel oils & other	853	15
Specialty products		
Lubricating oils	748	14
Solvents	485	8
Packaged & synthetic specialty products	313	5
Waxes	144	2
Other	38	1
Oil field services	368	6
Total	**5,791**	**100**

COMPETITORS

BP Lubricants USA	HollyFrontier
CITGO	Koch Industries Inc.
Chevron	Marathon Petroleum
ConocoPhillips	Motiva Enterprises
Delek US	San Joaquin Refining
Ergon	Sunoco
Exxon Mobil	Valero Energy

HISTORICAL FINANCIALS

Company Type: Public

Income Statement

FYE: December 31

	REVENUE ($ mil.)	NET INCOME ($ mil.)	NET PROFIT MARGIN	EMPLOYEES
12/14	5,791	(112)	—	2,200
12/13	5,421	3	0.1%	1,420
12/12	4,657	205	4.4%	1,250
12/11	3,134	43	1.4%	920
12/10	2,190	16	0.8%	650
Annual Growth	**27.5%**	**—**	**—**	**35.6%**

2014 Year-End Financials

Debt ratio: 54.92%	No. of shares (mil.): 70
Return on equity: —	Dividends
Cash ($ mil.): 8	Yield: 12.2%
Current ratio: 1.67	Payout: —
Long-term debt ($ mil.): 1,712	Market value ($ mil.): 1,588

STOCK PRICE ($)	P/E	PER SHARE ($)		
FY Close	High/Low	Earnings	Dividends	Book Value
12/14 22.41	— —	(1.80)	2.74	11.43
12/13 26.02	— —	(0.17)	2.70	15.03
12/12 30.39	10 6	3.50	2.30	15.16
12/11 20.16	25 16	0.98	1.94	13.86
12/10 21.30	51 34	0.46	1.83	17.93
Annual Growth 1.3%	— —	—	10.7%	(10.6%)

Camden National Corp. (ME)

Camden National Corporation is the holding company for Camden National Bank which boasts nearly 45 branches in about a dozen Maine counties and provides standard deposit products such as checking and savings accounts CDs and IRAs. Commercial mortgages and loans make up 50% of its loan portfolio while residential mortgages make up another 40% and consumer loans constitute the remainder. Subsidiary Acadia Trust provides trust fiduciary investment management and retirement plan administration services while Camden Financial Consultants offers brokerage and insurance services. The largest bank headquartered in Maine Camden National Bank was founded in 1875 and once issued its own US currency.

OperationsAbout 63% of Camden National's total revenue came from loan interest (including fees) in 2014 while another 15% came from interest on its US government and sponsored enterprise obligations (investment securities). The rest of its revenue came from deposit account service charges (5%) other service charges and fees (5%) income from fiduciary services (4%) brokerage and insurance commissions (2%) and other miscellaneous income sources. The bank had a staff of 471 employees at the end of 2014.Geographic Reach-Camden National has around 45 branches in 12 counties throughout Maine with one commercial loan office in Manchester New Hampshire. Its primary markets are in the counties of Androscoggin Cumberland Hancock Kennebec Knox Lincoln Penobscot Piscataquis Somerset Waldo Washington and York.Sales and MarketingThe company offers deposit and loan services to consumers institutions municipalities non-profits and commercial customers. Financial PerformanceThe company has struggled to consistently grow its revenues and profits in recent years mostly due to shrinking interest margins on loans amidst the low-interest environment. Camden National's revenue dipped by 3% to $112.8 million in 2014 mostly because the bank in 2013 had collected a non-recurring $2.7 million gain from the sale of its five Franklin County branches and because its mortgage banking income fell by $1.1 million as it decided to retain most of its 30-year fixed rate residential mortgage production in 2014. Despite revenue declines in 2014 the bank's net income jumped by 8% to $24.6 million mostly because in 2013 it had recorded a non-recurring $2.8 million goodwill impairment charge related to its financial services reporting unit. Camden's operating cash levels rose by 1% to $29.9 million for the year on higher cash earnings.StrategyThe bank competes with larger financial institutions by emphasizing customer service to build customer loyalty and long-term relationships. It also sometimes pursues acquisitions of banks and branches in its target markets in Maine to grow its loan and deposit business.Camden may also be expanding its franchise beyond Maine in future years. In 2014 it opened a commercial loan office in Manchester New Hampshire enabling it to serve more customers across northern New England.Mergers and AcquisitionsIn March 2015 Camden National Corporation agreed to purchase SBM Financial along with its subsidiary The Bank of Maine subsidiary. The deal expected to be completed in late 2015 would add $813 million in assets and make Camden National Bank Maine's largest community bank.In late 2012 the bank acquired 15 full-service branches from Bank of America for $12 million.

EXECUTIVES

Vice President Risk Management, Steve Matteo
EVP COO and CFO, Deborah A. Jordan, age 49, $223,327 total compensation
VP and Human Resources Manager, June B. Parent, age 51, $189,248 total compensation
EVP Risk Management, Joanne T. Campbell, age 52, $124,585 total compensation
President and CEO, Gregory A. (Greg) Dufour, age 54, $398,077 total compensation
SVP Information Technology, Scott Buckheit
EVP Commercial Lending, Timothy P. Nightingale, age 57, $213,846 total compensation
Vice President, Richard Nickerson
Vice President retail Regional Manager Southern, Nancy Tracy
Vice President, Craig Day
Assistant Vice President, Jody Landrith
Senior Vice President, Vera Roberts
Vice President Human Resources, Carolyn Crosby
Chairman Camden National Corporation and Camden National Bank, Karen W. Stanley, age 69
Auditors: Berry Dunn McNeil & Parker, LLC

LOCATIONS

HQ: Camden National Corp. (ME)
2 Elm Street, Camden, ME 04843
Phone: 207 236-8821   **Fax:** 207 236-6256
Web: www.camdennational.com

PRODUCTS/OPERATIONS

2014 Sales

	$ mil.	% of total
Interest		
Loans including fees	70	63
US government & agency securities	17	14
Other investments	0	1
Noninterest		
Service charges on deposit accounts & others	12	11
Income from fiduciary services	5	4
Brokerage and insurance commission	1	2
Other	5	5
Total	**112**	**100**

COMPETITORS

Bangor Savings Bank	People' s United
Bar Harbor Bankshares	Financial
KeyCorp	TD Bank USA
Northeast Bancorp	The First Bancorp
Norway Bancorp	

HISTORICAL FINANCIALS

Company Type: Public

Income Statement

FYE: December 31

	ASSETS ($ mil.)	NET INCOME ($ mil.)	INCOME AS % OF ASSETS	EMPLOYEES
12/14	2,789	24	0.9%	471
12/13	2,603	22	0.9%	481
12/12	2,564	23	0.9%	550
12/11	2,302	26	1.1%	425
12/10	2,306	24	1.1%	421
Annual Growth	4.9%	(0.2%)	—	2.8%

2014 Year-End Financials

Debt ratio: 2.69%
Return on equity: 10.32%
Cash ($ mil.): 60
Current ratio: —
Long-term debt ($ mil.): —
No. of shares (mil.): 7
Dividends
  Yield: 2.7%
  Payout: 35.5%
Market value ($ mil.): 296

	STOCK PRICE ($) FY Close	P/E High/Low	PER SHARE ($) Earnings	Dividends	Book Value
12/14	39.84	13 11	3.28	1.08	33.01
12/13	41.84	15 11	2.97	1.06	30.49
12/12	33.97	13 10	3.05	1.50	30.67
12/11	32.60	11 7	3.41	1.50	28.56
12/10	36.23	12 8	3.23	1.00	26.90
Annual Growth	2.4%	— —	0.4%	1.9%	5.2%

Cameron International Corp

Cameron International knows how to work under pressure. A leading manufacturer provider and servicer of oil and gas industry equipment the company makes products that control pressure at oil and gas wells including blowout preventers chokes controls wellheads and valves. Cameron sells its products which are used for offshore onshore and subsea applications under more than 60 brand names including Ajax Cameron Cooper-Bessemer Demco LeTourneau Natco Petreco and Willis. In 2015 Cameron agreed to be acquired rival Schlumberger in a transaction valued at $14.8 billion.

Geographic Reach

Cameron's Western Hemisphere are mainly located in North and South America; Eastern Hemisphere operations cover Norway the UK and on the European continent. It also has operations in Asia/Pacific and Middle East and West Africa (mainly Angola Algeria and Nigeria).In 2014 the US accounted for 45% of Cameron's revenues.

Operations

The company provides oil and gas production support systems through three separate business segments: Subsea Surface Drilling and Valves and Measurement (V&M).

The Subsea segment delivers integrated solutions products systems and services to the subsea oil and gas market including integrated subsea production systems involving wellheads subsea trees manifolds and flowline connectors subsea processing systems for the enhanced recovery of hydrocarbons control systems connectors and services designed to maximize reservoir recovery and extend the life of each field. The Subsea segment includes the operations of OneSubsea a business jointly owned by Cameron (60%) and Schlumberger (40%).Cameron's Surface segment designs and manufactures complete wellhead and Christmas tree systems for onshore and offshore topside applications (from conventional to high-pressure high temperature systems to specialized systems for dry completions and heavy oil.

The Drilling segment is one of the leading global suppliers of integrated drilling systems for onshore and offshore applications to shipyards drilling contractors exploration and production companies and rental tool companies. Drilling equipment designed and manufactured includes ram and annular BOPs control systems drilling risers drilling valves choke and kill manifolds diverter systems topdrives drawworks mud pumps pipe handling equipment other rig products and parts and services.

The V&M segment supplies valves and measurement systems primarily used to control direct and measure the flow of oil and gas as they are moved from wellheads to refineries petrochemical plants and industrial centers. Its products include gate valves ball valves butterfly valves plug valves globe valves check valves actuators chokes and measurement products such as totalizers turbine meters flow computers chart recorders and ultrasonic flow meters.

Sales and Marketing

Subsea products and services are marketed products under the Cameron Mars McEvoy and Willis brand names through a worldwide network of sales and marketing employees supported by agents in some international locations.The Surface segment has a portfolio of API 6A valves chokes actuators and artificial lift technologies is marketed primarily to oil and gas operators under the Cameron Camrod IC McEvoy Precision SBS Tundra Willis and WKM brands. One of the major services provided by the Surface segment is CAMSHALE Production Solutions which specializes in shale gas production.Drilling segment products are marketed by a staff of sales and marketing employees supported by an engineering group under the Cameron Guiberson H&H CUSTOM H&H Melco LeTourneau Lewco OEM Sense and Townsend brand names.Valves & Measurement products are sold through a network of wholesalers and distributors primarily in North America and to upstream markets in Asia-Pacific and the Middle East. This equipment and the related services are marketed through a worldwide network of combined sales and marketing employees as well as distributors and agents in selected international locations.Customers include oil and gas majors independent producers engineering and construction companies pipeline operators drilling contractors and major chemical petrochemical and refining companies.

Financial Performance

The company has seen its revenues rise over the last five years.In 2014 Cameron's net revenues increased by 6%.Subsea revenues increased primarily as a result of higher international project activity levels on large subsea projects offshore Brazil and Nigeria partially offset by certain subsea projects nearing completion in the Gulf of Mexico and the Asia-Pacific region as well as a moderate decline in custom processing equipment revenues.Surface revenues rose due mainly to higher activity levels as well as increased market penetration in various North American unconventional resource regions and higher deliveries to customers in the North Sea Saudi Arabia and Oman as well as higher sales to the Company's Drilling segment.Drilling revenues increased driven by the execution of orders from the segment's substantial beginning-of-the-year backlog levels and better project execution as well as an increased demand for the company's services.V&M revenues

for 2014 were relatively flat as increased sales of distributed valves and measurement products (stemming from continued strength in the North American market) were mostly offset by lower engineered and process valves sales due largely to project slippage order weakness and delayed timing of valve deliveries due to various customer changes.In 2014 Cameron's net income increased by 16% due to higher net sales lower other costs and income from discontinued operations.Cash from operating activities increased by 42%.

Strategy

In 2015 the company sold its Reciprocating Compression business to Ingersoll Rand for $850 million.

That year Cameron announced the execution of definitive agreements between OneSubsea Helix Energy Solutions and Schlumberger for a non-incorporated alliance formed to develop technologies and to deliver equipment and services designed to provide customers with more cost effective and more efficient subsea well intervention solutions particularly for deep and ultra-deepwater basins and high well pressure environments. Subsequently Schlumberger made a bid to acquire Cameron in a deal valued at $14.8 billion.

Cameron pursues a strategy of growth through joint ventures and the acquisition of companies that complement its existing core businesses.

North America continues to be important to Cameron accounting for nearly 64% of Cameron's revenues for the year ended December 31 2014 up from 61% in 2013 and 55% in 2012. Production and service facilities in North and South America Europe Asia the Middle East and West Africa provide the Company with the ability to serve the global marketplace.

In 2014 the company was rationalizing its business portfolio and sharpening its focus on the business segments that target the oil and gas equipment markets: markets that will be core to Cameron's future growth and that will provide synergies share common processes customers technologies as well as provide aftermarket services and growth opportunities.

Company Background

In 2013 Cameron and Schlumberger formed OneSubsea (60% owned by Cameron International) to manufacture and develop products systems and services for the subsea oil and gas market. The creation of OneSubsea allows the company to bring together Schlumberger's expertise in subsea processing and platform integration with its own capabilities in subsea equipment to allow customers to greatly increase their subsea reservoir recovery rates. (In 2014 OneSubsea Helix Energy Solutions and Schlumberger formed an alliance to develop technologies and deliver services to optimize the cost and efficiency of subsea well intervention systems.)

Cameron moved into the lucrative shale market in the US Northeast in 2011 through the acquisition of West Virginia-based Industrial Machine & Fabrication a leading aftermarket service provider for reciprocating engines and compressors.

That year it also expanded its drilling equipment portfolio buying LeTourneau Technologies Drillings Systems and Offshore Products divisions from Joy Global for $375 million.

In 2010 a BP rig in the Gulf of Mexico exploded and sank spewing oil into the Gulf. The blowout preventer on the system made by Cameron International failed to work properly. A board of inquiry was set up to find out the cause of the disaster and a separate government report found that the company's blowout preventer proved incapable of stopping the high-pressure flow from the doomed well. The company claimed that its equipment met industry standards and it was not found liable in any legal proceeding although it did pay $82.5 million

to settle with BP. (BP accounted for 12% of the company's revenues in 2010).

Cameron traces its roots to the mid-1800s when it made steam engines to generate power for plants and textile and rolling mills.

EXECUTIVES

SVP and CFO, Charles M. Sledge, age 50, $646,490 total compensation

Chairman and CEO, Jack B. Moore, age 62, $1,125,000 total compensation

President Process Systems, Steven W. Roll

VP Operational Excellence, Douglas E. (Doug) Meikle

President and COO, R. Scott Rowe, age 44, $486,338 total compensation

VP Marketing and CTO, Justin Rounce

Vice President Finance, Kevin Orme

Vice President Health Safety and Environment, Christopher (Chris) Tagoe

Vice President Sales and ENGRG OFFSHORE PRODUCTS, Julian F Bowes

Vice President North and South America, Mark Schubert

Vice President, Willy Findlay

Vice President Total Rewards, Amber Macksey

Auditors: Ernst & Young LLP

LOCATIONS

HQ: Cameron International Corp
1333 West Loop South, Suite 1700, Houston, TX 77027
Phone: 713 513-3300   **Fax:** 713 513-3320
Web: www.c-a-m.com

2014 Sales

	$ mil.	% of total
US	4,689	45
UK	964	9
Other countries	4,728	46
Total	10,381	100

PRODUCTS/OPERATIONS

2014 Sales

	$ mil.	% of total
Subsea	3,067	29
Drilling	3,049	28
Surface	2,411	23
V&M	2,125	20
Elimination	(271)	-
Total	10,381	100

Selected Mergers and Acquisitions

COMPETITORS

ABB Inc.
Aker Solutions
Atlas Copco
CIRCOR International
Dresser-Rand
Dril-Quip
Ebara
FMC
Flotek
GE Oil
Ingersoll-Rand Industrial Technologies
McDermott
National Oilwell Varco
Tyco
Weatherford International

HISTORICAL FINANCIALS

Company Type: Public

Income Statement

FYE: December 31

	REVENUE ($ mil.)	NET INCOME ($ mil.)	NET PROFIT MARGIN	EMPLOYEES
12/15	8,782	501	5.7%	23,000
12/14	10,381	811	7.8%	28,000
12/13	9,838	699	7.1%	29,000
12/12	8,502	750	8.8%	27,000
12/11	6,959	521	7.5%	22,500
Annual Growth	6.0%	(1.0%)	—	0.6%

2015 Year-End Financials

Debt ratio: 24.57%
Return on equity: 11.00%
Cash ($ mil.): 1,775
Current ratio: 2.22
Long-term debt ($ mil.): 2,542

No. of shares (mil.): 191
Dividends
  Yield: —
  Payout: —
Market value ($ mil.): 12,083

	STOCK PRICE ($) FY Close	P/E High/Low		PER SHARE ($) Earnings	Dividends	Book Value
12/15	63.20	27	16	2.60	0.00	23.82
12/14	49.95	19	11	3.96	0.00	23.36
12/13	59.53	23	18	2.87	0.00	26.43
12/12	56.46	19	13	3.02	0.00	22.56
12/11	49.19	29	19	2.09	0.00	19.17
Annual Growth	6.5%	—	—	5.6%	—	5.6%

Campbell Soup Co.

Soup boils down to M'm! M'm! Money! at the world's #1 soup maker Campbell Soup. The company's most popular selections among its 90-variety soup portfolio in the US include chicken noodle tomato and cream of mushroom. Campbell also makes many other simple foods snacks and beverages including SpaghettiOs canned pasta Pace picante sauce V8 beverages Aussie favorite Arnott's biscuits and Pepperidge Farm baked goods (including those popular tiny Goldfish crackers). Newer products for the soup company include Garden Fresh Gourmet salsas and dips and Bolthouse Farms carrots and organic baby foods. All told Campbell sells its products in 100-plus countries from facilities across the globe.

HISTORY

Campbell Soup Company began in Camden New Jersey in 1869 as a canning and preserving business founded by icebox maker Abram Anderson and fruit merchant Joseph Campbell. Anderson left in 1876 and Arthur Dorrance took his place. The Dorrance family assumed control after Campbell retired in 1894.

Arthur's nephew John Dorrance joined Campbell in 1897. The young chemist soon found a way to condense soup by eliminating most of its water. Without the heavy bulk of water-filled cans distribution was cheaper; Campbell products quickly spread.

In 1904 the firm introduced the Campbell Kids characters. Entering the California market in 1911 Campbell became one of the first US companies to achieve national distribution of a food brand. It bought Franco-American the first American soup maker in 1915.

The company's ubiquity in American kitchens made its soup can an American icon (consider Andy Warhol's celebrated 1960 print) and brought great wealth to the Dorrance family.

With a reputation for conservative management Campbell began to diversify acquiring V8 juice (1948) Swanson (1955) Pepperidge Farm (1961) Godiva Chocolatier (33% in 1966 full ownership in 1974) Vlasic pickles (1978) and Mrs. Paul's seafood (1982). It introduced Prego spaghetti sauce and LeMenu frozen dinners in the early 1980s.

Much of Campbell's sales growth in the 1990s came not from unit sales but from increasing its prices. In 1993 it took a $300 million restructuring charge and over the next two years it sold poor performers at home and abroad. John Sr.'s grandson Bennett Dorrance took up the role of vice chairman in 1993 becoming the first family member to take a senior executive position in 10 years.

Two years later Campbell paid $1.1 billion for Pace Foods (picante sauce) and acquired Fresh Start Bakeries (buns and muffins for McDonald's) and Homepride (popular cooking sauce in the UK). As part of its international expansion in 1996 the firm acquired Erasco a top German soup maker and Cheong Chan a food manufacturer in Malaysia. However back at home it sold Mrs. Paul's. In 1997 Campbell sold its Marie's salad dressing operations and bought Groupe Danone's Liebig (France's leading wet-soup brand). Also that year Dale Morrison a relative newcomer to the firm succeeded David Johnson as president and CEO. To reduce costs and focus on other core segments in 1998 Campbell spun off Swanson frozen foods and Vlasic pickles into Vlasic Foods International. (Vlasic later filed bankruptcy and was snapped up in a leveraged buyout.) In 1999 Campbell redesigned its soup can labels altering an American icon.

Morrison resigned abruptly as president and CEO in 2000; Johnson returned to the helm during the search for a permanent chief. In early 2001 Douglas Conant previously of Nabisco Foods joined Campbell as president and CEO. A fresh plan was introduced to spend up to $600 million on marketing product development and quality upgrades (at the expense of shareholder dividends). In 2001 Campbell also bought the Batchelors Royco and Heisse Tasse brands of soup as well as the OXO brand of stock cubes from Unilever for about $900 million. The deal made Campbell the leading soup maker in Europe. In 2003 Campbell bought Snack Foods Limited a leading snack food maker in Australia and Irish dry soup maker Erin Foods from Greencore.

Campbell reorganized its North American business in 2004 into the following units: US Soup Sauces and Beverages; Campbell Away From Home and Canada Mexico and Latin America; Pepperidge Farm; and Godiva Worldwide. (In response to dietary trends the company announced that year that it was removing all trans-fatty acids from its Pepperidge Farm breads.) The company retired the Franco-American brand in 2004; products that carried the brand (most notably SpaghettiOs) now bear the Campbell brand. Also that year company chairman George M. Sherman retired and was replaced by Harvey Golub.

In 2006 Campbell sold its UK and Irish businesses to Premier Foods for about $870 million. Brands involved in the sale included Homepride sauces OXO stock cubes and Batchelors McDonnells and Erin soups.In 2012 the company purchased Bolthouse Farms for about $1.55 billion from Madison Dearborn Partners. Bolthouse known for selling fresh carrots beverages and salad dressings was expected to further fuel Campbell's US beverage division which had benefited from the rising popularity of the V8 juice brand.

EXECUTIVES

President and CEO, Denise M. Morrison, age 61, $1,091,667 total compensation
VP and Controller, Anthony P. DiSilvestro, age 56, $587,733 total compensation
SVP and Chief Strategy Officer, Michael P. (Mike) Senackerib, age 49
SVP and CIO, Joseph C. (Joe) Spagnoletti, age 50
President Americas Simple Meals and Beverages, Mark R. Alexander, age 51, $657,875 total compensation
President Packaged Fresh, Jeffrey T. (Jeff) Dunn, $700,000 total compensation
SVP Integrated Global Services, Ed Carolan, age 46
President Global Biscuits and Snacks, Luca Mignini, age 52, $674,042 total compensation
SVP Global Research and Development, Carlos J Barroso, age 56, $470,000 total compensation
SVP and Chief Legal and Public Affairs Officer, Ellen Oran Kaden, age 62, $729,458 total compensation
SVP Global Supply Chain, David B. (Dave) Biegger
Vice President Marketing, Tom Wegmann
Vice President Industry Relations, Keith Olscamp
Vice President Consumer Customer Insights, Charles (Chas) Vila
Vice President Immediate Consumption, Kyle Jordan
Vice President Global Supply Chain Process Excellence, Pat Folan
Vice President Sales and Marketing North America Foodservice, Kevin Matier
Vice President Sales US Retail, Jim Sterbenz
Vice President Customer Planning and Category Strategy, Veeral Shah
Vice President Swanson Prego Pace Specialty Brands, Dale Clemiss
Vice President Supply Chain Campbell's North American Operations and US Retail Business Team, Alan (Al) Blake
Vice President Marketing and Sales Campbell's Fresh, Mark Rutledge
Vice President Corporate Audit, Tom Smith
Senior Vice President Finance, Tony Disilvestro
Chairman, Les C. Vinney, age 66
Auditors: PRICEWATERHOUSECOOPERS LLP

LOCATIONS

HQ: Campbell Soup Co.
  1 Campbell Place, Camden, NJ 08103-1799
Phone: 856 342-4800   **Fax:** 856 342-3878
Web: www.campbellsoupcompany.com

2015 Sales

	$ mil.	% of total
US	6,400	79
Australia	646	8
Other	1,036	13
Total	**8,082**	**100**

PRODUCTS/OPERATIONS

2015 Sales

	$ mil.	% of total
US Simple Meals	2,930	36
Global Baking & Snacking	2,375	29
International Simple Meals & Beverages	700	9
US Beverages	689	9
Bolthouse & Foodservice	1,388	17
Total	**8,082**	**100**

2015 Sales

	$ mil.	% of total
Simple Meals	4,446	55
Baked Snacks	2,502	31
Beverages	1,134	14
Total	**8,082**	**100**

Selected Brand Names

Domestic
  Away From Home

Bolthouse Farms
Campbell
Ecce Panis
Pace
Pepperidge Farm
Plum Organics
Prego
Select Harvest
StockPot
Swanson
V8 and V8 Splash
Wolfgang Puck
International
Arnott' s (Australia)

Selected Subsidiaries

Arnott' s Biscuits Limited (Australia)
Bolthouse Holding Corp. (US)
Ecce Panis Inc.
Pepperidge Farm Incorporated
Players Group Limited (Australia)
Sinalopasta S.A. de C.V. (Mexico)
Stockpot Inc.

COMPETITORS

Associated British	Hanover Foods
Foods	Harry' s Fresh Foods
B&G Foods	Heinz
Barbara' s Bakery	Hormel
Baxters	Kellogg U.S. Snacks
Beech-Nut	Mondelez International
Big Heart Pet Brands	Morgan Foods
Bush Brothers	NORPAC
Canyon Creek Food	Nestl©
ConAgra	Odwalla
Dole Food	Pacific Coast
Faribault Foods	Producers
Frito-Lay	Peter Rabbit Farms
General Mills	Red Gold
Gerber Products	Reily Foods
Golden Enterprises	Ren©e' s Gourmet Foods
Grimmway Enterprises	Snyder' s-Lance
H. J. Heinz Limited	Unilever
Hain Celestial	Walkers Snack Foods

HISTORICAL FINANCIALS

Company Type: Public

Income Statement

FYE: August 2

	REVENUE ($ mil.)	NET INCOME ($ mil.)	NET PROFIT MARGIN	EMPLOYEES
08/15	8,082	691	8.5%	18,600
08/14*	8,268	818	9.9%	19,400
07/13	8,052	458	5.7%	20,000
07/12	7,707	774	10.0%	17,700
07/11	7,719	805	10.4%	17,500
Annual Growth	1.2%	(3.7%)	—	1.5%

*Fiscal year change

2015 Year-End Financials

Debt ratio: 50.62%
Return on equity: 46.27%
Cash ($ mil.): 253
Current ratio: 0.75
Long-term debt ($ mil.): 2,552

No. of shares (mil.): 310
Dividends
  Yield: 0.0%
  Payout: 56.4%
Market value ($ mil.): 15,286

	STOCK PRICE ($) FY Close	P/E High/Low		PER SHARE ($) Earnings	Dividends	Book Value
08/15	49.31	22	19	2.21	1.25	4.45
08/14*	41.96	18	15	2.59	1.25	5.16
07/13	47.07	33	22	1.44	1.16	3.90
07/12	33.12	14	12	2.41	1.16	2.88
07/11	33.05	15	13	2.42	1.15	3.40
Annual Growth	10.5%	—	—	(2.2%)	2.2%	7.0%

*Fiscal year change

CANDID COLOR SYSTEMS INC.

LOCATIONS

HQ: CANDID COLOR SYSTEMS INC.
  1300 METROPOLITAN AVE, OKLAHOMA CITY, OK
  731082042
Phone: 4059478747
Web: WWW.OKLAHOMAPARTYPICS.COM

HISTORICAL FINANCIALS

Company Type: Private

Income Statement

FYE: July 31

	REVENUE ($ mil.)	NET INCOME ($ mil.)	NET PROFIT MARGIN	EMPLOYEES
07/07	21,742	2,534	11.7%	300
07/05	22	1	8.3%	—
07/04	21	2	10.9%	—
07/03	21	0	—	—
Annual Growth	467.2%	—	—	—

2007 Year-End Financials

Debt ratio: ——
Return on equity: 11.70%
Cash ($ mil.): 2
Current ratio: 1.70
Long-term debt ($ mil.): —

Dividends
  Yield: —
  Payout: —
Market value ($ mil.): —

Capital Bank Financial Corp

Capital Bank Financial Corporation (formerly North American Financial Holdings) ownsÂnearly 20% of Capital Bank NA which operatesÂmore thanÂbranches in Florida North Carolina South Carolina Tennessee and Virginia. TheÂbank offersÂstandardÂsavings and checking accounts as well as mortgagesÂconsumer and commercial loans and other financial products and services. Formed in 2009 Capital Bank Financial went public in 2012. The company plans to use the proceeds from the offering (about $180 million) to fund future acquisitions and for general corporate purposes and working capital.ÂTo that end it acquiredÂSouthern Community Financial Corp. for about $47 million in cashÂin late 2012.

Winston-Salem-based Southern Community Financial adds another 22 branches in North Carolina to its new parent' s holdings. Since 2009 Capital Bank Financial has raised some $900 million (mostly through private placement of its stock) to acquire its banks the majority of which were distressed or failed institutions operating in what the company deems to be attractive fast-growing metropolitan markets. The company acquired five banks in 2009 and 2010 including Capital Bank Metro Bank Turnberry Bank TIB Bank and First National Bank of the South. It bought a sixth Green Bankshares in 2011. The latest deal nearly doubled NAFH' s branch network and expanded the company' s presence in Tennessee. GreenBank was merged into Capital Bank NA after the transaction was complete.

While Capital Bank Financial may continue to acquire additional banks in the region it also intends to grow through organic means including opening additional branches in existing markets and focusing on commercial and consumer lending as a way to fuel growth. It is also concentrating on controlling costs and has among other cost-cutting measures reorganized its banks and reduced personnel as a way to eliminate expenses.

EXECUTIVES

Executive Vice President And General Counsel,
  Vincent Lichtenberger
Senior Vice President, Edward (Ed) Tietjen
Auditors: Crowe Horwath LLP

LOCATIONS

HQ: Capital Bank Financial Corp
  121 Alhambra Plaza Suite 1601, Coral Gables, FL 33134
Phone: 305 670-0200
Web: www.capitalbank-us.com

COMPETITORS

BB&T	JPMorgan Chase
Bank of America	Pinnacle Financial
Citigroup	Partners
CommunityOne Bancorp	RBC Financial Group
EverBank Financial	Regions Financial
Fifth Third	South State
First Citizens	SunTrust
Bancorporation	Synovus
First Horizon	TD Bank
First South Bancorp	U.S. Bancorp
(NC)	Wells Fargo
First South Bancorp	
(SC)	

HISTORICAL FINANCIALS

Company Type: Public

Income Statement

FYE: December 31

	ASSETS ($ mil.)	NET INCOME ($ mil.)	INCOME AS % OF ASSETS	EMPLOYEES
12/14	6,831	50	0.7%	1,515
12/13	6,617	38	0.6%	1,610
12/12	7,295	51	0.7%	1,588
12/11	6,587	6	0.1%	1,480
12/10	3,496	12	0.3%	—
Annual Growth	18.2%	43.4%	—	—

2014 Year-End Financials

Debt ratio: 2.04%
Return on equity: 4.68%
Cash ($ mil.): 188
Current ratio: —
Long-term debt ($ mil.): —

No. of shares (mil.): 47
Dividends
  Yield: —
  Payout: —
Market value ($ mil.): 1,275

	STOCK PRICE ($) FY Close	P/E High/Low		PER SHARE ($) Earnings	Dividends	Book Value
12/14	26.80	26	21	1.02	0.00	22.35
12/13	22.75	32	21	0.73	0.00	21.36
12/12	17.07	17	16	1.06	0.00	20.70
Annual Growth	11.9%	—	—	(1.0%)	—	1.9%

Capital City Bank Group, Inc.

Capital City Bank Group is the holding company for Capital City Bank (CCB) which serves individuals businesses and institutionsÂfrom some 70 branches in Florida Georgia and Alabama.ÂCCB offers checking savings and money market accounts; CDs; IRAs; Internet banking; and debit and credit cards. Commercial real estate mortgages account for aboutÂ40% of its loan portfolio;Âresidential real estate loans also hover near 40%. The bank alsoÂoriginates business loans andÂconsumer loans including credit cards. Capital City alsoÂperforms data processing services for other financial institutions in its market area.

Geographic Reach

Florida is CCB's largest market accounting for about 78% of its revenue. Georgia and Alabama account for 21% and 1% respectively.

Operations

In addition to its CCB bank subsidiary which accounts for about 94% of Capital City Bank Group's total revenue the holding company operates three other subsidiaries: Capital City Trust a provider of trust and asset management services; Capital City Banc Investments which offers investments retirement plans and life and long-term care insurance through an agreement with third-party provider INVEST Financial Corporation a subsidiary of Jackson National Life Insurance Company; and data processor Capital City Services Co.

Financial Analysis

Capital City Bank Group's revenue has slid since the onset of the recession and housing crisis which battered the Florida market and during the uneven recovery. Revenue fell 5% in 2011 vs. 2010 marking the fourth consecutive year of decline. Indeed revenue plunged 74% between 2007 and 2011. However in 2011 the group returned to profitability with net income of $4.9 million following losses in 2010 and 2009.

Interest income decreased by 10% while non-interest income increased 4% in 2011 vs. 2010. Lower interest and fees on loans contributed to the decline in interest income. Growth in bank card and retail brokerage fees contributed to the rise in non-interest income.

Strategy

Capital City Bank Group was founded in 1982 to acquire six banks and has never looked back. While its growth has slowed the company has continued its acquisition strategy buying 15 banks since 1984; it has also expanded by opening new offices. However its home state of Florida was one of the hardest hit during the recession. High unemployment levels contributed to an increase in nonperforming loans in the bank's portfolio which in turn translated to net losses in 2009 and 2010. (Nonperforming loans totaled $75 million or 4.6% of the company's total loan portfolio at the end of 2011.) Capital City is focusing on diversifying its portfolio and reducing problem assets.

Ownership

Chairman and CEO William Smith Jr. and his brother Robert own about 20% of Capital City Bank Group.

EXECUTIVES

Vice President, Karen Love
EVP and CFO, J. Kimbrough (Kim) Davis, age 61, $260,000 total compensation
Chairman President and CEO, William G. (Bill) Smith, age 61, $350,000 total compensation

Credit Administration, Dale A. Thompson
Chief People Officer and President Capital Services Company, Bethany H. (Beth) Corum
President Capital City Banc Investments; President Capital City Trust Company, Bill Moor
President Leon County, Ed West
Residential Mortgage, Tom Allen
Commercial Banking, Ed Canup
Community Banking, Mitch Englert
Executive Vice President Marketing, Connie Odom
Vice President And Trust Officer, Janice White
Assistant Vice President, Lisa Elam
Assistant Vice President Community Banker, Brian Timmons
Senior Vice President Compliance and Security, Brian Wimpling
Senior Vice President, David Caldwell
Assistant Vice President, Leslie Samuelson
Assistant Vice President, Leitta Williamson
Vice President, Joel Ginaldi
Assistant Vice President, Cindy Richardson
Vice President Lender, Todd Troyer
Vice President, Cristie Garrett
Assistant Vice President Human Resources, Sharon Martin
Assistant Vice President, Janette Wagner
Assistant Vice President MIS Analysis, Canington Carol
Vice President Of Corporate Cm, Carol Brannen
Vice President Marketing, Walter Hoskins
Assistant Vice President, Sylvia White
Assistant Vice President, Edie Frasier
Vice President, Karen Meadows
Vice President Community Banking Specialist, Patsy McKenzie
Assistant Vice President And Community Banker, Janie Stewart
Vice President Information Security, Leanne Staalenburg
Executive Vice President Chief Financial Officer, Kim Davis
Senior Vice President Capital City Bank, Mark Strickland
Secretary And Treasurer, Evelyn Pridgeon
Auditors: Ernst & Young LLP

LOCATIONS

HQ: Capital City Bank Group, Inc.
217 North Monroe Street, Tallahassee, FL 32301
Phone: 850 402-7000
Web: www.ccbg.com

PRODUCTS/OPERATIONS

2014 Sales

	$ mil.	% of total
Interest		
Loans including fees	73	56
Investment securities	3	3
Funds sold	1	1
Noninterest income		
Service charges on deposit accounts	24	19
Bank card fees	10	8
Wealthmanagement fees	7	6
Mortgage Banking fees	3	2
Data processing fees	1	1
Other	4	4
Total	**130**	**100**

COMPETITORS

Ameris	Regions Financial
BBX Capital	SunTrust
Bank of America	Thomasville Bancshares
Delta Community Credit Union	

HISTORICAL FINANCIALS

Company Type: Public

Income Statement

FYE: December 31

	ASSETS ($ mil.)	NET INCOME ($ mil.)	INCOME AS % OF ASSETS	EMPLOYEES
12/14	2,627	9	0.4%	937
12/13	2,611	6	0.2%	927
12/12	2,633	0	0.0%	913
12/11	2,641	4	0.2%	959
12/10	2,622	(0)	—	975
Annual Growth	0.0%	—	—	(1.0%)

2014 Year-End Financials

Debt ratio: 3.58%	No. of shares (mil.): 17
Return on equity: 3.37%	Dividends
Cash ($ mil.): 385	Yield: 0.5%
Current ratio: —	Payout: 15.5%
Long-term debt ($ mil.): —	Market value ($ mil.): 271

	STOCK PRICE ($) FY Close	P/E High/Low		PER SHARE ($) Earnings	Dividends	Book Value
12/14	15.54	30	22	0.53	0.09	15.62
12/13	11.77	37	30	0.35	0.00	15.92
12/12	11.37	1169	651	0.01	0.00	14.33
12/11	9.55	47	33	0.29	0.30	14.68
12/10	12.60	—	—	(0.02)	0.49	15.15
Annual Growth	5.4%	—	—	—	(34.5%)	0.8%

Capital One Financial Corp

Capital One isn't just concerned with what's in your wallet; it's interested in your bank account as well. The company is best known as one of the largest issuers of Visa and MasterCard credit cards in the US but it also boasts a banking network of 900-plus branches in about half a dozen states (including New York and Texas) and the District of Columbia. Bolstered by its 2012 acquisition of ING Direct the bank also offers online and direct banking. Capital One which serves more than 50 million customers in the US Canada and the UK also has units that offer auto financing write home loans sell insurance and manage assets for institutional and high-net-worth clients.

HISTORY

Company BackgroundCapital One Financial is a descendant of the Bank of Virginia which was formed in 1945. The company began issuing products similar to credit cards in 1953 and was MasterCard issuer #001. Acquisitions and mergers brought some 30 banks and several finance and mortgage companies under the bank's umbrella between 1962 and 1986 when Bank of Virginia became Signet Banking.

Signet's credit card operations had reached a million customers in 1988 when the bank hired consultants Richard Fairbank and Nigel Morris (Fairbank is now chairman and CEO) to implement their "Information-Based Strategy." Under the duo's leadership the bank began using sophisticated data-collection methods to gather massive amounts of information on existing or prospective customers; it then used the information to design and mass-market customized products to the customer.

In 1991 —after creating an enormous database and developing sophisticated screening processes and direct-mail marketing tactics —Signet escalated the credit card wars luring customers from its rivals with its innovative balance-transfer credit card. The card let customers of other companies transfer what they owed on higher-interest cards to a Signet card with a lower introductory rate.

The new card immediately drew imitators (by 1997 balance-transfer cards accounted for 85% of credit card solicitations). After skimming off the least risky customers Fairbank and Morris began going after less desirable credit customers who could be charged higher rates. The result was what they call second-generation products —secured and unsecured cards with lower credit lines and higher annual percentage rates and fees for higher-risk customers.

The credit card business had grown to 5 million customers by 1994 but at a high cost to Signet which had devoted most of its resources to finding and servicing credit card holders. That year Signet spun off its credit card business as Capital One to focus on banking. (Signet was later acquired by First Union.)

The company moved into Florida and Texas in 1995 and into Canada and the UK in 1996; that year it established its savings bank mainly to offer products and services to its cardholders. In 1997 the company used this unit to move into deposit accounts buying a deposit portfolio from J. C. Penney. In 1998 the company began marketing its products to such clients as immigrants and high school students (whose parents must co-sign for the card). The company also expanded in terms of products and geography acquiring auto lender Summit Acceptance and opening a new office in Nottingham England.

In 1999 the firm's growth continued. The company stepped up its marketing efforts and was rewarded with significant boosts to its non-interest income and customer base. The next year the company launched The Capital One Place an Internet shopping site. In 2001 the company acquired AmeriFee which provides loans for elective medical and dental surgery; and PeopleFirst Inc. the nation's largest online provider of direct motor vehicle loans.

In response to industry-wide concern over subprime lending Capital One agreed in 2002 to beef up reserves on its subprime portfolio. Also in 2002 the company's UK operations proved profitable for the first time.

The company expanded into banking in 2005 and 2006 with the acquisitions of Hibernia and North Fork Bancorporation respectively. The deals gave it a boost in the banking sector expanding its presence both geographically in the Northeast and in the South and turning the company into one of the top bank holding companies in the US. The $13.2 billion stock-and-cash North Fork deal gave the company more than 300 bank branches in New York New Jersey and Connecticut.

The 2005 purchase of New Orleans-based Hibernia was a stock-and-cash transaction valued at some $5 billion nearly 10% less than the originally agreed-upon price. The transaction was delayed then renegotiated after Hurricane Katrina devastated Hibernia's home city. Hibernia which relocated to Houston adopted the Capital One moniker.

Capital One closed wholesale lender GreenPoint Mortgage Funding acquired as part of its acquisition of North Fork in 2007. The unit suffered from the credit woes that have plagued the subprime mortgage industry.

The company expanded its franchise into the Washington DC market in 2009 by buying Chevy Chase Bank for some $475 million in cash and stock.

EXECUTIVES

Evp, James R Tietjen
General Counsel and Corporate Secretary, John G. Finneran, age 65, $974,693 total compensation
Chairman and CEO, Richard D. (Rich) Fairbank, age 64
Vice President, Salvatore Chierico
Senior Vice President manager, Gerald (Jerry) Shepard
CFO, Stephen S. (Steve) Crawford, age 50, $1,526,538 total compensation
CIO, Robert M. Alexander, age 50
President Commercial Banking, Michael C. Slocum, age 58
President Financial Services, Sanjiv Yajnik, age 58, $912,923 total compensation
EVP Auto Finance, Ryan M. Schneider, age 45, $1,116,462 total compensation
President Retail and Direct Banking, Jonathan W. Witter, age 45, $870,769 total compensation
Chief Risk Officer, Kevin Borgmann, age 43
Senior Vice President, Nancy Stich
MVP, Suzette Prechter
Executive Vice President Head Of Strategy, Stephen Mugford
Vice President, Khary Scott
Vice President Human Resources, Sammy Duff
Executive Vice President, Michael (Mel) Wassmer
Vice President Commercial Real Estate, Frank Volpe
Senior Vice President, Jeff Lee
Vice President, Carol Anderson
Vice President, Ashish Tandon
Assistant Vice President, Michelle Morales
Assistant Vice President Information S, Carl Pomplon
Assistant Vice President, Disnalda Cuevas
Senior Vice President, Patrick (Paddy) Olinde
Senior Vice President Middle Atlantic Middle Market Banking, Richard (Dick) Amador
Vice President Administration, Regina Meskill
Vice President, Linda Walz
Vice President Underwriter, Allison Sardo
Senior Vice President, Anthony Fermo
Business Banker Assistant Vice President, Adam Kulikowski
Vice President, Brad Dolbec
Senior Vice President, Adam Ostrach Adam Ostrach
Assistant Vice President, Karla Lastrap
Vice President Brokerage Information Technology, Garrett Silver
Senior Vice President, Robert (Bob) Harvey
Executive Vice President, Murray Abrams
Vice President Compliance, Mike Lamberth
Senior Vice President, Roy Aksdal
Senior Vice President Card Marketing, Sherri Gilligan
Vice President, Ross Mazer
Vice President End User and Data Center Systems Integration, Beatricia Helou
Senior Vice President and Market President Commercial Banking, Edward (Ed) Waterfield
Vice President Human Resources, Guenet Beshah
Senior Vice President, Karen Bauer
Assistant Vice President Principal Recruiter Commercial Operations, Heather McAleavy
Vice President, Theodore McField
Vice President, Ehab Awadallah
Vice President In Us Card Recoveries Division, Amanda Aghdami
Vice President Information Technology, Patricia Elliott
Vice President Corporate Audit Services, Erika Ray
Vice President, Michael Lockery
Senior Vice President, Harry Golliday
Vice President Sales and Service Strategy, Shail Moorjani
Senior Vice President Middle Market New York, Ellen Marshall

Vice President Institutional Equity Sales, Andreas Argenti
Senior Vice President, Jon Oldham
Senior Vice President, Scott Fishbein
Senior Vice President Hedge Strategy Debt Capital Markets, Stephanie Tyner
Senior Vice President, Wilson Tam
Executive Vice President For Direct Businesses, Jim Kelly
Assistant Vice President Trust Assistant, James (Jamie) Brooks
Managing Vice President, Johan Gericke
Vice President, Yolanda Rodriguez
Senior Vice President, Stephen Block
Vice President, Shahram Elghanayan
Senior Vice President, John Blackwelder
Vice President, Jeff Holtshopple
Vice President Private Banking, Bob Sferrazza
Vice President, Joanne Gagliardi
Vice President Multifamily Lending, Todd Phillips
Senior Vice President, Gregory Horstman
Business Banker Assistant Vice President, Ellie Azar
Vice President Middle Atlantic Middle Market Banking, Peter (Pete) Schatz
Vice President Capital One Bank, Margaret (Peg) Kamba
Vice President Underwriter, Lawrence Cannariato
Vice President Business Banking, Sanjay Mukhi
Vice President Commercial Real Estate, Cynthia Forte
Assistant Vice President, David (Dave) Vitt
Senior Vice President, Elisa Depalma
Vice President Senior Compliance Officer, Elias Rizkallah
Vice President Business Banking, Nate Hoffman
Vice President, Paul Keagle
Senior Vice President, Bryan Pynchon
District Manager Vice President, Lisa Robbins
Senior Vice President Capital One Equipment Finance Corp, Ellen Barry
Assistant Vice President, Alexander (Al) Thezan
Vice President, Erin Coveny
Senior Vice President Retail Distribution, Kenneth (Ken) Kido
Vice President Business Banker, Michael (Mel) Dunn
Vice President Information Technology Integrated Production Support, John (Jack) Walker
Senior Vice President Retail Banking, William Luckert
Vice President, Michael Piazza
Vice President of End User Services, Martha Wilson
Senior Vice President, Paul Verdi
Vice President Business Banking, Maria Brosnahan
Vice President Bank Project Management Office, Jonathan (Jon) Topp
Senior Vice President Treasury Management, Shaleen Prakash
Vice President Segmentation Marketing, Raj Dutt
Vice President, Kim Dean
Assistant Vice President, Carter King
Senior Vice President Regional Sales Manager Treasury Manage, James (Jamie) Porr
Senior Vice President And Public Finance, Spencer Gagnet
Assistant Vice President, Marc Fridson
Assistant Vice President, Mirko Pefaure
Vice President Business Banking, Jeffrey (Jeff) Webster
Vice President, David Blasini
Vice President Strategy, Sarah Strauss
Vice President Us Card, Emilia Lopez
Vice President, Kara Lyons
Vice President Tax, Mark Servis
Vice President, Jorge Calderon
Vice President, John Villar
Vice President Finance Corporate Planning And Analysis, Chad Eisele

Vice President, Betty Waller
Vice President, Chris Shankle
Senior Vice President, Joseph Matusek
Vice President, Scott Zimmer
Vice President, Robbie Naquin
Vice President, Kader Ma
Senior Vice President Retail Banking Models and
  Project Management Bank, Keri Gohman
Vice President And Treasurer, Nicole Benoit
Assistant Vice President, Bill Manning
Vice President Business Banking, Dan Sullivan
Senior Vice President Sales And Service, Daniel
  (Dan) Caretta
Vice President Human Resources Client
  Consulting, Laura Baron Bellome
Senior Vice President Bank External Fraud Risk
  Management, Yu Huang
Vice President, Michelle Khalili
Vice President, Patrick Gemmell
Vice President Enterprise mobile and emerging
  channels, Toby Russell
Vice President Of Human Resources, Joel Martinez
Vice President Investor Real Estate, Kevin Lemoine
Assistant Vice President, Lawren Allen
Senior Vice President, Michael Fink
Assistant Vice President, Karen Eleser
Executive Vice President Southeast Commercial
  Banking, William Herrington
Vice President Human Resources, Meghan Welch
Senior Vice President, Stuart Schulman
Senior Vice President Commercial Real Estate,
  Jeff Wallace
Vice President, Edward Kang
Executive Vice President Marketing, Ashley Taylor
Vice President Internet Services, Marie Kraus
Assistant Vice President Small Business Banker,
  Andrei Barros
Vice President Senior Business Banker, Richard
  Ziegler
Vice President, Drew Scrivener
Vice President Business Development, Don
  Chapman
Auditors: Ernst & Young LLP

LOCATIONS

HQ: Capital One Financial Corp
  1680 Capital One Drive, McLean, VA 22102
Phone: 703 720-1000
Web: www.capitalone.com

PRODUCTS/OPERATIONS

2014 Sales

	$ mil.	% of total
Interest		
Loans held for investment	17,662	74
Investment securities	1,628	7
Other	107	-
Noninterest		
Interchange fees	2,021	8
Service charges & other customer fees	1,867	8
Other	608	3
Adjustments	(48)	-
Total	23,869	100

2014 Segment Sales

	% of total
Credit card	61
Consumer banking	29
Commercial banking	10
Total	100

COMPETITORS

American Express	HSBC USA
Bank of America	JPMorgan Chase
Citigroup	PNC Financial
Credit Acceptance	Regions Financial
Discover	Wells Fargo
GM Financial	

HISTORICAL FINANCIALS

Company Type: Public

Income Statement

FYE: December 31

	ASSETS ($ mil.)	NET INCOME ($ mil.)	INCOME AS % OF ASSETS	EMPLOYEES
12/14	308,854	4,428	1.4%	46,000
12/13	297,048	4,159	1.4%	41,951
12/12	312,918	3,517	1.1%	39,593
12/11	206,019	3,147	1.5%	31,542
12/10	197,503	2,743	1.4%	27,826
Annual Growth	11.8%	12.7%	—	13.4%

2014 Year-End Financials

Debt ratio: 15.69%
Return on equity: 10.20%
Cash ($ mil.): 7,242
Current ratio: —
Long-term debt ($ mil.): —

No. of shares (mil.): 553
Dividends
  Yield: 1.4%
  Payout: 16.4%
Market value ($ mil.): 45,682

	STOCK PRICE ($) FY Close	P/E High/Low		PER SHARE ($) Earnings	Dividends	Book Value
12/14	82.55	11	9	7.59	1.20	81.41
12/13	76.61	11	7	6.96	0.95	72.89
12/12	57.93	10	7	6.16	0.20	69.56
12/11	42.29	8	5	6.80	0.20	64.50
12/10	42.56	8	6	6.01	0.20	58.07
Annual Growth	18.0%	—	—	6.0%	56.5%	8.8%

Capitol Federal Financial Inc

Dorothy and Toto may not be in Kansas anymore but Capitol Federal Financial is. The holding company owns Capitol Federal Savings Bank the largest bank headquarted there. The savings bankÂserves metropolitan areasÂof the Sunflower StateÂ as well asÂ Kansas City Missouri throughÂaboutÂ45 branches includingÂnearly aÂdozen inside retail stores such asÂTarget Price Chopper and Dillons. Serving consumers and commercial customers theÂthrift offers standard servicesÂsuch as mortgages and loans depositsÂand retail investments. Its Capitol Agency affiliate sells life liability homeowners renters and vehicle insurance.Â

Capitol Federal Financial became a stock form holding companyÂthrough a 2010 offeringÂthat brought in more than $1 billion in capital. Before the conversion a mutual holding company Capitol Federal Savings Bank MHC owned about 70% of the company's shares.

Capitol Federal Savings concentrates onÂretail consumers. About 95% of its loan portfolio isÂmade up ofÂmortgagesÂsecured by owner-occupied residences. The bankÂalso writes consumer loans construction loans and other real estateÂloans. Thanks to its conservative underwriting standards theÂcompany has been able to maintain relatively low levels of nonperformingÂloans compared to many ofÂits peers since the credit crisis. HoweverÂits net income fell by nearly 45% from $67.8 million in fiscal 2010 to $38.4 million in 2011Âas Capital Federal Financial contributed $40 million to its charitable foundation as part of its corporate reorganization. A decline in interest income from lending also hampered the company's results.

Capitol Federal is lookingÂto expand in all of its markets though theÂKansas CityÂarea isÂof particular focus forÂthe company. It opened three new branches there in fiscal 2010.

EXECUTIVES

Chairman President and CEO, John B. Dicus, age 54, $581,484 total compensation
SVP and Controller, Kent G. Townsend, age 53, $303,991 total compensation
EVP and Chief Lending Officer, Rick C. Jackson, $163,690 total compensation
EVP Corporate Services, Carlton A Ricketts
EVP General Counsel, Natalie Haag
EVP Retail Operations, Frank H. Wright, $202,362 total compensation
Assistant Vice President, Sharon Dodd
Vice President, Jennifer (Jen) Raine
Auditors: Deloitte & Touche LLP

LOCATIONS

HQ: Capitol Federal Financial Inc
  700 Kansas Avenue, Topeka, KS 66603
Phone: 785 235-1341
Web: www.ir.capfed.com

PRODUCTS/OPERATIONS

2011 Sales

	$ mil.	% of total
Interest		
Loans receivable	251	68
Mortgage-backed securities	71	19
Investment securities	19	5
Other	4	1
Noninterest		
Retail fees & charges	15	4
Other	9	3
Total	371	100

COMPETITORS

Bank of America	Landmark Bancorp
Commerce Bancshares	U.S. Bancorp
First Federal of Olathe	UMB Financial

HISTORICAL FINANCIALS

Company Type: Public

Income Statement

FYE: September 30

	ASSETS ($ mil.)	NET INCOME ($ mil.)	INCOME AS % OF ASSETS	EMPLOYEES
09/14	9,865	77	0.8%	716
09/13	9,186	69	0.8%	724
09/12	9,378	74	0.8%	738
09/11	9,450	38	0.4%	734
09/10	8,487	67	0.8%	753
Annual Growth	3.8%	3.4%	—	(1.3%)

2014 Year-End Financials

Debt ratio: —
Return on equity: 4.97%
Cash ($ mil.): 810
Current ratio: —
Long-term debt ($ mil.): —

No. of shares (mil.): 140
Dividends
  Yield: 8.2%
  Payout: 192.1%
Market value ($ mil.): 1,666

	STOCK PRICE ($) FY Close	P/E High/Low		PER SHARE ($) Earnings	Dividends	Book Value
09/14	11.82	24	21	0.56	0.98	10.59
09/13	12.43	27	24	0.48	1.00	11.04
09/12	11.96	26	22	0.47	0.40	11.63
09/11	10.56	53	43	0.24	0.83	11.58
Annual Growth	2.9%	—	—	23.6%	4.4%	(2.2%)

Cardinal Financial Corp

Cardinal Financial can help you keep out of the red. The holding company owns Cardinal Bank which operates nearly 30 branches in northern Virginia and the Washington DC metropolitan area. Serving commercial and retail customers it offers such deposit options as checking savings and money market accounts; IRAs; and CDs as well as trust services. Commercial real estate loans make up more than 40% of Cardinal Financial's loan portfolio; residential mortgages construction loans business loans and home equity and consumer loans round out the bank's lending activities. Subsidiary Cardinal Wealth Services provides brokerage and investment services through an alliance with Raymond James Financial.

Operations

Other units include money manager Wilson/Bennett Capital Management which focuses on value-oriented investing and large-cap stocks and George Mason Mortgage which originates residential mortgages for sale into the secondary market through about 15 branches in Cardinal Bank's market area.

Financial Performance

The company's revenue has been up and down in recent fiscal years. Its revenue decreased in fiscal 2013 compared to the prior year. The company reported revenue of $144 million for fiscal 2013 down from $178.4 million in fiscal 2012 but up from the $137.2 million it reported for revenue in fiscal 2011.

More concerning than the dip in total annual revenue during fiscal 2013 was the drop in net income compared to fiscal 2012. Cardinal Financial reported net income of $25 million in fiscal 2013 down from $45 million in fiscal 2012.

However despite the decreased annual revenue and net income the company's cash flow recovered from negative levels in fiscal 2012 to positive territory by the close of fiscal 2013.

EXECUTIVES

EVP Retail Banking Human Resources and Marketing Cardinal Bank, Eleanor D. Schmidt, age 51
Acting President and CEO, Christopher W. Bergstrom, age 55, $346,667 total compensation
Regional President Cardinal Bank, F. Kevin Reynolds, age 55, $263,000 total compensation
EVP and COO, Alice P. Frazier, age 49, $346,667 total compensation
EVP and Chief Lending Officer, Dennis M. Griffith, age 66, $154,985 total compensation
EVP and CFO Cardinal Financial Corporation and Cardinal Bank, Mark A. Wendel, age 56, $223,667 total compensation
President and CEO George Mason Mortgage LLC, Bob Brower
Chairman Cardinal Financial Corporation and Cardinal Bank, Bernard H. Clineburg, age 66
Auditors: Yount, Hyde & Barbour, P.C.

LOCATIONS

HQ: Cardinal Financial Corp
8270 Greensboro Drive, Suite 500, McLean, VA 22102
Phone: 703 584-3400
Web: www.cardinalbank.com

COMPETITORS

Access National	PNC Financial
BB&T	SunTrust
Bank of America	United Bankshares
Burke & Herbert Bank	Virginia Commerce
Capital One	Bancorp
Millennium Bankshares	

HISTORICAL FINANCIALS

Company Type: Public

Income Statement

FYE: December 31

	ASSETS ($ mil.)	NET INCOME ($ mil.)	INCOME AS % OF ASSETS	EMPLOYEES
12/14	3,399	32	1.0%	733
12/13	2,894	25	0.9%	809
12/12	3,039	45	1.5%	706
12/11	2,602	28	1.1%	510
12/10	2,072	18	0.9%	417
Annual Growth	13.2%	15.4%	—	15.1%

2014 Year-End Financials

Debt ratio: 0.72%	No. of shares (mil.): 32
Return on equity: 9.37%	Dividends
Cash ($ mil.): 20	Yield: 1.7%
Current ratio: —	Payout: 39.5%
Long-term debt ($ mil.): —	Market value ($ mil.): 636

	STOCK PRICE ($) FY Close	P/E High/Low		PER SHARE ($) Earnings	Dividends	Book Value
12/14	19.83	20	16	1.00	0.34	11.76
12/13	17.99	22	18	0.82	0.28	10.57
12/12	16.30	11	7	1.51	0.20	10.19
12/11	10.74	13	9	0.94	0.12	8.83
12/10	11.63	19	14	0.62	0.08	7.75
Annual Growth	14.3%	—	—	12.7%	43.6%	11.0%

Cardinal Health, Inc.

When your local pharmacy runs low on drugs or supplies it probably calls Cardinal Health. The company is a top distributor of pharmaceuticals and other medical supplies and equipment in the US. Its pharmaceutical division provides supply chain services including branded and generic prescription and OTC drug distribution. It also franchises Medicine Shoppe retail pharmacies. Its medical division parcels out medical laboratory and surgical supplies and provides logistics consulting and data management. Customers include retail pharmacies hospitals nursing homes doctor's offices and other health care businesses. International markets for Cardinal Health include China.

HISTORY

Cardinal Health harks back to Cardinal Foods a food wholesaler named for Ohio's state bird. In 1971 Robert Walter then 26 and with the ink still fresh on his Harvard MBA acquired Cardinal in a leveraged buyout. He hoped to grow Cardinal by acquisitions but was frustrated when he found that the food distribution industry was already highly consolidated.

In 1980 Cardinal moved into pharmaceuticals distribution with the acquisition of Zanesville. It went public in 1983 as Cardinal Distribution and Walter began looking for more acquisitions. Cardinal soon expanded nationwide by swallowing other distributors. During the 1980s these purchases included two pharmaceuticals distributors headquartered in New York and a Massachusetts-based pharmaceuticals and food distributor.

In 1988 Cardinal sold its food group including Midland Grocery and Mr. Moneysworth to Roundy's and narrowed its focus to pharmaceuticals.

Drug distributors joined the rest of the pharmaceutical industry in its rush toward consolidation during the 1990s. Cardinal's acquisitions in those years included Ohio Valley-Clarksburg (1990 the Mid-Atlantic) Chapman Drug Co. (1991 Tennessee) PRN Services (1993 Michigan) Solomons Co. (1993 Georgia) Humiston-Keeling (1994 Illinois) and Behrens (1994 Texas).

One of Cardinal's most important acquisitions during this period was its cash purchase of Whitmire Distribution in 1994. Formerly Amfac Health Care Whitmire had been a subsidiary of Amfac one of Hawaii's "Big Five" landholders. When Amfac Health Care was spun off in 1988 its president Melburn Whitmire led a management group that acquired a majority interest. When Cardinal bought it Whitmire was the US's #6 drug wholesaler; the purchase bumped Cardinal up to #3. At that time the company changed its name to Cardinal Health and Melburn Whitmire became Cardinal's vice chairman.

In 1995 Cardinal made its biggest acquisition yet when it purchased St. Louis-based Medicine Shoppe International the US's largest franchisor of independent retail pharmacies. Founded by two St. Louis obstetricians in 1970 the Medicine Shoppe had 987 US outlets and 107 abroad at the time of its purchase by Cardinal (for $348 million in stock).

Over the next few years Cardinal continued to grow through acquisitions including automatic drug-dispensing system maker Pyxis pharmaceutical packaging company PCI Services and pharmacy management services company Owen Healthcare (which became Cardinal Health Pharmacy Management).

EXECUTIVES

Vice President for Enterprise Solutions and Architect Cardinal Health, Greg Boggs
EVP Customer Care Shared Services and CIO, Patricia B. (Patty) Morrison, age 55
Chairman and CEO, George S. Barrett, age 60, $1,314,630 total compensation
President Nuclear Pharmacy Services, Tiffany P. Olson, age 56
President Cardinal Health at Home, Michael B. Petras
President Specialty Solutions, Meghan M. FitzGerald, age 44
CFO, Michael C. (Mike) Kaufmann, age 52, $647,699 total compensation
CEO Medical Segment, Donald M. (Don) Casey, age 56, $647,699 total compensation
Chief Legal and Compliance Officer, Craig S. Morford, age 56, $508,466 total compensation
President Cardinal Health Specialty Solutions, Joseph I. DePinto, age 48
President Medical Products, Mike Duffy
EVP General Counsel and Corporate Secretary, Stephen T. (Steve) Falk, age 50
CEO Pharmaceutical Segment, Jon Giacomin, age 50
President Hospital Sales and Services, Steve Inacker
EVP Global Sourcing, Craig Cowman
EVP Enterprise Corporate Accounts, G. Brian Ellis
Vice President Indirect Procurement Facilities and Real Estate, Marino Colatruglio
Vice President Information Technology, Scot Lindsey
Senior Vice President Government and Community Relations, Connie Woodburn
Senior Vice President General Counsel, Susan (Sue) Jacobson
Vice President Alternate Care Sales, Jim Scott
Pharmd, Sheryl Sunnongmuang
Pharmacy Manager, Michael Teaster
Senior Vice President Health Information Services, Nick Augustinos
Corp Vice President, Victor Ruiz

Senior Vice President Global Sourcing, Stefan Grunwald
Pharmacy Manager, John Miller
Vice President Strategic PLNG Execution, Steve Thompson
Vice President Generic Product Management, Scott Decker
Vice President Business Development, Jody Rogers
Vice President Strategic Sourcing and Product Management, Sanjeeth Pai
Vice President of Sales and Marketing, Dan Farrell
Global Vice President Legal Affairs And Human Resources, Mindy Stobart
Vice President of Marketing and Product Management, Marc DeLorenzo
Senior Vice President Public Relations, Debbie Mitchell
Executive Vice President, Kirk Bantz
Vice President Of Pharmaceutical Sciences, Diane Beatty
Vice President, Shaden Marzouk
Vice President And Associate General Counsel Healthcare Supply Chain Services, Eric Christensen
Vice President Strategic Accounts, Eric Bolling
Vice President Sales, Douglas Katz
Vice President Operations, Micheal Brown
Vice President National Account Customer Support, Don Lyle
Vice President Operations Support, Rick Boykin
Vice President Managing Counsel, Jessica Mayer
Vice President Regulatory Affairs, Gary Cacciatore
Vice President Sales, Michael (Mel) Marusa
Vice President Global Trade Operations, Warren Hastings
Pharmacy Manager, Susan (Sue) Morgan
Senior Vice President Sales and Marketing, Marc Mullen
Vice President MW Region Operations, Brian Bejarano
Senior Vice President Finance Medical, Dennis Braun
Vice President Account Management, Paul Farnin
Vice President Tax, Mark Stauffer
Vice President Application Design and Development, Shauna Latshaw
Vice President Of Operations, Sean McCaffrey
Director of Pharmacy, Allen (Al) Johnson
Director Of Pharmacy, Laurie Sobas
Vice President Platform and Enterprise Information Technology Shared Services, Lori Havlovitz
Director Of Pharmacy, Jill Ashworth
Vice President Marketing And Product Management, David P (Dave) Mitchell
Vice President Health Systems, Erik Lilje
Vice President General Manager, Guru Gurushankar
Vice President Strategic Accounts, Phyllis Jarrett
Executive Vice President, Gilberto Quintero
Vice President ISF of Sales Opps, Todd Cameron
Vice President Compensation, Melanie Filas
Vice President Qra, David (Dave) Ticker
Vice President Sales Training and Effectiveness, Cindy Davidson
Vice President Quality Operations, Michael Groesbeck
Senior Vice President Marketing and Customer Solutions, Christi Pedra
Vice President, Bob Glover
Vice President Of Sales, Ryan Cox
Vice President Warehouse Operations, Kevin Kannally
Vice President Of Operational Excellence, Alan Deutschendorf
Regional Vice President, Peter Brennan
Vice President Of Government Accounts, Kate Spirko
Vice President Sales, Stephen Karavitch
Vice President M and A (attorney), Patrick (Paddy) Belville

National Vice President Sales, Brad Wilson
Strategic Account Vice President, Linda Lockyer
Senior Vice President Cardinal Health, Ramon Gregory
Vice President, Tim Copeland
Vice President, Mike Scholze
Vice President, Karen McNeal
Vice President Transportation and Logistics, Mike Good
Pharmacy Manager, Michael Wyant
Vice President Services And Operations, Carola Endicott
Vice President, Ronald Schultz
Vice President Pharmaceutical Sales, Thompson Kevin
Vice President Marketing and Product Management, Myles Hoover
Vice President of General, Thomas (Thom) Burke
Vice President Inventory Management, Andy Keller
Medical Director, Kevin J Soden
Pharmacy Manager, Tally Townsend
Vice President, Lisa Patterson
Vice President Marketing, Don Cere
Vice President, Jamie Mathews
Director of Pharmacy, Robert (Bob) Shuminski
Executive Vice President Enterprise Architecture and Chief Information Security Officer, Talvis Love
Director Of Pharmacy, Gregory Blank
Vice President Sales Operations Pricing andcontracting, Bruce Krarup
Director Of Pharmacy, Jeremy Bymaster
Director Of Pharmacy, Michelle Dalton
Vice President, Colleen McGuffin
MW Strategic Account Group Vice President, Gregg Brewster
Vice President Retail Sales, Jeff Brannon
Vice President, Steve Hyland
Vice President, Judy Hiscocks
Vice President, Constance Mantel
Vice President Medical Business Transformation, Cathy King
Vice President, Rick Buechner
Senior Vice President Corp Development and Strategy, Joshua T (Josh) Gaines
Vice President and Associate General Counsel, Charles (Chas) Aragon
Vice President, Robert Doren
Vice President Supply Chain Services, Kelly Parkey
Vice President Software Engineering, Tim Heller
Vice President Operations (UroMed), Terrie Sommers
Vice President, Brian Waeltz
Vice President EIT Client Services, Michael (Mel) Scrase
Vice President Financial Planning and Analysis for E.I.T., Todd Williams
Vice President of Human Resources, Ola Snow
Group Vice President Health Systems, Therese Grossi
Rph, Vanessa Vallejo
Vice President Human Resources, Lisa Finneran
Vice President Sales, Mark Mitchell
Executive Vice President Packaging Service Group, Renard Pawlak
Vice President Transportation Medical Segment Hospital Sales and Services, Scott Wagner
Vice President Cardinal Health, Robert Larkin
Vice President Telecommunications, Debbie Partyka
Senior Vice President Sales And Distribution International Business Machines Corporation, Colleen Arnold
Vice President Distribution and Warehouse, Brian Merrill
Pharmacy Manager, Jay Dyer
Vice President, Kent Oakley
Director Of Pharmacy, Brad Morris
Pharmacy Manager, Todd Lamb
Vice President Of Sales, Chris Lanctot

Director Of Pharmacy, Todd Worsham
Vice President Marketing Management, Emily Gallo
Vice President Fin PLNG And Analysis, Jason Buehler
Vice President Strategic Accounts, Lisa Dunkley
Pharmacy Manager, Joann Fitch
Vice President Finance Management, Gira Shah
Pharmacy Manager, Ann Shea
Director Of Pharmacy, Lynn Staggs
Vice President Fin PLNG And Analysis, Justin Schomaker
National Account Manager, Alan Pinyerd
National Account Manager, Marcy Cassaro
Pharmacy Manager, John Miano
Director Of Pharmacy, Jessica Hoover
Director Of Pharmacy, Sharon Greasheimer
Auditors: Ernst & Young LLP

LOCATIONS

HQ: Cardinal Health, Inc.
7000 Cardinal Place, Dublin, OH 43017
Phone: 614 757-5000
Web: www.cardinalhealth.com

2015 Sales

	$ mil.	% of total
US	98,435	96
Other countries	4,096	4
Total	**102,531**	**100**

PRODUCTS/OPERATIONS

2015 Sales

	$ mil.	% of total
Pharmaceutical	91,116	89
Medical	11,395	11
Corporate	20	-
Total	**102,531**	**100**

COMPETITORS

AmerisourceBergen	Medline Industries
Ansell	Molnlycke
CVS	Moore Medical
Deroyal Industries	Omnicare
Franz Haniel	Owens & Minor
H. D. Smith Wholesale Drug	PSS World Medical
Henry Schein	PharMerica
Kimberly-Clark	Quality King
McKesson	Rite Aid
Medical Action Industries	Thermo Fisher Scientific
	Walgreen

HISTORICAL FINANCIALS

Company Type: Public

Income Statement

FYE: June 30

	REVENUE ($ mil.)	NET INCOME ($ mil.)	NET PROFIT MARGIN	EMPLOYEES
06/15	102,531	1,215	1.2%	34,500
06/14	91,084	1,166	1.3%	34,000
06/13	101,093	334	0.3%	33,600
06/12	107,552	1,069	1.0%	32,500
06/11	102,644	959	0.9%	31,900
Annual Growth	**(0.0%)**	**6.1%**	**—**	**2.0%**

2015 Year-End Financials

Debt ratio: 18.22%	No. of shares (mil.): 328
Return on equity: 19.20%	Dividends
Cash ($ mil.): 4,616	Yield: 1.6%
Current ratio: 1.26	Payout: 41.4%
Long-term debt ($ mil.): 5,211	Market value ($ mil.): 27,437

	STOCK PRICE ($) FY Close	P/E High/Low	PER SHARE ($) Earnings	Dividends	Book Value
06/15	83.65	25 19	3.62	1.41	19.07
06/14	68.56	22 14	3.38	1.25	18.99
06/13	47.20	50 39	0.97	1.09	17.63
06/12	42.00	15 12	3.06	0.88	18.20
06/11	45.42	17 11	2.72	0.80	16.66
Annual Growth	16.5%	— —	7.4%	15.3%	3.4%

Carmax Inc.

To the greatest extent possible CarMax helps drivers find late-model used autos. Typically selling vehicles that are less than six years old with less than 60000 miles the US's largest specialty used-car retailer buys reconditions and sells cars and light trucks through more than 140 superstores in 70-plus metropolitan markets mainly in the Southeast and Midwest. CarMax also operates seven new-car franchises and sells older vehicles through more than 350000 in-store auctions each year at some 50 stores. Additionally it sells older cars and trucks with higher mileage via its ValuMax program and offers vehicle financing through its CarMax Auto Finance unit.

Operations

CarMax operates through two business segments: CarMax Sales Operations and CarMax Auto Finance (CAF). CarMax Sales Operations which sells more than 500000 used cars per year represents the nation's largest used-car retailer. The company's finance arm CAF offers financing solely to CarMax customers and financed 41% of the company's retail vehicle unit sales in fiscal 2015 (ended February). CAF also serviced 619000 customer accounts in its $8.46 billion portfolio of managed receivables.The company's used vehicle sales generated 82% of total revenue in fiscal 2015 while wholesale vehicle sales and new vehicle sales made up 14% and 2% of total sales respectively.Geographic ReachWhile Richmond-based CarMax sells cars in 34 US states it sells most of its vehicles in Florida Texas Southern California Virginia and the Washington DC/Baltimore area.

Sales and Marketing

CarMax markets and sells its cars in a relaxed "no-haggle" dealing environment. In fiscal 2015 the company sold a total of 582282 used cars and 376186 wholesale vehicles at its in-store auctions (with an average auction sales rate of 97%). The average used car sold for $19800 during the year.

CarMax focuses on developing brand awareness and detailing the advantages of shopping at its stores. It reaches customers through TV and radio broadcasts carmax.com Internet search engines the likes of Google and Yahoo! and online classified listings such as Pandora and Hulu. Additionally it looks to connect with consumers through Facebook Twitter and mobile apps. A fiscal 2015 company survey found that 89% of customers who purchased a CarMax vehicle had first visited its online website.Consumers have been taking advantage of the company's transfer option which allows a customer to get a vehicle of their choice relocated to a more-local CarMax store. In fiscal 2015 about 31% of vehicles sold were transferred via customer request.Overall CarMax spent $124 million on advertising in fiscal 2015 up from $114 million and $108.2 million in fiscal 2014 and fiscal 2013 respectively.

Financial Performance

CarMax has enjoyed healthy revenue and profit growth for the past several years as discretionary incomes have improved in the strengthening economy and as consumers have flocked to used vehicles to save money in the post-recession years. CarMax's revenue grew by 13% to a record $14.27 billion in fiscal 2015 (ended February) thanks mostly to continued double-digit growth in used vehicle sales driven by a combination of 10% sales volume growth and a 2.5% increase in average retail vehicle selling price. The dealer's comparable store used unit sales grew by 4.4% for the year while new store openings also helped contribute to the its top line growth. Carmax's wholesale vehicle revenue also surged by 12% for the year thanks to higher appraisal buy rates and growth in its store base. The CarMax Auto Finance division's income grew by 9% as its average managed receivables balance grew by 18% to $7.86 billion for the year.Higher revenue and strong cost controls in fiscal 2015 drove Carmax's net income up by 21% to a record $597.36 billion marking the company's sixth straight year of profit growth. Despite higher earnings Carmax's cash from operations fell sharply for the year mostly because the company spent more toward building its car inventory in anticipation of seasonal sales opportunities. It also used more cash toward financing customer auto loans through its CAF business.

Strategy

CarMax's main strategy is to "revolutionize the used auto retail market" by resolving the major sources of complaint that customers face at traditional auto retailers with superior customer service offerings. Some of these offerings include the 5-day money-back guarantee and the vehicle transfer service which allows a customer to get a vehicle of their choice relocated from a distant CarMax store to a more local one. Leveraging its successful "no-haggle" pricing business model CarMax has been aggressively expanding its geographic footprint over the past several years. The auto dealer has already more than doubled its store count from 58 locations in 2005 to 144 stores in 2015 and plans to open between 13 and 16 new locations annually through fiscal 2018. CarMax opened 13 stores in fiscal 2015 after opening 13 stores in fiscal 2014 and 10 stores in fiscal 2013 focusing on markets in Virginia Georgia Texas California Tennessee Maryland Missouri Delaware and Pennsylvania. The company's used-vehicle sales focus has been a buffer for the firm since the economic downturn and credit crisis which had decimated new-car dealer sales. Indeed used vehicles still account for more than 80% of CarMax's total sales while new vehicles make up less than 2%.

HISTORY

Looking for new retailing channels to conquer in 1993 Circuit City Stores began test-driving the used-car concept when it opened its first CarMax outlet in Richmond Virginia. Richard Sharp who was named Circuit City's CEO in 1986 became the chairman and CEO for CarMax Group as well.

A pioneer in the car industry CarMax offered computerized shopping play areas for children and no-haggle pricing. Competing car dealers criticized CarMax's TV ads which tarred rivals with a stereotype of sleaze and greed. Some dealers disputed CarMax's low-price claims.

The company extended its geographical reach into North Carolina Georgia and Florida in 1995 and 1996. In 1996 CarMax began selling new cars at an Atlanta store.

No longer riding it as a test-drive Circuit City spun off about 25% of CarMax to the public in 1997. The following year it moved into Illinois.

Also in 1998 CarMax bought a new-car Toyota dealership in Maryland and the multi-make Mauro Auto Mall of Wisconsin. It entered South Carolina that year and added a Georgia Mitsubishi dealership in early 1999. The company acquired two new-car franchises in the competitive Los Angeles market in mid-1999.

In mid-2001 Circuit City reduced its share in CarMax from 75% to about 65% having sold some stock to help remodel the company's electronics stores. Circuit City then spun off CarMax as an independent company in October 2002. President Austin Ligon took the CEO title at that time (Sharp remained chairman).

CarMax opened five superstores but sold four new-car dealerships in 2003.

EXECUTIVES

Vice President Information Technology, Barbara (Barb) Harvill
Vice President Marketing CarMax, Rob Sorenson
Region Vice President Merchandising Florida Region, William L (Bill) McChrystal
Region Vice President Service Operations Southwest Region, Brian Dunne
Assistant Vice President Investor Relations, Katharine Kenny
SVP CarMax Auto Finance, Angela (Angie) Chattin
President and CEO, Thomas J. (Tom) Folliard, $1,129,175 total compensation
VP Advertising, Laura R. Donahue
EVP and CFO, Thomas W. (Tom) Reedy, $570,230 total compensation
EVP Human Resources and Administration, William D. (Bill) Nash, $492,806 total compensation
EVP Stores, William C. (Cliff) Wood, $570,229 total compensation
VP Auction Services and Merchandising Development, Joe Wilson
SVP and CIO, Shamim Mohammad, age 46
VP Information Technology, Dave Banks
Vice President Human Resources, Peggy Philips
Vice President Of Information Technology, Michelle Ellwood
Vice President Operations, John Davis
Assistant Vice President Sales Development, Brian Stone
Assistant Vice President Management Information Systems, Troy Downs
Senior Vice President, Fred Hayton
Assistant Vice President Process Engineering, Gary Sheehan
Assistant Vice President Consumer Finance, Rusty Jordan
Assistant Vice President CarMax Auto Finance, Mike Callahan
Vice President Finance, Enrique Mayor-mora
Vice President Of Human Resources, Jean Dixon
Vice President Sales, Cliff Wood
Assistant Vice President Talent Acquisition at Carmax, Donna Schaar
Assistant Vice President Treasurer, Andrew (Andy) McMonigle
Vice President, Patricia (Pat) Gangwer
Legal Secretary, Kim Wickens
Assistant Vice President Account Services, Jeff Austin
Assistant Vice President Assistant Controller, Veronica Hinckle
Vice President Treasurer, Tom Reedy
Vice President of Business Strategy, Anu Agarwal
Vice President For The Atlanta Region, Kevin Cox
Vice President Sales and Marketing, Chris Bartee
Vice President Real Estate, K Moyers
Senior Vice President Human Resources and Adminis, Bill Nash
Assistant Vice President and Deputy General Counsel, Michelle (Mitch) Halasz
Vice President Regional Sales, Dan Johnston

Senior Vice President, Richard (Dick) Smith
Chairman, William R. Tiefel
Auditors: KPMG LLP

LOCATIONS

HQ: Carmax Inc.
12800 Tuckahoe Creek Parkway, Richmond, VA 23238
Phone: 804 747-0422
Web: www.carmax.com

2015 Stores

	No.
California	18
Texas	14
Florida	13
Virginia	10
North Carolina	9
Georgia	8
Tennessee	7
Illinois	6
Maryland	6
Ohio	5
Wisconsin	4
Alabama	3
Arizona	3
Colorado	3
Missouri	3
Nevada	3
Pennsylvania	3
South Carolina	3
Connecticut	2
Indiana	2
Kansas	2
Kentucky	2
Mississippi	2
Oklahoma	2
Oregon	2
Delaware	1
Iowa	1
Louisiana	1
Massachusetts	1
Nebraska	1
New Mexico	1
New York	1
Utah	1
Washington	1
Total	**144**

PRODUCTS/OPERATIONS

2015 Sales

	$ mil.	% of total
Used vehicles	11,674	82
Wholesale vehicles	2,049	14
New vehicles	240	2
Other sales & revenue	305	2
Total	**14,268**	**100**

COMPETITORS

Asbury Automotive	Holman Enterprises
AutoNation	Internet Brands
AutoTrader	JM Family Enterprises
Brown Automotive	KAR Auction Services
Cox Automotive	McCombs Enterprises
Danner Company	Penske Automotive
DriveTime Automotive	Group
Ed Morse Auto	Serra Automotive
Group 1 Automotive	Sonic Automotive
Hendrick Automotive	

HISTORICAL FINANCIALS

Company Type: Public

Income Statement

FYE: February 28

	REVENUE ($ mil.)	NET INCOME ($ mil.)	NET PROFIT MARGIN	EMPLOYEES
02/15	14,268	597	4.2%	22,064
02/14	12,574	492	3.9%	20,171
02/13	10,962	434	4.0%	18,111
02/12	10,003	413	4.1%	16,460
02/11	8,975	380	4.2%	15,565
Annual Growth	**12.3%**	**11.9%**	**—**	**9.1%**

2015 Year-End Financials

Debt ratio: 69.02%	No. of shares (mil.): 208
Return on equity: 18.45%	Dividends
Cash ($ mil.): 27	Yield: —
Current ratio: 2.61	Payout: —
Long-term debt ($ mil.): 8,818	Market value ($ mil.): 14,017

	STOCK PRICE ($) FY Close	P/E High/Low		PER SHARE ($) Earnings	Dividends	Book Value
02/15	67.11	25	15	2.73	0.00	15.11
02/14	48.43	24	17	2.16	0.00	14.96
02/13	38.41	21	13	1.87	0.00	13.36
02/12	30.69	19	13	1.79	0.00	11.77
02/11	35.37	22	11	1.67	0.00	10.15
Annual Growth	**17.4%**	**—**	**—**	**13.1%**	**—**	**10.5%**

Casey's General Stores, Inc.

Casey's General Stores makes sure that small towns in the Midwest get their fill of convenient shopping. It operates about 1850 company-owned convenience stores in more than a dozen states primarily in the Midwest and all within about 500 miles of its Iowa headquarters and distribution center. Towns with 5000 people or fewer where rent is low are home to about 60% of the chain's stores. Casey's sells lots of gasoline (some 70% of total sales) as well as beverages groceries and fresh prepared foods including from-scratch pizza donuts and hot sandwiches. It also sells tobacco products automotive goods and other nonfood items such as ammunition and photo supplies.

Geographic Reach

Casey's operates stores in 14 states including its largest markets —Iowa Illinois and Missouri —as well as Wisconsin Indiana Oklahoma Arkansas Tennessee and North Dakota. New markets for the chain include Kentucky and Tennessee.

Financial Performance

Fiscal 2014 (ends April) sales at Casey's General Stores peaked at a record-breaking $7.8 billion in 2014 and remained around that mark during 2015. Profits surged 34% from $135 million in 2014 to $181 million in 2015 primarily due to a steady fall in wholesale costs midyear.

The flat revenue for 2015 was due to a decline in fuel sales partially offset by increased sales from its prepared food and fountain operations. Casey's experienced a 15% decrease in the average price of a gallon of gas which was offset by a spike in the number of gallons sold.

Strategy

Casey's seeks to meet the needs of its small town clientele by combining the features of a general store and convenience store. The stores which offer more than 3000 food and nonfood products carry a broader selection than a typical convenience store. It addition to low-margin food and grocery items the stores offer lots of prepared foods which sell at higher markups. Indeed while sales of products other than gasoline account for about 30% of its total revenue they contribute nearly 80% of the chain's gross profit.

To make more room for food the convenience store operator has been opening larger (about 3800 sq. ft.) "O-shaped" stores. The format (launched in 2008) devotes additional space to food and beverages allowing for a wider selection of beer energy drinks and other high-margin items.

The company's annual goal is to increase its store count by 4% to 6%. To that end Casey's has been building and acquiring new stores including about 70 in fiscal 2014. About 45 stores were newly constructed and it closed nine stores in fiscal 2015. Also in 2015

Mergers and Acquisitions

Casey's purchased 36 stores in 2015 through a variety of single store and multi-store transactions with several unrelated third parties. Of the 36 stores acquired 32 were re-opened as a Casey's store during the year three were closed permanently and one will be opened during 2016.

Company Background

Donald Lamberti who had run his family's grocery store founded Casey's General Stores with Kurvin C. "K. C." Fish. The men converted a gas station into the first Casey's convenience store in 1968. To expand and build brand recognition the company began franchising outlets two years later. By focusing on small towns the company avoided competition and expensive building and property costs. A significant growth spurt in 1979 took Casey's from 119 stores to 226. Fish retired the following year and the company went public in 1983.

EXECUTIVES

SVP and CFO, William J. (Bill) Walljasper, $520,000 total compensation
VP Marketing, Michael R. (Mike) Richardson, $195,000 total compensation
Chairman and CEO, Robert J. (Bob) Myers, age 69, $1,050,000 total compensation
President and COO, Terry W. Handley, $700,000 total compensation
SVP Logistics and Acquisitions, Sam J. Billmeyer, $520,000 total compensation
SVP Corporate General Counsel and Human Resources, Julie L. Jackowski, $490,000 total compensation
IT Director, Rich Schappert
Auditors: KPMG LLP

LOCATIONS

HQ: Casey' s General Stores, Inc.
One Convenience Boulevard, Ankeny, IA 50021
Phone: 515 965-6100
Web: www.caseys.com

PRODUCTS/OPERATIONS

2015 Sales

	$ mil.	% of total
Fuel	5,144	66
Grocery & other merchandise	1,794	23
Prepared food & fountain	780	10
Other	47	1
Total	**7,767**	**100**

Selected Merchandise

Ammunition
Automotive products
Beverages
Food including fresh foods
Gasoline (self-service)
Health and beauty aids
Housewares
Pet products
Photo supplies
School supplies
Tobacco products

COMPETITORS

7-Eleven	Kroger
CVS	Kwik Trip
Chevron	Martin & Bayley
Couche-Tard	McDonald' s
Exxon Mobil	Pizza Hut

Holiday Companies   QuikTrip
Hy-Vee   Royal Dutch Shell
IGA   Walgreen
Krause Gentle

HISTORICAL FINANCIALS

Company Type: Public

Income Statement

FYE: April 30

	REVENUE ($ mil.)	NET INCOME ($ mil.)	NET PROFIT MARGIN	EMPLOYEES
04/15	7,767	180	2.3%	31,766
04/14	7,840	134	1.7%	29,749
04/13	7,250	110	1.5%	27,079
04/12	6,987	116	1.7%	24,726
04/11	5,635	94	1.7%	22,157
Annual Growth	8.4%	17.5%	—	9.4%

2015 Year-End Financials

Debt ratio: 34.56%
Return on equity: 22.65%
Cash ($ mil.): 48
Current ratio: 0.84
Long-term debt ($ mil.): 838

No. of shares (mil.): 38
Dividends
  Yield: 0.9%
  Payout: 18.9%
Market value ($ mil.): 3,196

	STOCK PRICE ($) FY Close	P/E High/Low	PER SHARE ($) Earnings	Dividends	Book Value
04/15	82.18	20 14	4.62	0.80	22.51
04/14	68.66	22 16	3.46	0.72	18.69
04/13	57.91	22 16	2.36	0.66	15.70
04/12	56.35	19 13	3.04	0.60	13.27
04/11	39.03	20 16	2.22	0.51	10.64
Annual Growth	20.5%	— —	20.1%	12.2%	20.6%

Caterpillar Inc.

Whether digging loading paving or moving Caterpillar does it all. The company is the world's #1 manufacturer of construction and mining equipment which includes excavators loaders and tractors as well as forestry paving and tunneling machinery. It also manufactures diesel and natural gas engines industrial gas turbines and diesel-electric locomotives. Subsidiary Caterpillar Financial Services offers a slew of financing leasing insurance and warranty products and services for dealers and customers. Among Caterpillar's other services are remanufacturing through Caterpillar Remanufacturing Services and rail-related upgrade repair and maintenance services through Progress Rail Services.

Geographic Reach

Caterpillar sells its products and services in North America Asia/Pacific Europe Africa & Middle East (EAME) and Latin America. Sales from each of these segments is fairly well dispersed with two-thirds of revenue coming from non-North American markets.

Operations

Caterpillar's construction mining and power equipment manufacturing operations are conducted in facilities scattered across the US. It also operates a technical center in Mossville Illinois. Additionally the company has marketing and operating locations in the US Switzerland Japan China Singapore and Brazil. Parts distribution centers are located in the US Mexico Belgium Russia China Singapore Australia South Africa United Arab Emirates and Brazil.

Caterpillar is organized into five operating segments that fall under two categories. Machinery

Energy and Transportation consists of Resource Industries Construction Industries Energy and Transportation and All Other. The All Other segment's operations consist of remanufacturing services primarily the refurbishment and restoration of used machinery and technologies for automotive and industrial OEMs as well as for the defense industry.

Caterpillar's second business category and fifth operating segment Financial Products consists of subsidiaries Caterpillar Financial Services Corporation (Cat Financial) Caterpillar Insurance Holdings Inc. (Cat Insurance) and their respective subsidiaries.

Sales and Marketing

Caterpillar machinery is distributed primarily through a worldwide network of dealers many of which provide sales rental service and aftermarket support. Most are independently owned and operated though Caterpillar owns and operates three of its own dealerships in Japan. Within its global dealer network about 50 are located in the US and an additional 130 are located outside of the US. This network serves more than 180 countries. Caterpillar engines are sold through the dealer network and to other manufacturers for use in their products.

Caterpillar serves several different customer segments including those using machinery in mine and quarry applications (Resource Industries); those using machinery in building construction and infrastructure applications (Construction Industries); those using reciprocating engines and turbines in industries serving electric power industrial marine and petroleum applications as well as those needing the provision of rail services (Energy and Transportation); and retail and dealer customers needing financing leasing and insurance for their equipment (Financial Products). At the front end of a purchase Caterpillar provides financing to its customers; at the back end it offers support for the purchase and lease of its equipment.

Financial Performance

After posting record-setting revenue and profit totals for 2012 Caterpillar saw its revenues fall 15% to hover around the $55 billion mark for both 2013 and 2014. The static revenue for 2014 was fueled by a 24% drop from Resource Industries and an 8% drop from customers outside the US. Aftermarket part sales also declined in 2014 as some companies continue to extend proactive maintenance schedules and delay major overhauls when possible.

Profits too were flat from 2013 to 2014 remaining at $3.7 billion. This was fueled by the nonfluctuating revenues levels coupled with a spike in selling general and administrative expenses. In addition Caterpillar's operating cash flow declined from $10.2 billion in 2013 to $8.1 billion in 2014.

Strategy

As part of its Vision 2020 strategy Caterpillar sets forth multiple goals that it is striving to achieve by 2015. It seeks to accelerate aftermarket parts and services growth; excel at product development; simplify cost structure; achieve profits; expand its leadership in the mining quarry and aggregates markets; grow its Power Systems segment within the rail power conversion and alternative fuel markets; and become a leader in China while growing its position in India Russia and other parts of Asia that are developing their infrastructure.

With China being an important part of Caterpillar's long-term strategy the company in early 2013 opened a new power train production facility for earthmoving and mining machinery and completed expansion of another facility that produces hydraulic cylinders both in Wuxi to bring the total number of operating factories in China to 24.

Mergers and Acquisitions

In line with its goal of expanding its role as an equipment and services provider throughout Europe in 2013 the company acquired Johan Walter Berg AB (Berg) headquartered in Öckerö Islands Sweden. Berg is a manufacturer of mechanically and electrically driven propulsion systems and marine controls for ships. With the acquisition Caterpillar transitioned from selling only engines and generators to providing complete marine propulsion package systems.

HISTORY

In 1904 in Stockton California combine maker Benjamin Holt modified the farming tractor by substituting a gas engine for steam and replacing iron wheels with crawler tracks. This improved the tractor's mobility over dirt.

The British adapted the "caterpillar" (Holt's nickname for the tractor) design to the armored tank in 1915. Following WWI the US Army donated tanks to local governments for construction work. The caterpillar's efficiency spurred the development of earthmoving and construction equipment.

Holt merged with Best Tractor in 1925. The company renamed Caterpillar moved to Peoria Illinois in 1928. Cat expanded into foreign markets in the 1930s and phased out combine production to focus on construction and road-building equipment.

EXECUTIVES

VP and Chief Procurement Officer, Frank J. Crespo
Vp Finance Services Division, Mike Dewalt
Chairman and CEO, Douglas R. (Doug) Oberhelman, age 63, $1,600,008 total compensation
Group President Resource Industries, Edward J. (Ed) Rapp, age 58, $755,202 total compensation
EVP Law and Public Policy and Chief Legal Officer, James B. (Jim) Buda, age 68
VP; President and CEO Progress Rail Services, William P. (Billy) Ainsworth, age 59
VP; President Caterpillar Financial Services, Kent M. Adams
Group President and CFO, Bradley M. (Brad) Halverson, age 55, $755,202 total compensation
VP Product Development and Global Technology and CTO, Gwenne A. Henricks
Group President Customer and Dealer Support, Robert B. (Rob) Charter, age 52
President Energy and Transportation, D. James (Jim) Umpleby, age 56, $755,202 total compensation
Group President Construction Industries, Thomas (Tom) Pellette
VP; President Solar Turbines, Pablo M. Koziner
VP and CIO, Julie A. Lagacy
Vp Human Services Division And Chief Human Resources Officer, Kimberly S Hauer
Vp Marine And Petroleum Power Division, Tom Frake
Vice President, Dennis Smith
Vice President Remanufacturing Division, Steven (Steve) Fisher
Vice President Asia Pacific Manufacturing Operations, Thomas (Thom) Bluth
Auditors: PricewaterhouseCoopers LLP

LOCATIONS

HQ: Caterpillar Inc.
100 N.E. Adams Street, Peoria, IL 61629
Phone: 309 675-1000   **Fax:** 309 675-4332
Web: www.caterpillar.com

2014 Sales

	$ mil.	% of total
Inside United States	21,122	38
Outside United States	34,062	62
Total	55,184	100

PRODUCTS/OPERATIONS

2014 Sales

	$ mil.	% of total
Energy & Transportation	21,727	39
Construction Industries	19,362	35
Resource Industries	8,921	16
Financial Products Segment	3,313	6
All Other Segments	2,251	4
Corporate Items and Eliminations	(390)	0
Total	**55,184**	**100**

Selected Products

Engines
  Engines for Caterpillar machinery
  Engines for electric power generation systems
  Engines for marine petroleum construction industrial
  and agricultural applications
  Engines for on-highway trucks and locomotives
Financing and insurance services
  Financing to customers and dealers
  Insurance to customers and dealers
Machinery
  Articulated trucks
  Backhoe loaders
  Log loaders
  Log skidders
  Mining shovels
  Motor graders
  Off-highway trucks
  Paving products
  Pipelayers
  Related parts
  Skid steer loaders
  Telescopic handlers
  Track and wheel excavators
  Track and wheel loaders
  Track and wheel tractors
  Wheel tractor-scrapers
Mining
  Surface mining
  Draglines
  Drills
  Electric mining shovels
  Highwall miners
  Hydraulic excavators
  Off-highway haul trucks
  Underground mining
  Longwall equipment
  Armored face conveyors
  Automated plow systems
  Hydraulic roof supports
  Longwall shearers
  Room and pillar mining
  Continuous haulage systems
  Continuous miners
  Feeder breakers
  Underground haulage and utility vehicles

Selected Brands

CAT
Caterpillar
Electro-Motive
FG Wilson
MaK
MWM
Olympian
Perkins
Progress Rail
SEM
Solar Turbines

COMPETITORS

ALSTOM	MAN
Atlas Copco	Mitsubishi Heavy
Bombardier	Industries
Charles Machine Works	Navistar International
Cummins	Nortrak
DEUTZ	Rolls-Royce
Deere	Rolls-Royce Power
Detroit Diesel	Systems
Doosan Infracore	Sandvik
GE	Sany Heavy Industry
GE Capital	Siemens Energy
Generac Holdings	Sumitomo Heavy
Hitachi Construction	Industries
Machinery	Terex
Hyundai Heavy	Volvo

Industries	Vossloh
J C Bamford Excavators	Weichai Power
Joy Global	Wells Fargo Equipment
Kohler	Finance
Komatsu	Wärtsilö
Kubota	

HISTORICAL FINANCIALS

Company Type: Public

Income Statement

FYE: December 31

	REVENUE ($ mil.)	NET INCOME ($ mil.)	NET PROFIT MARGIN	EMPLOYEES
12/15	47,011	2,102	4.5%	105,700
12/14	55,184	3,695	6.7%	114,233
12/13	55,656	3,789	6.8%	118,501
12/12	65,875	5,681	8.6%	125,341
12/11	60,138	4,928	8.2%	125,099
Annual Growth	**(6.0%)**	**(19.2%)**	**—**	**(4.1%)**

2015 Year-End Financials

Debt ratio: 48.53%
Return on equity: 13.32%
Cash ($ mil.): 6,460
Current ratio: 1.31
Long-term debt ($ mil.): 25,247

No. of shares (mil.): 582
Dividends
  Yield: 4.3%
  Payout: 60.8%
Market value ($ mil.): 39,575

	STOCK PRICE ($) FY Close	P/E High/Low		PER SHARE ($) Earnings	Dividends	Book Value
12/15	67.96	26	18	3.50	2.94	25.43
12/14	91.53	19	14	5.88	2.60	27.63
12/13	90.81	17	14	5.75	2.24	32.63
12/12	89.61	13	9	8.48	2.48	26.76
12/11	90.60	15	9	7.40	1.80	19.90
Annual Growth	**(6.9%)**	**—**	**—**	**(17.1%)**	**13.0%**	**6.3%**

Cathay General Bancorp

Cathay General Bancorp is the holding company for Cathay Bank which mainlyÅserves Chinese and Vietnamese communities from someÅ30 branches in California and about 20 more in Illinois New Jersey New YorkÅMassachusetts Washington and Texas. It also hasÅa branch in Hong Kong and offices in Shanghai and Taipei. Catering to small to medium-sized businesses and individual consumers the bank offersÅstandard deposit services and loans. Commercial mortgageÅloans account for more than half of the bank's portfolio; business loans comprise nearly 25%. The bank'sÅCathay Wealth Management unit offers online stock tradingÅmutual funds and other investment products and services through an agreement withÅPrimeVest.

Geographic Reach

California state-chartered Cathay Bank has branches in California Illinois Massachusetts New Jersey New York Texas and Washington. Overseas it has a branch in Hong Kong and offices in Shanghai and Taipei.

Financial Performance

The bank's revenue is on a downward trend. In 2012 revenue declined more than 5% vs. 2011 after posting a 3% decline in the previous annual comparison. Indeed between 2008 and 2012 revenue dipped by about 17% on lower interest income and dividend income. However the bank's profit picture is improving with net income up in 2012 for the third consecutive year.

Strategy

With 60% of its branches in California —a state hard hit by the downturn in the housing market — Cathay Bank's real estate secured loan portfolio has suffered as the value of the underlying collateral plummeted. In 2010 the company entered into a memorandum of understanding with the FDIC to reduce its concentration of commercial real estate loans improve its capital ratios reduce overall risk and strengthen asset quality. The moves have helped the company to cut its losses. The bank has also been successful growing deposits.

However under the terms of its deal with the FDIC Cathay General is restricted from opening new branches or entering new business lines until the memorandum is lifted. (Prior to the entering into the agreement with the FDIC Cathay Bank expanded beyond California mainly through acquisitions. The company bought New York's Great Eastern Bank and Illinois-based New Asia Bancorp in 2006 while the 2007 purchase of United Heritage Bank gave the company its first branch in New Jersey.

EXECUTIVES

Senior Vice President, Perry Oei
SEVP and COO, Irwin Wong, age 66, $297,273 total compensation
EVP and Director, Anthony M. Tang, age 62, $313,000 total compensation
Chairman President and CEO, Dunson K. Cheng, age 71, $1,003,846 total compensation
EVP CFO and Treasurer, Heng W. Chen, age 63, $376,861 total compensation
President and Director Cathay Bank, Pin Tai, $334,681 total compensation
EVP and Chief Risk Officer Cathy Bank, Kim R. Bingham, age 58
Vice President Human Resources, Geri Santoro
Assistant Vice President Collections Officer, Jon Delgado
Senior Vice President, Gregory Badura
Assistant Vice President, Sushma Malhotra
Assistant Vice President Debit Card Atm Services, Jyoti Bhojak
Vice President, Susan (Sue) Yang
Assistant Vice President Senior Training and Development Officer, Joyce Kwok
Assistant Vice President Marketing, Chris Lu
Assistant Vice President Security, Kim Morris
Vice President, Ales Susmel
Senior Vice President Human Resources, Jennifer Powells
Vice President, Ebrahim Sharaki
Vice President Credit Risk Officer, William (Bill) Summers
Senior Vice President And Chief Inform, Bob Romero
Vice President, Donna Lew
Assistant Vice President, Peggy Chan
Vice President, Jennifer (Jen) Linh
Assistant Vice President, Kai Cheng
Auditors: KPMG LLP

LOCATIONS

HQ: Cathay General Bancorp
  777 North Broadway, Los Angeles, CA 90012
Phone: 213 625-4700
Web: www.cathaybank.com

2011 Branch Offices

	No.
California	31
New York	8
Illinois	3
Washington	3
Texas	2
Massachusetts	1
New Jersey	1
Hong Kong	1
Total	**50**

PRODUCTS/OPERATIONS

2014 Sales

	$ mil.	% of total
Interest & dividends		
Loans receivable	390	86
Taxable investment securities	24	5
Other	4	-
Noninterest		
Net securities gains	6	1
Letter of credit commissions	6	1
Depository service fees	5	1
Other	22	6
Total	**459**	**100**

COMPETITORS

BBCN	Grandpoint Bank
Bank of America	Hanmi Financial
Citibank	U.S. Bancorp
East West Bancorp	Wilshire Bancorp
Far East National Bank	

HISTORICAL FINANCIALS

Company Type: Public

Income Statement
FYE: December 31

	ASSETS ($ mil.)	NET INCOME ($ mil.)	INCOME AS % OF ASSETS	EMPLOYEES
12/14	11,516	137	1.2%	1,074
12/13	10,989	123	1.1%	1,132
12/12	10,694	117	1.1%	1,092
12/11	10,644	100	0.9%	1,018
12/10	10,801	11	0.1%	1,010
Annual Growth	**1.6%**	**85.8%**	**—**	**1.5%**

2014 Year-End Financials

Debt ratio: 1.21%	No. of shares (mil.): 79
Return on equity: 9.00%	Dividends
Cash ($ mil.): 666	Yield: 1.1%
Current ratio: —	Payout: 17.2%
Long-term debt ($ mil.): —	Market value ($ mil.): 2,042

	STOCK PRICE ($) FY Close	P/E High/Low	PER SHARE ($) Earnings	Dividends	Book Value
12/14	25.59	16 13	1.72	0.29	20.08
12/13	26.73	19 13	1.43	0.08	18.33
12/12	19.53	15 12	1.28	0.04	20.58
12/11	14.93	18 10	1.06	0.04	19.16
12/10	16.70	— —	(0.06)	0.04	18.18
Annual Growth	**11.3%**	**— —**	**—**	**64.1%**	**2.5%**

CBRE Group Inc

CBRE (formerly CB Richard Ellis Group) is all about location location location —not to mention ubicación l'emplacement posizione and Standort. One of the world's largest commercial real estate services companies CBRE provides property and facilities management leasing brokerage appraisal and valuation asset management financing and market research services from around 370 offices worldwide and manages 1.5 billion sq. ft. of commercial space for third-party owners and occupants. Subsidiary Trammell Crow provides property development services for corporate and institutional clients primarily in the US. CBRE Global Investors manages real estate investments for institutional clients.

HISTORY

Company BackgroundColbert Coldwell and Albert Tucker started real estate brokerage Tucker Lynch & Coldwell in 1906 in San Francisco. In 1922 the company expanded to Los Angeles where it began developing real estate in 1933 with a 60-acre subdivision in the burgeoning city.

Having profited from California's rapid growth in the 1950s and 1960s the firm expanded out of state. The partnership incorporated in 1962 as Coldwell Banker which went public in 1968. Sears Roebuck & Co. bought the company in 1981 for 80% above its market price. But by 1991 Sears had abandoned aims to become a financial services giant and sold Coldwell Banker's commercial operations to The Carlyle Group as CB Commercial Real Estate Services Group.

Free of Sears but $56 million in the red the company didn't return to profitability until 1993. Two years later it embarked on a shopping spree in real estate services buying tenant representatives Langon Rieder and Westmark Realty. In 1996 the company went public and bought mortgage banker L. J. Melody & Company (which was renamed CBRE | Melody); it purchased Koll Real Estate Services in 1997.

In 1998 the company widened its global scope with the acquisition of REI Limited the non-UK operations of Richard Ellis; it was renamed CB Richard Ellis Services. CB Richard Ellis also bought Hillier Parker May & Rowden (now operating in the UK as CB Hillier) a London-based provider of commercial property services.

CB Richard Ellis experienced a revenue crunch in 1999 and responded by restructuring its North American operations into three divisions (transaction financial and management services) and cutting management ranks by 30%. Growth continued in 1999 with the purchase of Pittsburgh-based Gold & Co. the addition of an office in Venezuela and a fat contract to manage more than 1100 locations for Prudential.

In 2000 the company committed significant resources to the Internet inking a deal to offer the lease management services of MyContracts.com and investing in Canadian real estate transaction tracker RealNet Canada.

A group of investors including then-CEO Ray Wirta chairman Richard Blum (and his BLUM Capital Partners) and Freeman Spogli took the company private in 2001. Blum Capital Partners bought the 60% of publicly traded CBRE that it did not already own forming CBRE Holding. Three years later the company went public once again.

In 2003 CBRE merged with top commercial real estate broker and property manager Insignia Financial. The next year the company changed its name to CB Richard Ellis Group and went public. It bought rival Trammell Crow in 2006 as well as a dozen or so other companies as it sought to fill in its holdings. The acquisitions deepened CBRE's outsourcing services especially project and facilities management for corporate and institutional clients in the US.

CBRE spun off former subsidiary Realty Finance Corporation in 2008 after the real estate investment trust continued to post losses in a troubled credit market.

Also in 2008 it opened its first offices in Bahrain and joined forces with Vanke to provide residential property management services in China. The following year CBRE expanded its existing UK-based investment banking business (advisory and restructuring services for real estate hospitality and gaming companies) to the Americas.

In November 2012 CBRE acquired EA Shaw. a independent commercial and residential property partnership specializing in central London. The purchase significantly enhanced the firm's business in central London.

EXECUTIVES

President CEO and Director, Robert E. (Bob) Sulentic, age 59, $875,000 total compensation

President Global Corporate Services, William F. (Bill) Concannon, age 59

President Americas Brokerage and Capital Markets, Christopher R. Ludeman

President U.S. Eastern Division, James A. (Jim) Reid

CFO and Global Director of Corporate Development., James R. (Jim) Groch, $675,000 total compensation

CEO Americas, Calvin W. (Cal) Frese, age 59, $600,000 total compensation

Global President Debt and Structured Finance, Brian F. Stoffers

CEO Asia Pacific, Steven A. (Steve) Swerdlow

COO, Michael J. (Mike) Lafitte, age 54, $600,000 total compensation

Chairman Asia Pacific, Robert (Rob) Blain, age 60, $560,000 total compensation

Chairman Europe Middle East and Africa (EMEA), Michael J. (Mike) Strong, age 67, $472,115 total compensation

Global President Valuation and Advisory Services, Michael L. (Mike) Gerard

EVP and General Counsel, Laurence H. Midler, age 50, $325,000 total compensation

CIO, Mandy Edwards

Global President Asset Services, Tony Long

Vice Chairman Occupier Advisory and Transaction Services Group, Lynn Williams

CEO CBRE Global Investors, Matt Khourie

COO CBRE Global Investors, Daniel (Danny) Queenan

President Transaction Services, Jack Durburg

Managing Director CBRE/Buffalo, Shana Stegner

Vice Chairman Law Firm Services Mid-Atlantic, Robert O. Copito

Vice Chairman Retail Services, Richard B. Hodos

EVP Occupier Advisory and Transaction Services Group, Jeffrey Welch

CEO CBRE Europe Middle East and Africa (EMEA), Martin Samworth

President Florida and Latin America, Mary Jo Eaton

Chairman Global Retail Executive Committee, Anthony Buono

COO and Managing Director CBRE Deutschland, Mark Spangenberg

Senior Vice President, Thom Cooley

Senior Vice President, Chris Cozby

Vice President, Trent Snarr

Executive Vice President, Tim Swan

Vice President Research and Development, Joane Noiseux

Vice President, Erik Wanland

Senior Vice President Tenant Representation Global Corporate Services, Dennis Hearst

Senior Vice President, Patrick (Paddy) Cavanagh

First Vice President, Craig Lillibridge

Vice President, Bob C Patterson

Vice President, Nita Stewart

Senior Vice President, Blake Mirkin

First Vice President and Senior Counsel (2006), Karen L Greenberg

First Vice President, Gerald (Jerry) Harvey

First Vice President, John (Jack) Vandenbark

Senior Vice President, Mindy Lissner

First Vice President, John (Jack) Suerth

Vice President Senior, Mary O'Connor

Vice President, Mario Melone

Senior Vice President, Marc Sallette

Senior Vice President And Partner, Robert (Bob) Daglio

Senior Vice President, Kim Sior

Vice President, Jason Levendusky
Vice President, Scott Halloran
Senior Vice President, David (Dave) Durbin
Senior Vice President, Steven (Steve) Brabant
Vice President, Dennis Jimenez
First Vice President Industrial Specialist, Chris Bates
Spqrea Senior Vice President, Maurice Nieman
Executive Vice President, Jeffrey C (Jeff) Babikian
Senior Vice President, David (Dave) Nixon
Senior Vice President, Bob Healey
Vice President, Larry Tanji
Vice President Senior, Mark Guthrie
Executive Vice President and Partner, Andrew (Andy) Majewski
Senior Vice President, Erik Mclaughlin
Senior Vice President, Steve Cosby
Senior Vice President, Timothy (Tim) Vaughan
First Vice President, Ron McWherter
Senior Vice President, Will Adams
Senior Vice President, Mark Darrington
Senior Vice President, Nick Psyllos
Vice President, Michael (Mel) Quinn
Vice President Chief Vice President, Robert (Bob) Morton
Senior Vice President, Cynthia Kamin
Vice President, Jamie Shafer
Executive Vice President, Rob Faktorow
Vice President Global Corporate Services, Thomas (Thom) Boyd
Senior Vice President of Office Brokerage Services, Troy Holme
Vice President, Steve Brown
Vice President, Conrad Mceachern
Vice President Portfolio Manager, Shay Sims
Senior Vice President, Chris Reynolds
Vice President, Ben Lazzareschi
Vice President, Chad Lesley
SP Senior Vice President, Terry Kittleson
Vice President, Wood Thornton
Vice President, David Ccim
Senior Vice President, John Brewer
First Vice President, Phillip Linton
Spqrea Vice President, Chris van Keulen
Vice President, Lisa Ferrazza
Vice President, Craig Hall
Vice President Brokerage Services, Michael Mitchell
Senior Vice President, William Hearn
Vice President, Matthew (Matt) Taylor
Vice President, Robert (Bob) Doxsee
First Vice President, Joshua Kleinberg
Legal Secretary, Carol Evans
First Vice President, Robert Dubbins
Vice President, Frank Galleher
SP Vice President, Dan Wengert
Senior Vice President, Jim Koenig
Spqrea First Vice President, Michael (Mel) Liss
Vice President, Scott Williams, age 74
Vice President Global Compensation and Benefits, Karina Pettengill
Vice President Tax, Becky Younger
Vice President, Robert (Bob) Gibson
Vice President, Richard (Dick) Schmidt
Vice President, Bruce Suppes
Vice President of Project Management, Paul Ureneck
Vice President, Patrick Greene
First Vice President Partner, Michael (Mel) Svoboda
Senior Vice President Finance, Len Santoro
Vice President, Bryan Graham
Senior Vice President, Jim Lighthizer
Vice Presidenl, Julius Tabert
Vice President Information Technology, Mike Washington
Executive Vice President, Donald Crigger
Senior Vice President, Ned Burns
Vice President North America Sales, Melanie Keo
Vice President Retail Services, Donna Hovey
Senior Vice President, Joe Moriarty
First Vice President, Paul Barker

Vice President Debt and Structured Finance, Erik Binkowski
Executive Vice President Partner Global Corporate Services, Mary Marino
Vice President Valuation and Advisory Services, Haydon Burns
Senior Vice President Brokerage Services Office, Warren Savery
Senior Vice President Global Compliance, Tyson Avery
Senior Vice President, Bradley Gingerich
Senior Vice President, Pat O'Keefe
Senior Vice President, Bert Kempfert
Vice President, Colleen Johnson
First Vice President, David Hartsook
Senior Vice President, William Tyler
Senior Vice President, Frank Tomasulo
Vice President Investment Real Estate, Ned Coyle
Senior Vice President, Kim McGuire
Vice President, Bradley Wilford
Executive Vice President, Sean Sullivan
Vice President Of Sales And Leasing, Ben Rojas
Senior Vice President, Patrick Scruggs
Executive Vice President, William Waxman
Executive Vice President, Jeffrey Babikian
Vice President Strategic Sourcing, Dan Lenze
Vice President, Mitchell Stravitz
Senior Vice President, Jack Hoskins
Senior Vice President, Jesse Weber
Firsl Vice President, Todd Folger
First Vice President, Kenneth Sweeney
Vice President, Neil Kolatkar
Senior Vice President, Brian Fiumara
Executive Vice President, Thomas Bohlinger
Auditors: KPMG LLP

LOCATIONS

HQ: CBRE Group Inc
400 South Hope Street, 25th Floor, Los Angeles, CA 90071
Phone: 213 613-3333
Web: www.cbre.com

2014 Sales

	$ mil.	% of total
Americas	5,203	57
Europe Middle East & Africa	2,344	26
Asia/Pacific	967	11
Global investment management	468	5
Development services	65	1
Total	**9,049**	**100**

2014 Sales

	$ in mil.
% of total	
US	56
UK	18
Other countries	26
Total	**100**

PRODUCTS/OPERATIONS

Selected Subsidiaries

CBRE Inc.
CBRE Capital Markets Inc.
CBRE Capital Markets of Texas LP
CBRE Global Holdings SARL
CBRE Global Investors LLC
CBRE Limited
CBRE Services Inc.
Norland Managed Services Ltd.
Trammell Crow Company LLC

COMPETITORS

BGC Partners	HFF
Cassidy Turley	Inland Group
Colliers International	Jones Lang LaSalle
Cushman & Wakefield	Lincoln Property
Eastdil Secured	Mitsui Fudosan
FirstService	Savills Studley

HISTORICAL FINANCIALS

Company Type: Public

Income Statement

FYE: December 31

	REVENUE ($ mil.)	NET INCOME ($ mil.)	NET PROFIT MARGIN	EMPLOYEES
12/14	9,049	484	5.4%	52,000
12/13	7,184	316	4.4%	44,000
12/12	6,514	315	4.8%	37,000
12/11	5,905	239	4.0%	34,000
12/10	5,115	200	3.9%	31,000
Annual Growth	15.3%	24.7%	—	13.8%

2014 Year-End Financials

Debt ratio: 31.70%	No. of shares (mil.): 332
Return on equity: 23.32%	Dividends
Cash ($ mil.): 740	Yield: —
Current ratio: 1.23	Payout: —
Long-term debt ($ mil.): 1,852	Market value ($ mil.): 11,405

	STOCK PRICE ($) FY Close	P/E High/Low	PER SHARE ($) Earnings	Dividends	Book Value
12/14	34.25	24 17	1.45	0.00	6.79
12/13	26.30	27 21	0.95	0.00	5.71
12/12	19.90	21 15	0.97	0.00	4.66
12/11	15.22	40 17	0.74	0.00	3.51
12/10	20.48	33 19	0.63	0.00	2.81
Annual Growth	13.7%	— —	23.2%	—	24.7%

CBS Corp

You might say this company has a real eye for broadcasting. CBS Corporation is a leading mass media conglomerate with television radio online content and publishing operations. Its portfolio is anchored by CBS Broadcasting which operates the #1 rated CBS television network along with a group of local TV stations. CBS also owns cable network Showtime and produces and distributes TV programming through CBS Television Studios and CBS Television Distribution. Other operations include CBS Radio CBS Interactive and book publisher Simon & Schuster. Chairman Sumner Redstone controls CBS Corporation through National Amusements.

HISTORY

The company that would eventually become CBS Corporation began as Viacom in 1970. It was the result of numerous mergers and acquisitions dating back nearly 90 years combining everything from a movie studio to a company that made car bumpers. CBS launched Viacom after the FCC ruled that TV networks could not own cable systems and TV stations in the same market. Viacom took over CBS's program syndication division and bought TV and radio stations in the late 1970s and early 1980s. In 1978 it co-founded pay-TV network Showtime. Viacom became full owner in 1982 and combined Showtime with The Movie Channel the following year to form Showtime Networks. Viacom also began producing TV series and bought MTV Networks in 1986.

After a bidding war with renowned financier Carl Icahn and a Viacom management group Sumner Redstone's National Amusements bought 83% of Viacom in 1987. Viacom bought King's Entertainment (theme parks) shortly thereafter and followed that with two mega-deals in 1994: it bought Paramount Communications for about $10 billion (which included Simon & Schuster) and Block-buster for $8.4 billion (which included Spelling Entertainment). The next year along with Chris-Craft Viacom launched UPN (United Paramount Network) the fifth commercial-broadcast TV network in the US.

Chiseling away at a mountain of debt Viacom dumped its radio stations and sold its share in USA Networks (now named IAC/InterActiveCorp) to Universal for $1.7 billion in 1997. In 1998 it sold the reference and education publishing divisions of Simon & Schuster to Pearson for $4.6 billion and unloaded the unprofitable Blockbuster Music chain to Wherehouse Entertainment for $115 million.

Viacom created an Internet division (MTV Networks Online) in 1999 to house its MTV VH1 and Nickelodeon Web sites (later decentralized into The MTVi Group and Nickelodeon Online). Later that year it sold 18% of Blockbuster in an IPO and sold 10% of MTVi to TCI Music (later Liberty Digital) in exchange for the SonicNet websites.

Viacom bought Chris-Craft's 50%-stake in the struggling UPN Network for a paltry $5 million in 2000 by exercising a buy-sell clause in the contract. BHC Communications (Chris-Craft's 80%-owned subsidiary that actually owned the stake in UPN) filed suit to block Viacom's merger with CBS claiming that it violated a non-compete clause in the contract but the New York Supreme Court ruled in Viacom's favor. Its $45 billion merger with CBS went through (reuniting two companies split apart by the government 30 years ago) and Viacom was given one year to sell UPN. However a federal law prohibiting ownership of more than one TV network was overturned in 2001 allowing Viacom to keep the network.

Later that year Viacom's victory over Chris-Craft turned to sour grapes when News Corp. agreed to buy Chris-Craft. The deal could have forced UPN to fold if News Corp. had turned Chris-Craft's large-market UPN stations into FOX affiliates (a new pact later signed with Chris-Craft keeps UPN as the stations' network).

In 2001 Viacom bought the rest of Infinity Broadcasting that it didn't already own as well as Black Entertainment Television (the media company targeting African-Americans) for $3 billion. It also folded MTVi back into parent MTV Networks. Other cost cutting measures in 2002 included combining the business operations of UPN and CBS and placing Simon & Schuster under the same division as its film and TV production holdings.

Two years later Viacom finally sold its majority stake in Blockbuster which never really fit in with Viacom's other media properties. The media firm also didn't want to deal with the new challenges facing Blockbuster such as stiff competition from video on demand services the cheap DVD market and mail order video rental company Netflix.

In a move designed to simplify the firm's operations and re-focus the company on its core assets in late 2005 Viacom split into two separately traded firms –one called CBS Corporation consisting of traditional television and radio broadcasting operations and headed by former co-COO Les Moonves; and the other called the "new" Viacom made up of cable television and film operations and headed by former co-COO Tom Freston. (Freston resigned in 2006.) Redstone retained his title as chairman of both firms as well as his majority control.

Shortly after the split CBS Corp. sold Paramount Parks to Cedar Fair for $1.2 billion. A newly formed network called The CW a combination of UPN and The WB debuted in 2006. The following TV season the CBS network fell from first place in the ratings for the first time in six years. CBS Corp. expanded its online publishing operations in 2008 with the $1.8 billion acquisition of CNET Networks.

In 2011 production on the eighth season of its hit comedy Two and a Half Men ceased as a result of the erratic behavior of actor Charlie Sheen. CBS fired Sheen and has put the show on hiatus for an undetermined period of time.

In 2014 the company spun off its CBS Outdoor Americas advertising business.

EXECUTIVES

Executive Vice President Office Of The Chairman, Carl D Folta

Chairman President and CEO, Leslie (Les) Moonves, age 65, $3,513,461 total compensation

SEVP and Chief Communications Officer, Gil Schwartz, age 64

SEVP Chief Administrative Officer and Chief Human Resources Officer, Anthony G. Ambrosio, age 55, $878,365 total compensation

SEVP and Chief Legal Officer, Lawrence P. (Larry) Tu, age 61, $1,204,615 total compensation

EVP Government Affairs, John Orlando

EVP Investor Relations, Adam Townsend

COO, Joseph R. Ianniello, age 48, $2,509,615 total compensation

EVP Deputy General Counsel and Secretary, Angeline C. Straka, age 70

EVP General Tax Counsel and Chief Veteran Officer, Richard M. Jones, age 50

SVP and CTO, Douglas (Doug) Rousso

Executive Vice President Labor Relations, Harry Isaacs

Vice President Advertising and Promotion Finance, Tracey Kimball

Vice President Production, Al Kennedy

Vice President Advertising and Promotion, Michael (Mel) Pollack

Vice President Operations Internal Audit Department, Jeff Meyer

Vice President Sales, Alan Clack

Senior Vice President Human Resources, Jeff Ryan

Vice President, Robert Noethiger

Assistant Vice President Platform Infrastructure, Clay Webster

Vice President Director Broadcast Operations And Engineering, Tom Schnecke

Vice President Finance, Bill Crupe

Senior Vice President Current Programs, Jeanne Mau

Vice President Human Resources, Cassie Thomas

Vice President Finance At CBS Television Network, David (Dave) Strouse

Vice President, Debra Wichser

Vice President Business Affairs, Deanna O'Toole

Senior Vice President Strategic Events And Partnerships, Amy Stevens

Senior Vice President Programming, Greg Trager

Vice President, Rich Landesman

Senior Vice President Corporate Security, Thomas Cruthers

Senior Vice President Corporate Development, Bryon Rubin

Vice President Of Information Technology, Michael Grant

Vice President Operations and Engineering, Paul Puccio

Senior Vice President Information Systems Director, Brelinda Snoddy

Executive Vice President Marketing and Media Relations, John (Jack) Wentworth

Vice President Senior Tax Counsel, Kenneth Koen

Vice President Special Projects On air Promotion, Chris Cranner

Vice President Env Projects Env Rem, Dottie Alke

Senior Vice President General Manager Entertainmen, Marc Debevoise

Vice President of Business Sysems, Stuart (Stu) Lepkowsky

Senior Vice President Creative, Jorge Ferreiro

Vice President Of Personnel TV Stations, Robin Bona

Vice President National Sports Sales, Bob Malmgren

Seniorvice President, Sue Lamphear

Senior Vice President Workforce Development, Jennifer Suarez

Vice President Assistant General Co, Andrew Siegel

Vice President of Detroit Sales, Joe Butkovich

Vice President Assistant General Co, Jonathan Sternberg

Vice President Finance, Steve Grosso

Vice President Research, Patti Cohen

Vice President, Laura Franco

Senior Vice President Sales, Barry Chamberlain

Senior Vice President Regional Sales Manager, John Holdridge

Executive Vice President, Larry Jenkins

Vice President, Edy Mendoza

Senior Vice President And Director Of Sales Analysis Operations, Bob Kaplan

Vice President Finance And Administration, AL Lipson

Vice President Business Development, Amy Young

Vice President Of Sales, Kevin Barth

Senior Vice President Sales Prime, Linda Rene

Senior Vice President Of Manufacturing, Marilyn Levatino

Vice President, Max Flisi

Vice President, George Lewis

Vice President Distribution, Ken Hinshaw

Vice President Mergers And Acquisitions, Ed Schwartz

Senior Vice President Sales, Marty Daly

Vice President, Katie Kulik

Vice President Of Casting, Amy Herzig

Vice President Market Resources, Vinnie Della Valle

Vice President National Digital Sales, John Vilade

Senior Vice President Sales Training And Development, Sheila Kirby

Vice President Ad Operations, Mark Halstead

Vice President Executive Creative Director, James Shefcik

Vice President of Business Affairs, Alison Choi

Vice President Technical Operations King World Productions, Rich Cervini

Vice President On Air Promotion, Paul Friedman

Vice President Executive Creative Director, James (Jamie) Shefcik

Vice President Corporate Finance and International Treasury CBS Corporation, Jd Karabas

Vice President Business Development at CBS Interactive, Adam London

Senior Vice President Publicity and National Partnerships and Promotions, Christine Batista

Vice President Sales West Coast CBS Interactive, Chris Fix

Senior Vice President Controller and Chief Accounting Officer, Larry Liding

Senior Vice President And Associate General Counsel Litigation, Anthony Bongiorno

Vice President Corporate Communications, Judy Dehaven

Vice President Group Sales, Brian Murphy

Vice President Current Programming, Amanda Schweitzer

Senior Vice President for Standards and Special Projects, Linda Mason

Vice Chair, Shari E. Redstone, age 61

Vice President Senior Counsel Securities and Assistant Secretary, Kimberly Pittman

Vice President And Assistant Treasurer, Jim Morrison

Auditors: PricewaterhouseCoopers LLP

LOCATIONS

HQ: CBS Corp
51 W. 52nd Street, New York, NY 10019
Phone: 212 975-4321
Web: www.cbscorporation.com

PRODUCTS/OPERATIONS

2014 Sales

	$ mil.	% of total
Advertising	7,204	52
Content	3,990	29
Affiliate fees & subscriptions	2,362	17
Other	250	2
Total	**13,806**	**100**

2014 Sales

	$ mil.	% of total
Entertainment	8,309	58
Local broadcasting	2,756	20
Cable networks	2,176	16
Publishing	778	6
Adjustments	(213)	-
Total	**13,806**	**100**

Selected Operations

Entertainment
  CBS Films (motion picture production)
  CBS Interactive (online content)
  BNET
  CBS.com
  CBSSports.com
  CNET
  GameSpot
  TV.com
  CBS Studios International (international program syndication)
  CBS Television Distribution (domestic programming syndication)
  CBS Television Network (broadcast television network)
  CBS Entertainment
  CBS News
  CBS Sports
  CBS Television Studios (television production)
  The CW Network (50% broadcast television network)
Local broadcasting
  CBS Radio
  CBS Television Stations
Outdoor advertising
  CBS Outdoor
Cable networks
  CBS College Sports Network
  Showtime (pay-TV service)
Publishing
  Simon & Schuster

COMPETITORS

21st Century Fox	Penguin Random House
AOL	SIRIUS XM
Cumulus Media	Sony Pictures
Disney	Entertainment
JCDecaux	Time Warner
Lamar Advertising	Yahoo!
NBCUniversal	iHeartCommunications

HISTORICAL FINANCIALS

Company Type: Public

Income Statement

FYE: December 31

	REVENUE ($ mil.)	NET INCOME ($ mil.)	NET PROFIT MARGIN	EMPLOYEES
12/15	13,886	1,413	10.2%	16,260
12/14	13,806	2,959	21.4%	17,310
12/13	15,284	1,879	12.3%	19,490
12/12	14,089	1,574	11.2%	20,930
12/11	14,245	1,305	9.2%	20,915
Annual Growth	**(0.6%)**	**2.0%**	**—**	**(6.1%)**

2015 Year-End Financials

Debt ratio: 35.55%	No. of shares (mil.): 463
Return on equity: 22.55%	Dividends
Cash ($ mil.): 323	Yield: 1.2%
Current ratio: 1.61	Payout: 20.7%
Long-term debt ($ mil.): 8,226	Market value ($ mil.): 21,821

	STOCK PRICE ($) FY Close	P/E High/Low	PER SHARE ($) Earnings	Dividends	Book Value
12/15	47.13	22 13	2.89	0.60	12.02
12/14	55.34	13 9	5.27	0.54	13.75
12/13	63.74	21 12	3.01	0.48	16.72
12/12	38.05	15 11	2.39	0.44	16.21
12/11	27.14	15 10	1.92	0.35	15.22
Annual Growth	**14.8%**	**— —**	**10.8%**	**14.4%**	**(5.7%)**

CDW Corp

LOCATIONS

HQ: CDW Corp
200 N. Milwaukee Avenue, Vernon Hills, IL 60061
Phone: 847 465-6000
Web: www.cdw.com

HISTORICAL FINANCIALS

Company Type: Public

Income Statement

FYE: December 31

	REVENUE ($ mil.)	NET INCOME ($ mil.)	NET PROFIT MARGIN	EMPLOYEES
12/14	12,074	244	2.0%	7,211
12/13	10,768	132	1.2%	7,000
12/12	10,128	119	1.2%	6,800
12/11	9,602	17	0.2%	—
12/10	8,801	(29)	—	—
Annual Growth	**8.2%**	**—**	**—**	**—**

2014 Year-End Financials

Debt ratio: 52.30%	No. of shares (mil.): 172
Return on equity: 29.72%	Dividends
Cash ($ mil.): 344	Yield: 0.5%
Current ratio: 1.67	Payout: 13.0%
Long-term debt ($ mil.): 3,174	Market value ($ mil.): 6,056

	STOCK PRICE ($) FY Close	P/E High/Low	PER SHARE ($) Earnings	Dividends	Book Value
12/14	35.17	25 16	1.42	0.20	5.44
12/13	23.36	29 22	0.84	0.04	4.14
Annual Growth	**10.8%**	**— —**	**14.0%**	**46.4%**	**7.1%**

Celanese Corp (DE)

Celanese Corporation gets a lot of good ink about its acetates. The global technology and specialty materials company's primary operations include the manufacture of building block chemicals like acetic acid and vinyl acetate monomers. Those chemicals are used in everything from inks and paints to agricultural products and chewing gum. Canadian subsidiary Acetex the majority of whose sales come from Europe is the world's largest acetyls manufacturer. Other products include acetate tow (in cigarette filters) which accounted for 16% of the company's total sales in 2013; industrial specialties like ethylene vinyl acetate; and engineered plastics.

Geographic Reach

The company has 28 global production facilities and an additional eight strategic affiliate production facilities. In addition to manufacturing sites in the US Celanese also has properties plants or other operations in Belgium Brazil Canada China France Germany Malaysia Mexico the Netherlands South Korea Spain Sweden Singapore and the UK. The US accounted for 28% of the company's revenues in 2014.

Operations

The company is one of the world's largest producers of acetyl products as well as a top global producer of engineered polymers.

Celanese operates through four business segments: Advanced Engineered Materials (specialty polymers for application in automotive medical and electronics products as well as other consumer and industrial applications); Consumer Specialties (acetate products and the Nutrinova businesses which serve consumer-driven applications); Industrial Specialties (emulsions and EVA performance polymers businesses); and Acetyl Intermediates (acetic acid vinyl acetate monomer acetic anhydride and acetate esters used as starting materials for colorants paints adhesives coatings and medicines).

Celanese also indirectly owns a 25% interest in National Methanol Company affiliate through CTE Petrochemicals Company a joint venture with Texas Eastern Arabian Corporation Ltd. The remaining interest in Ibn Sina is held by Saudi Basic Industries Corporation (SABIC). SABIC and CTE entered into the Ibn Sina joint venture agreement in 1981. Ibn Sina is constructing a 50000 ton per year polyacetal production facility in Saudi Arabia and the term of the joint venture agreement extends until 2032.

Acetyl Intermediates accounted for 47% of Celanese's total revenues in 2014; Advanced Engineered Materials 20%; Industrial Specialties 17%; and Consumer Specialties 16%.

Sales and Marketing

Celanese markets its products both directly to customers and through distributors. Sales to major global customers in a wide range of industries are usually made under multi-year contracts. The company serves a broad range of industries including consumer and industrial adhesives paints and coatings textiles food and beverage automotive applications consumer and medical applications performance industrial applications filter media paper and packaging chemical additives and construction applications.

Financial Performance

In 2014 Celanese's net revenues grew by 4% due to higher vinyl acetate monomer (VAM) and acetic acid pricing in the Acetyl Intermediates segment and higher volume globally in the Advanced Engineered Materials segment fueled by growth in automotive medical and industrial applications.Revenues from Advanced Engineered Materials increased primarily due to higher volume globally partially offset by lower pricing for polyoxymethylene and GUR due to shifts in product and geographic sales mix. In Europe volume increased due to strong growth in nearly all product lines. Consumer Specialties revenues decreased as the result of lower acetate tow volume globally and lower acetate flake pricing under a legacy contract slightly offset by an increase in acetate tow pricing reflecting favorable shifts in customer mix higher acetate flake volume. and higher volume in food ingredients business primarily related to sorbates.Revenues from Industrial Specialties rose due to higher pricing and volume. In the emulsion polymers business pricing increased primarily due to higher raw material costs for VAM in Europe Asia and North America. Volume increases were driven by a targeted strategy in Asia primarily in adhesive and construction products and paints and coatings products and by higher demand in Europe.Acetyl Intermediates revenues increased due to higher VAM pricing resulting from permanent capacity reductions in Europe and planned and unplanned industry outages slightly offset by lower volume. Net sales also benefited from higher acetic acid pricing resulting from planned and unplanned industry outages as well as higher acetic anhydride pricing.In 2014 Celanese's net income decreased by 43% due to higher selling general and administrative expenses.Selling general and administrative expenses rose primarily due to an increase in pension and other postretirement plan net periodic benefit cost of $379 million higher functional and project spending of $43 million and an increase in incentive compensation costs of $25 million.In 2014 Celanese's cash from operating activities increased by 26% as a result of stronger earnings performance an increase in value-added tax refunds increase in dividends received from its cellulose derivatives ventures partially offset by an increase in pension plan and other postretirement benefit plan contributions.

Strategy

Celanese's strategy is to grow the company through expansion into emerging regions particularly China; to offer innovation through developing new products and applications; increase its productivity through energy reduction business process improvements and manufacturing optimization; and boost its portfolio by growing its business through both acquisitions or internal growth. It s also eyeing Europe as a growth market.

In 2014 the company teamed up with Mitsui & Co. forming a joint venture for the production of methanol at its integrated chemical plant in Clear Lake Texas. The total investment in the methanol facility (with a planned annual capacity of 1.3 million tons) is estimated to be $800 million. To better serve key customers in Japan in 2014 Celanese Japan Limited and Setsunakasei Co. Ltd. (Setsunan) signed a deal whereby Setsunan will compound Celanese engineered polymers in Setsunan's facilities in Japan. That year Indian Oil and Celanese agreed to explore the potential of a joint investment in a fuel ethanol plant to be built in India based on Celanese's TCX Technology.

In 2014 Celanese expanded its compounding capabilities at its integrated chemical complex in Nanjing China to include polyphenylene sulfide and expansion of the Florence Kentucky facility and expansion of the Suzano Brazil facility to include long-fiber reinforced thermoplastics production to serve customers in Brazil and Latin America.That year it introduced a family of low-friction and low-wear thermoplastic polymers for medical devices that enables the device to operate smoothly providing a high degree of patient comfort and consistency. It also commercially launched its CelFX technology for the Japanese market and launched the Commercial Technology Center in Seoul Korea tosupport customer growth in South Korea and advance the technical capabilities of our product portfolio.It also opened a new sales center in Istanbul Turkey to support customer growth of their intermediate chemistry engineered materials and emulsion polymers businesses in Turkey and the greater European region.In 2014 Celanese formed Fairway Methanol LLC (a joint venture with Mitsui & Co.) for the production of methanol at the company's integrated chemical plant in Clear Lake Texas. The methanol unit will have an annual capacity of 1.3 million tons.

Mergers and Acquisitions

In 2014 the company acquired Rhode Island-based Cool Polymers to accelerate Celanese's growth in the conductive polymers market by building on Cool Polymers' strong product portfolio and technical know how. Cool Polymers is a top compounder of conductive polymers with expertise in the LED (light-emitting diode) market

Company BackgroundIn 2013 the company announced the expansion of its polyacetal manufacturing footprint in Asia to support its customers including the expansion of its joint venture agreements with Polyplastics in Malaysia Korea Engineering Plastics (KEP) in Korea and SABIC in Saudi Arabia.

Strengthening its European distribution channels in 2013 appointed Krahn Chemie as its distributor for Celanese Emulsions GmbH in Germany. It also appointed Innovia Solutions Ltd as a distributor in the UK and Ireland.

On the product innovation side in 2013 the company introduced a new generation of Thermx PCT grades that provide outstanding initial reflectance and reflectance stability under heat and light (as required in LED lighting packages found in display backlight and general lighting).

In 2012 the company teamed up with Indonesia's Pertamina forming a joint venture to develop fuel ethanol projects in that country.

To grow its emulsion polymers business in 2011 the company acquired two product lines Vinac and Flexbond from Ashland. The acquisition is expected to speed up growth of the company's emulsion polymers operations throughout the Americas —especially in the adhesives textiles coatings and paper segments.

Celanese Corporation was created in 2004 by the Blackstone Group which had acquired a majority share in Celanese AG turned it private and then flipped it in a 2005 public offering. Blackstone finally divested its remaining holdings in Celanese in 2007.

EXECUTIVES

Senior Vice President, Mark Oberle
Chairman and CEO, Mark C. Rohr, age 64, $1,088,462 total compensation
SVP Human Resources, Lori Johnston, $464,615 total compensation
EVP; President Acetyl Chain, Patrick D. (Pat) Quarles, age 47
SVP Business Strategy Development Procurement and Advanced Fuels Technology, Jay C. Townsend, age 56, $553,077 total compensation
SVP and General Counsel, Gjon N. Nivica, age 50, $520,385 total compensation
EVP; President Materials Solutions, Scott Sutton
VP and CIO, Mike Jackson
SVP Finance and CFO, Christopher W. (Chris) Jensen, age 48, $430,769 total compensation
VP and General Manager Europe Acetyl Chain and Acetyl Chain Global Sales, Mark Murray
Executive Vice President General Counsel and Corporate Secretary, Curtis Shaw
Sr V Pres Operations, John Wardzel
Executive Vice President and President Chemicals americas, Rick Shaw
Vice President Europe Region, Amy Hebert
Vice President and General Manager Global Sales, Todd Elliott
Vice President Business Development, Marcel Van Amerongen
Vice President Human Resources and Employment Law, Joe Fox
Vice President Global Communications and Corporate Social Responsibility, Gretchen Rosswurm
Vice President Human Resources, David Dart

Vice President Global Corporate Strategy And Manda, Patrick (Paddy) Schumacher
Executive Vice President, Stephen Cushard
Senior Corporate Vice President, Jon Nivica
Vice President Shared Services, Darren Major
Vice President U S. Public Affairs, Stephanie Daigle
Vice President Of Human Resources, Jim Coppens
Vice President Corporate Sales, Rick Hall
Vice President Manufacturing and Technology, Bek Humelsine
Vice President And Deputy General Counsel, Jay Felkins
Senior Vice President Supply Management, William Antonace
Senior Vice President Chief Financial Officer, Steven (Steve) Sterin
Sales Vice President, Bob Walters
Treasurer, Divya Kottayil
Assistant Treasurer, Thomas (Thom) Liu
Auditors: KPMG LLP

LOCATIONS

HQ: Celanese Corp (DE)
222 W. Las Colinas Blvd., Suite 900N, Irving, TX 75039-5421
Phone: 972 443-4000
Web: www.celanese.com

2014 Sales

	$ mil.	% of total
Germany	2,156	31
US	1,899	28
China	996	15
Singapore	632	9
Belgium	480	7
Canada	204	3
Mexico	259	4
Others	176	3
Total	**6,802**	**100**

PRODUCTS/OPERATIONS

2014 Sales

	$ mil.	% of total
Acetyl Intermediates	3,493	47
Advanced Engineered Materials	1,459	20
Consumer Specialties	1,160	16
Industrial Specialties	1,224	17
Adjustments	(534)	-
Total	**6,802**	**100**

Selected Products

Acetyl Intermediates
  Acetate esters
  Acetic acid
  Acetic anhydride
  Carboxylic acids
  Methanol
  Vinyl acetate monomer (VAM)
Industrial Specialties
  Emulsions
Consumer Specialties
  Acetate tow
  Sunett sweetener
Advanced Engineered Materials
  Polyacetal products (POM)
  Polyphenylene sulfide (Forton)
  UHMW-PE (GUR)

Selected Brand Names

AOPlus
BuyTiconaDirect
Celanex
Celcon
Celstran
Celvolit
Clarifoil
Compel
Erkol
GUR
Hostaform
Impet
Mowilith
Nutrinova
Riteflex

Sunett
Thermx
Vandar
Vectra
Vinamul

COMPETITORS

Asahi Kasei	LANXESS
BASF SE	Methanex
DSM	NutraSweet
Daicel Chemical	Rhodia
Dow Chemical	SABIC Innovative
DuPont	Plastics
Eastman Chemical	Solvay
Hexion	

HISTORICAL FINANCIALS

Company Type: Public

Income Statement

FYE: December 31

	REVENUE ($ mil.)	NET INCOME ($ mil.)	NET PROFIT MARGIN	EMPLOYEES
12/15	5,674	304	5.4%	7,081
12/14	6,802	624	9.2%	7,468
12/13	6,510	1,101	16.9%	7,430
12/12	6,418	605	9.4%	7,550
12/11	6,763	607	9.0%	7,600
Annual Growth	(4.3%)	(15.9%)	—	(1.8%)

2015 Year-End Financials

Debt ratio: 34.72%
Return on equity: 11.70%
Cash ($ mil.): 967
Current ratio: 1.80
Long-term debt ($ mil.): 2,468

No. of shares (mil.): 146
Dividends
  Yield: 1.7%
  Payout: 33.8%
Market value ($ mil.): 9,883

	STOCK PRICE ($) FY Close	P/E High/Low		PER SHARE ($) Earnings	Dividends	Book Value
12/15	67.33	36	26	2.00	1.15	16.20
12/14	59.96	16	12	4.00	0.93	18.43
12/13	55.31	8	6	6.91	0.53	17.20
12/12	44.53	14	9	3.79	0.27	10.84
12/11	44.27	15	8	3.82	0.22	8.57
Annual Growth	11.1%	—	—	(14.9%)	51.2%	17.3%

Celgene Corp.

Celgene lines up cells and genes to create good health. The biopharmaceutical company's lead product is Revlimid which is approved in the US Europe and other select markets as a treatment for multiple myeloma (bone marrow cancer). Revlimid also is used to treat a blood disorder called myelodysplastic syndrome (MDS). The company's second-biggest seller is another treatment for MDS called Vidaza; the drug is also approved to treat leukemia in Europe. Other products include Thalomid used to treat patients newly diagnosed with multiple myeloma as well as breast cancer treatment Abraxane and lymphoma drug Istodax. The firm has other drugs in development that combat inflammatory diseases and cancer.

Operations

Revlimid is by far the company's biggest seller making up some two-thirds of Celgene's annual sales. Its other top selling products –Vidaza Thalomid Pomalyst and Abraxane –make up most of its remaining revenues. The newly developed product Pomalyst was approved by the FDA in 2013 to treat multiple myeloma in patients that have not responded well to other medications.

Outside of blood cancers and diseases Celgene receives royalties on sales of ADHD drugs Focalin Focalin XR and Ritalin LA which are licensed to and sold by global drugmaker Novartis. The company also makes a small amount of revenues from its Cellular Therapeutics subsidiary which is is researching stem cell therapies for diseases such as cancer and multiple sclerosis and its Lifebank USA unit which operates a blood bank in which parents may choose to store their newborn's cord and placenta stem cells as a way to combat possible blood diseases the child might contract later.

The company is developing novel small molecules that target PDE4 an intracellular enzyme that regulates the production of multiple pro-inflammatory and anti-inflammatory mediators. Other therapies in the works include CC-122 and CC-220 which are being tested for hematological and solid tumor cancers and other diseases.

Geographic Reach

The US is the company's largest market accounting for about 60% of revenues with Europe accounting for most of the rest of sales. However Celgene is working to expand its global presence. Its products reach customers in more than 50 countries.

In addition to global sales and service locations Celgene operates manufacturing plants in the US (Phoenix) and Switzerland (Boudry and Zofingen) that meet a majority of its needs though some of the firm's products are made by third-party manufacturers. The company also has sales and research offices in California Florida Kansas Massachusetts New Jersey North Carolina and Washington DC.

Sales and Marketing

Celgene sells its products through a global direct sales force as well as via independent representatives in select markets (primarily in Latin America). In the US products are distributed primarily to wholesalers and in the case of Revlimid Pomalyst and Thalomid specialty pharmacies (the drugs must be handled under special risk-management programs due to blood clot risks associated with the drugs). In international markets the company's products are distributed to hospitals clinics and retailers.

Financial Performance

The company's strategies of making select acquisitions finding new uses for existing drugs and conducting proprietary R&D to keep its pipeline well-stocked seem to be paying off. Celgene has achieved rapidly climbing revenues and profits in recent years as its product offerings grew including an 18% revenue increase (to $7.7 billion) and a 38% net income jump (to nearly $2 billion) in 2014 due to increased sales of Revlamid Abraxane Otezla and Pomalyst. That growth was partially offset by declines in revenue from Vidaza and Thalomid.

Cash flow from operations has followed rising revenues and profits over the past few years. In 2014 operating cash flow rose 26% to $2.8 billion.

Strategy

Key focus areas for the company include hematology oncology inflammation and immunology. Though Celgene has a little breathing room before it loses market exclusivity on most of its products the firm is still working avidly to avoid the dips in revenue that go hand-in-hand with patent losses by adding or developing new drugs and pipeline candidates through internal development collaborations and acquisitions. Vidaza's patent expired in the US in 2011 for instance though no competing generic versions of the drug have been approved so far. In 2013 Celgene contracted with Sandoz to sell a generic version of Vidaza in the US; the drug's regulatory exclusivity is expected to continue in Europe through 2018. Celgene's other major drug patents aren't set to expire for several years.

Many of the firm's internal programs are focused on getting its marketed drugs approved for other indications. For instance Revlimid is in clinical trials to treat ailments including forms of non-Hodgkin's lymphoma and chronic lymphatic leukemia as well as to treat newly diagnosed multiple myeloma patients and Istodax is under development for solid tumor cancers.

The company is looking to gain US approval for Vidaza to treat acute myeloid leukemia (AML); it is already used for AML indications in Europe. Abraxane is being tested to treat skin lung bladder and other cancers. Other candidates target additional hematological cancers solid tumors anemia and inflammatory conditions. In 2015 Otezla was granted approval by the European Commission for the treatment of psoriasis and psoriatic arthritis.

In the largest up-front payment for a biotechnology licensing agreement to date Celgene in 2015 paid $1 billion to gain access to innovative cancer treatments being developed by Juno Therapeutics. The collaboration deal gives Celgene the option to partner with Juno on the commercialization of its cancer drugs and cell therapies for the treatment of autoimmune diseases; Juno will retain responsibilities for R&D and commercialization in North America while Celgene will take on the development and commercialization duties in the rest of the world. The deal also gives Celgene a 10% stake in Juno.

Mergers and Acquisitions

In 2015 the company moved to expand its position in the field of innovative cancer therapies when it agreed to buy privately held Quanticel Pharmaceuticals for some $100 million. Through the deal Celgene will gain access to Quanticel's platform for the single-cell genomic analysis of cancer and its lead programs targeting epigenetic modifiers. Also that year Celgene bought Receptos gaining that firm's ozanimod candidate for the treatment of multiple ailments including relapsing multiple sclerosis. That deal was valued at $7.2 billion.

Company Background

Celgene was founded in 1986 as a spinoff entity; it was formerly part of Celanese Corporation.

EXECUTIVES

EVP; President Celgene Research and Early Development, Thomas O. (Tom) Daniel, $691,500 total compensation

EVP and CFO, Peter N. Kellogg, age 59, $400,000 total compensation

President and COO, Jacqualyn A. (Jackie) Fouse, age 53, $803,250 total compensation

CEO Celgene Cellular Therapeutics, Perry A. Karsen, age 60, $666,500 total compensation

EVP General Counsel and Corporate Secretary, Gerald F. Masoudi

President Global Inflammation and Immunology, Scott Smith, age 53, $546,246 total compensation

CEO, Mark J. Alles, age 55, $767,917 total compensation

SVP and CIO, Richard Williams

Vice President And General Manager, Joseph (Jo) Kaminiski

Corporate Vice President Head Of Global Drug Safety and Risk Management, John (Jack) Freeman

Vice President Finance, Hunter Smith

Vice President Talent Leadership Development, Joe Garbus

Vice President Research and Development Informatics, John (Jack) Apathy

Vice President Clinical and Medical Affairs, Steven (Steve) Fischkoff

Vice President Investor Relations, Patrick Flanigan
Corporate Vice President Head Us Commercial
  Inflammation and Immunology, Terrie Curran
Vice President Head Us Medical Affairs, Peg Squier
Medical Director Europe, Kamel Djazouli
Senior Vice President Sales and Marketing, Joanna
  Forester
Executive Vice President, Beatriz C Mateos
Medical Director, Aysen Karayal
Vice President, Tom Tomayko
Senior Vice President, Pauline Vinnicombe
Senior Vice President, Joe Camardo
National Account Manager, Mitch Marks
Vice President, Oliver Kong
National Account Manager, Greg Walls
Medical Director, Ahmet Hasaligil
Vice President, Allison Nance
Vice President Patient Advocacy, Joel Beetsch
Vice President Global Marketing Inflammation
  and Immunology, Mark Kreston
Vice President, Ross Davis
Senior Vice President Operations, Jeffrey Silverman
Vice President Corporate Communications,
  William (Bill) Westlin
Vice President of Clinical Trial Operations, Patricia
  (Pat) Moenaert
Vice President Of Finance, Lori Kudzma
Vice President, Deborah Tady
National Sales Manager, Jacinta Lawson
National Account Manager, Jeff Wunderlich
Corporate Vice President Chief Compliance
  Officer, John (Jack) Soriano
Vice President Regulatory Affairs Emea, Patricia
  Pallier
Payer National Account Manager, Todd Hood
Vice President Clinical Research And
  Development, Patricia Rohane
Pharmd CPH Mrpharms, Arti Lynn
Vice President, Robert (Bob) Knight
Chairman, Robert J. (Bob) Hugin, age 60
Treasurer, Cathy Marino
Board Member, Stacy Deserio
Assistant Treasurer, Sandra Alves
Board Member, Simona Bortolazzi
Auditors: KPMG LLP

LOCATIONS

HQ: Celgene Corp.
  86 Morris Avenue, Summit, NJ 07901
Phone: 908 673-9000
Web: www.celgene.com

2014 Sales

	$ mil.	% of total
US	4,482	59
Europe	2,310	30
Other regions	876	11
Total	7,670	100

PRODUCTS/OPERATIONS

2014 Sales

	$ mil.	% of total
Products		
Revlimid	4,980	65
Abraxane	848	11
Pomalyst/Imnovid	679	9
Vidaza	611	8
Thalomid	221	3
Azacitidine for injection	78	1
Otezla	69	1
Istodax	65	1
Other	9	-
Other	106	1
Total	7,670	100

Selected Products

Approved
  Abraxane (breast cancer treatment)
  Istodax (cancer treatment gained through Gloucester
  buy)

Revlimid (multiple myeloma myelodysplastic
  syndromes)
Pomalyst (multiple myeloma)
Thalomid (complications from leprosy multiple
  myeloma)
Vidaza (myelodysplastic syndromes)

Selected Acquisitions

COMPETITORS

Abbott Labs	Johnson & Johnson
Allergan	Merck
Amgen	Millennium: The Takeda
Astex Pharmaceuticals	Oncology Company
AstraZeneca	Novartis
Baxter International	Onyx Pharmaceuticals
Biogen	Pfizer
Bristol-Myers Squibb	Roche Holding
CTI BioPharma	Sanofi
Eisai	Shire
Eli Lilly	Takeda Pharmaceutical

HISTORICAL FINANCIALS

Company Type: Public

Income Statement

FYE: December 31

	REVENUE ($ mil.)	NET INCOME ($ mil.)	NET PROFIT MARGIN	EMPLOYEES
12/15	9,256	1,602	17.3%	6,971
12/14	7,670	1,999	26.1%	6,012
12/13	6,493	1,449	22.3%	5,100
12/12	5,506	1,456	26.4%	4,700
12/11	4,842	1,318	27.2%	4,460
Annual Growth 17.6%		5.0%	—	11.8%

2015 Year-End Financials

Debt ratio: 52.68% No. of shares (mil.): 786
Return on equity: 25.75% Dividends
Cash ($ mil.): 4,880 Yield: —
Current ratio: 4.77 Payout: —
Long-term debt ($ mil.): 14,250 Market value ($ mil.): 94,203

	STOCK PRICE ($) FY Close	P/E High/Low	PER SHARE ($) Earnings	Dividends	Book Value
12/15	119.76	69 52	1.94	0.00	7.52
12/14	111.86	69 33	2.39	0.00	8.15
12/13	168.97	98 45	1.69	0.00	6.82
12/12	78.47	49 35	1.65	0.00	6.78
12/11	67.60	47 34	1.43	0.00	6.30
Annual Growth 15.4%		— —	8.0%	—	4.5%

Centene Corp

Centene is sensitive to the needs of those enrolled in government-assisted health programs. The company provides managed care and related services in more than a dozen states under names such as Managed Health Services (Wisconsin and Indiana) Superior HealthPlan (Texas) and Buckeye Community Health Plan (Ohio). Centene provides services to some 2.7 million low-income elderly and disabled people receiving benefits from programs including Medicaid Supplemental Security Income (SSI) and state Children's Health Insurance Program (CHIP). Centene also offers specialty services in areas such as behavioral health (through Cenpatico) vision benefits (OptiCare) and pharmacy benefits management (US Script).

Operations

The company operates in two primary segments: Managed Care and Specialty Services.

Centene's Medicaid managed care contracts account for three-fourths of revenues. Its largest contracts are with the state of Texas which accounts for about a quarter of revenues. The company provides services through Medicaid CHIP SSI LTC (long-term care) foster care and ABD (aged blind and disabled) programs.

The company has expanded its specialty services to include telehealth advisory (NurseWise) case management (CaseNet) and disease and wellness management (Nurtur). Centene's Celtic Insurance subsidiary specializes in providing low-cost consumer-directed insurance policies to uninsured customers nationwide and its Bridgeway Health Solutions provides long-term care policies in select territories.

Geographic Reach

Centene's health plans provide services through a network of more than 59000 primary care physicians 178000 specialists and 2000 hospitals in 22 states: Arizona Arkansas California Florida Georgia Illinois Indiana Kansas Kentucky Louisiana Massachusetts Minnesota Mississippi Missouri New Hampshire Ohio South Carolina Texas Tennessee Vermont Washington and Wisconsin.

Sales and Marketing

Most of Centene's revenue comes under contract or subcontract with state Medicaid managed care programs. Its largest markets are Texas (25% of revenue in 2014 –that percentage has declined from 40% in 2012) and Florida (14%).

Financial Performance

Centene's steady revenue growth (25% in 2013) continued in 2014 when it hit $16.6 billion a 52% jump. The increase was attributed to geographic expansion growth in its specialty pharmacy unit AcariaHealth and acquisitions. After years of net income growth Centene in 2012 reported a 98% drop as expenses rose across the board. Since then profits have more than rebounded and in 2014 they rose 64% to $271 million (driven by the higher revenues). Cash flow from operations increased 220% that year to $1.2 billion.

Strategy

Centene's primary growth strategies are to enter new markets and expand in existing markets via acquisitions and by gaining new contracts with state Medicaid agencies. For example the company was granted a contract to begin providing Medicaid services in Kansas at the start of 2013. Centene is benefiting from the growing number of mandated managed care plans in states that are looking to control Medicaid spending.

In 2014 the company entered the international market with its investment in Spanish health management group Ribera Salud.

In addition to geographic expansion the company looks to grow its membership by adding new services in its existing state markets such as small business health plans and low-income individual plans. It also evaluates opportunities to grow in new fields such as health-related information technology and non-Medicaid health plans. In 2013 it began a joint venture with MHM Services called Centurion to move into the correctional facility managed care market. Centene purchased specialty pharmacy AcariaHealth expanded in Florida and Mississippi and started a new contract with Texas Health and Human Services Commission the same year.

Centene also occasionally divests or exits operations in smaller service areas to focus on its core growth regions. For instance the company terminated its Kentucky Medicaid contract in mid-2013 due to disappointing financial results in the region.

Mergers and Acquisitions

In 2015 the company announced plans to buy insurer Health Net in a $6.3 billion deal that will broaden its presence in the Medicare Advantage and Medicaid programs. The move follows other consolidation efforts in the insurance industry as companies adjust to federal health care reforms. Other deals that year included agreements to purchase Oregon-based Agate Resources the rest of LiveHealthier (health management solutions) it didn't already own and Fidelis SecureCare of Michigan.

Centene paid $213 million in 2014 for management services organization US Medical Management; that unit provides in-home health services for patients with multiple complex conditions. It also bought a stake in Spanish health management firm Ribera Salud.

In 2013 Centene acquired Specialty Therapeutic Care Holdings (known as AcariaHealth) a specialty pharmacy services provider for some $152 million. The purchase added a sister business for Centene's US Script operations allowing it to offer pharmacy services to patients with complex medical conditions including hemophilia and cancer.

EXECUTIVES

Vice President Of Information Technology, Keith Bernier
Executive Vice President Operations and CIO, Donald G (Don) Imholz
Chairman President and CEO, Michael F. Neidorff, age 72, $1,200,000 total compensation
EVP and Chief Administrative Officer, Carol E. Goldman, age 57, $550,000 total compensation
EVP and Chief Business Development Officer, Jesse N. Hunter, age 39, $600,000 total compensation
EVP CFO and Treasurer, William N. Scheffel, age 61, $720,000 total compensation
EVP, Cary D. Hobbs
EVP Secretary and General Counsel, Keith H. Williamson, age 62
EVP, Holly Benson
CFO, Jeffrey A Schwaneke, age 40
EVP Insurance Group Business Unit, K. Rone Baldwin, age 56, $425,000 total compensation
COO Sunshine Health, Nathan Landsbaum
EVP, Brandy Burkhalter
Vice President Finance, Holly Mayer
Svp Operations, Patricia (Pat) Darnley
Regional Vice President Ophthalmology Services, Karen Fraider
Vice President And Director, Kim Owens
Senior Vice President Business Development, Brent Layton
Vice President And Director, Julie Boulch
Senior Vice President Patient Services, Susan Ekvall
Vice President and Director, Linda Taylor
Vice President And Director, Marian Williams
Vice President Network Development And Provider Relations, Irene Armendariz
Vice President Network Development and Contract, Randall Guillory
Vice President And Director, Tiffany Smith
Senior Vice President Network Development and Contract, Michael (Mel) Diel
Vice President Medical Management, Terry Johnson
Vice President And Director, Deborah (Deb) Robbins
Vice President Network Strategy, Jim Messina
Vice President And Director, Michelle (Mitch) Whitener
Medical Director, Sherman Podolsky
Vice President Of Operations, Eric Ruschmann
Vice President Of Operations, Sherry Wolter
Vice President And Director, Melissa (Mel) Johnson
Vice President and Director, Thomas (Thom) Welch
Vice President For Complex Programs, Gale Arden
Medical Director, David (Dave) Gilchrist
Vice President Operations, Krisitine Cusimano
Vice President, Jared Wolfe
Vice President And Director, James (Jamie) Robson
Division President, Elizabeth Griffin

Vice President And Director, Janie Fauconneau
Vice President and Director, Marie Downing
Vice President Member and Provider Solutions, Jennifer (Jen) Weigand
Vice President Network Development And Contracting, Clyde White
Vice President and Director, Rebecca Hahn
Senior Vice President Business Development, Debra Cooper
Vice President And Director, Cara Larose
Vice President Contracting and Network Development, Jill Anderson
Vice President And Director, Jennifer (Jen) Clark
Vice President Development And Integr, Bob Nolan
Vice President Of Human Resources, Jalie Cohen
Executive Vice President International Operations And Business Integration, Cindy Brinkley
Vice President Of Human Resources, Mary-katherine Kutac
Vice President Information Technology, Steele Sloane
Vice President Compliance, Katie Rogers
Regional Vice President Finance Centene subsidiaries CelitCare and New Hampshire Healthy Families, Alida Dodd
Vice President Network Development and Contracting, David (Dave) Willard
Vice President Clinical Programs, Amy Poole-yaeger
Vice President Medical Management, Ann Cahill
Vice President Of Medical Management, Wendy Faust
Vice President Network Development and Contracting, Christopher (Chris) Merrill
Vice President Operations Business Proces, Leon Luttschwager
Vice President Of Operations, Kristine Cusimano
Vice President ??? Corporate Community Relations, Joyce Larkin
Vice President Human Resources, Stephanie Hall
Vice President Of Payment Innovation, Ananth Lalithakumar
Vice President Of Operations, Tanya Hester
Medical Director, Steve Dziabis
Vice President Internal Audit, Karen Fain
Vice President Corporate Controller, Alaine Heselmeyer
Senior Vice President CCP Operations, Esmeralda Baig
Vice President and Director, Carolyn Thomas
Vice President Information Technology, Ellen McCahon
Senior Vice President Innovation and Product Development, Aparna Abburi
Vice President and Director, Melissa (Mel) Chenault
Vice President Of Long Term Care, David Wagner
Vice President and Director, Joyce Edwards
Vice President Operations, James Sefcik
Vice President And Director, Matt Schmitt
Vice President And Director, Helen Bryson
Senior Vice President And Chief Communications Officer, Marcela Manjarrez-williams
Vice President Pharmacy Operations, Justin Weiss
Medical Director, Amy Yaeger
Vice President Network Contracting, Gary Strong
Vice President Facility Management And Construction, Andrea Cruce
Vice President of Enrollment Operations, Michael (Mel) Boone
Vice President Operations OptiCare Managed Vision, Tara Price
Executive Vice President Specialty Company Business Unit, Jason M Harrold
Vice President Health Plan Operations, Kevin OToole
Executive Vice President, Mark Eggert
Vice President Compliance, Jeff Torres
Director of Pharmacy, James Frank (Jamie) Reynolds
Vice President Customer Service, Rodney (Rod) Long

Director of Pharmacy Operations, Martha Exton
Vice President Pharmacy Operations Federal Programs, Jeff Borowiecki
Vice President of Medical Management New Business, Judy Bauer
Auditors: KPMG LLP

LOCATIONS

HQ: Centene Corp
7700 Forsyth Boulevard, St. Louis, MO 63105
Phone: 314 725-4477   **Fax:** 314 725-5180
Web: www.centene.com

PRODUCTS/OPERATIONS

2014

	% of total
Managed Care	74
Specialty Services	26
Total	**100**

2014 Sales

	$ mil.	% of total
Premiums	14,198	86
Services	1,469	9
Premium tax & health insurer fees	893	5
Total	**16,560**	**100**

Selected Acquisitions

COMPETITORS

AMERIGROUP
Aetna
Anthem
Blue Cross and Blue Shield of South Carolina
Blue Cross and Blue Shield of Texas
CIGNA
Coventry Health Care
Health Net
Humana
Kaiser Foundation Health Plan
Molina Healthcare
Schaller Anderson Inc
Scott & White Health Plan
Security Health Plan of Wisconsin
UCare Minnesota
UnitedHealth Group
WellCare Health Plans

HISTORICAL FINANCIALS

Company Type: Public

Income Statement

FYE: December 31

	REVENUE ($ mil.)	NET INCOME ($ mil.)	NET PROFIT MARGIN	EMPLOYEES
12/14	16,560	271	1.6%	13,400
12/13	10,863	165	1.5%	8,800
12/12	8,667	1	0.0%	6,800
12/11	5,340	111	2.1%	5,300
12/10	4,448	94	2.1%	4,200
Annual Growth	**38.9%**	**30.0%**	**—**	**33.6%**

2014 Year-End Financials

Debt ratio: 15.30%
Return on equity: 18.20%
Cash ($ mil.): 1,610
Current ratio: 1.05
Long-term debt ($ mil.): 888

No. of shares (mil.): 118
Dividends
  Yield: —
  Payout: —
Market value ($ mil.): 12,299

	STOCK PRICE ($) FY Close	P/E High/Low	PER SHARE ($) Earnings	Dividends	Book Value
12/14	103.85	46 24	2.25	0.00	14.73
12/13	58.95	44 27	1.47	0.00	11.15
12/12	41.00	25401342	0.02	0.00	9.11
12/11	39.59	37 23	1.06	0.00	9.20
12/10	25.34	27 18	0.94	0.00	8.00
Annual Growth	**42.3%**	**— —**	**24.4%**	**—**	**16.5%**

CenterPoint Energy Resources Corp.

EXECUTIVES

Chb-pres-ceo, Scott M Prochazka
Auditors: Deloitte & Touche LLP

LOCATIONS

HQ: CenterPoint Energy Resources Corp.
1111 Louisiana, Houston, TX 77002
Phone: 713 207-1111
Web: www.centerpointenergy.com

HISTORICAL FINANCIALS

Company Type: Public

Income Statement

	REVENUE ($ mil.)	NET INCOME ($ mil.)	NET PROFIT MARGIN	EMPLOYEES
12/14	6,367	323	5.1%	4,581
12/13	5,522	64	1.2%	4,714
12/12	4,901	137	2.8%	4,842
12/11	6,102	316	5.2%	4,701
12/10	6,569	300	4.6%	4,725
Annual Growth	(0.8%)	1.9%	—	(0.8%)

FYE: December 31

2014 Year-End Financials

Debt ratio: 22.83%
Return on equity: 7.60%
Cash ($ mil.): 2
Current ratio: 1.15
Long-term debt ($ mil.): 2,469

No. of shares (mil.): 0
Dividends
  Yield: —
  Payout: 125.3%
Market value ($ mil.): —

CenterPoint Energy, Inc

CenterPoint Energy pivots around its core operations which include power and gas distribution utilities and natural gas pipeline gathering and marketing operations. CenterPoint Energy's regulated utilities distribute natural gas to 3.4 million customers in six US states and electricity to more than 2.1 million customers on the Texas Gulf Coast. The company's main stomping ground is Texas where it has regulated power distribution operations through subsidiary CenterPoint Energy Houston Electric. CenterPoint Energy operates more than 50717 miles of power distribution lines 20000 miles of interstate gas pipeline and 3700 miles of gas gathering pipeline. It also provides natural gas field services.

Geographic Reach

The company's natural gas distribution subsidiaries serve customers in Arkansas Indiana Louisiana Minnesota Mississippi Oklahoma and Texas. (Texas accounted for about 49% of CenterPoint Energy's natural gas distribution customers in 2014). The company's electric distribution assets are all in Texas.

Operations

CenterPoint Energy's six reportable business segments are led by Electric Transmission and Distribution and Natural Gas Distribution.

The Competitive Natural Gas Sales and Services segment is engaged in unregulated gas sales and services.

Other segments include Interstate Pipelines (interstate natural gas pipeline operations); Field Services (non-rate regulated natural gas gathering processing and treating); and Other Operations (corporate support operations).

CenterPoint Energy markets natural gas and related services to more than 17960 commercial industrial and wholesale customers located primarily in the eastern US. It also provides HVAC and other energy-related services through its gas division. In 2014 58% of gas operations' throughput was to commercial and industrial customers; 42% to residential customers.

Natural Gas Distribution accounted for 35% of CenterPoint Energy's 2014 revenues; Energy Services 34%; and Electric Transmission & Distribution 31%.

Sales and Marketing

CenterPoint Energy distributes electricity via substations and delivers electricity to end users through distribution feeders and sells natural gas directly to commercial and industrial customers and metered sales.

The company's customers including biofuel companies government entities manufacturers small businesses refineries and utilities. NRG Energy accounted for 37% of CenterPoint Energy's revenues in 2014; Energy Future Holdings 10%.

Financial Performance

In 2014 CenterPoint Energy's net revenues increased by 13.8% due to growth in Natural Gas Distribution Electric Transmission & Distribution and Natural Gas Distribution driven by higher natural gas prices (due to weather conditions spiking demand) and other changes in natural gas use.

That year the company reported a 96.5% jump in net income due to higher revenues lower income tax expense an increase in equity earnings of unconsolidated affiliates a decrease in the loss on indexed debt securities lower interest expense and higher other income. These were partially offset by a lower operating income decrease on the gain on marketable securities.In 2014 net cash provided by operating activities decreased by 13% due to higher net tax payments and net margin deposits decreased cash provided by fuel cost recovery cash related to gas storage inventory cash from non-trading derivatives and cash provided by net regulatory assets and liabilities. These were partially offset by increased distributions from equity method investments and a growth in cash provided by net accounts receivable/payable.

Strategy

CenterPoint Energy's strategy is focused on enhancing and expanding its existing core operations while acquiring complementary and synergistic businesses and teaming up with other major entities to enhance its operations.

The company continued to grow organically in electric and natural gas service territories in 2014 adding 55000 new metered customers (a growth rate of more than 2%). The company continued to build out their intelligent electric grid and invest to support customer growth and invested $525 million of capital in its natural gas utilities to support growth improve the safety and reliability of their systems and to improve service to customers.In 2015 CenterPoint Energy launched a new pilot program in Minnesota to decouple its rates from the volume of natural gas consumed. (Innovative rate designs help align the company's interests with those of its communities and supports energy efficiency).

In 2013 CenterPoint Energy OGE Energy and ArcLight Capital Partners formed a partnership that includes CenterPoint Energy's interstate pipelines and field services businesses and the midstream business of Enogex. The general partner is a CenterPoint Energy/OGE joint venture.That year it also signed a deal with XTO Energy to gather XTO's crude oil production through a new crude oil gathering and transportation pipeline system (with a capacity of up to 19500 barrels per day) in the Bakken play in North Dakota.

HISTORY

CenterPoint Energy's earliest predecessor Houston Electric Lighting and Power was formed in 1882 by a group including Emanuel Raphael cashier at Houston Savings Bank and Mayor William Baker. In 1901 General Electric's financial arm United Electric Securities Company took control of the utility which became Houston Lighting & Power (HL&P). United Electric sold HL&P five years later; by 1922 HL&P ended up in the arms of National Power & Light Company (NP&L) a subsidiary of Electric Bond & Share (a public utility holding company that had been spun off by General Electric).

In 1942 NP&L was forced to sell HL&P in order to comply with the 1935 Public Utility Holding Company Act. As the oil industry boomed in Houston after WWII so did HL&P.

HL&P became the managing partner in a venture to build a nuclear plant on the Texas Gulf Coast in 1973. Construction on the South Texas Project with partners Central Power and Light and the cities of Austin and San Antonio began in 1975. In 1976 Houston Industries (HI) was formed as the holding company for HL&P.

By 1980 the nuke was four years behind schedule and over budget. HL&P and its partners sued construction firm Brown & Root in 1982 and received a $700 million settlement in 1985. (The City of Austin also sued HL&P for damages but lost.) The nuke was finally brought online in 1988 with the final cost estimated at $5.8 billion.

Meanwhile HI diversified into cable TV in 1986 by creating Enrcom (later Paragon Communications) through a venture with Time Inc. Two years later it bought the US cable interests of Canada's Rogers Communications. HI left the cable business in 1995 selling out to Time Warner.

Developing Latin fever HI joined a consortium that bought 51% of Argentinean electric company EDELAP in 1992. (However in 1998 HI sold its stake to AES.) On a roll HI acquired 90% of Argentina's electric utility EDESE (1995); joined a consortium that won a controlling stake in Light a Brazilian electric utility (1996); bought a stake in Colombian electric utility EPSA (1997); and bought interests in three electric utilities in El Salvador (1998). It also won a permit to develop and operate a natural gas system in Mexico (1998).

Back in the US HI acquired gas dealer NorAm for $2.5 billion in 1997. The next year it bought five generating plants in California from Edison International and laid plans to build merchant plants in Arizona (near Phoenix) Illinois Nevada (near Las Vegas in partnership with Sempra Energy) and Rhode Island. Overseas HI finished a power plant in India in 1998. It also bought a 65% interest in Colombian electric utilities Electricaribe and Electrocosta; EPSA bought about 55% of CET in Colombia and Light bought about 75% of Metropolitana (São Paulo Brazil).

In 1999 HI became Reliant Energy and HL&P became Reliant Energy HL&P. That year the company bought a 52% stake in Dutch power generation firm UNA; it bought the remaining 48% the next year. Also in 2000 Reliant Energy paid Sithe Energies (now a part of Dynegy) $2.1 billion for 21 power plants in the mid-Atlantic states. It sold its operations in Brazil Colombia and El Salvador that year and transferred all of its nonregulated operations to subsidiary Reliant Resources. Reliant Energy also announced plans to spin off Reliant Resources that year.

Reliant Energy netted about $1.7 billion in 2001 from the sale to the public of nearly 20% of Reliant Resources. Later that year Reliant Resources announced that it would acquire US independent power producer Orion Power Holdings in a $4.7 billion deal; the deal was completed in 2002. Deregulation took effect in Texas that year and Reliant Energy transferred its retail power supply business to Reliant Resources.

As the finances of wholesale energy companies came under scrutiny in 2002 the SEC issued a formal investigation into "round-trip" energy trades completed by Reliant Resources. These activities artificially inflated the company's trading volumes and led it to restate its 1999 2000 and 2001 financial results; it also reduced its energy marketing and trading workforce by about 35%.

Reliant Energy announced plans in 2001 to form a new holding company (CenterPoint Energy) for itself and Reliant Resources; it completed the name change in 2002.

CenterPoint Energy changed its name in 2002 in preparation for the spin-off of its 83% stake in Reliant Resources (now GenOn Energy) a global independent power producer and energy marketer; the spinoff was completed later that year. (Reliant Resources changed its name to Reliant Energy in 2004.) CenterPoint Energy transferred its nonregulated Texas retail power supply business to Reliant Resources before spinning off the unit.

EXECUTIVES

Vice President Marketing, Kevin J Blase
Division Vice President and General Counsel (2003), Mark Charles Schroeder
EVP and President Gas Division, Joseph B. (Joe) McGoldrick, $428,500 total compensation
SVP Information Technology and CIO, Gary Hayes
EVP and President Electric Division, Tracy B. Bridge, $422,750 total compensation
President and CEO, Scott M. Prochazka, $900,000 total compensation
SVP Electric Utility Business, Kenneth M. Mercado
SVP Gas Operations, Richard A. (Rick) Zapalac
EVP and CFO, William D. (Bill) Rogers, age 54
Vice President Regulatory Affairs, Carol Helliker
Vice President Strategic and Financial Planning, Ray Ehmer
Division Vice President Operations, Frank Antoine
Division Vice President and Chief Risk Officer, Lee C Ferrell
Vice President, Calvin Roberts
Vice President of Audit Services, Carla Kneipp
Senior Vice President and Chief Human Resources Officer, Susan (Sue) Ortenstone
Vice President Customer And Market Services, Susan (Sue) Coronado
Senior Vice President, Joe Hamm
Vice President Vice President Transmission and Substation Operations, John (Jack) Houston
Vice President Operations, John Slanina
Vice President Marketing, Carol Burchfield
Vice President Tax, Kimberly Johnston
Senior Vice President, Roy Medina
Vice President Of Sales, Tom Gros
Vice President Marketing and Sales, Debbie Koreneck
Executive Vice President, Thomas (Thom) Standish
Division Vice President Engineering and Technical Services, Jeff Goetzman
Board Member, Walter Ferguson, age 60
Chairman, Milton Carroll
Assistant Treasurer, Linda Geiger
SECRETARY Division, Shantala Epps
Vice Chairman, Jeremy Bloch
Secretary, Vilma Chapa
Auditors: Deloitte & Touche LLP

LOCATIONS

HQ: CenterPoint Energy, Inc
  1111 Louisiana, Houston, TX 77002
Phone: 713 207-1111
Web: www.centerpointenergy.com

PRODUCTS/OPERATIONS

2014 Sales

	$ mil.	% of total
Natural Gas	3,271	35
Energy Service	3,095	34
Electric Transmission and Distribution	2,845	31
Interstate Pipeline	0	0
Field services	0	0
Others	15	0
Total	**9,226**	**100**

2014 Sales

	$ mil.	% of total
Retail gas	5,049	55
Electric delivery	2,845	31
Wholesale gas	1,159	13
Energy products & services	135	1
Gas transportation and processing	38	2
Total	**9,226**	**100**

COMPETITORS

AEP	Exelon
AEP Texas Central	Koch Industries Inc.
AEP Texas North	Mississippi Power
Ameren	OGE Energy
Avista	ONEOK
CMS Energy	Progress Energy
Cleco	Southern Company
Constellation Energy Group	Southwestern Electric Power
Dominion Resources	Southwestern Energy
Duke Energy	Williams Companies
Energy Future	Xcel Energy
Entergy	

HISTORICAL FINANCIALS

Company Type: Public

Income Statement

FYE: December 31

	REVENUE ($ mil.)	NET INCOME ($ mil.)	NET PROFIT MARGIN	EMPLOYEES
12/14	9,226	611	6.6%	8,540
12/13	8,106	311	3.8%	8,591
12/12	7,452	417	5.6%	8,720
12/11	8,450	1,357	16.1%	8,827
12/10	8,785	442	5.0%	8,843
Annual Growth	**1.2%**	**8.4%**	**—**	**(0.9%)**

2014 Year-End Financials

Debt ratio: 38.18%
Return on equity: 13.77%
Cash ($ mil.): 298
Current ratio: 0.94
Long-term debt ($ mil.): 8,009

No. of shares (mil.): 430
Dividends
  Yield: 4.0%
  Payout: 74.8%
Market value ($ mil.): 10,075

	STOCK PRICE ($) FY Close	P/E High/Low	PER SHARE ($) Earnings	Dividends	Book Value
12/14	23.43	18 15	1.42	0.95	10.58
12/13	23.18	34 26	0.72	0.83	10.09
12/12	19.25	22 19	0.97	0.81	10.05
12/11	20.09	7 5	3.17	0.79	9.91
12/10	15.72	16 12	1.07	0.78	7.52
Annual Growth	**10.5%**	**—**	**7.3%**	**5.1%**	**8.9%**

Centerstate Banks, Inc.

CenterState Banks is the holding company for CenterState Bank of Florida which serves the Sunshine State through about 60 branches. The bank offers standard deposit products such as checking and savings accounts money market accounts and CDs. Real estate loans primarily residential and commercial mortgages make up 85% of the company's loan portfolio while the rest is made up of business loans and consumer loans. The bank's correspondent division provides bond securities accounting and loans to small and mid-sized banks across the Southeast and Texas. It also sells mutual funds annuities and other investment products.

OperationsAbout 65% of CenterState Banks' total revenue came from loan interest in 2014 while another 10% came from interest on its investment securities. The rest of the bank's revenue came form correspondent banking capital markets revenue and related revenue (11%) deposit account service charges (5%) debit/ATM and merchant card fees (3%) wealth management fees (2%) and other miscellaneous income sources. The company had a staff of 785 employees by the end of 2014.Geographic ReachCenterState has nearly 60 branches across 20 counties in central southeast and northeast Florida. Its loan production offices are in Tampa Gainesville Crystal River and Ft. Meyers.Sales and MarketingCenterState offers consumer and commercial banking services to individuals businesses and industries across Florida.Financial PerformanceThe company has struggled to consistently grow its revenues in recent years due to shrinking interest margins on loans amidst the low-interest environment. Its profits however have been rising thanks to declining loan loss provisions as its loan portfolio's credit quality has improved with higher property valuations in the strengthened economy.CenterState had a breakout year in 2014 however with its revenue jumping 22% to $164.5 million thanks to higher interest income stemming from new loan business from its acquisitions of First Southern Bancorp and Gulfstream Bancshares during the year. Higher revenue and stable costs in 2014 also drove the bank's net income higher by 6% to a record $12.96 million. CenterState's operating cash levels plummeted by 90% to $1.4 million after adjusting its earnings for non-cash items mostly related to the net proceeds from its trading securities sales.Strategy

CenterState Banks continues to seek out additional acquisition opportunities to boost its loan and deposit business and expand into more markets across Florida. To this end the bank's 2014 acquisitions extended its reach into Broward Palm Beach and Martin counties for the first time while adding more than $1.3 billion in new deposits and over $600 million in new loan business to its books.Struggling to grow its revenues the bank has also worked to become more efficient and profitable through selective branch closures. During 2014 the company closed seven smaller branches and a standalone drive-thru facility to free up resources for more profitable bank acquisitions.Mergers and AcquisitionsIn June 2014 CenterState purchased First Southern Bancorp which expanded its market reach into Broward County after adding a net of seven new branches. The deal also added some $600 million in new loan assets and $853 million in deposits. In January 2014 the company expanded into Palm Beach and Martin counties after buying Gulfstream Bancshares and its four branches with $479 million in deposits.

EXECUTIVES

SVP and CFO, James J. Antal, age 64, $312,750 total compensation
Senior Vice President, Rick Alspaugh
President CEO and Director CenterState Banks Inc. and Centerstate Bank of Florida, John Corbett, age 46, $420,250 total compensation
Corporate Chief Risk Officer, Daniel E. Bockhorst, $217,500 total compensation
Treasurer, Stephen Young, $278,333 total compensation
Vice President, Anita Stasiak
First Vice President Business Development, Chris Wright
Senior Vice President County Executive, Hershel Hensley
Vice President, Dianne Wood
First Vice President Business Development, Jim Gatherum
Vice President, Todd Patrick
First Vice President, Erik Bagwell
Vice President, Scott Wools
Senior Vice President, Parker Grubbs
First Vice President Business Development, Casey Christopher
Vice President Commercial Lending, Dan Jackson
Assistant Vice President Assistant Branch Manager, Jani Lowdell
Vice President, Gary Smith
Vice President Division Controller, John Rust
Senior Vice President, Michael (Mel) Crowell
Vice President Retail Service Leader, Annette Fortunato-diaz
Vice President Manager Of Eservices, Christina Zenchak
Vice President Commercial Lender, Patrick (Paddy) Jacks
Vice President Information Technology, Gerri Cook
Senior Vice President And Commercial Lending Officer, Bill Daniels
Senior Vice President Capital Markets, Jim Bigger
Assistant Vice President Merchant Services Divison, Deborah Joyce
Assistant Vice President Business Analyst Ii, Chante Carlson
Senior Vice President Loan Review Officer, Tom Sheffield
Assistant Vice President Commercial Banker, Angel K Gonzalez
First Vice President, Stacey A Dunn
Vice President Finance and Accounting, Michael (Mel) Fleming
Chairman, Ernest S. (Ernie) Pinner, age 67
Treasurer, Brett Rawls
Auditors: Crowe Horwath LLP

LOCATIONS

HQ: Centerstate Banks, Inc.
42745 U.S. Highway 27, Davenport, FL 33837
Phone: 863 419-7750
Web: www.centerstatebanks.com

PRODUCTS/OPERATIONS

2011 Sales

	$ mil.	% of total
Interest		
Loans	65	36
Investment securities available for sale	15	9
Other	0	-
Noninterest		
Bargain purchase gain	57	31
Correspondent banking & bond sales	24	13
Service charges on deposit accounts	6	3
Net gain on sale of securities	3	2
Other	10	6
Total	**184**	**100**

COMPETITORS

BB&T	Regions Financial
BBX Capital	Seacoast Banking
Bank of America	SunTrust
Fifth Third	Wells Fargo
JPMorgan Chase	

HISTORICAL FINANCIALS

Company Type: Public

Income Statement

FYE: December 31

	ASSETS ($ mil.)	NET INCOME ($ mil.)	INCOME AS % OF ASSETS	EMPLOYEES
12/14	3,776	12	0.3%	785
12/13	2,415	12	0.5%	693
12/12	2,363	9	0.4%	689
12/11	2,284	7	0.3%	655
12/10	2,063	(5)	—	600
Annual Growth	**16.3%**	—	—	**6.9%**

2014 Year-End Financials

Debt ratio: 0.63%
Return on equity: 3.57%
Cash ($ mil.): 158
Current ratio: —
Long-term debt ($ mil.): —

No. of shares (mil.): 45
Dividends
Yield: 0.3%
Payout: 20.0%
Market value ($ mil.): 540

	STOCK PRICE ($) FY Close	P/E High/Low		PER SHARE ($) Earnings	Dividends	Book Value
12/14	11.91	37	31	0.31	0.04	9.98
12/13	10.15	26	18	0.41	0.04	9.08
12/12	8.53	27	20	0.33	0.04	9.09
12/11	6.62	31	19	0.26	0.04	8.74
12/10	7.92	—	—	(0.20)	0.04	8.42
Annual Growth	**10.7%**	—	—	—	**(0.0%)**	**4.3%**

Central Pacific Financial Corp

When in the Central Pacific do as the islanders do. This may include doing business with Central Pacific Financial the holding company for Central Pacific Bank which operates more than 35 branch locations and 110 ATMs across the Hawaiian Islands. Targeting individuals and local businesses the $5 billion bank provides such standard retail banking products as checking and savings accounts money market accounts and CDs. About 70% of the bank's loan portfolio is made up of commercial real estate loans residential mortgages and construction loans though it also provides business and consumer loans.

OperationsCentral Pacific Financial operates through two core segments. The Banking Operations segment provides construction and real estate development loans commercial loans residential mortgage loans consumer loans trust services retail brokerage services and traditional banking products and services. The Treasury segment manages the company's investment securities portfolio and wholesale funding activities.Boasting total assets of $5 billion Central Pacific Bank ranked as the fourth-largest bank by deposits in the state of Hawaii in 2014. The bank makes nearly 60% of its total revenue from interest and fees on loans and leases and nearly 20% from interest and dividends on its investment securities. It makes about 10% on service charges on deposit accounts and

other charges and fees while the small remainder of its revenue comes from a mix of loan servicing fees gains on sales of residential loans and foreclosed assets income from fiduciary activities and income from bank-owned life insurance.Central Pacific Financial's other wholly-owned subsidiaries include CPB Capital Trust II; CPB Statutory Trust III; CPB Capital Trust IV; and CPB Statutory Trust V. Central Pacific Bank holds 50% stakes in Pacific Access Mortgage Gentry HomeLoans and Island Pacific HomeLoans. Geographic Reach-Honolulu-based Central Pacific boasts more than 35 branches and 110 ATMs across Hawaii. The island of Oahu holds 28 branches while the Maui Hawaii and Kauai islands host the remaining branches.Sales and MarketingCentral Pacific Financial spent $2.34 million on advertising in 2014 compared to $2.67 million and $3.52 million in 2013 and 2012 respectively.Financial PerformanceCentral Pacific Financial's revenue performance has been mixed in recent years. Its mortgage banking business has suffered from lower residential mortgage origination volumes while its loan business has been growing at a healthy clip thanks to higher loan balances from added assets.Following two years of modest top-line growth driven by growing loan business Central Pacific's revenue dipped by 1% to $193.63 million in 2014 as it collected lower net gains on sales of foreclosed assets and lower net gains on sales of residential mortgage loans. The bank's interest income from loans continued to grow however as the bank added more than $403 million in new loan assets.Central Pacific's net income declined by 76% to $40.45 million in 2014 mostly because in 2013 the bank received a $112.25 million income tax benefit as it reversed a significant portion of its valuation allowance for its doubtful accounts from 2009. Beyond this non-recurring event the bank managed to cut its salaries and employee benefit expenses by 22% saving about $8 million for the year.The bank's operating cash also fell by 15% during the year to $71.43 million primarily due to lower cash earnings. StrategyCentral Pacific reiterated in 2015 that its strategy is to continue growing its loan business particularly focusing on providing more commercial loans and mortgages as well as construction loans and leases to small and mid-sized companies business professionals and real estate developers. Though its residential mortgage and consumer loans made up just 25% of its loan portfolio that year the bank will also continue its focus on extended those loans to more local homebuyers and individuals. The bank's key to drumming up its commercial loan business has traditionally come from its community-oriented commercial real estate team and banking officers which are able to develop deep relationships with local communities and industries that they serve.

EXECUTIVES

President and CEO, A. Catherine Ngo, age 55, $285,833 total compensation
Chairman, John C. Dean, age 68, $325,000 total compensation
EVP Corporate Services, Denis K. Isono, age 64, $270,000 total compensation
EVP and Chief Risk Officer, Raymond W. (Bill) Wilson, age 58, $262,917 total compensation
President and Chief Banking Officer, Lance A. Mizumoto, age 56, $287,500 total compensation
EVP CFO and Treasurer, David S. Morimoto, age 47
Senior Vice President Risk Management, David (Dave) Hudson
Vice President And Asset And Liability Manager, Dayna N Matsumoto
Assistant Vice President And Branch Manager, Sharlene Chae
Senior Vice President, John Taira
Auditors: KPMG LLP

LOCATIONS

HQ: Central Pacific Financial Corp
220 South King Street, Honolulu, HI 96813
Phone: 808 544-0500   **Fax:** 808 531-2875
Web: www.centralpacificbank.com

PRODUCTS/OPERATIONS

2014 Sales

	$ mil.	% of total
Interest income		
Loans and leases	112	58
Securities	37	19
Non-interest income		
Other service charges and fees	11	6
Service Charges on deposit accounts	8	4
Loan Servicing fees	5	3
Others	18	10
Total	**193**	**100**

COMPETITORS

American Savings Bank	Mitsubishi UFJ
BancWest	Financial Group
Bank of Hawaii	Territorial Bancorp
First Hawaiian Bank	

HISTORICAL FINANCIALS

Company Type: Public

Income Statement   FYE: December 31

	ASSETS ($ mil.)	NET INCOME ($ mil.)	INCOME AS % OF ASSETS	EMPLOYEES
12/14	4,852	40	0.8%	841
12/13	4,741	172	3.6%	903
12/12	4,370	47	1.1%	948
12/11	4,132	36	0.9%	935
12/10	3,938	(250)	—	921
Annual Growth	**5.4%**	—	—	**(2.2%)**

2014 Year-End Financials

Debt ratio: 1.91%	No. of shares (mil.): 35
Return on equity: 6.59%	Dividends
Cash ($ mil.): 86	Yield: 1.6%
Current ratio: —	Payout: 37.8%
Long-term debt ($ mil.): —	Market value ($ mil.): 758

	STOCK PRICE ($) FY Close	P/E High/Low		Earnings	PER SHARE ($) Dividends	Book Value
12/14	21.50	20	16	1.07	0.36	16.12
12/13	20.08	5	4	4.07	0.16	15.68
12/12	15.59	14	11	1.13	0.00	12.06
12/11	12.92	10	0	3.31	0.00	10.93
12/10	1.53	—	—	(171.13)	0.00	43.26
Annual Growth	**93.6%**	—	—	—	—	**(21.9%)**

Century Bancorp, Inc.

Century Bancorp is the holding company for Century Bank and Trust which serves Boston and surrounding parts of northeastern Massachusetts from more than 25 branches. Boasting some $3.6 billion in total assets the bank offers standard deposit products including checking savings and money market accounts; CDs; and IRAs. Nearly two-thirds of its loan portfolio is comprised of commercial and commercial real estate loans. while residential mortgages and home equity loans make up around 30%. The bank also writes construction and land development loans business loans and personal loans. It offers brokerage services through an agreement with third-party provider LPL Financial.

OperationsCentury Bank also provides cash management short-term financing and transaction processing services to municipalities in Massachusetts and Rhode Island. It offers automated lockbox collection services to its municipal customers as well as commercial clients. The bank also continues to open new branches in its traditional market area in metropolitan Boston.The bank gets more than 80% of its revenue in the form of interest income (mostly from loans). It generated 32% of its total revenue from taxable loans in 2014 while another 18% came from non-taxable loans and 35% came from interest income on the bank's investment securities. On the non-interest side the bank made 8% of its overall revenue from service charges on deposit accounts 3% from lockbox fees and a negligible amount on brokerage commissions and gains on sales of securities or mortgage loans.Geographic ReachThe bank operates more than 25 branches in 20 cities and towns across Massachusetts ranging from Braintree in the South to Andover in the northern part of the state.Sales and MarketingMost of Century Bank's business comes from small and medium-sized businesses needing commercial loans though the bank also serves retail customers as well as local governments and other institutions throughout Massachusetts. The bank spent $1.79 million on advertising in 2014 compared to $1.75 million and $1.85 million in 2013 and 2012 respectively. Financial PerformanceCentury Bancorp's revenues and profits have been steadily rising over the past few years thanks to increased loan business and declining loan loss provisions as its loan portfolio's credit quality has been improving in the strengthening economy. The bank's revenue rose by more than 2% to a record $100.64 million in 2014 mostly as it collected more interest income from long-term securities and non-taxable loans during the year. The bank's earning securities assets grew by 8.5% during the year while the size of its loan business swelled by double-digits with increased tax-exempt lending and residential second mortgage lending; all of which boosted interest income during the year. Higher revenue lower interest expenses on deposits and a continued dip in loan loss provisions in 2014 pushed Century's net income higher by 9% to a record $21.86 million. The bank's operating cash also grew by 7% to $22.39 million thanks to higher cash earnings.StrategyCentury Bancorp has been growing organically through new branch openings and digital bank product launches in recent years. In 2014 for example the bank opened its new branch in Woburn Massachusetts and launched its all-new Century Bank Mobile App which boosted customer convenience and allowed the bank to better compete with larger banks with more expansive branch networks.Showcasing its strong financial capitalization the bank received an "A" rating from the Standard and Poor's credit ratings agency in 2015 making Century Bank the only regional bank in the state to receive such a rating.

EXECUTIVES

EVP Century Bank and Trust Company, Paul A. Evangelista, age 51, $337,614 total compensation
EVP Century Bank and Trust Company, David B. Woonton, age 59, $337,614 total compensation
President CEO and Director, Barry R. Sloane, age 60, $569,207 total compensation
CFO and Treasurer, William P. Hornby, age 48, $294,708 total compensation
EVP Century Bank and Trust Company, Linda Sloane Kay, age 53, $294,708 total compensation
EVP Century Bank and Trust, Brian J. Feeney, age 54, $294,708 total compensation
Assistant Vice President Electronic Services, Toni Chardo
Auditors: KPMG LLP

LOCATIONS

HQ: Century Bancorp, Inc.
400 Mystic Avenue, Medford, MA 021255
Phone: 781 391-4000
Web: www.centurybank.com

PRODUCTS/OPERATIONS

2014 Sales

	$ mil.	% of total
Interest		
Loans	50	50
Securities	2	3
Other	32	32
Noninterest		
Service charges on deposit accounts	8	8
Lockbox fees	3	3
Gains on sales of Mortgage loans	2	3
Other	1	1
Total	**100**	**100**

COMPETITORS

Boston Private	Eastern Bank
Brookline Bancorp	Middlesex Savings
Cambridge Financial	Peoples Federal
Capital Crossing	Bancshares Inc.
Central Bancorp	Sovereign Bank
Citizens Financial Group	

HISTORICAL FINANCIALS

Company Type: Public

Income Statement   FYE: December 31

	ASSETS ($ mil.)	NET INCOME ($ mil.)	INCOME AS % OF ASSETS	EMPLOYEES
12/14	3,624	21	0.6%	440
12/13	3,431	20	0.6%	428
12/12	3,086	19	0.6%	418
12/11	2,743	16	0.6%	405
12/10	2,441	13	0.6%	380
Annual Growth	**10.4%**	**12.7%**	—	**3.7%**

2014 Year-End Financials

Debt ratio: 11.91%	No. of shares (mil.): 5
Return on equity: 11.85%	Dividends
Cash ($ mil.): 305	Yield: 1.2%
Current ratio: —	Payout: 12.5%
Long-term debt ($ mil.): —	Market value ($ mil.): 223

	STOCK PRICE ($) FY Close	P/E High/Low		Earnings	PER SHARE ($) Dividends	Book Value
12/14	40.06	8	7	3.93	0.48	34.57
12/13	33.25	9	7	3.61	0.48	31.76
12/12	32.95	8	6	3.43	0.48	32.40
12/11	28.24	10	7	3.01	0.48	28.98
12/10	26.79	11	7	2.45	0.48	26.18
Annual Growth	**10.6%**	—	—	**12.5%**	**(0.0%)**	**7.2%**

CenturyLink, Inc.

CenturyLink would like to be your communications hook-up for more than the next 100 years. Historically a regional wireline local and long-distance telephone provider it's connecting with the times by transforming into a broadband and network services provider for residential business and government clients. The company is the third-largest US wireline telecom company by total access lines and is the incumbent local carrier in 37 states though three-quarters of its lines are in just a dozen mostly in the West and Midwest. Additionally CenturyLink provides wireless service through Verizon and paid television service through its own Prism TV (in selected markets) with satellite provider DIRECTV.

Operations

CenturyLink operates two segments: Business and Consumer.

The Business segment 65% of sales consists of private line broadband Ethernet MPLS Voice over Internet Protocol network management services colocation managed hosting and cloud hosting services for enterprise wholesale and governmental customers including other communication providers.

The Consumer segment 35% of sales offers broadband wireless and video services including Prism TV services. It also offers local and long-distance service.

Geographic Reach

CenturyLink operates almost 74% of its total access lines in portions of Arizona Colorado Florida Iowa Minnesota Missouri New Mexico Nevada North Carolina Oregon Utah and Washington.

It also provides local service in parts of Alabama Arkansas California Georgia Idaho Illinois Indiana Kansas Louisiana Ohio Michigan Mississippi Montana Nebraska New Jersey North Dakota Oklahoma Pennsylvania South Carolina South Dakota Tennessee Texas Virginia Wisconsin and Wyoming.

The company operates nearly 58 data centers throughout North America Europe and Asia.

Financial Performance

CenturyLink's revenue dropped from about $18.1 billion in 2013 to $18.03 billion in 2014 on decreases in both business segments. Loss of access lines as traditional wirelines are replaced by wireless phones helped cut Business revenue by about 1% in 2014. On the Consumer side revenue fell 1% in 2014 on losses in local and long distance service.

With net income a $1.1 billion changed turned 2013's $239 loss into 2014's $772 million profit. The company had lower operating costs in 2014. Also the 2013 results felt the impact of a goodwill impairment and a litigation settlement. Cash flow from operations dropped to $5.2 billion in 2014 from $5.56 billion in 2013.

Strategy

CenturyLink is expanding its services particularly those oriented toward cloud computing. In 2015 the company made its public cloud service available in the Asia Pacific region through its date center in Singapore. The company also opened a cloud development center in Seattle to work with developers.

Mergers and Acquisition

In 2014 CenturyLink acquired Cognilytics a provider of advanced predictive analytics and Big Data to mid-sized and large enterprises. The acquisition will allow CenturyLink to offer more services that help customers collect and analyze data.

HISTORY

CenturyLink began as CenturyTel in 1930 when Marie and William Clarke Williams bought the Oak Ridge Telephone Company in Oak Ridge Louisiana. In 1946 they gave the 75-line company as a wedding present to their son Clarke who launched a course of growth by acquisition buying the Marion Louisiana telephone exchange in 1950 (Clarke Williams remained active in the company until his death in 2002). The company was renamed Century Telephone Enterprises in 1971; it went public in 1978.

The company has expanded into net geographies and technologies mainly through acquisitions over the years.

EXECUTIVES

EVP CFO and Assistant Secretary, R. Stewart Ewing, age 63, $650,000 total compensation
President and CEO, Glen F. Post, age 62, $1,100,000 total compensation
Senior Vice President Marketing, Shirish Lal
Senior Vice President Business Service Delivery And Operations, Todd Schafer
President Sales and Marketing, Dean J. Douglas, age 59
EVP General Counsel and Secretary, Stacey W. Goff, age 49, $520,890 total compensation
President Global IT Services and Solutions, Girish K. Varma
EVP and CTO, Aamir Hussain, $85,892 total compensation
EVP Network Services, Maxine L. Moreau, age 53
EVP Human Resources, Scott A. Trezise, age 46
SVP and Chief Information Officer, William E. (Bill) Bradley
Vice President Wholesale Sales Account Management, Craig Davis
Vice President External Relations, Jeff Glover
Vice President Of Sales, Harman Steve
Vice President Core Networks, Jason Gutenschwager
Vice President Supply Chain Management, Brent Vanderark
Vice President Sales, Graylen Allen
Vice President, Christopher Denzin
Vice President Customer Service, Katherine (Kate) Victory
National Account Manager, Karl Engert
Senior Vice President Information Technology, Alfonso Rivera
Vice President Business Markets Group North East, Bruce Smith
Vice President and General Counsel, Laurie Korneffel
Assistant Vice President, Michael (Mel) Sadler
Vice President Engineering And Construction, Greg Edmoundson
National Sales Manager, Thomas Allison
Wholesale Markets Sales Area Vice President, Monte Johnson
Vice President and General Manager, Guy Gunther
Vice President Engineering And Construction, Trent Clausen
National Account Manager, Joseph (Jo) Stumpf
Executive Vice President, Daniel Davis
Vice President General Manager, Gerald Piper
Vice President and General Manager Cloud Business Unit, Suku Krishnaraj
Vice President Cloud Strategy and Business Development, Jonathan (Jon) King
Vice President Sales Midwest Region, Richard (Dick) Buyens
Regional Vice President, Christie Kestler
Vice President Of Finance Of Finance, Sharon Wallace
National Account Manager, Frank Palazzo
Vice President of External Relations Middle Atlantic Region, William (Bill) Hanchey
Area Vice President Sales Engineering, Loughran Brad
Area Vice President Business Markets Group, Kim Baker
Vice President Of Information Technology Security, Tim Kelleher
Vice President Data, Doug Pershing
Vice President Of Corporate Development And Strategy, Kenneth Dunn
Vice President General Manager South Florida, Taylor Chestnut
Senior Vice President Operations Support, Dave Cole

Vice President, Steve Campbell
Vice President Talent Acquisition, Brett Blair
Vice Chairman, Harvey P. Perry, age 70
Chairman, William A. (Bill) Owens, age 74
Executive Board Member, Brandi Johnston
Assistant Treasurer, Glynn Williams
Auditors: KPMG LLP

LOCATIONS

HQ: CenturyLink, Inc.
 100 CenturyLink Drive, Monroe, LA 71203
Phone: 318 388-9000   **Fax:** 318 789-8656
Web: www.centurylink.com

PRODUCTS/OPERATIONS

2014 Sales by Category

	$ mil.	% of total
Strategic services	9,200	51
Legacy services	7,138	40
Data integration	690	4
Other	1,003	5
Total	**18,031**	**100**

2014 Sales

	% of total
Consumer	65
Business	35
Total	**100**

COMPETITORS

AT&T	Level 3 Communications
Cavalier Telephone	NTELOS
Comcast	Nsight
Cox Communications	Sprint Communications
DISH Network	Telephone & Data
Equinix	Systems
FairPoint	Time Warner Cable
Communications Inc.	Verizon
Farmers	XO Holdings
Telecommunications	
Frontier	
Communications	

HISTORICAL FINANCIALS

Company Type: Public

Income Statement

FYE: December 31

	REVENUE ($ mil.)	NET INCOME ($ mil.)	NET PROFIT MARGIN	EMPLOYEES
12/14	18,031	772	4.3%	45,000
12/13	18,095	(239)	—	47,000
12/12	18,376	777	4.2%	47,000
12/11	15,351	573	3.7%	49,200
12/10	7,041	947	13.5%	20,300
Annual Growth	**26.5%**	**(5.0%)**	**—**	**22.0%**

2014 Year-End Financials

Debt ratio: 41.22%
Return on equity: 4.79%
Cash ($ mil.): 128
Current ratio: 0.91
Long-term debt ($ mil.): 20,121

No. of shares (mil.): 568
Dividends
 Yield: 5.4%
 Payout: 153.1%
Market value ($ mil.): 22,502

	STOCK PRICE ($) FY Close	P/E High/Low	PER SHARE ($) Earnings	Dividends	Book Value
12/14	39.58	31 21	1.36	2.16	26.42
12/13	31.85	— —	(0.40)	2.16	29.45
12/12	39.12	34 29	1.25	2.90	30.83
12/11	37.20	44 30	1.07	2.90	33.67
12/10	46.17	15 11	3.13	2.90	31.62
Annual Growth	**(3.8%)**	**— —**	**(18.8%)**	**(7.1%)**	**(4.4%)**

CFJ PROPERTIES LLC

LOCATIONS

HQ: CFJ PROPERTIES LLC
5508 LONAS DR, KNOXVILLE, TN 379093221
Phone: 8016241000
Web: WWW.CRYSTALINNS.COM

HISTORICAL FINANCIALS

Company Type: Private

Income Statement
FYE: January 31

	REVENUE ($ mil.)	NET INCOME ($ mil.)	NET PROFIT MARGIN	EMPLOYEES
01/09	7,672	157	2.1%	6,250
01/07	6,769	50	0.7%	
Annual Growth	6.5%	77.6%	—	—

2009 Year-End Financials

Debt ratio: ——
Return on equity: 2.10%
Cash ($ mil.): 37
Current ratio: 0.40
Long-term debt ($ mil.): —
Dividends
Yield: —
Payout: —
Market value ($ mil.): —

CGB ENTERPRISES INC.

The farmer in the delta relies on CGB Enterprises. Located in Louisiana near the shores of Lake Pontchartrain and the mouth of the Mississippi River the agricultural company provides US farmers with a range of services including grain handling storage and merchandising. It offers inland grain transportation by barge rail and truck and also markets and sells seeds agricultural chemicals and insurance. CGB's Consolidated Terminals and Logistics Co. (CTLC) subsidiary provides transportation logistics and bulk commodity services for both agricultural and non-agricultural customers. The company operates more than 95 locations across the US. Japanese trading conglomerates ITOCHU and ZEN-NOH own CGB.

Geographic Reach

From its headquarters in the city of Mandeville Louisiana CGB operates its business through more than 95 locations nationwide including 74 grain elevators across the Midwest. It boasts grain facilities in nearly 10 states including Nebraska Oklahoma Arkansas Iowa Illinois Indiana Ohio Kentucky and Missouri. The company's fertilizer operations span Ohio Illinois Arkansas and Michigan.

Sales and Marketing

Besides its core services of inland grain transportation via barge rail and truck CGB markets and sells seeds agricultural chemicals and insurance as part of its operations.

Strategy

CGB has expanded its CTLC business in recent years. To give the unit an extended reach CTLC now serves the transportation bulk commodity and logistics needs of a global base of customers rather than just CGB's core businesses.

CGB also regularly invests in its own holdings. The company is constructing a rail shipment facility in Defiance Ohio to boost its production capacity and existing transportation system. In 2014 CGB began building a new facility on the Ohio River near Brandenburg Kentucky.

Mergers and Acquisitions

In mid-2014 CGB Enterprises acquired a grain storage facility in Savage Minnesota from Ceres Global Ag Corp. Under the terms of the deal Ceres will lease back 3.5 million bushels of storage capacity from CGB for a six-year term. The purchase of the grain storage facility in Savage brings new customers to CGB which also plans to expand its fertilizer diversified services and other divisions in the Minnesota market. Also CGB acquired Oklahoma's W.B. Johnston Grain (WBJ) in April 2014. WBJ operates 19 grain elevators in Oklahoma and Texas including two grain terminals.

Strengthening its foothold on the Mississippi River CGB acquired the grain and fertilizer assets of Twomey based in Smithshire Illinois. The deal consummated in 2011 added valuable loading capacity on the river and offered CGB with a solid customer base in northwestern Illinois.

Company Ownership

CGB is owned by a pair of Japanese trading conglomerates: ITOCHU and ZEN-NOH.

EXECUTIVES

President CEO, Kevin D. Adams
General Manager Diversified Services, Rodney L. Clark
General Manager Agri Financial Services, Alan Singleton
Manager BioEnergy Services, Steve Burbrink
Manager Information Systems, Sean Goodgion
General Manager Feed Ingredients, Marc Cruse
Director of Sales & Marketing, Brent Mahana
Vice President Manager Director, Cindi Ernest
Vice President Administration, Mike Merkel
Vice President, Osamu Yako
Vice President Human Resources, Mark Berry
Vice President And Controller, Michael (Mel) Smith
Auditors: KPMG LLP NEW ORLEANS LA

LOCATIONS

HQ: CGB ENTERPRISES INC.
1127 HWY 190 E SERVICE RD, COVINGTON, LA 704334929
Phone: 9858673500
Web: WWW.CGB.COM

PRODUCTS/OPERATIONS

Selected Business Units
Feed Ingredients
Fertilizer
Financial Services
Grain
Marine
Premium Grains
Risk Management
Soybean Processing
Terminals

COMPETITORS

ADM	Crosby Tugs
Ag Processing Inc.	Jimmy Sanders
Alabama Farmers Cooperative	Kirby Corporation
Canal Barge Company	Southern States
Cargill	Tennessee Farmers Co-op

HISTORICAL FINANCIALS

Company Type: Private

Income Statement
FYE: May 31

	REVENUE ($ mil.)	NET INCOME ($ mil.)	NET PROFIT MARGIN	EMPLOYEES
05/14	7,227	53	0.7%	1,250
05/13	6,212	30	0.5%	
05/12	6,108	53	0.9%	
05/11	5,202	0	—	
Annual Growth	11.6%	—	—	—

2014 Year-End Financials

Debt ratio: ——
Return on equity: 0.70%
Cash ($ mil.): 16
Current ratio: 0.30
Long-term debt ($ mil.): —
Dividends
Yield: —
Payout: —
Market value ($ mil.): —

CH2M Hill Companies Ltd

LOCATIONS

HQ: CH2M Hill Companies Ltd
9191 South Jamaica Street, Englewood, CO 80112-5946
Phone: 303 771-0900

HISTORICAL FINANCIALS

Company Type: Public

Income Statement
FYE: December 31

	REVENUE ($ mil.)	NET INCOME ($ mil.)	NET PROFIT MARGIN	EMPLOYEES
12/14	5,468	(181)	—	25,000
12/13	5,931	118	2.0%	—
12/12	6,224	92	1.5%	—
Annual Growth	(6.3%)	—	—	—

2014 Year-End Financials

Debt ratio: 17.44%
Return on equity: (-43.37%)
Cash ($ mil.): 131
Current ratio: 1.03
Long-term debt ($ mil.): 508
No. of shares (mil.): 27
Dividends
Yield: —
Payout: —
Market value ($ mil.): —

	STOCK PRICE ($) FY Close	P/E High/Low	PER SHARE ($) Earnings	Dividends	Book Value
12/14	0.00	— —	(6.42)	0.00	7.79
12/13	0.00	— —	3.96	0.00	21.69
Annual Growth	—	— —	—	—	(40.1%)

CH2M HILL COMPANIES LTD.

CH2M HILL's name is a bit tricky but the engineering and construction firm is all up front. The firm (named for its founders Cornell Howland Hayes and Merryfield) operates five main market-oriented divisions: Environment and Nuclear Water Transportation Energy and Industrial and Urban Environments. CH2M Hill's top client is the US Government which contributes more than one-fifth of the company's annual revenue. Public sector clients include the US Department of Energy and the Department of Defense. CH2M HILL also works for state and local governments building water and wastewater systems airports highways and other transportation projects. Founded in 1946 the firm is owned by its employees.

Operations

Since reorganizing its business lines in January 2015 CH2M HILL operates five business segments based on market type: Environment and Nuclear Energy Water Transportation and Industrial and Urban Environments. The Environment and Nuclear division which made up 25% of total revenue in 2014 provides consulting design build engineering operations and maintenance construction management and program management services. The segment is comprised of the Environmental business the Government Facilities and Infrastructure business and the Nuclear business.

Its Energy division (20% of revenue) provides similar construction and design services as the company's Environmental and Nuclear segment. The division is comprised of the Oil Gas and Chemicals business as well as the Power business. The Water division (23% of revenue) works on various water-related projects for the wastewater drinking water industrial water conveyance and storage water resources and ecosystem management and intelligent water services markets. CH2M HILL's Transportation division (18% of revenue) provides horizontal and vertical infrastructure development services for the Aviation Highway and Bridge Ports and Maritime and Transit and Rail market sectors. The Industrial and Urban Environments division (15% of revenue) provides similar design and construction services to the company's Energy division and is made up of the Industrial and Advanced Technology business the Buildings business and the Urban Environments business.

In 2014 CH2M HILL derived 33% of its total revenues from fixed price and guaranteed maximum price contracts.

Geographic Reach

Colorado-based CH2M HILL gets about 70% of its revenue from the US while about 10% comes from the UK. The remainder comes from Asia Australia/New Zealand Canada Europe Latin America and the Middle East and Africa: some 120 countries in all.

Sales and Marketing

The company's clients include US federal and foreign government agencies state and local governments private sector companies and utilities. The US government (and federally-regulated agencies) is the company's largest client generating approximately 21% of total revenues in 2014.

Financial Performance

CH2M HILL has experienced slowly declining revenue since 2012. The firm's revenue fell by 8% to $5.47 billion in 2014 mostly due to declines in its Energy and Industrial and Urban Environments divisions. The Energy division drove most of the total revenue declines shrinking by 29% after the business completed four of its domestic design-build power plant projects. The Industrial and Urban Environments business also shrank by 14% due to lower demand for new projects in the US electronics and manufacturing industries and because of a decline in planning support services in the Middle East for US armed forces. Further adding to its revenue decline the company decided that it would no longer pursue fixed-price design-build contracts in the Government Facilities sector. Lower revenue and higher impairment losses on goodwill and intangibles in 2014 led HC2M HILL to a net loss of $318.30 million (compared to a $131.15 million profit in 2013). Cash from operations also declined by 43% mostly due to lower cash earnings.

Strategy

CH2M HILL announced in 2014 that it would be restructuring the company to improve efficiency reduce risk and create more opportunity for profitable growth. The restructuring aims to gain over $100 million in operational efficiencies and will include cutting the company's workforce by about 5% (about 1200 people). As part of this plan the company in January 2015 organized its business into five key integrated markets and six core regions in order to more effectively serve the infrastructure needs of its clients: Energy Environment & Nuclear Industrial & Urban Environment Transportation and Water. Reducing its dependence on the US Federal Government the company decided in 2014 that it would no longer pursue fixed-price design-build contracts in the Government Facilities sector. It's also begun to do more projects abroad. In 2015 for example the company partnered with the Singapore Public Utilities Board (PUB) and Singapore Cooperation Enterprise to provide technical and integrated water management services to the Rajasthan state government for the four-million-person city of Jaipur India. CH2M HILL occasionally acquires similar businesses to bolster its own service lines. In 2014 it purchased certain assets of Canada-based TERA Environmental Consultants an employee-owned environmental consulting firm that specializes in environmental assessment planning siting and permitting as well licensing services for the oil & gas pipeline and electrical transmission industries. Company Background

In November 2011 the company acquired Halcrow Group a London-based specialist in environmental infrastructure and transport projects for an estimated $192 million. The deal helped boost CH2M HILL's facilities and infrastructure revenues and expanded the company's global reach adding Halcrow's extensive client list and about 100 offices worldwide.

In 2011 CH2M HILL expanded its public transit business when it acquired the state and local government transit consulting business of Booz Allen Hamilton.

The company which is owned by its employees was founded in 1946.

EXECUTIVES

EVP Chief Operational Excellence Officer and Chief Delivery Officer, Michael A. Szomjassy, age 64, $500,011 total compensation
Vice President CH2M HILL OMI, Elisa Speranza
EVP Client Solutions and Sales, Lisa Glatch, age 52, $328,852 total compensation
EVP and CFO, Gary L. McArthur, age 55, $223,080 total compensation
EVP and Chief Human Resources Officer, John A. Madia, age 59, $453,003 total compensation
President Global Business Groups, Gregory T. (Greg) McIntyre, age 56
SVP and Regional Managing Director Middle East North Africa and India, Neil Reynolds
EVP Sales and Risk, Frank C. Gross
President Water Business Group, Peter G. Nicol
SVP and Regional Managing Director Latin America, Manuel E. Aguirre, age 56
Corporate VP and President Global Regions, Mark D. Fallon
Chairman and CEO, Jacqueline C. Hinman, age 53, $889,919 total compensation
Corporate VP and Global President Transportation, Terry A. Ruhl
Global President Environment and Nuclear, Chris Shea
SVP and Regional Managing Director United States, Patrick O'Keefe
SVP and Managing Director Tunnels and Earth Engineering, Martin Knights
SVP and Managing Director Operations Management Services, Steve Meininger
SVP and Regional Managing Director Asia/Pacific, Steven J. Nye
Acting Regional Managing Director Europe, Mark Thurston

EVP General Counsel and Corporate Secretary, Thomas M. (Tom) McCoy, age 64
Business Group President Industrial and Urban Environments, Thomas L. Pennella
SVP and Regional Managing Director - Canada, Alan Cary
Vice President, Didier Menard
Senior Vice President Of Corporate Development, Matthew (Matt) Mcgowan
Vice President, Sidney A (Sid) Faas
Vice President Of Information Systems, Rick Robertson
Executive Vice President Marketing, Gail Chamberlain
Regional Vice President Project Delivery, Gary Wood
Senior Vice President, Ken Miller
Vice President for National Security Programs, Rob Hood
Executive Vice President Marketing, Henry (Hal) Abiera
Vice President of Technology Systems, Kathryn Benson
Vice President Bd for Strategic Carbon and Energy Management, Ronald (Ron) Rudolph
Division Executive Vice President, Courtney Brown
Executive Vice President Marketing, Erika Powell
Vice President Navy and Utility Programs, James (Jamie) Kovalcik
Executive Vice President Marketing, Grace Wachira
Vice President Sales, William (Bill) Hannah
Executive Vice President Marketing, Gary Colgan
Vice President Of Information Systems, Donna Riley
Vice President Of Information Technology, Kristina Nygaard
Vice President Creative, Rosemarie Gumba
Vice President Bd Energy And Chemicals, Sun Pao
Senior Vice President Operations Energy And Chemicals, Pete Wiggin
Vice President, Mike Tilchin
Vice President of Technology, Cathy Zou
Vice President, Tony Omobono
Vice President, Christopher (Chris) Thomas
Senior Vice President; Managing Director Strategic Consulting, Scott Haskins
Vice President, Russell Bowen
Senior Vice President, Craig Pierrotti
Vice President Of Information Technology, Rick Riker
Vice President, Pete Butler
Vice President, Scott Yenzer
Vice President of Municipal Services, Rick Hirsekorn
Executive Vice President Marketing, James (Jamie) Gorham
Vice President Sales, Andrew Barash
Executive Vice President Marketing, James (Jamie) Maughan
Vice President, Alan (Al) Ispass
SeniorVice President Corporate Secretary and Chief Legal Officer, Mark Boedigheimer
Vice President Sales, Aaron Hall
Vice President Sales, Anja Schoenberger
Vice President of Information Technology, Birsen Zeyrek
Senior Vice President, Jhan Schmitz
Executive Vice President Marketing, Gregg Thompson
Vice President, David Hackworth
Vice President Of Operations, Randy Bender
Executive Vice President Marketing, Gregg Hughes
Vice President Of Marketing, Joseph Arnold
Vice President Of Business Development, Karen Wiemelt Karen Wiemelt
Vice President Of Information Technology, Louise Lella
Vice President Of Finance, David (Dave) Bechler
Vice President, Steve Gelman
Vice President, Meg Ibison

Vice President Of Information Technology, Tim Constantine
Vice President Of Tax, John-Bauer Martinez
Senior Vice President, George Powell
Executive Vice President Marketing, Emilio Candanoza
Vice President Director Of Aviation, Jerry Farrar
Senior Vice President, Jan Walstrom
Regional Sales Vice President, James (Jamie) Mcpherson
Vice President Sales, Alan Teare
Vice President, Gwendolyn Buchholz
Vice President Of Information Technology, Thomas Higgins
Vice President, Ted Garrish
Regional Business Group Manager Vice President, Rod Brauer
Executive Vice President Marketing, Gerald Simpson
Vice President Of Information Systems, Michael Fiaksel
Vice President Engineering, Tom Heinemann
Vice President And Area Manager, Deron Huck
Executive Vice President Marketing, Ileana Ruiz
Group Vice President Finance, Steven (Steve) Betts
Executive Vice President Marketing, Fair Yeager
Vice President International Government Affairs, Theresa Loar
Technology Vice President, Korkud Egrican
Vice President, Gary Swanson
Vice President, Scott Weikert
Executive Vice President Marketing, Imad Feghali
Executive Vice President Marketing, Gretchen Engel
Executive Vice President Marketing, Ginger Moore
Vice President, Jonathan Goldstick
Vice President Site Management, Saeed Khan
Vice President Finance, Todd Heskett
Executive Vice President Marketing, Jay McRae
Executive Vice President Marketing, Elizabeth (Beth) Bryant
Vice President, Leofwin Clark
Vice President, Laurens Tak
Vice President, George Gunn
Executive Vice President Marketing, Howard Thomas
Senior Vice President, Michael Rengel
Vice President Sales, Benjamin Romero
Executive Vice President Marketing, Greg Eldridge
Vice President, Joe Cazares
Vice President Business Development And Nuclear Business Group, Cathy Hickey
Executive Vice President, Gerard Orozco
Executive Vice President, Mike Bracken
Vice President Sales, Angela Lee
Executive Vice President Marketing, Iosefa Matagi
Vice President, Tom Price
Vice President Tunnels, Mark Johnson
Vice President North West Regional Business Manager, Vicki Bogenberger
Senior Vice President Latin America Region Energy And Chemicals, Jose Montalvo
Vice President ??? International, Dan Baublis
Vice President Of Information Technology, Stuart Jeffcoat
Vice President And Business Manager, Brent Diemer
Vice President Of Community Investment And Director Of Ch2m Hill Foundation, Ellen Sandberg
Vice President, Jerry Notte
Vice President, Elizabeth French
Global Vice President And Director Of Wastewater Market Segment, Liliana Maldonado
Senior Vice President, Keith Ogden
Vice President, Jim Hunter
Vice President Program Manager, Robert Hayden
Vice President Senior Program Manager, Daniel Wetstein

Vice President (Business Development), Chris Coggans
Vice President International Operations Director, Matthew (Matt) Radek
Executive Vice President Marketing, Emilee Edginton
Vice President Sales, Anne Lynch
Vice President, Paul Wobma
Vice President of Water Supply, Bill Bellamy
Vice President Product Marketing, Morgan Hanscom
Vice President of Information Technology, Jonathan (Jon) James
Vice President Information Technology, Dana Raughton
Vice President Waste Management Market Segment Director, John J (Jack) Wood
Regional Vice President Project Delivery, Ted Constantine
Vice President, Mel Hatcher
Board Member, Bill Farmer
Board Member, Paul Davis
Assistant Treasurer, Allan Chow
Board Member, Don Lewissecretary
Secretary, Franklin Judy
Board Member, Hank Postrozny
Auditors: KPMG LLP DENVER COLORADO

LOCATIONS

HQ: CH2M HILL COMPANIES LTD.
  9191 S JAMAICA ST, ENGLEWOOD, CO 801125946
Phone: 3037710900
Web: WWW.CH2M.COM

2014 Sales

	% of total
US	70
International	30
Total	**100**

PRODUCTS/OPERATIONS

2014 Sales

	$ mil.	% of total
Environment and Nuclear	1,377	24
Water	1,243	23
Energy	1,055	20
Transportation	947	18
Facilities and Urban Environment	789	15
Total	**5,413**	**100**

Selected Subsidiaries

CH2M HILL Alaska Inc.
CH2M HILL Canada Inc.
CH2M HILL Constructors Inc.
CH2M Hill Energy Ltd.
CH2M HILL Engineers Inc.
CH2M HILL Hanford Inc.
CH2M HILL Inc.
CH2M HILL International Ltd.
Halcrow Group Ltd.
HEBL Inc.

COMPETITORS

AECOM	Jacobs Engineering
Amec Foster Wheeler	KBR
Balfour Beatty	MWH Global
Bechtel	Parsons Brinckerhoff
Black & Veatch	Parsons Corporation
ERM	Tetra Tech
Fluor	Tutor Perini

HISTORICAL FINANCIALS
Company Type: Private

Income Statement

FYE: December 31

	REVENUE ($ mil.)	NET INCOME ($ mil.)	NET PROFIT MARGIN	EMPLOYEES
12/14	5,468	(318)	—	26,000
12/13	5,931	131	2.2%	—
12/12	6,224	98	1.6%	—
12/11	5,555	0	—	—
Annual Growth	**(0.5%)**	**—**	**—**	**—**

2014 Year-End Financials

Debt ratio: ——
Return on equity: (-5.80%)
Cash ($ mil.): 131
Current ratio: 1.00
Long-term debt ($ mil.): —

Dividends
  Yield: —
  Payout: —
Market value ($ mil.): —

CHALMETTE REFINING L.L.C.

LOCATIONS

HQ: CHALMETTE REFINING L.L.C.
  500 W SAINT BERNARD HWY, CHALMETTE, LA 700434821
Phone: 5042799481
Web: WWW.CHALMETTEREFINING.COM

HISTORICAL FINANCIALS
Company Type: Private

Income Statement

FYE: December 31

	REVENUE ($ mil.)	NET INCOME ($ mil.)	NET PROFIT MARGIN	EMPLOYEES
12/07	5,647	364	6.4%	600
12/06	5,020	423	8.4%	—
12/05	3,462	264	7.6%	—
12/04	3,130	0	—	—
Annual Growth	**21.7%**	**—**	**—**	**—**

2007 Year-End Financials

Debt ratio: ——
Return on equity: 6.40%
Cash ($ mil.): 302
Current ratio: 0.50
Long-term debt ($ mil.): —

Dividends
  Yield: —
  Payout: —
Market value ($ mil.): —

Charter Communications Inc

Charter Communications navigates the waters of US cable services largely by making itself a bigger boat. The cable system operator has almost 6 million mostly-residential subscribers (many brought on board through acquisitions) in more than two dozen states making it one of the top national cable companies behind Comcast Time Warner Cable and Cox Communications. In addition to 4.2 million video customers (92% opting for digital service) Charter also boasts 4.4 million broadband Internet subscribers and 2.3 million digital phone users. Its Charter Business provides Internet access data networking phone and wireless backhaul services to about 500000 commercial clients. In addition Charter sells local advertising on such cable networks as MTV CNN and ESPN. In 2015 Charter agreed to buy one of its competitors Bright House Networks for $10.4 billion. But wait there's more: in May 2015 Charter agreed to buy Time Warner Cable for $55 billion creating the second biggest cable company.

Operations

While Charter reports in one segment —broadband —it reports revenue in the elements that comprise the segment. Video is the biggest revenue generator with 49% followed by Internet 28% Commercial 11% Voice 6% with Advertising and other 6%.

Geographic ReachCharter's reach is national in scope with its key markets in the south Alabama Georgia the Carolinas Louisiana and Tennessee; the northeast New England states; the Midwest Michigan Wisconsin Minnesota and Nebraska; the southwest Texas; and the west California and several Mountain states. The company has some 300 call-handling offices across the US

Sales and Marketing

Charter markets its services via direct sales outbound telemarketing its online presence and Charter stores. The company appeals to new and existing customers with its multi-service bundled packages. It spent $529 million on marketing and $380 million on advertising in 2014 which were higher than its 2013 marketing and ad spending.

Financial Performance

Charter dialed up a an 11.7% revenue increase in 2014 from 2013 to reach $9.11 billion. The increase came from several sources including a rising number of residential Internet and triple play customers and business customers. Annual rate increases played a part too. As is the case throughout the industry Charter is losing basic video customers.The company has a history of losses and 2014 was no exception - Charter reported a loss of $183 million compared to the $169 million loss in 2013. Its sales are not enough to cover operating expenses debt-related interest (the company has $14.2 billion in debt) and the investments needed to keep its network up-to-date. It had more cash flow from operations $2.36 billion in 2014 from $2.16 billion in 2013.

Strategy

Charter continues to pursue a strategy popular with its competitors providing voice Internet access and other data services as a complete package. Similar to the results of rival cable companies it has seen rises in telephone Internet and enterprise customers while video subscribers have dwindled among both residential and business clients. It does however continue to see upticks in the move to digital video services.

Keeping its network and services current requires substantial investment. The company had $2.2 billion in capital expenditures in 2014 up from $1.8 billion in 2013. About half of the 2014 capital spending went to customer-premise equipment which includes costs incurred at the customer residence to secure new customers such customer installation costs and set-top boxes and cable modems. The company has upgraded its network to the DOCSIS 3.0 high-speed data capability standard which is in place for some 97% of homes it has passed and allows Internet speeds up to 100 megabits per second. That deployment will help as it continues to pursue enterprise clients. Charter has also invested in switched digital video (SDV) technology to increase the number of HD

channels it offers and is experimenting with a cloud-based user interface for its set-top boxes.

Charter also is moving some of its customer-related operations to the cloud to offer common user interfaces across its network and to effect quick updates.

Mergers and Acquisitions

Charter's acquisition of Time Warner Cable for $55 billion would position the company as a strong competitor to industry leader Comcast. The combination of Charter and Time Warner Cable does not have the same elements that scuttled Comcast's bid for Time Warner which could lessen regulatory opposition. The new company would not be the market leader nor would it provide content such as Comcast's NBCUniversal unit does.

Even with the Time Warner Cable deal Charter intends to maintain its deal for Bright House Networks for $10.4 billion. Bright House is the sixth largest provider serving markets that mostly don't compete with those served by Charter.

In 2013 the company increased its offerings and expand into new markets purchasing Optimum West/Bresnan from Cablevision for about $1.6 billion. Optimum West serves more than 360000 customers through cable systems in fast-growing regions of Colorado Montana Wyoming and Utah.

Company Background

Driven by dreams of creating a "wired world" chairman Paul Allen (a co-founder of Microsoft) reportedly poured more than $12 billion into Charter since 1998 and the billionaire saw most of that investment evaporate. After expanding through the purchase of a slew of small-town cable assets that needed extensive infrastructure upgrades Charter experienced ongoing subscriber losses financial losses and a debt load in excess of $20 billion. Faced with legal opposition from some of its lenders the company's 2009 bankruptcy reorganization plan eliminated about $8 billion of debt reduced annual interest expenses by about $830 million and left Allen controlling about one-third of the company (a stake that has since fallen to less than 10%).

HISTORY

Early History

Crown Media bought St. Louis-based Cencom Cable in 1992. Rather than relocate to Crown's Dallas home Cencom CEO Howard Wood joined with fellow executives Barry Babcock and Jerry Kent to form Charter Communications as a cable acquisition and management company in St. Louis. With an investment from Crown owned by Hallmark Cards the trio partnered with LEB Communications in 1994 to manage Charter's growth. And grow it did.

In 1994 Charter paid about $900 million for a majority stake in Crown. Charter spent $3 billion on 15 cable acquisitions in its first four years. It had more than 1 million subscribers by early 1997 and began offering high-speed cable Internet access and paging services in some of its markets.

Charter went into acquisition overdrive in 1998 when Microsoft co-founder Paul Allen took control with his $4.5 billion investment. The deal closely followed Allen's $2.8 billion takeover of Dallas-based Marcus Cable; Marcus was merged with Charter. The combined company based in St. Louis with Kent as CEO was the #7 US cable business with 2.5 million subscribers. Also that year the company teamed up with Wink and WorldGate to offer TV Internet services with set-top boxes.

Before the ink was dry on the merger papers Allen was at it again. The company's 1999 acquisitions included Falcon Communications (1 million cable subscribers) and Fanch Cablevision (more than 500000); it also bought cable systems from

Helicon InterMedia Partners Avalon Cable Inter-Link Communications Renaissance Media and Rifkin. Charter said it would spend $3.5 billion upgrading its systems over three years after raising that amount in a major junk bond sale. Months later the company raised $3.2 billion in its IPO.

In 2000 Charter completed its purchase of Bresnan Communications (700000 subscribers) and bought a system from Cablevision to form a major cluster in Michigan Minnesota and Wisconsin. The next year the company gained 554000 subscribers by swapping noncore cable systems and $1.8 billion in cash to AT&T Broadband in exchange for systems serving the St. Louis area parts of Alabama and the Reno area of Nevada and California.

Also in 2001 Kent resigned from the company and its board of directors and was replaced as CEO by former Liberty Media executive Carl Vogel. Vogel stayed on the job until 2005 at which point he also retired. Former AOL executive Neil Smit replaced Vogel later that year. Several other executive departures followed and a subsequent securities investigation led to convictions against former COO Dave Barford (sentenced to one year in prison) and former CFO Kent Kalkwarf (14 months in prison).

The company in 2006 sold nearly $900 million in assets including systems in Illinois and Kentucky to New Wave Communications and systems in West Virginia and Virginia to Cebridge Connections. Shedding more assets Charter also sold cable TV systems serving nearly 70000 customers in the western US to subsidiaries of Orange Broadband Holding Company.

EXECUTIVES

COO, John R. Bickham, age 63, $1,375,001 total compensation

President and CEO, Thomas M. (Tom) Rutledge, age 61, $1,999,999 total compensation

EVP and President Commercial Services, Donald F. (Don) Detampel, age 59, $617,999 total compensation

EVP Customer Operations, Kathleen Mayo, $133,269 total compensation

EVP General Counsel and Corporate Secretary, Richard R. Dykhouse, age 51, $397,475 total compensation

EVP Government Affairs, Catherine Bohigian, $176,923 total compensation

EVP and President Business Enterprise Services, Philip G. Meeks

EVP and CFO, Christopher L. (Chris) Winfrey, age 39, $566,500 total compensation

EVP Engineering and Information Technology, James A. (Jim) Blackley, $82,211 total compensation

EVP and Chief Marketing Officer, Jonathan Hargis, $552,385 total compensation

EVP Network Operations, Scott Weber

EVP Field Operations, Thomas E. (Tom) Adams

EVP Business Planning, James Nuzzo

EVP and President Media Sales, David Kline

EVP Product and Strategy, Richard J. DiGeronimo

Vice President Investor Relations, Stefan Anninger

Vice President Direct Marketing and Customer Engagement, Geoff Boytos

Svp-govt Affairs, Adam Falk

Vice President Billing and Collections, Mike Ciszek

Vice President Marketing and Sales Operations, Madeline Marcus

Vice President General Manager, Melissa (Mel) Morris

Vice President Service Delivery and Support, Ashok Kuthyar

Vice President, Thaddeus Vickers

Vice President Customer Care Operations, Bob Calabro

Vice President Finance, Peggy Giaminetti

Vice President Field Operations Strategy, Thomas (Thom) Monaghan
Vice President and Associate General Counsel Regulatory Affairs, Michael (Mel) Moore
Regional Vice President of Finance, Bob Rubery
Executive Vice President, Jim Blackley
Vice President of Sales, David (Dave) Hall
Chairman, Eric L. Zinterhofer, age 43
Auditors: KPMG LLP

LOCATIONS

HQ: Charter Communications Inc
400 Atlantic Street, Stamford, CT 06901
Phone: 203 905-7801
Web: www.charter.com

PRODUCTS/OPERATIONS

2014 Sales

	$ mil.	% of total
Video	4,443	49
High-speed Internet	2,576	28
Commercial	993	11
Telephone	575	6
Advertising sales	341	4
Other	180	2
Total	**9,108**	**100**

COMPETITORS

AT&T	Netflix
Amazon.com	RCN Corporation
Apple Inc.	SONIFI Solutions Inc.
Bright House Networks	Skype
Cablevision Systems	Sprint Communications
Comcast	Suddenlink
Cox Communications	Communications
DIRECTV	T-Mobile USA
DISH Network	Time Warner Cable
EarthLink	United Online
Frontier	Verizon
Communications	Vonage
Hulu	YouTube
Mediacom	
Communications	

HISTORICAL FINANCIALS

Company Type: Public

Income Statement

FYE: December 31

	REVENUE ($ mil.)	NET INCOME ($ mil.)	NET PROFIT MARGIN	EMPLOYEES
12/15	9,754	(271)	—	23,800
12/14	9,108	(183)	—	23,200
12/13	8,155	(169)	—	21,600
12/12	7,504	(304)	—	17,800
12/11	7,204	(369)	—	16,000
Annual Growth	**7.9%**	**—**	**—**	**10.4%**

2015 Year-End Financials

Debt ratio: 90.86%
Return on equity: (-542.00%)
Cash ($ mil.): 5
Current ratio: 0.17
Long-term debt ($ mil.): 35,723

No. of shares (mil.): 112
Dividends
  Yield: —
  Payout: —
Market value ($ mil.): 20,588

	STOCK PRICE ($) FY Close	P/E High/Low	PER SHARE ($) Earnings	Dividends	Book Value
12/15	183.10	— —	(2.43)	0.00	(0.41)
12/14	166.62	— —	(1.70)	0.00	1.30
12/13	136.76	— —	(1.65)	0.00	1.42
12/12	76.24	— —	(3.05)	0.00	1.47
12/11	56.94	— —	(3.39)	0.00	4.07
Annual Growth	**33.9%**	**— —**	**—**	**—**	**—**

Chemical Financial Corp

Chemical Financial has banking down to a science. It's the holding company for Chemical Bank which provides standard services such as checking and savings accounts CDs and IRAs credit and debit cards and loans and mortgages to individuals and businesses through nearly 190 branches in the lower peninsula of Michigan. The majority of the bank's loan portfolio is made up of commercial loans while consumer loans make up the remainder. Boasting assets of $9 billion Chemical is the second largest bank in Michigan. The company also offers trust investment management brokerage and title insurance services through subsidiaries.

OperationsIts Wealth Management division which has some $4 billion in assets under custody offers trust services estate planning investment management and employee benefit programs. Chemical Financial Advisors offers mutual funds and marketable securities while CFC Title Services issues title insurance for mortgage properties. CFC Capital manages the company's municipal investment securities portfolio.About 72% of Chemical Financial's total revenue came from loan interest (including fees) in 2014 while another 6% came from interest on its investment securities. The rest of its revenue came from deposit account service charges and fees (8%) wealth management revenue (6%) mortgage banking income (2%) and other miscellaneous sources of income. Sales and MarketingChemical Financial spent $3.45 million on advertising in 2014 up from $2.97 million and $3.11 million in 2013 and 2012 respectively.Financial PerformanceChemical Financial's revenues and profits have been rising over the past few years thanks growing loan and deposit business from acquisitions lower interest expenses on deposits and declining loan loss provisions as its loan portfolio's credit quality has improved with higher property valuations in the strengthened economy. The bank's revenue rose by 6% to $290.4 million in 2014 as the bank as its acquisition of Northwestern Bancorp boosted its loan business during the year. Higher revenue lower interest expenses and a continued decline in loan loss provisions drove the bank's net income up by 9% to a record $62.1 million. The bank's operating cash levels inched higher to $89.9 million on higher cash earnings.StrategyThe bank follows an aggressive acquisition strategy to boost its loan and deposit business while expanding its branch network into key parts of Michigan. Indeed its acquisitions in 2015 and 2014 boosted the bank's presence in northwestern Michigan and along the Michigan-Indiana border. By the end of 2014 the bank had acquired some 21 community banks and 36 branch bank offices. Mergers and AcquisitionsIn June 2015 it acquired Lake Michigan Financial Corporation along with its The Bank of Holland and The Bank of Northern Michigan subsidiaries and branches for some $187.4 million. The acquisition added $1.2 billion in assets $959 million in loans and $956 million in deposits to Chemical's books.In April 2015 Chemical Financial purchased Monarch Community Bancorp and its Monarch Community Bank subsidiary for $27.2 million which grew the company's presence and market share along the Michigan-Indiana border. The deal also added $174 million in assets $130 million in new loan assets and $142 million in new deposits. In October 2014 Chemical Financial bought Northwestern Bancorp and its Northwestern Bank sub-

sidiary for $121 million representing its largest expansion into northwestern Michigan to date.

Company BackgroundIn late 2012 the company acquired 21 branches in northeastern Michigan and Battle Creek from Independent Bank. That more than $8-million transaction further expands Chemical Bank's presence geographically. Additional acquisitions including FDIC-assisted takeovers of failed banks are possible.

EXECUTIVES

First Vice President Corporate Human Resources, Joseph (Jo) Torrence
Chairman President and CEO, David B. Ramaker, age 59, $569,042 total compensation
EVP CFO and Treasurer, Lori A. Gwizdala, age 57, $297,924 total compensation
First VP and Director of Branch Administration, Kenneth W. Johnson, age 53, $265,534 total compensation
President South Region, Richard J. DeVries, age 59
EVP and COO Business Operations, Leonardo Amat
EVP and Chief Risk Management Officer, Lynn Kerber
EVP General Counsel and Secretary, William Collins, age 62
Regional President - West Region Chemical Bank, Joel Rahn
EVP and COO Customer Experience, Robert S. Rathbun
SVP and Senior Investment Officer, Pavel Konecny
SVP and CIO, Greg Meidt
Vice President of Information Technology Operations, Tad Sumner
Vice President Of Information Technology Operations, Ted Sumner
Vice President Of Human Resources, Kim Butcher
Senior Vice President Head of Personal Trust, James (Jamie) Blanchard
Vice President Commercial Loan Officer, Jeff Hyde
Assistant Vice President Branch Manager Ii, Anita Merchant
Executive Vice President Marketing, Dawn Dryer
Senior Vice President Senior Lender, Mike Williams
Vice President, Carl Ahearn
Vice President Iso, Laurie Soren
Senior Vice President and Trust Officer, Jude Patnaude
Vice President Information Technology, Barb Mechem
Executive Vice President Marketing, Todd Elby
Vice President Senior Financial Advisor East Region Sales Manager, Brenda Rajewski
Vice President and Community Reinvestment Act Officer, Robert (Bob) BurgessJr
Vice Chairman, Thomas W. Kohn, age 61
Auditors: KPMG LLP

LOCATIONS

HQ: Chemical Financial Corp
235 E. Main Street, Midland, MI 48640
Phone: 989 839-5350
Web: www.chemicalbankmi.com

PRODUCTS/OPERATIONS

2014 Sales

	$ mil.	% of total
Interest		
Loans including fees	209	72
Investment securities	17	6
Other	0	-
Non-interest		
Service charges on deposit accounts	22	8
Wealth management revenue	16	6
Other customer service charges & fees	18	6
Other	6	2
Total	**290**	**100**

HISTORICAL FINANCIALS

Company Type: Public

Income Statement

FYE: December 31

	ASSETS ($ mil.)	NET INCOME ($ mil.)	INCOME AS % OF ASSETS	EMPLOYEES
12/14	7,322	62	0.8%	2,000
12/13	6,184	56	0.9%	1,700
12/12	5,917	51	0.9%	1,859
12/11	5,339	43	0.8%	1,700
12/10	5,246	23	0.4%	1,608
Annual Growth	8.7%	28.1%	—	5.6%

2014 Year-End Financials

Debt ratio: —	No. of shares (mil.): 32
Return on equity: 8.32%	Dividends
Cash ($ mil.): 183	Yield: 3.0%
Current ratio: —	Payout: 47.7%
Long-term debt ($ mil.): —	Market value ($ mil.): 1,004

	STOCK PRICE ($) FY Close	P/E High/Low	PER SHARE ($) Earnings	Dividends	Book Value
12/14	30.64	17 13	1.97	0.94	24.32
12/13	31.67	16 12	2.00	0.87	23.38
12/12	23.76	13 10	1.85	0.82	21.69
12/11	21.32	15 9	1.57	0.80	20.82
12/10	22.15	28 21	0.88	0.80	20.41
Annual Growth	8.4%	— —	22.3%	4.1%	4.5%

Chemours Co (The)

Auditors: PricewaterhouseCoopers LLP

LOCATIONS

HQ: Chemours Co (The)
1007 Market Street, Wilmington, DE 19899
Phone: 302 773-1000

HISTORICAL FINANCIALS

Company Type: Public

Income Statement

FYE: December 31

	REVENUE ($ mil.)	NET INCOME ($ mil.)	NET PROFIT MARGIN	EMPLOYEES
12/14	6,432	400	6.2%	9,000
12/13	6,859	423	6.2%	—
12/12	7,365	1,057	14.4%	—
Annual Growth	(6.5%)	(38.5%)	—	—

Chesapeake Energy Corp.

Chesapeake Energy (named after the childhood Chesapeake Bay haunts of a company founder) builds oil and natural gas reserves through the acquisition and development of oil and gas assets across the US. In 2014 the company had estimated proved reserves of 10.7 trillion cu. ft. of natural gas equivalent. Chesapeake has exploration and production assets in Appalachia the Mid-Continent the Barnett Bossier and Haynesville shale plays the Permian Basin and the Rockies. In 2014 Chesapeake had 45100 producing oil and natural gas wells that produced 729000 barrels of oil equivalent per day the bulk of which was natural gas.

Geographic Reach

The company has natural gas resources in the Haynesville and Bossier Shales in northwestern Louisiana and East Texas; the Marcellus Shale in the northern Appalachian Basin of West Virginia and Pennsylvania; the Barnett Shale in the Fort Worth Basin of north-central Texas; and the Pearsall Shale in South Texas. In addition it has built leading positions in the liquids-rich resource plays of the Eagle Ford Shale in South Texas; the Utica Shale in Ohio and Pennsylvania; the Granite Wash Cleveland Tonkawa and Mississippi Lime plays in the Anadarko Basin in western Oklahoma and the Texas Panhandle; the Bone Spring Avalon Wolfcamp and Wolfberry plays in the Permian and Delaware Basins in West Texas and southern New Mexico; and the Niobrara Shale in the Powder River Basin in Wyoming.

Operations

Chesapeake is the second-largest producer of natural gas and the 10th largest producer of oil and natural gas liquids (NGLs) in the US. The company has two reportable operating segments exploration and production (which is responsible for finding and producing oil natural gas and NGLs) and marketing gathering and compression (which is engaged in marketing gathering and compression of oil natural gas and NGLs).

Sales and Marketing

Chesapeake Energy Marketing provides natural gas oil and NGL marketing services including commodity price structuring contract administration and nomination services for Chesapeake its partners and other producers. By aggregating volumes it seeks to increase the value of products to be sold to in various intermediary markets end markets and pipelines. Chesapeake's oil and NGL production is sold under market sensitive short-term or spot price contracts while its natural gas production is sold to purchasers under spot price contracts or percentage-of-proceeds and percentage-of-index contracts.

Sales to Exxon Mobil and Plains Marketing accounted for 12% and 11% respectively of Chesapeake revenues in 2014 and 2012 respectively. There were no sales to individual customers constituting 10% or more of total revenues for the year 2013.

Financial Performance

In 2014 net sales increased by 20% due to higher sales from oil natural gas and NGL and marketing gathering and compression segments partially offset by a decline in oilfield services revenues. Revenues and operating expenses from marketing business increased substantially in 2014 and 2013 primarily as a result of an increase in a variety of purchase and sales contracts it entered into with third parties for various commercial pur-

poses including credit risk mitigation and to help meet certain of its pipeline delivery commitments. Net income increased by 165% due to increased revenue decreased oilfield service expense and Restructuring and other termination costs partially offset by increased Deferred income taxes. As a result of the spin-off of oilfield services business in June 2014 the company did not have oilfield services revenues and expenses in the second half of the year. Cash provided by operating activities increased by $20 million that year.

Strategy

With substantial leasehold positions in most of the premier US onshore resource plays Chesapeake is focused on finding and producing hydrocarbons in a responsible and efficient manner that seeks to maximize shareholder returns.

In 2014 the company completed the spin-off of its oilfield services business which it previously conducted through its indirect wholly owned subsidiary Chesapeake Oilfield Operating L.L.C. into an independent publicly traded company called Seventy Seven Energy.

That year Chesapeake agreed to sell its assets in the Southern Marcellus Shale and a portion of the Eastern Utica Shale in West Virginia to Southwestern Energy for $5.4 billion. It also sold its interest in Chaparral Energy for $215 million and its crude oil hauling assets for $44 million.

In 2013 it also sold assets in the Northern Eagle Ford Shale and Haynesville Shale to an EXCO Resources subsidiary for $1 billion. In 2013 the company sold its 50% undivided interest in 850000 acres in northern Oklahoma (its Mississippi Lime joint venture with Sinopec International Petroleum Exploration and Production) for $1.02 billion. Other asset sales in 2013 included Granite Wash Midstream Gas Services (to a subsidiary of MarkWest Energy Partners for $252 million) and its interests in certain gathering system assets in Pennsylvania to Western Gas Partners for $134 million.

Mergers and Acquisitions

In 2014 Chesapeake repurchased all of the outstanding preferred shares of its subsidiary CHK Utica L.L.C. from third-party preferred shareholders for $1.25 billion.

HISTORY

Aubrey McClendon (who grew up near Maryland's Chesapeake Bay) and Tom Ward had been non-operating partners in about 600 wells in Oklahoma before forming their own company in 1989 to develop new fields in Texas and Oklahoma during the 1990s. The firm went public in 1993. In 1995 the company acquired oil and gas acreage in Louisiana as well as Princeton Natural Gas an Oklahoma City-based gas marketing firm.

Oil finds in Louisiana and strong production from its Texas and Oklahoma wells helped lift Chesapeake's sales in 1996. That year it acquired Amerada Hess' (later renamed Hess) half of their joint operations in two Oklahoma fields. In 1997 chairman McClendon and president Ward acquired control of Chesapeake.

The company's success was based on its "growth through the drillbit" strategy —developing new wells. But after a 1997 loss Chesapeake modified its strategy and sought to grow by acquiring other companies. That year it bought energy company AnSon Production. Chesapeake subsequently bought oil and gas explorer-producer Hugoton Energy and energy company DLB Oil & Gas.

In 1998 the company acquired a 40% stake in Canadian oil producer Ranger Oil and paid Occidental Petroleum $105 million for natural gas reserves in the Texas Panhandle. Chesapeake then began to transform itself from a hotshot driller to an acquirer of natural gas properties almost tripling its proved reserves. The company suffered a huge loss that year in part from the acquisitions and continuing lower gas prices.

With gas prices soaring again the company continued its buying spree into 2000 when it agreed to buy midcontinent natural gas producer Gothic Energy for $345 million in stock and assumed debt. The deal closed in 2001. The company also sold its Canadian assets that year in order to focus on its core US properties.

In 2002 Chesapeake acquired oil and gas producer Canaan Energy for about $118 million. Later that year the company announced plans to sell or trade its Permian Basin assets.

Chesapeake acquired in 2003 a 25% stake in Pioneer Drilling (which it subsequently sold). In 2004 the company acquired Barnett Shale assets from Hallwood Energy for $292 million. That year it also bought privately owned Concho Resources for $420 million. The next year the company acquired privately held BRG Petroleum which held assets of more than 450 wells with proved reserves of more than 275 billion cu. ft. of natural gas for $325 million.

In 2005 Chesapeake acquired 20% of Gastar Exploration (reduced to 15% by 2007). That year in a major move the company acquired Columbia Natural Resources for $2.2 billion.

To get better financial returns the company is selling assets to secure capital. Hurt by continuing low natural gas prices the company sold its midstream assets in 2012 and 2013 for $4.9 billion in three separate deals. As part of this move in 2012 the company sold its limited partner units and its general partner interests in Chesapeake Midstream Partners to Global Infrastructure Partners for $2 billion. That year the company also sold about $6.9 billion of its Permian basin properties in order to pay down debt.

To simplify its operations in 2012 Chesapeake spun off its oilfield service affiliate Chesapeake Oilfield Services.

EXECUTIVES

Vice President Information Technology, Dale Wildman

SVP Information Technology and CIO, Cathlyn L. (Cathy) Tompkins, age 54

EVP and CFO, Domenic J. (Nick) Dell'Osso, age 39, $725,000 total compensation

EVP Exploration Technology and Land, Frank J. Patterson

EVP General Counsel and Secretary, James R. Webb, $595,192 total compensation

President and CEO, Robert D. (Doug) Lawler, $1,250,000 total compensation

EVP Operations Northern Division, M. Christopher (Chris) Doyle, $566,346 total compensation

EVP Operations Southern Division, Mikell J. (Jason) Pigott, $519,231 total compensation

Vice President AandD, Brian Exline

Vice President Marketing and Corporate Business Development, Bryan Lemmerman

Vice President Marine Information Technology, Steve A Melton

Vice President Human Resources, James Hawkins

Vice President Crude Oil Marketing, John Caldwell

Legal Secretary, Johna Dodson

Vice President Tax, Bobby Mattice

Second Vice President, Mandy Duane

Vice President Information Technology, Steve Evans

Vice President Geoscience Technology, Todd Stephenson

Vice President Internal Audit, Lacie Wilson

Senior Vice President Of Provider Solutions, Clint Martin

Vice President Investor Relations Communications, Brad Sylvester

Senior Vice President Information Technology, Cathy Tompkins

Vice President Geosciences Northern Divison, John (Jack) Kapchinske

Vice President of Human Resources, Jay (james) Hawkins

Senior Vice President Operations, Jason Pigott

Vice President Geology Eastern Division, H Dewitt

Treasurer, Martha Burger

Chairman, Archie W. Dunham, age 76

Auditors: PricewaterhouseCoopers LLP

LOCATIONS

HQ: Chesapeake Energy Corp.
6100 North Western Avenue, Oklahoma City, OK 73118
Phone: 405 848-8000
Web: www.chk.com

PRODUCTS/OPERATIONS

2014 Sales

	$ mil.	% of total
Marketing gathering & compression	12,225	58
Natural gas Oil and NGL	8,180	39
Service operations	546	3
Total	**20,951**	**100**

COMPETITORS

Adams Resources	Koch Industries Inc.
Anadarko Petroleum	Noble Energy
Apache	OGE Energy
Ashland Inc.	Occidental Petroleum
BP	Par Petroleum
Bonanza Creek	Patterson-UTI Energy
Chevron	Pioneer Natural
ConocoPhillips	Resources
Exxon Mobil	SandRidge Energy
Freeport-McMoRan Oil &	Southwestern Energy
Gas LLC	Unit Corporation

HISTORICAL FINANCIALS

Company Type: Public

Income Statement

FYE: December 31

	REVENUE ($ mil.)	NET INCOME ($ mil.)	NET PROFIT MARGIN	EMPLOYEES
12/14	20,951	1,917	9.1%	5,500
12/13	17,506	724	4.1%	10,800
12/12	12,316	(769)	—	12,000
12/11	11,635	1,742	15.0%	12,600
12/10	9,366	1,774	18.9%	10,000
Annual Growth	22.3%	2.0%	—	(13.9%)

2014 Year-End Financials

Debt ratio: 28.38%	No. of shares (mil.): 663
Return on equity: 11.65%	Dividends
Cash ($ mil.): 4,108	Yield: 1.7%
Current ratio: 1.27	Payout: 44.3%
Long-term debt ($ mil.): 11,184	Market value ($ mil.): 12,981

	STOCK PRICE ($) FY Close	P/E High/Low		PER SHARE ($) Earnings	Dividends	Book Value
12/14	19.57	16	9	1.87	0.35	25.48
12/13	27.14	40	23	0.73	0.35	24.08
12/12	16.62	—	—	(1.46)	0.35	23.44
12/11	22.29	14	9	2.32	0.25	25.21
12/10	25.91	11	8	2.51	0.30	23.34
Annual Growth	(6.8%)	—	—	(7.1%)	3.9%	2.2%

Chevron Corporation

Chevron has earned its stripes as the #2 integrated oil company in the US behind Exxon Mobil. In 2014 it reported proved reserves of 11.1 billion barrels of oil equivalent and a daily production of 2.6 million barrels of oil equivalent 5550 miles of oil and gas pipeline and a refining capacity of 2 million barrels of oil per day. Chevron also owns interests in chemicals mining and power production businesses. The company owns or has stakes in 8060 gas stations in the US (and 8600 outside the US) that operate mainly under the Chevron and Texaco brands. Chevron also owns 50% of chemicals concern Chevron Phillips Chemical.

HISTORY

Thirty years after the California gold rush a small firm began digging for a new product —oil. The crude came from wildcatter Frederick Taylor's well located north of Los Angeles. In 1879 Taylor and other oilmen formed Pacific Coast Oil attracting the attention of John D. Rockefeller's Standard Oil. The two competed fiercely until Standard took over Pacific Coast in 1900.

When Standard Oil was broken up in 1911 its West Coast operations became the stand-alone Standard Oil Company (California) which was nicknamed Socal and sold Chevron-brand products. After winning drilling concessions in Bahrain and Saudi Arabia in the 1930s Socal summoned Texaco to help and they formed Caltex (California-Texas Oil Company) as equal partners. In 1948 Socony (later Mobil) and Jersey Standard (later Exxon) bought 40% of Caltex's Saudi operations and the Saudi arm became Aramco (Arabian American Oil Company).

Socal exploration pushed into Louisiana and the Gulf of Mexico in the 1940s. In 1961 it bought Standard Oil Company of Kentucky (Kyso). The 1970s brought setbacks: Caltex holdings were nationalized during the OPEC-spawned upheaval and the Saudi Arabian government claimed Aramco in 1980.

In 1984 Socal was renamed Chevron and doubled its reserves with its $13 billion purchase of Gulf Corp. which had origins in the 1901 Spindletop gusher in Texas. Gulf became an oil power by developing Kuwaiti concessions but was hobbled when those assets were nationalized in 1975. After Gulf was rocked by disclosures that it had an illegal political slush fund Socal stepped in. The deal loaded the new company with debt and it cut 20000 jobs and sold billions in assets.

Chevron bought Tenneco's Gulf of Mexico properties in 1988 and in 1992 swapped fields valued at $1.1 billion for 15.7 million shares of Chevron stock owned by Pennzoil. It also moved into the North Sea in 1994.

In the 1990s Chevron gave its retailing units a tune-up. It allied with McDonald's (1995) to combine burger stands and gas stations in 12 western states. In addition the company sold 450 UK gas stations and a refinery to Shell (1997). Meanwhile Chevron sold its natural gas operation in 1996 for a stake in Houston-based NGC (later Dynegy; sold in 2007) and it signed an onshore exploration contract in China the next year.

Poor economic conditions in Asia and slumping oil prices in 1998 forced Chevron to shed some US holdings including California properties. Looking for growth overseas in 1999 it bought Rutherford-Moran Oil increasing its interests in Thailand and Petrolera Argentina San Jorge Argentina's #3 oil company.

Chevron trimmed about 10% of its workforce in 1999 and 2000 in an effort to cut costs. As the rest of the industry consolidated Chevron discussed merging with Texaco but the talks collapsed in 1999. Later that year CEO Ken Derr retired and vice chairman Dave O'Reilly replaced him.

In 2000 Chevron formed a joint venture with Phillips Petroleum (later ConocoPhillips) that combined the companies' chemicals businesses as Chevron Phillips Chemical. That year talks with Texaco were revived and Chevron agreed to acquire its Caltex partner for about $35 billion in stock and about $8 billion in assumed debt. The deal completed in 2001 formed ChevronTexaco.

Part of the 2001 deal to acquire Texaco required Chevron to sell exclusive rights to the Texaco brand for a period of three years. A division of Royal Dutch Shell owned rights to the Texaco brand until 2004 and changed the name of the service stations to Shell. Once Chevron regained the rights to the Texaco name it revitalized the brand name by adding about 400 Texaco stations in the western US.

In 2002 ChevronTexaco divested its stakes in US downstream joint ventures Equilon (to Shell) and Motiva (to Shell and Saudi Aramco). It also sold part of a Gulf of Mexico pipeline and two natural gas plants in Louisiana to Duke Energy and its 12.5% stake in a natural gas liquids fractionator to Enterprise Products Partners. In 2004 ChevronTexaco sold 150 US natural gas and oil properties to XTO Energy for $912 million. The company changed its name to Chevron Corporation in 2005.

Chevron acquired Unocal in 2005 for more than $16 billion boosting its proved reserves by about 15%. Equally attractive to Chevron was the strategic position of Unocal's operations; at a time when industries are trying to get a foothold in China the reserves in Southeast Asia could easily be transported not only there but also to a surging India as well. Unocal's other operations easily supplied the US (from the Gulf of Mexico) and Europe (Caspian Sea) with gas and oil. Chevron bought a 5% stake in Indian refiner Reliance Petroleum for about $300 million in 2006. That year a company-led group of exploration firms announced a new successful oil strike in the Gulf of Mexico.

The company has also been growing its natural gas assets. In 2008 it announced plans to construct a $3.1 billion natural gas project in the Gulf of Thailand. The project will have the capacity to meet 14% of Thailand's natural gas needs.

Ultrapar acquired Chevron's Texaco-branded fuel distribution business in Brazil for $720 million in 2008 and the next year Chevron sold its Nigerian fuel marketing business.

A leading producer of viscous heavy oil in 2010 a Chevron-led consortium was awarded the rights to 40% of a heavy oil project in Venezuela's Orinoco Oil Belt.

In 2010 in the wake of the BP oil rig disaster in the Gulf of Mexico Chevron announced it was forming a $1 billion joint venture with Exxon Mobil Royal Dutch Shell and ConocoPhillips to create a rapid-response system capable of capturing and containing up to 100000 barrels of oil from an oil spill in water depths of 10000 feet.

Looking to develop a deepwater area unaffected by US regulations in 2010 the company acquired a 70% stake in three concessions in Liberia in West Africa. Other deepwater exploration asset acquisitions that year included purchases in China and the Turkish Black Sea.

In 2010 the company began to cut its US refining and marketing business staff by 20% and as part of this realignment it sold its 23% stake in Colonial Pipeline to a KKR affiliate.

In a major move in 2011 Chevron acquired Atlas Energy in a $4.3 billion deal. The acquisition is part

the company's strategy of finding new reserves to replace reserves lost from declining fields. It also marked Chevron's move to become a major player in the prolific Marcellus Shale play in Pennsylvania where a number of majors are seeking to cash in on the improved drilling technology that has made the exploitation of unconventional gas finds more commercially viable. The purchase gave Chevron Atlas Energy's 850 billion cu. ft. of proved natural gas reserves and 80 million cu. ft. of daily natural gas production. It also complements Chevron's earlier acquisitions of shale gas assets in Canada Poland and Romania as well as its purchase of an additional 228000 acres in the Marcellus Shale from Chief Oil & Gas LLC and Tug Hill Inc. (The acquisitions added up to 5 trillion cubic feet of natural gas resources to Chevron's existing Marcellus Shale operations.)

An earlier chapter of Chevron's history reemerged in 2011 when the company was slapped with a bill for $18 billion in fines and charges by a court in Ecuador regarding environmental damages allegedly caused by Texaco (acquired in 2001) in the 1970s and 1980s. Chevron challenged the findings as illegitimate and unenforceable.

Restructuring its refinery and retail businesses to cut costs in 2011 Chevron sold its Chevron Ltd. UK unit which operated the Pembroke refinery to Valero for $730 million. In addition Valero agreed to pay more that $1 billion for other Chevron Ltd. assets including 1000 gas stations. That year Chevron also sold its fuels marketing and aviation businesses in 16 countries in the Caribbean and Latin America and some marketing businesses in five African countries.

In 2012 the company signed a 20-year deal with Tohoku Electric Power for the delivery of liquefied natural gas (LNG) from the Chevron-operated Wheatstone natural gas project in Australia.

EXECUTIVES

Chairman and CEO, John S. Watson, age 59, $1,825,500 total compensation
VP and CFO, Patricia E. (Pat) Yarrington, age 59, $1,035,417 total compensation
EVP Downstream and Chemicals, Michael K. (Mike) Wirth, age 55, $1,063,600 total compensation
VP Finance Global Downstream, Pierre R. Breber, age 51
Managing Director Nigeria/Mid-Africa Strategic Business Unit, Jay R. Pryor, age 58
VP and General Counsel, R. Hewitt (Hew) Pate, age 53, $842,708 total compensation
Managing Director IndoAsia, Stephen W. (Steve) Green, age 58
VP Health Environment and Safety, Wesley E. (Wes) Lohec, age 56
EVP Technology Projects and Services, Joseph C. (Joe) Geagea, age 55
EVP Upstream, James W. (Jay) Johnson, age 56
President Chevron Bangladesh, Kevin Lyon
VP Strategic Planning, Joseph M. Naylor
Vice President and Treasurer, Paul Bennett
Vice President Procurement And Global Downstream, Maria Lindenberg
Vice President, Greg Wagner
Senior Vice President Marketing, Bradley Smith
Vice President Deepwater Exploration, Stephen Thurston
Vice President, David Taber
Vice President, Robert Kimmel
Vice President Chevron Natural Gas Trading, Brent Faulk
Vice President, Roberto Soto
Vice President Finance and Shared Services, John (Jack) Wilcox-Black
Senior Vice President of Asset Management for Cpl, William (Bill) Lacobie

Vice President, Mark Skalinski
Vice President Marketing, Jose Parra
Vice President, Eugene Luzietti
Medical Director, Ana Luis
Senior Vice President Operations, Karen Figenshu
Vice President Responsible Care And Engineering, Oscar Pena
Vice President Sales, Bill Gilliam
Vice President, Jay Byers
Vice President Strategy And Planning, Nicola Woods
Vice President Finance, Craig Isom
Vice President Of Finance, Uriel Ose
Senior Execution Manager Jvp Relations, Tom Koren
Vice President Asia Pacific, Farrukh Saeed
Vice President Marketing, Rod Knoll
Assistant Vice President Loan Administrator, Carl Okpattah
Vice President, Michael Fleck
Vice President, Petros Papazis
Vice President Health ENVIRONMENT and SAFETY, Rhonda Zygocki
Vice President Finance, Uriel Oseguera
Vice President, Larry Buster
Senior Vice President, Jim Tosh
Vice President Inside Sales Marketing, Joe Reid
Vice President, Bachtiar Fatah
Vice President Marketing, Jeff Petro
Vice President and General Counsel, Dotson John
Vice President Of Finance, Kathy Carnevale
Vice President Global Real Estate Services, Steven Berg
Vice President Sustainability, Thomas Schuttish
Senior Vice President Asset Management, Charles Hall
Partner Vice President Production Manager, Jacques A Oosthuizen
Vice President and General Counsel, Hew Pate
Vice President Marketing Gorgon Project, Geoff Hegney
Vice President, Alan Levine
Vice President Of Marketing, Idowu Okunzua
Vice President, Ken Smyth
Vice President Human Resources, Juan Garcia
Vice President, Paul Allinson
Vice President Business Development, Don Haley
Vice President, Mark Macleod
Vice President And General Counsel Land, Wendy Daboval
Executive Vice President Sales and Marketing, Gabriel Diaz
Vice President, Paul Fontenot
Vice President, David (Dave) Smith
Executive Vice President Technology and Services, John (Jack) Caw
Vice President Of Montgomery Operations, Julia Martin
Vice President Human Resources, Pete Vincent
Vice President Commercial and Business Development, Martin (Marti) Isoje
Senior Vice President, Jennifer M (Jen) Papier
Vice President Engineering, Paul Donald
Vice President, Dorcus Chu
Vice President Marketing, Jeanne H Waguespack
Senior Vice President Operations, Ted Etchison
Vice President Policy Government And Public Affairs, David (Dave) Macinnis
Vice President, Frank Bilotti
Senior Vice President Marketing, Kevin Masson
Vice President, Michael Kisucky
Medical Director, Julie Allred
Vice President Retail Distribution Network, Desmond Cecil
Vice President Marketing, Eddie Toro
Vice President, Jesus Carbonell
Vice President Alternate Channels, Yolanda Mosley
Vice President Of Global Exploration, Robert Ryan
Vice President, Prerna Singh
National Account Manager, Steve Faggard

Vice President Communications, Stanfield Kim
Vice President, Peter Martin
Vice President General Manager, Jackie Hebert
Vice President Of Membership, Yolanda Peria
Vice President Global Manufacturing, Brant Fish
Vice President Operations, Jill Seal
Vice President, Jose Velazquez
Vice President, David Brewster
Vice President, Maud Faulmann
Vice President, Peter Fung
Vice President, Richard Kirk
Vice President, Hugo Velasco
Vice President North America, Peter Roden
National Account Manager, Bryan Kempf
Canadian Area Vice President, Bob Bradbury
Vice President Business Development Portfolio
  Management, Martin (Marti) Donohue
Vice President, Brian Edgar
Vice President Finance, Stephen (Steve) Farrand
Vice President Of Collections, John Randall
Executive Vice President, Sandy Cab
Vice President, Stephen Switzer
Vice President, Girish Desai
Vice President Gulf Of Mexico Business Unit,
  Melody Meyer
Executive Vice President Global Downstream,
  Patricia (Pat) Woertz
Vice President Finance, Brenda Young
Vice President Public Sector Sales Western
  Region, Tim Veale
Vice President, Nathan Kuhle
National Account Manager, Marcella Love
Vice President of Business Development, Alicia
  Boutan
Vice President, J J Miller
Executive Vice President Technology and
  Services, James (Jamie) Blackwell
Vice President Human Resources Medical and
  Security, Joe Laymon
Executive Vice President Downstream and
  Chemicals, Mike Wirth
Vice President and Comtroller, Matthew (Matt)
  Foehr
Vice President Information Technology, Barb
  Burger
Vice Chairman Of The Board, Glenn F Tilton
Board Member, Teresa Brown
Board Member, Thomas (Thom) Hebert
Secretary, Tim Brown
Board Member, David Minor
Board Member, Lisa Nelson
Assistant TREASURER Corporate Strategic and
  Financing, Robert (Bob) Gordan
Freelance Writer And Secretary, Jan Steegstra
Treasurer and Director, Brady Pierce
Board Member, Karen Kubenka
Board Member, Olivier Andrieux
Pac Treasurer, Lydia Wylie
Board Member, Thomas Gottseger
Secretary, H Xun
Treasurer, M Ring
Auditors: PricewaterhouseCoopers LLP

LOCATIONS

HQ: Chevron Corporation
  6001 Bollinger Canyon Road, San Ramon, CA 94583-
  2324
Phone: 925 842-1000   Fax: 925 894-6017
Web: www.chevron.com

2014 Sales

	$ mil.	% of total
US	103,243	40
International	146,186	56
Equity income and others	11,476	4
Adjustments	(48935)	-
Total	211,970	100

PRODUCTS/OPERATIONS

2014 Sales

	$ mil.	% of total
Downstream	177,846	68
Upstream	69,825	27
Equity income and others	11,476	4
Other	1,758	1
Adjustments	(48935)	-
Total	211,970	100

Selected Mergers and Acquisitions

COMPETITORS

Anadarko Petroleum	Koch Industries Inc.
BP	PEMEX
ConocoPhillips	PETROBRAS
Devon Energy	Petrleos de
Eni	Venezuela
Exxon Mobil	Repsol
Hess Corporation	Royal Dutch Shell
Imperial Oil	TOTAL

HISTORICAL FINANCIALS

Company Type: Public

Income Statement

FYE: December 31

	REVENUE ($ mil.)	NET INCOME ($ mil.)	NET PROFIT MARGIN	EMPLOYEES
12/14	211,970	19,241	9.1%	64,700
12/13	228,848	21,423	9.4%	64,600
12/12	241,909	26,179	10.8%	62,000
12/11	253,706	26,895	10.6%	61,000
12/10	204,928	19,024	9.3%	62,000
Annual Growth	0.8%	0.3%	—	1.1%

2014 Year-End Financials

Debt ratio: 10.46%
Return on equity: 12.65%
Cash ($ mil.): 12,793
Current ratio: 1.32
Long-term debt ($ mil.): 24,028
No. of shares (mil.): 1,879
Dividends
Yield: 3.7%
Payout: 41.5%
Market value ($ mil.): 210,859

	STOCK PRICE ($) FY Close	P/E High/Low	PER SHARE ($) Earnings	Dividends	Book Value
12/14	112.18	13 10	10.14	4.21	82.48
12/13	124.91	11 10	11.09	3.90	77.92
12/12	108.14	9 7	13.32	3.51	70.13
12/11	106.40	8 7	13.44	3.09	61.27
12/10	91.25	10 7	9.48	2.84	52.34
Annual Growth	5.3%	— —	1.7%	10.3%	12.0%

CHS Inc

CHS goes with the grain. The company is a leading publicly traded cooperative marketer of grain oilseed and energy resources in the US. It represents farmers ranchers and co-ops from the Great Lakes to Texas. CHS trades grain and sells farm supplies through its stores to members. The group processes soybeans for use in food and animal feeds and grinds wheat into flour. Through joint ventures and a variety of business segments it sells soybean oil and crop nutrient products and markets grain. CHS also provides insurance financial and risk-management services and operates petroleum refineries to sell Cenex-brand fuels lubricants and other energy products.

HISTORY

To help farmers through the Great Depression the Farmers Union Terminal Association (a grain marketing association formed in 1926) created the Farmers Union Grain Terminal Association (GTA) in 1938. With loans from the Farmers Union Central Exchange (later known as CENEX) and the Farm Credit Association the organization operated a grain elevator in St. Paul Minnesota. By 1939 GTA had 250 grain-producing associations as members.

GTA leased terminals in Minneapolis and Washington and built others in Wisconsin and Montana in the early 1940s. It then took over a Minnesota flour mill and created Amber Milling. GTA also began managing farming insurance provider Terminal Agency. In 1958 the association bought 57 elevators and feed plants from the McCabe Company.

Adding to its operations in 1960 GTA bought the Honeymead soybean plant. The next year the co-op acquired Minnesota Linseed Oil. In 1977 it acquired Jewett & Sherman (later Holsum Foods) which helped transform the company into a provider of jams jellies salad dressings and syrups.

In 1983 GTA combined with North Pacific Grain Growers a Pacific Northwest co-op incorporated in 1929 to form Harvest States Cooperatives. Harvest States grew in the early and mid-1990s by acquiring salad dressing makers Albert's Foods Great American Foods and Saffola Quality Foods; soup stock producer Private Brands; and margarine and dressings manufacturer and distributor Gregg Foods.

The company started a joint venture to operate the Ag States Agency agricultural insurance company in 1995. The next year the co-op's Holsum Foods division and Mitsui & Co.'s edible oils unit Wilsey Foods merged to form Ventura Foods a distributor of margarines oils spreads and other food products.

Harvest States merged in 1998 with Minnesota-based CENEX a 16-state agricultural supply co-op that had been founded in 1931 as Farmers Union Central Exchange. (Among CENEX's major operations was a farm inputs services marketing and processing joint venture with dairy cooperative Land O'Lakes formed in 1987.) CENEX CEO Noel Estenson took the helm of the resulting co-op Cenex Harvest States Cooperatives which soon formed a petroleum joint venture called Country Energy with Farmland Industries.

CHS members rejected a proposed merger with Farmland Industries in 1999. Also that year Cenex/Land O'Lakes Agronomy (it became Agriliance in 2000 when Farmland Industries joined the joint venture) bought Terra Industries' $1.7 billion distribution business (400 farm supply stores seed and chemical distribution operations partial ownership of two chemical plants).

CHS bought the wholesale propane marketing operations of Williams Companies in 2000 and the co-op paid $14 million for tortilla and tortilla chip maker Sparta Foods. Additionally Estenson retired that year and company president John Johnson took over as CEO. CHS launched an agricultural e-commerce site (Rooster.com) in conjunction with Cargill and DuPont in 2000. The site was shut down the next year however because of a lack of funds. Also in 2001 the cooperative became the full owner of Country Energy by purchasing Farmland Industries' share.

In 2002 CHS acquired Agway's Grandin North Dakota-based sunflower business and formed a wheat-milling joint venture (Horizon Milling) with Cargill. In 2003 the company changed its name from Cenex Harvest States Cooperatives to CHS Inc. and began trading on the NASDAQ. It used the proceeds from the stock offering to repay its short-term debts.

In 2004 CHS purchased all of bankrupt Farmland Industries' ownership of Agriliance thus giving CHS a 50% ownership of Agriliance (with Land O'Lakes owning the other 50%). With an eye to this growing energy sector CHS acquired a 28% ownership of ethanol producer and marketer US BioEnergy Corporation in 2005. Also that year it sold off its Mexican foods business and sold 81% of its 20% ownership of crop-nutrient manufacturer CF Industries in an initial public offering.

CHS and Land O'Lakes realigned the businesses of their 50-50 joint venture Agriliance in 2007 with CHS acquiring its crop-nutrients wholesale-products business and Land O'Lakes acquiring the crop-protection products business. Canadian ag cooperative La Coop fédérée purchased Agriliance's retail agronomy operation the following year. Adding to its lubricants offerings in 2007 the company acquired two Minnesota companies: Nor-Lakes Services Midwest and The Farm-Oyl Company. In 2008 it sold off all its remaining shares of CF.

Recognizing the growing demand for soy-based food products and in turn to increase shareholder value the company in 2008 acquired Legacy Foods maker of Ultra Soy and TSP brands of textured soybean products for use by both human food and pet food manufacturers. Legacy's operations are overseen by CHS's oilseed processing division.

On the energy front CHS became the sole owner of Provista Renewable Fuels Marketing in 2008 by purchasing US BioEnergy's 50% interest in the biofuels maker. (VeraSun Energy bought out US BioEnergy later that year.

In 2009 CHS acquired Winona River & Rail including 90000 tons of dry-fertilizer storage capacity a dedicated river dock and a 65-car railroad track capacity. The acquisition of the Minnesota operations bolstered the company's storage capacity and rail access in the midwestern and upper Mississippi River regions. Later that year it formed a joint venture with Russia's farm operation Agrico Group (called ACG) in order to manage the export and worldwide marketing of its wheat and feed grains. In turn it gave CHS access to the Russian grain market and improved its ability to serve its global customers.

Also in 2009 CHS formed another of its joint ventures this time at home. It joined with Nebraska's Central Valley Ag Cooperative (CVA) to form Advanced Energy Fuels to provide customers with an industry-leading fuel delivery system.

EXECUTIVES

EVP and COO Energy and Foods, Jay D. Debertin, age 55, $628,524 total compensation
President and CEO, Carl M. Casale, age 54, $960,600 total compensation
EVP Business Solutions, Lisa Zell, age 47
EVP Country Operations, Lynden E. Johnson, age 55
EVP and COO Ag Business and Enterprise Strategy, Shirley Cunningham, age 54
EVP and CFO, Timothy Skidmore, age 53, $459,000 total compensation
VP Enterprise Marketing and Communications, Beth LaBreche
Vice President Propane, Darin Hunoff
Vice President And General Manager, Roger Baker
Senior Vice President Oilseed Processing, Dennis Wendland
First Vice Chairman, Dennis Carlson, age 54
Director, David Bielenberg, age 65
Second Vice Chairman, Steve Fritel, age 60
Auditors: PricewaterhouseCoopers LLP

LOCATIONS

HQ: CHS Inc
   5500 Cenex Drive, Inver Grove Heights, MN 55077
Phone: 651 355-6000
Web: www.chsinc.com

PRODUCTS/OPERATIONS

2014 Sales

	% of total
Ag	66
Energy	33
Others	1
Adjustments	-
Total	**100**

Selected Operations

Ag business
   Grain exporter
   Grain merchandising in Argentina
   Grain merchandising in Europe
   Grain merchandising in Spain
   Grain procurement and merchandising in Russia
   Grain procurement and merchandising in Ukraine
   Retail distribution of agronomy products
   Soybean procurement in Brazil
Corporate and Other
   Finance company
   Insurance agency
   Insurance brokerage
   Risk management products broker
Energy
   Crude oil transportation
   Finished product transportation
   Petroleum refining
Processing
   Food manufacturing and distribution
   Wheat milling in Canada
   Wheat milling in US

COMPETITORS

ACH Food Companies	Helena Chemical
ADM	JR Simplot
Ag Processing Inc.	Koch Industries Inc.
Agrium	Land O' Lakes Purina
AmeriGas Partners	Feed
Andersons	Louis Dreyfus Group
BP	Marathon Petroleum
Bartlett and Company	Marzetti
Bunge Limited	Mondelez International
C.F. Sauer	Mosaic Company
CF Industries	Nestl©
CGC	Riceland Foods
CITGO	Ridley Inc.
Cargill	Scoular
Columbia Grain	Shell Oil Products
ConAgra	Smucker
ConocoPhillips	U.S. Venture
Dakota Growers	US Soy
ExxonMobil Chemical	Unilever NV
Ferrellgas Partners	Valero Energy
Flint Hills	Western Petroleum
GROWMARK	Whole Harvest Foods
Gavilon Group	Wilbur-Ellis

HISTORICAL FINANCIALS

Company Type: Public

Income Statement

FYE: August 31

	REVENUE ($ mil.)	NET INCOME ($ mil.)	NET PROFIT MARGIN	EMPLOYEES
08/15	34,582	781	2.3%	12,511
08/14	42,664	1,081	2.5%	11,824
08/13	44,479	992	2.2%	10,716
08/12	40,599	1,260	3.1%	10,216
08/11	36,915	961	2.6%	9,562
Annual Growth	**(1.6%)**	**(5.1%)**	**—**	**7.0%**

2015 Year-End Financials

Debt ratio: 17.05%—
Return on equity: 11.07%
Cash ($ mil.): 1,226
Current ratio: 1.52
Long-term debt ($ mil.): 1,260
Dividends
Yield: 5.0%
Payout: —
Market value ($ mil.): —

	STOCK PRICE ($) FY Close	P/E High/Low	PER SHARE ($) Earnings	Dividends	Book Value
08/15	27.28	— —	(0.00)	1.34	(0.00)
Annual Growth	—		—	—	—

Cigna Corp

With a significant position in the US health insurance market CIGNA covers some 14.5 million Americans with its various medical plans. The firm's offerings include PPO HMO point-of-service (POS) indemnity and consumer-directed products as well as specialty coverage in the form of dental vision pharmacy and behavioral health plans. It also sells group accident life and disability insurance. Customers include employers government entities unions Medicare recipients and other groups and individuals in North America. Internationally CIGNA sells life accident and health insurance in parts of Europe and Asia and provides health coverage to expatriate employees of multinational companies. It is being acquired by rival Anthem.

HISTORY

The Insurance Company of North America (INA) was founded in 1792 by Philadelphia businessmen. INA was the US's first stock insurance company and its first marine insurer. It later issued life insurance fire insurance and coverage for the contents of buildings. In 1808 it began using agents outside Pennsylvania. INA grew internationally in the late 1800s appointing agents in Canada as well as in London and Vienna in Europe. It was the first US company to write insurance in China beginning in Shanghai in 1897.

In 1942 INA provided both accident and health insurance for men working on the Manhattan Project which developed the atomic bomb. It introduced the first widely available homeowner coverage in 1950. In 1978 INA bought HMO International which was then the largest publicly owned health maintenance organization in the US. INA merged with Connecticut General in 1982 to form CIGNA.

Connecticut General began selling life insurance in 1865 and health insurance in 1912. It wrote its first group insurance (for the Hartford Courant newspaper) in 1913 and the first individual accident coverage for airline passengers in 1926. In the late 1930s Connecticut General was a leader in developing group medical coverage. The company offered the first group medical coverage for general use in 1952 and in 1964 added group dental insurance.

After the merger CIGNA bought Crusader Insurance (UK 1983; sold 1991) and AFIA (1984). To begin positioning itself as a provider of managed health care the company sold its individual insurance products division to InterContinental Life in 1988 and its Horace Mann Cos. (individual financial services) to an investor group in 1989. To further its goal in 1990 CIGNA bought EQUICOR an HMO started by Hospital Corporation of America (now part of HCA Inc.) and what is now AXA Equitable Life Insurance.

In the early 1990s it began to withdraw from the personal property/casualty business to focus on small and midsized commercial clients in the US cutting sales overseas and combining them with life and health operations. It also exited such areas as airline insurance and surety bonds.

CIGNA expanded internationally in the mid-1990s opening a Beijing office in 1993 43 years after its departure from China. The next year the company bought 60% of an Indonesian insurance company. It also acquired 45% of Mediplan a managed health care organization in Mexico.

Reeling from unforeseen environmental liabilities (chiefly related to asbestos) CIGNA in 1995 split its remaining property/casualty business between a healthy segment that continued to write new policies and one for run-off business. Four years later it finally sold these operations (including Cigna Insurance Co. of Europe) to ACE Limited (later renamed Chubb Limited) in order to fund internal growth and acquisitions.

In the late 1990s the company continued to cultivate its health care segment acquiring managed care provider Healthsource in 1997. The company expanded its group benefits operations to India Brazil and Poland; at home it cut its payroll by 1300 in the US to counter rising costs. The company sold its domestic individual life insurance and annuity business in 1998 but began offering investment and pension products in Japan in 1999. In 2000 CIGNA settled a federal lawsuit over Medicare billing fraud. It also sold its reinsurance businesses that year to a subsidiary of Swiss Reinsurance Company while continuing to maintain some previous reinsurance policies on a runoff basis.

EXECUTIVES

Chief Medical Officer, Alan M. Muney, age 62
EVP Human Resources and Services, John M. Murabito, age 57, $592,250 total compensation
EVP and Global CIO, Mark L. Boxer, age 56
President and CEO, David M. Cordani, age 49, $1,125,185 total compensation
President U.S. Commercial Markets and Global Health Care Operations, Matthew G. (Matt) Manders, age 53, $585,667 total compensation
President Cigna-HealthSpring, Herbert A. (Herb) Fritch, age 65, $1,000,000 total compensation
EVP and General Counsel, Nicole S. Jones, age 44, $545,065 total compensation
EVP and CFO, Thomas A. (Tom) McCarthy, age 58, $637,037 total compensation
President International Markets, Jason D. Sadler, age 46, $554,977 total compensation
EVP and Global Chief Marketing Officer, Lisa R. Bacus, age 50
President Tennessee Market, Greg Allen, age 45
CEO Middle East and North Africa (Mena), Howard Gough
Vice President Sales and Business Development, Robert (Bob) Matura
Vice President Corporate Communications At Cigna, Jon Sandberg
Vice President National Account Executive, Jean Chadbourne
Vice President, Colin M Hill
Vice President Sales, Sean Hughes
Assistant Vice President, Rosemary Sullivan
Senior Vice President, Jack Wright
Vice President Information Technology, Gerald Sweeney
Vice President, Tom Garvey
Vice President Pharmaceutical Contracting, Alex Krikorian
Vice President, Marc Wiersma
Vice President, Judy Chechuck

Vice President, Jim Dwyer
Senior Vice President Services Operations, DavidChristian Ruff
Vice President, Lisa Kimbrough
Vice President Product Management, Meg Woolley
Vice President Talent Optimization, Charlene Parsons
Vice President, Carol Bafford
Vice President Supplier Account Management, Rob Johnson
Vice President National Accounts Dental, Karen Wever
Assistant Vice President Provider Contracting, Richard (Dick) White
Vice President Of Sales, Theresa Hall
Vice President, Antoinette Bonacci
Vice President, Sarah Portugal
Vice President, Tamika Holmes
Vice President, James Guemple
Vice President, Michelle Bailey
Vice President, Joan Mastropaolo
Vice President, Sylvia Garza
Vice President Information Technology Application Development Cigna Voluntary, Milton Mattox
Vice President, Craig Martin
Vice President, Rachel Salerno
Assistant Vice President Compensation, Edward Miller
Vice President Pharmacy Voluntary Technology, Aaron Crosson
Regional Vice President, Tom Golias
Vice President Sales and Account Management, Ron Jordan
Vice President, Lynn Withrow
Vice President, Tony Sumner
Vice President, Lynn Rossitto
Vice President, Phyllis Petro
Vice President, John Palmieri
Vice President, Don Falkenstine
Assistant Vice President Of Clinical Operation, Jeffrey (Jeff) Nielsen
Vice President, Angel Burrage
Vice President, Jana Walker
Vice President, John Clark
Vice President, Bob McNamara
Vice President National Account Executive, Melanie McCoy
Vice President Global Internet Strategy Leader, William Gagnon
Medical Director, Ramnik Singh
Vice President, Deserea Bullock
Vice President Business Development, Mike Greer
Vice President, Monica Johnson
Vice President, Toni Hopson
Vice President, Linda Toolen
Vice President, Sue Register
Vice President, David Harman
Medical Director, Hundt John
Vice President Global Marketing Customer Relationship Management, Michele Paige
Vice President National Accounts, Alan Gates
Vice President, Joe Turgeon
Vice President Client Consulting and Analytics, Brent Mulberry
Senior Vice President, Ian Glew
Assistant Vice President Global Storage And Backup Engineer, Anthony Szwankowski
Vice President, Alan Carkner
Vice President National Accounts, Steve Gallacher
Vice President Of Sales, David Rather
Senior Vice President And Chief Actuary Cigna Supplemental Benefits, Tracy Maples
Senior Vice President And Associate Chief Counsel, Teresa Jordan
Vice President National Accounts, Michael Conrad
Vice President, Sanjiv Awasthi
Assistant Vice President Product Management, Craig Iredell

Vice President Network Management San Antonio Tx Markets, David (Dave) Dupree
Vice President Regional Sales GA and AL, Kirk Erickson
Domain Architect Avice President, Michelle (Mitch) Zaremskas
Assistant Vice President Operational Effectivness, Kevin Hutt
Vice President Service Operations Claims, Tom Philibotte
Vice President National Segment Pharmacy Go to Market Lead, Tamara Marshall-Igunbor
Vice President National Accounts Market Leader, Bryan Holgerson
Vice President consumer Health Engagement, Joan Kennedy
Vice President Public Policy, William (Bill) Hoagland
Vice President and Chief Accounting Officer, Mary Hoeltzel
Vice President, Janice Fleshman
Vice President Sales and Account Management, Matt Alberico
Vice President Information Management, J Oates
Vice President Strategy and Marketing, Thor Kayeum
Vice President Actuary, Scott D Schneider
Vice President Group and Voluntary Products, David (Dave) Underhill
Assistant Vice President Network Operations, Maryanne Bourdier
Vice President Information Strategy and Solutions, Daniel (Dan) Carmody
RVP Network Contracting, Susan (Sue) Dennis-Buss
Assistant Vice President Delivery System Innovation and Collaboration, Conway Brew
Chairman, Isaiah (Ike) Harris, age 62
Auditors: PricewaterhouseCoopers LLP

LOCATIONS

HQ: Cigna Corp
900 Cottage Grove Road, Bloomfield, CT 06002
Phone: 860 226-6000   **Fax:** 860 226-6741
Web: www.cigna.com

2014 Sales

	% of total
US	90
Other countries	10
Total	**100**

PRODUCTS/OPERATIONS

2014 Sales

	$ mil.	% of total
Global health care	27,290	79
Global disability & life	3,970	11
Global supplemental benefits	3,005	9
Other operations	510	1
Realized investment gains	154	-
Corporate	(15)	-
Total	**34,914**	**100**

Selected Products and Services

Health care
  Behavioral health care benefits
  CareAllies (disease management and health advocacy)
  CIGNA Choice Fund (consumer-directed products)
  CIGNA Tel-Drug (mail order pharmacy)
  Dental insurance
  Managed care health plans (HMO PPO POS)
  Medicare Part D (prescription drug coverage)
  Prescription drug coverage
  Stop-loss coverage
  Voluntary plans
Disability and life
  Group disability insurance
  Group term life insurance
  Leave management services
  Workers' compensation case management
International
  Expatriate insurance
  Life accident and supplemental health insurance

AEGON
AIG
AMERIGROUP
AXA
Aetna
Allianz
Allstate
Anthem
Aon
BUPA
Blue Cross
CNA Financial
CVS
Centene
Coventry Health Care
Express Scripts
Health Net
Highmark

Humana
ING
John Hancock Financial
  Services
Kaiser Foundation
  Health Plan
MassMutual
MetLife
Molina Healthcare
New York Life
Northwestern Mutual
Principal Financial
Prudential
The Hartford
UnitedHealth Group
Unum Group
WellCare Health Plans

HISTORICAL FINANCIALS

Company Type: Public

Income Statement
FYE: December 31

	ASSETS ($ mil.)	NET INCOME ($ mil.)	INCOME AS % OF ASSETS	EMPLOYEES
12/14	55,896	2,102	3.8%	37,200
12/13	54,336	1,476	2.7%	36,500
12/12	53,734	1,623	3.0%	35,800
12/11	51,047	1,327	2.6%	31,400
12/10	45,682	1,345	2.9%	30,600
Annual Growth	5.2%	11.8%	—	5.0%

2014 Year-End Financials

Debt ratio: 8.95%
Return on equity: 19.70%
Cash ($ mil.): 1,420
Current ratio: —
Long-term debt ($ mil.): —

No. of shares (mil.): 259
Dividends
Yield: 0.0%
Payout: 0.5%
Market value ($ mil.): 26,682

	STOCK PRICE ($) FY Close	P/E High/Low		PER SHARE ($) Earnings	Dividends	Book Value
12/14	102.91	13	9	7.83	0.04	41.55
12/13	87.48	17	10	5.18	0.04	38.35
12/12	53.46	10	7	5.61	0.04	34.18
12/11	42.00	11	7	4.84	0.04	29.22
12/10	36.66	8	6	4.89	0.04	24.44
Annual Growth	29.4%	—	—	12.5%	(0.0%)	14.2%

Cincinnati Financial Corp.

Cincinnati Financial Corporation (CFC) serves up a whole menu of insurance —plain and simple or with extras if you like. The company's flagship Cincinnati Insurance (operating through four property/casualty subsidiaries) sells commercial property liability excess and surplus auto bond and fire insurance; personal lines include homeowners auto and liability products. Subsidiary Cincinnati Life sells life disability income and annuities. The company's CFC Investment subsidiary provides commercial financing leasing and real estate services to its independent insurance agents. Its CSU Producers Resources offers insurance brokerage services to independent agencies. The Schiff family formed CFC in 1968.

Operations

CFC operates through five segments: Commercial Lines Insurance Personal Lines Insurance Excess and Surplus Lines Insurance Life Insurance and Investments. Commercial Lines Insurance which accounts for about 60% of total sales provides coverages including commercial property/casualty workers' compensation and management liability. Personal Lines Insurance accounting for some 20% of sales writes personal automobile and homeowner products.

Subsidiaries include standard property/casualty insurers Cincinnati Casualty Company and Cincinnati Indemnity Company Cincinnati Life Insurance Company and Cincinnati Specialty Underwriters Insurance Company.

Geographic Reach

CFC markets its policies in 49 states the District of Columbia and Puerto Rico. The company writes some 20% of its business in Ohio and is strong in Illinois Indiana and Pennsylvania. Its commercial lines segment targets primarily small to mid-sized businesses. CFC has tied its growth to expanding the territories in which it markets and increasing the number of new agencies with which it strikes new relationships.

Sales and Marketing

The company maintains a force of some 1300 field associates who provide local service to some 1460 distributing independent agencies and policy holders.

Cincinnati Insurance launched its first-ever national television ad in 2015.

Financial Performance

CFC revenue which has been on the rise for the past five years rose 9% to $4.9 billion in 2014 on higher earned premiums fee revenues and investment earnings. Increased renewal rates for commercial and property/casualty products as well as price increases led to the growth as did higher new business written premiums. Additionally gains in excess and surplus lines and life insurance sales contributed to the rise.

Due to the company's growing revenues net income has also been on the rise. In 2014 it increased 2% to $525 million. Cash flow from operations increased 10% to $873 million that year.

Strategy

Going forward the company plans to wring more profit out of policies by raising deductibles and conducting more site inspections of properties it insures. CFC also works on developing new products and helping its independent and captive agents better market existing policies. To further broaden its operations the company works toward deepening its penetration into each market it serves. For example it has been introducing workers' compensation coverage in more states.

Cincinnati Insurance is also expanding its products and services for wealthy individuals. It plans to launch these offerings in additional states including Texas California Massachusetts and New Jersey.

HISTORY

Jack Schiff spent three years with the Travelers Company before he joined the Navy in WWII. He returned to Cincinnati to start his own independent insurance agency in 1946 and was joined by his younger brother Robert; both were Ohio State graduates whose affection for the Buckeyes led them in later years to close company banquets with the school fight song. The brothers incorporated Cincinnati Insurance with $200000 from investors.

Under Harry Turner the company's first president the company offered property/casualty insurance to small businesses and homeowners through its network of agents. By 1956 the company had spread into neighboring Kentucky and Indiana. During the next decade Cincinnati Insurance expanded its products and network adding auto burglary and commercial all-risk lines and enlisting agents throughout the Midwest.

In 1963 Turner took the chairman's seat and Jack Schiff became president introducing a more aggressive leadership style. In 1969 the company reorganized and went public forming Cincinnati Financial Corporation as a holding company for the insurance operation. CFC used the money to pay off debts and buy new businesses forming two subsidiaries: CFC Investment Company in 1970 to deal in commercial real estate and financing; and Queen City Indemnity (later named The Cincinnati Casualty Company) in 1972 to offer direct-bill personal policies.

By 1973 operations included The Life Insurance Company of Cincinnati Queen City Indemnity and fellow Cincinnati giant Inter-Ocean Insurance Company. That year Jack Schiff added CEO to his title.

CFC continued to grow throughout the 1970s with a new emphasis on independent investments. In 1982 Cincinnati Financial veteran Robert Morgan became president and CEO. The company's conservative roots and investment base helped it shake off the early-1980s recession and a string of natural disasters that left many other insurers dangling in the wind.

Also during the 1980s the company started to shift its focus from personal to commercial lines. In 1988 it reorganized its life insurance subsidiaries under the Cincinnati Life banner and formed The Cincinnati Indemnity Company to offer workers' compensation and personal insurance. In 1998 a string of storms (reminiscent of others earlier in the decade) dampened the company's earnings.

EXECUTIVES

Senior Vice President of Operations, Timothy (Tim) Timmel

Svp Commercial Lines Cincinnati Insurance, Charles (Chas) Stoneburner

President CEO and Director, Steven J. Johnston, age 55, $922,846 total compensation

Vice President Commercial, Anthony Henn

EVP and Chief Insurance Officer Cincinnati Insurance, Jacob F. Scherer, age 62, $845,942 total compensation

President and COO Cincinnati Life Insurance, David H. Popplewell, age 71, $376,750 total compensation

SVP and CIO Cincinnati Insurance Company, John S. Kellington, age 53

SVP and Chief Claims Officer Cincinnati Insurance, Martin J. Mullen, age 59

SVP and Chief Risk Officer Cincinnati Insurance, Teresa C. Cracas, age 49

SVP CFO and Treasurer, Michael J. (Mike) Sewell, age 51, $753,658 total compensation

SVP Chief Investment Officer Assistant Secretary and Assistant Treasurer, Martin F. Hollenbeck, age 55, $617,769 total compensation

Assistant Vice President Bond and Executive Risk, Ted W Doughman

Vice President, Matt Laws

Vice President, Craig Forrester

National Sales Manager, Doug Mundt

Assistant Vice President Marketing Director, Mark McBeath

Vice President Commercial Lines, Mark Wietmarschen

Assistant Vice President For Education, Bradleybrad Delaney

Vice President Of Personal Lines, Stephen Leibel

Assistant Vice President, Bill Clevidence

Svp Personal Insurance, Will Van Den Heuvel

Vice President Personnel Property Casualty Insurance Subsidiar, Greg Ziegler
Vice President, Tom Scheid
Vice President Data Management, Carol Oler
Vice President And Manager Target Markets, Ronald (Ron) Klimkowski
Vice President Marketing, Mike Terrell
Assistant Vice President, David Hartkemeier
Legal Secretary, Rebecca Alexander
Vice President Sales And Marketing, Duane Swanson
Vice President Of Business Development, Phil Howard
Vice President Corporate Accounting The Cincinnati Insurance C, Todd Pendery
Senior Vice President Chief Underwriter The Cincinnati Life Insurance Company, Brad Behringer
Assistant Vice President Director of Worksite Marketing, Eric Taylor
Vice President nformation Technology, Bill Geir
Vice President Field Claims, Ron Robinson
Senior Vice President and Director Cincinnati Ins Co, Larry Plum
Legal Secretary, Amanda Turner
Vice President Commercial Lines Director of Underwriting, Rick Ferris
Chairman, Kenneth W. (Ken) Stecher, age 68
Secretary field Claims, Jack Kelley
Assistant Secretary, Mark Rutherford
Secretary Life and Health Claims Cincinnati Life Insurance Company, Ann Binzer
Assistant Secretary Information Technology, Michael (Mel) Hingsbergen
Assistant Secretary And Underwriting Manager Contract Surety, Nick Wright
Assistant Secretary Information Technology The Cincinnati Life Insurance Company, Michelle (Mitch) Kyle
Assistant Secretary Information Technology The Cin, Michelle (Mitch) Kye
Secretary, Julie Sweeney
Secretary, William Gregory
Secretary of Special Investigations Unit, George Grossenbaugh
Assistant Secretary Bond And Executive R, Scott R Boden
Assistant Secretary, Sean Givler
Treasurer, Theresa Hoffer
Auditors: Deloitte & Touche LLP

LOCATIONS

HQ: Cincinnati Financial Corp.
6200 S. Gilmore Road, Fairfield, OH 45014-5141
Phone: 513 870-2000
Web: www.cinfin.com

PRODUCTS/OPERATIONS

2014 Sales

	$ mil.	% of total
Property/casualty insurance		
Commercial	2,860	58
Personal	1,043	21
Investment income	682	14
Life Insurance	204	4
Excess & surplus insurance	148	3
Other income	8	-
Total	**4,945**	**100**

Selected Subsidiaries

CFC Investment Company
CSU Producer Resources Inc.
The Cincinnati Insurance Company
  The Cincinnati Casualty Company
  The Cincinnati Indemnity Company
  The Cincinnati Life Insurance Company
  The Cincinnati Specialty Underwriters Insurance Company

COMPETITORS

Allied Group	Ohio Casualty
American Financial Group	OneBeacon
CNA Financial	Progressive Corporation
Erie Indemnity	Selective Insurance
Farmers Group	The Hartford
Great American Insurance Company	Travelers Companies
Indiana Insurance	Westfield Insurance
	Zurich American

HISTORICAL FINANCIALS

Company Type: Public

Income Statement
FYE: December 31

	ASSETS ($ mil.)	NET INCOME ($ mil.)	INCOME AS % OF ASSETS	EMPLOYEES
12/14	18,753	525	2.8%	4,305
12/13	17,662	517	2.9%	4,163
12/12	16,548	421	2.5%	4,057
12/11	15,668	166	1.1%	4,067
12/10	15,095	377	2.5%	4,060
Annual Growth	**5.6%**	**8.6%**	**—**	**1.5%**

2014 Year-End Financials

Debt ratio: 4.67%
Return on equity: 8.30%
Cash ($ mil.): 591
Current ratio: —
Long-term debt ($ mil.): —

No. of shares (mil.): 163
Dividends
  Yield: 3.4%
  Payout: 60.6%
Market value ($ mil.): 8,485

	STOCK PRICE ($) FY Close	P/E High/Low	PER SHARE ($) Earnings	Dividends	Book Value
12/14	51.83	16 14	3.18	1.76	40.15
12/13	52.37	17 12	3.12	1.66	37.24
12/12	39.16	16 12	2.57	1.62	33.45
12/11	30.46	34 24	1.02	1.61	31.20
12/10	31.69	14 11	2.31	1.59	31.06
Annual Growth	**13.1%**	**— —**	**8.3%**	**2.6%**	**6.6%**

Cisco Systems, Inc.

Cisco Systems routes packets and routs competitors with equal efficiency. Dominating the market for Internet Protocol-based networking equipment the company makes and sells routers servers security devices Internet conferencing systems set-top boxes and other networking equipment to businesses and government agencies. The company also provides consulting services and offers products for a growing array of household industrial medical and other gadgets that connect to the Internet. Cisco sells its products primarily to large enterprises and telecommunications service providers but it also markets products designed for small businesses. Cisco Systems was founded in 1984 by Stanford University graduates.

Operations

The meat-and-potatoes of Cisco is its switching equipment which generates 30% of the company's revenue. Its next-generation networking routing gear accounts for 16% of revenue. Some 23% of revenue comes from Cisco's services business. In 2015 (ended July) the company's fastest growing area was its data center products up 22% for the year. Cisco has experienced momentum in data center and cloud environments with orders from current customers building out their data centers as well as orders from new customers.

Geographic Reach

While the Americas is Cisco's largest market accounting for some 60% of its sales about half its employees reside outside of the US. Cisco's US headquarters is in San Jose California. It also has regional headquarters in Amsterdam and Singapore. Cisco has a Globalization Center East campus in Bangalore India. The company has other significant operations in Belgium China France Germany India Israel Italy Japan Norway and the UK.

Financial Performance

Cisco's revenue rebounded 4% higher in 2015 (ended July) to $49 billion compared to $47 million in fiscal 2014 (which was a 3% drop from 2013). Cisco saw revenue gains in the Americas segment due to higher sales to the US federal government and stronger sales to state and local governments.

The revenue increase drove a 14% rise in net income which was $8.9 billion for 2015.

Cash flow from operations closed out 2015 at $12.5 billion which was slightly stronger than that of 2014.

Strategy

Cisco entered into a deep partnership with Ericsson the biggest telecom equipment maker. The companies intend to cooperate to develop products and services in areas such as 5G cloud computing Internet protocol and the Internet of Things. Their goal is to add $1 billion in revenue for each company by 2018. With their strategic partnership announced in 4Q 2015 the companies will cooperate on developing networks through reference architectures and joint development systems-based management and control a broad reseller agreement and collaboration in key emerging market segments. The companies will work together specifically on virtualization technologies and software-defined networks. In Ericsson Cisco gets a partner with complementary strengths in technologies and in markets around the world.

The deal helps Cisco counter the merger of Alcatel-Lucent and Nokia which if concluded would be the second biggest provider (Huawei is #1) of telecom equipment.

Cisco's dominant market position in switches and routing and aggressive pricing strategy have helped it to gain market share from rivals such as Juniper Networks. In addition to the core routing and switching products Cisco is developing products and services for data center software security and the cloud. It is restructuring engineering and sales units to foster a more comprehensive view toward developing and marketing products. Geographically the company is investing in emerging markets such as Russia China Brazil Mexico and India.

The company adheres to an aggressive growth strategy making numerous acquisitions in high-growth segments such as cloud and mobile.

Mergers and Acquisitions

Cisco is actively acquisitive company bolstering its offerings with purchases both large and small.

In 2015 Cisco acquired real-time communications startup Tropo. Cisco intends to use Tropo's technology to provide a user-friendly collaboration platform. The company added another collaboration technology in late 2015 with its $700 million purchase of Acano based in the UK. Acano will become part of Cisco's Collaboration Technology Group.

In another 2015 acquisition Cisco bought OpenStack provider Piston Cloud Computing to help accelerate the development and capabilities of Cisco Intercloud Services.

Cisco added to its security offerings with its acquisition of Lancope for $425 million in 2015. The companies have worked together but with the acquisition they can integrate their products more tightly with the goal to detect networks threats faster.

In mid-2014 it paid $175 million for Tail-f Systems a Swedish company that provides multi-vendor network service orchestration for traditional and virtual networks. The acquisition will boost Cisco's cloud virtualization offerings.

Cisco also acquired Metacloudwhich deploys and operates private clouds for organizations. Metacloud's OpenStack-based cloud platform will push Cisco's strategy to build the world's largest global Intercloud.

HISTORY

Early History

Cisco Systems was founded by Stanford University husband-and-wife team Leonard Bosack and Sandra Lerner and three colleagues in 1984. Bosack developed technology to link his computer lab's network with his wife's network in the graduate business school. Anticipating a market for networking devices Bosack and Lerner mortgaged their house bought a used mainframe put it in their garage and got friends and relatives to work for deferred pay. They sold their first network router in 1986. Originally targeting universities the aerospace industry and the government the company in 1988 expanded its marketing to include large corporations. Short of cash Cisco turned to venture capitalist Donald Valentine of Sequoia Capital who bought a controlling stake and became chairman. He hired John Morgridge of laptop maker GRiD Systems as president and CEO.

Cisco whose products had a proven track record had a head start as the market for network routers opened up in the late 1980s. Sales leapt from $1.5 million in 1987 to $28 million in 1989.

The company went public in 1990. That year Morgridge fired Lerner with whom he had clashed and Bosack quit. The couple sold their stock for about $200 million giving most to favorite causes including animal charities and a Harvard professor looking for extraterrestrials.

With competition increasing Cisco began expanding through acquisitions. Purchases included networking company Crescendo Communications (1993) and Ethernet switch maker Kalpana (1994). Cisco also surpassed the $1 billion revenue mark in 1994. In 1995 EVP John Chambers succeeded Morgridge as president and CEO; Morgridge became chairman (and Valentine vice chairman).

EXECUTIVES

Vp Application Delivery Business Unit, George Kurian, age 49

Svp Worldwide Partner Organization, Bruce Klein

Vice President of Sales Strategy and Planning, Inder Sidhu

EVP and Chief Development Officer, Pankaj S. Patel, $700,000 total compensation

EVP Operations Processes and Systems, Randy Pond, age 61, $815,385 total compensation

SVP Enterprise Products and Solutions, Robert (Rob) Soderbery

EVP Industry Solutions and Chief Globalization Officer, Wim Elfrink, age 63, $729,169 total compensation

SVP and CTO Platforms and Solutions., Zorawar Biri Singh

CEO and Director, Charles H. (Chuck) Robbins, age 49

President Asia Pacific, Owen Chan

SVP and Chief Operations, Rebecca J. Jacoby

SVP and General Manager Collaboration Technology Group, Rowan M. Trollope

President Cisco Capital, Kristine A. (Kris) Snow, age 55

SVP Services, Joe Cozzolino

SVP Cisco Consulting Services, Martin McPhee

President Latin America Theater, Jordi Botifoll

President Smart+Connected Communities and Deputy Chief Globalization Officer, Anil Menon

SVP Cloud Infrastructure and Managed Services Organization, Faiyaz Shahpurwala

SVP and General Manager Cisco Security Solutions, Bryan Palma

EVP and CFO, Kelly A. Kramer

SVP Chief Technology and Strategy Officer, Hilton Romanski

SVP and CIO, Guillermo Diaz

SVP and Chief Marketing Officer, Karen Walker

SVP and Chief Digital Officer, Kevin Bandy

Svp And General Manager Service Provider Video Technology Group, Jesper Andersen

Vice President Customer Advocacy, Hans Hwang

Svp And General Manager Collaboration Technology Group, Barry O'Sullivan

SVP and Chief Technology Officer Global Government Solutions, Gregory Akers

Vice President Marketing South Florida, Marcelo Weiss

Vice President Worldwide Customer Advocacy, Jay Pederson

Senior Vice President Software Enterprise Networking Group, R Chandrasekaran

Vice President Rcbu, Rick McConnell

Vice President Middle East and Turkey Operat, Mike Weston

Vice President Of Public Relations, Tom Wesselman

Vice President Global Service Provider Segment, Kit Beall

Vice President, Ole Troan

Vice President Technology, Frank Cowell

Vice President Product Management And Product Marketing, John Hanahan

Vice President Finance, Ken Mesuda

Vice President Marketing, Roman Schmid

Vice President General Manager Dial Platforms, Hoss Christensen

Vice President and General Manager Cisco Home Networking, Brett Wingo

Vice President Of Business Development, Mario Mastromattei

Vice President Sales, Hunter Haverty

Vice President Of Service Provider Marketing, Suraj Shetty

Senior Vice President Corporate Controller and Chief Accounting Officer, Prat Bhatt

Area Vice President Us Sales, Tom Wilburn

Vice President of Business Development, Bonnie Yang

Vice President And General Manager Mobile Internet Technology Group, Mike Iandolo

Vice President General Manager Digital Media Systems, Sean Parham

Vice President General Manager Eag, Larry Birenbaum

Vice President For Worldwide Security, George Strowmeyer

Customer Support Engineer VPN, Nehal Naik

Vice President.Strategic Planning, Mark Patterson

Vice President, Bruce Laird

Vice President Canadian Services Operations, Derek Mak

Vpam Small Business Washington DC Maryland Virginia Pennsylvania, Rosemary Campbell

Assistant Vice President us Sales, John (Jack) Shelnutt

Vice President World Wide Financial Operations, Ward Dickson

UK Vice President Technology, Simon Parnall

Vice President Strategic Accounts, Peter (Pete) Lynskey

Data Center VPSS, Lisa Brown

Vice President, Amy Christen

Vice President Marketing, Jim McHugh

Vice President Service Delivery, Rick Hamilton

Vice President And Site Executive, Paul Bosco

Vice President Marketing Manager, Donna Cox

Vice President Of Information Technology, Billot Luc

Vice President of Product Management, Gennady Sirota

S Assistant Vice President And Gm Ip Video Bu, Joe Chow

Vice President Plant, Don McClaughlin

Area Vice President.Sp Sales, Jesper Knutsson

Senior Vice President, David (Dave) Chai

Vice President Manufacturing. Elob, Tony Banta

Vpam Small Business Missouri Iowa Nebraska Iowa Minnesota ND SD Kansas, Derrick Jett

AREA Vice President US Sales, Jim Walsh

Vice President of Mobility, Chris Spain

Regional Vice President Cisco Systems Administrator, Mark Guerrazzi

Vice President and General Manager, Sandeep Vohra

Vice President Of Marketing, Christoph Caspar

Vice President Advanced Services, Flint Brenton

Vice President General Manager Of Otbu, Terry Brown

Vice President Of Webex Connect, David McKnight

Vice President of Engineering, Andy Bechtolsheim

Vice President, Murray Kirk

Vice President of Engineering, Krishna Doddapaneni

Vice President Marketing, Zack Urlocker

Vice President Global Corporate Marketing and Branding, Michele Janes

Linksys Senior Vice President General Manager, Mike Pocock

Vice President of Worldwide Channel Account Managers, Mary Iverson

Vice President of North America Sales, Ken Werner

Vice Presidentproduct Management, Steve Chazin

Area Vice President Us Sales, Georges Antoun

Vice President of Talent, Annmarie Neal

Vice President General Manager Content Switching Tcnlgs, Chin-cheng Wu

Vice President And General Manager Of Network Mana, Bill McVey

Major Vice President Marketing Cisco Systems, Scott Curtis

Vice President Of Engineering, Ayman Sayed

Vpam Small Business Fl South North Carolina South Carolina, Richard Hinkley

Vpss Flexpod, Cesar Hurtado

Vice President of Customer Service and Energy Delivery, Ania Nachajska

Vice President Business Development, Mitch Zenger

Vice President Market Development, Paul Kosac

Vice President Systems Engineering, Michael (Mel) Koons

Area Sales Vice President Central, Mark Houska

Vice President Of Customer Support, Dallas Williams

Vice President Customer Value Chain Management, David Ashley

Vice President Software Engineeting, Richard (Dick) Heaton

Vice President Sales, Clarence Jasin

Vice President Engineering, Steve Phillips

Vice President Federal Operations, Ed McCrossen

Vice President, Randy Harrell

Vice President Customer Value Chain Management, Jeff Devine

Vice President New Business Ventures, Sanjay Pol

Vice President Finance Operations, Debbie Normington

Area Vice President Us Sales, Roxann Swanson

Vice President, Cindy Duquette

Vice Presidentibsg, Richard Cantwell

Vice President Finance, Phil Roush

Senior Vice President and Chief Human Resources Officer, Kathleen A Weslock
Vice President Us Channels, Bob Gault
Vice President Strategy, Inder Singh
Vice President of Business Development, Rick Jansky
Vice President Information Technology Customer Strategy and Success, Lance Perry
Consulting Systems Engineer Northeast Security VPN Cisco Representative, Ken Kaminski
Vice President and General Manager Optical Transport Business Unit, Bill Gartner
Virtual Sales Vpam, Sue Joseph
Vice President Broker, Rajeev Grover
Vice President Human Resources, Tim Grace
Vice President Marketing, Ron Czinski
Bill Swifts Assistant: Vice President of Engineering Crbu Cisco, Stacey Hilton
Vice President Information Technology, Ginna Raahauge
Vice President Engineering Network Software and Systems, Amit S Phadnis
Vice President Of Marketing, Andy Blackburn
Vice President Product Strategy and Development, Jeff Seebeck
Vice President of Software Engineering, Ramesh Bodapati
Vice President Sales, Timothy Hannon
Vice President, Parvesh Sethi
Vice President, Marie Higa
Vice President Sales and Marketing, Leon Baranovsky
Vice President Sales, Jeff Towson
Kfir Pravda IMTC Vice President of Marketing, Cary Bryan
Vice President Engineering and Architecture, Edward (Ed) Haynes
Area Vice President Commercial Sales S, David (Dave) Ruggiero
Senior Vice President General Counsel and Corporate Secretary, Jon Brown
Vice President Subscriber Networks Sector, Robert (Bob) Beebe
Vice President Service Provider Video, Yves Padrines
Vice President Engineering, John Wakerly
Senior Vice President Sales And Marketing, Jacob Verhagen
Vice President Consumer Marketing, Ken Wirt
Major Vice President Marketing Cisco Systems, Mitch Connor
Auditors: PricewaterhouseCoopers LLP

LOCATIONS

HQ: Cisco Systems, Inc.
170 West Tasman Drive, San Jose, CA 95134-1706
Phone: 408 526-4000
Web: www.cisco.com

2015 Sales

	$ mil.	% of total
Americas	29,655	60
Europe the Middle East & Africa	12,322	25
Asia-Pacific region Japan & China	7,184	15
Total	**49,161**	**100**

PRODUCTS/OPERATIONS

2015 Sales

	$ mil.	% of total
Product		
Switching	14,741	30
NGN Routing	7,704	16
Service provider video	3,555	7
Collaboration	4,000	8
Data Center	3,220	7
Wireless	2,542	5
Security	1,747	4
Other	241	-
Service	11,411	23
Total	**49,161**	**100**

Selected Products

Access servers
Blade servers
Cable modems
Cables and cords
Content delivery devices
Customer contact software
Digital video recorders
Ethernet concentrators hubs and transceivers
Interfaces and adapters
Network management software
Networked applications software
Optical platforms
Power supplies
Routers
Security components
Switches
Telephony access systems
Television set-top boxes
Video networking
Virtual private network (VPN) systems
Voice integration applications
Wireless networking

Selected Acquisitions

COMPETITORS

ARRIS	Huawei Technologies
Alcatel-Lucent	IBM
Amazon.com	Juniper Networks
Aruba Networks	LogMeIn
Avaya	MRV Communications
Belden	Meru Networks
Brocade Communications	Microsoft
CA Inc.	Motorola Mobility
Check Point Software	NETGEAR
Ciena	Nokia Siemens Networks
Citrix Systems	Pace
D-Link	Palo Alto Networks
Dell	Polycom
ECI Telecom	Riverbed Technology
Ericsson	Symantec
Extreme Networks	Technicolor
F5 Networks	Tellabs
Fortinet	VMware
HP	ZTE
Harris Corp.	

HISTORICAL FINANCIALS

Company Type: Public

Income Statement

FYE: July 25

	REVENUE ($ mil.)	NET INCOME ($ mil.)	NET PROFIT MARGIN	EMPLOYEES
07/15	49,161	8,981	18.3%	71,833
07/14	47,142	7,853	16.7%	74,042
07/13	48,607	9,983	20.5%	75,049
07/12	46,061	8,041	17.5%	66,639
07/11	43,218	6,490	15.0%	71,825
Annual Growth	**3.3%**	**8.5%**	**—**	**0.0%**

2015 Year-End Financials

Debt ratio: 22.34%—
Return on equity: 15.48%
Cash ($ mil.): 6,877
Current ratio: 3.23
Long-term debt ($ mil.): 21,457

Dividends
 Yield: 0.0%
 Payout: 45.7%
Market value ($ mil.): —

	STOCK PRICE ($) FY Close	P/E High/Low		PER SHARE ($) Earnings	Dividends	Book Value
07/15	28.40	17	13	1.75	0.80	11.74
07/14	25.97	18	13	1.49	0.72	11.09
07/13	25.50	14	8	1.86	0.62	10.97
07/12	15.69	14	9	1.49	0.28	9.68
07/11	15.97	21	13	1.17	0.12	8.69
Annual Growth	**15.5%**	—	—	**10.6%**	**60.7%**	**7.8%**

CIT Group, Inc.

If you haven't heard of CIT Group then you're O-U-T of the proverbial loop. On the big-business landscape for about a century CIT is a financial holding company that offers lending leasing debt restructuring equipment financing and advisory services to small- and mid-sized businesses in such industries as energy healthcare retail communications manufacturing IT services and sports. The company also operates CIT Bank in Utah which offers commercial financing and leasing as well as online deposit products such as CDs. CIT has some $35 billion in assets and serves clients in more than 20 countries.

HISTORY

Company BackgroundHenry Ittleson founded CIT Group as Commercial Credit and Investment Trust in St. Louis in 1908. Initially financing horse-drawn carriages it moved to New York in 1915 as Commercial Investment Trust (CIT) to participate in one of the milestones of modern consumer debt: Its auto financing program launched in collaboration with Studebaker was the first of its kind.

CIT diversified into industrial financing during the 1920s and went public in 1924 on the NYSE. Cars remained a strong focus though: When Ford Motor Co. ran into difficulties in 1933 it sold financing division Universal Credit Corp. to CIT. CIT continued to expand into industrial financing incorporating its industrial business as CIT Financial Corp. in 1942.

During the post-WWII boom CIT began financing manufactured home sales and offering small loans. In 1964 it consolidated factoring operations into Meinhard-Commercial Corp. By the end of the 1960s the firm started to retreat from auto financing focusing instead on industrial leasing factoring and equipment financing.

In 1980 RCA bought CIT seeking to buy financing to develop its other businesses. RCA found the debt from the purchase unwieldy however and sold CIT to Manufacturers Hanover Bank (Manny Hanny) in 1984. The bank bought CIT to expand outside its home state of New York: Though it could not open banks out of state Manny Hanny could still offer financial services through CIT which became The CIT Group in 1986.

Manny Hanny executives tried to bring aggressive management to staid top-heavy CIT. The company sold its Inventory Finance division in 1987 divested the consumer loan business in 1988 and consolidated the Meinhard-Commercial and Manufacturers Hanover factoring units in 1989. By then Manny Hanny was cash-strapped over losses incurred from foreign loans so it sold a 60% stake in CIT to The Dai-Ichi Kangyo Bank of Japan.

CIT gave Dai-Ichi entrée into US financial services and it began expanding CIT's range of services again including equity investment (1990) credit finance (from its purchase of Fidelcor Business Credit in 1991) and venture capital (1992). CIT also reentered the consumer loan market (including home equity lending) with a new Consumer Finance group (1992).

In 1995 Chemical Bank (Manny Hanny's successor; now part of JPMorgan Chase) sold an additional 20% share to Dai-Ichi bumping the Japanese bank's holdings to 80% and arranging to sell its remaining shares to Dai-Ichi. In 1997 instead of Dai-Ichi buying the rest of Chase's shares CIT bought them and spun them off to the public. In 1998 Dai-Ichi reduced its stake.

In 1999 CIT bought Newcourt Credit Group North America's #2 equipment finance and leasing firm; it also bought Heller Financial's commercial services unit. In 2000 the firm worked on integrating Newcourt and sold its Hong Kong consumer finance unit.

Tyco International bought CIT in 2001 renaming the new subsidiary Tyco Capital. Under Tyco's umbrella it sold its manufactured home loan portfolio to Lehman Brothers and recreational vehicle portfolio to Salomon Smith Barney in an effort to exit noncore businesses. Tyco however expanded too far too fast and the next year announced an about-face on its financial services subsidiary deciding to spin off the division and return it to its CIT identity.

Jeff Peek took the reins of the company from longtime chairman and CEO Al Gamper in 2004. CIT Group's Student Loan Xpress unit was one of several companies in the student-lending industry that came under investigation for business practices in 2007. It discontinued its private student loans that year and in 2008 it stopped originating government-guaranteed student loans.

Amid losses the company also exited the consumer finance business to focus on commercial lending. In 2008 it sold its home loan unit to Lone Star Funds and its manufactured housing portfolio to Vanderbilt Mortgage and Finance. The previous year it sold its construction lending unit to Wells Fargo and its 30% stake in Dell Financial Services to Dell.

CIT was hit hard in the economic recession which nearly shut down the credit markets. The company struggled to stay afloat as liquidity levels sank (a situation exacerbated as nervous customers drew on their credit lines). It exited money-losing businesses sold units and secured $3 billion from company bondholders including PIMCO and Oaktree Capital. The company also converted to a bank holding company enabling it to access government bailout funds. Still struggling CIT filed for Chapter 11 in November 2009. The restructuring lasted six weeks and helped the company eliminate more than $10 billion in debt. None of CIT's operating subsidiaries were included in the bankruptcy.

Jeffrey Peek who oversaw CIT's untimely expansion activities stepped down as CEO in early 2010. He was succeeded by John Thain who has also led Merrill Lynch and New York Stock Exchange. No stranger to turning ailing companies around Thain is credited with bringing the NYSE into the modern era with electronic trading. He also merged NYSE with Euronext establishing the first trans-Atlantic exchange.

EXECUTIVES

EVP General Counsel and Secretary, Robert J. (Bob) Ingato, age 54, $406,731 total compensation
Chairman and CEO, John A. Thain, age 59, $1,003,846 total compensation
Co-President CIT Group Inc. and Vice Chairman CIT Bank N.A., Nelson J. Chai, age 50, $752,885 total compensation
Co-President CIT Group Inc. and CEO and President CIT Bank N.A., Joseph M. Otting, age 58
EVP and Head Communications and Government Relations, Margaret D. Tutwiler, age 64
Vice Chairman CIT Group Inc. and Chairman CIT Bank N.A., Steven T. (Steve) Mnuchin, age 52
President CIT Transportation and International Finance, C. Jeffrey (Jeff) Knittel, age 56, $501,923 total compensation
EVP and Chief Administrative Oficer, Andrew T. Brandman, age 45
EVP and CIO, Stacey Goodman
President CIT Rail, George D. Cashman
Group Head and Managing Director CIT Corporate Finance Entertainment Gaming Sports and Media, Wade Layton

Group Head and Managing Director CIT Corporate Finance Communications Information Services and Technology, Tom Westdyk
President CIT Communications Media and Entertainment, James L. (Jim) Hudak, $487,885 total compensation
President CIT Commercial Services, Jonathan A. (Jon) Lucas
EVP and Chief Risk Officer, Lisa K. Polsky, age 58, $501,923 total compensation
EVP and Chief Credit Officer, Robert C. Rowe, age 54
EVP and CFO, Carol Hayles, age 54
EVP and Chief Auditor, Robert (Bob) Hart
Managing Director CIT Canada, Blake Macaskill
Group Head and Managing Director CIT Maritime Finance, Svein Engh
President CIT International Finance, Rich Green
Group Head and Managing Director CIT Business Aircraft Finance, Mike Kahmann
Group Head and Managing Director CIT Corporate Finance Energy, Mike Lorusso
Group Head and Managing Director CIT Capital Markets, Neil Wessan
EVP and Chief Human Resources Officer, Bryan Allen
President Nacco, Dan DiStefano
President CIT Commercial Air, Tony Diaz
President CIT Corporate Finance Commercial and Industrial, Burt Feinberg
President CIT Real Estate Finance, Matthew E. Galligan
President CIT Asia, Markus Weinseiss
EVP and Treasurer, Israel Kaufman
Group Head and Managing Director CIT Corporate Finance Healthcare, William Douglass
EVP CIT Corporate and Specialty Banking, Grant Ahern
Senior Vice President, Monahan Mike
Vice President, Karl Carlstrom
Senior Vice President Rail Resources, Jeff Lytle
Assistant Vice President Senior Business Analyst BI, Jennifer (Jen) Repik
Vice President, Michael Aufrichtig
Senior Vice President, John Edel
Vice President, Howard Botwinick
Assistant Vice President Data Analyst, Brendan Nolan
Vice President, Julianne Allen
Vice President And Assistant General Counsel, Ira Finkelson
Vice President Strategic Marketing, Ann Crater
Assistant Vice President Global Accounting Operation, Betty Ciesla
Executive Vice President And Controller, William (Bill) Taylor
Vice President Of Internal Audit, Jim Baumgartner
Senior Vice President Global Information Technology Infrastructure Director, Frank Nazzaro
Assistant Vice President Corporate Compliance Officer, Todd Hawkins
Assistant Vice President Credit Scoring, Xiaoman Wang
Vice President Dealer Service, Rob Sureda
Vice President, Jeff Rushnak
Vice President New Aircraft, Craig McIntyre
Senior Vice President Bsa Aml And Ofac Sanctions Compliance Head, Michelle Goodsir
Vice President, George Fikaris
Assistant Vice President of Systems Software, Ken Porowski
Senior Vice President National Manager, Kenneth Wendler
Vice President Information Technology Infrastructure Solutions, Michael Discala
Vice President, Joel Wolitzer
Assistant Vice President In Corporate Risk Management, Lara Thompson
Vice President New Business, Alan Horton

Vice President Collections, Denise Byrd
Assistant Vice President Financial Analyst, Darby Marasigan
Vice President Secondary Marketing, Ronald Rouse
Vice President and Director Channel Sales, Louis Fortunato
Vice President National Accounts Manager, Mike Loconsolo
Vice President, Maria Contino
Assistant Vice President, Joe Przytula
Capital Management Treasury Vice President, Frederik Sziszak
Vice President, Ross Evangelista
Vice President, Ronald Gibney
Executive Vice President Chief Credit And Risk Officer Corporate Credit Risk Management, Nancy Foster
Assistant Vice President Sales, Jeanette Moreno
Vice President Aml Compliance, Rachel Benjamin
Vice President Communications and Government Relations Information Technology Lead, Steven (Steve) Zahner
Assistant Vice President, Joshua Hare
Assistant Vice President, Rosalyn Jones
Vice President Flow Credit, Sean Cokeley
Assistant Vice President, Brent Huffman
Vice President, Sohail Khan
Vice President Sox, Doreen Chambers
Assistant Vice President, Soheir Krauss
Vice President, Debra Brown
Vice President, Young Hsu
Senior Vice President and General Manager Locomotives, Kenneth (Ken) Pierson
Assistant Vice President Cit Corporate Finance, Nadira Prescott
Vice President International Client Services, Mary Farley
Assistant Vice President Global Operations Center Team Lead, Diego Acevedo
Assistant Vice President Sales Support, Haley Werle
Assistant Vice President Account Executive Client Service Officer, Chu Enriquez
Vice President, Patricia Matos
Vice President Operations, David Howson
Vice President Enterprise Architecture, Woodie Westbrook
Assistant Vice President Finance, Sean Malone
Senior Vice President Information Technology, John (Jack) Smith
Vice President, Yolanda Lopez
Vice President Corporate Recruiter, Ann Rosenblum
Vice President Enterprise Portfolio Manager, Katherine (Kate) Mahoney
Vice President Director of Marketing and Customer Integration, Paul Carmedelle
Vice President, Kai Liang
Vice President Head Of Contracts (Cit Aerospace), Susan Geitzenauer
Vice President Corporate Compliance, Khyati Desai
Vice President Corporate Finance Heathcare, Francois Delangle
Vice President, Jim Condina
Assistant Vice President Events, James (Jamie) Spencer
Senior Vice President Corporate Planning, Taylor Kamp
Senior Vice President, Eugene Schwartz
Vice President National Account Mannager Cit Tech, James Bailey
Vice President Consumer Finance Operations, Krista Neal
Executive Vice President And Chief Sales Officer, James Conheeneya
Vice President Employment Human, Tammy Haynie
Vice President Threat And Vulnerability Management Information, Roman Brozyna

Assistant Vice President Financial Planning and
Analysis, Dean Cook
Vice President Sales, Thomas Gonnella
Executive Vice President, Kenneth Brown
Vice President Finance, Frederick Rick
Operation Manager Vice President, Marvin Daniel
Senior Vice President, Munish Gupta
Vice President, Kristin Appelbaum
Vice President Finance (Vendor LATAM Reg
Reporting Data quality), Raul Santoyo
Assistant Vice President, Adam Schacter
Senior Vice President, Joe Lux
Assistant Vice President Of New Aircraft
Programs, Howard Mitchell
Assistant Vice President Internal Audit, Ana
Almeida
Vice President Communications Media And
Entertainment, Jennifer Mitchell
Vice President Cit Healthcare, Kirk Strittmatter
Vice President Qrm Treasury Support, Leonard
Gray
Executive Vice President CIT Syndicated Loan
Group, Pete Connolly
Executive Vice President, Lisa Zonino
Vice President of Financial Operations, Pam Mac
Executive Vice President and Treasurer, Glenn
Alan Votek
Executive Vice President and Chief Audit
Executive, Bob Hart
Assistant Vice President Corporate Finance, Nicole
C Rapport
Vice President Project and Service Management,
Russell (Russ) Hansen
Vice Chairman, Ellen R. Alemany
Auditors: PricewaterhouseCoopers LLP

LOCATIONS

HQ: CIT Group, Inc.
11 West 42nd Street, New York, NY 10036
Phone: 212 461-5200
Web: www.cit.com

2014 Sales

	$ mil.	% of total
US	2,174	60
Europe	857	24
Rest of the world	592	16
Total	**3,624**	**100**

PRODUCTS/OPERATIONS

2014 Sales

	$ mil.	% of total
Interest income		
Interest & fees on loans	1,191	33
Interest & dividends on interest-bearing deposits & investments	35	1
Non-interest income		
Rental income on operating leases	2,093	58
Other income	305	8
Total	**3,624**	**100**

Selected Subsidiaries

Aireal Technologies of Harrisburg LLC
ATMOR Properties Inc.
Capita Colombia Holdings Corp.
Education Lending Services Inc.
Education Loan Servicing Corporation
The Equipment Insurance Company
Flex Holdings LLC
Flugzeug Limited (Ireland)
Imaginarium LLC
North Romeo Storage Corporation
Waste to Energy II LLC
Wellington Capital Corporation (Barbados)

COMPETITORS

Ally Financial	ILFC
Citigroup	JPMorgan Chase
Deutsche Bank	ORIX
GE Capital	

HISTORICAL FINANCIALS

Company Type: Public

Income Statement

FYE: December 31

	ASSETS ($ mil.)	NET INCOME ($ mil.)	INCOME AS % OF ASSETS	EMPLOYEES
12/14	47,880	1,130	2.4%	3,360
12/13	47,139	675	1.4%	3,240
12/12	44,012	(588)	—	3,560
12/11	45,235	31	0.1%	3,526
12/10	50,958	521	1.0%	3,778
Annual Growth	**(1.5%)**	**21.3%**	**—**	**(2.9%)**

2014 Year-End Financials

Debt ratio: 38.55%
Return on equity: 12.62%
Cash ($ mil.): 7,119
Current ratio: —
Long-term debt ($ mil.): —

No. of shares (mil.): 180
Dividends
 Yield: 1.0%
 Payout: 9.4%
Market value ($ mil.): 8,653

	STOCK PRICE ($) FY Close	P/E High/Low		Earnings	PER SHARE ($) Dividends	Book Value
12/14	47.83	9	7	5.96	0.50	50.13
12/13	52.13	15	11	3.35	0.10	44.78
12/12	38.64	—	—	(2.95)	0.00	41.49
12/11	34.87	377	224	0.13	0.00	44.30
12/10	47.10	18	11	2.58	0.00	44.48
Annual Growth	**0.4%**	**—**	**—**	**23.3%**	**—**	**3.0%**

Citigroup Inc

This is the Citi that never sleeps. One of the largest financial services firms known to man Citigroup (also known as Citi) has some 200 million customer accounts and serves clients around the globe. It offers deposits and loans (mainly through Citibank) investment banking brokerage wealth management and other financial services. Few other banks can equal Citigroup's global reach: In addition to Citibank it owns stakes in several international regional banks and has more than 100 million Citi-branded credit cards in circulation. However Citi has been selling dozens of underperforming and noncore businesses in the aftermath of the financial crisis in order to refocus on its original mission —traditional banking.

HISTORY

Company BackgroundEmpire builder Sanford "Sandy" Weill who helped build brokerage firm Shearson Loeb Rhoades sold the company to American Express (AmEx) in 1981. Forced out of AmEx in 1985 Weill bounced back in 1986 buying Control Data's Commercial Credit unit.

Primerica caught Weill's eye next. Its predecessor American Can was founded in 1901 as a New Jersey canning company; it eventually expanded into the paper and retail industries before turning to financial services in 1986. The firm was renamed Primerica in 1987 and bought brokerage Smith Barney Harris Upham & Co.

Weill's Commercial Credit bought Primerica in 1988. In 1993 Primerica bought Shearson from AmEx as well as Travelers taking its name and logo.

Weill set about trimming Travelers. He sold life subsidiaries and bought Aetna's property/casualty business in 1995. In 1996 he consolidated all property/casualty operations to form Travelers Property Casualty and took it public. The next year

Travelers bought investment bank Salomon Brothers and formed Salomon Smith Barney Holdings (now Citigroup Global Markets).

Weill sold Citicorp chairman and CEO John Reed on the idea of a merger in 1998 in advance of the Gramm-Leach-Bliley act which deregulated the financial services industry in the US. By the time the merger went through a slowed US economy and foreign-market turmoil brought significant losses to both sides. The renamed Citigroup consolidated in 1998 and 1999 laying off more than 10000 employees. So many executives (including co-chairmen and co-CEOs Weill and Reed) were paired through "co" titling that the company was dubbed "the ark."

In 1999 Citigroup moved deeper into subprime lending. Also that year former Treasury Secretary Robert Rubin joined Citigroup as a co-chairman.

In 2000 Reed retired and the company bought the investment banking business of British firm Schroders. Citigroup also bought subprime lender Associates First Capital (now part of CitiFinancial) for approximately $27 billion to expand its consumer product lines and its international presence. The deal however also brought Citigroup federal scrutiny regarding perceived predatory lending tactics. In 2001 the company bought New York-based European American Bank from ABN AMRO and purchased Grupo Financiero Banamex one of Mexico's biggest banks.

The company parlayed the $4 billion it netted from the 2002 spinoff of 20% of Travelers Property Casualty (it distributed most of the remaining stock to Citigroup shareholders) into a $5.8 billion purchase of California-based Golden State Bancorp the parent of the then-third-largest thrift in the US Cal Fed.

Also that year Citigroup paid some $215 million to settle federal allegations that Associates First Capital made customers unwittingly purchase credit insurance by automatically billing for the service. The agreement was one of the largest consumer-protection settlements ever.

The company also became embroiled in the Enron mess as regulators scrutinized short-term loans that Citigroup floated to the energy trader and were possibly used by Enron in transactions with offshore entities to mask debt and inflate cash flow figures. Citigroup neither confirmed nor denied allegations that it helped fudge Enron's books but in 2003 remitted more than $100 million earmarked to pay victims who lost money because of Enron's malfeasance.

A landmark ruling by the SEC in 2003 implied that Citigroup issued favorable stock ratings to companies in exchange for investment banking contracts (predictably the company neither confirmed nor denied the allegations). Also as part of the ruling erstwhile star analyst Jack Grubman agreed to pay some $15 million in fines for his overly rosy stock reports and accepted a lifetime ban from working in the securities industry. Citigroup forked over $400 million in fines the largest portion of a total of some $1.4 billion levied against 10 brokerage firms regarding conflicts of interest between analysts and investment bankers.

Amid the investigations Citigroup separated its stock-picking and corporate advisory businesses creating a retail brokerage and equity research unit called Smith Barney. In the SEC's 2003 ruling such a "Chinese Wall" between bankers and analysts was later made mandatory at all firms. Still Citigroup raked in net profits of nearly $18 billion (on revenues in excess of $94 billion) in 2003 one of the largest-ever yearly takes in US corporate history.

In 2004 the company —while admitting no wrongdoing —paid $2.65 billion to investors who were burned when WorldCom went bankrupt amid an accounting scandal. (Citigroup was one of the lead underwriters of WorldCom stocks and bonds.) The settlement was one of the largest ever for alleged securities fraud and compelled Citigroup to set aside an additional $5 billion to cover legal fees for this case and others involving Enron and spinning. The company eventually paid $2 billion in mid-2005 to investors who lost money on publicly traded Enron stocks and bonds again settling the matter while denying it broke any laws. Enron shareholders had argued that Citigroup helped Enron to set up offshore companies and shady partnerships to exaggerate the energy trader's cash flow.

In Japan where Citigroup is one of the leading foreign banks regulators pulled the plug on the company's private banking operations in 2004 after determining that Citigroup misled customers regarding the sale of certain structured bonds. The closures led to the forced resignation of three top executives in the company's asset management and private banking units about a month later.

Citigroup sold The Travelers Life and Annuity Company (now MetLife Life and Annuity Company of Connecticut) plus most of its international insurance business to MetLife in 2005. Later that year a convoluted deal with Legg Mason netted Citigroup that company's retail brokerage and capital markets business (and $1.5 billion of Legg Mason stock) in exchange for most of Citigroup's asset management and mutual fund division; Citigroup concurrently sold Legg Mason's capital markets operations to Stifel Financial.

Seeking growth internationally Citigroup was part of a consortium that acquired a controlling stake in Guangdong Development Bank in 2006. Also that year the company opened more than 800 bank branches and consumer finance offices outside the US.

Weill ended years of speculation in 2003 by anointing corporate and investment bank head Chuck Prince as his successor. Weill retired as chairman in 2006 and Prince assumed that title as well. Prince resigned in 2007 as Citigroup dealt with losses on mortgage-related securities and other investments.

Prince was succeeded by Vikram Pandit a Morgan Stanley veteran who came to Citigroup when it acquired hedge fund and private equity manager Old Lane Partners in 2007. Pandit was at Citigroup only a few months before he was named CEO but during that time he oversaw the company's alternative investments and led its institutional clients group. The following year Citigroup disbanded Old Lane and wound up its flagship fund.

Citigroup further expanded its fund services operations via its 2007 acquisition of BISYS. As part of the deal the company sold BISYS' insurance services division to investment firm J.C. Flowers & Co.

Also that year it picked up remnants of the subprime mortgage collapse when it acquired ACC Capital Holding's wholesale mortgage origination operations as well as the servicing rights to some $5 billion in home loans. It also bought ABN AMRO Mortgage Group and shelled out more than $1 billion to buy Egg one of the largest online-only banks in the world from Prudential plc. The deal boosted its UK consumer operations by adding some 3 million customers.

The company sold its trademark red umbrella logo back to insurance firm Travelers which began using the symbol nearly 150 years before. Citigroup acquired the iconic logo when it bought the insurance company in 1993 and held onto it after it spun off Travelers in 2002. But the company ultimately decided that customers associated the umbrella with insurance and sold it in 2007.

In order to shore up its balance sheet Citigroup sold some 5% of itself to the Abu Dhabi Investment

Authority a Middle Eastern sovereign fund for $7.5 billion in 2007. It later raised more than $12 billion by selling preferred shares to investors including a Singapore government-owned investment fund former CEO Sandy Weill and Saudi investor Prince Al-Walid bin Talal who owns roughly 5% stake of Citigroup.

Citigroup bought a majority stake in one of Japan's largest brokerages Nikko Cordial in 2007. It acquired the remaining shares of Nikko Cordial in early 2008 and merged it with Citigroup Japan Holdings to form Nikko Citi Holdings.

In 2008 Citigroup sold several of its commercial finance lines to GE Capital. It sold its German consumer banking business to French bank Groupe Crédit Mutuel.

As the global credit crisis mounted in 2008 the US government injected some $700 billion into the nation's banking industry including $45 billion investment in Citigroup. It further stepped in to aid the faltering bank by backing more than $300 in loans and securities to boost confidence in the bank and protect its investments. In exchange the government took a 34% stake in Citigroup. The company received approval to pay the funds back in 2009 and the government began reducing its ownership.

Citigroup shed numerous noncore operations (grouped into its new Citi Holdings division) to raise money to repay the government bailout funds. In 2009 it sold Japanese brokerage Nikko Cordial (now SMBC Nikko) and other parts of Nikko Citi Holdings for $8.7 billion to Sumitomo Mitsui Financial Group. Also in 2009 Citigroup combined its Smith Barney and Quilter wealth management units with those of Morgan Stanley to create Morgan Stanley Smith Barney taking a 49% of the combined firm.

Sales in 2010 include its $1.93 billion Canadian MasterCard portfolio (to CIBC) a $3.5 billion real estate loan portfolio (to JPMorgan Chase) a $3.2 billion auto loan portfolio (to Santander) and a $1.6 billion portfolio of retail credit card assets (to GE). In 2011 it sold a $1.7 billion private equity portfolio to AXA. Also in 2010 the company spun off Primerica in an IPO selling remaining shares by 2011.

Furthermore Citigroup exited the student loan business in the wake of federal legislation eliminating subsidies for private lenders: It sold its 80% stake in Student Loan Corporation and much of its private student loans portfolio to Discover Financial Services and Sallie Mae. The company also sold three hedge fund businesses with a combined $4.2 billion in assets under management to New York-based SkyBridge Capital.

The firm began withdrawing from the consumer lending business in Europe by selling its Egg UK credit card business to Barclays in 2011 and its UK/Ireland Diners Club business to Affiniture Cards in 2012.

EXECUTIVES

Branch Manager Vice President, Thomas (Thom) Simon
Vice President Big Data Platform Engineering, Peter Burns
Vice President, Sandip Sen
Vice President Information Technology, Michael (Mel) Griffin
CEO Citibank N.A., Barbara J. Desoer, age 62
CEO North America, William J. (Bill) Mills, age 59
President and CEO Institutional Clients Group, James A. (Jim) Forese, age 52, $475,000 total compensation
CEO, Michael L. Corbat, age 55, $1,500,000 total compensation
Global Head Markets and Securities Services, Paco Ybarra

CFO, John C. Gerspach, age 62, $500,000 total compensation
CEO Global Consumer Bank, Stephen Bird, age 48
CEO Grupo Financiero Banamex, Javier Arrigunaga
CEO Citi Holdings, Francesco Vanni d'Archirafi
Head Operations and Technology, Don Callahan, age 58
EVP Global Public Affairs, Edward Skyler, age 41
CEO Latin America, Jane Fraser
Head EMEA Markets Institutional Clients Group, James C. Cowles
CEO Citi Cards, Jud Linville
CEO Asia Pacific, Francisco Aristeguieta Silva
Chief Risk Officer, Bradford Hu
CEO Qatar; Head Private Bank Gulf and Egypt, Carmen Haddad
Chairman Nordic Countries and Head of Nordic Investment Banking, Eirik Winter
Country Officer Sweden and Head of Nordic Corporate Banking, Mikkel Gr.nlykke
Chairman and Managing Director China Investment Banking, Catherine Cai
CEO Citi Nigeria, Akin Dawodu
CEO Citi Mexico and Banco Nacional de M©xico (Banamex), Ernesto Torres Cantu
CEO Citi FinTech, Heather Cox
Chairman EMEA Leverage Finance, Paul Simpkin
Head of Lebanon, Elissar Farah Antonios
Vice President, Susan (Sue) Krimigis
Senior Vice President, Brad Sandstrom
Senior Vice President Global Wealth Management, Richard (Dick) Harding
Senior Vice President Financial Centger Manager, Robert (Bob) Manley
Vice President Digital Product Management, Edward (Ed) Kim
Vice President, Katherine E Marschall
Senior Vice President Human Resources, Noreen Chin
Assistant Vice President Citigroup Procurement Services, Nicole Loiselle
Senior Vice President, Justin Skeels
Vice President, Steven Gross
Vice President, Lynnea Olsen
Vice President Project Management and Infrastructure Development, William (Bill) Lee
Vice President of Asian Marketing, Arthur (Art) Chiu
Vice President Human Resources, John (Jack) Taylor
Senior Vice President Manager Compensation, David (Dave) Cohen
Vice President Operational Risk, Jim Krenowicz
Assistant Vice President And Business Information Security Officer, Veena Srinivasan
Senior Vice President, Eugene Bai
Vice President, Jervis Smith
Vice President Executive Recruiter, Rebecca Barber
Senior Vice President Data Assets and List Acquisitions, Coleen Rozzi
Vice President Global Markets, Lucciola John
Senior Vice President Finance, Ravindra Pradhan
Senior Vice President Asset Management, Gustav Gollisz
Vice President Technology, Kevin Yu
Vice President Compensation Lead Analyst, Angela (Angie) Tsui
Real Estate Analyst Assistant Vice President, Alexander (Al) Koutrouby
Vice President Marketing, Scott Saltzman
Securities Finance Trader Senior Vice President, Frances (Fran) Man
Senior Vice President, John Abato
Information Technology Management: Vice President, Robin Rekowski
Vice President Marketing, Carlissa Louther
Vice President Operations, Scott McGuane
Vice Presidenttechnical Information Officer At Citibank Tiso At Citigro, Syed Rahat

Vice President Specialized Analytics Manager, Renee Jackson

Vice President, Elyse Milun

Senior Vice President Country Operations And Technology Head, Peter (Pete) Lemoucheux

Vice President and Agency Finance, Thomas (Thom) Coenen

Senior Vice President Project Strategy Office, Allison Flynn

Vice President Information Technology Business Analyst, Faith Reyes

Senior Vice President Marketing Strategy Citi Retail Services, Rob Engelman

Vice President Information Technology Project Technical Specialist, Amr Hambazaza

Executive Vice President, Gregg Morton

Assistant Vice President, Scott Ward

Vice President Account Managementdepositary Receipt Services, Maria Perez

Vice President, Darrell Fiala

Vice President Credit And Risk Latmex, Andrea Di Fabio

Vice President Of Human Resources, Sara Melloni

Senior Vice President Compensation And Benefits, Martha Callum

Vice President Information Technology Business Tech Specialist Global Risk and Fraud, Kevin Foley

Vice President Of Sales, Bill Power

Senior Vice President, Nathaniel Halsey

Vice President Product Head Cards Business, Amit Vasudev

Senior Vice President Data Governance Policies and Practices (Chief Data Office), Paul Christakos

Vice President, Stephen (Steve) Trent

Senior Vice President regional Credit Director, Regis Garcia

Senior Vice President Digital Marketing Partnerships, Maja Lapcevic

Vice President Senior Ciient Manager, Manuela Draqan

Senior Vice President Technology, Jan Beccia

Vice President Technology Citigroup Inc, Charles (Chas) Kim

Assistant Vice President Cash Management Implementation Manager, Zachi Rosenberg

Senior Vice President Global Events Marketing, Andrea Conner

Vice President, Noah Meely

Senior Vice President Technology, Sean Holton

Vice President Treasury Sales Consultant, Kathy Palmer

Vice President, Casey Pimenta

Vice President Human Resources, Venus Tse

Senior Vice President Information Technology Risk and Control Management, Boris Shakhmurov

Senior Vice President Citibank Commerc, Tom Harris

Vice President Information Technology, Zeshan Jalali

Senior Vice President Information Technology, John Dybus

Senior Business Analyst Assistant Vice President, Pravin Pathak

Senior Vice President, Judy Bassanello

Assistant Vice President, Rizwan Sharif

Vice President, Edmond Lee

Executive Vice President Business Development, Rick Cunningham

Senior Vice President Global Network Strategy and Business Development, David (Dave) McDowell

Senior Vice President, John (Jack) Sangiorgio

Assistant Vice President information Technology and Services, Ganesh Bhat

Vice President, David (Dave) Gubitosi

Vice President Relationship Manager Commercial Banking, Johnny Srivastava

Senior Vice President, Maureen Baker

Senior Vice President Corporate Sponsorships and Marketing, Tina Davis

Vice President Client Development Consumer Opl, Michael (Mel) Stark

Vice President Market Data, Darren Donegan

Vice President Cti Portfolio Manager, Andrew (Andy) Sato

Vice President, Marbel Ugando

Vice President Creative Director, David Lockhart

Vice President Treasury, Shawn Stolar

Vice President Business Development and Strategic Accounts, Jeremy A Flinchbaugh

Vice President Finance, Steve Kincheloe

Senior Vice President and General Coun, James (Jamie) Garner

Assistant Vice President, Feng Wang

Senior Vice President Director Decision Management, David (Dave) Sapuppo

Vice President Prime Broker Account Manager, Jason Friedman

Short Sale Negotiator Vice President, Federico Moran

Vice President, Bruce Gaudino

Vice President, Kimberly Jenkins

Vice President Technical Specialist And Project Lead, Zhong Yang

Vice President, Zac Costello

Assistant Vice President Technology Operations Manager, David (Dave) Kiraly

Senior Vice President Commercial Banking, Jack Crowley

Vice President Business Finance, Pamela Frederick

Vice President Regional Sales Manager, Dan Brennan

Executive Vice President Control and Supplier Risk Manageme, Paul Pitre

Assistant Vice President Telecommunications, Julie Moomaw

Senior Vice President, Joellen Onesios

Vice President Senior Apps Dev Manager, Vasi Rahaman

Senior Vice President Mobile Marketing, Jason Brunstein

Senior Vice President, Philip Waterman

Vice President Marketing Research, Rochelle Ohring

Senior Vice President ficc Technology, Firas Aljallad

Assistant Vice President Information Technology, Reginald Thompson

Vice President, Jenny Flores

Senior Vice President Marketing Director, Kevin Crimmins

Vice President Information Technology, Lisa Gresham

First Vice President, David (Dave) Breakstone

Vice President Marketing, Mary Redick

Vice President Senior Technology Manager, Stephen Sackstein

Vice President Corporate Marketing, Kasia Jakubowska

Vice President, Jennifer Kelso

Vice President Global Operations Risk Management, David (Dave) Harrington

Auditors: KPMG LLP

LOCATIONS

HQ: Citigroup Inc
399 Park Avenue, New York, NY 10022
Phone: 212 559-1000
Web: www.citigroup.com

PRODUCTS/OPERATIONS

2014 Sales

	$ mil.	% of total
Interest		
Loans including fees	44,776	49
Investments including dividends	7,195	8
Trading account assets	5,880	6
Federal funds sold & securities purchased under resale agreements	2,366	3
Deposits with banks	959	1
Other	507	1
Noninterest		
Commissions & fees	13,032	15
Principal transactions	6,698	7
Administration & other fiduciary fees	4,013	4
Insurance premiums	2,110	2
Realized gains on sales of investments	570	1
Other	2,890	3
Adjustments	(424)	-
Total	90,572	100

2014 Assets

	% of total
Net loans	628,641
Investments	333,443
Trading accounts	296,786
Federal funds	242,570
Cash and deposits	160,197
Other	180,893
Total	1,842,530

COMPETITORS

American Express	Goldman Sachs
Bank of America	HSBC
Bank of New York Mellon	JPMorgan Chase
	Mizuho Financial
Barclays	U.S. Bancorp
Capital One	UBS
Deutsche Bank	USAA
FMR	Wells Fargo
GE	

HISTORICAL FINANCIALS

Company Type: Public

Income Statement

FYE: December 31

	ASSETS ($ mil.)	NET INCOME ($ mil.)	INCOME AS % OF ASSETS	EMPLOYEES
12/14	1,842,530	7,313	0.4%	241,000
12/13	1,880,382	13,673	0.7%	251,000
12/12	1,864,660	7,541	0.4%	259,000
12/11	1,873,878	11,067	0.6%	266,000
12/10	1,913,902	10,602	0.6%	260,000
Annual Growth	(0.9%)	(8.9%)	—	(1.9%)

2014 Year-End Financials

Debt ratio: 12.11%—
Return on equity: 3.53%
Cash ($ mil.): 160,197
Current ratio: —
Long-term debt ($ mil.): —

Dividends
Yield: 0.0%
Payout: 1.8%
Market value ($ mil.): —

	STOCK PRICE ($) FY Close	P/E High/Low		PER SHARE ($) Earnings	Dividends	Book Value
12/14	54.11	26	21	2.20	0.04	69.62
12/13	52.11	12	9	4.35	0.04	67.46
12/12	39.56	16	10	2.44	0.04	62.42
12/11	26.31	12	1	3.63	0.03	60.81
12/10	4.73	1	1	3.50	0.00	56.26
Annual Growth	83.9%	—	— (11.0%)	—	5.5%

Citizens Financial Group Inc (New)

Paper plastic or coin? No matter —Citizens Financial Group can handle it all. The company formerly known as RBS Citizens Financial Group is the parent of Citizens Bank which boasts some 1370 branches —many of which are located in supermarkets —across a dozen US states in the Northeast and the Midwest. The banks offer standard retail and commercial services as well as investment services insurance and employer-sponsored retirement plans. Citizens Financial also operates a network of non-branch banking offices in more than 30 states. Formerly owned by Royal Bank of Scotland RBS sold its remaining stake in Citizens in late 2015.

IPO

Royal Bank of Scotland (RBS) sold a 25% ownership interest or 140 million shares of the regional US bank for $21.50 each (below the company's expected range of $23 to $25 per share) in September 2014. The deal which valued Citizens Financial Group (CFG) at $3 billion was one of the largest bank IPOs on record. In October 2015 RBS sold its remaining stake (the last 20.9% of Citizens common stock) for $23.38 per share raising some $2.6 billion.

Operations

In select markets nationwide Citizens Financial Group offers customers mortgage lending auto lending student lending and commercial banking services. Altogether its portfolio includes 1370 branches 80 non-branch offices and more than 3500 ATMs.

Geographic Reach

Rhode Island-based Citizens Financial Group operates branches in New England and in the Mid-Atlantic and the Midwest. Its largest markets are Boston Philadelphia Providence and Pittsburgh.

Sales and Marketing

Citizens Financial Group which boasts some 5 million customers serves a variety of consumers including individuals small businesses middle-market companies large corporations and institutions.

Financial Performance

Citizens Financial Group logged $5.13 billion in revenue in fiscal 2013 representing a $380 million drop as compared to 2012. The company points to a decrease in both interest and non-interest income for the decline. Continued low interest rates conspired to reduce loan yields and deposit spreads. Additionally net impairment losses (recognized in earnings) and a decrease in mortgage banking fees dragged down revenue. During the reporting period the financial firm posted a $3.42 billion net loss compared to net income of $643 million in 2012.

Strategy

To create a more unified brand name Citizens Financial Group in 2014 rolled out a plan focused on growth and enhanced performance that involves rebranding more than 200 Charter One branches in Michigan and Ohio under that Citizens Bank banner by mid-2015. The move aims to create a consistent presence across the company's 11-state retail footprint. Also in Michigan and Ohio Citizens Financial Group launched its Premier Banking business in 2014. It's extending its personalized services to Charter One's top customers with investable assets of $500000.

Citizens Financial Group is also selling certain assets and deposits associated with its Chicago-area retail branches small business relationships and select middle-market relationships to U.S. Bancorp. The 2014 deal comprises 103 branches that altogether boasted $5.3 billion in deposits and $1.1 billion in loans as of December 31 2013.

Company Background

After being bought by RBS in 1988 Citizens Financial went on an acquisition spree making more than two dozen deals. Since 2000 the company gobbled up Mellon's retail banking network Medford Bancorp and Port Financial in Massachusetts and Pennsylvania's Commonwealth Bancorp and Thistle Group Holdings among others. The company expanded into the Midwest by buying super-regional bank Charter One in 2004. Following its

acquisition of Charter One its largest deal yet Citizens Financial retained the Charter One Bank name in Midwestern markets but converted the bank's branches to Citizens Bank in New York and Pennsylvania. That was the company's last major acquisition however.

Like many banks the company was hamstrung by the mortgage crisis. It posted a nearly $1 billion loss in 2008 as its nonperforming loans roughly doubled. The developments compelled the company to re-evaluate its acquisition strategy and it has reversed its field: Citizens Financial sold 18 of its branches in northern New York to Community Bank System in 2008 and all 65 Charter One branches in Indiana to Old National Bancorp the following year. The company also pegged certain operations as noncore including its dealer finance program and portions of its auto lending business. In 2012 Citizens Financial unloaded more branches selling nearly 60 supermarket locations to People's United Financial. In 2013 it opted to unload its Chicago branches.

EXECUTIVES

Vice Chairman; Head Business Services, David Bowerman
Chief Risk Officer, Nancy Shanik
Head Distribution Consumer Banking, Michael Cleary
Chairman and CEO, Bruce Van Saun
Head Corporate Strategy, Beth Johnson
Regional Director Technology Services, Brian OÅConnell
Interim Co-Head Commercial Banking, Robert C. Rubino
Chief Risk Officer, Nancy L. Shanik
Interim Co-Head Commercial Banking, Stephen R. Woods
CFO, Eric Aboaf
Head of Treasury Solutions, Michael Cummins
Senior Vice President Human Resources, Joanna Robbins
Executive Vice President Head Of Customer Service Operations, Peg Marty
Senior Vice President, Richard (Dick) Urban
Senior Vice President Director Business Lending, Rich Henderson
Vice President Corporate Banking, Gary Hatfield
Senior Vice President Senior Counsel, Miriam Dowd
Senior Vice President Market Manager, Catherine (Cathy) Milioti
Vice President Senior Risk Manager, Jeanne Medeiros
Executive Vice President ne Regional Director, Patrick (Paddy) Burns
Senior Vice President, Joseph (Jo) Hoffmn
Vice President Senior Risk Manager, Pat Coutu
Vice President Principal Architect ETL DataStage Administrator, Kevin Murphy
Assistant Vice President Operations Manager, Alicia Carl
Vice President Treasury Solutions, Kellea Russell
Senior Finance Manager Vice President, Jennifer (Jen) Gobeil
Senior Vice President Middle Atlantic, Edward (Ed) Kloeker
Vice President Head of Executive Recruiting, Robert (Bob) Drury
Senior Vice President Contact Centers, Kevin Dunne
Vice President Senior Team Leader, Matthew (Matt) Correia
Vice President District Lending Manager, Ed Negron
Vice President Education Finance, Simon Lowenthal
Vice President and REGULATORY LIAISON LAW Department, Pam Brown

Vice President Ohio Market Small Business Leader, Jeff Bier
Vice President Senior Public Relations Manager, Jason Guy
Assistant Vice President Risk Manager, Tracy Borges
Vice President Education Finance, Kannan Mani
Vice President Risk Management, Shawn Wilks
Vice President Senior Risk Manager, Daiena Matson
Vice President Information Security Specialist, Marc Ayotte
Vice President Senior Merchandising Manager Corporate Marketing, Annette Badali
Senior Vice President Head of Marketing Analytics, Mark Conces
Vice Chairman and Head Commercial Banking, Donald H. (Don) McCree, age 48
Group Executive Vice President and Treasurer, Joe Dewhirst
Auditors: Deloitte & Touche LLP

LOCATIONS

HQ: Citizens Financial Group Inc (New)
One Citizens Plaza, Providence, RI 02903
Phone: 401 456-7000   **Fax:** 401 455-5927
Web: www.citizensbank.com

PRODUCTS/OPERATIONS

2013 Sales

	$ mil.	% of total
Interest income		
Interest on loans & fees	3,013	58
Investment securities	488	9
Non-interset income		
Service charges and fees	640	12
Card fees	234	5
Mortgage banking fees	153	3
Trust & investment services fees	149	3
Securities gains & losses	144	3
Other	312	7
Total	**5,133**	**100**

Selected Subsidiaries

CCO Investment Services Corp.
Citizens Automobile Finance
Citizens Bank of Pennsylvania
RBS Asset Finance Inc.
RBS Card Services
RBS Citizens Business Capital
RBS Citizens N.A.

COMPETITORS

Bank of America	M&T Bank
Bank of New York Mellon	PNC Financial
Citigroup	People' s United Financial
Fifth Third	Sovereign Bank
HSBC USA	TD Bank USA
Huntington Bancshares	U.S. Bancorp
JPMorgan Chase	Wintrust Financial
KeyCorp	

HISTORICAL FINANCIALS

Company Type: Public

Income Statement

FYE: December 31

	ASSETS ($ mil.)	NET INCOME ($ mil.)	INCOME AS % OF ASSETS	EMPLOYEES
12/14	132,857	865	0.7%	18,310
12/13	122,154	(3,426)	—	18,160
12/12	127,053	643	0.5%	—
12/11	0	0	—	—
12/09	147,681	(740)	—	—
Annual Growth	(2.1%)	—	—	—

City Holding Co.

Take Me Home Country Roads may be the (unofficial) state song of West Virginia but City Holding hopes all roads lead to its City National Bank of West Virginia subsidiary which operates more than 80 branches in the Mountaineer State and in neighboring areas of southern Ohio eastern Kentucky and northern Virginia. Serving consumers and regional businesses the nearly $4 billion bank offers standard deposit products loans credit cards insurance trust and investment services. Residential mortgages and home equity loans constitute more than half of City Holding's $2.5 billion loan portfolio though the bank also writes commercial industrial commercial mortgage and installment consumer loans.

OperationsCity National Bank (CNB) operates four main business divisions: Commercial banking Consumer Banking Mortgage Banking and Wealth Management and Trust Services. Commercial Banking provides traditional banking products commercial and industrial loans and different kinds of real estate loans to corporations and other business customers. Consumer Banking provides deposit products installment loans and real estate loans and lines of credit. The bank's Mortgage Banking division offers fixed and adjustable-rate mortgages construction financing production of conventional and government-backed mortgages secondary marketing and mortgage servicing. Wealth Management and Trust Services offers personal trust and estate administration investment management and investment and custodial services for commercial and individual customers. This includes management of investment accounts for individuals employee benefit plans and charitable foundations.Altogether the company earned 62% of its total revenue from interest and fees on loans in 2014 plus another 7% from interest on its investment securities. About 14% of revenue came from service charges 8% came from bankcard revenue and 2% came from trust and investment management fee income. Geographic ReachCity boasts around 80 branches in four US states including more than 55 branches in West Virginia nearly 15 in Virginia around 10 in Kentucky and less than a handful of branches in Ohio.Sales and MarketingThe bank spent $3.27 million on advertising in 2014 compared to $2.67 million and $2.59 million in 2013 and 2012 respectively.Financial PerformanceCity Holding's revenues and profits have mostly been on the uptrend in recent years as the bank has grown its loan business through acquisitions. The bank's revenue dipped by 4% to $188.29 million in 2014 mostly because it generated less in loan interest due to an expected drop in accretion from fair value adjustments related to its recent Virginia Savings Bank and Community Bank acquisitions. Interest margins also shrank

amidst the low interest environment which caused further headwinds to interest income. The bank did have some bright spots with 16% growth in trust and investment fee income and 11% growth in bankcard revenue as it continued to push those services.Despite lower revenue in 2014 City Holdings net income jumped by 10% to $52.96 million —the highest its profit has been since 2007. The rise was mostly thanks to a combination of a non-income based tax rebate (non-recurring) decreased legal and professional fees from lower legal settlements a $2.7 million decline in loan loss provisions as the credit quality of the bank's loan portfolio improved and a $1.3 million reduction in interest expense on deposits.City's operating cash fell to $53.35 million despite higher earnings during the year primarily because the bank used more of its cash toward purchasing assets and generated less net cash proceeds from its loans held for sale.StrategyCity Holding's flagship subsidiary City National Bank has been growing its loan business and branch network in target markets through acquisitions in recent years. In mid-2015 for example the bank agreed to acquire three bank branches in Lexington Kentucky from American Founders Bank boosting CNB's presence in the state to 11 branches while adding $164.2 million in new deposits and $125 billion in performing loans to its books. Beyond buying just select branches the bank has also been known to buy smaller community banks outright in its target markets. To free up resources for more investment in its core business City National sold its insurance operations to The Hilb Group in early 2015 netting an after-tax gain of $5.80 million.Mergers and AcquisitionsIn January 2013 City Holding acquired Community Financial Corporation holding company of the 11-branch Community Bank in Virginia.In 2012 the company entered a new market in Virginia through its acquisition of Virginia Savings Bank which had five branches in the northern part of the state.

EXECUTIVES

EVP Marketing Human Resources and Retail Banking, Craig G. Stilwell, age 59, $330,000 total compensation
President and CEO, Charles R. (Skip) Hageboeck, age 52, $500,000 total compensation
EVP Commercial Banking, John A. DeRito, age 65, $250,000 total compensation
CFO, David L. Bumgarner, age 50, $207,000 total compensation
CIO, Jeffrey D. (Jeff) Legge, $175,000 total compensation
Vice President And Trust Investment Of, Jason Rogers
Executive Vice President, William Butcher
Senior Vice President, Tim Quinlan
Vice President Risk Management, Kevin Thomas
Executive Vice President Customer Service, Jack Cavender
Executive Vice President Marketing, Carolyn Hays
Senior Vice President Investor Relations, Victoria Evans
Vice President, Madison Sayre
Assistant Vice President, Patricia Davis
Vice President Sales, Mark Davis
Vice President, Steve Clark
Vice President Systems, Susie Robinson
Senior Vice President, Todd Taylor
Senior Vice President Director Of Security, Joe Flueckiger
Vice President, Robert Nagy
Vice President, Sharon Hughes
Executive Vice President Marketing, Craig Young
Vice President, Keith Unger
Senior Vice President, Massie Boster

Vice President Treasury Management, Dewey Kuhns
Assistant Vice President of Information Technology Data Management, Michael (Mel) Myers
Senior Vice President Information Technology, Abigal Scott
Senior Vice President cco, Tim Whittaker
Senior Vice President Retail Administration, Terry Childers
Assistent Vice President, Christina Pocrnich
Board President, Becky Linton
Chairman, Philip L. McLaughlin, age 74
Treasurer Secretary Vice President Systems Staff Finance Other Personnel, Jack Cipoletti
Auditors: Ernst & Young LLP

LOCATIONS

HQ: City Holding Co.
25 Gatewater Road, Charleston, WV 25313
Phone: 304 769-1100
Web: www.bankatcity.com

PRODUCTS/OPERATIONS

2014 Sales

	$ mil.	% of total
Interest		
Loans including fees	116	62
Investment securities & other	13	7
Noninterest		
Service charges	265	14
Bankcard revenue	15	8
Other	171	9
Total	**188**	**100**

COMPETITORS

1st West Virginia Bancorp	Huntington Bancshares
BB&T	Ohio Valley Banc
Fifth Third	Premier Financial Bancorp
First Community Bancshares	United Bankshares
	WesBanco

HISTORICAL FINANCIALS

Company Type: Public

Income Statement

FYE: December 31

	ASSETS ($ mil.)	NET INCOME ($ mil.)	INCOME AS % OF ASSETS	EMPLOYEES
12/14	3,461	52	1.5%	889
12/13	3,368	48	1.4%	923
12/12	2,917	38	1.3%	843
12/11	2,777	40	1.5%	795
12/10	2,637	38	1.5%	805
Annual **Growth**	7.0%	8.0%	—	2.5%

2014 Year-End Financials

Debt ratio: 0.48%
Return on equity: 13.61%
Cash ($ mil.): 148
Current ratio: —
Long-term debt ($ mil.): —

No. of shares (mil.): 15
Dividends
  Yield: 3.3%
  Payout: 48.3%
Market value ($ mil.): 705

	STOCK PRICE ($) FY Close	P/E High/Low	Earnings	PER SHARE ($) Dividends	Book Value
12/14	46.53	14 12	3.38	1.57	25.79
12/13	46.33	16 11	3.04	1.46	24.61
12/12	34.85	14 12	2.61	1.40	22.47
12/11	33.89	14 10	2.67	1.36	21.05
12/10	36.23	15 11	2.47	1.36	20.31
Annual **Growth**	6.5%	— —	8.2%	3.7%	6.2%

Clorox Co (The)

Bleach is the cornerstone of Clorox. The company's namesake household cleaning products are world leaders but the Clorox business reaches far beyond bleach. While it makes laundry and cleaning items (Formula 409 Pine-Sol Green Works) its vast products portfolio extends into dressings/sauces (Hidden Valley KC Masterpiece) plastic wrap and containers (Glad) cat litters (Fresh Step Scoop Away) and infection control items (HealthLink Aplicare Soy Vay). Other items include filtration systems (Brita in the Americas) charcoal briquettes (Kingsford Match Light) and natural personal care items (Burt's Bees). Clorox makes and sells its products worldwide.

HISTORY

Known first as the Electro-Alkaline Company The Clorox Company was founded in 1913 by five Oakland California investors who put up $100 apiece to make bleach using water from salt ponds around San Francisco Bay. The next year the company registered the brand name Clorox (the name combines the bleach's two main ingredients chlorine and sodium hydroxide). At first the company sold only industrial-strength bleach but in 1916 it formulated a household solution.

With the establishment of a Philadelphia distributor in 1921 Clorox began national expansion. The company went public in 1928 and built plants in Illinois and New Jersey in the 1930s; it opened nine more US plants in the 1940s and 1950s. In 1957 Procter & Gamble (P&G) bought Clorox. The Federal Trade Commission raised antitrust questions and litigation ensued over the next decade. P&G was ordered to divest Clorox and in 1969 Clorox again became an independent company.

Following its split with P&G the firm added household consumer goods and foods acquiring the brands Liquid-Plumr (drain opener 1969) Formula 409 (spray cleaner 1970) Litter Green (cat litter 1971) and Hidden Valley (salad dressings 1972). Clorox entered the specialty food products business by purchasing Grocery Store Products (Kitchen Bouquet 1971) and Kingsford (charcoal briquettes 1973).

Henkel a large West German maker of cleansers and detergents purchased 15% of Clorox's stock in 1974 as part of an agreement to share research. Beginning in 1977 Clorox sold off subsidiaries and brands such as Country Kitchen Foods (1979) to focus on household goods.

During the 1980s Clorox launched a variety of new products including Match Light (instant-lighting charcoal 1980) Tilex (mildew remover 1981) and Fresh Step (cat litter 1984). Clorox began marketing Brita water filtration systems in the US in 1988 (adding Canada in 1995). In 1990 it paid $465 million for American Cyanamid's household products group including Pine-Sol cleaner and Combat insecticide. (It sold Combat and Soft Scrub to Henkel in 2004.)

Clorox left the laundry detergent business in 1991 (begun in 1988) after it was battered by heavyweights P&G and Unilever. Household products VP Craig Sullivan became CEO the next year (stepping down in December 2003). In 1993 Clorox dumped its frozen food and bottled water operations. It began marketing its liquid bleach in Hungary through a Henkel subsidiary in 1994 and also bought S.O.S soap pads from Miles Inc.

A string of acquisitions brought the company into new markets as it built on existing brands. Clorox bought Black Flag and Lestoil in 1996 and

car care product manufacturer Armor All in 1997. With its 1999 purchase of First Brands –for about $2 billion in stock and debt –Clorox added four more brands of cat litter and diversified into plastic products (Glad).

Despite adding 115 new products in 2000 the company said it would put more emphasis on core brands going forward; it pushed its struggling Glad brand with more trade promotions and coupons.

Clorox in January 2001 announced a joint venture with Bombril Brazil's leading name in steel wool to form Detergentes Bombril; however Clorox canceled the agreement in April 2001 claiming that various conditions of the deal had not been met. A year later Clorox further distanced itself from the Brazilian market selling its SBP insecticides business to Reckitt Benckiser. In 2002 Clorox announced that due to the difficult economic environment in the region it was selling its Brazil business.

In 2003 it jumpstarted a joint venture with Procter & Gamble to take advantage of P&G's manufacturing acumen to improve its Glad products. P&G received a 10% stake in Glad. Clorox also sold its Jonny Cat Litter business to Oil-Dri Corporation of America and Black Flag operations in 2003.

In January 2004 Robert Matschullat the company's nonexecutive chairman replaced Sullivan upon his retirement. Matschullat stepped down as chairman and became a director in January 2005; he passed the title to Jerry Johnston. Matschullat reclaimed the titles of chairman and CEO on an interim basis when Johnston suffered a heart attack and retired in 2006. Former Coca-Cola executive Donald Knauss was named chairman and CEO in late 2006; Matschullat remained a director.

Chemical giant Henkel once owned nearly 30% of Clorox but Clorox bought it back in 2004 through an asset swap valued at $2.8 billion. The transaction involved Henkel's purchase of Clorox's 20% stake in Henkel Iberica a joint venture between the two firms operating in Portugal and Spain. Henkel also bought Clorox's stake in a pesticide company.

In late 2004 though P&G boosted its share in the joint venture (with $133 million) from 10% to 20% which is the maximum it can invest according to the agreement.

In 2010 Clorox began to explore strategic alternatives for its $300-million-in-sales car-care brands (Armor All STP) culminating in their sale to private equity firm Avista Capital Partners for $780 million.

EXECUTIVES

EVP New Business Development, Frank A. Tataseo, age 61, $534,672 total compensation

EVP and General Counsel, Laura Stein, age 54, $545,875 total compensation

EVP Human Resources and Corporate Affairs, Jacqueline P. (Jackie) Kane, age 63

CEO, Benno Dorer, age 51, $522,669 total compensation

EVP and CFO, Stephen M. (Steve) Robb, age 50, $491,731 total compensation

EVP Product Supply Enterprise Performance and IT, James Foster, age 52

SVP and Chief Innovation Officer, Denise Garner

SVP International Division, Michael Costello, age 48

SVP; General Manager Specialty Division, Jon Balousek, age 46

EVP and COO Cleaning International and Professional Products, Dawn Willoughby, age 46

EVP and COO Household Lifestyle and Core Global Functions, Nikolaos (Nick) Vlahos, age 47

SVP and Chief Marketing Officer, Eric Reynolds

Senior Vice President Human Resources Clorox Executive Committee, Jackie Kane

Vice President Brand Development, Doug Milliken

Chairman, George J. Harad, age 71

Auditors: Ernst & Young LLP

LOCATIONS

HQ: Clorox Co (The)
1221 Broadway, Oakland, CA 94612-1888
Phone: 510 271-7000
Web: www.thecloroxcompany.com

2014 Sales

	% of total
United States	80
International	20
Total	**100**

PRODUCTS/OPERATIONS

2014 Sales

	$ mil.	% of total
Cleaning	1,776	32
Household	1,706	31
International	1,170	20
Lifestyle	936	17
Total	**5,591**	**100**

Selected Mergers & Acquisitions

FY 2007

Latin American and Canadian bleach brands (Javex Agua Jane Nevex) from Colgate-Palmolive Company ($126 million plus inventory)

Burt's Bees line of natural skin and hair-care products ($925 million)

FY 2006

Tom's of Maine natural oral care products

Selected Food-Related Products

Brita
Glad
Glad Press ' n Seal
GladWare
Hidden Valley
K.C. Masterpiece

Selected Household & Professional Cleaning Products

Aplicare
Clorox
Clorox 2
Clorox Clean-Up
Clorox Disinfecting Wipes
Clorox Dispatch
Clorox FreshCare
Clorox Healthcare
Clorox Oxi Magic
Clorox ReadyMop
Clorox Toilet Bowl Cleaner
Formula 409
Formula 409 Carpet Cleaner
Green Works
Handi-Wipes
HealthLink
Lestoil
Liquid-Plumr
Pine-Sol
S.O.S
Stain Out
Tilex
ToiletWand
Tuffy
Ultra Clorox Bleach

Selected International Products

Agua Jane (bleach Uruguay)
Ant Rid (insecticides)
Arela (waxes)
Astra (disposable gloves)
Bluebell (cleaners)
Chux (cleaning tools)
Clorisol (bleach)
Clorox Gentle (color-safe bleach)
Glad (containers)
Glad-Lock (resealable bags)
Guard (shoe polish)
Gumption (cleaners)
Home Mat (insecticides)
Home Keeper (insecticides)

Javex (bleach Canada)
Mono (aluminum foil)
Nevex (bleach Venezuela)
OSO (aluminum foil)
Prestone (coolant)
Selton (insecticides)
S.O.S (cleaners)
Super Globo (bleach)
XLO (sponges)
Yuhanrox (bleach)

Selected Specialty Products
BBQ Bag
Burt's Bees
EverClean
EverFresh
Fresh Step
Fresh Step Scoop
Kingsford
Match Light
Rain Dance
Scoop Away
Son of a Gun!
Tuff Stuff

COMPETITORS

Alticor	Kiss My Face
Big Heart Pet Brands	McBride plc
Blistex	Mondelez International
Bonne Bell	Natural Health Trends
CalCedar	Nature's Sunshine
Campbell Soup	Newman's Own
Church & Dwight	Oil-Dri
Colgate-Palmolive	Pactiv
ConAgra	Procter & Gamble
Diversey	Reckitt Benckiser
Dow Chemical	S.C. Johnson
Dr. Bronner's	Seventh Generation
Est©e Lauder	The Dial Corporation
Forever Living	Unilever
Kiehl's	

HISTORICAL FINANCIALS

Company Type: Public

Income Statement

FYE: June 30

	REVENUE ($ mil.)	NET INCOME ($ mil.)	NET PROFIT MARGIN	EMPLOYEES
06/15	5,655	580	10.3%	7,700
06/14	5,591	558	10.0%	8,200
06/13	5,623	572	10.2%	8,400
06/12	5,468	541	9.9%	8,400
06/11	5,231	557	10.6%	8,100
Annual Growth	2.0%	1.0%	—	(1.3%)

2015 Year-End Financials

Debt ratio: 52.62%
Return on equity: 426.47%
Cash ($ mil.): 382
Current ratio: 1.02
Long-term debt ($ mil.): 1,796

No. of shares (mil.): 128
Dividends
  Yield: 2.8%
  Payout: 70.1%
Market value ($ mil.): 13,378

	STOCK PRICE ($) FY Close	P/E High/Low		PER SHARE ($) Earnings	Dividends	Book Value
06/15	104.02	25	19	4.37	2.96	0.92
06/14	91.40	22	19	4.23	2.84	1.20
06/13	83.14	20	16	4.30	2.56	1.12
06/12	72.46	18	15	4.09	2.40	(1.04)
06/11	67.44	18	15	4.02	2.20	(0.66)
Annual Growth	11.4%	—	—	2.1%	7.7%	—

CMS Energy Corp

Michigan consumers rely on CMS Energy. The energy holding company's utility Consumers Energy has a generating capacity of 8766 MW (primarily fossil-fueled) and distributes electricity and natural gas to more than 6.6 million of Michigan's 10 million residents. CMS Enterprises operates the non-utility businesses of CMS Energy and is an operator of independent power generating plants; its independent power plants (coal- gas- and biomass-fired) have a capacity of 2619 MW and are primarily located in Michigan but also in North Carolina. Subsidiary EnerBank USA provides unsecured home improvement payment option programs for homeowners.

HISTORY

In the late 1880s W. A. Foote and Samuel Jarvis formed hydroelectric company Jackson Electrical Light Works in Jackson Michigan. After building plants in other Michigan towns Foote formed utility holding company Consumers Power. In 1910 the firm merged with Michigan Light to create Commonwealth Power Railway and Light (CPR&L) and began building a statewide transmission system.

Foote died in 1915 and after nine years of acquisitions successor Bernard Cobb sold the rail systems and split CPR&L into Commonwealth Power (CP) and Electric Railway Securities. In 1928 Cobb bought Southeastern Power & Light (SP&L) and merged CP with Penn-Ohio Edison to form Allied Power & Light. Commonwealth and Southern (C&S) was then created as the parent of Allied and SP&L.

In 1932 future GOP presidential nominee Wendell Willkie took the helm and became a national political figure by opposing the Public Utility Holding Company Act of 1935 which began 60 years of regulated monopolies. Consumers Power was divested from C&S after WWII.

Consumers brought a nuclear plant on line in 1962 and the next year began buying Michigan oil and gas fields. In 1967 it formed NOMECO (now CMS Oil and Gas) to guide its oil and gas efforts.

The completion of the Palisades nuke in 1971 began a 13-year run of chronic problems and lengthy shutdowns. Cost overruns and an environmental lawsuit killed the firm's third nuke (Midland) in 1984 —after $4.1 billion was spent.

A rate hike and new CEO William McCormick set the firm on a new path in 1985. McCormick formed a subsidiary to develop and invest in independent power projects in 1986 and created holding company CMS (short for "Consumers") Energy the next year. CMS Gas Transmission was formed in 1989.

Midland Cogeneration Venture (CMS Energy and six partners) completed converting Midland to a natural gas-fueled cogeneration plant in 1990 and CMS Energy wrote off $657 million from its losses at the former nuke. It regained profitability in 1993.

McCormick split the utilities into electric and gas divisions in 1995 and also issued stock for its gas utility and transmission businesses Consumers Gas Group. The next year CMS Energy formed an energy marketing arm.

In 1996 and 1997 CMS Energy invested in power plants in Morocco and Australia and bought a stake in a Brazilian electric utility. The next year it began developing a gas-fired plant in Ghana and won a bid to build a plant in India. CMS Energy also bought gas gathering and processing firms

Continental Natural Gas and Heritage Gas Services in 1998.

Michigan's public service commission (PSC) issued utility restructuring orders in 1997 and 1998 but in 1999 the state Supreme Court ruled that the PSC lacked restructuring authority. Facing less-favorable proposed legislation CMS Energy and DTE Energy moved to implement competition per the PSC's guidelines.

CMS Energy bought Panhandle Eastern Pipe Line from Duke Energy for $2.2 billion in 1999. It also grabbed a 77% stake in another Brazilian utility and began building its Powder River Basin gas pipeline. In 2000 the company partnered with Marathon Ashland Petroleum (now Marathon Petroleum) and TEPPCO to operate a pipeline transporting refined petroleum from the US Gulf Coast to Illinois. Later that year CMS Energy announced plans for an IPO for its CMS Oil and Gas unit; however the IPO was withdrawn in 2001.

CMS Energy agreed in 2001 to sell Consumers' high-voltage electric transmission assets to independent transmission operator Trans-Elect for about $290 million; the deal which was the first of its kind in the US was completed in 2002. That year the company sold its Equatorial Guinea (West Africa) oil and gas assets to Marathon Oil for about $1 billion. Also that year McCormick stepped down amid controversy over "round trip" power trades that artificially inflated the company's sales and trading volume; CMS Energy later announced that it would restate its 2000 and 2001 financial results to eliminate the effects of the trades.

Later in 2002 the company exited the exploration and production business. It sold CMS Oil and Gas' North American and African assets to private French energy firm Perenco for $167 million and it sold the unit's Colombian properties to Spanish energy firm Compañía Española de Petróleos (Cepsa) for $65 million. CMS Energy sold its CMS Panhandle companies which together operated an 11000-mile pipeline system to Southern Union for $1.8 billion in 2003.

CMS Energy's nonregulated operations grew to account for more than half of sales in 2001 and 2002; however as the wholesale power marketing industry has experienced a downturn the company has refocused on its regulated energy distribution operations. The company has exited the speculative wholesale energy-trading business which was conducted through its CMS Energy Resource Management (formerly CMS Marketing Services and Trading) unit; it has sold its wholesale natural gas trading book to Sempra Energy and has sold its electricity trading book to Constellation Energy Commodities Group (formerly Constellation Power Source).

EXECUTIVES

EVP and CFO, Thomas J. (Tom) Webb, age 63, $685,000 total compensation
VP Governmental and International Affairs CMS Energy and Consumers Energy, David G. Mengebier, age 58, $375,000 total compensation
President and CEO CMS Energy and Consumers Energy, John G. Russell, age 58, $1,110,000 total compensation
SVP Energy Resources, Daniel J. (Dan) Malone, $440,000 total compensation
SVP and General Counsel, Catherine M. Reynolds
VP and CIO, Brian F. Rich
SVP CMS and Consumers, John M. Butler, $435,000 total compensation
SVP Distribution Operations Engineering and Transmission, Patricia K. (Patti) Poppe, age 47
Vice President, Dennis Dobbs
Chairman, David W. Joos, age 62
Auditors: PRICEWATERHOUSECOOPERS LLP

HQ: CMS Energy Corp
  One Energy Plaza, Jackson, MI 49201
Phone: 517 788-0550
Web: www.cmsenergy.com

PRODUCTS/OPERATIONS

2014 Sales

	$ mil.	% of total
Electric utility	4,436	62
Gas utility	2,363	33
Enterprises	299	4
Other reconciling items	81	1
Total	**7,179**	**100**

Selected Subsidiaries

Consumers Energy Company (electric and gas utility)
CMS Capital
  EnerBank USA (banking services)
CMS Enterprises Company (nonutility holding company)
Dearbon Industrial Generations LLC
EnerBank USA

COMPETITORS

AEP	NextEra Energy
AES	NiSource
Alliant Energy	ONEOK
Ameren	Progress Energy
Atmos Energy	Resources Corp.
Calpine	SCANA
CenterPoint Energy	SEMCO ENERGY
Con Edison	Sempra Energy
DTE	TECO Energy
Duke Energy	Tractebel Engineering
Dynegy	WEC Energy
Edison International	Xcel Energy
Eversource Energy	

HISTORICAL FINANCIALS

Company Type: Public

Income Statement

FYE: December 31

	REVENUE ($ mil.)	NET INCOME ($ mil.)	NET PROFIT MARGIN	EMPLOYEES
12/15	6,456	525	8.1%	7,394
12/14	7,179	479	6.7%	7,388
12/13	6,566	454	6.9%	7,781
12/12	6,253	382	6.1%	7,514
12/11	6,503	415	6.4%	7,727
Annual Growth	**(0.2%)**	**6.1%**	**—**	**(1.1%)**

2015 Year-End Financials

Debt ratio: 45.55%	No. of shares (mil.): 277
Return on equity: 13.80%	Dividends
Cash ($ mil.): 266	Yield: 3.2%
Current ratio: 1.01	Payout: 62.3%
Long-term debt ($ mil.): 8,559	Market value ($ mil.): 10,001

	STOCK PRICE ($) FY Close	P/E High/Low		PER SHARE ($) Earnings	Dividends	Book Value
12/15	36.08	20	17	1.89	1.16	14.21
12/14	34.75	21	15	1.74	1.08	13.34
12/13	26.77	18	14	1.66	1.02	12.98
12/12	24.38	17	15	1.42	0.96	12.09
12/11	22.08	13	10	1.58	0.84	11.92
Annual Growth	**13.1%**	**—**	**—**	**4.6%**	**8.4%**	**4.5%**

CNA Financial Corp.

CNA Financial provides cross-continental coverage. The company is an umbrella organization for a wide range of insurance providers including Continental Casualty and Continental Insurance. It primarily provides commercial policies such as workers' compensation auto and general liability. CNA also sells specialty insurance including professional liability (doctors lawyers and architects) and vehicle warranty service contracts. The firm offers commercial surety bonds (through CNA Surety) risk management claims administration and information services. Its products are sold by independent agents and brokers in the US and through partners abroad. Holding company Loews owns 90% of CNA which was formed in 1897.OperationsIn late 2014 the company realigned its core property/casualty segments to Specialty (40% of sales) Commercial (40% of sales) and International. Its non-core business segments are Life & Group Non-Core and Corporate & Other Non-Core.The Specialty segment provides professional financial and specialty products and services through independent agents brokers and managing general underwriters. The Commercial segment includes products sold to small and mid-market organizations primarily through an independent agency distribution system; it also sells commercial insurance and risk management products to large corporations primarily through insurance brokers. Meanwhile the International segment offers management and professional liability products and services outside of the US; distribution is via a network of brokers independent agencies and managing general underwriters. It also sells on the Lloyd's marketplace.Most of CNA Financial's non-core insurance products are in run-off including a few remaining life annuity and pension products as well as accident and health insurance.Geographic ReachCNA is headquartered in Chicago and has offices throughout the US and Canada; it also has locations in Europe and Asia.Sales and MarketingIn the US independent agents and brokers market CNA products while partners handle the coverage abroad. It primarily targets companies in the health care manufacturing education financial services and construction industries.Financial AnalysisCNA's revenue has seen slow growth over the past few years. In 2014 revenue decreased 2% to $9.6 billion on decreases in the Commercial segment which saw net written premiums decline $143 million. That slowdown was indicative of a lower level of new business in an increasingly competitive market although offset by rate increases. The decline in Commercial was partially offset by a $43 million increase in the Specialty segment. Net written premiums in the International segment fell $79 million largely due to changes in the recently acquired London-based Hardy subsidiary and the termination of a specialty product managing general underwriter relationship in Canada.The lower revenue as well as a $211 million loss from discontinued operations from the 2014 sale of Continental Assurance Company led to a 26% decline in net revenue (to $691 million).Cash flow from operations rose 20% to $1.4 billion in 2014 on lower net claim payments and other factors.StrategyCNA is focused on strengthening its core commercial operations through both enhanced customer retention efforts and new customer additions. In 2015 it expanded its Allied Vendor Program for law firms by adding three companies offering services to strengthen customers' risk control programs. Also that year the company expanded its specialty lines business into Canada.CNA partnered with equipment mainte-

nance and asset management service provider Remi in 2014. The company intends to offer a program to manage the risk of equipment maintenance and repair.In 2014 the company began efforts to sell its run-off and pension deposit business. It also sold Continental Assurance Company a structured settlement and group annuity subsidiary.

HISTORY

When merchant Henry Bowen could not find the type of fire insurance he wanted he began Continental Insurance. Bowen assembled a group of investors and started with about $500000 in capital. In 1882 Continental Insurance added marine and tornado insurance. Seven years later Francis Moore became president; he was developer of the Universal Mercantile Schedule a system of assessing fire hazards in buildings.

About the time Continental Insurance was writing the book on fire insurance several midwestern investors were having trouble assessing risk in their own insurance field —disability. In 1897 this group founded Continental Casualty in Hammond Indiana. In the early years its primary clients were railroads. Continental Casualty eventually merged with other companies in the field and by 1905 had branch offices in nine states and Hawaii and was writing business in 41 states and territories.

Both Continentals added new insurance lines in 1911: Continental Insurance went into personal auto and Continental Casualty formed subsidiary Continental Assurance to sell life insurance. By 1915 Continental Insurance had four primary companies; spurred by growing prewar patriotism they were called the America Fore Group. Both Continentals rose to the challenges presented by the World Wars and the Depression; they entered the 1950s ready for new growth.

In the 1960s the companies began to diversify. Continental Insurance added interests in Diners Club and Capital Financial Services; in 1968 it formed holding company Continental Corp. Meanwhile Continental Assurance (which had formed its own holding company CNA Financial) went even farther afield adding mutual fund consumer finance nursing home and residential construction companies.

By the early 1970s CNA was on the ropes because of the recession and setbacks in the housing business. In 1974 Robert and Laurence Tisch bought most of the company and cut costs ruthlessly. Continental had its own problems in the 1970s including an Iranian joint venture that got caught up in the revolution.

Both companies suffered losses arising from Hurricane Andrew in 1992 but CNA which did its housecleaning in the 1970s was better able to deal with the blow than Continental which entered the 1990s in need of restructuring.

Rising interest rates in 1994 hurt Continental whose merger with CNA in 1995 made CNA one of the US's top 10 insurance companies. CNA consolidated the two operations cutting about 5000 jobs.

CNA bought Western National Warranty in 1995 followed by managed care provider CoreSource the next year. In 1997 the company spun off its surety business in a deal with Capsure Holdings and formed CNA Surety. Taking advantage of outsourcing trends CNA created CNA UniSource (payroll and human resources services) and bought its payroll servicer Interlogic Systems the next year.

CNA pursued a global strategy buying majority interests in an Argentine workers' compensation carrier and a British marine insurer but with 1998 sales flat and earnings down the tube the company did more slashing than accumulating. It cut 2400 jobs and exited such lines as agriculture and entertainment insurance.

The company exited the personal insurance business to focus on the commercial market: It transferred its personal insurance lines including its auto and homeowners coverage to Allstate in 1999. Then in 2000 CNA sold its life reinsurance operations to a subsidiary of Munich Re.

As part of a restructuring effort (the company reshuffled itself into three major segments: property/casualty life and group) CNA fired some 10% of its workforce in 2001. In 2002 CNA paid out more than $450 million in claims related to the attacks on the World Trade Center.

CNA Financial restated its earnings in 2002 after being questioned by the SEC over the accounting treatment of investment losses.

Freeing up some much needed capital CNA sold its group benefits business to The Hartford in 2003 for some $530 million. To better focus on its remaining property/casualty lines the company sold its individual life insurance segment to Swiss Re Life & Health in 2004.

EXECUTIVES

EVP General Counsel and Secretary, Jonathan D. (Jon) Kantor, $800,000 total compensation
Chairman CEO and Chairman CNA Insurance Company Limited (CNA Europe), Thomas F. (Tom) Motamed, $1,000,000 total compensation
EVP and Chief Administration Officer, Thomas (Tom) Pontarelli, $697,917 total compensation
President and COO CNA Canada, Gary J. Owcar
President and COO CNA Specialty, Mark Herman, $675,000 total compensation
President CNA Surety, John F. Welch
EVP and CFO, D. Craig Mense, $825,000 total compensation
Central Zone Officer, Gregory M. (Greg) Vezzosi
Chief Executive Hardy, David J. (Dave) Brosnan
Southeastern Zone Officer, James R. (Rob) Huber
Chairman and CEO, Dino E. Robusto, age 57
EVP Worldwide Property and Casualty Claim, George R. Fay
EVP and Chief Actuary, Larry A. Haefner, $367,628 total compensation
Mid-Atlantic Zone Officer, Bob McCarty
Northern Zone Officer, Steve Wachtel
President and COO CNA Canada, John Hennessy
SVP and CIO, Ray Oral
President Worldwide Field Operations, Timothy J. (Tim) Szerlong, $698,125 total compensation
Northeastern Zone Officer, Jim Romanelli
SVP and Chief Risk Officer, Mark Verheyen
SVP Worldwide Operations, Katie Cunning
SVP Ceded Reinsurance, Peter Lies
Director of Underwriting Hardy Underwriting Bermuda Ltd., Patrick Gage
Western Zone Officer, Steve Marohn
President Long-Term Care, Al Miralles
President and COO CNA Commercial, Kevin Leidwinger
Auditors: DELOITTE & TOUCHE LLP

LOCATIONS

HQ: CNA Financial Corp.
333 South Wabash, Chicago, IL 60604
Phone: 312 822-5000   **Fax:** 312 822-6419
Web: www.cna.com

PRODUCTS/OPERATIONS

2014 Sales

	$ mil.	% of total
Commercial		
Middle market	1,631	17
Small business insurance	709	7
Other commercial insurance	1,343	14
Specialty		
Management & professional	2,818	29
Surety	509	5
Warranty & alternative risks	381	4
International		
Hardy	365	4
CNA Europe	335	3
Canada	273	3
Life & Group	1,279	13
Corporate & other	56	1
Adjustments	(7)	-
Total	**9,692**	**100**

Selected Solutions

Business interruption
Cargo (ocean marine)
CNA connect
CNA paramount
Commercial auto
Commercial general liability
Cyber liability
Directors & officers (d&o)
Employment practices liability (epl)
Epack extra
Equipment breakdown
Fidelity and crime insurance
Inland marine
International
Kidnap ransom and extortion
Professional liability (errors & omissions)
Property
Surety
Umbrella liability
Warranty
Workers' compensation

COMPETITORS

ACMAT	Nationwide
AIG	Old Republic
American Financial Group	State Farm
	The Hartford
Aspen Insurance	Travelers Companies
Assurant	United Fire
Berkshire Hathaway	W. R. Berkley
Cincinnati Financial	White Mountains
Everest Re	Insurance Group
Liberty Mutual	Zurich Insurance Group

HISTORICAL FINANCIALS

Company Type: Public

Income Statement

FYE: December 31

	ASSETS ($ mil.)	NET INCOME ($ mil.)	INCOME AS % OF ASSETS	EMPLOYEES
12/14	55,566	691	1.2%	6,900
12/13	57,194	937	1.6%	7,035
12/12	58,522	628	1.1%	7,500
12/11	55,179	614	1.1%	7,600
12/10	55,331	690	1.2%	8,000
Annual Growth	0.1%	0.0%	—	(3.6%)

2014 Year-End Financials

Debt ratio: 4.61%
Return on equity: 5.43%
Cash ($ mil.): 190
Current ratio: —
Long-term debt ($ mil.): —

No. of shares (mil.): 269
Dividends
 Yield: 5.1%
 Payout: 75.7%
Market value ($ mil.): 10,451

	STOCK PRICE ($) FY Close	P/E High/Low		PER SHARE ($) Earnings	Dividends	Book Value
12/14	38.71	17	14	2.55	2.00	47.39
12/13	42.89	12	8	3.47	0.80	46.90
12/12	28.01	13	11	2.33	0.60	45.71
12/11	26.75	14	9	2.28	0.40	42.92
12/10	27.05	13	10	2.28	0.00	40.70
Annual Growth	9.4%	—	—	2.8%	—	3.9%

CNO Financial Group Inc

Have a modest but stable income? Graying at the temples? CNO Financial Group finds that especially attractive and has life insurance and related products targeted at you and 4 million other customers. With a focus on middle-income working families and seniors the holding company's primary units include Bankers Life & Casualty which provides Medicare supplement life annuities and long-term care insurance; Washington National which offers specified disease insurance accident insurance life insurance and annuities; and Colonial Penn which offers life insurance to consumers. CNO Financial operates nationwide.

Operations

The health and life offerings of the Bankers Life division account for about 70% of CNO's annual revenues. The Washington National division accounts for more than 20% of sales.

Geographic Reach

With operations throughout the US CNO counts Florida California Texas and Pennsylvania among its largest markets; together the four states accounted for about a quarter of CNO's total premiums.

Sales and Marketing

Bankers Life sells products through its own team of career agents; it also markets Medicare Advantage plans through distribution arrangements with Humana and United HealthCare and Medicare Part D plans through an arrangement with Coventry Health Care. Washington National uses a combination of brokers independent agents and worksite marketing programs. The smaller Colonial Penn unit sells policies through direct sales efforts including advertising mail telemarketing and online sales campaigns.

Financial Performance

CNO has reported several years of steady single-digit revenue growth including in 2013 when revenue rose 3% to $4.5 billion. However revenue decreased 7% to $4.1 billion in 2014 due to a decline in the Bankers Life division and the sale of Conseco Life Insurance Company (CLIC). Premiums collected on long-term care policies decreased 6.3% reflecting the run-off of that business and the continuing shift towards short-term care sales.

Net income which has fluctuated for the past five years plummeted 89% to $51.4 million due to losses on the CLIC sale and reinsurance transactions. Cash flow from operations which has also been up and down followed suit and declined 83% to $122 million.

Strategy

CNO believes its target markets of seniors and middle-income families are often overlooked and underserved giving the company opportunity in the senior market which is expected to double over the next decade. The company is interested in both organic growth and strategic acquisitions. It launched a whole life product for minors in 2013 and Colonial Penn began targeting Hispanics in 2014. Also that year Bankers Life added 11 new sales offices bringing its total number of branches and satellite offices to 312.

In addition CNO is revamping some of its distribution channels to increase efficiency and reach. It is also working to reduce unnecessary costs across the entire organization while expanding its agent salesforce and number of locations. In 2014 it sold life insurance subsidiary Conseco Life Insurance Company (CLIC) which primarily consisted of closed block life insurance and annuities to Wilton

Reassurance. In 2015 the company struck up a partnership with Cognizant to improve its information technology processes and enable more rapid innovatoin.

Company Background

In 2010 the company changed its name from Conseco to CNO Financial Group to reflect a broader identity. (The firm also sought to distance itself from historical financial instabilities associated with the Conseco brand.) The name change came after several years' worth of management efforts to conserve capital reduce complexity and debt and sequester or divest less profitable operations.

HISTORY

The company evolved from Security National an Indiana insurance company formed in 1979 by Stephen Hilbert. The former encyclopedia salesman and Aetna executive believed most insurance companies were bloated and the industry itself overcrowded as well as ripe for consolidation by a smart lean organization.

In 1982 it began a growth-by-acquisition strategy with the purchase of Executive Income Life Insurance (renamed Security National Life Insurance). The next year it bought Consolidated National Life Insurance and renamed the expanded company Conseco.

The firm went public in 1985 using the proceeds to fund an acquisitions spree that included Lincoln American Life Insurance Lincoln Income Life (sold 1990) Bankers National Life Insurance Western National Life Insurance (sold 1994) and National Fidelity Life Insurance.

In 1990 the company formed Conseco Capital Partners (with General Electric and Bankers Trust) to finance acquisitions without seeming to burden the parent company with debt. This device financed the purchase of Great American Reserve and the 1991 acquisition of Beneficial Standard Life. The former Conseco bought Bankers Life Insurance in 1992 then sold 67% of it the next year. Also in 1993 the company formed the Private Capital Group to invest in noninsurance companies.

In 1994 the company tried to acquire the much larger Kemper Corp. but shied away from the debt load that the $2.6 billion deal would have entailed. The aborted deal cost $36 million in bank and accounting fees and spelled the end of the company's relationship with Merrill Lynch which had underwritten the company's IPO when a Merrill Lynch analyst downgraded its stock after the fiasco.

Meanwhile Private Capital's success led the company to form Conseco Global Investments. Other investments included stakes in racetrack and riverboat gambling operations in Indiana.

In 1996 and 1997 the firm absorbed eight life health property/casualty and specialty insurance companies and raised its interest in American Life Holdings to 100%.

Itching to move beyond insurance in 1998 the company bought Green Tree Financial the US's #1 mobile home financier. Charges of Green Tree's own fuzzy accounting practices helped torpedo the company's quest for a federal thrift charter. But the troubles had just begun. The mobile home finance industry took a dive as customers refinanced at lower rates and prepayments slammed Green Tree Financial reducing Conseco's earnings.

The company tried to recoup in 1999 by launching an ad campaign portraying the company as the "Wal-Mart of financial services." It also continued the acquisition spree. But Green Tree Financial (renamed Conseco Finance that year) couldn't stanch the flow of red ink: Buyers grew wary of the quality of the finance unit's loan securities and changes in accounting methods cost the parent company a $350 million charge against earnings for 1999.

In 2002 due to its financial woes Gary Wendt stepped down as CEO the NYSE suspended trading in the company and its stock was moved to the OTC. The company also filed for Chapter 11 protection in 2002. As part of the reorganization agreement it agreed to sell Conseco Finance. The company's insurance operations were not subject to the Chapter 11 agreement.

In 2003 it finally unloaded the Conseco Finance unit to CFN Investment Holdings LLC an investor group and General Electric Co.'s consumer finance unit for $1 billion. The company emerged from bankruptcy in September 2003.

The company agreed to pay a fine of $6.3 million in 2008 after an investigation determined that its long-term care insurance business Conseco Senior Health had wrongly denied claims and mishandled complaints and that some sales and marketing practices at Banker's Life did not comply with industry standards. To put what it could in the past in late 2008 the firm spun off its closed block of long-term care insurance. The new entity was named Senior Health Insurance Company of Pennsylvania and consisted entirely of policies in run-off.

EXECUTIVES

EVP COO and CTO, Bruce K. Baude, age 51, $483,334 total compensation
Chief Investment Officer and President 40|86 Advisors, Eric R. Johnson, age 55, $500,000 total compensation
CEO and Director, Edward J. (Ed) Bonach, age 61, $1,000,000 total compensation
EVP Human Resources, Susan L. (Sue) Menzel, age 50
President Bankers Life and Casualty Company, Scott L. Goldberg, age 44
Chief Business Officer, Scott R. Perry, age 53, $573,583 total compensation
EVP and Chief Actuary, Christopher J. (Chris) Nickele, age 59, $387,790 total compensation
EVP and General Counsel, Matthew J. (Matt) Zimpfer, age 48
President Colonial Penn Life Insurance Company, Gerardo Monroy, age 48
President Washington National, Barbara S. (Barb) Stewart, age 56
Interim CFO and SVP and Chief Accounting Officer, John R. Kline
Vice President Technical Support, Gevan Arnett
Vice President Product Management Worksite Health and Specified Disease, Blake Westerfield
Senior Vice President Investor Relations, Erik Helding
Vice President Finance, John (Jack) Rizzo
Vice President Compensation and Benefits, Grace Brothers
Vice President Of Information Technology, Adiza Caldwell
Assistant Vice President of Networks, Aaron Delprince
Vice President Communications, Barbara Ciesemier
Senior Vice President Health Product Man, Richard (Dick) Garner
Vice President, Jeremy Williams
Assistant Vice President Internet T Senior Director Customer Service, Ming Tong
Assistant Vice President, John McKain
Vice President Enterprise Information Technology Strategy and Services, Kuldip Mohanty
Senior Vice President, Richard James
Senior Vice President Operations, Chris McKee
Senior Vice President Investor Relations, Erik Carol Untrauer
Vice President, Joe Calvin
Vice President It, Mohammed Alhaffar

Vice President Information Technology, Lynn Murphy
Vice President Life Prodcut Development, Greg Turner
Senior Vice President and Valuation Actuary, Mark Billingsley
Assistant Vice President, Paul Okerson
Assistant Vice President Director Field Support Services, Shawn Ardizone
Senior Vice President, Tim Bischof
Vice President general Auditor, Thomas (Thom) Kleyle
Chairman, Neal C. Schneider, age 71
Secretary, Karl Kindig
Auditors: PricewaterhouseCoopers LLP

LOCATIONS

HQ: CNO Financial Group Inc
11825 N. Pennsylvania Street, Carmel, IN 46032
Phone: 317 817-6100
Web: www.cnoinc.com

PRODUCTS/OPERATIONS

2014 Sales

	$ mil.	% of total
Bankers Life	2,638	64
Washington National	903	22
Colonial Penn	288	7
Net investment income	14	-
Fee and other income	6	-
Net realized investment gains	33	1
Revenue related to certain non-strategic investments	33	1
Fee revenue related to transition and support services agreements	15	-
Revenues of CLIC prior to be sold	210	5
Total	**4,144**	**100**

COMPETITORS

Aetna	Mutual of Omaha
Aflac	Northwestern Mutual
American General	Protective Life
Lincoln Financial Group	Prudential
MassMutual	Securian Financial
MetLife	Torchmark
Monumental Life	Unum Group

HISTORICAL FINANCIALS

Company Type: Public

Income Statement

FYE: December 31

	ASSETS ($ mil.)	NET INCOME ($ mil.)	INCOME AS % OF ASSETS	EMPLOYEES
12/14	31,184	51	0.2%	4,200
12/13	34,780	478	1.4%	4,250
12/12	34,131	221	0.6%	4,200
12/11	33,332	382	1.1%	3,800
12/10	31,899	284	0.9%	3,680
Annual Growth	(0.6%)	(34.8%)	—	3.4%

2014 Year-End Financials

Debt ratio: 11.54%	No. of shares (mil.): 203
Return on equity: 1.07%	Dividends
Cash ($ mil.): 679	Yield: 1.3%
Current ratio: —	Payout: 72.7%
Long-term debt ($ mil.): —	Market value ($ mil.): 3,501

	STOCK PRICE ($) FY Close	P/E High/Low		Earnings	PER SHARE ($) Dividends	Book Value
12/14	17.22	80	65	0.24	0.24	23.06
12/13	17.69	8	4	2.06	0.11	22.49
12/12	9.33	11	6	0.83	0.06	22.80
12/11	6.31	5	3	1.31	0.00	20.86
12/10	6.78	6	4	0.99	0.00	17.23
Annual Growth	26.2%	—	—	(29.8%)	—	7.6%

CoBiz Financial Inc

CoBiz Financial is reaching new heights in the Rockies and in the Valley of the Sun. It's the holding company for CoBiz Bank which operates as Colorado Business Bank and Arizona Business Bank. The former operates more than 10 branches in the Denver Boulder and Vail areas; the latter has about a half-dozen branches in and around Phoenix. CoBiz's locations operate as separate community banks each with a local president who has decision-making authority. The company offers investment banking services through subsidiary Green Manning & Bunch insurance through CoBiz Insurance and wealth management through CoBiz Investment Management CoBiz Trust and Financial Designs.

Operations

Residential and commercial real estate mortgages make up approximately half of CoBiz's loan portfolio; business loans are more than a third.

Sales and Marketing

CoBiz courts professionals high-net-worth individuals and families small and midsized business clients as the company believes that it is able to provide more personalized services than its larger competitors while offering more sophisticated products than smaller banks. It looks to extend its relationships with customers often requiring borrowers to procure other products and services from the bank such as deposit accounts or treasury management. Other initiatives include growing its wealth management operations and other fee-based activities opening new branches and acquiring other financial institutions throughout the West.

Financial Performance

The company's revenue increased slightly in fiscal 2013 compared to the previous year. It reported $137 million in revenue for fiscal 2013 after claiming $136.7 million in revenue for fiscal 2012 and $147.2 million in revenue for fiscal 2011.

Net income increased from $24.5 million in fiscal 2012 up to $27.6 million for fiscal 2013. The company's cash on hand decreased by about $5 million in fiscal 2013 compared to fiscal 2012 levels.

Strategy

The company had been growing its portfolio of commercial real estate and operating loans but as with many of its peers during the economic downturn its loan volume slowed and asset quality deteriorated.

EXECUTIVES

EVP and CFO, Lyne B. Andrich, age 48, $300,000 total compensation
EVP and COO, Richard J. Dalton, age 58, $275,000 total compensation
Chairman Colorado Business Bank and Arizona Business Bank, Jonathan C. Lorenz, age 63, $380,000 total compensation
Chairman and CEO, Steven Bangert, age 58, $522,500 total compensation
CEO Colorado Business Bank and Arizona Business Bank, Scott E. Page, $297,500 total compensation
Vice President Bsa Manager And Bsa Officer, Bonnie Sajczuk
Assistant Vice President Operations Mana, Stacy Willems
Assistant Vice President, Eric Curry
Executive Vice President, Margaret (Peg) Battiste
Vice President, Greg Grote
Vice President, Mike Jezier
Assistant Vice President Portfolio Manager, Michael Godo

Executive Vice President, Margaret D'Emery
First Vice President Public Finance, Logan McKenzie
Vice President Public Finance, Derek Peters
Auditors: Crowe Horwath LLP

LOCATIONS

HQ: CoBiz Financial Inc
  821 17th Street, Denver, CO 80202
Phone: 303 312-3400
Web: www.cobizbank.com

COMPETITORS

BBVA Compass Bancshares	KeyCorp
Bank of America	U.S. Bancorp
FirstBank Holding Company	Vectra Bank
	Wells Fargo

HISTORICAL FINANCIALS

Company Type: Public

Income Statement

FYE: December 31

	ASSETS ($ mil.)	NET INCOME ($ mil.)	INCOME AS % OF ASSETS	EMPLOYEES
12/15	3,351	26	0.8%	532
12/14	3,062	29	0.9%	534
12/13	2,800	27	1.0%	513
12/12	2,653	24	0.9%	512
12/11	2,423	33	1.4%	546
Annual Growth	**8.4%**	**(6.1%)**	**—**	**(0.6%)**

2015 Year-End Financials

Debt ratio: 3.91%	No. of shares (mil.): 41
Return on equity: 8.95%	Dividends
Cash ($ mil.): 67	Yield: 1.2%
Current ratio: —	Payout: 24.6%
Long-term debt ($ mil.): —	Market value ($ mil.): 552

	STOCK PRICE ($) FY Close	P/E High/Low	PER SHARE ($)		
			Earnings	Dividends	Book Value
12/15	13.42	22 17	0.62	0.17	6.65
12/14	13.13	19 14	0.70	0.15	7.57
12/13	11.96	18 11	0.66	0.12	6.96
12/12	7.47	13 10	0.55	0.07	6.46
12/11	5.77	9 6	0.76	0.04	5.93
Annual Growth	**23.5%**	**— —**	**(5.0%)**	**43.6%**	**2.9%**

Coca-Cola Co (The)

Coke is it —it being the #1 nonalcoholic beverage company as well as one of the world's most recognizable brands. The Coca-Cola Company is home to 20 billion-dollar-brands including four of the top five soft drinks: Coca-Cola Diet Coke Fanta and Sprite. Other top brands include Minute Maid Powerade and vitaminwater. All told the company owns or licenses and markets more than 500 beverage brands mainly sparkling drinks but also waters juice drinks energy and sports drinks and ready-to-drink teas and coffees. With the world's largest beverage distribution system The Coca-Cola Company reaches thirsty consumers in more than 200 countries.

HISTORY

Atlanta pharmacist John Pemberton invented Coke in 1886. His bookkeeper Frank Robinson named the product after two ingredients coca leaves (later cleaned of narcotics) and kola nuts. By 1891 druggist Asa Candler had bought The Coca-Cola Company and within four years the soda-fountain drink was available in all states; it was in Canada and Mexico by 1898.

Candler sold most US bottling rights in 1899 to Benjamin Thomas and John Whitehead of Chattanooga Tennessee for $1. The two designed a regional franchise bottling system that created more than 1000 bottlers within 20 years. In 1916 Candler retired to become Atlanta's mayor; his family sold the company to Atlanta banker Ernest Woodruff for $25 million in 1919. Coca-Cola went public that year.

The firm expanded overseas and introduced the slogans "The Pause that Refreshes" (1929) and "It's the Real Thing" (1941). To keep WWII soldiers in Cokes at a nickel a pop the government built 64 overseas bottling plants. Coca-Cola bought Minute Maid in 1960 and began launching new drinks —Fanta (1960) Sprite (1960) TAB (1963) and Diet Coke (1982).

In 1981 Roberto Goizueta became chairman. Four years later with Coke slipping in market share the firm changed its formula and introduced New Coke which consumers soundly rejected (thus Coca-Cola Classic was born). In 1986 it consolidated the US bottling operations it owned into Coca-Cola Enterprises and sold 51% of the new company to the public. Goizueta also engineered the company's purchase of Columbia Pictures in 1982. (Columbia earned Coke a $1 billion profit when it sold the studio to Sony in 1989.)

In 1995 it bought Barq's root beer. Goizueta died of lung cancer in 1997; while he was at the helm the firm's value rose from $4 billion to $145 billion. Douglas Ivester the architect of Coca-Cola's restructured bottling operations succeeded him. An agreement to buy about 30 Cadbury Schweppes beverage brands —including Canada Dry Dr Pepper and Schweppes —outside the US and France was scaled down because of antitrust concerns. Completed in 1999 the deal also excluded Canada much of continental Europe and Mexico. (Cadbury in 2008 spun off its beverage division which became Dr Pepper Snapple Group.)

A battered Ivester resigned in 2000; president and COO Douglas Daft was named chairman and CEO. Coca-Cola began its largest cutbacks ever slashing nearly 5000 jobs and later agreed to pay nearly $193 million to settle a race-discrimination suit filed by African-American workers.

To fortify its portfolio in the fast-growing noncarbonated drinks segment Coca-Cola acquired Mad River Traders (teas juices sodas) and Odwalla (juices and smoothies) in 2001. The company also bought a 35% interest (San Miguel Corporation owned the rest) in bottler Coca-Cola Philippines from Coca-Cola Amatil. (In 2005 Coke bought the remaining percentage of the Philippine bottler.) The company announced the creation of a huge beverage and snack distribution joint venture with Procter & Gamble but the multibillion-dollar operation fell apart before it could begin. Coca-Cola also announced that it would invest $150 million to build bottling facilities in China.

In 2002 Coca-Cola introduced Vanilla Coke its biggest new product launch since the disastrous New Coke debacle. The company also secured distribution rights to Danone's Evian brand in North America and paid about $128 million when it formed a joint venture (CCDA Waters LLC) with Danone to produce market and distribute Danone's bottled water in the North America (including Dannon and Sparkletts brands under license). Also in 2002 Steven Heyer president and COO of Coca-Cola Ventures and Coca-Cola Latin America was named Coca-Cola's new president and COO. (The company's former president Jack Stahl had left after a reorganization in 2001.)

As part of the restructuring initiated by Daft in 2000 another 1000 employees (half in Atlanta) were laid off in 2003 after the company decided to combine several business units under the Coca-Cola North America umbrella. The company laid off 2800 employees worldwide in 2003.

Those layoffs led one former employee to sue claiming the soft drink maker improperly accounted for funds discriminated against minorities and in 2000 rigged test marketing of frozen Coca-Cola at a Virginia Burger King. Coca-Cola said it does not violate general accounting principles and does not discriminate. However the company said it had already disciplined employees involved in the Burger King tests and Coke executive Thomas Moore who led the fountain drinks division responsible for the questionable tests resigned. Coke also agreed to pay Burger King as much as $21 million to settle the matter. Coke said in 2003 it would reduce its revenue by $9 million to make up for accounting errors from the fountain drinks division that managed the troubled tests. Coke later settled its dispute with the former employee who first raised concerns about Coke's conduct agreeing to pay $500000 in severance and legal costs.

Later in 2003 trouble broke out for the company overseas. Claims surfaced in India that both Coke and Pepsi bottled in that country contain traces of DDT malathion and other pesticides that exceed government limits. Both Coke and Pepsi denied the reports in a joint press conference. Government labs cleared the colas saying the drinks were safe but not before both soft drink companies saw sales dip by as much as 50% in a two-week period.

Trying to boost the younger consumer's interest in its flagship cola Coca-Cola launched new marketing and ad campaigns in 2003. Efforts included changing graphics on Coke bottles and cans back to a more traditional look. However Coca-Cola took the opposite tactic to spur interest in Sprite unveiling Sprite Remix a tropical-flavored version of the soft drink. Minute Maid unveiled Minute Maid Premium Heart Wise which claims to lower cholesterol as long as people consistently drink two glasses a day.

Coca-Cola rolled out a lime version of its Diet Coke in 2004. (The non-diet version came out in 2005.) The flavor joined diet cherry lemon and vanilla. In making the announcement Coca-Cola said it also had reformulated its lemon flavor so that it tastes "lighter." Also in 2004 Coke opened an online music store in the UK called MyCokemusic.com. A month later Coke began selling its Dasani bottled water in the UK and 19 other countries. Later in 2004 the company recalled Dasani water in Europe because of elevated levels of bromate. In addition Daft retired as Coca-Cola's chairman and CEO in 2004 and former Coca-Cola HBC CEO E. Neville Isdell replaced him.

Responding to the growing awareness by consumers of health problems associated with obesity and inactive lifestyles in 2004 Coca-Cola created The Beverage Institute for Health & Wellness a beverage research and educational operation which the company hopes will lead to the creation of more healthful beverage products.

Having introduced Minute Maid products in Russia in 2004 Coke furthered its juice presence in the country with the 2005 purchase of Russian juice maker Multon. Coke bought the company in conjunction with Coca-Cola Hellenic Bottling Co. Later that year Coke began test marketing a Mountain Dew-like drink named Vault in Alabama North Carolina and Tennessee. (Surge a previous Mountain Dew competitor tried by Coke failed in testing.) In 2005 the company announced the phasing out of Vanilla Coke and introduction of Black Cherry Coke.

In 2005 Coke bought Danone's 49% stake in their North American bottled-water venture for about $100 million. The joint venture never turned a profit during its three-year run but Coke hopes full ownership of the Dannon and Sparkletts brands will prove profitable. Coke still shares North American import and marketing rights of Danone's premier water brand Evian which although the world's top-selling bottled water has seen declining in US sales.

The company's rivalry with PepsiCo goes beyond soda to juice products (Coca-Cola's Minute Maid vs. PepsiCo's Tropicana) bottled water (Dasani vs. Aquafina) and other noncarbonated products. Feeling pressure to stay competitive with these faster selling beverages Coca-Cola introduced an energy drink Full Throttle in 2005.

Also in 2005 Coke also announced a revamping of its global marketing team announcing the retirement of Sandy Allen president of its European division. In an effort to expand its international product offerings later that same year it acquired Brazilian juice maker Sucos Mais for some $48 million.New drinks introduced in 2006 included Vault (a Mountain Dew knock-off). That year Blak a coffee-flavored Coke (with half the calories and twice the caffeine of a regular Coke that was in development for two years) was first test-marketed in France and subsequently introduced in the US. (The pricey soda —$1.99 for an 8-ounce bottle —was discontinued in the US in 2007 due to poor sales.)Boosting its drinks in the reduced-calorie category in 2006 the company introduced a so-called "calorie-burning" drink called Enviga a green-tea-based drink. It is marketed through a joint venture with Nestlé . (The joint venture called Beverage Partners Worldwide primarily focuses on black tea drinks.)The company also launched a new line of premium coffee and tea beverages called Far Coast in 2006. The drinks were launched in Canada along with Far Coast concept stores where consumers can taste test the flavors. The company expanded its reach into coffee further with a deal with coffeehouse chain Caribou Coffee. Coca-Cola and Caribou created a new line of ready-to-drink iced coffee beverages.

EXECUTIVES

Executive Vice President, Joseph (Jo) Gladden
EVP and Chief Administrative Officer, Alexander B. (Alex) Cummings, age 59, $700,000 total compensation
EVP Supply Chain; President Bottling Investments Group, Irial Finan, age 58, $869,022 total compensation
EVP and CTO, Alan Boehme
EVP and President Coca-Cola North America, J. Alexander M. (Sandy) Douglas, age 54, $682,711 total compensation
EVP and Chief Marketing Officer, Marcos de Quinto
EVP and President Coca-Cola International, Ahmet C. Bozer, age 55, $721,000 total compensation
President Latin America Group, Brian J. Smith
President and COO, James R. Quincey, age 51
Group President Asia, Atul Singh
Chairman and CEO, Muhtar Kent, age 62, $1,600,000 total compensation
EVP and CFO, Kathy N. Waller, age 57, $641,890 total compensation
President Eurasia & Africa Group, Nathan Kalumbu
VP; President The McDonald's Division, Javier C. Goizueta
Vice President Customer Solutions Large Store North and South, Kraig Adams
Chief Customer and Commercial Leadership Officer, Julie Hamilton

Vice President Field Operations Coca, Charles (Chas) Holmes
Senior Vice President GMCL Business Services Center, John (Jack) Hackett
Vice President Finance National Retail CCR, Jennifer (Jen) Finley
Senior Vice President Global Community Connections, Ingrid Jones
Vice President Marketing Venturing and Emerging Brands, Mary-Ann Somers
Vice President Network Optimization and Strategy, Scott Boze
Vice President Public Affairs and Communications, Scott Williamson
Vice President, Jerry Rodriguez
Vice President and Controller, Steve Vonderhaar
Vice President Of Region Marketing, David Preston
Senior Vice President Human Resources, Stevens Sainte-rose
Senior Vice President and Northwest Region General Manager, Bill O'Brien
Vice President Community Relations, Lori Georgebillingsley
Vice President Community Relations, Lori Billingsley
Vice President SC Operations, Luis Viso
Vice President And Investor Relations Officer, Jackson Kelly
Vice President Human Resources, Kelly Holmes
Vice President General Tax Counsel, Robert (Bob) Jordan
Vice President National Sales, Jim Andrist
Vice President, Dan Dejournette
Vice President Human Resources Brazil, Jose Hernandez
Vice President Government Relations, Connell Stafford
Vice President Of Tamacc, Ish Arebalos
Vice President Sprite Flavors, Kim Venkatesh
Vice President Environment, Jefferson Seabright
Vice President Manufacturing, Pat Paya
National Account Manager, Dean Crozier
Vice President Sales Operations Refreshments, Dawn Kirk
Vice President Engineering Coca Cola, Marc Katz
Vice President Purchasing And Information Technologist, Janine Shearer
Vice President of Strategic Projects, Ben Shanley
Vice President Procurement Indirect Goods and Services, Christina Ruggiero
VP and Chief of Internal Audit, Steven J (Steve) Vonderhaar
Vice President Of Latin Affairs, Rudy Beserra
Vice President Demand Management and Supply Chain Planning, Jeff Messer
Vice President corporate Communications, Ben Deutsch
Vice President Market Unit Field Operations, Mike Bonham
Vice President, Alex Zigliara
Senior Vice President of Business Development, Mike Ohmstede
Vice President Region Manager Coca Cola Nor, Doug Coffed
Vice President Global Information, Daniel (Dan) Dilucchio
Vice President Environmental Communications, Lisa Manley
Region Vice President Public Affairs and Communications, Percy Wells
Refreshments Houston Vice President of Field Operations, Hector Amaya
Vice President International Government Relations, Michael (Mel) Goltzman
Vice President Customer Engagement, Michael J (Mel) Slocum
Vice President and Managing Director Asia Pacific Mid, Adam Juszynski
Vice President and Director Mergers and Acquisitions, Marie D Quintero Johnson

Vice President, Gary Azar
Group Director and Vice President Supply Chain, Steve Buffington
Executive Director and Vice President, Xue Guoping
Assistant Vice President Contract Manufacturing, Binoo George
Vice President Total Beverage Team, Tony Ferlauto
Vice President Distribution Management, Mike Hagen
Vice President and General Manager, Tim Mckay
Vice President of Marketing, Barry Thomas
Assistant Vice President Hispanic Marketing, Reinaldo O Padua
Vice President of Ccna Business Systems, John (Jack) Murphy
Vice President Chief Scientific and Regulatory Officer, Rhonda Applebaum
Vice President, B Shotts
Executive Vice President Director of Opr Latin America, Glenn Jordan
Vice President of Breakthrough Innovation, David (Dave) Butler
Vice President Strategic Planning, John (Jack) Farrell
Executive Vice President And Chief Finan, Gary Fayard
Senior Vice President Chief Customer and Commercial Officer, Jerry Wilson
Vice President Environment And Sustainability, Bruce Karas
Vice President For Sales Maryland Market Unit, Brendan Walshe
Information Controller Vice President, Steve Whaley
Vice President Global Health and Wellbeing Initiatives, L Bottorff
Vice President Environmental and Water Resources, Jeff Seabright
Vice President Secretary, Silvi Alzetta-Reali
Auditors: Ernst & Young LLP

LOCATIONS

HQ: Coca-Cola Co (The)
One Coca-Cola Plaza, Atlanta, GA 30313
Phone: 404 676-2121   **Fax:** 404 676-6792
Web: www.coca-colacompany.com

2014 Sales

	$ mil.	% of total
US	19,763	43
Other countries	26,235	57
Total	**45,998**	**100**

2014 Unit Sales

	% of total
North America	47
Europe	11
Asia Pacific	11
Latin America	10
Eurasia & Africa	6
Bottling investments	15
Total	**100**

PRODUCTS/OPERATIONS

2014 Sales

	% of total
Finished product operations	62
Concentrate operations	38
Total	**100**

Selected Brands

Sparkling Beverages
 Core sparkling
 Barq's
 Coca-Cola
 Coca-Cola Zero/Coke Zero
 Diet Coke/Coca-Cola Light
 Fanta
 Fresca
 Inca Kola

Lift
Schweppes
Sprite
Thums Up
Energy drinks
 Burn
 Nos
 Real Gold
Still Beverages
 Coffee & teas
 Ayataka teas
 Dogadan teas
 Georgia coffees
 Leão/Matte Leão teas
 Nestea teas
 Sokenbicha teas
 Juices and juice drinks
 Cappy
 Del Valle
 Dobriy
 Hi-C
 Minute Maid
 Minute Maid Pulpy
 Simply
 Other still beverages
 glaceau vitaminwater
 Fuze
 Sports drinks
 Aquarius
 Powerade
 Waters
 Bonaqua/Bonaqa
 Ciel
 Dasani
 Ice Dew
 Kinley
 ZICO Pure Premium Coconut Water

Selected Anchor Bottlers

Coca-Cola Amatil Limited (29%; Australia Fiji Indonesia New Zealand and Papua New Guinea)
Coca-Cola FEMSA S.A.B. de C.V. (29%; parts of Argentina Brazil Colombia Costa Rica Guatemala Mexico Nicaragua Panama and Venezuela)
Coca-Cola Hellenic Bottling Company S.A. (23%; Armenia Austria Belarus Bosnia-Herzegovina Bulgaria Croatia Cyprus the Czech Republic Estonia Greece Hungary Italy Latvia Lithuania Macedonia Moldova Montenegro Nigeria Northern Ireland Poland Republic of Ir

Selected Subsidiaries

Atlantic Manufacturing
Caribbean Refrescos Inc.
CCDA Waters LLC
Coca-Cola China Industries Ltd.
Coca-Cola Refreshments USA Inc.
Energy Brands Inc.
Hindustan Coca-Cola Beverages Private Limited
Odwalla Inc.

COMPETITORS

American Beverage	Kraft Foods Group Inc.
Aquaterra Corporation	Lassonde
Big Heart Pet Brands	Leading Brands
Britvic	Monarch Beverage (GA)
Chiquita Brands	Mountain Valley
Citrus World	Naked Juice
Clearly Canadian	National Beverage
Clement Pappas	Naumes
Cott	Nestl©
Cranberries Limited	Ocean Spray
Danone	Old Orchard
Dole Food	PepsiCo
Dr Pepper Snapple Group	Pernod Ricard
	Red Bull
Faygo	Silver Springs
Fiji Water	South Beach Beverage
Fresh Del Monte Produce	Southern Gardens Citrus
Great Western Juice	Sun-Rype
Hawaiian Springs	Sunny Delight
Hornell Brewing	Suntory Holdings
IZZE	Tree Top
Impulse Energy USA	True Drinks
Jamba	Unilever
Jones Soda	Welch's
Kirin Holdings Company	Wet Planet Beverages

HISTORICAL FINANCIALS
Company Type: Public

Income Statement

				FYE: December 31
	REVENUE ($ mil.)	NET INCOME ($ mil.)	NET PROFIT MARGIN	EMPLOYEES
12/14	45,998	7,098	15.4%	129,200
12/13	46,854	8,584	18.3%	130,600
12/12	48,017	9,019	18.8%	150,900
12/11	46,542	8,572	18.4%	146,200
12/10	35,119	11,809	33.6%	139,600
Annual Growth	**7.0%**	**(11.9%)**	**—**	**(1.9%)**

2014 Year-End Financials

Debt ratio: 45.36%—
Return on equity: 22.36%
Cash ($ mil.): 8,958
Current ratio: 1.02
Long-term debt ($ mil.): 19,063
Dividends
 Yield: 2.8%
 Payout: 76.2%
Market value ($ mil.): —

	STOCK PRICE ($) FY Close	P/E High/Low	PER SHARE ($) Earnings	Dividends	Book Value
12/14	42.22	28 23	1.60	1.22	6.94
12/13	41.31	22 19	1.90	1.12	7.54
12/12	36.25	41 18	1.97	1.02	7.34
12/11	69.97	38 33	1.85	0.94	6.99
12/10	65.77	26 20	2.53	0.88	6.76
Annual Growth	**(10.5%)**	**— —**	**(10.8%)**	**8.5%**	**0.7%**

Coca-Cola Enterprises Inc

Scientists at The Coca-Cola Company concoct the secret syrup but it's up to Coca-Cola Enterprises (CCE) to do the heavy lifting. CCE buys it combines it with other ingredients then bottles and distributes Coke products in Western Europe. One of the world's largest Coca-Cola bottlers by volume CCE bottles and distributes energy drinks sports drinks still and sparkling waters (Dr Pepper Snapple's Schweppes Abbey Well) juices and coffees and teas. The company's European reach includes distribution in Belgium France the Netherlands Norway Sweden and the UK. All told CCE operates more than 15 production and about 50 distribution facilities in Europe.

Operations
CCE is one of the largest Coca-Cola bottlers in the world handling some 8% of the Coca-Cola system's global volume in 2014. The company operates under licensing bottling and distribution agreements with The Coca-Cola Company; it has 10-year bottling agreements through 2020 with the right to request 10-year renewals.CCE makes money by marketing producing and distributing nonalcoholic beverages. Indeed the company sold approximately 12 billion bottles or cans of its beverages in 2014. It manufactures about 95% of the finished product it sells from syrups and concentrates that it purchases while the rest is purchased and sold in finished form. Coca-Cola trademark beverages accounted for nearly 70% of CCE's net sales in 2014 while Sparkling flavors and energy drinks accounted for 18% and juices isotonics and other drinks accounted for 10%.

Geographic Reach
Coca-Cola Enterprises (CCE) serves about 170 million consumers in Belgium France Luxembourg

Monaco the Netherlands Norway Sweden and the UK. The UK is CCE's largest market accounting for about a third of total unit sales. France is next with about 30% followed by Belgium (15%). The Nordic countries and Luxembourg and Monaco account for the remainder.

Sales and Marketing

The Coca-Cola Company (TCCC) and other suppliers of product to CCE advertise across all major media to promote beverage sales in local markets. CCE and TCCC have established a Global Marketing Fund agreement where TCCC pays CCE $45 million annually through the end of 2015 except under select circumstances. CCE's Share a Coke campaign in which the Coca-Cola logo was replaced with a popular names from various regions met with success in 2013 and 2014. The company plans to campaign on new opportunities around the Rugby World Cup in Great Britain in the fall of 2015 along with other similar events. CCE previously participated in the 2014 World Cup.

Financial Performance

CCE's sales and profits have remained mostly flat in recent years. Revenue inched up by less than 1% to $8.26 billion in 2014 thanks to favorable foreign currency exchange rates though overall volumes remained stagnant and bottle and can pricing per case declined by 0.5% for the year amidst a difficult retail environment and increasingly competitive landscape. Product-wise the Coca-Cola and Diet Coke/Coca-Cola Light product sales volumes shrank by 1% while Coca-Cola Zero sales volumes rose by double-digits. CCE's Sprite Fanta and Schweppes sales declined slightly for the year while its Monster and Relentless energy drink brands grew by 6.5% for the year. Despite slightly higher revenue in 2014 CCE's net income dipped by 1% to $663 million for the year as it paid higher income taxes when it repatriated some of its foreign earnings to the US during the year. The company's cash from operations rose by 18% despite lower cash earnings in 2014 mostly thanks to higher cash earnings after adjusting for income tax expenses and because CCE sold off more of its inventory.

Strategy

CCE reiterated its long-term strategy in 2015 to introduce new initiatives for its core brand portfolio (including its Coca-Cola Zero Fanta and Sprite Brands) strengthen its focus on high-growth brands and continue to promote brand and package innovations. It also planned to introduce its newer brands —which include Coca-Cola Life Smartwater and Finley —into more territories. Additionally the company planned to grow its energy brands by continuing to build its partnership with Monster.Its marketplace strategy which it also outlined in 2015 planned to tackle both the home and cold channels. For the home channel it planned to introduce a price and package diversification strategy with price-specific programs for large plastic products new multi-pack products providing extra consumer value and smaller plastic packages and multi-pack cans. For the cold channels the company planned to increase the visibility of its products on store shelves for maximum consumer presence. Expanding its product line in 2014 CCE launched a low-calorie fruit-based sparkling drink for adults called Finley in France. On the packaging front in 2013 the company introduced slimline 250ml cans of Coke products in several markets and 150ml mini-cans in Norway.

To cut operational costs CCE launched a restructuring initiative in 2012 designed to improve its operating model and create a platform for driving sustainable growth. The company planned to streamline and reduce the cost structure of its finance support function which includes the establishment of a new centralized shared services center. CCE also began restructuring its sales and

marketing organization to better align central and field sales and began deploying standardized channel-focused organization within each of its territories. CCE expected to complete the restructuring initiative by the end of 2014 for a cost of approximately $240 million.

Company Background

CCE was formed when its predecessor company also called Coca-Cola Enterprises Inc. merged with The Coca-Cola Company (TCCC) in fall 2010 and separated its European operations. As part of the $12 billion transformation CCE was established as a new company to focus on the western European Coke business. CCE's international business further expanded with the takeover of TCCC's bottling operations in Norway and Sweden soon after. CCE remains at the original Coca-Cola Enterprises headquarters in Atlanta. Although it took over its predecessor's NYSE ticker the original shareholders were issued new stock and $10 a share.

EXECUTIVES

EVP Supply Chain, William W. (Bill) Douglas, age 54, $565,000 total compensation
Chairman and CEO, John F. Brock, age 66, $1,200,000 total compensation
SVP and CIO, Yahya Esat (Esat) Sezer, age 52
EVP; President European Group, Hubert Patricot, age 55, $676,163 total compensation
COO, Damian Gammell
VP; General Manager Northern Europe, Stephen Moorhouse
VP; General Manager France, Ben Lambrecht
SVP and CFO, Manik H. (Nik) Jhangiani, age 49, $554,275 total compensation
VP; General Manager Great Britain, Leendert Den Hollander
Vice President Financial Strategy and Analysis, Jon Paton-Smith
Vice President Human Resources North America, Brian Wynne
Vice President National Logistics, Chris Gaffney
Vice President and Secretary, Scott Holloway
Senior Vice President And Chief Information Office, Lisa Cochran
Vice President Sales And Marketing, Bernie Roy
Senior Vice President Sales Marketing, Carletta Ooton
Vice President And General Manager France Business Unit European Group, Jean-pierre Bagard
Vice President, Dave Wassenich
Vice President Information Technology, Dana Johnson
Region Vice President Sales FSOP, Todd Bourgeois
Vice President Global Development Depl, Anthony Nuzzo
Vice President of Target Team, Mike Cinque
Vice President Engineering and Manufacturing, Stan Kaplita
Vice President of Sales, Ray Faust
Vice President of Foodservice Gaming Lodging Sales, Trent Goluboff
Vice President Internal Audit, Suzanne Patterson
Senior Vice President, Jerry S Wilson
Vice President Operations Engineering, L Otto Jeffrey
Auditors: Ernst & Young LLP

LOCATIONS

HQ: Coca-Cola Enterprises Inc
2500 Windy Ridge Parkway, Atlanta, GA 30339
Phone: 678 260-3000
Web: www.cokecce.com

2014 Sales

	% of total
UK	34
France	30

Belgium	15
Netherlands	8
Norway	7
Sweden	6
Total	**100**

PRODUCTS/OPERATIONS

2014 Sales

	% of total
Coca-Cola trademark	69
Sparkling flavors & energy	18
Juices isotonics & other	10
Water	3
Total	**100**

Top Five Brands by Volume
Coca-Cola
Diet Coke/Coca-Cola light
Coca-Cola Zero
Fanta
Capri-Sun

COMPETITORS

AG Barr	Nichols plc
Britvic	Ocean Spray
Cott	Orchard House Foods
Danone	PepsiCo
Fraser & Neave	Red Bull
Mondelez International	Snapple
Nestl©	

HISTORICAL FINANCIALS

Company Type: Public

Income Statement

FYE: December 31

	REVENUE ($ mil.)	NET INCOME ($ mil.)	NET PROFIT MARGIN	EMPLOYEES
12/15	7,011	596	8.5%	11,492
12/14	8,264	663	8.0%	11,650
12/13	8,212	667	8.1%	11,750
12/12	8,062	677	8.4%	13,000
12/11	8,284	749	9.0%	13,250
Annual Growth	(4.1%)	(5.6%)	—	(3.5%)

2015 Year-End Financials

Debt ratio: 50.73%
Return on equity: 49.92%
Cash ($ mil.): 170
Current ratio: 0.95
Long-term debt ($ mil.): 3,407

No. of shares (mil.): 227
Dividends
  Yield: 2.2%
  Payout: 48.0%
Market value ($ mil.): 11,194

	STOCK PRICE ($) FY Close	P/E High/Low	PER SHARE ($) Earnings	Dividends	Book Value
12/15	49.24	21 16	2.54	1.12	4.21
12/14	44.22	18 15	2.63	1.00	5.98
12/13	44.13	18 13	2.44	0.80	8.85
12/12	31.73	14 11	2.25	0.64	9.55
12/11	25.78	13 10	2.29	0.51	9.51
Annual Growth	17.6%	— —	2.6%	21.7%	(18.4%)

Cognizant Technology Solutions Corp.

Cognizant Technology Solutions is aware of the state of your technology and where it should be in becoming digital. The information technology services provider helps customers digitize operations and provides application maintenance services business intelligence data warehousing software and systems development and integration and re-engineering services for legacy systems. Its customers are primarily corporations from the Forbes Global 2000 and it targets customers in the financial services health care manufacturing retail and logistics sectors. Most of Cognizant's software development centers and employees are located in India although it has other development and delivery facilities around the world.

Operations

Cognizant serves more than 820 clients across the chief segments of financial services (42% of sales) health care (26%) and the combined industries of manufacturing retail and logistics (20%). Its Other segment accounts for the remaining industries.

Cognizant continues to work on providing capabilities in customer relationship management enterprise resource planning data warehousing and business intelligence software testing infrastructure management and vertically-oriented business and knowledge process outsourcing. Cognizant's biggest growth drivers have been infrastructure management and business and knowledge process outsourcing.

Cognizant also offers a mix of on-site and near-shore and offshore service. Unlike competitors that provide no on-site assistance Cognizant typically locates technical and account management teams at its customers' locations with development work handled at dedicated development centers offshore. This boosts Cognizant's bottom line by taking advantage of cheaper labor costs while maintaining a close connection with its customers.

Geographic Reach

Cognizant has 50 delivery centers worldwide and operations in Australia Argentina Canada China Europe Ireland Malaysia Singapore the UK and the US. It generates about 80% of its revenues in North America.

Sales and Marketing

The company markets and sells through its direct sales force which operates from 32 offices in the US and around the world The sales process can last between two months to a year depending on the products or services being negotiated. Of Cognizant's 1200 customers it considers 271 of them to be strategic which means they have the potential to bring in $5 million to $50 million a year.

Financial Performance

Cognizant has posted robust revenue and profit growth over the last seven years. Revenues surged by 16% from $8.8 billion in 2013 to $10.2 billion in 2014. Profits jumped 17% from $1.2 million in 2013 to $1.4 billion in 2014.

The year-over-year increase in revenue across all segments is due to its continued expansion of existing customer relationships as well as revenue contributed by new customers. Business from new customers contributed $298 million in 2013 up 21% from 2013. Cognizant's acquisition of TriZetto added $81 million in revenue for the last two months of 2014. The rise in profits was driven by higher revenue and a lower loss from foreign exchange rates.

Cash flow from operations increased from $1.4 billion in 2013 to $1.47 billion in 2014. The increase came from the rise in net income and more efficient use of working capital.

Strategy

The company's long-term growth is aimed at the Middle East and Asia/Pacific especially Japan India Australia and Singapore.

In 2014 Cognizant was chosen by the National Association for Public Health Statistics and Information Systems (NAPHSIS) further develop its Electronic Verification of Vital Events (EVVE) system to help businesses and government agencies verify birth and death records and prevent identity theft.

Much of the company's growth has been the result of increasing demand for offshore IT software and services and business process outsourcing as the market place grows more confident in the effectiveness and security of such services. Cognizant has also capitalized on its customer relationships by successfully cross-selling. Additionally despite the general concerns in Europe spending on IT projects has risen.

Mergers and Acquisitions

In 2014 Cognizant shelled out $2.7 billion for TriZetto Corporation a privately held provider of healthcare IT software. In another 2014 acquisition the company bought Cadient Group a digital marketing agency with customers in the pharmaceutical biotechnology consumer health and medical device industries. In a third 2014 purchase Cognizant bought Odecee a digital services provider to enterprises in Australia and New Zealand.

Company Background

Cognizant Technology Solutions began as an in-house technology center for Dun & Bradstreet in 1994 and was spun off from D&B in 1996. Two years later Cognizant reorganized and spun off its market research operations into two public companies IMS Health and Nielsen Media Research in order to focus on IT services.

EXECUTIVES

President, Gordon J. Coburn, age 51, $595,500 total compensation
CEO IT Services, Rajeev (Raj) Mehta, age 48, $508,000 total compensation
SVP Marketing and Strategy, Malcolm Frank, age 48, $382,200 total compensation
EVP and Chief Legal and Corporate Affairs Officer, Steven Schwartz, age 48, $353,600 total compensation
Executive Vice Chairman Cognizant India, Ramakrishnan Chandrasekaran, age 57, $152,925 total compensation
CFO, Karen McLoughlin, age 50, $372,000 total compensation
CEO and Director, Francisco D'Souza, age 46, $626,000 total compensation
COO, Sridhar Thiruvengadam, age 51
SVP and CTO, Raj Bala
EVP and President Banking and Financial Services, Ramakrishna Prasad Chintamaneni, age 45
EVP and President Healthcare and Life Sciences, Venkat Krishnaswamy
EVP and President Technology Solutions, Debashis Chatterjee, age 49
EVP and President Client Services, Dharmendra Kumar Sinha, age 52
EVP and President Industry Solutions, Sumithra Gomatam, age 47
Vice President Global Insurance Practice Leader, Michael (Mel) Kim
Senior Vice President, Mark Livingston
Vice President Director Manager Inform, Jude Francis
Assistant Vice President Projects, Ronald Trella
Senior Vice President Information Technology, Vinod Ranganathan
Vice President finance, Karen Mclaughlin
Vice President Projects, Robert (Bob) Fritz
Assistant Vice President and Senior Associate Gen, Dana Gilbert
Vice President Consulting, Edward (Ed) Merchant
Assistant Vice President Projects, Ramkumar Balagopal
Assistant Vice President Crm, Rajarshi Chatterjee
Assistant Vice President BPO, Aniket Maindarkar
Assistant Vice President Global Tax, Desmond O'Brien
Assistant Vice President, Raja Renganathan
Senior Vice President Chief Technology Officer, Bill Strain
Assistant Vice President Enterprise Application Services, Praveen Desai
Vice President Corporate Communications, Rick Lacroix
Assistant Vice President Consulting, Timothy (Tim) Pare
Vice Chairman, Lakshmi Narayanan, age 62
Chairman, John E. Klein, age 73
Auditors: PricewaterhouseCoopers LLP

LOCATIONS

HQ: Cognizant Technology Solutions Corp.
Glenpointe Centre West, 500 Frank W. Burr Blvd., Teaneck, NJ 07666
Phone: 201 801-0233   **Fax:** 201 801-0243
Web: www.cognizant.com

2014 Sales

	$ mil.	% of total
North America	7,879	77
Europe	1,883	18
Other	499	5
Total	**10,262**	**100**

PRODUCTS/OPERATIONS

2014 Sales

	$ mil.	% of total
Financial services	4,285	42
Health care	2,689	26
Manufacturing retail & logistics	2,093	20
Other	1,194	12
Total	**10,262**	**100**

Selected Services

Application design development integration and re-engineering
  Complex custom systems development
  Customer relationship management (CRM)
  Data warehousing/Business intelligence (BI)
  Enterprise resource planning (ERP)
  Software testing services
IT consulting and technology services
  Business and knowledge process consulting
  IT strategy consulting
  Program management consulting
  Technology consulting
Outsourcing services
  Application maintenance
  Business and knowledge process outsourcing
  Cloud
  CRM and ERP maintenance
  Custom application maintenance
  IT infrastructure outsourcing
  Mobility

Selected Mergers and Acquisitions

FY2011
  CoreLogic Global Services (business processing services)
FY2010
  Galileo Performance (IT testing)
  The PIPC Group (management consulting)
FY2009
  UBS India Service Centre (financial-services outsourcing)
  Pepperweed Advisors (IT consulting)
  Active Intelligence (systems integration)
Industries
Banking & Financial Services
Communications
Consumer Goods
Education
Energy & Utilities
Healthcare
Information Services
Insurance
Life Sciences
Manufacturing
Media & Entertainment
Retail
Technology
Transportation & Logistics
Travel & Hospitality

3i Infotech	Infosys
Accenture	Mastek
Capgemini	MindTree
Computer Sciences Corp.	MphasiS
	Ness Technologies
HCL Technologies	Tata Consultancy
HP Enterprise Services	Wipro
IBM Global Services	Zensar Technologies
ITC Infotech India	

HISTORICAL FINANCIALS

Company Type: Public

Income Statement

FYE: December 31

	REVENUE ($ mil.)	NET INCOME ($ mil.)	NET PROFIT MARGIN	EMPLOYEES
12/14	10,262	1,439	14.0%	211,500
12/13	8,843	1,228	13.9%	171,400
12/12	7,346	1,051	14.3%	156,700
12/11	6,121	883	14.4%	137,700
12/10	4,592	733	16.0%	104,000
Annual Growth	22.3%	18.4%	—	19.4%

2014 Year-End Financials

Debt ratio: 13.97%	No. of shares (mil.): 609
Return on equity: 20.74%	Dividends
Cash ($ mil.): 2,010	Yield: —
Current ratio: 2.60	Payout: —
Long-term debt ($ mil.): 937	Market value ($ mil.): 32,091

	STOCK PRICE ($) FY Close	P/E High/Low		PER SHARE ($) Earnings	Dividends	Book Value
12/14	52.66	45	18	2.35	0.00	12.70
12/13	100.98	49	30	2.02	0.00	10.10
12/12	73.88	45	32	1.72	0.00	8.05
12/11	64.31	57	37	1.43	0.00	6.52
12/10	73.29	61	35	1.19	0.00	5.90
Annual Growth	(7.9%)	—	—	18.7%	—	21.1%

Colgate-Palmolive Co.

Colgate-Palmolive takes a bite out of grime. The company is a top global maker and marketer of toothpaste and soap and cleaning products. Colgate-Palmolive also offers pet nutrition products through subsidiary Hill's Pet Nutrition which makes Science Diet and Prescription Diet pet foods. Many of its oral care products fall under the Colgate brand and include toothbrushes mouthwash and dental floss. Its Tom's of Maine unit covers the natural toothpaste niche. Personal and home care items include Ajax brand household cleaner Palmolive dishwashing liquid Softsoap shower gel and Sanex and Speed Stick deodorants. The company has operations in 70-plus countries and sells its products in more than 200 countries.

HISTORY

William Colgate founded The Colgate Company in Manhattan in 1806 to produce soap candles and starch. Colgate died in 1857 and the company was passed to his son Samuel who renamed it Colgate and Company. In 1873 the company introduced toothpaste in jars and in 1896 it began selling Colgate Dental Cream in tubes. By 1906 Colgate was making 160 kinds of soap 625 perfumes and 2000 other products. The company went public in 1908.

In 1898 Milwaukee's B. J. Johnson Soap Company (founded 1864) introduced Palmolive a soap made of palm and olive oils rather than smelly animal fats. It became so popular that the firm changed its name to The Palmolive Company in 1916. Ten years later Palmolive merged with Peet Brothers a Kansas City-based soap maker founded in 1872. Palmolive-Peet merged with Colgate in 1928 forming Colgate-Palmolive-Peet (shortened to Colgate-Palmolive in 1953). The stock market crash of 1929 prevented a planned merger of the company with Hershey and Kraft.

During the 1930s the firm purchased French and German soap makers and opened branches in Europe. Colgate-Palmolive-Peet introduced Fab detergent and Ajax cleanser in 1947 and the brands soon became top sellers in Europe. The company expanded to Asia in the 1950s and by 1961 foreign sales were 52% of the total.

Colgate-Palmolive introduced a host of products in the 1960s and 1970s including Palmolive dishwashing liquid (1966) Ultra Brite toothpaste (1968) and Irish Spring soap (1972). During the same time the company diversified by buying approximately 70 other businesses including Kendall hospital and industrial supplies (1972) Helena Rubinstein cosmetics (1973) Ram Golf (1974) and Riviana Foods and Hill's Pet Products (1976). The strategy had mixed results and most of these acquisitions were sold in the 1980s.

Reuben Mark became CEO of Colgate-Palmolive in 1984. The company bought 50% of Southeast Asia's leading toothpaste Darkie in 1985; it changed its name to Darlie in 1989 following protests of its minstrel-in-blackface trademark. Both Palmolive automatic dishwasher detergent and Colgate Tartar Control toothpaste were introduced in 1986. That year Colgate-Palmolive purchased the liquid soap lines of Minnetonka the most popular of which is Softsoap. In 1992 the company bought Mennen maker of Speed Stick (the leading US deodorant).

Increasing its share of the oral care market in Latin America to 79% in 1995 Colgate-Palmolive acquired Brazilian company Kolynos (from Wyeth for $1 billion) and 94% of Argentina's Odol Saic. The company also bought Ciba-Geigy's oral hygiene business in India increasing its share of that toothpaste market. At home however sales and earnings in key segments were dismal so in 1995 Colgate-Palmolive began a restructuring that included cutting more than 8% of its employees and closing or reconfiguring 24 factories in two years.

The company introduced a record 602 products in 1996 and continued to expand its operations in countries with emerging economies. In 1997 Colgate-Palmolive took the lead in the US toothpaste market for the first time in 35 years (displacing P&G).

In 1999 the company sold the rights to Baby Magic (shampoos lotions oils) in the US Canada and Puerto Rico to Playtex Products retaining the rights in all other countries. Two years later the company sold its heavy-duty laundry detergent business in Mexico (primarily the Viva brand) to Henkel one of Europe's leading detergent producers.

In 2002 Colgate-Palmolive introduced a teethwhitening gel Simply White to compete with rival P&G's Crest Whitestrips. The company saw success that year when its Hill's Pet Nutrition subsidiary launched new specialty foods for cats and dogs; one of its dog foods reportedly slows brain aging in canines.

In late 2004 Colgate-Palmolive implemented a four-year restructuring plan. Its three primary objectives were to increase profit reallocate resources to promising growth areas and leverage global market efficiencies. It implemented the plan by reducing its global workforce by some 12% closing

about 25 of its 78 factories and focusing on core units. Colgate-Palmolive also built new state-of-the-art plants to produce toothpaste in the US and Poland. The company believed that its savings estimated at $500 million altogether would allow it to fund investments in its key businesses as well as provide for new product development.

By selling its North American laundry detergent brands in 2005 Colgate-Palmolive began focusing on the high-margin pearly whites (with bite) of its portfolio —oral care and pet care. The company's purchase of natural oral-care products maker Tom's of Maine in 2006 marked its effort to target the natural niche. It bought some 84% of the firm for about $100 million.

Chairman and CEO Reuben Mark handed over the title of CEO to then-president and COO Ian Cook in July 2007 and the title of chairman to Cook in January 2009; Mark retired at the end of 2008.

Colgate-Palmolive in early 2010 sold its Code 10 brand which boasted about a 10% market share. Indian consumer goods maker Marico acquired the Malaysian hair-styling name; the move was intended to allow Colgate-Palmolive to focus on its oral personal and pet care businesses.

EXECUTIVES

VP and Controller, Dennis J. Hickey, age 66, $820,000 total compensation
Chairman President and CEO, Ian M. Cook, age 63, $1,273,333 total compensation
Vice President Of Global Human Resources, Martin Collins
Vice President, Panagiotis Tsourapas
Senior Vice President Global Human Resources, Daniel Marsili
Vice President Information Technology, Tom Greene
Vice President, Malcolm Williams
COO Tom's of Maine, Tom O'Brien
President and General Manager Hill's Pet Nutrition Europe and Russia, Antonio Caro
COO Emerging Markets and Business Development, Franck J. Moison, age 62, $845,567 total compensation
COO Global Innovation and Growth Europe/South Pacific and Hill's Pet Nutrition, Fabian T. Garcia, age 55, $913,833 total compensation
President Global Oral Care, Suzan F. Harrison
VP and General Manager Colgate South Pacific, Chris E. Pedersen
VP Greece, Ricardo (Ricky) Ramos
President Colgate Latin America, Noel R. Wallace
VP Colgate-US, James A. Napolitano
VP and General Manager Hawley and Hazel Taiwan, Louis Ruggiere
President and CEO Hill's Pet Nutrition, Peter Brons-Poulsen
President Colgate North America and Global Sustainability, P. Justin Skala, age 56
VP and General Manager Global Personal Care, Michael Sload
VP and General Manager Colgate U.S., Derek A. Gordon
VP and General Manager Colgate South Africa, Bradley Farr
VP and General Manager Colgate Caribbean, Bernal Saborio
VP and General Manager Colgate Western Europe, Jean-Luc Fischer
VP and General Manager Colgate Central Europe East, Wojciech Krol
VP and General Manager Colgate Southern Cone Region, Andrea Lagioia
VP and General Manager Colgate Venezuela, Francisco Munoz Ramirez
CTO, Patricia Verduin, age 55

VP and General Manager Colgate Mexico, Juan
Pablo Zamorano
President Hill's Pet Nutrition North America,
Kostas Kontopanos
VP and General Manager Colgate UK and Ireland,
Massimo Poli
VP; General Manager Colgate-Venezuela, Ruben
Young
VP; General Manager Colgate-Italy, Vinod Nambiar
VP and General Manager Colgate Russia, Burc
Cankat
VP and General Manager Colgate U.S., Philip
Durocher
CIO, Mike Crowe
VP and General Manager Colgate India and South
Asia, Issam Bachaalani
President Colgate Africa Eurasia, Prabha
Parameswaran
VP and General Manager Greater China, Arvind
Sachdev
VP and General Manager Colgate Central America,
David Scharf
VP and General Manager Colgate Central Europe
West, Dany Schmidt
VP and General Manager Colgate Southern
Europe, Natasha Chen
VP and General Manager Colgate Philippines,
Stephen Lau
VP and General Manager Colgate U.S., Bill Van de
Graaf
VP and General Manager Global Home Care, Lucie
Claire Vincent
VP and General Manager Colgate East-West Africa
Region, Scott Geldart
VP and GM Colgate Andina Region, Hector Pedraza
Vice President Global Legal, Nadine P Flynn
Vice President and General Manager Pers Care,
John (Jack) Kooyman
Vice President Human Resources, Roland Heincke
Vice President, Sally Phipps
Vice President of Promotions Management, John
(Jack) Simone
Vice President Call Center, Lou Mancinelli
Vice President Sourcing, Katherine (Kate) Freeley
National Account Manager, Crystal Harris
Vice President Deputy General Counsel
Operations, Rosemary Nelson
Vice President of Hills Pet Nutrition, Neil Stout
Vice President, Donghui Wu
Vice President Finance, Freddy Alejandro
Vice President, Ron Meyer
Vice President, Vicky Chaparro
Vice President, Steve Renard
Vice President, Ebba Bartz
Vice President Corporate Communications, Jan
Guifarro
National Account Manager, Jim Webb
Vice President Global Oral Care, Anthony Volpe
National Sales Manager, Tom Finnerty
Vice President Worldwide Shopper Marketing,
Steve Fogarty
National Sales Manager, Donna Ellis
Vice President, Marty Stern
Vice President Supply Chain, Rick Spann
Vice President Director Of Manufacturing, Dennis
Quinn
Vice President IT Finance, Gary Palmietto
Vice President Colgate Africa Middle East, Robert
Tatera
Vice President, Ralph Hadley
Vice President Of Operations, Fran Rao
Vice President, Phil Gorlin
Assistant Vice President of Real Estate Division,
Parul Patel
Vice President Human Resources, Rodolfo
Montalvo
Vice President, Mike Stranick
Vice President Retail Marketing, Marie-agnes
Daumas
Vice President Global Oral Care, Marsha Butler

Vice President Chief Patent Counsel, Ellen Park
Vice President And General Manager Colgate Oral
Pharmaceuticals, Maria Carvajal
Vice President Personal Care Research and
Development, Robert C (Bob) Pierce
Vice President Asia, Orlando Tenorio
Vice President, Debbie Peru
Vice President, Rich Cuprys
Vice President, Andrea Motyka
Vice President Global Finance, Malcolm Jones
Vice President General Manager US Personal
Care, Bill Graaf
Vice President, Betty Kong
Vice President, Joe Vazquez
Vice President Colgate Europe and South Pacific,
Victoria Dolan
Vice President, Ps Venkatachalam
Vice President Global Research and Development,
Raj Kohli
Vice President, Kathy Weida
Vice President Global Supply Chain, Linda Topping
Assistant Treasurer, Mercedes Michel
Assistant Treasurer, Elaine Paik
Auditors: PricewaterhouseCoopers LLP

LOCATIONS

HQ: Colgate-Palmolive Co.
300 Park Avenue, New York, NY 10022
Phone: 212 310-2000   Fax: 212 310-3284
Web: www.colgatepalmolive.com

2014 Sales

	$ mil.	% of total
Oral personal & home care		
Latin America	4,769	28
Europe/South Pacific	3,406	20
North America	3,124	18
Asia	2,515	14
Africa/Eurasia	1,208	7
Pet nutrition	2,255	13
Total	**17,277**	**100**

PRODUCTS/OPERATIONS

2014 Sales

	$ mil.	% of total
Oral personal & home care	15,022	87
Pet nutrition	2,255	13
Total	**17,277**	**100**

Selected Brands

Home Care
  Ajax
  Fabuloso
  Murphy Oil Soap
  Palmolive
  Suavitel
Oral Care
  Colgate
Personal Care
  Afta
  Irish Spring
  Sanex
  Skin Bracer
  Softsoap
  Speed Stick
Pet Nutrition
  Prescription Diet
  Science Diet

COMPETITORS

Amden	Mars Petcare
Avon	McBride plc
Church & Dwight	Nestl©
Clorox	Nu Skin
Dr. Fresh	Philips Oral
GlaxoSmithKline	Procter & Gamble
Hain Celestial	Reckitt Benckiser
Henkel	S.C. Johnson
Johnson & Johnson	Sun Products
Kiss My Face	Unilever
L' Or©al USA	

HISTORICAL FINANCIALS

Company Type: Public

Income Statement

	REVENUE ($ mil.)	NET INCOME ($ mil.)	NET PROFIT MARGIN	EMPLOYEES
				FYE: December 31
12/14	17,277	2,180	12.6%	37,700
12/13	17,420	2,241	12.9%	37,400
12/12	17,085	2,472	14.5%	37,700
12/11	16,734	2,431	14.5%	38,600
12/10	15,564	2,203	14.2%	39,200
Annual Growth	2.6%	(0.3%)	—	(1.0%)

2014 Year-End Financials

Debt ratio: 45.68%
Return on equity: 126.38%
Cash ($ mil.): 1,089
Current ratio: 1.23
Long-term debt ($ mil.): 5,644
No. of shares (mil.): 906
Dividends
  Yield: 2.0%
  Payout: 62.2%
Market value ($ mil.): 62,735

	STOCK PRICE ($) FY Close	P/E High/Low		PER SHARE ($) Earnings	Dividends	Book Value
12/14	69.19	30	25	2.36	1.42	1.26
12/13	65.21	52	23	2.38	1.33	2.51
12/12	104.54	43	34	2.58	1.22	2.34
12/11	92.39	38	30	2.47	1.14	2.47
12/10	80.37	39	33	2.16	1.02	2.70
Annual Growth	(3.7%)	—	—	2.3%	8.8%	(17.3%)

Columbia Banking System, Inc.

Columbia Banking System (CBS) is the holding company for Columbia State Bank (also known as Columbia Bank). The regional community bank has about 155 branches in Washington from Puget Sound to the timber country in the southwestern part of the state as well as in northern Oregon where it also operates as Bank of Astoria. Targeting retail and small and medium-sized business customers the bank offers standard retail services such as checking and savings accounts CDs IRAs credit cards loans and mortgages. Commercial business and real estate loans make up more than 75% of the company's loan portfolio. CBS is increasing its presence in the Pacific Northwest through acquisitions of other community banks.

Geographic Reach

Tacoma-based Columbia Banking System has bank branches in 38 countries in Washington and Oregon.

Operations

The bank's Columbia Private Banking division offers customized financial services for businesses and affluent families. Subsidiary CB Financial Services provides investment products through a pact with third-party provider PrimeVest.

Financial Performance

Columbia Bank's revenue increased 17% in 2013 versus 2012 to $323.6 million. Net income rose 30% over the same period to $60 million. The bank's merger with West Coast Bank in early 2013 had a positive impact on its financial performance. Columbia's total assets at the end of 2013 were $7.16 billion compared with $4.9 billion at year end 2012 primarily due to the purchase of West Coast.

Strategy

Columbia Banking System has taken advantage of the rash of bank failures in recent years to increase its presence in the region. It added more than 30 branches in 2010 when it acquired most of the deposits and assets of failed banks Columbia River Bank and American Marine Bank a week apart. In similar transactions in 2011 it acquired most of the operations of the failed institutions Summit Bank First Heritage Bank and Bank of Whitman. Those deals added more than a dozen branches in Washington. More recently it acquired its smaller competitor West Coast Bank in spring 2013. Columbia plans to rebrand West Coast under its own name. Also Bank of Astoria will rebrand as Columbia State Bank to create a unified presence in the market.

Mergers and Acquisitions

In April 2013 Columbia acquired West Coast Bancorp –the parent company of West Coast Bank which operates nearly 60 bank branches in Oregon and Washington. The cash-and-stock deal included $264 million in cash and 12.8 million shares of its stock which were paid to West Coast shareholders. The purchase boosted Columbia's total assets to more than $7 billion and furthered Columbia's goal of becoming the leading regional community bank in the Pacific Northwest.

EXECUTIVES

President and CEO; President and CEO Columbia Bank, Melanie J. Dressel, age 63, $452,283 total compensation

EVP and Chief Banking Officer Columbia Bank, Mark W. Nelson, age 64, $253,073 total compensation

EVP and Chief Credit Officer, Andrew L. (Andy) McDonald, age 56, $209,998 total compensation

EVP and CFO, Clint E. Stein, $174,667 total compensation

EVP and COO, Hadley Robbins, age 54

Vice President Senior Financial Advisor with CB Financial, John (Jack) Brunk

Vice President, Michelle (Mitch) Claeys

Vice President Cheryl Dorman works, Cheryl Dorman

Chairman and Interim CEO Columbia Banking System; Chairman Columbia Bank, William T. Weyerhaeuser, age 72

Auditors: Deloitte & Touche LLP

LOCATIONS

HQ: Columbia Banking System, Inc.
1301 A Street, Tacoma, WA 98402-2156
Phone: 253 305-1900
Web: www.columbiabank.com

2013 Branches

	No.
Washington	86
Oregon	71
Total	**157**

COMPETITORS

BECU	JPMorgan Chase
Bank of America	KeyCorp
Banner Corp	U.S. Bancorp
Heritage Financial	Washington Federal
HomeStreet	Wells Fargo

HISTORICAL FINANCIALS

Company Type: Public

Income Statement

FYE: December 31

	ASSETS ($ mil.)	NET INCOME ($ mil.)	INCOME AS % OF ASSETS	EMPLOYEES
12/14	8,578	81	1.0%	1,844
12/13	7,161	60	0.8%	1,695
12/12	4,906	46	0.9%	1,198
12/11	4,785	48	1.0%	1,256
12/10	4,256	30	0.7%	1,092
Annual Growth	**19.2%**	**27.6%**	**—**	**14.0%**

2014 Year-End Financials

Debt ratio: 0.10%	No. of shares (mil.): 57
Return on equity: 7.15%	Dividends
Cash ($ mil.): 188	Yield: 3.4%
Current ratio: —	Payout: 60.2%
Long-term debt ($ mil.): —	Market value ($ mil.): 1,586

	STOCK PRICE ($) FY Close	P/E High/Low	PER SHARE ($) Earnings	Dividends	Book Value
12/14	27.61	19 16	1.52	0.94	21.38
12/13	27.49	23 14	1.21	0.41	20.55
12/12	17.94	20 14	1.16	0.98	19.25
12/11	19.27	18 11	1.21	0.27	19.22
12/10	21.06	34 22	0.72	0.04	17.97
Annual Growth	**7.0%**	**— —**	**20.5%**	**120.2%**	**4.4%**

Comcast Corp

Comcast is the biggest pay-TV provider in the US with about 22 million video subscribers for its core cable division. The company downloads the bulk of its revenue from its cable services offered in 39 states and the District of Columbia. Its broadband Internet service has about 21 million subscribers and its XFINITY computer telephony service has about 11 million customers. Comcast also owns NBCUniversal which includes the NBC TV network Universal Studios and the Universal theme parks. Comcast ended its $45 billion bid to acquire Time Warner Cable in the face of regulatory opposition.

HISTORY

In 1963 Ralph Roberts Daniel Aaron and Julian Brodsky bought American Cable Systems in Tupelo Mississippi. The company soon expanded throughout the state. In 1969 the company got a new name: Comcast combining "communications" and "broadcast." Two years later Comcast acquired franchises in western Pennsylvania and when it went public in 1972 it moved to Philadelphia.

Comcast bought up local operations nationwide through the early 1980s and gained its first foreign cable franchise in 1983 in London (it sold its affiliate there to NTL –now Virgin Media –in 1998). It took a 26% stake in the large Group W Cable in 1986. Roberts also lent financial support that year to a fledgling home-shopping channel called QVC –for "quality value and convenience."

A big step into telecommunications came in 1988 when Comcast bought American Cellular Network with Delaware and New Jersey franchises. Two years later Roberts' son Brian –who had trained as a cable installer during a summer away from college –became Comcast's president.

In 1992 Comcast bought Metromedia's Philadelphia-area cellular operations and began investing in fiber-optic and wireless phone companies. By then the company was a major QVC shareholder. With an eye toward Comcast's programming needs Brian persuaded FOX network head Barry Diller to become QVC's chairman. But when Diller tried to use QVC to take over CBS Comcast bought control of QVC in 1994 to quash the bid which went against cross-ownership bans. To pay for QVC Comcast had to sell its 20% stake in cable firm Heritage Communications in 1995. Diller left the company to oversee for a time InterActiveCorp parent of QVC's archrival HSN). Also in 1995 Comcast funded former Disney executive Richard Frank to launch the C3 (Comcast Content and Communication) programming company.

Comcast TCI and Cox sold Teleport their local phone venture to AT&T in 1998 but Comcast turned around and bought long-distance service provider GlobalCom (now Comcast Telecommunications). That year Sprint Spectrum –Comcast's PCS venture with Sprint Cox and the former TCI –was rolled into Sprint PCS under Sprint's management.

Comcast sold its cellular operations to SBC Communications for $1.7 billion in 1999. The company also agreed to acquire rival MediaOne in 1999 but soon after the $54 billion deal was struck AT&T weighed in with a $58 billion offer. Comcast dropped its bid for MediaOne when AT&T offered to sell Comcast 2 million cable subscribers. More than a million of those subscribers came from Pennsylvania cable operator Lenfest Communications which Comcast bought in 2000 from AT&T and the Lenfest family in a $7 billion deal. Also that year Comcast took full ownership of Jones Intercable in which it already had a controlling interest.

In 2001 Comcast completed a systems swap with Adelphia Communications and completed the $2.75 billion purchase of systems in six states from AT&T. Also that year Comcast offered to buy the rest of AT&T's cable operations for $44.5 billion in stock and $13.5 billion in assumed debt. AT&T's board rejected the offer but left the door open for another bid. That December after it had heard proposals from Time Warner and Cox AT&T agreed to sell its cable unit to Comcast for $47 billion in stock and $25 billion in assumed debt. C. Michael Armstrong came from AT&T to Comcast and was named chairman. Challenged with the task of absorbing AT&T Broadband's assets Comcast struggled to meet its numbers. About 18 months after the AT&T Broadband deal Comcast had reduced its headcount by 10000 people.

Also in 2001 Comcast sold its 57% stake in QVC to Liberty Media for about $7.7 billion. Prior to the sale the online retailer had been responsible for bringing in a third of Comcast's sales.

When Armstrong stepped down as chairman in 2004 president and CEO Brian Roberts was named successor. The same year Comcast made an offer to buy The Walt Disney Company but withdrew it after getting a chilly reception. The following year the company joined a consortium that bought film studio MGM.

Comcast acquired TechTV for about $300 million which it merged with its video game-centric G4 network. Comcast's majority-owned subsidiary G4 Media operates the new network now called G4 - Video Game Television. Other Comcast interests include a two-thirds stake in Comcast Spectacor a venture that owns the Flyers the 76ers and arena management firm Global Spectrum among others.

Even though Comcast's 2004 bid for The Walt Disney Company didn't work out the two companies have forged a sizeable distribution deal that brought Disney-owned content to Comcast's broadband Internet subscribers. In 2006 Comcast bought Disney's nearly 40% stake in E! Entertainment Television in a deal valued at nearly $1.25

billion (Comcast already owned 60%). The deal included a multiyear distribution agreement that allows Comcast to offer Disney programming through its video-on-demand service.

Comcast had owned a 21% stake in rival Time Warner Cable (TWC) which made for strange bedfellows but the companies managed to unwind their relationship in mid-2006. The two rivals purchased all of troubled Adelphia Communications' cable television assets. Adelphia shareholders received about $9 billion from TWC and $3.5 billion in cash from Comcast which also contributed its TWC stake to the deal. Comcast no longer owns any part of TWC.

In 2006 the company expanded broadband cable operations through the acquisition of Susquehanna Communications which has operations primarily in Maine Mississippi New York and Pennsylvania (Comcast previously held a 30% stake in the company). Operating as SusCom the firm has 230000 basic cable subscribers along with 86000 broadband Internet customers and had recently introduced cable-based phone services.

In 2007 the company purchased Patriot Media & Communications a small New Jersey cable operator for about $483 million. Also that year in a bid to boost its video entertainment holdings Comcast purchased movie tickets Web site Fandango. Meanwhile the company expanded its stable of regional sports channels with the purchase of two networks from Cablevision Systems. The $570 million deal included a 60% stake in FSN Bay Area and gave Comcast full ownership of FSN New England which became part of Comcast SportsNet.

Comcast made an investment in its cable TV subscription business with the 2008 purchase of Insight Midwest for about $1.3 billion. The deal added about 700000 subscribers in Illinois and Indiana. Other purchases included the acquisition of additional interest in cable channel Comcast SportsNet Bay Area and of the remaining interest in Los Angeles-based cable and satellite channel G4 that it did not already own.

In 2010 MGM filed for Chapter 11 bankruptcy protection. The prepackaged plan of reorganization wiped out the ownership interests of the consortium (which included Comcast) that bought the film studio in 2005.

EXECUTIVES

SEVP and CEO NBCUniversal, Stephen B. (Steve) Burke, age 56, $2,652,500 total compensation
Executive Vice President Strategy and Development, Samuel H (Sam) Schwartz
Chairman and CEO, Brian L. Roberts, age 56, $2,857,315 total compensation
Chairman NBC News and MSNBC, Andrew R. (Andy) Lack, age 68
EVP and Chief Accounting Officer, Lawrence J. Salva, age 59
Chairman and CEO Universal Parks & Resorts (UPR), Thomas L. (Tom) Williams, age 67
Chairman NBC Sports Group, Mark H. Lazarus, age 52
EVP and COO Comcast Cable, David N. (Dave) Watson
Chairman NBC Broadcasting NBCUniversal, Ted Harbert
Chairman NBCUniversal Cable Entertainment Group, Bonnie Hammer, age 64
President Comcast Spotlight, Charlie Thurston
SEVP, David L. Cohen, age 60, $1,399,137 total compensation
EVP General Counsel and Secretary, Arthur R. Block, age 60, $900,000 total compensation
SVP and Managing Director and Head of Funds Comcast Ventures, Amy L. Banse

EVP; President and CEO Comcast Cable, Neil Smit, age 55, $1,568,546 total compensation
Chairman NBC Entertainment, Robert (Bob) Greenblatt
EVP and Chief Communications Officer, D'Arcy F. Rudnay
President and COO Comcast-Spectator, David A. (Dave) Scott
SEVP and CFO, Michael J. (Mike) Cavanagh, age 48
President and CEO CNBC, Mark Hoffman
President Comcast Business Services, William R. (Bill) Stemper
Chairman NBCUniversal International, Kevin MacLellan
Chairman NBCUniversal International Group and NBCUniversal Telemundo Enterprises, Cesar Conde, age 40
EVP Global Corporate Development and Strategy, Alexander D. (Alex) Evans
Chairman Universal Filmed Entertainment Group, Jeff Shell
SVP Global Chief Information Security Officer (GCISO), Myrna Soto
Vice President of Engineering, Dale Kirk
Vice President Finance and Business Operations, Meena Soleiman
Senior Vice President Marketing Communications, Peter (Pete) Intermaggio
Svp Strategic Services Communc, Susan Jin (Sue) Davis
Svp-legal Regulatory Affairs, Lynn Charytan
Evp-consumer Services, Marcien Jenckes
Vice President Competitive and Business Analytics, Michael A (Mel) Kelman
Vice President Business Services Eastern Massachusetts Region, Peter (Pete) Marsh
Vice President Business Development and Strategy, Jon Kaplowitz
National Sales Manager, Rose Davis
Vice President Business Development, Scott McGill
Vice President Government and Regulatory Affairs, Nick Leuci
Legal Secretary, Leonard (Len) Rodriguez
Vice President Customer Journeyman and Insights, Graham Tutton
National Sales Manager Comcast Spotlight, Trevor Clements
Vice President Real Estate, Jerry O'Brien
National Sales Manager Roanoke Lynchburg Comcast Spotlight, Tom White
Vice President Procurement, Jeur Abeln
Region Vice President Business Services, Shawn Adamson
Senior Vice President General Manager Online, John Williamson
Division Vice President, Dave Kowolenko
Vice President Finance and Accounting, Chris Lawler
Vice President Engineering Operations, Thomas (Thom) Carroll
Vice President Labor Relations, Patrick Battel
Vice President Brand Development And Communications, Todd Arata
Vice President Product Management Broadband Home Security, Bill Horrocks
Corporate Vice President Field Compensation, Karen Baker
Vice President Operations, Patrick (Paddy) Oliver
Vice President of Mortgage Lending, Reynaldo Perez
Vice President Finance and Accounting, Maureen Hines
Vice President of Marketing and Sales, Janet Uthman
Vice President of Marketing, Michael (Mel) Volosin
Executive Vice President, George Tidd
Clinical Director Licensed Professional Counselor Supervisor, Mark McKelvey
Senior Vice President Of Finance, Mark Coffey

National Sales Manager Comcast Spotlight, Julie Areford
Senior Vice President Finance and Accounting, John (Jack) Iadanza
Senior Vice President Group Technical Advisor, Theresa Hennesy
Senior Vice President Sales Partner, Brenda Alarcon
Vice President Mile High Region Comcast Business Services, Jay Dirkmaat
Senior Vice President, Kenneth (Ken) Walkinshaw
Vice President Business Development, Rachel Archuleta
Vice President Talent Acquisition, Raul Valentin
Vice President Of Marketing Operations, Jason Wicht
Vice President Business Operations and Finance, Dave Sartori
Vice President Information Technology Comcast Business Services, Christer Peltomaa
Vice President Of Technical Operations, Jeff Cardoso
National Sales Manager Comcast Spotlight, Mary Butler
National Sales Manager, Christopher Schubert
Executive Vice President Sales Marketing and Business Development, Barbara (Barb) Allen
Vice President Patent Engineering, Jingyu Zhou
Senior Vice President Human Resources, Tina Simmons
Vice President Advanced Advertising Sales, Chip Meehan
Vice President Federal Government Affairs, Melissa (Mel) Maxfield
Area Vice President of Human Resources Comcast Spotlight Inc, Jeff Hamstad
Vice President of Human Resources, Michael (Mel) Cindric
National Sales Manager, David (Dave) Klein
Vice President of VOD Western Division, Esteban Sandino
Regional Vice President Marketing And Sales, Chip Goodman
Vice President New Products and Operations, Rob Klippel
Vice President Operations Nfc, Pete Petrizzio
Regional Vice President Human Resources, Suzy Persutti
Vice President Product Development Comcast Cable, Jonathan (Jon) Palmatier
Vice President Technology, Mark Vickers
Vice President Finance and Administration Comcast Cable Comcast Spotlight, Bill Haase
Vice President Deputy General Counsel, Kathryn Koles
Senior Vice President of Customer Experience at Comcast, Tom Karinshak
Vice President Video Products, John (Jack) Vonk
National Sales Manager Comcast Spotlight, Wendy Eaby
Vice President Affiliate Finance, Victor Viola
National Sales Manager Comcast Spotlight, Bob Kucharczuk
Vice President, Bill Revell
Vice President Call Center, Lisa Walker
EXECUTIVE VICE PRESIDENT, Dave Watson
Vice President, Hank Oster
Senior Vice President Programming and Scheduling, Andrew (Andy) Beecham
Senior Vice President Customer care, Cahterine Kilstrom
National Account Manager, Mike Mullin
Region Vice President Cable Operations, Paul Navin
Senior Vice President Finance, Greg Brennen
Vice President Product Deployment, Rich Massi
Vice President Finance, Sarah Gustashaw
Vice President Finance, Randall Sylvan
Senior Vice President Finance, Michael (Mel) Mcgreevy

Vice President Information Technology, Derek
 Brown
Regional Senior Vice President, Amy Smith
Vice President Network Architecture, Robert (Bob)
 Howald
Vice President Finance, Kathleen DeAmicis
Vice President Finance, Thomas (Thom) Jelinek
Vice President 1 Customer Service Strategy and
 Operations, Tonya Webster
Vice President Technology Assessment and
 Strategy, Dan Wang
Vice President Retail Global Industry Leader
 Global Business Services, Laurie Armstrong
Vice President Big Data Initiatives, Matthew (Matt)
 Hull
Board Member, Kenneth (Ken) Styduhar
Advisory Board Member, Nancy Kaminski
Board Member, Les Wadleigh
Chairman Emeritus, Ralph Roberts
Secretary and Manager, Monique Wilson
Board Member, Robert (Bob) Peronto
Auditors: DELOITTE & TOUCHE LLP

LOCATIONS

HQ: Comcast Corp
 One Comcast Center, Philadelphia, PA 19103-2838
Phone: 215 286-1700
Web: www.comcastcorporation.com

PRODUCTS/OPERATIONS

2014 Sales

	$ mil.	% of total
Cable Communications	44,140	64
NBC Universal		
Cable Networks	9,563	13
Broadcast Television	8,542	12
Filmed Entertainment	5,008	7
Theme parks	2,623	4
Headquarters & others	13	-
Eliminations	(321)	-
Corporate and others	709	-
Eliminations	(1502)	-
Total	**68,775**	**100**
Cable Networks		
Bravo		
Chiller		
Cloo (form		
CNBC		
CNBC World		
E!		
G4		
Golf Channel		
MSNBC		
NBC Sports		
Oxygen		
Style		
Syfy		
Universal HD		
USA Network		

COMPETITORS

21st Century Fox	EVINE Live
AT&T	EarthLink
Cablevision Systems	Liberty Interactive
CenturyLink	Netflix
Charter Communications	RCN Corporation
Cox Communications	Time Warner Cable
DIRECTV	Verizon
DISH Network	Viacom
Disney	

HISTORICAL FINANCIALS
Company Type: Public

Income Statement
FYE: December 31

	REVENUE ($ mil.)	NET INCOME ($ mil.)	NET PROFIT MARGIN	EMPLOYEES
12/15	74,510	8,163	11.0%	141,000
12/14	68,775	8,380	12.2%	139,000
12/13	64,657	6,816	10.5%	136,000
12/12	62,570	6,203	9.9%	129,000
12/11	55,842	4,160	7.4%	126,000
Annual Growth	**7.5%**	**18.4%**	**—**	**2.9%**

2015 Year-End Financials

Debt ratio: 31.59%—
Return on equity: 15.55%
Cash ($ mil.): 2,295
Current ratio: 0.68
Long-term debt ($ mil.): 48,994

Dividends
 Yield: 1.7%
 Payout: 30.5%
Market value ($ mil.): —

	STOCK PRICE ($) FY Close	P/E High/Low	PER SHARE ($) Earnings	Dividends	Book Value
12/15	56.43	20 16	3.24	0.98	21.40
12/14	58.01	18 15	3.20	0.87	20.74
12/13	51.97	20 14	2.56	0.78	19.45
12/12	37.36	16 11	2.28	0.65	18.70
12/11	23.71	18 13	1.50	0.54	17.47
Annual Growth	**24.2%**	**— —**	**21.2%**	**15.7%**	**5.2%**

Comerica, Inc.

If you have a cosigner Comerica will be your
copilot. The holding company owns Comerica
Bank which has around 480 branches in about a
dozen states across the US. The company is organized into three main segments. The Business Bank
division is the largest offering loans deposits and
capital markets products to middle-market large
corporate and government clients. The Retail Bank
serves small businesses and consumers while the
Wealth Management arm provides private banking
investment management financial advisory investment banking brokerage insurance and retirement
services. Comerica has total assets of nearly $70
billion.

Operations

Broadly speaking Comerica generates nearly
60% of its revenue from loan interest and almost
10% from interest on investment securities and
short-term investments. The remainder of the
bank's revenue is fee-based coming mostly from
service charges on deposit accounts fiduciary income and commercial lending and card-related
fees. The bank divides its operations into several
segments: The Business Bank (commercial loans
and lines of credit to middle market businesses
multinational corporations and government agencies) The Retail Bank (small business banking and
personal financial services) and Wealth Management (fiduciary services private banking and retirement and investment management services). In
addition to these segments Comerica manages a
securities portfolio and offers asset and liability
management services.

Geographic Reach

Comerica boasts 482 branches in about a dozen
states and another 80 trust services locations loan
production or other financial services offices primarily in Texas Michigan California Florida and
Arizona. Michigan and California are its largest

markets generating 60% of net income in 2014. It
also has primary markets in Arizona and Florida
and international locations in Canada and Mexico.

Sales and Marketing

Comerica spent $23 million on advertising and
marketing campaigns in 2014 up from $21 million
in 2013. The bank licenses its brand for the Comerica Park in Detroit home to the Detroit Tigers
baseball team.

Financial Performance

Comerica's revenues have remained relatively
flat at around $2.6 billion for the past five years.
Revenue inched up by less than 1% to $2.62 billion in 2014 mostly as the bank collected more
non-interest revenue from fiduciary income card
fees and foreign exchange income. While the
bank's average earning asset balances grew its
loan yields continued to shrink in the low interest
rate environment causing interest income to fall by
2%.Despite flat revenues the bank's profits have
been rising for the past several years. Net income
jumped by 10% to $593 million in 2014 mostly because Comerica paid less in litigation-related
charges and less in employee-related pension and
deferred compensation expenses. Cash from operations declined by 24% to $639 million mostly due
to unfavorable changes in the bank's working capital.

Strategy

Comerica hopes to leverage its established business banking relationships to cross sell more financial products. In 2014 it launched several key initiatives to do just that including the "Trusted
Advisor" initiative which gives its customer-facing
relationship bankers and others in the Business
bank the tools they need to build customer relationships with tailor-fit growth cash risk and
wealth-related services. It has also been moving
into digital banking technology to shrink its costlybranch network and courting higher-net-worth
clients in its wealth management segment.Comerica continues to support its already-strong presence in the fast-growing and large states of California and Texas. In 2014 the bank beefed up its
Middle Market Banking staff in Houston Dallas
and Austin to bolster its position as the largest US
commercial bank headquartered in the state.

Company Background

In 2011 the company acquired Sterling Bancshares to strengthen its franchise in Texas. The
deal which carried a price tag in excess of $1 billion added nearly 60 branches mainly in the Dallas/Fort-Worth Houston and San Antonio metropolitan areas.

HISTORY

Company BackgroundComerica traces its history to 1849 when Michigan governor Epaphroditus Ransom tapped Elon Farnsworth to found the
Detroit Savings Fund Institute. At that time Detroit
was a major transit point for shipping between
Lakes Huron and Erie as well as between the US
and Canada. The bank grew with the town and in
1871 became Detroit Savings Bank.

By 1899 Detroit was one of the top 10 US manufacturing centers and thanks to a group of local
tinkerers and mechanics that included Henry Ford
was on the brink of even greater growth. Detroit
Savings grew also fueled by the deposits of workers whom Ford paid up to $5 a day. Detroit Savings was not however the beneficiary of significant
business with the auto makers; for corporate banking they turned first to eastern banks and then to
large local banks in which they had an interest.

Detroit boomed during the 1920s as America
went car-crazy but after the 1929 crash Detroiters
defaulted on mortgages by the thousands. By 1933
Michigan's banks were in such disarray that the
governor shut them down three weeks prior to the

federal bank holiday. Detroit Savings was one of only four Detroit banks to reopen. None of the major banks associated with auto companies survived.

A few months later Manufacturers National Bank backed by a group of investors that included Edsel Ford (Henry's son) was founded. Although its start was rocky Manufacturers National was on firm footing by 1936; around the same time Detroit Savings Bank renamed itself the Detroit Bank to appeal to a more commercial clientele.

WWII and the postwar boom put Detroit back in gear. In the 1950s and 1960s both banks thrived. In the 1970s statewide branching was permitted and both banks formed holding companies (DETROITBANK Corp. and Manufacturers National Corp.) and expanded throughout Michigan. As they grew they added services; when Detroit's economy was hit by the oil shocks of the 1970s these diversifications helped them through the lean years.

DETROITBANK opened a trust operation in Florida in 1982 to maintain its relationship with retired customers and renamed itself Comerica to be less area-specific. Manufacturers National also began operating in Florida (1983) and made acquisitions in the Chicago area (1987). Comerica went farther afield buying banks in Texas (1988) and California (1991).

Following the national consolidation trend in 1992 Comerica and Manufacturers National merged (retaining the Comerica name) but did not fully integrate until 1994 when the new entity began making more acquisitions. To increase sales and develop its consumer business the company reorganized in 1996. It sold its Illinois bank and its Michigan customs brokerage business and acquired Fairlane Associates to expand its property/casualty insurance line.

As part of its strategy to have operations in all three NAFTA countries Comerica opened a bank in Mexico in 1997 and one in Canada in 1998. That year it dropped $66 million for the naming rights to the Detroit Tigers' baseball stadium which opened as Comerica Park in 2000. It also started a Web-based payment system for its international trade business.

To fortify its business lending operations in California Comerica bought Imperial Bancorp in 2001. At the beginning of 2002 chairman Eugene Miller handed the CEO reins to Ralph Babb who had been CFO. Later that year Babb became chairman as well.

In 2009 Comerica sold its institutional retirement plan recordkeeping operations which served some 250 retirement plans to Wells Fargo. The company did not consider the business as part of its core operations.

EXECUTIVES

Senior Vice President Business Affairs, Linda Forte

Chairman President and CEO Comerica Incorporated and Comerica Bank, Ralph W. Babb, age 66, $1,261,154 total compensation

EVP Governance Regulatory Relations and Legal Affairs and Corporate Secretary Comerica Incorporated and Comerica Bank, Jon W. Bilstrom, age 69, $565,308 total compensation

Executive Vice President Chief Credit Of, John (Jack) Killian

President Comerica Bank (California Market), Judith S. Love, age 58

EVP and Chief Risk Officer, Michael H. Michalak, age 57

EVP and Director of Operations Services, Paul R. Obermeyer, age 57

EVP and General Auditor Comerica Incorporated and Comerica Bank, David E. Duprey, age 57

President Comerica Incorporated and Comerica Bank, Curtis C. Farmer, age 52, $625,692 total compensation

President Comerica Bank Michigan Market, Michael T. Ritchie, age 46

EVP and Chief Human Resources Officer Comerica Incorporated and Comerica Bank, Megan D. Burkhart, age 43

EVP and Haed of Business Bank, J. Patrick (Pat) Faubion, age 61

Vice Chairman and CFO, Karen L. Parkhill, age 49, $618,154 total compensation

EVP and Chief Credit Officer, Peter W. Guilfoile, age 54

Vice President Texas Market, Greg Wilcox

Executive Vice President Chief Accounting Officer, Muneera Carr

First Vice President Corporate Information Security Services, Kenneth (Ken) Schaeffler

Vice President And Manager Corporate Learning, Laurie Goetz

Vice President Financial Systems Support, William Grace

Vice President Of Corporate Purchasing, Susan V (Sue) Newman

Vice President, Lake McGuire

Vice President Of Product Development, Elizabeth Siewert

Senior Vice President, Mark Renfro

Vice President Network Planning, Nilesh Patel

Assistant Vice President, Daniel (Dan) Backer

Vice President International Finance, Louis Zedan

Assistant Vice President, Deanna Fietzer

Vice President, Jeff Treadway

Vice President Technology and Life Sciences, Jeff Hasselman

Assistant Vice President Information Systems, Ken Lootens

Vice President CBO, Angela (Angie) Knight

Assistant Vice President Business Support Services, Jackie Parker

Vice President, Sharon Walsh Sharon Walsh

Vice President Human Resources Staffing, Dan Dunn

Vice President, Daniel (Dan) Roesner

Senior Vice President Western Market, Michael Silva

Vice President, Jon E Haffner

Vice President Marketing, Jason Logan

Assistant Vice President Network Services, Christine Chevalier

Vice President Middle Market Banking, Paul Russo

Senior Vice President Western Market, Sheila Mussone

Vice President Business Finance, Matthew (Matt) Griffin

Vice President, Kelly McConnell

Senior Vice President, Cynthia Jordan

Senior Vice President Texas Market, Kenny Barhanovich

Vice President End User Technology Ser, Kim Martin

Vice President Information Technology Process Services, Joe Taubitz

Assistance Vice President, Daphne Berry

Vice President, Geoffrey Rossi Geoffrey Rossi

Vice President Treasury Management Sales Texas, Marcia Graves

First Vice President, Keith W Maruska

Vice President Buseness Development Healthcar, Christopher (Chris) Healy

Executive Vice President, Lisa Zarzycki

Vice President and Treasurer, Brad Bell

Vice President, Indiresha Maktal

Assistant Vice President Letter of Credit Specialist, Gail Matheson

Vice President Senior Information Security Risk An, Lisa Graye

Vice President And Assistant Chief Appraiser, Marc Farmer

Vice President Technology and Life Sciences Division, Paul Gerling

Senior Vice President Group Manager Business Banking, Lane Allen

Senior Vice President, David P (Dave) Cagle

Senior Vice President Senior Wealth Advisor, Matthew (Matt) Orth

Vice President International Finance Department, Aryan Dokht

Vice President Middle Market Banking, Kimberly Kersten

Vice President Private Banker, Julie Pausch

Assistant Vice President Financial Consultant, Tony Stefani

Senior Vice President And North Texas Director Of Business Banking, David (Dave) Milton

Banking Center Manager Vice President, Ruth Bonilla

Vice President, Rhonda D Dantzler

Vice President, Andrea Krzemien-Roy

Private Banking Vice President, Jennifer J (Jen) Zuniga

Vice President, Josie Fenech

Vice President, Lynn M Hough

Vice President Private Banking, Gary J Beyer

Assistant Vice President, Dave Samra

Treasury Management Vice President, Danette R Hames

Vice President Retail Bank Support, Glenda Vicari

Vice President Middle Market Banking, Rob Rosati

Vice President Middle Market Banking, Bryan L Johnston

Vice President Process Manager, Mary Hammond

Vice President, Marc P Abello

Senior Vice President Regional Private Banking, William (Bill) Osbach

Vice President, Yvonne Auyang

Senior Vice President Chief Investment Officer, Bob Griffin

Vice President, Lesley B (Les) Higginbotham

Senior Vice President Equity Fund Services, Steve Kattner

Vice President And Alternate Group Manager Commercial Real Estate, Cynthia V Porter

Vice President, Debbie Watson

Banking Center Manager And Assistant Vice President, Alfonso J Ugarte

Vice President, SI Rowlett

Vice President, Debbie Tuftee

Assistant Vice President Regional Operations Manager, Bruce E Neville

Vice President, Christine Mccamont

Assistant Vice President, James (Jamie) Robinson

Assistant Vice President, Carole Condon

Assistant Vice President Asset Based Auditing, Christopher (Chris) Anthony

Global Corporate Product Management Assistant Vice President, Angie Roche

Vice President, Amanda T Cecil

Vice President Personal Banker, Frank Gormley

Vice President And Banking Center Manager, John (Jack) Edwards

Vice President And Banking Center Manager, Jeremy Farr

Vice President Loan Officer Mlo, Sam L Braswell

Vice President, Sheila Ausberry

Assistant Vice President Treasury Management, Pamela G (Pam) Porter

Senior Vice President And Alternate Credit Administration Officer, Mike Hammond

Assistant Vice President, Reba L Mounzer

Vice President, Kristy Denby

Vice President Middle Market Banking, Kelly L Mione

Vice President Estate Administration, Angela W (Angie) Aycock

Banking Center Manager Assistant Vice President, Ron Davis

Vice President of Marketing, Melissa (Mel) David-Rosenberg

Vice President Lakeshore District, Christopher (Chris) Scott
Vice President District Manager, Jason Abate
Vice President western Division FX Operations Manager Global Capital Markets, Barbara (Barb) Isaacs
Vice President, Tien G Huynh
Vice President And Alternate Group Manager, Stephen G (Steve) Wells
Vice President Market Planning, Kevin Cornell
Banking Center Manager Vice President, Linda Wagner
Vice President western Market Treasury Management Officer, Sharon Slofkosky
Assistant Vice President, Christian Sporl
Banking Center Manager Assistant Vice President, Teresa Nolasco
Vice President, John (Jack) McKee
Vice President U S. Banking Midwest, Mark Leveille
Senior Vice President, Dick Lundin
Banking Center Manager Vice President, Gordon McKinley
Senior Vice President middle Market Banking Iv, Steven (Steve) Swiftney
Banking Center Manager Assistant Vice President, Lisa Thompson
Vice President, Chris Bauchan
Vice President, Paul Orsborn
Vice President, Laura Wrocklage
Senior Vice President Management Accounting, Jan Dominick
Vice President western Market Coastal Region, Angela (Angie) Reed
Vice President, Cynthia Walters
Vice President Institutional Trust Client Administration, Daniel (Dan) Molnar
Vice President Alt. Group Manager Environmental Services Group, Matthew (Matt) Breight
Vice President National Real Estate Services, Matt Maberry
Vice President and Team Leader Treasury Management Sales, Andrea Uhlian
Vice President Business Banking, Patricia (Pat) Alexander
First Vice President Assistant Secretary and General Counsel, Nicole Gersch
Senior Vice President, Eric Kraft
Vice President, Ann Day-Salo
Assistant Vice President western Division Senior Auditor Asset Based Auditing, Diane Chang
Vice President, Mina Castaneda
Vice President and Consultant Treasury Management Service, Liana Sanchez
Regional President, Kennedy Fillar
Vice President National Developers, Casey Stevenson
Banking Center Manager Vice President, Raffi Khelghatian
Vice President, Gary P Mach
Vice President Commercial Banking, Jason Syrinek
Vice President, Chris Scott
Auditors: Ernst & Young LLP

LOCATIONS

HQ: Comerica, Inc.
Comerica Bank Tower, 1717 Main Street, MC 6404, Dallas, TX 75201
Phone: 214 462-6831
Web: www.comerica.com

2014 Banking Centers

	No.
Michigan	214
Texas	135
California	104
Other Markets	
Arizona	18
Florida	9
Canada	1
Total	**481**

Selected Markets

Arizona
California
Colorado
Florida
Illinois
Michigan
Nevada
Ohio
Texas
Washington

PRODUCTS/OPERATIONS

2014 Sales

	$ mil.	% of total
Interest		
Loans including fees	1,525	58
Investment securities	211	8
Short-term investments	14	1
Noninterest		
Service charges on deposit accounts	215	8
Fiduciary income	180	7
Commercial lending fees	98	4
Card fees	80	3
Letter of credit fees	57	2
Foreign exchange	40	2
Bank-owned life insurance	39	1
Brokerage fee	17	1
Others	142	5
Total	**2,618**	**100**

Selected Subsidiaries

Comerica Bank
Comerica Bank & Trust National Association
Comerica Capital Advisors Incorporated
Comerica Equities Incorporated
Comerica Financial Incorporated
Comerica Holdings Incorporated
Comerica Insurance Group Inc.
Comerica Insurance Services Inc.
Comerica International Corporation
Comerica Investment Services Inc.
Comerica Investments LLC
Comerica Leasing Corporation
Comerica Merchant Services Inc.
Comerica Securities Inc.
Wilson Kemp & Associates Inc.
World Asset Management Inc.

COMPETITORS

Bank of America	MUFG Americas Holdings
Citigroup	SVB Financial
Cullen/Frost Bankers	SunTrust
Fifth Third	TCF Financial
Huntington Bancshares	U.S. Bancorp
JPMorgan Chase	Wells Fargo

HISTORICAL FINANCIALS

Company Type: Public

Income Statement

FYE: December 31

	ASSETS ($ mil.)	NET INCOME ($ mil.)	INCOME AS % OF ASSETS	EMPLOYEES
12/14	69,190	593	0.9%	9,115
12/13	65,227	541	0.8%	9,207
12/12	65,359	521	0.8%	9,306
12/11	61,008	393	0.6%	9,757
12/10	53,667	277	0.5%	9,365
Annual Growth	**6.6%**	**21.0%**	**—**	**(0.7%)**

2014 Year-End Financials

Debt ratio: 3.87%
Return on equity: 8.15%
Cash ($ mil.): 6,071
Current ratio: —
Long-term debt ($ mil.): —
No. of shares (mil.): 179
Dividends
  Yield: 1.6%
  Payout: 26.6%
Market value ($ mil.): 8,385

	STOCK PRICE ($) FY Close	P/E High/Low	PER SHARE ($) Earnings	Dividends	Book Value
12/14	46.84	16 13	3.16	0.79	41.35
12/13	47.54	16 10	2.85	0.68	39.24
12/12	30.34	13 10	2.67	0.55	36.87
12/11	25.80	21 10	2.09	0.40	34.80
12/10	42.24	50 33	0.88	0.25	32.81
Annual Growth	**2.6%**	**— —**	**37.7%**	**33.3%**	**5.9%**

Commerce Bancshares, Inc.

Commerce Bancshares owns bank branch operator Commerce Bank. The financial institution boasts a network of more than 360 locations across several US states including Missouri Kansas Illinois Oklahoma and Colorado. The bank focuses on retail and commercial banking services such as deposit accounts mortgages loans and credit cards. Commerce Bank also runs a wealth management division that offers asset management trust private banking brokerage and estate planning services and also manages proprietary mutual funds. As part of its operations Commerce Bank has subsidiaries devoted to insurance leasing and private equity investments.OperationsThe company operates three main segments: Consumer Commercial and Wealth. The Commercial segment which collects roughly 65% of the bank's total revenue provides corporate lending merchant and commercial bank card products leasing and international services as well as business and government deposit and cash management services. Fixed income investments are sold to individuals and institutional investors through the segment's Capital Markets Group. Another 20% of bank revenue is generated through the Consumer segment which includes the retail branch network consumer installment lending personal mortgage banking and consumer debit and credit bank card activities. It provides services through a network of more than 200 full-service branches a 400-machine ATM network and alternative delivery channels such as extensive online banking and telephone banking services. The remaining bank revenue (around 15%) comes from the Wealth segment which manages investments with a market value of $20.4 billion and administers an additional $14.8 billion in non-managed assets provides traditional trust and estate tax-planning services brokerage services and advisory and discretionary investment portfolio management services targeted to personal and institutional corporate customers. The Wealth segment also manages Commerce Bank's proprietary mutual funds.Broadly speaking interest income from the bank's portfolio of loans make up more than 40% of total revenue. Roughly 60% of the portfolio is comprised of commercial loans (mostly business real estate loans but also construction and land loans and other business-related loans). Personal banking loans make up the remaining 40% of the portfolio and mostly include real estate loans and consumer lines of credit but also consumer credit cards revolving home equity loans and some overdraft lines of credit. Geographic ReachCommerce Bancshares through its Commerce Bank business operates more than 360 branch banks in five central US states with major focus in Peoria and Bloomington Illinois; St. Louis; Kansas City and Wichita Kansas; Denver; Tulsa Oklahoma; Nashville; Cincinnati; and Dallas. The bank also has commercial offices in Cincinnati Nashville and Dallas. The company's two largest markets include St. Louis and Kansas City. To this end the cities serve as the central hubs for its operation.Sales and MarketingThe bank spent $14.2 million on marketing in fiscal 2013 down 6% from $15.1 million in 2012 and down 15% from the $16.8 million it spent on marketing in 2011.Financial PerformanceIn the recent low interest environment Commerce Bancshares has seen its revenue slowly decline over the past few years from declining interest income from its loans and investment securities. In fiscal 2013 revenue fell by $8.9 million to $1.08 billion as the bank earned lower rates on investment securities and loans (from smaller interest margins) despite higher loan balances and lower rates paid on deposits. The bank was able to offset some of its revenue losses by earning $18.8 million more from bank card transaction trust and brokerage fees.The bank's net income also dipped by $8.4 million (or 3%) to $261 million in 2013. This is mostly from the drop in revenue but also because the bank paid $6 million more toward employee salaries and benefits (from higher salaries) and $4.4 million more toward data processing and software expenses as bank card processing costs went up. Profits are still up significantly from the bank's recovery period in 2009 and 2010 when it earned $169.1 million and $221.7 million respectively.The amount of cash provided from operations fell for the third straight year to $360.9 million in 2013 down 6% from the $383.1 million provided in 2012. This was primarily because of lower net income but also because it paid $11.7 million more toward its income tax obligations than in the prior year.Unlike its revenue and earnings Commerce's assets have been growing. Total loans were $10.96 billion in 2013 representing an increase of $1.13 billion or 11% over balances in 2012. While loan assets have increased across the board business loan assets contributed the most growing by $580.5 million in 2013 to a total of $3.7 billion. Deposit assets also rose by 4% to $19.05 billion in 2013.StrategyCommerce Bancshares serves its local retail markets through relationship banking and high touch service. It works to grow its core revenue by expanding new and existing customer relationships leveraging improved technology and enhancing customer satisfaction. To respond to changes in consumer banking preferences the bank will work to improve its distribution strategy by de-emphasizing the central role of traditional branch banking and providing more customers access to its services through ATMs call centers mobile and house lines internet. It will also work to develop new products and focus on expense reductions wherever possible to improve the company's bottom line.To grow its commercial business segment which already provides two-thirds of all bank revenue Commerce plans to invest in distinctive lower-risk/higher return businesses to increase its loan business. In addition it intends to deepen its relationships with existing commercial customers and provide more products to them to increase profitability while taking on little additional risk or cost.Thanks to higher brokerage and trust fees Commerce Bancshares' Wealth division saw the largest segment revenue growth in 2013. The bank is optimistic that its new hires in the division will contribute to higher sales productivity over the next few years particularly in the institutional and St. Louis Family Office. In addition management believes that the improving US economy and booming stock market will improve investor confidence and M&A activity which should help grow the segment in the years ahead. Mergers and AcquisitionsCommerce Bancshares in May 2013 inked a merger agreement with Summit Banc-

shares whereby Summit merged into a wholly-owned subsidiary of Commerce Bancshares. The transaction valued at approximately $40.6 million consisted entirely of Commerce Bancshares' stock and added more than $200 million in new loans to the bank's portfolio. The deal significantly boosted Commerce Bank's foothold in the Tulsa Oklahoma market and allowed it to enter the Oklahoma City market.

EXECUTIVES

SVP; Director Operations and Information Services, Robert J. Rauscher, age 57
CFO, Charles G. (Chuck) Kim, age 55, $415,080 total compensation
EVP Commercial Line of Business; President and COO Commerce Bank Kansas City Region, Kevin G. Barth, age 55, $408,705 total compensation
EVP; Chief Human Resources Officer and Director Internal Support Services, Sara E. Foster, age 55
Chairman and CEO, David W. Kemper, age 64, $896,073 total compensation
EVP Trust Line of Business; President The Commerce Trust Company a division of Commerce Bank, V. Raymond (Ray) Stranghoener, age 64, $235,900 total compensation
EVP; Chief Credit Officer and Chief Risk Officer, Daniel D. Callahan
SVP; Director Commercial Card and Merchant Services, Jeff Burik
SVP; Director Community Bank Administration, Michael J. Petrie
President and COO, John W. Kemper, $462,287 total compensation
Vice President Of Human Resources, Betty Maes
Vice President Of Commercial Lending, Jeffrey Hotop
Vice President Commercial Marketing, Liz Lewis
Senior Vice President, Mary McClain
Vice President, James Roman
Vice President Marketing Product Manager, Winona Murray
Vice President Credit Manager, Stephen (Steve) Savage
Vice President Business Banking Team Leader, Gregory Kendall
Vice President, Susan (Sue) Doyle
Vice President Treasury Sales, Chuck Peterson
Vice President Server Operations Manager Information Technology, Wanda Edgmond
Assistant Vice President Information Technology Manager, Chad Boline
Vice President, Mark Bond
Vice President, Clive Veri
Senior Vice President; Director Commercial Card And Merchant Services, Jeffrey (Jeff) Burik
Vice President, Carissa Albers
Vice President Human Resources, Robert Heflin
Vice President, Susan McGee
Vice President Commercial Lending, Pam Hill
Regional Vice President Corporate Banking, Matt Crossing
Vice President Information Technology, Thomas (Thom) Cook
Vice President, Lance Wright
Senior Vice President; Director Community Bank Administration, Michael (Mel) Petrie
Vice President Interest Rate Swaps Marketing, Jessie Kelley
Assistant Vice President Computer Operations Information Technology, Matt Pflugradt
Vice President Product Development, Bruce Bienhoff
Assistant Vice President Small Business Banking Specialist, Darin Crump
Vice President Mortgage Technology Manager, Sarah Vande
Vice Chairman, Seth M. Leadbeater, age 64

Vice Chairman, Jonathan M. Kemper, age 62
Treasurer, Michael (Mel) Bude
Auditors: KPMG LLP

LOCATIONS

HQ: Commerce Bancshares, Inc.
1000 Walnut, Kansas City, MO 64106
Phone: 816 234-2000   **Fax:** 816 234-2369
Web: www.commercebank.com

2012 Sales by Market

	% of total
St. Louis	33
Kansas City	28
Other regions	39
Total	**100**

PRODUCTS/OPERATIONS

Selected Services
Commercial Banking
    Financing
    Treasury Services
    Commercial Card Products
    Merchant Services
    International Services
    Capital Markets
    Investment Management
    Corporate Trust
Personal Banking
    Checking Accounts
    Savings Accounts
Money Mark
Borrowing
    Mortgages
    Credit Cards
    Check Cards & Prepaid Cards
    Online Banking Services & Mobile Banking
Small Business Banking
    Small Business Checking Accounts
    Small Business Online Services
    Small Business Loans
    Business Credit Cards & Check Cards
    Business Resource Center
    Merchant Services
Wealth Management
    The Commerce Trust Company
    Investment Management
    Private Banking Services
    Financial Advisory Services
    Trust Services
    Institutional Trust Services
    Corporate Trust
    Brokerage Services
    Insurance Services

Selected Subsidiaries
Capital for Business Inc.
CBI-Kansas Inc.
CFB Partners LLC
CFB Venture Fund L.P.
Clayton Financial Corp.
Clayton Holdings LLC
Clayton Realty Corp.
Commerce Bank National Association
Commerce Brokerage Services Inc.
Commerce Insurance Services Inc.
Commerce Investment Advisors Inc.
Commerce Mortgage Corp.
Illinois Financial LLC
Illinois Realty LLC
Tower Redevelopment Corporation

COMPETITORS

BOK Financial	First National of
Bank of America	Nebraska
Bank of the West	Great Western Bancorp
Capitol Federal	INTRUST
Financial	U.S. Bancorp
Dickinson Financial	UMB Financial
First Banks	Wells Fargo

HISTORICAL FINANCIALS

Company Type: Public

Income Statement

FYE: December 31

	ASSETS ($ mil.)	NET INCOME ($ mil.)	INCOME AS % OF ASSETS	EMPLOYEES
12/14	23,994	261	1.1%	4,866
12/13	23,072	260	1.1%	4,889
12/12	22,159	269	1.2%	4,878
12/11	20,649	256	1.2%	4,860
12/10	18,502	221	1.2%	5,005
Annual Growth	6.7%	4.2%	—	(0.7%)

2014 Year-End Financials

Debt ratio: 0.43%
Return on equity: 11.53%
Cash ($ mil.): 1,083
Current ratio: —
Long-term debt ($ mil.): —

No. of shares (mil.): 101
Dividends
　Yield: 1.9%
　Payout: 32.8%
Market value ($ mil.): 4,405

	STOCK PRICE ($) FY Close	P/E High/Low	PER SHARE ($) Earnings	Dividends	Book Value
12/14	43.49	19　17	2.49	0.82	23.01
12/13	44.91	19　14	2.47	0.78	20.88
12/12	35.06	17　14	2.51	1.99	20.45
12/11	38.12	19　14	2.32	0.72	20.01
12/10	39.73	22　18	1.97	0.70	18.27
Annual Growth	2.3%	—　—	5.9%	3.9%	5.9%

Commercial Metals Co.

Man of Steel wanted: Commercial Metals (CMC) manufactures recycles and sells enough steel and metal to test even Superman. CMC operates via five segments: Americas Recycling its metal processing plants in the US Southwest shreds and pulverizes scrap for sale to steel mills. Americas Mills turn out reinforcing bar flats rounds fence post and other shapes. A fabrication arm shapes produces and treats steel bar and angles. International business (rolling and finishing mills recycling and fabrication plants) churn out reinforcing bar and mesh. CMC's marketing and distributing segment sells products in 200 locations in more than 20 countries to the construction energy and transportation markets.

Geographic Reach

The US generates 70% of the company's total sales. Other major markets include Europe and Asia representing about 15% and 10% of sales respectively. CMC has locations in Africa Asia North America Europe and Oceania.

Sales and Marketing

CMC sells its products directly to customers primarily manufacturers in the steel nonferrous metals metal fabrication chemical refractory construction and transportation sectors.

Financial Performance

CMC's revenues fell 15% from $7.04 billion in 2014 to $5.99 billion in 2015 while its net income increased 23% over that same time period. (Note: the company's 2014 annual revenues were restated due to the recent divestiture of its Australian steel business.)

The revenue dip for 2015 was fueled by a decrease in tons shipped and a decrease in average selling prices across its Americas Recycling Americas Mills International Mill and International Marketing and Distribution segments. The decrease also reflected unfavorable foreign currency impacts for its International Mill and International Marketing and Distribution segments.

In 2015 CMC's operating cash flow skyrocketed by 129% to $313 million. The upswing was attributed to changes in accounts receivable due to lower net sales and a decrease in inventory levels for its international marketing and distribution segment.

Strategy

CMC has responded to its turbulent balance sheet by lowering inventory costs maximizing internal purchases and opening new mills. Throughout 2015 the company sold its Australian steel distribution business.

In the summer of 2015 the company announced plans to build a new mini-mill in Durant Oklahoma to better serve a growing North Texas market as well as expand into markets in Arkansas Kansas Missouri Nebraska and Oklahoma.

Company Background

Russian immigrant Moses Feldman moved to Dallas in 1914 and founded scrap metal company American Iron & Metal the next year. In the 1920s Feldman suffered a heart attack and his son Jake helped out with the business. Low metal prices hurt the company during the Depression. In 1932 Jake formed a two-man brokerage firm Commercial Metals Company (CMC) which was combined as a partnership with his father's scrap metal operations. Moses Feldman died in 1937. CMC was incorporated in 1946 and began buying related businesses during the 1950s. It was listed on the American Stock Exchange in 1960.

EXECUTIVES

COO, Barbara R. Smith, age 56, $535,685 total compensation
Chairman President and CEO, Joseph (Joe) Alvarado, age 63, $926,468 total compensation
SVP and President CMC Americas, Tracy L. Porter, $545,685 total compensation
SVP and President CMC International, John C. Elmore, $550,000 total compensation
VP and Chief Human Resources Officer, Terry P. Hatten, $266,827 total compensation
VP and CFO, Mary A. Lindsey, age 60
Vice President Business Development Military and Government, Jure Bevanda
Vice President Marketing, Billy Milligan
Vice President, Stefan Henne
Vice President Construction Services, Scott Williams
Vice President, Joel Kahn
Senior Vice President Compliance, Keith Wright
Assistant Vice President, Robert (Bob) Rodriguez
Executive Vice President Finance, Robert Cundiff
Vice President Sales, Timothy Day
Human Resources Director Or Vice President Of Human Resources, Rod Austin
Vice President, Adam Batchelor
Vice President and Treasurer, Carey Dubois
Auditors: Deloitte & Touche LLP

LOCATIONS

HQ: Commercial Metals Co.
　6565 North MacArthur Blvd, Irving, TX 75039
Phone: 214 689-4300　　Fax: 214 689-5886
Web: www.cmc.com

2015 Sales

	$ mil.	% of total
US	4,199	70
Europe	1,006	17
Asia	578	10
Australia & New Zealand	121	2
Other regions	82	1
Total	5,988	100

PRODUCTS/OPERATIONS

2015 Sales

	$ mil.	% of total
Americas		
Mills	1,841	26
Fabrication	1,624	23
Recycling	1,022	15
International		
Marketing and distribution	1,897	27
Mill	626	9
Corporate	0	—
Eliminations	(1024.8)	-
Total	5,988	100

2015 Sales

	$ mil.	% of total
Steel products	4,084	68
Industrial materials	566	10
Nonferrous scrap	536	9
Ferrous scrap	428	7
Construction materials	220	4
Nonferrous products	10	-
Other	142	2
Total	5,988	100

Selected Services

Fabrication
Marketing and Distribution
Metals Recycling
Mill Products
Services
　Heat Treating
　Structural Engineering

COMPETITORS

AK Steel Holding Corporation
BHP Billiton
Blue Tee
Connell LP
David J. Joseph
Gerdau Ameristeel
Indel
Keywell
Metals USA
Mueller Industries
Nucor
OmniSource

Quanex Building Products
Roanoke Bar Division
Ryerson
Schnitzer Steel
Simec
Steel Dynamics
Tube City IMS
United States Steel
Universal Forest Products
Worthington Industries

HISTORICAL FINANCIALS

Company Type: Public

Income Statement

FYE: August 31

	REVENUE ($ mil.)	NET INCOME ($ mil.)	NET PROFIT MARGIN	EMPLOYEES
08/15	5,988	141	2.4%	9,126
08/14	7,039	115	1.6%	9,293
08/13	6,889	77	1.1%	9,411
08/12	7,828	207	2.7%	9,860
08/11	7,918	(129)	—	11,422
Annual Growth	(6.7%)	—	—	(5.5%)

2015 Year-End Financials

Debt ratio: 38.79%
Return on equity: 10.62%
Cash ($ mil.): 485
Current ratio: 3.74
Long-term debt ($ mil.): 1,277

No. of shares (mil.): 115
Dividends
　Yield: 3.0%
　Payout: 31.1%
Market value ($ mil.): 1,815

	STOCK PRICE ($) FY Close	P/E High/Low	PER SHARE ($) Earnings	Dividends	Book Value
08/15	15.70	15　11	1.20	0.48	11.41
08/14	17.28	21　15	0.97	0.48	11.44
08/13	14.88	26　19	0.66	0.48	10.85
08/12	12.74	9　5	1.78	0.48	10.71
08/11	11.75	—　—	(1.13)	0.48	10.04
Annual Growth	7.5%	—　—	—	(0.0%)	3.2%

Community Bank System, Inc.

Community Bank System is right up front about what it is. The holding company owns Community Bank which operatesÂ about 180 branches acrossÂnearly 30Âcounties in upstate New York and five counties in northeastern Pennsylvania where it operates as First Liberty Bank and Trust. Focusing on small underserved towns the bank offers standard products and services suchÂas checking and savings accountsÂ certificates of depositÂandÂloans and mortgagesÂto consumer business and government clients.ÂThe bank's loan portfolio is divided more or less equally among business loans residential mortgages and consumer loans.

Community Bank System also owns subsidiaries that offer employee benefits administration (Benefit Plan Administrative Services) wealth management and brokerage (Community Investment Services) institutional and individual investment advisory (Nottingham Advisors) and insurance (CBNA Insurance Agency).

The company has grown mostly through acquisitions of smaller banks or branches in non-urban areas. The latest was its mid-2012 purchase of about 20 locations in upstate New York from HSBC. The deal which was made to satisfy antitrust concerns regarding First Niagara's purchase of 195 branches in New York from HSBC strengthens Community Bank Systems' geographic footprint. The company bought bank holding company The Wilber Corporation in 2011 adding about 20 locations in the Catskills Mountains region of central New York.

Community Bank System has also expanded its trust and benefits administration business through acquisitions including firms outside the bank's traditional market area in cities such as Houston Philadelphia and Pittsburgh. In 2011 it bought retirement plan administrator CAI Benefits which has offices in New York and Northern New Jersey.

Community Bank System enjoyed upticks in profitability in 2010 and 2011 (53% and 16% respectively) thanks to several factors including higher electronic banking revenue more favorable interest rate spreads and an increase in fees from benefit trust administration and consulting.

EXECUTIVES

EVP and CFO, Scott A. Kingsley, age 50, $411,012 total compensation
President CEO and Director, Mark E. Tryniski, $674,040 total compensation
EVP and Chief Banking Officer, Brian D. Donahue, age 59, $334,050 total compensation
SVP and Senior Operations Officer, Timothy J. (Tim) Baker, age 63
CTO, J. Michael Wilson, age 44
SVP Retail Banking Sales and Marketing, Harold M. (Harry) Wentworth, age 50
SVP and Chief Investment Officer, Joseph J. Lemchak, age 53
President Pennsylvania Banking, Robert P. Matley, age 63
SVP Central New York Region-Banking, Joseph E. Sutaris, age 47
SVP and Retail Banking Administrator, Richard M. (Dick) Heidrick, age 56
SVP and Senior Commercial Lending Officer Northern New York, Nicholas S. (Nick) Russell, age 47
SVP and Chief Credit Administrator, Stephen G. Hardy, age 60

EVP and General Counsel, George J. Getman, $364,900 total compensation
SVP and Chief Risk Officer, Paul J. Ward
SVP and Chief Credit Officer, Joseph Serbun, $241,467 total compensation
SVP and Pennsylvania Retail Banking Manager, Robert A. Cirko
Assistant Vice President Marketing an, Mary K Barnette
Executive Vice President Marketing, Aaron Kurtz
Senior Vice President, Matthew (Matt) Dougherty
Vice President, Michael Brassard
Executive Vice President Marketing, Deborah Fitch
Executive Vice President Marketing, Caryn Wake
Vice President Marketing, Art Gentry
Senior Vice President Director Of Sales And Marketing, Hal Wentworth
Vice President Director Mortgage Lending, George J Burke
Vice President Finance, Richard (Dick) Chatin
Vice President Cash Management Product and Sales Manager, Cindy Lefko
Senior Vice President and CHRO, Bernadette Barber
Senior Vice President and Chief Credit Officer, Joe Serbun
Assistant Vice President Hris Projects Manager, Lorie Semmel
Director, Nicholas A. DiCerbo, age 68
Auditors: PricewaterhouseCoopers LLP

LOCATIONS

HQ: Community Bank System, Inc.
5790 Widewaters Parkway, DeWitt, NY 13214-1883
Phone: 315 445-2282
Web: www.communitybankna.com

PRODUCTS/OPERATIONS

2013 Sales

	$ mil.	% of total
Interest		
Loans including fees	188	41
Taxable investments	55	12
Nontaxable investments	21	5
Noninterest		
Deposit service fees	49	11
Employee benefit services	38	9
Wealth management	15	3
Other	86	19
Adjustments	(87.3)	-
Total	**366**	**100**

Selected Subsidiaries & Affiliates

Benefit Plans Administrative Services Inc.
Benefit Plans Administrative Services LLC
Brilie Corporation
CBNA Insurance Agency Inc.
CBNA Preferred Funding Corp.
CBNA Treasury Management Corporation
Community Bank N.A. (also dba First Liberty Bank & Trust)
Community Investment Services Inc.
First of Jermyn Realty Company
First Liberty Service Corporation
Flex Corporation
Hand Benefit & Trust Company
Hand Securities Inc.
Harbridge Consulting Group LLP
Nottingham Advisors Inc.
Town & Country Agency LLC
Western Catskill Realty Inc.

COMPETITORS

Arrow Financial	First Niagara
Bank of America	Financial
Canandaigua National	HSBC USA
Chemung Financial	JPMorgan Chase
Citizens Financial	KeyCorp
Group	M&T Bank
Elmira Savings Bank	NBT Bancorp
Financial Institutions	

HISTORICAL FINANCIALS

Company Type: Public

Income Statement

FYE: December 31

	ASSETS ($ mil.)	NET INCOME ($ mil.)	INCOME AS % OF ASSETS	EMPLOYEES
12/14	7,489	91	1.2%	2,182
12/13	7,095	78	1.1%	2,215
12/12	7,496	77	1.0%	2,188
12/11	6,488	73	1.1%	2,030
12/10	5,444	63	1.2%	1,627
Annual Growth	**8.3%**	**9.6%**	**—**	**7.6%**

2014 Year-End Financials

Debt ratio: 5.88%	No. of shares (mil.): 40
Return on equity: 9.80%	Dividends
Cash ($ mil.): 138	Yield: 3.0%
Current ratio: —	Payout: 52.2%
Long-term debt ($ mil.): —	Market value ($ mil.): 1,554

	STOCK PRICE ($) FY Close	P/E High/Low		PER SHARE ($) Earnings	Dividends	Book Value
12/14	38.13	18	15	2.22	1.16	24.24
12/13	39.68	21	14	1.94	1.10	21.66
12/12	27.36	15	13	1.93	1.06	22.78
12/11	27.80	14	11	2.01	1.00	20.94
12/10	27.77	15	9	1.89	0.94	18.23
Annual Growth	**8.2%**	**—**	**—**	**4.1%**	**5.4%**	**7.4%**

Community Health Systems, Inc.

Community Health Systems (CHS) isn't much of a city dweller. The hospital operator prefers small-town America owning or leasing more than 200 hospitals mostly in rural areas or small cities in 29 states. Its hospitals (which house roughly 31000 beds) typically act as the sole or primary acute health care provider in a service area and offer a variety of medical surgical and emergency services (though a handful are specialty centers). The hospitals generally have ancillary facilities including doctors' offices surgery centers and diagnostic imaging facilities as well as home health and hospice agencies. CHS' Quorum Health Resources subsidiary provides management services to around 150 non-affiliated hospitals.

Operations

CHS operates two segments: hospital operations (the bulk of the company's business) and home care agency operations. (Prior to Q1 2013 hospital management services represented its own segment but that business' financials have since been rolled into Hospital Operations.) The hospital operations segment includes inpatient centers and their related outpatient care facilities and accounts for about 99% of annual revenues. Meanwhile the home care agency segment operates some 65 home health agencies and 21 hospice agencies primarily in markets where the firm also runs a medical center. Now part of hospital operations Quorum Health Resources provides executive management and consulting services.

Altogether CHS employs some 22000 physicians and their medical staffs. Combined the company's hospitals provided care for 1 million inpatients and processed nearly 5 million emergency visits in 2013.

Geographic Reach

CHS has hospitals in 29 states with its largest market concentrations in Florida Indiana Texas and Pennsylvania.

Sales and Marketing

CHS receives about 35% of its revenues from Medicare and Medicaid reimbursements for patient services. Another 50% comes from commercial insurance companies with which it has managed care contracts and the rest is attributed to self-pay patients.

Financial Performance

As it has expanded its network of facilities over the years CHS' revenues have likewise shown steady growth (with the exception of 2013 when a decline in admissions cut into earnings). In 2014 revenue rose 43% to $18.6 billion primarily driven by the system's acquisition of hospital operator and consulting firm Health Management Associates. Same-store net operating revenues also increased that year as a result of a favorable shift in payor mix with charity care and self-pay discounts declining.

Profits have fluctuated in the past five years with peaks in 2010 and 2012 and valleys in 2011 and 2013. Net income fell again in 2014 decreasing 35% to $92 million on higher operating expenses including salaries and benefits as well as costs related to integrating the operations of newly purchased Health Management Associates.

Cash flow from operations has also been generally on the rise and in 2014 it grew 48% to $1.6 billion. This was largely due to an increase in cash provided by supplies and other current assets accounts payable and income taxes.

Strategy

In addition to adding new hospitals and clinics through acquisitions CHS looks to grow revenue and profitability at its existing facilities. Its strategy focuses on recruiting primary care doctors and specialists; expanding services; investing in technology and facility improvements; and controlling costs through among other things centralizing certain business operations. For instance CHS trims supply costs through its membership in group purchasing organization HealthTrust.

CHS adds complex services to its line-up —including orthopedics cardiovascular care and urology —to make its facilities more attractive to physicians and patients. It is also undertaking a number of quality and safety initiatives to meet regulatory standards and improve resource utilization including the implementation of electronic health record (EHR) technology. In 2014 company spent approximately $166 million on 58 major construction projects —new emergency rooms cardiac catheterization laboratories surgical suites etc. —that were completed that year.

To further expand its services CHS often forms partnerships with other area organizations. For instance in 2013 it teamed up with Cleveland Clinic to enhance patient care services reduce expenses and increase operational efficiencies in the Ohio operating territory.

In addition the company sometimes divests facilities it deems as not core to its strategy. The company sold several smaller hospitals in 2014 and it plans to sell more as required by the FTC as a condition of the $7.6 billion acquisition of rival health system Health Management Associates that year. In 2015 it sold Arizona-based Payson Regional Medical Center for $22 million; it also sold its interests in two South Carolina hospitals and one Arkansas hospital and plans to sell two hospitals in Florida.

In another restructuring move CHS in 2015 announced plans to spin off nearly 40 of its hospitals along with hospital management unit Quorum Health Resources forming a new public company to be named Quorum Health Corporation.

The firm expects its earnings to increase in coming years thanks to an aging population. It also hopes to benefit from reform measures that aim to increase the number of insured patients in the US which could cut down on self-pay patients and reduce the amount of bad debt its hospitals carry.

Mergers and Acquisitions

You don't become one of the largest for-profit hospital operators in the nation without a pretty aggressive acquisition strategy and CHS certainly has that. CHS target hospitals in non-urban locations poised for growth. Because such areas have fewer people they generally have fewer hospitals (meaning less competition for patients and for managed care contracts). CHS typically purchases a number of small community hospitals each year though it also sometimes conducts larger acquisitions of hospital operating groups.

CHS boosted its operational footprint significantly in 2014 when it acquired Health Management Associates in a deal worth some $7.6 billion (including $3.7 billion in debt). The merger of the two hospital operators —both of which share a focus on community medical centers —created a system with more than 200 hospitals (with a total of some 31000 beds) in 29 states. Other acquisitions that year included hospitals in Mississippi South Carolina and Pennsylvania.

HISTORY

Community Health Systems (CHS) was founded in 1985.

In 1996 it was acquired by investment firm Forstmann Little & Co. in a leveraged buyout transaction worth some $1.1 billion. It also moved its headquarters from Houston to Nashville Tennessee that year.

CHS once again became a public entity through an IPO in 2000. It engaged is engaged in a flurry of acquisition activity of small regional hospitals each year following its IPO.

However CHS limited its purchases somewhat after plunking down $7 billion in 2007 to acquire Triad Hospitals (and its more than 50 hospitals). After conducting integration efforts at the former Triad hospitals CHS fully resumed its acquisition activity when it purchased five hospitals during 2010 including the Marion Regional Hospital in South Carolina the Forum Health (later ValleyCare) hospitals in Ohio and the Bluefield Hospital in West Virginia.

Buoyed by those purchases CHS launched a campaign to acquire fellow hospital operator and rival Tenet in late 2010 in a deal worth some $7.3 billion in cash stock and debt. However after much back and forth between the firms —including lawsuits and hostile tender offers —CHS halted its acquisition attempts the following year due to a lack of response from Tenet's shareholders and board members.

CHS instead completed several smaller purchases that year including the acquisition of the Mercy Health Partners Scranton operations in Pennsylvania from Catholic Health Partners. The company also purchased Tomball Regional Medical Center (TRMC) located near Houston.

As part of its periodic practice of divesting non-core centers in 2011 it sold two Oklahoma facilities SouthCrest Hospital and Claremore Regional Hospital to Ardent Health Services' Hillcrest HealthCare System unit for an undisclosed price. It also sold a Texas hospital Cleveland Regional Medical Center that year to New Directions Health Systems.

Vice President, Christine Galanda
Director Of Surgery Services, Craig Hiott
Director Of Pharmacy, Kathryn Jost
Clinical Director, Tammy Cooper
Vice President Investor Relations, Michael Culotta
Vice President Of Operations, Kim Needham
**Director of Surgery Director of Surgery Services
Operating Room Director,** Amber Jones
Medical Director, Scott Wagner
Vice President Of Hospitalist Services, Garen
Throneberry
Vice President Finance Division I Operations..,
Eric Roach
Vice President Of Human Resources, Mike Meeks
Clinic Manager, Stephanie Thompson
Clinic Manager, Amanda Anderton
Vice President, Laurence Bludau
Vice President and Director of Aviation, Thomas
(Thom) Tate
Vice President Physician Business Services, Dan
Adkins
Vice President Investor Relations, Lib Schuler
**Vice President Corporate Controller And Chief
Accounting Officer,** T Buford
Vice Presidents Business Development, Kristine
Burnell
**Vice President Division Iii Operations Division Iv
Operations Leadership,** Neil Heatherly
Assistant Treasurer, Ted Lomicka
Board Member, Margaret Bass
Auditors: Deloitte & Touche LLP

LOCATIONS

HQ: Community Health Systems, Inc.
4000 Meridian Boulevard, Franklin, TN 37067
Phone: 615 465-7000
Web: www.chs.net

Selected Facilities

Alabama
 Cherokee M
 Crestwood
 Dekalb Reg
 Flowers Ho
 Gadsden Re
 L.V. Stabl
 Medical Ce
 South Bald
 Trinity Me
Alaska
 Mat-Su Reg
Arizona
 Northwest
 Northwest
 Payson Reg
 Western Ar
Arkansas
 Forrest Ci
 Harris Hos
 Helena Reg
 Medical Ce
 Northwest
 Northwest
 Siloam Spr
 Willow Cre
California
 Barstow Co
 Fallbrook
 Watsonvill
Florida
 Lake Wales
 North Okal
Georgia
 Fannin Reg
 Trinity Ho
Illinois
 Crossroads
 Galesburg
 Gateway Re
 Heartland
 MetroSouth
 Red Bud Re
 Union Coun
 Vista Medi
Indiana

Bluffton R
Dupont Hos
Dukes Memo
Kosciusko
Lutheran H
Lutheran M
Porter Hos
St. Joseph
Kentucky
 Kentucky R
 Parkway Re
 Three Rive
Louisiana
 Byrd Regio
 Northern L
 Women and
Mississippi
 River Regi
 Wesley Med
Missouri
 Moberly Re
 Northeast
Nevada
 Mesa View
New Jersey
 Memorial H
New Mexico
 Alta Vista
 Carlsbad M
 Eastern Ne
 Lea Region
 Mimbres Me
 MountainVi
North Carolina
 Martin Gen
Ohio
 Affinity M
  ValleyCare Health System
 Northside
 Trumball M
 Hillside R
Oklahoma
 Deaconess
 Ponca City
  Woodward Regional Hospital
Oregon
 McKenzie-W
Pennsylvania
 Berwick Ho
 Brandywine
 Chestnut H
 Easton Hos
 First Hosp
 Jennersvil
 Lock Haven
 Phoenixvil
 Memorial H
  Moses Taylor Health System
 Mid-Valley
 Moses Tayl
 Pottstown
 Regional Hospital of Scranton (Scranton formerly
  Mercy Hospital of Scranton)
 Special Care Hospital (Nanticoke formerly Mercy
  Special Care Hospital)
 Sunbury Co
 Tyler Memorial Hospital (Tunkhannock formerly
  Mercy Tyler Hospital)
 Wyoming Va
South Carolina
 Carolinas
 Chesterfie
 Marion Reg
 Marlboro P
 Mary Black
 Springs Me
Tennessee
 Heritage M
 Dyersburg
 Gateway Me
 Haywood Pa
 Henderson
 Lakeway Re
 McKenzie R
 McNairy Re
 Regional H
 Sky Ridge
 Volunteer
Texas
 Abilene Re
 Big Bend R

Brownwood
Cedar Park
College St
DeTar Hosp
DeTar Hosp
Hill Regio
Lake Granb
Laredo Med
Longview R
Navarro Re
San Angelo
Scenic Mou
South Texa
Tomball Re
Weatherfor
Woodland H
Utah
 Mountain W
Virginia
 Southampto
 Southern V
 Southside
West Virginia
 Bluefield
 Greenbrier
 Plateau Me
Wyoming
 Evanston R

PRODUCTS/OPERATIONS

2014 Sales

	% of total
Managed care & commercial	51
Medicare & Medicaid	36
Self-pay	13
Total	**100**

2014 Sales

	$ mil.	% of total
Hospital	18,399	100
Corporate & other	240	-
Total	**18,639**	**100**

Selected Acquisitions

COMPETITORS

Adventist Health
Adventist Health System Sunbelt Healthcare
Ascension Health
Banner Health
CHRISTUS Health
Carolinas HealthCare System
Catholic Health Initiatives
Dignity Health
HCA
HealthSouth
LifePoint Health
Mercy Health
Mercy Health (OH)
SSM Health Care
SunLink Health Systems
Sutter Health
Tenet Healthcare
Texas Health Resources
Trinity Health (Novi)
Universal Health Services
University Health Services
WellStar Health System

HISTORICAL FINANCIALS
Company Type: Public

Income Statement

FYE: December 31

	REVENUE ($ mil.)	NET INCOME ($ mil.)	NET PROFIT MARGIN	EMPLOYEES
12/14	18,639	92	0.5%	167,000
12/13	12,997	141	1.1%	87,000
12/12	13,028	265	2.0%	96,000
12/11	13,626	201	1.5%	88,000
12/10	12,986	279	2.2%	87,000
Annual Growth	9.5%	(24.3%)	—	17.7%

Debt ratio: 61.69% No. of shares (mil.): 116
Return on equity: 2.60% Dividends
Cash ($ mil.): 509 Yield: —
Current ratio: 1.55 Payout: —
Long-term debt ($ mil.): 16,681 Market value ($ mil.): 6,294

	STOCK PRICE ($) FY Close	P/E High/Low		PER SHARE ($) Earnings	Dividends	Book Value
12/14	53.92	70	43	0.82	0.00	34.29
12/13	39.27	34	20	1.51	0.00	32.29
12/12	30.74	11	6	2.96	0.25	29.70
12/11	17.45	19	7	2.23	0.00	26.47
12/10	37.37	14	9	3.01	0.00	23.63
Annual Growth	9.6%	—	—	(27.8%)	—	9.8%

Community Trust Bancorp, Inc.

Community Trust Bancorp is the holding company for Community Trust Bank one of the largest Kentucky-based banks. It operates 70-plus branches throughout the state as well as in northeastern Tennessee and southern West Virginia. The bank offers standard services to area businesses and individuals including checking and savings accounts credit cards and CDs. Loans secured by commercial properties and other real estate account for nearly 70% of the bank's portfolio which also includes business consumer and construction loans. Subsidiary Community Trust and Investment Company provides trust estate retirement brokerage and insurance services through a handful of offices in Kentucky and Tennessee.

Geographic Reach

Kentucky-based Community Trust Bancorp operates more than 70 banking locations across Kentucky West Virginia and Tennessee. Its trust offices are located in Kentucky and Tennessee.

Operations

Community Trust Bancorp's lending activities include making commercial construction mortgage and personal loans. It also offers lease-financing lines of credit revolving lines of credit term loans and other specialized loans including asset-backed financing.

Some 69% of Community Trust Bancorp's portfolio of loans is secured real estate (36% of which consists of commercial real estate).

Sales and Marketing

Community Trust Bancorp specializes in serving both small and medium-sized businesses.

Mergers and Acquisitions

Community Trust Bancorp bought LaFollette First National Corporation the holding company for First National Bank of LaFollette for some $16 million. The 2010 acquisition gave the company its first four bank branches and first trust office in Tennessee.

Community Trust is considering additional acquisitions of smaller competitors. It also grows by opening new branches.

Financial Performance

Despite weak loan demand Community Trust Bancorp has grown its revenue from 2009 to 2011 followed by a marginal decline in 2012. Thanks to a decline in both interest expenses and provisions for loan losses Community Trust Bancorp has seen its net income rise during the past five years.

While Community Trust Bancorp logged marginal decreases (1%) in revenue in fiscal 2012 vs. 2011 the financial institution posted net income increases of 16% to $45 million during the reporting period.

EXECUTIVES

Vice President Of Loans, Michael S Wasson
Chairman President and CEO; Chairman Community Trust Bank, Jean R. Hale, age 69, $483,846 total compensation
EVP and CFO; EVP and Treasurer Community Trust Bank, Kevin J. Stumbo, age 55, $190,385 total compensation
EVP; EVP and Chief Credit Officer Community Trust Bank, James J. (Jim) Gartner, age 74
EVP; EVP Operations Community Trust Bank, James B. (Jim) Draughn, age 56, $210,154 total compensation
Executive Vice President, Ricky D. Sparkman, age 52
EVP; EVP and Eastern Region President Community Trust Bank, Richard W. (Rick) Newsom, age 60
Executive Vice President, Larry W. Jones, age 68, $219,231 total compensation
EVP; EVP and Chief Internal Audit and Risk Officer Community Trust Bank, Steven E. (Steve) Jameson, age 58
EVP; President North East Region Community Trust Bank Inc., Andrew Jones
President and CEO Community Trust and Investment Company, Andy D. Waters
Assistant Vice President Technology, Brian Hatmaker
Senior Vice President credit Administrator, Anita Justice
Vice President, Barbara Maynard
Vice President Assistant Controller, Philip Smith
Vice President Business Development, Deborah Baber
Senior Vice President Operations And Compliance Manager, Sandra K Payne
Vice President Of Marketing, Zachary Cantrell
Vice President Of Market Research, Jeremy Rigney
Assistant Vice President, Alicia Bullock
Executive Vice President Marketing, Bridgett Fields
Vice President Of Human Resources, Kevin Burford
Executive Vice President Marketing, Daryl Slone
Vice President Marketing, Carl Tristchler
Vice President Rom, Linda Miracle
Vice President And Security Officer, Jim Brown
Vice President Information Technology, Darrell Stepp
Vice President and Branch Manager, Linda Smith
Senior Vice President, Rhonda S Longmire
Vice President Manager, Tammy R Provost
Vice President, Jeannine Petell
Senior Vice President, Stephen Belcher
Vice President Market Second Officer, Cathy Taylor
Vice President Of Commercial Lending, Larry Forester
Vice President Technology, Thomas (Thom) McCoy
Senior Vice President, Billie Dollins
Vice President, Sandy Payne
Senior Vice President General Counsel Secretary and Treasurer, Christy Emerson
Vice President Of Human Resources, Jim Draughn
Executive Vice President Marketing, Carl Tritschler
Senior Vice President, J Carol McDonald
Senior Vice President Controller, Stacey Watson
Build Treasurer, Julie Clark
Auditors: BKD, LLP

LOCATIONS

HQ: Community Trust Bancorp, Inc.
346 North Mayo Trail, Pikeville, KY 41501
Phone: 606 432-1414
Web: www.ctbi.com

PRODUCTS/OPERATIONS

2012 Revenue

	% of total
Interest	77
Non-interest	23
Total	**100**

Selected Products & Services

Business Banking
  Business CDs
  Business Checking
  Corporate Services
  Lending
  Merchant Services
  Online Services
  Savings & Money Market
Financial Services
Personal Banking
  Card Services
  CDs & IRAs
  Consumer Loans
  Home Equity
  Interest Checking
  Mobile Banking
  Mortgages
  Personal Checking
  Savings & Money Market
Wealth & Trust Management

COMPETITORS

BB&T	Premier Financial
Farmers Capital Bank	Bancorp
Fifth Third	Republic Bancorp
Home Federal	U.S. Bancorp

HISTORICAL FINANCIALS

Company Type: Public

Income Statement FYE: December 31

	ASSETS ($ mil.)	NET INCOME ($ mil.)	INCOME AS % OF ASSETS	EMPLOYEES
12/14	3,723	43	1.2%	1,012
12/13	3,581	45	1.3%	1,022
12/12	3,635	44	1.2%	1,035
12/11	3,591	38	1.1%	1,015
12/10	3,355	33	1.0%	1,041
Annual Growth	2.6%	7.0%	—	(0.7%)

2014 Year-End Financials

Debt ratio: 1.65% No. of shares (mil.): 17
Return on equity: 10.05% Dividends
Cash ($ mil.): 108 Yield: 3.2%
Current ratio: — Payout: 47.8%
Long-term debt ($ mil.): — Market value ($ mil.): 639

	STOCK PRICE ($) FY Close	P/E High/Low		PER SHARE ($) Earnings	Dividends	Book Value
12/14	36.61	18	13	2.49	1.18	25.64
12/13	45.16	17	12	2.62	1.27	23.70
12/12	32.78	14	11	2.63	1.25	23.31
12/11	29.42	13	10	2.30	1.12	21.61
12/10	28.96	16	11	1.96	1.21	20.15
Annual Growth	6.0%	—	—	6.1%	(0.6%)	6.2%

Computer Sciences Corp.

Computer Sciences Corporation (CSC) is one of the world's leading providers of systems integration and other information technology services. It offers application development data center management communications and networking development IT systems management and business consulting. It also provides business process outsourcing (BPO) services in such areas as billing and payment processing customer relationship management (CRM) and human resources. CSC boasts 2500 clients in more than 70 countries. CSC generated about a third of its revenue from US federal agencies through its public sector division which was spun off as CSRA in late 2015.

Operations

Prior to the CSRA spinoff CSC divided its business into three main service lines: Global Business Services (GBS) Global Infrastructure Services (GIS) and North American Public Sector (NPS). GBS (33% of revenue) addresses key business challenges such as consulting applications services and software. GIS (34% of revenue) provides IT infrastructure services such as managed and virtual desktop solutions unified communications and collaboration services data center management cyber security and cloud-based offerings. NPS was responsible for 33% of revenue.

Geographic Reach

CSC has major operations throughout North America Europe Asia and Australia. The company has clients in some 70 countries however 60% of total company sales are made in the US.

Sales and Marketing

CSC's clients have included hospital system Ascension Health transportation giant Bombardier diversified manufacturer Textron and defense contractor Raytheon.

Financial Performance

During fiscal 2015 (year-end March) CSC's revenue decreased for the sixth straight year. In 2015 it reported $12.17 billion in revenue down 6% from $13 billion in 2013. The pace of new business in the company's commercial sector didn't keep up with the completion of contracts. The company also saw contract terms adjust downward part of an industry trend toward smaller contract awards. NPS revenue fell due to decreases on both US Department of Defense (DOD) and civil agencies contracts. Sales fell in all geographic markets save for the UK which eked out a 1% sales increase. The reduced revenue combined with higher costs resulted in an $8 billion loss for 2015. The company has turned a $674 million profit in 2014.

Cash flow also fell down 8% to $1.4 billion.

Strategy

CSC had been working on several fronts to turn itself around and increase sales before it took the big step of breaking the company up. The company like others in the computer services business has had a hard time maintaining revenue levels in the switch to cloud and Software-as-a-Service offerings in which revenue comes from subscriptions.

One rationale for the split is that the new companies will be better able to more tightly focus on their core customers. But one problem in the American public sector has been a tightening of government purse strings which has affected many companies with a government customer base. Companies selling toward the international market have an uneasy economic environment with slow growth around the world and tensions around the European Union.

CSC isn't the first technology company to turn to an alternate corporate structure in the face of waning revenue. Several others including Hewlett-Packard and eBay have split and other companies such as Dell BMC and CompuWare have gone private with the help of private equity firms.

Before the breakup CSC formed partnerships with Amazon Web Services (AWS) and IBM to expand its cloud computing offerings With AWS CSC will collaborate on Centers of Excellence to develop applications big data analytics cyber security and AWS services and support. The IBM-CSC alliance is to help clients speed adoption of hybrid cloud mobile and big data.

Mergers and Acquisitions

On the acquisition front CSC boosted the NPS unit in buying Autonomic Resources a provider of cloud computing infrastructure for $14 million. The Autonomic addition helps CSC offer cloud services under the Federal Risk and Authorization Management Program to federal state and local governments.

In mid-2014 CSC paid $282 million for ServiceMesh an enterprise cloud services management company with operations in the Australia the UK and the US. Earlier in the year it paid $27 million for big data Platform-as-a-Service provider Infochimps. In fiscal 2013 it paid $35 million for 42Six Solutions which makes software for big data processing and analytics. 42Six Solutions counts the US Department of Defense (DOD) among its customers.

HISTORY

Early History

Computer Sciences Corporation (CSC) was founded in Los Angeles in 1959 by Fletcher Jones and Roy Nutt to write software for manufacturers such as Honeywell. In 1963 CSC became the first software company to go public. Three years later it signed a $5.5 million contract to support NASA's computation laboratory. Annual sales had climbed to just over $53 million by 1968.

In 1969 CSC agreed to merge with Western Union but the deal ultimately fell through. When Jones died in a plane crash in 1972 William Hoover a former NASA executive who had come aboard eight years earlier became chairman and CEO. Under Hoover CSC began transforming itself into a systems integrator. In 1986 when federal contracts still accounted for 70% of sales the company started diversifying into the commercial sector.

CSC signed a 10-year $3 billion contract in 1991 with defense supplier General Dynamics. In 1995 Hoover after more than three decades with CSC stepped down as CEO (remaining chairman until 1997); he was succeeded by president and COO Van Honeycutt. Also that year CSC bought Germany's largest independent computer services company Ploenzke. In 1996 CSC acquired insurance services provider Continuum Company for $1.5 billion.

EXECUTIVES

Vice President and Co Director E Business, Chris Davis

EVP and General Counsel, William L. (Bill) Deckelman, age 58, $539,700 total compensation

EVP and CFO, Paul N. Saleh, age 58, $700,000 total compensation

EVP and General Manager Global Business Services, James R. (Jim) Smith, age 48, $650,000 total compensation

EVP and General Manager Global Industries, Romil Bahl, age 46, $606,846 total compensation

EVP and General Manager Americas Region, David W. (Dave) Zolet, age 54, $532,692 total compensation

CIO, Doug S. Tracy, age 54

Chairman President and CEO, J. Michael (Mike) Lawrie, age 62, $1,250,000 total compensation

CTO, Dan Hushon, age 47

EVP and General Manager Emerging Business Group, Ashish Mahadwar, $470,615 total compensation

EVP and General Manager Global Infrastructure Services, Stephen Hilton

EVP and General Manager North American Public Sector, Larry Prior

Vice President, David (Dave) Levitt

Vice President Business Development SRA International Inc Civil Sector, Debbie Granberry

Vice President Finance, Paul Sturm

Senior Vice President, Paul Hebert

Vice President, Pat McCaffrey

Vice President Deputy General Counsel, Laura Heltebran

Vice President Marketing, Mark Dieterle

Vice President Us Shared Services, Diane Schroeder

Senior Information Technology Management Vice President Director, Diana Pohl

Vice President, Kevin Kelley

Vice President and ECSS Program Executive, Jack Gallagher

North American Public Sector Business Development Vice President, Sally Sullivan

Vice President CIVIL Division, Elaine Dauphin

Vice President Human Resources, Dennis McCabe

Vice President, Ken Dalgleish

Vice President CSC, Tom Robinson

Vice President and General Manager, James (Jamie) Hanley

Vice President and General Manager Diversified, Carlos Lopez-Abadia

Corp Vice President, Michael (Mel) Shove

Vice President Finance and Corporate Treasurer at Computer Sciences Corporation, Charlie Diao Charlie Diao

Vice President, Don Durbin

Vice President Information Technology, Richard Sandler

Vice President Cyber Operations, John (Jack) Osterholz

Senior Vice President The Americas Insurance Division, John Connell

Vice President At Csc, Jim Kennedy

Vice President General Manager Enforcement Security And Intelligence, Hal Smith

Vice President General Manager Western Region, Richard Jennings

Vice President, Mark Hurwich

Vice President FirstPoint Products, Brad Wright

Vice President Information Technology, Atul Gupta

Vice President Finance and Business, Kevin Appleton

Vice President Financial Services Sector, Durai Velan

Vice President, Ramaswamy Rajagopal

Vice President And General Manager Mission Services, John Desimone

Vice President Program Executive, Dave White

Vice President GBS Customer Program Delivery, Chris Donohue

Vice President, Debbie Carver

Vice President Homeland Security, Michael Przepiora

Vice President, Deborah Williams

Vice President, Lyn Burchfield

Vice President, Jeannie Maul

Vice President Technology And Consumer, Dave Baldwin

Vice President Treasurer, Gary Larson

Vice President, Chris Weaver

Senior Vice President, Karen Kraynak

Division Director Deputy Vice President General Manager, Richard Morrow
Vice President Global Offerings Sales, Stefano Baroni
Director Media Relations, Chris Grandis
Vice President Global Legal Compliance (1988), Harvey N Bernstein
Vice President Business Development, Marcie Smith
Vice President Corporate Development, Randy Phillips
Vice President, Jack Norton
Vice President, Irv Halter
Vice President Info Infrastructure Advisory, Guy Copeland
Vice President Acquisition Prgrams and SETA Support, Thomas (Thom) McGinnis
Vice President Global Applications Portfolio Executive, Rick Wilcox
Vice President Global Computing, Chris Helme
Board Member, Rama M Pasala
Treasurer, Marc A Kirsch
Secretary, Jennifer (Jen) Suda
Treasurer, Karen Williams
Board Member, Michael (Mel) Trettel
Auditors: Deloitte & Touche LLP

LOCATIONS

HQ: Computer Sciences Corp.
3170 Fairview Park Drive, Falls Church, VA 22042
Phone: 703 876-1000
Web: www.csc.com

2015 Sales

	% of total
US	60
Europe	
UK	14
Other countries	16
Other regions	10
Total	**100**

PRODUCTS/OPERATIONS

2015 Sales

	$ mil.	% of total
Global Business Services	4,080	34
North American Public Sector	4,057	33
Global Infrastructure Services	4,036	33
Total	**12,173**	**100**

Selected Service Areas

Application outsourcing
Business process outsourcing
Customer relationship management
Data hosting
Enterprise application integration
Knowledge management
Management consulting
Risk management
Security
Supply chain management

Selected Solutions

Application Services
Big Data & Analytics
Business & Technology Consulting
Cloud Solutions & Services
Cybersecurity
Industry Software & Solutions
Infrastructure Services
Managed Services & Outsourcing
Mobility Solutions

COMPETITORS

ADP
Accenture
Atos
Booz Allen
CACI International
CIBER
Capgemini

Cognizant Tech Solutions
Computacenter
Convergys
Deloitte Consulting
Dimension Data
General Dynamics Information Technology
Getronics
HCL Technologies
HP Enterprise Group
HP Enterprise Services
Honeywell International
IBM Global Services
Infosys
Leidos
Lockheed Martin Information Systems
ManTech
NTT Data
Northrop Grumman
Northrop Grumman Info Systems
Siemens AG
Tata Consultancy
Tech Mahindra
Unisys
Wipro
Wipro Technologies

HISTORICAL FINANCIALS

Company Type: Public

Income Statement

FYE: April 3

	REVENUE ($ mil.)	NET INCOME ($ mil.)	NET PROFIT MARGIN	EMPLOYEES
04/15*	12,173	(8)	—	70,000
03/14	12,998	674	5.2%	79,000
03/13	14,993	961	6.4%	90,000
03/12	15,877	(4,242)	—	98,000
04/11	16,042	740	4.6%	91,000
Annual Growth	(6.7%)	—	—	(6.3%)

*Fiscal year change

2015 Year-End Financials

Debt ratio: 26.16%
Return on equity: (-0.23%)
Cash ($ mil.): 2,098
Current ratio: 1.36
Long-term debt ($ mil.): 1,765

No. of shares (mil.): 138
Dividends
  Yield: 0.0%
  Payout: 1,871.4%
Market value ($ mil.): 9,073

	STOCK PRICE ($) FY Close	P/E High/Low		Earnings	Dividends	Book Value
04/15*	65.38	—	—	(0.05)	0.92	21.05
03/14	60.29	14	9	4.47	0.80	26.88
03/13	49.23	8	4	6.18	0.80	20.88
03/12	29.94	—	—	(27.37)	0.80	17.91
04/11	49.38	12	8	4.73	0.70	48.58
Annual Growth	7.3%	—	—	—	7.1%	(18.9%)

*Fiscal year change

ConAgra Foods, Inc.

ConAgra Foods fills the refrigerators freezers and pantries of most households. The company makes and markets name-brand packaged and frozen foods that are sold in most retail outlets. ConAgra's cornucopia of America's best-known brands includes Banquet Chef Boyardee Egg Beaters Healthy Choice Hunt's Marie Callender Orville Redenbacher's PAM Peter Pan Reddi-Wip Slim Jim Snack Pack and Van Camp's. It is also one of the biggest producers of seasoning and grain ingredients for the US food service food manufacturing and industrial markets. ConAgra Foods sold its private-label food business to TreeHouse Foods for $2.7 billion in February 2016.

HISTORY

Company BackgroundAlva Kinney founded Nebraska Consolidated Mills in 1919 by combining the operations of four Nebraska grain mills. It did not expand outside Nebraska until it opened a mill and feed processing plant in Alabama in 1942.

Consolidated Mills developed Duncan Hines cake mix in the 1950s. But Duncan Hines failed to raise a large enough market share and the company sold it to Procter & Gamble in 1956. Consolidated Mills used the proceeds to expand opening a flour and feed mill in Puerto Rico the next year. In the 1960s while competitors were moving into prepared foods the firm expanded into animal feeds and poultry processing. By 1970 it had poultry processing plants in Alabama Georgia and Louisiana. In 1971 the company changed its name to ConAgra (Latin for "in partnership with the land"). During the 1970s it expanded into the fertilizer catfish and pet accessory businesses.

Poorly performing subsidiaries and commodity speculation caused ConAgra severe financial problems until 1974 when Mike Harper a former Pillsbury executive took over. Harper trimmed properties to reduce debt and had the company back on its feet by 1976. ConAgra stayed focused on the commodities side of the business but was thus tied to volatile price cycles. In 1978 it bought United Agri Products (agricultural chemicals).

ConAgra moved into consumer food products in the 1980s. It bought Banquet (frozen food 1980) and within six years had introduced almost 90 new products under that label. Other purchases included Singleton Seafood (1981) Armour Food Company (meats dairy products frozen food; 1983) and RJR Nabisco's frozen food business (1986). ConAgra became a major player in the red meat market with the 1987 purchases of E.A. Miller (boxed beef) Monfort (beef and lamb) and Swift Independent Packing.

Confident it had found the right path ConAgra continued with acquisitions of consumer food makers including Beatrice Foods (Orville Redenbacher's popcorn Hunt's tomato products) in 1991. In 1997 the company agreed to pay $8.3 million to settle federal charges of wire fraud and watering down grain. That year ConAgra named vice chairman and president Bruce Rohde as CEO; he became chairman in 1998. Also in 1998 the company bought GoodMark Foods maker of Slim Jim and Nabisco's Egg Beaters and table spread unit(Parkay). ConAgra bought Holly Ridge Foods (pastries) in 1999 and announced a major restructuring.

ConAgra bought Emerge an agricultural and land-use information software provider from Litton Industries in 2000. It also acquired Seaboard's poultry division and refrigerated meat alternatives maker Lightlife (Tofu pups Smart Dogs) before buying major brand holder International Home Foods from HM Capital Partners (known as Hicks Muse Tate & Furst at the time) for about $2.9 billion. The company then became ConAgra Foods.

During 2001 the company drew SEC attention and was forced to restate earnings for the previous three years due to accounting no-no's in its United Agri Products division.

In 2002 the USDA forced ConAgra to recall 19 million pounds of ground beef because of possible E. coli contamination making it the second-largest food recall in US history. (The largest recall occurred in 1997 when Hudson Foods later purchased by Tyson Foods withdrew 35 million pounds of beef.) Later in 2002 ConAgra sold its fresh beef and pork processing business —one of the largest in the US –to Booth Creek Management and HM Capital Partners and it was renamed Swift & Company Swift & Company. (Swift was acquired by Brazilian beef giant JBS in 2007.)

In 2003 the company began supplying packaged meat products for grilling to George Foreman Foods which sells them via its Web site. That year it sold its Bumble Bee canned seafood business to members of Bumble Bee management and private investment firm Centre Partners Management and its blue cheese brands (Treasure Cave Nauvoo) to Canada's Saputo Inc. for undisclosed prices. It also sold its chicken processing business to Pilgrim's Pride for a stock and cash deal worth about $550 million in 2003.

Also in 2003 ConAgra agreed to pay $1.5 million in cash and job offers to settle an EEOC lawsuit charging bias against disabled workers at the company's California-based Gilroy Foods plant. The agreement involves the largest disability settlement in the agriculture industry. The dispute dated back to 1999 when Gilroy Foods then owned by Basic Vegetable Products (ConAgra bought the facility in 2000) after a strike failed to recall disabled workers who were on leaves of absence due to illness or pregnancy or who had a history of illness or injury.

In keeping with its strategy to focus on its branded and value-added food business in 2003 ConAgra sold United Agri Products to Apollo Management for stock and securities. The deal was worth about $600 million. In 2004 it sold its minority interest in the beef and pork processing operations of Swift Foods to HM Capital Partners. The deal was worth $194 million. ConAgra also sold Swift's feedlot operations to Smithfield Foods for an undisclosed amount.

ConAgra sold its turkey hatchery and breeding business to Ag Forte in 2004. It sold its Canadian and US crop inputs businesses and its Spanish feed and Portuguese poultry businesses that year as well. In addition it sold Casa de Oro Foods (the US's third-largest tortilla maker) to the Plaza Belmont Fund II. Also that year ConAgra introduced Golden Cuisine a line of frozen meals designed for seniors. The company began manufacturing and supplying Golden Cuisine to Meals On Wheels which distributes the meals which are formulated for seniors to the homebound elderly. That year ConAgra also introduced a high-fiber flour called Ultragrain that has the taste and texture of refined flour but the nutrition of whole grain.

In 2005 ConAgra sold its remaining 15 million shares of Pilgrim's Pride to that company for about $480 million. That year CEO Bruce Rhode retired. His replacement was former chairman and CEO of PepsiCo Beverages and Foods North America Gary Rodkin who began a company-wide restructuring. The company reorganized its business structure from three channels to two: Foodservice was merged with Food Ingredients and became ConAgra Foods Commercial; the ConAgra Retail channel remained the same.

ConAgra agreed to pay a $14 million shareholder settlement in 2005 regarding a lawsuit claiming fictitious sales and mis-reported earnings at its former subsidiary United Agri Products.

In a move to demonstrate its commitment to the humane treatment of animals in 2006 ConAgra urged its poultry suppliers to consider slaughtering chickens in a more humane manner called controlled-atmosphere killing. The process which ConAgra has only suggested to its suppliers is approved by the People for the Ethical Treatment of Animals.

Rodkin continued the company redo focusing on portfolio trimming when in early 2006 he announced plans to sell a large part of ConAgra's refrigerated-meats business. The brands involved in the sale include some of the company's best-known: Armour Butterball and Eckrich. (The Brown 'N Serve Healthy Choice Hebrew National Pemmican and Slim Jim brands were not included in the portfolio reduction.) It sold its Cook's ham business to Smithfield Foods for $260 million that year.

Not long after that it agreed to sell of the rest of its refrigerated meats business that it had for sale to Smithfield as well. The deal which became final in October 2006 cost Smithfield $571 million in cash. That same month it sold its Butterball Turkey unit to Carolina Turkeys for $325 million. (Carolina subsequently changed its company name to Butterball LLC.)

Divesting almost faster than one can keep track of one day after the Butterball deal was completed ConAgra sold its MaMa Rosa's Pizza operations to investment firm the Plaza Belmont Management Group. (MaMa Rosa's is refrigerated —not frozen pizza —and competes in a different market than other pizzas albeit frozen powerhouses such as Di Giorno Tombstone or Tony's.)

In another move to improve long-term operating performance ConAgra announced its intention to sell off its seafood and domestic and imported cheese businesses. To that end the company sold its surimi business including the Louis Kemp brand to Trident Seafoods and its Singleton Seafood and Meridian Seafood to Singleton Fisheries. It sold its specialty and imported cheese operation Swissrose International to investment company Fairmount Food Group. Late in 2006 the company sold its oat-milling business to investment companies Sequel Holdings and Falcon Investment Advisors.

The company added to its Lamb Weston branded potato products with the 2008 acquisition of Watts Brothers. With operations in Washington and Oregon Watts is a vegetable-processing company that has annual sales of some $100 million. It has retail foodservice and industrial customers throughout the US as well as in Mexico Japan China and other Far East countries. The deal also included Watts' organic dairy fertilizer cold storage packaging and agricultural farming businesses.

In early 2007 salmonella was found in some of the company's Peter Pan and Great Value (a Wal-Mart product) brands of peanut butter forcing a nationwide recall of the peanut butter bearing the product code involved. Salmonella food poisoning was linked to some 600 people in 47 states. No deaths related to the peanut better were confirmed. The recall eventually included products made as far back as October 2004. ConAgra shut down the Sylvester Georgia plant that was involved in the outbreak and reopened it in Auguts 2007 having spent $15 million on renovation which included repairing the roof installing new equipment and creating a manufacturing process that better separated raw materials from the finished peanut butter.

Just two months later the company voluntarily stopped production at the Missouri plant that makes its Banquet and generic brands of frozen turkey and chicken pot pies after learning that the were linked to some 140 cases of salmonella in 30 states. ConAgra did not recall the pies but offered mail-in refunds and store returns. The USDA began an investigation and advised consumers not to eat the pies.

As part of its strategy to add to its brand-name offerings in 2007 ConAgra acquired Alexia Foods a maker of natural frozen potatoes appetizers and artisan breads for about $50 million in cash. Later that year the company paid a penalty of $45 million in the wake of SEC charges that alleged the company had misreported its profits for the fiscal years 1999 2000 and 2001.

The company acquired Lincoln Snacks Company in 2007. Lincoln's well-known brands such as Fiddle Faddle and Poppycock extended ConAgra's name-brand lineup which is in line with company strategy. That year it also announced the removal of the chemicals from its microwave popcorn products that are suspected of causing lung ailments in popcorn-plant workers.

ConAgra sold its trading and merchandising operations (ConAgra Trade Group) in 2008 to a group of investors that included the Ospraie Special Opportunities Fund for $2.8 billion. The sale was part of the company's long-term strategy to exit the commodities business and concentrate on its consumer food products. Saying it couldn't give the brand the attention it needs in 2008 the company sold its Knott's Berry Farm jam and jelly business to J. M. Smucker.

In a tragedy that made the evening news three ConAgra workers were killed and some 40 were injured in an explosion and fire at a company Slim Jim manufacturing plant in Garner North Carolina in June 2009. It was later determined that the blast was caused by a natural-gas leak. ConAgra partnered with the United Way forming the Garner Plant Fund that raised money to assist the victims and their families. The company also continued to pay workers salaries while the plant remained closed for investigation. ConAgra was fined $106000 by the government in 2010 and the plant was eventually closed.

During 2010 ConAgra unloaded its Gilroy Foods & Flavors business-to-business unit to Olam International for $250 million. The sale excluded Gilroy's seasonings and flavors businesses.

In 2011 ConAgra Foods made an unsolicited takeover bid to buy Ralcorp Holdings a leading maker of private-label snack foods cereals and condiments. After proffering an initial bid of $82 per share ConAgra ultimately offered $94 (valuing Ralcorp at more than $5 billion). However Ralcorp spurned all bids saying they were not in the best interests of shareholders.

In May 2012 the company completed the acquisition of Odom's Tennessee Pride the #2 producer of frozen breakfast sandwiches in the US.

In January 2013 ConAgra completed its $6.8 billion purchase of Ralcorp Holdings.

EXECUTIVES

Vice President Information Systems And Chief Information Officer, Andre J Hawaux

Senior Vice President and Chief Litigation Counsel, Leo Knowles

Vice President Financial Planning, Brad Muse

Senior Vice President Corporate Controller, Robert (Bob) Wise

Vice President Business Development Dairy, Jim Donzelli

EVP General Counsel and Corporate Secretary, Colleen Batcheler, age 41, $494,615 total compensation

EVP and CFO, John F. Gehring, age 54, $589,904 total compensation

EVP and Chief Human Resources Officer, Nicole B. Theophilus, age 45

CEO, Sean M. Connolly

EVP and Chief Strategy Officer, Andrew G. Ross, age 47

President Consumer Foods, Thomas M. (Tom) McGough, age 50

EVP and President Sales, Derek De La Mater

President Commercial Foods, Tom Werner

Vice President Compensation and Benefits, Charles Salter

Vice President Marketing and New Ventures, Pablo Heyman

Vice President of Sales Foodservice at, John (Jack) Sivilla

Vice President Manufacturing, Dave Hall

National Account Manager, Greg Demain

Vice President General Manager Meats and Seeds, Jill Rahman

National Account Manager, Tom Soffera

Vice President Finance Frozen Foods, Shannon Kennedy
National Account Manager, Kimberly Henderson
Vice President Manufacturing food ingredients, Brad Allen
Vice President Quality, Scott Tylski
Vice President of Production Inc., Karl Henschel
Vice President Quality Senior Director Food Safety And Quality, Chris Fosse
National Account Manager, Keith Chapman
Vice President Codes and Standards Compliance, Ricky Draehn
Vice President Customer Development Frozen, Ken Lahey
Vice President General Manager Store brands, Chris Wilkins
Vice President Of Shopper Marketing, Rachael Norton
National Account Manager, Robert Butler
National Accounts Manager, Sherri Poole
Vice President Finance, Doug Kooren
Vice President Of Marketing, Shari Kobela
Systems Data Processing Director, Tim Hardy
Vice President Technology Partnerships, Pat Canzonere
National Account Manager, Les Manis
National Account Manager, Sherry Ford-lyman
Vice President Contract Manufacturing, Tim Kelly
National Account Manager, Robert Sheehan
Vice President Human Resources, Rick Hansen
National Account Manager, Nicole Sterling
Division Vice President Central, Wes Upchurch
Vice President Of Operations, Jim West
Vice President Human Resources, Kelly Schaefer
Executive Vice President, Doug Ricketts
Vice President Of Human Resources Operations, Jeff Welter
Vice President General Manager, Taylor Strubell
Vice President Organization Development, Lucy Dinwiddie
SLS Vice President, Matt Materazo
Vice President National Accounts, Rob Kirkpatrick
Vice President Of Marketing, Andy Johnston
National Account Manager, Chad Yuza
Vice President Research Quality And Innovation, Christian Rhynalds
Vice President General Manager Spicetec, Mark Duffy
Vice President Processing, Jeff Korengel
Vice President Of Marketing For Popcorn Business, Stan Jacot
Vice President Human Resources Private Brands, Lura Lentz
Senior Vice President Marketing, Karen E Carey
National Account Manager, Dennis Grymes
Vice President Information Technology, Matthew Spyers
Vice President, Mike Henderson
National Account Manager, Stephanie Biesterveld
Vice President Internal Audit, Allen Cooper
Senior Vice President National Specialty Programs, Carolyn Davis
Vice President research and Development, Julie Luby
Executive Vice President Research Quality and Innovation, Albert D (Al) Bolles
Vice President Media Digital and Social Marketing, Brett Groom
Vice President Human Resources, Angela (Angie) Jones
Vice President Compensation and Benefits, Charlie Salter
National Account Manager, Chuck Albers
National Account Manager, Eric Sosa
National Account Manager, Karen Loughran
Vice President Finance, Javier Alarcon
National Accounts Manager, Greg Ashford
Vice President Internal Audit, Mark Warner
Vice President Packaging and Sustainability, Robert (Bob) Weick

Senior Vice President Procurement, D K Singh
National Account Manager, Mark Kiltau
Chairman, Steven F. (Steve) Goldstone, age 70
Board Member, Jennifer Hudson
Treasurer, Rob Wise
Auditors: KPMG LLP

LOCATIONS

HQ: ConAgra Foods, Inc.
  One ConAgra Drive, Omaha, NE 68102-5001
Phone: 402 240-4000
Web: www.conagrafoods.com

PRODUCTS/OPERATIONS

2015 Sales

	% of total
Consumer foods	46
Commercial foods	28
Private brands	26
Total	**100**

2015 Sales

	% of total
Consumer Foods	
Grocery	25
Frozen	14
International	6
Other Brands	1
Commercial Foods	
Specialty potatoes	18
Food services & flavors	10
Private Brands	
Snacks sauces & spreads	8
Retail bakery	5
Bars & coordinated	5
Pasta	3
Cereal	3
Condiments	2
Total	**100**

Selected Brands

Commercial foods
  ConAgra Mills
  Lamb Weston
  Spicetec Flavors & Seasonings
Consumer foods
  Act II
  Alexia
  Banquet
  Bertolli
  Blue Bonnet
  Chef Boyardee
  DAVID Seeds
  Egg Beaters
  Healthy Choice
  Hebrew National
  Hunt' s
  Marie Callender' s
  Odom' s Tennessee Pride
  Orville Redenbacher' s
  PAM
  Peter Pan
  P.F. Chang' s
  Reddi-wip
  Slim Jim
  Snack Pack
  Swiss Miss
  Van Camp' s
  Wesson

COMPETITORS

American Pop Corn	Jenny Craig
B&G Foods	Kellogg
Big Heart Pet Brands	Kraft Foods Group Inc.
Boulder Brands	Link Snacks
Bush Brothers	MOM Brands
Campbell Soup	Manischewitz Company
Clorox	McCain Foods
Eden Foods	McIlhenny
Frito-Lay	Monterey Gourmet Foods
General Mills	Mott' s
Gilster-Mary Lee	Nestl©
Goya	Newman' s Own
H. J. Heinz Limited	Nutrisystem

Hain Celestial	Pinnacle Foods
Hanover Foods	Schwan' s
Heinz	Seneca Foods
Hormel	Slim-Fast
Inventure foods	Smucker
J-OIL MILLS	Snappy Popcorn
JR Simplot	Weaver Popcorn Company

HISTORICAL FINANCIALS

Company Type: Public

Income Statement   FYE: May 31

	REVENUE ($ mil.)	NET INCOME ($ mil.)	NET PROFIT MARGIN	EMPLOYEES
05/15	15,832	(252)	—	32,900
05/14	17,702	303	1.7%	32,800
05/13	15,491	773	5.0%	34,840
05/12	13,262	467	3.5%	26,100
05/11	12,303	817	6.6%	23,200
Annual Growth	6.5%	—	—	9.1%

2015 Year-End Financials

Debt ratio: 45.06%	No. of shares (mil.): 428
Return on equity: (-5.08%)	Dividends
Cash ($ mil.): 183	Yield: 0.0%
Current ratio: 1.11	Payout: —
Long-term debt ($ mil.): 6,888	Market value ($ mil.): 16,533

	STOCK PRICE ($) FY Close	P/E High/Low	PER SHARE ($) Earnings	Dividends	Book Value
05/15	38.61	— —	(0.60)	1.00	10.57
05/14	31.61	52 39	0.70	1.00	12.46
05/13	34.77	19 13	1.85	0.99	12.55
05/12	25.25	24 20	1.12	0.95	10.89
05/11	25.04	13 11	1.88	0.89	11.45
Annual Growth	11.4%	— —	—	3.0%	(2.0%)

ConnectOne Bancorp Inc (New)

ConnectOne Bancorp (formerly Center Bancorp) is the holding company for ConnectOne Bank which operates some two dozen branches across New Jersey. Serving individuals and local businesses the bank offers such deposit products as checking savings and money market accounts; CDs; and IRAs. It also performs trust services. Commercial loans account for about 60% of the bank's loan portfolio; residential mortgages account for most of the remainder. It also has a subsidiary that sells annuities and property/casualty life and health coverage. The former Center Bancorp acquired rival community bank ConnectOne Bancorp in 2014 and took that name.

Geographic Reach
ConnectOne has 24 branches in Bergen Essex Hudson Manhattan Mercer Monmouth Morris and Union Counties in New Jersey.

Mergers and Acquisitions
In 2014 Center Bancorp acquired ConnectOne Bancorp in an all-stock deal valued at approximately $243 million. The merged bank with nearly $4 billion in assets now does business under the ConnectOne brand name.

EXECUTIVES

Executive Vice President Chief Compliance Officer, Laura C Criscione

Executive Vice President Chief Lending Officer,
Elizabeth Magennis, age 46
Svp And Chief Relationship Officer, Laurel Merse
Vice President Finance, Christopher (Chris) Gorey
Auditors: Crowe Horwath LLP

LOCATIONS

HQ: ConnectOne Bancorp Inc (New)
301 Sylvan Avenue, Englewood Cliffs, NJ 07632
Phone: 201 816-8900
Web: www.centerbancorp.com

COMPETITORS

BCB Bancorp	New York Community
Bank of America	Bancorp
Citizens Financial	Oritani Financial
Corp.	PNC Financial
Fulton Financial	Provident Financial
Hudson City Bancorp	Services
Investors Bancorp	Sovereign Bank
JPMorgan Chase	Valley National
Kearny Financial	Bancorp
Lakeland Bancorp	Westamerica

HISTORICAL FINANCIALS

Company Type: Public

Income Statement

FYE: December 31

	ASSETS ($ mil.)	NET INCOME ($ mil.)	INCOME AS % OF ASSETS	EMPLOYEES
12/14	3,448	18	0.5%	—
12/13	1,673	19	1.2%	166
12/12	1,629	17	1.1%	178
12/11	1,432	13	1.0%	163
12/10	1,207	7	0.6%	159
Annual Growth	30.0%	27.6%	—	—

2014 Year-End Financials

Debt ratio: 14.52%	No. of shares (mil.): 29
Return on equity: 6.04%	Dividends
Cash ($ mil.): 126	Yield: 1.5%
Current ratio: —	Payout: 33.7%
Long-term debt ($ mil.): —	Market value ($ mil.): 564

	STOCK PRICE ($) FY Close	P/E High/Low	PER SHARE ($) Earnings	Dividends	Book Value
12/14	19.00	25 21	0.79	0.30	15.03
12/13	18.76	16 10	1.21	0.26	10.30
12/12	11.58	11 9	1.05	0.17	9.83
12/11	9.77	14 10	0.80	0.12	8.32
12/10	8.15	21 16	0.43	0.12	7.43
Annual Growth	23.6%	— —	16.4%	25.7%	19.3%

ConocoPhillips

Proudly combining the two venerable oil industry names of Conoco and Phillips ConocoPhillips is the world's largest independent exploration and production company based on reserves and oil production. Once a fully integrated oil company (upstream and downstream) ConocoPhillips now focuses on exploration and production. The company explores for produces transports and sells crude oil bitumen natural gas liquefied natural gas (LNG) and natural gas liquids (NGLs) around the world. ConocoPhillips explores for oil and gas in 27 countries and in 2013 it had proved reserves of 8.9 billion barrels of oil equivalent. It produced about 1.6 million barrels per day in 2013.

Geographic Reach

ConocoPhillips has oil and gas assets in Asia Australia Europe and North America. In 2013 the US accounted for 53% of the company's revenues.

Operations

The company manages its operations through six operating segments: Alaska Lower 48 (where it holds 13.1 million net acres of onshore conventional and unconventional acreage) and Latin America Canada Europe Asia Pacific and Middle East and Other International.

Sales and Marketing

ConocoPhillips' worldwide commodity portfolio (natural gas crude oil bitumen NGLs and LNG) is marketed through offices in the US Canada Europe and Asia. Commodity sales (made at prevailing market prices) are boosted through the purchase of third-party volumes for better economies of scale in trading transactions.

Natural gas is sold to a diverse client portfolio which includes local distribution companies; gas and power utilities; large industrial enterprises; oil and gas exploration and production companies; and marketing companies.

Crude oil bitumen and natural gas liquids are sold under contracts with prices based on market indices adjusted for location quality and transportation.

Financial Performance

In 2012 revenues fell by 75% primarily as the result of the divestiture of the company's Downstream Business but also from lower natural gas and NGL prices partly offset by higher LNG prices. In 2013 the company's revenue dipped by a further 6% due to lower natural gas volumes and lower crude oil prices partly offset by higher natural gas prices.ConocoPhillips' net income increased by 9% due to a decline in operating costs and income from continuing operations.In 2013 the company's operating cash inflow increased to $16.09 billion (from $13.92 billion in 2012) due to higher net income and a change in working capital as a result of cash generated from accounts and notes receivable.

Strategy

To raise cash to pay down debt that year the company sold its 8.4% interest in the North Caspian Sea Production Sharing Agreement (Kashagan) for $5.4 billion. In 2013 it also agreed to sell more than $1 billion in oilfield assets in Montana and North Dakota to Denbury Resources and its Clyden oil sands assets in Canada to Imperial Oil and ExxonMobil Canada for $720 million. The deals both raises cash and allows the company to focus on its core US shale assets.

In 2013 ConocoPhillips announced an oil discovery in the deepwater Gulf of Mexico.

In a major strategic reorganization in 2012 ConocoPhillips spun off its refining and marketing unit as Phillips 66. Prior to that event the then-integrated company had a refining capacity of more than 2.2 million barrels per day. The company also had 8300 retail outlets in the US under the 76 Conoco and Phillips 66 brands and at 1700 owned or dealer-owned gas stations in Europe. The Phillips 66 company absorbed the refining and marketing midstream and chemicals businesses freeing up ConocoPhillips as a pure exploration and production play.

The spin off was seen as a way to add more value for investors by creating two public traded companies with separate strategic businesses - ConocoPhillips (upstream activities) and Phillips 66 (midstream and downstream activities).

HISTORY

The roots of ConocoPhillips go back more than a century and run deep into the history of the US oil industry.

Isaac Elder Blake an Easterner who had lost everything on a bad investment came to Ogden Utah and founded Continental Oil & Transportation (CO&T) in 1875. In 1885 CO&T merged with Standard Oil's operations in the Rockies and was reincorporated in Colorado as Continental Oil. Continental tightened its grip on the Rocky Mountain area and by 1906 had taken over 98% of the western market. Its monopoly ended in 1911 when the US Supreme Court ordered Standard to divest several holdings: Continental was one of 34 independent oil companies created in 1913.

Seeing opportunity in autos Continental built a gas station in 1914. Two years later it got into oil production when it bought United Oil and by 1924 it had become fully integrated by merging with Mutual Oil which owned production refining and distribution assets. Continental's biggest merger came in 1929 when it merged with Marland Oil of Oklahoma.

Continental diversified in the 1960s acquiring American Agricultural Chemicals in 1963 and Consolidation Coal (Consol) in 1966. Restructuring in the 1970s into Conoco Chemical Consol and two petroleum divisions the company ramped up oil exploration and entered ventures to develop uranium. In 1979 it changed its name to Conoco.

In the late 1970s Conoco began joint ventures with chemical titan DuPont. The companies worked together well and in 1981 Conoco was acquired by DuPont to forestall hostile takeover attempts by Mobil and Seagram. DuPont sold off $1.5 billion of Conoco's assets and absorbed Conoco Chemical. In 1998 however DuPont spun off Conoco in what was the US's largest-ever IPO at the time (DuPont had completely divested its 70% stake by the next year).

Conoco expanded its natural gas reserves in 2001 by buying Gulf Canada Resources for $4.3 billion in cash and $2 billion in assumed debt. Also that year Conoco agreed to merge with Phillips Petroleum.

The story of Phillips Petroleum begins with Frank Phillips a prosperous Iowa barber who married a banker's daughter in 1897 and began selling bonds. When a missionary who worked with Native Americans in Oklahoma regaled him with stories about the oil patch Phillips migrated to Bartlesville Oklahoma and established Anchor Oil in 1903.

Anchor's first two wells were dry but the next one —the Anna Anderson No. 1 —was the first of a string of 81 successful wells. Phillips and his brother L. E. doubling as bankers in Bartlesville transformed Anchor into Phillips Petroleum in 1917.

With continued success on Native American lands in Oklahoma Phillips moved into refining and marketing. In 1927 the company opened its first gas station in Wichita Kansas. Frank Phillips retired after WWII and died in 1950.

During the 1980s Phillips became a target of takeover attempts. To fend off bids from corporate raiders T. Boone Pickens (1984) and Carl Icahn (1985) Phillips repurchased stock and ran its debt up to $9 billion. It then cut 8300 jobs and sold billions of dollars' worth of assets; strong petrochemicals earnings kept it afloat.

As part of an industry trend to share costs of less-profitable operations Phillips and Conoco flirted with the idea of merging their marketing and refining operations in 1996 but the talks failed. Discussions between Phillips and Ultramar Diamond Shamrock about merging the companies' North American oil refining and marketing operations broke down in 1999.

James Mulva took over as CEO in 1999 and Phillips decided to shift its focus to its upstream operations. The company combined its natural gas gathering and processing operations with those of

Duke Energy in 2000 and received a minority stake in a new company Duke Energy Field Services. Also that year Phillips acquired ARCO's Alaska assets for $7 billion and merged its chemicals division with that of Chevron (later Chevron-Texaco and still later Chevron once again).

In 2001 however Phillips elected to expand its refining and marketing operations rather than spin them off and the company bought Tosco for about $7.3 billion in stock and $2 billion in assumed debt. Big as it was the Tosco deal was eclipsed the next year by the merger of Phillips and Conoco.

In 2003 as part of its plan to exit the retail business the company sold its Circle K gas station chain to Alimentation Couche-Tard for $812 million.

In 2006 to boost its reserves base ConocoPhllips acquired Burlington Resources for about $36 billion.

LOCATIONS

HQ: ConocoPhillips
600 North Dairy Ashford, Houston, TX 77079
Phone: 281 293-1000   **Fax:** 281 661-7636
Web: www.conocophillips.com

HISTORICAL FINANCIALS

Company Type: Public

Income Statement

FYE: December 31

	REVENUE ($ mil.)	NET INCOME ($ mil.)	NET PROFIT MARGIN	EMPLOYEES
12/14	55,517	6,869	12.4%	19,100
12/13	58,248	9,156	15.7%	18,400
12/12	62,004	8,428	13.6%	16,900
12/11	251,226	12,436	5.0%	29,800
12/10	198,655	11,358	5.7%	29,700
Annual Growth	(27.3%)	(11.8%)	—	(10.4%)

2014 Year-End Financials

Debt ratio: 19.36%
Return on equity: 13.21%
Cash ($ mil.): 5,062
Current ratio: 1.31
Long-term debt ($ mil.): 22,383
No. of shares (mil.): 1,231
Dividends
   Yield: 4.1%
   Payout: 37.6%
Market value ($ mil.): 85,037

	STOCK PRICE ($) FY Close	P/E High/Low	PER SHARE ($) Earnings	Dividends	Book Value
12/14	69.06	16 11	5.51	2.84	42.16
12/13	70.65	10 8	7.38	2.70	42.49
12/12	57.99	12 8	6.72	2.64	39.33
12/11	72.87	9 7	8.97	2.64	50.73
12/10	68.10	9 6	7.62	2.15	46.72
Annual Growth	0.4%	— —	(7.8%)	7.2%	(2.5%)

Consolidated Edison Co. of New York, Inc.

Consolidated Edison Company of New York (Con Edison of New York) keeps the nightlife pulsing in The Big Apple. The utility a subsidiary of Consolidated Edison distributes electricity throughout most of New York City and Westchester County. The company distributes electricity to 3.4 million residential and business customers in New York City; it also delivers natural gas to about 1.1 million customers. The utility also provides steam services to 1703 customers in portions of the New York metropolitan area. Con Edison of New York

owns and operates more than 133900 miles of overhead and underground power distribution lines.
Operations
Other assets include more than 4300 miles of gas distribution mains a gas liquefaction and storage facility and electric and steam generating stations. It also owns a range of power transmission assets which are operated by the New York Independent System Operator. Con Edison of New York's electric generating facilities consist of plants located in New York City with an aggregate capacity of 698 MW.
Financial Performance
After experiencing a slight dip in revenues in 2012 due to a decline in the electric gas and steam revenues in 2013 Con Edison of New York's revenues increased by 2% due to higher gas and steam revenues. Gas revenues grew by 14% as a result of an increase in gas purchased for resale costs and higher revenues from the gas rate plan. Steam revenues increased by 15% due to a favorable weather impact and higher rates.In 2013 Con Edison of New York delivered 56918 million kWhs of electricity (0.5% down on 2012) 139046 mdths of gas (19.4% up) and 21923 MMlbs of steam (up 11.1%).The company's net income increased to $1.02 billion in 2013 (from $1.01 billion in 2012) primarily due to higher revenues and investment and other income.Con Edison of New York's operating cash inflow increased to $2.64 billion in 2013 (from $2.35 billion) due to higher net income and a change in current assets and liabilities.
Strategy
In 2014 Con Edison of New York was in the middle of a four-year $1 billion storm hardening program in the wake of 2012's Superstorm Sandy. Investments include the installation of 3000 devices that isolate and clear temporary faults on overhead electric systems and more than 150 smart switches that minimize outages caused by fallen trees. More than a mile of flood walls and 260 pieces of submersible equipment also have been installed. For its efforts the utility was named as the winner of the 2014 Outstanding System Reliability Award by the PA Consulting Group. The award recognizes the PA Consulting Group ReliabilityOne regional award recipient that demonstrated superior annual system-wide reliability performance for its customers. Con Edison of New York was also named best in the Northeast Region.
Company Background
Citing a 20% growth rate during the 2000s Con Edison of New York in 2011 spent almost $1.8 billion ($2 billion in 2010) to upgrade the company's aging electrical delivery systems (new high-voltage transmission cables) in New York City and surrounding areas. In 2010 Con Edison of New York and sister company Orange and Rockland also received $200 million in federal grants to install smart grid technology (automated more efficient meters and other systems) across their service area. By mid-2011 the company had also supported the installation of 8.5 MW of solar power units across its service region.

EXECUTIVES

Svp Gas Operations, Claude Trahan, age 63
Chairman and CEO, Kevin Burke, age 65, $1,107,200 total compensation
SVP and CRO, Robert N. Hoglund, age 54, $584,200 total compensation
President of Consolidated Edison Company of New York; Inc., Craig S. Ivey, age 52
President and CEO Orange and Rockland Utilities Inc., John T. McAvoy, age 54
Owner, Linda Goldberg
Auditors: PricewaterhouseCoopers LLP

LOCATIONS

HQ: Consolidated Edison Co. of New York, Inc.
4 Irving Place, New York, NY 10003
Phone: 212 460-4600
Web: www.coned.com

PRODUCTS/OPERATIONS

2013 Sales

	$ mil.	% of total
Electric	8,131	78
Gas	1,616	15
Steam	683	7
Total	**10,430**	**100**

COMPETITORS

Commerce Energy Group	New York Power
Delmarva Power	Authority
Green Mountain Energy	Public Service
Integrys Energy	Enterprise Group
Services	Rochester Gas and
NYSEG	Electric
National Grid USA	

HISTORICAL FINANCIALS

Company Type: Public

Income Statement

FYE: December 31

	REVENUE ($ mil.)	NET INCOME ($ mil.)	NET PROFIT MARGIN	EMPLOYEES
12/14	10,786	1,058	9.8%	13,200
12/13	10,430	1,020	9.8%	13,235
12/12	10,187	1,017	10.0%	13,130
12/11	10,484	989	9.4%	13,605
12/10	10,573	904	8.6%	—
Annual Growth	0.5%	4.0%	—	—

2014 Year-End Financials

Debt ratio: 28.29%
Return on equity: 9.60%
Cash ($ mil.): 647
Current ratio: 1.11
Long-term debt ($ mil.): 10,864
No. of shares (mil.): 235
Dividends
   Yield: —
   Payout: 67.3%
Market value ($ mil.): —

Consolidated Edison, Inc.

Utility holding company Consolidated Edison (Con Edison) is the night light for the city that never sleeps. Con Edison's main subsidiary Consolidated Edison Company of New York distributes electricity to 3.4 million residential and business customers in New York City; it also delivers natural gas to about 1.1 million customers and steam service in parts of Manhattan. Subsidiary Orange and Rockland Utilities serves more than 400000 electric and gas customers in three Northeast states. Con Edison's nonutility operations include retail and wholesale energy marketing independent power production and infrastructure project development.

HISTORY

Several professionals led by Timothy Dewey formed The New York Gas Light Company in 1823 to illuminate part of Manhattan. In 1884 five other gas companies joined New York Gas Light to form the Consolidated Gas Company of New York.

Thomas Edison's incandescent lamp came on the scene in 1879 and The Edison Electric Illuminating Company of New York was formed in 1880 to build the world's first commercial electric power station (Pearl Street) financed by a group led by J.P. Morgan. Edison supervised the project and in 1882 New York became the first major city with electric lighting.

Realizing electricity would replace gas Consolidated Gas acquired electric companies including Anthony Brady's New York Gas and Electric Light Heat and Power Company (1900) which joined Edison's Illuminating Company in 1901 to form the New York Edison Company. More than 170 purchases followed including that of the New York Steam Company (1930) a cheap source of steam for electric turbines.

The Public Utility Holding Company Act of 1935 ushered in the era of regulated regional monopolies. The next year New York Edison combined its holdings to form the Consolidated Edison Company of New York (Con Ed).

Con Ed opened its first nuclear station in 1962. By then Con Ed had a reputation for inefficiency and poor service and shareholders were angry about its slow growth and low earnings. Environmentalists joined the grousers in 1963 when Con Ed began constructing a pumped-storage plant in Cornwall near the Hudson River. Charles Luce a former undersecretary with the Department of Interior was recruited to rescue Con Ed in 1967. He added power plants and beefed up customer service.

In the 1970s inflation and the energy crisis drove up oil prices (Con Ed's main fuel source) and in 1974 Luce withheld dividends for the first time since 1885. He persuaded the New York State Power Authority to buy two unfinished power plants saving Con Ed $200 million. In 1980 Luce ended the Cornwall controversy and donated the land for park use. He retired in 1982.

The utility started buying power from various suppliers and in 1984 began a two-year price freeze a boon to rate-hike-weary New Yorkers. The New York State Public Service Commission didn't approve another rate increase until 1992.

In 1997 Con Ed government officials consumer groups and other energy firms outlined the company's deregulation plan which included the formation of the Consolidated Edison Inc. holding company (known as Con Edison) and a power marketing unit in 1998. The next year Con Edison sold New York City generating facilities to KeySpan Northern States Power and Orion Power for a total of $1.65 billion.

Also in 1999 Con Edison bought Orange and Rockland Utilities for $790 million to increase its New York base and expand into New Jersey and Pennsylvania. In an effort to push into New England the company that year agreed to buy Northeast Utilities (NU since renamed Eversource Energy) for $3.3 billion in cash and stock and $3.9 billion in assumed debt. But the deal broke down in 2001. NU accused Con Edison of improperly trying to renegotiate terms while Con Edison accused NU of concealing information about unfavorable power supply contracts.

Con Edison's Indian Point Unit 2 nuclear plant was shut down temporarily in 2000 after a radioactive steam leak; later that year it agreed to sell Indian Point Units 1 and 2 to Entergy for $502 million. The sale was completed in 2001. That year Con Edison also incurred an estimated $400 million in costs related to emergency response and asset damage from the September 11 terrorist attacks on New York City.

EXECUTIVES

President Shared Services CECNY, William G. Longhi, age 62, $529,192 total compensation
Vice President Human Resources, Claude Trahan, age 63
SVP and CFO Con Edison and CECONY, Robert N. Hoglund, age 54, $679,742 total compensation
President CECONY, Craig S. Ivey, age 52, $748,058 total compensation
Chairman and CEO ConEd and CECONY, John T. McAvoy, age 54, $1,140,000 total compensation
President and CEO Orangle & Rockland Utilities, Timothy P. Cawley
SVP and General Counsel Consolidated Edison and CECONY, Elizabeth D. Moore, age 60, $573,017 total compensation
Office Of The Vice President Central Engineering, Laurens Irizarry
Auditors: PricewaterhouseCoopers LLP

LOCATIONS

HQ: Consolidated Edison, Inc.
4 Irving Place, New York, NY 10003
Phone: 212 460-4600
Web: www.conedison.com

PRODUCTS/OPERATIONS

2014 Sales

	$ mil.	% of total
Electricity	9,114	70
Gas	1,933	15
Steam	628	5
Non-utility	1,244	10
Total	**12,919**	**100**

Selected Subsidiaries

Consolidated Edison Company of New York Inc. (utility)
Consolidated Edison Development Inc. (investments in power generation projects)
Consolidated Edison Energy Inc. (wholesale energy marketing and trading)
Consolidated Edison Solutions Inc. (retail energy marketing and services)
Orange and Rockland Utilities Inc. (utility)

COMPETITORS

AEP	National Fuel Gas
Accent Energy	National Grid USA
Avangrid	New York Power
CH Energy	Authority
CMS Energy	PPL Corporation
Delmarva Power	Public Service
Duke Energy	Enterprise Group
Enbridge	South Jersey
Eversource Energy	Industries
Green Mountain Energy	USPowerGen
NSTAR	Viridis Energy Inc

HISTORICAL FINANCIALS

Company Type: Public

Income Statement

FYE: December 31

	REVENUE ($ mil.)	NET INCOME ($ mil.)	NET PROFIT MARGIN	EMPLOYEES
12/14	12,919	1,092	8.5%	14,601
12/13	12,354	1,062	8.6%	14,648
12/12	12,188	1,141	9.4%	14,529
12/11	12,938	1,062	8.2%	13,605
12/10	13,325	1,003	7.5%	15,180
Annual Growth	**(0.8%)**	**2.1%**	**—**	**(1.0%)**

2014 Year-End Financials

Debt ratio: 27.51%
Return on equity: 8.80%
Cash ($ mil.): 707
Current ratio: 1.02
Long-term debt ($ mil.): 11,631
No. of shares (mil.): 292
Dividends
   Yield: 3.8%
   Payout: 59.5%
Market value ($ mil.): 19,333

	STOCK PRICE ($) FY Close	P/E High/Low	PER SHARE ($) Earnings	Dividends	Book Value
12/14	66.01	18 14	3.71	2.52	42.94
12/13	55.28	18 15	3.61	2.46	41.81
12/12	55.54	17 14	3.86	2.42	40.53
12/11	62.03	17 14	3.57	2.40	39.77
12/10	49.57	15 12	3.47	2.38	38.66
Annual Growth	**7.4%**	**— —**	**1.7%**	**1.4%**	**2.7%**

CONSOLIDATED GRAIN & BARGE COMPANY

Auditors: KPMG LLP NEW ORLEANS LA

LOCATIONS

HQ: CONSOLIDATED GRAIN & BARGE COMPANY
WASHINGTON & WATER ST, WAYNE CITY, IL 62895
Phone: 6188952181
Web: WWW.CGB.COM

HISTORICAL FINANCIALS

Company Type: Private

Income Statement

FYE: May 31

	REVENUE ($ mil.)	NET INCOME ($ mil.)	NET PROFIT MARGIN	EMPLOYEES
05/14	7,093	44	0.6%	650
05/12	5,996	50	0.8%	—
05/08	4,386	31	0.7%	—
05/07	2,849	0	—	—
Annual Growth	**13.9%**	**—**	**—**	**—**

2014 Year-End Financials

Debt ratio: ——
Return on equity: 0.60%
Cash ($ mil.): 5
Current ratio: 0.40
Long-term debt ($ mil.): —
Dividends
   Yield: —
   Payout: —
Market value ($ mil.): —

Constellation Brands Inc

Thinking about alcohol makes this company starry-eyed. Constellation Brands is the world's largest premium wine producer. It offers more than 100 brands including Robert Mondavi Clos du Bois and Manischewitz. The company is also the nation's third largest beer distributor and the sole US distributor for Mexican beer giant Grupo Modelo the brewer of Corona Modelo Especial Negra Modelo and other beers. Constellation Brands also markets premium spirits including Black Velvet whiskey and SVEDKA vodka. Constellation Brands' wine beer and spirits are sold in some 100 countries. Brothers Richard and Robert Sands control the company which was founded by the late Marvin Sands.

Operations

Constellation Brands reports its business in two main segments: Beer and Wine and Spirits. The beer segment has an exclusive license to import and sell Grupo Modelo's Corona Modelo and other brands while wine and spirits covers a wide range of wine types brands and price points.

Constellation Brands generated 53% of its total revenue from Beer sales in fiscal 2015 (ended February) while its Wine and Spirit sales contributed 42% and 5% to total revenue for the year respectively.

Geographic Reach

New York-based Constellation Brands sells its products in roughly 100 countries. It gets about 90% of its sales from the US while most of the rest comes from Canada. The company is also a leading wine company in New Zealand. Constellation operates 40 wineries worldwide with 19 in California eight in Canada four in New Zealand and five in Italy.Sales and MarketingConstellation Brands staffs in-house marketing sales and customer service teams to increase its sales. These teams deploy a variety of marketing strategies conducting market research consumer and trade advertising price promotions point-of-sale materials event sponsorship on-premise promotions and public relations activities.The company spent $406.1 million on advertising in fiscal 2015 (ended February) compared to $278.5 million and $121.9 million in fiscal 2014 and 2013 respectively.

Financial Performance

Constellation reversed its multi-year sales declines in 2014 when it greatly expanded into the beer business with the acquisition of Crown Imports. In fiscal 2015 (ended February) Constellation Brands' sales shot up 24% to a record $6.03 billion thanks again to the product contributions from its recent Beer Business acquisition combined with organic volume growth within the company's Mexican beer portfolio. Beer sales grew by 12% thanks to higher sales volumes from continued customer demand an increase in advertising and favorable impacts from pricing. Spirit sales rose by 8% thanks to higher sales volumes while Wine sales fell by 1% as sales volumes for branded and non-branded wines fell and due to unfavorable foreign currency exchange rates.Despite higher revenue in FY2015 the company's profit took a dive for the year mostly because it didn't enjoy the $1.64 billion worth of non-recurring revaluation benefits that stemmed from its Beer Business acquisition in fiscal 2014. Constellation's gross profits grew by 29% during the year as the company kept tight control on its production costs. Constellation Brand's cash from operations rose by 31% to $1.08 billion in FY2015 mostly thanks to increased cash inflows from the freshly acquired Beer Business and higher cash income from the Mexican beer portfolio.

Strategy

Constellation Brands reiterated in 2015 that its long-term growth strategy involved: increasing its mix of premium brands (especially in the Wine and Spirits segment) through acquisitions improving profit margins expanding the distribution of its key brands and creating operating efficiencies to boost profits. Responding to changes in drinking patterns in the US Constellation Brands has doubled down on the beer market acquiring its joint venture partner Group Modelo's 50% share of Crown Imports in mid-2013. The deal gave Constellation Brands perpetual license to distribute Modelo beer brands in the US and ownership of the Modelo brewery in the state of Coahuila Mexico. Thirsty for growth Constellation plans to double production at the Mexico brewery by the end of 2016 to meet future demand expectations.

Constellation has also been strategically acquiring agricultural glass and other manufacturing facilities with the goal of cost-effectively boosting its bottling production and profit margins. In 2014 for example Constellation spent roughly $300 million to acquire Anheuser-Busch InBev's glass production plant located in Nava Mexico. It also planned to expand the production capacity space in the Nava facility by 25% to boost overall output to 25 million hectoliters.

Mergers and Acquisitions

In September 2014 to further broaden its premium spirits offerings Constellation Brands purchased the Casa Noble tequila brand and all inventories. The Casa Noble family of tequilas which had experienced consistent double-digit growth included the Casa Noble Crystal Reposado and Anejo tequilas as well as limited production of some high-end Casa Noble tequilas. In June 2013 Constellation Brands completed its acquisition of Grupo Modelo's US beer business from Anheuser-Busch InBev for approximately $5.23 billion. The transaction included full ownership of Crown Imports LLC which provides Constellation with complete independent control of all aspects of the US commercial business; a state-of-the-art brewery in Nava (Piedras Negras) Mexico; exclusive perpetual brand license in the US to import market and sell Corona and the Modelo brands. The deal gave Constellation ownership of six of the top 20 imported beer brands in the US.

In 2012 expanding its high-end wine product line the company purchased the premium wine brand Mark West for $159.3 million.

HISTORY

Marvin Sands the son of winemaker Mordecai (Mack) Sands exited the Navy in 1945 and entered distilling by purchasing an old sauerkraut factory in Canandaigua New York. His business Canandaigua Industries struggled while making fruit wines in bulk for local bottlers in the East. Aiming at regional markets the company began producing its own brands two years later. Marvin opened the Richards Wine Cellar in Petersburg Virginia in 1951 and put his father in charge of the unit. In 1954 Marvin developed his own brand of "fortified" wine –boosted by 190-proof brandy –and named it Richards Wild Irish Rose after his son Richard.

The company slowly expanded buying a number of small wineries in the 1960s and 1970s. It went public in 1973 changing its name to Canandaigua Wine. A year later the company expanded to the West Coast thus gaining access to the growing varietal market.

Canandaigua continued to grow through acquisitions and new product introductions in the early 1980s. In 1984 when wine coolers became popular the company introduced Sun Country Coolers doubling sales to $173 million by 1986.

The short-lived wine cooler fad made Canandaigua realize that its distribution network could handle more volume so it began looking for additional brands. After a flurry of acquisitions in the late 80s and 90s the company changed its name in 1997 to Canandaigua Brands.

Founder Marvin Sands died in 1999. His son Richard who had been CEO since 1993 succeeded his father as chairman. In 2000 the firm changed its name to Constellation Brands.

EXECUTIVES

President and CEO, Robert S. (Rob) Sands, age 56, $1,247,454 total compensation
President Wine and Spirits Division, William A. (Bill) Newlands, age 56
EVP and General Counsel, Thomas J. (Tom) Mullin, age 64, $497,663 total compensation
President Beer, F. Paul Hetterich, age 52, $495,667 total compensation

President Canadian Business, John A. (Jay) Wright, age 57, $608,168 total compensation
President Pacific Wine Partners, Ben Dollard
EVP and President Beer Division, William F. (Bill) Hackett, $565,366 total compensation
SVP and CIO, Joseph D. (Joe) Bruhin
EVP and Chief Human Resources Officer, Thomas M. (Tom) Kane
EVP and CFO, David Klein
Vice President Benefits and Wellness, Jeffrey (Jeff) Viviano
Vice President And Controller, Deb Price
Senior Vice President Finance, Peter Bruno
Senior Vice President, Lou Applebaum
Vice President Strategic Accounts, Phil Parker
Vice President Assistant Treasurer, Sandy Dominach
Vice President General Manager Central Coast, Steve Smit
Zone General Manager sales Texas Vice President, Harry Markley
Vice President of Marketing and Global Imports, Diana Pawlik
Vice President Organizational Development and Learning, Barb Egenhofer
Vice President Engineering Services, Curtis Robinson
Vice President Operations East Coast, Terry Wolcott
Vice President Engineering, Michael (Mel) Drewel
Ea For Chris Stenzel Senior Vice President, Andrea Hurteau
Senior Vice President Operations, Martin (Marti) Van Der Merwe
Chairman, Richard Sands, age 64
Auditors: KPMG LLP

LOCATIONS

HQ: Constellation Brands Inc
207 High Point Drive, Building 100, Victor, NY 14564
Phone: 585 678-7100
Web: www.cbrands.com

2015 Sales

	$ mil.	% of total
US	5,360	89
International	668	11
Total	**6,028**	**100**

PRODUCTS/OPERATIONS

2015 Sales

	$ mil.	% of total
Beer	3,188	53
Wine	2,523	42
Spirit	316	5
Adjustments - -		
Total	**6,028**	**100**

Selected Subsidiaries and Operations

Constellation Spirits Inc.
Constellation Wines U.S.
Crown Imports LLC (beer)
Vincor International Inc. (wine Canada)

Selected Brands

Wine
  Arbor Mist
  Black Box
  Blackstone
  Clos du Bois
  Estancia
  Franciscan Estate
  Inniskillin
  Kim Crawford
  Mark West
  Mount Veeder
  Nobil
  Ravenswood
  Rex Goliath
  Robert Mondavi
  Ruffino
  SIMI

Toasted Head
Wild Horse
Beer
  Corona Extra
  Corona Light
  Modelo Especial
  Negra Modelo
  Pacifico
Spirits
  Black Velvet Canadian Whisky
  SVEDKA Vodka

COMPETITORS

Andrew Peller	MillerCoors
Anheuser-Busch InBev	Patrn Spirits
Bacardi	Pernod Ricard
Beam Suntory	SABMiller
Boston Beer	Scheid Vineyards
Bronco Wine Co.	Sebastiani Vineyards
Brown-Forman	Taittinger
Carlsberg	Terlato Wine
Diageo	Treasury Wine Estates
E. & J. Gallo	Americas
GIV	Trinchero Family
Halewood	Estates
Heineken	W.J. Deutsch
Jackson Family Wines	Willamette Valley
Korbel	Vineyards
LVMH	Wine Group
Lion	

HISTORICAL FINANCIALS

Company Type: Public

Income Statement

FYE: February 28

	REVENUE ($ mil.)	NET INCOME ($ mil.)	NET PROFIT MARGIN	EMPLOYEES
02/15	6,028	839	13.9%	7,200
02/14	4,867	1,943	39.9%	6,300
02/13	2,796	387	13.9%	4,500
02/12	2,654	445	16.8%	4,400
02/11	3,332	559	16.8%	4,300
Annual Growth	16.0%	10.7%	—	13.8%

2015 Year-End Financials

Debt ratio: 48.52%
Return on equity: 15.61%
Cash ($ mil.): 110
Current ratio: 2.57
Long-term debt ($ mil.): 7,137

No. of shares (mil.): 194
Dividends
  Yield: —
  Payout: —
Market value ($ mil.): 22,318

	STOCK PRICE ($) FY Close	P/E High/Low		PER SHARE ($) Earnings	Dividends	Book Value
02/15	114.72	26	18	4.17	0.00	29.66
02/14	81.03	8	4	9.83	0.00	26.02
02/13	44.24	21	9	2.04	0.00	15.48
02/12	21.84	10	8	2.13	0.00	12.47
02/11	20.32	8	6	2.62	0.00	12.08
Annual Growth	54.1%	—	—	12.3%	—	25.2%

Consumers Energy Co.

Consumers Energy Company makes sure that the energy consumers in Michigan have the power to crank up their heaters and the gas to fire up their stoves. The company's operating area includes all 68 counties of Michigan's lower peninsula. All told Consumers Energy (the primary operating unit of CMS Energy) has a generating capacity of 6130 MW (primarily fossil-fueled) and distributes electricity to 1.8 million customers and natural gas to 1.7 million customers. Included in the utility's arsenal of power production is electricity generated from fossil-fueled nuclear wind and hydroelectric power plants. Utility customers are aÂmix of residential commercial and diversified industrial clients.

Geographic ReachConsumers Energy provides electric service toÂ275 cities and villages in 61 counties in Michigan. Principal cities served are Battle Creek Bay City Cadillac Flint Grand Rapids Jackson Kalamazoo Midland Muskegon and Saginaw. It provides natural gas service in 44 of the 68 counties in Michigan's Lower Peninsula. It serves an area that includes 215 cities and villages. Among the principal cities served are Bay City Flint Jackson Kalamazoo Lansing Macomb Midland Royal Oak Saginaw and Warren. More than one-half of the utility's gas customers are in metro Detroit.OperationsConsumers Energy's electric utility operations include the generation purchase distribution and sale of electricity. Its gas utility operations include the purchase transmission storage distribution and sale of natural gas.The company's electric distribution system has 66065 miles of lines and the gas distribution system delivers of 337 billion cubic feet of natural gas per year.In addition to its electric and gas utility service the companyÂ operates 12 coal-fired and two oil-fired generating plants 13 hydroelectric plants a pumped storage generating plant and several combustion-turbine plants that produce electricity when needed during peak demand periods.Financial PerformanceConsumers Energy's revenues increased by 2% on 2011 and its net income increased by 8%. Except for a revenues slump in 2009 caused by the global recession crimping demand the company saw an upward trend in revenues from 2007 to 2011.

To improve its bottom line and the efficiency of its operations and in an effort to stem the tide of commercial and residential customers jumping ship for other electricity providers Consumers EnergyÂis looking at options to reform its rate structures.Strategy

The company is being guided by its "Balanced Energy Initiative" a comprehensive 20 year plan (introduced in 2007). The plan calls for the utility to develop new power plants increase the efficiency of its operations and expand its renewable energy projects.

As part of its commitment to reduce greenhouse gas emissions in 2010 Consumers Energy acquired access to about 60000 acres for the development of Lake Winds Energy Park in Mason County Michigan which beganÂoperatingÂin 2012. Cross Winds Energy Park in Tuscola and Huron countiesÂare scheduledÂto come on streamÂin two phases in 2015 and 2017.

In 2012 itÂbegan installingÂsmart meters (advanced meters that allow customers to have better control over their energy use) across its electric power distribution system.

Ownership
Consumers Energy is a subsidiary of CMS Energy.

EXECUTIVES

EVP and CFO, Thomas J. (Tom) Webb, age 63
President Electric and Gas, John G. Russell, age 58
VP and CIO, Mamatha Chamarthi
SVP Distribution Operations Engineering and Transmission, Patricia K. (Patti) Poppe, age 47
Chairman, David W. Joos, age 62
Auditors: PRICEWATERHOUSECOOPERS LLP

LOCATIONS

HQ: Consumers Energy Co.
  One Energy Plaza, Jackson, MI 49201
Phone: 517 788-0550
Web: www.consumersenergy.com

PRODUCTS/OPERATIONS

2011 Sales

	$ mil.	% of total
Electric	3,913	63
Gas	2,340	37
Total	**6,253**	**100**

COMPETITORS

DTE Electric	SEMCO ENERGY
DTE Gas Company	We Energies
Indiana Michigan Power	Xcel Energy

HISTORICAL FINANCIALS

Company Type: Public

Income Statement

FYE: December 31

	REVENUE ($ mil.)	NET INCOME ($ mil.)	NET PROFIT MARGIN	EMPLOYEES
12/15	6,165	594	9.6%	7,394
12/14	6,800	567	8.3%	7,388
12/13	6,321	534	8.4%	7,435
12/12	6,013	439	7.3%	7,205
12/11	6,253	467	7.5%	7,435
Annual Growth	(0.4%)	6.2%	—	(0.1%)

2015 Year-End Financials

Debt ratio: 31.05%
Return on equity: 10.98%
Cash ($ mil.): 50
Current ratio: 1.11
Long-term debt ($ mil.): 5,324

No. of shares (mil.): 84
Dividends
  Yield: 4.6%
  Payout: 80.0%
Market value ($ mil.): 8,158

	STOCK PRICE ($) FY Close	P/E High/Low	PER SHARE ($) Earnings	Dividends	Book Value
12/15	97.00	— —	(0.00)	4.50	65.95
12/14	104.51	— —	(0.00)	4.50	62.75
12/13	96.32	— —	(0.00)	4.50	57.75
12/12	93.74	— —	(0.00)	4.50	54.48
12/11	91.45	— —	(0.00)	4.50	52.25
Annual Growth	1.5%	— —	—	(0.0%)	6.0%

Core Mark Holding Co Inc

Smokes and snacks are at the center of Core-Mark Holding's cosmos. The company distributes packaged consumables (including cigarettes and other tobacco products candy snacks grocery items perishables nonalcoholic beverages and health and beauty aids) to about 31000 convenience stores; mass merchandisers; supermarkets; and drug liquor and specialty retailers. Cigarettes and other tobacco products are its top sellers generating about three-quarters of net sales. Through nearly 30 distribution facilities Core-Mark serves customers in all 50 US states and five Canadian provinces. Its 10 biggest clients (which include Couche-Tard and CST Brands) contribute about 35% of sales.

Operations
Core-Mark supplies its customers with consumable items from a network of nearly 30 distribu-

tion centers in the US and Canada. It also operates dedicated facilities for its largest customers Couche-Tard and CST Brandsin Phoenix and San Antonio respectively.

Geographic Reach

South San Francisco-based Core-Mark operates in the US where it generates 88% of its revenue. The company's remaining revenue comes from Canada.

Sales and Marketing

Canadian convenience store operator Couche-Tard is Core-Mark's largest customer representing 15% of sales in 2014.

Financial Performance

Core-Mark's sales have been on the rise since 2010 and they increased another 5% in 2014. Incremental sales increases along with higher cigarette prices drove the result countered by a drop in cigarette sales. Profits have also been rising and continued to with a 3% increase in 2013 due to higher sales.

Strategy

Core-Mark hopes to offset the decline in cigarette smoking by gaining a larger share of the shrinking market and growing its non-cigarette categories like fresh foods. To grow food sales Core-Marked has expanded its "Fresh and Local" food program to more than 92000 stores. The program offers freshly made sandwiches salads baked goods fruits vegetables and dairy items. Core-Mark distributes Jamba Juice's "Grab 'n Go" line of fresh deli wraps salads and sandwiches bolstering its fresh offering to convenience stores. (Core-Mark also supplies coffee and coffee brewing equipment and other food-to-go programs to its customers.) As consumers increase their purchases of fresh food and dairy products at convenience stores Core-Mark has focused on offering customers more fresh merchandise which has the added benefit of returning higher margins. To keep perishables fresh on the way to market the company has upgraded its refrigerated capacity and invested in chilling docks and other systems designed to deliver fresh goods quickly.

In mid-2014 Core-Mark opened a new distribution center in Glenwillow Ohio expanding its presence in the Midwest. The new distribution center serves about 1000 new stores and 1000 existing stores transferred from other Core-Mark divisions. Start-up costs for the new facility totaled approximately $1.5 million and capital expenditures about $16 million. It's expected to reduce transportation costs by making it more efficient to serve customers in the region.

In a big win for the company Core-Mark in May 2013 signed a three-year distribution agreement with Turkey Hill a subsidiary of grocery giant Kroger and the largest of its convenience store divisions. The agreement specifies that Core-Mark will service all of Turkey Hill's convenience stores which are located in Pennsylvania Ohio and Indiana. With the addition of Turkey Hill Core-Mark now services about 700 of Kroger's convenience stores. Also as drugstores sell more food Core-Mark formed a new business relationship with Rite Aid in mid-2014 to supply its stores with frozen refrigerated and fresh food. Core-Mark was already supplying some 800 Rite Aid stores on the West Coast.

Mergers and Acquisitions

To grow market share and extend its geographic reach Core-Mark has been active on the acquisition front. In 2015 it paid $8 million for the assets of Karrys Bros a regional distributor in Ontario and surrounding provinces.

Company Background

The company's roots reach back to 1888 when it was known as Glaser Bros. a family-run candy and tobacco distribution business in San Francisco.

EXECUTIVES

Vice President, Michael (Mel) Beach
SVP US Distribution West, Christopher L. Walsh, age 50, $282,894 total compensation
SVP Business Operations and Strategic Opportunities, Scott E. McPherson, age 45, $270,348 total compensation
President and CEO, Thomas B. Perkins, age 56, $480,000 total compensation
SVP and CFO, Stacy Loretz-Congdon, age 55, $322,313 total compensation
President Core-Mark Canada, Eric J. Rolheiser, age 44
SVP Sales and Marketing, Christopher K. (Chris) Hobson, age 46, $257,500 total compensation
SVP US Distribution East, William G. Stein, age 45, $230,000 total compensation
Vice President Merchandising, David (Dave) Dresser
National Account Manager, Monica Lucchese
Chairman, Randolph I. Thornton, age 69
Auditors: Deloitte & Touche LLP

LOCATIONS

HQ: Core Mark Holding Co Inc
395 Oyster Point Boulevard, Suite 415, South San Francisco, CA 94080
Phone: 650 589-9445
Web: www.core-mark.com

2014 Sales

	$ mil.	% of total
US	8,989	88
Canada	1,250	12
Corporate	40	—
Total	**10,280**	**100**

PRODUCTS/OPERATIONS

2014 Sales

	$ mil.	% of total
Cigarettes	6,942	68
Food	1,462	14
Candy	534	5
Other tobacco products	827	8
Health beauty & general	361	4
Beverages	151	1
Equipment/other	1	—
Total	**10,280**	**100**

COMPETITORS

800-JR Cigar	McLane
AMCON Distributing	Roundy's
Associated Food	SUPERVALU
BJ's Wholesale Club	Sam's Club
C&S Wholesale	Southern Wine &
Coca-Cola	Spirits
Costco Wholesale	Stephenson Wholesale
Eby-Brown	Company
Frito-Lay	Unified Grocers
GSC Enterprises	Wal-Mart
H. T. Hackney	

HISTORICAL FINANCIALS

Company Type: Public

Income Statement

FYE: December 31

	REVENUE ($ mil.)	NET INCOME ($ mil.)	NET PROFIT MARGIN	EMPLOYEES
12/14	10,280	42	0.4%	5,933
12/13	9,767	41	0.4%	5,617
12/12	8,892	33	0.4%	5,225
12/11	8,114	26	0.3%	4,852
12/10	7,266	17	0.2%	4,399
Annual Growth	**9.1%**	**24.6%**	**—**	**7.8%**

2014 Year-End Financials

Debt ratio: 6.62%	No. of shares (mil.): 23
Return on equity: 9.54%	Dividends
Cash ($ mil.): 14	Yield: 0.7%
Current ratio: 1.83	Payout: 25.1%
Long-term debt ($ mil.): 68	Market value ($ mil.): 1,429

	STOCK PRICE ($) FY Close	P/E High/Low	PER SHARE ($) Earnings	Dividends	Book Value
12/14	61.93	50 23	1.83	0.46	19.99
12/13	75.93	42 25	1.79	0.40	18.84
12/12	47.35	34 25	1.46	0.45	17.48
12/11	39.60	35 26	1.12	0.09	16.55
12/10	35.59	45 31	0.78	0.00	16.31
Annual Growth	**14.9%**	**— —**	**24.0%**	**—**	**5.2%**

Corning, Inc.

The source of Corning's revenue and profits transparently obvious: it's glass. Once known for its kitchenware and lab products the company manufactures glass ceramic and other components for a variety of products in the consumer electronics telecommunications automotive and life sciences industries among others. Its products include substrates for flat-panel displays and computer monitors optical fiber and cable substrates and filters for automotive emissions control products labware and scientific equipment and glass and optical materials for a wide range of industries. Corning has about 90 manufacturing and processing facilities across more than a dozen countries. About 60% of its sales come from the Asia/Pacific region.

HISTORY

Amory Houghton started Houghton Glass in Massachusetts in 1851 and moved it to Corning New York in 1868. By 1876 the company renamed Corning Glass Works was making several types of technical and pharmaceutical glass. In 1880 it supplied the glass for Thomas Edison's first lightbulb. Other early developments included the red-yellow-green traffic light system and borosilicate glass (which can withstand sudden temperature changes) for Pyrex oven and laboratory ware.

Joint ventures have been crucial to Corning's success. Early ones included Pittsburgh Corning (with Pittsburgh Plate Glass 1937 glass construction blocks) Owens-Corning (with Owens-Illinois 1938 fiberglass) and Dow Corning (with Dow Chemical 1943 silicones).

By 1945 the company's laboratories had made it the undisputed leader in the manufacture of specialty glass. Applications for its glass technology included the first mass-produced television tubes freezer-to-oven ceramic cookware (Pyroceram Corning Ware) and car headlights.

After WWII Corning emphasized consumer product sales and expanded globally. In the 1970s the company pioneered the development of optical fiber and auto emission technology (now two of its principal products).

Seeing maturing markets for such established products as lightbulbs and television tubes Corning began buying higher-growth laboratory services companies —MetPath in 1982 Hazleton in 1987 Enseco in 1989 and G.H. Besse-laar in 1989. Vice chairman James Houghton the great-great-grandson of Corning's founder was named chairman and CEO in 1983.

Corning established international joint ventures with Siemens Mitsubishi and Samsung. In 1988 the company bought Revere Ware (cookware). The next year Corning dropped Glass Works from its name.

In 1994 Corning and Siecor (joint venture with Siemens) acquired several fiber and cable businesses from Northern Telecom (now Nortel Networks) expanding the company's presence in Canada.

Joint venture Dow Corning under assault from thousands of women seeking damages because of leaking breast implants entered Chapter 11 bankruptcy protection in 1995 (and exited it in 2004). The massive losses incurred by Dow Corning due to litigation and a downturn in Corning's lab products sales prompted the company to recast itself. Corning began selling off its well-known consumer brands and putting greater emphasis on its high-tech optical and display products through acquisitions and R&D.

Company veteran Roger Ackerman was named chairman and CEO in 1996 replacing Houghton. He moved quickly to transform the company from a disjointed conglomerate to a high-tech optics manufacturer. That year the company spun off its laboratory testing division to shareholders creating Covance and Quest Diagnostics.

After deals to sell a stake in Corning Consumer Products to AEA Investors fell through in 1997 Corning sold a majority stake in the housewares unit to KKR the next year. In 1999 Corning bought UK-based BICC Group's telecom cable business.

In 2000 Corning made more than $5 billion worth of acquisitions to expand its optical fiber and hardware business. It bought Siemens' optical cable and hardware operations and the remaining 50% of the companies' Siecor joint venture. Corning acquired Oak Industries (optical components) for $1.8 billion and NetOptix (optical filters) for $2.15 billion and purchased the 67% of microelectromechanical systems specialist IntelliSense it didn't already own. Continuing its spending spree the company bought part of Pirelli's fiber-optic telecom components business for about $3.6 billion; it also acquired Cisco's 10% stake in the business.

In 2001 Ackerman retired as chairman and CEO of the company. COO John Loose was named CEO and Houghton was again appointed chairman.

In the early 21st century Corning suffered from slowing sales of telecommunications products but a realignment of its businesses allowed the company to regain its financial footing. That year the company moved to expand the segment through its acquisition of Optimum Manufacturing Corporation which makes precision machined components for the aerospace communications medical military and scientific markets.

Slowing demand prompted Corning to lay off about 25% of its staff shut down plants and discontinue its glass tubing operations that year. Houghton returned to the position of chief executive after Loose retired in 2002. That year the company made more layoffs closed plants and sold several noncore operations; it also bought rival Lucent's fiber-optic and cable facilities in China where demand was relatively strong. The following year Corning sold its photonic components business to Avanex (now part of Oclaro). In 2004 it sold its quartz crystal frequency-control products business.

Corning president Wendell Weeks succeeded Houghton as CEO in 2005. Houghton remained chairman and retired again in 2006 becoming non-executive chairman. Houghton became chairman emeritus in 2007 and remained on the board as a director. Weeks was elected chairman of the board.

Corning set plans in 2006 to build an LCD glass substrate finishing plant in Beijing the first to be constructed on the Chinese mainland. The facility was completed and opened in 2008.

Through all of the changes in Corning's business model and strategic priorities the company kept Steuben Glass as a subsidiary for 90 years. The fine-glass firm was named for Steuben County New York where Steuben maintained its design studio and glassworks. In 2007 Corning put the business up for sale after a decade of financial losses at Steuben Glass. The parent company in 2008 sold Steuben Glass to Schottenstein Stores; it kept an equity stake of nearly 20% in the fine-glass firm.

In 2007 it committed $795 million over five years to build a glass manufacturing plant at Sharp's new LCD production complex in Sakai Japan. Sharp began making large glass panels for LCD TVs at the Sakai plant in 2009. The company then started making Gen 10 LCD glass substrate sizes for Sharp with its EAGLE XG glass-making process at the new plant.

The company continued to focus on emerging technologies. Gorilla Glass a damage-resistant cover glass was introduced in 2008 for use in mobile phones notebook computers and for touch-screen technologies. The company's Green Laser technology rivals light-emitting diodes (LEDs) by offering improved images on mobile devices. It began developing better silicon on glass (SiOG) technology which adds pure crystalline silicon uniformly to computer chips and devices. The company also began work on a filter that would remove mercury released at coal-fired power plants. Other innovations include the Gen 10 (10th generation) LCD glass ClearCurve optical fiber and DuraTrap emissions-control solutions.

In 2008 Corning created its fifth operating segment Specialty Materials which includes semiconductors and optical sensors for aerospace and defense. To expand the segment the company acquired Optimum Manufacturing Corporation which made precision machined components for the aerospace communications medical military and scientific markets.

In 2009 the company acquired California-based Axygen BioScience a manufacturer and distributor of laboratory research plastic ware and benchtop equipment. Corning purchased the company and its subsidiaries from American Capital for about $400 million. Axygen BioScience was integrated into its Life Sciences segment and boosted Corning's portfolio of life sciences products. The acquisition also widened the door to promising global opportunities which will be channeled through Axygen's two manufacturing locations in Asia.

EXECUTIVES

Director; President Corning Optical Communications, Wendell P. Weeks, age 56, $1,261,923 total compensation
Vice Chairman and Corporate Development, Lawrence D. (Larry) McRae, age 57, $647,615 total compensation
SVP and CFO, R. Tony Tripeny, age 56
EVP and Corning Innovation Officer, Martin J. (Marty) Curran
EVP Corning Optical Telecommunications, Clark S. Kinlin
President Corning Glass Technologies (CGT), James P. Clappin, age 58, $641,692 total compensation
EVP Corning Technologies and International, Eric S. Musser, age 56
SVP Corporate Research, David L. Morse, age 63
Vice President Sales and Marketing, Aparna Krishnamurthy
Vice President Flat Glass Photovoltaics Program, Marc Giroux

Vice President New Opportunity Development New Business Development, Robert Ritchie
Vice President Information Technology, Charles Krotje
Vice President And General Manager Life Sciences, Mark A Beck
Vice President of Sales, Allen (Al) Smith
Vice President of Tax, Susan (Sue) Ford
Vice President Of Sales, Eric Marinakis
Vice President Of Product Management, Jeff Kunst
Vice President, Kevin McManus
Vice President Information Technology Service Delivery, Mark Clark
Vice President And General Manager Corni, Stephen (Steve) Miller
Vice President, Donna Gardjulis
Senior Vice President, Johann-Peter Hegemann
Division Vice President, John Sharkey
Vice President Marketing, Dan Krawiec
Vice President Of Chemical Engineering, Thomas Capek
Vice President and General Manager Automotive Technologies, Thomas (Thom) Appelt
Vice President Of Human Resources, Christine Pambianchi
Vice President Sales, Peter King
Vice President Marketing, Stephen Cohen
Senior Vice President, Alan (Al) Eusden
Vice President, Adriane Brown
Vice President Sales, Kevin Hussey
Senior Vice President Human Resources, Amy Kazmierczak
Vice President Sales, Dave Johnson
Vice President Of Communications, Joe Dunning
Division Vice President and Director Intellectual Property Department and Assistant Secretary, Mark Lauroesch
Vice President, Daniela Lavric
Senior Vice President, David Bassett
Senior Vice President cao corp Controller, R T Tripeny
Vice President Of Corporate Communications, Daniel (Dan) Collins
International Treasurer, Bengt Elvinsson
Board Member, Darlene Salvagin
Treasurer, Lee Starnes
Us Treasurer, Ida Meadows
Secretary, Kathy McClure
Auditors: PricewaterhouseCoopers LLP

LOCATIONS

HQ: Corning, Inc.
  One Riverfront Plaza, Corning, NY 14831
Phone: 607 974-9000
Web: www.corning.com

2014 Sales

	$ mil.	% of total
Asia/Pacific		
China	1,893	20
Korea	1,882	20
Taiwan	1,092	11
Japan	608	6
Other	308	3
North America		
United States	2,275	23
Canada	311	3
Mexico	35	-
Europe		
Germany	397	4
UK	187	2
France	81	1
Other	369	4
Latin America		
Brazil	67	
Other	35	1
Other regions	175	2
Total	**9,715**	**100**

PRODUCTS/OPERATIONS

2014 Sales

	$ mil.	% of total
Display technologies	3,851	40
Optical communications	2,652	27
Specialty materials	1,205	12
Environmental technologies	1,092	11
Life sciences	862	9
Other	53	1
Total	**9,715**	**100**

Selected Products

Display technologies
  Liquid crystal displays (LCD)
  Organic light-emitting diode (OLED) displays
Telecommunications
  Optical fiber and cable
  Optical networking components
Environmental technologies
  Industrial and stationary emissions products
  Mobile emissions and automotive catalytic converter
  products
Life sciences
  Genomics and laboratory equipment
Specialty Materials
  Gorilla Glass
Other
  Polarized glass
  Semiconductor materials

COMPETITORS

3M	Nikon
Alcatel-Lucent	Nippon Electric Glass
Amphenol	Nippon Sheet Glass
Asahi Glass	Nortel Networks
Becton Dickinson	Oerlikon
Belden	Prysmian
Carl-Zeiss-Stiftung	SCHOTT
CommScope	SWCC SHOWA
DENSO	Saint-Gobain
Dai Nippon Printing	Shin-Etsu Chemical
Draka Holding	Sumitomo Electric
Fujikura Ltd.	Superior Essex
Furukawa Electric	TE Connectivity
General Cable	Thermo Fisher
Heraeus Holding	Scientific
Hoya Corp.	Thomas & Betts
IBIDEN	Toppan Printing
NGK INSULATORS	Viavi Solutions

HISTORICAL FINANCIALS

Company Type: Public

Income Statement

FYE: December 31

	REVENUE ($ mil.)	NET INCOME ($ mil.)	NET PROFIT MARGIN	EMPLOYEES
12/15	9,111	1,339	14.7%	35,700
12/14	9,715	2,472	25.4%	34,600
12/13	7,819	1,961	25.1%	30,400
12/12	8,012	1,728	21.6%	28,700
12/11	7,890	2,805	35.6%	28,800
Annual Growth	3.7%	(16.9%)	—	5.5%

2015 Year-End Financials

Debt ratio: 15.70%
Return on equity: 6.63%
Cash ($ mil.): 4,500
Current ratio: 2.94
Long-term debt ($ mil.): 3,910

No. of shares (mil.): 1,130
Dividends
  Yield: 2.6%
  Payout: 32.0%
Market value ($ mil.): 20,656

	STOCK PRICE ($) FY Close	P/E High/Low		PER SHARE ($) Earnings	Dividends	Book Value
12/15	18.28	25	16	1.00	0.48	16.63
12/14	22.93	13	9	1.73	0.40	16.94
12/13	17.82	13	9	1.34	0.39	15.13
12/12	12.62	13	9	1.15	0.32	14.62
12/11	12.98	13	7	1.77	0.23	13.91
Annual Growth	8.9%			— — (13.3%)	20.9%	4.6%

Costco Wholesale Corp

Wal-Mart isn't a behemoth in every business. Operating more than 680 membership warehouse stores Costco is the nation's largest wholesale club operator (ahead of Wal-Mart's SAM'S CLUB). Primarily under the Costco Wholesale banner it serves more than 71 million members in 40-plus US states and Puerto Rico as well as in Canada Mexico the UK Japan South Korea Taiwan and Spain. Stores offer discount prices on an average of about 4000 products (many in bulk packaging) ranging from alcoholic beverages and appliances to fresh food pharmaceuticals and tires. Certain club memberships also offer products and services such as car and home insurance mortgage and real estate services and travel packages.

Operations

Costco generates revenue from six major product categories: sundries hardlines softlines food fresh food and ancillary and other. It generated 57% of its revenue in fiscal 2015 (ended August) from sundries food and fresh food. Another 16% came from hardline product sales (such as electronics appliances jewelry etc.) while 11% came from softline product sales (such as clothing footwear and other apparel). Serving the retail stores is Costco Wholesale Industries a division of the company that operates manufacturing businesses including special food packaging optical labs meat processing and jewelry distribution. To shop at Costco customers must be members —a policy the company believes reinforces customer loyalty and provides a steady source of fee revenue (2% of FY2015 sales). Three types of annual memberships are available: Business ($55 each); Gold Star ($55 for individuals and their spouses): and Executive ($110 allows members to purchase products and services including insurance mortgage services and long-distance phone service at reduced rates). Costco also operates the e-commerce site costco.com which offers products not found in its stores.

Geographic Reach

Costco Wholesale's 480 US stores rang up 73% of its total sales in FY2015 while the company's 89 stores in Canada accounted for 15% of sales. Other countries —including Mexico the UK Japan Korea Taiwan Australia and Spain —contributed the rest of its revenue. Costco operates in Taiwan and Korea through majority-owned subsidiaries.

Sales and Marketing

Costco uses several marketing and promotional tactics to reach existing and prospective members. It typically promotes new warehouse openings sends direct mail pieces to potential new members and employs a regular direct-marketing program. The program which targets existing members to promote selected merchandise consists of The Costco Connection magazine coupon mailers handouts and emails from costco.com costco.ca and costco.co.uk.

Financial Performance

The warehouse club operator's revenues and profits have been rising over the past several years as it's expanded its store count and in-store amenities. The wholesaler's revenue grew 3% to $116.2 billion in fiscal 2015 (ended August) driven by new store openings in 2014 and 2015 and a 1% increase in same-store sales at the company's warehouse stores. Membership fee income increased by 4% thanks to new member sign-ups and members upgrading to higher-fee executive membership program. Geographically sales in the US grew by 5% while sales in Canada declined by 3% due to a poorer economy there. Sales elsewhere grew by 2% during the year.Higher revenue

in FY2015 boosted Costco's net income by 16% to $2.38 billion for the year. Its operating cash levels rose by 8% to $4.28 billion as its cash earnings rose.

Strategy

Costco aims to offer its members a broad range of high-quality merchandise at consistently lower prices than they can find elsewhere. To keep inventory costs low its merchandising strategy is to limit certain items to fast-selling models sizes and colors. By doing this Costco is able to limit its number of stock keeping units (SKUs) to about 3700 per warehouse; enabling it to hold significantly fewer items than other discount retailers supermarkets and supercenters. Facing competition from no-fee discounters like Wal-Mart and Target as well as from rivals SAM'S CLUB and BJ's Wholesale Costco has been busy expanding and retrofitting its warehouses (which average about 144000 sq. ft.) to accommodate fresh food sections and other ancillary units such as gas stations optical departments pharmacies and food counts. It also continues to offer new customer loyalty programs such as the co-branded rewards credit card it established with Visa and Citi in early 2015. Indeed thanks to efforts like these Costco in FY2015 boasted a 91% renewal rate in North America and 88% worldwide despite intense competition.Costco is also aggressively expanding its portfolio of stores in both the US and overseas. On the international front the retailer is looking to take advantage of rising consumer demand in developing markets especially in Asia in the key markets of Japan Korea and Taiwan. Altogether the wholesaler planned to open 34 new warehouses in FY2015 (about the same as in FY2014 and up from 26 in FY2013) to boost its total square footage by 5% including 20 new stores in the US four in Mexico three in Japan two each in Australia and Korea and one each in Canada the UK and Taiwan.

HISTORY

Company BackgroundFrom 1954 to 1974 retailer Sol Price built his Fed-Mart discount chain into a $300 million behemoth selling general merchandise to government employees. Price sold the company to Hugo Mann in 1975 and the next year with son Robert Rick Libenson and Giles Bateman opened the first Price Club warehouse in San Diego to sell in volume to small businesses at steep discounts.

Posting a large loss its first year prompted Price Club's decision to expand membership to include government utility and hospital employees as well as credit union members. In 1978 it opened a second store in Phoenix. With the help of his father Sol's other son Laurence began a chain of tire-mounting stores (located adjacent to Price Club outlets on land leased from the company and using tires sold by the Price Clubs).

The company went public in 1980 with four stores in California and Arizona. Price Club moved into the eastern US with its 1984 opening of a store in Virginia and continued to expand including a joint venture with Canadian retailer Steinberg in 1986 to operate stores in Canada; the first Canadian warehouse opened that year in Montreal.

Two years later Price Club acquired A. M. Lewis (grocery distributor Southern California and Arizona) and the next year it opened two Price Club Furnishings offering discounted home and office furniture.

Price Club bought out Steinberg's interest in the Canadian locations in 1990 and added stores on the East Coast and in California Colorado and British Columbia. However competition in the East from ensconced rivals such as SAM'S CLUB and PACE forced the closure of two stores two years later. A 50-50 joint venture with retailer Controladora Comercial Mexicana led to the opening of two Price Clubs in Mexico City one each in 1992 and 1993.

Price Club merged with Costco Wholesale in 1993. Founded in 1983 by Jeffrey Brotman and James Sinegal (a former EVP of Price Company) Costco Wholesale went public in 1985 and expanded into Canada.

In 1993 Price/Costco opened its first warehouse outside the Americas in a London suburb. Merger costs led to a loss the following year and Price/Costco spun off its commercial real estate operations as well as certain international operations as Price Enterprises (now Price Legacy). In 1995 the company launched its Kirkland Signature brand of private-label merchandise. Two years later the company changed its corporate name to Costco Companies.

Costco began online sales and struck a deal to buy two stores in South Korea in 1998 and opened its first store in Japan in 1999. Under industrywide pressure over the way members-only chains record fees Costco took a $118 million charge for fiscal 1999 to change accounting practices. That year the company made yet another name change to Costco Wholesale (emphasizing its core warehouse operations).

In 2000 the company purchased private retailer Littlewoods' 20% stake in Costco UK increasing Costco's ownership to 80%. Costco began expanding into the Midwest in 2001 as part of plans to open 40 new clubs a year including ones in China.

During fiscal 2002 Costco opened 29 new warehouse clubs. In December 2002 the retailer opened its first home store –called Costco Home –in Kirkland Washington stocked with mostly high-end furniture. A second Costco Home store opened in Tempe Arizona in December 2004.

Costco increased its equity interest in Costco Wholesale UK in October 2003 to 100% when it purchased Carrefour Nederland's 20% stake.

In 2006 Costco began offering more than 200 generic prescription medicines (100 count) for $10 or less. The following year Costco.com logged sales in excess of $1 billion.

In July 2009 Costco shuttered its two Costco Home stores which were located in Washington and Arizona. The retailer cited the weak economy and market for home furnishings and the fact that the concept didn't fit with its expansion plans for their closure. In August the company opened its first warehouse club in Australia.

CEO Jim Sinegal stepped down in 2012 after more than 20 years at the helm. Sinegal who together with chairman Jeffrey Brotman founded Costco in 1983 handed the reins to Craig Jelinek a 28-year veteran and former president and COO of the company.In 2012 Costco bought the remaining 50% stake in Costco Mexico for $789 million from its joint venture partner Controladora Comercial Mexicana.

EXECUTIVES

EVP Costco Wholesale Industries, Timothy L. Rose, age 62

EVP Information Systems and CIO, Paul G. Moulton, age 64, $602,519 total compensation

EVP Administration and Human Resources, Franz E. Lazarus, age 68

EVP and COO Eastern and Canadian Divisions, Joseph P. (Joe) Portera, age 63, $644,712 total compensation

President and CEO, W. Craig Jelinek, age 63, $650,000 total compensation

EVP and COO Southwest and Mexico Divisions, Dennis R. Zook, age 66, $627,443 total compensation

EVP and CFO, Richard A. Galanti, age 59, $682,785 total compensation

EVP International, James P. (Jim) Murphy, age 62

EVP and COO Northern and Midwest Division, John D. McKay, age 58

SVP and General Manager Northeast Region, Jeffrey R. Long

SVP and General Manager Bay Area Region, Dennis A. Hoover

SVP and General Manager Midwest Region, John B. Gaherty

SVP and General Manager Mexico, Jaime Gonzalez

SVP and General Manager Los Angeles Region, Bruce A. Greenwood

SVP and General Manager San Diego Region, Robert D. Hicok

EVP and COO Merchandising, Douglas W. (Doug) Schutt, age 56

SVP E-Commerce and Publishing, Ginnie M. Roeglin

SVP and General Manager Southeast Region, Yoram Rubanenko

SVP and General Manager Eastern Canada Region, Pierre Riel

SVP and General Manager Western Canada Region, Russ Miller

SVP and General Manager Northwest Region, Ron Vachris

Pharmacy Manager, Hassan Awada

Vice President Real Estate, Larry Farren

Senior Vice President Depot Operations, John (Jack) Thelan

Vice President of Operations for the Auto Program Costco Wholesale Corp., Rick Borg

Senior Executive Vice President, Richard (Dick) Dicerchio

Vice President, Erin Haag

Chairman, Jeffrey H. (Jeff) Brotman, age 73

Board Member, Annetta Knight

Auditors: KPMG LLP

LOCATIONS

HQ: Costco Wholesale Corp
999 Lake Drive, Issaquah, WA 98027
Phone: 425 313-8100
Web: www.costco.com

2015 Locations

	No.
US & Puerto Rico	480
Canada	89
Mexico	36
UK	27
Japan	23
Taiwan	11
Korea	12
Australia	7
Spain	1
Total	**686**

2015 Sales

	$ mil.	% of total
US	84,351	73
Canada	17,341	15
Other international	14,507	12
Total	**116,119**	**100**

PRODUCTS/OPERATIONS

2015 Sales

	% of total
Sundries (including candy snacks beverages cleaning products & tobacco)	21
Food (dry & institutionally packaged)	22
Hardlines (including major appliances electronics & office & auto supplies)	16
Fresh food (meat bakery deli & produce)	14
Softlines (including apparel housewares media home furnishings & jewelry)	11
Other (including pharmacy optical photo & gas stations)	16
Total	**100**

2015 Sales

	$ mil.	% of total
Sales	113,666	98
Membership fees	2,533	2
Total	**116,199**	**100**

Selected Products and Services

Alcoholic beverages
Apparel
Appliances
Automotive insurance products (tires batteries)
Automobile sales
Baby products
Books
Cameras film and photofinishing
Candy
Caskets
CDs
Checks and form printing
Cleaning and institutional supplies
Collectibles
Computer hardware and software
Computer training services
Copying and printing services
Credit card processing
DVDs
Electronics
Eye exams
Flooring
Floral arrangements
Fresh foods (bakery deli meats produce seafood)
Furniture
Gasoline
Gifts
Glasses and contact lenses
Groceries and institutionally packaged foods
Hardware
Health and beauty aids
Hearing aids
Home insurance
Housewares
Insurance (automobile small-business health home)
Jewelry
Lighting supplies
Mortgage service
Office equipment and supplies
Outdoor living products
Payroll processing
Pet supplies
Pharmaceuticals
Plumbing supplies
Real estate services
Snack foods
Soft drinks
Sporting goods
Tobacco
Tools
Toys
Travel packages and other travel services
Video games and systems
Private Label
Kirkland Signature

COMPETITORS

1-800 CONTACTS	Kohl's
ALDI	Kroger
Amazon.com	Lowe's
Army and Air Force Exchange	Mattress Firm
	Office Depot
Aurora Wholesalers	PETCO
AutoZone	PetSmart
BJ's Wholesale Club	Safeway
Barnes & Noble	Staples
Best Buy	Target Corporation
Big Lots	Toys ''R'' Us
CVS	Trader Joe's
Dollar General	Wal-Mart
Family Dollar Stores	Walgreen
Home Depot	Whole Foods
Kmart	

HISTORICAL FINANCIALS

Company Type: Public

Income Statement

FYE: August 30

	REVENUE ($ mil.)	NET INCOME ($ mil.)	NET PROFIT MARGIN	EMPLOYEES
08/15	116,199	2,377	2.0%	205,000
08/14*	112,640	2,058	1.8%	195,000
09/13	105,156	2,039	1.9%	184,000
09/12	99,137	1,709	1.7%	174,000
08/11	88,915	1,462	1.6%	164,000
Annual Growth	6.9%	12.9%	—	5.7%

*Fiscal year change

2015 Year-End Financials

Debt ratio: 18.38%	No. of shares (mil.): 437
Return on equity: 20.80%	Dividends
Cash ($ mil.): 4,801	Yield: 0.0%
Current ratio: 1.05	Payout: 121.2%
Long-term debt ($ mil.): 4,864	Market value ($ mil.): 61,291

	STOCK PRICE ($) FY Close	P/E High/Low	PER SHARE ($) Earnings	PER SHARE ($) Dividends	PER SHARE ($) Book Value
08/15	139.95	29 22	5.37	6.51	24.24
08/14*	121.08	27 23	4.65	1.33	28.11
09/13	111.87	26 20	4.63	8.17	24.80
09/12	97.87	25 20	3.89	1.03	28.59
08/11	77.21	25 17	3.30	0.89	27.64
Annual Growth	16.0%	— —	12.9%	64.5%	(3.2%)

*Fiscal year change

Crown Holdings Inc

Crown Holdings wants to pop a top on profits. The company is a leading global manufacturer of consumer packaging; steel and aluminum food and beverage cans and related packaging are Crown's primary lines. Its portfolio includes aerosol cans and various metal vacuum closures marketed under brands Liftoff SuperEnd and Easylift as well as specialty packaging such as novelty containers and industrial cans. Crown also supplies can-making equipment and parts. Its roster of customers has included Coca-Cola Cadberry Schweppes Heinz Nestl&e SC Johnson Unilever and Procter & Gamble which owns Gillette another customer.

Geographic Reach

Crown operates 150 plants in 41 countries with about 75% of net sales coming from outside the US.

Operations

Crown's performance is driven by an unwavering focus to build segment income worldwide; it therefore segments its business along geographic lines. Its main divisions comprise the Americas Europe and Asia/Pacific. Crown is fighting back with heavy investments in international markets particularly those promising urban growth such as Latin America Asia and South and Central Europe.

The company believes that technological innovation will help mitigate for usual risks and cycles. Not happy to just make containers the same old way Crown Holdings operates research development and engineering centers in the US and the UK. Its mission is to design cost-efficient manufacturing processes reduce material content while maintaining freshness and develop new products with the application of new technologies. Some of its innovative closures include Orbit Closure (all-metal vacuum closure for glass jars) SuperEnd (metal ends using reduced material) and Easylift food ends (improved tab access).

Sales and Marketing

Crown markets and sells products to customers through its own sales and marketing staffs. In some instances contracts with customers are centrally negotiated but products are ordered through and distributed directly by its local facilities. Its top 10 global customers collectively represented 29% of its overall revenue in 2014.

Financial Performance

Crown's revenues increased 5% from $8.7 billion in 2013 to peak at a record-setting $9.1 billion in 2014. Its profits also increased 19% from $324 million in 2013 to $387 million in 2014.

The historic growth in 2014 was fueled by additional revenue from previous acquisitions. Crown was particularly helped by a 25% rise in European Food sales mostly due to a 73% spike in sales from Spain. The company's operating cash flow has also steadily surged the last several years jumping from $885 million in 2013 to $912 million in 2014.

Strategy

Crown grows its businesses in specific international growth markets while improving its operations and results in more mature markets through disciplined pricing and improvements in manufacturing and productivity. However with international expansion Crown like its rivals risks exposure to unfavorable foreign-currency exchange rates of the euro pound sterling and Canadian dollar as well as cyclical consumer spending on food and beverages. Its net sales are also impacted by the rise or decrease in the cost of aluminum and steel which is passed on to customers.

The company is specifically targeting Asia/Pacific as a region ripe with growth opportunities. In 2013 it commercialized second beverage can lines in Putian China; and Bangi Malaysia. It also commercialized new beverage can plants in Sihanoukville Cambodia; Danang Vietnam; and Bangkok Thailand.

Mergers and Acquisitions

Crown has been earning additional revenue in key markets through the use of acquisitions. Looking to Europe in 2014 Crown purchased Spain-based Mivisa the largest food can producer in both the Iberian Peninsula and Morocco. Primarily serving the vegetable fruit fish and meat segments Mivisa has 10 manufacturing facilities including six in Spain and one in Morocco. Mivisa was purchased for $1.7 billion and the deal helped Crown to achieve a revenue milestone of $9.1 billion in 2014.

In early 2015 Crown acquired acquire EMPAQUE a leading Mexican manufacturer of aluminum cans and ends bottle caps and glass bottles for the beverage industry. Crown purchased EMPAQUE from Heineken N.V. in a cash transaction valued at $1.23 billion. The acquisition will significantly enhance Crown's strategic position in beverage cans both regionally and globally. As a result of the deal Crown is now the second-largest beverage can producer in North America supplying over 24 billion units annually to a balanced portfolio of beer and soft drink customers.

HISTORY

Formed as Crown Cork & Seal Co. (CC&S) of Baltimore in 1892 the company was consolidated into its present form in 1927 when it merged with New Process Cork and New York Patents. The next year CC&S expanded overseas and formed Crown Cork International. In 1936 CC&S acquired Acme Can and benefited from the movement at the time from home canning to processed canning. A decade later the company launched its new product in 1946 —the first aerosol can.

EXECUTIVES

President CEO and Director, Timothy J. Donahue, age 53, $615,000 total compensation
Vice President, Richard L Krzyzanowski
President Americas Division, Raymond L. McGowan, age 64, $595,000 total compensation
SVP and CFO, Thomas A. Kelly, age 56, $480,000 total compensation
EVP Corporate Technology and Regulatory Affairs and President Crown Packaging Technology, Daniel A. Abramowicz
President Asia Pacific, Jozef Salaerts, age 60, $478,021 total compensation
President - CROWN Europe, Gerard H (Jerry) Gifford, age 60, $550,000 total compensation
President Crown Aerosol Packaging North America, C. Anderson (Andy) Bolton
President Crown Latin America and Caribbean, Ramiro (Barney) Dussan
President Crown Food Packaging North America Crown Closures and Specialty Packaging, James D. Wilson
President Americas Division, Djalma Novaes, age 54
President CROWN Beverage Packaging South America, Wilmar Arinelli
President Colombiana, Juan Carlos Turjillo
President CROWN Beverage Packaging Mexico, Abel Coello Quintanilla
President CROWN Beverage Packaging North America, Timothy J. Lorge
Vice President Sales and Marketing Beverage Packaging, Thomas (Thom) Fisher
Senior Vice President Corporate Controller, Fred Dermody
Vice President Operations, Rick Schneider
Division Vice President, George Fernandez
Vice President Marketing, Anthony White
Vice President, Martin (Marti) Reynolds
Vice President, Randall Chaffins
Vice President Sales Closures and Speciality Packaging, Eric Meyer
Senior Vice President Finance, Edward (Ed) Bisno
Vice President Thailand, Patrick Lee
Vice President Logistics, David Watkins
Vice President Sourcing, Richard Nunn
Regional Vice President Sales, Michelle (Mitch) Hinton
Vice President, Ian Carmichael
Vice President Sales Crown Beverage Packaging, Janice Dunphy
Vice President Manufacturing, Dominic Capretta
Vice President Sales, Ralph Menichini
Executive Vice President, Ronald (Ron) Thoma
Senior Vice President General Counsel Secretary, William T (Bill) Gallagher
Vice President Of Sales beverage, Tom Fischer
Vice President Of Marketing, Dahlgren Brad
Vice President Sales North America Aerosol Division, Bradley Dahlgren
Vice President Crown Closure Europe, Peter (Pete) Collier
Vice President, Geelen Eddy
Chairman, John W. Conway, age 69
Auditors: PricewaterhouseCoopers LLP

LOCATIONS

HQ: Crown Holdings Inc
One Crown Way, Philadelphia, PA 19154-4599
Phone: 215 698-5100
Web: www.crowncork.com

2013 Sales

	$ mil.	% of total
US	2,414	27
UK	759	9
France	547	6
Other regions	5,136	58
Total	**8,656**	**100**

PRODUCTS/OPERATIONS

2013 Sales

	$ mil.	% of total
Metal beverage cans & ends	4,824	56
Metal food cans & ends	2,339	27
Other metal packaging	1,211	14
Other products	282	3
Total	**8,656**	**100**

2013 Sales by Segment

	$ mil.	% of total
Americas beverage	2,289	26
European food	1,751	20
European beverage	1,731	20
Asia Pacific	1,189	14
North America food	845	10
Non-reportable segments	851	10
Total	**8,656**	**100**

Selected Products

Metal packaging
  Aerosol cans
  Beverage cans
  Closures and caps
  Crowns
  Ends
  Food cans
Plastics packaging
Other products
  Can making equipment and spares

Selected Markets

Food and beverage
Health and beauty
Household
Industrial

COMPETITORS

Alcoa	Owens-Illinois
Amcor	Rexam
AptarGroup	Silgan
BWAY	Sonoco Products
Ball Corp.	Tetra Laval
Berry Plastics	
Metal Container	
Corporation	

HISTORICAL FINANCIALS

Company Type: Public

Income Statement

FYE: December 31

	REVENUE ($ mil.)	NET INCOME ($ mil.)	NET PROFIT MARGIN	EMPLOYEES
12/14	9,097	387	4.3%	23,000
12/13	8,656	324	3.7%	21,300
12/12	8,470	557	6.6%	21,900
12/11	8,644	282	3.3%	20,700
12/10	7,941	324	4.1%	20,500
Annual Growth	**3.5%**	**4.5%**	**—**	**2.9%**

2014 Year-End Financials

Debt ratio: 54.17%	No. of shares (mil.): 139
Return on equity: 629.27%	Dividends
Cash ($ mil.): 965	Yield: —
Current ratio: 1.24	Payout: —
Long-term debt ($ mil.): 5,007	Market value ($ mil.): 7,075

	STOCK PRICE ($) FY Close	P/E High/Low	PER SHARE ($) Earnings	Dividends	Book Value
12/14	50.90	19 14	2.79	0.00	0.86
12/13	44.57	19 16	2.30	0.00	0.03
12/12	36.81	10 9	3.75	0.00	(1.13)
12/11	33.58	22 16	1.83	0.00	(3.19)
12/10	33.38	17 11	2.00	0.00	(0.62)
Annual Growth	**11.1%**	**— —**	**8.7%**	**—**	**—**

CST Brands Inc

CST Brands is hoping to corner the market on convenience stores. The holding company spun off from energy giant Valero in 2013 operates more than 1000 gas stations/convenience stores in the US under the Corner Store moniker. Its gasoline is sold under the Valero and Diamond Shamrock brands while its stores are located in 10 US states and sell the usual –snacks drinks tobacco products health and beauty products automotive products and other convenience items. CST Brands has another 850 Dépanneur du Coin stores in eastern Canada (mostly in French-speaking Quebec); however the majority of its Canadian stores are operated by independent dealers.

OperationsBy product CST Brands generated 83% of its total revenue in 2014 from motor fuel sales while merchandise sales accounted for 13%. Some of its private-label products are Fresh Choices soda U Force sports drinks Cibolo Mountain coffee and Flavors2Go fountain drinks. Much of its store merchandise comes from distributor Core-Mark. CST Brands operates three business segments: US Retail Canada Retail and CrossAmerica.The company's US Retail segment which generated 59% of its total revenue in 2014 is comprised of roughly 1020 convenience store and motor fuel sales businesses across 10 US states. More than 60% of the stores are in Texas while Colorado California Arizona New Mexico New York Louisiana Arkansas Wyoming and Oklahoma hold the rest.The Canadian Retail segment which brought in 37% of overall revenue in 2014 counts about 860 company-owned and operated convenience stores as well as commission agents cardlocks and heating oil operations across a handful of Canadian provinces. About 60% of these stores are located in Quebec while the rest are in Ontario Maritimes Newfoundland and Labrador.The remainder of revenue comes from the CrossAmerica segment which gets its business mostly from wholesale distribution of motor fuel through CrossAmerica Partners LP to lessee and independent dealers as well as CST's US Retail Segment sub-wholesalers and retail commission agents. Geographic Reach

The US accounts for about 60% of sales while Canada takes in the other 40%. In Canada most of its money is only made on fuel sales as the convenience stores are operated by independent dealers.Sales and MarketingCST Brands sells its products via wholesale retail and distribution centers. It also has an agreement with Core-Mark International to provide merchandise expertise purchasing power and efficient distribution services in its US Retail segment.The company's average convenience store size is about 2200 sq. ft.

Financial Performance

CST Brands' sales have remained relatively flat in recent years as its retail business has matured. Its revenue barely rose in 2014 to $12.76 billion as both its Canadian and US Retail businesses declined due to weakness in the Canadian dollar (versus the US dollar) and lower gas prices respectively. Merchandise sales rose by 5% however with growth in both regions thanks to new store openings while motor fuel sales grew in Canada thanks to higher fuel prices resulting from higher excise taxes. The company's new Cross America business added another revenue stream helping to offset most of the losses from the other two business segments for the year.CST Brand's net income rebounded by 44% to $200 million in 2014 thanks to higher revenue and lower costs of sales stemming from lower crude oil and wholesale gasoline

prices and the weakening of the Canadian dollar. The company also made about $32 million in gains on the sale of its assets during the year.Despite higher earnings in 2014 the company's cash from operations declined by 19% to $355 million mostly because in 2013 it had enjoyed a non-recurring cash benefit resulting from its payment terms on motor fuel purchased from Valero.

Strategy

CST Brands reiterated in 2015 that its growth strategies include: growing organically by building more convenience stores in the US and Canada; expanding into new geographic markets through strategic acquisitions of retail convenience stores; bolstering and expanding its wholesale fuel distribution business; developing new convenience store brands to improve same-store profit; and maximizing its gross profit margins on its merchandise.

Pursuant to its strategy of expanding via acquisitions CST in late 2015 said it would purchase about 164 convenience stores from The Jones Company for about $425 million. The deal also includes Jones' distribution and fuel supply companies about a dozen real estate sites set for convenience store development and 21 quick service restaurants. The restaurants are mostly located in the convenience stores and operate under Krystal Dairy Queen Subway Taco Bell and McDonald's banners. Its retail strategy is to pull customers away from the supermarket. Hoping that as supermarkets get larger and customers become more likely to use convenience stores for quick trips CST Brands aims to attract buyers with a large selection of products and proprietary brands. To this end in 2015 the company announced that it would be remodeling and/or re-branding some of its existing stores and would add between 35 and 40 new stores during the year under its US Retail business to grow its Corner Store brand value. Management also announced that it would keep expanding its Canadian Retail business by adding 10 to 12 new stores in 2015 in the region.

Aiming for a more full-service operation some of CST Brands' more than 1850 stores in North America offer car washes lottery games money orders vehicle air/water/vacuums video and game rentals and ATMs. Nearly 40 US stores even have Subway franchises and another 45 in Canada have Country Style coffee shops. CST Brands also uses customer loyalty programs such as coupons discounts and promotions to encourage repeat business.

Mergers and Acquisitions

In January 2015 CST Brands partnered with Cross America to purchase 22 convenience stores from Landmark Industries. CST purchased the personal property working capital and convenience store operations for $20 million while CrossAmerica purchased the real estate property and certain wholesale fuel distribution assets for $44 million.In February 2015 CrossAmerica purchased Erickson Oil Products for $85 million resulting in the acquisition of 64 retail sites located in Minnesota Michigan Wisconsin and South Dakota.In November 2014 the company acquired Nice N Easy Grocery Shoppes which operated nearly 80 convenience stores in New York. The move marked an expansion into new territory for CST adjacent to its Canadian network.In October 2014 CST purchased the General Partner and IDRs of CrossAmerica for a total of $17 million giving CST Brands access to more capital through the master limited partnership (MLP) and expanding its wholesale fuel supply business.

EXECUTIVES

SVP and CFO, Clay E. (Clay) Killinger, age 54, $558,372 total compensation

SVP and Chief Marketing Officer, Charles H. (Hal) Adams, age 55, $359,630 total compensation
SVP and Chief Development Officer, Stephan F. (Steve) Motz, age 56, $359,630 total compensation
Chairman President and CEO, Kimberly S. (Kim) Lubel, age 50, $851,755 total compensation
SVP and COO, Anthony P. (Tony) Bartys, age 58, $416,414 total compensation
VP Brand Marketing, Peter Brodnitz
SVP Canadian Retail, Christian Houle
SVP and CIO, James Maxey
VP Wholesale, Warren Maynard
VP Regional Retail Operations, Pete Linton
VP Home Heat, Martin Longpre
Regional VP Retail, Mario Sauv ©
SVP Real Estate and Construction, Paul Clark
VP Regional Retail Operations, David Mock
VP Regional Retail Operations, Jeff Truman
Vice President Controller, Tammy Floyd
Auditors: KPMG LLP

LOCATIONS

HQ: CST Brands Inc
One Valero Way, Building D, Suite 200, San Antonio, TX 78249
Phone: 210 692-5000
Web: www.CSTBrands.com

2014 Sales

	$ mil.	% of total
U.S.Retail	7,482	59
Canada Retail	4,702	37
CrossAmerica	587	4
Elimination	(13)	-
Total	**12,758**	**100**

U.S Location 2014

	Stores
Texas	612
Colorado	138
California	79
Arizona	62
New Mexico	38
New York	32
Louisiana	28
Arkansas	27
Wyoming	3
Oklahoma	2
Total	**1,021**

CrosAmerica Location 2014

	Stores
Pennsylvania	131
New Jersey	107
Virginia	83
Ohio	76
Massachusetts	70
Tennessee	50
Florida	46
New York	32
New Hampshire	21
West Virginia	14
Illinois	8
Maine	8
Kentucky	7
Indiana	3
Delaware	1
Maryland	1
Total	**658**

Canada Retail Store 2014 Location

	Stores
Quebec	536
Ontario	140
Maritimes	117
Newfoundland and Labrador	68
Total	**861**

PRODUCTS/OPERATIONS

2014 Sales

	$ mil.	% of total
Motor fuel sales	10,580	83
Merchandise	1,617	13
Other	561	4
Total	**12,758**	**100**

COMPETITORS

7-Eleven	Exxon Mobil
Alon Brands	Hess Corporation
BP	Kwik Trip
CITGO	Murphy USA
Casey' s General Stores	QuikTrip
Chevron	Racetrac Petroleum
ConocoPhillips	Royal Dutch Shell
Couche-Tard	The Pantry

HISTORICAL FINANCIALS

Company Type: Public

Income Statement

FYE: December 31

	REVENUE ($ mil.)	NET INCOME ($ mil.)	NET PROFIT MARGIN	EMPLOYEES
12/14	12,758	200	1.6%	13,496
12/13	12,777	139	1.1%	12,321
12/12	13,135	210	1.6%	11,640
12/11	12,863	214	1.7%	—
12/10	10,371	193	1.9%	—
Annual Growth	**5.3%**	**0.9%**	**—**	**—**

2014 Year-End Financials

Debt ratio: 35.81%	No. of shares (mil.): 77
Return on equity: 27.78%	Dividends
Cash ($ mil.): 368	Yield: 0.5%
Current ratio: 1.45	Payout: 13.5%
Long-term debt ($ mil.): 1,227	Market value ($ mil.): 3,365

	STOCK PRICE ($) FY Close	P/E High/Low	PER SHARE ($) Earnings	Dividends	Book Value
12/14	43.61	17 11	2.63	0.25	10.54
12/13	36.72	20 16	1.84	0.13	8.32
Annual Growth	**4.4%**	**— —**	**9.3%**	**18.9%**	**6.1%**

CSX Corp

CSX banks on the railway as the right way to make money. Its main subsidiary CSX Transportation (CSXT) operates a major rail system of some 21000 route miles in the eastern US. The freight carrier links 23 states 70 ports 240 short-line railroads the District of Columbia and two Canadian provinces (Ontario and Quebec). Freight hauled by the company includes a wide variety of merchandise (food chemicals and consumer goods) coal and automotive products. CSX also transports via intermodal containers and trailers (Intermodal freight hauling uses multiple modes of transportation). CSX's rail segment also includes units that operate motor vehicle distribution centers and bulk cargo terminals.

Geographic Reach

CSX operates in two dozen states primarily in the Eastern US and along the Eastern Seaboard. It also operates in Washington DC.

Operations

CSX's transportation services operate through three lines of businesses: merchandise (its largest segment by revenue) coal and intermodal. The company's subsidiary CSX Real Property handles real estate sales leasing acquisition and management and development activities. CSX Intermodal Terminals provides intermodal terminal and trucking services though more than 50 terminals across the eastern US.

CSXT operates with a fleet of more than 4250 locomotives (98% are owned by CSXT) and around 84000 railcars (gondolas hoppers and box/flat cars). Other CSX holdings include Total Distribution Services a storage and distribution company for the automotive industry; Transflo Terminal Services a logistics company for transferring shipments from rail to truck; and CSX Technology which provides IT services to its parent company.

Sales and MarketingCSX operates sales representative offices in strategic parts of the world including Mexico City Monterrey Buenos Aires Sao Paolo Rio de Janeiro and Munich. Noteworthy customers include Ascend Performance Materials Aux Sable Liquid Products Cargill Dow Corning MarkWest Hydrocarbon SABIC Americas and United Refining.

Financial Performance

CSX has recognized unprecedented growth over the last few years. Its revenues peaked at $12.7 billion in 2014 a historic milestone for the company. Its profits increased to $1.93 billion in 2014 also a high-point. Its cash flow from operations increased 2% to $2.34 billion in 2014.

The historic growth for 2014 was due to a 6% rise in volumes across most markets. The merchandise segment experienced growth from the chemical markets resulting from higher energy-related shipments that included crude oil liquefied petroleum gas (LPG) and frac sand. This was offset by its coal segment decreasing by 2% during 2014.

Strategy

Citing fuel prices and environmental efficiency CSX hopes to persuade more shippers to shift freight from trucks to trains especially for cross-country journeys. It has invested almost $400 million and is working with several states and the federal government to outfit tunnels bridges and overpasses to accommodate the taller railcars.

CSX is building new terminals and increasing its network capacity to enhance its intermodal operations and broaden its market presence in key growth areas. During 2013 it opened or expanded terminals in Columbus Ohio; Louisville Kentucky; Atlanta; and Worcester Massachusetts. CSX in 2014 opened new terminals in Winter Haven Florida; and Quebec Canada. In 2015 it began construction on a new terminal near Pittsburgh.

The company also plans to capitalize on the economic growth in developing countries like India China and Brazil which have generated a long-term demand for coal. Demand for coal used in electric power generation is also projected to increase as more countries become urbanized. These increases in global coal demand are expected to prominently be met by export shipments originating from the US. CSX has positioned itself to capitalize on this surge in growth through its relationship with coal suppliers and network of multiple port facilities.

HISTORY

Company Background

CSX Corporation was formed in 1980 when Chessie System and Seaboard Coast Line (SCL) merged in an effort to improve the efficiency of their railroads. Chessie's oldest railroad the Baltimore & Ohio (B&O) was chartered in 1827 to help Baltimore compete against New York and Philadelphia for freight traffic. By the late 1800s the railroad served Chicago Cincinnati New York City St. Louis and Washington DC. Chesapeake & Ohio (C&O) acquired it in 1962.

C&O originated in Virginia with the Louisa Railroad in 1836. It gained access to Chicago Cincinnati and Washington DC and by the mid-1900s was a major coal carrier. After B&O and C&O acquired joint control of Baltimore-based Western Maryland Railway (1967) the three railroads became subsidiaries of newly formed Chessie System (1973).

One of SCL's two predecessors Seaboard Air Line Railroad (SAL) grew out of Virginia's Portsmouth & Roanoke Rail Road of 1832. SCL's other predecessor Atlantic Coast Line Railroad (ACL) took shape between 1869 and 1893 as William Walters acquired several southern railroads. In 1902 ACL bought the Plant System (railroads in Georgia Florida and other southern states) and the Louisville & Nashville (a north-south line connecting New Orleans and Chicago) giving ACL the basic form it was to retain until 1967 when it merged with SAL to form SCL.

EXECUTIVES

EVP Law and Public Affairs General Counsel and Corporate Secretary, Ellen M. Fitzsimmons, age 55, $550,000 total compensation
Vice President Chief Human Resources Officer, Diana Sorfleet
President, Clarence W. Gooden, age 63, $650,000 total compensation
Chairman and CEO, Michael J. Ward, age 65, $1,200,000 total compensation
VP and Chief Transportation Officer, Cindy M. Sanborn, age 50
EVP and CFO, Frank A. Lonegro
EVP and Chief Sales and Marketing Officer, Fredrik J. Eliasson, age 45, $550,000 total compensation
President TRANSFLO Terminal Services Inc., Brian Ward
President CSX Real Property, Richard Hood
Vice President Network Operations, Steve Potter
Vice President Sales and Marketing, Derrick Smith
Vice President Regulatory Affairs, Brian Hammock
Assistant Vice President Network, Mark Hinsdale
Information Technology Management Vice President, Matthew (Matt) Charron
Regional Vice President of Public Affairs, Tom Drake
Assistant Vice President, Sean Craig
Assistant Vice President Operations Compliance, Tom Murta
Assistant Vice President, David Biggs
Assistant Vice President Engineering, Dale Ophardt
Assistant Vice President Operations Process Excellence, John (Jack) Murphy
Assistant Vice President Process Improvement CSX Corporation, Bob Gutman
Assistant Vice President Load Engineering, Mitch Hobbs
Vice President Regulatory Affairs, Peter Shudtz
Vice President Engineeringandfacilities Management, Michele Mastrean
Resident Vice President, Sharon Daboin
Assistant Vice President Information Technology Operations, Duard Williams
Vice President Customer Service, Shelley Mast
Executive Vice President Information Services, Wendy Hausler
Vice President Information Security, Greg Bissette
Vice President of Operations Research and Planning, John (Jack) Gibson
Assistant Vice President Talent Management, Terri Baumgardner
Vice President Finance Commercial, Fred Eliasson
Vice President and Chief Transportation Officer, Cindy Sandborn
Vice President Network Operations, Cary Helton
Senior Vice President, Carl Gerhardstein
Assistant Vice President Network Operations Locomotive Management, Peter (Pete) Burrus
Assistant Vice President Of Real Estate Sales, Rick Hood
Auditors: Ernst & Young LLP

LOCATIONS

HQ: CSX Corp
500 Water Street, 15th Floor, Jacksonville, FL 32202
Phone: 904 359-3200
Web: www.csx.com

PRODUCTS/OPERATIONS

Selected Services
Container/trailer shipping
Freight shipping by rail
Intermodal transportation
Logistics
Property/real estate (buying/leasing property for commercial or rail)
Salvage sales (distressed cargo sales)

COMPETITORS

APL Logistics	Hub Group
Burlington Northern Santa Fe	J.B. Hunt
Canadian National Railway	Norfolk Southern
	Schneider National
	Union Pacific
Canadian Pacific Railway	Washington Companies

HISTORICAL FINANCIALS

Company Type: Public

Income Statement

FYE: December 25

	REVENUE ($ mil.)	NET INCOME ($ mil.)	NET PROFIT MARGIN	EMPLOYEES
12/15	11,811	1,968	16.7%	29,000
12/14	12,669	1,927	15.2%	31,511
12/13	12,026	1,864	15.5%	31,254
12/12	11,756	1,859	15.8%	32,120
12/11	11,743	1,822	15.5%	31,344
Annual Growth	0.1%	1.9%	—	(1.9%)

2015 Year-End Financials

Debt ratio: 30.55%
Return on equity: 17.31%
Cash ($ mil.): 628
Current ratio: 1.52
Long-term debt ($ mil.): 10,683
No. of shares (mil.): 965
Dividends
  Yield: 0.0%
  Payout: 35.0%
Market value ($ mil.): 25,229

	STOCK PRICE ($) FY Close	P/E High/Low	PER SHARE ($) Earnings	Dividends	Book Value
12/15	26.13	19 12	2.00	0.70	12.07
12/14	36.68	20 13	1.92	0.63	11.25
12/13	28.29	16 11	1.83	0.59	10.39
12/12	19.43	13 11	1.79	0.54	8.81
12/11	21.06	48 11	1.67	0.45	8.06
Annual Growth	5.5%	— —	4.6%	11.9%	10.6%

Cullen/Frost Bankers, Inc.

One of the largest independent bank holding companies in Texas Cullen/Frost Bankers owns Frost Bank and other financial subsidiaries through a second-tier holding company The New Galveston Company. The community-oriented bank serves individuals and local businesses as well as clients in neighboring parts of Mexico through 120-plus branches in Texas metropolitan areas. It offers commercial and consumer deposit products and loans trust and investment manage-

ment services mutual funds insurance brokerage and leasing. Subsidiaries include Frost Insurance Agency Frost Brokerage Services Frost Investment Advisors and investment banking arm Frost Securities. Cullen/Frost has total assets of $26.5 billion.

Geographic Reach

San Antonio-based Cullen/Frost Bankers has branches throughout Texas including the Austin Corpus Christi Dallas Fort Worth Houston Permian Basin the Rio Grande Valley and San Antonio regions.

Financial Performance

Cullen/Frost reported revenue of $945.3 million in 2013 an increase of 3% versus 2012 on increased interest income on loans and deposits and an increase in trust and investment management fees. Net income was $237.9 a flat comparison with the prior year. 2013 marked the third consecutive year of rising revenue following a dip in 2010. The bank's fortunes are rising along with the thriving energy and technology sectors in Texas.

Strategy

Cullen/Frost has built its insurance business through acquisitions in recent years; since 2009 it has bought agencies in Dallas Houston San Antonio and San Marcos that provide group employee benefit plans. The company continues to seek out acquisition opportunities while it also looks for ways to expand and diversify within its existing markets. To reduce its reliance on interest rate spreads Cullen/Frost wants to grow its income from fees such as insurance commissions trust investment fees and service charges on deposit accounts.

Mergers and Acquisitions

In June 2014 Frost Bank acquired Odessa Texas-based Western National Bank (WNB) increasing its presence in the oil-rich Permian Basin Midland and Odessa markets in West Texas. Seven of WNB's eight branches were converted to the Frost name (an office in San Antonio was closed) increasing the number of Frost branches statewide to more than 120. The acquisition of WNB added $1.8 billion in assets $1.6 billion in deposits and $668 million in total loans to Cullen/Frost. The purchase of WNB was the first time in nearly seven years that Frost acquired another bank.

EXECUTIVES

Chairman and CEO; Chairman and CEO Frost Bank, Richard W. (Dick) Evans, age 68, $830,000 total compensation
President, Phillip D. Green, age 60, $440,000 total compensation
Director; President Frost Bank, Patrick B. (Pat) Frost, age 55, $362,000 total compensation
President and Chief Business Banking Officer Frost Bank, David W. (Dave) Beck, age 64, $390,000 total compensation
Chief Banking Officer, Paul H. Bracher, age 58, $387,000 total compensation
Group EVP Chief Credit Officer and Chief Risk Officer Frost Bank, William L. (Bill) Perotti, age 57
Group EVP and Executive Trust Officer Frost Bank, Richard Kardys, age 68, $387,000 total compensation
Group EVP eCommerce Operations Research and Strategy, Robert A. (Bobby) Berman, age 52
Group EVP Consumer Banking Frost Bank, Paul J. Olivier, age 62
Group EVP Human Resources, Emily A. Skillman, age 70
CFO, Jerry Salinas
SEVP and Corporate HR Manager, Annette Alonzo
Group EVP Technology and Operations, Gary McKnight
Group EVP Culture and People Development, Candace Wolfshohl
Vice President, Stephanie Conti

Executive Vice President Information Technology Division, Carl Bush
Vice President of Marketing, Linda Hopkins
Vice President of Marketing, Howard Kasanoff
Senior Vice President It, Harvey Gutierrez
Senior Vice President And Chief Appraiser, Michael (Mel) Cleary
Senior Executive Vice Presiden, William Sirakos
Senior Vice President Director Of Investor Relatio, Greg Parker
Vice President Community Development, Betty Davis
Assistan Vice President, Maralessa Gonzales
Executive Vice President, Mark Freeman
Senior Vice President Treasury Management, Darlene Selsor
Executive Vice President Human Resources, Janet Lane
Senior Vice President, Andrew Merryman
Vice President of Operation, David (Dave) Perdue
Senior Vice President And Portfolio Manager For The Dallas Region, John M (Jack) Hind
Vice President, Liz Gonzaba
Senior Vice President, Miltie Devin
Executive Vice President, Cliff McCauley
Vice President Of Finance, Gregory Dreier
Vice President, Oscar Molina
Vice President of Marketing, Cathy Garison
Vice President, Casey Maxfield
Vice President Corporate Communications, Sheri Rosen
Vice President Of Finance, Mike Benson
Senior Vice President, Charles Plummer
Senior Vice President, Matt Bryant
Vice President, Robert (Bob) Bernal
Vice President Executive Benni, Darleen Schauer
Senior Vice President, Jill Stacy
Vice President Sales, Talal Tay
Senior Vice President eCommerce, Wendy Erickson
Vice President of Operation, Rocky McAshan
Vice President of Finance, Wayne Baker
Vice President Marketing, Ericka Pullin
Senior Vice President, Michael Cain
Senior Vice President, Edward Porras
Executive Vice President Credit Administration Support, Jimmy Locke
Senior Vice President, James Valdez
Senior Vice President, John Harris
Senior Vice President, Michael D (Mel) Falk
Assistant Vice President, Kelly Shanteau
Executive Vice President, Matt Henson
Vice President Marketing, Erica Noriega
Senior Vice President Capital Markets, Mark Brell
Senior Vice President Information Technology Project Management Office, Roger Lind
Senior Vice President, Gene Witter
Vice President, Clay Jones
Vice President Private Banking Officer, Beverly Hankinson
Vice President Of Information Technology, Diane Madalin
Assistant Vice President Marketing, Monica Barrera
Senior Vice President, Terrie Ramirez
Senior Vice President, Leigh Olejer
Vice President Collections, Alan (Al) McCabe
Vice President Research and Strategy Marketing Department RB7, Tammy Herrera
Senior Vice President, Michael Nutter
Senior Vice President, Mike Davis
Vice President, Susan (Sue) Carruthers
Vice President Internal Audit, Natalie McCabe
Vice President, Jane Verette
Assistant Vice President, Austin Burns
Vice President, Larry Inman
Vice President, Matt Badders
Senior Vice President Institutional Trust Administration, Steven A (Steve) Klein
Senior Vice President, Terry Frank
Vice President, Letty Dominguez

Senior Vice President Community Leader, Jeff Fuller
Vice President Technology Infrastructure, Robert (Bob) Jacobs
Vice President Trust, John (Jack) Sands
Assistant Vice President, Justin Shoemaker
Executive Vice President, Stan Richard
Vice President, Stella Villarreal
Assistant Vice President Corporate Banking, Derek Rosson
Senior Vice President Corporate Banking, Susie Howell
Senior Vice President, Victor Quiroga
Vice President Treasury Management, Paige Bowlin
Vice President of Marketing, Daryl Hoffmann
Executive Vice President, Sue Turnage
Senior Vice President Marketing, Mike Witsken
Community Leader And Assistant Vice President, Travis Buchanan
Senior Vice President Of Investment Division, Jeanne Glorioso
Vice President, Kristie Cherry
Senior Vice President, Michael (Mel) Williams
Senior Vice President Application Support, Jeff Sanders
Assistant Vice President Regulatory Compliance Officer, Tracie Gaiser
Assistant Vice President, Elsie Boone
Executive Vice President, Robert Harvey
Senior Vice President Investments, Linnie Phebus
Executive Vice President Marketing, Debbie Danmeter
Vice President External Reporting, Ben Kavanagh
Senior Vice President, Carey Womble
Assistant Vice President, Laura Cook
Senior Vice President Deposit Service, Gloria Navarro
Vice President, Omar Quintanilla
Vice President Sales, Anthony Vallejo
Vice President, Kris Walsh
Senior Vice President, Carol Lampier
Assistant Vice President, Beth Pence
Assistant Vice President Employee Benefits, Brenda Smith
Vice President, Julie Crockett
Assistant Vice President, Rene Ramirez
Vice President of Project Management, Terri Ramirez
Senior Vice President Philanthropic Programs, Melissa (Mel) Adams
Executive Vice President Information Technology Division, Carl Pachalska
Vice President Of Finance, Vance Arnold
Vice President Energy Finance, Alex Zemkoski
Vice President Change Management, Brenda Gonzales
Vice President Public Finance, Duncan Morrow
Vice President Corporate Banking, Michelle Zamora
Senior Vice President Special Assets, Betsy Gleiser
Assistant Vice President Corporate Banking, Jim Dixon
Regional President, Paul Koch
Vice President, Zada Cisneros
Executive Vice President, Roderick Washington
Vice President Of Marketing, John Greenwood
Executive Vice President Compliance Manager, Cindy Reeves
Senior Vice President Compliance, Verna Fletcher
Vice President, Stephen Spears
Vice President, Wayne Thompson
Vice President of Finance, James (Jamie) Allen
Executive Vice President, Louis Barton
Senior Vice President, Stacy Flores
Senior Vice President Of Private Trust Services, Debbie Eippert
Senior Vice President, Jerry Colwell
Vice President Commercial Middle Market Banking, Colin Jones
Senior Vice President, Mark Ritter
Vice President, Chris Brower

Executive Vice President Retail Loans, Genny Rakowitz
Assistant Vice President, Ben Brandenburg
Vice President, Ken Orsburn
Assistant Vice President, Patricio Perez
Assistant Vice President, Lauren Urban
Assistant Vice President Commercial Banking, Jennifer Grimes
Assistant Vice President, Yolanda Gonzales
Assistant Vice President, Nathaniel Ellis
Senior Vice President, Daniel O'Connor
Assistant Vice President, Norma Adame
Auditors: Ernst & Young LLP

LOCATIONS

HQ: Cullen/Frost Bankers, Inc.
100 W. Houston Street, San Antonio, TX 78205
Phone: 210 220-4011   Fax: 210 220-5578
Web: www.frostbank.com

PRODUCTS/OPERATIONS

2013 Sales

	% of total
Interest	
Loans including fees	44
Securities	23
Other	1
Noninterest	
Trust fees	9
Service charges on deposit accounts	8
Insurance commissions & fees	5
Other charges commissions & fees	4
Other	6
Total	**100**

Selected Subsidiaries

Carton Service Corporation
Cullen BLP Inc.
Cullen/Frost Capital Trust II
Frost Bank
Frost Brokerage Services Inc.
Frost Insurance Agency Inc.
Frost Investment Advisors Inc.
Frost Securities Inc.
Main Plaza Corporation
Tri-Frost Corporation

COMPETITORS

BBVA Compass Bancshares	JPMorgan Chase
Bank of America	Lone Star Bank
Broadway Bancshares	PlainsCapital
Capital One	Prosperity Bancshares
Comerica	Texas Capital Bancshares
Extraco	Wells Fargo
First Financial Bankshares	Woodforest Financial
International Bancshares	

HISTORICAL FINANCIALS

Company Type: Public

Income Statement

	ASSETS ($ mil.)	NET INCOME ($ mil.)	INCOME AS % OF ASSETS	EMPLOYEES
12/15	28,567	279	1.0%	4,211
12/14	28,277	277	1.0%	4,154
12/13	24,312	237	1.0%	3,979
12/12	23,124	237	1.0%	3,878
12/11	20,317	217	1.1%	3,848
Annual Growth	**8.9%**	**6.5%**	**—**	**2.3%**

FYE: December 31

2015 Year-End Financials

Debt ratio: 0.83%
Return on equity: 9.73%
Cash ($ mil.): 3,524
Current ratio: —
Long-term debt ($ mil.): —
No. of shares (mil.): 61
Dividends
  Yield: 3.5%
  Payout: 46.7%
Market value ($ mil.): 3,719

	STOCK PRICE ($) FY Close	P/E High/Low	PER SHARE ($) Earnings	Dividends	Book Value
12/15	60.00	19 14	4.28	2.10	46.63
12/14	70.64	19 16	4.29	2.03	45.15
12/13	74.43	20 14	3.80	1.98	41.51
12/12	54.27	16 14	3.86	1.90	39.32
12/11	52.91	18 12	3.54	1.83	37.27
Annual Growth	3.2%	— —	4.9%	3.5%	5.8%

Cummins, Inc.

If it's comin' around the mountain it could have a Cummins' engine powering it. The company makes about half of its revenues from its Engine segment which makes diesel and natural gas powered engines for the heavy and mid-duty truck RV automotive and industrial markets along with marine rail mining and construction. Its other complementary business segments include Components (filtration products and fuel systems); Power Generation (vehicle and residential generators); and Distribution (product distributors and servicing). Major customers include OEMs Chrysler Daimler Ford Komatsu PACCAR and Volvo. More than half of Cummins' sales are from outside the US.

Geographic Reach

Cummins has main domestic operating facilities in Columbus Indiana; Franklin and Nashville Tennessee; and Washington DC. Key international locations reside in Beijing; Shanghai; Pune India; and Staines and Stanton UK.

It serves customers in 190 countries through a network of more than 600 company owned and independent distributor locations and 7200 dealer locations. The US generates about 52% of its total sales. China Brazil India Mexico Canada and the UK collectively account for nearly 24%.

Operations

The company's 49 to 5100 horsepower engines are made under the Cummins brand name. The Components segment manufactures products that are complementary to commercial diesel applications; more than 8300 filtration products are offered some branded as Fleetguard. Other products within this segment include turbo technologies for air handling in engines and exhaust after-treatment technology as well as new used and remanufactured fuel systems.

Power Generation's standby power products (alternators transfer switches and controls) serve commercial and consumer needs as well as those of the military. Brands include Onan (generator sets) and Stamford (alternators). Cummins' Distribution segment comprises a network of more than 600 company-owned and independent distributors that serve 190 countries worldwide.

Sales and Marketing

Major customer PACCAR accounted for 14% of the company's consolidated sales in 2014.

Financial Performance

After experiencing flat revenues the previous two years Cummins achieved unprecedented growth in 2014 with revenues peaking at a record-setting $19.2 billion. Profits also climbed 11% to reach almost $1.7 billion in 2014. In addition its operating cash flow has risen over the years jumping by $177 million to $2.2 billion in 2014.

The historic growth for 2014 was fueled by a 38% spike in Distribution segment sales due to acquisitions of North American distributors. Engine segment sales spiked by 9% due to higher demand in the North American on-highway markets. Components segment sales also increased by 18% primarily due to higher demand in on-highway markets in North America Europe and China.

Strategy

The company's fortunes are shaped in large part by the cyclical booms and busts of the on-highway construction and industrial markets. Its customers are particularly sensitive to the general economic climate interest rates and access to credit as well as regulatory issues (environmental and emissions standards) and political shifts.

In an effort to mitigate a slump in demand in any one market or region Cummins is continuing to transform itself from a company concentrated in North America to one whose business is seizing up opportunities in developing countries. Following the US China Brazil and India are Cummins' largest markets. Despite the potential for tapping these markets Cummins has acknowledged the higher risks involved when it comes to foreign currency translations and political economic and regulatory shifts. The company intends to continue acquiring its partially-owned North American distributors which will increase its distribution segment revenues.

To increase its market penetration the company relies on joint ventures that allow it to reduce capital spending streamline its supply chain management and boost its technology development. Some of the partnering companies include Dongfeng Automotive and Beijing Foton Motor in China Tata Motors in India Japan's Komatsu Hyundai Heavy Industries in South Korea Westport Innovations based in Canada and US-based Mercury Marine.

In 2014 Cummins began construction of a global technical center office for the high-horsepower engine business in Seymour Indiana.

HISTORY

Chauffeur Clessie Cummins believed that Rudolph Diesel's cumbersome and smoky engine could be improved for use in transportation. Borrowing money and work space from his employer —Columbus Indiana banker W. G. Irwin —Cummins founded Cummins Engine in 1919. Irwin invested more than $2.5 million and in the mid-1920s Cummins produced a mobile diesel engine. Truck manufacturers were reluctant to switch from gas to diesel so Cummins used publicity stunts (such as racing in the Indianapolis 500) to advertise his engine.

The company was profitable by 1937 the year Irwin's grandnephew J. Irwin Miller took over. During WWII the Cummins engine was used in cargo trucks. Sales jumped from $20 million in 1946 to more than $100 million by 1956. That year Cummins started its first overseas plant in Scotland and bought Atlas Crankshafts in 1958. By 1967 it had 50% of the diesel engine market.

EXECUTIVES

Vice President Human Resources, Jill Cook
Vice President PowerCare, Robert (Bob) Hutchinson
VP MidRange Engine Sales Engine Business, Dave Crompton, age 59
Chairman and CEO, N. Thomas (Tom) Linebarger, age 52, $1,250,000 total compensation
President and COO, Richard J. (Rich) Freeland, age 58, $730,208 total compensation
VP and President Power Generation, Livingston L. (Tony) Satterthwaite, age 55, $550,000 total compensation
Group VP China and Russia, Steven M. (Steve) Chapman
CIO, Sherry A. Aaholm

Managing Director International India, Anant Talaulicar, age 54, $537,500 total compensation
VP and CFO, Patrick J. (Pat) Ward, age 51, $680,000 total compensation
President — Cummins Turbo Technologies (CTT), Tracy Embree
VP Global Supply Chain and Manufacturing, Lisa Yoder
VP and CTO, Jennifer Rumsey
Vice President Sales and Support Engine Business, Jeff Jones
Vice President and GM Fuel Systems, Ray Amlung
Vice President Of Internal Audit, Luther Peters
V P- Bus Dev, Donald W Trapp
Vpi Manufacturing Engineer, Rajan Gandhi
Vpi Engineer, Nathan Wager
CE VPI Support team Lead, Mark Bosserman
HHP Vice President Rebuild, Terry Wham
Vice President Ecommerce, Lillia Bromley
Evu Vpi Process Owner Incoming, Rob Heathcote
Vice President Industrial Sales And Distribution, Norbert Nusterer
Vice President Chief Financial Officer Cummins Power Systems, Kelley Tate
Vice President Information Technology, Joe Mills
Vpi Sourcing Manager Engine Business Global Purchasing, Kurt Metzloff
Vice President Sales, Barry Kreuzer
Vice President Midrange Engineering, Jeff Weikert
Vice President mining Market, Kevin Spiller
VPI Sourcing Director, Michelle (Mitch) Stall
Vpi Sourcing Manager, Richard (Dick) Landshut
Second Vice President Corporate Development, Jeff Lawrence
Vpi Sourcing Specialist, Julie Franklin
Advanced Sourcing Vpi Team, Greg Thomas
Vpi Sourcing Specialist, Ryan Ingalls
Vpi Manufacturing Engineer, Mark Schoolfield
National Account Manager, Jim Schreiber
Vpi Manufacturing Program Manager, Hamilton Harper
Vpi Sourcing Manager, Susie Baker-Coy
Senior Vice President, Pam Fischvogt
Vice President Engine Business Quality, Robert Weimer
Vice President, Bruce Carver
Vice President Information Technology, Gail Farnsley
Vice President Customer Support, David Taylor
Human Resource Vice President Director Manager, Pam Donohoe-Duncan
Asq Cqe Vpi Sqe, Tao Gan
Vice President, Scot Lenger
Vice President Operations, Rick Miller
Vice President Of Sales, Roger Morrison
Vpi Sourcing Manager, Ashley Schultz
Vice President, Michael Kearney
Vice President General Manager, Merritt Becker
Vice President, Herman Van Niekerk
National Account Manager, Jeff Poferl
Vice President Oem S Human Resources Manager, Robert Shockman
XPI VPI Sourcing Manager, Holli Barger
Vice President Power Generation, David Hagewood
Executive Vice President; President Power Generation, Thomas (Thom) Linebarger
Executive Vice President President Power Generation Business, Thomas (Thom) Linebarge
Vice President Truck and Business OEM Business, Lori Thompson
Vice President Human Resource, Sean Huddleston
Vice President General Counsel, Sharon Barner
Vice President Corporate Strategy and Business Development, Thad Ewald
Vpi Service Engineer, Ian Ezard
Vice President Taxes, Joseph (Jo) Bernot
VPi Procurement Sqie, Neil Shah
Vice Chair, John C. Wall, age 64
Secretary, Cheryl Quisenberry
Secretary, Pedro Silva

LOCATIONS

HQ: Cummins, Inc.
500 Jackson Street, P.O. Box 3005, Columbus, IN 47202-3005
Phone: 812 377-5000   **Fax:** 812 377-4937
Web: www.cummins.com

2014 Sales

	$ mil.	% of total
US	10,058	52
China	1,446	8
Canada	4	
Brazil	730	4
Mexico	561	3
India	546	3
UK	479	2
Other countries	4,630	24
Total	**19,221**	**100**

PRODUCTS/OPERATIONS

2014 Sales

	$ mil.	% of total
Engine	10,962	46
Distribution	5,174	21
Components	5,118	21
Power generation	2,896	12
Adjustments	(4929)	-
Total	**19,221**	**100**

Selected Products

Components business
  Emission solutions
  Filtration (heavy-duty air fuel hydraulic and lube filtration and chemicals)
  Fuel systems (new fuel systems remanufactured electronic control modules)
  Turbo technologies (turbochargers)
Emissions solutions
Engine business
  Bus engines
  Heavy- and medium-duty truck engines
  Industrial engines for construction mining agricultural rail and marine equipment
  Light commercial vehicle engines
  Marine diesels (recreational and commercial)
Filtration business
  Air system
  Cooling system (crankcase ventilation)
  Diesel emission additives
  Fuel system (hydraulic)
  Lube system (transmission)
Fuel systems
  CELECT electronically controlled unit injection system
  Common rail pump
  Extreme pressure injection system
  High Pressure Injection (HPI) system
  Remanufactured products
Power generation business
  Diesel and alternative-fuel electrical generator sets (PowerCommand Onan Newage AVK SEG G-Drive)
Turbo technologies Holset (medium and heavy-duty diesel engines)

COMPETITORS

BorgWarner	Isuzu
Briggs & Stratton	Kohler
Power Products	MAN
CLARCOR	Mack Trucks
Caterpillar	Mitsubishi Heavy
China Yuchai	Industries
DENSO	Navistar International
DEUTZ	Parker-Hannifin
Detroit Diesel	Regal Beloit
Donaldson Company	Robert Bosch
Emerson Electric	Rolls-Royce Power
Fiat Chrysler	Systems
Ford Motor	Tenneco

Hino Motors	Textron
Honeywell	UD Trucks
International	Volvo
Illinois Tool Works	W.W. Grainger
Ingersoll-Rand	Weichai Power

HISTORICAL FINANCIALS
Company Type: Public

Income Statement
FYE: December 31

	REVENUE ($ mil.)	NET INCOME ($ mil.)	NET PROFIT MARGIN	EMPLOYEES
12/15	19,110	1,399	7.3%	55,200
12/14	19,221	1,651	8.6%	54,600
12/13	17,301	1,483	8.6%	47,900
12/12	17,334	1,645	9.5%	46,000
12/11	18,048	1,848	10.2%	43,900
Annual Growth	**1.4%**	**(6.7%)**	**—**	**5.9%**

2015 Year-End Financials

Debt ratio: 10.83%
Return on equity: 18.46%
Cash ($ mil.): 1,711
Current ratio: 2.09
Long-term debt ($ mil.): 1,576

No. of shares (mil.): 175
Dividends
  Yield: 3.9%
  Payout: 37.5%
Market value ($ mil.): 15,419

	STOCK PRICE ($) FY Close	P/E High/Low		PER SHARE ($) Earnings	Dividends	Book Value
12/15	88.01	19	11	7.84	3.51	42.27
12/14	144.17	18	14	9.02	2.03	42.53
12/13	140.97	18	13	7.91	2.25	40.22
12/12	108.35	15	10	8.67	1.80	34.79
12/11	88.02	13	8	9.55	1.33	28.60
Annual Growth	**(0.0%)**	**—**	**—**	**(4.8%)**	**27.6%**	**10.3%**

Customers Bancorp Inc

Customers Bancorp makes it pretty clear who they want to serve. The bank holding company operates about 15 locations in Pennsylvania New York and New Jersey. It offers personal and business checking savings and money market accounts as well as loans certificates of deposit credit cards and concierge or appointment banking (they come to you seven days a week). Customers has about $2 billion in assets; its loan portfolio is about a third commercial and half warehouse lending (short-term loans to mortgage lenders) with consumer loans making up the balance. It was formed in 2010 as a holding company for Customers Bank which was created in 1994 as New Century Bank.

Customers' strategy is to become a leading regional bank. Its acquisition area includes its current operating area as well as Maryland Delaware and Connecticut. Customers focuses on serving small business not-for-profit and consumer clients. It also specializes in warehouse lending which it sees as a wide open segment since so many companies exited the mortgage market after the housing crash.

In late 2011 Customers purchased Berkshire Bancorp and picked up five branches in Berks County Pennsylvania for about $11.3 million. Per its growth strategy Customers made several acquisitions in 2010. It picked up some at a bargain compared to the fair market value of the targets' assets leading Customers to record a $40 million bump in net income. Year-end results for 2011 look weak in comparison but are actually on track for continued recovery since the 2009 recession.

EXECUTIVES

Chairman and CEO, Jay S. Sidhu, age 63, $300,000 total compensation
President and COO, Richard A. Ehst, age 69, $225,000 total compensation
Executive Vice President President of Community Banking, Warren Taylor, age 57, $190,000 total compensation
EVP and Chief Credit Officer, Thomas Jastrem
EVP and Chief Administrative Officer, Jim Collins
EVP and Chief Lending Officer, Timothy D. Romig
EVP and President Special Assets Group, Robert A. White
EVP and CFO, James D. Hogan
EVP and Director Multi-Family and Investment CRE Lending, Kenneth A. Keiser
Senior Vice President and Director Consumer Lending, John (Jack) Ricca
Svp General Counsel And Corporate Secretary, Trudy Hackney
Executive Vice President And General Counsel, Glenn Yeager
Executive Vice President Market Chief Lending Officer, George Maroulis
Vice President of Operations, Richard (Dick) Kirk
Vice President Retail Banking Operations, Tim Monahan
Auditors: BDO USA LLP

LOCATIONS

HQ: Customers Bancorp Inc
1015 Penn Avenue, Suite 103, Wyomissing, PA 19610
Phone: 610 933-2000
Web: www.customersbank.com

COMPETITORS

Bank of America	Huntington Bancshares
Capital One	JPMorgan Chase
Citigroup	KeyCorp
Comerica	PNC Financial
Fifth Third	U.S. Bancorp
HSBC	Wells Fargo

HISTORICAL FINANCIALS
Company Type: Public

Income Statement
FYE: December 31

	ASSETS ($ mil.)	NET INCOME ($ mil.)	INCOME AS % OF ASSETS	EMPLOYEES
12/14	6,825	43	0.6%	426
12/13	4,153	32	0.8%	388
12/12	3,201	23	0.7%	255
12/11	2,077	4	0.2%	—
12/10	0	23	—	—
Annual Growth	**—**	**16.2%**	**—**	**—**

2014 Year-End Financials

Debt ratio: 2.90%
Return on equity: 10.42%
Cash ($ mil.): 371
Current ratio: —
Long-term debt ($ mil.): —

No. of shares (mil.): 26
Dividends
  Yield: —
  Payout: —
Market value ($ mil.): 520

	STOCK PRICE ($) FY Close	P/E High/Low		PER SHARE ($) Earnings	Dividends	Book Value
12/14	19.46	14	11	1.55	0.00	16.57
12/13	20.46	15	11	1.30	0.00	14.51
12/12	14.50	11	6	1.57	0.00	13.27
Annual Growth	**7.6%**	**—**	**—**	**(0.4%)**	**—**	**5.7%**

CVB Financial Corp.

CVB Financial is into the California Vibe Baby. The holding company's Citizens Business Bank offers community banking services to primarily small and midsized businesses but also to consumers through nearly 50 branch and office locations across central and southern California. Boasting more than $7 billion in assets the bank offers checking money market CDs and savings accounts trust and investment services and a variety of loans. Commercial real estate loans account for about two-thirds of the bank's loan portfolio which is rounded out by business consumer and construction loans; residential mortgages; dairy and livestock loans; and municipal lease financing.

Operations

In addition to its 40 business financial centers CVB operates seven Commercial Banking Centers (CBCs). The CBCs operate primarily as sales offices and focus on business clients professionals and high-net-worth individuals. The bank also has three trust offices.

Citizens Business Bank provides auto and equipment leasing and brokers mortgage loans through its Citizens Financial Services Division; CitizensTrust offers trust and investment services.Overall the bank made 63% of its total revenue from interest income on loans and leases in 2014 with another 24% of total revenue coming from interest income on the bank's investment securities. About 5% of total revenue came from service charges on deposit accounts and 3% came from trust and investment services income. Geographic ReachCVB Financial has 40 Business Financial Centers located in the Inland Empire Los Angeles County Orange County San Diego County and the Central Valley regions in California.Sales and MarketingCVB Financial provides services to companies from a variety of industries including: industrial and manufacturing dairy and livestock agriculture education nonprofit entertainment medical professional services title and escrow government and property management.

Financial Performance

CVB's revenue has been in decline in recent years due to shrinking interest margins on loans amidst the low-interest environment. The firm's profits however have been rising thanks to declining loan loss provisions as its loan portfolio's credit quality has been improving in the strengthening economy.CVB enjoyed a breakout year in 2014 with revenue rebounding by 12% to $289.32 million mostly thanks to higher interest income as the bank grew its loan and lease assets by 7% during the year and grew its investment security assets by 18%. Most of its loan growth came from commercial real estate loans while SFR mortgage loans consumer loans and construction loans also helped boost the company's top line. The bank's non-interest income also jumped by 44% during the year thanks to a $6 million gain on loans held-for-sale and a net $3.6 million decrease in its FDIC loss sharing asset.Higher revenue and a $16.1 million loan loss provision recapture in 2014 also drove the bank's net income higher by 9% to $104.02 million. Despite higher earnings for the year CVB's operating cash levels shrank by 22% to $87.70 million as the bank used more cash toward employee payments and income taxes.

Strategy

CVB Financial continues to seek out acquisitions of smaller banking trust and investment companies to grow its loan and deposit business as well as its geographic reach in key markets in (mostly Southern) California. With its 2014 acquisition of American Security Bank for example CVB boosted its assets by 6% to over $7 billion while adding branches in more than a handful of key markets in Southern California.

Remaining profitable throughout the economic downturn CVB Financial credits its success in part to its strict loan underwriting standards. The bank targets family-owned or other privately held businesses with annual revenues of up to $200 million with the goal of maintaining its client relationships for decades.Mergers and AcquisitionsIn March 2014 CVB Financial through its Citizens Business Bank (CBB) subsidiary purchased Southern California-based American Security Bank (the flagship subsidiary of American Bancshares) for a total of $57 million. The deal would add American Security Bank's $431 million in assets and boost CBB's branch presence across key markets in Newport Beach Corona Laguna Niguel Lancastar Victorville and Apple Valley.

Ownership

Chairman George Borba who led the founding of Citizens Business Bank owns about 11% of CVB Financial through a family trust.Company Background

In 2009 CVB Financial healthier than most California banks acquired the failed San Joaquin Bank after the FDIC took it over. The deal added five branches banking centers in the Bakersfield area.

EXECUTIVES

Senior Vice President And Regional Manager, Vince Gottuso

EVP and General Counsel CVB Financial Corporation and Citizens Business Bank, Richard H. Wohl, age 56

President CEO and Director CVB Financial and Citizens Business Bank, Christopher D. (Chris) Myers, age 52, $750,000 total compensation

EVP and CIO Information Technology Division, Elsa I. Zavala

EVP and Dairy and Livestock Industries Group Manager Citizens Business Bank, G. Larry Zivelonghi

SVP and Regional Manager Citizens Business Bank, David A. Brager, $189,116 total compensation

EVP and COO Citizens Business Bank, David C. Harvey

EVP and Chief Credit Officer Citizens Business Bank, James F. Dowd

EVP and CFO CVB Financial Corp. and Citizens Business Bank, Richard C. Thomas

EVP and Head of CitizensTrust, R. Daniel Banis

EVP and Chief Risk Officer Citizens Business Bank, Yamynn De Angelis

Vice President Relationship Manager, Nadine Ortega

Vice President Senior Product Manager, John (Jack) Outwater

Vice Chairman, George A. Borba, age 82

Chairman, Raymond V. OÅBrien

Auditors: KPMG LLP

LOCATIONS

HQ: CVB Financial Corp.
701 North Haven Ave., Suite 350, Ontario, CA 91764
Phone: 909 980-4030
Web: www.cbbank.com

Selected Branch Locations

Fresno County
Kern County
Los Angeles County
Madera County
Orange County
Riverside County
San Bernardino County
Tulare County

PRODUCTS/OPERATIONS

2014 Sales

	$ mil.	% of total
Interest		
Loans including fees	181	62
Investment securities	68	24
Other	2	1
Noninterest		
Service charges on deposit accounts	15	5
Trust & investment services	8	3
Bankcard services	3	1
BOLI income	2	1
Other	10	3
Adjustments	(3.6)	-
Total	**289**	**100**

COMPETITORS

Bank of America	Popular Inc.
Bank of the West	Provident Financial
City National	Holdings
Comerica	U.S. Bancorp
JPMorgan Chase	Wells Fargo
MUFG Americas Holdings	

HISTORICAL FINANCIALS

Company Type: Public

Income Statement

FYE: December 31

	ASSETS ($ mil.)	NET INCOME ($ mil.)	INCOME AS % OF ASSETS	EMPLOYEES
12/14	7,377	104	1.4%	—
12/13	6,664	95	1.4%	784
12/12	6,363	77	1.2%	810
12/11	6,482	81	1.3%	811
12/10	6,436	62	1.0%	819
Annual Growth	3.5%	13.4%	—	—

2014 Year-End Financials

Debt ratio: 0.97%	No. of shares (mil.): 105
Return on equity: 12.61%	Dividends
Cash ($ mil.): 132	Yield: 2.5%
Current ratio: —	Payout: 40.8%
Long-term debt ($ mil.): —	Market value ($ mil.): 1,696

	STOCK PRICE ($) FY Close	P/E High/Low	PER SHARE ($) Earnings	Dividends	Book Value
12/14	16.02	17 14	0.98	0.40	8.29
12/13	17.07	19 11	0.91	0.39	7.33
12/12	10.40	17 13	0.74	0.43	7.27
12/11	10.03	13 10	0.77	0.26	6.84
12/10	8.67	19 11	0.59	0.34	6.07
Annual Growth	16.6%	— —	13.5%	4.1%	8.1%

CVR Energy Inc

CVR Energy's CV says that it puts its energy into oil refining and ammonia production. It operates a 115000 barrels-per-day-throughput-capacity oil refinery in Coffeyville Kansas and a 70000 barrels-per day refinery in Oklahoma and a crude oil gathering system in Kansas and Oklahoma. CVR Energy's Coffeyville refinery has 1.4 million barrels of storage tanks and it also has 2.8 million barrels of leased storage capacity in Cushing Oklahoma. It has asphalt and refined fuels storage and terminalling plants in Phillipsburg Kansas. The company controls public traded CVR Refining (refining assets) and CVR Partners LP (a producer of ammonia and urea ammonium nitrate fertilizers).

Geographic Reach

The petroleum business focuses its Coffeyville petroleum product marketing efforts in the central Mid-continent and Rockies because of its proximity to the refinery and pipeline access also has access to the Rocky Mountain area. The company also directly supplies customers in close geographic proximity to the refinery through tanker trucks and customers at throughput terminals on the refined products distribution systems of Magellan and NuStar. The company has its headquarters in Texas and a presence in Kansas and Oklahoma.

Operations

The company has two businesses: Petroleum (the petroleum and related businesses operated by CVR Refining); and Nitrogen Fertilizer (the nitrogen fertilizer business operated by the CVR Partners). Most nitrogen fertilizer producers use more expensive natural gas. CVR Partners operates the only nitrogen fertilizer plant in North America that uses coke gasification (superheating using low cost petroleum coke to generate the hydrogen used in fertilizer production). About 85% of the company's nitrogen products are for agricultural use. e petroleum business accounted for 97% of total net sales in fiscal 2014 and the remaining was accounted for by its nitrogen business.

Sales and Marketing

Customers include other refiners convenience store chains railroads and farm cooperatives. CVR Energy's major customers include CHS Dyno Nobel MFA National Cooperative Refinery Association and Transammonia.In 2014 the company's top five ammonia customers accounted for 41% of the nitrogen fertilizer business' ammonia sales. The nitrogen fertilizer business' top two customers (Gavilon Fertilizer and United Suppliers) accounted for 17% and 10% respectively of the CVR Energy's nitrogen fertilizer business revenues.

Financial Performance

CVR Energy's net sales have been on an upward trend since 2010.In 2014 net sales increased by 1% due to higher sales from the petroleum business partially offset by lower nitrogen fertilizer sales.Petroleum sales grew due to higher overall sales volumes largely offset by lower sales prices for gasoline and distillates.Nitrogen fertilizer sales decreased by $25 million due to lower UAN sales prices a drop in ammonia sales volumes and lower ammonia sales prices partially offset by higher UAN sales volumes. In 2014 CVR Energy's net income decreased by $196.8 million due to higher products costs partially offset by increased sales. Consolidated cost of products sold increase of $502.8 million primarily resulting from an increase of $486.7 million in cost of petroleum products sold due to higher costs of consumed crude oil and higher refined fuels purchased for resale. The increase in consumed crude costs was due to higher consumed volumes.The nitrogen fertilizer segment cost of products sold increased by $13.9 million as a result of higher distribution costs due to increased railcar regulatory inspections and repairs and a growth in ammonia purchases.Net cash provided by the operating activities increased by 45% due to change in accounts receivable and inventories.

Strategy

Both the petroleum business and the nitrogen fertilizer business are considering pursuing acquisitions and expansion projects in order to continue to grow and increase profitability.

Company Background

To improve shareholder return and raise cash to pay down debt in 2013 CVR Energy spun off its refining assets as CVR Refining for about $600 million. The Nitrogen Fertilizer Partnership will continue to expand the nitrogen fertilizer business' existing asset base to execute its growth strategy. The growth strategy includes expanding produc-

tion of UAN and acquiring additional infrastructure and production assets. The Nitrogen Fertilizer Partnership completed a significant two-year plant expansion in 2013 which increased its UAN production capacity by 400000 tons or approximately 50% per year.

The UAN expansion provides the nitrogen fertilizer business with the ability to upgrade substantially all of its ammonia production to UAN. If the premium that UAN currently earns over ammonia decreases this expansion project may not yield the economic benefits and accretive effects that the nitrogen fertilizer business currently anticipates.

In 2012 investor Carl Icahn (and 82% owner) made a $2.6 billion bid to acquire CVR Energy claiming that it could be sold to a larger oil company for up to $7 billion. The board of directors and stockholders rejected the offer. (Icahn subsequently succeed in spinning off the refining unit).

In 2011 the company spun off its CVR Partners unit (formed in 2007 to operate its nitrogen fertilizer business) for $307 million.

Seeking to expand its refining base in 2011 the company acquired Denver-based independent Gary-Williams Energy and its Wynnewood Oklahoma refinery for $593 million. The refinery has the capacity to produce 70000 barrels per day of crude oil. With the acquisition CVR Energy bumped up its processing capacity to 185000 barrels per day.

The company traces its roots to the National Refining Company which in 1906 built a refinery in Coffeyville. The completed refinery was the second largest in the US at the time.

EXECUTIVES

Vice President Environmental Health Safety, Janice T Develasco

Vice President Corporate Communications, Steve Eames

Senior Vice President General Counsel Secretary, John (Jack) Walter

Vice President of Human Resources, Jerry Reed

Vice President Human Resources, Alicia Skalnik

Vice President Refined Products And Risk Management, Michael (Mel) Puddy

Vice President Logistics, Reed Copeland

Vice President And Chief Accounting Officer, Susan (Sue) Ball

Senior Vice President General Counsel and Secretary, Edmund S Gross

Vice President Economics and Planning, David (Dave) Landreth

Auditors: Grant Thornton LLP

LOCATIONS

HQ: CVR Energy Inc
 2277 Plaza Drive, Suite 500, Sugar Land, TX 77479
Phone: 281 207-3200
Web: www.cvrenergy.com

PRODUCTS/OPERATIONS

2014 Sales

	$ mil.	% of total
Petroleum	8,829	97
Nitrogen fertilizer	298	3
Adjustments	(18.9)	-
Total	**9,109**	**100**

COMPETITORS

Agrium	National Cooperative
CF Industries	Refinery Association
ConocoPhillips	Phillips 66
Flint Hills	Potash Corp
HollyFrontier	Sinclair Oil
Koch Industries Inc.	Valero Energy

HISTORICAL FINANCIALS

Company Type: Public

Income Statement

FYE: December 31

	REVENUE ($ mil.)	NET INCOME ($ mil.)	NET PROFIT MARGIN	EMPLOYEES
12/14	9,109	173	1.9%	1,298
12/13	8,985	370	4.1%	1,192
12/12	8,567	378	4.4%	1,091
12/11	5,029	345	6.9%	764
12/10	4,079	14	0.4%	695
Annual Growth	22.2%	86.8%	—	16.9%

2014 Year-End Financials

Debt ratio: 19.49%
Return on equity: 15.98%
Cash ($ mil.): 753
Current ratio: 3.44
Long-term debt ($ mil.): 673

No. of shares (mil.): 86
Dividends
 Yield: 12.9%
 Payout: 221.2%
Market value ($ mil.): 3,361

	STOCK PRICE ($) FY Close	P/E High/Low		PER SHARE ($) Earnings	Dividends	Book Value
12/14	38.71	25	18	2.00	5.00	11.38
12/13	43.43	16	8	4.27	14.25	13.69
12/12	48.79	11	5	4.33	0.00	17.56
12/11	18.73	7	4	3.94	0.00	13.27
12/10	15.18	90	40	0.16	0.00	7.98
Annual Growth	26.4%	—	—	88.0%	—	9.3%

CVR Refining, LP

Oil refinery Coffeyville Resources may be located in Coffeyville Kansas but new parent CVR Refining is thinking "We're not just in Kansas anymore." CVR Refining was formed by CVR Energy in September 2012 as an indirect wholly owned subsidiary to take over its downstream operations. CVR Refining is taking ownership of the 115000 barrels-per-day Coffeyville refinery and a 70000 barrels-per-day refinery in Wynnewood Oklahoma both of which are not too far from a crude oil hub at Cushing Oklahoma. In addition CVR Refining will control 350 miles of pipeline 125 oil tanker trucks tank farms and 6 million barrels of storage capacity. CVR Refining went public in 2013 with an offering worth $600 million.

IPO

The company is using proceeds from the IPO to pay down debt for Coffeyville Resources fund capital expenditures through 2014 and pay for maintenance and upgrades to the Wynnewood refinery. (CVR Energy bought Gary-Williams Energy Corporation the owner of the Wynnewood refinery in December 2011 for $525 million).

Sales and Marketing

CVR Refining's customers include retailers railroads and farm cooperatives. Generally customers in the energy industry are not tied to long-term contracts as the price of commodities always changes. But the top five customers for the Coffeyville refinery accounted for about half of its sales in 2011. At the Wynnewood refinery the top five customers made up about 35% of sales.

Financial Performance

With the cost of a barrel of oil steadily on the rise CVR Refining saw revenues for its refinery operations grow in 2012 by 74% due to higher overall sales volume and higher product prices. The higher sales volume included a full year of Wynnewood refinery revenues.

In 2012 the company's net income increased by 24% as the huge increase net sales outpaced higher operating costs.

Ownership

CVR Refining is controlled by subsidiaries of CVR Energy.

Strategy

CVR Energy created CVR Refining LP in order to reduce risk and tax obligations. CVR Refining LP is organized as a Delaware limited partnership which means it isn't personally liable for any of the partnership's debt. That responsibility falls to the general partner CVR Refining GP LLC which is owned by CVR Refining Holdings LLC another indirect subsidiary of CVR Energy. With all roads leading back to CVR Energy the risk to CVR Refining LP is limited. CVR Refining LP is exempt from paying federal income tax. Previously CVR Energy organized its fertilizer operations as CVR Partners under the same concept. CVR Partners went public in April 2011.

EXECUTIVES

Vice President Crude Oil Supply, Bill Copeland
Executive Vice President Refining Operations, Robert (Bob) Haugen
Vice President Economics Planning, David (Dave) Landreth
Auditors: Grant Thornton LLP

LOCATIONS

HQ: CVR Refining, LP
2277 Plaza Drive, Suite 500, Sugar Land, TX 77479
Phone: 281 207-3200
Web: www.cvrrefining.com

PRODUCTS/OPERATIONS

2012 Sales

	% of total
Gasoline	52
Distillate	43
Other	5
Total	**100**

COMPETITORS

BP	Marathon Petroleum
Blueknight Energy	Motiva Enterprises
Partners	National Cooperative
Chevron	Refinery Association
El Dorado Refinery	Phillips 66
Exxon Mobil	Shell Oil Products
HollyFrontier	Valero Energy

HISTORICAL FINANCIALS

Company Type: Public

Income Statement

FYE: December 31

	REVENUE ($ mil.)	NET INCOME ($ mil.)	NET PROFIT MARGIN	EMPLOYEES
12/14	8,829	358	4.1%	982
12/13	8,683	590	6.8%	891
12/12*	8,281	595	7.2%	832
09/12	0	0	—	800
12/11	4,752	480	10.1%	—
Annual Growth	**22.9%**	**(9.3%)**	**—**	**—**

*Fiscal year change

2014 Year-End Financials

Debt ratio: 24.05%	No. of shares (mil.): 147
Return on equity: —	Dividends
Cash ($ mil.): 370	Yield: 17.4%
Current ratio: 2.31	Payout: 121.0%
Long-term debt ($ mil.): 580	Market value ($ mil.): 2,480

	STOCK PRICE ($) FY Close	P/E High/Low		PER SHARE ($) Earnings	Dividends	Book Value
12/14	16.80	12	7	2.43	2.93	9.82
12/13	22.62	10	6	3.47	3.23	10.31
Annual Growth	(9.4%)	—	—	(11.2%)	(3.2%)	(1.6%)

CVS Health Corporation

Size matters to CVS Health Corp. (formerly CVS Caremark) the nation's #2 drugstore chain and a leading pharmacy benefits manager with nearly 65 million plan members. With more than 7800 retail and specialty drugstores under the CVS Navarro and Longs Drug banners it trails rival Walgreen (8300) in store count. In addition to its stand alone pharmacy operations the company operates CVS locations inside Target stores and runs a prescription management company Caremark Pharmacy Services. The growing company also offers walk-in health services through its retail network of MinuteClinics that are located in more than 900 CVS stores. In mid-2015 it acquired Omnicare in a $12.7 billion mega deal.

HISTORY

Brothers Stanley and Sid Goldstein who ran health and beauty products distributor Mark Steven branched out into retail in 1963 when they opened up their first Consumer Value Store in Lowell Massachusetts with partner Ralph Hoagland.

The chain grew rapidly amassing 17 stores by the end of 1964 (the year the CVS name was first used) and 40 by 1969. That year the Goldsteins sold the chain to Melville Shoe to finance further expansion.

Melville had been founded in 1892 by shoe supplier Frank Melville. Melville's son Ward grew the company creating the Thom McAn shoe store chain and later buying its supplier. By 1969 Melville had opened shoe shops in Kmart stores (through its Meldisco unit) launched one apparel chain (Chess King sold in 1993) and purchased another (Foxwood Stores renamed Foxmoor and sold in 1985).

In 1972 CVS bought the 84-store Clinton Drug and Discount a Rochester New York-based chain. Two years later when sales hit $100 million CVS had 232 stores —only 45 of which had pharmacies. The company bought New Jersey-based Mack Drug (36 stores) in 1977. By 1981 CVS had more than 400 stores.

CVS's sales hit $1 billion in 1985 as it continued to add pharmacies to many of its older stores. In 1987 Stanley's success was recognized companywide when he was named chairman and CEO of CVS's parent company which by then had been renamed Melville.

CVS bought the 490-store Peoples Drug Stores chain from Imasco in 1990 giving it locations in Maryland Pennsylvania Virginia West Virginia and Washington DC. CVS created PharmaCare Management Services in 1994 to take advantage of the growing market for pharmacy services and managed-care drug programs. Pharmacist Tom Ryan was named CEO that year.

With CVS outperforming Melville's other operations in 1995 Melville decided to concentrate on the drugstore chain. By that time Melville's holdings had grown to include discount department store chain Marshalls and furniture chain This End Up both sold in 1995; footwear chain Footaction spun off as part of Footstar in 1996 along with Meldisco; the Linens 'n Things chain spun off in 1996; the Kay-Bee Toys chain sold in 1996; and Bob's Stores (apparel and footwear) sold in 1997.

Melville was renamed CVS in late 1996. Amid major consolidation in the drugstore industry in 1997 CVS —then with about 1425 stores —paid $3.7 billion for Revco D.S. which had nearly 2600 stores in 17 states mainly in the Midwest and Southeast. The next year the company bought Arbor Drugs (200 stores in Michigan later converted to the CVS banner) for nearly $1.5 billion.

CVS opened about 180 new stores and relocated nearly 200 in 1998 as it shifted from strip malls to freestanding stores. (It also closed nearly 160 stores.) Stanley retired as chairman in 1999 and was succeeded by Ryan.

In 1999 the company bought online drugstore pioneer Soma.com renamed CVS.com. It also launched the CVS ProCare pharmacy to serve customers in need of complex drug therapies. A year later CVS bought Stadtlander Pharmacy of Pittsburgh from Bergen Brunswig (now Amerisource-Bergen) for $124 million.

In early 2001 Wolverine Equities paid $288 million for 96 stores which CVS said it would continue to operate. In 2001 CVS opened 43 stores in new markets including Miami and Fort Lauderdale Florida; Las Vegas; and Dallas Houston and Fort Worth Texas. As part of a strategic restructuring begun in 2001 CVS closed more than 200 stores and moved others from strip malls to freestanding locations.

In July 2002 CVS was among the winning bidders for the remaining assets of bankrupt rival Phar-Mor. CVS acquired the majority of Phar-Mor's prescription lists. In October CVS named KB Toys as the exclusive toy supplier to its drugstores. CVS opened 266 new stores in 2002 and another 150 new stores in 2003.

In April 2003 specialty pharmacy division CVS ProCare changed its name to PharmaCare Specialty Pharmacy.

With those store closings behind it the drugstore chain began opening stores in Minneapolis the 10th-largest drugstore market in the US in 2004. CVS opened about 10 stores in the Los Angeles area in 2004 marking the drugstore chain's return to Southern California after a 12-year absence. CVS is also targeting other high-traffic markets including Chicago Florida Las Vegas Phoenix and Texas for expansion.

In July 2004 CVS completed the acquisition of 1260 Eckerd stores Eckerd Health Services (which included Eckerd's $1 billion mail order and pharmacy benefits management businesses) and three distribution centers from J. C. Penney Company for $2.15 billion. The acquisition of the Eckerd stores (622 in Florida) gave CVS more stores than archrival Walgreen. CVS completed the conversion of Eckerd stores in Alabama Arizona Colorado Florida Kansas Louisiana Mississippi Missouri New Mexico Oklahoma and Texas to its own banner within about a year.

In June 2005 CVS agreed to pay $110 million to settle a shareholders' lawsuit filed in 2001 that alleged the company had made misleading statements to artificially raise its stock price and violated accounting practices. CVS denied the charges and said the settlement was "purely a business decision."

In June 2006 CVS completed the acquisition of some 700 stand-alone Sav-On and Osco drugstores from Albertson's. CVS was part of a consortium that bought the nation's #2 supermarket chain and split it up amongst themselves. The transaction gave CVS access to Southern California and key Midwest markets. In September the company purchased the retail-based health clinic operator MinuteClinic for an undisclosed amount. The acquisition allowed CVS to provide in-store care to its customers for minor ailments.

In March 2007 CVS changed its name to CVS Caremark Corporation following its acquisition of the pharmacy benefits manager Caremark RX after months of bidding between CVS and Express Scripts. Ultimately CVS paid about $26.5 billion for Caremark. In November CEO Ryan added the chairman's title to his job description following the retirement of Mac Crawford.

In October 2008 CVS Caremark acquired Longs Drug Stores for about $2.9 billion. Longs Drug operates 521 pharmacies in California Hawaii Nevada and Arizona. The purchase included Long's Rx America subsidiary a pharmacy benefits management service to more than 8 million members. Also in 2008 the company opened about 190 new retail pharmacies.

In 2008 CVS settled a lawsuit regarding drug-switching allegations for $36.7 million. The company had been accused of switching Medicaid customers to a more expensive capsule form of Zantac from a tablet form; CVS denied the allegations.

In June 2009 CVS agreed to pay almost $1 million to settle allegations stemming from the sale of expired OTC medications infant formula and dairy products.

CVS Caremark in early 2011 won a contract to administer Aetna's retail pharmacy network. CVS Caremark is managing both purchasing and prescription filling for Aetna's mail-order and specialty pharmacy operations. Prior to his retirement in May 2011 Ryan assumed the title of non-executive chairman in March when Larry Merlo took over as president and CEO of CVS.

In 2012 CVS opened drugstores in four new states: Arkansas Colorado Oregon and Washington.

In September 2014 the company changed its name to CVS Health Corporation to reflect its broader commitment to health care. The corporate name change coincided with the cessation of tobacco sales at its retail stores in September.

EXECUTIVES

EVP Health Plans, Tracy L. Bahl, age 52
President and CEO, Larry J. Merlo, age 59, $1,350,000 total compensation
EVP; President CVS/pharmacy, Helena B. Foulkes, age 50, $850,000 total compensation
SVP and CIO, Stephen J. Gold, age 56
EVP, Per G. H. Lofberg, age 67, $900,000 total compensation
EVP Pharmaceutical Contracting Purchasing and Network Administration, Matthew J. Leonard
EVP and Chief Human Resources Officer, Lisa Bisaccia, age 59
EVP Specialty Pharmacy CVS/caremark, Alan M. Lotvin, age 53
EVP and Chief Medical Officer, Troyen A. Brennan, age 61, $637,500 total compensation
EVP Retail Operations, Scott Baker
EVP; President CVS/caremark, Jonathan C. Roberts, age 59, $900,000 total compensation
EVP and CFO, David M. (Dave) Denton, age 50, $825,000 total compensation
EVP and Associate Chief Medical Officer; President CVS/minuteclinic, Andrew J. (Andy) Sussman, age 49
EVP Sales and Marketing CVS/caremark, J. David Joyner, age 50
EVP Chief Health Strategy Officer and General Counsel, Thomas M. Moriarty, age 52, $670,000 total compensation
EVP Strategy Corporate Development and Government Affairs, Mary Langowski

SVP Corporate Social Responsibility and Philanthropy; President CVS Health Foundation, Eileen Howard Boone
EVP Pharmacy Services, Joshua (Josh) Flum
Vice President Of Information Technology, Jennifer (Jen) Davin
Vice President Government Services Information Technology, Roshan Navagamuwa
Executive Vice President Sales and Marketing Cvs Caremark, David J (Dave) Joyner
Auditors: Ernst & Young LLP

LOCATIONS

HQ: CVS Health Corporation
One CVS Drive, Woonsocket, RI 02895
Phone: 401 765-1500   **Fax:** 401 762-2137
Web: www.cvshealth.com

PRODUCTS/OPERATIONS

2013 Retail Sales

	% of total
Prescription drugs	69
Over-the-counter & personal care	11
Beauty/cosmetics	5
General merchandise & other	15
Total	**100**

2013 Sales

	% of total
Pharmacy services	54
Retail pharmacy	46
Adjustments	-
Total	**100**

COMPETITORS

A&P	Kroger
Aetna	MedImpact
Ahold U.S.A.	Medicine Shoppe
Anthem	OptumRx
BioScrip	Prime Therapeutics
CIGNA	Rite Aid
Costco Wholesale	Target Corporation
Express Scripts	UnitedHealth Group
H-E-B	Wal-Mart
Humana	Walgreen
Kmart	

HISTORICAL FINANCIALS

Company Type: Public

Income Statement

FYE: December 31

	REVENUE ($ mil.)	NET INCOME ($ mil.)	NET PROFIT MARGIN	EMPLOYEES
12/15	153,290	5,237	3.4%	243,000
12/14	139,367	4,644	3.3%	297,800
12/13	126,761	4,592	3.6%	286,000
12/12	123,133	3,877	3.1%	280,000
12/11	107,100	3,461	3.2%	280,000
Annual Growth	**9.4%**	**10.9%**	**—**	**(3.5%)**

2015 Year-End Financials

Debt ratio: 29.32%	No. of shares (mil.): 1,101
Return on equity: 13.94%	Dividends
Cash ($ mil.): 2,459	Yield: 1.4%
Current ratio: 1.31	Payout: 31.5%
Long-term debt ($ mil.): 26,267	Market value ($ mil.): 107,645

	STOCK PRICE ($) FY Close	P/E High/Low		PER SHARE ($) Earnings	Dividends	Book Value
12/15	97.77	24	20	4.63	1.40	33.78
12/14	96.31	25	16	3.96	1.10	33.30
12/13	71.57	19	13	3.74	0.90	32.15
12/12	48.35	16	14	3.03	0.65	30.63
12/11	40.78	16	12	2.57	0.50	29.32
Annual Growth	**24.4%**	—	—	**15.9%**	**29.4%**	**3.6%**

Dana Holding Corp

When it comes to building cars it starts with the parts and Dana makes the parts that carmakers use to piece together new vehicles. In addition to its core offerings which include driveline products (axles driveshafts transmissions) it provides power technologies (sealing thermal-management products) and service parts. It makes products for vehicles in the light medium/heavy (commercial) and off-highway markets. The company's products carry brand names that include Spicer Victor Reinz and Long. Dana also supplies companies that make commercial and off-highway vehicles such as Deere Navistar Ford and PACCAR.

Geographic Reach

Dana manufactures its products in about 100 facilities in 26 countries in North America Europe South America and Asia/Pacific. The company also has engineering centers located throughout the world.

North America accounts for 47% of its revenue while Europe contributes 30%. South America generates around 12% and the Asia/Pacific region accounts for the remaining amount.

Operations

Dana divides its operations across four business segments: Light vehicle driveline (38% of total sales in 2014) commercial vehicle (27%) off-highway (19%) and power technologies (16%).

Sales and Marketing

Ford accounted for 18% of Dana's total revenue in 2014 while PACCAR accounted for 9%. Other large customers include OEMs such Hyundai Tata Motors and Volkswagen AG.

Financial Performance

Dana's revenues have gradually dropped the last several years declining 2% from $6.8 billion in 2013 to $6.7 billion in 2014. Profits however climbed 31% from $244 million to $319 million over that same time period due to lower expenses. The company's operating cash flows decreased by 11% to $510 million in 2014 due to cash outflows incurred from accounts receivable and inventories.

The 2014 revenue decline was fueled by international currency fluctuations along with weaker demand in the company's global off-highway business and the South America medium and heavy truck market. Light vehicle sales also fell by 2% mostly due to unfavorable exchange rates.

Strategy

Desiring to reduce its dependence on any one geographic market the company is expanding into growth regions with a particular emphasis on the Asia/Pacific region especially India and China. In 2014 it invested roughly $30 million to open its 15th facility in India. The new center supports Dana's Indian operations along with other markets like Europe Thailand Australia Indonesia and other parts of the US.

EXECUTIVES

EVP and CFO, William G. (Bill) Quigley, age 53, $615,000 total compensation
President Light Vehicle Driveline Technologies, Robert (Bob) Pyle, age 48
EVP and Group President On-Highway Driveline Technologies, Mark E. Wallace, age 48, $565,000 total compensation
President and CEO, James K. (Jim) Kamsickas
Chief Technical and Quality Officer, George T. Constand, age 56
President Off-Highway Technologies, Aziz S. Aghili, age 56, $460,000 total compensation
Chief Administrative Officer, Jeffrey S. (Jeff) Bowen, age 57, $475,000 total compensation

President Power Technologies, Dwayne E.
Matthews, age 55
Vice President Finance Chief Accounting Officer,
Rodney (Rod) Filcek
Senior Vice President Human Resources, Ari
Papadakos
Vice President Operations, Ed Kopkowski
Chairman, Joseph C. (Joe) Muscari, age 68
Auditors: PricewaterhouseCoopers LLP

LOCATIONS

HQ: Dana Holding Corp
    3939 Technology Drive, Maumee, OH 43537
Phone: 419 887-3000   Fax: 419 887-5200
Web: www.dana.com

2014 Sales

	$ mil.	% of total
North America	3,126	47
Europe	1,978	30
South America	771	12
Asia/Pacific	742	11
Total	**6,617**	**100**

PRODUCTS/OPERATIONS

2014 Sales

	$ mil.	% of total
Light vehicle driveline	2,496	38
Commercial vehicle	1,838	28
Off-highway	1,231	18
Power technologies	1,052	16
Total	**6,617**	**100**

Selected Products

Automotive (light vehicle driveline)
  Axles (front and rear)
  Differentials
  Driveshafts
  Modular assemblies
  Side rails
  Torque couplings
Commercial vehicle (medium-heavy)
  Axles
  Driveshafts
  Steering shafts
  Suspension and tire management systems
Off-highway
  Axles
  Driveshafts
  Electronic controls
  Torque converters
  Transaxles
  Transmissions
Power technologies
  Cooling and heat transfer
  Cover modules
  Engine sealing systems
  Heat shields
  Gaskets
Structures (for light and medium/heavy)
  Cradles
  Frames
  Side rails

COMPETITORS

AISIN World Corp.
American Axle &
  Manufacturing
AxleTech International
Boler
BorgWarner
Carraro
DENSO
Dayco Products
ElringKlinger
FCA US
Federal-Mogul
Freudenberg-NOK
GKN
Hitachi Automotive
  Systems Americas

Magna International
Mahle International
Martinrea
  International
Meritor
Metaldyne
Modine Manufacturing
Neapco
Tower International
Valeo
Visteon
Wanxiang
ZF Friedrichshafen

HISTORICAL FINANCIALS

Company Type: Public

Income Statement

FYE: December 31

	REVENUE ($ mil.)	NET INCOME ($ mil.)	NET PROFIT MARGIN	EMPLOYEES
12/14	6,617	319	4.8%	22,600
12/13	6,769	244	3.6%	23,000
12/12	7,224	300	4.2%	23,300
12/11	7,592	219	2.9%	24,500
12/10	6,109	10	0.2%	22,500
Annual Growth	**2.0%**	**137.7%**	**—**	**0.1%**

2014 Year-End Financials

Debt ratio: 34.04%
Return on equity: 26.71%
Cash ($ mil.): 1,121
Current ratio: 2.34
Long-term debt ($ mil.): 1,613

No. of shares (mil.): 164
Dividends
  Yield: 0.9%
  Payout: 13.7%
Market value ($ mil.): 3,576

	STOCK PRICE ($) FY Close	P/E High/Low		Earnings	PER SHARE ($) Dividends	Book Value
12/14	21.74	12	9	1.84	0.20	6.57
12/13	19.62	—	—	(0.09)	0.20	9.01
12/12	15.61	9	6	1.40	0.20	12.43
12/11	12.15	15	8	1.02	0.00	11.79
12/10	17.21	—	—	(0.16)	0.00	11.69
Annual Growth	**6.0%**			**—**	**—**	**—(13.4%)**

Danaher Corp.

Danaher is a well-diversified industrial and medical conglomerate whose products test analyze and diagnose. Its subsidiaries design manufacture and market products and offer services geared at worldwide professional medical industrial and commercial markets. Danaher operates through five segments: Life Sciences & Diagnostics (research and clinical tools) Test & Measurement (electronic measurement instruments) Industrial Technologies (product identification motion control equipment and sensors) Environmental (turbine pumps and air/water analysis and treatment equipment) and Dental (orthodontic bracket systems and lab products).

Change in Company Type

Danaher agreed to acquire Pall Corporation a major supplier of filtration separation and purification technologies for $13.8 billion in mid-2015. Upon completion of the deal Danaher plans to separate the combined company into two independent publicly traded companies: a science and technology company which will retain the Danaher name (and will include Pall); and a diversified industrial company which will comprise Danaher's test and measurement instruments operations.

Geographic Reach

Danaher has around 270 manufacturing and distribution facilities worldwide. Almost 140 of these facilities are located in the US in more than 25 states; roughly 130 locations reside outside the US in over 50 other countries throughout Asia Europe North America South America and Australia. The company generates almost half of its revenue from North America primarily the US (43% of sales).

Operations

Built largely through acquisitions Danaher's five business segments reflect a well balanced portfolio. Top segments Life Sciences and Test & Meas-

urement accounted for 36% and 18% of revenues in fiscal 2014 respectively. Life Sciences products include imaging systems acute care equipment (blood gas measurement devices) pathology diagnostics (tissue embedding and chemical reagents) and instrumentation (microscopes).

Key Danaher subsidiaries include Beckman Coulter Matco Tools Corporation Jacobs Vehicle Systems Tektronix X-Rite EskoArtwork Linx Printing Technologies Fluke Corporation Keithley Instruments Sybron Dental Specialties Trojan Technologies Gems Sensors Gilbarco and Sea-Bird Electronics.

Financial Performance

Danaher has enjoyed five straight years of unprecedented growth. Its revenues rose by 4% from $19.1 billion in 2013 to peak at a record-setting $19.9 billion in 2014. Profits remained relatively flat however falling 4% from $2.7 billion in 2013 to $2.6 billion in 2014 due to higher income taxes and the selling of certain marketable equity securities. The company's operating cash flow has also trended upwards the last few years rising 5% in 2014.

The company's historic growth for 2014 was led by a 7% increase in Environmental segment sales resulting from growth in analytical instrumentation product lines in North America China Europe and Latin America. Life Sciences & Diagnostics sales spiked 5% due to growth in demand of its existing businesses across China and other high-growth markets along with additional revenue from a previous acquisition. Dental segment sales also grew 5% resulting from increased demand for imaging products instruments and implant products along with modest growth in dental consumables.

Strategy

Already its top segment Danaher is working to get an even larger foothold in the life sciences sector whose growth is being driven by such factors as aging populations increased preventive health care and US health care reforms. It is also seeking opportunities to beef up its industrial business. To this end Danaher uses a combination of divestitures and acquisitions.

In its largest potential acquisition to date Danaher agreed to acquire Pall Corporation a major supplier of filtration separation and purification technologies for $13.8 billion in mid-2015. Upon completion of the deal Pall will operate as a subsidiary in Danaher's portfolio and will maintain its brand. Danaher also has announced its intention to separate the combined company into two independent publicly traded companies: a science and technology company which will retain the Danaher name (and will include Pall); and a diversified industrial company which will comprise Danaher's test and measurement instruments operations.

In 2015 Danaher purchased Nobel Biocare Holding for $2.2 billion. The deal is expected to significantly widen Danaher's market presence in the global dental industry. Headquartered in Zurich Switzerland Nobel Biocare serves customers in 80 markets globally supplying dental implant systems high-precision individualized prosthetics and biomaterials and digital diagnostics products.

Danaher sold most of its communications unit —composed of Tektronics Fluke Networks and Arbor Networks —to NetScout in 2014.

HISTORY

Danaher (from the Celtic word dana meaning "swift flowing") is named for a fishing stream off the Flathead River in Montana. The term is also an appropriate description of the spotlight-averse Rales brothers. The two have proven to be fishers not only of trout but also of companies buying underperforming companies with strong market shares and recognizable brand names.

Once dubbed "raiders in short pants" by Forbes Steven and Mitchell Rales began making acquisitions in their 20s. In 1981 they bought their father's 50% stake in Master Shield a maker of vinyl building products. The brothers bought tire manufacturer Mohawk Rubber the following year. In 1983 they acquired control of publicly traded DMG a distressed Florida real-estate firm; the next year they sold DMG's real estate holdings and folded Mohawk and Master Shield into the company which they renamed Danaher.

EXECUTIVES

Senior Vice President, Henk Van Duijnhoven
EVP and CFO, Daniel L. Comas, age 52, $782,250 total compensation
President and CEO, Thomas P. Joyce, age 55, $847,585 total compensation
President Fluke Corporation, James A. (Jim) Lico, age 50, $661,500 total compensation
EVP, William K. (Dan) Daniel, age 50, $650,000 total compensation
Vice President Global Procurement, Bob Mahlik
Group Vice President Finance Chief Financial Officer, Henry (Hal) Carroll
Vice President Finance, Emily Weaver
Vice President Compensation, Joe Cavallaro
Vice President Supply Chain Management, Mike Sandridge
Vice President Internal Audit, Christopher Sandberg
Vice President Environment Health, Stephen Evanoff
Vice President Global Benefits and Human Resources Mergers and Acquisitions, Rich King
Vice President Human Resources, Angie Lalor
Vice President Investor Relations, Matthew (Matt) Gugino
Vice President Finance Automation, Mike Morrison
Group Vice President Finance, Dave Bergmann
Chairman, Steven M. Rales, age 64
Auditors: Ernst & Young LLP

LOCATIONS

HQ: Danaher Corp.
2200 Pennsylvania Avenue, N.W., Suite 800W, Washington, DC 20037-1701
Phone: 202 828-0850   **Fax:** 202 828-0860
Web: www.danaher.com

2013 Sales

	$ mil.	% of total
US	8,109	42
China	1,631	9
Germany	1,182	6
Japan	777	4
Other countries	7,416	39
Total	**19,118**	**100**

PRODUCTS/OPERATIONS

2013 Sales by Segment

	$ mil.	% of total
Life sciences & diagnostics	6,856	36
Industrial technologies	3,432	18
Test & measurement	3,417	18
Environmental	3,316	17
Dental	2,094	11
Total	**19,118**	**100**

2013 Sales by Product Group

	$ mil.	% of total
Medical & dental products	8,958	47
Analytical & physical instrumentation	6,278	33
Motion & industrial automation controls	1,559	8
Product identification	1,551	8
Other	770	4
Total	**19,118**	**100**

Selected Mergers & Acquisitions
FY2012

X-Rite Incorporated ($625 million; Grand Rapids Michigan; provider of color-science products that include spectrophotometers and colorimeter)
IRIS International Inc. ($338 million; Chatsworth California; automated in-vitro diagnostic systems maker)
FY2011
EskoArtwork ($470 million; Belgium; printing and packaging software provider)
Beckman Coulter Inc. ($5.8 billion; Brea California; diagnostic testing systems and supplies)
FY2010
Genetix Group PLC ($82 million; UK; cell imaging and screening systems maker)
Keithley Instruments Inc. ($300 million; Solon Ohio; digital multimeters semiconductor parametric test and device characterization systems signal analyzers and generators)

Selected Products
Color measurement
  Color formulation (ColorMail)
  Colorimeters (color accuracy testing)
  Densitometers (optical and photographic density measurement)
  Ink formulations software
  Paint matching systems
  Sensitometers (photographic exposure control)
Dental
  Digital imaging
  Implant systems
  Impression bonding and restorative materials
  Infection control products
  Orthodontic brackets and lab products
Environmental
  Analytical instruments
  Fuel dispensers
  Monitoring and leak detection systems
  Submersible turbine pumps
  Ultraviolet disinfection systems
  Vapor recovery equipment
  Water treatment systems
Industrial Technologies
  Aerospace and defense
  Electrical power generation systems
  Electronic security systems
  Smoke detection and fire suppression
  Submarine periscopes and related sensors
  Motion
  Controls
  Drives
  Mechanical components (linear bearings clutches/brakes and linear actuators)
  Standard and custom motors
  Product identification equipment
  Sensors and controls
  Monitoring and control instruments (temperature position quantity level flow and time)
Life Sciences & Diagnostics
  Acute care
  Blood gas and immunochemistry instruments (Radiometer brand)
  Life sciences instrumentation
  Compound microscopes
  Laser scanning
  Pathology diagnostics
  Chemical and immuno-staining instruments
  Slide coverslipping
  Tissue embedding
Test and Measurement
  Video test measurement and monitoring products
Tools and Components
  Mechanics hand tools

COMPETITORS

ABB	Parker-Hannifin
Bosch Rexroth Corp.	PerkinElmer
Datamax-O' Neil	Rockwell Automation
Emerson Electric	SPX
GE	Schneider Electric
Greenlee Textron	Siemens Water
Hitachi	Technologies
Johnson & Johnson	Snap-on
Medical	Stanley Black and
Johnson Controls	Decker
Labfacility	Thermo Fisher
Makita	Scientific
Mettler-Toledo	Wayne

HISTORICAL FINANCIALS
Company Type: Public

Income Statement
FYE: December 31

	REVENUE ($ mil.)	NET INCOME ($ mil.)	NET PROFIT MARGIN	EMPLOYEES
12/14	19,913	2,598	13.0%	71,000
12/13	19,118	2,695	14.1%	66,000
12/12	18,260	2,392	13.1%	63,000
12/11	16,090	2,172	13.5%	59,000
12/10	13,202	1,793	13.6%	48,200
Annual Growth	**10.8%**	**9.7%**	**—**	**10.2%**

2014 Year-End Financials

Debt ratio: 9.39%
Return on equity: 11.36%
Cash ($ mil.): 3,005
Current ratio: 1.75
Long-term debt ($ mil.): 3,401

No. of shares (mil.): 704
Dividends
  Yield: 0.4%
  Payout: 11.0%
Market value ($ mil.): 60,366

	STOCK PRICE ($) FY Close	P/E High/Low		PER SHARE ($) Earnings	Dividends	Book Value
12/14	85.71	24	19	3.63	0.40	33.19
12/13	77.20	20	14	3.80	0.10	32.07
12/12	55.90	16	14	3.36	0.10	27.66
12/11	47.04	17	13	3.11	0.09	24.58
12/10	47.17	32	13	2.64	0.08	20.89
Annual Growth	**16.1%**	**—**	**—**	**8.3%**	**49.5%**	**12.3%**

Darden Restaurants, Inc.

Darden Restaurants is the #1 casual-dining operator (in terms of revenue) with about 1535 restaurants in the US and Canada. Its flagship chain is Italian-themed concept Olive Garden. Olive Garden caters to families by offering mid-priced menu items themed interiors and primarily suburban locations. Darden also operates the LongHorn Steakhouse chain with about 430 outlets. Other dining concepts include The Capital Grille (upscale steakhouse) Bahama Breeze (Caribbean food and drinks) and Seasons 52 (casual grill and wine bar). In 2015 it spun off a chunk of its real estate portfolio as Four Corners Property Trust; the portfolio includes about 425 US restaurants that are all leased to Darden subsidiaries.

Geographic Reach

Darden is looking outside of the US for growth including plans to develop Olive Garden and Long-Horn Steakhouse locations in Brazil Colombia the Dominican Republic Panama and Puerto Rico. Most of the company's international growth emphasis has been on its Olive Garden and LongHorn Steakhouse chains. Darden has been remodeling many of its domestic Olive Garden and LongHorn Steakhouse units in lieu of adding new locations.

Sales and Marketing

Olive Garden has come to epitomize the chain restaurant experience. Olive Garden offer a version Italian cuisine designed for mass appeal and affordability.

Darden spends heavily on research and development in order to roll out a succession of new menu items that are heavily promoted through television advertising. The chains also utilize discount pricing and special offers to win business against the competition including Applebee's Chili's (operated by Brinker International) and Outback Steakhouse (OSI Restaurant Partners).

Financial Performance

During fiscal 2015 Darden's revenue increased by 8% to almost $6.7 billion compared to $6.2 billion in fiscal 2014. The increase in revenue was primarily due to the addition of 33 new company-owned restaurants and a same-restaurant sales increase at most of the company's locations. Olive Garden's sales increase for fiscal 2015 was driven by revenue from nine new locations while Long-Horn Steakhouse's sales increase during fiscal 2015 was driven by revenue from 16 new restaurants.

Darden's net income has been declining in recent fiscal years. However the company's net income increased by 148% to $709.5 million in fiscal 2015 compared to a net income of $286.2 million in fiscal 2014. The increased net income was primarily due to the company's increased gross annual revenue.

Strategy

Darden has built its dining empire without the aid of franchising a strategy that allows the company the highest degree of control for maintaining food and service quality. The major downside is the cost of operating and maintaining all those restaurants. The company is constantly focused on improving margins by negotiating lower prices for food and other ingredients and by adjusting its workforce to reduce labor costs.

The recession of recent years has posed serious challenges for most casual dining operators but Darden's chains fared better than some of the company's competitors thanks to intense customer loyalty. The company did sell off the struggling Red Lobster chain to focus more on getting Olive Garden back to growth and profitability.

Darden has also been working to consolidate its various restaurant brands onto a single digital technology platform.

EXECUTIVES

Vice President Quality Assurance, Ana J Hooper
Senior Vice President Operations, Brian Foye
Senior Vice President Finance, Dave Lothrop
CEO and Director, Eugene I. (Gene) Lee, age 54, $891,462 total compensation
President Olive Garden, David C. (Dave) George, age 59, $558,296 total compensation
President Specialty Restaurant Group, Harald Herrmann, age 50, $452,492 total compensation
SVP and CIO, Patti Reilly-White
Director, William (Bill) Lenehan
SVP and Chief Marketing Officer, Matt Park
SVP and CFO, Jeffrey (Jeff) Davis, age 52
President LongHorn Steakhouse, Todd Burrowes
Vice President Information Technology (Red Lobster Seafood Company), Lou Grande
Vice President Information Technology, Norma Sica
Senior Vice President, Melissa Baker
Senior Vice President Division, Sam Pereira
Senior Vice President Culinary and Beverage Red Lobster, John (Jack) Fadool
Vice President Accounting and Corporate Planning, Dan Williams
Vice President, Kathy Janiga
Senior Vice President Division, Paula Britton
Vice President Quality Assurance, Ana Hooper
Senior Vice President Group Human Resources, Ronald (Ron) Bojalad
Senior Vice President Operations, Kathy Nahlovsky
Senior Vice President Operations RED LOBSTER PARADISE Division, Jim McKeating
Vice President Culinary and Beverage Operations Olive Garden, Tim Blaise
Chairman, Jeffrey C. Smith

Vice President General Counsel and Secretary, Barbara (Barb) Posada
Auditors: KPMG LLP

LOCATIONS

HQ: Darden Restaurants, Inc.
1000 Darden Center Drive, Orlando, FL 32837
Phone: 407 245-4000
Web: www.darden.com

PRODUCTS/OPERATIONS

2014 Sales

	$ mil.	% of total
Olive Garden	3,789	56
LongHorn Steakhouse	1,544	23
Fine Dining	500	7
Other Business	929	14
Total	**6,764**	**100**

COMPETITORS

Bob Evans	Hooters
Brinker	OSI Restaurant
Carlson Restaurants	Partners
Cheesecake Factory	Perkins & Marie
Cracker Barrel	Callender's
Denny's	Ruby Tuesday
DineEquity	

HISTORICAL FINANCIALS

Company Type: Public

Income Statement

FYE: May 31

	REVENUE ($ mil.)	NET INCOME ($ mil.)	NET PROFIT MARGIN	EMPLOYEES
05/15	6,764	709	10.5%	150,000
05/14	6,285	286	4.6%	206,489
05/13	8,551	411	4.8%	206,000
05/12	7,998	475	5.9%	180,000
05/11	7,500	476	6.4%	178,380
Annual Growth	**(2.5%)**	**10.5%**	**—**	**(4.2%)**

2015 Year-End Financials

Debt ratio: 24.48%
Return on equity: 31.09%
Cash ($ mil.): 535
Current ratio: 0.88
Long-term debt ($ mil.): 1,452

No. of shares (mil.): 126
Dividends
  Yield: 0.0%
  Payout: 40.2%
Market value ($ mil.): 8,304

	STOCK PRICE ($) FY Close	P/E High/Low	PER SHARE ($) Earnings	Dividends	Book Value
05/15	65.54	13 8	5.47	2.20	18.42
05/14	49.55	25 21	2.15	2.20	16.30
05/13	52.83	18 14	3.13	2.00	15.81
05/12	53.06	15 11	3.57	1.72	14.28
05/11	50.92	15 11	3.39	1.28	14.38
Annual Growth	**6.5%**	**— —**	**12.7%**	**14.5%**	**6.4%**

DaVita HealthCare Partners Inc

DaVita HealthCare Partners gives life in the form of dialysis treatments to patients suffering from end-stage renal disease (chronic kidney failure). Through its Kidney Care division the firm is one of the US' largest providers of dialysis providing administrative services to 2200 outpatient centers across the US; it serves some 170000 patients. The company also offers home-based dialysis services as well as inpatient dialysis in about 1000 hospitals. It operates two clinical laboratories that specialize in routine testing of dialysis patients and serve the company's network of clinics. Subsidiary HealthCare Partners (HCP) operates primary care clinics and physician practices in several states.

HISTORY

Hospital chain National Medical Enterprises (NME now Tenet) formed Medical Ambulatory Care in 1979 to run its in-hospital dialysis centers. The unit bought other centers in NME's markets. In 1994 the subsidiary's management backed by a Donaldson Lufkin & Jenrette —now Credit Suisse First Boston (USA) —investment fund bought the dialysis business and renamed it Total Renal Care (TRC).

To become a leader in its consolidating field TRC began buying other centers and soon added clinical laboratory and dialysis-related pharmacy services and home dialysis programs. It went public in 1995.

The next year the firm added 66 facilities 32 from its acquisition of Caremark International's dialysis business. In 1997 TRC expanded abroad buying UK-based Open Access Sonography (vein care) and partnering with UK-based Priory Hospitals Group.

In 1998 TRC bought Renal Treatment Centers nearly doubling its size. But the acquisition costs caused a loss that year and sparked shareholder lawsuits (settled in 2000) over alleged misleading statements. The firm also became embroiled in a reimbursement dispute with Florida's Medicare program. Problems continued into 1999 as the company struggled to meld operations. The company took a charge to cover a billing shortfall and chairman and CEO Victor Chaltiel and COO/CFO John King resigned. New management began improving billing procedures and took other cost-cutting measures.

The company changed its name in 2000 to DaVita an Italian phrase loosely translated as "he/she gives life." It also sold its international operations to competitor Fresenius.

In 2005 the company acquired Gambro's US dialysis operations for about $3 billion adding some 565 dialysis clinics to its operations. To meet FTC requirements for the deal DaVita sold about 70 clinics to RenalAmerica a company founded by former Gambro Healthcare executive Michael Klein.

In 2007 DaVita expanded its health care offerings by acquiring a majority stake in HomeChoice Partners a provider of home infusion services. The company added about 80 new centers through acquisitions in 2009.

DaVita significantly widened its domestic network of dialysis centers when it acquired regional dialysis chain DSI Renal for $690 million in 2011. To secure approval for the deal from the FTC DaVita agreed to divest 30 clinics but overall the acquisition added more than 100 dialysis centers to its holdings.

Elsewhere around the world DaVita entered Germany with the 2011 purchase of DV Care. It also expanded into the Middle East through the acquisition of a majority stake in Lehbi Care a leading Riyadh-based kidney care company with three clinics.

The company has also been looking to branch out into new areas of health care including medical practice management a mission it accomplished through the 2012 purchase of private medical group management firm HealthCare Partners through a merger transaction worth some $4.4 billion.

Following the deal the company changed its legal name from DaVita to DaVita HealthCare Partners to reflect its broadened operations; the dialysis division continues to operate under the DaVita name while HealthCare Partners operates as an independent subsidiary of DaVita HealthCare Partners. The two companies both count California and Florida as key markets and DaVita HealthCare Partners has used HealthCare Partners' integrated care model to help it offer a wider range of health care services.

Internationally the company entered China in 2012 through a joint venture to provide dialysis services with Chinese biotech company 3SBio.

EXECUTIVES

Co-Chairman and CEO, Kent J. Thiry, age 60, $1,200,000 total compensation

COO HealthCare Partners, Joseph C. (Joe) Mello, age 56, $700,003 total compensation

Group VP Purchasing and Public Affairs, LeAnne M. Zumwalt, age 56

Interim CFO and Chief Accounting Officer, James K. (Jim) Hilger, age 53, $326,925 total compensation

President HealthCare Partners, Dennis L. Kogod, age 55, $800,000 total compensation

CEO Kidney Care, Javier J. Rodriguez, age 44, $800,000 total compensation

Chief Medical Officer Kidney Care, Allen R. Nissenson, age 68

COO Kidney Care, Michael D. Staffieri, $515,385 total compensation

President HealthCare Partners Colorado, Mark Price

President and CEO Florida Market, Lorie Glisson

Vice President Clinical Integrated Services, Steve McMurray

Vice President Of Medical Affairs, Robert Provenzano

Evp Global Operations, Atul Mathur

Division Vice President, Kurt Koptish

Vice President Clinical Affairs Home Dialysis, Martin (Marti) Schreiber

Vice President Corporate Development, Asher Royal

Vice President Clinical Risk Support, Robert Merrell

Vice President Business Development, Eduardo Cisneros

Vice President Of Enterprise Data, Jed Summerton

Vice President, Rebecca Griggs

Senior Vice President Strategy, James Rechtin

Vice President Wisdom, Dave Hoerman

Director Of Clinical Services, Karen Maier

Group Vice President, Ray Follett

Divisional Vice President, Vicki Burrier

Vice President Integration, Douglas Allen

Vice President, Sibito Morley

Vice President Marketing And Strategy, Samuel (Sam) Awuah

Auditors: KPMG LLP

LOCATIONS

HQ: DaVita HealthCare Partners Inc
2000 16th Street, Denver, CO 80202
Phone: 303 405-2100
Web: www.davita.com

PRODUCTS/OPERATIONS

2014 Revenues by Payer

	% of total
Government-based programs	
Medicare & Medicare-assigned plans	58
Medicaid	6
Other government-based programs	3
Commercial	33
Total	**100**

2014 Dialysis Revenues

	% of total
Outpatient hemodialysis centers	79
Peritoneal dialysis and home-based hemodialysis	16
Hospital inpatient hemodialysis	5
Total	**100**

2014 Sales

	$ mil
% of total	
US dialysis and related lab services	64
HCP	27
Other-ancillary services	9
Eliminations	-
Total	**100**

Selected Operations

Astro Hobby West Mt. Renal Care Limited Partnership
Austin Dialysis Centers L.P.
Beverly Hills Dialysis Partnership
Brighton Dialysis Center LLC
Capital Dialysis Partnership
Carroll County Dialysis Facility L.P.
Central Carolina Dialysis Centers LLC
Chicago Heights Dialysis LLC
Continental Dialysis Center Inc.
Dallas-Fort Worth Nephrology L.P.
Dialysis of Des Moines LLC
Dialysis Specialists of Dallas Inc.
Downriver Centers Inc.
Downtown Houston Dialysis Center L.P.
Durango Dialysis Center LLC
DVA Healthcare of Maryland Inc.
East End Dialysis Center Inc.
Elberton Dialysis Facility Inc.
Empire State DC Inc.
Greenwood Dialysis LLC
Hawaiian Gardens Dialysis LLC
HealthCare Partners LLC
HuntingtonPark Dialysis LLC
Indian River Dialysis Center LLC
Jedburg Dialysis LLC
Kidney Centers of Michigan L.L.C.
Lincoln Park Dialysis Services Inc.
Mason-Dixon Dialysis Facilities Inc.
Middlesex Dialysis Center LLC
Natomas Dialysis
Nephrolife Care (India) Pte. Ltd.
North Colorado Springs Dialysis LLC
Open Access Lifeline LLC
Palomar Dialysis LLC
Physicians Choice Dialysis of Alabama LLC
Physicians Dialysis of Houstin LLP
Renal Life Link Inc.
Renal Treatment Centers Inc.
RMS Lifeline Inc.
Rocky Mountain Dialysis Services LLC
Shining Star Dialysis Inc.
Soledad Dialysis Center LLC
Summit Dialysis Center L.P.
Tortugas Dialysis LLC
Total Renal Care Inc.
Total Renal Laboratories Inc.
Total Renal Research Inc.
TRC West Inc.
Tulsa Dialysis Center LLC
Upper Valley Dialysis L.P.

COMPETITORS

Apria Healthcare	LabCorp
Critical Care Systems	Lincare Holdings
International	Molina Healthcare
Dialysis Clinic Inc	Quest Diagnostics
FMCNA	U.S. Renal Care
Gentiva	UnitedHealth Group

HISTORICAL FINANCIALS

Company Type: Public

Income Statement

FYE: December 31

	REVENUE ($ mil.)	NET INCOME ($ mil.)	NET PROFIT MARGIN	EMPLOYEES
12/14	12,795	723	5.7%	57,900
12/13	11,764	633	5.4%	57,400
12/12	8,186	536	6.5%	53,400
12/11	6,731	478	7.1%	41,000
12/10	6,447	405	6.3%	36,500
Annual Growth	18.7%	15.5%	—	12.2%

2014 Year-End Financials

Debt ratio: 47.39%
Return on equity: 15.06%
Cash ($ mil.): 965
Current ratio: 1.86
Long-term debt ($ mil.): 8,383

No. of shares (mil.): 215
Dividends
  Yield: —
  Payout: —
Market value ($ mil.): 16,333

	STOCK PRICE ($) FY Close	P/E High/Low	PER SHARE ($) Earnings	Dividends	Book Value
12/14	75.74	23 18	3.33	0.00	23.98
12/13	63.37	43 18	2.95	0.00	20.79
12/12	110.53	41 28	2.74	0.00	17.84
12/11	75.81	35 24	2.48	0.00	11.43
12/10	69.49	37 28	1.97	0.00	10.30
Annual Growth	2.2%	— —	14.0%	—	23.5%

Dean Foods Co.

Dean Foods is the nation's largest milk bottler. The company's Fresh Dairy Direct business markets fluid milk ice cream cultured dairy products and beverages (juices teas and bottled water) under more than 50 local regional and private-label brands including Borden Pet Country Fresh-Meadow Gold and TruMoo a leading national flavored milk brand. Following the spinoff of most of its WhiteWave Foods business Dean Foods still holds about 20% of WhiteWave which makes coffee creamers (International Delight) dips ice cream butter cottage cheese and specialty dairy products. Dean Foods owns and operates a number of smaller dairy companies including Berkeley Farms and Garelick Farms.

Geographic ReachDallas-based Dean Foods rings up 99% of its sales in the US where it operates more 68 manufacturing facilities. Overseas the dairy giant has operations in Europe (Belgium France the Netherlands and the UK).Operations-Following the sale of its Morningstar Foods division and the spinoff of WhiteWave in 2013 Dean Foods was left with Fresh Dairy Direct. The company manufactures markets and distributes a wide variety of branded and private label dairy case products including milk ice cream cultured dairy products creamers ice cream mix and other dairy products to retailers distributors foodservice outlets educational institutions and governmental entities across the US.Sales and MarketingDean Foods markets its products through advertising and other promotions including media coupons trade shows and other promotional activities. The company spent about $27.5 million on advertising in 2014 about $22 million in 2013 and $28.6 million in 2012. Dean's customers include food retailers distributors foodservice operators educational institutions and governmental entities throughout the US. Wal-Mart and its subsidiaries including

Sam's Club is Dean Foods' largest customer. The company's products are sold primarily on a local or regional basis through local and regional sales forces although some national customer relationships are coordinated by a centralized corporate sales department. Financial Performance In 2014 Dean Foods' net sales increased by 5% due to higher pricing as a result of the pass-through of higher dairy commodity costs. On average the Class I price was 24% above prior-year levels. The company incurred a net loss of $20.2 million (compared to net income of $813.2 million in 2013). The primary reason was due to increased cost of sales absence of gain on disposition of White Wave common stock loss from discontinued operations and decreased gain on sale of discontinued operations net of tax partially offset by higher revenues. Cost of sales increased due to higher dairy commodity costs. In 2014 Dean Foods' net cash provided by the operating activities was 152.9 million (compared to cash outflow of $316.6 million in 2013) due to a change in accounts payables and accrued expenses and income taxes receivables/payables. Strategy After diversifying into higher-margin businesses (and piling on debt in the process) Dean Foods has reversed course to get on a sounder financial footing and has become essentially a pure-play in low-margin fluid milk and traditional diary products. Its current strategy is to build on its unique capabilities and cost reduction opportunities to create a leading positions as a low-cost fluid milk producer. After selling a 20% stake in WhiteWave-Alpro to the public for $391 million in fall 2012 it spun off the rest in 2013. (The purchase of Alpro in 2009 and its combination with WhiteWave Foods gave Dean Foods a firm presence in Europe and furthered its ambition of becoming a global brand. WhiteWave's reconfiguration also separated the Dean Foods' more traditional lower-margin businesses from the higher-margin organic and value-added businesses. Indeed WhiteWave-Alpro was considered by many to be the most valuable part of Dean Foods. The company's standard dairy products and its large private-label business are more vulnerable to volatility in commodity prices and consumers' dwindling appetitive for milk and other dairy foods). While Dean Foods has been focused intently on acquisitions it has recently made some disposals. In the company 2013 sold its Morningstar Foods division to Canada's #1 dairy processor Saputo for $1.45 billion.

HISTORY

Investment banker Gregg Engles formed a holding company in 1988 with other investors including dairy industry veteran Cletes Beshears to buy the Reddy Ice unit of Dallas-based Southland (operator of the 7-Eleven chain). The company also bought Circle K's Sparkle Ice and combined it with Reddy Ice. By 1990 it had acquired about 15 ice plants.

The company changed its name to Suiza Foods when it bought Suiza Dairy in 1993 for $99 million. The Puerto Rican dairy was formed in 1942 by Hector Nevares Sr. and named for the Spanish word for "Switzerland." By 1993 it was Puerto Rico's largest dairy controlling about 60% of the island's milk market.

Suiza Foods bought Florida's Velda Farms manufacturer and distributor of milk and dairy products in 1994. The company went public in 1996 the same year it bought Swiss Dairy (dairy products California and Nevada) and Garrido y Compañía (coffee products Puerto Rico).

The company became one of the largest players in the North American dairy industry through its acquisitions in 1997. It paid $960 million for Morn-

ingstar (Lactaid brand lactose-free milk Second Nature brand egg substitute) which —like Suiza Foods itself —was a Dallas-based company formed in 1988 through a Southland divestiture. The company entered the Midwest with its $98 million purchase of Country Fresh and the Northeast with the Bernon family's Massachusetts-based group of dairy and packaging companies including Garelick Farms and Franklin Plastics (packaging).

Suiza Foods strengthened its presence in the southeastern US in 1998 with its $287 million acquisition of Land-O-Sun Dairies operator of 13 fluid-dairy and ice-cream processing facilities. Also that year Suiza Foods purchased Continental Can (plastic packaging) for about $345 million and sold Reddy Ice to Packaged Ice for $172 million.

After settling an antitrust lawsuit brought by the US Department of Justice in 1999 Suiza Foods bought dairy processors in Colorado Ohio and Virginia. That year Suiza Foods combined its US packaging operations with Reid Plastics to form Consolidated Containers retaining about 40% of the new company.

In 2001 Suiza Foods announced it had agreed to purchase rival Dean Foods for $1.5 billion and the assumption of $1 billion worth of debt. Dean Foods had begun as Dean Evaporated Milk founded in 1925 by Sam Dean a Chicago evaporated-milk broker. By the mid-1930s it had moved into the fresh milk industry. The company went public in 1961 and was renamed Dean Foods in 1963.

Suiza Foods completed the acquisition and took on the Dean Foods name later in 2001. The new Dean Foods bought out Dairy Farmers of America's interest in Suiza Dairy and merged it with the "old" Dean's fluid-dairy operations to create its internal division Dean Dairy Group.

Along with the purchase of "old" Dean came a 36% ownership of soy milk maker WhiteWave and in 2002 Dean Foods purchased the remaining 64% for approximately $189 million. By the end of the year Dean had sold off some smaller businesses (boiled peanuts and contract hauling) and its Puerto Rico operations for $119 million in cash.

EXECUTIVES

EVP and COO, Ralph P. Scozzafava, age 56
CEO, Gregg A. Tanner, age 59, $1,000,000 total compensation
EVP General Counsel Corporate Secretary and Government Affairs, Marc L. Kesselman
EVP Human Resources, Kimberly (Kim) Warmbier, age 53, $375,000 total compensation
EVP and CFO, Chris Bellairs, age 54, $465,000 total compensation
SVP and CIO, Brian Murphy, age 48, $300,000 total compensation
SVP Operations and Procurement, C. Shay Braun, age 48, $375,000 total compensation
SVP Logistics, S. Craig McCutcheon, age 54
Vice President Legal, Mark Niermann
Vice President Continuous Improvement, Craig McCutheon
Vice President Total Rewards, Jose Motta
Vice President Purchasing, Don Klein
Vice President It Operations, Shaun Young
Vice President Sales Small Format Channel Products For Resale, Jeff Springer
Vice President Finance, Kim Lechner
Vice President, Kristy Waterman
Vice President Research And Development Fresh Dairy Direct, Kathleen Dacunha
Vice President Finance, Eddie Tollison
Vice President, Scott Toth
Vice President Legal, Nancy Davis
Vice President Sales South Region, Marvin Monroe
Vice President Prc, Gary Tritt

Vice President Corporate Development, Steve Schultz
Vice President Human Resources, Terry Hatten
Vice President Tax Planning, Shan Luton
Vice President Private Brands, Jay Altizer
Senior Vice President Logistics, Tony Brooks
Board Member, Janet Hill
Auditors: Deloitte & Touche LLP

LOCATIONS

HQ: Dean Foods Co.
2711 North Haskell Avenue, Suite 3400, Dallas, TX 75204
Phone: 214 303-3400
Web: www.deanfoods.com

2013 Sales

	% of total
Domestic	99
Foreign	1
Total	**100**

PRODUCTS/OPERATIONS

2014 Fresh Dairy Direct Sales

	% of total
Private-label brands	53
Company brands	47
Total	**100**

2014 Fresh Dairy Direct Sales

	% of total
Fluid dairy	
Fresh milk	73
Ice cream	9
Other	2
Cultured dairy	4
Other beverages	5
Fresh cream	4
ESL & ESL creamers	3
Total	**100**

Selected Brands

Alpro (Europe)
Alta Dena
Berkeley Farms
Borden (licensed)
Brown Cow
Brown' s Dairy
Dean' s
Garelick Farms
Gandy' s
Hershey' s (licensed)
Horizon Organic
Knudsen (licensed)
LAND O' LAKES (licensed)
Oak Farms
Over the Moon
Pet (licensed)
Provamel (Europe)
Robinson Dairy
Silk
Swiss Premium
Tru Moo
Tuscan
WhiteWave

Selected Products

Bottled waters
Eggnog
Eggs
Cottage cheese
Half-and-half
Ice cream
Juice
Milk
Pudding
Sour cream
Soymilk
Whipping cream

COMPETITORS

Associated Milk Producers
Aurora Organic Dairy

Ben & Jerry' s
Blue Bell
Brewster Dairy
California Dairies Inc.
ConAgra
Crystal Farms Refrigerated Distribution Company
Dairy Farmers of America
Danone
Darigold Inc.
Dreyer' s
Foster Dairy Farms
Friendly' s Ice Cream
Galaxy Nutritional Foods
Grupo LALA
HP Hood
Hain Celestial
Hiland Dairy
Lactalis
Lifeway Foods
Maryland & Virginia Milk Producers
Mondelez International
National Dairy
Nestl© USA
Northwest Dairy
Organic Valley
Prairie Farms Dairy
Quality Chekd
Rockview Dairies
Stonyfield Farm
Tillamook County Creamery Association
Vitasoy International

HISTORICAL FINANCIALS

Company Type: Public

Income Statement

FYE: December 31

	REVENUE ($ mil.)	NET INCOME ($ mil.)	NET PROFIT MARGIN	EMPLOYEES
12/14	9,503	(20)	—	17,246
12/13	9,016	813	9.0%	18,040
12/12	11,462	158	1.4%	21,915
12/11	13,055	(1,575)	—	24,066
12/10	12,122	91	0.8%	25,780
Annual Growth	(5.9%)	—	—	(9.6%)

2014 Year-End Financials

Debt ratio: 33.12%
Return on equity: (-3.03%)
Cash ($ mil.): 16
Current ratio: 1.49
Long-term debt ($ mil.): 916

No. of shares (mil.): 94
Dividends
  Yield: 1.4%
  Payout: —
Market value ($ mil.): 1,823

	STOCK PRICE ($) FY Close	P/E High/Low		PER SHARE ($) Earnings	Dividends	Book Value
12/14	19.38	—	—	(0.22)	0.28	6.67
12/13	17.19	2	1	8.58	0.00	7.53
12/12	16.51	11	6	1.70	0.00	3.85
12/11	11.20	—	—	(17.18)	0.00	(1.13)
12/10	8.84	19	7	1.00	0.00	16.46
Annual Growth	21.7%	—	—	—	—	(20.2%)

Deere & Co.

Deere & Co. is interested in seeing its customers go to seed and grow. The company one of the world's largest makers of farm equipment is also a major producer of construction forestry and commercial and residential lawn care equipment. Deere operates through three business segments: the agriculture and turf and construction and forestry segments make up its equipment operations; a credit segment provides financial services. Deere

famous for its "Nothing Runs Like A Deere" marketing sells John Deere and other brands through retail dealer networks and also makes products for outlets Home Depot and Lowes.

Geographic Reach

North America accounts for around 65% of Deere's revenue each year. The company owns nine facilities housing one centralized parts distribution center and eight regional parts depots and distribution centers throughout North America. The company also owns centralized parts distribution centers in Brazil Germany India and Russia and regional parts depots and distribution centers located in Argentina Australia China Mexico South Africa Sweden and the UK.

Operations

Deere's largest operating segment is agriculture and turf which accounts for 68% of revenue. Consolidated into five product platforms —crop harvesting turf and utility hay and forage crop care and tractors —the segment makes such products as loaders combines corn pickers cotton and sugarcane pickers and even golf course equipment and outdoor power products. Besides John Deere brands include Frontier Green Systems as well as SABO in Europe and Benye in China.

The company's construction and forestry segment represents 21% of its total revenue. Making 90% of the types of equipment used in North America this segment distributes backhoe loaders crawler dozers motor graders log skidders and skid-steer loaders.

Besides equipment the company's other main operational division financial services provides credit services for Deere dealers and wholesalers.

Sales and Marketing

Deere operates through roughly 25 sales and marketing locations and nearly 20 warehousing locations spanning 15 countries including Argentina Australia Brazil Chile China Ecuador France India Israel Italy Mexico Russia Spain Turkey and the US.

Through US and Canadian facilities Deere markets products to approximately 2381 dealer locations most of which are independently owned and operated. Of these about 1522 sell agricultural equipment while approximately 427 sell construction earthmoving material handling and/or forestry equipment. Nortrax owns some of the 427 dealer locations. Outside the US and Canada Deere agriculture and turf equipment is also sold to distributors and dealers for resale.

Financial Performance

Deere has seen its revenues drop the last two years. From 2014 to 2015 revenues declined 20% from $36 billion to $29 billion and profits plunged 29% from $3.2 billion to $1.9 billion.

Deere attributed the declines to a large dip in agriculture and turf sales fueled by lower shipment volumes and the unfavorable effects of currency translations. The erosion of profits was also fueled by higher production costs primarily related to the impact of engine emission programs in the company's equipment operations.

Strategy

Deere is focused on enhancing its operations as strong demand for agricultural commodities continues. To keep manufacturing in sync with demand Deere increases production during the second and third quarters when customers are buying more.

In 2014 Deere made a move to expand in an important emerging market when it opened two new manufacturing facilities in Brazil. Also that year Deere acquired Auteq Telematica an onboard software and computer company located in Sao Paulo Brazil. The acquisition provided the company with additional expertise in the sugarcane market and the ability to develop products and services to help customers leverage the data produced by onboard

computers in equipment used for planting crop care and harvesting in sugarcane production.

HISTORY

Vermont-born John Deere moved to Grand Detour Illinois in 1836 and set up a blacksmith shop. Deere and other pioneers had trouble with the rich black soil of the Midwest sticking to iron plows designed for sandy eastern soils so in 1837 Deere used a circular steel saw blade to create a self-scouring plow that moved so quickly it was nicknamed the "whistling plow." He sold only three in 1838 but by 1842 he was making 25 a week.

Deere moved his enterprise to Moline in 1847. His son Charles joined the company in 1853 beginning a long tradition of family management. (All five Deere presidents before 1982 were related by blood or marriage.) Charles eventually set up an independent dealership distribution system and added wagons buggies and corn planters to the product line.

EXECUTIVES

Vice President Information Technology, Daniel (Dan) McCabe
Vice President Corporate Business Development, Ganesh Jayaram
Senior Vice President Engineering and, Randal Sergesketter
Vice President Worldwide Supply Management Logistics, Thomas (Thom) Knoll
Chairman President and CEO, Samuel R. (Sam) Allen, age 62, $1,495,204 total compensation
Comptroller, James M. Field, age 52, $646,353 total compensation
VP Engineering and Manufacturing (Worldwide Construction & Forestry Division & Deere Power Systems Group), Max A. Guinn
Group President John Deere Financial Services Global HR and Public Affairs, Michael J. Mack, age 59, $656,147 total compensation
President Agriculture and Turf Europe Asia Africa and Global Tractor Platform, Mark von Pentz, age 52
SVP and CFO, Rajesh (Raj) Kalathur, $525,437 total compensation
President Agricultural Solutions and CIO, John C. May
VP Information Technology, Patrick W. Webber
VP Global Supply Management and Logistics, Pierre Guyot
Vice President Sales and Marketing, Christoph Wigger
Senior Vice President And Finance Director John Deere Credit Worldwide, Michael (Mel) Matera
Vice President Engineering, Brian Rauch
Vice President Management Information Systems, Lisa Herrig
Vice President of Sales and Marketing, Michael (Mel) Triplett
Vice President Marketing, Jim Anderson
Senior Vice President Global Marketing Services, Cory Reed
Vice President Sales and Marketing, Wigger Chris
Vice President Information Services, Daniel Weber
Vice President Worldwide Supply Management, David (Dave) Nelson
Senior Vice President Operations, Frank Bates
Vice President Of Finance, Carolyn Clementes
Vice President Interactive Marketing, James Heseman
Vice President Engineering And Manufacturing, Mike Weinert
Vice President Marketing, Chris Arnold
Vice President Of Manufacturing Engineering, Pete Zimmerman
Senior Vice President Information Technology, Randy Sergesketter

Vice President Sales And Marketing, John (Jack) Lagemann
Vice President Sales, Vanessa Stiffler-claus
Vice President Technology and Information Solutions Intelligent Solutions Group, Pat Pinkston
Vice President Corporate Textile Accounts, Paul Bauer
Vice President Finance Water Technologies, Ken Stephens
Vice President, Lawrence Sidwell
Vice President, Craig Purvis
Vice President Information Systems, Ray Lybarger
National Account Manager, Todd Vantilburg
Finance Vice President, Mark Theuerkauf
Vice President Purchasing, Chuck Dupree
Vice President, Barry Nelson
Executive Vice President Operations And Technology Whitney Holding And Whitney National Bank, Karrie Fuhr
Vice President and Deputy General Counsel International, James H (Jamie) Becht
Vice President Manufacturing, Bernhard Haas
Vice President Marketing, David (Dave) Plaster
Vice President of Marketing, Jeffrey (Jeff) Peterson
Senior Vice President Technology and Human Resources, Johnathan Lawson
Vice President Information Services, Pat Weber
Vice President Information Systems, Raymond Lybarger
Vice President Global Platform Services Agriculture And Turf Division, Patrick (Paddy) Pinkston
Vice President of Sales and Marketing, Stefan Von Stegmann
Vice President Information Technology, Morgan Kurk
Vice President Information Technology, Nimesh Rastogi
Vice President and Controller, James (Jamie) MField
Vice President Training, Scott Clarke
Assistant Treasurer, Jeff Trahan
Board Member, Brandt Boland
Board Member, Sherry Smith
Treasurer, John (Jack) Mann
Auditors: DELOITTE & TOUCHE LLP

LOCATIONS

HQ: Deere & Co.
One John Deere Place, Moline, IL 61265
Phone: 309 765-8000   Fax: 309 765-9929
Web: www.johndeere.com

2015 Sales

	$ mil.	% of total
US & Canada	18,750	65
Outside U.S. and Canada	9,616	33
Other	497	2
Total	**28,863**	**100**

PRODUCTS/OPERATIONS

2015 Sales

	$ mil.	% of total
Agriculture & turf	19,812	68
Construction & forestry	5,963	21
Financial services	2,591	9
Other	497	2
Total	**28,863**	**100**

Selected Products and Services

Agricultural and turf equipment
  Balers
  Combines
  Cotton harvesting equipment
  Golf course equipment
  Harvesters
  Hay and forage equipment
  Irrigation
  Landscape and nursery
  Loaders

Mowers (commercial riding lawn equipment and walk-behind mowers)
Planting and seeding equipment
Power products (outdoor)
  Sprayers
  Tillage
  Tractors (large medium and utility)
  Utility vehicles
Construction and forestry equipment
  Articulated dump trucks
  Backhoe loaders
  Crawler dozers
  Crawler loaders
  Excavators
  Landscape loaders
  Log skidders and loaders
  Material handling equipment
  Motor graders
  Skid-steer loaders
Credit
  Leasing
  Retail and wholesale financing
Power systems
  Diesel and natural gas engines (marine industrial mining)
  Powertrain components
  Transmissions

COMPETITORS

AGCO	Kubota
Buhler Industries	Mahindra
Caterpillar	Navistar International
Great Plains Manufacturing	Terex
	Toro Company
Honda	Valmont Industries
Komatsu	Volvo

HISTORICAL FINANCIALS

Company Type: Public

Income Statement

FYE: October 31

	REVENUE ($ mil.)	NET INCOME ($ mil.)	NET PROFIT MARGIN	EMPLOYEES
10/15	28,862	1,940	6.7%	57,200
10/14	36,066	3,161	8.8%	59,623
10/13	37,795	3,537	9.4%	67,044
10/12	36,157	3,064	8.5%	66,900
10/11	32,012	2,799	8.7%	61,300
Annual Growth	**(2.6%)**	**(8.8%)**	**—**	**(1.7%)**

2015 Year-End Financials

Debt ratio: 63.59%	No. of shares (mil.): 316
Return on equity: 24.55%	Dividends
Cash ($ mil.): 4,162	Yield: 0.0%
Current ratio: 0.61	Payout: 41.5%
Long-term debt ($ mil.): 23,833	Market value ($ mil.): 24,702

	STOCK PRICE ($) FY Close	P/E High/Low		PER SHARE ($) Earnings	Dividends	Book Value
10/15	78.00	17	13	5.77	2.40	21.29
10/14	85.54	11	9	8.63	2.22	26.23
10/13	81.84	10	9	9.09	1.99	27.46
10/12	85.44	12	9	7.63	1.79	17.64
10/11	75.90	15	9	6.63	1.52	16.75
Annual Growth	**0.7%**			**(3.4%)**	**12.1%**	**6.2%**

Delek US Holdings Inc

Delek US Holdings' US petroleum business is a delectable mix of refining fuel marketing and retail operations. The company a subsidiary of Israeli-based conglomerate Delek Group operates refineries in Tyler Texas and El Dorado Arkansas

with a total production capacity of 140000 barrels per day. Delek US Holdings' marketing segment sells refined products on a wholesale basis in west Texas through company-owned and third-party operated terminals. On the retail side its MAPCO Express unit manages almost 380 convenience store/gas stations (156 company operated) under MAPCO Express East Coast Discount Food Mart and other names in several southern US states.

Geographic Reach
Delek US Holdings has operations in Alabama Arkansas Georgia Kentucky Mississippi Tennessee and Virginia.

Operations
Delek US Holdings operates the 60000 barrels-per-day Tyler Texas refinery and the Lion Oil Company (which owns a 100000 barrels-per-day refinery in El Dorado Arkansas) as well as other pipeline and product assets. The El Dorado refinery operational capacity is 80000 barrels per day. It also has a 55000 barrels-per-day vacuum unit a 20000 barrels-per-day FCC unit and a 15300 barrels-per-day continuous regenerative catalytic reforming unit.

The company also owns five light product distribution terminals (in Nashville and Memphis Tennessee; and in Big Sandy San Angelo and Abilene Texas) and sells wholesale fuel and operates a chain of retail gas stations.

Sales and Marketing
Delek US Holdings sells refined products on a wholesale basis to inter-company and third-party customers in Arkansas Tennessee Texas and the Ohio River Valley. The logistics unit provides products terminalling services to independent third parties at its light products terminal in Nashville markets light products using terminals in Abilene and San Angelo and markets light products via third-party terminals in Aledo Big Spring Frost and Odessa Texas.

In 2011 the company's largest customer accounted for 21.3% of marketing segment net sales and its top ten customers accounted for 61.3%. The logistics segment's customers including major oil companies independent refiners and marketers jobbers distributors and retail fuel operators as well as transportation companies and utilities.

Financial Performance
Delek US Holdings revenue jumped by 21% in 2012 due to the 2011 acquisition of the El Dorado refinery and higher fuel sales prices (which lifted logistics and retail sales) and stronger logistics segment sales volumes. Overall revenues would have been higher save for lower sales volumes due to decreased refining throughputs and production.

The El Dorado refinery purchase lifted refining revenues by 31% in 2012 while logistic segment revenues grew by 8% due to higher diesel prices and an increase in West Texas wholesale marketing business volumes and the 2011 acquisitions of the Lion Pipeline System and SALA Gathering System.The acquisitions and strong prices helped the company report net income of $272.8 in 2012 a 72% jump over the previous year.

With the exception of the the recession driven revenue slump in 2009 Delek US Holdings has reported strong revenue growth in recent years.

Strategy
Delek US Holdings has historically grown by pursuing complementary acquisitions and by upgrading its retail business and its refinery assets.

In 2015 it acquired 48% of Alon USA Energy.

To generate cash in 2012 the company spun off wholly-owned crude oil and refined products logistics and marketing subsidiary Delek Logistics Partners LP.

The company is pursuing a retrofitting program to physically improve and upgrade the appearance of its convenience stores and gas stations in order to boost market share. During 2011 it spent $23.4

million on renovating 51 stores and constructing two new stores.

Delek US Holdings is upgrading its light product distribution terminals located in Big Sandy Texas to provide additional logistical support to the Tyler refinery by the end of 2013.

Mergers and Acquisition

Growing its assets in 2013 the company agreed to buy a biodiesel production (12 million gallons per year capacity) plant in Cleburne Texas from EQM Technologies & Energy Inc. for $5.3 million.

In 2012 it bought the Nettleton Pipeline from Plains for $12.3 million. The 35-mile long pipeline will ship crude oil from tank farms around Nettleton to the Tyler refinery. That year it also has bought a light petroleum products terminal located in Big Sandy Texas from Sunoco Partners Marketing & Terminals L.P. for $11 million.

To grow its refinery operations in 2011 the company bought Ergon's 54% stake in Lion Oil boosting its ownership of that company to 88%. Later that year it boosted its holdings in Lion Oil to 100%.That year Delek US Holdings also acquired Paline Pipeline Company LLC from Ergon Terminaling for $50 million. The 185-mile Paline Pipeline System is crude oil pipeline that runs between Nederland Texas and Longview Texas.

Ownership

Delek Group owns 53% of the company.

EXECUTIVES

EVP Refining Operations, Frederec C. Green, age 50, $280,000 total compensation
Chairman President and CEO, Ezra Uzi Yemin, age 47, $635,723 total compensation
EVP Marketing and Supply of Refined Products, Pete Daily, age 66, $250,000 total compensation
EVP and CFO, Assaf (Assi) Ginzburg, age 40, $280,000 total compensation
EVP General Counsel and Secretary, Kent B. Thomas, age 47, $250,000 total compensation
EVP Human Resources, Donald Holmes, $219,231 total compensation
EVP Tesoro, Mark D Smith
EVP, Daniel L. Gordon
Vice President Strategic Planning, Assi Ginzburg
Executive Vice President Commercial Operations, Mark Smith
Vice President, Avigal Soreq
Vice President Of Organizational Development, Jennifer Boulton
Vice President and Corporate Controller, Paul Stone
Vice President Delek Logistics, John Laing
Vice President of Sales and Merchandising MAPCO Express, Tony Miller
Treasurer and Vice President, Greg Intemann
Auditors: Ernst & Young LLP

LOCATIONS

HQ: Delek US Holdings Inc
7102 Commerce Way, Brentwood, TN 37027
Phone: 615 771-6701
Web: www.Delekus.com

PRODUCTS/OPERATIONS

2012 Sales

	$ mil.	% of total
Refining	6,070	70
Retail	1,877	22
Logistics	775	8
Other	2	-
Total	**8,726**	**100**

Selected Mergers and Acquisitions 2012 Nettleton Pipeline ($12.3 million; crude oil pipeline) That year it also has bought aA light petroleum products terminal ($11 million; Big Sandy

Texas)2011Lion Oil (El Dorado Arkansas; oil refinery)Paline Pipeline Com

COMPETITORS

7-Eleven	Motiva Enterprises
CITGO	Murphy Oil
Chevron	Publix
ConocoPhillips	Racetrac Petroleum
Costco Wholesale	The Pantry
Cumberland Farms	Wal-Mart
Exxon Mobil	Winn-Dixie
Gate Petroleum	

HISTORICAL FINANCIALS

Company Type: Public

Income Statement

FYE: December 31

	REVENUE ($ mil.)	NET INCOME ($ mil.)	NET PROFIT MARGIN	EMPLOYEES
12/14	8,324	198	2.4%	4,361
12/13	8,706	117	1.4%	4,366
12/12	8,726	272	3.1%	4,033
12/11	7,198	158	2.2%	3,801
12/10	3,755	(79)	—	3,395
Annual Growth	**22.0%**	**—**		**6.5%**

2014 Year-End Financials

Debt ratio: 20.39%
Return on equity: 20.51%
Cash ($ mil.): 444
Current ratio: 1.46
Long-term debt ($ mil.): 533

No. of shares (mil.): 57
Dividends
Yield: 3.6%
Payout: 38.1%
Market value ($ mil.): 1,562

	STOCK PRICE ($) FY Close	P/E High/Low		PER SHARE ($) Earnings	Dividends	Book Value
12/14	27.28	11	8	3.35	1.00	17.49
12/13	34.41	20	10	1.96	0.95	15.79
12/12	25.32	6	2	4.57	0.50	15.08
12/11	11.41	6	2	2.78	0.33	11.26
12/10	7.28	—	—	(1.47)	0.15	8.15
Annual Growth	**39.1%**			**—**	**60.7%**	**21.0%**

Delta Air Lines, Inc. (DE)

Delta Air Lines is one of the world's largest airlines by traffic. Through its regional carriers (including subsidiary Comair) the company serves about 330 destinations in about 60 countries and it operates a mainline fleet of 770-plus aircraft as well as maintenance repair and overhaul (MRO) and cargo operations. The airline serves nearly 170 million customers each year and offers more than 15000 daily flights. Delta is a founding member of the SkyTeam marketing and code-sharing alliance (airlines extend their networks by selling tickets on one another's flights) which includes carriers Air France KLM and Alitalia.

Geographic Reach

Delta operates from domestic hubs in Atlanta Boston Cincinnati Detroit Los Angeles Minneapolis/St. Paul New York Seattle and Salt Lake City. Delta has international hubs in Amsterdam Paris and Tokyo.

OperationsOther Delta businesses include Delta TechOps which provides maintenance and engineering services for the Delta fleet as well as more than 150 other aviation customers and Delta

Global Services which provides staffing for about 150 clients. Another unit MLT Vacations wholesales vacation packages.Delta divides its operations into two chief segments: airline and refinery. The airline segment provides scheduled air transportation for passengers and cargo throughout the US and around the world and other ancillary airline services including maintenance and repair services for third parties.The refinery segment provides jet fuel to the airline segment from its own production and through jet fuel obtained through agreements with Phillips 66 and BP. The costs included in the refinery segment are primarily for the benefit of the airline segment.Sales and Marketing

Delta serves nearly 170 million customers each year. Its tickets are sold through various distribution channels including telephone reservations Delta.com and traditional brick and mortar and on-line travel agencies. It spends about $200 million each year on advertising.

Financial Performance

Delta has achieved unprecedented growth over the years with revenues climbing 7% from $37.8 billion in 2013 to $40 million in 2014 a company milestone. Delta's profits however nosedived 94% from $10.5 billion in 2013 to $659 million in 2014.

The historic revenue growth for 2014 was driven by a spike in passenger revenue resulting from a 2% bump in passenger mile yield on 4% higher traffic. Geographically domestic services increased by 8% resulting from a strong performance from its hubs in Atlanta New York-LaGuardia and Seattle. In addition its international revenues climbed by 3% fueled by a capacity growth in the Latin America region.

The massive fall in profits for 2014 was attributed to a sharp rise in fuel expenses unfavorable adjustments on fuel hedges and an increase of $413 million paid in income taxes. In 2014 its operating cash flows increased by 10% to $4.95 billion due to a rise in cash inflows from fuel inventory prepaid expenses and accounts payable.

Strategy

The airline industry is fueled by strategic alliances that allow individual carriers to extend their service without physically flying into new territory. In 2013 Delta acquired the 49% stake Singapore Airlines owns in Virgin Atlantic for $360 million. The new alliance will strengthen Delta's flight services between North America and the UK especially the New York London market.

Delta's alliance with SkyTeam allows the airline's reach to extend to more than 900 destinations in 170-plus countries around the globe. Looking to become the preferred carrier in New York City Delta expanded a hub at LaGuardia Airport in 2012 to provide flights to almost all top domestic destinations. The company also redeveloped its facility at JFK International in 2013 with a focus on more transcontinental and international service. The company gets a boost in global coverage with airlines around the world coming aboard the SkyTeam alliance. Besides the SkyTeam alliance Delta offers more international service through a joint venture with Air France-KLM and Alitalia. The airlines share revenue and split the cost of trans-Atlantic flights between North America and Europe Africa the Middle East India and Latin America.

HISTORY

Delta Air Lines was founded in Macon Georgia in 1924 as the world's first crop-dusting service Huff-Daland Dusters to combat boll weevil infestation of cotton fields. It moved to Monroe Louisiana in 1925. In 1928 field manager C. E. Woolman and two partners bought the service and renamed it Delta Air Service after the Mississippi Delta region it served. About 80 years later Delta became one of the world's largest airlines by traffic after its $2.8 billion acquisition of Northwest Airlines in 2008.

EXECUTIVES

Director, Richard H. Anderson, age 59, $790,625 total compensation

Executive Vice President Human Resources And Labor Relations, Michael Campbell

President and Director, Edward H. (Ed) Bastian, age 58, $618,750 total compensation

EVP and Chief Revenue Officer, Glen W. Hauenstein, age 54, $523,750 total compensation

President Delta TechOps MRO Services, Jack M. Arehart, age 59

SVP Delta Connections; President Delta Global Services and Delta Private Jets, Cyril J. Turner, age 53

EVP and CFO, Paul A. Jacobson, age 43, $496,875 total compensation

EVP and Chief Legal Officer, Richard B. (Ben) Hirst, age 70

SEVP and COO, Wayne G. (Gil) West, $496,875 total compensation

EVP and Chief Human Resources Officer, Joanne Smith

SVP and CIO, Rahul Samant

EVP Global Sales and President International, Steve Sear

V Pres, Harold Bevis

Senior Vice President Flight Operations Delta Air Lines, Stephen Dickson

Vice President Community and Public Affairs, Tad Hutcheson

Vice President corporate Real Estate, Jones Donald

Vice President Finance and Chief Risk Officer, Christopher (Chris) Duncan

Senior Vice President Government Affairs, Andrea Newman

Aa To Vice President, Deborah (Deb) Tuma

Senior Vice President Corporate Strategy and Real Estate, Holden Shannon

Vice President Learning, Sharon Mickelson

Vice President skymiles, Robertson Jeffrey

Vp Sales, Ranjan Goswami

Vice President Consumer Technology and Innovation, Matthew (Matt) Muta

Vice President, Andrew Zarras

Senior Vice President Flight Operations, Bill Lentsch

Senior Vice President Human Resources, Elizabeth (Beth) Johnston

Senior Vice President Delta Techops, Anthony Charaf

Aa To Vice President, Sue Ebdon

Aa To Vice President, Lynn Gordon

Vice President, Rex Christensen

Vice President, Cherylope Taylor

Vice President Domestic Pricing and Revenue Management, Eric Phillips

Senior Vice President Maintenance Operations, John Laughter

Vice President, Patrick Redahan

Vice President Reservations Sales And Customer Care, Perry Cantarutti

Aa To Senior Vice President, Maylin Martin

Assistant Vice President Retail Information Technology, Timothy Harms

Senior Vice President, Robert Rivkin

Vice President Governance Systems Operations And Information Security And Privacy Office, Richardson Harry

Vice President Information Systems, Robert Olson

Senior Vice President Delta Connection, Don Bornhurst

Senior Vice President Delta Connection, Donald Bornhorst

Senior Vice President Fuels Optimization, Graeme Burnett

Vice President, Shreve Lee

Vice President Marketing and Business Development, Brett Mannion

Executive Vice President and Chief Ope, Steve Gorman

Vice Chairman, Roy J. Bostock, age 75

Chairman, Daniel A. (Dan) Carp, age 66

Board Of Directors, Annie Larkin

Auditors: Ernst & Young LLP

LOCATIONS

HQ: Delta Air Lines, Inc. (DE)
Post Office Box 20706, Atlanta, GA 30320-6001
Phone: 404 715-2600
Web: ir.delta.com

2013 Sales

	$ mil.	% of total
Domestic	24,857	66
Atlantic	6,446	17
Pacific	4,086	11
Latin America	2,384	6
Total	**37,773**	**100**

PRODUCTS/OPERATIONS

2013 Sales

	$ mil.	% of total
Passenger		
Mainline	26,534	70
Regional carriers	6,408	18
Cargo	937	2
Other	3,894	10
Total	**37,773**	**100**

COMPETITORS

Air Canada	Qantas
AirTran Airways	SAS
American Airlines Group	Singapore Airlines
British Airways	Southwest Airlines
Cathay Pacific	US Airways
Japan Airlines	United Continental
JetBlue	Virgin Atlantic
Lufthansa	Airways

HISTORICAL FINANCIALS

Company Type: Public

Income Statement

FYE: December 31

	REVENUE ($ mil.)	NET INCOME ($ mil.)	NET PROFIT MARGIN	EMPLOYEES
12/15	40,704	4,526	11.1%	83,000
12/14	40,362	659	1.6%	80,000
12/13	37,773	10,540	27.9%	78,000
12/12	36,670	1,009	2.8%	74,000
12/11	35,115	854	2.4%	78,392
Annual Growth	**3.8%**	**51.7%**	**—**	**1.4%**

2015 Year-End Financials

Debt ratio: 15.68%
Return on equity: 46.04%
Cash ($ mil.): 1,972
Current ratio: 0.52
Long-term debt ($ mil.): 6,766

No. of shares (mil.): 778
Dividends
  Yield: 0.8%
  Payout: 12.6%
Market value ($ mil.): 39,477

	STOCK PRICE ($) FY Close	P/E High/Low		PER SHARE ($) Earnings	Dividends	Book Value
12/15	50.69	9	7	5.63	0.45	13.93
12/14	49.19	62	35	0.78	0.30	10.68
12/13	27.47	2	1	12.29	0.12	13.67
12/12	11.87	10	7	1.19	0.00	(2.50)
12/11	8.09	13	6	1.01	0.00	(1.65)
Annual Growth	**58.2%**	—	—	**53.7%**	—	—

Devon Energy Corp.

Despite its name independent oil and gas producer Devon Energy puts its energy into oil and gas fields far from England's southwestern coast. It focuses on exploration and production assets in Oklahoma Texas Wyoming and western Canada. In 2014 Devon Energy reported proved reserves of almost 3 billion barrels of oil equivalent. Devon Energy produces about 2.4 billion cu. ft. of of gas equivalent a day (3% of all the gas consumed in North America). It also has midstream and marketing assets. The company is the largest producer and lease holder in the Barnett Shale (Texas) and is looking to replicate its success there in other unconventional plays.

HISTORY

Larry Nichols (a lawyer who clerked for US Supreme Court Chief Justice Earl Warren) and his father John founded Devon Energy in 1969. John Nichols was a partner in predecessor company Blackwood and Nichols an oil partnership formed in 1946.

In 1981 the company bought a small stake in the Northeast Blanco Unit of New Mexico's San Juan Basin. To raise capital Devon formed the limited partnership Devon Resource Investors and took it public in 1985. In 1988 Devon consolidated all of its units into a single publicly traded company.

The firm increased its stake in Northeast Blanco in 1988 and again in 1989 ending up with about 25%. By 1990 Devon had drilled more than 100 wells in the area and had proved reserves of 58 billion cu. ft. of natural gas.

During the 1990s the company launched a major expansion program using a two-pronged strategy: acquiring producing properties and drilling wells in proven fields. In 1990 it bought an 88% interest in six Texas wells; two years later Devon snapped up the US properties of Hondo Oil & Gas. After its 1994 purchase of Alta Energy which operated in New Mexico Oklahoma Texas and Wyoming Devon had proved reserves of more than 500 billion cu. ft. of gas.

Between 1992 and 1997 the company also drilled some 840 successful wells. Buoyed by new seismic techniques that raise the odds of finding oil Devon devoted more resources to pioneering fields in regions where it already had expertise.

Continuing its buying spree Devon bought Kerr-McGee's onshore assets in 1997. Two years later it bought Alberta Canada-based Northstar for $775 million creating a company with holdings divided almost evenly between oil and gas.

Also in 1999 Devon grabbed its biggest prize when it purchased PennzEnergy of Houston in a $2.3 billion stock-and-debt deal that analysts called a bargain. PennzEnergy spun off from Pennzoil in 1998 dates back to the Texas oil boom after WWII. In addition to new US holdings the deal gave Devon a number of international oil and gas assets in such places as Azerbaijan Brazil Egypt Qatar and Venezuela.

On a roll Devon in 2000 bought Santa Fe Snyder for $2.35 billion in stock and $1 billion in assumed debt. The deal increased Devon's proved reserves by nearly 400 million barrels of oil equivalent.

In 2001 the company agreed to a major deal to supply Indonesian natural gas to Singapore. It also made an unsuccessful bid for rival Barrett Resources that was trumped by a bid from Williams Companies. Undaunted that year Devon acquired Anderson Exploration for $3.4 billion in cash and

$1.2 billion in assumed debt. It also purchased Mitchell Energy & Development for $3.1 billion in cash and stock and $400 million in assumed debt.

As part of its strategy to refocus on core operations in 2002 the company sold its Indonesian assets to PetroChina for $262 million. By mid-year the company had raised about $1.2 billion through the disposition of oil properties worldwide.

Over this decade Devon Energy bought its way into the big leagues as a North American producer through a series of multibillion-dollar acquisitions of oil and gas producers including Ocean Energy in 2003 for $3.5 billion and US-based Chief Holdings LLC in 2006 for $2.2 billion.

In 2007 Devon began to divest all of its assets in West Africa. It sold its oil and gas business in Egypt to Dana Petroleum for $375 million and its Gabon assets for $206 million. In 2008 it sold its oil and gas business in Côte d'Ivoire to Afren plc for $205 million and in Equatorial Guinea (to that country's national oil company GE Petrol) for $2.2 billion.

In 2010 it sold most of its remaining international assets to BP for $7 billion. As part of this deal BP sold undeveloped oil sand leases in Canada to Devon Energy for $500 million and formed a joint venture with the company to exploit them. The company also sold its Panyu field offshore China to China National Offshore Oil for $515 million.

Consolidating its North American assets to just its onshore properties In 2010 Devon Energy sold its stakes in the Cascade Jack and St. Malo fields in the Gulf of Mexico (about 200 million barrels of estimated recoverable reserves) to AP Moller-Maersk's oil unit for $1.3 billion. It also sold its remaining Gulf of Mexico shelf assets to Apache for $1 billion.

In 2012 it sold its last international offshore asset in Angola for about $71 million.

Boosting its financial resources in 2012 Devon Energy secured a commitment from Sinopec International Petroleum Exploration & Production for the Chinese company to invest $2.2 billion in exchange for one-third of Devon's interest in five new joint venture plays in the Tuscaloosa Marine Shale Niobrara Mississippian Ohio Utica Shale and the Michigan Basin.

That year it also closed a similar $1.4 billion joint venture deal with Sumitomo Corp. to develop 650000 net acres in the Cline Shale and the Midland-Wolfcamp Shale in West Texas.

EXECUTIVES

EVP and CFO, Thomas L. Mitchell, age 55, $454,808 total compensation

EVP Marketing Facilities Pipeline and Supply Chain, Darryl G. Smette, age 68, $715,231 total compensation

EVP Human Resources, Frank W. Rudolph, age 59

EVP Administration, R. Alan Marcum, age 49

President and CEO, David A. (Dave) Hager, age 59, $895,385 total compensation

EVP and General Counsel, Lyndon C. Taylor, age 57, $550,000 total compensation

VP and CIO, Ben Williams, age 43

EVP Exploration and Production, Tony D. Vaughn, age 58, $634,615 total compensation

VP Midland Basin Business Unit, Andy Coolidge, age 52

SVP Canadian Division and President Devon Canada, Rob Dutton, age 45

VP Southern Business Unit, Gregg Jacob, age 54

VP Anadarko Basin Business Unit, Todd Moehlenbrock, age 50

VP Delaware Slope Business Unit, Frank Schroeder, age 44

VP Rockies Business Unit, Phil Cook, age 54

VP Delaware Basin Business Unit, Rick Gideon, age 40

VP North Texas Business Unit, Kevin Lafferty, age 40

Vice President Acquisitions and Divestitures, Jeff Ritenour

Senior Vice President Retail Banking and Business Development, Klaholt Kimker

Vice President EHS, Richard (Dick) Luedecke

Vice President Project Development, Jimmy Turnini

Senior Vice President Marketing, Sue Alberti

Vp Planning And Evaluation, Terry Shyer

Vice President, Curtis Kantenberger

Vice President Delaware Basin Business Unit, Tom Hooper

First Vice President, Gilbert Horton

Vice President Rockies Business Unit, Dale Fritz

Business Analyst; Vice President Programs, Tricia Hillman

Senior Vice President Exploration Product, Michael (Mel) Lacey

Executive Vice President Administration, R Alan Marcum

Vice President Corporate Governance, Carla Brockman

Vice Chairman, John Richels, age 64

Chairman, J. Larry Nichols, age 73

Auditors: KPMG LLP

LOCATIONS

HQ: Devon Energy Corp.
333 West Sheridan Avenue, Oklahoma City, OK 73102-5015
Phone: 405 235-3611
Web: www.devonenergy.com

2014 Sales

	$ mil.	% of total
US	14,862	76
Canada	2,063	11
EnLink	2,641	13
Total	**19,566**	**100**

PRODUCTS/OPERATIONS

2014 Sales

	$ mil.	% of total
Oil gas & natural gas liquids	9,910	51
Marketing & midstream	7,667	39
Oil gas & natural gas liquids derivatives	1,989	10
Total	**19,566**	**100**

COMPETITORS

Abraxas Petroleum	Exxon Mobil
Apache	Hess Corporation
BP	JKX
Bonanza Creek	Jones Energy
Cabot Oil & Gas	Marathon Oil
Chesapeake Energy	Occidental Petroleum
Chevron	Royal Dutch Shell
ConocoPhillips	Williams Companies
EOG	XTO Energy
Encana	

HISTORICAL FINANCIALS

Company Type: Public

Income Statement

FYE: December 31

	REVENUE ($ mil.)	NET INCOME ($ mil.)	NET PROFIT MARGIN	EMPLOYEES
12/14	19,566	1,607	8.2%	6,600
12/13	10,397	(20)	—	5,900
12/12	9,502	(206)	—	5,700
12/11	11,454	4,704	41.1%	5,200
12/10	9,940	4,550	45.8%	5,000
Annual Growth	**18.4%**	**(22.9%)**	**—**	**7.2%**

2014 Year-End Financials

Debt ratio: 22.24%	No. of shares (mil.): 409
Return on equity: 7.65%	Dividends
Cash ($ mil.): 1,480	Yield: 1.5%
Current ratio: 1.09	Payout: 17.3%
Long-term debt ($ mil.): 9,830	Market value ($ mil.): 25,035

	STOCK PRICE ($) FY Close	P/E High/Low		PER SHARE ($) Earnings	Dividends	Book Value
12/14	61.21	20	13	3.91	0.94	52.66
12/13	61.87	—	—	(0.06)	0.86	50.49
12/12	52.04	—	—	(0.52)	0.80	52.41
12/11	62.00	8	5	11.25	0.67	53.08
12/10	78.51	8	6	10.31	0.64	44.62
Annual Growth	**(6.0%)**	**—**	**—**	**(21.5%)**	**10.1%**	**4.2%**

Dick's Sporting Goods, Inc

See Dick's shoppers run putt dunk dribble –and buy. Dick's Sporting Goods operates about 690 stores in 45-plus states. The stores usually contain five smaller shops ("stores within a store") that feature sporting goods apparel and footwear for leisure pursuits ranging from football golf and cycling to hunting and camping. In addition to brands including NIKE and adidas Dick's carries Ativa Walter Hagen Top-Flite and others exclusive to the firm. The company also operates more than 75 Golf Galaxy stores in 30 states as well as 10 Field & Stream and three True Runner stores. Dick's was founded in 1948 when Dick Stack father of company chairman and CEO Edward Stack opened a bait and tackle shop.

Sales and Marketing

Dick's sells its products through retail stores — its primary sales channel —and e-commerce sites.

The retailer spent $249 million on advertising in fiscal 2015 up from $224 million and $201 million in 2014 and 2013 respectively. Its media plan includes television direct mail and digital and print advertising. In recent years Dick's has focused on growing its brand through fully integrated campaigns across all mediums. It's optimizing its media mix by using more efficient and effective marketing channels and by leveraging extensive customer relationship marketing data gleaned from its ScoreCard Rewards and Advantage Club loyalty programs. To build its brand Dick's is also actively involved in sponsoring thousands of local teams.

Historically the company's marketing strategy has involved promoting its selection of brand-name products at competitive prices using newspaper advertising direct mail pieces and seasonal ads on local and national television and radio. While Dick's continues to enlist the help of traditional channels to market its merchandise assortment the sporting goods retailer has reduced its spending on newspaper advertising. Instead it's spending on developed brand-building marketing campaigns that work to build passion and loyalty to the Dick's Sporting Goods brand. The company's advertising mix is also heavier on the digital marketing side and includes emphasis on digital platforms and digital-exclusive marketing campaigns. To further enhance its customers' mobile and in-store experience Dick's in 2013 launched a comprehensive mobile application for both iPhone and Android smartphones.

In 2015 Nike and Under Armour its largest vendors accounted for 19% and 12% of merchandise sales respectively.

Financial Performance

Dick's reported $6.8 billion in revenue for fiscal 2015. That was an increase of more than $600 million compared to the prior fiscal period. The company claimed a net income of $344.1 million for fiscal 2015 which was an increase of $6.6 million (or 2%) compared to its fiscal 2014 net income.

Dick's ended fiscal 2015 with about $605 million in cash on hand. That was increase of more than $200 million compared to the company's fiscal 2014 cash levels.

Strategy

Believing that the sporting goods retailing market can bear at least 1100 Dick's locations nationwide the company has been focused on expanding its retail footprint east of the Mississippi River in Atlanta Chicago and the corridor between New York and Washington DC.

EXECUTIVES

EVP and COO, Andr ©. Hawaux, age 55, $750,000 total compensation

Chairman and CEO, Edward W. (Ed) Stack, age 60, $1,000,000 total compensation

SVP Merchandising, Ronald E. (Ron) Baime, age 50

EVP Product Development and Planning Allocations and Replenishment, Lee J. Belitsky, age 54, $462,952 total compensation

SVP and Chief Marketing Officer, Lauren R. Hobart, age 46, $416,827 total compensation

President Field & Stream, Steven A. (Steve) Clemente

SVP Information Technology and CIO, Kurt J. Schnieders

EVP Inventory Supply Chain and eCommerce, Michele B. Willoughby, age 49, $500,000 total compensation

EVP and CFO, Teri L. List-Stoll

SVP Human Resources, Deborah M. Victorelli, age 52, $382,524 total compensation

SVP Supply Chain, George P. Giacobbe

SVP and General Manager Athletic Apparel Licensed and Accessories Footwear Outerwear Apparel DICK'S Golf and Golf Galaxy and True Runner, Alexander L. (Alex) Tomey

Executive Vice President, John (Jack) Duken

Vice President Application Development, Bob Pecina

Executive Vice President And Chief Ope, Joseph (Jo) Schmidt

Vice President Information Technology, Andrew (Andy) Truini

Vice President of Store Planning Construction and Purchasing, Scott Blyze

Vice President Product Development Private Brands, Dave D'Angelo

Vice President Tax, Todd Hipwell

Vice Chairman, William J. (Bill) Colombo, age 59

Auditors: Deloitte & Touche LLP

LOCATIONS

HQ: Dick's Sporting Goods, Inc
345 Court Street, Coraopolis, PA 15108
Phone: 724 273-3400
Web: www.DICKS.com

PRODUCTS/OPERATIONS

2015 Sales

	% of total
Hardlines	44
Apparel	36
Footwear	19
Other	1
Total	**100**

Selected Categories

Archery
Backpacking
Baseball
Basketball
Boating
Bowling
Camping
Cycling
Exercise
Fishing
Football
Golf
Hockey (ice and roller)
Hunting
In-line skating
Lacrosse
Optics/telescopes
Paintball
Racquetball/squash
Running
Skateboarding
Snow sports
Soccer
Tennis
Volleyball
Water sports

COMPETITORS

Academy Sports	Hibbett Sports
Big 5	J. C. Penney
Cabela's	Kmart
Callaway Golf	L.L. Bean
Costco Wholesale	Modell's
Dunham's	Olympia Sports
Eastern Mountain Sports	REI
Finish Line	Sears
Foot Locker	Sports Authority
Gander Mountain	Target Corporation
Golfsmith	Wal-Mart
	Winmark

HISTORICAL FINANCIALS

Company Type: Public

Income Statement
FYE: January 31

	REVENUE ($ mil.)	NET INCOME ($ mil.)	NET PROFIT MARGIN	EMPLOYEES
01/15*	6,814	344	5.1%	37,600
02/14	6,213	337	5.4%	34,300
02/13	5,836	290	5.0%	29,800
01/12	5,211	263	5.1%	28,400
01/11	4,871	182	3.7%	26,700
Annual Growth	8.8%	17.3%	—	8.9%

*Fiscal year change

2015 Year-End Financials

Debt ratio: 0.19%	No. of shares (mil.): 118
Return on equity: 19.59%	Dividends
Cash ($ mil.): 221	Yield: 0.0%
Current ratio: 1.65	Payout: 17.6%
Long-term debt ($ mil.): 5	Market value ($ mil.): 6,100

	STOCK PRICE ($) FY Close	P/E High/Low	PER SHARE ($) Earnings	Dividends	Book Value
01/15*	51.65	20 14	2.84	0.50	15.51
02/14	52.50	21 16	2.69	0.50	13.99
02/13	47.90	23 17	2.31	2.50	12.90
01/12	41.16	19 14	2.10	0.50	13.46
01/11	35.80	24 14	1.50	0.00	11.48
Annual Growth	9.6%	— —	17.3%	—	7.8%

*Fiscal year change

Dillard's Inc.

Tradition is trying to catch up with the times at Dillard's. Sandwiched between retail giant Macy's and discount chains such as Kohl's Dillard's is rethinking its strategy and trimming its store count. The department store chain operates about 270 locations (down from 330 in 2005) in some 30 US states covering the Sunbelt and the central US. Its stores cater to middle- and upper-middle-income women selling name-brand and private-label merchandise with a focus on apparel and home furnishings. Women's apparel and accessories account for nearly 40% of its sales. Founded in 1938 by William Dillard family members through the W. D. Company control the company.

Operations

Dillard's exclusive brand lines include Antonio Melani Gianni Bini GB Roundtree & York and Daniel Cremieux. By product line the company generated 22% of its sales from ladies' apparel in fiscal 2015 (ended January) and another 16% from ladies' accessories and lingerie. Another 17% of sales came from men's apparel and accessories while the rest of sales came from shoes (16%) cosmetics (14%) juniors' and children's apparel (9%) and home and furniture products (4%). Beyond department stores Dillard's owns CDI Contractors a Little Rock Arkansas-based construction firm that was started to build and remodel its stores. It also owns Acumen Brands the operator of a dozen online retailers including scrubschopper.com (medical uniforms) and countryoutfitter.com (western wear) which assists in its e-commerce operations.

Geographic Reach

Texas and Florida are the Arkansas-based department store chain's two largest markets accounting for about a third of total stores. In 2015 the company operated 272 Dillard's stores and 25 clearing centers —representing more than 50 million sq. ft. of space —in 29 states.

Sales and Marketing

Dillard's markets its products in shopping malls and open-air centers. The retailer spent $56 million on advertising in FY2015 down from $65 million in FY2014 and $77 million in FY2013.

In 2014 the company launched a partnership with Time Inc.'s Southern Living franchise to produce home products (bath bedding tabletop candles ceramic accessories) available exclusively at Dillard's stores. Later that year Dillard's entered a new agreement with James Avery to provide that company's jewelry at more than 40 store locations.

Financial Performance

Dillard's sales and profits have remained mostly flat over the past few years as its rising comparable store sales have been offset by its shrinking net store count. The retailer's sales inched up 1% to $6.78 billion in fiscal 2015 (ended January) thanks to a 1% increase in comparable store sales with sales increases for all of its product lines except for cosmetics which remained flat and home and furniture which declined significantly. Sales transactions decreased 2% while average dollars per transaction increased 3%.

Higher sales in FY2015 drove Dillard's net income up 3% to $331.85 million. The retailer's operating cash levels climbed 22% to $611.6 million for the year thanks to favorable working capital changes mostly related to increases in trade accounts payable and accrued expenses.

Strategy

To try and reverse falling sales the department store chain has moved "up market" positioning itself above Macy's and Belk and below high-end chains such as Nordstrom and Bloomingdale's. To attract more customers Dillard's is focusing on adding more fashion much like J. C. Penney has done in recent years. The firm's new direction is inspired on the success of specialty stores with their edited displays or merchandise in boutique-like settings rather than an endless sea of apparel racks. New stores are smaller (averaging 170000 sq. ft.) and located in open-air lifestyle centers rather than enclosed malls. Dillard's which has been averse to marking down merchandise but has been forced to discount by its lower-end competitors hopes its move up market will stop the markdowns.

Dillards also continues to shrink its net store count as it shutters underperforming locations in attempt to cut operating expenses and generate property gains. During 2014 for example it closed its Southgate Mall location in Sarasota Florida for a gain of $6.3 million and sold a store in Longmont Colorado for $14.5 million in proceeds.

HISTORY

Company BackgroundAt age 12 William Dillard began working in his father's general store in Mineral Springs Arkansas. After he graduated from Columbia University in 1937 the third-generation retailer spent seven months in the Sears Roebuck manager training program in Tulsa Oklahoma.

With $8000 borrowed from his father William opened his first department store in Nashville Arkansas in 1938. Service was one of the most important things he had to offer he said and he insisted on quality —he personally inspected every item and would settle for nothing but the best. William sold the store in 1948 to finance a partnership in Wooten's Department Store in Texarkana Arkansas; he bought out Wooten and established Dillard's the next year.

Throughout the 1950s and 1960s the company became a strong regional retailer developing its strategy of buying well-established downtown stores in small cities; acquisitions in those years included Mayer & Schmidt (Tyler Texas; 1956) and Joseph Pfeifer (Little Rock Arkansas; 1963). Dillard's moved its headquarters to Little Rock after buying Pfeifer. When it went public in 1969 it had 15 stores in three states.

During the early 1960s the company began computerizing operations to streamline inventory and information management. In 1970 Dillard's added computerized cash registers which gave management hourly sales figures.

The chain continued acquiring outlets (more than 130 over the next three decades including stores owned by Stix Baer & Fuller Macy's Joske's and Maison Blanche). In a 1988 joint venture with Edward J. DeBartolo Dillard's bought a 50% interest in the 12 Higbee's stores in Ohio (buying the other 50% in 1992 shortly after Higbee's bought five former Horne's stores in Ohio).

In 1991 Vendamerica (subsidiary of Vendex International and the only major nonfamily holder of the company's stock) sold its 8.9 million shares of Class A stock (25% of the class) in an underwritten public offering.

Dillard's purchase of 12 Diamond stores from Dayton Hudson in 1994 gave it a small-event ticket-sales chain in the Southwest which it renamed Dillard's Box Office. A lawsuit filed by the FTC against Dillard's that year claiming the company made it unreasonably difficult for its credit card holders to remove unauthorized charges from their bills was dismissed the following year.

Dillard's continued to grow; it opened 11 new stores in 1995 and 16 more in 1996 (entering Georgia and Colorado). The next year it opened 12 new stores and acquired 20 making its way into Virginia California and Wyoming.

William retired in 1998 and William Dillard II took over the CEO position while brother Alex became president. The company then paid $3.1 billion for Mercantile Stores which operated 106 apparel and home design stores in the South and Midwest. To avoid redundancy in certain regions Dillard's sold 26 of those stores and exchanged seven others for new Dillard's stores. The assimilation of Mercantile brought distribution problems that cut into earnings for fiscal 1999. In late 2000 with a slumping stock price and declining sales Dillard's said it would de-emphasize its concentration on name-brand merchandise and offer deep discounts on branded items already in stock. Despite these efforts sales and earnings continued to slide in 2001.

Founder and patriarch William Dillard (the company's guiding force) died in February 2002. Son William II became chairman of the company which has been family-controlled for half a century. Dillard's opened four new stores and closed nine in 2002. Sales declined 3% versus the previous year.

In 2003 Dillard's shuttered 10 stores and opened five new store locations.

In November 2004 Dillard's completed the sale of Dillard National Bank the retailer's credit card portfolio to GE Consumer Finance for about $1.1 billion (plus debt). Dillard's had said it would use the proceeds to reduce debt repurchase stock and to achieve general corporate purposes.

In the spring of 2005 Dillard's shuttered the last of 16 home and furniture stores acquired when the department store chain acquired Mercantile Stores Co. in 1998. Hurricanes Katrina Rita and Wilma took a toll on Dillard's in 2005 interrupting business in about 60 of the company's stores at various times.

In August 2008 Dillard's purchased the 50% stake in the Arkansas-based construction firm CDI Contractors that it didn't already own for about $9.8 million. CDI is a general contactor that also builds stores for Dillard's. In November Dillard's announced 500 job cuts including about 60 at headquarters.

Amid falling sales and rising investor discontent Dillard's bowed to pressure from hedge funds Barington Capital Group and Clinton Group and appointed four new directors in April 2008 to avoid a proxy fight.

In February 2012 Dillard's acquired Acumen Brands an e-commerce company located in Fayetteville Arkansas.

EXECUTIVES

EVP, Drue Matheny, age 68, $710,000 total compensation
SVP and CFO, James I. Freeman, age 65, $775,000 total compensation
EVP, Mike Dillard, age 63, $710,000 total compensation
President, Alex Dillard, age 65, $1,000,000 total compensation
Chairman and CEO, William (Bill) Dillard, age 70, $1,000,000 total compensation
Vice President and Treasurer, Sherrill Wise
Vice President Transportation and Distrabution, Tony Bolte
Regional Vice President, Michael Hubbell
Vice President Advertising, Christine Rowell
Vice President of Mens, Jim Northup
Upper Management Vice President, Kristin Jacobson
Assistant Vice President for Sponsored Programs, Theodore (Theo) Callier
Vice President, Samantha Carrasco
Vice President, Mike Shields
Vice President, James Stockman
Vice President Accounting, Steve Gelwix
Executive Vice President and Director, Drue Corbusier

Vice President Advertising, Roger Williams
Vice President Merchanising, Mike McNiff
Vice President Accessories, Kay White
Vice President Merchandising ST Louis Division, Mark Killingsworth
Vice President Sales Promotion, Louise Platt
Secretary, Ann Niccoli
Secretary, Suzanne Stewart
Secretary, Shirley Wallace
Auditors: KPMG LLP

LOCATIONS

HQ: Dillard's Inc.
1600 Cantrell Road, Little Rock, AR 72201
Phone: 501 376-5200
Web: www.dillards.com

2015 Stores

	No.
Texas	59
Florida	42
Arizona	17
North Carolina	14
Ohio	14
Louisiana	14
Georgia	12
Alabama	10
Oklahoma	10
Missouri	10
Tennessee	10
Arkansas	8
Colorado	7
South Carolina	8
Kansas	6
Virginia	6
Kentucky	6
Mississippi	6
New Mexico	6
Utah	5
Iowa	5
Nevada	5
California	3
Illinois	3
Indiana	3
Nebraska	3
Idaho	2
Montana	2
Wyoming	1
Total	**297**

PRODUCTS/OPERATIONS

2015 Sales

	% of total
Ladies' apparel	22
Men's apparel & accessories	17
Shoes	16
Ladies' accessories & lingerie	16
Cosmetics	14
Juniors' & children's apparel	9
Home & furniture	4
Construction segment	2
Total	**100**

COMPETITORS

Abercrombie & Fitch	Macy's
American Eagle Outfitters	Mattress Firm
	Men's Wearhouse
Ann Taylor	Neiman Marcus
Bed Bath & Beyond	Nordstrom
Belk	Sears
Bon-Ton Stores	Stein Mart
Burlington Coat Factory	TJX Companies
	Talbots
Caleres	Target Corporation
Eddie Bauer LLC	The Gap
Foot Locker	Tuesday Morning Corporation
J. C. Penney	
J. Crew	Von Maur
Kohl's	Walgreen
Lands' End	

Income Statement

FYE: January 31

	REVENUE ($ mil.)	NET INCOME ($ mil.)	NET PROFIT MARGIN	EMPLOYEES
01/15*	6,780	331	4.9%	40,000
02/14	6,691	323	4.8%	40,000
02/13	6,751	335	5.0%	38,000
01/12	6,399	463	7.2%	38,900
01/11	6,253	179	2.9%	38,900
Annual Growth	2.0%	16.6%	—	0.7%

*Fiscal year change

2015 Year-End Financials

Debt ratio: 19.70%	No. of shares (mil.): 41
Return on equity: 16.59%	Dividends
Cash ($ mil.): 403	Yield: 0.0%
Current ratio: 2.13	Payout: 3.0%
Long-term debt ($ mil.): 820	Market value ($ mil.): 4,679

	STOCK PRICE ($) FY Close	P/E High/Low		PER SHARE ($) Earnings	Dividends	Book Value
01/15*	113.60	16	11	7.79	0.24	49.02
02/14	87.30	14	11	7.10	0.22	45.33
02/13	85.41	13	6	6.87	5.20	41.24
01/12	46.14	7	4	8.52	0.19	41.50
01/11	40.21	16	6	2.67	0.16	34.79
Annual Growth	29.6%	—	—	30.7%	10.7%	8.9%

*Fiscal year change

nancial PerformanceDime Community's revenue has been in decline in recent years due to shrinking interest margins on loans amidst the low-interest environment. The firm's profits however have been rising since 2012 thanks to declining loan loss provisions as its loan portfolio's credit quality has improved with the strengthened economy.Dime's revenue dipped by less than 1% to $182 million in 2014 as the bank's interest income continued to decline on shrinking interest margins on both real estate loans and mortgage-backed securities. The bank blamed fierce mortgage refinancing competition for much of the 49 basis point-reduction of interest yields on its loan portfolio which led to lower interest income.Despite lower revenue in 2014 the company's net income rose by nearly 2% to $44.25 million thanks to a continued decline in the provision for loan losses. Dime Community's operating cash fell by 23% to $47.26 million during the year due to lower cash earnings.StrategyDime Community Bancshares has been moving toward digital banking channels that are quickly taking the industry by storm allowing the bank to slow expensive branch-expansion plans and cut operating costs significantly while giving customers faster access to banking services. In 2014 as part of its eBanking platform initiative to expand into online banking mobile banking bill pay and remote deposit the bank launched its Dime Mobile Banking platform which allowed customer to deposit checks pay bills transfer funds and check account balances and status from their smartphones.

EXECUTIVES

EVP and Chief Risk Officer, Timothy B. King, age 56, $300,000 total compensation

President and COO, Kenneth J. Mahon, age 64, $450,400 total compensation

Chairman and CEO, Vincent F. Palagiano, age 74, $388,500 total compensation

EVP and Chief Retail Officer, Terence J. Mitchell, age 62

EVP and Chief Accounting Officer, Michael Pucella, age 61, $307,500 total compensation

Secretary, Lance J. Bennett

EVP and Chief Investment Officer, Robert Volino

EVP and CTO, Timothy Lenhoff

Vice President Of Facilities, Marie Twomey

Vice President, Tom Dippolito

Vice Chairman, Michael P. Devine, age 68

Auditors: Crowe Horwath LLP

LOCATIONS

HQ: Dime Community Bancshares, Inc
209 Havemeyer Street, Brooklyn, NY 11211
Phone: 718 782-6200
Web: www.dime.com

PRODUCTS/OPERATIONS

2014 Sales

	$ mil.	% of total
Interest		
Loans secured by real estate	169	93
Mortgage-backed securities	0	1
Other	2	1
Noninterest		
Service charges & other fees	3	2
Bank-owned life insurance	1	1
Other	4	2
Total	182	100

COMPETITORS

Astoria Financial	HSBC
Carver Bancorp	JPMorgan Chase
Citigroup	Valley National
First of Long Island	Bancorp
Flushing Financial	

Dime Community Bancshares, Inc

Dime Community Bancshares is in a New York state of mind. It is the holding company for The Dime Savings Bank of Williamsburgh which boasts $4.5 billion in assets and operates more than 25 branches in Brooklyn Queens and the Bronx as well as Nassau County on Long Island. Founded in 1864 the bank provides standard products and services including checking savings retirement money market and club accounts accounts. Multifamily residential and commercial real estate loans comprise the vast majority of the bank's loan portfolio. Subsidiary Dime Insurance Agency (formerly Havemeyer Investments) offers life policies fixed annuities and wealth management services.

OperationsMultifamily residential real estate loans accounted for 80% of Dime Savings' $4 billion loan portfolio in 2014; most of these were secured by properties in Brooklyn Queens and Manhattan. Another 18% of the portfolio was made up of commercial real estate loans. The community-oriented bank believes that multifamily residential and mixed-use loans in the New York City area produce higher yields than securities with similar maturities. The bank generated 93% of its total revenue from interest income on loans secured by real estate in 2014 while interest on mortgage-backed securities service charge fees mortgage banking income and other miscellaneous fees made up the rest of revenues.Geographic ReachThe Brooklyn-based bank operates 25 branches in New York City in the boroughs of Brooklyn Queens and the Bronx as well as in Nassau County in New York.Sales and MarketingDime Community's primary lending area is in the New York Metro area though its total lending area spans 50 miles from its headquarters' radius.Fi-

Income Statement

FYE: December 31

	ASSETS ($ mil.)	NET INCOME ($ mil.)	INCOME AS % OF ASSETS	EMPLOYEES
12/14	4,497	44	1.0%	409
12/13	4,028	43	1.1%	413
12/12	3,905	40	1.0%	421
12/11	4,021	47	1.2%	435
12/10	4,040	41	1.0%	442
Annual Growth	2.7%	1.7%	—	(1.9%)

2014 Year-End Financials

Debt ratio: —	No. of shares (mil.): 36
Return on equity: 9.88%	Dividends
Cash ($ mil.): 78	Yield: 3.4%
Current ratio: —	Payout: 47.4%
Long-term debt ($ mil.): —	Market value ($ mil.): 600

	STOCK PRICE ($) FY Close	P/E High/Low		PER SHARE ($) Earnings	Dividends	Book Value
12/14	16.28	14	11	1.23	0.56	12.47
12/13	16.92	14	11	1.23	0.56	11.86
12/12	13.89	13	11	1.17	0.56	10.96
12/11	12.60	11	7	1.40	0.56	10.28
12/10	14.59	12	9	1.24	0.56	9.50
Annual Growth	2.8%	—	—	(0.2%)	(0.0%)	7.0%

Discover Financial Services

Seems cardholders aren't the only ones getting paid to discover. Discover Financial Services is best known for issuing Discover-brand credit cards which are used by more than 25 million members. The company's cards which include several levels of business and consumer accounts repay cardholders a percentage of the purchase price each time they use their cards. Discover also licenses Diners Club credit cards which are accepted in more than 185 countries. But there's more to this business than just plastic. The company also offers direct banking services makes student and personal loans including mortgages and runs the PULSE Network ATM system. Morgan Stanley spun off Discover Financial Services in 2007.

Operations

DFS has two operating segments. Direct Banking is the largest accounting for about 95% of annual revenue. It includes Discover-branded credit cards issued to individuals and small businesses as well as other consumer products and services such as private student loans personal loans home loans prepaid cards and other consumer lending and deposit products. DFS began offering home mortgages and related services in 2012. The company's Payment Services segment includes PULSE the automated teller machine debit and electronic funds transfer network; and Diners Club.The PULSE network of ATMs and POS terminals operates from more than 7200 financial institutions across the US and has a direct relationship with more than half of them. PULSE also provides cash from more than 1.6 million ATMS in 130 countries.

Sales and Marketing

The direct banking and payment services company markets its credit cards and other loans products via direct mail media advertising and merchant or partner relationships. DFS reported advertising costs of $194 million $208 million and $172 million in the fiscal years ended November 30 2014 2013 and 2012 respectively.

Financial Performance

The card issuer has enjoyed multiple years of revenue growth as customers carry higher balances with revenue rising by 3% to $9.61 billion in 2014. Driving the rise in revenue was a 7% increase in the company's core Direct Banking segment revenues thanks to higher average balances on credit card loans personal loans and private student loans combined with higher yields on credit card loans and PCI student loans. Despite higher revenue net income dipped 6% over the same period to $2.32 billion mostly because the company incurred higher provisions for loan losses and spent more on employee compensation and benefits marketing and business development and professional fee expenses.Discover's cash flow from operations however jumped by 9% to $3.83 billion in 2014 mostly because it wrote off more for its loan loss provisions accrued expenses and other liabilities.

Strategy

DFS has also been busy building its international business to increase the acceptance of its cards worldwide. The company has reciprocity alliances with card issuers in countries such as Canada China France Germany Japan South Korea and the UK to increase its cards' acceptance in those markets and allow cardholders access to Discover's network anywhere in the world. In early 2015 the company's international Diner Club subsidiary partnered with payment specialist The Logic Group to grow Discover and Diners Card acceptance in the UK and Europe. In 2014 Diners Club extended its merchant acquiring service's reach into Thailand and Southeast Asia through an alliance with Bangkok Bank. In 2013 Discover inked a deal with Network International a top payment solutions provider in the Middle East that promotes the newly launched Mercury domestic card network. As part of their alliance Mercury network cards will be accepted on Discover Diners Club and PULSE networks for international purchases and cash access outside the United Arab Emirates. In 2012 Discover issued its first cards outside the US (in Ecuador) and entered into an alliance with National Payments Corporation to increase network acceptance in India. In past years the card issuer has also sought growth in its credit card and student and personal loan operations by acquiring new accounts and by purchasing other companies.

Mergers and Acquisitions

In 2012 DFS bought Home Loan Center the mortgage origination operations of Tree.com for nearly $56 million.

Company Background

To gain access to federal funds made available through the Troubled Asset Relief Program (TARP) Discover Financial converted to a bank holding company in 2009. It received $1.2 billion from the program which it repaid the following year.Discover boosted its lending operations in 2010 with its $600 million purchase of Citibank's 80% stake in Student Loan Corporation. It also acquired a $4.2 billion portfolio of private student loans from Citibank. The company later divested its portfolio of federal student loans after the government overhauled its lending program and became the sole provider of government-backed student loans in 2010. The following year Discover bought another $2.5 billion in student loans from Citibank.

EXECUTIVES

Chairman and CEO, David W. Nelms, age 54, $1,000,000 total compensation
President and COO, Roger C. Hochschild, age 51, $750,000 total compensation
EVP and CFO, R. Mark Graf, age 50, $625,000 total compensation
SVP and Chief Risk Officer, Steven E. Cunningham, age 45
EVP; President Payment Services, Diane E. Offereins, age 58, $650,000 total compensation
EVP; President Consumer Banking, Carlos Minetti, age 53, $650,000 total compensation
EVP General Counsel and Secretary, Kelly McNamara Corley, age 55
EVP; President Credit and Card Operations, James V. Panzarino, age 63
SVP and CIO, Glenn P. Schneider, age 53
SVP and Chief Marketing Officer, Julie Loeger
Vice President Information Technology Web Development, Larry Holstein
Senior Vice President Information Technology Operations, Denise Carlson
Vice President, Dana Traci
Vice President Technology Products, Joseph Bonefas
Vice President Of It Audit, Vesela Zlateva
Vice President Development and Support, John Williamson
Vice President Discover Network Strategic Development, Joe Hurley
Vice President International Acceptan, Gerry Wagner
Vice President Business Technology, Christine Watts
Vice President Of Marketing, Mark Scarborough
Senior Vice President Medical and Scientific Affairs Chief Marketing Officer, Ryan Lunt
Vice President Marketing, Steve Carmichael
Vice President and Assistant General Counsel, Simon Halfin
Assistant Vice President Predictive Sciences, Anna Liu
Vice President Banking Systems, Tristan Hoag
Vice President Corporate Planning and Procurement, Dan Capozzi
Vice President Risk, Shrikant Dash
Vice President Network Services, Rob Tourt
Executive Vice President, R Graf
Auditors: Deloitte & Touche LLP

LOCATIONS

HQ: Discover Financial Services
2500 Lake Cook Road, Riverwoods, IL 60015
Phone: 224 405-0900
Web: www.discover.com

PRODUCTS/OPERATIONS

2013 Sales

	$ mil.	% of total
Direct banking	9,040	96
Payment services	330	4
Total	**9,370**	**100**

2013 Sales

	$ mil.	% of total
Interest		
Credit card loans	5,978	64
Other loans	997	10
Investment securities	74	1
Other	15	-
Non-interest		
Net discount & interchange revenue	1,126	12
Protection products	350	4
Loan fees	320	3
Transaction processing	192	2
Gain on origination & salesof mortgage loans	144	2
Other	174	2
Total	**9,370**	**100**

COMPETITORS

Ally Financial	JPMorgan Chase
American Express	MasterCard
Bank of America	PNC Financial
Barclays Bank Delaware	Sallie Mae
Capital One	USAA
Citigroup	Visa Inc
First Data	Wells Fargo

HISTORICAL FINANCIALS

Company Type: Public

Income Statement

FYE: December 31

	ASSETS ($ mil.)	NET INCOME ($ mil.)	INCOME AS % OF ASSETS	EMPLOYEES
12/14	83,126	2,323	2.8%	14,676
12/13*	79,340	2,470	3.1%	14,128
11/12	75,283	2,345	3.1%	13,009
11/11	68,783	2,226	3.2%	11,650
11/10	60,784	764	1.3%	10,300
Annual Growth	**8.1%**	**32.0%**	**—**	**9.3%**

*Fiscal year change

2014 Year-End Financials

Debt ratio: 27.12%
Return on equity: 21.17%
Cash ($ mil.): 7,284
Current ratio: —
Long-term debt ($ mil.): —

No. of shares (mil.): 449
Dividends
Yield: 1.4%
Payout: 17.4%
Market value ($ mil.): 29,417

	STOCK PRICE ($) FY Close	P/E High/Low		PER SHARE ($) Earnings	Dividends	Book Value
12/14	65.49	14	11	4.90	0.92	24.79
12/13*	55.95	11	8	4.96	0.74	22.89
11/12	41.61	9	5	4.46	0.40	19.64
11/11	23.82	7	4	4.06	0.20	15.59
11/10	18.28	16	10	1.22	0.08	11.85
Annual Growth	**37.6%**	**—**	**—**	**41.6%**	**84.2%**	**20.3%**

*Fiscal year change

Discovery Communications, Inc.

Discovery Communications allows viewers to go on safari without ever having to leave their couch. It is the world's #1 non-fiction media company with more than 150 worldwide cable TV networks including Discovery Channel Animal Planet and The Learning Channel (TLC). Among its US joint venture networks are The Oprah Winfrey Network (OWN) The Hub and 3net (the first 24-hour 3D network). Discovery Communications reaches more than 2.2 billion subscribers in more than 220 countries. In addition the company offers educational products and services to school; a diverse set of digital media services; and online content through Discovery.com and AnimalPlanet.com.

HISTORY

John Hendricks a history graduate who wanted to expand the presence of educational programming on TV founded Cable Educational Network in 1982. Three years later he introduced the Discovery Channel. Devoted entirely to documentaries and nature shows the channel premiered in 156000 US homes. After dodging bankruptcy (it had $5000 cash and $1 million in debt to the BBC) within a year the Discovery Channel had 7 million subscribers and a host of new investors including Cox Communications and TCI (later AT&T Broadband). It expanded its programming from 12 hours to 18 hours a day in 1987.

Discovery continued to attract subscribers reaching more than 32 million by 1988. The next year it launched Discovery Channel Europe to more than 200000 homes in the UK and Scandinavia. The company began selling home videos in 1990 and entered the Israeli market. The following year Discovery Communications Inc. (DCI) was formed to house the company's operations and it bought The Learning Channel (TLC founded 1980). The company revamped TLC's programming and in 1992 introduced a daily six-hour commercial-free block of children's programs. The next year it introduced its first CD-ROM title In the Company of Whales based on the Discovery Channel documentary.

DCI increased its focus on international expansion in 1994 moving into Asia Latin America the Middle East North Africa Portugal and Spain. The next year the company introduced its website and began selling company merchandise such as CD-ROMs and videos. DCI solidified its move into the retail sector in 1996 with the acquisition of The Nature Company and Scientific Revolution chains (renamed Discovery Channel Store). Also that year it launched its third major cable channel Animal Planet.

The company continued expanding internationally throughout the mid-1990s establishing operations in Australia Canada India New Zealand and South Korea (1995); Africa Brazil Germany and Italy (1996); and Japan and Turkey (1997). DCI also added to its stable of cable channels with the purchase of 70% of the Travel Channel from Paxson Communications (later ION Media Networks) in 1997. (It acquired the remaining 30% interest in 1999.) The company's 1997 original production "Titanic: Anatomy of a Disaster" attracted 3.2 million US households setting a network ratings record.

The following year DCI and the BBC launched Animal Planet in Asia through a joint venture and agreed to market and distribute new cable channel BBC America. It also bought CBS's Eye on People renaming the channel Discovery People (DCI shut the channel down in 2000). DCI spent $330 million launching its new health and fitness channel Discovery Health in 1999 and formed partnerships with high-speed online service Road Runner (to provide interactive information and services to Road Runner customers) and Rosenbluth Travel (to provide vacation packages based on DCI programming).

DCI reorganized its Internet activities into one unit called Discovery.com in 2000 with plans to eventually take it public. Later that year the Discovery Channel set back-to-back records with the two highest-rated documentaries ever on cable "Raising the Mammoth" (10.1 million people) and "Walking With Dinosaurs" (10.7 million people). In 2001 the company cut about 50 jobs as part of a restructuring. Later that year Discovery Communications struck a three-year deal to lease time from NBC on Saturday mornings (paying $6 million per season) to show its Discovery Kids programs.

In 2002 the company launched a 24-hour high-definition television network called Discovery HD Theater. Two years later founder John Hendricks relinquished his CEO duties (he remained chairman). President Judy McHale replaced him.

DCI started off 2005 by rebranding its aviation-themed Discovery Wings channel as the Military Channel. Later that year former majority owner Liberty Media placed its stake in DCI into a new company called Discovery Holding which it then spun off to Liberty shareholders.

Early in 2007 former NBC Universal Cable executive David Zaslav was named CEO replacing McHale. DCI later bought out 25%-partner Cox Communications in exchange for $1.3 billion in cash along with such assets as the Travel Channel and Antenna Audio. It also began shuttering its chain of Discovery Channel Stores as part of a cost-cutting effort.

Joint venture partners Discovery Holding and Advance/Newhouse (an affiliate of Advance Publications) combined their stakes in Discovery Communications in 2008 spinning off DCI as a public company.

Over the next few years DCI worked diligently to launch new networks targeting a diverse selection of audience segments. In 2010 it rolled out The Hub a channel targeting kids ages 2-11. Another 50/50 joint venture with toy maker Hasbro The Hub offers programming based on many of Hasbro's popular brands including G.I. Joe Scrabble Tonka and Transformers.

In early 2011 the company helped launch OWN talk show host Oprah Winfrey's new network and 3net one of the first networks dedicated to providing 3D programming 24 hours a day.

EXECUTIVES

President CEO and Director, David M. Zaslav, age 56, $3,000,000 total compensation
Group President Discovery Channel Animal Planet and Science Channel, Rich Ross, age 54
President Advertising Sales, Joseph (Joe) Abruzzese
Co-President Oprah Winfrey Network and Harpo Studios, Erik Logan Toppenberg
Group President Investigation Discovery American Heroes Channel and Destination America, Henry S. Schleiff, age 66
CTO, John Honeycutt
President Global Business and Legal Affairs Production Management and Studios, Marc Graboff
President Discovery Networks International, Jean-Briac (JB) Perrette
SEVP and CFO, Andrew C. (Andy) Warren, age 48, $925,442 total compensation
CEO Domestic Content Distribution and President and CEO of Discovery Education, Bill Goodwyn
President Studios Group, Lee Bartlett
EVP Global Communications and Corporate Affairs, David C. Leavy
Co-President Oprah Winfrey Network and Harpo Studios, Sheri Salata
President Content Discovery Networks International, Marjorie Kaplan
EVP and General Manager TLC, Nancy Daniels
EVP and Managing Director Discovery Networks Latin America/U.S. Hispanic, Enrique R. (Henry) Mart nez
President and Managing Director Discovery Networks Northern Europe, Dee Forbes
President and Managing Director Discovery Networks Central & Eastern Europe Middle East and Africa, Kasia Kieli
President Sports Strategy and Development Discovery Networks International, Jean-Thierry Augustin
CEO Eurosport, Peter Hutton
President Domestic Distribution, Eric Phillips
President and Managing Director Discovery Networks Southern Europe, Marinella Soldi
Vice President Operations And Prod Development Partnerships, Kevin Malone
Vice President Operations, Toni Herbert
Vice President Financial Planning And Analysis, Matthew Deprey

Executive Vice President Advertising Sales Mtv Networks Kids And Family Group, Jim Perry
Vice President Technology, Jim Boyle
Carrie D Storer Senior Vice President Human Resources And Compliance Legal, Carrie Storer
Senior Vice President Of Operations, Veronica Cajigas
Vice President, John Saag
Vice President, Michela Giorelli
Senior Vice President Investor Relations, Craig Felenstein
Senior Vice President Distribution, Meg Lowe
Senior Vice President Us Media Operations, Don Johnson
Vice President Strategy And Account Management, Todd Richards
Chairman, Robert J. (Bob) Miron, age 78
Auditors: PricewaterhouseCoopers LLP

LOCATIONS

HQ: Discovery Communications, Inc.
One Discovery Place, Silver Spring, MD 20910
Phone: 240 662-2000
Web: www.corporate.discovery.com

2013 Sales

	$ mil.	% of total
US	3,071	55
International	2,464	45
Total	**5,535**	**100**

PRODUCTS/OPERATIONS

2014 Sales

	$ mil.	% of total
Advertising	3,089	49
Distribution	2,842	45
Other	334	5
Total	**6,265**	**100**

2013 Sales

	$ mil.	% of total
Advertising	2,739	49
Distribution	2,536	46
Other	260	5
Total	**5,535**	**100**

2013 Sales

	$ mil.	% of total
US networks	2,952	53
International networks	2,474	45
Education & other	114	2
Corporate & adjustments	(5)	-
Total	**4,487**	**100**

2014 Sales

	$ mil.	% of total
US networks	2,950	47
International networks	3,157	50
Education & other	160	3
Corporate & adjustments	(2)	-
Total	**6,265**	**100**

Selected Mergers and Acquisitions

FY2012
Revision3 ($30 million; San Francisco CA; digital video provider)

Selected Operations

Cable channels
Animal Planet
Discovery Channel
Discovery Kids
FitTV
HD Theater
Investigation Discovery
Military Channel
Planet Green
Science Channel
TLC (The Learning Channel)
Commerce and education
Discovery Education
DiscoveryStore.com
Business and Brands

U.S. Networks
Discovery Networks International
Discovery Education
Discovery Commerce
Discovery Digital Media
Revision3
Discovery Enterprises International
Discovery Studios

COMPETITORS

A&E Networks	NBCUniversal
AMC Networks	PBS
CBS Corp	Scripps Networks
Disney	Turner Broadcasting
E! Entertainment	Viacom
Television	

HISTORICAL FINANCIALS

Company Type: Public

Income Statement

FYE: December 31

	REVENUE ($ mil.)	NET INCOME ($ mil.)	NET PROFIT MARGIN	EMPLOYEES
12/14	6,265	1,139	18.2%	6,800
12/13	5,535	1,075	19.4%	5,700
12/12	4,487	943	21.0%	4,500
12/11	4,235	1,132	26.7%	4,600
12/10	3,773	653	17.3%	4,200
Annual Growth	13.5%	14.9%	—	12.8%

2014 Year-End Financials

Debt ratio: 44.67%	No. of shares (mil.): 439
Return on equity: 19.31%	Dividends
Cash ($ mil.): 367	Yield: —
Current ratio: 0.96	Payout: —
Long-term debt ($ mil.): 6,046	Market value ($ mil.): 15,132

	STOCK PRICE ($) FY Close	P/E High/Low	PER SHARE ($) Earnings	Dividends	Book Value
12/14	34.45	54 19	1.66	0.00	12.75
12/13	90.42	60 42	1.49	0.00	13.23
12/12	63.48	51 33	1.24	0.00	12.83
12/11	40.97	32 25	1.41	0.00	12.48
12/10	41.70	59 36	0.76	0.00	10.96
Annual Growth	(4.7%)	— —	21.6%	—	3.9%

Dish Network Corp

DISH Network serves up fare intended to whet everyone's appetite for televised entertainment. The #2 provider of satellite-based pay-TV in the US (behind DIRECTV) the company serves more than 14 million subscribers which include business clients in such industries as hospitality restaurant and retail. Programming includes premium movies SIRIUS radio on-demand video service regional and specialty sports local and international channels and pay-per-view in addition to basic video programming. It offers bundled voice and Internet services through partnerships with voice and data communications providers. DISH generates all of its sales in the US.

Operations

The company offers about 3100 local channels including standard definition channels in all US markets and HD channels in 190 of the some 210 national markets. It also carries 70 Sirius radio channels 30 premium movie channels 35 regional and specialty sports channels 300 Latino and international channels and 70 pay-per-view chan-

nels. Its DISH Anywhere service allows subscribers to watch more than 325000 movies TV shows clips and trailers online from personal computers smartphones and other mobile devices. Blockbuster@ Home provides streaming access to more than 10000 movies and TV shows to DISH customers on their TVs and online access to more than 25000 movies and TV shows by computer.

DISH provides its programming options via satellites that it owns or leases from satellite equipment and services provider EchoStar (spun off by DISH in 2008). The company distributes its programming from operations centers also owned by EchoStar. DISH subscribers access the service using a small satellite dish and digital set-top receivers.

Sales and MarketingThe company gains new subscribers through third parties including national retailers and telecommunications firms local and regional electronics stores and small satellite retailers among other channels. Customer acquisition costs dropped to $853 per customer in 2014 from $866 in 2013 while the average pay-TV bill increased to $83.77 in 2014 from $80.37 in 2013.

Financial PerformanceDISH has produced steady if unspectacular revenue growth in the past few years and 2014 was in line with that pattern. Revenue increased 5% to $16.6 million from $13.9 billion in 2013. The company added new subscribers at a slightly slower rate than it did in 2013. The number of broadband subscribers was also down in 2014.

Net income increased 17% to $944 million in 2014 from 2013. The increase came from the rise in revenue as well as a lack of costs for discontinued operations that ran at $47 million in 2013.

Driven by the rise in net income DISH's cash flow from operations climbed in 2014 to about $2.4 billion from $2.3 billion the previous year.

Strategy

While DISH has much on its plate with its satellite business it launched another version of pay-TV in 2015. The Sling TV streaming service offers a variety of channels for a $20 monthly subscription. Delivered over the Internet to computer mobile devices and services such as Roku Amazon Fire TV and Xbox One it offers live viewing of sought after cable channels HBO and ESPN and others. For additional fees Sling TV offers more tiers of programming of news and children's shows as well as a video on-demand programming library.The company successfully bid about $9 billion for a number of wireless spectrum licenses that the US Federal Communications Commission auctioned. The company has options to offer wireless telephone service sell it or wait to see if its value rises.

HISTORY

Early History

Charlie Ergen a former financial analyst for Frito-Lay founded a Denver company called Echosphere a retailer of large-dish C-band satellite TV equipment with his wife Cantey and James DeFranco in 1980. Echosphere evolved into a national manufacturer and distributor which in 1987 began its move toward the new direct broadcast satellite (DBS) delivery system. It filed for a DBS license and set up subsidiary EchoStar Communications Corporation to build launch and operate DBS satellites. In 1992 the FCC granted the company an orbital slot.

By 1994 Echosphere was the US's largest distributor of conventional home satellite equipment but the future clearly rested with DBS and EchoStar. A 1995 reorganization renamed the firm EchoStar Communications; the Echosphere distributor business became a subsidiary. EchoStar also created the DISH (Digital Sky Highway) Net-

work brand aiming for an easier-to-remember name than its rivals' "DSS" and "USSB."

EXECUTIVES

EVP Strategic Planning, Bernard L. (Bernie) Han, age 51, $495,193 total compensation
Executive Vice President Human Resources, Stephen Wood
EVP and Special Advisor to the CEO, James (Jim) DeFranco, age 63, $374,640 total compensation
Chairman and CEO, Charles W. Ergen, $900,000 total compensation
EVP Corporate Development, Thomas A. (Tom) Cullen, age 55, $450,000 total compensation
EVP Advanced Technologies and CEO Sling TV, Roger J. Lynch, age 52
EVP and Chief Human Resources Officer, Mike McClaskey
President and COO, W. Erik Carlson, age 45
EVP General Counsel and Secretary, R. Stanton Dodge, age 47, $296,155 total compensation
EVP and CTO, Vivek Khemka
EVP Operations, John Swieringa
EVP Customer Acquisition and Retention, Brian Neylon
SVP and CFO, Steve Swain
EVP Marketing Programming and Media Sales, Warren Schlichting
VP IT Application Development, Rob Dravenstott
Vice President and Corporate Controller, Paul W Orban
Senior Vice President Programming, David Shull
Vice President Of Business Development, Theodore Henderson
Vice President Of Programming, Andrew (Andy) Lecuyer
Vice President Wireless Development, David Zufall
Vice President Customer Care, Melissa Gonzalez
National Sales Manager, Jason Lefkowitz
Vice President DNS Operations, Dennis Newman
Vice President Of Operations, Darren Swanson
Vice President Of Finance, Kevin Gelston
National Sales Manager, Glen Smith
Vice President Human Resources, Aaron LaPoint
Vice President Associate General Counsel And Assistant Secretary, Brandon Ehrhart
National Account Manager, Christopher Guthery
Vice President Of Sales, Stan Kozlowski
Vice President Accounting, Douglas Mohr
Vice President Of Business Development, Robert (Bob) Grosz
National Sales Manager, Milena Bontcheva
Vice President Financial Planning And Analysis, Kathy Schneider
Vice President Dishlatino, Alfredo Rodriguez
National Sales Manager, Perry Crider
Vice President Of Software Engineering, Greg Goldey
Senior Vice President, Amir Ahmed
National Accounts Manager, Brett Mason
Vice President Program Management, Brian McIntyre
National Sales Manager Latino Sales, Juan Colmenares
National Accounts Manager, Stephen Butters
Vice President Of Marketing, Melanie Polvoriza
Vice President Corporate Initiatives, Rex Povenmire
Vice President Sales Operatio, Carolyn Crawford
Vice President Advertising, Stephanie Pence
Vice President Commercial Sales, Josh Costa
Vice President, Anthony Bowling
Call Center customer Service Director Vice President, Alex Greengold
Vice President Technology Development At Dish, Mariam Sorond
Vice President Tax, Karen Frank
Senior Vice President Programming, Dave Shull

Vice President and Associate General Counsel, Nick Sayeedi
Vice President, Nick Rossetti
Vice President Brand Marketing, Andy Cipra
Executive Vice President and Special Advisor to the Chief Executive Officer, Jim DeFranco
Senior Vice President Corporate Finance Group, Steven (Steve) Swain
Board Member, Hazel Quiambao
Auditors: KPMG LLP

LOCATIONS

HQ: Dish Network Corp
9601 South Meridian Boulevard, Englewood, CO 80112
Phone: 303 723-1000   Fax: 303 723-1499
Web: www.dishnetwork.com.

PRODUCTS/OPERATIONS

2014 Sales

	$ mil.	% of total
Subscriber-related revenue	14,495	99
Equipment sales & other	85	1
Equipment sales services - EchoStar	62	-
Total	**14,643**	**100**

2014 Sales

	$ mil.	% of total
DISH	14,643	100
Wireless	0	-
Total	**14,643**	**100**

COMPETITORS

AMC Networks	Grande Communications
AT&T	Hulu
Cablevision Systems	Netflix
Charter Communications	RCN Corporation
Comcast	Time Warner Cable
Cox Communications	Verizon
DIRECTV	

HISTORICAL FINANCIALS

Company Type: Public

Income Statement

FYE: December 31

	REVENUE ($ mil.)	NET INCOME ($ mil.)	NET PROFIT MARGIN	EMPLOYEES
12/14	14,643	944	6.5%	19,000
12/13	13,904	807	5.8%	25,000
12/12	14,266	636	4.5%	35,000
12/11	14,048	1,515	10.8%	34,000
12/10	12,640	984	7.8%	22,000
Annual Growth	3.7%	(1.0%)	—	(3.6%)

2014 Year-End Financials

Debt ratio: 65.42%
Return on equity: 63.19%
Cash ($ mil.): 7,104
Current ratio: 3.06
Long-term debt ($ mil.): 13,782

No. of shares (mil.): 461
Dividends
  Yield: —
  Payout: —
Market value ($ mil.): 33,655

	STOCK PRICE ($) FY Close	P/E High/Low		PER SHARE ($) Earnings	Dividends	Book Value
12/14	72.89	39	26	2.04	0.00	4.36
12/13	57.92	33	19	1.76	0.00	2.13
12/12	36.40	27	19	1.41	1.00	0.08
12/11	28.48	9	6	3.39	2.00	(0.94)
12/10	19.66	10	8	2.20	0.00	(2.56)
Annual Growth	38.8%	—	—	(1.9%)	—	—

Disney (Walt) Co. (The)

The monarch of this magic kingdom is no man but a mouse: Mickey Mouse. The Walt Disney Company is the world's largest media conglomerate with assets encompassing movies television publishing and theme parks. Its Disney/ABC Television Group includes the ABC television network and 10 broadcast stations as well as a portfolio of cable networks including ABC Family Disney Channel and ESPN (80%-owned). Walt Disney Studios produces films through imprints Walt Disney Pictures Disney Animation and Pixar. It also owns Marvel Entertainment and Lucasfilm two extremely successful film producers. In addition Walt Disney Parks and Resorts runs its popular theme parks including Walt Disney World and Disneyland.

HISTORY

After getting started as an illustrator in Kansas City Walt Disney and his brother Roy started Disney Brothers Studio in Hollywood California in 1923. Walt directed the first Mickey Mouse cartoon Plane Crazy in 1928 (the third Steamboat Willie was the first cartoon with a soundtrack). The studio produced its first animated feature film Snow White and the Seven Dwarfs in 1937. Walt Disney Productions went public in 1940 and later produced classics such as Fantasia and Pinocchio. The Disneyland theme park opened in 1955.

Roy Disney became chairman after Walt died of lung cancer in 1966. Disney World opened in Florida in 1971 the year Roy died. His son Roy E. became the company's principal individual shareholder. Walt's son-in-law Ron Miller became president in 1980. Two years later Epcot Center opened in Florida. In 1984 the Bass family of Texas in alliance with Roy E. bought a controlling interest in the company. New CEO Michael Eisner (from Paramount) and president Frank Wells (from Warner Bros.) ushered in an era of innovation prosperity and high executive salaries.

The company later launched The Disney Channel and opened new theme parks including Tokyo Disneyland (1984) and Disney-MGM Studios (1989; eventually renamed Hollywood Studios). In 1986 the company changed its name to The Walt Disney Company. The Disney Store retail chain debuted in 1987. Disneyland Paris (originally Euro Disney) opened in 1992. The following year Disney expanded its movie studio with the purchase of independent film company Miramax the brainchild of producers Bob and Harvey Weinstein.

Following Wells' death in a helicopter crash in 1994 boardroom infighting led to the acrimonious departure of studio head Jeffrey Katzenberg. (He was awarded $250 million in compensation in 1999.) The next year Eisner appointed Hollywood agent Michael Ovitz as president. (Ovitz left after 16 months with a severance package of more than $100 million.) Disney bought Capital Cities/ABC (now ABC Inc.) for $19 billion in 1996 and two years later it bought Web services firm Starwave from Microsoft co-founder Paul Allen. It later acquired 43% of Internet search engine Infoseek for $70 million and together they launched the GO Network in 1999. Disney bought the remaining 57% of Infoseek later that year and formed GO.com (later Disney Online) which began trading as a separate tracking stock.

In early 2000 ABC chairman Robert Iger was named Disney's president and COO. Later that year Time Warner Cable briefly suspended ABC broadcasts during a dispute over re-broadcasting rights drawing the ire of some 3.5 million cable customers. (The FCC later ruled that Time Warner violated rules against dropping a station from cable systems during sweeps periods.)

The company expanded its theme parks in Anaheim in 2001 opening Downtown Disney and Disney's California Adventure. It also announced a further restructuring of its Internet business including closing the GO.com search site and converting its Internet tracking stock back into Disney common stock. That year Disney formed a joint venture with Wenner Media (US Weekly LLC) and took a 50% stake in entertainment magazine US Weekly (sold in 2006). Later Disney bought Fox Family Channel which it renamed ABC Family from News Corporation and Haim Saban for $2.9 billion in cash and assumption of $2.3 billion in debt.

In 2003 Disney began its exit from the sports world by selling the Anaheim Angels. (The company had acquired a 25% stake in the baseball team in 1995 and purchased the remaining interest four years later.) At Disney's annual shareholder meeting in 2004 about 45% of stock owners voted to not re-elect the embattled Eisner to the board. In response Disney directors stripped Eisner of the chairman title and named director and former US senator George Mitchell to that position.

Disney sold its under-performing chain of Disney Store retail outlets to The Children's Place in 2004. Amid all the strife the company boosted its children's entertainment properties by purchasing the Muppet and Bear in the Big Blue House characters along with their film and television libraries from The Jim Henson Company.

Several big executive shakeups occurred at Walt Disney in late 2005. Eisner finally passed the CEO torch after more than 20 years to former COO Iger. That same year Disney Parks opened Hong Kong Disneyland the company's biggest foray into the world's most populated country. In addition the Weinstein brothers left Miramax to form The Weinstein Company ending two of the most successful tenures of the independent film movement. (Disney ceased the operations of Miramax in a cost-cutting move in 2010 and announced plans to sell the Miramax label later that year.)

In mid-2006 Walt Disney completed a crucial acquisition —the $7.4 billion purchase of Pixar Animation. Disney almost lost Pixar as a production partner in the animation house's blockbuster films but Iger successfully dodged the bullet. Disney Studios' release of Pirates of the Caribbean: Dead Man's Chest that year topped box office records when it brought in $132 million during its opening weekend. The mark was broken by the third installment of the series Pirates of the Caribbean: At World's End which took in $156 million when it was released the next year. Also in 2007 Disney spun off ABC's radio broadcasting operations to Citadel Broadcasting for $2.7 billion in cash and stock.

Disney re-acquired the Disney Store chain in 2008 from Hoop Holdings a subsidiary of retailer The Children's Place in an effort to save the stores from closing. Hoop Holdings had filed bankruptcy that year citing continued losses and rising debt. (The Children's Place was not involved in the bankruptcy filing.) Also in 2008 the company reorganized its digital holdings with the formation of Disney Interactive Media Group. The following year the company purchased a 30% stake in video streaming website Hulu.

Roy E. died in late 2009 at age 79. Also that year Disney acquired Marvel Entertainment bringing Spider-Man Iron Man and other comic book characters into the Magic Kingdom. The deal was worth a whopping $4 billion and changed the course of its movie-making strategy reducing the number of films the studio releases each year while significantly ramping up production of costly big-budget franchises.

In attempts to cut costs Disney Studios in 2010 sold its venerable Miramax production unit (producer of films as Pulp Fiction and Shakespeare in Love) in 2010 to a group of investors (including Ron Tutor private equity firm Colony Capital and Qatar Holdings) for some $663 million. Also that year the company spent $563.2 million to acquire Playdom a popular social game company on Facebook in order to boost its DIMG holdings. Meanwhile Pixar's Toy Story 3 was the top grossing summer release in 2010.

Jobs who stepped down as CEO of Apple in 2011 for medical reasons and died of pancreatic cancer later that year had been Disney's largest individual stockholder with a 7% stake he acquired when the company purchased Pixar. (Jobs had bought Pixar from Lucasfilm in 1986.) Upon his death his Disney shares were converted to the Steven P. Jobs Trust led by his widow Laurene Powell Jobs.

Disney's 2012 box office bomb John Carter lost some $200 million and is reported to be one of the biggest money-losing films of all time.

EXECUTIVES

EVP and Chief Communications Officer, Zenia Mucha

SEVP General Counsel and Secretary, Alan N. Braverman, age 66, $1,374,231 total compensation

Senior Vice President, Steven Bardwil

Senior Vice President, Dan Cohen

Senior Vice President Security, Ronald (Ron) Iden

Senior Vice President Investor Relations, Lowell Singer

Vice President Corporate Communications Europe Middle East And Africa, Matthew (Matt) Grossman

COO, Thomas O. (Tom) Staggs, age 54, $1,338,558 total compensation

Chairman and CEO, Robert A. (Bob) Iger, age 62, $2,500,000 total compensation

President ESPN and Co-Chairman Disney Media Networks, John Skipper

SVP and Treasurer, Christine M. McCarthy, age 59, $588,606 total compensation

Chairman The Walt Disney Studios, Alan F. Horn

Chairman Walt Disney Parks and Resorts, Robert (Bob) Chapek

Chairman Walt Disney International, Andy Bird, age 52

EVP Corporate Strategy and Business Development, Kevin A. Mayer, age 52, $925,981 total compensation

Co-President Disney Interactive Media Group, James A. (Jimmy) Pitaro

EVP and Chief Human Resources Officer, Mary Jayne Parker, age 53, $722,269 total compensation

Co-Chair Disney Media Networks and President Disney/ABC Television Group, Ben Sherwood

Vice President of Advertising Sales, Rita Ferro

President Consumer Products, Leslie Ferraro

Vice President Human Resources, Steven (Steve) Milovich

Senior Vice President Marketing, Brendan Ryan

Vice President Marketing, Frank Keating

Executive Vice President Sales, John Ryan

Vice President Publicity, Lillian Matulic

Senior Vice President Of Marketing, David Sameth

Vice President Operations and Sales Development, Helen Faust

Vice President Compensation and Human Resources Operations, Rochelle Holden

Vice President, Kristin Burr

Senior Vice President Business and Legal Affairs, Denise Brown

Vice President Global Sales Planning and Analytics, Dominic Hougham

Vice President Construction Management, Jeremy Chaston

Vice President Human Resources, Janet Pate

Senior Vice President Of Marketing Operations, Steven Bushong

Executive Vice President Of Global Licensing, Josh Silverman

Vice President Global Public Policy, James (Jamie) Filippatos

Vice President of Technology and Innovation, Chris Heatherly

Vice President Global Security Operations, Grant Crabtree

Vice President, Kris Theiler

Vice President Of Publicity, Charlotte Tudor

Vice President and CMO The Walt Disney Company Uk And GM Disney Channels Uk, Anna Hill

Vice President WorldWide Post Production, Stephen (Steve) Swofford

Vice President Porfolio Development, Cynthia Derick

Senior Vice President, Barrie Godwin

Vice President Of International Publicity, Maggie Todd

Senior Vice President Marketing and Sales Strategy, Lisa Becket

Senior Vice President International, Ron Kollen

Vice President, Ted Skidmore

Vice President Of Lodging, Mark Rucker

Vice President International Treasury, Gregory Belzer

Senior Vice President Digital Media Disney ABC, Karin Timpone

Vice President Of Global Engineering, Jeff Vahle

Senior Vice President Programming Strategy, Paul Debenedittis

Senior Vice President Human Resources, Marjorie Randolph

Vice President Technology, Andy Grosz

Lawn and Garden Global Finance Vice President, Julia Gatewood

Executive Vice President of Casting, Keli Lee

Senior Vice President Advertising Sales Disney Online, Spencer Moseska

Senior Vice President of Enterprise Infrastructure Services, Charles (Chas) Weiner

Senior Vice President Finance, Tracy Wilson

Vice President Human Resources Business Partner, Josefina Leon

Vice President Business Affairs, Yvonne Shay

Vice President Parks Operations The Disneyland Resort, Jon Storbeck

Senior Vice President, Jerry Ketcham

Vice President Finance and Planning Disney Studios Home Entertainment, Daniel (Dan) Thein

Vice President Walt Disney Co. The, Vincent Vedrenne

Vice President Executive Compensation, Sandy Digilio

Vice President Theatrical Development, Michael (Mel) Jung

Vice President Human Resources, Tami L Garcia

Vice President of Marketing Creative Film Services, Ticole Richards

Vice President Production and Asset Management, David (Dave) Abdo

Vice President technical Development And Production Resource, Ted Carlsson

Senior Vice President VFX And Post Production, Todd London

Vice President And Director of Engineeri, Dave Converse

Vice President, Alannah Hall-smith

Vice President Operations Dcvi, Andrew (Andy) Aherne

Vice President Corporate Brand Management, Charlie Cain

Vice President Analytic Insights and Business Intelligence, Wayne Peacock

Senior Vice President Technology Risk Management and Security, Greg Wood

Senior Vice President, Ken Caldwell

Vice President of Marketing, Danielle Mullin

Vice President Applications Development, Michelle (Mitch) Kong

Vice President Business and Legal Affairs Motion Pictures, Jim Krauss

Vice President Labor Relations, Krysten Brennan

Vice President Marketing, Priya Girishankar

Vice President Finance and Accounting, Brian Simkin

Vice President Ratings Publicity, Jeff Lindsey

Vice President Information Technology Security and Compliance, Mitch Widman

Executive Vice President, Bob Weis

Vice President Human Resources Walt Disney Studio, Kathy Locketti

Vice President of Risk Mng, Steve Wilder

Vice President Counsel, Michael Rosenfeld

Vice President Magic Kingdom Park Walt Disney World Resort, Phil Holmes

Vice President, Ellen Blackler

Vice President Engineering Services Disney Technology Solutions and Services Team, Eric Lippke

Senior Vice President Creative Advertising, Jackson George

Vice President Government Relations, Bill J Bailey

Vice President Sales, Jeremiah Tachna

Vice President Sales Services and Administration, Cyndi Cruz

Vice President eCommerce and Digital Analytics, Narayan R Iyengar

Vice President Information Systems and Analytics, Kenny Funk

Vice President at The Walt Disney Company, Carmen Smith

Vice President, Becky Marquardt

Vice President Finance, Hilda Rivera

Imagineering Vice President Of Human Resources, Chris Trout

Vice President Shoreside Travel Operations At Disney Cruise Line, Jo-Ann Arndt

Vice President Finance And China, Tim Adam

Vice President Finance, Stephanie Harris

Senior Vice President Online, Vivek Sharma

Vice President Counsel, Steve Plotkin

Vice President Tax Planning, Gary Courtland

Vice President, Gilberto Kladt

Senior Vice President Deputy General Counsel, Suzanne Wilson

Vice President Of Business Development, Geoffrey Hamasaki

Vice President Management Audit, Gary D Hansen

Vice President Sourcing and Procurement, Derek Johnson

Senior Vice President Production, Susette Hsiung

Vice President animal Prog Environmental Initiatives, Jackie Ogden

Vice President Production Management, Jayne Bieber

Vice President Marketing and Promotion Daytime, Valerie (Val) McMichael

Vice President Compensation and HRIS, Eric Chaisson

Vice President Office Of The Chief Executive Officer, Agnes Chu

Vice President Legal Affairs Digital Distribution, Susan (Sue) Kigawa

Vice President Strategy at Walt Disney Media Networks, Mia Rondinella

Vice President Operations and Cashier, Kevin E Meyer

Vice President, Andrew Wu

Vice President of Stationery North Ame, Ralph Ayers

Vice President Of Operations, Janny Mulholland

Vice President Production, Amanda Ramey

Vice President Ad Sales Marketing, Laura Kuhn

Vice President Creative Film Services, Barbara (Barb) Lange
Vice President of Special Events Operations, Bob Gault
Vice President Human Resources and DI DCL and New Vacation Operations, Yvonne Sweeney
Vice President Manager Director, Chris Gray
Vice President Of Forecasting, Mark Haskell
Vice President Sales and Marketing, Jeff James
Executive Vice President Sales and Marketing Disney and ESPN Media Networks, Sean Bratches
Senior Creative Vice President, Joe A Lanzisero
Vice President Controller ABC, Nate Basile
Vice President Counsel, Tod Devine
Executive Vice President Marketing, Jason Taback
Vice President Marketing, Sandra Gomes
Vice President of Innovation, Christopher S (Chris) Taylor
Executive Vice President, Kim Theiss
VP Sales and Marketing Disney ABC Kids Networks, Kara Rousseau
Vice President Finance, Ryan McCollum
Vice President Global Facility Services and Support, Monica Stenberg
Svp Global Public Policy, Dorothy Attwood
Vice President Pension and Investments, Larry Goldsmith
Vice President Development, Osnat Shurer
Vice President Finance, Michelle (Mitch) Long-Knize
Auditors: PricewaterhouseCoopers LLP

LOCATIONS

HQ: Disney (Walt) Co. (The)
500 South Buena Vista Street, Burbank, CA 91521
Phone: 818 560-1000
Web: www.disney.com

2014 Sales

	$ mil.	% of total
US & Canada	36,769	75
Europe	6,505	13
Asia/Pacific	3,930	8
Latin America & other regions	1,609	4
Total	**48,813**	**100**

PRODUCTS/OPERATIONS

2014 Sales

	$ mil.	% of total
Media networks	21,152	43
Parks & resorts	15,099	31
Studio entertainment	7,278	15
Consumer products	3,985	8
Interactive media	1,299	3
Total	**48,813**	**100**

2014 Sales

	$ mil.	% of total
Service	40,246	82
Product	8,567	18
Total	**48,813**	**100**

Selected Operations

Consumer products
    Disney Publishing Worldwide
    Disney Stores (retail outlets)
Interactive media
    Disney Interactive Studios (video games)
    Club Penguin (social networking for children)
    Disney Online
    Disney.com
    DisneyFamily.com
Media networks
    A&E Television Networks (42%)
    A&E
    Bio (The Biography Channel)
    The History Channel
    History International
    Lifetime
    Lifetime Movie Network
    Lifetime Real Women
    The Military History Channel
    ABC Family Channel

ABC Television Network
Disney Channel
ESPN (80%)
ESPN2
ESPN Classic
ESPNEWS
JETIX Europe
SOAPnet
Television broadcast stations
    KABC (Los Angeles)
    KFSN (Fresno CA)
    KGO (San Francisco)
    KTRK (Houston)
    WABC (New York City)
    WJRT (Flint MI)
    WLS (Chicago)
    WPVI (Philadelphia)
    WTVD (Raleigh-Durham NC)
    WTVG (Toledo OH)
Toon Disney
Studio entertainment
    Dimension
    Disney Music Group (music production and distribution)
    Disney Theatrical Group (live entertainment events)
    Lucasfilm
    Marvel Entertainment
    Pixar
    Touchstone Pictures
    Walt Disney Pictures
Theme parks and resorts
    Adventures by Disney (vacation packages)
    Disney Cruise Line
    Euro Disney (40%)
    Disney Village
    Disneyland Paris
    The Walt Disney Studios Park (Marne-La-Vallee France)
    Disneyland Resort (Anaheim CA)
    Disneyland
    Disney' s California Adventure
    Hong Kong Disneyland (47%)
    Tokyo Disney Resort (owned and operated by Oriental Land Co.; Disney earns royalties)
    Tokyo Disneyland
    Tokyo DisneySea
    Walt Disney Imagineering (planning and development)
    Walt Disney World Resort (Orlando FL)
    Disney Vacation Club
    Disney' s Animal Kingdom
    Disney' s Hollywood Studios
    Disney' s Wide World of Sports
    Downtown Disney
    Epcot
    Magic Kingdom

COMPETITORS

21st Century Fox	MGM
AOL	SeaWorld
CBS Corp	Six Flags
Comcast	Sony Pictures
Discovery	Entertainment
Communications	Time Warner
DreamWorks Animation	Viacom
Liberty Interactive	Yahoo!

HISTORICAL FINANCIALS

Company Type: Public

Income Statement

FYE: October 3

	REVENUE ($ mil.)	NET INCOME ($ mil.)	NET PROFIT MARGIN	EMPLOYEES
10/15*	52,465	8,382	16.0%	185,000
09/14	48,813	7,501	15.4%	180,000
09/13	45,041	6,136	13.6%	175,000
09/12	42,278	5,682	13.4%	166,000
10/11	40,893	4,807	11.8%	156,000
Annual Growth	**6.4%**	**14.9%**	**—**	**4.4%**

*Fiscal year change

2015 Year-End Financials

Debt ratio: 19.66%	No. of shares (mil.): 1,600
Return on equity: 18.43%	Dividends
Cash ($ mil.): 4,269	Yield: 0.0%
Current ratio: 1.03	Payout: 36.9%
Long-term debt ($ mil.): 12,773	Market value ($ mil.): 164,800

	STOCK PRICE ($) FY Close	P/E High/Low		Earnings	PER SHARE ($) Dividends	Book Value
10/15*	103.00	25	17	4.90	1.81	27.83
09/14	88.74	21	15	4.26	0.86	26.34
09/13	65.19	20	14	3.38	0.75	25.24
09/12	52.28	17	9	3.13	0.60	22.34
10/11	30.16	17	12	2.52	0.40	21.21
Annual Growth	**35.9%**	**—**	**—**	**18.1%**	**45.8%**	**7.0%**

*Fiscal year change

Dollar General Corp

Dollar General's at ease with living off the crumbs of Wal-Mart. The fast-growing retailer boasts roughly 12200 discount stores in over 40 US states mostly in the South East the Midwest and the Southwest. It generates about 75% of its sales from consumables (including refrigerated shelf-stable and perishable foods) and another 10% from seasonal items. The stores also offer household products (cleaning supplies and health and beauty aids) and apparel. Pricing its items at $10 or less (and 25% of items at or under $1) Dollar General targets low- middle- and fixed-income shoppers. The no-frills stores typically measure about 7400 sq. ft. and are located in small towns that are off the radar of giant discounters.

Operations

Dollar General's massive stores network is supported by 13 distribution centers that are strategically located throughout its geographic footprint. Dollar General owns several trademarks including Dollar General Dollar General Market Clover Valley DG DG Guarantee Smart & Simple trueliving and Sweet Smiles. It also boasts a few licenses such as Bobbie Brooks and Fisher Price for clothing and Rexall for health and beauty aids.Geographic ReachThe company operated nearly 1200 stores in 43 US states in 2015. More than 10% of its stores were located in Texas while over 20% of stores were spread across the states of Florida Georgia Ohio and North Carolina.

Sales and Marketing

The retailer devotes its dollars to promotional circulars targeted circulars that support new stores television and radio advertising in-store signage and costs associated with the sponsorship of certain auto racing activities.Because Dollar General's customers typically live in small towns (with fewer than 20000 people) the company doesn't allocate ample amounts of money to advertising. It has spent increasingly more on advertising in recent years however as the company expands its stores footprint. The retailer spent $77.3 million on advertising in fiscal 2015 (ended January) up from $70.5 million and $61.7 million in fiscal years 2014 and 2013 respectively.

The retailer sells brand-name products from manufacturers the likes of Procter & Gamble Kimberly-Clark Unilever Kellogg's General Mills Nabisco Hanes PepsiCo and Coca-Cola.

Financial Performance

Dollar General's sales and profits have been rising for the past several years thanks to aggressive store expansion and increased same-store sales as its consumable item selection have become increasingly popular.

The retailer's revenues rose 8% to a record $18.91 billion in fiscal 2015 (ended January) driven by 3% growth in same-store sales and a 9% jump in Consumables product sales. Seasonal product and Home products sales grew by 8% and 4% respectively while Apparel product sales increased by 7%.Higher revenue in FY2015 drove Dollar General's net income up 4% to a record $1.1 billion. The retailer's operating cash levels climbed 8% to $1.3 billion mostly as its cash earnings rose.

Strategy

With its small-box stores typically measuring some 7400 sq. ft Dollar General targets cost-conscious consumers that prefer easier and quicker access to items than at super-sized competitors such as Wal-Mart and Costco (which are also often much farther away). Indeed Dollar General's strategy of catering to the value conscious has paid off big both during and after the recession. The discount retailer boasted its 25th consecutive year of same-store sales growth in FY2015 attributable to its compelling value and convenience proposition. Dollar General continues to aggressively open new stores in existing and new states to boost sales. It also continues to evaluate its long-term opportunities to best serve the needs of customers in new markets and more densely populated metropolitan areas. In 2015 it planned to open 730 new stores —including expanding into three new US states (Oregon Maine and Rhode Island) —while boosting its square footage by around 6% especially at legacy stores that haven't been converted to its current customer-centric format. During FY2013 it opened some 635 new stores including its first stores in the vast California market. Many of the new locations are Dollar General Market (DGM) stores which offer an expanded selection of groceries and perishables including fresh dairy products produce and meats. The company concentrates on serving customers in food deserts —areas not served by supermarkets or nearby grocers. Banking on its lucrative and growing consumables sales the retailer has initiatives underway to increase its margins on many items within its consumables category. To this end Dollar General anticipates adding more private-brand consumables each year and offer tobacco products in most of its locations. It's also been expanding its refrigerated food offerings in more than 1500 of its stores.

HISTORY

J. L. Turner was 11 when his father was killed during the 1890s in a Saturday night wrestling match. This forced J. L. to drop out of school and work on the family farm which was weighted by a mortgage. By his 20s J. L. who never learned to read well was running an area general store. Experiencing some success he branched out and purchased two stores of his own. They failed but J. L. rebounded going to work for a wholesaler. With the onset of the Depression J. L. found he could buy out the inventories of failing merchants for next to nothing using short-term bank loans that were quickly repaid.

In 1939 J. L. was joined by his son Cal. The two each put up $5000 to start a new Scottsville Kentucky-based dry goods wholesaling operation called not surprisingly J.L. Turner & Son. It was not until 1945 when the company experienced a glut of women's underwear that it expanded into retail. J.L. Turner & Son sold off the dainties in their first store located in Albany Kentucky. Within a decade the company was operating 35 stores. In 1956 J.L. Turner & Son introduced its first experimental Dollar General Store —all items priced less than a dollar —in Springfield Kentucky. Like the

company's first stores the dollar store concept would grow: Dollar General Stores numbered 255 a decade later.

Cal Jr. J. L.'s 25-year-old grandson joined the family business in 1965 and became a director in 1966. The company changed its name to Dollar General and went public two years later. In 1977 Cal Jr. was named president and CEO. That year Dollar General acquired Arkansas-based United Dollar Stores.

The early 1980s saw Dollar General continue its acquisition-powered growth. The company bought INTERCO's 280-store P.N. Hirsch chain and the 203-store Eagle Family Discount chain in 1983 and 1985 respectively. To cope with expanded distribution demands Dollar General opened an additional distribution center in Homerville Georgia in 1986 to help out the original Scottsville facility. The acquisitions led by Cal Jr.'s brother Steve ended up costing the company dearly; Dollar General's 1987 stock price dropped nearly 85%. The next year they also cost Steve his job: He was forced out by the company's new chairman Cal Jr. In addition to ousting Steve Cal Jr. replaced more than half of Dollar General's executives in 1988. The retailer began moving toward everyday low pricing (à la Wal-Mart) in the late 1980s.

Growth from then on was powered by internal expansion. In 1990 the company operated nearly 1400 stores; by 1995 it had more than 2000. To accommodate the growth Dollar General built a third distribution center in Ardmore Oklahoma in 1995 and another in South Boston Virginia in 1997.

While continuing to focus on small towns and neighborhoods Dollar General has expanded beyond the Southeast and Midwest opening its first stores in New York and New Jersey in 2001. In 2004 the company opened more than 700 locations and expanded into Arizona New Mexico and Wisconsin.

In April 2005 the company settled a Securities and Exchange Commission investigation into the circumstances that resulted in a $100 million earnings restatement for the years 1998 through 2000 with payment of a $10 million civil penalty.

To support its growth Dollar General opened a new distribution center in South Boston (its ninth) in 2006 and one in Union County South Carolina in mid-2005. Also in 2006 the retailer expanded its warehouse in Ardmore Oklahoma.

In July 2007 Dollar General was taken private by Kohlberg Kravis & Roberts GS Capital Partners (an affiliate of Goldman Sachs) and Citi Private Equity an investment arm of Citigroup in a deal valued at $7.3 billion.

In November 2009 the company went public with an offering valued at $716 million. The fast-growing chain opened its 9000th store in late July 2010.

Dollar General in August 2014 bid $78.50 per share for its smaller rival Family Dollar Stores. The all-cash offer which valued Family Dollar at about $9.7 billion topped a standing offer for Family Dollar from Dollar Tree of $74.50 in cash and stock. The addition of Family Dollar's 8200 stores would solidify Dollar General's standing as the largest in its industry. By July 2015 however Dollar Tree had prevailed in the bid and completed its acquisition that month. Before Dollar Tree's triumph Dollar General revealed that it may have had to sell between 1500 and 4000 stores prior to the deal closing in order to comply with regulators.

EXECUTIVES

Vice President, Susan S Lanigan
Chairman, Richard W. (Rick) Dreiling, age 62, $1,323,789 total compensation

Senior Vice President Global Strategic Sourcing, Gary Stephens
Senior Vice President And Chief Information Officer, Bruce Ash
EVP Store Operations, Gregory A. (Greg) Sparks, age 54, $635,676 total compensation
CEO and Director, Todd J. Vasos, age 53, $765,342 total compensation
EVP and Chief People Officer, Robert D. (Bob) Ravener, age 56, $441,599 total compensation
EVP Global Supply Chain, John W. Flanigan, age 64, $452,716 total compensation
EVP and General Counsel, Rhonda M. Taylor, age 47
EVP and Chief Merchandising Officer, David W. (Dave) D'Arezzo, age 56, $663,297 total compensation
EVP and CFO, John W. Garratt
Vice President Application Development, Dan Bruni
Vice President Real Estate, Tim Dearman
Divisional Vice President, Tom Balchak
Vice President Dmm Household, Brian Hartshorn
Vice President Dmm, Steve Jacobson
Vice President In Store Experience, Mark Banister
Vice President Store Operations, Jeff Owen
Vice President Internal Audit, Dave Fentress
Marketing Vice President, Ginny Evans
Vice President Of Asset Protection, David George
Vice President and Division Manager Store Operations, Steven (Steve) Brimner
Senior Vice President Store Operations, Steve Sunderland
Vice President Distribution, Anthony Roden
Vice President Operations, Bill Bass
Senior Vice President, Thomas Mitchell
Vice President Of Information Technology Operations, Bobby Aflatooni
Vice President, Debbie Combest
Vice President Government Affairs, Stephen Brophy
Vice President Investor Relations, Mary Pilkington
Vice President Marketing, Dave Steward
Auditors: Ernst & Young LLP

LOCATIONS

HQ: Dollar General Corp
  100 Mission Ridge, Goodlettsville, TN 37072
Phone: 615 855-4000   **Fax:** 615 855-5527
Web: www.dollargeneral.com

No of Stores

	No.
Texas	1,246
Florida	710
Georgia	675
Ohio	643
North Carolina	633
Other states	7,972
Total	**11,879**

PRODUCTS/OPERATIONS

2015 Sales

	$ mil.	% of total
Consumables	14,321	76
Seasonal	2,245	12
Home products	1,205	6
Apparel	1,038	6
Total	**18,909**	**100**

Selected Merchandise

Basic apparel
Cleaning supplies
Dairy products
Frozen foods
Health and beauty aids
Housewares
Packaged foods
Seasonal goods
Stationery

COMPETITORS

99 Cents Only	Kmart
Big Lots	Rite Aid
CVS	TJX Companies
Costco Wholesale	Target Corporation
Dollar Tree	Variety Wholesalers
Family Dollar Stores	Wal-Mart
Fred's	Walgreen

HISTORICAL FINANCIALS

Company Type: Public

Income Statement

FYE: January 30

	REVENUE ($ mil.)	NET INCOME ($ mil.)	NET PROFIT MARGIN	EMPLOYEES
01/15	18,909	1,065	5.6%	105,500
01/14*	17,504	1,025	5.9%	100,600
02/13	16,022	952	5.9%	90,500
02/12	14,807	766	5.2%	90,000
01/11	13,035	627	4.8%	85,900
Annual Growth	**9.7%**	**14.1%**	**—**	**5.3%**

*Fiscal year change

2015 Year-End Financials

Debt ratio: 24.42%	No. of shares (mil.): 303
Return on equity: 19.23%	Dividends
Cash ($ mil.): 579	Yield: —
Current ratio: 1.78	Payout: —
Long-term debt ($ mil.): 2,639	Market value ($ mil.): 20,349

	STOCK PRICE ($) FY Close	P/E High/Low	PER SHARE ($) Earnings	Dividends	Book Value
01/15	67.06	20 15	3.49	0.00	18.82
01/14*	56.32	20 14	3.17	0.00	17.04
02/13	46.28	19 14	2.85	0.00	15.24
02/12	41.94	19 12	2.22	0.00	13.83
01/11	28.40	18 12	1.82	0.00	11.90
Annual Growth	**24.0%**	**— —**	**17.7%**	**—**	**12.1%**

*Fiscal year change

Dollar Tree, Inc.

Dollars may not grow on trees but Dollar Tree stores work hard to bring in the green. The company operates more than 13200 Dollar Tree Deal$ Dollar Bills and Family Dollar discount stores in 48 US states and the District of Columbia and in five provinces in Canada. Stores carry a mix of housewares toys seasonal items food health and beauty aids gifts and books. At Dollar Tree shops most priced at $1 or less while Family Dollar merchandise is usually less that $10. The stores are located in high-traffic strip centers and malls often in small towns. It purchased fellow discounter Family Dollar in 2015.

Operations

In addition to its 5367 retail stores Dollar Tree has an e-commerce site —dollartreedirect.com — which allows customers to purchase large quantities of items from its stores. FamilyDollar.com offers tips for cooking on a budget ways to help local communities in need and access to local school supply lists.

The company's nationwide retail network is supplied by 21 distribution centers; 10 supply Dollar Tree locations and 11 belong to Family Dollar.

Family Dollar's 8000 small neighborhood stores are located in rural and urban areas near the fixed-low- and middle-income customers its serves. Most merchandise costs less than $10.

Geographic Reach

Virginia-based Dollar Tree rings up almost all of its sales in the US. The 180 Canadian stores —located in Alberta British Columbia Manitoba Ontario and Saskatchewan —do not contribute meaningfully to revenue.

Sales and Marketing

Advertising costs were approximately $18.1 million in fiscal 2015 up from $14.9 million in 2014 and $13.5 million in 2013 respectively.

Financial Performance

Dollar Tree along with other dollar store operators has thrived in recent years as the recession turned more and more shoppers into bargain hunters. Apparently those thrifty buying habits stuck as the chain continues to thrive despite the ongoing recovery of the US economy. In fiscal 2015 (ended January) the chain reported sales of $8.6 billion an increase of 9% versus the prior year. The increase was driven by the addition of new stores and a 4% rise in same-store sales as a result of increased sales mostly as well as a slight increase in prices. The company points to the addition of frozen and refrigerated foods as a key part of increased sales.

Despite the strong rise in sales net income only rose just $2.5 million in fiscal 2015 essentially remaining flat due to increased expenses. Net income the previous year had fallen 4%. Overall both profits and revenue have been trending upward since fiscal 2006 driven by rapid store growth before the profit stutter.

Strategy

The fast-growing chain has added about 1500 stores since 2009 both through acquisitions and opening new locations. In a deal that greatly expanded its size and consumed a key competitor in 2015 Dollar Tree bought Family Dollar Stores the operator of some 8200 stores in 46 states. Combined the two chains operate more than 13000 stores and ring up more than $18 billion in sales annually. The $8.5 billion cash-and-stock deal is expected to generate some $300 million a year in synergies in areas such as sourcing merchandise and expense reductions. Competitor Dollar General Corp had topped Dollar Tree's offer but Family Dollar said it prefers Dollar Tree's friendly approach to Dollar General's hostile offer. Dollar Tree satisfied anti-trust regulators by selling more than 300 Family Dollar stores across 35 states to private equity firm Sycamore Partners.

Dollar Tree and its rivals have transformed and expanded their businesses over the past decade or so by offering more consumables including frozen and refrigerated foods thereby stealing sales from convenience and grocery stores. Indeed consumables account for 50% of Dollar Tree's annual sales.

Mergers and Acquisitions

After nearly a year of wrangling in mid-2015 Dollar Tree beat out rival Dollar General and gained approval from the FTC to close its purchase of Family Dollar. The deal created a 13000 location discount behemoth with the size and scope to do battle with Wal-Mart and Dollar General.

Company Background

Founded in 1986 as Dollar Tree Stores the company later changed its name to Dollar Tree Inc.

EXECUTIVES

CFO, Kevin S. Wampler, age 52, $570,192 total compensation

President and COO Family Dollar, Gary M. Philbin, age 58, $830,769 total compensation

CEO, Bob Sasser, age 63, $1,505,769 total compensation

Chief Administrative Officer, Michael (Mike) Matacunas, age 48, $483,077 total compensation

Chief Merchandising Officer, Robert H. (Bob) Rudman, age 64, $656,154 total compensation

COO, Michael Witynski, age 52

Chairman, Macon F. Brock, age 72

Auditors: KPMG LLP

LOCATIONS

HQ: Dollar Tree, Inc.
  500 Volvo Parkway, Chesapeake, VA 23320
Phone: 757 321-5000
Web: www.dollartree.com

2015 US Stores

	No.
Texas	1,360
Florida	982
Ohio	673
North Carolina	627
California	604
Michigan	597
Georgia	592
New York	591
Pennsylvania	559
Illinois	443
Virginia	404
Louisiana	384
Tennessee	378
South Carolina	321
Indiana	316
Kentucky	295
Alabama	278
Arizona	249
Wisconsin	245
New Jersey	238
Mississippi	221
Missouri	219
Colorado	215
Massachusetts	211
Maryland	205
Oklahoma	187
Minnesota	176
Arkansas	165
New Mexico	157
West Virginia	152
Connecticut	115
Utah	109
Washington	96
Oregon	88
Maine	87
Kansas	82
Nevada	79
Idaho	70
Iowa	70
New Hampshire	62
Rhode Island	54
Nebraska	53
Delaware	52
Wyoming	42
South Dakota	34
North Dakota	26
Vermont	24
Montana	20
District of Columbia	5
Total	**13,212**

2015 Canadian Stores

	No.
Ontario	102
British Columbia	53
Alberta	34
Manitoba	11
Saskatchewan	10
Total	**210**

PRODUCTS/OPERATIONS

2015 Sales

	% of total
Consumables	49
Variety categories	47
Seasonal	4
Total	**100**

Store Names
Deal$
Dollar Bills
Dollar Giant
Dollar Tree
Dollar Tree Deal$
Family Dollar

Selected Products

Books
Candy
Cards
Food
Gifts
Health and beauty care products
Housewares
Party goods
Personal accessories
Seasonal goods
Stationery
Toys

COMPETITORS

99 Cents Only	Rite Aid
ALDI	Salvation Army
Big Lots	Save-A-Lot Food Stores
CVS	Savers Inc.
Dollar General	Target Corporation
Fred' s	Wal-Mart
Goodwill Industries	Walgreen
Grocery Outlet	Winn-Dixie
Kmart	

HISTORICAL FINANCIALS

Company Type: Public

Income Statement

FYE: January 31

	REVENUE ($ mil.)	NET INCOME ($ mil.)	NET PROFIT MARGIN	EMPLOYEES
01/15*	8,602	599	7.0%	90,000
02/14	7,840	596	7.6%	87,400
02/13	7,394	619	8.4%	81,920
01/12	6,630	488	7.4%	72,770
01/11	5,882	397	6.8%	63,860
Annual Growth	10.0%	10.8%	—	9.0%

*Fiscal year change

2015 Year-End Financials

Debt ratio: 21.22%	No. of shares (mil.): 205
Return on equity: 40.66%	Dividends
Cash ($ mil.): 864	Yield: —
Current ratio: 2.32	Payout: —
Long-term debt ($ mil.): 757	Market value ($ mil.): 14,624

	STOCK PRICE ($) FY Close	P/E High/Low	PER SHARE ($) Earnings	Dividends	Book Value
01/15*	71.10	25 17	2.90	0.00	8.68
02/14	50.52	22 14	2.72	0.00	5.62
02/13	40.12	42 14	2.68	0.00	7.42
01/12	84.64	42 24	2.02	0.00	5.82
01/11	50.99	41 26	1.55	0.00	5.91
Annual Growth	8.7%	— —	17.0%	—	10.1%

*Fiscal year change

Dominion Resources Inc

And darkness shall have no dominion .... as long as Dominion Resources powers lights across the territory it serves. Dominion is one of the top energy players in the US. Dominion Generation (its largest revenue generator) manages regulated and non-regulated power plants Through its Dominion Virginia Power unit the company transmits and distributes electricity across 57100 miles of electric distribution lines to 2.5 million customers and natural gas to 1.7 million customers. Subsidiary Dominion Energy trades and markets energy oversees natural gas transmission pipelines and operates underground gas storage facilities (928 billion cu. ft. of capacity.)

HISTORY

In 1781 the Virginia General Assembly established a group of trustees including George Washington and James Madison to promote navigation on the Appomattox River. The group (named the Appomattox Trustees) formed the Upper Appomattox Company in 1795 to secure its water rights. The company eventually began operating hydroelectric plants on the river and by 1888 it had added a steam-powered plant to its portfolio.

The Virginia Railway and Power Company (VR&P) led by Frank Jay Gould purchased the Upper Appomattox Company (which had changed its name) in 1909. The next year the firm acquired several electric and gas utilities as well as some electric streetcar lines.

In 1925 New York engineering company Stone & Webster acquired VR&P. The company became known as Virginia Electric and Power Company (Virginia Power) and was placed under Engineers Public Service (EPS) a new holding company. Virginia Power purchased several North Carolina utilities following its acquisition.

During the 1930s the Depression (and the popularity of the automobile) led the company to exit the trolley business. The Public Utility Holding Company Act of 1935 (repealed 2005) which ushered in an era of regulated utility monopolies forced EPS to divest all of its operations except Virginia Power. However the utility soon merged with the Virginia Public Service Company thus doubling its service territory.

The company added new power plants to keep up with growing customer demand in the 1950s. Always an innovator it also built an extra-high-voltage transmission system the first in the world.

In the 1970s Virginia Power's first nuclear plants became operational. By 1980 however the firm was near bankruptcy. That year William Berry who had completed a 23-year rise through the ranks to become president canceled two other nuclear units. He also became an early supporter of competition in the electric utility industry. In 1983 he formed Dominion Resources as a parent company for Virginia Power and halted nearly all plant construction. Two additional subsidiaries were soon formed: Dominion Capital in 1985 and Dominion Energy in 1987.

In 1990 the year Thomas Capps took over as CEO Dominion sold its natural gas distribution business and in 1995 Dominion Energy began developing natural gas reserves through joint ventures and by purchasing three natural gas exploration and production companies.

The company acquired UK utility East Midlands Electricity in 1997. However after it was hit by a hefty windfall tax by the newly elected Labour Party and its hopes for mergers with other UK utilities were dashed it sold East Midlands to PowerGen just 18 months after acquiring it.

In 1999 Dominion prepared for energy deregulation through reorganization. It separated its electricity generation activities from its transmission and distribution operations. In 2000 Dominion bought Consolidated Natural Gas (CNG) for $9 billion making it one of the largest fully integrated gas and electric power companies in the US; it then sold CNG's Virginia Natural Gas to AGL Resources and the two firms' combined Latin American assets to Duke Energy.

Virginia Power moved to head off state and federal lawsuits in 2000 by agreeing to spend $1.2 billion over 12 years to reduce pollution from coal-fired plants. The company also agreed to pay $1.3 billion for Eversource Energy's Millstone nuclear power complex that year (the deal closed in 2001). Also in 2000 Dominion changed its brand name from Dominion Resources to just Dominion and re-branded several of its subsidiaries as well.

In 2001 Dominion bought exploration and production company Louis Dreyfus Natural Gas for about $1.8 billion in cash and stock and $500 million in assumed debt; the acquisition added 1.8 trillion cu. ft. of natural gas equivalent to Dominion's proved reserves. The company also sold the assets of its financial services unit Dominion Capital that year.

The following year Dominion purchased a 500-MW Chicago power plant from US power producer Mirant (now GenOn Energy)for $182 million and it purchased the Cove Point LNG (liquefied natural gas) import facility from The Williams Companies for $217 million.

Dominion began to prepare for power deregulation implemented in most of its service territories by expanding its nonregulated electric operations. The company also divested its non-US operations to focus on its businesses in the Northeast Mid-Atlantic and Midwest. In 2004 it sold its telecom business to private firm Elantic Networks. The firm completed the acquisition of three fossil-fueled plants (2800 MW) from USGen New England a subsidiary of National Energy & Gas Transmission for $656 million in 2005. That was the same year Dominion purchased the 550-MW Kewaunee nuclear plant from WPS Resources subsidiary Wisconsin Public Service and Alliant Energy subsidiary Wisconsin Power & Light for $220 million.

At the end of 2006 Dominion Exploration & Production had proved reserves of 6.5 trillion cu. ft. of natural gas equivalent. The next year Dominion began to dismantle the unit selling its offshore operations in the Gulf of Mexico to Eni; its assets in Alabama Michigan and Texas to Loews Corp.; its Mid-Continent operations to Linn Energy; and operations in the Rocky Mountain and Gulf Coast regions to XTO Energy. Dominion Resources pocketed almost $14 billion from the sales.

To free up cash and hone its business focus the company has sold most of its exploration and production operations in recent years. In 2010 the company sold its remaining Appalachian exploration and production assets to CONSOL Energy for about $3.5 billion. The acquisition doubled CONSOL's natural gas reserves to 3 million cu. ft. (In 2007 Dominion sold the bulk of its oil and gas exploration and production assets —excluding its Appalachian operations because at the time they offered less risk —for nearly $14 billion.)

In a related move Dominion agreed to sell its Appalachian gas distribution companies The Peoples Natural Gas Company and Hope Gas located in Pennsylvania and West Virginia to investment firm SteelRiver Infrastructure Partners for $910 million. After receiving approval from Pennsylvania the deal was rejected in late 2009 by West Virginia saying the terms of the agreement were not in the public interest. The company then sold just Peoples Natural Gas to SteelRiver in 2010 for $780 million.

Dominion's divestments allow it to concentrate its efforts on its core power generation and gas and electricity distribution businesses along with its trading and marketing activities.

In 2012 Dominion announced plans to sell three fossil fuel-fired merchant power stations (one in Massachusetts and two in Illinois) as part of its transition to cleaner burning and renewable power plants.

On the gas side of the business in 2012 Dominion and Caiman Energy II LLC formed a $1.5 billion joint venture (Blue Racer Midstream LLC) to provide midstream services to natural gas producers operating in the Utica shale in Ohio and portions of Pennsylvania.

EXECUTIVES

EVP; CEO Energy Infrastructure Group and Dominion Virginia Power, Paul D. Koonce, age 55, $653,630 total compensation

Chairman President and CEO, Thomas F. Farrell, age 60, $1,411,744 total compensation

EVP and CFO, Mark F. McGettrick, age 57, $747,945 total compensation

EVP; CEO Dominion Generation Group, David A. Christian, age 60, $641,096 total compensation

President and Chief Nuclear Officer Dominion Nuclear, David A. Heacock, age 57, $492,632 total compensation

SVP Regulation Law Energy Solutions and Policy, Robert M. (Bob) Blue, age 47

SVP and CIO, P. Rodney Blevins

SVP Pipeline Services and Optimization, Anne E. Bomar

SVP Dominion Transmission, Diane G. Leopold, age 48

VP General Counsel and Chief Risk Officer, Mark O. Webb, age 50

SVP Power Generation, Katheryn B. (Kathy) Curtis

Vice President Distribution Operations, Rodney (Rod) Blevins

Auditors: Deloitte & Touche LLP

LOCATIONS

HQ: Dominion Resources Inc
120 Tredegar Street, Richmond, VA 23219
Phone: 804 819-2000   **Fax:** 804 775-5819
Web: www.dom.com

PRODUCTS/OPERATIONS

2014 Sales

	$ mil.	% of total
Dominion Virginia Power	7,665	62
Dominion Energy	1,918	15
Dominion Generation	1,718	14
Corporate & other	(12)	0
Adjustments	1,147	9
Total	**12,436**	**100**

Selected Subsidiaries and Business Units

Dominion Generation Corporation (power plant management)
Dominion Energy (energy marketing gas and power transmission)
Dominion Transmission Inc. (natural gas pipelines)
Dominion Virginia Power
 Consolidated Natural Gas
 Dominion East Ohio (or The East Ohio Gas Company gas distribution)
 Dominion Hope (or Hope Gas Inc. West Virginia gas distribution)
 Dominion North Carolina Power (or Virginia Electric and Power Company electricity distribution)
 Dominion Retail Inc. (retail energy marketing)
 Virginia Electric and Power Company (electricity distribution)

COMPETITORS

AEP	Exelon
CenterPoint Energy	Koch Industries Inc.
Duke Energy	NiSource
Entergy	Piedmont Natural Gas

HISTORICAL FINANCIALS

Company Type: Public

Income Statement

FYE: December 31

	REVENUE ($ mil.)	NET INCOME ($ mil.)	NET PROFIT MARGIN	EMPLOYEES
12/14	12,436	1,310	10.5%	14,400
12/13	13,120	1,697	12.9%	14,500
12/12	13,093	302	2.3%	15,500
12/11	14,379	1,408	9.8%	15,800
12/10	15,197	2,808	18.5%	15,800
Annual Growth	(4.9%)	(17.4%)	—	(2.3%)

2014 Year-End Financials

Debt ratio: 45.24%	No. of shares (mil.): 585
Return on equity: 11.17%	Dividends
Cash ($ mil.): 318	Yield: 3.1%
Current ratio: 0.78	Payout: 93.7%
Long-term debt ($ mil.): 21,805	Market value ($ mil.): 44,987

	STOCK PRICE ($) FY Close	P/E High/Low		PER SHARE ($) Earnings	Dividends	Book Value
12/14	76.90	36	28	2.24	2.40	19.75
12/13	64.69	23	18	2.93	2.25	20.48
12/12	51.80	104	93	0.53	2.11	18.79
12/11	53.08	22	17	2.45	1.97	20.53
12/10	42.72	9	8	4.76	1.83	21.09
Annual Growth	15.8%			— —(17.2%)	7.0%	(1.6%)

Domtar Corp

Leaving a paper trail is Domtar's business; the company is North America's #1 uncoated freesheet paper manufacturer and marketer. The majority of its sales are from paper comprising office commercial printing and publishing and converting and specialty papers. The lines include offset printing paper photocopying paper as well as fine and imaging (security) papers. Its top paper freesheet (coated and uncoated) is used for a range of printed materials with demanding image and press requirements such as food packaging medical and industrial applications. The company's distribution operations also buys stores and sells paper products made by Domtar and other manufacturers.

Geographic Reach

Domtar mainly has operations throughout Canada China Sweden and the US. It has eight pulp and paper mills in the US and two in Canada. The US accounts for 74% of its sales; Canada 12%.

Operations

Domtar's operations are divided into two chief segments: Pulp and Paper (90% of total sales) and Personal Care (10%).

Sales and Marketing

The company sells pulp to customers in North America through a North American sales force. Overseas sales to customers are made directly or through commission agents. Staples accounted for 10% of its total sales in 2013.

Financial Performance

Domtar's balance sheet has been stagnating over the course of the last three years. Revenues were down 2% from $5.48 billion in 2012 to $5.39 billion in 2013. Profits plunged 47% from $172 million in 2012 to $91 million in 2013.

The company attributes the downward momentum to a decrease in the average selling price for manufactured paper. Domtar also had lower revenue due to the selling of its Ariva distribution business in 2013. The erosion of profits for 2013 was due to higher expenses affiliated with an alternative fuel tax credit and litigation settlements.

Domtar's operating cash flow has spiraled downward over the last three years. In 2013 its operating cash flow decreased by $140 million primarily due to the decreased profitability in 2013.

Strategy

In order to adjust its cost structure Domtar has been disposing of several underperforming operations. In 2013 the company sold its Ariva paper distribution business to rival papermaker Central National-Gottesman.

Mergers and Acquisitions

Domtar intends to broaden its product offerings through business acquisitions and alliances. In early 2014 it obtained Laboratorios Indas S.A.U. a branded incontinence products manufacturer and marketer in Spain. Indas operates two manufacturing facilities in Spain.

In 2013 it purchased the US and Canadian paper and print media products business (coated and uncoated papers business forms carbonless and wide-format paper) of Xerox. Also that year it enhanced its Personal Care segment through the purchase of Associated Hygienic Products (AHP) a supplier of store brand infant diapers. AHP was previously owned by DSG International and has offices in Georgia Ohio and Texas.

In mid-2012 Domtar obtained EAM Corporation a maker of laminated absorbent cores used in hygiene adult incontinence baby diapers and medical packaging products. Domtar bought EAM for $61 million and the deal broadened its adult incontinence product portfolio and added to its newly created Personal Care business segment.

LOCATIONS

HQ: Domtar Corp
234 Kingsley Park Drive, Fort Mill, SC 29715
Phone: 803 802-7500
Web: www.domtar.com

HISTORICAL FINANCIALS

Company Type: Public

Income Statement

FYE: December 31

	REVENUE ($ mil.)	NET INCOME ($ mil.)	NET PROFIT MARGIN	EMPLOYEES
12/14	5,563	431	7.7%	9,800
12/13	5,391	91	1.7%	9,400
12/12	5,482	172	3.1%	9,300
12/11	5,612	365	6.5%	8,700
12/10	5,850	605	10.3%	8,500
Annual Growth	(1.2%)	(8.1%)	—	3.6%

2014 Year-End Financials

Debt ratio: 21.99%	No. of shares (mil.): 64
Return on equity: 15.20%	Dividends
Cash ($ mil.): 174	Yield: 3.4%
Current ratio: 1.80	Payout: 21.4%
Long-term debt ($ mil.): 1,181	Market value ($ mil.): 2,574

	STOCK PRICE ($) FY Close	P/E High/Low		PER SHARE ($) Earnings	Dividends	Book Value
12/14	40.22	17	5	6.64	1.40	45.15
12/13	94.34	70	48	1.36	2.10	42.91
12/12	83.52	42	29	2.38	1.70	41.28
12/11	79.96	23	14	4.54	0.65	40.44
12/10	75.92	12	7	7.00	0.75	37.72
Annual Growth	(14.7%)			— —(1.3%)	16.9%	4.6%

Donnelley (R.R.) & Sons Co.

If you can read it R.R. Donnelley & Sons can print it. A leading full-service printing company R.R. Donnelley produces magazines catalogs and books as well as advertising material business forms financial reports and telephone directories. The company offers graphics and prepress services in conjunction with printing. In addition it provides logistics distribution and business process outsourcing services related to getting printed material to its audience. Along with publishers R.R. Donnelley's customers include companies in the advertising financial services healthcare retail and technology industries.

HISTORY

In 1864 Canadian Richard Robert Donnelley joined Chicago publishers Edward Goodman and Leroy Church to form what eventually would become Lakeside Publishing and Printing. The company's building and presses were destroyed in the 1871 Chicago fire but soon were rebuilt.

By 1890 Richard Donnelley's son Thomas was leading the company which was incorporated as R.R. Donnelley & Sons. The company spun off its phone directory publishing subsidiary the Chicago Directory Company in 1916. (Renamed the Reuben H. Donnelley Corporation after another of Richard Donnelley's sons the business was acquired by Dun & Bradstreet —now D&B —in 1961 which spun it off as R.H. Donnelley now Dex One in 1998.)

R.R. Donnelley began printing Time in 1928 and LIFE in 1936. The company endured limits on commercial printing and paper shortages during WWII. It went public in 1956. Thomas Donnelley's son Gaylord steered the company from 1964 until 1975 when Charles Lake the first CEO who was not a member of the Donnelley family replaced him.

During the 1980s R.R. Donnelley developed the Selectronic process which allowed magazine publishers to tailor content and ads to different geographic audiences. The company acquired Metromail the largest US mailing list business in 1987. John Walter became CEO in 1988. R.R. Donnelley's South Side Chicago plant its oldest was shuttered in 1993 when Sears stopped publishing its catalogs.

R.R. Donnelley merged its software operations with Corporate Software to form Stream International (technical support software licensing and fulfillment) in 1995. That year Donnelley expanded internationally into Chile China India and Poland.

In 1996 Donnelley took both its Donnelley Enterprise Solutions subsidiary (IT services) and its Metromail subsidiary public retaining about 43% and 38% of each company respectively. Controversy erupted that year when it was revealed that Metromail had sold personal information in its customer database and through contracting had given prison inmates access to its database. In the wake of these revelations Walter resigned in 1996. Former Emerson Electric executive William Davis was appointed CEO in 1997.

Davis restructured the company reorganized Stream's operations and integrated digital printing into R.R. Donnelley's other operations. He also pushed the company to jettison underperforming units. In 1998 the company sold its interests in Metromail and Donnelley Enterprise Solutions.

Sharpening its focus in commercial printing R.R. Donnelley continued divesting in 1999 selling most of its stake in Stream International (which was later acquired by Solectron) and its stakes in software distributor Corporate Software & Technology and manufacturing and fulfillment firm Modus Media International. The company's Internet unit also unveiled ePublish a turnkey system enabling magazine publishers to publish on the Web.

In early 2000 the company doubled the size of its logistics unit when it bought business-to-home parcel mailer CTC Distribution Direct. It also expanded its digital services through the purchase of premedia services firm Iridio. In 2001 the company announced closures of a handful of plants as part of a streamlining effort. It also cut about 1700 jobs.

The company sold off its investments in two more companies MultiMedia Live and Global Directory Services in 2003. That same year it acquired distribution service provider Momentum Logistics and in 2004 it bought business forms and label printer Moore Wallace for about $2.8 billion. Moore Wallace CEO Mark Angelson took over leadership of the combined company. In its continuing efforts to divest itself of noncore assets R.R. Donnelley sold off its package logistics business including CTC Distribution Direct in 2004; it retained its print logistics and distribution businesses.

In 2005 R.R. Donnelley sold Peak Technologies a former Moore Wallace company that integrated and resold automated data capture and identification systems to Platinum Equity. R.R. Donnelley also acquired a number of regional printers in the US in 2005. It also bought The Astron Group a UK-based provider of outsourced document and information management services for $990 million. In 2006 the company acquired business process outsourcing company OfficeTiger for $250 million.

In 2007 Angelson retired in and CFO Thomas Quinlan replaced him as president and CEO. Also that year the firm acquired the business forms company Cardinal Brands for $130 million as well as rival Banta for $1.3 billion gaining printing operations in the US Europe and Asia and a supply chain management business that serves technology companies. Later in 2007 R.R. Donnelley completed the acquisition of magazine and catalog printer Perry Judd's Holdings for $176 million and textbook printer Von Hoffman for $413 million.

The following year it bought newspaper inserts printer Pro Line Printing in Irving Texas for about $120 million. Acquisitions in 2009 included Prospectus Central which provides electronic delivery of investment prospectuses and the assets of Santiago Chile-based PROSA a Web-based printing company.

Also in 2009 the company offered about $1.5 billion to take over the operations of rival printer Quebecor World which had filed for bankruptcy in 2008. Quebecor World rejected the bid however saying it was on track to emerge from bankruptcy protection by late summer. The following year R.R. Donnelley was able to buy Bowne & Co. a New York-based financial documents printer for about $480 million and Nimblefish Technologies a provider of software and services for managing direct marketing campaigns.

In 2011 R.R. Donnelley acquired LibreDigital a provider of digital distribution services. The following year it acquired Edgar Online a distributor of SEC documents.

EXECUTIVES

President and CEO, Thomas J. Quinlan, age 53, $1,000,000 total compensation
EVP General Counsel and Secretary, Suzanne S. Bettman, age 51, $450,000 total compensation
COO, Daniel L. (Dan) Knotts, age 51, $725,000 total compensation
EVP and CFO, Daniel N. Leib, age 49, $600,000 total compensation
SVP and Chief Accounting Officer, Andrew B. Coxhead, age 47, $325,000 total compensation
CIO, Ken O'Brien
Senior Vice President Sales, Scott Zornes
Vice President Sales, Gary Lake
Chairman, John C. (Jack) Pope, age 65
Auditors: Deloitte & Touche LLP

LOCATIONS

HQ: Donnelley (R.R.) & Sons Co.
35 West Wacker Drive, Chicago, IL 60601
Phone: 312 326-8000
Web: www.rrdonnelley.com

2014 sales

	$ mil.	% of total
U.S	8,974	78
Europe	983	8
Asia	860	7
Other	786	7
Total	**11,603**	**100**

PRODUCTS/OPERATIONS

2014 Sales

	$ mil.	% of total
Prosuct Sales	9,715	84
Services Sales	1,888	16
Total	**11,603**	**100**

2014 Sales

	$ mil.	% of total
Variable Print	3,767	32
Publishing and Retail Services	2,632	23
Strategic Services	2,607	23
International	2,595	22
Total	**11,603**	**100**

Selected Operations

US print and related services
Book (consumer religious educational and specialty and telecommunications)
Direct mail (content creation database management printing personalization finishing and distribution in North America)
Directories (yellow and white pages)
Logistics (consolidation and delivery of printed products; expedited distribution of time-sensitive and secure material; print-on-demand warehousing and fulfillment services)
Magazine catalog and retail inserts
Short-run commercial print (annual reports marketing brochures catalog and marketing inserts pharmaceutical inserts and other marketing retail point-of-sale and promotional materials and technical publications)
International
Business process outsourcing
Global Turnkey Solutions (product configuration customized kitting and order fulfillment)

COMPETITORS

Accenture	M & F Worldwide
Arandell	Merrill
Capgemini	Penn Lithographics
Cenveo	Quad/Graphics
Courier Corporation	St Ives
Dai Nippon Printing	St. Joseph
Deluxe Corporation	Communications
EBSCO	Taylor Corporation
Harte-Hanks	Toppan Printing
IBM Global Services	Transcontinental Inc.
Infosys	Valassis

HISTORICAL FINANCIALS

Company Type: Public

Income Statement

FYE: December 31

	REVENUE ($ mil.)	NET INCOME ($ mil.)	NET PROFIT MARGIN	EMPLOYEES
12/14	11,603	117	1.0%	68,000
12/13	10,480	211	2.0%	57,000
12/12	10,221	(651)	—	57,000
12/11	10,611	(122)	—	58,000
12/10	10,018	221	2.2%	58,700
Annual Growth	3.7%	(14.7%)	—	3.7%

2014 Year-End Financials

Debt ratio: 47.55%
Return on equity: 19.16%
Cash ($ mil.): 527
Current ratio: 1.42
Long-term debt ($ mil.): 3,429

No. of shares (mil.): 199
Dividends
  Yield: 6.1%
  Payout: 176.2%
Market value ($ mil.): 3,358

	STOCK PRICE ($) FY Close	P/E High/Low		PER SHARE ($) Earnings	Dividends	Book Value
12/14	16.81	35	25	0.59	1.04	2.97
12/13	20.28	18	8	1.15	1.04	3.48
12/12	8.99	—	—	(3.61)	1.04	0.29
12/11	14.43	—	—	(0.63)	1.04	5.84
12/10	17.47	22	14	1.06	1.04	10.77
Annual Growth (27.5%)	(1.0%)			— — (13.6%)	(0.0%)	

Dover Corp

The "D" in Dover could stand for diversity. Dover manages more than 30 companies that make equipment ranging from car wash systems to aerospace components. Dover operates in four segments: engineered systems (products for printing and identification transportation waste handling and industrial markets) energy (extraction and handling of oil and gas); fluids (fluid handling products for oil and gas chemical and hygienic markets); and refrigeration and food equipment (systems and products serving the commercial refrigeration and food service industries). Dover traces its historical roots back to 1955.

Geographic Reach

Dover has a significant worldwide presence and operates in Australia Brazil Canada China Eastern Europe France Germany India Malaysia Mexicothe Middle East the Netherlands Switzerland Sweden the UK and the US.

The US generates 60% of its revenue while Europe accounts for 16%. Other countries in the Americas generate 10% while Asia contributes 14%.

Operations

In 2014 Dover spun off its communications technologies operations (acoustic components microphones speakers receivers and transducers) into a new publicly traded company called Knowles Corporation. In conjunction with the move Dover reorganized its business structure into four new segments.

It now operates through the segments of engineered systems (products for printing and identification transportation waste handling and industrial markets); energy (extraction and handling of oil and gas); fluids (fluid handling products for oil and gas chemical and hygienic markets); and refrigeration and food equipment (systems and products serving the commercial refrigeration and food service industries).

Financial Performance

After posting a record-setting revenue total of $8.73 billion for 2013 Dover saw its revenues decline 11% to $7.75 billion in 2014. Its profits also dipped 23% from $1 billion in 2013 (also a milestone) to $775 million in 2014. (Note: the company restated its 2013 annual numbers due to discontinued operations.)

The declines for 2014 were primarily due to several operations –such as Datamax O'Neil a business previously within its printing and identification platform and Sargent Aerospace previously within its industrial operations –being reclassified as discontinued operations. The erosion of profits for 2014 was additionally fueled by the absence of income gains from these discontinued operations.

Dover's operating cash flow steadily increased for three straight years until 2013 when it dipped by $82 million. Cash flow also decreased 3% in 2014 due to higher investments in working capital of $43 million in 2014 relative to the prior year fueled by the timing impact of customer and vendor payments and higher revenue levels.

Strategy

Dover relies on a steady stream of divestitures and acquisitions as its principal means for growth. In 2015 Dover sold its Sargent Aerospace & Defense unit headquartered in Tucson Arizona to RBC Bearings for $500 million. It also divested its Datamax O'Neil unit headquartered in Orlando Florida to Honeywell for $185 million that year.In 2014 Dover sold its DEK Printing Machines unit to ASM Pacific Technology a Hong Kong listed company. Also that year Dover spun off its former communications technologies segment (acoustic components microphones speakers receivers and transducers) into a new publicly traded company called Knowles Corporation.

Mergers and Acquisitions

In 2014 Dover acquired Heidelberg CSAT GmbH a manufacturer of digital printing systems that are installed in-packaging-line for the identification of pharmaceutical and medical products located in Germany. It also picked up Italy-based MS Printing Solutions a manufacturer of digital ink jet printing systems for the textile and specialty material industries for $70 million. Both deals beefed up its engineering segment.

To fortify its energy segment Dover in 2014 bought Texas-based Timberline Manufacturing Company a maker of chemical injection and metering products for oil and gas producers. It also purchased The WellMark Company a manufacturer of valves instrumentation and chemical injection pumps serving the oil and gas industry located in Oklahoma. To enhance its international operations within its energy segment Dover in 2013 obtained Finder S.p.A. an Italy-based maker of engineered pumps and systems for the global energy market for $145 million.

HISTORY

George Ohrstrom a New York stockbroker formed Dover in 1955 and took it public that year. Originally headquartered in Washington DC Dover consisted of four companies: C. Lee Cook (compressor seals and piston rings) Peerless (space-venting heaters) Rotary Lift (automotive lifts) and W.C. Norris (components for oil wells). In 1958 Dover made the first of many acquisitions and entered the elevator industry by buying Shepard Warner Elevator.

EXECUTIVES

President and CEO Dover Fluids, William W. (Bill) Spurgeon, age 57, $650,000 total compensation
President and CEO, Robert A. (Bob) Livingston, age 61, $1,000,000 total compensation
President and CEO Dover Energy, Sivasankaran (Soma) Somasundaram, age 50
SVP and CFO, Brad M. Cerepak, age 56, $630,000 total compensation
President Asia, Michael Y. P. Zhang, age 51
President and CEO Dover Engineered Systems, C. Anderson Fincher, age 44, $495,282 total compensation
President and CEO Dover Refrigeration and Food Equipment, William C. Johnson, $491,346 total compensation
SVP Global Sourcing, Russell E. Toney
Vice President Operations, Dan Giesecke

Vice President Human Resources, Scott Greenhouse
Vice President human Resources refrigeration and Food Equipment, Gerry Vinci
Vice President Internal Audit, Cynthia Boumann
Chairman, Robert W. Cremin, age 75
Auditors: PricewaterhouseCoopers LLC

LOCATIONS

HQ: Dover Corp
  3005 Highland Parkway, Downers Grove, IL 60515
Phone: 630 541-1540
Web: www.dovercorporation.com

2014 Sales

	$ mil.	% of total
US	4,617	60
Europe	1,251	16
Other Americas	794	10
Asia	686	9
Others	401	5
Total	**7,752**	**100**

PRODUCTS/OPERATIONS

2014 Sales

	$ mil.	% of total
Engineered systems	2,385	31
Energy	2,017	26
Refrigeration & food Equipment	1,921	25
Fluids	1,430	18
Intra-segment eliminations	(2231)	-
Total	**7,752**	**100**

Selected Companies

Communication Technologies
  Colder Products
  Ceramic and Microwave Products
  Knowles
  Sargent Aerospace & Defense
  Vectron International
Energy
  Cook Compression
  Norris Production Solutions
  OPW
  TWG Power
  US Synthetic
  Waukesha Bearings
Engineered Systems
  Belvac Production Machinery
  Hill PHOENIX
  SWEP
  Tipper Tie
  Unified Brands
Printing and Identification
  Datamax O' Neil
  DEK
  Markem Imaje
  Multitest
  OK International

COMPETITORS

Alfa Laval	Oshkosh Truck
Carlisle Companies	PACCAR
Crane Co.	Paul Mueller
Danaher	RAKON LIMITED
Danfoss	SPX
Dayco Products	Schlumberger
Domino Printing	Sequa
Franklin Electric	Siemens AG
Gardner Denver	Smith Bits
Hussmann International	Snap-on
IDEX	Swagelok
Illinois Tool Works	Tatung
Ingersoll-Rand	Thermador Groupe
KEMET	Vesuvius
KSB AG	Wastequip
Kaydon	Weatherford
Lufkin Industries	International
Manitowoc	Weston EU
Middleby	Zebra Technologies
Navistar	

HISTORICAL FINANCIALS

Company Type: Public

Income Statement

FYE: December 31

	REVENUE ($ mil.)	NET INCOME ($ mil.)	NET PROFIT MARGIN	EMPLOYEES
12/15	6,956	869	12.5%	26,000
12/14	7,752	775	10.0%	27,000
12/13	8,729	1,003	11.5%	37,000
12/12	8,104	811	10.0%	35,000
12/11	7,950	895	11.3%	34,000
Annual Growth	(3.3%)	(0.7%)	—	(6.5%)

2015 Year-End Financials

Debt ratio: 32.12%
Return on equity: 23.68%
Cash ($ mil.): 362
Current ratio: 1.77
Long-term debt ($ mil.): 2,617

No. of shares (mil.): 155
Dividends
  Yield: 2.6%
  Payout: 29.5%
Market value ($ mil.): 9,503

	STOCK PRICE ($) FY Close	P/E High/Low		PER SHARE ($) Earnings	Dividends	Book Value
12/15	61.31	14	10	5.46	1.64	23.51
12/14	71.72	21	15	4.59	1.55	22.70
12/13	96.54	16	11	5.78	1.45	31.65
12/12	65.71	15	11	4.41	1.33	28.16
12/11	58.05	14	9	4.74	1.18	26.86
Annual Growth	1.4%	—	—	3.6%	8.6%	(3.3%)

Dow Chemical Co.

The Tao of Dow Chemical is its integrated production of plastics chemicals hydrocarbons and agrochemicals. The largest chemical company in the US and #2 worldwide behind BASF Dow also makes performance plastics (engineering plastics polyurethanes and materials) for Dow Automotive. It uses chlorine-based and hydrocarbon-based raw materials to make more than 6000 finished chemical products at 201 sites in 35 countries. The maker of Styrofoam insulation also is the world's #1 producer of chlorine and caustic soda and a top maker of ethylene dichloride and vinyl chloride monomer. Dow also owns 50% of silicone products maker Dow Corning. In late 2015 Dow agreed to merge with Dupont.

HISTORY

Herbert Dow founded Dow Chemical in 1897 after developing a process to extract bromides and chlorides from underground brine deposits around Midland Michigan. Its first product was chlorine bleach. Dow eventually overcame British and German monopolies on bleach bromides and other chemicals.

In the mid-1920s Dow rejected a takeover by DuPont. By 1930 the year of Herbert Dow's death sales had reached $15 million. Dow started building new plants around the country in the late 1930s.

Dow research yielded new plastics in the 1940s such as Saran Wrap the company's initial major consumer product. In 1952 Dow built a plant in Japan (Asahi-Dow) its first subsidiary outside North America. Plastics represented 32% of sales by 1957 compared with 2% in 1940. Strong sales of plastics and silicone products propelled the company into the top ranks of US firms. Dow entered the pharmaceutical field with the 1960 purchase of Allied Labs.

Dow suffered earnings drops from 1981 to 1983 from falling chemical prices. To limit the cyclical effect of chemicals on profits the company expanded its interests in pharmaceuticals and consumer goods. In 1989 it merged its pharmaceutical division with Marion Labs to create Marion Merrell Dow (it sold its 71% stake to Hoechst in 1995). Also in 1989 it formed DowElanco a joint venture with Eli Lilly to produce agricultural chemicals.

Following allegations that it had put a breast implant on the market without proper testing Dow Corning (a joint venture with glassmaker Corning Inc.) the #1 producer of silicone breast implants stopped making the devices in 1992. In 1995 a federal judge ordered Dow to pay a Nevada woman $14 million in damages —the first breast-implant verdict against the company as a sole defendant. Facing thousands of pending cases Dow Corning filed for bankruptcy protection. (In 1998 Dow Corning agreed to pay $3.2 billion to settle most breast-implant claims.) Dow Corning finally climbed out of bankruptcy in 2004.

Dow entered the polypropylene and polyethylene terephthalate markets with the 1996 purchase of INCA International a subsidiary of Italy's Enichem. It also bought a stake in seed developer Mycogen.

The company sold its 80% of Destec Energy in 1997 and bought Eli Lilly's 40% stake in DowElanco (renamed Dow AgroSciences 1998). That year Dow bought South Africa's Sentrachem (crop-protection products) but regulators made Dow sell part of it to Akzo Nobel.

In 1998 Dow sold its DowBrands unit —maker of bathroom cleaner (Dow) plastic bags (Ziploc) and plastic wrap (Saran Wrap) —to S.C. Johnson & Son. It also paid $322 million for the rest of Mycogen which became part of Dow AgroSciences.

The company paid $600 million in 1999 to purchase ANGUS Chemical (specialty chemicals) from TransCanada PipeLines. Dow also announced it planned to buy rival Union Carbide for $9.3 billion; it completed the acquisition early in 2001 after agreeing to divest some polyethylene assets to satisfy regulatory concerns.

In 2000 Dow acquired Flexible Products Company (polyurethane foam) and General Latex Chemical Corporation (rigid polyurethane foam). That year Michael Parker succeeded William Stavropoulos as president and CEO (Stavropoulos remained as chairman).

Dow acquired Rohm and Haas' agricultural chemicals (fungicides insecticides herbicides) business for $1 billion in 2001. That year it also acquired Celotex Corporation's rigid-foam insulation business and UK fine and specialty chemicals firm Ascot Plc.

A weakened economy high raw material costs and falling prices took a toll on Dow's sales and profits around the turn of the century. As a result of costs related to the Union Carbide takeover — such as the $830 million charge related to Union Carbide's exposure to asbestos claims —and the sputtering economy Dow recorded its first annual loss in nearly 10 years in 2001 then reported another loss in 2002. Parker was let go and William Stavropoulos returned to his post as both chairman and CEO. Stavropoulos went to work cutting jobs and closing plants in an effort to cut at least $1 billion in costs and make the company cash-flow positive in 2003.

From 2002 to 2004 the company cut nearly 7000 jobs or better than 13% of its entire workforce. By 2004 those moves coupled with a rebounding chemicals market had made Dow profitable again. Stavropoulos felt comfortable enough to relinquish the chief executive title and gave it to president and COO Andrew Liveris.

In the latter half of the decade the company began to switch its focus to more downstream products like performance plastics and systems. It acquired Bayer company Wolff Walsrode in 2007 and then more grandly specialty chemicals company Rohm and Haas in 2009.

Dow did take on significant debt during the Rohm and Haas transaction and as part of negotiations to close the deal Rohm and Haas sold salt-producing subsidiary Morton International to German company K+S. Dow also sold Rohm and Haas's powder coatings business to Akzo Nobel.

In 2010 Dow sold its Trinseo SA (then called Styron) unit to private investment group Bain Capital for $1.6 billion. Trinseo is a world leader in the production of plastics latex and rubber. Dow also sold its half of the Americas Styrenics joint venture with Chevron Phillips Chemical as part of the Trinseo deal.

That year Dow also formed a 50-50 joint venture with Mitsui to build a world-scale chlor-alkali plant at Dow's Freeport Texas manufacturing complex. The venture makes chlorine for feedstocks to supply Dow's downstream performance operations. Mitsui's share of the chlorine produced is converted to ethylene dichloride used primarily to make vinyl chloride monomer (VCM). VCM in turn is used to make polymers used in plastics and a range of both synthetic and natural materials.

Dow sold its polypropylene business to Brazil's Braskem in 2011 for $323 million. The deal involved two manufacturing plants in the US (Freeport and Seadrift Texas) and two in Germany (Wesseling and Schkopau) with a total annual polypropylene production capacity of 2.3 billion pounds.

To produce a new chlorocarbon for next-generation climate-friendly refrigerants Dow agreed to form a joint venture with Occidental Chemical Corporation in 2011. Known as HCC-1230xa the chlorocarbon will be used to produce the refrigerant known as HFO-1234yf which has low global-warming potential and zero ozone depletion potential. It will initially be used in air-conditioning systems in autos.

In 2011 Dow also formed an Advanced Electrolyte Technologies joint venture with Ube Industries to make electrolytes for lithium-ion batteries in energy storage applications.

Dow formed another joint venture in 2011 this time with Mitsui & Co. to develop biopolymers or organic plastics in Brazil. The 50-50 operation will use Dow's sugar cane production to develop biofuels and packaging materials offering a "green alternative" and replacement product for the flexible packaging hygiene and medical markets.

Investing in the Middle East Dow formed a joint venture in 2011 with Saudi Arabian Oil Company (Saudi Aramco) to build and operate a $20 billion chemicals complex in Jubail. Dow grew its presence in Saudi Arabia in 2012 with an investment in a plant at Jubail to make raw materials for paint and coating manufacturers in the region and for export markets.

In 2012 the company began a restructuring program designed to accelerate cost reductions. The program will cut 2400 positions or 5% of the global workforce and close down 20 manufacturing plants. Since 2009 Dow has divested non-core businesses representing $8 billion in revenues. Among other units Dow has targeted Polypropylene Licensing and Catalysts business unit and its Plastics Additives business unit for divestment.

In 2012 the company's Dow Electronic Materials unit acquired Lightscape Materials a spinoff of SRI International. US-based Lightscape Materials is a research company specializing in phosphor technology used in LED light-based systems. The acquisition enhances Dow's new LED Technologies unit (formed in 2011) because phosphors are used to enrich color quality in applications such as backlights for LCD displays.

In 2012 Dow formed a joint venture through its Dow Europe unit with Turkish acrylic fiber company Aksa Akrilik Kimya Sanayii. Called DowAksa Advanced Composites the venture will make carbon fiber and derivatives for industries such as transportation wind energy and construction.

In 2011 Dow agreed to form a joint venture with Chinese company Befar Group to produce perchloroethylene or PCE a key building block material for non-ozone depleting refrigerants used in industrial automotive and consumer applications. The companies will develop a PCE manufacturing facility in Shandong Province with a target capacity of 40000 to 80000 tons per year by 2014 to meet the growing needs of the Chinese market.

EXECUTIVES

Vice President, Fernando Ruiz
Chairman and CEO, Andrew N. Liveris, age 60, $1,921,433 total compensation
EVP General Counsel and Corporate Secretary, Charles J. Kalil, age 64, $1,024,661 total compensation
EVP; President Dow Europe Middle East and Africa, Heinz Haller, age 60, $765,146 total compensation
President and COO, James R. (Jim) Fitterling, $965,922 total compensation
Vice Chairman and CFO, Howard I. Ungerleider, $932,278 total compensation
Vice Chairman Market Businesses Chief Commercial Officer and Head of North America Latin America and Asia Pacific, Joe E. Harlan, age 55, $943,902 total compensation
VP Manufacturing and Engineering and Environment Health and Safety Operations, Peter Holicki
VP Business Services and CIO, Paula Tolliver
Corporate VP Human Resources and Aviation, Johanna S Söderström
Vice President Europe Latin America and Pacific Areas Dow AgroSciences, Tim Hassinger
Vice President Sustainability, Neil C Hawkins
Auditors: DELOITTE & TOUCHE LLP

LOCATIONS

HQ: Dow Chemical Co.
2030 Dow Center, Midland, MI 48674
Phone: 989 636-1000   **Fax:** 989 638 1740
Web: www.dow.com

2014 Sales

	$ mil.	% of total
Europe Middle East & Africa	19,671	34
US	19,449	33
Rest of the world	19,047	33
Total	**58,167**	**100**

PRODUCTS/OPERATIONS

2014 Sales

	$ mil.	% of total
Performance Plastics	22,386	38
Performance Materials	15,114	26
Infra-structure Solutions	8,429	14
Agricultural sciences	7,290	13
Consumer Solutions	4,639	8
Corporate Services	309	1
Total	**58,167**	**100**

Selected Products

Basic Plastics
  Polyethylene (resins including HDPE LDPE and LLDPE grades and catalysts and process technology)
  Polypropylene (resins and performance polymers)
  Styrenics (resins and styrenic alloys)
Performance Products

Engineering plastics (thermoplastic resins and elastomers advanced resins and crystalline polymers)
Emulsion polymers (synthetic latex)
Epoxy products and intermediates (acetone acrylic monomers epoxy resins glycerine and phenol)
Polyurethanes (Great Stuff foam sealant dispersions carpet backings polyurethane gloves roof adhesives and fiberboard products)
Performance Systems
  Dow Automotive (resins engineering plastic materials fluids adhesives sealants acoustical systems)
  Industrial chemicals (biocides surfactants and deicing fluids)
  Oxide derivatives (glycol ethers and amines)
  Specialty polymers (acrylic acid/acrylic esters epoxides dispersants vinyl resins specialty monomers)
  Wire and cable compounds (flame-retardant compounds wire and cable insulation compounds)
Health and Agricultural Sciences
  Fumigants
  Fungicides
  Herbicides
  Insecticides
Hydrocarbons and Energy
  Benzene
  Butadiene
  Butylene
  Cumene
  Ethylene
  Propylene
  Styrene
Coatings and Infrastructure
  Adhesives and Functional Polymers
  Dow Building and Construction
  Fabricated products (plastic film Styrofoam and Weathermate house wrap)
  Dow Coating Materials
Electronic and Specialty Materials
  Electronic Materials
  Antireflective coatings
  CMP slurries
  Immersion photoresists
  Specialty Materials
  Ion-exchange resins
  Nitroparaffins and nitroparaffin-based specialty chemicals
  Printing ink distillates
  Scale inhibitors
  UCAR emulsion systems (water-based emulsions)
  Water-soluble resins
Basic Chemicals
  Caustic soda
  Chlorine
  Ethylene glycol
  Ethylene oxide
  Vinyl chloride monomer
Other
  Property and casualty insurance (Liana Limited)

Selected Mergers and Acquisitions

COMPETITORS

Akzo Nobel	LANXESS
BASF SE	Lucite
Bayer AG	Mitsui Chemicals
Chevron Phillips	Monsanto Company
Chemical	Occidental Chemical
DuPont	Olin Chlor Alkali
Eastman Chemical	PPG Industries
ExxonMobil Chemical	SABIC
FMC	Shell Chemicals
Formosa Plastics	Syngenta
Koch Industries Inc.	Taminco

HISTORICAL FINANCIALS

Company Type: Public

Income Statement

FYE: December 31

	REVENUE ($ mil.)	NET INCOME ($ mil.)	NET PROFIT MARGIN	EMPLOYEES
12/15	48,778	7,685	15.8%	49,500
12/14	58,167	3,772	6.5%	53,000
12/13	57,080	4,787	8.4%	53,000
12/12	56,786	1,182	2.1%	54,000
12/11	59,985	2,742	4.6%	51,705
Annual Growth	**(5.0%)**	**29.4%**	**—**	**(1.1%)**

2015 Year-End Financials

Debt ratio: 25.05%	No. of shares (mil.): 1,116
Return on equity: 32.16%	Dividends
Cash ($ mil.): 8,577	Yield: 3.3%
Current ratio: 2.18	Payout: 44.4%
Long-term debt ($ mil.): 16,215	Market value ($ mil.): 57,500

	STOCK PRICE ($) FY Close	P/E High/Low		PER SHARE ($) Earnings	Dividends	Book Value
12/15	51.48	9	6	6.15	1.72	22.72
12/14	45.61	19	14	2.87	1.53	19.37
12/13	44.40	12	8	3.68	1.28	22.32
12/12	32.33	51	39	0.70	1.21	17.35
12/11	28.76	20	10	2.05	0.90	18.81
Annual Growth	**15.7%**	**—**	**—**	**31.6%**	**17.6%**	**4.8%**

Dr Pepper Snapple Group Inc

For many consumers it's a snap decision about which doctor to choose. Dr Pepper Snapple Group (DPS) is the bottler and distributor of Dr Pepper soda and Snapple drinks. Serving Canada Mexico and the US the company offers a vast portfolio of non-alcoholic beverages including flavored carbonated soft drinks and non-carbonated soft drinks along with ready-to-drink non-carbonated teas juices juice drinks and mixers. Among its brands are Dr Pepper and Snapple of course along with A&W Root Beer Hawaiian Punch Mott's and Schweppes. It has some cult favorites as well including Vernors Squirt and Royal Crown Cola. DPS is the #3 soda business in North America after #1 Coke and #2 Pepsi.

Operations

DPS's four core brands include: Canada Dry (the #1 ginger ale in the US); 7up (the #2 lemon-lime carbonated drink in the US); A&W (the #1 root beer in the US) and Sunkist (#1 orange carbonated drink in the US).

The company operates its business through three segments: Packaged Beverages Beverage Concentrates and Latin America Beverages.

Serving the US and Canada the Packaged Beverages segment generates more than 70% of total sales and makes and distributes finished beverages and other products including its own brands and third party brands through both direct-store and warehouse direct delivery. Wal-Mart is the segment's largest customer representing 16% of total net sales in 2014.

The Beverage Concentrates segment which accounts for roughly 20% of total sales sells branded concentrates and syrup to third-party bottlers primarily in the US and Canada. Most of the brands in this segment are carbonated soft drink brands. Pepsi and Coke are the Beverage Concentrates segment's largest customers accounting for some 27% and 21% of net sales respectively in 2014.

As its name suggests the Latin America Beverages segment serves the Mexico and Caribbean markets making and distributing concentrates syrup and finished beverages. It represents less than 10% of the beverage company's sales. About 90% of the segment's net sales are generated in Mexico.

Geographic Reach

Headquartered in Plano Texas the company operates nearly 155 administrative manufacturing and distribution facilities across the US which supply customers in the US and Canada. In Mexico it has more than a dozen sites through which it serves its customers in that country. In 2014 88% of the company's net sales were generated in the US while Mexico and the Caribbean generated some 8% of net sales. Canada generated the remaining 4%.

Sales and Marketing

DPS uses advertising sponsorships merchandising public relations promotions and social media to boost its brands. The company spent about $473 million on advertising and marketing in 2014 down from $486 million in 2013 and $481 million in 2012.

The company primarily serves bottlers (including quick-serve restaurants for syrups) and distributors as well as retailers. In 2013 its largest customer Wal-Mart accounted for 10% of total net sales. Its other retail customers include Kroger SUPERVALU Safeway Publix and Target. DPS also enjoys strong relationships with the largest bottlers and distributors such as Coca-Cola and PepsiCo the top customers of its Beverage Concentrates segment which generate about 21% and 27% respectively of the segment's sales. The company's largest foodservice customers include McDonald's Yum! Brands Burger King Sonic Wendy's Jack in the Box and Subway as well as convenience store customers the likes of 7-Eleven.

Its Beverage Concentrates brands are sold by its bottlers including its own Packaged Beverages segment through all major retail channels. Unlike the majority of its other carbonated soft drink brands 59% of DPS volumes are distributed through the Coca-Cola- and PepsiCo-affiliated bottler systems. The company's Packaged Beverages' products are made in multiple facilities nationwide and sold or distributed to retailers and their warehouses by its own distribution network or by third party distributors.

DPS sells its Packaged Beverages' products both through a Direct Store Delivery (DSD) system supported by a fleet of about 6000 vehicles and 19000 employees including sales representatives merchandisers drivers and warehouse workers as well as through its Warehouse Direct delivery system (WD) both of which include sales to all major retail channels.

In Mexico DPS makes and distributes its products through bottling operations and third-party bottlers and distributors. It also sells finished beverages through all major Mexican retail channels including local stores supermarkets hypermarkets and on premise channels. Further in Mexico it participates in a joint venture to manufacture Aguafiel brand water with Acqua Minerale San Benedetto. In the Caribbean it distributes products through third-party bottlers and distributors.

In 2014 the company entered a three-year sponsorship agreement with the San Francisco Giants. Through the arrangement Snapple's iced tea products will be sold at the baseball club's AT&T Park venue.

Financial Performance

DPS has enjoyed steady revenue and profit growth for the past several years thanks in large part to sales growth in its Latin America Beverages segment. Sales in 2014 rose by 2% to $6.12 billion thanks mostly to a 15% increase in the Latin America Beverages segment driven by a favorable product mix and higher sales volumes (particularly from the Penafiel 7UP and Clamato brands) and higher pricing as a result of the Mexican sugar tax. The Packaged Beverage segment also saw a slight (1%) increase in sales thanks to favorable product mix and higher branded sales volume (particularly from the Canada Dry Squirt and RC Cola brands) an increase in contract manufacturing and lower discounts. Higher revenue in 2014 also caused net income to jump by nearly 13% to $703 million (compared to $624 million in 2013). Cash from operations rose by 17% in 2014 to $1.02 billion thanks to a combination of higher earnings and an increase in other current liabilities mostly related to customer rebates and incentives and accrued compensation.

Strategy

The company might be #3 in overall North American sales but it wins the gold in one category. DPS is the #1 flavored carbonated soft drinks (CSD) company in the US. Dr Pepper its largest and namesake brand is the #2 flavored CSD in the US according to Nielsen and its Snapple brand is a leading ready-to-drink tea. DPS is the industry leader in flavored carbonated soft drinks (CSDs) with a 38.8% market share in the US for 2013 also according to Nielsen as measured by retail sales.

To this end DPS works to leverage the strength of its significant brands by launching innovations and brand extensions such as its Snapple Diet Half 'n Half. DPS has begun testing five new additions (7UP Sunkist soda A&W Canada Dry and RC Cola) to its TEN platform and launched these products nationally in early 2013. That year the company's CSD volume in the drugstore channel rose more than 8%.

Additionally DPS in 2013 inked a deal with Mondelez International to reacquire the distribution rights for Snapple and several other non-carbonated beverage brands in parts of the Asia/Pacific region to give DPS rights to distribute the Snapple brand in Australia Malaysia Singapore China Hong Kong Japan and South Korea. In Australia the company also will have distribution rights for Mott's Mr & Mrs T Clamato Mistic Holland House and Yoo-hoo. As part of the agreement DPS can explore opportunities for expanding the presence of Snapple and other non-carbonated brands.

Mergers and Acquisitions

In November 2014 DPS acquired Pennsylvania-based Davis Beverage Group and Davis Bottling Co. nearly doubling its direct store delivery footprint in Pennsylvania. The purchase included a 42-county distribution territory covering most of the eastern half of Pennsylvania excluding the Philadelphia area as well as western and central New Jersey.

In 2013 DPS acquired the assets and territory of Dr Pepper/7-Up Bottling Company of the West based in Reno Nevada. The purchase includes rights to the Dr Pepper/7-Up West territory and ownership of its distribution operation in Reno Chico California and Boise Idaho. The purchase is consistent with DPS's strategy of strengthening its route to market in the US.

EXECUTIVES

Vice President Corporate Communications, Tina Barry

President and CEO, Larry D. Young, age 60, $1,075,000 total compensation

CFO, Martin M. (Marty) Ellen, age 61, $568,462 total compensation

EVP Marketing, James R. (Jim) Trebilcock, age 57

President Packaged Beverages, Rodger L. Collins, age 57, $570,231 total compensation

EVP and General Counsel, James L. (Jim) Baldwin, age 54

EVP Supply Chain, Derry L. Hobson, age 64, $491,808 total compensation

President Beverage Concentrates and Latin American Beverages, James J. (Jim) Johnston, age 58, $570,770 total compensation

EVP Research and Development, David J. Thomas, age 53

EVP Human Resources, Lain Hancock

Vice President Packaging And Engineering, Kendall Yorn

Vice President Information Technology, Gerry Mecca

Vice President Fleet, Ted Phillips

Vice President Investor Relations, Heather Catelotti

Vice President Regional Accounts central, Tom Jerik

Vice President Finance and Accounting, Jeff Birch

Vice President Corporate Affairs, Vicki Draughn

Vice President National Accounts Walmart Sam's Team, Derek Dodge

Vice President Finance, Gregory Nestora

Vice President Human Resources Services and Consumer Relations, Deena Rembert

Vice President Burger King Team, Kelton Graham

Vice President Cold Drink Equipment and Equity, Mark Jackson

Vice President Supply Chain Planning and Logistics, Fernando Cortes

Vice President Finance Packaged Beverages, Brian Shepherd

Regional Vice President, Taylor Marcus

Vice President Mergers and Acquisitions, Lou Prignano

Vice President Sales Hispanic Markets, Pablo Guzman

Vice President Manufacturing, Dan Graham

Vice President of Sales and Market Development, Jeff Conrad

Vice President Sales, Rick Sweitzer

Vice President Licensing Operations, Rick Maiella

Vice President And Vice President Dp 7Up, John Kilduff

Vice President Regional Accounts, Jeff Vandenberg

Vice President Contract Manufacturing, Guy Mueller

Vice President, Roy Wright

Vice President National Accounts, Scott Johnson

Vice President Of Information Technology Bottling Group, Michael McKinney

Vice President West Zone Fountain Foodservice, Terry Molloy

Senior Vice President Manufacturing, Mike Chandler

Vice President Field Marketing, Phil Plummer

Zone Vice President, Dave Pitzer

Vice President Sales Operations, Mark Beaton

Vice President Quality, Kurt Martin

Vice President Human Resources, Linda Lumpkin

Vice President National Accounts Drug and Dollar, Eddie Hicks

Vice President Business Development and Marketing, James (Jamie) Collins

Vice President Finance Supply Chain, Jaime Garcia

Vice President of Enterprise Architecture and Infrastructure, Tom Farrah

Senior Vice President Controller, Angela (Angie) Stephens

Executive Vice President Human Resources Dr Pepper Snapple Group Inc., Lawrence Solomon

Senior Vice President of Commercial Finance, Greg Collins

Vice President of Enterprise Architecture and Support Services, Thomas (Thom) Farrah

Executive Vice President Human Resources, Larry
 Solomon
Vice President Human Resources Services, Deena
 Rembert-Neason
Vice President Corporate Audit, Ian Mutswiri
Vice President Sponsorships Travel and Events
 Marketing Capabilities, Hourigan Cindy
Chairman, Wayne R. Sanders, age 67
Auditors: Deloitte & Touche LLP

LOCATIONS

HQ: Dr Pepper Snapple Group Inc
 5301 Legacy Drive, Plano, TX 75024
Phone: 972 673-7000
Web: www.drpeppersnapplegroup.com

2014 Sales

	$ mil.	% of total
US	5,361	88
International	760	12
Total	**6,121**	**100**

PRODUCTS/OPERATIONS

2014 Sales

	$ mil.	% of total
Packaged Beverages	4,361	71
Beverage Concentrates	1,228	20
Latin America Beverages	532	9
Total	**6,121**	**100**

Selected Brands

7UP
A&W
Aguafiel (Mexico only)
Cadbury
Canada Dry
Clamato
Country Time (licensed)
Crush
Diet Rite
Dr Pepper
Hawaiian Punch
Holland House (licensed)
IBC
Margaritaville (licensed)
Mott' s
Mr & Mrs T
Nantucket Nectars
Orangina
Pe?afiel (Mexico only)
RC Cola
Rose' s (licensed)
Schweppes
Snapple
Squirt
Stewart' s (licensed)
Sundrop
Sunkist (licensed)
Sussex (Canada only)
Venom Energy
Vernors
Welch' s (licensed)
Yoo-Hoo

COMPETITORS

American Beverage
Austin Coca-Cola
Big Heart Pet Brands
Campbell Soup
Citrus World
Coca-Cola
Coca-Cola Bottling Consolidated
Coca-Cola Bottling company of southern california
Coca-Cola Bottling of Northern New England
Coca-Cola FEMSA
Coca-Cola North America
Coca-Cola Refreshments
Coca-Cola Tennessee
Coke United
Cott
Country Pure Foods
Dole Food
Faygo

G & J Pepsi-Cola Bottlers
Gatorade
Great Plains Coca-Cola
Great Western Juice
Hornell Brewing
IZZE
Jones Soda
Jugos del Valle
Kraft Foods Group Inc.
Lane Affiliated
Mondelez International
Monster Beverage
National Beverage
Nestl©
Ocean Spray
Odwalla
Old Orchard
Pepsi Bottling Ventures
Pepsi-Cola Bottling Company of NY
Pepsi-Cola Bottling of Central Virginia
Pepsi-Cola of Ft. Lauderdale
PepsiCo
Philadelphia Coca-Cola
Red Bull
Reed' s
South Beach Beverage
Sunny Delight
Swire Coca-Cola
Tree Top
Tropicana
Wet Planet Beverages
Wonderful Company

HISTORICAL FINANCIALS

Company Type: Public

Income Statement

FYE: December 31

	REVENUE ($ mil.)	NET INCOME ($ mil.)	NET PROFIT MARGIN	EMPLOYEES
12/14	6,121	703	11.5%	19,000
12/13	5,997	624	10.4%	19,000
12/12	5,995	629	10.5%	19,000
12/11	5,903	606	10.3%	19,000
12/10	5,636	528	9.4%	19,000
Annual Growth	2.1%	7.4%	—	0.0%

2014 Year-End Financials

Debt ratio: 31.32%
Return on equity: 30.76%
Cash ($ mil.): 237
Current ratio: 1.17
Long-term debt ($ mil.): 2,588

No. of shares (mil.): 192
Dividends
 Yield: 2.2%
 Payout: 45.9%
Market value ($ mil.): 13,831

	STOCK PRICE ($) FY Close	P/E High/Low	PER SHARE ($) Earnings	Dividends	Book Value
12/14	71.68	21 13	3.56	1.64	11.89
12/13	48.72	16 14	3.05	1.52	11.50
12/12	44.18	15 12	2.96	1.36	11.11
12/11	39.48	15 12	2.74	1.21	10.67
12/10	35.16	18 12	2.17	0.90	10.98
Annual Growth	19.5%	— —	13.2%	16.2%	2.0%

DTE Electric Company

Ford Motors is not the only powerhouse operating in Detroit –DTE Electric is another. The utility (formerly known as Detroit Edison) generates and distributes electricity to 2.1 million customers in Michigan. The company a unit of regional power player DTE Energy has almost 11000 MW of generating capacity from its interests in primarily fossil-fueled nuclear and hydroelectric power plants.

It operates more than 46000 circuit miles of distribution lines and owns and operates more than 670 distribution substations. DTE Electric also sells excess power to wholesale customers and provides coal transportation services.

Geographic Reach

The company serves customers across a 7600-sq. ml. service area in southeastern Michigan.

Operations

The largest electric utility in Michigan DTE Electric has a 1 million utility poles 671 distribution substations and 430600 line transformers.

The utility operates nine fossil fuel-(coal and oil) fired generating plants and one nuclear power plant (which accounts for 30% of Michigan's nuclear power output). It also co-owns a hydroelectric pumped storage plant with Consumers Energy.

Financial Performance

Reflecting a stronger economy and growing demand in 2012 DTE Electric's revenues increased by 3% to $5.3 billion due to an 8% jump in residential segment sales 11% growth in commercial segment revenues and a 13% increase in industrial segment sales. Net income increased 11% in 2012 due to stronger sales and a 13% jump in other income.

The company has seen consistent revenue growth over the past five years.

Strategy

To meet the state requirements for reducing carbon emissions in 2009 the company announced plans to add 1200 MW of renewable power by 2015 half through contracts with third-parties and the remainder through its own renewable energy projects (primarily wind farms). In 2011 the company was working on developing a 200 MW wind farm.

In 2010 the company began operating a 60-kW solar energy plant in Scio Township in Washtenaw County the first installation to produce power for the grid under DTE Electric's SolarCurrents program. Its 270 solar panels include 60 that track the sun's movement.

Ownership

DTE Electric is a direct wholly owned subsidiary of DTE Energy.

EXECUTIVES

EVP and CFO DTE Energy, David E. Meador, age 57
VP Corporate Secretary and Director, Susan M. Beale
Chairman, Anthony F. Earley Jr., age 64
SVP Customer Service, Joyce V. Hayes-Giles
Group President; President and Chief Operating Officer of Detroit Edison, Steven E. Kurmas, age 58
VP Distribution Operations DTE Energy, Trevor F. Lauer, age 49
Senior Vice President - Finance, Peter Oleksiak
Corporate Secretary, Lisa Muschong
Director, Bruce D. Peterson
SVP Electrical Operations DTE Energy, Paul Fessler, age 61
CIO DTE Energy, Steve Ambrose, age 48
EVP CFO and Director, David E. Meador, age 56
Director, Bruce D. Peterson
Auditors: PricewaterhouseCoopers LLP

LOCATIONS

HQ: DTE Electric Company
 One Energy Plaza, Detroit, MI 48226-1279
Phone: 313 235-4000
Web: www.dteenergy.com

2012 Sales

	$ mil.	% of total
Residential	2,354	44
Commercial	1,898	36
Industrial	784	15
Interconnection sales	105	2
Other	150	3
Total	**5,291**	**100**

COMPETITORS

Consumers Energy	SEMCO ENERGY
ITC Holdings Corp.	We Energies
Indiana Michigan Power	Xcel Energy

HISTORICAL FINANCIALS

Company Type: Public

Income Statement

FYE: December 31

	REVENUE ($ mil.)	NET INCOME ($ mil.)	NET PROFIT MARGIN	EMPLOYEES
12/14	5,282	532	10.1%	4,900
12/13	5,197	487	9.4%	4,800
12/12	5,291	486	9.2%	4,800
12/11	5,152	437	8.5%	4,800
12/10	4,993	441	8.8%	4,700
Annual Growth	1.4%	4.8%	—	1.0%

2014 Year-End Financials

Debt ratio: 28.48%	No. of shares (mil.): 138
Return on equity: 10.59%	Dividends
Cash ($ mil.): 14	Yield: —
Current ratio: 1.43	Payout: 69.5%
Long-term debt ($ mil.): 5,144	Market value ($ mil.): —

DTE Energy Co.

Detroit's economy may be lackluster but DTE Energy still provides a reliable spark. The holding company's main subsidiary DTE Electric (formerly Detroit Edison) distributes electricity to some 2.1 million customers in southeastern Michigan. The utility's power plants (mainly fossil-fueled) have a generating capacity of more than 10418 MW. The company's DTE Gas (formerly Michigan Consolidated Gas) unit distributes natural gas to 1.2 million customers. DTE Energy's nonregulated operations (in more than 20 states) include energy marketing and trading; coal transportation and procurement; energy management services for commercial and industrial customers; and independent and on-site power generation.

HISTORY

DTE Energy's predecessor threw its first switch in 1886 when George Peck and local investors incorporated the Edison Illuminating Company of Detroit. Neighboring utility Peninsular Electric Light was formed in 1891 and both companies bought smaller utilities until they merged in 1903 to form Detroit Edison. A subsidiary of holding company North American Co. Detroit Edison was incorporated in New York to secure financing for power plants.

Detroit's growth in the 1920s and 1930s led the utility to build plants and buy others in outlying areas. Detroit Edison acquired Michigan Electric Power which had been divested from its holding company under the Public Utility Holding Company Act of 1935 and was itself divested from North American in 1940.

The post-WWII boom prompted Detroit Edison to build more plants most of them coal-fired. In 1953 it joined a consortium of 34 companies to build Fermi 1 a nuclear plant brought on line in 1963. Still strapped for power Detroit Edison built the coal-fired Monroe plant which began service in 1970. In 1972 Fermi 1 had a partial core meltdown and was taken off line.

Detroit Edison began shipping low-sulfur Montana coal through its Wisconsin terminal in 1974 which reduced the cost of obtaining the fuel. The next year it began building another nuke Fermi 2. The nuke had cost more than $4.8 billion by the time it went on line in 1988. That year the utility began its landfill gas recovery operation (now DTE Biomass Energy).

A recession pounded automakers in the early 1990s leading to cutbacks in electricity purchases. In 1992 Congress passed the Energy Policy Act allowing wholesale power competition. In 1993 a fire shut down Fermi 2 for almost two years. Michigan's public service commission (PSC) approved retail customer-choice pilot programs for its utilities in 1994. Detroit Edison and rival Consumers Energy (now CMS Energy) took the PSC to court.

DTE Energy became Detroit Edison's holding company in 1996. The next year it formed DTE Energy Trading (to broker power) and DTE-CoEnergy (to provide energy-management services and sell power to large customers). It also formed Plug Power with Mechanical Technology to develop fuel cells that convert natural gas to power without combustion.

In 1997 and 1998 the PSC bolstered by state court decisions issued orders to restructure Michigan's utilities. The transition to retail competition began in 1998. That year DTE Energy and natural gas provider Michigan Consolidated Gas (Mich-Con) began collaborating on some operations including billing and meter reading. DTE and GE formed a venture to sell and install Plug Power fuel cell systems.

A higher court shot down the PSC's restructuring orders in 1999 but DTE Energy and CMS Energy decided to implement customer choice using PSC guidelines. That year the US Department of Energy selected DTE Energy to install the world's first super power-cable which could carry three times as much electricity as conventional copper. Also in 1999 DTE Energy agreed to acquire MCN Energy MichCon's parent.

In 2000 DTE Energy formed subsidiary International Transmission (ITC) to hold Detroit Edison's transmission assets; the next year ITC joined the Midwest Independent System Operator which began to manage ITC's network. It also completed its $4.3 billion purchase of MCN Energy in 2001. Full deregulation of Michigan's electricity market was completed in 2002. International Transmission was sold in 2003 to affiliates of Kohlberg Kravis Roberts and Trimaran Capital Partners for $610 million.

In 2007 it sold its Michigan Antrim Shale gas exploration and production assets to Atlas Energy Resources (which later was acquired by Chevron) for about $1.3 billion. That year due to the expiration of synthetic fuel production tax credits DTE Energy exited the synfuels business. In 2010 it sold its rail service unit (DTE Rail Services) to FreightCar America for $23 million.

In 2012 DTE Energy signed a deal with Spectra Energy and Enbridge to jointly develop the NEXUS Gas Transmission system a 250-mile long pipeline project to transport the growing supplies of Ohio Utica shale gas to markets in Michigan Ohio and Ontario.

To raise cash to pay down debt and to focus on its core businesses in 2012 the company sold its Unconventional Gas Production business (88000 acres of gas and oil production assets in the western Barnett and Marble Falls shale areas of Texas) for $255 million.

EXECUTIVES

SVP Energy Distribution Detroit Edison, Ron A. May, age 64

Chairman and CEO, Gerard M. Anderson, $1,243,269 total compensation

President and COO, Steven E. Kurmas, $623,077 total compensation

President DTE Gas and Oil and DTE Gas Resources, Richard L. Redmond, age 58

VP Public Affairs and President DTE Energy Foundation, Faye A. Nelson, age 62

President and COO DTE Electric and DTE Group President, Gerardo (Jerry) Norcia, $583,654 total compensation

VP Gas Sales and Supply Michigan Consolidated Gas Company, Mark W. Stiers, age 53

VP Distribution Engineering, Vincent G. Dow

President DTE Energy Services, David Ruud, age 48

SVP and CFO, Peter B. Oleksiak, age 49, $435,385 total compensation

President DTE Energy Trading, Steven Mabry

VP and CIO, Steve Ambrose, age 49

VP Fossil Generation, Frank Warren

President DTE Gas Storage and Pipelines, David Slater

Vice President Customer Credit Service, Gail Fielder

Vice President, Sakinah Howard

Vice President Performance Management, Kay Moore

Vice President Sales and Distribution, Doug Brown

Vice President Corporate Services DTE Coal Services, Stephen (Steve) Braverman

Vice President Senior Pre Construction Manager, Pamela Key

Vice President of Marketingn++, Jeffrey T (Jeff) Parks

Network Vpn Engineer, Carl Henrichs

Vice President Corporate Communications, Paula Silver

Assistant Vice President Of Communications, Pam Francis

Vice President Of Sales Operations For Apj, Kofi Antwih

Vice President Of Operations, Gary Quantock

Vice President DTE Methane Resources, Jan Stewart

Vice President Regulatory Affairs, Daniel (Dan) Brudzynski

Vice Chairman and Chief Administrative Officer, David E. (Dave) Meador, age 58

Assistant Treasurer, David R Murphy

Auditors: PricewaterhouseCoopers LLP

LOCATIONS

HQ: DTE Energy Co.
One Energy Plaza, Detroit, MI 48226-1279
Phone: 313 235-4000
Web: www.dteenergy.com

PRODUCTS/OPERATIONS

2014 Sales

	$ mil.	% of total
Electric utility	5,283	40
Gas utility	1,636	12
Non-utility operations		
Energy trading	3,762	29
Power & industrial products	2,289	17
Gas storage & pipeline	203	2
Adjustments	(874)	-
Corporate and Other	2	
Total	**12,301**	**100**

HISTORICAL FINANCIALS

Company Type: Public

Income Statement

FYE: December 31

	REVENUE ($ mil.)	NET INCOME ($ mil.)	NET PROFIT MARGIN	EMPLOYEES
12/15	10,337	727	7.0%	10,000
12/14	12,301	905	7.4%	10,000
12/13	9,661	661	6.8%	9,900
12/12	8,791	610	6.9%	9,900
12/11	8,897	711	8.0%	9,800
Annual Growth	3.8%	0.6%	—	0.5%

2015 Year-End Financials

Debt ratio: 34.13%	No. of shares (mil.): 179
Return on equity: 8.50%	Dividends
Cash ($ mil.): 37	Yield: 3.5%
Current ratio: 1.02	Payout: 53.6%
Long-term debt ($ mil.): 8,835	Market value ($ mil.): 14,392

	STOCK PRICE ($) FY Close	P/E High/Low	PER SHARE ($) Earnings	Dividends	Book Value
12/15	80.19	23 18	4.05	2.84	48.88
12/14	86.37	18 13	5.10	2.69	47.05
12/13	66.39	19 16	3.76	2.59	44.73
12/12	60.05	17 15	3.55	2.42	42.78
12/11	54.45	13 11	4.18	2.32	41.41
Annual Growth	10.2%	— —	(0.8%)	5.2%	4.2%

Du Pont (E.I.) de Nemours & Co

E. I. du Pont de Nemours (also known simply as DuPont) wants to coat your car feed your crops and decrease your dependence on fossil fuels. A top US chemical maker (along with Dow and ExxonMobil Chemicals) the company consists of 13 businesses that are divided into eight segments each of which serves a diverse set of markets. Using its expertise in science-based development it offers products materials and services that are applied in everything from agriculture apparel and construction to electronics nutrition and safety. DuPont operates worldwide with most of its sales coming from outside of the US. To raise cash in 2013 sold its Performance Coatings business.

Geographic Reach

DuPont has operations in more than 90 countries worldwide. The majority are located in Europe while other operations can be found in North America Latin America the Middle East Africa and Asia. In 2013 the US accounted for 40% of the company's revenues.

Operations

DuPont's eight business segments are Agriculture Electronics & Communications Industrial Biosciences Nutrition and Health Performance Chemicals Performance Materials (which it plans to sell)

Safety & Protection and Pharmaceuticals. The company's largest segment Agriculture consists of the Pioneer Hi-Bred International and DuPont Crop Protection businesses offering a slew of products and services aimed at improving crop yields and productivity. Products include Pioneer brand seeds as well as other insecticide fungicide and herbicide brands.

Performance Chemicals (fluorine products and white pigments) and Performance Materials (a wide range of polymers) round out DuPont's top three segments which all together generate about two-thirds of the company's sales.

Sales and Marketing

The company serves companies in a rage of industries including Agriculture Automotive Building and Construction Chemicals Electronics Energy Food and Beverage Government and Public Sector and Health Care and Medical.

Financial Performance

In 2013 DuPont's revenues grew by 2% due to a 5% increase in worldwide sales volume with growth in all segments. Agriculture segment sales increased by 13% due to higher global seed prices and volumes increased global insecticide and fungicide volumes and the benefit of increased ownership in Pannar Seed (Pty) Ltd. These gains were slightly offset by negative currency transactions. Growth in seeds reflected strong corn sales in North America and Brazil; higher insecticide volumes were driven by demand for Rynaxypyr particularly in Latin America; while fungicide volume increases were led by demand for picoxytstrobin in North America and Latin America. Industrial Biosciences revenues increased by 4%; Safety & Protection2%; Nutrition & Health1%; and Performance Materials segments 1%.After experiencing net income drop in 2012 due to lower revenues and increased operating cost in 2013 the company's net income increased by 76% due to higher revenues and income from discontinued operations.In 2013 the DuPont's operating cash inflow decreased to $3.18 billion (from $4.85 billion in 2012 was due a major change in working capital as a result of cash used for accrued interest and income taxes.

Strategy

DuPont's general strategy for growth is to use its expertise in science and technology to launch products that will address global needs for food cleaner energy (mainly reducing dependence on fossil fuels) and keeping people and the environment safe.

The company is undergoing a shift from being a chemical maker known for paints plastics and industrial chemicals to a company that is trying to grow in certain high-growth high-margin markets such as agriculture and nutrition advanced materials and biotechnology.

DuPont has a five-year plan with annual growth targets of 7% for sales and 12% for earnings through 2015. The company also plans to get 40% of its sales by 2015 from developing markets which include China India and countries in Latin America Eastern and Central Europe the Middle East Africa and Southeast Asia.

In 2014 DuPont Protection Technologies today announced the new DuPont Kevlar brand platform Dare Bigger and a sponsorship of ESPN X Games through 2015.

In 2013 the company entered into a definitive agreement to sell Glass Laminating Solutions/Vinyls a part of Packaging & Industrial Polymers to Kuraray for $543 million plus the value of the inventories.

To raise cash to pay down debt and focus on its core businesses in 2013 DuPont sold one of its larger units Performance Coatings to The Carlyle Group for $4.9 billion.

In a further portfolio reorganization that year DuPont also announced plans to spin off its Performance Chemicals unit in 2015.

HISTORY

Company Background

Eleuth ̈ re Ir ⓝ ⓔ du Pont de Nemours fled to America in 1800 after the French Revolution. Two years later he founded a gunpowder plant in Delaware. Within a decade the DuPont plant was the largest of its kind in the US. After Ir ⓝ ⓔ's death in 1834 his sons Alfred and Henry took over. DuPont added dynamite and nitroglycerine in 1880 guncotton in 1892 and smokeless powder in 1894.

In 1902 three du Pont cousins bought DuPont. By 1906 the company controlled most of the US explosives market but a 1912 antitrust decision forced it to sell part of the powder business. WWI profits were used to diversify into paints plastics and dyes.

DuPont acquired an interest in General Motors in 1917; the stake increased to 37% by 1922 (the company surrendered its stake in 1962 due to antitrust regulations). In the 1920s the firm bought and improved French cellophane technology and began producing rayon. DuPont's inventions include neoprene synthetic rubber (1931) Lucite (1937) nylon (1937) Teflon (1938) and Dacron. The last du Pont to head the company resigned as chairman in 1972. DuPont got into the energy business by acquiring Conoco for $7.6 billion in 1981.

In 1991 DuPont and Merck created DuPont Merck Pharmaceutical to focus on non-US markets. After record earnings in 1994 DuPont spent $8.8 billion the next year to buy back shares of the corporation from Seagram. In 1997 DuPont purchased Protein Technologies International (soy proteins) from Ralston Purina and Imperial Chemical's polyester-resins and intermediates operations (1997) and polyester-film business (1998).

DuPont president Chad Holliday became CEO in early 1998. That year DuPont purchased a 20% stake in Pioneer Hi-Bred International (corn seed) for $1.7 billion and Merck's 50% stake in DuPont Merck Pharmaceutical for $2.6 billion. DuPont's public offering of Conoco in 1998 raised $4.4 billion the largest US IPO at the time.

In 1999 DuPont bought the Herberts paints and coatings unit from Hoechst. It also bought the remaining 80% of Pioneer Hi-Bred for $7.7 billion and biotechnology research firm CombiChem for $95 million. Making a clean break with its oil business DuPont sold its remaining 70% stake in Conoco.

EXECUTIVES

EVP, James C. Borel, age 59

President Nutrition and Health, Craig F. Binetti, age 59

Chairman and CEO, Ellen J. Kullman, age 58, $703,685 total compensation

President Latin America, Eduardo W. Wanick, age 57

SVP Integrated Operations and Engineering, Jeffrey A. Coe, age 62

VP Operations North America, Willie C. Martin

VP Global Supply Chain Performance Polymers, Francine C. Shaw, age 59

President Performance Polymers, Diane H. Gulyas, age 58

EVP and Chief Innovation Officer, Thomas M. (Tom) Connelly Jr., age 62, $638,600 total compensation

VP Finance and Treasurer, Susan M. Stalnecker, age 61

VP Agriculture Biotechnology Pioneer Hi-Bred, John Bedbrook, age 64

President and CFO Canada, Michael J. (Mike) Oxley

President Electronics and Communications, David B. Miller, age 57

President Korea, Cheoroo Won, age 60

President Packaging and Industrial Polymers, William J. (Bill) Harvey, age 64

SVP Chief Science and Technology Officer, Douglas W. (Doug) Muzyka, age 59

SVP Corporate Strategy, David G. Bills, age 52

VP Business Process Excellence and Corporate Champion DuPont Six Sigma, Don R. Linsenmann

SVP Corporate Productivity and Business Process Simplification, Richard C. Olson, age 57

SVP General Counsel and Member Office of the Chief Executive, Thomas L. Sager, age 64

VP Sourcing and Logistics and Chief Procurement Officer, Shelley Stewart Jr., age 61

President Titanium Technologies, Boo Ching (BC) Chong, age 53

VP BioMaterials Group, John P. Ranieri

VP Government Marketing and Government Affairs, Barry M. Granger

EVP, Mark P. Vergnano, age 56

VP Pioneer Hi-Bred - China, William S. (Bill) Niebur, age 57

EVP and CFO, Nicholas C. (Nick) Fanandakis, age 58

President Protection Technologies, Thomas G. (Tom) Powell, age 54

President Industrial Biosciences, James C. Collins Jr., age 51

VP Tax and Business Finance, Robert E. Giblin, age 61

Media Relations, Tara Stewart

VP Corporate Planning and Analyses, Linda B. West, age 55

President and CEO Capital Management, Valerie J. Sill

President East Asia, Carl J. Lukach, age 57

VP Safety Health and Environment and Chief Sustainability Officer, Linda J. Fisher, age 61

VP Strategic Planning Pioneeer Hi-Bred, Peter C. Hemken

President Performance Coatings, John G. McCool, age 61

VP Technology Protection Technologies, Roger K. Siemionko, age 58

President K.K. Japan, Minoru Amoh

VP and Controller, Barry J. Niziolek, age 57

President Europe Middle East and Africa; President International SA Geneva, Ian Hudson

Senior Vice President ? Integrated Operations & Engineering, Gary W. Spitzer, age 56

President South Asia, Balvinder S. Kalsi, age 56

VP Global Operations Corporate Supply Chains, Donald D. (Don) Wirth

VP and Assistant General Counsel, Martha L. Rees

President Building Innovations, Timothy P. (Tim) McCann, age 57

VP Investor Relations, Karen A. Fletcher

President Sustainable Solutions, James R. Weigand, age 59

SVP Human Resources and Member Office of the Chief Executive, Benito Cachinero-Sanchez, age 55

President Pioneer, Paul E. Schickler, age 63

Chief Marketing and Sales Officer, Scott Coleman, age 50

VP Information Technology and CIO, Phuong Tram, age 60

VP General Auditor and Chief Ethics and Compliance Officer, Donna H. Grier, age 55

Chief Engineer and VP DuPont Engineering Facilities and Real Estate, Jocelyn E. Scott

CEO Solae, Torkel Rhenman

VP Human Resources, Maritza J. Poza-Grise

Chairman and President Taiwan; Sales Excellence Leader Titanium Technologies Asia Pacific, Steve Chen

VP Supply Chain Performance Coatings, K. Peter Hurd

Director Media Relations, Anthony Farina

Media Relations, Marie Beletti

VP Protection Technologies North America, William F. Weber, age 54

VP Global Technology Performance Coatings, Lewis E. Manring

VP Supply Chain DuPont Chemicals & Fluoroproducts, Janet H. Waters

VP and Assistant General Counsel, Hinton J. Lucas Jr.

VP Supply Chain Pioneer Hi-Bred Crop Protection Nutrition & Health and Applied BioSciences, John W. (Bill) Mooney

VP Regulatory and Product Stewardship, James C. Romine

Secretary and Corporate Counsel, Mary E. Bowler

President Greater China, Tony H.S. Su, age 57

President Chemicals & Fluoroproducts, Thierry F. J. Vanlancker, age 50

President Crop Protection, Rik L. Miller, age 57

Director Global Automotive Technology, David A. Glasscock

VP Integrated Business Management, David L. Peet

Leader Media Relations, Mike Hanretta

Media Relations, Dan Turner

Global IT Planning Manager DuPont Information Technology, Vicki L. Garrison

President Industrial Biosciences, William Feehery, age 44

President Protection Technologies, Marc Doyle

Director, Alexander M. (Sandy) Cutler, age 62

Director, Richard H. (Dick) Brown, age 66

Director, Curtis J. Crawford, age 66

Director, Bertrand P. Collomb, age 71

Director, Lois D. Juliber, age 65

Director, William K. Reilly, age 74

Director, Robert A. Brown, age 62

Director, Eleuthere I. (There) du Pont, age 47

Director, Marillyn A. Hewson, age 60

Independent Director, Eleuthere Pont

Independent Director, Lee Thomas

Auditors: PricewaterhouseCoopersLLP

LOCATIONS

HQ: Du Pont (E.I.) de Nemours & Co
974 Centre Road, Wilmington, DE 19805
Phone: 302 774-1000
Web: www.dupont.com

HISTORICAL FINANCIALS

Company Type: Public

Income Statement

	REVENUE ($ mil.)	NET INCOME ($ mil.)	NET PROFIT MARGIN	EMPLOYEES
				FYE: December 31
12/15	25,130	1,953	7.8%	52,000
12/14	36,046	3,625	10.1%	63,000
12/13	36,144	4,848	13.4%	64,000
12/12	35,310	2,788	7.9%	70,000
12/11	38,719	3,474	9.0%	70,000
Annual Growth	(10.2%)	(13.4%)	—	(7.2%)

2015 Year-End Financials

Debt ratio: 21.39%
Return on equity: 16.75%
Cash ($ mil.): 5,300
Current ratio: 1.71
Long-term debt ($ mil.): 7,642

No. of shares (mil.): 871
Dividends
  Yield: 2.5%
  Payout: 79.6%
Market value ($ mil.): 58,032

	STOCK PRICE ($) FY Close	P/E High/Low	PER SHARE ($) Earnings	Dividends	Book Value
12/15	66.60	37 22	2.16	1.72	11.47
12/14	73.94	19 15	3.92	1.84	14.72
12/13	64.97	12 9	5.18	1.78	17.51
12/12	44.98	18 14	2.95	1.70	10.81
12/11	45.78	15 10	3.68	1.64	9.28
Annual Growth	9.8%	— —	(12.5%)	1.2%	5.4%

Duke Energy Carolinas LLC

LOCATIONS

HQ: Duke Energy Carolinas LLC
526 South Church Street, Charlotte, NC 28202-1803
Phone: 704 382-3853

HISTORICAL FINANCIALS

Company Type: Public

Income Statement

	REVENUE ($ mil.)	NET INCOME ($ mil.)	NET PROFIT MARGIN	EMPLOYEES
				FYE: December 31
12/14	7,351	1,072	14.6%	—
12/13	6,954	976	14.0%	—
12/12	6,665	865	13.0%	—
12/11	6,493	834	12.8%	—
Annual Growth	4.2%	8.7%	—	—

2014 Year-End Financials

Debt ratio: 24.83%—
Return on equity: 10.08%
Cash ($ mil.): 13
Current ratio: 1.26
Long-term debt ($ mil.): 7,884

Dividends
  Yield: —
  Payout: —
Market value ($ mil.): —

	STOCK PRICE ($) FY Close	P/E High/Low	PER SHARE ($) Earnings	Dividends	Book Value
12/14	0.00	— —	(0.00)	0.00	(0.00)
Annual Growth	—	— —	—	—	—

Duke Energy Corp

Duke Energy is a John Wayne-sized power business. It serves electric and gas customers in the South and Midwest. Its US Franchised Electric and Gas unit operates through its Duke Energy Carolinas Duke Energy Ohio Progress EnergyDuke Duke Energy Progress Duke Energy Florida Duke Energy Indiana and Duke Energy Kentucky regional businesses. The company has 57500 MW of electric generating capacity from diverse mix of coal nuclear natural gas oil and renewable resources. Duke Energy also has domestic commercial and international power assets. The company serves 7.3 million electric retail customers in the Southeast and Midwest. It also has some limited insurance real estate and telecom assets.

HISTORY

Surgeon Gill Wylie founded Catawba Power Company in 1899; its first hydroelectric plant in South Carolina was on line by 1904. The next year Wylie and James "Buck" Duke (founder of the American Tobacco Company and Duke University's namesake) formed Southern Power Company with Wylie as president.

In 1910 Buck Duke became president of Southern Power and organized Mill-Power Supply to sell electric equipment and appliances. He also began investing in electricity-powered textile mills which prospered as a result of the electric power and continued to bring in customers. He formed the Southern Public Utility Company in 1913 to buy other Piedmont-region utilities. Wylie died in 1924 the same year the company was renamed Duke Power; Buck Duke died the next year.

Growing after WWII the company went public in 1950 and moved to the NYSE in 1961. It also formed its real estate arm Crescent Resources in the 1960s. Insulating itself from the 1970s energy crises Duke invested in coal mining and three nuclear plants the first completed in 1974.

In 1988 Duke began to develop power projects outside its home region and it also bought neighboring utility Nantahala Power and Light. The next year it formed a joint venture with Fluor's Fluor Daniel unit to provide engineering and construction services to power generators. Mill-Power Supply was sold in 1990.

By the 1990s Duke had moved into overseas markets acquiring an Argentine power station in 1992. It also tried its hand at telecommunications creating DukeNet Communications in 1994 to build fiber-optic systems and in 1996 it joined oil giant Mobil to create a power trading and marketing business. As the US power industry traveled toward deregulation Duke also sought natural gas operations. It targeted PanEnergy which owned a major pipeline system in the eastern half of the US. Duke Power bought PanEnergy in 1997 to form Duke Energy Corporation.

Seeing an opportunity in 1998 Duke formed Duke Communication Services to provide antenna sites to the fast-growing wireless communications industry. It also acquired a 52% stake in Electroquil an electric power generating company in Guayaquil Ecuador. That year it purchased a pipeline company in Australia from PG&E; it also bought three PG&E power plants to compete in California's deregulated electric utility marketplace.

Duke merged its pipeline business Duke Energy Trading and Transport with TEPPCO Partners and acquired gas processing operations from Union Pacific Resources. It sold Panhandle Eastern Pipe Line and gas-related assets in the Midwest to CMS Energy in 1999 to reduce operations in the region and made plans to build a pipeline extending from Alabama to Florida (completed in 2002).

To further enhance natural gas operations in other regions Duke bought El Paso's East Tennessee Natural Gas pipeline unit in 2000 and a 20% stake in Canadian 88 Energy; it also purchased $1.4 billion in South American generation assets including assets from Dominion Resources and the gas trading operations of Mobil (now Exxon Mobil) in the Netherlands. Also in 2000 Duke and Phillips Petroleum (now ConocoPhillips) merged their gas gathering and processing and NGL operations into Duke Energy Field Services.

In 2001 Duke announced the $8 billion acquisition of Westcoast Energy; the purchase which was completed in 2002 added more than a million natural gas customers and 6900 miles of gas pipeline in Canada. That year Duke sold its Duke Engineering & Services unit to Framatome ANP and its DukeSolutions unit to Ameresco. Duke Energy Field Services purchased Chevron's 33%

stake in Discovery Producer Services which operates a Gulf of Mexico gas pipeline and nearby processing facilities.

Duke set out to sell $1.5 billion in assets in 2003 to focus on core operations. The company sold its Empire State Pipeline subsidiary to National Fuel Gas for $240 million and sold its stakes in the Alliance Pipeline Alliance Canada Marketing and the Aux Sable refinery to Enbridge and Fort Chicago Energy Partners for $245 million. Also that year Duke sold its stake in Foothills Pipe Lines to TransCanada for $181 million and it sold $300 million in renewable energy facilities to privately owned Highstar Renewable Fuels.

In 2004 the company sold an Indonesian power plant to Freeport-McMoRan in a $300 million deal and it sold its 30% interest in the Vector Pipeline to Enbridge and DTE Energy for $145 million. It also sold the assets of its merchant finance business (Duke Capital Partners) and its stake in Canadian 88 Energy (now Esprit Exploration). Following this trend in 2005 Duke Energy sold its 620-MW Grays Harbor facility (Washington) to an affiliate of Invenergy for $21 million.

In 2006 Duke sold a 50% stake in its real estate subsidiary Crescent Resources to Morgan Stanley Real Estate. That year the company bought an 825-MW power plant in Rockingham County North Carolina from Dynegy for $195 million.

In a major industry power move in 2006 the company bought energy provider Cinergy in a $9 billion stock swap. Reorganizing its business lines to focus on its US power businesses that year Duke Energy sold its commercial marketing and trading businesses to Fortis and in 2007 it spun off its natural gas transmission business as Spectra Energy. The company also exited the European energy marketing business; it also left the proprietary (third-party) energy trading business in North America (primarily made up of Duke Energy North America or DENA sold to LS Power Equity Partners for a reported $1.5 billion). Duke also wound down its energy-trading joint venture with Exxon Mobil.

In 2008 Duke moved to strengthen its alternative energy assets by buying wind energy producer Catamount Energy for about $240 million plus assumed debt. Catamount had about 500MW of renewable energy in operation.

That year as part of its refocusing on its energy businesses the company stopped reporting on its Crescent Resources unit (a joint venture with Morgan Stanley Real Estate Fund which manages land holdings and develops real estate projects).

It acquired its first solar project Blue Wing Solar now a 14-MW solar farm in San Antonio from juwi solar in January 2010.

That year it formed a partnership with Integrys Energy Services and Smart Energy Capital to build solar projects across the US. In 2010 Duke Energy also teamed up with Areva to build a $250 million biomass-fueled power plant in Shelton in Washington state.

To raise cash that year Duke Energy sold its 50% stake in DukeNet communications to investment firm Alinda Capital Partners for $137 million.

Boosting its role in the transmission sector in 2011 Duke Energy formed a transmission utility joint venture with American Transmission. Duke-American Transmission Co. builds owns and operates new power transmission infrastructure across North America.

Through its Duke Energy Renewables unit in 2011 the company acquired the Shirley Wind Power Project a 20-MW wind farm in Wisconsin from Central Hudson Energy Group. The project has a 20-year contract to sell its output to Wisconsin Public Service Corp.

In late 2011 the Renewables unit acquired three commercial solar projects in southwestern North

Carolina. It bought the photovoltaic projects from ESA Renewables and the power from each solar farm is sold through Blue Ridge Mountain EMC to the Tennessee Valley Authority. The unit has four other commercial solar farms in North Carolina all located outside of Duke Energy's regulated service territories in the state. That year it also snapped up two solar farms in Arizona (in Ajo and Bagdad) from Recurrent Energy doubling its portfolio of commercial solar projects in operation and expanding its footprint further into the western US.

Not neglecting its international growth markets in 2012 Duke Energy International acquired CGE Group's Iberoamericana de Energía Ibener S.A. subsidiary in Chile including hydroelectric generating assets with 140 MW capacity for $415 million. Chile is Duke's the fourth largest non-US country in terms of generating capacity.

In a major US expansion in 2012 Duke acquired Progress Energy in a $32 billion deal. The acquisition created a more than $100 billion enterprise with the US' largest regulated customer base and was aimed at securing major costs savings in fuel purchasing power generating plant operations and other economies of scale benefits.

In 2012 Duke had almost 1300 MW of wind and solar powered plants in operation.

EXECUTIVES

Senior Vice President Corporate Tax, Keith Butler
Vice President Legal Corporate Legal Services, Catherine (Cathy) Stempien
Vice President Duke Energy Foundation and Community Affairs, Richard (Dick) Williams
Senior Vice President, Michael A Lewis
EVP and CFO, Steven K. Young, age 55, $535,418 total compensation
EVP Startegic Services, A. R. Mullinax
EVP Chief Legal Officer and Corporate Secretary, Julie S. Janson
SVP Global Risk Management and Insurance; Chief Risk Officer, Dwight L. Jacobs
EVP Regulated Utilities, Lloyd M. Yates, $585,833 total compensation
Vice Chairman President and CEO, Lynn J. Good, $1,200,000 total compensation
EVP External Affairs and Strategic Policy, Jennifer L. Weber
EVP and President Midwest and Florida, Douglas F. (Doug) Esamann, age 57
EVP and President Regulated Generation, Dhiaa M. Jamil, $650,000 total compensation
President Duke Energy International, Andrea Bertone
SVP Midwest Distribution Operations, Melody Birmingham-Byrd
Vice President Foundation and Community Affairs, Alisa McDonald
State President North Carolina, David B. Fountain
State President Florida, R. Alexander Glenn
State President Ohio and Kentucky, James P. (Jim) Henning
State President South Carolina, Clark S. Gillespy
SVP and Chief Nuclear Officer, John W. (Bill) Pitesa
VP and CIO, Christopher B. (Chris) Heck
SVP and Chief Procurement Officer, Jeffrey A. Corbett
President Commercial Portfolio, Greg Wolf
Vice President Information Technology, Larry Eiser
Vice President Chief Compliance Officer, Joe Crapster
Vice President Legal and Assistant Corporate Secretary, David (Dave) Maltz
Vice President Of Marketing, Jack Farley
National Sales Manager Convention Center, Justin Markle
Vice President Environment Health and Safety, James (Jamie) Hendricks

Senior Vice President Midwest Generation Portfolio, Phillip (Phil) Grigsby
Vice President Human Resources Business Partners, Jim O'Connor
Vice President Commercial Human Resources, Jackie Salinas
Vice President, Brandon Starnes
MIRM Vice President of Marketing, Jim Doyle
Vice President Fossil Stations, Donald (Don) Faulkner
Vice President of Sales Information Technology, Charles (Chas) Underwood
Vice President Information Technology, Mike Jones
Vice President, Karen Monday
Executive Vice President Regulated Utilities, John McArthur
Senior Vice President merchant Finance, John (Jack) Thomas
Senior Vice President Nuclear Operations, Bill Pitesa
Vice President Nuclear Human Resources, Jeana Sheehan
Vice President Field Operations, Al Ritchie
Vice President, Ben Zhang
Vice President Human Resources, Ann Morgan
Vice President Total Rewards, Jay Alvaro
Vice President, Bob Duncan
Vice President US Marketing Information technology, Chris Green
Vice President, Ben Waldrep
Occupational Medicine, Terry Hayes
Vice President, Theodore Bright
Vice President Human Resources, Davie Goode
Vice President Community Relations For N.c., Mike Hughes
Vice President, Leslie Pomaville
Vice President, Lisa Bridges
Vice President Transmission Design Engineering and Asset Management, Rick Bagley
Vice President Retail Programs, Michael Luhrs
Vice President Structured Finance, James (Jamie) Lance
Senior Vice President Of Federal Gover, William (Bill) Tyndall
Senior Vice President, Phil Grigsby
Vice President Power Generation Carolinas West, Harry Sideris
Vice President Catawba Nuclear, Kelvin Henderson
Vice President Portfolio Risk Management, Salil Pradhan
Vice President Generation Engineering, Bob Ellis
Vice President Customer Operations Services, Sipes Robert
Vice President Legal Commercial BusandOperations, Kodwo Ghartey-Tagoe
Vice President, Macey Austin
Senior Vice President Power Generation Operations, Charlie Gates
Vice President, Stephanie Todd
Vice President Power Generation Services, Paul Draovitch
Vice President Human Resources, Joseph Lentz
Vice President Operations, Al Smith
Vice President Corporate EHS Services, Mitchell (Mitch) Griggs
Vice President, Sally Whitney
Vice President Non Regulated Accounting, Gwen Pate
Vice President, Lauren Bosse
Vice President of Health and Safety, Carol Barajas
Vice President, John Barquin
Vice President, Richard Harrell
Vice President, Katie Mcclure
Vice President, Angeline Clinton
Vice President Rates (Ohio Kentucky), Don Wathen
CC Ct Operations Regulated Vice President, Albert (Al) Smith
Vice President Operations And Finance, Michael (Mel) Lambert

Vice President Finance, Ken Chaisson
Vice President Finance, Mike Gecox
Vice President Marketing, Matthew Walz
Vice President Finance, Patti Reeder
Vice President Of Engineering, Wayne Crowe
Vice President Finance, Bill Dickey
Vice President Finance, Randy Brashier
Vice President Business Development, John Upchurch
Vice President Business Development, Francis Wills
Vice President, James Hackett
Senior Vice President Financial Re Engineering and Financial IT, Sara S Whitney
Senior Vice President Information Technology Database Services, Betryn Byrd
Regional Vice President and General Manager, Anita McDaniel
Vice President Planning And Integration Commercial Businesses, Stacey Schrader
Vice President, Jeff Stone
Site Vice President, Dave Baxter
Vice President, Mike Robinson
Vice President Energy Efficiency, Ted Schultz
Vice President Environment Health Safety, Mitch Griggs
Executive Vice President and President Commercial Portfolio, Marc Manly
Vice President Environmental Policy, John (Jack) Stowell
Vice President Customer Strategy and Innovation, Jared Lawrence
Executive Vice President Startegic Services, A Mullinax
Vice President Human Resources Spectra Energy US, Jim Haynes
Vice President, Karen Feld
Vice President and Chief Sustainability Officer, Shawn Heath
Vice President Supply Chain, Lee Mazzocchi
Vice President, Neal Alexander
Vice President Internal Audit and Chief Ethics and Compliance Officer, Jeffrey (Jeff) Stone
Senior Vice President Portfolio Management and Strategic Planning, Cheryl Lipshutz
Senior Vice President and Chief Human Resources Officer, Weber Jennifer
Vice President Controller And Chief Accounting Officer, Brian Savoy
Vice President, John (Jack) Elnitsky
Vice President Construction And Maintenance, Harrall JR
Vice President, Ernie Kapopoulos
Vice President, Jim Henning
Vice President Business Relations and Development, Kirk Hobbs
Vice President Legal executive Compensation And Benefits, Robert (Bob) Ringel
Senior Vice President Strategy And Plannin, Robert (Bob) Mohr
Chairman, Ann Maynard Gray, age 69
Treasurer Senior Software Engineer, Robert Combs
Treasurer and Group Vice President Mergers and Acquisitions, Guy Buckley
Pac Treasurer, William Mayhew
Advisory Board Member, Amy Bolin
Secretary, Carl Yount
Auditors: Deloitte & Touche LLP

LOCATIONS

HQ: Duke Energy Corp
550 South Tryon Street, Charlotte, NC 28202-1803
Phone: 704 382-3853
Web: www.duke-energy.com

2014 Sales

	$ mil.	% of total
US	22,508	94
Latin America	1,417	6
Total	**23,925**	**100**

PRODUCTS/OPERATIONS

2014 Sales

	$ mil.	% of total
Regulated electric	22,271	93
Commercial Power	255	1
International Energy & others	1,522	6
Adjustments	(123)	-
Total	**23,925**	**100**

Selected Mergers and Acquisitions

COMPETITORS

AEP	Exelon
AES	Koch Industries Inc.
Avista	PG&E Corporation
CenterPoint Energy	Piedmont Natural Gas
Constellation Energy Group	SCANA
	SemGroup
Dynegy	Southern Company
Energy Future	TVA
Entergy	Tractebel Engineering
Enterprise Products	Williams Companies

HISTORICAL FINANCIALS

Company Type: Public

Income Statement

FYE: December 31

	REVENUE ($ mil.)	NET INCOME ($ mil.)	NET PROFIT MARGIN	EMPLOYEES
12/14	23,925	1,883	7.9%	28,344
12/13	24,598	2,665	10.8%	27,948
12/12	19,624	1,768	9.0%	27,885
12/11	14,529	1,706	11.7%	18,249
12/10	14,272	1,320	9.2%	18,440
Annual Growth	**13.8%**	**9.3%**	**—**	**11.3%**

2014 Year-End Financials

Debt ratio: 35.24%	No. of shares (mil.): 707
Return on equity: 4.58%	Dividends
Cash ($ mil.): 2,036	Yield: 3.7%
Current ratio: 1.03	Payout: 90.2%
Long-term debt ($ mil.): 37,213	Market value ($ mil.): 59,063

	STOCK PRICE ($) FY Close	P/E High/Low	Earnings	PER SHARE ($) Dividends	Book Value
12/14	83.54	33 25	2.66	3.15	57.81
12/13	69.01	20 17	3.76	3.09	58.54
12/12	63.80	22 7	3.07	1.53	58.18
12/11	22.00	6 4	3.84	2.97	51.13
12/10	17.81	6 5	3.00	2.91	50.84
Annual Growth	**47.2%**	**— —**	**(3.0%)**	**2.0%**	**3.3%**

E*TRADE Financial Corp.

E*TRADE wants you to use its services for nearly E*VERYTHING financial. Known for its brokerage services the firm provides the products tools services and advice to individual investors and stock plan participants wanting to manage their own investments. For corporate clients it offers market making trade clearing and employee stock option plan admin services. Subsidiary E*TRADE Bank offers deposits savings and credit cards online and from 30 financial centers in major US cities. E*TRADE Clearing offers securities clearing and settlement while E*TRADE Securities the bank's broker-dealer arm offers mutual funds options fixed income products exchange-traded funds and portfolio management services.

Operations

E*TRADE operates two main business segments. Trading and Investing which makes up more than 70% of the firm's total revenue includes its retail brokerage products and services investor-focused banking products and corporate services. The Balance Sheet Management segment which makes up the remainder of E*TRADE's revenue manages asset allocation loans originated by the company or from third-parties deposits and customer payables and manages credit liquidity and interest rate risk.More broadly E*TRADE makes nearly 60% of its revenue from interest income which is generated from a fairly-even mix of loans available-for-sale and held-to-maturity securities margin receivables and borrowed securities assets. Nearly 25% of the firm's revenue comes from commission income while fees and service charges make up another roughly 10% of revenue.

Geographic Reach

New York-based E*TRADE Financial has 30 branch offices across the US. E*TRADE currently maintains about a dozen retail brokerage websites in Europe the Middle East and the Pacific Rim in addition to the US.Sales and MarketingThe company sells and provides customer support from its branches online and by telephone. Its financial advisors also promote the firm's products and services. E*TRADE spent $120 million on advertising and marketing development in 2014 compared to $108 million and $139 million in 2013 and 2012 respectively.

Financial Performance

E*TRADE's revenues have seen a slow decline over the past years as low interest rates in the US have eaten away at the firm's interest margins on loans and investment securities. Profits however have been on the rise as thanks to declining loan loss provisions as its loan portfolio's credit quality has improved with the strengthened economy. The firm had a breakout year in 2014 with its revenue rebounding by 2% to $2 billion mostly thanks to double-digit interest income growth as it purchased more interest-earning assets such as held-to-maturity securities securities borrowed and margin receivables and as interest margins steadied during the year. E*TRADE's commission income also rose by 9% as daily average revenue per trade (DART) volumes increased by double digits while fee and service charge income grew by 20% thanks to higher trading volumes and assets under management (AUM) growth.E*TRADE's profit more than tripled to $293 million in 2014 thanks to a combination of higher revenue and the absence of a $142 million goodwill impairment charge that the firm incurred in 2013 after it exited the market making business that year. The brokerage's operating cash declined by more than 30% to $701 million mostly as its margin receivables more than doubled during the year.

Strategy

E*TRADE in 2015 reiterated its focus on growing the market share of its retail brokerage business with competitive pricing and a wide variety of corporate services to attract new customers and grow existing relationships via cross-selling. It's also committed to "strengthening its overall financial and franchise position."As part of its refocusing efforts in shedding non-core business lines and amid declining sales and profits E*TRADE sold its Chicago-based market-making unit G1 Execution Services to Susquehanna International for some $76 million in 2014. The sale came after a long string of bad luck at the firm and seven CEOs since 2007.

E*TRADE continues its interest in mobile innovation to attract new customers as well. In addi-

tion to launching its custom Apple Watch market data app in 2015 E*TRADE in 2014 launched an iOS 8 app providing market and watch list information and featuring cutting-edge technologies such as finger print ID log in a new browser trading web application allowing users to trade directly from research pages an enhanced online robo-advisor tool and new technical indicator features. Company BackgroundA disastrous decision to move more strongly into banking (originally aiming to triple its loan business) just as the credit crisis struck down banks and lenders around the world led to large losses at the company. The firm was forced to hoard reserves to counter loan losses and exited both its wholesale lending and direct lending operations. The company also shuttered its institutional brokerage business. Its strategy to do improve results revolves around focusing on its online brokerage business and enhancing its position in retirement and investing while continuing to mitigate credit losses in its loan portfolio.

HISTORY

Company BackgroundIn 1982 physicist William Porter created Trade Plus an electronic brokerage service for stockbrokers; clients included Charles Schwab & Co. and Fidelity Brokerage Services. A decade later subsidiary E*TRADE Securities became CompuServe's first online securities trader.

In 1996 E*TRADE moved from the institutional side to retail when it launched its website. Christos Cotsakos (a Vietnam and FedEx veteran) became CEO and took the firm public. But there were problems: E*TRADE covered $1.7 million in customer losses and added backup systems after computer failure stymied user access. In 1997 it formed alliances with America Online and BANK ONE and ended the year with 225000 accounts.

The firm began to position itself globally in 1997 and 1998 opening sites for Australian Canadian German Israeli and Japanese customers. It offered its first IPO (Sportline USA) in 1997. Volume grew as Internet trading increased but technical glitches dogged E*TRADE. In 1999 day trading became fashionable and the company began running ads promoting prudent trading to counter criticism that online trading fosters a get-rich-quick mentality.

The company also continued to add services. In 1999 it teamed with Garage.com to offer affluent clients venture capital investments in young companies and launched online investment bank E*OFFERING with former Robertson Stephens & Co. chairman Sanford Robertson. (E*TRADE sold its stake in the bank to Wit Soundview —which later became SoundView Technology Group —the next year.) It also bought TIR Holdings which executes and settles multi-currency securities transactions.

Retail banking was a major focus in 2000. The company bought Telebanc Financial (now E*TRADE Financial) owner of Telebank an online bank with more than 100000 depositors and started E*TRADE Bank which offers retail banking products on the E*TRADE website. To provide clients with "real-world" access to their money it bought Card Capture Services an operator of more than 9000 ATMs across the US.

Continuing to expand its global reach E*TRADE bought the part of its E*TRADE UK joint venture it didn't already own; acquired Canadian firm VERSUS Technologies a provider of electronic trading services; and teamed with UBS Warburg to allow non-US investors to buy US securities without needing to trade in dollars. Later its E*Trade International Capital announced plans to offer IPOs to European investors.

In 2001 E*TRADE entered consumer lending when it bought online mortgage originator Loans-

Direct (now E*TRADE Mortgage). Also that year the company bought online brokerage Web Street and moved to the NYSE. In late 2002 E*TRADE Bank purchased Ganis Credit Corp. (a US-based unit of Germany's Deutsche Bank) to boost its consumer finance business.

E*TRADE purchased the online trading operations of Tradescape in mid-2002. The deal which cost E*TRADE $280 million had hashed out the previous April –just days after rival Ameritrade announced its acquisition of online brokerage Datek.

Cotsakos resigned in early 2003 days after the company issued a gloomy forecast (he also had been criticized for his 2001 pay of $80 million although he subsequently gave up about $20 million). He was replaced by company president Mitch Caplan who had been viewed as instrumental in the company's effort to integrate brokerage and banking operations.

In 2005 E*TRADE bought US-based online brokerage Harrisdirect from Bank of Montreal as well as the former J.P. Morgan Invest unit BrownCo which served experienced online traders. The acquisitions expanded its client base and helped the company to keep pace with TD Ameritrade (the result of the 2006 merger of rivals Ameritrade and TD Waterhouse).

E*TRADE built its wealth management operations in 2005 and 2006 by purchasing several money managers including Boston-area investment advisory firm Kobren Insight Management.

After E*TRADE got snared in the subprime mortgage crisis in 2007 Caplan stepped down. He was replaced in 2008 by Donald Layton a former executive with JPMorgan Chase.Layton retired the following year. Company director Robert Druskin took over as chairman while Steven Freiberg became CEO. Freiberg was formerly a co-CEO of Citigroup's global consumer operations.To raise additional cash it sold its Canadian operations to Scotiabank for more than $440 million in 2008. The following year it raised some $733 million in three separate stock offerings and exchanged another $1.7 billion in debt for convertible debentures.

EXECUTIVES

President, Navtej S. Nandra, age 48, $792,500 total compensation

EVP General Counsel and Corporate Secretary, Karl A. Roessner, age 47, $800,000 total compensation

CEO, Paul T. Idzik, age 54, $1,000,000 total compensation

EVP and Chief Administrative Officer, Michael E. Foley, age 63, $535,000 total compensation

CFO, Michael A. Pizzi

Acting Chief Risk Officer, Paul W. Brandow

Vice President Web Channel, Hiram Veciana

Chairman, Rodger A. Lawson, age 68

Board Member, Lewis Randall

Auditors: Deloitte & Touche LLP

LOCATIONS

HQ: E*TRADE Financial Corp.
1271 Avenue of the Americas, 14th Floor, New York, NY 10020
Phone: 646 521-4300
Web: www.etrade.com

PRODUCTS/OPERATIONS

2014 Sales

	$ mil.	% of total
Operating interest income		
Loans	297	15
Available-for-sale securities	288	14
Held-to-maturity securities	328	16
Margin receivables	264	13

Securities borrowed & other		116	6
Commissions		456	23
Fees & service charges		186	9
Principal transactions		10	0
Gains on loans and securities net		36	2
Net impairment		0	0
Adjustments		38	2
Total		**2,019**	**100**

Selected Subsidiaries

E*TRADE Bank (federally chartered savings bank)
E*TRADE Clearing LLC (clearing house)
E*TRADE Securities (registered broker-dealer)
G1 Execution Services LLC (registered broker-dealer and market maker)

COMPETITORS

Charles Schwab	ShareBuilder
FMR	Siebert Financial
Morgan Stanley	TD Ameritrade
Scottrade	UBS Financial Services

HISTORICAL FINANCIALS

Company Type: Public

Income Statement

FYE: December 31

	ASSETS ($ mil.)	NET INCOME ($ mil.)	INCOME AS % OF ASSETS	EMPLOYEES
12/14	45,530	293	0.6%	3,200
12/13	46,279	86	0.2%	3,009
12/12	47,386	(112)	—	3,000
12/11	47,940	156	0.3%	3,240
12/10	46,373	(28)	—	2,962
Annual Growth	(0.5%)	—	—	2.0%

2014 Year-End Financials

Debt ratio: 5.85%	No. of shares (mil.): 289
Return on equity: 5.73%	Dividends
Cash ($ mil.): 2,338	Yield: —
Current ratio: —	Payout: —
Long-term debt ($ mil.): —	Market value ($ mil.): 7,016

	STOCK PRICE ($) FY Close	P/E High/Low	PER SHARE ($) Earnings	Dividends	Book Value
12/14	24.26	25 19	1.00	0.00	18.58
12/13	19.64	65 30	0.29	0.00	16.90
12/12	8.95	— —	(0.39)	0.00	17.14
12/11	7.96	30 13	0.54	0.00	17.27
12/10	16.00	— —	(0.13)	0.00	18.35
Annual Growth	11.0%	— —	—	—	0.3%

Eagle Bancorp Inc (MD)

For those nest eggs that need a little help hatching holding company Eagle Bancorp would recommend its community-oriented EagleBank subsidiary. The bank serves businesses and individuals through more than 15 branches in Washington DC and its suburbs. Deposit products include checking savings and money market accounts; certificates of deposit; and IRAs. Commercial real estate and construction real estate loans combined represent about 70% of its loan portfolio. The bank which has significant expertise as a Small Business Administration lender also writes business consumer and home equity loans. EagleBank offers insurance products through an agreement with The Meltzer Group.

Financial Performance

Eagle Bancorp's revenue and net income have been trending up year-over-year. Its annual rev-

enue increased in fiscal 2013 compared to the prior year. Eagle Bancorp reported $182 million in revenue for fiscal 2013 up from $163.3 million in fiscal 2012.

The company's net income also increased in fiscal 2013 versus the previous fiscal period. It reported $47 million in net income for fiscal 2013 up from $35 million in fiscal 2012.

Eagle Bancorp's cash on hand spiked from $15 million in fiscal 2012 up to more than $258 million by the end of fiscal 2013.

Strategy

The company has been focused on growing within its existing markets. Its strategy for further growth includes continuing to seek opportunities to open or acquire new banking locations while waiting out record low interest rates. Eagle's strict loan underwriting standards –it didn't write subprime residential mortgages and didn't buy securities backed by subprime mortgages –has helped it have fewer problem loans the downfall for many banks.

EXECUTIVES

EVP and CFO, James H. Langmead, $300,500 total compensation
EVP, Susan G. Riel, $365,500 total compensation
President Community Banking of EagleBank, Thomas D. Murphy, $289,200 total compensation
Chairman President and CEO, Ronald D. Paul, $667,000 total compensation
EVP and COO, Michael T. Flynn, $236,080 total compensation
EVP and General Counsel, Laurence E. Bensignor
Executive Vice President, Susan Schumacher
Vice President Of Marketing, Jane Cornett
Senior Vice President Commercial Banking Team Leader, Derek Whitwer
Vice President Commercial Real Estate Lender, Timothy Annett
Senior Vice President, Elizabeth Ferrenz
Vice President, Renee Aldrich
Assistant Vice President Business Relationship Manager, Pfashema Faber
Vice President, Clarice Ribeiro
Vice President Commercial Lending, Len Rann
Vice President, Samantha Perry
Assistant Vice President Branch Service Manager, Rosalind Alexander
Vice President Facilities Operations Manager, Shawn Cox
Vice President, Jacqueline Ames
Executive Vice President CandI Chief Lending Officer, Lindsey Rheaume
Vice Chairman, Robert P. Pincus
Vice President Treasurer, Scott Clark
Auditors: Stegman & Company

LOCATIONS

HQ: Eagle Bancorp Inc (MD)
7830 Old Georgetown Road, Third Floor, Bethesda, MD 20814
Phone: 301 986-1800
Web: www.eaglebankcorp.com

PRODUCTS/OPERATIONS

Selected Subsidiaries

EagleBank
  Bethesda Leasing LLC
  Eagle Insurance Services LLC
  Fidelity Mortgage Inc.
Eagle Commercial Ventures LLC

COMPETITORS

BB&T	OBA Financial Services
Bank of America	PNC Financial
Capital One	Sandy Spring Bancorp

M&T Bank	SunTrust

HISTORICAL FINANCIALS

Company Type: Public

Income Statement

FYE: December 31

	ASSETS ($ mil.)	NET INCOME ($ mil.)	INCOME AS % OF ASSETS	EMPLOYEES
12/14	5,247	54	1.0%	427
12/13	3,771	47	1.2%	386
12/12	3,409	35	1.0%	393
12/11	2,831	24	0.9%	338
12/10	2,089	16	0.8%	292
Annual Growth	25.9%	34.3%	—	10.0%

2014 Year-End Financials

Debt ratio: 1.51%	No. of shares (mil.): 30
Return on equity: 10.70%	Dividends
Cash ($ mil.): 252	Yield: —
Current ratio: —	Payout: —
Long-term debt ($ mil.): —	Market value ($ mil.): 1,071

	STOCK PRICE ($) FY Close	P/E High/Low	PER SHARE ($) Earnings	Dividends	Book Value
12/14	35.52	18 15	1.95	0.00	20.60
12/13	30.63	18 11	1.76	0.00	15.22
12/12	19.97	14 10	1.46	0.00	13.86
12/11	14.54	14 11	1.04	0.00	12.15
12/10	14.43	21 14	0.70	0.00	9.45
Annual Growth	25.3%	— —	29.2%	—	21.5%

East West Bancorp, Inc

East West Bancorp banks in both hemispheres of the world. It's the holding company for East West Bank which provides standard banking services and loans through more than 130 branches in major US metropolitan areas and about 10 offices across in China Hong Kong and Taiwan. Boasting $29 billion in assets East West Bank focuses on making commercial and industrial real estate loans which account for the majority of the company's loan portfolio. Catering to the Asian-American community it also provides international banking and trade financing to importers/exporters doing business in the Asia/Pacific region. East West Bank offers multilingual service in English Cantonese Mandarin Vietnamese and Spanish.

Operations

East West Bancorp operates two business segments. The commercial banking segment (which generated 62% of its total revenue in 2014) includes commercial industrial and commercial real estate primarily generates commercial and industrial real estate loans and offers a wide variety of international finance and trade services and products. The retail banking segment (33% of total revenue) focuses primarily on retail operations through the East West Bank's branch network. The bank also offers insurance products through East West Insurance.Broadly speaking the bank made 93% of its revenue from loan interest (including fees) in 2014 and another 7% from interest on investment securities investment in Federal Home Loan Bank and Federal Reserve Bank Stock and short-term investments. It had a staff of roughly 2700 employees at the end of 2014.Geographic ReachEast West's bank network in the US is mainly in California (in and around Los Angeles the San Francisco Bay area Orange County and Silicon Valley) and in the Atlanta Boston Houston New York and Seattle metropolitan areas. Internationally the bank has five branches in Hong Kong and Greater China (Shanghai Shantou and Shenzhen) and five representative offices in Beijing Chongqing Guangzhou Xiamen and Taiwan.Sales and MarketingEast West Bancorp caters its banking and loan business to companies in the manufacturing wholesale trade and service sectors.Financial PerformanceThe bank has struggled to consistently grow its revenues in recent years due to shrinking interest margins on loans amidst the low-interest environment. Its profits however have been rising thanks to declining loan loss provisions as its loan portfolio's credit quality has improved with higher property valuations in the strengthened economy.East West had a breakout year in 2014 as its revenue climbed by 17% to $1.14 billion mostly thanks to an increase in non-covered loan volumes. Higher revenue in 2014 drove East West Bancorp's net income higher by 16% to $342.5 million. Lower income tax provisions resulting from additional purchases of affordable housing partnerships and tax-credited investments also help pad the bank's bottom line. The bank's operating cash levels dipped by 8% to $392.9 million mostly due to unfavorable working capital changes related to accrued interest receivables and other asset balances.

Strategy

East West Bancorp's long-term vision reiterated in 2015 is to "serve as the financial bridge between the United States and Greater China" by reaching more customers with its cross-border products and capabilities. Its full-service branches in Greater China offer traditional letters of credit and trade finance between businesses while also providing the bank a way to serve existing clients and establish new business relationships.Toward its international expansion plans the company opened two new branches in Greater China's Shenzhen and Shanghai Pilot Free Trade Zone during 2014 which would better position it to help its customers and facilitate their financial needs between Greater China and the US. The bank may also occasionally pursue acquisitions of other banks to broaden its market reach and grow its loan and deposit business. Mergers and AcquisitionsIn 2014 East West Bancorp expanded its presence in Texas and California after it purchased Metrocorp along with its 19 MetroBank and Metro United Bank branches in the Houston Dallas and San Diego markets. The deal also added $1.7 billion in assets and $1.4 billion in new loan assets.

Company Background

East West Bancorp was founded in 1998.

In 2009 the company acquired more than 60 branches and most of the banking operations of larger rival United Commercial Bank which had been seized by regulators. The deal gave East West Bank about 40 more California branches plus some 20 additional US locations beyond the state.

EXECUTIVES

President and COO East West Bancorp and East West Bank, Julia S. Gouw, age 55, $580,667 total compensation
Chairman and CEO East West Bancorp and East West Bank, Dominic Ng, age 56, $1,000,000 total compensation
Vice Chairman East West Bancorp and East West Bank, John Lee, age 83
EVP and CFO, Irene Oh, $359,228 total compensation
Vice President Senior Relationship Manager, Steve Smith
Vice President, Sue Chao

Executive Vice President Cro General Counsel And Secretary, Douglas (Doug) Krause
Auditors: KPMG LLP

LOCATIONS

HQ: East West Bancorp, Inc
135 N. Los Robles Ave., 7th Floor, Pasadena, CA 91101
Phone: 626 768-6000
Web: www.eastwestbank.com

PRODUCTS/OPERATIONS

2011 Sales

	$ mil.	% of total
Commercial lending	619	57
Retail banking	358	33
Other& adjustments	112	10
Total	**1,091**	**100**

COMPETITORS

BBCN	Comerica
Bank of America	Hanmi Financial
Bank of East Asia	JPMorgan Chase
Cathay General Bancorp	U.S. Bancorp
Citibank	Wells Fargo
City National	Wilshire Bancorp

HISTORICAL FINANCIALS

Company Type: Public

Income Statement

FYE: December 31

	ASSETS ($ mil.)	NET INCOME ($ mil.)	INCOME AS % OF ASSETS	EMPLOYEES
12/14	28,738	342	1.2%	2,709
12/13	24,730	295	1.2%	2,542
12/12	22,536	281	1.2%	2,306
12/11	21,968	245	1.1%	2,329
12/10	20,700	164	0.8%	2,131
Annual Growth	**8.5%**	**20.1%**	**—**	**6.2%**

2014 Year-End Financials

Debt ratio: 0.79%	No. of shares (mil.): 143
Return on equity: 13.14%	Dividends
Cash ($ mil.): 1,039	Yield: 1.8%
Current ratio: —	Payout: 31.5%
Long-term debt ($ mil.): —	Market value ($ mil.): 5,558

	STOCK PRICE ($) FY Close	P/E High/Low		PER SHARE ($)		
				Earnings	Dividends	Book Value
12/14	38.71	16	13	2.38	0.72	19.85
12/13	34.97	17	10	2.10	0.60	17.18
12/12	21.49	13	10	1.89	0.40	16.98
12/11	19.75	15	9	1.60	0.16	15.48
12/10	19.55	23	16	0.83	0.04	14.23
Annual Growth	**18.6%**	**—**	**—**	**30.1%**	**106.0%**	**8.7%**

Eastman Chemical Co.

Eastman Chemical can recall its past through photos —it was once part of film giant Eastman Kodak. The company is now a major producer of chemicals fibers plastics rubber materials polymers and solvents. The chemicals and materials manufacturer is one of the world's largest suppliers of acetate tow for cigarette filters. Eastman's products include such items as food and medical packaging films and toothbrushes. In 2014 the US accounted for 46% of company's revenues; Asia Pacific 27%;

Europe Middle East and Africa 22%; and Latin America 5%.

HISTORY

Eastman Chemical went public in 1994 but the company traces its roots to the 19th century. George Eastman after developing a method for dry-plate photography established the Eastman Dry Plate and Film Company in 1884 in Rochester New York (the name was changed to Eastman Kodak in 1892).

In 1886 Eastman hired scientist Henry Reichenbach to help create and manufacture new photographic chemicals. As time passed Reichenbach and the company's other scientists came up with chemicals that were either not directly related to photography or had uses in addition to photography.

Eastman bought a wood-distillation plant in Kingsport Tennessee in 1920 and formed the Tennessee Eastman Corporation to make methanol and acetone for the manufacture of photographic chemicals. The company by this time called Kodak introduced acetate yarn and Tenite a cellulose ester plastic in the early 1930s. During WWII the company formed Holston Defense to make explosives for the US armed forces.

Kodak began to vertically integrate Tennessee Eastman's operations during the 1950s acquiring A. M. Tenney Associates Tennessee Eastman's selling agent for its acetate yarn products in 1950. It also established Texas Eastman opening a plant in Longview to produce ethyl alcohol and aldehydes raw materials used in fiber and film production. At the end of 1952 Kodak created Eastman Chemical Products to sell alcohols plastics and fibers made by Tennessee Eastman and Texas Eastman. Also that year Tennessee Eastman developed cellulose acetate filter tow for use in cigarette filters. In the late 1950s the company introduced Kodel polyester fiber.

Kodak created Carolina Eastman Company in 1968 opening a plant in Columbia South Carolina to produce Kodel and other polyester products. It also created Eastman Chemicals Division to handle its chemical operations.

In the late 1970s Eastman Chemicals Division introduced polyethylene terephthalate (PET) resin used to make containers. It acquired biological and molecular instrumentation manufacturer International Biotechnologies in 1987.

Eastman Chemicals Division became Eastman Chemical Company in 1990. In 1993 it exited the polyester fiber business. When Kodak spun off Eastman Chemical in early 1994 the new company was saddled with $1.8 billion in debt.

Eastman's 1996 earnings were reduced when oversupply lowered prices for PET. Eastman opened plants in Argentina Malaysia and the Netherlands in 1998.

Eastman added to its international locations in 1999 by opening a plant in Singapore and an office in Bangkok. It also bought Lawter International (specialty chemicals for ink and coatings) with locations in Belgium China and Ireland. In 2000 the company began restructuring into two business segments (chemicals and polymers) and acquired resin and colorant maker McWhorter Technologies.

In 2001 Eastman acquired most of Hercules' resins business. In November the company announced that it had postponed plans to split into two companies (one focusing on specialty chemicals and plastics the other concentrating on polyethylene plastics and acetate fibers) until mid-2002 due to the weak economy. In early 2002 the company announced that it had cancelled those plans altogether and would operate the two as separate divisions.

The following year Eastman announced it would split off part of its coatings adhesives specialty polymers and inks (CASPI) segment. The division had been underperforming and had been hit particularly hard by the high costs of raw materials and a general overcapacity in the marketplace. Eastman sold a portion of CASPI to investment firm Apollo Management for $215 million. Businesses included in the sale were composites inks and graphic arts raw materials liquid and powder resins and textile chemicals. (Apollo called the acquired businesses Resolution Specialty Materials and then joined RSM with Resolution Performance Products and another of its chemical companies Borden Chemical to form the new Hexion Specialty Chemicals in 2005.)

It restructured its divisional alignment in 2006 in an attempt to group together related product groups and technologies. In the process Eastman disbanded its former Voridian Division.

At the end of 2007 the company decided to divest its PET facilities in the UK and the Netherlands as well as its Dutch PTA plants. Eastman sold the facilities to Indorama for about $330 million.

Chairman and CEO Brian Ferguson retired in 2009 after nearly seven years as CEO. James Rogers who had been president of the company and head of the chemicals and fibers group became his successor and Ferguson became executive chairman.

In 2009 the company joined with SK Chemicals in a joint venture to construct a cellulose acetate tow facility in Ulsan South Korea. Eastman owns 80% of the JV and operates the plant. It also bought a facility in China in 2010 in a joint venture with Mazzucchelli 1849 SPA. The previous year Eastman had expanded an acetate tow facility it owns in the UK.

Eastman Chemical acquired Genovique Specialties Corporation a global provider of benzoate plasticizers from Arsenal Capital Partners in 2010. Genovique produces benzoic acid sodium benzoate and specialty plasticizers with operations in North America Europe and Asia.

Eastman bought Houston-based Sterling Chemicals for $100 million in 2011. The company plans to use Sterling's plasticizers manufacturing plant to produce its own line of non-phthalate plasticizers Eastman 168 for its PCI segment. The non-phthalate plasticizers used to soften vinyl are an alternative to phthalates which have seen restrictions because of safety concerns.

To raise cash for core businesses in 2011 Eastman sold its Texas-based TX Energy unit to Zero Emission Energy Plants. The TX Energy facility will convert petroleum coke an oil refining waste product into hydrogen and pipeline-quality carbon dioxide.

Eastman Chemicals completed its exit of its Performance Polymers segment in 2011 by selling its polyethylene terephthalate (PET) business to DAK Americas LLC for about $600 million. Eastman Chemicals had been a top producer of PET a plastic used to make packaging for soft drinks food and water.

In a major move in 2012 Eastman acquired US-based chemicals firm Solutia in a $4.7 billion cash-and stock deal. With the addition of Solutia Eastman became a top-tier specialty chemicals company. Its products include rubber materials specialty polymers (synthetic plastics) solvents adhesives plasticizers (additives to soften plastics such as PVC) and specialty fluids.

The Solutia purchase not only broadened Eastman Chemicals' portfolio but also its geographic reach. The addition was a significant step in the company's growth strategy particularly in the Asia/Pacific region and other emerging markets and the company expected the transaction to accelerate the expansion of its businesses worldwide.

That year Eastman also bought Dynaloy a specialty chemical company in Indianapolis. Dynaloy sells cleaning products used in the manufacture of semiconductors and the acquisition supports Eastman's efforts to expand its CASPI segment.

In 2012 Eastman's joint venture with Sinopec Yangzi Petrochemical announced plans to build a major hydrogenated hydrocarbon resin plant in Nanjing China capable of producing 50000 metric tons of Eastman's Adhesives and Plasticizers segment's Regalite hydrocarbon resins.

EXECUTIVES

EVP and CFO, Curtis E. (Curt) Espeland, age 50, $627,087 total compensation
COO, Ronald C. Lindsay, age 56, $751,024 total compensation
Chairman and CEO, Mark J. Costa, age 48, $987,316 total compensation
SVP and Chief International Ventures Officer, Michael H.K. Chung, age 61
SVP and CTO, Stephen G. (Steve) Crawford, age 50
EVP Additives & Functional Products and Advanced Materials, Brad A. Lich, age 47, $551,348 total compensation
SVP Chief Manufacturing and Engineering Officer, Mark K. Cox, age 49
Vice President, Don Cleek
Vice President Corporate Strategy, Robert (Bob) Lurie
National Account Manager Retail Channel Performance Films Division, Rose Dygard
Vice President and General Manager Advanced Interlayers, Eric Nichols
Vice President Finance, Mary Dean Hall
Board Member, Laurie Paulonis
Auditors: PricewaterhouseCoopers LLP

LOCATIONS

HQ: Eastman Chemical Co.
200 South Wilcox Drive, Kingsport, TN 37662
Phone: 423 229-2000
Web: www.eastman.com

2014 Sales

	$ mil.	% of total
US & Canada	4,384	46
Asia/Pacific	2,540	27
Europe Middle East & Africa	2,091	22
Latin America	512	5
Total	**9,527**	**100**

PRODUCTS/OPERATIONS

2014 Sales

	$ mil.	% of total
Specialty Fluids & Intermediates	2,490	26
Advanced Materials	2,378	25
Additives & Functional Products	1,821	19
Additives & Plasticzers	1,363	14
Fibers	1,457	15
Other	18	1
Total	**9,527**	**100**

Selected Brands and Products

ABALYN rosin resins
ABITOL hydroabietyl alcohols
ADMEX plasticizers
ASPIRA family of resins
BENZOFLEX plasticizers
BIOEXTEND high performance additives
CADENCE resins for calendered films
CELLOLYN synthetic resins
CHROMSPUN acetate yarn
CRYSTEX insoluble sulfur
CYPHREX microfibers
DRESINATE rosin soaps
DURASTAR polymer
DYMEREX rosins
EASTAPURE electronic chemicals
EASTAR copolyesters

EASTEK polymer dispersion
EASTMAN AQ polymers
EASTMAN cellulose esters
EASTMAN coalescents
EASTMAN G polymers
EASTMAN low volatile pure monomer resins
EASTMAN NPG glycol
EASTMAN plasticizers
EASTMAN solvents
EASTMAN TXIB formulation additive
EASTOFLEX amorphous polyolefins
EASTOTAC resins
ECDEL elastomers
EMBRACE family of resins
ENDEX hydrocarbon resins
ENERLOGIC low-e window film
ESTRON acetate yarn
FLEXVUE film
FORAL hydrogenated rosins
FORALYN hydrogenated rosin esters
FORMULAONE high performance auto tint
GILA DIY window film
HUPER OPTIK & DESIGN film
IQUE film
KRISTALEX hydrocarbon resins
LLUMAR window film
METALYN rosin esters
NANOLUX film
NEOSTAR elastomer
OPTIFILM family of products
PAMOLYN fatty acids
PENTALYN synthetic resins
PERENNIAL WOOD
PERMALYN resins
PICCO hydrocarbon resins
PICCOLASTIC hydrocarbon resins
PICCOTAC hydrocarbon resins
PICCOTEX hydrocarbon resins
PLASTOLYN hydrocarbon resins
POLY-PALE rosin resins
PROBENZ sodium benzoate
PROVISTA copolymer
REGALITE hydrocarbon resins
REGALREZ hydrocarbon resins
SAFLEX PVB polymers
SANTOFLEX antidegradants
SKYDROL aviation hydraulic fluids
SKYKLEEN solvents
SOLUS performance additive
SPECTAR copolyester
STAYBELITE-E hydrogenated rosins
SUN-X film
SUSTANE SAIB
TACOLYN resin dispersions
TENITE cellulosics
TENOX antioxidants
TEXANOL ester alcohol
THE GLASS POLYMER
THERMINOL heat transfer fluids
TiGLAZE copolyester
TMPD glycol
TRITAN copolyester
VANCEVA PVB polymers
VELATE coalescents
VISTA window film
V-KOOL film
XIR coated PET

Selected Mergers and Acquisitions

COMPETITORS

Akzo Nobel	Dow Chemical
BASF SE	DuPont
Celanese	ExxonMobil Chemical
Clariant	Huntsman Corp
DIC Corporation	Solvay
DSM	

HISTORICAL FINANCIALS

Company Type: Public

Income Statement

FYE: December 31

	REVENUE ($ mil.)	NET INCOME ($ mil.)	NET PROFIT MARGIN	EMPLOYEES
12/14	9,527	751	7.9%	15,000
12/13	9,350	1,165	12.5%	14,000
12/12	8,102	437	5.4%	13,500
12/11	7,178	696	9.7%	10,000
12/10	5,842	438	7.5%	10,000
Annual Growth	13.0%	14.4%	—	10.7%

2014 Year-End Financials

Debt ratio: 46.97%
Return on equity: 20.56%
Cash ($ mil.): 214
Current ratio: 1.57
Long-term debt ($ mil.): 7,248

No. of shares (mil.): 148
Dividends
Yield: 1.9%
Payout: 20.5%
Market value ($ mil.): 11,273

	STOCK PRICE ($) FY Close	P/E High/Low	PER SHARE ($) Earnings	Dividends	Book Value
12/14	75.86	18 14	4.97	1.45	23.62
12/13	80.70	11 8	7.44	1.25	24.91
12/12	68.05	22 13	2.93	1.08	19.12
12/11	39.06	22 7	4.86	0.99	13.66
12/10	84.08	28 17	2.96	0.90	11.51
Annual Growth	(2.5%)	— —	13.8%	12.8%	19.7%

eBay Inc.

I got it on eBay has barreled its way into the lexicon of the new millennium placing a cyber-grin on the corporate face of this online auctioneer. Trading goods every second of every day eBay offers an online forum for selling merchandise worldwide from fine antiques to the latest video games. eBay generates revenue through listing and selling fees and through advertising and boasts more than 155 million users. Its e-commerce platforms include StubHub and Half.com. eBay also has a mobile version of its service and owns e-commerce services provider GSI Commerce as well as a minority stake in online classifieds service craigslist.

HISTORY

Pierre Omidyar created a flea market in cyberspace when he launched online auction service Auction Web on Labor Day weekend in 1995. Making a name for itself largely through word of mouth the company incorporated in 1996 the same year it began to charge a fee to auction items online. That year it enhanced its service with Feedback Forum (buyer and seller ratings).

The company changed the name to eBay in 1997 and began promoting itself through advertising. By the middle of that year eBay was boasting nearly 800000 auctions each day and Benchmark Capital came on board as a significant financial backer.

Margaret ("Meg") Whitman a former Hasbro executive replaced Omidyar as CEO in early 1998. EBay made a blockbuster debut as a public company later that year. The company moved closer to household name status the same year by launching a national ad campaign and inking alliance deals with AOL and WebTV.

eBay showed its acquisitive streak in 1999 with purchases of Alando (online auctions in Germany) and Billpoint (person-to-person credit card technol-

ogy). It also made one of its first investments in an outside company with the purchase of 6% of TradeOut.com an online seller of corporate surplus materials. The company set the jewel in its 1999 acquisition crown when it acquired upscale auction house Butterfield & Butterfield (now just Butterfields). eBay also expanded down under through a joint venture with Australia-based ecorp (formerly PBL Online). A bit of the bloom came off the rose in 1999 when online service interruptions (one "brownout" in June persisted for 22 hours) revealed a chink in eBay's armor. The company called its top 10000 users to convey its apologies and pledged to improve its website's performance.

In 2000 eBay agreed to develop person-to-person and merchant-to-person auction sites for Disney's GO Network began distributing information through wireless products and joined with banking giant Wells Fargo to offer eBay sellers the option of accepting online checks. Also that year the US Department of Justice began an investigation to determine if eBay had violated antitrust laws in its dealings with competitors. In other legal news a class-action lawsuit was filed against the company claiming that eBay was an auctioneer and therefore must authenticate the items on its site. (A trial court dismissed the case in early 2001.)

Also in 2000 the company expanded into Japan through eBay Japan with computer firm NEC acquiring 30% of the Japanese subsidiary and eBay owning the rest; it also launched Canadian and Austrian sites. In addition eBay took an equity stake in online used-car dealer AutoTrader.com and launched a co-branded used-car auction website and it acquired online trading community Half.com.

eBay strengthened its European position in 2001 through the purchase of French Internet auction firm iBazar. It also launched sites in Ireland New Zealand and Switzerland. eBay made a deal that year to provide its e-commerce capabilities to Microsoft developers and to add business-to-business auctions to its consumer operations. In addition the company began offering virtual storefronts for retailers to sell fixed-price items and purchased auctioneer of foreclosed property HomesDirect. In late 2001 eBay sold its iBazar's Brazilian subsidiary to MercadoLibre Latin America's leading auction site in exchange for a 19.5% stake (now 18%) in MercadoLibre.

Disappointed with the performance of eBay Premiere (fine art and other high-end merchandise) in 2002 the company partnered with Sotheby's in a deal that moved Sotheby's entire online business into the eBay website replacing eBay Premiere (Sotheby's later pulled out of the deal citing lagging sales). eBay also sold its traditional auction house Butterfields and shuttered its eBay Japan operations after its dismal performance in that market. In 2003 the company continued to grow through acquisitions with its purchases of EachNet (after acquiring a minority stake in the Chinese e-commerce company in 2002) FairMarket and Internet Auction.

In 2004 eBay took several steps toward diversifying its business. It expanded its international presence through acquisitions in China and India and spent heavily to establish operations there. Three years later eBay shifted its China strategy entering into a joint venture with Chinese Internet gaming firm TOM Online.

The company purchased about a 25% stake in online classifieds provider craigslist and announced plans to offer a music downloading service. Overall in 2004 more than 60% of eBay's new registered users were in the international business.

2005 was a particularly acquisitive year for eBay. That year it picked up Internet listing site Rent.com for about $415 million. Then eBay's international classifieds group Kijiji (Swahili for "village") ac-

quired London-based Gumtree.com and Spain's LoQUo.com a community-based listings website that operates sites for several Spanish cities alongside ones for France Germany Norway Portugal and the UK. Kijiji next acquired opusforum a local classifieds website based in Germany for an undisclosed sum.

Later in 2005 eBay closed on three major deals. It acquired Shopping.com —a provider of online comparison shopping and consumer reviews with sites in France the UK and the US —for about $635 million. It also purchased PayPal VeriSign's payment gateway business for about $370 million. Also in 2005 eBay acquired start-up online telecom service provider Skype of Luxembourg for nearly $3 billion. Skype's Web-based software allowed its 220 million registered users to make phone calls over the Internet. The acquisition proved costly however. eBay took about $1.5 billion in Skype-related charges in the third quarter of 2007.

Keeping the acquisitions rolling in 2006 eBay snatched up the leading Swedish online auctioneer Tradera.com for $48 million; eBay made the purchase to strengthen its Swedish trading opportunities in the future. Later in 2006 Internet powerhouse Yahoo! and eBay entered an agreement to join forces on advertising Web searches online payments (through eBay's PayPal platform) and a co-branded toolbar. Key elements of the arrangement's design included Yahoo! providing advertisements throughout eBay's site and the integration of PayPal into Yahoo!'s e-commerce infrastructure.

eBay bought German auction management software company Via-Online in 2007. Via-Online operated sales tool Afterbuy.com and eBay made the deal to ramp up support for its Germany sellers. Looking to diversify its online marketplace operations also that year eBay acquired ticket seller StubHub for about $310 million. The company followed that up with the significant $900 million purchase of Bill Me Later in 2008.

In 2008 eBay settled its long-running patent dispute with MercExchange agreeing to buy the three MercExchange patents it had been accused of violating. MercExchange had sued eBay in 2001 claiming that eBay's "Buy It Now" option infringed on its patent technology. A federal judge ruled that eBay should pay MercExchange $30 million in damages in the case. Terms of the settlement were not disclosed.

Later in 2008 eBay announced it would end its arrangement with LiveAuctioneers.com that allowed customers to participate in live auctions hosted by other companies. eBay said ending the deal allowed it to better concentrate on growing listings in its core product.

To encourage further growth in its auctions the company reduced fees and rolled out an improved matching feature in 2008. The feature implemented a ranking system that took into account time remaining feedback scores quality of listing pictures and other criteria.

Whitman who led eBay for a decade stepped down as president and CEO of the company in 2008. She was succeeded by John Donahoe who previously led the company's highest revenue-producing unit eBay Marketplaces. Also that year eBay acquired the California-based visual media company VUVOX Network to further develop rich media capabilities in the eBay marketplace.

In a program that ran through the bulk of 2009 eBay partnered with resurrected automaker General Motors to sell new cars online. Prospective buyers could place bids for vehicles from more than 225 GM dealers in California at gm.ebay.com. The program did not move as many cars as anticipated however prompting the automaker to halt sales and shift its attention to marketing. eBay in 2009 paid about $1 billion for a majority stake

(99.2%) in Gmarket a leading online marketplace in South Korea.

eBay also sold a majority of Skype in 2009. Four years after investing in the service eBay acknowledged that Skype did not complement the rest of its operations. It sold off a 70% stake in Skype to investors led by the private-equity firm Silver Lake in a deal involving $1.9 billion in cash and a $125 million note. As part of the agreement eBay retained a 30% interest in the Skype. (eBay had purchased Skype for nearly $3 billion but in 2007 it took a write-down for about half that amount.) eBay sold its share in Skype to Microsoft in 2011.

In 2010 eBay acquired popular German shopping site Brands4Friends for about $200 million. It made the deal to become a leading online fashion destination in Europe. The company continued its shopping spree in Germany the following year when it bolstered PayPal assets by acquiring the German company BillSAFE adding over 15 million accounts. The deal gave eBay purchase-on-invoice capabilities that are popular to merchants and consumers in Austria German the Netherlands and Switzerland.

eBay bought mobile software application developer Critical Path in 2010. Critical Path had worked with eBay to develop several of its applications for Apple's iPhone. The acquisition doubled the size of eBay's mobile team which is working to capitalize on the growing numbers of consumers who are shopping on their smart phones.

In its largest acquisition since purchasing Skype in 2011 eBay bought GSI Commerce a provider of such services as website development and maintenance order fulfillment and digital advertising for $2.4 billion.

In 2012 eBay sold Rent.com to PRIMEDIA. eBay spun off PayPal in 2015.

EXECUTIVES

Senior Vice President, Alan (Al) Marks
President and CEO, Devin N. Wenig, age 48, $823,077 total compensation
President StubHub, Scott Cutler
SVP eBay North America, Hal Lawton
SVP and CTO, Steve Fisher
SVP and CFO, Scott Schenkel
VP Global Operations, Wendy Jones
SVP eBay Europe, Paul Todd
SVP eBay Asia Pacific, Jay Lee
SVP and Chief Product Officer, RJ Pittman
Vice President Chief Accounting Officer, Brian Doerger
Vice President Finance, Peter (Pete) Wade
Vice President eBay Fashion, Michael (Mel) Mosser
Senior Vice President Operations Client Services, Tom Barone
Executive Vice President, Molly Smith
Vice President marketing Solutions, Stephen (Steve) Denton
Vice President And General Counsel, Paul Cataldo
Vice President Global Customer Optimization and Data, Zoher Karu
Vice President Talent Acquisition Management And Development, Lou Sanchez
Vice President Business Development X Commerce, Sharon Meers
Senior Vice President Information Technology, Andre Tozzi
Vice President Product Development, Raji Arasu
Vice President, Greg Fant
Vice President Technology Finance and Analytics, Joe Billante
Vice President Sales, Todd Pearson
National Account Manager, Jessica Schrenker
Vice President For Public Relations, Al Stewart
National Sales Manager at eBay Motors, Roy Daves

Vice President Enterprise Sales And Service At Ebay Enterprise, Scott Hardy
Vice President Product Development, Jay Hanson
Senior Vice President Finance Chief Financial Officer, Bob Swan
Senior Vice President Human Resources, Kristin Yetto
Department Head, Beth Gomez
Vice President, Don Albert
Vice President Global Customer Experience Ebay Europe, Jean-marc Codsi
Vice President Investor Relations, Thomas Hudson
Vice President Of Enabling Functions Tech., Dan Morales
Vice President Of Database Services, Ramesh Murugan
Vice President Legal, John Muller
Senior Vice President Of Quality And Service Information Technology, Yuemin Wang
Vice President Uk Marketplaces, Tanya Lawler
Vice President Of Business Development At Paypal Unit, Garrett Price
Executive Vice President and General Counsel, Michael (Mel) Jacobson
Vice President Information Technology, Omar Jabbar
Executive Vice President Finance, John (Jack) Kim
Senior Vice President And Chief Product Officer, R J Pittman
Chairman, Thomas J. (Tom) Tierney, age 61
Assistant Treasurer, Omar Paz
Treasurer, Louise Curtis
Board Member, Max Stanford
Auditors: PricewaterhouseCoopers LLP

LOCATIONS

HQ: eBay Inc.
  2065 Hamilton Avenue, San Jose, CA 95125
Phone: 408 376-7400
Web: www.ebay.com

2014 Sales

	$ mil.	% of total
US	8,495	47
UK	2,633	15
Germany	2,107	12
Rest of world	4,667	26
Total	**17,902**	**100**

COMPETITORS

AKQA	HSN
Alibaba.com	NexTag
Amazon.com	OnlineAuction
Blast Radius Inc.	Overstock.com
Buy.com	PriceGrabber.com
Costco Wholesale	Shopzilla
Digital River	Spectrum Group
DigitasLBi	Target Corporation
Etsy	Tickets.com
Google	Walmart.com

HISTORICAL FINANCIALS

Company Type: Public

Income Statement

FYE: December 31

	REVENUE ($ mil.)	NET INCOME ($ mil.)	NET PROFIT MARGIN	EMPLOYEES
12/15	8,592	1,725	20.1%	11,600
12/14	17,902	46	0.3%	36,500
12/13	16,047	2,856	17.8%	33,500
12/12	14,072	2,609	18.5%	31,500
12/11	11,651	3,229	27.7%	27,770
Annual Growth	(7.3%)	(14.5%)	—	(19.6%)

2015 Year-End Financials

Debt ratio: 38.12%	No. of shares (mil.): 1,184
Return on equity: 13.03%	Dividends
Cash ($ mil.): 1,832	Yield: —
Current ratio: 3.49	Payout: —
Long-term debt ($ mil.): 6,779	Market value ($ mil.): 32,536

	STOCK PRICE ($) FY Close	P/E High/Low	PER SHARE ($) Earnings	Dividends	Book Value
12/15	27.48	46 17	1.42	0.00	5.55
12/14	56.12	1483 1197	0.04	0.00	16.26
12/13	54.87	26 22	2.18	0.00	18.27
12/12	51.00	26 15	1.99	0.00	16.12
12/11	30.33	14 11	2.46	0.00	13.94
Annual Growth	(2.4%)	— —	(12.8%)	—	(20.5%)

Ecolab, Inc.

Ecolab cleans up by cleaning up. The company offers cleaning sanitation pest-elimination and maintenance products and services to energy healthcare hospitality industrial and other customers. Its cleaning and sanitizing operations serve hotels schools commercial and institutional laundries and quick-service restaurants. Other units focus on products for textile care water care health care food and beverage processing and pest control. It also makes chemicals used in water treatment for industrial processes including in the paper and energy industries. The company is expanding its services to the offshore and international energy market.

HISTORY

Salesman Merritt Osborn founded Economics Laboratory in 1924 as a specialty chemical maker; its first product was a rug cleaner for hotels. It added industrial and institutional cleaners and consumer detergents in the 1950s. The company went public in 1957. By 1973 it had been organized into five divisions: industrial (cleaners and specialty chemical formulas) institutional (dishwasher products sanitation formulas) consumer (dishwasher detergent and laundry aids coffee filters floor cleaners) food-processing (detergents) and international (run by future CEO Fred Lanners).

At the time household dishwasher detergent was Economics Laboratory's top seller second to Procter & Gamble in the US and #1 overseas. The company began offering services and products as packages in the early 1970s including on-premise laundry services for hotels and hospitals and sanitation and cleaning services for the food industry.

E. B. Osborn son of the founder retired in 1978 and Lanners became the company's first CEO outside the Osborn family. Sales of dishwashing detergent had fallen while the institutional cleaning business had become its primary segment quadrupling in sales between 1970 and 1980. International sales were growing rapidly. In 1979 the company bought Apollo Technologies (chemicals and pollution-control equipment) to improve its share of the industrial market.

A depressed industrial sector caused Apollo's sales to drop in early 1980. The man expected to save Apollo Richard Ashley succeeded Lanners in 1982 but died in a car crash that year. Sandy Grieve became CEO in 1983 and shut down Apollo. Meanwhile debt was up the institutional market had shrunk and the company was slipping in the dishwashing-detergent market. Grieve sold the firm's coffee-filters unit and several plants laid off employees and began new packaging processes. The company changed its name to Ecolab in 1986 and in 1987 it sold its dishwashing-detergent unit and bought lawn-service provider ChemLawn. (ChemLawn was sold in 1992.)

As 1990 neared Grieve introduced what's now known as "Circle the Customer –Circle the Globe" the aim being to become a worldwide leader in core businesses and broaden product offerings. The company concentrated on building its presence in Africa the Asia/Pacific region Latin America and the Middle East. In 1991 Ecolab also began a highly successful joint venture Henkel-Ecolab with German consumer-products company Henkel to better exploit European markets.

Ecolab acquired Kay Chemical (cleaning and sanitation products for the fast-food industry 1994) Monarch (cleaning and sanitation products for food processing 1996) Huntington Laboratories (janitorial products 1996) and Australia-based Gibson (cleaning and sanitation products 1997). In 1995 Grieve stepped down and president Allan Schuman became CEO. Adding a few more degrees to its circle of services in 1998 Ecolab bought GCS Service (commercial kitchen equipment repair).

The company further secured footholds in Asia and South America in 2000 by acquiring industrial and institutional cleaning firms Dong Woo Deterpan (South Korea) Spartan de Chile and Spartan de Argentina. At home it bought kitchen-equipment companies ARR/CRS and Southwest Sanitary Distributing. Late in 2000 Ecolab sold its Johnson dish machines unit to Endonis and announced a restructuring that was soon followed by the departure of several top executives including president and COO Bruno Deschamps.

In 2001 Ecolab purchased the 50% of Henkel-Ecolab that it didn't own from Henkel for about $435 million; the move greatly expanded the company's international business.

Schuman stepped down as CEO in 2004 (retaining the chairman's role); president Doug Baker took over and became a director in addition to his role as president and CEO. Two years later Schuman retired as chairman ending his 49-year tenure with Ecolab. The company named Baker to replace him.

In 2007 Ecolab made an acquisition to expand its operations in the health care field buying Microtek Medical Holdings which makes infection control products for health care facilities for about $275 million. The next year it paid $210 million for Ecovation a company that treats wastewater solid waste and air pollution primarily for food and beverage companies.

In 2011 Ecolab completed its acquisition of O.R. Solutions a privately held Virginia company that makes warming and cooling systems for surgical fluids for $260 million. The business became part of the US Cleaning and Sanitizing segment.

The company began a major financial restructuring of its European operations in 2011 expecting to save about $120 million over a three-year period. The plan includes changes to the division's supply chain administrative operations and other functions as well as a 12% reduction in workforce. As a part of the restructuring it rolled out its Ecolab Business System platform a common set of business processes and systems for its European operations. The EBS platform is designed to streamline the organization improve efficiency and competitiveness and more rapidly improve the region's profitability.

In 2011 Ecolab acquired Nalco in a $5.4 billion cash and stock deal. Following this purchase Ecolab continued restructuring and cutting costs in 2012 including cutting back on its global workforce and streamlining its supply chain. With the merging of both companies' operations Ecolab emerged as a global leader in water hygiene and energy technologies and services.

EXECUTIVES

Chairman and CEO, Douglas M. (Doug) Baker, age 57, $1,103,277 total compensation
EVP Latin America, James H. (Jim) White
CFO, Daniel J. (Dan) Schmechel, age 55, $487,500 total compensation
EVP and CIO, Stewart H. McCutcheon
President and COO, Thomas W. (Tom) Handley, age 60, $595,000 total compensation
EVP; President Global Institutional, Michael A. (Mike) Hickey, age 53, $486,250 total compensation
EVP and CTO, Larry L. Berger, age 54
EVP; President International Regions, Christophe Beck, age 47
EVP; President Global Water and Process Services, Timothy P. Mulhere, age 52
EVP Human Resources, Laurie M. Marsh, age 51
EVP; President Global Energy, Stephen M. (Steve) Taylor, age 53, $518,818 total compensation
EVP; President Global Services and Specialty, Roberto D. (Bobby) Mendez
EVP General Counsel and Secretary, James J. (Jim) Seifert, age 58
EVP and President Global Healthcare, Martha Goldberg Aronson, age 47
EVP and President Europe, Darrell Brown
EVP Global Textile Care, Andreas Weilinghoff
EVP; President Global Food and Beverage, Jill S. Wyant, age 43
EVP and Chief Supply Chain Officer, Alex Blanco, age 54, $450,000 total compensation
SVP Global Marketing and Communications, Elizabeth A. (Beth) Simermeyer
VP Middle East and Africa, Vishal Sharma
EVP Asia Pacific, Sean Toohey
Assistant Vice President Of Corporate Accounts For, Greg Cocchiarella
Vice President Finance, Dave Beehler
Vice President Of Finance, Anil Arcalgud
Vice President Human Resources Talent, Sue Metcalf
Vice President Human Resources Global Operations, Michael (Mel) Larson
Kay Assistant Vice President Corporate, Philip Perry
Vice President Marketing And Business, Tom Arata
Vice President and General Manager Anz TC HC FRS and VC, Paul Smith
Vice President Global Benefits, Suzanne Hanson
Vice President Marketing Food and Beverage Asia Pacific and Latin America, David (Dave) Anton
Assistant Vice President Corporate Accounts TCD, Thomas (Thom) Harrington
Assistant Vice President Corporate Accounts, Nick Degregorio
VPandSegment Manager, Kurt Huelsman
Vice President Marketing Institute Strat PlnandCat Management, Tina Dear
Vice President Corporate Planning and Analysis, Jeffrey (Jeff) Mains
Auditors: PricewaterhouseCoopers LLP

LOCATIONS

HQ: Ecolab, Inc.
370 Wabasha Street North, St. Paul, MN 55102
Phone: 800 232-6522
Web: www.ecolab.com

2014 Sales

	% of total
North America	
US	51
Canada	5
EMEA	24
Asia/Pacific	12
Latin America	8
Total	100

PRODUCTS/OPERATIONS

2014 Sales

	$ mil.	% of total
Global Industrial	4,886	34
Global Institutional	4,314	30
Global Energy	4,283	30
Other	750	6
Adjustments	45	-
Total	14,280	100

Selected Services

Equipment Care
Facility Cleaning
Food Retail Solutions
Food Safety Specialties
Foodservice Water Management
Front and Back of House
Housekeeping — Guest Rooms
HVAC Performance Services
Laundry
Pest Elimination
Pool and Spa
Restaurants
Restroom
Water Safety
Water Treatment

COMPETITORS

3M Purification	ISS A/S
Ashland Inc.	Medline Industries
CPAC	Rollins Inc.
Chemed	STERIS
Diversey	ServiceMaster
GE Water and Process Technologies	Unilever
	Zep Inc.
Healthcare Services	

HISTORICAL FINANCIALS

Company Type: Public

Income Statement

FYE: December 31

	REVENUE ($ mil.)	NET INCOME ($ mil.)	NET PROFIT MARGIN	EMPLOYEES
12/14	14,280	1,202	8.4%	47,430
12/13	13,253	967	7.3%	45,415
12/12	11,838	703	5.9%	40,860
12/11	6,798	462	6.8%	40,200
12/10	6,089	530	8.7%	26,494
Annual Growth	23.7%	22.7%	—	15.7%

2014 Year-End Financials

Debt ratio: 33.75%
Return on equity: 16.41%
Cash ($ mil.): 209
Current ratio: 1.11
Long-term debt ($ mil.): 4,864
No. of shares (mil.): 299
Dividends
  Yield: 1.1%
  Payout: 30.7%
Market value ($ mil.): 31,341

	STOCK PRICE ($) FY Close	P/E High/Low		PER SHARE ($) Earnings	Dividends	Book Value
12/14	104.52	29	24	3.93	1.16	24.40
12/13	104.27	33	22	3.16	0.97	24.39
12/12	71.90	30	24	2.35	0.83	20.62
12/11	57.81	30	23	1.91	0.73	19.41
12/10	50.42	23	18	2.23	0.64	9.16
Annual Growth	20.0%	—	—	15.2%	15.9%	27.8%

Edison International

Edison International has been around the world but its largest subsidiary is Southern California Edison (SCE) which distributes electricity to a population of almost 14 million people in central coastal and southern California; it is also the top purchaser of renewable energy in the US. The utility's system consists of more than 12780 circuit miles of transmission lines and more than 91800 circuit miles of distribution lines. SCE also has 6287 MW of generating capacity from interests in nuclear hydroelectric and fossil-fueled power plants. Through Edison Energy the company owns and operates solar power projects.

Geographic Reach

Southern California Edison (SCE) is a regulated electric utility serving Southern California. SCE's service territory includes about 430 cities and communities with a total customer base of about 5 million residential and business accounts. SCE has facilities in Catalina Island and Redlands in California and in Phoenix Arizona.

Operations

SCE maintains a more than $20 billion grid including 1.5 million power poles 700000 transformers and 103000 miles of distribution and transmission lines.

Subsidiary Edison Energy provides new products and services in the fast-changing energy marketplace and invests in and partners with technology leaders in the energy market.Its SoCore Energy unit is a market leader in commercial and industrial solar portfolio development. With hundreds of solar solutions designed and installed across 19 states SoCore offers multisite retailers REITs and industrial companies portfolio-wide solar systems.Edison Transmission a subsidiary of Edison Energy pursues competitive electric transmission projects across the US.

Sales and Marketing

In 2014 SCE got 42.4% of its revenues from commercial customers 36.1% from residential customers 5.7% from agricultural and other customers 5.6% from industrial customers 5.1% from public authorities and 5.1% from resale sales.

Financial Performance

The company's net revenues increased between 2010 and 2014. Edison International's net revenue increased by 7% due to increase in California Public Utilities Commission-related revenues related to the higher rates. In 2014 Edison International's net income increased by 76% due to higher net revenues and decrease in impairment and other charges associated with the San Onofre OII Settlement Agreement (nuclear plant closure).

The company's cash inflow increased by 9% in 2014.

Strategy

Edison International's strategy is to focus on the financially more secure US power market. It is investing in upgrading its traditional power infrastructure and expanding its portfolio of solar projects to make the company compliant with increasingly stringent state and federal carbon emission requirements.

In 2015 the company signed a commercial agreement with Tesla as part of its launch of a new line of Tesla Energy products. SCE and SoCore Energy are developing energy storage projects (battery systems) that feature Tesla Powerpacks.

In 2014 the company signed contracts for 2221 MW of power from diverse new resources to meet its customers' long-term electricity needs. The new contracts result from a plan recommended by SCE in response to state forecasts of local reliability needs due to the closure of the San Onofre Nuclear

Generating Station and anticipated retirement of older natural gas generation plants along the Southern California coastline that rely on ocean water for their cooling needs. In 2014 Edison International announced that its Edison Mission Energy (EME) subsidiary's plan of reorganization was approved by the US Bankruptcy Court whereby all of Edison Mission Energy's assets will be sold to NRG Energy. (EME marketed energy in the US and Turkey and had interests in more than 40 power plants in the US and one in Turkey that gave it a net physical generating capacity of about 10780 MW. EME filed for bankruptcy protection in 2012 citing high operating losses due to low realized energy and capacity prices high fuel costs and low generation at its Midwest Generation plants).

In 2013 SCE decided to permanently retire Units 2 and 3 of its San Onofre Nuclear Generating Station. Unit 2 was taken out of service January 2012 for a planned routine outage. Unit 3 was also taken offline a few weeks later after station operators found a small leak in a tube inside a steam generator.

To compensate SCE was taking measures in 2013 to make up for the power generation loss by making critical infrastructure improvements to its transmission systems.

Mergers and Acquisitions

In 2013 Edison Energy acquired SoCore Energy a Chicago-based solar portfolio development and commercial rooftop installation company focusing on the solar energy needs of multisite retailers REITs and industrial clients and bought a minority stake in Clean Power Finance a financial services and software provider for the solar industry.

HISTORY

In 1896 a group including Elmer Peck and George Baker organized West Side Lighting to provide electricity in Los Angeles. The next year the company merged with Los Angeles Edison Electric which owned the rights to the Edison name and patents in the region and Baker became president. Edison Electric installed the first DC-power underground conduits in the Southwest.

John Barnes Miller took over the top spot in 1901. During his 31-year reign the firm bought many neighboring utilities and built several power plants. In 1909 it took the name Southern California Edison (SCE).

SCE doubled its assets by buying Southern California electric interests from rival Pacific Light & Power in 1917. However in 1912 the City of Los Angeles had decided to develop its own power distribution system and by 1922 SCE's authority in the city had ended. A 1925 earthquake and the 1928 collapse of the St. Francis Dam severely damaged SCE's facilities.

SCE built 11 fossil-fueled power stations (1948-1973) and moved into nuclear power in 1963 when it broke ground on the San Onofre plant with San Diego Gas & Electric (brought online in 1968). It finished consolidating its service territory with the 1964 purchase of California Electric Power. In the late 1970s SCE began to build solar geothermal and wind power facilities.

Edison Mission Energy (EME) was founded in 1986 to develop buy and operate power plants around the world. The next year investment arm Edison Capital was formed as well as a holding company for the entire group SCEcorp. EME began to build its portfolio in 1992 when it snagged a 51% stake in an Australian plant and bought hydroelectric facilities in Spain. In 1995 it bought UK hydroelectric company First Hydro; it also began building plants in Italy Turkey and Indonesia.

The 1994 Northridge earthquake that cut power to a million SCE customers was nothing compared to the industry's seismic shifts. In 1996 SCEcorp became the more worldly Edison International. California's electricity market opened to competition in 1998 and the utility began divesting SCE's generation assets; it sold 12 gas-fired plants. Overseas EME picked up 25% of a power plant being built in Thailand and a 50% stake in a cogeneration facility in Puerto Rico.

SCE got regulatory approval to offer telecom services in its utility territory in 1999. That year EME snapped up several plants in the Midwest from Unicom for $5 billion. Overseas it purchased two UK coal-fired plants from PowerGen (which it sold to American Electric Power in 2001 for $960 million). The next year EME CEO Edward Muller (who had held the post since 1994) abruptly resigned and Edison bought Citizens Power from the Peabody Group.

In 2000 SCE got caught in a price squeeze brought on in part by deregulation. Prices on the wholesale power market soared but the utility was unable to pass along the increase to customers because of a rate freeze. The company gained some prospect of relief in 2001 when California's governor signed legislation to allow a state agency to buy power from wholesalers under long-term contracts. In addition the California Public Utilities Commission (CPUC) approved a substantial increase in retail electricity rates and the Federal Energy Regulatory Commission approved a plan to limit wholesale energy prices during periods of severe shortage in 11 western states.

To reduce debt Edison International agreed to sell its transmission grid to the state for $2.8 billion. While the California legislature debated the agreement however the CPUC announced a settlement in which SCE would be allowed to keep its current high rates in place until its debts are paid off. The settlement which was approved in 2002 eliminated the need for the sale of the company's transmission grid.

Also in 2001 the company sold most of its Edison Enterprises businesses including home security services unit Edison Select which was sold to ADT Security Services.

In 2004 Edison International committed to taking a lead position in developing comprehensive national programs to reduce greenhouse gas emissions primarily carbon dioxide.

In 2006 SCE signed the largest wind energy deal ever completed by a US utility providing for 1500 MW of wind power from plants in the Tehachapi area of California.

EXECUTIVES

Chairman President and CEO, Theodore F. (Ted) Craver, age 64, $1,200,000 total compensation
President Edison Energy, Ronald L. Litzinger, age 56, $597,529 total compensation
Vice President Human Resources, Patricia (Pat) Miller
President Southern California Edison (SCE), Pedro J. Pizarro, age 50, $450,000 total compensation
VP and CIO Southern California Edison, Todd L. Inlander
EVP CFO and Treasurer, William J. (Jim) Scilacci, $600,000 total compensation
President and Treasurer Edison Transmission LLC, Steven D. Eisenberg
President SoCore Energy, Pete Kadens
EVP and General Counsel, Adam S. Umanoff
Vice President Controller, Chris Dominski
Svp Corporate Communications, Janet Clayton
Vice President Human Resources, Jenene Wilson
Executive Vice President Generation, Harold Ray
Executive Vice President, David Schiada
Vice President Customer Service, Abdou Hassaine

LOCATIONS

HQ: Edison International
2244 Walnut Grove Avenue, P.O. Box 976, Rosemead, CA 91770
Phone: 626 302-2222
Web: www.edisoninvestor.com

PRODUCTS/OPERATIONS

Selected Subsidiaries
Edison Energy (solar power activities)
Southern California Edison Company (SCE electric utility)

COMPETITORS

AES	NRG Energy
Avista	NV Energy
Berkshire Hathaway Energy	NextEra Energy
CMS Energy	PG&E Corporation
Calpine	PacifiCorp
Constellation Energy Group	Portland General Electric
Electricit© de France	Sacramento Municipal Utility
Los Angeles Water and Power	Sempra Energy

HISTORICAL FINANCIALS

Company Type: Public

Income Statement

FYE: December 31

	REVENUE ($ mil.)	NET INCOME ($ mil.)	NET PROFIT MARGIN	EMPLOYEES
12/14	13,413	1,612	12.0%	13,690
12/13	12,581	915	7.3%	13,677
12/12	11,862	(183)	—	16,593
12/11	12,760	(37)	—	19,930
12/10	12,409	1,256	10.1%	20,117
Annual Growth	2.0%	6.4%	—	(9.2%)

2014 Year-End Financials

Debt ratio: 23.97%
Return on equity: 15.43%
Cash ($ mil.): 132
Current ratio: 0.73
Long-term debt ($ mil.): 10,234

No. of shares (mil.): 325
Dividends
  Yield: 2.2%
  Payout: 32.6%
Market value ($ mil.): 21,334

	STOCK PRICE ($) FY Close	P/E High/Low		PER SHARE ($) Earnings	Dividends	Book Value
12/14	65.48	14	9	4.89	1.48	33.64
12/13	46.30	19	16	2.78	1.37	30.50
12/12	45.19	—	—	(0.56)	1.31	28.95
12/11	41.40	—	—	(0.11)	1.29	30.86
12/10	38.60	10	8	3.82	1.27	32.48
Annual Growth	14.1%	—	—	6.4%	4.0%	0.9%

EMC Corp. (MA)

EMC has its head in the cloud ... and rightly so for a company that's helping businesses build Web-based computing systems with its data storage products and services. Its hardware and software platforms enable enterprises to store manage protect and analyze massive volumes of data. EMC also offers data security products through its RSA Security business and virtualization software through majority-owned VMware. The company serves both large FORTUNE 500 organizations and smaller businesses across many industries. Banks government agencies ISPs and manufacturers are among its customers. EMC serves a global client base from facilities and partners worldwide; it generates nearly half its sales outside the US. In October 2015 EMC agreed to be bought by Dell Inc. for $67 billion.

Change in Company Type

The combination of Dell and EMC creates a nearly full-service IT operation. The company would provide PCs services IT services and storage filling gaps for each company. The deal does carry risk. It is highly leveraged with debt although the money to finance the deal is being borrowed when interests rates are at rock bottom. And while getting a major storage provider the reason for the deal for Dell it exposes the company to the volatility of the storage market. The acquisition is expected to be completed in mid-2016.

OperationsEMC divides its business into five segments: Information Storage Enterprise Content Division RSA Information Security Pivotal and VMware Virtual Infrastructure.

Information Storage packs in 68% of EMC's revenue and VMware Virtual Infrastructure accounts for about a quarter revenue.

Infrastructure which generates 68% of total sales includes information storage (enterprise data management devices and software from entry-level to data center-class that support storage back-up and recovery).

The VMware Virtual Infrastructure segment 24% of revenue includes EMC's about 80% stake in VMware a leading provider of virtualization and cloud infrastructure products and services that are designed to help customers aggregate multiple servers and networks together into shared pools of capacity in the search for improved efficiency and manageability particularly for data center purposes.

Geographic ReachThe US is the company's largest market accounting for nearly 52% of sales. The EMEA (Europe Middle East and Africa) and Asia-Pacific regions contributed about 29% and about 13% respectively. EMC saw growth across in the US and Europe in 2014 but sales were flat in Asia-Pacific and dropped slightly in the company's reporting segment for Latin America Mexico and Canada.

Sales and MarketingEMC markets its products directly as well as through a network of distributors systems integrators resellers and OEMs. Participants in the company's selling partner program generate more than half of sales.

Financial Performance

EMC maintained a string of increasingly sales with a 5% rise in 2014 to just about $25 billion as it took advantage of opportunities in the cloud mobile social media and Big Data trends. Revenue from service operations with higher demand for professional services and in putting together products and software from EMC's segments. The company attributed a 6% decline in net income to $2.7 billion to higher income taxes.

Cash flow from operations dropped by about $400 million to $6.52 billion for 2014.

Strategy

The growing trends of cloud computing and big data are transforming information technology requiring companies to find new partners and invest in new products. EMC sees this as a huge growth opportunity and is focused on creating a product and services portfolio to meet these emerging needs. Research and development expenses in 2014 were about 12% of revenue on par with spending from the previous two years.

The company released a new hybrid cloud product in 2014 that combines EMC and VMware technologies. The EMC Enterprise Hybrid Cloud Solution integrates hardware software and services from EMC and VMware to offer advantages of private (security) and public cloud (flexibility). The company beefed up its hybrid cloud technologies through the acquisition of Cloudscaling a provider of OpenStack-powered Infrastructure-as-a-Service).

EMC maintains a number of strategic alliances including one with Cisco with whom EMC (along with VMware and Intel) created and funds Virtual Computing Environment Company (VCE). VCE develops and markets new cloud products to push to the adoption of multi-tenant cloud infrastructure by commercial and government enterprises. Multi-tenant cloud infrastructure allows for sharing of resources while still maintaining secure levels of isolation.

Mergers and Acquisitions

In order to expand into new markets EMC invested about $14 billion in acquisitions from 2003 to 2010. The company has since maintained an acquisitive strategy spending $1.7 billion in 2014. The latest acquisitions including Cloudscaling and two other cloud technology companies Maginatics and Spanning Cloud Apps. The VMware unit bought AirWatch wihc develops enterprise mobile and security software. That deal alone was cor $1.2 billion. EMC also bought DSSD which develops storage tools to run Big Data workloads more efficiently in data centers.

HISTORY

Early History

Former Intel executive Dick Egan and his college roommate Roger Marino founded EMC in 1979. (Their initials gave the company its name.) Egan a feisty entrepreneur whose first job was shining shoes served as a Marine in Korea and later worked at MIT on the computer system for NASA's Apollo program. Egan also helped found Cambridge Memory Systems (later Cambex).

EMC was started with no business plan only the idea that Egan and Marino would be better off working for themselves. At first they sold office furniture which in short order led to contacts at technology companies and recognition of the niche market for add-on memory boards for minicomputers.

EMC grew steadily throughout the early 1980s and went public in 1986. Two years later Michael Ruettgers a former COO of high-tech publishing and research company Technical Financial Services joined the company as EVP of operations. Ruettgers spent his first year and a half at EMC dealing with a crisis that almost ruined the company: Defective disk drives in some of its products were losing customers' files. Ruettgers stepped up quality control and guided EMC through the crisis period. In 1989 he became the company's president and COO.

In the late 1980s EMC expanded into data storage developing a system that employed small hard disks rather than larger more expensive disks and tapes used in IBM mainframes. EMC then separated itself from competitors by providing systems with a large cache –a temporary storage area used for quicker data retrieval.

In 1990 EMC pioneered redundant array of independent disks (RAID) storage and eliminated nearly a dozen major product lines focusing on storage for large IBM computers in a bid to beat Big Blue by undercutting prices. The company introduced its original Symmetrix system based on the new integrated cached disk array technology that held data from a variety of computer types. Marino left the company in 1990.

Ruettgers became CEO in 1992. The next year the company acquired Epoch Systems a provider of data management software and in 1994 it bought storage products company Array Technology as well as Magna Computer a leader in tape storage technology for IBM computers. EMC also introduced its first storage product for open systems the Centriplex series and its sales passed the $1 billion mark.

EMC increased its presence in this fast-growing data switching and computer connection market with the 1995 acquisition of McDATA. The next year it launched a digital video storage and retrieval system for the TV and film industry and introduced software that let its systems work on networks instead of requiring file servers for data storage management.

In 1997 the company began managing Web sites for customers. Expanding its international service presence EMC in 1998 bought French technology services provider Groupe MCI and in 1999 opened an Internet services office in Ireland. Also that year the company moved into the market for midrange storage when it acquired data storage and server specialist Data General.

EXECUTIVES

SVP and General Counsel, Paul T. Dacier, age 57
Chairman and CEO, Joseph M. (Joe) Tucci, age 68, $1,000,000 total compensation
CEO EMC Information Infrastructure, David I. Goulden, age 55, $850,000 total compensation
President and COO Global Enterprise Services, Howard D. Elias, age 57, $750,000 total compensation
EVP, Harry L. You, age 56, $523,391 total compensation
President Products and Marketing, Jeremy Burton, age 48, $768,750 total compensation
President Global Sales and Customer Operations, William F. (Bill) Scannell, $700,000 total compensation
SVP and Chief Risk Officer, Irina Simmons
President Europe Middle East and Africa, Adrian McDonald
President RSA, Amit Yoran, age 43
EVP and Advisor CEO, Amitabh Srivastava
EVP and CFO, Zane C. Rowe, age 44, $167,308 total compensation
President Core Technologies Division, Guy Churchward
Chief Accounting Officer and Chief Operating Officer Finance, Denis G. Cashman, age 55
President Emerging Technologies Division, Chirantan (CJ) Desai
SVP and CTO, John Roese
EVP Enterprise Business Solutions and CIO, Vic Bhagat
President EMC Americas Sales and Customer Operations, John F. Hanlon
SVP and President Asia Pacific and Japan, David Webster
COO Global Services, Mike Koehler
President South East Asia, Paul Henaghan
President Enterprise Content Division, Rohit Ghai
President VCE, Chad Sakac

Vice President Of Business Development and Marketing, Barry Ruditsky
Vice President Software Engineering, Rebek Duhaime
Network Solutions Global Delivery Manager Global Solutions Architect VPlex, Robert Bixby Robert (Bob) Bixby
National Sales Manager Cloud Service Providers At EMC, Robert (Bob) Bland
Vice President Performance Research, Amnon Naamad
Vice President, Jon Fay
Area Vice President, Michael Steed
Executive Vice President Corporate Marketing, Verna Dallaire
Vice President, Mike Lewis
Vice President Technology Alliances, Marc Burckin
Vice President Global Alliances, George Ackels
Vice President Software Engineering EMC Corp., Ed Sullivan
Vice President of Storage Product Marketing, Barbara (Barb) Robidoux
Vice President Recovery Point And Vplex Business Unit, Beth Phalen
Vice President of Marketing Backup Recovery Systems Division, Shane Jackson
Vice President Global Sales Strategy and GTM, Denise Millard
Vice President Sales, Chris Carlsen
Vice President Leasing, Norman (Norm) Mike
Vice President, Rob Crowley
Vice President Corporate Consulting, Malte Bernholz
Executive Vice President, Rob Salmon
Vice President Product Marketing, Jonathan (Jon) Siegal
Vice President, Mike Lee
Vice President Engineering, Percy Tzelnic
Vice President Engineering, Uday Gupta
Vice President Sales, Wayne Turnbow
Vice President Of Global Customer Operations, Kathie Lyons
Vice President Product Marketing, Richard Blaschke
Vice President General Manager Worldwide Purchasin, Bo Andersson
Vice President, Anthony Takazawa
Business Development OEM Sales Vice President of Marketing at Kashya, Mehran Hadipour
National Account Manager, Terry Baldwin
Vice President Human Resources, Aissa Chorki
Vice President Technology Partners, Bill Burckin
Vice President Engineering, John Woods
Senior Vice President Of Global Inside Sales, Linda Connly
Medical Director, John Howe
Vice President Product Development, Salvatore Desimone
Senior Vice President Of Tsg, Mary Krakauer
Vice President Product Management Vplex, Elizabeth (Beth) Phalen
Senior Vice President Sales and Merchandising, Dave Norton
Vice President Hardware Development, Williambill Depatie
Area Vice President, Matthew (Matt) Bauer
Vice President, Kevin Connolly
Vice President; Customer Support Services, Gordon Winters
Vice President Eservices, Julie Larsen
Executive Vice President Sales And Marketing, John (Jack) Egan
Vice President World Wide Sales, Jeff Brooks
Vice President Storage, Richard Napolitano
Regional Vice President Sales, Bill Rowan
Senior Vice President, Belinda Marcotte
Vice President Marketing and Product Management, Sam Grocott
Vice President Nas Engineering Emc Corp, John Ywoskus

National Accounts Manager, Peter (Pete) DeFreece
Area Vice President, Gary Abbagnaro
Vice President Global Channel Marketing, Fred Kohout
Vice President Of Sales, Debbie Bates
Vice Presidentfleneml Manager, Jennifer (Jen) Axt
Vice President Global Market Development, Richard Vita
Executive Vice President+Of+Marketing, Dan Saad
Vice President Engineering Operations, John Giubileo
Vice President Global Pre Sales, Mithu Bhargava
Vice President Americas Sales, Andrew O'Brien
Vice President of Sales, Tom Darnley
Vice President Of Advanced Solutions, Patricia Florissi
Vice President Information Technology, John (Jack) Peirce
Vice President International Tax, Mark Colabella
Vice President Global Compensation And Benefits, Kevin Close
Vice President Strategy and Operations, Arthur (Art) Min
Vice President Information Technology, John (Jack) Herrera
Channel Partner (Sales Training Vice President), Scott Crossman
Vice President Cloud based data protection, Gaurav Khanna
National Account Manager, Jim Frank
Vice President Global Services Marketing, Nina Hargus
Regional Vice President, Erik Hardy
Vice President, David Reinsel
Vice President Global Corporate Affairs and Public Policy, Christopher E (Chris) Goode
Vice President Corporate Financial Planning And Analysis, Cherie Dentiste
Vice President of Sales, Robert (Bob) Douglas
Vice President Sales Americas Channel, Scott Millard
Vice President Operations, James Smith
Vice President Customer Service Operations, Michael Clarke
Global Vice President, Michael (Mel) Wing
Vice President, Jaya Bhanot
Vice President and General Manager, Sean Lanagan
Vice President, Rich Pellizzi
Vice President Business Development and Advocacy, Edith Pfister
Vice President Business Development, Steve Fulton
Vice President Customer Service Marketing, Walter Reitz
Senior Vice President CLARiiON Software Development, Rona Newmark
Vice President, Gil Shapira
Vice President Business Development and Alliances, Paul Suffredini
Executive Vice President, David Wright
Vice President Of Marketing, Jeff Wright
Senior Vice President President Japan, Steven (Steve) Fitz
Vice President Engineering Emc Corp, Lee Muise
Vice President Inside Sales, Blake Yule
Vice President Global Sales Cloud Business Directors, John Theberge
Vice President of Human Resources for the Software IIG Division, Eva Andres
Regional Vice President Americas Sales, George Kotsiantos
Vice President Marketing, Brent McKinley
Vice President Sales, Trisa Rivera
Executive Vice President Finance, Yazmin Aguirre
Senior Vice President business Strategy and Operations, Kevin Roche
Vice President Global Supply Chain Management, Tom Smith
Vice President Of Sales Bura, Ray Lipsky
Vice President Of Sales, Michael Piccininni

Vice President Engineering, Ron Morita
Vice President of Sales, George Joseph
Vice President Human Resources, Betsy Sutter
Vice President Global Sales, Michael Hoff
Vice President Engineering Network Attached Stor, Uresh Vahalia
Vice President Global Internal Audit, Melanie Payne
Sales Vice President, Brian Barrass
Area Vice President, Tom Gelbach
Vice President Product Marketing, Jeff Gustafson
Vice President, Jim Pearson
Vice President Brs Emea Division, Luc Esprit
Vice President Sales and Marketing, Jennifer (Jen) Sutton
Executive Assistant to the Vice President of Channel Sales and Vice President of Worldwide Sales, Charlene Woock
New York New Jersey Area Vice President Sales, Polaski Greg
Vice President Finance Global Shared Services, Erin Champlin
Vice President Field Operations Europe Middle East and Africa, Michael (Mel) Sptter
Senior Vice President Global Product Operarians, Mike Kerouac
Vice President Enterprise Programs, Anthony Pagliarulo
Senior Vice President, Bill Scanell
Vice President Professional Services, John (Jack) Omelia
Vice President Corporate Strategy, Mike Phelan
Auditors: PricewaterhouseCoopers LLP

LOCATIONS

HQ: EMC Corp. (MA)
176 South Street, Hopkinton, MA 01748
Phone: 508 435-1000   Fax: 508 435-5222
Web: www.emc.com

2014 Sales

	$ mil.	% of total
US	12,835	52
Europe Middle East & Africa	6,981	29
Asia Pacific	3,191	13
Latin America Mexico & Canada	1,433	6
Total	24,440	100

PRODUCTS/OPERATIONS

2014 Sales

	$ mil.	% of total
EMC Information Infrastructure		
Information storage	16,542	68
RSA information security	1,035	4
Enterprise Content Division	640	3
VMware Virtual Infrastructure	5,996	24
Pivotal	227	1
Total	24,440	100

Selected Product Areas

Storage
Backup and Recovery
Cloud
Big Data
Security
Content Management
Infrastructure Managment
Archiving

Selected Acquisitions

COMPETITORS

CA Inc.	Microsoft
Citrix Systems	NetApp
Dell	Oracle
Fujitsu	Quantum Corporation
HP	Symantec
Hitachi Data Systems	Teradata
IBM	Western Digital
McAfee	Xyratex

HISTORICAL FINANCIALS

Company Type: Public

Income Statement

FYE: December 31

	REVENUE ($ mil.)	NET INCOME ($ mil.)	NET PROFIT MARGIN	EMPLOYEES
12/14	24,440	2,714	11.1%	70,000
12/13	23,222	2,889	12.4%	63,900
12/12	21,713	2,732	12.6%	60,000
12/11	20,007	2,461	12.3%	53,600
12/10	17,015	1,900	11.2%	48,500
Annual Growth	9.5%	9.3%	—	9.6%

2014 Year-End Financials

Debt ratio: 11.98%
Return on equity: 12.28%
Cash ($ mil.): 6,343
Current ratio: 1.34
Long-term debt ($ mil.): 5,495

No. of shares (mil.): 1,985
Dividends
  Yield: 1.5%
  Payout: 36.4%
Market value ($ mil.): 59,034

	STOCK PRICE ($) FY Close	P/E High/Low	PER SHARE ($) Earnings	Dividends	Book Value
12/14	29.74	23 18	1.32	0.45	11.03
12/13	25.15	19 15	1.33	0.20	11.04
12/12	25.30	23 17	1.23	0.00	10.61
12/11	21.54	24 17	1.10	0.00	9.25
12/10	22.90	25 18	0.88	0.00	8.41
Annual Growth	6.8%	— —	10.7%	—	7.0%

EMCOR Group, Inc.

Electrical and mechanical construction is at the core of EMCOR Group. One of the world's largest specialty construction firms EMCOR designs installs operates and maintains complex mechanical and electrical systems. These include systems for power generation and distribution lighting water and wastewater treatment voice and data communications fire protection plumbing and heating ventilation and air-conditioning (HVAC). EMCOR also provides facilities services including management and maintenance support. Through some 70 subsidiaries and joint ventures the company serves a range of commercial industrial institutional and utility customers. EMCOR exited the UK market in 2014 to focus on the US.

OperationsEMCOR Group operates five main business segments based on service type. Its US mechanical construction and facilities services and US building services divisions are the two largest each generating around 30% of the company's annual revenue. The three other segments include the company's United States electrical construction and facilities services segment (generating roughly 25% of revenue); United States industrial services (roughly 10%); and its soon-to-be discontinued United Kingdom building services (around 5%).The company's United States mechanical construction and facilities services division the largest of all five segments involves systems for central air refrigeration and clean-room process ventilation; fire protection; plumbing and piping; controls and filtration; water and wastewater treatment and central plant heating and cooling; cranes and rigging; and steel-related work. Its United States building services business offers operation maintenance and services for everything from a company's electrical and mechanical systems for commercial and government site-based operations and maintenance to janitorial services landscaping and snow removal services. Its United States electrical construction and facilities services division deals with systems for electrical power; premises electrical and lighting systems; low-voltage systems such as fire alarm security and process control; voice and data communication; roadway and transit lighting; and fiber optic lines.Geographic Reach

More than 95% of EMCOR's revenue comes from work performed in the US. The remainder is derived from the UK through EMCOR Group (UK) though the company announced in 2014 that it would be discontinuing its business in the UK.

Sales and Marketing

Some of EMCOR's largest institutional industrial and commercial projects include water treatment plants hospitals correctional facilities research labs manufacturing plants oil refineries data centers hotels shopping malls and office buildings. Many of these projects exceed $10 million and can span several years. Clients include Microsoft the US Department of Veteran Affairs and Hard Rock Hotel & Casino in Las Vegas.

Financial Performance

EMCOR has struggled to grow its business in recent years. Revenue in 2014 barely rose to $6.42 billion mostly thanks to sales contributions from the company's 2013 acquisitions as well as 61% growth in its US industrial services segment and the UK building services segment. The company's three largest segments (electrical mechanical and building services in the US) each declined between 3% to 7% with the mechanical business offsetting the bulk of the company's top-line growth as major projects were completed in 2013 and not replaced.Profit in 2014 rebounded sharply by 36% to $168.66 million thanks to the company's strong cost controls reduced loss from its discontinued operations and gains on building sales. Cash levels also jumped sharply thanks to higher cash earnings and a reduction in accounts receivables balances. In 2013 profit and cash levels had dipped due to restructuring charges −including employee and lease terminations −related to EMCOR's exiting of the construction business in the UK.

Strategy

EMCOR has been retreating from international markets while growing its core US business. Just a few years after selling its Canadian subsidiary Comstock in August 2011 EMCOR in 2014 ceased its construction business in the UK after disappointing losses and a bleak market outlook there.

EMCOR has grown by diversifying its services and expanding geographically within the US. With the US economy on the upswing EMCOR is reaping the benefits of being a more efficient operator. In 2013 to capitalize on growth markets in the US the company acquired RepconStrickland Inc. (RSI) a provider of turnaround and specialty services to the North American refinery and petrochemical markets.

Mergers and Acquisitions

In late 2013 EMCOR acquired RepconStrickland Inc. for $455 million in cash folding RepconStrickland into its existing Ohmstede operations to give it greater access to high-margin high-growth industrial markets. EMCOR made the deal to enhance its earnings power for several years.

In 2012 EMCOR acquired North Carolina-based industrial services contractor Southern Industrial Constructors. In 2011 the firm purchased industrial services provider Bahnson Holdings and USM Services further expanding its facilities maintenance offerings.

HISTORY

Company BackgroundEMCOR's forerunner Jamaica Water Supply Co. was incorporated in 1887 to supply water to some residents of Queens and Nassau Counties in New York. In 1902 it bought

Jamaica Township Water Co. and by 1906 it was generating revenue —reaching $1.6 million by 1932. Over the next 35 years the company kept pace with the population of its service area.

In 1966 the enterprise was acquired by Jamaica Water and Utilities which then bought Sea Cliff Water Co. In 1969 and 1970 it acquired Welsbach (electrical contractors) and A to Z Equipment (construction trailer suppliers); it briefly changed its name in 1974 to Welsbach Corp. before becoming Jamaica Water Properties in 1976.

Diversification proved unprofitable however and in 1977 Martin Dwyer and his son Andrew took over the management of the struggling firm. Despite posting million-dollar losses in 1979 it was profitable by 1980.

The Dwyers acquired companies in the electrical and mechanical contracting security telecommunications computer energy and environmental businesses. In 1985 Andrew Dwyer became president and the firm changed its name the next year to JWP.

Between 1986 and 1990 JWP acquired more than a dozen companies including Extel (1986) Gibson Electric (1987) Dynalectric (1988) Drake & Scull (1989) NEECO and Compumat (1990) and Comstock Canada (1990).

In 1991 JWP capped its strategy of buying up US computer systems resellers by acquiring Businessland. It then bought French microelectronics distributor SIVEA. Later that year JWP bought a 34% stake in Resource Recycling Technologies (a solid-waste recycler).

JWP's shopping spree extended the firm's reach but the company began to struggle when several sectors turned sour. A price war in the information services business and a weak construction market led to a loss of more than $600 million in 1992. That year president David Sokol resigned after questioning JWP's accounting practices. He turned over to the SEC a report that claimed inflated profits.

Cutting itself to about half its former size the company sold JWP Information Services in 1993. (JWP Information Services later became ENTEX Information Services which was acquired by Siemens in 2000.) However JWP continued to struggle and in early 1994 it filed for bankruptcy. Emerging from Chapter 11 protection in December 1994 the reorganized company took the name EMCOR. That year Frank MacInnis former CEO of electrical contractor Comstock Group stepped in to lead EMCOR.

In 1995 the SEC using Sokol's information charged several former JWP executives with accounting fraud claiming they had overstated profits to boost the value of their company stock and their bonuses. EMCOR later reached a non-monetary settlement with the SEC. The company sold Jamaica Water Supply and Sea Cliff in 1996; it also achieved profitability that year.

Focusing on external growth EMCOR acquired a number of firms in 1998 and 1999 including Marelich Mechanical Co. and Mesa Energy Systems BALCO Inc. and the Poole & Kent group of mechanical contracting companies based in Baltimore and Miami. To meet increased demands for facilities services in 2000 EMCOR consolidated the operations of three of its mechanical contractors (BALCO J.C. Higgins and Tucker Mechanical) into one company EMCOR Services which operates in New England.

That year about six years after emerging from bankruptcy EMCOR began trading on the New York Stock Exchange. In 2002 EMCOR bought 19 subsidiaries from its financially troubled rival Comfort Systems USA including its largest unit Shambaugh & Son. Later that year it expanded its facilities services operations with the acquisition of

Consolidated Engineering Services (CES) an Archstone-Smith subsidiary that operated in 20 states. EMCOR broadened its facilities services operations by acquiring the US facility management services unit of Siemens Building Technologies in 2003; in 2005 it added Fluidics Inc. a mechanical services company based in Philadelphia.

In 2007 EMCOR acquired FR X Ohmstede Acquisitions Co. a leading provider of aftermarket maintenance and repair services and replacement parts for oil refinery equipment.

The company added to its industrial services operations by acquiring South Carolina-based facilities maintenance provider MOR PPM in 2008.

In 2009 EMCOR bought LT Mechanical of North Carolina a leading plumbing and mechanical contractor. The following year it bought Pennsylvania-based engineering and facilities services firm Scalise Industries broadening its mechanical services business..

EXECUTIVES

EVP and CFO, Mark A. Pompa, age 51, $630,000 total compensation
EVP Shared Services, R. Kevin Matz, age 57, $500,000 total compensation
EVP General Counsel and Corporate Secretary, Sheldon I. (Shelly) Cammaker, age 76, $520,000 total compensation
CEO Emcor UK, Keith Chanter, age 56
President CEO and Director, Anthony J. (Tony) Guzzi, age 50, $1,010,000 total compensation
VP Marketing and Communications, Mava K. Heffler
President and CEO EMCOR Construction Services, Michael J. (Mike) Parry, age 66
President and CEO EMCOR Building Services, Michael P. (Mike) Bordes
President and CEO EMCOR Industrial Services and Ohmstede, Bill Reid
Executive Vice President General Counsel and Secretary, Shelly Cammaker
Vice President Of Sales And Marketing Emcor Group Inc, Jeff Budzinski
Vice President Information Systems and Technology, Peter (Pete) Baker
Chairman, Stephen W. Bershad, age 73
Auditors: Ernst & Young LLP

LOCATIONS

HQ: EMCOR Group, Inc.
301 Merritt Seven, Norwalk, CT 06851-1092
Phone: 203 849-7800
Web: www.emcorgroup.com

PRODUCTS/OPERATIONS

2014 Sales

	$ mil.	% of total
US electrical mechanical construction and facilities services	2,219	34
US building Services	1,762	27
US electrical construction & facility services	1,326	21
US industrial services	842	13
UK construction & building Services	350	5
Intersegment revenue	(76.6)	-
Total	**6,425**	**100**

Selected Operations

Mechanical and Electrical Construction
Building plant and lighting systems
Data communications systems
Electrical power distribution systems
Energy recovery
Heating ventilation and air-conditioning (HVAC) systems
Lighting systems
Low-voltage systems (alarm security communications)
Piping and plumbing systems
Refrigeration systems
Voice communications systems

Facilities Services
Facilities management
Installation and support for building systems
Mobile maintenance and service
Program development and management for energy systems
Remote monitoring
Site-based operations and maintenance
Small modification and retrofit projects
Technical consulting and diagnostic services

Selected Subsidiaries

Dyn Specialty Contracting Inc.
EMCOR Construction Services Inc.
EMCOR-CSI Holding Co.
EMCOR Facilities Services Inc.
EMCOR Group (UK) plc
EMCOR International Inc.
EMCOR (UK) Limited
EMCOR Mechanical/Electrical Services (East) Inc.
EMCOR (UK) Limited
FR X Ohmstede Acquisitions Co.
MES Holdings Corporation

COMPETITORS

ABM Industries	Jacobs Technology
AECOM	Johnson Controls
APi Group	Jones Lang LaSalle
CBRE Group	Limbach Facility
Carillion	Services
Comfort Systems USA	MYR Group
Dycom	MasTec
Fluor	Quanta Services
Hoffman Corporation	Schneider Electric
Honeywell	Siemens AG
International	SteelFab
Integrated Electrical	Trane Inc.
Services	Tutor Perini

HISTORICAL FINANCIALS

Company Type: Public

Income Statement

FYE: December 31

	REVENUE ($ mil.)	NET INCOME ($ mil.)	NET PROFIT MARGIN	EMPLOYEES
12/14	6,424	168	2.6%	27,000
12/13	6,417	123	1.9%	27,000
12/12	6,346	146	2.3%	26,000
12/11	5,613	130	2.3%	25,000
12/04	4,747	33	0.7%	26,000
Annual Growth	**3.1%**	**17.6%**	**—**	**0.4%**

2014 Year-End Financials

Debt ratio: 9.90%	No. of shares (mil.): 62
Return on equity: 11.70%	Dividends
Cash ($ mil.): 432	Yield: 0.7%
Current ratio: 1.47	Payout: 12.5%
Long-term debt ($ mil.): 316	Market value ($ mil.): 2,802

	STOCK PRICE ($) FY Close	P/E High/Low	PER SHARE ($) Earnings	Dividends	Book Value
12/14	44.49	19 15	2.52	0.32	22.48
12/13	42.44	24 19	1.82	0.49	21.92
12/12	34.61	16 12	2.16	0.51	20.10
12/11	26.81	17 9	1.91	0.05	18.58
12/04	45.18	86 63	0.53	0.00	9.23
Annual Growth	**(0.2%)**	**— —**	**16.8%**	**—**	**9.3%**

Emerson Electric Co.

Ralph Waldo Emerson's adage "Make yourself necessary to somebody" holds true for Emerson Electric. The company makes a slew of electrical electromechanical and electronic products many of which are used to control gases liquids and electricity. Its InSinkErator is a maker of food waste disposers and hot water dispensers. Emerson pursues an aggressive acquisition strategy coupled with select divestitures in building up its global presence. The company gathers its business units and divisions under five business segments. It has more than 235 manufacturing locations with about 160 outside of the US. International markets make up 60% of Emerson's sales.

Geographic Reach

North America is Emerson's largest market representing 46% of its total sales. Asia generates 22% of its revenue while Europe accounts for 20%. Other targeted markets include Latin America (6%) and the Middle East and Africa (6%). The company has 230 manufacturing locations worldwide and a marketing presence in more than 150 countries. Of this amount 155 are located outside the US.

Operations

The company operates through five primary segments. Process management (36% of total sales) provides products and services for precision measurement control monitoring and other functions for oil and gas reservoirs power plants and plants for processing products that include food and paper. Its network power segment (20%) serves power and telecommunications networks and data centers with products that include embedded power supplies control devices and inbound power systems.

Emerson's industrial automation operations (20%) provide products that aid the manufacturing process including motors fluid controls and materials joining equipment. Climate technologies (16%) offers products and services for residential heating and cooling commercial air conditioning and commercial and industrial refrigeration. Finally commercial & residential solutions its smallest segment (8%) sells professional tools commercial storage products food waste disposers and appliances such as ceiling fans and compact electric water heaters.

Across all segments the company has dozens of brand names including AMS ASCO Bettis Dixell Fisher Go Switch Kato Engineering Liebert Sealmaster Stratos Therm-O-Disc and White-Rodgers. Consumer-facing brands include ClosetMaid Flo Healthcare InSinkErator Lionville MedDispense and ProTeam.

Financial Performance

Emerson's revenues decreased marginally by 0.5% from 24.6 billion in 2013 $24.5 billion in 2014. This was primarily driven by an 18% drop in network power segment sales and lower sales in Asia (7%) and Latin America (3%). The company's profits spiked 7% from $2 billion in 2013 to $2.15 billion due to a decrease in cost of sales fueled by divestitures. In addition Emerson's operating cash flow has remained consistent the last few years rising slightly from $3.65 billion in 2013 to $3.69 billion in 2014.

Strategy

Emerson has a history of achieving growth through acquisitions and by divesting underperforming non-core units. In late 2013 it sold 51% of its embedded computing and power business to Platinum Equity and in 2014 sold its connectivity solutions business for $99 million to Bel Fuse. In another large deal in early 2015 Emerson sold its power transmission solutions operations to Regal Beloit for $1.44 billion. Emerson sold the operations (part of its industrial automation segment) to focus on its core operations.

Mergers and Acquisitions

In early 2014 Emerson acquired the 44% of EGS Electrical Group (electrical products for industrial hazardous and adverse environments) it didn't already own from SPX Corporation and integrated it into the industrial automation segment under the Appleton Group name. The transaction tightened Emerson's focus on the growing oil gas and chemical industries as those markets have grown to more than half of ESG's revenue.

In late 2013 the company paid $506 million and assumed $76 million in debt to acquire Virgo Valves and Controls (ball valves and automation systems) and Enardo (tank and terminal safety equipment) for its process management segment.

HISTORY

Emerson Electric was founded in 1890 in St. Louis by brothers Alexander and Charles Meston inventors who developed uses for the alternating-current electric motor which was new at the time. The company was named after former Missouri judge and US marshal John Emerson who financed the enterprise and became its first president. Emerson's best-known product was an electric fan introduced in 1892. Between 1910 and 1920 the company helped develop the first forced-air circulating systems.

EXECUTIVES

SEVP and Director, Charles A. Peters, age 59, $635,000 total compensation
SVP and CTO, Randall D. Ledford, age 66
Chairman and CEO, David N. Farr, age 61, $1,300,000 total compensation
Vice President Engineering, Keith Calhoun
Vice President Planning, Steve J Pelch
Vice President Global Logistics, Greg Fromknecht
EVP; Business Leader Commercial and Industrial Solutions, James J. (Jim) Lindemann, age 59
EVP Emerson Charitable Trust and Corporate Travel Vehicle and Sales, Patrick J. (Pat) Sly
Vice President Finance, Mark Pentz
Vice President Quality Assurance, Andy Kolbeck
EVP and CFO, Frank J. Dellaquila, age 57, $600,000 total compensation
President, Edward L. Monser, age 64, $700,000 total compensation
EVP; Business Leader Emerson Industrial Automation, Mark J. Bulanda
COO, Edgar M. (Ed) Purvis
EVP and President Emerson Process Management, Steven A. (Steve) Sonnenberg, age 63
EVP; Business Leader Emerson Network Power (Systems), D. Scott Barbour
VP Profit Planning, Robert T. Sharp
Vice President Sales, Jim Davis
Vice President Deputy General Counsel, Victor A Lazzaretti
Vice President Engineering, Kent Ross
Vice President Marketing Liebert Services, Kevin McCalla
Vice President Procurement, Bill Estes
Vice President Human Resources, Cathy Bevan
Vice President of Sales Americas, Don Fregelette
Vice President and General Counsel Emerson Network Power, Matthew (Matt) Dean
Vice President Development, Michael (Mel) Molloy
Vice President and Treasurer, David (Dave) Rabe
Vice President Finance Embedded Computing, Trevor Zillwood
Vice President Financial Planning, Scot Roemer
Vice President Product Safety, Steve Bryant
Executive Vice President, Ted Peachee
National Sales Manager, Dan Myers
Vice President Of Marketing, Brad Gossard
Vice President Sales, Roy Clingman
Vice President Marketing, Greg Dalton
Vice President Business Development, Matthew (Matt) Fox
Vice President, Ronald (Ron) Barker
Vice President Operations, Shannon Moss

Vice President Sales And Business Development Proteam DIV., Matt Reimers
Vice President Finance, Brian McGinnis
Vice President operations, Frank Jackson
Vice President Lp Gas Equipment, Tim Backs
Vice President Engineering, Scott Rose
Vice President Information Technology Risk Management, Jim Loge
Vice President Engineering, Steve Blackwell
Vice President, Andy Wang
Vice President Marketing Excellence Europe, Steve Brown
Vice President Operations, Brad Schwartz
Vice President Sales, Doug Butler
Vice President Information Technology, Nirav Patel
Vice President Sales, Mark Rezac
Vice President Assistant General Counsel, David (Dave) Hancock
Vice President Middle East And Africa, Phillip (Phil) Bond
Vice President Business Development and Marketing, Mike Nugent
Vice President Audit, Lisa Flavin
Vice President Sales, Scott Whitley
Vice President Of Sales, Douglas Pennington
Vice President of Process Development at Emerson Process Management, Charles (Chas) Bruce
Vice President Government Affairs, Rob McDonald
Vice President Asia Pacific, Chris Miller
Vice President Of Marketing, Andy Duffy
Vice President Sales Operations and Customer Service, Coryn DeGrands
Vice President Of Human Resources, Barbara Gandy
Vice President Tax, David (Dave) Moon
Vice President Engineering, Robert (Bob) Jantz
National Sales Manager, Keith Gilomen
Vice President Technical Support, Natalie McVeigh
Vice President Human Resources for the Process Analytic Division, Kevin Rhodes
Vice President Account Sales, Kevin Meyer
Vice President Marketing, Tim Flinn
Vice President of Research and Development, Chris Hanson
Vice President Information Technology, Jeff Dymond
Vice President Marketing and Sales Americas, Bob M Brown
Vice President Product Marketing, Michael Johnson
Vice President Marketing O Z Gedney, Timothy (Tim) Rooney
Vice President Of Business Development, Wayne Wehber
Vice President Mea, Jeff Householder
Vice President Operations, Karen Isaacson
Vice President Sales, Tom Stovall
Senior Vice President, Ed Feeney
Vice President of Operations at Emerson Climate Technologies, Martin (Marti) Staples
Senior Vice President, James Switzer
Vice President Human Resources, Jill Lutes
Vice President Lifecycle Services Process Systems and Sol, Sean Sims
Vice President Sales, Dennis Hyland
Vice President General Manager, Chenfai Chung
Vice President Service, Augie Digiovanni
Vice President Information Systems, Michael Morgan
Senior Vice President Worldwide Marketing, Richard Dubois
Vice President Operations, Kent Schultz
Vice President Finance, Dan Owens
National Account Manager, Traci Olmstead
Vice President Development, Russell (Russ) Browning
Emerson Executive Vice President, Scott Barbour
Vice President Global Strategic Accounts and Hyperscale Solutions, Michael (Mel) Rockwell
Vice President Pension Investments, Michael Neal

Vice President International, Kim Emerson
Vice President Global Supply Chain, Ken Poczekaj
Vice President Labor Relations, Alan Lebon
Vice President Sales Latin America, Trini Lopez
Vice President Finance Chief Financial Officer, Jack Frazier
Vice President Tax Planning (007), Phillip G (Phil) Conrad
Vice President Marketing and Business Development, Andy Schwegel
Vice President Global Oem Sales, Steve Merrifield
Vice President Human Resources and General Manager, Phil Lamb
Vice President of Technology and Product Development, Graham Ross
Assistant Vice President, John Bell
Vice President Engineering, Robert Jantz
Vice President of Sales, Jerry Born
Vice President Electronics Engineering, Sai Krishnan
Vice President Worldwide Communications, Bill Morrison
Vice President Of Information Technology, Larry Siebeerg
Vice President Global Marketing, Gary Niederpruem
Vice President Global Logistics, Ross Harris
Vice President of Benefits, Jan L Bansch
Vice President of Marketing, Kathy Buttonbell
Vice President of Marketing, Lori Moser
Vice President of Information Technology, Ted Doering
Vice President Global Logistics, Ga Fromknecht
Senior Vice President Human Resources, Phil Hutchison
Vice President Global Supply Electrical Products, Mike Kitson
Vice President Finance, Scott Garfield
Vice President Finance Liebert Europe, David (Dave) Noonan
Vice President Sales, Mike McDonald
Senior Vice President Human Resources, P Hutchison
Vice President Employee Relations, M G Rohret
Vice President Sales, Mark Downie
General Associate Vice President Attorney, Steven (Steve) Chelesnik
Vice President and Associate General Counsel, Mike Sheldon
Vice President Manufacturing, Fred Cox
Vice President Information Technology, Lisa Nelson
Vice President tax, D C Moon
Vice President Product Engineering, Jim Anderson
Vice President And Deputy General Counsel, D J Green
Vice President Information Technology, Paulo Michael
Vice President Sales and Marketing NA, Roger Hager
Vice President Global Sales, Robert (Bob) Walker
Vice President Planning, Dave Bersaglini
Vice President And Treasurer, D J Rabe
Vice President Sales, Carlos Batista
Vice President of Sales Northeast Area, Doug Taylor
Vice President and General Manager of Component Test Division Kobe, Afton Coleman
Vice President Marquee Accounts, Mike Rockwell
Treasurer, Anita Cotton
Assistant Treasurer, Jim Thomasson
Board Member, Joe Morris
Secretary, Candy Vogt
Treasurer, Alan (Al) Mielcuszny
Assistant Treasurer and Director Investor Relations, Chris Tucker
Assistant Treasurer and Director Investor Relations, LM Maxeiner
Auditors: KPMG LLP

LOCATIONS

HQ: Emerson Electric Co.
8000 W. Florissant Avenue, P.O. Box 4100, St. Louis, MO 63136
Phone: 314 553-2000
Web: www.emerson.com

2014 Sales

	$ mil.	% of total
US & Canada	11,262	46
Asia	5,483	22
Europe	4,815	20
Latin America	1,508	6
Middle East/Africa	1,469	6
Total	**24,537**	**100**

PRODUCTS/OPERATIONS

2014 Sales

	$ mil.	% of total
Process management	9,189	36
Network power	5,073	20
Industrial automation	4,990	20
Climate technologies	4,109	16
Commercial & Residential Solutions	1,924	8
Adjustments	(748)	-
Total	**24,537**	**100**

Selected Products and Services

Process Management
  Actuators
  Measurement and analytical instrumentation
  Software services and systems
  Regulators
  Valves
Network Power
  Electrical switching equipment
  Embedded power supplies
  Integrated infrastructure monitoring & management systems
  Power conditioning & uninterruptible AC & DC power supplies
  Precision cooling systems
Industrial Automation
  Commercial & industrial motors & drives
  Electrical distribution equipment
  Fluid power & control mechanisms
  Low medium & high voltage alternators
  Materials joining products
  Power transmission & materials handling equipment
  Precision cleaning products
Climate Technologies
  Compressors
  Flow controls
  Remote monitoring services
  Temperature sensors & controls
  Thermostats
Tools & Storage
  Appliance products
  Home & commercial storage systems
  Tools for professionals & homeowners

COMPETITORS

ABB	Parker-Hannifin
AMETEK	Raytheon
Cummins	Rexnord
Dana Holding	Rockwell Automation
Danaher	Rolls-Royce
Dayco Products	SPX
Endress + Hauser	Siemens AG
GE	Sino-American
Hitachi	Electronic
Honeywell	Snap-on
International	Stanley Black and
Illinois Tool Works	Decker
Ingersoll-Rand	TE Connectivity
Interpump	Tecumseh Products
Johnson Controls	Toshiba
Lennox	Trippe Manufacturing
McDermott	United Technologies
NEC	Yokogawa Electric
Nidec Kinetek	

HISTORICAL FINANCIALS

Company Type: Public

Income Statement

FYE: September 30

	REVENUE ($ mil.)	NET INCOME ($ mil.)	NET PROFIT MARGIN	EMPLOYEES
09/15	22,304	2,710	12.2%	110,800
09/14	24,537	2,147	8.8%	115,100
09/13	24,669	2,004	8.1%	131,600
09/12	24,412	1,968	8.1%	134,900
09/11	24,222	2,480	10.2%	133,200
Annual Growth	(2.0%)	2.2%	—	(4.5%)

2015 Year-End Financials

Debt ratio: 30.98%
Return on equity: 29.78%
Cash ($ mil.): 3,054
Current ratio: 1.29
Long-term debt ($ mil.): 4,289

No. of shares (mil.): 654
Dividends
  Yield: 4.2%
  Payout: 52.3%
Market value ($ mil.): 28,914

	STOCK PRICE ($) FY Close	P/E High/Low		PER SHARE ($) Earnings	Dividends	Book Value
09/15	44.17	16	11	3.99	1.88	12.34
09/14	62.58	23	20	3.03	1.72	14.53
09/13	64.70	24	17	2.76	1.64	14.98
09/12	48.27	20	15	2.67	1.60	14.22
09/11	41.31	19	13	3.27	1.38	14.07
Annual Growth	1.7%	—	—	5.1%	8.0%	(3.2%)

Employers Holdings Inc

Because workers' compensation is nothing to gamble with small business owners can turn to Employers Holdings. The Reno-based holding company provides workers' compensation services including claims management loss prevention consulting and care management to small businesses in low hazard industries including retailers and restaurants. The company provides workers' compensation through its Employer Insurance Company of Nevada (EICN) and Employers Compensation Insurance Company. Employers Holdings also operates Employers Assurance and Employers Preferred Insurance Company both of which also offer workers' compensation.

Geographic Reach

While it distributes its products in more than 30 states and the District of Columbia more than half of its premiums come from California.

Sales and Marketing

Employers Holdings uses independent agents and brokers to bring its wares to the public. It also markets its products along with ADP's payroll services in several states and with Anthem Blue Cross of California's group health insurance products in California. They each contribute about 10% of in-force premiums. Employers Holdings is forging additional distribution partners in other markets.

Financial Performance

After weathering a few rough years during the economic downturn Employers Holdings has seen multiple years of revenue growth. In 2013 revenue rose about 25% from $579.2 million to $723.6 million due to increased net premiums as the company issued more policies expanded existing policies and earned higher rates. Net income however dropped 40% from $107 million to $64 million as losses increased. Buoyed by the increased premiums cash flow increased by $32 million from $132 million to $164 million even though the company paid more for claims and in commissions.

Strategy

Employers Holdings maintains a strategy of engaging in low-to-medium hazard industries in order to try to keep its losses under control. Its top types of insureds include restaurants the clerical side of physician offices automobile service or repair centers and colleges (professional employees and clerical). The company also spreads its risk around and is not dependent upon any one customer for a significant portion of its income.

HISTORY

EICN was the successor to Nevada's public workers' compensation fund. The state-run system which was deeply in debt and on the verge of collapse was officially privatized in 2000 under the guidance of CEO Douglas Dirks. In 2004 EICN reorganized into a mutual insurance company which took the name EIG Mutual Holdings and included EICN as its subsidiary.

In 2006 EIG Mutual Holdings filed its initial public offering to convert from a mutual insurance holding company to a publicly traded corporation. When the company's members approved the conversion in early 2007 the name changed to Employers Holdings Inc. Eligible members received shares of the new company; non-eligible members took home just their share of the proceeds raised.

EXECUTIVES

President and CEO, Douglas D. Dirks, $808,387 total compensation
EVP Chief Legal Officer and General Counsel, Lenard T. Ormsby, $439,151 total compensation
EVP Corporate and Public Affairs, Ann W. Nelson, $218,963 total compensation
EVP and Chief Administrative Officer, John P. Nelson, $334,391 total compensation
EVP and COO, Stephen V. Festa, $329,363 total compensation
EVP and CFO, William E. Yocke, $439,151 total compensation
SVP and Regional Manager Western Region, T. Hale Johnston
SVP and General Manager Strategic Partnerships and Alliances, David M. Quezada
Interim CIO, Richard P. Hallman
SVP and Chief Actuary, Bryan Ware
SVP and Chief Underwriting Officer, Cecelia M. Abraham
SVP and Regional Manager Eastern Region, Mark R. Hogle
EVP and CFO, Terry Eleftheriou
Vice President Corporate Marketing, Ty Vukelich
Senior Vice President Chief Underwriting Officer, Larry Rogers
Vice President Deputy General Counsel, Mary Lynn
Vice President Investor Relations, Vicki Erickson
Svp Claims, Barry J Vogt
Vice President Of Premium Audit, Sharon Morgan
Vice President Of Sales Strategic Partnerships and Alliances, David (Dave) Morton
Chairman, Robert J. Kolesar
Auditors: Ernst & Young LLP

LOCATIONS

HQ: Employers Holdings Inc
10375 Professional Circle, Reno, NV 89521
Phone: 888 682-6671

2013 Premiums In-force

	% of total
California	60
Illinois	5
Georgia	4
Florida	3

North Carolina	3
Other states	25
Total	**100**

PRODUCTS/OPERATIONS

2013 Sales

	$ mil.	% of total
Net premiums earned	642	89
Net investment income	70	10
Realized gains on investments & adjustment	9	1
Other income	1	-
Total	**723**	**100**

Selected Subsidiaries

AmSERV Inc.
EIG Services Inc.
Elite Insurance Services Inc.
Employers Assurance Company
Employers Compensation Insurance Company
Employers Group Inc.
Employers Insurance Company of Nevada
Employers Occupational Health Inc.
Employers Preferred Insurance Company
Pinnacle Benefits Inc.

COMPETITORS

AMERISAFE	Republic Indemnity
AmTrust Financial	Safety Insurance
Baldwin & Lyons	SeaBright Insurance
Berkshire Hathaway	Selective Insurance
CNA Financial	State Auto Financial
Donegal	State Compensation
EMC Insurance	Insurance Fund
Harleysville Group	The Hartford
Liberty Mutual	TowerGroup
Meadowbrook Insurance	Travelers Companies
Navigators	United Fire
ProAssurance	Zurich Insurance Group
RLI	

HISTORICAL FINANCIALS

Company Type: Public

Income Statement

FYE: December 31

	ASSETS ($ mil.)	NET INCOME ($ mil.)	INCOME AS % OF ASSETS	EMPLOYEES
12/14	3,769	100	2.7%	709
12/13	3,643	63	1.8%	723
12/12	3,511	106	3.0%	667
12/11	3,481	48	1.4%	651
12/10	3,480	62	1.8%	699
Annual Growth	**2.0%**	**12.5%**	**—**	**0.4%**

2014 Year-End Financials

Debt ratio: 2.44%	No. of shares (mil.): 31
Return on equity: 16.04%	Dividends
Cash ($ mil.): 114	Yield: 1.0%
Current ratio: —	Payout: 8.8%
Long-term debt ($ mil.): —	Market value ($ mil.): 740

	STOCK PRICE ($) FY Close	P/E High/Low		PER SHARE ($) Earnings	Dividends	Book Value
12/14	23.51	10	6	3.14	0.24	21.81
12/13	31.65	16	10	2.00	0.24	18.17
12/12	20.58	6	5	3.37	0.24	17.53
12/11	18.09	16	8	1.29	0.24	14.37
12/10	17.48	12	8	1.51	0.24	12.58
Annual Growth	**7.7%**	**—**	**—**	**20.1%**	**(0.0%)**	**14.7%**

Enbridge Energy Partners, L.P.

Head of the class in transporting petroleum around the Great Lakes is Enbridge Energy Partners which owns the 2211-mile US portion (Lakehead System) of the world's longest liquid petroleum pipeline. When combined with the Canadian segment (owned and operated by Enbridge Inc.) the pipeline system spans some 5100 miles across North America. Other midstream assets include 5300 miles of crude oil gathering and transportation lines and 34 million barrels of crude oil storage and terminaling capacity and 11100 miles of natural gas gathering and transportation pipelines. Enbridge's US unit Enbridge Energy Management owns a 23% stake in the company.

Operations

In 2014 Enbridge Energy Partners changed its reporting segments. The Marketing segment was combined with the Natural Gas segment to form one new segment called Natural Gas. There was no change to the Liquids segment. As a result the company conducts its business through two business segments: Natural Gas and Liquids.

Natural gas (74% of total sales in 2014) operates three major natural gas systems —Anadarko East Texas and North Texas Systems. These systems collectively comprise about 11100 miles of natural gas gathering and transmission pipelines as well as 26 processing plants and 10 treating plants. Its marketing activities includes transactions with various counter-parties to provide natural gas supply transportation balancing storage and sales services primarily in Texas and Oklahoma.

The natural gas segment business includes natural gas and NGL gathering and transportation pipeline systems natural gas processing and treating facilities and NGL fractionation facilities as well as trucking rail and liquids marketing operations. It delivers the NGLs produced at its processing and fractionation facilities to intrastate and interstate pipelines for transportation to the NGL market hubs in Mont Belvieu Texas and Conway Kansas. The Natural Gas segment's trucking and marketing business markets natural gas NGLs and condensate from Enbridge Energy Partners' gathering processing and transportation systems.

The liquids segment (26% of 2014 sales) operates through its Lakehead North Dakota and Mid-Continent systems which consists primarily of crude oil and liquid petroleum common carrier pipelines and terminal assets in the Great Lakes and Midwest. The Lakehead system together with the Enbridge system in Canada forms the Mainline system the longest liquid petroleum pipeline system in the world. The Mainline system serves all the major refining centers in the US Great Lakes and Midwest regions and in Ontario Canada.

Sales and Marketing

Enbridge Energy Partners sells and delivers natural gas to wholesale customers such as distributors refiners fractionators utilities chemical facilities and power plants.

Financial Performance

The company's net revenues increased by 12% in 2014 due to higher natural gas and liquids sales.

Natural gas revenues rose primarily due to on-cash mark-to-market gains on NGL hedges. Liquids revenues increased due to higher rates for the Lakehead North Dakota and Ozark systems; Lakehead system expansion projects placed into service in 2014 and a full year of revenues for Lakehead and North Dakota expansion projects placed into service during 2013.Enbridge Energy Partners' net income increased by 361% in 2014 due to higher net revenues and decrease in environmental costs related to the Line 6B crude oil release.The company's cash inflow decreased by 33% as the result of changes in working capital (receivables trade and other accounts payable and other and accrued receivables).

Strategy

Enbridge Energy Partners' business strategy is to focus on maintaining and expanding its core pipelines business while developing additional transportation and storage assets.

To raise cash to pay down debt in 2014 the company sold an additional 12.6% limited partner interest in Midcoast Operating to MEP for $350.0 million reducing its ownership of Midcoast Operating from 61% to 48.4%.

In 2013 the company in tandem with Enterprise Products Partners Anadarko Petroleum and DCP Midstream Partners began service on the Texas Express natural gas liquids pipeline from Skellytown Texas to the NGL fractionation and storage complex in Mont Belvieu Texas. The Texas Express Pipeline operated by Enterprise gives producers in West and Central Texas the Rocky Mountains southern Oklahoma the Mid-continent and the Denver-Julesburg basin much-needed takeaway capacity for growing NGL volumes and improved access to the largest NGL trading hub on the Gulf Coast.

Mergers and Acquisitions

In 2015 Enbridge Energy Partners agreed to buy New Gulf Resources' natural gas gathering system in Leon Madison and Grimes Counties Texas for $85 million.

Company Background

The company was formed in 1991 initially to own and operate the Lakehead system.

EXECUTIVES

Senior Vice President Operations, Rich Adams
EVP Liquids Pipelines, Stephen J. (Steve) Wuori, age 58, $700,019 total compensation
President and Principal Executive Officer, Mark A. Maki, age 51, $383,336 total compensation
SVP Operations, Richard L. Adams, age 50, $303,644 total compensation
EVP, Leon A. Zupan, age 59, $411,557 total compensation
VP Finance, Stephen J. Neyland, age 48, $257,788 total compensation
VP Natural Gas Marketing, Janet L. Coy, age 58
Vice President Systems Staff Finance Other Personn, Mike Howell
Vice President, Stephen Merritt
Vice President Engineering and Operations Gathering and Processing, Kerry Puckett
Vice President EPC and Project Services, Andrew J (Andy) Harrington
Vice President Engineering, Rick Adams
Vice President Operations and Technologies, R L Adams
Chairman, Jeffrey A. Connelly, age 69
Auditors: PricewaterhouseCoopers LLP

LOCATIONS

HQ: Enbridge Energy Partners, L.P.
1100 Louisiana Street, Suite 3300, Houston, TX 77002
Phone: 713 821-2000
Web: www.enbridgepartners.com

PRODUCTS/OPERATIONS

2014 Sales

	$ mil.	% of total
Natural gas	5,894	74
Liquids	2,070	26

Total	7,964	100

COMPETITORS

Buckeye Partners	Martin Midstream
DCP Midstream Partners	Partners
Duke Energy	ONEOK Partners
Dynegy	Sunoco Logistics
Enron	TransCanada
Koch Industries Inc.	Williams Companies
Magellan Midstream	

HISTORICAL FINANCIALS

Company Type: Public

Income Statement
FYE: December 31

	REVENUE ($ mil.)	NET INCOME ($ mil.)	NET PROFIT MARGIN	EMPLOYEES
12/14	7,964	740	9.3%	—
12/13	7,117	160	2.3%	—
12/12	6,706	550	8.2%	—
12/11	9,109	677	7.4%	—
12/10	7,736	(137)	—	—
Annual Growth	0.7%	—	—	—

2014 Year-End Financials

Debt ratio: 38.45%
Return on equity: —
Cash ($ mil.): 197
Current ratio: 0.50
Long-term debt ($ mil.): 6,823

No. of shares (mil.): 396
Dividends
  Yield: 5.5%
  Payout: 327.9%
Market value ($ mil.): 15,818

	STOCK PRICE ($) FY Close	P/E High/Low		Earnings	PER SHARE ($) Dividends	Book Value
12/14	39.90	61	40	0.67	2.20	12.92
12/13	29.87	—	—	(0.39)	2.17	17.56
12/12	27.90	26	21	1.27	2.15	14.69
12/11	33.19	34	13	1.99	2.09	14.65
12/10	62.38	—	—	(1.09)	2.02	13.56
Annual Growth	(10.6%)	—	—	—	2.1%	(1.2%)

Energy Future Holdings Corp

Energy Future Holdings has seen the future and it works —with electricity. It operates the largest nonregulated retail electric provider in Texas (TXU Energy) with more than 1.7 million customers and its Luminant unit has a generating capacity of more than 15400 MW from its interests in nuclear and fossil-fueled power plants in the state. Energy Future Holdings has regulated power transmission and distribution operations through 80%-owned Oncor Electric Delivery which operates the largest regulated distribution and transmission system in Texas providing power to more than 3.2 million electric delivery points over 119000 miles of transmission and distribution lines. The company filed for bankruptcy in 2014.

HISTORY

The first North Texas electric power company was founded in Dallas in 1883. Another was built in 1885 in Fort Worth. From these and other small power plants three companies grew to serve most of the state: Texas Power & Light (TP&L incorporated in 1912) Dallas Power & Light (DP&L 1917) and Texas Electric Service (TES 1929). Texas Utilities Company called TU was formed in 1945 as a holding company for the three utilities.

In the 1940s TU began leasing large lignite coal reserves and in 1952 formed Industrial Generating to mine lignite and operate a coal-fired power plant. TU after pioneering lignite-burning technology in the 1960s opened the first of nine large lignite units in 1971. In 1974 it began building the Comanche Peak nuclear plant near Fort Worth.

DP&L TES TP&L and Industrial Generating joined in 1984 as Texas Utilities Electric (TU Electric). The mining company was renamed Texas Utilities Mining.

The Nuclear Regulatory Commission wouldn't license Comanche Peak in 1985 citing design and construction faults but finally granted the license in 1990. TU bought out its construction partners after much wrangling over multibillion-dollar cost overruns.

In 1993 TU bought Southwestern Electric Service (now TXU SESCO) another Texas electric utility. Accounting changes resulted in a loss for TU in 1995. However it did gain entry to the telecom arena buying a 20% stake in the Texas operations of wireless PCS provider PrimeCo. (The company sold the PrimeCo stake in 1999.) TU expanded its telecom holdings in 1997 when it acquired phone company Lufkin-Conroe (now part of TXU Communications).

TU headed down under in 1996 buying Australian electric company Eastern Energy (now part of TXU Electricity). It purchased gas dealer ENSERCH (now TXU Gas) which brought substantial energy services and trading assets on board including Texas' largest gas utility Lone Star Gas.

Despite a windfall tax levied by the UK's Labor Party TU bought British utility The Energy Group (now TXU Europe) for about $10 billion in 1998. TU sold Energy Group's Citizens Power a US power marketer and Peabody Coal the #1 US coal producer to the investment arm of Lehman Brothers.

In 1999 the company bought Australian state-owned natural gas distributors Westar (now TXU Networks (Gas) Pty. Ltd.) and Kinetic Energy (now TXU Pty. Ltd.). TU also joined a consortium to build undersea power lines connecting Tasmania to the Australian mainland.

Back in Texas the 1999 Legislature approved retail competition for the electric industry beginning in 2002. Also in 1999 Texas Utilities restructured its operations and began using the name TXU Corp. It officially changed its name the next year.

Also in 2000 TXU acquired Norweb Energi United Utilities' electricity and gas supply business which added some 1.8 million electricity customers and 400000 gas customers in the UK. TXU also contributed the stock of its telecommunications companies to Pinnacle One Partners in exchange for a 50% stake and about $960 million which was earmarked for TXU's debt. Other efforts to reduce debt and streamline operations included TXU's sale of its natural gas processing operations UK gas metering business and interests in a Czech utility and North Sea gas fields.

After raising its stake in Spanish utility Hidroeléctrica del Cantábrico to 19% TXU sold its interest to a consortium led by Electricidade de Portugal and Spanish bank Caja de Ahorro de Asturias in 2001. That year TXU also acquired a 50% stake in Stadtwerke Kiel its first utility in Germany (where TXU Europe was already trading energy) and it agreed to sell two gas-fired power plants (2300 MW) in Texas to Exelon for $443 million (completed in 2002). TXU Europe sold two UK power stations (3000 MW) in 2001 and sold its Eastern Electricity distribution unit and its interest in joint venture 24seven in 2002.

In 2002 retail electric competition began in Texas and TXU responded by separating TXU Electric's regulated and nonregulated operations. TXU Electric's name was changed to TXU US Holdings which also took over TXU SESCO's electric operations.

TXU sold TXU Europe's retail supply and generation operations to UK utility Powergen in late 2002 due to poor market conditions. Shortly after TXU Europe filed for bankruptcy protection and TXU wrote off its investment in the unit. The following year TXU sold the northeastern US gas marketing operations of TXU Energy to UGI. In 2004 TXU Australia was sold to Singapore Power for $1.9 billion in cash and $1.7 billion in assumed debt.

Continuing with its effort to reduce debt and focus on core utility businesses TXU sold subsidiary TXU Communications to private telecom firm Consolidated Communications for $527 million and its TXU Fuel (gas transportation) unit to Energy Transfer Partners for approximately $500 million.

The company sold TXU Gas to Atmos Energy for $1.9 billion in 2004; the transaction included the company's gas transportation and storage assets. It has also agreed to sell its Oncor Utility Solutions unit to utility consulting firm UMS Group. Due to market conditions the firm has retired or temporarily shut down some of its power plants in Texas; the company is also considering the sale of its nuclear power generation assets. As a result of its narrowed focus the company has restructured its operations and reorganized its management.

The company announced plans to form a wholesale energy marketing joint venture with Credit Suisse First Boston in 2004; however the two firms later decided not to pursue the venture. Energy Future Holdings also outsourced its information technology functions to Capgemini Energy LP a unit of Capgemini.

In 2006 the company teamed up with InfrastruX Group to form the InfrastruX Energy Services joint venture in a 10-year $8.7 billion agreement to provide for utility infrastructure and management services.

In 2007 TXU was acquired in a $45 billion leveraged buyout by an investor group led by Goldman Sachs Kohlberg Kravis Roberts and Texas Pacific Group and became Energy Future Holdings. To help raise capital in 2008 Energy Future Holdings sold a 20% stake in Oncor to an investor group led by Borealis Infrastructure Management for $1.2 billion.

EXECUTIVES

Vice President Internal Audit and Risk, Andrew (Andy) Cameron
President and CEO, John F. Young, $1,350,000 total compensation
SVP and CIO, Kevin Chase
CEO Luminant, Mac A. McFarland, $675,000 total compensation
CEO TXU Energy, James A. (Jim) Burke, $675,000 total compensation
EVP Human Resources, Carrie Kirby
EVP and CFO, Paul M. Keglevic, $735,000 total compensation
EVP and General Counsel, Stacey Dor ©$600,000 total compensation
Vice President For Contact Center Operations, Jeff Camp
Vice President and Associate General Counsel, Andrew (Andy) Wright
Vice President and Assistant Treasurer, Kristopher Moldovan
Vice President Internal Audit, Drew Cameron

Vice President Human Resources, Debbie Dennis
Executive Vice President human Resources, Richard (Dick) Landy
Vice President Human Resources, Pitt Pittman
Senior Vice President Public Policy And External Affairs, John (Jack) O%27BRIEN
Chairman, Donald L. Evans
Auditors: Deloitte & Touche LLP

LOCATIONS

HQ: Energy Future Holdings Corp
1601 Bryan Street, Dallas, TX 75201-3411
Phone: 214 812-4600
Web: www.energyfutureholdings.com

PRODUCTS/OPERATIONS

2014 Sales

	$ mil.	% of total
Retail electricity		
Residential	2,970	50
Small business	701	12
Large business & other	742	12
Wholesale electricity	1,267	21
Amortization of intangibles	23	0
Other	275	5
Total	**5,978**	**100**

COMPETITORS

AEP	Entergy
AEP Texas Central	First Choice Power
AEP Texas North	Gexa Energy
AES	Green Mountain Energy
Atmos Energy	NRG Energy
Brazos Electric	NextEra Energy
Calpine	ONEOK
CenterPoint Energy	Southwestern Electric
Direct Energy	Power
Duke Energy	Texas Gas Transmission
El Paso Electric	

HISTORICAL FINANCIALS

Company Type: Public

Income Statement

FYE: December 31

	REVENUE ($ mil.)	NET INCOME ($ mil.)	NET PROFIT MARGIN	EMPLOYEES
12/14	5,978	(6,406)	—	8,920
12/13	5,899	(2,218)	—	9,000
12/12	5,636	(3,360)	—	9,100
12/11	7,040	(1,913)	—	9,300
12/10	8,235	(2,812)	—	9,200
Annual Growth	(7.7%)	—	—	(0.8%)

2014 Year-End Financials

Debt ratio: 23.77%
Return on equity: —
Cash ($ mil.): 3,428
Current ratio: 2.83
Long-term debt ($ mil.): 6,953

No. of shares (mil.): 1,669
Dividends
　Yield: —
　Payout: —
Market value ($ mil.): —

Energy Transfer Equity LP

Energy Transfer Equity transfers natural gas and other energy resources through its massive pipelines running across the country. The company acts as the general partner of Energy Transfer Partners and Regency Energy Partners. Through

these operations and through Sunoco and Southern Union the company owns natural gas pipelines all over the country and a crude oil pipeline with the capacity of around 12800 miles. All in all Energy Transfer Equity's family of companies owns more than 71000 miles of natural gas natural gas liquids refined products and crude pipelines. In 2015 Energy Transfer Equity agreed to buy Tulsa-based Williams Companies in a $37.7 billion merger deal.

Geographic Reach

Energy Transfer Equity has more than 400 locations in about 40 US states.

Operations

The company divides its revenues across six channels. Refined product sales accounted for 35% of its revenues in 2014 while crude sales generated 29%. Other segments include natural gas (10%); NGL sales (10%); gathering transportation and other fees (7%); and other (9%).Through its Energy Transfer Partners GP unit Energy Transfer Equity owns a 2% general partnership stake in Energy Transfer Partners (ETP) and about 26% of common stock. Energy Transfer Equity is managed by general partner LE GP LLC. ETP operates as a conglomerator in the fragmented pipeline and propane industries. It has more than 45000 miles of natural gas pipelines and 30.7 billion cu. ft. per day of natural gas transportation capacity.Energy Transfer Equity's family of companies owns and operates 71000 miles of natural gas natural gas liquids refined products and crude oil pipelines. Regency Energy Partners of which Energy Transfer Equity is the general partner is a publicly traded partnership engaged in the gathering processing contract compression treating and transportation of natural gas and the transportation fractionation and storage of NGLs. Its operations are run through about eight segments: Intrastate Transportation and Storage Midstream NGL Transportation and ServicesRetail Marketing and Sunoco and Regency Energy Partners.During 2014 Energy Transfer Equity's consolidated subsidiaries Trunkline LNG Company LLC Trunkline LNG Export LLC and Susser Petroleum Partners LP changed their names to Lake Charles LNG Company LLC Lake Charles LNG Export LLC and Sunoco LP respectively.

Sales and Marketing

ETP's retail marketing business operations are conducted through various wholly-owned subsidiaries as well as through Sunoco LP which ETP controls through its ownership of the general partner. ETP's counterparties consist of a diverse portfolio of customers across the energy industry including petrochemical companies commercial and industrial manufacturers oil and gas producers municipalities gas and electric utilities and midstream companies.The company sells natural gas to utilities industrial consumers other marketers and pipeline companies. Its retail marketing segment sells gasoline and diesel in addition to a broad mix of merchandise such as groceries fast foods and beverages at its convenience stores. A portion of our gasoline and diesel sales are to wholesale customers on a consignment basisETP's retail marketing and wholesale distribution operations include the following activities conducted in 30 US states: the sale of motor fuel (gasoline and diesel) and merchandise at company-operated retail locations and branded convenience stores ;and the distribution of gasoline diesel and other petroleum products to convenience stores independent dealers distributors and other commercial customers. The unit's retail marketing operations have a portfolio of outlets operating under three channels of trade: company-operated dealer-operated and distributor-operated sites.

Financial Performance

Energy Transfer Equity has seen a very strong increase in net revenues over the last five years. In 2014 the company's revenues increased by 15%. ETP's gross margin increased primarily as a result of increase in retail marketing operations increased due to the acquisition of Susser and MACS. In addition transportation and services operations increased due higher volume transported to west Taxes due to the completion of expansion projects and the completion of Lone Star's fractionators. Midstream operations increased due to increase in fee-based revenues driven by increased production from assets recently placed in service in the Eagle Ford Shale. Regency's gross margin increased primarily due to increased volumes in Regency's south and west Texas and north Louisiana gathering and processing operations as well as an increase from the PVR Eagle Rock and Hoover acquisitions. Lake Charles LNG derives all of its revenues from a contract with a non-affiliated gas marketer. In 2014 Energy Transfer Equity's net income increased by 223% due to higher net sales a decrease in goodwill impairments a gain on sale of AmeriGas common units a decrease in losses on extinguishments of debt and an absence of non-operating environmental remediation driven primarily by Sunoco's recognition of environmental obligations related to closed sites. Cash from operating activities increased by 31%.

Strategy

The company has grown through large complementary acquisitions.

ETP and Regency each have strategies that contemplate growth through the development and acquisition of a wide range of midstream and other energy infrastructure assets. These strategies include constructing and acquiring additional assets and businesses to enhance their ability to compete effectively and diversify their respective asset portfolios thereby providing more stable cash flow. ETP and Regency regularly consider and enter into discussions regarding the acquisition of additional assets and businesses stand-alone development projects or other transactions that ETP and Regency believe will present opportunities to realize synergies and increase cash flow.

In 2014 Energy Transfer Equity ETP and Phillips 66 formed two joint ventures to develop the previously announced Dakota Access Pipeline and Energy Transfer Crude Oil Pipeline projects. ETP and ETE hold an aggregate interest of 75% in each joint venture and ETP operates both pipeline systems. Phillips 66 owns the remaining 25% interests and funds its proportionate share of the construction costs.

Mergers and Acquisitions

In a major industry consolidation move in 2015 Energy Transfer Equity agreed to buy Williams Companies in a $37.7 billion merger deal.

In 2015 ETP and Regency entered into a definitive merger agreement pursuant to which Regency will merge with a wholly-owned subsidiary of ETP with Regency continuing as the surviving entity and becoming a wholly-owned subsidiary of ETP.

In 2015 ETP acquired Susser Holdings Corporation for $1.8 billion. By acquiring Susser Holdings ETP will own the general partner interest and the incentive distribution rights in Susser (50.2 % of its shares) and Susser's existing retail operations (630 convenience stores).

In 2014 Regency acquired Eagle Rock's midstream business for $1.3 billion. This acquisition complements Regency's core gathering and processing business and further diversifies Regency's basin exposure in the Texas Panhandle east Texas and south Texas. Regency acquired PVR for 5.7 billion in 2014. The PVR acquisition enhanced Regency's geographic diversity with a strategic presence in the Marcellus and Utica shales in the Ap-

palachian Basin and the Granite Wash in the Mid-Continent region.

Company Background

In 2012 Energy Transfer Equity bought diversified gas player Southern Union for $9.4 billion (including $3.7 billion in debt). The acquisition made Energy Transfer Equity one of the largest natural gas infrastructure companies in the US.

That year the company also completed a $2 billion merger of a wholly owned Energy Transfer Partners subsidiary with and into Southern Union subsidiary CrossCountry Energy LLC which owns an indirect 50% interest in Citrus Corp. the owner of the Florida Gas Transmission pipeline system. After the merger CrossCountry Energy remained as the surviving entity a wholly owned subsidiary of Energy Transfer Partners.

In 2010 Energy Transfer Equity acquired the general partner stake of Regency Energy Partners and sold a 49.9% stake in its Midcontinent Express Pipeline to that company. The move was seen as a way for the company to diversify its general partner operations with the aim of getting a better return for shareholders. Regency Energy Partners focuses on the gathering processing marketing and transportation of natural gas and natural gas liquids in Arkansas Kansas Louisiana and Texas.

Energy Transfer Equity was formed in 2002 as La Grange Energy a Texas limited partnership. In early 2005 it changed its name to Energy Transfer Company. In August 2005 it converted from a Texas limited partnership to a Delaware limited partnership and became Energy Transfer Equity.

EXECUTIVES

President, John W. McReynolds, age 63, $550,000 total compensation
CFO, Thomas E. (Tom) Long, age 59
President and COO ETP, Marshall S. (Mackie) McCrea, $619,137 total compensation
Vice President Commercial, Steven Breckon
Vice President Operations, Robert Truesdell
Vice President Operations Support, Jeffrey (Jeff) Whippo
Executive Vice President Head Of Tax, Brad Whitehurst
Vice President Refined Products Logistics Asset Marketing, Bob Young
Vice President Operations Engineering, Rodney (Rod) Rogers
Vice President Process Engineering, Jim McCaleb
Vice President Human Resources and Admin in Houston Texas, Robert (Bob) Kerrigan
Vice President, James (Jamie) Dowden
Auditors: Grant Thornton LLP

LOCATIONS

HQ: Energy Transfer Equity L P
3738 Oak Lawn Avenue, Dallas, TX 75219
Phone: 214 981-0700
Web: www.energytransfer.com

PRODUCTS/OPERATIONS

2014 Sales

	$ mil.	% of total
Refined product sales	19,437	35
Crude sales	16,416	29
Natural gas sales	5,386	10
NGL Sales	5,845	10
Gathering transportation & other fees	3,733	7
Other	4,874	9
Total	**55,691**	**100**

2014 Sales

	$mil.
% of total	
Investment in ETP	92
Investment in Regency	8

Investment in lake Charles LNG   216
Adjustments

| **Total** | **100** |

Selected Subsidiaries and Operating Units

EASTERN GULF CRUDE ACCESS LLC
ETP- Energy Transfer Partners L.P.
ETP GP- Energy Transfer Partners GP L.P. the general partner of ETP
ETP LLC- Energy Transfer Partners L.L.C. the general partner of ETP GP
Holdco- ETP Holdco Corporation
Regency GP- Regency Energy Partners GP LP the general partner of Regency
Regency LLC- Regency Energy Partners GP LLC the general partner of Regency GP
Regency- Regency Energy Partners LP
Southern Union- Southern Union Company
Sunoco Logistics- Sunoco Logistics Partners L.P.
Sunoco- Sunoco Inc.

COMPETITORS

AmeriGas Partners	Enbridge
Atmos Energy	Ferrellgas Partners
Crestwood Midstream Partners LP	Star Gas Partners
	Suburban Propane
DCP Midstream Partners	

HISTORICAL FINANCIALS

Company Type: Public

Income Statement   FYE: December 31

	REVENUE ($ mil.)	NET INCOME ($ mil.)	NET PROFIT MARGIN	EMPLOYEES
12/14	55,691	633	1.1%	27,605
12/13	48,335	196	0.4%	13,573
12/12	16,964	304	1.8%	14,433
12/11	8,240	309	3.8%	2,477
12/10	6,598	192	2.9%	6,229
Annual Growth	**70.4%**	**34.6%**	**—**	**45.1%**

2014 Year-End Financials

Debt ratio: 47.56%
Return on equity: 1,947.69%
Cash ($ mil.): 847
Current ratio: 0.91
Long-term debt ($ mil.): 29,653

No. of shares (mil.): 1,080
Dividends
  Yield: 2.6%
  Payout: 130.4%
Market value ($ mil.): 62,006

	STOCK PRICE ($) FY Close	P/E High/Low	PER SHARE ($)		
			Earnings	Dividends	Book Value
12/14	57.38	146 69	0.58	0.75	0.65
12/13	81.74	471260	0.18	0.65	0.99
12/12	45.48	169122	0.28	0.63	1.95
12/11	40.58	133 92	0.35	0.59	0.14
12/10	39.07	188131	0.22	0.54	0.21
Annual Growth	**10.1%**	**— —**	**27.9%**	**8.6%**	**31.6%**

Energy Transfer Partners LP

Auditors: Grant Thornton LLP

LOCATIONS

HQ: Energy Transfer Partners LP
8111 Westchester Drive, Suite 600, Dallas, TX 75225
Phone: 214 981-0700   **Fax:** 214 981-0703
Web: www.energytransfer.com

Company Type: Public

Income Statement
FYE: December 31

	REVENUE ($ mil.)	NET INCOME ($ mil.)	NET PROFIT MARGIN	EMPLOYEES
12/14	51,158	1,336	2.6%	25,682
12/13	46,339	456	1.0%	12,450
12/12	15,702	1,569	10.0%	13,847
12/11	6,850	668	9.8%	1,946
12/10	5,884	617	10.5%	5,433
Annual Growth	71.7%	21.3%	—	47.5%

2014 Year-End Financials

Debt ratio: 40.11%	No. of shares (mil.): 405
Return on equity: —	Dividends
Cash ($ mil.): 639	Yield: 5.8%
Current ratio: 0.90	Payout: 213.8%
Long-term debt ($ mil.): 18,332	Market value ($ mil.): 26,369

	STOCK PRICE ($) FY Close	P/E High/Low	PER SHARE ($) Earnings	PER SHARE ($) Dividends	PER SHARE ($) Book Value
12/14	65.00	38 30	1.77	3.79	29.75
12/13	57.25	— —	(0.18)	3.59	30.05
12/12	42.93	12 9	4.42	3.58	22.94
12/11	45.85	50 36	1.10	3.58	25.38
12/10	51.82	43 36	1.19	3.58	24.55
Annual Growth	5.8%	— —	10.4%	1.4%	4.9%

Entergy Corp.

Entergy is into energy. The integrated utility holding company's subsidiaries distribute electricity to 2.8 million customers in four southern states (Arkansas Louisiana Mississippi and Texas) and provide natural gas to 196000 customers in Louisiana. Entergy operates 15500 miles of high-voltage transmission lines and 1500 transmission substations. In addition the company has interests in regulated and nonregulated power plants in North America that have a combined generating capacity of about 30000 MW (including nearly 10000 MW of nuclear power). Entergy is one of the largest nuclear power generators in the US.

Geographic Reach

Entergy performs operations across a 114000 square mile area in Arkansas Louisiana Mississippi and Texas.

Operations

The company operates primarily through two business segments: Utility and Wholesale Commodities.

The utility segment includes the generation transmission distribution and sale of electric power in Arkansas Mississippi Texas and Louisiana including the City of New Orleans. It also operates a small natural gas distribution business. Entergy's wholesale commodities segment owns and operates six nuclear power plants (10000 MW of capacity) in the northern US and sells power from these plants (and from its interests in non-nuclear power plants) to wholesale customers. It also provides services to other nuclear power plant owners.

Entergy's major subsidiaries include Entergy Arkansas Inc. Entergy Gulf States Louisiana L.L.C. Entergy Louisiana LLC Entergy Mississippi Inc. Entergy New Orleans Inc. Entergy Texas Inc. Entergy Nuclear Inc. Entergy Wholesale Commodities

Entergy Solutions District Cooling LP and Entergy Thermal LLC.

Financial Performance

In 2014 the company's net revenues increased by 10% due to an increase in utility sales thanks to rate hikes at Entergy Arkansas Entergy Mississippi Entergy Texas and Entergy Louisiana.Entergy's net income increased by 32% in 2014 due to higher net revenues a decrease in asset write-offs and impairments (including property plant and equipment impairments and related charges) and changes in other regulatory charges.The company's cash inflow increased by 22% that year.

Strategy

The company expecting that the diverse industrial base in the Gulf South region including chemicals primary metals wood products and petrochemicals will deliver significant utility sales growth through 2017.

Entergy publicized several transmission projects in 2014 and early 2015 in Louisiana and Texas including the Lake Charles transmission project. It also announced an accelerated gas pipe replacement program to replace about 100 miles of pipe in Baton Rouge over the next 10 years.

To raise cash in 2015 the company sold a natural gas-fired power plant in New England to the Carlyle Group or $490 million.

To save operating costs in 2014 Entergy Louisiana and Entergy Gulf States Louisiana asked the Louisiana Public Service Commission for permission to merge into a single utility.

In another move to improve operating efficiency that year Entergy broke ground on a new $23-million Transmission Operations Center in Little Rock that will be a nerve center where employees monitor the status of the Arkansas transmission system coordinate line outages for maintenance or repair and remotely operate switches and breakers at substations.

Growing its non-nuclear power assets in 2013 Entergy Gulf States Louisiana signed a deal with Sempra Energy's Cameron LNG unit to supply up to 200 MW of additional power to the proposed Cameron LNG liquefaction project in Hackberry.

HISTORY

Arkansas Power & Light (AP&L founded in 1913) consolidated operations with three other Arkansas utilities in 1926. Also that year New Orleans Public Service Inc. (NOPSI founded in 1922) merged with two other Big Easy electric companies. Louisiana Power & Light (LP&L) and Mississippi Power & Light (MP&L) were both formed in 1927 also through consolidation of regional utilities.

AP&L LP&L MP&L NOPSI and other utilities were combined into a Maine holding company Electric Power and Light which was dissolved in 1949. A new holding company Middle South Utilities emerged that year to take over the four utilities' assets.

In 1971 the company bought Arkansas-Missouri Power. In 1974 it brought its first nuclear plant on line and formed Middle South Energy (now System Energy Resources) to develop two more nuclear facilities Grand Gulf 1 and 2. Unfortunately Grand Gulf 1 was completed behind schedule and about 400% over budget. When Middle South tried to pass on the costs to customers controversy ensued. Construction of Grand Gulf 2 was halted and the CFO Edwin Lupberger took charge in 1985. Two years later nuke-related losses took the company to the brink of bankruptcy.

The company moved to settle the disputes by absorbing a $900 million loss on Grand Gulf 2 in 1989. To distance itself from the controversy Middle South changed its name to Entergy. In 1991

NOPSI settled with the City of New Orleans over Grand Gulf 1 costs.

That year Entergy anticipating deregulation branched out into nonregulated industries and looked abroad for growth opportunities. In 1993 a consortium including Entergy acquired a 51% interest in Edesur a Buenos Aires electric utility. In 1995 Entergy agreed to buy a 20% stake in a power plant under construction in India but the state government soon halted the project accusing the participating US companies of exploiting India.

Entergy completed its acquisition of CitiPower an Australian electric distributor in 1996 and the next year it bought the UK's London Electricity.

But diversification had drained funds. Lupberger resigned in 1998 and a new management team began selling noncore businesses such as CitiPower and London Electricity. NYMEX began trading electricity futures in 1998 using Entergy and Cinergy as contract-delivery points.

EXECUTIVES

President and CEO Entergy Arkansas, Hugh McDonald, age 56, $319,286 total compensation

EVP Nuclear Operations and Chief Nuclear Officer Entergy Nuclear, Jeff S. Forbes, age 58, $547,548 total compensation

Group President Utility Operations, Theodore H. (Theo) Bunting, age 57, $350,448 total compensation

Chairman and CEO, Leo P. Denault, age 56, $1,103,173 total compensation

SVP and COO, Paul D. Hinnenkamp

EVP and Chief Administrative Officer, Roderick K. (Rod) West, age 47, $623,854 total compensation

Acting Chief Nuclear Officer, Tim Mitchell

President and CEO Entergy Mississippi Inc, Haley R. Fisackerly, $248,346 total compensation

President Entergy Wholesale Commodities, William M. (Bill) Mohl, age 55, $568,141 total compensation

EVP and CFO, Andrew S. (Drew) Marsh, age 42, $512,721 total compensation

President and CEO Entergy New Orleans Inc, Charles Rice

EVP and General Counsel, Marcus V. Brown, age 53

President and CEO Entergy Texas Inc, Sallie Rainer

President and CEO Entergy Louisiana LLC and Entergy Gulf States Louisiana L.L.C., Phillip R. May

Vice President General Auditor, Lee Randall

Exec V Pres, Jerry D Jackson

Executive Vice President External Affairs, Curtis Hebert

Senior Vice President Of Nuclear Business Development, Randy Hutchinson

Vice President Engineering, Michael (Mel) Knight

Vice President, Charles Fink

Divisional Vice President, Joel Ferguson

Vice President Of Marketing, Liz Gaiennie

Vice President In Charge Of Marketing Information Technology And Business Development, Dena Willis

Vice President, Terry Roberts

Vice President, Gary Serio

Vice President Plant Operations Solid Fuel, Gerard Fontenot

Vice President, Howard Kenneth

Vice President, William Maguire

Vice President Transmission Regulatory Compliance, Richard (Dick) Riley

Vice President, Dan Turton

Vice President, Wilkerson Jean

Vice President Of Loss Prevention Services, Debbie Riggan

Vice President Of Customer Operations, Napoleon Johnson

Group Vice President Corporate, Necole Merritt

Vice President, Michela Darville

Vice President Comm, Phil Miracle
Vice President, Kimberly Buckhalter
Vice President, David (Dave) Landeche
Senior Vice President, Horace Webb
Senior Vice President, Kimberly Despeaux
Vice President, Byron Young
Vice President, Robert (Bob) Sloan
Vice President, Michele Lopiccolo
Vice President, Peter (Pete) Norgeot
Vice President Information Technology Delivery,
  Christine Maimaron
Vice President, Chantana Funchess
Vice President, Harriett Thehpope
Vice President Regulatory Affairs, Robert (Bob)
  Hall
Vice President, Donald (Don) Vinci
Executive Vice President and General Counsel,
  Brionn Stephens
Vice President Information Technology, Mark
  Serpa
Site Vice President, Anthony Vitale
Vice President Finance, Noradeen Farlakas
Vice President Of Human Resources, Peter Proulx
Executive Vice President Human Resources And
  Administration, Erenae Conley
Vice President Operations Grand Gulf, C
  Hutchinson
Vice President, Ed Davis
Senior Vice President, Joseph (Jo) Henderson
Vice President Federal Governmental Affairs,
  Daniel (Dan) Turton
Vice President, Michael (Mel) Kansler
Vice President and Treas, Steven (Steve) McNeal
Vice President Public Affairs, John (Jack) Arledge
Site Vice President, Bob Smith
Vice President Strategic Planning, Drew Marsh
Site Vice President, John (Jack) Ventosa
Vice President, Michael T (Mel) Twomey
New Orleans Reg Affairs Vice President, Tracie
  Boutte
Vice President Corporate Comm and Public
  Relations, Cyril Guerrera
Vice President and Associate Broker, Mike Wilson
Cash Manager And Assistant Treasurer, Mary Ann
  Valladares
Secretary, Gwen Hymel
Secretary, Shirley Weston
Secretary, Julie Mullet
Board Member, Perry Rodrigue
Board Member, Charles Watkins
Board Of Directors, Dave McElwee
Auditors: Deloitte & Touche LLP

LOCATIONS

HQ: Entergy Corp.
  639 Loyola Avenue, New Orleans, LA 70113
Phone: 504 576-4000
Web: www.entergy.com

PRODUCTS/OPERATIONS

2014 Sales

	$ mil.	% of total
Electric	9,591	77
Competitive businesses	2,721	22
Natural gas 181.8		1
Total	12,494	100

2014 Sales

	$ mil.	% of total
Utility	9,773	78
Entergy wholesale commodities	2,719	22
Others	1	-
Adjustment	(0.1)	-
Total	12,494	100

Selected Subsidiaries

Entergy Arkansas Inc. (electric utility)
Entergy Gulf States Inc. (electric and gas utility)
Entergy Louisiana LLC. (electric utility)
Entergy Mississippi Inc. (electric utility)

Entergy New Orleans Inc. (electric and gas utility)
Entergy Nuclear Inc. (nuclear plant operation)
Entergy Operations Inc. (plant management and
  maintenance for Entergy utilities)
Entergy Services Inc. (management services for Entergy
  utilities)
Entergy Solutions District Cooling LP
Entergy Thermal LLC.
Entergy Wholesale Commodities (wholesale power sales
  and marketing)
System Energy Resources Inc. (plant management and
  supply to Entergy utilities)
System Fuels Inc. (fuel storage and delivery to Entergy
  utilities)

Selected Mergers and Acquisitions

COMPETITORS

AEP	El Paso Electric
AES	Energy Future
Atmos Energy	Exelon
Avista	NextEra Energy
Berkshire Hathaway	OGE Energy
Energy	PG&E Corporation
Brazos Electric	Peabody Energy
CenterPoint Energy	Progress Energy
Cleco	Sempra Energy
Constellation Energy	Southern Company
Group	TVA
Dominion Resources	Williams Companies
Duke Energy	Xcel Energy
Edison International	

HISTORICAL FINANCIALS

Company Type: Public

Income Statement

FYE: December 31

	REVENUE ($ mil.)	NET INCOME ($ mil.)	NET PROFIT MARGIN	EMPLOYEES
12/14	12,494	960	7.7%	13,393
12/13	11,390	730	6.4%	13,808
12/12	10,302	868	8.4%	14,625
12/11	11,229	1,367	12.2%	14,682
12/10	11,487	1,270	11.1%	15,000
Annual Growth	2.1%	(6.8%)	—	(2.8%)

2014 Year-End Financials

Debt ratio: 30.15%
Return on equity: 9.48%
Cash ($ mil.): 1,422
Current ratio: 1.14
Long-term debt ($ mil.): 12,529

No. of shares (mil.): 179
Dividends
  Yield: 3.8%
  Payout: 61.6%
Market value ($ mil.): 15,680

	STOCK PRICE ($) FY Close	P/E High/Low	PER SHARE ($) Earnings	Dividends	Book Value
12/14	87.48	17 12	5.22	3.32	57.53
12/13	63.27	18 15	3.99	3.32	55.71
12/12	63.75	15 13	4.76	3.32	53.30
12/11	73.05	10 8	7.55	3.32	52.40
12/10	70.83	13 10	6.66	3.24	49.27
Annual Growth	5.4%	— —	(5.9%)	0.6%	4.0%

Enterprise Financial Services Corp

Enterprise Financial Services wants you to
boldly bank where many have banked before. It's
the holding company for Enterprise Bank & Trust
which mostly targets closely-held businesses and
their owners but also serves individuals in the St.

Louis Kansas City and Phoenix metropolitan areas.
Boasting $3.5 billion in assets and 15 branches En-
terprise offers standard products such as checking
savings and money market accounts and CDs.
Commercial and industrial loans make up over
half of the company's lending activities while real
estate loans make up another 45%. The bank also
writes consumer and residential mortgage loans.
Bank subsidiary Enterprise Trust offers wealth
management services.

OperationsEnterprise Trust the company's
wealth management unit targets business owners
wealthy individuals and institutional investors providing financial planning business succession planning and related services. The unit also invests in
Missouri state tax credits from funds for affordable
housing development which it then sells to clients
and others. About 82% of Enterprise Financial's
total revenue came from loan interest (including
fees) in 2014 while another 7% came from interest on its taxable and tax-exempt investment securities. The rest of its revenue came from wealth
management income (4%) service fees (3%) gains
on state tax credits (1%) and other miscellaneous
income sources. The bank had a staff of 452 full-
time employees at the end of 2014.Geographic
Reach

Enterprise Bank & Trust operates eight banking locations in or around Kansas City six banking locations and a support center in the St. Louis
area and two banking locations in the Phoenix
metro area.Financial PerformanceThe company
has struggled to consistently grow its revenues in
recent years mostly due to shrinking interest margins on its loans amidst the low-interest environment. Its profits however have mostly trended
higher thanks to declining loan loss provisions as
its loan portfolio's credit quality has improved with
higher property valuations in the strengthened
economy. Enterprise Financials' revenue fell by
9% to $148.4 million in 2014 mostly due to dou-
ble-digit declines in interest income as its purchased credit-impaired (PCI) loan balances and accelerated payments declined and as interest
margins on its loans continued to shrink. The
bank's portolio loan balances increased however
helping to offset some of its interest income de-
cline.Lower revenue and higher loan loss provisions (it received a loan loss benefit of $642 thou-
sand in 2013) in 2014 caused the bank's net
income to dive 18% to $27.2 million. Enterprise Fi-
nancial's operating cash levels rose by 7% to $31.5
million despite lower earnings for the year mostly
thanks to favorable changes in its working capital
related to a $12-million change in other asset bal-
ances.   StrategyEnterprise Financial Services
planned in 2015 to continue its long-term strategy
of keeping a "relationship-oriented distribution and
sales approach"; growing its fee income and niche
businesses; practicing "prudent" credit and interest
rate risk management; and using advanced technology and controlled-expense growth. The company added that it planned on "operating branches
with larger average deposits and employing experienced staff who are compensated on the basis of
performance and customer service."

Though it just had two branches in Phoenix in
2015 the bank believes the fast-growing Phoenix
market offers long-term growth opportunities for
the company with its underlying demographic and
geographic factors. Indeed at the end of 2014 the
market had over 90000 privately-held businesses
and 80000-plus households each with investible
assets of more than $1 million.
Company Background

In a restructuring move Enterprise Financial
Services sold life insurance arm Millennium Brokerage in 2010 five years after investing in the
company.

Enterprise Products Partners L.P.

Both enterprising and productive Enterprise Products Partners is a leading player in the North American natural gas natural gas liquids (NGL) and crude oil industries with a range of processing transportation and storage services. Operations include natural gas processing NGL fractionation petrochemical services and crude oil transportation including 51300 miles of pipelines 14 billion cu. ft. of natural gas storage and 225 million barrels of NGL refined products and crude oil storage capacity. It also has about 22 NGL fractionators and some 131 barges and 63 tow boats. The hub of Enterprise Products Partners' business is Houston's Mont Belvieu refinery complex.

Operations

Enterprise provides midstream energy services to producers and consumers of natural gas NGLs crude oil refined products and petrochemicals. It has five reportable segments: NGL Pipelines and Services; Onshore Natural Gas Pipelines and Services; Onshore Crude Oil Pipelines and Services; Offshore Pipelines and Services; and Petrochemical and Refined Products Services.

Its services include: natural gas gathering treating processing transportation and storage; NGL transportation fractionation and storage; LPG import and export terminals; crude oil gathering and transportation storage and terminals; and offshore production platforms; petrochemical and refined products transportation and services. The company also has a marine transportation business that operates primarily on in inland and Intracoastal Waterway systems in the US and in the Gulf of Mexico.

The NGL Pipelines and Services segment (40% of Enterprise's 2014 sales) includes natural gas processing plants and related NGL marketing activities 19300 miles of NGL pipelines NGL and related product storage facilities and 15 NGL fractionators. It also includes the company's NGL import and LPG export terminal operations. NGL marketing activities use a fleet of 740 railcars most of which are leased from third parties.

The Onshore Natural Gas Pipelines and Services business segment (43% of 2014 sales) is engaged in gathering and transportation of natural gas in Colorado Louisiana New Mexico Texas and Wyoming.

The Offshore Pipelines and Services business segment serves some of the most active drilling and development regions including deepwater production fields in the northern Gulf of Mexico offshore Texas Louisiana Mississippi and Alabama.

Sales and Marketing

NGL is sold to industrial and commercial customers and distribute through local gas distribution companies and other customers of natural gas purchased from producers regional natural gas processing plants and the open market. Refined products terminal customers are typically billed a fee per unit of volume loaded.

Royal Dutch Shell is the company's largest non-affiliated customer accounting for 8.5% of Enterprise's revenues in 2014.

Financial Performance

In 2014 Enterprise's net revenues edged up by about 0.5% in 2014.Higher prices lifted revenues from natural gas and refined products partially offset by lower refined products sales volumes. Revenues from the marketing of crude oil decreased due to lower prices partially offset by volumes. NGL sales declined due to lower prices and lower

sales volumes (caused by unscheduled plant maintenance outages). Midstream services revenues increased due to the ongoing expansion of its operations. (Recently completed assets such as the ATEX pipeline and the Rocky Mountain expansion of our Mid-America Pipeline System as well as certain assets in the Eagle Ford Shale and at their Mont Belvieu complex contributed $400 million of this increase). Revenues from Oiltanking also contributed to the slight increase in net revenues.

In 2014 net income increased by 9% due to higher net sales and a lower provision for income taxes due to changes in accruals for state tax obligations under the Revised Texas Franchise Tax.Enterprise's cash from operating activities increased by 8% in 2014.

Strategy

Enterprise's strategy is focused on building and managing an integrated network of midstream energy assets (including salt domes and fractionation and natural gas processing plants) to take advantage of growing US market demand for natural gas NGLs crude oil and refined products.

The company's business strategies are to capitalize on expected increases in the production of natural gas NGLs and crude oil from development activities in various US production basins. Part of this strategy involves expansion through growth capital projects. It plans to continue to expand its assets through the construction of new facilities and to capitalize on expected increases in natural gas NGL and crude oil production resulting from development activities in the Rocky Mountains Mid-Continent Northeast and US Gulf Coast regions including the Niobrara Barnett Eagle Ford Permian Haynesville Marcellus and Utica Shale plays and deepwater Gulf of Mexico production fields.

To raise cash to fund expansion and pay down debt in 2015 the company sold its offshore Gulf of Mexico pipelines and services business to Genesis Energy for $1.5 billion.

In 2015 Enterprise announced plans to build a new rude oil and condensate pipeline from Midland to Houston Texas and a natural gas processing facility in the Delaware Basin through a 50/50 joint venture with an affiliate of Occidental Petroleum Corporation.

In 2014 it announced plans to construct a new cryogenic natural gas processing plant in Eddy County New Mexico and associated natural gas and NGL pipeline infrastructure to facilitate growing production of NGL-rich natural gas in the Delaware Basin (a prolific production area in West Texas and southern New Mexico). In addition it also announced plans to build a ninth NGL fractionator at its Mont Belvieu complex.

In 2014 the company teamed up with Plains All American Pipeline to jointly begin building a new condensate gathering system into their Three Rivers terminal and doubling the mainline capacity on their Eagle Ford Joint Venture Pipeline from Three Rivers to Corpus Christi Texas.

That year Enterprise also completed construction of the first segment of the Aegis pipeline between Mont Belvieu and Beaumont Texas. Supplying petrochemical customers this 60-mile segment of 20-inch diameter pipeline is part of the 270-mile Aegis ethane pipeline that will create a 500-mile header system from Corpus Christi to the Mississippi River in Louisiana.

In 2014 the company developed two refined products export facilities to meet the growing demand for additional refined products export capability on the US Gulf Coast. The Beaumont marine terminal will initially handle Panamax size vessels. Subsequently its expanded marine terminal on the Houston Ship Channel will handle up to Aframax class vessels.

Mergers and Acquisitions

Growing its Eagle Ford assets in 2015 the company a bought a pipeline and processing company in Texas from Pioneer Natural Resources and Reliance Industries for $2.15 billion.

Growing its portfolio in 2014 the company acquired the general partner and related incentive distribution rights 15899802 common units and 38899802 subordinated units in Oiltanking Partners L.P. held by Oiltanking Holding Americas Inc. for $4.41 billion. Oiltanking Partners is a major storage provider of crude oil liquid chemicals and gas product

Company Background

The company is investing heavily in serving shale plays especially the Eagle Ford in South Texas and is building midstream facilities to serve the surge in natural gas production. In 2012 it opened a fifth NGL fractionator at its Mont Belvieu facility to process Eagle Ford hydrocarbons and a fifth in 2012.

That year Enterprise joined Enbridge Energy Partners and Anadarko Petroleum in advancing development of the Texas Express Pipeline by the companies' joint venture. The 20-inch diameter pipeline will extend about 580 miles from Skellytown Texas to the Mont Belvieu NGL fractionation complex. The pipeline also provides access to other producers in several regions: West Texas the Rocky Mountains southern Oklahoma and the Mid-continent area.

In 2010 in a move to increase its footprint in the lucrative Haynesville/Bossier Shale play Enterprise acquired two natural gas gathering and treating systems in northwest Louisiana and East Texas from M2 Midstream LLC for $1.2 billion.

In a major expansion move in 2009 the company acquired rival TEPPCO Partners L.P. in a $26 billion all-stock deal which boosted its pipelines and oil refined products and NGL storage capacity. The TEPPCO Partners purchase made the company the largest publicly traded energy partnership in the US. The expanded company's assets include 60 liquid storage terminals 25 natural gas storage facilities 17 fractionation facilities and six offshore hub platforms.

That year the company acquired Enterprise GP Holdings which controlled the general partner of Enterprise. The $8 billion deal was aimed at reducing long-term capital costs and simplifying the business structure of Enterprise Products Partners.

The family of Chairman Dan Duncan controls a 35% stake in Enterprise.

EXECUTIVES

CEO and Director, A. James (Jim) Teague, age 69, $753,788 total compensation
Group SVP Engineering, Leonard W. Mallett, age 57
Group SVP Unregulated NGLs Crude and Natural Gas Assets, William (Bill) Ordemann, age 56, $433,400 total compensation
SVP and CFO, Bryan F. Bulawa, age 46
Group SVP, G. R. (Jerry) Cardillo, age 57
SVP and CIO, Paul G. Flynn
Group SVP Operations and Environmental Health Safety and Training, Graham W. Bacon, age 51
General Counsel and Group SVP, Craig W. Murray, age 67
Chairman, Randa D. Williams, age 53
Auditors: Deloitte & Touche LLP

LOCATIONS

HQ: Enterprise Products Partners L.P.
1100 Louisiana Street, 10th Floor, Houston, TX 77002
Phone: 713 381-6500
Web: www.enterpriseproducts.com

PRODUCTS/OPERATIONS

2014 Sales

	$ mil.	% of total
Onshore crude oil pipelines & services	32,863	43
NGL pipelines & services	30,806	40
Petrochemical & refined products services	8,096	10
Onshore natural gas pipelines & services	5,310	7
Offshore pipeline & services	163	0
Elimination	(29288.0)	0
Total	**47,951**	**100**

COMPETITORS

Crestwood Midstream Partners LP	Exxon Mobil
Duke Energy	Huntsman International
Dynegy	Occidental Petroleum
Equistar Chemicals	Spectra Energy
	Williams Companies

HISTORICAL FINANCIALS

Company Type: Public

Income Statement

FYE: December 31

	REVENUE ($ mil.)	NET INCOME ($ mil.)	NET PROFIT MARGIN	EMPLOYEES
12/14	47,951	2,833	5.9%	—
12/13	47,727	2,607	5.5%	—
12/12	42,583	2,428	5.7%	—
12/11	44,313	2,088	4.7%	—
12/10	33,739	320	1.0%	—
Annual Growth	**9.2%**	**72.4%**	**—**	**—**

2014 Year-End Financials

Debt ratio: 45.36%	No. of shares (mil.): 1,937
Return on equity: —	Dividends
Cash ($ mil.): 74	Yield: 3.9%
Current ratio: 0.70	Payout: 94.7%
Long-term debt ($ mil.): 19,157	Market value ($ mil.): 69,976

	STOCK PRICE ($) FY Close	P/E High/Low	PER SHARE ($) Earnings	Dividends	Book Value
12/14	36.12	53 21	1.47	1.43	9.32
12/13	66.30	45 35	1.41	1.35	8.13
12/12	50.08	39 33	1.36	1.27	7.30
12/11	46.38	37 30	1.19	1.20	6.83
12/10	41.61	76 52	0.58	1.14	6.70
Annual Growth	**(3.5%)**	**— —**	**26.4%**	**5.8%**	**8.6%**

EOG Resources, Inc.

EOG Resources' geographic focus is determined by where it can locate primary energy resources — natural gas natural gas liquids and oil. In recent years that focus has been on exploiting shale plays in the US. The independent oil and gas company is engaged in exploring for natural gas and crude oil and developing producing and marketing those resources. In 2014 EOG's total estimated net proved reserves was 2.5 billion barrels of oil equivalent of which 1.1 billion barrels was crude oil and condensate reserves and 5 trillion cubic feet was natural gas reserves.

Geographic Reach

EOG is developing major shale plays in the US —the Eagle Ford Shale and Barnett Shale in Texas and the Bakken Formation in North Dakota. EOG also has operations in Canada offshore Trinidad the UK North Sea and East Irish Sea and Sichuan Basin in China.

In 2014 the US accounted for some 97% of the company's proved reserves.

Operations

EOG is the largest oil producer in the lucrative Eagle Ford Shale play in South Texas producing 202700 barrels of oil equivalent per day in 2014.

That year it also drilled and participated in 62 net wells in the Permian Basin to develop its liquids-rich Leonard and Wolfcamp plays. The company has 80000 net acres in the Leonard Shale and 140000 net acres in the Wolfcamp Shale all within the Permian's Delaware Basin. Additionally EOG has acreage in the Wolfcamp Shale within the Midland Basin.

Sales and Marketing

The company sell its North American wellhead crude oil and condensate production to local markets and (by pipeline rail and truck) to downstream markets and its natural gas production to local markets or via pipeline to downstream markets.

EOG's major sales points include Cushing Oklahoma St. James Louisiana and other points along the Gulf Coast. In 2014 two purchasers each accounted for more than 10% of EOG's total wellhead crude oil and condensate NGLs and natural gas revenues and gathering processing and marketing revenues. In 2014 and 2013 all natural gas from EOG's Trinidad operations was sold to the National Gas Company of Trinidad and Tobago and all natural gas from EOG's China operations was sold to PetroChina.

In 2014 EOG processed certain of its natural gas production to extract NGLs. Most of the wellhead natural gas volumes from Trinidad were sold under contracts that year. All wellhead natural gas volumes from the UK were sold on the spot market. The wellhead natural gas volumes from China were sold at regulated prices based on the purchaser's pipeline sales volumes to various local market segments.

Financial Performance

The company's revenues have grown steadily since 2010. In 2014 EOG's revenues increased by 24% due to higher revenues from natural gas liquids crude oil and condensate and natural gas and from a gain on the disposal of assets. Natural Gas liquids revenues grew by 21% due to an increase in NGL deliveries and higher wellhead crude oil and condensate deliveries. Both reflected increased volumes in the Eagle Ford and the Permian Basin. In 2014 EOG also recognized net gains on the mark-to-market of financial commodity derivative contracts of $834 million which included net cash received from settlements of crude oil and natural gas financial derivative contracts of $34 million. The company's net income increased by 33% in 2014 due to an increase in revenues and operating income. In 2014 EOG's net cash provided by operating activities rose by 18% due to increased net income and a change in inventories and accounts payable.

Strategy

EOG's strategy is to focus on organic growth of its North American shale plays and making complementary acquisitions of properties in North America and internationally. The company puts an emphasis on developing advanced technology associated with maximizing production from shale plays (especially in the Eagle Ford and Permian Basin) including reservoir simulation models improved drill bits mud motors for horizontal drilling and horizontal completion methods.

EOG implements its strategy by emphasizing the drilling of internally generated prospects in order to find and develop low-cost reserves. It also looks to maintain the lowest possible operating cost structure that is consistent with prudent and safe operations.

In 2014 EOG expanded its inventory of crude oil plays with successful drilling results in the Second Bone Spring Sand which underlies its extensive Leonard Shale acreage position in Lea and Eddy counties New Mexico.To raise cash for general purpose use in 2014 EOG sold all of its assets in Manitoba and the majority of its assets in Alberta for $410 million.

HISTORY

In 1987 Enron formed Enron Oil & Gas from its existing InterNorth and Houston Natural Gas operations to concentrate on exploration for oil and natural gas and their production. Enron maintained full ownership until 1989 when it spun off 16% of Enron Oil & Gas to the public raising about $200 million. Later offerings reduced its holdings to just over 50%.

Enron Oil & Gas in 1992 was awarded a 95% working interest in three fields off Trinidad that previously had been held by government-owned companies. Two years later the company assumed the operations of three drilling blocks off Bombay (including the Tapti field) as well as a 30% interest in them. Natural gas prices fell in the winter of 1994 causing Enron Oil & Gas to focus its 1995 drilling on crude oil exploitation and the enhancement of its natural gas reserves. Natural gas prices rebounded in 1996. That year Enron Oil & Gas was awarded a 90% interest in an offshore area of Venezuela. In 1997 the company inked a 30-year production contract with China. The company made a major discovery of natural gas in offshore Trinidad in 1998. That year Mark Papa succeeded Forrest Hoglund as CEO (Papa became chairman in 1999).

In 1999 Enron traded most of its remaining stake in Enron Oil & Gas to the company in exchange for Enron Oil & Gas' operations and assets in India and China. Consequently the company changed its name from Enron Oil & Gas to EOG Resources.

The next year EOG won contracts to develop properties in Canada's Northwest Territories. It also moved into the Appalachian Basin in 2000 through the acquisition of Somerset Oil & Gas. Buoyed by a strong performance that year the company increased its capital spending on North American exploration by more than 30% and in 2001 it bought Energy Search a small natural gas exploration and production company that operated in the Appalachian Basin.

EXECUTIVES

Chairman and CEO, William R. Thomas, age 63, $906,731 total compensation
President and COO, Gary L. Thomas, age 66, $791,154 total compensation
Executive Vice President and General Manager Denver, Kurt Doerr
VP and CIO, Sandeep Bhakhri
VP and CFO, Timothy K. Driggers, age 54, $458,077 total compensation
EVP and General Manager Denver, Robert K. Garrison, age 63, $362,761 total compensation
VP and General Manager Oklahoma City, Tony C. Maranto
VP and General Manager Corpus Christi, Kenneth E. Dunn
EVP Exploration and Production, Lloyd W. (Bill) Helms, age 57, $448,077 total compensation
VP Drilling, Robert C. Smith
Managing Director EOG Resources Trinidad Limited, Sammy G. Pickering
VP and General Manager Tyler, Ernest J. LaFlure
EVP Exploration and Production, David W. Trice, age 44

VP and General Manager Forth Worth, J. Pat Woods
VP and General Manager Midland, Ezra Y. Yacob
VP Exploration, John J. Chapman
VP and General Manager San Antonio, John J. Boyd
VP and General Manager Fort Worth and Pittsburgh, Ronald D. Oden
VP Land, Steven D. Wentworth
Vice President Human Resources, Bryan Baldwin
Vice President Information Technology, Jim Coleman
Vice President Operations, Richard Ott
Vice President, Kevin Hanzel
Vice President Engineering, Cory Helms
Vice President, Keith Trasko
Vice President Accounting, Ann Janssen
Vice President Sales And Marketing, Pat Woods
Vice President, Sara Miller
Vice President, Chad Weisenburger
Vice President, Matthew (Matt) Garrison
Senior Vice President Investor Relations, Cedric Burgher
Secretary And Membership Chairman Eog Resources, Lorraine Baline
Board Member, Megan Lewis
Secretary, Natalie Brown
Auditors: Deloitte & Touche LLP

LOCATIONS

HQ: EOG Resources, Inc.
 1111 Bagby, Sky Lobby 2, Houston, TX 77002
Phone: 713 651-7000
Web: www.eogresources.com

2014 Sales

	$ mil.	% of total
US	16,792	93
Canada	706	4
Trinidad	518	3
Other countries	18	0
Total	**18,035**	**100**

PRODUCTS/OPERATIONS

2014 Sales

	$ mil.	% of total
Crude oil & condensate	9,742	54
Gathering processing & marketing	4,046	22
Natural gas	1,916	11
Natural gas liquids	934	5
Gain on assets dispositions	507	3
Others	54	-
Gains (Losses) on Mark-to-Market commodity derivative contracts	834	5
Total	**18,035**	**100**

COMPETITORS

Adams Resources	Murphy Oil
Anadarko Petroleum	Occidental Petroleum
Apache	Pioneer Natural
BP	Resources
Cabot Oil & Gas	Royal Dutch Shell
Chevron	Sonde Resources Corp.
Exxon Mobil	Talisman Energy

HISTORICAL FINANCIALS

Company Type: Public

Income Statement

FYE: December 31

	REVENUE ($ mil.)	NET INCOME ($ mil.)	NET PROFIT MARGIN	EMPLOYEES
12/14	18,035	2,915	16.2%	3,000
12/13	14,487	2,197	15.2%	2,800
12/12	11,682	570	4.9%	2,650
12/11	10,126	1,091	10.8%	2,550
12/10	6,099	160	2.6%	2,290
Annual Growth	**31.1%**	**106.4%**	**—**	**7.0%**

2014 Year-End Financials

Debt ratio: 17.00%	No. of shares (mil.): 548
Return on equity: 17.60%	Dividends
Cash ($ mil.): 2,087	Yield: 0.5%
Current ratio: 1.60	Payout: 9.1%
Long-term debt ($ mil.): 5,903	Market value ($ mil.): 50,482

	STOCK PRICE ($) FY Close	P/E High/Low		PER SHARE ($) Earnings	Dividends	Book Value
12/14	92.07	35	15	5.32	0.51	32.30
12/13	167.84	46	28	4.02	0.73	28.23
12/12	120.79	117	79	1.06	0.67	24.45
12/11	98.51	58	33	2.05	0.32	23.49
12/10	91.41	355	271	0.32	0.61	20.13
Annual Growth	**0.2%**	**—**	**—**	**102.7%**	**(4.3%)**	**12.5%**

Erie Indemnity Co.

Erie Indemnity may be near a lake but it prefers pools. Founded in 1925 as an auto insurer it now provides management services that relate to the sales underwriting and issuance of policies of one customer: Erie Insurance Exchange. The Exchange is a reciprocal insurance exchange that pools the underwriting of several property/casualty insurance firms. It offers coverage ranging from homeowners to boat policies through independent representatives with a reach that extends to about a dozen states east of the Mississippi River. Erie Indemnity charges a management fee of 25% of all premiums written or assumed by the Exchange. It is the only publicly traded part of the Erie Insurance Group.OperationsThe company operates through four reporting segments: management operations property and casualty insurance operations life insurance operations and investment operations. Its management operations segment comprises its acting as attorney-in-fact for the Exchange. The property and casualty insurance operations includes personal and commercial lines while the life insurance operations includes traditional and universal individual life products and and fixed annuities; both utilize the same independent agency force.The Exchange and its subsidiaries operate as a property/casualty insurer and are collectively referred to as the Property and Casualty Group.In 2014 Erie Indemnity's earned premiums and fees on insurance operations made up about 90% of its revenues with investment operations making up the other 10%. About one-third of revenues are derived from premiums from the property/casualty lines insurance business which includes homeowners renters business owners and auto coverage. The Erie Insurance family of companies serves a total of some 5 million property/casualty policyholders as well as 330000 life insurance and annuity customers.Geographic ReachThe property and casualty group operates in a dozen midwestern mid-Atlantic and southeastern states (Illinois Indiana Kentucky Maryland New York North Carolina Ohio Pennsylvania Tennessee Virginia West Virginia and Wisconsin) as well as in the District of Columbia. Erie Indemnity's largest markets are Pennsylvania Maryland North Carolina Ohio and Virginia making up more than 70% of net written premiums.The Erie Insurance Group operates 25 field offices in its market.Sales and MarketingErie Indemnity distribution network includes about 2200 agencies and independent agents.Financial PerformanceErie Indemnity has shown increased revenues over the last five years with the exception of a marginal (1%) decline in

2011 and a 2% decline in 2014. Most recently revenues fell 2% to $6 billion primarily due to a 44% decline in investment earnings but partially offset by increases in the other segments.In 2014 net income rose 3% to $168 million due largely to a decline in provisions for income taxes. Cash flow from operations peaked in 2013 but declined 14% the following year as losses loss expenses agent commissions and bonuses and underwriting and acquisition costs rose.StrategyThrough careful risk selection and pricing practices as well as by maintaining a diverse product mix Erie Indemnity seeks to maintain long-term underwriting profit growth for the Exchange. It also seeks to provide consistent support services to policyholders and agents. Towards that end the company is upgrading its technology platforms.Erie Indemnity plans for growth also include increasing its property/casualty group premiums and improving its competitive position in the marketplace by expanding the size of its agency force and increasing market penetration in existing territories. It also intends to expand geographically and broaden the types of products it offers.For example in 2014 it introduced its Rate Lock protection to Maryland and rolled out its ErieSecure Home offering in North Carolina. Commercially it began offering restaurant-specific lines and data breach coverage. Other newer offerings include more customized homeowners' protection and even auto coverage for customers providing rideshare services through Lyft or Uber.Company BackgroundErie Indemnity's structure and relationship to other parts of the larger Erie Insurance Group are complex to say the least. The company operated as a property/casualty insurer through its wholly-owned subsidiaries Erie Insurance Co. Erie New York and Erie Insurance Property and Casualty throughout 2010. At year-end however Erie Indemnity sold all of its outstanding capital stock and voting shares of these subsidiaries to the Exchange. As a result now all of its former property/casualty insurance operations are owned by the Exchange and Erie Indemnity serves as the management company. The sale of the subsidiaries did not affect its pooling agreement. The company also sold its approximate 22% ownership in Erie Family Life to the Exchange which became its full parent.

EXECUTIVES

EVP and CIO, Robert C. (Bob) Ingram, age 56, $412,692 total compensation
EVP Services, George D. (Chip) Dufala, age 43, $418,462 total compensation
President CEO and Director, Terrence W. Cavanaugh, age 61, $935,000 total compensation
EVP Sales and Marketing, John F. Kearns, age 55
EVP Products, Richard F. (Rick) Burt, age 51, $388,462 total compensation
EVP Secretary and General Counsel, Sean McLaughlin, age 60
SVP and Controller, Gregory (Greg) Gutting
Vice President Claim Manager, Kristine Musselman
Vice President Internal Audit, Jim Stoik
Vice President And Claims Manager, Gregory Green
Chairman, Thomas B. Hagen, age 79
Auditors: Ernst & Young LLP

LOCATIONS

HQ: Erie Indemnity Co.
100 Erie Insurance Place, Erie, PA 16530
Phone: 814 870-2000
Web: www.erieinsurance.com

PRODUCTS/OPERATIONS

2014 Revenues

	$ mil.	% of total
Premiums earned	5,344	87
Investment income	446	7
Realized investment gains	193	3
Equity in earnings of limited partnerships	113	2
Other income	32	1
Net impairment losses	(4)	-
Total	**6,124**	**100**

2014 Revenues

	$ mil.	% of total
Property & casualty insurance	5,260	70
Management operations	1,407	19
Investment operations	764	10
Life insurance	87	1
Adjustments	(1394)	-
Total	**5,124**	**100**

COMPETITORS

ACE USA	Old Republic
Alleghany Corporation	PMA Companies
Gallagher	Transatlantic Holdings
Marsh & McLennan	Travelers Companies
Navigators	

HISTORICAL FINANCIALS

Company Type: Public

Income Statement

FYE: December 31

	ASSETS ($ mil.)	NET INCOME ($ mil.)	INCOME AS % OF ASSETS	EMPLOYEES
12/14	17,758	168	0.9%	4,700
12/13	16,676	163	1.0%	4,450
12/12	15,441	160	1.0%	4,400
12/11	14,348	169	1.2%	4,300
12/10	14,344	162	1.1%	4,200
Annual Growth	5.5%	0.9%	—	2.9%

2014 Year-End Financials

Debt ratio: —
Return on equity: 23.38%
Cash ($ mil.): 514
Current ratio: —
Long-term debt ($ mil.): —
No. of shares (mil.): 46
Dividends
  Yield: 2.8%
  Payout: 74.9%
Market value ($ mil.): 4,193

	STOCK PRICE ($) FY Close	P/E High/Low	PER SHARE ($) Earnings	Dividends	Book Value
12/14	90.77	26 19	3.18	2.54	15.22
12/13	73.12	24 20	3.08	4.37	15.80
12/12	69.22	23 18	2.99	4.80	13.69
12/11	78.16	23 18	3.08	2.06	16.32
12/10	65.47	21 12	2.85	1.92	18.22
Annual Growth	8.5%	— —	2.8%	7.2%	(4.4%)

ERP OPERATING LIMITED PARTNERSHIP

LOCATIONS

HQ: ERP OPERATING LIMITED PARTNERSHIP
2 N RIVERSIDE PLZ STE 400, CHICAGO, IL 606062624
Phone: 3124741300

HISTORICAL FINANCIALS

Company Type: Private

Income Statement

FYE: December 31

	ASSETS ($ mil.)	NET INCOME ($ mil.)	INCOME AS % OF ASSETS	EMPLOYEES
12/14	22,950	658	2.9%	3,600
12/13	22,834	1,905	8.3%	—
12/12	17,201	881	5.1%	—
Annual Growth	15.5%	(13.5%)	—	—

2014 Year-End Financials

Debt ratio: ——
Return on equity: 25.20%
Cash ($ mil.): 40
Current ratio: ——
Long-term debt ($ mil.): ——
Dividends
  Yield: —
  Payout: —
Market value ($ mil.): —

Essendant Inc

Don't think that Essendant (formerly United Stationers) is just another paper pusher. The company is a leading pure wholesale distributor of office supplies and equipment in North America offering more than 160000 of its own and national brand products to about 30000 reseller customers. Through subsidiaries Essendant supplies such items as business machines computer products and peripherals janitorial supplies and office products and furniture. It also offers office furniture for such markets as education and health care. The company sells primarily to resellers through catalogs and over the Internet as well as through its direct sales force.

HISTORY

Company BackgroundMorris Wolf and Harry Hecktman former office supply salesmen and Israel Kriloff a grocer purchased Utility Supply Company (founded in 1906) and began selling office supplies in downtown Chicago in 1921. Weathering the Depression Utility Supply's business grew steadily during the 1930s. In 1935 the company published its first catalog and it opened its first retail store in downtown Chicago two years later. The partners bought out Kriloff in 1939.

WWII created a scarcity of raw materials and Utility Supply had difficulty in obtaining merchandise. The company tried selling non-office products unsuccessfully. Fortunately the war's end brought an end to the inventory drought. During the postwar era Utility Supply began mailing a series of catalogs to retailers nationwide. By 1948 mail-order business accounted for 40% of sales. A wholesale division to sell products to independent resellers was created in the 1950s.

In 1960 the company adopted the name United Stationers Supply and the retail stores became the Utility Stationery Stores. Business increased as independent retailers began to appreciate the advantages of ordering through a wholesaler instead of a manufacturer —purchasing goods on an as-needed basis. Howard Wolf the founder's son became CEO in 1967 and began emphasizing computers and automation to track inventory and costs.

Wholesale trade accounted for about two-thirds of sales by 1970. United Stationers introduced a series of abridged catalogs targeting specific groups and marketing segments such as furniture and electronics. The following year United Stationers developed regional redistribution centers that offered overnight delivery. The company sold its retail outlets in 1978.

Three years later United Stationers went public. During the 1980s the advent of warehouse clubs and office supply superstores threatened independent retailers. The company developed marketing concepts to help its independent resellers even as it aggressively targeted mail-order houses and superstores. The downsizing trend in the late 1980s caused the corporate market to shrink and United Stationers lowered prices; it instituted a decentralization plan in 1990.

The next year the company expanded into Canada opening its first non-US subsidiary and it acquired archrival Stationers Distributing and its distribution centers across the US in 1992. In 1994 it established its United Facility Supply unit to distribute maintenance supplies.

Investment firm Wingate Partners which controlled rival Associated Stationers bought United Stationers in 1995 and combined the operations of the two companies under the United Stationers name. United Stationers acquired janitorial supplies wholesaler Lagasse Bros. in 1996. In 1998 the company acquired the US and Mexican operations of Abitibi-Consolidated including Azerty. (It acquired Azerty Canada in 2000.)

United Stationers launched a venture with E-Commerce Industries in 1999 to help customers sell products over the Internet. The next year the company started The Order People a third-party call center fulfillment business aimed at online retailers; however the dot-com bust and higher losses than planned led United Stationers to curtail operations in 2001. Also that year it bought Peerless Paper Mills (merging the wholesale distributor of janitorial and paper products into Lagasse).

The company sold its Canadian operations in 2006 following an accounting scandal. United Stationers discovered that its Canadian operation was incorrectly accounting for supplier allowances and other receivables.

United Stationers acquired ORS Nasco a wholesale distributor of industrial supplies for about $180 million in 2007.

In 2008 it purchased Emco Distribution a New Jersey-based business product distributor for $15 million.

United Stationers promoted P. Cody Phipps its president and COO to the position of CEO in May 2011 when CEO Richard Gochnauer retired.

EXECUTIVES

Vice President Treasurer, Robert (Bob) Kelderhouse
President and CEO, Robert B. (Bob) Aiken, age 52
SVP and CFO, Todd A. Shelton, age 48, $440,000 total compensation
COO, Timothy P. (Tim) Connolly, age 51, $402,000 total compensation
COO ORS Nasco, Paul J. Barrett
President On-Line and New Channels, Richard D. (Ric) Phillips, age 44, $375,000 total compensation
SVP Merchandising, Joseph G. (Joe) Hartsig, age 51, $390,000 total compensation
SVP and CIO, Janet Zelenka

Vice President Information Technology, Marshall Lancaster
Vice President Of Marketing, Laura Gale
Vice President Of Logistics, Bill Stark
Vice President IDC Sales, Harry Dochelli
Vice President Sales, Mike Miller
Vice President Human Resources, Julie Rose
Vice President Sales and Marketing for Azerty, Kevin Bowman
Vice President Marketing, Diane Hund
Vice President Supply Chain Logistics, Stan Becraft
Vice President Digital Marketing, Oi Eng-crandus
Vice President Supply Chain Analytics, Henrik Danford-klein
Vice President Of Finance At Ors Nasco, Fred Heger
Vice President Global Sourcing, Peter Dehio
Senior Vice President Human Resources, Barbara (Barb) Kennedy
Senior Vice President General Counsel and Secretary, Eric Blanchard
Chairman, Charles K. Crovitz, age 61
Treasurer, Jason Crawford
Auditors: Ernst & Young LLP

LOCATIONS

HQ: Essendant Inc
One Parkway North Boulevard, Suite 100, Deerfield, IL 60015-2559
Phone: 847 627-7000   **Fax:** 847 627-7001
Web: www.unitedstationers.com

PRODUCTS/OPERATIONS

2014 Sales

	$ mil.	% of total
Janitorial & breakroom supplies	1,448	27
Technology products	1,437	27
Traditional office products	1,331	25
Industrial supplies	638	12
Office furniture	309	6
Freight revenue	121	2
Other	39	1
Total	**5,327**	**100**

Selected Products

Technology products
  Computer monitors
  Copiers and fax machines
  Data storage
  Digital cameras
  Printers and printer cartridges
Traditional office products
  Calendars
  Organizers
  Paper products
  Writing instruments
Office furniture
  Computer furniture
  Leather chairs
  Vertical and lateral file cabinets
  Wooden and steel desks
Janitorial and sanitation products
  Food service disposables
  Janitorial and sanitation supplies
  Paper and packaging supplies
  Safety and security items
Industrial supplies
  Hand and power tools
  Safety and security supplies
  Janitorial equipment and supplies
  Maintenance repair and operations items
  Oil field and welding supplies

COMPETITORS

D & H Distributing	S.P. Richards
Gould Paper	SED International
Ingram Micro	Staples
Newell Rubbermaid	Supplies Network

HISTORICAL FINANCIALS

Company Type: Public

Income Statement

FYE: December 31

	REVENUE ($ mil.)	NET INCOME ($ mil.)	NET PROFIT MARGIN	EMPLOYEES
12/14	5,327	119	2.2%	6,500
12/13	5,085	123	2.4%	6,100
12/12	5,080	111	2.2%	6,100
12/11	5,005	109	2.2%	5,950
12/10	4,832	112	2.3%	5,950
Annual Growth	2.5%	1.4%	—	2.2%

2014 Year-End Financials

Debt ratio: 30.12%
Return on equity: 14.18%
Cash ($ mil.): 20
Current ratio: 2.47
Long-term debt ($ mil.): 713
No. of shares (mil.): 38
Dividends
  Yield: 1.3%
  Payout: 18.3%
Market value ($ mil.): 1,632

	STOCK PRICE ($) FY Close	P/E High/Low	PER SHARE ($)		
			Earnings	Dividends	Book Value
12/14	42.16	15 12	3.05	0.56	22.11
12/13	45.89	15 10	3.06	0.56	20.78
12/12	30.99	13 9	2.73	0.53	18.31
12/11	32.56	30 10	2.42	0.52	16.72
12/10	63.81	28 18	2.34	0.00	16.45
Annual Growth	(9.8%)	— —	6.9%	—	7.7%

Eversource Energy

Eversource Energy (formerly Northeast Utilities) uses Yankee ingenuity power and gas to keep customers happy. The largest utility in New England Eversource operates six electric and gas utilities in Connecticut Massachusetts and New Hampshire and serves more than 3.6 million electric and gas customers. It has 3880 miles of power transmission lines 48486 miles electric distribution lines and 6400 miles of gas distribution lines. Subsidiaries include Connecticut Light and Power Public Service Company of New Hampshire and Western Massachusetts Electric. Eversource's Yankee Gas supplies natural gas to 220000 customers in 71 cities and towns in Connecticut.

HISTORY

In 1966 three old intertwined New England utilities merged. One was The Hartford Electric Light Company (HELCO) founded in 1883 by Austin Dunham in Hartford Connecticut. In 1915 the company signed the first power exchange agreement in the US with Connecticut Power (CP) which HELCO acquired in 1920.

The second founded in 1886 was Western Massachusetts Electric (WMECO) which merged with Western Counties in the 1930s to become WMECO. The third was Connecticut Light and Power (CL&P). Founded as Rocky River Power in 1905 it took the CL&P name in 1917. In 1929 it built the US's first large-scale pumped-storage hydroelectric plant.

In the 1950s HELCO formed Yankee Atomic Electric with CL&P WMECO and others to build an experimental nuclear reactor. In 1965 members of the group began jointly building the Connecticut Yankee nuke (on line in 1968). After years of cooperation CL&P HELCO and WMECO merged in 1966 and Northeast Utilities (NU) was born. It was the first multistate utility holding company created since the Public Utility Holding Company Act of 1935 had broken up the old utility giants. Holyoke Water Power joined NU the following year.

The 1970s energy crisis spurred NU to continue building nukes including Maine Yankee Vermont Yankee and two Millstone units. But by the 1980s construction delays had raised the cost of the final unit Millstone 3.

Regulators forced CL&P to spin off its gas utility Yankee Energy System in 1989. The next year NU acquired bankrupt utility Public Service Company of New Hampshire (PSNH) and its new Seabrook nuke. (PSNH emerged from bankruptcy in 1991.)

The 1995 shutdown of Millstone 1 began NU's nuclear troubles. In 1996 regulators closed all of its nukes except Seabrook because of safety concerns and NU mothballed Connecticut Yankee. The next year Michael Morris replaced CEO Bernard Fox who left after federal regulators ordered NU to comply with regulations and fix management problems —NU managers had routinely retaliated against whistleblowers —the first time a utility had been given such an order. New managers came in including a former whistleblower but NU couldn't avoid a record-setting $2.1 million fine. NU received permission to restart the Millstone units in 1998-99. But it had to absorb the $1 billion in power replacement associated with the shutdown.

Meanwhile as deregulation loomed NU created a retail marketer (now Select Energy) and a telecommunications arm (Mode 1 Communications) in 1996. Two years later retail competition began in Massachusetts and deregulation legislation was passed in Connecticut (deregulation went into effect there in 2000).

In 1999 NU sold its Massachusetts plants to New York's Consolidated Edison and auctioned off its non-nuclear plants in Connecticut to its subsidiary Northeast Generation and Northern States Power (now Xcel Energy). NU agreed to plead guilty to 25 federal felony counts and pay $10 million in penalties for polluting water near Millstone and lying to regulators.

That year Consolidated Edison agreed to buy NU for $3.3 billion in cash and stock and $3.9 billion in assumed debt. The deal broke down in 2001 however; Con Edison charged NU with misrepresenting information about power-supply contracts and NU charged Con Edison with improperly attempting to renegotiate the terms of the acquisition.

Bringing an old family member home NU bought Yankee Energy System for $679 million in 2000. Later that year Dominion Resources which had helped NU restart Millstone 2 and Millstone 3 (Millstone 1 had been taken out of service) agreed to buy the Millstone complex for $1.3 billion. The sale closed in 2001.

Also in 2001 NU subsidiary Select Energy bought Niagara Mohawk's energy marketing unit NU sold the distribution business of its Holyoke Water Power utility to the City of Holyoke for $18 million and retail electric competition began in New Hampshire. The company agreed to sell CL&P's 10% stake in the Vermont Yankee nuclear facility to Entergy in 2001; the deal was completed the following year.

NU sold its 40% interest in the Seabrook Nuclear Generating facility in 2002 to FPL Group.

In 2006 NU sold nonregulated subsidiary Select Energy which marketed and traded energy to wholesale and retail customers to Hess Corporation. That year the company also sold its competitive generation assets in Connecticut and Massachusetts to Energy Capital Partners for $1.34 billion.

In 2007 Connecticut Light and Power Company completed the installation of electric service to Yan-

kee Gas Services Company's new liquefied natural gas facility in Waterbury.

To give better access and service to its customers in 2009 NU relocated its headquarters from Berlin Connecticut to a larger building in downtown Hartford.

The 2012 acquisition of NSTAR (with 1.1 million power and 300000 gas customers) for $4.2 billion boosted the financial resources of Eversource to pay for planned transmission projects aimed at bringing cleaner power from northern New England and Canada to population centers in southern New England. The "merger of equals" (NSTAR and Eversource) created a major energy player in the US Northeast which serves more than half the total utility customers in New England. NSTAR shareholders hold about 44% of the expanded company.

EXECUTIVES

EVP and COO, Werner J. Schweiger, age 55, $538,950 total compensation

EVP and CFO NU CL&P NSTAR Electric NSTAR Gas PSNH WMECO Yankee Gas and NUSCO, James J. (Jim) Judge, age 59, $587,975 total compensation

Chairman President and CEO and Chairman CL&P NSTAR Electric NSTAR Gas PSNH WMECO and Yankee Ga, Thomas J. (Tom) May, age 68, $1,196,325 total compensation

EVP Enterprise Energy Strategy and Business Development, Leon J. (Lee) Olivier, age 66, $617,225 total compensation

EVP and Chief Administrative Officer NU CL&P NSTAR Electric NSTAR Gas PSNH WMECO Yankee Gas and NUSCO, David R. McHale, age 54, $587,643 total compensation

Senior Vice President, Gregory Butler

Vice President Operations Executive, Robert S (Bob) Coates

Auditors: Deloitte & Touche LLP

LOCATIONS

HQ: Eversource Energy
   300 Cadwell Drive, Springfield, MA 01104
Phone: 413 785-5871
Web: www.eversource.com

PRODUCTS/OPERATIONS

2014 Sales

	$ mil.	% of total
Utilities		
Distribution		
Electric	5,663	73
Gas	1,007	13
Transmission	1,018	13
Competitive businesses --		
Other & adjustments	53	1
Total	**7,741**	**100**

Selected Subsidiaries

The Northeast Utilities System (regulated utilities)
   Connecticut Light and Power Company (CL&P electric utility)
   NSTAR Electric (electric utility Massachusetts)
   Public Service Company of New Hampshire (PSNH electric utility)
   Western Massachusetts Electric Company (WMECO electric utility)
   Yankee Energy System Inc. (natural gas utility Connecticut)
   Yankee Gas Services Company (retail natural gas service)
Other Operations
   Northeast Utilities Service Company (administrative services for NU subsidiaries)
   NU Enterprises Inc. (nonutility operations)
   Hopkinton LNG Corp. (LNG services)

COMPETITORS

AEP
Avangrid
Bangor Hydro-Electric
Con Edison
Green Mountain Power
Massachusetts Municipal Wholesale Electric
National Grid USA
NiSource
PG&E Corporation
Public Service Enterprise Group
Southern Company
USPowerGen
Unitil

HISTORICAL FINANCIALS

Company Type: Public

Income Statement

	REVENUE ($ mil.)	NET INCOME ($ mil.)	NET PROFIT MARGIN	EMPLOYEES
12/14	7,741	819	10.6%	8,248
12/13	7,301	786	10.8%	8,697
12/12	6,273	525	8.4%	8,842
12/11	4,465	394	8.8%	6,063
12/10	4,898	387	7.9%	6,182
Annual Growth	**12.1%**	**20.6%**	**—**	**7.5%**

FYE: December 31

2014 Year-End Financials

Debt ratio: 32.94%
Return on equity: 8.37%
Cash ($ mil.): 38
Current ratio: 0.86
Long-term debt ($ mil.): 8,606
No. of shares (mil.): 316
Dividends
   Yield: 2.9%
   Payout: 64.3%
Market value ($ mil.): 16,965

	STOCK PRICE ($) FY Close	P/E High/Low	PER SHARE ($) Earnings	Dividends	Book Value
12/14	53.52	22 16	2.58	1.57	31.47
12/13	42.39	18 16	2.49	1.47	30.49
12/12	39.08	21 18	1.89	1.60	29.41
12/11	36.07	16 14	2.22	1.10	22.65
12/10	31.88	15 11	2.19	1.03	22.26
Annual Growth	**13.8%**	**— —**	**4.2%**	**11.2%**	**9.0%**

Exelon Corp.

The City of Brotherly Love meets the Windy City and The Greatest City in America in utility and power generating holding company Exelon. It distributes electricity and gas to 7.8 million customers in Illinois Maryland and Pennsylvania through subsidiaries Baltimore Gas and Electric Commonwealth Edison and PECO Energy. Exelon Generation holds power assets of 32265 MW (19316 MW of which is nuclear). Exelon Power Team is a top wholesale energy marketer and Exelon Energy markets retail power and offers other energy-related services. The company's Constellation unit serves 2.5 million retail customers. In a major expansion in 2014 Exelon agreed to buy Pepco for $6.8 billion.

HISTORY

Thomas Dolan and local investors formed the Brush Electric Light Company of Philadelphia in 1881 to provide street and commercial lighting. Competitors sprang up and in 1885 Brush merged with the United States Electric Lighting Company of Pennsylvania to form a secret "electric trust" or holding company. Dolan became president in 1886 and bought four other utilities.

In 1895 Martin Maloney formed Pennsylvania Heat Light and Power to consolidate the city's electric companies. By the next year it had acquired among other businesses Columbia Electric Light Philadelphia Edison and the electric trust. In 1899 a new firm National Electric challenged Maloney by acquiring neighboring rival Southern Electric Light. Before retiring Maloney negotiated the merger of the two firms forming Philadelphia Electric in 1902.

Demand rose rapidly into the 1920s fueled in part by the company's promotion of electric appliances. In 1928 the year after it completed the Conowingo Hydroelectric Station Philadelphia Electric was absorbed by the much larger United Gas Improvement. United Gas avoided large layoffs during the Depression but passage of the Public Utility Holding Company Act (PUHCA) in 1935 sounded its death knell. (PUHCA was repealed in 2005.) In 1943 the SEC forced United Gas to divest Philadelphia Electric.

Philadelphia Electric built several plants in the 1950s and 1960s in response to a postwar electricity boom. A small experimental nuclear reactor was completed at Peach Bottom Pennsylvania in 1967 and in 1974 the company placed two nuclear units in service at the plant. The Salem (New Jersey) nuke (Unit 1) followed in 1977. The company relied on these plants during the OPEC oil crisis. Another one Limerick Unit 1 began operations in 1986 and Unit 2 went on line in 1990 but the Peach Bottom plant was shut down from 1989 to 1991 because of management problems (later resolved).

The company began reorganizing in 1993 and changed its name the next year to PECO Energy Company. It also sold Maryland retail subsidiary Conowingo Power retaining the hydroelectric plant. In 1995 rival PP&L rejected PECO's acquisition bid citing PECO's nuclear liabilities.

A year later PECO teamed with AT&T Wireless to offer PCS in Philadelphia (service was launched in 1997). EnergyOne a national venture formed in 1997 by PECO UtiliCorp United (now Aquila) and AT&T offered consumers a package of power phone and Internet services on one bill. However the slow deregulation process caused the venture to fail.

PECO also joined with British Energy in 1997 to form AmerGen hoping to buy nukes at rock-bottom prices from utilities eager to unload them. AmerGen purchased three nuclear facilities in 1999 and 2000: Unit 1 of the Three Mile Island (Pennsylvania) facility; a plant in Clinton Illinois; and an Oyster Creek (New Jersey) location.

In 1999 PECO announced plans to acquire Chicago's Unicom the parent company of Commonwealth Edison (ComEd). After the deal was completed in 2000 the combined company took the name Exelon and established its headquarters in Chicago.

Pennsylvania's utility markets were fully deregulated in 2000. To expand its power generation business Exelon that year bought 49.9% of Sithe Energies for $682 million. In 2001 Exelon agreed to buy two gas-fired power plants (2300 MW) in Texas from TXU for $443 million; the deal was completed in 2002.

Also in 2002 Exelon purchased Sithe Energies' stakes in six New England power plants with 2000 MW of capacity (plus 2400 MW under construction) for $543 million plus the assumption of $1.15 billion in debt. The company also sold its Philadelphia PCS venture interest to former partner AT&T Wireless Services (now part of AT&T Mobility). Sithe Energies was sold to Dynegy in 2005 for $135 million.

To focus on core utility operations the company sold its infrastructure construction business InfraSource and its facility and infrastructure management business Exelon Solutions. Exelon then completed the sale of its interest in telecommunications joint venture PECO TelCove which provides voice and data services to its partner TelCove and sold its district heating and cooling division (Thermal Chicago).

In 2008 in a move to expand its geographic reach Exelon made a $6.2 billion bid to buy NRG Energy. Though the offer to buy NRG met with resistance Exelon had kept up its pursuit of the company. Toward the end of 2008 it announced an exchange offer for NRG's shares. By the expiration date of the offer early the next year it had acquired just more than 50% of those shares. In addition to announcing another extension of the offer Exelon said it hoped NRG's Board would allow it to do due diligence and begin negotiations for an acquisition. But an NRG proxy vote rejection in 2009 led Exelon to terminate its offer.

In 2010 in a bid to grow its renewable energy segment and lower its carbon emissions the company acquired wind power developer John Deere Renewables for about $860 million. The deal added 735 MW of operating wind power capacity (and 230 MW under development) to Exelon's generation assets.

To meet stricter environmental regulations the company has been bulking up its non-fossil fuel generating assets. Growing its cleaner-burning plant fleet in Texas in 2011 the company bought Wolf Hollow a 720 MW combined-cycle natural gas-fired power plant in north Texas from Sequent Wolf Hollow for $305 million.

Expanding its green energy assets that year the company also acquired Antelope Valley Solar Ranch One from First Solar. The 230-MW solar power project is under development in northern Los Angeles County. The $1.4 billion investment complements Constellation Energy's solar power holdings and marks Exelon's first move into the California merchant power market.

In 2012 the company bought Constellation Energy in a $7.9 billion stock deal. The acquisition part of an industry-wide consolidation trend gives Exelon access to Constellation's major retail operations in Maryland enabling it to grow its retail profile.

The US Department of Justice required Exelon and Constellation to divest three electricity generating plants in Maryland to proceed with the merger. It contended that combining the companies' assets would potentially enable the merged firm to raise wholesale electricity prices and reduce output.

EXECUTIVES

President and CEO, Christopher M. (Chris) Crane, age 56, $1,200,000 total compensation
President Exelon Power, Ronald J. (Ron) DeGregorio, age 52
EVP; COO Excelon Generation, Michael J. Pacilio, age 54
SEVP and CFO, Jonathan W. (Jack) Thayer, age 43, $717,597 total compensation
President and CEO ComEd, Anne R. Pramaggiore, age 56
SEVP and Chief Commercial Officer and President and CEO Exelon Generation, Kenneth W. (Ken) Cornew, age 49, $815,769 total compensation
EVP and CEO Constellation, Joseph (Joe) Nigro
EVP and General Counsel, Darryl M. Bradford, age 59
SEVP and Chief Strategy Officer, William A. (Bill) Von Hoene, age 61, $736,710 total compensation

President and Chief Nuclear Officer Exelon Nuclear, Bryan C. Hanson, age 49
EVP; President and CEO PECO, Craig L. Adams, age 62
CEO Baltimore Gas and Electric, Calvin G. Butler, age 44
EVP and Chief Enterprise Risk Officer, Paymon Aliabadi
EVP Governmental and Regulatory Affairs and Public Policy, Joseph Dominguez, age 51
SEVP and CEO Exelon Utilities, Denis P. OABrien, age 54, $761,534 total compensation
SVP and Chief Information and Innovation Officer, Sunil (Sonny) Garg, age 48
SVP and Chief Supply Officer, M. Bridget Reidy
Senior Vice President Operations Support, Christopher Mudrick
Vice President, Chris Symonds
Vice President Congressional Affairs, David C Brown
Vice President Corporate Communications, Laura Duda
Vice President Licensing and Regulatory Affairs, Keith Jury
Vice President, Dennis Murphy
Vice President, Dean Hengst
Vice President Regulatory Affairs and General Counsel PECO Energy, Paul R Bonney
Chairman, Mayo A. Shattuck, age 60
Auditors: PricewaterhouseCoopers LLP

LOCATIONS

HQ: Exelon Corp.
10 South Dearborn Street, P.O. Box 805379, Chicago, IL 60680-5379
Phone: 800 483-3220
Web: www.exeloncorp.com

PRODUCTS/OPERATIONS

2014 Sales

	$ mil.	% of total
Generation	17,393	59
ComEd	4,564	15
PECO	3,094	11
BGE	3,165	11
Other	1,285	4
Adjustments	(2072)	-
Total	**27,429**	**100**

Selected Operating Units Subsidiaries and Affiliates

Exelon Energy Delivery
Baltimore Gas and Electric (BGE electric and gas utility)
   Commonwealth Edison Company (ComEd electric utility)
   PECO Energy Company (PECO electric and gas utility)
Constellation
Exelon Generation Company LLC
   Exelon Power
   Exelon Hydro
   Exelon Solar
   Exelon Wind
   Exelon Power Team
   Exelon Energy (nonregulated retail power sales)
   Exelon Nuclear (nuclear power generation)
Exelon Transmission Company

COMPETITORS

AES	Dynegy
Alliant Energy	Entergy
Ameren	FirstEnergy
American Transmission	Green Mountain Energy
CenterPoint Energy	NextEra Energy
Delmarva Power	Nicor Gas
Dominion Resources	PPL Corporation
Duke Energy	UGI
Duquesne Light Holdings	

HISTORICAL FINANCIALS

Company Type: Public

Income Statement

FYE: December 31

	REVENUE ($ mil.)	NET INCOME ($ mil.)	NET PROFIT MARGIN	EMPLOYEES
12/15	29,447	2,250	7.6%	29,762
12/14	27,429	1,820	6.6%	28,993
12/13	24,888	1,729	6.9%	25,829
12/12	23,489	1,171	5.0%	26,057
12/11	18,924	2,495	13.2%	19,267
Annual Growth	11.7%	(2.6%)	—	11.5%

2015 Year-End Financials

Debt ratio: 27.59%
Return on equity: 9.22%
Cash ($ mil.): 6,502
Current ratio: 1.68
Long-term debt ($ mil.): 24,286

No. of shares (mil.): 919
Dividends
  Yield: 4.4%
  Payout: 55.1%
Market value ($ mil.): 25,546

	STOCK PRICE ($) FY Close	P/E High/Low	PER SHARE ($) Earnings	Dividends	Book Value
12/15	27.77	15 10	2.54	1.24	28.25
12/14	37.08	20 14	1.88	1.24	26.52
12/13	27.39	19 13	2.00	1.46	26.74
12/12	29.74	30 20	1.42	2.10	25.40
12/11	43.37	12 11	3.75	2.10	21.82
Annual Growth	(10.5%)	— —	(9.3%)	(12.3%)	6.7%

Exelon Generation Co LLC

Exelon Generation Company has built an excellent reputation by generating electricity. The company a subsidiary of Exelon Corporation is one of the largest electric wholesale and retail power generation companies in the US. In 2013 Exelon Generation had a generation capacity of more than 44560 MW (primarily nuclear but also fossil-fired and hydroelectric and other renewable energy-based plants). Subsidiary Exelon Nuclear operates the largest fleet of nuclear power plants in the US. Exelon Generation's Exelon Power unit oversees a fleet of more than 100 fossil- and renewable-fueled plants (more than 15875 MW of capacity) in Illinois Maryland Massachusetts Pennsylvania and Texas. Geographic ReachThe Mid-Atlantic represents operations in the eastern half of PJM and accounted for 37% of Exelon Generation's generating capacity in 2013; Midwest (western half of PJM the entire US footprint of MISO34%); New England (the operations within the ISO-NE 8%); New York (ISO-NY 3%); ERCOT (Texas) 12%; and Other areas 6%).The Mid-Atlantic region includes Pennsylvania New Jersey Maryland Virginia West Virginia Delaware the District of Columbia and parts of North Carolina. Midwest includes portions of Illinois Indiana Ohio Michigan Kentucky and Tennessee; and the United States footprint of MISO excluding MISO's Southern Region which covers all or most of North Dakota South Dakota Nebraska Minnesota Iowa Wisconsin and the remaining parts of Illinois Indiana Michigan and Ohio not covered by PJM; and parts of Montana Missouri and Kentucky.New England represents the operations within ISO-NE covering the states of Connecticut Maine Massachusetts New Hampshire Rhode Island and Vermont. New York represents

the operations within ISO-NY which covers the state of New York in its entirety. ERCOT represents operations within Electric Reliability Council of Texas covering most of the state of Texas. "Other Regions" is an aggregate of other geographic regions not considered individually significant.OperationsThe company operates as an integrated business leveraging its owned and contracted electric generation capacity to market and sell power to wholesale and retail customers. It has ownership interests in eleven nuclear generating stations currently in service consisting of 19 units with an aggregate of 17263 MW of capacity. It also owns a 50% interest in CENG a joint venture with EDF. CENG is governed by a board of ten directors five of which are appointed by Generation and five by EDF.Sales and MarketingExelon Generation's customers include distribution utilities municipalities cooperatives financial institutions and commercial industrial governmental and residential customers in competitive markets. The company also sells natural gas and renewable energy and other energy-related products and services and engages in natural gas exploration and production activities.Financial PerformanceThe company's revenues increased by 8% in 2013 primarily due to increased capacity prices and higher nuclear volume partially offset by lower realized energy prices higher nuclear fuel costs and lower mark-to-market gains.Net income increased by 90% in 2013 primarily due to higher revenues net of purchased power and fuel expense lower operating and maintenance expense and higher earnings from Exelon Generation's interest in CENG; partially offset by impairment of certain generating assets and higher depreciation costs property taxes and interest expenses.StrategyExelon Generation leverages owned and contracted electric generation capacity to market and sell power wholesale. The company's integrated business operations include the physical delivery and marketing of power obtained through its generation capacity and through long-term intermediate-term and short-term contracts. Exelon Generation maintains an effective supply strategy through ownership of generation assets and power purchase and lease agreements. The company has also contracted for access to additional generation through bilateral long-term power agreements.Exelon Generation's electricity generation strategy is to pursue opportunities that provide generation to load matching and that diversify the generation fleet by expanding Generation's regional and technological footprint. The company leverages its energy generation portfolio to ensure delivery of energy to both wholesale and retail customers under long-term and short-term contracts and in wholesale power markets.In 2012 a subsidiary of Exelon Generation sold three coal-fired plants (Brandon Shores and H.A. Wagner generating station in Anne Arundel County Maryland and the C.P. Crane plant in Baltimore County Maryland) to Raven Power Holdings LLC a subsidiary of Riverstone Holdings LLC to comply with certain of the regulatory approvals required by the company's merger with Constellation Energy for net proceeds of $371 million which resulted in a pre-tax loss of $272 million.Exelon Nuclear operates the largest nuclear fleet in the US (10 stations with 17 nuclear units) and has about 20% of the industry's total capacity. Exelon Generation has submitted an application to the Nuclear Regulatory Commission to build a new nuclear generating facility in Texas. The company hasn't made the decision to build the facility but wanted to get a start on the potentially onerous process. The last license to result in the construction of a new nuclear facility in the US was granted in 1973. However the Fukushima nuclear plant disaster in early 2011 placed nuclear power expansion plans

under serious scrutiny from regulators.Mergers and AcquisitionsIn a major move to grow its retail operations in 2012 parent Exelon Corporation bought Constellation Energy in a $7.9 billion stock deal. The purchase of Constellation Energy (which gets 17% of its power from nuclear plants) helped the company boost its nuclear-generated power plant assets.Company BackgroundGrowing its cleaner-burning plant fleet in Texas in 2011 Exelon Corporation bought the 720 MW capacity Wolf Hollow plant in north Texas from Sequent Wolf Hollow for $305 million.In 2010 to grow its renewable energy unit the company acquired wind power developer John Deere Renewables for about $860 million. The purchase adds 735 MW of operating wind power capacity to its generation capacity.

EXECUTIVES

Svp And President And Chief Nuclear Officer Exelon Nuclear, Bryan C Hanson, age 50
Auditors: PricewaterhouseCoopers LLP

LOCATIONS

HQ: Exelon Generation Co LLC
  300 Exelon Way, Kennett Square, PA 19348-2473
Phone: 610 765-5959
Web: www.exeloncorp.com

PRODUCTS/OPERATIONS

2013 Sales

	% of total
Mid-Atlantic	33
Midwest	27
New England	8
ERCOT	8
Other Regions	6
New York	5
Others	13
Total	**100**

COMPETITORS

AES	Duke Energy
AMP	NextEra Energy
Buckeye Power	Wolverine Power Supply
CMS Energy	

HISTORICAL FINANCIALS

Company Type: Public

Income Statement

FYE: December 31

	REVENUE ($ mil.)	NET INCOME ($ mil.)	NET PROFIT MARGIN	EMPLOYEES
12/14	17,393	835	4.8%	14,370
12/13	15,630	1,070	6.8%	11,973
12/12	14,437	562	3.9%	12,116
12/11	10,308	1,771	17.2%	9,586
12/10	10,025	1,972	19.7%	9,595
Annual Growth	14.8%	(19.3%)	—	10.6%

2014 Year-End Financials

Debt ratio: 17.08%—
Return on equity: 6.56%
Cash ($ mil.): 780
Current ratio: 1.71
Long-term debt ($ mil.): 7,652

Dividends
  Yield: —
  Payout: —
Market value ($ mil.): —

Expedia Inc

These days expediting your vacation begins online. As the market leader in online travel services (ahead of rival Priceline) Expedia offers online trip-planning tools that allow users to book airline tickets hotel reservations car rentals cruises and vacation packages. Its portfolio of brands includes flagship Expedia.com accommodations manager Hotels.com travel discounter Hotwire travel booker Orbitz luxury package provider Classic Vacations and Chinese travel service eLong among others. Launched in 1996 the company serves travelers in North America Europe and the Asia/Pacific region. In late 2015 Expedia purchased vacation rental site operator HomeAway.

Operations

Expedia operates through two reportable segments: Leisure and Egencia. Its primary business which generates 93% of revenue is the Leisure segment. Leisure provides a full range of travel and advertising services to customers. It does so through several brands including Expedia.com and Hotels.com in the US and localized Expedia and Hotels.com websites globally as well as Expedia Affiliate Network Hotwire.com Venere eLong Orbitz and Classic Vacations.

The company provides travelers with access to nearly 435000 hotels through its websites that include Trivago and some 400 airlines in about 200 countries worldwide. About 70% of Expedia's revenue came from the booking of hotel reservations in 2014 with 8% from airline ticket sales.

The Egencia segment which accounts for the 8% of revenue not from Leisure provides managed travel services to corporate customers in North America Europe and the Asia/Pacific region.

Geographic Reach

Based in Bellevue Washington Expedia has offices throughout the Americas Europe and Asia/Pacific regions and operates in about 200 countries. The US accounts for about 53% of revenue.

Financial Performance

Expedia's revenue growth trajectory continued in 2014 increasing about 21% to $5.76 billion. Worldwide hotel revenue rose 18% in 2014 driven by a 26% increase in room nights stayed. Worldwide air revenue was up 22% with a 28% increase in air tickets sold. Expedia also had robust growth in its corporate travel business.

Net income soared like Expedia customers on a trip to Hawaii rising 71% to $398 million in 2014. Besides the sales growth Expedia benefited income from interest expenses and provision for taxes including absence of acquisition-related charges.

Strategy

International customers accounted for 47% of 2014 revenue up significantly from 30% in 2008. Building its image globally and expanding its brand portfolio have been key in its efforts to reach a wide slice of consumers (including budget-conscious luxury and business travelers). Expedia gained more international exposure with its agreement to add Sixt's international rental vehicle fleet to its listings.

Expedia has expanded in India by establishing a global technology center in Gurgaon to operate alongside its 42000-sq.-ft Indian subsidiary office there. The center will house several of the region's functions such as sales and marketing research and development and travel supply support services activities in support of the Expedia brand Expedia.co.in the Hotels.com-brand and the Egencia businesses. The Gurgaon center is one of Expedia's largest facilities outside of Bellevue Washington. Activities at the center include developing travel applications for local and global markets as well as company-wide technology development initiatives across all brands and platforms.

Mergers and Acquisitions

In 2015 Expedia bought key competitor Travelocity from its parent Sabre Corporation for $280 million in cash. The acquisition cemented a relationship Expedia and Travelocity had since 2013 in which Expedia provided technology platforms for Travelocity's US and Canadian websites and access to its supply and customer service program. Next it grabbed competitor Orbitz Worldwide for about $1.6 billion to bring its travel-booking technology aboard. Later in the year Expedia paid about $4 billion for "alternative accommodations" company HomeAway.

Expedia has also grown by focusing on international expansion as an increasing portion of its revenue is generated by bookings outside the US. To that end in November 2014 Expedia acquired Australia-based Wotif.com Holdings for A$703 million ($613.7 million). Wotif.com is an online travel company offering hotel rooms airline tickets and vacation packages in about 70 countries.

In July 2014 Expedia acquired Auto Escape Group a leading online car rental reservation company with offices in France and Germany to add to its CarRentals.com business.

In 2013 Expedia purchased a majority stake in trivago a European travel site based in Dusseldorf Germany for about €477 million ($632 million). Trivago is an online metasearch site which compares hotel rates from more than 600000 hotels on 140-plus booking sites worldwide.

Company Background

Originally a division of Microsoft Expedia was sold to IAC/InterActiveCorp which acquired the computer maker's majority stake in 2002 and the minority interest it did not already own in 2003. Two years later IAC spun off Expedia into a separate publicly traded firm.

EXECUTIVES

President CEO and Director, Dara Khosrowshahi, age 45, $1,000,000 total compensation
President eCommerce Platform, J. Tucker Moodey
President Hotwire Group, Henrik V. Kjellberg, age 45
President Hotels.com Brand and Venere.com, Johan Svanstrom, age 44
President Expedia Lodging Partner Services, Cyril Ranque
EVP Human Resources, Connie Symes
President Egencia, Rob Greyber
EVP Operations and CFO, Mark D. Okerstrom, $644,712 total compensation
EVP General Counsel and Secretary, Robert Dzielak, $450,000 total compensation
President Brand Expedia Group, Aman Bhutani, age 39
Vice President Of Employee Engagement, Kristin Graham
Vice President, Scott Grove
Senior Vice President Marketing Packages And Canada, Sean C Shannon
Vice President Market Management, Ariane Gorin
Vice President And Associate Corporate Counsel, Angela Niemann
Vice President Global Supply Operations, Sean Huberty
Senior Vice President Head Of Corporate, Eric Hart
Vice President Sales Egencia, Wendy Aird
Vice President Finance Egencia, Paolo De Ruggiero
Vice President Supplier Relations, Chris Vukelich
Vice President Emerging Markets Emea, Fabrizio Giulio
Vice President Associate General Counsel, Ronen Elad
Vice President And General Manager, Tom Colandrea
Vice President Transport Americas, Julie Kyse
Vice President Global Financial Operations, Frank Zijlstra
Vice President Transport Emea, Ian Davies
Vice President Planning and Talent Analytics, Dave Sutherland
Senior Vice President Egencia Americas, Mark Hollyhead
Vice President Business Initiatives and Development, Nicolas (Nick) Dagousset
Vice President Of Enterprise Information Security, Darren Challey
Senior Vice President Sales, Bruce Freeman
Vice President Human Resources, Nikki Krish
Vice President of Finance, Bank Rec
Vice Chairman, Victor A. Kaufman, age 71
Chairman, Barry Diller, age 73
Auditors: Ernst & Young LLP

LOCATIONS

HQ: Expedia Inc
333 108th Avenue N.E., Bellevue, WA 98004
Phone: 425 679-7200
Web: www.expediainc.com

2014 Sales

	$ mil.	% of total
US	3,046	53
Other countries	2,716	47
Total	**5,763**	**100**

PRODUCTS/OPERATIONS

2014 Sales

	$ mil.	% of total
Merchant	3,749	65
Agency	1,535	27
Advertising & media	479	8
Total	**5,763**	**100**

2014 Sales

	$ mil.	% of total
Leisure	5,363	93
Egencia	400	7
Total	**5,763**	**100**

Reportable Segments
Leisure
  CarRentals.com
  Classic Vacations
eLong (Chi
  Expedia.com
  Expedia Affiliate Network
  Expedia CruiseShipCenters
  Expedia Local Expert
  Hotels.com
  Hotwire.com
  trivago
  Venere.com
Egencia

Selected Expedia.com Features

Airline flight information and booking
E-mail notifications
Frequent flyer management tools
Hotel reservations
Maps
Personalized Web page
Price matching tools
Vacation packages

Selected Subsidiaries

Classic Vacations LLC
eLong Inc. (66%)
Egencia LLC
Hotels.com L.P.
Hotwire Inc.
Interactive Affiliate Network LLC
Premier Getaways Inc.
travago GmbH
Travelscape LLC
Venere Net S.p.A.
WWTE Inc.

COMPETITORS

Amadeus IT	Priceline
American Express	Sabre
BCD Travel	Travelport
Carlson Wagonlit	Uniglobe Travel
GetThere	WorldRes
Pegasus Solutions	ebookers.com
Prestige Travel	last minute network

HISTORICAL FINANCIALS

Company Type: Public

Income Statement

FYE: December 31

	REVENUE ($ mil.)	NET INCOME ($ mil.)	NET PROFIT MARGIN	EMPLOYEES
12/15	6,672	764	11.5%	18,730
12/14	5,763	398	6.9%	18,210
12/13	4,771	232	4.9%	14,570
12/12	4,030	280	7.0%	12,330
12/11	3,449	472	13.7%	9,480
Annual Growth	17.9%	12.8%	—	18.6%

2015 Year-End Financials

Debt ratio: 20.65%
Return on equity: 23.00%
Cash ($ mil.): 1,676
Current ratio: 0.50
Long-term debt ($ mil.): 3,201

No. of shares (mil.): 150
Dividends
Yield: 0.6%
Payout: 13.2%
Market value ($ mil.): 18,677

	STOCK PRICE ($) FY Close	P/E High/Low		PER SHARE ($) Earnings	Dividends	Book Value
12/15	124.30	23	13	5.70	0.84	32.37
12/14	85.36	30	20	2.99	0.66	14.04
12/13	69.66	40	26	1.67	1.08	16.54
12/12	61.44	30	14	2.00	0.96	16.85
12/11	29.02	9	6	3.41	0.56	16.47
Annual Growth	43.9%	—	—	13.7%	10.7%	18.4%

Expeditors International of Washington, Inc.

Need your goods moved expeditiously? Freight forwarder Expeditors International of Washington can help. As a freight forwarder the company purchases air and ocean cargo space on a volume basis and resells that space to its customers at lower rates than they could obtain directly from the carriers. The company also acts as a customs broker for air and ocean freight shipped by its customers and offers supply chain management services. Customers include global businesses engaged in retailing/wholesaling electronics and manufacturing. Founder Peter Rose used $55000 in seed money to establish Expeditors International of Washington in 1979.

Geographic Reach

Expeditors operates from more than 250 facilities in about 60 countries. Regional international headquarters reside in Beirut London Sao Paulo and Shanghai. Half of the company's total sales come from Asia and the US accounts for around 25% of sales.

Operations

Expeditors' airfreight services segment 42% of revenue represents airlines as an agent in addition to providing freight consolidation for shippers. The consolidation of airfreight owned by several shippers is a valuable service because increasing the weight of an air shipment decreases its cost per pound/kilo or cubic inch/centimeter. Besides shipping on scheduled flights the company sometimes charters aircraft for the delivery of backlogs. By not purchasing its own aircraft the company avoids the costs of large capital expenditures and operating costs.

Ocean freight and ocean services 33% of revenue operates as a non-vessel operating common carrier which is a contractor with ocean shipping lines for a set amount of containers. Expeditors also obtains less-than container load freight to fill containers. The segment additionally provides such order management services as document management and SKU visibility. Similar to the strategy of the airfreight services segment the ocean freight segment does not own its own vessels.

Customs brokerage and other services 25% of revenue aids in the movement of shipments across borders by providing such services as adding up duties and taxes and arranging inspections. Beyond the border entry the segment provides additional services including warehousing product distribution and time-definite transportation. Expeditors provides these services not only for its own shipping customers but also for businesses that have not hired the company as a forwarder a class of client that accounts for a significant portion of the segment's revenue.

Sales and Marketing

Expeditors caters to its customers' supply chains. Therefore its marketing efforts target people in their company's logistics international and domestic transportation customs compliance and purchasing departments. It employs district managers who are responsible for marketing sales coordination and implementation in the area in which he or she is located. The company primarily targets the aviation and aerospace health care oil and energy and retail sectors.

Financial Performance

Expeditors saw its revenues climb 8% from $6.08 billion in 2013 to a record-setting $6.6 billion in 2014. Its profits also jumped 8% from nearly $349 million in 2013 to $377 million in 2014. After experiencing an increase in operating cash flow for 2013 Expeditors saw its operating cash flow decrease 3% to $395 million driven by an increase of outflows in accounts receivable caused by a spike in cash advances.

The historic growth for 2014 was driven by a 9% bump in airfreight services due to an increase in tonnage that was offset by lower sell rates in response to competitive market conditions in North America and Asia Pacific. Its ocean freight and ocean services operations increased due to an 11% rise in container volume. Expeditors in 2014 was also aided by a spike in customs brokerage and other services which was fueled by higher volumes from existing and new customers.

Strategy

In its rapid development Expeditors has favored internal growth over expansion by acquisition (though it has also selectively made some strategic acquisitions) and the company continues to open new offices and to invest in its information technology infrastructure. By eschewing acquisitions as its main form of growth the company has been able to develop a common hardware platform that lets the entire company use the same accounting and transportation software.

Going forward in 2015 and beyond the company is focused on diversifying its product mix through focused investments in its distribution services transcon and ocean export products. It also aims to diversify its market verticals by investing further in the pharmaceutical and automotive markets.

EXECUTIVES

EVP Europe, Timothy C. Barber, age 55, $100,000 total compensation
EVP Global Services, Eugene K. Alger, age 54
President Global Geographies and Operations, Philip M. Coughlin, age 54, $112,731 total compensation
SVP and CFO, Bradley S. (Brad) Powell, age 55, $100,000 total compensation
VP Imports, Rosanne Esposito, age 63
President Global Products, Daniel R. Wall, age 46
President and CEO, Jeffrey S. Musser, age 49, $100,000 total compensation
SVP Global Transcon Services, William A. Romberger
SVP The Americas, Richard H. Rostan
Regional VP Northwest Region North America, Jose A. Ubeda
SVP Global Distribution Services, Bruce J. Krebs
SVP and CIO, Christopher J. McClincy, age 40
SVP Africa Near/Middle East and Indian Subcontinent, Murali Krishnamurthy
SVP South Asia, Khoon Ling Lim
SVP Global Sales and Marketing, J. Jonathan Song
SVP North Asia, Allen Wang
Vice President Research and Development, Bret Backman
Chairman, Peter J. Rose, age 71
Auditors: KPMG LLP

LOCATIONS

HQ: Expeditors International of Washington, Inc.
1015 Third Avenue, 12th Floor, Seattle, WA 98104
Phone: 206 674-3400   **Fax:** 206 674-3459
Web: www.expeditors.com

2013 Sales

	$ mil.	% of total
Asia/Pacific	3,112	49
North America		
US	1,651	26
Other North America	227	4
Europe & Africa	888	14
Middle East & India	318	5
Latin America	107	2
Eliminations	(224.3)	-
Total	6,080	100

PRODUCTS/OPERATIONS

2013 Sales

	$ mil.	% of total
Airfreight services	2,633	43
Ocean freight & ocean services	1,958	32
Customs brokerage & other services	1,488	25
Total	6,080	100

Selected Products and Services

Air consolidation
Air forwarding
Cargo insurance
Customs
Distribution management
Ocean shipment
Purchase order management

COMPETITORS

APL Logistics	NYK Line
C.H. Robinson	Nippon Express
Worldwide	Panalpina
CEVA Logistics	Schenker
DHL	Sino-Global
FedEx Trade Networks	Sinotrans
Kintetsu World Express	UPS Supply Chain
Kuehne + Nagel	Solutions
International	Yamato Holdings
Mitsui-Soko	

HISTORICAL FINANCIALS
Company Type: Public

Income Statement
FYE: December 31

	REVENUE ($ mil.)	NET INCOME ($ mil.)	NET PROFIT MARGIN	EMPLOYEES
12/14	6,564	376	5.7%	14,670
12/13	6,080	348	5.7%	13,910
12/12	5,980	333	5.6%	13,700
12/11	6,150	385	6.3%	13,590
12/10	5,967	344	5.8%	12,880
Annual Growth	2.4%	2.3%	—	3.3%

2014 Year-End Financials

Debt ratio: —	No. of shares (mil.): 191
Return on equity: 19.07%	Dividends
Cash ($ mil.): 927	Yield: 1.4%
Current ratio: 2.33	Payout: 35.3%
Long-term debt ($ mil.): —	Market value ($ mil.): 8,550

	STOCK PRICE ($) FY Close	P/E High/Low	PER SHARE ($) Earnings	Dividends	Book Value
12/14	44.61	24 20	1.92	0.64	9.75
12/13	44.25	28 21	1.68	0.60	10.29
12/12	39.55	30 22	1.57	0.56	9.82
12/11	40.96	30 22	1.79	0.50	9.45
12/10	54.60	35 20	1.59	0.40	8.21
Annual Growth	(4.9%)	— —	4.8%	12.5%	4.4%

Express Scripts Holding Co

Express Scripts Holding knows that its customers like their medicine delivered quickly. The company administers more than a billion prescription drug benefits of tens of millions of health plan members in the US and Canada. Members have access to a network of about 69000 retail pharmacies as well as the company's own mail-order pharmacies. On behalf of its insurer clients Express Scripts processes claims for prescriptions designs drug benefit plans and offers such services as specialty drug delivery disease management programs and consumer drug data analysis. The firm merged with rival Medco Health Solutions in 2012 creating the largest pharmacy benefits management (PBM) company in North America.

HISTORY

In 1986 St. Louis-based drugstore chain Medicare-Glaser and HMO Sanus joined forces to create Express Scripts which would manage the HMO's prescription program. Express Scripts began managing third-party programs in 1988 and later developed other operations: mail-order prescription infusion therapy and vision services. New York Life bought Sanus and picked up the rest of Express Scripts in 1989 when Medicare-Glaser went into bankruptcy.

In 1992 Express Scripts went public. The next year the company formed subsidiary Practice Patterns Science to begin profiling providers and tracking treatment outcomes.

In the late 1990s the company continued to expand adding customers in Canada (1996) and building operations –with varying success. A 1996 expansion of its eye care management services

was abandoned in 1998. Express Scripts has traditionally grown through big-ticket contracts such as its 1997 pact with RightCHOICE Managed Care and through acquisitions. For example it boosted its PBM operations with its 1998 acquisition of Columbia/HCA's (now HCA) ValueRx unit and its 1999 purchase of SmithKline Beecham's Diversified Pharmaceutical Services (DPS); however it lost DPS's largest customer when United Healthcare began moving its more than 8 million enrollees to Merck-Medco in 2000.

The company suffered another setback in 2000 when it wrote down its 20% interest in online pharmacy PlanetRx. It had bought into the company in 1999 when dot-coms were soaring transferring its own Internet pharmacy operations (YourPharmacy.com) into the fledgling company. In 2001 Express Scripts joined rivals AdvancePCS and Merck-Medco (now Medco Health Solutions) to form RxHub to create technology to allow physicians to file prescriptions electronically.

In 2001 the firm began a bit of an acquisition spree. That year it bought Phoenix Marketing Group one of the biggest prescription drug sample fulfillment companies in the US. National Prescription Administrators a top private pharmacy benefits management company in the US joined the family in 2002. Express Scripts expanded its specialty pharmacy capabilities with the purchases of CuraScript a leading specialty pharmacy in 2004 and biopharmaceutical pharmacy and distributor Priority Healthcare in 2005.

In 2007 Express Scripts acquired ConnectYourCare a third-party administrator of consumer-directed health plans which link a high-deductible plan with tax-sheltered savings accounts. The company expanded again in 2008 by purchasing the pharmacy services division of Medical Services Company for $251 million. The acquired business specialized in managing pharmacy benefits for workers' compensation insurers.

To focus on its core distribution operations the company divested its CuraScript Infusion Pharmacy business which operated infusion therapy centers in six states to Walgreen's Option Care subsidiary in 2008.

In 2009 the company expanded its contract with the US Department of Defense adding a number of services beyond its existing management of the pharmacy network of the TRICARE military health care program. The contract now includes home delivery specialty pharmacy claims management and other integrated offerings.

The company grew substantially at the end of 2009 with the acquisition of NextRx the PBM business of Blue Cross Blue Shield (BCBS) licensee Anthem for about $4.7 billion. As part of the acquisition the company gained a 10-year contract to provide PBM services to Anthem the nation's largest health insurer. The purchase launched Express Scripts closer to its top two rivals (Medco and Caremark Pharmacy Services) by increasing its claims processing load from 500 million to more than 750 million prescriptions per year. It also enhanced the company's online generic drug and mail delivery service offerings. Revenues from Express Scripts' PBM division jumped from $23 billion in 2009 to $43 billion in 2010 primarily due to the NextRx acquisition.

Express Script has also divested some operations that it determined were not core to its growth initiatives. In late 2010 the company spun off its Rx Outreach business which provides access to prescription drugs for low income and uninsured patients. Following the spinoff Rx Outreach applied for federal recognition as a not-for-profit organization. Also in 2010 Express Scripts sold its Phoenix Marketing Group business which provided outsourced distribution and verification services to pharmaceutical manufacturers.

Through a 2012 $29 billion merger transaction with rival PBM Medco Express Scripts became the largest PBM in the US. Following the transaction the company changed its name to Express Scripts Holding.

EXECUTIVES

Chairman and CEO, George Paz, $1,235,385 total compensation
EVP and CFO, Eric R. Slusser
EVP and General Counsel, Keith J. Ebling, $660,385 total compensation
SVP and Chief Medical Officer, Steven (Steve) Miller
SVP Clinical Research & New Solutions, Glen D. Stettin
SVP and CIO, Gary Wimberly
President and CEO, Tim Wentworth, $815,303 total compensation
SVP Specialty and Supply Chain, David Norton
EVP Finance, Jim Havel
SVP Operations, Christine Houston
Auditors: PricewaterhouseCoopers LLP

LOCATIONS

HQ: Express Scripts Holding Co
One Express Way, St. Louis, MO 63121
Phone: 314 996-0900
Web: www.express-scripts.com

PRODUCTS/OPERATIONS

2014 Sales

	$ mil.	% of total
Product		
Network	58,468	58
Home delivery & specialty	38,663	38
Other	2,203	2
Service	1,582	2
Total	100,887	100

Selected Products and Services Pharmacy Benefits Management (PBM) Benefit design consultation Biopharma management Compliance management programs for members Drug formulary management Drug utilization review Electronic claims processing Fertility drug distributi

COMPETITORS

Aetna	Magellan Health
Allscripts	MedImpact
Argus	NationsHealth
BioScrip	Omnicare
CIGNA	OptumRx
Caremark Pharmacy Services	PharMerica
	Prime Therapeutics
First Health Group	Rite Aid
HealthTrans	Wal-Mart
Humana	Walgreen

HISTORICAL FINANCIALS
Company Type: Public

Income Statement
FYE: December 31

	REVENUE ($ mil.)	NET INCOME ($ mil.)	NET PROFIT MARGIN	EMPLOYEES
12/15	101,751	2,476	2.4%	25,900
12/14	100,887	2,007	2.0%	29,500
12/13	104,098	1,844	1.8%	29,975
12/12	93,858	1,312	1.4%	30,215
12/11	46,128	1,275	2.8%	13,120
Annual Growth	21.9%	18.0%	—	18.5%

Debt ratio: 29.29%
Return on equity: 13.23%
Cash ($ mil.): 3,186
Current ratio: 0.70
Long-term debt ($ mil.): 13,946

No. of shares (mil.): 676
Dividends
  Yield: —
  Payout: —
Market value ($ mil.): 59,168

	STOCK PRICE ($) FY Close	P/E High/Low	PER SHARE ($) Earnings	Dividends	Book Value
12/15	87.41	26 22	3.56	0.00	25.67
12/14	84.67	32 24	2.64	0.00	27.62
12/13	70.24	31 23	2.25	0.00	28.23
12/12	54.00	36 26	1.76	0.00	28.58
12/11	44.69	24 14	2.53	0.00	5.10
Annual Growth	18.3%	— —	8.9%	—	49.7%

Exxon Mobil Corp.

It's not necessarily the oil standard but Exxon Mobil is one of the world's largest integrated oil companies (with Royal Dutch Shell and BP). Exxon Mobil engages in oil and gas exploration production supply transportation and marketing. In 2014 it had proved reserves of 25.2 billion barrels of oil equivalent including major holdings in oil sands through Imperial Oil. Exxon Mobil's 30 refineries in 17 countries have a throughput capacity of 5.2 million barrels per day and lubricant basestock manufacturing capacity of 131000 barrels per day. It supplies refined products to more than 19000 gas stations worldwide (including almost 10000 in the US). Exxon Mobil is also a major petrochemical producer.

HISTORY

Exxon's 1999 acquisition of Mobil reunited two descendants of John D. Rockefeller's Standard Oil Company. Rockefeller a commodity trader started his first oil refinery in 1863 in Cleveland. Realizing that the price of oil at the well would shrink with each new strike Rockefeller chose to monopolize oil refining and transportation. In 1870 he formed Standard Oil and in 1882 he created the Standard Oil Trust which allowed him to set up new ostensibly independent companies including the Standard Oil Company of New Jersey (Jersey Standard); Rochester New York-based Vacuum Oil; and Standard Oil of New York (nicknamed Socony).

Initially capitalized at $70 million the Standard Oil Trust controlled 90% of the petroleum industry. In 1911 after two decades of political and legal wrangling the Supreme Court broke up the trust into 34 companies the largest of which was Jersey Standard.

Walter Teagle who became president of Jersey Standard in 1917 secretly bought half of Humble Oil of Texas (1919) and expanded operations into South America. In 1928 Jersey Standard joined in the Red Line Agreement which reserved most Middle East oil for a few companies. Teagle resigned in 1942 after the company was criticized for a prewar research pact with German chemical giant I.G. Farben.

The 1948 purchase of a 40% stake in Arabian American Oil Company combined with a 7% share of Iranian production bought in 1954 made Jersey Standard the world's #1 oil company at that time.

Meanwhile Vacuum Oil and Socony reunited in 1931 as Socony-Vacuum and the company adopted the Flying Red Horse (Pegasus —representing speed and power) as a trademark. The fast-growing diversifying company changed its name to Socony Mobil Oil in 1955 and became Mobil in 1976.

Other US companies still using the Standard Oil name objected to Jersey Standard's marketing in their territories as Esso (derived from the initials for Standard Oil). To end the confusion in 1972 Jersey Standard became Exxon a name change that cost $100 million.

Nationalization of oil assets by producing countries reduced Exxon's access to oil during the 1970s. Though it increased exploration that decade and the next Exxon's reserves shrank.

Oil tanker Exxon Valdez spilled some 11 million gallons of oil into Alaska's Prince William Sound in 1989. Exxon spent billions on the cleanup and in 1994 a federal jury in Alaska ordered the company to pay $5.3 billion in punitive damages to fishermen and others affected by the spill. (Exxon appealed and in 2001 the jury award was reduced to $2.5 billion and in 2008 to $507.5 million).

With the oil industry consolidating Exxon merged its worldwide oil and fuel additives business with that of Royal Dutch/Shell in 1996. The next year under FTC pressure Exxon agreed to run ads refuting claims that its premium gas enabled car engines to run more efficiently. Another PR disaster followed in 1998 when CEO Lee Raymond upset environmentalists by publicly questioning the global warming theory.

Still Exxon was unstoppable. It acquired Mobil for $81 billion in 1999; the new company had Raymond at the helm and Mobil's Lucio Noto as vice chairman. (Noto retired in 2001.) To get the deal done Exxon Mobil had to divest $4 billion in assets. It agreed to end its European gasoline and lubricants joint venture with BP and to sell more than 2400 gas stations in the US.

In 2000 Exxon Mobil sold 1740 East Coast gas stations to Tosco for $860 million. It sold a California refinery and 340 gas stations to Valero Energy for about $1 billion.

More than a decade after the Exxon Valdez wreaked environmental havoc off the shores of Alaska Exxon Mobil attempted to atone in 2001 by joining the California Fuel Cell Partnership a group studying possible alternatives to and supplements for gasoline in fuel-burning engines. That year Exxon Mobil also announced that it was proceeding with a $12 billion project (with Japanese Indian and Russian partners) to develop oil fields in the Russian Far East.

In 2002 Exxon Mobil sold its 50% stake in a Colombian coal mine as part of its strategy to divest coal assets in order to focus on its core businesses. That year the company sold its Chilean copper mining subsidiary (Disputada de Las Condes) to mineral giant Anglo American for $1.3 billion. Exxon Mobil sold its 3.7% stake in China Petroleum & Chemical Corp. (Sinopec) in early 2005. Later that year the company was ordered to pay $1.3 billion to about 10000 gas station owners for overcharges dating back to 1983; the average amount for each station owner was about $130000.

Shortages caused by Hurricane Katrina prompted Exxon Mobil to receive a 6 million barrel of crude oil loan primarily from the US Strategic Petroleum Reserve and increase gasoline production at its Baton Rouge facility.

Exiting the low-margin retail gasoline business in order to focus on its other operations in 2008 the company began to sell to distributors its remaining 820 company-owned US gas stations and another 1400 outlets operated by dealers.

In 2009 the company signed up to partner with TransCanada to jointly develop the $26 billion Alaska Pipeline Project. A long-term project if and when built the pipeline will deliver natural gas from Alaska's North Slope to US markets.

Also in 2009 it made its first major investment in developing biofuels agreeing to spend $600 million in an algae-to-fuel project with biotech firm Synthetic Genomics.

In a move to replace the decline of oil reserves from its mature fields in 2010 Exxon Mobil acquired XTO Energy. The $41 billion all-stock deal sharply boosted Exxon shale properties in the continental US including the Haynesville shale. Exxon followed up by acquiring Ellora Energy that same year for $695 million which further solidified Exxon's Haynesville position in Texas and Louisiana.

In 2010 in response to the BP oil rig disaster in the Gulf of Mexico Exxon Mobil joined forces with other US oil companies to create a $1 billion rapid-response joint venture capable of capturing and containing some 100000 barrels of oil in water depths of 10000 feet.

In 2011 the company reported a major oil find in the Gulf with potentially 700 million barrels of recoverable oil equivalent.

That year Exxon Mobil acquired two Pittsburgh-area natural gas producers (Phillips Resources and TWP) for $1.7 billion giving the company access to hundreds of thousands of leased acres of the Marcellus Shale in southwestern Pennsylvania.

In 2012 Saudi Basic Industries Corporation and Exxon Mobil agreed to build a world-scale specialty elastomers facility (to be completed in 2015) at the Al-Jubail Petrochemical Company manufacturing joint venture in Saudi Arabia.

To raise cash to pay down debt in 2012 the company sold its North Sea assets to Apache for $1.25 billion.

EXECUTIVES

Vice President, Lucille Cavanaugh
Chairman and CEO, Rex W. Tillerson, age 62, $2,867,000 total compensation
SVP and Principal Financial Officer, Andrew P. (Andy) Swiger, age 59, $1,142,500 total compensation
President ExxonMobil Research and Engineering Company, T.J. Wojnar
President ExxonMobil Chemical Company, Neil A. Chapman
VP and President ExxonMobil Fuels Lubricants and Specialties Marketing Company, Allan J. Kelly, age 58
President ExxonMobil Development Company, Neil W. (Neil) Duffin, age 59
VP and President ExxonMobil Production Company, Thomas R. (Tom) Walters, age 60
President ExxonMobil Gas and Power Marketing Company, Robert S. Franklin, age 57
President ExxonMobil Upstream Research, Sara N. Ortwein
VP and President ExxonMobil Exploration Company, Stephen M. Greenlee
President XTO Energy Inc, Randy J. Cleveland
President and Director, Darren W. Woods, age 50
President ExxonMobil Refining and Supply Company, D.G. (Jerry) Wascom, age 59
President ExxonMobil Global Services Company, Bryan W. Milton
Vice President Treasury Department, Hugh Comer
Vice President Information Technology, Nigel Searle
Executive Vice President, Marcel Vanderzee
Executive Vice President, Anantha Sundaram
Vice President Finance, Simon Ashton
Vice President Drilling, Joel Kiker
Vice President, Chris Erickson
Vice President Commercial, Paul Dubetz
Process Vice President, Mike Coker
Svp, Mark W Albers

Svp, Jack Williams
Vice President Legal Services, Dave Raaf
Vice President, Annette Moore
Vice President, Pat Doolan
Vice President Apparel Merchandise, Doug Blake
Engineering Vice President, Carol Lloyd
Vice President Of Information Technology, Terri Dosch
Vice President Of Sales, Jim Hennessy
Vice President, Roger Higham
Vice President Global Supply Chain, Kurt Aerts
Vice President Land, Patrick Murphy
Vice President Information Technology, Bob Fentress
Senior Vice President, Matthew Aguiar
National Account Manager, Richard Bowen
Vice President, Stephen Karner
Vice President, William Espegren
Vice President, Taye Akewusola
Department Head, Michael Hotaling
Vice President Executive Assistant Senior Staff Admin, Vivian Winston
Vice President, S Lance Jackson
Vice President Purchasing And Equipment, Espen Hillmann
Senior Vice President Of Natural Gas Operations, Idora Abdulmalek
Vice President planning, Kevin Barnes
Vice President Operations Production Manufacturing, Nic Harker
Vice President, Robert (Bob) Mccormack
Vice President Information Technology, James (Jamie) Weaver
Assistant Treasurer exxonmobil Chemical America, Beth Casteel
Treasurer???s ??? Benefits Finance And Investments, Cindy Kessel
Cis Treasurer, Rico S Burch
Treasurer, Razi Asaduddin
Assistant Treasurer, Julio Tamacas
Treasurer, Scott Darling
Secretary, Suzanne Manahan-smith
Credit Analyst Downstream Treasurer's Credit, Veena Atmaramani
Treasurer's Credit Assistant Manager, Andrea Benith
Upstream Treasurers, Tanya Gordon
Board Member, Charles Weatherington
Board Member, Gloria Archambault
Advisory Board Member, Anne Courtiright
Board Member, Pin Oak
Vice Chair, Harleen Chhabra
L And S Downstream Treasurers Credit Analyst, Patricia Beckwith
Financial Advisor Upstream Treasurers, Todd Norman
Assistant Treasurer, Kate Shae
Secretary Offsites Division, Anita H Vasilda
Upstream Treasurers, Mark Terry
Auditors: PricewaterhouseCoopers LLP

LOCATIONS

HQ: Exxon Mobil Corp.
5959 Las Colinas Boulevard, Irving, TX 75039-2298
Phone: 972 444-1000   **Fax:** 972 444-1505
Web: www.exxonmobil.com

2014 Sales

	% of total
Non-U.S.	62
U.S.	38
Total	**100**

PRODUCTS/OPERATIONS

Selected Acquisitions

COMPETITORS

7-Eleven	Marathon Oil
Ashland Inc.	Norsk Hydro ASA
BHP Billiton	Occidental Petroleum
BP	PEMEX
Chevron	PETROBRAS
ConocoPhillips	Petrleos de
Costco Wholesale	Venezuela
Dow Chemical	Racetrac Petroleum
DuPont	Repsol
Eastman Chemical	Royal Dutch Shell
Eni	Saudi Aramco
Hess Corporation	Sunoco
Huntsman International	TOTAL
JX Holdings	Valero Energy
Koch Industries Inc.	

HISTORICAL FINANCIALS

Company Type: Public

Income Statement

FYE: December 31

	REVENUE ($ mil.)	NET INCOME ($ mil.)	NET PROFIT MARGIN	EMPLOYEES
12/14	411,939	32,520	7.9%	75,300
12/13	438,255	32,580	7.4%	75,000
12/12	482,295	44,880	9.3%	76,900
12/11	486,429	41,060	8.4%	82,100
12/10	383,221	30,460	7.9%	83,600
Annual Growth	1.8%	1.6%	—	(2.6%)

2014 Year-End Financials

Debt ratio: 8.33%—
Return on equity: 18.67%
Cash ($ mil.): 4,658
Current ratio: 0.82
Long-term debt ($ mil.): 11,653

Dividends
Yield: 2.9%
Payout: 33.9%
Market value ($ mil.): —

	STOCK PRICE ($) FY Close	P/E High/Low		PER SHARE ($) Earnings	Dividends	Book Value
12/14	92.45	14	11	7.60	2.70	41.51
12/13	101.20	14	12	7.37	2.46	40.14
12/12	86.55	10	8	9.70	2.18	36.84
12/11	84.76	10	8	8.42	1.85	32.61
12/10	73.12	12	9	6.22	1.74	29.49
Annual Growth	6.0%	—	—	5.1%	11.6%	8.9%

F.N.B. Corp.

F.N.B. Corporation is the holding company for First National Bank of Pennsylvania which serves consumers and small to midsized businesses though more than 270 bank branches in Pennsylvania northeastern Ohio and Maryland. The company also has more than 50 consumer finance offices operating as Regency Finance in those states as well as Tennessee and Kentucky. In addition to community banking and consumer finance F.N.B. also has segments devoted to insurance and wealth management. It also offers leasing and merchant banking services. F.N.B. has extended its reach in its target states through acquisitions of banks including Metro Bancorp Annapolis Bancorp and PVF Capital Corp.

Mergers and AcquisitionsIn early 2016 F.N.B. Corporation purchased Metro Bancorp along with its $3 billion in assets and more than 30 Metro

Bank branches in south-central Pennsylvania. The deal effectively merged Metro Bank into F.N.B.'s First National Bank of Pennsylvania subsidiary. In October 2013 F.N.B. moved to expand its presence in the greater Cleveland area by purchasing PVF Capital Corp. which owned Park View Federal Savings Bank with some 20 offices in Cleveland and northeastern Ohio.In April 2013 F.N.B. purchased Annapolis Bancorp the parent company of BankAnnapolis in an all-stock transaction valued at about $51 million. The deal expanded F.N.B.'s reach into Maryland. Company Background

F.N.B. which moved its headquarters from Pennsylvania to Florida in 2001 spun off First National Bankshares of Florida at the start of 2004 and returned to the Pittsburgh area. F.N.B. still operates two loan offices in Florida but these primarily manage the company's legacy loan portfolio there.

The bank is again rooted firmly in the Keystone State and bordering markets. After returning it expanded via several acquisitions prior to the Parkvale deal including bank holding companies NSD Bancorp Slippery Rock Financial North East Bancshares Omega Financial and Iron and Glass Bancorp. In 2011 F.N.B. expanded in northeastern Pennsylvania through the acquisition of Comm Bancorp. The deal valued at some $70 million brought in 15 branches.

EXECUTIVES

SVP and Corporate Controller, Timothy G. Rubritz, age 62, $215,016 total compensation
Chief Legal Officer, James G. Orie, age 56, $165,000 total compensation
CFO, Vincent J. Calabrese, age 52, $385,008 total compensation
Chief Credit Officer, Gary Guerrieri, age 54, $350,016 total compensation
President and CEO; CEO First National Bank, Vincent J. (Vince) Delie, age 50, $770,016 total compensation
President First National Bank, John C. Williams, $385,008 total compensation
Senior Vice President Market Manager, Doug Williamson
Vice President Planning Reporting Manager, Michael (Mel) Cope
Vice President, Tom Miles
Vice President, Nick Gates
Senior Vice President Corporate Strategies Coordinator And Group Man, David (Dave) Yates
Executive Vice President, Louise Lowrey
Vice President Treasury Management Sales Officer, Tracie Elza
Auditors: Ernst & Young LLP

LOCATIONS

HQ: F.N.B. Corp.
One North Shore Center, 12 Federal Street, Pittsburgh, PA 15212
Phone: 800 555-5455
Web: www.fnbcorporation.com

PRODUCTS/OPERATIONS

2013 Sales by Segment

	$ mil.	% of total
Community banking	493	86
Consumer finance	40	7
Wealth management	28	5
Insurance	13	2
Total	**576**	**100**

2013 Sales

	$ mil.	% of total
Interest		
Loans including fees	391	67
Securities including dividends	49	9
Other	0	

Noninterest		
Service charges	68	12
Trust Services	16	3
Insurance commissions & fees	16	3
Securities commissions & fees	11	2
Other	22	4
Total	**576**	**100**

Selected Subsidiaries

F.N.B. Capital Corporation (merchant banking)
First National Bank of Pennsylvania
  Bank Capital Services LLC (also dba F.N.B. Commercial Leasing)
  First National Trust Company
  F.N.B. Investment Advisors
  First National Investment Services Company
First National Insurance Agency LLC
Regency Finance Company
  Citizens Financial Services Inc.
  F.N.B. Consumer Discount Company
  Finance and Mortgage Acceptance Corporation

COMPETITORS

Bank of America	Glen Burnie Bancorp
Citizens Financial Group	Huntington Bancshares
Dollar Bank	M&T Bank
Fifth Third	Northwest Bancshares
First Commonwealth Financial	PNC Financial
First Niagara Financial	S&T Bancorp
Fulton Financial	Sandy Spring Bancorp
	Sovereign Bank
	United Community Financial

HISTORICAL FINANCIALS

Company Type: Public

Income Statement

FYE: December 31

	ASSETS ($ mil.)	NET INCOME ($ mil.)	INCOME AS % OF ASSETS	EMPLOYEES
12/14	16,127	144	0.9%	3,145
12/13	13,563	117	0.9%	3,103
12/12	12,023	110	0.9%	2,975
12/11	9,786	87	0.9%	3,015
12/10	8,959	74	0.8%	2,718
Annual Growth	**15.8%**	**17.9%**	**—**	**3.7%**

2014 Year-End Financials

Debt ratio: 0.88%
Return on equity: 7.59%
Cash ($ mil.): 287
Current ratio: —
Long-term debt ($ mil.): —
No. of shares (mil.): 173
Dividends
  Yield: 3.6%
  Payout: 60.0%
Market value ($ mil.): 2,318

	STOCK PRICE ($) FY Close	P/E High/Low	PER SHARE ($) Earnings	Dividends	Book Value
12/14	13.32	17 14	0.80	0.48	11.62
12/13	12.62	16 13	0.80	0.48	11.16
12/12	10.62	16 13	0.79	0.48	10.02
12/11	11.31	16 12	0.70	0.48	9.51
12/10	9.82	15 10	0.65	0.48	9.29
Annual Growth	**7.9%**	**— —**	**5.3%**	**(0.0%)**	**5.7%**

Facebook, Inc.

When it comes to social networking it's wise to put your best face forward. Facebook the social networking juggernaut lets users share information post photos and videos play games and otherwise connect with one another through online profiles. The site which allows outside developers to build apps that integrate with Facebook boasts more than a billion total users. The firm was launched in 2004 by Harvard student Mark Zuckerberg as an online version of the Harvard Facebook. (The name comes from books of freshmen's faces majors and hometowns that are distributed to students.) In 2012 Facebook began publicly trading after filing one of the largest IPOs in US history.

IPO

The company and its underwriters priced shares at $38 valuing Facebook at a staggering $104 billion. The deal represented the biggest technology IPO to date and the third biggest IPO ever (behind General Motors and Visa).

Geographic Reach

Global in its reach Facebook generated almost half of its revenue outside the US in fiscal 2012. The majority of its international business comes from customers located in western Europe Canada and Australia. The company sees Brazil and India in particular as key sources of growth. As emerging markets they suffer from less social media saturation and Faceook can also benefit from their large populations.

Financial Performance

Facebook has experienced exponential growth over the past few years enabling it to dominate the social networking world as the most trafficked site of its kind in the US. Its revenue of more than $5 billion in fiscal 2012 represented an increase of nearly $2.4 billion compared to its 2011 take. Net income suffered however due to higher operating expenses acquisitions and other large investments and costs related to its IPO.

Strategy

Facebook owes the bulk of its growth to its ability to lure more and more visitors to its site and keeping them engaged. The site then stores data about its users and sells that info to advertisers and marketers. The growth in Facebook's advertising business driven by mobile ads customized for individuals has been staggering.

Mergers & Acquisitions

In 2012 Facebook announced its largest acquisition to date —the purchase of Instagram for a whopping $1 billion in cash and stock. Facebook has been slower in developing its mobile services and Instagram has developed a popular mobile photo-sharing app famous for its filters that give digital photos an "old-timey" look. Instagram is attracted to Facebook's large user base which it will use to spread its app and brand to more people. Instagram has about 30 million iPhone users; it added an Android offering just a week before the Facebook acquisition announcement and received more than a million Android users in 12 hours.

Ownership

Facebook's IPO made billions for its investors. Zuckerberg owns more than 65% of the company (with 54% voting power). His former roommate at Harvard Dustin Moskovitz owns about 10%.

EXECUTIVES

COO, Sheryl K. Sandberg, age 46, $592,885 total compensation
VP Business and Marketing Partnerships, David B. Fischer, age 42
Chairman and CEO, Mark Zuckerberg, age 31, $1 total compensation
CTO, Michael (Mike) Schroepfer, age 40, $535,577 total compensation
CFO, David M. (Dave) Wehner, age 46, $418,051 total compensation
Chief Product Officer, Christopher K. (Chris) Cox, age 32, $533,654 total compensation
Managing Director Southeast Asia (SEA), Kenneth Bishop
Vice President National Sales, Brandon Pierce
Vice President National Ad Sales, Jorissen Alexandra
Vice President of Global Marketing Solutions, Grady Burnett
Vice President Sales Emerging Markets, Blake Chandlee
Vice President Global Communication Marketing and Public Policy Facebook Inc, Elliot Schrage
Vice President Engineering, Mike Schroepfer
Second Vice President, Pam Zinn
Senior Vice President Production Services, Ellis Collins
Vice President Partnerships and Platform Marketing, Daniel (Dan) Rose
Auditors: Ernst & Young LLP

LOCATIONS

HQ: Facebook, Inc.
  1601 Willow Road, Menlo Park, CA 94025
Phone: 650 543-4800
Web: www.facebook.com

2014 Sales

	$ mil.	% of total
US	5,649	45
International	6,817	55
Total	**12,466**	**100**

PRODUCTS/OPERATIONS

2014 Sales

	$ mil.	% of total
Advertising	11,492	92
Payments & other fees	974	8
Total	**12,466**	**100**

Selected Products and Features

Products for Users
  Timeline
  News feed
  Photos & videos
  Messages
  Groups
  Lists
  Events
  Places
  Notifications
  Facebook Pages
Products for Developers
  Open Graph
  Social plugins
  Like button
  Recommendations
  Comments
  Facebook Payments
  Apps on Facebook
Products for Advertisers & Marketers
  Facebook Ads
  Sponsored Stories
  Ad analytics

COMPETITORS

Apple Inc.	Memory Lane
Bebo	Microsoft
Digg	Myspace
Friendster	TheSquare
Google	Tribe Networks
IAC	Twitter
LinkedIn	Yelp
LiveJournal	YouTube
Meetup	craigslist

HISTORICAL FINANCIALS

Company Type: Public

Income Statement

FYE: December 31

	REVENUE ($ mil.)	NET INCOME ($ mil.)	NET PROFIT MARGIN	EMPLOYEES
12/15	17,928	3,688	20.6%	12,691
12/14	12,466	2,940	23.6%	9,199
12/13	7,872	1,500	19.1%	6,337
12/12	5,089	53	1.0%	4,619
12/11	3,711	1,000	26.9%	3,539
Annual Growth	48.3%	38.6%	—	37.6%

2015 Year-End Financials

Debt ratio: 0.23%—
Return on equity: 9.18%
Cash ($ mil.): 4,907
Current ratio: 11.25
Long-term debt ($ mil.): 107

Dividends
Yield: —
Payout: —
Market value ($ mil.): —

	STOCK PRICE ($) FY Close	P/E High/Low	PER SHARE ($) Earnings	Dividends	Book Value
12/15	104.66	83 57	1.29	0.00	15.54
12/14	78.02	73 48	1.10	0.00	12.91
12/13	54.65	93 37	0.60	0.00	6.07
12/12	26.62	1912886	0.01	0.00	4.95
Annual Growth	40.8%	—	—237.0%	—	33.1%

Fannie Mae

The Federal National Mortgage Association or Fannie Mae has helped more than 50 million low- to middle-income families realize the American Dream. Like its brother Freddie Mac the government-supported enterprise (GSE) provides liquidity in the mortgage market by buying mortgages from lenders and packaging them for resale transferring risk from lenders and allowing them to offer mortgages to those who may not otherwise qualify. It owns or guarantees about $10.7 trillion in home loans or more than a quarter of all outstanding mortgages in the US. Due to losses caused largely by the subprime mortgage crisis the government seized both Fannie and Freddie in 2008. It plans to wind the GSEs down over time.

HISTORY

Company BackgroundIn 1938 President Franklin Roosevelt created Fannie Mae as part of the government-owned Reconstruction Finance Corporation; its mandate was to buy FHA (Federal Housing Administration) loans. Fannie Mae began buying VA (Veterans Administration) mortgages in 1948. It was rechartered as a public-private mixed-ownership corporation in 1954.

The Housing Act of 1968 divided the corporation into the Government National Mortgage Association (Ginnie Mae which retained explicit government backing) and Fannie Mae which went public (with only an implicit US guarantee). Fannie Mae retained its treasury backstop authority whereby the secretary of the treasury can purchase up to $2.24 billion of the company's obligations.

The company introduced uniform conventional loan mortgage documents in 1970 began to buy conventional mortgages in 1972 and started buying condo and planned-unit development mortgages in 1974. By 1976 it was buying more conventional loans than FHA and VA loans.

As interest rates rose in the 1970s Fannie Mae's profits declined and by 1981 it was losing more than $1 million a day. Then it began offering mortgage-backed securities (MBSs) —popular as an investment product because of their implicit guarantee from the government. By 1982 the company funded 14% of US home mortgages.

Fannie Mae began borrowing money overseas and buying conventional multifamily and co-op housing loans in 1984. The next year it tightened credit rules and began issuing securities aimed at foreign investors such as yen-denominated securities. Fannie Mae issued its first real estate mortgage investment conduit (REMIC) securities (shares in mortgage pools of specific maturities and risk classes) and introduced a program to allow small lenders to pool loans with other lenders to create MBSs in 1987.

After CEO David Maxwell's 1991 retirement with a reported $29 million pension package Fannie Mae's powerful Washington lobby squelched calls to limit executive salaries. Other attempts to make the company more competitive with private concerns were more successful. In 1992 Fannie Mae's capital requirements were raised; a new mandate also required the organization to lend greater support to inner-city buyers. A new client/server computer system helped the company handle the deluge of new and refinanced loans that came in 1993 (Fannie Mae had struggled to improve its information systems in the 1980s pouring more than $100 million into a mainframe system that was obsolete before it went online).

In 1997 Fannie Mae officially adopted its longtime nickname. The next year Fannie Mae named White House budget chief Franklin Raines to succeed CEO James Johnson.

Fannie Mae is no stranger to bad news or bad press. In 1999 the Department of Housing and Urban Development began investigating charges that the company's automated underwriting systems were racially biased. The next year the agency released a study that found it to be negligent in promoting homeownership in low-income neighborhoods. In response Fannie Mae eased credit requirements in an effort to boost minority homeownership (1999) and announced plans to loan some $2 trillion to minority and low-income homebuyers (2000). This move however invoked criticism that the company was exposing itself to increased risk from buyers more likely to default.

Following the lead of rival Freddie Mac in 2000 Fannie Mae offered securities for sale over the Internet. In 2002 it tightened standards for mortgage refinance cash-out loans it would buy as mortgage defaults rose (even as home sales and mortgage refinancings were helping prop up the sagging US economy).In response to those who thought it was in bed with the federal government Fannie Mae kicked off the covers and put one foot on the floor. In 2003 it fulfilled a voluntary commitment to register its common stock with the SEC and came permanently under that organization's disclosure and oversight requirements.But the move did not stop controversy from swirling around the lender. Chairman and CEO Franklin Raines CFO Timothy Howard and auditor KPMG were ousted in December 2004 after the SEC determined Fannie Mae had violated accounting rules. The inquiry was prompted by accusations Fannie Mae had manipulated earnings; earnings from 2001 through 2003 were restated and those from 2004 and 2005 were each released more than a year late.

In 2006 federal regulators hit the firm with a whopping $400 million fine. Investigators claimed that its former executives willfully overstated earnings by more than $10 billion —and then tried to impede an investigation into the discrepancies —in order to reap performance bonuses. Chairman Stephen Ashley and CEO Daniel Mudd who'd been brought in to replace Franklin Raines in late 2004 were brought to task by the Senate Banking Committee in regard to accounting misdeeds.

Though the Justice Department eventually dropped criminal charges against the firm Fannie Mae agreed to major changes in its accounting internal controls and management practices. It additionally agreed to appoint an independent chief risk officer as well as an organizational review overseen by a compliance committee. Meanwhile the lender suspended its home construction loan program —worth about $10 billion —while it got its financial house in order.Fannie suffered huge losses in 2007 and 2008 as a result of the subprime mortgage crisis which saw a tremendouse increase in loan defaults. The government stepped in loans and in 2008 seized both Fannie and Freddie. It also shuffled their management teams: Fannie CEO Mudd was replaced by Herbert Allison former TIAA-CREF. Allison was later tapped by the Obama administration to run the Treasury Department's financial recovery program. Former COO Michael Williams was named CEO in 2009.

The Federal Housing Finance Agency (FHFA) was created in 2008 to oversee both Fannie and Freddie as well as the 12 Federal Home Loan Banks. The FHFA was granted more authority than its predecessor agencies the Federal Housing Finance Board and the Office of Federal Housing Enterprise Oversight.

EXECUTIVES

Vice President, William B (Bill) Senhauser
Vice President Accounting Systems, James (Jamie) Horne
President CEO and Director, Timothy J. (Tim) Mayopoulos, age 56, $600,000 total compensation
SVP and Head Multifamily Mortgage Business, Jeffery R. Hayward, age 59
SVP and Treasurer Capital Markets, David C. Benson, age 56, $600,000 total compensation
EVP Single-Family Underwriting Pricing and Capital Markets, Andrew Bon Salle, $475,769 total compensation
EVP and Chief Risk Officer, John R. Nichols, age 52, $450,000 total compensation
SVP Operations and Technology, Pascal Boillat
EVP General Counsel and Corporate Secretary, Brian P. Brooks
Executive Vice President and Chief Business Officer, Robert (Bob) Levin
Vice President, Steve Spies
Vice President Risk Management, Carlos Perez
Vice President Multifamily Operations, Angela Benton
Vice President Operations Eastern Business Center, Cheryl Croxton
Vice President Finance And Corporate Technology, Ramon Richards
Vice President Information Technology, Beth Applegate
Vice President Corporate Governance Deputy General Counsel, Christine Reddy
Vice President Of Internal Audit Technology, Don Farineau
Executive Vice President Enterprise Operations and Securities, Linda Knight
Vice President Multifamily E Business, Caroline Blakely
Chairman, Egbert L. J. Perry, age 59
Auditors: Deloitte & Touche LLP

LOCATIONS

HQ: Fannie Mae
  3900 Wisconsin Avenue, N.W., Washington, DC 20016
Phone: 202 752-7000
Web: www.fanniemae.com

Selected Locations

Atlanta
Chicago
Dallas
Pasadena
Philadelphia
Washington DC

PRODUCTS/OPERATIONS

2014 Sales

	% of total
Interest income	
Mortgage loans	92
Available-for-sale securities	2
Trading securities	
Others	-
Non interest income	
Fee and other income	5
Fair value losses	-
Investment	1
Others	-
Total	**100**

2014 Sales

	% of total
Single-Family	48
Capital Markets	43
Multifamily	5
Others	4
Total	**100**

Selected Business Segments

Single-Family Credit Guaranty
Multifamily
Capital Markets

COMPETITORS

FHLB Atlanta

HISTORICAL FINANCIALS

Company Type: Public

Income Statement

	ASSETS ($ mil.)	NET INCOME ($ mil.)	INCOME AS % OF ASSETS	EMPLOYEES
12/14	3,248,176	14,208	0.4%	7,600
12/13	3,270,108	83,963	2.6%	7,400
12/12	3,222,422	17,224	0.5%	7,200
12/11	3,211,484	(16,855)	—	7,000
12/10	3,221,972	(14,014)	—	7,300
Annual Growth	0.2%	—	—	1.0%

2014 Year-End Financials

Debt ratio: 99.20%
Return on equity: 214.93%
Cash ($ mil.): 22,023
Current ratio: —
Long-term debt ($ mil.): —

No. of shares (mil.): 1,158
Dividends
  Yield: —
  Payout: —
Market value ($ mil.): 2,380

	STOCK PRICE ($) FY Close	P/E High/Low		PER SHARE ($) Earnings	Dividends	Book Value
12/14	2.06	—	—	(0.19)	0.00	3.18
12/13	3.01	—	—	(0.25)	0.00	8.24
12/12	0.26	2	1	0.24	0.00	6.20
12/11	0.20	—	—	(4.61)	0.00	(3.99)
12/10	0.30	—	—	(3.81)	0.00	(2.32)
Annual Growth	61.8%	—	—	—	—	—

FARM CREDIT SERVICES ILLINOIS ACA

LOCATIONS

HQ: FARM CREDIT SERVICES ILLINOIS ACA
  1100 FARM CREDIT DR, MAHOMET, IL 618538532
Phone: 2175902200
Web: WWW.FCSILLINOIS.COM

HISTORICAL FINANCIALS

Company Type: Private

Income Statement

FYE: December 31

	ASSETS ($ mil.)	NET INCOME ($ mil.)	INCOME AS % OF ASSETS	EMPLOYEES
12/13	3,338	63	1.9%	165
12/12	3,304	63	1.9%	—
12/11	2,843	56	2.0%	—
12/10	2,607	0	—	—
Annual Growth	8.6%	—	—	—

FARM CREDIT SERVICES OF AMERICA PCA/FLCA

LOCATIONS

HQ: FARM CREDIT SERVICES OF AMERICA PCA/FLCA
  5015 S 118TH ST, OMAHA, NE 681372210
Phone: 4023483554
Web: WWW.FCSAMERICA.COM

HISTORICAL FINANCIALS

Company Type: Private

Income Statement

FYE: December 31

	ASSETS ($ mil.)	NET INCOME ($ mil.)	INCOME AS % OF ASSETS	EMPLOYEES
12/13	21,274	0	—	10,000
12/04	8,475	294	3.5%	—
12/03	7,633	114	1.5%	—
12/02	6,976	0	—	—
Annual Growth	10.7%	—	—	—

2013 Year-End Financials

Debt ratio: ——
Return on equity: —
Cash ($ mil.): 86
Current ratio: —
Long-term debt ($ mil.): —

Dividends
  Yield: —
  Payout: —
Market value ($ mil.): —

FARM CREDIT WEST

LOCATIONS

HQ: FARM CREDIT WEST
  1478 STONE POINT DR # 450, ROSEVILLE, CA 956612869
Phone: 9167244800

HISTORICAL FINANCIALS

Company Type: Private

Income Statement

FYE: December 31

	ASSETS ($ mil.)	NET INCOME ($ mil.)	INCOME AS % OF ASSETS	EMPLOYEES
12/13	6,925	156	2.3%	165
12/12	6,668	151	2.3%	—
12/11	6,282	176	2.8%	—
12/10	6,129	0	—	—
Annual Growth	4.2%	—	—	—

FBL Financial Group, Inc.

Insurance holding company FBL Financial Group (FBL) is the parent of Farm Bureau Life Insurance Company. Through its subsidiary the firm sells life insurance annuities and investment products to farmers ranchers and agricultural businesses. Farm Bureau Life sells insurance and annuities through an exclusive network of about 2000 agents across some 15 states in the Midwest and West. (In Colorado it operates as Greenfields Life Insurance.) The company markets its products through an affiliation with the American Farm Bureau Federation. FBL also manages for a fee two Farm Bureau-affiliated property/casualty insurance companies. The Iowa Farm Bureau Federation owns close to 60% of the company.

Operations

FBL divides its business into two segments annuity and life insurance. Traditional and universal life insurance products sold primarily in Iowa Kansas and Oklahoma account for about 60% of sales. Annuities including fixed rate and index are also big in Iowa and Kansas and account for about 30% of revenue.

The two Farm Bureau-affiliated property/casualty insurers that FBL manages are Farm Bureau Property & Casualty and Western Agricultural Insurance. The two affiliates underwrite auto crop and other property/casualty policies for individuals and groups under FBL's corporate and other segment which accounts for about 10% of revenue.

Geographic Reach

FBL offers its services in 15 western and midwestern states. Iowa Kansas Oklahoma and Wyoming are key markets.

Financial Performance

After a few rocky years FBL has been back on track the last two years. In 2013 it reported a 5% increase in revenue from $656 million to $691 million as both annuity and life segments reported increases in the volume of business. Net income has been on a steady rise and increased 36% in 2013 from $80 million to $109 million due to the improved revenue and increased equity income. Cash from operations however has been declining for years and continued its trend with a $24 million drop to $182 million due to cash used for paying out and administering claims.

Strategy

Strategically FBL expands its penetration in both the life and property/casualty markets by encouraging existing policyholders to purchase other insurance products through the agents they already know. Its cross-selling technique has led the industry as a whole. Additionally FBL depends on the talent of the agents it engages and its overall ability to provide products that meet changing needs as well as superior customer service and market knowledge. It continually invests in training and supporting existing agents and recruiting new ones. FBL also launches new products like index annuities in 2012 and takes steps like decreasing commissions for some products that aren't profitable during this time of low interest rates.

EXECUTIVES

EVP Farm Bureau Life, JoAnn W. Rumelhart, age 61, $287,426 total compensation
Chief Executive Officer Chief Financial Officer Chief Administrative Officer Treasurer, James P. (Jim) Brannen, age 53, $432,900 total compensation
VP Information Technology, Douglas W. Gumm, age 60
EVP Marketing and Distribution, Kevin R. Slawin, $400,000 total compensation
Chief Operating Officer - Life Companies, Richard J. (Rich) Kypta, age 63, $381,063 total compensation
CFO and Treasurer, Donald J. (Don) Seibel, age 51
EVP and Chief Investment Officer, Charles T. Happel, age 53, $291,500 total compensation
COO Life Companies, Raymond W. Wasilewski, age 56
Commercial Ag Vice President, Ryan Albers
Securities Vice President, Herman Riva
Vice President Marketing Research, Dan Koster
Vice Chairman, Jerry L. Chicoine, age 72
Chairman, Craig D. Hill, age 59
Auditors: Ernst & Young LLP

LOCATIONS

HQ: FBL Financial Group, Inc.
5400 University Avenue, West Des Moines, IA 50266-5997
Phone: 515 225-5400
Web: www.fblfinancial.com

Selected Areas of Operation
Farm Bureau Life Insurance Company
  Multi-line (life and property/casualty)
    Arizona
    Iowa
    Kansas
    Minnesota
    Nebraska
    New Mexico
    South Dakota
    Utah
  Life only
    Idaho
    Montana
    North Dakota
    Oklahoma
    Wisconsin
    Wyoming
Farm Bureau Property & Casualty Insurance Company and Western Agricultural Insurance Company
  Arizona
  Iowa
  Kansas
  Minnesota
  Nebraska
  New Mexico
  South Dakota
  Utah

PRODUCTS/OPERATIONS

2013 Revenues

	$ mil.	% of total
Life Insurance	385	56
Annuity	197	29
Gains on derivatives	13	2
Losses on investments	(2.0)	-
Corporate & other	96	13
Total	**691**	**100**

Selected Subsidiaries
Insurance
  Farm Bureau Life Insurance Company
Noninsurance
  5400 Holdings L.L.C.
  FBL Assigned Benefit Company
  FBL Financial Group Capital Trust
  FBL Financial Group Capital Trust II
  FBL Financial Services Inc.
  FBL Investment Management Services Inc.
  FBL Leasing Services Inc.
  FBL Marketing Services L.L.C.

COMPETITORS

AIG
Allstate
American Equity Investment Life Holding Company
American Farmers & Ranchers Mutual Insurance Co.
COUNTRY Financial
Farm Family Holdings
Farmers & Merchants Investment
Great American Financial Resources
MetLife
Midland National Life
Nationwide
Nationwide Agribusiness
Prudential
State Farm
Thrivent Investment Management

HISTORICAL FINANCIALS
Company Type: Public

Income Statement
FYE: December 31

	ASSETS ($ mil.)	NET INCOME ($ mil.)	INCOME AS % OF ASSETS	EMPLOYEES
12/14	9,064	109	1.2%	1,628
12/13	8,461	108	1.3%	1,589
12/12	8,417	79	0.9%	1,582
12/11	8,225	31	0.4%	1,570
12/10	15,334	120	0.8%	1,679
Annual Growth	**(12.3%)**	**(2.3%)**	**—**	**(0.8%)**

2014 Year-End Financials

Debt ratio: 1.07%
Return on equity: 9.57%
Cash ($ mil.): 76
Current ratio: —
Long-term debt ($ mil.): —

No. of shares (mil.): 24
Dividends
  Yield: 2.4%
  Payout: 32.3%
Market value ($ mil.): 1,434

	STOCK PRICE ($) FY Close	P/E High/Low		PER SHARE ($) Earnings	Dividends	Book Value
12/14	58.03	13	8	4.39	1.40	50.69
12/13	44.79	11	8	4.21	2.52	42.20
12/12	34.21	13	9	2.87	0.40	47.58
12/11	34.02	35	25	1.00	0.29	41.70
12/10	28.67	7	4	3.92	0.25	37.05
Annual Growth	**19.3%**	**—**	**—**	**2.9%**	**53.8%**	**8.2%**

Federal Agricultural Mortgage Corp

Farmer Mac (Federal Agricultural Mortgage Corporation) is Fannie Mae and Freddie Mac's country cousin. Like its city-slicker kin it provides liquidity in its markets (agricultural real estate and rural housing mortgages) by buying loans from lenders and then securitizing the loans into Farmer Mac Guaranteed Securities. Farmer Mac buys both conventional loans and those guaranteed by the US Department of Agriculture. Farmer Mac was created by Congress in 1987 to establish a secondary market for agricultural mortgage and rural utilities loans. It is a stockholder-owned publicly-traded corporation based in Washington DC with an underwriting office in Iowa.

Financial Performance

Farmer Mac's revenue increased 18% to $268 million in 2012 versus 2011 primarily due to a decline in losses on financial derivatives and hedging activities. The revenue growth was partially offset by the decline in investments and cash equivalents and loans in interest income. Net income grew 181% to $47 million in 2012 versus 2011 on higher non-interest income. Underpinning the company's strong financial performance in 2012 was the continuing growth and strength of the agricultural economy and a near-record year in terms of farm income. The fundamentals underlying the strong agricultural economy led to increasing land values and an attractive investment environment for agricultural producers and lenders.

Strategy

Farmer Mac seeks to improve the availability of long-term credit at stable interest rates to rural communities. To this end its primary strategy for managing interest rate risk is to fund asset purchases with liabilities that have similar duration and cash flow characteristics so that they will perform similarly as interest rates change.

EXECUTIVES

President and CEO, Timothy L. (Tim) Buzby, age 46, $643,750 total compensation
EVP CFO and Treasurer, R. Dale Lynch, age 48, $375,950 total compensation
SVP Agricultural Finance, J. Curtis Covington, age 59
SVP General Counsel and Secretary, Stephen P. Mullery, age 48, $340,930 total compensation
Senior Vice President Agricultural Finance, Curt Covington
Chairman, Lowell L. Junkins, age 71
Vice Chairman, Myles J. Watts, age 64
Auditors: PricewaterhouseCoopers LLP

LOCATIONS

HQ: Federal Agricultural Mortgage Corp
1999 K Street, N.W., 4th Floor, Washington, DC 20006
Phone: 202 872-7700   **Fax:** 202 872-7713
Web: www.farmermac.com

PRODUCTS/OPERATIONS

Selected Operations
Farm & Ranch (Farmer Mac I)
USDA Guarantees (Farmer Mac II)
Rural Utilities

COMPETITORS

AgFirst	Fannie Mae
AgStar	Farm Credit Services
AgriBank	of Mid-America
Bank of America	Freddie Mac
Citigroup	

HISTORICAL FINANCIALS

Company Type: Public

Income Statement

FYE: December 31

	ASSETS ($ mil.)	NET INCOME ($ mil.)	INCOME AS % OF ASSETS	EMPLOYEES
12/14	14,287	48	0.3%	71
12/13	13,361	75	0.6%	67
12/12	12,622	46	0.4%	64
12/11	11,883	16	0.1%	62
12/10	9,479	31	0.3%	58
Annual Growth	10.8%	10.7%	—	5.2%

2014 Year-End Financials

Debt ratio: 89.76%
Return on equity: 10.95%
Cash ($ mil.): 1,363
Current ratio: —
Long-term debt ($ mil.): —

No. of shares (mil.): 10
Dividends
  Yield: 1.8%
  Payout: 16.6%
Market value ($ mil.): 332

	STOCK PRICE ($) FY Close	P/E High/Low		PER SHARE ($) Earnings	Dividends	Book Value
12/14	30.34	10	8	3.37	0.56	49.90
12/13	34.25	6	4	6.41	0.48	30.55
12/12	32.50	8	4	3.98	0.40	32.81
12/11	18.02	17	11	1.28	0.20	30.19
12/10	16.32	11	3	2.08	0.20	23.05
Annual Growth	16.8%	—	—	12.8%	29.4%	21.3%

Federal Home Loan Bank New York

Federal Home Loan Bank of New York (FHLBNY) provides funds for residential mortgages and community development to more than 330 member banks savings and loans credit unions and life insurance companies in New York New Jersey Puerto Rico and the US Virgin Islands. One of a dozen Federal Home Loan Banks in the US it is cooperatively owned by its member institutions and supervised by the Federal Housing Finance Agency. FHLBNY like others in the system is privately capitalized; it receives no taxpayer funding. The bank instead raises funds mainly by issuing debt instruments in the capital markets.

Geographic Reach

Based in New York FHLBNY serves not only New York but New Jersey Puerto Rico and the US Virgin Islands.

Operations

FHLBNY is a secured lender that requires collateral for its advances which are typically used by members to underwrite residential mortgages or to invest in US Treasury and agency securities mortgage-backed securities and other real estate-related assets.

A large part of FHLBNY's business is in making collateralized loans or advances to members. It serves the public through its mortgage programs. Three members —Citibank (25%) Met Life (14%) and New York Community Bank (11%) — accounted for half of total advances.

Sales and Marketing

FHLBNY caters to more than 330 member banks credit unions life insurance companies and savings and loans.

Financial Performance

Revenue dropped by 14% to $801 million in fiscal 2013 from 2012's $934.9 million. FHLBNY at-

tributes the decline to a decrease in interest income and other income. Net income also dropped some 16% in 2013 to $304.6 million vs. $360.7 million in 2012. It attributes net income decreases to declining revenue and rising other expenses. Operating cash flow decreased in fiscal 2013 to $525.6 million compared to 2012's $678.9 million.

Strategy

Credit unions are a possible area of growth for FHLBNY. The bank has identified more than 50 credit unions and banks that are not members but are eligible. To be under consideration an institution must have more than $50 million in assets ($100 million for banks) be an established wholesale lender maintain a high deposit-to-loan ratio and have management that has done business with an FHLB in the past.

Beginning in 2014 it's also funding —with the help of $35.5 million in subsidies —48 affordable housing initiatives throughout New Jersey New York Puerto Rico the US Virgin Islands Florida Maryland and Pennsylvania. The effort involves the creation or rehabilitation of more than 3000 affordable housing units.

EXECUTIVES

Vice President Director Of Human Resources, Mildred Tse-Gonzalez
Senior Vice President, Paul Heroux
Senior Vice President, Steve Christatos
Assistant Vice President, Diahann Rothstein
Assistant Vice President, Claudia Kim
Vice President, Edwin Bird
Senior Vice President, Paul Roux
Vice President Director Of Trading, Philip Scott
Assistant Vice President Calling Officer, Angel Santos
Vice President Sales And Marketing And C, Alfred O'Connell
Vice President Manager Business Research, John Brandon
Vice President, Phil Scott
Vice President Senior Manager Business Research and Development, Maria Lopes
Vice Chairman, Joseph (Jo) Ficalora
Auditors: PricewaterhouseCoopers LLP

LOCATIONS

HQ: Federal Home Loan Bank New York
101 Park Avenue, New York, NY 10178
Phone: 212 681-6000
Web: www.fhlbny.com

PRODUCTS/OPERATIONS

2013 Sales

	$ mil.	% of total
Interest		
Advances	444	55
Long-term securities	244	30
Mortgage loans held for portfolio	68	9
Available-for-sale securities	16	2
Other	14	2
Non-interest	13	2
Total	**801**	**100**

HISTORICAL FINANCIALS

Company Type: Public

Income Statement

FYE: December 31

	ASSETS ($ mil.)	NET INCOME ($ mil.)	INCOME AS % OF ASSETS	EMPLOYEES
12/14	132,825	314	0.2%	258
12/13	108,332	304	0.2%	258
12/12	102,988	360	0.4%	272
12/11	97,662	244	0.3%	276
12/10	100,212	275	0.3%	271
Annual Growth	7.3%	3.4%	—	(1.2%)

2014 Year-End Financials

Debt ratio: 55.36%
Return on equity: 4.84%
Cash ($ mil.): 6,458
Current ratio: —
Long-term debt ($ mil.): —

No. of shares (mil.): 55
Dividends
  Yield: —
  Payout: 73.6%
Market value ($ mil.): —

Federal Home Loan Bank Of San Francisco

The city by the bay is the home to the Federal Home Loan Bank of San Francisco one of a dozen regional banks in the Federal Home Loan Bank System chartered by Congress in 1932 to provide credit to residential mortgage lenders. The government-sponsored enterprise is privately owned by its members which include some 400 commercial banks credit unions industrial loan companies savings and loans insurance companies and housing associates headquartered in Arizona California and Nevada. The bank links members to worldwide capital markets which provide them with low-cost funding. Members then pass these advances along to their customers in the form of affordable home mortgage and economic development loans.

FHLB San Francisco and its counterparts around the country are governed by the Federal Housing Finance Agency which recently gave eligible community development financial institutions approval to become FHLB members. In addition to providing its member institutions with advances the bank also acquires residential mortgage-backed securities (RMBS) from its members.

Although FHLB San Francisco has remained profitable through the economic downturn it has been dealing with the ill effects of the crash which has severely impacted the states of Arizona California and Nevada in particular. In 2011 the bank's revenues fell 35% to $1.1 billion while net income fell 46% to $216 million. Demand for loans remains low in the stagnant economy and FHLB San Francisco's interest earnings fell 20% that year. Additionally the value of its RMBS portfolio has declined in the downturn.

EXECUTIVES

Svp And General Counsel Corporate Secretary, Suzanne Titus-Johnson
Senior Vice President and Director Human Resources, Gregory Fontenot
Senior Vice President External and Legislative Affairs, Lawrence Parks
Senior Vice President Sales and Marketing, Patricia (Pat) Remch
Vice President Marketing, Cynthia Lopez
Vice President Mortgage, Tom Wilson
Managing Director Mortgage Finance, John (Jack) McCormack
Assistant Vice President, Kevin Blackburn
Assistant Vice President Operations and Compliance Risk Management, Katy Liu
Assistant Vice President Secondary Marketing and Collateral Development, Paschal Greene
Vice President and Treasurer, Tony Ruscitti
Auditors: PricewaterhouseCoopers LLP

LOCATIONS

HQ: Federal Home Loan Bank Of San Francisco
600 California Street, San Francisco, CA 94108
Phone: 415 616-1000
Web: www.fhlbsf.com

PRODUCTS/OPERATIONS

2013

	$ mil.	% of total
Interest income	1,086	97
Other income	5	3
Total	**1,091**	**100**

HISTORICAL FINANCIALS

Company Type: Public

Income Statement

FYE: December 31

	ASSETS ($ mil.)	NET INCOME ($ mil.)	INCOME AS % OF ASSETS	EMPLOYEES
12/14	75,807	205	0.3%	255
12/13	85,774	308	0.4%	262
12/12	86,421	491	0.6%	264
12/11	113,552	216	0.2%	274
12/10	152,423	399	0.3%	304
Annual Growth	(16.0%)	(15.3%)	—	(4.3%)

2014 Year-End Financials

Debt ratio: 90.83%
Return on equity: 3.60%
Cash ($ mil.): 3,920
Current ratio: —
Long-term debt ($ mil.): —

No. of shares (mil.): 33
Dividends
  Yield: —
  Payout: 117.0%
Market value ($ mil.): —

Federal Reserve Bank of Atlanta, Dist. No. 6

One of 12 regional banks in the Federal Reserve System the Federal Reserve Bank of Atlanta oversees Fed member banks and thrifts and their holding companies throughout the Southeast including Alabama Florida Georgia and parts of Louisiana Mississippi and Tennessee. It conducts examinations and investigations of member institutions distributes cash issues savings bonds and Treasury securities and assists the Fed in setting monetary policy such as interest rates. The bank also processes checks and acts as a clearinghouse for payments between banks. Fed Reserve Banks are independent arms within the government and return earnings (gleaned mostly from investments in government bonds) to the US Treasury.

Geographic Reach

The Federal Reserve Bank of Atlanta has branch offices in Birmingham Jacksonville Miami Nashville and New Orleans.

Operations

Of the 12 regional banks in the Federal Reserve System only the Atlanta bank processes both paper and electronic checks for the system.

Financial Performance

In 2012 FRB Atlanta reported about $5.5 billion in total current income about 7% of the $81.6 billion in total income for the Federal Reserve System.

Company Background

The Federal Reserve Bank of Atlanta was established in 1914.

EXECUTIVES

Vice President, Robert Schaub
Executive Vice President, Oliver Rich
Vice President Marketing, Anita Brown
Vice President Information Technology, Vicki Kosydor
Vice President Supervision And Regulation Division, Cynthia C Goodwin
Senior Vice President Retail Payments Product Manager, Richard (Dick) Oliver
Vice President Marketing, Rob Lilly
Assistant Vice President, Paige Harris
Assistant Vice President, Christina Wilson
Assistant Vice President Human Resources, Clifford (Cliff) Stanford
Assistant Vice President, Molly Willison
Assistant Vice President And Public Information Officer, Pierce Nelson
Senior Vice President, Christopher (Chris) Brown
Assistant Vice President, Gregory Fuller
Assistant Vice President For Community And Economi, Todd Greene
Assistant Vice President, Robert (Bob) Hawkins
Vice President Marketing, Hanh Dong
Vice President And Assistant General Counsel, Richard Fraher
Assistant Vice President Supervision and Regulation, Lani Mauriello
Vice President, Nellie Liang
Vice President Marketing, Lane Smith
Assistant Vice President of Facilities Management Facilities Management and Law Enforcement, Blake Lyons
Vice President, Mary Kepler
Assistant Vice President Of Public Affairs, Robin Ratliff
Vice President And Branch Manager, Jay Curry
Vice President Marketing, Christopher (Chris) Oakley
Assistant Vice President and Assistant Branch Manager, Annita Moore
Vice President of International Supervision, Robert (Bob) Schenck
Board Of Directors, D Jones
Auditors: Deloitte & Touche LLP

LOCATIONS

HQ: Federal Reserve Bank of Atlanta, Dist. No. 6
1000 Peachtree Street, N.E., Atlanta, GA 30309-4470
Phone: 404 498-8500
Web: www.frbatlanta.org

HISTORICAL FINANCIALS

Company Type: Public

Income Statement

FYE: December 31

	REVENUE ($ mil.)	NET INCOME ($ mil.)	NET PROFIT MARGIN	EMPLOYEES
12/14	6,861	156	2.3%	—
12/13	6,105	89	1.5%	—
12/12	6,317	135	2.1%	—
12/11	7,222	(6,450)	—	—
12/10	8,205	(7,567)	—	—
Annual Growth	(4.4%)	—	—	—

2014 Year-End Financials

Debt ratio: 72.74%
Return on equity: 4.86%
Cash ($ mil.): 258,652
Current ratio: 3.85
Long-term debt ($ mil.): 191,944

No. of shares (mil.): 32
Dividends
  Yield: —
  Payout: —
Market value ($ mil.): —

Federal Reserve Bank of Chicago, Dist. No. 7

The Federal Reserve Bank of Chicago regulates banks and bank holding companies in northern Illinois northern Indiana southern Wisconsin the Lower Peninsula of Michigan and all of Iowa. It supervises more than 850 bank holding companies and state member banks distributes money issues savings bonds and Treasury securities and assists the Fed in setting monetary policy. The Chicago Fed also processes checks and acts as a clearinghouse for payments between banks. Like the 11 other regional banks in the Federal Reserve System it returns its profits (earned largely from investments in government and federal agency securities) to the US Treasury.

Geographic Reach

The Chicago Fed serves the Seventh Federal Reserve District a region that includes all of Iowa and most of the states of Illinois Indiana Michigan and Wisconsin. The bank's head office is in Chicago and it has a branch office in Detroit. Overall it has 2230 depository institutions across its district; these include banks credit unions savings and loans institutions and others.

Financial Performance

From 2011 to 2012 the bank's total revenues dropped by 3% from nearly $5.6 billion to $5.4 billion. However its net income surged by nearly 30% increasing from $94 million to $122 million during that same time period. Treasury securities accounted for 57% of its total revenue in 2012 while federal agency mortgage-backed securities generated nearly 40%.

Company Background

The Federal Reserve Bank of Chicago is one of the 12 Federal Reserve Banks created by Congress under the Federal Reserve Act of 1913 which established the central bank of the US.

EXECUTIVES

Vice President, Richard Anstee
Assistant Vice President, Todd Aadland
Vp National Sales And Marketing, Laura J Hughes
Senior Vice President Of Central Bank Services Accounting And Procurement, Valerie J Van Meter
Senior Vice President And Director Of, Daniel G Sullivan
Vice President and Economic Advisor Macroeconomic Policy Research, Spencer D Krane, age 60
Vice President Financial Markets Group, Adrian DSilva
Assistant Vice President, Jennifer Whiteman
Executive Vice President Customer Relations And Support Office, Ellen J Bromagen
Senior Vice President Financial Markets, David (Dave) Marshall
Senior Vice President Fac Management, Jerome F John
Senior Vice President Strategic Planning, Barbara (Barb) Benson
Vice President, Douglas (Doug) Tillett
Senior Research Advisor Financial Markets Vice President, Ed Nosal
Vice President, Ted Kurdes
Assistant Vice President Large Financial Institution Learning Officer, Kristin LaPorte
Vice President Risk Management Bank Supervision, Richard (Dick) Cahill
Vice President Operations, Douglas Kasl
Assistant Vice President Of Accounting, Mike Keppler
Vice President, Wayne Baxter

Vice President Community Bank, Mark Kawa
Assistant Vice President, Daniel (Dan) Gonzalez
Assistant Vice President Hospitality Services,
Cynthia Castillo
Special Assistant President And First Vice
President, Jamica Quillin
Assistant Vice President Office Of Diversity And
Inclusion, Deborah Baldwin
Vice President Of Marketing, Brian Mantel
Vice President Payments Research, Richard Porter
Vice President Of Finance Division, Kelly Emery
Senior Vice President, James Bluemle
Senior Vice President And General Counsel,
Elizabeth Knospe
Vice President Of Information Technology, Kelly
McMillan
Assistant Vice President, Craig Priebe
Vice President, Yurii Skorin
Vice President; Senior Operational Risk
Specialist, Ryan Metcalfe
Assistant Vice President, Charles Luse
Senior Vice President Of Supervision And
Regulation, Cathy Lemieux
Vice President, Doug Tillett
Assistant Vice President, Jason Adams
Assistant Vice President Wholesale Credit Risk,
Nancy Beebe
Managing Director Of Economic Development,
Jeremiah Boyle
Vice President Technology, Dan Reiman
Vice President And Monetary And Financial Policy
Advisor, Hesna Genay
Assistant Vice President National, Connie Theien
Vice President and Senior Economist Financial
Mar, Douglas (Doug) Evanoff
Senior Vice President Supervision Regulation
Department, James (Jamie) Nelson
Assistant Vice President, Jon Sudduth
Vice President, Michael Hoppe
Senior Vice President Financial, Robert Wiley
Senior Vice President Supervision Regulation,
Steve Durfey
Vice President, Jeffery Anderson
Assistant Vice President applications and
Enforcement, Colette Fried
Auditors: Deloitte & Touche LLP

LOCATIONS

HQ: Federal Reserve Bank of Chicago, Dist. No. 7
230 South La Salle Street, P.O. Box 834, Chicago, IL
60690-0834
Phone: 312 322-5322
Web: www.chicagofed.org

HISTORICAL FINANCIALS

Company Type: Public

Income Statement

	REVENUE ($ mil.)	NET INCOME ($ mil.)	NET PROFIT MARGIN	EMPLOYEES
			FYE: December 31	
12/14	5,176	66	1.3%	—
12/13	5,001	(12)	—	—
12/12	5,409	122	2.3%	—
12/11	5,586	5,026	90.0%	—
12/10	6,541	6,068	92.8%	—
Annual Growth	(5.7%)	(67.7%)	—	—

2014 Year-End Financials

Debt ratio: 49.36%
Return on equity: 4.33%
Cash ($ mil.): —
Current ratio: 2.01
Long-term debt ($ mil.): 90,946
No. of shares (mil.): 15
Dividends
Yield: —
Payout: —
Market value ($ mil.): —

Federal Reserve Bank of New York, Dist. No. 2

The Federal Reserve Bank of New York is the largest in the Federal Reserve System to oversee US bank activities. It issues currency clears money transfers and lends to banks in its district. In addition to the duties it shares with 11 other regional Federal Reserve Banks the New York Fed trades US government securities to regulate the money supply intervenes on foreign exchange markets and stores monetary gold for foreign central banks and governments. The New York Fed's district is relatively small (made up of New York Puerto Rico the US Virgin Islands northern New Jersey and Fairfield County Connecticut) but the bank is the largest in the Federal Reserve System in assets and volume of transactions.

Operations

Secured in a vault 80 feet below street level in the New York Fed's Manhattan headquarters is billions of dollars worth of gold —some 25% to 30% of the world's official monetary gold reserves. The vault rests on Manhattan Island's bedrock considered to be one of the few foundations adequate enough to support the weight of the vault and its contents.

Financial Performance

The New York Fed's total revenue for 2012 was $56.4 billion a 42% increase in the $39.7 billion in revenue it collected for 2011. Treasury securities generate 55% of the New York Fed's total interest income while government sponsored mortgage securities generate almost 40%.

EXECUTIVES

Senior Vice President Deputy General Counsel
And Secretary, Michael A Held
Senior Vice President, Jean Bolwell
Svp Development Studies And Foreign Research
Emerging Markets And International Affairs,
John J Clark
Vice President of Data Center Operations, Len Len
Myrie Myrie
Senior Vice President Risk and Policy Financial
Institution Supervision, Arthur (Art) Angulo
Vice President Central Bank and International
Account Services, Betty Lau
Vice President Investment Support Office, Helen
Mucciolo
EVP and Head Emerging Markets and
International Affairs Group, Terrence J. Checki
Sr V Pres - Public Information, Peter Bakstansky
First Vice President, Christine M. Cumming
Executive Vice President, Roseann Stichnoth
Executive Vice President Risk Group, Sandra C.
(Sandy) Krieger
EVP and Head Research and Statistics Group,
James J. McAndrews
EVP Markets Group, Brian P. Sack
EVP and General Auditor, Edward C. Smith
EVP Corporate, Edward F. Murphy
President and CEO, William C. Dudley, age 63
Executive Vice President, William T. Christie
Executive Vice President, Susan W. Mink
EVP and Head Communications, Krishna Guha
Executive Vice President Markets Group, Simon M.
Potter
Chief of Staff and Vice President, James P. Bergin
Svp Financial Sector Analysis Financial
Institution Supervision, Kevin J Stiroh
Vice President And Counsel, Stephanie Heller
Assistant Vice President Large Domestic Banks,
Homer C Hill
Vice President, Rae Rosen

Vice President Human Resources Analytics and
Information Systems, Christina Miller
Senior Vice President And Deputy General
Counsel, Raleigh Tozer
Assistant Vice President Emerging Markets And
International Affairs Group, Matthew Higgins
Assistant Vice President, Donald (Don) Morgan
Vice President, Catherine Kung
Assistant Vice President And Markets Group
Contingency Officer, Denley Chew
Assistant Vice President of Special Investments
Management Group, Anna Chang
Executive Vice President, Dona Wong
Vice President Special Investment Management,
Zachary Taylor
Assistant Vice President, Matthew Wagner
Deputy General Counsel And Senior Vice
President, Joyce Hansen
Vp Financial Risk Management Credit And
Payments Risk, Adam Ashcraft
Vice President, Jonathan Polk
Assistant Vice President, Nick Marlin
Senior Vice President Relationship Management
Bank Supervision Grou, Dianne Dobbeck
Svp Statistics, Ken Lamar
Assistant Vice President, Linda Ricci
Vice President, Haeran Kim
Vice President Information Technology, Harry
Pringle
Vice President, Jennifer Zara
Vice President Of Protection Department Of Legal
G, Robert Sama
Vice President Senior Operational Risk Analyst
Basel Ii, Julie Heo
Assistant Vice President Of Legal Group, Sean
Omalley
Assistant Vice President Markets Group
Automation Services, Michael (Mel) Burk
Assistant Vice President, Michael Mowbray
Vice President Customer Service, Andrew Danzig
Vice President Legal And Compliance Risk, John G
(Jack) Ricketti
Assistant Vice President And Financial
Institutions Supervision Officer, Bettyann Griffith
Assistant Vice President, Sarah Adelson
Vice President, Robert Kraus
Assistant Vice President Of Financial Institution
Supervision Group, Brian Hefferle
Assistant Vice President, Dina Maher
Vice President Chief Procurement Officer, Maria
Frangelaki
Assistant Vice President, Rosalie Yee
Senior Vice President Federal Reserve Police,
Nicholas Proto
Assistant Vice President Of Financial Institution
Supervision Group, Louis Braunstein
Vice President Financial Institution Supervision
Group, Vic Chakrian
Vice President Engineering, Jason Stern
Vice President, Richard Cahill
Assistant Vice President Portfolio Management,
Pamela Yip
Senior Vice President Technology Strategy, Jeff
Weinstein
Assistant Vice President, Louis Scenti
Vice President, Jan Voigts
Assistant Vice President Of Credit And, Jhankhna
Varma
Vice President Strategy And Architecture, Carlos
Fuentes
Vice President, Bruce Richards
Assistant Vice President Service Strategy And
Oversight, John Mosquera
Vice President Purchasing, Todd Greenberg
Vice President, Richard Peach
Assistant Vice President Of Financial Institution
Supervision Group, Marilyn Arbuthnott
Vice President Wholesale Product Office, Robyn
Brandow

Assistant Vice President Of Emerging Markets And International Affairs Group, Idanna Appio
Internal Communications Vice President, Nick Balamaci
Assistant Vice President Of Human Resources Group, Danielle Levitt
Counsel And Assistant Vice President, Candace Jones
Assistant Vice President And Head Of Media Relations And Public Affairs, Andrea Priest
Assistant Vice President Senior Financial Analyst Global Wealth And Investment Management, Scott Nesson
Senior Vice President Of Chief Of Staffs Office Executive Office, Margaret McConnell
Assistant Vice President Of Financial Institution Supervision Group, Jacqueline McCormack
Vice President Financial Services, Chris Armstrong
Executive Vice President, Tamara Marcopulos
Vice President Information Security Automation And Systems Services Group, Roy Thetford
Assistant Vp Business Systems Development, Chin Yeh
Vice President Foreign Financial Institutions, Dana Green
Vice President And Counsel In The Legal Group, Richard Charlton
Senior Vice President Money And Payments Studies Research And Statistics Group, Kenneth Garbade
Assistant Vice President, Matthew Lieber
Assistant Vice President Emerging Markets Group, Tricia Kissinger
Assistant Vice President And Senior Advisor, Ethan Buyon
Assistant Vice President And Business Continuity Officer, Tami Daughdrill
Senior Executive Specialist Executive Vice President, Marlene Williams
Assistant Vice President Foreign Exchange And Investments, Robert Lerman
Assistant Vice President Business Process Excellence Office, Zachery Brice
Assistant Vice President Supervisory Policy, Kristin Malcarney
Vice President International Research Research And Statistics, Thomas Klitgaard
Assistant Vice President Of Financial Institution Supervision Group, Karen Kahrs
Assistant Vice President, Marsha Takagi
Senior Vice President Bank Supervision, Daniel Muccia
Vice President Of Data Center Operations, Len Myrie
Vice President, Daniel Hulse
Associate Vice President, Grace Sone
Vice President Customer Service, Tom Piderit
Senior Vice President, Steven Manzari
Assistant Vice President, Thomas Reilly
Vice President, Robert (Bob) Galletta
Vice President Market Operations, Anna Nordstrom
Vice President Of Group Shared Services Markets Group, Michele Walsh
Vice President Regional Affairs, Erica Groshen
Vice President Of Bank Supervision Group, Lance Auer
Department Head Monetary Policy And Economic Survey Department Statistics Function, Lessa Gomez
Vice President Payments Policy, Lucinda Brickler
Senior Vice President Bank Supervision Group, Vivek Alix
Vice President Wholesale Credit Risk Financial Institution Supervision Group, Eric Parsons
Assistant Vice President, Mayra Gonzalez
Assistant Vice President Of Financial Institution Supervision Group, Glen Reppy
Vice President, Smejkal Peter
Senior Vice President, Nancy Bercovici

Assistant Vice President Public Information, Margaret Carmody
Senior Vice President Statistics, Leon Taub
Assistant Vice President Markets Architecture, Max Hrabrov
Vice President, Lorie Logan
Senior Vice President, Christopher Calabia
Assistant Vice President, Patrick Coyne
Vice President Information Technology, Dianne Klein
Assistant Vice President Of Legal Group, Brett Phillips
Assistant Vice President Of Markets Group, Frank Keane
Chairman, Lee C. Bollinger, age 69
Chairman, Emily K. Rafferty, age 66
Assistant Treasurer, Angela O'Connor
Treasurer, Oliver Giannotti
Auditors: Deloitte & Touche LLP

LOCATIONS

HQ: Federal Reserve Bank of New York, Dist. No. 2
33 Liberty Street, New York, NY 10045-0001
Phone: 212 720-5000
Web: www.newyorkfed.org

Selected Offices
Buffalo New York
East Rutherford New Jersey
New York City
Utica New York

PRODUCTS/OPERATIONS

2012 Total Interest Income

	$ mil.	% of total
Treasury securities net	24,774	56
US government federal agency & government sponsored-enterprise securities	16,671	38
Government-sponsored enterprise debt securities net	1,395	3
Investments held by consolidated variable interest entities	1,110	3
Central bank liquidity swaps	76	-
Other	129	1
Total	**44,155**	**100**

HISTORICAL FINANCIALS

Company Type: Public

Income Statement

	REVENUE ($ mil.)	NET INCOME ($ mil.)	NET PROFIT MARGIN	EMPLOYEES
12/14	68,824	2,398	3.5%	—
12/13	50,355	(1,397)	—	—
12/12	56,361	525	0.9%	—
12/11	39,655	35,026	88.3%	—
12/10	43,290	39,761	91.8%	—
Annual Growth	**12.3%**	**(50.4%)**	**—**	**—**

FYE: December 31

2014 Year-End Financials

Debt ratio: 15.22%
Return on equity: 13.28%
Cash ($ mil.): 2,716,096
Current ratio: 1.51
Long-term debt ($ mil.): 418,319
No. of shares (mil.): 184
Dividends
Yield: —
Payout: —
Market value ($ mil.): —

Federal Reserve Bank of Richmond, Dist. No. 5

One of 12 regional banks in the Federal Reserve System the Federal Reserve Bank of Richmond oversees the Fifth District's system member banks and bank holding companies in Virginia; Maryland; the Carolinas; Washington DC; and most of West Virginia from branches in Maryland North Carolina and Virginia. It conducts examinations and investigations of member institutions distributes money issues savings bonds and Treasury securities and assists the Federal Reserve SystemÂin setting monetary policy. The bank also processes checks and acts as a clearinghouse for payments between banks. Federal Reserve Banks return earnings (mostly from investments in government bonds) to theÂUS Treasury.

Operations

The Richmond Fed employs economists scholars and research associates to conduct economic study regarding the Fifth District economy and also to support the Federal Reserve System's policymakers. It was organized in 1914 subsequent to the enactment of the Federal Reserve Act in 1913.

EXECUTIVES

Senior Vice President Research Director, John (Jack) Weinberg
Vice President, Malissa Ladd
Vice President Federal Reserve Information Technology Audit, Gregory Johnson
Assistant Vice President, Edward B Norfleet
President and CEO, Jeffrey M. (Jeff) Lacker, age 60
First VP and COO, Mark L. Mullinix
SVP and CTO, Roland Costa
CFO, Michael L. (Mike) Wilder
SVP and Regional Executive Baltimore, David E. (Dave) Beck
SVP Supervision Regulation and Credit, Jennifer J. Burns
SVP and CIO, Janice E. Clatterbuck
SVP and Regional Executive Charlotte, Matthew A. Martin
Assistant Vice President Support Services, James (Jamie) Hayes
Assistant Vice President, Hattie Barley
Assistant Vice President, Steven (Steve) Bareford
Assistant Vice President Information Technology Client and Computing Services, Johnnie Moore
Assistant Vice President, Christopher (Chris) Cook
Assistant Vice President, Cathy Howdyshell
Vice President Head of Risk Specialist Division, Carl Tannenbaum
Vice President, Linwood A Gill
Assistant Vice President, Doug Sampson
Assistant Vice President, Kim Nguyen
General Auditor Senior Vice President, Robert E (Bob) Wetzel
Assistant Vice President, Victoria Riendeau
Vice President, David Alfano
Vice President, Kevin Kckenna
Assistant Vice President, Devon Kistler
Assistant Vice President Deputy Central Point Of Contact, Joshua R%2E (Josh) Daulton
Assistant Vice President Information Technology, Keith Malatesta
Vice President Information Technology, Valerie Freund
Assistant Vice President, Julie Severson
Vice President, Howard Whitehead

Assistant Vice President, Gwen Byer
Vice President, R Ahern
Vice President And Chief Human Resources,
 Wendi L Hickman
Chairman, Russell C. (Rusty) Lindner, age 59
Deputy Chairman, Margaret G. Lewis, age 61
Assistant Vice President and Secretary, Page
 Marchetti
Treasurer, Cindy Bullington
Auditors: Deloitte & Touche LLP

LOCATIONS

HQ: Federal Reserve Bank of Richmond, Dist. No. 5
 Post Office Box 27622, Richmond, VA 23261
Phone: 804 697-8000
Web: www.richmondfed.org

HISTORICAL FINANCIALS

Company Type: Public

Income Statement

	REVENUE ($ mil.)	NET INCOME ($ mil.)	NET PROFIT MARGIN	EMPLOYEES
12/14	6,148	1,202	19.6%	—
12/13	5,666	284	5.0%	—
12/12	7,799	542	6.9%	—
12/11	10,043	9,222	91.8%	—
12/10	7,178	6,241	86.9%	—
Annual Growth	(3.8%)	(33.8%)	—	—

FYE: December 31

2014 Year-End Financials

Debt ratio: 35.99%
Return on equity: 9.78%
Cash ($ mil.): 247,334
Current ratio: 1.72
Long-term debt ($ mil.): 91,935
No. of shares (mil.): 131
Dividends
 Yield: —
 Payout: —
Market value ($ mil.): —

Federal Reserve Bank of San Francisco, Dist. No. 12

One of 12 regional banks in the Federal Reserve System the Federal Reserve Bank of San Francisco through four branch offices oversees hundreds of banks and thrifts in nine western states and American Samoa Guam and the Northern Mariana Islands - the largest of the 12 districts. It conducts examinations and investigations of member institutions distributes money issues savings bonds and Treasury securities and assists the Federal Reserve in setting monetary policy. The bank also processes checks and acts as a clearinghouse for payments between banks. Federal Reserve Banks are not-for-profit and return earnings (mostly from investments in government bonds) to the US Treasury.

Geographic Reach

The bank oversees the Twelfth Federal Reserve District which includes the nine western states of Alaska Arizona California Hawaii Idaho Nevada Oregon Utah and Washington and also the American Samoa Guam and the Commonwealth of the Northern Mariana Islands.

Branch offices reside in Los Angeles; Portland Oregon; Salt Lake City; and Seattle. It also has a cash processing center in Phoenix.

EXECUTIVES

First VP and COO, Mark A. Gould
President and CEO, John C. Williams
SVP, Teresa M. Curran
SVP Information and Technology and CIO, Gopa
 Kumar
Group Vice President and Deputy, David (Dave)
 Walker
Vp, Scott Turner
Vice President, Kevin Zerbe
Group Vice President, Clifford Croxall
Vice President Risk, Tom Cunningham
Senior Vice President, Stephen Hoffman
Vice President, Tracy Basinger
Group Vice President, Patrick (Paddy) Loncar
Senior Vice President, Jim Narron
Chairman, Roy A. Vallee, age 63
Deputy Chairman, Alexander R. (Alex) Mehran
Auditors: Deloitte & Touche LLP

LOCATIONS

HQ: Federal Reserve Bank of San Francisco, Dist. No. 12
 101 Market Street, San Francisco, CA 94105
Phone: 415 974-2000
Web: www.frbsf.org

HISTORICAL FINANCIALS

Company Type: Public

Income Statement

	REVENUE ($ mil.)	NET INCOME ($ mil.)	NET PROFIT MARGIN	EMPLOYEES
12/14	11,704	470	4.0%	—
12/13	8,507	323	3.8%	—
12/12	8,357	26	0.3%	—
12/11	8,863	8,071	91.1%	—
12/10	8,622	7,890	91.5%	—
Annual Growth	7.9%	(50.6%)	—	—

FYE: December 31

2014 Year-End Financials

Debt ratio: 30.41%
Return on equity: 5.75%
Cash ($ mil.): 469,398
Current ratio: 1.46
Long-term debt ($ mil.): 165,853
No. of shares (mil.): 83
Dividends
 Yield: —
 Payout: —
Market value ($ mil.): —

Federal Reserve System

Where do banks go when they need a loan? To the Federal Reserve System which sets the discount interest rate the base rate at which its member banks may borrow. Known as the Fed the system oversees a network of 12 Federal Reserve Banks located in major US cities; these in turn regulate banks in their districts and ensure they maintain adequate reserves. The Fed also clears money transfers issues currency and buys or sells government securities to regulate the money supply. Through its powerful New York bank the Fed conducts foreign currency transactions trades on the world market to support the US dollar's value and stores gold for foreign governments and international agencies.

Operations

By setting the discount rate and the federal funds rate (the rate at which banks borrow from each other) the Board influences the pace of lending and many believe the pace of the economy it-

self. In response to the economic downturn in 2008 the Fed aggressively cut the discount interest rate in an effort to jump-start the US economy.

Fed board members are appointed by the US president and confirmed by the Senate for one-time 14-year terms staggered at two-year intervals to prevent political stacking. Seven governors comprise the majority of the 12-person Federal Open Market Committee which determines monetary policy. The five remaining members are reserve bank presidents who rotate in one-year terms with New York always holding a place. National member banks must own stock in their Federal Reserve Bank though it is optional for state-chartered banks.

A seven-member Board of Governors oversees the Fed's activities. The board was chaired by Alan Greenspan from the Reagan administration until 2006. As chairman under four different presidents Greenspan wielded more power than perhaps any Fed chief in history and securities markets rose and fell on his every word. Greenspan was replaced by former chairman of President George W. Bush's Council of Economic Advisers and Fed board member Ben Bernanke whose second term as chairman ends January 31 2014.

Financial Performance

The Reserve Banks' income in 2012 was $81.6 billion. Sources of income come from interest earnings from the portfolio of government securities ($49 billion) and federal agency mortgage-backed securities ($31.4 billion). The total expenses for the entire Federal Reserve System for 2012 were $3.7 billion.

HISTORY

When New York's Knickerbocker Trust Company failed in 1907 it brought on a panic that was stemmed by J. P. Morgan who strong-armed his fellow bankers into supporting shaky New York banks. The incident showed the need for a central bank.

Morgan's actions sparked fears of his economic power and spurred congressional efforts to establish a central bank. After a six-year struggle between Eastern money interests and populist monetary reformers the 1913 Federal Reserve Act was passed. Twelve Federal Reserve districts were created but New York's economic might ensured it would be the most powerful.

New York bank head Benjamin Strong dominated the Fed in the 1920s countering the glut of European gold flooding the US in 1923 by selling securities from the Fed's portfolio. After he died in 1928 the Fed couldn't stabilize prices. Such difficulty along with low rates encouraging members to use Fed loans for stock speculation helped set the stage for 1929's crash.

During the Depression and WWII the Fed yielded to the demands of the Treasury to buy bonds. But after WWII it sought independence using Congress to help free it from Treasury demands. This effort was led by chairman William McChesney Martin with the assistance of New York bank president Alan Sproul (also a rival for the chairmanship). Martin diluted Sproul's influence by governing by consensus with the other bank leaders.

The Fed managed the economy successfully in the postwar boom but it was stymied by inflation in the late 1960s. In the early 1970s the New York bank also faced the collapse of the fixed currency exchange-rate system and the growth of currency trading. Its role as foreign currency trader became even more crucial as the dollar's value eroded amid rising oil prices and a slowing economy.

The US suffered from double-digit inflation in 1979 as President Jimmy Carter appointed New York Fed president Paul Volcker as chairman. Volcker believing that raising interest rates a few points would not suffice allowed the banks to raise their discount rates and increased bank reserve requirements to reduce the money supply. By the time inflation eased Ronald Reagan was president.

During the 1980s and 1990s US budget fights limited options for controlling the economy through spending decisions so the Fed's actions became more important. Its higher profile brought calls for more access to its decision-making processes. Alan Greenspan took over as chairman in 1987 after being designated by Reagan (and reappointed by presidents George H. W. Bush Bill Clinton and George W. Bush). He stepped down during the second Bush administration and was replaced by Ben Bernanke.

While the US economy seemed immune to the Asian currency crisis of 1997 and 1998 the Federal Reserve remained relatively quiescent. But when Russia defaulted on some of its bonds in 1998 leading to the near-collapse of hedge fund Long-Term Capital Management the New York Federal Reserve Bank brokered a bailout by the fund's lenders and investors.

This led in 1999 to new guidelines for banks' risk management. The next year the Fed faced up to the Internet age taking a look at e-banking supervision. After raising interest rates to stave off inflation during the go-go late 1990s the Fed cut rates an unprecedented 11 times in 2001 (to a 40-year low of 1.75%) to help spur the flagging post-boom economy.

Rate changes and subsequent economic changes continued with a low of 1% in 2003. In all rates were adjusted a total of 18 times between 2002 and 2006.

In 2008 the US faced an economic crisis as severe as any seen since the Great Depression that claimed numerous victims including Bear Stearns (the Fed brokered and assisted its purchase by JP-Morgan Chase) and Lehman Brothers. Together with former Secretary of the Treasury Henry Paulson chairman Ben Bernanke pushed for the passage of a $700 billion rescue plan —the largest in history. Through the plan the government purchased toxic assets including troubled mortgages and distressed properties. As his predecessor did during the economic downturn earlier this decade Bernanke also agressively cut the discount interest rate in an effort to jumpstart the economy.

EXECUTIVES

President Federal Reserve Bank of Philadelphia, Charles I. Plosser, age 64

President Federal Reserve Bank of Atlanta, Dennis P. Lockhart, age 66

President Federal Reserve Bank of Chicago, Charles L. (Charlie) Evans, age 58

President Federal Reserve Bank of Richmond, Jeffrey M. (Jeff) Lacker, age 60

Chairman, Janet L. Yellen, age 69

President Federal Reserve Bank of Dallas, Richard W. Fisher

President Federal Reserve Bank of Boston, Eric S. Rosengren, age 57

President and CEO Federal Reserve Bank of St. Louis, James B. Bullard, age 54

President Federal Reserve Bank of New York, William C. Dudley, age 63

President Federal Reserve Bank of Minneapolis, Narayana Kocherlakota

President Federal Reserve Bank of Kansas City, Ester George

President Federal Reserve Bank of San Francisco, John C. Williams

President Federal Reserve Bank of Cleveland, Loretta J. Mester

Vice President Information Technology, Jeffrey (Jeff) Blye

Vice President Corporate Support Services, Bruce Grinnell

Assistant Vice President And Economist, Troy Davig

Vice President Financial Management Lawson Cbaf, Kasandra Goulding

Executive Vice President And Research Director, Jeffrey Fuhrer

Assistant Vice President IT, Isaac Obstfeld

Senior Vice President (Senior Vice President) Corporate Strategy And Operations, Christina Kite

Vice Chairman, Stanley Fischer

Auditors: Deloitte & Touche LLP

LOCATIONS

HQ: Federal Reserve System
20th Street and Constitution Avenue N.W., Washington, DC 20551
Phone: 202 452-3245   **Fax:** 202 728-5886
Web: www.federalreserve.gov

Federal Reserve Banks
Atlanta
Boston
Chicago
Cleveland
Dallas
Kansas City Missouri
Minneapolis
New York
Philadelphia
Richmond Virginia
St. Louis
San Francisco

HISTORICAL FINANCIALS

Company Type: Public

Income Statement

FYE: December 31

	REVENUE ($ mil.)	NET INCOME ($ mil.)	NET PROFIT MARGIN	EMPLOYEES
12/14	114,299	4,363	3.8%	—
12/13	90,540	(492)	—	—
12/12	100,526	2,151	2.1%	—
12/11	88,027	78,538	89.2%	—
12/10	89,816	81,689	91.0%	—
Annual Growth	6.2%	(51.9%)	—	—

2014 Year-End Financials

Debt ratio: 28.87%
Return on equity: 7.78%
Cash ($ mil.): 4,425,400
Current ratio: 1.70
Long-term debt ($ mil.): 1,298,725

No. of shares (mil.): 574
Dividends
  Yield: —
  Payout: —
Market value ($ mil.): —

Federal-Mogul Holdings Corp

For Federal-Mogul the sum of the parts is greater than the whole. The company makes components used in cars trucks and commercial vehicles as well as in energy industrial and other transportation equipment. Its products include pistons spark plugs ignition coils bearings gaskets seals and brake pads sold under brand names such as Champion Federal-Mogul Fel-Pro Glyco and Moog. Federal-Mogul has manufacturing and distribution facilities in 34 countries worldwide; customers include global automakers BMW Ford General Motors and Volkswagen. Federal-Mogul also distributes its own and other company's auto parts to aftermarket customers. About 60% of sales come from outside the US.

Geographic Reach

Federal-Mogul operates almost 175 worldwide manufacturing facilities technical and distribution centers as well as sales and administration offices in 35 countries. The US represents its largest market generating 39% of its total revenue; Germany is next in line representing 17% of sales.

Operations

In 2012 Federal-Mogul restructured its operations into two segments to focus on two distinct customer sets. Its new powertrain segment makes and sells original equipment products for automotive heavy duty and industrial applications. The vehicle components segment distributes products in the global vehicle aftermarket and also serves original equipment (OE/OES) manufacturers with vehicle products like brakes chassis wipers and other vehicle components.

Financial Performance

The company has worked to rebuild its health after a rough decade. Its total sales decreased by 4% from $6.9 billion to $6.7 billion during 2011 to 2012. After earning a profit of $161 million in 2010 Federal-Mogul suffered a net loss of $90 million in 2011 and a net loss of $117 million in 2012.

Its net loss for 2012 was the result of the lower net revenue higher restructuring expenses and lower demand for its products in Europe. Since nearly 60% of its total sales derive from outside the US the company experienced decreased reported sales of about $288 million as a result of the strengthened US dollar against the euro during 2012.

Strategy

Federal-Mogul is taking steps to maintain its flexibility and reduce its dependence on cars trucks and commercial vehicles by applying its core products in other areas. For example it has expanded into the aerospace (brake products for airplanes) railroad (piston rings for locomotives) and offshore and marine markets (large bore rings and seals). Its push into power generation (large bearings for windmills) has included acquisitions of piston ring suppliers which has expanded Federal-Mogul's presence in commercial engines and wind energy.

Federal-Mogul has a number of joint ventures and alliances allowing it to expand its geographic reach into emerging markets including the BRIC (Brazil Russia India China) countries as well as South Korea and Turkey. Federal-Mogul maintains a controlling interest in just over half of its almost 30 joint ventures in 13 countries. These partnerships also allow the company to lower manufacturing costs broaden its customer base and develop and extend its product lines. Federal-Mogul works closely with customers to develop products specific to their needs utilizing its research and development centers in major global auto manufacturing locations including the US Germany UK France China and Japan.

To boost its business in China the company's Powertrain unit opened a new systems protection manufacturing facility in Changshu China —measuring some 7000-sq.-meters —to support domestic customers in the automotive high-speed rail and aviation sectors.

Mergers and Acquisitions

In 2012 Federal-Mogul purchased the spark plug business belonging to BorgWarner. The deal improved the company's European market share by adding new spark plug manufacturing sites located in France and Germany.

Ownership

Billionaire investor and chairman Carl Icahn owns a little more than 77% of Federal-Mogul.

HISTORY

In 1899 J. Howard Muzzy and Edward Lyon formed the Muzzy-Lyon Company and later subsidiary Mogul Metal Company. The two modified a printer's typecasting machine and developed a process for making die-cast engine bearings. Their first big order came in 1910 when Buick ordered 10000 connecting rod bearings for the Buick 10. In 1924 Mogul Metal merged with Federal Bearing and Bushing to become Federal-Mogul Corporation.

In 1941 Federal-Mogul had about 50 factories dedicated to the war effort and by 1945 sales had doubled from prewar levels. In 1955 the company acquired Bower Roller Bearing Company and changed its name to Federal-Mogul-Bower Bearings Inc. By the late 1950s it had nearly 100 distribution centers and sales had quadrupled in 10 years.

The company began investing in foreign manufacturing plants during the 1960s to safeguard against lower US car exports as more foreign cars entered the global market. It changed its name back to Federal-Mogul in 1965 and moved its headquarters from Detroit to Southfield Michigan the following year. After a recession in the mid-1970s Federal-Mogul realized that it was too dependent on the big automakers and began diversifying. It acquired the Mather Company a maker of high-performance sealing products in 1985. The next year it bought Carter Automotive (fuel pumps) and Signal-Stat (lighting and safety components).

In 1989 Dennis Gormley became CEO. He continued the diversification strategy and led the company into the automotive aftermarket. Gormley proposed a push into retail in 1992 and that year Federal-Mogul bought the aftermarket business of TRW Inc. In its effort to become the Pep Boys of the third world the company sold parts of its manufacturing business to finance its retail ventures. By 1996 it owned about 130 retail stores primarily in Latin America. The company lost money and that year Gormley resigned. His successor Dick Snell put an immediate end to the retail fiasco.

By 1998 Federal-Mogul had sold all of its retail holdings and was concentrating on providing parts for entire engine systems. That year it made two major acquisitions: Fel-Pro a domestic maker of gaskets and other sealing products for $720 million and T&N plc a British maker of bearings pistons and brake pads and Europe's largest asbestos maker during the 1980s. T&N was picked up on the cheap as its stock was depressed by looming asbestos lawsuits. The decision would prove a grave one for Federal-Mogul.

Driving further into the aftermarket Federal-Mogul paid $1.9 billion for the automotive business of Cooper Industries (Champion spark plugs windshield wipers steering and suspension parts brake parts). UK-based LucasVarity rejected Federal-Mogul's $6.4 billion buyout offer in 1999 in favor of a $7 billion offer from TRW.

In 2000 Federal-Mogul announced plans to close 22 North American replacement parts warehouses and consolidate 18 manufacturing plants in Europe and Asia. Despite the proposed cutbacks aimed at revitalizing the company CEO Richard Snell stepped down that year. Federal-Mogul director Robert Miller replaced Snell as chairman and became the interim CEO.

Early in 2001 Frank Macher a former Ford and ITT Automotive executive was named CEO. Not long after in the midst of the economic slowdown Federal-Mogul announced that it would cut its salaried workforce by almost 9%. In August the company acquired 85% of WSK Gorzyce a Polish piston maker.

After an ill-advised acquisitions bender which more than tripled the size of the company Federal-Mogul was forced into bankruptcy in 2001. The company entered Chapter 11 bankruptcy protection as a result of asbestos claims related to its acquisition of T&N plc. Following six years in bankruptcy in 2007 Federal-Mogul became the first of the leading suppliers of auto parts to emerge from Chapter 11. Competitors Dana (exited 2008) and Delphi (exited 2009) followed suit.

Federal-Mogul sold its Signal-Stat lighting business to Truck-Lite (a subsidiary of Penske) for $23 million in 2002. Early the next year the company sold its original equipment molded lighting assembly operations to Magna International for $19 million.

The company sold its large bearing operations in South Africa and Germany as well as its Dayton Ohio transmission operations in 2004. In 2005 the company named José Maria Alapont as CEO. Carl Icahn was appointed chairman in 2008 after acquiring an additional 50% stake in Federal-Mogul.

By the time 2008 rolled around the global financial markets were beginning to show signs of stress as the economic crisis was first rearing its ugly head. Between 2008 and 2010 the company implemented restructuring activities including a workforce reduction of more than 9% and a number of facility closures.

EXECUTIVES

SVP Global Chassis and Service, Bradley Norton
Co-CEO; CEO Vehicle Component Solutions, Daniel A. (Dan) Ninivaggi, age 51
SVP Global Marketing Vehicle Components Segment, James (Jay) Burkhart, age 58
President Asia Pacific Vehicle Components Segment, Paul Jefferson
SVP and CFO, Jerome Rouquet, age 48
SVP Global Sealing and Engine, Andrew Sexton
Senior Vice President and General Manager Global Pistons, Bernhard Motel
Senior Vice President and General Manager Sealing and Gaskets and Systems Protection, Janice Maiden
President Motorparts Europe Middle East and Africa (EMEA), Martin Hendricks
Sr. Vice President and General Manager Rings and Liners Valve Seats and Guides, Michael Hedderich
VP and General Manager Chassis and Service, Paul Stanecki
Senior Vice President and General Manager Bearings and Ignition, Richard (Rick) Llope
SVP Sales and Marketing Powertrain Segment, Horst Fischer
Vice President, Steve Gaut
Vice President, Brett Pynnonen
Auditors: Grant Thornton LLP

LOCATIONS

HQ: Federal-Mogul Holdings Corp
27300 West 11 Mile Road, Southfield, MI 48034
Phone: 248 354-7700
Web: www.federalmogul.com

2012 Sales

	$ mil.	% of total
US	2,584	39
Germany	1,163	17
France	436	7
Italy	312	5
Belgium/Switzerland	288	4
Mexico	286	4
UK	263	4
China	260	4
India	229	3
Other countries	843	13
Total	**6,664**	**100**

PRODUCTS/OPERATIONS

2012 Sales

	$ mil.	% of total
Powertrain	4,118	58
Vehicle component solutions	2,937	42
Adjustments	(391)	-
Total	**6,664**	**100**

Selected Products

Global Aftermarket
  Bearings and seals
  Camshafts
  Chassis
  Driveline
  Engine bearings
  Filters
  Friction products (brake drums linings pads and rotors)
  Fuel pumps
  Gaskets
  Ignition products
  Lighting products
  Oil pumps
  Performance additives
  Piston rings
  Pistons
  Spark plugs
  Steering and suspension products
  Timing components
  Valvetrain components
  Wipers
Powertrain Energy
  Camshafts
  Connecting rods
  Cylinder liners
  Engine pistons
  Ignition products
  Piston pins
  Piston rings
  Valve seats and guides
Powertrain Sealing and Bearings
  Aluminum engine bearings
  Bonded piston seals
  Bronze engine bearings
  Bushings and washers
  Combustion and exhaust gaskets
  Dynamic seals
  Engine and industrial bearings
  Heat shields
  Metallic filters
  Sintered engine and transmission components
  Static gaskets and seals
  Transmission components
Vehicle Safety and Protection
  Brake disc pads
  Brake linings and blocks
  Brake shoes
  Chassis parts (ball joints tie rod ends sway bar links idler arms and pitman arms)
  Dic pads (light vehicle and railway)
  Element resistant sleeving systems (protection products for wires hoses sensors and mechanical components)
  Flexible heat shields
  Fuel pumps
  Lighting (interior and exterior lighting components)
  Railway brake blocks
  Windshield wipers

Selected Brand Names

Abex (brake products)
AE (bearings piston rings pistons timing belts and kits and valves)
ANCO (wiper blades washer pumps and wiper arms)
Atlas (gaskets for diesel engines and heavy-duty equipment in Mexico)
Beral (brake linings and disc brake pads for commercial vehicles and trailers)
Carter (fuel pumps)
Champion (spark plugs filters and wiper blades)
DURON (brake products for commercial vehicles in Europe)
Fel-Pro (sealing products)
Ferodo (brake discs brake fluids brake pads and shoes motorcycle products and racing products)
FP Diesel (engine parts and gaskets for vehicles used in agricultural construction gas compression industrial marine mining and trucking sectors)
Glyco (bearings)

Goetze (piston rings and cylinder liners)
Moog (steering and suspension parts)
National (wheel end products)
Necto (brake products for vehicles in Spain)
Nüral (pistons)
Payen (gaskets cylinder head bolts and oil seals)
PowerMAX (spark plug wires)
Precision (universal joints)
Raimsa (clutch-release bearings hanger bearings and
    kingpins for vehicles in Mexico)
Sealed Power (camshafts engine bearings oil pumps
    pistons piston rings timing components and valvetrain
    products)
Speed-Pro (high-performance engine components)
Wagner Brake Products (brake products for passenger
    cars and medium-duty commercial vehicles)
Wagner Lighting

COMPETITORS

Affinia	Kolbenschmidt Pierburg
Aisin Seiki	Linamar Corp.
Akebono Brake	MAN
American Trim	Mahle International
BERU	Meritor
Bendix Commercial	Miba
Vehicle Systems	NGK SPARK PLUG
Bosch Corp.	Nippon Piston Ring
Continental AG	OSRAM Licht
Cooper-Standard	Remy International
Automotive	Riken Corporation
DENSO	Robert Bosch
Daido Steel	SPX
Dana Holding	Stanadyne
Delphi Automotive	Standard Motor
Systems	Products
Edelbrock	Stant Manufacturing
ElringKlinger	Timken
EnPro	Trico Products
Freudenberg-NOK	UCI International
GE	Universal
GKN	Manufacturing
Hastings Manufacturing	Valeo
Hella	Visteon
Hitachi Automotive	ZF TRW Automotive
Systems Americas	
Honeywell	
International	

HISTORICAL FINANCIALS
Company Type: Public

Income Statement
FYE: December 31

	REVENUE ($ mil.)	NET INCOME ($ mil.)	NET PROFIT MARGIN	EMPLOYEES
12/14	7,317	(168)	—	48,600
12/13	6,786	41	0.6%	44,275
12/12	6,664	(117)	—	45,000
12/11	6,910	(90)	—	45,000
12/10	6,219	161	2.6%	42,700
Annual Growth	4.1%	—	—	3.3%

2014 Year-End Financials

Debt ratio: 38.06%
Return on equity: (-14.63%)
Cash ($ mil.): 332
Current ratio: 1.74
Long-term debt ($ mil.): 2,563

No. of shares (mil.): 150
Dividends
  Yield: —
  Payout: —
Market value ($ mil.): 2,414

	STOCK PRICE ($) FY Close	P/E High/Low	PER SHARE ($) Earnings	Dividends	Book Value
12/14	16.09	— —	(1.12)	0.00	5.37
12/13	19.68	64 15	0.33	0.00	9.93
12/12	8.02	— —	(1.18)	0.00	7.33
12/11	14.75	— —	(0.91)	0.00	9.64
12/10	20.65	13 7	1.62	0.00	12.91
Annual Growth	(6.0%)	— —	—	—	(19.7%)

FedEx Corp

Holding company FedEx hopes its package of subsidiaries will keep delivering significant market share. Its FedEx Express unit is the world's #1 express transportation provider delivering about 3.5 million packages daily to more than 220 countries and territories from about 1800 FedEx Office shops. It maintains a fleet of about 650 aircraft and more than 56000 motor vehicles and trailers. To complement the express delivery business FedEx Ground provides small-package ground delivery in North America and less-than-truckload (LTL) carrier FedEx Freight hauls larger shipments. FedEx Office stores offer a variety of document-related and other business services and serve as retail hubs for other FedEx units.

Operations

FedEx offers a broad portfolio of transportation e-commerce and business services through subsidiary companies which operate independently and are managed collaboratively under the FedEx brand. These companies are included in four business segments:

FedEx Express: The world's largest express transportation company. Its business operations include FedEx Trade Networks (international trade services) and FedEx SupplyChain Systems (supply chain solutions.)

FedEx Ground: A leading North American provider of small-package ground delivery services. This segment includes FedEx SmartPost (business-to-consumer package delivery using the US Postal Service.)

FedEx Freight: Less-than-truckload freight services. This unit's offerings include FedEx Freight Priority FedEx Freight Economy. The FedEx Freight segment also offers freight delivery service throughout Canada and Mexico and includes FedEx Custom Critical which offers time-specific critical shipment services.

FedEx Services: Sales marketing information technology communications and back-office support for other FedEx companies. This unit includes FedEx TechConnect (US billings and collections support) and FedEx Office and Print Services (document and business services for FedEx Express and FedEx Ground shipping services.)

Geographic Reach

Fed Ex operates in or delivers goods to more than 220 countries and territories from over 1800 locations. The US accounts for roughly 70% of net sales each year.

Financial Performance

FedEx has achieved five straight years of unprecedented growth. Revenues jumped 4% from $45.6 billion in 2014 to $47.5 billion in 2015 –a historic milestone for the company. The company in 2015 was helped by a 12% increase in FedEx Ground sales and a 8% uptick in sales for its FedEx Freight operations.

Profits however fell 50% from $2.1 billion in 2014 to $1.1 billion in 2015. This was attributed to higher retirement plans adjustment expenses salaries and employee benefits. FedEx's cash flow from operating activities increased by 26% in 2015 primarily due to favorable changes in accounts payable and other liabilities and pension and postretirement health care assets and liabilities.

Mergers and AcquisitionsFedEx has achieved historic growth over the years through the use of acquisitions. In 2015 it agreed to acquire rival TNT Express for a purchase price of $4.8 billion in a major deal that will vastly improve its European footprint.

Previously in 2015 it expanded its e-commerce and supply chain portfolio through the purchase of GENCO a leading North American third-party logistics provider for $1.4 billion. The deal bolstered FedEx's expertise in the targeted vertical markets of technology health care and retail.In 2013 the company completed its acquisitions of Rapidão Cometa Logística e Transporte S.A. a Brazilian transportation and logistics company for $398 million. It also purchased TATEX a French express transportation company for $55 million and Opek Sp. z o.o. a Polish domestic express package delivery company for $54 million.

HISTORY

Company BackgroundFrom his undergraduate classes at Yale and his experience as a charter airplane pilot Fred Smith got the idea that increased automation of business processes would create the need for a reliable overnight delivery service and he presented his case in a term paper in 1965. After serving in the Marine Corps in Vietnam Smith began raising money to develop the overnight delivery idea. He founded Federal Express in 1971 with $4 million inherited from his father and $80 million from investors. Overnight and second-day delivery to two dozen US cities began in 1973.Several factors contributed to FedEx's early success: Airlines turned their focus from parcels to passengers; United Parcel Service (UPS) union workers went on strike in 1974; and competitor REA Express went bankrupt. FedEx went public in 1978.

EXECUTIVES

EVP Market Development and Corporate Communications, T. Michael Glenn, age 59, $833,364 total compensation
EVP and CFO, Alan B. Graf, age 59, $902,784 total compensation
Chairman President and CEO, Frederick W. (Fred) Smith, age 71, $1,266,960 total compensation
President and CEO FedEx Express, David J. Bronczek, age 61, $942,096 total compensation
EVP Information Services and CIO, Robert B. (Rob) Carter, age 55, $762,960 total compensation
President and CEO FedEx Freight, Michael L. Ducker, age 62
EVP General Counsel and Secretary, Christine P. Richards, age 60, $617,640 total compensation
President and CEO FedEx Ground, Henry J. Maier
Vice President, Shannon Brown
Senior Vice President Human Resources Emea, Jerry Tims
Senior Sales Vice President Analyst, Lynn Stuart
Vice President Administration. IT Operations, Lisa Coterillo
Vice President Operations northern Europe, Diamond Psarianos
Vice President Administration, Caroline Clarkson
Vice President Sox Compliance, Mike Callender
Vice President Administration to Belinda Watkins Network Computing and Information Technology Operat, Denise Alexander
Vice President Human Resources, Donna Humphreys
Vice President Administration EC Marketing, Shana Hyman
Executive Vice President, Rosa Rangel
Senior Vice President Human Resources, Mark Bishop
Executive Vice President, Marilyn Dasilva
Vice President Corporate Sales, Michael Moriarty
Corporate Vice President, Gina Adams
Vice President Sales and LAC, Steven (Steve) Goddard
Vice President Sales, Alan Grayson
Vice President Information Technology, Steve Moore

Senior Sales Analyst Vice President US Sales Northeast, Karen Kehrli
Vice President Digital Access Marketing, Tom Wicinski
Vice President Sales, Larry Labelle
Senior Sales Vice President Analyst, Theresa McKee
Vice President Marketing, Lawrence Lanier
Vice President Legal And Regulatory Fedex Express Latin America and Caribbean Division, Marilyn Blanco-reyes
Executive Vice President, Dottie Berry
Senior Vice President Of Sales, David Edmonds
Vice President Marketing, Malcolm Sullivan
Vice President Sales, Tobin Thomson
Senior Sales Vice President Analyst, Karen James
Vice President Applications, Jim Bowman
Vice President Ground Services, Scott Depoy
Vice President Of The Southern Region, Robert Holcombe
Vice President of Sales and Marketing, Rick Bateman
Vice President Sourcing, Susan Spence
Vice President Sales, Jerry Beyl
Vice President Government Affairs, Rick Rodgers
Security Coordinator Wpvp, Katrina Cole-Duncan
Vice President Risk Management and Business Transactions (1993), Cary S Blancett
Vice President Express Finance Planning, Elise Jordan
Volunteer Treasurer, David (Dave) Triplett
Secretary, Rona Foye
Auditors: Ernst & Young LLP

LOCATIONS

HQ: FedEx Corp
  942 South Shady Grove Road, Memphis, TN 38120
Phone: 901 818-7500
Web: www.fedex.com

2015 Sales

	% of total
US	72
Other countries	28
Total	**100**

PRODUCTS/OPERATIONS

2015 Sales

	$ mil.	% of total
FedEx Express	27,239	57
FedEx Ground	12,984	27
FedEx Freight	6,191	13
FedEx Services	1,545	3
Corporate eliminations and other	(506)	-
Total	**47,453**	**100**

Services
FedEx Trade Networks
FedEx Supply Chain Systems
FedEx SmartPost
GENCO

COMPETITORS

ABF Freight System	Pitney Bowes
Allegra Network	PostNL
AlphaGraphics	Ricoh USA
ArcBest	Ryder System
Canada Post	TNT Express
DHL	The UPS Store
Japan Post	UPS
Nippon Express	US Postal Service
Office Depot	Xerox
Old Dominion Freight	YRC Worldwide

HISTORICAL FINANCIALS

Company Type: Public

Income Statement

FYE: May 31

	REVENUE ($ mil.)	NET INCOME ($ mil.)	NET PROFIT MARGIN	EMPLOYEES
05/15	47,453	1,050	2.2%	166,000
05/14	45,567	2,097	4.6%	162,000
05/13	44,287	1,561	3.5%	160,700
05/12	42,680	2,032	4.8%	149,000
05/11	39,304	1,452	3.7%	143,000
Annual Growth	**4.8%**	**(7.8%)**	**—**	**3.8%**

2015 Year-End Financials

Debt ratio: 19.61%
Return on equity: 6.94%
Cash ($ mil.): 3,763
Current ratio: 1.84
Long-term debt ($ mil.): 7,249

No. of shares (mil.): 282
Dividends
  Yield: 0.0%
  Payout: 21.9%
Market value ($ mil.): 48,923

	STOCK PRICE ($) FY Close	P/E High/Low		PER SHARE ($) Earnings	Dividends	Book Value
05/15	173.22	49	38	3.65	0.80	53.09
05/14	144.16	21	14	6.75	0.60	48.04
05/13	96.34	22	17	4.91	0.56	54.71
05/12	89.14	15	10	6.41	0.52	46.46
05/11	93.64	21	15	4.57	0.48	48.01
Annual Growth	**16.6%**	**—**	**—**	**(5.5%)**	**13.6%**	**2.5%**

Fidelity & Guaranty Life

LOCATIONS

HQ: Fidelity & Guaranty Life
  Two Ruan Center, 601 Locust Street, 14th Floor, Des Moines, IA 50309
Phone: 800 445-6758
Web: www.fglife.com

HISTORICAL FINANCIALS

Company Type: Public

Income Statement

FYE: September 30

	ASSETS ($ mil.)	NET INCOME ($ mil.)	INCOME AS % OF ASSETS	EMPLOYEES
09/15	24,925	118	0.5%	220
09/14	24,152	162	0.7%	200
09/13	22,429	347	1.6%	175
09/12	20,990	344	1.6%	—
09/11	0	176	—	—
Annual Growth	**—**	**(9.6%)**	**—**	**—**

2015 Year-End Financials

Debt ratio: 1.20%
Return on equity: 7.47%
Cash ($ mil.): 502
Current ratio: —
Long-term debt ($ mil.): —

No. of shares (mil.): 58
Dividends
  Yield: 1.0%
  Payout: 11.9%
Market value ($ mil.): 1,432

	STOCK PRICE ($) FY Close	P/E High/Low		PER SHARE ($) Earnings	Dividends	Book Value
09/15	24.54	13	10	2.02	0.26	25.74
09/14	21.35	8	6	2.90	0.20	28.39
Annual Growth	**3.5%**	**—**	**—**	**(8.6%)**	**7.5%**	**(2.4%)**

Fidelity National Financial Inc

To make sure that buying a dream home doesn't become a nightmare Fidelity National Financial (also known as FNF) provides title insurance escrow home warranties and other services related to real estate transactions. It is now the biggest dog in the residential and commercial title insurance sectors (the next largest player is First American) and accounts for 35% of all title insurance policies in the US. The company operates through underwriters including Fidelity National Title Company Chicago Title Commonwealth Land Title Alamo Title and National Title of New York. It sells its products both directly and through independent agents. Fidelity National has also grown its holdings in casual restaurant chains.

Operations

The company is organized into two segments: FNF Core Operations which accounts for more than 80% of revenues and includes title insurance and related closing services; and FNF Ventures which includes its other investments.

Title insurance is typically one of the most stable types of insurance written. It is folded into the piles of paperwork homebuyers sign during closings with little or no fuss. Even when US home sales become sluggish the company stays busy from the brisk pace of refinancing of existing mortgages. Through Black Knight Financial and ServiceLink Fidelity National Financial provides mortgage technology and transaction services utilizing subsidiary Lender Processing Services' or LPS' MSP system (the largest residential mortgage servicing technology platform in the country). Fidelity National Financial acquired LPS in early 2014 and it plans to make similar acquisitions going forward.

Title insurance premiums account for about three-fourths of Fidelity National Financial's revenues but the company also maintains a small handful of other operations completely outside of the title insurance industry. These include a 32% stake in Ceridian a payroll and HR services firm. It has also committed to expanding its holdings in casual and upscale dining restaurants though its 55% ownership of American Blue Ribbon Holdings and its 87% stake in J. Alexander's.

Geographic Reach

Fidelity National Financial's insurance businesses operate exclusively within the US. Naturally the biggest markets are in states with the greatest populations: California Texas and Florida account for more than a third of its title insurance premiums. The company has international operations in the Asia/Pacific Europe and the Americas through its minority interest in an auto parts manufacturing business.

The company primarily leases offices in 41 states and Washington DC as well as in Canada India Mexico and Puerto Rico.

Sales and Marketing

Fidelity National Financial uses direct sales representatives and independent agents to market its title and escrow products to residential and commercial real estate customers. The company maintains some 1200 retail offices to provide residential title insurance. It markets its commercial title insurance though a network of 5000 agents in major urban real estate markets.

Financial Performance

While the company is basically sound Fidelity National Financial's revenues can be hampered by stiffness in the residential mortgage lending market. Recent earnings had trended upward until 2014 when revenue declined 6% to $8 billion (versus $8.6 billion in 2013). The decline was primarily due to lower title insurance earnings which fell as closing volumes decreased –especially refinance transactions.

Despite the decline in revenue net income rose 48% to $583 million in 2014 due to equity in earnings of unconsolidated affiliates such as Ceridian and FleetCor.

Cash flow from operations grew 17% to $567 million that year due to such factors as increased earnings from operations lower claims payments and a tax refund on the acquisition of LPS.

Strategy

Fidelity National Financial is now so dominant within the title insurance industry that any attempt to grow larger there would draw the scrutiny of regulators. While keeping its eye on strengthening its existing title insurance operations the company is focused on diversifying by buying up non-insurance related businesses. After bulking up on restaurant operations through recent acquisitions Fidelity National Financial aims to increase same-store sales and guest counts and reach long-term profit growth within its restaurant operations. The company is conducting some consolidation efforts within the division to assist with these goals.

To raise cash for more diversification the company sometimes sells its stakes in its investments. For example in 2014 it spun off its stake in auto parts manufacturer Remy International. In 2015 it sold its 70% stake in Cascade Timberlands to Whitefish Cascade Forest Resources for $85 million.

Mergers and Acquisitions

In a move to further expand its presence in the real estate world in 2014 the company acquired Lender Processing Services for $3.4 billion. The company's MPS real estate services platform is the leading such system in the US. Later that year FNF acquired a majority stake in LandCastle Title which had suffered from substantial escrow account violations. The bailout allowed Fidelity National Financial to further grow its title operations while preventing LandCastle's collapse.

Company Background

Like all title insurers Fidelity National Financial shivered when the big chill hit the real estate market in 2008. But while the company slowed it remained quick enough to take advantage of opportunities. When its ailing rival LandAmerica Financial Group filed Chapter 11 in 2008 the company bought up the choicer bits for $235 million. This purchase helped make it into the largest title insurer in the US and caught the attention of the FTC prompting the company to divest a few holdings to soothe the agency's nerves. The 2009 sale of Fidelity National Capital only brought in $50 million but took $214 million of debt off company ledgers. The 2010 sale of its 32% stake in Sedgwick Claims Management brought in some $225 million.

The current company arose in 2006 when a previous company also named Fidelity National Financial split apart its title insurance operations from its information services business. What had been Fidelity National Title Group took on its former parent's name while Fidelity National Information Services took on the former parent's remaining operations. The two companies share a history and some stray holdings but are otherwise separate.

EXECUTIVES

EVP and Chief Legal Officer, Peter T. Sadowski, age 61, $431,671 total compensation
Vice President Customer Care, Cynthia Fitzgerald

CEO, Raymond R. (Randy) Quirk, age 69, $769,133 total compensation
Vice President, Richard L Cox
Senior Vice President, Connie Mahoney
EVP General Counsel and Corporate Secretary, Michael L. (Mike) Gravelle, age 54, $495,984 total compensation
EVP, Brent B. Bickett, age 51, $550,558 total compensation
EVP and CFO, Anthony J. (Tony) Park, age 49, $435,069 total compensation
CIO, John Crowley
President, Mike Nolan
Vice President, James Johnson
Vice President Of Advanced Technology Solutions, Stella Painter
Senior Vice President Director Technology Services, Lenny Smith
Assistant Vice President Law, Greg Williamson
Senior Vice President Government Relations, Sherwood Girion
Executive Vice President, James E Sindoni
Vice President Finance, Karen Schwartz
Vice President Regional Controller, Sylvia Freyling
Managing Director Senior Vice President, Michael (Mel) Erwin
Assistant Vice President And Administrative Assistant, Jennifer (Jen) Edwards
Vice President Finance, Steven Pierce
Senior Vice President Major Claims, Joe Ward
Vice President Financial Analyst for Raymond R. Quirk Chief Executive Officer, Rene Strickland
Vice President County Manager, Nancilee Boslau
Vice President Associate Counsel, Paul Kleidman
Vice President Banking Administration, Don Eppley
Vice President Assistant Controller, Edward Peebles
Assistant Vice President Business Development, Scott Nordell
Assistant Vice President Division Counsel, Arthur (Art) Maroney
Assistant Vice President Product Development, Robin Guinee
Senior Vice President New Solutions Development, Greg Cleveland
Assistant Vice President Branc, Kim Barr
Assistant Vice President, Jose Flores
Vice President US Customer Relationships and Implementations Automotive Finance Division, Joyce Fletcher
Vice President Enterprise Strategy, Greg McCrery
Vice President, Jennifer Gehr
Vice President of Sales And Marketing, Marty Romain
Assistant Vice President Human Resources and Acco, Kavi Shankar
Senior Vice President Data Center Operations, Brian Hann
Vice President Marketing and Communications, Laura Buser
Assistant Vice President, Sandy Dow
Assistant Vice President, Don Todd
Assistant Vice President Agency Auditor, Mary Rooney
Senior Vice President And Associate General Counsel, Marc Mayo
Assistant Vice President Corporate Technology, Ellen Gander
Assistant Vice President Escrow Administrator, Brenda Betz
Assistant Vice President, Erin Searcy
Vice President Kitsap Operations, Mary Schofield
Senior Vice President Enterprise Technology Services, Mike Williams
Vice President Information Technology, Steve Murnin
Vice President Information Technology, Dan Leisle
Vice President, George Tellez

Senior Vice President National Business Development, Mark Till
Vice President In House Litigation Director, Joseph (Jo) Tucker
Vice President North and Central Florida Area Agency Services Manager, Jason Somers
Vice President Human Resources Employee Training and Development, Karen Harper
Assistant Vice President, Jill Wright
Vice President, Claire Manning
Vice President Legal Department, Lottie Skarnulis
Vice President Regional Agency Audit Director, Chuck Hart
Assistant Vice President, Denise Presley
Assistant Vice President, Elaine Lovit
Assistant Vice President Of Human Resource, Carla Farmer
Vice President Agency Counsel, Thomas (Thom) Bartlett
Vice President, Lewis Dunton
Vice President Regional Manager, Jeffrey Wolff
Assistant Vice President And Director 401K Plan, Eva Chavis
Vice President, Amy Tueckes
Vice President Commercial Title Officer, Eric Bowen
Assistant Vice President, David (Dave) Scott
Senior Vice President Fidelity National Title, John (Jack) Tonelli
Senior Claims Counsel And Vice President, Scott Aronowitz
Vice President And Business Development Representative, Terri Griswold
Vice President Of Inbound Sales, Susan Apodaca
Vice President, Debby Boyd
Vice President Commercial Underwriting, Jeffrey Yearwood
Vice President Sales and Major Accounts, Ginger McCully
Vice President, Stephanie Barteky
Vice President, Marty Clinkaberry
Southeast Regional Vice President, Dave Myers
Assistant Vice President Regional Accounting Manger, Holly A Odonnell
Assistant Vice President Team Lead Order Management, Joanne Passantino
Vice President Of Sales And Marketing, Lisa Capes
Vice President Regional Escrow, Heidi Cassel
Assistant Vice President Technology Program Manager, Jamie Baker
Senior Vice President Corporate Finance, David Ducommun
Vice President Product Management, Dottie Yates
Vice President, Jim Petropoulos
Vice President Of Business Development, Ryan Pulliam
Vice President, Tabitha Campbell
Executive Vice President Regional Manager, Don Dubois
Vice President and Indemnified Credit Risk Underwriter Title Insurance, Keith Dager
Assistant Vice President Asset Accounting Manager, Melissa (Mel) Garcia
Vice President Senior Counsel, Vanessa Elliott
Senior Vice President, Maggie Vogeler
Vice President, Roger Shiffermiller
Vice President, Stacey Krone
Assistant Vice President Senior Project Manager FIS Project Management Office, Avis Sweet
Assistant Vice President Counsel, Natalie Bray
Assistant Vice President Branch Manager, Rita Abbey
Managing Counsel Vice President, Ray Aaronian
Assistant Vice President, Kristin Wyckoff
Vice President Of Operations, Christine Martin
Executive Vice President, Phil Shea
Assistant Vice President, Paul Brown
Senior Vice President, Kevin Gallagher
Executive Vice President, Jim Herleman
Assistant Vice President, Pati Walter

Assistant Vice President And Escrow Officer, Yvonne Ahsing
Vice President Sales, Ron Nyeholt
Vice President, Gregory Thomas
Assistant Vice President Marketing and Business Development, Deborah (Deb) Bayha
Assistant Vice President, Annie Grogan
Vice President Assistant Controller, John King
Executive Vice President Fidel, Joe Grealish
Assistant Vice President, James Carels
Senior Vice President Mergers And Acquisitions, Greg S Lane
Vice President Sales, John Ravita
Assistant Vice President Branch Manager, Diane Nelson
Assistant Vice President, Jacque Ryan
Assistant Vice President, Sue Davila
Assistant Vice President Associate Couns, Janelle Rosenbaum
Assistant Vice President, Phyllis Miller
Assistant Vice President, Pat Dove
Assistant Vice President Escrow Closer, Vickie Zackery
Vice President Director Regulatory LIC, Trudy Beck
Assistant Vice President Associate Branch Counsel, Francis (Fran) Hoffman
Executive Vice President, Marvin Zindler
Assistant Vice President, Filmon Berhe
Executive Vice President Human Resources, Donnette Peacock
Assistant Vice President, Brandie Cho
Assistant Vice President And Senior Account Executive, Chris Newman
Vice President Business Development, Eileen Saul
Assistant Vice President Analyst Corporate Compliance, Gina Stanley
Legal Assistant Assistant Vice President, Patricia (Pat) Jandrue
Assistant Vice President Senior NCS Coordinator, Suzanne Rippel
Vice President, Dorry Bragg
Assistant Vice President Escrow Officer, Catherine Dean
Vice President Sales, Betty Carter
Assistant Vice President Sales Representative, Mitch Perez
Vice President, Gerry Grady
Assistant Vice President, Lois Watson
Vice President Of Sales, Isabelle Pullis
Assistant Vice President And Agency Account Manager, John Stilla
Vice President, Sam Kitamura
Vice President Senior Trial Attorney, Nate Bernstein
Vice President Senior Claims Counsel, Reece Wilson
Assistant Vice President Senior Recoupment Counsel, Christopher (Chris) Wasson
Auditors: KPMG LLP

LOCATIONS

HQ: Fidelity National Financial Inc
601 Riverside Avenue, Jacksonville, FL 32204
Phone: 904 854-8100
Web: www.fnf.com

PRODUCTS/OPERATIONS

2014 Revenues

	$ mil.	% of total
FNF Core		
Title operations	5,652	70
BKFS	852	11
FNF Corporate & other	(14)	-
FNFV		
Restaurant group	1,423	18
FNF Corporate & other	111	1
Total	**8,024**	**100**

COMPETITORS

American Coast Title
American Home Shield
DENSO
Denny's
DineEquity
Equity Title Company
First American
Gracy Title A Stewart Company
Investors Title
Motorcar Parts
North American Title
OSI Restaurant Partners
Old Republic
Old Republic National Title
Perkins & Marie Callender's
Robert Bosch
Stewart Information Services
Title Resource Group
United General Title Insurance

HISTORICAL FINANCIALS

Company Type: Public

Income Statement
FYE: December 31

	ASSETS ($ mil.)	NET INCOME ($ mil.)	INCOME AS % OF ASSETS	EMPLOYEES
12/14	13,868	583	4.2%	56,883
12/13	10,524	402	3.8%	63,861
12/12	9,902	606	6.1%	60,451
12/11	7,862	369	4.7%	17,396
12/10	7,887	370	4.7%	18,200
Annual Growth	**15.2%**	**12.0%**	—	**33.0%**

2014 Year-End Financials

Debt ratio: 20.38%
Return on equity: 10.54%
Cash ($ mil.): 700
Current ratio: —
Long-term debt ($ mil.): —

No. of shares (mil.): 371
Dividends
  Yield: 1.0%
  Payout: 36.2%
Market value ($ mil.): 12,808

	STOCK PRICE ($) FY Close	P/E High/Low	PER SHARE ($) Earnings	Dividends	Book Value
12/14	34.45	47 34	0.75	0.37	16.12
Annual Growth	—	— —	—	—	—

Fidelity National Information Services Inc

At Fidelity National Information Services (FIS) the check will never get lost in the mail. FIS provides software outsourcing and IT consulting for the financial services industry. For banks and other financing entities the company's offerings address financial functions such as core processing decision and risk management and retail channel operations as well as payment services such as electronic funds transfer check and ticket processing and credit card production and activation. The company's 14000 customers aren't just the largest private financial institutions but also small businesses and government entities and are in more than 100 countries.

Operations FIS is divided three product/service segments: payment solutions financial solutions and an international segment. Payment solutions and financial solutions each generate about 40% of the company's total sales. International solutions makes up the remainder of sales and provides services outside North America primarily in Brazil

Germany the UK and India. The company's NYCE Payments Network operates a network of more than 360000 ATMs serving more than 90 million cardholders. Its Capco subsidiary offers strategic consulting services when it comes to complex technology and large-scale integration projects.

Geographic Reach

FIS operates through 140 owned or leased locations in Africa Asia Australia Europe the Middle East the Caribbean Latin America and the US. It operates 27 service centers around the world.

Financial Performance FIS broke through the $6 billion mark in revenue for the first time in 2013 and posted its sixth straight year of revenue growth. Revenue rose about 4.5 % from 2012 because of growth in transactions and professional and consulting services higher termination fees and incremental revenues from acquisitions made in 2013 and 2012.

Net income rose about 7% in 2013 to $493 million buoyed by the higher revenue and decreased interest expense. Cash flow from operations ticked up in 2013 to $1.06 billion from $1.05 billion in 2012.

Strategy

FIS has been aggressive in expanding internationally and it has been especially active in India. Muthoot Finance tapped FIS to provide fully managed ATM services and switching which enables Muthoot to place its branded ATMs across India. FIS also installed its EFT switching platform and comprehensive card management product for Bank of Maharashtra. Further Shivalik Mercantile Cooperative Bank Ltd selected FIS to provide its Profile core banking product.

Brazil is another international growth area for FIS where its joint venture partner Banco Bradesco accounts for 23% of revenue for international solutions. The venture currently processed more than 50 million credit cards for clients in Brazil and provides call center cardholder support and collection services for their card portfolios.

Mergers and Acquisitions

FIS continues to bank on acquisitions to strengthen its offerings and broach new markets. With the purchase of Reliance Financial Corporation FIS Wealth Management Services an FIS subsidiary can quickly expand the company's retirement and trust offerings. In consumer lending FIS acquired CMSI a provider of consumer loan origination software and services. Adding CMSI's underwriting automation strengthens FIS' consumer lending services. The acquisition of Brussels-based Clear2Pay added corporate payment products payments managed services and payments processing utilities bolstering FIS' global payments offerings.

In 2012 FIS purchased mFoundry a mobile banking software provider for both retailers and banks. The deal gave FIS access to a broader client base and kept up its momentum in the important mobile growth market.

EXECUTIVES

Corporate Executive Vice President Strategic Solutions, Francis (Fran) Sanchez
Senior Vice President Customer Delivery Automotive Finance, Linda Mae Southerland
Executive Vice President And Chief Financial Officer Fis, Jeffrey (Jeff) Carbiener
EVP Global Financial Solutions (GFS), Rob Heyvaert
CIO, Ido Gileadi
President Integrated Financial Solutions, Gary A. Norcross, age 50, $850,000 total compensation
EVP Integrated Financial Solutions (IFS), Anthony Jabbour
EVP and Chief Product Officer; Head Enterprise Product Organization, Nancy Langer

EVP General Counsel and Corporate Secretary, Michael P. Oates, age 56, $475,000 total compensation
EVP and CFO, James W. (Woody) Woodall, age 45, $500,000 total compensation
EVP and Chief Risk Officer, Greg Montana, $365,000 total compensation
SVP and CTO, Troy Bradley
Senior Vice President Global Commercial Services Supply Chain and Real Estate, Kevin Gouin
Vice President Account Management, Jaspreet Kondal
Senior Vice President and Treasurer, Michael E (Mel) Sax
Executive Vice President, Kay Nichols
Senior Vice President%2c+strategy+%26+business+development, Ijaz Anwar
Senior Vice President Engineering And Product Management, Cayford Burrell
Vice President Sales CSF Division, Brian Paulson
Senior Vice President, Tere Brun
Senior Vice President, Duncan Mitchell
Vice President Global Solutions, Glenn Bingham
Vice President Marketing, Linda Netherton
Vice President International Human Resources, Bart Ballew
Vice President, Doug French
Senior Vice President, Maria Schuld
Assistant Vice President Chargeback Services, Christine Sterling
Assistant Vice President, Marie Storey
Svp Marketing And Corporate Communications Enterprise Banking Solutions, Michelle (Mitch) Kersch
Executive Vice President, Steve Patterson
Vice President Global Real Estate Director, Sean Oliver
Vice President Product Management, Dominique Stevens
Vice President Marketing, Terry Blake
Vice President, Robert (Bob) Brennen
Senior Vice President Business Development, Debbie Laudermilk
Operations Vice President, David Smith
Vice President Solutions Consulting, Floyd Berus
Vice President Sales And Marketing, Robert Boitano
Senior Vice President Payments Strategy And Architecture, Barry Rhodes
Vice President Of Operations, Scott Daniel
Vice President Business Development, Thomas Carlton
Vice President Managing Director, Juan Aviles
Senior Vice President Loyalty Services, Robert (Bob) Legters
Senior Vice President Product Planning, Chris Knebel
Vice President Operations, John Oleon
Senior Vice President Credit Card, Barbara Hunter
Vice President Law, Debbie Segers
Vice President, Bradford Pineault
Vice President Head of Global Infrastructure and Delivery, Mike Williams
Senior Vice President Relationship Manager, Melissa (Mel) Tierney
Assistant Vice President Treasury, Alex Alley
Vice President Systems, Jim Hawley
Assistant Vice President, Kimberly Sadler
Vice President, William Peirce
Vice President Advanced Technology Solutions, Hank Godwin
Vice President Business Recovery Services Advanced Technology Solutions, Ovid Babb
Assistant Vice President Global Midrange Applications, Alex Pisieczko
Senior Vice President Operations, Mike Amble
Vice President Architecture Usability and Tools, James (Jamie) Joyce
Senior Vice President, Scott Stiegler

Assistant Vice President Chargeback Services, Cameron Arnold
Vice President Network Products, Ignacio Blanco
Vice President Channels Delivery, Sethu Thottikamath
Vice President Service Delivery Advanced Technology Solutions, Curtis Townsend
Senior Vice President Business Development Enterprise Banking Solutions, Frank Krause
Executive Vice President Chief Legal Officer and Corporate Secretary, Michael L (Mel) Gravelle
Vice President IT, Jon Parks
Vice President Marketing, Cynthia Knowles
Vice President Sales, Jan Whitfield
Vice President Infrastructure Delivery, Corey Maso
Vice President Sales and Marketing, Danny Amaral
Vice President Strategic Account Management, Kristen Wiley
Vice President of Software Development, Matt Lessig
Executive Vice President Finance, Al Stinson
Senior Vice President Financial Solutions, Pete Van Sistine
Network Vice President, Zahoor Elahi
Vice President Operations, John G (Jack) Oleon
Senior Vice President Sales Automotive Finance, Cliff Thompson
Vice President and Chief Division Counsel, Pamela (Pam) Green
Chairman, Frank R. Martire, age 67
Auditors: KPMG LLP

LOCATIONS

HQ: Fidelity National Information Services Inc
601 Riverside Avenue, Jacksonville, FL 32204
Phone: 904 438-6000
Web: www.fisglobal.com

PRODUCTS/OPERATIONS

2014 Sales

	$ mil.	% of total
Payment solutions	2,454	40
Financial solutions	2,344	39
International solutions	1,273	21
Corporate & other	(2.5)	-
Total	**6,070**	**100**

Selected Products and Operations
Biller Direct
Card
Commercial Treasury
Core Banking
Document Output
eBanking
ePayment
Fraud Management
Governance Risk and Compliance
Government
Hardware Solutions
Image
Lending
Loyalty
Mobile
NYCE Payments Network
Payment Network Solutions
Retail Payments
Risk Management
Sales and Service
Technology Platforms
Wealth Management Solutions

COMPETITORS

ACI Worldwide	Jack Henry
Accenture	MasterCard
Alliance Data Systems	Misys
D+H USA	Open Solutions
DST Systems	Oracle Financial
First Data	Services Software
Fiserv	SEI Investments
Global Payments	SunGard
HP Enterprise Services	TEMENOS Group AG

Heartland Payment Systems
IBM
Infosys
TeleCheck
Total System Services
Visa Inc

HISTORICAL FINANCIALS
Company Type: Public

Income Statement
FYE: December 31

	REVENUE ($ mil.)	NET INCOME ($ mil.)	NET PROFIT MARGIN	EMPLOYEES
12/14	6,413	679	10.6%	40,000
12/13	6,070	493	8.1%	38,000
12/12	5,807	461	7.9%	35,000
12/11	5,745	469	8.2%	33,000
12/10	5,269	404	7.7%	33,000
Annual Growth	**5.0%**	**13.8%**	**—**	**4.9%**

2014 Year-End Financials

Debt ratio: 34.90%
Return on equity: 10.34%
Cash ($ mil.): 492
Current ratio: 1.55
Long-term debt ($ mil.): 5,054

No. of shares (mil.): 284
Dividends
Yield: 1.5%
Payout: 50.0%
Market value ($ mil.): 17,721

	STOCK PRICE ($) FY Close	P/E High/Low	PER SHARE ($) Earnings	Dividends	Book Value
12/14	62.20	27 21	2.35	0.96	23.01
12/13	53.68	31 20	1.68	0.88	22.64
12/12	34.81	23 17	1.55	0.80	22.58
12/11	26.59	22 14	1.53	0.20	22.20
12/10	27.39	26 19	1.15	0.20	21.21
Annual Growth	**22.8%**	**— —**	**19.6%**	**48.0%**	**2.1%**

Fidelity Southern Corp

Fidelity Southern Corp. is the holding company for Fidelity Bank which boasts over $3 billion in assets and some 45 branches in the Atlanta metro and in northern Florida markets. The bank offers traditional deposit services such as checking and savings accounts CDs and IRAs. Consumer loans primarily indirect auto loans which the company purchases from auto franchises and independent dealers throughout the Southeast make up more than 50% of its loan portfolio. Real estate construction commercial real estate business residential mortgage and other consumer loans round out Fidelity Southern's lending activities. Subsidiary LionMark Insurance Company offers consumer credit-related insurance products.

OperationsAbout 50% of Fidelity Southern's total revenue came from loan interest (including fees) in 2014 while another 2% came from interest on its investment securities. The rest of its revenue came from mortgage banking income (28%) indirect lending activities (9%) SBA Lending (3%) service charges on deposit accounts (2%) and other miscellaneous income sources. The bank had a staff of roughly 1040 employees at the end of 2014.Geographic ReachWhile the company mostly has a branch presence in Georgia and Florida it also offers mortgage loans indirect auto loans and Small Business Administration (SBA) loans in a dozen Southern states.Sales and MarketingFidelity Southern mostly serves individuals and small to medium-sized businesses. The company spent $2.34 million on advertising and promotions in 2014 up from $1.69 million and $1.13 million in 2013 and 2012 respectively.Financial

PerformanceFidelity Southern's revenues and profits have risen over the past several years thanks to growing loan and deposit business from branch openings and acquisitions lower interest expenses and declining loan loss provisions as its loan portfolio's credit quality has improved with higher property valuations in the strengthened economy. The company's revenue inched higher by 1% to $197 million in 2014 mostly as its loan balances grew organically by 8% during the year with higher loan originations and market expansion.Higher revenue and lower interest expenses in 2014 boosted Fidelity Southern's net income by 9% to a record $30 million. Its cash levels plummeted during the year with operations using a net $141 million for the year after adjusting its earnings for non-cash items related to its net proceeds from its loans held for sale.Strategy

Fidelity Southern has focused on building and diversifying its loan portfolio including originating more residential mortgages commercial loans and consumer installment loans. The bank has been opening new branches as part of this organic growth strategy. During 2014 it opened 12 new branches including five in Georgia and seven in Florida.It's also pursued small bank and branch acquisitions to grow its loan and deposit business while expanding its geographic reach in Florida and Georgia.Mergers and AcquisitionsIn October 2015 the Fidelity Bank agreed to purchase The Bank of Georgia including its $295 million in total assets $280 million in deposits and seven branches in Peachtree City Fayetteville Tyrone Sharpsburg Newnan and Fairburn. September 2015 Fidelity Southern purchased eight branches in Florida from First Bank including $154 million in deposits and $31.6 million in loans. The deal expanded Fidelity's presence in counties surrounding Bradenton Palmetto and Longboat Key.In September 2014 the company purchased six branches of CenterState Bank of Florida including $174.2 million in deposits. The deal expanded Fidelity's presence in counties surrounding Orlando and Jacksonville.

HISTORY

Company BackgroundWWII veteran Clark Harrison and five others founded Fidelity National Bank in 1973. The first office opened in downtown Decatur Georgia the next year. Fidelity National Bank opened its second branch and formed Fidelity Southern Corporation as a holding company in 1979; it formed Fidelity National Mortgage a year later. In 1984 the company received trust powers opened two new branches and began a major credit card marketing program.

The acquisition of two branches from the Resolution Trust Corporation in 1992 brought the number of branches to 10 and increased assets to $257 million. Fidelity National Capital Investors a retail brokerage was incorporated that year. In 1993 Fidelity National Bank began a consumer sales finance department to buy auto loans from car dealers.

The company opened an office in Jacksonville in 1995 to offer mortgage car and construction lending. Also that year the firm changed the name of its holding company to Fidelity National Corporation.

Fidelity National acquired Friendship Community Bank in Florida and bought six branches from First Union and NationsBank in 1996; rapid expansion and unexpectedly high credit card chargeoffs that year slashed earnings and prevented Fidelity National from opening three of its newly acquired branches. Under the scrutiny of federal regulators the bank discontinued its high-default card program the next year and shored up its finances raising capital through a stock offering.

In 1998 Fidelity National focused on maintaining capital levels and recovering from its losses while other banks expanded. Fidelity National Bank finally gained regulatory approval to open the three remaining branches acquired from NationsBank and First Union later that year. Regulators released the bank from capital and dividend restrictions in 1999 but Fidelity National had to restate its earnings for 1997 citing overestimation of an asset's value.

Fidelity National experienced moderate growth in 2001. Inspections by the Federal Reserve Board in 2000 and 2001 led to Fidelity National's adoption of a resolution that prohibits Fidelity National from redeeming its capital stock paying dividends on its common stock or incurring debt without prior approval of the Federal Reserve Board. In light of a softening economy in 2001 Fidelity National placed greater significance on credit risk management and building the secured portion of its consumer loan portfolio. The company sold its credit card business to Bank One in December.

In 2003 the company changed its name back to Fidelity Southern Corporation and its branches converted to the shortened Fidelity Bank; the bank also switched from a national to a state charter.

EXECUTIVES

President; Secretary and Treasurer LionMark Insurance Company, H. Palmer Proctor, age 47, $500,000 total compensation

Chairman and CEO, James B. Miller, age 75, $750,000 total compensation

VP; EVP Fidelity Bank; President LionMark Insurance Company, David Buchanan, age 57, $400,000 total compensation

CFO, Stephen H. Brolly, age 52, $250,000 total compensation

Human Resources Director and Vice President, Jimmy Trimble

Vice President Commercial Banking, Kevin Lubitz

Auditors: Ernst & Young LLP

LOCATIONS

HQ: Fidelity Southern Corp
3490 Piedmont Road, Suite 1550, Atlanta, GA 30305
Phone: 404 639-6500

PRODUCTS/OPERATIONS

2014 Sales

	$ mil.	% of total
Interest		
Loans including fees	96	50
Investment securities	4	2
Federal funds sold & bank deposits	0	.
Noninterest		
Mortgage banking activities	55	28
Indirect lending activities	18	9
SBA lending activities	5	3
Service charges on deposit accounts	4	2
Bank owned life insurance	1	1
Other fees & charges	4	2
Other	5	3
Total	**197**	**100**

COMPETITORS

BB&T	SunTrust
Bank of America	Synovus
Citizens Bancshares	Wells Fargo
Regions Financial	

HISTORICAL FINANCIALS

Company Type: Public

Income Statement

FYE: December 31

	ASSETS ($ mil.)	NET INCOME ($ mil.)	INCOME AS % OF ASSETS	EMPLOYEES
12/14	3,085	30	1.0%	1,038
12/13	2,564	27	1.1%	890
12/12	2,477	25	1.0%	774
12/11	2,234	11	0.5%	174
12/10	1,945	10	0.5%	559
Annual Growth	**12.2%**	**31.2%**	**—**	**16.7%**

2014 Year-End Financials

Debt ratio: 1.50%	No. of shares (mil.): 21
Return on equity: 11.99%	Dividends
Cash ($ mil.): 71	Yield: 1.8%
Current ratio: —	Payout: 27.0%
Long-term debt ($ mil.): —	Market value ($ mil.): 344

	STOCK PRICE ($) FY Close	P/E High/Low		PER SHARE ($)		
		High	Low	Earnings	Dividends	Book Value
12/14	16.11	12	9	1.28	0.30	12.40
12/13	16.61	13	7	1.21	0.05	11.07
12/12	9.55	7	4	1.34	0.00	13.05
12/11	6.08	13	9	0.59	0.02	12.56
12/10	6.98	14	5	0.57	0.00	13.04
Annual Growth	**23.3%**	**—**	**—**	**22.4%**	**—**	**(1.2%)**

Fifth Third Bancorp (Cincinnati, OH)

Fifth Third Bancorp strives to be first in the hearts and minds of its customers (not fifth or third). The holding company of Fifth Third Bank boasts assets of nearly $140 billion and more than 1300 branches across Ohio Michigan Florida and several other states in the Midwest and Southeast. Fifth Third operates through four segments: branch banking (deposit accounts and loans for consumers and small businesses) commercial banking (lending leasing and syndicated and trade finance for corporations) consumer lending (residential mortgages home equity loans and credit cards) and investment advisers (private banking brokerage and asset management).

Operations

Fifth Third owns 23% of Vantiv one of the country's largest payment processing firms.

The bank generated 51% of its revenue from interest and fees on loans and leases in 2014 and 11% from interest on securities. Its non-interest income stemmed from service charges on deposits (8%) corporate banking income (7%) investment advisory revenue (6%) and mortgage banking revenue (5%) among other sources.

Geographic Reach

Fifth Third has 15 affiliates with 1303 full-service Banking Centers —including nearly 105 Bank Mart locations open seven days a week inside select grocery stores —and 2640 ATMs in the states of Ohio Kentucky Indiana Michigan Illinois Florida Tennessee West Virginia Pennsylvania Missouri Georgia and North Carolina.Sales and MarketingIn addition to retail customers and affluent individuals Fifth Third targets provides financial services to agribusinesses dealers government agencies healthcare-related companies US financial institutions and to businesses seeking energy financing.It spent $98 million on advertising in 2014 compared to $114 million and $128 million in 2013 and 2012 respectively.

Financial Performance

Fifth Third has struggled to grow its annual revenues much past the $7 billion mark in recent years which is a far cry from its revenue high of $9.45 billion in 2009. Following two years of top-line growth the bank's revenue fell by 10% to $6.50 billion in 2014 mostly because its mortgage banking business shrank by 56% as new residential mortgage loan originations and refinancing volumes fell compared to the prior year. The bank also didn't make as much from its business divestitures compared to the prior year even though it sold nearly one-third of its non-controlling stake in Vantiv.Revenue declines in 2014 caused Fifth Third's profits to reverse course after four years of bottom-line growth with net income plummeting by 19% to $1.48 billion. Cash from operations also dove by 55% to $2.08 billion as the company's mortgage banking division generated fewer net proceeds from sales of its loans held for sale.

Strategy

Fifth Third Bancorp's strategy for growth includes strengthening its presence in core markets expanding into contiguous markets and broadening its product offerings while conducting due diligence activities in connection with possible transactions. In addition to strengthening its loan portfolio Fifth Third is on the lookout for strategic growth opportunities through opening new branches establishing partnerships or by buying other banks or bank branches. To this end in 2014 in an exclusive partnership with RaceTrac Petroleum Fifth Third installed 228 of its ATMs in RaceTrack convenience stores across its key markets of Georgia and Florida (74 in Georgia and 154 in Florida); effectively expanding its ATM network by almost 10%. Also that year the company opened a new office in London to serve as its European representative location.Fifth Third Bancorp has also targeted private banking treasury management and small business services as areas ripe for growth. In 2014 Fifth Third bolstered its Fifth Third Securities subsidiary's expertise by inducting Challenger Capital Group's team of M&A professionals which boasted a successful track record of advising middle-market businesses in M&A and other strategic capital market transactions.Company Background

Fifth Third spun off part of its payment processing unit formerly named Fifth Third Processing Solutions in 2009 as part of a plan to create a stand-alone payment processing business. Two years later Fifth Third Processing changed its name to Vantiv in preparation for taking itself public in 2012.

HISTORY

In 1863 a group of Cincinnati businessmen opened the Third National Bank inside a Masonic temple to serve the Ohio River trade. Acquiring the Bank of the Ohio Valley (founded 1858) in 1871 the firm progressed until the panic of 1907. Third National survived and in 1908 consolidated with Fifth National forming the Fifth Third National Bank of Cincinnati. The newly organized bank acquired two local banks in 1910.

A second bank consolidation in 1919 resulted in Fifth Third's affiliation with Union Savings Bank and Trust Company permitting the bank to establish branches theretofore forbidden by regulators. The company acquired the assets and offices of five more banks and thrifts that year operating them as branches.

In 1927 the bank merged its operations with the Union Trust Company forming the Fifth Third Union Trust. With its combined strength it weathered the Great Depression and acquired three more banks between 1930 and 1933. However the Depression also brought massive banking regulations to the industry limiting Fifth Third's acquisitions.

In the postwar years and during the 1950s and 1960s the bank expanded its consumer banking services offering traveler's checks. Under CEO Bill Rowe son of former CEO John Rowe the firm emphasized the convenience of its locations and increased hours of operations.

In the 1970s Fifth Third shifted its lending program's emphasis from commercial loans to consumer credit and launched its ATM and telephone banking services. Aware that the bank was technologically unprepared for the onslaught of electronic information Fifth Third expanded its data processing and information services resources forming the basis for its Midwest Payment Systems division.

The company formed Fifth Third Bancorp a holding company and began to branch within Ohio (branching had previously been limited to the home county) in 1975. Ten years later more deregulation allowed the bank to move into contiguous states. Focused on consumer banking and with cautious underwriting policies Fifth Third weathered the real estate bust and leveraged-buyout problems of the 1980s and acquired new outlets cheaply by buying several small banks as well as branches from larger banks. It acquired the American National Bank in Kentucky and moved further afield with its purchase of the Sovereign Savings Bank in Palm Harbor Florida in 1991.

The company continued to expand buying several banks and thrifts in Ohio in 1997 and 1998. In 1999 Fifth Third moved into Indiana in a big way with its purchase of CNB Bancshares then solidified its position in the state with the acquisition of Peoples Bank of Indianapolis. Fifth Third also moved into new business areas buying mortgage banker W. Lyman Case broker-dealer The Ohio Company (1998) and Cincinnati-based commercial mortgage banker Vanguard Financial (1999). The company began to offer online foreign exchange via its FX Internet Trading Web in 2000.

In 2001 Fifth Third bought money manager Maxus Investments and added some 300 bank branches with its purchase of Capital Holdings (Ohio and Michigan) and Old Kent Financial (Michigan Indiana and Illinois) its largest-ever acquisition.

Fifth Third exited the property/casualty insurance brokerage business in 2002 selling its operations to Hub International. Also that year Fifth Third arranged to enter Tennessee via its planned purchase of Franklin Financial. But the deal was stalled as industry regulators investigated Fifth Third's risk management procedures and internal controls. A moratorium on acquisitions was placed on the bank during the investigation. It was lifted in 2004 and the purchase of Franklin was completed not long afterwards. That opened the door for Fifth Third's acquisition of First National Bankshares of Florida in 2005. Two years later it continued growing with its purchase of R-G Crown Bank from R&G Financial which added some 30 branches in Florida in addition to locations in Georgia.

EXECUTIVES

Senior Vice President, Mark Bitter
President and CEO, Greg D. Carmichael, age 54, $709,203 total compensation
EVP, Robert A. (Bob) Sullivan, age 60, $570,003 total compensation
EVP and COO, Lars C. Anderson, age 54
EVP and Chief Risk Officer, Frank R. Forrest, $144,234 total compensation

Regional President Fifth Third Bank (Indiana), Steven Alonso, age 54
EVP, Gregory L. (Greg) Kosch, age 55
EVP, Philip R. McHugh
EVP and CIO, Joseph R. Robinson
EVP and Chief Administrative Officer, Teresa J. Tanner, age 46
EVP and CFO, Tayfun Tuzun, age 50, $425,006 total compensation
SVP and Chief Marketing Officer, Maria Veltre
EVP, Chad M. Borton
President Fifth Third Mortgage Company, Michelle Van Dyke
President and CEO Fifth Third Bank (Georgia), Hal Clemmer
Vice PresidentandManager The Foundation Office, Heidi Jark
Vice President of Information Technology, Don Powell
Vice President Of Benefits, James Girton
Vice President Finance, Dan Flanigan
Vice President Information Technology, Ken Valentine
Senior Vice President Finance, Jamie Leonard
Vice President, Robert Weaver
Assistant Vice President, Guy Manaugh
Senior Vice President National Sales Manager, Richard (Dick) Maxwell
Vice President Risk Management, William Thurman
Vice President Finance, Shawn Manns
Vice President Loan Officer, Chris Fink
Vice President Structured Finance Group, Scott Kilgore
Assistant Vice President, Allison Mulhern
Vice President, Rich Skrodzki
Vice President Recruiting, Nancy Pinckney
Vice President Of Enterprise Architecture, Greg Mindrum
Executive Vice President, James Hudepohl
Vice President Public Relations, Jeff Kursman
Vice President Other Than Information Technology Management, Sherry McDarty
Vice President Acquisitions, Jim Rose
Vice President, Tim Kelly
Assistant Vice President Branch Manager, Cory Kent
Vice President, Morris Marlin
Vice President, Jerry Knott
Assistant Vice President Quality Systems, Jason Parigen
Vice President Treasury Management, Kevin Zgonc
Vice President Mortgage, Alisa Hunter
Executive Vice President Consumer Marketing, Winston Wilkinson
Vice President, Daniel Plumert
Assistant Vice President, Michelle (Mitch) Knight
Vice President Legal Counsel, Shannon Barrow
Vice President Compliance, Mike Bell
Senior Vice President, Doug Riddle
Vice President, Thomas Merkle
Vice President, Daniel Hunt
Vice President Chief Operational Risk Officer, John Wallace
Vice President, Michael Cole
Assistant Vice President, Mark Zink
Financial Center Manager Assistant Vice President, Jim Hunter
Vice President And Trust Officer, David Garber
Vice President Director Of Private Wealth Planning., Bryan Havighurst
Assistant Vice President Financial Center Manager III, John (Jack) Slavik
Vice President Project Management, Jennifer (Jen) Kaufman
Vice President Of Enterprise Architecture, Gary Schnettler
Vice President, Greg Vollmer
Vice President, Tab Demita
Vice President And Director Commercial Analytics, Stephen Boras

Vice President, Ronald (Ron) Keller
Assistant Vice President, Patrick Kavanaugh
Assistant Vice President and Manager
Information Technology Consumer, Glenn Yeager
Treasury Management Assistant Vice President,
Mike Eifert
Vice President Commercial Leasing dire, Gerald
(Jerry) Whitfield
Vice President, Charles Arkin
Vice President Director and Head of Commodity
Derivatives Trading, Timothy (Tim) Lyons
Vice President And Chief Financial Officer Of
Eastern Michigan, John Worthington
Vice President Manager Financial Services,
Terrence Lyons
Vice President Of Finance, Kurt Krebs
Vice President Information Technology
Compliance, Jeffrey Jones
Vice President, Alfred Mancuso
Vice President Dealer Development
Representative, Steve Sudnick
Assistant Vice President Corporate Banking, Kevin
Mataway
Vice President Information Technology, David
(Dave) Williams
Vice President Corporate Banking, William Whitley
Vice President Treasury Management Officer,
Alicia Mattice
Vice President Correspondent Banking
Department, Lisa Lyman
Treasurer Vice President, Melanie Chakor
Vice President, Brian Gardner
Vice President Corporate Facilities, Mark Jaconette
Assistant Vice President Commodities Derivatives
Marketing, Peter (Pete) Richards
Vice President, Tim Tierney
Vice President, Lauren Grodin
Vice President, David Schmitz
Vice President, William Hummel
Assistant Vice President, Jackie DeJonckheere
Vice President Sales, Brad Boersma
Vice President Commercial Loan Workout, Glenn
McEachern
Vice President, Joann Oeters
Vice President, Keith Goodpaster
Vice President, Polly Robinson
Vice President, David (Dave) Gottman
Assistant Vice President, David Cox
Assistant Vice President, Maher Kaddoura
Vice President, Libby Chapin
Assistant Vice President, Brandon Wallace
Vice President, Craig Ellis
Senior Vice President Of Sales, Benjamin Heckert
Vice President, Steven Slee
Senior Vice President of Upper Middle Market
Group, William (Bill) Behe
Assistant Vice President, Derrick Theetge
Vice President Foreign Exchange, Joe Areddy
Vice President, Mark Telles
Vice President Syndication Team Lead, Douglas
(Doug) Lusco
Senior Vice President Director of Business
Banking Strategy and Sales Effectiveness,
Elizabeth (Beth) Isphording
Vice President Financial Center Manager,
Stephanie Aguila
Vice President Commercial Lender, Kathleen
Mekesa
Vice President, Kelly Soller
Vice President Customer Service Team Lead
Portfoli, Michele Mullins
Vice President, Gary Losey
Assistant Vice President Information Technology
Projects, Michele McDonel
Vice President, Amy Deger
Vice President Indirect Originations, Edward (Ed)
Mcelveen
Vice President, Dean Haberkamp
Assistant Vice President Ftam, Tom Eldridge

Assistant Vice President In Global Treasury
Management, Megan Anderson
Vice President, Matthew Sheehan
Vice President, Christopher Bell
Vice President Senior Treasury Product Manager,
Suzanne Pierce
Vice President, Dan Driscoll
Vice President, Paulette Kosorski
Assistant Vice President Financial Center
Manager Ii, Deena Reynolds
Vice President Global Payments, Jason Dement
Senior Vice President Managing Directo, Ken Flierl
Vice President, Donald Mitchell
Assistant Vice President, Gregory Hahn
Vice President Legal Counsel, Peter (Pete) Jurs
Vice President, Jennifer Dunigan-wernke
Vice President, Clinton Long
Vice President, Rimantas Aukstuolis
Vice President Director of Accounting Policy and
Reporting, Jeff Lopper
Vice President Area Sales Manager, Scott Hazel
Assistant Vice President, Chad Rudzik
Vice President, Jody Promer
Assistant Vice President, Laura Balside
Vice President, Kip Heekin
Vice President, Matt Rodgers
Vice President Business Banking, Tracey
Siarkowski
Vice President Commercial Banking, Tim Egloff
Vice President Special Assets Group, Kristof
Schneider
Vice President National Healthcare Finance,
William (Bill) Priester
Vice President Commercial, Brett Hughes
Financial Center Manager vice Presiden, Mikki
Smith
Operations Vice President, Gary Loucks
Vice President Commercial Banking, Mary Weldon
Vice President, Bill Szlinis
Vice President Commercial Portfolio Manager,
Jonathan Roe
Auditors: Deloitte & Touche LLP

LOCATIONS

HQ: Fifth Third Bancorp (Cincinnati, OH)
Fifth Third Center, Cincinnati, OH 45263
Phone: 800 972-3030
Web: www.53.com

Selected Markets
Florida
Georgia
Indiana
Illinois
Kentucky
Michigan
Missouri
North Carolina
Ohio
Pennsylvania
Tennessee
West Virginia

PRODUCTS/OPERATIONS

2014 Sales

	$ mil.	% of total
Interest		
Loans & leases including fees	3,298	51
Securities & other	732	11
Noninterest		
Service charges on deposits	560	8
Corporate banking revenue	430	7
Investment advisory revenue	407	6
Mortgage banking net revenue	310	5
Card & processing revenue	295	5
Other	472	7
Total	6,504	100

Selected Subsidiaries
Fifth Third Capital Trust VII
Fifth Third Financial Corporation

Fifth Third Bank
GNB Management LLC
GNB Realty LLC
Fifth Third Asset Management Inc.
Fifth Third Funding LLC
Fifth Third Holdings LLC
Fifth Third Insurance Agency Inc.
Fifth Third International Company
Fifth Third Trade Services Limited (Hong Kong)
Fifth Third Equipment Finance Company (formerly
The Fifth Third Leasing Company)
The Fifth Third Auto Leasing Trust
Fifth Third Mortgage Company
Fifth Third Real Estate Investment Trust Inc.
Fifth Third Real Estate Capital Markets Company
Fifth Third Securities Inc.
Old Kent Mortgage Services Inc.
Fifth Third Community Development Corporation
Fifth Third New Markets Development Co. LLC
Fifth Third Investment Company
Fountain Square Life Reinsurance Company Ltd.
(Turks and Caicos Islands)
Vista Settlement Services LLC

COMPETITORS

Bank of America	JPMorgan Chase
Citigroup	KeyCorp
Comerica	Northern Trust
FirstMerit	PNC Financial
Harris	U.S. Bancorp
Huntington Bancshares	Wells Fargo

HISTORICAL FINANCIALS
Company Type: Public

Income Statement
FYE: December 31

	ASSETS ($ mil.)	NET INCOME ($ mil.)	INCOME AS % OF ASSETS	EMPLOYEES
12/14	138,706	1,481	1.1%	18,351
12/13	130,443	1,836	1.4%	19,446
12/12	121,894	1,576	1.3%	20,798
12/11	116,967	1,297	1.1%	21,334
12/10	111,007	753	0.7%	20,838
Annual Growth	5.7%	18.4%	—	(3.1%)

2014 Year-End Financials

Debt ratio: 10.76%	No. of shares (mil.): 824
Return on equity: 9.80%	Dividends
Cash ($ mil.): 3,451	Yield: 2.5%
Current ratio: —	Payout: 30.3%
Long-term debt ($ mil.): —	Market value ($ mil.): 16,790

	STOCK PRICE ($) FY Close	P/E High/Low		PER SHARE ($) Earnings	Dividends	Book Value
12/14	20.38	14	11	1.66	0.51	18.96
12/13	21.03	10	7	2.02	0.47	17.06
12/12	15.20	9	7	1.66	0.36	15.55
12/11	12.72	13	8	1.18	0.28	14.35
12/10	14.68	24	15	0.63	0.04	17.65
Annual Growth	8.5%			— — 27.4%	89.0%	1.8%

Financial Institutions Inc.

Financial Institutions may not have a luxurious
name but they specialize in five star service. The
holding company owns Five Star Bank which provides standard deposit products such as checking
and savings accounts CDs and IRAs to retail and
business customers through some 50 branches

across western and central New York. Indirect consumer loans originated through agreements with area franchised car dealers account for the largest percentage of the company's loan portfolio (35%) followed by commercial mortgages. The company also sells insurance while its Five Star Investment Services subsidiary offers brokerage and financial planning services.

OperationFinancial Institutions operates through two business segments: banking which includes the bank's retail and commercial banking operations; and insurance which sells insurance to both personal and business clients through its Scott Danahy Naylon Co (SDN) subsidiary.About 65% of the company's total revenue came from loan interest (including fees) in 2014 while another 15% came from interest on its investment securities. The rest of its revenue came from deposit account service charges (7%) ATM and debit card fees (4%) insurance income (2%) investment advisory (2%) and other miscellaneous income sources. Geographic ReachFive Star Bank boasts 50 branches and an ATM network across Western and Central New York in the counties of Allegany Cattaraugus Cayuga Chautauqua Chemung Erie Genesee Livingston Monroe Ontario Orleans Schuyler Seneca Steuben Wyoming and Yates.Sales and MarketingThe company offers financial and banking services to individuals municipalities and businesses in Western and Central New York.Financial PerformanceFinancial Institution's revenues and profits have been rising over the past few years thanks to growing loan business (organically and from 2012 acquisitions) lower interest expenses and rising fee-based revenue.The company's revenue rose by 2% to $126.4 million in 2014 mostly thanks to the addition of insurance income from stemming from the bank's acquisition of SDN. Financial's loan interest grew by 1% on organic loan business growth while interest on investment securities grew by 7% as it purchased more interest-earning assets. Higher revenue and a decline in loan loss provisions from a more credit-worthy loan portfolio in 2014 drove Financial Institution's net income higher by 15% to a record $29.4 million. The company's operating cash levels dipped by 5% to $35.2 million during the year due to unfavorable changes in working capital related to its contributions to its defined benefit pension plan. StrategyFinancial Institutions' long-term strategy reiterated in 2015 has been to "maintain a community bank philosophy which consists of focusing on and understanding the individualized banking needs of individuals municipalities and businesses of the local communities surrounding their primary service area." The firm believes this focus will enable it to better respond to customer needs and provide a higher level of personalized services giving it a competitive advantage over larger competitors.The company has also pursued acquisitions to bolster its service lines to grow its non-interest business. Its 2014 acquisition of a New-York based full-service insurance agency for example launched it beyond banking into the insurance business. Mergers and AcquisitionsIn January 2015 Financial Institutions bolstered its investment service business after acquiring Courier Capital which offers customized investment management investment consulting and retirement plan services to some 1100 individuals businesses and institutions. In 2014 Financial Institutions expanded its services into the insurance business after acquiring Buffalo-based Scott Danahy Naylon Co. (SDN) a full-service insurance agency for a total of $16.9 million plus a promise of $3.4 million in future payments contingent on SDN meeting revenue performance goal targets through 2017.Company Background

In 2012 Five Star Bank acquired four retail branches owned by HSBC Bank and four owned by First Niagara Bank in upstate New York. Five Star Bank was formed in 2005 when the company consolidated its four banking subsidiaries (First Tier Bank & Trust National Bank of Geneva Wyoming County Bank and Bath National Bank) into a single entity. First Tier Bank & Trust absorbed the other three banks and changed its name to Five Star Bank.

EXECUTIVES

Vice President, Mitchell (Mitch) Mclaughlin
EVP CFO and Treasurer, Kevin B. Klotzbach, age 62, $230,000 total compensation
SVP and Senior Retail Lending Administrator, Richard J. Harrison, age 69, $280,500 total compensation
President and CEO, Martin K. Birmingham, $420,000 total compensation
EVP Commercial Executive and Regional President, Jeffrey P. Kenefick, $209,100 total compensation
SVP and Director of Human Resources and Enterprise Planning, Paula D. Dolan, $140,000 total compensation
EVP and Chief Risk Officer, Kenneth V. Winn
Vice President of Commercial Lending, Robert (Bob) McFadden
Vice President, Karen Urban
Vice President, Richard W (Dick) Simpson
Vice President, Amy Mathis
Senior Vice President And Manager Work, Steven Ambrose
Chairman, Robert N. Latella, age 72
Auditors: KPMG LLP

LOCATIONS

HQ: Financial Institutions Inc.
220 Liberty Street, Warsaw, NY 14569
Phone: 585 786-1100
Web: www.fiiwarsaw.com

PRODUCTS/OPERATIONS

2013 Sales

	$ mil.	% of total
Interest income		
Loans including fees	81	66
Investment securities	17	14
Noninterest income		
Service charges on deposits	9	9
ATM & debit card	5	4
Investment advisory	2	2
Other	7	5
Total	**123**	**100**

COMPETITORS

Astoria Financial	First Niagara
Citibank	Financial
Community Bank System	HSBC USA
ESL Federal Credit	KeyCorp
Union	M&T Bank

HISTORICAL FINANCIALS

Company Type: Public

Income Statement

FYE: December 31

	ASSETS ($ mil.)	NET INCOME ($ mil.)	INCOME AS % OF ASSETS	EMPLOYEES
12/14	3,089	29	1.0%	645
12/13	2,928	25	0.9%	645
12/12	2,764	23	0.8%	662
12/11	2,336	22	1.0%	613
12/10	2,214	21	1.0%	616
Annual Growth	**8.7%**	**8.4%**	**—**	**1.2%**

2014 Year-End Financials

Debt ratio: —	No. of shares (mil.): 14
Return on equity: 10.99%	Dividends
Cash ($ mil.): 58	Yield: 3.0%
Current ratio: —	Payout: 38.5%
Long-term debt ($ mil.): —	Market value ($ mil.): 355

	STOCK PRICE ($) FY Close	P/E High/Low		PER SHARE ($) Earnings	Dividends	Book Value
12/14	25.15	13	10	2.00	0.77	19.80
12/13	24.71	15	10	1.75	0.74	18.43
12/12	18.63	12	10	1.60	0.57	18.41
12/11	16.14	13	9	1.49	0.47	17.18
12/10	18.97	12	7	1.61	0.40	19.40
Annual Growth	**7.3%**	**—**	**—**	**5.6%**	**17.8%**	**0.5%**

First American Financial Corp

First American Financial knows that when you're buying real estate you'll probably want some insurance to go along with it. In addition to good old title insurance from its First American Title subsidiary the company's financial services arm also provides specialty property/casualty insurance and home warranties through its First American Home Buyers Protection business. Its First American Trust offers banking and trust services to the escrow and real estate industries. Other offerings include settlement title plant management record keeping valuation and investment advisory services.

Operations

First American Financial is one of the largest title insurers in the US. Its title insurance and services segment accounts for more than 90% of revenues. The unit is focused on issuing title insurance for commercial and residential real estate transactions in the US and abroad; it also provides escrow closing exchange documentation banking and other title insurance-related services. The company also provides real property-related data services to mitigate risk and facilitate transactions.

The remainder of revenue comes from the specialty insurance segment which offers property/casualty policies including homeowners renters and property hazard coverage. It also markets home warranties.

In response to challenges in the US real estate market in recent years the company has exited its information services and industrial banking operations.

Geographic Reach

With headquarters in California First American Financial serves customers in about 70 countries around the globe. The US market where the specialty business is licensed in all 50 states and the District of Columbia accounts for more than 90% of revenues.

It has regional offices in countries including Australia Canada and the UK. Through acquisitions (partial and total) of existing businesses and through partnerships with local companies First American Financial is carefully moving into emerging markets in central and eastern Europe.

Sales and Marketing

First American Financial distributes its title insurance and related products through a direct sales force and agent channels. For residential products it markets to real estate agents and brokers as well as mortgage originators and brokers real estate attorneys homebuilders and escrow service providers. Refinance business is marketed to mortgage originators and servicers and government-sponsored entities. Commercial lines are primarily marketed to investors including real estate investment trusts (REITs) as well as law firms banks investment banks mortgage brokers and commercial property owners.

Financial Performance

While the company has mostly held steady tension in the domestic mortgage credit market has impacted real estate sales in recent years thereby crimping First American Financial's revenues. Earnings also have been impacted by asset sales.

After slight declines each year from 2009 to 2011 the company showed a large boost (19%) in revenues to more than $4.5 billion in 2012.The growth trend continued the following year with revenue increasing by 9% to $5 billion in 2013. However in 2014 revenue declined 6% to $4.7 billion due to a decline in the title insurance and services segment as fewer orders closed. Net investment income also decreased 22% that year primarily due to higher impairment losses and lower equity in earnings. Agent premiums and information services additionally saw declines in 2014. The specialty insurance segment was the only unit that saw growth rising 9% that year.

Net income grew 25% to $233 million in 2014 as personnel costs premiums retained by agents and provisions for policy losses went down. Cash flow from operations decreased 5% to $360 million due to an increase in cash used for accounts payable and accrued income receivable.

Strategy

Strategically First American Financial is making its way in the slowly recovering real estate and mortgage markets through strict control of its expenses and by enhancing operational efficiencies. Additionally the company continues to pursue targeted organic and non-organic growth opportunities that complement its core title insurance and settlement services businesses.

First American Financial is conducting a number of technology enhancements including the launch of its new myFirstAm commercial real estate portal. The company also made its existing myFirstAm system available on mobile devices. In 2014 it launched a new multilingual website and online video library to serve a more diverse set of customers.

Also in 2014 the company's mortgage solutions group became a distributor of Freddie Mac's Home Value Suite which offers valuation modeling tools automating and streamlining the cost of collateral valuation in the housing market. That move should lower products for mortgage customers.

Mergers and Acquisitions

The company continues to grow through a number of strategic acquisitions. In 2014 First American Financial purchased California-based Interthinx a mortgage loan analytics and review services from Verisk Analytics. That company's services will help financial institutions comply with load-quality regulations passed in the wake of the mortgage meltdown.

In 2015 First American Financial bought New York-based firm TitleVest Holdings.

Company Background

Previously known as First American Corporation the company spun off its real estate information services into CoreLogic in 2010.

Chairman Parker Kennedy is a descendant of the founder of the company C. E. Parker.

HISTORY

In 1889 when Los Angeles was on its way to becoming a real city the more countrified residents to the south (including The Irvine Company's founding family) formed Orange County a peaceful realm of citrus groves where land transactions were assisted by title companies Orange County Abstract and Santa Ana Abstract. In 1894 the firms merged under the leadership of local businessman C. E. Parker. For three decades the resulting Orange County Title limited its business to title searches.

In 1924 as real estate transactions became more complex (in part because of mineral-rights issues related to Southern California's oil boom) Orange County Title began offering title insurance and escrow services. The company remained under Parker family management until 1930 when H. A. Gardner took over and guided it through the Depression. In 1943 the company returned to Parker family control.

In 1957 the company began a major expansion beyond Orange County. The new First American Title Insurance and Trust name acknowledged the firm's expansion into trust and custody operations. Donald Kennedy (C. E. Parker's grandson) took over in 1963 and took the company public the next year.

In 1968 First American Corporation was formed as a holding company for subsidiaries First American Title Insurance and First American Trust. This structure facilitated growth as the firm began opening new offices and buying all or parts of other title companies including Title Guaranty Co. of Wyoming Security Title & Trust (San Antonio) and Ticore Inc. (Portland Oregon) all purchased in 1968.

The 1970s were a quiet time for the company but it began growing again in the 1980s as savings and loan deregulation jump-started the commercial real estate market in Southern California. First American diversified into home warranty and real estate tax services. In 1988 on the brink of the California meltdown the company bought an industrial loan corporation to make commercial real estate loans.

EXECUTIVES

EVP, Kenneth D. DeGiorgio, $725,000 total compensation
CEO and Director, Dennis J. Gilmore, $900,000 total compensation
COO First American Title Insurance Company, Christopher M. Leavell, $675,000 total compensation
SVP and CIO, Larry W. Godec
EVP and CFO, Mark E. Seaton, $520,192 total compensation
VP and Chief Accounting Officer, Matthew F. Wajner, $260,000 total compensation
President First American Property and Casualty Insurance Group, James J. Court
Vice President Southern California Area Operations Director, Chris Clemens
Vice President, Myron Schuster
Senior Vice President Human Resources, Mark Rutherford
Vice President Corporate Information Technology, Desai Priti
Vice President Suburban Metro Area Manager, Mary Glavac
Vice President And National Counsel, Michelle Owens
Vice President, Sharon Yarber
Vice President Nevada Division Escrow Officer Branch Manager, Crystal Ferrari
Vice President Controller And Assistant Treasurer, Ted Misogas
Vice President National Accounts, Valerie Kolytiris

Vice President Underwriting, Ken Guillaume
Senior Vice President Sales, Caitlin Stearns
Vice President, Deborah Gibson
Vice President Sales, Marie Hom
Title Operations Manager Vice President, Dwayne Rudisill
Vice President, Trish Brown
Assistant Vice President, Mark Sarber
Assistant Vice President, Joseph Rishel
Vice President Human Resources, Gretchen Demartini
Vice President Homebuilder Services Northern California, Dorian McCoy
Assistant Vice President And Senior Underwriter Alaska Oregon And Washington, Michael Gilbertson
Vice President Escrow Area Manager, Frank La Blanc
Assistant Vice President Trust Services, Kathy Vian
Assistant Vice President Application Development, Rahul Goel
Chairman, Parker S. Kennedy
Auditors: PricewaterhouseCoopers LLP

LOCATIONS

HQ: First American Financial Corp
1 First American Way, Santa Ana, CA 92707-5913
Phone: 714 250-3000 **Fax:** 714 250-3151
Web: www.firstam.com

2014 Title Insurance & Services Revenues

	% of total
US	92
International	8
Total	**100**

PRODUCTS/OPERATIONS

2014 Revenues

	$ mil.	% of total
Title insurance & services	4,304	92
Specialty insurance	368	8
Corporate & other	6	-
Elimination	(1.6)	-
Total	**4,677**	**100**

2014 Revenues

	$ mil.	% of total
Direct premiums & escrow fees	2,115	45
Agent premiums	1,841	39
Information & other	619	13
Investment income	71	2
Investment gains	31	1
Impairment losses (1.7)		
Total	**4,677**	**100**

Selected Services

Property/Casualty Insurance
  Home Warranty
Title Insurance and Services
  1031 Tax-Deferred Exchange Services
  Banking and Investment Management
  Default Services
  Homebuilder Services
  National Commercial Services
  Origination Services
  Professional Real Estate Services
  Property Information and Recorded Documents
  Title Insurance and Closing Services
  Title Technology Solutions
  UCC Insurance Search and Filing Services
  Valuation Services

COMPETITORS

American Home Shield	North American Title
Fidelity National	Old Republic
Financial	Stewart Information
Home Buyers Warranty	Services
Investors Title	Ticor Title Co.

Income Statement
FYE: December 31

	ASSETS ($ mil.)	NET INCOME ($ mil.)	INCOME AS % OF ASSETS	EMPLOYEES
12/14	7,666	233	3.0%	17,103
12/13	6,520	186	2.9%	17,292
12/12	6,050	301	5.0%	17,312
12/11	5,370	78	1.5%	16,117
12/10	5,821	127	2.2%	16,879
Annual Growth	7.1%	16.3%	—	0.3%

2014 Year-End Financials

Debt ratio: 7.66%	No. of shares (mil.): 107
Return on equity: 9.29%	Dividends
Cash ($ mil.): 1,190	Yield: 2.4%
Current ratio: —	Payout: 44.4%
Long-term debt ($ mil.): —	Market value ($ mil.): 3,646

	STOCK PRICE ($) FY Close	P/E High/Low	PER SHARE ($) Earnings	Dividends	Book Value
12/14	33.90	16 11	2.15	0.84	23.92
12/13	28.20	16 12	1.71	0.48	23.16
12/12	24.09	9 5	2.77	0.36	21.90
12/11	12.67	23 14	0.73	0.24	19.24
12/10	14.94	13 10	1.20	0.40	18.96
Annual Growth	22.7%	— —	15.7%	20.4%	6.0%

First Bancorp

Not to be confused with North Carolina's First Bancorp this First BanCorp is the holding company for FirstBank Puerto Rico which provides business and retail banking services through more than 50 branches in Puerto Rico and about two dozen more in Florida and the Virgin Islands. Puerto Rico's second-largest bank gets more than one-third of its business from its Commercial and Corporate Banking loans and services. Residential mortgages make up nearly one-third of First-Bank's $9 billion loan portfolio while commercial mortgages make up another one-fifth. First BanCorp also owns FirstBank Insurance Agency Firstbank Puerto Rico Securities and the consumer loan company Money Express La Financiera.

OperationsGenerating more than 80% of its revenue from loan interest First BanCorp operates through six business segments: Commercial and Corporate Banking; Consumer (Retail) Banking; Mortgage Banking; Treasury and Investments; United States Operations; and Virgin Islands Operations.Commercial and Corporate Banking which made up roughly 35% of the company's total revenue in 2014 provides lending and other services for organizations in the public sector as well as for large and specialized middle-market businesses operating in a variety of industries. The Consumer (Retail) Banking segment (22% of revenue) provides consumer lending and deposit services mainly through FirstBank's branch network and loan centers in Puerto Rico. FirstBank's loans include auto boat and personal loans credit cards and lines of credit.The Mortgage Banking (18% of revenue) business buys and sells home loans through FirstBank and the company's mortgage origination subsidiary First Mortgage. Treasury and Investments (1% of revenue) manages securities and lends funds to the company's three banking segments to finance their respective lending ac-

tivities. It also borrows from those segments and from the United States Operations segment.United States Operations (20% of revenue) consists of FirstBank's 10 retail and corporate banking businesses in the US mainland mostly in southern Florida. Virgin Islands Operations (3% of revenue) counts FirstBank's banking business (mostly consumer commercial lending and deposit account activities) in the US Virgin Islands (USVI) and British Virgin Islands (BVI) through 12 branches in the USVI (St. Thomas St. Croix and St. John and the islands) and the BVI (Tortola and Virgin Gorda).Geographic ReachSan Juan-based First-Bank boasts more than 50 branches across Puerto Rico around a dozen branches in the USVI and BVI and 10 US branches in southern Florida. The bank also has 27 First First Federal Finance Corp (dba Money Express La Financiera) offices in Puerto Rico.Financial PerformanceFirst BanCorp ended its multi-year revenue decline in 2014 with revenue rebounding by 10% to $695.3 million for the year. This is mostly because the bank in 2013 had suffered more than $200 million from a combination of losses on sales from non-performing assets and losses from a write-off of assets pledged as collateral to Lehman Brothers Inc. Despite earning lower interest income during 2014 the bank's net interest income managed to climb slightly thanks to lower interest expenses on deposits amidst the continued low-interest environment.The company's profit jumped sharply to $392.29 million in 2014 (compared to a net loss of $164.49 million in 2013) mostly thanks to a drop in loan loss provisions as its loan portfolio's credit quality improved as the economy strengthened but also thanks to a combination of higher revenue and lower interest and non-interest expenses. Despite higher earnings in 2014 First BanCorp's operating cash declined as the company generated less cash from proceeds on its loans held for sale.StrategyFirst BanCorp has followed an acquisition strategy to grow its loan business and bank clientele in recent years. In early 2015 for example flagship subsidiary FirstBank purchased 10 bank branches in Puerto Rico from its rival Doral Bank which added some $600 million in new deposits $300 million in new mortgage loan business and 140000 new clients. The acquisition also grew FirstBanCorp's total branch network by 20% while expanding its market presence in geographic areas with room for deposit and mortgage loan business growth. The year before in 2014 FirstBank expanded its loan business through the purchase of a $242-million portfolio of mortgage loans from Doral for some $232.9 million.

Company Background

Scotiabank a Canadian bank with operations throughout the Caribbean acquired a 10% stake in First BanCorp in 2007.

EXECUTIVES

EVP Business Group Executive, Cassan Pancham, age 55, $399,815 total compensation
EVP and Chief Risk Officer, Nayda Rivera-Batista, age 41
President and CEO, Aurelio Aleman-Bermudez, $850,102 total compensation
EVP and CFO, Orlando Berges-Gonzalez, $600,101 total compensation
EVP and Florida Region Executive, Calixto Garcia-Velez, $486,115 total compensation
EVP and COO, Donald L. Kafka
EVP Retail and Business Banking Executive, Ginoris Lopez-Lay
EVP and Chief Lending Officer, Emilio Martino-Valdes
EVP and Business Group Director, Michael McDonald

EVP; General Counsel and Secretary, Lawrence Odell, $550,110 total compensation
EVP and Consumer Lending Business Executive, Carlos Power Pietrantoni
Senior Vice President Commercial Lending, Alfred Massheder
Assistant Vice President, Esther Cremades
Assistant Vice President, Hiram Rivas
Senior Vice President Chief Accounting Officer, Pedro Romero
Vice President Of Investments Department, Javier Cabrera
Vice President, Rafael Perez
Senior Vice President Commercial Mortgage Lending, Jose Aponte
Vice President Of Commercial Department, Francisco Pascual
Vice President, Manuel Muchacho
Chairman, Roberto R. Herencia, age 55
Auditors: KPMG LLP

LOCATIONS

HQ: First Bancorp
1519 Ponce de Leon Avenue, Stop 23, Santurce 00908
Phone: 787 729-8200
Web: www.firstbankpr.com

PRODUCTS/OPERATIONS

2014 Sales

	$ mil.	% of total
Interest		
Loans	579	82
Investment securities	52	8
Money market investments	1	-
Noninterest		
Service charges on deposit accounts	16	2
Mortgage banking activities	14	2
Insurance income	6	1
Others	30	5
Adjustments	(7.7)	-
Total	**695**	**100**

2014 Sales by Segments

	% of total
Commercial and corporate banking	35
Consumer(Retail) banking	22
United State Operations	21
Mortgage Banking	18
Virgin Island Operations	3
Treasury and Investments	1
Total	**100**

Selected Subsidiaries

FirstBank Puerto Rico
  FirstBank Overseas Corporation
  FirstBank Puerto Rico Securities Corp.
  First Federal Finance Corp. (d/b/a Money Express La Financiera)
  First Insurance Agency Inc.
  First Mortgage Inc.
FirstBank Insurance Agency Inc.
Grupo Empresas de Servicios Financieros (d/b/a PR Finance)

COMPETITORS

Citigroup	Popular Inc.
OFG Bancorp	Santander BanCorp

HISTORICAL FINANCIALS
Company Type: Public

Income Statement
FYE: December 31

	ASSETS ($ mil.)	NET INCOME ($ mil.)	INCOME AS % OF ASSETS	EMPLOYEES
12/14	12,727	392	3.1%	2,617
12/13	12,656	(164)	—	2,458
12/12	13,099	29	0.2%	2,512
12/11	13,127	(82)	—	2,490
12/10	15,593	(524)	—	2,518
Annual Growth	(4.9%)	—	—	1.0%

Debt ratio: 1.82%	No. of shares (mil.): 212		
Return on equity: 27.17%	Dividends		
Cash ($ mil.): 796	Yield: —		
Current ratio: —	Payout: —		
Long-term debt ($ mil.): —	Market value ($ mil.): 1,250		

	STOCK PRICE ($) FY Close	P/E High/Low		PER SHARE ($) Earnings	Dividends	Book Value
12/14	5.87	3	2	1.87	0.00	7.85
12/13	6.19	—	—	(0.80)	0.00	5.87
12/12	4.58	33	22	0.14	0.00	7.20
12/11	3.49	3	0	2.18	0.00	7.04
12/10	0.46	—	—	(10.79)	0.00	49.66
Annual Growth	**89.0%**	—	—	—		—(36.9%)

First Bancorp (NC)

First things first: Don't confuse this First Bancorp with Virginia's First Bancorp or First BanCorp in Puerto Rico. This one is the holding company for First Bank which operates about 100 branch locations in east-central North Carolina east South Carolina and western Virginia (where it operates under the name First Bank of Virginia). In addition to offering standard commercial banking services such as deposit accounts and lending the bank offers investment products and discount brokerage services. Another subsidiary First Bank Insurance Services offers property/casualty products. First Bank focuses its lending on mortgages which account for more than half of its loan portfolio.

First Bancorp's strategy for growth includes buying banks in or near its existing market areas or banks that offer new business lines. (It entered South Carolina through its 2008 purchase of Great Pee Dee Bancorp.) In late 2011 the company arranged to purchase nearly a dozen branches in coastal portions of the Carolinas from Waccamaw Bank.

In addition to buying healthy banks the company has also been able to take advantage of the glut of bank failures by participating in FDIC-assisted transactions. Also in 2011 First Bancorp bought the assets and liabilities of The Bank of Asheville a five-branch bank in a new North Carolina market. Previously it took over the assets of the failed Cooperative Bank and its Lumina Mortgage subsidiary in a deal that added two dozen branches.

The acquisitions especially in respect to Cooperative Bank also added to First Bank's loan losses as a result of foreclosed properties assumed with the purchases. The bank's market area is slowly recovering from the effects of the recession and battered property values and it could be another couple of years before volatility in the region subsides. Overall the company has struggled with the lackluster economic recovery which has depressed loan and deposit levels. Revenues in 2011 slipped some 3% from the year before to $182 million but net income jumped 27% largely as a result of gain related to the Bank of Asheville acquisition. (Net FDIC indemnification asset income accounted for some 10% of the company's revenues that year.)

First Bancorp provided electronic data processing to external customers through its Montgomery Data Services subsidiary until 2010 when its last remaining client terminated its service agreement. The bank absorbed Montgomery's data processing operations that year.

EXECUTIVES

Chief Information Officer; Executive Vice President of First Bank, David G. Grigg, age 64, $91,000 total compensation
EVP COO and Secretary First Bancorp and First Bank, Anna G. Hollers, age 64, $265,356 total compensation
EVP and CFO First Bancorp and First Bank, Eric P. Credle, age 46, $214,000 total compensation
Executive Vice President; Director of the Company and First Bank, John F. Burns, age 68, $207,027 total compensation
President; Director of First Bank; Director, Jerry L. Ocheltree, age 55, $340,000 total compensation
President and CEO and Director, Richard T. Moore
President of First Bank, Michael Mayer
Vice President Operations First Bank, Patricia Lynch
Chairman of the Board, Mary Capel
Auditors: Elliott Davis Decosimo, PLLC

LOCATIONS

HQ: First Bancorp (NC)
300 S.W. Broad Street, Southern Pines, NC 28387
Phone: 910 246-2500
Web: www.localFirstbank.com

COMPETITORS

BB&T	NewBridge Bancorp
BNC Bancorp	PNC Financial
Bank of America	South Street Financial
CommunityOne Bancorp	SunTrust
First Citizens	Wells Fargo
BancShares	

HISTORICAL FINANCIALS

Company Type: Public

Income Statement

FYE: December 31

	ASSETS ($ mil.)	NET INCOME ($ mil.)	INCOME AS % OF ASSETS	EMPLOYEES
12/14	3,218	25	0.8%	825
12/13	3,185	20	0.6%	873
12/12	3,244	(23)	—	852
12/11	3,290	13	0.4%	849
12/10	3,278	9	0.3%	794
Annual Growth	**(0.5%)**	**25.8%**	—	**1.0%**

2014 Year-End Financials

Debt ratio: 3.62%	No. of shares (mil.): 19		
Return on equity: 6.58%	Dividends		
Cash ($ mil.): 252	Yield: 1.7%		
Current ratio: —	Payout: 28.3%		
Long-term debt ($ mil.): —	Market value ($ mil.): 364		

	STOCK PRICE ($) FY Close	P/E High/Low		PER SHARE ($) Earnings	Dividends	Book Value
12/14	18.47	16	13	1.19	0.32	19.67
12/13	16.62	17	12	0.98	0.32	18.90
12/12	12.82	—	—	(1.54)	0.32	18.11
12/11	11.15	38	18	0.44	0.32	20.41
12/10	15.31	48	34	0.35	0.32	20.51
Annual Growth	**4.8%**	—	—	**35.8%**	**(0.0%)**	**(1.0%)**

First Banks, Inc. (MO)

First Banks keeps it in the family. The holding company for First Bank it is owned by chairman James Dierberg and his family; many of the bank's branches and ATMs are located in Dierbergs Markets a Missouri-based grocery chain owned by relatives of the chairman. First Bank has about 130 branches in California Florida Illinois and Missouri with a concentration in metropolitan markets such as Los Angeles San Diego San Francisco Sacramento and St. Louis. The bank offers standard services like deposits mortgages and business and consumer loans. Additional services include brokerage insurance trust and private banking as well as commercial treasury management and international trade services.

Geographic Reach
St. Louis-based First Banks has First Bank branches in Missouri California Florida and Illinois. Southern California accounts for about a third of deposits. The St. Louis metro area accounts for about a quarter of total deposits.

Operations
The bank operates 130 branches with 163 ATM machines in four states. First Bank offers a variety of financial services including commercial and personal deposit products commercial and consumer loans. Other services include mortgage banking debit cards brokerage services Internet banking remote deposit mobile banking telephone banking safe deposit boxes and trust and private banking services.

Financial Performance
First Bank reported net income of $241.7 million in 2013 versus $26.3 million in 2012. The fourth quarter of 2013 marked the eighth consecutive quarter of profitability for the bank after three years deep in the red. The bank's return to profitability resulted from a reduction in size of its branch network and problem loan portfolio and asset sales. The bank sold branches and subsidiaries and received a $125 million capital infusion from its the Dierberg family. First Bank had $5.9 billion in assets at the end of 2013.

Driving profits in 2013 was strong loan production in all of First Bank's markets. Loan volume increased 86% in 2013 over 2012 to $562.2 million.

Strategy
Since early 2008 the bank has been working to strengthen its capital ratios and improve its financial performance. Under its Capital Plan it has reduced nonperforming assets and potential problem loans in its portfolio and sold merged or closed bank branches. In May 2014 the Federal Reserve Board ended the regulatory supervision that First Banks and its First Bank subsidiary were under. The bank has been subject to a written agreement since March 2010 to improve its banking practices.

In November 2013 the bank sold its Association Bank Services (ABS) business to Union Bank for a gain of $28.6 million. ABS provided services to homeowners associations and community management companies. The proceeds from the sale were invested in First Bank's core commercial retail mortgage and wealth management activities.

To raise capital First Banks in 2010 sold some two-dozen branches in the Chicago area to FirstMerit; the deal came after First Banks sold most of its asset-based lending portfolio to the Ohio-based bank. It also sold about 10 branches in northern Illinois to First Mid-Illinois Bancshares and sold investment adviser Missouri Valley Partners to Stifel Financial. First Banks also sold its Texas locations to Prosperity Bancshares in 2010.

Before the company hit its rough patch that resulted in three years of record losses First Banks had been growing through both the acquisitions of other bank holding companies as well as by opening new branches and purchasing non-bank financial services companies. The company has made nearly 20 acquisitions since 2003 including the troubled Coast Financial Holdings in 2007 which gave First Bank an entrance into Florida. Holding company First Banks has since put the brakes on further purchases amid the difficult economic environment.

EXECUTIVES

Senior Vice President, Laura Ramsey
Vice President, Jackie Wilson
Vice President Manager Insurance Services, Debbie Porter
Senior Vice President Director, Michael Johnson
Evp And Coo, Jason W Steris
Vice President, Ed Cagle
Vice President And Commercial Lender And Branch Manager, Roger Foster
Vice President and Retail Banking Manager Community Banking Group Southern Illinois First Bank, Kathryn Theen
Vice President Commerical Banking Systems, Theodore (Theo) Gribat
Senior Vice President Mortgage Banking First Bank, Kathy Alexander
Vice President Accounting, Cathy Studer
Senior Vice President Compliance Officer, Gayle Davison
Vice President, Carol Nelson
Vice Chairman, Michael J Dierberg, age 44
Auditors: KPMG LLP

LOCATIONS

HQ: First Banks, Inc. (MO)
135 North Meramec, Clayton, MO 63105
Phone: 314 854-4600
Web: www.firstbanks.com

2013 Branches

	No.
Southern California	37
St. Louis metro area	34
Southern Illinois	20
Northern California	19
Missouri (excludingSt. Louis metro area)	12
Florida	8
Total	**130**

PRODUCTS/OPERATIONS

2013 Sales

	$ mil.	% of total
Interest		
Loans including fees	118	50
Investment securities	52	22
Other	2	1
Noninterest		
Service charges on deposit accounts & customer service fees	34	14
Loan servicing fees	7	3
Net gain on sale of other real estate and repossessed assets	6	3
Gain on loans sold & held for sale	5	2
Other	12	5
Total	**237**	**100**

Selected Services

Brokerage
Commercial Banking
Home loans
Personal Banking
Small business

Selected Subsidiaries

The San Francisco Company
First Bank
FB Holdings LLC (53%)
First Bank Business Capital Inc.
NT Rosolution Corporation
SBRHC Inc
Small Business Loan Source LLC

COMPETITORS

Bank of America	JPMorgan Chase
Capital One	Regions Financial
Citigroup	U.S. Bancorp
Comerica	UMB Financial
Commerce Bancshares	Wells Fargo

HISTORICAL FINANCIALS

Company Type: Public

Income Statement

FYE: December 31

	ASSETS ($ mil.)	NET INCOME ($ mil.)	INCOME AS % OF ASSETS	EMPLOYEES
12/14	5,935	21	0.4%	1,167
12/13	5,918	241	4.1%	1,147
12/12	6,509	26	0.4%	1,177
12/11	6,608	(41)	—	1,171
12/10	7,378	(191)	—	1,380
Annual Growth	**(5.3%)**	**—**	**—**	**(4.1%)**

2014 Year-End Financials

Debt ratio: 5.97%
Return on equity: 5.33%
Cash ($ mil.): 205
Current ratio: —
Long-term debt ($ mil.): —
No. of shares (mil.): 0
Dividends
  Yield: —
  Payout: —
Market value ($ mil.): —

First Busey Corp

First Busey Corporation keeps itself busy taking care of deposits and making loans. It's the holding company for Busey Bank which boasts $4 billion in assets and 40 branches across Illinois Florida and Indiana. The bank offers standard deposit products and services using funds from deposits to originate primarily real estate loans and mortgages. Subsidiary Busey Wealth Management which manages $5 billion in assets provides asset management trust brokerage and related services to individuals businesses and foundations while FirsTech provides retail payment processing services. Most of Busey Bank's branches are located in downstate Illinois.

OperationsFirst Busey Corporation operates three business segments Busey Bank which generated more than 99% of its total revenue in 2014 and serves retail and corporate customers; FirsTech which provides remittance processing for online bill payments lock box and walk-in payments; and Busey Wealth Management which provides asset management tax preparation philanthropic advisory services and investment and fiduciary services to individuals businesses and foundations. Real estate loans including commercial and residential mortgages accounted for 70% of the bank's loan portfolio in 2014 while commercial loans (25%) construction loans (4%) and consumer installments and other loans (0.5%) comprised the rest. About 55% of First Busey's total revenue came from loan interest (including fees) while another 10% came from interest income on taxable and non-taxable investment securities. The rest of its revenue came from trust fees (11%) deposit account service charges (7%) remittance processing fees (6%) commissions and brokers' fees (2%) and various types of gains on securities and loan sales.

Geographic ReachBusey Bank has nearly 30 branches in Illinois seven locations in southwest Florida and another office in Indianapolis. Its FirsTech subsidiary accepts payments from its 3000 agent locations across 36 US states.Sales and MarketingThe bank which staffed 801 employees at the end of 2014 serves individuals businesses and foundations.Financial PerformanceFirst Busey's revenues have declined in recent years due to shrinking interest margins on loans amidst the low-interest environment. Its profits however have been rising thanks to lower interest expenses

on deposits and declining loan loss provisions as its loan portfolio's credit quality has improved with higher property valuations in the strengthened economy.The bank's revenue dipped by 2% to $167 million mostly as it collected smaller gains from loan sales due to lower refinancing volumes as interest rates began to rise. The bank's loan interest income also continued to decline with lower yields on loan and security assets in the low-interest environment.Despite generating less revenue in 2014 First Busey's net income jumped by 14% to $32.8 million thanks to continued declines in interest expenses on deposits and lower loan loss provisions. The company's operating cash levels fell by 31% to $68.1 million after adjusting its earnings for non-cash items related to its net proceeds from its loans held-for-sale.   StrategyFirst Busey sometimes strategically acquires smaller banks in its target markets to boost its market share broaden its service offerings and boost its loan and deposit business.Mergers and Acquisitions In December 2015 First Busey Corporation expanded into Missouri for the first time after it agreed to buy Pulaski Financial Corporation –along with its $1.5 billion in assets (including $1.3 billion in loans $1.1 billion in deposits) and 13 Pulaski Bank branches in the St. Louis metro area –for around $210.7 million.In January 2015 First Busey boosted its market share in Illinois after purchasing Pekin-based Herget Financial and its three Herget Bank branches in the area. The $34.1 million-deal extended Busey Bank's presence in Pekin and the greater Peoria market added Herget Financials "dominant" deposit market position in its community and bolstered its service offerings with trust estate and asset management services as well as competitive commercial loan and mortgage offerings.

EXECUTIVES

EVP and Chief Risk Officer, Barbara J. Harrington, age 55
President CEO and Director, Van A. Dukeman, age 56, $537,308 total compensation
EVP COO and Chief Credit Officer; President and CEO Busey Wealth Management, Robert F. (Bob) Plecki, age 54, $268,654 total compensation
CIO and President and CEO FirsTech Inc., Howard F. Mooney, age 50, $240,216 total compensation
EVP and Regional President Busey Bank, Christopher M. (Chris) Shroyer, age 49, $268,654 total compensation
EVP and General Counsel, John J. Powers
EVP and CFO, Robin N. Elliott, $256,731 total compensation
Chairman, Gregory B. (Greg) Lykins, age 67
Auditors: McGladrey LLP

LOCATIONS

HQ: First Busey Corp
100 West University Avenue, Champaign, IL 61820
Phone: 217 365-4544
Web: www.busey.com

PRODUCTS/OPERATIONS

2014 Sales

	$ mil.	% of total
Interest		
Loans including fees	92	55
Interest & dividends on securities	15	10
Noninterest		
Trust fees	19	11
Service charges on deposit accounts	12	7
Remittance processing	9	6
Gain on sales of loans	4	3
Commissions and broker's fees net	2	2
Other	10	6
Total	**167**	**100**

COMPETITORS

Bank of America	First Midwest Bancorp
CIB Marine Bancshares	JPMorgan Chase
Fifth Third	Mercantile Bancorp
First Mid-Illinois Bancshares	PNC Financial
	Wintrust Financial

HISTORICAL FINANCIALS

Company Type: Public

Income Statement

FYE: December 31

	ASSETS ($ mil.)	NET INCOME ($ mil.)	INCOME AS % OF ASSETS	EMPLOYEES
12/14	3,665	32	0.9%	801
12/13	3,539	28	0.8%	849
12/12	3,618	22	0.6%	948
12/11	3,402	29	0.9%	888
12/10	3,605	23	0.6%	866
Annual Growth	0.4%	9.0%	—	(1.9%)

2014 Year-End Financials

Debt ratio: 1.50%
Return on equity: 7.72%
Cash ($ mil.): 339
Current ratio: —
Long-term debt ($ mil.): —

No. of shares (mil.): 28
Dividends
Yield: 0.1%
Payout: 51.3%
Market value ($ mil.): 188

	STOCK PRICE ($) FY Close	P/E High/Low		PER SHARE ($) Earnings	Dividends	Book Value
12/14	6.51	6	5	1.11	0.57	14.98
12/13	5.80	7	5	0.87	0.36	14.36
12/12	4.65	8	6	0.66	0.00	14.15
12/11	5.00	6	5	0.87	0.00	14.17
12/10	4.70	7	4	0.81	0.00	15.94
Annual Growth	8.5%	—	—	8.2%	—	(1.5%)

First Citizens BancShares, Inc. (NC)

First Citizens BancShares knows commercial banking. It owns First-Citizens Bank which operates about 400 branches in 17 states mainly in the southeastern and western US and urban areas scattered nationwide. The bank provides standard services such as deposits loans mortgages and trust services in addition to processing and operational support to other banks. Subsidiary First Citizens Investor Services offers investments and discount brokerage services to bank clients. Real estate loans including commercial residential and revolving mortgages and construction and land development loans comprise most of its loan portfolio.

Geographic Reach

First Citizens BancShares has 401 offices in 17 states (Arizona California Colorado Florida Georgia Kansas Maryland Missouri New Mexico North Carolina Oklahoma Oregon Tennessee Texas Virginia Washington and West Virginia) and Washington DC.

Operations

The company provides consumer business and commercial banking wealth investments and insurance through a network of branch offices internet banking mobile banking telephone banking and ATMs.

Sales and Marketing

First Citizens BancShares serves both individuals and commercial entities in its market areas. In 2013 it spent $8.3 million for advertising costs compared to $3.4 million in 2012.

Financial Performance

After experiencing a slight revenue decrease in 2012 First Citizens BancShares' revenues declined by 11% in 2013 due to a decrease in the interest income as a result of lower accreted loan discounts resulting from payments on acquired loans. Accretion income will continue to decrease in future periods as acquired loan balances continue to decline.However the company's net income increased by 25% in 2013 due to a decline in interest expenses as a result of a 22 basis point decrease in the rate and a $387.7 million drop in average interest-bearing liabilities. Interest expense declined for the fourth consecutive year during 2013. The rate on all interest-bearing liabilities fell to 0.41 percent during 2013 compared to 0.63 percent during 2012 and 0.96 percent during 2011.In 2013 First Citizens BancShares' operating cash flow increased to $331.0 million compared to $201.3 million in 2012 primarily due to a profit from provision for loan and lease losses and a gain on the sale of processing services.

Mergers and Acquisitions

Growing its assets and geographic reach in 2014 First Citizens BancShares and First Citizens Bancorporation merged Columbia South Carolina-based First Citizens Bancorporation and its banking subsidiary First Citizens Bank and Trust Company into Raleigh North Carolina-based First Citizens BancShares and its banking subsidiary First Citizens Bank.

Company Background

First Citizens BancShares has been fortifying its presence along the West Coast by snapping up failed financial institutions. Since 2009 it has acquired most of the banking operations of Temecula Valley Bank Washington-based Venture Bank and First Regional Bank in Southern California. It also acquired the failed Florida-based bank Sun American and entered Colorado through the acquisitions of United Western Bank and Colorado Capital Bank. All were FDIC-assisted transactions and each acquired institution became branches of First-Citizens Bank. The deals added about 50 branches to the bank's network. First Citizens BancShares continues to seek out acquisitions of other seized institutions.

Though the company has been able to grow geographically thanks to the economic downturn its IronStone Bank division which focused on business customers suffered from weakened markets in Florida and Georgia. (First Citizens Bancshares merged IronStone into First-Citizens Bank in 2011 to increase efficiency and unify the company's brand.) It has remained profitable thanks in part to its acquisitions which include loss-sharing agreements with the FDIC but has had to increase its provisions for loan losses each of the last five years. The Holding family which occupies several positions in the company's board room and executive suite controls First Citizens BancShares.

EXECUTIVES

COO BancShares and First-Citizens Bank & Trust Company, Edward L. (Ed) Willingham, age 60, $585,125 total compensation

President and Corporate Sales Executive of BancShares and First-Citizens Bank & Trust Company, Peter M. Bristow, age 49

Executive Vice President, Carol Yochem

Chairman and CEO First Citizens BancShares First-Citizens Bank & Trust and IronStone Bank, Frank B. Holding, age 54, $902,875 total compensation

EVP Finance and CFO, Craig L. Nix, age 43

EVP Business Banking Segment Manager and Director First-Citizens Bank & Trust; President IronStone Bank, Hope Holding Connell, age 52, $563,750 total compensation

EVP and Chief Human Resources Officer First-Citizens Bank & Trust, Lou J. Davis, age 62

Chief Credit Officer and Executive Vice President of FCB, Ricky T. Holland, age 61

Executive Vice President and General Auditor of FCB, Donald Preskenis

Vice President Financial Sales Manager, Karen Carver

Vice President Financial Services Manager, Benny Lisk

Assistant Vice President Service Manager, Loretta Bischoff

Senior Vice President, David (Dave) Morrison

Vice President Chief Legal Officer; Executive Vice President and Chief Legal Officer of FCB, Barry Harris

Vice President Marketing, Christine Thompson

Vice President, Scott German

Vice President, Tina Partin

Vice President, Shelly Mohabir

Vice President, Parenty Paul

Senior Vice President, Rich Smith

Vice President Branch Operations Manager, Joseph (Jo) Williams

Vice President, Shirley Fitzpatrick

Vice President Business Banking, Michael (Mel) Caldwell

Vice President, Edwards Malarie

Vice President Financial Sales Manager III, Ricardo Siordia

Senior Vice President Credit Resolution Group, John (Jack) Mecklenburg

Financial Sales Manager Assistant Vice President, Cynthia Dendy

Vice President Financial Sales Manager, David (Dave) Reed

Assistant Vice President Senior Information Technology Recruiting Specialist, Jesse Harris

Vice President and Business Banker, Luz Cooper

Vice President And Financial Services, Rich Irons

Senior Vice President and Senior Counsel, John (Jack) Fleming

Vice President, Sandy Mitchell

Senior Vice President Executive Project Director, Julie Sizer

Vice President Business Banking, Robert (Bob) Spector

Vice President, Lynn Kershner

Auditors: Dixon Hughes Goodman LLP

LOCATIONS

HQ: First Citizens BancShares, Inc. (NC)
4300 Six Forks Road, Raleigh, NC 27609
Phone: 919 716-7000
Web: www.firstcitizens.com

2013 Branches

	No.
North Carolina	253
Virginia	48
California	21
Florida	18
Georgia	14
Washington	7
Texas	7
Colorado	6
Tennessee	6
West Virginia	5
Arizona	2
New Mexico	2
Oklahoma	2
Oregon	2
District of Columbia	1
Kansas	1
Maryland	1
Missouri	1
Total	**397**

PRODUCTS/OPERATIONS

2013 Sales

	$ mil.	% of total
Interest		
Loans & leases	757	72
Investment securities including dividends	36	3
Overnight investments	2	-
Noninterest		
Service charges on deposit accounts	60	5
Wealth management services	59	5
Merchant services	56	4
Cardholder services	48	4
Fees from processing services	22	1
Other service charges and fees	15	1
Adjustments	(72.3)	-
Other	72	5
Total	**1,060**	**100**

COMPETITORS

BB&T	JPMorgan Chase
BBVA Compass Bancshares	PNC Financial
	Regions Financial
Bank of America	SunTrust
Capital One	Synovus
Citibank	Wachovia Corp
First Horizon	Wells Fargo

HISTORICAL FINANCIALS

Company Type: Public

Income Statement
FYE: December 31

	ASSETS ($ mil.)	NET INCOME ($ mil.)	INCOME AS % OF ASSETS	EMPLOYEES
12/14	30,075	138	0.5%	6,440
12/13	21,199	167	0.8%	4,875
12/12	21,283	134	0.6%	4,821
12/11	20,881	195	0.9%	5,077
12/10	20,806	193	0.9%	5,135
Annual Growth	**9.6%**	**(8.0%)**	**—**	**5.8%**

2014 Year-End Financials

Debt ratio: 3.46%	No. of shares (mil.): 12
Return on equity: 5.82%	Dividends
Cash ($ mil.): 2,329	Yield: 0.4%
Current ratio: —	Payout: 11.2%
Long-term debt ($ mil.): —	Market value ($ mil.): 3,036

	STOCK PRICE ($) FY Close	P/E High/Low		PER SHARE ($) Earnings	Dividends	Book Value
12/14	252.79	20	16	13.56	1.20	223.77
12/13	222.63	13	9	17.43	1.20	215.89
12/12	163.50	14	12	13.11	1.20	193.75
12/11	174.99	11	7	18.80	1.20	180.97
12/10	189.05	11	9	18.50	1.20	166.08
Annual Growth	**7.5%**	**—**	**—**	**(7.5%)**	**(0.0%)**	**7.7%**

First Commonwealth Financial Corp. (Indiana, PA)

First Commonwealth Financial is the holding company for First Commonwealth Bank which provides consumer and commercial banking services from nearly 115 branches across 15 central and western Pennsylvania counties as well as in Columbus Ohio. The bank's loan portfolio mostly consists of commercial and industrial loans including real estate operating agricultural and construction loans. It also issues consumer loans such as education automobile and home equity loans and offers wealth management insurance financial planning retail brokerage and trust services. The company has total assets exceeding $6 billion with deposits of roughly $4.5 billion.

OperationsThe bank made 65% of its total revenue from interest and fees on loans in 2014 while another 12% came from interest and dividends on its investments. Another 6% of First Commonwealth's revenue came from service charges on deposit accounts while trust income and insurance and retail brokerage commissions each made up 2% of the bank's total revenue.Geographic ReachThe bank boasts nearly 115 branch offices in western and central Pennsylvania and Columbus Ohio. It also has loan production offices in downtown Pittsburgh Pennsylvania and Cleveland Ohio.Sales and MarketingFirst Commonwealth Financial spent $2.95 million on advertising in 2014 compared to $3.13 million and $4.16 million in 2013 and 2012 respectively.Financial PerformanceFirst Commonwealth's revenues have been slowly decline over the past few years due to shrinking interest margins on loans amidst the low-interest environment. The firm's profits however have been rising thanks to declining loan loss provisions as its loan portfolio's credit quality has been improving in the strengthening economy. The bank's revenue dipped by more than 1% to $263.04 million in 2014 mostly as interest margins on loans continued to decline as it issued new loans with lower rates in the low-interest environment.Despite lower revenue in 2014 the bank's net income jumped by 7% to $44.45 million for the year mostly thanks to further decreases in loan loss provisions with a strengthening credit portfolio and lower interest expenses on deposits. First Commonwealth's operating cash fell by 4% to $82.14 million despite higher earnings mostly as the bank collected less in cash proceeds from the sales of its mortgage loans held for sale.Strategy First Commonwealth Financial has historically expanded its branch reach through the acquisition smaller banks and thrifts in its market area. However in recent years the company has also been adding non-banking businesses such as insurance firms to bolster its existing non-banking service lines. Mergers and AcquisitionsIn 2014 subsidiary First Commonwealth Bank entered the Columbus Ohio market for the first time with its purchase of the Ohio-based First Community Bank for $14.75 million cash.Also in 2014 the bank bolstered its insurance business through its acquisition of Thompson/McLay Insurance Associates which boasted long-term client relationships in the home auto commercial and specialty insurance lines. The deal added the insurance firm's experienced sales and account management personnel as well as the popular Thompson/McLay Insurance Associates brand which it would keep as a division of its own insurance agency.

EXECUTIVES

EVP and Chief Revenue Officer, Jane Grebenc, $355,833 total compensation
EVP and Chief Credit Officer, I. Robert (Bob) Emmerich, $274,500 total compensation
President and CEO, Thomas Michael (Mike) Price, age 52, $435,567 total compensation
EVP CFO and Treasurer, James R. Reske, $237,372 total compensation
EVP and Chief Audit Executive, Leonard V. Lombardi, age 55
EVP Business Integration, Norman J. Montgomery, $261,792 total compensation

EVP Chief Risk Officer General Counsel and Secretary, Matthew C. (Matt) Tomb
EVP Human Resources, Carrie Riggle
Vice President, Homer Starr
Vice President of Networking Security, Sheila Hoover
Assistant Vice President, Molly Russell
Vice President, Terry Lingenfelter
Assistant Vice President, Scott Repine
Senior Vice President Information Technology, Brad Bellas
Vice President, Kevin Cribbs
Vice President, Stephen Orban
Senior Vice President, William Bonner
Senior Vice President Relationship Manager, Doug Sako
Assistant Vice President, Suzanne Johnson
Assistant Vice President Corporate Bkng, William (Bill) Buchanan
Vice President And Commercial Real Estate, Brian Pukylo
Assistant Vice President Operations, Mona Straw
Executive Vice President And Chief Credit Officer, I Emmerich
Chairman, David S. (Dave) Dahlmann, age 65
Auditors: KPMG LLP

LOCATIONS

HQ: First Commonwealth Financial Corp. (Indiana, PA) 601 Philadelphia Street, Indiana, PA 15701
Phone: 724 349-7220
Web: www.fcbanking.com

PRODUCTS/OPERATIONS

2014 Sales

	$ mil.	% of total
Interest		
Loans including fees	171	65
Taxable investments	31	12
Noninterest		
Service charges on deposit accounts	15	7
Insurance & retail brokerage commissions	6	2
Trust income	6	2
Others	32	12
Total	**263**	**100**

Selected Subsidiaries

First Commonwealth Bank
First Commonwealth Insurance Agency
First Commonwealth Home Mortgage LLC (49.9%)
First Commonwealth Financial Advisors Incorporated

COMPETITORS

Allegheny Valley Bancorp	Fidelity Bancorp (PA)
AmeriServ Financial	First Niagara Financial
Citizens Financial Group	Northwest Bancshares
Dollar Bank	PNC Financial
F.N.B. (PA)	S&T Bancorp

HISTORICAL FINANCIALS

Company Type: Public

Income Statement
FYE: December 31

	ASSETS ($ mil.)	NET INCOME ($ mil.)	INCOME AS % OF ASSETS	EMPLOYEES
12/14	6,360	44	0.7%	1,363
12/13	6,214	41	0.7%	1,437
12/12	5,995	41	0.7%	1,482
12/11	5,841	15	0.3%	1,506
12/10	5,812	22	0.4%	1,622
Annual Growth	**2.3%**	**17.9%**	**—**	**(4.3%)**

2014 Year-End Financials

Debt ratio: 1.13%	No. of shares (mil.): 91
Return on equity: 6.23%	Dividends
Cash ($ mil.): 74	Yield: 3.0%
Current ratio: —	Payout: 57.1%
Long-term debt ($ mil.): —	Market value ($ mil.): 846

	STOCK PRICE ($) FY Close	P/E High/Low		PER SHARE ($)		
			Earnings	Dividends	Book Value
12/14	9.22	20 16	0.48	0.28	7.81
12/13	8.82	22 16	0.43	0.23	7.47
12/12	6.82	19 14	0.40	0.18	7.49
12/11	5.26	49 24	0.15	0.12	7.23
12/10	7.08	30 17	0.25	0.06	7.15
Annual Growth	6.8%	— —	17.7%	47.0%	2.2%

First Community Bancshares, Inc. (NV)

First Community Bancshares doesn't play second fiddle to other area banks. The firm is the holding company for First Community Bank which provides traditional services like checking and savings accounts CDs and credit cards and serves communities through some 55 branches across Virginia West Virginia North Carolina and Tennessee. Commercial real estate loans make up 45% of its loan portfolio while commercial business loans make up another 5%. First Community Bancshares offers insurance through subsidiary Greenpoint Insurance and wealth management and investment advisory services through Trust Services and First Community Wealth Management.

OperationsFirst Community Bancshares operates through four main business activities: commercial and consumer banking lending activities wealth management and insurance services. Its Trust Services and First Community Wealth Management subsidiary had managed assets with a market value of nearly $700 million in 2014.The bank which had a staff of 678 employees at the end of 2014 generated 70% of its total revenue from loan interest (including fees and loans held for investment) in 2014 and another 8% from interest on taxable and non-taxable securities. The rest of its revenue came from deposit account service charges (9%) insurance commissions (4%) wealth management (1%) and other miscellaneous sources of income.Sales and MarketingThe bank serves individuals and businesses across several industries including: manufacturing mining services construction retail healthcare military and transportation.Financial PerformanceThe company has struggled to grow its revenues in recent years due to shrinking interest margins on loans amidst the low-interest environment. Its profits however have been rising thanks to falling interest expenses and declining loan loss provisions as its loan portfolio's credit quality has improved with higher property valuations in the strengthened economy.First Community Bancshares's revenue dipped by 2% to $136.1 million in 2014 as its interest income on loans and securities declined with fewer assets and because it took on a $1.39 million loss from the sale of its investment securities during the year. Despite revenue declines in 2014 the bank's net income jumped 9% to $25.5 million thanks to continued declines in interest expenses on deposits and loan loss provisions. First Community's oper-

ating cash levels fell by 6% to $41.7 million for the year after adjusting its earnings for non-cash items related to its loan loss provisions and the proceeds of its mortgage loan sales.StrategyFaced with shrinking revenues in recent years First Community has been strategically changing its geographic positioning selling off some of its branches in certain areas and acquiring new branches in others. In late 2014 it acquired seven branches from Bank of America in Southwestern Virginia and Central North Carolina and sold 13 of its branches to Charleston-based CresCom Bank including 10 of its branches in Southeastern North Carolina and three in South Carolina.Mergers and AcquisitionsIn 2014 First Community purchased seven branches from Bank of America including six branches in Southwestern Virginia and one in Central North Carolina. The deal also added $318.9 million in new deposits as well as real estate and assumed leases associated with the branches.Company BackgroundAfter slowing its acquisition activity during the economic downturn First Community resumed in 2012 buying Peoples Bank of Virginia which added four branches in the Richmond area. The company also acquired the failed Waccamaw Bank in a FDIC-facilitated transaction. That deal brought in 16 branches in North Carolina.

EXECUTIVES

EVP and COO, E. Stephen (Steve) Lilly, age 56, $252,000 total compensation
Chairman and CEO, William P. Stafford, age 51, $200,013 total compensation
CFO, David D. Brown, age 40, $225,000 total compensation
President; CEO First Community Bank, Gary R. Mills, $300,000 total compensation
President First Community Bank, Martyn A. Pell, $255,000 total compensation
Vice President Director Of Operations, Garry Stutts
Vice President Finance, Jason Belcher
Assistant Vice President Credit Administration, Jeff Noble
Senior Vice President On The Corporate Staff, John Spracher
Assistant Vice President Regulatory Compliance Officer, Jonathan (Jon) Conway
Auditors: Dixon Hughes Goodman LLP

LOCATIONS

HQ: First Community Bancshares, Inc. (NV)
P.O. Box 989, Bluefield, VA 24605-0989
Phone: 276 326-9000
Web: www.fcbinc.com

PRODUCTS/OPERATIONS

2011 Sales

	$ mil.	% of total
Interest		
Loans including fees	80	61
Securities	13	10
Deposits in banks	0	-
Noninterest		
Service charges on deposit accounts	13	10
Insurance commissions	6	5
Net gains on sales of securities	5	4
Wealth management	3	3
Other service charges commissions & fees	5	4
Other	3	3
Adjustments	(2.3)	-
Total	**129**	**100**

COMPETITORS

BB&T	Huntington Bancshares
Bank of America	SunTrust

City Holding	United Bankshares
First Citizens BancShares	WesBanco
Highlands Bankshares Inc.	

HISTORICAL FINANCIALS

Company Type: Public

Income Statement

FYE: December 31

	ASSETS ($ mil.)	NET INCOME ($ mil.)	INCOME AS % OF ASSETS	EMPLOYEES
12/14	2,607	25	1.0%	678
12/13	2,602	23	0.9%	729
12/12	2,728	28	1.0%	760
12/11	2,164	20	0.9%	633
12/10	2,244	21	1.0%	683
Annual Growth	3.8%	3.9%	—	(0.2%)

2014 Year-End Financials

Debt ratio: 0.69%	No. of shares (mil.): 18
Return on equity: 7.50%	Dividends
Cash ($ mil.): 40	Yield: 3.0%
Current ratio: —	Payout: 39.3%
Long-term debt ($ mil.): —	Market value ($ mil.): 303

	STOCK PRICE ($) FY Close	P/E High/Low		PER SHARE ($)		
			Earnings	Dividends	Book Value
12/14	16.47	13 10	1.31	0.50	19.09
12/13	16.70	16 13	1.11	0.48	17.75
12/12	15.97	11 8	1.40	0.43	17.77
12/11	12.48	14 9	1.07	0.40	17.13
12/10	14.94	14 9	1.23	0.40	15.11
Annual Growth	2.5%	— —	1.6%	5.7%	6.0%

First Data Corp (New)

Paper plastic or digital —in whatever form First Data moves the money. One of the world's largest electronic payments processors First Data serves more than 6 million merchants and some 4000 card issuers in some 35 countries. It provides a variety of secure funds transfer and related services including credit card payment processing fraud protection and authentication check guarantee (through subsidiary TeleCheck) electronic bill payment management and point-of-sale (POS) services. First Data operates through three primary segments: retail and alliance services financial services and international. It owns a majority stake in Bank of America Merchant Services. The company went public in late 2015.

HISTORY

Company BackgroundBoth predecessors of today's First Data (First Financial Management and First Data Resources) developed from in-house data processing operations that became independent profit centers for their parent companies and were then spun off.

The older of the two companies First Financial Management arose out of the data processing department of the Georgia Railroad Bank & Trust. By the time it went public in 1983 First Financial was the largest banking data processor in the Southeast. It grew rapidly in a consolidating industry and in 1987 entered the credit card transaction processing business with the purchase of Na-BANCO.

That year American Express created First Data Resources a separate unit for its transaction processing functions under the leadership of Henry Duques. Duques had built up the unit during the 1980s to process a variety of transactions for American Express' charge card processing business and its burgeoning financial services operations. While First Data was growing First Financial remained active buying Georgia Federal Bank in 1989 to facilitate the growth of its bank card business.

As the 1990s dawned American Express' dreams of a financial services empire were crumbling. The businesses did not fit well with American Express diverting attention from its core lines. However First Data had become the largest bank card processing company in the US and a significant power in mutual fund transactions. In 1992 it was spun off.

First Financial began sharpening its focus on merchant (rather than bank) services. It bought TeleCheck (check authorization) in 1992 and began divesting its banking and bank services holdings.

In 1994 First Data and First Financial Management went head-to-head vying for Western Union (founded 1855) from bankrupt parent New Valley. First Financial was the victor in the bruising bidding war (which also included Forstmann Little).

Although First Data's $6.5 billion merger with First Financial in 1995 raised antitrust concerns the deal went through with only the stipulation of selling the MoneyGram (money transfer) services business. The new union gave First Data a 30% share of the fragmented credit card processing market and moved it into new service areas many of which it began divesting in efforts to focus on financial support.

First Data won a 10-year contract in 1996 to process credit and debit transactions for retail giant Wal-Mart —more than 5 billion transactions each year. A 1997 pact with BANK ONE and its First USA subsidiary added another 6 million accounts. First Data also expanded its geographical presence that year agreeing to provide credit card processing for HSBC Holdings' banks in the UK the US and Hong Kong (First Data pulled out of Hong Kong the following year).

In 1999 First Data and BANK ONE strengthened their relationship: First Data took a stake in BANK ONE subsidiary Paymentech and folded it into an existing joint venture with BANK ONE (Banc One Payment Services). To refocus on its electronic payment and commerce services First Data sold its Investor Services Group.

In 2000 the company slashed some 400 management jobs and made other workforce cuts. First Data continued to grow through acquisitions (including Cardservice International and PaySys) and alliances (with such entities as JPMorgan Chase and Deutsche Post) in 2001.

The US Department of Justice challenged First Data's 2004 purchase of rival Concord EFS over antitrust concerns but later approved the deal when First Data agreed to divest ATM network NYCE in a sale to Metavante.

The Concord EFS acquisition was notable both because of its size and because it brought First Data's credit and debit processing strengths together with Concord EFS' PIN-debit network. However it did not bring about the expected synergies and First Data struggled for the next few years to absorb its new prize. CEO Charlie Fote left the company in 2005 and was replaced by his predecessor Ric Duques who had led the company from 1992 to 2002.

Duques led the company through a restructuring in 2006 spinning off its Western Union operations as well as related units Orlandi Valuta and Vigo Remittance to shareholders.

Investment firm KKR acquired First Data in 2007 and Duques handed over the company reins to former Compaq and MCI exec Michael Capellas following the acquisition. The $26 billion deal was the largest leveraged-buyout transaction to date but the timing was less than ideal. After the acquisition the economy took a nosedive and payments declined in volume and number. Consumers began using debit cards rather than credit cards another trend that lowered the company's revenues. Facing billions in debt from the buyout First Data sold some operations to raise capital and discontinued others that weren't performing. The company also restructured merging its commercial and financial services segments and cutting operational costs. In 2008 First Data strengthened its European business by forming card processing joint venture AIB Merchant Services with Allied Irish Banks and through the acquisition of a 50% stake in the interbank processing business of multibank entity Trionis (formerly European Savings Banks Financial Services or EUFISERV). Also that year First Data announced plans to buy prepaid gift card provider Interactive Communications but purchase negotiations stalled and the company instead inked a distribution deal to sell InComm's cards. In 2009 First Data moved its headquarters office back to Atlanta —near Banc of America Merchant Services and other payments industry companies including customers —after some eight years of being headquartered in the Denver area. First Data retained its Colorado office as its administrative headquarters.

EXECUTIVES

EVP and Director Finance, Michael K. (Mike) Neborak, age 58, $279,615 total compensation
Chairman and CEO, Frank J. Bisignano, age 55, $1,500,000 total compensation
EVP and Head of Latin America and Mexico (LATAM) Region, Gustavo C. Marin, age 57
EVP and Head of Human Resources, Anthony S. (Tony) Marino, age 52
EVP and Head of Network and Security Solutions, Barry C. McCarthy, age 51
President, Guy Chiarello, age 55, $481,410 total compensation
EVP and Head of Corporate and Business Development, Christopher M. Foskett, age 57
EVP Global Financial Solutions, Sanjiv Das, age 52, $523,077 total compensation
EVP General Counsel and Secretary, Adam L. Rosman, age 50
EVP and COO, Christine E. Larsen, age 53, $396,667 total compensation
EVP Strategy Planning and Business Development, Himanshu A. Patel, age 39, $305,128 total compensation
CIO, Christopher (Chris) Augustin
EVP and Co-Head of Global Financial Solutions, Andrew Gelb, age 44
EVP and Chief Control Officer, Cynthia (Cindy) Armine-Klein, age 53, $320,192 total compensation
EVP and Head of Global Business Solutions, Daniel J. (Dan) Charron, age 50
EVP and COO (Global Business Solutions), Jeffrey I. (Jeff) Hack, age 50
EVP and Chief Administrative Officer, Thomas (Tom) Higgins, age 56
Vice Chairman, Joseph J. (Joe) Plumeri, age 71
Auditors: Ernst & Young LLP

LOCATIONS

HQ: First Data Corp (New)
225 Liberty Street, 29th Floor, New York, NY 10281
Phone: 800 735-3362
Web: www.firstdata.com

2014 Sales

	$ mil.	% of total
US	9,427	85
International	1,724	15
Total	**11,151**	**100**

PRODUCTS/OPERATIONS

2014 Sales

	$ mil.	% of total
Transaction & processing fees		
Merchant-related services	4,060	37
Card services	1,817	16
Check services	264	2
Other	513	5
Reimbursable debit network feespostage & other	3,603	32
Product sales & other	892	8
Total	**11,151**	**100**

COMPETITORS

Atos	Fiserv
Cardtronics	Global Payments
Chase Paymentech Solutions	Heartland Payment Systems
Discover	MasterCard
ECHO Inc.	Total System Services
Elavon	Visa Inc
Fidelity National Information Services	

HISTORICAL FINANCIALS

Company Type: Public

Income Statement

FYE: December 31

	REVENUE ($ mil.)	NET INCOME ($ mil.)	NET PROFIT MARGIN	EMPLOYEES
12/14	11,151	(457)	—	23,000
12/13	10,808	(869)	—	23,000
12/12	10,680	(700)	—	24,000
12/11	10,713	(516)	—	24,000
12/10	10,380	(1,021)	—	24,500
Annual Growth	1.8%	—	—	(1.6%)

2014 Year-End Financials

Debt ratio: 60.91%
Return on equity: —
Cash ($ mil.): 358
Current ratio: 1.04
Long-term debt ($ mil.): 20,711
No. of shares (mil.): 0
Dividends
Yield: —
Payout: —
Market value ($ mil.): —

First Financial Bancorp (OH)

First Financial Bancorp spreads itself thick. The holding company's flagship subsidiary First Financial Bank operates nearly 110 branches in Ohio Indiana and Kentucky. Founded in 1863 the bank offers checking and savings accounts money market accounts CDs credit cards private banking and wealth management services through its First Financial Wealth Management subsidiary. Commercial loans including real estate and construction loans make up more than 50% of First Financial's total loan portfolio; the bank also offers residential mortgage and consumer loans. First Financial Bancorp boasts more than $7 billion in assets including nearly $5 billion in loans.

OperationsThe company's private banking business First Financial Wealth Management had $2.4 billion in assets under management in early

2015.Sales and MarketingFirst Financial spent $3.60 million on marketing in 2014 compared to $4.27 million and $5.55 million in 2013 and 2012 respectively.Financial PerformanceFirst Financial's revenue has been in decline in recent years due to shrinking interest margins on loans amidst the low-interest environment. The company has also struggled to grow its profits much past the $65 million-mark though profit levels are more than twice as high as they were prior to 2009.The company's revenue dipped by 2% to $311.82 million in 2014 mostly as its loan interest income declined by nearly 4% as interest margins continued to shrink in the low-interest environment. First Financial's non-interest income fell by double-digits mostly due to lower FDIC loss sharing income lower income from the accelerated discount on prepaid covered loans and smaller gains on investment securities sales.Despite lower revenue in 2014 First Financial's net income rebounded by 34% to $65 million for the year mostly thanks to an 80% reduction in loan and lease loss provisions as the bank's loan portfolio's credit quality improved with the strengthening economy. The company's non-interest expenses also declined by double-digits mostly because the bank in 2013 incurred a nonrecurring $22.4 million FDIC indemnification valuation adjustment. First Financial's operating cash declined by 66% to $56.65 million after adjusting its earnings for non-cash items related to the indemnification asset decrease and net sales proceeds on its loans held for sale.

Strategy

First Financial has been focusing on branch expansion (on its own or through acquisitions) in three core metropolitan markets: Cincinnati Dayton and Indianapolis. In 2014 for example First Financial acquired three Ohio-based banks and their branches in 2014 expanding its branch network in Central Ohio while adding new loan and deposit business at the same time.Mergers and AcquisitionsIn 2014 to expand further into key markets in Columbus and Central Ohio First Financial purchased The First Bexley Bank which served commercial and consumer bank clients from its one branch location in Bexley Ohio. Similarly that year it purchased Insight Bank operated a branch in Worthington Ohio and a mortgage origination office in Newark Ohio; and bought Worthington-based Guernsey Bancorp and its three branches in Central Ohio. Company Background In the past the bank acquired 16 branches in western Ohio from Liberty Savings Bank and bought 22 Indianapolis-area branches from Flagstar Bank in 2011. Together the two acquisitions furthered the bank's growth strategy for the key markets of Dayton and Indianapolis.

EXECUTIVES

President Western Markets Commercial Banking and Wealth Management, C. Douglas (Doug) Lefferson

President and CEO, Claude E. Davis

President and COO, Anthony M. (Tony) Stollings

Chief Credit Officer, Richard S. Barbercheck

SVP and CFO, John Gavigan

President Eastern Markets and Consumer Banking, Kevin T. Langford

President Mortgage Banking, Jill A. Stanton

EVP and Chief Compliance Officer, Holly M. Foster

President Corporate Banking, Brad Ringwald

Marketing Vice President, Peter Austin

Vice President Commercial Underwriter, Brian Englert

Vice President Commercial Lending, Ray McCleese

First Vice President Commercial Banking, Stephen Murphy

Assistant Vice President Sales Center Manager III, Diana Bravo

Sales Center Manager Assistant Vice President Beckett Park Branch, Kristi Wilson

Assistant Vice President, Jeremy Fuller

First Vice President Information Technology, Bard Lowry

Assistant Vice President Sales Center Manager III, Cooley Andrew

Vice President Commercial Banking, Thomas (Thom) Gabrielson

Vice President Commercial Underwriter, David (Dave) Brown

Assistant Vice President Mortgage Operations Manager, Tammy Kinser

Vice President Enterprise Information Security Officer, Dan Polly

Chairman, Murph Knapke

Vice Chairman, J. Wickliffe Ach

Auditors: Crowe Horwath LLP

LOCATIONS

HQ: First Financial Bancorp (OH)
255 East Fifth Street, Suite 700, Cincinnati, OH 45202
Phone: 877 322-9530
Web: www.bankatfirst.com

PRODUCTS/OPERATIONS

2014 Sales

	$ mil.	% of total
Interest		
Loans including fees	208	66
Investment securities	44	14
(Adjustment)	(5.5)	-
Noninterest		
Service charges on deposit accounts	20	7
Trust and wealth management fees	13	5
Bankcard income	10	3
Net gains from sales on loans	4	1
Accelerated discount on covered/formerly covered loans	4	1
Others	10	3
Total	**311**	**100**

COMPETITORS

AMB Financial
Commercial Bancshares
Farmers National
Fifth Third
First Defiance Financial
First Franklin
LCNB
Liberty Capital
Logansport Financial
MutualFirst Financial
PNC Financial
Peoples Community Bancorp
Peoples-Sidney
SB Financial Group
U.S. Bancorp

HISTORICAL FINANCIALS

Company Type: Public

Income Statement

FYE: December 31

	ASSETS ($ mil.)	NET INCOME ($ mil.)	INCOME AS % OF ASSETS	EMPLOYEES
12/14	7,217	65	0.9%	1,442
12/13	6,417	48	0.8%	1,422
12/12	6,497	67	1.0%	1,547
12/11	6,671	66	1.0%	1,656
12/10	6,250	59	0.9%	1,664
Annual Growth	**3.7%**	**2.3%**	**—**	**(3.5%)**

2014 Year-End Financials

Debt ratio: 0.36%
Return on equity: 8.87%
Cash ($ mil.): 132
Current ratio: —
Long-term debt ($ mil.): —

No. of shares (mil.): 61
Dividends
  Yield: 3.2%
  Payout: 70.9%
Market value ($ mil.): 1,142

	STOCK PRICE ($) FY Close	P/E High/Low		PER SHARE ($) Earnings	Dividends	Book Value
12/14	18.59	17	14	1.09	0.61	12.76
12/13	17.43	21	17	0.83	0.94	11.86
12/12	14.62	16	12	1.14	1.18	12.24
12/11	16.64	16	12	1.14	0.78	12.22
12/10	18.48	21	14	0.99	0.40	12.01
Annual Growth	**0.1%**	**—**	**—**	**2.4%**	**11.1%**	**1.5%**

First Financial Bankshares, Inc.

Texas hold 'em? Well sort of. First Financial Bankshares is the holding company forÂelevenÂbanksÂconsolidated under the First Financial brand all of which are located in small and midsized markets in Texas. Together they have about 50 locations. The company maintains a decentralized management structure with each of the subsidiary banks having their own local leadership and decision-making authority.ÂIts First Financial Trust & Asset Management subsidiary administers retirement and employee benefit plans in addition to providing trust services.ÂFirst Financial BanksharesÂ also owns anÂ insurance agency.Real estate mortgages account for approximatelyÂhalf ofÂthe company'sÂloan portfolio whileÂcommercial financial and agricultural loans account for about another third. The banks also offer construction and consumer loans as well as deposit products like checking and savings accounts and CDs. Some locations offer brokerage services through arrangements with third parties.First Financial Bankshares has grown both organically and through acquisitions. In 2010 the companyÂbought Huntsville Texas-based Sam Houston Financial Corporation the parent of The First State Bank. The deal worth moreÂthan $22 million expanded First Financial Bankshares' footprint in East Texas. The following year The First State Bank changed its name to First Financial Bank bringing all of the company's banks under the same banner.First Financial Bankshares continues to open new branches andÂseek out acquisitions of other banks in TexasÂwith a continued focus on burgeoning smaller markets where competition is less intense than metropolitan areas. The company whose earnings have increasedÂeach year for a quarter-centuryÂhas benefitted from the Texas economy which was not nearly as hard-hit by the recession as other regions andÂis one of the fastest-growing in the country. First Financial Bankshares has alsoÂgotten a boost by investing its capital wisely;Âa relatively large proportion of its revenues —more than 25% — comes from interest-earning assets such as mortgage-backed securities state and municipal bonds and government agency securities.

EXECUTIVES

Chairman President and CEO; Chairman First Financial Bank N.A., F. Scott Dueser, age 62, $626,666 total compensation

EVP and CFO, J. Bruce Hildebrand, age 60, $395,000 total compensation

EVP Operations; Chairman First Technology Services Inc., Gary L. Webb, age 58, $316,666 total compensation

EVP and Chief Administrative Officer, Ronald D. (Ron) Butler, age 54, $355,000 total compensation
EVP Lending, Marna Yeriga
EVP and CIO, Thomas S. (Stan) Limerick
EVP and Senior Lending Officer, Gary S.Gragg, $316,666 total compensation
Vice President Wires, Sandra Holt
Senior Vice President, Kay Berry
Senior Vice President, Dennis Tarrant
Executive Vice President of Commercial Loans, Marelyn Shedd
Assistant Vice President Human Resources, Racheal Carter
Vice President, Fernando Quintana
Executive Vice President Lending, Brad Seay
Assistant Vice President, Mary Hopkins
Vice President, Russell Phillips
Lending Officer Vice President, Chris Cregger
Vice President Mortgage Loans, Corie Oconnor
Vice President Consumer Lending, Ryan Sonntag
Assistant Vice President, Lori Davis
Assistant Vice President, Brad Magers
Executive Vice President Cashier and Chief Financial Officer, Charles (Chas) Tennesson
Executive Vice President, David Bailey
Vice President, Kevin Shipman
Senior Vice President, Mike Hopkins
Executive Vice President, Robert (Bob) Lemons
Assistant Vice President, Janet Johnson
Vice President Senior Consumer Lender, Lani White
Vice President, Jesse Villarreal
Central Doc Prep Manager Assistant Vice President, Carmen Williams
Vice President, Murielle Gillet
Vice President Application Analyst Manager, Mark Murray
Senior Vice President, Mark Pierce
Vice President and Branch Manager, Britt Stuart
Vice President .consumer Lending, Blayne Baley
Vice President, Isabel Montoya
Vice President Credit Adminstration, Clay Trumble
Vice President Alternative Delivery Channels, Jeff Casey
Assistant Vice President, Faye Dodson
Senior Vice President Appraisal Services, Brandon Harris
Vice President, Wade Spain
Vice President, Raquel Garza
Senior Vice President San Angelo, Chuck Shore
Vice President Treasury Management, Kelly Jones
Executive Vice President, Robert (Bob) Pate
Executive Vice President Lending, Marna Yerigan
Vice President, Kathy Bushnell
Senior Vice President, Cindi LaChance
Auditors: Ernst & Young LLP

LOCATIONS

HQ: First Financial Bankshares, Inc.
400 Pine Street, Abilene, TX 79601
Phone: 325 627-7155
Web: www.ffin.com

PRODUCTS/OPERATIONS

2011 Sales

	$ mil.	% of total
Interest		
Loans including fees	98	47
Investment securities	60	28
Other	1	1
Noninterest		
Service charges on deposit accounts	17	8
ATM & credit card fees	13	6
Trust fees	12	6
Other	7	4
Total	**211**	**100**

Selected Subsidiaries

First Financial Bank National Association (Abilene)
First Financial Bank National Association (Cleburne)
First Financial Bank National Association (Eastland)
First Financial Bank National Association (Hereford)
First Financial Bank National Association (Huntsville)
First Financial Bank National Association (Mineral Wells)
First Financial Bank National Association (San Angelo)
First Financial Bank National Association (Southlake)
First Financial Bank National Association (Stephenville)
First Financial Bank National Association (Sweetwater)
First Financial Bank National Association (Weatherford)
First Financial Insurance Agency Inc.
First Financial Trust & Asset Management Company National Association

COMPETITORS

BBVA Compass Bancshares	JPMorgan Chase
Bank of America	Wells Fargo
Cullen/Frost Bankers	Woodforest Financial

HISTORICAL FINANCIALS

Company Type: Public

Income Statement

FYE: December 31

	ASSETS ($ mil.)	NET INCOME ($ mil.)	INCOME AS % OF ASSETS	EMPLOYEES
12/14	5,848	89	1.5%	1,140
12/13	5,222	78	1.5%	1,100
12/12	4,502	74	1.6%	1,000
12/11	4,120	68	1.7%	980
12/10	3,776	59	1.6%	1,000
Annual Growth	**11.6%**	**10.7%**	**—**	**3.3%**

2014 Year-End Financials

Debt ratio: —	No. of shares (mil.): 63
Return on equity: 14.11%	Dividends
Cash ($ mil.): 261	Yield: 1.8%
Current ratio: —	Payout: 40.1%
Long-term debt ($ mil.): —	Market value ($ mil.): 1,899

	STOCK PRICE ($) FY Close	P/E High/Low	Earnings	Dividends	Book Value
12/14	29.88	47 20	1.39	0.55	10.72
12/13	66.11	54 31	1.24	1.03	9.26
12/12	39.01	35 26	1.18	0.99	8.92
12/11	33.43	51 23	1.09	0.47	8.15
12/10	51.25	58 46	0.95	0.91	7.09
Annual Growth	**(12.6%)**	— —	**9.9%**	**(11.7%)**	**10.9%**

First Financial Corp. (IN)

Which came first the First Financial in Indiana Ohio South Carolina or Texas? Regardless this particular First Financial Corporation is the holding company for First Financial Bank which operates more than 60 branches in west-central Indiana and central Illinois. The bank offers traditional services such checking and savings accounts CDs and credit cards. It also provides trust private banking wealth management and investment services. First Financial sells personal and commercial insurance through regional agency subsidiary Forrest Sherer. Another unit Morris Plan originates indirect auto loans through some 70 dealerships in the bank's market area.

In 2011 First Financial bought Freestar Bank adding more than a dozen branches in central Illinois. It was the largest acquisition in the company's history. The bank also grows by opening new branches.

First Financial has remained profitable throughout the economic turmoil that began in earnest during 2008; not only that it has grown its net income each of the last three fiscal years including an increase of nearly 33% in 2011 when the company reported record earnings. Though the bank recorded fewer provisions for loan losses that year its amount of charged-off loans remained elevated compared to pre-recession levels. Commercial loans and mortgages account for more than half of the company's loan portfolio which also includes residential mortgage and consumer loans

With roots dating back to 1834 First Financial Bank is not only one of the oldest banks in Indiana but also the entire country. It is also one of the oldest continually operating businesses in its hometown of Terre Haute. Another local business Princeton Mining Company owns nearly 10% of First Financial Corporation.

EXECUTIVES

Vice Chairman and CEO, Norman D. Lowery, age 47, $630,297 total compensation
Vice President, Richard White
Vice President and Marketing Director, Terry Tevlin
Vice President, Brad Williams
Assistant Vice President Marketing, Sally Whitehurst
Vice President Collections, Jeff Nickels
Executive Vice President, Curtis Brighton
Vice President Special Assets Officer, Bart Duesdieker
Personal Trust Department Assistant Vice Presiden, Carol Myers
Vice President, Steve Herndon
First Vice President, Gloria Curry
Vice President Marketing, David (Dave) Cowley
Vice President, Thom Frantz
Vice President, Rosselli Teresa
Senior Executive Vice President General Counsel and Corporate Secretary, Warren Troupe
Executive Vice President, Marelyn Shedd
Commercial Relationship Manager Vice President, Robert (Bob) Kocot
Vice President Treasury Operations, Teresa Moon
Executive Vice President, Tom Boecking
Assistant Vice President Consumer Lender, Thea Serrano
Vice President Human Resources, Racheal Carter
Chairman, B. Guille Cox
Auditors: Crowe Horwath LLP

LOCATIONS

HQ: First Financial Corp. (IN)
One First Financial Plaza, Terre Haute, IN 47807
Phone: 812 238-6000
Web: www.first-online.com

PRODUCTS/OPERATIONS

2011 Sales

	$ mil.	% of total
Interest		
Loans including related fees	91	61
Securities	22	15
Other	2	1
Noninterest		
Service charges & fees on deposit accounts	9	6
Other service charges & fees	8	6
Insurance commissions	7	5
Trust & financial services	4	3
Other	4	3
Total	**149**	**100**

COMPETITORS

FFW	Huntington Bancshares
Fifth Third	JPMorgan Chase
First Midwest Bancorp	MainSource Financial
First Robinson	Old National Bancorp
Financial	PNC Financial

HISTORICAL FINANCIALS

Company Type: Public

Income Statement

FYE: December 31

	ASSETS ($ mil.)	NET INCOME ($ mil.)	INCOME AS % OF ASSETS	EMPLOYEES
12/14	3,002	33	1.1%	952
12/13	3,018	31	1.0%	954
12/12	2,895	32	1.1%	928
12/11	2,954	37	1.3%	932
12/10	2,451	28	1.1%	813
Annual Growth	5.2%	4.8%	—	4.0%

2014 Year-End Financials

Debt ratio: —	No. of shares (mil.): 12
Return on equity: 8.65%	Dividends
Cash ($ mil.): 78	Yield: 2.7%
Current ratio: —	Payout: 38.6%
Long-term debt ($ mil.): —	Market value ($ mil.): 461

	STOCK PRICE ($) FY Close	P/E High/Low	PER SHARE ($) Earnings	Dividends	Book Value
12/14	35.62	14 12	2.55	0.97	30.46
12/13	36.56	16 12	2.37	0.96	28.94
12/12	30.24	15 11	2.48	0.95	28.01
12/11	33.28	12 9	2.83	0.94	26.29
12/10	35.14	17 12	2.14	0.92	24.46
Annual Growth	0.3%	— —	4.5%	1.3%	5.6%

First Horizon National Corp

First Horizon National would like to be on banking consumers' horizons in the Volunteer State and beyond. The bank holding company operates more than 170 First Tennessee Bank branches in its home state and neighboring markets. Boasting roughly $26 billion in total assets it offers traditional banking services like loans deposit accounts and credit cards as well as trust asset management financial advisory and investment services. Subsidiary FTN Financial performs securities sales and trading fixed-income underwriting and other investment banking services through more than 25 offices in more than 15 states as well as in Hong Kong.

OperationsFirst Horizon operates two core business segments: Regional Banking and Capital Markets. Regional Banking is the company's largest division (it generated 73% of the bank's total revenue in 2014) and provides traditional banking products and services to retail and commercial customers mostly in Tennessee but also in neighboring markets. The division also provides investments financial panning trust services and asset management as well as correspondent banking services such as credit depository and other banking related services for financial institutions.The Capital Markets segment which contributed 18% to total revenues in 2014 serves mainly institutional clients in the US and overseas. Its services

consist of fixed-income sales trading loan sales portfolio advisory and derivative sales.First Horizon's two non-core segments include a Corporate division which collects gains and losses related to the bank's debt and investment activities; and the non-strategic segment (11% of total revenues in 2014) which consists of the wind down of the company's national consumer lending activities its legacy mortgage banking elements including service fees its trust preferred loan portfolio and exited businesses.The company has diversified revenue streams generating about 56% of its total revenue from interest income (mostly from loans) in 2014 16% from capital markets-related fees nearly 10% from deposit transactions and cash management fees about 6% from its Mortgage Banking business and 6% from a combination of brokerage fees and trust services and management fees.Geographic ReachFirst Horizon National boasts more than 180 branch locations across seven US states. More than 90% of the branches are in Tennessee while just over a dozen are in the states of Georgia (northwestern) Mississippi (northwestern) North Carolina Virginia South Carolina and Florida. It also has more than 25 financial offices in 16 states across the US plus a financial office in Hong Kong.Sales and MarketingThe company spent $18.68 million on advertising and public relations in 2014 up from $18.24 million and $17.44 million in 2013 and 2012 respectively.Financial PerformanceFirst Horizon's revenue has been in decline in recent years due to shrinking interest margins on loans amidst the low-interest environment. The firm's profits however have been rising thanks to declining loan loss provisions as its loan portfolio's credit quality has been improving in the strengthening economy. The company's revenue fell by 4% to $1.26 billion in 2014 mostly as the Capital Markets business shrank by 26% as fixed-income markets suffered from low rates low market volatility and uncertainty around the Federal Reserve's monetary policy. The bank's interest income also fell by 3% despite rising commercial loan business mostly due to a combination of continued run-off of non-strategic loan portfolios lower-yielding commercial loans and lower strategic loan balances. Offsetting some of the top-line decline First Horizon's mortgage banking revenue more than doubled for the year mostly thanks to a nearly $40 million gain on the sale of its mortgage loans held-for-sale. Despite revenue declines in 2014 First Horizon's net income skyrocket nearly sevenfold to $219.52 million thanks to a combination of lower interest and non-interest expenses and a significant decline in loan loss provisions as its loan portfolio's credit condition improved. The company's operating cash also jumped by 63% to $704.7 million during the year as cash earnings rose and as net cash proceeds from the bank's mortgage loans held-for-sale increased.StrategyFirst Horizon National's flagship First Tennessee Bank has been expanding its geographic reach in recent years through both branch openings and strategic acquisitions of smaller banks and branches in target markets. In 2014 the bank opened its first office in Florida (in Jacksonville) as it continued its plans for growth in the Mid-Atlantic region which includes North Carolina South Carolina Virginia and northern parts of Florida. Also that year the bank agreed to purchase 13 bank branches located in the Middle and East Tennessee for a total of nearly $438 million which would add some $437 million worth of new deposits and expand its reach in its home state. Mergers and AcquisitionsIn 2014 First Horizon agreed to purchase TrustAtlantic Financial Corporation along with its five TrustAtlantic Bank branches in North Carolina (mostly in the Raleigh-Cary metro area). The deal matched First Horizon's objectives to expand in North Carolina's fast-growing Research

Triangle region of the state.In mid-2013 First Tennessee bank acquired Mountain National Bank from the FDIC adding 12 new branch locations in Sevier and Blount counties in Eastern Tennessee as well as $249 million in loan assets and $362 million in deposits. In 2012 the company added to FTN Financial with the purchase of Las Vegas-based Main Street Capital Advisors which provides investment management and consulting services mainly to state and local municipalities.Company Background

At the start of the recession First Horizon began selling non-core assets and refocused growth closer to home. First Horizon exited the Baltimore-Washington DC and Atlanta markets. The company also sold some 230 First Horizon Home Loan offices as well as the unit's loan origination and servicing operations outside of Tennessee to MetLife. After the sale First Horizon Financial outsourced some its mortgage origination processing and servicing operations within Tennessee to PHH Mortgage.

In 2008 the bank discontinued its specialty construction and consumer lending activities beyond Tennessee. It exited the institutional equity research business in 2010 and sold its First Horizon Insurance unit to Brown & Brown the following year. Also in 2011 First Horizon sold a subsidiary that provided administrative services for health savings accounts.

EXECUTIVES

EVP and Chief Human Resources Officer, John M. Daniel, age 60

President and COO, David T. Popwell, $450,000 total compensation

Chairman President and CEO, D. Bryan Jordan, age 53, $760,000 total compensation

EVP and General Counsel, Charles T. Tuggle, age 66, $475,000 total compensation

Executive Vice President of Corporate Communications, Kimberley C. (Kim) Cherry

EVP and CIO, Bruce Livesay

EVP and CFO, William C. (BJ) Losch, age 44, $425,000 total compensation

EVP and Chief Risk Officer, Yousef A. Valine, age 55

President FTN Financial, Michael E. Kisber, age 55, $450,000 total compensation

EVP and Chief Credit Officer, Susan Springfield

EVP; Chief Operating and Financial Officer FTN Financial, Michael K. Waddell

EVP Consumer Banking, David W. Miller

EVP Corporate Banking, Steve J. Hawkins

Vice President Of Corporate Strategy, Dane P Smith

Vice President Corporate Procurement, Michael Anderson

Senior Vice President Facilities Management, Stephen Bieber

Vice President Risk Management, Kathleen Mooney

Vice President Manager Customer Data Corporate And Internal Systems, Donna Linton

Vice President Risk Management, Aaron Townsend

Senior Vice President Corporate Risk Management model Validation Group, Walter Person

Senior Vice President And Chief Investment, Karen Kruse

Vice President Business Process Service, Gerri Bailey

Senior Vice President Bank Operations, Janet Honeycutt

Vice President Bus Continuity, Ronnie Smith

Executive Vice President, James Blasingame

Auditors: KPMG LLP

LOCATIONS

HQ: First Horizon National Corp
165 Madison Avenue, Memphis, TN 38103
Phone: 901 523-4444
Web: www.firsthorizon.com

PRODUCTS/OPERATIONS

2014 Sales

	$ mil.	% of total
Interest		
Loans including fees	571	45
Investment securities	93	7
Trading securities	32	3
Loans held for sale	11	1
Other	1	-
Noninterest		
Capital markets	200	16
Deposit transactions & cash management	112	9
Mortagage banking	71	6
Brokerage management fees & commissions	49	4
Trust services and investment management	27	2
Bankcard income	23	2
Bank owned life insurance	16	1
Other	49	4
Total	**1,259**	**100**

COMPETITORS

Athens Federal Community Bank	JPMorgan Chase
	Regions Financial
BB&T	SunTrust
Bank of America	Trustmark
Citigroup	Wells Fargo

HISTORICAL FINANCIALS

Company Type: Public

Income Statement
FYE: December 31

	ASSETS ($ mil.)	NET INCOME ($ mil.)	INCOME AS % OF ASSETS	EMPLOYEES
12/14	25,672	219	0.9%	4,310
12/13	23,789	29	0.1%	4,340
12/12	25,520	(27)	—	4,514
12/11	24,789	131	0.5%	4,809
12/10	24,698	50	0.2%	5,487
Annual Growth	1.0%	44.6%	—	(5.9%)

2014 Year-End Financials

Debt ratio: 7.32%
Return on equity: 9.75%
Cash ($ mil.): 1,971
Current ratio: —
Long-term debt ($ mil.): —
No. of shares (mil.): 234
Dividends
Yield: 1.4%
Payout: 21.9%
Market value ($ mil.): 3,181

	STOCK PRICE ($) FY Close	P/E High/Low	Earnings	PER SHARE ($) Dividends	Book Value
12/14	13.58	15 12	0.91	0.20	9.80
12/13	11.65	126 97	0.10	0.20	9.33
12/12	9.91	— —	(0.11)	0.04	9.09
12/11	8.00	25 11	0.50	0.04	9.28
12/10	11.78	— —	(0.25)	0.00	9.05
Annual Growth	3.6%	— —	—	—	2.0%

First Interstate BancSystem, Inc.

This Treasure State bank wants to be your treasury. First Interstate BancSystem is the holding company for First Interstate Bank which has about 80 branches in Montana western South Dakota and Wyoming. Serving area consumers businesses and municipalities the bank provides traditional services including deposit accounts wealth management and loans. Commercial loans including mortgages make up more than half of the bank's loan portfolio; residential real estate agricultural and construction loans round out its lending activities. On the wealth management side the bank has more than $8 billion in trust assets held in a fiduciary or agent capacity.

Financial Performance

The company's revenue decreased in fiscal 2013 compared to the previous period. It reported $369.3 million in revenue for fiscal 2013 down from $388.8 million in fiscal 2012. However despite the decreased annual revenue the company's net income increased in fiscal 2013 to $86 million up from a net income of $58 million the prior fiscal year. Cash flow increased by about $15 million in fiscal 2013 compared to 2012 levels.

Strategy

The company is always looking for opportunities for expansion including organic growth as well as growth through acquisitions.

EXECUTIVES

EVP and CFO, Terrill R. Moore, age 62, $271,522 total compensation
President CEO and Director, Edward Garding, age 65, $553,330 total compensation
SVP and CIO, Kevin J. Guenthner, age 51, $205,385 total compensation
SVP and Chief Credit Officer, Robert M. Cerkovnik, age 56, $185,962 total compensation
EVP and Chief Banking Officer, Michael G. Huston, age 47, $241,229 total compensation
Chairman, James R. Scott, age 65
Auditors: McGladrey LLP

LOCATIONS

HQ: First Interstate BancSystem, Inc.
401 North 31st Street, Billings, MT 59116-0918
Phone: 406 255-5390
Web: www.fibk.com

COMPETITORS

Bank of the West	Great Western Bancorp
Crazy Woman Creek	U.S. Bancorp
Eagle Bancorp	Wells Fargo
Glacier Bancorp	

HISTORICAL FINANCIALS

Company Type: Public

Income Statement
FYE: December 31

	ASSETS ($ mil.)	NET INCOME ($ mil.)	INCOME AS % OF ASSETS	EMPLOYEES
12/14	8,609	84	1.0%	1,705
12/13	7,564	86	1.1%	1,635
12/12	7,721	58	0.8%	1,683
12/11	7,325	44	0.6%	1,677
12/10	7,500	37	0.5%	1,723
Annual Growth	3.5%	22.6%	—	(0.3%)

2014 Year-End Financials

Debt ratio: 1.40%
Return on equity: 9.87%
Cash ($ mil.): 798
Current ratio: —
Long-term debt ($ mil.): —
No. of shares (mil.): 45
Dividends
Yield: 2.3%
Payout: 34.7%
Market value ($ mil.): 1,274

	STOCK PRICE ($) FY Close	P/E High/Low	Earnings	PER SHARE ($) Dividends	Book Value
12/14	27.82	16 13	1.87	0.64	19.85
12/13	28.37	15 8	1.96	0.54	18.15
12/12	15.43	12 10	1.27	0.61	17.35
12/11	13.03	17 10	0.96	0.46	17.94
12/10	15.24	20 13	0.85	0.45	17.21
Annual Growth	16.2%	— —	21.8%	9.2%	3.6%

First Merchants Corp.

First Merchants is the holding company that owns First Merchants Bank which operates more than 100 branches in Indiana Illinois and western Ohio. Along with its Lafayette Bank & Trust and Commerce National Bank divisions the bank provides standard consumer and commercial banking services including checking and savings accounts CDs check cards and loans and mortgages. First Merchants Corporation also owns First Merchants Trust Company which provides trust and asset management services and First Merchants Insurance Group which sells personal property/casualty and employee benefit coverage. Founded in 1982 First Merchants has nearly $6 billion worth of consolidated assets.

OperationsFirst Merchants operates under three different bank brands including: First Merchants Bank which serves Indiana Illinois and Ohio; Lafayette Bank & Trust serving customers in six Indiana counties; and Commerce National Bank which serves customers in Franklin county in Ohio.Commercial real estate loans made up nearly 50% of the bank's loan portfolio while residential and commercial & consumer loans split the remaining 50%.

Geographic Reach

The Muncie Indiana-based holding company's 100-plus bank branches are located across Indiana and in two counties each in Illinois and Ohio.Sales and MarketingFirst Merchant spent $3.46 million on marketing in 2014 which is 55% more than in 2013 and 60% more than in 2012.

Financial Performance

Revenue jumped by 22% to a record-high of $274.6 million in 2014 mostly thanks to higher interest income from more loan business and more investment security income following the bank's recent acquisitions of CFS Bancorp and Community Bancshares. The bank also collected significantly more non-interest income from deposit account service charges electronic card fees and investment brokerage fees as it grew its customer base with the recent acquisitions.Net income also spiked by 35% to a record-high $60.2 million in 2014 thanks mostly to higher revenue and lower provisions for loan losses as the credit of the bank's loan portfolio improved with a strengthening housing market.Operations provided $75.84 million or 59% less cash than in 2013 returning to cash levels seen between 2010 and 2012. Cash from operations reached a recent high in 2013 as the bank was able to decrease its "other" receivables accounts by more than $110 million which was an non-occurring event.

Strategy

A key part of the bank holding company's growth strategy is to expand geographically through more branch openings in new areas. In 2014 the bank expanded its reach into Tennessee through opening a new branch in Davidson

County and by purchasing land in Williamson County for another branch location in the future. In early 2014 the bank opened its second location in Shelbyville IndianaIt's also been expanding through strategic acquisitions. In early 2015 First Merchants acquired C Financial Corporation and its handful of Cooper State Bank locations to create the second-largest financial holding company based in Indiana. In late 2014 the company bought Community Bancshares and acquired 10 more branches in the central Indiana region. In late 2013 First Merchants purchased CFS Bancorp. to increase its branch network in Indiana and Illinois by 20 branches. In 2012 it acquired certain loans and core deposits of Shelby County Bank which was seized by the FDIC. The deal included four branches in Shelby County Indiana a new market for First Merchants.Mergers and AcquisitionsIn January 2015 First Merchants agreed to purchase C Financial Corporation along with its handful of Cooper State Bank branches in exchange for $15.5 million in cash for all outstanding shares of C Financial common stock. Both C Financial and Cooper State Bank adopted the First Merchant brand name as part of the deal.

In November 2014 First Merchants purchased Community Bancshares for $49.2 million in cash and common stock which added 10 full-service branches in central Indiana to its network.In November 2013 First Merchants Corp. (FMC) acquired Munster Indiana-based CFS Bancorp. a holding company for Citizens Financial Bank (CFB) with about 20 branches in Indiana and Illinois including parts of the Chicago metro area in a transaction valued at about $135.6 million. CFB branches were rebranded as First Merchants Bank in early 2014.

EXECUTIVES

SVP and CIO, Robert R. Connors, age 65, $206,433 total compensation
EVP and CFO, Mark K. Hardwick, age 44, $269,936 total compensation
President CEO and Director, Michael C. (Mike) Rechin, age 56, $372,500 total compensation
EVP and Chief Banking Officer, Michael J. (Mike) Stewart, age 49, $266,369 total compensation
Executive Vice President and Chief Credit Officer, John J. Martin, age 48, $197,981 total compensation
Vice President of the Mortgage Department, Tracie Simon
Business Banking Officer Assistant Vice President, Ryan Mooney
First Vice President and Director Investor Relations, David (Dave) Ortega
Vice President Special Asset Officer, Patrick (Paddy) Berghoff
Vice President Corporate Banking, Joseph Munhall
Assistant Vice President Software Developer, Chris Horton
Vice President and Trust Officer, Rhonda King
Assistant Vice President Manager Of Deposit Services, Donna Coulson
Vice President Of Loans, Christopher Allen
Vice President, Derek Jones
Senior Vice President Employee Benefits, Kevin Mandrell
Vice President Account Executive, Mark Lehan
Vice President Marketing Manager, Dana Talaga
Vice President Cash Management, Jennifer (Jen) Wehrly
Vice President, Tonya Gooden
Vice President Special Assets, Chris Cossell
Vice President Retail Market Leader, Theresa Mudd
Executive Vice President Mortgage Operations, Debra Rynearson
Senior Vice President Human Resources, Leslie Holland
Vice President Administration, Lisa Brothers

Vice President Loans, Patricia Hudson
Vice President, David Benjamin
Vice President, Joseph Keyler
Vice President and Manager Trust Accounting, Candy Shannon
Vice President, Rhonda Davis
Vice President, Margaret Hoke
Senior Vice President Product Management, John Ditmars
Senior Vice President, David E (Dave) Mooney
Vice President, Dale Clapp
Vice President Special Assets Officer, Jeffrey (Jeff) Jex
Senior Vice President and Director of Human Resources, Kim A Ellington
Vice President Retail Market Leader, Roberta Salway
Vice President, Dave Decraene
Vice President, Daniel Gick
Executive Vice President, Mike Gilbert
Vice President, James F (Jamie) Zimmerman
Assistant Vice President, Tammy Hall
Vice President, Jeffrey (Jeff) Lorentson
Chairman, Charles E. Schalliol, age 68
Board Member, David Forbes
First Vice President And Corporate Treasurer, Brad Davis
Board Member, Lee Elzemeyer
ABM, Michael (Mel) Patton
Treasurer, Sherri Beabout
Auditors: BKD, LLP

LOCATIONS

HQ: First Merchants Corp.
   200 East Jackson Street, Muncie, IN 47305-2814
Phone: 765 747-1500

PRODUCTS/OPERATIONS

2014 Sales

	$ mil.	% of total
Interest		
Loans	172	63
Investment Securities	34	12
Others	2	1
Non-interest		
Service charges on deposits	15	6
Fiduciary activities	9	3
Commission income	7	3
Others	33	12
Total	**274**	**100**

COMPETITORS

Ameriana Bancorp	MutualFirst Financial
Bank of America	NorthWest Indiana
Citigroup	Bancorp
Harris	Old National Bancorp
JPMorgan Chase	STAR Financial Group
MainSource Financial	U.S. Bancorp

HISTORICAL FINANCIALS

Company Type: Public

Income Statement

FYE: December 31

	ASSETS ($ mil.)	NET INCOME ($ mil.)	INCOME AS % OF ASSETS	EMPLOYEES
12/14	5,824	60	1.0%	1,415
12/13	5,437	44	0.8%	1,449
12/12	4,304	45	1.0%	1,149
12/11	4,173	25	0.6%	1,144
12/10	4,170	6	0.2%	1,178
Annual Growth	**8.7%**	**71.8%**	**—**	**4.7%**

2014 Year-End Financials

Debt ratio: 2.18%	No. of shares (mil.): 37
Return on equity: 8.84%	Dividends
Cash ($ mil.): 166	Yield: 1.2%
Current ratio: —	Payout: 17.5%
Long-term debt ($ mil.): —	Market value ($ mil.): 857

	STOCK PRICE ($) FY Close	P/E High/Low		PER SHARE ($) Earnings	Dividends	Book Value
12/14	22.75	14	12	1.65	0.29	19.29
12/13	22.72	16	10	1.41	0.18	17.68
12/12	14.84	11	6	1.41	0.10	19.25
12/11	8.47	29	20	0.34	0.04	18.01
12/10	8.86	20	11	0.48	0.04	17.77
Annual Growth	**26.6%**	**—**	**—**	**36.2%**	**64.1%**	**2.1%**

First Midwest Bancorp, Inc. (Naperville, IL)

There's a lot of cabbage in corn country. Just ask First Midwest Bancorp the holding company for First Midwest Bank. Through nearly 110 branches the bank mainly serves suburban Chicago though its market extends into central and western Illinois and neighboring portions of Iowa and Indiana. Focusing on area small to mid-sized businesses it offers deposit products loans trust services wealth management insurance and retirement plan services; it has $7.2 billion of client trust and investment assets under management. Commercial real estate loans account for more than half of the company's portfolio.

Operations

More than 85% of the company's loan portfolio consists of corporate loans (the majority of which are secured by commercial real estate) while the remainder of the portfolio consists of consumer loans (which include home equity loans lines of credit and 1-4 family mortgages). Illustrative of its commitment to business lending First Midwest does not originate sub-prime lending or investment banking activities. The bank's subsidiaries include: equipment leasing and commercial financier First Midwest Equipment Finance Co.; investment security managers First Midwest Securities Management LLC and First Midwest Holdings Inc.; Section 8 housing venture investor LIH Holdings; and Synergy Property Holdings LLC which manages the bank's OREO properties.

Geographic Reach

The company operates 109 banking offices largely located in various communities throughout the suburban metropolitan Chicago market as well as central and western Illinois and eastern Iowa. It owns 145 automated teller machines most of which are housed at banking locations. First Midwest and Allpoint together provide access to more than 50000 free ATMs worldwide.

Sales and Marketing

The company serves different industry segments including manufacturing health care pharmaceutical higher education wholesale and retail trade service and agricultural. First Midwest spent about $8.2 million on advertising and promotions in 2014 up from $7.8 million in 2013 and $5.1 million in 2012.

Financial Performance

Following a modest rebound in 2013 First Midwest's revenue in 2014 dipped by less than 1% to $426.48 million mostly because of a 76% drop in net securities gains as the bank in 2013 was able to collect a non-recurring equity investment sale gain of $34 million. Lower mortgage banking income resulting from lower market pricing also contributed to the modest dip in revenue. The bank did however report higher interest income as its loan business grew higher wealth management fees with growth in assets under management and higher service charge fees as deposit accounts grew.After healthy profit growth in 2013 net income fell by nearly 13% to $69.31 million in 2014 mostly as the bank incurred higher costs associated with the acquisition and integration of Popular and Great Lakes and because the bank had higher loan loss provision expenses. In 2013 First Midwest had posted a large jump in net income thanks to higher revenue a decrease in the provision for loan and covered loan losses and lower interest and non-interest expenses.Continuing its annual cash declines the bank's operations provided $122.93 million (or 10% less cash than in 2013) mostly due to lower earnings.

Mergers and Acquisitions

In 2014 First Midwest agreed to acquire south suburban Chicago-based Great Lakes Financial Resources Inc. the holding company for Great Lakes Bank National Association. As part of the $58 million deal the company will acquire eight locations $490 million in deposits and $234 million in loans. That year it also bought the Chicago banking operations of Popular Community Bank a subsidiary of Popular Inc. (twelve full-service retail branches and its small business and middle market commercial lending activities in the Chicago metropolitan area which included $726 million in deposits and $562 million in loans).Company Background

First Midwest capitalized on the rash of bank failures that have occurred in the Chicago area amid the recessionary economy. Its relative financial soundness put it in a position to acquire three failed Illinois banks through separate FDIC-facilitated transactions in 2009 and 2010: First DuPage Bank Peotone Bank and Trust and Palos Bank and Trust. The deals which included loss-sharing agreements with the regulator added a total of nearly 10 branches. In 2012 the company acquired the deposits and loans of Waukegan Savings Bank in another FDIC-assisted deal that added two more branches to its network. First Midwest will continue to consider acquisitions of failed banks in the Chicago area.

EXECUTIVES

Executive Vice President Business Institutional Services, Stephanie Wise
President CEO and Director; Chairman and CEO First Midwest Bank, Michael L. Scudder, age 54, $720,000 total compensation
Executive Vice President Director of Retail Sales & Service, Janet M. Viano, age 60
EVP CIO and COO First Midwest Bank, Kent S. Belasco, age 64, $224,000 total compensation
Executive Vice President and Senior Credit Officer of the Bank, Michael J. Kozak, age 64
EVP and CFO First Midwest Bancorp Inc. & First Midwest Bank, Paul F. Clemens, age 63, $356,000 total compensation
SEVP and COO; President and Chief Operating Officer First Midwest Bank, Mark G. Sander, age 56, $507,000 total compensation
EVP and Director Commercial Banking First Midwest Bank, Victor P. Carapella, $325,000 total compensation
EVP and Treasurer First Midwest Bancorp Inc. & First Midwest Bank, James P. Hotchkiss, age 58
EVP and Director of Wealth Management First Midwest Bank, Robert P. Diedrich

EVP and Chief Risk Officer First Midwest Bancorp Inc. & First Midwest Bank, Kevin L. Moffitt
EVP and Director Retail Banking First Midwest Bank, Thomas M. Prame, $191,827 total compensation
Executive Vice President Corporate Secretary and General Counsel, Nicholas J. Chulos
Executive Vice President Director of Employee Resources First Midwest Bank, Caryn J. Guinta
Vice President Compliance Review Manager, Beth Uhlir
Vice President Human Resources, Joe Hoffman
Senior Vice President Head of Mortgage, Dave Hilger
Vice President Marketing Product, Robert (Bob) Hohe
Vice President Group Sales Manager, Cynthia Perry
Senior Vice President, Rob Schultz
Vice President, Dan Stevenson
Vice President, Susan (Sue) Koski
Chairman, Robert P. (Bob) O'Meara, age 77
Auditors: Ernst & Young LLP

LOCATIONS

HQ: First Midwest Bancorp, Inc. (Naperville, IL)
One Pierce Place, Suite 1500, Itasca, IL 60143-9768
Phone: 630 875-7450
Web: www.firstmidwest.com

PRODUCTS/OPERATIONS

2014 Sales

	$ mil.	% of total
Interest		
Loans	256	60
Investment securities	31	7
Covered loans	8	2
Other	3	1
Noninterest		
Service charges on deposit accounts	36	9
Wealth managment fees	26	6
Card based fee	24	6
Marchant servicing fees	11	3
Net securities gains	8	2
Others	19	4
Total	**426**	**100**

COMPETITORS

Bank of America	Meta Financial Group
BankFinancial	Northern Trust
Cummins-Allison	PrivateBancorp
Fifth Third	QCR Holdings
First Busey	West Suburban Bancorp
Harris	Wintrust Financial
JPMorgan Chase	

HISTORICAL FINANCIALS

Company Type: Public

Income Statement

FYE: December 31

	ASSETS ($ mil.)	NET INCOME ($ mil.)	INCOME AS % OF ASSETS	EMPLOYEES
12/14	9,445	69	0.7%	1,788
12/13	8,253	79	1.0%	1,647
12/12	8,099	(21)	—	1,707
12/11	7,973	36	0.5%	1,768
12/10	8,146	(9)	—	1,820
Annual Growth	**3.8%**	**—**	**—**	**(0.4%)**

2014 Year-End Financials

Debt ratio: 2.13%
Return on equity: 6.59%
Cash ($ mil.): 606
Current ratio: —
Long-term debt ($ mil.): —

No. of shares (mil.): 77
Dividends
Yield: 1.8%
Payout: 27.1%
Market value ($ mil.): 1,329

	STOCK PRICE ($) FY Close	P/E High/Low	PER SHARE ($) Earnings	Dividends	Book Value
12/14	17.11	19 17	0.92	0.31	14.17
12/13	17.53	17 11	1.06	0.16	13.34
12/12	12.52	— —	(0.28)	0.04	12.57
12/11	10.13	38 20	0.35	0.04	12.93
12/10	11.52	— —	(0.27)	0.04	15.01
Annual Growth	**10.4%**	**— —**	**—**	**66.8%**	**(1.4%)**

First National Bank Alaska

First National Bank Alaska is a financial anchor in Anchorage. Founded in 1922 the bank is one of the state's oldest and largest financial institutions. With about 30 branches throughout The Last Frontier (and about 20 ATMs in rural communities) the bank offers traditional deposit products such as checking and savings accounts CDs and IRAs as well as loans and mortgages credit and debit cards and trust and investment management services. The family of longtime president Daniel Cuddy owns a majority of First National Bank Alaska; he took the helm of the bank in 1951.

Geographic Reach

In order to help serve clients in remote locales First National Bank Alaska opened its first branch with a full-service customer kiosk at a joint air force/army base outside of Anchorage where customers can make routine banking transactions without teller assistance. The bank may add such kiosks at other branches.

Financial Performance

The company's total annul revenue has slowly declining across recent fiscal years. However it has managed to stay profitable.

EXECUTIVES

Vice President Information Systems, Larry Chen
Senior Vice President Commercial Lending, Bill Inscho
Senior Vice President, Doug Longacre
Vice President, Dustin Hofeling
Senior Vice President, Sue Foley
Svp And Regional Manager Kenai Peninsula, Charles (Chas) Weimer
Vice President Corporate Lending, Joe Gelione
Assistant Vice President, Casey Neill
Assistant Vice President, Debra Archey
Senior Vice President Compliance Officer And Consumer Loan Officer, David (Dave) Lawer
Auditors: Crowe Horwath LLP

LOCATIONS

HQ: First National Bank Alaska
101 West 36th Avenue, Post Office Box 100720, Anchorage, AK 99510-0720
Phone: 907 777-4362   **Fax:** 907 265-3528
Web: www.FNBAlaska.com

COMPETITORS

Alaska Pacific Bancshares	KeyCorp
Alaska USA	Northrim BanCorp
	Wells Fargo

HISTORICAL FINANCIALS
Company Type: Public

Income Statement
FYE: December 31

	ASSETS ($ mil.)	NET INCOME ($ mil.)	INCOME AS % OF ASSETS	EMPLOYEES
12/14	3,312	32	1.0%	—
12/13	3,102	32	1.0%	—
12/12	3,015	40	1.3%	—
12/11	2,870	34	1.2%	662
12/10	2,725	40	1.5%	—
Annual Growth	5.0%	(5.2%)	—	—

2014 Year-End Financials

Debt ratio: 0.00%
Return on equity: 7.05%
Cash ($ mil.): 95
Current ratio: —
Long-term debt ($ mil.): —

No. of shares (mil.): 0
Dividends
  Yield: 3.1%
  Payout: 49.3%
Market value ($ mil.): 509

	STOCK PRICE ($) FY Close	P/E High/Low		PER SHARE ($) Earnings	Dividends	Book Value
12/14	1,588.00 1,472.07	17	16	101.37	50.00	
12/13	1,751.00 1,403.84	18	17	99.80	50.00	
12/12	1,675.00 1,416.40	14	12	122.51	50.00	
12/11	1,540.00 1,347.05	18	14	105.17	50.00	
12/10	1,800.00 1,272.19	16	14	121.61	200.00	
Annual Growth	(3.1%)	—	—	(4.4%)	(29.3%)	3.7%

First NBC Bank Holding Co.

First NBC Holding Company is a new kid in the Old South. The bank holding company was created in 2006 to help revive New Orleans after Hurricane Katrina. First NBC Holding Company operates through subsidiary First NBC Bank which has about 30 branches in New Orleans neighboring Jefferson Parish and the surrounding suburban parishes north of Lake Ponchartrain. Its retail operation offers standard checking saving and money market accounts to individuals and businesses. In addition the company has a loan production office in Gulfport Mississippi and offers trust and wealth management services. First NBC Holding Company went public in 2013.

IPO

The company plans to use the net proceeds of its $100 million IPO to support organic growth and for other general corporate purposes.

Geographic Reach

First NBC Bank has 32 branches in Orleans Jefferson Tangipahoa St. Tammany Livingston and Washington parishes (counties) and a loan production office in Gulfport Mississippi.

Sales and Marketing

The bank attracts new customers from competitors more by word-of-mouth advertising rather than market growth for banking services in New Orleans. However it did spend $2.4 million on advertising in 2013.

Financial Performance

First NBC Bank makes most of its money on interest income from loans made to small and mid-

sized businesses real estate owners and private banking clients. In 2013 overall sales grew 15% to $137 million. Ninety percent of its income came from interest; non-interest income such as ATM and bank account fees accounted for 10% of sales. Profits also shot up 41% to $40 million due to the higher income and a $20 million income tax benefit.

Strategy

Old banking institutions in New Orleans traditionally held the most market share until Katrina hit in 2005. After that national banks began entering the market when longtime bank Hibernia was bought by Capital One and Whitney Bank was bought by Hancock. Even Chase Bank only entered the New Orleans market in 2004 when it bought Bank One.

First NBC Bank aims to separate itself from its larger competitors by positioning itself as a community bank with a focus on customer service. It offers low-risk Small Business Administration and US Dept. of Agriculture loans to borrowers who might not otherwise qualify for lending services. Commercial mortgages make up about half of its loan portfolio and other commercial loans make up another 35%. The remaining 15% is made up on construction loans and consumer mortgages.

Mergers and Acquisitions

First NBC Bank has stepped in and bought other struggling community banks over the years that contributed to its inorganic growth. In 2008 it bought Dryades Saving Bank (founded 1913) and its four branches. Later that year it bought Statewide Bank which has one branch in Jefferson Parish. In 2011 it bought the 17-branch Central Progressive Bank which expanded the company's presence to the Northshore or the suburban parishes north of Lake Ponchartrain.

EXECUTIVES

President Chief Executive Officer and Chairman of the Board of First NBC Bank Holding Company and First NBC Bank, Ashton J. Ryan, age 68, $450,000 total compensation
Senior Executive Vice President & Chief Credit Officer First NBC Bank Holding Company and First NBC Bank, William J. Burnell, age 65, $260,000 total compensation
Senior Executive Vice President & Chief Compliance Officer First NBC Bank Holding Company and First NBC Bank, Marsha S. Crowle, age 53, $260,000 total compensation
EVP and CFO First NBC Bank Holding Company and First NBC Bank, Mary Beth Verdigets, age 47, $205,000 total compensation
Senior Vice President, Michael Lulich
Auditors: Ernst & Young LLP

LOCATIONS

HQ: First NBC Bank Holding Co.
  210 Baronne Street, New Orleans, LA 70112
Phone: 504 566-8000

PRODUCTS/OPERATIONS

2013 Sales

	$ mil.	% of total
Interest income		
Loans including fees	111	81
Investment securities	8	6
Investment in short-term receivables & other	4	3
Noninterest income		
Community development entity fees	2	2
Income from sales of state tax credits	2	2
Service charges on deposit accounts	2	2
ATM fees	.8	
Gain on assets sold net	1	1
Gain on sale of loans net	0	1
Other	1	1
Total	**137**	**100**

Selected Services
Business Banking
Business Checking Savings and MMA Rate Sheet
Business Loans & Lines of Credit
Cash Management
CD Rate Sheet
Certificates of Deposit
Checking Accounts
Convenience Services
Money Market Accounts
Savings Accounts
Personal Banking
CD Rate Sheet
CDs & IRAs
Checking Accounts
Consumer Loans & Lines of Credit
Convenience Services
Money Market Account
Personal Checking Savings and MMA Rate Sheet
Savings Accounts
Trust Services
Custodial Services
Investment Services
Class Action Settlement Account Services
Retirement Services

COMPETITORS

Capital One
Hancock Holding
IBERIABANK
Investar

JPMorgan Chase
Louisiana Bancorp
Regions Financial

HISTORICAL FINANCIALS
Company Type: Public

Income Statement
FYE: December 31

	ASSETS ($ mil.)	NET INCOME ($ mil.)	INCOME AS % OF ASSETS	EMPLOYEES
12/14	3,750	55	1.5%	486
12/13	3,286	40	1.2%	494
12/12	2,670	28	1.1%	433
12/11	2,216	19	0.9%	—
12/10	0	10	—	—
Annual Growth	—	53.3%	—	—

2014 Year-End Financials

Debt ratio: 1.07%
Return on equity: 13.59%
Cash ($ mil.): 32
Current ratio: —
Long-term debt ($ mil.): —

No. of shares (mil.): 18
Dividends
  Yield: —
  Payout: —
Market value ($ mil.): 654

	STOCK PRICE ($) FY Close	P/E High/Low		PER SHARE ($) Earnings	Dividends	Book Value
12/14	35.20	13	10	2.84	0.00	23.49
12/13	32.30	14	10	2.32	0.00	20.63
Annual Growth	2.2%	—	—	5.2%	—	3.3%

First Niagara Financial Group, Inc.

A lot of water and a few barrels have gone over Niagara Falls since First Niagara Bank was founded. Tracing its roots to 1870 the flagship subsidiary of acquisitive First Niagara Financial operates nearly 400 branches in upstate New York Connecticut Massachusetts and Pennsylvania. Boasting $39 billion in assets the bank offers financial services like deposits loans insurance investments and wealth management. Commercial real estate loans business loans and residential mortgages account for most of the bank's loan portfolio. Subsidiary First Niagara Risk Management offers insurance risk management and claims investigations. KeyCorp agreed to acquire the bank in 2015.

Change in Company OwnershipIn October 2015 Cleveland-based KeyCorp agreed to purchase First Niagara Bank. The $4.1 billion merger deal was expected to close in the third-quarter of 2016 and lead to annual cost savings of $400 million for KeyCorp beginning in 2017. KeyCorp also estimated that the deal would lead to an internal rate of return of around 15%. OperationsCommercial real estate and business loans made up 61% of First Niagara's loan portfolio in 2014. About 55% of the company's total revenue came from loan interest (including fees) during the year while another 23% came from interest on its investment securities. The rest of its revenue came from deposit service charges (6%) insurance commissions (5%) wealth management services (4%) merchant and card fees (3%) and other miscellaneous income sources.Geographic ReachFirst Niagara boasts around 400 branches in the Northeastern US with about half of them in New York (mostly in Buffalo Rochester Syracuse and Albany) roughly 120 in Pennsylvania (mostly around Philadelphia Pittsburgh Erie and Warren) nearly 85 in Connecticut (around New Haven and Hartford) and a dozen in Western Massachusetts (near Springfield).Sales and MarketingThe bank serves individuals families and businesses.Financial PerformanceFirst Niagara's revenues and profits have been rising in recent years thanks to growing loan business lower interest expenses in the low-interest environment and declining loan loss provisions as its loan portfolio's credit quality has improved with higher property valuations in the strengthened economy. The company's revenue dipped by 4% to $1.52 billion in 2014 mostly as its non-interest revenues from deposit service charges capital markets income and other income fell during the year. Its interest income also fell on shrinking interest margins on loans.First Niagara's suffered a loss of $715 million after incurring some $1.1 billion worth of (non-recurring) goodwill impairment charges stemming after the bank compared its fair value of its assets to its carrying values. The company's operating cash levels dropped 32% to $484 million as it collected less in cash earnings.StrategyFirst Niagara Financial has been moving toward digital banking channels that are quickly taking the industry by storm allowing the bank to slow expensive branch-expansion plans and cut operating costs significantly while giving customers faster access to banking services. To this end in 2015 the bank introduced a new feature for its web banking customers allowing them to apply for and open their own accounts online in "around 5 minutes for most products and customers" according to the bank. In 2014 it launched new features for its mobile banking app (released in January 2013) which enjoyed some 140000 unique mobile banking users.Company BackgroundFirst Niagara has a history of making large acquisitions. In one of its largest the company bought nearly 200 HSBC branches in upstate New York and Connecticut for some $1 billion in 2012.

EXECUTIVES

Executive Vice President, John Hoffman
Senior Executive Vice President and Chief Banking Officer, Daniel E. Cantara, age 56, $511,058 total compensation
Interim President and Chief Executive Officer, Gary M. Crosby, age 61, $587,716 total compensation
Executive Vice President Retail Banking, Mark R. Rendulic

SEVP and CFO, Gregory W. Norwood, $511,058 total compensation
Executive Vice President - Corporate Development, Oliver H. Sommer, age 46, $488,462 total compensation
Executive Vice President; Chief Risk Officer, Richard M. Barry
Executive Vice President Consumer Finance, Andrew D. Fornarola
President New England Region, Jeff L. Hubbard
Senior Vice President Central Underwriting Credi, John (Jack) Kenefick
Vice President Operations, Cheryl Malicki
Executive Vice President Commercial Lending Services, Joseph (Jo) Saffire
Vice President Employee Benefits Manager, Marylisa Oross
Vice President, Gail Maccleverty
Vice President, Ryan Casullo
Vice President Secondary Marketing, Jim McEvoy
Vice President Commercial Real Estate, Ryan Crouthamel
Fvp Manager Product Strategy and Analytics, David (Dave) Cushing
Vice President, Joy Rogers
Vice President Human Resources, Patty Swan
Assistant Vice President Quality Assurance Information Technology Solutions Delivery, Aaron Berger
First Vice President, John Allenson
Assistant Vice President Loan Review Specialist, Mark Hudson
Assistant Vice President, Richard (Dick) McDermott
Fvp Compliance Intelligence and Analytics Manager, Gary Smith
Senior Vice President Director Corporate Insurance, Robert (Bob) Brewer
Vice President Business Development Finance, Bill Kuhn
Vice President, Gus Kasparis
Senior Vice President Lender Relations, Rick Kuhn
Small Business Banker Vice President, Jerry Dorn
Vice President, Frank Cipriano
First Vice President, Donald (Don) Rotzien
Assistant Vice President And Trust Officer, Deborah (Deb) Henninger
Assistant Vice President, Dan Giannuzzi
Vice President, John (Jack) Bodine
Vice President, Noreen O'neill
Assistant Vice President And Associate Counsel, Shane Sclichter
Vice President, John Berry
Assistant Vice President And Senior Portfolio Underwriter, Jack Finkle
Assistant Vice President, Lynn Conway
First Vice President, Don Mishler
Assistant Vice President, Jeff Wright
Vice President Senior Counsel, Marc Krawiec
Financial Consultant Vice President, Kat Genovese
Vice President Branch Manager, Gary Turku
Vice President and Senior Account Executive, Christopher (Chris) Clark
Assistant Vice President, Kelli Griffin
Vice President, Kris Volpatti
Vice President, Lori Weatherman
Assistant Vice President Compliance Manager, Sara Loeser
Vice President, Francie Bacon
Vice President, Daniel (Dan) Hooper
Solutions Delivery Lead ?? Information Technology Retail ?? Assistant Vice President, Paul Fiegl
First Vice President Assistant General Counsel, Sam Burruano
Vice President Associate Counsel, David (Dave) Aldous
Senior Vice President Information Technology Governance Risk And Compliance, Kerry Ruhl
Assistant Vice President Information Technology Vendor Management, Jason Cwiklinski

Senior Vice President Information Technology, Lesley Norris
Vice President Consumer Finance, Wayne Morlock
Vice President, Tim Glass
First Vice President And Team Leader, Marc Wegener
Vice President, Maurice Fry
Vice President Relationship Manager, Joe Bifolco
Vice President International Trade Finance, Ralph Bocchino
Complex Asset Specialist And Vice President, Franz Ross
Vice President Corporate Banking, Steve Yantz
Vice President, Peter Hausherr
Vice President, Frederick Parker
Vice President Branch Manager, Steven (Steve) Goykhman
Vice President Enterprise Project Management Office And Business Change Management, Kate Mohr
Enterprise Sales Leader Senior Vice President, Kim McGillicuddy
Vice President Finance Manager ALM, Joseph (Jo) Ondesko
Vice President LPL Financial Advisor, William (Bill) Winsman
Vice President Consumer Finance, Rich Loecher
Vice President Online Banking and eCommerce, Anthony Parisi
Assistant Vice President Sales Equipment Finance, Krista Bailey
Vice President, Nancy Cinfio
Vice President Finance Solutions Manager, Daniel (Dan) Rath
Vice President Credit, Lynn Sciog
Vice President Information Technology, Chris Good
Vice President Business Banking, John (Jack) Jepson
Senior Vice President, R Buford Sears
Vice President, Jennifer (Jen) Schade
Vice President, Amanda Snyder
Vice President, Daniel (Dan) Losowski
Vice President, Tarinee Pefley
Vice President Infrastructure Architecture, Edward (Ed) Case
Vice President Senior Product Development Manager, Keith Kozlowski
Senior Vice President Business Banking, John (Jack) Golding
Vice President Small Business Banking, Judy Colone
Vice President Regional Sales Manager, Andrew (Andy) Rubino
First Vice President Area Manager, Janice Yusza
Vice President Commercial Real Estate, Randy Cornelius
Vice President Product Manager, Thomas (Thom) Arena
Vice President, Alex Salafia
Vice President, Gregory Pocius
Vice President, Matthew (Matt) Lowery
Vice President Product Manager, Christopher (Chris) Hahn
Assistant Vice President Marketing Manager, Morgan Seegert
Vice President, Lisa Hackett
Assistant Vice President, Randall Upper
Vice President, Frank Sardina
Vice President Architecture Enterprise Shared Services Delivery Manager II, Abdennour Laaroubi
Vice President Branch Sales Manager, Brion Robert
Vice President Quality Program Manager, Natalie Dickinson
Assistant Vice President of Marketing Operations and Communications, Kristen Lopez
Chairman, G. Thomas Bowers, age 72
Board Member, Christa Hall
Board Member, Susan (Sue) Harnett
Auditors: KPMG LLP

LOCATIONS

HQ: First Niagara Financial Group, Inc.
726 Exchange Street, Suite 618, Buffalo, NY 14210
Phone: 716 819-5500
Web: www.firstniagara.com

PRODUCTS/OPERATIONS

2014 Sales

	$ mil.	% of total
Interest		
Loans & leases	847	55
Investment securities & other	361	23
Non-interest		
Deposit service charges	90	7
Insurance commissions	66	4
Wealth management services	61	4
Merchant and card fees	50	3
Capital markets income	18	1
Others	25	3
Total	**1,517**	**100**

COMPETITORS

Capital One	KeyCorp
Citigroup	M&T Bank
Citizens Financial	NBT Bancorp
Group	PNC Financial
Community Bank System	SEFCU
HSBC USA	TD Bank USA
JPMorgan Chase	

HISTORICAL FINANCIALS

Company Type: Public

Income Statement

FYE: December 31

	ASSETS ($ mil.)	NET INCOME ($ mil.)	INCOME AS % OF ASSETS	EMPLOYEES
12/15	39,918	224	0.6%	5,428
12/14	38,551	(715)	—	5,572
12/13	37,628	295	0.8%	5,807
12/12	36,806	168	0.5%	5,927
12/11	32,810	173	0.5%	4,827
Annual Growth	**5.0%**	**6.5%**	**—**	**3.0%**

2015 Year-End Financials

Debt ratio: 1.84%
Return on equity: 5.45%
Cash ($ mil.): 672
Current ratio: —
Long-term debt ($ mil.): —

No. of shares (mil.): 354
Dividends
  Yield: 2.9%
  Payout: 52.4%
Market value ($ mil.): 3,849

	STOCK PRICE ($) FY Close	P/E High/Low	PER SHARE ($) Earnings	Dividends	Book Value
12/15	10.85	20 14	0.54	0.32	11.63
12/14	8.43	— —	(2.13)	0.32	11.58
12/13	10.62	15 10	0.75	0.32	14.11
12/12	7.93	26 18	0.40	0.32	13.97
12/11	8.63	24 13	0.64	0.64	13.64
Annual Growth	**5.9%**	**— —**	**(4.2%)**	**(15.9%)**	**(3.9%)**

First of Long Island Corp.

When it comes to banking The First of Long Island wants to be the first thing on Long Islanders' minds. The company owns The First National Bank of Long Island which offers a variety of lending investment and deposit services through more than 30 commercial and retail branches on New York's Long Island and in Manhattan. Loans secured by real estate including residential and commercial mortgages and home equity loans make up more than 90% of the bank's loan portfolio. To a lesser extent the bank also writes business and consumer loans. Other services include checking and savings accounts IRAs CDs and credit cards. Subsidiary The First of Long Island Agency sells mutual funds and annuities.

Operations

The First National Bank of Long Island also operates an investment management division that offers trust and investment management estate and custody services.

Financial Performance

The company's revenue decreased in fiscal 2013 compared to the prior year. It reported $81.9 million in revenue for fiscal 2013 down from $86.4 million in fiscal 2012.

Despite the drop in total annual revenue the company's net income increased in fiscal 2013 compared to the previous fiscal period. It reported net income of $21.3 million in fiscal 2013 up from $20.3 million in fiscal 2012.

The company's cash on hand also increased by almost $5 million in fiscal 2013 compared to fiscal 2012 levels.

Strategy

The bank has been expanding by opening new branches and it has plans for more openings. The growth has helped it increase its portfolio of interest-earning assets.

EXECUTIVES

SVP and EVP and Senior Lending Officer Commercial Lending The First National Bank Long Island, Donald L. Manfredonia, age 63, $222,500 total compensation
SVP, Richard Kick, age 57, $230,100 total compensation
SVP and Treasurer; EVP CFO and Cashier The First National Bank of Long Island, Mark D. Curtis, age 60, $242,700 total compensation
President and CEO The First of Long Island Corporation and The First National Bank of Long Island, Michael N. Vittorio, age 62, $468,000 total compensation
SVP and Secretary; SEVP The First National Bank of Long Island, Sallyanne K. Ballweg, age 59, $264,000 total compensation
EVP and Chief Risk Officer First National Bank of Long Island, Christopher Becker
Senior Vice President Of Commercial, Paul Daley
Vice President, Jane Reed
Assistant Vice President, Giuseppe Sparacino
Vice President, Robert Eisen
Vice President Sales Manager, Rick Hughes
Vice President Director Of Human Resources, Sue Hempton
Chairman The First of Long Island Corporation and The First National Bank of Long Island, Walter C. Teagle, age 65
Auditors: Crowe Horwath LLP

LOCATIONS

HQ: First of Long Island Corp.
10 Glen Head Road, Glen Head, NY 11545
Phone: 516 671-4900
Web: www.fnbli.com

COMPETITORS

Astoria Financial	JPMorgan Chase
Bank of America	New York Community
Citibank	Bancorp
Dime Community	Ridgewood Savings Bank
Bancshares	Suffolk Bancorp
Flushing Financial	

HISTORICAL FINANCIALS

Company Type: Public

Income Statement

FYE: December 31

	ASSETS ($ mil.)	NET INCOME ($ mil.)	INCOME AS % OF ASSETS	EMPLOYEES
12/14	2,721	23	0.8%	284
12/13	2,399	21	0.9%	260
12/12	2,108	20	1.0%	255
12/11	2,022	19	1.0%	251
12/10	1,711	18	1.1%	249
Annual Growth	**12.3%**	**5.8%**	**—**	**3.3%**

2014 Year-End Financials

Debt ratio: 1.65%
Return on equity: 10.46%
Cash ($ mil.): 32
Current ratio: —
Long-term debt ($ mil.): —

No. of shares (mil.): 13
Dividends
  Yield: 2.4%
  Payout: 65.0%
Market value ($ mil.): 394

	STOCK PRICE ($) FY Close	P/E High/Low	PER SHARE ($) Earnings	Dividends	Book Value
12/14	28.37	26 14	1.65	0.71	16.80
12/13	42.87	28 18	1.55	1.02	15.06
12/12	28.32	21 16	1.51	1.19	15.21
12/11	26.32	20 15	1.47	0.60	14.35
12/10	28.76	19 15	1.53	0.84	12.00
Annual Growth	**(0.3%)**	**— —**	**1.9%**	**(4.2%)**	**8.8%**

First Republic Bank (San Francisco, CA)

No not the original Roman Republic but rather a modern-day haven for the elite. Founded in 1985 First Republic Bank offers private banking wealth management trust and brokerage services for businesses and high-net-worth clients though about 70 branches. Its main geographic focus is on urban markets including San Francisco Los Angeles New York Boston Portland and San Diego. The bank's lending focuses on commercial and residential real estate and personal loans including vacation home mortgages and aircraft and yacht financing. Trust services are offered through the bank's First Republic Trust Company division. First Republic Bank has some $41.6 billion of assets under management.

Geographic Reach

The company operates 73 offices 66 of which are Preferred Banking locations in Boston; Los Angeles; New York; Newport Beach California; Palm Beach Florida; Palo Alto California; Portland Oregon; San Diego San Francisco and Santa Barbara California. In 2014 it opened an additional Preferred Banking office in downtown San Diego. The other seven locations offer lending wealth management or trust services.

Sales and Marketing

First Republic Bank advertises via digital media and newspaper and radio ads; its primary marketing goal is to attract deposits in its Preferred Banking offices. In 2013 the company spent $25.5 million on advertising and marketing slightly up from $25.1 million in 2012 (but down from $28.8 million in 2011).

Financial Performance

The bank has seen stable growth in earnings since 2010. In 2013 revenue grew 10% to $1.6 billion (compared to $1.5 billion in 2012) as both interest and noninterest income rose. Higher interest rates brought added income on both loans and investments while fees increases on investment advisory services net loan servicing deposits and foreign exchanges also contributed to the revenue growth. However a decline in gains on sales of loans slightly offset those improvements.

Net income which has also been on the rise grew 15% to $462.1 million in 2013 (versus $401.2 million in 2012) primarily as a result of the year's higher revenues. In turn the profit growth helped contribute to a rise of cash flow from operations which grew 28% to $562.2 million.

Strategy

A conservative lender First Republic has been relatively unscathed by the financial problems plaguing the banking industry. The company has a solid asset portfolio with few delinquencies. First Republic is focused on growing its business banking and wealth management business which spurs fee income. The bank is expanding its wealth management unit through hiring and cross-selling. The bank also caters to film and television companies by offering lending deposit and wealth management services.

EXECUTIVES

EVP Secretary and General Counsel, Edward J. Dobranski, age 64
President CEO and Director, James H. Herbert
EVP and Chief Credit Officer, David B. Lichtman
EVP Deposit Sales Product and Strategy, Joseph M. (Joe) Petitti
President First Republic Securities Company, David Tateosian
SEVP and Chief Banking Officer, Michael D. (Mike) Selfridge, age 47
President First Republic Trust Company, Michael J. Harrington
President Private Wealth Management, Bob Thornton
EVP and Chief Marketing Officer, Dianne Snedaker
SVP and Chief Investment Officer, Hafize Gaye (Gaye) Erkan
EVP and CFO, Michael J. (Mike) Roffler
EVP; Chief BSA and AML and Security Officer, Bill Ward
EVP and CIO, Dale A. Smith
EVP and COO, Jason C. Bender
President First Republic Trust Company, Kelly Johnston
Senior Vice President, Sam Heshmati
Vice President Compliance Risk Manager, Steven Sears
Vice President Engineering and Technology Operations, Michael (Mel) Campbell
Vice President, Thomas Ehrhardt
Vice President Residential Lending, Lionel Antunes
Vice President, Michael Curley
Vice President, Todd Brantley
Vice President, Margaret Zywicz
Vice President, Karen Conway
Vice President First Republic Investment Management, Reynolds Ospina
Vice President, Monika Mugg
Vice President Investments And Private Wealth Management Risk Officer, Sam Franco
Senior Vice President Deputy General Counsel, Jonathan Santelli
Vice President Of Retail Marketing, Gwenn Murphy
Vice President, Peter Chang
Vice President Digital Banking, Adam Devlin
Vice Chairman, Katherine August-deWilde, age 64
Assistant Treasurer, Thomas Lacher
Auditors: KPMG LLP

LOCATIONS

HQ: First Republic Bank (San Francisco, CA)
111 Pine Street, 2nd Floor, San Francisco, CA 94111
Phone: 415 392-1400
Web: www.firstrepublic.com

PRODUCTS/OPERATIONS

2013 Sales

	% of total
Interest income other	85
Noninterest income	15
Total	**100**

Selected Affiliates

First Republic Investment Management Inc.
First Republic Securities Company LLC
First Republic Trust Company

COMPETITORS

Bank of Marin	City National
Bank of New York Mellon	JPMorgan Private Bank
Boston Private	MUFG Americas Holdings
Citigroup Private Bank	Morgan Stanley
	TriState Capital

HISTORICAL FINANCIALS

Company Type: Public

Income Statement

FYE: December 31

	ASSETS ($ mil.)	NET INCOME ($ mil.)	INCOME AS % OF ASSETS	EMPLOYEES
12/14	48,353	487	1.0%	2,506
12/13	42,112	462	1.1%	2,388
12/12	34,387	402	1.2%	2,110
12/11	27,791	352	1.3%	1,821
12/10	22,377	142	0.6%	1,502
Annual Growth	**21.2%**	**36.0%**	**—**	**13.7%**

2014 Year-End Financials

Debt ratio: 11.81%
Return on equity: 10.90%
Cash ($ mil.): 817
Current ratio: —
Long-term debt ($ mil.): —
No. of shares (mil.): 138
Dividends
Yield: 1.0%
Payout: 18.1%
Market value ($ mil.): 7,207

	STOCK PRICE ($) FY Close	P/E High/Low	PER SHARE ($) Earnings	Dividends	Book Value
12/14	52.12	18 14	3.07	0.54	34.56
12/13	52.35	16 10	3.10	0.46	31.33
12/12	32.78	12 10	2.76	0.30	25.89
12/11	30.61	13 8	2.65	0.00	19.46
12/10	29.12	26 24	1.12	0.00	16.59
Annual Growth	**15.7%**	**— —**	**28.7%**	**—**	**20.1%**

FirstEnergy Corp.

FirstEnergy's first goal is to generate and deliver power but its second goal is to stay profitable in a market undergoing deregulation. Its ten utilities provide electricity to 6 million customers in the Midwest and the Mid-Atlantic. The company's domestic power plants have a total generating capacity of more than 17000 MW most generated by coal-fired plants. Subsidiary FirstEnergy Solutions trades energy commodities in deregulated US markets. FirstEnergy's other nonregulated operations include electrical and mechanical contracting and energy planning and procurement.

Geographic Reach

The company operates and serves customers in an service area of 65000 square miles in Illinois Maryland Michigan New Jersey New York Ohio Pennsylvania and West Virginia.

Operations

FirstEnergy has power regulated generation transmission and distribution operations. Through FirstEnergy Solutions it is also engaged in competitive generation and electricity sales. As part of its assets FirstEnergy has 2400 MW of renewable energy (primarily generated by wind farms) and 24136 miles of high-voltage transmission lines.

The Regulated Distribution segment distributes electricity through FirstEnergy's ten utilities which serve 6 million customers and a combined population of 13.5 million. It purchases power in Ohio Pennsylvania New Jersey and Maryland and controls 3790 MWs of generation capacity.The Regulated Transmission segment transmits electricity through transmission facilities owned and operated by American Transmission Systems Trans-Allegheny Interstate Line Company and a number of FirstEnergy's utilities and the regulatory asset associated with the abandoned PATH project.The Competitive Energy Services segment supplies electricity through retail and wholesale arrangements including competitive retail sale to customer primarily in Ohio Pennsylvania Illinois Michigan New Jersey and Maryland and the provision of partial Provider of Last Resort and default service for some utilities in Ohio Pennsylvania and Maryland. It controls 14068 MW of capacity including 885 MWs of capacity scheduled to be deactivated in 2015.

Financial Performance

In 2014 the company's revenues were restated due to reflect the divestiture of 11 hydroelectric power stations.FirstEnergy's 2014 revenues increased by 1% due to higher Regulated Distribution revenues as the result of a $331 million increase in wholesale generation sales volumes resulting from Harrison/Pleasants asset transfer of 1476 MW of generation capacity.The company's net income decreased by 24% in 2014 due higher operating expenses as a result of increase in FirstEnergy's Pension and OPEB mark-to-market adjustment partially offset by the absence of impairment charges on regulatory assets and long lived assets ($1.1 billion recognized in 2013).Cash inflow increased by 632% as a result of changes in working capital as a result of changes in receivables prepayments and other current assets and accounts payable.

Strategy

In 2015 the company planned to focus on to develop the transmission business strengthen the regulated utilities and manage overall risk within the competitive business The core of this strategy is the $4.2 billion energizing the Future investment plan. This program is focused on a large number of small projects within the existing 24000 mile service territory that improve service to customers. The company has identified $15 billion in transmission investment opportunities across its system beyond 2014-2017.In 2015 the company completed multiple transmission projects that will further enhance electric service for customers throughout northern Ohio. The new facilities are designed to ensure system reliability following the retirement of coal-fired power plants in the region. The company spent nearly $800 million on transmission projects to support plant retirements along Lake Erie. FirstEnergy expects to spend $1.2 billion through 2019 on projects related to plant retirements across its entire transmission system. The completed projects represent a significant milestone in the company's Energizing the Future initiative and include new 138- and 345-kV transmission lines and new substations.

As part of its ongoing efforts to help enhance service reliability in 2014 Mon Power installed new automated switching equipment on a 47-mile 69000 volt transmission line serving nearly 6000 customers in the Marlinton and Snowshoe Mountain Resort areas of Pocahontas County.To raise cash to pay down debt in 2014 FirstEnergy sold 11 hydroelectric power stations to Harbor Hydro for $395 million. The hydroelectric power stations had a total capacity of 527 MW (less than 3% of FirstEnergy's generation fleet output).

As states push to reduce carbon emissions FirstEnergy has been expanding its renewable energy operations and reducing its fossil-fuel power plants. In 2013 the company announced plans to deactivate two coal-fired power plants in Pennsylvania reducing its overall power generating capacity from more than 20000 MW to more than 18000 MW.

HISTORY

FirstEnergy came to light in 1893 as the Akron Electric Light and Power Company. After several mergers the business went bankrupt and was sold in 1899 to Akron Traction and Electric Company which became Northern Ohio Power and Light (NOP&L).

In 1930 Commonwealth and Southern (C&S) bought NOP&L and merged it with four other Ohio utility holding companies to form Ohio Edison. The new firm increased sales during the Depression by selling electric appliances.

The Public Utility Holding Company Act of 1935 (passed to rein in uncontrolled utilities) caught up with C&S in 1949 forcing it to divest Ohio Edison. Rival Ohio Public Service was also divested from its holding company and in 1950 Ohio Edison bought it.

In 1967 after two decades of expansion Ohio Edison and three other Ohio and Pennsylvania utilities formed the Central Area Power Coordination Group (CAPCO) to share new power-plant costs including the construction of the Beaver Valley nuclear plant (1970-76). Although the CAPCO partners agreed in 1980 to cancel four planned nukes in 1985 Ohio Edison took part in building the Perry Unit 1 and Beaver Valley Unit 2 nuclear plants.

The federal Energy Policy Act of 1992 allowed wholesale power competition and to satisfy new federal requirements Ohio Edison formed a six-state transmission alliance in 1996 with fellow utilities Centerior Energy Allegheny Power System and Dominion Resources' Virginia Power to coordinate their grids.

Ohio Edison paid about $1.5 billion in 1997 for Centerior Energy formed in 1986 as a holding company for Toledo Edison and Cleveland Electric. Ohio Edison and Centerior both burdened by high-cost generating plants merged to cut costs and the expanded energy concern was renamed FirstEnergy Corp.

Looking toward deregulation FirstEnergy began buying mechanical construction contracting and energy management companies in 1997 including Roth Bros. and RPC Mechanical. In 1998 it added nine more. FirstEnergy then ventured into natural gas operations by purchasing MARBEL Energy. The company also created separate subsidiaries for its nuclear and transmission assets.

In 2000 FirstEnergy agreed to acquire New Jersey-based electric utility GPU in an $11.9 billion deal; it became one of the largest US utilities in 2001 when it completed the acquisition which added three utilities (Jersey Central Power & Light Metropolitan Edison and Pennsylvania Electric) serving 2.1 million electricity customers.

Beefing up its generation assets in 2011 the company acquired Allegheny Energy in a $8.5 bil-

lion deal. The acquisition increased FirstEnergy's power generation capacity by 70% and its customer base by 35% dramatically boosting its position as a leading regional energy provider focused on both regulated utility operations and a competitive generation business.

EXECUTIVES

President Maryland Operations, James A. Sears
Vice President, Michael (Mel) Dowling
Regional President Pennsylvania Electric Company, James (Jamie) Napier
Associate General Counsel, Leila L. Vespoli, age 56, $690,769 total compensation
Plant Manager, Donald R. (Donny) Schneider, age 54
SVP Corporate Services and CIO, Bennett L. Gaines
Regional President The Cleveland Electric Illuminating Company, Dennis M. Chack
President CEO and Director, Charles E. (Chuck) Jones, age 60, $607,212 total compensation
EVP and CFO, James F. (Jim) Pearson, age 61, $507,212 total compensation
EVP and President FirstEnergy Generation, James H. (Jim) Lash, age 64, $554,327 total compensation
Regional President The Cleveland Electric Illuminating Company, John E. Skory
Regional President Metropolitan Edison Company, Edward L. Shuttleworth
Regional President Ohio Edison Company, Randall A. Frame
Regional President West Penn Power Company, David W. McDonald
President Jersey Central Power and Light, James V. Fakult
Regional President Pennsylvania Electric Company, Scott R Wyman
President West Virginia Operations, Holly C Kauffman
President Pennsylvania Operations, Linda L. Moss, age 50
SVP and COO FirstEnergy Nuclear Operating Company, Samuel L. Belcher
Executive Vice President, Charles (Chas) Lasky
Vice President, Rick Collings
Vice President Corporate Affairs and Community Involvement, Dee Lowery
Vice President Engineering, Dave Rencurrel
Vice President Energy Policy, Marty Hall
Executive Vice President, Charles Lasky
Vice President Contract Admin And Admin, Marvin Davis
Vice President, Robert Ehasz
Regional Vice President, Jeffrey (Jeff) Elser
Executive Vice President and General Counsel, Anthony Alexander
Vice President and General Counsel, Bob Reffner
Regional President Toledo Edison, Trent Smith
Vice President fossil Engineering and Construction, George Farah
Non-Executive Chairman, George M. Smart, age 69
Auditors: PricewaterhouseCoopers LLP

LOCATIONS

HQ: FirstEnergy Corp.
76 South Main Street, Akron, OH 44308
Phone: 800 736-3402
Web: www.firstenergycorp.com

PRODUCTS/OPERATIONS

2014 Sales

	$ mil.	% of total
Regulated Distribution	9,102	59
Regulated Transmission	769	5
Competitive Energy Services	5,470	36
Corporate/Other	(146)	-
Reconciling Adjustments	(146)	-
Total	**15,049**	**100**

2014 Sales

	$ mil.	% of total
Electric utilities	9,871	66
Unregulated businesses	5,178	34
Total	**15,049**	**100**

Electric Utility Subsidiaries
American Transmission Systems Inc.
The Cleveland Electric Illuminating Company (The Illuminating Company)
Jersey Cen
Metropolit
Ohio Edison Company
Pennsylvan
Pennsylvan
The Toledo Edison Company
West Penn Power Company The Potomac Edison Company Monongahela Power Company (formerly Allegheny Power)

Selected Unregulated Subsidiaries

FirstEnergy Nuclear Operating Co. (nuclear generation facilities)
FirstEnergy Properties Inc.
FirstEnergy Securities Transfer Company
FirstEnergy Service Company
FirstEnergy Solutions Corp. (retail and wholesale energy marketing and management services)
FirstEnergy Ventures Corp.
GPU Diversified Holdings LLC
GPU Nuclear Inc. (nuclear plant management and decommissioning)

Selected Mergers and Acquisitions

COMPETITORS

AEP	Exelon Energy
Avista	National Fuel Gas
CMS Energy	NiSource
Constellation Energy	PG&E Corporation
Group	PPL Corporation
DPL	PSEG Energy Holdings
Delmarva Power	Peabody Energy
Dominion Resources	Peoples Natural Gas
Duke Energy	Pepco Holdings
Duquesne Light	Public Service
Duquesne Light	Enterprise Group
Holdings	Southern Company
Dynegy	TVA
EnergySolve	Vectren
Exelon	WGL Holdings

HISTORICAL FINANCIALS

Company Type: Public

Income Statement

FYE: December 31

	REVENUE ($ mil.)	NET INCOME ($ mil.)	NET PROFIT MARGIN	EMPLOYEES
12/15	15,026	578	3.8%	15,781
12/14	15,049	299	2.0%	15,557
12/13	14,917	392	2.6%	15,754
12/12	15,303	770	5.0%	16,495
12/11	16,258	885	5.4%	17,257
Annual Growth	**(2.0%)**	**(10.1%)**	**—**	**(2.2%)**

2015 Year-End Financials

Debt ratio: 42.28%	No. of shares (mil.): 423
Return on equity: 4.65%	Dividends
Cash ($ mil.): 131	Yield: 4.5%
Current ratio: 0.54	Payout: 123.0%
Long-term debt ($ mil.): 19,192	Market value ($ mil.): 13,440

	STOCK PRICE ($) FY Close	P/E High/Low		PER SHARE ($) Earnings	Dividends	Book Value
12/15	31.73	30	21	1.37	1.44	29.33
12/14	38.99	57	43	0.71	1.44	29.49
12/13	32.98	50	34	0.94	2.20	30.32
12/12	41.76	27	22	1.84	2.20	31.29
12/11	44.30	21	16	2.21	2.20	31.75
Annual Growth	**(8.0%)**		**—**	**— (11.3%)**	**(10.1%)**	**(2.0%)**

FirstMerit Corp

FirstMerit Corporation is the holding company for FirstMerit Bank which provides retail and commercial banking services through more than 360 branches in five US states primarily in the Midwest. Serving local consumers and small to midsized businesses the bank provides standard services such as deposit accounts credit and debit cards and loans as well as wealth management and trust services. Subsidiaries offer investment and brokerage services financial planning commercial lease financing life and title insurance annuities and mortgage servicing. Huntington Bancshares agreed to buy FirstMerit for $3.4 billion in January 2016.

Geographic Reach

About three-fourths of FirstMerit's bank branches are located in Ohio and Michigan. It has 40-plus branches in both Wisconsin and Illinois (the Chicago area) as well as four branches in Western Pennsylvania.

Financial Performance

After a few years of flat or declining revenue FirstMerit reported growth of more than 40% in 2013 as revenue hit $1 billion. In addition net income was up almost an equal amount topping $180 million. Those results were powered primarily by the 2013 acquisition of Citizens Republic Bancorp which doubled the bank's number of branches and extended its reach into new markets. On the strength of the acquisition total interest income rose 50% year-over-year; non-interest income grew by a slightly more modest 20%.

The company's net income has been on a strong growth trajectory over the past five years more than doubling since 2009. Cash flow from operations has been on a similar path jumping from about $90 million in 2009 to $173 million in 2013.

Strategy

FirstMerit emphasizes relationship banking and local decision-making with credit authority appropriate to specific markets and branches staffed by bankers with deep community ties. In 2013 it was focused on both organic growth and acquisitions. Organically that year the company saw commercial loan production in legacy markets grow 14%. The transformational event of the year however was the purchase of Citizens Republic.

Mergers and Acquisitions

In April 2013 FirstMerit completed the acquisition of Flint Michigan-based Citizens Republic Bancorp for $912 million in stock. The deal which is the largest in FirstMerit's history doubled its branch locations and ATM network strengthened its presence in northeastern Ohio and expanded its operations into Michigan and Wisconsin. The company completed its brand roll-out by mid-2013 and had converted operating systems in the new branches by year's end.

EXECUTIVES

Senior Executive Vice President & Chief Financial Officer, Terrence E. Bichsel, age 65, $387,125 total compensation
President and CEO Akron Region, Nicholas V. Browning
Executive Vice President; Treasurer, Mark N. DuHamel
Chairman President and CEO FirstMerit and FirstMerit Bank, Paul G. Greig, age 59, $791,250 total compensation
President and CEO Columbus Region, Sue E. Zazon
SVP and Chief Marketing Officer, Julie C. Tutkovics
EVP & CIO, Mark D. Quinlan, age 54
EVP and Chief Credit Officer, William P. (Bill) Richgels, age 64, $387,125 total compensation

EVP of Retail, N. James (Jim) Brocklehurst
SEVP Chief Commercial Banking Officer, David G. Goodall, $326,000 total compensation
EVP Wealth Management Services, Michael G. Robinson
Vice Chairman FirstMerit Corporation; Chairman and CEO FirstMerit Michigan, Sandra L. Pierce
Vice President Director of Commercial Marketing Channel Management, Jay Dobkowski
Vice President Systems Manager Strategic Information Group, Douglas (Doug) Turner
Executive Vice President, Robert Morlan
Senior Vice President of Marketing, Eugene Lucci
Vice President Business Development, Jason Hanes
Vice President, Kevin Reid
Vice President, Tari Detzler
Vice President, Bonnie Coponen
Senior Vice President Head Of Asset Based Lending, Douglas (Doug) Winget
Senior Vice President District Manager, Thomas (Thom) Jalette
Vice President Private Banker, Kimberly Miller
Vice President, David Olenik
Vice President, Edward Longville
Vice President, James Garland
Vice President, Shawn Lavetter
Vice President Of Systems Programming, Mark Hanna
Senior Vice President, Wendy J Bolas
Executive Vice President Marketing, Beth Birone
Assistant Vice President International Credit Risk Officer, Innara Goldstein
Executive Vice President Director of Retail Banking, Jim Brocklehurst
Vice President, Dan Ranger
Vice President, Jason Bierlein
Vice President, Marilee Wright
Vice President, Darla Kolomak
Vice President, David Janowicz
Vice President, Carpenter Robert
Vice President, Kyle Donato
Vice President Commercial Banking, Joe McNeill
Vice President Commercial Banking, Doug Brashler
Vice President Customer Service, Lynn Myers
Vice President Finance, Steven Lick
Vice President Treasury Management, Alison Kavulich
Vice President Client Advisor, Lou Lajoe
Senior Vice President and Team Leader Commercial Banking, James A (Jamie) Eckelberry
Vice President, Mark Seryak
Senior Vice President And Manager New Business Development, Joseph Kwasny
Vice President, Michelle Del Rio-keller
Vice President Commercial Loan, Mattie Jones-hollowell
Vice President Commercial Appraisal Environmental and Quality Assurance, Carol Krozek
Group Manager Senior Vice President, June Courtney
Vice President, Thomas Heidy
Senior Vice President Manager Core Business Banking Michigan, Patrick (Paddy) Reardon
Assistant Vice President, Phil Long
Vice President, Norman Lange
Vice President Commercial Lending, Phillip Hohler
Vice President Commercial Banking, Chris Doyle
Vice President Systems Development Group, Amy Fadeley
Vice President, Manjit Khuban
Vice President, Joe Pelle
Vice President, Mona Sarkar
Senior Vice President, Mary Patton
Vice President Business Banking Relationship Manager, Donna Wells
Senior Vice President Private Banking, Kristine Movsesian
Senior Vice President And Manager Dealer Services, Eric Earvin

Vice President, Allyson Vanderhaar
Auditors: Ernst & Young LLP

LOCATIONS

HQ: FirstMerit Corp
III Cascade Plaza, 7th Floor, Akron, OH 44308
Phone: 330 996-6000
Web: www.firstmerit.com

2013 Branch Locations

	No.
Ohio	156
Michigan	153
Wisconsin	47
Illinois	44
Pennsylvania	4
Total	**404**

PRODUCTS/OPERATIONS

2013 Sales

	$ mil.	% of total
Interest		
Loans	635	61
Investment securities	129	13
Noninterest		
Service charges on deposits	74	7
Credit card fees	50	5
Trust department	34	3
Loan sales & servicing		**23.1**
2		
ATM & other service fees	19	2
Bank-owned life insurance	16	2
Investment services & insurance	12	1
Other	41	4
Investment securities losses net	(2.8)	-
Total	**1,036**	**100**

Selected Subsidiaries

Citizens Savings Corporation of Stark County
FirstMerit Bank National Association
  FirstMerit Advisors Inc.
  FirstMerit Equipment Finance Inc.
  FirstMerit Financial Services Inc.
  FirstMerit Insurance Agency Inc.
  FirstMerit Insurance Group Inc.
  FirstMerit Mortgage Corporation
  FirstMerit Mortgage Reinsurance Company Inc.
  FirstMerit-Moss Creek Ventures LLC
  FirstMerit Securities Inc.
  FirstMerit Title Agency Ltd.
  Midwest Financial and Investment Services Inc.
FirstMerit Community Development Corporation

COMPETITORS

Associated Banc-Corp	PNC Financial
Fifth Third	Park National
First Midwest Bancorp	Peoples Bancorp (OH)
Harris	TFS Financial
Huntington Bancshares	U.S. Bancorp
JPMorgan Chase	Wells Fargo
KeyCorp	Wintrust Financial
MB Financial	

HISTORICAL FINANCIALS

Company Type: Public

Income Statement

FYE: December 31

	ASSETS ($ mil.)	NET INCOME ($ mil.)	INCOME AS % OF ASSETS	EMPLOYEES
12/14	24,902	237	1.0%	4,419
12/13	23,909	183	0.8%	4,570
12/12	14,913	134	0.9%	2,836
12/11	14,441	119	0.8%	3,177
12/10	14,136	102	0.7%	3,058
Annual Growth	**15.2%**	**23.3%**	**—**	**9.6%**

Debt ratio: 3.75%		No. of shares (mil.): 165
Return on equity: 8.59%		Dividends
Cash ($ mil.): 697		Yield: 3.3%
Current ratio: —		Payout: 46.0%
Long-term debt ($ mil.): —		Market value ($ mil.): 3,124

	STOCK PRICE ($) FY Close	P/E High/Low	PER SHARE ($) Earnings	Dividends	Book Value
12/14	18.89	17 12	1.39	0.64	17.14
12/13	22.23	20 12	1.18	0.64	16.38
12/12	14.19	14 11	1.22	0.64	15.00
12/11	15.13	18 9	1.10	0.64	14.33
12/10	19.79	24 16	1.02	0.64	13.86
Annual Growth	(1.2%)	— —	8.0%	(0.0%)	5.5%

Fiserv, Inc.

Fiserv gives financial companies the tech services they need to run. The company provides core processing systems electronic billing and payment systems ATM management and loan processing services to banks thrifts credit unions and other financial institutions. It also provides licensed software consulting and other support services to round out its offerings. Fiserv serves customers of all sizes but its bread and butter has traditionally been small to midsized banks without in-house processing units. Other clients include insurance companies merchants leasing firms and government agencies. Founded in 1984 Fiserv serves some 14500 clients in 100-plus countries.

HISTORY

When First Bank System of Minneapolis bought Milwaukee-based Midland Bank in 1984 the head of Midland's data processing operation George Dalton bought the unit and then merged that operation with Sunshine State Systems a newly independent Florida processing company headed by Leslie Muma. Christened Fiserv the company went public in 1986. It grew by providing outsourcing services to small banks and thrifts.

In the 1990s Fiserv began targeting larger clients. But industry consolidation sometimes hurt the company as when the 12-year term of a 1995 contract with Chase Manhattan was reduced to three after Chase and Chemical Bank merged in 1996.

As banks moved into new areas Fiserv went along. In the late 1990s it acquired BHC Financial and Hanifen Imhoff Holdings (securities transaction processing). Other purchases that broadened its service list included Automated Financial Technology (credit union software) and Network Data Processing (administrative software for insurance companies). The push into software continued with 1999 purchases in the field of workers' compensation systems.

Also in 1999 Fiserv bolstered its client list by buying QuestPoint's check servicing business. It moved into retirement plan administration with the purchase of a unit from what is now SunAmerica Financial Group. In 2000 a deal to provide back-office services for American Express' online Membership Banking unit fell apart but Fiserv recovered its momentum with enhanced mortgage servicing offerings and an agreement to provide technology services to cahoot the online banking unit of the UK's Abbey National (which was ac-

quired by Spanish group Banco Santander in 2004).

Fiserv continued its acquisitive activities in 2001 buying Benefit Planners (a leading employee benefit program administrator with operations in Europe the Middle East South America and the US) Facilities and Services Corporation (a California-based insurance software maker) NCSI (information and services targeting the flood insurance industry) and the bank processing operations of NCR Corporation. The company that year also sold its Human Resources Information Services unit to buyout firm Gores Group.

Fiserv boosted its ATM and electronic funds transfer (ETF) business with the 2002 purchase of the Consumer Network Services unit of Electronic Data Systems (now HP Enterprise Services).

The company embarked on a series of sales in the next few years. It sold its securities clearing operations to a unit of FMR in 2005. Three years later it sold most of its health business to UnitedHealth for some $480 million. The sale included Fiserv Health Plan Administration Fiserv Health Plan Management Innoviant Pharmacy Avidyn Health and other units but not WorkingRx (workers' compensation) and CareGain (technology) which remained with Fiserv.The company also sold the bulk of its Fiserv Trust Company (also known as Fiserv Investment Support Services or Fiserv ISS) business including advisor services and institutional retirement services to TD AMERITRADE. In a separate transaction the newly formed Trust Institution Bank (headed by former Fiserv ISS management) acquired most of the company's investment administration services business.Fiserv acquired one of the largest electronic payments firms CheckFree in 2007 boosting its capabilities in the payments landscape. In a smaller deal Fiserv bought payment processor i_Tech from First Interstate BancSystem in 2008.All of the acquisition activity led the company to higher debt levels which it began paying down through a combination of cost-cutting measures and divesting non-core operations. In 2008 it sold most of its health business to UnitedHealth and the bulk of Fiserv Trust Company to TD AMERITRADE. The following year it sold 51% of Fiserv Insurance Services (now StoneRiver) to investment firm Stone Point Capital for some $540 million. It also sold Loan Fulfillment Solutions a provider of mortgage-related services including settlement and title certification. As it added new operations and jettisoned others the company introduced a new marketing strategy in 2009 to unify its brands under the Fiserv banner.In 2010 Fiserv acquired AdviceAmerica which provides desktop technology for financial advisers. It also introduced ZashPay a peer-to-peer platform available to consumers.

EXECUTIVES

EVP and COO, Mark A. Ernst, age 56, $575,000 total compensation
EVP and Group President International, Steven (Steve) Tait, age 55
President CEO and Director, Jeffery W. Yabuki, age 54, $840,000 total compensation
EVP Human Resources, Kevin P. Pennington
EVP CFO and Treasurer, Thomas J. Hirsch, age 51, $500,000 total compensation
Group President Depository Institution Services, Byron C. Vielehr, age 51, $470,000 total compensation
EVP and Chief Sales Officer, Shawn M. Donovan
EVP and Group President Billing and Payments, Rahul Gupta, age 55, $470,000 total compensation
Group President Digital Banking, Kevin J. Schultz, age 57
EVP General Counsel and Secretary, Lynn S. McCreary, age 55

President Biller Solutions, Michael O'Laughlin
Group President Enterprise Technology, Clifford A. Skelton
Group President Financial Institutions, Kevin P. Gregoire
Vice President And Director Of Account Executives, Tracy Brewster
Vice President Client Management, Erik Swenson
Vice President, Rebekkah Wilson
Assistant Vice President, Jerome Linderman
Senior Vice President, Jed Delker
Senior Vice President, Doug Lees
Senior Vice President, Douglas Hanson
Executive Vice President, Cliff Skelton
Chairman, Daniel P. Kearney, age 75
Auditors: Deloitte & Touche LLP

LOCATIONS

HQ: Fiserv, Inc.
255 Fiserv Drive, Brookfield, WI 53045
Phone: 262 879-5000 **Fax:** 262 879-5013
Web: www.fiserv.com

PRODUCTS/OPERATIONS

2014 Sales

	$ mil.	% of total
Payments		
Processing & services	2,030	40
Products	717	14
Financial		
Processing & services	2,195	43
Product	172	3
Adjustments	(48)	-
Total	**5,066**	**100**

Selected Subsidiaries

BillMatrix Corporation
CheckFree Corporation
CheckFreePay Corporation
Data-Link Systems LLC
Fiserv Automotive Solutions Inc.
Fiserv CIR Inc.
Fiserv (Europe) Limited (UK)
Information Technology Inc.
ITI of Nebraska Inc.
USERS LLC
XP Systems Corp.

COMPETITORS

Accenture	Intuit Financial
Banc of America	Services
Merchant Services	Jack Henry
CGI Group	MasterCard
D+H USA	SunGard
DST Systems	Total System Services
Fidelity National	Visa Inc
Information Services	Western Union
First Data	

HISTORICAL FINANCIALS

Company Type: Public

Income Statement

	REVENUE ($ mil.)	NET INCOME ($ mil.)	NET PROFIT MARGIN	EMPLOYEES
12/14	5,066	754	14.9%	21,000
12/13	4,814	648	13.5%	21,000
12/12	4,482	611	13.6%	20,000
12/11	4,337	472	10.9%	20,000
12/10	4,133	496	12.0%	19,000
Annual Growth	5.2%	11.0%	—	2.5%

2014 Year-End Financials

Debt ratio: 40.73%		No. of shares (mil.): 240
Return on equity: 21.92%		Dividends
Cash ($ mil.): 294		Yield: —
Current ratio: 1.00		Payout: —
Long-term debt ($ mil.): 3,711		Market value ($ mil.): 17,054

	STOCK PRICE ($)	P/E	PER SHARE ($)		
	FY Close	High/Low	Earnings	Dividends	Book Value
12/14	70.97	24 18	2.98	0.00	13.71
12/13	59.05	46 23	2.44	0.00	13.97
12/12	79.03	36 26	2.22	0.00	12.81
12/11	58.74	39 30	1.64	0.00	11.63
12/10	58.56	37 27	1.64	0.00	10.99
Annual Growth	4.9%	— —	16.2%	—	5.7%

Flagstar Bancorp, Inc.

Flagstar Bancorp is the holding company for Flagstar Bank which operatesÂ about 115Âbranches (including some in retail stores)Âin Michigan.Â Home loans are a major focus for Flagstar. The thrift originates purchases and servicesÂ residential mortgages in all 50 states through a network of brokers andÂcorrespondents as well as nearly 30 of its own loan offices in more than a dozen states. More than three-quarters of the company's revenue (after interest expenses) isÂlinked toÂresidential lending but the reliance on this business hurtÂFlagstar during the housing bust. Expanding its commercial lending operations the firm in 2011 opened four full-service branches in Massachusetts Connecticut and Rhode Island.

Flagstar is broadening its reach beyond mortgage lending. The company is transforming its branches into full-service community banks and focusing on cross-selling an expanded suite of retail commercial and government banking services. It has also recently introduced a line of consumer loans such as credit cards and home equity lines of credit and added services for small and midsized businesses like treasury management and specialty lending. Additionally the bank formally expanded its commercial lending business into New England. While home mortgage lending remains key to Flagstar the company hopes to diversify its revenue streams so the business eventually accounts for about a third of sales.

The shift likely has something to do with the company's exposure to the miserable mortgage market. Flagstar has reported annual losses every year since 2007 since which it has lost a total of nearly $1.4 billion. Revenues fell 11% to $851 million in 2011 while losses that year totaled $182 million. Both interest and noninterest earnings declined that year as as the credit markets remained challenged. The company has been slowing its losses down though and despite reporting another quarter in the red in 2012 expects to return to profitability for the year. Flagstar has also lowered its provision for loan losses thanks to a decline in charge-offs.

To raise capital the company sold 27 bank branches in the suburbs north of Atlanta along with their deposits to PNC in 2011. The company also sold its 22 Indiana branches to First Financial Bancorp in late 2011. In addition to bringing in some cash the divestitures help Flagstar focus on its Michigan operations.

MP Thrift an affiliate of private equity firm MatlinPatterson Global Advisors assumed a controlling stake of Flagstar in 2009. Today it owns 64% of the company.

EXECUTIVES

EVP and Director Performing Servicing, Mark Landschulz, age 50

President Mortgage Banking, Leonard (Len) Israel

President CEO and Director, Alessandro P. DiNello, age 60

EVP and Senior Deputy General Counsel, Paul D. Borja, age 54, $749,982 total compensation

EVP and Treasurer, Brian D.J. Boike, age 38

EVP and COO, Lee M. Smith

EVP and CFO, James K. Ciroli

EVP and Chief Risk Officer, Steve Figliuolo

EVP and Director MIS and Analytics, William D. Belekewicz

EVP and CIO, Tony Buttrick

EVP Secondary Marketing, Palmer T. Heenan

EVP and Director Mortgage Fulfillment, Donna M. Krall

EVP and Chief Lending Officer Commercial Banking, Thomas R. Kuslits

EVP and Chief Human Resources Officer, Cynthia M. Myers

EVP and Chief Credit Officer, Joseph M. Redoutey

EVP and Chief Compliance Officer, Karen A. Sabatowski

Chairman, John D. Lewis

Auditors: PricewaterhouseCoopers LLP

LOCATIONS

HQ: Flagstar Bancorp, Inc.
5151 Corporate Drive, Troy, MI 48098-2639
Phone: 248 312-2000
Web: www.flagstar.com

PRODUCTS/OPERATIONS

2014 Sales

	$ mil.	% of total
Interest income		
Loans	245	37
Securities	39	6
Other	0	-
Noninterest income		
Net gain on loan sales	205	31
Loan fees & charges	73	11
Loan administration income	24	4
Net return on mortgage serving assets	24	4
Other	43	7
Adjustments	(10.0)	-
Total	**646**	**100**

2014 Sales

	% of total
Mortgage originations	52
Community Banking	28
Mortgage Servicing	13
Others	7
Total	**100**

COMPETITORS

Bank of America	JPMorgan Chase
Comerica	KeyCorp
Fifth Third	Northern Trust
Harris	PNC Financial
Huntington Bancshares	

HISTORICAL FINANCIALS

Company Type: Public

Income Statement

FYE: December 31

	ASSETS ($ mil.)	NET INCOME ($ mil.)	INCOME AS % OF ASSETS	EMPLOYEES
12/14	9,839	(69)	—	2,739
12/13	9,407	266	2.8%	3,253
12/12	14,082	68	0.5%	3,328
12/11	13,637	(181)	—	3,136
12/10	13,643	(374)	—	3,279
Annual Growth	**(7.8%)**	**—**		**(4.4%)**

2014 Year-End Financials
Debt ratio: 3.37%
Return on equity: (-4.96%)
Cash ($ mil.): 136
Current ratio: —
Long-term debt ($ mil.): —
No. of shares (mil.): 56
Dividends
Yield: —
Payout: —
Market value ($ mil.): 886

	STOCK PRICE ($)	P/E	PER SHARE ($)		
	FY Close	High/Low	Earnings	Dividends	Book Value
12/14	15.73	— —	(1.72)	0.00	24.37
12/13	19.62	5 3	4.37	0.00	25.40
12/12	19.40	22 1	0.87	0.00	20.75
12/11	0.51	— —	(3.60)	0.00	19.43
12/10	1.63	— —	(24.40)	0.00	22.77
Annual Growth	76.3%	— —	—	—	1.7%

Florida Power & Light Co.

Florida Power & Light (FPL) sheds extra light onto the Sunshine State. The company is a subsidiary of utility holding company NextEra Energy serves some 4.6 million electricity customers in eastern and southern Florida. FPL has more than 74160 miles of transmission and distribution lines as well as interests in fossil-fueled nuclear and solar power plants that give it a generating capacity of about 24100 MW. Its 73 natural gas units and 3 coal plants accounted for 86% of the power it generated in 2012. FPL also purchases and sells energy commodities to wholesale customers.

Financial Performance

FPL reported a 5% decreases in revenues in 2012 primarily due to lower fuel cost recovery revenues.Net income went up by 16% in 2012 primarily driven by investments in plant in service which resulted in a higher use of FPL's surplus depreciation credit (to earn an 11% regulatory return on equity on its retail rate base) as well as an increase in cost recovery clause results and higher Allowance For Funds Used During Construction equity.

Strategy

The company's 10-year strategic plan (initiated in 2012) for meeting Florida's energy needs relies on building additions to its existing generating plants while ramping up renewable energy sources in order to avoid building four medium-sized fossil-fueled power plants (called for by an earlier plan).

In 2013 FPL began installing solar panels at about 100 schools in 23 counties. It also agreed to a plan whereby more than 400 homes being built or refurbished by Habitat for Humanity and other non-profits would be fitted with solar-powered water heaters.

Between 2011 to 2013 FPL invested $9 billion to strengthen and improve its electric generation and delivery system. The company has revived a $2 billion plan to convert a plant in Port St. John and a plant in Riviera Beach from heavy fuel to natural gas. It also got a further 510 MW of capacity from its Turkey Point and St. Lucie nuclear power plants in 2012 and 2013.

The company also has long-term purchased power agreements for 1963 MW of power with expiration dates ranging from 2015 through 2032.

Company Background

In 2010 the Florida Public Service Commission turned down the company's proposed 30% retail rate hike or $1.3 billion. FPL adjusted its expansion programs accordingly.

Moving further to meet federal requirements for green energy production in 2010 the company commissioned the Space Coast Next Generation Solar Energy Center at the Kennedy Space Center three solar farms built in tandem with NASA to produce 10 MW of clean energy enough to serve 1100 homes. It also brought into service the 75-MW Martin Next Generation Solar Energy Center designed to power about 11000 homes. The hybrid facility connects more than 190000 solar thermal mirrors to an existing combined-cycle natural gas power plant.

EXECUTIVES

EVP Engineering Construction and Corporate Services, Robert L. (Bob) McGrath, age 62
EVP Finance and CFO, Moray P. Dewhurst, age 60
EVP, Charles E. Sieving, age 42
President and CEO, Eric E. Silagy
EVP Human Resources, Shaun J. Francis
Vice President Distr, Keith Hardy
Vice President Transmission And Substation, Manny Miranda
Vice President Human Resources Nuclear Division, Mike Bryce
Vice President Nuclear Transition, Art Stall
Site Vice President Turkey Point Nuclear Power Plant, Michael (Mel) Kiley
Vice President of Human Resources, Jim Poppell
Medical Director, Ron Gazze
Chairman, Lewis (Lew) Hay, age 59
Assistant Treasurer, Andrew (Andy) Kushner
Auditors: Deloitte & Touche LLP

LOCATIONS

HQ: Florida Power & Light Co.
  700 Universe Boulevard, Juno Beach, FL 33408
Phone: 561 694-4000
Web: www.nexteraenergy.com

PRODUCTS/OPERATIONS

2012 Operating Revenues

	% of total
Residential	51
Commercial	43
Industrial	3
Industrial power	1
Other	2
Total	**100**

2012 Sales

	$ mil.	% of total
Fuel cost recovery	4,246	42
Retail base	3,815	38
Other	2,053	20
Total	**10,114**	**100**

COMPETITORS

AGL Resources	Progress Energy
Clay Electric	Florida
Florida Public	Seminole Electric
Utilities	Sumter Electric
Gulf Power	Tampa Electric
JEA	
Orlando Utilities	
Commission	

HISTORICAL FINANCIALS
Company Type: Public

Income Statement
FYE: December 31

	REVENUE ($ mil.)	NET INCOME ($ mil.)	NET PROFIT MARGIN	EMPLOYEES
12/14	11,421	1,517	13.3%	8,700
12/13	10,445	1,349	12.9%	8,900
12/12	10,114	1,240	12.3%	9,700
12/11	10,613	1,068	10.1%	9,800
12/10	10,485	945	9.0%	10,000
Annual Growth	**2.2%**	**12.6%**	**—**	**(3.4%)**

2014 Year-End Financials

Debt ratio: 27.01%
Return on equity: 11.56%
Cash ($ mil.): 14
Current ratio: 0.76
Long-term debt ($ mil.): 9,413

No. of shares (mil.): 0
Dividends
  Yield: —
  Payout: —
Market value ($ mil.): —

Florida Power Corp.

Sometimes the sunshine state just isn't bright enough and that's when Florida Power (doing business as Progress Energy Florida) really shines. The utility transmits and distributes electricity to 1.6 million customers and oversees 10025 MW of generating capacity from interests in 14 nuclear and coal- oil- and gas-fired power plants. Additionally Florida Power purchases about 20% of the energy it provides. Florida Power operates 5100 miles of transmission lines and 52000 miles of overhead and 18700 miles of underground distribution cable. It also has 500 electric substations. A subsidiary of holding company Duke Energy the company also sells wholesale power to other utilities and marketers.

Geographic Reach

Florida Power's service territory covers 20000 square miles in west-central Florida and includes the densely populated areas around Orlando as well as the cities of St. Petersburg and Clearwater.

Operations

The company is a regulated public utility primarily engaged in the generation transmission distribution and sale of electricity. Its power grid is interconnected with 22 municipal power systems and with nine rural electric cooperative systems.

Sales and Marketing

The company's wholesale customers include Seminole Electric Cooperative Reedy Creek Improvement District the city of Gainesville the city of Winter Park and the city of Homestead.

Financial Performance

Revenue decreased by 17% in 2011 primarily due to the unfavorable impact of weather and lower wholesale base revenues. The unfavorable impact of weather was driven by 61% lower heating-degree days than in the previous year.

Net income decreased by 31% in 2011 primarily due to the charge for the amount to be refunded to customers through the fuel clause in accordance with a settlement agreement and the less favorable impact of weather.

Ownership

Florida Power is a subsidiary of Duke Energy.

EXECUTIVES

Vice President Nuclear Plant Development, John (Jack) Elnitsky
Vice President, Laura Boisvert
Auditors: Deloitte & Touche LLP

LOCATIONS

HQ: Florida Power Corp.
  299 First Avenue North, St. Petersburg, FL 33701
Phone: 704 382-3853   **Fax:** 727 866-4990

COMPETITORS

AGL Resources	JEA
Florida Power & Light	Orlando Utilities
Florida Public	Commission
Utilities	Seminole Electric
Gulf Power	Tampa Electric

HISTORICAL FINANCIALS
Company Type: Public

Income Statement
FYE: December 31

	REVENUE ($ mil.)	NET INCOME ($ mil.)	NET PROFIT MARGIN	EMPLOYEES
12/14	4,975	548	11.0%	—
12/13	4,527	325	7.2%	—
12/12	4,689	266	5.7%	—
12/11	4,369	314	7.2%	4,000
12/10	5,254	453	8.6%	4,000
Annual Growth	**(1.4%)**	**4.9%**	**—**	**—**

2014 Year-End Financials

Debt ratio: 31.32%
Return on equity: —
Cash ($ mil.): 8
Current ratio: 0.98
Long-term debt ($ mil.): 4,298

No. of shares (mil.): 0
Dividends
  Yield: —
  Payout: 22.6%
Market value ($ mil.): —

	STOCK PRICE ($) FY Close	P/E High/Low	PER SHARE ($) Earnings	Dividends	Book Value
12/14	0.00	— —	(0.00)	0.00	
52,220,000.00					
12/13	0.00	— —	(0.00)	1.42	
47,970,000.00					
12/12	97.50	— —	(0.00)	4.60	
48,330,000.00					
Annual Growth	**—**	**— —**	**—**	**—**	**2.0%**

Fluor Corp.

From the ground up Fluor is one of the world's largest international design engineering and contracting firms. Through subsidiaries it provides engineering procurement construction and maintenance (EPCM) as well as project management services for a variety of industrial sectors around the world. Its construction portfolio includes manufacturing plants refineries pharmaceutical facilities health care buildings power plants and telecommunications and transportation infrastructure. Oil and gas projects account for more than 50% of sales. The group also provides operations and maintenance services for its projects as well as administrative and support services to the US government.

HISTORY

Company BackgroundFluor's history began in 1890 when three Fluor brothers immigrants from Switzerland opened a Wisconsin lumber mill under the name Rudolph Fluor & Brothers. In 1912 John Simon Fluor formed a construction firm in Santa Ana California. Fluor's company soon began a relationship with Southern California Gas which led it to specialize in oil and gas construction. The company incorporated as Fluor Construction in 1924 later began making engine mufflers. In 1930 it expanded outside of California with a contract to build Texas pipelines.

After WWII Middle East oil reserves were aggressively developed by Western companies. Fluor cashed in on the stampede winning major contracts in Saudi Arabia. During the early 1960s it continued to emphasize oil and gas work establishing a contract drilling unit and in the 1970s it began work on giant energy projects.

In 1977 Fluor made its biggest purchase: Daniel International a South Carolina engineering and construction firm with more than $1 billion in annual revenues. The contracting firm founded by Charles Daniel in 1934 initially did construction work for the textile industry then later worked for the chemical pharmaceutical metal and power industries.

Flush with cash Fluor bought St. Joe Minerals in 1981. A drop in oil prices in the 1980s killed demand for the big projects that were its bread and butter. As metal prices fell St. Joe didn't help the bottom line either. John Robert Fluor the last of the founding family to head the firm died in 1984.

When David Tappan stepped in as CEO he faced a $573 million loss the first year. The white-haired son of missionaries to China Tappan —known as the Ice Man —dumped subsidiaries and halved the payroll. In 1986 he merged Daniel into Fluor's engineering unit forming Fluor Daniel.

Leslie McCraw succeeded Tappan as CEO in 1991. McCraw saw Fluor as overly conservative and three years later he began setting up offices around the world while decentralizing Fluor's structure and adding new business such as temporary staffing and equipment leasing. Fluor also shed some of its commodity companies including its lead business in 1994. In 1996 Fluor's environmental services unit merged with Groundwater Technology and was spun off as a public company Fluor Daniel GTI.

Fluor saw mixed results from its expansion. Amid fierce competition and pricing pressure Fluor Daniel began cutting its overhead in early 1997 by reorganizing and selling noncore businesses.

Ill with cancer McCraw stepped down in 1998 and Philip Carroll who had overhauled Shell Oil took over as CEO. Carroll reorganized Fluor into four business units and tagged $90 million to rebuild its internal information management systems. Fluor also unloaded its 52% stake in Fluor Daniel GTI to The IT Group for $36 million.

Fluor in 1999 cut 5000 jobs further streamlined operations and focused on growth industries such as biotechnology and telecommunications. The next year the company split its construction and coal mining operations into two separate publicly traded companies one to concentrate on engineering and construction and one on coal mining. Former Fluor subsidiary A. T. Massey Coal was spun off as Massey Energy.

Carroll his restructuring job complete announced in December 2001 that he would retire the following February. That year the company also made plans to dispose of noncore operations of the company's construction equipment and temporary staffing businesses. Alan Boeckmann who had been president and COO succeeded Carroll in 2002.

The next year Fluor acquired Del-Jen a provider of outsourced services to US military bases and to the US Department of Labor. It also picked up five specialty operations and maintenance business groups from Philip Services. And in 2003 the company decided to dissolve its Duke/Fluor Daniel joint venture.

Fluor moved its headquarters from California to Dallas in 2006. The move resulted in the elimination of about 100 jobs. That year the company also entered the health care construction market.

In 2007 the company saw growth in all of its business segments with the exception of its government contracts in part because of the conclusion of projects for FEMA and in Iraq. The following year Fluor formed Fluor Offshore Solutions which is dedicated to global oil and gas clients in the offshore market. The company's construction segment acquired two private engineering companies in Europe —Belgium's UNEC Engineering N.V. and Spain's Europea de Ingenieria y Asesoramiento —increasing Fluor's ability to support its clients from a local level.

In early 2011 Alan Boeckmann retired as CEO after nearly a decade at the helm. He was succeeded by longtime company executive David Seaton who previously led Fluor's energy and chemicals global sales and China operations among others.

EXECUTIVES

Vice President and Controller, Gary G Smalley
Executive Vice President Business Development And Strategy, David (Dave) Dunning
EVP Chief Legal Officer and Corporate Secretary, Carlos M. Hernandez, age 60, $607,084 total compensation
EVP and CFO, Biggs C. Porter, age 62, $812,240 total compensation
Group President Government, Bruce A. Stanski, age 54, $474,834 total compensation
EVP Systems and Supply Chain, Ray F. Barnard, age 57
EVP Project Support Services, Garry W. Flowers, age 64
Chairman and CEO, David T. Seaton, age 54, $1,228,310 total compensation
EVP Human Resources and Administration, Glenn C. Gilkey, age 57
COO, Peter W. B. Oosterveer, $650,798 total compensation
President Energy and Chemicals Americas, Jim Brittain
President Energy and Chemicals Asia Pacific, Ken R. Choudhary
President Energy and Chemicals Europe Africa and Middle East (EAME), Taco de Haan
President Industrial Services, Juan G. Hern˜ndez
President Mining and Metals, Rick Koumouris
President Power, Matthew McSorley
President Infrastructure, Terry Towle
SVP Information Technology and CIO, Robert C. Taylor
EVP Business Development and Strategy, Jose Bustamante
Chief Procurement Officer, Mike Wheeler
Senior Vice President Project Management, Steve Andersen
Vice President Corporate Finance, Kenneth Lockwood
Senior Vice President Govenment Affair, David (Dave) Marventano
Vice President of Operations FLUOR AUSTRALIA, Joe McAneny
Senior Vice President, Jim Heavner
Vice President of Prime Contract Management, Eleanor Spector
Vice President Of Technology, Bonita Hamilton
Vice President Business Development, Matt Johnson
Vice President ??? Government Group, Kevin Leonard
Vice President Project Management, Stewart Cameron
Senior Vice President Proj. Director, Otto Kjos
Vice President Life Sciences Sales, Juan Hernandez
Vice President, Paul Koppel
Vice President Project Director, Pervaiz Chowdhry

Senior Vice President of Power Services Business Line, Rick Graves
Vice President, Joanna Oliva
Vice President North America Operations AMECO, Tracey Cook
Vice President, Malla Reddy
Vice President Operation, Carl Fletcher
Vice President Corporate Communication, Lee Tashjian
Vice President, Bob Armstrong
Hanford Vice President, Pete Knollmeyer
Vice President, Drew Wilson
Vice President Finance, Shields Scott
Vice President, Shawn West
Construction Vice President, David (Dave) Gates
Vice President and Managing Director, Ruth Wismeg
Vice President Sales Nuclear, Brad Porlier
Vice President, Lee Richardson
Vice President Project Management, Denis Menegaz
Vice President Of Power Group, James Mackey
Executive Vice President, John Carlson
Senior Vice President Global Sales and Marketing, Michael (Mel) Pears
Senior Vice President, Mark A Stevens
Board Member, Shay Gray
Senior Vice President and Treasurer, Robyn Volpe
Assistant Treasurer, Enrique Calderon
Auditors: Ernst & Young LLP

LOCATIONS

HQ: Fluor Corp.
6700 Las Colinas Boulevard, Irving, TX 75039
Phone: 469 398-7000
Web: www.fluor.com

2014 Sales

	$ mil.	% of total
United States	7,466	34
Canada	4,133	19
Middle East and Africa	2,799	13
Asia Pacific	2	12
Central and south America	2,494	12
Europe	2,070	10
Total	**21,531**	**100**

PRODUCTS/OPERATIONS

2014 Sales by Segment

	$ mil.	% of total
Oil & Gas	11,368	52
Industrial & Infrastructure	6,061	28
Government	2,511	12
Power	1,004	5
Global Services	585	3
Total	**21,531**	**100**

Selected Services

Construction management
Design
Engineering procurement and construction (EPC)
Operations and maintenance
Program management
Project development and finance
Project management
Staffing

Selected Industries Served

Biotechnology
Chemicals and petrochemicals
Commercial and institutional
Equipment
Gas processing
Government
Manufacturing
Mining
Oil and gas production
Petroleum refining
Pharmaceuticals
Power generation
Telecommunications
Transportation

Selected Subsidiaries

American Equipment Company Inc.
  American Construction Equipment Company Inc.
Fluor Constructors International Inc.
Fluor Enterprises Inc.
  Daniel International Corporation
  Del-Jen Inc.
  Fluor Daniel Mexico S.A.
  ICA-Fluor Daniel S. de R.L. de C.V. (49% Mexico)
Fluor Holding Company LLC
TRS Staffing Solutions Inc.

COMPETITORS

AECOM	Hyundai Engineering
ARCADIS	and Construction
Amec Foster Wheeler	JGC
Balfour Beatty	Jacobs Engineering
Construction	KBR
Bechtel	McDermott
Bilfinger	POSCO
Black & Veatch	Parsons Corporation
Bouygues	Raytheon
CH2M HILL	Technip
Chicago Bridge & Iron	Tetra Tech
Chiyoda Corp.	WorleyParsons Corp.

HISTORICAL FINANCIALS

Company Type: Public

Income Statement

FYE: December 31

	REVENUE ($ mil.)	NET INCOME ($ mil.)	NET PROFIT MARGIN	EMPLOYEES
12/14	21,531	510	2.4%	37,508
12/13	27,351	667	2.4%	38,129
12/12	27,577	456	1.7%	41,193
12/11	23,381	593	2.5%	43,087
12/10	20,849	357	1.7%	39,329
Annual Growth	0.8%	9.3%	—	(1.2%)

2014 Year-End Financials

Debt ratio: 12.45%
Return on equity: 14.88%
Cash ($ mil.): 1,993
Current ratio: 1.73
Long-term debt ($ mil.): 991

No. of shares (mil.): 148
Dividends
  Yield: 1.3%
  Payout: 29.4%
Market value ($ mil.): 9,012

	STOCK PRICE ($) FY Close	P/E High/Low		PER SHARE ($) Earnings	Dividends	Book Value
12/14	60.63	26	17	3.20	0.84	20.93
12/13	80.29	19	13	4.06	0.64	23.29
12/12	58.74	23	17	2.71	0.64	20.58
12/11	50.25	22	13	3.40	0.50	20.09
12/10	66.26	33	21	1.98	0.50	19.82
Annual Growth	(2.2%)	—	—	12.8%	13.8%	1.4%

Flushing Financial Corp.

Flush with cash? You could keep it at Flushing Financial Corp. (FFC). The holding company's Flushing Savings Bank operates more than 15 branches in the Brooklyn Manhattan and Queens boroughs of New York City and in nearby Nassau County. The bank offers services catering to the sizable populations of Asians and other ethnic groups in its market. Deposit products include CDs and checking savings passbook money market and NOW accounts. Mortgages secured by multifamily residential commercial and mixed-use real estate account for most of the company's loan portfolio.

Operations

The company's other offerings include single-family mortgages construction loans business loans and taxi medallion loans.

Financial Performance

The company's revenue decreased in fiscal 2013 compared to the previous fiscal period. It reported revenue of $210.1 million for fiscal 2013 down from $222.8 million in revenue for fiscal 2012.

However despite the dip in annual revenue the company's net income increased in fiscal 2013 compared to the prior year. FFC reported $37.75 million in net income for fiscal 2013 up from $34.3 million in net income for fiscal 2012.

The company's cash flow increased by about $3 million in fiscal 2013 compared to fiscal 2012 levels.

Strategy

The bank has shifted its strategy from operating as a traditional thrift to a more commercial slant focusing on such offerings as business lending and cash management services as well as commercial lending.

Flushing Savings tightened its lending practices after seeing a rise in bad loans during the financial crisis. It has also reduced the number of construction loans and commercial mortgages it originates as they typically carry a higher risk. As a result the bank has been originating and purchasing fewer loans than it did before the downturn started. However higher-yielding multifamily mortgages remain a key strategic focus for the company.

EXECUTIVES

SEVP and Chief of Real Estate Lending Flushing Financial and Flushing Savings Bank, Francis W. (Frank) Korzekwinski, age 52, $418,111 total compensation

President CEO and Director Flushing Financial and Flushing Savings Bank, John R. Buran, age 65, $899,176 total compensation

SEVP COO and Corporate Secretary Flushing Financial and Flushing Savings Bank, Maria A. Grasso, age 50, $481,222 total compensation

EVP Residential Mixed-Use and Small Multi-Family Real Estate Lending, Jeoung (A. J.) Jin, age 48

EVP and CIO, Allen M. Brewer, age 62

EVP and Chief Audit Officer, Robert G. (Bob) Kiraly, age 59

EVP and Director of Government Banking, Patricia Mezeul, age 55

EVP Commercial Real Estate Lending, Ronald Hartmann, age 59

EVP Business Banking Flushing Financial and Flushing Savings Bank, Theresa Kelly, age 53, $285,704 total compensation

EVP and Chief Risk Officer, Gary P. Liotta, age 55

EVP CFO and Treasurer, Susan Cullen

EVP and Director of Distribution and Client Development, Michael Bingold, age 52

EVP and Chief of Staff, John F. Stewart

SVP and Chief Investment Officer, Frank J. Akalski, age 60

Senior Vice President; Controller, Astrid Burrowes

Svp Asian Markets, Paul Ho

Vice President Information Technology Security, Salvatore Mannino

Vice President Management Information Systems, Sal Mannino

Assistant Vice President Education And Devel Manager, Margaret (Peg) Coniglio

Vice President Business Development, Frank Pelliccione

Senior Vice President and Director of Strategic Development and Delivery, Caterina dePasquale

Vice President Business Banking, Steven (Steve) Arzt

Chairman Flushing Financial and Flushing Savings Bank, John E. Roe, age 81

Auditors: BDO USA, LLP

LOCATIONS

HQ: Flushing Financial Corp.
220 RXR Plaza, Uniondale, NY 11556
Phone: 718 961-5400

COMPETITORS

Apple Bank for Savings	First of Long Island
Astoria Financial	HSBC USA
Bank of America	JPMorgan Chase
Bank of New York	Korea Exchange Bank
Mellon	New York Community
Citigroup	Bancorp
Dime Community	
Bancshares	

HISTORICAL FINANCIALS

Company Type: Public

Income Statement

FYE: December 31

	ASSETS ($ mil.)	NET INCOME ($ mil.)	INCOME AS % OF ASSETS	EMPLOYEES
12/14	5,077	44	0.9%	424
12/13	4,721	37	0.8%	378
12/12	4,451	34	0.8%	385
12/11	4,287	35	0.8%	394
12/10	4,324	38	0.9%	379
Annual Growth	4.1%	3.3%	—	2.8%

2014 Year-End Financials

Debt ratio: 0.57%
Return on equity: 9.96%
Cash ($ mil.): 34
Current ratio: —
Long-term debt ($ mil.): —

No. of shares (mil.): 29
Dividends
  Yield: 2.9%
  Payout: 39.7%
Market value ($ mil.): 596

	STOCK PRICE ($) FY Close	P/E High/Low		PER SHARE ($) Earnings	Dividends	Book Value
12/14	20.27	14	12	1.48	0.60	15.52
12/13	20.70	17	12	1.26	0.52	14.36
12/12	15.34	14	11	1.13	0.52	14.39
12/11	12.63	13	9	1.15	0.52	13.49
12/10	14.00	11	8	1.28	0.52	12.48
Annual Growth	9.7%	—	—	3.7%	3.6%	5.6%

FMC Technologies, Inc.

FMC Technologies' name is a vestige of its early years as a food machinery maker but today this company's bread and butter is oil and gas equipment. FMC Technologies offers subsea drilling and production systems for the exploration and production of oil and gas. It also offers similar equipment and services for onshore oil production. In addition the company's energy infrastructure segment makes fluid control measurement marine loading separation material handling blending systems and other equipment. Its offerings are divided into three chief segments: subsea technologies surface technologies and energy infrastructure.

Geographic Reach

FMC Technologies operates 24 facilities in 14 countries. The US accounted for 28% of its 2014 sales; Norway 13%; Angola 10%; Brazil 10%; and Nigeria 8%.

Operations

FMC Technologies is the world's largest manufacturer of "Christmas Trees" an assembly of control valves gauges and chokes that control oil and gas flow in an underwater or subsea oil well. The trees are a crucial component of the company's subsea systems that direct the flow of oil and gas to processing stations on land or on the offshore production platforms.

Its operations are divided into three segments. Subsea technologies (products and systems used underwater for the exploration of crude oil and natural gas) accounted for 66% of total 2014 sale. Surface technologies (27%) makes equipment used on land and offshore exploration while energy infrastructure (7%) makes liquid and gas measurement and transportation equipment and systems.

Sales and Marketing

Subsea Technologies sells its products via its own technical sales organization.In 2014 about 72% of total sales came from outside the US where it has targeted opportunities in West Africa Brazil the North Sea and the Asia-Pacific region because of the offshore drilling potential in these regions.

The company's largest customers include Statoil (14% of 2014 revenues) Royal Dutch Shell BP and Anadarko.

Financial Performance

FMC Technologies has enjoyed five straight years of unprecedented growth. In 2014 its revenues increased by 11%.

Revenue from Subsea Technologies' revenue increased by 11% despite the unfavorable impact of foreign currency translation. Despite the late 2014 decline in crude oil prices the company had solid order activity during 2014 from high demand for subsea systems and services. The year-over-year increase in revenues was attributable to the conversion of backlog and solid order activity in 2014.Surface Technologies' revenues increased $323.9 million in 2014 driven by international growth in the surface wellhead business primarily in the Middle East and Europe regions. Additionally revenues in North America increased as the North American shale markets had higher activity compared to the prior year which drove additional demand for well service pumps and flowline products in the fluid control business and surface wellhead products and services. Energy Infrastructure's revenues declined by $59.8 million in 2014 due to the sale of its Material Handling Products business.

FMC Technologies has recorded an increasing trend in net income over the last five years. This increase was mainly due to higher net sales.In 2014 cash from operating activities grew by 12%.

Strategy

The company develops close working relationships with its customers. The Subsea Technologies business results reflect their ability to build long-term alliances with oil and natural gas companies that are actively engaged in offshore deepwater development and to provide solutions for their needs in a timely and cost-effective manner.

FMC Technologies' long-term strategy is to maintain its subsea market leadership continuing to invest in the technologies required to develop its customers' challenging assets and further expand its capabilities focused on increasing reservoir production over the life of the field. It continues to focus on subsea processing and subsea services as key long-term growth platforms so that it can expand its role as life-of-field partners with customers by lowering their costs and improving their recovery.Surface Technologies has prepared for decreased North American land activity in 2015 which will affect the company's surface wellhead

fluid control and completion services businesses in North America.

The company forms joint ventures and uses acquisitions to add additional revenue streams to its impressive balance sheet.

In 2015 FMC Technologies and Technip received all regulatory approvals to make their 50/50 joint venture Forsys Subsea legal and operational. The joint venture is part of a broader alliance between FMC Technologies and Technip that unites the skills and capabilities of two subsea leaders to redefine the way subsea fields are designed delivered and maintained.

In 2014 FMC Technologies signed an agreement with Anadarko BP ConocoPhillips and Shell to jointly develop a new generation of standardized subsea production equipment and systems designed to meet the challenges of producing oil and gas from deepwater reservoirs with pressures of up to 20000 psi and temperatures of 350°F at the mudline.

That year it also signed a long term frame agreement with Wintershall Norge AS to supply subsea production systems for its developments offshore Norway.In 2013 the company signed a four-year deal with PETROBRAS to provide subsea services for its fields offshore Brazil and renewed a deal with Statoil to provide subsea operations services for its developments on the Norwegian Continental Shelf. That year FMC Technologies also signed a five-year agreement with Tullow Ghana Ltd. to provide subsea services for its developments in the Jubilee field offshore Ghana.

Company Background

In 2012 FMC Technologies formed a joint venture with Edison Chouest Offshore LLC to provide integrated vessel-based subsea services for offshore oil and gas companies globally.

Expanding its portfolio FMC Technologies in 2012 acquired Calgary-based Pure Energy Services Ltd. for approximately $285 million. FMC acquired Pure Energy which provides frac flowback and wireline services for oilfields in North America to complement its Surface Technologies segment. The combination provides an integrated set of well site products and services which should increase value for customers.

Other key 2012 acquisitions include the purchase of Control Systems International a major supplier of control and automation systems for the oil and gas industry for an undisclosed price and the purchase of Schilling Robotics which produces remotely operated vehicles and other control systems for oil and gas subsea production.

FMC Technologies was formed as subsidiary of FMC Corporation in 2000 and went public as an independent unit the next year. It spun off its industrial food equipment and airport systems unit into a separate company called John Bean Technologies in 2008.

FMC Technologies traces its roots to 1884 when inventor John Bean developed a new type of spray pump to combat San Jose scale in California's orchards and formed the Bean Spray Pump Company to commercialize it.

EXECUTIVES

Vice President Energy Infrastructure, Barry Glickman
Chairman and CEO, John T. Gremp, age 63, $974,167 total compensation
SVP Subsea Technologies, Tore H. Halvorsen, age 60, $524,021 total compensation
EVP and CFO, Maryann T. Seaman, age 53, $548,297 total compensation
VP Technology, Bradley D. Beitler, age 61
President and COO, Douglas J. (Doug) Pferdehirt, age 51, $737,179 total compensation

Vice President Surface Technologies, Johan Pfeiffer
Vice President Administration, Mark Scott
National Account Manager, Andrew Kadavy
Vice President Internal AudIT, Matthew (Matt) Acosta
Vice President Business Development, Sanjay Bhatia
National Accounts Manager, Lynn Grayson
Vice President Information Technology, Robert (Bob) Potter
Executive Vice President, William (Bill) Schumann
Senior Vice President General Counsel Secretary, Jeffrey (Jeff) Carr
Auditors: KPMG LLP

LOCATIONS

HQ: FMC Technologies, Inc.
5875 N. Sam Houston Parkway West, Houston, TX 77086
Phone: 281 591-4000
Web: www.fmctechnologies.com

2014 Sales

	$ mil.	% of total
US	2,245	28
Norway	1,023	13
Brazil	831	10
Nigeria	627	8
Angola	406	6
Other countries	2,808	35
Total	**7,942**	**100**

PRODUCTS/OPERATIONS

2014 Sales

	$ mil.	% of total
Subsea technologies	5,266	66
Surface technologies	2,130	27
Energy infrastructure	557	7
Adjustments	(11.9)	-
Total	**7,942**	**100**

COMPETITORS

Aker Solutions	John Wood Group
Baker Hughes	McDermott
Cameron International	National Oilwell Varco
Dril-Quip	Weatherford
GE Oil	International

HISTORICAL FINANCIALS

Company Type: Public

Income Statement

FYE: December 31

	REVENUE ($ mil.)	NET INCOME ($ mil.)	NET PROFIT MARGIN	EMPLOYEES
12/14	7,942	699	8.8%	20,300
12/13	7,126	501	7.0%	19,300
12/12	6,151	430	7.0%	18,400
12/11	5,099	399	7.8%	14,200
12/10	4,125	375	9.1%	11,500
Annual Growth	17.8%	16.8%	—	15.3%

2014 Year-End Financials

Debt ratio: 18.24%	No. of shares (mil.): 231
Return on equity: 29.32%	Dividends
Cash ($ mil.): 638	Yield: —
Current ratio: 1.59	Payout: —
Long-term debt ($ mil.): 1,297	Market value ($ mil.): 10,845

	STOCK PRICE ($) FY Close	P/E High/Low		PER SHARE ($) Earnings	Dividends	Book Value
12/14	46.84	21	14	2.95	0.00	10.61
12/13	52.21	28	20	2.10	0.00	9.83
12/12	42.83	30	21	1.78	0.00	7.75
12/11	52.23	58	22	1.64	0.00	5.99
12/10	88.91	58	31	1.53	0.00	5.47
Annual Growth	(14.8%)	—	—	17.8%	—	18.0%

Foot Locker, Inc.

Foot Locker leads the pack in the race to capture the biggest share of the global athletic footwear market. The company is a leading retailer of athletic shoes and apparel with more than 3400 specialty stores mostly in US malls but also in 20-plus countries in North America and Europe as well as in Australia and New Zealand. Its 1830-store namesake Foot Locker chain is the #1 seller of name-brand (NIKE) athletic footwear in the US. The company also operates stores under the Lady Foot Locker Kids Foot Locker Footaction Champs Sports and CCS banners. Beyond its bricks-and-mortar business Foot Locker markets sports gear through its direct-to-customer unit which consists of catalog retailer Eastbay and Footlocker.com.

HISTORY

Company BackgroundWith the idea of selling merchandise priced at no more than five cents Frank Woolworth opened the Great Five Cent Store in Utica New York in 1879; it failed. That year he moved to Lancaster Pennsylvania and created the first five-and-dime. Woolworth moved his headquarters to New York City (1886) and spent the rest of the century acquiring other dime-store chains. He later expanded to Canada (1897) England (1909) France (1922) and Germany (1927).

The 120-store chain with $10 million in sales incorporated as F.W. Woolworth & Company in 1905 with Woolworth as president. In 1912 the company merged with five rival chains and went public with 596 stores making $52 million in sales the first year. The next year paying $13.5 million in cash Woolworth finished construction of the Woolworth Building then the world's tallest building (792 feet). When he died in 1919 the chain had 1081 stores with sales of $119 million.

Woolworth became more competitive after WWII by advertising establishing revolving credit and self-service moving stores to suburbs and expanding merchandise selections. In 1962 it opened Woolco a US and Canadian discount chain.

From the 1960s through the 1980s the company grew by acquiring and expanding in the US and abroad. It picked up Kinney (shoes 1963) Richman Brothers (men's clothing 1969) Holtzman's Little Folk Shop (children's clothing 1983) Champs Sports (sporting goods 1987) and Mathers (shoes Australia 1988).

The company introduced Foot Locker the athletic shoe chain in 1974 later developing Lady Foot Locker (1982) and Kids Foot Locker (1987). In 1993 Woolworth launched an ambitious restructuring plan focusing on specialty stores (mostly apparel and shoes). It also closed 400 US stores and sold 122 Canadian Woolco stores to Wal-Mart that year. Former Macy's president Roger Farah became CEO in 1994. Farah eliminated 16 divisions and dozens of executives.

A year later the firm sold its Kids Mart/Little Folks children's wear chain. In 1996 Woolworth began a major remodeling program that included removing its venerable lunch counters. (Another alleged renovation at the Woolworth chain –the firing of older workers who were replaced by teenagers –led to an Equal Employment Opportunity Commission lawsuit against the company in 1999.) The changes failed and the next year the company closed its US Woolworth stores and bought athletic-products catalog company Eastbay.

In 1998 Woolworth changed its name to Venator Group and sold the Woolworth Building a national landmark (headquarters remained in the building). The company then shed itself of more than 1400 stores including Kinney shoes and Footquarters (both closed).

Internet site eVenator was launched in 1999 to sell Eastbay Champs and Foot Locker merchandise. Venator came out the champ in a proxy fight against investment group Greenway Partners in July 1999. Shortly thereafter Farah was replaced as CEO (he remained chairman) by president Dale Hilpert.

In 2000 Venator slashed 7% of its workforce in the US and Canada (a small part of the planned 30% cut) and closed 465 stores. COO Matt Serra became president and Hilpert became chairman when Farah resigned later that year.

In March 2001 Hilpert resigned replaced by Carter Bacot as chairman and Serra added CEO to his title. Venator later sold its Canadian Northern Group unit to investment firm York Management Services and closed its Northern Reflections stores in the US. Venator changed its name to Foot Locker in November. It also sold gift retailer San Francisco Music Box Co. and its hospitality division's fast-food franchises before the end of the year.

In early 2004 chairman Bacot become lead director and president and CEO Serra added chairman to his title.

In 2004 Foot Locker capitalizing on the Chapter 11 filing of Footstar Inc. purchased from the company 350 of its Footaction stores. The company also acquired 11 stores in Ireland from Champion Sports Group later in the same year.

The company's short-lived family footwear retail concept –called Footquarters –launched in early 2007 but was quickly discontinued due to poor performance. The locations were converted to Foot Lockers and Champs Sports outlet stores. Also in early 2007 Foot Locker made an unsolicited $1.2 billion bid for rival Genesco that was rejected by Genesco's board. Foot Locker closed about 275 mostly underperforming stores in 2007.

In 2008 the company reduced its store count by about 145 locations across its five chains in a bid to boost profitability by focusing on its most profitable locations and improving operations. In November Foot Locker acquired the CCS brand from dELiA*s for about $103 million. The CCS brand includes skateboarding and snowboarding equipment apparel and footwear targeting primarily teenage boys.

J.C. Penney executive Kenneth Hicks was recruited to succeed Serra as president and CEO in August 2009. Serra who had held the CEO title since 2001 retained the chairman's title until his retirement in January 2010. At that time Hicks became chairman.

In July 2013 Foot Locker acquired Germany's Runners Point Group a specialty athletic store and online retailer based in Recklinghausen.

EXECUTIVES

EVP and CFO, Lauren B. Peters, age 53, $561,250 total compensation
Vice President Real Estate, Jack Lehner
SVP Real Estate, Jeffrey L. Berk, age 59, $488,524 total compensation
EVP Operations Support, Robert W. McHugh, age 56, $668,500 total compensation
President and CEO, Richard A. (Dick) Johnson, age 57, $931,250 total compensation
President and CEO Footlocker.com/Eastbay, Dowe S. Tillema
President and CEO Champs Sports, Byron W. Milburn
President and CEO Foot Locker Europe, Lewis P. Kimble
VP and General Manager Lady Foot Locker/ SIX:02, Natalie M. Ellis

President and CEO Foot Locker North America, Stephen D. Jacobs
Managing Director Foot Locker Asia/Pacific, Phillip G. Laing
Managing Director Foot Locker Canada, Nicholas Jones
SVP and Chief Human Resources Officer, Paulette R. Alviti, age 44, $461,250 total compensation
SVP and CIO, Pawan Verma
VP and General Manager Runners Point Group, Bart de Wilde
VP and General Manager Footaction, Kenneth W. Side
Vice President, Don Yost
Vice President Information Technology, Steven Dinndorf
Vice President Finance Lady Foot Locker, Richard (Dick) Aneser
Vice President Merchandise, Rusty Dewitt
Vice President, Tom McNiff
Regional Vice President, John (Jack) Wompey
Vice President G.m., Larry Remmington
Vice President Of Public Relations, Lori Kober
Vice President Logistics, Joseph Bongiorno
Experience Champs Sports Vice President Marketing, Dave Lokes
Vice President, Mike Owens
Regional Vice President, Christina Sarrat
Vice President Integrated Brand Marketing, Francine Feder
Vice President Supply Chain, Saadi Majzoub
Vice President Public Relations, Lori Casavina
Vice President Merchandise Logistics, Patricia Kowalski
Vice President Finance and Accounting Logistics, Patrick (Paddy) Meister
Vice President Of Benefits, Julie Blume
Vice President Risk Management, Bernard Steenman
Senior Vice President Of Sales, Arnie Knipp
Senior Vice President Of Sales, Vicki Schwallenberg
Regional Vice President, Martin Lucas
Senior Vice President Leasing, John Pawley
Vice President, George Davitt
Vice President Accounting, Pete Gorman
Vice President Logistics, John Matta
Vice President Global Sourcing, Jenny Sim
Vice President Leasing, Tj Jensen
Senior Vice President Real Estate, Jeff Berke
Vice President Of Marketing, Cunningham Stacy
Vice President, Rob Rainer
Vice President Brand Marketing Lady Foot Locker Six02, Kirta Carroll
Senior Vice President Real Estate, Jeff Berk
Vice President Chief Financial Officer Foot Locker Canada, Phil Reiprich
Vice President of Leasing, Gregg Mathieu
Treasurer, John (Jack) Maurer
Chairman, Nicholas (Nick) DiPaolo, age 73
Treasurer, Stacy Cunningham
Board Member, Matthew (Matt) Serra
Auditors: KPMG LLP

LOCATIONS

HQ: Foot Locker, Inc.
  112 West 34th Street, New York, NY 10120
Phone: 212 720-3700
Web: www.footlocker-inc.com

2014 Sales

	$ mil.	% of total
US	4,567	70
International	1,938	30
Total	**6,505**	**100**

2015 Sales

	$ mil.	% of total
US	4,976	70
International	2,175	30
Total	**7,151**	**100**

PRODUCTS/OPERATIONS

2015 Stores

	No.
Foot Locker US	1,015
Foot Locker Europe	603
Foot Locker Canada	126
Foot Locker Asia Pacific	91
Lady Foot Locker	213
Kids Foot Locker	357
Footaction	272
Champs Sports	547
Runners Point Group	116
Sidestep	83
Total	**3,423**

2015 Sales

	$ mil.	% of total
Athletic Stores	6,286	88
Direct-to-Customers	865	12
Total	**7,151**	**100**

COMPETITORS

Academy Sports	Modell's
Caleres	Pacific Sunwear
DSW	Quiksilver
Dick's Sporting Goods	Sears
Dillard's	Shoe Carnival
FGL Sports	Sports Authority
Finish Line	TJX Companies
Genesco	Target Corporation
Hibbett Sports	The Gap
J. C. Penney	Wal-Mart
Kmart	Zappos.com
L.L. Bean	shoebuy.com
Macy's	

HISTORICAL FINANCIALS

Company Type: Public

Income Statement

FYE: January 31

	REVENUE ($ mil.)	NET INCOME ($ mil.)	NET PROFIT MARGIN	EMPLOYEES
01/15*	7,151	520	7.3%	44,568
02/14	6,505	429	6.6%	43,518
02/13	6,182	397	6.4%	40,639
01/12	5,623	278	4.9%	39,077
01/11	5,049	169	3.3%	38,007
Annual Growth	**9.1%**	**32.4%**	**—**	**4.1%**

*Fiscal year change

2015 Year-End Financials

Debt ratio: 3.75%	No. of shares (mil.): 140
Return on equity: 20.89%	Dividends
Cash ($ mil.): 967	Yield: 0.0%
Current ratio: 3.53	Payout: 24.7%
Long-term debt ($ mil.): 132	Market value ($ mil.): 7,497

	STOCK PRICE ($) FY Close	P/E High/Low		Earnings	Dividends	Book Value
01/15*	53.22	16	10	3.56	0.88	17.72
02/14	38.60	14	11	2.85	0.80	17.16
02/13	34.56	14	10	2.58	0.72	15.84
01/12	26.44	15	9	1.80	0.66	13.92
01/11	17.77	18	10	1.07	0.60	13.10
Annual Growth	**31.6%**			**35.1%**	**10.0%**	**7.9%**

*Fiscal year change

Ford Motor Co. (DE)

Ford Motor began a manufacturing revolution with mass production assembly lines in the early 20th century but today it is one of the world's largest automakers. The carmaker's staple of brands and models includes the Ford Mustang the F-Series pickup Focus Lincoln Fiesta and Taurus. In addition finance unit Ford Motor Credit is one of the US's leading auto finance companies and accounted for 6% of Ford's sales in 2014. Ford owns a small stake in Mazda and operates about 65 plants worldwide. The company generated 65% of its sales from North America in 2014.

Geographic Reach

Ford global reach is vast and it generates 57% of its total sales from the US. Other sizable markets include Canada (7% of sales) the UK (8%) and Germany (5%).

Operations

Ford manages its global operations through joint ventures. It has partnered with companies in China Germany Taiwan Turkey and Vietnam among others. Ford Otosan Ford's joint venture with Turkey-based Koç Holding supplies the Ford Transit Connect and distributes Ford cars in Turkey.

Sales and Marketing

Ford's vehicles parts and accessories are marketed through retail dealers in North America and through distributors and dealers outside of North America. Most of the dealerships are independently owned. In 2014 Ford had a network of more than 11980 dealerships worldwide. Its advertising expenses were $4.3 million in 2014 $4.4 million in 2013 and $4 million in 2012.

Financial Performance

Ford's 2014 revenues decreased by 2% driven by a 3% decline in its automotive sales (a collective 6% drop from North America); this decline offset a 10% surge in financial services sales during 2014.

The company's net income in 2014 also plummeted 55% from $7.2 billion in 2013 to $3.2 billion in 2014 primarily due to an additional $1.2 billion it paid in income taxes. Ford's operating cash flow in 2014 increased to $14.5 billion compared to 2013 primarily due to increases in accounts payable.

Strategy

Reflecting a growing global auto market in 2014 Ford embarked on its most aggressive product launch schedule in its history with the launch of 24 all-new or significantly refreshed vehicles around the world (Ford will continue with 15 new global product launches in 2015).

In a bold design move in 2014 it launched an aluminum body version of its best-selling Ford-150 model. The new lighter-weight 2015 F150s offer increased gas mileage. Ford has worked to improve vehicle fuel efficiency in other areas launching hybrid models such as the 2013 Fusion available with hybrid and plug-in hybrid powertrains. The company is also promising upgraded engines and powertrain transmissions such as the 2.0 liter EcoBoost.

Like many other car makers the company is also looking to emerging economies for growth particularly Brazil Russia India and China where cars sales are forecast to grow more rapidly than in mature markets. Ford is building new plants in India Thailand and especially China to meet more demand in the region. In 2013 Ford entered the South Asia market of Myanmar which it views as a key strategic location between India and China next to a shared border with Thailand.In 2013 Ford accelerated its growth plan in Russia with a

$274 million New Engine Plant in Elabuga Tatarstan (the first passenger car engine plant in the region) and Launch of Ford EcoSport SUV. In the same year it also increased its North American capacity by 200000 Units reduced its summer shutdown and invested $150 million in its Buffalo Stamping Plant (adding some 350 new jobs at the facility to support future product growth).

Mergers and Acquisitions

To accelerate innovation in 2013 Ford acquired Michigan-based software development startup Livio enabling both companies to work toward developing an industry standard for smartphone-to-vehicle communications.

HISTORY

Henry Ford started the Ford Motor Company in 1903 in Dearborn Michigan. In 1908 Ford introduced the Model T produced on a moving assembly line that revolutionized both carmaking and manufacturing. By 1920 some 60% of all vehicles on the road were Fords.

After Ford omitted its usual dividend in 1916 stockholders sued. Ford responded by buying back all of its outstanding shares in 1919 and didn't allow outside ownership again until 1956.

Ford bought Lincoln Motor Company in 1922 and discontinued the Model T in 1927. Its replacement the Model A came in 1932. With Henry Ford's health failing his son Edsel became president that year. Despite the debut of the Mercury (1938) market share slipped behind General Motors and Chrysler. After Edsel's death in 1943 his son Henry II took over and decentralized Ford following the GM model. Henry Ford died in 1947 at the age of 83. In 1950 the carmaker recaptured second place. Ford rolled out the infamous Edsel line in 1958 and launched the Mustang in 1964.

Ford acquired Hertz in 1994 and two years later bought #3 rental agency Budget Rent a Car (sold 1997). Also in 1996 it sold a 19% stake in finance unit Associates First Capital in an IPO and increased its stake in Mazda to one-third. The next year Ford sold its heavy-duty truck unit to Daimler's Freightliner subsidiary (since renamed Daimler Trucks North America) for about $200 million and spun off 19% of Hertz in an IPO. Also in 1997 it launched automotive systems supplier Visteon (formerly Ford Automotive Products Operations) at the Frankfurt Motor Show.

Decades later in order to focus on its struggling automotive operations Ford sold its Hertz car rental business in 2005 to a private equity group made up of Clayton Dubilier & Rice The Carlyle Group and Merrill Lynch Global Private Equity for $5.6 billion and the assumption of nearly $10 billion of Hertz debt.

In mid-2009 the US Department of Energy approved $5.9 billion in low-interest loans to Ford for converting its US plants to making cleaner more efficient engines transmissions and vehicles. As a result Ford reported it would spend $550 million to convert its Michigan Assembly Plant where Ford Expedition and Lincoln Navigator SUVs were produced into a modern facility for making its next-generation Focus small car. The new Focus rolled off the assembly line in 2010 with an all-electric version of the Focus to follow in 2011. Ford consolidated operations from its Wayne Assembly Plant as part of the project and worked with the UAW on more flexible work rules for the Michigan Assembly Plant. In addition Ford converted its Cuautitlan Assembly Plant in Mexico from SUV production to assembly of small cars commencing in 2011. The Mexican plant began building the new Fiesta subcompact in 2010.

With the automotive industry reeling from the Great Recession companies made decisions to streamline their operations for survival. In mid-

2010 Ford sold all of Volvo Car Corporation to Geely Automotive a subsidiary of China-based Zhejiang Geely Holding Group. Volvo's headquarters and manufacturing operations remain in Sweden and Belgium with Stefan Jacoby (former CEO of Volkswagen Group of America) serving as president and CEO of Volvo Cars. At the onset of 2011 Ford's Mercury model production was discontinued.

EXECUTIVES

Group Vice President Human Resources and Corporate Services, Felicia J Fields
EVP and CFO, Robert L. (Bob) Shanks, age 62, $798,750 total compensation
President CEO and Director, Mark Fields, age 55, $1,662,500 total compensation
Group VP and Chairman and CEO Ford Motor Credit Company, Bernard B. Silverstone, age 60
EVP Global Marketing Sales and Service, Stephen T. Odell, age 60
EVP and President Europe Middle East and Africa, James D. (Jim) Farley, age 53, $868,750 total compensation
EVP; President Americas, Joseph R. (Joe) Hinrichs, age 49, $936,250 total compensation
Group VP and President Asia Pacific, Dave Schoch, age 63
President Changan Ford Mazda Automobile (CFMA), Marin Burela
VP and President Ford South America, Steven Armstrong
VP and President Lincoln, A. Kumar Galhotra
Executive Director Material Planning & Logistics, Frederiek Toney, age 59
EVP Product Development and CTO, Raj Nair, age 50
Chairman and CEO Ford Motor China, John Lawler
VP Research and Development and CTO, Kenneth (Ken) Washington
VP and CIO, Marcy Klevorn, age 56
VP Sales Ford Australia/New Zealand, Graeme Whickman
Vice President Of Finance, Jane Carnarvon
Vice President Manufacturing, Gary Johnson
RIC PTE NAVP Portfolio Manager Vehicle Solutions, Mark Anders
Vice President Sales and Marketing, Gabriella Bruno
Vice President, Frank Froio
Vice President, Anurag Mehrotra
Manager Technical Service Information Devp, John (Jack) Norton
Vice President Marketing, Patty Riggio
Vice President Human Resources, Rex Johnson
Vice President, Linda Garrison
Vice President of Construction Excellence Vice President of Construction Excellence, Jim Swoish
Senior Vice President, Greg Bell
Vice President Of Retail Operations, Randy Houston
Vice President Of Aila's Philadelphia Chapter, Jason Medley
Vice President Branches and Divisions, Susan (Sue) Barnosky
Global Vice President Cycle Plan Manager At Ford Motor Company, David (Dave) Schaefer
Division Vice President, Jeffrey Gorrall
Senior Vice President, Jean Kwapis
Vp Us Sales & Marketing, Mark Laneve
Vice President Of Global Communications, Brenda Hines
Vice President, Ed Diegel
Executive Vice President, Marco Rios
Vice President, Craig Kuberski
National Account Manager, Catherine (Cathy) Morrissey
Vice President Supply Chain Management, Michael Goodin

Vice President Operations and Quality Systems, Raymundo Balderrama
National Account Manager, Rory Cashman
Vice President, Scott Collins
Vice President Global Quality Assurance, Ronald Domas
Vice President and Controller, Michael (Mel) Seneski
Vice President Of Purchasing, Sam Casabene
Vice President Of Marketing, David Herman
Vice President of Communications, Chris Pitchford
Vice President Sales Effectiveness And Global Alignment, Duane Martin
Vice President General Counsel And Secretary, Shawn Murphy
Vpe Foward Model Manager, Lyn Wagner-Ditzhazy
National Account Manager, Steve Shier
Vice President, Neil Schloss
National Account Manager, Vic Kachel
Vice President Sales And Marketing, Robert (Bob) Gerrard
Vice President Purchasing, Alan Draper
National Accounts Manager, Chris Trewin
Vice President Supply Chain, Estella Slone
Vice President Strategic Development, Stacey Coopes
Senior Vice President Chief Customer Officer, Jim Bacon
Group Philippines Assistant Vice President, Anika Salceda-Wycoco
Sta Engineer FVP, Alex Milshteyn
Executive Vice President and President Europe Middle East and Africa, Jim Farley
Senior Vice President, Keith Sprain
Executive Vice Chairman, William C. (Bill) Ford, age 57
Financial Sec'y Treasurer, Mike Susalla
Assistant Treasurer, Marion Harris
Board Member, Ana Querol
Board Member, Abel Ortiz
Financial Strategy Treasurers Office, Mark Turner
Board Member, Elvis Harrell
Board Member, Luis Canseco
Portfolio Management Department Treasurers Office, Devra Thuss
Board Member, Mike Learman
Vice Chairman, David Waterman
Board Member, S Cambra
Auditors: PricewaterhouseCoopers LLP

LOCATIONS

HQ: Ford Motor Co. (DE)
One American Road, Dearborn, MI 48126
Phone: 313 322-3000
Web: www.corporate.ford.com

2014 Sales

	$ mil.	% of total
North America		
US	82,665	57
United Kingdom	11,742	8
Canada	9,409	7
Germany	7,487	5
Mexico	1,757	1
All Others	31,017	22
Total	**144,077**	**100**

PRODUCTS/OPERATIONS

Selected Products

Cars
  Fiesta
  Focus
  Fusion
  Mustang
  Taurus
Crossovers
  Edge
  Flex
Commercial trucks
  Chassis Cab
  E-Series Cutaway
  E-Series Van
  E-Series Wagon

F-650
F-750
Stripped Chassis
Super Duty Pickup
Transit Connect
Electric v
Transit Connect EV
Hybrids
  Escape Hybrid
  Fusion Hybrid
Sport util
  Escape
  Expedition
  Explorer
Trucks
  E-Series Wagon
  F-150
  Ranger
  Super Duty
  Transit Connect

Selected Auto Brands

Ford
Lincoln
2014 Sales

	$ mil.	% of total	
Automotive	135782	94	
Financial services	8295	6	
Total	144077	100	

COMPETITORS

Adam Opel	Kia Motors
AutoNation	Mazda
BMW	Mitsubishi Motors
Bank of America	Navistar International
Citigroup	Nissan
Daimler	Peugeot
FCA US	Renault
Fiat Chrysler	Suzuki Motor
General Motors	Tata Motors
Honda	Toyota
Hyundai Motor	Vauxhall
Isuzu	Volkswagen
JPMorgan Chase	Volvo

HISTORICAL FINANCIALS

Company Type: Public

Income Statement

FYE: December 31

	REVENUE ($ mil.)	NET INCOME ($ mil.)	NET PROFIT MARGIN	EMPLOYEES
12/15	149,558	7,373	4.9%	199,000
12/14	144,077	3,187	2.2%	187,000
12/13	146,917	7,155	4.9%	181,000
12/12	144,252	5,665	4.2%	171,000
12/11	136,264	20,213	14.8%	164,000
Annual Growth	2.4%	(22.3%)	—	5.0%

2015 Year-End Financials

Debt ratio: 59.07%—
Return on equity: 27.59%
Cash ($ mil.): 14,272
Current ratio: 0.56
Long-term debt ($ mil.): 89,856

Dividends
  Yield: 4.2%
  Payout: 50.0%
Market value ($ mil.): —

	STOCK PRICE ($) FY Close	P/E High/Low		PER SHARE ($) Earnings	Dividends	Book Value
12/15	14.09	9	7	1.84	0.60	7.22
12/14	15.50	22	17	0.80	0.50	6.27
12/13	15.43	10	7	1.76	0.40	6.69
12/12	12.95	9	6	1.42	0.20	4.07
12/11	10.76	4	2	4.94	0.05	3.83
Annual Growth	7.0%	—	—	(21.9%)	86.1%	17.1%

Fortress Investment Group LLC

Fortress Investment Group protects its investors' money. The global investment firm manages private equity and hedge funds for institutional investors wealthy individuals and on its own behalf. Its private equity arm buys long-term controlling stakes in undervalued or distressed companies and credit assets; it also manages real estate investors Newcastle Investment and Eurocastle Investment. The hedge fund arm invests in liquid markets. Fortress offers traditional asset management through Logan Circle Partners. Fortress earns fees performance-based incentive revenues and investment income on its own investments. The firm has more than $67 billion in assets under management.

OperationsFortress operates its management and investment business through six main segments differentiated by strategy including: Private Equity Funds Permanent Capital Vehicles Liquid Hedge Funds Credit Hedge Funds Credit Private Equity Funds and Logan Circle.The company generated nearly 35% of its total revenue from management fees (tied to assets under management) in 2014 while incentive income (based on alternative investment performance) and expense reimbursements made up another roughly 20% and 10% respectively. Fortress made 35% of its total revenue from its non-managed investments including nearly 20% from Advertising company investments 10% from Circulation companies and the small remainder of revenues from a mix of commercial printing and rental revenue.Geographic ReachThe investment firm has headquarters in New York City and roughly 15 offices in the US Europe and Asia. Specifically its offices are in San Francisco Philadelphia London Tokyo Dallas Frankfurt Portland Los Angeles Plano Tampa Summit Sydney New Canaan Atlanta Luxembourg City Singapore Rome Lake Oswego Shanghai Dubai Hong Kong and Tel Aviv.Sales and MarketingFortress serves more than 1700 institutional clients and private investors worldwide. Financial PerformanceFortress Investment Group's revenues and profits have been on the uptrend in recent years mostly as its assets under management have risen with the appreciating financial markets. The firm's revenue jumped by more than 40% to $1.81 billion in 2014 thanks to a $626.2 million revenue increase from the consolidation of its New Media and New Senior investments held in its NewCastle Investment real estate investor division. Beyond this non-recurring transaction overall revenue declined with the company's incentive income revenue falling by nearly $100 million for the year due to lower returns and performance from its hedge funds credit hedge funds and liquid hedge fund managed accounts. The firm's management fee income however rose by nearly $14 million (around 2%) as assets under management grew during the year.Fortress' net income plummeted by 50% to $99.96 million mostly because of a $621.3 million expense related to its consolidation of its New Media and New Senior holdings though investment manager expenses also swelled by $95 million due to higher compensation and benefits and increased general administrative and other expenses. Fortress' operating cash also dove by 45% to $239.87 million mostly due to a decline in cash earnings.Strategy

Fortress reiterated in 2015 that its main strategy is to grow its fee-paying assets under management with an eye toward generating strong risk-adjusted returns from its funds over the long haul. To boost its assets under management the firm plans to entice new investors to invest in its funds by regularly introducing new investment products. To this end during 2014 Fortress raised $6.4 billion in new third-party capital and launched four new funds. That year the company also attracted some $5.4 billion in net client inflows in its traditional asset management business. On the real estate management side Fortress eyes new investments in a variety of sectors including in the hospitality transportation senior living and financial services sectors. In 2015 for example the firm's Japan Opportunity Fund which specializes in real estate investments in the region agreed to purchase Rihga Royal Hotel Kyoto one of Japan's most prestigious hotels with plans to enhance the facilities and update its rooms with more modern features while keeping its classic look intact. In late 2013 Fortress acquired more than 50 senior-housing properties from Holiday Acquisition Holdings for more than $1 billion.

EXECUTIVES

Managing Director Fortress Investment Group LLC (UK), Jonathan Ashley, age 49
Managing Director Shanghai, Lilly H. Donohue
Chief Executive Officer Co-Founder Principal and Director, Randal A. Nardone, age 60, $200,000 total compensation
Principal and Director; Co-Chief Investment Officer of the Fortress Macro Fund and the Drawbridge Global Macro Fund, Michael E. Novogratz, age 51, $200,000 total compensation
President Liquid Markets; Senior Managing Director Strategy, Stuart H. (Stu) Bohart, age 48
Managing Director Private Equity Group, Joseph P. Adams, age 57
CFO, Daniel N. Bass, age 49, $200,000 total compensation
Managing Director Chief Executive Officer and Chief Investment Officer Fortress Partners Funds Fortress Investment Group LLC, Alexander M. Cook
Managing Director Co-Chief Investment Officer of the Credit Funds at Fortress Investment Group LLC, Constantine M. (Dean) Dakolias
Managing Director Private Equity and Chief Operating Officer Permanent Capital Business Group, Andrew P. Dempsey
Managing Director President and Chief Operating Officer Credit Funds at Fortress Investment Group LLC, Marc K. Furstein
Managing Director Capital Formation Group, A. Todd Ladda
Managing Director San Francisco, Andrew A. McKnight
Managing Director Tokyo Chief Investment Officer Fortress Real Estate (Asia) GK, Thomas W. Pulley
Managing Director Deputy President and Chief Risk Officer Fortress Liquid Markets, Sherif Sweillam
Managing Director Global Chief Operating Officer Liquid Markets Hedge Fund, Louis D. Thorne
Managing Director Credit Funds, Anthony B. Tufariello
Vice President, Robyn Gewanter
Vice President, Rory Vandamme
Vice President, Scott Silvers
Vice President, Suvin Malik
Vice President, Peter Stone
Vice President Controller, Michael (Mel) Sabatell
Vice President, Josh Bonacci
Vice President Vice President, Thomas (Thom) Garbaccio
Vice President, David (Dave) Scheible
Vice President Senior Accountant, Maritza Munoz
Vice President, Adam Bodenstein

Vice President Of Tax Compliance Credit Funds, Johnery Laurimore
Vice President, Christopher Frey
Vice President, Solange Tsutsui
Senior Vice President Controller, Kristina Samuelsen
Vice President, Michael Richman
Vice President Credit Funds, Roman Mendoza
Vice President, Madhu Kutty
Vice President, Michael Mucciolo
Senior Vice President, Andrew Miller
Vice President, Cristina Gonzalez
Senior Vice President, Scott Schwarmann
Vice President, Carrie Sin
Vice President, Victoria Hartman
Vice President, Peter Kobliska
Vice President, Leigh Maranuk
Vice President, Jason Okeefe
Vice President Accounts Payable, Karen Kotik
Vice President, Yoni Shtein
Vice President, Brittain Rogers
Vice President Private Equity Global Sourcing, Jeanmarie Rall
Vice President, Neil Carter
Vice President Vice President, Brannen McElmurray
Senior Vice President Counsel, Alex Gillette
Vice President, Jennifer Story
Vice President, Ed Montolio
Vice President Tax, Brian McGrath
Vice President, Steven Brogden
Vice President, Steven Willemin
Vice President, John Kwaak
Vice President, Aaron Slan
Vice President Controller, Jane Li
Vice President, Stacey Griffin
Vice President, Patrick Diaz
Vice President, Jared Kanefsky
Vice President, Marc Sottile
Vice President, Ryan Muller
Vice President, Mike Wou
Vice President, Phat Loc
Vice President Accounting, Tom Kelly
Vice President, Micah Kaplan
Vice President Capital Formations Group Investor Relations, Diana Bellizzi
Vice President, Justin Bogan
Vice President Trading Counsel, David (Dave) Sims
Vice President, Walker Kidd
Vice President, Scott Werthamer
Senior Vice President Operations Director, Harriett Gordon
Vice President, Robert (Bob) China
Senior Vice President Head of Expense Management and Operations, Scott Min
Vice President, Sergey Dyakin
Vice President, Joseph Pontrello
Vice President Compensation And Benefits Counsel, Wonda Quinn
Vice President, Peter Leibman
Vice President Software Engineer, Jay Cheng
SPQREA Vice President, Dana D'Ascoli
Vice President, Lance Sherer
Vice President, Nils Wilson
Vice President, Joseph Hayek
Vice President Sales And Marketing, Judy Godinho
Vice President Senior Business Analyst, Todd Mangel
Vice President, Marc Blanchette
Vice President, Misty Shores
Vice President Senior Financial Analyst, Brian Nicholson
Vice President, Ana Fratila
Vice President, Patrick Schulz
Vice President, David Fasano
Vice President. Trader Equity Markets, Jeff Jackson
Vice President Client Service Manager, Michael (Mel) Green
Vice President Fund Counsel, Christine Putek
Vice President Operations Analyst, Chris D Magnus

Vice President Trader And Research Analyst,
Kevin Hendrickson
Vice President Compensation Controller, Paul
Petrsoric
Vice President, Andrew Armstrong
Vice President, Timothy Bailey
Vice President Trader And Research Analyst,
Stephen (Steve) Kelly
Vice President, Rhonda Ramparas
Vice President Vice President, Susan Givens
Senior Vice President, Jim Daly
Senior Vice President Senior Tax, Fran Benoit
Vice President Vice President, Greg Kleczek
Vice President Vice President, Peter (Pete) SU
Vice President, David Schneider
Vice President, Neil Thompson
Vice President, Anthony Barwacz
Vice President Controller, Miki Ortiz
Vice President Senior Portfolio Manager, Nikolai
Walter
Vice President Senior Portfolio Manager, Torsten
Baeppler
Vice President Controller, Junko Nakamura
Vice President, Andrey Tsetlin
Vice President, Andrew (Andy) Webber
Vice President Assistant Controller, Eileen Ying
Shen
Principal and Co-Chairman, Wesley R. (Wes) Edens,
age 53
Principal and Co-Chairman, Peter L. Briger, age 52
Secretary, Marisol Sanchez
Auditors: Ernst & Young LLP

LOCATIONS

HQ: Fortress Investment Group LLC
1345 Avenue of the Americas, New York, NY 10105
Phone: 212 798-6100

PRODUCTS/OPERATIONS

2014 Sales

	% of total
Investment Manager	65
Non-investment manager	
Advertising	19
Circulation	10
Commercial printing and others	4
Rental revenue resident fees and services	2
Total	**100**

COMPETITORS

American Capital	Investcorp
Apollo Investment	PineBridge Investments
Bessemer Trust	RREEF Funds
Blackstone Group	Schroders
Integrated Asset	Soros Fund Management
Management	

HISTORICAL FINANCIALS

Company Type: Public

Income Statement

FYE: December 31

	ASSETS ($ mil.)	NET INCOME ($ mil.)	INCOME AS % OF ASSETS	EMPLOYEES
12/14	5,934	99	1.7%	2,860
12/13	2,674	200	7.5%	2,324
12/12	2,161	78	3.6%	1,996
12/11	2,220	(431)	—	979
12/10	2,076	(284)	—	900
Annual Growth	**30.0%**	**—**	**—**	**33.5%**

2014 Year-End Financials

Debt ratio: 26.23%
Return on equity: 13.61%
Cash ($ mil.): —
Current ratio: —
Long-term debt ($ mil.): —
No. of shares (mil.): 434
Dividends
Yield: 6.2%
Payout: 68.4%
Market value ($ mil.): 3,488

	STOCK PRICE ($) FY Close	P/E High/Low	PER SHARE ($) Earnings	Dividends	Book Value
12/14	8.02	19 13	0.43	0.50	1.48
12/13	8.56	11 5	0.79	0.24	1.68
12/12	4.39	16 10	0.27	0.20	1.35
12/11	3.38	— —	(2.36)	0.00	0.98
12/10	5.70	— —	(1.83)	0.00	0.88
Annual Growth	**8.9%**	**— —**	**—**	**—**	**14.0%**

Franklin Resources, Inc.

Franklin Resources believes a penny saved is a penny lost —if it's not wisely invested. Operating as Franklin Templeton Investments the firm manages more than 100 mutual funds that invest in international and domestic stocks; taxable and tax-exempt money market instruments; and corporate municipal and US government bonds. Franklin Resources also offers separately managed accounts closed-end funds insurance product funds and retirement and college savings plans. Its investment products are sold through more than 1600 banks securities firms and financial advisors under the Franklin Templeton Mutual Series Bissett Darby and Fiduciary Trust banners.

OperationsMost of Franklin Resources' revenues come from investment management fees which account for more than 65% of company revenue and are directly tied to its assets under management.

Sales and distribution fees generate another 30% of revenue and are made up of sales charges and commissions derived from sales and distribution of the company's sponsored investment products (SIPs). In addition to its core business Franklin Resources also provides shareholder services and manages investments for high-net-worth clients and institutional investors. These services make up less than 5% of overall revenue.Retail banking private banking auto finance and trust services are offered through Franklin Templeton Bank & Trust Franklin Capital Fiduciary Trust Company International and other subsidiaries. Serving more than 24 million shareholder accounts Franklin Resources and its subsidiaries boast nearly $899 billion in assets under management.Geographic ReachBased in California Franklin Resources boasts an extensive global presence with offices in some 35 countries and clients reaching across 150-plus countries. The firm has operations in North America South America Europe Asia Pacific the Middle East and Africa. The company's business in the US accounts for about 60% of revenue while Luxembourg contributes another 25%. Sales and MarketingFranklin Resources sells its investment products and services under a variety of brand names such as Franklin Templeton Mutual Series Bissett Fiduciary Trust Darby Balanced Equity Management and K2. The company also advertises in major financial publications television Internet through sporting even sponsorship and social media marketing to promote brand recognition and to assist its distribution network. Its advertising and promotion expenses reached $4.5 million in 2014.

The company plans to keep its advertising spend steady and may increase it faster than the rate of revenue growth or decrease it more slowly than the rate of potential revenue declines in the future.Financial PerformanceFranklin has enjoyed rising revenues for the past few years as its assets under management (AUM) have steadily grown with a fa-vorable stock market. Revenue grew by 6% to $8.49 billion in fiscal 2014 thanks to another year of double-digit growth in average AUM across all regions and across all product lines (except for tax-free fixed income investments). The increase in overall managed assets combined with a higher mix of equity and hybrid AUM (which generate higher fees) also led to a 6% boost in sales and distribution fees.Higher revenue also boosted the company's net income for a fifth straight year with profit reaching a record-high $2.38 billion in fiscal 2014. Higher investment and other income also helped increase the company's bottom line.The boost in net income was the primary reason behind improved cash levels with operations providing $2.14 billion or 5% more cash than in fiscal 2013. The company' receivables and prepaid expense balance also rose less than in 2013 which helped improve its operating cash flow.StrategyThanks to healthy stock market growth over the past six years and thanks to piqued interest in the market to invest Franklin assets under management have enjoyed double-digit growth for the past few years. Looking at fiscal years 2014 and 2013 in particular the company's AUM grew by 10% and 15% respectively which resulted in healthy revenue growth across the board among its regions and product lines.To expand its investment offerings the company has been acquiring investment groups with promising strategies in recent years. In 2013 Franklin Resources secured a 100% controlling interest in Pelagos Capital Management a Boston-based investment advisor that employs commodity managed futures and hedge fund replication strategies. Further enhancing its alternative investments and multi-asset solutions platforms Franklin Resources acquired a 69% equity stake in K2 Advisors Holdings LLC.The company also continues to expand its geographic reach. It still gets most of its business in North America but has been growing its assets under management in Europe and the Asia-Pacific region as well. Since 2008 the company has been establishing asset management groups or joint ventures in countries such as Brazil China Dubai India Japan and Vietnam. All told Franklin Resources now has offices in some 35 countries and has clients in more than 150.

HISTORY

Rupert Johnson Sr. founded Franklin Distributors (capitalizing on Benjamin Franklin's reputation for thrift) in New York in 1947; it launched its first fund Franklin Custodian in 1948. Custodian grew into five funds including conservatively managed equity and bond funds. In 1968 Johnson's son Charles (who had joined the firm in 1957) became president and CEO. The company went public in 1971 as Franklin Resources.

In 1973 Franklin bought San Mateo-based investment firm Winfield & Co. and relocated to the Golden State. The buy provided additional products including the Franklin Gold Fund (made possible by the end of the prohibition in the US against private interests owning commodity gold). With interest rate spikes in the late 1970s and early 1980s money drained from savings accounts was poured into more lucrative money market mutual funds.

The Franklin Money Fund launched in 1975 fueled the firm's tremendous asset growth in the 1980s. In 1981 the Franklin Tax-Free Income Fund (introduced in 1977) began investing solely in California municipal bonds. The fund's success led Franklin to introduce 43 tax-free income funds in later years.

In 1985 Franklin bought Pacific Union Bank and Trust (now Franklin Bank) allowing it to offer consumers such services as credit cards and to compete with financial services supermarkets such as Merrill Lynch. It also bought real estate firm Property Resources (now Franklin Properties).

The 1987 stock crash and the California real estate slump forced Franklin to focus on its funds businesses. In 1992 it bought Bahamas-based Templeton Galbraith & Hansberger the manager of Templeton Funds a major international funds business. The Templeton deal added an aggressive investment management unit to complement the conservatively managed Franklin funds.

In 1940 Sir John Templeton gained control of investment company Templeton Dobbrow and Vance (TDV). TDV launched Templeton Growth Fund in 1954. In 1969 Templeton sold his interest in TDV but continued to manage the Templeton Growth Fund. John Galbraith became president of Securities Fund Investors (SFI) the distribution company for Templeton Growth Fund in 1974. In 1977 Galbraith bought SFI from Templeton and began building the Templeton funds broker-dealer network in the US. The Templeton World Fund was formed in 1978. Templeton Investment Counsel was launched to provide investment advice in 1979. In 1986 these companies were combined to form Templeton Galbraith & Hansberger Ltd.

In 1996 Franklin bought Heine Securities previous investment adviser to Mutual Series Fund Inc. Max Heine a leading investor had established Mutual Shares Corp. in 1949. Heine Securities was formed in 1975. Following the purchase Franklin set up subsidiary Franklin Mutual Advisers as the investment adviser for Mutual Series Fund.

In 1997 the weak Asian economy hurt Templeton's international funds prompting liquidation of a Japanese stocks-based fund. Franklin cut jobs and shuffled management in 1999; the restructuring acknowledged the clash between the firm's value-investing style and investors' bull-market optimism.

In 2000 the firm gained a foothold in Canada with its purchase of Bissett & Associates Investment Management. Franklin's purchase of Fiduciary Trust the following year gave the firm greater access to institutional investors and affluent individuals.

Franklin Resources boosted its alternative investment offerings with the 2003 acquisition of Darby Overseas which focuses on private equity mezzanine and fixed-income investment products and specializes in Asian and Latin American fixed-income securities.

Chairman Charles Johnson retired from the CEO's office in 2004 turning the reins over to a new generation; his son Gregory was named CEO. Also that year Franklin Resources agreed to pay $50 million to settle market-timing allegations and reached a $20 million settlement with the SEC and an $18 million settlement with the state of California over commissions paid to brokers for mutual fund sales.The company continued its international growth with the acquisitions of stakes in Dubai's Algebra Capital (in 2007) and Brazilian asset manager Bradesco Templeton (in 2006) since renamed Franklin Templeton Investimentos (Brasil).

EXECUTIVES

Chairman President and CEO, Gregory E. Johnson, $780,132 total compensation

EVP and COO, Jennifer M. Johnson, $525,000 total compensation

EVP and CFO, Kenneth A. Lewis, $525,000 total compensation

EVP Alternative Strategies, William Y. Yun, age 56, $525,000 total compensation

EVP Investment Management, John M. Lusk, $525,000 total compensation

EVP and General Counsel, Craig S. Tyle

Co-President, Vijay C. Advani, $525,000 total compensation

SVP and CIO, Priscilla Moyer

Senior Vice President, Frank Felicelli

Senior Vice President, Roger Bayston

Vice President, Evan Mcculloch

Vice President Research Analyst, James Lucas

Vice President Retirement Marketing, Michael (Mel) Doshier

Senior Vice President, John (Jack) Mcgee

Senior Vice President, Scott Lee

Vice President of Human Resources, Allison Katz

Executive Vice President Technology and Operations, Jennifer (Jen) Bolt

Vice President Senior Advisor Consultant, Roy Tirakayos

Senior Vice President Portfolio Manager, Jim Conn

Senior Vice President Institutional Marketing Support, Tracy Harrington

Vice President Portfolio Manager, Stella Wong

Vice President Product Manager, Stan Hong

Vice President Portfolio Manager, Tony Coffey

Senior Vice President And Managing Director, Sheila Amoroso

Vice President global Product Marketing, Bethany Hollrah

Vice Chairman, Rupert H. Johnson

Treasurer, Debbie Bettencourt

Auditors: PRICEWATERHOUSECOOPERS LLP

LOCATIONS

HQ: Franklin Resources, Inc.
One Franklin Parkway, San Mateo, CA 94403
Phone: 650 312-2000 **Fax:** 650 312-3655
Web: www.franklinresources.com

2013 Sales

	$ mil.	% of total
North America		
US	5,389	68
Bahamas	1,049	13
Canada	323	4
Asia-Pacific	661	8
Europe Middle East & Africa	547	7
Latin America	13	-
Total	**7,985**	**100**

PRODUCTS/OPERATIONS

2013 Sales

	$ mil.	% of total
Investment management fees	5,071	63
Sales & distribution fees	2,516	32
Shareholder servicing fees	303	4
Other	93	1
Total	**7,985**	**100**

2013 Assets Under Management

	% of total
Fixed-income	43
Equity	40
Hybrid	16
Cash management	1
Total	**100**

Selected Subsidiaries

Balanced Equity Management Pty. Limited
C&EE General Partner Ltd.
Darby Administração de Investimentos Ltda.
Darby Asia Founder Partner L.P.
Darby Asia Investors (HK) Ltd.
Darby Asia Investors (India) Private Limited
Darby Asia Investors Ltd.
Darby Asia Mezzanine Fund II Management Co. Ltd.
Darby Asia Opportunities Fund III GP L.P.

COMPETITORS

AllianceBernstein	Legg Mason
American Century	Morgan Stanley
BlackRock	Old Mutual (US)
Capital Group	PIMCO
Dodge & Cox	Principal Financial
FMR	Putnam
Invesco	T. Rowe Price
John Hancock Financial Services	The Vanguard Group

HISTORICAL FINANCIALS

Company Type: Public

Income Statement

FYE: September 30

	REVENUE ($ mil.)	NET INCOME ($ mil.)	NET PROFIT MARGIN	EMPLOYEES
09/15	7,948	2,035	25.6%	9,500
09/14	8,491	2,384	28.1%	9,300
09/13	7,985	2,150	26.9%	9,000
09/12	7,101	1,931	27.2%	8,600
09/11	7,140	1,923	26.9%	8,500
Annual Growth	**2.7%**	**1.4%**	**—**	**2.8%**

2015 Year-End Financials

Debt ratio: 13.19%
Return on equity: 17.38%
Cash ($ mil.): 8,368
Current ratio: 8.33
Long-term debt ($ mil.): 2,155

No. of shares (mil.): 603
Dividends
  Yield: 2.9%
  Payout: 29.4%
Market value ($ mil.): 22,487

	STOCK PRICE ($) FY Close	P/E High/Low		PER SHARE ($)		
			Earnings	Dividends	Book Value
09/15	37.26	18 11	3.29	1.10	19.62
09/14	54.61	15 13	3.79	0.48	18.60
09/13	50.55	50 13	3.37	1.39	15.97
09/12	125.07	43 30	2.98	1.03	14.45
09/11	95.64	48 34	2.87	1.00	13.05
Annual Growth	**(21.0%)**	**— —**	**3.4%**	**2.4%**	**10.7%**

Freddie Mac

These siblings know there's no place like home. Government-sponsored enterprises (GSEs) Freddie Mac (officially Federal Home Loan Mortgage Corporation) and Fannie Mae were established to buy residential mortgages and boost the housing market. They do so by purchasing mortgages from lenders and packaging them for resale thereby mitigating risk and allowing lenders to provide mortgages to those who may not otherwise qualify. The agency also provides assistance for affordable rental housing. Together Fannie and Freddie guarantee some 70% of all new home loans in the US. Due to losses related to the subprime mortgage crisis the government seized Fannie and Freddie in 2008. It now plans to wind the GSEs down.

HISTORY

Ah the '60s –free love great tunes and a war nobody wanted to pay for with taxes. By the '70s inflation was rising and real income was starting to fall. To divert a construction industry recession Congress created a new entity to buy home mortgages and boost the flow of money into the housing market.

Fannie Mae had been buying mortgages since 1938 but focused on Federal Housing Administration (FHA) and Veterans Administration loans. In 1970 Congress created Freddie Mac and enlarged Fannie Mae's field of action to include conventional mortgages. Still rising interest rates in the 1970s were brutal to the US real estate market.

In the early 1980s dealers devised a way to securitize the company's loans –seen as somewhat frumpy investments –by packaging them into more alluring bond-like investments made even sexier by the implicit government guarantee. When three major government securities dealers collapsed in 1985 ownership of some Freddie Mac securities was in doubt and the Federal Reserve Bank of New York quickly automated registration of government securities.

In 1984 Freddie Mac issued shares to members of the Federal Home Loan Bank (the overseer of US savings and loans). By 1989 the shares had been converted to common stock and were traded on the NYSE. Freddie Mac's board expanded from three political appointees to 18 members.

Nationwide real estate defaults (rampant in the wake of the late 1980s crash) kindled concern about Freddie Mac's reserve levels and whether it might need to tap its US Treasury line of credit. In response Congress in 1992 created the Office of Federal Housing Enterprise Oversight to regulate Freddie Mac and Fannie Mae. Initial examinations sounded no alarms. A 1996 Congressional Budget Office report questioned whether the government should continue its implicit guarantees of the pair's debt securities.

In 1997 Freddie Mac officially adopted its long-time nickname. The next year it launched a system to cut loan approval time from weeks to minutes (it agreed to develop a similar version for the FHA). The streamlining was crucial to pacts in which mortgage lenders (including one of the US's largest Wells Fargo) promised to sell Freddie Mac their loan originations. In 1999 Freddie Mac hired former House Speaker Newt Gingrich as a consultant.

Freddie Mac made a major Internet push in 2000 with its first online taxable bond offering. A wired venture involving Freddie Mac Microsoft and such big lenders as Chase Manhattan (now part of JPMorgan Chase & Co.) Bank of America and Wells Fargo drew fire from small banks that said it would push them out of the online lending business.

In 2001 Freddie Mac bought Tuttle Decision Systems a loan-pricing software system provider. Critics responded that Freddie Mac overstepped its government charter with such a move.

In a move initiated by its auditor Freddie Mac re-audited its earnings from 2000 to 2003 uncovering accounting irregularities and employee misconduct. Further investigations executive oustings restructuring and numerous lawsuits followed. In late 2003 Freddie Mac announced the findings of its re-audit. The company admitted to understating earnings by $4.4 billion between 2000 and 2002 and overstating profits by $989 million in 2001 all in an attempt to smooth out results and show steady profit growth.

In 2006 the company paid a record $3.8 million fine to settle allegations by the Federal Election Commission that the company made illegal campaign contributions to members of the US House Financial Services Committee. It also agreed to pay $4.65 million to settle a lawsuit related to its employee 401(k) plan. Freddie Mac did receive good news that year though when the Department of Justice dropped criminal charges against the company for misstating earnings from 2000 to 2002.

As the subprime mortgage crisis began heating up in 2007 and 2008 Freddie Mac announced plans to stop purchasing risky subprime mortgages. However the company tried to help restore stability to the teetering mortgage market by investing in billions of dollars in new jumbo mortgages raising its loan limits to more than $700000.

Although the government stepped in with loans to help Freddie the company still struggled with subprime mortgage losses. The government seized Fannie Mae and Freddie Mac in 2008 and placed them in conservatorship. Freddie Mac's leadership was also shaken up. David Moffat resigned as CEO in 2009 and chairman John Koskinen stepped in to serve as his interim replacement. Later that year Charles Haldeman Jr. the former head of Putnam Investments was selected to lead the company.

The Federal Housing Finance Administration (FHFA) was created in 2008 to oversee Fannie and Freddie as well as the 12 Federal Home Loan Banks. The FHFA was granted more authority than its predecessor agencies the Federal Housing Finance Board and the Office of Federal Housing Enterprise Oversight.

EXECUTIVES

Executive Vice President Community Relations, Ralph F Boyd
CEO, Donald H. (Don) Layton, age 64
Senior Vice President of Multifamily Loan Production, Robert (Bob) Tsien
Vice President, James (Jamie) Bowden
EVP and Chief Administrative Officer, Jerry Weiss, age 54, $450,000 total compensation
EVP Multifamily Business, David M. Brickman
EVP Single-Family Business, David B. (Dave) Lowman, age 54
EVP and CFO, James G. Mackey, age 48
EVP General Counsel and Corporate Secretary, William McDavid
EVP and CIO, Robert (Rob) Lux
EVP Investments and Capital Markets, Michael Hutchins
Senior Vice President Corporate Contro, Robert (Bob) Mailloux
Executive Vice President Of Operations And Technology, Andrew (Andy) Dolan
Vice President Call Centers, Jeanmarie Puglisi
Executive Vice President General Counsel Corporate Secretary, Robert (Bob) Bostrom
Vice President Servicer Relationship, William Maguire
Vice President Industry And State Relations, Jeffrey (Jeff) Markowitz
Vice President Accounting Policy, Timothy (Tim) Kviz
Vice President Information Technology, David Munford
Vice President Sourcing, Sally Baker
Vice President, James Berkovec
Vice President Finance, Joseph (Jo) Amato
Vice President Of Client Services, Sanjiv Nathwani
Senior Vice President Multifamily Sourcing, Michael (Mel) May
Vice President, James Bowden
Vice President of Tax Accounting and Compliance, Michael (Mel) Culhane
Vice President External Operations Risk Manager, Mike Wade
Chairman, Christopher S. Lynch, age 57
Auditors: PricewaterhouseCoopers LLP

LOCATIONS

HQ: Freddie Mac
  8200 Jones Branch Drive, McLean, VA 22102-3110
Phone: 703 903-2000
Web: www.freddiemac.com

PRODUCTS/OPERATIONS

2014 Revenue

	% of total
Interest Income Total	80
Investments in Securities	8
Other —	
Non-interest Income	12
Total	**100**

COMPETITORS

FHLB Atlanta

HISTORICAL FINANCIALS

Company Type: Public

Income Statement

	ASSETS ($ mil.)	NET INCOME ($ mil.)	INCOME AS % OF ASSETS	EMPLOYEES
				FYE: December 31
12/14	1,945,539	7,690	0.4%	5,007
12/13	1,966,061	48,668	2.5%	5,112
12/12	1,989,856	10,982	0.6%	5,017
12/11	2,147,216	(5,266)	—	4,921
12/10	2,261,780	(14,025)	—	5,309
Annual Growth	(3.7%)	—	—	(1.5%)

2014 Year-End Financials

Debt ratio: 99.18%
Return on equity: 99.32%
Cash ($ mil.): 19,463
Current ratio: —
Long-term debt ($ mil.): —

No. of shares (mil.): 650
Dividends
  Yield: —
  Payout: —
Market value ($ mil.): 1,339

	STOCK PRICE ($) FY Close	P/E High/Low	PER SHARE ($)		
			Earnings	Dividends	Book Value
12/14	2.06	— —	(0.72)	0.00	4.08
12/13	2.90	— —	(1.09)	0.00	19.74
12/12	0.26	— —	(0.64)	0.00	13.58
12/11	0.21	— —	(3.63)	0.00	(0.22)
12/10	0.30	— —	(6.09)	0.00	(0.62)
Annual Growth	61.2%	— —	—	—	—

Freeport-McMoRan Inc

Freeport-McMoRan (FCX formerly Freeport-McMoRan Copper & Gold) digs its profits from copper and precious metal mines and from oil and gas assets. In 2014 FCX's proven and probable reserves totaled 103.5 billion pounds of copper 28.5 million ounces of gold and 282.9 million ounces of silver. Subsidiary PT Freeport Indonesia (PT-FI) operates the vast Grasberg gold copper and silver mine in Indonesia. FCX is also engaged in smelting and refining via PT-FI's 25% stake in PT Smelting a copper smelter in Indonesia. In 2014 the company reported estimated proved oil and natural gas reserves of 390 million barrels of oil equivalent. In 2016 it agreed to sell 13% of its Morenci (US) copper mine for $1 billion.

HISTORY

The Freeport Sulfur Company was formed in Texas in 1912 by Francis Pemberton banker Eric Swenson and several investors to develop a sulfur field. The next year Freeport Texas was formed as a holding company for Freeport Sulfur and other enterprises.

During the 1930s the company diversified. In 1936 Freeport pioneered a process to remove hydrocarbons from sulfur. The company joined Consolidated Coal in 1955 to establish the National Potash Company. In 1956 Freeport formed an oil and gas subsidiary Freeport Oil.

Internationally Freeport formed an Australian minerals subsidiary in 1964 and a copper-mining subsidiary in Indonesia in 1967. The company changed its name to Freeport Minerals in 1971 and merged with Utah-based McMoRan Oil & Gas (formerly McMoRan Explorations) in 1982.

McMoRan Explorations had been formed in 1969 by William McWilliams Jim Bob Moffett and Byron Rankin. In 1973 McMoRan formed an exploration and drilling alliance with Dow Chemical and signed a deal with Indonesia to mine in the remote Irian Jaya region. McMoRan went public in 1978.

Moffett became chairman and CEO of Freeport-McMoRan in 1984. The company formed Freeport-McMoRan Copper in 1987 to manage its Indonesian operations. The unit assumed the Freeport-McMoRan Copper & Gold name in 1991. Two years later Freeport-McMoRan acquired Rio Tinto Minera a copper-smelting business with operations in Spain.

To support expansion in Indonesia Freeport-McMoRan spun off its copper and gold division in 1994. In 1995 Freeport-McMoRan Copper & Gold (FCX) formed an alliance with the UK's RTZ Corporation to develop its Indonesian mineral reserves. Local riots that year closed the Grasberg Mine and FCX's political risk insurance was canceled. Despite these setbacks higher metal prices and growing sales in 1995 helped the company double its operating income.

An Indonesian tribal leader filed a $6 billion lawsuit in 1996 charging FCX with environmental human rights and social and cultural violations. The company called the suit baseless but offered to set aside 1% of its annual revenues or about $15 million to help local tribes. Tribal leaders rejected the offer and in 1997 a judge dismissed the lawsuit.

In 1997 FCX pulled out of Bre-X Minerals' Busang gold mine project which independent tests later proved to be a fraud of historic proportions. Amid widespread rioting Indonesia's embattled president Suharto was forced out of office in 1998. The new government investigated charges of cronyism involving FCX.

FCX received permission from the Indonesian government in 1999 to expand the Grasberg Mine and increase ore output up to 300000 metric tons per day. However the next year an overflow accident killed four workers in Grasberg and as a result of the accident the Indonesian government ordered FCX to reduce its production at the mine by up to 30%. Normal production at the mine resumed in early 2001.

FM Services (administrative legal and financial services) was added as a subsidiary in 2002. In 2003 FCX bought an 86% stake in PT Puncakjaya Power a supplier of power to PT-FI.

The $26 billion acquisition of Phelps Dodge in 2007 brought that company's global copper gold and molybdenum business into the fold. The deal placed FCX in a position to thrive as a global competitor in the rank just below metals and mining giants such as BHP Billiton Rio Tinto and Vale. A year later FCX sold the wire and cable business it acquired in the Phelps Dodge deal to General Cable Corporation for $735 million.

Following the acquisition —and benefiting from high copper prices and a good business climate — the company began to invest in its development projects. It was also able to retire a sizable portion of its debt much of it accumulated from the Phelps Dodge acquisition.

Political and environmental controversy in Indonesia has been a problem for FCX since its major protector former President Suharto was forced to resign in 1998 after more than 30 years in power. Sectarian violence in Indonesia where FCX is one of the largest employers also makes the company vulnerable to work stoppages. Anglo-Australian mining giant Rio Tinto is jointly involved with FCX in developing mineral properties in Indonesia's politically and environmentally sensitive Papua region. The company's Tenke Fungume copper and gold mine named Too is lo-

cated in the Democratic Republic of Congo which also can be an unstable environment in which to do business. Tenke Fungume is jointly owned with Lundin Mining and the Congolese government. It began production in 2009.

EXECUTIVES

EVP and Chief Administrative Officer, Michael J. Arnold, age 63, $550,000 total compensation
Vice Chairman President and CEO, Richard C. Adkerson, age 68, $1,354,167 total compensation
Vice Chairman; President and CEO Freeport-McMoRan Oil & Gas, James C. (Jim) Flores, age 56, $1,354,167 total compensation
Vice President Taxes, Hugh O Donahue
Vice President of Corporate Communications, Peter (Pete) Faur
EVP CFO and Treasurer, Kathleen L. Quirk, age 51, $650,000 total compensation
VP and CIO, Bertrand (Bert) Odinet
Advertising Vice President, Gay Cole
Senior Vice President Morenci Operations, Josh Olmsted
General Vice President Manager, Mark Albertsen
Vice President Systems President, Gordon Carlson
Vice President Settlement and Regulatory Affairs, Don Stoneberger
Vice President Global Supply Chain, Brian Esser
Vice President Of Public Relations, Spencer Davis
Chairman, Gerald J. Ford, age 71
Auditors: Ernst & Young LLP

LOCATIONS

HQ: Freeport-McMoRan Inc
333 North Central Avenue, Phoenix, AZ 85004-2189
Phone: 602 366-8100
Web: www.fcx.com

2014 Sales by Destination

	$ mil.	% of total
US	10,311	48
Indonesia	1,792	8
Japan	1,573	7
Spain	1,208	6
China	968	5
Switzerland	800	4
Chile	687	3
Turkey	484	2
Korea	383	2
Other countries	3,232	15
Total	**21,438**	**100**

PRODUCTS/OPERATIONS

2014 Sales

	$ mil.	% of total
Refined copper products	9,451	44
Oil	4,233	20
Copper in concentrates	3,366	16
Gold	1,584	7
Molybdenum	1,207	6
Other products	1,597	7
Total	**21,438**	**100**

Selected Subsidiaries and Affiliates

Atlantic Copper Holding SA (smelting and refining Spain)
Chino Mines Company
Climax Molybdenum Company
FM Service Company (administrative and financial services)
Missouri Lead Smelting Company
Plains Exploration & Production (oil and gas US)
PT Freeport Indonesia Co. (91% mining)
   PT Smelting (Gresik) Co. (25% smelting Indonesia)
PT Irja Eastern Minerals Corp. (mining Indonesia)
PT Puncakjaya Power (86% supplies power to PT Freeport Indonesia)

COMPETITORS

Anadarko Petroleum	Exxon Mobil
Antofagasta	Goodrich Petroleum
Apache	Newmont Mining
BHP Billiton	Petrohawk Energy
BP	Pioneer Natural
Barrick Gold	Resources
Cabot Oil & Gas	Regency Energy
Chesapeake Energy	Rio Tinto Limited
Chevron Mining	Royal Dutch Shell
Codelco	Southern Copper
Devon Energy	Vale Limited
EOG	
Encana Oil & Gas (USA) Inc.	

HISTORICAL FINANCIALS

Company Type: Public

Income Statement

FYE: December 31

	REVENUE ($ mil.)	NET INCOME ($ mil.)	NET PROFIT MARGIN	EMPLOYEES
12/14	21,438	(745)	—	35,000
12/13	20,921	3,441	16.4%	36,100
12/12	18,010	3,980	22.1%	34,000
12/11	20,880	5,747	27.5%	31,800
12/10	18,982	5,544	29.2%	29,700
Annual Growth	3.1%	—		4.2%

2014 Year-End Financials

Debt ratio: 32.26%
Return on equity: (-3.80%)
Cash ($ mil.): 464
Current ratio: 1.75
Long-term debt ($ mil.): 18,492
No. of shares (mil.): 1,039
Dividends
   Yield: 5.3%
   Payout: 57.8%
Market value ($ mil.): 24,271

	STOCK PRICE ($) FY Close	P/E High/Low		PER SHARE ($) Earnings	Dividends	Book Value
12/14	23.36	—	—	(1.26)	1.25	17.60
12/13	37.74	14	10	2.64	2.25	20.17
12/12	34.20	15	10	3.19	1.19	18.49
12/11	36.79	25	6	4.78	1.50	16.50
12/10	120.09	26	12	4.57	0.95	13.23
Annual Growth	(33.6%)	—	—	—	7.1%	7.4%

Fulton Financial Corp. (PA)

Fulton Financial is a $17 billion financial holding company that owns six community banks which together operate more than 250 branches in rural and suburban areas of Pennsylvania Maryland Delaware New Jersey and Virginia. The banks offer standard products such as checking and savings accounts CDs IRAs and credit cards. While commercial mortgage and construction loans account for about 45% of the company's loan portfolio home loans are also available through subsidiary Fulton Mortgage Company. Other non-bank units include investment management and trust services provider Fulton Financial Advisors and Fulton Insurance an agency selling life insurance and related products.

Operations

Fulton Financial's six subsidiary banks include the $9.5 billion Fulton Bank (Fulton's largest with more than 100 branches in Pennsylvania and Delaware) The Columbia Bank FNB Bank Fulton Bank of New Jersey Lafayette Ambassador Bank and Swineford National Bank. Geographic Reach-Fulton Financial and its subsidiary banks operate more than 250 branches in suburban and semi-rural markets in the states of Pennsylvania Delaware Maryland New Jersey and Virginia.Sales and MarketingFulton spent $7.7 million on advertising in 2013 or 6% less than it spent in 2012.

Financial Performance

Fulton Financial's revenue has been in decline since 2007 and fell by another 4% to $763.5 million in 2014 mostly from a combination of lower interest income from loans as interest margins shrunk less fee income from deposit service charges and smaller gains from mortgage sales as the bank had a lower balance of loan commitments. Lower revenue caused net income to dip by 2% to $157.9 million in 2014 but lower interest expenses on deposits less risk-related losses and lower salary and employee benefit costs from recent cost-savings initiatives all helped to buoy profits some.Cash provided by operations fell by 30% to $210.4 million in 2014 mostly because the company generated smaller gains from the sales of its held-for-sale mortgage loans and used more cash toward other assets related to tax credit partnerships and commercial interest rate swaps.Company BackgroundThe company had owned more than a dozen banks as recently as 2007 but consolidated some of them in the hopes of creating operating and marketing efficiencies. Maryland-based Hagerstown Trust Company and The Peoples Bank of Elkton merged into The Columbia Bank in 2009 and Delaware National Bank which had a dozen branches in the state became part of Fulton Bank the following year. In 2011 Fulton Financial merged two more banks New Jersey-based The Bank and Skylands Community Bank to form Fulton Bank of New Jersey which has some 70 branches throughout the state.

EXECUTIVES

Chairman and CEO, R. Scott Smith, age 68, $809,007 total compensation
CFO and SEVP, Charles J. Nugent, age 67, $502,889 total compensation
Senior Vice President Finance, Jeffrey Peeling
SEVP Human Resources Corporate Communication and Administrative Services, Craig H. Hill, age 60, $231,365 total compensation
SEVP Community Banking, Craig A. Roda, $402,782 total compensation
SEVP and Chief Risk Officer, Philmer H. Rohrbaugh, $483,315 total compensation
EVP, David Hostetter
SEVP; President and COO Fulton Bank, Curtis J. Myers
SEVP and Chief Credit Officer, Meg R. Mueller
SEVP CIO and Information Technology Manager, Angela M. Sargent
Senior Vice President Employment Manager, Lori Berquist
Vice President, Thomas (Thom) Fasnacht
Vice President Senior Leasing Sales Officer, Neil Wiker
Vice President Ancillary Services Manager, Doug Tshudy
Vice President Of Loan Administration, Patricia (Pat) Royer
Vice President Of Marketing, Jobeth Mauriello
Vice President Senior Cash Management Sales Officer, Steve Schreiber Steve Schreiber
Executive Vice President General Counsel And Corporate Secretary, Dan Stolzer
Vice President, Forest Crigler
Vice President Cash Management Operations, Rose Derr
Senior Vice President, Wood John
Senior Vice President Director Of Retail, Randy Metz
Senior Vice President Funds Management, Keith Paich

Senior Executive Vice President Director Strategic Initatives And Bank Operations, David (Dave) Campbell
Vice President And Mortgage Sales Manager, Stephen (Steve) Warrington
Vice President And Corporate Training Director, William Glover
Senior Vice President Loan Documentation, Beth Bowers
Vice President, Alan (Al) Brayman
Board Member, Joe Ballard
Auditors: KPMG LLP

LOCATIONS

HQ: Fulton Financial Corp. (PA)
One Penn Square, P.O. Box 4887, Lancaster, PA 17604
Phone: 717 291-2411
Web: www.fult.com

PRODUCTS/OPERATIONS

2013 Sales

	$ mil.	% of total
Interest		
Loans including fees	540	68
Investment securities	65	8
Other	3	-
Noninterest		
Service charges on deposit accounts	55	7
Investment management & trust services	41	5
Other service charges & fees	37	5
Mortgage banking income	30	4
Other	22	3
Total	**797**	**100**

2013 Branches

	No.
Fulton Bank (PA)	119
Fulton Bank of New Jersey	71
The Columbia Bank (MD)	38
Lafayette Ambassador Bank (PA)	23
FNB Bank (PA)	8
Swineford National Bank (PA)	7
Total	**266**

COMPETITORS

First Commonwealth Financial	Mid Penn Bancorp
	PNC Financial
Investors Bancorp	Sovereign Bank
M&T Bank	TD Bank USA

HISTORICAL FINANCIALS

Company Type: Public

Income Statement

FYE: December 31

	ASSETS ($ mil.)	NET INCOME ($ mil.)	INCOME AS % OF ASSETS	EMPLOYEES
12/14	17,124	157	0.9%	3,560
12/13	16,934	161	1.0%	3,620
12/12	16,528	159	1.0%	3,570
12/11	16,370	145	0.9%	3,530
12/10	16,275	128	0.8%	3,530
Annual Growth	**1.3%**	**5.3%**	**—**	**0.2%**

2014 Year-End Financials

Debt ratio: 3.28%
Return on equity: 7.78%
Cash ($ mil.): 463
Current ratio: —
Long-term debt ($ mil.): —
No. of shares (mil.): 178
Dividends
Yield: 2.7%
Payout: 39.5%
Market value ($ mil.): 2,212

	STOCK PRICE ($) FY Close	P/E High/Low	PER SHARE ($) Earnings	Dividends	Book Value
12/14	12.36	15 12	0.84	0.34	11.16
12/13	13.09	16 11	0.83	0.32	10.71
12/12	9.61	13 11	0.80	0.30	10.45
12/11	9.81	16 10	0.73	0.20	9.95
12/10	10.34	20 14	0.59	0.12	9.45
Annual Growth	**4.6%**	**— —**	**9.2%**	**29.7%**	**4.3%**

Gallagher (Arthur J.) & Co.

Arthur J. Gallagher knows all about risky business. The company provides insurance brokerage and risk management services through a network of subsidiaries and agencies. It places traditional and niche property/casualty lines in addition to offering retirement solutions and managing employee benefits programs. Risk management services include claims management loss control consulting and workers' compensation investigations. Gallagher UK places insurance with the Lloyd's of London exchange. The global company operates 650 sales and service locations in about 30 nations and through correspondent brokers and consultants does business in more than 140 countries.

Operations

Gallagher has grown to become one of the world's top five insurance brokers based on revenue as well as a top property/casualty claims administrator. It also ranks among the top employee benefits consulting firms.

The brokerage division which provides both retail and wholesale services accounts for more than 60% of annual revenues. A majority of Gallagher's brokerage income comes from commissions paid by insurance companies (upon placement of their policies). Retail insurance brokerage accounts for more than 80% of the segment's revenues.

Meanwhile the smaller risk management business (14% of sales in 2014) earns fees from insurance companies and self-insured clients; it provides contract claim settlement and administration services for enterprises. The division's business is largely related to workers' compensation claims (which account for more than 70% of revenues) as well as auto liability and property claims.

Gallagher's corporate segment accounts for about a quarter of total revenues; it primarily generated income in 2014 from the consolidation of refined fuel operations. Its managed investments include a 46.5% stake in pollutant reduction firm Chem-Mod and a 12% stake in private carbon dioxide emissions reduction outfit C-Quest Technology.

Geographic Reach

The company gets more than 70% of its revenues from the US but it is working to expand its international operations. Its largest overseas markets include Australia Bermuda Canada New Zealand Singapore and the UK.

Sales and Marketing

Most of the brokerage business comes from retail customers which include commercial industrial not-for-profit government and religious organizations. Gallagher's wholesale brokerage centers provide insurance placement assistance to affiliated and independent agents.

The company manages its brokerage operations through a network of more than 650 sales and service offices. It manages its third-party claims adjusting operations through a network of 100 offices across the US and in Australia Canada New Zealand and the UK.

Financial Performance

Gallagher's growth efforts in both the brokerage segment and the risk management segment have helped the company to increase new customer volumes and has created substantial annual revenue increases in recent years including a 46% jump in 2014. Revenue growth that year came from acquisitions ($595 million) as well as from new businesses and renewal rate growth. Additionally a 23% revenue spike in clean coal activities including earnings from consolidated clean coal production plants and royalties from clean coal licenses contributed to the jump. The company's net income grew by 13% in 2014 thanks to higher revenues and benefits from income taxes outstripping a rise in expenses. In 2013 Gallagher's operating cash flow increased by 15% to $402 million due to factors including an increase in accrued compensation and a net change in premiums receivable.

Strategy

In addition to growth through acquisitions Gallagher has influenced the growth of its business by expanding and strengthening its relationships with independent brokerage partners increasing cross-selling opportunities and pursuing niche markets such as employee benefit risk management. It also seeks to expand its geographic presence through organic and acquisitive growth efforts.

Mergers and Acquisitions

The company grows through the acquisition of small regional insurance agencies and benefits consulting firms; it completed 339 acquisitions between 2002 and 2014 (including 60 purchases made in 2014). Purchases typically cost between $1 million and $50 million although in 2014 it completed three large deals with a combined purchase price in excess of $1.7 billion; they typically target strong sales organizations with a focus on middle-market clients or expertise in niche property/casualty lines (such as aviation energy hospitality and health care).

The company made two of its largest acquisitions to date in 2013 when it acquired Bollinger for some $277 million which expanded Gallagher's presence in the Northeast market and The Giles Group of Companies for $365 million which boosted Gallagher's portfolio of services in the UK.

Larger deals continued into 2014. That year Gallagher acquired the UK's Oval Group of Companies for some $338 million adding more than 1000 employees and boosting its retail client base in the middle market. It also bought Wesfarmers' Crombie/OAMPS brokerage operations for $952 million making that the largest deal in the firm's history. That purchase added 1700 employees in Australia New Zealand and the UK. The company also acquired an 89% stake in Canada's Noraxis Capital Corporation for some $420 million.

Company Background

Gallagher is led by J. Patrick Gallagher grandson of founder Arthur Gallagher who formed the company back in 1927.

EXECUTIVES

Corporate VP and President U.S. Wholesale Brokerage, David E. (Dave) McGurn, age 61, $550,008 total compensation

Corporate VP and President Employee Benefit Brokerage Operation, James W. Durkin, age 65, $725,000 total compensation

Chairman President and CEO, J. Patrick Gallagher, age 62, $1,000,000 total compensation

Area Vice President, Kathy Betts
Global Chief Information Officer, Sean P. Connelly, age 44
Area Senior Vice President, Laurie S Miller
Senior Vice President, Norman Henley
Corporate VP and CFO, Douglas K. (Doug) Howell, age 53, $750,000 total compensation
CEO International Brokerage, Grahame D. (Chily) Chilton, age 56
Corporate VP and President Retail Property/Casualty Brokerage Operation, James S. Gault, age 63, $800,000 total compensation
Chief Marketing and Communications Officer, Richard Tallo
Corporate VP and President and CEO Risk Management Operation, Scott R. Hudson, age 53
Corporate VP and Chairman International Brokerage, Thomas J. Gallagher, age 57, $700,000 total compensation
Area Senior Vice President, Mark A Russ
Regional Vice President, John Neumaier
Executive Vice President And Managing Director, Marcia L Hahn
Area Vice President Surety, Harold Miller
Executive Vice President, Mike Temple
Area Assistant Vice President, Roland Castro
Area Executive Vice President, Lynn Tu
Vice President, George V Baus
Area Senior Vice President, Karen W Petty
Area Executive Vice President, Scott McAdams
Assistant Vice President, Josephine Digiacomo
Area Vice President Marketing Executive, Mary Chiu
Area Assistant Vice President, Rose M Unruh
Area Vice President Indiana, Kathy Kebo
Area Vice President, Nancy Snell
Area Vice President, Christina Caughlin
Area Senior Vice President Compliance Counsel, Sally Wineman
Area Vice President;Client Devel, Brian Lomas
Area Vice President Consulting Services, Bill McCann
Area Vice President, Scott Maceachen
Division President, Jeff Kassal
Area Assistant Vice President m, Walt Larkin
Vice President, Scott Baldwin
Area Vice President, Sue O'Connor
Area Assistant Vice President, Cody E Vicknair
Global Vice President of Talent Management, Eric Tolman
Vice President Client Management, Rich Hemmerich
Vice President Quality Assurance and Compliance, Tory Mayhue
Area Vice President, Katie Lau
Area Assistant Vice President, Josinica R Gonzales
Senior Area Vice President, Gayle Czeizler
Area Senior Vice President, Ryan Pfeiffer
Vice President Analytics, Ravi Singhvi
Area Senior Vice President Technology Practice director, Joe Inge
Area Vice President, Richard Waldman
Area Senior Vice President, Allen (Al) Brooks
Area Executive Vice President, Stuart (Stu) Wallace
Area Vice President, Vinny Catalano
Vice President, John Fitzgerald
Senior Area Vice President, Bill Dickenson
Vice President, Mike Hargis
Assistant Vice President, Scott Spangler
Area Vice President Marketing, Kevin Groba
Area Assistant Vice President, Laura Tharp
Area Vice President, Walter Viteri
Vice President Marketing, Linda McCall
Area Executive Vice President, Steven (Steve) Kahl
Vice President, Judy Graf
Assistant Vice President, Phil Fabrizio
Area President, Ken Evelyn
Area Vice President, Doug Myers
Corporate Vice President, Peter (Pete) Durkalski
Vice President Marketing, Craig Der Voort

Area Senior Vice President, Gregg Aleman
Area Vice President, Kelly Peltz
Area Vice President, Anne Scialabba
Area Assistant Vice President, Kip Walby
Area Vice President, Ken Urrutia
Area Vice President Employee Benefits, Robert (Bob) Salcedo
Area Vice President, Mark Nolan
Area Vice President, David (Dave) Mcneil
Senior Vice President, Stephanie Giannini
Area Vice President, Richard (Dick) Ryan
Area Vice President and Loss Contr, Chuck Goodman
Area Senior Vice President, Mark Smith
Area Vice President, Jori van der Voort
Assistant Vice President, Lawrence Healey
Executive Vice President, John Grob
Area Assistant Vice President, Ilene Abella
Area Vice President, Jonathan Gleason
Area Vice President, Peter Deheulle
Area Senior Vice President, John (Jack) Barry
Execuitve Vice President, Bill Holland
Area Vice President, Mike Howell
Vice President, Eric Elbell
Corporate Vice President, James (Jamie) Agnew
Area Senior Vice President, Richard (Dick) Fieldman
Area Senior Vice President, Richard (Dick) Terlecki
Area Vice President Insurance Broker, Joe Hunter
Area Vice President Global Human Resources Services, Kristin M Sampson
Area Vice President, Eric Pearson
Area Senior. Vice President, Greg Martin
Area Senior Vice President, David D (Dave) Kempton
Area Executive Vice President, James Mandel
Area Executive Vice President Claims, Greg Bradley
Area Vice President, Scott Santos
Area Executive Vice President, Pete Coyle
Area Senior Vice President, Adam Cottini
Area Senior Vice President, Barb Galuppi
Area Vice President Operations, Kathy Wright
Area Executive Vice President, Bob McWeeney
Area Senior Vice President, Debbie Russell
Area Senior Vice President, Ray Hussey
Area Vice President, Ron D'Ambrosi
Area Senior Vice President, David D (Dave) White
Senior Vice President, Miles Shepp
Area Executive Vice President, Todd Burke Todd Burke
Division Vice President, Brandon Rich
Vice President Of Claims, Daniel Summa
Area Vice President, Chris Gleason
Area Executive Vice President, Dirk Peterson
Area Executive Vice President, Martin (Marti) Stair
Area Vice President, Darlene Ames
Area Senior Vice President, Evan Kraus
Senior Vice President, Theresa Balaszi
Area Senior Vice President, Warren Meyer
Vice President Mergers and Acquisitions, Kevin Doyle
Vice President, Judy Koch
Area Senior Vice President, Kinsey Carpenter
Area Senior Vice President Client Management, Jennifer (Jen) Barth
Vice President Professional Standards, Whitney Harrison
Area Assistant Vice President, Jill M Kizyma
Area Vice President, Steve Surber
Vice President Manager Director Information Technology, Sandhya Patel
Area Vice President, Brian Oneill
Vice President, Steve Springer
Area Senior Vice President Operations, Karen Pielow
Area Assistant Vice President, Nathan Mitzner
Area Senior Vice President, Derek van der Voort
Area Senior Vice President, Ron Bensyl
Senior Vice President, Bob Walker
Area Senior Vice President, Betty Woodruff
Senior Vice President, Rob Russell

Area Vice President, Gregg Murawsky
Senior Area Vice President, Michael (Mel) Long
Area Senior Vice President, Phil Algozino
Area Executive Vice President, Brian Selna
Area Vice President, Loann Le
Area Vice President, Rob Winn
Area Senior Vice President, James (Jamie) Tobenfeld
Area Vice President Chief Compliance Officer And Area Assistant Counsel, Natalie Kossak
Assistant Vice President, Heidi Roberts
Vice President of Operations Oklahoma, Chris Mangum
Assistant Vice President, John Zimmermann
Area Vice President, Richard McClure
Area Vice President, Emily Loupee
Area Vice President Operations, Donna Dailly
Vice President Business Intelligence, Mark Tainton
Auditors: Ernst & Young LLP

LOCATIONS

HQ: Gallagher (Arthur J.) & Co.
Two Pierce Place, Itasca, IL 60143-3141
Phone: 630 773-3800
Web: www.ajg.com

2014 Sales

	$ mil.	% of total
US	3,454	75
UK	726	16
Other countries	445	9
Total	**4,626**	**100**

PRODUCTS/OPERATIONS

2014 Sales

	$ mil.	% of total
Brokerage		
Commissions	2,083	45
Fees	595	13
Supplemental commissions	104	2
Contingent commissions	84	2
Investment income & other brokerage	47	1
Risk management		
Fees	663	14
Investment income	1	-
Corporate		
Clean energy & other investment income	1,047	23
Total	**4,626**	**100**

Selected Subsidiaries

AJG Financial Services Inc.
  AJG Coal Inc.
Arthur J. Gallagher & Co. (Bermuda) Limited (insurance & reinsurance placement captive risk services)
  Artex Risk Solutions (Bermuda) Ltd.
Arthur J. Gallagher & Co. (Canada) Ltd.
Arthur J. Gallagher Australasia Holdings Pty Ltd (Australia)
  Australis Group (Underwriting) Pty Ltd
  Interpacific Underwriting Agencies Pty Ltd
Arthur J. Gallagher Brokerage & Risk Management Services LLC
  Arthur J. Gallagher Risk Management Services Inc.
  Manning & Smith Insurance Inc.
Arthur J. Gallagher Service Company
Arthur J. Gallagher (UK) Limited (Lloyd's of London brokerage)
  Risk Management Partners Ltd. (customized insurance & risk management)
Gallagher Bassett Services Inc. (risk analysis)
  Gallagher Bassett International Ltd. (UK)
  Gallagher Bassett Services Pty Ltd. (Australia)
Gallagher Benefit Services Inc. (employee benefit program management)
Heath Lambert Limited (Gallagher Heath UK)
Protected Insurance Company
Risk Placement Services Inc.

COMPETITORS

ACE USA	Marsh & McLennan
AIG	Sedgwick Claims
AmWINS Group	Management Services
Aon	Swett & Crawford

Bollinger Inc.	The Hartford
BroadSpire	The Lockton Companies
Brown & Brown	UMR
CRC Insurance	USI
Fiserv	Wells Fargo Insurance Services
Fortegra Financial	
General Re	Willis Towers Watson
Hub International	Zurich American
Jardine Lloyd	

HISTORICAL FINANCIALS

Company Type: Public

Income Statement

FYE: December 31

	REVENUE ($ mil.)	NET INCOME ($ mil.)	NET PROFIT MARGIN	EMPLOYEES
12/15	5,392	356	6.6%	21,500
12/14	4,626	303	6.6%	20,200
12/13	3,179	268	8.4%	16,400
12/12	2,520	195	7.7%	13,700
12/11	2,134	144	6.8%	12,400
Annual Growth	**26.1%**	**25.4%**	**—**	**14.8%**

2015 Year-End Financials

Debt ratio: 22.51%
Return on equity: 10.39%
Cash ($ mil.): 480
Current ratio: 1.03
Long-term debt ($ mil.): 2,075
No. of shares (mil.): 176
Dividends
  Yield: 3.6%
  Payout: 74.3%
Market value ($ mil.): 7,242

	STOCK PRICE ($) FY Close	P/E High/Low		PER SHARE ($) Earnings	Dividends	Book Value
12/15	40.94	24	19	2.06	1.48	20.57
12/14	47.08	25	22	1.97	1.44	19.62
12/13	46.93	23	17	2.06	1.40	15.61
12/12	34.65	23	20	1.59	1.69	13.21
12/11	33.44	26	19	1.28	1.32	10.84
Annual Growth	**5.2%**	**—**	**—**	**12.6%**	**2.9%**	**17.4%**

GameStop Corp

GameStop holds the top score in video game retailing. The largest retailer of new and used games hardware entertainment software and accessories boasts over 4100 GameStop EB Games and Micromania branded stores in the US and 1500-plus stores in Europe Australia and Canada. Its stores and e-commerce websites stock more than 5000 video game related items with more than half of its sales coming from new video game hardware and software. GameStop also sells downloadable add-on content from publishers operates nearly 500 smartphone retail locations (under the AT&T Cricket Wireless Simply Mac and Spring Mobile banners) and publishes video game magazine Game Informer.

HISTORY

NeoStar Retail Group resulted from the 1994 combination of software retailers Babbage's and Software Etc. Babbage's had been founded by James McCurry and Gary Kusin in 1983. Named for 19th-century mathematician Charles Babbage (considered the father of the computer) it went public in 1988.

Software Etc. began as a division of B. Dalton Bookseller in 1984. Bookstore chain Barnes & Noble and Dutch retailer Vendex acquired B. Dalton two years later. Software Etc. went public in 1992.

Both companies focused on mall retailing: Babbage's on game software and Software Etc. on a broader variety of PC software. Both saw growth spurred by the rising popularity of Nintendo and Sega game systems and by falling PC prices. The two merged in 1994 in an effort to stave off growing competition from big retail chains such as Best Buy and Wal-Mart. NeoStar opened 122 stores in 1995.

Amid flat sales the following year several senior executives left. Also in 1996 NeoStar lost its contract to operate software departments at 136 Barnes & Noble sites and it soon filed for Chapter 11. Late that year a group led by Barnes & Noble's head honcho Leonard Riggio purchased about 460 of NeoStar's 650 stores for $58.5 million and renamed the company Babbage's Etc. Former Software Etc. chief Dick Fontaine was named CEO.

By 1997 the company began concentrating on popular games and software and in 1999 it formed its e-commerce site GameStop.com. In late 1999 Barnes & Noble paid Riggio's group $210 million for Babbage's Etc. In June 2000 the company fortified its position and became the #1 US video game retailer with the purchase of rival game retailer Funco (about 400 stores) for $161.5 million. The company changed its name to GameStop in August 2001 and filed to go public which it accomplished in February 2002. Though public it was still under the majority control of Barnes & Noble until 2004 when GameStop bought back its shares.

GameStop bought rival Electronics Boutique in 2005 more than doubling its size from 2000 to about 4500 stores. Steven R. Morgan a former executive with Electronics Boutique became president of GameStop later that year.

A new CEO took the controls at GameStop in 2008 —its first CEO change since the company's inception in 1996. Dick Fontaine gave up the title of chief executive to Daniel DeMatteo who had served as COO since 1996 and vice chairman of the company since 2004. Also Paul Raines formerly with Home Depot joined the company as COO in September 2008. Fontaine retained the chairman's title and focused on international operations and acquisitions.

GameStop focused on international expansion in 2008 driven primarily by a pair of acquisitions. The largest of those was its $629 million purchase of video game retailer Micromania which brought with it some 330 stores in France. South of the equator GameStop acquired The Gamesman the largest independent gaming retailer in New Zealand. The deal included eight Gamesman video game stores and brought GameStop's total store count in the country to 38.

In June 2010 DeMatteo was promoted to executive chairman of the company while Raines was named CEO.

EXECUTIVES

COO, Tony D. Bartel, age 51, $821,865 total compensation
CEO, J. Paul Raines, $1,201,346 total compensation
EVP and CFO, Robert A. (Rob) Lloyd, $853,558 total compensation
VP Marketing, Mike Hogan, $499,717 total compensation
EVP and President U.S. Stores, Mike Buskey
SVP Technology Brands, Jason Ellis
President Kongregate, Emily Greer
EVP and President GameStop International, Michael K. (Mike) Mauler, $545,077 total compensation
President Simply Mac, Steve Bain
SVP Information Technology and CIO, Michael Cooper
Vice President Of Merchandising, Bob Puzon

Divisional Vice President Refurbishment Reverse Logistics, John (Jack) Daugherty
Vice President Stores, Kyle Leonard
Regional Vice President, Rory Rhodes
Regional Vice President, Matt Koch
Divisional Vice President Merchandising, Darron Nielsen
DVP International Information Technology Strategic Initiatives, Luigi Grosoli
Vice President Marketing And Sales, Art Doud
Regional Vice President, Mike Terlecky
Senior Vice President Customer Support, Bruce Kulp
Vice President, Blayne White
Vice President Stores Western U S, Jason Cochran
Vice President and Managing Director Europe, Jim Kirk
Vice President Treasurer, Michael (Mel) Nichols
DVP of Tax, Aj Cobb
Chairman, Daniel A. DeMatteo
Secretary, Scott Shaver
Treasurer, Sara Chho
Board Member, Asim Naqvi
Treasurer, Michael (Mel) Hogan
Auditors: Deloitte & Touche LLP

LOCATIONS

HQ: GameStop Corp
625 Westport Parkway, Grapevine, TX 76051
Phone: 817 424-2000
Web: www.gamestop.com

2015 Sales

	% of total
US	66
Europe	18
Australia	7
Canada	5
Technology brand	4
Total	**100**

2015 Stores

	No.
US	4,138
Europe	1,316
Australia	421
Canada	331
Technology Brand	484
Total	**6,690**

PRODUCTS/OPERATIONS

2015 Sales

	% of total
New video game software	33
Pre-owned video game products	26
New video game hardware	22
Other	19
Total	**100**

Selected Mergers & Acquisitions

FY2011
Spawn Labs (peer-to-peer game streaming technology developer)
Impulse (online distribution platform)
FY2010
Kongregate (social gaming site)

Selected Websites

www.ebgames.com.au
www.gamestop.ca
www.gamestop.co.uk
www.gamestop.com
www.gamestop.com/pcgames
www.gamestop.de
www.gamestop.es
www.gamestop.ie
www.gamestop.it
www.kongregate.com
www.micromania.fr

Selected Merchandise

Accessories
PC entertainment accessories
Video game accessories
Other
Internet streaming technology & digital distribution
Online games
PC entertainment software & other software
Used video games
Video game hardware
Video game software

COMPETITORS

Amazon.com	Kmart
Best Buy	RadioShack
Buy.com	Target Corporation
Carrefour	Toys ' ' R ' ' Us
Costco Wholesale	Wal-Mart
Fry' s Electronics	Zones
GameFly	eBay

HISTORICAL FINANCIALS

Company Type: Public

Income Statement

FYE: January 31

	REVENUE ($ mil.)	NET INCOME ($ mil.)	NET PROFIT MARGIN	EMPLOYEES
01/15*	9,296	393	4.2%	73,000
02/14	9,039	354	3.9%	69,000
02/13	8,886	(269)		65,000
01/12	9,550	339	3.6%	71,000
01/11	9,473	408	4.3%	68,000
Annual Growth	**(0.5%)**	**(0.9%)**	**—**	**1.8%**

*Fiscal year change

2015 Year-End Financials

Debt ratio: 8.38%
Return on equity: 18.25%
Cash ($ mil.): 610
Current ratio: 1.26
Long-term debt ($ mil.): 350

No. of shares (mil.): 107
Dividends
Yield: 0.0%
Payout: 38.0%
Market value ($ mil.): 3,796

	STOCK PRICE ($) FY Close	P/E High/Low		PER SHARE ($) Earnings	Dividends	Book Value
01/15*	35.25	13	9	3.47	1.32	19.20
02/14	35.07	19	8	2.99	1.10	19.53
02/13	24.69	—	—	(2.13)	0.80	19.34
01/12	24.32	12	8	2.41	0.00	22.24
01/11	20.98	9	6	2.65	0.00	19.84
Annual Growth	**13.9%**	**—**	**—**	**7.0%**	**—**	**(0.8%)**

*Fiscal year change

General Cable Corp. (DE)

General Cable keeps power flowing and communication going. The company designs manufactures and distributes copper aluminum and fiber optic wire and cable products that are used in electrical transmission and distribution power generation and voice and data communications. Major brands include BICC (energy cables) Carol (temporary power cables) and NextGen (data communication cables). General Cable's products are sold to commercial industrial electric utility telecom military and government retail and OEM distributor customers worldwide. The company also makes copper and aluminum rod for other wire and cable manufacturers and it integrates and installs high voltage systems on land and under water.

Geographic Reach

General Cable has more than 35 manufacturing facilities in some 22 countries around the world. The US accounts for 34% of its net sales.

Operations

With global R&D engineering and manufacturing operations General Cable divides its business into four geographic segments: North America Europe Latin America and Africa/Asia Pacific. These segments account for fairly balanced portions of revenue. Each segment also operates high-tech laboratories that engage in everything from material compounding and electrical testing to specialty cable product development and rod fabrication.

Sales and Marketing

General Cable has a regionally coordinated global direct sales force. Certain businesses operate under supply agreements for varying lengths of time. These agreements are generally strategic alliances with major utility customers around the world. General Cable is heavily dependent on its primary customer base of independent distributors and retailers which account for a substantial share of it sales; contractors and OEMs account for a smaller portion. The company spent almost $14 million on advertising during 2014.

Financial Performance

After experiencing three straight years of steady growth General Cable saw its revenues fall 7% to $5.98 billion in 2014. The company's net losses significantly grew from $10 million in 2013 to $643 million in 2014.

The revenue decline for 2014 was fueled by reduced sales from almost all of its segments. Its decrease in metal-adjusted net sales was primarily due to decreased volume unfavorable foreign currency exchange rate changes and an unfavorable selling price and product mix. Volume as measured by metal pounds sold decreased by 4% in 2014 compared to 2013.

Its larger net loss for 2014 was attributed to a goodwill impairment charge of $155 million and intangible asset impairment charges of $98 million related to its global restructuring plan. General Cable's operating cash flow has fluctuated wildly the last few years increasing by 95% in 2014 due to gains on the disposal of a subsidiary and a decrease in accounts payable and accrued and other liabilities.

Strategy

After experiencing net losses for 2013 and 2014 General Cable is working to cut costs. Throughout 2014 the company implemented a restructuring program designed to improve profitability in each of its reportable segments. The restructuring program is expected to result in ongoing annual savings of approximately $75 million beginning in 2014 with full realization starting in early 2016. The restructuring program involves the closure of certain underperforming assets as well as the consolidation and realignment of other facilities.

HISTORY

General Cable originated from some of the oldest names in the wiring business: Standard Underground Cable (founded by George Westinghouse) and Phillips Wire and Safety Cable Company both founded in the 1800s. The companies supplied wire for historic events such as Samuel Morse's first telegram between Baltimore and Washington DC in 1844 the lighting of the Statute of Liberty in 1886 and the first Chicago World's Fair in 1892.

The company's best-known brand of nonmetallic sheathed cable Romex was invented at the company's Rome New York facility in 1922. Five years later Phillips Wire and Standard Underground Cable joined to form General Cable Corporation. In 1935 the company's cables were used for power lines connecting the Hoover Dam to Los Angeles.

EXECUTIVES

SVP and CIO, Elizabeth W. (Coco) Taliaferro

EVP General Cable Corporation and President and CEO General Cable North America, Gregory J. Lampert, age 47, $476,538 total compensation

EVP and CFO, Brian J. Robinson, age 46, $480,000 total compensation

President CEO and Director, Michael T. McDonnell, age 58

EVP General Cable Corporation and President and CEO General Cable Asia Pacific, Peter A. Campbell, age 54, $314,562 total compensation

EVP General Cable Corporation and President and CEO General Cable Europe, Robert D. (Bob) Kenny, age 49, $283,538 total compensation

EVP and Chief Human Resources Officer, Sonya Reed, age 41

Assistant Vice President Systems and Network Administrator Team Lead, Cory Thompson

Vice President Internal Audit, Glen Gustafson

Vice President Marketing and Business Development, Howard H Atkins

Vice President Human Resources, Matt Austin

National Accounts Manager, Ralph Perricelli

Vice President Quality, Bill Wilson

Vice President Finance and Global Treasurer, Steve Skerl

Vice President And General Manager Electric Utility Cables, Jay Lahman

Executive Vice President Group President, Greg Lampert

Vice President Operations, Duncan McIver

Chairman, John E. Welsh, age 64

Board Of Directors, Charles G McClure

Secretary, Robert (Bob) Siverd

Auditors: Deloitte & Touche LLP

LOCATIONS

HQ: General Cable Corp. (DE)
4 Tesseneer Drive, Highland Heights, KY 41076-9753
Phone: 859 572-8000   **Fax:** 859 572-8458
Web: www.generalcable.com

2014 Sales

	$ mil.	% of total
US	2,049	34
Canada	467	8
Brazil	457	8
France	383	6
Spain	218	4
Other	2,403	40
Total	**5,979**	**100**

PRODUCTS/OPERATIONS

2014 Sales by Product

	$ mil.	% of total
Electric utility	2,006	33
Electrical infrastructure	1,589	27
Construction	1,440	24
Communications	570	10
Non-Operating revenue bridges	373	6
Total	**5,979**	**100**

Selected Markets

Automotive
Commercial Audio/Video
Construction
Data Communications Distribution
Electrical Distribution
Electronics Distribution
Energy
Industrial Automation
Industrial Distribution
Military
Mining
Oil Gas & Petrochemical
Professional A/V and Broadcast
Renewables
Telecommunications
Transit

Selected Brands

Anaconda
BICC
Brand Rex
Carol
GenSPEED
Gepco
NextGen
NSW
NUAL
Phelps Dodge
Prestolite Wire
Silec
STABILOY

Selected Products

Automotive Products
Broadcast and Pro/Com A/V
Building Wire
Central Office Cables
Cord and Cordset Products
Datacom Cables
Electric Utility Cables
Electronic Cables
Fiber Optic Cables
Gepco Products
Industrial Cables
Military Cables
Mining Cables
Nuclear Cables
Offshore and Marine Shipboard Cables
Solar Energy Cables
Specialty Wire Harnesses
Telecommunications Cables
Transit Cables
Wind Energy Cables
X-tract ESP Cables

COMPETITORS

Belden	Owl Wire & Cable
Coleman Cable	Quabbin Wire
CommScope	Southwire
Corning	Standard Motor
Encore Wire	Products
Hubbell	Sumitomo Electric
Kalas Manufacturing	Superior Essex
LEONI	Volex
Nexans	

HISTORICAL FINANCIALS

Company Type: Public

Income Statement

FYE: December 31

	REVENUE ($ mil.)	NET INCOME ($ mil.)	NET PROFIT MARGIN	EMPLOYEES
12/14	5,979	(643)	—	13,000
12/13	6,421	(10)	—	15,000
12/12	6,014	9	0.2%	14,000
12/11	5,866	85	1.5%	12,000
12/10	4,864	76	1.6%	11,700
Annual Growth	**5.3%**	—	—	**2.7%**

2014 Year-End Financials

Debt ratio: 39.72%
Return on equity: (-74.24%)
Cash ($ mil.): 205
Current ratio: 1.62
Long-term debt ($ mil.): 933

No. of shares (mil.): 48
Dividends
  Yield: 4.8%
  Payout: —
Market value ($ mil.): 725

	STOCK PRICE ($) FY Close	P/E High/Low	PER SHARE ($) Earnings	Dividends	Book Value
12/14	14.90	— —	(12.86)	0.72	9.29
12/13	29.41	— —	(0.37)	0.72	25.81
12/12	30.41	356247	0.08	0.00	27.23
12/11	25.01	30 13	1.57	0.00	28.14
12/10	35.09	27 16	1.31	0.00	28.44
Annual Growth	**(19.3%)**	— —	—	—	**(24.4%)**

General Dynamics Corp.

Generally dynamic General Dynamics is a prime military contractor to the Pentagon (the US government accounts for about 60% of sales). The company's military operations include information systems and technology (information technology and collection as well as command control systems); marine systems (warships commercial tankers and nuclear submarines); and combat systems (battle tanks wheeled combat/tactical vehicles munitions and rockets and gun systems). Its aerospace unit which is composed of Gulfstream Aerospace and Jet Aviation designs makes and refurbishes business jets primarily for civilian customers.

Geographic Reach

General Dynamics operates around the world serving government and commercial customers on six continents spanning more than 40 countries. The US represents its largest market generating 75% of sales in 2014.

Operations

Unlike some of its rivals who cater only to the military market that is at the mercy of government budgetary fluctuations General Dynamics caters to military and civilian sectors manufacturing both combat systems and high-tech systems with each side buffering the other in times of market downturn. The Combat Systems division is composed of Armament and Technical Products; European Land Systems; Land Systems; and Ordnance and Tactical Systems.

General Dynamic's Marine Systems group is a major shipbuilder for the US Navy and it provides MRO (maintenance/repair/overhaul) services to keep those vessels ship-shape. Marine systems manufactures the Virginia-class nuclear-powered submarine the Arleigh Burke-class guided-missile destroyer (DDG-51) and the Lewis and Clark-class dry cargo/ammunition combat-logistics ship (T-AKE). Subsidiary Electric Boat builds nuclear submarines (Seawolf Ohio and Los Angeles classes) while Bath Iron Works builds DDG-51 and DDG-1000 destroyers.

On the civilian side of the business the company's Aerospace segment produces mid- and large-cabin business jet aircraft for which the company provides maintenance refurbishment and outfitting.

Last but not least –serving both the military and civilian sides –the company's Information Systems and Technology business unit provides cyber security tactical communication systems sensors and cameras ruggedized computers (for use in harsh environments such as those with strong vibrations extreme temperatures and wet or dusty conditions) and antennas to customers in the DoD the Department of Homeland Security the intelligence community federal civilian agencies and international customers.

Sales and MarketingGeneral Dynamics' main customer is the US Department of Defense (DoD). The company conducts business with government customers around the world with operations in Australia Brazil Canada France Germany Mexico Spain Switzerland and the United Kingdom. Throughout 2014 58% of its revenues were from the US government 17% came from US commercial customers 11% from international defense customers and the remaining 14% stemmed from international commercial customers.

Financial Performance

After enjoying years of growth General Dynamics has seen its revenues slowly decline over the last few years. Revenues declines marginally by 1% from 2013 to 2014. The company achieved a

7% spike in net income from 2013 to 2014 due to major cost reductions stemming from its Information Systems and Technology group. (Note: the company's 2013 annual financials were restated due to the early 2015 sale of its AxleTech business.)

The revenue dip was attributed to the selling of its axle operations coupled with an 11% decline in Information Systems and Technology sales resulting from lower volume across several programs including commercial wireless work. The small revenue decline for 2014 was also due to lower volumes within its Combat Systems business as a result of decreased US Army spending and delays in international orders.

The company has recorded consistent operating cash flow over the years increasing by 20% in 2014 due to the rise in net income coupled with cash inflows in changes in accounts receivable and a rise in customer advances and deposits.

Strategy

With US defense spending in decline General Dynamics' business strategy addresses programs that the military continues to emphasize including the need for warfighters and the need to replace resources lost in Iraq and Afghanistan. As the first US submarine to be configured for a post-Cold War defense landscape General Dynamics' Virginia-class submarine continues to meet the needs of the US Navy.

General Dynamics is also working to tighten up its balance sheet and cut down on costs. In early 2015 the company sold its AxleTech International subsidiary to The Carlyle Group. Also in 2015 the company integrated its two business units Advanced Information Systems and C4 Systems into a new Mission Systems business to improve cost competitiveness leverage the businesses' complementary capabilities and increase responsiveness to customers.

HISTORY

In 1899 John Holland founded Electric Boat Company a New Jersey ship and submarine builder. The company built ships PT boats and submarines during WWII but when faced with waning postwar orders CEO John Jay Hopkins diversified with the 1947 purchase of aircraft builder Canadair. Hopkins formed General Dynamics in 1952 merging Electric Boat and Canadair and buying Consolidated Vultee Aircraft (Convair) a major producer of military and civilian aircraft in 1954.

EXECUTIVES

Vice President & General Manager Of Nassco, Kevin M Graney

Vice President Administration, Raymond E Kozen

EVP Marine Systems, John P. Casey, age 61, $685,000 total compensation

VP; President Bath Iron Works and NASSCO, Frederick J. (Fred) Harris, age 68

VP; President Ordnance and Tactical Systems, Michael S. Wilson, age 65

Chairman and CEO, Phebe N. Novakovic, age 58, $1,560,000 total compensation

VP; President C4 Systems, Christopher (Chris) Marzilli, age 56

VP; President Electric Boat, Jeffrey S. Geiger, age 53

President Gulfstream Aerospace Corp., Mark L. Burns, age 56

President Jet Aviation, Robert E. (Rob) Smith

EVP Combat Systems, Mark C. Roualet, age 57, $612,500 total compensation

EVP General Dynamics Information Systems and Technology Group; President General Dynamics Information Technology, S. Daniel (Dan) Johnson, age 68

VP; President European Land Systems, Alfonso J. Ramonet

SVP and CFO, Jason W. Aiken, age 42, $625,000 total compensation

VP; President Land Systems, Gary L. Whited, age 54

CIO General Dynamics Information Technology, Jim Knapp

Vice President Supply Chain Management, Kevin Mooney

Vice President President Land Systems, Mark Smith

Vice President Internal Audit, Wayne Maiers

Vice President GSA GWAC Programs, Vic Bukowski

Vice President Of International Development, Sheldon Summers

Vice President And General Manager For Army Infrastructure, Daniel (Dan) Busby

Vice President Contracts, Duane Piper

Vice President Engineering Manufacturing And Mission Assurance, Jim Stockdale

VPGM, Michael (Mel) Kent

Vice President Strategic Planning, Marion T Davis

Vice President Of Information Technology, Lashawn Taylor

Vice President Financial Planning, Mark Rayha

Vice President, Markeba Gregory

Vice President, Tommy Augustsson

Vice President and General Manager, Steve Elgin

Director Of Surgery, Todd Tarby

Vice President Gm, Jim Losse

Vice President, Charles Prouty

Vice President, Mike Garrity

Senior Vice President Service Delivery for AIS, Tom Carstenbrock

Vice President, Billy Statham

Staff Vice President And Associate General Counsel, Jim Murphy

Vice President Human Resources And Admistration, Jack Picker

Executive Vice President Combat Systems, Charles (Chas) Hall

Vice President, Asha Wiethers

Vice President Communications Information Technology, Mark Meudt

Vice President Business Development, Brian Lass

VPGM ISR Systems, Kirstan Rock

Vice President Maritime Information Systems, Bob Browning

Vice President, Alan Lovelace

Senior Vice President Production Delivery And Sustainment, Rick Gillette

Vice President Tax, Ken Hayduk

Vice President Real Estate, Jeffrey (Jeff) Kudlac

Vice President and Treasurer, David H (Dave) Fogg

Executive Vice President Aerospace, Joseph T (Jo) Lombardo

Senior Vice President General Counsel Secretary, David A (Dave) Savner

Vice President; President Advanced Information Systems, Thomas (Thom) Kirchmaier

Vice President Business Development, Dave Bristow

Vice President Business Development, Tony Cothron

Board Member, William Fricks

Secretary, Regina Pedroso

Treasurer, Bob Selee

Auditors: KPMG LLP

LOCATIONS

HQ: General Dynamics Corp.
2941 Fairview Park Drive, Suite 100, Falls Church, VA 22042-4513
Phone: 703 876-3000
Web: www.generaldynamics.com

2013 Sales

	% of total
North America	83
Europe	9
Asia/Pacific	5
Other	3
Total	**100**

PRODUCTS/OPERATIONS

2013 Sales by Segment

	$ mil.	% of total
Information systems & technology	10,268	33
Aerospace	8,118	26
Marine systems	6,712	21
Combat systems	6,120	20
Total	**31,218**	**100**

2013 Sales by Customer

	% of total
US government	62
US commercial	18
International commercial	13
International defence	7
Total	**100**

Selected Operations

Aerospace
  Gulfstream Aerospace
  G150 (Midsize range of 3000 nautical miles 4 passengers)
  G280 (Super midsize range 3600 nautical miles 4 passengers)
  G350 (Large-cabin range of 3800 nautical miles 8 passengers)
  G450 (Large-cabin range of 4350 nautical miles 8 passengers)
  G500 (Large-cabin range of 5800 nautical miles 8 passengers)
  G550 (Large-cabin range of 6750 nautical miles 8 passengers)
  G650 (Ultra-large-cabin range of 7000 nautical miles 8 passengers)
Combat systems
  Armament & technical products
  Advanced materials (composites)
  Armament systems
  AxleTech
  European land systems
  Ammunition
  Artillery
  Bridge systems
  Tracked vehicles
  Wheeled vehicles
  Land systems
  Abrams tank
  MRAP combat vehicle
  Stryker combat vehicle
  Ordnance and tactical systems
  Artillery projectiles
  Bomb bodies
  Combat systems
  Munitions
  Mortar weapons
Information systems and technology
  Advanced information systems
  C4 Systems
  Information technology
Marine systems
  Bath Iron Works Corp.
  Arleigh Burke (DDG 51) destroyer
  Zumwalt (DDG 1000) destroy
  Electric Boat
  Virginia submarine
  Seawolf submarine
  NASSCO (ship construction and repair)

COMPETITORS

Airbus	Leidos
BAE SYSTEMS	Lockheed Martin
Boeing	Motorola Solutions
Bombardier	Navistar International
Cisco Systems	Nokia
DRS Technologies	Northrop Grumman
Dassault Aviation	Orbital ATK
Day & Zimmermann	Peugeot

FLIR Systems	Raytheon
HP Enterprise Services	Renco
Harris Corp.	Rockwell Collins
ITT Corp.	Textron
L-3 Communications	United Technologies

HISTORICAL FINANCIALS
Company Type: Public

Income Statement
FYE: December 31

	REVENUE ($ mil.)	NET INCOME ($ mil.)	NET PROFIT MARGIN	EMPLOYEES
12/15	31,469	2,965	9.4%	99,900
12/14	30,852	2,533	8.2%	99,500
12/13	31,218	2,357	7.6%	96,000
12/12	31,513	(332)	—	92,200
12/11	32,677	2,526	7.7%	95,100
Annual Growth	(0.9%)	4.1%	—	1.2%

2015 Year-End Financials

Debt ratio: 10.62%
Return on equity: 26.28%
Cash ($ mil.): 2,785
Current ratio: 1.17
Long-term debt ($ mil.): 2,898

No. of shares (mil.): 312
Dividends
Yield: 1.9%
Payout: 30.6%
Market value ($ mil.): 42,992

	STOCK PRICE ($) FY Close	P/E High/Low	PER SHARE ($) Earnings	Dividends	Book Value
12/15	137.36	17 14	9.08	2.69	34.31
12/14	137.62	19 12	7.42	2.42	35.61
12/13	95.55	14 10	6.67	2.19	41.03
12/12	69.27	— —	(0.94)	2.51	32.20
12/11	66.41	11 8	6.87	1.83	37.12
Annual Growth	19.9%	— —	7.2%	10.1%	(2.0%)

General Electric Co

From turbines and TVs to aircraft engines and power plants General Electric (GE) is plugged in to businesses that shape the modern world. The company produces —take a deep breath —aircraft engines locomotives and other transportation equipment lighting electric control equipment generators and turbines and medical imaging equipment. GE also owns mega-financial company GE Capital which offers commercial finance commercial aircraft leasing real estate and energy financial services. GE's other segments include Aviation Home & Business Solutions and Transportation. GE looks to sell its GE Capital and home appliances businesses to focus on its core industrial business.

HISTORY

Company BackgroundGeneral Electric (GE) was established in 1892 in New York the result of a merger between Thomson-Houston and Edison General Electric. Charles Coffin was GE's first president and Thomas Edison who left the company in 1894 was one of the directors.

GE's financial strength (backed by the Morgan banking house) and its research focus contributed to its initial success. Early products included such Edison legacies as light bulbs elevators motors toasters and other appliances under the GE and Hotpoint labels. In the 1920s GE joined AT&T and Westinghouse in a radio broadcasting venture Radio Corporation of America (RCA) but GE sold

off its RCA holdings in 1930 because of an antitrust ruling.

By 1980 GE had reached $25 billion in revenues from plastics consumer electronics nuclear reactors and jet engines. But it had become rigid and bureaucratic. Jack Welch became president in 1981 and shook up the company. He decentralized operations and adopted a strategy of pursuing only high-achieving ventures and dumping those that didn't perform. GE shed air-conditioning (1982) housewares (1984) and semiconductors (1988) and with the proceeds acquired Employers Reinsurance (1984); RCA including NBC (1986 but sold RCA in 1987); CGR medical equipment (1987); and investment banker Kidder Peabody (1990).

In the early 1990s GE grew its lighting business. It bought mutual fund wholesaler GNA in 1993 and GE Investment Management (now GE Financial Network) began selling mutual funds to the public.

GE sold scandal-plagued Kidder Peabody to Paine Webber in 1994. General Electric Capital Services (GECS) expanded its lines buying Amex Life Insurance (Aon's Union Fidelity unit) and Life Insurance Co. of Virginia in 1995 and First Colony the next year. The company sold its struggling GEnie online service in 1996 and formed an NBC and Microsoft venture the MSNBC cable news channel. In 1997 GE Engine Services bought aircraft engine maintenance firms Greenwich Air Services and UNC.

GE acquired Lockheed Martin's medical imaging unit in 1997 and added to the medical systems business with the 1998 purchase of Marquette Medical Systems. In 1998 GECS became the first foreign company to enter Japan's life insurance market when it bought assets from Toho Mutual Life Insurance and set up GE Edison Life.

In 1999 GECS bought the 53% of Montgomery Ward it didn't already own along with the retailer's direct-marketing arm as Montgomery Ward emerged from bankruptcy. (Ward declared bankruptcy again in 2000.) In 2000 it reorganized GE Information Systems to form an e-commerce unit Global eXchange Services (GXS). (GE sold 90% of GXS to buyout firm Francisco Partners in 2002.)

Later in 2000 the company announced its biggest acquisition of the Welch era. Moving in at the last minute GE trumped a rival bid from United Technologies and agreed to pay $45 billion in stock for manufacturing giant Honeywell International and to assume $3.4 billion in Honeywell debt.

Welch by then viewed as one of the best corporate leaders in the US had agreed to postpone his retirement from April 2001 until the end of that year in order to oversee the completion of the Honeywell acquisition. But European regulators concerned about the potential strength of the combined GE-Honeywell aircraft-related businesses blocked the Honeywell deal that summer. Welch then stepped down and Jeff Immelt formerly president and CEO of GE Medical Systems succeeded him in September 2001.

Immelt initially set about reshaping GE by spinning off its life and mortgage insurance businesses into a new entity Genworth Financial which went public in 2004 (completely divested in 2006). GE acquired UK-based Amersham a medical diagnostics and life sciences company since renamed GE Healthcare Medical Diagnostics.

In 2006 GE sold off most of its remaining insurance businesses including GE Insurance Solutions and Employers Reinsurance in a sale to Swiss Re. The company kept its US life reinsurance business.

Citing rising commodities costs GE sold its advanced materials unit which produced silicone quartz and ceramics products to Apollo Manage-

ment and sold its GE Plastics unit (now SABIC Innovative Plastics) to SABIC for more than $11 billion in 2007. Also that year GE shut down the operations of wholesale subprime lender WMC Mortgage.

At the same time GE built some of its traditional businesses through acquisitions. In early 2007 the company's aviation division acquired aircraft systems manufacturer Smiths Aerospace from Smiths Group. GE Energy bought oil and gas production equipment supplier Vetco Gray and the US retail natural gas distribution network of Knight (then named Kinder Morgan).

In 2011 GE sold a controlling stake in NBCUniversal to Comcast. GE retained a 49% stake in the media venture.

In late 2015 GE terminated its agreement to sell its household appliances business to the world's second-largest appliance maker Electrolux for $3.3 billion in after a year of opposition from US regulators over concerns about competition.

EXECUTIVES

Vice Chairman and Chairman and CEO GE Capital, Keith S. Sherin, age 56, $2,300,000 total compensation
SVP and CFO, Jeffrey S. (Jeff) Bornstein, $1,450,000 total compensation
SVP and President and CEO GE Europe and CEO GE Germany, Ferdinando F. (Nani) Beccalli-Falco
SVP and Director GE Global Research and CTO, Mark M. Little, age 62
VP Corporate Communications, Elizabeth J. (Beth) Comstock, age 54
VP and Senior Counsel Litigation and Legal Policy, Brackett B. Denniston, age 67, $1,775,000 total compensation
Vice Chairman and Head of Global Operations, John G. Rice, age 58, $2,450,000 total compensation
Chairman and CEO, Jeffrey R. (Jeff) Immelt, age 59, $3,750,000 total compensation
President and CEO GE Healthcare, John L. Flannery, age 53
President and CEO GE Capital International, Richard A. (Rich) Laxer
President and CEO GE Lighting, Maryrose T. Sylvester
SVP and President and CEO GE Aviation, David L. Joyce, age 58
Head of Global Research, Victor (Vic) Abate, age 46
SVP and President and CEO GE Power and Water, Steve Bolze, age 52
President and CEO GE Transportation, Jamie S. Miller, age 46
President and CEO GE Africa, Jay W. Ireland
President and CEO GE Asset Management, Dmitri L. Stockton, age 51
President and CEO Synchrony Financial, Margaret M. Keane, age 56
President and CEO GE Appliances and Lighting, Charles P. (Chip) Blankenship, age 49
SVP and COO GE Hitachi, Jay Wileman
President and CEO Power Generation Services GE Power and Water, Paul A. McElhinney
President and CEO GE Oil and Gas, Lorenzo Simonelli, age 42
President and CEO GE Healthcare China, Rachel Duan, age 41
President and CEO GE Transportation, Russell Stokes, age 44
CEO GE Onshore Wind, Anne M. McEntee, age 45
Chief Digital Officer, Bill Ruh, age 54
President and COO GE Capital, Tom Gentile
President and CEO GE Capital Americas, Dan Henson
CIO, Jim Fowler
VP and CEO Russia/CIS, Ron Pollett
CEO GE Vietnam and Cambodia, Pham Hong Son

CEO GE Sustainable Healthcare Solutions, Terri Bresenham
CEO GE Offshore Wind, Anders Soe Jensen
CEO GE Hydro, Yves Rannou
Vice President Of Marketing, Peter Lysogorski
Vice President Management, Alexander Kloet
Vice President, Kevin Czarnecki
Senior Vice President CAO, Sean Looney
Assistant Vice President, Valerie Bouchereau
Vice President Marketing and Global Product Management Lighting, Steve Briggs
Senior Vice President, Philip Carfora
Vice President Senior Account Manager, Kevin O'Connor
Senior Vice President Advanced Technology, Anil Duggal
Second Vice President, Delaine Ferrell
Senior Vice President Bank Loan Group, James (Jamie) Persico
Vice President Of It, Jeff Brousseau
Senior Vice President Of Brand Marketing, Chris Matthews
Senior Vice President, Timothy Perusek
Vice President, Jason Piorkowski
Senior Vice President Sales, Wren K Rex
Vice President Fraud Risk, Richard (Dick) Cooney
Vice President And Assistant Treasurer Short Term Funding, Mark Barber
Assistant Vice President, Andrew Eversfield
Vice President Supply Chain Services, Jay Eisenmenger
Vice President Media Digital and Social Marketing, Bob Bishop
Senior Vice President risk, Karen Burston
Vice President Human Resources, Melissa Reinke
Vice President, William Hayburn
Vice President of Field Marketing Services, Andy Hermo
Vice President Marketing, Louisa Ostrowski
Vice President Chief Engineers Engineering and Technology Aviation Systems, Mark Beatson
National Sales Manager Retail, Ned Butler
Vice President Patent Licensing, Daniel Potvin
Senior Vice President Commercial Excellence, Anthony Sabino
Vice President, Scott Klayman
Assistant Vice President, Nicole Cipriani
Vice President Missouri, Rich Lynn
Senior Vice President Structured Finance, Michelle Demita
Vice President Of Equity Derivatives, Charmaine Altmann
Senior Vice President Fleet Services, Andy Rubin
Cvpe, Jacqueline Sears
Vice President Corporate Risk and Retail Finance, Stephen (Steve) Bakonyi
Assistant Vice President, Anthony Pope
Vice President Of Sales, Michael Sylstra
Vice President Of Operations, Chris Wentland
Senior Vice President, Steve Decarlo
Vice President, Mike Schlessinger
Senior Vice President Strategic Marketing GE Finance, Brian Fedigan
Vice President International Programs, Richard (Dick) Douglas
Vice President Aerospace Business, Lynn A Saunders
Vice President, Robert Wagner
Vice President For Clinical And Regulatory Affairs, Mei Barselou
Vice President Customer Support and Services, Brian Lonergan
Vice President Finance, Paul Hanounik
Senior Vice President, Thomas (Thom) Bruce
Vice President Of Gaming Operations, Julie Kutchin
Vice President, Jodi Groth
Vice President, Martin Miller
Vice President Operations, Marianne Mallon

Vice President Marketing and Sales, Jeffrey (Jeff) Davis
Vice President Of Human Resources, Richard (Dick) Croll
Assistant Vice President of Marketing, Bryan Clark
Commercial Vice President, Jeff Glenn
Senior Vice President, Darren Dixon
Senior Vice President Product Development, Hector Chaviano
Senior Vice President Global Sales and Business Development, Ryan Aquino
Vice President Global Manufacturing, Gary Powell
Vice President Enterprise and Operational Risk, Joseph (Jo) Beal
Senior Vice President Of Music, Jan Scholzen
Senior Vice President Sponsor Business Development, Rod P Bollins
Regional Vice President Sales, Bjorn Gidner
Vice President Business Operations, Jennifer Taylor
Vice President Of Industry Solutions, Debbie Mackey
Vice President Bank Marketing, Joseph Lyons
Vice President Strategic Initiatives, Allison Garrigan
Vice President Strategic Operations, Ralph Passarelli
Vice President Marketing Operations Strategic Business Development, Ron Rozier
Region Vice President, Joe Gasque
National Account Manager, Kennith Miller
Vice President Marketing, Peter Ehrenheim
Vice President, Deborah (Deb) Zajac
Vice President Of Marketing, Ron Gladish
Vice President Finance, Stephani Cunningham
Senior Vice President, Savant Ahmed
Vice President Marketing and Product Marketing, Barbara (Barb) Veneklase
Assistant Vice President Brand and Corporate Communications Indonesia, Dendi Danianto
Vice President, Rena Stanislovaitis
Assistant Vice President Risk, Andrew Lackner
National Account Manager, Travis Hayman
Senior Vice President Vice Public Relations, Rene Buhay
Vice President Transmission and Distribution GE Energy, Bob Gilligan
Vice President Corporate Investor Communications, Trevor Schauenberg
Vice President And General Manager Customer Collaboration Business Unit, Jessica Braun
Vice President License And Certifictions, Luke Fields
Vice President Customer Intelligence, William Whymark
Assistant Vice President Customer Service Manager, Robert Kircher
Executive Vice President Of Washington Operations, Myron Van Ert
Senior Vice President GC and ChiefComplianceOff, David D (Dave) Nelson
Senior Vice President Environmental Affairs, Ron Burke
National Sales Manager, Mikhail Yakunkin
Vice President Controller Chief Accounting Officer, Kelly Tracy
Vice President Of Risk Management, Irina Moore
Vice President, Gunjan Bhartia
Senior Vice President Capital Markets, Sean Obranski
Vice President Advance Technology, Rohan Kelkar
Vice President Strategic Marketing, John Padgett
Senior Vice President, Kathleen Chomienne
Vice President Investor, Keith Jack
Vice President, Mary Gaede
Vice President Engineering And Technology, Joe Krisciunas
Vice President Marketing, Caimin Dolphin
Vice President And Director, Pupinder Bhutiani
Vice President Risk Manager, Peter Wielgos

Assistant Vice President, Jason Embleton
Vice President Marketing Operations, Dermot Manifold
Vice President Marketing, Gilberto Peralta
Vice President Marketing, Maran Nalluswami
Assistant Vice President, Paul Sleet
Vice President, John Critelli
Vice President, Keith Tornichia
Legal Secretary, Marlene Gerardi
Auditors: KPMG LLP

LOCATIONS

HQ: General Electric Co
  3135 Easton Turnpike, Fairfield, CT 06828-0001
Phone: 203 373-2211   **Fax:** 203 373-3131
Web: www.ge.com

2014 Sales

	% of total
Americas	
US	48
Other Countries	9
Non-US	
Europe	17
Asia	16
Middle East & Africa	10
Total	**100**

PRODUCTS/OPERATIONS

2014 Sales

	$ mil.	% of total
GE Capital	42,725	28
Power & Water	27,564	18
Aviation	23,990	15
Oil & Gas	18,676	12
Healthcare	18,299	12
Appliances & Lighting	8,404	6
Energy Management	7,319	5
Transportation	5,650	4
Corporate items & eliminations	(4038)	-
Total	**148,589**	**100**

COMPETITORS

ALSTOM	ITT Corp.
Agilent Technologies	JPMorgan Chase
Bank of America	Johnson Controls
CIGNA	Raytheon
Capital One	Rockwell Automation
Caterpillar	Rolls-Royce
Citigroup	Siemens AG
Deutsche Bank	Textron
Electrolux	ThyssenKrupp
General Re	Toshiba
HSBC	United Technologies
Hitachi	

HISTORICAL FINANCIALS

Company Type: Public

Income Statement

FYE: December 31

	REVENUE ($ mil.)	NET INCOME ($ mil.)	NET PROFIT MARGIN	EMPLOYEES
12/14	148,589	15,233	10.3%	305,000
12/13	146,045	13,057	8.9%	307,000
12/12	147,359	13,641	9.3%	305,000
12/11	147,300	14,151	9.6%	301,000
12/10	150,211	11,644	7.8%	287,000
Annual Growth	(0.3%)	6.9%	—	1.5%

2014 Year-End Financials

Debt ratio: 41.98%—
Return on equity: 11.78%
Cash ($ mil.): 90,208
Current ratio: 0.86
Long-term debt ($ mil.): 200,414

Dividends
  Yield: 3.5%
  Payout: 59.3%
Market value ($ mil.): —

	STOCK PRICE ($)	P/E	PER SHARE ($)		
	FY Close	High/Low	Earnings	Dividends	Book Value
12/14	25.27	19 16	1.50	0.89	12.74
12/13	28.03	22 16	1.27	0.79	12.98
12/12	20.99	18 14	1.29	0.70	11.82
12/11	17.91	17 12	1.23	0.61	11.01
12/10	18.29	18 13	1.06	0.46	11.20
Annual Growth	8.4%	— —	9.1%	17.9%	3.3%

General Mills, Inc.

General Mills gets its Kix vying for the top spot among cereal makers. Every year it jockeys with Kellogg to be #1 in that market with a brand arsenal that includes kid-friendly Kix as well as Chex Cheerios Lucky Charms and Wheaties. Much more than a cereal maker General Mills is one of the world's largest food companies. Some of its #1 and #2 market-leading brands include Betty Crocker dessert mixes Gold Medal flour Green Giant vegetables Pillsbury cookie dough and Yoplait yogurt. While most of the firm's sales come from the US General Mills is working to extend the reach and position of its brands globally. It picked up natural foods maker Annie's in 2014.

HISTORY

Cadwallader Washburn built his first flour mill in 1866 in Minneapolis which eventually became the Washburn Crosby Company. After winning a gold medal for flour at an 1880 exposition the company changed the name of its best flour to Gold Medal Flour.

In 1921 advertising manager Sam Gale created fictional spokeswoman Betty Crocker so that correspondence to housewives could go out with her signature. The firm introduced Wheaties cereal in 1924. James Bell named president in 1925 consolidated the company with other US mills in 1928 to form General Mills the world's largest miller. The companies operated independently of one another with corporate headquarters coordinating advertising and merchandising.

General Mills began introducing convenience foods such as Bisquick (1931) and Cheerios (1941). During WWII it produced war goods such as ordnance equipment and developed chemical and electronics divisions.

When Edwin Rawlings became CEO in 1961 he closed half of the flour mills and divested non-profitable lines as electronics. This cost $200 million in annual sales but freed resources for such acquisitions as Kenner Products (toys 1967) and Parker Brothers (board games 1968) which made General Mills the world's largest toy company.

During the next 20 years the company made many acquisitions including Gorton's (frozen seafood 1968) Monet (jewelry 1968) Eddie Bauer (outerwear 1971) and The Talbots (women's clothing 1973). It bought Red Lobster in 1970 and acquired the US rights to Yoplait yogurt in 1977. When the toy and fashion divisions' profits fell in 1984 they were spun off as Kenner Parker Toys and Crystal Brands (1985). Reemphasizing food in 1989 the firm sold many businesses including Eddie Bauer and Talbots.

To expand into Europe General Mills struck two important joint ventures: Cereal Partners Worldwide (with Nestlé in 1989) and Snack Ventures Europe (with PepsiCo in 1992).

As part of a cereal price war in 1994 the company cut coupon promotion costs by $175 million and lowered prices on many cereals. But some retailers did not pass on the price cuts to consumers due to shortages that developed after the FDA found an unauthorized pesticide in some cereals. General Mills destroyed 55 million boxes of cereal at a cost of $140 million. Stephen Sanger became CEO in 1995. That year the company sold Gortons to Unilever and spun off its restaurant businesses as Darden Restaurants.

Focused on a food-only future in the late 1990s General Mills picked up several smaller businesses including Ralcorp Holdings' Chex snack and cereal lines and Gardetto's Bakery snack mixes as well as the North American rights to Olibra an appetite suppressant food additive made by Scotia Holdings. Entering the natural foods market in 2000 General Mills launched Sunrise organic cereal and bought organic foods producer Small Planet Foods.

Big changes came in 2001 when General Mills became the #1 cereal maker in the US overtaking Kellogg for the first time since 1906. The company then completed its $10.5 billion purchase of Pillsbury from Diageo in October 2001. A month later General Mills sold competing product lines to International Multifoods. Also that year the company launched a 50-50 joint venture with DuPont to develop soy beverages marketed under the 8th Continent brand name. While busily integrating Pillsbury in 2002 General Mills saw its income fall and watched as Kellogg regained the lead in the cereal market. In 2003 the SEC began an investigation into the company's sales and accounting practices (which it terminated in 2005 taking no action against General Mills).

In 2004 General Mills filed a universal shelf registration with the SEC the result of which is that Diageo had to register the common shares of General Mills that it owns before it could sell those shares in a public offering. Also as a result of the shelf registration two Diageo-designated members of General Mills' board (including Diageo CEO Paul Walsh) resigned as a result of a change in the two companies' stockholders agreement that terminated Diageo's right to designate two General Mills' board members. Diageo sold part of its approximate 20% stake in General Mills. General Mills in turn sold an $835 million stake to an affiliate of Lehman Brothers Holding and used $750 million to buy back the Diageo shares and $85 million to pay down debt.

Also in 2004 the company sold its US Häagen-Dazs ice cream shop franchise business to Dreyer's Grand Ice Cream. In 2005 it sold its stake in Snack Ventures Europe joint venture to PepsiCo for $750 million. That year the company introduced Yoplait Healthy Heart which contains cholesterol-lowering plant sterols.

Diageo sold two-thirds of its 20% stake in General Mills in 2005. Later that year General Mills announced the sale of Lloyd's barbecue business to Hormel Foods. In 2006 Cereal Partners Worldwide (its joint venture with Nestlé) acquired the Australian breakfast cereal operations of Uncle Tobys from Burns Philp.

After more than 10 years of being ignored the Jolly Green Giant came out of retirement in 2005 as part of a multi-million dollar marketing campaign by General Mills to up its veggie sales. The next year General Mills declined to renew its licensing agreement with Archer Daniels Midland regarding the sale and marketing of Pillsbury Bakery Flour to the industrial and foodservice sectors. General Mills integrated the brand which consists of mixes and frozen bakery products into its bakery ingredients segment.

In order to develop healthier products in 2006 the company entered a supply agreement for DHA (an omega-3 fatty acid said to play a role in mental and cardiovascular health) with Martek Biosciences maker of DHA (which is already widely used in infant formula).

General Mills pulled its reduced-sugar children's cereal from the market in 2007 due to poor sales. Sweetened with SPLENDA the cereals never took off with consumers perhaps due to resistance to the sugar replacement. (Kellogg and Kraft use sugar in their reduced-sugar cereal offerings.) That year the company acquired UK chilled pastry company Saxby Bros.

Also in 2007 CEO Sanger stepped down. President and COO Ken Powell replaced him. The following year General Mills and DuPont sold their soy-milk joint venture 8th Continent to Stremicks Heritage Foods.

To better focus on its core brands and foodservice offerings the company in mid-2010 sold its Delicity chain of bakeries in Argentina to Tentissimo Group which also operates restaurants under the Tentissimo banner in the country. The deal included the Delicity brand five company-owned bakeries and franchiser rights which apply to the roughly 55 bakery locations operated by franchisees. General Mills also agreed to continue supplying dough products to the chain. It had owned Delicity since acquiring Pillsbury in 2001.

In 2008 the company sold its Pop·Secret operations to Diamond Foods for some $190 million in cash. Pop·Secret is the second-largest-selling branded popcorn in the US after Orville Redenbacher which is made by ConAgra. (ConAgra also makes Act II microwaveable popcorn.) While General Mills said it is concentrating its efforts on increasing the sales of its more lucrative core brands the high price of corn most probably also figured into the decision to jettison Pop·Secret.

General Mills made no divestures in 2009 but in 2010 the company ceased making Perfect Portions refrigerated biscuits and exited the kids' refrigerated yogurt beverage and microwave soup segments in its US retail operations; internationally it also stopped the manufacture of foodservice breadcrumbs with the sale of its Brazilian bread and pasta plant for $6 million. These product cessations were made in response to its declining financial results particularly in its international segment.

To better focus on its retail sales channels in late 2010 General Mills sold its Croissant King (acquired in 2005) and van den Bergh's (acquired in 1999) frozen bakery business in Australia to Ireland's Kerry Group. The sale includes frozen dough and pastry products sold to professional bakers.

Following that divestiture General Mills in 2011 acquired Australia's Pasta Master a maker of chilled Italian meals pasta and sauces. The purchase valued at nearly $40 million broadened General Mills' ready-to-cook pasta offerings.

To help offset weakness in its core cereal business General Mills is beefing up its yogurt empire through acquisitions such as its $1.2 billion purchase of a controlling stake in Yoplait in 2011 a brand that it had licensed for several decades. The company acquired the 50% stake in Yoplait owned by French investment firm PAI Partners plus 1% from dairy cooperative Social. Additionally General Mills acquired a 50% share of a related firm that owns Yoplait's global branding rights. General Mills aims to expand Yoplait's operations in France Europe and the rest of the world. Also in 2011 General Mills acquired Dean Foods' Mountain High all-natural yogurt business for about $85 million. The brand became part of General Mills' Yoplait USA division.

In line with its strategy to grow its business in global markets General Mills acquired Parampara's ready-to-cook spice and sauce mixes made and marketed in India and also exported to the US Canada and Japan. In 2012 it bought Brazilian food maker Yoki Alimentos which makes and markets more than 600 items under nine brands including Yoki and Kitano. The deal doubles General Mills' annual sales in Latin America.

EXECUTIVES

Chairman and CEO, Kendall J. (Ken) Powell, age 62, $1,165,717 total compensation
Senior Vice President, Mike Davis
EVP General Counsel Chief Compliance and Risk Management Officer and Secretary, Roderick A. (Rick) Palmore, age 64, $645,150 total compensation
SVP; CEO Cereal Partners Worldwide, David P. (Dave) Homer
EVP and COO International, Christopher D. (Chris) O'Leary, age 56, $653,417 total compensation
SVP External Relations; President General Mills Foundation, Kimberly A. (Kim) Nelson, age 52
SVP and Chief Marketing Officer, Ann W. H. Simonds
SVP; President Greater China, Gary Chu
VP Treasurer, Donal L. (Don) Mulligan, age 55, $653,417 total compensation
SVP; President Big G Cereals, James H. (Jim) Murphy
EVP Supply Chain, John R. Church, age 49
SVP; President Meals, Michele S. Meyer
SVP; President Sales and Channel Development, Shawn P. O'Grady, age 51
EVP; COO US Retail, Jeffrey L. Harmening, age 49
EVP Innovation Technology and Quality, Peter C. Erickson, age 54
SVP; President General Mills Canada, David E. Dudick
VP; President Häagen-Dazs Strategic Business Unit, Rebecca L. (Becky) O'Grady
SVP; President Latin America, Sean N. Walker
SVP; President Europe Australia and New Zealand, Jonathon J. (Jon) Nudi
VP; President Snacks, Anton Vincent
VP; President Yoplait International, Olivier Faujour
VP; President Asia Middle East and Africa, Christina Law
VP; President Yoplait USA, David Clark
VP; President Convenience and Foodservice, Bethany C. Quam
VP; President Baking, Elizabeth Nordlie
VP and Chief Investment Officer, Marie C. Pillai
Vice President, Jerald (Jerry) Young
Vice President General Manager, Tim Fieldhouse
Vice President Marketing Big G, John (Jack) Haugen
Vice President, Laurie Downs
Vice President Consumer Insight, Gayle Fuguitt
Vice President Of Government Relations, Mary Catherinetoker
Vice President Chief Staffing Officer, Stephanie Lilak
Vice President Of Human Resources, Peter (Pete) Mcdonald
Vice President Health and Wellness Initiatives, Andy Haversack
Vice President Investor Relations, Kristin Wenker
Vice President Human Resources, Sandy Olson
Vice President Of Human Resources, Mark Innis
National Account Manager, Karyna Rooke
Vice President, Dave Dudick
Vice President Of Labor Relations, Brian McMenamin
Vice President Yoplait, Camille Gibson
Vice President Global Health Services and Chief Medical Officer, Julia Halberg
Vice President Of Marketing, Doug McGillivray
Vice President Human Resources, Michael (Mel) Davis
Vice President Human Resources, Beth Flynn

Vice President Manufacturing, Kevin Schoen
Vice President Government Relations, Mary Toker
Vice President Marketing Pillsbury, Katy Dickson
Vice President, Dave Johnson
Vice President Information Technology, James Rohe
Vice President Of Human Resources, Randy Schwing
Vice President Of Customer Marketing, Pat Simmons
Vice President Of Human Resources, Liz Bosman
Vice President Of Human Resources, Victor Huang
Vice President Sales Admin, Ruth Welter
Vice President Infrastructure General Mills Inc., Suzanne Simonett
Vice President Supply Chain Logistics Strategy and Grain Operations, Tim Coats
Vice President, Kim Nelson
Vice President of Strategic Planning, Lohr Lesueur
Assistant Treasurer, Gerald (Jerry) Morris
Secretary, Christopher (Chris) Rauschl
Treasurer, Jake Osterberg
Auditors: KPMG LLP

LOCATIONS

HQ: General Mills, Inc.
Number One General Mills Boulevard, Minneapolis, MN 55426
Phone: 763 764-7600   **Fax:** 763 764-8330
Web: www.generalmills.com

2015 Sales

	$ mil.	% of total
US	12,501	71
International		
Europe	2,126	12
Canada	1,105	6
Asia/Pacific	1,023	6
Latin America	873	5
Total	**17,630**	**100**

PRODUCTS/OPERATIONS

2015 Sales

	$ mil.	% of total
US Retail	10,507	60
International	5,128	29
Convenience Stores & Foodservice	1,995	11
Total	**17,630**	**100**

2015 Sales

	$ mil.	% of total
Snacks	3,392	19
Yogurt	2,938	17
Cereal	2,771	16
Convenient meals	2,810	16
Baking mixes & integrates	1,867	11
Dough	1,877	11
Vegetables	937	5
Super-premium ice cream	769	4
Other	266	1
Total	**17,630**	**100**

Selected Brands

Dessert and baking mixes
  Betty Crocker
  Bisquick
  Gold Medal
  SuperMoist
  Warm Delights
Dry dinners and shelf stable and frozen vegetable products
  Annie' s
  Bac*O' s
  Betty Crocker
  Chicken Helper
  Diablitos
  Green Giant
  Hamburger Helper
  Old El Paso
  Potato Buds
  Simply Steam
  Suddenly Salad
  Valley Selections

  Tuna Helper
  Wanchai Ferry
Frozen pizza and pizza snacks
  Jeno' s
  Party Pizza
  Pillsbury Pizza Minis
  Pillsbury Pizza Pops
  Pizza Rolls
  Totino' s
Grain fruit and savory snacks
  Annie' s
  Bugles
  Chex Mix
  Fiber One
  Fruit By The Foot
  Fruit Roll-Ups
  Gardetto' s
  Gushers
  Lärabar
  Nature Valley
  Stickerz
Ice cream and frozen desserts
  Häagen-Dazs
Organic products
  Annie' s
  Cascadian Farm
  Muir Glen
Ready-to-eat cereals
  Basic 4
  Cheerios
  Chex
  Cinnamon Toast Crunch
  Clusters
  Cocoa Puffs
  Cookie Crisp
  Fiber One
  Golden Grahams
  Kix
  Lucky Charms
  Oatmeal Crisp
  Reese' s Puffs
  Total
  Trix
  Wheaties
Ready-to-serve soup
  Progresso
Refrigerated and frozen dough products
  Big Deluxe
  Golden Layers
  Grands!
  Jus-Rol
  La Salte?a
  Latina
  Pasta Master
  Pillsbury
  Savorings
  Toaster Scrambles
  Toaster Strudel
  V.Pearl
  Wanchai Ferry
Refrigerated yogurt
  Go-GURT
  Fiber One
  Mountain High
  Trix
  Yoplait
  Yoplait Kids
  Yoplait Whips!
  YoPlus

COMPETITORS

B&G Foods	Hain Celestial
Barbara' s Bakery	Hanover Foods
Bay State Milling	Heinz
Ben & Jerry' s	Kellogg
Big Heart Pet Brands	King Arthur Flour
Birds Eye	Lakeside Foods
Blue Bell	MOM Brands
Bob' s Red Mill Natural Foods	Manischewitz Company
Campbell Soup	McKee Foods
Carvel	Mondelez International
Chelsea Milling	Mrs. Fields
Cold Stone Creamery	Nature' s Path
ConAgra	Nestlé
Dairy Queen	Pinnacle Foods
Danone	Pro-Fac
Dole Food	Procter & Gamble
	Ralston Food

Dreyer's	Seneca Foods
Fresh&ns	Stonyfield Farm
Friendly's Ice Cream	Unilever
Frito-Lay	Victoria Packing
Gilster-Mary Lee	YoCream

HISTORICAL FINANCIALS

Company Type: Public

Income Statement

FYE: May 31

	REVENUE ($ mil.)	NET INCOME ($ mil.)	NET PROFIT MARGIN	EMPLOYEES
05/15	17,630	1,221	6.9%	42,000
05/14	17,909	1,824	10.2%	43,000
05/13	17,774	1,855	10.4%	41,000
05/12	16,657	1,567	9.4%	35,000
05/11	14,880	1,798	12.1%	35,000
Annual Growth	4.3%	(9.2%)	—	4.7%

2015 Year-End Financials

Debt ratio: 41.99%	No. of shares (mil.): 598
Return on equity: 20.84%	Dividends
Cash ($ mil.): 334	Yield: 0.0%
Current ratio: 0.77	Payout: 84.7%
Long-term debt ($ mil.): 7,607	Market value ($ mil.): 33,617

	STOCK PRICE ($) FY Close	P/E High/Low	PER SHARE ($) Earnings	PER SHARE ($) Dividends	PER SHARE ($) Book Value
05/15	56.15	28 24	1.97	1.67	8.35
05/14	53.81	19 16	2.83	1.55	10.67
05/13	48.98	18 13	2.79	1.32	10.41
05/12	39.08	17 14	2.35	1.22	9.90
05/11	39.29	27 12	2.70	1.12	9.87
Annual Growth	9.3%	— —	(7.6%)	10.5%	(4.1%)

General Motors Co.

General Motors (GM) one of the world's largest auto manufacturers makes cars and trucks with well known brands such as Buick Cadillac Chevrolet and GMC. GM also builds cars through its GM Daewoo Opel Vauxhall and Holden units. The company operates through five business segments: GM North America GM Europe GM International Operations and GM South America. Financing activities are primarily conducted by General Motors Financial Company. The current iteration of GM traces its roots to mid-2009 when the former GM was split into two companies after it emerged from Chapter 11 bankruptcy protection: General Motors and Motors Liquidation (the name for leftover assets).

Geographic Reach

GM has more than 100 locations in the US (excluding automotive financing operations and dealerships) and 15 locations in Canada. It has assembly manufacturing distribution office or warehousing operations in 61 other countries. GM Financial has 46 facilities of which 22 are located in the US. Its major facilities outside the US are in Canada the UK Brazil and Spain.

The US generated around 60% of its total sales in 2014.

Operations

The company operates through four automotive segments. GM North America (GMNA) generates 65% of its total sales and has operations in Canada Central America Mexico the Caribbean and the US. GM International Operations (GMIO) operates in the Asia/Pacific Eastern Europe and Africa and

generates 9% of sales. GM Europe (GME) 14% of sales caters to Europe and Russia. GM South America (GMSA) 8% of sales has operations in Argentina Bolivia Brazil Chile Columbia Ecuador Paraguay Peru Uruguay and Venezuela.

Financial services unit GM Financial accounts for the remainder of revenues.

Sales and Marketing

The company sells cars and trucks to fleet customers including daily rental car companies commercial fleet customers leasing companies and governments. GM markets its vehicles worldwide primarily through a network of independent distributors dealers and authorized sales service and parts outlets with a network of over 20700 dealerships. It spends about $5 billion each year on advertising.

Financial Performance

The company has seen an upward trend in its revenues since 2010 (following GM's emergence from bankruptcy protection).In 2014 net revenues eased up by 0.3% due to increased revenues from GM Financial and GMNA partially offset by lower sales in the GMIO and GMSA segments.GM Financial revenues increased thanks to finance charge income of $0.9 billion due to the acquisition of Ally Financial international operations and increased leased vehicle income of $0.5 billion due to a larger lease portfolio. GMNA's sales increase due to vehicle pricing higher wholesale volumes and mix related to full-size pick-ups and full-size SUVs and the Chevrolet. Colorado Corvette Malibu and Impala models; increased operating lease revenues related to daily rental vehicles sold with guaranteed repurchase obligations; and higher parts and accessories sales.GMIO's revenues declined due to decreased wholesale volumes related to discontinuing sales of the Chevrolet Spark Aveo Cruze Captiva and Orlando in Europe and lower sales of older version SUVs and trucks and other car models. Unfavorable net foreign currency transactions were also a factor.GMSA segment revenues decreased due to lower wholesale volumes in Brazil associated with weaker demand for the Chevrolet Celta Classic and Agile and decreases across Argentina and Venezuela caused by difficult economic conditions; and unfavorable net foreign currency conditions.In 2014 GM's net income decreased by $1.3 billion due to higher automotive cost of sales partially offset by lower increased revenues. The cost of sales increased due to recall campaigns a catch-up adjustment recorded related to the change in estimate for recall campaigns and a charge stemming from the ignition switch recall compensation program. That year GM's net cash provided by the operating activities decreased by $2.5 billion due to reduced net income and change in other operating assets and liabilities.

Strategy

The company's strategic plan includes several major initiatives to help to achieve 9-10% margins by the early 2020s. The initiatives include a strong product pipeline to retain customers; leading the industry in quality and safety; taking a lead in product design with light-weight and mixed material body structures and in leading edge technology; growing its brands (especially the Cadillac brand); and to continuing to develop GM Financial as its captive automotive financing company.

Like most auto makers GM is also focusing on its growth in China. It aims to increase the number of nameplates under the Buick Chevrolet and Cadillac brands in China and continue to grow its business under the Baojun Jiefang and Wuling brands.In 2014 GM launched its watershed education program in seven new communities across Canada the largest international expansion in the initiative's 25-year history. The GM Global Rivers Environmental Education Network now comprises

53 GM facilities including all of the company's US and Canadian manufacturing plants.

GM's efforts to improve its products include developing energy-saving models such as the Chevrolet Volt an electric car powered by a lithium-ion battery introduced in late 2010. The company introduced the Chevrolet Spark electric car in 2013. GM also formed a partnership with Segway to develop a two-wheeled two-seat electric vehicle. GM also has about 20 FlexFuel cars available in the US.

In late 2013 GM company announced plans to cease mainstream distribution of its Chevrolet brand in Western and Central Europe in 2015 due to the challenging business model and difficult economic situation in Europe. The company believes the move will improve its European operations through a further strengthening of its Opel and Vauxhall brands and reduce the market complexity within those regions.

Mergers and Acquisitions

Growing its financial services operations in 2015 GM Financial acquired Ally Financial's 40% stake in SAIC-GMAC in China for $1 billion.

In 2013 GM Financial bought Ally Financial's European and Latin American automotive finance operations for $3.3 billion.

Company Background

In the early years of the auto industry hundreds of carmakers each produced a few models. William Durant who bought a failing Buick Motors in 1904 reasoned that manufacturers could benefit from banding together and formed the General Motors Company in Flint Michigan in 1908.

The auto giant went through a six-week period of bankruptcy protection in 2009. GM was split into two companies when it emerged from Chapter 11 —General Motors and Motors Liquidation (the name for leftover assets). In 2011 Motors Liquidation sold the majority of its assets which encompassed almost 90 industrial sites in 14 states which cleared the way for GM bondholders to receive stock in the new company.

EXECUTIVES

President and CEO GM Financial, Daniel E. (Dan) Berce, age 62

EVP and General Counsel, Craig B. Glidden, age 57

EVP Consolidated International Operations, Stefan Jacoby, age 57

EVP; President Europe, Karl-Thomas Neumann, age 54, $822,133 total compensation

EVP; President Cadillac, Johan de Nysschen, age 50

EVP Global Product Development Purchasing and Supply Chain, Mark L. Reuss, age 51, $846,212 total compensation

Chairman and CEO, Mary T. Barra, age 54, $1,567,803 total compensation

EVP; President GM China, Matthew (Matt) Tsien

EVP and President South America, Barry Engle, age 52

EVP; President North America, Alan Batey

President, Daniel (Dan) Ammann, age 43, $990,530 total compensation

SVP Global Information Technology and CIO, Randall D. (Randy) Mott

EVP and CFO, Charles K. (Chuck) Stevens, $691,667 total compensation

President South-East Asia, Tim Zimmerman

EVP Global Manufacturing, James B. (Jim) DeLuca

President and Managing Director South Africa sub-Saharan Africa and Israel, Ian Nicholls

Vp Global Purchasing And Supply Chain, Robert E Socia, age 62

Vice President Of Management Information Systems, Joe Wamsley

GMNA Vice President Communications, Tony Cervone

Vice President Communications, Selim Bingol

Vice President, Carlos Diaz

Treasurer's Office, Nick Coupe
Auditors: DELOITTE & TOUCHE LLP

LOCATIONS

HQ: General Motors Co.
  300 Renaissance Center, Detroit, MI 48265-3000
Phone: 313 556-5000
Web: www.gm.com

2014 Sales

	% of total
Automotive	
US	60
Non - US	37
GM Financial	
US	2
Non - US	1
Total	**100**

PRODUCTS/OPERATIONS

2014 Sales

	$ mil.	% of total
GMNA	101,199	65
GME	22,235	14
GMIO	14,392	9
GMSA	13,115	8
Corporate & eliminations	151	1
Automotive	151,092	97
GM Financial	4,837	3
Total	**155,929**	**100**

Selected Brands

Buick
Cadillac
Chevrolet
GMC
Holden
Isuzu
Opel
Vauxhall

COMPETITORS

BMW	Mazda
Daimler	Mitsubishi Motors
FCA US	Navistar International
Fiat Chrysler	Nissan
Ford Motor	Peugeot
Fuji Heavy Industries	Renault
Honda	Suzuki Motor
Hyundai Motor	Tata Motors
Kia Motors	Toyota
Land Rover	Volkswagen

HISTORICAL FINANCIALS

Company Type: Public

Income Statement

FYE: December 31

	REVENUE ($ mil.)	NET INCOME ($ mil.)	NET PROFIT MARGIN	EMPLOYEES
12/15	152,356	9,687	6.4%	215,000
12/14	155,929	3,949	2.5%	216,000
12/13	155,427	5,346	3.4%	219,000
12/12	152,256	6,188	4.1%	213,000
12/11	150,276	9,190	6.1%	207,000
Annual Growth	**0.3%**	**1.3%**	**—**	**1.0%**

2015 Year-End Financials

Debt ratio: 32.44%
Return on equity: 25.72%
Cash ($ mil.): 23,401
Current ratio: 1.09
Long-term debt ($ mil.): 43,549

No. of shares (mil.): 1,544
Dividends
  Yield: 4.0%
  Payout: 50.5%
Market value ($ mil.): 52,528

	STOCK PRICE ($) FY Close	P/E High/Low		PER SHARE ($) Earnings	Dividends	Book Value
12/15	34.01	6	4	5.91	1.38	25.81
12/14	34.91	23	17	1.65	1.20	22.02
12/13	40.87	15	10	2.38	0.00	26.80
12/12	28.83	9	6	2.92	0.00	26.53
12/11	20.27	8	4	4.58	0.00	24.36
Annual Growth	**13.8%**	**—**	**—**	**6.6%**	**—**	**1.5%**

Genuine Parts Co.

What do spark plugs hydraulic hoses paper clips and magnet wire have in common? They're all Genuine Parts. The diversified company is the sole member and majority owner of National Automotive Parts Association (NAPA) a voluntary trade association that distributes auto parts nationwide. Genuine Parts Company (GPC) operates about 1100 NAPA Auto Parts stores in more than 45 US states. North of the border NAPA Canada runs some 700 auto parts and TRACTION stores supplied by UAP. GPC's Auto Todo operates eight stores and tire centers in Mexico. Other subsidiaries include auto parts distributor Balkamp industrial parts supplier Motion Industries and office products distributor S.P. Richards.

HISTORY

Company BackgroundGenuine Parts Company (GPC) got its start in Atlanta in 1928 when Carlyle Fraser bought a small auto parts store. That year GPC had the only loss in its history. Three years earlier a group that included Fraser had founded the National Automotive Parts Association (NAPA) an organization of automotive manufacturers remanufacturers distributors and retailers.

The Depression was a boon for GPC because fewer new-car sales meant more sales of replacement parts. During the 1930s GPC's sales rose from less than $350000 to more than $3 million. One tool it developed to spur sales during the Depression was its monthly magazine Parts Pups which featured pretty girls and corny jokes (discontinued in the 1990s). GPC acquired auto parts rebuilder Rayloc in 1931 and established parts distributor Balkamp in 1936.

WWII boosted sales at GPC because carmakers were producing for the war effort but scarce resources limited auto parts companies to producing functional parts. GPC went public in 1948.

The postwar boom in car sales boosted GPC's sales in the 1950s and 1960s. It expanded during this period with new distribution centers across the country. GPC bought Colyear Motor Sales (NAPA's West Coast distributor) in 1965 and introduced a line of filters and batteries in 1966 that were the first parts to carry the NAPA name.

GPC moved into Canada in 1972 when it bought Corbetts a Calgary-based parts distributor. That acquisition included Oliver Industrial Supply. During the mid-1970s GPC began to broaden its distribution businesses adding S.P. Richards (office products 1975) and Motion Industries (industrial replacement parts 1976). In the late 1970s GPC acquired Bearing Specialty and Michigan Bearing as part of Motion Industries.

In 1982 the company introduced its now familiar blue-and-yellow NAPA logo. Canadian parts distributor UAP (formerly United Auto Parts) and

GPC formed a joint venture UAP/NAPA in 1988 with GPC acquiring a 20% stake in UAP.

During the 1990s GPC diversified its product lines and its geographic reach. Its 1993 acquisition of Berry Bearing made the company a leading distributor of industrial parts. The next year GPC formed a joint venture with Grupo Auto Todo of Mexico.

NAPA formed an agreement in 1995 with Penske Corporation to be the exclusive supplier of auto parts to nearly 900 Penske Auto Centers. GPC purchased Horizon USA Data Supplies that year adding computer supplies to S.P. Richards' product mix.

A string of acquisitions in the late 1990s increased GPC's industrial distribution business (including Midcap Bearing Power Drives & Bearings and Amarillo Bearing).

GPC paid $200 million in 1998 for EIS a leading wholesale distributor of materials and supplies to the electrical and electronics industries. Late in 1998 after a 10-year joint venture it bought the remaining 80% of UAP it didn't already own. GPC continued to expand its auto parts distribution network in 1999 acquiring Johnson Industries an independent distributor of auto supplies for large fleets and car dealers. GPC also acquired Oklahoma City-based Brittain Brothers a NAPA distributor that serves about 190 auto supply stores in Arkansas Missouri Oklahoma and Texas.

In 2000 the company bought a 15% interest in Mitchell Repair Information (MRIC) a subsidiary of Snap-on Incorporated that provides diagnostic and repair information services. The next year Johnson Industries acquired Coach and Motors a distribution center in Detroit.

GPC acquired NAPA Hawaii which serves more than 30 independently owned NAPA stores and four company-owned ones in Hawaii and Samoa in 2003. Also that year the company sold its interest in the partnership that distributes industrial parts in Mexico Refacciones Industriales de México.

President Thomas Gallagher became the company's fourth CEO in more than 75 years when he was named to the position in August 2004. Former CEO Larry Prince remained as chairman until early in 2005 when Gallagher was elected chairman; Prince remains on the board. Also during 2005 the company acquired a 25% interest in Altrom Canada Corp.

GPC subsidiary Motion Industries in mid-2006 acquired Lewis Supply Co. a provider of casters cutting tools machinery accessories and other general mill supplies. In October the company merged HorizonUSA Data Supplies previously a wholly owned subsidiary of S.P. Richards into S.P. Richards.

In early 2008 the company sold its Johnson Industries subsidiary which provided automotive supplies to fleets and new car dealers. In October GPC's S.P. Richards unit acquired ActionEmco's business assets in the midwestern US including its Grand Rapids Michigan distribution center. Also that year Motion Industries acquired Texas-based Drago Supply Company Mill Supply Corp. and Monroe Rubber and Plastic Supply.

In 2009 GPC added eight companies to its industrial and automotive operations for about $70 million and snapped up the remaining 11% interest in Balkamp that it did not already control for some $60 million making it a wholly owned subsidiary. These deals compare to a broader acquisition strategy in 2008 which added a dozen companies to all four of GPC's business segments (automotive industrial office products and electrical and electronic) for nearly $135 million.

Also in 2010 it acquired Canada's BC Bearing a distributor of bearing and power transmission components.

EVP CFO and Corporate Secretary, Carol B.
Yancey, age 52, $430,000 total compensation
Chairman and CEO, Thomas C. (Tom) Gallagher, age
68, $1,091,750 total compensation
President and CEO Motion Industries, William J.
(Bill) Stevens, age 66, $512,151 total compensation
SVP Human Resources, James R. (Jim) Neill, age 53,
$287,500 total compensation
**President Genuine Parts and U.S. Automotive
Parts Group,** Paul D. Donahue, age 59, $612,000
total compensation
SVP Technology and CIO, Charles A. Chesnutt, age
55
Assistant Vice President Corporate Controller,
David (Dave) Haskett
Vp Internal Audit Comp & Risk, Robert (Bob)
Swann
**Group Vice President Business and Systems
Solutions,** Gerald (Jerry) Sourbeer
Secretary, Carol Yancy
Auditors: Ernst & Young LLP

LOCATIONS

HQ: Genuine Parts Co.
2999 Circle 75 Parkway, Atlanta, GA 30339
Phone: 770 953-1700   **Fax:** 770 956-2211
Web: www.genpt.com

2014 Sales

	$ mil.	% of total
US	12,565	82
Canada	1,583	10
Australasia	1,133	7
Mexico	127	1
Adjustments	(68.2)	-
Total	**15,341**	**100**

PRODUCTS/OPERATIONS

2014 Sales

	$ mil.	% of total
Automotive	8,096	53
Industrial	4,771	31
Office products	1,802	11
Electrical & electronic materials	739	5
Adjustments	(68.2)	-
Total	**15,341**	**100**

Selected Operations

Automotive Parts Group
  Altrom Canada Corp. (distribution of import
  automotive parts Canada)
  Balkamp (majority-owned subsidiary; distribution of
  replacement parts and accessories for cars heavy-duty
  vehicles motorcycles and farm equipment)
  Grupo Auto Todo S.A. de C.V. (Mexico)
  UAP Inc. (auto parts distribution Canada)
Electrical/Electronic Materials Group
  EIS Inc. (products for electrical and electronic
  equipment including adhesives copper foil and
  thermal management materials)
Industrial Parts Group
  Motion Industries (Canada) Inc.
  Motion Industries Inc.
Office Products Group
  S.P. Richards Company

COMPETITORS

Advance Auto Parts	General Parts
Applied Industrial	Gould Paper
Technologies	Graybar Electric
Arrow Electronics	Hahn Automotive
AutoZone	Ingersoll-Rand
Avnet	Kaman Industrial
CARQUEST	Technologies
Coast Distribution	MSC Industrial Direct
Cole Office Products	O' Reilly Automotive
Complete Office	Office Depot
D & H Distributing	Pep Boys
Essendant	Staples
Ford Motor	W.W. Grainger
General Motors	

HISTORICAL FINANCIALS
Company Type: Public

Income Statement
FYE: December 31

	REVENUE ($ mil.)	NET INCOME ($ mil.)	NET PROFIT MARGIN	EMPLOYEES
12/14	15,341	711	4.6%	39,000
12/13	14,077	684	4.9%	37,500
12/12	13,013	648	5.0%	31,900
12/11	12,458	565	4.5%	29,800
12/10	11,207	475	4.2%	29,500
Annual Growth	**8.2%**	**10.6%**	**—**	**7.2%**

2014 Year-End Financials

Debt ratio: 9.77%	No. of shares (mil.): 153
Return on equity: 21.39%	Dividends
Cash ($ mil.): 137	Yield: 2.1%
Current ratio: 1.56	Payout: 49.8%
Long-term debt ($ mil.): 540	Market value ($ mil.): 16,317

	STOCK PRICE ($) FY Close	P/E High/Low		Earnings	PER SHARE ($) Dividends	Book Value
12/14	106.57	23	17	4.61	2.30	21.56
12/13	83.19	19	14	4.40	2.15	21.78
12/12	63.58	16	14	4.14	1.98	19.36
12/11	61.20	17	13	3.58	1.80	17.88
12/10	51.34	17	12	3.00	1.64	17.72
Annual Growth	**20.0%**	**—**	**—**	**11.3%**	**8.8%**	**5.0%**

Genworth Financial, Inc. (Holding Co)

What's a Genworth? Insurance and investment
specialist Genworth Financial might ask what your
nest egg is worth. The company specializes in life
insurance and retirement investments in the US
market. Internationally Genworth offers mortgage
insurance and other payment protection products.
The firm also provides private residential mortgage insurance in the US. Genworth focuses its retirement investment products including fixed annuities and mutual funds on affluent individuals.
Genworth serves over 15 million customers in 25
countries.

Operations

The company operates in three segments: US
Life Insurance Global Mortgage Insurance and
Corporate and Other (which includes international
protection and runoff operations).

Genworth's largest source of income is its US
Life Insurance segment which accounts for about
70% of annual revenues; it sells life insurance long-
term care policies and fixed annuities. The Global
Mortgage Insurance segment makes up about 15%
of sales and includes the mortgage insurance operations in the US and abroad. The Corporate and
Other segment also contributes about 15% and includes the international protection and runoff
(products that are no longer actively marketed including Medicare supplement variable annuity variable life and corporate-owned life) operations. The
firm divested its wealth management segment in
2013.

Geographic Reach

While US operations account for more than
three-fourths of revenues Genworth's international
operations include significant mortgage insurance
businesses in Australia Canada Mexico and parts

of Europe. The firm is looking to expand its mortgage insurance operations into emerging markets.

In 2014 the company raised a bit of cash by
spinning off a minority stake (about 35%) in its
Australian mortgage insurance business through
an IPO. The following year it sold another small
stake retaining 52% of the unit.

Sales and Marketing

Genworth's products are sold through direct
sales brokerage general agencies and independent
marketing organizations as well as by banks and
financial advisors. Long-term care insurance products are sold through a variety of sales channels —
independent producers financial intermediaries
and sales specialists.

Financial Performance

Genworth's sales and profits have fluctuated
over the past few years. In 2014 revenue increased
2% to $9.6 billion on higher US life insurance
sales. A favorable impact of foreign exchange rates
also helped boost earnings. However that was partially offset by a decline in the International Mortgage Insurance segment.

The company had a net loss of $1.2 billion that
year due to increases in benefits and other changes
in policy reserves as well as goodwill impairment
expenses incurred. Cash flow from operations
which has been fluctuating rose 74% to $2.4 bil-
lion on lower claim payments and cash collateral
received from counterparties.

Strategy

Genworth is streamlining its operations through
asset sales which allow the company to improve its
cash position and focus on its core offerings. Genworth is focused on increasing the value of new
and existing policies through pricing initiatives and
changes in product distribution and design practices across all of its business units. It is also working to improve returns in the global mortgage unit
by balancing risk through measures including reducing exposure in European markets —it agreed
to sell its European mortgage insurance business
to AmTrust Financial in 2015 —and sold part of
the Australian unit. Also in 2015 it sold its European lifestyle protection insurance business to
France's AXA for some $510 million. In early
2016 Genworth sold certain blocks of term life insurance policies to Protective Life Insurance Company.

Previously Genworth stopped selling long-term
care insurance to AARP members in 2013; Genworth had served as the exclusive provider of
AARP long-term care policies since 2007.

Other divestitures include the early 2013 sale of
the Liberty Home Equity Solutions (reverse mortgage) business to Ocwen Financial Corporation
for $22 million. Later that year the company com-
pleted the sale of its wealth management businesses including Genworth Financial Wealth Management and the Altegris companies for some
$412.5 million to an investment partnership be-
tween Aquiline Capital and Genstar Capital; proceeds from the sale were used to pay down debt.

To boost its core operations the company has
realigned and expanded its sales team dedicated to
serving mortgage originators. In 2014 Genworth
introdced a new fixed index annuity with a lifetime
income rider. It is designed for consumers from the
age of 45 on.

HISTORY

Company BackgroundThe company was formed
in 2004 to acquire certain insurance and financial
services business from General Electric (GE). GE
retained a controlling stake in Genworth Financial
after its stock offering but sold its remaining stake
in 2006.During the downturn in the US housing
market (starting in 2008) the company faced losses
in its US mortgage insurance segment. After con-

sidering divestitures Genworth instead simply yanked hard on those operations making its underwriting criteria more stringent and restricting new business. The company also conducted extensive restructuring programs including a 15% workforce reduction in 2009 and a de-risking of its investment portfolio to recover from the economic downturn. Nonetheless the company saw income and cash flow losses during those years as a result of poor returns on investments.In 2009 the company launched an IPO of its Canadian mortgage insurance business.In late 2010 Genworth expanded its asset management operations with the purchase of hedge fund and managed futures producer Altegris Capital. The purchase brought in alternative investments and $2.2 billion in assets under management.Despite steady growth in the sales of its Medicare supplemental products in 2011 the company sold the block of products (held by the former Continental Life Insurance Company unit) to Aetna for $290 million. In addition in 2011 the company stopped offering mortgage insurance policies in New Zealand.

EXECUTIVES

President and CEO, Thomas J. (Tom) McInerney, age 59, $996,803 total compensation
President US Mortgage Insurance, Rohit Gupta
EVP Human Resources, Michael S. Laming, age 64
EVP and CIO, Scott J. McKay, age 54
COO, Kevin D. Schneider, age 53, $636,520 total compensation
President International Protection, Robert J. (Bob) Brannock
President Long-Term Care Insurance, Elena K. Edwards
CEO and Managing Director Australia, Ellie F. Comerford
President and CEO Canada, Stuart Levings
President Life and Annuities, Lou E. Hensley, age 51
EVP and Chief Investment Officer, Daniel J. (Dan) Sheehan, $582,746 total compensation
President Mortgage Insurance Europe, Angel G. Mas
EVP and Chief Risk Officer, Lori M. Evangel, $455,271 total compensation
EVP and General Counsel, Ward E. Bobitz
President Distribution, Anthony Vossenberg
CFO, Kelly Groh
Vice President and Director of Practice Management Genworth Financial Wealth Management Inc., Matthew (Matt) Matrisian
Vice President Public Relations, Alfred Orendorff
Vice President Technical Services Chief Technology Officer Genworth Mortgage, Bob McKeown
Divisional Vice President Wholesale Western Region, Karen Palmquist
Chairman, James S. (Jim) Riepe, age 72
Auditors: KPMG LLP

LOCATIONS

HQ: Genworth Financial, Inc. (Holding Co)
6620 West Broad Street, Richmond, VA 23230
Phone: 804 281-6000
Web: www.genworth.com

2014 Revenues

	$ mil.	% of total
US	7,488	78
Canada	669	7
Australia	537	6
Other countries	871	9
Total	**9,565**	**100**

PRODUCTS/OPERATIONS

2014 Revenues

	$ mil.	% of total
US Life	6,587	69
International mortgage	1,240	13
International protection	837	9
US Mortgage Insurance	639	6
Runoff	275	3
Corporate & other	(13)	-
Total	**9,565**	**100**

2014 Revenues

	$ mil.	% of total
Premiums	5,431	57
Net Investment income	3,242	34
Net investment losses	(20)	-
Insurance & investment product fees & other	912	9
Total	**9,565**	**100**

Selected Products and Services

Fixed annuities
Life insurance
Long-term care insurance
Mortgage
Retirement solutions
Wealth management solutions

COMPETITORS

AEGON USA	MetLife
AIG	Nationwide
Great American Financial Resources	New York Life
	Northwestern Mutual
John Hancock Financial Services	PMI Group
	Prudential
MGIC Investment	Radian Group
MassMutual	The Hartford
Medamerica Insurance	

HISTORICAL FINANCIALS

Company Type: Public

Income Statement

FYE: December 31

	ASSETS ($ mil.)	NET INCOME ($ mil.)	INCOME AS % OF ASSETS	EMPLOYEES
12/14	111,358	(1,244)	—	5,300
12/13	108,045	560	0.5%	5,000
12/12	113,312	323	0.3%	6,300
12/11	114,302	122	0.1%	6,400
12/10	112,395	142	0.1%	6,500
Annual Growth	**(0.2%)**	**—**	**—**	**(5.0%)**

2014 Year-End Financials

Debt ratio: 5.96%
Return on equity: (-8.49%)
Cash ($ mil.): 4,918
Current ratio: —
Long-term debt ($ mil.): —
No. of shares (mil.): 497
Dividends
  Yield: —
  Payout: —
Market value ($ mil.): 4,225

	STOCK PRICE ($) FY Close	P/E High/Low		Earnings	Dividends	Book Value
12/14	8.50	—	—	(2.51)	0.00	30.03
12/13	15.53	14	7	1.12	0.00	29.08
12/12	7.51	14	6	0.65	0.00	33.61
12/11	6.55	57	20	0.25	0.00	33.69
12/10	13.14	65	37	0.29	0.00	28.29
Annual Growth	**(10.3%)**	**—**	**—**	**—**	**—**	**1.5%**

Georgia Power Co.

Bigger than a giant peach Georgia Power is the largest subsidiary of US utility holding company Southern Company. The regulated utility provides electricity to about 2.4 million residential commercial and industrial customers throughout most of Georgia. It has interests in about 20 fossil-fueled 2 nuclear and 20 hydroelectric power plants that give it about 22000 MW of generating capacity. When necessary the company purchases excess power from nine small power producers. Georgia Power sells wholesale electricity to several cooperatives and municipalities in the region. The utility also offers energy efficiency surge protection and outdoor lighting products and services.

Geographic Reach

The company serves retail customers in Georgia. It also sells power to wholesale customers across the US Southeast.

Operations

Georgia Power generates purchases transmits distributes and sells electricity in Georgia. It generates power from coal and natural gas as well as from renewable sources such as solar hydroelectric and wind.

In 2012 the company purchased about 440 kilowatt hours of power from other providers.

On the financing front the company invests in domestic equity international equity fixed income trust-owned life insurance special situations real estate investments and private equity.

Financial Performance

Georgia Power's revenues grew by 3% in 2013 due to increase in retail base revenues as the result of higher rates (to help pay for placing new generating units at Plant McDonough-Atkinson in service and collecting financing costs related to the construction of Plant Vogtle Units 3 and 4 as well as higher market-driven contributions from commercial and industrial customers.Net income was flat in 2013 at stayed at $1.2 million as an increase in operating expenses (the result of a 9.9% increase in the volume of KWHs generated as a result of higher prices for purchased power and an 8.1% increase in the average cost of fuel per KWH generated for all types of fuel generation) was offset by a decrease in other expenses due to the decline in interest expenses as a result of refinancing activity.

Strategy

As part of the company's integrated resource plan in addition to a renewables push it is looking to building two additional nuclear power units at its power plant in Vogtle near Waynesboro Georgia (the country's first nuclear power plants in more than 30 years). In 2012 it secured US Nuclear Regulatory Commission approval to go ahead and build these units.

To upgrade its coal plants between 1990 and 2015 Georgia Power plans to invest $7 billion on environmental control technologies.

The company is committed to diversifying its portfolio to include more green energy. To that end in 2013 it signed a contract with EDP Renewables North America for 250 MW of wind energy which it will begin receiving in 2016. That year Georgia Power opened its Water Research Center that will look for ways to reduce its power plant water use and improve the quality of water it releases from plants.

In 2012 it opened the Piedmont Green Power Plant in Barnesville Georgia and signed a 20-year agreement with Rollcast Energy to purchase about 54 MW of biomass energy.

Company Background

The company was founded in 1927.

EXECUTIVES

EVP Nuclear Development, Joseph A. (Buzz) Miller, age 53
EVP Customer Service and Operations, Anthony L. Wilson

EVP Customer Service Organization, Mickey A. Brown, age 68, $357,813 total compensation
EVP CFO and Treasurer, Ronnie R. Labrato, age 60
EVP External Affairs, W. Craig Barrs, age 57
SVP Metro Atlanta Region, Richard L. Holmes, age 61
VP Chief Accounting Officer and Comptroller, W. Ron Hinson, age 58
Chairman President and CEO, Paul Bowers
Vice President Of South Region, Terri Lupo
Vice President Customer Services, Gerald (Jerry) Johnson
Vice President Resource Planning and Nuclear Development, Oscar Harper
Vice President Controller, Robert Morris
Vice President, Doug Page
Vice President Information Technology Audit, Courtney Williams
Vice President, Lenn Chandler
Vice President of Human Resources, Sloane Evans
Vice President Human Resources, Leonard Owens
Transmission Vice President, Leslie Sibert
Vice President of Systems and Data Processing, Brian Ivey
Executive Vice President, Joesph Miller
Auditors: Deloitte & Touche LLP

LOCATIONS

HQ: Georgia Power Co.
241 Ralph McGill Boulevard, N.E., Atlanta, GA 30308
Phone: 404 506-6526
Web: www.georgiapower.com

PRODUCTS/OPERATIONS

2013 Sales

	$ mil.	% of total
Retail		
Residential	3,058	37
Commercial	3,077	37
Industrial	1,391	17
Other retail	94	1
Wholesale	301	4
Other	353	4
Total	**8,274**	**100**

2013 Fuel Mix

	% of total
Gas	39
Coal	35
Nuclear	23
Hydro	3
Total	**100**

COMPETITORS

AGL Resources	Oglethorpe Power
Atmos Energy	Progress Energy
Duke Energy Progress	SCANA
Inc.	Sawnee EMC
Energen	South Carolina
Entergy	Electric & Gas
Flint Energies	TECO Energy
MEAG Power	Walton EMC

HISTORICAL FINANCIALS

Company Type: Public

Income Statement

FYE: December 31

	REVENUE ($ mil.)	NET INCOME ($ mil.)	NET PROFIT MARGIN	EMPLOYEES
12/14	8,988	1,242	13.8%	7,909
12/13	8,274	1,191	14.4%	7,886
12/12	7,998	1,185	14.8%	8,094
12/11	8,800	1,162	13.2%	8,310
12/10	8,349	967	11.6%	8,330
Annual Growth	**1.9%**	**6.5%**	**—**	**(1.3%)**

2014 Year-End Financials

Debt ratio: 32.20%
Return on equity: 12.09%
Cash ($ mil.): 24
Current ratio: 0.70
Long-term debt ($ mil.): 8,683

No. of shares (mil.): 9
Dividends
  Yield: 5.5%
  Payout: 77.8%
Market value ($ mil.): 985

	STOCK PRICE ($) FY Close	P/E High/Low	PER SHARE ($) Earnings	Dividends	Book Value
12/14	106.40	— —	(0.00)	1.53	1,153
12/13	100.40	— —	(0.00)	6.50	1,064
12/12	112.00	— —	(0.00)	1.53	1,029
12/11	109.60	— —	(0.00)	6.50	1,002
12/10	105.00	— —	(0.00)	6.50	972.52
Annual Growth	**0.3%**	**— —**	**—**	**(30.3%)**	**4.4%**

Gilead Sciences, Inc.

Gilead Sciences has biotech balms for infectious diseases including hepatitis HIV and infections related to AIDS. The company's HIV franchise includes Truvada a combination of two of its other drugs Viread and Emtriva. It co-promotes another HIV treatment called Atripla in the US and Europe with Bristol-Myers Squibb (BMS). Other products on the market include AmBisome used to treat systemic fungal infections such as those that accompany AIDS or kidney disease; and hepatitis B antiviral Hepsera. Beyond HIV/AIDS Gilead also markets cardiovascular drugs Letairis and Ranexa as well as respiratory and ophthalmic medicines.OperationsGilead primarily focuses on producing treatments for HIV liver diseases including hepatitis B and hepatitis C cancer and inflammation and cardiovascular and respiratory conditions. Although the company is steadily working to expand in medicines in various fields its main source of revenue continues to be its antiviral franchise which contributes more than 90% of product sales and primarily consists of HIV medications.Aside from the Atripla partnership with BMS Gilead has collaborations with other companies including Japan Tobacco which promotes HIV drugs Truvada Viread and Emtriva in Japan; and with GlaxoSmithKline which markets Hepsera Viread and Volbris in select international markets. Additionally Gilead Sciences receives royalties on influenza treatment Tamiflu which it developed with Roche and on Macugen an ophthalmologic drug developed by Eyetech using Gilead's technology. In addition to distributing AmBisome in Canada and the US Astellas pays royalties on US sales of Lexiscan which is used in stress tests for coronary artery disease.Gilead continues to advance its R&D pipeline; the company had some 225 active clinical studies at the end of 2014. In 2013 it advanced its momelotinib product to Phase 3 (Gilead has more than 50 trials in Phase 3).The company's portfolio of 19 marketed products contains a number of firsts such as the first complete treatment regimens for HIV and chronic hepatitis C available in a once-daily single pill.Geographic ReachThe US market accounts for some 70% of Gilead's annual revenues. The company operates in more than 30 countries worldwide with a significant presence in Europe (France the UK Spain Italy Germany and Switzerland); it also operates in Africa South America and the Asia/Pacific region.Gilead has R&D facilities in Oceanside and Fremont California; Branford Connecticut; Alberta; and Seattle. It has manufacturing sites in San Dimas California; and Cork Ireland. Commercial operations are located in 20 offices throughout Europe seven in Asia one in South America and another in North America.Sales and Marketing-Gilead promotes its antiviral drugs through its own commercial infrastructure in North America some European and Asian countries and in Australia and New Zealand; products are promoted through third-party distributors and partnerships in other regions. Gilead sells and distributes products including Atripla Sovaldi and Viread exclusively through wholesale channels in the US; Letairis and Cayston are distributed through specialty pharmacies. Customers include physicians hospitals clinics and other health care facilities. The company's product distribution processes are handled primarily by wholesalers including Cardinal Health (14% of revenues) McKesson (24%) and AmerisourceBergen (25%).In 2014 Gilead spent $393 million on advertising up from $216 million in 2013 and $160 million in 2012.Financial PerformanceIncreased sales of antiviral products have provided healthy revenue increases for Gilead in recent years. Overall revenue more than doubled in 2014 to $24.9 billion (versus $11 billion in 2013 primarily due to a 145% increase in antiviral product sales. The company's Sovaldi and Stribild products have especially shown growth particularly in the US and Europe as has sales of the new hepatitis treatment Harvoni (introduced in 2014). US product sales increased to $18.1 billion in 2014 as compared to $6.6 billion in 2013 thanks to the successes of Sovaldi Harvoni Stribild and Complera.In Europe product sales rose 54% to $5.1 billion driven primarily by sales of Sovaldi Stribild and Eviplera.Other new products that have driven up earnings include Letairis Ranexa AmBiosome and Zydelig.Net income nearly tripled in 2014 rising to $12 billion primarily as a result of growth in revenue. Cash flow from operations also spiked rising 312% to $12.8 billion (largely due to higher profits and cash generated from accrued liabilities).StrategyOne of the pitfalls of the pharma manufacturing business is patent expirations where older medications see a decline in sales as they begin to face generic competition. Other medications struggle to penetrate highly saturated markets. To offset potential losses from these challenges Gilead is working to increase sales of top selling products in new territories. With partner BMS the firm is especially focused on increasing international commercialization of Atripla. In addition Gilead works to get existing medications approved for new medical indications.The company also works to launch new or next-generation drugs to freshen its lineup of patent-protected offerings. The company's development programs include potential treatments for viral infections liver disease respiratory and cardiovascular ailments and various cancers. Gilead also conducts R&D efforts through collaborations; for instance it has a development partnership with Japan Tobacco on new HIV drugs.Gilead continues to build up its existing portfolio through internal discovery and clinical development as well as by acquiring or in-licensing products.In 2013 the company received FDA approval of hepatitis C drug Sovaldi; it also expanded its HIV product offerings with the launch of once-a-day tablet Stribild. The EMA also approved Vitekta for the treatment of HIV-1 infection. The following year the European Commission gave marketing approval for Zydelig (idelalisib) a treatment for incurable blood cancers chronic lymphocytic (CLL) leukemia and follicular lymphoma. Sovaldi was also given the go-ahead in Europe; the FDA granted approvals for Harvoni Tybost and Zydelig for the treatment of hepatitis HIV and cancer respectively. Harvoni was approved in Europe in 2014.The company is focused on expanding access to Sovaldi and Harvoni in the US as well as launching Harvoni in additional markets in Europe and elsewhere. In 2014 Gilead signed licensing agreements with nine India-based generic pharmaceutical manufacturers to increase access to its chronic hepatitis C medications (including Sovaldi) in more than 90 developing nations.Other new partnerships entered into in 2014 are the license agreement with Ono Pharmaceutical to develop and commercialize GS-4059 a BTK inhibitor for the treatment of B-cell malignancies; and an agreement with Janssen R&D Ireland for the development of a new HIV treatment containing compounds from both companies.Mergers and AcquisitionsAs yet another way of fending off losses from patent expirations Gilead Sciences has diversified its product line through acquisitions.In early 2013 Gilead purchased YM BioSciences for some $510 million. The purchase added clinical development programs for oncology therapies in the field of hematologic cancers.The company entered into an agreement with Phenex Pharmaceuticals in 2015; under the deal Gilead will acquire Phenex's FXR program for the treatment of liver diseases. That transaction will accelerate Gilead's efforts to develop new treatments for fibrotic liver diseases.Also in 2015 Gilead acquired EpiTherapeutics a developer of novel cancer drugs based on epigenetics for $65 million.

HISTORY

Dr. Michael Riordan started Gilead Sciences in 1987 backed by venture capital firm Menlo Ventures. The name was derived from the Biblical phrase "Is there no balm in Gilead?" In 1990 Glaxo Wellcome (now GlaxoSmithKline) agreed to fund Gilead's research into code-blocking treatments for cancer. Gilead went public in 1992.

In 1994 the company formed an alliance with American Home Products' Storz Instruments (now part of Bausch & Lomb) to develop and market a topical treatment for an ophthalmic virus. Two years later Gilead joined forces with Roche to develop treatments for influenza.

Vistide was approved in the US in 1996 and in Europe in 1997. But more-effective HIV therapies brought declining demand for Vistide.

The company bounced back with Tamiflu (the fruit of its Roche partnership) which was approved in 1999. Sales were brisk during that flu season. Also that year Gilead expanded its pipeline and geographic reach with the $550 million all-stock acquisition of NeXstar Pharmaceuticals which focused on antifungals antibiotics and cancer treatments.

In 2000 Gilead sought approval for Tamiflu in Japan and Europe (it withdrew the European application after regulators there asked for more information) and also sought approval for pediatric uses for the drug which was granted. The following year it resubmitted Tamiflu for approval in Europe.

Chairman Donald Rumsfeld resigned in 2001 to become US secretary of defense and was replaced by retired Sears Roebuck executive James Denny. Perhaps the Defense connection helped: Vistide became one of the many drugs that researchers began studying as possible alternatives to vaccines should a smallpox bio-attack occur in the US.

EXECUTIVES

EVP Pharmaceutical Development and Manufacturing, Taiyin Yang, age 61
EVP Research and Development and Chief Scientific Officer, Norbert W. Bischofberger, age 59, $920,647 total compensation
Chairman and CEO, John C. Martin, age 63, $1,605,017 total compensation
President and COO, John F. Milligan, age 54, $1,046,898 total compensation

SVP and CFO, Robin L. Washington, age 52, $797,601 total compensation
EVP Corporate and Medical Affairs, Gregg H. Alton, age 49, $814,300 total compensation
EVP Commercial Operations, Paul R. Carter, age 54
EVP Clinical Research, John G. McHutchison
Vice President Sales and Marketing, David (Dave) Johnson
Svp R&d Strategy/corp Dev't, Muzammil Mansuri
Vice President Global Safety, Tobias Peschel
Vice President Legal Affairs, Brett Pletcher
Medical Director, Belinda Jump
Vice President Of U S Marketing And Sales, Jean Kress
Pharmd, Tracey Rezak
V P Risk Management, Marti Dodson
Vice President, Choung Kim
Vice President Information Technology, Mark Hill
Vice President of Human Resources, Eva Sanchez
Vice President Policy and Public Health, David (Dave) Gollaher
Vice President of Medical Affairs and HIV Global Medical Director, Bill Guyer
Vice President Analytical Operations, Gary Visor
Auditors: Ernst & Young LLP

LOCATIONS

HQ: Gilead Sciences, Inc.
  333 Lakeside Drive, Foster City, CA 94404
Phone: 650 574-3000
Web: www.gilead.com

2014 Sales

	$ mil.	% of total
US	18,182	73
Europe	5,442	22
Other countries & regions	1,266	5
Total	**24,890**	**100**

PRODUCTS/OPERATIONS

2014 Sales

	$ mil.	% of total
Antiviral products		
Sovaldi	10,328	41
Atripla	3,470	14
Truvada	3,340	13
Harvoni	2,127	9
Complera/Eviplera	1,228	5
Stribild	1,197	5
Viread	1,058	4
Other antiviral	88	
Other products		
Letaris	595	2
Ranexa	510	2
AmBisome	388	2
Zydelig	23	-
Other	167	1
Royalties Contract & other	416	2
Total	**24,890**	**100**

Selected Products

Antiviral
  Atripla (HIV with Bristol-Myers Squibb)
  Complera/Eviplera (HIV)
  Emtriva (HIV)
  Harvoni (HCV infection)
  Hepsera (hepatitis B)
  Sovaldi (HCV infection)
  Stribild (HIV)
  Tamiflu (flu treatment royalties from Roche)
  Truvada (fixed-dose combination of Viread and Emtriva for HIV)
  Viread (HIV chronic hepatitis B with liver disease)
  Vistide (AIDS-related cytomegalovirus retinitis)
Other products
  AmBisome (antifungal with Astellas)
  Cayston (cystic fibrosis)
  Flolan (pulmonary hypertension)
  Letairis (pulmonary arterial hypertension)
  Lexiscan/Rapiscan (cardiovascular with Astellas)
  Macugen (age-related macular degeneration royalties from Eyetech)
  Ranexa (chronic angina)

Products in development
  Aztreonam (cystic fibrosis)
  Cobicistat (HIV/AIDS)
  Elvitegravir (HIV/AIDS)
  GS-1101 (leukemia and lymphoma)
  GS-7977 (hepatitis C)
  Intesgrase (HIV)
  Ranolazine (cardiovascular diabetes)

Selected Acquisitions

COMPETITORS

AbbVie	Enzon
Abbott Labs	GlaxoSmithKline
Actelion	Janssen
AstraZeneca	Pharmaceuticals
Bausch & Lomb	Merck
BioCryst	Novartis
Pharmaceuticals	Pfizer
Boehringer Ingelheim	Roche Holding
Bristol-Myers Squibb	Shire

HISTORICAL FINANCIALS

Company Type: Public

Income Statement

FYE: December 31

	REVENUE ($ mil.)	NET INCOME ($ mil.)	NET PROFIT MARGIN	EMPLOYEES
12/14	24,890	12,101	48.6%	7,000
12/13	11,201	3,074	27.4%	6,100
12/12	9,702	2,591	26.7%	5,000
12/11	8,385	2,803	33.4%	4,500
12/10	7,949	2,901	36.5%	4,000
Annual Growth	**33.0%**	**42.9%**	**—**	**15.0%**

2014 Year-End Financials

Debt ratio: 35.78%
Return on equity: 90.32%
Cash ($ mil.): 10,027
Current ratio: 3.07
Long-term debt ($ mil.): 11,921

No. of shares (mil.): 1,499
Dividends
  Yield: —
  Payout: —
Market value ($ mil.): 141,296

	STOCK PRICE ($) FY Close	P/E High/Low		PER SHARE ($) Earnings	Dividends	Book Value
12/14	94.26	14	8	7.35	0.00	10.29
12/13	75.10	39	20	1.81	0.00	7.41
12/12	73.45	45	24	1.64	0.00	6.13
12/11	40.93	24	20	1.78	0.00	4.47
12/10	36.24	29	19	1.66	0.00	3.66
Annual Growth	**27.0%**	**—**	**—**	**45.1%**	**—**	**29.5%**

Glacier Bancorp, Inc.

Glacier Bancorp is on a Rocky Mountain high. The holding company owns about a dozen community bank divisions with about 100 locations in Montana Idaho Utah Washington Colorado and Wyoming. Serving individuals small to midsized businesses not-for-profits and public entities the banks offer traditional deposit products and credit cards in addition to retail brokerage and investment services through agreements with third-party providers. Its lending activities consist of commercial real estate loans (about half of the company's loan portfolio) as well as residential mortgages business loans and consumer loans.

Financial Performance

The company's revenue increased in fiscal 2013 compared to the prior fiscal period. It reported revenue of $356.6 million for fiscal 2013 up from $345.3 million in revenue for fiscal 2012. Net income also increased in fiscal 2013 compared to the prior year. The company reported net income of $95 million for fiscal 2013 up from $75 million in fiscal 2012.

Glacier Bancorp's cash on hand also increased in fiscal 2013 compared to fiscal 2012 levels.

Strategy

Glacier Bancorp hopes to capitalize on additional acquisition opportunities that it expects to arise as small banks deal with new industry regulations. To this end the bank agreed in 2014 to buy Montana Community Banks for $25 million to expand its Western Montana presence.

The company is also banking on organic growth with the populations of the states in its market area growing faster than the national average thanks to an influx of retiring Baby Boomers and an increase in energy- and natural resource-related jobs.

EXECUTIVES

President and CEO and Director, Michael J. (Mick) Blodnick, age 62, $334,183 total compensation
EVP and CFO, Ronald J. (Ron) Copher, age 58, $201,571 total compensation
EVP and Chief Administrative Officer, Don J. Chery, $201,571 total compensation
Senior Vice President Real Estate Manager, Mike Smith
Vice President Compliance, April Kelso
Vice President, Ryan Screnar
Senior Vice President Real Estate Manager, Michael (Mel) Smith
Senior Vice President Business Development, Don Lloyd
Assistant Vice President Internal Auditor, Becky Turner
Assistant Vice President, Judy Gohsman
Senior Vice President Human Resources, Robin S Roush
Vice President Compliance CRA Officer, Karin Hergesheimer
Branch President, Lin Aikie
Vice President Project Office Manager, Grant Orr
Vice President and Internal Auditor, Jessica Rice
Vice President Information Security, Samuel (Sam) Mauch
Vice President Internal Auditor, Leslie Thompson
Chairman, Dallas I. Herron, age 70
Auditors: BKD, LLP

LOCATIONS

HQ: Glacier Bancorp, Inc.
49 Commons Loop, Kalispell, MT 59901
Phone: 406 756-4200
Web: www.glacierbank.com

PRODUCTS/OPERATIONS

Selected Bank Divisions
1st Bank (Wyoming)
Bank of th
Big Sky We
Citizens C
First Bank of Montana
First Nati
First Secu
Glacier Ba
Mountain W
Valley Ban
Western Se

COMPETITORS

BancWest	First Interstate
Eagle Bancorp	U.S. Bancorp
First Citizens Banc	Wells Fargo
Corp	Zions Bancorporation

HISTORICAL FINANCIALS
Company Type: Public

Income Statement
FYE: December 31

	ASSETS ($ mil.)	NET INCOME ($ mil.)	INCOME AS % OF ASSETS	EMPLOYEES
12/14	8,306	112	1.4%	2,030
12/13	7,884	95	1.2%	1,919
12/12	7,747	75	1.0%	1,753
12/11	7,187	17	0.2%	1,653
12/10	6,759	42	0.6%	1,674
Annual Growth	5.3%	27.8%	—	4.9%

2014 Year-End Financials

Debt ratio: 1.51%
Return on equity: 11.32%
Cash ($ mil.): 441
Current ratio: —
Long-term debt ($ mil.): —
No. of shares (mil.): 75
Dividends
Yield: 2.4%
Payout: 45.3%
Market value ($ mil.): 2,083

	STOCK PRICE ($) FY Close	P/E High/Low		PER SHARE ($) Earnings	Dividends	Book Value
12/14	27.77	20	16	1.51	0.68	13.70
12/13	29.79	24	11	1.31	0.60	12.95
12/12	14.71	15	12	1.05	0.66	12.52
12/11	12.03	66	38	0.24	0.52	11.82
12/10	15.11	31	21	0.61	0.52	11.66
Annual Growth	16.4%	—	—	25.4%	6.9%	4.1%

Global Partners LP

Global Partners (formerly Global Companies) imports petroleum products from global sources but its marketing is largely regional. The company wholesales heating oil residual fuel oil diesel oil kerosene distillates and gasoline to commercial retail and wholesale customers in New England and New York. A major player in the regional home heating oil market Global Partners operates storage facilities at 25 bulk terminals each with a storage capacity of more than 50000 barrels and with a collective storage capacity of 11.2 million barrels. It also owns and supplies a network of gasoline stations. Wholesale revenues accounts for the bulk of the company's sales.

EXECUTIVES

COO, Mark A. Romaine, age 46, $500,000 total compensation
EVP Chief Accounting Officer and Co-Director Mergers and Acquisitions, Charles A. (Chuck) Rudinsky, age 67, $273,000 total compensation
SVP Marketing, Joseph (Joe) DeStefano
President CEO and Director, Eric Slifka, age 49, $800,000 total compensation
EVP General Counsel and Secretary, Edward J. Faneuil, age 62, $376,000 total compensation
CFO, Daphne H. Foster, age 57, $300,000 total compensation
EVP Director and President Alliance Gasoline, Andrew Slifka, age 46, $425,000 total compensation
SVP Information Technology, Bill Gifford
Vice President of Business Development, Bruce Atkins
Vice President Project Management and Development, Jack Frost
Vice President Business Development, Jennifer (Jen) Culver
Vice President Heavy Oil Marketing, Dennis Bowersox

Vice President Credit, Robert (Bob) Fraczkiewicz
Vice President Environmental Health and Safety Operations, Tom Keefe
Senior Vice President Marketing, Joe Destefano
Vice President of Human Resources, Barbara (Barb) Rosenbloom
Vice President Marketing, Ray Gincavage
Chairman, Richard Slifka, age 74
Auditors: Ernst & Young LLP

LOCATIONS

HQ: Global Partners LP
P.O. Box 9161, 800 South Street, Waltham, MA 02454-9161
Phone: 781 894-8800
Web: www.globalp.com

PRODUCTS/OPERATIONS

2014 Sales

	$ mil.	% of total
Wholesale	12,896	74
Gasoline distribution & station operations	3,407	20
Commercial	967	6
Total	17,270	100

Selected Products
Biofuels
Bunker oil
Diesel oil
Distillates
Gasoline
Home heating oil
Kerosene
Residual fuel oil

Selected Mergers and Acquisitions

COMPETITORS

Bayside Fuel	Highlands Fuel
Exxon Mobil	Delivery
George Warren	Koch Industries Inc.
Getty Petroleum	Sprague Resources
Marketing	Tauber Oil
Gulf Oil	Warren Equities

HISTORICAL FINANCIALS
Company Type: Public

Income Statement
FYE: December 31

	REVENUE ($ mil.)	NET INCOME ($ mil.)	NET PROFIT MARGIN	EMPLOYEES
12/14	17,269	114	0.7%	1,154
12/13	19,589	42	0.2%	943
12/12	17,626	46	0.3%	788
12/11	14,835	19	0.1%	264
12/10	7,801	27	0.3%	286
Annual Growth	22.0%	43.5%	—	41.7%

2014 Year-End Financials

Debt ratio: 29.54%
Return on equity: —
Cash ($ mil.): 22
Current ratio: 1.36
Long-term debt ($ mil.): 601
No. of shares (mil.): 30
Dividends
Yield: 7.6%
Payout: 71.0%
Market value ($ mil.): 1,017

	STOCK PRICE ($) FY Close	P/E High/Low		PER SHARE ($) Earnings	Dividends	Book Value
12/14	32.99	11	8	3.95	2.53	19.03
12/13	35.39	28	18	1.42	2.34	15.10
12/12	25.35	16	12	1.71	2.06	15.85
12/11	21.87	34	17	0.87	2.00	14.47
12/10	27.40	17	12	1.59	1.96	14.49
Annual Growth	4.8%	—	—	25.5%	6.6%	7.1%

Goldman Sachs Group, Inc.

Goldman Sachs has traditionally possessed the Midas touch in the investment banking world. A global leader in mergers and acquisitions advice and securities underwriting Goldman offers a gamut of investment banking and asset management services to corporate and government clients worldwide as well as institutional and wealth individual investors. It owns Goldman Sachs Execution & Clearing one of the largest market makers on the NYSE and a leading market maker for fixed income products currencies and commodities. Through affiliates Goldman Sachs is also one of the largest private equity investors in the world. Goldman Sachs was founded in 1869.

HISTORY

German immigrant-cum-Philadelphia retailer Marcus Goldman moved to New York in 1869 and began buying customers' promissory notes from jewelers to resell to banks. Goldman's son-in-law came aboard in 1882 and the firm became Goldman Sachs & Co. in 1885.

Two years later Goldman Sachs began offering US-UK foreign exchange and currency services. To serve such clients as Sears Roebuck it expanded to Chicago and St. Louis. In 1896 it joined the NYSE.

While the firm increased its European contracts Goldman's son Henry made it a major source of financing for US industry. In 1906 it co-managed its first public offering United Cigar Manufacturers (later General Cigar). By 1920 it had underwritten IPOs for Sears B.F. Goodrich and Merck.

Sidney Weinberg made partner in 1927 and stayed until his death in 1969. In the 1930s Goldman Sachs entered securities dealing and sales. After WWII it became a leader in investment banking co-managing Ford's 1956 IPO. In the 1970s it pioneered buying blocks of stock for resale.

Under Weinberg's son John Goldman Sachs became a leader in mergers and acquisitions. The 1981 purchase of J. Aron gave the firm a significant commodities presence and helped it grow in South America.

Seeking capital after 1987's market crash Goldman Sachs raised more than $500 million from Sumitomo for a 12% nonvoting interest in the firm (since reduced to 3%). The Kamehameha Schools/Bishop Estate of Hawaii an educational trust also invested.

The 1994 bond crash and a decline in new debt issues led Goldman Sachs to cut staffing for the first time since the 1980s. But problems went deeper. Partners began leaving and taking their equity. Cost cuts a stronger bond market and the long bull market helped the firm rebound; firm members sought protection through limited liability partnership status. The firm also extended the period during which partners can cash out (slowing the cash drain) and limited the number of people entitled to a share of profits. Overseas growth in 1996 and 1997 focused on the UK and Asia.

After three decades of resistance the partners in 1998 voted to sell the public a minority stake in the firm but market volatility led to postponement. Goldman Sachs also suffered from involvement with Long-Term Capital Management ultimately contributing $300 million to its bailout.

In 1999 Jon Corzine then co-chairman and co-CEO announced that he would leave the group after seeing it through its IPO and Goldman Sachs finally went public that year in an offering valued at close to $4 billion. In 2000 Corzine was elected to a US Senate seat. The New Jersey Democrat spent more than $64 million on his campaign (a record) nearly $61 million of it from his own personal wealth (also a record). Corzine went on to win New Jersey's gubernatorial race in 2005.

In early 2004 Goldman president and COO John Thain left the firm to assume the helm of the New York Stock Exchange. Lloyd Blankfein was named his successor and became chairman and CEO in 2006 when his predecessor Henry "Hank" Paulson was named secretary of the US Treasury.At the height of the economic crisis Goldman Sachs converted to a bank holding company. It formed subsidiary Goldman Sachs Bank USA (GS Bank USA) to manage bank loan trading mortgage originations and other activities. The Federal Reserve mandated the change for Goldman Sachs and fellow investment bank Morgan Stanley. The shift marked a monumental change on Wall Street as it put an end to the independent brokerage firm model that had been a mainstay in the US since reform measures were implemented during the Great Depression. Rivals Merrill Lynch Lehman Brothers and Bear Stearns had already merged with larger banks or filed for bankruptcy. The bank holding company structure brought increased regulation but allowed Goldman Sachs to acquire commercial banks –all in an effort to shore up the company's balance sheet.In the days following the Federal Reserve announcement Warren Buffett's Berkshire Hathaway invested $5 billion in Goldman Sachs and acquired an option to assume $5 billion more of the company's common shares. Goldman Sachs made an additional $5 billion worth of stock available in a public offering. Additionally the US government stepped in with funding for Goldman Sachs in late 2008 when it announced an economic stimulus plan to buy some $250 billion worth of preferred shares of the nation's top banks; approximately $10 billion went to Goldman Sachs.The capital infusions helped but didn't completely shield Goldman Sachs from the financial crisis the effects of which were felt worldwide. To cut costs the company trimmed some 10% of its workforce. It eventually returned to profitability in 2009 and paid back the money it received from the government but still drew ire from politicians over what have been perceived to be extravagant pay packages for its top employees. (The firm's extravagant year-end bonuses had become the stuff of legend.)

Goldman Sachs opened a new $1.8-billion headquarters building in New York City's lower Manhattan in 2009.

In January 2013 Goldman sold approximately 45% of its ordinary shares of ICBC.

EXECUTIVES

Head Merchant Banking Division, Richard A. Friedman, age 57
EVP General Counsel and Secretary, Gregory K. Palm, age 66
CEO Goldman Sachs Bank USA, Esta E. Stecher, age 58
CIO, R. Martin Chavez, age 51
Chairman and CEO, Lloyd C. Blankfein, age 60, $2,000,000 total compensation
Vice Chairman; Chairman Goldman Sachs Asia/Pacific, Mark Schwartz, age 60, $1,850,000 total compensation
EVP and Global Head of Compliance, Alan M. Cohen, age 64
Co-CEO Goldman Sachs International; Co-Head Investment Banking Division, Richard J. Gnodde
Co-Head Investment Banking Division, David M. Solomon
President Goldman Sachs Japan, Masanori Mochida

Vice Chairman; Co-CEO Goldman Sachs International, Michael S. Sherwood, age 49, $1,850,000 total compensation
President Asia/Pacific Outside Japan, Kenneth W. Hitchner
EVP Chief of Staff and Secretary, John F. W. Rogers, age 58
President and COO, Gary D. Cohn, age 54, $1,850,000 total compensation
Global Co-Head Investment Management Division, Timothy J. O'Neill
EVP and Global Head Human Capital Management, Edith W. Cooper, age 53
Head Business Selection and Conflicts Resolution Group, Gwen R. Libstag
EVP and CFO, Harvey M. Schwartz, age 50, $1,850,000 total compensation
Global Co-Head Securities Division, Isabelle Ealet
Global Co-Head Securities Division, Pablo J. Salame
Head Global Investment Research, Steven H. Strongin
Co-Head Global Mergers and Acquisitions, Gene T. Sykes
Global Co-Head Investment Management Division, Eric S. Lane
Chief Strategy Officer and Head Latin America, Stephen M. Scherr
Global Co-Head Securities Division, Ashok Varadhan
Chief Risk Officer, Craig W. Broderick
Co-Head Investment Banking Division, John Waldron
Global Head Credit Trading, Justin G. Gmelich
Vice President Legal, Peter Morreale
Vice President Information Technology, Stephen McConville
Vice President In Information Technology, Paul Frio
Vice President, Elaine Young
Vice President and Chief of Staff Federation Technology, Jonathan (Jon) Wolfe
Vice President Portfolio Manager, Michael (Mel) Desantis
Vice President, Richard Wilson
Vice President Operations, Michael (Mel) Lapetina
Vice President, Adam Rosenberg
Vice President, Anand Kulkarni
Vice President, Ward McLanahan
Vice President, Sean Hockens
Vice President, Will Acree
Vice President Global Head of Bank Relations and Market Infrastructure, Jeffrey (Jeff) Hole
Vice President Equity Research Brokers Market STR, Daniel (Dan) Harris
Vice President Equities Technology, Drew Gutstein
Vice President, Jill Toporek
Vice President Equities Division, Michael Triunfo
Vice President, John Nixon
Vice President, Molly Decker
Vice President Regional Director, Evan Recht
Vice President, Samantha Kell
Vice President, Tara McCarton
Vice President, Derek Johnson
Vice President, Roger Gardiner
Vice President, Ilya Gaysinskiy
Vice President, Tom Healy
Vice President, Heather Conlan-katz
Vice President Information Technology, Milind Sapre
Vice President Insurance Management Finance Division, Jenny Chin
Vice President, Martin Dailerian
Vice President, Lisa Levine
Vice President Prime Brokerage, Tracy Hennes
Vice President GSAM Operations, Smriti Jha
Vice President, Richard (Dick) Case
Vice President Corporate Service RE, Michael (Mel) Butkiewicz
Vice President, Douglas Tansey

Vice President, Sean Brenan
Vice President, Anuraag Verma
Vice President, Joe Duffy
Vice President Technology, Krishnamurthy Vaidyanathan
Vice President, Curtis Ambrose
Vice President Brand Marketing Group Corporate Communications, Thomas (Thom) Croft
Vice President, Joshua (Josh) Matheus
Vice President, Neil Kaufman
Vice President, Ovadiah Jacob
Vice President Global Securities Services, Caitlin Walsh
Vice President, Kavita Kotte
Vice President, Molly Carleton
Vice President, Temitayo Olajide
Senior Vice President Ibd, Jim Gabriel
Vice President, Phillip Han
Vice President Corporate Engagement, Brad Weinstein
Vice President, Anisha Malhotra
Vice President, Joyce Young
Vice President Assistant General Counsel, Teresa De Turris
Vice President, Rohan John
Vice President, Jarrett Fisher
Vice President FX Ecommerce Product Management, Soomin Hu
Vice President Goldman Private Wealth, Michael (Mel) Duffy
Vice President Investment Banking Division, Arden Lee
Vice President, Timothy Driscoll
Vice President Private Wealth Management Investment Management Division, Cristin Dalecki
Vice President Prime Brokerage Sales, Gabriela Gargano
Vice President Leveraged Finance Investment Banking, Jamie Tam
Vice President, Tim Halladay
Vice President, Karen Ho
Vice President, Jason Danziger
Vice President Information Technology, Chris Muller
Vice President, Manoj Susarla
Vice President, Vincent Saulys
Vice President, Doreen Fattore
Vice President, Mark Lambert
Vice President Investment Banking Division, Robert Schatzman
Vice President, Jessica Yurocko
Vice President Of Legal Technology, Danielle Cherence
Vice President, Ian Taylor
Vice President, Suresh Thumma
Vice President, Michael (Mel) Parrish
Vice President MD, Richard (Dick) Kleter
Vice President, Brian Riley
Vice President, Albert Elkind
Vice President, Justin Portnoy
Vice President, Jessica LI
Vice President, Puneet Awasthi
Vice President, Patti Nalipi
Vice President, Melinda Robertson
Vice President, Carrie Gannon
Vice President, Gitika Gumbar
Vice President, Gina Lytle
Vice President, Andrew Dubinsky
Vice President Implementation and Transition Group, Elke Schlafrig
Vice President, Maureen Hill
Vice President Global Securities Lending, James (Jamie) Conti
Vice President, Matt Levin
Vice President, Emily Baker
Vice President, Sean McGee
Vice President Information Technology Manager, Greg Killeen
Vice President, Kate Thomas
Vice President, David Rothenberg

Vice President Information Technology, Robert Brosnan
Vice President, Shlomit Perry
Vice President, Krishnan Narayanan
Vice President Information Technology, Igor Shubov
Vice President, Seth Greengrass
Vice President Securities Compliance Information Technology, Peter Ferns
Vice President, Jessie Sinden
Vice President, John Dipalo
Vice President, Hui Wang
Vice President, Barbara Williams
Vice President, Alex Topkins
Vice President, Dmitriy Furer
Vice President, Yumi Son
Vice President Credit Risk Management And Advisory, Dennis Halliwell
Vice President, Deanna Lamirata
Vice President Human Capital Management, Stefanie Morris
Vice President, Gary Godshaw
Vice President Senior Technical Architect Market Risk, Rafael Gonzalez
Vice President, Jeannie Kang
Vice President, Cynthia Klein
Vice President Fixed Income Currency and Commodities Division, Doug Penick
Vice President Principal Investing, David (Dave) Goldburg
Vice President, Philip Vehec
Auditors: PricewaterhouseCoopers LLP

LOCATIONS

HQ: Goldman Sachs Group, Inc.
200 West Street, New York, NY 10282
Phone: 212 902-1000   Fax: 212 902-3000
Web: www.gs.com

2014 Sales

	% of total
Americas	58
Europe the Middle East & Africa	26
Asia	16
Total	**100**

PRODUCTS/OPERATIONS

2014 Sales

	$ mil.	% of total
Interest income	9,604	24
Market making	8,365	22
Investment banking	6,464	16
Investment management	5,748	14
Commissions & fees	3,316	8
Other	6,588	16
Total	**40,085**	**100**

2014 Sales

	% of total
Institutional Client Services	44
Investing & Lending	20
Investment Banking	19
Investment Management	17
Total	**100**

Selected Subsidiaries

Goldman Sachs & Co.
Goldman Sachs Bank USA
Goldman Sachs Credit Partners L.P. (Bermuda)
Goldman Sachs Financial Markets L.P.
Goldman Sachs International (UK)
Goldman Sachs Japan Co. Ltd.
Goldman Sachs Mortgage Company
GSTM LLC
Goldman Sachs Execution & Clearing L.P.
J. Aron & Company

COMPETITORS

BMO Capital Markets	FMR
Barclays	JPMorgan Chase
CIBC World Markets	Lazard
Citigroup Global Markets	Merrill Lynch
	Morgan Stanley
Credit Suisse	Nomura Securities
Credit Suisse (USA)	RBC Capital Markets
Deutsche Bank	UBS

HISTORICAL FINANCIALS

Company Type: Public

Income Statement

FYE: December 31

	ASSETS ($ mil.)	NET INCOME ($ mil.)	INCOME AS % OF ASSETS	EMPLOYEES
12/14	856,240	8,477	1.0%	34,000
12/13	911,507	8,040	0.9%	32,900
12/12	938,555	7,475	0.8%	32,400
12/11	923,225	4,442	0.5%	33,300
12/10	911,332	8,354	0.9%	35,700
Annual Growth	**(1.5%)**	**0.4%**	**—**	**(1.2%)**

2014 Year-End Financials

Debt ratio: 25.17%
Return on equity: 10.51%
Cash ($ mil.): 109,316
Current ratio: —
Long-term debt ($ mil.): —

No. of shares (mil.): 430
Dividends
Yield: 1.1%
Payout: 13.1%
Market value ($ mil.): 83,397

	STOCK PRICE ($) FY Close	P/E High/Low		PER SHARE ($) Earnings	Dividends	Book Value
12/14	193.83	11	9	17.07	2.25	192.44
12/13	177.26	11	8	15.46	2.05	175.79
12/12	127.56	9	6	14.13	1.77	162.78
12/11	90.43	37	19	4.51	1.40	144.97
12/10	168.16	13	9	13.18	1.40	152.42
Annual Growth	**3.6%**	**—**	**—**	**6.7%**	**12.6%**	**6.0%**

Goodyear Tire & Rubber Co.

When the rubber hits the road most years are good years for Goodyear Tire & Rubber. Through a global alliance with Sumitomo Rubber Industries Goodyear is working to unseat tire industry leaders Bridgestone and Michelin (by total sales). Goodyear sells mainly new tires under the Goodyear Dunlop Kelly Fulda Debica and Sava brand names. With Sumitomo Goodyear makes markets and sells Dunlop tires in North America and Western Europe. In Japan the tire makers own businesses that sell tires separately to OEMs and to aftermarket companies. Goodyear sells some 58% of its products outside the US.

HISTORY

In 1898 Frank and Charles Seiberling founded a tire and rubber company in Akron Ohio and named it after Charles Goodyear (inventor of the vulcanization process 1839). The debut of the Quick Detachable tire and the Universal Rim (1903) made Goodyear the world's largest tire maker by 1916.

Goodyear began manufacturing in Canada in 1910 and over the next two decades it expanded into Argentina Australia and the Dutch East Indies. The company established its own rubber plantations in Sumatra (now part of Indonesia) in 1916.

Financial woes led to reorganization in 1921 and investment bankers forced the Seiberlings out. Succeeding caretaker management Paul Litchfield began three decades as CEO in 1926 a time in which Goodyear emerged to become the world's largest rubber company.

Goodyear blimps served as floating billboards nationwide by the 1930s. During that decade Goodyear opened company stores acquired tire maker Kelly-Springfield (1935) and began producing tires made from synthetic rubber (1937). After WWII Goodyear was an innovative leader in technologies such as polyester tire cord (1962) and the bias-belted tire (1967).

By 1980 Goodyear had introduced radial tire brands such as the all-weather Tiempo the Eagle and the Arriva as it led the US market.

Thwarting British financier Sir James Goldsmith's takeover attempt in 1986 CEO Robert Mercer raised $1.7 billion by selling the company's non-tire businesses (Motor Wheel Goodyear Aerospace) and by borrowing heavily.

Recession overcapacity and price-cutting in 1990 led to hard times for tire makers. After suffering through 1990 its first money-losing year since the Depression Goodyear lured Stanley Gault out of retirement. He ceased marketing tires exclusively through Goodyear's dealer network by selling tires through Wal-Mart Kmart and Sears. Gault also cut costs through layoffs plant closures and spending reductions and returned Goodyear to profitability in 1991.

The company increased its presence in the US retail market in 1995 when it began selling tires through 860 Penske Auto Centers and 300 Montgomery Ward auto centers. President Samir Gibara succeeded chairman Gault as CEO in 1996. That year Goodyear bought Poland's leading tire maker T C Debica and a 60% stake in South African tire maker Contred (acquiring the rest in 1998).

In 1997 Goodyear formed an alliance with Sumitomo Rubber Industries under which the companies agreed to make and market tires for one another in Asia and North America. The next year Goodyear sold its Celeron Oil subsidiary which operated the All American Pipeline and acquired the remaining 26% stake in tire distributor Brad Ragan (commercial and retail outlets in the US) for $20.7 million.

The company acquired Sumitomo Rubber Industries' North American and European Dunlop tire businesses in 1999. The acquisition returned Goodyear to its #1 position in the tire-making industry. However the company recorded drastically low profits that year because it had cut tire production and was unable to meet supplier demands.

To improve profitability Goodyear increased tire prices in 2000 and began consolidating its manufacturing operations. Goodyear also announced plans to combine its commercial tire service centers with those of Treadco through a joint venture named Wingfoot Commercial Tire Systems. Despite record sales in 2000 the company's profits hit some hard road prompting Goodyear to lay off 10% of its workforce and implement other cost-cutting efforts.

Early in 2001 the company announced that it would close its Mexican tire plant. The same year the company agreed to replace Firestone Wilderness AT tires with Goodyear tires for Ford owners as part of Ford's big Firestone tire recall.

Early in 2002 Goodyear announced that its recent job cuts and manufacturing consolidation resulted in an $85 million decrease in annual operating costs. Later in the year the tire maker became embroiled in an age discrimination lawsuit claiming unfair job evaluations for the company's older employees. Blaming a slow US economy Goodyear announced plans to cut 450 jobs at its Union City Tennessee manufacturing plant. The job cuts were just the beginning of what would be a series of operational adjustments made as part of a Capital Structure Improvement Plan formally launched in 2003.

Although Goodyear once owned about 10% of its Sumitomo Rubber Industries it sold more than 20 million shares of its Japanese counterpart stock back to the tire maker in 2003. Later in the year as the company was embroiled in a lengthy debate with the United Steelworkers union it was announced that the Huntsville Alabama tire manufacturing plant would be closed. Goodyear also announced that it would cut 500 non-union salaried employees in North America. Later that same year it was announced that Goodyear was chosen by Volvo to be the truck manufacturer's primary tire supplier in North America; Goodyear had a similar contract with Mack Trucks.

Qantas Airways announced in early 2004 that it chose Goodyear to provide tires for the Australia-based company's Jetstar Airways. Later in the year Goodyear acquired the shares of Slovenia-based Sava Tires it did not already own and the company's Goodyear Dunlop Tires Europe unit purchased the Sweden-based Dackia retail tire stores. The company announced more job cuts in the non-tire sector in 2004 affecting Goodyear's engineered products and chemical units.

In 2005 Goodyear sold its stake in Goodyear Sumatra Plantations (rubber plantations in Indonesia) to rival Bridgestone for $62 million. Later that year the company sold its Wingtack adhesive resin business to Sartomer Company Inc. (a subsidiary of France's TOTAL S.A.) for about $65 million. As 2005 wound to a close the company sold its farm tire business to Titan International for $100 million.

Goodyear called off plans to sell its Chemical Products division. Instead the company integrated its chemical operations with those of its North American Tire division to take greater advantage of operational synergies. The company did however move forward with plans to jettison its Engineered Products division. In 2005 Goodyear secured the services of J.P. Morgan Securities and Goldman Sachs to help it explore opportunities for the sale of Engineered Products. The company struck a deal for The Carlyle Group in 2007 to buy its Engineered Products division for about $1.5 billion.

In 2011 Goodyear sold its tire reinforcement wire business (located in Luxembourg and North Carolina) to South Korea-based Hyosung for $50 million. The same year it sold its farm tire business in Latin America to a Titan International unit for $99 million. In 2010 Goodyear had agreed to sell its farm tire business in Europe as well as Latin America to Titan but the European part of the deal fell through and Goodyear does not have a time frame for making that sale. (In 2005 Titan had purchased Goodyear's North American farm tire business.) Also in 2011 Goodyear closed a facility in Union City Tennessee.

Intent on making more tires at lower-cost facilities Goodyear relocated its tire-making operations from Dalian China to Pulandian China in 2012. Additionally Goodyear is expanding or modernizing plants in Brazil Chile Germany and the US.

EXECUTIVES

Executive Vice President Of Human Resources, Joe Ruocco

Chairman President and CEO, Richard J. (Rich) Kramer, age 51, $1,083,333 total compensation

EVP and CFO, Laura K. Thompson, age 51, $508,333 total compensation

President Americas, Steve McClellan, age 50, $500,000 total compensation

SVP and CTO, Joe Zekoski, age 63

SVP Global Operations, Gregory L. (Greg) Smith, age 51, $541,667 total compensation

President Asia Pacific, Chris Delaney, age 54

President President Europe Middle East and Africa (EMEA), Jean-Claude Kihn, age 56

President Asia Pacific, Daniel (Dan) Smytka, age 53

SVP Global Sales and Marketing, Richard Kellam, age 54

SVP Strategy and Business Development, Scott King

VP Global Manufacturing, Marcelo Toscani, age 57

President Nippon Goodyear, Yujiro Kanahara

Vice President General Manager of North American Tire unit, Johann Finkelmeier

National Sales Manager, Phil Waters

Vice President of Human Resources, Gary Vanderlind

Vice President Director Manager, Carol Archer

Senior Vice President General Counsel Secretary, Thomas Harvie

Vice President Global Project Management, Sherry Neubert

Vice President Supply Chain, Patrick (Paddy) Hurley

Vice President Total Rewards At The Goodyear Tire And Rubber Company, Annie Granchi

Vice President Consumer Tires Asia Pacific, Mike Rytokoski

Vice President FleetHQ, Roy Sutfin

Vice President Sales Financial Advisor, Bertram Bell

Vice President Director Manager, Attila Nagy

Vice President Information Technology Financial Advisor, David (Dave) Bialosky

Country Vice President Manufacturing, Frank Turner

Vice President Sales and Marketing, Mark Totten

Auditors: PricewaterhouseCoopers LLP

LOCATIONS

HQ: Goodyear Tire & Rubber Co.
200 Innovation Way, Akron, OH 44316-0001
Phone: 330 796-2121   **Fax:** 330 796-4099
Web: www.goodyear.com

2014 Sales

	$ mil.	% of total
North America	8,085	45
Europe Middle East & Africa	6,180	34
Asia/Pacific	2,077	11
Latin America	1,796	10
Total	**18,138**	**100**

2014 Sales

	$ mil.	% of total
US	7,558	42
Germany	2,288	12
Other countries	8,292	46
Total	**18,138**	**100**

PRODUCTS/OPERATIONS

Selected Products

Automotive repair services
Chemical products
Natural rubber
Tires
    Automotive
    Aviation
    Buses
    Construction
    Farm
    Mining
    Motorcycles
    Trucks
Tread rubber
Wholesale tires

Selected Subsidiaries

Celeron Corporation
Dapper Tire Co. Inc.
Dunlop Grund und Service Verwaltungs GmbH (Germany)
Dunlop Tyres Limited (UK)

Goodyear Canada Inc.
Goodyear Dalian Tire Company Ltd. (China)
Goodyear de Chile S.A.I.C.
Goodyear de Colombia S.A.
Goodyear do Brasil Productos de Borracha Ltda (Brazil)
Goodyear Dunlop Tires Austria GmbH
Goodyear Dunlop Tires Belgium N.V.
Goodyear Dunlop Tires Czech s.r.o.
Goodyear Dunlop Tires Danmark A/S
Goodyear Dunlop Tires Espana S.A. (Spain)
Goodyear Dunlop Tires Finland OY
Goodyear Dunlop Tires Hellas S.A.I.C. (Greece)
Goodyear Dunlop Tires Hungary Ltd.
Goodyear Dunlop Tires Ireland Ltd
Goodyear Dunlop Tires Italia SpA (Italy)
Goodyear Dunlop Tires Polska Sp z.o.o. (Poland)
Goodyear Dunlop Tires Portugal Unipessoal Lda
Goodyear Dunlop Tires Slovakia s.r.o.
Goodyear Dunlop Tires Suisse S.A. (Switzerland)
The Kelly-Springfield Tyre Company Ltd (UK)
Wingfoot Corporation

COMPETITORS

Bridgestone	Pep Boys
Continental AG	Pirelli
Cooper Tire & Rubber	Sime Darby
Hankook Tire	Titan International
Kumho Tire	Toyo Tire & Rubber
Marangoni	Yokohama Rubber
Michelin	Zeon
Midas	

HISTORICAL FINANCIALS

Company Type: Public

Income Statement

FYE: December 31

	REVENUE ($ mil.)	NET INCOME ($ mil.)	NET PROFIT MARGIN	EMPLOYEES
12/15	16,443	307	1.9%	66,000
12/14	18,138	2,452	13.5%	67,000
12/13	19,540	629	3.2%	69,000
12/12	20,992	212	1.0%	69,000
12/11	22,767	343	1.5%	73,000
Annual Growth	(7.8%)	(2.7%)	—	(2.5%)

2015 Year-End Financials

Debt ratio: 35.01%	No. of shares (mil.): 267
Return on equity: 8.15%	Dividends
Cash ($ mil.): 1,476	Yield: 0.7%
Current ratio: 1.24	Payout: 2.4%
Long-term debt ($ mil.): 5,120	Market value ($ mil.): 8,723

	STOCK PRICE ($) FY Close	P/E High/Low		PER SHARE ($) Earnings	Dividends	Book Value
12/15	32.67	31	21	1.12	0.25	14.68
12/14	28.57	3	2	8.78	0.22	13.40
12/13	23.85	10	5	2.28	0.05	6.48
12/12	13.81	20	13	0.74	0.00	1.51
12/11	14.17	14	7	1.26	0.00	3.06
Annual Growth	23.2%	—	—	(2.9%)	—	48.0%

Grainger (W.W.) Inc.

Grainger is no stranger to those in need of a wide variety of industrial products. W.W. Grainger distributes more than 1.2 million industrial products from supplies to equipment and tools. The short list has electrical devices fasteners fleet maintenance equipment hand tools hardware janitorial lighting office supplies power and plumbing tools and safety security and test instruments. Its some two million customers are contractors maintenance and repair shops manufacturers and commercial government and educational facilities. Grainger sells through a network of branches distribution centers catalogs and websites.

Geographic Reach

About 78% of Grainger's sales are made in the US 11% in Canada and rest in Europe Asia and Latin America. With locations in all 50 states the US business has about 380 branches and 19 distribution centers and 51 contact centers.

The company has 709 branches and 33 distribution centers and operates in about 25 countries.

Operations

Grainger's US business is its largest operating segment. The segment's product lines include lighting and electrical equipment power and hand tools pumps and plumbing and cleaning and maintenance supplies. The US business purchases products from more than 2500 key suppliers most of which are manufacturers.

Acklands-Grainger the company's core Canadian business focuses on distributing industrial and safety products via about 180 domestic branches and distribution centers.

Through a global sourcing operation Grainger procures competitively priced high-quality products produced outside the US from some 400 suppliers.

Besides a wide range of products Grainger also provides services that include inventory management and energy efficiency assistance for lower maintenance costs. The company's KeepStock program offers on-site services and vendor-managed inventory. Since the program's launch in 2006 KeepStock has grown to serve more than 18000 customers. It completed more than 13000 installations in 2014.

Sales and Marketing

Grainger offers its services to a range of industries such as manufacturing hospitality transportation government retail healthcare and education. It markets its products through sales representatives direct marketing materials catalogs and eCommerce and also through contact centers inventory management and its branches. The company also operates its international business through Fabory a European distributor of fasteners tools and industrial supplies; and in Japan through its 51% stake in MonotaRO Co.

Its Zoro Tools unit an online distributor serving US businesses and consumers through its website Zorotools.com.

Its advertising expense was $169 million $178 million and $173 million for 2014 2013 and 2012 respectively.

Financial Performance

Grainger has enjoyed five straight years (2010-2014) of unprecedented growth. Revenues were up by 6% in 2014 due to organic growth and incremental sales from Zoro Tools Brazil and Mexico while the company saw sales outside of Canada and the US grow by 9%. It also saw sales growth in heavy and light manufacturing and diversified commercial services markets. Net income has followed the same trend as net sales. In 2014 its net income grew by 1% due to higher revenues and a drop in interest expense due to lower interest rates. In 2014 Grainger's operating cash flow decreased by $26.7 million due to higher inventory purchases an increase in prepaid expenses and other assets and decline in cash provided by trade accounts payable.

Strategy

Grainger occasionally pursues business acquisitions and joint ventures that promise sustainable opportunities and broaden its offerings.

In 2014 Grainger bought of 96 acres of land in Bordentown Township New Jersey and announced plans to build a 1.3 million square-foot distribution center on this property. Scheduled to open in 2016 the center will allow the company to deleiver more products next day to customers in the US Northeast. In late 2014 the company announced plans to close its operations Brazil during 2015.

In 2013 it transitioned Grainger.com to a new web platform launched a Spanish language website and introduced new applications for mobile devices. That year the company also added more than 200 new sales representatives in North America bolstered its inventory management services across the Americas and Europe and added more than 300000 new products to Grainger.com. Growing its physical assets in 2013 Grainger opened a 1 million sq. ft. highly automated distribution center in the Chicago area. It also opened its new branch in Williston North Dakota to support customers in the Bakken oil fields. In 2013 Grainger divested four direct marketing brands at the end of the fourth quarter which included Gempler's Ben Meadows AW Direct and McFeely's. Mergers and Acquisitions

In 2014 it acquired WFS Enterprises a distributor of tools and supplies to industrial markets in Southern Ontario (and select US locations) for $87 million. In 2013 the company acquired E&R Industrial Sales (a distributor of metalworking production supplies and materials to manufacturers and industrial customers) for $116 million; and Safety Solutions Inc. (a distributor of safety footwear supplies and services with a focus on the manufacturing sector) for $30 million.

That year it also acquired the remaining non controlling interest it did not own in Grainger Colombia for $10 million. Grainger's 2013 acquisitions added 21 branches to the company's portfolio.

HISTORY

In 1919 William W. Grainger a motor designer and salesman saw the opportunity to develop a wholesale electric-motor sales and distribution company. He set up an office in Chicago in 1927 and incorporated the business a year later. With sales generated primarily through postcard mailers and an eight-page catalog called MotorBook Grainger started shipping motors to mail-order customers.

Utilities and factories began to shift from direct-current to alternating-current power systems in the late 1920s. Uniform DC-powered assembly lines gave way to individual workstations each powered by a separate AC motor. This burgeoning market opened the way for distributors such as W.W. Grainger to tap into segments that high-volume manufacturers found difficult to reach. In the early 1930s W.W. Grainger opened offices in Atlanta Dallas Philadelphia and San Francisco; by 1936 it had 15 sales branches.

W.W. Grainger entered a boom period after WWII and by 1949 it had branches in 30 states. The company continued to expand in the 1950s and 1960s then went public in 1967.

William Grainger retired in 1968 and his son David succeeded him as CEO. The company expanded into electric motor manufacturing with the purchase of the Doerr Companies in 1969. Ten years later it opened its 150th branch.

Grainger's distribution became decentralized with the 1983 opening of its 1.4-million-sq.-ft. automated regional distribution center in Kansas City. The next year Grainger surpassed $1 billion in sales. The company sold its Doerr Electric subsidiary to Emerson Electric in 1986. It added 91 branches in 1987 and 1988.

After a 17-year hiatus the company started making acquisitions again buying Vonnegut Industrial Products in 1989; Bossert Industrial Supply and Allied Safety in 1990; Ball Industries a distributor of sanitary and janitorial supplies in 1991; and

Lab Safety Supply in 1992. Grainger began integrating its sanitary supply business with its core activities in 1993.

For the first time in company history no Grainger held the CEO position when president Richard Keyser was appointed in 1995 replacing David Grainger. That year the company moved its headquarters to Lake Forest Illinois.

EXECUTIVES

Chairman President and CEO, James T. (Jim) Ryan, age 57, $1,123,500 total compensation

VP Finance Industrial Supply Division, Ronald L. Jadin, age 55, $685,125 total compensation

SVP and CIO, Michael Ali

SVP and Group President Americas, Court D. Carruthers, age 42, $576,261 total compensation

COO, Donald G. (D.G.) Macpherson, age 48, $659,750 total compensation

Senior Vice President and Chief Human Resources Director Officer, Joseph (Jo) High

Vice President Information Technology, Carol Pilz

Vice President Technology, Chris Chapman

Vice President of Corporate and Major Account Business, Michael (Mel) DuBose

Regional Sales Vice President, Daniel Moscaritolo

Vice President Marketing, Jim Penvillo

Regional Sales Vice President, Lloyd Peterson

Vice President Sales Pacific Mountain Region, Brian W Norris

Vice President of International Market Development, Bonnie McLntyre

Vice President Human Resources Operations, Sam Nadda

Vice President Information Technology, Nefertira Rogers

Vice President Corporate Mergers and Acquisitions, Jon Skelly

Vice President and Secretary, Gloria Sinclair

Vice President US Ecommerce, Samuel (Sam) Kim

Regional Sales Vice President, Gerry Frank

Vice President Solutions Delivery, John (Jack) Hill

Regional Sales Vice President, Sergio Sanchez

National Sales Manager, Martin (Marti) Johnsson

National Account Manager, Paula Rupiper

Regional Sales Vice President, Mark Busbee

National Account Manager, Helen McMullen

Regional Sales Vice President Government, Rob Laughlin

Regional Sales Vice President Middle Atlantic Commercial Sales, Jeff Collier

Vice President U.S. Mergers and Acquisitions, Bill Koenig

Vice President Corporate Strategy And Analytics, Brian Walker

Auditors: Ernst & Young LLP

LOCATIONS

HQ: Grainger (W.W.) Inc.
100 Grainger Parkway, Lake Forest, IL 60045-5201
Phone: 847 535-1000   **Fax:** 847 535-0878
Web: www.grainger.com

2014 Sales

	$ mil.	% of total
US	7,780	78
Canada	1,074	11
Other countries	1,109	11
Total	**9,965**	**100**

2013 Sales

	$ mil.	% of total
US	7,290	77
Canada	1,126	12
Other countries	1,020	11
Total	**9,437**	**100**

PRODUCTS/OPERATIONS

2014 Sales

	$ mil.	% of total
US-based businesses	7,714	77
Canada-based businesses	1,075	11
Other businesses	1,174	12
Total	**9,965**	**100**

Selected Products

Adhesives
Air compressors
Air-filtration equipment
Electric motors
Electrical products
Fasteners
Fleet and vehicle maintenance products
Hand tools
Heating and ventilation equipment
Janitorial and plumbing supplies
Lab supplies
Library equipment
Lighting equipment
Material handling
Pneumatics and hydraulics
Power tools
Pumps
Safety products
Security products
Spray paints
Test Instruments

COMPETITORS

Ace Hardware	International Library
Applied Industrial	Furniture
Technologies	Kaman Industrial
Fastenal	Technologies
Genuine Parts	Lowe' s
Gexpro	MSC Industrial Direct
Graybar Electric	McMaster-Carr
Industrial	WESCO International
Distribution Group	Wilson

HISTORICAL FINANCIALS

Company Type: Public

Income Statement

FYE: December 31

	REVENUE ($ mil.)	NET INCOME ($ mil.)	NET PROFIT MARGIN	EMPLOYEES
12/14	9,964	801	8.0%	23,600
12/13	9,437	797	8.4%	23,700
12/12	8,950	689	7.7%	22,400
12/11	8,078	658	8.2%	21,400
12/10	7,182	510	7.1%	18,500
Annual Growth	**8.5%**	**11.9%**	—	**6.3%**

2014 Year-End Financials

Debt ratio: 9.18%
Return on equity: 24.82%
Cash ($ mil.): 226
Current ratio: 2.35
Long-term debt ($ mil.): 404

No. of shares (mil.): 67
Dividends
  Yield: 1.6%
  Payout: 36.2%
Market value ($ mil.): 17,188

	STOCK PRICE ($) FY Close	P/E High/Low	PER SHARE ($) Earnings	Dividends	Book Value
12/14	254.89	23 20	11.45	4.17	47.60
12/13	255.42	24 18	11.13	3.59	47.21
12/12	202.37	23 18	9.52	3.06	43.52
12/11	187.19	21 14	9.07	2.52	37.57
12/10	138.11	20 14	6.93	2.08	31.79
Annual Growth	**16.6%**	— —	**13.4%**	**19.0%**	**10.6%**

Graybar Electric Co., Inc.

There's no gray area when it comes to Graybar Electric: it's one of the largest distributors of electrical products in the US. The employee-owned company distributes more than 1 million electrical communications and data networking products through a network of around 260 distribution facilities. Its diversified lineup includes a myriad of wire cable and lighting products from thousands of manufacturers and suppliers. It also offers supply chain management and logistics services. Affiliate Graybar Financial Services provides equipment leasing and financing. Graybar Electric sells to construction contractors industrial plants power utilities and telecommunications providers primarily in the US.

Geographic Reach

Graybar's business is primarily based in the US as its headquarters are located in St. Louis Missouri. Other operations include distribution facilities in Canada and Puerto Rico. The company serves its customers through a a network of over 260 locations across the US and Canada. It also operates in 13 geographical districts in the US each of which maintains multiple distribution facilities that consist primarily of warehouse space. The number of facilities excluding distribution centers in its designated districts varies from 10 to 22 totaling 215 for all districts.

Sales and Marketing

Among the company's strengths is a diverse and large customer base with more than 130000 clients. Graybar gets nearly half of its sales from electrical contractors. Other customers come from the institutional commercial and government (22%) and industrial and utility (21%) sectors. The company has expanded its sales presence to support its government business which continues to see strong growth.

Financial Performance

The company's revenue climbed 6% from $5.7 billion in 2013 to a record-setting $5.9 billion in 2014. The historic growth for 2014 was fueled by a 5% surge in sales from its construction vertical and an 8% uptick from the industrial and utility markets. In addition Graybar's profits increased 8% to $87 million during 2014. Its net cash provided by operating activities also increased by 49% in 2014 compared to 2013 primarily due to changes in accrued payroll and benefit costs and other liabilities.

Strategy

Graybar plans to continue adding physical locations to expand its presence and service offerings. In addition Graybar is broadening its e-commerce and mobility capabilities to enhance its online presence and expand its digital marketing to grow sales with new and existing customers.

In 2015 Graybar announced the opening of a branch in Utah and two branches in California. The company in 2014 opened a branch in Texas two in North Dakota and one in Oregon.

HISTORY

After serving as a telegrapher during the Civil War Enos Barton borrowed $400 from his widowed mother in 1869 and started an electrical equipment shop in Cleveland with George Shawk. Later that year Elisha Gray a professor of physics at Oberlin College who had several inventions (including a printing telegraph) to his credit bought Shawk's interest in the shop and the firm of Gray

& Barton moved to Chicago where a third partner joined.

The company incorporated as the Western Electric Manufacturing Co. in 1872 with two-thirds of the company's stock held by two Western Union executives. As the telegraph industry took off the enterprise grew rapidly providing equipment to towns and railroads in the western US.

Western Electric then formed a new distribution business in 1926 Graybar Electric Co. (from "Gray" and "Barton") the world's largest electrical supply merchandiser. In 1929 employees bought the company from Western Electric for $3 million in cash and $6 million in preferred stock. During the 1930s it marketed a line of appliances and sewing machines under the Graybar name.

EXECUTIVES

SVP North American Business, Robert C. Lyons, age 59, $268,435 total compensation
SVP Sales and Marketing, William P. Mansfield, age 53
SVP and CFO, Randall R. Harwood, age 59, $246,534 total compensation
Chairman President and CEO, Kathleen M. Mazzarella, age 56, $696,774 total compensation
SVP Secretary and General Counsel, Matthew W. Geekie, age 53, $283,143 total compensation
VP and CIO, David Meyer
SVP Supply Chain Management, Scott S. Clifford, age 44
Vice President and Treasurer, Jon N Reed
District Vice President Phoenix Direct, Craig Mead
Vice President Manager Director, Ray Schneider
Vice President, Leigh Graff
Vice President Education Graybar Electric, Chris Althauser
Vice President Manager Director, Byron Bennett
National Sales Manager Graybar Financial Services, Stuart (Stu) Jaeger
Vice President Human Resources, Vicki Hall
Vice President Of Marketing, Rob Bezjak
District Vice President, Joseph Lamotte
District Vice President, Joseph (Jo) Lamotte
Auditors: Ernst & Young LLP

LOCATIONS

HQ: Graybar Electric Co., Inc.
34 North Meramec Avenue, St. Louis, MO 63105
Phone: 314 573-9200
Web: www.graybar.com

2014 Sales

	% of total
US	94
Other countries	6
Total	**100**

PRODUCTS/OPERATIONS

2014 Sales

	% of total
Construction	55
Commercial Institutional and Government	23
Utility & Industrial	22
Total	**100**

Selected Products

Ballasts
Batteries
Cable
Conduit
Connectors
Emergency lighting
Enclosures
Fiber-optic cable
Fittings
Fluorescent lighting
Fuses
Hand tools

Hangers/fasteners
Heating and ventilating equipment
Industrial fans
Lighting
Lubricants
Paints
Patch cords
Smoke detectors
Testing and measuring instruments
Timers
Transfer switches
Transformers
Utility products
Wire

Selected Subsidiaries

Commonwealth Controls Corporation
Distribution Associates Inc.
Graybar Business Services Inc.
Graybar Canada Limited
Graybar Commerce Corporation
Graybar Electric Canada Limited
Graybar Financial Services Inc.
Graybar International Inc.
Graybar Services Inc.

COMPETITORS

Anixter International	Rexel Canada
Border States Electric	Rexel Inc.
Communications Supply	Richardson Electronics
Consolidated Electrical	SUMMIT Electric Supply
Gexpro	Sonepar USA
HD Supply	United Electric Supply
HWC	W.W. Grainger
Premier Farnell	WESCO International

HISTORICAL FINANCIALS

Company Type: Public

Income Statement

FYE: December 31

	REVENUE ($ mil.)	NET INCOME ($ mil.)	NET PROFIT MARGIN	EMPLOYEES
12/14	5,978	87	1.5%	8,250
12/13	5,659	81	1.4%	7,600
12/12	5,413	86	1.6%	7,500
12/11	5,374	81	1.5%	7,400
12/10	4,616	42	0.9%	7,000
Annual Growth	**6.7%**	**20.1%**	**—**	**4.2%**

2014 Year-End Financials

Debt ratio: 4.34%	No. of shares (mil.): 15
Return on equity: 12.99%	Dividends
Cash ($ mil.): 33	Yield: —
Current ratio: 1.44	Payout: 72.4%
Long-term debt ($ mil.): 11	Market value ($ mil.): —

Great Southern Bancorp, Inc.

Despite its name Great Southern Bancorp is firmly entrenched in the heartland. It is the holding company for Great Southern Bank which operates more than 75 branches in Missouri plus more than two dozen locations in Iowa Kansas Nebraska and Arkansas. Founded in 1923 the bank offers checking and savings accounts CDs IRAs and credit cards. The firm's Great Southern Travel division is one of the largest travel agencies in Missouri. It serves both leisure and corporate travelers through about a dozen offices. Among other units Great Southern Insurance offers property/ca-

sualty and life insurance while Great Southern Financial provides investment products and services through an agreement with Ameriprise.

Operations

Great Southern's lending activities primarily consist of originating and buying real estate loans: Commercial real estate mortgages and construction and land development loans account for around half of its loan portfolio while single-family residential mortgages make up another 15%. The bank also writes consumer (including home equity) construction and business loans.

Sales and Marketing

The bank introduced a smartphone banking application in early 2012. The addition of mobile banking services allows it to better compete with larger technologically advanced banks.

Financial Performance

The company's revenue decreased in fiscal 2013 compared to the prior year. It reported revenue of $184.1 million for fiscal 2013 down from $258.2 million in fiscal 2012.

The company's net income also decreased in fiscal 2013 compared to the previous fiscal period. It netted $33.7 million in fiscal 2013 down from $48.7 million in fiscal 2012. Great Southern's cash on hand also dipped by more than $50 million in fiscal 2013 compared to fiscal 2012 levels.

EXECUTIVES

VP Operations and Secretary Great Southern Bank, Douglas W. (Doug) Marrs, age 57, $122,602 total compensation
Vice President and Director of Human Resources Great Southern Bank, Matt Snyder
Vice President, Brian Fogle
SVP and Chief Lending Officer of the Bank, Steven G. Mitchem, age 63, $227,429 total compensation
President CEO and Director Great Southern Bancorp and Great Southern Bank, Joseph W. (Joe) Turner, age 50, $299,237 total compensation
SVP and CFO Great Southern Bank, Rex A. Copeland, age 50, $235,201 total compensation
VP Information Systems, Linton J. (Lin) Thomason, age 58
Vice President Sales And Marketing, Teresa S Chasteen
Vice President, Jennifer (Jen) Cook
Assistant Vice President, Kim Warren
Vice President, Scott Brekke
Vice President, Cal Glasco
Chairman Great Southern Bancorp and Great Southern Bank, William V. Turner, age 82
Auditors: BKD, LLP

LOCATIONS

HQ: Great Southern Bancorp, Inc.
1451 E. Battlefield, Springfield, MO 65804
Phone: 417 887-4400
Web: www.greatsouthernbank.com

COMPETITORS

BancorpSouth	Hawthorn Bancshares
Bank of America	NASB Financial
Commerce Bancshares	U.S. Bancorp
First Bancshares (MO)	UMB Financial
Guaranty Federal	Wells Fargo

HISTORICAL FINANCIALS
Company Type: Public

Income Statement
FYE: December 31

	ASSETS ($ mil.)	NET INCOME ($ mil.)	INCOME AS % OF ASSETS	EMPLOYEES
12/14	3,951	43	1.1%	1,252
12/13	3,560	33	0.9%	1,163
12/12	3,955	48	1.2%	1,164
12/11	3,790	30	0.8%	1,256
12/10	3,411	23	0.7%	1,086
Annual Growth	3.7%	16.2%	—	3.6%

2014 Year-End Financials

Debt ratio: 0.78%	No. of shares (mil.): 13
Return on equity: 10.88%	Dividends
Cash ($ mil.): 218	Yield: 2.0%
Current ratio: —	Payout: 27.7%
Long-term debt ($ mil.): —	Market value ($ mil.): 546

	STOCK PRICE ($) FY Close	P/E High/Low		PER SHARE ($) Earnings	Dividends	Book Value
12/14	39.67	13	9	3.10	0.80	30.52
12/13	30.41	13	9	2.42	0.72	27.84
12/12	25.45	9	6	3.54	0.90	27.20
12/11	23.59	12	8	1.93	0.72	24.08
12/10	23.59	17	13	1.46	0.72	22.60
Annual Growth	13.9%		—	20.7%	2.7%	7.8%

Great West Life & Annuity Insurance Co - Insurance Products

Great-West Life & Annuity Insurance is the southern arm of a northern parent. The company a subsidiary of Canada's Great-West Lifeco and a member of the Power Financial family represents the Great-West group's primary US operations. It offers life insurance and annuities to individuals and employer groups. Under the Great-West Retirement Services brand it administers employer-sponsored retirement products including defined-benefit pension and 401(k) plans. Additional Great-West services include investment consulting and fund management. Great-West Life & Annuity markets products through its sales representatives and regional offices as well as independent brokers.

Geographic Reach

Great-West Life & Annuity has offices in more than 50 locations throughout the US Puerto Rico Guam and the US Virgin Islands.

Operations

Great-West Life & Annuity also distributes its individual life insurance and annuity products through partnerships with banking institutions and financial advisors including Bank of America Citigroup and Charles Schwab. Outside of its own retirement products which are marketed to corporate not-for-profit health care educational and government organizations the Great-West Retirement Services unit provides business services including record-keeping for plans offered by other financial institutions. Its recordkeeping subsidiary FASCore LLC serves 4.7 million participant accounts. Great-West Life & Annuity's Individual Markets Division

offers individual retirement accounts (IRAs) individual term and single-premium life insurance individual annuity products as well as executive benefits and business-owned life insurance products.

In 2012 the company had 540000 individual accounts and had $201.5 billion in assets under administration.

Sales and Marketing

Great-West Life & Annuity markets its products and services through sales and service professionals brokers consultants advisors financial institutions and third-party administrators.

Financial Performance

Great-West Life & Annuity's revenues grew by 3% in 2012 thanks to its portfolio of diverse products expanded partnerships and enhanced tools. IRA sales grew 50% as part of a push to provide enhanced distribution education services to terminated group plan participants. This initiative gained $916 million in roll-ins to existing plans.The company's net income jumped by 18% in 2012 thanks to higher revenues and a drop in expenses.

Strategy

Growing it product portfolio in 2012 the company launched two retail retirement income products securing selling agreements with five distribution partners.

Ownership

Great-West Life & Annuity is an indirect wholly owned subsidiary of Great-West Lifeco. Its ultimate parent is the Power Corporation of Canada.

Company Background

In 2008 the company sold its Great-West Healthcare division to CIGNA for $1.5 billion; the segment offered group life and medical insurance products to US businesses with an emphasis on self-funded programs for small and midsized employers. The divestiture of its health care unit was part of Great-West's strategy of focusing its efforts in the financial services arena.

EXECUTIVES

EVP Individual Markets, Robert K. Shaw, age 60, $458,100 total compensation
SVP and Chief Investment Officer General Account, Ernie Friesen
SVP and Chief Investment Officer Separate Accounts, Catherine S. Tocher
President and CEO, Robert L. Reynolds
President Empower Retirement, Edmund F. Murphy
EVP Great West Lifeco U.S. Inc., Charles B. McDevitt
SVP and CIO, Jeffrey W. Knight
SVP and CFO, Louis J. Mannello
SVP Product Management, David G. McLeod
National Account Manager, Brad Dzurovchin
Assistant Vice President Information Systems, Camilla Langenfeld
Regional Vice President, Brian Sugrue
Assistant Vice President, Renee Graham
Auditors: Deloitte & Touche LLP

LOCATIONS

HQ: Great West Life & Annuity Insurance Co - Insurance Products
8515 East Orchard Road, Greenwood Village, CO 80111
Phone: 303 737-3000
Web: www.greatwest.com

PRODUCTS/OPERATIONS

Selected Products and Services
Annuities
Life insurance
Retirement services
Retirement plans for government corporate and not-for-profit employers

Communication and education services
Enrollment services
Investment options
Third-part

COMPETITORS

AXA Financial
Allstate
Industrial Alliance Insurance and Financial Servic
John Hancock Financial Services
Liberty Mutual
Lincoln Financial Group
Manulife Financial
MetLife
Mutual of Omaha
Nationwide Financial
Pacific Mutual
Prudential
State Farm
Sun Life
The Hartford

HISTORICAL FINANCIALS
Company Type: Public

Income Statement
FYE: December 31

	ASSETS ($ mil.)	NET INCOME ($ mil.)	INCOME AS % OF ASSETS	EMPLOYEES
12/14	58,348	317	0.5%	4,500
12/13	55,323	128	0.2%	3,300
12/12	52,818	238	0.5%	3,300
12/11	48,336	214	0.4%	3,200
12/10	47,627	202	0.4%	3,100
Annual Growth	5.2%	11.9%	—	9.8%

2014 Year-End Financials

Debt ratio: 0.94%	No. of shares (mil.): 7
Return on equity: 15.82%	Dividends
Cash ($ mil.): 12	Yield: —
Current ratio: —	Payout: 99.7%
Long-term debt ($ mil.): —	Market value ($ mil.): —

Great Western Bancorp Inc

LOCATIONS

HQ: Great Western Bancorp Inc
100 North Phillips Avenue, Sioux Falls, SD 57104
Phone: 605 334-2548
Web: www.greatwesternbank.com

HISTORICAL FINANCIALS
Company Type: Public

Income Statement
FYE: September 30

	ASSETS ($ mil.)	NET INCOME ($ mil.)	INCOME AS % OF ASSETS	EMPLOYEES
09/15	9,798	109	1.1%	1,475
09/14	9,371	104	1.1%	1,492
09/13	9,134	96	1.1%	1,486
09/12	9,008	73	0.8%	—
Annual Growth	2.8%	14.3%	—	—

2015 Year-End Financials

Debt ratio: 6.86%
Return on equity: 7.57%
Cash ($ mil.): 237
Current ratio: —
Long-term debt ($ mil.): —

No. of shares (mil.): 55
Dividends
  Yield: 1.4%
  Payout: 20.2%
Market value ($ mil.): 1,401

	STOCK PRICE ($)	P/E		PER SHARE ($)		
	FY Close	High/Low	Earnings	Dividends	Book Value
09/15	25.37	14 9	1.90	0.36	26.43
09/14	0.00	— —	1.81	1.76	24.55
Annual Growth	—	— —	1.6%	(41.1%)	2.5%

GREENSTONE FARM CREDIT SERVICES ACA

One of the largest associations in the Farm Credit System GreenStone offers FARM CREDIT SERVICES (FCS) providesÅshort intermediate and long-term loans; equipment and building leases; appraisal services; and life and crop insurance to farmers in Michigan and Wisconsin. ItÂserves about 15000 members and has nearlyÅ40 locations. Through an alliance with AgriSolutions a farm software and consulting company Greenstone provides income tax planning and preparation services farm business consulting and educational seminars. FCS Mortgage provides residential loans for rural properties as well as loans for home improvement construction and refinancing.

Dairy and cash crop loans each account for nearly a quarter of GreenStoneÂFCS' loan portfolio which is rounded out by rural residential real estate andÅgreenhouses hogs and other commodities.

EXECUTIVES

Exec V Pres, Melissa (Mel) Stolicker
Exec V Pres, Peter Lemmer
Vice President Human Resources, Bethany Barker
Regional Vice President, Erin Dubois
Vice President Commercial Lending, Tyson Lemon
Regional Vice President, David Ballman
Regional Vice President, Tim McTigue
Senior Vice President Sales, Brad Henion
Vice President Credit, Kevin Emison
Senior Vice President Chief Credit Off, Paul Anderson
Senior Vice President Capital Markets, Al Compton
Vice President of Marketing and Public Relations, Melissa (Mel) Rogers
Vice President Financial Services, Leo Pasch
Vice President Commercial, Dana Kirk
Senior Vice President Commercial Lending, John Jones
Vice President Commercial Credit, Gayle Olson
Vice President Credit, Steve Kluemper
Vice President Commercial Lending, Larry Urban
Vice President Credit, Thomas (Thom) Urban
Vice President of Sales and Customer Relations, Ben Mahlich
Second Vice President, Shane Kenner
Regional Vice President Northeast Region, Carl Treml
Vice President Commercial Lending, Thomas (Thom) Wilson
Senior Vice President Chief Human Resources, Sphr B Barker
Auditors: PRICEWATERHOUSECOOPERS LLP MI

LOCATIONS

HQ: GREENSTONE FARM CREDIT SERVICES ACA
3515 WEST RD, EAST LANSING, MI 488237312
Phone: 5173240213
Web: WWW.GREENSTONEFCS.COM

COMPETITORS

COUNTRY Financial   Rabobank Group
FB BanCorp

HISTORICAL FINANCIALS

Company Type: Private

Income Statement

FYE: December 31

	ASSETS ($ mil.)	NET INCOME ($ mil.)	INCOME AS % OF ASSETS	EMPLOYEES
12/07	4,317	69	1.6%	380
12/06	3,691	63	1.7%	—
Annual Growth	17.0%	8.9%	—	—

Group 1 Automotive, Inc.

Group 1 Automotive is only one in a group of firms (AutoNation and Penske Automotive Group are the largest) striving to consolidate US auto sales. The company owns and operates more than 145 franchises at about 115 dealerships as well as about 28 collision service centers in about 15 US states. More than half of Group 1's dealerships are located in Texas Oklahoma and California. Group 1 Automotive also has 25 franchises at about 20 dealerships and several collision centers in the UK and 20 franchises at dealerships and five collision centers in Brazil. The company's dealerships offer new (more than 55% of sales) and used cars and light trucks under some 30 different brands. It also offers financing provides maintenance and repair services and sells replacement parts.

Operations

Group 1 Automotive's operations include five core business segments: New Vehicles (58% of sales) Used Vehicles (23%) Parts & Service (11%) Used Vehicles wholesale (4%) and Finance & Insurance. In the UK the auto dealer operates through its subsidiary Group 1 Automotive UK Ltd.

Geographic Reach

The auto dealer rings up about 80% of its sales in the US; the remainder comes from the UK and Brazil. In Britain it has locations in Brighton Chelmsford Chingford Farnborough Hailsham Harold Wood Hindhead Southend Stansted and Worthington.

Sales and Marketing

About 70% of Group 1's 2014 new vehicle sales came from Toyota Honda Ford BMW and Nissan. Sales of new vehicles bearing Toyota/Scion/Lexus nameplates accounted for more than a quarter of new vehicle unit sales in 2014.

Group 1 spent $73.8 million $59.0 million and $54.1 million in 2014 2013 and 2012 respectively.

Financial Performance

Group 1 has reported consistently rising revenue since 2010 and in 2014 it grew another 11% compared to the previous year. Increased sales of all vehicle groups particularly luxury models lead to the improvement. Net income has also been on the rise but dipped 20% in 2014 due to increased sales commission costs as the company sold more cars.

2013 sales jumped 19% versus 2012 to $8.9 billion (a company high) while net income climbed 14% over the same period to almost $114 million. Driving its strong financial performance were double-digit gains on new and used vehicle retail sales and in its used vehicle wholesale business. Stronger consumer confidence and more dealerships contributed to the increases. Finance and insurance sales jumped about 14% while parts and service sales climbed 7%. Cash flow from operations rose to $52 million in 2013 on higher net income gain on dispositions and a favorable change in working capital.

Strategy

Like its rival AutoNation Group 1 Automotive is focusing on acquiring import and luxury brand dealerships. The Houston-based auto dealer is also expanding internationally both in the UK (where it already has an established presence) and in Brazil a relatively new market for the company. Those countries accounted for 18% of sales in 2014. The company's strategy also includes growing its higher margin parts and services business growing its share of the new and used vehicle market taking advantage of its size to boost efficiency and continuing to make strategic acquisitions. In recent years Group 1 has seen import and luxury brands account for an increased share of its business.

Mergers and Acquisitions

In 2015 Group 1 continued to add to its dealership roster though not at the pace it did in 2014. It added Audi and Mercedes-Benz dealerships in Texas as well as one of the nation's top Audi dealerships Prestige Audi of North Miami Beach.

The company in 2014 acquired the Alex Rodriguez Mercedes-Benz dealership in the Houston suburb of League City. Also in the Houston area the company expanded its Hyundai operations opening a new South Loop Hyundai dealership. In Southern California Group 1 bought Heller Ford and Heller Hyundai. Group 1 scooped up the Munday Chevrolet and Mazda operations in Houston Texas. Up the road the company bought South Point Kia in Austin where it owns Maxwell Ford Town North Nissan and Round Rock Nissan.

Overseas the company acquired three Elms BMW/MINI dealerships in the UK. The dealership are in Bedford Cambridge and Stansted.

EXECUTIVES

VP Human Resources, J. Brooks O'Hara, age 59, $309,200 total compensation
President and CEO, Earl J. Hesterberg, age 62, $1,000,000 total compensation
VP Financial Services Manufacturer Relations and Public Affairs, Peter C. DeLongchamps, age 54, $443,000 total compensation
Regional VP West Region, Frank Grese
SVP and CFO, John C. Rickel, age 54, $566,500 total compensation
VP and General Counsel, Darryl M. Burman, age 57, $427,500 total compensation
VP Information Systems, James R. Druzbik
Regional VP UK, Ian Twinley
Regional VP East Region, Daryl Kenningham, age 51
Vice President Finance, Kim Craig
Regional Vice President, David (Dave) Hult
Director, John L. Adams, age 70
Auditors: Ernst & Young LLP

LOCATIONS

HQ: Group 1 Automotive, Inc.
800 Gessner, Suite 500, Houston, TX 77024
Phone: 713 647-5700   **Fax:** 713 647-5858
Web: www.group1auto.com

2014 Sales

	$ mil.	% of total
U.S.	8,175	82
U.K.	987	10
Brazil	775	8
Total	**9,937**	**100**

PRODUCTS/OPERATIONS

2014 Sales

	$ mil.	% of total
New vehicle retail	5,741	58
Used vehicle retail	2,324	23
Used vehicle wholesale	379	4
Parts & service	1,125	11
Finance insurance & other	366	4
Total	**9,937**	**100**

Selected Brands

Domestic
  Ford
  Chevrolet
  Dodge
  Jeep
  GMC
  Chrysler
  Buick
Import
  Toyota
  Nissan
  Honda
  Volkswagen
  Hyundai
  Mazda
  Subaru
  Scion
  Kia
  Fiat
  Mitsubishi
Luxury
  BMW
  Acura
  MINI
  Audi
  Infiniti
  Volvo
  Cadillac
  Lincoln
  Porsche
  Maybach
  Sprinter
  smart

COMPETITORS

Ancira
Asbury Automotive
AutoNation
CarMax
David McDavid Auto
  Group
Herb Chambers
Lithia Motors

Lookers
Pendragon
Penske Automotive
  Group
Phil Long Dealerships
Sonic Automotive
Sytner

HISTORICAL FINANCIALS

Company Type: Public

Income Statement

FYE: December 31

	REVENUE ($ mil.)	NET INCOME ($ mil.)	NET PROFIT MARGIN	EMPLOYEES
12/14	9,937	93	0.9%	11,978
12/13	8,918	113	1.3%	11,510
12/12	7,476	100	1.3%	9,343
12/11	6,079	82	1.4%	8,267
12/10	5,509	50	0.9%	7,454
Annual Growth	**15.9%**	**16.6%**	—	**12.6%**

2014 Year-End Financials

Debt ratio: 59.65%
Return on equity: 9.11%
Cash ($ mil.): 40
Current ratio: 1.06
Long-term debt ($ mil.): 1,008

No. of shares (mil.): 24
Dividends
  Yield: 0.7%
  Payout: 19.2%
Market value ($ mil.): 2,181

	STOCK PRICE ($) FY Close	P/E High/Low	PER SHARE ($) Earnings	Dividends	Book Value
12/14	89.62	24 16	3.60	0.70	40.18
12/13	71.02	17 12	4.32	0.65	43.77
12/12	61.99	15 10	4.19	0.59	39.28
12/11	51.80	15 10	3.47	0.48	35.54
12/10	41.76	19 10	2.16	0.10	32.97
Annual Growth	**21.0%**	— —	**13.6%**	**62.7%**	**5.1%**

GROWMARK INC.

Retail farm-supply and grain-marketing cooperative GROWMARK can mark its growth by the grain. A member-owed agricultural co-op GROWMARK has more than 100000 members. Under the FAST STOP name the co-op runs more than 250 fuel stations and convenience stores in the Midwest. Its Seedway subsidiary sells commercial vegetable seed and farm seed for turf and grains including alfalfa corn wheat and soybeans. GROWMARK also offers fertilizer seeds ethanol biodiesel and farm financing. Its MID-CO COMMODITIES subsidiary trades grain and offers advice regarding futures and options.

Geographic Reach

GROWMARK is headquartered in Bloomington Illinois and serves customers in more than 40 states and Ontario Canada. SEEDWAY maintains eight office and warehouse locations in Vermont New York Pennsylvania and Florida.

Strategy

Cooperation is important within and among agricultural cooperatives. A strong believer in the latter part of this principle GROWMARK has marketing agreements and alliances with among others fertilizer maker and distributor CF Industries pet-food producer PRO-PET agribusiness company Syngenta and rural financial services provider CoBank.

Mergers and Acquisitions

GROWMARK acquires fertilizer storage terminals and transportation infrastructure on a regular basis.

EXECUTIVES

Vice President, Jim Spradlin
Vice Chairman, John Reifsteck
CEO, Jeff Solberg
Vice President General Counsel, Brent Bostrom
VP Eastern Retail Operations, Steve Buckalew
VP and CFO, Marshall Bohbrink
VP Energy, Kevin Carroll
VP Midwest Retail and Acquisitions, Shelly Kruse
VP Grain, Brent Ericson
Vice President Human Resources & Compliance, Gary Swango
VP Agronomy, Mark Orr
VP Financial and Risk Management, Mike Woods
VP Member Services, Denny Worth
Vice President Information Technology, George Key
Vice President Information Systems, Marvin Weisert
National Account Manager, Norman Frank

Vice President Information Technology, George Mueller
Vice President Of Information Technology, Rick Norton
Vice President Member Services, Dennis Farmer
Vice President, Paul Eckhart
Vice President Finance, Jeffrey (Jeff) Solberg
Vice Chairman, Rick Nelson
Vice Chairman, Chet Esther
Assistant Treasurer, John Fruin
Auditors: ERNST & YOUNG LLP CHICAGO IL

LOCATIONS

HQ: GROWMARK INC.
1701 TOWANDA AVE, BLOOMINGTON, IL 617012057
Phone: 3095576000
Web: WWW.GROWMARK.COM

PRODUCTS/OPERATIONS

Selected Retail Products and Operations

COMFORT PRO (propane heating oil)
  FAST STOP
  FS (farm s
  Green Yard (turf seed fertilizer)
  Seedway (farm turf and vegetable seed)

Selected Member Cooperatives and Subsidiaries

AgVantage FS Inc.
AgView Grain LLC
Evergreen FS Inc.
GROWMARK FS LLC
MID-CO COMMODITIES
Northern Grain Marketing LLC
Seedway LLC
Total Grain Marketing LLC
Western Grain Marketing LLC

COMPETITORS

ADM
AGRI Industries
Ag Processing Inc.
BP
Barkley Seed
Bayer CropScience
CHS
Cargill
Chevron
Costco Wholesale
DeBruce Grain
Exxon Mobil

Marathon Oil
NC Hybrids
Orscheln Farm and Home
Pfister Hybrid Corn
Pioneer Hi-Bred
Rabo AgriFinance
Sakata Seed
Seed Enterprises
Southern States
Terra Nitrogen
Wal-Mart
Wilbur-Ellis

HISTORICAL FINANCIALS

Company Type: Private

Income Statement

FYE: August 31

	REVENUE ($ mil.)	NET INCOME ($ mil.)	NET PROFIT MARGIN	EMPLOYEES
08/14	10,372	166	1.6%	1,036
08/13	10,171	189	1.9%	—
08/12	10,057	249	2.5%	—
08/11	8,597	0	—	—
Annual Growth	**6.5%**	—	—	—

2014 Year-End Financials

Debt ratio: ——
Return on equity: 1.60%
Cash ($ mil.): 83
Current ratio: 0.80
Long-term debt ($ mil.): —

Dividends
  Yield: —
  Payout: —
Market value ($ mil.): —

Halliburton Company

One of the largest oilfield services companies in the world Halliburton serves the upstream oil and gas industry in 80 countries with a complete range of services from the location of hydrocarbons to the production of oil and gas. It operates in two segments: Drilling and Evaluation and Completion and Production. Services include providing production optimization drilling evaluation fluid services and oilfield drilling software and consulting. It combines tried-and-true well drilling and optimization techniques with high-tech analysis and modeling software and services. In a major expansion in 2014 the company agreed to acquire Baker Hughes for about $35 billion.

HISTORY

Erle Halliburton began his oil career in 1916 at Perkins Oil Well Cementing. He moved to oil boomtown Burkburnett Texas to start his Better Method Oil Well Cementing Company in 1919. Halliburton used cement to hold a steel pipe in a well which kept oil out of the water table strengthened well walls and reduced the risk of explosions. Though the contribution would later be praised his technique was considered useless at the time.

In 1920 Halliburton moved to Oklahoma. Incorporating Halliburton Oil Well Cementing Company in 1924 he patented its products and services forcing oil companies to employ his firm if they wanted to cement wells.

Erle died in 1957 and his company grew through acquisitions between the 1950s and the 1970s. In 1962 it bought Houston construction giant Brown & Root an expert in offshore platforms. After the 1973 Arab oil embargo Halliburton benefited from the surge in global oil exploration and later as drilling costs surged it became a leader in well stimulation.

When the oil industry slumped in 1982 the firm halved its workforce. Three years later a suffering Brown & Root coughed up $750 million to settle charges of mismanagement at the South Texas Nuclear Project.

In the 1990s Halliburton expanded abroad entering Russia in 1991 and China in 1993. The next year Brown & Root was named contractor for a pipeline stretching from Qatar to Pakistan. Halliburton drilled the world's deepest horizontal well (18860 ft.) in Germany in 1995.

That year Dick Cheney a former US defense secretary became CEO. Brown & Root began providing engineering and logistics services to US Army peacekeeping troops in the Balkans in 1995 and won a major contract to develop an offshore Canadian oil field the next year.

In 1997 Halliburton completed a major reorganization started in 1993 uniting 10 businesses under the Halliburton Energy Services umbrella. The company nearly doubled in size in 1998 with its $7.7 billion acquisition of oil field equipment manufacturer Dresser Industries. The purchase coupled with falling oil prices in 1998 and 1999 prompted Halliburton to ax more than 9000 workers. (Even after oil prices rebounded in 2000 Halliburton had to wait for the effects of the upturn to reach the oil field services sector.)

Brown & Root Energy Services won a contract to provide logistics support for the US Army in Albania in 1999. Halliburton also invested in oil field emergency-response firm Boots & Coots and took a stake in Japanese engineering firm Chiyoda.

The company began to sell off portions of its Dresser acquisition in 1999. Partner Ingersoll-Rand bought Halliburton's stake in Ingersoll-Dresser Pump for $515 million and bought its stake in Dresser-Rand (industrial compressors) for $579 million in 2000. Cheney resigned as chairman and CEO that year after he was chosen as George W. Bush's vice presidential running mate. President and COO David Lesar was named to succeed him.

A group consisting of investment firms First Reserve and Odyssey Investment Partners and Dresser managers paid $1.55 billion in 2001 for Dresser Equipment Group. That year a number of multimillion-dollar verdicts against Halliburton in asbestos cases sparked rumors that the company was going to file for bankruptcy (flatly denied by Halliburton) and caused the firm's stock price to tumble.

In 2002 in part to protect the company's assets from the unresolved asbestos claims issue Lesar announced plans to restructure Halliburton into two independent subsidiaries separating the Energy Services Group from Halliburton's KBR engineering and construction operations. Halliburton took a $483 million (pretax) charge against earnings in the second quarter of 2002 to cover its estimated asbestos liability.

Halliburton settled more than 300000 asbestos-related lawsuits by paying about $4 billion in cash and in stock. As a result Halliburton placed its subsidiaries Dresser Industries and Kellogg Brown & Root under Chapter 11 bankruptcy protection. Later that year in an effort to boost its newly formed Energy Services unit Halliburton purchased Pruett Industries a fiber optic sensor technology company.

In 2003 Halliburton announced plans to divest its noncore assets in an effort to return its focus to its main operating divisions. The company began its disposal of assets with the sale of its mono pumping businesses to National-Oilwell. The company sold its Wellstream business to European buyout firm Candover Partners for $136 million. It also completed the sale of its interests in European Marine Contractors Bredero-Shaw and its Subsea operations. The company's Halliburton Measurement Systems subsidiary was sold to NuFlo Technologies.

In 2004 the company's KBR subsidiary was awarded nearly $1.4 billion worth of contracts to aid in the repair and restoration of Iraq's oil fields during the US-led invasion of Iraq. The US Army Corps of Engineers later withdrew the contracts after allegations that they were awarded to the subsidiary due to Halliburton's relationship to Cheney. KBR also came under fire when the Pentagon claimed the company overcharged US taxpayers $61 million to supply fuel to Iraq. After an investigation by the US Army Corp of Engineers Halliburton was cleared of any wrongdoing. The investigation was picked up by the Pentagon's criminal investigative unit and the US State Department. Following an internal audit Halliburton repaid $6 million after discovering an overcharge from one of its subcontractor companies.

Later that year Halliburton enhanced its Fluids division by acquiring ITS Drilling Services' SU-PAVAC unit. It also restructured its Engineering and Construction group into two divisions: Energy and Chemicals and Government and Infrastructure. In anticipation of selling off its KBR unit the company reorganized its management team promoting KBR CEO Andrew Lane to COO for Halliburton and placing him in charge of all Halliburton subsidiaries.

The company agreed to pay more than $4 billion in cash and stock to settle more than 300000 asbestos and silica-related personal injury lawsuits filed against its DII Industries and KBR subsidiaries. Halliburton reorganized its DII and KBR subsidiaries and finalized its asbestos settlements. DII and KBR emerged from Chapter 11 bankruptcy protection in January 2005. The company also completed the sale of its 50% stake in Subsea 7 to joint venture partner Siem Offshore for $200 million.

In 2006 Halliburton was awarded a multimillion-dollar contract by Saudi Aramco as part of the Khurais oilfield development project the largest in the region since the 1950s. The same year it spun off KBR to the public.

Establishing a new product service line (intervention services and pressure control) in 2010 the company acquired well control specialist and industry innovator Boots & Coots for $240 million in cash and stock. Halliburton has combined its global hydraulic workover and coiled tubing deployed technologies with Boots & Coots' operations to provide customers with a wider range of services to help increase well production.

Earlier in 2010 the company was involved in cementing operations to cap a well on the ill-fated BP's Deepwater Horizon rig. The rig exploded and sank spewing oil into the Gulf of Mexico. A board of inquiry found fault with the company's cementing procedures.

In 2011 Halliburton acquired Multi-Chem a leading provider of oilfield production and completion chemicals and services.

In 2012 Halliburton signed a strategic agreement with Russian gas giant Gazprom to jointly develop new oil and gas technologies to support global exploration and production projects.

In 2012 the company formed a 40%-owned joint venture with Schlumberger OneSubsea to make and develop products systems and services for the subsea oil and gas market. Cameron will contribute its existing subsea division and receive $600 million from Schlumberger. Schlumberger will contribute its Framo Surveillance Flow Assurance and Power and Controls businesses.

Expanding its portfolio in 2012 Halliburton acquired Petris Technology a leading US-based global supplier of data-management and integration solutions.

EXECUTIVES

LOCATIONS

2014 Sales

	$ mil.	% of total
North America	17,698	53
Latin America	3,875	12
Europe/Africa/CIS	5,490	17
Middle East/Asia	5,807	18
Total	**32,870**	**100**

PRODUCTS/OPERATIONS

2014 Sales

	$ mil.	% of total
Completion & production	20,253	62
Drilling & evaluation	12,617	38
Total	**32,870**	**100**

Selected Mergers and Acquisitions

COMPETITORS

Baker Hughes	Superior Energy
Cudd Energy Services	Technip
GE Oil	Transocean
RPC	Weatherford
Saipem	International
Schlumberger	Wild Well Control

HISTORICAL FINANCIALS

Company Type: Public

Income Statement
FYE: December 31

	REVENUE ($ mil.)	NET INCOME ($ mil.)	NET PROFIT MARGIN	EMPLOYEES
12/15	23,633	(671)	—	65,000
12/14	32,870	3,500	10.6%	80,000
12/13	29,402	2,125	7.2%	77,000
12/12	28,503	2,635	9.2%	73,000
12/11	24,829	2,839	11.4%	68,000
Annual Growth	(1.2%)	—	—	(1.1%)

2015 Year-End Financials

Debt ratio: 41.54%
Return on equity: (-4.23%)
Cash ($ mil.): 10,077
Current ratio: 4.03
Long-term debt ($ mil.): 14,687

No. of shares (mil.): 856
Dividends
Yield: 2.1%
Payout: 240.0%
Market value ($ mil.): 29,138

	STOCK PRICE ($) FY Close	P/E High/Low		Earnings	PER SHARE ($) Dividends	Book Value
12/15	34.04	—	—	(0.79)	0.72	18.06
12/14	39.33	18	9	4.11	0.63	19.18
12/13	50.75	24	15	2.36	0.53	16.00
12/12	34.69	14	9	2.84	0.36	16.97
12/11	34.51	19	9	3.08	0.36	14.33
Annual Growth	(0.3%)	—	—	—	18.9%	6.0%

Hancock Holding Co.

Hancock Holding holds its own as a Gulf Coast financial force. It is the holding company of Mississippi-based Hancock Bank and Louisiana-based Whitney Bank. Together the banks have about 250 branches and 300 ATMs throughout the Gulf South from Florida to Texas. The community-oriented banks offer traditional products and services such as deposit accounts trust services and consumer and business lending. Hancock Holding also has subsidiaries or business units that offer insurance discount brokerage services mutual funds and consumer financing.

EXECUTIVES

President CEO and Director, John M. Hairston, age 52, $707,000 total compensation
Chief Retail Banking Officer, Richard T. Hill, $375,000 total compensation
Chief Wealth Management Officer, Clifton J. Saik, $384,961 total compensation
Chief Commercial Banking Officer, Edward G. Francis
COO, D. Shane Loper
CFO, Michael M. Achary, $400,000 total compensation
President Whitney Bank, Joseph S. Exnicios
Chief Credit Officer Whitney Bank, Suzanne C. Thomas
Chief Credit Officer, Samuel B. Kendricks
Chief Risk Officer, Michael K. Dickerson
Business Intelligence Manager Assistant Vice President, Edgar Ruiz
Vice President, Sandy Porter
Senior Vice President And Director, Scott L Erlichman
Vice President, Spencer Wiggins
Vice President And Private Banker, Larry Cuervo
Senior Vice President Financial And Estate Planner, Emile Koury
Assistant Vice President, Kim Gibson
Assistant Vice President, Jimmy Campbell
Vice President Consumer Credit Risk Analytics, Alan Eads
Vice President Senior Product Manager, John (Jack) Fox
Vice President Portfolio Manager, Thom Swanson
Vice President, Kristy Oehms
Assistant Vice President Technology, Roland Pittman
Chairman, James B. Estabrook, age 71
Auditors: PricewaterhouseCoopers LLP

LOCATIONS

HQ: Hancock Holding Co.
One Hancock Plaza, P.O. Box 4019, Gulfport, MS 39501
Phone: 228 868-4000
Web: www.hancockbank.com

2013 Sales

	$ mil.	% of total
Whitney	571	59
Hancock	337	35
Other	63	6
Adjustment	(4.6)	-
Total	**968**	**100**

PRODUCTS/OPERATIONS

2013 Sales

	$ mil.	% of total
Interest		
Loans including fees	630	65
Securities	90	10
Other	1	-
Noninterest		
Service charges on deposit accounts	79	8
Bank card and ATM fees	45	5
Trust fees	38	4
Investment and annutiy fees	19	2
Insurance commissions and fees	15	1
Secoudary mortgage market operations	12	1
Other	35	4
Total	**968**	**100**

Subsidiaries
Berwick LLC
Community First Inc.
Dudley Ventures Hancock Fund LLC
Gulf South Technology Center LLC
The Gulfport Building Inc.
Hancock Bank
Hancock Bank of Alabama
Hancock Bank Securities Corporation II
Hancock Community Investment Corporation
Hancock Enterprise Investment Fund LLC
Hancock Insurance Agency

Hancock Insurance Agency of Alabama
Hancock Insurance Agency of Florida
Hancock Investment Services of Alabama Inc.
Hancock Investment Services of Florida Inc.
Hancock Investment Services of Louisiana Inc.
Hancock Investment Services of Mississippi Inc.
Hancock Investment Services Inc.
Harrison Finance Company
Harrison Loan Company
HBSC LLC
HMC LLC
Invest-Sure Inc.
J Everett Eaves Inc.
Lighthouse Services Corporation
Peoples First Transportation Inc.
Town Properties Inc.
Whitney Bank

COMPETITORS

BancorpSouth	Investar
Capital One	MidSouth Bancorp
First Horizon	Regions Financial
First NBC Bank	Renasant
IBERIABANK	Trustmark

HISTORICAL FINANCIALS

Company Type: Public

Income Statement
FYE: December 31

	ASSETS ($ mil.)	NET INCOME ($ mil.)	INCOME AS % OF ASSETS	EMPLOYEES
12/14	20,747	175	0.8%	3,794
12/13	19,009	163	0.9%	3,978
12/12	19,464	151	0.8%	4,235
12/11	19,774	76	0.4%	4,745
12/10	8,138	52	0.6%	2,271
Annual Growth	26.4%	35.4%	—	13.7%

2014 Year-End Financials

Debt ratio: 1.80%
Return on equity: 7.18%
Cash ($ mil.): 1,158
Current ratio: —
Long-term debt ($ mil.): —

No. of shares (mil.): 73
Dividends
Yield: 3.1%
Payout: 47.0%
Market value ($ mil.): 2,253

	STOCK PRICE ($) FY Close	P/E High/Low		Earnings	PER SHARE ($) Dividends	Book Value
12/14	30.70	18	14	2.10	0.96	33.70
12/13	36.68	19	14	1.93	0.96	29.49
12/12	31.73	21	16	1.75	0.96	28.91
12/11	31.97	31	22	1.15	0.96	27.95
12/10	34.86	32	19	1.40	0.96	23.22
Annual Growth	(3.1%)	—	—	10.7%	(0.0%)	9.8%

HanesBrands Inc

Hanesbrands can't wait 'til it gets its Hanes on you. The company designs makes and sells bras hosiery men's boxers socks and other intimate apparel under brand names such as Bali Champion barely there Just My Size Hanes L'eggs Playtex and Wonderbra. Its bras are tops in the US; its underwear legwear and activewear units are market leaders as well. Hanesbrands also makes basic outerwear such as T-shirts and licensed logo apparel for collegiate bookstores legwear for Donna Karan and underwear for Polo Ralph Lauren. The lineup is sold to wholesalers major retail chains (Wal-Mart Target and Kohls) and through Hanesbrands' value outlets and Internet site. It acquired Maidenform in 2013.

Operations

Hanesbrands divides its operations into four segments including innerwear (intimate apparel men's and children's underwear and socks) activewear direct to consumer and international. Innerwear is the largest by far accounting for more than 50% of revenue while Activewear generates more than 25%.The company operates nearly 39 distribution centers with 14 of the in the US and 25 located internationally near manufacturing regions.

Geographic Reach

Hanesbrands sells in roughly 35 countries and rings up roughly 85% of its sales in the US. Its largest international markets include Europe Canada Japan Mexico Brazil and Australia.

Sales and Marketing

Wal-Mart Target and Kohls are the company's largest customers accounting for 24% 17% and 5% of 2014 sales respectively. Mass merchandise stores are vital to the company's performance accounting for about half of Hanesbrands' total sales. Hanesbrands also allies with mid-tier stores including J. C. Penney Macy's and Kohls which are adding its lower-priced labels. It's L'eggs and Hanes brand underwear are also sold in food drug and variety stores. Hanesbrands also sell apparel to the US military for sale to soldiers and through discount chains including Dollar General and Family Dollar Stores.

Financial Performance

Hanesbrand's revenue grew for a second straight year jumping by 15% to $5.3 billion in fiscal 2014 (ended January 2015) with sales growth across all segments. The top-line growth was driven by the acquisitions of Maidenform and DBA which led to a 61% jump in international sales for the year. The company also enjoyed higher Innerwear product sales thanks to higher product price and licensed product sales and higher Activewear sales due to a combination of higher sales volume higher point-of-sale activity at the retail level gains from retailers and new products.Higher revenue also pushed net income higher by 22% to $404.52 million despite higher selling general and administration costs associated with acquisition integration and other action-related costs. Operations provided $508.1 million or 14% less cash than in 2013 mostly because it used more cash toward building its inventories.

Strategy

Looking to grow abroad in 2014 Hanesbrands acquired DBApparel Group of France a maker of intimate apparel in Europe from investment firm Sun Capital Partners. DBApparel holds the license to manufacture and sell apparel under the Wonderbra and Playtex trademarks in the European Union as well as several other nations in Europe and South Africa.

Hanesbrands hopes to identify and capitalize on the long-term megatrends related to their top product lines over the next five to 10 years. To this end in early 2015 the company purchased Knights Apparel to expand its sports licensed collegiate apparel business with a goal of appealing to college students as that market grows over the next years and decades. Hanesbrands has also been reducing production costs by improving operating efficiencies in using a low-cost global supply chain based upon a combination of owned contracted and sourced manufacturing. It has successfully started and increased production at a textile plant in China its first company-owned facility in Asia. Hanesbrands meanwhile shuttered about 10 manufacturing plants and three distribution centers. The closings include the company's last large knit-fabric textile plant in the US.

Mergers and Acquisitions

In October 2013 looking to boost earnings Hanesbrands purchased Maidenform for $547 million. The move gave Hanesbrands a brands portfolio with greater depth (adding the Maidenform Flexees and Self Expressions brands) to better compete with rivals such as Victoria's Secret and Spanx who are changing the landscape of the bra and underwear niche of the apparel industry with frilly and shapewear options.

Less than a year after buying Maidenform Brands HanesBrands traveled across the Atlantic to acquire DBApparel a maker of intimate apparel hosiery and underwear in Europe for €400 million ($528 million) in late 2014. DBApparel's brands include DIM Playtex and Wonderbra.

In 2015 the company bought Knights Apparel a leading retailer of licensed collegiate logo apparel to enrich its own Gear for Sports licensed collegiate apparel business.

EXECUTIVES

Chairman and CEO, Richard A. (Rich) Noll, age 58, $1,200,000 total compensation
CFO, Richard D. Moss, age 57, $575,000 total compensation
COO, Gerald W. Evans, age 56, $750,000 total compensation
Group President Innerwear Americas, W. Howard Upchurch, age 51, $515,000 total compensation
Vice President Planning and Global Sourcing, Micky Swaim
Vice President Marketing, Richard Heller
Vice President Global Comp Benefits, Annamarie D'Souza
Vice President Human Resources International Asia, Thomas Tom (Thom) Payne
Vice President of Information Technology, Pete Bobalik
Vice President Information Technology Compliance and Project Management Office, Allison Norton-Rimron
Vice President Customer Operations, Jack Sutton
Vice President Commodity Risk Management, Vern Tyson
Vice President Sales, Scott Somerville
Vice President Division, Mike Phelps
Vice President Mens Underwear, Jay Turner
Vice President Tax, Mike Caminiti
Vice President Marketing mass Markets, Jennifer (Jen) Armstrong
Vice President Distribution And Customer Service, Todd Nelson
Vice President Audit Services, George Korn
Vice President Of Sales, Sonya Hemingway-marion
Vice President Human Resources, Fred Johnson
Senior Vice President And General Manager Of Casualwear, John (Jack) Marsh
Vice President, Carol Davis
Vice President Operations, Marilyn Hanes
Vice President Textiles E Hilos, Keith Huskins
Vice President Supply Chain Finance Asia, Tom Kerr
Executive Vice President General Counsel And Corporate Secretary, Joia Johnson
Senior Vice President of External Communications, Matt Hall
Vice President International Marketing, Larry French
Vice President Global Supply Chain Finance, Craig Swecker
Vice President Information Technology Infrastructure, Johnathan Zaski
Assistant Vice President Risk Management, David (Dave) Bowers
Senior Vice President General Manager Innerwear, Howie Upchurch
Board Member, John Bradburn
Treasurer, Donald Cook
Auditors: PricewaterhouseCoopers LLP

LOCATIONS

HQ: HanesBrands Inc
1000 East Hanes Mill Road, Winston-Salem, NC 27105
Phone: 336 519-8080
Web: www.Hanes.com

2014 Sales

	$ mil.	% of total
US	4,525	85
Europe	302	6
Canada	140	3
Japan	107	2
Mexico	74	1
Brazil	48	1
China	9	—
Central America & the Caribbean Basin	3	—
Other	113	2
Total	**5,324**	**100**

PRODUCTS/OPERATIONS

Selected Brands

Bali
barely there
C9 by Champion
Champion
Gear for Sports
Just My Size
Hanes
L'eggs
Maidenform
Outer Banks
Playtex
Rinbros
Sol y Oro
Wonderbra
Zorba

COMPETITORS

Calvin Klein	Russell Brands
Frederick's of Hollywood Group	The Gap
	Tommy Hilfiger
Fruit of the Loom	Top Form
Gerber Childrenswear	Triumph Apparel
Gildan Activewear	Under Armour
J. Crew	Victoria's Secret Stores
Jockey International	
L Brands	Wacoal
PremiumWear	Warnaco Group
Redcats USA	Warnaco Swimwear

HISTORICAL FINANCIALS

Company Type: Public

Income Statement

FYE: January 2

	REVENUE ($ mil.)	NET INCOME ($ mil.)	NET PROFIT MARGIN	EMPLOYEES
01/16	5,731	428	7.5%	65,300
01/15*	5,324	404	7.6%	59,500
12/13	4,627	330	7.1%	49,700
12/12	4,525	164	3.6%	51,500
12/11	4,637	266	5.8%	53,300
Annual Growth	5.4%	12.6%	—	5.2%

*Fiscal year change

2016 Year-End Financials

Debt ratio: 46.71%	No. of shares (mil.): 391
Return on equity: 32.30%	Dividends
Cash ($ mil.): 319	Yield: 0.0%
Current ratio: 1.94	Payout: 37.7%
Long-term debt ($ mil.): 2,254	Market value ($ mil.): 11,527

	STOCK PRICE ($) FY Close	P/E High/Low	PER SHARE ($) Earnings	Dividends	Book Value
01/16	29.43	120 25	1.06	0.40	3.26
01/15*	110.61	86 48	1.32	0.30	4.61
12/13	69.35	64 32	1.08	0.15	4.12
12/12	34.98	66 39	0.55	0.00	3.01
12/11	21.86	37 24	0.90	0.00	2.33
Annual Growth	7.7%	— —	4.3%	—	8.8%

*Fiscal year change

Hanmi Financial Corp.

No hand-me-down operation Hanmi Financial is headquartered in a penthouse suite along Los Angeles' Wilshire Boulevard. The company owns Hanmi Bank which serves California's Korean-American community and others in the multi-ethnic Los Angeles San Diego San Francisco Bay and Silicon Valley areas. Hanmi Bank offers retail and small business banking with an emphasis on the latter from more than 25 California branches and loan offices throughout the US. Commercial and industrial loans including SBA and international trade finance loans account for about 60% of its loan portfolio; real estate loans make up most of the rest.

Financial Performance

After five straight years of declines Hanmi's revenue grew 6% in 2013 to $153 million. The financial and housing crises particularly acute in California hurt Hanmi's customers many of whom operate small businesses and consequently the bank's finances. As loan volume begins to increase and bring higher yields on investment securities the company's interest income has slowly risen. While non-interest income such as insurance commissions is also on the rise other types of non-interest income such as service charges on deposit accounts is declining as customers demand lower-cost banking products and services.

In 2013 it earned $39.9 million in profit down from $90.4 million in 2012. The decrease was due to the absence of the reversal of the deferred tax asset valuation allowance which contributed an income tax benefit of $47.4 million in 2012.

Strategy

Hanmi and Korean bank Woori Finance called off plans to merge in mid-2011 instead forming a business alliance. Two years later Hanmi is still actively looking for a partner to merge with. It hopes to find a South Korean financial institution looking to establish a presence in the US.

In order to focus on its business banking in 2014 the bank sold its insurance subsidiaries Chun-Ha Insurance Services and All World Insurance Services to Chunha Holding Corporation. The two companies sold life and property/casualty insurance plans.

Mergers and Acquisitions

In its first foray outside of California in late 2013 Hanmi agreed to acquire Central Bancorp Inc. the parent of Texas-based United Central Bank. United Central Bank serves multi-ethnic communities in Texas Illinois Virginia California New York and New Jersey through some two dozen branches. Once the acquisition is complete Hanmi will have about 50 branches and two loan production offices serving a broad range of ethnic communities in California Texas Illinois New York New Jersey Virginia and Georgia.

EXECUTIVES

SEVP and COO, Bonita I. (Bonnie) Lee, age 52
EVP and Chief Risk Officer, Jean Lim
EVP and CFO, Michael W. McCall
President CEO and Director, Chong Guk (C. G.) Kum
EVP and Chief Credit Officer, Randall G. Ewig
EVP and Chief Administrative Officer, Greg D. Kim
EVP and Chief Banking Officer, Peter Yang
EVP and Chief Lending Officer, Anthony Kim
Chairman, Joseph K. Rho, age 74
Auditors: KPMG LLP

LOCATIONS

HQ: Hanmi Financial Corp.
3660 Wilshire Boulevard, Penthouse Suite A, Los Angeles, CA 90010
Phone: 213 382-2200
Web: www.hanmi.com

PRODUCTS/OPERATIONS

2013 Sales

	$ mil.	% of total
Interest income	122	80
Non-interest income	31	20
Total	**153**	**100**

COMPETITORS

BBCN	Far East National Bank
Bank of America	JPMorgan Chase
Broadway Financial	Wilshire Bancorp
Cathay General Bancorp	Woori
East West Bancorp	

HISTORICAL FINANCIALS

Company Type: Public

Income Statement
FYE: December 31

	ASSETS ($ mil.)	NET INCOME ($ mil.)	INCOME AS % OF ASSETS	EMPLOYEES
12/14	4,232	49	1.2%	699
12/13	3,055	39	1.3%	499
12/12	2,882	90	3.1%	470
12/11	2,744	28	1.0%	483
12/10	2,907	(88)	—	499
Annual Growth	**9.8%**	—	—	**8.8%**

2014 Year-End Financials

Debt ratio: 0.44%	No. of shares (mil.): 31
Return on equity: 11.65%	Dividends
Cash ($ mil.): 158	Yield: 1.2%
Current ratio: —	Payout: 19.5%
Long-term debt ($ mil.): —	Market value ($ mil.): 696

	STOCK PRICE ($) FY Close	P/E High/Low	PER SHARE ($) Earnings	Dividends	Book Value
12/14	21.81	16 12	1.56	0.28	14.21
12/13	21.89	18 11	1.26	0.14	12.63
12/12	13.59	5 3	2.87	0.00	12.01
12/11	7.40	6 1	1.38	0.00	9.07
12/10	1.15	— —	(7.44)	0.00	9.17
Annual Growth	**108.7%**	— —	—	—	**11.6%**

Hanover Insurance Group Inc

The Hanover Insurance Group is an all-around property/casualty insurance holding company. Through Hanover Insurance Company it provides personal and commercial automobile homeowners and workers' compensation coverage as well as commercial multi-peril insurance and professional liability coverage. The group sells its products through a network of 2000 independent agents throughout the US but Michigan Massachusetts and New York account for about 40% of its business. In Michigan it operates as Citizens Insurance Company. Hanover's Opus Investment Management subsidiary provides institutional investment

management services and it operates internationally through UK subsidiary Chaucer Holdings.

Operations

Primarily through the Hanover Insurance Company unit Hanover writes some $4.5 billion in premiums and handles about 200000 claims each year. Commercial policies account for about 45% of annual revenues while personal lines account for about 30%. Subsidiary Chaucer operates two Lloyd's of London syndicates which manage and underwrite global property/casualty policies; the subsidiary also offers specialty insurance and reinsurance coverage. (In 2014 Chaucer generated $1.3 billion or about one-quarter of the group's consolidated operating revenues.)

Hanover's Other segment comprises Opus which provides investment advisory services to affiliates; it also manages approximately $1.4 billion in assets for unaffiliated clients including insurance companies retirement plans and foundations.

Geographic ReachMichigan is Hanover's largest market accounting for nearly a quarter of all commercial and personal lines. Massachusetts and New York account for 10% and 9% respectively while California and New Jersey contribute an additional 8% and 5%. US operations account for three-fourths of annual premiums.

In addition to its headquarters in Worcester Massachusetts the company has regional offices in cities across the US (40 in all) and eight overseas including those in Argentina (Buenos Aires) Denmark (Copenhagen) Norway (Oslo) the UK (London) and Singapore.

The majority of processing support for those locations takes place in Worcester Massachusetts; Howell Michigan; Salem Virginia; and Windsor Connecticut.

Sales and Marketing

Hanover sells through a network of agents and brokers including some 2000 independent representatives. The company's customers include individuals families and businesses.

Chaucer the international segment distributes primarily via Lloyd's as well as through underwriting agencies.

Financial PerformanceHanover has reported several years for revenue growth including in 2014 when it increased 6% to $5.1 billion from $4.8 billion due to increased premium revenue from Chaucer and commercial lines. Chaucer casualty premiums rose primarily as a result of expanded underwriting capabilities growth in the marine line and a favorable impact of foreign exchange rates. Growth in commercial lines was driven by rate increases higher retention rates and new business.

Normal 0   false false false   EN-US X-NONE X-NONE

Net income grew $31 million to $282 million due to the higher revenue.

Cash flow from operations increased 47% to $565 million in 2014 due to a change in loss loss adjustment expense and unearned premium reserves.

Strategy

The company has increased its operations through acquisitions and geographic expansion; it also works to build partnerships with other insurers and agents. Hanover pursues growth in a conservative manner to preserve long-term financial and operational stability. In addition the company is working to increase efficiencies through technology upgrades.

Hanover's written premiums are balanced between its personal and commercial products but competition is fierce in personal insurance so the company has placed more emphasis on expanding its commercial offerings. It has launched several niche insurance programs such as coverage for not-for-profit youth organizations community services organizations and religious institutions.Wriggling into a niche is one method of expanding and Hanover has moved into several areas of specialty insurance in recent years such as health care and engineering. It partnered with OMS National Insurance in 2013 to provide coverage for maxillofacial and oral surgeons. In 2014 Hanover expanded into more medical facilities and broadened its health offerings. Health care is a key growth field as the aging US population creates a stronger demand for health services.

HISTORY

In 1842 a group of Worcester Massachusetts businessmen tried to form a mutual life insurance company. After a failed first attempt they succeeded with the help of lobbyist Benjamin Balch. In 1844 the State Mutual Life Assurance Co. of Worcester set up business in the back room of secretary Clarendon Harris' bookstore. The first president was John Davis a US senator. The company issued its first policy in 1845.

In the early years State Mutual reduced risk by issuing policies only for residents of such "civilized" areas as New England New Jersey New York Pennsylvania and Ohio. It also restricted movement requiring policyholders to get permission for travel outside those areas. By the 1850s the company had begun issuing policies in the Midwest (with a 25% premium surcharge) the South (for 30% extra) and California (for a pricey extra $25 per $1000) with a maximum coverage of $5000.

The Civil War was a problem for many insurers who had to decide what to do about Southern policyholders and payment on war-related claims. State Mutual chose to pay out its Northern policyholders' benefits despite the extra cost. In 1896 the firm began offering installment pay-out plans for policyholders concerned that their beneficiaries would fritter away the whole payment.

The first 30 years of the 20th century were for the company a time of growth that was stopped short by the Depression. But despite a great increase in the number of policy loans and surrenders for cash value State Mutual's financial footing remained solid.

After WWII the company entered group insurance and began offering individual sickness and accident coverage. In 1957 it was renamed State Mutual Life Assurance Co. of America. The firm added property/casualty insurance in the late 1950s through alliances with such firms as Worcester Mutual Fire Insurance. During the 1960s State Mutual continued to develop property/casualty buying interests in Hanover Insurance and Citizens Corp.

The firm followed the industrywide shift into financial services in the 1970s adding mutual funds a real estate investment trust and an investment management firm. This trend accelerated in the 1980s and State Mutual began offering financial planning services as well as administrative and other services for the insurance and mutual fund industries (the mutual fund administration operations were sold in 1995). Managing this growth was another story: Its acquisitions left it bloated and disorganized. Technical systems were in disarray by the early 1990s and the agency force had grown to more than 1400. In response the company began a five-year effort to upgrade systems cut fat and reduce sales positions.

In view of its shifting focus State Mutual became Allmerica Financial in 1992. Three years later it demutualized. In 1997 it bought the 40% of Allmerica Property & Casualty it didn't already own.

EXECUTIVES

President CEO and Acting CFO, Frederick H. (Fred) Eppinger, age 56, $1,000,000 total compensation
EVP and General Counsel, J. Kendall Huber, age 60, $468,077 total compensation
EVP Corporate Development and President Specialty Insurance, Andrew S. Robinson, age 49, $451,538 total compensation
President International Operations and CEO Chaucer, Robert A. (Bob) Stuchbery, age 58, $610,500 total compensation
SVP and Chief Claims Officer, Mark Welzenbach, age 55
EVP and President Business Insurance and Filed Operations, John C. (Jack) Roche, age 51
Chief Underwriting Officer Chaucer Holdings PLC(, Bruce B. Bartell, age 58
EVP Chief Marketing Officer and President Personal Lines, Richard (Dick) Lavey
SVP and Chief Investment Officer and President Opus Investment Management, Ann K. Tripp, age 56
Assistant Vice President Investor Relations, Oksana Lukasheva
Vice President Personal Lines, Tammy Hessberger
Vice President Senior Counsel, John L (Jack) Mcdonough
Vice President Lead Actuary, Kathleen Cunningham
Vice President Field Finance and Marketing Analytics, Rob Lachance
Senior Vice President Human Resources, Christine Bilotti-Peterson
Assistant Vice President Cl Operations, Karen Andrade
Assistant Vice President Technology, Sandi Maldonado
Assistant Vice President Allied Healthcare, Eric Paynter
Assistant Vice President Cl Uw Processes, Erin A Fenlon
Chief Compliance Officer and Vice President, Donald P (Don) Wayman
Assistant Vice President Technology, James (Jamie) Marengo
Assistant Vice President Business Operations And Quality, Richard F (Dick) Tackett
Vice President Engineering and Product Development, Chris Kosak
Vice President of Information Technology, Patty Kularski
Assistant Vice President Medical Strategy, Karen Malone
Vice President Sales and Marketing, Dave Bradford
Vice President, Andrew R (Andy) Knipfer
Vice President business Development, Daniel (Dan) Mastrototaro
Vice President And Director Information Technology, Debbie Lewis
Vice President, Eric Simonsen
Chairman, Michael P. Angelini, age 72
Auditors: PricewaterhouseCoopers LLP

LOCATIONS

HQ: Hanover Insurance Group Inc
440 Lincoln Street, Worcester, MA 01653
Phone: 508 855-1000   **Fax:** 508 855-6332
Web: www.hanover.com

2014 Gross Written Premiums

	% of total
US	78
UK	6
Other countries	16
Total	**100**

PRODUCTS/OPERATIONS

2014 Revenue

	$ mil.	% of total
Insurance		
Commercial lines	2,239	44
Personal lines	1,491	29
Chaucer	1,279	25
Other	7	.
Investment gains	50	2
Total	**5,067**	**100**

Selected Products

Personal Lines
  Auto Insurance
  Companion Products
  Dwelling Fire
  Home Care Services
  Homeowners Insurance
  Identity Integrity
  Umbrella
  Valuable Items
  Watercraft
Small Commercial and Middle Market Core Products
  Business Owner' s Policy
  Commercial Automobile
  Commercial Package
  General Liability
  Property
  Umbrella
  Workers' Compensation
Specialized Products
  AIX Specialty Programs
  Commercial Umbrella and Excess
  Healthcare
  Industrial Property Risk
  Management Liability
  Marine (inland and ocean)
  Professional Liability
  Surety (commercial and contract)

COMPETITORS

Allstate	Markel Insurance
American Automobile	Nationwide
Association (AAA)	Progressive
American Financial	Corporation
Group	State Farm
Auto-Owners Insurance	Travelers Companies
GEICO	USAA
Liberty Mutual	

HISTORICAL FINANCIALS

Company Type: Public

Income Statement

FYE: December 31

	ASSETS ($ mil.)	NET INCOME ($ mil.)	INCOME AS % OF ASSETS	EMPLOYEES
12/14	13,759	282	2.0%	5,100
12/13	13,378	251	1.9%	5,100
12/12	13,484	55	0.4%	5,100
12/11	12,624	37	0.3%	5,100
12/10	8,569	154	1.8%	4,400
Annual Growth	12.6%	16.2%	—	3.8%

2014 Year-End Financials

Debt ratio: 6.57%
Return on equity: 10.37%
Cash ($ mil.): 373
Current ratio: —
Long-term debt ($ mil.): —

No. of shares (mil.): 43
Dividends
  Yield: 2.1%
  Payout: 26.0%
Market value ($ mil.): 3,131

	STOCK PRICE ($) FY Close	P/E High/Low		PER SHARE ($) Earnings	Dividends	Book Value
12/14	71.32	11	8	6.28	1.52	64.78
12/13	59.71	11	7	5.59	1.36	59.37
12/12	38.74	33	27	1.23	1.23	58.59
12/11	34.95	60	38	0.81	1.13	56.27
12/10	46.72	14	12	3.34	1.00	54.80
Annual Growth	11.2%	—	—	17.1%	11.0%	4.3%

Harley-Davidson Inc

Four wheels move the body. Two wheels move the soul. Harley-Davidson is a major US maker of motorcycles and seller of heavyweight cruisers. The company offers touring and custom Harleys through a worldwide network of more than 1400 dealers. The company manufactures and markets six families of motorcycles: Touring Dyna Softail Street Sportster and V-Rod. It also makes three-wheeled motorcycles. Harley-Davidson sells attitude with its brand-name products which include a line of clothing and accessories (MotorClothes). Harley-Davidson Financial Services (HDFS) offers financing to dealers and consumers in the US and Canada.

Geographic Reach

Harley-Davidson generates around 70% of its total sales from the US. Its operations are located in the Asia/Pacific Europe the Middle East Africa Latin America and the US.

Operations

The company operates through two segments. Its core motorcycle manufacturing operations generate around 90% of its revenue each year; Harley-Davidson Financial Services contributes the remainder of revenue.

Harley-Davidson's Touring Dyna Softail Street and Sportster are equipped with air-cooled twin-cylinder engines (in a 45-degree "V" configuration) while its V-Rod sports a 60-degree "V" configuration twin-cylinder engine that is liquid cooled.

The company also makes special editions for peace officers and firefighters. Its products and related lifestyle are supported by H.O.G. (Harley Owners Group). Harley also supports a rental and tour program market and a rider training program known as Riders Edge.

Sales and Marketing

Harley-Davidson's motorcycles are sold to customers through a network of independent distributors. The company spends around $107 million each year on advertising. Its products are marketed to retail customers worldwide primarily through advertising and promotional activities via various broadcast print and electronic channels. The company targets young adults ages 18-34 women African-Americans and Hispanics as well as Caucasian men ages 35-plus.

Financial Performance

Harley-Davidson has enjoyed five straight years of steady growth. Revenues increased by 6% from $5.9 billion in 2013 to peak at a record-setting $6.2 billion in 2014. Profits were up 15% from $734 million in 2013 in $845 million in 2014 due to the higher revenue coupled with a decline in interest expense.

The company's revenue growth for 2014 was primarily attributed to a 6% increase within its motorcycles segment sales. It experienced an increase in US retail sales impacted by strong sales of Rushmore and Street motorcycles. In 2014 international retail sales grew in the Asia Pacific Latin America (mostly in Mexico) and EMEA regions. The company was also helped by growth in financial services revenues due to higher interest income.

After declining from 2011 to 2012 Harley-Davidson's operating cash flow increased two straight years jumping 17% from $977 million in 2013 to $1.2 billion in 2014.

Strategy

Harley-Davidson is focused on growing internationally. To support this initiative it has two CKD (complete knock down) assembly plants which assemble motorcycles from component kits produced by its US plants and by its suppliers. Its first CKD plant is located in Brazil and has been in operation since 1999 and its second CKD resides in India and has been in operation since 2011.

As a primary means of growth the company adds new dealerships to its network each year. In 2013 it added 118 new international dealerships and in 2014 it added 18 new international dealers.

Harley-Davidson also grows by introducing new product models. In 2013 it introduced the new Street motorcycles designed for young urban riders around the world. In 2014 it launched a Harley-Davidson electric motorcycle.

HISTORY

In 1903 William Harley and the Davidson brothers (Walter William and Arthur) of Milwaukee sold their first Harley-Davidson motorcycle which essentially was motor-assisted bicycle that required pedaling uphill. Demand was high and most sold before leaving the factory. Six years later the company debuted its trademark two-cylinder V-twin engine. By 1913 it had 150 competitors.

EXECUTIVES

President and COO Harley-Davidson Financial Services, Lawrence G. Hund, age 58, $525,000 total compensation
VP General Counsel and Secretary, Paul J. Jones, age 45, $456,667 total compensation
President and CEO, Matthew S. (Matt) Levatich, age 50, $669,167 total compensation
SVP and CFO, John A. Olin, age 54, $585,000 total compensation
VP Human Resources; President Harley-Davidson Foundation, Tonit M. Calaway, age 47
VP and CIO, Dave Cotteleer
CTO, Sean McCormack
VP and Managing Director EMEA, Rob Lindley
VP and Managing Director Asia Pacific, Marc McAllister
VP and Managing Director North America, Mike Kennedy
SVP Global Demand, Sean J. Cummings
Vice President and Information Technology Manager, Brad Rose
Chairman, Richard I. (Dick) Beattie, age 76
Auditors: Ernst & Young LLP

LOCATIONS

HQ: Harley-Davidson Inc
   3700 West Juneau Avenue, Milwaukee, WI 53208
Phone: 414 342-4680   **Fax:** 414 343-4621
Web: www.harley-davidson.com

2014 Sales

	$ mil.	% of total
US	4,400	71
EMEA	875	14
Canada	218	3
Japan	197	3
Australia	190	3
Other	346	6
Total	**6,228**	**100**

PRODUCTS/OPERATIONS

2014 Sales

	$ mil.	% of total
Motorcycle & related parts	5,567	89
Financial services	660	11
Total	**6,228**	**100**

Selected Motorcycles

Harley-Davidson
   CVO (custom vehicle operations)
   Road Gllide Ultra
   Softail Convertible
   Street Glide
   Ultra Classic Electroglide
   Dyna
   Fat BOB
   Street BOB
   Super Glide Custom
   Wide Glide
   Softail
   Black Line
   Cross Bones
   Fat Boy
   Heritage Softail Classic
   Night Train
   Rocker C
   Softail Deluxe
   Sportster
   883 (Low and Custom)
   1200 (Custom and Low)
   Forty Eight
   Iron 883
   Nightster
   SuperLow
   XR1200X
   Touring
   Electra Glide (Standard Classic and Ultra Classic)
   Road Glide Ultra
   Road King (and Classic)
   Street Glide
   Tri Glide Ultra Classic
   Trike
   Street Glide Trike
   Tri Glide Ultra Classic
   VRSC
   Night Rod Special
   V-Rod (and V-Rod Muscle)

Selected Operations

Motorcycles
   Harley-Davidson Motor Company
Financial services
   Harley-Davidson Financial Services Inc.
   Harley-Davidson Credit
   Harley-Davidson Insurance

COMPETITORS

BMW	Polaris Industries
Ducati	Triumph Motorcycles
Honda	Ultra Motorcycle
Indian Motorcycle	Viper Motorcycle

HISTORICAL FINANCIALS

Company Type: Public

Income Statement

FYE: December 31

	REVENUE ($ mil.)	NET INCOME ($ mil.)	NET PROFIT MARGIN	EMPLOYEES
12/14	6,228	844	13.6%	6,500
12/13	5,899	733	12.4%	6,400
12/12	5,580	623	11.2%	5,800
12/11	5,311	599	11.3%	6,600
12/10	4,859	146	3.0%	6,900
Annual Growth	6.4%	54.9%	—	(1.5%)

2014 Year-End Financials

Debt ratio: 57.77%
Return on equity: 28.54%
Cash ($ mil.): 906
Current ratio: 1.65
Long-term debt ($ mil.): 3,761
No. of shares (mil.): 211
Dividends
   Yield: 1.6%
   Payout: 28.4%
Market value ($ mil.): 13,965

	STOCK PRICE ($) FY Close	P/E High/Low		PER SHARE ($) Earnings	Dividends	Book Value
12/14	65.91	19	14	3.88	1.10	13.73
12/13	69.24	21	15	3.28	0.84	13.68
12/12	48.83	19	14	2.72	0.62	11.31
12/11	38.87	18	12	2.55	0.48	10.50
12/10	34.67	56	34	0.62	0.40	9.37
Annual Growth	17.4%	—	—	58.2%	28.8%	10.0%

Harman International Industries, Inc.

Harman International Industries is loud and clear. It makes high-end stereo and audio equipment for consumer and professional markets. The company makes loudspeakers CD and DVD players CD recorders and amplifiers under such brands as Mark Levinson JBL Harman/Kardon Revel AKG Infinity Logic 7 and others. Harman's auto unit sells branded audio systems through several carmakers including Toyota Lexus and BMW. Its professional unit makes audio equipment such as monitors amplifiers microphones and mixing consoles for recording studios cinemas touring performers and others. Harman also offers computer software and development tools to the automotive energy medical and telecom industries.

HISTORY

Sidney Harman and his partner Bernard Kardon left their engineering jobs at a public address system company to found Harman/Kardon in 1953. The two marketed their home audio components to the general public instead of to the traditional audio buff. Their novel concept was to package amplifiers and a tuner in a single unit (called a receiver) that appealed to average consumers. Kardon cashed out in a 1956 IPO that left Harman with about 33% of the firm. Harman/Kardon acquired the respected JBL speaker business in 1969.

Harman was also interested in internal growth. He introduced new management techniques emphasizing workers' quality of life allowing employees to redesign their jobs and leave work after meeting production quotas. His projects which had varying degrees of success attracted the attention of President Carter's administration which brought Harman on board as undersecretary of commerce in 1977. Harman sold the company to Beatrice Foods that year to avoid a conflict of interest. The company did poorly under the conglomerate and Harman bought much of it back in 1980 taking it private. He then changed the name to Harman International Industries.

Through acquisitions he quickly expanded the business into the auto OEM market acquiring Essex Loudspeaker from United Technologies (1981) then moving into the professional audio equipment market with his purchase of Infinity (1983). In the mid-1980s Harman signed exclusive deals to supply JBL speakers to Ford (ended in 1995) and Chrysler (now DaimlerChrysler) and in 1985 it bought back the Harman/Kardon trade name (Beatrice Foods had sold it to Japanese company Shin Shirasuna). The company went public again the next year.

In 1991 Harman went into a tailspin (losing $20 million laying off 500) caused by a worldwide recession poor auto sales and four soured acquisitions. Harman who had been living in Washington DC with his politician wife Jane moved back to California site of the company's largest plant. President Donald Esters quit in 1992 and Harman set about reorganizing the firm.

The company bought AKG a leading Austrian microphone maker in 1993. Signaling its interest in the new digital age Harman created a new business unit Harman Interactive the following year to focus on PC and home theater systems.

It acquired Becker supplier of audio systems to Mercedes and high-end equipment manufacturer Madrigal Audio Laboratories in 1995. Harman expanded its customer base by selling to home electronics superstores and specialty stores for audiophiles.

A year later the company began supplying speakers for a Compaq line of computers. In 1997 it boosted its car audio business with new agreements to supply audio systems to certain models of BMW Toyota Hyundai and Peugeot and it purchased two car loudspeaker makers (Oxford International and Audio Electronic Systems).

In the 1990s Harman trimmed its consumer product lines from 2000 to 200. With its sales to Asia down and European sales ailing as well it closed plants and laid off workers in 1998. That year president Bernard Girod succeeded Harman as CEO. Also in 1998 the company created a remote control with Microsoft and divested several of its international distribution companies to focus on manufacturing and marketing. Harman sold its Orban broadcasting-products business in 1999 and replaced it with Crown International (maker of high-powered amplifiers) in 2000. (Crown has since ceased operations.)

EXECUTIVES

EVP and Chief Human Resource Officer, John Stacey, age 51
Chairman President and CEO, Dinesh C. Paliwal, age 57, $1,193,513 total compensation
EVP and President Automotive Services, David J. Slump, age 47, $380,000 total compensation
VP and CIO, Marty O'Brien
EVP and President Services Division, Sanjay Dhawan
EVP and President Professional Division, Blake W. Augsburger, age 52, $484,500 total compensation
EVP Operational Excellence, Herbert K. Parker, age 57, $560,000 total compensation
EVP and General Counsel, Todd A. Suko, age 48
EVP and Chief Marketing Officer, Ralph Santana
EVP and CFO, Sandra E. (Sandy) Rowland, age 44
EVP and President Lifestyle Division, Michael Mauser, age 52, $518,990 total compensation
EVP and CTO, I. P. Park
EVP and President Infotainment, Phillip Eyler
Vice President and General Manager Americas, Dave Rogers
Vice President And General Manager Mmandamp;h Sbu, Andy Trott
Vice President Of Tax, Dennis Hamilton
Vice President Legal Lifestyle Division and Compliance, Vahe Tazian
Vice President, Paula Davis
Vice President and General Manager, Alon Atsmon
Vice President Western Region USA Canada, Sean Olive
Vice President Global Supply Chain, Karney Yakmalian
Vice President Target Setting And People Continuity, Russe Krystolovich
Vice President Engineering, Marc Dissosway
Vice President Sale Loudspeaker SBU, John (Jack) Powell
Vice President Finance, Marc Marlatt
National Sales Manager, Ty Deville
National Account Manager, Michael Knese
Global Vice President Strategic, Gayle Papadopoulos
Vice President Systems (Automotive), Klaus Beck
Vice President Customer Business Unit Bmw, Wolfram Kohl
Vice President And Controller, Bernd Vogt
Vice President Atg Lifestyle, Gerhard Pfaffinger
Senior Vice President Human Resources, Udo Huels
Department Head, Jack Zou
Vice President Customer Program Management Daimler Project Management Office Eu, Mario Topel
Vice President And General Manager Cbu Daimler, Jens Tillner
National Account Manager, David (Dave) Guido
Vice President Engineering Services, Manfred Schedl
Vice President And GM Global Car Audio, Jeffery Fay
Executive Vice President Chief Financial Officer and Secretary, Frank Meredith
Auditors: KPMG LLP

LOCATIONS

HQ: Harman International Industries, Inc.
  400 Atlantic Street, Suite 1500, Stamford, CT 06901
Phone: 203 328-3500
Web: www.harman.com

2014 Sales

	$ mil.	% of total
Europe		
Germany	1,722	32
Other countries	969	18
US	1,626	31
Other regions	1,029	19
Total	**5,348**	**100**

PRODUCTS/OPERATIONS

2014 Sales

	$ mil.	% of total
Infotainment	2,838	53
Lifestyle	1,656	31
Professional	853	16
Other	0	—
Total	**5,348**	**100**

Selected Products

Automotive
  Audio systems
  Information and entertainment systems
Professional
  Audio amplifiers
  Audio headphones
  Broadcasting studio equipment
  Cinema audio systems
  Digital audio workstations
  Equalizers
  Loudspeakers
  Microphones
  Mixing consoles
  Signal processing systems
  Sound reinforcement systems
  Special effects units
  Surround sound systems
Consumer
  Audio amplifiers
  Audio and video receivers
  CD players
  Digital signal processors
  DVD players
  Home theater systems
  Loudspeakers
  PC audio systems

Selected Brands

AKG
Becker
BSS
Crown
dbx
DigiTech
Harman/Kardon
Infinity
JBL
JBL Professional
Lexicon
Logic 7
Mark Levinson
Martin Professional
Revel
Selenium
Soundcraft
Studer

COMPETITORS

ASK	JVC KENWOOD
Aisin Seiki	Klipsch
Altec Lansing	Krell
Audio Research	LOUD Technologies
Avid Technology	Logitech
BSH Bosch und Siemens	Macintosh Retail Group
Hausgeräte	Marshall Amplification
Bang & Olufsen	Meyer Sound
Bosch Communications	Mitsubishi Electric &
Systems	Electronics
Bose	Onkyo
Boston Acoustics	Panasonic Corporation
Continental Automotive	of North America
Group	Peavey Electronics
Creative Technology	Pioneer Corporation
D&M	Polk Audio
DENSO	QSC Audio
Delphi Automotive	Sennheiser
Systems	Shure
Denon Electronics	Sony
Fender Musical	TASCAM
Instruments	TomTom
Foster Electric	Visteon
(U.S.A.)	Yamaha
Harris Corp.	

HISTORICAL FINANCIALS

Company Type: Public

Income Statement

FYE: June 30

	REVENUE ($ mil.)	NET INCOME ($ mil.)	NET PROFIT MARGIN	EMPLOYEES
06/15	6,155	342	5.6%	24,197
06/14	5,348	234	4.4%	14,202
06/13	4,297	142	3.3%	12,221
06/12	4,364	329	7.6%	11,366
06/11	3,772	135	3.6%	10,103
Annual Growth	13.0%	26.0%	—	24.4%

2015 Year-End Financials

Debt ratio: 18.32%
Return on equity: 16.45%
Cash ($ mil.): 649
Current ratio: 1.39
Long-term debt ($ mil.): 1,080

No. of shares (mil.): 71
Dividends
Yield: 1.1%
Payout: 29.7%
Market value ($ mil.): 8,471

	STOCK PRICE ($) FY Close	P/E High/Low	PER SHARE ($) Earnings	Dividends	Book Value
06/15	118.94	30 17	4.84	1.32	33.34
06/14	107.43	33 16	3.36	1.20	26.33
06/13	54.20	26 18	2.04	0.60	24.17
06/12	39.60	11 6	4.57	0.30	22.73
06/11	45.57	27 15	1.90	0.05	20.36
Annual Growth	27.1%	— —	26.3%	126.7%	13.1%

Harris Corp.

Harris has ways to make its customers communicate. The company which develops communications products for government and commercial customers in more than 125 countries makes radio-frequency (RF) and satellite communications and other wireless network transmission equipment; air traffic control systems; and digital network management systems. Harris also offers specialized IT services. Harris' commercial clients come from the construction energy health care maritime oil transportation and utilities industries.

Operations

Harris' two largest segments are government communications and RF communications. Government communications systems 36% of revenue provides advanced communications and information equipment to government civil national intelligence and defense programs. Civil settings include aviation and weather; national intelligence applications provide tracking surveillance cyber security and other functions; defense programs offers communications and information processing in support of missions and other defense operations.

RF communications 34% of sales offers radio communications and encryption technology for the US DoD international tactical communications and public safety and professional communications.

The integrated network solutions unit 25% of sales offers IT services managed satellite and terrestrial communications and health care interoperability and image management.

Through an acquisition Harris added another segment Exelis which accounted for 5% of sales. Exelis provides instruments solutions for positioning and navigation sensors air traffic management image processing and distribution communications and information systems.

In 2015 Harris restructured its reporting segments. Starting with its 2016 fiscal year it will report results for Communication Systems Critical Networks Electronic Systems and Space and Intelligence Systems.

Geographic Reach

Harris operates 260 locations in Canada Europe the Middle East Central and South America Africa Asia Caribbean Latin American and the US which generates 92% of its overall revenue.

Sales and Marketing

Its primary customers are US government agencies including prime contractors and supported foreign militaries accounting for about 65% of sales.

Financial Performance

Harris reported slightly higher revenue in 2015 (ended July) while net income tumbled. Revenue inched up 1.4% in 2014 to $5.08 billion. The Exelis acquisition contributed to higher revenue was did an increase in government communications systems. Sales of the Integrated Network Solutions segment dropped 14% with few US government orders.

The 2015 net income of $334 million was off 37% from 2013 when revenue was inflated by a decline in losses from discontinued operations.

Harris maintained its steady cash flow from operations posting $854 million for 2015 compared to $849 in 2014.

Strategy

Harris considers its greatest opportunities for growth to be in managed satellite communications public safety and professional communications health care IT and emerging national markets. Affected sectors include energy maritime and government. The continued global deployment of the wireless 4G LTE standard will help fuel growth.

Mergers and AcquisitionsHarris also grows through the use of acquisitions. In a potentially significant deal in 2015 it agreed to purchase Exelis provider of communications products catering to the government in a transaction worth $4.7 billion. The deal will beef up Harris' presence in the government sector and would create a combined company with more than $8 billion in sales.

HISTORY

Early History

Harris was founded in Niles Ohio in 1895 by brothers Alfred and Charles Harris both jewelers and inventors. Among their inventions was a printing press that became Harris Automatic Press Company's flagship product.

Harris remained a small family-run company until 1944 when engineer George Dively was hired as general manager. Under Dively the company began manufacturing bindery typesetting and paper converting equipment while remaining a leading supplier of printing presses. In 1957 Harris merged with typesetter maker Intertype and became known as Harris-Intertype Corporation.

During the 1960s and 1970s Harris-Intertype grew through acquisitions. In 1967 it bought electronics and data processing equipment maker Radiation a company heavily dependent on government contracts and relocated to Radiation's headquarters in Melbourne Florida. The company also bought RF Communications (two-way radios 1969) General Electric's broadcast equipment line (1972) and UCC-Communications Systems (data processing equipment 1972).

The company changed its name to Harris Corporation in 1974. In 1980 Harris bought Farinon a manufacturer of microwave radio systems and Lanier Business Products the leading maker of dictating equipment. In 1983 it sold its printing equipment business.

EXECUTIVES

Vice President Harris Caprock General Counsel, Alan (Al) Aronowitz
Chairman President and CEO, William M. (Bill) Brown, age 52, $921,154 total compensation
SVP and Chief Global Business Development Officer, Dana A. Mehnert, age 53, $493,208 total compensation
SVP Integration and Engineering, Sheldon J. Fox, age 57, $436,154 total compensation
VP Environmental-Energy Solutions Business Government Communications Systems Division, Carl D'Alessandro
SVP Human Resources and Administration, Robert L. Duffy, $433,846 total compensation
CIO, Henry Debnam
President Electronic Systems, Ed Zoiss
President Space and Intelligence Systems, Bill Gattle
President Communication Systems, Chris Young
SVP and CFO, Rahul Ghai, age 43
Senior Vice President Of Business Development, Alex Heidt
Vice President Corporate Technology, Kent Buchanon
Vice President Corporate Strategy, George Kirov
Vice President Controller, Daniel Heneghan
Vice President Operations, Paul North
Vice President Sales, John Koening
Broker And Vice President, George Hurst
Vice President Products And Systems, Shawn Baerlocher
Vice President Large Account Sales, Kevin Lombardo
Senior Vice President, Neal Serven
Vice President And Chief Technology Officer (Chief Technology Officer), Oscar Diaz
Vice President And Deputy General Counsel, Anthony Deglomine
Senior Vice President Resident Sales Director, Phil Wenzel
Vice President Information Technology, Michele St Mary
Vice President And General Manager Of Harris Videotek Test And Measurement Solutions, Dave Guerrero
Vice President, Brett Kleefisch
Vice President, Daniel Flugstad
Vice President General Counsel, Eugene Cavallucci
Vice President Information Technology, Mark Gawron
Vice President, Paul Eisner

Vice President Human Resources, Ken Laprade
Vice President Lean Six Sigma, Phil Burroughs
Vice President Of North American Sales And
  Geno Viviano Director, Walt Paskowski
Vice President Finance Public Safety And
  Professional Communications, William Cullen
Vice President General Manager Texas Region,
  Paige Herr
Vice President, Erick Sanz
Vice President General Counsel And, Scott Mikuen
Engineering Team Manager Treasurer, David
  Bruder
Treasurer, Steve Thompson
Treasurer, Harmon David
Auditors: Ernst & Young LLP

LOCATIONS

HQ: Harris Corp.
  1025 West NASA Boulevard, Melbourne, FL 32919
Phone: 321 727-9100
Web: www.harris.com

2014 Sales

	$ mil.	% of total
US	4,589	92
Other countries	422	8
Total	**5,012**	**100**

PRODUCTS/OPERATIONS

2014 Sales

	$ mil.	% of total
RF communications	1,828	36
Government communications systems	1,801	35
Integrated network solutions	1,462	29
Adjustments	(80.1)	-
Total	**5,012**	**100**

Selected Product Groups

Government Communications Systems
  Civil programs
  Aviation
  Weather
  IT services
  Mission command-and-control
  National intelligence programs
Radio-frequency (RF) Communications
  Antennas and accessories
  Information assurance
  Internet protocol voice and data networks
  Public safety
  Tactical radio communications

COMPETITORS

Advisory Board	Leidos
Aetna	Lockheed Martin
Airbus Group	ManTech
Alcatel-Lucent	Motorola Solutions
Amper	NCI
Avid Technology	NEC
BAE Systems Inc.	Nokia Siemens Networks
Boeing	Nortel Networks
CACI International	Northrop Grumman
Ceragon Networks	Orion HealthCorp
ChyronHego	Pilat Media
Cisco Systems	Raytheon
Computer Sciences	RigNet
Corp.	Rockwell Collins
Dell	Rohde & Schwarz
Elbit Systems	SELEX SI
Ericsson	Sony
Exelis	Technicolor
General Dynamics	Tektronix
Globecomm	Telos
HP	Thales
Harmonic	UNICOM Government
IBM	Vizrt
L-3 Communications	WideOrbit

HISTORICAL FINANCIALS

Company Type: Public

Income Statement

FYE: July 3

	REVENUE ($ mil.)	NET INCOME ($ mil.)	NET PROFIT MARGIN	EMPLOYEES
07/15*	5,083	334	6.6%	22,300
06/14	5,012	534	10.7%	14,000
06/13	5,111	113	2.2%	14,000
06/12	5,451	30	0.6%	15,200
07/11	5,924	588	9.9%	16,900
Annual Growth	(3.8%)	(13.2%)	—	7.2%

*Fiscal year change

2015 Year-End Financials

Debt ratio: 39.73%	No. of shares (mil.): 123
Return on equity: 12.58%	Dividends
Cash ($ mil.): 481	Yield: 0.0%
Current ratio: 1.54	Payout: 60.4%
Long-term debt ($ mil.): 5,053	Market value ($ mil.): 9,615

	STOCK PRICE ($) FY Close	P/E High/Low	PER SHARE ($) Earnings	Dividends	Book Value
07/15*	77.74	26 20	3.11	1.88	27.47
06/14	75.98	16 10	4.95	1.68	17.31
06/13	49.25	51 40	1.01	1.48	14.60
06/12	41.85	176 128	0.26	1.22	17.29
07/11	45.55	11 9	4.60	1.00	20.32
Annual Growth	14.3%	— —	(9.3%)	17.1%	7.8%

*Fiscal year change

Hartford Financial Services Group Inc.

Despite its name at its heart The Hartford Financial Services Group is an insurer with a range of commercial and personal property/casualty insurance and financial products. Its commercial operations include auto liability workers' compensation policies as well as group benefits and specialty commercial coverage for large companies. The Hartford also offers consumer homeowners and auto coverage. It has been the direct auto and home insurance writer for AARP's members for more than 30 years. Through its mutual fund division the company offers wealth management products and services. The Hartford in business since 1810 sells products through a network of independent agents and brokerages.

HISTORY

In 1810 a group of Hartford Connecticut businessmen led by Walter Mitchell and Henry Terry founded the Hartford Fire Insurance Co. Frequent fires in America's wooden cities and executive ignorance of risk assessment and premium-setting often left the firm on the edge of insolvency. (In 1835 stockholders staged a coup and threw management out.) Still each urban conflagration —including the Great Chicago Fire of 1871 —gave The Hartford an opportunity to seek out and pay all its policyholders thus teaching the company to underwrite under fire as it were and to use such disasters to refine its rates.

The company's stag logo was initially a little deer as shown on a policy sold to Abraham Lincoln in 1861. A few years later however Hartford began using the majestic creature (from a Landseer painting) now familiar to customers. By the 1880s Hartford operated nationwide as well as in Canada and Hawaii.

The company survived both world wars and the Depression but emerged in the 1950s in need of organization. It set up new regional offices and added life insurance buying Columbian National Life (founded 1902) which became Hartford Life Insurance Co.

In 1969 Hartford was bought by ITT (formerly International Telephone and Telegraph) whose CEO Harold Geneen was an avid conglomerateur. Consumer advocate Ralph Nader strongly opposed the acquisition —he fought the merger in court for years and felt vindicated when ITT spun off Hartford in 1995. Others opposed it too because ITT had engineered the merger based on an IRS ruling (later revoked) that Hartford stockholders wouldn't have to pay capital gains taxes on the purchase price of their stock.

Insurance operations consolidated under the Hartford Life Insurance banner in 1978. Through the 1980s Hartford Life remained one of ITT's strongest operations. A conservative investment policy kept Hartford safe from the junk bond and real estate manias of the 1980s.

Hartford reorganized its property/casualty operations along three lines in 1986 and in 1992 it organized its reinsurance business into one unit. The company faced some liability in relation to Dow Corning's breast-implant litigation but underwriting standards after 1985 reduced long-term risk. In 1994 the company began selling insurance products to AARP members under an exclusive agreement. In 1996 the company finished its spin-off from ITT which was acquired by Starwood Hotels & Resorts two years later.

To grow its reinsurance operation Hartford acquired the reinsurance business of Orion Capital (now Royal & SunAlliance USA) in 1996. It posted a loss of $99 million due in large part to asbestos and pollution liabilities. Late that year the firm changed its name to The Hartford Financial Services Group.

To shore up reserves and fund growth in 1997 the company spun off 19% of Hartford Life. The Hartford expanded into nonstandard auto insurance in 1998 by buying Omni Insurance Group (since sold in 2006). The company also sold its London & Edinburgh Insurance Group in 1998 to Norwich Union (now part of Aviva formerly CGNU). In 1999 The Hartford acquired the reinsurance business of Vesta Fire Insurance a subsidiary of Vesta Insurance Group.

In 2000 Hartford bought back the part of Hartford Life it had spun off. The Hartford also bought the financial products and excess and surplus specialty insurance lines of Reliance Group Holdings. Assurances Générales de France bought the company's Dutch subsidiary Zwolsche Algemeene. In 2001 the company bought Fortis Financial a US subsidiary of Belgian insurer Fortis and sold Hartford Seguros its Spanish subsidiary to Liberty Mutual.

Before the financial crisis hit Hartford Life invested in its data management with the acquisition of a defined contribution recordkeeping business (Princeton Retirement Group 2007) and a web-based technology company (TopNoggin 2008). Following the same strategy The Hartford acquired Sun Life's US 401K plan administration business.

Like so many others in the insurance and financial services industry The Hartford had its share of losses during the 2008 financial crisis due to its investment holdings in Fannie Mae Freddie Mac and Lehman Brothers. In mid-2009 the US Treasury stepped in and offered The Hartford and other major life insurers access to its Troubled Asset Relief Program (TARP). The Hartford borrowed $3.4

billion to shore up its capital reserves. As the company and the economy stabilized the loan was repaid by early 2010 including an additional $21.7 million dividend payment.

Prior to the creation of TARP funds the Treasury first made money available to banks through its Capital Purchase Program (CPP). To make itself more eligible The Hartford worked quickly to transform itself into a bank –at least on paper. In 2009 The Hartford acquired Federal Trust Corporation a regional bank holding company for $10 million. However shortly thereafter TARP funds became available and The Hartford readily accepted them and the strings attached. Two years later the company recognized that banking was not among its core competencies or passions and made arrangements to sell Federal Trust Corporation to CenterState Banks.

Chairman and CEO Ramani Ayer had planned on retiring at the end of 2008 but agreed to stay at the helm through 2009. His final year was marked by efforts to stem the company's losses stemming from the global economic and financial crisis that began in 2008. Former head of consumer banking at Bank of America Liam McGee was appointed as the company's new CEO in late 2009.

The Hartford then conducted restructuring measures including exiting international markets and disposing of non-core assets. It ended sales of variable annuities in Japan and the UK in 2009 and sold its Canadian mutual funds business and its Brazilian joint venture in 2010. In early 2011 The Hartford also sold off its third-party claims administration business Specialty Risk Services (SRS) unit to Sedgwick Claims Management Services for $278 million. In addition in late 2011 the company formed an agreement with Wellington Management which took over management of several of Hartford's mutual funds.

During 2010 the company reshaped its reporting segments into the commercial markets consumer markets and wealth management categories. In 2011 it also also placed a number of operations into a separate runoff segment including its exited international operations and its discontinued institutional annuities and private placement life insurance operations.

Despite all of its efforts to recover from the financial crisis of 2008-2009 (which caused heavy investment losses for The Hartford) via cost-cutting and restructuring measures in early 2012 the company began facing investor pressure to separate its life and property/casualty operations through spinoff or asset sale transactions. After reviewing its options The Hartford soon gave in to the demands. While it retained its mutual funds business the firm exited its annuity business and sold the bulk of its life insurance operations (including individual life retirement plans and Woodbury Financial Services units) in 2012 and 2013. It also sold Hartford Life Insurance KK in 2014.

EXECUTIVES

Senior Vice President and Head Hartford Financial Products, Michael (Mel) Dandini

Reg Vice President Chicago Regional Offic, Jeff Lange

President, Douglas G. (Doug) Elliot, age 55, $825,000 total compensation

Chairman and CEO, Christopher J. Swift, age 55, $912,500 total compensation

Chief Investment Officer, Brion Johnson, age 55, $458,333 total compensation

CFO, Beth A. Bombara, age 47, $560,000 total compensation

EVP Human Resources, Martha (Marty) Gervasi, age 53

President The Hartford Mutual Funds, James E. (Jim) Davey, age 50

EVP and Chief Risk Officer, Robert R. Rupp, age 62, $600,000 total compensation

EVP Operations and Technology, William A. (Bill) Bloom, age 51

SVP and Secretary, David C. Robinson

EVP Personal Lines, Raymond J. (Ray) Sprague, age 56

Vice President And Assistant General Counsel, Jonathan (Jon) Hatch

Svp And Secretary, Ricardo Anzaldua

Assistant Vice President Service Strategy, Sue Sweeney

Vice President Talent Management Diversity and Inclusion, Jennifer (Jen) Centrone

Assistant Vice President Human Resources, Daniel (Dan) O'Shea

Assistant Vice President Corporate Communications, Paula McGinley

Senior Vice President Product and Strategy, Mike Fish

Vice President Group Benefit Field Claims, Michael (Mel) Cleveland

Assistant Vice President and LOB Manager Workers Compensation, Sashi Aiyathurai

Assistant Vice President Senior Counsel and Assistant Secretary, Terence Shields

Vice President, Anthony Retartha

Vice President Assistant General Counsel, Richard (Dick) Alleyne

Assistant Vice President Large Loss Liability Claim, Michele A Vitali

Assistant Vice President, Mark T Wilson

Vice President Executive Communications, Peter (Pete) Schwartz

Senior Counsel and Assistant Vice President, Ian Veitzer

Vice President Of Communications, Donna Gendreau

National Account Manager Group Benefits, Sarah Berard

Assistant Vice President Tax Reporting and Compliance, Susan (Sue) Faenza

Assistant Vice President Group Benefits Relationship Management, Alison Colli

Assistant Vice President Workers Compensation Product Manager, Matt Lyon

Assistant Vice President Corporate Communications, Pat Riso

Vice President Internal Audit, Michael (Mel) Hession

Assistant Vice President Uw Small Comm, Kenneth Zygiel

Vice President Commercial Auto Product A, Jeanne Fenster

Assistant Vice President, Scott Cochrane

Assistant Vice President Information Security, Tim Carling

Vice President Houston, Jeffrey (Jeff) Lange

Mbr 1St Vice President, Mayer Goldberger

Division Manager Vice President, Robert (Bob) Larence

Vice President International Development, Lynne Urban

Assistant Vice President Group Benefit Claims, Jeanette Zenner

Legal Secretary, Sandra Branz

Assistant Vice President Assistant General Counsel, Liz Steigman

Legal Secretary, Nancy Ley

Legal Secretary, Amy Loboda

Assistant Vice President Enterprise Risk Management, Dan Oconnell

Senior Vice President, Michael Hotaling

Regional Vice President, Mark Gromek

Assistant Vice President Commercial Markets Technology, Ann Nemphos

Vice President Executive Communication, Leila Bryner

Assistant Vice President Litigation Management, Kevin Mohr

Assistant Vice President Head of Quantitative Analysis Market Risk Management, Greg Slone

Vice President Sales and Distribution Operations, Matthew (Matt) Montminy

Assistant Vice President, Lee Siegel

Vice President Claims Cio For Commercial Markets Technology, Michael Lipka

Assistant Vice President Counsel, Brian Fresher

Senior Tax Counsel Assistant Vice President, William (Bill) Elwell

Vice President Assistant General Counsel, Andrew (Andy) Diaz-Matos

Assistant Vice President, Susan Bencher

Vice President And General Counsel, Danielle Woolsey

Assistant Vice President Senior Counsel, Cedric Delacruz

Vice President Associate GC Litigation, Rochelle Cummings

Assistant Vice President Counsel, Robin Linker

Assistant Vice President Finance Business Lead, Steven Paccioretti

Vice President and Director Corporate Risk Management, Chris Mango

Regional Vice President, Mark Shears

Senior Vice President Director of Litigation, Heavner James

Vice President Auto and Property Strategy, Mike Lawlor

Executive Vice President and General Counsel, Alan (Al) Kreczko

Senior Vice President of Enterprise Services, Michael Knipper Michael (Mel) Knipper

Assistant Vice President and Assistant Treasurer, Mike Fixer

Vice President Internal Audit, Robin Generous

Senior Vice President Investor Relations, Richard (Dick) Costello

Assistant Vice President Senior Counsel, Cedric G Delacruz

Assistant Vice President Information Security, Timothy (Tim) Carling

Assistant Vice President Information Technology, Len Fiorilli

Assistant Vice President Product Management, Chad Mirock

Vice President Government Affairs, Cliff Leach

Vice President Research, Isaac Adams

Divisional Vice President, Brian Garrette

Assistant Vice President Product Management, Chris DiMartino

Vice President and Assistant General Counsel, Kevin LaFreniere

Assistant Vice President and Counsel, Andrew (Andy) Daly

Vice President Asset Strategy, Ellen Hall

Vice President Marketing Strategy and Relationship Management, Sarah Sledge Cook

Assistant Vice President Information Technology Operations and Back Office, Sam Balasubramaniyam

Assistant Vice President Executive Communications, Courtney Nogas

Vice President, Dave Akers

Assistant Vice President Information Technology Quality, Dianne Bertolet-Duff

Assistant Vice President Internal Communication, Kristin Tetreault

Assistant Vice President Marketing Consumer Markets, Pat Browne

Assistant Vice President Middle Market Division Management, Rob Sullivan

Senior Vice President Head of Investment Operations, Sunil Bhatt

Assistant Vice President WC Field Operations, Debbie Kane

Vice President WC Underwriting and Product Operations, Joseph (Jo) Wells

Assistant Vice President Department Manager
  Financial Services Group, Marc Berner
Vice President Strategy and Business
  Performance Management, Robert (Bob) Wentling
Assistant Vice President Middle Market and
  Specialty Commercial Project Management and
  Execution, Bob Leyden
Assistant Vice President Business Readiness and
  Performance Enablement, Corey Johnson
Auditors: Deloitte & Touche LLP

LOCATIONS

HQ: Hartford Financial Services Group Inc.
One Hartford Plaza, Hartford, CT 06155
Phone: 860 547-5000
Web: www.thehartford.com

PRODUCTS/OPERATIONS

2014 Revenues

	$ mil.	% of total
Earned premiums fees & other		
Commercial lines	6,289	34
personal lines	3,806	20
Group benefits	3,095	17
Talcott Resolution (runoff)	1,407	8
Mutual funds	723	3
Corporate	11	-
Net investment income	3,154	17
Net realized capital gains (losses)	16	-
Other revenues	113	1
Total	**18,614**	**100**

COMPETITORS

AIG	Nationwide
Allstate	New York Life
Berkshire Hathaway	Prudential
CNA Financial	State Farm
Liberty Mutual	Travelers Companies
MetLife	Zurich Insurance Group

HISTORICAL FINANCIALS

Company Type: Public

Income Statement

FYE: December 31

	ASSETS ($ mil.)	NET INCOME ($ mil.)	INCOME AS % OF ASSETS	EMPLOYEES
12/14	245,013	798	0.3%	17,500
12/13	277,884	176	0.1%	18,800
12/12	298,513	(38)	—	22,500
12/11	304,064	662	0.2%	24,400
12/10	318,346	1,680	0.5%	26,800
Annual Growth	(6.3%)	(17.0%)	—	(10.1%)

2014 Year-End Financials

Debt ratio: 2.31%
Return on equity: 4.24%
Cash ($ mil.): 399
Current ratio: —
Long-term debt ($ mil.): —

No. of shares (mil.): 424
Dividends
  Yield: 1.5%
  Payout: 42.3%
Market value ($ mil.): 17,694

	STOCK PRICE ($) FY Close	P/E High/Low		PER SHARE ($) Earnings	Dividends	Book Value
12/14	41.69	23	18	1.73	0.66	44.11
12/13	36.23	99	61	0.34	0.50	41.71
12/12	22.44	—	—	(0.18)	0.40	51.45
12/11	16.25	22	11	1.30	0.40	51.77
12/10	26.49	11	7	2.49	0.20	45.69
Annual Growth	12.0%	—	—	(8.7%)	34.8%	(0.9%)

Hartford Life Insurance Co

Auditors: Deloitte & Touche LLP

LOCATIONS

HQ: Hartford Life Insurance Co
200 Hopmeadow Street, Simsbury, CT 06089
Phone: 860 547-5000
Web: www.thehartford.com

HISTORICAL FINANCIALS

Company Type: Public

Income Statement

FYE: December 31

	ASSETS ($ mil.)	NET INCOME ($ mil.)	INCOME AS % OF ASSETS	EMPLOYEES
12/14	191,775	676	0.4%	—
12/13	202,715	465	0.2%	—
12/12	215,891	554	0.3%	—
12/11	222,537	244	0.1%	—
12/10	231,752	744	0.3%	—
Annual Growth	(4.6%)	(2.4%)	—	—

2014 Year-End Financials

Debt ratio: —
Return on equity: 7.71%
Cash ($ mil.): 258
Current ratio: —
Long-term debt ($ mil.): —

No. of shares (mil.): 0
Dividends
  Yield: —
  Payout: —
Market value ($ mil.): —

HCA Holdings Inc

HCA dispenses TLC for a profit. HCA Holdings through its HCA Inc. (Hospital Corporation of America) unit operates 166 hospitals comprising 162 acute care centers three psychiatric facilities and one rehabilitation hospital in the US and UK. It also runs more than 110 ambulatory surgery centers —as well as cancer treatment urgent care and outpatient rehab centers —that form health care networks in many of the communities it serves. In total its hospitals are home to some 43000 beds. HCA's facilities are located in 20 states; roughly half of its hospitals are in Florida and Texas. The HCA International unit operates the company's hospitals and clinics in the UK.

HISTORY

In 1987 Dallas lawyer Rick Scott and Fort Worth Texas financier Richard Rainwater founded Columbia Hospital Corp. to buy two hospitals in El Paso Texas. The partners eventually sold 40% of the hospitals to local doctors hoping that ownership would motivate physicians to increase productivity and efficiency.

The company entered the Miami market the next year and by 1990 had four hospitals. After merging with Smith Laboratories that year Columbia went public and then acquired Sutter Laboratories (orthopedic products). By the end of 1990 it had 11 hospitals.

Columbia moved into Florida in 1992 with the purchase of several hospitals and facilities. The next year it acquired Galen Health Care which operated 73 hospitals and had been spun off from

health plan operator Humana earlier in the year. The merger thrust the hospital chain into about 15 new markets.

Columbia bought Hospital Corporation of America (HCA) in 1994. Thomas Frist his son Thomas Frist Jr. and Jack Massey (former owner of Kentucky Fried Chicken now part of TRICON) founded HCA in Nashville Tennessee in 1968. By 1973 the company had grown to 50 hospitals.

Meanwhile the medical industry was changing — insurers Medicare and Medicaid began scrutinizing payment procedures while the growth of HMOs (which aimed to restrict hospital admissions) cut hospital occupancy rates. HCA began paring operations in the late 1980s selling more than 100 hospitals. In 1989 the younger Frist led a $5.1 billion leveraged buyout of the company. He sold more assets and in 1992 took HCA public again but losses and a tumbling stock price made it a takeover target.

Later in 1994 the newly christened Columbia/HCA acquired the US's largest operator of outpatient surgery centers Dallas-based Medical Care America. A year later it bought 117-hospital HealthTrust a 1987 offshoot of HCA. Columbia/HCA was unstoppable in 1996 with some 150 acquisitions.

In 1997 the government began investigating the company's business practices. After executive indictments the company fired Scott and several other top officers. Frist Jr. became chairman and CEO pledging to shrink the company and tone down its aggressive approach. Columbia/HCA sold its home care business more than 100 of its less-desirable hospitals and almost all the operations of Value Health a pharmacy benefits and behavioral health care management firm it had recently bought.

The trimming continued in 1998: The company sold nearly three dozen outpatient surgery centers and more than a dozen hospitals. That year Columbia/HCA sued former financial executive Samuel Greco and several vendors accusing them of defrauding the company of several million dollars. In 1999 it spun off regional operators LifePoint Health (23 facilities) and Triad Hospitals (34) to trim its holdings. The next year it sold some 120 medical buildings to MedCap Properties a joint venture formed with First Union Capital Partners.

During 2000 the company bought out partner Sun Life and Provincial Holdings' (now AXA UK) interest in several London hospitals and bought three hospitals there from St. Martins Healthcare. It also renamed itself HCA - The Healthcare Company. While continuing a strategy of consolidating and streamlining operations (and resolving remaining legal matters) in 2001 the company streamlined its name even further to simply HCA Inc.

By 2002 HCA began shaking off its shaky past. Profits stabilized allowing it to reinvest millions into modernizing facilities and equipment at its hospitals and surgery centers. It entered the Kansas City market in 2003 by acquiring a local hospital chain.

The company finally closed the books during 2003 on the numerous government investigations launched in 1997 into its business practices. In the five years leading up to 2003 HCA paid out some $2 billion in settlements for Medicare fraud and other claims. These settlements took their toll on the firm's bottom line.

To expand its outpatient services HCA beginning in 2004 began purchasing imaging centers. In early 2005 the firm acquired Tampa Florida's Total I Imaging and its five centers that offer diagnostic services. In 2005 HCA's iMage1 Network part of HCA's outpatient services group bought more than a handful of imaging centers located in the Tampa Florida area from Ultra Open MRI Corp.

The devastating hurricane season of 2005 hit HCA's operations hard as they are concentrated in the southern US. When Hurricane Katrina hit HCA evacuated its Tulane University Hospital and Clinic (it reopened in early 2006). Hurricane Rita spurred HCA to evacuate three Houston-area hospitals (Mainland Medical Center in Texas City East Houston Regional Medical Center in Houston and Clear Lake Regional Medical Center in Webster) and partially evacuate two others.

In 2006 a group of investors — including Thomas Frist Jr. as well as Bain Capital Kohlberg Kravis Roberts and the private equity arm of Merrill Lynch —took HCA private in a $30 billion leveraged buyout. In 2009 Richard Bracken became CEO of the company.

The hospital operator maintained its private status for several years until it once again went public in 2011 as a way to pay off some debt.

Normal 0   false false false   EN-US X-NONE X-NONE

EXECUTIVES

Chairman and CEO, R. Milton Johnson, age 58, $1,099,979 total compensation
COO, Samuel N. (Sam) Hazen, age 55, $899,983 total compensation
President Service Line and Operations Integration, A. Bruce Moore, age 55, $574,989 total compensation
EVP and CFO, William B. (Bill) Rutherford, age 51, $599,989 total compensation
President American Group, Jon M. Foster, age 53, $748,736 total compensation
President Clinical Services and Chief Medical Officer, Jonathan B. (Jon) Perlin, age 54, $699,987 total compensation
President National Group, Charles J. (Chuck) Hall, age 62, $750,000 total compensation
SVP and CIO, P. Martin (Marty) Paslick
President Physician Services Group, Michael Cuffe
SVP and Chief Nursing Officer, Jane Engelbright
Director Of Physical Therapy Physical Therapy Director, Angie Brown
Assistant Vice President Of Technical Services, Tom Morris
Physical Therapy Director, Mary B Peterson
Assistant Vice President Strategic Resource Group, Joseph Cazayoux
Vice President Investor Relations, Mark Kimbrough
Vice President, Michael Marotta
Director Of Radiology Services, Phyllis Barker
Vice President Field Operations, Jay Levy
Assistant Vice President Operations East Group, Martin (Marti) Plevak
Vice President Strategic Planning, Brittney Powlesson
Assistant Vice President, William Wright
Assistant Vice President Business Development, Kristin Gence
Assistant Vice President Technical Services, Bill Fitzgerald
Assistant Vice President Development, Bobby Stokes
Vice President Physician Recruitment, Tim Watson
Assistant Vice President Owned Hospitals, Ron Redding
Vice President Investments, James Glasscock
Senior Vice President Marketing and Engagement H2u, Cheryl Carlson
Vice President Physician Services, Patrick Kueny
Vice President Of Operations, Carol Smith
Director Of Pharmacy, Ron Nagata
Assistant Vice President, Sherri Neal
Vice President Corporate Communications and Marketing, Jana Davis
Vice President Operations Improvement, Adam Rudd
Director Of Surgery Services, Ann Carr

Assistant Vice President, William Blaufuss
Vice President Sales and Marketing, Doug Swanson
Assistant Vice President Information Technology Strategy and Planning, David (Dave) Catino
Vice President Chief Architect, Tom Doyle
Vice President Supply Chain Operations, David Welch
Vice President Human Resources Operations Support, Yonnie Chesley
Assistant Vice President, Connie Glover
Nursing Director, Nathan Thorne
Assistant Vice President, Chris Mayfield
Vice President Insurance, Shirley Fuller-cooper
Vice President, Pamella Tucker
Director Of Him, Mary Merritt
Vice President Human Resources Midwest Division, Rich Lowe
Vice President Information Technology, Cyndi Talley
Assistant Vice President, Lana Henry
Vice President Design and Construction, Greg Stein
Assistant Vice President, Mary Speciale
Vice President Internal Audit Vice President Internal Audit, Rodney (Rod) Bennett
Vice President Of Operations, Daniel Winkler
Vice President Physician Sales, Michael John
Vice President Of Sales Tristar Division, Patrick Steed
Vice President Of Operations, Ted Johnson
Vice President Sales, Lori Marshall
Vice President, Jay Dhingra
Director Of Radiology, Darlene Debrillo
Senior Vice President Developmemt, Carl George
Assistant Vice President Coding Operations HCA Physician Services, Julie Appleton
Assistant Vice President External Customers, Glenn Greiner
Vice President Employee Relations, Samuel J (Sam) Coulter
Vice President Marketing and Communications, JC Sadler
Treasurer, Michael (Mel) Bray
Auditors: Ernst & Young LLP

LOCATIONS

HQ: HCA Holdings Inc
One Park Plaza, Nashville, TN 37203
Phone: 615 344-9551
Web: www.hcahealthcare.com

2014 Locations

	No.
US	
Florida	42
Texas	36
Tennessee	13
Virginia	10
Georgia	7
Colorado	7
Utah	8
Missouri	5
Louisiana	5
California	5
Kansas	4
Nevada	3
South Carolina	3
Idaho	2
Kentucky	2
New Hampshire	2
Oklahoma	2
Alaska	1
Indiana	1
Mississippi	1
UK	7
Total	**166**

Selected US Facilities

Alaska
  Alaska Regional Hospital (Anchorage)
California
  Good Samaritan Hospital (San Jose)
  Los Robles Medical Center (Thousand Oaks)
  Regional Medical Center of San Jose

Riverside Community Hospital
West Hills Hospital & Medical Center
Colorado
  Centrum Surgical Center (Greenwood Village)
  Medical Center of Aurora
  North Suburban Medical Center (Thornton)
  Presbyterian/St. Luke' s Medical Center (Denver)
  Rose Medical Center (Denver)
  Sky Ridge Medical Center (Lone Tree)
  Spalding Rehabilitation Hospital (Aurora)
  Swedish Medical Center (Englewood)
Florida
  Aventura Hospital and Medical Center
  Blake Medical Center (Bradenton)
  Brandon Regional Hospital
  Capital Regional Medical Center (Tallahassee)
  Central Florida Regional Hospital (Sanford)
  Columbia Hospital (West Palm Beach)
  Doctors Hospital of Sarasota
  Edward White Hospital (St. Petersburg)
  Fawcett Memorial Hospital (Port Charlotte)
  Gulf Coast Medical Center (Panama City)
  JFK Medical Center (Atlantis)
  Kendall Regional Medical Center (Miami)
  Lake City Medical Center
  Largo Medical Center
  Memorial Hospital Jacksonville
  Memorial Hospital of Tampa
  North Florida Regional Medical Center (Gainesville)
  Northwest Medical Center (Margate)
  Ocala Regional Medical Center
  Osceola Regional Medical Center (Kissimmee)
  Palms of Pasadena Hospital (St. Petersburg)
  Palms West Hospital (Loxahatchee)
  South Bay Hospital (Sun City Center)
  St. Lucie Medical Center (Port St. Lucie)
  Town and Country Hospital (Tampa)
  Twin Cities Hospital (Niceville)
  University Hospital and Medical Center (Tamarac)
  West Florida Hospital (Pensacola)
  Westside Regional Medical Center (Plantation)
Georgia
  Atlanta Outpatient Surgery Center (Atlanta)
  Cartersville Medical Center
  Coliseum Medical Centers (Macon)
  Doctors Hospital (Augusta)
  Eastside Medical Center (Snellville)
  Fairview Park Hospital (Dublin)
  Northlake Surgical Center (Tucker)
  Polk Medical Center (Cedartown)
  Redmond Regional Medical Center (Rome)
Idaho
  Eastern Idaho Regional Medical Center (Idaho Falls)
  West Valley Medical Center (Caldwell)
Indiana
  Terre Haute Regional Hospital
Kansas
  Allen County Hospital (Iola)
  Galichia Heart Hospital (Wichita)
  Menorah Medical Center (Overland Park)
  Overland Park Regional Medical Center
  Wesley Medical Center (Wichita)
Kentucky
  Frankfort Regional Medical Center
  Greenview Regional Hospital (Bowling Green)
Louisiana
  Dauterive Hospital (New Iberia)
  Lafayette Surgicare
  Lakeview Regional Medical Center (Covington)
  Rapides Regional Medical Center (Alexandria)
  Tulane Medical Center (Metarie)
  Tulane University Hospital & Clinic (New Orleans)
  Women' s & Children' s Hospital (Lafayette)
Mississippi
  Garden Park Medical Center (Gulfport)
Missouri
  Centerpoint Medical Center (Independence)
  Lafayette Regional Health Center (Lexington)
  Lee' s Summit Hospital
  Research Medical Center (Kansas City)
  Research Psychiatric Center (Kansas City)
Nevada
  Flamingo Surgery Center (Las Vegas)
  MountainView Hospital (Las Vegas)
  Southern Hills Hospital and Medical Center (Las Vegas)
  Sunrise Hospital and Medical Center (Las Vegas)
New Hampshire
  Parkland Medical Center (Derry)
  Portsmouth Regional Hospital
  Salem Surgery Center

Oklahoma
  Edmond Medical Center
  Oklahoma Surgicare (Oklahoma City)
  Oklahoma University Medical Center (Oklahoma City)
South Carolina
  Colleton Medical Cemter (Walterboro)
  Grand Dunes Surgery Center (Myrtle Beach)
  Grand Strand Regional Medical Center (Myrtle Beach)
  Summerville Medical Center
  Trident Regional Medical Center (Charleston)
Tennessee
  Centennial Medical Center (Nashville)
  Hendersonville Medical Center
  Horizon Medical Center (Dickson)
  Parkridge East Hospital (Chattanooga)
  Parkridge Valley Hospital (Chattanooga)
  Skyline Medical Center (Nashville)
  StoneCrest Medical Center (Smyrna)
  Summit Medical Center (Hermitage)
Texas
  Bailey Square Surgery Center (Austin)
  Bayshore Medical Center (Pasadena)
  Clear Lake Regional Medical Center (Webster)
  Conroe Regional Medical Center
  Corpus Christi Medical Center
  Del Sol Medical Center (El Paso)
  Denton Regional Medical Center
  Green Oaks Hospital (Dallas)
  Kingwood Medical Center
  Las Colinas Medical Center (Irving)
  Mainland Medical Center (Texas City)
  Medical Center of Arlington
  Medical Center of Lewisville
  Medical Center of McKinney
  Medical Center of Plano
  Medical City Dallas Hospital
  Methodist Hospital (San Antonio)
  Metropolitan Methodist Hospital (San Antonio)
  North Austin Medical Center
  North Hills Hospital (North Richland Hills)
  Plaza Medical Center of Fort Worth
  Rio Grande Regional Hospital (McAllen)
  Round Rock Medical Center
  South Austin Hospital
  St. David' s Medical Center (Austin)
  Valley Regional Medical Center (Brownsville)
  West Houston Medical Center
  Woman' s Hospital of Texas (Houston)
Utah
  Brigham City Community Hospital
  Lakeview Hospital (Bountiful)
  Ogden Regional Medical Center
  St. Mark' s Hospital (Salt Lake City)
  Timpanogos Regional Hospital (Orem)
Virginia
  CJW Medical Center (Richmond)
  Dominion Hospital (Falls Church)
  Henrico Doctors' Hospital (Richmond)
  John Randolph Medical Center
  LewisGale Medical Center (Salem)
  Pulaski Community Hospital
  Reston Hospital Center
  Spotsylvania Regional Medical Center (Fredricksburg)

Selected International Facilities
UK
  Harley Street Clinic (London)
  Lister Hospital (London)
  London Bridge Hospital (London)
  The Portland Hospital for Women and Children (London)
  Princess Grace Hospital (London)
  The Wellington Hospital (London)

PRODUCTS/OPERATIONS

2014 Revenue

Payer sources	$ mil.	% of total
Managed care & other insurers	20,066	50
Medicare	8,354	21
Managed Medicare	3,614	9
Managed Medicaid	1,923	5
Medicaid	1,848	4
International (managed care & commercial insurers)	1,311	3
Uninsured & other	2,971	8
Adjustments (provisions for doubtful accounts)	(3269)	-
Total	36,918	100

2014 Revenues

	$ mil.	% of total
American Group	17,532	47
National Group	17,325	47
Corporate & other	2,061	6
Total	36,918	100

COMPETITORS

Adventist Health
Adventist Health System Sunbelt Healthcare
AmSurg
Ascension Health
Banner Health
CHRISTUS Health
Catholic Health Initiatives
Children' s Medical Center of Dallas
Community Health Systems
HealthSouth
LifePoint Health
SSM Health Care
Saint Thomas Midtown Hospital
Sutter Health
Tenet Healthcare
Texas Health Resources
Trinity Health (Novi)
United Surgical Partners
Universal Health Services

HISTORICAL FINANCIALS
Company Type: Public

Income Statement
FYE: December 31

	REVENUE ($ mil.)	NET INCOME ($ mil.)	NET PROFIT MARGIN	EMPLOYEES
12/14	36,918	1,875	5.1%	225,000
12/13	34,182	1,556	4.6%	215,000
12/12	33,013	1,605	4.9%	204,000
12/11	29,682	2,465	8.3%	199,000
12/10	30,683	1,207	3.9%	194,000
Annual Growth	4.7%	11.6%	—	3.8%

2014 Year-End Financials

Debt ratio: 95.02%	No. of shares (mil.): 420
Return on equity: —	Dividends
Cash ($ mil.): 566	Yield: —
Current ratio: 1.63	Payout: —
Long-term debt ($ mil.): 29,307	Market value ($ mil.): 30,859

	STOCK PRICE ($) FY Close	P/E High/Low	PER SHARE ($) Earnings	Dividends	Book Value
12/14	73.39	17 11	4.16	0.00	(18.77)
12/13	47.71	14 9	3.37	0.00	(18.81)
12/12	30.17	9 6	3.49	6.50	(21.80)
12/11	22.03	7 3	4.97	0.00	(18.88)
Annual Growth	35.1%	— —	(4.4%)	—	—

HD Supply Holdings Inc

Do-it-yourselfers shop Home Depot or Lowe's but the pros do business at HD Supply. One of the largest industrial distributors in North America (and formerly the professional services division of Home Depot) HD Supply provides building materials and tools and installation services to professionals in the specialty construction; maintenance repair and operations (MRO); and infrastructure and power markets through 500-plus locations across 48 US states and six Canadian provinces. It operates more than a handful of business units including HD Supply Facilities Maintenance Waterworks Construction & Industrial - White Cap In-

terior Solutions and Home Improvement Solutions. HD Supply went public in 2013.
  Operations
  The industrial distributor operated its business through four segments during fiscal 2015 (ended February 1 2015): Facilities Maintenance (which made up 28% of FY2015 revenue) Waterworks (27%) Power Solutions (22%) and White Cap (17%). Corporate and Other comprise the rest of HD Supply's revenue.
  Top segment Facilities Maintenance distributes maintenance repair and operations (MRO) products provides value-add services and fabricates custom products to multifamily hospitality healthcare and institutional facilities. Within the segment products include electrical and lighting items plumbing HVAC products appliances janitorial supplies hardware kitchen and bath cabinets window coverings textiles and guest amenities healthcare maintenance and water and wastewater treatment products.
  The company's Waterworks segment is focused on distributing water and wastewater transmission products. It primarily serves contractors and municipalities in the water and wastewater industries for non-residential and residential uses. HD Supply's smaller White Cap segment distributes specialized hardware tools engineered materials and safety products to non-residential and residential contractors.
  The Power Solutions segment –which the company sold in October 2015 to Anixter for $825 million –distributed electrical transmission and distribution products power plant MRO supplies and smart-grid products. It also arranged materials management and procurement outsourcing for the power generation and distribution industries.
  Geographic Reach
  HD Supply primarily operates its business in the US but extends its reach into Canada through its Facilities Maintenance segment.
  Sales and Marketing
  The company which boasts 14000 associates and carries a broad range of products and offers value-added services serves some 500000 professional customers who boast leadership positions in numerous sectors such as maintenance repair and operations infrastructure power and specialty construction. As part of its services HD Supply provides jobsite delivery will call or direct-ship of its products as well as diversified logistics. It ships products through an internal fleet or to a lesser extent by third-party carriers.
  HD Supply markets products through a range of sales channels including through its outside and inside sales forces call centers various business unit websites and branch-supported direct marketing programs that utilize market-tailored product catalogs. The company spent $33 million on advertising in fiscal 2015 (ended February 1 2015) compared to $35 million and $34 million in fiscal years 2014 and 2013 respectively.
  Financial Performance
  HD Supply's revenues have been rising over the past several years with sales growth from the strengthening construction and home building markets as well as through acquisitions. It has also slowly climbed out of years of losses after cutting its overhead costs through restructuring measures and paying down its long-term debt which has resulted in lower interest payments.The company's net sales rose by 8% to $654 million in fiscal 2015 (ended February 1 2015) thanks to growth initiatives in each of its businesses and partially thanks to an increase in market volume. Most of the growth was driven by near double-digit sales increases in the Facilities Maintenance (from investments in personnel products and technology) and Waterworks (from growth initiatives new locations and higher sales volumes) segments and a 15%

sales jump in the Construction & Industrial - White Cap segment (mostly driven by growth initiatives including its Managed Sales approach and direct marketing strategies). Higher sales in FY2015 combined with lower depreciation and amortization and interest expenses led to HD Supply to its first profit in years with a net income of $3 million (compared to a loss of $218 million in FY2014). The company's operating cash levels spiked to $295 million (operations used $367 million in FY2014) for the year partly thanks to higher earnings but mostly because in FY2014 it had spent a significant amount of its cash on extinguishing its long-term debt and had paid more in interest payments during the year.

Strategy

HD Supply's strategy includes entering new markets and expanding its product lines to grow its customer base. It also seeks to streamline and upgrade its supply chain processes and technological capabilities. Aside from its focus on organic growth HD Supply works to expand its business by seeking tuck-in acquisitions in core and adjacent markets to supplement its product set geographic footprint and other capabilities.

To boost profitability and free up resources HD Supply has also strategically sold off its non-core business lines in recent years. In October 2015 it sold its Power Solutions business to Anixter for $825 million. Also in 2015 HD Supply sold its Hardware Solutions business sold fasteners business hardware plumbing etc. the unit's largest customer (and the company's former parent) Home Depot for $198 million. In 2014 the company sold Litemor a specialty lighting distributor within their HD Supply Canada business for a loss on disposal of between $10 million and $25 million.The company regularly opens new distribution centers to boost supply in hot markets and hasten delivery times. In 2014 it opened its newest distribution center in Houston followed by the relocation of its corporate headquarters and training facility in St. Louis to better serve customers and position the company for sustainable long-term growth. In the same year it also opened a new combined Waterworks and White Cap 25000 square-foot facility located in Manchester New Hampshire. In mid-2013 it opened a 50000-sq.-ft. facility in Secaucus New Jersey as well as a distribution center in Calera Alabama to improve its local support for customers in the Southeast including Alabama Tennessee Mississippi Louisiana and the Florida panhandle.

Company Background

HD Supply went public in 2013. It aimed to raise $1 billion in the IPO but it walked away with $957 million which would be used to pay down debt.In 2012 the company's HD Supply Waterworks division purchased RAMSCO a waterworks distributor specializing in water sanitary and storm sewer materials and services. The addition of RAMSCO which is based in New York State extended Waterworks' service to customers in the US Northeast.

Also in 2012 HD Supply purchased Water Products of Oklahoma Arkansas Water Products and Municipal Water Works Supply for $48 million. Additionally it bought Georgia-based Peachtree Business Products (a specialist in customizable business and property marketing supplies serving residential and commercial property managers medical facilities schools and universities churches and funeral homes) for $196 million.

HD Supply was formed in 1997 when Home Depot acquired Maintenance Warehouse. Before going public in 2013 it was owned by three of the world's leading private equity firms: Bain Capital The Carlyle Group and Clayton Dubilier & Rice each held about a 19% stake in the company.

EXECUTIVES

Chairman and CEO, Joseph J. (Joe) DeAngelo, $1,000,000 total compensation

SVP and President Interior Solutions and Home Improvement Solutions, Joseph C. (Joe) Izganics, age 53

Executive President HD Supply; President HD Supply Construction and Industrial; White Cap, John A. Stegeman, $743,404 total compensation

CEO HD Supply Waterworks, Jerry L. Webb, $383,281 total compensation

President and CEO HD Supply Facilities Maintenance, Anesa Chaibi, $743,404 total compensation

President HD Supply Waterworks, Steve LeClair

SVP and CFO, Evan J. Levitt, $352,946 total compensation

President HD Supply Power Solutions, John Tisera

CIO, Brad Cowles

Auditors: PricewaterhouseCoopers LLP

LOCATIONS

HQ: HD Supply Holdings Inc
3100 Cumberland Boulevard, Suite 1480, Atlanta, GA 30339
Phone: 770 852-9000
Web: www.hdsupply.com

PRODUCTS/OPERATIONS

2015 Sales

	$ mil.	% of total
Facilities maintenance	2,510	28
Waterworks	2,427	27
Power Solutions	1,913	22
White Cap	1,481	17
Corporate & others	551	6
Total	**8,882**	**100**

Selected Businesses

Creative Touch Interiors
HD Supply Canada
HD Supply Crown Bolt
HD Supply Electrical
HD Supply Industrial PVF
HD Supply Facilities Maintenance
HD Supply Repair & Remodel
HD Supply Utilities
HD Supply Waterworks
HD Supply White Cap

COMPETITORS

84 Lumber
ABC Supply
BMC
BlueLinx
Builders FirstSource
Fastenal
Ferguson Enterprises
Guardian Building Products Distribution
MSC Industrial Direct
PrimeSource Building
Pro-Build
Rexel Inc.
Stock Building Supply
W.W. Grainger
Watsco
Wesco
WinWholesale

HISTORICAL FINANCIALS

Company Type: Public

Income Statement

FYE: February 1

	REVENUE ($ mil.)	NET INCOME ($ mil.)	NET PROFIT MARGIN	EMPLOYEES
02/15	8,882	3	0.0%	15,000
02/14	8,487	(218)	—	15,500
02/13*	8,035	(1,179)	—	15,000
01/12	7,028	(543)	—	—
01/11	6,449	(619)	—	—
Annual Growth	**8.3%**	—	—	—

*Fiscal year change

2015 Year-End Financials

Debt ratio: 86.75% No. of shares (mil.): 196
Return on equity: — Dividends
Cash ($ mil.): 85 Yield: —
Current ratio: 2.02 Payout: —
Long-term debt ($ mil.): 5,223 Market value ($ mil.): 5,652

	STOCK PRICE ($) FY Close	P/E High/Low		PER SHARE ($) Earnings	Dividends	Book Value
02/15	28.83	1509	1045	0.02	0.00	(3.88)
02/14	21.47	—	—	(1.31)	0.00	(3.97)
Annual Growth	**7.6%**	—	—	—	—	—

Health Net, Inc.

Health Net has woven together a web of health plan services. The company provides managed health care medical coverage to about 6 million members. The company's health plan services unit offers HMO PPO Medicare and Medicaid plans as well as vision dental care and pharmacy benefit programs to customers in Arizona California Oregon and Washington. Health Net's Managed Health Network subsidiary provides behavioral health substance abuse and employee assistance to employer groups and traditional health plan customers. The company also provides administration services for self-funded medical plans. Medicaid insurer Centene plans to buy Health Net for $6.3 billion.

Operations

The Health Net core health plan business makes up the company's western region operations segment which accounts for more than 90% of sales. The segment also includes Medicare and Medicaid offerings life and health insurance entities pharmaceutical service units and some behavioral health operations. The Managed Health Network behavioral health unit serves about 7.1 million customers many of which also are health plan members.

The company's government contracts division is primarily made up of the Health Net Federal Services subsidiary which holds a contract with the government's TRICARE program to provide health benefits to some 3 million military members in the northern US. TRICARE serves employees within the US Department of Defense the US State Department and the US Department of Veterans' Affairs. Other government divisions provide behavioral mental and traditional health care services.

Geographic Reach

Health Net's core health plan business is firmly focused on the western US with California comprising its largest health plan market. HN California Health Net's California HMO is part of the Children's Health Insurance Program (known as

Healthy Families) and insures more than 140000 children. Other key states include Arizona Oregon and Washington.

Sales and Marketing

Health Net's products are marketed to commercial clients through its sales force agents and external brokers. Individual plans are sold mostly through independent agents. Products are also sometimes marketed via consultants on the Internet and the new Affordable Care Act-mandated exchanges.

It offers its services through group individual Medicare (including Medicare Part D) Medicaid dual-eligible US Department of Defense (including TRICARE) and US Department of Veterans Affairs programs.

Commercial payments accounted for 39% of the health plan services premiums in 2014; Medicaid accounted for 34% and Medicare accounted for 22%.

Financial Performance

In recent years Health Net's earnings had softened due in part to inking a smaller TRICARE contract as well as from making select divestitures and experiencing losses in its non-core markets. However in 2014 Health Net's revenues increased 11% to $14 billion (over $11 billion in 2013) primarily due to 29% growth in the West. This was driven by an increase in Medicaid membership numbers under the Affordable Care Act; government contracts also rose marginally that year.

Despite the revenue growth net income declined 14% to $146 million (after two successive years of growth). The decline was primarily due to asset impairment expenses related to property and equipment goodwill and internally developed software.

Meanwhile cash flow from operations spiked by 710% that year due to growth in the Medicaid business and other factors including a change in accounts payable.

Strategy

The company is increasingly focused on creating tailored products targeting specific groups of people. Like traditional HMO networks (in which a provider is given a set fee per patient regardless of service performed) these new products are intended to lower costs (and co-pays) while still offering comprehensive benefits and a broad provider network.

Its HMO Silver Network is one such product and is a network of doctors specialists and hospitals in 10 counties in California. Another tailored network product Salud con Health Net has plans targeted at the Latino community in Southern California. In 2015 Health Net launched new palliative care programs in Oregon and California.

Also that year the company's California arm joined together with John Muir Health to form an Accountable Care Organization (ACO) serving Contra Costa Solano and Alameda counties. In a separate agreement entered into in 2014 its Arizona unit partnered with Banner Health Network to provide patient care services in Maricopa and Pinal counties.

Health Net in 2014 sold its technology platform including software assets and related intellectual property to Cognizant Healthcare Services which will under a master services agreement provide Health Net with consulting technology and administrative services related to claims management medical management support and other areas.

In 2015 Health Net agreed to be acquired by Centene Corporation in a $6.3 billion transaction. The deal will expand Centene's Medicaid and Medicare Advantage operations important areas for growth as federal health care reforms continue.

HISTORY

Foundation Health started as the not-for-profit Foundation Community Health Plan in the 1960s. In 1984 it was bought by AmeriCare Health which had HMOs in six states. The acquisition was a coup: Foundation Health soon accounted for the bulk of AmeriCare's sales.

AmeriCare went public in 1985. The next year it lost to another firm the rights to that name. Redubbed Foundation Health the company expanded into new states and unrelated businesses: commercial real estate silk flowers and furniture.

In late 1986 senior management led a $140 million LBO that left Foundation Health hobbled with debt when the industry started to slide. A 1988 Department of Defense (DOD) CHAMPUS contract brightened prospects but the five-year $3 billion contract to provide health care to 860000 military retirees and dependents in California and Hawaii provided little short-term relief against the effects of high debt and rapid growth: The company lost money again.

The CEO slot had been vacant a year when Dan Crowley a trained accountant with a good turnaround record came aboard in 1989. He cut staff slashed budgets sold unrelated and nonperforming units and kicked off a huge sales effort. To satisfy bankers and the DOD which was threatening to rescind its contract Crowley refinanced Foundation's debt. In a little over a year Foundation Health recorded its best results ever. In 1990 the company went public.

Back on solid ground the company expanded its services and markets buying such firms as Western Universal Life Insurance (renamed Foundation Health Benefit Life Insurance 1991) Occupational Health Services (employee assistance and substance abuse programs 1992) and California Compensation Insurance (workers' compensation insurance 1993).

Foundation Health lost the DOD Hawaii/California contract (almost half its revenues) in 1993 but managed to cope until it regained the business — by then worth $2.5 billion —two years later. Also that year Foundation Health won DOD's five-year $1.8 billion managed-care contract for Oklahoma and parts of Arkansas Louisiana and Texas.

Meanwhile the company had formed Integrated Pharmaceutical Services and bought CareFlorida Health Systems Intergroup Healthcare and Thomas-Davis Medical Centers in 1994.

In 1995 the company dropped an offer to buy Health Systems International. The next year it added behavioral health and employee assistance programs with the purchase of Managed Health Network.

Renewed discussions with Health Systems International resulted in the companies merging to become Foundation Health Systems in 1997. Crowley —whose aggressive style garnered profits but was denounced as brutal by some critics —resigned after the merger.

In 1998 the company pushed into the Northeast buying Connecticut-based HMO Physicians Health Services. It then sold its workers' compensation insurance operations. Chairman Malik Hasan (founder of Health Systems' nucleus QualMed) resigned that year partly because president Jay Gellert planned to focus on Arizona and California health plans CHAMPUS and behavioral health and pharmacy benefit management.

The financial aftershocks of the companies' merger continued and FHS pruned its operations in 1999 and 2000 exiting such states as Colorado New Mexico and Texas; trimming its Medicare operations; and selling certain non-core administrative business lines. In 2000 the California Medical Association sued the company under RICO statutes claiming it coerced doctors and interfered

in doctor-patient relationships. Later that year the company changed its name to Health Net in its effort to build a national brand name.

EXECUTIVES

President and CEO, Jay M. Gellert, age 62, $1,214,137 total compensation
President Health Net Pharmaceutical Services, John P. Sivori, age 51
EVP COO CFO and Interim Treasurer, James E. (Jim) Woys, age 57, $755,026 total compensation
President Government Programs, Steven D. (Steve) Tough, age 64, $552,800 total compensation
President Western Region Health Plan, Steven J. (Steve) Sell, age 49, $534,094 total compensation
SVP Chief Administration Officer and BPaaS Transformation Officer, Juanell Hefner, $523,597 total compensation
President Health Net Health Plan of Oregon, Chris Ellertson, age 47
President Managed Health Network Inc., Larry Tallman
Health Care Services Officer, Scott D. Law, age 50, $490,979 total compensation
President Health Net of Arizona, Rose Megian
Chief Actuarial Officer, Rich Hall
Chief State Health Programs and Regulatory Relations Officer, Patricia T. Clarey
Vice President Real Estate Corporate Business Planning, Dennis Bell
Vice President Information Technology, Makini Enakaya
Senior Vice President, Marie Montgomery
Vice President and Controller, Steve Miller
Vice President Of Operations, Susan Burkhart
Vice President Provider Management Senior Products Division, Jennifer (Jen) Moore
Medical Director, Michael Chan
Pharmacy Manager, Rodney (Rod) Gedey
Vice President of Marketing, John (Jack) Rindlaub
Vice President Information Systems, Matt Cleveland
Vice President Chief Information Security Officer, Lou Desorbo
National Account Manager, Susan Franklin
Vice President Finance, Brian Tweten
Vice President Business Solutions, Michael (Mel) Sobetzko
Vice President Product, Jennifer Barrows
Vice President Hedis Management, Eileen O'Connor
Vice President Of Underwriting, Jody Giordano
Vice President Legal Affairs, Anne Schlueter
Vice President Marketing, Arild Hovland
Vice President Application Technology, Jeff Flynn
Regional Vice President Operations, Nate Nygaard
Vice President, Raul Baeza
Vice President Of Human Resources, Debbie Cholea
Vice President Information Technology, Jack Marstellar
Senior Vice President Operations, Phil Hunt
Vice President Contact Center And Aandg, Gary Neiman
Vice President Leadership Devel. and Talent Management, Andy Ortiz
Vice President, Daniel (Dan) Tyler
Senior Vice President Human Resources, Karin Mayhew
Vice President Of State Health Programs Health Net, Dave Meadows
Senior Vice President Corporate, Pat Claery
Vice President Investor Relations and Corporate Communications, Peter (Pete) O'Neill
Vice President Finance, Alida Dodd
Regional Vice President Sales, Anne Hanlon
Chairman, Roger F. Greaves, age 78
Treasurer, Randy McClaran
Auditors: Deloitte & Touche LLP

LOCATIONS

HQ: Health Net, Inc.
  21650 Oxnard Street, Woodland Hills, CA 91367
Phone: 818 676-6000
Web: www.healthnet.com

PRODUCTS/OPERATIONS

2014 Sales

	$ mil.	% of total
Western region operations	13,361	95
Government contracts	604	4
Net investment income	45	1
Administrative services fees and other income	(1.7)	-
Total	**14,008**	**100**

2014 Membership

	% of total
Tricare	47
Medicaid	28
Commercial	20
Medicare	5
Duals	-
Total	**100**

COMPETITORS

Aetna	Magellan Health
Anthem	Moda Health
Anthem Blue Cross	PacificSource
Blue Cross	Providence Health &
Blue Cross Blue Shield	Services
of Arizona	Regence BlueCross
CIGNA	BlueShield of Oregon
Humana	UnitedHealth Group
LifeWise Health Plan	ValueOptions
of Oregon	

HISTORICAL FINANCIALS

Company Type: Public

Income Statement
FYE: December 31

	REVENUE ($ mil.)	NET INCOME ($ mil.)	NET PROFIT MARGIN	EMPLOYEES
12/14	14,008	145	1.0%	8,014
12/13	11,053	170	1.5%	7,659
12/12	11,289	122	1.1%	7,378
12/11	11,901	72	0.6%	7,471
12/10	13,619	204	1.5%	8,169
Annual Growth	0.7%	(8.1%)	—	(0.5%)

2014 Year-End Financials

Debt ratio: 9.26%	No. of shares (mil.): 78
Return on equity: 8.73%	Dividends
Cash ($ mil.): 869	Yield: —
Current ratio: 1.53	Payout: —
Long-term debt ($ mil.): 499	Market value ($ mil.): 4,179

	STOCK PRICE ($) FY Close	P/E High/Low	PER SHARE ($) Earnings	Dividends	Book Value
12/14	53.53	30 16	1.80	0.00	21.89
12/13	29.67	16 11	2.12	0.00	20.48
12/12	24.30	27 12	1.47	0.00	19.15
12/11	30.42	42 26	0.80	0.00	17.61
12/10	27.29	14 10	2.06	0.00	17.90
Annual Growth	18.3%	— —	(3.3%)	—	5.2%

Heartland Financial USA, Inc. (Dubuque, IA)

Heartland Financial USA brings heart-felt community banking to nation's heartland. The $5.9 billion multi-bank holding company owns flagship subsidiary Dubuque Bank & Trust and nine other banks that together operate more than 75 branches in 55-plus communities in the Midwest and Southwest US. In addition to standard deposit loan and mortgage services the banks also offer retirement wealth management trust insurance and investment services including socially responsible investing. Heartland Financial USA also owns consumer lender Citizens Finance which has about a dozen offices in Illinois Iowa and Wisconsin.

OperationsHeartland operates two main segments: Community and Other Banking and Retail Mortgage Banking. The Community and Other Banking business generates revenue from interest earned on loans and investment securities and fees from deposit services. Its Retail Mortgage Banking collects revenue from interest from mortgage loans held for sale gains on sales of loans on the secondary market the servicing of mortgage loans for investors and loan origination fee income. Approximately 70% of Heartland Financial's loan portfolio comes from commercial loans and mortgages but in keeping with the bank's Midwestern identity it also makes agricultural residential mortgage and consumer loans.Heartland Financial USA's subsidiaries include: Dubuque Bank and Trust Company Galena State Bank & Trust Co. Illinois Bank & Trust Wisconsin Bank & Trust Morrill & Janes Bank and Trust New Mexico Bank & Trust Arizona Bank & Trust. It also owns multi-line insurance company DB&T Insurance Inc. and runs the community development company DB&T Community Development Corp.Geographic Reach-Heartland operates more than 75 branches in local communities in Arizona Colorado Illinois Iowa Kansas Montana Minnesota Missouri New Mexico and Wisconsin. It also has loan production offices in California Idaho Nevada North Dakota Oregon Washington and Wyoming. About 40% of the company's assets are based in Western markets.Sales and MarketingHeartland offers its banking services to businesses public sector and non-profit entities and individuals. In total the bank serves some 120000 business and consumer households. Heartland spent $5.52 million on advertising in 2014 about 4% more than it spent in 2013.Financial PerformanceHeartland's revenue was up for a second straight year jumping by 10% to $319.3 million in 2014. The boost was mostly driven by interest income from loan growth and additional investment security income as the company increased its earning assets by 18% during the year. The bank's non-interest income sources however lagged as the bank netted fewer gains on its loans held for sale and its investment security sales.The company's net income also rose in 2014 by 14% to $41.9 million rebounding from last year's dip thanks to higher revenue and because it paid lower interest on its deposits.Operations provided $80.4 million or 40% less cash than in 2013 mostly as the bank collected less in proceeds from the net sales of its loans-held-for-sale and because it used more cash toward its prepaid expenses.StrategyHeartland Financial's main growth strategy is to expand its presence in the West with the goal of making the region home to half of its total assets and balancing growth in those markets with the stability of the Midwest. In line with this the bank seeks to expand its subsidiaries through acquisitions and grow its customer base organically in its existing markets.

Consistent with this strategy in early 2015 Heartland purchased the Community Banc-Corp of Sheboygan Inc. (the parent company of Community Bank & Trust) which added 10 branches in Wisconsin and some $410 million worth of loan assets. In 2013 Heartland purchased Morrill Bancshares Inc. along with its Morrill & Janes Bank and Trust Company subsidiary effectively expanding its reach into Kansas and growing its loan assets and deposits by nearly $378 million and $665 million respectively. That year Heartland also bought Freedom Bank and its three branches which expanded its reach into Illinois and enriched its service offerings to business agri-business and consumer banking clients.Mergers and AcquisitionsIn January 2015 Heartland acquired the Community Banc-Corp of Sheboygan Inc. along with all 10 of its Community Bank & Trust branches along with $530.4 million worth of assets $410 million in loans and $429 million in deposits; in exchange for $52 million in an all-stock transaction. The Community Bank & Trust bank was folded into Wisconsin Bank & Trust under the deal.In 2013 the company acquired Morrill Bancshares Inc. the holding company of the Kansas-based Morrill & Janes Bank and Trust Company along with $377.7 million in total loans and $665.3 million worth of deposits. The Morrill & Janes Bank and Trust Company became one of Heartland's independent bank subsidiaries.In 2012 Heartland Financial acquired Heritage Bank N.A. a Phoenix-based commercial bank in an all-cash deal valued at about $16 million consistent with its goal of expansion in the West.

EXECUTIVES

Vice President Marketing, Dawn Oelke
President and CEO Minnesota Bank & Trust, Catherine T. (Kate) Kelly
Chairman of the Board President and Chief Executive Officer Heartland Financial USA Inc.; Vice Chairman of the Board Dubuque Bank & Trust., Lynn B. Fuller, age 65, $470,000 total compensation
Executive Vice President Chief Credit Officer, Kenneth J. Erickson, age 62, $263,000 total compensation
Executive Vice President Lending, Douglas J. Horstmann, age 61, $250,000 total compensation
President and CEO New Mexico Bank & Trust, R. Greg Leyendecker
President Heartland Business Bank, Kevin Tenpas
President, Bruce K. Lee, age 55
Executive Vice President Human Resources, Mark Murtha
Chairman and President Wisconsin Community Bank, Thomas J. (Tom) Wilkinson
President Centennial Bank and Trust, Steven E. Ward
EVP Wealth Management, Bruce J. Rehmke
President Citizens Finance Co., Al H. Green
Executive Vice President Commercial Sales, Frank Walter
Executive Vice President Senior General Counsel Corporate Secretary, Michael Coyle
Executive Vice President - Marketing & Sales, John J. Berg, age 63
Executive Vice President Operations, Brian J. Fox, $190,000 total compensation
Executive Vice President Chief Risk Officer, Rodney L. Sloan
Chief Financial Officer, Bryan McKeag
Executive Vice President Finance, David L. Horstmann
President and CEO Galena State Bank & Trust Company, Robert Eby

President and CEO Arizona Bank & Trust, Jerry L. Schwallier

President and CEO Rocky Mountain Bank, Curtis Chrystal

President Summit Bank & Trust, John Rhoades

President and CEO Morrill & Janes Bank and Trust Co., Kurt M. Saylor

EVP and Private Client Services, Kelly Johnson

President and CEO Illinois Bank and Trust, Jeff Hultman

Vice President Finance, Sandra Wild

Vice President Administrative Services, Joseph V (Jo) Berretta

Vice President Finance, Jacquie Manternach

Vice President Loan Operations, Kate Barth

Vice President Deposit Operations Manager, Doris Hannan

Vice President, Jean Harkey

Mortgage Servicing Vice President, Tony Newkirk

Vice President Loan Imaging Manager, Marie Koerperich

Vice President Corporate Training Director, Bonnie Bollin

Assistant Vice President Commercial Services, Lynn Stoffregen

Vice President Operations and Finance, Bret Tuley

Senior Vice President Director Retail Banking, Tut Fuller

Vice President, Rachel Steiner

Vice President Information Technology, Les Oelke

Vice President Credit Administration, Ted Kraft

Senior Vice President Small Business Loan Center Manager, Jeff Ciochetto

Senior Vice President, Julie Shanahan

Vice President Retail Sales, Lu Bowman

Senior Vice President Special Assets REO, John (Jack) Hawkins

Assistant Vice President Senior Research Analyst, Troy Steger

Vice President, Cheri Wheelan

Vice President, Craig Sciara

Vice President, Rod Sloan

Executive Vice President Finance, Dave Horstmann

Senior Vice President Credit Administration, Brian McCarthy

Vice President General Counsel, David (Dave) Kapler

Senior Vice President Head of Loan Operations, Dan Tabraham

Vice Chairman of the Board of Heartland Financial USA Inc.; Chairman and Director of Dubuque Bank and Trust, Mark C. Falb, age 67

Vice Chairman of the Board of Heartland Financial USA Inc.; Director and Vice Chairman of the Board of Dubuque Bank and Trust, Thomas L. Flynn, age 59

Auditors: KPMG LLP

LOCATIONS

HQ: Heartland Financial USA, Inc. (Dubuque, IA)
1398 Central Avenue, Dubuque, IA 52001
Phone: 563 2000   **Fax:** 563 589-2011
Web: www.htlf.com

PRODUCTS/OPERATIONS

2014 Sales

	$ mil.	% of total
Interest		
Loans & leases including fees	194	61
Securities & other	43	13
Noninterest		
Gains on sales of loans	31	10
Service charges and fees	20	7
Trust fees	13	4
Loan serving income	5	2
Brokerage & insurance commissions	4	1
Security gains	3	1
Other	4	1
Total	**319**	**100**

Selected Subsidiaries

Arizona Bank & Trust
Citizens Finance Co. (consumer lending)
Dubuque Bank and Trust (IA)
  DB&T Insurance Inc.
  DB&T Community Development Corp.
First Community Bank (IA)
Galena State Bank & Trust Co. (IL)
New Mexico Bank & Trust
Minnesota Bank & Trust (80%)
Riverside Community Bank (IL)
Rocky Mountain Bank (MT)
Summit Bank & Trust (87% CO)
Wisconsin Community Bank

COMPETITORS

Associated Banc-Corp
BBVA Compass Bancshares
Bank of America
Bank of the West
First Banks
U.S. Bancorp
Wells Fargo
Zions Bancorporation

HISTORICAL FINANCIALS

Company Type: Public

Income Statement

				FYE: December 31
	ASSETS ($ mil.)	**NET INCOME** ($ mil.)	**INCOME AS % OF ASSETS**	**EMPLOYEES**
12/14	6,052	41	0.7%	1,631
12/13	5,923	36	0.6%	1,676
12/12	4,990	49	1.0%	1,498
12/11	4,305	28	0.7%	1,195
12/10	3,999	23	0.6%	1,066
Annual Growth	**10.9%**	**15.1%**	**—**	**11.2%**

2014 Year-End Financials

Debt ratio: 4.73%
Return on equity: 8.96%
Cash ($ mil.): 76
Current ratio: —
Long-term debt ($ mil.): —

No. of shares (mil.): 18
Dividends
  Yield: 1.4%
  Payout: 18.2%
Market value ($ mil.): 502

	STOCK PRICE ($) FY Close	**P/E** High/Low		**PER SHARE ($)** Earnings	Dividends	Book Value
12/14	27.10	13	10	2.19	0.40	26.81
12/13	28.79	14	11	2.04	0.50	23.88
12/12	26.15	10	5	2.77	0.50	23.88
12/11	15.34	15	10	1.23	0.40	21.24
12/10	17.46	18	12	1.13	0.40	20.04
Annual Growth	**11.6%**	**—**	**—**	**18.0%**	**(0.0%)**	**7.6%**

Heritage Financial Corp. (WA)

Heritage Financial is ready to answer the call of Pacific Northwesterners seeking to preserve their heritage. Heritage Financial is the holding company for Heritage Bank which operates more than 65 branches throughout Washington and Oregon. Boasting nearly $4 billion in assets the bank offers a range of deposit products to consumers and businesses such as CDs IRAs and checking savings NOW and money market accounts. Commercial and industrial loans account for over 50% of Heritage Financial's loan portfolio while mortgages secured by multi-family real estate comprise about 5%. The bank also originates single-family mortgages land development construction loans and consumer loans.

OperationsThe bank also does business under the Central Valley Bank name in the Yakima and Kittitas counties of Washington and under the Whidbey Island Bank name on Whidbey Island.About 79% of Heritage Financial's total revenue came from loan interest (including fees) in 2014 while another 7% came from interest on its investment securities. The rest of its revenue came from service charges and other fees (8%) Merchant Visa income (1%) and other miscellaneous fees. The company had a staff of 748 employees at the end of that year.Geographic ReachThe Olympia-based bank operates more than 65 branches across Washington and the greater Portland area. It has additional offices in eastern Washington mostly in Yakima county.Sales and MarketingHeritage targets small and medium-sized businesses along with their owners as well as individuals. Financial PerformanceFueled by loan and deposit growth from a series of bank acquisitions Heritage Financial's revenues and profits have been on the rise in recent years.The company's revenue jumped 70% to a record $137.6 million in 2014 mostly thanks to new loan business stemming from its acquisition of Washington Banking Company. Deposit service charge income also increased thanks to new deposit business from the acquisition.Higher revenue in 2014 allowed Heritage Financial's net income to more than double to a record $21 million while its operating cash levels rose 66% to $51.3 million on higher cash earnings and net proceeds from the sale of its loans.StrategyThe bank reiterated in 2015 that it would continue to pursue strategic acquisitions of community banks to grow market share across the Pacific Northwest (its region of expertise) expand its business lines and grow its loan and deposit business. With its focus on business and commercial lending the bank also in 2015 emphasized the importance of seeking high asset quality loans lending to familiar markets that have a historical record of success. Recruiting and retaining "highly competent personnel" to execute its strategies was also key to its long-term agenda.Mergers and AcquisitionsIn May 2014 Heritage acquired Washington Banking Company and its Whidbey Island Bank subsidiary for $265 million which "significantly expanded and enhanced" its product offerings across its core geographic market.

In July 2013 the bank acquired Puyallup Washington-based Valley Community Bancshares and its eight Valley Bank branches for $44 million.In January 2013 the company purchased Lakewood Washington-based Northwest Commercial Bank along with its two branch locations in Washington state for $5 million.

EXECUTIVES

President CEO and Director; CEO Heritage Bank; Vice Chairman and CEO Central Valley Bank, Brian L. Vance, age 60, $238,200 total compensation

EVP Community Banking Heritage Bank, Gregory D. Patjens, age 66, $147,840 total compensation

President Central Valley Bank, D. Michael Broadhead, age 70, $156,765 total compensation

SVP and CIO Heritage Bank, Lisa A. Welander

SVP and CFO Heritage Financial Corporation Heritage Bank and Central Valley Bank, Donald J. Hinson, age 54, $131,280 total compensation

EVP; EVP and COO Heritage Bank, Jeffrey J. (Jeff) Deuel

Owner, Jane Skinner

Owner, Daniel Phillips

Owner, Charlie McManus

Senior Vice President Commercial Lending, Charles M Folsom

Vice President And Financial Reporting Manager, Patrice Hernandez

Vice President Information Technology Manager, Mike Rand
Chairman Heritage Financial Corporation
Heritage Bank and Central Valley Bank, Donald V. (Don) Rhodes, age 78
Auditors: Crowe Horwath LLP

LOCATIONS

HQ: Heritage Financial Corp. (WA)
   201 Fifth Avenue SW, Olympia, WA 98501
Phone: 360 943-1500
Web: www.HF-WA.com

PRODUCTS/OPERATIONS

2014 Sales

	$ mil.	% of total
Interest income		
Interest and fees on loans	110	79
Investment securities	10	7
Others	0	-
Non-interest income		
Service charges and others	11	8
Merchant Visa income	1	1
Others	4	5
Total	**137**	**100**

COMPETITORS

Bank of America	U.S. Bancorp
Columbia Banking	Washington Federal
FS Bancorp	Wells Fargo
KeyCorp	

HISTORICAL FINANCIALS

Company Type: Public

Income Statement

FYE: December 31

	ASSETS ($ mil.)	NET INCOME ($ mil.)	INCOME AS % OF ASSETS	EMPLOYEES
12/14	3,457	21	0.6%	748
12/13	1,659	9	0.6%	373
12/12	1,345	13	1.0%	363
12/11	1,368	6	0.5%	354
12/10	1,367	13	1.0%	321
Annual Growth	**26.1%**	**12.0%**	**—**	**23.6%**

2014 Year-End Financials

Debt ratio: 0.55%	No. of shares (mil.): 30
Return on equity: 6.27%	Dividends
Cash ($ mil.): 121	Yield: 2.8%
Current ratio: —	Payout: 84.7%
Long-term debt ($ mil.): —	Market value ($ mil.): 531

	STOCK PRICE ($) FY Close	P/E High/Low	PER SHARE ($) Earnings	Dividends	Book Value
12/14	17.55	23 19	0.82	0.50	15.02
12/13	17.10	29 22	0.61	0.42	13.31
12/12	14.69	18 14	0.87	0.80	13.16
12/11	12.56	36 25	0.42	0.38	13.10
12/10	13.92	16 12	1.04	0.00	12.99
Annual Growth	**6.0%**	**— —**	**(5.8%)**	**—**	**3.7%**

Hershey Company (The)

The Hershey Company works to inspire Almond Joy and lots of Kisses. As a global leader and North America's top chocolate producer the company has built a big business manufacturing such well-known chocolate and candy brands as Hershey's Kisses Reese's peanut butter cups Twizzlers licorice and under license Mounds candy bar York peppermint pattie and Kit Kat wafer bar. Hershey also makes grocery goods including baking chocolate chocolate syrup cocoa mix cookies snack nuts breath mints and bubble gum. Products from the chocolate king are sold to a variety of wholesale distributors and retailers throughout North America and exported overseas.

Operations

The company's operations consist of two business segments in which more than 80 name brands are made marketed sold and distributed. Many product types sold under the Hershey's Kisses and Reese's names are included in the company's chocolate business unit. Other popular brand franchises –such as Twizzlers Mounds York Kit Kat Ice Breakers and Bubble Yum –fall within the company's sweets and refreshment business unit.

Hershey also has a retail presence. Referred to as The Hershey Experience the company's retail operations comprise Hershey's Chocolate World (Hershey Pennsylvania) and stores in New York City San Francisco Chicago Niagara Falls (Ontario) Shanghai Dubai and Singapore.

Geographic Reach

Hershey's business focuses on three regions. The US is the company's largest market. The Americas its second region consists of Canada Mexico Brazil Central America Puerto Rico and global exports. Hershey also operates a third region in Asia Europe the Middle East and Africa. The company markets its products in about 70 countries worldwide. While the US is a top revenue generator sales outside the US from developing regions have contributed about 19% of its total revenue.

Financial Performance

Hershey has achieved historic revenue growth over the last few years. Revenues climbed 7% to peak at a record-setting $7.4 billion in 2014 while profits jumped 3% to reach a company milestone of $847 million in 2014. Cash generated from operations however decreased by 29% from 2013 to 2014 after increasing the previous period.

The growth for 2014 reflected core brand sales increases and incremental sales of new products in the US and its international businesses. Additional sales from a previous acquisition also contributed to the historic growth. Its profit increase was driven by the bump in revenue coupled with a decline in selling marketing and administrative expenses.

Strategy

To drive sales growth Hershey is investing in its five core brands –Hershey's Reese's Hershey's Kisses Jolly Rancher and Ice Breakers –in both the US and key international markets. As a result the confectionery company aims to meet new long-term targets of sales growth in the 7% to 9% range.

It's also looking to build out its existing infrastructure in China and chase after the country's growing middle class there through a new initiative to grow its international operations to 25% of its business by 2017. As part of this effort Hershey opened an Asia Innovation Center in Shanghai in mid-2013 and has announced plans to build a $250 million confectionery manufacturing plant in Malaysia. It also debuted the new Lancaster line of caramels in early 2013 and aims to roll out its US version which is manufactured in Canada in the states in the near future.

Mergers and Acquisitions

Hershey's strategic focus is on expanding its global presence as it jockeys for market share from rivals Mars and Kraft which owns Cadbury. In 2014 it purchased The Allan Candy Company a North American manufacturer of confectionery products based in Ontario Canada. Allan Candy is known across Canada for its iconic confectionery brands including Allan Big Foot Hot Lips and Laces. More than half of Allan Candy's current manufacturing capacity is used to make Hershey Sweets & Refreshment products such as Jolly Rancher hard candy and Lancaster caramels for North America.

Also in 2014 Hershey significantly enhanced its Asian footprint when it obtained 80% of Shanghai Golden Monkey Food Joint Stock Co. Ltd. (SGM) a privately held confectionery company based in Shanghai China. SGM manufactures markets and distributes Golden Monkey branded products including candy chocolates protein-based products and snack foods in China.

Sales and Marketing

Among its significant customers wholesale distribution giant McLane Company accounted for 25% of Hershey's sales in 2014. It's the primary distributor of Hershey products to Wal-Mart. Hershey leverages a staff of full-time sales representatives and food brokers to peddle its products to customers. In general the confectionary company counts wholesale distributors chain drug stores vending companies wholesale clubs convenience stores dollar stores concessionaires and department stores among its vast customer set. Hershey's distribution network ships its products from its manufacturing plants to strategically located distribution centers using common carriers to deliver products from there to customers.

The company makes a point to launch new versions of old favorites such as Jolly Rancher lollipops and bite-size bits of chocolate bars. Although chocolate bars take center stage most recently premium dark varieties it introduced sugar-free chocolate to tempt the growing number of diabetic and overweight consumers. Moving into the snack aisle Hershey has rolled out cookies 100-calorie treats and granola bars.

In 2014 Hershey spent about $570 million on advertising compared to $582 million in 2013.

HISTORY

The Hershey Company is the legacy of Milton Hershey of Pennsylvania Dutch origin. Apprenticed in 1872 at age 15 to a candy maker Hershey started Lancaster Caramel Company at age 30. In 1893 at the Chicago Exposition he saw a new chocolate-making machine and in 1900 he sold the caramel operations for $1 million to start a chocolate factory.

The factory was completed in 1905 in Derry Church Pennsylvania and renamed Hershey Foods the next year. Chocolate Kisses individually hand-wrapped in silver foil were introduced in 1907. Two years later the candy man founded the Milton Hershey School an orphanage; the company was donated to a trust in 1918 and for years existed solely to fund the school. Hershey went public in 1927.

EXECUTIVES

Vice President Investor Relations, Mark K Pogharian
Senior Vice President, Thomas Hernquist
Chairman President and CEO, John P. (J.P.) Bilbrey, age 58, $1,164,462 total compensation
President North America, Michele G. Buck, age 54, $642,461 total compensation
SVP Chief Knowledge Strategy and Technology Officer, Waheed Zaman, age 54
SVP and Chief Supply Chain Officer, Terence L. O'Day, age 65, $567,172 total compensation
SVP and CFO, Patricia A. Little, age 55
President China and Asia, Steven C. Schiller

Senior Vice President Chief Comml Officer
  Global, Mike Wege
Senior Vice President General Counsel, Burton
  McCallion
Vice President Logistcis, Carole Rich
Vice President Finance Canada, David (Dave) Hulays
Vice President Logistics, Michael Wells
Vice President Us Finance, Todd Cunfer
Vice President, Joe Beck
Senior Vice President and Chief People Officer,
  Kevin Walling
National Account Manager, Mike Jauch
Vice President Insights, Robert Goodpaster
Vice President Global Ethics and Compliance,
  Adrian D Mebane
Vice President Customer Innovation, Bernard
  Banas
Vice President, Thomas (Thom) Smuda
Vice President Us Finance And Planning,
  Montgome Garrabrant
Vice President Finance, Gayla Bush
Vice President of Marketing, Michael D (Mel) Wege
Vice President Global Applications and
  Infrastructure Services, Joseph (Jo) Zakutney
Vice President North American Chocolate Product
  Development, Jim St John
Assistant Secretary, Vincent R Clempson
Assistant Treasurer, James G (Jamie) Nolan
Member Board Of Directors, James (Jamie) Mead
Vice President and Treasurer, Rosa Stroh
Vice Chairman For Finance And Informatics,
  Doug Eggli
Assistant Secretary, Kathleen Purcell
Auditors: KPMG LLP

LOCATIONS

HQ: Hershey Company (The)
  100 Crystal A Drive, Hershey, PA 17033
Phone: 717 534-4200   Fax: 717 531-6161
Web: www.hersheys.com

2014 Sales

	% of total
US	81
Other countries	19
Total	**100**

PRODUCTS/OPERATIONS

Selected Brands
Confectionery
  Hershey' s
  Air Delight
  Bliss
  Cookies &#
  Drops
  Extra dark
  Hugs
  Milk chocolate
  Miniatures
  Nuggets
  Pot of Gold
  Sugar free
  Kisses
  Air Delight
  Milk chocolates
  Special Dark
  Reese' s
  Big Cup
  Fast Break
  Nutrageous
  Peanut butter cups
  Pieces
  Reesesticks
  Sugar free
  Wafer bars
  Whipps
  Other
  5th Avenue
  Almond Joy (worldwide license from Cadbury)
  Cadbury (USA license from Cadbury)
  Caramello (USA license from Cadbury)
  Chipits (C

Eat More (
Glosette (
Godrej (In
  Good & Plenty (worldwide license from
    Huhtamäki)
  Heath (worldwide license from Huhtamäki)
IO-IO (Bra
  Jolly Rancher (worldwide license from
    Huhtamäki)
  Kit Kat (US license from Nestlé)
  Lancaster (China since 2013 US in 2014)
  Milk Duds (worldwide license from Huhtamäki)
  Mounds (worldwide license from Cadbury)
  Mr. Goodbar
Nutrine (I
Oh Henry!
  Payday (worldwide license from Huhtamäki)
Pelón
  Pot Of Gold
  Rolo (US license from Nestlé)
  Scharffen Berger
  Skor
  Special Dark
  Symphony
  Take5
  Thingamajig
  Twizzlers
  Van Houten (under license in Asia and the Middle
    East)
  Whatchamacallit
  Whoppers (worldwide license from Huhtamäki)
  York (worldwide license from Cadbury)
  Zagnut
  Zero
Food and beverage enhancers
  Bake Shoppe
  Goodnight Hugs
  Goodnight Kisses
  Granola Bars
  Toppings
Pantry items
  Heath
  Hershey' s
  Hershey' s Bliss
  Reese' s
  Scharffen Berger
Premium products
  Dagoba natural and organic chocolate
  Scharffen Berger high-cacao dark chocolate
Refreshment products
  Breath Savers
  Bubble Yum
  Ice Breakers
Snack products
  Hershey' s 100 calorie bars
  Mauna Loa macadamia snack nuts

COMPETITORS

Annabelle Candy
Anthony-Thomas Candy
Asher' s Chocolates
Betsy Ann Candies
Chase General
Chocolates □la Carte
Chupa Chups
Endangered Species
  Chocolate
Enstrom
Fazer Konfektyr
Ferrero
Flowers Foods
Ghirardelli Chocolate
Godiva Chocolatier
Goetze' s Candy
Guittard
Harry London Candies
Jelly Belly Candy
Kellogg
Laura Secord

Lindt & Sprngli
Mars Incorporated
Mondelez International
Nestl©
Otis Spunkmeyer
Perfetti Van Melle
Purdy' s Chocolates
Rocky Mountain
  Chocolate
Russell Stover
See' s Candies
Smucker
Spangler Candy
Sweet Shop USA
Tootsie Roll
Warrell Corporation
World' s Finest
  Chocolate
Wrigley
Zachary Confections

HISTORICAL FINANCIALS
Company Type: Public

Income Statement
FYE: December 31

	REVENUE ($ mil.)	NET INCOME ($ mil.)	NET PROFIT MARGIN	EMPLOYEES
12/14	7,421	846	11.4%	22,450
12/13	7,146	820	11.5%	14,800
12/12	6,644	660	9.9%	14,200
12/11	6,080	628	10.3%	13,800
12/10	5,671	509	9.0%	13,500
Annual Growth	7.0%	13.5%	—	13.6%

2014 Year-End Financials

Debt ratio: 38.80%   No. of shares (mil.): 221
Return on equity: 55.36%   Dividends
Cash ($ mil.): 374   Yield: 1.9%
Current ratio: 1.16   Payout: 55.4%
Long-term debt ($ mil.): 1,548   Market value ($ mil.): 22,973

	STOCK PRICE ($) FY Close	P/E High/Low	PER SHARE ($) Earnings	Dividends	Book Value
12/14	103.93	28 23	3.77	2.04	6.58
12/13	97.23	27 19	3.61	1.81	7.17
12/12	72.22	25 20	2.89	1.56	4.63
12/11	61.78	22 16	2.74	1.38	3.77
12/10	47.15	23 16	2.21	1.28	3.97
Annual Growth	21.8%	— —	14.3%	12.4%	13.4%

Hertz Global Holdings Inc

If you've ever said "Don't worry about it it's just a rental" guess who hurts: Hertz a world leader in car rental. On its own and through agents and licensees Hertz operates about 11555 rental locations in about 150 countries under the Hertz Dollar and Thrifty brands. About 70% of its US revenues come from airport locations. Its fleet includes approximately 524500 cars from Ford General Motors Toyota and other manufacturers. While car rental accounts for about 80% of its sales Hertz also rents a variety of heavy equipment through about 335 locations in North America Europe and China.

HISTORY

In 1918 22-year-old John Jacobs opened a Chicago car rental business with 12 Model T Fords that he had repaired. By 1923 when Yellow Cab entrepreneur John Hertz bought Jacobs' business it had revenues of about $1 million. Jacobs continued as top executive of the company renamed Hertz Drive-Ur-Self System. Three years later General Motors acquired the company when it bought Yellow Truck from John Hertz. Hertz introduced the first car rental charge card in 1926 opened its first airport location at Chicago's Midway Airport in 1932 and initiated the first one-way (rent-it-here/leave-it-there) plan in 1933. The company expanded into Canada in 1938 and Europe in 1950.

Omnibus bought Hertz from GM in 1953 sold its bus interests and focused on vehicle leasing and renting. The next year Omnibus changed its name to The Hertz Corporation and was listed on the NYSE. Also in 1954 the company purchased Metropolitan Distributors a New York-based truck leasing firm. In 1961 Hertz began operations in South America.

The company formed its Hertz Equipment Rental subsidiary in 1965. RCA bought Hertz two years later but allowed the company to maintain its board of directors and management. In 1972 it introduced the first frequent traveler's club the #1 Club which allowed the rental location to prepare a rental agreement before the customer arrived at the counter. Three years later Hertz began defining the company's image through TV commercials featuring former football star O. J. Simpson running through airports. (Hertz canceled Simpson's contract in 1994 after his arrest on murder charges –the TV ads had stopped in 1992.) Frank Olson became CEO in 1977 after serving in the same position at United Airlines.

United Airlines bought Hertz from RCA in 1985 then sold it in 1987 for $1.3 billion to Park Ridge which had been formed by Hertz management and Ford Motor specifically for the purchase. (Hertz was Ford's largest customer.) In 1988 Ford which held 80% of Park Ridge sold 20% to Volvo North America for $100 million. (Ford later reduced its stake to 49% when it sold shares to Volvo.) Also that year Hertz sold its stock in the Hertz Penske truck leasing joint venture for $85.5 million and issued Penske a license to use its name.

Ford bought all the shares of Hertz it didn't already own in 1994. The next year it formed a unit to provide replacement cars for insurance companies. Taking advantage of heightened investor interest in rental car companies (stemming in part from the purchases of some competitors) Ford sold 17% of Hertz to the public in 1997.

Hertz acquired several equipment rental companies in 1998 including the Boireau Group (France) and Matthews Equipment (Canada). In 1999 the company's European acquisitions included French car rental franchise SST and German van rental company Yellow Truck. Also in 1999 Hertz created a referral network with Toyota Japan's #1 car dealer.

Lackluster performance of Hertz stock in 2001 prompted Ford to pay about $735 million to buy back shares held by the public –once again making the car rental company a wholly owned Ford subsidiary. Also that year Hertz opened about 200 new suburban rental locations. In April 2001 Hertz eliminated commissions for negotiated corporate and government accounts in the US and Canada.

The decline in air travel that followed the terrorist attacks of September 11 2001 hampered Hertz's business during 2001 and 2002. As part of an effort to strengthen its balance sheet and focus on its core automotive manufacturing operations Ford sold Hertz to a group of investment firms –Clayton Dubilier & Rice The Carlyle Group and Merrill Lynch Global Private Equity –in December 2005 for $5.6 billion and nearly $10 billion in assumed debt.

Ford had filed for an IPO of the car rental company in June 2005 but that offering was withdrawn in favor of a new proposed IPO in July 2006. Proceeds of the offering which was completed in November 2006 were to be used to reduce debt –including a $1 billion loan taken out by the company in June 2006 –and to pay an additional dividend to the investment firms.

Hertz acquired Advantage Rent A Car out of bankruptcy for nearly $33 million in early 2009. Advantage added about 45 rental locations in the US and Europe and more than a dozen affiliates in Latin America and the Caribbean to Hertz's rental network and bolstered its position in the leisure travel market.

After more than two years Hertz persuaded a reluctant Dollar Thrifty Automotive Group (DTG) to succumb to its advances. Indeed in a deal valued at $2.3 billion DTG in 2012 was acquired by Hertz after rejecting a lower bid from the company in 2010 and a rival bid from Avis Budget Group.

EXECUTIVES

Senior Vice President North America Car Rental Operations, Daniel Flynn
Vice President Revenue Management, Charles Vuono
Executive Vice President; President Rent A Car International, Michel Taride
Auditors: PricewaterhouseCoopers LLP

LOCATIONS

HQ: Hertz Global Holdings Inc
 999 Vanderbilt Beach Road - 3rd Floor, Naples, FL 34108
Phone: 239 552-5800
Web: www.hertz.com

2014 Sales by Point of Rental

	% of total
US	
Airport	72
Off-airport	28
Total	**100**
International	
Airport	55
Off-airport	45
Total	**100**

2014 Sales

	$ mil.	% of total
US	8,158	74
International	2,888	26
Total	**11,046**	**100**

PRODUCTS/OPERATIONS

2014 Sales

	$ mil.	% of total
Car rental	8,907	81
Equipment rental	1,571	14
Other	568	5
Total	**11,046**	**100**

2014 Type of Car Rental

	% of total
US	
Leisure	65
Business	35
100	
International	
Business	59
Leisure	41
100	

Selected Subsidiaries

CCL Vehicle Rentals Ltd. (UK)
Dollar Thrifty Automotive Group Inc.
Eileo Inc.
Hertz Equipment Rental Corp.
Hertz Entertainment Services Corp.
Hertz Equipment Rental International
Simply Wheelz LLC (dba Advantage Rent A Car)
The Hertz Corp. (dba Hertz Car Sales Hertz Rent-A-Car)

COMPETITORS

Avis Budget	Neff
Caterpillar	Sixt
Enterprise Rent-A-Car	Sunbelt Rentals
HD Supply	United Rentals
Lei Shing Hong	Zipcar
NES Rentals	

HISTORICAL FINANCIALS

Company Type: Public

Income Statement

FYE: December 31

	REVENUE ($ mil.)	NET INCOME ($ mil.)	NET PROFIT MARGIN	EMPLOYEES
12/14	11,046	(82)	—	33,000
12/13	10,771	346	3.2%	30,400
12/12	9,020	243	2.7%	30,200
12/11	8,298	176	2.1%	23,900
12/10	7,562	(48)	—	22,900
Annual Growth	**9.9%**	**—**	**—**	**9.6%**

2014 Year-End Financials

Debt ratio: 66.68%	No. of shares (mil.): 459
Return on equity: (-3.13%)	Dividends
Cash ($ mil.): 490	Yield: —
Current ratio: 1.19	Payout: —
Long-term debt ($ mil.): 15,993	Market value ($ mil.): 11,447

	STOCK PRICE ($) FY Close	P/E High/Low		PER SHARE ($) Earnings	Dividends	Book Value
12/14	24.94	—	—	(0.18)	0.00	5.37
12/13	28.62	34	20	0.76	0.00	6.22
12/12	16.27	29	18	0.54	0.00	5.95
12/11	11.72	41	19	0.40	0.00	5.36
12/10	14.49	—	—	(0.12)	0.00	5.11
Annual Growth	**14.5%**	**—**	**—**	**—**	**—**	**1.2%**

Hess Corp

Oil and gas company Hess has exploration and production operations worldwide. In 2014 Hess reported proved reserves totaling more than 1.4 billion barrels of oil equivalent. In 2014 51% of the company's total proved reserves were located in the US; 61% of its crude oil and natural gas liquids production and 32% of its natural gas production came from US operations. In a major shift in strategy Hess has sold all its its downstream businesses (refining and petroleum product and energy marketing) in order to focus on its higher margin exploration and production activities.

Geographic Reach

Hess has operations in Algeria Australia Azerbaijan Brunei China Denmark Equatorial Guinea France Gabon Ghana Indonesia Kurdistan (Iraq) Libya Malaysia Norway Russia Thailand the UK and the US.

Operations

In 2014 Hess operated 17 rigs drilled 261 wells and completed 230 wells and began production at 168 wells bringing the total number of operated production wells to 982. In 2015 it planned to bring onstream a further 210 wells primarily in the Bakken shale in the US. Its offshore production on the Gulf of Mexico principally comes from a handful of fields in which it which holds stakes –Shenzi (Hess 28%) Llano (50%) Conger (38%) Baldpate (50%) Hack Wilson (25%) and Penn State (50%).

Financial Performance

Hess' revenues have been restated due to divestiture of its business which includes sale of Angola assets and Norway business.

In 2014 the company's net revenues decreased by 53% due to the strategic decision to dispose of its retail energy marketing terminal energy trading and refining operations. Hess' net income declined by 54% due to lower revenues an increase in depreciation depletion and amortization and changes in income tax requirements. The company's cash inflow decreased by 8% in 2014 primarily due to lower net income and changes in working capital.

Strategy

The company has exited its retail energy marketing and energy trading businesses in order to focus on a higher growth lower-risk portfolio of exploration and production assets primarily in the US. It plans to be a more focused pure-play exploration and production company with an average annual production growth of 5% to 8% through 2017 from its 2012 pro forma production of 289000 barrels of oil equivalent per day.In 2015 the company forecast production to average between 350000 and 360000 barrels of oil equivalent per day excluding Libya. In the near term this growth will be underpinned by the Bakken Tubular Bells and the Utica Shale play. Longer term growth will benefit from the North Malay Basin project in Malaysia and from Stampede both of which are currently under development. In 2014 Hess sold its retail marketing business (1260 retail gasoline stations most of which had convenience stores) to Marathon Petroleum for $2.6 billion. It also sold two joint venture investments in natural gas-fueled electric generating projects in Newark and Bayonne New Jersey. The company sold all downstream businesses except for the energy trading joint venture HETCO which was sold in February 2015 and its former refinery HOV-ENSA which will be shut down in 2015.

In 2014 the company sold of its Pangkah asset to a subsidiary of PT Saka Energi Indonesia. The Indonesian asset produced an average of 9000 barrels of oil equivalent per day for Hess in 2013.

In 2014 Hess also announced plans to divest its exploration and production assets in Thailand.

Hess' former refinery in the US Virgin Islands was operated as a joint venture with Venezuela's state oil company Petróleos de Venezuela S.A (PDVSA). However the loss-making HOVENSA refinery was shut down in 2012 and converted to an oil storage terminal. In 2013 Hess announced that it completed its exit from the refining business by closing its Port Reading New Jersey refinery.

As part of its strategy of unwinding its refining and marketing assets in 2013 Hess sold Russian subsidiary Samara-Nafta to LUKOIL for $2.05 billion. It also sold its energy marketing business to Direct Energy for a $1.2 billion.

To raise cash it also sold its 2.7% interest in in India's Azeri Chirag and Guneshli Fields and its 2.4% stake in the associated BTC pipeline to ONGC Videsh for $1 billion. It also sold its Indonesian oil and gas assets for $1.3 billion.

That year it also sold 20 liquid petroleum products terminals along the US East Coast with total storage capacity of 39 million barrels to Buckeye Partners for $850 million.

The Utica Shale in Ohio was a growth area. However in 2014 low gas prices prompted Hess agreed to sell 74000 acres of dry gas acreage in the Utica Shale for $924 million in order to focus on more lucrative oil plays.

That year it also sold its oil and gas assets in Thailand to PTT Exploration and Production for $1 billion.Asset sales in 2013 include its interest in the Natuna A Field offshore Indonesia for $656 million; its stakes in the Azeri-Chirag-Guneshli fields (3%) offshore Azerbaijan in the Caspian Sea and the associated Baku-Tbilisi-Ceyhan oil transportation pipeline company (2%) for $884 million; and its holdings in the Beryl fields and the Scottish Area Gas Evacuation System in the UK North Sea for $442 million.

HISTORY

In 1919 British oil entrepreneur Lord Cowdray formed Amerada Corporation to explore for oil in North America. Cowdray soon hired geophysicist Everette DeGolyer a pioneer in oil geology research. DeGolyer's systematic methods helped Amerada not only find oil deposits faster but also pick up fields missed by competitors. DeGolyer became president of Amerada in 1929 but left in 1932 to work independently.

After WWII Amerada began exploring overseas and during the 1950s entered pipelining and refining. It continued its overseas exploration through Oasis a consortium formed in 1964 with Marathon Shell and Continental to explore in Libya.

Leon Hess began to buy stock in Amerada in 1966. The son of immigrants he had entered the oil business during the Depression selling "resid" — thick refining leftovers that refineries discarded — from a 1929 Dodge truck in New Jersey. He bought the resid cheap and sold it as heating fuel to hotels. Hess also speculated buying oil at low prices in the summer and selling it for a profit in the winter. He later bought more trucks a transportation network refineries and gas stations and went into oil exploration. Expansion pushed up debt so in 1962 Leon's company went public as Hess Oil and Chemical after merging with Cletrac Corporation.

Hess acquired Amerada in 1969 after an ownership battle with Phillips Petroleum. During the Arab oil embargo of the 1970s Amerada Hess began drilling on Alaska's North Slope. Oilman T. Boone Pickens bought up a chunk of Amerada Hess stock during the 1980s spurring takeover rumors. They proved premature.

Amerada Hess completed a pipeline in 1993 to carry natural gas from the North Sea to the UK. In 1995 Leon Hess stepped down as CEO (he died in 1999) and his son John took the position. Amerada Hess sold its 81% interest in the Northstar oil field in Alaska to BP and the next year Petro-Canada bought the company's Canadian operations. In 1996 the company acquired a 25% stake (sold in 2002) in UK-based Premier Oil.

The company teamed with Dixons Stores Group in 1997 to market gas in the UK. It also purchased 66 Pick Wick convenience store/service stations.

In 1998 Amerada Hess signed production-sharing contracts with a Malaysian oil firm as part of its strategy to move into Southeast Asia and began to sell natural gas to retail customers in the UK.

To offset losses brought on by depressed oil prices Amerada Hess sold assets worth more than $300 million in 1999 including its southeastern pipeline network gas stations in Georgia and South Carolina and Gulf Coast terminals. It also moved into Latin America acquiring stakes in fields in offshore Brazil.

In 2000 Amerada Hess acquired Statoil Energy Services which markets natural gas and electricity to industrial and commercial customers in the northeastern US. It also announced its intention to buy LASMO a UK-based exploration and production company before Italy's Eni topped the Amerada Hess offer.

Undeterred in 2001 the company bought Dallas-based exploration and production company Triton Energy for $2.7 billion in cash and $500 million in assumed debt. Amerada Hess also acquired the Gulf of Mexico assets of LLOG Exploration Company for $750 million. That year however stiff competition prompted Amerada Hess to put its UK gas and electricity supply business on the auction block. The unit was sold to TXU (now Energy Future Holdings) in 2002.

In 2003 Amerada Hess sold 26 oil and gas fields in the Gulf of Mexico to Anadarko Petroleum. Am-

erada Hess was granted permission by the Equatorial Guinea government in 2004 to develop 29 new wells in that country. That year Amerada Hess acquired a 65% stake in Trabant Holdings International a Russia-based production and exploration company.

The company re-entered its former oil and gas production operations in the Waha concessions in Libya in 2006. Also that year it changed its name to Hess Corporation.

Looking to grow its position in the lucrative Bakken oil shale play in North Dakota in 2010 the company acquired American Oil and Gas in a $450 million stock deal that added 85000 net acres to Hess' holdings. It also bought 167000 acres in the Bakken play from TRZ Energy LLC for $1 billion.

In late 2008 Hess expanded its electricity marketing business in its core US retail market acquiring power assets in the northeastern US from RRI Energy (now GenOn Energy).

EXECUTIVES

CEO, John B. Hess, age 61, $1,500,000 total compensation

SVP and CFO, John P. Rielly, age 52, $775,000 total compensation

COO; President Exploration and Production, Gregory P. (Greg) Hill, age 53, $1,100,000 total compensation

SVP Onshore, Michael R. Turner, age 55, $575,000 total compensation

SVP Services and CIO, Zhanna Golodryga

SVP Offshore, Brian D. Truelove, age 56

SVP Global Drilling Completions and Development, Richard Lynch

SVP Exploration, Barbara Lowery-Yilmaz, age 58

Vice President, Paul Fejer

Vice President Commercial Development, Deborah (Deb) Loeblein

Executive Vice President, David Chaimengyew

Vice President and General Counsel, Toni Hennike

Vice President Sales and Marketing, Brandon Herda

Vice President EandP Planning and Strategy, Rob Fast

Vice President Global Supply Chain, Dennis Creech

Vice President Secretary And Deputy General Coun, George Barry

Vice President Investor Relations And Corporate Communications, Ryan McCready

Vice President Controller, Dan Devine

Vice President Natural Gas Sales, Todd Porter

Senior Vice President Finance And Corporate Development, John Scelfo John (Jack) Scelfo

Senior Vice President Administration, Doris Moore

Executive Assistant Vice President Global Supply Chain, Robin T Hensley

Vice President of Sales and Marketing, Patrick A (Paddy) Dunn

Vice President Production Asia Pacific, Brock Hajdik

Vice President Crude Oil Supply And Logistics, Chris Allen

Vice President Refining And Marketing Shared Servi, William Hanna

Vice President Accounting, Gilbert Depaul

Vice President Exploration, Bob Spinieo

Vice President Investor Relations, Jay Wilson

Vice President Information Technology, Carl Gerard

Vice President, Toomey Joseph

Vice President, Stuart Lake

Vice President Human Resources Operations, Helena Deal

Executive Vice President Exploration And Productio, Eloise Castillo

Vice President Information Technology and Knowledge Management, Marfiza Muhammad

Vice President Retail Field Operations, David Klavsons

Senior Vice President Development And Technical Su, Janice Flaherty

Vice President Of Environmental Health, Mary Mata

Vice President Specialist Information Security Engineer, Hamish Brown

Vice President Information Technology, Jeffrey Sauber

Senior Vice President, Howard Paver

Senior Vice President Operations and Marketing, Gillian Bond

Vice President International Exploration, Grant Gilchrist

Vice President, Michael Gregg

Vice President Mobile Communications, Bambang Prasodjo

Senior Vice President Operations And Marketing, Joseph Serafino

Vice President It, Damon Bastin

Executive Vice President President Exploration Production, Greg Hill

Vice President Global Government Affairs And Public Policy, Drew Maloney

Vice President Controller, Daniel (Dan) Devine

Vice President Marketing Asphalt and Specialty, Michael (Mel) Lambraia

Chairman, Mark R. Williams, age 63

Assistant Treasurer, Eric S Fishman

Sec Treas, Ben Davis

Assistant Secretary, Randy Pharr

Auditors: Ernst & Young LLP

LOCATIONS

HQ: Hess Corp
1185 Avenue of the Americas, New York, NY 10036
Phone: 212 997-8500
Web: www.hess.com

2014 Sales

	% of total
US	58
Europe	15
Africa	19
Asia & other regions	8
Total	**100**

PRODUCTS/OPERATIONS

2014 Sales

	% of total
Crude oil & natural gas liquids	88
Natural gas	12
Other operating revenues	-
Total	**100**

COMPETITORS

Abraxas Petroleum	Exxon Mobil
BP	Gastar Exploration
CMA CGM	Koch Industries Inc.
Chevron	Marathon Oil
ConocoPhillips	Norsk Hydro ASA
Continental Energy	Occidental Petroleum
Desire Petroleum	PEMEX
Devon Energy	PETROBRAS
Dominion Resources	Petrleos de
Double Eagle Petroleum	Venezuela
ERHC	Pioneer Oil and Gas
Encana Oil & Gas (USA)	Royal Dutch Shell
Inc.	Serica Energy
Eni	TOTAL

HISTORICAL FINANCIALS

Company Type: Public

Income Statement

FYE: December 31

	REVENUE ($ mil.)	NET INCOME ($ mil.)	NET PROFIT MARGIN	EMPLOYEES
12/14	11,439	2,317	20.3%	3,045
12/13	24,421	5,052	20.7%	12,225
12/12	38,373	2,025	5.3%	14,775
12/11	37,871	1,703	4.5%	14,350
12/10	34,613	2,125	6.1%	13,800
Annual Growth	**(24.2%)**	**2.2%**	**—**	**(31.5%)**

2014 Year-End Financials

Debt ratio: 15.52%	No. of shares (mil.): 285
Return on equity: 9.88%	Dividends
Cash ($ mil.): 2,444	Yield: 1.3%
Current ratio: 1.38	Payout: 7.5%
Long-term debt ($ mil.): 5,919	Market value ($ mil.): 21,100

	STOCK PRICE ($) FY Close	P/E High/Low		PER SHARE ($)		
				Earnings	Dividends	Book Value
12/14	73.82	13	9	7.53	1.00	77.68
12/13	83.00	6	4	14.82	0.70	75.99
12/12	52.96	11	7	5.95	0.40	61.75
12/11	56.80	17	10	5.01	0.40	54.46
12/10	76.54	12	8	6.47	0.40	49.42
Annual Growth	**(0.9%)**	—	—	**3.9%**	**25.7%**	**12.0%**

Hewlett Packard Enterprise Co

Hewlett-Packard is slimming down to flex its muscle in big data cloud computing and security. HP provides one of the tech world's most comprehensive portfolios of hardware software and services. It is the world's second-largest provider of PCs (Lenovo is #1); other products include servers storage devices printers and networking equipment. The company's services unit offers IT and business process outsourcing application development consulting systems integration and other technology services. HP generates software sales through enterprise IT management big data and security applications. The 75-year-old company which serves customers worldwide in 2014 announced plans to split into two companies taking its restructuring to the ultimate level.

HISTORY

Encouraged by Stanford professor Frederick Terman (considered the founder of Silicon Valley) in 1938 engineers Bill Hewlett and David Packard started Hewlett-Packard (HP) in a garage in Palo Alto California with $538. Hewlett was the idea man while Packard served as manager; the two were so low-key that the company's first official meeting ended with no decision on exactly what to manufacture. Finding good people took priority over finding something to sell. The first product ended up being an audio oscillator. Walt Disney Studios one of HP's first customers bought eight to use in the making of Fantasia.

Demand for HP's electronic testing equipment during WWII spurred sales growth from $34000 in 1940 to nearly $1 million just three years later. HP went public in 1957. The company expanded

beyond the US during 1959 establishing a marketing organization in Switzerland and a manufacturing plant in West Germany. HP entered the medical field in 1961 by acquiring Sanborn and the analytical instrumentation business in 1965 with the purchase of F&M Scientific. In 1969 Packard left the company to serve as deputy defense secretary under President Nixon for two years.

The company pioneered personal computing with the world's first handheld scientific calculator in 1972. Under the leadership of John Young the founders' chosen successor (named CEO in 1978) HP introduced its first PCs the first desktop mainframe and the LaserJet printer. Its initial PCs were known for their rugged build tailored for factory operations. They were also more expensive than rival versions and consequently didn't enjoy strong sales.

By 1986 a five-year $250 million R&D project — the company's largest at the time —produced a family of HP computers based on the reduced instruction set computing (RISC) architecture. Hewlett retired in 1987 (he died in 2001); sons of both Hewlett and Packard were named that year to the company's board of directors. HP became a leader in workstations with the 1989 purchase of market pioneer Apollo Computer despite technology delays with the merger that resulted in the loss of nearly $750 million in new business.

HP acquired Texas Instruments' line of UNIX-based computers in 1992 and committed to product cost-cutting. Lewis Platt an EVP since 1987 was named president and CEO that year. Packard retired in 1993 (he died in 1996). HP combined its varied computer operations in 1995. Continuing expansion through acquisition HP bought electronic commerce firm VeriFone in 1997.

Two years later HP formed Agilent Technologies for its test and measurement and other non-computer operations and spun off 15% of the company to the public. (HP distributed to its shareholders its remaining 85% in 2000). Also in 1999 Platt retired and HP became one of the first major US corporations to be headed by a woman when it appointed Lucent executive Carly Fiorina president and CEO. She was named chairman the following year.

The company acquired application server specialist Bluestone Software in 2001; the acquisition helped form HP's Netaction operations. Later that year the company sold its VeriFone division to high-tech acquisition specialist Gores Technology Group (now Gores Group). Soon after HP agreed to pay $400 million to Pitney Bowes to settle a 1995 patent infringement case related to printer technology.

After an unsuccessful bid for the IT services unit of equipment leasing company Comdisco HP acquired StorageApps for $350 million in stock. HP said in 2002 that it was cutting about 6000 jobs. Soon after it acquired network performance software maker Trinagy.

Next came the announcement of a blockbuster deal: HP agreed to buy rival Compaq Computer in a stock transaction initially valued at about $25 billion. The highly contentious deal eventually met with shareholder approval in 2002 after months of heated volleys between merger advocates and dissenters. At the time of closing the deal was valued at approximately $19 billion. Integration efforts included a workforce reduction of roughly 10% as the company eliminated redundant product groups.

Fiorina soon had to address the clash of disparate corporate cultures and subsequent morale problems without Michael Capellas; the former Compaq CEO who initially served as president under Fiorina and helped champion the deal left HP in 2002 to become CEO of troubled telecom giant WorldCom (later renamed MCI and acquired by Verizon).

While managing the challenge of merging operations and maintaining customer focus HP continued to make acquisitions. It bought Consera Software and Novadigm in 2004 and shortly after it purchased TruLogica.

Fiorina's differences with HP's board over strategic direction finally came to a head in 2005 and she stepped down as chairman and CEO. HP's CFO Robert Wayman was named interim CEO and director Patricia Dunn took over as nonexecutive chairman. Mark Hurd the former CEO of NCR was named to lead HP that year. (Hurd resigned in August 2010 and was replaced by former SAP CEO L © Apotheker).

HP's leadership experienced another shakeup the following year this time prompted by negative attention related to tactics used in an investigation of boardroom leaks. The company's board came under fire after it was revealed that third-party investigators employed by HP impersonated board members and journalists to obtain their phone records (a practice known as "pretexting"). Dunn was asked to resign from the board in 2006 and Hurd replaced her as chairman. HP settled a related dispute with the California attorney general later that year agreeing to pay $14.5 million. ($13.5 million of the settlement was earmarked to create a Privacy and Piracy Fund to assist state prosecutors).

In 2007 HP announced a different business model for its camera business opting to outsource the design licensing and distribution of HP-branded devices to an OEM. HP gave its Business Technology Optimization (BTO) software portfolio a boost when it purchased Opsware a developer of data center automation software for approximately $1.6 billion in 2007.

In 2010 HP made an acquisition to complement its PC group buying smartphone maker and PDA pioneer Palm for about $1.2 billion. Palm the creator of the iconic Palm Pilot PDA had struggled to keep up with other vendors (most notably Apple HTC and BlackBerry) in the burgeoning smartphone market. HP made the purchase in an attempt to carve a niche for itself in the wireless market building a line of smartphones around Palm's nascent webOS mobile software platform. In addition the company threw its hat into the tablet computing ring with a tablet PC (TouchPad) also featuring webOS that targeted Apple's iPad and devices from other manufacturers. HP killed the short-lived phone and tablet lines the next year.

HP's software purchases in 2010 included Fortify Software a specialist in applications for analyzing source code to detect potential security risks. It also paid $1.5 billion that year for security software maker ArcSight a developer of applications used to track and monitor data flow throughout an organization in order to prevent network hacking theft and internal fraud. The fact that its products are used to guard networks and data centers made ArcSight an attractive target for HP as it expands its reach past the desktop PC.

EXECUTIVES

EVP and General Manager Enterprise Group, David A. (Dave) Donatelli, age 48
SVP and General Manager Palm Global Business Unit, Jonathan J. (Jon) Rubinstein, age 56
Interim Chairman, Ralph V. Whitworth, age 58
President and CEO, Margaret C. (Meg) Whitman, age 57
EVP HP Software, George Kadifa, age 54
VP Experience Marketing Personal Systems Group, Carlos O. Montalvo, age 56
EVP and General Manager HP Enterprise Group, Bill Veghte

EVP and Chief Customer Experience Officer, Martin (Marty) Homlish
Chairman, Raymond J. (Ray) Lane, age 67
EVP Imaging and Printing Group, Vyomesh (VJ) Joshi, age 59, $743,125 total compensation
Media Relations Contact Workstations Personal Systems Group, Jim Christensen
EVP Printing and Personal Systems Group, R. Todd Bradley, age 56, $743,125 total compensation
CTO and Director of HP Labs, Martin Fink
EVP Emerging Markets, Francesco Serafini
SVP and CIO, Craig Flower
SVP and General Manager Infrastructure Technology Outsourcing HP Enterprise Services, Pete Karolczak
SVP and General Manager HP StorageWorks; President and CEO 3PAR, David C. Scott, age 51
SVP Global Information Technology, Linda M. Dillman, age 56
General Manager China, Ruey-Bin Kao
EVP and CFO, Catherine A. (Cathie) Lesjak, age 54, $589,063 total compensation
SVP and General Manager HP Enterprise Services, Thomas J. (Tom) Iannotti, age 56
SVP Growth Markets Organization, Brian Humphries
EVP and Chief Marketing and Communications Officer, Henry Gomez
VP Technology Support Enterprise Americas, Paul Tsaparis
SVP and Global CIO, Ramon F. Baez
SVP Enterprise Business; Managing Director for HP Europe the Middle East and Africa, Yves de Talhouet
SVP and Treasurer, John McMullen, age 54
EVP Technology and Operations, John Hinshaw, age 44
SVP Controller and Principal Accounting Officer, James T. (Jim) Murrin, age 52
EVP General Counsel and Secretary, Michael J. (Mike) Holston, age 50
SVP Research; Director HP Laboratories, Prith Banerjee, age 52
EVP Human Resources, Tracy Keogh, age 52
VP Worldwide Developer Relations Palm Global Business Unit, Richard Kerris
SVP Global Information Technology, Ahmed Mahmoud
VP Global Government Affairs and Deputy General Counsel, Gregg R. Melinson
Enterprise Sales Lead HP Networking Group Asia Pacific and Japan excluding China, Jeff Healey
VP Global Government Affairs, Larry Irving, age 58
Interim Chief Communications Officer, Lynn Anderson
VP; Managing Director Russia, Aleksandr Mikoyan
Director New Business Initiatives; Chief MagClouder MagCloud, Andrew Bolwell
VP Investor Relations, James (Jim) Burns
SVP Operations Personal Systems Group, Anthony (Tony) Prophet
Manager Worldwide Solution Virtualization, Robert (Bob) Meyer
President and CEO Canada, Peter Galanis, age 46
Chief Strategy Officer, Mohamad S. Ali, age 43
EVP Global Sales and Enterprise Marketing, Jan Zadak
Director Emerging Technologies ProCurve Networking; Director Advanced Technology Solutions HP Networking, Lin Nease
VP IT Infrastructure, Ken Gray
VP HP IT Operations Control, James Cook
CIO Software Division, Saum Mathur
VP HP Product Development and Engineering IT, Michael Wolfe
VP Global Telecommunications Architecture & Engineering, Tony Bolton
Senior Director IT End User Services, Terry Criscione

Director Data Center Transformation, Grant Folsom
Director Operations Automation, Mahesh Shah
Director Asset Change and Configuration Management, Tim Benson
Manager Global Portfolio Management Office, Hiram Davis
Senior Portfolio Analyst, Rosalynn Tuggle
Worldwide Marketing Lead ? Application Transformation, Paul Evans
Director and Global Manager Data Center Transformation Technology Services, Ewald Comhaire
Director Investor Relations, Beth Howe
Director Investor Relations, Catriona Fallon
VP Investor Relations, Steve Fieler
Director Investor Relations, Amar Maletira
Director Investor Relations, Charly Kevers
VP Corporate Communications, Connie Guglielmo
Director Corporate/Innovation and International PR, Christina Schneider
Director General/Breaking News, Mylene Mangalindan
Strategic Advisor MagCloud, Udi Chatow
Chief Technologist MagCloud, Andy Fitzhugh
Chief of Awesome MagCloud, Derek Powazek
Chief Designologist MagCloud, James Goode
Media Relations Contact Cross-PSG Inquiries Personal Systems Group, Marlene Somsak
Media Relations Contact General/Breaking News, Michael Thacker
VP Global Telecommunications Delivery and Service Management, David E. Flanagin
EVP and General Manager of Enterprise Services, John Visentin
Worldwide Applications Development Leader, Srinivas (Srini) Koushik
CEO Autonomy Corporation PLC, Mike Lynch
EVP Enterprise Services, Mike Nefkens
EVP and General Counsel, John F. Schultz
EVP Printing and Personal Systems, Dion Weisler
Director, Gary M. Reiner, age 58
Director, Marc L. Andreessen, age 41
Director, John H. Hammergren, age 54
Director, Rajiv L. (Raj) Gupta, age 67
Director, Sari M. Baldauf, age 57
Director, Lawrence T. (Larry) Babbio Jr., age 68
President CEO and Director, Margaret C. (Meg) Whitman, age 57
Chairman, Raymond J. (Ray) Lane, age 67
Director, Patricia F. (Pat) Russo, age 60
Director, G. Kennedy (Ken) Thompson, age 62
Director, Ann M. Livermore, age 54
Director, Shumeet Banerji, age 53
Director, Dominique Senequier, age 59
Auditors: Ernst & Young LLP

LOCATIONS

HQ: Hewlett Packard Enterprise Co
  3000 Hanover Street, Palo Alto, CA 94304
Phone: 650 857-1501

HISTORICAL FINANCIALS

Company Type: Public

Income Statement

	REVENUE ($ mil.)	NET INCOME ($ mil.)	NET PROFIT MARGIN	EMPLOYEES
10/15	52,107	2,461	4.7%	240,000
10/14	55,123	1,648	3.0%	252,000
10/13	57,371	2,051	3.6%	—
10/12	61,042	(14,761)	—	—
Annual Growth	(5.1%)	—	—	—

FYE: October 31

2015 Year-End Financials

Debt ratio: 19.43%	No. of shares (mil.): 1,742	
Return on equity: —	Dividends	
Cash ($ mil.): 9,842	Yield: —	
Current ratio: 1.41	Payout: —	
Long-term debt ($ mil.): 15,103	Market value ($ mil.): 25,650	

	STOCK PRICE ($) FY Close	P/E High/Low	PER SHARE ($) Earnings	Dividends	Book Value
10/15	14.72	13 11	1.34	0.00	19.25
10/14	0.00	— —	(0.00)	0.00	(0.00)
Annual Growth	—	— —	—	—	—

Hexion Inc

Hexion (formerly Momentive Specialty Chemicals) is the world's largest thermosetting resins (or thermosets) maker ahead of competitor Georgia-Pacific. Thermosets add a desired quality (heat resistance gloss adhesion etc.) to a number of different paints coatings and adhesives. They include an array of resins: phenolic epoxy polyester acrylic and urethane. The company also is a leading producer of adhesive and structural resins and coatings. It serves several markets including paints consumer products and automotive coatings. Hexion (which changed its name in early 2015) is a subsidiary of Momentive Performance Materials Holdings.

Geographic Reach

Hexion operates 63 production sites around the world and serves more than 5200 customers in about 100 countries. It has US-based manufacturing plants in 14 US states and 36 in Australia Brazil Canada Colombia the Czech Republic Finland France Germany Italy Korea Malaysia Netherlands New Zealand Spain Thailand the UK and Uruguay.

In 2014 the company's non-US operations accounted for 57% of its total revenues.

Operations

The company has two main operating divisions: Forest Products Resins and Epoxy Phenolic and Coating Resins. Its business segments produce a wide variety of products. The Epoxy Phenolic and Coating Resins segment is the largest accounting for more than 60% of sales. It markets its products to the auto aerospace electronics and oil and gas industries. The epoxy resins are the fundamental components of many types of materials and are used in a number of products for their adhesion strength and durability properties –including protective coatings for the industrial flooring automotive coatings and industrial flooring industries. The unit also is one of the world's largest producers of versatic acids which are additives for finished coatings pharmaceuticals and personal care products.

Its next largest unit is the Forest Products Resins segment whose forest resins are use in the lumber plywood particle board and decorative laminates markets. It also has formaldehyde applications used in herbicides fungicides fabric softeners and oil and gas production.

Sales and Marketing

Hexion's products are sold to industrial users worldwide through a direct sales force (for larger customers) and third-party distributors (that more cost-effectively serve smaller customers). In 2014 the company's top ten customers accounted for 16% of net sales. The diverse markets include forest products architectural and industrial paints packaging consumer products and automotive coatings as well as higher growth markets such as composites and electrical components. Major industry sectors served by serve Momentive Specialty Chemicals include industrial/marine construction consumer/durable goods automotive wind energy aviation electronics architectural civil engineering repair/remodeling and oil and gas field support.

Financial Performance

In 2014 Hexion's net revenues rose by 5% due primarily to an increase in demand in oil field epoxy specialty North American formaldehyde and Latin American forest products resins businesses partially offset by price decreases in certain businesses driven by unfavorable product mix and an imbalance in supply and demand which outpaced raw-material-driven price increases in certain other businesses. Sales from Epoxy Phenolic and Coating Resins higher volumes positively impacted results primarily driven by increased demand within the oil field (a result of key customer wins and new product development) and epoxy (driven by improving demand in the Asian wind energy market) businesses. Sales from higher Forest Products Resins volumes positively impacted sales driven primarily by volume increases in North American forest products resins business driven by increases in US housing construction activity as well as volume increases in Latin American forest products resins business driven by increases in the furniture housing construction and industrial markets.

In 2014 the company recorded a net loss of $148 million compared to a loss of $633 million in 2013. This improvement was due to decrease in Income tax expense primarily as a result of income from certain foreign operations and decrease in asset impairments due to the likelihood that certain assets would be disposed of before the end of their estimated useful lives. Cash from operating activities used in 2014 was 163% down on 2013 due $172 million of net non-cash expense items of which $144 million was for depreciation and amortization $46 million related to unrealized foreign currency losses and $5 million was for non-cash asset impairments. These items were partially offset by gains on the sale of certain assets of $16 million and $2 million of deferred tax benefit. Increases in inventory and accounts receivable due to sales volume increases as well as decreases in accounts payable driven by the timing of vendor payments also impacted cash used in operating activities.

Strategy

Hexion's strategy for growth includes developing and marketing new products expanding in higher growth regions shifting to high-margin specialty products and continuing to pursue key add-on acquisitions and joint ventures.

The company is investing about $66 million to expand its Forest Products business by building two new formaldehyde plants in Louisiana. The plant in Luling Louisiana will supply Monsanto by providing formaldehyde through a direct pipeline into its adjacent manufacturing facility.

In 2014 Hexion expanded its specialty chemicals capability in Rayong Thailand. As part of continued focus on productivity Hexion begun executing a new $30 million cost savings program in 2014 that will structurally enhance its manufacturing and administrative cost profile by 2016 and realize $23 million in savings in 2015.

Growing its global footprint in 2013 the company opened new curing agent manufacturing capabilities at a plant in Tianjin China. The facility expands Hexion's regional capacity to produce amine curing agents for that fast growing market.

That year the company signed a deal with Kanoria Chemicals & Industries Limited to form a formaldehyde and phenolic specialty resins joint venture in India and a joint venture to construct a phenolic specialty resins manufacturing facility in China. In 2013 Hexion (as Momentive Specialty Chemicals) and MicroBlend based in Gilbert Arizona agreed to form a joint venture company located in Cali Colombia to support MicroBlend's revolutionary “Automated Paint Machine System” with the necessary liquid components for making fresh paint at the point of sale in Colombian home center stores. That year the company also teamed up with the Fraunhofer Project Center for Composites Research at Western University to develop high-volume lightweight composites for the North American automotive market.

Mergers and Acquisitions

In 2013 Momentive Specialty Chemicals Pty Ltd. acquired Dynea Chemical OY's stake in the Dynea Australia's joint venture with the Laminex Group (the leading marketer and manufacturer of premium decorative surfaces in Australia and New Zealand). The new joint venture known as Momentive Specialty Chemicals Australia is 50% owned by Momentive Specialty Chemicals and 50% by Laminex. The JV provides formaldehyde and urea formaldehyde resins to Laminex as well as other products to industrial customers in Western Australia.

Company Background

In 2012 the company's joint venture with China-based Shanxi Sanwei Group began production at a VeoVa-brand vinyl ester plant that supplies Momentive's monomer products for the coatings and adhesives industry. The monomer is used to provide a variety of qualities to water-based paints wood stains and coatings as well as to adhesives and powders used in construction.

That year the company also announced that it is building a new plant in Thailand to expand its production of acrylic-based resins used in coatings adhesives and building applications in the Southeast Asia region. The plant is part of the company's strategy for global growth.

In another expansion move in 2012 Momentive Speciality Chemicals and sister company Momentive Performance Materials opened a new research and development center and business headquarters in Bangalore to serve the India Middle East and Africa markets.

Momentive Specialty Chemicals also opened a joint venture plant in 2011 with China-based UPC Technology Corporation a maker of specialty chemicals and materials to produce specialty phenolic resins. The plant in Zhenjiang in Jiangsu Province produces specialty novolac and resole phenolic resins used in refractories friction and abrasives applications.

To raise cash in early 2011 Momentive Specialty Chemicals sold its IAR business which produced naturally derived resins for a variety of applications to Japan's Harima Chemicals for about $120 million. The unit had been one of the company's Coating and Inks' segments.

That year Momentive Specialty Chemicals also sold its North American composites and coating resins business to a subsidiary of Investindustrial a European investment group specializing in chemicals resins and intermediates.

The company was created after the former Hexion merged with Momentive Performance Materials in 2010. Under the terms of the merger Momentive Performance Materials and Momentive Specialty Chemicals became subsidiaries of the newly formed Momentive Performance Materials Holdings. The capital and legal structures of both companies remain separate entities under the holding company.

EXECUTIVES

Svp Finance And Treasurer, George Knight

EVP and CFO, William H. (Bill) Carter, age 61, $776,735 total compensation

Chairman President and CEO, Craig O. Morrison, age 59, $1,102,500 total compensation

EVP; President Epoxy Phenolic and Coating Resins Division, Joseph P. (Jody) Bevilaqua, age 59, $603,460 total compensation

EVP Human Resources, Judith A. (Judy) Sonnett, age 58, $425,000 total compensation

EVP Procurement, Nathan E. Fisher, age 49

EVP and General Counsel, Douglas A. (Doug) Johns, age 57, $486,200 total compensation

EVP; President Forest Products Division, Dale N. Plante, age 57, $402,756 total compensation

EVP Business Development and Strategy, Anthony B. Greene, age 55

EVP Environmental Health and Safety, Karen Koster

Vice President Epoxy Supply Chain, Bill Hoffman

Vice President Human Resources Business Processes, Kathy Tamber

Vice President Supply Chain, Kevin Fortier

Vice President Sales Operations, Daryl Johnson

Executive Vice President Chief Marketing Officer, Marcello Boldrini

Vice President Of Human Resources, Steven Brown

Vice President, Dave Snover

Vice President Of Human Resources, David Angel

Vice President Ehs Accounts Payable, Kimberly Iverson

Auditors: PricewaterhouseCoopers LLP

LOCATIONS

HQ: Hexion Inc
    180 East Broad St., Columbus, OH 43215
Phone: 614 225-4000
Web: www.momentive.com

2014 Sales

	$ mil.	% of total
US	2,189	43
Netherlands	856	17
Canada	429	8
Germany	282	5
Other countries	1,381	27
Total	**5,137**	**100**

PRODUCTS/OPERATIONS

2014 Sales

	$ mil.	% of total
Epoxy Phenolic & Coating Resins	3,277	64
Forest Products Resins	1,860	36
Total	**5,137**	**100**

COMPETITORS

Aditya Birla Chemicals	Huntsman International
Ashland Inc.	Nan Ya Plastics
BASF SE	Reichhold
Celanese	SI Group
Dow Chemical	Thermoset Resins
Dynea	Valspar
Georgia-Pacific	Wacker Chemie

HISTORICAL FINANCIALS

Company Type: Public

Income Statement

	REVENUE ($ mil.)	NET INCOME ($ mil.)	NET PROFIT MARGIN	EMPLOYEES
12/14	5,137	(148)	—	5,200
12/13	4,890	(633)	—	5,000
12/12	4,756	324	6.8%	5,100
12/11	5,207	118	2.3%	5,300
12/10	4,818	214	4.4%	6,000
Annual Growth	1.6%	—	—	(3.5%)

FYE: December 31

2014 Year-End Financials

Debt ratio: 143.49%
Return on equity: —
Cash ($ mil.): 172
Current ratio: 1.51
Long-term debt ($ mil.): 3,735

No. of shares (mil.): 82
Dividends
    Yield: —
    Payout: —
Market value ($ mil.): —

HILL/AHERN FIRE PROTECTION LLC

LOCATIONS

HQ: HILL/AHERN FIRE PROTECTION LLC
    11045 GAGE AVE, FRANKLIN PARK, IL 601311437
Phone: 8472885100
Web: WWW.HILLAHERN.COM

HISTORICAL FINANCIALS

Company Type: Private

Income Statement

	REVENUE ($ mil.)	NET INCOME ($ mil.)	NET PROFIT MARGIN	EMPLOYEES
12/11	5,669	185	3.3%	40
12/10	2,568	80	3.1%	—
Annual Growth	120.7%	130.7%	—	—

FYE: December 31

2011 Year-End Financials

Debt ratio: ——
Return on equity: 3.30%
Cash ($ mil.): 480
Current ratio: 2.30
Long-term debt ($ mil.): —

Dividends
    Yield: —
    Payout: —
Market value ($ mil.): —

Hilton Worldwide Holdings Inc

If you need a bed for the night Hilton has a few hundred thousand of them. The company is one of the world's largest hoteliers with a lodging empire that includes more than 4300 hotels and resorts in some 95 countries operating under such names as Doubletree Embassy Suites and Hampton as well as its flagship Hilton brand. Many of its hotels serve the mid-market segment though its Hilton and Conrad hotels offer full-service upscale lodging. In addition its Homewood Suites chain offers extended-stay services. The company franchises many of its hotels; it owns the Waldorf-Astoria brand and the New York Hilton. Hilton became a public company again in 2013.

IPO

After six years of being groomed by Blackstone for a return to the public market Hilton went public again in December 2013 and raised $2.35 billion. The company used the proceeds to pay down debt.

Geographic Reach

With a name like Hilton Worldwide the company has hotels in about 95 countries but it generates almost 75% of sales in the US. Through new man-

agement franchise and/or development contracts in recent years Hilton has added properties to its portfolio in Azerbaijan Bangladesh Brazil China Croatia Egypt Germany India Kazakhstan Mexico Nambia the Netherlands New Zealand Russia Saudi Arabia South Africa Turkey the UAE the UK the US and Vietnam.

Operations

With its extensive portfolio of brands Hilton seeks to serve multiple segments within the lodging sector. The company's largest chains Hampton Inn and Hampton Inn & Suites include about 2000 locations and target mid-market travelers with moderately priced rooms and limited amenities. Nearly all its Hampton hotels are operated by franchisees or by the company under management contracts with third-party owners.

At the other end of the scale the company's Conrad chain offers luxury services and distinctive locations while its Waldorf-Astoria Collection is a prestigious collection of hotels inspired by the New York landmark. The company's Hilton Grand Vacations subsidiary operates about 50 time-share vacation resorts with a concentration located in Florida.

Sales and Marketing

Hilton relies on traditional advertising and promotions along with a variety of direct marketing techniques such as email and postal mailings to drum up business. A fair amount of the company's hotel rooms get booked through internet travel intermediaries. Hilton pays commissions and transaction fees for sales of rooms through such services. The company also has a robust customer loyalty program it uses to try to generate return business.

Financial Performance

Hilton has maintained steady revenue growth for the past five years. In fiscal 2014 revenue increased by 8% compared to fiscal 2013 to $10.5 billion. The company experienced increased revenue across all segments and regions along with occupancy and rate increases in all regions except the Middle East and Africa.

The company's net income has been growing consistently over the past five fiscal years. Its net income was $673 million in fiscal 2014 an increase of $258 million or 62% compared to the prior fiscal period. The increased net income was the result of increased total revenue combined with decreased operating expenses.

Hilton's cash flow decreased by $735 million during fiscal 2014 but remained at a comfortable $1.36 billion.

Strategy

Hilton has been focused on expansion. Its current development pipeline includes a total of 1351 hotels with approximately 230000 rooms which are under construction or approved for development. With a focus on its global business more than half of the new hotels are located outside the US.

In 2015 Hilton sold its Waldorf Astoria New York hotel for $1.95 billion. The company used the proceeds from the sale to acquire five other hotel properties.

HISTORY

Conrad Hilton got his start in hotel management by renting out rooms in his family's New Mexico home. He served as a state legislator and started a bank before leaving for Texas in 1919 hoping to make his fortune in banking. Hilton was unable to shoulder the cost of purchasing a bank however but recognized a high demand for hotel rooms and made a quick change in strategy buying his first hotel in Cisco Texas. Over the next decade he bought seven more Texas hotels.

Hilton lost several properties during the Depression but began rebuilding his empire soon thereafter through the purchase of hotels in California (1938) New Mexico (1939) and Mexico (1942). He even married starlet Zsa Zsa Gabor in 1942 (they later divorced of course). Hilton Hotels Corporation was formed in 1946 and went public. The company bought New York's Waldorf-Astoria in 1949 (a hotel Hilton called "the greatest of them all") and opened its first European hotel in Madrid in 1953. Hilton paid $111 million for the 10-hotel Statler chain the following year.

Hilton took his company out of the overseas hotel business in 1964 by spinning off Hilton International and began franchising the following year to capitalize on the well-known Hilton name. Barron Hilton Conrad's son was appointed president in 1966 (he became chairman upon Conrad Hilton's death in 1979). Hilton bought two Las Vegas hotels (the Las Vegas Hilton and the Flamingo Hilton) in 1970 and launched its gaming division. The company returned to the international hotel business with Conrad International Hotels in 1982 and opened its first suite-only Hilton Suites hotel in 1989.

In the 1990s Hilton expanded its gaming operations buying Bally's Casino Resort in Reno in 1992 and launching its first riverboat casino the Hilton Queen of New Orleans in 1994. Two years later it acquired all of Bally Entertainment making it the largest gaming company in the world. Also that year Stephen Bollenbach the former Walt Disney CFO who had negotiated the $19 billion acquisition of Capital Cities/ABC was named CEO — becoming the first nonfamily-member to run the company.

Hilton formed an alliance with Ladbroke Group in 1997 (later Hilton Group owner of Hilton International and the rights to the Hilton name outside the US) to promote the Hilton brand worldwide. Hilton also put in a bid that year to acquire ITT owner of Sheraton hotels and Caesars World but was thwarted when ITT accepted a higher offer from Starwood Hotels & Resorts. Hilton was foiled once again in 1998 when a deal with casino operator Circus Circus (now part of MGM Resorts International) that would have separated Hilton's hotel and casino operations fell through. With a downturn in the gambling industry translating into sluggish results in Hilton's gaming segment the company spun off its gaming interests as Park Place Entertainment later that year.

In 1999 Hilton made a massive acquisition with the $3.7 billion purchase of Promus Hotel Corp. The following year Hilton sold its Flamingo Casino-Kansas City a remaining casino property left over from the Park Place spinoff to Isle of Capri Casinos for $33.5 million. In 2001 it sold 56 of its leases and management contracts to RFS Hotel Investors for about $60 million.

Hilton continued selling properties in 2002 with the sales of two Doubletree hotels and all 41 Red Lion locations to WestCoast Hospitality (now Red Lion Hotels) for about $51 million. It also sold its Harrison Conference Center portfolio (14 conference centers and university hotels) to ARAMARK for $55 million. At the end of that same year the company formed a $400 million venture with CNL Hospitality (now CNL Hotels & Resorts) to buy and refurbish hotel properties.

Following an extended downturn in the hospitality business brought on by recession and post-9/11 fears about terrorism Hilton began to invest in refurbishments for many of its properties and added about 150 locations in 2004.

Hilton Hotels acquired Hilton International from Hilton Group (now Ladbrokes) for about $5.7 billion in 2006. The deal re-unified the Hilton brand globally and added about 400 new locations to the company's portfolio. The year after the acquisition

Hilton Hotels sold its Scandic Hotels business to private equity firm EQT for $1.1 billion and later sold LivingWell Health Clubs to Bannatyne Fitness; both brands had been included in the Hilton International transaction.

Also in 2007 the company was taken private by The Blackstone Group through a $26 billion buyout. The acquisition included about $6 billion in debt. Christopher Nassetta later replaced Bollenbach as CEO. Hilton Hotels was renamed Hilton Worldwide in 2009. Through a financial restructuring in 2010 Hilton was able to cut about $4 billion of its $20 billion debt. In early 2011 its newest brand Home2 Suites by Hilton opened its first property.

EXECUTIVES

EVP and President Development Architecture and Construction, Ian R. Carter, age 53, $698,077 total compensation

President CEO and Director, Christopher J. (Chris) Nassetta, age 53, $1,142,201 total compensation

EVP and Chief Human Resources Officer, Matthew W. (Matt) Schuyler, age 49

SVP Hilton Brand Management, Jeffrey A. (Jeff) Diskin, age 53

EVP Global Sales and President Hilton Grand Vacations, Mark D. Wang, age 58, $623,654 total compensation

EVP & General Counsel, Kristin A. Campbell, age 53, $581,994 total compensation

EVP Global Brands, James E. (Jim) Holthouser, age 56

EVP and CFO, Kevin J. Jacobs, age 42, $663,820 total compensation

EVP and President Americas, Joe Berger

EVP and President Asia Pacific, Martin Rinck

President Europe Middle East & Africa, Simon Vincent

EVP and Chief Commercial Officer, Chris Silcock

Chairman, Jonathan D. Gray, age 45

Auditors: Ernst & Young LLP

LOCATIONS

HQ: Hilton Worldwide Holdings Inc
7930 Jones Branch Drive, Suite 1100, McLean, VA 22102
Phone: 703 883-1000
Web: www.hiltonworldwide.com

PRODUCTS/OPERATIONS

Selected Brands
Conrad Hot
Doubletree
Embassy Suites Hotels
Hampton Inn
Hampton In
Hilton
Hilton Garden Inn
Hilton Grand Vacations Club
Homewood Suites by Hilton

Selected Hotels
Chicago's Palmer House Hilton
Hilton Barcelona
Hilton Bora Bora Nui Resort & Spa
The Hilton Hawaiian Village on Waikiki Beach
Hilton Manchester Deansgate
Hilton Orlando
Hilton San Francisco on Union Square
Hilton Sedona
The New York Hilton
The Waldorf Astoria

COMPETITORS

Accor	Interstate Hotels
Best Western	Loews
Carlson Hotels	Marriott
Choice Hotels	Omni Hotels

FRHI Hotels and Resorts	Red Lion Hotels
Four Seasons Hotels	Ritz-Carlton
Hyatt	Starwood Hotels & Resorts
InterContinental Hotels	Wyndham Worldwide

HISTORICAL FINANCIALS
Company Type: Public

Income Statement
FYE: December 31

	REVENUE ($ mil.)	NET INCOME ($ mil.)	NET PROFIT MARGIN	EMPLOYEES
12/14	10,502	673	6.4%	157,000
12/13	9,735	415	4.3%	152,000
12/12	9,276	352	3.8%	151,000
12/11	8,783	253	2.9%	—
12/10	8,068	128	1.6%	—
Annual Growth	6.8%	51.4%	—	—

2014 Year-End Financials

Debt ratio: 44.75%
Return on equity: 14.77%
Cash ($ mil.): 566
Current ratio: 1.11
Long-term debt ($ mil.): 11,555

No. of shares (mil.): 984
Dividends
  Yield: —
  Payout: —
Market value ($ mil.): 25,689

	STOCK PRICE ($) FY Close	P/E High/Low	PER SHARE ($) Earnings	Dividends	Book Value
12/14	26.09	39 31	0.68	0.00	4.83
12/13	22.25	50 48	0.45	0.00	4.43
Annual Growth	4.1%	— —	10.9%	—	2.2%

HollyFrontier Corp.

HollyFrontier refines crude oil to produce gasoline diesel and jet fuel and sells it in erstwhile American frontier territories: the Southwest northern Mexico Kansas and the Rockies. Its major assets are a 52000 barrels-per-day refinery in Wyoming; the El Dorado Kansas refinery 135000 barrels; a Utah refinery 31000 barrels; a Tulsa refinery 125000 barrels and subsidiary Navajo Refining (New Mexico) which has a capacity of 100000 barrels a day. The company also has a 39% stake in Holly Energy Partners which operates crude oil and petroleum product pipelines. It also has owns 50% of Sabine Biofuels II LLC.

Geographic Reach

HollyFrontier's refinery operations (Cheyenne Wyoming; El Dorado Kansas; Navajo New Mexico; Tulsa Oklahoma; and Woods Cross Utah) serve customers in the US Mid-Continent Rocky Mountain and Southwest regions.

Operations

The independent petroleum refiner produces high-value products such as gasoline diesel fuel jet fuel specialty lubricant products and specialty and modified asphalt. It is operates in two reportable segments Refining and HEP. The Refining segment (98% of the company's revenues in 2014). It includes the operations of their El Dorado Tulsa Navajo Cheyenne and Woods Cross Refineries and NK Asphalt.

The company's five refineries have a total crude capacity of 443000 barrels per stream day. In 2014 gasoline diesel fuel jet fuel and specialty lubricants accounted for 50% 34% 4% and 2% respectively of the company's total refinery sales volumes. HollyFrontier also owns and operates NK Asphalt

Partners which manufactures and markets asphalt products from various terminals in Arizona and New Mexico.

The HEP segment generates revenues by charging tariffs for transporting petroleum products and crude oil through its pipelines.

Sales and Marketing

The company's principal customers for gasoline include other refiners convenience store chains independent marketers and retailers. Diesel fuel is sold to other refiners truck stop chains wholesalers and railroads. Jet fuel is sold for commercial airline use. Specialty lubricant products are sold in both commercial and specialty markets. LPG's are sold to LPG wholesalers and LPG retailers. They produce and purchase asphalt products that are sold to governmental entities paving contractors or manufacturers. Asphalt is also blended into fuel oil and is either sold locally or is shipped to the Gulf Coast.For 2014 gasoline diesel fuel jet fuel and specialty lubricants (excluding volumes purchased for resale) represented 47% 33% 7% and 4% respectively of HollyFrontier's Mid-Continent sales volumes. Sales to Shell Oil represented 22% of the El Dorado Refinery's total sales and 11% of HollyFrontier's sales. Sinclair Oil accounted for 30% of the Tulsa Refineries' sales and 10% of HollyFrontier's total revenues.

The primary markets for the El Dorado Refinery's refined products are Colorado and the Plains States. The Woods Cross Refinery's primary market is Utah. The Cheyenne Refinery primarily markets its products in eastern Colorado including metropolitan Denver eastern Wyoming and western Nebraska. It also sells a significant portion of its diesel directly from the truck rack at the refinery eliminating transportation costs.

Asphalt products are marketed in Arizona New Mexico Oklahoma Kansas Missouri Texas and northern Mexico. Products are shipped via third-party trucking companies to commercial customers that provide asphalt based materials for commercial and government projects.

Financial Performance

In 2014 net revenues decrease by 2% due to decrease in year-over-year sales prices partially offset by higher refined product sales volumes.HollyFrontier's 2014 net income decreased by 62% due to a lower cost or market inventory valuation adjustment attributable to a lower crude oil and refined products prices. An increase in depreciation and amortization expenses attributable to capitalized improvement projects and a loss on early extinguishment of debt also contributed to the drop in net income.In 2014 the company's cash from operating activities decreased by 13%.

Strategy

In 2014 the company announced plans to enter into the Mid-continent asphalt business by expanding its current Southwest asphalt production and marketing business into the Mid-continent asphalt paving markets.

That year HollyFrontier invested $485 million towards projects that included the Woods Cross refinery expansion ongoing work at the El Dorado refinery the Tulsa refinery modernization and work on Holly Energy Partners' crude gathering system expansion.An additional component of its growth strategy is to selectively acquire complementary assets for their refining operations in order to increase earnings and cash flow.

Building up its infrastructure to create greater efficiencies in 2013 HollyFrontier and Holly Energy Partners agreed to build a rail facility to enable crude oil loading and unloading near HollyFrontier's Artesia and/or Lovington New Mexico refining facilities. The rail project which will be connected to Holly Energy's crude oil pipeline transportation system in southeastern New Mexico will have a capacity of up to 70000 barrels per

day and will enable access to a variety of crude oil types.

Company Background

To expand market share in 2011 the company acquired regional rival Frontier Oil and Holly changed its corporate name to HollyFrontier.

The all-stock deal created an enterprise valued at $7 billion and added Frontier's Kansas and Wyoming refineries to the company's portfolio. The acquisition which boosted HollyFrontier's refining capacity to 443000 barrels a day is expected to create cost savings of at least $30 million per year.

The purchase was part of a multi-year strategy of expanding refinery capacity through selective acquisitions of complementary assets. (Earlier the company bought Sunoco's 85000-barrels-per-day Tulsa refinery. Building the largest refinery complex in the Midcontinent the company also acquired Sinclair Oil's 75000-barrels-per-day Tulsa refinery for $128.5 million).

BlackRock Inc. TCTC Holdings LLC and FMR LLC together own about 21% of HollyFrontier.

HISTORY

HollyFrontier was founded in 1947 as General Appliance Corp. to process other companies' crude oil; the current name was adopted in 1952. As Holly the company grew with the number of gas-guzzling cars in the 1950s and 1960s and in the 1970s it developed its Navajo refinery in New Mexico. In 1981 Holly began producing higher-grade gasoline and started an asphalt company at Navajo.

In 1984 Holly became a partner in Montana Refining and later bought the entire business. It upgraded the Navajo refinery in the early 1990s to meet the demand for unleaded gasoline. In 1995 Amoco Mapco and Holly formed a joint venture the 265-mile Rio Grande Pipeline (completed in 1997) to transport natural gas liquids to Mexico.

Also in 1997 FINA and Holly allied to expand and use Holly's pipelines in the southwestern US. A proposed merger with another southwestern refiner Giant Industries died in 1998 because of federal antitrust concerns and a billion-dollar lawsuit filed against Holly by Longhorn Partners Pipeline. Court papers revealed in 2000 that Holly had paid $4 million to fight Longhorn's request for a permit to transport gasoline in its Houston-to-El Paso pipeline. The permit if approved would compete with Holly's own interests in western Texas.

Later in 2000 Holly cut its workforce by about 10% mostly at Navajo Refining. The next year Navajo Refining secured a $122 million contract to provide JP-8 jet fuel to the Defense Department.

In a move to expand its production capacity in 2003 Holly acquired ConocoPhillips' Woods Cross refinery and related assets for $25 million. Holly agreed to be acquired by Frontier Oil for about $450 million that year but the companies terminated the agreement and litigation between the parties resulted.

In 2004 the company spun off its Navajo refinery-related refined petroleum pipeline and other distribution assets as Holly Energy Partners L.P.; it retains a 45% interest in the company.

In 2005 the Delaware Chancery Court ruled that Frontier Oil had not proved that Holly had repudiated the merger agreement and awarded Frontier Oil only $1 in damages. Also that year Holly acquired the remaining 51% of NK Asphalt Producers that it did not already own. The company sold its intermediate feedstock pipelines connecting two refining facilities in Lovington and Artesia New Mexico to Holly Energy Partners for $81.5 million.

To free up cash in 2008 it sold 136 miles of crude oil trunk lines and some tankage assets to Holly Energy Partners for $180 million.

To expand market share in 2011 the company acquired regional rival Frontier Oil and Holly changed its corporate name to HollyFrontier.

Responding to increased demand in 2012 HollyFrontier announced planned to expand the capacity of its Woods Cross Utah refinery from 31000 barrel per day to 45000 barrel per day by the end of 2014.

EXECUTIVES

Chairman HollyFrontier and President and CEO Holly Energy Partners, Michael C. Jennings, $1,060,000 total compensation

Vice President Sales and Marketing and Product Supply Holly Refining and Sales and Marketing, Gregory White

Vice President Corporate EHandS Holly Corporation, David (Dave) Jelmini

SVP Refining Operations, James M. Stump, $468,577 total compensation

EVP and CFO, Douglas S. Aron, $560,000 total compensation

President CEO and Director, George J. Damiris, $539,923 total compensation

SVP General Counsel and Secretary, Denise C. McWatters, age 55, $400,000 total compensation

VP Information Technology, Nellson D. Burns

Vice President Investor Relations, Julia Heidenreich

Assistant Vice President, Margaret (Peg) Schieffer

Senior Vice President General Counsel And Director, John (Jack) Glancy

Vice President, Scott Surplus

Vice President Business Development, Mark Plake

Vice President Engineering and Process Development Holly Refining and Marketing, Janusz Siwek

Vice President Of Information Technology, Ryan Kiernan

Vice President Accounting, Kathryn Walker

Vice President Investor Relations, Marcus Hickerson

Vice President Economics And Planning, Kent Bradbury

Vice President And Project Manager, Conrad Jenson

Vice President And Controller, John W (Jack) Gann

Vice President Acquisitions And Corporate Development, Paige Kester

Vice President, D G Blair

Vice President Environmental Affairs, Philip L Youngblood

Treasurer, Stephen (Steve) Wise

Auditors: Ernst & Young LLP

LOCATIONS

HQ: HollyFrontier Corp.
2828 North Harwood, Suite 1300, Dallas, TX 75201-1507
Phone: 214 871-3555
Web: www.hollyfrontier.com

PRODUCTS/OPERATIONS

2014 Sales

	$ mil.	% of total
Refining	19,706	98
HEP	332	2
Corporate & other	2	-
Adjustments	(276.6)	-
Total	**19,764**	**100**

COMPETITORS

BP	Sunoco
Crown Central	Tesoro
Exxon Mobil	Valero Energy
George Warren	Western Refining Inc.
Marathon Petroleum	Williams Companies

HISTORICAL FINANCIALS

Company Type: Public

Income Statement

FYE: December 31

	REVENUE ($ mil.)	NET INCOME ($ mil.)	NET PROFIT MARGIN	EMPLOYEES
12/14	19,764	281	1.4%	2,686
12/13	20,160	735	3.6%	2,662
12/12	20,090	1,727	8.6%	2,534
12/11	15,439	1,023	6.6%	2,382
12/10	8,322	103	1.2%	1,661
Annual Growth	24.1%	28.3%	—	12.8%

2014 Year-End Financials

Debt ratio: 11.43%
Return on equity: 4.88%
Cash ($ mil.): 567
Current ratio: 2.22
Long-term debt ($ mil.): 1,054

No. of shares (mil.): 196
Dividends
  Yield: 8.7%
  Payout: 114.7%
Market value ($ mil.): 7,349

	STOCK PRICE ($) FY Close	P/E High/Low		PER SHARE ($) Earnings	Dividends	Book Value
12/14	37.48	37	25	1.42	3.26	28.17
12/13	49.69	16	11	3.64	3.20	30.17
12/12	46.55	6	3	8.38	3.10	29.74
12/11	23.40	12	3	6.42	1.34	24.86
12/10	40.77	42	24	0.97	0.30	6.55
Annual Growth	(2.1%)	—	—	10.0%	81.6%	44.0%

Home BancShares Inc

At this Home you don't have to stash your cash under the mattress. Home BancShares is the holding company for Centennial Bank which operates about 150 branches in Arkansas Alabama and Florida. The bank offers traditional services such as checking savings and money market accounts; IRAs; and CDs. It focuses on commercial real estate lending including construction land development and agricultural loans which make up more than 55% of its lending portfolio. The bank also writes residential mortgage business and consumer loans. Nonbank subsidiaries offer trust and insurance services. Investments are available to customers through an agreement with third-party provider LPL Financial.

Geographic Reach

The Arkansas-based bank holding company's Centennial Bank operates 149 branches in Arkansas the Florida Keys southwestern Florida Central Florida the Florida Panhandle and south Alabama.

Financial Performance

Home BancShares reported $257.5 million in revenue in 2013 up 14% versus 2012. The rise in revenue was due primarily to increased interest income from a higher level of earning assets combined with higher yields on their covered loans.

Net income rose 6% over the same period to $66.5 million. The increase was primarily due to additional net income and other non-interest income resulting from acquisitions completed in 2012.

Strategy

The acquisitive bank holding company is expanding in its core Florida and Arkansas markets through the purchase of local managed community banks. Home continues to look for additional acquisitions including institutions seized by regu-

lators in and contiguous to its geographical markets.

Mergers and Acquisitions

In July 2014 Home BancShares completed the acquisition of Florida Traditions Bank (FTB) in a $43 million deal. FTB operated eight branches in central Florida. Post purchase Home had approximately $7 billion in total assets $5.5 billion in depositions $4.7 billion in loans and 149 branches.

In October 2013 the firm acquired the $2.8 billion holding company Liberty Bancshares Inc. parent company of 46-branch Liberty Bank of Arkansas. The Liberty purchase significantly increased Home's deposit market share in Arkansas making it the second largest bank holding company headquartered in Arkansas.Home BancShares entered another new market with the 2012 acquisition of Vision Bank from Park National. The deal included 17 branches along the Florida panhandle and Gulf Coast and gave Home BancShares its first locations in Alabama. Also in 2012 it bought Florida-based Premier Bank from Premier Bank Holding Company and Heritage Bank of Florida with offices in Tampa Lutz and Wesley Chapel.

EXECUTIVES

CFO and Treasurer and Director, Randy E. Mayor, age 50, $300,000 total compensation
President and CEO, C. Randall (Randy) Sims, age 60, $390,000 total compensation
Regional President Centennial Bank, Robert F. Birch, age 65, $290,000 total compensation
President and CEO Centennial Bank, Tracy M. French, age 53, $290,000 total compensation
Chief Lending Officer, Kevin D. Hester, age 51
COO Home BancShares Inc. and Centennial Bank, John (Stephen) Tipton
Vice President Security, Jenni Holbrook
Vice President, Brian Jackson
Senior Vice President Director Of Loan Review, Tish Cartwright
Chairman, John W. Allison, age 68
Vice Chairman, Robert H. Adcock, age 66
Auditors: BKD, LLP

LOCATIONS

HQ: Home BancShares Inc
719 Harkrider, Suite 100, Conway, AR 72032
Phone: 501 328-4770
Web: www.homebancshares.com

PRODUCTS/OPERATIONS

2013 Sales

	$ mil.	% of total
Interest		
Loans	198	74
Investment securities	18	7
Noninterest		
Service charges on deposit accounts	17	7
Other service charges & fees	16	6
Other income	6	2
Mortgage lending income	6	2
Insurance commission	2	1
Gain on OREO	1	1
FDIC indemnification accretion	(10.4)	-
Total	257	100

Selected Services

Personal Banking
Business Banking
ebanking
Investment & insurance
Trust Services

COMPETITORS

Arvest Bank	Bear State Financial
BB&T	Regions Financial
BBX Capital	Simmons First
Bank of America	Woodforest Financial
Bank of the Ozarks	

HISTORICAL FINANCIALS

Company Type: Public

Income Statement

FYE: December 31

	ASSETS ($ mil.)	NET INCOME ($ mil.)	INCOME AS % OF ASSETS	EMPLOYEES
12/14	7,403	113	1.5%	1,376
12/13	6,811	66	1.0%	1,497
12/12	4,242	63	1.5%	926
12/11	3,604	54	1.5%	774
12/10	3,762	17	0.5%	698
Annual Growth	18.4%	59.2%	—	18.5%

2014 Year-End Financials

Debt ratio: 0.82%
Return on equity: 12.18%
Cash ($ mil.): 112
Current ratio: —
Long-term debt ($ mil.): —

No. of shares (mil.): 67
Dividends
  Yield: 1.0%
  Payout: 24.1%
Market value ($ mil.): 2,173

	STOCK PRICE ($) FY Close	P/E High/Low		PER SHARE ($) Earnings	Dividends	Book Value
12/14	32.16	22	16	1.70	0.35	15.03
12/13	37.35	38	18	1.14	0.36	12.92
12/12	33.02	32	22	1.12	0.29	9.17
12/11	25.91	28	22	0.93	0.13	8.38
12/10	22.03	111	76	0.26	0.11	8.38
Annual Growth	9.9%	—	—	59.9%	34.0%	15.7%

Home Depot Inc

When embarking on household projects many start their journey at The Home Depot. As the world's largest home improvement chain and one of the largest US retailers the company operates nearly 2270 stores in the US Canada and Mexico as well as an online business. It targets the do-it-yourself (DIY) and professional markets with its selection of some 40000 items including lumber flooring plumbing supplies garden products tools paint and appliances. Home Depot also offers installation services for carpeting cabinetry and other products. After regaining its footing after the deep recession and housing crisis in the US Home Depot was stung by a massive payment data breach in 2014.

HISTORY

Company BackgroundBernard Marcus and Arthur Blank founded The Home Depot in 1978 after they were fired (under disputed circumstances) from Handy Dan Home Improvement Centers. They joined Handy Dan co-worker Ronald Brill to launch a "new and improved" home center for the do-it-yourselfer (DIY). In 1979 they opened three stores in the fast-growing Atlanta area and expanded to four stores in 1980.

Home Depot went public opened four stores in South Florida and posted sales of $50 million in 1981. The chain entered Louisiana and Arizona next. By 1983 sales were more than $250 million.

In 1984 Home Depot's stock was listed on the NYSE and the company acquired nine Bowater Home Centers in the South. Through subsequent stock and debenture offerings Home Depot continued to grow entering California (Handy Dan's home turf) with six new stores in 1985.

Back on track in 1986 sales exceeded $1 billion in the firm's 60 stores. Home Depot began the current policy of "low day-in day-out pricing" the following year achieving Marcus' dream of eliminating sales events. The company entered the competitive northeastern market with stores in Long Island New York in 1988 and opened its first EXPO Design Center in San Diego.

Home Depot's sales continued to rise during the 1990-92 recession and the retailer kept opening stores. It entered Canada in 1994 when it acquired a 75% interest in Aikenhead's a DIY chain that it converted to the Home Depot name (it bought the remaining 25% in 1998).

A series of gender-bias lawsuits plagued the company in 1994 as female workers claimed they were not treated on an equal basis with male employees. Home Depot reached a $65 million out-of-court settlement in 1997 but not before the company was ordered to pay another female employee $1.7 million in a case in California.

Troubles aside Home Depot roared past the 500-store mark in 1997. That year Blank succeeded Marcus as the company's CEO; Marcus remained chairman. Home Depot bought National Blind & Wallpaper Factory (a mail-order firm) and Maintenance Warehouse (a direct-mail marketer) that year.

The company introduced its 40000-sq.-ft. Villager's Hardware stores designed to compete with smaller hardware shops in 1999 in New Jersey. It also bought Georgia Lighting an Atlanta lighting designer distributor and retailer. Home Depot later began adding large appliances to some stores following competitor Lowe's (most stores had them by 2000).

In 2000 Home Depot bought Apex Supply (a 20-plus-location plumbing distributor in Georgia South Carolina and Tennessee) and opened a flooring-only test store in Texas. Later that year the company named General Electric executive Robert Nardelli as its president and CEO. Marcus and Blank were named co-chairmen.

The company opened 200 new stores in 2001 and bought Total HOME a home improvement chain with four stores in Mexico. Additionally Marcus was named chairman after Blank stepped down. Later in the year Marcus retired and Nardelli became chairman. Also that year the company said it was scrapping its Villager's Hardware experiment to test a small-store concept in urban areas.

In 2002 Home Depot opened its first small store a 61000-sq.-ft. outlet in New York City. Further increasing its presence in Mexico the company acquired the four-store Del Norte chain in Ciudad Juárez that year.

Also in 2002 Home Depot created a new subsidiary HD Builder Solutions through the acquisition of Floors Inc. Arvada Hardwood Floor Company and FloorWorks Inc. The next year the company acquired roofing installer IPUSA and replacement windows and siding installer RMA Home Services.

Home Depot expanded its business in the home-builder market in January 2004 by purchasing Creative Touch Interiors a floor and counter installer in California and Nevada. Additionally early that year Home Depot opened its largest store ever —205000 sq. ft. –in wealthy Anaheim Hills California. It also announced in February 2004 that it had partnered with AARP to hire people older than 50.

In addition that month Home Depot became the exclusive retailer of Maytag's SkyBox a home beverage dispenser. It acquired Home Mart a 20-unit Mexican chain in that June giving it a total of more than 40 stores in Mexico. Also in 2004 the company acquired White Cap Construction Supply; agreed to settle discrimination claims of some Col-

orado employees for $5.5 million; opened two trend-setting urban-oriented stores in Manhattan; and bought 18 stores from Kmart.

In mid-2005 Home Depot acquired National Waterworks Holdings (now National Waterworks Inc.) and Williams Bros. Lumber of Georgia and folded them both into its The Home Depot Supply business (called HD Supply until it was sold). In September Home Depot Direct launched 10 Crescent Lane a high-end home decorating catalog and Web site offering furniture lighting and decorative accessories housewares and more. While some Home Depot locations in Louisiana and Texas were temporarily shut down by hurricanes Katrina and Rita its stores (and those of rival Lowe's and other building suppliers) are among the first places people visited in the wake of the disaster. In the immediate aftermath of the storms Home Depot stocked nontraditional items such as food and diapers in affected areas. Also in 2005 the company shuttered 15 EXPO Design Center stores which cater to affluent homeowners and converted five others to The Home Depot format. In all in 2005 Home Depot spent about $2.5 billion to acquire 21 companies.

The company's direct-to-consumer division launched a pair of high-end catalogs in 2005: 10 Crescent Lane and Paces Trading Company. However the catalogs which featured home furnishings and lighting products were discontinued in 2006 and selected products were folded back into the main Home Depot store catalog and website.

In January 2006 Home Depot acquired carpet and upholstery cleaning franchisor Chem-Dry and folded it into its At-Home Services division. (Chem-Dry has some 4000 franchises worldwide including 2500 in the US). In March the company completed its largest acquisition to date: the construction repair and maintenance products distributor Hughes Supply Inc. for $3.2 billion. That purchase was followed in May by the acquisition of Cox Lumber Co. a Tampa-based provider of trusses doors and lumber-related products. Also Home Depot acquired Home Decorators Collection a company specializing in catalog and online sales of home decor merchandise in 2006. Lured by the growth potential of the vast Chinese market the retailer purchased a majority stake in Taiwan-based HomeWay for about $100 million in late 2006. HomeWay operates DIY warehouse stores in northern China.

Joining the trend of big-box retailers adding gasoline and convenience store services to fuel sales Home Depot opened its first Home Depot Fuel locations in Tennessee and Georgia in 2006.

In early 2007 Nardelli left the company and vice chairman and EVP Frank Blake took the top spot. Home Depot decided to close its handful of flooring-only stores that year. The apparent nail in Nardelli's coffin was his autocratic management style and hefty compensation package (strategically based on options rather than shareholder returns and estimated at $245 million over five years). Nardelli left Home Depot with a $210 million severance package.

The company sold its HD Supply business in 2007 to Bain Capital Carlyle Group and Clayton Dubilier & Rice. The retailer used the proceeds to help it make a $10 billion stock repurchase of more than 15% of its market capitalization.

The Home Depot closed two stores in China in fiscal 2011. In fiscal 2013 it closed the last of its big-box stores there.

EXECUTIVES

Senior Vice President Information Technology Store Field and Corporate Support, Cara Kinzey
EVP Corporate Services and CFO, Carol B. Tom © age 58, $1,019,231 total compensation

SVP and Chief Marketing Officer, Trish Mueller
President Mexico Division, Ricardo E. Saldivar, age 62
Chairman President and CEO, Craig A. Menear, age 57, $991,104 total compensation
EVP Supply Chain and Product Development, Mark Q. Holifield, age 58, $737,300 total compensation
EVP and CIO, Matthew A. (Matt) Carey, age 50, $690,846 total compensation
EVP Human Resources, Timothy M. (Tim) Crow, age 59, $586,308 total compensation
President Northern Division, Joseph (Joe) McFarland, age 47
SVP Operations, Marc D. Powers, age 53
President Southern Division, Ann-Marie Campbell
EVP Outside Sales and Service, Bill Lennie
EVP General Counsel and Corporate Secretary, Teresa W. Roseborough, age 56
President Western Division, Aaron Flowe
SVP; President Online, Kevin Hofmann
SVP Home Services, Lyne Castonguay
EVP Merchandising, Edward P. (Ted) Decker, age 52
Vice President Operations, Christopher (Chris) Duffy
Vice President, Scott Bohrer
Vice President, Dawn Melvin
Vice President, Christopher (Chris) Thornton
Vice President, Gervaise Tiernan
Vice President, Dana Martin
Vice President, Mark Trager
Vice President, Kelly Horn
Vice President, Santiago Bernardez
Vice President, Michelle (Mitch) Macomber
Vice President, Thomas (Thom) Testa
Vice President Of Finance, Mike Zizak
Vice President Ethics Standards Medical Education, Correen Lewis
Vice President Employment Practices and Associate Relations, Derek Bottoms
Vice President of Millwork, Marty Gallager
Vice President Real Estate, Bill Harris
Vice President of Talent Management and Diversity, Thomas (Thom) Spahr
Department Head Kitchen and Bath, Tim Morse
Vice President Information Technology, Daniel (Dan) Grider
Vice President Merchandising Operations, Mark Vedeer
Vice President, Dwaine Kimmet
Vice President of Marketing, Lisa Destefano Orebaugh
Vice President Corporate Communications, Brad Shaw
Vice President Of Finance, Andrew (Andy) Waslo
Senior Vice President Merchandising, Gordy Erickson
Vice President Merchandising Online, Mark Veeder
Auditors: KPMG LLP

LOCATIONS

HQ: Home Depot Inc
2455 Paces Ferry Road N.W., Atlanta, GA 30339
Phone: 770 433-8211   Fax: 770 431-2707
Web: www.homedepot.com

2014 Locations

	No.
US	1,977
Canada	180
Mexico	106
Total	**2,263**

PRODUCTS/OPERATIONS

2014 Sales

	% of total
Kitchen	10
Indoor garden	9
Paint	9
Outdoor garden	7

Lumber	7
Flooring	7
Building materials	7
Plumbing	7
Electrical	7
Tools	6
Hardware	6
Millwork	6
Bath	5
Lighting	3
Decor	3
Total	**100**

Selected Private Labels and Proprietary Brands

Behr Premium Plus (paint)
Glacier Bay (fixtures)
Hampton Bay (lighting)
Husky (hand tools)
Mill's Pride (cabinets)
Vigoro (lawn care products)

COMPETITORS

84 Lumber
Abbey Carpet
Ace Hardware
Amazon.com
B&Q
BMC
Best Buy
CCA Global
Costco Wholesale
Do it Best
F.W. Webb
Guardian Building Products Distribution
Improvement Direct
Kelly-Moore
Lowe's
Menard
Northern Tool
Pacific Coast Building Products
RONA
Sears Holdings
Sherwin-Williams
Stock Building Supply
Sutherland Lumber
Target Corporation
Tractor Supply
True Value
W.E. Aubuchon
Wal-Mart
WinWholesale
Wolseley

HISTORICAL FINANCIALS

Company Type: Public

Income Statement
FYE: February 1

	REVENUE ($ mil.)	NET INCOME ($ mil.)	NET PROFIT MARGIN	EMPLOYEES
02/15	83,176	6,345	7.6%	371,000
02/14	78,812	5,385	6.8%	365,000
02/13*	74,754	4,535	6.1%	340,000
01/12	70,395	3,883	5.5%	331,000
01/11	67,997	3,338	4.9%	321,000
Annual Growth	**5.2%**	**17.4%**	**—**	**3.7%**

*Fiscal year change

2015 Year-End Financials

Debt ratio: 43.05%
Return on equity: 58.25%
Cash ($ mil.): 1,723
Current ratio: 1.36
Long-term debt ($ mil.): 16,869
No. of shares (mil.): 1,307
Dividends
　Yield: 0.0%
　Payout: 39.9%
Market value ($ mil.): 136,477

STOCK PRICE ($)	P/E	PER SHARE ($)		
FY Close	High/Low	Earnings	Dividends	Book Value
02/15	104.42	23 16	4.71	1.88	7.13
02/14	76.85	22 17	3.76	1.56	9.07
02/13*	67.30	22 15	3.00	1.16	11.98
01/12	44.87	18 11	2.47	1.04	11.64
01/11	36.70	19 13	2.01	0.95	11.64
Annual Growth	**29.9%**	**— —**	**23.7%**	**18.8%**	**(11.5%)**

*Fiscal year change

HomeStreet Inc

HomeStreet brings community banking home to the Pacific Northwest and Hawaii. Its subsidiary HomeStreet Bank operates some 30 branches and 45 loan offices in the Pacific Northwest California and Hawaii. Serving individuals and businesses the bank offers standard services including checking savings and money market accounts CDs credit cards loans and mortgages and investments. The bank originates home loans both directly and through a joint venture Windermere Real Estate which operates about 40 offices in Washington and Oregon. HomeStreet also provides specialty financing for income-producing properties. It operates an insurance agency as well. HomeStreet went public in 2012.

IPO
HomeStreet went public in February 2012 with an offering worth $55 million. The company sold 1.6 million shares priced at $44 each. HomeStreet had postponed two previous attempts to go public in 2011 that had planned to sell many more shares. Proceeds from the 2012 IPO were used to meet capital-ratio requirements required by regulators in the wake of allegations that the bank engaged in unsafe practices.

Geographic Reach
Seattle-based HomeStreet operates bank branches in California Hawaii Oregon and Washington.

Operations
HomeStreet's primary subsidiaries are HomeStreet Bank and HomeStreet Capital Corp. (HCC). HCC sells and services multifamily mortgage loans in conjunction with HomeStreet Bank.

Financial Performance
HomeStreet reported total net revenue of $279.7 in 2013 a decline of 12% versus 2012 on declining net interest income and non-interest income. Net income declined from $82.1 million in 2012 to $23.8 million in 2013. Rising expenses including 37% growth in personnel related to the bank's expansion of its mortgage and commercial and consumer businesses put the squeeze on profits in 2013.

Strategy
HomeStreet which began as a small mortgage bank and grew into a full-service community bank that caters to consumers and businesses with some 30 branches was hit hard by the economic downturn and slowdown in the housing market. Trouble in its core mortgage lending business led to losses in 2009 and 2010 and the bank entered into agreements with regulators to improve its capital position earnings and management. It brought in a new management team and launched a turnaround plan to stabilize the business which included tightening its lending standards restructuring troubled loans when necessary and the sale of real estate backed by nonperforming loans. The

measures helped HomeStreet return to profitability in 2011 and remain in the black to date.

With a successful IPO behind it HomeStreet has begun acquiring other small community banks in its region in a bid to grow its business. With the housing market on the mend HomeStreet has begun residential lending again. With nearly $3.1 billion in assets under management the bank competes with financial services giants Bank of America JPMorgan Chase (successor to Washington Mutual Bank) and KeyBank.

Merger and Acquisitions
In November 2013 HomeStreet acquired Fortune Bank a community bank with two branches in Seattle and Bellevue for about $27 million. Concurrently it purchased YNB Financial Services Corp. the parent company of Yakima National Bank which operates four branches in Yakima Selah Sunnyside and Kennewick for about $10.3 million. The twin purchases along with the acquisition of two branches from AmericanWest Bank increased the number of retail deposit branches operates by HomeStreet to 29.

EXECUTIVES

Chairman President and CEO HomeStreet Inc. and HomeStreet Bank, Mark K. Mason, age 55, $500,000 total compensation
EVP Chief Administrative Officer General Counsel and Corporate Secretary Homestreet Inc. and HomeStreet Bank, Godfrey B. Evans, age 61, $247,200 total compensation
EVP Commercial Banking HomeStreet Bank, David H. Straus, age 68
EVP HomeStreet Inc. and EVP and Residential Lending Director HomeStreet Bank, Richard W. H. (Rich) Bennion, age 65, $203,000 total compensation
EVP and Chief Credit Officer HomeStreet Inc. and Homestreet Bank, Jay C. Iseman, age 55, $200,000 total compensation
EVP Chief Investment Officer and Treasurer HomeStreet Inc. and HomeStreet Bank, Darrell van Amen, age 49, $206,359 total compensation
EVP and Commercial Real Estate Lending Director HomeStreet Bank, Randy Daniels, age 53
EVP and Chief Accounting Officer HomeStreet Inc. and HomeStreet Bank, Cory D. Stewart, age 43
EVP and Mortgage Lending Director Homestreet Bank, Rose Marie David, age 51, $200,000 total compensation
EVP and Eastern Region President HomeStreet Bank, Jeffrey K. Newgard, age 43
EVP and Mortgage Lending Director, Rose David
Vice President Income Property Loan Officer, Katie Plett
Vice President Commercial Lending Manager, George Brace
Vice President Loan Officer, Carmen Esteban
Vice President Audit and Compliance, Annette Mumford
Vice President Income Property Credit Administrator, Mark Ahlstedt
Vice President and Relationship Manager, Todd Burchett
Auditors: Deloitte & Touche LLP

LOCATIONS

HQ: HomeStreet Inc
　601 Union Street, Suite 2000, Seattle, WA 98101
Phone: 206 623-3050
Web: www.homestreet.com

PRODUCTS/OPERATIONS

2013 Sales

	$ mil.	% of total
Interest		
Loans	76	28
Investment securities available for sale	12	4
Other	0	-
Noninterest		
Net gains on mortgage origination & sales activities	164	59
Mortgage servicing	17	6
Depositor & other retail banking fees	3	1
Gain on sale of investment securities available for sale	1	1
Insurance agency commission Income from WMS Series LLC and other	1	4
Total	**279**	**100**

Selected Services

Personal Banking
Home LoansInvestmentInsurancePrivate Bank
Commercial Banking
Builder Financing/Residential ConstructionCommercial LendingCommercial Real EstatePartnership Programs

COMPETITORS

American Savings Bank	KeyCorp
BancWest	Sound Financial
Bank of America	U.S. Bancorp
Bank of Hawaii	Umpqua Holdings
Banner Corp	Washington Federal
JPMorgan Chase	Wells Fargo

HISTORICAL FINANCIALS

Company Type: Public

Income Statement   FYE: December 31

	ASSETS ($ mil.)	NET INCOME ($ mil.)	INCOME AS % OF ASSETS	EMPLOYEES
12/14	3,535	22	0.6%	1,611
12/13	3,066	23	0.8%	1,502
12/12	2,631	82	3.1%	1,099
12/11	2,264	16	0.7%	613
12/10	2,485	(34)	—	—
Annual Growth	**9.2%**			

2014 Year-End Financials

Debt ratio: 1.75%
Return on equity: 7.84%
Cash ($ mil.): 30
Current ratio: —
Long-term debt ($ mil.): —

No. of shares (mil.): 14
Dividends
  Yield: 2.5%
  Payout: 29.5%
Market value ($ mil.): 259

	STOCK PRICE ($) FY Close	P/E High/Low	PER SHARE ($) Earnings	Dividends	Book Value
12/14	17.41	14 11	1.49	0.44	20.34
12/13	20.00	17 11	1.61	0.33	17.97
12/12	25.55	9 3	5.98	0.00	18.34
Annual Growth	**(9.1%)**	**— —**	**(29.3%)**	**—**	**2.6%**

HomeTrust Bancshares Inc.

LOCATIONS

HQ: HomeTrust Bancshares Inc.
  10 Woodfin Street, Asheville, NC 28801
Phone: 828 259-3939
Web: www.hometrustbanking.com

HISTORICAL FINANCIALS

Company Type: Public

Income Statement   FYE: June 30

	ASSETS ($ mil.)	NET INCOME ($ mil.)	INCOME AS % OF ASSETS	EMPLOYEES
06/15	2,783	8	0.3%	505
06/14	2,074	10	0.5%	471
06/13	1,583	9	0.6%	328
06/12	1,720	4	0.3%	314
06/11	1,637	(14)	—	290
Annual Growth	**14.2%**	**—**	**—**	**14.9%**

2015 Year-End Financials

Debt ratio: 0.07%
Return on equity: 2.15%
Cash ($ mil.): 582
Current ratio: —
Long-term debt ($ mil.): —

No. of shares (mil.): 19
Dividends
  Yield: —
  Payout: —
Market value ($ mil.): 327

	STOCK PRICE ($) FY Close	P/E High/Low	PER SHARE ($) Earnings	Dividends	Book Value
06/15	16.76	40 35	0.42	0.00	19.04
06/14	15.77	31 28	0.54	0.00	18.28
06/13	16.96	38 26	0.45	0.00	17.65
Annual Growth	**(0.3%)**	**— —**	**(1.7%)**	**—**	**1.9%**

Honeywell International Inc

Thermostats and jet engines seem worlds apart but they're the wind beneath Honeywell International's wings. More than a century old the company is a diverse industrial conglomerate with four segments the largest are Automation and Control Solutions (ACS —making HVAC and manufacturing process products) and Aerospace (turbo engines and flight safety and landing systems). Additional segments include Performance Materials and Technology (PMT formerly Honeywell Specialty Materials thermal switches fibers and chemicals) and Transportation Systems (engine boosting systems and brake materials).

Geographic Reach
Honeywell has approximately 1300 manufacturing research and sales offices and facilities; more than 40% of its products are manufactured in Asia and Europe and the US represents about 60% of sales. Other key international markets are Canada and Latin America.

Operations
Honeywell reorganized its segments during 2014 when it sold its Friction Materials business unit (part of its former Transportation Systems segment) to Federal-Mogul Corporation for $155 million. Transportation Systems was later folded into Aeropspace (39% of net sales). Other segments include Automation and Control Solutions (ACS; 36% of total sales) and Performance Materials and Technologies (PMT; 25%).

Sales and Marketing
Honeywell distributes its building control products through independent contractors and distributor channels throughout North America. Sales to the US government accounted for 9% of its total sales in 2014 while commercial aerospace OEMs generated 6%. Commercial aftermarket customers of aerospace products accounted for 11%.

Financial Performance
Honeywell has enjoyed four straight years of unprecedented growth. Its revenues rose by 3% from $39.1 billion in 2013 to $40.3 billion in 2014. Its net income climbed 8% from $3.9 billion in 2013 to $4.2 billion in 2014. Both these totals represented historic milestones for the company.

The historic revenue growth for 2014 was driven by increases in PMT (4%) and ACS (8%) due to acquisitions and organic growth. It also benefited from a 5% rise in non-US sales during 2014. The spike in net income was primarily the result of the milestone revenues for 2014.

Honeywell's operating cash flow has steadily grown over the last several years from $2.8 billion in 2011 to more than $5 billion in 2014. Cash flow increased by 16% in 2014 compared to 2013 primarily due to change in inventories other current assets and accrued liabilities.

Strategy
For all its segments Honeywell is focusing on several issues and initiatives including expanding in such emerging area as China India Eastern Europe Latin America and the Middle East; managing raw material costs through hedging; staying alert for liquidity issues among suppliers and customers; and controlling costs related to asbestos and environmental matters.Over the last few years it has launched new facilities in China Malaysia and India.

Honeywell's strategy for this growth also includes both acquisitions and the divestiture of under-performing units. In 2014 Honeywell sold its Friction Materials business unit (part of its former Transportation Systems segment) to Federal-Mogul Corporation for $155 million.

Spurred by an aggressive acquisition strategy (possibly spending $10 billion or more through 2018) the company hopes to increase its revenues to $59 billion by 2018.

Mergers and Acquisitions
In 2015 Honeywell completed its $185 million acquisition of Datamax-O'Neil a global manufacturer of fixed and mobile printers used in a variety of retail warehouse and distribution and health care applications. The addition of Datamax-O'Neil to its portfolio enhanced its position within the global barcode printing segment.

During 2013 Honeywell spent about $1 billion on acquisitions. Halfway through the year it acquired RAE Systems for $340 million. RAE Systems makes intelligent gas and radiation detection systems that allow for real-time safety and security threat detection. Months later Honeywell purchased Intermec a maker of bar code scanners RFID readers mobile and fixed vehicle computers printers and label media for $600 million. Both companies were integrated into Honeywell Analytics a part of Honeywell Life Safety in Honeywell Automation and Control Solutions.

HISTORY

During WWI Germany controlled much of the world's chemical industry causing dye and drug shortages. In response Washington Post publisher Eugene Meyer and scientist William Nichols organized the Allied Chemical & Dye Corporation in 1920.

Allied opened a synthetic ammonia plant in 1928 near Hopewell Virginia and became the world's leading producer of ammonia. After WWII Allied began making nylon refrigerants and other products. The company became Allied Chemical Corporation in 1958.

Seeking a supplier of raw materials for its chemical products Allied bought Union Texas Natural Gas in 1962. In the early 1970s CEO John Connor sold many of the firm's unprofitable businesses and invested in oil and gas exploration. By 1979 when Edward Hennessy became CEO Union Texas produced 80% of Allied's income.

Hennessy led the company into the electronics and technical markets. Under a new name Allied Corporation (1981) it bought the Bendix Corporation an aerospace and automotive company in 1983. In 1985 Allied merged with Signal Companies (founded by Sam Mosher in 1922) to form AlliedSignal. The company spun off more than 40 unprofitable chemical and engineering businesses over the next two years.

Larry Bossidy hired from General Electric in 1991 as the new CEO began to cut waste and buy growth businesses. In 1998 alone the company made 13 acquisitions. Late in 1999 the company acquired Honeywell (which dated back to 1906) in a deal valued at $15 billion and changed its name to Honeywell International. Honeywell after trying to make a go of it in the computer and telecommunications industries had refocused on its core products lines —thermostats security systems and other automation equipment.

EXECUTIVES

Chairman and CEO, David M. (Dave) Cote, age 62, $1,865,769 total compensation

VP Chief Strategy and Marketing Officer, Rhonda G. Germany

President and CEO Aerospace, Timothy O. (Tim) Mahoney, age 58, $878,365 total compensation

President and CEO Global High Growth Regions, Shane Tedjarati

President and CEO Transportation Systems, Terrence S. Hahn

President and CEO Automation and Control Solutions (ACS), Alexandre (Alex) Ismail, age 50

President Technology Solutions, Krishna Mikkilineni

SVP and CFO, Tom Szlosek, age 51, $754,750 total compensation

President and CEO Performance Materials and Technologies (PMT), Darius Adamczyk

President Southeast Asia, Briand Greer

Vice President and General Counsel, Anthony Kuznik

Vice President And General Counsel, Richard (Dick) Kent

National Sales Manager, Randy Lee

Vice President, Bill Mayor

Sales Vice President, David (Dave) Moniz

Vice President Business Development, Tom Hart

Vice President General Manager Resins And Chemicals, Qamar S Bhatia

Vice President, Terry Farley

Vice President Marketing, Brian Holliday

Vice President Electrical Sourcing, Lawrence Polizzotto

Vice President Data Processing, Johnathan Farrell

Vice President Marketing, Athanasios Karras

Vice President, Tom Odonnell

Vice President Americas Htt, Anthony Schultz

Vice President Honeywell Shared Services, Michael (Mel) Clark

Vice President Controller Worldwide Sales, Sherry Shapiro

Vice President Communications, Bill Kircos

Managing Vice President Public Finance, Jitendra Chandel

Operations Leader and Excecutive Vice President, Miguel Mendez

Vice President And General Manager Of, Rebecca Liebert

Vice President Sales North America, Bruce Kopp

CPG Information Technology Vice President, David (Dave) Richardson

Vice President of Human Resources, Jeff Tepperman

Vice President Business Development High Growth Regions, Eric Wagner

Vice President Purchasing, Bill Coleman

Vice President Program Management, Paul Ebertz

Vice President Sales EMEA, Orhan Genis

Vice President of Global Transitions, Laura Landriani

Vice President Eic, Andrew (Andy) Scher

Vice President ISC Strategy and Transition ACS, Victor Ramos

Vice President Global Sales Workflow Solutions, Marc Osgoodby

Vice President and General Manager Fine Chemicals, Robert (Bob) Wedinger

Vice President, John (Jack) Fatcheric

Vice President Strategy and Marketing, Eremy Eaton

Vice President Sales North America Ecc, Robert (Bob) Andersen

Vice President And General Manager, Ron Sieck

Vice President Marketing, Sim Reid

Vice President Sales, Sue Knight

Vice Chairman, Roger Fradin, age 61

President Environmental Combustion and Control Automation and Control Solutions, Andreas C. Kramvis, age 62

Secretary, Denise Brown

Auditors: PricewaterhouseCoopers LLP

LOCATIONS

HQ: Honeywell International Inc
115 Tabor Road, Morris Plains, NJ 07950
Phone: 973 455-2000   **Fax:** 973 455-4807
Web: www.honeywell.com

2014 Sales

	$ mil.	% of total
US	23,911	59
Europe	9,870	25
Rest of world	6,525	16
Total	**40,306**	**100**

PRODUCTS/OPERATIONS

2014 Sales

	$ mil.	% of total
Aerospace	15,598	39
Automation & control solutions	14,487	36
Performance materials & technologies	10,221	25
Total	**40,306**	**100**

2014 Sales

	$ mil.	% of total
Product sales	32,398	80
Service sales	7,908	20
Total	**40,306**	**100**

Selected Products

Aerospace
  Aircraft engines (turbine propulsion)
  Aircraft information systems
  Aircraft landing systems
  Aircraft and airport lighting
  Auxiliary power units
  Avionics systems
  Control products
  Guidance
  Radar
  Pressure
  Thermal
  Electric power systems
  Environmental control systems
  Inertial sensors
  Space products and subsystems
Automation and Control Solutions
  Building Solutions and Services
  Building information services
  Energy management
  Enterprise building integration
  HVAC and building control
  Security and asset management
  Environmental combustion controls and sensing controls
  Heating and air-conditioning controls
  Humidifiers and thermostats
  Indoor air quality products

Process Automation Products
  Analytical instrumentation
  Control software and industrial automation systems
  Industrial control equipment and systems
  Production management software
  Security and Life Safety Products
  Access controls and closed-circuit TV
  Emergency lighting
  Fire products and systems
  Gas-detection products
  Home health monitoring and nurse call systems
Specialty Materials
  Absorbents
  Advanced fibers and composites
  Catalysts
  Electronic chemicals
  Fluorine products
  Fluorocarbons
  Hydrofluoric acid
  Imaging chemicals
  Nuclear services
  Performance chemicals
  Renewable fuels and chemicals
  Research and fine chemicals
  Resins and chemicals
  Semiconductor materials and services
  Specialty additives and films
Transportation Systems
  Aluminum radiators
  Anti-lock brakes
  Brake components and materials
  Hydraulic components
  Pads
  Fluid
  Charge-air systems
  Friction materials
  Thermal systems
  Turbochargers

Selected Services

Aerospace
  Ground support
  Repair and overhaul
  Spare parts
  Training
Automation and Control Solutions
  Building information and energy management
  HVAC maintenance and repair

COMPETITORS

3M	Lockheed Martin
ABB AG	Lonza
Air Products	MSA Safety
Akebono Brake	Merck KGaA
Arkema	Mexichem
Asahi Glass	Modine Manufacturing
Astronautics	Motorola Solutions
BAE Systems Inc.	NGK SPARK PLUG
BASF SE	Northrop Grumman
Bechtel	Old World Industries
Boeing	Parker-Hannifin
BorgWarner	Pelco
Bosch Corp.	Raytheon
Clariant	Riken Corporation
Computer Sciences Corp.	Robert Bosch
DSM	Rockwell Automation
Daikin	Rolls-Royce
DuPont	SAFRAN
DynCorp International	Sauer-Danfoss
Eastman Chemical	Schneider Electric
Emerson Electric	Shinko Electric
Endress + Hauser	Siemens AG
Exxon Mobil	Sigma-Aldrich
Federal-Mogul	Sinochem
GE	Solvay
Garmin	Teijin
Halma	Thales
Hella	Thermo Fisher Scientific
ITT Corp.	Trimble Navigation
Ingersoll-Rand	Tyco
Jeppesen Sanderson	United Space Alliance
Johnson Controls	United Technologies
KVH Industries	Unitika
Kyocera	Universal Avionics
L-3 Communications	Valeo
LSI Industries	Yokogawa Electric
Leidos	

HISTORICAL FINANCIALS

Company Type: Public

Income Statement

FYE: December 31

	REVENUE ($ mil.)	NET INCOME ($ mil.)	NET PROFIT MARGIN	EMPLOYEES
12/15	38,581	4,768	12.4%	129,000
12/14	40,306	4,239	10.5%	127,000
12/13	39,055	3,924	10.0%	131,000
12/12	37,665	2,926	7.8%	132,000
12/11	36,529	2,067	5.7%	132,000
Annual Growth	1.4%	23.2%	—	(0.6%)

2015 Year-End Financials

Debt ratio: 24.47%
Return on equity: 26.16%
Cash ($ mil.): 5,455
Current ratio: 1.09
Long-term debt ($ mil.): 5,554

No. of shares (mil.): 770
Dividends
Yield: 2.0%
Payout: 37.5%
Market value ($ mil.): 79,790

	STOCK PRICE ($) FY Close	P/E High/Low		PER SHARE ($) Earnings	Dividends	Book Value
12/15	103.57	18	15	6.04	2.15	24.11
12/14	99.92	19	16	5.33	1.87	22.85
12/13	91.37	18	13	4.92	1.68	22.50
12/12	63.47	17	14	3.69	1.53	16.77
12/11	54.35	23	16	2.61	1.37	13.95
Annual Growth	17.5%	—	—	23.3%	11.9%	14.7%

Horace Mann Educators Corp.

Naming itself in honor of Horace Mann considered the father of public education Horace Mann Educators is an insurance holding company that primarily serves K-12 school teachers and other public school employees throughout the US. Through its operating subsidiaries the company offers homeowners auto (majority of revenue) and individual and group life insurance as well as retirement annuities. Horace Mann employs some 800 agents many of whom are former teachers themselves. Writing business in 48 states and Washington DC the company derives about a third of its direct premiums and contract deposits from five states - California North Carolina Texas Minnesota and Illinois.

Operations

Horace Mann maintains a long-standing relationship with the country's biggest education association the National Education Association which has more than 3 million members. It has also established a number of advertising and sponsorship agreements with a host of smaller educator groups as a way to drum up new business leads.

The company divides it business into property and casualty insurance annuities and life insurance. Property casualty is the largest contributor to revenue with auto being the largest component of that group.

Financial Performance

Horace Mann experienced a slight uptick in revenue for 2012 based on an increase in auto policies. That lead to a large (47%) jump in net income year-over-year as the company paid out fewer property losses partly due to fewer Florida sinkholes.

The reduced claims and improved revenue lead to a $6 million increase in cash flow.

Strategy

In recent years the company has moved away from single-person agency operations to an agency business model (ABM) with multiple sales agents licensed product specialists and other support personnel based together in outside offices. The company saw enough success with the ABM model that it began migrating agents over to an exclusive agent agreement through which the agents become independent contractors that only sell Horace Mann products. Nearly all its agents now operate in this manner.

EXECUTIVES

Executive Vice President Senior Vice President Vice President, Jeff Jaynes
Senior Vice President Finance, Dwayne Hallman
Executive Vice President Service and Technology Operations and Financial Services, George J Zock
Vice President Finance, Robert (Bob) Lee
EVP of Property and Casualty; Chief Marketing Officer, Stephen P. Cardinal, age 46, $393,812 total compensation
Vice President, Edward L Najim
Vice President Human Resources, Kathi Karr
Information Technology Of Vice President, Karen Ruffatto
Assistant Vice President tax Planning and Compliance, Diane M Barnett
Vice President, Kevin Littlejohn
Assistant Vice President Contact Center Generalist, Beth Smith
Assistant Vice President, Reid McClintock
Assistant Vice President and Assistant General Counsel, Cynthia Lamar
Vice President, Robert (Bob) Nevill
Assistant Vice President Communications Program and Public Relations, Marilyn Schaefer
Assistant Vice President Of Sales, Celestine Gates
Vice President Finance, Rick Bowers
Vice President Information Technology, Michael McCullough
Assistant Vice President Product Manager, Angel Plaza
Vice President and Tax Director, Craig Provenzano
Assistant Vice President Product Management, Joel Abrahamson
Assistant Vice President Product Management, Adam Wendling
Southeast Regional Vice President, Rick Leininger
Assistant Vice President Claims Training, Jill Kilroy
Vice President Communications and Market Research, Dick Madden
Vice President Of Marketing, Dawn Klintworth
Vice President Marketing Operations, David (Dave) Baumgardner
Assistant Vice President Category Management and Purchasing Operations, Scott Keeshin
Vice President Marketing, Margo Smith
Regional Claims Assistant Vice President, Randal Mickey
Assistant Vice President Casualty Claims, David (Dave) Ousley
Assistant Vice President Process Improvement, Jennifer (Jen) Turley
Svp-chief Hr Officer, John (Jack) McCarthy
Vice President Annuity Administration And Compliance, Bill Kelly
Assistant Vice President Information Technology, Joseph (Jo) Cooper
Assistant Vice President Human Resources Generalis, Debbie Cimarossa
Assistant Vice President, Charles Vijayawardhana
Assistant Vice President Auto Claims, Paul Riffel
Vice President Of Information Technology, Denise Rice

Vice President Property and Casualty Underwriting, Bill Pearse
Assistant Vice President Information Technology Bus, Hetal Desai
Executive Vice President Life, Matt Sharpe
Vice President, Dennis Duffin
Vice President, Debbie Thompson
Vice President and Chief Actuary, Richard (Dick) Atkinson
Vice President, James (Jamie) Henderson
Vice President, Larry Becker
Vice President Investor Relations, Ryan Greenier
Regional Claims Assistant Vice President, Robert (Bob) Ellison
Assistant Vice President Regional Auto Product Manager, Cpcu Eric Tawfall
Assistant Vice President Compensation, Tim Ellison
Assistant Vice President Talent Management, Audrey Tarter
Chairman, Gabriel L. Shaheen, age 62
Auditors: KPMG LLP

LOCATIONS

HQ: Horace Mann Educators Corp.
1 Horace Mann Plaza, Springfield, IL 62715-0001
Phone: 217 789-2500
Web: www.horacemann.com

PRODUCTS/OPERATIONS

2012 Sales

	$ mil.	% of total
Insurance premiums & contract charges earned	670	66
Net investment income	306	30
Net realized investment gains	27	3
Other income	7	1
Total	**1,010**	**100**

COMPETITORS

AIG	Nationwide
AXA	Progressive
Allstate	Corporation
Farmers Group	Security Benefit Group
GEICO	State Farm
ING Americas	TIAA-CREF
LSW	USAA
Liberty Mutual Agency	VALIC
MetLife	

HISTORICAL FINANCIALS

Company Type: Public

Income Statement

FYE: December 31

	ASSETS ($ mil.)	NET INCOME ($ mil.)	INCOME AS % OF ASSETS	EMPLOYEES
12/14	9,768	104	1.1%	2,008
12/13	8,826	110	1.3%	2,095
12/12	8,167	103	1.3%	2,058
12/11	7,483	70	0.9%	2,107
12/10	7,005	80	1.2%	2,121
Annual Growth	8.7%	6.6%	—	(1.4%)

2014 Year-End Financials

Debt ratio: 2.05%
Return on equity: 8.56%
Cash ($ mil.): 11
Current ratio: —
Long-term debt ($ mil.): —

No. of shares (mil.): 40
Dividends
Yield: 2.7%
Payout: 35.9%
Market value ($ mil.): 1,358

	STOCK PRICE ($)	P/E		PER SHARE ($)		
	FY Close	High/Low	Earnings	Dividends	Book Value
12/14	33.18	13 11	2.47	0.92	32.65
12/13	31.54	11 7	2.66	0.78	27.14
12/12	19.96	8 5	2.51	0.55	31.65
12/11	13.71	10 6	1.70	0.46	27.33
12/10	18.04	9 6	1.97	0.35	22.19
Annual Growth	16.5%	— —	5.8%	27.3%	10.1%

Hormel Foods Corp.

The maker of such thrifty pantry staples as SPAM lunch meat and Dinty Moore stew has turned sophisticated. Besides canned meats Hormel Foods produces a slew of refrigerated processed meats and deli items ethnic entrees and frozen foods sold under the Hormel brand as well as Don Miguel and MegaMex Mexican Country Crock (side dishes) and Lloyd's barbeque. Food service offerings include Hormel Natural Choice meats Café H ethnic Austin Blues barbeque and Bread Ready pre-sliced meats. Hormel is also a major US turkey and pork processor churning out Jennie-O turkey Cure 81 hams and Always Tender pork. More than 30 Hormel brands are ranked #1 or #2 in their respective markets.

HISTORY

George Hormel opened his Austin Minnesota slaughterhouse in an abandoned creamery in 1891. By 1900 Hormel had modernized his facilities to compete with larger meat processors. In 1903 the enterprise introduced its first brand name (Dairy Brand) and a year later began opening distribution centers nationwide. The scandal that ensued after the discovery in 1921 that an assistant controller had embezzled over $1 million almost broke the company causing Hormel to initiate tighter controls. By 1924 it was processing more than a million hogs annually. Hormel introduced canned ham two years later.

Jay Hormel George's son became president in 1929; under his guidance Hormel introduced Dinty Moore beef stew (1936) and SPAM (1937). A Hormel executive won a contest and $100 by submitting the name a contraction of "spiced ham." During WWII the US government bought over half of Hormel's output; it supplied SPAM to GIs and Allied forces.

In 1959 Hormel introduced its Little Sizzlers pork sausage and sold its billionth can of SPAM. New products rolled out in the 1960s included Hormel's Cure 81 ham (1963). By the mid-1970s the firm had more than 750 products.

The company survived a violent nationally publicized strike triggered by a pay cut in 1985. In the end only 500 of the original 1500 strikers returned to accept lower pay scales.

Sensing the consumer shift toward poultry Hormel purchased Jennie-O Foods in 1986. Later acquisitions included the House of Tsang and Oriental Deli (1992) Dubuque (processed pork 1993) and Herb-Ox (bouillon and dry soup mix 1993). After more than a century as Geo. A. Hormel & Co. the company began calling itself Hormel Foods in 1993 to reflect its expansion into non-pork foods. Former General Foods executive Joel Johnson was named president and CEO that year (and chairman two years later).

Hormel proved it could take a joke with the 1994 debut of its tongue-in-cheek SPAM catalog featuring dozens of SPAM-related products. But when a 1996 Muppets movie featured a porcine character named Spa'am Hormel sued Jim Henson Productions; a federal court gave Spa'am the go-ahead.

Also in 1996 Hormel teamed up with Mexican food processor Grupo Herdez to sell Herdez sauces and other Mexican food products in the US. It then formed a joint venture with Indian food producer Patak Spices (UK) to market its products in the US. Late that year Hormel paid $64 million for a 21% interest in Spanish food maker Campofrio Alimentacion.

Earnings fell in 1996 due in part to soaring hog prices. The company was hit hard again in 1998 when production contracts with hog growers meant it wound up paying premium rates despite a market glut. In 1998 the Smithsonian Institution accepted two cans of SPAM (one from 1937 the other an updated 1997 version) for its History of Technology collection.

SPAM sales soared in 1999 as nervous consumers stockpiled provisions for the millennium. To build its growing HealthLabs division Hormel acquired Cliffdale Farms (2000) and Diamond Crystal Brands nutritional products (a division of Imperial Sugar) in 2001 –boosting its share of the market for easy-to-swallow foods sold to hospitals and nursing homes.

In early 2001 Hormel acquired family-owned The Turkey Store for approximately $334 million and folded it into its Jennie-O division.

Hormel produced its 6 billionth can of SPAM in 2002 and traded $115 million in stock to acquire the rest of Imperial Sugar's Diamond Crystal Brands unit which packages single-serve packets of sugar sweeteners seasonings and plastic cutlery for the foodservice industry.

To further diversify in 2003 Hormel acquired food manufacturer Century Foods International (whey-based protein powders beverages and nutrition bars) and added it to its burgeoning specialty foods group. In 2004 Hormel sold off its stake in Campofrio to Smithfield Foods.

Its last act of business in 2004 was to purchase Southern California's Clougherty Packing for about $186 million. The pork processor's facilities help extend Hormel's capacity for further-processed foods in the southwestern US.

In 2005 the company purchased Mexican food manufacturer Arriba Foods for $47 million in cash. Later that year it bought Lloyd's Barbecue Company from General Mills.

Responding to the growing trend of the US population to dine out Hormel expanded its foodservice segment (which it refers to as its specialty foods business) with the 2005 purchase of foodservice food manufacturer and distributor Mark-Lynn Foods. Mark-Lynn's products include salt and pepper packets ketchup mustard sauces and salad dressings creamers and sugar packets as well as jellies desserts and drink mixes.

Adding to its grocery product offerings in 2006 the company acquired canned ready-to-eat chicken producer Valley Fresh Foods for $78 million. It also bought pepperoni and pasta maker Provena Foods and sausage and sliced meat maker Saag's Products. It added another to its list of countries in which it has joint ventures in 2006 when it formed a JV with San Miguel to raise and market hogs and animal feed in Vietnam. The JV is 49%-owned by Hormel.

Hormel acquired Burke Corporation a maker of pizza toppings and other fully cooked meat items in 2007 for $115 million in cash. The acquisition allowed Hormel to extend its pizza-topping operations into the foodservice sector. The following year it acquired Boca Grande Foods for $23.5 in

cash. Boca Grande makes Poco Pac branded jams jellies and pancake syrup portion-control products for foodservice operators.

EXECUTIVES

Group Vice President Specialty Foods, Michael (Mel) Tolbert
Executive Vice President Corporate Strategy, Ronald (Ron) Fielding
Vice President Meat Products Marketing, Joe Swedberg
EVP; President Hormel Business Units, Steven G. Binder, age 58, $466,380 total compensation
Group VP; President Consumer Products Sales, Larry L. Vorpahl, age 52
Chairman President and CEO, Jeffrey M. Ettinger, age 57, $1,000,220 total compensation
VP Foodservice Sales, Thomas R. Day, age 57, $315,120 total compensation
VP and Treasurer, Jody H. Feragen, age 59, $466,380 total compensation
VP Marketing Consumer Products-Refrigerated Foods, James M. Splinter, age 52
SVP Supply Chain, Bryan D. Farnsworth, age 58
Group VP Foodservice, Deanna T. Brady, age 50
Group VP Specialty Foods, Donald H. (Don) Kremin, age 55
Group VP; President Hormel Foods International, James P. Snee, age 47
Group VP; President Jennie-O Turkey Store, Glenn R. Leitch, age 54, $317,580 total compensation
VP Information Technology Services, Mark D. Vaupel
Vice President, Rebecca Smith
National Sales Manager, Kerry Wren
Vice President, Alan (Al) Rasell
Vice President, Brett Asleson
Vice President Finance, Don Hodapp
Vice President Of Finance, Brent Hood
Vice President Business Planning, Steve Althaus
Vice President of Marketing, Paul Sheehan
National Sales Manager Case Ready Meats, Jeff Schultz
National Sales Manager, Mark Engelhardt
National Sales Manager, Michael Dougherty
Senior Vice President Of Consumer Produc, Daniel Hartzog
Vice President Of Marketing, Scott Aakre
Vice President, Alan Rasell
Vice President Corporate Communications, Juile Craven
Vice President Research and Development, Kevin Myers
Treasurer controller, Eldon Quam
Auditors: Ernst & Young LLP

LOCATIONS

HQ: Hormel Foods Corp.
1 Hormel Place, Austin, MN 55912-3680
Phone: 507 437-5611 **Fax:** 507 437-5489
Web: www.hormel.com

2015 Sales

	$ mil.	% of total
US	8,721	94
Other	542	6
Total	9,263	100

PRODUCTS/OPERATIONS

2015 Sales by Segment

	$ mil.	% of total
Refrigerated Foods	4,372	47
Jennie-O Turkey Store	1,635	18
Grocery Products	1,617	17
Specialty Foods	1,103	12
International & Other	534	6
Total	9,263	100

Selected Products and Brands

Refrigerated
Country Crock Side Dishes
Hormel
Hormel Always Tender flavored pork and beef products
Hormel Black Label and Microwave Ready bacon
Hormel Cure 81 ham
Hormel Fresh Pantry meats
Hormel Little Sizzlers pork sausage
Hormel Natural Choice meats
Hormel pepperoni minis and stix
Hormel refrigerated entrees
Hormel Wranglers franks
Hormel Snac Cups
Lloyd's Barbeque products
Saag's sausages

Jennie-O Turkey Store
Bratwursts and breakfast/dinner sausages
Breast meat products
Deli
Di Lusso deli meats
Farmer John deli meats
Hormel 100 percent natural deli meats
Hormel Deli beef dry sausage ham and turkey
Hormel party trays
Ground turkey
Marinated turkey tenderloins
So-Easy Entrees
Turkey burger patties and franks
Whole turkeys

Grocery products
Dinty Moore stew Hearty Meals varieties microwave-ready products
Herb-Ox bouillon
Herdez Salsa
Hormel
Hormel bacon toppings
Hormel Chili Master
Hormel chunk meats
Hormel Compleats microwave meals
Hormel corned beef and roast beef with gravy
Hormel dried beef
Hormel Kid's Kitchen microwave cups
Hormel Mary Kitchen hash
Hormel microwave cups
Not-So-Sloppy-Joe sloppy joe sauce
Skippy peanut butter
SPAM products (classic hickory smoke flavored hot and spicy lite low-sodium spread singles and oven-roasted turkey)
Stagg chili
Valley Fresh chunk meats and broths

Specialty Foods
Century Foods International (dairy and vegetable proteins nutraceuticals)
Diamond Crystal Brands (salts sugar substitutes)
Hormel Foods Ingredients (sauces powders broths oils Omega-3 additives)
Private Label products (canned meats prepared foods and desserts bouillon sweeteners salts seasonings)

Other
MegaMex Mexican brands
Bufalo hot sauces
CHI-CHI'S Mexican hot sauces taco tubs dips seasoning mixes and tortillas
Do?a María Authentic Mexican products
Don Miguel burritos appetizers empanadas taquitos tacos flautas chimichangas enchiladas
El Torito sauces dressings and corn cakes
Embasa Mexican peppers salsas
Herdez imported salsas
La Victoria Mexican salsas taco sauces enchilada sauces green chile peppers
Wholly Guacamole
World Food ethnic brands
House of Tsang entrees sauces and oils
Marrakesh Express Mediterranean products (couscous risotto)
Peloponnese Greek foods olives

Selected Foodservice Brands

Always Tender Pork
Austin Blues barbeque meats
Authentic Barbeque
Bread Ready pre-sliced meats
Café H ethnic meats
Cure 81 Ham
Dry Sausage
Fast 'N Easy Fully Cooked Meats
Hormel Chili

Masterpieces Toppings
Natural Choice meats
Old Smokehouse bacon
Old Tyme breakfast sausage
Old Tyme ham
Special Recipe Sausage
Stagg Chili

COMPETITORS

B&G Foods	H. J. Heinz Limited
Boar's Head	JBS USA
Bob Evans	Kraft Foods Group Inc.
Bridgford Foods	Perdue Incorporated
Bush Brothers	Pilgrim's Pride
Butterball	Pinnacle Foods
Campbell Soup	Plainville Farms
Cargill	Sanderson Farms
ConAgra	Seaboard
Cooper Farms	Smithfield Foods
Eberly Poultry	Smucker
Foster Farms	The Dial Corporation
General Mills	Tyson Foods

HISTORICAL FINANCIALS

Company Type: Public

Income Statement

FYE: October 25

	REVENUE ($ mil.)	NET INCOME ($ mil.)	NET PROFIT MARGIN	EMPLOYEES
10/15	9,263	686	7.4%	20,700
10/14	9,316	602	6.5%	20,400
10/13	8,751	526	6.0%	19,800
10/12	8,230	500	6.1%	19,700
10/11	7,895	474	6.0%	19,500
Annual Growth	4.1%	9.7%	—	1.5%

2015 Year-End Financials

Debt ratio: 7.08%
Return on equity: 18.10%
Cash ($ mil.): 347
Current ratio: 1.70
Long-term debt ($ mil.): 250

No. of shares (mil.): 528
Dividends
Yield: 0.0%
Payout: 78.7%
Market value ($ mil.): 36,106

	STOCK PRICE ($) FY Close	P/E High/Low	PER SHARE ($) Earnings	Dividends	Book Value
10/15	68.33	53 39	1.27	1.00	7.57
10/14	52.54	46 37	1.12	0.80	6.84
10/13	43.62	44 30	0.98	0.68	6.28
10/12	29.34	32 29	0.93	0.60	5.36
10/11	29.95	58 29	0.87	0.51	5.03
Annual Growth	22.9%	— —	9.9%	18.3%	10.7%

Horton (D.R.) Inc.

When this Horton heard a Who it built the little guy a house. One of the largest homebuilding companies in the US D.R. Horton constructs single-family homes that range in size from 1000 sq. ft. to 4000 sq. ft. and sell for an average price of about $285700 under the D.R. Horton Emerald Homes Regent Homes and Express Homes brand names. Texas-based D.R. Horton is active in nearly 80 markets in 27 states and generates more than 75% of its revenue in the Southeast South Central and Western regions of the US. Beyond single-family detached homes which account for some 90% of sales D.R. Horton builds duplexes townhomes and condominiums. It also provides mortgage title and closing services.

Operations

The company operates through some 40 divisions which are somewhat autonomously led by presidents familiar with their geographic markets. The divisions report to one of four regional offices.
Geographic Reach
Fort Worth-based D.R. Horton is hammering away in 27 states. On a regional basis the homebuilder generated 27% of its sales in the Southeast 25% in the South Central US (in states including Texas Louisiana and Oklahoma) and 24% of its sales in the West (California and Hawaii) in FY2015 (ended September). Its home sales in the East accounted for 12% of total sales while sales in the southwest made up the remainder.Sales and MarketingThe builder markets and sells its homes under the D.R. Horton Emerald Homes and Express Homes brand names in most of its markets. Homes marketed under the Express Homes and Regent Homes brands represented 15% of its home closings and 10% of sales revenue in FY2015.D.R. Horton markets and sells homes mostly through commissioned employees and independent real estate brokers. It also markets through digital media (such as email search engine marketing social networking sites and the company website) and print media and advertisement formats such as billboards radio television magazine and newspaper advertising in local markets. Altogether the builder spent $42.4 million on advertising in FY2015 compared to $44 million and $33.2 million in fiscal years 2014 and 2013 respectively.

Financial Performance
D.R. Horton has enjoyed healthy revenue and profit growth over the past several years thanks to a strengthening housing market and higher demand for higher-end homes. Still the builder's revenues and profits are still well below their pre-recession levels; its revenue in 2014 was about two-thirds as high as in 2006 when sales exceeded $15 billion. The company's revenue jumped 35% to $10.82 billion during fiscal 2015 (ended September) thanks to higher home closing volumes and higher average home sale prices. The number of home closings rose 28% to 36648 for the year while average sale prices ticked up 5% to $285700 per home. Home sales grew in all regions though sales growth in the Southeast (resulting from its 2014 acquisition of Crown Communities and higher sales in Florida) and South Central region (resulting from higher sales in Houston Austin and Fort Worth) made the most impact to the company's top line.Higher revenue in FY2015 drove D.R. Horton's net income up 41% to $750.7 million for the year. The builder's operating cash levels skyrocketed to $700 million thanks to higher earnings and because in FY2014 it had used $918.2 million to boost its construction in progress and finished home inventory.

Strategy
D.R. Horton continues to acquire regional builders and their brands assets and home/lot inventories to grow looking to sell more homes at higher prices as the housing market has skyrocketed over the past few years.The builder has been expanding its home lines to capture a variety of different homebuyers and geographic markets in recent years. During FY2015 for example D.R. Horton capitalized on the affordable and entry-level homebuyer market by introducing its new Express Homes brand. It also continued to push its Emerald Homes brand line of higher-end move-up and luxury home communities to entice more affluent homebuyers.Shortly after the financial crisis D.R. Horton prepared for the housing rebound by strategically buying land at distressed prices seeking promising new markets to enter and renegotiating purchasing contracts —a strategy that has paid off handsomely through FY2015. As one of the nation's largest homebuilders the company

was able to survive the worst housing market in 25 years unlike many smaller builders with limited resources that went out of business or were acquired in recent years. As the recovery in the housing market gained momentum Horton began acquiring regional builders.

Mergers and Acquisitions

In May 2015 D.R. Horton purchased Seattle-based builder Pacific Ridge Homes —including its 350 lots 90 homes in inventory and 40 homes in sales order backlog —for some $72 million in cash. D.R. Horton also bought control of some 400 lots through option contracts. Pacific Ridge would operate as a separate division within D.R. Horton. In May 2014 D.R. Horton acquired the homebuilding assets of Crown Communities —including roughly a thousand homes that had been sold or remained in inventory as well as more than 2000 lots in Georgia South Carolina and Alabama —for $210 million. In October 2013 Horton acquired the homebuilding operations of Regent Homes for about $35 million in cash. Regent Homes operated in Charlotte Greensboro and Winston-Salem North Carolina. The purchase included approximately 240 homes in inventory 300 lots and control of some 600 additional lots through option contracts. Horton also acquired a sales order backlog of 213 homes valued at $31.1 million.Company BackgroundIn August 2012 the company acquired Breland Homes which operated in Alabama and along the Gulf Coast of Mississippi. The purchase included 320 homes in inventory and 1020 finished lots. The purchase gave Horton entry to the Huntsville Alabama and Mississippi Gulf Coast markets.Chairman Donald R. Horton founded the business in 1978.

HISTORY

Company BackgroundDonald R. Horton was selling homes in Fort Worth Texas when he hit upon a strategy for increasing sales —add options to a basic floor plan. In 1978 he borrowed $33000 to build his first home added a bay window for an additional charge and sold the home for $44000. Donald soon added floor plans and options that appealed to regional preferences.

The depressed Texas market drove the company to expand beyond the Dallas/Fort Worth area in 1987 when it entered the then-hot Phoenix market. It continued to expand into the Southeast Mid-Atlantic Midwest and West in the late 1980s and early 1990s. By 1991 Horton and his family owned more than 25 companies that were combined as D.R. Horton which went public in 1992.

D.R. Horton acquired six geographically diverse construction firms in 1994 and 1995. In 1996 the company started a mortgage services joint venture expanded its title operations and added three more firms.

In 1998 the company bought four builders including Scottsdale Arizona-based Continental Homes. Continental had been expanding beyond its Arizona and Southern California base and had entered the lucrative retirement community market. After the Continental purchase Donald Horton stepped down as president remaining chairman. Richard Beckwitt took over as president and Donald Tomnitz became CEO. In 1999 the company acquired Century Title and Midwest builder Cambridge Properties.

D.R. Horton sold its St. Louis assets to McBride & Son Enterprises in 2000 after spending five years trying to break into the St. Louis homebuilding market. Tomnitz also took over the duties of president in 2000 when Beckwitt retired.

D.R. Horton gained homebuilding operations in Houston and Phoenix when it bought Emerald Builders in 2001. In February 2002 the company acquired Schuler Homes for $1.2 billion including debt.

Sales continued to climb in fiscal 2003 and 2004. D.R. Horton experienced its 27th consecutive year of earnings and revenue growth in 2004 and broke records by being the first residential homebuilder to sell more than 45000 homes in the US in a fiscal year; in fiscal 2005 the company closed 51172 homes. By 2007 however it was evident that the heady days were over with a rise in cancellations and a larger value of backlog orders.

CEO Donald Tomnitz summed up the housing market crash when he said "I don't want to be too sophisticated here but '07 is going to suck all 12 months of the calendar year." Indeed the company suffered a loss that year and the next when sales orders declined and cancellation rates rose due to tightened mortgage markets and severe liquidity shortages. Adding to homebuilders' difficulties an influx of foreclosed homes on the market brought down the demand for new homes.

D.R. Horton responded to the downturn in 2008 by reducing land and housing inventory controlling construction and inventory costs and using its cash to reduce debt. Despite drops in many markets D.R. Horton saw improvements in its eastern market where home affordability and employment led to a higher demand for new homes.

EXECUTIVES

President West Region, J. Matt Farris
President North Region, George W. Seagraves, $175,000 total compensation
EVP and CFO, William W. (Bill) Wheat, age 49, $500,000 total compensation
President Financial Services, Randall C. (Randy) Present
VP and CIO, Rick Rawlings
President Central Region, Rick Horton
President Southeast Region, David V. Auld, age 58, $500,000 total compensation
SVP Busienss Development, Michael Murray
President East Region, Tom Hill
Vice President Purchasing, Jonathan (Jon) Smith
Vice President, Robert (Bob) Coltin
Vice President Purchasing, Chris Jurgens
Vice President Land Development, Dennis Hudspeth
Assistant Vice President and Environmental Manager, Edward (Ed) Perez
Division President, Todd McCrory
Vice President Land Acquisition, Eric Taylor
Vice President, William Mayer
Vice President Oahu Development Group, Robert (Bob) Bruhl
Assistant Vice President Real Estate Counsel, Tracy Burks
Vice President Construction, Robert (Bob) White
Vice President of Operations, Chris Green
Chairman, Donald R. Horton, age 65
Auditors: PricewaterhouseCoopers LLP

LOCATIONS

HQ: Horton (D.R.) Inc.
301 Commerce Street, Suite 500, Fort Worth, TX 76102
Phone: 817 390-8200
Web: www.drhorton.com

2015 Homebuilding Sales by Region and financial services

	% of total
West	24
South central	25
Southeast	27
East	12
Midwest	6
Southwest	3
Financial Services revenue	3
Total	**100**

PRODUCTS/OPERATIONS

2015 Sales

	$ mil.	% of total
Homebuilding		
Home sales	10,469	97
Landlot sales &other	89	1
Financial services	265	2
Total	**10,824**	**100**

COMPETITORS

Beazer Homes	Meritage Homes
CalAtlantic	NVR
David Weekley Homes	PulteGroup
Gehan Homes	Ryan Building
Hovnanian Enterprises	Toll Brothers
KB Home	Weyerhaeuser Real
Lennar	Estate
M.D.C.	

HISTORICAL FINANCIALS

Company Type: Public

Income Statement
FYE: September 30

	REVENUE ($ mil.)	NET INCOME ($ mil.)	NET PROFIT MARGIN	EMPLOYEES
09/15	10,824	750	6.9%	6,230
09/14	8,024	533	6.6%	5,621
09/13	6,259	462	7.4%	4,609
09/12	4,354	956	22.0%	3,477
09/11	3,636	71	2.0%	3,010
Annual Growth	31.3%	79.8%	—	19.9%

2015 Year-End Financials

Debt ratio: 34.18%	No. of shares (mil.): 368
Return on equity: 13.64%	Dividends
Cash ($ mil.): 1,383	Yield: 0.8%
Current ratio: 11.95	Payout: 13.5%
Long-term debt ($ mil.): 3,811	Market value ($ mil.): 10,823

	STOCK PRICE ($) FY Close	P/E High/Low		PER SHARE ($) Earnings	Dividends	Book Value
09/15	29.36	16	10	2.03	0.25	15.99
09/14	20.52	16	11	1.50	0.14	14.03
09/13	19.43	19	12	1.33	0.30	12.57
09/12	20.63	7	3	2.77	0.15	11.19
09/11	9.04	59	39	0.23	0.15	8.29
Annual Growth	34.2%	—	—	72.4%	13.6%	17.8%

Host Hotels & Resorts Inc

Host Hotels & Resorts will leave the chandelier on for you. It's the nation's largest hospitality real estate investment trust and one of the top owners of luxury and upscale hotels. It owns about 115 luxury and "upper upscale" hotels mostly in the US but also in Canada Australia New Zealand Chile Mexico and Brazil totaling some 60000 rooms. Properties are managed by third parties; most operate under the Marriott brand and are managed by sister firm Marriott International. Other brands include Hyatt Ritz-Carlton Sheraton and Westin. To maintain its status as a real estate investment trust (REIT) which carries tax advantages Host operates through majority-owned Host Hotels & Resorts LP.

HISTORY

Company Background That's right —The Four Seasons started as a root beer stand.

Newlyweds John and Alice Marriott left Marriott Utah (founded by John's grandparents) in 1927 and opened a root beer stand in Washington DC. As a way to attract customers during the winter they began selling tamales and tacos —recipes came from a cook at the Mexican Embassy. Dubbed the Hot Shoppe the Marriotts built the business into a regional chain.

In 1937 the Marriotts began providing boxed lunches for airlines. Hot Shoppes entered the hospital food service business in 1955 and two years later opened its first hotel in Arlington Virginia. John and Alice's son Bill became president in 1964. The company which operated four hotels 45 Hot Shoppes and the airline catering business became Marriott-Hot Shoppes.

In the 1960s the company acquired Bob's Big Boy restaurant chain (sold 1987) started Roy Rogers fast-food restaurants (sold 1990) and changed its name to Marriott Corp. Later Marriott bought an Athenian cruise line (Oceanic; sold 1987). Bill became CEO in 1972.

Marriott diversified its hotel operations in the 1980s moving into limited-service middle-priced hotels with the launch of Courtyard by Marriott in 1983. To accelerate growth the company began building hotels for sale retaining their control through management contracts. In 1987 it acquired Residence Inn Co. which targeted extended-stay travelers. The company also expanded its airline catering business and moved into retirement facilities. To fund the expansion Marriott formed limited partnerships and issued corporate bonds; when the late 1980s recession hit the company was deeply in debt.

In 1993 Marriott Corp. divided into Marriott International (hotel management services) and Host Marriott (real estate and food service) leaving Host Marriott with most of the corporation's debt. Host Marriott began focusing on full-service hotels. It raised money to buy more hotels (many of which belonged to its old limited partnerships) by taking loans from Marriott International and selling assets (including 14 retirement properties and 30 Fairfield Inns). In late 1995 the company further refined its focus by spinning off its food service and concessions business as Host Marriott Services (later acquired by Italy-based restaurant operator Autogrill).

Host Marriott acquired three Ritz-Carlton hotels in 1995 through Marriott International which owns the Ritz-Carlton name and in 1997 acquired the Forum Group owner of 29 retirement communities. The next year it spun off Crestline Capital (now Barcelo Crestline Corp.) to own its retirement properties and to lease its hotels.

In 1999 the company expanded its hotel brands adding controlling stakes in 13 luxury Ritz-Carlton Four Seasons Swissôtel and Hyatt properties bought from the Blackstone Group investment firm in exchange for a stake in Host Marriott. It also restructured as a real estate investment trust or REIT.

Host Marriott and Marriott International were slapped with an investor fraud lawsuit in 2000 relating to its capital-raising efforts in the late 1980s; they reached a tentative settlement under which they would buy back the partnerships. The bulk of the settlements were awarded to about 2000 investors in two of the six limited partnerships in question. That year Marriott matriarch Alice died.

Host Marriott's New York Marriott World Trade Center hotel located at Three World Trade Center was completely devastated on September 11 2001. Two blocks south the New York Marriott Financial Center hotel sustained heavy damage.

Even before September 11 brought the hotel industry to a screeching halt the company had curtailed the buying binge that saw it add more than 100 hotels to its portfolio since 1994. It decided to sell less posh noncore hotels and focus on renovating remaining holdings. Crashing per-room revenue had the company waiting for the slow return of the health of the industry and when it had the company began a cautious acquisition spree.

After a tourism industry downturn made worse by the September 11 2001 terrorist attacks the company made a key acquisition in 2006: It purchased a portfolio of 25 domestic and 3 international hotels from Starwood Hotels & Resorts for more than $4 billion and changed its name to Host Hotels & Resorts in conjunction with that buy. The package expanded the company's reach into Europe South America and the South Pacific.

In 2009 Host sold its leasehold interest in CBM Joint Venture Partnership which owned 115 Courtyard by Marriott hotels. The deal earned Host about $13 million.

In late 2011 the company sold its 95% interest in the Toronto Airport Marriott Hotel for CAD$30.6 million ($30.7 million).

EXECUTIVES

President CEO and Director, W. Edward (Ed) Walter, age 59, $925,000 total compensation

EVP; Managing Director Europe, James F. Risoleo, age 59, $500,000 total compensation

EVP and CFO, Gregory J. (Greg) Larson, age 50, $475,000 total compensation

EVP General Counsel and Secretary, Elizabeth A. Abdoo, age 56, $460,000 total compensation

EVP Asset Management, Minaz B. Abji, age 61, $515,000 total compensation

EVP Human Resources, Joanne G. Hamilton, age 57

Vice President Asset Management, Georgina Sussan

Senior Vice President Development Desi, Gerard Haberman

Vice President Asset Management, Patrick Webber

Vice President Asset Management, Christopher (Chris) Ford

Senior Vice President Chief Development Officer, Matthew (Matt) Richardson

Vice President, Matthew (Matt) Ahrens

Vice President Human Resources, Doug McLeod

Vice President Asset Management, Jeff Gross

Vice President Hotel Reporting and Analysis, Joanne Ballin

Vice President Business Intelligence, Sourav Ghosh

Vice President Controller, Alison Gendron

Senior Vice President Taxes and General Tax Counsel, Jeff Clark

Vice President Human Resources, Lisa Whittington

Vice President of Tax, Doug Link

Vice President Asset Management, Christopher (Chris) Ostapovicz

Vice President, Rusty Allen

Senior Vice President Asset Management, D Eric Habermann

Chairman, Richard E. Marriott, age 76

Auditors: KPMG LLP

LOCATIONS

HQ: Host Hotels & Resorts Inc
6903 Rockledge Drive, Suite 1500, Bethesda, MD 20817
Phone: 240 744-1000
Web: www.hosthotels.com

2014 Sales

	$ mil.	% of total
US	5,077	95
Canada	87	2
Others	190	3
Total	**5,354**	**100**

PRODUCTS/OPERATIONS

2014 Sales

	% of total
Rooms	64
Food & Beverage	29
Other	7
Total	**100**

2014 Brands

	No. of hotels
Marriott	54
Starwood:	
Westin	13
Sheraton	8
W	3
St. Regis	1
The Luxury Collection	1
Hyatt	9
Ritz-Carlton	7
Hilton/Embassy Suites	3
Swissoetel	1
Fairmont	1
Accor:	
ibis	4
Novotel	5
Others	4
Total	**114**

COMPETITORS

Ashford Hospitality Trust
Carlson Companies
FelCor
Hospitality Properties Trust
InterContinental Hotels
LaSalle Hotel Properties
Lodgian
Pebblebrook
Strategic Hotels
Sunstone Hotel Investors

HISTORICAL FINANCIALS

Company Type: Public

Income Statement

				FYE: December 31
	REVENUE ($ mil.)	NET INCOME ($ mil.)	NET PROFIT MARGIN	EMPLOYEES
12/14	5,354	732	13.7%	251
12/13	5,166	317	6.1%	242
12/12	5,286	61	1.2%	233
12/11	4,998	(15)	—	219
12/10	4,437	(130)	—	203
Annual Growth	4.8%	—	—	5.4%

2014 Year-End Financials

Debt ratio: 32.70%
Return on equity: 10.05%
Cash ($ mil.): 684
Current ratio: 2.30
Long-term debt ($ mil.): 3,992

No. of shares (mil.): 755
Dividends
  Yield: 3.1%
  Payout: 93.7%
Market value ($ mil.): 17,965

	STOCK PRICE ($) FY Close	P/E High/Low		PER SHARE ($) Earnings	Dividends	Book Value
12/14	23.77	25 19		0.96	0.75	9.71
12/13	19.44	45 36		0.42	0.46	9.58
12/12	15.67	216172		0.08	0.30	9.42
12/11	14.77	— —		(0.02)	0.14	9.47
12/10	17.87	— —		(0.21)	0.04	9.33
Annual Growth	7.4%	— —		—	108.1%	1.0%

HOVENSA LLC

HOVENSA brings together US and Latin American know-how and operations to handle oil products in the US Virgin Islands. HOVENSA is a joint venture of Hess and Venezuelan oil giant PDVSA (its major crude oil supplier). Once the largest private employer in the US Virgin Islands the company operated a 500000-barrels-per-day crude oil refinery on St. Croix along with two specialized oil processing complexes a 150000-barrels-per-day fluid catalytic cracking unit and a 58000-barrels-per-day delayed coker unit. However the St. Croix refinery had run up losses for years; it was shut down in 2012 and was put up for sale in 2013.

Strategy

Citing high operating and maintenance costs (the refinery was fueled by oil not the cheaper natural gas) and the growth of lower-cost refineries in emerging markets HOVENSA has posted $1.3 billion in losses since 2009. As a result the company decided to cut its losses by converting the refinery into an oil storage terminal which can take advantage of St. Croix's strategic location. Its 55-ft. deep harbor enables it to receive crude oil tanker deliveries from Venezuela and around the world. The storage terminal employs about 100 workers. The shutdown of the refinery resulted in more than 2000 employes being laid off.

Company Background

In 2009 the global economic downturn depressed demand for oil caused a dip in production and prompted the company to lay off 270 employees (about 21% of its total contract workers).

Crude thoughput has declined steadily at HOVENSA due to weaker refining margins and planned and unplanned maintenance from 402000 barrels per day (bpd) in 2009 to 390000 bpd in 2010 to 284000 bpd in 2011.

EXECUTIVES

President and COO, Lawrence J. (Larry) Kupfer
EVP, Alexander A. (Alex) Moorehead
VP and Deputy COO, Marco Crovesi
VP Environmental Health and Safety, Richard (Dick) Smullen
VP Refinery Operations, Peter (Pete) Barba
Finance Manager, Mike Fennessey
Purchasing Manager, Gary Miller
President Chief Operating Officer of HOVENSA, Brian K. Lever
Auditors: ERNST & YOUNG LLP NEW YORK N

LOCATIONS

HQ: HOVENSA LLC
1 ESTATE HOPE, CHRISTIANSTED, VI 00820
Phone: 3406923000
Web: WWW.HOVENSALLC.COM

COMPETITORS

Chevron	Royal Dutch Shell
ConocoPhillips	Sunoco
Exxon Mobil	Valero Energy
Marathon Oil	

HISTORICAL FINANCIALS

Company Type: Private

Income Statement

FYE: December 31

	REVENUE ($ mil.)	NET INCOME ($ mil.)	NET PROFIT MARGIN	EMPLOYEES
12/09	10,048	(451)	—	1,300
12/08	17,479	94	0.5%	—
Annual Growth	(42.5%)	—	—	—

2009 Year-End Financials

Debt ratio: ——
Return on equity: (-4.50%)
Cash ($ mil.): 77
Current ratio: 0.20
Long-term debt ($ mil.): —

Dividends
Yield: —
Payout: —
Market value ($ mil.): —

HP Inc

Making a hard copy takes a device often a personal computer to create a document or presentation and a printer to transfer words and images to paper. That's pretty much the business of HP Inc. one of two companies created from the breakup of Hewlett-Packard Co. HP makes 60% of its revenue from personal systems (notebook computers and desktops) and 40% from printers and supplies such as ink. It's the No. 1 printer company and No. 1 commercial PC maker in the world (Lenovo is tops overall). About half of revenue comes from customers in the Americas. Even after the breakup HP and sibling HP Enterprise (HPE) would rank in the Fortune 100.

OperationsSales of notebook computers account for a third of HP Inc.'s revenue followed by printer supplies such as ink cartridges at 26% of revenue. The business of actually selling printers is 16% of HP's revenue and its split between 10% for commercial printers and 6% from consumer printers. Desktop computer sales bring in about a fifth of revenue and workstations about 6%.

Geographic ReachSome 46% of HP Inc.'s revenue comes from sales to customers in the Americas. Customers in the Europe Middle East and Africa region generate 25% with the Asia-Pacific region and Japan accounting for 19%.

Sales and MarketingHP markets its products directly as well as through a wide range of third-party channels including retailers resellers and distributors and original equipment manufacturers and systems integrators.

Financial PerformanceMost financials aren't available from HP Inc. yet but when it was part of the former Hewlett-Packard its revenue was $57.3 billion (compared to HPE's $53 million revenue). Moreover the high-margin printer business was the former company's biggest profit maker.

StrategyFortunately for HP Inc. the vision for the paperless office hasn't come true. The company pegs the printer market at $234 billion and still growin. People in offices and homes still want to print documents and images and many of them do it with HP printers and HP ink. For years the printer business profits helped pay for other Hewlett-Packard units that had a hard time finding traction. Now HP Inc. can take some of that money and invest in research and development. With its Multi Jet Fusion 3D printer HP is moving beyond images and words on a page to objects. It also is looking at what are called A3 printers that handle 11 inch by 17 inch sized paper as well as the standard 8 ½ by 11 inch pages. Managed-print services is another area receiving serious attention from HP.

The PC side isn't as cheery. Overall PC shipments have declined for several years for just about all PC makers. The state of the PC has even driven HP and competitors such as Dell and Lenovo to run an advertising campaign touting new capabilities for PCs running the Microsoft Windows operating system (Microsoft also is part of the campaign).

HISTORY

Early History

Encouraged by Stanford professor Frederick Terman (considered the founder of Silicon Valley) in 1938 engineers Bill Hewlett and David Packard started Hewlett-Packard (HP) in a garage in Palo Alto California with $538. Hewlett was the idea man while Packard served as manager; the two were so low-key that the company's first official meeting ended with no decision on exactly what

to manufacture. Finding good people took priority over finding something to sell. The first product ended up being an audio oscillator. Walt Disney Studios one of HP's first customers bought eight to use in the making of Fantasia.

Demand for HP's electronic testing equipment during WWII spurred sales growth from $34000 in 1940 to nearly $1 million just three years later. HP went public in 1957. The company expanded beyond the US during 1959 establishing a marketing organization in Switzerland and a manufacturing plant in West Germany. HP entered the medical field in 1961 by acquiring Sanborn and the analytical instrumentation business in 1965 with the purchase of F&M Scientific. In 1969 Packard left the company to serve as deputy defense secretary under President Nixon for two years.

The company pioneered personal computing with the world's first handheld scientific calculator in 1972. Under the leadership of John Young the founders' chosen successor (named CEO in 1978) HP introduced its first PCs the first desktop mainframe and the LaserJet printer. Its initial PCs were known for their rugged build tailored for factory operations. They were also more expensive than rival versions and consequently didn't enjoy strong sales.

By 1986 a five-year $250 million R&D project — the company's largest at the time —produced a family of HP computers based on the reduced instruction set computing (RISC) architecture. Hewlett retired in 1987 (he died in 2001); sons of both Hewlett and Packard were named that year to the company's board of directors. HP became a leader in workstations with the 1989 purchase of market pioneer Apollo Computer despite technology delays with the merger that resulted in the loss of nearly $750 million in new business.

EXECUTIVES

Chief Supply Chain Officer, Stuart C. Pann, age 56
COO, Jon E. Flaxman, age 58
President 3D Printing Business, Stephen (Steve) Nigro
CTO, Shane D. Wall, age 50
President Personal Systems Business, Ron Coughlin
CFO, Catherine A. (Cathie) Lesjak, age 56, $850,033 total compensation
VP and General Manager Inkjet Commercial Division HP Imaging and Printing Group; Site Manager Barcelona, Enrique Lores, age 50
President Americas, Christoph Schell
President Asia Pacific and Japan (APJ), Richard Bailey
President and CEO, Dion J. Weisler, $831,251 total compensation
President Europe Middle East and Africa (EMEA), Nick Lazaridis
Vice President and General Manager Inkjet High speed Production Solutions, Aurelio Maruggi
Executive Vice President, John (Jack) Hinshaw
Vice President Marketing and Business Development Americas Personal Systems Group, John (Jack) Dayan
Vice President HPN Business Strategy and Operations, Monique Nolk
Vice President Big Data, Pankaj Dugar
Vice President Information Technology Infrastructure And Operations, Rich Gilbert
Vice President Of Corporate Communications, Howard Clabo
Vice President Of Product Marketing, Jay Jamison
Vice President Product Marketing, Roy Ritthaler
Vice President Of Sales, Deborah Kostrzeski
Vice President Americas Channels And Alliances, Archie Miller
Vice President Customer Solution Center Americas, Bernie Woods

Senior Vice President Hp Technology Services, Jean-Paul Wagner

Vice President Information Technology, Albert Werner

Vice President Automotive Aerospace And Defense High Tech Life Sciences, Stephen Mason

Vice President Meaning Based Governance, Dominic Brown

European Vice President of Marketing, Luciana Broggi

Vice President Enterprise Group Marketing Apj, Karen Holland

Vice President Enterprise Server Sales, Robin Adler

Vice President Manager Director, Barbara Cofsky

Vice President Marketing, Kimberly Millier

Vice President Of Marketing, Paul Barker

Vice President Strategy and Planning, Lorna Heynike

Vice President Decision Support And Analytics Services, Prithvijit Roy

Vice President Marketing, Richard Swingle

Vice President Sales, Rodney Moore

Vice President Human Resources, Jason Wilkinson

Vice President Of Marketing, Gregory Poole

Vice President Of Mobile, Christopher Wu

Vice President Information Technology Principal, Rod Walker

Vice President and General Manager, Bill Mannel

Vice President Advanced Platforms Group, Louis Kim

Vice President And General Manager BSM, Christoph Pfister

HP Helion VPC Engineer, David (Dave) Mineo

Vice President Global Security Director, Bob Moore

Vice President, Mike Klaus

Vice President And Social Business Application Services, Franklin Grosvenor

Vice President Content Strategy and Marketing Programs, Michelle (Mitch) Tolod

Vice President Americas Server Sales, Leslie Maher

Vice President Worldwide Software Operations and Strategy, Deven Waghani

Vice President Strategy Solutions and Technical Marketing, Yogesh Agrawal

Vice President Sales Strategy and Operations Enterprise Group Americas, Jeff DiLullo

Vice President and Global Practice Lead, Claude Ferguson

Senior Vice President Strategy and Operations Enterprise Services, Kreg Nichols

Vice President Federal Civilian Business Development, Jackie Everett

Vice President Strategy and GWAC Project Management Office, Connie Theroux

Vice President and General Manager US Consumer Sales, Christoph Ruef

Vice President Other Line of Business, Jo Dennis

Vice President, Brian Cumbra

Vice President Product Marketing, Derrick Runcie

Vice President Hardware Systems and Technology, Ric Lewis

Vice President Worldwide ESP Inside Sales, Ingrid Steinbergs

Senior Vice President and General Manager Business Critical Systems, Martin (Marti) Fink

Vice President Investor Relations, Rob Binns

Vice President Worldwide Total Rewards HP Enterprise Busines, Jake Parker

National Account Manager, Amy Hilfiker

Executive Vice President Enterprise Services, Mike Nefkens

Vice President Global, Gregg Melinson

Senior Vice President Software, Yazmin Martinez

Vice President Consumer and Brand Strategy, Boby Joseph

Vice President Human Resources, Missy Ballew

Vice President, M Johnson

Vice President Technology Services Marketing, Bob Conklin

Vice President And General Manager: Enterprise Services Americas, Charles (Chas) Salameh

Vice President Supply Chain Delivery, Kk Narayanan

Vice President Marketing Business Desktop Pc Business Unit, Jeff Groudan

Vice President Account Executive NASA, Robert (Bob) Pearson

Vice President Finance Strategy, Michael (Mel) Bordoni

Senior Vice President Deputy General Counsel Corporate Securities and Mergers and Acquisitions, Rishi Varma Rishi Varma

Vice President Global Digital Marketing, Natalie Malaszenko Natalie Malaszenko

Vice President Sales, Alex Langer

Senior Vice President HP Cloud, Kerry Bailey

Chairman, Margaret C. (Meg) Whitman, age 59

Auditors: Ernst & Young LLP

LOCATIONS

HQ: HP Inc
1501 Page Mill Road, Palo Alto, CA 94304
Phone: 650 857-1501
Web: www.hp.com

2014 Sales

	$ mil.	% of total
US	38,805	35
Other countries	72,649	65
Total	**111,454**	**100**

PRODUCTS/OPERATIONS

2014 Sales

	$ mil.	% of total
Products	73,726	66
Services	37,327	34
Financing income	401	-
Total	**111,454**	**100**

2014 Sales

	$ mil.	% of total
Personal systems	34,303	31
Enterprise servers storage & networking	27,814	24
Printing	22,979	20
Services	22,398	19
Software	3,933	3
Financial services	3,498	3
Investments	302	-
Adjustments	(3773)	-
Total	**111,454**	**100**

Selected Products and Services

Personal Systems
   Calculators
   Desktop PCs
   Digital entertainment centers
   DVD writers
   Handheld computers
   Notebook computers
   Televisions (LCD plasma)
   Workstations
Imaging and Printing
   Commercial printing
   Digital presses
   Printers
   Digital imaging
   Projectors
   Scanners
   Personal printing
   All-in-ones (copier fax printer scanner)
   Ink jet printers
   Laser printers
   Shared printing
   Networked inkjet laser and multifunction printers
   Office all-in-ones
   Services
   Supplies

Selected Acquisitions2011Autonomy (UK; data repurposing software)Printelligent (managed print

services)2010ArcSight (security software)3PAR (storage software and hardware)Fortify Software (data security software)Stratavia (database and application automa

COMPETITORS

ADP	Hitachi
ASUSTeK	IBM
Acer	Konica Minolta
Apple Inc.	Lenovo
Brother Industries	Lexmark
CA Inc.	Microsoft
CACI International	NCR
CGI Group	NEC
Canon	Oc©
Cisco Systems	Oki Electric
Computer Sciences	Oracle
Corp.	Panasonic Corp
Dell	Ricoh Company
Eastman Kodak	Samsung Electronics
Epson	Sharp Corp.
First Data	Sony
Fiserv	Symantec
Fuji Xerox	Teradata
Fujitsu	Toshiba
Fujitsu Technology	Unisys
Solutions	Wipro Technologies
Heidelberger	Xerox
Druckmaschinen	

HISTORICAL FINANCIALS

Company Type: Public

Income Statement

FYE: October 31

	REVENUE ($ mil.)	NET INCOME ($ mil.)	NET PROFIT MARGIN	EMPLOYEES
10/15	103,355	4,554	4.4%	287,000
10/14	111,454	5,013	4.5%	302,000
10/13	112,298	5,113	4.6%	317,500
10/12	120,357	(12,650)	—	331,800
10/11	127,245	7,074	5.6%	349,600
Annual Growth	**(5.1%)**	**(10.4%)**	**—**	**(4.8%)**

2015 Year-End Financials

Debt ratio: 23.08%	No. of shares (mil.): 1,803
Return on equity: 16.71%	Dividends
Cash ($ mil.): 17,433	Yield: 0.0%
Current ratio: 1.23	Payout: 27.1%
Long-term debt ($ mil.): 21,780	Market value ($ mil.): 48,628

	STOCK PRICE ($) FY Close	P/E High/Low		PER SHARE ($) Earnings	Dividends	Book Value
10/15	26.96	16	10	2.48	0.67	15.39
10/14	35.88	14	9	2.62	0.61	14.53
10/13	24.37	10	4	2.62	0.55	14.29
10/12	13.85	—	—	(6.41)	0.50	11.43
10/11	26.61	14	7	3.32	0.40	19.40
Annual Growth	**0.3%**	**—**	**—**	**(7.0%)**	**13.8%**	**(5.6%)**

HRG Group Inc

HRG Group (formerly Harbinger Group) has zapped its former image as an oil and gas company and instead looks to pump up its portfolio. Like an investment firm the holding company acquires businesses across a diverse array of industries. Harbinger Group makes most of its revenue from the sale of branded consumer products such as residential locksets consumer batteries grooming and personal products small household appliances and pest control products. It also deals in life insurance and annuities provides asset-backed loans and owns energy assets. The company was co-founded in 1953 by former US President George H. W. Bush under the name Zapata.

Operations

HRG Group operates through four segments: Consumer Products (Spectrum Brands which generates nearly 75% of total revenue); Insurance (FGL and Front Street nearly 25% of revenue) Energy (Compass Production Partners 2% of revenue) and Asset Management (Salus Five Island EIC and CorAmerica).

Geographic Reach

New York-based HRG Group enjoys a global reach with operations in North America Latin America and Europe.Sales and MarketingBecause of consolidation within the retail industry the company's Spectrum Brand products are sold through a limited group of retailers including: Wal-Mart The Home Depot Lowe's Target Carrefour PetSmart PetCo Canadian Tire and Gigante. In 2014 Spectrum Brands' sales to Wal-Mart made up 16% of net sales. The company spent $22 million on advertising costs in 2014; down from $23 million in 2013 but up from $20.7 million in 2012.

Financial Performance

HRG Group has enjoyed rising revenues from its portfolio holdings over the past several years thanks to organic growth and growth through acquisitions. Revenue jumped nearly 8% to $5.96 billion in fiscal 2014 (ended September) mostly thanks to increased revenue from the company's 2013 acquisition of Spectrum Brands' residential hardware and home improvement (HHI) businesses but also thanks to higher sales of Spectrum's home and garden and consumer battery products. The company's Energy division also grew by 63% thanks to new oil and natural gas revenue from the company's 2013 share acquisition of Compass while its asset management division grew by nearly 20% thanks to new business activity.Despite higher revenue the company suffered a second year of losses though it managed to cut them considerably to a $10.3 million loss in 2014 thanks to higher revenue and a decline in income tax expenses. Leading to the company's loss in 2014 were higher corporate expenses related to higher stock-based compensation and bonus expenses and higher impairment charges in the Energy segment as oil prices fell.Cash from operations grew by 16% to $607.9 million in 2014 mostly driven by lower inventories and accounts receivables and lower acquisition integration and restructuring costs.

Strategy

HRG Group works to acquire operating businesses across a range of industries such as consumer products insurance and financial products telecommunications agriculture power generation and water and natural resources.

HRG Group acquired a majority interest in consumer goods firm Spectrum Brands in 2011. Spectrum Brands expanded its business in 2012 by acquiring the residential hardware and home improvement business of Stanley Black & Decker. The move gave the consumer products company additional brands names such as Kwikset Weiser Baldwin and National Hardware. It also purchased certain assets of Tong Lung Metal Industry Co. Ltd. a Taiwan company that specializes in producing residential locks in 2013.

The company purchased Old Mutual U.S. Life Holdings from Old Mutual for $350 million rebranding them as Fidelity & Guaranty Life Insurance Company and Fidelity & Guaranty Life Insurance Company of New York. Harbinger Group then acquired a minority stake in North American Energy Partners which primarily provides construction and pipeline services to the Canadian oil sands market.

HRG Group also owns almost all of Zap.Com Corporation; however it is a public shell company with no business operations. Zap.Com is seeking investments or it may develop a new business so that it can become an operating company.Mergers and AcquisitionsIn late 2014 HGR's subsidiary HGI Energy Holdings purchased the remaining 25.5% in share interest that it didn't own in Compass Production Partners LP from EXCO Resources for $118.75 million in cash.In mid-2014 through its subsidiary HGI Funding purchased 62% interest in women's apparel retailer Frederick's of Hollywood. Also around that time the company entered an agreement to purchase a controlling stake in commercial real estate firm CorAmerica to expand its asset management division. In April 2013 the company acquired the residential hardware and home improvement (HHI) businesses from Stanley Black & Decker which consisted of certain assets of TLM Taiwan.Company Background

Under its former name Zapata Corporation the company sold its energy businesses in the 1990s and became a producer of marine protein through its holdings in Omega Protein. Omega's facilities suffered major hurricane damage in 2005 and Zapata sold Omega the next year.

HISTORY

Named for the movie Viva Zapata! Zapata was formed by the 1953 merger of the young George H. W. Bush's Bush-Overby oil company and another oil firm run by Hugh and Bill Liedtke. After going public in 1955 Bush and the Liedtkes split the company in 1959 with Bush taking over Zapata Off-Shore. He sold his stake in Zapata in 1966 after being elected to Congress. In 1973 the company bought fish processor Haynie Products. Zapata struggled through the oil slump of the 1980s sold assets and converted debt to stock to avoid bankruptcy.

Investor Malcolm Glazer took control of the company in 1993. He became CEO and chairman the following year and shifted the company's focus away from energy. In 1995 Zapata sold the natural gas compression business and acquired Glazer's 31% share of money-losing food packaging manufacturer Envirodyne (increased to 40% in 1996 and renamed Viskase Companies in 1998). In 1997 it sold its Bolivian operations the last of the energy holdings to Tesoro.

The company expanded its fishing business by purchasing two competitors in 1997 but it didn't hold them for long. The next year it spun off its fishing businesses to the public as Omega Protein retaining a majority stake.

Excited by the Internet's possibilities Zapata in 1998 resuscitated two e-zines that had been spiked by Icon CMT and it formed Zap.com to hold those and other Web sites that it planned to buy. Despite having few significant assets and no revenues in 1999 the company spun off Zap.com to its shareholders; Zapata retained nearly 98%. Also that year the company moved its headquarters from Houston to Rochester New York.

Zapata recorded big losses in 1999 mostly due to sluggish sales at Omega Protein which suffered from a glut in the protein meal and edible oil markets. In addition Viskase which has been struggling and selling operations for a few years sold its shrink film business in 2000 to help retire debt. Also that year Viskase announced that it was selling its plastics business. Zapata announced in 2000 that it would begin a new focus for Charged including expansion into wireless animation and creative multimedia. In 2001 however the company shut down both Zap.com and its Charged Productions operations. In September 2001 Zapata sold its interest in Viskase.

In 2003 Zapata rejected an unsolicited $108 million cash take-over bid from merger and acquisition group Hollingsworth Rothwell & Roxford. Later that year Zapata bought additional shares of Safety Components International bringing its ownership of the company to about 80%; however it sold its shares in Safety Components in 2005.

In late 2006 it began selling its holdings in Omega Protein. Omega bought back 36% of Zapata's shares for $47.5 million in November of that year. Zapata announced the sale of the last of its Omega holdings to a group of private investors for about $29 million in December 2006.

In 2009 the company changed its name to Harbinger Group.

EXECUTIVES

EVP and CFO, Thomas A. (Tom) Williams, age 55, $500,000 total compensation
EVP Investments and Managing Director, David M. Maura, $500,000 total compensation
President CEO and Director, Omar M. Asali, $500,000 total compensation
Managing Director Investments, Phil Gass
Senior Vice President Deputy General Counsel And Corporate Secretary, Ehsan Zargar
Vice President Investments, Tyler Kolarik
Chairman, Joseph S. Steinberg, age 71
Auditors: KPMG LLP

LOCATIONS

HQ: HRG Group Inc
450 Park Avenue, 29th Floor, New York, NY 10022
Phone: 212 906-8555
Web: www.harbingergroupinc.com

PRODUCTS/OPERATIONS

2014 Revenue

	% of total
Net consumer product sales	75
Net investment income	14
Net investment gains (losses)	7
Oil & natural gas	2
Insurance premiums	1
Insurance & investment product fees & other	1
Total	**100**

2014 Revenue by Segment

	% of total
Consumer products	74
Insurance	23
Energy	2
Asset Management	1
Total	**100**

COMPETITORS

Apollo Global Management	Hellman & Friedman
	KKR
Berkshire Hathaway	Lightyear Capital LLC
Blackstone Group	Onex
Brookfield Asset Management	TPG

HISTORICAL FINANCIALS

Company Type: Public

Income Statement

FYE: September 30

	REVENUE ($ mil.)	NET INCOME ($ mil.)	NET PROFIT MARGIN	EMPLOYEES
09/15	5,815	(556)	—	15,922
09/14	5,963	(10)	—	14,427
09/13	5,543	(45)	—	13,742
09/12	4,480	89	2.0%	6,019
09/11	3,477	34	1.0%	6,009
Annual Growth	**13.7%**	**—**	**—**	**27.6%**

2015 Year-End Financials

Debt ratio: 19.74%
Return on equity: (-54.90%)
Cash ($ mil.): 1,197
Current ratio: 2.46
Long-term debt ($ mil.): 6,382

No. of shares (mil.): 201
Dividends
  Yield: —
  Payout: —
Market value ($ mil.): 2,362

	STOCK PRICE ($) FY Close	P/E High/Low		PER SHARE ($) Earnings	Dividends	Book Value
09/15	11.73	—	—	(2.81)	0.00	2.91
09/14	13.12	—	—	(0.51)	0.00	7.13
09/13	10.37	—	—	(0.67)	0.00	7.40
09/12	8.43	69	27	0.15	0.00	10.68
09/11	5.07	92	57	0.04	0.00	8.47
Annual Growth	23.3%	—	—	—	—	—(23.4%)

HSBC Finance Corp

Auditors: KPMG LLP

LOCATIONS

HQ: HSBC Finance Corp
26525 North Riverwoods Boulevard, Suite 100,
Mettawa, IL 60045
Phone: 224 880-7000
Web: www.us.hsbc.com

HISTORICAL FINANCIALS

Company Type: Public

Income Statement

FYE: December 31

	ASSETS ($ mil.)	NET INCOME ($ mil.)	INCOME AS % OF ASSETS	EMPLOYEES
12/14	31,960	523	1.6%	1,700
12/13	37,872	536	1.4%	2,200
12/12	46,778	(845)	—	2,537
12/11	63,469	(1,408)	—	5,350
12/10	76,532	(1,916)	—	6,650
Annual Growth	(19.6%)	—	—	(28.9%)

2014 Year-End Financials

Debt ratio: 73.13%
Return on equity: 7.59%
Cash ($ mil.): 2,157
Current ratio: —
Long-term debt ($ mil.): —

No. of shares (mil.): 0
Dividends
  Yield: 6.2%
  Payout: —
Market value ($ mil.): 0

	STOCK PRICE ($) FY Close	P/E High/Low		PER SHARE ($) Earnings	Dividends	Book Value
12/14 104,750,000.00	25.34	—	—	(0.00)	1.59	
12/13 97,955,882.00	22.90	—	—	(0.00)	1.59	
12/12 89,779,411.00	25.06	—	—	(0.00)	1.59	
12/11 101,852,941.00	21.25	—	—	(0.00)	1.59	
12/10 116,969,696.00	22.84	—	—	(0.00)	1.59	
Annual Growth	2.6%	—	—	—	(0.0%)	(2.7%)

HSBC USA, Inc.

HSBC USA a subsidiary of British banking behemoth HSBC Holdings operates HSBC Bank USA one of the biggest foreign-owned banks in the country by assets. With about 240 offices (including 155 in New York City) the bank has one of the largest branch networks in New York State plus more than 100 additional locations in about a dozen other states and Washington DC; California New Jersey and Florida are its next largest markets. The bank offers personal commercial and mortgage banking services. Its personal financial services segment provides mutual funds investments and insurance. HSBC Bank USA also offers investment banking private banking brokerage and trust services.

Geographic Reach

HSBC USA serves customers nationwide with the highest concentration of its bank branches located in New York California and Florida.

Operations

Boasting one of New York's largest bank networks HSBC USA offers personal commercial and mortgage banking services as well as investment banking brokerage and trust services.

HSBC USA operates foreign branches and representative offices in the Caribbean Canada Latin America Europe and Asia.

Sales and Marketing

HSBC USA serves a variety of customers such as individuals (including high net worth individuals) small businesses corporations institutions and governments. It boasts some 3 million customers 36% of which live in New York and 26% in California.

In 2013 HSBC USA spent about $43 million on advertising down from 2012's $47 million.

Strategy

The firm is focused on security. HSBC USA in 2014 became one of the nation's first major banks to roll out a new fraud protection device which employs two-factor authentication for its personal Internet customers.

Financial Performance

HSBC USA posted $4.8 billion in revenue in fiscal 2013 down $343 million —or 7% —vs. 2012's results. Lower interest rates and lower average outstanding balances contributed to the declines as well as a decrease in credit card fees in both 2013 and 2012. Additionally the financial institution logged a net loss of $338 million thanks to continued revenue declines and the provision for loan losses. Change in the working capital and asset and liabilities as well as net losses conspired against HSBC USA gaining ground. Indeed during fiscal 2013 the firm posted a cash outflow of $1.36 billion after having logged a cash inflow of $8.37 billion in 2012.

Company Background

HSBC and HSBC USA restructured their operations in 2011 which included divesting operations and cutting staff. As part of the restructuring HSBC sold 195 retail branches in New York and Connecticut to First Niagara for $1 billion. Through HSBC USA and its HSBC Finance affiliate HSBC also sold its card and retail services business to Capital One Financial. In 2010 HSBC USA exited its noncore wholesale banknotes business. The company also closed and consolidated about a dozen branches in Connecticut and New Jersey. The moves are part of the company's strategy to focus more on commercial and corporate banking in New York and other key urban markets itself part of HSBC's restructuring to create a leaner group.

EXECUTIVES

Senior Executive Vice President and Regional Head of Insurance, Patrick A. Cozza, age 59
EVP and Secretary, Patrick D. Schwartz, age 57
SEVP Head of Retail Banking and Wealth Management, Kevin R. Martin, age 54
Executive Vice President - Communications, Lisa M. Sodeika, age 51
SEVP and CFO, John T. McGinnis, age 48, $463,077 total compensation
Executive Vice President Head of Strategy and Planning, Loren C. Klug, age 54
Senior Executive Vice President and Regional Head of Wholesale & Market Risk, Mark A. Hershey, age 62
EVP and Head Private Banking, Marlon Young, age 59, $389,423 total compensation
President CEO and Director, Irene M. Dorner, age 60, $700,000 total compensation
Executive Vice President and Chief Accounting Officer, Eric K. Ferren
SEVP and General Counsel, Stuart Alderoty, age 56
Senior Executive Vice President and Chief Operating Officer USA, Gregory Zeeman
Executive Vice President Head of Human Resources USA, Mary E. Bilbrey
Senior Executive Vice President and Chief Risk Officer, Steven G. Ekert
Senior Executive Vice President Chief Compliance Officer and Head of Regulatory Compliance and Financial Crimes Compliance, Gary E. Peterson
Senior Executive Vice President Head of Commercial Banking, Steven A. Bottomley
Senior Executive Vice President Head of Global Banking and Markets Americas, Patrick M. Nolan
Senior Vice President Compensation, Deanna Larkin
Assistant Vice President Portfolio Manager, David Freeman
Auditors: KPMG LLP

LOCATIONS

HQ: HSBC USA, Inc.
452 Fifth Avenue, New York, NY 10018
Phone: 212 525-5000

PRODUCTS/OPERATIONS

2013 Sales

	$ mil.	% of total
Interest		
Loans	1,876	39
Securities	876	19
Other	227	4
Non-interest		
Other fees & commissions	706	14
Trading revenue	474	9
Servicing and other fees from HSBC affiliates	202	4
Other securities gains	202	4
Trust income	123	3
Other	150	4
Total	**4,836**	**100**

COMPETITORS

Astoria Financial	KeyCorp
Bank of America	M&T Bank
Capital One	New York Community
Citibank	Bancorp
Citizens Financial	PNC Financial
Group	TD Bank USA
JPMorgan Chase	Wells Fargo

HISTORICAL FINANCIALS

Company Type: Public

Income Statement

FYE: December 31

	ASSETS ($ mil.)	NET INCOME ($ mil.)	INCOME AS % OF ASSETS	EMPLOYEES
12/14	185,539	354	0.2%	6,400
12/13	185,487	(338)	—	6,500
12/12	196,567	(1,045)	—	7,000
12/11	210,280	1,018	0.5%	9,000
12/10	183,813	1,564	0.9%	12,000
Annual Growth	0.2%	(31.0%)	—	(14.5%)

2014 Year-End Financials

Debt ratio: 14.30%
Return on equity: 2.12%
Cash ($ mil.): 52,790
Current ratio: —
Long-term debt ($ mil.): —

No. of shares (mil.): 0
Dividends
  Yield: 6.4%
  Payout: —
Market value ($ mil.): 0

	STOCK PRICE ($) FY Close	P/E High/Low	PER SHARE ($) Earnings	Dividends	Book Value
12/14	22.60 23,796,633	— —	(0.00)	1.63	
12/13	18.60 23,091,164	— —	(0.00)	1.63	
12/12	21.75 25,015,427	— —	(0.00)	1.63	
12/11	15.30 25,985,955	— —	(0.00)	0.89	
12/10	21.29 23,501,404	— —	(0.00)	1.63	
Annual Growth	1.5%		—	(0.0%)	0.3%

Humana Inc.

Medicare has made Humana a big-time player in the insurance game. One of the country's largest Medicare providers and a top health insurer Humana provides Medicare Advantage plans and prescription drug coverage to more than 5 million members throughout the US. It also administers managed care plans for other government programs including Medicaid plans in Florida and Puerto Rico and TRICARE (a program for military personnel) in 10 southern states. Additionally Humana offers commercial health plans and specialty (life dental and vision) coverage; it also provides health management services and operates outpatient care clinics. All told it covers about 20 million members in the US. Aetna is buying Humana for $37.1 billion.

HISTORY

In 1961 Louisville Kentucky lawyers David Jones and Wendell Cherry bought a nursing home as a real estate investment. Within six years their company Extendicare was the largest nursing home chain in the US (with only eight homes).

Faced with a glutted nursing home market the partners noticed that hospitals received more money per patient per day than nursing homes so they took their company public in 1968 to finance hospital purchases (one per month from 1968 to 1971). The company then sold its 40 nursing homes. Sales rose 13 times over in the next five years and in 1973 the firm changed its name to Humana.

By 1975 Humana had built 27 hospitals in the South and Southwest. It targeted young privately insured patients and kept its charity caseload and bad-debt expenses low. Three years later #3 for-profit hospital operator Humana moved up a notch when it bought #2 American Medicorp.

In 1983 the government began reimbursing Medicare payments based on fixed rates. Counting on its high hospital occupancy in 1984 the company launched Humana Health Care Plans rewarding doctors and patients who used Humana hospitals. However hospital occupancy dropped and the company closed several clinics. When its net income fell 75% in 1986 the firm responded by lowering premiums to attract employers.

In 1991 co-founder Cherry died. With hospital profits down in 1993 Jones spun off Humana's 76 hospitals as Galen Healthcare which formed the nucleus of what is now HCA - The Healthcare Company. Humana used the cash to expand its HMO membership buying Group Health Association (an HMO serving metropolitan Washington DC) and CareNetwork (a Milwaukee HMO). The next year Humana added 1.3 million members when it bought EMPHESYS and the company's income which had stagnated since the salad days of the late 1980s and early 1990s seemed headed in the right direction.

In the mid-1990s cutthroat premiums failed to cover rising health care costs as members' hospital use soared out of control particularly in the company's new Washington DC market. Profits dropped 94% and Humana's already tense relationship with doctors and members worsened. President and COO Wayne Smith and CFO Roger Drury resigned as part of a management shake-up and newly appointed president Gregory Wolf offered to drop the company's gag clause after the Florida Physicians Association threatened to sue.

A reorganized Humana rebounded in 1997. The company pulled out of 13 unprofitable markets including Alabama (though it did not drop TRICARE its military health coverage program in that state) and Washington DC. Refocusing on core markets in the Midwest and Southeast Humana bought Physician Corp. of America (PCA) and ChoiceCare a Cincinnati HMO. Wolf replaced Jones as CEO in 1997.

To cut costs Humana agreed in 1998 to be bought by United HealthCare (now UnitedHealth Group). The deal was abandoned however when United HealthCare took a $900 million charge in advance of the purchase. Humana found savings by pruning its Medicare HMO business.

Humana did everything but party in 1999. The company faced RICO charges for allegedly overcharging members for co-insurance; it agreed to repay $15 million in Medicare overpayments to the government; and it became the first health insurance firm to be slapped with a class-action suit over its physician incentives and other coverage policies.

Humana sold PCA in 2000 saying that it had paid too much for the company; subsidiary PCA Property & Casualty was also sold marking the company's exit from the workers' compensation business. That year Humana also sold its underperforming Florida Medicaid HMO to Well Care HMO and agreed to pay more than $14 million to the government for submitting false Medicare payment information.

In 2001 Humana bought a unit of Anthem that provides health benefits to the military. Expanding its holdings in the southeast Humana acquired Louisiana's Ochsner Health Plan in 2004.

It further grew its product line with the 2007 acquisition of Atlanta-based CompBenefits a provider of dental and vision benefits to nearly 5 million members. The acquisition gave Humana a full-service vision offering and expanded its dental benefits operations. Later that year the company bought KMG America a life and health insurer and third-party administrator for more than 1 million members. Humana combined CompBenefits KMG America and its previous dental benefits operations into a new unit in 2008 called Humana Specialty Benefits.

In 2008 Humana acquired about 25000 Medicare Advantage members in Nevada from UnitedHealth which was divesting the operations as part of its merger deal with Sierra Health Services for $225 million. And later that year it acquired smaller Florida-based Medicare Advantage provider Metcare Health Plans from Metropolitan Health Networks.

Additional acquisitions include the 2008 acquisition of OSF HealthPlans an Illinois-based managed care company belonging to OSF Healthcare. The deal worth about $90 million gave Humana another 60000 commercial members as well as some new Medicare customers in Illinois. The company had already wrapped up its acquisition of Tennessee-based PHP Companies (which does business as Cariten Healthcare) from Covenant Health. Humana spent $250 million in late 2008 to gain Cariten's managed care operations in East Tennessee adding 70000 commercial customers and 45000 Medicare members.

One of Humana's competitive TRICARE contracts was awarded to another party in 2009; however after Humana objected and bids were re-evaluated the decision was reversed in 2011 (with no negative impact on the company's operations).

In 2010 Humana moved into an all new specialty business area with its acquisition of Concentra a provider of occupational medicine urgent care and wellness programs from Welsh Carson Anderson & Stowe for some $790 million. Humana made the purchase to bolster its consumer-focused initiatives and provide a platform for future service-offering expansion efforts.

To widen its cost-control services and advance its IT offerings Humana partnered with software firm Anvita Health in 2010. The analytics firm provided analytics capabilities to identify at-risk members and also served other insurers benefit managers health care professionals and electronic health record providers. (Humana wound up acquiring Anvita in late 2011.)

Early in 2012 Humana purchased MD Care a Medicare Advantage provider serving some 15000 members in four Southern California counties. It also acquired Arcadian Management Services a Medicare Advantage HMO with some 64000 members in 15 states including California. To complete its acquisition of Arcadian Humana was required to sell select Medicare Advantage plans serving some 12000 former Arcadian members to CIGNA (in Texas and Arkansas) and WellCare Health Plans (in Arizona).

EXECUTIVES

EVP and COO, James E. (Jim) Murray, age 60, $786,184 total compensation
Senior Vice President, Thomas T Noland
President and CEO, Bruce D. Broussard, age 52, $1,118,954 total compensation
SVP and Chief Consumer Officer, Jody L. Bilney, age 52
SVP and Chief Medical Officer, Roy A. Beveridge, age 56
SVP and CIO, Brian P. LeClaire, age 53
SVP and Chief Human Resources Officer, Timothy S. (Tim) Huval, age 47, $540,750 total compensation
SVP and CFO, Brian A. Kane, age 42, $323,076 total compensation
SVP and Chief Strategy Officer, Christopher H. (Chris) Hunter, age 45, $465,865 total compensation
Segment Vice President, Mark A McCullough
Vice President Marketing, Phyllis Anderson

Vice President and Chief Clinical Strategies, Melissa (Mel) Weaver

Vice President Operations, John Brown

Vice President, William (Bill) Hauser

Vice President Marketpoint Sales, Jim Van Valin

Vice President Information Technology Operations, Kristy Stivers

Senior Vice President Human Resources CHRO, Bonny Hatclatk

Vice President Of Accounting, Anita Poole

Vice President, Bill Niehaus

Vice President, Brian Schwaniger

Vice President Information Technology, Margaret Houston

Field Vice President, Ryan O Catignani

Vice President, Douglas (Doug) Stoss

Vice President, Paul Davis

Vice President, Tim Moorhead

Vice President Provider Development Central Region, Lori Mallory

Medical Director, Richard Fernandez

Assistant Vice President, Kimberly Brown

Vice President Of Federal Affairs, Doug Stoss

Medical Director, Lourdes Pila-collazo

Field Vice President, Stacy Taylor

National Account Manager, Monique Clay

Medical Director, Joseph Migliozzi

Vice President, Michelle Wilfong

Vice President Network Management, Linda Bowers

Vice President, Colleen Pamperin

Field Vice President, Eric Bohannon

Vice President of Regulatory Affairs Corporate Compliance Officer, Carin A Mandarino

National Account Manager, Aimee Walter

Vice President Information Technology, Michael Richmond

Third Vice President, Tom Ryan

Regional President, Larry Costello

Vice President Information Technology, Kevin Obryan

Medical Director, Arthur Tomases

Medical Director, Harris Blackman

Medical Director, Mary Lawlor

Health Services Director, Marlene Spicer

Medical Director, Mayo Gilson

Vice President, Thomas Nelson

Vice President, Steve Chick

Vice President Group Sales, Rick Remmers

Health Services Director, Yvonne Shell

Executive Vice President Marketing, Jennifer (Jen) Bazante

Medical Director, Rae Godsey

Medical Director, Michael Richman

Medical Director Senior Products, Amarin Alexander

Executive Vice President Digital Center Of Excellence, Jeff Reid

Vice President, John Barger

Segment Vice President, John Delorimier

Health Services Director, Ricardo Menchaca

Medical Director, Earl Jackman

Medical Director, Teresita Hernandez

Vice President, Lois Gargotto

Market Vice President, Anita Holloway

National Account Manager, Melissa Staton

Regional Vice President, Cal Cullinan-james

Vice President Information Technology Transformation And Shared Services, Faheem Zuberi

Regional President Senior Products, Kevin Meriwether

Vice President, Gary Williams

Vice President of Finance Lifesynch, Jonathon Curlett

Segment Vice President, Michael J (Mel) Bellissimo

Ohio Indiana Vice President Network Contracting, Rich Gunza

Field Vice President, Mayra Torres

Vice President of Market Development Northeast Region, Denise Smith

Vice President and Controller Principal Accounting Officer, Steven E (Steve) McCulley

Vice President of Marketing, Jd Denny

Health Care Director, C Robertson

Chairman, Kurt J. Hilzinger, age 54

Secretary, Marisol Rivera

Board Member, Jerry Valentine

Assistant Treasurer, Alan Bailey

Board Member, Larry Pereiro

Secretary Treasurer, Jeff Fernandez

Auditors: PricewaterhouseCoopers LLP

LOCATIONS

HQ: Humana Inc.
  500 West Main Street, Louisville, KY 40202
Phone: 502 580-1000
Web: www.humana.com

PRODUCTS/OPERATIONS

2014 Sales

	$ mil.	% of total
Premiums		
Medicare Advantage	31,431	65
Fully insured commercial	8,604	18
Medicare stand-alone PDP	3,404	7
Specialty commercial	1,354	3
Military	19	—
Medicaid & other premiums	1,147	2
Services	2,164	4
Investment income	377	1
Total	**48,500**	**100**

2014 Sales

	$ mil.	% of total
Retail	34,069	50
Healthcare services	20,015	30
Employer group	12,419	19
Other	611	1
Adjustments	(18614)	-
Total	**48,500**	**100**

Selected Acquisitions

COMPETITORS

AMERIGROUP	First Health Group
Aetna	Florida Blue
Anthem	HCSC
Assurant	Health Net
Blue Cross and Blue Shield of Texas	HealthSpring
	Highmark
CIGNA	Kaiser Foundation
Caremark Pharmacy Services	Health Plan
	Molina Healthcare
Centene	UnitedHealth Group
Coventry Health Care	Universal American
Express Scripts	WellCare Health Plans

HISTORICAL FINANCIALS

Company Type: Public

Income Statement

FYE: December 31

	ASSETS ($ mil.)	NET INCOME ($ mil.)	INCOME AS % OF ASSETS	EMPLOYEES
12/14	23,466	1,147	4.9%	57,000
12/13	20,735	1,231	5.9%	52,000
12/12	19,979	1,222	6.1%	43,400
12/11	17,708	1,419	8.0%	40,000
12/10	16,103	1,099	6.8%	35,200
Annual Growth	**9.9%**	**1.1%**	**—**	**12.8%**

2014 Year-End Financials

Debt ratio: 16.30%
Return on equity: 12.10%
Cash ($ mil.): 1,935
Current ratio: —
Long-term debt ($ mil.): —

No. of shares (mil.): 149
Dividends
  Yield: 0.7%
  Payout: 17.8%
Market value ($ mil.): 21,488

	STOCK PRICE ($) FY Close	P/E High/Low		Earnings	PER SHARE ($) Dividends	Book Value
12/14	143.63	20	13	7.36	1.11	64.48
12/13	103.22	13	8	7.73	1.07	60.48
12/12	68.63	13	8	7.47	1.03	55.88
12/11	87.61	10	6	8.46	0.75	49.16
12/10	54.74	9	7	6.47	0.00	41.10
Annual Growth	**27.3%**	**—**	**—**	**3.3%**	**—**	**11.9%**

Hunt (J.B.) Transport Services, Inc.

When it comes to hauling freight J.B. Hunt Transport Services knows how to deliver. Its inter-modal unit the company's largest maintains about 4000 tractors 4750 drivers and more than 73000 pieces of trailing equipment and moves customers' cargo by combinations of truck and train. JBI's dedicated contract services unit supplies customers with drivers and equipment; it operates about 6500 company-owned trucks. The company's truckload transportation unit provides dry freight transportation with a fleet of about 1300 tractors. A fourth business segment integrated capacity solutions (ICS) manages freight transportation via third-party carriers as well as J.B. Hunt equipment.

Geographic Reach

The Company's corporate headquarter is located in Lowell Arkansas and its principal facilities are located throughout the US. Its JBI segment offers intermodal freight services to customers in the US Canada and Mexico.

Operations

Freight transported by J.B. Hunt includes automotive parts building materials chemicals food and beverages forest and paper products and general merchandise. The company divides its operations across four segments. JBI offers intermodal freight services to customers in Canada Mexico and the US; it generated almost 60% of J.B. Hunt's total sales in 2014.

Dedicated contract services (DCS) provides supply chain services supplementing a variety of different types of transportation and accounted for almost 20% of total sales. Other segments include JBT (trucking) and ICS (integrated capacity solutions). The latter segment often arranges specialty trucking services such as transporting freight that requires the use of flatbed or refrigerated trailers.

Sales and Marketing

J.B. Hunt markets its services through a nation-wide sales and marketing network. It uses a specific sales force within its DCS segment due to the length and complexity of the sales cycle. In addition the ICS segment utilizes its own local branch of salespeople. Traditionally one of the company's top customers has been its Arkansas neighbor Wal-Mart.

Financial Performance

The company has enjoyed unprecedented growth in the receding wake of the recession. From 2013 to 2014 its revenues increased 10% from $5.6 billion to a record-setting $6.2 billion. Profits also surged 10% from $342 million to a milestone $375 million.

J.B. Hunt attributes the historic growth for 2014 to increases in demand across its JBI (7%) DCS (13%) and ICS (34%) segments. Higher load counts new contracts and a focus on cost reduction initiatives proved beneficial to the trucking company throughout the year.

Strategy

J.B. Hunt hopes to continue its pathway to growth by concentrating on its operating segments as separate but overlapping businesses and by selling more value-added services to its customers. It has continued to expand its intermodal unit which has agreements with major North American railroads including Burlington Northern Santa Fe and Norfolk Southern railways. The arrangement also allows J.B. Hunt to cut down on costs.

J. B. Hunt also plans to invest closer to 75% of its projected cash flow to support growth and increase replacement activity. In 2014 the company acquired three new operating center locations located in Alliance Texas; Edgerton Kansas (Kansas City); and San Bernardino California.

HISTORY

Johnnie Bryan (J.B.) Hunt's life was a classic tale of rolling from rags to riches —with a little help from a Rockefeller. Hunt grew up in a family of sharecroppers during the Depression and he left school at age 12 to work for his uncle's Arkansas sawmill. In the late 1950s after driving trucks for more than nine years Hunt noticed that the rice mills along his eastern Arkansas route were burning rice hulls. Believing the hulls could be used as poultry litter Hunt got a contract to haul away the hulls and began selling them to chicken farmers.

In 1961 he began the J.B. Hunt Company with help from future Arkansas governor Winthrop Rockefeller who owned Winrock grass company where Hunt bought sod for one of his side businesses. Hunt developed a machine to compress the rice hulls which made their transportation profitable and within a few years the company was the world's largest producer of rice hulls for poultry litter.

Still looking for new opportunities Hunt bought some used trucks and refrigerated trailers in 1969 though the company continued to focus on its original business. In the 1980s J.B. Hunt's trucking division grew dramatically and became lucrative as the trucking industry was being deregulated. In 1981-82 the Hunt trucking business had higher margins than most trucking firms. In 1983 when J.B. Hunt Transport Services went public Hunt sold the rice hull business to concentrate on trucking.

EXECUTIVES

EVP Operations and COO, Craig Harper, age 58, $375,000 total compensation
President and CEO, John N. Roberts, age 50, $695,000 total compensation
Vice President Finance, Richie Henderson
EVP and CIO, Stuart L. Scott
EVP and President Intermodal, Terrence D. (Terry) Matthews, age 57, $442,589 total compensation
EVP Finance and Administration CFO and Corporate Secretary, David G. Mee, age 55, $437,845 total compensation
EVP; President Integrated Capacity Solutions, Shelley Simpson, age 43, $371,635 total compensation
EVP and President Dedicated Contract Services, Nick Hobbs, age 52
Vice President Of Sales, Mark Calcagni
Vice President Finance, Jack Krupka
Senior Vice President Marketing Network Development, Greg Breeden
National Account Manager, Korey Christian
National Account Manager, Ron Sweeney
National Account Manager, Stuart Townsley
Vice President Sales, David (Dave) Simpson
National Sales Manager, David Zych

Vice President Business Development, Brian Webb
Vice President Intermodal Operations, Darren Field
National Sales Manager, Micah Ansley
National Sales Manager, Carrie Smith
Vice President Personnel, Sherry Moncrief
Vice President driver Personnel, Stan Hampton
National Sales Manager, Paul Staudinger
Vice President Memphis, John Flynt
Vice President Of Pricing, Ryan McGuire
National Account Manager, Chris Putnam
National Sales Manager, Josh Francis
National Accounts Manager, Chris Wylie
National Account Manager, Michelle Timmermans
National Sales Manager, Keith Brown
Vice President Marketing, Cecilia Gann
Vice President of Sales and Marketing, Will Johnson
National Account Manager, Kevin Boortz
Senior Vice President Operations, Brad Hicks
Vice President Business Development, Paul Bingham
Vice President Of Business Development, Rodney Nye
National Account Manager, John Ferebee
Vice President Business Development, Jason Fountain
National Account Manager, Linda Peak
Vice President, Tracy Black
National Account Manager, Chad Glascock
Vice President Business Development, Raul Cavazos
Vice President Operations, Thomas (Thom) Lastovica
Assistant Vice President Operations, John McKuin
Senior Vice President Marketing, Tom Williams
Vice President Security and Audits, Johnie Wood
Senior Vice President Operations, Mike Taylor
National Account Manager, Christopher Trout
Vice President National Accounts, Bill Copelin
Senior Vice President Marketing, Jeff Franco
National Sales Manager, Ande Cason
National Account Manager, Scott Woodell
Vice President, Jay Johnson
National Accounts Manager, Todd Witt
Vice President Intermodal, Mike Dougherty
National Sales Manager, Scott Coleman
Vice President International, John Hammond
Vice President Sales, Spencer Frazier
National Sales Manager, Bill Gasaway
Vice President, John (Jack) Kuhlow
Chairman, Kirk Thompson, age 62
Auditors: Ernst & Young LLP

LOCATIONS

HQ: Hunt (J.B.) Transport Services, Inc.
615 J.B. Hunt Corporate Drive, Lowell, AR 72745
Phone: 479 820-0000
Web: www.jbhunt.com

PRODUCTS/OPERATIONS

2014 Sales

	$ mil.	% of total
Intermodal (JBI)	3,676	60
Dedicated contract services (DCS)	1,394	22
Integrated capacity solutions (ICS)	718	12
Trucking (JBT)	386	6
Adjustments	(20)	-
Total	**6,165**	**100**

Selected Trucking Services

Dedicated
Expedited
Final Mile
Flatbed
Intermodal
Less Than Truckload
Refrigerated
Truckload

COMPETITORS

APL Logistics	Ryder System
CSX	Schneider National
Canadian National Railway	Swift Transportation
Hub Group	U.S. Xpress
Kansas City Southern	Union Pacific
Landstar System	Werner Enterprises
	YRC Worldwide

HISTORICAL FINANCIALS

Company Type: Public

Income Statement
FYE: December 31

	REVENUE ($ mil.)	NET INCOME ($ mil.)	NET PROFIT MARGIN	EMPLOYEES
12/14	6,165	374	6.1%	20,158
12/13	5,584	342	6.1%	18,467
12/12	5,054	310	6.1%	16,475
12/11	4,526	257	5.7%	15,631
12/10	3,793	199	5.3%	16,233
Annual Growth	**12.9%**	**17.1%**	**—**	**5.6%**

2014 Year-End Financials

Debt ratio: 27.48%	No. of shares (mil.): 116
Return on equity: 33.81%	Dividends
Cash ($ mil.): 5	Yield: 0.9%
Current ratio: 1.14	Payout: 26.5%
Long-term debt ($ mil.): 683	Market value ($ mil.): 9,821

	STOCK PRICE ($) FY Close	P/E High/Low		PER SHARE ($) Earnings	Dividends	Book Value
12/14	84.25	27	22	3.16	0.80	10.33
12/13	77.30	27	20	2.87	0.60	8.64
12/12	59.71	23	17	2.59	0.71	6.74
12/11	45.07	23	16	2.11	0.52	4.85
12/10	40.81	26	19	1.56	0.48	4.72
Annual Growth	**19.9%**	**—**	**—**	**19.3%**	**13.6%**	**21.7%**

Huntington Bancshares, Inc

Huntington Bancshares is the holding company for The Huntington National Bank which operates about 700 branches in Ohio Michigan and four other Midwestern and Northeastern states. In addition to traditional retail and commercial banking services the bank offers mortgage banking capital market services equipment leasing brokerage services wealth and investment management trust and estate services and personal and business insurance. The company's automobile finance business provides car loans to consumers and real estate and inventory finance to car dealerships throughout the Midwest and Northeast. Founded in 1966 the company boasts total assets of more than $65 billion.

HISTORY

Company BackgroundPelatiah Webster (P. W.) Huntington descendant of both a Revolutionary War leader and a Declaration of Independence signer went to work at sea in 1850 at age 14. He returned to go into banking and in 1866 founded what would become Huntington National Bank of Columbus. As the business grew he conscripted four of his five sons. The bank took a national charter in 1905 and became The Huntington National Bank of Columbus. It survived the hard times of 1907 and 1912 through the Huntington philosophy of sitting on piles of cash.

P. W. died in 1918 and his son Francis became president. Francis expanded the company into trust services. Unlike many bankers in the 1920s he refused to make speculative loans based on the stock market. Francis died in 1928 and was succeeded by brother Theodore. By 1930 Huntington's trust assets accounted for more than half of the total. The family's conservative philosophy helped the bank sail through the 1933 bank holiday although when it reopened the amount of cash it could pay out was restricted to 10% of deposits.

P. W.'s son Gwynne chaired the bank during its post-WWII expansion. His death in 1958 ended the Huntington family reign. The bank began opening branches and adding new services such as mortgage and consumer loans. In 1966 in order to expand statewide the bank formed a holding company Huntington Bancshares. In the 1960s and 1970s the corporation added new operations including mortgage and leasing companies and an international division to help clients with foreign exchange.

In 1979 the company consolidated its 15 affiliates into The Huntington National Bank. Three years later the company bit off more than it could chew with the acquisitions of Reeves Banking and Trust Company of Dover and Union Commerce Corporation of Cleveland. The latter purchase loaded the company with debt. Nevertheless it continued to expand particularly after 1985 when banking regulations allowed interstate branch banking and it soon had operations in Florida Indiana Kentucky Michigan and West Virginia.

Huntington Bancshares was largely insulated from the real estate problems of the late 1980s and early 1990s thanks to its continuing conservative lending policies. But the company was at risk from the nationwide consolidation of the banking industry which made it a potential takeover target. It increased its service offerings and bolstered its place in the market through acquisitions. In 1996 Huntington Bancshares bought life insurance agency Tice & Associates and began cross-selling bank and insurance products. Important banking acquisitions in 1997 included First Michigan Bank and several Florida companies.

Also in 1997 the company took advantage of deregulation to consolidate its interstate operations (except for The Huntington State Bank) into a single operating company. In 1998 Huntington Bancshares continued to build its Huntington insurance services unit with the acquisition of Pollock & Pollock. In 1999 the bank launched a mortgage program aimed at wealthy clients and sold its credit card receivables portfolio to Chase Manhattan (now JPMorgan Chase & Co.). In 2000 the company bought Michigan's Empire Banc Corporation.

Former BANK ONE executive Thomas Hoaglin was named president and CEO in 2001. Later that year he became chairman when Frank Wobst retired after leading the company for 20 years.

In 2002 the company consolidated some branches in the Midwest to cut costs and exited the retail banking market in Florida selling some 140 retail branches there to SunTrust. After the mid-2007 acquisition of Sky Financial Sky's CEO Marty Adams became president and COO of Huntington Bancshares. He retired at the end of 2007 and Hoaglin resumed the president's role until his own retirement in 2009; Stephen Steinour then took the helm.

EXECUTIVES

President Northwest Ohio Region, Sharon S. Speyer

Chairman President and CEO, Stephen D. (Steve) Steinour, age 57, $1,000,000 total compensation

EVP and Manager Dealer Sales, Nicholas G. (Nick) Stanutz, age 60, $465,000 total compensation

SEVP Retail and Business Banking, Mary W. Navarro, age 59, $528,333 total compensation

SEVP and Chief Risk Officer, Helga S. Houston, age 54, $460,000 total compensation

SEVP and Director Regional Banking and The Huntington Private Client Group, James E. (Jim) Dunlap, age 62, $518,333 total compensation

Region President Central Ohio/West Virginia, James E. Kunk

SEVP Corporate Operations and Huntington Insurance, Mark E. Thompson, age 56, $315,340 total compensation

President West Virginia Region, Andrew J. Paterno

President Western Pennsylvania and Ohio Valley Region, Susan (Susie) Baker Shipley

SEVP and CFO, Howell D. (Mac) McCullough, age 56, $400,000 total compensation

President Huntington Asset Services Inc. (HASi), Jeff Young

President Greater Cleveland Region, Renee R. Csuhran

President Central Indiana The Huntington National Bank, Michael W. (Mike) Newbold

VP Commercial Banking Greater Akron/Canton Region, William C. Shivers

SEVP and Chief Credit Officer, Daniel J. Neumeyer, age 55

SEVP Chief Technology and Operations Officer, Paul G. Heller, age 51, $525,000 total compensation

EVP and Chief Communications Officer, Barbara Benham, age 43

President West Michigan Region, John Irwin

President Southern Ohio and Northern Kentucky Region, Kevin Jones

Assistant Vice President Senior Marketing Specialist, Stacy Oberman

Vice President Commercial Banking Treasury Management, Robin Triplett

Senior Vice President, Brad Smith

Senior Vice President, Andy Arduini

Vice President, Bill Cosby

Vice President, Alison Noall

Vice President Of Enterprise Systems, Audrey Hanscel

Senior Vice President, Steve Roberts

Vice President Sales Executive, Barry Mintzer

Senior Vice President Business Banking Rm, Connie Condo

Vice President, Sarah Gigliello

Senior Vice President Chief Sourcing Officer, Debbie Manos-Mchenry

Senior Vice President Direct Loan Operations Document Management And Loan Servicing, Connie Mckee

Vice President Sales and Service Specialist, Natalie Johns

Senior Vice President Senior Segment Risk Manager, Chuck Peirano

Vice President Employee Benefits At Huntington National Bank, Kristin Janutolo

Vice President Of Human Resources, Rob Nussbaum

Vice President Risk Management, John St-germain

Vice President, Ryan Kroge

Vice President, Bruce Sautter

Vice President, Couturier Jan

Vice President, Robert Storbeck

Vice President, Geoffrey Mowery

Assistant Vice President Mutual Funds And Income, Dan Luke

Assistant Vice President Corporate Trust Administration, Ellen Campbell

Vice President, Paul Koscik

Business Systems Analyst Senior Assistant Vice President, Michael (Mel) Roach

Assistant Vice President Principal Architect, Tom Hill

Senior Vice President, Clint Sommer

Vice President, James Matousek

Vice President Associate Counsel, Dana Farthing

Vice President Marketing, Everett Jones

Assistant Vice President Section Manager, Gayla Strickler

Vice President Corporate Trust Department, James (Jamie) Schultz

Senior Vice President, Edward (Ed) Kitchen

Assistant Vice President Facility Services, Gene Freeman

Executive Vice President Private Banking, Andrew Livingston

Vice President of Retail Distribution, Tom Wesolowski

Vice President National Sales Manager And Key Accounts, Patrick Prato

Assistant Vice President Mortgage Lending, James Boots

Senior Vice President Director of Strategic Distribution, Michael (Mel) Bassani

Vice President, Bret Haggy

Vice President, Cindy Hauer

Vice President I Business Banking, Kevin Dougherty

Vice President I Treasury Management Industry Solutions, Brett Bailey

Senior Vice President Treasury Management, Jim Mele

Assistant Vice President, Rob Larger

Vice President Digital Marketing Acquisition, Trisha Jackson

Assistant Vice President, Brock Mcfann

Business Banker Assistant Vice President, Andrew (Andy) Ziegler

Vice President Finance, Jim Posani

Assistant Vice President, Diane Clingerman

Senior Vice President Market Manager, Geoffrey Sale

Assistant Vice President Senior Marketing Specialist, Lisa Brinker

Senior Vice President, Mike Corsi

Senior Vice President Marketing, Tony Monago

Senior Vice President Currency Risk Management, Adam Ravens

Assistant Vice President, Brad Udy

Assistant Vice President 1 Portfolio Manager, Nick Markovich

Assistant Vice President, Cary Hager

Assistant Vice President Aml Bsa, Katherine (Kate) Orkis

Senior Vice President Regional Banking Process Solutions, Steven (Steve) Clemens

Vice President, Sheryl Palmer

Senior Vice President, Neil S Clark, age 63

Vice President, Jennifer Parsons

Vice President Marketing Business Banking, Ginger Pettit

Executive Vice President Human Resources Director, Craig Wilkins

Senior Vice President, Adam Rohrig

Assistant Vice President Treasury Group Finance Manager, Erik Kyre

Vice President Region Marketing Manager, Patricia (Pat) Barton

Vice President, Todd Sawyers

Vice President I Healthcare Banking Relationship Manage I, Maureen Hands

Vice President, James Mathias

Vice President, William Slutz

Vice President Regional Credit Manager New England Market, Al Fry

Vice President, Robin Washienko

Assistant Vice President, Karissa Hendricks

Vice President Strategic Distributing Channels, James (Jamie) Sias

Assistant Vice President, Paulette Helm

Vice President, Amy Klarer

Senior Vice President Sales, Jon Greenwood
Vice President Home Lending Marketing, Amy Tyler
Vice President Commercial Portfolio Manager senior, Nikki Shaffer
Senior Vice President Credit Risk Management, Tim Barber
Assistant Vice President, Robbin Flis
Vice President and Controller, Scott Dupler
Vice President Comml Loan Review, Boggs Michael
Vice President, Walt Tomich
Assistant Vice President, Sandra Clarke
Senior Vice President Managing Director Mortgage, Henry (Hal) Crall
Vice President, Rob Koogler
Vice President Of Commercial Lending, Leslie Caruso
Assistant Vice President, Brian Linn
Vice President, Theresa Davis
Vice President, Mike Flis
Vice President, Chris Shimala
Vice President, John Tremoulis
Senior Vice President, Jay Plum
Vice President, Michael Crawford
Vice President General Manager, Eric George
Vice President IT Governance and Project Management Center, Deb Abner
Vice President, Harry Farver
Vice President Huntington Private Financial Group, Darryl Lycourt
Vice President, Joseph Ahee
Executive Vice President Senior Commercial Credit Approval Officer, Josh Eichenhorn
Senior Vice President, Terence Dorgan
Senior Vice President Treasury Management, Steve Veach
Assistant Vice President, Terry Kuney
Assistant Vice President Home Lending Compliance Section Manager, Omar Ramsay
Vice President, Josh Bond
Vice President Retail Sales and Service Specialist, Christie Hall
Vice President Treasury Relationship Manager, Richard (Dick) Ryba
Avice President Process Improvement Specialist, Jane (Ginny) Jamison
Vice Presicent Business Analyst 3, Andrew (Andy) Mace
Vice President Human Resources Senior Staffing Specialist, Karis Spence
Vice President Senior Sourcing Manager, Jay Gomer
Senior Vice President, Perrie Scott
Senior Vice President Retail Marketing, Karen Maruna
Vice President, Kimberly Harrison
Assistant Vice President, Tony Ruberg
Vice President Business Banking, Jerry Prestopine
Vice President Wealth Marketing, Mark Leskowyak
Vice President Government Banking, Cheryl Schultz
Vice President, Nancy Clevenger
Assistant Vice President, Cindy Ramsey
Vice President Special Assets Department, David Kirkley
Vice President Regional Banking Communications, Tim Dirrim
Vice President Front End Collections, Dave Mortenson
Senior Vice President Auto Finance, Brad Norman
Senior Vice President, Betsy Lambert
Assistant Vice President Regional Facililty Manager, Cheryl A Pitzer
Auditors: PricewaterhouseCoopers LLP

LOCATIONS

HQ: Huntington Bancshares, Inc
41 South High Street, Columbus, OH 43287
Phone: 614 480-8300
Web: www.huntington.com

2014 Bank Branches

	No.
Ohio	404
Michigan	179
Pennsylvania	48
Indiana	43
West Virginia	31
Kentucky	10
Total	**715**

PRODUCTS/OPERATIONS

2014 Sales

	$ mil.	% of total
Interest		
Loans & leases	1,674	57
Securities	288	10
Other	13	-
Noninterest		
Service charges on deposit accounts	273	9
Trust services	116	4
Electronic banking	105	4
Mortgage banking income	84	3
Brokerage income	68	2
Insurance	65	2
Bank-owned life insurance	57	2
Capital markets fees	43	1
Gain on sales of loans	21	1
Net gains on sales of securities	17	1
Other	126	4
Total	**2,955**	**100**

COMPETITORS

Citizens Financial Group	PNC Financial
Comerica	Park National
Fifth Third	Regions Financial
FirstMerit	TFS Financial
JPMorgan Chase	U.S. Bancorp
KeyCorp	Wells Fargo

HISTORICAL FINANCIALS

Company Type: Public

Income Statement

FYE: December 31

	ASSETS ($ mil.)	NET INCOME ($ mil.)	INCOME AS % OF ASSETS	EMPLOYEES
12/14	66,298	632	1.0%	11,873
12/13	59,476	638	1.1%	11,964
12/12	56,153	641	1.1%	11,806
12/11	54,450	542	1.0%	11,245
12/10	53,819	312	0.6%	11,341
Annual Growth	**5.4%**	**19.3%**	**—**	**1.2%**

2014 Year-End Financials

Debt ratio: 5.40%
Return on equity: 10.18%
Cash ($ mil.): 1,285
Current ratio: —
Long-term debt ($ mil.): —

No. of shares (mil.): 811
Dividends
  Yield: 2.0%
  Payout: 29.1%
Market value ($ mil.): 8,537

	STOCK PRICE ($) FY Close	P/E High/Low	PER SHARE ($) Earnings	Dividends	Book Value
12/14	10.52	15 12	0.72	0.21	7.80
12/13	9.65	13 9	0.72	0.19	7.34
12/12	6.39	10 8	0.71	0.16	6.87
12/11	5.49	13 8	0.59	0.10	6.27
12/10	6.87	38 19	0.19	0.04	5.77
Annual Growth	**11.2%**	**— —**	**39.5%**	**51.4%**	**7.8%**

Huntington Ingalls Industries, Inc.

For 40 years Huntington Ingalls Industries (HII) —formerly a Northrop Grumman subsidiary —has been the sole builder of the US Navy's nuclear air-craft carriers. Rivaling nuclear submarine builder General Dynamics HII is the largest naval ship-builder in the world; it also maintains refuels and repairs nuclear aircraft carriers and submarines. In addition HII supplies expeditionary warfare ships surface combatants submarines commercial oil hull tankers and Coast Guard surface ships as well as provides aftermarket fleet support. Almost off its offerings are sold to the US government. Northrop Grumman spun off HII in spring 2011.

Geographic Reach

The company's principal properties are located in San Diego; Broomfield Colorado; Avondale (New Orleans) Louisiana; Gulfport and Pascagoula Mississippi; Houston; Hampton Newport News Suffolk and Virginia Beach Virginia; and Washington DC. Some of the properties comprising its Other segment reside in Waggaman Louisiana; Calgary Aberdeen Scotland; and San Juan Trinidad; and Tobago.

Operations

The shipbuilder divides its work between a few divisions: Newport News (nuclear-powered submarines; 65% of net sales) Ingalls (warship production for the US Navy; 33%) and Other (2%). In addition subsidiary AMSEC offers a wide variety of naval architecture and marine engineering services.

Its carrier Gerald R. Ford (CVN 78) is the first ship of its class and is scheduled for delivery to the Navy in 2016. Its last-of-the-Nimitz-class predecessor the USS George H.W. Bush was commissioned in early 2009.

In addition to the US Navy for which it has built 70% of the current surface combatant fleet HII serves the US Coast Guard (8% of total sales) and navies from other countries. It also provides fleet repair maintenance and technology upgrade services to companies in the energy and petrochemical industries.

Financial Performance

HII has achieved unprecedented growth over the years with revenues climbing 2% from $6.82 billion in 2013 to peak at a record-setting $6.96 billion in 2014. Profits also surged 30% from $261 million to $368 million another company milestone during that same time period.

The historic growth for 2014 was attributed to a 4% rise in Newport News sales and a 22% spike in service revenues. This was driven by higher sales volumes in energy programs and submarines coupled with additional revenue from acquisitions.

The surge in profits for 2014 was fueled by a decline in cost of product sales due to performance improvements and risk retirements from certain programs. HII's operating cash flow increased from $236 million in 2013 to $480 million in 2014 due to decreases from retirement benefit funding and the absence of an insurance settlement charge.

Strategy

HII is currently constructing its DDG-113 John Finn and DDG-114 Ralph Johnson ships scheduled for delivery in 2016 and 2017 respectively. In 2013 the company was awarded a multi-year contract totaling $3.3 billion for the construction of five additional DDG-51 Arleigh Burke-class destroyers as a part of a larger US Navy order for nine DDG-51 Arleigh Burke-class destroyers.

Mergers and Acquisitions

HII often uses acquisitions in order to bolster its core offerings. In mid-2015 HII acquired the engineering solutions division of The Columbia Group in a deal that enabled it to compete more strongly in the unmanned underwater vehicle market.

In 2014 it acquired The S.M. Stoller Corp. a provider of technical environmental ecological waste management remediation and consultation services to private sector companies and the US government. The deal positioned its Newport News segment for expanded growth within the Department of Energy environmental management and commercial nuclear services markets.Also in 2014 HII purchased Houston-based UniversalPegasus International Holdings (UPI) a provider of engineering and project management services to the domestic and international energy markets.

EXECUTIVES

President and CEO, C. Michael (Mike) Petters, age 56, $950,000 total compensation
Corporate VP and President Newport News Shipbuilding, Matthew J. (Matt) Mulherin, age 55, $512,115 total compensation
Corporate VP Business Management and CFO, Barbara A. (Barb) Niland, age 56, $563,327 total compensation
Corporate VP and President Ingalls Shipbuilding, Brian Cuccias, $376,677 total compensation
Corporate VP Business Management and CFO, Christopher D. Kastner, age 51
Corporate VP Government and Customer Relations, Mitchell D. (Mitch) Waldman
Corporate VP and President UniversalPegasus International (UPI), Philip Luna
Corporate Vice President General Counsel, Bruce N Hawthorne
Corporate Vice President Litigation, Chad N Boudreaux
Corp Vice President Benefits and Compensatio, Jim Taylor
Vice President Human Resources And Administration, Edmond Hughes
Corporate Vice President Chro, Bill Ermatinger
Corporate Vice President Government and Customers Relations, Mitch Waldman
Corporate Vice President Communications, Jerri Fuller Dickseski
Vice President Senior Vice President, Thomas (Thom) Johnston
Chairman, Thomas B. Fargo, age 67
Corporate Director of Risk Mangement and Assistant Treasurer, Michael (Mel) Burton
Auditors: Deloitte & Touche LLP

LOCATIONS

HQ: Huntington Ingalls Industries, Inc.
4101 Washington Avenue, Newport News, VA 23607
Phone: 757 380-2000
Web: www.huntingtoningalls.com

PRODUCTS/OPERATIONS

2014 Sales

	$ mil.	% of total
Products	5,712	82
Services	1,245	18
Total	**6,957**	**100**

2014 Sales

	$ mil.	% of total
Newport News	2,286	65
Ingalls	4,536	33
Other	137	2
Intersegment eliminations	(2)	0
Total	**6,957**	**100**

Selected Products

Aircraft carriers (nuclear-powered)
Amphibious assault ships
Coast Guard cutters
Destroyers
Fleet services
Submarines (nuclear-powered)

COMPETITORS

BAE SYSTEMS
Direction des Constructions Navales
Electric Boat
General Dynamics
Northrop Grumman
Todd Shipyards

HISTORICAL FINANCIALS

Company Type: Public

Income Statement

FYE: December 31

	REVENUE ($ mil.)	NET INCOME ($ mil.)	NET PROFIT MARGIN	EMPLOYEES
12/14	6,957	338	4.9%	38,000
12/13	6,820	261	3.8%	3,800
12/12	6,708	146	2.2%	37,000
12/11	6,575	(94)	—	38,000
12/10	0	0	—	39,000
Annual Growth	—	—	—	(0.6%)

2014 Year-End Financials

Debt ratio: 27.12%
Return on equity: 23.42%
Cash ($ mil.): 990
Current ratio: 1.94
Long-term debt ($ mil.): 1,592
No. of shares (mil.): 48
Dividends
  Yield: 0.8%
  Payout: 13.1%
Market value ($ mil.): 5,432

	STOCK PRICE ($) FY Close	P/E High/Low	PER SHARE ($) Earnings	Dividends	Book Value
12/14	112.46	17 13	6.86	1.00	28.26
12/13	90.01	17 8	5.18	0.50	31.23
12/12	43.34	15 11	2.91	0.10	13.45
12/11	31.28	— —	(1.93)	0.00	17.86
Annual Growth	**37.7%**	— —	—	—	12.2%

Huntsman Corp

Huntsman Corporation has a long track record of successfully stalking profits in the world's chemical marketplace. The global chemical manufacturer operates its businesses through subsidiary Huntsman International. Its broad range of products include MDI (methylene diphenyl diisocyanate) amines surfactants epoxy-based polymers and polyurethanes. Huntsman's chemicals are sold worldwide to a variety of customers in the adhesives construction products electronics medical and packaging industries. Huntsman operates manufacturing and research and development facilities in more than 30 countries worldwide. It gets 53% of its revenues from the US.

EXECUTIVES

EVP and CFO, J. Kimo Esplin, $640,025 total compensation
President and CEO, Peter R. Huntsman, $1,600,000 total compensation
President Huntsman Performance Products Division (HPP), Monte G. Edlund, age 57
CEO Asia/Pacific; Division President Polyurethanes, Anthony P. Hankins, $813,625 total compensation
Division President Advanced Materials, James H. Huntsman
Division President Textile Effects, Paul G. Hulme, $508,531 total compensation
EVP General Counsel Chief Compliance Officer and Secretary, David Stryker, $475,500 total compensation
Division President Pigments, Simon Turner, $468,944 total compensation
VP and CIO, Maria Csiba-Womersley
Vice President Human Resources, Wade Rogers
Vice President And General Manager, Eric Phillips
Vice President Engineering, Brandon Buckner
Vice President Director, Valter Musso
Vice President Information Systems, Bob Peck
Vice President Finance and Division Controller, Felicia Pang
Vice President Global Finance And Controller, Phil Lister
Finance Vice President, Duncan Emerson
Division President Performance Products, Stewart Monteith
Vice President, Tom Fisher
Executive Vice President Of Information Technology, Edwin Clement
Executive Vice President Strategic, Paige Peterson
Vice President, Russell (Russ) Healy
Vice President, Russell Healy
Vice President And Associate General Counsel For Intellectual Property, Ron Brown
Vice President Research and Technology Textile Effects Division, Sarada Namhata
Senior Vice President Purchasing, Brian Ridd
Vice President Administration, Thomas (Thom) Muir
National Sales Manager, D Dodd
Vice President IR, Kurt Ogden
Vice Chairman, Nolan D. Archibald
Executive Chairman and Director, Jon M. Huntsman
Board Member, Patrick (Paddy) Harker
Vice President Of Finance And Treasurer, Brian Lee
Auditors: DELOITTE & TOUCHE LLP

LOCATIONS

HQ: Huntsman Corp
500 Huntsman Way, Salt Lake City, UT 84108
Phone: 801 584-5700
Web: www.huntsman.com

2013 Sales

	$ mil.	% of total
US	3,319	30
China	1,081	10
Mexico	853	8
Germany	586	5
Italy	437	4
Other	4,803	43
Total	**11,079**	**100**

2014 Sales

	$ mil.	% of total
US	6,116	53
China	1,626	14
Mexico	960	8
Germany	921	8
Italy	522	5
Other	1,433	12
Total	**11,578**	**100**

PRODUCTS/OPERATIONS

2014 Sales

	$ mil.	% of total
Polyurethanes	5,032	42
Performance Products	3,072	27
Advanced Materials	1,248	11
Textile Effects	896	7
Pigments and additives	1,549	13
Adjustments (219) (1)		
Total	**11,578**	**100**

Segments & Selected Products

Polyurethanes
- Aniline
- MDI (methylene diphenyl diisocyanate)
- MTBE (methyl tertiary-butyl ether)
- PG (propyl
- PO (propyl
- Polyols
- TPU (therm

Performance Products
- Ethylene glycol
- Ethylene oxide
- Ethanolamines
- Ethyleneamines
- Maleic anhydride
- Polyetheramines
- Surfactants

Materials
- Adhesives
- Acrylic
- Polyurethane-based
- Epoxy
- Epoxy resin compounds

Pigments
- Titanium dioxide

Selected Mergers and Acquisitions

COMPETITORS

Akzo Nobel	Evonik Degussa
BASF SE	Hexion
Bayer AG	Kronos Worldwide
Dow Chemical	LyondellBasell
DuPont	National Titanium
Eastman Chemical	Dioxide Company

HISTORICAL FINANCIALS

Company Type: Public

Income Statement
FYE: December 31

	REVENUE ($ mil.)	NET INCOME ($ mil.)	NET PROFIT MARGIN	EMPLOYEES
12/15	10,299	93	0.9%	15,000
12/14	11,578	323	2.8%	16,000
12/13	11,079	128	1.2%	12,000
12/12	11,187	363	3.2%	12,000
12/11	11,221	247	2.2%	12,000
Annual Growth	(2.1%)	(21.7%)	—	5.7%

2015 Year-End Financials

Debt ratio: 48.84%
Return on equity: 5.78%
Cash ($ mil.): 257
Current ratio: 2.00
Long-term debt ($ mil.): 4,626

No. of shares (mil.): 237
Dividends
Yield: 4.4%
Payout: 250.0%
Market value ($ mil.): 2,696

	STOCK PRICE ($) FY Close	P/E High/Low	PER SHARE ($) Earnings	Dividends	Book Value
12/15	11.37	64 25	0.38	0.50	6.08
12/14	22.78	22 16	1.31	0.50	7.30
12/13	24.60	46 30	0.53	0.50	8.24
12/12	15.90	11 6	1.51	0.40	7.44
12/11	10.00	20 8	1.02	0.40	7.05
Annual Growth	3.3%	— —	(21.9%)	5.7%	(3.6%)

HY-VEE INC.

Give Hy-Vee a high five for being one of the largest privately owned US supermarket chains despite serving some modestly sized towns in the Midwest. The company runs some 235 stores in eight Midwestern states. About half of its supermarkets are in Iowa as are most of its 20-plus Hy-Vee drugstores. It distributes products to its stores through several subsidiaries including Lomar Distributing (specialty foods) and Perishable Distributors of Iowa (fresh foods). Other activities include construction and specialty pharmacies. Charles Hyde and David Vredenburg founded the employee-owned firm in 1930. It takes its name from a combination of its founders' names.

Geographic Reach

Hy-Vee's stores are located in Illinois Iowa Kansas Minnesota Missouri Nebraska South Dakota and Wisconsin. The company supplies its stores from distribution centers in Chariton and Cherokee Iowa.

Operations

In addition to its food and drug retail operations Hy-Vee offers customers financial products. Adding to its menu of financial services Hy-Vee subsidiary Midwest Heritage Bank in 2011 acquired Iowa-based L&K Insurance a full-line insurance agency. L&K changed its name to Midwest Heritage Insurance Services post sale.

Financial Performance

Hy-Vee's 235 stores ring up more than $8 billion in annual sales.

Strategy

Hy-Vee is gradually expanding in several key markets in the Midwest including Chicago Minneapolis-St. Paul and Madison Wisconsin. To that end the regional grocery chain in 2014 announced plans to enter the Twin Cities market. In 2013 the chain opened its second supermarket in Madison after entering the Madison market in 2009. To cater to local tastes the company says the 80000-sq.-ft. Madison store has the largest cheese selection of any Hy-Vee supermarket. Hy-Vee is also testing a smaller-format store (about 20000-25000 sq. ft. with no pharmacies) in select locations. It's also adding stores in its core Iowa market with a supermarket slated to open in Winterset in 2014.

Going beyond traditional grocery fare Hy-Vee in 2013 acquired its joint venture partner's stake in Hy-Vee Weitz Company a construction firm based in Des Moines. The grocery store operator renamed the company Hy-Vee Construction and plans to expand the in-house construction management group. The company also teamed up with specialty pharmacy operator Amber Pharmacy to form a new company (called Hy-Vee Pharmacy Solutions) to provide services for patients with complex and chronic health problems including Crohn's disease hemophilia psoriasis and other chronic ailments. The grocery chain has also been focusing on adding Hy-Vee Gas convenience units (some 80 locations include these) wine and spirits stores pharmacies and Hy-Vee HealthMarket departments.

Ric Jurgens in 2012 retired as chairman and CEO after 43-years with Hy-Vee. He was succeeded by president and COO Randy Edeker.

EXECUTIVES

EVP and Chief Merchandising Officer, Jon S. Wendel, age 52
Chairman President and CEO, Randy Edeker, age 53
EVP and Chief Customer Officer, Sheila Laing
EVP CFO and Treasurer, Mike Skokan
Vice Chairman EVP and Chief Administrative Officer, Andy McCann
EVP Western Region, Brett Bremser
EVP and COO, Jay Marshall
EVP Eastern Region, Darren Baty
Rph, Helen Eddy
Vice President Retail Information Technology, Julie Proffitt
Assistant Vice President Sec, Angie Rosenberger
Assistant Vice President Of Operations, Rob Eslick
Assistant Vice President Bakery Operations, Tony Byington
Senior Vice President Of Purchasing, Ken Waller
Assistant Vice President Construction, Mark Brauer
Assistant Vice President Engineering and Construction, Dave Kozak
Assistant Vice President Meat Operations, Kenan Judge
Director of Pharmacy Technology, Michael (Mel) Wilson
Assistant Vice President Marketing Communications, Donna Tweeten
Assistant Vice President Operations NorthEast, Dan Wampler
Vice President Sales, Katie Graham
Assistant Vice President, Tony Kaska
Assistant Vice President Audit Services, Juli Egeland
Assistant Vice President Store, Mark Millsap
Vice President Distribution, Tod Hockenson
Vice President, Karl Kruse
Assistant Vice President risk Management, Janet Crocker
Vice President Human Resources, Leigh Walters
Assistant Vice President Retail Systems, Christy Myers
Assistant Vice President Human Resources, Kate Wolfe
Assistant Vice President Operations Bakery, Don Wilkens
Assistant Vice President Brand Image, Wendy Hiatt
Senior Vice President Secretary and General Counsel, Steve Meyer
Vice President Store Development, Jeff Markey
Assistant Vice President Distribution, Rob Douglas
Assisant Treasurer, Jeff Pierce
Secretary to Greg Frampton, Stacey Groff

LOCATIONS

HQ: HY-VEE INC.
5820 WESTOWN PKWY, WEST DES MOINES, IA 502668223
Phone: 5152672800
Web: WWW.HY-VEE.COM

PRODUCTS/OPERATIONS

2012 Stores

	No.
Supermarkets	212
Drugstores	22
Total	**234**

Selected Subsidiaries

D & D Foods Inc. (salads dips and meats)
Florist Distributing Inc. (flowers plants and florist supplies)
Hy-Vee Construction L.C. (construction)
Hy-Vee Pharmacy Solutions (specialty pharmacy services)
Hy-Vee Weitz Construction L.C. (construction)
Lomar Distributing Inc. (specialty foods)
Midwest Heritage Bank FSB (banking)
Perishable Distributors of Iowa Ltd. (meat fish seafood and ice cream)

COMPETITORS

ALDI	Niemann Foods
Associated Wholesale Grocers	Rite Aid
Ball' s Food	Roundy' s
CVS	SUPERVALU
Casey' s General Stores	Save-A-Lot Food Stores
Fareway Stores	Target Corporation
Kmart	Wal-Mart
Kroger	Walgreen

HISTORICAL FINANCIALS

Company Type: Private

Income Statement

FYE: September 28

	REVENUE ($ mil.)	NET INCOME ($ mil.)	NET PROFIT MARGIN	EMPLOYEES
09/14	8,014	0	—	62,000
09/13	8,014	0	—	—
09/12*	7,682	0	—	—
10/11	0	0	—	—
Annual Growth	—	—	—	—

*Fiscal year change

2014 Year-End Financials

Debt ratio: ——
Return on equity: —
Cash ($ mil.): 7
Current ratio: 0.20
Long-term debt ($ mil.): —

Dividends
Yield: —
Payout: —
Market value ($ mil.): —

IBERIABANK Corp

IBERIABANK Corp. serves up financial services with a Cajun flare. Through its flagship bank subsidiary also called IBERIABANK the holding company operates some 267 branches in Louisiana and five other southern states. It also has about 21 title insurance offices in Louisiana and Arkansas in addition to some 61 mortgage loan offices in a dozen states. Offering deposit products such as checking and savings accounts CDs and IRAs the bank uses funds gathered mainly to make loans. Commercial real estate and business loans make up nearly three-quarters of the company's loan portfolio which also includes consumer loans and residential mortgages. IBERIABANK Corp. has $13.4 billion in assets.

Geographic Reach

The company operates 267 combined offices including 172 bank branch offices and four loan production offices in Louisiana Arkansas Florida Alabama Tennessee Georgia and Texas 21 title insurance offices in Arkansas and Louisiana and mortgage representatives in 61 locations in 12 US states.

Operations

IBERIABANK Corp. has eight wholly-owned nonbank subsidiaries including brokerage unit Iberia Financial Services IBERIABANK Insurance Services Acadiana Holdings IBERIABANK Mortgage Company Little Rock Arkansas-based Lenders Title Company and several investment funds.

IB Aircraft Holdings LLC owns a fractional share of an aircraft used by management of the company and its subsidiaries. IAM provides wealth management and trust services for commercial and private banking clients. CDE is engaged in the purchase of tax credits.

Financial Performance

After enjoying two straight years of revenue increase in 2013 IBERIABANK Corp.'s revenues decreased by 2% due to lower interest and noninterest income. Noninterest income decreased as a result of a drop in the valuation of the company's mortgage-related derivatives and a lower margin on the sales of mortgage loans both of which negatively impacted mortgage income. However IBERIABANK Corp. had a $2.9 million increase in broker commissions as well as a growth of $2 million in service charges that partially offset the mortgage income decrease. After experiencing a huge

net income increase in 2012 due to a decrease in the provision for loan loss and interest expenses in 2013 the company's net income declined by 15% to $65.1 million due to increased noninterest expenses as a result of a higher impairment of FDIC loss share receivables and other long-lived assets. This was partially offset by a decline in the provision for loan losses and interest expenses.In 2013 IBERIABANK Corp.'s operating cash inflow increased to $309.8 million (compared to cash out flow of $12.2 million in 2012) primarily due to a huge decline in the provision for loan losses and change in the assets and liabilities.

Strategy

Acquisitions have been a big part of IBERIABANK Corp.'s growth strategy since 2003. All of the acquisition activity has expanded the company's assets and branch network helped it enter new markets such as Florida and Texas and strengthen its presence in existing ones.

As part of IBERIABANK's growth through acquisition strategy in late 2014 it purchased Georgia Commerce Bank as part of a merger deal for $195 million which expanded IBERIABANK's reach into the Atlanta Georgia market for the first time. Earlier that same year the bank also acquired First Private Holdings Inc. the holding company of First Private Bank of Texas a Dallas Texas-based bank with two branch locations; Florida Bank Group; and certain assets of the Memphis Tennessee operations of Trust One Bank a division of Synovus Bank.

Company Background

In 2012 IBERIABANK Corp. struck an agreement to buy Florida Gulf Bank. In 2011 the bank completed three acquisitions: OMNI Bank with 14 offices in New Orleans and Baton Rouge Louisiana; Cameron State Bank with 22 offices in Lake Charles Louisiana; and the assets of Florida Trust Company a subsidiary of the failed Bank of Florida Corporation. (Between 2003 and 2010 the bank completed 13 acquisitions with combined total assets of more than $6 billion.)

The company was founded in 1887.

EXECUTIVES

President and CEO, Daryl G. Byrd, age 60, $1,015,000 total compensation
Evp-dir Organizational Devt, Barry F Berthelot
SEVP Mergers and Acquisitions Finance and Investor Relations; Director Financial Strategy and Mortgage, John R. Davis, age 54, $456,154 total compensation
Vice Chairman and Managing Director of Brokerage Trust and Wealth Management, Jefferson G. (Jeff) Parker, age 62, $480,192 total compensation
SEVP and Director Communications Facilities and Human Resources, Elizabeth A. (Beth) Ardoin, age 46
SEVP and CFO, Anthony J. Restel, age 45, $480,385 total compensation
Vice Chairman; SEVP and COO, Michael J. (Mike) Brown, age 51, $598,269 total compensation
President and CEO IberiaBank Mortgage, Bill Edwards
EVP and Director Retail Small Business and Mortgage, Robert M. (Bob) Kottler, age 56
EVP and Executive Credit Officer, H. Spurgeon Mackie, age 64
EVP and Chief Risk Officer, J. Randolph Bryan, age 47
EVP Corporate Secretary and General Counsel, Robert B. Worley, age 55
President and CEO Lender's Title Company, David B. Erb
Vice President, Mark Herpin
Vice President, David A Doherty
Vice President Mortgage Executive, Ted Nusenow

Branch Manager And Assistant Vice President, Lauren V Schreiber
Vice President Business Banker, Lori Buhs
Vice President, Bill Neal
Senior Vice President Commercial Relationship Manager, Steve Krueger
Vice President Commercial Relationship Manager, Chuck Kramer
Assistant Vice President, Dolores Hernandez
Commercial Relationship Manager Senior Vice President, Brandon Cooper
Vice President, Tom Chelewski
Vice President Commercial Relationship Manager, Douglas (Doug) Webster
Senior Vice President, James (Jamie) Currie
Vice President, Mike Barnes
Vice President Human Resources Manager, Kevin Robinson
Vice President, Bruce Reid
Vice President Private Banker, Ken Brown
Assistant Vice President, Misty Labat
Vice President Business Credit Services Retail Officer, Mary Rice
Vice President Treasury Management Se, Diane Dame
Vice President, Jack Avery
Senior Vice President Network Support Manager, Chris Berthaut
Executive Vice President Business Banking, Bob Tusa
Vice President, Nancy Dost
Senior Vice President Bank Owned Assets, Mark Collier
Vice President Commercial Relationship Manager, Susan (Sue) Pereira
Executive Vice President Managing Director, Jason Waters
Senior Vice President, Missy Krantz
Vice President, Craig Peak
Vice President, Greg Mendez
Senior Vice President Of The Commercial Banking GR, John (Jack) Everett
Vice President Community Banking, Randall Rojas
Vice President Of Product Management, Paula Allred
Senior Vice President, Eric Movassaghi
Vice President Business Banking, Angela Velardi
Vice President, Steve Barnes
Vice President Business Credit Services, Brian Buczko
Vice President Manager of Financial Analytics, Stephanie Verret
Vice President, Nancy Wooten
Senior Vice President Corporate Banking, C Mizelle
Vice President, Michael Hallmark
Senior Vice President, David Warlick
Assistant Vice President, Andy Gaines
Vice President Retail Bank Manager, Christopher Lebato
Assistant Vice President, Keaton Smith
Vice President Assistant Branch Manager, Sandra Parks
Vice President, Barbara Riggin
Vice President Retail Administration, Robin Bordelon
Vice President Branch Manager Business Development Officer, Pedro Diaz
Assistant Vice President And Branch Manager, Heidi Young
Vice President Business Credit Services Officer, Michael Schaefer
Vice President Business Credit Services, Timothy Wilson
Executive Vice President Director of Organizational Deve, Donna Domick
Vice President, Janet Patton
Assistant Vice President Branch Manager, Dawn Primeaux

Vice President Senior Network Engineer, Jon Luckett

Vice President, Pauline Sampson

Vice President Private Banker, Christina Blake

Senior Vice President Corporate Accounting, David Sparacio

Vice President: Business Banker, Ryan Eustis

Chenal Branch Manager Assistant Vice President, Tyler Treadway

Vice President Construction Lending Manager, Montreen Badeaux

Senior Vice President Project Management, Gina Stritzinger

Executive Vice President, Barry Kilpatrick

Senior Vice President, Stephen Durrett

Vice President Finance, Joel Jewell

Senior Vice President, Steve Kelly

Vice President Human Resources And Employee Development And Training, Mike Pelletier

Vice President And Chatham County Market Executive, Michael Carper

Vice President Controllera, Angela Robert

Vice President Business Banking Relationship Manager, Jason Kern

Senior Vice President, Pat Yates

Vice President Business Credit Services, David Krage

Assistant Vice President Financial Reporting and Analytics, Chasity Dupuy

Senior Vice President, Mary Guidry

Vice President Applications Programmera, Carole Peck

Assistant Vice President And Senior Relationship Banker, Darlene Nicks

Executive Vice President Senior Credit Officer, Robin Kavanaugh

Executive Vice President IBERIA Corporate Services Capital Markets Manager, David (Dave) Shutley

Senior Vice President, Jill Merkl

Executive Vice President and Executive Credit Officer, H Mackie

Vice President, Winifred K Stamps

E Commerce Product Manager Assistant Vice President, Shelby Maloney

Chairman, William H. Fenstermaker, age 66

Auditors: Ernst & Young LLP

LOCATIONS

HQ: IBERIABANK Corp
200 West Congress Street, Lafayette, LA 70501
Phone: 337 521-4003
Web: www.iberiabank.com

PRODUCTS/OPERATIONS

2013 Sales

	$ mil.	% of total
Interest		
Loans including fees	488	70
Securities	38	5
Other	8	1
Adjustments	(97.8)	-
Noninterest		
Mortgage income	64	9
Service charges on deposit accounts	28	5
Title revenue	20	3
Brokerage Commissions	16	2
ATM/debit card fees	9	1
Income from bank owned life insurance	3	1
Others	25	3
Total	606	100

COMPETITORS

Bank of America	Investar
Bank of the Ozarks	JPMorgan Chase
Capital One	Louisiana Bancorp
First NBC Bank	MidSouth Bancorp
Hancock Holding	Regions Financial
Home Bank	Teche Holding

HISTORICAL FINANCIALS
Company Type: Public

Income Statement
FYE: December 31

	ASSETS ($ mil.)	NET INCOME ($ mil.)	INCOME AS % OF ASSETS	EMPLOYEES
12/14	15,758	105	0.7%	2,825
12/13	13,365	65	0.5%	2,638
12/12	13,129	76	0.6%	2,758
12/11	11,757	53	0.5%	2,645
12/10	10,026	48	0.5%	2,193
Annual Growth	12.0%	21.2%	—	6.5%

2014 Year-End Financials

Debt ratio: 1.22%	No. of shares (mil.): 33
Return on equity: 6.23%	Dividends
Cash ($ mil.): 548	Yield: 2.1%
Current ratio: —	Payout: 43.7%
Long-term debt ($ mil.): —	Market value ($ mil.): 2,169

	STOCK PRICE ($) FY Close	P/E High/Low	PER SHARE ($) Earnings	Dividends	Book Value
12/14	64.85	22 18	3.30	1.36	55.39
12/13	62.85	29 20	2.20	1.36	51.40
12/12	49.12	21 17	2.59	1.36	51.88
12/11	49.30	32 23	1.87	1.36	50.48
12/10	59.13	33 26	1.88	1.36	48.50
Annual Growth	2.3%	— —	15.1%	(0.0%)	3.4%

Icahn Enterprises LP

Icahn Enterprises has a can-do attitude when it comes to making money. The holding company has stakes in firms in a diverse array of industries including metals manufacturing energy real estate gaming and home fashion. Holdings include car parts maker Federal-Mogul; energy refinery and production company CVR; PSC Metals one of the largest scrap yard operators in the US; residential developer Bayswater which is active in Florida and Massachusetts; and WestPoint Home a maker of bed bath and other home products. Billionaire corporate raider Carl Icahn and his affiliates control his namesake firm.

Operations

Icahn Enterprises is a holding company with subsidiaries in several industries ranging from investment and automotive to energy metals and railcars. Icahn's energy subsidiary (CVR which owns CVR Refining and CVR Partners) and its automotive segment (which includes Federal-Mogul and Uni-Select USA) make up its two largest segments generating 37% and 47% of the firm's total revenue in 2014 respectively.

The company also holds stakes in gaming food packaging real estate and home fashion companies. Its portfolio includes significant positions in such enterprises as Apple Forest Laboratories eBay Netflix Talisman Energy and Navistar International.Geographic Reach

The New York-headquartered company owns stakes in a number of companies operating worldwide. Primary subsidiary Federal-Mogul operates more than 170 locations globally including manufacturing facilities technical centers distribution centers and administration offices.Sales and MarketingThe firm's Federal-Mogul customers include automotive and heavy-duty vehicle manufacturers agricultural off-highway marine railroad aerospace high performance and industrial application man-

ufacturers. The subsidiary has well-established relationships with nearly all major American European and Asian automotive OEs.Its CVR subsidiary's petroleum customers include retailers railroads and farm cooperatives while its nitrogen fertilizer customers include retailers and distributors (for UAN products) and agricultural and industrial businesses (for ammonia products). Some of its largest customers in 2014 included Gavilon Fertilizer United Suppliers Crop Production Services J.R. Simplot Interchem and MFA. Its WestPoint Home subsidiary sells home fashion products to catalog retailers chain stores mass merchants department stores specialty stores and warehouse clubs worldwide. Signaling a highly-concentrated customer base the subsidiary's top customer contributed 29% of its net sales in 2014 while its top four customers accounted for 67% of its net sales that year.

Financial Performance

Icahn Enterprises has reported steady revenue growth over the past several years as its strategy of buying and holding undervalued equity positions for the long term has helped the company report strong results. Icahn's sales reversed course in 2014 however as revenue fell by 7% to $19.68 billion mostly from losses in its Investment and Metals segments. Icahn's investment segment drove most of the decline as it incurred heavy losses from its short equity exposure mostly through broad market hedges and from its long equity positions particularly in energy which was hit by oil price plunges. Ichan's Metal segment shrank by 23% as ferrous and non-ferrous shipment volumes and prices fell while its Home Fashions revenue dipped by 4% due to lower sales volumes and low-margin programs. In 2013 revenue had jumped to a record $20.67 billion thanks to growth in the firm's investment automotive energy and food packaging segments.Revenue declines in 2014 pushed Icahn Enterprises into the red for the first time since 2008 with losses of $373 million for the year (compared to a record-profit of $1.03 billion in 2013 thanks to record revenues and an income tax benefit). Cash levels also decreased significantly with operations using $390 million (as opposed to in 2013 when operations provided $717 million).

Strategy

The company's strategy —known as The Icahn Formula. named after its lead investment strategist —is to seek undervalued assets (including firms in bankruptcy) improve their operations and enhance their value for possible sale. As an example of this in 2013 the company reduced its stake in Netflix but not before seeing a return of more than four times its original investment in 14 months. The firm typically purchases substantial stakes in companies with an eye toward gaining control of them often by waging proxy battles for seats on their boards of directors. Mr. Icahn —famous for his activism —is known for his ability to force underperforming management teams to maximize value for shareholders.

Icahn Enterprises' diversification across multiple industries and geographies acts as a natural hedge against cyclical and general economic swings. Through its investment segment the firm has held significant positions in various companies including Dell Inc. HerbalifeChesapeake Energy Hain Celestial Group Forest laboratories and Transocean.

In 2013 Icahn Enterprises and Mr. Icahn entered into a joint venture agreement to establish American Railcar Leasing (which includes the American Railcar Industries business); the venture was expected to generate more than $120 million for the company.Mergers and AcquisitionsIn February 2015 Icahn Enterprises agreed to purchase Uni-Select USA (the US auto parts assets of auto parts distributor Uni-Select Inc.) and Beck/Arnley

Worldparts Inc. for a purchase price of $340 million. The firm acquired all 39 distribution centers and satellite locations and 240 corporate-owned jobber stores in the US. The business became part of Icahn Enterprises' automotive segment with Federal Mogul. Also in February 2015 Icahn Enterprises agreed to buy certain assets of the engine components business of TRW Automotive Holdings for $313 million adding another product line to Federal-Mogul's portfolio and making it a stronger core engine component developer and supplier for customers looking to improve fuel economy and reduce emissions.

Ownership

Affiliates of founder and chairman Carl Icahn own approximately 91% of the firm's outstanding depository units.

EXECUTIVES

CFO, SungHwan Cho, age 40, $513,466 total compensation
Chief Accounting Officer, Peter Reck, age 48, $280,000 total compensation
President CEO and Director, Keith Cozza, age 36, $1,505,567 total compensation
Chairman, Carl C. Icahn, age 79
Treasurer, John Saldarelli
Auditors: Grant Thornton LLP

LOCATIONS

HQ: Icahn Enterprises LP
   767 Fifth Avenue, Suite 4700, New York, NY 10153
Phone: 212 702-4300
Web: www.ielp.com

PRODUCTS/OPERATIONS

2014 Sales

	% of total
Energy	47
Automotive	37
Gaming	4
Ralicar	4
Metals	4
Food packing	2
Home Fashion	1
Real Estate	1
Investment	-
Holding Company	-
Total	**100**

Selected Subsidiaries

Ace Nevada Corp.
American Entertainment Properties Corp.
AREP Oil & Gas Holdings LLC
AREP Real Estate Holdings LLC
AREP Sands Holdings LLC
Atlantic Coast Entertainment Holdings Inc.
Bayswater Development LLC
The Bayswater Group LLC
Federal-Mogul Corporation
Icahn Capital LP
Icahn Capital Management LP
Icahn Enterprises Holdings L.P.
Icahn Offshore LP
Icahn Onshore LP
New Seabury Properties L.L.C.
PSC Metals Inc.
Tropicana Entertainment Inc.
Viskase Companies Inc.
WestPoint Home LLC

COMPETITORS

Apollo Global Management	Leucadia National
Berkshire Hathaway	Loews
Blackstone Group	MSD Capital
Clark Enterprises	Soros Fund Management
D. E. Shaw	The Trump Organization
KKR	Vulcan
	Wesco Financial

Income Statement

FYE: December 31

	REVENUE ($ mil.)	NET INCOME ($ mil.)	NET PROFIT MARGIN	EMPLOYEES
12/14	19,157	(373)	—	66,559
12/13	20,682	1,025	5.0%	59,565
12/12	15,654	396	2.5%	60,665
12/11	11,855	750	6.3%	59,559
12/10	9,119	199	2.2%	56,647
Annual Growth	**20.4%**	**—**		**4.1%**

2014 Year-End Financials

Debt ratio: 32.39%	No. of shares (mil.): 123
Return on equity: —	Dividends
Cash ($ mil.): 4,347	Yield: 6.4%
Current ratio: 2.15	Payout: —
Long-term debt ($ mil.): 11,588	Market value ($ mil.): 11,383

	STOCK PRICE ($) FY Close	P/E High/Low		PER SHARE ($) Earnings	Dividends	Book Value
12/14	92.47	—	—	(3.08)	6.00	44.21
12/13	109.41	16	5	9.07	4.50	52.56
12/12	44.70	13	10	3.75	0.40	44.53
12/11	35.80	5	4	8.23	0.94	43.38
12/10	35.26	22	13	2.31	0.99	37.13
Annual Growth	**27.3%**	**—**	**—**	**—**	**57.0%**	**4.5%**

iHeartMedia Inc

iHeartMedia loves the advertising-supported consumer-focused business of show business. The firm formerly known as CC Media owns and operates more than 850 radio stations in about 150 markets through iHeartCommunications. With more than 245 million listeners a month iHeart-Media is the #1 radio company in the US. The company also owns outdoor advertising giant Clear Channel Outdoor Holdings. Clear Channel Outdoor Holdings sells advertising space on billboards public transportation buildings and other outdoor environments throughout the US and more than 30 other countries.

Geographic Reach

iHeartMedia's broadcast stations are available on AM/FM HD digital radio satellite radio Internet smartphones iPads and tablets auto dashboards smart TVs and gaming consoles. Its iHeartRadio has more than 50 million registered users.

The company does business throughout North and South America Europe and the Asia/Pacific region. Its media and entertainment executive operations are located in San Antonio and New York City. The headquarters of Americas outdoor is in Phoenix and the headquarters of International outdoor is in London. The majority of revenue comes from the Americas.

Operations

In addition to its large stable of radio statios iHeartMedia now includes iHeartMedia Digital with its more than 90 million digital monthly uniques; Premiere Networks which syndicates 90 radio programs and services to more than 5500 radio affiliates; the Total Traffic and Weather Network. iHeartMedia also owns Katz Media Group a full-service media representation business. Katz Media is part of the company's media and entertainment holdings.

Sales and Marketing

iHeartMedia gets much of its revenue from advertising but the company also spent $133.7 million on advertising and promotional activities during fiscal 2013.

Financial Performance

iHeartMedia's revenue decreased slightly in fiscal 2013 compared to the previous fiscal period but its revenue has been remarkably consistent year-over-year. The company reported $6.243 billion in fiscal 2013 after claiming $6.246 billion in fiscal 2012 and $6.161 billion in fiscal 2011.

iHeartMedia suffered a net loss of $606.8 million in fiscal 2013. That was an increase of 43% compared to the $424.4 million loss it claimed in fiscal 2012. Net loss spiked due to increased direct operating expenses higher promotional and sponsorship costs and the impact of divesting the company's international neon business during 2012. The company's cash on hand dipped along with the net loss and increased expenses during fiscal 2013 compared to the previous year.

Strategy

iHeartMedia's growth strategy includes investing in digital platforms. It is developing the next generation of iHeartRadio an integrated digital radio platform. The company is also working on the ongoing deployment of more digital outdoor displays.

During fiscal 2013 the company divested some of its outdoor advertising assets in Times Square for approximately $18.7 million. It also sold five radio stations in the Green Bay market for about $17.6 million. In addition CC Media sold its shares of Sirius XM Radio for $135.5 million.In fiscal 2012 the company's International outdoor segment sold its international neon business and its outdoor advertising business in Romania resulting in an aggregate gain of $39.7 million

Mergers and Acquisitions

During fiscal 2012 the company acquired WOR-AM in New York City for $30 million and WFNX in Boston for $14.5 million. In fiscal 2011 the company acquired the Metro Traffic division of Dial Global (then called Westwood One). It made the deal to expand its Total Traffic Network business. Before the deal closed Metro Networks had approximately 1500 affiliates across the US while Total Traffic served more than 100 metro areas worldwide.

EXECUTIVES

President COO and CFO, Richard J. Bressler, age 57, $1,200,000 total compensation
President of Entertainment Enterprises, John Sykes, age 54
Chairman and CEO, Robert W. (Bob) Pittman, age 61, $1,193,939 total compensation
CEO Clear Channel International, C. William Eccleshare, age 59, $1,123,012 total compensation
CEO Clear Channel Outdoor America, Scott R. Wells, age 45
EVP and Chief Communications Officer, Wendy Goldberg, age 51
EVP and Chief Marketing Officer, Gayle Troberman, age 51
EVP Business Development and Corporate Strategy, Steven Cutler
EVP General Counsel and Secretary, Robert H. Walls, age 54, $750,000 total compensation
President Digital Revenue Strategy, Carter Brokaw
President Springfield Market, Matt Saunders
President Wichita Market, Jeffery McCausland
President Charlotte Market, Keith Hotchkiss
CIO, Steve Mills
President Denver, Tim Hager
President Louisville, Earl Jones
Senior Vice President And Engineering, Tom Cox
Vice President Quality Management, Dean Brown
Vice President of Sales Atlanta Division, Jonathan (Jon) Graviss

Executive Vice President Regional Managing
Director, John (Jack) Duong
Executive Vice President Distribution Clear
Channel Radio, Jeff Littlejohn
Vice President Of Sales, Namon Jones
I Vice President National Sales, David (Dave)
Steiner
Vice President and Sales, Tracey Wommack
Vice President Sales and Marketing, Pat Coyne
Vice President Business Operations, Barbara
(Barb) Caraballo
Vice President Corporate Reporting, Katrin
Ordnung
Vice President Product Management, R O Catalfo
Vice President And Market Manager, Jackie Rinker
Vice President Human Resources Ccr, Kim Heintz
Vice President Marketing Solutions, Tara Adamos
Vice President Government and Public Affairs,
Mitchell (Mitch) Schwartz
Vice President Of Marketing, Eileen Woodbury
Vice President Regional Finance, Meagan Schaller
Vice President of Marketing, Justin Tanis
Vice President Las Vegas Operations and
Partnerships, Edward (Ed) Sheftel
Vice President Product (Web), Rob Rowe
Vice President Business Development, Larry
Linietsky
Senior Vice President Strategic Dev, John (Jack)
Tippit
Vice President of Sales, Pat Connor
SVP and President CC Media Holdings Inc., John
(Jack) Hogan
Senior Vice President Chief Accounting Officer,
Scott Hamilton
Vice President and Market Manager, Bill Hurley
Vice President and Sales, Damon Gunkel
Vice President Director of Sales, Matthew (Matt)
Bailey
Vice President Director of Sales, Dan Smith
Vice President Public Affairs, Bridge Barbara
Vice President of Sales, Jeff Luckoff
Executive Vice President Programming
Operations, Jon Zellner
Vice President of Urban Programming, Doc Wynter
Treasurer Secretary, Crystal Duncan
Auditors: Ernst & Young LLP

LOCATIONS

HQ: iHeartMedia Inc
200 East Basse Road, Suite 100, San Antonio, TX
78209
Phone: 210 822-2828
Web: www.iheartmedia.com

PRODUCTS/OPERATIONS

2014 Sales

	$ mil.	% of total
iHM	3,161	49
Americas Outdoor Advertising	1,253	20
Internationl Outdoor Advertising	1,708	27
Other	260	4
Adjustments	(65.1)	-
Total	**6,318**	**100**

COMPETITORS

CBS Corp
Cumulus Media
JCDecaux
Lamar Advertising
Radio One Inc.

HISTORICAL FINANCIALS

Company Type: Public

Income Statement

FYE: December 31

	REVENUE ($ mil.)	NET INCOME ($ mil.)	NET PROFIT MARGIN	EMPLOYEES
12/14	6,318	(793)	—	19,200
12/13	6,243	(606)	—	20,800
12/12	6,246	(424)	—	20,800
12/11	6,161	(302)	—	21,200
12/10	5,865	(479)	—	20,283
Annual Growth	**1.9%**	**—**		**(1.4%)**

2014 Year-End Financials

Debt ratio: 144.77%
Return on equity: —
Cash ($ mil.): 457
Current ratio: 1.60
Long-term debt ($ mil.): 20,322

No. of shares (mil.): 88
Dividends
Yield: —
Payout: —
Market value ($ mil.): 651

	STOCK PRICE ($) FY Close	P/E High/Low	PER SHARE ($) Earnings	Dividends	Book Value
12/14 (111.61)	7.35	— —	(9.46)	0.00	
12/13 (102.05)	6.53	— —	(7.31)	0.00	
12/12	3.40	— —	(5.23)	6.08	(96.88)
12/11	4.39	— —	(3.70)	0.00	(96.20)
12/10	9.00	— —	(5.94)	0.00	(92.55)
Annual Growth	**(4.9%)**	**— —**	**—**	**—**	**—**

Illinois Tool Works, Inc.

Illinois Tool Works (ITW) hammers out more than just tools and it operates well beyond the Land of Lincoln. With operations in about 60 countries ITW manufactures and services equipment for the automotive construction electronics food/beverage power system decorative surfaces and medical (adhesives) industries. The largest of its segments is Transportation which provides metal and plastic fasteners fluids and body repair putties as well as truck remanufacturing. Second in sales Power Systems & Electronics churns out arc welding equipment and airport ground support equipment.

HISTORY

In the early years of the 20th century Byron Smith founder of Chicago's Northern Trust Company recognized that rapid industrialization was outgrowing the capacity of small shops to supply machine tools. Smith encouraged two of his four sons to launch Illinois Tool Works (ITW) in 1912. Harold C. Smith became president of ITW in 1915 and expanded its product line into automotive parts.

ITW developed the Shakeproof fastener the first twisted-tooth lock washer in 1923. When Harold C. died in 1936 the torch passed to his son Harold B. who decentralized the company and exhorted salesmen to learn customers' businesses so they could develop solutions even before the customers recognized the problems. Smith plowed profits back into research as WWII spurred demand.

In the 1950s the company began exploring plastics and combination metal and plastic fasteners as well as electrical controls and instruments to become a leader in miniaturization. Its major breakthrough came in the early 1960s with the devel-

opment of flexible plastic collars to hold six-packs of beverage cans. This item under a new division called Hi-Cone was ITW's most-profitable offering.

Silas Cathcart became CEO in 1970. Smith's son another Harold B. was president and COO until 1981 (he remained on the board of directors and served as chairman of the board's executive committee). By the early 1980s ITW had become bureaucratic and susceptible to foreign competition. It was forced to lower prices to hold on to customers. Wary after the 1982 recession ITW hired John Nichols as CEO.

Nichols broadened the company's product line introduced more-effective production methods and doubled ITW's size by buying 27 companies the largest being Signode Industries bought for $524 million (1986). Nichols broke Signode into smaller units to speed development of 20 new products.

ITW purchased Ransburg Corporation (electrostatic finishing systems 1989) and the DeVilbiss division of Eagle Industries (1990) and merged the two to form its Finishing Systems and Products division. In 1992 the company introduced the Ring Leader Recycling Program to recycle its plastic six-pack rings.

Through a stock swap ITW acquired ownership of the Miller Group (arc welding equipment and related systems) in 1993. An 11% increase in car building in Europe in 1994 caused revenues of the company's engineered-components segment to grow dramatically; that year 76% of ITW's international sales came from European operations.

In 1995 ITW named president James Farrell as CEO. He replaced Nichols as chairman in 1996. ITW acquired Hobart Brothers (welding products) and Medalists Industries (industrial fasteners) in 1996 and made 28 acquisitions and joint ventures in 1997. It entered the domestic spray-painting equipment business in 1998 by acquiring Binks Sames (now Sames Corporation) for $106 million.

ITW gained the technology to make bar-code printers in 1999 when it acquired industrial inkjet maker Trident International in a $107 million deal. Other purchases that year included a polyester film-processing plant from South Korea's SKC Duo-Fast (pneumatic nailing and stapling tools) and for $3.5 billion Premark International (consumer products which it began selling off in 2002). ITW sold its Irathane Systems urethane linings and moldings division to Industrial Rubber Products.

The company added to its ink-jet operations in 2000 with the acquisition of Imaging Technologies LLC. Through its Hobart subsidiary ITW also acquired Trilectron Industries (ground support equipment) from HEICO in a deal worth about $57 million. Early in 2001 the company added to its welding operations by buying four welding component businesses from Dover Corporation. Later in the year it acquired hot stamp foil company Foilmark. In early 2002 ITW's board of directors gave its stamp of approval for the divestiture of ITW's consumer products segment. That decision led to the sale of its Precor fitness equipment business to Finland's Amer Sports in October for about $180 million.

Farrell retired as CEO in 2005 though he remained chairman; he was replaced by president David Speer. Farrell retired as chairman in 2006 and was succeeded by Speer in that post. EVP Thomas Hansen was elevated to vice chairman as well.

ITW purchased the Wynn Oil segment of industrial products maker Parker Hannifin in early 2005. Wynn Oil manufactures chemical car care products and maintenance technology for the auto industry. It also bought Rippey Corporation a maker of polyvinyl alcohol (PVA) cleaning products for the semiconductor industry that year. ITW continued its streak of diverse acquisitions later in 2005 with the purchase of instrumentation maker Instron from investment group Kirtland Capital Partners. Instron's products include instruments software and services designed to test materials and structures. And the company rolled on into 2006 with more acquisitions with the purchase of Alpine Engineered Products a maker of connectors design software and related machinery from Stonebridge Partners which had just acquired the company in the middle of 2005. Alpine fit in well with other ITW companies like Truswal and Pryda.

Also in 2006 ITW acquired CFC International (multilayer coatings for a variety of markets including furniture) for about $90 million in cash. In mid-2006 ITW bought BagCo (plastic recloseable packaging) and Kester (solder and related materials). The company then acquired Click Commerce a developer of supply chain management software for about $292 million in cash. ITW saw the software company with its 1500 customers having strengths in industries served by ITW. In late 2006 ITW purchased Speedline Technologies a manufacturer of printed circuit board assembly and semiconductor packaging equipment.

In 2007 the acquisitive company accumulated another 52 firms following a record set in 2006 that picked up more than 50 companies at a cumulative investment of around $1.7 billion. Also that same year ITW acquired the assets of Avery Berkel a venerable manufacturer of retail scales and other food processing equipment from Avery Weigh-Tronix. The company bought the rest of Avery Weigh-Tronix in 2008.

Trymer was among the 50 businesses acquired worldwide in 2008; the maker of rigid foam products expanded ITW's mechanical insulation offerings in its industrial packaging segment as well as sports a plant in La Porte Texas. Trymer's product applications run from mechanical and panel insulation to floral arrangements and crafts. Its lines like many of ITW's products are sold under their original owner's name.

In late 2009 ITW acquired the assets of South Carolina-based Hartness International a manufacturer of conveyor systems and line automation for the beverage and food industries. The acquisition complements ITW's packaging business in a lower cost geography. Nineteen other acquisitions were made in 2009 including a savvy negotiation for Ride Rite an inflatable paper dunnage (packing) bag manufacturer from recession hit KapStone Paper and Packaging.

ITW also divested a number of companies that didn't pan out for growth. In mid-2009 it jettisoned its Click Commerce a business with a buffet of industrial software applications to private equity Marlin Equity Partners. Marlin bought three software divisions from Requisite Technology (formerly Click Commerce) and raked away Service Network Solutions Research and Healthcare Solutions and Contract Service and Management operations as well as the Click Commerce nameplate.

The company pushed to unload an automotive components business on the sale rack since 2007. Instead the business was reclassified as discontinued along with an automotive machinery business and two consumer packaging businesses. Its consumer products holdings (appliances and cookware exercise equipment and ceramic tile acquired with Premark International) were also curbed. In a surprise move ITW's decorative surfaces segment which could not find a buyer was revived in 2009 as a continuing business.

In 2010 ITW acquired Accessories Marketing (dba Slime) a maker of tire care products and accessories from private equity Friend Skoler & Co. Slime brings a flagship brand green Slime tire sealants and a lineup of tire gauges tire repair kits portable air compressors and self-healing tire tubes sold in more than 60000 retail stores worldwide.

To build on its automotive aftermarket business in 2011 the company purchased Shell's SOPUS Products unit a car care product distributor for Pennzoil-Quaker State brands such as Rain-X (window rain repellent) Black Magic (liquid wax) and Gumout (fuel system cleaner). SOPUS (an acronym for Shell Oil Products US) made about $300 million in annual sales.

Also in 2011 Minnesota-based Despatch Industries joined ITW. The acquisition expanded ITW's presence in thermal processing equipment for the solar carbon fiber and other thermal technology sectors —a high-growth market.

ITW in late 2012 sold 51% of its Decorative Surfaces segment to Clayton Dubilier & Rice for about $1.05 billion. The divestment allowed ITW to focus on core segments while retaining some value in Decorative Surfaces which is expected to enjoy more sales as the construction sector strengthens. ITW in spring 2012 sold its finishing group of businesses to fluid-handling equipment specialist Graco for $650 million. Included in the sale were ITW companies such as Binks (spray guns) and Gema which made paint and spray systems for industrial applications. The company also sold its electronic components business in the power systems and electronics segment and it is divesting its consumer packaging operations in the "all other" segment.

EXECUTIVES

Vice President and Treasurer, Felix Rodriguez
EVP Test and Measurement and Electronics, Steven L. (Steve) Martindale, age 59
Chairman and CEO, E. Scott Santi, age 53, $1,083,525 total compensation
EVP Specialty Products, Roland M. Martel, age 61, $512,871 total compensation
EVP Polymers and Fluids, Juan Valls, age 54
SVP and CFO, Michael M. Larsen, $650,000 total compensation
EVP Automotive OEM, Sundaram (Naga) Nagarajan, age 52
EVP Welding, John R. Hartnett, age 55
VP Information Technology and Services, Mike Parisi
EVP Construction Products, Michael R. Zimmerman
Vice President, James H Wooten
Executive Vice President, Jane (Ginny) Warner
Vice President Marketing Financial Advisor, John (Jack) Brooklier
Vice President Research and Development, Lei Schlitz
Vice President Financial Planning Revenue Division, George Mondane
Executive Vice President Construction Products, Mike Zimmerman
Vice President Research and Development, Laurel Stein
Vice President of Sales and Purchasing Financial Advisor, Craig Hindman
Vice Chairman, David C. Parry, age 62
Vice Chairman, Christopher (Chris) O'Herlihy, age 52
Auditors: DELOITTE & TOUCHE LLP

LOCATIONS

HQ: Illinois Tool Works, Inc.
155 Harlem Avenue, Glenview, IL 60025
Phone: 847 724-7500
Web: www.itw.com

2014 Sales

	$ mil.	% of total
North America		
US	6,191	42
Other North America	993	7
Europe Middle East and Africa	4,319	30
Asia Pacific	2,427	17
South America	554	4
Total	**14,484**	**100**

PRODUCTS/OPERATIONS

2014 Sales

	$ mil.	% of total
Automotive OEM	2,590	18
Test & measurement & Electronics	2,204	15
Food Equipment	2,177	15
Specialty Products	2,055	14
Polymers & Fluids	1,927	14
Welding	1,850	13
Construction Products	1,707	12
Adjustments	(26)	.
Total	**14,484**	**100**

Selected Products

Construction products
  Anchors for concrete applications
  Anchors for retail
  Fasteners concrete applications
  Fasteners for retail
  Fasteners for wood and metal applications
  Metal plate truss components
  Packaged hardware for retail
Decorative surfaces
  Decorative high-pressure laminate for furniture office and retail space and countertops
  High-pressure laminate worktops
Food equipment
  Cooking equipment
  Ovens
  Ranges
  Broilers
  Food processing equipment
  Slicers
  Mixers
  Scales
  Kitchen exhaust systems
  Pollution-control systems
  Refrigeration equipment
  Refrigerators
  Freezers
  Prep tables
  Ventilation Systems
  Warewashing equipment
Industrial packaging
  Metal jacketing
  Paper products that protect goods in transit
  Plastic products that protect goods in transit
  Plastic strapping
  Plastic stretch film
  Steel strapping
Polymers and fluids
  Adhesives
  Industrial
  Construction
  Consumer
  Chemical fluids that clean or add lubrication to machines
  Epoxy and resin-based coating products for industrial applications
  Hand wipes and cleaners for industrial applications
  Pressure-sensitive adhesives and components
  Telecommunications
  Electronics
  Medical
  Transportation
  Resin-based coating products for industrial applications
Power systems and electronics
  Airport ground support equipment
  Arc welding equipment
  Component packaging
  Electronic components
  Equipment for microelectronics assembly
  Metal arc welding consumables
  Metal solder materials for PC board fabrication
Transportation
  Fillers for auto body repair
  Fluids for auto aftermarket maintenance and appearance
  Metal components for automobiles and light trucks
  Patch products for the marine industry
  Plastic components for automobiles and light trucks
  Polyester coatings for the marine industry
  Polymers for auto aftermarket maintenance and appearance
  Putties for auto body repair
Other
  Equipment and related software for testing and measuring of materials and structures

Film used to decorate consumer products
Foil used to decorate consumer products
Plastic reclosable packaging for consumer food storage
Plastic consumables that multi-pack cans and bottles and related equipment
Plastic for appliances and industrial applications
Metal fasteners for appliances and industrial applications

COMPETITORS

3M	Marmon Group
BASF SE	NCH
Cummins	Nordson
DuPont	Park-Ohio Holdings
ESAB	PennEngineering
Emerson Electric	Snap-on
Federal Screw Works	Stanley Black and
GE	Decker
Graco	Textron
IBIDEN	TriMas
Johnson Controls	Victor Technologies
Koch Enterprises	W. R. Grace
Lincoln Electric	ZF TRW Automotive
Manitowoc	

HISTORICAL FINANCIALS

Company Type: Public

Income Statement

FYE: December 31

	REVENUE ($ mil.)	NET INCOME ($ mil.)	NET PROFIT MARGIN	EMPLOYEES
12/15	13,405	1,899	14.2%	48,000
12/14	14,484	2,946	20.3%	49,000
12/13	14,135	1,679	11.9%	51,000
12/12	17,924	2,870	16.0%	60,000
12/11	17,786	2,071	11.6%	65,000
Annual Growth	(6.8%)	(2.1%)	—	(7.3%)

2015 Year-End Financials

Debt ratio: 47.03%	No. of shares (mil.): 363
Return on equity: 31.54%	Dividends
Cash ($ mil.): 3,090	Yield: 2.2%
Current ratio: 2.84	Payout: 40.6%
Long-term debt ($ mil.): 6,896	Market value ($ mil.): 33,709

	STOCK PRICE ($) FY Close	P/E High/Low	PER SHARE ($) Earnings	Dividends	Book Value
12/15	92.68	19 16	5.13	2.07	14.36
12/14	94.70	13 10	7.28	1.81	17.81
12/13	84.08	22 16	3.74	1.60	22.55
12/12	60.81	10 8	6.06	1.48	23.21
12/11	46.71	14 10	4.19	1.40	20.71
Annual Growth	18.7%	— —	5.2%	10.3%	(8.7%)

Independent Bank Corp. (MA)

Independent Bank wants to rock the northeast. Its banking subsidiary Rockland Trust operates almost 75 retail branches as well as investment and lending offices in Eastern Massachusetts and Rhode Island. Serving area individuals and small to midsized businesses the bank offers standard services such as checking and savings accounts CDs and credit cards in addition to insurance products financial planning trust services. Commercial loans including industrial construction and small business loans make up more than 70% of Rockland Trust's loan portfolio. Incorporated in 1985

the bank boasts total assets of nearly $7 billion including over $5 billion in deposits and $5 billion in loans.

Operations

About 28% of Independent Bank's loan portfolio is made up of consumer real estate loans which include residential mortgages and home equity loans and lines; while personal loans and auto loans make up around 1% of the portfolio. Through an agreement with LPL Investment Holdings Rockland Trust offers investment products such as securities and insurance. Independent Bank generated 70% of its total revenue from interest and fee income on loans in 2014 and another 6% from interest and dividends on investment securities. Investment management fees made up 6% of total revenue for the year while deposit account fees and interchange and ATM fees combined made up 11%.Geographic ReachRockland Trust boasts nearly 75 retail branches and three limited-services branches located in Eastern Massachusetts in the counties of Barnstable Bristol Middlesex Norfolk Plymouth and Worcester. Sales and MarketingThe company's borrowers include consumers and small-to-medium sized businesses with credit needs up to $250000 and revenues of less than $2.5 million. Independent Bank spent $3.86 million on advertising in 2014 compared to $4.28 million and $3.95 million in 2013 and 2012 respectively.Financial PerformanceIndependent Bank Corp's revenues and profits have trended higher in recent years thanks to continued loan business growth from both acquisitions and through organic expansion higher deposit account and ATM fee income from customer base growth and thanks to a decline in loan loss provisions as the credit quality of its loan portfolio has improved with the strengthened economy.The bank's revenue rose by 5% to $286.40 million in 2014 mostly thanks to higher interest income as its loan business growth continued to outpace the margin-eating impacts of low interest rates. Independent's non-interest income also rose by 3% thanks to a combination of higher interchange and ATM fees and investment management fees.Higher revenue and lower interest expenses on deposits in 2014 drove Independent Bank Corp's net income up by 19% to $59.85 million. Despite higher earnings the company's operating cash dove sharply primarily because of working capital changes related to its loans held for sale and changes in other assets.StrategyIndependent Bank planned in 2015 to grow its loans organically between 4-6% for the year while growing its deposits between 3% and 4%. The company has also been expanding its fee-based revenue business especially in its investment management segment with expectations of growing the business by another 3% to 4% in 2015. In addition to organic growth in other financial services areas Independent Bank has expanded via acquisitions.

Mergers and Acquisitions

In 2015 in expanding its Eastern Massachusetts presence and strengthening its position in the greater Boston market Independent Bank Corp purchased Peoples Federal Bancshares along with its flagship subsidiary Peoples Federal Savings Bank for $130.6 million. The deal added $606 million in total assets $435 million in deposits and $497 million in new loan business.In November 2013 Independent Bank acquired Mayflower Bancorp along with Mayflower Co-operative Bank for a total of $40.3 million adding deposits and loan assets and expanding its product and service offerings.In 2012 the company agreed to buy Central Bancorp parent of Central Bank. That deal added nine branches in Maryland's Middlesex County.Company BackgroundIn past years Independent Bank launched institutional asset managers Bright Rock Capital Management (2010)

and Compass Exchange Advisors (2006) and formed a handful of mutual funds.

EXECUTIVES

Executive Vice President Director of Retail Delivery Business Banking & Home Equity Lending, Jane L. Lundquist, age 58, $262,981 total compensation
President CEO and Director Independent Bank Corp. and Rockland Trust, Christopher (Chris) Oddleifson, age 56, $589,616 total compensation
CFO, Robert D. Cozzone
Executive Vice President Commercial Banking, Gerard F. Nadeau, age 57, $322,308 total compensation
Chief Information Officer, Barry Jensen
Vice President Regional Manager, Thomas Banks
Vice President Marketing Segment Manager, Elizabeth (Beth) Lynch
Vice President Product Development, John Barron
Senior Vice President, Joel Cavness
Senior Vice President, Kyle Spears
Senior Vice President Of Cash Management Division, Tracey Scalata
Vice President and Director, Scott Ewing
Vice President Sales and Marketing, Debbie Carroll
Vice President Commercial Banking, Nick Noorani
Regional President, Charlie Rigney
Vice President Business Development, Jeanne Barnett
Vice President of Retail Branch Sales, Kerri Pigott
Vice President Of Commercial Lending, William Zawacki
Senior Vice President Director Residential Lending, Kevin Inkley
Senior Vice President Deposit Operations and Branch Operations, Debbie Smith
Vice President and Compensation Benefits and Payroll Manager, Melanie D Whitney
Chairman, Donna L. Abelli
Auditors: Ernst & Young LLP

LOCATIONS

HQ: Independent Bank Corp. (MA)
2036 Washington Street, Hanover, MA 02339
Phone: 781 878-6100
Web: www.RocklandTrust.com

PRODUCTS/OPERATIONS

2012 Sales

	$ mil.	% of total
Interest		
Loans	178	69
Taxable securities including dividends	16	6
Other	1	-
Noninterest		
Service charges on deposit accounts	16	6
Wealth management	14	6
Interchange & ATM fees	9	4
Other	21	9
Adjustments	(0.1)	-
Total	**258**	**100**

COMPETITORS

Bank of America	Hingham Institution
Chicopee	for Savings
Citizens Financial	Sovereign Bank
Group	TD Bank USA
Eastern Bank	

Income Statement
FYE: December 31

	ASSETS ($ mil.)	NET INCOME ($ mil.)	INCOME AS % OF ASSETS	EMPLOYEES
12/14	6,364	59	0.9%	980
12/13	6,099	50	0.8%	984
12/12	5,756	42	0.7%	998
12/11	4,970	45	0.9%	909
12/10	4,695	40	0.9%	919
Annual Growth	7.9%	10.4%	—	1.6%

2014 Year-End Financials

Debt ratio: 2.96%	No. of shares (mil.): 24
Return on equity: 9.71%	Dividends
Cash ($ mil.): 178	Yield: 2.2%
Current ratio: —	Payout: 42.1%
Long-term debt ($ mil.): —	Market value ($ mil.): 1,027

	STOCK PRICE ($) FY Close	P/E High/Low	PER SHARE ($) Earnings	Dividends	Book Value
12/14	42.81	17 14	2.49	0.96	26.69
12/13	39.12	18 13	2.18	0.88	24.85
12/12	28.95	16 13	1.96	0.84	23.24
12/11	27.29	14 10	2.12	0.76	21.82
12/10	27.05	15 11	1.90	0.72	20.78
Annual Growth	12.2%	— —	7.0%	7.5%	6.5%

Ingram Micro Inc.

The only things micro about Ingram are some of the smaller electronic components it sells. The world's largest wholesale distributor of information technology products Ingram Micro provides thousands of products —desktop and notebook PCs servers storage devices monitors printers and software —to more than 200000 customers in some 160 countries worldwide. Its sells products from more than 1700 suppliers including many of the world's top manufacturers; Hewlett-Packard is the company's largest supplier. Ingram Micro also offers a wide range of services to its resellers and suppliers including supply chain management business intelligence financing logistics cloud computing and network support services. The company rings up 61% of sales outside North America.

Operations

The computer seller's Ingram Micro Services division provides managed services such as network security application hosting and remote monitoring under the Seismic brand along with professional services such as consulting staffing and warranty contract management. Through acquisitions the company has bolstered its offering with mobile device lifecycle services and logistics and a range of cloud-computing services.

Geographic Reach

Beyond the US and Canada California-based Ingram Micro has operations in 38 countries throughout Asia Europe Africa and Latin America.

Sales and Marketing

About 14% of Ingram Micro's 2014 sales were generated by products purchased from Hewlett-Packard Co.

Financial Performance

Ingram Micro's sales reached higher in 2014 to $46.4 billion a 9% increase from the $42.5 billion it recorded in 2013. Sales were higher in North America and Europe. North American revenue benefited from a better than 100% increase in its mobility business.

Net income however dropped 7% in 2014 to $266 million from $310.5 million in 2013. Ingram Micro in 2014 had higher administrative costs an increase in amortization expense stemming from acquisition and costs associated with a reorganization. Changes in trade accounts receivable inventory and accrued expenses drove cash out of the business to the tune of $490 million in 2014 compared to positive cash flow of $466 million in 2013.

Strategy

The fast-growing firm has acquired more than 20 companies over the past decade expanding its geographic reach as well as its menu of products and services. Ingram Micro's long-term strategy is to expand its business in high-growth geographic markets and product segments such as mobile technology. To that end it's looking to emerging markets including the Middle East (where it recently acquired an IT distribution business) and Africa where total IT spending is projected to reach $80 billion by 2015.

Besides mobile devices and services Ingram Micro has increased its offerings in another hot sector: cloud-computing services and resources. It has aggregated 224 cloud products from 74 vendors and in 2015 expanded its Ingram Micro Cloud Marketplace in New Zealand and throughout Europe in 2015.

Challenges facing the company include raising its razor-thin margins in a cutthroat pricing environment and more vendors selling directly to end users reducing the need for Ingram's services. More than just a reseller of IT peripherals systems software and networking products Ingram offers its vendors and customers a variety of services including supply chain management and technical support and training which provide higher profit margins and help distinguish it from its rivals. In 2014 it partnered with electronics case makers OtterBox and LifeProof to offer enterprise customers a line of protective cases for smart phones and tablets.

Another possible challenge comes from the break up of Hewlett-Packard into two companies. HP has been the biggest provider of products for resale and distribution through Ingram Micro. While channels will remain open at the split formalizes in late 2015 any HP hiccups could have an impact at Ingram Micro.

Ingram Micro reorganized in early 2014 to align costs and resources and to move into faster growing higher margin businesses. The reorg cost about $94000 in employee termination benefits and a write off of an acquired brand name.

Mergers and Acquisitions

Ingram Micro made acquisitions in 2015 that expanded its services and its geographic reach.

It added to its mobility assets with the purchases of CANAI Group and Clarity Technology. CANAI based in the UK specializes in retail carrier and web-based trade-in processes sustainable recovery reuse and recycling of electronic products. Clarity which operates from Portugal provides mobility services that include reverse logistics repairs parts and accessory management and diagnostics and repair avoidance.

In broadening its reach in the Middle East and Africa Ingram Micro Inc. acquired Arabian Applied Technology the largest value-added technology distributor in Saudi Arabia. The business will operate as Aptec Saudi Arabia as a part of Ingram Micro's Middle East Turkey & Africa region.

HISTORY

Micro D was founded in Fountain Valley California in 1979 by husband-and-wife entrepreneurs Geza Csige and Lorraine Mecca. As the company grew Mecca sought to merge the computer distributor with a partner that could take over daily operations. She relinquished control of Micro D to Linwood "Chip" Lacy in 1986 and sold her 51% share of the company to minority shareholder Ingram Distribution Group.

Sales bottomed out for Micro D that year. Lacy tightened Micro D's belt and took huge charges for outdated inventory it sold at a discount and overdue payments from customers that had gone bankrupt.

At the same time Ingram Industries was busy merging recently acquired Ingram Software Distribution Services of Buffalo New York with Compton California-based Softeam. The merger made the company one of the nation's largest wholesale distributors of computer software. Lacy saw Ingram's purchase of Micro D shares as a conflict of interest but he was too busy returning Micro D to profitability —centralizing its marketing and distribution functions cutting costs and expanding its market to include more small retailers which provided higher margins. Micro D went from the fourth-largest distributor of microcomputer products to #1 in just one year.

The surging PC market in the late 1980s fueled Micro D's growth. By 1988 the firm had expanded outside the US for the first time acquiring Canadian company Frantek Computer Products.

Ingram Industries offered to acquire the 41% of outstanding Micro D stock it did not own in 1988 but Lacy resisted preferring to let Ingram wait. Though Ingram owned a majority of Micro D stock it only controlled three of seven seats on the board. Ingram was forced to play Lacy's game and finally acquired the company at a higher cost in 1989. The new company which controlled 20% of the computer distribution market was called Ingram Micro D. The merger was anything but smooth and several Micro D executives jumped ship.

As the PC took hold in the US in the 1990s Ingram Micro D became the dominant industry player but relations between Lacy and the Ingram family never improved. The company shortened its name to Ingram Micro in 1991 and two years later as it was hitting stride Lacy announced plans to leave. To keep him Ingram Industries CEO Bronson Ingram (much to his distaste) promised to let Lacy take the company public.

Bronson Ingram died in 1995 and the next year his widow Martha forced Lacy's resignation. Lacy was replaced by Jerre Stead formerly CEO of software maker LEGENT (bought by CA) who devised a compensation package for himself consisting solely of stock options (no salary) and listed "Head Coach" on his business card. Ingram went public a few months after Stead took over.

In 1998 Ingram Micro forged a distribution alliance with Japanese computer giant SOFTBANK and bought a majority stake in German computer products distributor Macrotron. It also expanded into build-to-order PC manufacturing. Amid softer PC sales industrywide Ingram Micro in 1999 terminated nearly 600 employees as part of a worldwide realignment and signed a deal (worth an estimated $10 billion) with CompUSA to be its primary PC manufacturer and distributor.

Later in 1999 Stead —with Ingram Micro's sales slipping and its stock slumping —made plans to step down as CEO. The search for his replacement ended in 2000 when the company named GTE veteran Kent Foster to the post.

Ingram Micro expanded its portfolio of services for enterprises and began offering more extensive network and product support services. The company outsourced certain IT infrastructure operations along with the related personnel to Affiliated Computer Services (ACS) in 2002. Ingram Micro continued to expand international operations that year acquiring the 49% of a Singapore exporter it did not previously own and purchasing operations in Belgium and the Netherlands. In a move to expand its presence in the Asia/Pacific region Ingram acquired Australian distributor Tech Pacific in 2004.

Company president Greg Spierkel replaced Foster as CEO in 2005. Ingram Micro also acquired certain assets of consumer electronics distributor AVAD. The following year it expanded its reach in Northern Europe when it purchased the assets of SymTech Nordic. It also formed a North American services division focused on professional IT services warranty contract management and managed services. Ingram purchased consumer electronics distributor DBL Distributing for $96 million in 2007.

In 2009 Ingram Micro bought certain assets of Computacenter Distribution (CCD) a distributor of server storage and networking equipment in the UK that was previously a division of Computacenter.

Ingram Micro acquired BrightPoint for $9.90 per share in cash in October 2012. The acquisition of BrightPoint supported Ingram Micro's long-term growth strategy to expand its business in high growth markets.

EXECUTIVES

Vice President Of Business Development, Bob Laclade
EVP General Counsel and Secretary, Larry C. Boyd, age 62, $464,406 total compensation
EVP and Group President, Michael (Mike) Zilis
CFO, William D. Humes, age 50, $708,750 total compensation
EVP and President Mobility and Lifecycle Services, Shailendra Gupta, age 52, $650,741 total compensation
CEO, Alain Moni Çage 64, $992,307 total compensation
EVP and CEO U.S. and Miami Export, Paul Bay
EVP Business Development and Strategy, John Soumbasakis
President and COO, Paul Read, age 48, $747,115 total compensation
EVP Finance, Gina Mastantuono
EVP Human Resources, Scott D. Sherman, age 49
EVP and President Europe Technology Solutions, Gerhard Schulz
EVP Global Cloud Computing, Nimesh Dave
EVP and CIO, Ramesh Nair
EVP Commerce and Fulfillment Solutions, Ken Beyer
Vice President Marketing North America, Jennifer (Jen) Anaya
Executive Vice President Marketing, Brian Stelmach
National Account Manager, Tom Gordon
Senior Vice President, Chris Loomis
Senior Vice President Operations, Terry Tysseland
Executive Vice President Human Resources, Lynn Jolliffe
Senior Executive Vice President Corporate, Alain Maquet
Vice President and General Manager Ingram Micro Canada, Mark Snider
Vice President Marketing, Mary Whittle
Senior Vice President Sales, Andrew Weinzler
Vice President Controller North America, Thomas (Thom) Balding
Vice President Distribution And Customer Services, Bruce Reizman
National Account Manager, Jan Markelin
National Account Manager, David (Dave) Tanner
Vice President, Rainer Kozlik
Vice President Ingram Micro And President, Damon Schechter

Vice President Central And Eastern European Region, Thomas Maurer
Vice President Internal Audit, Jeanette Hughes
Vice President North American Operations, Bill Ross
National Account Manager, Shelly Stephens
Senior Vice President Corporate Controller, James Agnew
Vice President Tax, Jerry Thompson
Senior Vice President Finance Global, Vince Hassel
Vice President Of Managed Services, Renee Bergeron
Executive Vice President, Mario Leone
Chairman, Dale R. Laurance
Treasurer Secretary, John Somers
Treasurer, Hiren Patel
Auditors: PricewaterhouseCoopers LLP

LOCATIONS

HQ: Ingram Micro Inc.
3351 Michelson Drive, Suite 100, Irvine, CA 92612-0697
Phone: 714 566-1000   **Fax:** 714 566-7604
Web: www.ingrammicro.com

2014 Sales

	$ mil.	% of total
North America	19,929	43
Europe	14,263	31
Asia/Pacific	9,991	21
Latin America	2,303	5
Total	**46,487**	**100**

2014 $ mil %		
US	18,245	39
International	28,242	61
Total	**46,487**	**100**

PRODUCTS/OPERATIONS

Selected Products

IT Peripheral/CE/AIDC/POS/Mobility and Others
  Barcode/card printers
  Cell phones
  Components
  Digital cameras
  Digital signage products
  Digital video disc players
  Game consoles
  Mass storage
  Printers
  Projectors
  Scanners
  Supplies and accessories
  Televisions
Networking
  Network interface cards
  Storage
  Switches hubs and routers
  Wireless local area networks
Software
  Business application software
  Developer software tools
  Entertainment software
  Middleware
  Operating system software
  Security software
  Storage software
Systems
  Desktops
  Personal digital assistants
  Portable personal computers
  Rack tower and blade servers

COMPETITORS

ASI Computer Technologies	New Age Electronics
Agilysys	Redington Group
Arrow Electronics	SED International
Avnet	SHI International
Black Box	SYNNEX
Brightstar Corp.	ScanSource
Computacenter	Schindler Holding
	Softmart

D & H Distributing	Supercom
DHL	TESSCO
Digiland	Tech Data
Digital China	UNICOM Government
Dimension Data	UPS Supply Chain
Essendant	Solutions
Intcomex	Westcon
Menlo Worldwide	

HISTORICAL FINANCIALS

Company Type: Public

Income Statement

FYE: December 31

	REVENUE ($ mil.)	NET INCOME ($ mil.)	NET PROFIT MARGIN	EMPLOYEES
12/14	46,487	266	0.6%	21,700
12/13	42,553	310	0.7%	21,800
12/12	37,827	305	0.8%	20,800
12/11*	36,328	244	0.7%	15,500
01/11	34,588	318	0.9%	15,650
Annual Growth	**7.7%**	**(4.3%)**	**—**	**8.5%**

*Fiscal year change

2014 Year-End Financials

Debt ratio: 11.45%
Return on equity: 6.52%
Cash ($ mil.): 692
Current ratio: 1.54
Long-term debt ($ mil.): 1,096

No. of shares (mil.): 156
Dividends
  Yield: —
  Payout: —
Market value ($ mil.): 4,318

	STOCK PRICE ($) FY Close	P/E High/Low	PER SHARE ($) Earnings	Dividends	Book Value
12/14	27.64	18 13	1.67	0.00	26.67
12/13	23.38	12 8	1.99	0.00	25.59
12/12	16.54	10 7	1.99	0.00	24.02
12/11*	18.19	14 10	1.53	0.00	21.89
01/11	19.09	10 8	1.94	0.00	20.42
Annual Growth	**9.7%**	**— —**	**(3.7%)**	**—**	**6.9%**

*Fiscal year change

Ingredion Inc

Sweet sodas and diet desserts alike get their taste from Ingredion's ingredients. The company makes food ingredients and industrial products from corn and other starch-based raw materials. It serve 60 markets including food beverage brewing and pharmaceutical companies. More than 40% of sales come from sweeteners including high-fructose corn syrup which is used by just about every beverage maker and a good many food companies to sweeten their products. Ingredion also produces corn starch (a thickener for processed foods) corn oil and corn gluten (for animal feed). Ingredion operates manufacturing plants throughout Africa Asia Europe and North and South America.

Geographic Reach

Ingredion has 36 manufacturing plats as well as R&D and sales offices in more than 40 countries. The company serves customers in more than 60 markets in over 100 countries.

North America (Canada Mexico and the US) is Ingredion's largest market accounting for about 55% of the firm's 2014 sales. South America contributes about 21% of sales followed by the Asia Pacific region (14%) and Europe the Middle East and Africa (10%).

Operations

Ingredion organizes its operations geographically. To this end its business segments include

North America South America Asia Pacific and EMEA.

Sales and Marketing

The company supplies a range of customers including the food beverage brewing pharmaceutical paper and corrugated products textile and personal care industries as well as the global animal feed and corn oil markets. Ingredion sells its products through its own sales force directly to manufacturers and distributors.

Financial Performance

Ingredion reported continuous growth in revenues until 2012 followed by a 3% decline in 2013 and a 10% drop in 2014. The decline for 2014 was highlighted by a decrease in net sales in North America driven by lower raw material costs (primarily corn). South American sales decreased 10% as the company also experienced weaker foreign currencies.

Ingredion experienced net losses in 2013 and 2014. The loss for 2014 was attributed to an impairment charge of $33 million to write-off goodwill at its Southern Cone of South America reporting unit and $2 million in after-tax costs related to a pending acquisition. Cash provided by operations increased 18% in 2014 reflecting improved cash flow associated with working capital activities and an increase in accounts payable and accrued liabilities associated.Strategy

Beyond acquisitions Ingredion is also growing organically broadening its ingredient portfolio and geographic coverage. Outside North America the company's second-largest market is South America. To support its growth there the company is investing up to $100 million to expand its operations in Brazil –its biggest market in the region. Ingredion currently operates about a half a dozen manufacturing plants and two ingredient development facilities there.

In 2014 Ingredion entered an agreement with Alliance Grain Traders (AGT) to be AGT's distributor of that company's pulse flours protein and bran ingredients a move that complements three of Ingredion's growth platforms - wholesome ingredients texturizers and nutritional ingredients.

Mergers and Acquisitions

Ingredion in March 2015 acquired Iowa-based Penford Corp. a maker of carbohydrate-based specialty starches used by the paper packaging and food industries for $19 per share in cash. The deal was valued at around $340 million and extended Ingredion's core offerings and geographical footprint; Penford has offices and plants in Colorado Idaho Iowa Pennsylvania South Carolina Washington and Wisconsin.

EXECUTIVES

EVP and CFO, Jack C. Fortnum, age 58, $571,500 total compensation

EVP Global Specialties; President North America and EMEA, James P. Zallie, age 53, $532,500 total compensation

Chairman President and CEO, Ilene S. Gordon, age 61, $1,121,668 total compensation

SVP and President South America, Ernesto Peres Pousada, age 48

CIO, Ronald E. (Ron) Lejcar

SVP and President Asia Pacific and EMEA, Jorgen Kokke, age 46

Vice President Human Resources north America, Becky Tinkham

Vice President Corporate Controller, Matt Galvanoni

Senior Vice President General Counsel and Corporate Secretary, Christine Castellano

Vice President Innovation And Strategy, Igor Playner

Vice President Global Technology, Manish Shah

Vice President and Managing Director Canada, Robert (Bob) Kee

Vice President Applications Research And Technical Services, Ron Deis

Senior Vice President Operational Excellence, Robert Stefansic

Vice President Global Beverage And General Manager Sweetener And Industrial Solutions, Larry Fernandes

Vice President Strategic Planning, Rick Kyle

Vice President Safety and Health, Ron McCrimmon

Vice President Us Canada Industrial Solutions, John (Jack) Keaveney

Assistant Treasurer, Dorsey Lewis

Auditors: KPMG LLP

LOCATIONS

HQ: Ingredion Inc
5 Westbrook Corporate Center, Westchester, IL 60154
Phone: 708 551-2600   **Fax:** 708 551-2700
Web: www.ingredion.com

2014 Sales

	$ mil.	% of total
North America	3,093	55
South America	1,203	21
Asia Pacific	794	14
EMEA	578	10
Total	**5,668**	**100**

PRODUCTS/OPERATIONS

2014 Sales

	% of total
Starch products	43
Sweetener products	39
Co-products & others	18
Total	**100**

Selected Products

Sweetener products
  Dextrose
  Glucose corn syrups
  High fructose corn syrup
  High maltose corn syrup
  Maltodextrins
  Polyols
Starch products
  Corn starch (consumer and industrial)
  Specialty Starches
Co-products and others
  Corn gluten feed
  Corn gluten meal
  Refined corn oil
Speciality Ingredients
Delivery systems
Green Solutions
Nutrition
Sweetness
Texture
Wholesome

Selected Subsidiaries

Canada Starch Company Inc.
Colombia Millers Ltd.
CP Ingredients Limited (UK)
Derivados del Maiz S.A. (95% Peru)
Feed Products Limited
Globe Ingredients Nigeria Limited
GTC Oats Inc.
National Starch LLC

COMPETITORS

ACH Food Companies	Malt Products
ADM	Corporation
Ajinomoto	Merisant
Cargill	Nordzucker
Cumberland Packing	NutraSweet
DSM	PureCircle
Faultless Starch	Roquette Frères
Global Bio-chem	Sweet Green Fields
Grain Processing	Sdzucker
Corporation	Tate & Lyle
Henkel	Ingredients
Imperial Sugar	Yamazaki Baking

HISTORICAL FINANCIALS

Company Type: Public

Income Statement

FYE: December 31

	REVENUE ($ mil.)	NET INCOME ($ mil.)	NET PROFIT MARGIN	EMPLOYEES
12/14	5,668	355	6.3%	11,400
12/13	6,328	396	6.3%	11,300
12/12	6,532	428	6.6%	11,200
12/11	6,219	416	6.7%	11,100
12/10	4,367	169	3.9%	10,700
Annual Growth	**6.7%**	**20.4%**	**—**	**1.6%**

2014 Year-End Financials

Debt ratio: 35.89%	No. of shares (mil.): 71
Return on equity: 15.50%	Dividends
Cash ($ mil.): 580	Yield: 1.9%
Current ratio: 2.97	Payout: 35.4%
Long-term debt ($ mil.): 1,804	Market value ($ mil.): 6,051

	STOCK PRICE ($) FY Close	P/E High/Low		PER SHARE ($)		
				Earnings	Dividends	Book Value
12/14	84.84	18	12	4.74	1.68	30.52
12/13	68.46	14	12	5.05	1.56	32.35
12/12	64.43	12	8	5.47	0.92	31.64
12/11	52.59	11	7	5.32	0.66	27.73
12/10	46.00	21	12	2.20	0.56	25.99
Annual Growth	**16.5%**	**—**	**—**	**21.2%**	**31.6%**	**4.1%**

Insight Enterprises Inc.

With Insight Enterprises around the end of your technology woes could be in sight. The company distributes computer hardware and software and provides IT services for businesses schools and government agencies and departments. Insight offers thousands of products from major manufacturers (including Hewlett-Packard IBM and Cisco) and it provides networking and communications services through subsidiaries Insight Networking in the US and UK-based MINX. The company uses direct telesales field sales agents and an e-commerce site to reach its clients in North America and about 200 other countries across Europe the Middle East Africa and the Asia/Pacific region.

OperationsHardware accounted for more than half of the company's 2014 revenues; software 43%.In 2013 Insight purchased products and software from 3600 partners.

In North America and Western Europe Insight sells hardware software and services. Ih the rest of the world it's just software and related services.Geographic ReachInsight rings up more than two-thirds of its sales in North America. Second in importance is Europe the Middle East and Africa (EMEA) which contributes almost 30%. The Asia-Pacific (APAC) region accounts for the rest.Sales and MarketingMicrosoft accounted for 31% of Insight's revenues in 2014; HP 14%; and Cisco 10%The company's advertising expenses were $31.2 million $29.4 million and $27.6 million for the years 2014 2013 and 2012 respectively.Financial PerformanceAfter experiencing a slight dip in revenue in 2013 Insight returned to its five-year trend and reported a modest growth in revenue for 2014. The 3% increase was driven by higher sales across all segments in North America and mostly hardware and services in EMEA. Net income which has fluctuated in recent years rose by 7% on higher revenue and lower severance restructuring and interest expenses.StrategyInsight is growing at home and abroad by upgrading its technology expanding its product line entering new markets and making acquisitions.In 2014 the company announced plans to migrate its APAC operations to the same IT system platform it uses in North America. During 2013 Insight deployed all countries in its EMEA segment onto a separate single new IT system platform that gives them the capability to expand their sales of hardware and services (in addition to software) to clients in that region. That year it also announced the expansion of its InsightCloud Solutions Center with the addition of Cloud Business Provisioning powered by dinCloud.

HISTORY

Eric Crown worked for a small computer retail chain in the mid-1980s before leaving to market PCs. In 1986 he and his brother Tim pooled $2000 from credit cards and $1300 in savings and anticipating a drop in hard drive prices placed an ad for low-cost hard drives in a computer magazine. The ad pulled in $20000 worth of sales and since costs did indeed drop the profit was enough to start a new company Hard Drives International. In 1988 they changed the name to Insight Enterprises; by 1991 the Crowns also sold Insight-branded PCs software and peripherals (discontinued in 1995). The company passed the $100 million revenue mark in 1992.

Insight shifted its marketing focus to catalogs in 1993 and had a circulation of more than 7 million by 1995. The company went public that year and entered an alliance with Computer City (acquired by CompUSA in 1998) to handle its mail-order fulfillment. It also launched its website. The next year subsidiary Insight Direct began to offer on-site service warranties and in 1997 retailing subsidiary Direct Alliance was chosen to provide product fulfillment for Internet software firm Geo Publishing. That year the company began sponsoring the Copper Bowl a college football game played in Arizona which was renamed the Insight.com Bowl (and later the Insight Bowl).

Looking beyond the US in 1998 Insight established operations in Canada and acquired direct marketers Choice Peripherals (UK) and Computerprofis Computersysteme (Germany). At home it added direct marketer Treasure Chest Computers. Sales passed the billion-dollar mark that year.

The company formed an alliance with Daisytek International in 1999 that expanded its product line by more than 10000. Soon thereafter Insight walked away from a merger with UK-based computer wholesaler Action Computer Supplies when Action's profits slumped.

Insight withdrew its planned IPO and spinoff of Direct Alliance in 2001 due to poor market conditions. Also that month Eric became chairman and Tim became CEO (they had previously shared the title of co-CEO). Insight ended up buying Action Computer Supplies in 2001. It also shut down its German operations and acquired computer direct marketers in both the UK and Canada in late 2001.

In April 2002 Insight acquired Comark a leading private reseller of computers peripherals and computer supplies in the US and began integrating its operations into Insight North America's existing operational structure.

Tim stepped down as president and CEO and became chairman in late 2004 while Eric assumed the title of chairman emeritus. The company appointed IBM veteran Richard Fennessy to the position of president and CEO. That year Insight spun off its UK-based Internet service provider PlusNet.

In 2006 Insight Enterprises bought software and mobile solutions firm Software Spectrum.

EXECUTIVES

President and CEO, Kenneth T. (Ken) Lamneck, age 60, $709,172 total compensation
CIO, Michael Guggemos, age 50, $355,374 total compensation
CFO, Glynis A. Bryan, age 56, $443,679 total compensation
President Insight US, Steven W. Dodenhoff, age 52, $433,370 total compensation
President Insight EMEA, Wolfgang Ebermann, age 50, $578,315 total compensation
Vice President Sales, Jason Sullivan
Vice President Of Finance, John Carnahan
Vice President Finance, Michael Kasen
Assistant Vice President Marketing Div, Karla Herder
Senior Vice President Na And Apac Software, Andrea Mattea
Chairman, Timothy A. (Tim) Crown, age 51
Auditors: KPMG LLP

LOCATIONS

HQ: Insight Enterprises Inc.
6820 South Harl Avenue, Tempe, AZ 85283
Phone: 480 333-3000
Web: www.insight.com

2014 Sales

	$ mil.	% of total
North America	3,562	67
Europe Middle East & Africa	1,540	29
Asia/Pacific	213	4
Total	**5,316**	**100**

2014

	$ mil.	% of total
US	3,368	63
Foreign	1,947	37
Total	**5,316**	**100**

PRODUCTS/OPERATIONS

2014 Sales

	$ mil.	% of total
Hardware	2,760	52
Software	2,298	43
Services	257	5
Total	**5,316**	**100**

Selected Products

Computer memory and processors
Desktop computers
Monitors
Networking equipment
Notebook computers
Printers and printing consumables
Servers
Software
Storage devices

Selected Services

Business optimization software
  Business productivity
  Core infrastructure
  Software asset management
Collaboration
  Call/contact center
  Unified communications/messaging
  Video collaboration/conferencing
Cloud services
  Collaboration
  Infrastructure
  Messaging
  Security
Data center
  Infrastructure solutions
  Server solutions
  Storage solutions
Infrastructure and security
  Network infrastructure
  Security infrastructure
Managed services
  Business process outsourcing
  Connected real estate and sports
  Financing and leasing

IT asset disposal
Maintenance
Product provisioning
Remote network operations
Telecom expense management
Warehouse/integration

COMPETITORS

Amazon.com	Microsoft
Best Buy	Newegg
Buy.com	Office Depot
CDW	OfficeMax
CompuCom	PC Connection
Convergys	PC Mall
Dell	PFSweb
Digital River	RadioShack
Fry' s Electronics	SHI International
Gateway Inc.	Softchoice
HP	Staples
HP Enterprise Services	Symantec
IBM	Systemax
Lenovo	Zones
Micro Electronics	

HISTORICAL FINANCIALS

Company Type: Public

Income Statement

FYE: December 31

	REVENUE ($ mil.)	NET INCOME ($ mil.)	NET PROFIT MARGIN	EMPLOYEES
12/14	5,316	75	1.4%	5,406
12/13	5,144	71	1.4%	5,202
12/12	5,301	92	1.7%	5,045
12/11	5,287	100	1.9%	5,386
12/10	4,809	75	1.6%	5,115
Annual Growth	**2.5%**	**0.1%**	**—**	**1.4%**

2014 Year-End Financials

Debt ratio: 3.25%	No. of shares (mil.): 40
Return on equity: 10.53%	Dividends
Cash ($ mil.): 164	Yield: —
Current ratio: 1.51	Payout: —
Long-term debt ($ mil.): 62	Market value ($ mil.): 1,039

	STOCK PRICE ($) FY Close	P/E High/Low		PER SHARE ($) Earnings	Dividends	Book Value
12/14	25.89	17	11	1.83	0.00	17.96
12/13	22.71	15	10	1.64	0.00	17.06
12/12	17.37	11	7	2.07	0.00	15.82
12/11	15.29	9	6	2.18	0.00	13.59
12/10	13.16	10	7	1.61	0.00	11.76
Annual Growth	**18.4%**	**—**	**—**	**3.3%**	**—**	**11.2%**

Intel Corp

Intel has followed the law —Moore's Law that is —to the top spot in manufacturing and selling semiconductors. Company co-founder Gordon Moore determined in 1965 (making 2015 the 50th anniversary of the law) that microprocessors would regularly get more powerful smaller and less expensive. Intel has followed that formula to grab about 80% of the market share for microprocessors that go into desktop and notebook computers smartphones tablets and computer servers. The company also makes embedded semiconductors for the industrial medical and in-vehicle infotainment markets. The company's technology roadmap calls for releasing a new Core processor and a Xeon processor every two years. Most computer makers use Intel processors. In late 2015 Intel bought chipmaker Altera for $16.7 billion.

Operations

Intel is indeed inside millions of personal computers and that's why is PC Client Group segment accounted for 62% of the company's revenue in 2014. The Data Center Group brought in 26% of revenue. A third segment the recently organized unit devoted to processors and software for the Internet of Things was responsible for 4%.

The company's subsidiaries include Shiva Corporation Chips and Technologies Intel Technology India Intel Corporation UK Intel China Wind River Systems McAfee IM Flash Technologies and Havok.com.

Geographic Reach

Intel has more than 150 locations around the globe with assembly and test facilities in China Costa Rica Malaysia and Vietnam. Singapore and China generate 21% and 20% of Intel's total sales respectively. The US accounts for 17%.

Sales and Marketing

Intel sells its products primarily to OEMs and original design manufacturers (ODMs). ODMs provide design and manufacturing services to branded and unbranded private label resellers. In addition Intel products are sold to makers of a wide range of industrial and communications equipment.

Its customers also include those who buy PC components and other products through distributor reseller retail and OEM channels. Intel's worldwide reseller sales channel consists of thousands of indirect customers (systems builders that purchase its microprocessors and other products from their distributors).

In 2014 Hewlett-Packard accounted for 18% of the company's sales while Dell contributed 16% and Lenovo accounted for 12%. Intel's advertising expenses were $1.8 billion in in 2014.

Financial Performance

After two years of declining revenue and profit Intel reported growth in both in 2014. Revenue increased 6% to nearly $56 billion for the year a record high. Intel's traditional PC and server businesses had higher sales as worldwide PC sales stabilized. Sales for the mobile and communications segment however dropped 85% in 2014.

Higher revenue translated into a 22% increase in net income of $11.7 billion for 2014. A turnaround in interest on other income also helped push profit higher even as the company had operating expenses that were $1 billion higher in 2014 from 2013.

The company's cash flow from operations was 2% lower in 2014 with higher receivables and a decline in accounts payable.

Strategy

While Intel has long dominated the chip market for personal computers and servers it was late to the game for smart phones and tablets and that cost it sales and profit. The company is looking to catch up in mobile and establish leadership in other areas such as the Internet of Things and cloud computing.

In addressing the mobile market the company released its M Core family of processors which boost graphics and battery life. Intel shipped 40 million processors for tablets in 2014 better than its goal for the year. For 2015 it will introduce its SoFIA system-on-a-chip for mobile.

In late 2014 Intel announced its Intel IoT Platform a platform designed to unify and simplify connectivity and security for the Internet of Things (IoT). The company drew on software developed by its recent acquisitions Wind River and McAfee for the platform. The platform is to make it easier to develop applications and to connect the “things” effectively and securely with the Internet.

In its main processor business Intel's has released and is nearing release on several rounds of processor upgrades that offer higher performance while using less energy. They include the Intel Xeon E5 and Xeon E7 processors as well as the Intel Xeon Phi coprocessors. The Phi coprocessors are designed to act as power boosters in supercomputers enabling trillions of calculations per second.

Mergers and Acquisitions

The acquisition of Altera provides Intel with key technology for dealing with data center cloud and the Internet of Things. Altera makes chips that can be reprogrammed after installation. Intel will combine its powerful Xeon processors which handle dedicated tasks with Altera's more chips to give customers more flexibility.

In 2105 Intel completed the acquisition of Lantiq a supplier of broadband access and home networking technologies. With the acquisition Intel moves further into DSL and fiber markets.

For 2014 Intel spent $963 million on eight acquisitions. The biggest was the $650 million purchase of the Axxia networking business of Broadcom. The Axxia acquisition is intended to quicken Intel's push into mobile wireless base stations. In 2013 Intel shelled out about $925 million on a dozen companies. With Stonesoft Intel will expand its network security products.

HISTORY

Early History

The founding of Intel is one of the legendary stories of Silicon Valley. In 1968 three engineers from Fairchild Semiconductor created Intel in Mountain View California to develop technology for silicon-based chips. ("Intel" is a contraction of "integrated electronics.") The trio consisted of Robert Noyce (who co-invented the integrated circuit or IC in 1958) Gordon Moore and Andy Grove.

Intel initially provided computer memory chips such as DRAMs (1970) and EPROMs (1971). These successes funded the microprocessor designs that revolutionized the electronics industry. In 1971 Intel introduced the 4004 microprocessor promoted as "a micro-programmable computer on a chip."

In 1979 Moore became Intel's chairman and Grove its president. (Grove became CEO in 1987.) When Intel's 8088 chip was chosen for IBM's PC in 1981 Intel secured its place as the microcomputer standard-setter.

Cutthroat pricing by Japanese competitors forced Intel out of the DRAM market in 1985; in a breathtaking strategy shift that became the subject of countless business school case studies the company refocused on microprocessors. It licensed its 286 chip technology to Advanced Micro Devices (AMD) and others in an effort to create an industry standard. Reacting to AMD's escalating market share (which stood at more than half by 1990) Intel fiercely protected the technology of its 386 (1985) and 486 (1989) chips; AMD sued for breach of contract.

EXECUTIVES

EVP and President Intel Capital, Arvind Sodhani, age 61, $225,000 total compensation

Corporate VP and General Manager Datacenter Engineering Group, Stephen L. Smith

EVP and General Manager Technology and Manufacturing Group, William M. (Bill) Holt, age 62, $641,000 total compensation

VP Sales and Marketing Group; Co-President Intel Americas, Thomas M. (Tom) Kilroy, age 58, $625,000 total compensation

Corporate VP and General Manager Europe Middle East Africa, Christian Morales

CEO and Director, Brian M. Krzanich, age 55, $1,000,000 total compensation

SVP and General Manager Sales and Marketing Group, Gregory R. Pearson, age 55

EVP and CFO, Stacy J. Smith, age 53, $673,000 total compensation

VP Intel Communications Group; General Manager Network Processor Division, Douglas L. (Doug) Davis, age 54

Corporate VP and General Manager Mobile and Communications Group, Hermann Eul, age 56

General Manager Software Products Division Software and Solutions Group, Jonathan (Jon) Khazam, age 53

SVP and General Manager Non-Volatile Memory Solutions Group, Robert B. Crooke

SVP and General Manager Perceptual Computing; President Intel Israel, Shmuel (Mooly) Eden

Corporate VP and General Manager New Devices Group, Michael A. Bell

VP and CIO, Kimberly S. (Kim) Stevenson

Corporate VP and General Manager Global Supply Management, Robert E. Bruck, age 59

VP Sales and Marketing Group; General Manager Microsoft Program Office, Ren @ J. James, age 50, $850,000 total compensation

SVP and General Manager Data Center Group, Diane M. Bryant, age 54

Corporate VP and General Manager Intellectual Property Blocks and Technologies, Ron Friedman, age 59

SVP and General Manager New Technology Group, Joshua M. (Josh) Walden, age 53

Corporate VP and President Intel China, Xu (Ian) Yang

SVP and Co-General Manager Platform Engineering Group, Amir Faintuch

VP and President Intel Americas Inc., Christopher J. (CJ) Bruno

SVP and General Manager Software and Services Group, Douglas W. (Doug) Fisher

SVP and General Manager PC Client Group, Kirk B. Skaugen

Corporate VP and Managing Director Intel Labs, Wen-Hann Wang

Corporate VP and Co-General Manager Platform Engineering Group, Aicha S. Evans

SVP and General Manager Intel Security Group, Christopher Young

Corporate VP and President Mergers and Acquisitions, Wendell Brooks

EVP and President Client and Internet of Things (IoT) Businesses and Systems Architecture Group, Venkata (Murthy) Renduchintala, age 50

Vice President And GM Datacenter Platform Engineering Group, Lisa Graff

Intel Information Technology vPro AMT Product Manager, Omer Livne

Vice President Of Education, Rich Leonard

Senior Vice President, Arun Chandrasekhar

Marketing Vice President, Horst Pratsch

Northeast Regional Vice President, Praveen Kundurthy

Vice President, Jamie Urwin

Vice President Of Finance, Norma Dore

Vice President Of Product Development, Michael Munger

Senior Vice President Communications, Chuck Brabenac

Senior Vice President, Davidx Oh

National Sales Manager, Simon Chan

Vice President New Devices General Manager Software, Philippe Gaglione

Vice President Data Center Groupgeneral Manager Workstations And High Performance Computing, Charles (Chas) Wuischpard

Doctor VPG Planning, Connie Martin

Vice President, Lei Shao

Vice President, Sandra Rardon

Vice President Of Professional Services, Craig Quinn

Vice President and General Manager Engineering De, Gary Weiss

Vice President, Scott Zych

Vice President Of Programs, Michael Deangelis

Vice President Of Sales, Michael Jakubowski

Vice President Of Sales And General Manager Of Asi, Navin Shenoy

Vice President Tmg, Tim Hendry

Vice President of Customer Operations, Gary Niekerk

Division Vice President, Tom Horvath

Medical Director, Christopher Baruffi

Vice President Of Human Resources, Michael Hill

Vice President Software and Services Sales Organization Sales and Marketing Group, Jeff Paul

Vice President Technology and Manufacturing Group, Koushik Banerjee

Vice President, Steven Holmes

Vice President Finance, Ching Ng

Vice President Corporate Communications, Jolly Wang

Vice President Engineering Co Founder, George Chaltas

Vice President Operations And Finance, Evgenia Abramov

Vice President And Regional Manager Louisiana Arkansas And Missouri Regions, Myra J McDonnell

Executive Vice President, Russell Haugan

Vice President Marketing And Business Development, James A (Jamie) Johnson

Vice President Secretary Treas, Kelvin Thompson

Vice President Technology and Manufacturing Group Director Portl, Niraj Anand

Tech Advs To Vice President At Intel, Mahendra Tadikonda

Senior Vice President, Kimberly Liss

Vice President Of Finance, Kay Phamdo

Legal Secretary, Eyal Laufer

Vice President, Dale Hicks

Executive Vice President, Frederico Carvalho

VPG Hardware, Anita Rao

Vice President Sustainability Initiatives, Joan C Garcia

Vice President Of Interactive Merchandising, Roshni Das

Vice President Data Center Group, Dave Patterson

Technical Asssistant for MDO Vice President, Gaston Suarez

Vice President Legal And Corporate Director Antitrust And Commercial Litigation, Darren Bernhard

Vice President Operations, Steve Allen

Vice President Finance, Diana Romo

Vice President, Matt Brenner

Senior Vice President, Shashi Jain

Vice President Director Manager, Ulf Hofemeier

Vice President Business Development, Chaim Rand

Vice President Technology And Manufacturing Group Director Logic Technology Integration0, Kaizad Mistry

vPro Product Specialist, Tal Elgar

Vice President and General Manager Content and Services Division Intel Media, Eric Free

Vice President Tmg Plant Manager Nm Site Fab 11X, Kirby Jefferson

Vice President Technology and Manufacturing Group Director Manufacturing and Operations, Ralph Schweinfurth

Vice President and General Manager Supply Chain Information Technology, Lisa Davis

Vice President and President Intel Foundation, Justin Rattner

Vice President Global Public Policy, Peter (Pete) Cleveland

Vice President; GM Software and Solutions Group, Renee J James

Vice President SSG and GM Visual Computing Software Intel Corporation, Elliot Garbus

Vice President TMG and GM Design and Tech Solutions Intel Corporation, Siva Yerramilli

Vice President Intel Capital, Raheel A Shah

Vice President Sales And Marketing, Kazumasa Yoshida

Senior Vice President and General Counsel, A Melamed

Vice President and Deputy General Counsel, Suzan A Miller

Vice President Piston Pin Operations, Lornax Egan

Vice President Global Creative Director, Teresa Herd

Chairman, Andy D. Bryant, age 64

Treasurer, Ravi Jacob

Board Member, Richard Powell

Vice Chair, Lalitha Immaneni

Treasurer, Lloyd Herring

Club Treasurer, Varun Setlur

Treasurer, Amanda Hamlin

TOWN Clerk Treasurer, David (Dave) Hinderliter

Board Member, Kristen Guy

Board Member, Izhar Hofshi

Treasurer, Sharad Khetan

Board Member, Haripriya Prakasam

Treasurer, Mahendra Malliwal

Board Member, Peggy A Hill

Board Member, Prakash Sarangapani

Assistant Treasurer, Shannon Thompson

Board Member, Elaine Marc

Board Member, Glen Dueck

Board Member, Kai Wang

Secretary, Bryan Hsieh

Regional Treasurer, Robert (Bob) Yenko

Board Member, Ron Bedard

Board Member, Gary Berger

Board Member, Carolyn Hasker

Auditors: Ernst & Young LLP

LOCATIONS

HQ: Intel Corp
2200 Mission College Boulevard, Santa Clara, CA 95054-1549
Phone: 408 765-8080   Fax: 408 765-2633
Web: www.intc.com

2014 Sales

	$ mil.	% of total
Singapore	11,573	21
China	11,197	20
US	9,828	17
Taiwan	8,955	16
Japan	2,776	5
Other	11,541	21
Total	**55,870**	**100**

PRODUCTS/OPERATIONS

2014 Sales

	$ mil.	% of total
PC Client Group	34,669	62
Data Center Group	14,387	26
internet of Things Groups	2,142	4
Software & services	2,216	4
Mobile communication & others	2,456	4
Total	**55,870**	**100**

Selected Products

Chipsets (communications consumer electronics desktop embedded handheld netbook notebook server storage workstation)

Communication infrastructure components
Network processors
Networked storage products

Device software optimization products (embedded handheld)

Digital home (chips for cable modems digital TVs high-definition media players set-top boxes and home network integration)

Microprocessors (communications consumer electronics desktop embedded handheld network netbook notebook server storage workstation)
Atom
Celeron
Centrino
Core i3 i5 i7
Core Duo
Core Quad
Itanium
Pentium
Xeon

Motherboards (desktop server workstation)

NAND flash memory (all-in-one desktop digital camera memory card portable memory storage device solid-state drive tablet computer)

Software products (software development tools middleware operating systems software tools)

Ultra-Mobility (chips for high-end smartphones handheld devices)

Wired and wireless connectivity components (embedded wireless cards network adapters)

COMPETITORS

AMD	Oracle
ARM Holdings	QUALCOMM
Apple Inc.	SK Hynix
Atmel	STMicroelectronics
Cisco Systems	Samsung Electronics
Conexant Systems	SanDisk
Fujitsu Semiconductor	Silicon Integrated
GLOBALFOUNDRIES	Systems
IBM	Sony
Maxim Integrated	Symantec
Products	TSMC
MediaTek	Texas Instruments
Microchip Technology	Toshiba Semiconductor
Micron Technology	& Storage Products
NVIDIA	VIA Technologies

HISTORICAL FINANCIALS

Company Type: Public

Income Statement

FYE: December 26

	REVENUE ($ mil.)	NET INCOME ($ mil.)	NET PROFIT MARGIN	EMPLOYEES
12/15	55,355	11,420	20.6%	107,300
12/14	55,870	11,704	20.9%	106,700
12/13	52,708	9,620	18.3%	107,600
12/12	53,341	11,005	20.6%	105,000
12/11	53,999	12,942	24.0%	100,100
Annual Growth	**0.6%**	**(3.1%)**	**—**	**1.8%**

2015 Year-End Financials

Debt ratio: 22.00%—
Return on equity: 19.29%
Cash ($ mil.): 15,308
Current ratio: 2.58
Long-term debt ($ mil.): 20,036

Dividends
Yield: 0.0%
Payout: 41.2%
Market value ($ mil.): —

	STOCK PRICE ($) FY Close	P/E High/Low		PER SHARE ($) Earnings	Dividends	Book Value
12/15	34.98	16	11	2.33	0.96	13.12
12/14	37.55	16	10	2.31	0.90	11.96
12/13	25.60	13	10	1.89	0.90	11.73
12/12	20.23	13	9	2.13	0.87	10.36
12/11	24.25	10	8	2.39	0.78	9.18
Annual Growth	**9.6%**	**—**	**—**	**(0.6%)**	**5.2%**	**9.3%**

INTERMOUNTAIN HEALTH CARE INC

If you whoosh down the side of one of Idaho's majestic mountains and take a nasty spill Intermountain Health Care (dba Intermountain Healthcare) will pick you up and put you back together. From air ambulance services to urgent care clinics and general hospitals Intermountain has all the tools to mend skiers (and non-skiers alike) in Utah and southern Idaho. With about 1100 physicians the not-for-profit health system operates 22 hospitals and 185 urgent care clinics as well as home health care agencies and rehabilitation centers. Its hospitals have a combined total of about 2700 licensed beds.

Operations

Its hospitals range from general surgical to specialty care including orthopedic and pediatric facilities. Along with the full spectrum of physical health care services Intermountain also offers comprehensive mental health and substance abuse programs for patients of all ages. The organization's spectrum of care includes acute inpatient residential treatment day treatment chemical dependency inpatient/detoxification and intensive outpatient programs. To serve the region's uninsured and low-income residents Intermountain owns or supports 15 community and school primary care clinics.

The organization conducts cancer research through its partnership with Huntsman Cancer Institute at the University of Utah. The two share data best practices funding and co-conduct clinical trials. They also operate a number of cancer-specific treatment centers including multi-disciplinary tumor-specific clinics designed to provide one-stop service for cancer patients to meet with different cancer specialists on the same day for a more comprehensive treatment plan. Other areas of research include cardiovascular intensive medicine surgical care and behavioral health.

On the physician side the Intermountain Medical Group administers multi-specialty health care services in clinics located throughout the region. The group also operates urgent care clinics under the ExpressCare InstaCare and KidsCare banners.

Entering itself into the "what doesn't Intermountain do?" category the health system also provides health and dental insurance plans through its SelectHealth division. SelectHealth provides coverage for large and small employer groups runs the state Children's Health Insurance Program and administers a high-risk insurance pool for the state of Utah.

In 2013 Intermountain reported 474450 emergency room visits; 133973 acute patient admissions; 39552 inpatient surgeries; and 30972 births. Insurance provider SelectHealth had 660000 members.

Geographic Reach

Intermountain serves the health care needs of Utah and Idaho residents.

Sales and Marketing

Commercial insurance accounted for about 60% of the system's net patient revenues in 2013; payments received under the Medicare and Medicaid programs accounted for 26% and 12% respectively while self-pay accounted for 5%.

Financial Performance

In 2013 revenues grew 7% to $5 billion due to an increase in premiums and admission fees (but partially offset by an increase in provision for bad debts). Net income more than doubled that year growing 183% to $1.5 billion. Factors leading to the rise included increases in investment returns and unrecognized changes in funded status of post-retirement benefit plans.

Cash flow from operations fell 5% to $671 million in 2013 due to increases in salaries benefits supplies and other operating expenses.

Strategy

Intermountain uses its dedicated supply chain organization to continuously improve system efficiency. In addition to delivering medical supplies the unit also oversees hospital vehicles and recently switched them all to natural gas.

In 2013 it teamed up with several leading IT companies (including Xi3 Intel Dell and NetApp) to form Intermountain's Healthcare Transformation Lab on the campus of its flagship hospital Intermountain Medical Center in Murray Utah. The lab researches develops and measures new ideas to improve patient care. The same year it worked with GE to established a research center to reduce radiation during tomography procedures.

Intermountain has also joined peers Mayo Clinic Cleveland Clinic and others in the High Value Healthcare Collaborative to share information to improve health care manage and save costs and extend best practices out to physicians clinics and hospitals throughout the US. In 2015 the company announced a partnership with hospital Uintah Basin Medical Center to bring the Intermountain Life Flight program to Roosevelt bringing trauma and specialty care to residents of all of eastern Utah. This marked the company's first partnership with a non-Intermountain facility.

The company is also collaborating with the Centers for Medicare & Medicaid Services and other health systems to examine ways to improve health care safety and reduce costs by preventing patient injuries and complications.

In 2014 Intermountain introduced its mobile application Health Hub. One of its features is GermWatch which tells users which diseases are active in Utah communities.

Company Background

Intermountain was formed in 1975 when the Church of Jesus Christ of Latter Day Saints donated 15 hospitals to local communities.

EXECUTIVES

Vice President Community Benefit, Mikelle Moore
CEO Intermountain Medical Group, Linda C. Leckman
President and CEO SelectHealth, Patricia R. Richards
EVP and CFO, Bert R. Zimmerli
EVP and COO, Laura S. Kaiser
VP and CIO, Marc Probst
Chief Development Officer, David L. Flood
President and CEO, Charles W. Sorenson
VP Supply Chain and Support Services; Chief Purchasing Officer, Brent Johnson
VP Clinical Operations and Chief Nursing Officer, Kim Henrichsen
Chief Medical Officer, Brent E. Wallace
CEO Primary ChildrenÂ's Medical Center, Katherine A. (Katy) Welkie
President Weber State University, Ann Millner
Director Patient Care Nursing, Paul Blad
Vice President Revenue Cycle Organization, Todd Craghead
Medical Director, David (Dave) Pombo
Medical Director, Terry Clemmer
Medical Director, Keith Robbins
Pharmacy Manager, Robert Dengg
Assistant Vice President Communications, Tom Vitelli
Assistant Vice President, Kathleen Konishi
Vice President Of Engineering, Craig Bedford
Assistant Vice President Compensation and Benefits, David (Dave) Adams
Pharmacy Manager, Brenda Winger
Vice President Management, Jim Darrington
Vice President Marketing and Communication, Todd Frehse
Medical Director Utah County Region, Gordon Harkness
Pharmacy Manager, Tom Shelley
Medical Director, Gregory Gochnour
Medical Director, Scott Hansen
Vice President Marketing, Jerry Edgington
Medical Director, James Orme
Director Of Admissions, Louise Green
Director Of Pharmacy, Scott Yardley
Medical Director, Justin Abbott
Director Media Relations, Daron Cowley
Director Media Relations, Jess Gomez
Vice President Information Technology, Matt Weed
Medical Librarian, Don McFall
Clinic Manager, Rebecca Beck
Pharmacy Manager, Beth Johnson
Medical Director, Scott Whittle
Clinic Manager, Summer Patterson
Clinic Manager, Teri Roberts
Clinic Manager, Amy Tippets
Clinic Manager, Laurie Clayton
Pharmacy Manager, Elizabeth Burnham
Clinic Manager, Brock Place
Clinic Manager, Maribel Olmos
Medical Director US Synthetic Clinic, Spencer Scoville
Medical Director Epilepsy Program, Tawnya Constantino
Medical Director Adult Service, Craig Shane
Medical Director, Wayne Cannon
Director Of Radiology, Susan Raymond
Medical Director of The Anticoagulation, Kory Anderson
Medical Director, Eugene Worth
Medical Director, Kristian Kemp
Clinic Manager, Gay Tregaskis
Medical Director Intermountain Medical Group And Kidscare, Mark Briesacher
Medical Director Hospitals Urban Central Region, William Hamilton
Vice President, Eric Cannon
Vice President Business Ethics and Compliance, Suzie Draper
Vice President Human Resources, Dan Zuhlke
Vice President Information Technology, Karl West
Vice President And General Counsel, Doug Hammer
Assistant Vice President Financial, Craig Jacobsen
Vice President Strategic Planning, Gregory Pou Poulsen
Assistant Vice President Clinical Inform, Tammy Madsen
Medical Director, Donald (Don) Lappe
RPH, Rob Tadje
Vice Chairman, Bruce T. Reese
Chairman, A. Scott Anderson
Secretary, Nicole Houghton
Secretary, Jeri Lay
Secretary, Sheri Jones
Secretary, Elise Reeves
Secretary, Candyce Penman
Secretary, Rene Warner
Secretary, Maxine Buhler
Secretary, Terri Bowen
Treasurer, Kent Johnson
Board Member, Cody Thornock
Secretary, Kenna Thiriot
Secretary, Leah Church
Secretary, Lisa Mjos
Auditors: KPMG LLP SALT LAKE CITY UTAH

LOCATIONS

HQ: INTERMOUNTAIN HEALTH CARE INC
36 S STATE ST STE 1600, SALT LAKE CITY, UT
841111441
Phone: 8014422000
Web: WWW.INTERMOUNTAINHEALTHCARE.ORG

PRODUCTS/OPERATIONS

Selected Hospitals
Alta View
American F
Bear River
Cassia Reg
Delta Comm
Dixie Regional Medical Center (St. George UT)
Fillmore C
Garfield M
Heber Valley Medical Center (Heber City UT)
Intermount
LDS Hospital (Salt Lake City)
Logan Regi
McKay-Dee
  McKay-Dee Behavioral Health Institute
Orem Commu
Park City Medical Center (Park City UT)
Primary Children's Medical Center (Salt Lake City)
Riverton H
Sanpete Valley Hospital (Mt. Pleasant UT)
Sevier Val
TOSH - The
Utah Valle
Valley View Medical Center (Cedar City UT)

Selected Other Facilities
Northern Idaho and Utah
  Clinics
  Bear River Clinic
  Budge Clinic
  Canyon View Orthopedics & Associates
  Isom Plastic Surgery
  Logan Clinic
  South Cache Valley Clinic
  Summit Clinic
  Home Health Hospice and Home Medical Equipment
  Cassia
  Logan
  Tremonton
  InstaCare and KidsCare
  Logan InstaCare
  WorkMed
  Burley
  Logan
  Tremonton
Davis - Weber
  Clinics
  Bountiful Clinic
  Calton/Harrison Orthopedic Clinic
  Endocrine Diabetes
  Herefordshire Clinic
  Layton Clinic
  McKay-Dee Cardiology Clinic
  McKay-Dee Dermatology & Plastic Surgery
  McKay-Dee ENT Clinic
  McKay-Dee Foot and Ankle Clinic
  McKay-Dee Internal Medicine Clinic
  McKay-Dee Rheumatology Clinic
  McKay-Dee Urogynecology Clinic
  North Ogden Clinic
  Northern Utah Pediatrics
  Northern Utah Surgeons
  Ogden Cardiovascular Associates
  South Ogden Clinic
  Sports Medicine Specialists - Bountiful
  Summit Orthopedics
  Syracuse Clinic
  Wasatch OB/GYN
  Home Health Hospice and Home Medical Equipment
  Ogden
  InstaCare and KidsCare
  Bountiful InstaCare
  Bountiful KidsCare
  Herefordshire InstaCare
  Layton InstaCare
  Layton KidsCare
  North Ogden InstaCare
  North Ogden KidsCare
  South Ogden InstaCare
  Syracuse InstaCare

ExpressCare
Smith's Food & Drug - Farmington
WorkMed
Layton
Ogden
Greater Salt Lake Valley
  Clinics
  Alta View Specialty Clinic
  Avenues Specialty Clinic
  Bryner Clinic
  Central Valley ENT Head & Neck Surgery
  Central Valley Thyroid & Parathyroid Clinic
  Cottonwood Endocrine & Diabetes Center
  Cottonwood Family Practice
  Cottonwood Internal Medicine
  Gorang Family Practice
  Heart and Lung Surgical Associates
  Hillcrest Pediatrics
  Holladay Clinic
  Holladay Pediatrics
  Holladay Pediatrics - North
  Internal Medicine Associates
  Medical Tower Family Practice
  Memorial Clinic
  Mountain View Pediatrics
  Noyes Surgical Oncology
  Obstetrics & Gynecology Specialists
  Orthopedic Specialty Group Clinics
  Park City Specialty Clinic
  Plastic Surgery Center
  Pulmonology Clinic
  Salt Lake Clinic
  Sandy Clinic
  Sandy OB/GYN
  South Jordan Clinic
  South Sandy Clinic
  Southridge Clinic
  Southridge OB/GYN
  Southridge Pediatrics
  Surgical Specialists
  Taylorsville Clinic
  Utah Heart Clinic
  Urological Institute Clinics
  West Jordan Clinic
  Home Health Hospice and Home Medical Equipment
  Salt Lake City
  InstaCare and KidsCare
  Holladay InstaCare
  Memorial InstaCare
  Memorial KidsCare
  Mountain View Pediatrics KidsCare
  Murray InstaCare
  Sandy InstaCare
  Southridge InstaCare
  Southridge KidsCare
  Taylorsville InstaCare
  Taylorsville KidsCare
  West Jordan InstaCare
  West Jordan KidsCare
  ExpressCare
  Smith's Food & Drug - Draper
  Smith's Food & Drug - Salt Lake City
  WorkMed
  Murray
  Salt Lake City
Greater Utah Valley
  Clinics
  American Fork Internal Medicine & Dermatology
  American Fork Pulmonary Clinic
  American Fork Surgical Associates
  Central Orem Clinic
  Heber Valley Clinic
  Highland Clinic
  Legacy OB/GYN Clinic
  North Canyon Family Practice
  North Orem Clinic
  North Valley Pediatrics
  Physical Medicine & Rehabilitation
  Provo Neurological Clinic
  Saratoga Springs Clinic
  Springville Clinic
  Utah Valley Ear Nose & Throat
  Utah Valley Heart & Lung Surgical Associates
  Utah Valley Internal Medicine Clinic
  Utah Valley Orthopaedics & Sports Medicine
  Utah Valley Pediatric Specialists
  Utah Valley Pulmonary Clinic
  Utah Valley Vein Clinic
  Home Health Hospice and Home Medical Equipment
  Heber City
  Orem

Urgent Care
Highland InstaCare
North Orem InstaCare
Provo InstaCare
Saratoga Springs InstaCare
Springville InstaCare
WorkMed
Orem
Springville
Central Utah
  Clinics
  Ephraim Clinic
  Fillmore Clinic
  Manti Family Clinic
  Moroni Clinic
  Mt. Pleasant Clinic
  North Sevier Medical Clinic
  Richfield Family Practice
  Sevier Valley Family Practice
  Home Health Hospice and Home Medical Equipment
  Delta
  Fillmore
  Mt. Pleasant
  Richfield
  WorkMed
  Moroni
  Mt. Pleasant
Southern Utah
  Clinics
  Canyon View Family Practice
  Cardiovascular & Thoracic Surgery - St. George
  Cedar City Clinic
  Dixie Plastic & Reconstructive Surgery
  Hurricane Valley Clinic
  Pulmonary Medicine Clinic - St. George
  Redrock Pediatrics
  Rim Rock Orthopaedics & Sports Medicine
  River Road Family Practice
  River Road Internal Medicine
  Southern Utah Behavioral Health
  Southern Utah Surgical Associates
  Southwest Cardiology - St. George
  Southwest Neurology Associates
  Southwest Regional Cancer Clinic
  Southwest Rheumatology Associates
  Southwest Spine & Pain Center
  Sunset Clinic
  Valley View Heart Clinic
  Women's Health Specialists
  Zion Orthopaedics & Sports Medicine
  Home Health Hospice and Home Medical Equipment
  Cedar City
  St. George
  InstaCare and KidsCare
  Cedar City InstaCare
  Hurricane Valley InstaCare
  River Road InstaCare
  Sunset InstaCare
  WorkMed
  Cedar City
  St. George

COMPETITORS

CHRISTUS Health	Regence BlueCross
HCA	BlueShield of Utah
HealthSouth	St. Mark's
Iasis Healthcare	University of Utah
LifePoint Health	Hospitals & Clinics
Ogden Regional Medical Center	

HISTORICAL FINANCIALS
Company Type: Private

Income Statement
FYE: December 31

	REVENUE ($ mil.)	NET INCOME ($ mil.)	NET PROFIT MARGIN	EMPLOYEES
12/13	5,041	1,546	30.7%	23,000
12/12	4,700	546	11.6%	—
12/11	4,049	6	0.2%	—
12/10	4,381	0	—	—
Annual Growth	4.8%	—	—	—

Debt ratio: ——
Return on equity: 30.70%
Cash ($ mil.): 607
Current ratio: 0.80
Long-term debt ($ mil.): —

Dividends
Yield: —
Payout: —
Market value ($ mil.): —

International Bancshares Corp.

International Bancshares Corp.Âis leading post-NAFTA banking in South Texas.Â One of the largest bank holding companies in Texas it does business throughÂ International Bank of Commerce (IBC) and Commerce Bank in Texas and Oklahoma through nearly 220 locations. The company facilitates trade between the US and Mexico and serves Texas' growing Hispanic population; aboutÂ30% of its deposits come from south of the border. In addition to commercial and international banking services International Bancshares provides retail deposit services insurance and investment products and mortgages and consumer loans. The bulk of the company's portfolio is made up of business and construction loans.

Geographic Reach

Based in the border city of Laredo Texas IBC has many customers living in Mexico especially northern Mexico.

Financial Analysis

IBC's 2011 revenue declined nearly 9% vs. 2010 on a decrease in both interest and non-interest income. Net incomeÂfell by about 2% over the same period. Indeed 2011 was the fourth consecutive year of falling revenue for the bank as interest and fees declined on its shrinking loan portfolio. Income on taxable investment securities declined as well in 2011 vs. 2010.

Cash flow increased by nearly $92 million is 2011 vs. 2010 due to cash provided by investing activities as compared to cash used in 2010.

Strategy

IBC maintains a decentralized structure in which local advisory boards made up of members of the communities inÂthe bank is located direct operations of its branches including recruiting prospective clients and developing products and services to meet local customers' needsÂÂHowever in 2012 IBC closed most of its bank branches inside grocery stores (H-E-B KrogerÂRandalls)Âin response to an amendment to the Dodd-Frank Act that gutted overdraft charges and interchange fees that banks charge when a consumer swipes a debit card suppressing revenue at fee-focused in-store branches. The company is replacing theÂunprofitable grocery store branches with more expensive but lucrative brick-and-mortar branches in Houston and other cities.

In addition to the tougher regulatory environment the increasing preference by consumers for online and mobile banking is causing IBC to shrink it branch network in Texas and Oklahoma.

Ownership

Founder and director Antonio (Tony) R. Sanchez aÂone-time candidate for Texas governor and his family own around 14% of International Bancshares. WithÂa large number ofÂHispanic shareholders International Bancshares is one of the largest minority-owned banks in the nation.Â

EXECUTIVES

Executive Vice President, Idaloia Ramirez
VP and Director; President and CEO International Bank of Commerce McAllen, R. David Guerra, age 62, $226,123 total compensation
Chairman and President; President and CEO International Bank of Commerce, Dennis E. Nixon, age 72, $650,245 total compensation
Treasurer; SEVP International Bank of Commerce, Imelda Navarro, age 57, $199,496 total compensation
Vice President Area Sales Manager, Rene Arriaga
First Vice President Auditor, Ramiro Herrera
Vice President And Corp. BSA Coordinator Cams, Jessica Mendiola
Senior Vice President Information Technology Operations, Chris Loehr
Vice President, Jennifer (Jen) Alvarado
Vice President Marketing, Jessica Neikirk
Vice President, Julie L Tarvin
Senior Vice President Of It, Hector Vasquez
Vice President Of Accounting, Alvaro Martinez
Executive Vice President, Carlos Moreno
Assistant Vice President, Brian Lindsey
Vice President Human Resources, Rosie Ramirez
Vice President, Natividad Lozano
Senior Vice President, Eddie Aldrete
Executive Vice President, Dalia Martinez
Assistant Vice President Support Services, Fernando Santos
Auditors: McGladrey LLP

LOCATIONS

HQ: International Bancshares Corp.
1200 San Bernardo Avenue, Laredo, TX 78042-1359
Phone: 956 722-7611
Web: www.iboc.com

PRODUCTS/OPERATIONS

2011 Sales

	$ mil.	% of total
Interest		
Loans including fees	292	47
Taxable investment securities	113	18
Other	11	2
Noninterest		
Service charges on deposit accounts	98	16
Other service charges commissions & fees	58	9
Net investment securities transactions	17	3
Other investments net	16	3
Other	12	2
Total	**619**	**100**

COMPETITORS

BancFirst	JPMorgan Chase
Bank of America	Lone Star National
Broadway Bancshares	Bancshares
Citigroup	Midland Financial
Cullen/Frost Bankers	Wells Fargo
Falcon Bancshares	
First Victoria	
National Bank	

HISTORICAL FINANCIALS

Company Type: Public

Income Statement

FYE: December 31

	ASSETS ($ mil.)	NET INCOME ($ mil.)	INCOME AS % OF ASSETS	EMPLOYEES
12/14	12,196	153	1.3%	3,256
12/13	12,079	126	1.0%	3,223
12/12	11,882	107	0.9%	3,259
12/11	11,739	127	1.1%	3,388
12/10	11,943	130	1.1%	3,747
Annual Growth	**0.5%**	**4.2%**	**—**	**(3.5%)**

Debt ratio: 10.24%
Return on equity: 10.19%
Cash ($ mil.): 255
Current ratio: —
Long-term debt ($ mil.): —

No. of shares (mil.): 66
Dividends
Yield: 1.9%
Payout: 22.7%
Market value ($ mil.): 1,764

	STOCK PRICE ($) FY Close	P/E High/Low		PER SHARE ($) Earnings	Dividends	Book Value
12/14	26.54	12	9	2.28	0.52	23.78
12/13	26.36	14	10	1.88	0.43	21.19
12/12	18.09	16	12	1.39	0.40	21.37
12/11	18.34	12	7	1.69	0.38	23.78
12/10	20.03	14	9	1.72	0.36	21.56
Annual Growth	**7.3%**	—	—	**7.3%**	**9.6%**	**2.5%**

International Business Machines Corp.

International Business Machines (IBM) is the world's top provider of computer products and services. Called Big Blue for a reason the company is among the leaders in almost every market in which it competes. It focuses primarily on its services business which accounts for nearly 60% of sales. While IBM made its name in computer hardware (think mainframes) the company's information technology business services and software units are now among the largest in the world. While it has moved from hardware to a large degree the company maintains its industry-leading enterprise server and data storage products lines. IBM is transforming its operations as it deals with a rapidly changing technology environment.

HISTORY

In 1914 National Cash Register's star salesman Thomas Watson left to rescue the flagging Computing-Tabulating-Recording (C-T-R) Company the pioneer in US punch card processing that had been incorporated in 1911. Watson aggressively marketed C-T-R's tabulators supplying them to the US government during WWI and tripling company revenues to almost $15 million by 1920. The company became International Business Machines (IBM) in 1924 and soon dominated the global market for tabulators time clocks and electric typewriters. It was the US's largest office machine maker by 1940.

IBM perfected electromechanical calculation (the Harvard Mark I 1944) but initially dismissed the potential of computers. When Remington Rand's UNIVAC computer (1951) began replacing IBM machines IBM quickly responded.

The company unveiled its first computer in 1952. With its superior research and development and marketing IBM built a market share near 80% in the 1960s and 1970s. Its innovations included the STRETCH systems which eliminated vacuum tubes (1960) and the first compatible family of computers the System/360 (1964). IBM also developed floppy disks (1971) and the first laser printer for computers (1975). The introduction of the IBM PC in 1981 ignited the personal computer industry sparking a barrage of PC clones. Through it all IBM was the subject of a 12-year government antitrust investigation that ended in 1982.

The shift to smaller open systems along with greater competition in all of IBM's segments caused wrenching change. Instead of responding to the market need for cheap PCs and practical business applications IBM stubbornly stuck with mainframes and rivals began capitalizing on Big Blue's technology. After posting profits of $6.6 billion in 1984 the company began a slow slide. It sold many noncomputer businesses including its copier division to Kodak in 1988 and its Lexmark typewriter business in 1991. Closing the book on its heritage IBM shuttered the last of its punch card plants that year.

In 1993 CEO John Akers was replaced by Louis Gerstner the first outsider to run IBM. He began to turn the ailing antiquated company around by slashing costs and nonstrategic divisions cutting the workforce shaking up entrenched management and pushing services. His $1 billion R&D budget cut caused an exodus of IBM scientists and created an operation geared more toward quick turnaround than lengthy research (however the company still leads the business world in patents each year). In 1994 Big Blue reported its first profit in four years. It also began making computer chips that year.

A pioneer in server operating system software IBM made an early move into messaging and network management software with its acquisitions of spreadsheet pioneer Lotus Development in 1995 and network management specialist Tivoli the next year. Expanding its Web focus to include small businesses IBM in 1999 bought Internet communications server maker Sequent. That year IBM exited the networking hardware market selling related intellectual property to Cisco Systems.

Hoping to turn around its ailing PC business IBM in 1999 axed manufacturing staff and halted sales of its PCs through US retailers. The following year the head of its server business Samuel Palmisano was named president and COO; the change fueled speculation that IBM's emperor had found his heir.

In a move intended to bolster its data management division IBM in 2001 purchased the database software unit of Informix for $1 billion. It also bought longtime partner CrossWorlds Software a maker of application integration products the next year.

Streamlining efforts in 2002 included increased outsourcing of manufacturing and refurbishing activities to Sanmina-SCI and Solectron (acquired by Flextronics in 2007); each had acquired manufacturing facilities from IBM. Also that year the company formed a joint venture with Hitachi to combine the companies' disk drive operations. After an initial investment of about $2 billion from Hitachi combined with further payments to IBM over the next three years Hitachi eventually took on full ownership of the business. Additionally IBM combined its Technology (microchips) and Systems (servers storage) groups.

Looking to extend its lead in technology and business services IBM also acquired PricewaterhouseCoopers' consulting and IT services unit PwC Consulting for an estimated $3.5 billion in 2002. While presenting IBM with a significant integration challenge the transaction served the dual purpose of augmenting IBM's standard array of outsourcing maintenance and integration services while moving the company into high-end management consulting. Palmisano succeeded Gerstner as CEO that year.

In 2003 IBM acquired development tool maker Rational Software for $2.1 billion and it acquired supply chain software developer Trigo Technologies early in 2004. Also that year the company purchased Daksh eServices one of India's largest call center businesses and the Business Continuity Services unit of Schlumberger.

The company in 2005 sold its PC business —a segment that had begun to yield little profit for the company — to Chinese manufacturing partner Lenovo. IBM received a minority ownership stake in the expanded Lenovo as part of the deal but it subsequently sold its shares.

Also in 2005 it expanded the presence of its service arm in the health care market when it acquired Healthlink as well as software partner Candle. In 2005 it acquired Ascential Software for about $1.1 billion. The next year the company bought FileNet a maker of content management software for $1.6 billion.

In 2007 IBM spent about $1 billion on 12 acquisitions; half of those were software companies that included Vallent Corporation Softek Storage Solutions Watchfire and DataMirror (for which it paid $161 million).

Continuing the trend of divesting its hardware operations IBM in 2007 sold its digital business-printer operations –through a 49% stake in a new printing joint venture known as InfoPrint Solutions (between itself and Japan-based printing and imaging giant Ricoh) –for about $725 million. Ricoh acquired the remaining 49% of the venture in 2010.

Among the 15 purchases made by the company in 2008 (up from 12 the previous year) was software developer Cognos. IBM paid about $5 billion for Cognos in a bid to increase its portfolio of so-called business process optimization applications. The deal helped the company gain ground against enterprise software industry leaders Oracle and SAP specifically in the areas of business intelligence and performance management.

Another notable acquisition that year was the $885 million purchase of business process optimization and embedded systems software specialist Telelogic. The deal complemented the embedded systems capabilities of IBM's Rational Software as IBM worked to meet demand for such technology in sectors that included auto manufacturing. The company's key purchase for 2009 was of analytics provider SPSS for about $1.2 billion in cash. IBM integrated the SPSS software into its Business Analytics and Optimization consulting organization.

Its 2010 purchase of Unica for about $480 million added more tools for managing targeted marketing and advertising efforts. Meanwhile the company sold its declining product lifecycle management software business to Dassault Systèmes in 2010 for $600 million in order to focus on core products.

IBM acquired the Sterling Commerce subsidiary of AT&T in 2010 for about $1.4 billion in cash and integrated the business with its software development operations. Sterling Commerce made software that helped businesses create and integrate networks of customers partners and suppliers. The Sterling Commerce deal complemented IBM's portfolio of applications that enable customers to automate and manage business processes across functions such as marketing selling ordering and fulfillment. It also provided IBM with a more complete platform for business process automation by adding to its selection of middleware the code that connects disparate software components and applications.

In 2010 IBM bought Web analytics software maker Coremetrics data compression tool developer Storwize and document digitization and data management application maker Datacap. Its other data-centric purchases that year were of Netezza which makes data analytics appliances used in data warehouses for about $1.7 billion and blade server and Ethernet switch maker BLADE Network Technologies. BLADE which became part of IBM's Systems and Technology group also developed virtualization software used to integrate and simplify networks in cloud computing environments.

IBM also that year acquired OpenPages a developer of financial risk and compliance management software that has partnered with IBM for several years as well as Texas-based business process management software maker Lombardi. The company also acquired PSS Systems a developer of software used to analyze and automate information governance policies for large volumes of business data while also automating the disposal of unneeded information. Additionally in 2010 IBM acquired Toronto-based Clarity Systems a developer of software used to collect and prepare financial statements for electronic filing with the SEC and other regulatory agencies.

Among its 2011 acquisitions IBM paid $387 million to acquire Toronto-based risk analysis software developer Algorithmics to extend its analytics expertise for financial services clients in particular. Algorithmics specializes in tools used to manage market liquidity credit operational and insurance risk among other areas. Also that year IBM acquired software developer Q1 Labs as part of an ongoing effort to build its network and data security holdings. Q1 a specialist in data analysis tools used to detect abnormal or suspicious network behavior became a part of IBM's new security systems division led by Q1's CEO; the unit also comprises ten other security businesses acquired by IBM including Tivoli and Rational as well as other security product and service operations.

The company named its first female CEO in 2012 hiring SVP and group executive of sales marketing and strategy Virginia "Ginni" Rometty as president and CEO. Former CEO Samuel Palmisano stayed on as chairman.

EXECUTIVES

Vice President ISC Engineering, Sophie Bechu
Vice President Of Legal, Martha Rendeiro
SVP Solutions Portfolio and Research, John E. Kelly, age 62, $638,000 total compensation
Managing Partner IBM Business Consulting Services, Virginia M. (Ginni) Rometty, age 57, $1,500,000 total compensation
EVP IBM Software and Systems, Steven A. (Steve) Mills, age 64, $730,500 total compensation
CIO Transformation and Operations, Jeff S. Smith
SVP IBM Sales and Distribution, Colleen F. Arnold, age 57
SVP Cloud, Robert J. LeBlanc, age 56
SVP and Director IBM Research, Arvind Krishna, age 52
General Manager IBM Commerce, Deepak Advani, age 52
SVP IBM Sales and Distribution, Erich Clementi, age 56
SVP and CFO, Martin J. Schroeter, age 50, $660,000 total compensation
SVP IBM Watson Group, Michael D. (Mike) Rhodin, age 54
SVP IBM Systems, Thomas W. (Tom) Rosamilia, age 54
SVP IBM Analytics, Robert J. (Bob) Picciano
SVP Transformation and Operations, James J. Kavanaugh, age 48
SVP Global Business Services, Bridget A. van Kralingen, age 51
Chief Executive UK and Ireland, David Stokes
Managing Director IBM India Private Limited, Vanitha Narayanan
SVP Corporate Strategy, Ken M. Keverian, age 58, $450,000 total compensation
SVP IBM Global Technology Services, Martin Jetter
General Manager Global Travel and Transportation Industry, Dee K. Waddell
Vice President, David Smith
Vice President Sales, Brad Kindorf
Vice President Business Analytics And Mathematical Sciences, Robert (Bob) Sutor

Vice President Strategic and Executive Communications, Mike Wing
Vice President Business Analytics And Mathematical Sciences And Fellow, Brenda Dietrich
Vice President, Joel Cawley
Vice President Marketing, Steve Wilkins
Vice President Strategic Alliance And Chief Technologist Officer, Bernard Meyerson
Vice President, Theo Fletcher
Vice President Of Sales Information Management Ind, Robert Massie
Vice President Mergers And Acquisitions, Kareem Yusuf
Vice President Finance And Operations Ibm Channels, David Colistra
Vice President Ww Sales Unix(sales Used To Work With Borman), Gary Lancaster
Vice President Technology, Alex Cocq
Executive Vice President, Pari Sadasivan
Vice President Finance And Director, James W Boyken
Vice President And Treasurer, Jesse J Greene
Vice President Global Site and Facility Services, Steven (Steve) Sams
Vice President, Scott Hebner
Vice President Sales, Judy Buchholz
Vice President, Moshe Cohen
Vice President of Sales and Marketing, Steven (Steve) Canepa
Vice President Of Strategy For Smarter Cities, Michael Littlejohn
Executive Vice President, Surjit Chana
Vice President Marketing, Annie Cheung
Vice President Tools and Tech, Bob Kemper
Vice President Sales, Kevin Nunnally
Vice President of Sales Operations, Bill Lintner
Sales Vice President, Thomas (Thom) Geisel
Vice President Cloud Managed Services, Fausto Bernardini
Senior Vice President Middleware Software Ibm Soft, Robert (Bob) Sera
Vice President Strategic Services, Randall Dalia
Vice President Of North American Sales, Paul Resten
Vice President Telecommunications Industry Americas, Dave Mancl
Vice President Ww Integrated Marketing Communicati, Liz Baird
Vice President Global Channels And Solutions Marketing, Michael Gerentine
Vice President Software Sales And Marketing Central Region, Bete Demeke
Vice President Partner Application Innovation Services, Roger Letalien
Senior Vice President Legal And Regulatory Affairs General Counsel, Robert (Bob) Weber
Vice President Software Business Partners And Midmarket, Mark Register
Vice President, Veronica Dwyer
Vice President Latin America, Carla Ciperski
Vice President of Marketing, Kristen Lauria
North American Sales Vice President Mindspan Learning, David (Dave) Hatch
Vice President Communications, Greg Golden
Vice President Product Marketing, Paul Vandenberg
Vice President Of Hardware Development, Erich Baier
Vice President Sales, Arlene Garcia
Vice President, Gilbert Molinar
Vice President Manager Director, Laura Schimke
Vice President of Marketing, Jack Brown
Vice President Finance Software Group, Guy Desanctis
Vp Cross Industry Alliances, Jay Ennesser
Executive Vice President, Kari Barbar
Vice President Business Development, Mark Bytner
Senior Vice President, Joseph (Jo) Sweeney

Vice President And Assistant General Counsel, Richard Kaplan
Vice President, Timothy (Tim) Donofrio
Vice President Marketing And Communications, Robyn Bennett
Vice President, Don Jue
Vice President Brand System Programs, Matthew McMahon
Vice President Global Workforce Diversity, Ron Glover
Vice President, Roland Hagan
Vice President Business Partner Midmarket Marketing, Heidi Dethloff
Vice President Government Programs, Christopher G (Chris) Caine
Vice President, Marianne Cooper
Senior Vice President Of Worldwide Marketing, Michael Broos
Vice President Alternative And Emerging Technology, Cheryl Dalby
Vice President, Michael Healy
Vice President For Information Technology And Wireless Convergence, Radha Ratnaparkhi
Senior Vice President Of Marketing, Neeraj Chandra
Vice President Of Information Technology, John (Jack) Giametta
Vice President Semiconductor Research And Development Center, Gary Patton
Vice President Strategic Alliances And Vendor Programs, Mark Young
Vice President of Marketing, Ann Rubin
Vice President Technology, Jay Cook
Vice President Solution Architects, Thanhia Sanchez
Vice President Marketing, Deon Newman
Vice President, David Simms
Vice President, Juhi Jotwani
Vice President Network And Systems Operations, Simon Alves
Vice President Human Resources Software Group, Thomas (Thom) Fleming
Vice President of Purchasing and Operations, Roger McKnight
Vice President Integrated Marketing Communications, Ed Abrams
Vice President Field Marketing, Sandra Brogie
Vice President Marketing And Communications, Maria Reeves Hayes
Vice President Sales, Janet Schultz
Creative Vice President, Clarisse Renaldo
Senior Vice President Marketing Storage Technologies, Jim Kely
Vice President Marketing, Mary Garrett
Group Vice President of the Transportation Unit, Lillian Hanson
Vice President Partner Enablement, William Liebler
Vice President Information Management Strategy Market Management, Andrew Warzecha
Senior Vice President, Bob Moffat
Vice President Iseries Marketing, Peter Bingaman
Vice President Information Security Strategy, John Hsieh
Vice President Workforce Strategy, Domenic Tripoli
Vice President Federal Systems Integrators, Kevin Costello
Vice President Homeland Security, Courtney Bromley
Vice President, Julie Curry
Vice President Marketing Cloud and Global Technology Services North America, David (Dave) Lapp
Senior Vice President Human Resources, Jonathan Zalisk
Vice President Global Pe American Express, Carolyn Maher
Vice President Marketing And Communications, Glen Thomas
Vice President of Storage, Terri Green

Information Technology Information Systems Vice President Director, Sadie Williams
Senior Management (Senior Vice President General Manager Director), Ganesh Krishnamurthy
Vice President PCD Sales, John (Jack) Brantley
Vice President Marketing, Bill Bartow
Vice President of Marketing and Communications, Staunton Brooks
Vice President Systems and Technology Group, Nigel Beck
Vice President Of Global Community Initiatives, Paula Baker
Vice President Market Strategy, Martin Duggan
Vice President World Wide Brand System, Kevin Bishop
Vice President Information Technology, Dennis Jay
Assistant Vice President Services Overall, Jen Noble
Vice President And Business Line Executive Ibm System X And Bladecenter, Alex Yost
Worldwide Vice President Business Partners Sales IBM Software Group, Vincent Zandvliet
Vice President Project Financing, Judd Ficklen
Vice President Global Delivery, Richard (Dick) Patterson
Vice President Product Management Watson Health, Cory Wiegert
Vice President Global Services, James (Jamie) Kast
Vice President Marketing, Kevin Taylor
Vice President Of Worldwide Marketing, William Scull
Vice President Innovation And University Relations, Gina Poole
Vice President of Mobile Brand Marketing, Rick McGee
Vice President Marketing, Caroline Layne
Vice President Security Growth Initiatives Security Services, Shelley Westman
Vice President Sales Western Region, Scott Ferber
Auditors: PricewaterhouseCoopers LLP

LOCATIONS

HQ: International Business Machines Corp.
One New Orchard Road, Armonk, NY 10504
Phone: 914 499-1900   Fax: 914 765-4190
Web: www.ibm.com

2014 Sales

	$ mil.	% of total
US	32,021	35
Japan	8,382	9
Other countries	52,390	56
Total	92,793	100

PRODUCTS/OPERATIONS

2014 Sales

	% of total
Global technology services	40
Software	28
Global business services	19
Systems & technology	11
Global financing	2
Other	-
Total	100

2014 Sales

	$ mil.	% of total
Services	55,673	60
Sales	35,063	38
Financing	2,057	2
Total	92,793	100

Selected Services

Business services
    Application management
    E-business
    Strategic consulting
    Systems integration
Financing
Technology services
    Business process outsourcing

Infrastructure
Maintenance
Outsourcing
Software integration
Systems management
Web hosting
Training

Selected Products
Printing systems
Servers
Software
  Application development
  Database and data management
  E-commerce
  Graphics and multimedia
  Groupware
  Networking and communication
  Operating systems
  Product life cycle management
  Security
  Speech recognition
  System management
  Transaction system
  Web application servers
Storage
  Hard drive systems
  Optical libraries
  Storage networking
  Tape drives systems and libraries

Selected Acquisitions
Alchemy API (2015 data collection and analysis)
Lighthouse Security (2014 cloud computing)
Cloudant (2014 cloud computing)
Silverpop (2014 cloud computing)
CrossIdeas (2014 security software)
Aspera (2013 high-speed data transfer)
SoftLayer (2013 cloud-computing infrastructure)
Fiberlink Communications (2013 mobile management)
Xtify (2013 cloud-based mobile messaging)
Kenexa (2012 cloud-based recruiting and talent
  management)
Tealeaf Technology (2012 customer experience analytics
  software)
Vivisimo (2012 analytics software)
TRIRIGA (2011 real estate management software)
Netezza (2010 data storage and analysis devices)
BLADE Network Technologies (2010; network servers
  switches and software)
OpenPages (2010 financial risk and compliance
  management software)
Clarity Systems (2010 financial data management
  software)
PSS Systems (2010 legal software)
Unica (2010 enterprise marketing software)
Storwize (2010 data compression software)
Sterling Commerce (2010 business integration software)
Datacap (2010 document digitization and data
  management software)
Coremetrics (2010 Web analytics software)
BigFix (2010 corporate security software)
Lombardi (2010 business process management software)
SPSS (2009 enterprise data analysis software)
ILOG (2008 enterprise resource management software)
Telelogic (2008 embedded systems software)
Cognos (2008 business intelligence software)
Softek Storage Solutions (2007 storage management
  software)
NovusCG (2007 enterprise resource planning software)
DataMirror (2007 data integration software)
WebDialogs (2007 Web conferencing services)
Princeton Softech (2007 data management software)
Watchfire (2007 website management software)
Vallent (2007 network management software)
Consul Risk Management (2007 risk management
  software)

COMPETITORS
Accenture	HP Enterprise Services
Alcatel-Lucent	Hitachi
BMC Software	Infosys
CA Inc.	Intel
Capgemini	Lexmark
Cisco Systems	Microsoft
Cognizant Tech	Motorola Solutions
Solutions	NEC
Computer Sciences	NTT DATA
Corp.	Novell

Dell	Oracle
Deloitte Consulting	Panasonic Corp
Deloitte Global	Ricoh Company
Services	SAP
EMC	Sony
Epson	TSMC
Ericsson	Tata Consultancy
Fujitsu	Texas Instruments
GE	Toshiba
HCL Technologies	Unisys
HP	Wipro Technologies

HISTORICAL FINANCIALS
Company Type: Public

Income Statement
FYE: December 31

	REVENUE ($ mil.)	NET INCOME ($ mil.)	NET PROFIT MARGIN	EMPLOYEES
12/14	92,793	12,022	13.0%	379,592
12/13	99,751	16,483	16.5%	431,212
12/12	104,507	16,604	15.9%	434,246
12/11	106,916	15,855	14.8%	433,362
12/10	99,870	14,833	14.9%	426,751
Annual Growth	(1.8%)	(5.1%)	—	(2.9%)

2014 Year-End Financials
Debt ratio: 34.72%
Return on equity: 69.37%
Cash ($ mil.): 8,476
Current ratio: 1.25
Long-term debt ($ mil.): 35,073

No. of shares (mil.): 990
Dividends
  Yield: 2.6%
  Payout: 35.7%
Market value ($ mil.): 158,920

	STOCK PRICE ($) FY Close	P/E High/Low	PER SHARE ($) Earnings	Dividends	Book Value
12/14	160.44	17 13	11.90	4.25	11.98
12/13	187.57	14 11	14.94	3.70	21.62
12/12	191.55	15 12	14.37	3.30	16.88
12/11	183.88	15 11	13.06	2.90	17.31
12/10	146.76	13 10	11.52	2.50	18.77
Annual Growth	2.3%	— —	0.8%	14.2%	(10.6%)

International Paper Co

For International Paper (IP) business is a global paper chase. It is one of the world's largest manufacturers of printing papers. Products include uncoated paper used in printers market pulp for making towels and tissues and coated paper and uncoated bristols (heavyweight art paper). In the US IP is #1 in containerboard production 70% of which is used in industrial corrugated boxes. A consumer packaging arm makes board to box cosmetics and food. IP owns recycling plants mainly in the US and a pulp and paper business in Russia via a 50/50 venture with Ilim Holding.

Geographic Reach

IP has manufacturing operations in Asia Europe Latin America North America North Africa and Russia. In the US it operates nearly 25 pulp paper and packaging mills roughly 180 converting and packaging plants some 20 recycling plants and three bag facilities. In Europe Asia Latin America and South America the company operates 16 pulp paper and packaging mills 69 converting and packaging plants and two recycling plants.

The US is by far its largest market representing nearly 70% of its total sales each year. EMEA is its second-largest market generating around 11% followed by the Asia/Pacific 8%.

Operations

IP divides its operations into three segments: industrial packaging (62% of total sales in 2014) printing papers (24%) and consumer packaging (11%). It divested its former distribution segment (the remaining 19% of sales) in 2014.

Sales and Marketing

IP sells packaging products paper products and other products directly to end users and converters as well as through agents resellers and paper distributors.

Financial Performance

Over the last five years the company has maintained steady revenue growth —until fiscal 2014. In 2014 revenues dipped slightly to fall to $23.6 billion. Its bottom line was affected by the 2014 sale of its distribution segment along with positive results from industrial packaging (contributing 62%) which increased by 1% from acquisitions. (Note the company restated its 2013 operations due to the divestiture of its distribution business.)

IP experienced a massive drop in profits from 2013 to 2014 ($1.4 billion to $555 million) due to the reduced revenue along with the increased expenses associated from restructuring charges affiliated with the sale of the distribution segment and an uptick in taxes. In addition the company's operating cash flows steadily peaked at $3.1 billion in 2014 due to reduced outflows in accounts receivables and accounts payable.

Strategy

IP has grown over the years through selective acquisitions and divestitures. In a major move to adjust its cost structure in mid-2014 IP merged its xpedx operations with Unisource and created a new publicly traded company called Veritiv Corporation. Both xpedx and Unisource were business-to-business distributors of printing packaging and facility supplies.

In 2013 IP and a Brazilian corrugated packaging producer formed Orsa International Paper Embalagens S.A. The new entity includes three containerboard mills and four box plants. The investment ($470 million) is part of IP's strategy to grow its packaging business globally especially in South America. It initially held a 75% stake but it purchased the remaining 25% of Orsa in 2014.

HISTORY

In 1898 nearly 20 northeastern pulp and paper firms consolidated to lower costs. The resulting International Paper had 20 mills in Maine Massachusetts New Hampshire New York and Vermont. The mills relied on forests in New England and Canada for wood pulp. When Canada enacted legislation to stop the export of pulpwood in 1919 International Paper formed Canadian International Paper.

During the 1940s and 1950s the company bought Agar Manufacturing (shipping containers 1940) Single Service Containers (Pure-Pak milk containers 1946) and Lord Baltimore Press (folding cartons 1958). It diversified in the 1960s and 1970s buying Davol (hospital products 1968; sold to C. R. Bard 1980) American Central (land development 1968; sold to developers 1974) and General Crude Oil (gas and oil 1975; sold to Mobil Oil 1979).

Decades later International Paper picked up Shorewood Packaging for $850 million in 2000. That year it made an unsolicited $6.2 billion bid for Champion International —which had previously agreed to be acquired by UPM-Kymmene —igniting a bidding war. UPM withdrew its offer however and International Paper acquired Champion for about $9.6 billion.

After surviving the Great Recession IP made one of its most significant acquisitions to date in 2012 when it acquired Temple-Inland one of North America's top producers of corrugated packaging in a transaction valued at $4.5 billion.

EXECUTIVES

SVP Container The Americas, William P. (Bill) Hoel, age 58

SVP and CFO, Carol L. Roberts, age 56, $742,500 total compensation

SVP Human Resources Communications and Government Relations, Thomas G. (Tom) Kadien, age 59, $629,167 total compensation

SVP Industrial Packaging, Timothy S. (Tim) Nicholls, age 54, $710,000 total compensation

Chairman and CEO, Mark S. Sutton, age 54, $880,708 total compensation

SVP Manufacturing Technology EHS&S and Global Sourcing, Tommy S. Joseph, age 55, $575,250 total compensation

SVP and President Europe Middle East Africa and Russia, Jean-Michel Ribieras, age 52, $420,000 total compensation

SVP and President IP Latin America, Glenn R. Landau

SVP North American Papers and Pulp and Consumer Packaging, W. Michael Amick, age 51

Vice President Industry Strategy and Marketing, Marge Forrester

Vice President Marketing Development, Jean Wall

Vice President And General Manager Xpedx Illinois Division, Thomas Plath

Vice President Commercial Printing, Teri Shanahan

Vice President, Brian McDonald

Carolinas Vice President Operations, John (Jack) Hash

Vice President Manufacturing Coated Paper Board, Kirt Cuevas

Vice President Compensation and Benefits, Mark Azzarello

Vice President Finance, Mary Davis

Senior Vice President Human Resources and Communications, Paul Karee

Senior Vice President President Ip Asia, Thomas (Thom) Gestrich

Senior Vice President Strategic Planning, Mark Nellessen

Secretary of Union Committee, Arnetta Graham

Auditors: Deloitte & Touche LLP

LOCATIONS

HQ: International Paper Co
6400 Poplar Avenue, Memphis, TN 38197
Phone: 901 419-7000
Web: www.internationalpaper.com

2014 Sales

	$ mil.	% of total
Americas		
US	16,645	71
Other countries	1,748	7
EMEA	3,273	14
Pacific Rim & Asia	1,951	8
Total	**23,617**	**100**

PRODUCTS/OPERATIONS

2014 Sales

	$ mil.	% of total
Industrial packaging	14,944	62
Printing papers	5,720	24
Consumer packaging	3,403	14
Adjustments	(450)	-
Total	**23,617**	**100**

Selected Operations and Products

Consumer Packaging
Cold cups and lids
Consumer-ready packaging (Shorewood Packaging folding carton set-up box)
Folding carton board
Food buckets and lids
Hot cups and lids
Milk container and lids
Starcote tobacco board

Distribution North America (xpedx)
Building services and away-from-home markets with facility supplies
Commercial printers with printing papers and graphic pre-press printing presses post press equipment
Manufacturers with packaging supplies and equipment
Warehousing and delivery services
Industrial Packaging
Automotive packaging
Corrugated pallet
Die-cut package
Flapless
Kraft linerboard
Laminated bulk bin
Liquid bulk
Litho lamination
Medium paper
Retail displays
Saturating kraft
Slotted container
White top liner
Papers
HP (Hewlett-Packard) home and commercial papers
Office papers
Pulp
Fluff pulp
Paper and tissue pulp
Recycling products
Old corrugated containers and kraft corrugated cuttings
Old newspaper

COMPETITORS

Alcoa	Louisiana-Pacific
Amcor	M-real
Cascades Inc.	Mondi
Domtar	Nippon Paper
ENCE Energia y	Packaging Corp. of
Celulosa SA	America
Environmental Mill &	Smurfit Kappa
Supply	Stora Enso
Georgia-Pacific	UPM-Kymmene

HISTORICAL FINANCIALS

Company Type: Public

Income Statement

FYE: December 31

	REVENUE ($ mil.)	NET INCOME ($ mil.)	NET PROFIT MARGIN	EMPLOYEES
12/14	23,617	555	2.4%	58,000
12/13	29,080	1,395	4.8%	69,000
12/12	27,833	794	2.9%	70,000
12/11	26,034	1,341	5.2%	61,500
12/10	25,179	644	2.6%	59,500
Annual Growth	**(1.6%)**	**(3.7%)**	**—**	**(0.6%)**

2014 Year-End Financials

Debt ratio: 32.68%
Return on equity: 8.40%
Cash ($ mil.): 1,881
Current ratio: 1.62
Long-term debt ($ mil.): 8,631

No. of shares (mil.): 420
Dividends
  Yield: 2.7%
  Payout: 112.4%
Market value ($ mil.): 22,512

	STOCK PRICE ($) FY Close	P/E High/Low		PER SHARE ($) Earnings	Dividends	Book Value
12/14	53.58	43	35	1.29	1.45	12.17
12/13	49.03	16	13	3.11	1.25	18.58
12/12	39.84	22	15	1.80	1.09	14.33
12/11	29.60	11	7	3.07	0.98	15.15
12/10	27.24	19	13	1.48	0.40	15.62
Annual Growth	**18.4%**	**—**	**—**	**(3.4%)**	**38.0%**	**(6.0%)**

Interpublic Group of Companies Inc.

Subsidiaries of this company come between brands and the general public. The Interpublic Group of Companies is one of the world's largest advertising and marketing services conglomerates. Its flagship creative agencies include McCann Worldgroupand Lowe & Partners while such firms as Campbell-Ewald Deutsch and Hill Holliday are leaders in the US advertising business. Interpublic also offers direct marketing media services and public relations through such agencies as Initiative and Weber Shandwick. Its largest have clients included General Motors Johnson & Johnson Microsoft Samsung and Unilever.

HISTORY

Standard Oil advertising executive Harrison McCann opened the H. K. McCann Company in 1911 and signed Standard Oil of New Jersey (later Exxon) as his first client. McCann's ad business boomed as the automobile became an integral part of American life. His firm merged with Alfred Erickson's agency (created 1902) in 1930 forming the McCann-Erickson Company. At the end of the decade the firm hired Marion Harper a top Yale graduate as a mailroom clerk. Harper became president in 1948.

Harper began acquiring other ad agencies and by 1961 controlled more than 20 companies. That year he unveiled a plan to create a holding company that would let the ad firms operate separately allowing them to work on accounts for competing products but giving them the parent firm's financial and information resources. He named the company Interpublic Inc. after a German research company owned by the former H. K. McCann Co. The conglomerate continued expanding and was renamed The Interpublic Group of Companies in 1964. Harper's management capabilities weren't up to the task however and the company soon faced bankruptcy. In 1967 the board replaced him with Robert Healy who saved Interpublic and returned it to profitability. The company went public in 1971.

The 1970s were fruitful years for Interpublic; its ad teams created memorable campaigns for Coke ("It's the Real Thing" and "Have a Coke and a Smile") and Miller Beer ("Miller Time" and Miller Lite ads). After Philip Geier became chairman in 1980 the company gained a stake in Lowe Howard-Spink (1983; it later became The Lowe Group) and bought Lintas International (1987). Interpublic bought the rest of The Lowe Group in 1990.

Interpublic bought Western International Media (now known as Initiative) and Ammirati & Puris (which was merged with Lintas to form Ammirati Puris Lintas) in 1994. As industry consolidation picked up in 1996 Interpublic kept pace with acquisitions of PR company Weber Group and Draft-Worldwide. Interpublic bought a majority stake in artist management and film production company Addis-Wechsler & Associates (now Industry Entertainment) in 1997 and later formed sports marketing and management group Octagon.

Interpublic acquired US agencies Carmichael Lynch and Hill Holliday Connors Cosmopulos in 1998. It also boosted its PR presence with its purchase of International Public Relations (UK) the parent company of public relations networks Shandwick and Golin/Harris. Interpublic strengthened its position in the online world in 1999 when it bought 20% of Stockholm-based Internet services company Icon Medialab International. That year the company merged agencies Ammirati and Lowe & Partners Worldwide to form Lowe Lintas & Partners Worldwide (in 2002 they changed the name to just Lowe & Partners Worldwide).

Interpublic bought market research firm NFO Worldwide for $580 million in 2000 and merged Weber Public Relations with Shandwick International to form Weber Shandwick Worldwide one of the world's largest PR firms. Later that year the company bought ad agency Deutsch for about $250 million. John Dooner took the position of chairman and CEO at the end of the year after Geier resigned. His first move proved a big one: Interpublic acquired True North Communications for $2.1 billion in stock in 2001.

The honeymoon was short lived; facing a recession the mounting debt from its buying spree and with the revelation of accounting discrepancies at McCann-Erickson WorldGroup (renamed McCann Worldgroup in 2004) Dooner stepped aside as chairman and CEO in 2003. Interpublic chose vice chairman David Bell (former CEO of True North) as Dooner's replacement. After almost two years of work to improve Interpublic's balance sheet Bell was replaced by former MONY Group chief Michael Roth.

In 2005 Roth was tasked with straightening out Interpublic's financial controls and improving its balance sheet. Later that year the company revealed extensive bookkeeping problems primarily in its overseas operations leading to a financial restatement going back to 2000.

In order to simplify its operating structure in 2006 Interpublic integrated direct marketer Draft Inc. with advertising agency Foote Cone & Belding (forming DraftFCB). A year later it restructured its vast network of media brands to report under a single management structure (Mediabrands).

Looking to India in mid-2007 Interpublic bought all the shares of FCB Ulka a top-five ad agency in the country that operated from six offices. Interpublic integrated the Indian agency with its DraftFCB operations. At the same time it acquired the remaining 51% stake it didn't hold in Lintas India Private Limited at a cost of $50 million in cash and integrated it into its Lowe Worldwide network.

In 2010 Interpublic acquired Brazilian creative advertising strategy firm CUBOCC and London-based marketing agency Delaney Lund Knox Warren & Partners (DLKW). During 2011 the company acquired several marketing agencies. In early 2012 Interpublic obtained German consumer lifestyle agency Nicole Weber Communications (NWC) and UK-based digital and interactive agency FUSE.

EXECUTIVES

Senior Vice President Business Development, David J Weiss
SVP and Managing Director, Terry D. Peigh
Chairman and CEO, Michael I. Roth, age 69, $1,400,000 total compensation
EVP and CFO, Frank Mergenthaler, age 54, $1,000,000 total compensation
EVP Chief Strategy and Talent Officer, Philippe Krakowsky, age 53, $800,000 total compensation
SVP and Managing Director Interpublic Group, Peter Leinroth
SVP General Counsel and Secretary, Andrew Bonzani, $700,000 total compensation
SVP Controller and Chief Accounting Officer, Christopher Carroll, $565,110 total compensation
SVP and CIO, John Halper
Auditors: PricewaterhouseCoopers LLP

LOCATIONS

HQ: Interpublic Group of Companies Inc.
1114 Avenue of the Americas, New York, NY 10036
Phone: 212 704-1200
Web: www.interpublic.com

2014 Sales

	% of total
US	56
Asia Pacific	12
Continental Europe	11
United Kingdom	9
Latin America	6
Other	6
Total	**100**

PRODUCTS/OPERATIONS

2014 Sales

	% of total
IAN	81
CMG	19
Total	**100**

Selected Operations

Advertising and marketing services
  Advertising agencies
  Austin-Kelly
  Avrett Free Ginsberg
  Campbell-Ewald
  Campbell Mithun
  Carmichael Lynch
  Dailey & Associates
  Deutsch
  Gotham
  Hill Holiday
  Jay Advertising
  Lowe & Partners (UK)
  The Martin Agency
  McCann Erickson Worldwide
  Mullen
  Tierney Communications
  TM Advertising
  Marketing agencies
  DraftFCB
  The Hacker Group
  MRM Partners
  Momentum
  Rivet
  Translation Consulting + Brand Imaging
  Media services
  Initiative Media
  MAGNA Global
  Universal McCann
Public relations and corporate communications
  DeVries Public Relations
  MWW Group
  Weber Shandwick

COMPETITORS

Dentsu	Omnicom
Dentsu Aegis	Publicis Groupe
Hakuhodo	WPP
Havas	

HISTORICAL FINANCIALS

Company Type: Public

Income Statement

FYE: December 31

	REVENUE ($ mil.)	NET INCOME ($ mil.)	NET PROFIT MARGIN	EMPLOYEES
12/14	7,537	477	6.3%	47,400
12/13	7,122	267	3.8%	45,400
12/12	6,956	446	6.4%	43,300
12/11	7,014	532	7.6%	42,000
12/10	6,531	261	4.0%	41,000
Annual Growth	**3.6%**	**16.3%**	**—**	**3.7%**

2014 Year-End Financials

Debt ratio: 13.59%
Return on equity: 22.03%
Cash ($ mil.): 1,660
Current ratio: 1.05
Long-term debt ($ mil.): 1,623
No. of shares (mil.): 413
Dividends
Yield: 1.8%
Payout: 45.2%
Market value ($ mil.): 8,595

	STOCK PRICE ($) FY Close	P/E High/Low		PER SHARE ($) Earnings	Dividends	Book Value
12/14	20.77	18	14	1.12	0.38	5.11
12/13	17.70	28	18	0.61	0.30	5.22
12/12	11.02	12	9	0.94	0.24	5.80
12/11	9.73	12	6	0.99	0.24	5.48
12/10	10.62	19	11	0.47	0.00	5.17
Annual Growth	**18.3%**	**—**	**—**	**24.2%**	**—**	**(0.3%)**

INTL FCStone Inc.

Going global is the name of the game for securities broker INTL FCStone and its subsidiaries. The company specializes in niche international markets offering commodity risk management consulting and international securities. It offers clearing and execution services of listed futures and options on futures. Its INTL FCStone Securities subsidiary is a wholesale market-maker for some 800 foreign securities. The company also offers asset management and commodity financing and facilitation. INTL FCStone serves financial institutions corporations charitable organizations and other institutional investors in the US and abroad.

Geographic Reach

INTL FCStone serves 11000 customers in about 100 countries around the world. The company operates through a network of about 20 offices in the US. International offices are located in Argentina Australia Brazil Canada China Ireland Paraguay Singapore the UAE the UK and Uruguay.

Sales and Marketing

Customers are served through a direct sales force of risk management consultants who are organized by commodity verticals such as agriculture energy metals and livestock as well as geographic areas such as Latin America/Brazil or China.

Financial Performance

INTL FCStone reported a 5% increase in operating revenue in 2013 (the financial gauge measures income from the company's everyday business operations). That increase was attributed to a spike in operating revenues in the company's securities segment offset by a decline in its consulting and risk management segment. Operating revenues declined in the consulting and risk management segment from decreases in OTC contract volumes in the soft commodities product line primarily in Brazil Mexico and other countries in Latin America.

Strategy

INTL FCStone is focused on broadening its customer base in new markets by offering more services. The company is zeroing in on midsized commercial entities as many are relatively underserved and seeking risk management services. Key growth areas for INTL FCStone include Latin America Canada Asia Europe and Australia.

Mergers and Acquisitions

Acquisitions play a big part in INTL FCStone's growth strategy. In the past several years the company has bought other firms that have helped broaden its geographic reach and service capabilities. In 2014 it bought Sinclair & Company an introducing broker in Twin Falls Idaho that focuses on dairy grains and livestock. A 2013 deal to buy Cleartrade Exchange and significantly expand its commodities derivatives trading in Asia fell through amid regulatory changes in foreign ownership. That year it did buy certain customer accounts from First American Capital and Trading and in 2012 bought certain institutional accounts from Tradewire Securities and UK brokerage and clearing firm TRX Futures which targets coffee and cocoa customers as well as the energy and financial industries.

In 2011 INTL FCStone bought Ambrian Commodities Limited a London metals exchange from Ambrian Capital and the metals division of bankrupt MF Global. However in 2013 the company exited the physical base metals business after a change in management strategy.

Company Background

INTL FCStone which traces its roots to 1924 was created after the 2009 merger of FCStone Group and International Assets Holding.

EXECUTIVES

President and CEO, Sean M. O'Connor, age 53, $400,000 total compensation
CFO, William J. (Bill) Dunaway, age 44, $275,000 total compensation
COO, Xuong Nguyen, age 47
Chief Risk Officer, Tricia Harrod
CEO INTL FCStone Ltd, Philip A. Smith, age 43, $314,761 total compensation
CEO INTL FCStone Securities Inc., Charles Lyon, age 40, $150,000 total compensation
CEO Asia Operations, Malcolm Wilde, age 64
Vice President Emerging Market Debt Capital Markets, Rodrigo Steiner
Vice President Equity Trading, Thomas (Thom) Moore
Assistant Vice President Financial Operations, Marcelo Taborda
Assistant Vice President Trading, Gary Esterman
Vice President Asian Trading, Shaun Finnerty
Vice President Equity Trading, Al Barbella
Senior Vice President Base Metals Lead, Tom Gramlich
Vice President Equity Trading, Albert (Al) Barbella
Chairman, John Radziwill
Board Member, Bruce Krehbiel
Board Member, Brent Bunte
Treasurer, Bruce Fields
Auditors: KPMG LLP

LOCATIONS

HQ: INTL FCStone Inc.
708 Third Avenue, Suite 1500, New York, NY 10017
Phone: 212 485-3500
Web: www.intlfcstone.com

2013 Sales

	% of total
US	66
Asia	34
Total	**100**

PRODUCTS/OPERATIONS

2013 Sales

	% of total
Sales of physical commodities	99
Trading gains net	1
Total	**100**

Selected Subsidiaries

Blackthorn Mult-Advisor Fund LP
FCC Futures Inc.
FCC Investments Inc.
FCStone Advisory Inc.
FCStone Asia Pte. Ltd.

FCStone Australia Pty Ltd.
FCStone Canada ULC
FCStone Carbon LLC
FCStone Commodities Services (Europe) Ltd.
FCStone do Brazil Ltda.
FCStone Financial Inc.
FCStone Forex LLC
FCStone Group
FCStone Information LLC
FCStone International LLC
FCStone Investments Inc.
FCStone Merchant Services LLC
FCStone Paraguay S.R.L.
FCStone LLC
Gainvest Asset Management Ltd.
Gainvest S.A. Sociedad Gerente de Fondos Comunes de Inversion
Gainvest Uruguay Asset Management S.A.
Gletir S.A.
Hanley Alternative Trade Group LLC
HGC Advisory Services LLC
HGC Asset Management LLC
HGC Office Services LLC
HGC Trading LLC
IAHC Bermuda Ltd
INTL Asia Pte. Ltd
INTL Capital and Treasury Global Services Ltd. (Nigeria)
INTL Capital Limited (Dubai UAE)
INTL Capital S.A. (Argentina)
INTL CIBSA Sociedad de Bolsa S.A.
INTL Colombia Ltda.
INTL Commodities DMCC
INTL Commodities Inc.
INTL Commodities Mexico S de RL de CV
INTL FCStone Commodities Inc.
INTL FCStone (Europe) Ltd.
INTL FCStone (Netherlands) B.V.
INTL FCStone SA
INTL Gainvest Capital Assessoria Financeira Ltda. (formerly Gainvest do Brasil Ltda.).
INTL Global Currencies Ltd.
INTL Hanley LLC
INTL Hencorp Futures LLC
INTL Holding (U.K.) Limited
INTL Netherlands B.V.
INTL Participacoes Ltda.
INTL Provident Inc.
INTL Sieramet LLC
INTL Trading Inc.
INTL Universal Commercial (Shanghai) Co. Ltd.
Risk Management Incorporated
RMI Consulting Inc.
Westown Commodities LLC

Selected Mergers & Acquisitions

COMPETITORS

BGC Partners
CAPIS
Citigroup Global Markets
Credit Suisse (USA)
Goldman Sachs
ICAP
Interactive Brokers
J.P. Morgan Clearing
Morgan Stanley
Newedge
Rosenthal Collins
Susquehanna International Group LLP

HISTORICAL FINANCIALS

Company Type: Public

Income Statement

FYE: September 30

	REVENUE ($ mil.)	NET INCOME ($ mil.)	NET PROFIT MARGIN	EMPLOYEES
09/15	34,676	55	0.2%	1,231
09/14	34,011	19	0.1%	1,141
09/13	43,755	19	0.0%	1,094
09/12	69,249	15	0.0%	1,074
09/11	75,486	37	0.0%	904
Annual Growth	**(17.7%)**	**10.5%**	**—**	**8.0%**

2015 Year-End Financials

Debt ratio: 1.72%
Return on equity: 15.00%
Cash ($ mil.): 593
Current ratio: 0.75
Long-term debt ($ mil.): —

No. of shares (mil.): 18
Dividends
Yield: —
Payout: —
Market value ($ mil.): 464

	STOCK PRICE ($) FY Close	P/E High/Low		PER SHARE ($) Earnings	Dividends	Book Value
09/15	24.69	13	6	2.87	0.00	21.11
09/14	17.32	21	17	0.98	0.00	18.29
09/13	20.45	20	16	0.97	0.00	17.46
09/12	19.06	35	23	0.75	0.00	16.81
09/11	20.76	13	9	1.96	0.00	15.89
Annual Growth	**4.4%**	**—**	**—**	**10.0%**	**—**	**7.4%**

Investors Bancorp Inc (New)

Investors Bancorp is the holding company for Investors Savings Bank which serves New Jersey and New York from more than 130 branch offices. Founded in 1926 the bank offers such standard deposit products as savings and checking accounts CDs money market accounts and IRAs. Nearly 40% of the bank's loan portfolio is made up of residential mortgages while multi-family loans and commercial real estate loans make up more than 50% combined. The bank also originates business industrial and consumer loans. Founded in 1926 Investors Bancorp's assets now exceed $20 billion.

OperationsAbout 86% of Investors Bancorp's revenue came from interest income from loans and loans held-for sale in 2014 while another 8% came from interest income on the bank's mortgage-backed securities municipal bonds and other debt. The remainder of its revenue came from fees and service charges (3%) and other miscellaneous income sources. Investors Bancorp boasted a staff of more than 1700 at the end of 2014.Geographic ReachBased in Short Hills New Jersey Investors Bancorp has more than 130 branches across New Jersey and New York. It also has lending offices in New York City Short Hills Spring Lake Newark Astoria and Brooklyn. Its operation center is in Iselin New Jersey.Sales and MarketingThe company offers retail and commercial banking services to individuals professional service firms municipalities small and middle-market companies commercial and industrial firms and other businesses.Financial PerformanceInvestors Bancorp's revenues and profits have been rising thanks to strong loan growth from bank acquisitions falling interest expenses on deposits and declining loan loss provisions as its loan portfolio's credit quality has improved with higher property valuations in the strengthened economy.The bank's revenue jumped by 21% to a record $702.7 million in 2014 mostly thanks to loan asset growth stemming from the bank's 2014 acquisition of Gateway Community Financial. Higher revenue and a continued decline in loan loss provisions in 2014 drove the bank's net income higher by 18% to a record $131.7 million. Investor Bancorp's operating cash levels spiked by 58% to $277.4 million for the year on higher cash earnings and favorable changes in its working capital.StrategyInvestors Bancorp continues to expand its geographic reach in its core New Jersey and New York markets and boost its loan and deposit business mainly through select bank and branch acquisitions. Indeed the bank noted in 2015 that it had made eight bank or branch acquisitions since 2008 adding that they have counted for "a significant portion" of the bank's historic growth.The company's 2014 and 2013 bank acquisitions bolstered its expansion in New Jersey into the suburbs of Philadelphia the boroughs of New York City the Nassau and Suffolk Counties on Long Island and historic markets throughout New Jersey.Mergers and Acquisitions.In January 2014 Investors Bancorp purchased Gateway Community Financial Corp along with its four branches in Gloucester County New Jersey. The deal added nearly $255 million in customer deposits and $195 million in new loan business to its books.In December 2013 the company bought Roma Financial Corporation and its 26 branches in Burlington Ocean Mercer Camden and Middlesex counties in New Jersey. The deal added $1.34 billion in deposits and $991 million in loan assets while expanding the company's reach into the Philadelphia suburbs of New Jersey.Company Background.In late 2012 the company acquired Marathon Banking Corporation (a subsidiary of Greece-based Piraeus Bank) for $135 million adding 13 branches in the New York metro area and more than doubling its branches in New York. The deal also would mark Investors Bancorp's entry into Manhattan and Staten Island.

EXECUTIVES

SEVP and COO, Domenick A. Cama, age 59, $621,000 total compensation

President and CEO, Kevin Cummings, age 60, $935,000 total compensation

EVP and Chief Lending Officer, Richard S. Spengler, age 53, $400,000 total compensation

EVP and Chief Retail Banking Officer, Paul Kalamaras, $375,000 total compensation

SVP and CFO, Sean Burke

Vice President Payroll Manager, Mary Ward

Senior Vice President, William (Bill) Cosgrove

Senior Vice President Information Technology, Sergio Alonso

Chairman, Robert M. Cashill, age 72

Auditors: KPMG LLP

LOCATIONS

HQ: Investors Bancorp Inc (New)
101 JFK Parkway, Short Hills, NJ 07078
Phone: 973 924-5100
Web: www.myinvestorsbank.com

PRODUCTS/OPERATIONS

2014 Sales

	$ mil.	% of total
Interest		
Loans receivable and held-for-sale	603	86
Mortgage-backed securities	44	6
Federal Home Loan Bank stock	6	1
Municipal bonds & other debt	5	1
Other	0	-
Non-interest		
Fees & service charges	19	3
Gain on loan transaction	5	2
Others	17	1
Total	**702**	**100**

COMPETITORS

Bank of America	M&T Bank
Bank of New York Mellon	New York Community Bancorp
Citigroup	OceanFirst Financial
ConnectOne Bancorp	PNC Financial
Fulton Financial	

HISTORICAL FINANCIALS

Company Type: Public

Income Statement

FYE: December 31

	ASSETS ($ mil.)	NET INCOME ($ mil.)	INCOME AS % OF ASSETS	EMPLOYEES
12/14	18,773	131	0.7%	1,708
12/13	15,623	112	0.7%	1,597
12/12	12,722	88	0.7%	1,219
12/11	10,701	78	0.7%	982
12/10	9,602	62	0.6%	892
Annual Growth	**18.2%**	**20.7%**	**—**	**17.6%**

2014 Year-End Financials

Debt ratio: 14.73%
Return on equity: 5.36%
Cash ($ mil.): 230
Current ratio: —
Long-term debt ($ mil.): —

No. of shares (mil.): 358
Dividends
 Yield: 0.7%
 Payout: 21.0%
Market value ($ mil.): 4,019

	STOCK PRICE ($) FY Close	P/E High/Low	PER SHARE ($) Earnings	Dividends	Book Value
12/14	11.23	74 26	0.38	0.08	9.99
12/13	25.58	64 44	0.40	0.00	3.78
12/12	17.78	58 42	0.32	0.00	3.74
12/11	13.48	53 42	0.29	0.00	3.42
12/10	13.12	64 47	0.22	0.00	3.13
Annual Growth	**(3.8%)**	**— —**	**14.7%**	**—**	**33.7%**

iStar Inc

iStar Financial is a real estate investment trust (REIT) that acts as a private banker for owners of high-end commercial real estate in the US and abroad. Its financing activities include first mortgages senior and mezzanine real estate debt and corporate capital net lease financing and equity investments. The REIT's loans typically range in size from $20 million to $150 million and are mainly secured by apartments or other residential properties office complexes land hotels or industrial retail entertainment or mixed-use properties. Office or industrial properties make up 25% of its secured assets while land makes up another 20%.

Operations

iStar operates four business segments based on portfolio strategy. The Real Estate Finance portfolio is primarily comprised of senior and mezzanine real estate loans that may be either fixed-rate or variable-rate. It also includes senior and subordinated loans to corporations. The Net Lease portfolio is made up of company-owned properties leased to tenants where the properties are subject to long-term leases. The Operating Properties portfolio represent a diverse pool of assets across a broad range of geographies and property types. The commercial properties within this portfolio include office retail and hotel properties. The residential properties within this portfolio are generally luxury condominium projects. iStar seeks to reposition or redevelop these assets with the objective of maximizing their value through the infusion of capital and/or intensive asset management efforts. Finally the Land portfolio is made up of master planned communities as well as waterfront and urban infill land parcels.The REIT makes more than 50% of its revenue from operating lease income which the firm gets from its net lease assets and commercial operating properties. About 25% of iStar's revenue comes from interest income

from its financing services.Geographic ReachThe New York-based company has regional offices in Atlanta; Dallas; Hartford Connecticut; San Francisco and Los Angeles. Its properties are located across 33 US states with about 25% of property assets in the Northeast 20% in the West 15% in the Mid-Atlantic 15% in the Southeast and 13% in the Southwest.Sales and MarketingSome iStar's customers include AT&T Drake Hotel Landmark Apartment Trust Marina Palms La Kapolei Van Dyke Commons The Ilikai Hotel Paramount Bay Ocean House University Technical Institute (UTI) and Solo Cup.

Financial Performance

iStar's revenue has been on the uptrend in recent years mostly thanks to rising operating lease income as the firm has acquired more property assets charged higher rent and increased occupancy rates over time. iStar's revenue jumped by 18% to $462 million in 2014 mostly as it made a $19.5 million gain on sales of non-performing loans and $16.5 million on asset-related settlements. Additionally the firm enjoyed 4% growth in operating lease income from higher rental prices and occupancy rates during the year as well as 14% growth in interest income as the firm originated more investments and financed a higher volume of loans during the year.Following three years of losses stemming from the company's high interest expenses iStar reported a profit of $16.45 million in 2014 mostly as interest expenses declined sharply during the year as it continued to reduce its long-term debt . In addition the firm's equity method investment gains increased by $50 million compared to the prior year further padding its bottom line. iStar's operating cash also improved sharply thanks to higher cash earnings.

Strategy

As its Net Lease property business continues to grow even driving the company to a profit in 2014 for the first time since 2010 iStar has been looking for more ways to make money in the landlord business. In 2014 for example the company partnered with a sovereign wealth fund to form its Net Lease Venture with plans to invest $500 million in equity to acquire and develop up to $1.25 billion worth of net lease assets. iStar would own a majority non-controlling interest in the venture.

Struggling to dig out of liabilities stemming from the real estate slump the company's core strategy is to sell non-core assets and raise capital (including secured and unsecured debt financing debt exchanges asset sales issuances of equity joint ventures and other third party capital arrangements) and invest in its core business. Accordingly the firm often divests in properties to lock in gains for future investments. In 2013 iStar sold its 24% stake in LNR Property LLC for $220 million. During 2012 the company sold a portfolio of 12 net lease assets for a gain of $24.9 million. It also sold net lease assets for a gain of $2.4 million and sold commercial properties valued at $29.3 million and land assets ($72.1 million).

On the growth side of the business in 2013 the company sold the entire inventory of homes in phase two of its VIVE luxury townhome community project in Asbury Park New Jersey.

Company Background

The economic recession that began in 2008 impacted iStar in two critical ways. The tightening credit markets made it more difficult for the company to secure both debt and equity financing for its commercial real estate lending and investment activities. And the deterioration of the real estate markets caused the firm's nonperforming loans to balloon. iStar began limiting its new investments while focusing on resolving non-performing loans and improving credit quality.

EXECUTIVES

Chairman and CEO, Jay Sugarman, age 53, $1,000,000 total compensation
EVP iStar Asset Services Inc, Barbara (Barb) Rubin, $400,000 total compensation
EVP Land, Steven P. Magee
EVP Chief Investment Officer and Chief Legal Officer, Nina B. Matis, age 64, $500,000 total compensation
EVP Investments, Barclay G. Jones, age 54
EVP Investments and Head Capital Markets, Michelle M. Mackay, $400,000 total compensation
EVP Credit, Chase S. Curtis
EVP Investments, Vernon B. Schwartz, age 60
CFO, David M. DiStaso, $400,000 total compensation
EVP Land, Karl Frey
Vice President Information Technology, Chris Beach
Vice President Information Technology Security, Phil Burke
Executive Vice President Investments, Cabot Lodge
Senior Vice President, Anthony Burns
Vice President, Eric Brooks
Auditors: PricewaterhouseCoopers LLP

LOCATIONS

HQ: iStar Inc
1114 Avenue of the Americas, 39th Floor, New York, NY 10036
Phone: 212 930-9400   **Fax:** 212 930-9494
Web: www.istarfinancial.com

2014 Assets

	% of total
US	
Northeast	26
West	19
Southeast	15
Mid-Atlantic	15
Southwest	13
Central	5
Other	4
Other countries	1
Strategic Investments	2
Total	**100**

PRODUCTS/OPERATIONS

2014 Sales

	% of total
Interest	53
Operating lease income	27
Other	20
Total	**100**

2014 Property Distribution

Property/Collateral Type	% of total
Office/Industrial	26
Land	22
Mixed Use/Mixed Colleteral	13
Entertainment/Leisure	11
Hotel	9
Retail	6
Condominim	5
Strategic Investments	2
Others	6
Total	**100**

COMPETITORS

Annaly Capital Management	Dynex Capital
CIFC	MFA Financial
Capital Trust	NovaStar Financial
Capstead Mortgage	Redwood Trust

HISTORICAL FINANCIALS

Company Type: Public

Income Statement

FYE: December 31

	ASSETS ($ mil.)	NET INCOME ($ mil.)	INCOME AS % OF ASSETS	EMPLOYEES
12/14	5,463	16	0.3%	182
12/13	5,642	(111)	—	175
12/12	6,150	(239)	—	170
12/11	7,517	(22)	—	184
12/10	9,174	79	0.9%	200
Annual Growth	**(12.2%)**	**(32.6%)**	**—**	**(2.3%)**

2014 Year-End Financials

Debt ratio: 73.63%
Return on equity: 1.35%
Cash ($ mil.): 472
Current ratio: —
Long-term debt ($ mil.): —

No. of shares (mil.): 85
Dividends
Yield: —
Payout: —
Market value ($ mil.): 1,163

	STOCK PRICE ($) FY Close	P/E High/Low		Earnings	PER SHARE ($) Dividends	Book Value
12/14	13.65	—	—	(0.40)	0.00	14.05
12/13	14.27	—	—	(1.83)	0.00	14.85
12/12	8.15	—	—	(3.26)	0.00	14.79
12/11	5.29	—	—	(0.70)	0.00	18.66
12/10	7.82	20	6	0.39	0.00	17.85
Annual Growth	**14.9%**	**—**	**—**	**—**	**—**	**(5.8%)**

Jabil Circuit, Inc.

Jabil Circuit makes a jabillion different kinds of electronics. The company is one of the leading providers of outsourced electronics manufacturing services (EMS) in the world. It makes electronics components and parts on a contract basis for computers smartphones printers and other consumer electronics as well as more complex specialized products for the aerospace automotive and healthcare industries. The company's services range from product design and component procurement to product testing order fulfillment and supply chain management. Jabil Circuit operates some 90 plants in about 25 countries across the Americas Asia and Europe.

Operations
Jabil Circuit conducts business in two segments: Electronics Manufacturing Services (EMS) and Diversified Manufacturing Services (DMS). The EMS segment (60% of revenue) focuses on IT supply chain design and engineering for all things electronic. Customers' products are used in applications for automotive digital home industrial and energy networking and telecommunications point of sale printing and storage.

The DMS segment (40% of revenue) focuses on manufacturing services for material sciences and technologies. It works with customers to develop and manufacture products for consumer lifestyles and wearable technologies defense and aerospace emerging growth healthcare mobility and packaging.

Geographic Reach Jabil Circuit's 90 plants are located in low-cost countries such as Argentina Brazil China Colombia Czech Republic Hungary India Japan Malaysia Mexico Poland Russia Singapore South Korea Taiwan Turkey Ukraine United Arab Emirates and Vietnam as well as in high-cost countries such as Austria Belgium Canada France Germany Ireland Israel Italy Scotland The Netherlands the UK and the US.

Singapore and China are its largest markets accounting for about 28% and 2% of sales respectively. Customers in Mexico and the US generate 14% and 12% of revenue respectively. **Sales and Marketing** Jabil Circuit depends on a small number of customers for a significant percentage of revenue – five customers account for 50% of sales. Its top customer is Apple (24% of sales) and other significant customers are Cisco Systems LM Ericsson General Electric Ingenico NetApp Sony Mobile Communications Valeo and Zebra Technologies. In 2014 Jabil decided it would no longer work with BlackBerry which accounted for about 15% of revenue in 2013.

Financial Performance Overall sales rose 13.5% to about $18 billion in 2015 (ended August) as the DMS segment's revenue increased 39%. EMS revenue was flat year-to-year. The mobility business within DMS was particularly strong in 2015.

Profits rose 17.7% in 2015 from 2014 to reach $284 million. Increased revenue coupled with lower restructuring charges boosted Jabil's earnings.

Cash flow from operations surged to $1.2 billion in 2015 from $499 billion in 2014. Factors in the increase included a $984 million increase in accounts payable accrued expenses and other liabilities $529 million in non-cash depreciation and amortization expense a $113 million decrease in prepaid expenses and other current assets and $62 million of recognized stock-based compensation expense and related charges. The increase in accounts receivable was primarily driven by the timing of sales and collections activity coupled with higher sales levels.

Strategy Jabil Circuit continued restructuring in 2014 most notably with its decision to discontinue its work for Nokia. The business accounted for 12% of revenue in 2013 but Jabil Circuit rebounded in 2015. Jabil Circuit also expanded manufacturing capacity in Malaysia and Vietnam.

To compete in a rapidly consolidating industry Jabil provides production on a global scale and operates through semi-autonomous business units that are dedicated to individual customers. The company continues to add services and to expand globally through acquisitions including deals to acquire manufacturing operations from customers looking to reduce costs through outsourcing. The company tends to place manufacturing plants close to its customers. **Mergers and Acquisitions** In 2015 Jabil's healthcare and packaging division Nypro acquired Plasticos Castella a molder of plastic lids for condiments. Nypro's acquisition of Plasticos Castella expands smart packaging capabilities by combining design engineering and manufacturing facilities in Spain and Hungary with the services of Nypro's six North American plants.

HISTORY

Early History
Jabil Circuit was named for founders James Golden and Bill Morean. The duo who originally ran an excavation business started Jabil in suburban Detroit in 1966 to provide assembly and reworking services to electronics manufacturers. Jabil incorporated in 1969 and began making printed circuit boards for Control Data Corporation (later renamed Control Data Systems) that year.

William D. Morean the founder's son who had worked summers at Jabil while in high school joined the company in 1977. The next year the younger Morean took over Jabil's day-to-day operations. The company had entered the automotive electronics business in 1976 through a $12 million contract with General Motors.

During the 1980s Jabil began building computer components adding such customers as Dell NEC Sun Microsystems and Toshiba. Jabil moved its headquarters to St. Petersburg Florida in 1983. William Morean became Jabil's chairman and CEO in 1988.

EXECUTIVES

EVP Strategic Planning and Development, Joseph A. (Joe) McGee, age 53, $510,000 total compensation
CEO, Mark T. Mondello, age 51, $1,000,000 total compensation
COO, William D. (Bill) Muir, age 47, $640,000 total compensation
EVP and CEO Nypro, Courtney J. Ryan, age 45
CFO, Forbes I. J. Alexander, age 55, $635,000 total compensation
VP Business Development, Steven D. (Steve) Borges
SVP Materials Technology, Hwai Hai (HH) Chiang, $445,000 total compensation
SVP and Chief Supply Chain Officer Manufacturing Services, Erich Hoch
SVP High Velocity, Michael J. Loparco, age 44
EVP and CEO Enterprise and Infrastructure, Alessandro Parimbelli, age 47
President, William E. (Bill) Peters, age 52, $640,000 total compensation
SVP and CIO, Gary L. Cantrell
EVP Human Resources and Human Development, Scott D. Slipy, age 47
SVP Sales Enablement and Marketing, Joanne Moretti
Vice President Global Mechanicals and Enclosures EMS Division, John D (Jack) Caltabiano
Vice President Of Business Development, Kip Ferris
Assistant Vice President and Systems Manager, Mahesh Rakte
Vice President, David Dunlop
Executive Vice President National Operations, Mark Butler
Vice President Of Finance After Market Services Division, Brian Greff
Vice President Human Resources, Tom Minneo
Vice President Information Technology, Marco Garcia
Vice President Finance and Divisional Chief Financial Officer, David (Dave) Beamer
Vice President, Justyna Czech
Vice President And General Manager, Ed Traupman
Vice President, Mitch Jones
Vice President Of Operations, George Campbell
Vice President Of Strategic Development, John Dargan
Vice President of Customer Services, Queenie Vu
Vice President Global Operations Services, Gonzalo Gonzalez
Vice President Operations Europe, Roger Shahnazarian
Vice President After Market Services, Hartmut Liebel
Assistant Vice President Sales National Accounts, Dennis Maddock
Vice President Information Technology Jabil Global Services, Erik Carlson
Vice President Global Business Units, Emanuele Cavallaro
Vice President Of Finance, Mike Dastoor
Vice President Operations (Asia), KC Ong
Chairman, Timothy L. (Tim) Main, age 58
Vice Chairman, Thomas A. Sansone, age 66
Board Member, Armando Ochoa
Assistant Treasurer, Greg Hebard
Auditors: Ernst & Young LLP

LOCATIONS

HQ: Jabil Circuit, Inc.
10560 Dr. Martin Luther King, Jr. Street North, St. Petersburg, FL 33716
Phone: 727 577-9749
Web: www.jabil.com

2015 Sales

	% of total
Singapore	28
China	22
Mexico	14
US	12
Malaysia	7
Hungary	5
Brazil	2
Other	10
Total	**100**

PRODUCTS/OPERATIONS

2015 Sales

	$ mil.	% of total
Electronics manufacturing services	10,777	60
Diversified Manufacturing Services	7,121	40
Total	**17,899**	**100**

Services
Component selection sourcing and procurement
Design and prototyping
Engineering
Order fulfillment
Printed circuit board and backplane assembly
Product testing
Repair and warranty
Systems assembly
Test development
Tooling design (molds and dies)

COMPETITORS

ASUSTeK	Key Tronic
BenQ	Plexus
Benchmark Electronics	SMTC Corp.
Celestica	Sanmina
Compal Electronics	Sparton
Flextronics	Venture Corp.
Hon Hai	Wistron
Inventec	

HISTORICAL FINANCIALS

Company Type: Public

Income Statement

FYE: August 31

	REVENUE ($ mil.)	NET INCOME ($ mil.)	NET PROFIT MARGIN	EMPLOYEES
08/15	17,899	284	1.6%	161,000
08/14	15,762	241	1.5%	142,000
08/13	18,336	371	2.0%	177,000
08/12	17,151	394	2.3%	141,000
08/11	16,518	381	2.3%	121,000
Annual Growth	**2.0%**	**(7.1%)**	**—**	**7.4%**

2015 Year-End Financials

Debt ratio: 17.39%	No. of shares (mil.): 192
Return on equity: 12.47%	Dividends
Cash ($ mil.): 913	Yield: 1.6%
Current ratio: 1.03	Payout: 35.5%
Long-term debt ($ mil.): 1,346	Market value ($ mil.): 3,717

	STOCK PRICE ($) FY Close	P/E High/Low		PER SHARE ($) Earnings	Dividends	Book Value
08/15	19.35	17	12	1.45	0.32	12.05
08/14	21.58	20	13	1.19	0.32	11.55
08/13	22.82	13	9	1.79	0.32	11.49
08/12	22.78	14	8	1.87	0.32	10.22
08/11	16.85	13	6	1.73	0.28	9.18
Annual Growth	**3.5%**	**—**	**—**	**(4.3%)**	**3.4%**	**7.0%**

Jacobs Engineering Group, Inc.

Jacobs Engineering fuels its rise up the ladder with oil gas and chemicals. The group provides technical professional and construction services for industrial government and commercial clients primarily in the US the UK and Canada. Jacobs handles project design and engineering construction operations maintenance and scientific consultation. Typical projects include oil refineries manufacturing plants and roads and highways. The company's largest single customer is the US government (about 20% of revenues) for which it chiefly performs aerospace and defense work. Founded in 1947 Jacobs Engineering has more than 200 offices in more than 25 countries.

Operations

The company divides its operations into four major categories: project services (including engineering and architectural design); construction services; operations and maintenance; and process scientific and systems consulting services. Its specialty consulting segment includes pricing studies project feasibility reports and automation and control system analysis.

Geographic Reach

California-based Jacobs Engineering's largest market is the US home to nearly 60% of its annual revenue. Europe contributes nearly 20% followed by Canada with 15%. The firm also has operations in Africa Asia India Australia Mexico the Middle East and South America.

Financial Performance

Jacobs Engineering's fiscal 2013 (ended September) sales increased 8.5% versus the prior year to an all-time high of $11.8 billion. Net earnings increased $44.1 million nearly 12% from $379 million in fiscal 2012 to $423.1 million in 2013. The growth in earnings was primarily driven by a strong performance in the Chemicals and Polymers industry. With the exception of the US and Canada which posted annual sales increases in the mid-single digit range all of Jacobs Engineer's markets posted double-digit gains led by South America and Mexico with a 53% gain in sales.

Indeed following a slump in construction activity during the global recession Jacobs is riding the boom in oil and gas and chemicals industries. Fiscal 2013 marked the third consecutive year of steadily increasing sales profits and cash flow for the firm.

Strategy

One of Jacobs' strengths is its roster of long-term clients. The group gets jobs and keeps jobs for the long term and a main strategy is to build on long-standing business relationships —some that have spanned around 60 years. Nearly all of Jacobs' business comes from repeat clients. For example US government agencies involved in defense and aerospace programs have been pivotal to the company's growth. The Air Force's Arnold Engineering Development Center (AEDC) has been a key client for 50 years. Another long-term client is NASA for which the company has a 40-year history of contract work.

Overseas Jacobs U.K. works on several projects for the Ministry of Defense and the Nuclear Decommissioning Authority. In 2010 the company added to its defense and aerospace business in the UK with the acquisition of Sula Systems. Jacobs earned its second contract with the Hong Kong government in 2012 for which it will provide management and operating services for a new public works laboratory.

The group also participates in the environmental restoration of former weapons production and defense sites. Jacobs' strategy to speed up environmental cleanup at the Department of Energy's Oak Ridge site has earned it contracts to help accelerate cleanup at other major DOE facilities. The company has also been providing services for the Air Force Center for Environmental Excellence (AFCEE) to help the agency with its environmental cleanup goals since 1991.

Acquisitions are also part of Jacobs' growth strategy. The company grows by entering new markets and services lines via strategic mergers and acquisitions allowing it to offer one-stop services.

Mergers and Acquisitions

In February 2014 Jacobs acquired Eagleton Engineering LLC a Houston-based design engineering firm with clients in the oil and gas and petrochemical industries. The purchase expands Jacobs' capabilities in midstream and upstream pipeline engineering design and field surveying services. In late 2014 it bought Virginia-based Federal Network Systems which concentrates on the intelligence community Department of Defense and federal civilian customers.

In November 2013 the firm acquired California-based MARMAC Field Services a privately held engineering and design services firm with clients in the oil and natural gas industry. In June of the same year Jacobs purchased Compass Technology Services in Atlanta Georgia. The purchase bolstered the firm's capabilities in wireless telecommunications infrastructure design and construction and its presence in the Southeast.   Normal 0 false false false   EN-US X-NONE X-NONE

Beyond the US the company in late 2013 added Ilitha Projects and Ilitha Staffing –two Cape Town South Africa-based professional services companies –through its South African joint venture Jacobs Matasis (Proprietary) Limited. Also in 2013 it acquired a stake in Rio de Janeiro's Guimar Engenharia a privately held engineering services and project management/construction management (PMCM) company.

HISTORY

Joseph Jacobs graduated from the Polytechnic Institute of Brooklyn in 1942 with a doctorate in engineering. He went to work for Merck designing processes for pharmaceutical production. Later he moved to Chemurgic Corp. near San Francisco where he worked until 1947 when he founded Jacobs Engineering as a consulting firm. Jacobs also sold industrial equipment avoiding any apparent conflict of interest by simply telling his consulting clients.

When equipment sales outstripped consulting work by 1954 Jacobs hired four salesmen and engineer Stan Krugman who became his right-hand man. Two years later the company got its first big chemical design job for Kaiser Aluminum. Jacobs incorporated his sole proprietorship in 1957.

In 1960 the firm won its first construction contract to design and build a potash flotation plant and Jacobs Engineering became an integrated design and construction firm. In 1967 it opened its first regional office but kept management decentralized to replicate the small size and hard-hitting qualities of its home office. Three years later Jacobs Engineering went public.

The firm merged with Houston-based Pace Companies which specialized in petrochemical engineering design in 1974. Also that year the firm became Jacobs Engineering Group and began building its first major overseas chemical plant in Ireland.

By 1977 sales had reached $250 million. A decade of lobbying paid off that year when the firm won a contract for the Arab Potash complex in Jordan. Jacobs began to withdraw from his firm's operations in the early 1980s but the 1982-83 recession and poor management decisions pounded earnings. Jacobs returned from retirement in 1985 fired 14 VPs cut staff in half and pushed the firm to pursue smaller process-plant jobs and specialty construction.

After abandoning a 1986 attempt to take the company private Jacobs began making acquisitions to improve the firm's construction expertise. In 1992 he relinquished his role as CEO to president Noel Watson. The next year the company expanded its international holdings by acquiring the UK's H&G Process Contracting and H&G Contractors.

The firm's $38 million purchase of CRS Sirrine Engineers and CRSS Constructors in 1994 was the company's largest buy at that point and added new markets in the paper and semiconductor industries. By 1995 Jacobs Engineering was working on a record backlog.

Continuing its acquisition drive the company bought a 49% interest in European engineering specialist Serete Group in 1996; it bought the rest the next year. Also in 1997 it gained control of Indian engineering affiliate Humphreys & Glasgow (now Jacobs H&G) increasing its 40% stake to 70% and bought CPR Engineering a pulp and paper processing specialist. It also formed a joint venture with Krupp UHDE to provide design engineering and construction management services in Mexico.

In 1999 the company paid $198 million for St. Louis construction and design firm Sverdrup which had completed projects in some 65 countries. The next year Jacobs Engineering purchased half of Dutch firm Stork Engineering's business (it acquired the rest in 2001). But the company's bid to buy the assets of bankrupt power plant construction company Stone & Webster in 2000 was topped by Shaw Group.

After being accused of overcharging the US government Jacobs Engineering settled a whistle-blower lawsuit (for $35 million) in 2000 while continuing to deny the allegations. However the next year Jacobs continued to receive federal contracts including contracts for boosting security at the US Capitol complex and providing logistics to the US Special Operations Command. Jacobs completed its acquisition of the UK-based GIBB unit of engineering consulting firm LawGibb Group in 2001 as well as the purchase of McDermott Engineers and Constructors (Canada).

EXECUTIVES

Executive Vice President Of Operations, Thomas Hammond
Group Vice President, Walter Barber
Vice President, Nazim G Thawerbhoy
Senior Vice President Information Technology, Michael (Mel) Miller
SVP Information Technology, Cora L. Carmody, age 58
President and CEO, Steven J. Demetriou, age 56, $125,000 total compensation
EVP and CFO, Kevin C. Berryman, age 56, $544,832 total compensation
President Industrial, Robert V. (Bob) Pragada, age 47
President Petroleum and Chemicals, Joseph G. Mandel, age 55, $699,996 total compensation
EVP Operations, Phillip J. Stassi, age 60, $639,423 total compensation
President Aerospace and Technology, Terence D. Hagen, age 50
Vice President Marketing and Consumer Affairs, Michelle (Mitch) Jones

Vice President Business Development, Terry Hagen
Vice President Of Human Resources, Mark Cooper
Senior Vice President Business Development, Julian Tai
Vice President and Shop Management, Ben Bortey
Senior Vice President, Nicholas Hallett
Vice President, Michael Zuniga
Division Vice President, Ford Hubbard
Vice President Business Development, James (Jamie) Smith
Senior Vice President Global Human Resources, Lori Sundberg
Vice President Community Investment Officer, Jane (Ginny) Allen
Vice President, Phil Sheridan
Vice President, Jannette Funderburk
Senior Vice President General Counsel, William (Bill) Markley
Executive Vice President Operations, Craig Landry
Vice President and Corporate Secretary, Mike Udovic
Vice President Operations, Jeffrey (Jeff) Stiles
Group Vice President federal Operations, Michael (Mel) Higgins
Executive Vice President, Greg Landry
Vice President, David (Dave) Parsons
Gvp Consulting Operations, Robert McWhinney
Vice President Sales Support, Mary Bloom
Vice President Information Technology, Pete Young
Vice President, Tom Mack
Vice President Global Supply Management, Susan (Sue) Steele
Division Vice President Director Construction Services, Joseph Franco
Vice President, Albert Pozotrigo
Gvp Federal Operations, James Thiesing
Senior Vice President, Roy Hearnsberger
Executive Vice President Operations, Santo Rizzuto
Vice President Corporate and Real Estate Investments, Frank McCaskell
Senior Vice President, Gary Brasser
Vice President Business Development, Michael Jones
Vice President Of Finance, Linda Duckworth
Vice President Facilities, John Stewart
Vice President Business Development, Philip Luna
Vice President Project Controls Western Region, Harry Greenberg
Vice President Global Litigation, Joanne Caruso
Senior Vice President Public Sector Sales, William (Bill) Birkhofer
Executive Vice President, Sy Exter
Vice President Federal Civilian, Marietta Hannigan
Vice President Legal Services Americas, Michael (Mel) Bante
Vice President, Tom Nielsen
Executive Vice President Finance and Administration Treasurer, John (Jack) Prosser
Vice President Project Controls, Dennis Helliwell
Vice President Global Risk Management, James (Jamie) Durree
Vice President National Design Build Leader, Kevin Walker
Chairman, Noel G. Watson, age 78
Board Member, Frank Way
Treasurer, Michael (Mel) Hogan
Board Member, Lewis Morgan
Vice Chairman North Information Technology Projects Manager, Brian Burkhard
Secretary, William Nordstrom
Board Member, Julie Ellis
Auditors: Ernst & Young LLP

LOCATIONS

HQ: Jacobs Engineering Group, Inc.
155 North Lake Avenue, Pasadena, CA 91101
Phone: 626 578-3500   **Fax:** 626 568-7144
Web: www.jacobs.com

2013 Sales

	$ mil.	% of total
US	6,993	59
Europe	2,148	18
Canada	1,652	14
Middle East & Africa	277	2
South America & Mexico	241	2
Asia	204	2
India	158	2
Australia	141	1
Total	**11,818**	**100**

PRODUCTS/OPERATIONS

2013 Sales by Industry

	$ mil.	% of total
Chemicals & polymers	2,391	20
Downstream refining	2,337	20
National government programs	2,284	19
Infrastructure	1,015	9
Upstream oil & gas	915	8
Buildings	738	6
Mining & minerals	712	6
Pharmaceuticals & biotechnology	523	4
Industrial & other	899	8
Total	**11,818**	**100**

2013 Sales by Service

	$ mil.	% of total
Project services	5,977	51
Construction	3,825	32
Operations & maintenance	1,308	11
Process scientific & systems consulting	705	6
Total	**11,818**	**100**

COMPETITORS

AECOM	HOK
Aker Solutions	KBR
Amec Foster Wheeler	Leidos
BWX Technologies	Lockheed Martin
Bechtel	Parsons Brinckerhoff
CH2M HILL	Technip
Computer Sciences	Tetra Tech
Corp.	Turner Construction
Fluor	WS Atkins
HDR	Weston Solutions
HNTB Companies	WorleyParsons Corp.

HISTORICAL FINANCIALS

Company Type: Public

Income Statement

FYE: October 2

	REVENUE ($ mil.)	NET INCOME ($ mil.)	NET PROFIT MARGIN	EMPLOYEES
10/15*	12,114	302	2.5%	64,000
09/14	12,695	328	2.6%	66,300
09/13	11,818	423	3.6%	66,500
09/12	10,893	378	3.5%	63,400
09/11	10,381	331	3.2%	62,000
Annual Growth	3.9%	(2.2%)	—	0.8%

*Fiscal year change

2015 Year-End Financials

Debt ratio: 7.68%
Return on equity: 6.80%
Cash ($ mil.): 460
Current ratio: 1.66
Long-term debt ($ mil.): 584

No. of shares (mil.): 123
Dividends
　Yield: —
　Payout: —
Market value ($ mil.): 4,606

	STOCK PRICE ($) FY Close	P/E High/Low	PER SHARE ($) Earnings	Dividends	Book Value
10/15*	37.40	20 15	2.40	0.00	34.85
09/14	49.68	27 20	2.48	0.00	33.92
09/13	57.79	19 12	3.23	0.00	32.00
09/12	40.43	16 11	2.94	0.00	28.65
09/11	32.29	20 12	2.60	0.00	25.93
Annual Growth	3.7%	— —	(2.0%)	—	7.7%

*Fiscal year change

Jarden Corp

More than 120 brands of consumer products for inside and outside the home make Jarden beam. It makes a wide variety of branded consumer products including Sunbeam and Oster appliances Coleman outdoor gear and First Alert home safety products. It also makes Ball canning jars Diamond matches and plastic cutlery Loew-Cornell art supplies K2 snowboards and Bee and Bicycle brand playing cards. Jarden sells its products primarily to retailers such as Wal-Mart Dick's Sporting Goods and Target. It also supplies copper-plated zinc penny blanks to the US Mint and the Royal Canadian Mint. To further diversify its products portfolio Jarden acquired The Yankee Candle Co. in 2013.

Operations

Jarden operates its business through four segments: Branded Consumables Outdoor Solutions Consumer Solutions and Process Solutions. Its largest business (36% of 2014 sales) is Branded Consumables which concentrates on the basics such as brooms brushes kitchen matches arts and crafts paint brushes home canning jars and smoke and carbon monoxide alarms. Outdoor Solutions (33%) focuses on making and marketing active lifestyle and outdoor-related products such as air beds camping stoves tents inflatable boats team sports equipment and all-terrain vehicle gear among other items. Jarden's Consumer Solutions segment (26% of sales) is responsible for manufacturing and distributing household products for making coffee purifying the air and slow-cooking meals. Process Solutions (about 5% of sales) makes and distributes a range of plastic products including closures contact lens packaging medical disposables and plastic cutlery.

Geographic Reach

New York-based Jarden Corporation rings up about 61% of its sales in the US. The company manufactures its products in China Europe Latin America and North America. It also sources goods from third parties primarily in Asia.

Sales and Marketing

Wal-Mart Stores which purchases products from all of Jarden's business segments is the company's #1 customer accounting for about 15% of annual sales. Other leading customers include: Academy Sports & Outdoors Amazon.com Bed Bath & Beyond Canadian Tire Costco The Home Depot Lowe's and Target.

Advertising expenses in 2014 $189 million up from $172 million in 2013 and $156 million in 2012.

Financial Performance

Jarden has seen its revenues rise consistently since 2010.In 2014 its net sales grew due by 12.7% thanks to increased Branded Consumables and Consumer Solutions sales.Excluding the impact of the The Yankee Candle Co. (YCC) acquisition and the Rexair Acquisition net sales increased due to higher demand and sell-through in certain product categories favorable weather conditions and increased seasonal demand for certain product categories expanded product offerings and increased demand internationally in certain product categories.Net sales in the Branded Consumables segment increased due to higher sales in certain product categories in the home care leisure and entertainment and safety and security businesses including the food preservation category.

Consumer Solutions sales rose on 2014 due to increased international demand primarily in Latin America due to expanded product offerings in the small appliance category expanded distribution and an increase in sales.In 2014 Jarden's net income increased by 19% due to higher sales and lower income tax partially offset by increased selling general and administrative expenses as the result of the impact of the YCC acquisition an increase in Venezuela foreign exchange-related charges an increase in acquisition-related and other costs and higher marketing and product development costs related to the company's investment in brand equity. Net cash provided by the operating activities decreased by $41.5 million in 2014 due to a change in accounts receivable inventory and accounts payable.

Strategy

Jarden's growth strategy is based on introducing new products as well as on expanding existing product categories which is supplemented through opportunistically acquiring businesses that reflect its core strategy often with highly-recognized brands within the categories they serve innovative products and multi-channel distribution.The company's objective is to increase profitability cash flow and revenues while enhancing its position as a leading manufacturer marketer and distributor of branded consumer products “used in and around the home” and “home away from home.” Its strategy for achieving these objectives includes further penetrating existing distribution channels; introducing new products; pursuing strategic acquisitions; further expanding internationally and focusing on operating margin improvements.It seeks to further penetrate existing distribution channels to drive organic growth by leveraging its strong existing customer relationships and attracting new customers. To drive organic growth from its existing businesses it intends to continue to leverage our strong brand names customer relationships and proven capacity for innovation to develop new products and product extensions in each of its major product categories.

Pumping out new products is what keeps Jarden's bottom line healthy. In 2013 its Coleman brand expanded its line of grills and launched a line of NFL licensed coolers. For skiers the company's Völkl brand introduced a new line of carbon fiber-reinforced alpine skis. Jarden also continued to develop products in food preparation entertaining pet care and health and wellness. Overseas the company entered the baby cosmetics category with balms creams and lotions under the NUK brand.

While new products are important for growth the company can fall back on long-established brands some in continuous use for more than 100 years such as Ball Bee Coleman and Sunbeam. Acquisitions such as the purchase of Yankee Candle in 2013 also play a part in Jarden's strategy as does extending its distribution reach overseas.Consistent with its historical acquisition strategy the company intends to focus on buying businesses with product offerings that provide geographic or product diversification or expansion into related categories that can be marketed through its existing distribution channels or provide it with new distribution channels for its existing products.

Mergers and Acquisitions

Jarden has maintained a steady pace of acquiring companies with noteworthy names to add value to its stable of brands.

In 2015 the company acquired Waddington a leading maker and marketer of premium disposable tableware for commercial foodservice and retail markets for $1.35 billion. The deal expands Jarden's product offerings and distribution channels and creates cross-selling opportunities. It also purchased Visant Holding the parent of Jostens which makes class rings and other school and sports memorabilia. In 2014 Jarden bought Rexair Holdings (a global provider of premium vacuum cleaning systems sold primarily under the Rainbow brand name) for $349 million.

The company acquired YCC from private equity firm Madison Dearborn Partners for about $1.8 billion in cash in 2013. Yankee Candle sells scented candles and home fragrance products through more than 500 stores in the US and Canada. Previously Jarden purchased Paris-based Mapa Spontex for $415 million. The French manufacturer's baby care products (such as baby bottles and nipples) carry the NUK Tigex and Lillo brands its household cleaning items (sponges rubber gloves) bear the Mapa and Spontex names and its health care segment makes condoms under the Billy Boy name. The purchase has exposed Jarden to new product segments and helped to boost revenue from foreign markets extending the firm's presence beyond North America to include Europe and Latin America (Brazil and Argentina).

EXECUTIVES

Vice Chairman and President, Ian G. H. Ashken, age 54, $1,011,982 total compensation

CEO, James E. (Jim) Lillie, age 54, $1,011,982 total compensation

EVP Operations, Richard T. Sansone, age 49, $554,875 total compensation

EVP and CFO, Alan W. (Al) Lefevre, age 55, $309,615 total compensation

EVP Administration General Counsel and Secretary, John E. Capps, age 51, $554,875 total compensation

VP Information Technology, David Armstrong

President and CEO Jarden Consumer Solutions, Andy Hill

President and CEO Jarden Branded Consumables, Chris Scherzinger

President and CEO Jarden Process Solutions, Chuck Villa

Vice President Of Operations Supply Chain, Dale Sexton

Vice President of Team Sales Rawlings Sporting Goods Worth Sports, Greg Bialis

Chairman, Martin E. Franklin, age 50

Auditors: PricewaterhouseCoopers LLP

LOCATIONS

HQ: Jarden Corp
 1800 North Military Trail, Boca Raton, FL 33431
Phone: 561 447-2520
Web: www.jarden.com

2014 Sales

	$ mil.	% of total
Domestic	5,085	61
International	3,201	39
Total	**8,287**	**100**

PRODUCTS/OPERATIONS

2014 Sales

	$ mil.	% of total
Branded consumables	2,993	36
Outdoor solutions	2,739	33
Consumer solutions	2,211	26
Process solutions	427	5
Adjustments	(84.8)	-
Total	**8,287**	**100**

Selected Products

Branded consumables
 Baby bottles soothers and nipples
 Candles
 Canning jars
 Clothespins
 Condoms (Billy B)
 Cord and twine
 Food preparation kits
 Fire safety equipment (First Alert)
 Home appliances (Mr. Coffee Oster Sunbeam)
 Infant accessories
 Kitchen matches
 Outdoor gear (Coleman Aero)

Plastic cutlery
Rope
Rubber gloves
Sponges
Toothpicks
Consumer Solutions
 Panini grills
 Vacuum packaging systems
 Waffle makers
Plastic Consumables
 Closures
 Contact lens packaging
 Plastic cutlery
 Refrigerator door liners
 Shotgun shell casings
 Surgical devices
 Syringes
Other
 Zinc strip and fabricated products

Selected Brands

Aviator
Ball
Bee
Bernardin
Bicycle
Campingaz
Coleman
Crawford
Diamond
First Alert
FoodSaver
Forster
Health o meter
Hoyle
Java Log
K2
Kerr
Lehigh
Leslie-Locke
Loew-Cornell
Mr. Coffee
Oster
Sunbeam
Ugly Stick
Villawear
XTools
Yankee Candle Co.

COMPETITORS

AZZ	Johnson Outdoors
Academy Sports	Kaz
Amazon.com	Kellwood
Amer Sports	Lasko Products
Andis	Lifetime Brands
BRG Sports	Lowe's
BWAY	MEGA Brands
Bass Pro Shops	Mattel
Bauer Hockey	Mayborn Group
Bed Bath & Beyond	Mizuno
Burton	NACCO Industries
Cabela's	NIKE
CalCedar	New Balance
Canadian Tire	Newell Rubbermaid
Carrefour	Owens-Illinois
Church & Dwight	Patch Products
Conair Consumer	Philips Avent
Products	Procter & Gamble
Costco Wholesale	Quiksilver
Crayola	REI
Daiwa	Richco
De' Longhi	Rollerblade
Deswell	Rossignol
Dick's Sporting Goods	Russell Hobbs
EBSCO	SEB
Edgewell Personal Care	Sealy
Elmer's Products	Simmons
Evenflo	Spectrum Brands
Female Health	Suncast
Gaming Partners	Target Corporation
International	Tecnica
Gerber Products	UTC Climate Controls &
Habasit America	Security
Hamilton Beach	Universal Security
Hanesbrands	Instruments
Head N.V.	VF Corporation
Hillerich & Bradsby	W.C. Bradley Co.

HoMedics	Wahl Clipper
Home Depot	West Pharmaceutical
Honeywell ACS	Services
Igloo Products	Whirlpool
Intex DIY	Worthington Industries
Johnson & Johnson	adidas

HISTORICAL FINANCIALS

Company Type: Public

Income Statement

FYE: December 31

	REVENUE ($ mil.)	NET INCOME ($ mil.)	NET PROFIT MARGIN	EMPLOYEES
12/14	8,287	242	2.9%	33,000
12/13	7,355	203	2.8%	33,000
12/12	6,696	243	3.6%	25,000
12/11	6,679	204	3.1%	23,000
12/10	6,022	106	1.8%	24,000
Annual Growth	**8.3%**	**22.8%**	**—**	**8.3%**

2014 Year-End Financials

Debt ratio: 46.84%	No. of shares (mil.): 192
Return on equity: 9.40%	Dividends
Cash ($ mil.): 1,164	Yield: —
Current ratio: 2.08	Payout: —
Long-term debt ($ mil.): 4,464	Market value ($ mil.): 9,193

	STOCK PRICE ($) FY Close	P/E High/Low	PER SHARE ($) Earnings	Dividends	Book Value
12/14	47.88	52 33	1.28	0.00	13.59
12/13	61.35	53 35	1.18	0.00	13.18
12/12	51.70	40 21	1.38	0.12	10.00
12/11	29.88	35 25	1.03	0.15	9.35
12/10	30.87	66 48	0.53	0.15	8.81
Annual Growth	**11.6%**	**— —**	**24.7%**	**—**	**11.4%**

JetBlue Airways Corp

JetBlue Airways is counting on more than low fares to make its ledgers jet-black. The carrier offers one-class service —with leather seats satellite TV from DIRECTV satellite radio from XM and movies —to more than 32 million passengers a year and taking them to more than 90 cities. It has 825 daily flights in more than 25 US states Puerto Rico Mexico and about a dozen countries in the Caribbean and Latin America. Most of its flights arrive or depart from Boston; Los Angeles; New York; Orlando and Fort Lauderdale Florida; and San Juan Puerto Rico. JetBlue's fleet of more than 190 aircraft consists mainly of Airbus A320s and A321s but also includes Embraer 190s.

HISTORY

JetBlue took to the skies in 2000 as the third airline start-up for founder and CEO David Neeleman. The first airline Neeleman helped create Morris Air was formed in 1984. Named after his business partner June Morris the discount airline was operating 22 planes out of Salt Lake City by 1993. While with Morris Air Neeleman pioneered ticketless travel which a decade later would become an industry standard.

Impressed with Morris Air's efficient and strategic network its e-ticket system and Neeleman Southwest Airlines acquired its smaller rival in 1993. Neeleman left Southwest after just six months but not without signing a non-compete clause that prevented him from attempting to repeat his Morris Air success in the US for five years.

Not willing to sit still for long (a characteristic he attributes to attention deficit disorder) Neeleman partnered with David Evans to create Open Skies an integrated e-ticket Internet booking and sales management tool that they began to market to smaller airlines.

Meanwhile Neeleman had skirted the terms of his non-compete agreement to help the founders of Canadian low-fare carrier WestJet get their project off of the ground serving as a consultant and a board member.

In 1999 a year after his non-compete agreement expired Neeleman sold Open Skies to Hewlett-Packard and set to work creating a new airline. In a matter of weeks he had managed to gather $130 million the most ever raised for a start-up airline from investors that included Chase Capital and financier George Soros. Neeleman immediately began acquiring new Airbus A320 jets and fitting them with satellite TV.

JetBlue's first flight was from New York to Fort Lauderdale in 2000. During the year the airline added nine more destinations in California Florida New York Utah and Vermont. By 2001 the airline was operating 20 new A320s with an ambitious 131 on order.

On September 11 of that year terrorists commandeered four passenger aircrafts and turned them into instruments of destruction killing some 3000 people. The events shocked the world and crippled the airline industry. Despite the climate however JetBlue continued to expand its network and it went public in 2002.

The industry star took some heat in 2003 for violating its own privacy policy when it gave the personal information of 1.1 million customers to the Department of Defense as part of anti-terrorism project.

JetBlue added nine new destinations in 2004 including Boston —a major market not dominated by a single carrier and lacking what the company deemed to be sufficient low-fare domestic service.

Consecutive losses in the fourth quarter of 2005 and the first quarter of 2006 —caused in part by rising fuel costs—led the carrier to raise fares on some routes redouble its efforts to keep expenses down and slow some of its expansion plans.

As part of the effort to improve the company's operations JetBlue's board in May 2007 asked David Neeleman to step down as CEO in favor of former president Dave Barger. Neeleman remained with the company as nonexecutive chairman until May 2008.

To grow JetBlue increased capacity at its base at New York's JFK airport with the opening of a new terminal in October 2008. The 630000 sq. ft. Terminal 5 has 26 gates solely used by JetBlue and can accommodate 250 daily departures. The $875 million renovation took three years; it has the largest single security checkpoint in the US and an adjacent 1500-space parking lot.

JetBlue expanded service in 2009 to Bogota Colombia and the Caribbean islands of St. Maarten and Jamaica.

In 2010 JetBlue ink a limited partnership with AMR Corp.'s legacy airline American; the two are sharing activities in New York and Boston including customer "interline" service one-stop booking and check-in and bag transfers for connecting flights. The partnership gives the younger low-cost carrier eight pairs of the Texas-based carrier's take-off and landing slots at Ronald Reagan Washington National Airport and swells American Airlines' New York market with 12 pairs of JetBlue's slots at John F. Kennedy International Airport.

In early 2011 the airline signed an interline agreement with Virgin Atlantic that allows passengers to make connecting flights on transatlantic routes using a single itinerary and baggage check.

EXECUTIVES

Vice President, Jim Hnat
CFO, Mark D. Powers, age 61, $423,000 total compensation
EVP Corporate Affairs General Counsel and Secretary, James G. (Jim) Hnat, age 45, $423,000 total compensation
President and CEO, Robin Hayes, age 49, $490,000 total compensation
EVP Customer Experience, Joanna Geraghty
EVP Operations, Jeff Martin
CIO, Eash Sundaram
EVP People, Mike` Elliott
EVP Commercial and Planning, Marty St. George
Vice President Crew and Values Relations, Michael S (Mel) Elliott
National Account Manager, Emily Forsyth
Vp-communications, Nancy Elder
Senior Vice President Marketing, Martin (Marti) St George
Vice President Technical Operations, Tony Lowery
Vice President of Founders Investment Banking, Eugene Wilson
Vice President Network Planning, Scott D Laurence
Vice President Airports, Alex Battaglia
Vice President Government Affairs Assoc Gen Counsl, Robert C (Bob) Land
Vice President Of Sales, Marc Rabinowitz
Vice President Customer Support, Frankie Littleford
Vice President Safety, John (Jack) Allen
Vice Chairman, Frank V. Sica, age 64
Chairman, Joel C. Peterson, age 68
Senior Vice President Treasurer, James (Jamie) Leddy
Board Member, Bret Anthony
Board Of Directors, Sandhya Kumar
Auditors: Ernst & Young LLP

LOCATIONS

HQ: JetBlue Airways Corp
27-01 Queens Plaza North, Long Island City, NY 11101
Phone: 718 286-7900
Web: www.jetblue.com

2014 Sales

	$ mil.	% of total
Domestic	4,093	70
Caribbean & Puerto Rico	1,724	30
Total	**5,817**	**100**

PRODUCTS/OPERATIONS

2014 Sales

	$ mil.	% of total
Passenger	5,343	92
Other	474	8
Total	**5,817**	**100**

COMPETITORS

AirTran Airways	Southwest Airlines
Alaska Air	US Airways
American Airlines Group	United Continental
Delta Air Lines	Virgin America
Frontier Airlines	WestJet

HISTORICAL FINANCIALS

Company Type: Public

Income Statement

FYE: December 31

	REVENUE ($ mil.)	NET INCOME ($ mil.)	NET PROFIT MARGIN	EMPLOYEES
12/14	5,817	401	6.9%	15,334
12/13	5,441	168	3.1%	14,883
12/12	4,982	128	2.6%	14,347
12/11	4,504	86	1.9%	14,022
12/10	3,779	97	2.6%	12,948
Annual Growth	**11.4%**	**42.6%**	**—**	**4.3%**

2014 Year-End Financials

Debt ratio: 28.49%
Return on equity: 17.20%
Cash ($ mil.): 341
Current ratio: 0.62
Long-term debt ($ mil.): 1,968
No. of shares (mil.): 309
Dividends
  Yield: —
  Payout: —
Market value ($ mil.): 4,915

	STOCK PRICE ($) FY Close	P/E High/Low		PER SHARE ($) Earnings	Dividends	Book Value
12/14	15.86	12	6	1.19	0.00	8.16
12/13	8.54	15	10	0.52	0.00	7.22
12/12	5.72	14	9	0.40	0.00	6.72
12/11	5.20	23	11	0.28	0.00	6.24
12/10	6.61	21	13	0.31	0.00	5.61
Annual Growth	**24.5%**	**— —**		**40.0%**	**—**	**9.8%**

Johnson & Johnson

It's difficult to get well without Johnson & Johnson (J&J). The diversified health care giant operates in three segments through more than 265 operating companies located in some 60 countries. Its Medical Devices division offers surgical equipment monitoring devices orthopedic products and contact lenses among other things. J&J's Pharmaceuticals division makes drugs for an array of ailments such as neurological conditions blood disorders autoimmune diseases and pain. Top sellers are psoriasis drug Remicade and cancer medication Velcade. Its Consumer business makes over-the-counter drugs and products for baby skin and oral care as well as first-aid and nutritional uses.

HISTORY

Brothers James and Edward Mead Johnson founded their medical products company in 1885 in New Brunswick New Jersey. In 1886 Robert joined his brothers to make the antiseptic surgical dressings he developed. The company bought gauze maker Chicopee Manufacturing in 1916. In 1921 it introduced two of its classic products the Band-Aid and Johnson's Baby Cream.

Robert Jr. became chairman in 1932 and served until 1963. A WWII Army general he believed in decentralization; managers were given substantial freedom a principle still used today. Product lines in the 1940s included Ortho (birth control products) and Ethicon (sutures). In 1959 Johnson & Johnson bought McNeil Labs which launched Tylenol (acetaminophen) as an OTC drug the next year. Foreign acquisitions included Switzerland's Cilag-Chemie (1959) and Belgium's Janssen (1961). The company focused on consumer products in the 1970s gaining half the feminine protection market and making Tylenol the top-selling painkiller.

J&J bought Iolab a developer of intraocular lenses used in cataract surgery in 1980. Trouble struck in 1982 when someone laced Tylenol capsules with cyanide killing eight people. The company's response is now a damage-control classic: It immediately recalled 31 million bottles and totally redesigned its packaging to prevent future tampering. The move cost $240 million but saved the Tylenol brand. The next year prescription painkiller Zomax was linked to five deaths and was pulled.

New products in the 1980s included ACUVUE disposable contact lenses and Retin-A. The company bought LifeScan (blood-monitoring products for diabetics) in 1986. In 1989 it began a joint venture with Merck to sell Mylanta and other drugs bought from ICI Americas.

The firm continued its acquisition and diversification strategy in the 1990s. After introducing the first daily-wear disposable contact lenses in 1993 it bought skin-care product maker Neutrogena (1994) to enhance its consumer lines. To diversify its medical products and better compete for hospital business it bought Mitek Surgical Products (1995) and heart disease product maker Cordis (1996). The FDA cleared J&J's Renova wrinkle and fade cream in 1996. The company also began selling at-home HIV test Confide but pulled it the next year after low sales and other problems.

EXECUTIVES

Corporate Vice President Public Affairs and Corporate Communication, Raymond Jordan

VP Finance and CFO, Dominic J. Caruso, age 58, $878,115 total compensation

Worldwide Chairman Consumer Group, Jorge S. Mesquita, age 54

Group Worldwide Chairman Consumer Group of Companies Supply Chain and Information Technology, Sandra E. Peterson, age 57, $841,346 total compensation

Chairman and CEO, Alex Gorsky, age 55, $1,500,000 total compensation

Chief Scientific Officer and Worldwide Chairman Pharmaceuticals, Paul Stoffels, $1,075,423 total compensation

Worldwide Chairman Pharmaceuticals, Joaquin Duato

Worldwide Chairman Medical Devices, Gary Pruden

Chairman Johnson & Johnson China, Jesse J. Wu

Worldwide Vice President Human Resources, Peter (Pete) Fasolo

Vice President Human Resources, Kaye Foster-Cheek

Legal Secretary, Michelle (Mitch) Dmochowski

Vice President of Information Technology, Mike Haas

Vice President Franchise Medical Leader, Christopher (Chris) Nessel

Vice President Clinical Trials, Mark Travers

Vice President Global Corporate Affairs, Michael (Mel) Sneed

Vice President Device Development Team Leader Cordis, Terri Jollymour

Vice President of Human Resources, Teresa Vaughn

Vice President Finance, Will Stevens

Vice President, Bart Talloen

Vice President of Sales and Marketing, Kuldeep Pandit

Vice President Of Market Research, Lisa Gaynor

Vice President Pharmaceutical Development Diabetes and Obesity, Hamish Ross

Vice President Human Resources Janssen EMEA, Els Vandecandelaere

Vice President Infectious Diseases Global Medical Affairs, Alan (Al) Tennenberg

Vice President Of Operation, Kira Lajeunesse

Senior Vice President Of Marketing, Alexandre Andrade

Vice President Human Resources Strategy and Services, Laura Famular

Corporate Vice President Worldwide Government Affairs And Policy, Clifford Holland

Vice President Global Innovation, Steve Lamonte

Vice President Global Compensation, Donna Ng

Vice President, Joyce Hansen

Vice President Human Resources, Shawn Oconnor

Vice President North America for Global Marketing Group, Darryl Nicholson

Vice President, Bill Stevens

Vice President, Matt Devito

Vice President And General Manager Nor, Lisa Roy

National Account Manager, Jeff Fujioka

Vice President Worldwide Media, Kim Kadlec

Vice President Patent Law, Verne Kreger

Vice President, Gaetan Rouleau

Vice President Finance Asia Pacific Pharmaceutical Group, Jose Azevedo

Vice President Oncology Sci Innovation, Pamela Carroll

Vice President Baby Research And Development And Consumer Sciences, Tara Glasgow

Vice President Therapeutic Clinical Quality Assurance, Lisa Schmitt

Vice President Territory Sales, Michael (Mel) McIntyre

Pharmacist PharmD, Leena Jindia

Vice President, Laurence Halimi

Vice President Human Resources, Chris Harris

Vice President Human Resources, Stella Strazdas

Vice President Global Regulatory Affairs, Sandra Rattray

Vice President Leadership Development And Learning, Michael (Mel) Ehret

Vice President Research And Development Healthcare Compliance, Frank Konings

Vice President Information Technology, David Decker

Vice President Clinical Research, Daniel (Dan) Baker

Vice President Business Development, Michael Grissinger

Legal Secretary, Mary Farley

Vice President, Ed Kuffner

Legal Secretary, Theresa Kerekgyarto

Legal Secretary, Margaret Commisso

Vice President, Kendall Obrien

Vice President Operations, Jeffrey Jones

Pharmd, Karin Hoogendoorn

Vice President Reimbursement and Disability Association Relations, Gregg Howard

Vice President, Karen Manson

Worldwide Vice President Pharmaceutical Group, Heng Wong

Vice President Of Quality, John Trentacosti

Vice President Global Procurement, Anu Hans

Vice President Sales Operations, Lynn Owen

Vice President of Quality At Ees, Rick Sedlatschek

Vice President Finance, Wendy Smith

Vice President Manufacturing, Pierre Dionne

Vice President Global Medical Affairs, Craig Tendler

Vice President Of Risk Management, Wayne Klokis

Vice President Marketing, Bill Adams

Vice President Comm And Public Affairs Med Dev, Tom Sanford

Medical Director Neuroscience Therapeutic Area, Ella Daly

Vice President Human Resources, Sandra Heymann

Vice President Global Procurement, William Korbich

Vice President Communications and Public Affairs, Stefan Gijssels

Vice President Global Regional Affairs, Robin Keen

Vice President Global Engineering, Michael Maggio

Vice President Group Finance, Annie Lo

Medical Director, Przemyslaw Bochenski

Vice President Of Communications, Sheri Woodruff

Vice President Business Transformation, Angie Caswell

National Sales Manager, Antonio Morenilla

Vice President Global Oral Care Franchise, Michael (Mel) Marquis

Area Vice President Northeast, Travis Williams

Ww Vice President Research And Development McNeil Nutritionals, Tom Ells

Vice President, Dayao Zhao

Vice President Compliance Policy Management, Michael (Mel) Higgins

Regional Vice President, David Atkins

Vice President Of Global Health, Scott Ratzan

Vice President Marketing Cardio, Patricia (Pat) Torr

Vice President Sales And Marketing, Gloria Ramos

Secretaria Executiva Vice President, Rosemar Cholak

Vice President Global Head Of Lead Disco, Peter Tummino

Legal Secretary, Joy Johnson

Vice President Application Services Supply Chain, Stephen Sorensen

Vice President Prod Stewardship, Susan Nettesheim

Vice President Procurement Global Surger, Maureen Paredes

Vice President Global System Quality Assurance, Steve Berry

Vice President Of Information Systems, Erin Carney

Vice President Finance Leadership Development, Katherine (Kate) Fitzpatrick

Vice President Operations Global Surgery, Joe Nuzzolese

Vice President Global Oral Healthcare, Josh Ghaim

Vice President Global Finance Standardis, Leo Van Ginckel

Vice President, Stephen Manich

Vice President Disease Area Leader Mood, Wayne Drevets

Vice President Quality Assurance J And J Consumer Group Of Companies, Teresa Gorecki

Vice President Global Account Management, Jack Gelman

Vice President of Sales and Customer Development, Sue Wetzel

Vice President Human Resourci Global Bea, Helaine Catalano

Vice President Sales Mrktg Primary Care, Kathleen Chupa

Vice President Global Pharmaceutical Communications, Craig Rothenberg

Vice President Sterile Process Technolog, Rainer Newman

Vice President Senior Vice President Finance Director, Philip Campbell

Vice President Director Manager, Ken Solognier

Executive Vice President Global Marketing, Ann Rewey

Senior Vice President Pharmaceutical Compliance And Global Regulatory Affairs, Georgia Keresty

Vice President Strategic Business Support, James Rider

Vice President Development CHAMPION, Carol Harding

Vice President Biotherapeutics Discovery, William (Bill) Strohl

Vice President Medical AFF Chief CMPL, Tony Cutshall

Vice President Evidence Based Medicine, Farup Christina

Vice President Global Health Partnershps, Benedict Plumley

Vice President Discovery Regul and Medical Affairs, Mark Dreher

Vice President Biology and Early Development Drug Discovery, Tim Lovenberg

Vice President Medical Affairs, Anthony Temple

Vice President Specialty Skin Care, Margaret (Peg) Aleles

Vice President Geriatric Affairs Clinical Affairs Division, Thomas (Thom) Gibson

Vice President Sales and Marketing, Gary Fischetti

Worldwide Vice President Global Medical Affairs, Fiona Dunbar

Vice President IT Operations Center, Sanjay Mandloi

Vice President Information Technology Security and Networking, George Tarantino

Vice President Corporate Controller, Stephen (Steve) Cosgrove

Vice President Quality Assurance Regulatory Affairs, Carol Montandon

Vice President Human Resources, Tim Raher

Vice President World Wide manufacturing, Hans Van Hees

Vice President, Michelle (Mitch) Dejonge

Vice President Tibotec virco Research Early Development, Kenneth (Ken) Simmen

Senior Vice President Head Worldwide Hematology Oncology Research and Development, William (Bill) Hait

Vice President Business Development, Denise McGinn

Vice President of Specialty Pharmaceuticals, Partick Ciccone

Senior Vice President Head Global Clinical Operations, Luc TruyenMDPh

Vice President Logistics, Julie Smith-Harris

Vice President Health Plan Sales, Steven (Steve) White

Vice President Venture Investments, Kadir Kadhiresan

Vice President Finance, John (Jack) Mahony

Vice President Strategic Marketing and Access, Gisella Boarato

Auditors: PricewaterhouseCoopers LLP

LOCATIONS

HQ: Johnson & Johnson
One Johnson & Johnson Plaza, New Brunswick, NJ 08933
Phone: 732 524-0400   Fax: 732 214-0332
Web: www.jnj.com

2014 Sales

	$ mil.	% of total
US	34,782	47
Europe	18,947	25
Asia/Pacific & Africa	13,442	18
Western Hemisphere excluding US	7,160	10
Total	71,312	100

PRODUCTS/OPERATIONS

2014 Sales

	$ mil.	% of total
Pharmaceuticals	32,313	43
Medical Devices	27,522	37
Consumer	14,496	20
Total	74,331	100

Selected Products

Medical devices
  AcuVue contact lenses (Vistakon)
  Advanced sterilization products
  Animas insulin pump (LifeScan)
  DePuy Mitek sports medicine products
  DePuy Orthopaedics hip and knee replacement products
  DePuy Spine repair products
  Electrophysiology products (Biosense Webster)
  Ethicon women's health and urology
  Harmonic scalpel (plastic surgery)
  OneTouch blood glucose monitor (LifeScan)
  Vitros diagnostic instrumentation systems (Ortho-Clinical)
Pharmaceuticals
  Aciphex/Pariet (acid reflux)
  Concerta (ADHD)
  Duragesic/Fentanyl transdermal (pain management Durogesic outside the US)
  Edurant (HIV)

Intelence (HIV)
Invega (schizophrenia)
Invega Sustenna (injectable Invega)
Levaquin/Floxin (anti-infective)
Nucynta (pain)
Ortho Evra (patch contraceptive)
Ortho Tri-cyclen (oral contraceptive)
Prezista (HIV)
Procrit/Eprex (anemia Eprex outside the US)
Remicade (rheumatoid arthritis psoriasis and Crohn's disease)
Risperdal (schizophrenia and bipolar)
Risperdal Consta (injectable Risperdal)
Simponi (rheumatoid arthritis)
Stelara (psoriasis)
Topamax (epilepsy and migraines)
Velcade (multiple myeloma)
Xarelto (blood clots)
Zytiga (prostate cancer)
Consumer
  Aveeno skin care products
  Band-Aid bandages
  Benecol food products
  Clean & Clear skin care products
  Imodium A-D antidiarrheal
  Johnson's adult skin care products
  Johnson's baby care products
  Lactaid nutritional products
  Listerine mouthwash
  Motrin IB analgesic
  Mylanta gastrointestinal aid
  Neutrogena skin and hair care products
  Pepcid AC gastrointestinal aid (marketed with Merck)
  Reach toothbrushes
  Rembrandt toothpaste
  RoC skin care products
  Splenda non-caloric sugar substitute
  Sudafed cold flu and allergy medications
  Tylenol acetaminophen pain medicines
  Viactiv calcium supplements
  Zyrtec allergy products

COMPETITORS

3M Health Care	Genzyme
Abbott Labs	GlaxoSmithKline
Alcon	Kimberly-Clark Health
Allergan	L'Or©al USA
Allergan plc	Medtronic
Amgen	Mentholatum Company
ArthroCare	Merck
AstraZeneca	Mylan
B. Braun Melsungen	Novartis
Bard	NutraSweet
Bausch & Lomb	Perrigo
Baxter International	Pfizer
Bayer AG	Procter & Gamble
Beckman Coulter	Roche Holding
Becton Dickinson	Sanofi
Biogen	Shire
Boehringer Ingelheim	Smith & Nephew
Boston Scientific	St. Jude Medical
Bristol-Myers Squibb	Stryker
Chattem	Terumo
Colgate-Palmolive	Teva
Cook Incorporated	The Dial Corporation
Dr. Reddy's	UCB
Edwards Lifesciences	Unilever
Eli Lilly	Zimmer Biomet

HISTORICAL FINANCIALS

Company Type: Public

Income Statement

FYE: December 28

	REVENUE ($ mil.)	NET INCOME ($ mil.)	NET PROFIT MARGIN	EMPLOYEES
12/14	74,331	16,323	22.0%	126,500
12/13	71,312	13,831	19.4%	128,100
12/12*	67,224	10,853	16.1%	127,600
01/12	65,030	9,672	14.9%	117,900
01/11	61,587	13,334	21.7%	114,000
Annual Growth	4.8%	5.2%	—	2.6%

*Fiscal year change

2014 Year-End Financials

Debt ratio: 14.31%—
Return on equity: 22.76%
Cash ($ mil.): 14,523
Current ratio: 2.36
Long-term debt ($ mil.): 15,122

Dividends
Yield: 0.0%
Payout: 48.4%
Market value ($ mil.): —

	STOCK PRICE ($) FY Close	P/E High/Low		PER SHARE ($) Earnings	Dividends	Book Value
12/14	105.06	19	15	5.70	2.76	25.06
12/13	92.35	19	14	4.81	2.59	26.25
12/12*	69.48	18	16	3.86	2.40	23.33
01/12	65.58	19	16	3.49	2.25	20.95
01/11	61.85	14	12	4.78	2.11	20.66
Annual Growth	14.2%	—	—	4.5%	6.9%	4.9%

*Fiscal year change

Johnson Controls Inc

Johnson Controls (JCI) wants to put you in the driver's seat —an environmentally conscious one. The company makes car batteries and interior parts for combustion engine and hybrid electric vehicles as well as energy-efficient HVAC systems for commercial buildings. Products include seating instrument panels and a slew of electronics. OEM customers include GM Daimler and Ford. The battery unit supplies car batteries for retailers such as Advance Auto Parts AutoZone Pep Boys and Wal-Mart. The building efficiency unit makes installs and services mechanical equipment that controls HVAC lighting security and fire systems in commercial buildings. The unit also offers on-site facility management.

Geographic Reach

JCI operates through more than 1300 locations worldwide. Nearly 45% of its total sales come from the US; other major markets include Germany (9%) and other countries in Europe (20%).

Operations

JCI operates through 230 wholly- and majority-owned manufacturing or assembly plants. Its building efficiency business segment designs control systems and mechanical equipment as well as services non-residential properties in about 52 countries. About half of this segment's sales are derived from HVAC products and control systems for construction and retrofit markets and the other half from services. Branded products include the Metasys control system and York chillers. This segment is looking to such emerging markets as China and the Middle East for strong sales.

The company's power solutions business claims it is the largest lead-acid automotive battery producer in the world. JCI holds an edge over other battery companies as it is not locked into an alliance with any specific automaker allowing it to play the field. Its 60 manufacturing and assembly facilities are located in about 22 countries and produce lead-acid batteries as well as AGM (absorbent glass mat) battery technology and lithium-ion batteries used in hybrid vehicles. About 75% of the company's batteries are sold in the automotive replacement sector with the rest going to OEMs. Power solutions is ready to benefit from vertical integration for lead recycling and a shift in its product mix to AGM technology.

Automotive experience designs and manufactures interior products and systems for passenger cars and light trucks including vans pick-up trucks and sport/crossover utility vehicles. The business produces automotive interior systems for OEMs and operates approximately 230 wholly- and majority-owned manufacturing or assembly plants with operations in 32 countries worldwide.

Sales and Marketing

JCI's main customers include the biggest names in the industry: Ford Daimler Fiat Chrysler Toyota and GM.

Financial Performance

After enjoying four straight years of revenue growth JCI posted a 13% drop in net sales from 2014 to 2015. The revenue decline for 2015 was triggered by a 9% decline in automotive experience sales (from seating and interiors products) coupled with a 30% decline from sales in Europe.

Profits surged by 29% during that same period from $1.22 billion to $1.56 billion primarily due to additional revenue from discounted operations and decreased cost of sales. JCI's operating cash flow has decreased the last two years dropping by $795 million from 2015 to 2014 primarily due to changes in receivables and accounts payables and accrued liabilities.

Strategy

JCI is looking to streamline its business by selling and spinning off non-core operations. In late 2015 it completed the sale of its Global Workplace Solutions (GWS) business to CBRE Group for $1.5 billion. GWS is a worldwide provider of facilities management services.

In addition the company has announced a potential spin-off for its automotive experience segment.

Mergers and AcquisitionsThe company often grows its product portfolio through the use of acquisitions. In a sweeping move for the home-products industry in early 2016 JCI announced it was acquiring Tyco International for $16.5 billion. The combined company will boast revenues of up to $32 billion. Once the deal goes through JCI plans to move its global headquarters to Tyco's main office in Cork Ireland in order to lower its tax bill.

In 2014 JCI acquired Air Distribution Technologies (ADT) one of the largest independent providers of air distribution and ventilation products in North America for approximately $1.6 billion. ADT produces a broad range of air distribution products under well-known brands such as Ruskin Titus Hart & Cooley Krueger PennBarry Tuttle & Bailey and many others.

HISTORY

Professor Warren Johnson developed the electric telethermoscope in 1880 so that janitors at Whitewater Wisconsin's State Normal School could regulate room temperatures without disturbing classrooms. His device the thermostat used mercury to move a heat element that opened and shut a circuit. Milwaukee hotelier William Plankinton believed in the invention and invested $150000 to start production.

The two men formed Johnson Electric Service Company in 1885. They sold the marketing installation and service rights to concentrate on manufacturing. Johnson also invented other devices such as tower clocks and he experimented with the telegraph before becoming intrigued with the automobile and beginning production of steam-powered cars. He won the US Postal Service's first automotive contract but never gained support within his own company. Johnson continued to look elsewhere for financing until his death in 1911.

The renamed Johnson Services regained full rights to its thermostats in 1912 and sold its other businesses. During the Depression it produced economy systems that regulated building temperatures. Johnson Services became a public company in 1940. During WWII it aided the war effort building weather-data gatherers and radar test sets.

In the 1960s Johnson Services began developing centralized control systems for temperature fire alarm lighting and security regulation. The company was renamed Johnson Controls in 1974.

EXECUTIVES

EVP and Chief Human Resources Officer, Susan F. Davis, age 62

Vice President Corporate Communication, Jacqueline Strayer

VP Vice Chairman Asia Pacific and President Automotive Experience, Beda-Helmut Bolzenius, age 59, $855,000 total compensation

Vice Chairman and EVP, R. Bruce McDonald, age 55, $881,000 total compensation

VP; VP and General Manager North America Systems and the Middle East Controls Group, Alex A. Molinaroli, age 56, $1,400,000 total compensation

EVP and CFO, Brian J. Stief, age 59, $536,000 total compensation

VP and Chief Procurement Officer, Michael Bartschat

VP and CIO, Jeffrey (Jeff) Augustin

Vice President President Controls Group, Brian J Stark

Vice President Wholesale Distribution, Dan Autey

Vice President, Mark Flynn

Vice President Information Technology, Lenny Joseph

Vice President Human Resources, Janice Stein

Vice President Of Equipment Technology, Michael R (Mel) Anderson

Vice President General Manager GWS Advanced Solutions, Tom Bourke

Vice President Human Resource, Mike Pollos

Vice President General Manager, Jim Rist

Vice President, Eric Scaff

Vice President, Bob Ellis

Vice President of Sales and Marketing, Mark Katz

Executive Vice President Gc And Secretary; Group Counsel, Michael (Mel) Hanson

Vice President and GC Systems and Service Emea, David (Dave) Kirtley

General Vice President Manager, Armando Martinez

Vice President Human Resources, Kimberly Reed

Vice President Procurement Powers Solutions, Joseph (Jo) Maalouf

Vice President And General Manager Aftermarket Parts North America, Elizabeth (Beth) Haggerty

Vice President HVAC Operations Systems North America, Corrie Prunuske

Vice President Operations Power Solutions Emea, Jose Domingo

Vice President and General Manager US and Canada, Kevin Pasqua

Vice President Global, Clayton Nesler

Regional Corporate Treasurer Latam, Marcio Righetti

Auditors: PricewaterhouseCoopers LLP

LOCATIONS

HQ: Johnson Controls Inc
5757 North Green Bay Avenue, Milwaukee, WI 53209
Phone: 414 524-1200
Web: www.johnsoncontrols.com

2015 Sales

	$ mil.	% of total
US	16,841	45
Europe		
Germany	3,375	9
Other European countries	7,320	20
Mexico	1,933	5
Rest of the world	7,710	21
Total	**37,179**	**100**

PRODUCTS/OPERATIONS

2015 Sales

	$ mil.	% of total
Automotive experience	20,079	54
Building efficiency	10,510	28
Power solutions	6,590	18
Total	**37,179**	**100**

Selected Products

Automotive experience
  Electronics
  Body electronics
  Driver information
  HomeLink (wireless car-to-home connectivity)
  Infotainment and connectivity
  Interiors
  Cockpits and instrument panels
  Door panels
  Floor consoles
  Overhead products
  Seating
  Climate seat systems
  Foam
  Metal structures and mechanisms
  Seat safety
  Trim
Building efficiency
  Building management systems
  Fire safety products
  HVAC systems
  Refrigeration
  Security products
  Snowmaking equipment
  York equipment
Power solutions
  Absorbent glass mat technology
  Lead-acid batteries
  Lithium-ion batteries

COMPETITORS

3M	Goodyear Tire & Rubber
A123 Systems	Honeywell
Addison	International
Alcoa	Illinois Tool Works
Caterpillar	Inci Ak□
Comfort Systems USA	International Paper
DENSO	Lear Corp
Deere	Lennox
Delphi Automotive	Lockheed Martin
Systems	Magna International
Dow Chemical	Northrop Grumman
DuPont	Paloma Group
Eagle-Picher	Raytheon
East Penn	Rieter Automotive
Manufacturing	North America
Eaton	Robert Bosch
Emerson Electric	SPX
Exide	Trane Inc.
Faurecia	United Technologies
GS Yuasa	Valeo
General Dynamics	Visteon
General Motors	Whirlpool
Goodman Global	Yazaki North America

HISTORICAL FINANCIALS

Company Type: Public

Income Statement

FYE: September 30

	REVENUE ($ mil.)	NET INCOME ($ mil.)	NET PROFIT MARGIN	EMPLOYEES
09/15	37,179	1,563	4.2%	139,000
09/14	42,828	1,215	2.8%	168,000
09/13	42,730	1,178	2.8%	170,000
09/12	41,955	1,226	2.9%	170,000
09/11	40,833	1,624	4.0%	162,000
Annual Growth	(2.3%)	(1.0%)	—	(3.8%)

2015 Year-End Financials

Debt ratio: 22.28%
Return on equity: 14.41%
Cash ($ mil.): 597
Current ratio: 1.06
Long-term debt ($ mil.): 5,745

No. of shares (mil.): 647
Dividends
Yield: 2.5%
Payout: 45.4%
Market value ($ mil.): 26,775

	STOCK PRICE ($) FY Close	P/E High/Low	PER SHARE ($) Earnings	Dividends	Book Value
09/15	41.36	22 16	2.36	1.04	16.03
09/14	44.00	29 22	1.80	0.88	17.00
09/13	41.50	25 15	1.71	0.76	17.99
09/12	27.40	20 13	1.78	0.72	16.94
09/11	26.37	18 11	2.36	0.64	16.23
Annual Growth	11.9%	— —	(0.0%)	12.9%	(0.3%)

Jones Lang LaSalle Inc

Jones Lang LaSalle (JLL) provides real estate without borders. Its services include commercial leasing real estate brokerage management advisory and financing through more than 230 corporate offices in more than 80 countries. It focuses on three main geographic areas: the Americas; Europe Middle East and Africa (EMEA); and Asia Pacific. The company's LaSalle Investment Management arm is a diversified real estate management firm with about $50 billion in assets under management. Jones Lang LaSalle has commercial real estate expertise across office retail hotel health care industrial cultural and multifamily residential properties. It manages approximately 3.5 billion sq. ft. worldwide.

HISTORY

Company BackgroundJones Lang Wootton had roots in London's Paternoster Row auction houses in 1783. LaSalle Partners originally known as IDC Real Estate was founded in El Paso Texas in 1968. The two companies could not have started out in a more disparate fashion yet their combined force is now one of the largest real estate services firms in the world.

Richard Winstanley opened an auction house in 1783 and his son James joined him in that business in 1806. In 1840 the Joneses entered the picture —the Winstanleys created a partnership with one James Jones. The business moved to King Street (in the Guildhall section of London) in 1860 and remained in that location for some 100 years in various incarnations —James' son Frederick took over the business renaming it Frederick Jones and Co. When James retired in 1872 the firm was again renamed to Jones Lang and Co. and was controlled by C. A. Lang. Jones Lang merged with Wootton and Son in 1939 becoming Jones Lang Wootton and Sons.

Jones Lang Wootton was active in redrawing the property lines in London after the Blitz. In 1945 the firm began contacting small landowners and by combining small parcels of land secured development leasing and/or purchase contracts. When the rebuilding of London began in 1954 Jones Lang Wootton was in a secure place to be right at the forefront of that new development. The firm began engaging in speculative development in the West End and in the City of London.

The year 1958 saw the expansion of Jones Lang Wootton into Australia; the firm had offices throughout the Asia/Pacific region by 1968. Further expansion took place closer to home in Scot-

land (1962) and Ireland (1965) and the first continental European office in Brussels (also 1965). The firm moved into the Manhattan market in 1975.

On the other side of the story IDC Real Estate (the name change to LaSalle Partners came in 1977) was a group of partnerships initially focused on investment banking investment management and land. The firm began offering development management services in 1975; it moved into property management leasing and tenant representation in 1978 and facility management operations in 1980.

It built market share by buying other firms including Kleinwort Benson Realty Advisors Corp. (1994) and UK-based investment adviser CIN Property Management (1996).

The firm leveraged its experience and long-term client base to pursue an acquisition strategy taking advantage of trends shaping commercial real estate —globalization consolidation and merchant banking. LaSalle went public in 1997 amalgamating the Galbreath Company (a property and development management firm with which it merged that year) with its other partnerships and becoming a corporation.

In 1998 it acquired the project management business of Satulah Group and two retail management business units from Lend Lease and took real estate investment trust LaSalle Hotel Properties public. In 1999 the firm strengthened its world position by merging with Jones Lang Wootton; the company was renamed Jones Lang LaSalle.

The merger with Jones Lang Wootton combined Wootton's strength in Asia and Europe with LaSalle Partners' large presence in North America to create a worldwide real estate services firm. In 2006 the company acquired Spaulding & Slye strengthening operations in the Mid-Atlantic and New England. Also that year it opened an office in Dubai and acquired RSP Group which operates in North Africa and the Middle East. In 2007 Jones Lang LaSalle bought German property advisory firm Kemper's Holding and took a stake in the former Trammell Crow Meghraj one of the largest private real estate companies in India.

The company broadened its presence in key North American markets when it acquired The Staubach Company in 2008. Jones Lang LaSalle paid $613 million for the rival real estate services firm which was founded by football legend and former Dallas Cowboys quarterback Roger Staubach.

Jones Lang LaSalle slowed its acquisition pace during the economic recession. But managed to cut a few deals. In 2009 Jones Lang LaSalle teamed up with Real Estate Disposition to begin offering online auction sales a product to help customers quickly sell commercial property and other distressed assets.

In another deal Jones Lang LaSalle acquired the third-party leasing and management duties of General Growth Properties in 2010 as part of the mall owner's restructuring efforts. The deal added about 20 shopping centers to Jones Lang LaSalle's management portfolio.

EXECUTIVES

Vice President Information Technology, Susan Nuccio
Executive Vice President, David (Dave) Hendrickson
Vice President, Jeffery Miller
President CEO and Director, Colin Dyer, age 62, $750,000 total compensation
Chairman Global Retail Leasing Board, C. David Zoba, age 63
CEO Americas, Gregory P. (Greg) O'Brien, age 52, $350,000 total compensation
CEO LaSalle Investment Management, Jeff A. Jacobson, age 53, $350,000 total compensation

CEO Asia Pacific, Alastair Hughes, age 49, $408,462 total compensation
EVP and Global CIO, David A. Johnson, age 52
CEO Europe Middle East and Africa, Christian Ulbrich, age 49, $316,202 total compensation
CFO, Christie B. Kelly, age 53, $400,000 total compensation
EVP Corporate Solutions Marketing, Heather MacLeod
Chairman and Country Head India, Anuj Puri, age 48
CEO Southern Europe and Maghreb, Benoit du Passage
Managing Director France, Charles Boudet
President Retail Brokerage JLL Americas, Naveen Jaggi
Vice Chairman JLL NewYork Brokerage, Patrick Smith
Vice President, Diane Roberts
Senior Vice President, James Wenk
Vice President, John (Jack) Walters
Vice President Finance, Bill Grice
Executive Vice President, Patsy Capbarat
Vice President, Aaron Ellison
Senior Vice President, Bob Gross
Senior Vice President Information Technology, David (Dave) Laduke
Senior Vice President Project And Development Services, Tim Gilmour
Vice President, Mike Zimmerman
Vice President Research, Lauren Picariello
Vice President Information Systems, Darryl Asack
Executive Vice President, Christoph Rle
Executive Vice President, Philip Lipper
Senior Vice President, Jake Lancaster
Vice President, Ray White
Senior Vice President New York, George Ladyman
Senior Vice President, Gary McCabe
Senior Vice President Of Engineering, Miles Anderson
Assistant Vice President Business Development; Markets, Sudha Prabhu
Senior Vice President, Mike Chionchio
Senior Vice President, Doug Mueller
Executive Vice President, Eric Kunkel
Senior Vice President Dire, Sally Hertz
Executive Vice President Capital Markets Group, Jason Schmidt
Executive Vice President Investment Sales, Mark Durran
Senior Vice President Investment Sales, Nihat Ercan
Vice President, Christine Tong
Vice President Global Client Applications Senior Business Analyst, Craig Parrish
Vice President, Rick Benoy
Assistant Vice President, Clayton Kline
Assistant Vice President, Jon Compitello
Vice President, Anne Huffington
Vice President Information Technology, Howard Kramer
Vice President Tenant Representation, Ned Tarbox
Vice President Industrial And Logistics Division, Wick Udy
Vice President, Jeannette Davis
Executive Vice President, Sior Stout
Executive Vice President Jones Lang Lasalle Americas, Matt Perrigue
Executive Vice President, Dennis McConnell
Vice President Marketing, Carol O'Grady
Vice President, Dean Brody
Vice President, Brian Means
Vice President, Dave Goldstein
Senior Vice President, George Gemelos
Executive Vice President, Ellen Herman
Vice President, Eric Vayle
Executive Vice President, David Matthews
Executive Vice President, Tom Turley
Senior Vice President, Ned Roberts
Vice President, Nick Wigoda

Senior Vice President, Peter Richardson
Senior Vice President Healthcare, Allison Maher
Vice President, Jeremiah Riordan
Senior Vice President, Guy Ponticiello
Vice President, Michael Sharapata
Vice President Compensation, Ryan Devlin
Executive Vice President, Wade Clark
Senior Vice President, Scott Vinett
Senior Vice President Brokerage, Julie Steffen
Senior Vice President, John Perkins
Senior Vice President Human Resources, Darline Scelzo
Vice President, John Ream
Senior Vice President, Mauricio Lozano
Vice President Public Relations, Paige Steers
Senior Vice President Strategic Consulting, James (Jamie) Rice
Executive Vice President, Daryl Mullin
Vice President, Kevin Kelley
Executive Vice President Industrial, Robert Kossar
Senior Vice President, Jon Vidaurri
Vice President, James Stockdale
Executive Vice President, George Kotrogiannis
Senior Vice President, Christopher J (Chris) Coccaro
Vice President Retail Leasing, Charlie Owens
Vice President Project and Development Services JLL, Kelly Kilboy
Vice President, Douglas Gottschalk
Executive Vice President, Dan Jessup
Vice President, Peter Beugg
Vice President, Mike Parlato
Senior Vice President, Robert Dmytryk
Senior Vice President, Brendan Callahan
Senior Vice President, Holly H Jones
Vice President, Sylvia Rojas
Executive Vice President, Jeff Adkison
Vice President Finance, Greg Sheehan
Senior Vice President, Marti Nemer
Vice President, Kenyattah Robinson
Senior Vice President, Brian Gorz
Vice President, Ryan Matthews
Executive Vice President, Shawn McDonald
Vice President Strategic Sourcing West Region, Tim Hamill
Vice President, Paul Ratkovic
Vice President, Kevin Morrison
Vice President And General Manager, Jennifer (Jen) Christakes
Vice President, Paul Schuler
Executive Vice President, Randall Wood
Senior Vice President, Bruce Kimbrew
Vice President, Rodney (Rod) Davidson
Vice President, Karen Eltz
Vice President, Gregg Christoffersen
Vice President, Mark Georgas
Senior Vice President, Mike Brown
Vice President, Brad Crosley
Senior Vice President, Erik C Charton
Vice President, Michael Carpenter
Vice President Regional Manager., Mary Stanton
Vice President Retail, Mike Horner
Senior Vice President Hotels, John L (Jack) Strauss
Executive Vice President And National Leader, Nick Joosten
Vice President, Michele Barkinge
Vice President, Erik Vonegger
Senior Vice President, Jorg Mast
Senior Vice President, Mark Collins
Vice President, Andy Koenig
Vice President, Chester Ellis
Vice President Of Investment Sales, Steven Echelson
Vice President, Carolina Lacerda
Vice President, Ben Bischmann
Senior Vice President, Jodi Prentice
Senior Vice President, Tom Fox
Vice President Industrial, Scott Duerkop
Vice President Business Develo, Jim Sadler
Senior Vice President, Brent Styles

Vice President Industrial And Logistics Division, Andy Wheeler
Vice President, Clare Berrang
Vice President, Zach Anderson
Vice President, Matt Kiehne
Vice President Engineering Regional Manager, Russell (Russ) Binggeli
Vice President, Gil Canton
Vice President, David Otis
Senior Vice President, Brian Tisbert
Vice President, Matt Nowaczyk
Senior Vice President, Travis D'Amato
Vice President, Anneke Greco
Auditors: KPMG LLP

LOCATIONS

HQ: Jones Lang LaSalle Inc
200 East Randolph Drive, Chicago, IL 60601
Phone: 312 782-5800   Fax: 312 782-4339
Web: www.jll.com

2014 Sales by Segment

	% of total
Americas	43
Europe Middle East Africa	30
Asia Pacific	20
Investment management	7
Total	**100**

PRODUCTS/OPERATIONS

2014 Sales

	% of total
Real Estate Services	
Leasing	28
Property and facility management	20
Capital Markets and hotels	15
Advisory consulting and other	9
Project and development services	8
LaSalle Investment Management	7
Gross contract costs	13
Total	**100**

Selected Services

Investor services
  Agency leasing
  Property management
  Valuations and consulting
Occupier services
  Facilities management
  Project and development services
  Tenant representation
Construction management
Capital markets
Energy and sustainability services
Hotel advisory
Money management
Strategic consulting

COMPETITORS

BGC Partners	Inland Group
CBRE Group	Lend Lease
Colliers International	Newmark Knight Frank
Cushman & Wakefield	Savills Studley
Hines	Shorenstein

HISTORICAL FINANCIALS

Company Type: Public

Income Statement

FYE: December 31

	REVENUE ($ mil.)	NET INCOME ($ mil.)	NET PROFIT MARGIN	EMPLOYEES
12/14	5,429	386	7.1%	58,100
12/13	4,461	269	6.0%	52,700
12/12	3,932	208	5.3%	48,000
12/11	3,584	164	4.6%	45,500
12/10	2,925	153	5.3%	40,300
Annual Growth	**16.7%**	**25.9%**	**—**	**9.6%**

2014 Year-End Financials

Debt ratio: 7.45%
Return on equity: 16.91%
Cash ($ mil.): 250
Current ratio: 1.03
Long-term debt ($ mil.): 275

No. of shares (mil.): 44
Dividends
  Yield: 0.3%
  Payout: 6.4%
Market value ($ mil.): 6,721

	STOCK PRICE ($) FY Close	P/E High/Low	PER SHARE ($) Earnings	PER SHARE ($) Dividends	PER SHARE ($) Book Value
12/14	149.93	18 12	8.52	0.48	53.24
12/13	102.39	17 13	5.98	0.44	49.04
12/12	83.94	18 13	4.63	0.40	44.29
12/11	61.26	28 12	3.70	0.30	38.90
12/10	83.92	24 16	3.48	0.20	36.78
Annual Growth	**15.6%**	**— —**	**25.1%**	**24.5%**	**9.7%**

JPMorgan Chase & Co

Boasting some $2.6 trillion in assets JPMorgan Chase is the largest bank holding company in the US. With more than 5600 branches in about two dozen states (and counting) it is also among the nation's top mortgage lenders and credit card issuers (it holds some $131 billion in credit card loans). Active in 60 countries the bank also boasts formidable investment banking and asset management operations through its prestigious JPMorgan Private Bank and institutional investment manager JPMorgan Asset Management (with $2.4 trillion in assets under supervision) subsidiaries respectively.

HISTORY

JPMorgan Chase & Co.'s roots are in The Manhattan Company created in 1799 to bring water to New York City. A provision buried in its incorporation documents let the company provide banking services; investor and future US Vice President Aaron Burr brought the company (eventually the Bank of Manhattan) into competition with The Bank of New York founded by Burr's political rival Alexander Hamilton. JPMorgan Chase still owns the pistols from the notorious 1804 duel in which Burr mortally wounded Hamilton.

In 1877 John Thompson formed Chase National naming it for Salmon Chase Abraham Lincoln's secretary of the treasury and the architect of the national bank system. Chase National merged with John D. Rockefeller's Equitable Trust in 1930 becoming the world's largest bank and beginning a long relationship with the Rockefellers. Chase National continued growing after WWII and in 1955 it merged with the Bank of Manhattan. Christened Chase Manhattan the bank remained the US's largest into the 1960s.

When soaring 1970s oil prices made energy loans attractive Chase invested in Penn Square an obscure oil-patch bank in Oklahoma and the first notable bank failure of the 1980s. (The legal aftereffects of Penn Square's 1982 failure dragged on until 1993.) Losses following the 1987 foreign loan crisis hit Chase hard as did the real estate crash. In 1995 the bank went looking for a partner. After talks with Bank of America it settled on Chemical Bank.

Chemical Bank opened in 1824 and was one of the US's largest banks by 1900. As with Chase Chemical Bank began as an unrelated business (New York Chemical Manufacturing) in 1823 largely in order to open a bank (it dropped its chemical operations in 1844). Chemical would merge with Manufacturers Hanover in 1991.

After its 1996 merger with Chase Chemical Bank was the surviving entity but assumed Chase's more prestigious name. Initial cost savings from the merger were substantial as jobs and branch offices were eliminated. In 1997 Chase acquired the credit business of The Bank of New York and the corporate trustee business of Mellon Financial but underwent another round of belt-tightening the next year when it took a $320 million charge and cut 4500 jobs. The bank also suffered losses related to its involvement with the ill-starred Long-Term Capital Management hedge fund.

In 1999 Chase focused on lending buying two mortgage originators and forming a marketing alliance with subprime auto lender AmeriCredit (now General Motors Financial Company). Chase also bought Mellon Financial's residential mortgage unit and Huntington Bancshares' credit card portfolio. It bought UK investment bank Robert Fleming Holdings in 2000.

In 2001 it closed its $30 billion buy of J.P. Morgan and renamed itself JPMorgan Chase & Co. The new firm eliminated some 10% of its combined workforce as a result of the merger. Chairman Sandy Warner (who ran J.P. Morgan) retired at year-end and was replaced by former Chase Manhattan leader CEO William Harrison.

JPMorgan Chase had more than $1 billion in exposure to Enron but in 2003 recovered some $600 million after a court battle with the failed energy trader's insurers which claimed the losses stemmed from loans by JPMorgan Chase disguised as oil and gas transactions. Nonetheless JPMorgan Chase ended up paying some $135 million to settle actions relating to the questionable loans.

In 2004 JPMorgan Chase joined forces with venerable investment bank Cazenove; the joint venture called JPMorgan Cazenove handles corporate finance and capital markets activities in the UK.

The next year JPMorgan Chase and its investment banking arm J.P. Morgan Securities avoided a trial by paying some $2 billion to settle claims from investors who lost money on bonds that the firm underwrote in 2000 and 2001 for scandal-ridden WorldCom which eventually declared bankruptcy (WorldCom became MCI and later was acquired by Verizon Communications).

On the heels of the its massive BANK ONE buy in 2004 JPMorgan Chase made several smaller purchases including global trade management and logistics software maker Vastera (renamed JPMorgan Chase Vastera) trading technology firm Neovest and the credit card business of Sears Canada. JPMorgan Chase also sold online brokerage subsidiary J.P. Morgan Invest and its BrownCo unit to E*TRADE. The following year the company acquired student lender Collegiate Funding Services which JPMorgan Chase combined with its existing Chase Education Finance division. The company also got the go-ahead from the FTC and bought Kohl's $1.6 billion credit card portfolio.

Enron continued to haunt the company: in 2005 it forked over $2.2 billion to settle part of an investor class-action suit over fraud charges related to the Enron debacle and paid another $350 million to the infamous energy trading firm which asserted that JPMorgan Chase and about 10 other banks aided and abetted the company's collapse. However the next year the company got some good news regarding its alleged involvement with the collapse of Enron when the class action suit against it was dismissed.

Also in 2006 the company cut ties with private equity investment arm J.P. Morgan Partners which divided into two companies CCMP Capital and Panorama Capital. JPMorgan Chase retained the former private equity operations of BANK ONE One Equity Partners.

In keeping with the lesson learned regarding its $2 billion fine to settle claims in the WorldCom debacle in 2006 the bank was quick to settle its part of another class-action lawsuit this time brought by investors claiming they were cheated in the dotcom IPO boom. JPMorgan Chase paid $425 million to settle that case. It paid a much smaller settlement of $3.8 million for its part in the demise of the ill-fated telecom Global Crossing.

All was not lawsuits and settlements in 2006 however: that year it swapped its corporate trust business for Bank of New York's nearly 340-branch network in the New York metropolitan area. Both units were valued at about $2 billion with JPMorgan Chase paying Bank of New York around $150 million more to make up the difference.

William Harrison retired as chairman at the end of 2006; he was succeeded by president and CEO (and the CEO of BANK ONE when it was acquired) Jamie Dimon.

As one of the largest mortgage and home equity providers in the country JPMorgan Chase was hurt by the subprime mortgage crisis and subsequent fall in home values in 2007. About a third of its loans were home equity loans and it had to write off more than $500 million in home equity loans that year.

In 2008 the bank assumed full ownership of payments processor Chase Paymentech Solutions which had been a joint venture with First Data. First Data assumed 49% of Chase Paymentech's assets and clients in the deal.

Also that year as part of a plan to stimulate the economy the US government invested in JPMorgan Chase and other banks. The bank got $25 billion of the $700 billion taxpayer-funded bailout package that was approved in late 2008 with the stipulation that the banks use the money and not hoard it. The investment came with restrictions on executive pay and other rules and JPMorgan returned the money the following year saying it was doing just fine without it.

Led by CEO Jamie Dimon JPMorgan Chase closed a couple of very high profile deals as the economic crisis claimed numerous victims. It acquired Bear Stearns one of Wall Street's top investment banks and the operations of Washington Mutual (WaMu) the largest bank to fail in US history. Both deals closed in 2008.

Initially JPMorgan Chase made a bargain-basement offer of $270 million (around $2 a share) for the struggling Bear Stearns which was drowning in subprime mortgage investment debt. It ultimately raised its offer to around $10 a share or some $1.2 billion. The deal came after the Fed extended a $30 billion lifeline to Bear Stearns to keep the firm afloat; JPMorgan Chase was one of the lenders.

The company also stepped in to buy WaMu when that bank failed and was seized by regulators. It paid $1.9 billion for the bank's operations and assumed some $31 billion in losses. JPMorgan began integrating WaMu's branches with its own retail network phasing out the WaMu brand and closing about 10% of the combined branches (especially in markets where there was overlap). Shortly after the acquisition JPMorgan cut 9200 WaMu jobs –about 20% of its workforce.

In 2009 JPMorgan Chase sold specialist firm Bear Wagner acquired in the Bear Stearns deal to Barclays Capital.

JPMorgan Chase agreed to pay more than $153 million to the Securities and Exchange Commission in order to settle a claim that it misled investors during the 2007 housing market crash. The company was among others that were investigated for improper sales practices.

In 2010 JPMorgan acquired the European and Asian segments of RBS Sempra Commodities the

energy trading joint venture between Royal Bank of Scotland and Sempra Energy. The $1.6 billion deal did not include RBS Sempra's more valuable North American segment. JPMorgan integrated the business into the bank's existing global commodities business doubling its corporate client numbers.

Also in 2010 the company bought the private equity administration services of Schroders. That deal added more than $6 billion in committed capital. J.P. Morgan Worldwide Securities Services already had some $15.3 trillion in assets under custody. In 2011 the company sold its 41% stake in mutual fund company American Century to CIBC for some $848 million.

EXECUTIVES

Vice President of Facilities Vip, Gerard Vanella

Chairman JPMorgan Securities plc, Winfried F. W. (Win) Bischoff, age 74

Vice President, Brian Coats

Vice President Information Technology Architecture, Douglas (Doug) Schwarz

Vice President, John Bradley

Senior Vice President, Steven (Steve) Smith

Chairman and CEO, James (Jamie) Dimon, age 59, $1,500,000 total compensation

CEO Consumer and Community Banking, Gordon A. Smith, age 56, $500,000 total compensation

CIO, Dana S. Deasy, age 54

CEO Corporate and Investment Bank, Daniel E. Pinto, age 52, $7,415,796 total compensation

COO, Matthew E. Zames, age 44, $750,000 total compensation

Global Chairman Financial Institutions Group (FIG), Therese Esperdy

Chairman Mergers and Acquisitions, Kurt Simon

CEO Commercial Banking and Executive Committee Member, Douglas B. (Doug) Petno, age 49

CEO Asset Management, Mary Callahan Erdoes, age 47, $750,000 total compensation

CFO, Marianne Lake, age 45, $750,000 total compensation

Chairman Europe the Middle East and Africa, Vittorio Grilli

President JPMorgan Chase Bank (China) Company, Brett Krause

Chief Risk Officer, Ashley Bacon, age 45

CEO Business Banking Consumer and Community Banking, Jennifer Piepszak

Chairman Banking Japan, Katsuyuki Kuki

Head of Investment Banking Japan, Masataka Yamada

Chief Investment Officer and Treasurer, John Horner

Head of Investor Services, James Kenny

Head of Macro Trading, Troy Rohrbaugh

Vice Chairman Investment Banking, Lauren Camp

Vice President, Josephine Norris

First Vice President District Manager, Sean Cummings

Vice President Information Technology, Sunil Gosain

Vice President Technology RMMFS, Daniel (Dan) Lynch

Vice President Director Of Information Technology Treasury And Securities Services, Karen Santelli

Vice President Technology Program Director, Mark Koban

Vice President Of Network, Gerard Trollo

Vice President Information Security Officer, Todd Bailey

Vice President Human Resources, Jim Odonnell

Vice President Of Information Technology, Paul Rosenberg

Vice President Of It, Alex Kayzerman

Senior Vice President MD, Jonathan (Jon) Teplitz

Vice President Middle Market Market Manager Long Island, Anthony Abbate

Vice President Assistant General Counsel, Catherine (Cathy) Hasenzahl

Vice President Marketing And Public Relations, John Johmann

Vice President, Michael Green

Vice President Of Technology, Tracey Ball

Vice President Market Risk Technology, Kevin Ford

Vice President, Jason Klein

Vice President Of Public Finance, David Elmquist

Vice President Controller, Jeptha Gibbs

Senior Vice President Middle Market Banking, Jim Nicholas

Vice President Of Information Systems, Frank Robbins

Vice President financial Advisor, Brian Terner

Vice President Training Manager, John (Jack) Majeski

Vice President Strategic Event Marketing, Lisl Stanton

Asisitant Vice President, Cameron Truhn

Vice President, Troy Hargrove

Vice President Information Technology Audit, Eric Bowers

Vice President, Richard Hixson

Creative Service Manager Assistant Vice President, Linda Paskey

Vice President Marketing Strategy Manager Home Lending, Jacki Karnap

Assistant Vice President Business Banker, Jason Silbaugh

Vice President Marketing China, James Katek

Vice President Human Resources, Jeanne Thomas

Vice President Global Investment Banking, Michael (Mel) Shaw

Vice President, Arthur (Art) Jackson

Vice President Field Marketing Manager, Adilia Linero

Vice President Of Information Technology, Brian Zitterkopf

Senior Vice President Technology Director, Richard Ward

Vice President Mortgage Banking Technology, John Jocson

Vice President, Douglas (Doug) Savage

Senior Vice President, Dan Howat

Assistant Vice President Marketing Analytics At Jpmorgan Chase And Co, Victor Triolo

Vice President Securitized Products Group, Gene Huang

Vice President Investment Banking Technology Med, Vikram Pandit

Vice President Finance, Charles (Chas) Peruski

Vice President, David (Dave) Bell

Vice President HARDWARE Technology, Glenn Magnan

Vice President, Harvey Klyce

Senior Vice President Dealer Commercial Services, Jeff Johns

Vice President, Manu Mahajan

Vice President Business Banking, Asma Kader

Vice President Ib Human Resources, Sarah Allese

Vice President, John (Jack) Zanetti

Vice President, Robert Locurto

Vice President Human Resources And Employee Development And Training, Sophia Chu

First Vice President Relationship Manager, Keith Potter

Vice President Client Advisor, Dan Brown

Assistant Vice President Banker, Javier Varela

Vice President Country Risk Management, Diego Vidal

Senior Vice President Risk Management, Patrick (Paddy) Carr

Vice President, Bruce Goldberg

Vice President, Donna Kopelman

Vice President, Nishant Dhamija

Executive Vice President, Miashillene Aponte

Vice President Biotech Equity Research, Matthew (Matt) Lowe

Vice President Finance, Laurie Goodman

Vice President Deputy Director Of Cyber Investigat, George Rettas

Vice President, Eileen Roberts

Vice President Marketing and Customer, John (Jack) Glazer

Vice President Human Resources Business, Helen Dubowy

Vice President Network Services, Stephen Gannon

Vice President Senior Relationship Manager, Michelle (Mitch) Erny

Vice President And Senior Market Wholesaler, Shawna Edwards

Vice President Assistant General Counsel, Philipp Von Turk

Assistantvice President Relationship Manager, John (Jack) Morris

Executive Vice President, Allison Hannam

Tulsa Middle Market Senior Vice President, Jennifer (Jen) Kalvaitis

Vice President, Nazli Beirne

Vice President Equity Research, Tyler Langton

Vice President Information Risk, Danny Laver

Executive Vice President, Bryne Hurley

Vice President Sourcing and Procurement Services, Marc Genovese

Senior Vice President The Apparel Group, Britt O'Rourke

Vice President, Monica M Mack

Vice President Object Technology, James (Jamie) Schneider

Vice President Technology, Viswanathan Hariharan

Vice President Corporate Internet Group, Jim Heiman

Vice President Of Infrastructure, Michael Knight

Vice President, Angelo Brattoli

Vice President Of Technology, Rick Schomburg

Vice President Crm Retention Management, Gail Timmerman

Vice President Banker, David (Dave) Sagers

Associate Vice President, Linda Murphy

Vice President Global Corporate Bank, Juan Trujillo

Vice President, Gregory Walker

Vice President, Steve Waldman

Vice President, Gino Disaverio

Senior Vice President, James (Jamie) Schroeder

Vice President Senior Etf Product Manager, James McGowan

Vice President Sourcing And Procurement Services, Anthony Caruso

Vice President Commercial Banking, Bill Cook

Senior Vice President Online and Mobile Products, Ravi Acharya

Vice President, Chris Collins

Vice President, William (Bill) Bardusch

Senior Vice President, Paul O'Neill

No. Utah Area Manager Vice President, Ryan Benson

Vice President Retail Information Technology, Lily Toner

Vice President Of Technology, Miguel Choto

First Vice President Product Management Chase Retail Products, Mark Colucy

Vice President Unified Communications And Collaboration, Mark Chilewitz

Vice President Architect Lead Treasury and Security Services, Rajiv Kewalramani

Vice President Digital Marketing, Lauren Coulston

Vice President Project Management, Radhika Chakravarthy

Vice President Human Resources Program Management, Jenny Blanco

Vice President Information Technology, Jason Tucker

Assistant Vice President Information Technology Production Assurance Analyst, Jarrod Holt

Assistant Vice President, Jessica Mignatti

Vice President, Jason Gies

Vice President Information Technology, Gregory Sampson

Vice President Relationship Manager, Pankaj Nath

Vice President Technical Operations Application Manager, Daniel (Dan) Meeks

Vice President Of Information Technology, Mark Sanelli

Vice President Executive Recruiter, Mary Reilly

Auditors: PricewaterhouseCoopers LLP

LOCATIONS

HQ: JPMorgan Chase & Co
270 Park Avenue, New York, NY 10017
Phone: 212 270-6000
Web: www.jpmorganchase.com

PRODUCTS/OPERATIONS

2014 Sales

	$ mil.	% of total
Interest		
Loans	32,218	31
securities	9,040	8
Trading assets	7,312	7
Federal funds sold & securities purchased under resale agreements	1,642	2
Deposits with banks	1,157	1
Securities borrowed	(501)	-
Other	663	1
Noninterest		
Asset management administration & commissions	15,931	16
Principal transactions	10,531	11
Investment banking fees	6,542	6
Credit card income	6,020	6
Lending- and deposit-related fees	5,801	6
Mortgage fees and related income	3,563	3
Securities gains	77	-
Other	2,106	2
Total	**102,102**	**100**

2014 Sales

	% of total
Consumer and Community Banking	46
Corporte and Investment	35
Asset Management	12
Commercial Banking	7
Total	**100**

COMPETITORS

American Express	Goldman Sachs
Bank of America	HSBC
Bank of New York	Morgan Stanley
Mellon	PNC Financial
Barclays	RBC Financial Group
CIBC	State Bank Financial
Capital One	Corporation
Citigroup	SunTrust
Citigroup Global	TD Bank USA
Markets	UBS
Credit Suisse (USA)	Wells Fargo
Deutsche Bank	

HISTORICAL FINANCIALS

Company Type: Public

Income Statement

FYE: December 31

	ASSETS ($ mil.)	NET INCOME ($ mil.)	INCOME AS % OF ASSETS	EMPLOYEES
12/14	2,573,126	21,762	0.8%	241,359
12/13	2,415,689	17,923	0.7%	251,196
12/12	2,359,141	21,284	0.9%	258,965
12/11	2,265,792	18,976	0.8%	260,157
12/10	2,117,605	17,370	0.8%	222,316
Annual Growth	**5.0%**	**5.8%**	**—**	**2.1%**

2014 Year-End Financials

Debt ratio: 8.23%—
Return on equity: 9.82%
Cash ($ mil.): 512,308
Current ratio: —
Long-term debt ($ mil.): —

Dividends
Yield: 2.4%
Payout: 28.8%
Market value ($ mil.): —

	STOCK PRICE ($) FY Close	P/E High/Low	PER SHARE ($) Earnings	Dividends	Book Value
12/14	62.58	12 10	5.29	1.56	62.47
12/13	58.48	13 10	4.35	1.36	56.22
12/12	43.97	9 6	5.20	1.15	53.65
12/11	33.25	11 6	4.48	0.80	48.66
12/10	42.42	12 9	3.98	0.20	45.04
Annual Growth	10.2%	— —	7.4%	67.1%	8.5%

KAISER FOUNDATION HOSPITALS INC

Kaiser Foundation Hospitals is on a roll. The hospital group operates 38 acute care hospitals and almost 630 medical offices in eight states (California Colorado Georgia Hawaii Maryland Oregon Virginia and Washington) and Washington D.C. The company's largest presence is in California where the majority of its hospitals are located. Hawaii and Oregon are home to one hospital each. Specialty facilities include three behavioral health and chemical dependency clinics the Denver area and more than a dozen dental clinics in Oregon and Washington.

Operations

Its doctors group is controlled by Permanente Medical Groups and its HMO is offered through Kaiser Foundation Health Plan. Altogether about 9.6 million members are enrolled in its HMO. The company has more than 17425 doctors.

Sales and Marketing

Kaiser Foundation Hospitals and Kaiser Foundation Health Plan's Capital spending in 2014 was $2.8 billion compared to $3.3 billion in 2013.

Company Background

The company was founded in 1945.

EXECUTIVES

Executive Vice President, Arthur (Art) Southam
EVP Kaiser Foundation Hospitals and Health Plan; Group President Kaiser Permanente Northern California and Mid-Atlantic States; President Kaiser Permanente Northern California, Gregory A. Adams
EVP Kaiser Foundation Hospitals and Health Plan; Group president Kaiser Permanente Southern California and Hawaii; President Kaiser Permanente Southern California, Benjamin K. Chu
Chairman Southern California Permanente Medical Group and Executive Medical Director, Edward Ellison
Medical Director Hospitalists, Scott Ediger
OperationSenior Vice President, Terri Pagelow
Vice President Business Information Officer (CIO) Middle Atlantic Region Kaiser Permanente, Harry Fox
Associate Medical Director clinical Process Improvement colorado Permanente Medical Group, Bill Marsh
Vice President Of Engineering, Anne Dench
Vice President It, Susannah Patton
Vice President, Yvonne Webb

National Vice President, Elisa Mendel
Vice President Of Health Insurance Exchanges, Bill Wehrle
Senior Vice President, Barry A Wolfman
Medical Director of Radiology, Chris Jensen
Vice President Business Information Officer Health Plan, Diane Comer
Vice President Business Development, Vicky Choi
Vice President Outpatient Pharmacy Services, Joseph (Jo) Douglas
Senior Vice President Of Financial Operations, Michael (Mel) McAnder
Vice President Strategic Planning, Vivian Tan
Vice President Engineering, Jeffrey Stiger
Vice President For Operations, Rame Hemstreet
Regional President, Barbara West
Vice President of Information Technology, Kathy Scheirman
Director of Nursing Services, Glenda Totten
Managing Director public Equity, Robert (Bob) Blagden
Vice President Learning And Organizational Development, Robert Sachs
Vice President Nursing Pt Care, Anita Zuniga
Vice President Finance, William Glitsch
Exec V Pres, Patrick (Paddy) Courneya
Medical Director, Andrew Lum
Vice President of Sales and Broker Relations, Tom Carter
Vice President Sales and Account Management Labor and Trust, Chris Blass
Medical Director, Gregory Shay
Vice President Quality And Service, Ellie Godfrey
Vice President Compensation, Debora Catsavas
Vice President Financial Services Operations, Marlene Foster
Clinical Director, Jessica Mantoani
Vice President Communications, Nancy Cartwright
Vice President Financial Systems, Lynette Seid
Senior Vice President Area Manager, Gerald (Jerry) Mccall
Vice President, Richard Frias
Vice President Supplier Service Management, June Burgett
Vice President, Robb Munson
Vice President Finance, Janice Murphy
Senior Vice President Chief Strategic Planning Officer, Paul Swenson
Vice President Of Internal Audit, Cindy Overmyer
Vice President Chief Financial Officer National Medicare and Medicaid Finance, Shawn Freeman
Vice President Marketing Sales and Business Development, Chris Hause
Vice President, Jill Rivers
Senior Vice President, Christopher (Chris) Boyd
Senior Vice President, Larry Wilson
Senior Vice President, Jed Weissberg
Vice President Enterprise Architecture, Simon Nazarian
Vice President Workplace Safety and Environmental Stewardship Officer, Kathy Gerwig
Radiology Director, Michael (Mel) Bruse
Supervisor of Medical Records, Sharon Merrill
Senior Management Senior Vice President General Manager Director, Anne Mcnealis
Vice President Direct Sales Individual and Family Plans, Evelyn Shaffer
Vice President Information Technology Finance Portfolio, Steve Stock
Vice President Information Technology, Julie Miller-phipps
Clinic Supervisor, Jacquie McCurdy
Vice President Risk Adjustment and Information Management, Hovannes Daniels
Physical Therapy, Leah Nelson
Vice President Account Management and Sales, Tina Bartelmay
Pharmd, Mena Shaker
Pharmd, Eric Cohen

Vice President Shared Application Services, Ken Goltara
Ambulatory Services Director, Janet Lundberg
Vice President Pharmacy Operations and Services, Suzanne Shea
Vice President of Primary Care and Medical Specialties, Ginny McLain
Assistant Treasurer and Director Cash Management, Robert (Bob) Venema

LOCATIONS

HQ: KAISER FOUNDATION HOSPITALS INC
1 KAISER PLZ STE 2600, OAKLAND, CA 946123673
Phone: 5102715800
Web: WWW.HEALTHY.KAISERPERMANENTE.ORG

PRODUCTS/OPERATIONS

Selected Hospitals

Antioch Medical Center
Fremont Medical Center
Fresno Medical Center
Hayward Medical Center
Manteca Medical Center
Modesto Medical Center
Oakland Medical Center
Redwood City Medical Center
Richmond Medical Center
Roseville Women and Children's Center
San Jose Medical Center
Santa Clara Medical Center
Sacramento Medical Center
South San Francisco Medical Center
South Sacramento Trauma Center
Santa Rosa Medical Center
San Francisco Medical Center
San Rafael Medical Center
Vacaville Medical Center
Vallejo Medical Center
Walnut Creek Medical Center
Baldwin Park Medical Center
Downey Medical Center
Fontana Medical Center
Los Angeles Medical Center
Moreno Valley Community Hospital
Orange County - Anaheim Medical Center
Orange County - Irvine Medical Center
Panorama City Medical Center
Riverside Medical Center
San Diego Medical Center
Harbor City (South Bay Medical Center)
Woodlands Hills Medical Center
West Los Angeles Medical Center
Sunnyside Medical Center (Portland Oregon area)
Moanalua M

COMPETITORS

Adventist Health	HCA
Ascension Health	LifePoint Health
Banner Health	Mercy Health (OH)
CHRISTUS Health	Sutter Health
Catholic Health Initiatives	Tenet Healthcare
Community Health Systems	The Cleveland Clinic
Dignity Health	Universal Health Services

HISTORICAL FINANCIALS

Company Type: Private

Income Statement

FYE: December 31

	REVENUE ($ mil.)	NET INCOME ($ mil.)	NET PROFIT MARGIN	EMPLOYEES
12/09	14,795	429	2.9%	175,668
12/08	0	0	99.0%	—
12/05	9,852	774	7.9%	—
Annual Growth	10.7%	(13.7%)	—	—

2009 Year-End Financials

Debt ratio: —
Return on equity: 2.90%
Cash ($ mil.): 57
Current ratio: —
Long-term debt ($ mil.): —

Dividends
Yield: —
Payout: —
Market value ($ mil.): —

Kansas City Life Insurance Co. (Kansas City, MO)

It's not just standing on the corner of 12th Street and Vine... it is moving across America with insurance policies. Kansas City Life Insurance and subsidiary Sunset Life provide insurance products throughout the US to individuals (life and disability coverage and annuities) and to groups (life dental vision and disability insurance). Subsidiary Old American Insurance focuses on burial and related insurance. The insurance companies sell through more than 2500 independent agents brokers and third-party marketers. Kansas City Life also operates its own insurance and investment brokerage network through its Sunset Financial Services unit. Chairman and CEO R. Philip Bixby and his family control the company.

Operations

Kansas City Life offers both universal and variable life policies. The company operates in three business segments: Individual Insurance Group Insurance and Old American.The Individual Insurance segment (68% of the company's revenues in 2014) consists of individual insurance products for both Kansas City Life and Sunset Life as well as the coinsurance and reinsurance transactions.

Old American (19% of Kansas City Life's revenues in 2014) sells final expense traditional life insurance products for the senior market (50-85 years old) principally through final arrangements planning (burial and related insurance).The Group Insurance segment (13% of the company's revenues in 2014) is operated as part of Kansas City Life and its administrative and accounting operations are part of the company's home office. It has two primary markets: groups with between two and nine employees and groups with 10 or more employees.

Geographic Reach

The company operates in 49 US states and Washington DC. Some of its largest state markets include Missouri Texas Kansas California and Colorado.

Sales and Marketing

Kansas City Life markets its products through a nationwide sales force of independent general agents agents brokers and third-party marketing arrangements. Old American uses direct response marketing to supply agents with leads.

Financial Performance

The company saw marginal revenue increases in 2012 and 2013 followed by a 4% decline to $465 million in 2014. That decline was primarily due to declines in individual insurance premiums new immediate annuity premiums fixed annuity renewal deposits and universal life renewal deposits. However the company saw increases in group insurance and Old America premiums as well as renewal premiums.

Kansas City Life reached its historic peak of $40 million in net income in 2012 but that was followed by a 26% decline in 2013 due to a reduction in net realized investment gains. In 2014 net income remained relatively flat due to revenue declines (partially offset by declines in income taxes paid).

Cash flows from operations have also declined as of late —except in 2013 when cash flow increased by $41 million and touched its historic peak of $56 million as a result of cash generated from future policy benefits. In 2014 cash flow from operations fell 32% to $38 million due to an increase in cash used in reinsurance recoverables and a decline in cash provided by future policy benefits.

Strategy

The company is looking to grow by acquiring other life insurance companies expanding its product portfolio moving into new markets and by enhancing technology.It also targets strategic growth opportunities through assumed reinsurance. In 2013 the Company completed a 100% modified coinsurance agreement for separate accounts a 100% coinsurance agreement for the fixed fund general account and a servicing agreement for a block of variable universal life insurance policies and variable annuity contracts from American Family.

The company is focused on expanding its individual life insurance operations by widening its distribution network and enhancing its marketing efforts. For instance it has marketing agreements with health plan provider American Republic Insurance and property/casualty firm GuideOne Insurance which distribute the life policies of Kansas City Life to their respective members and policyholders.

Expanding its individual insurance product portfolio in 2013 the company began to offer an indexed universal life product.Old American is expanding its sales territories with a focus on the recruitment and development of new agencies and agents. Group Insurance is looking to deliver more effective electronic and automated support through interactive delivery sites.

Company Background

The Bixby family owns about 60% of the company through trusts and investment partnerships.

Founded in 1895 the company built up its operations through a number of historical acquisitions including GuideOne Life (2003) Old American (1991) and Sunset Life (1974). The company exited its banking operations (Generations Bank) in 2007.

EXECUTIVES

SVP and Actuary, Mark A. Milton, age 56, $316,080 total compensation
Chairman President and CEO, R. Philip Bixby, age 61, $760,008 total compensation
Vice Chairman and EVP; President Old American Insurance Company, Walter E. (Web) Bixby, age 56, $339,480 total compensation
SVP Finance, Tracy W. Knapp, age 52, $313,140 total compensation
SVP Sales and Marketing, Donald E. Krebs, age 57, $292,680 total compensation
VP Operations, Stephen E Ropp
Assistant Vice President and Associate Actuary Product Management, Brenna Gardino
Assistant Vice President Group Sales And Marketing, Talva Parker
Regional Vice President, Tom Morgan
Medical Director, Charlotte Lee
Regional Vice President, Bill Browning
Assistant Vice President, Dawn Roy
Regional Vice President, Ryan Beasley
Vice President, Timothy Knott
Assistant Vice President Cusotmer Services And Claims, Anne Snoddy
Vice President Of Customer Service, Richard (Dick) Ropp
Assistant Vice President Of Marketing, Kris Jones
Vice President Of Customer Service, Richard Ropp
Vice President, Kathryn Church
Vice President Information Technology, Rob Fisher
Secretary, Matthew (Matt) O'Connor
Senior Vice President General Counsel Secretary, Craig Mason
Auditors: KPMG LLP

LOCATIONS

HQ: Kansas City Life Insurance Co. (Kansas City, MO)
3520 Broadway, Kansas City, MO 64111-2565
Phone: 816 753-7000
Web: www.kclife.com

PRODUCTS/OPERATIONS

2014 Sales

	$ mil.	% of total
Individual insurance	319	68
Old American	87	19
Group insurance	58	13
Adjustments	(0.4)	-
Total	**465**	**100**

2014 Sales

	$ mil.	% of total
Insurance	384	61
Net Investment income	164	35
Realized investment gains	3	1
Other	12	3
Total	**465**	**100**

Selected Subsidiaries

Old American Insurance Company
Sunset Financial Services
Sunset Life Insurance Company of America

COMPETITORS

AEGON USA	MassMutual
Advance Insurance of Kansas	MetLife
American Equity Life	National Western
American Heritage Life Insurance	Nationwide
American National Insurance	New York Life
Americo	Northwestern Mutual
Citizens Inc.	Phoenix Companies
Delphi Financial Group	Primerica
FBL Financial	Protective Life
Homesteaders Life	Prudential
Kemper Corp	Security Benefit Group
	The Hartford
	Torchmark
	Universal American

HISTORICAL FINANCIALS

Company Type: Public

Income Statement

FYE: December 31

	ASSETS ($ mil.)	NET INCOME ($ mil.)	INCOME AS % OF ASSETS	EMPLOYEES
12/14	4,571	29	0.7%	436
12/13	4,514	29	0.7%	446
12/12	4,525	39	0.9%	443
12/11	4,398	26	0.6%	444
12/10	4,333	22	0.5%	446
Annual Growth	1.3%	7.7%	—	(0.6%)

2014 Year-End Financials

Debt ratio: —	No. of shares (mil.): 10
Return on equity: 4.09%	Dividends
Cash ($ mil.): 11	Yield: —
Current ratio: —	Payout: 39.0%
Long-term debt ($ mil.): —	Market value ($ mil.): —

KBR Inc

KBR builds big projects for the US government. But the engineering and construction services company also lends its capabilities to the hydrocarbon energy minerals civil infrastructure and power and industrial markets. The company is widely known for its service to the government and infrastructure sector; however that figure is slowly declining as the military pulls its presence in the Middle East. KBR is increasingly focused on projects in the oil and gas industry. It has designed many of world's liquefied natural gas production facilities and develops new technologies such as coal gasification. Operations outside the US account for two-thirds of KBR's revenue.

Operations

Since its reorganization in 2014 KBR operates three business segments: Engineering & Consulting (E&C) Technology & Consulting (T&C) and Government Services. The E&C segment generates more than 70% of the company's revenue and provides engineering procurement construction (EPC) commissioning and maintenance services for customers operating in the oil and gas refining petrochemicals and chemicals sectors. The group is managed in separate geographic regions to ensure locality to customers. The Government Services division (10% of revenues) specializes in long-term service contracts (with annuity streams) mostly with the UK Australian and US governments. The T&C segment (around 5% of revenues) provides KBR-licensed technologies and consulting services to the oil and gas value chain; providing early planning and project lifecycle support from the wellhead stage to crude refining and specialty chemicals production.

Geographic Reach

Houston-based KBR has operations in more than 70 countries spanning the US Australia Africa the UK Asia and the Middle East. The US is its largest market accounting for nearly 40% of the company's revenue followed by Australia which provides more than 20%. Business in Canada Europe and the Middle East each contribute about 10% to the company's revenue while Africa contributes nearly 5%.

Sales and Marketing

The company's diverse customer base includes international oil and gas companies such as Chevron (17% of total revenue in 2014) petrochemical producers fertilizer producers and the US government.

Financial Performance

KBR's revenues and profits have been trending downward in recent years as military budgets have been shrinking with fewer global conflicts. Indeed the company's revenue has declined by nearly 40% since 2010. The company's revenue shrank by 12% to $6.4 billion in 2014 with business declines across all segments except the T&C division. The E&C segment (KBR's largest) revenues sank by 8% during the year with lower EPC activity in the LNG/GTL markets as projects neared completion and as construction project activity declined in the US market. KBR's Government Services division revenues plummeted by over 30% after the March 31 2014 completion of activities supporting the US military and Department of State for the war in Iraq and after troop reductions on the UK Ministry of Defence (MoD) and NATO contracts in Afghanistan. KBR also suffered a net loss of $1.26 billion in 2014 (compared to a profit of $229 million in 2013) mostly as its razor-thin profit margins were met with a $446 million impairment charge related to the company's goodwill on its Roberts and Schaefer (R&S) and BE&K acquisi-

tions. KBR's operating cash also fell sharply mostly due to losses.

Strategy

With revenues continuing to dwindle as military spending winds down KBR has begun to refocus operations toward its businesses that have a competitive edge. In 2014 the company began targeting growth in its two core markets: global hydrocarbons and international government services. Emphasizing its new strategic direction KBR in 2015 sold its KBR Building Group subsidiary to Pernix Building Group for $22 million; and its Infrastructure Americas division to American design firm Stantec. The growing hydrocarbons market in particularly has improved considerably with energy demand contributing to the company's long-term growth for projects in the offshore oil and gas production liquefied natural gas (LNG) biofuels motor fuels chemicals and fertilizer markets. To capitalize on this market KBR regularly enters joint ventures to diversify its income streams and expand its global reach. During 2014 for example the company partnered with JGC and Chiyoda to design procure fabricate construct commission and test the Ichthys Onshore LNG export facility in Darwin Australia. It also formed its KJVG venture (consisting of JGC Hatch Associates Clough Projects Australia and KBR) for similar activities on the LNG project on Barrow Island near Western Australia. Shale gas supplies in North America also represent opportunities for KBR to grow at home. It also inked a five-year Master Services Agreement with DuPont Engineering in 2014 to provide engineering procurement and construction management services for most DuPont facilities in the US and Mexico.

On the international government services front KBR in 2014 formed its Aspire Defence Holdings Limited joint venture to upgrade and provide services to the British Army's garrisons at Aldershot and Salisbury Plain in the UK. To expand into new service markets KBR similarly formed partnerships in 2015 with Bernhard Capital Partners to form Brown & Root Industrial Services which would provide maintenance services to the industrial services industry; and forged an alliance with its subsidiary Granherne and Subsea 7 to deliver Concept and Front End Engineering and Design (FEED) services to the global offshore oil and gas industry.

Company Background

Former parent Halliburton spun off about 20% of KBR through an IPO in 2006 and divested the rest in 2007. KBR's link to Halliburton brought the company trouble in 2009. KBR pleaded guilty to foreign bribery charges for its participation in a decade-long scheme to bribe Nigerian officials in exchange for government contracts. The company was ordered to pay a $402 million fine.

Additionally the company (along with Halliburton) was fined $177 million for violating SEC anti-bribery rules. Halliburton agreed to pay most of the fines leaving KBR paying about $20 million to the Department of Justice. In 2012 a former KBR chief executive was sentenced to 30 months in prison for his role in the bribe scheme.

EXECUTIVES

EVP and CFO, Brian K. Ferraioli, age 59, $650,021 total compensation
President Government Services, Andrew Pringle
President and CEO; Group President Engineering & Construction, Stuart J.B. Bradie, $538,474 total compensation
President Engineering & Construction Americas, Roy B. Oelking, age 62, $628,050 total compensation
President Technology and Consulting, John Derbyshire

President Onshore Engineering & Construction Americas, David Zelinski
EVP Commercial, Farhan Mujib
President Engineering & Construction Europe Middle East and Africa, Jan Egil Braendeland
EVP and General Counsel, Eileen G. Akerson
President Engineering & Construction Middle East and North Africa, Jay Ibrahim
EVP Human Resources, Ian Mackey
Chairman, Loren K. Carroll
Board Member, Richard (Dick) D'Souza
Auditors: KPMG LLP

LOCATIONS

HQ: KBR Inc
601 Jefferson Street, Suite 3400, Houston, TX 77002
Phone: 713 753-3011
Web: www.kbr.com

2014 Sales

	$ mil.	% of total
US	2,324	37
Australia	1,380	22
Canada	752	12
Middle East	707	11
Europe	624	10
Africa	251	4
Other countries	328	4
Total	**6,366**	**100**

PRODUCTS/OPERATIONS

2014 Sales

	$ mil.	% of total
Engineering and Construction	4,584	72
Government Services	638	10
Technology and Consulting	353	6
Non-Strategic Business	791	12
Total	**6,366**	**100**

Selected Services

Advanced Chemical Engineering
  Advanced Simulation
  Operations Management Systems
  Operator Training Simulators
  Technical Services
Construction and Design Build
  Commissioning and Start-up Services
  Construction Management
  Major Construction
  Module and Pipe Fabrication
  Segmented Construction (Mechanical E/I)
  Small and Mid-Capital Construction
Engineering
  Engineering Procurement and Construction
  Front End Engineering Designs (FEED)
  Grassroots Facilities and Revamps
Lifecycle Services
  Process Improvement Services
Logistics Support
  Rapid Response Delivery
Operations and Maintenance
  Facilities Management Services
  Special Facility Services
Procurement
  Global Procurement Services
  Inspection Services
  Logistics Optimization and Management
  Materials Management
  Procurement Management
  Subcontracts Services
  Supply Chain Management
Project and Program Management
  Construction Management
  Job Order Contracting
  Process and Industrial Services
  Project Oversight
  Risk Management
Special Facility Services

COMPETITORS

AECOM	JGC
ARB	Jacobs Engineering
Aker Solutions	John Wood Group

Amec Foster Wheeler	Kiewit Offshore
American Bridge	McDermott
Company	Parsons Corporation
Bechtel	Performance
Bechtel National	Contractors
CH2M HILL	Peter Kiewit Sons'
Chicago Bridge & Iron	Petrofac
Chiyoda Corp.	Saipem
DynCorp International	Technip
Fluor	Tutor Perini
Grunley Construction	Yates Companies
Hyundai Heavy	
Industries	

HISTORICAL FINANCIALS

Company Type: Public

Income Statement
FYE: December 31

	REVENUE ($ mil.)	NET INCOME ($ mil.)	NET PROFIT MARGIN	EMPLOYEES
12/14	6,366	(1,262)	—	25,000
12/13	7,283	229	3.1%	27,000
12/12	7,921	144	1.8%	27,000
12/11	9,261	480	5.2%	27,000
12/10	10,099	327	3.2%	35,000
Annual Growth	(10.9%)	—	—	(8.1%)

2014 Year-End Financials

Debt ratio: 1.74%
Return on equity: (-70.92%)
Cash ($ mil.): 970
Current ratio: 1.26
Long-term debt ($ mil.): 63

No. of shares (mil.): 144
Dividends
  Yield: 1.8%
  Payout: 800.0%
Market value ($ mil.): 2,455

	STOCK PRICE ($) FY Close	P/E High/Low	PER SHARE ($) Earnings	Dividends	Book Value
12/14	16.95	— —	(8.66)	0.32	6.50
12/13	31.89	23 18	1.54	0.32	17.66
12/12	29.92	39 24	0.97	0.20	17.22
12/11	27.87	12 7	3.16	0.20	16.84
12/10	30.47	15 8	2.07	0.20	14.86
Annual Growth	(13.6%)	— —	—	12.5%	(18.7%)

Kellogg Co

From the company's home base in Battle Creek Michigan Kellogg Company is in a constant battle for the #1 spot in the US cereal market with its main rival General Mills. Kellogg founded in 1906 boasts many familiar brand names including Kellogg's Corn Flakes Frosted Flakes Corn Pops and Rice Krispies. While the company works to fill the world's cereal bowls it supplements its bottom line with snacks and cookies (Keebler Cheez-It and Famous Amos) along with convenience foods such as Eggo waffles and Nutri-Grain and Bear Naked cereal bars. Its products are sold worldwide.

Operations

Kellogg operates through several segments based on product category and geographic location. They include US Morning Foods & Kashi (23% of sales) US Snacks (24% of sales) US Specialty North American Other Europe Latin America and Asia Pacific. Kellogg's international business focuses almost exclusively on cereal and wholesome snacks.

The US Morning Foods segment includes cereal toaster pastries health and wellness bars and beverages. US Snacks includes cookies crackers cereal bars savory snacks and fruit-flavored snacks. US Specialty primarily represents non-residential food operations including food service convenience vending Girl Scouts and food manufacturing.

Geographic Reach

The food company manufactures its products in 19 countries marketing them in more than 180 countries. It generates 61% of its revenues in the US.

The company's manufacturing facilities in the US include four cereal plants and warehouses in Battle Creek Michigan; Lancaster Pennsylvania; Memphis Tennessee; and Omaha Nebraska. Its other facilities are mostly in Georgia Kentucky Michigan and Ohio. Outside the US Kellogg has additional manufacturing locations (some with warehousing facilities) in about 20 countries in Europe Asia Africa and South America.

Sales and Marketing

Kellogg's largest customer is Wal-Mart which accounted for more than 20% of its consolidated net sales in fiscal 2015. The company's top five customers generated some 33% of Kellogg's total sales that year. The company's dependence on just a few companies makes it vulnerable to the loss of or weakness at any one of these retailers. It's also vulnerable to competition from lower-priced private-label cereal brands which consumers typically flock to during tough times.

The company markets its cereal products in general under the recognizable Kellogg's name as well as its "healthy" brand Kashi. Products are sold to supermarkets through a direct sales force model for resale to consumers. Kellogg uses broker and distributor arrangements for certain products in retail stores restaurants and other food service establishments. These particular arrangements are leveraged to market its products in less-developed areas or in markets outside its focus.

Kellogg's advertising expense in fiscal 2015 was $1.09 billion compared to $1.13 billion a year earlier.

Financial Performance

After posting sales declines between 2008 and 2010 Kellogg logged positive sales growth until 2013. However in fiscal 2015 (year ended January) revenues decreased by a marginal 1% due to a 4% decline in US Morning Foods as a result of a decline in sales of Special K and Kashi and a 3% drop in North America and Asia Pacific each due to soft demand for cereal.

After reaching a peak of $1.8 billion in 2013 the company's net income fell by 65% in fiscal 2015 due to increased selling general and administrative expenses and cost of goods sold (including adjustments for pension plans and commodity contracts).

Strategy

The company is focused on winning the breakfast segment increasing the size of its global snack business expanding its frozen-food business and increasing its investment in emerging markets. In this latter regard in 2014 Kellogg formed a joint-venture for cereal and snacks in China. It is also building a major halal snack plant in Malaysia. Kellogg is also focused on creating new simpler foods including cereals that meet the USDA's standard for organic food as well as cereals that are Non-GMO Project Verified new granolas gluten-free Special K and cereals offering progressive nutrition such as Kashi Sprouted Grains organic cereal. The company has started to invest in new brand-building programs designed to engage consumers and remind them of the health benefits that can result from the consumption of cereal.

To boost capacity and profits Kellogg is in the midst of a four-year global retooling of its manufacturing facilities which involves the closing of an 89-year-old facility in Ontario Canada as well as the closing of an Australian snack factory and the expansion of a plant in Thailand. Kellogg anticipates that it will return to its ongoing operating model. In recent years it has invested in the business adjusted its strategy to focus more on growth and acquired Pringles. It expects to realize growth through increased investment in advertising and continued investment behind a strong lineup of innovation launches.

Kellogg is also looking for continued growth from its vegetarian business particularly its Morningstar Farms and Worthington Foods brands of meat alternatives as the veggie business has performed well as consumers look for healthier foods.

The company's global signature cause (launched in 2013) aims to provide 1 billion servings of cereal and snacks to children and families worldwide by the end of 2016. Through 2014 the company had already provided more than 700 million servings.

Mergers and Acquisitions

To further enhance its global snacks business Kellogg acquired a majority stake in Bisco Misr the largest biscuit company in Egypt in 2015.

In 2012 in a major move the company bought Procter & Gamble's Pringles canned chip business for some $2.7 billion in cash. The deal propelled Kellogg to the second-largest snack food company in the world behind PepsiCo.

HISTORY

Will Keith (W. K.) Kellogg first made wheat flakes in 1894 while working for his brother Dr. John Kellogg at Battle Creek Michigan's famed homeopathic sanitarium. While doing an experiment with grains (for patients' diets) the two men were interrupted; by the time they returned to the dough it had absorbed water. They rolled it anyway toasted the result and accidentally created the first flaked cereal. John sold the flakes via mail order (1899) in a partnership that W. K. managed. In 1906 W. K. started his own firm to produce corn flakes.

As head of the Battle Creek Toasted Corn Flake Company W. K. competed against 42 cereal companies in Battle Creek (one run by former patient C. W. Post) and roared to the head of the pack with his innovative marketing ideas. A 1906 Ladies' Home Journal ad helped increase demand from 33 cases a day earlier that year to 2900 a day by year-end. W. K. soon introduced Bran Flakes (1915) All-Bran (1916) and Rice Krispies (1928). International expansion began in Canada (1914) and followed in Australia (1924) and England (1938).

EXECUTIVES

Vice President Procurement and Demand Planning, Kim Stumm
Vice President, Stacey Ring-Sanders
Vice President Transporation and Distribution, Steven (Steve) Smith
Vice President Global Procurement Cpo, Michele Tyler
Vice President Nutrition, Guy Johnson
Vice President core Technology and Cost Optimization, Paul Pezzoli
Vice President and Treasurer, Joel Vanderkooi
Vice President Treasury and Investor Relations, Joel R Wittenberg
Senior Vice President Morning Foods Supply Chain, George Chumakov
National Account Manager, Gina Ray
Vice President Cross Channel Operation and Business Development, Russell (Russ) Hockin
Senior Vice President Operations and Distribution Snacks, Sharron Moss-Higham
Vice President Kellogg North America Quality, Richard (Dick) Yacovoni
Senior Vice President Customer and Logistics Services, Wayne Skinner
Vice President Treasurer, Michael (Mel) Gaines
Vice President Government Relations, BrigitteSchmidt Gwyn
Vice President Human Resources, Xavier Boza
Vice President US Sales, Rick Davis
Vice President of Supply Chain Capability, David (Dave) Cowperthwait
Vice President and Director Information Technology, Joseph (Jo) Dante
Senior Vice President Global Sales, Darcey Macken
Vice President of Human Resources, Bruce Crockett
Senior Vice President Global Supply Chain Shared Services, Jeff Arnold
Senior Vice President Snack Marketing, MichaelA Allen
Auditors: PricewaterhouseCoopers LLP

LOCATIONS

HQ: Kellogg Co
One Kellogg Square, P.O. Box 3599, Battle Creek, MI 49016-3599
Phone: 269 961-2000   Fax: 616 961-2871
Web: www.kelloggcompany.com

2015 Sales

	$ mil.	% of total
United States	8,876	61
International	5,704	39
Total	**14,580**	**100**

PRODUCTS/OPERATIONS

2015 Sales

	$ mil.	% of total
US Morning Foods & Kashi	3,338	23
US Snacks	3,495	24
US Specialty	1,198	8
North America other	1,468	10
Europe	2,887	20
Latin America	1,205	8
Asia Pacific	989	7
Total	**14,580**	**100**

Selected Cereal Brands

Asia and Australia
  BeBig
  Cerola
  Chex
  Frosties
  Goldies
  Kellogg' s Iron Man Food
  Nutri-Grain
  Rice Bubbles
  Sultana Bran
Canada
  Vector
  Vive

Europe
  Choco Pops
  Chocos
  Country Store
  Frosties
  Fruit ‘n' Fibre
  Honey Loops
  Kellogg' s Crunchy Nut Corn Flakes
  Kellogg' s Crunchy Nut Red Corn Flakes
  Kellogg' s Extra
  Muslix
  Optima
  Pops
  Ricicles
  Smacks
  Start
  Sustain
Latin America
  Choco Krispis
  Choco Zucaritas
  Crusli Sucrilhos
  Musli
  NutriDia
  Sucrilhos Chocolate
  Vector
  Zucaritas
US
  All-Bran
  Apple Jacks
  Bran Buds
  Cinnamon Crunch
  Cocoa Krispies
  Complete Bran Flakes
  Complete Wheat Flakes
  Corn Pops
  Cracklin' Oat Bran
  Crispix
  Crunch
  Cruncheroos
  Froot Loops
  Frosted Krispies
  Frosted Mini-Wheats
  Just Right
  Kellogg' s Corn Flakes
  Kellogg' s Frosted Flakes
  Kellogg' s Low-Fat Granola
  Kellogg' s Raisin Bran
  Mueslix
  Pops
  Product 19
  Raisin Bran
  Rice Krispies
  Smacks/Honey Smacks
  Smart Start
  Special K
  Special K Red Berries

Selected Other Brands

Cereal Bars and Granola
  All-Bran
  Bear Naked
  Choco Krispies
  Froot Loops
  GoLean
  Kashi
Convenience Foods
  Austin
  Cheez-It
  Chips Deluxe
  Club
  Crouettes Croutons
  E. L. Fudge
  Famous Amos
  Fudge Shoppe
  Hi-Ho
  Keebler
  Kellogg' s Corn Flake Crumbs
  Krispy Munch' Ems
  Murray
  Pop-Tarts
  Pop-Tarts Pastry Swirls
  Pop-Tarts Snak-Stix
  Pringles
  Ready Crust
  Rice Krispies Squares
  Rice Krispies Treats
  Right Bites
  Sandies
  Soft Batch
  Stretch Island
  Sunshine

  Toasteds
  Town House
Frozen Waffles and Pancakes
  Eggo
  Froot Loops
  Nutri-Grain
  Special K
Water and Water Mixes
  Special K
  Special K2O
Meat and Egg Alternatives
  Gardenburger
  Loma Linda
  Morningstar Farms
  Natural Touch
  Worthington

COMPETITORS

Amy' s Kitchen	McKee Foods
Barbara' s Bakery	Mondelez International
Bob' s Red Mill Natural Foods	Nestl©
Boca Foods	Patty King
Campbell Soup	PepsiCo
ConAgra	Pinnacle Foods
Frito-Lay	PowerBar
General Mills	Ralston Food
Gilster-Mary Lee	Schulze and Burch
Goodman Fielder	Snyder' s-Lance
Hain Celestial	Weetabix
J & J Snack Foods	Wellness Foods
Jordans & Ryvita	Wessanen
MOM Brands	granoVita

HISTORICAL FINANCIALS

Company Type: Public

Income Statement

FYE: January 3

	REVENUE ($ mil.)	NET INCOME ($ mil.)	NET PROFIT MARGIN	EMPLOYEES
01/15*	14,580	632	4.3%	29,790
12/13	14,792	1,807	12.2%	30,277
12/12	14,197	961	6.8%	31,006
12/11	13,198	1,231	9.3%	30,700
01/11	12,397	1,247	10.1%	30,645
Annual Growth	**4.1%**	**(15.6%)**	**—**	**(0.7%)**

*Fiscal year change

2015 Year-End Financials

Debt ratio: 48.64%
Return on equity: 19.63%
Cash ($ mil.): 443
Current ratio: 0.77
Long-term debt ($ mil.): 5,935
No. of shares (mil.): 356
Dividends
  Yield: 0.0%
  Payout: 108.5%
Market value ($ mil.): 23,311

	STOCK PRICE ($) FY Close	P/E High/Low		PER SHARE ($) Earnings	Dividends	Book Value
01/15*	65.48	39	32	1.75	1.90	7.83
12/13	60.98	14	11	4.94	1.80	9.77
12/12	55.33	21	17	2.67	1.74	6.70
12/11	50.57	17	14	3.38	1.67	4.93
01/11	51.08	17	14	3.30	1.56	5.90
Annual Growth	**6.4%**	**—**	**—**	**(14.7%)**	**5.1%**	**7.3%**

*Fiscal year change

Kelly Services, Inc.

These days a lot of "Kelly Girls" are men. Once a business that supplied only female clerical help Kelly Services has expanded to include male and female temporary employees in light industrial technical and professional sectors including information technology specialists engineers and accountants. It also places lawyers (Kelly Law Registry) scientists (Kelly Scientific Resources) substitute teachers (Kelly Educational Staffing) nurses and other medical staff (Kelly Healthcare Resources) and teleservices personnel (KellyConnect). Kelly Services assigns some 555000 temporary employees around the world each year. Chairman Terence Adderley owns a controlling stake in the company.

Geographic Reach

Kelly caters to customers in three chief regions: the Americas (63% of total sales); Europe the Middle East and Africa (EMEA 19%); and the Asia/Pacific (18%).

Operations

The company provides additional personnel in areas such as electronics (Kelly Electronic Assembly Services) merchandising (Kelly Marketing Services) and catering (Kelly Catering and Hospitality). It also offers career transition outplacement and human resources consulting services through its Ayers Group division (which makes up its Outsourcing and Consulting Group segment or OCG).

Financial Performance

Like most companies involved in the employment industry Kelly has seen its balance sheet fluctuate. After experiencing a revenue decline in 2013 the company saw its revenues jump 3% to $5.56 billion in 2014. Profits however nosedived 60% from $59 million in 2013 to $24 million in 2014 due to an increase in cost of services and additional selling general and administrative expenses.

The revenue growth for 2014 was fueled by a 15% surge in sales from its OCG segment and increases from virtually all other segments. Kelly was also helped by an increase in bill rates in the commercial America region as APAC Services revenue increased to reflect a 10% uptick in the number of hours worked.

Kelly's operating cash flow plummeted by 185% from $115 million in 2013 to a negative cash flow of 70% during 2014. This was the result of $20 million the company paid related to the timing of supplier payments a $5 million effect of the correction of the error from prior periods and lower working capital requirements.

Strategy

The staffing firm's strategy for growth entails maintaining its core strengths in the commercial staffing market while also growing its professional and technical staffing capabilities. Kelly also plans to recognize additional revenue by growing its Outsourcing and Consulting Group segment and by targeting specialized niche markets which require staffing services.

HISTORY

William Russell Kelly a college dropout and former car salesman went to Detroit after WWII to seek his fortune. An owner of modern business equipment he set up Russell Kelly Office Service in 1946 to provide copying typing and inventory services for other businesses; first-year sales from 12 customers totaled $848.

Although companies began to acquire their own machines Kelly knew that they still needed people to work at their offices. He reincorporated his rapidly expanding business as Personnel Service in 1952 and opened the company's first branch office in Louisville Kentucky in 1955; by the end of that year he had 35 offices throughout the US. In 1957 the company was renamed Kelly Girl Service to reflect its all-female workforce.

In the 1960s Kelly ventured beyond office services and began placing convention hostesses blue-collar workers data processors door-to-door marketers and drafters among others. Kelly Girl went public in 1962 boasting 148 branches at the time.

In 1966 the company adopted the name Kelly Services. It opened its first non-US office in Toronto in 1968 and one in Paris followed in 1972.

EXECUTIVES

Executive Vice President and General Manager Americas, Michael (Mel) Webster
President and CEO, Carl T. Camden, age 60, $1,000,000 total compensation
EVP and COO, George S. Corona, age 56, $655,000 total compensation
SVP and General Manager US Operations, Steve S. Armstrong
SVP Centers of Excellence and General Manager Outsourcing and Consulting Group, Teresa S. Carroll
SVP General Counsel and Assistant Secretary, Peter W. Quigley, $419,250 total compensation
CIO, Judy Snyder
SVP; General Manager EMEA and APAC Regions; COO North Asia, Natalia Shuman
SVP Corporate Controller and Chief Accounting Officer, Olivier Thirot
Executive Vice President Senior Vice President Vice President, John (Jack) Healy
Vice President corp Controller Chief Accounting, Laura Lockhart
Senior Management (Senior Vice President General Manager Director), Mike Berich
Vice President Marketing Information, Maureen Kowalski
Vp-prod Ctrs Of Excellence, Nicola Soares
Territory Vice President, Brittna Valenzuela
Vice President Administration, Bonnie Huber
Vice President Finance, Mary Macherzak
Territory Vice President, Melissa (Mel) King
Vice President Global Solutions and Services, Brian Pauley
Vice President Pro Practice Lead, Tom Kaminsky
National Sales Manager, Yasikaan Chairoongrojsakul
Senior Vice President Outsourcing and Consulting Group Global Administration, James (Jamie) Bradley
Vice President Of Operations, Ginny Scaduto
Vice President And District Manager Ak, Rich Struble
Vice President Global Solutions Life Sciences, Kevin Duffy
Vice President And District Manager, Eileen Candels
Vice President Global Implementation, Kent Schomer
Regional Vice President, Cheryl Courier
Vice President and Science Product Leader Kelly Services, Jamie Stacey
Vice President and Operations Lead, Chris Gardiner
Vice President Human Resources, Dave Charlip
National Account Manager, Mara Krumins
Chairman President and CEO, Terence E. (Terry) Adderley, age 81
Auditors: PricewaterhouseCoopers LLP

LOCATIONS

HQ: Kelly Services, Inc.
999 West Big Beaver Road, Troy, MI 48084
Phone: 248 362-4444
Web: www.kellyservices.com

2014 Sales

	$ mil.	% of total
US	3,535	64
International	2,026	36
Total	**5,562**	**100**

PRODUCTS/OPERATIONS

Selected Services

CGR/seven (creative services staffing)

Kelly Cate
Kelly Educ
Kelly Electronic Assembly Services
Kelly Engi
Kelly Fina
Kelly Government Solutions (US federal government staffing)
Kelly Healthcare Resources (nurses medical technicians)
Kelly Information Technology Resources
Kelly Law Registry
Kelly Light Industrial
Kelly Marketing Services
Kelly Offi
Kelly Scie
KellyConnect (call center staffing)
KellyDirect (permanent placement service)
KellySelec

2014 Sales

	$ mil.	% of total
Americas		
Commercial	2,609	46
Professional & Technical	956	17
EMEA		
Commercial	894	16
Professional & Technical	190	3
APAC		
Commercial	351	6
Professional & Technical	40	1
Outsourcing & Consulting Group	586	11
Adjustments	(66.9)	-
Total	**5,562**	**100**

COMPETITORS

ATC Healthcare	Randstad Holding
Adecco	Robert Half
Allegis Group	Technical Aid
Insperity	Corporation
ManpowerGroup	TrueBlue
On Assignment	Volt Information

HISTORICAL FINANCIALS

Company Type: Public

Income Statement

FYE: December 28

	REVENUE ($ mil.)	NET INCOME ($ mil.)	NET PROFIT MARGIN	EMPLOYEES
12/14	5,562	23	0.4%	563,300
12/13	5,413	58	1.1%	548,100
12/12*	5,450	50	0.9%	568,100
01/12	5,551	63	1.1%	558,200
01/11	4,950	26	0.5%	538,000
Annual Growth	**3.0%**	**(2.4%)**	**—**	**1.2%**

*Fiscal year change

2014 Year-End Financials

Debt ratio: 4.79%	No. of shares (mil.): 37
Return on equity: 2.87%	Dividends
Cash ($ mil.): 83	Yield: 0.0%
Current ratio: 1.50	Payout: 32.7%
Long-term debt ($ mil.): —	Market value ($ mil.): 641

	STOCK PRICE ($) FY Close	P/E High/Low		PER SHARE ($) Earnings	Dividends	Book Value
12/14	17.00	42	25	0.61	0.20	22.10
12/13	25.29	17	10	1.54	0.20	21.98
12/12*	15.55	13	9	1.32	0.20	19.93
01/12	13.68	13	6	1.69	0.10	18.30
01/11	18.80	28	15	0.71	0.00	16.99
Annual Growth	**(2.5%)**	**—**	**—**	**(3.7%)**	**—**	**6.8%**

*Fiscal year change

Kemper Corp. (DE)

Kemper is among the largest property and casualty insurance groups in the nation. The company operates through two operating segments: Property and Casualty Insurance and Life and Health Insurance. The Property and Casualty Insurance segment's principal products are personal automobile insurance both standard and non-standard risk homeowners insurance other personal insurance and commercial automobile insurance. The Life and Health Insurance segment's principal products are individual life accident health and property insurance. The company operates in the southern midwestern and western US.

Geographic Reach

Kemper primarily sells its policies in 50 US states and Washington DC. Its largest markets include New York North Carolina California Washington and Texas. The Kemper Home Services Companies unit operates in 25 states.

Operations

The Kemper family of companies specializes in property and casualty insurance and life and health insurance products for individuals families and small businesses. Property and Casualty Insurance accounted for 60% of the company's 2014 revenues. The life and health insurance division accounted for 37% of sales primarily from its Kemper Home Service Companies unit. The smaller Reserve National unit sells specialty individual accident life and health insurance policies including illness and hospitalization plans.

Kemper Home Service Companies focuses on providing individual life and supplemental accident and health insurance products to customers of limited incomes who desire basic protection for themselves and their families.

Sales and Marketing

The company offers its services through more than 20000 independent agencies. Kemper Home Services used a network of 2600 career agents while Reserve National used about 300 independent agents. Property & Casualty Insurance segment's products are offered by 15300 independent insurance agents and brokers. Kemper Direct sells auto and home by phone and online.

Financial Performance

Kemper's revenues have declined over the past five years including a drop of 10% in 2014 that was attributed to lower earned premiums and a decline in net realized gains on sales of investments. Earned premium declined due to lower volume (driven primarily by personal automobile insurance and homeowners insurance in property and casualty segment and a lower volume of insurance as a drop of $12.6 million from life insurance products offered by the Kemper Home Service Companies.Kemper's net investment income decreased by $5.6 million in 2014 due primarily to $17.4 million in lower net investment income from equity method limited liability investments and $8.1 million of lower net investment income from interest and dividends on fixed maturities.Profits have fluctuated over the last few years with net income decreasing by 47% in 2014 due to lower revenues.

Kemper's operating cash flow continued its uptrend in 2014. It grew by 9% due to a decrease in cash used in insurance reserves and accrued expenses and other liabilities.

Strategy

The company is focused on increasing brand awareness and diversifying its operations and growing through acquisitions. Kemper also seeks to reduce catastrophe exposure through reinsurance (risk sharing) agreements and selective underwriting practices.

Its strategy includes expanding its shared services model. By concentrating key skill sets that support its businesses Kemper plans ro increase its levels of expertise and effectiveness while maintaining a more efficient cost structure. It will continue to invest in technology brand people and analytics enhance customer experience support its agents and deliver the shareholder returns.

In 2014 Kemper realigned its Property and Casualty segments and consolidated its Kemper Preferred Kemper Specialty and Kemper Direct into the Property and Casualty segment. As a result the company operates through two segments: property and casualty insurance and life and health insurance.

To broaden its operations the company launched a new Kemper Benefits line of voluntary benefit offerings in 2013.

Mergers and Acquisitions

Expanding its private passenger nonstandard auto insurance presence in California in 2015 Kemper acquired Alliance United Group (and its subsidiaries Alliance United Insurance Company and Alliance United Insurance Services) for $71 million. Alliance United distributes its products through producers and its extensive presence in Southern California complements Kemper Specialty California's more Northern California base. Additionally Alliance United brings valuable expertise in serving the growing Hispanic market.

Company Background

The company changed its name from Unitrin Inc. to Kemper Corp. in August 2011; it also rebranded several its business units under the Kemper name. The name change followed a downsizing where the company shed or shuttered several operations. Its Fireside Bank subsidiary which purchased (sub-prime) loan contracts from used automobile dealers halted lending activities in 2009 and ceased banking operations in 2012. Kemper also explored options to sell its Reserve National subsidiary but instead narrowed the unit's focus on specialized life and health policies.

Kemper's disposal-heavy strategy followed a period of expansion in its traditional consumer insurance options. The company enriched its property/casualty business segment through acquisitions of smaller companies.

James Kemper founded National Underwriters insurance exchange in 1913 to provide supplementary fire insurance for lumbermen.

EXECUTIVES

Executive Vice President Chief Financial Officer A, Eric Draut

Senior Vice President General Counsel, Scott Renwick

SVP and Chief Investment Officer, John M. Boschelli, age 47, $367,500 total compensation

President CEO and Director, Joseph P. (Joe) Lacher, age 46

CIO, Shawn R. Crawford

VP and Property and Casualty Group Executive, Denise I. Lynch, age 48, $461,250 total compensation

SVP and CFO, Frank J. Sodaro, age 46, $406,250 total compensation

EVP and General Manager Kemper Specialty California, Timothy D. Bruns

President Kemper Home Services Companies, Thomas D. Myers

President Reserve National Insurance Company, Andrew F. Schallhorn

EVP and General Manager Alliance United Group, David Mandel

Vp Of Investor Relations & Cor, Diana Hickert-Hill

Assistant Vice President, Lance Haukedahl

Vice President of Corporate Administrations and Head of Human Resources and Investor Relations, Edward (Ed) Konar

Senior Vice President Sales and Distribution, Paul Reissner

Senior Vice President Actuary, Stephen (Steve) Marsden

Assistant Vice President Information Technology Enterprise, Lisa Love

Vice President Senior Human Resources Manager, Rick Hammett

Assistant Vice President Real Estate and Administration, Calvin (Cal) Nash

Vice President, Christopher (Chris) Moses

Vice President, Lance Haukedhel

Vice President of Sales and Marketing, Jennifer (Jen) Griffin

Senior Vice President Sales and Marketing, Sharon Shofner-Meyer

Senior Vice President and Treasurer At Unitrin Career Agency Companies, Myers Thomas

Chairman, Robert J. (Bob) Joyce

Auditors: Deloitte & Touche LLP

LOCATIONS

HQ: Kemper Corp. (DE)
One East Wacker Drive, Chicago, IL 60601
Phone: 312 661-4600
Web: www.kemper.com

PRODUCTS/OPERATIONS

2014 Revenues

	$ mil.	% of total
Property & casualty insurance	1,322	60
Life & health insurance	832	37
Net realized gains on the sales of investments	39	2
Other	17	1
Net impairment losses recognized in earning	(15.2)	-
Total	**2,196**	**100**

Selected Insurance Options

Auto
Boat
Collectibles
Commercial Auto
Condo
Home
Identity Fraud
Life and Health
Package
Personal Catastrophe Liability
Personal Valuables
Renters

COMPETITORS

Allstate	Penn-America
Citizens Financial	Security National
Citizens Inc.	Financial
GEICO	State Farm
Liberty Mutual Agency	USAA
Nationwide	

HISTORICAL FINANCIALS

Company Type: Public

Income Statement

FYE: December 31

	ASSETS ($ mil.)	NET INCOME ($ mil.)	INCOME AS % OF ASSETS	EMPLOYEES
12/15	8,036	85	1.1%	5,600
12/14	7,833	114	1.5%	5,350
12/13	7,656	217	2.8%	6,100
12/12	8,009	103	1.3%	6,075
12/11	8,085	83	1.0%	—
Annual Growth	(0.2%)	0.6%	—	—

2015 Year-End Financials

Debt ratio: 9.34%	No. of shares (mil.): 51
Return on equity: 4.20%	Dividends
Cash ($ mil.): 161	Yield: 2.5%
Current ratio: —	Payout: 35.0%
Long-term debt ($ mil.): —	Market value ($ mil.): 1,912

	STOCK PRICE ($) FY Close	P/E High/Low	PER SHARE ($) Earnings	Dividends	Book Value
12/15	37.25	25 21	1.65	0.96	38.82
12/14	36.11	19 16	2.12	0.96	39.88
12/13	40.88	11 8	3.80	0.96	36.86
12/12	29.50	19 16	1.74	0.96	36.98
12/11	29.21	23 16	1.38	0.96	36.78
Annual Growth	6.3%	— —	4.6%	(0.0%)	1.4%

KeyCorp

Financial services giant KeyCorp unlocks its customers' monetary potential. With a focus on retail operations flagship subsidiary KeyBank operates nearly 1000 branches and 1300 ATMs in a dozen states in the Northeast the Midwest the Rocky Mountains and the Pacific Northwest including Alaska. Its operations are divided into two groups: Key Community Bank offers traditional services such as deposits loans credit cards and financial planning; while Key Corporate Bank provides investment banking services real estate capital equipment financing and capital markets services to large corporate clients nationwide.

OperationsBoasting around $94 billion in total assets KeyCorp is the US' third largest servicer of commercial and multifamily loans. The bank makes about 50% of its revenue from loan interest mostly from commercial financial and agricultural and commercial real estate loans (including commercial mortgage and construction loans) as well as commercial leases. Another roughly 20% of its revenue came from trust and investment services fee income and Investment banking and debt placement fee income.Geographic Reach

Cleveland-based KeyCorp has more than 990 US branches in Ohio Alaska Indiana Michigan New York Oregon Washington and throughout New England. One quarter of these branches are concentrated in the Pacific states while about one-third are split between the Eastern New York and Eastern Ohio regions.Sales and MarketingKey Community Bank provides traditional banking services to individuals and small to mid-sized businesses while Key Corporate Bank provides its investment banking services to middle-market clients in seven industry sectors including: consumer energy healthcare industrial public sector real estate and technology. The bank spent $49 million on advertising in 2014 down from the $51 million and $68 million it spent in 2013 and 2012 respectively.Financial PerformanceKeyCorp's revenue has been slowly declining over the past few years while profit has been mostly flat. Revenue in 2014 dipped by less than 1% to $4.35 billion mostly because the bank collected less in loan interest as asset yields shrank (though loan volumes grew for the year) in the low-interest environment. The bank's investment banking business however grew by nearly 20% for the year after its Pacific Crest Securities acquisition boosted its reach into the technology sector. Lower revenue in 2014 caused net income to fall by around 1% to $900 million while cash from operations declined by 15%.StrategyKeyCorp's main strategy which it initiated in 2014 and followed through 2015 is to grow its customer base and grow its business with existing clients by leveraging and cross selling its variety of financial products and services. In addition Keycorp has been focused on controlling costs and reducing expenses from the front to the back office

embracing digital banking platforms and cutting costly branch operations. The bank closed some 34 branches in 2014 bringing its total branch network size down to 994 (compared to 1088 branches in 2012).

The bank has also exited several non-core lines of business including education lending to focus on its core banking business in recent years. In 2014 for example it exited its international leasing business due to limited scale and cross-sell potential with its other businesses. In July 2013 KeyCorp sold its investment management business Victory Capital Management and its broker dealer affiliate Victory Capital Advisers to private equity firm Crestview Partners in order to focus on consumer and corporate banking.Keycorp is not opposed to strategic asset acquisitions to grow its business lines. In late 2014 the company purchased Pacific Crest Securities to expand its investment banking and capital markets business in the fast-growing technology sector. In 2013 KeyCorp purchased a commercial real estate serving portfolio and special servicing business that brought in more than $1 billion in low-cost escrow deposits and bolstered its existing servicing platforms.Mergers and Acquisitions

In October 2015 KeyCorp agreed to purchase First Niagara Financial and its bank subsidiaries. The $4.1 billion-merger deal expected to close in the third quarter of 2016 would add nearly 400 new branches to KeyCorp's network in New York state (boosting its existing total branch network by about 40%) and lead to annual cost savings of $400 million beginning in 2017. KeyCorp also estimated that the deal would lead to an internal rate of return of around 15%. In late 2014 Keycorp bought Pacific Crest Securities a technology sector-focused investment bank and capital markets firm as part of its broader investment banking growth strategy and to better serve middle-market companies.In 2012 KeyCorp acquired nearly 40 branches in the Buffalo and Rochester New York areas from First Niagara which is divesting the branches in order to satisfy antitrust concerns related to its acquisition of nearly 200 branches in upstate New York from HSBC USA.

HISTORY

Company BackgroundKeyCorp predecessor Commercial Bank of Albany was chartered in 1825. In 1865 it joined the new national banking system and became National Commercial Bank of Albany. After WWI National Commercial consolidated with Union National Bank & Trust as National Commercial Bank and Trust which then merged with First Trust and Deposit in 1971.

In 1973 Victor Riley became president and CEO. Under Riley National Commercial grew during the 1970s and 1980s through acquisitions. Riley sought to make the company a regional powerhouse but was thwarted when several New England states passed legislation barring New York banks from buying banks in the region.

As a result the company renamed Key Bank in 1979 turned west targeting small towns with less competition. Thus situated it prospered despite entering Alaska just in time for the 1986 oil price collapse. Its folksy image and small-town success earned it a reputation as the "Wal-Mart of banking."

Meanwhile in Cleveland Society for Savings followed a different path. Founded as a mutual savings bank in 1849 the institution succeeded from the start. It survived the Civil War and postwar economic turmoil and built Cleveland's first skyscraper in 1890. It continued to grow even during the Depression and became the largest savings bank outside the Northeast in 1949.

In 1955 the bank formed a holding company Society National. Society grew through the acquisitions of smaller banks in Ohio until 1979 when Ohio allowed branch banking in contiguous counties. Thereafter Society National opened branches as well. In the mid-1980s and the early 1990s the renamed Society Corporation began consolidating its operations and continued growing.

A 1994 merger of National Commercial with Society more than doubled assets for the surviving KeyCorp; compatibility of the two companies' systems and software simplified consolidation. KeyCorp sold its mortgage-servicing unit to NationsBank (now Bank of America) in 1995 and over the next year bought investment management finance and investment banking firms.

In 1997 KeyCorp began trimming its branch network divesting 200 offices including its 28-branch KeyBank Wyoming subsidiary. It expanded its consumer lending business that year by buying Champion Mortgage. In cooperation with USF&G (now part of The St. Paul Travelers Companies) and three HMOs KeyCorp began offering health insurance to the underserved small-business market.

In 1998 the company bought Leasetec which leases computer storage systems globally through its StorageTek subsidiary; it also bought McDonald & Company Investments (now McDonald Investments; sold in 2007) with an eye toward reaching its goal of earning half of its revenues from fees. Also in 1998 KeyCorp began offering business lines of credit to customers of Costco Wholesale the nation's largest wholesale club.

As part of a restructuring effort KeyCorp sold 28 Long Island New York branches to Dime Bancorp in 1999. The next year the company sold its credit card portfolio to Associates First Capital (now part of Citigroup) and bought National Realty Funding a securitizer of commercial mortgages. In 2001 it acquired Denver-based investment bank The Wallach Company.

The company expanded further in the Denver area with its 2002 purchase of Union Bankshares. Two years later KeyCorp bought Seattle-area bank EverTrust Financial Group.

In 2007 the company bought Tuition Management Systems which provides outsourced tuition billing accounting and counseling services for schools and colleges; the unit was later merged into its Key Education Resources operations. Also that year KeyCorp sold investment bank and brokerage McDonald Investments to UBS Financial Services.

The company bought New York-based U.S.B. Holding Co. and its Union State Bank subsidiary for some $550 million in early 2008. The deal added more than 30 branches nearly doubling KeyCorp's presence in the Hudson River Valley region.

EXECUTIVES

Executive Vice President General Counsel Secretary and Director, Paul Harris

Executive Vice President of IT Devlopment, Vernon L (Vern) Patterson

Vice President, Daniel (Dan) Stolzer

President Key Corporate Bank; Chairman and CEO KeyBank, Christopher M. (Chris) Gorman, age 54, $600,000 total compensation

President KeyBank Mortgage, Mark R. Danahy, age 56

CFO, Donald R. Kimble, age 55, $600,000 total compensation

President Cincinnati Market, John Marrocco

Co-President Key Community Bank, E. J. Burke, $533,127 total compensation

EVP EPMO Marketing and Client Insights and Data Management, Robert A. DeAngelis

SEVP and Chief Risk Officer, William L. (Bill) Hartmann, $500,000 total compensation
Chairman and CEO, Beth E. Mooney, age 59, $1,000,000 total compensation
Co-President Key Community Bank, Dennis A. Devine, $528,846 total compensation
CIO, Amy G. Brady
EVP and Director Corporate Center, Katrina M. (Trina) Evans
Executive Vice President Marketing, Bonnie Squadere
Vice President Technology Internal Audit, Lisa Evans
Vice President Database Marketing, Jonathan (Jon) Boyer
Vice President, Alison Sammon
Senior Vice President Institutional Fx, David Renta
Assistant Vice President, Grace Moyano
Senior Vice President Enterprise Technology, Karol Higaki
Assistant Vice President, Paul Pace
Vice President Marketing, Hannah Costin
Vice President Application Systems Manager, Nancy Walser
Senior Vice President, Helen France
Vice President Healthcare Products, Victoria Terekhova
Assistant Vice President Senior Financial Analyst Planning and Forecasting, Danny Pho
Vice President Global Trade Services, Robert Kurek
Senior Vice President Business Technology Executive, Douglas (Doug) Kanouff
Vice President Information Technology, Anurag Sharma
Senior Vice President, Kim Monson
Vice President Senior Business Analyst, Karen Mahoney
Executive Vice President Marketing, Darlene Kohring
Vice President Financial Risk Governance Manager, Anna Norcross
Vice President, Rachel Venezuela
Senior Vice President Commercial Credit Risk Review, David Navy
Vice President Compliance Manager, Benjamin Zlatin
Senior Vice President, David (Dave) Herron
Vice President Business Development, Carol Schafer
Vice President Finance, Patrick Mayo
Vice President Manager Of Information Services, Kelly McNamara
Senior Vice President and Manager West Region Government Relations, Thomas (Thom) Hosea
Senior Vice President Community Development Banking, Poppie Parish
Vice President, Melissa (Mel) Werner
Senior Vice President, Fred Villao
Executive Vice President, Bruce Murphy
Senior Vice President, Henry Alonso
SVPDirector Employee Relations and Human Resources Compliance, Katie Ladd
Senior Vice President Central Ohio District, Thomas (Thom) Spilman
Vice President, Marcella Pardo
Assistant Vice President Corporate Information Security, Rick Snevel
Senior Vice President Payment Deposit, Dominic Cugini
Senior Vice President Financial Planning, Jack Zugay
Senior Vice President Of Marketing Strategy, Marta Blase
Vice President Web Infrastructure Management, Thomas Krizsa
Senior Vice President Business Banking Market Executive, Randy Riffle
Senior Vice President Capital Planning, Jay Luzar
Vice President, Greg Endres

Vice President Database Marketing and Analytics, Ellen Shefner
Vice President Information Technology, Michael (Mel) Evans
Senior Vice President, Karen Grexa
KCM Vice President, Kelly Crawford
Executive Vice President Marketing, Denise Almeida
Senior Vice President Compliance, Ken Fox
Senior Treasury Services Sales Officer Vice President, Anwar Smiley
Executive Vice President, Cindy P Crotty
Vice President Client Relations Manager, Laura Karter
Vice President Finance, Linda Kacenjar
Vice President Commercial Banker, Yong Lee
Vice Preseident, Dora Johnson
Vice President Senior Relationship Manager Commercial Banking, Daniel (Dan) Jacques
Vice President Consumer Channel Sales, Colleen Dugarte
Vice President Sales, Joseph (Jo) Callahan
Vice President Agency and Media Director, Michael (Mel) Varvaro
Senior Vice President Asset Recovery Group, Dale Clayton
Vice President Of Loans, Margot J Copeland
Vice President, Nicholas Stuart
Vice President Marketing, Mark Knierim
Executive Vice President, George Emmons
Senior Financial Planner Vice President, Matthew (Matt) Stewart
Vice President, Adam Aufdenkampe
Senior Vice President Channel Technology Capability And Integration, Khalil Rahman
Marketing Vice President, Bradley Thomas
Vice President Senior Managing Appraisal Officer, Mark T Figley
Vice President Originations Specialty Finance And Syndications, Ric Andersen
Vice President Consumer Finance, Dan Sukys
Vice President Strategic Communications and Governance, Alison Altre-Kerber
Vice President Product Manager, Brian Guess
Vice President and Trust Team Lead Real Estate, Emily Mogen
Credit Executive Senior Vice President, Brett Swanson
Senior Vice President Market Manager Private Bank, Elizabeth Vealey
Vice President Of Marketing Strategist, Jill Dalton
Vice President Senior Business Banker, John Marriott
Vice President Senior Human Resources Business Partner, Amy Hoyer
Senior Vice President Public Sector, Lara Deleone
Vice President Credit Officer, Jimmy Cefalo
Vice President Compliance and Operational Risk Officer, Amy Brown
Assistant Vice President Business Banking, Mark Hingson
Senior Vice President Manager, Robert Likes
Assistant Vice President Retail Banking, Michael Emerson
Senior Vice President And Finance Director, William Shaw
Vice President And Manager, Janet Jaros
Vice President Credit Risk Reviewer, Greg Newhouse
Vice President Investments, Christopher Walker
Senior Vice President Commercial Banking, Stephen Markley
Market Manager Senior Vice President, Brendon Tripodo
Vice President Private Banking, Andrew Bowen
Vice President, Joseph (Jo) Vayda
Vice President Team Leader, Pete Dunbar
Vice President Senior Asset Manager, Thomas Wainscott
Senior Vice President, James Harnett

Vice President Manager, Larissa Tadiello
Executive Vice President Of Corporate Strategy, Clark Khayat
Vice President Regional Compliance Manager, Randy McCall
Vice President Product Manager, Natalie Treibatch
Vice President Foreign Exchange Sales, Rick Moskowitz
Vice President Senior Relationship Manager, Justin Williams
Vice President Senior Business Banking Relationship Manager, Michael (Mel) Rowland
Vice President Regional Marketing, Sherry Brown
Senior Vice President, Deborah Brady
Vice President Division Manager zEnterprise Systems Management, Robert (Bob) Bellanti
Vice President Senior Portfolio Manager, Jeff Stegeman
Senior Vice President Regional Financial Planning Manager And National Strategic Advice Leader, Brian Jaros
Vice President, Brice Stammen
Vice President And Senior Banker, Brian Heagler
Vice President Senior Portfolio Manager, Paul Olszewski
Senior Vice President Enterprise Architecture, Mike Onders
Vice President Business Development, Alice Karn
Vice President Senior Appraisal Officer, Scott Tomak
Senior Vice President Private Bank Sales Leader, Lucia Pileggi
Vice President Senior Treasury Advisor Institutional Banking, Michael Thomas
Vice President Client Services Consumer Segment, Cheryl Towns
Vice President Risk Reviewer IV Enterprise Risk Management Audit, Michael (Mel) Kemp
Vice President Risk Reviewer IV Operations Audit, Grant Kerner
Vice President District Operations Manager, Monica Cichon
Senior Cash Management Advisor And Assistant Vice President Treasury Services, Kristina Simpson
Vice President Manager Credit Risk Management, Frank Jancar
Vice President And Senior Trust Officer, Daryl Hembry
Senior Vice President Manager Derivatives Hedging and Trading, Fred White
Vice President Compliance And Security Operations, Anthony Rini
Senior Vice President Real Estate Finance, Craig Younggren
Vice President Investor Reporting Manager, Elizabeth Michalski
Assistant Vice President Senior Treasury Management Advisor, Markee Jones
Assistant Vice President Atm Applications Support, Gary Knott
Vice President Community Bank Sales Systems, Robert Brzezinski
Senior Vice President Corporate Bank Technology And Sales Tool Team Manager, Brian Utrup
Vice President And Trust Officer, Chris Dietz
Vice President Senior Commercial Reviewer, Caryn Blauser
Anti Money Laundering Vice President, Jackie Koellner
Senior Asset Manager Assistant Vice President, Daniel Last
Vice President and Manager Enterprise Business Resiliency Operations, Shelley Christensen
Auditors: Ernst & Young LLP

LOCATIONS

HQ: KeyCorp
127 Public Square, Cleveland, OH 44114-1306
Phone: 216 689-3000
Web: www.key.com

PRODUCTS/OPERATIONS

2014 Sales

	$ mil.	% of total
Interest		
Loans	2,110	49
Securities	422	9
Other	22	1
Noninterest		
Trust & investment services	403	9
Investment banking and debt placement fees	397	9
Service charges on deposits	261	6
Corporate Service income	178	4
Cards and payments income	166	4
Corporate owned life insurance income	118	3
Operating lease income and other leasing gains	96	2
Net gains from principal investing	78	2
Mortagage service fees and Others	56	1
Others	44	1
Total	**4,354**	**100**

COMPETITORS

Bank of America	Huntington Bancshares
Citigroup	JPMorgan Chase
Citizens Financial Group	M&T Bank
	Northern Trust
Comerica	PNC Financial
Fifth Third	Sovereign Bank
Flagstar Bancorp	U.S. Bancorp
HSBC USA	Wells Fargo

HISTORICAL FINANCIALS

Company Type: Public

Income Statement

FYE: December 31

	ASSETS ($ mil.)	NET INCOME ($ mil.)	INCOME AS % OF ASSETS	EMPLOYEES
12/14	93,821	900	1.0%	13,853
12/13	92,934	910	1.0%	14,783
12/12	89,236	858	1.0%	15,589
12/11	88,785	920	1.0%	15,381
12/10	91,843	554	0.6%	15,610
Annual Growth	**0.5%**	**12.9%**	**—**	**(2.9%)**

2014 Year-End Financials

Debt ratio: 8.18%	No. of shares (mil.): 859
Return on equity: 8.64%	Dividends
Cash ($ mil.): 1,403	Yield: 1.8%
Current ratio: —	Payout: 26.0%
Long-term debt ($ mil.): —	Market value ($ mil.): 11,946

	STOCK PRICE ($) FY Close	P/E High/Low		PER SHARE ($)		
				Earnings	Dividends	Book Value
12/14	13.90	14	12	0.99	0.25	12.25
12/13	13.42	14	9	0.97	0.22	11.57
12/12	8.42	10	8	0.89	0.18	11.09
12/11	7.69	11	7	0.87	0.10	10.39
12/10	8.85	20	12	0.44	0.04	12.62
Annual Growth	**11.9%**			**22.5%**	**58.1%**	**(0.7%)**

Kimberly-Clark Corp.

Nobody knows noses and bottoms better than Kimberly-Clark. One of the world's largest makers of personal paper products the company operates through three business segments: personal care consumer tissue and K-C Professional. Kimberly-Clark's largest unit personal care makes products such as diapers (Huggies Pull-Ups) feminine care items (Kotex) and incontinence care products (Poise Depend). Through its consumer tissue seg-

ment the manufacturer offers facial and bathroom tissues paper towels and other household items under the names Cottonelle Kleenex Viva and Scott (plus the Scott Naturals line). Kimberly-Clark's professional unit makes WypAll commercial wipes among other items.

Geographic Reach

Kimberly-Clark maintains a broad global presence as part of its growth strategy. It boasts some 110 manufacturing facilities in about 40 countries across the US Canada Europe Asia and Latin America. Products reach about 175 countries.

Developing regions Asia Latin America and others now generate 40% of the company's revenue due to expansion efforts such as building a $40 million plant in Singapore and acquisitions such as the remaining 31% of its Bogota Colombia-based subsidiary Colombiana Kimberly Colpapel (CKC). The deal secured the company's foothold in the developing markets of Bolivia Colombia Ecuador Peru and Venezuela. Kimberly-Clark also holds Kimberly-Clark Kenko Industria e Comercio Ltda based in Brazil.

Operations

Amid a slow global economy that has put pressure on cash-strapped consumers and inflated the cost of fuel pulp and paper Kimberly-Clark has managed to hold on to the #1 or #2 position in 80-plus countries. Personal Care accounted for about 50% of total sales in 2014; Consumer Tissue 34%; and K-C Professional 17%.

Sales and Marketing

Kimberly-Clark sells its household items directly to supermarkets mass merchandisers drugstores warehouse clubs variety and department stores and other retail outlets as well as through distributors and e-commerce. For the away-from-home market it serves the company sells through distributors and directly to high-volume public facilities and to manufacturing lodging office building food service and health care establishments.

To gain recognition for its brands the company has averaged about $780 million in advertising expenses each year. In 2014 Kimberly-Clark logged $767 million in ad spending. As business and economic conditions improve the consumer paper company will spend more aggressively on advertising and promoting its products.

Its largest customer über worldwide retailer Wal-Mart represented about 13% of sales in 2014 2013 and 2012.

Financial Performance

Kimberly-Clark's revenues have seen an upward trend over past few years. However revenues fell 7% to $19.7 billion in 2014 primarily due to the company's spin-off of its health care business. (Note: the company's 2013 financial numbers have been restated due to these discontinued operations.)

Its profits decreased 29% from nearly $2.2 billion in 2013 to $1.5 billion in 2013 due to a bump in other expenses and a decline in income from discontinued operations related to the spin-off of its health care business. The company's operating cash flow declined 6% to $2.8 billion in 2014 due to the lower profits and an increase in cash used in accrued income taxes.

Strategy

Kimberly-Clark's strategy includes building upon its well-branded position in the personal care and consumer tissue space. Notable introductions are Huggies Little Movers Slip-On Diapers Poise Hourglass Shape Pads and Kleenex Cool Touch Facial Tissue among several others. The company has simultaneously moved into making higher-margin disposable medical products. It produces sterilization wrap face masks surgical drapes and gowns and closed-suction respiratory products.

Its health care unit has logged increasingly higher year-over-year sales volumes helped by ac-

quisitions. Among them Kimberly-Clark took over Baylis Medical's pain management business which focuses on chronic spinal pain and I-Flow a developer and marketer of drug-delivery systems for post-surgical pain relief and surgical site care. To get better shareholder returns in 2014 Kimberly-Clark spun off its health care business into a standalone company known as Halyard Health. To offset $85 million in overhead costs associated with the pending spinoff the company announced plans to eliminate up to 1300 jobs by the end of 2015 in an effort to save $120 million to $140 million by the end of 2017.

In 2014 Kimberly-Clark spent $370 million on research and development directed toward new or improved personal care tissue wiping safety and health care products and nonwoven materials.

HISTORY

John Kimberly Charles Clark Havilah Babcock and Frank Shattuck founded Kimberly Clark & Company in Neenah Wisconsin in 1872 to manufacture newsprint from rags. The company incorporated as Kimberly & Clark Company in 1880 and built a pulp and paper plant on the Fox River in 1889.

In 1914 the company developed cellu-cotton a cotton substitute used by the US Army as surgical cotton during WWI. Army nurses used cellu-cotton pads as disposable sanitary napkins and six years later the company introduced Kotex the first disposable feminine hygiene product. Kleenex the first throwaway handkerchief followed in 1924. Kimberly & Clark joined with The New York Times Company in 1926 to build a newsprint mill (Spruce Falls Power and Paper) in Ontario Canada. Two years later the company went public as Kimberly-Clark.

EXECUTIVES

Chairman President and CEO, Thomas J. (Tom) Falk, age 57, $1,300,000 total compensation
CFO, Maria Henry
President Global Brands and Innovation, Anthony J. (Tony) Palmer, age 55, $622,500 total compensation
President Kimberly-Clark North America, Michael Hsu, age 51, $746,250 total compensation
President Kimberly-Clark Professional, Kim Underhill
Group President Kimberly-Clark International, Elane B. Stock, age 51, $718,750 total compensation
Vice President of Sales, Michael (Mel) Dana
Vice President Corporate Finance And Strategy Analysis, Joe Kupka
Vice President Tax, Dave Bernard
Vice President Walmart International Development, John Scholes
Vice President Human Resources, Rick Purdy
Vice President Global Health Care Qualit, Mizanu Kebede
Assistant Secretary, Jackie Bates
Auditors: DELOITTE & TOUCHE LLP

LOCATIONS

HQ: Kimberly-Clark Corp.
P.O. Box 619100, Dallas, TX 75261-9100
Phone: 972 281-1200
Web: www.kimberly-clark.com

2014 Sales

	$ mil.	% of total
North America	9,400	49
Asia Latin America & other	7,961	37
Europe	2,717	14
Intergeographic sales	(354)	-
Total	**19,724**	**100**

PRODUCTS/OPERATIONS

2014 Sales

	$ mil.	% of total
Personal Care	9,635	49
Consumer Tissue	6,645	34
K-C Professional	3,388	17
Corporate & other	56	-
Total	**19,724**	**100**

2014 Sales

	% of total
Baby & child care products	36
Consumer tissue products	33
Away-from-home professional products	17
All other	14
Total	**100**

Selected Products and Brands

Medical
  Closed-suction respiratory products
  Examination gloves
  Safeskin
  Face masks
  Infection-control products
  Scrub suits and apparel
  Sterile wrap
  Kimguard
  Surgical drapes and gowns
Personal Care
  Baby wipes
  Huggies
  Disposable diapers
  GoodNites
  Huggies
  Pull-Ups
  Feminine hygiene products
  Kotex
  Lightdays
  New Freedom
  Incontinence products
  Depend
  Poise
  Swimpants
  Little Swimmers
Tissue-Based
  Bathroom tissue
  Cottonelle
  Scott
  Commercial wipes
  Kimwipes
  WypAll
  Facial tissue
  Kleenex
  Paper napkins
  Scott
  Paper towels
  Kleenex
  Scott
  Viva

COMPETITORS

3M	Georgia-Pacific
Ansell	Johnson & Johnson
Becton Dickinson	Medline Industries
Bristol-Myers Squibb	Nice-Pak Products
CCA Industries	Potlatch
Cardinal Health	Procter & Gamble
Medical	SSI Surgical Services
DSG International Ltd	Suominen
Edgewell Personal Care	

HISTORICAL FINANCIALS

Company Type: Public

Income Statement

FYE: December 31

	REVENUE ($ mil.)	NET INCOME ($ mil.)	NET PROFIT MARGIN	EMPLOYEES
12/15	18,591	1,013	5.4%	43,000
12/14	19,724	1,526	7.7%	43,000
12/13	21,152	2,142	10.1%	57,000
12/12	21,063	1,750	8.3%	58,000
12/11	20,846	1,591	7.6%	57,000
Annual Growth	**(2.8%)**	**(10.7%)**	**—**	**(6.8%)**

2015 Year-End Financials

Debt ratio: 52.39%
Return on equity: 293.20%
Cash ($ mil.): 619
Current ratio: 0.85
Long-term debt ($ mil.): 6,106

No. of shares (mil.): 360
Dividends
  Yield: 2.7%
  Payout: 214.6%
Market value ($ mil.): 45,943

	STOCK PRICE ($) FY Close	P/E High/Low	PER SHARE ($) Earnings	Dividends	Book Value
12/15	127.30	47 37	2.77	3.52	(0.30)
12/14	115.54	29 25	4.04	3.36	2.19
12/13	104.46	20 15	5.53	3.24	12.94
12/12	84.43	20 16	4.42	2.96	14.22
12/11	73.56	18 16	3.99	2.80	14.65
Annual Growth	**14.7%**	**— —**	**(8.7%)**	**5.9%**	**—**

Kinder Morgan Inc.

Kinder Morgan Inc. (KMI formerly Kinder Morgan Holdco) is the top layer of a large oil and gas cake. The company owns Kinder Morgan Management which manages the general partner of Kinder Morgan Energy Partners (KMP). KMP operates pipeline that transport natural gas crude oil gasoline and other products along with terminals used to store chemicals and petroleum products and other items (including coal and steel). It produces carbon dioxide (CO2) which is used in oil field production. KMI owns stakes in or operates 84000 miles of pipelines and 180 terminals. It also holds 51% of El Paso Pipeline Partners.

Geographic Reach

KMI has operations in the US Canada. and Mexico. The US accounted for 96% of the company's revenues in 2014.

Operations

The company is a leader in petroleum product transportation terminal operations and coke and CO2 transportation.

It holds 48000 miles of natural gas transmission pipelines and gathering lines plus natural gas storage treating and processing facilities and through KMP 9000 miles of refined petroleum products pipelines and 1500 miles of CO2 pipelines. It also owns or operates seven oil fields in West Texas and a 450-mile crude oil pipeline system in West Texas.Its terminal business owns or operates 122 liquids and bulk terminal facilities and 10 rail transloading and materials handling facilities in the US and Canada. The business transloads and store refined petroleum products crude oil condensate and bulk products including coal petroleum coke cement alumina salt and other bulk chemicals. The segment also owns and operates Jones Act tankers.

Kinder Morgan Canada transports crude oil and refined petroleum products through across 713 miles of pipelines (and five associated product terminal facilities) from Alberta Canada to marketing terminals and refineries in British Columbia Washington State the Rockies and the Central US.

KMI also owns 51% of El Paso Pipeline Partners and about 20% of natural gas pipeline NGPL PipeCo.

Sales and Marketing

The Texas intrastate natural gas pipeline group buys and sells significant volumes of natural gas in Texas; the CO2 business segment also sells natural gas. Total revenues from the sales of natural gas from the Natural Gas Pipelines and CO2 business segments in 2014 accounted for 25% KMI's total revenues.

Financial Performance

KMI's revenues have increased consistently over the past few years. In 2014 revenues grew by 15% driven by Natural Gas Pipelines sales (mainly from external customers in both natural gas and CO2 business segments). Terminal segment revenues grew thanks to increased volumes.In 2014 KMI's net income decreased by 14% due to higher sales costs and other operating expenses related to major acquisitions.

Cash from operating activities increased by 8% in 2014 due to higher net income a decline in case reserve payments and net changes in working capital items and non-current assets and liabilities.

Strategy

KMI's strategy is focused on building and maintaining energy transportation and storage assets which are central components to a growing natural gas and petroleum products infrastructure across North America. Its business strategy includes acquiring additional businesses expanding existing assets and constructing new facilitiesIn 2015 KMI's joint venture with Keyera agreed to build a new crude oil storage terminal (4.8 million barrels of crude oil capacity) in Edmonton Alberta. KMI's investment in the joint venture terminal is approximately C$342 million ($385 million) for an initial 12 tank build.

In 2014 El Paso Pipeline Partners agreed to buy KMI's 50% stake in Ruby Pipeline 50% interest in Gulf LNG and 47.5% stake in Young Gas Storage for $2 billion. As a result KMI plans to reduce its debt while continuing to participate in the cash flows from these assets through its general and limited partner interests in El Paso Pipeline Partners.That year KMI also announced plans to invest $671 million to grow its carbon dioxide infrastructure in southwestern Colorado and New Mexico.

Mergers and Acquisitions

Growing its assets in 2015 KMI acquired Hiland Partners for an aggregate consideration of more than $3 billion. That year it also purchased three Vopak terminals and one undeveloped site for $158 Million. The acquisition which covers a 36-acre storage complex at Galena Park Texas will increase KMI's liquids storage capacity by more than 2.2 million barrels and 115 tanks while adding critical dock capacity on the Houston Ship Channel and in Wilmington.

In 2014 the company consolidated its oil-and-gas pipeline holdings into a single company with KMI acquiring KMP Kinder Morgan Management and El Paso Pipeline Partners in a $44 billion deal.

Significantly expanding its midstream services portfolio in 2013 KMI acquired Houston-based Copano Energy for $5 billion.

Company Background

In a major move to become the largest natural gas pipeline and midstream enterprise in North America (with about 75000 miles of natural gas pipeline and 180 terminals) in 2012 KMI acquired El Paso Corp. (which had 44000 miles of natural gas pipeline) for about $38 billion. To comply with FTC requirements in completing the deal in 2012 KMI sold KMP's FTC Natural Gas Pipelines disposal group to Tallgrass Energy Partners L.P. for $1.8 billion.

Apart from greatly expanding the company's size and scope the El Paso Corp. deal is expected to save KMI more than $400 million of cost savings per year through the integration of the two organizations and the elimination of redundancies.

In mid-2013 it paid $5 billion for Copano Energy a midstream company with interests in almost 7000 miles of natural gas pipeline in Oklahoma Texas and Wyoming. The acquisition expands Kinder Morgan's operations in the Eagle Ford shale and Barnett shale in Texas and the Mississippi Lime and Woodford shales in Oklahoma.

Growing its operations in other shale areas in 2013 Kinder Morgan Energy Partners L.P. and MarkWest Utica EMG L.L.C. agreed to form a joint venture to build a cryogenic processing complex and the infrastructure to support producers in the Utica and Marcellus shales in Ohio Pennsylvania and West Virginia.

Chairman and CEO Richard D. Kinder led a group of investors in taking KMI private in 2007. It then adopted the Knight name. To take advantage of its better-known brand it reverted to the Kinder Morgan name in 2009. Kinder Morgan went public in 2011 and changed its name to Kinder Morgan Inc (KMI). IPO proceeds went to the aforementioned selling shareholders.

EXECUTIVES

President and CEO, Steven J. (Steve) Kean, age 54, $1 total compensation
VP and CFO, Kimberly Allen (Kim) Dang, age 46, $348,077 total compensation
President Kinder Morgan Canada, Ian D. Anderson, age 58
VP and President Natural Gas Pipelines, Thomas A. (Tom) Martin, $348,077 total compensation
President Products Pipelines, Ronald G. (Ron) McClain
President Terminals, John W. Schlosser
VP and CIO, Mark Huse
President CO2, Jesse Arenivas
VP and General Counsel, David R. DeVeau, $348,077 total compensation
VP Human Resources Information Technology and Administration, Lisa M. Shorb
Vice President Purchasing, Tom Martin
Vice President Business Development Products Pipelines, Karen Kabin
Power Operations Vice President, Larry Stoddard
Vice President Pipeline Scheduling, Holly Breaux
Executive Vice President And Chief Operating Officer, Scott Stoness
Vice President Corporate Security and Business Continuity, Jay Montgomery
Vice President Corporate Planning, Kristin Tatum
Vice President of Source and Transportation, Ken Havens
Vice President Land and ROW, McGee Johnny
Vice President Deputy General Counsel, Shelia Tweed
Vice President Financial Planning Midstream, Joe Joyce
Vice President Kinder Morgan Natural Gas Pipelines, Kevin Howard
Board Vice President, Randy Ramsey
Vice President Land and Right of way, Johnny McGee
Vice President Finance, Da Sanders
Senior Vice President E and P Operations, John (Jack) Jensen
Vice President and Chief Compliance Officer, Charles (Chas) Schwager
Executive Chairman, Richard D. (Rich) Kinder, age 71
Treasurer, Anthony Ashley
Auditors: PricewaterhouseCoopers LLP

LOCATIONS

HQ: Kinder Morgan Inc.
1001 Louisiana Street, Suite 1000, Houston, TX 77002
Phone: 713 369-9000
Web: www.kindermorgan.com

2014 Sales

	$ mil.	% of total
US	15,605	96
Canada	437	3
Mexico	184	1
Total	**16,226**	**100**

PRODUCTS/OPERATIONS

2014 Sales

	$ mil.	% of total
Natural Gas Pipelines	10,168	63
CO2 - KMP	1,960	12
Products Pipelines - KMP	2,068	12
Terminals - KMP	1,718	11
Kinder Morgan Canada - KMP	292	2
Other	36	0
Less: total intersegment revenue	(16)	0
Total	**16,226**	**100**

COMPETITORS

AltaGas	K-Sea Transportation
BC Hydro	Koch Industries Inc.
Buckeye Partners	Plains All American
Canadian Utilities	Pipeline
Colorado Interstate	Royal Vopak
Gas	Spectra Energy
Dynegy	Sunoco Logistics
EnLink Midstream	TransMontaigne
Partners	Williams Companies
Enterprise Products	

HISTORICAL FINANCIALS

Company Type: Public

Income Statement

FYE: December 31

	REVENUE ($ mil.)	NET INCOME ($ mil.)	NET PROFIT MARGIN	EMPLOYEES
12/15	14,403	253	1.8%	11,290
12/14	16,226	1,026	6.3%	11,535
12/13	14,070	1,193	8.5%	11,075
12/12	9,973	315	3.2%	10,685
12/11	8,264	594	7.2%	8,120
Annual Growth	**14.9%**	**(19.2%)**	**—**	**8.6%**

2015 Year-End Financials

Debt ratio: 51.40%—
Return on equity: 0.73%
Cash ($ mil.): 229
Current ratio: 0.69
Long-term debt ($ mil.): 42,406

Dividends
Yield: 12.9%
Payout: 428.8%
Market value ($ mil.): —

	STOCK PRICE ($) FY Close	P/E High/Low		PER SHARE ($) Earnings	Dividends	Book Value
12/15	14.92	446	145	0.10	1.93	15.75
12/14	42.31	48	35	0.89	1.70	16.03
12/13	36.00	36	28	1.15	1.56	12.70
12/12	35.33	114	88	0.35	1.34	13.39
12/11	32.17	43	32	0.74	0.74	4.13
Annual Growth	**(17.5%)**	**—**	**—**	**(39.4%)**	**27.1%**	**39.7%**

Kindred Healthcare Inc

Families unable to provide 24-hour care to their kin can at least turn to Kindred Healthcare. As a leading provider of long-term health care Kindred operates more than 100 nursing and rehabilitation centers and some 100 long-term acute care hospitals in the US. In addition Kindred's RehabCare business provides contract rehabilitation therapy services at more than 1900 facilities. The firm also runs sub-acute and inpatient rehabilitation centers as well as home health and hospice agencies. Its facilities have a combined capacity of more than 35000 beds and span 47 states. In 2015 the company bought Gentiva Health Services in a $1.8 billion transaction; the deal nearly doubled Kindred's size.

HISTORY

After a stint as Kentucky's commerce secretary in the 1980s Bruce Lunsford was approached by respiratory therapist Michael Barr with the idea of establishing long-term hospitals for ventilator-dependent patients. Barr said these hospitals would be cheaper to run than full-service facilities which require additional equipment. Lunsford (who became chairman president and CEO) and Barr (who was COO) founded Vencare in 1983 with backing from Gene Smith (a wealthy political associate of Lunsford). They bought a money-losing 62-bed Indiana hospital and soon turned the operation around.

Vencare expanded into Florida and Texas and by the end of the 1980s operated more than 420 beds in seven facilities. Revenues jumped from less than $1 million in 1985 to $54 million by 1989 the year it changed its name to Vencor.

During the early 1990s Vencor added facilities in Arizona California Colorado Georgia and Missouri. Vencor ran 29 facilities by the end of 1993 the same year it launched its Vencare respiratory care program.

Vencor acquisitions in 1995 included hospital respiratory and cardiopulmonary departments in seven states. Later that year it bought the much-larger Hillhaven the US's #2 nursing home operator at that time. (In 1990 Hillhaven had been spun off from what is now Tenet Healthcare.) When Vencor bought it Hillhaven owned 310 nursing homes 60 pharmacies and 23 retirement communities. The buy furthered Lunsford's vision of creating a network of long-term-care facilities and services. Vencor also debuted VenTouch an electronic-pad-based record-keeping system for its facilities in 1995.

In 1996 Vencor spun off its assisted and independent living properties as Atria Communities; as part of the Hillhaven assimilation it also consolidated its MediSave pharmacy unit into its hospital operations and sold 34 nursing homes to Lennox Healthcare.

Vencor's 1997 buys included TheraTx (216 rehabilitation centers 28 nursing centers 16 occupational health clinics) and Transitional Hospitals (long-term acute care hospitals). That year Vencor formed an alliance with insurer CNA to develop an insurance product for long-term care.

In 1998 the company split into Ventas (real estate) and Vencor (operations). It also sold most of its remaining interest in an assisted living company (now called Atria Senior Quarters) it had spun off in 1996. To attract wealthier residents it also launched a program in 1998 to turn away —and turn out —Medicaid patients. Vencor soon abandoned the plan amid heated attacks from advocacy groups. (Welcoming back the evictees didn't stop

Florida regulators from fining Vencor.) Several other states and the federal government also began probing Vencor's practices; in 1999 the affair prompted Congressional action designed to protect Medicaid patients. Lunsford and Barr were ousted in the turmoil. The government also demanded that Vencor return $90 million in overpayments over 60 months ($2 million a month) or risk losing Medicare payments.

The company filed for Chapter 11 bankruptcy later in 1999. Despite bankruptcy protection the Justice Department in 2000 filed claims for more than $1 billion from Vencor for Medicare fraud since 1992. Vencor settled the majority of these claims the next year. The company emerged from bankruptcy in April 2001 and changed its name to Kindred Healthcare. In 2003 the company sold all of its Texas and Florida nursing center operations. Kindred Healthcare began operating its contract rehabilitation business as a separate division in 2004.

In 2006 the company bought the long-term care operations of Commonwealth Communities Holdings gaining six long-term acute care hospitals and 11 nursing homes in Massachusetts. The company entered lease agreements for eight nursing homes in San Francisco in 2007.

In 2007 Kindred spun off its Kindred Pharmacy Services unit which distributed drugs to long-term care facilities. The unit was combined with the institutional pharmacy unit of AmerisourceBergen to form a new entity named PharMerica. Kindred Pharmacy Services contributed more than 40 institutional pharmacies in 26 states to the combined company.

EXECUTIVES

EVP and President Care Management Division, William M. Altman, age 56, $402,278 total compensation
EVP and CFO, Stephen D. Farber, age 41, $442,318 total compensation
President CEO and Director, Benjamin A. Breier, age 44, $758,230 total compensation
EVP and COO, Kent H. Wallace, age 60
EVP and President RehabCare, Jon B. Rosseau
President Nursing Center Division, Michael W. Beal
President Hospital Division, Peter K. Kalmey
Vice President Talent Management, Kathi Eldridge
Director Of Health Information, Debra Patterson
Vice President Information Technology, Michael (Mel) Bean
Senior Vice President Clinical Operations prs, Mary van de Kamp
Vice President Director Manager, Renay Thommen
Senior Vice President Sales and Marketing, David (Dave) Mikula
Vice President Corporate Finance, Mark Laemmle
Respiratory Therapy Director, Cynthia Tinker
Cota, Janice Paradise
Admissions Director, Ivette Robinson
Senior Vice President Human Resources Operations, Jeffrey (Jeff) Jasnoff
Regional Vice President Chief Clinical Officer Wes, Heather Sebanc
Director Of Medical Records, Roxanne Keith
Director of Physical Therapy, Julie Westphal
Div Vice President Rehab prs, David (Dave) Tate
Division Vice President of Case Management, Tami Johnson
Senior Vice President, Suzanne Riedman
Admissions Director, Kelli Collins
Vice President Of Liability Claims, Hans Koehler
Director Of Respiratory Therapy, Daniel Simon
Director Of Nursing Services, Merry Dalahmeh
Director Of Respiratory Therapy, Michael Arellano
Vice President of Operations, Michelle (Mitch) Brown

Director Of Nursing, Ashley Collins
Director of Physical Therapy, Mathu Hanson
Director Of Nursing, Janet Jorgensen
Vice President and Chief Counsel Nursing Center Division, Kelly Priegnitz
Director Of Nursing, Melissa Cappuccino
Vice President Of Labor Relations, Edward Goddard
Divison Vice President at Rehab Care, Martin (Marti) Ardron
Vice President Finance, Joyce Simmons
Cota, Judy Kaufman
Director of Pharmacy Management, Aimee Snyder
Nursing Services Director, Mark Norman
Vice President Corporate Communications and Events, Susan (Sue) Moss
Cota, Barbara Stewart
Vice President Of Facilities, Tony Dickamore
Manager Of Laboratory Services, Dianna Denton
Director of Nursing, Michelle (Mitch) Kelczewski
Regional Vice President Of Finance, Doug Roth
Director Of Nursing, Kellie Kennedy
Director Of Physical Therapy, Adila Millwala
Nursing Director, Phillip Lindsay
Division Vice President Hospital Division, Julie Feasel
Senior Vice President Corporate Legal Affairs and Corporate Secretary, Joseph (Jo) Landenwich
Senior Vice President and Chief Medical Officer Hospital Division, Sean Muldoon
Vice President of Clinical Systems Development, Denny Ertel
Senior Vice President Clinical Operations, Tony Disser
Vice President of Rehab, Vonda Black
Director of Medical Records, Antaria Hill-Steele
Vice President and Real Estate Counsel, Cristina E O'Brien
Vice President Of Operations and Telecommunications, Charles (Chas) Wardrip
Executive Vice Chairman, Paul J. Diaz, age 54
Chairman, Phyllis R. Yale, age 58
Auditors: PricewaterhouseCoopers LLP

LOCATIONS

HQ: Kindred Healthcare Inc
680 South Fourth Street, Louisville, KY 40202-2412
Phone: 502 596-7300
Web: www.kindredhealthcare.com

PRODUCTS/OPERATIONS

2014 Sales

	$ mil.	% of total
Hospital division	2,525	48
Nursing center division	1,062	20
Rehabilitation division		
Skilled nursing rehabilitation services	1,007	19
Hospital rehabilitation services	299	6
Care management division	349	7
Eliminations	(215.2)	-
Total	**5,027**	**100**

Selected Acquisitions

COMPETITORS

Ascension Health	NHC
Covenant Care	Omnicare
Ensign Group	Paradigm Management
Extendicare	Services
Five Star Quality Care	Physiotherapy
Genesis Healthcare	Associates
Golden Horizons	SavaSeniorCare
HCA	Select Medical
HCR ManorCare	Sunrise Senior Living
HealthSouth	Tenet Healthcare
Life Care Centers	U.S. Physical Therapy
Mercy Health (OH)	

HISTORICAL FINANCIALS

Company Type: Public

Income Statement

FYE: December 31

	REVENUE ($ mil.)	NET INCOME ($ mil.)	NET PROFIT MARGIN	EMPLOYEES
12/14	5,027	(79)	—	61,500
12/13	4,900	(168)	—	63,300
12/12	6,181	(40)	—	78,000
12/11	5,521	(53)	—	77,800
12/10	4,359	56	1.3%	56,800
Annual Growth	**3.6%**	**—**	**—**	**2.0%**

2014 Year-End Financials

Debt ratio: 50.90%
Return on equity: (-6.32%)
Cash ($ mil.): 164
Current ratio: 1.62
Long-term debt ($ mil.): 2,852

No. of shares (mil.): 69
Dividends
Yield: 2.6%
Payout: —
Market value ($ mil.): 1,272

	STOCK PRICE ($) FY Close	P/E High/Low	PER SHARE ($) Earnings	Dividends	Book Value
12/14	18.18	— —	(1.36)	0.48	20.60
12/13	19.74	— —	(3.23)	0.24	19.99
12/12	10.82	— —	(0.78)	0.00	23.58
12/11	11.77	— —	(1.16)	0.00	24.73
12/10	18.37	14 8	1.43	0.00	26.12
Annual Growth	**(0.3%)**	**— —**	**—**	**—**	**(5.8%)**

KNIGHTS OF COLUMBUS

Good Knight! The Knights of Columbus is a formidable volunteer group boasting 15000 councils made up of 1.9 million Roman Catholic male members in the US Canada Mexico Cuba the Philippines Poland and several other countries. The fraternal organization is also a force to be reckoned with in the insurance world providing life insurance annuities and long-term care insurance to its members and their families. In addition the group manages the Knights of Columbus Museum in New Haven Connecticut featuring exhibits of religious art and history.

Geographic Reach
The Knights of Columbus comprises more than 14900 local councils throughout the US Canada Mexico Puerto Rico Guam and the U.S. Virgin Islands. It also has councils in the Bahamas Cuba the Dominican Republic Guatemala Panama the Philippines Poland and Saipan.

Operations
The Knights of Columbus was formed to render financial aid to members and their families. Mutual aid and assistance are offered to sick disabled and needy members and their families. Social and intellectual fellowship is promoted among members and their families through educational charitable religious social welfare war relief and public relief works. is also engaged in religious education the support of public policy issues (including immigration reform marriage protection opposing abortion) and charitable activities such as disaster relief.The entity is a Catholic family fraternal service organization. This theme permeates the entire Service Program: all Church community council family culture of life and youth activities. The Service Program is designed to establish each council as an influential and important force within the community elevate the status of the programming personnel provide more meaningful and relevant

programs of action establish direct areas of responsibility build leadership and ensure the success of council programs.

Strategy

In 2015 The Knights of Columbus created a new class of mutual funds that will invest based on Catholic values and will be marketed to faith-based institutions such as orders of nuns dioceses or Catholic universities. The New Haven-based Knights also created a new investment adviser firm Knights of Columbus Asset Advisors.

Expanding internationally in 2014 the Knights of Columbus opened a new branch in South Korea to support that country's growing Catholic population. (It also established a presence in Ukraine and Lithuania in 2013).In 2014 The Knights of Columbus funded the purchase of an ultrasound machine for a Baltimore area pregnancy center making it the 500th such gift by the Knights to a pregnancy center dedicated to helping women keep and care for their unborn babies. It also expanded its successful Coats for Kids program by teaming up with the New Haven Police Department providing officers with coats to distribute as they encounter children and families in need. The Knights of Columbus has established a new scholarship program to help fund the education of seminarians preparing to become Catholic chaplains in the US Armed Forces. The program will distribute $1 million in scholarship money to the Archdiocese for the Military Services USA over a period of five years at a rate of $200000 per year.

During 2014 the organization launched its new Long-Term Care Plus product across 40 states Canada (excluding Quebec) and Puerto Rico.

Company Background

The Knights of Columbus was founded in New Haven by Father Michael J. McGivney in 1882 and has been selling insurance since its founding

EXECUTIVES

Supreme Knight, Carl A. Anderson
Deputy Supreme Knight, Logan T. Ludwig
Supreme Treasurer, Michael J. O'Connor
Supreme Chaplain, William E. Lori
Assistant Vice President Of Application Development, Niki Kratzert
Vice President For Communications, Patrick Korten
Vice President Certified and Support Services, Lynn Hussey
Vice President, Anthony Minopoli

LOCATIONS

HQ: KNIGHTS OF COLUMBUS
1 COLUMBUS PLZ STE 1700, NEW HAVEN, CT
065103326
Phone: 2037524000
Web: WWW.EASTONKOFC.ORG

PRODUCTS/OPERATIONS

2013 Charitable Contributions

	% of total
State & local affiliates	79
Supreme Council	21
Total	**100**

HISTORICAL FINANCIALS

Company Type: Private

Income Statement

FYE: December 31

	ASSETS ($ mil.)	NET INCOME ($ mil.)	INCOME AS % OF ASSETS	EMPLOYEES
12/13	20,534	113	0.6%	2,300
12/12	19,401	127	0.7%	—
12/11	18,026	81	0.4%	—
12/10	16,861	0	—	—
Annual Growth	6.8%			

2013 Year-End Financials

Debt ratio: ——
Return on equity: 5.40%
Cash ($ mil.): 192
Current ratio: —
Long-term debt ($ mil.): —

Dividends
  Yield: —
  Payout: —
Market value ($ mil.): —

Kohl's Corp.

Kohl's wants its prices to be easy on shoppers and tough on competition. The clothing retailer operates about 1160 department stores in 49 states with nearly half of stores in the Midwest and West. Competing with discount and mid-level department stores it sells moderately priced name-brand and private-label apparel shoes accessories and housewares through centrally located cash registers designed to speed checkout and keep staff costs down. Merchandising relationships allow Kohl's to carry top brands (NIKE Levi's OshKosh B'Gosh) not always available to discounters; it's able to sell them for lower prices by controlling costs. A typical store spans 88000 sq. ft. and serves markets with 150000 to 200000 people.

OperationsBy product Kohl's generated 31% of its sales from women's clothing in fiscal 2015 (ended January) while 19% of sales came from men's clothing. The rest of the retailer's sales came from home products (18% of sales) children's clothing (13%) accessories (10%) and footwear (9%). About 50% of its sales were products tied to national brands while the other half of sales were tied to private & exclusive brands.Geographic Reach

While the retailer operates in 49 US states nearly one-third of its stores are in the states of California Texas Illinois Ohio and Florida.To support its brick-and-mortar and online businesses Wisconsin-based Kohl's maintains a network of more than a dozen distribution centers nationwide in Findlay Ohio; Winchester Virginia; Blue Springs Missouri; Corsicana Texas; Mamakating New York; San Bernardino California; Macon Georgia; Patterson California; and Ottawa Illinois. Facilities that cater to the Kohl's e-commerce business are located in Monroe Ohio; San Bernardino California; Edgewood Maryland; and DeSoto Texas. The company also operates design studios in New York City and in Santa Monica California.

Sales and Marketing

Kohl's has been boosting its ad spending in recent years particularly on promotional activities and typical costs related to television and radio broadcasts direct mail and newspaper circulars. It spent $1024 million in fiscal 2015 (ends January) up from $1013 million and $993 million in fiscal years 2014 and 2013 respectively. This represented 5.4% 5.3% and 5.2% of its total sales for each of those years respectively.

The company sells its products through its stores (91% of sales) online (9%) and through in-store kiosks that offer customers free shipping to their homes. Kohl's purchases its merchandise from both domestic and foreign suppliers. A third-party purchasing agent supplies about 30% of the company's merchandise.

Financial Performance

Kohl's revenues have been flat over the past few years with few new store openings and sluggish comparable store sales growth. Its profits have also been in a slow decline as rising merchandise costs have caused margins to shrink and as it's been spending more on investments in IT and marketing to support growth. The retailer's revenue dipped by less than 1% to $19.02 billion in fiscal 2015 (ended January) as sales volumes per transaction fell with higher prices of items (as it began pushing more expensive national brand items). By product sales increased for children's (especially toys) and men's clothing and footwear while sales underperformed in the home and women's product categories. Active-type clothing was the strongest performer in all of these categories. By geography sales rose in the West Southeast and Midwest while sales declined in the Northeast Mid-Atlantic and South Central regions.

Sales declines and a continued uptick in costs of merchandise from shipping costs in FY2015 caused the retailer's net income to tumble 2% to $867 million. Kohl's operating cash levels climbed 7% to $2 billion for the year as it reduced its store inventory by 2% and units per store by 3% and because its accounts payable balances increased from higher receipt volumes and the timing of payments to certain vendors.

Strategy

Kohl's announced in fall of 2015 that it would be tweaking its multi-year "Greatness Agenda" strategy (introduced in late 2014) which was designed to drive organic top-line growth by focusing on five pillars: amazing product incredible savings easy experience personalized connections and winning teams. After receiving feedback from customers and associates during the strategy's first year the company planned to support its five pillars by leveraging several strategies including: creating custom store assortments according to local market tastes focusing more on women's apparel launching new formats and distribution centers to boost sales driving traffic in stores through online buying and in-store pick up and by continuing to promote its Yes2You rewards program (which had 33 million members after one year) especially after the firm discovered that 80% of its sales were tied to repeat customers. Recognizing that national brands drive traffic the firm also continued its pivot toward pushing new key national brands like FitBit Madden Girl Columbia Samsung Bliss and other brands especially in the popular active and wellness categories. The retailer has been tweaking its store layout to boost same-store sales in recent years remodeling stores and increasing the number of small and urban stores in its portfolio to tailor its size to new markets. In late 2015 it planned to open "10 to 15" of its "smaller more nimble" prototype stores (with around 35000 sq. ft. of selling space) in underserved markets through 2016. The chain also planned to remodel around 30 stores after remodeling some 50 stores in FY2014. Company Background

Kohl's own brands were key to Kohl's merchandising strategy in past years. In 2012 in a bid to emulate its "cheap chic" rival Target and also long-time competitor J. C. Penney Kohl's began enlisting big-name designers to produce merchandise exclusively for its stores. In building its "Available Only at Kohl's" business the discounter offered a low-cost collection named Simply Vera in stores and online as the result of the deal with designer

Vera Wang. It inked a similar alliance with upscale jeans maker Rock & Republic Food Network LC Lauren Conrad and FILA Sport as well as "Desig-Nation" limited-edition collections from designers Narcisco Rodriguez in 2012 Derek Lam in spring 2013 and Catherine Malandrino in fall 2013.

HISTORY

Max Kohl (father of Sen. Herbert Kohl of Wisconsin) opened his first grocery store in Milwaukee in the late 1920s. Over the years he and his three sons developed it into a chain and in 1938 Kohl's incorporated.

Kohl opened a department store (half apparel half hard goods) in 1962 next door to a Kohl's grocery. In the mid-1960s he hired William Kellogg a twentysomething buyer in the basement discount department at Milwaukee's Boston Store for his expertise in budget retailing. Kellogg came from a retailing family (his father was VP of merchandising at Boston Store; the younger Kellogg had joined that firm out of high school). Kohl and Kellogg began developing the pattern for the store carving out a niche between upscale department stores and discounters (offering department store quality at discount store prices).

EXECUTIVES

Vice President of Operations, John (Jack) Worthington
Chairman President and CEO, Kevin B. Mansell, age 62, $1,352,700 total compensation
SEVP and CFO, Wesley S. (Wes) McDonald, age 53, $838,600 total compensation
SEVP and Chief Administrative Officer, Richard D. (Rick) Schepp, age 54, $834,800 total compensation
SEVP Logistics, Kenneth (Ken) Bonning, age 57, $726,500 total compensation
Chief Merchandising and Customer Officer, Michelle Gass, age 47, $932,600 total compensation
Vice President Customer Relationship Management, Brian Miller
Vice President, Amy Leschke-kahle
Senior Vice President Human Resources, Genny Shields
Vice President Application Development, Lawrence Mikels
Senior Vice President Assistant General Counsel, Jason Kelroy
Executive Vice President Multi Channel E Commerce, Krista Berry
Vice President Of Application Development, Aaron Johnson
Vice President Regional Manager, Brian Giles
Vice President Financial Planning And Reporting, Debbie Granger
Vice President of Product Services, Richard (Dick) Zielinski
Vice President Information Systems, Shelley Mathwick
Vice President Credit Marketing, Brent Cook
Vice President Regional Manager, Nick Vanella
Vice President Management Information Systems, Linn Allison
Vice President Information Systems, Peter Ciriscioli
Vice President Executive, Julie Persich
Vice President District Manager, Mickey Cockrell
Regional Vice President, Blaine Predmore
Vice President of Facilities Logistics, John (Jack) Fojut
Senior Vice President Ecommerce, Mike Molitor
Senior Vice President, Laurie Hummel
Vice President Product Development, Scott Conant
Executive Vice President Marketing, William Setliff
Vice President Real Estate Western Region, Bill Moreland
Vice President, Anne Sterling

Executive Vice President GMM of Ladies, Nancy Feldman
Vice President Brand And Consumer Insight, Joseph Bagby
Senior Vice President divisional Merchandise Manager, Carol Baiocchi
Regional Vice President, Doug Arnoldi
Vice President Supply Chain, Troy Carrothers
Senior Vice President Business Development, Stephen Walmsley
Senior Vice President DMM Womens, Marianne Stone
Executive Vice President Marketing, Debby Fisher
Vice President dmm E Commerce, Chad Melnick
Exectuvie Vice President Product Development, Carol Williams
Vice President, Sunil Bhardwaj
Vice President of Finance and Operations, Santa Paul
Vice President Information Technology, Greg Heinz
Vice President Communications, Colleen Wegner
Senior Vice President Communications and PR, Bevin Bailis
Vice President of Training, Nancy Blok-Anderson
Vice President of Application Development, Dan Mueller
Senior Vice President Of Product Development, Judi Langley
Executive Vice President, Will Setliff
Vice President Staffing and Finance, Kevin Mantz
Vice President Tax, Tom Taugher
Senior Vice President Product Development, Michael Gilbert
Vice President District Manager, Shane Knoy
Vice President Divisional Merchandise Manager, Scott Kolsky
Senior Vice President Assistant General Counsel, Steve Thomas
Vice President Production, Ron Katanick
Vice President Human Resources, Tim Kuckelman
Vice President, Deb Kuczora
Vice President Product Management Intern, Amanda Travis
Vice President of Property Development Law, Mark D Griepentrog
Senior Executive Vice President In Charge Of Store Operations And Information Technology, Tom Kingsbury
Vice President Of Loss Prevention, Paul Figarotta
Vice President, Annette Adams
Vice President of Trend, Sofia Wacksman
Vice President Operations, Steven Karl
Vice President, Greg Harned
Regional Vice President, Mark Grudecki
Vice President Dmm, Chris Candee
Executive Vice President, Teresa Sabish
Vice President Administration, Gregg Bartel
Executive Vice President General Merchandise Mana, Rick Seeger
Vice President Finance, Debbie Grainger
Senior Vice President Loss Prevention, Randy Meadows
Regional Vice President, Tim McLarty
Executive Vice President General Merchandise Manager Men's and Young Men's, Jeff Manby
Vice President Finance, Kelli Johnson
Vice President, Jeffrey (Jeff) Kellan
Executive Vice Presi, Ken Bonning
Vice President And District Manager, Dave Schmidt
Vice President Of MP, Michael (Mel) Donohue
Senior Vice President General Manager E commmerce, Ronald (Ron) Murray
Auditors: Ernst & Young LLP

LOCATIONS

HQ: Kohl's Corp.
N56 W17000 Ridgewood Drive, Menomonee Falls, WI 53051
Phone: 262 703-7000   **Fax:** 262 703-6373
Web: www.kohls.com

2013 Stores

	No.
California	128
Texas	84
Illinois	65
Ohio	58
Florida	53
New York	51
Michigan	45
Pennsylvania	48
Wisconsin	40
Indiana	38
New Jersey	38
Georgia	35
North Carolina	31
Virginia	30
Arizona	26
Minnesota	26
Colorado	24
Missouri	26
Massachusetts	24
Maryland	23
Tennessee	20
Connecticut	21
Washington	18
Kentucky	16
Iowa	16
South Carolina	15
Alabama	13
Utah	12
Nevada	12
Kansas	12
Oklahoma	10
Oregon	10
New Hampshire	10
Arkansas	8
Nebraska	7
West Virginia	7
Louisiana	6
Delaware	5
Idaho	5
Maine	5
Mississippi	5
New Mexico	5
North Dakota	3
Rhode Island	3
South Dakota	3
Montana	2
Wyoming	2
Alaska	1
Vermont	1
Total	**1,146**

2014 Stores

	No.
California	126
Texas	85
Illinois	66
Ohio	58
Florida	53
New York	50
Michigan	45
Pennsylvania	50
Wisconsin	40
Indiana	39
New Jersey	38
Georgia	35
North Carolina	31
Virginia	30
Arizona	26
Minnesota	26
Colorado	24
Missouri	26
Massachusetts	25
Maryland	23
Tennessee	20
Connecticut	22
Washington	19
Kentucky	17
Iowa	18
South Carolina	16
Alabama	14
Utah	12
Nevada	12

Kansas	12
Oklahoma	11
Oregon	11
New Hampshire	11
Arkansas	8
Nebraska	7
West Virginia	7
Louisiana	8
Delaware	5
Idaho	5
Maine	5
Mississippi	5
New Mexico	5
North Dakota	4
Rhode Island	3
South Dakota	3
Montana	2
Wyoming	2
Alaska	1
Vermont	1
Total	**1,162**

PRODUCTS/OPERATIONS

2015 Sales

	% of total
Private & exclusive brands	50
National brands	50
Total	**100**

2015 Sales

	% of total
Women's	31
Men's	19
Home	18
Children's	13
Accessories	10
Footwear	9
Total	**100**

2014 stores

	No.
Mid-Atlantic	115
Midwest	306
Northeast	155
South Central	150
Southeast	191
West	245
Total	**1,162**

Selected National Brands

adidas
apt. 9
Arrow
Calphalon
Candies
Carter's
Chaps
Columbia
Cuisinart
Daisy Fuentes
Dickies
Dockers
everGirl
George Foreman
Gloria Vanderbilt Home
Gold Toe
Haggar
Hanes
Healthtex
Henckels
HoMedics
Jockey
Jumping Beans
KitchenAid
Krups
Laura Ashley Lifestyles
Lee
l.e.i.
Levi's
Mudd
NIKE
Nine & Company
Oneida
OshKosh B' Gosh
Pfaltzgraff
Pyrex
Reebok
Skechers

Speedo
Unionbay
Urban Pipeline
Villager

Selected Private-label Brands

Apt. 9
Bobby Flay
ELLE
Jennifer Lopez
Jumping Beans
Marc Anthony

COMPETITORS

BJ's Wholesale Club	Old Navy
Bed Bath & Beyond	Ross Stores
Belk	Saks
Dillard's	Sears
J. C. Penney	Shopko Stores
Kmart	TJX Companies
Macy's	Target Corporation
Men's Wearhouse	Wal-Mart

HISTORICAL FINANCIALS

Company Type: Public

Income Statement

FYE: January 31

	REVENUE ($ mil.)	NET INCOME ($ mil.)	NET PROFIT MARGIN	EMPLOYEES
01/15*	19,023	867	4.6%	137,000
02/14	19,031	889	4.7%	137,000
02/13	19,279	986	5.1%	135,000
01/12	18,804	1,167	6.2%	142,000
01/11	18,391	1,114	6.1%	136,000
Annual Growth	0.8%	(6.1%)	—	0.2%

*Fiscal year change

2015 Year-End Financials

Debt ratio: 32.99%
Return on equity: 14.53%
Cash ($ mil.): 1,407
Current ratio: 1.99
Long-term debt ($ mil.): 4,651

No. of shares (mil.): 201
Dividends
  Yield: 0.0%
  Payout: 36.7%
Market value ($ mil.): 12,004

	STOCK PRICE ($) FY Close	P/E High/Low	PER SHARE ($) Earnings	Dividends	Book Value
01/15*	59.72	15 11	4.24	1.56	29.81
02/14	50.63	14 11	4.05	1.40	28.33
02/13	46.01	13 10	4.17	1.28	27.24
01/12	46.69	13 10	4.30	1.00	26.35
01/11	51.20	16 12	3.65	0.00	27.84
Annual Growth	3.9%	— —	3.8%	—	1.7%

*Fiscal year change

Kroger Co (The)

Kroger is still the US's largest traditional grocer despite Wal-Mart overtaking the chain as the nation's largest seller of groceries years ago. It operates some 3800 stores including 2600-plus supermarkets and multi-department stores under two dozen banners across 35 states. It also runs 780-plus convenience stores (under the Quik Stop Kwik Shop and other brands) around 330 jewelry stores and nearly 40 food processing plants in the US. Kroger's Fred Meyer Stores subsidiary operates around 130 supercenters that offer groceries merchandise and jewelry in the western US. While Kroger has added other amenities to its mix groceries still make up over 70% of its sales while fuel sales make up another 20%.

HISTORY

Bernard Kroger was 22 when he started the Great Western Tea Company in 1883 in Cincinnati. Kroger lowered prices by cutting out middlemen sometimes by making products such as bread. Growing to 40 stores in Cincinnati and northern Kentucky the company became Kroger Grocery and Baking Company in 1902. It expanded into St. Louis in 1912 and grew rapidly during the 1910s and 1920s by purchasing smaller cash-strapped companies. Kroger sold his holdings in the company for $28 million in 1928 the year before the stock market crash and retired.

The company acquired Piggly Wiggly stores in the late 1920s and bought most of Piggly Wiggly's corporate stock which it held until the early 1940s. The chain reached its largest number of stores –a whopping 5575 –in 1929. (The Depression later trimmed that total.) A year later Kroger manager Michael Cullen suggested opening self-service low-price supermarkets but company executives demurred. Cullen left Kroger and began King Kullen the first supermarket. If he was ahead of his time at Kroger it wasn't by much; within five years the company had 50 supermarkets.

During the 1950s Kroger acquired companies with stores in Texas Georgia and Washington DC. It added New Jersey-based Sav-on drugstores in 1960 and it opened its first SuperRx drugstore in 1961. The company began opening larger supermarkets in 1971; between 1970 and 1980 Kroger's store count grew just 5% but its selling space nearly doubled.

In 1983 the grocer bought Kansas-based Dillons Food Stores (supermarkets and convenience stores) and Kwik Shop convenience stores. Kroger sold most of its interests in the Hook and SuperRx drug chains (which became Hook-SupeRx) in 1987 and focused on its food-and-drugstores. (It sold its remaining stake to Revco in 1994.) The next year it faced two separate takeover bids from the Herbert Haft family and from Kohlberg Kravis Roberts. The company warded off the raiders by borrowing $4.1 billion to pay a special dividend to shareholders and to buy shares for an employee stock plan.

To reduce debt Kroger sold most of its equity in Price Saver Membership Wholesale Clubs and its Fry's California stores. In 1990 the company made its first big acquisition since the 1988 restructuring by buying 29 Great Scott! supermarkets. Joseph Pichler became CEO that year.

Kroger sold its Time Saver Stores unit in 1995. In 1999 Kroger acquired Fred Meyer operator of about 800 stores mainly in the West in a $13 billion deal. Late in 1999 it announced it was buying nearly 75 stores (mostly in Texas) from Winn-Dixie Stores; the deal was called off in 2000 shortly after the FTC withheld its approval. But the company kept buying –acquisitions included 20 former Hannaford stores in Virginia in 2000 as well as 16 Nebraska food stores bought from food distributor Fleming and seven New Mexico stores bought from Furrs Supermarkets in 2001.

Kroger acquired 17 supermarkets (16 in the Houston area) from Albertson's (now Albertsons LLC) and another seven stores from Winn-Dixie in the Dallas/Fort Worth area in 2002.

In April 2003 Kroger introduced Naturally Preferred its own brand of some 140 natural and organic items including baby food pastas cereal snacks milk and soy products.In 2012 with pharmacies in many of its stores nationwide Kroger purchased specialty pharmacy company Axium Pharmacy Holdings based in Florida. The move satisfied Kroger's long-term growth plans and allowed the grocery chain to serve customers that require complex drug therapies.

EXECUTIVES

Chairman and CEO, W. Rodney McMullen, age 54, $1,123,393 total compensation
EVP and CFO, J. Michael Schlotman, age 57, $745,313 total compensation
President Harris Teeter Supermarkets, Frederick J. (Fred) Morganthall, age 63
Sr V Pres, James (Jamie) Thorne
President Harris Teeter Supermarkets, Rodney C. (Rod) Antolock
EVP and CIO, Christopher T. (Chris) Hjelm, age 53
EVP Merchandising, Michael J. (Mike) Donnelly, age 56, $651,315 total compensation
President Central Division, Katie Wolfram, age 60
President and COO, Michael L. (Mike) Ellis, age 56, $785,194 total compensation
VP and Chief Supply Chain Officer, Kevin M. Dougherty, age 62
VP Merchandising QFC, Marlene Stewart, age 59
President Fred Meyer Division, Jeffrey D. (Jeff) Burt, age 53
VP Manufacturing, Erin S. Sharp, age 57
VP Non-Perishables, Robert W. Clark
President Dillons division, Joe Grieshaber
President Delta Division, Tim Brown, age 55
President Delta Division, Scot Hendricks, age 57
President Nashville Division, Zane Day
Senior Vice President of Human Resources, Kathleen Barclay
Vice President, Jeremy Stover
Pharmacy Manager, Carmen K Taylor
Pharmacy Manager, Eric Manchester
Pharmacy Manager, Clayton Williams
Vice President for Natural Foods Procurement and Merchandising, Nancy Moon-Eilers
Vice President Of Produce Operation, Adam Haarstad
Vice President Store Development, Patti Taylor
Director Of Surgery, Frank L Zagar
Vice President Merchandising, Joe Fey
Vice President Pension Investments, Edward (Ed) Waldvogel
Senior Executive Assistant At Kroger Reporting To Group Vice President Chief Supply Chain Officer, Cindy Saunders
Vice President, Bruce Gack
Vice President Distribution, Scott Palmer
Vice President Clinical, Foster Ratliff
Vice President merchandising Middle Atlantic Division, Valerie (Val) Jabbar
Group Vice President Human Resources, Peter (Pete) Barth
Vice President Finance Controller Quik Stop Division, Jim Bradshaw
Vice President Clinical, Peggy Jones
Senior Vice President Of Retail Divisions, Mark Tuffin
Pharmacy Manager, Joey Smith
Vice President Of Marketing, Barbara White
Vice President Operations, Gary Raymond
Vice President Of Tax, Joe Bradley
Vice President Engineering, Mike Kurzendoerfer
Vice President Store Development, Bryan Smith
Vice President Of Retail Operations, Mike Purdum
Pharmacy Manager, Kelly Thornburg
Vice President, Dennis Hackett
Vice President and Controller, Elizabeth (Beth) Van Olfen
Vice President Human Resources, Carl Wojciechowski
Vice President, Heather Coleman
Vice President Non Foods, Jim Wetta
Vice President Corporate Human Resources, Mark Roberts
Pharmacy Manager, Matthew Rafa
Vice President Of Talent Development, Tim Massa
Vice President, Steve Jones
Pharmacy Manager, Peggy Gilligan
Vice President Purchasing, Rick Krafels
Vice President MIS 8 90, Jack Hudson

Vice President Marketing Services, Jeff Talbot
Pharmacy Manager, Diane Chance
Pharmacy Manager, Anna Loyd
Vice President Customer Solutions and Services, Annette Franke
Senior Vice President, Pete Williams
Vice President Of Produce Operation, Terri Heidinger
Vice President, Don Barnett
Director Of Pharmacy, Tracy Ward
Vice President, Deanna Golden
Vice President of Operations of the New Nashville Division, Laurie King
Vice President Of Procurement, Keith Scott
Vice President, Joe Rother
Vice President, Barbara (Barb) Beumer
Executive Vice President Chief Financial Officer, Chris Hjelm
Vice President Director of Customer Experience, Sara Shelton
Vice President, Jim Hodge
Executive Vice President Secretary And General C, Paul Heldman
Pharmacy Manager, Mary Travis
Pharmacy Manager, Ralph Rodriguez
Senior Vice President, R Williams
Vice President of Marketing, Trey Powell
Vice President, Richard (Dick) Donaldson
Group Vice President and President Manufacturing, Calvin (Cal) Kaufman
Director and Assistant Treasurer, Caren Fike
Board Member, Carol Mclemore
Assistant Treasurer, Kathy Hanna
Vice Chairman, Rodney (Rod) McMullen
Auditors: PricewaterhouseCoopers LLP

LOCATIONS

HQ: Kroger Co (The)
1014 Vine Street, Cincinnati, OH 45202
Phone: 513 762-4000   **Fax:** 513 762-1400
Web: www.thekrogerco.com

PRODUCTS/OPERATIONS

2015 Sales

	$ mil.	% of total
Supermarket	86,281	80
Supermarket fuel sales	18,850	17
Other stores & manufacturing	3,334	3
Total	**108,465**	**100**

2015 Stores

	No.
Supermarkets & multidepartment stores	2,625
Convenience stores	782
Jewelry	326
Total	**3,733**

2015 Sales

	% of total
Non-perishable	50
Perishable	22
Fuel	18
Pharmacy	8
Other	2
Total	**100**

Selected Kroger Stores

Multidepartment stores
  Fred Meyer
Supermarkets
  Baker's
  City Market Food & Pharmacy
  Dillon Food Stores
  Fry's Food & Drug Stores
  Gerbes Supermarkets
  Harris Teeter Supermarkets
  Jay C Food Stores
  King Soopers
  Kroger
  Kroger Fresh Fare
  Owen's

Pay Less Super Markets
Quality Food Centers (QFC)
Ralphs
Scott's Food & Pharmacy
Smith's Food & Drug Centers
Warehouse stores
  Food 4 Less
  FoodsCo
Convenience stores
  Kwik Shop
  Loaf 'N Jug
  Quik Stop Markets
  Tom Thumb Food Stores
  Turkey Hill Minit Markets
Jewelry stores
  Barclay Jewelers
  Fox's Jewelers
  Fred Meyer Jewelers
  Littman Jewelers
Food Production
Bread and other baked goods
Cheese
Coffee
Crackers
Cultured products (cottage cheese yogurt)
Deli products
Fruit juices and fruit drinks
Ice cream
Juice
Meat
Milk
Nuts
Oatmeal
Peanut butter
Snacks
Soft drinks
Spaghetti sauce
Water

Selected Private-Label Brands

Bath & Body Therapies (body and bath)
Banner brands (Kroger Ralphs King Soopers)
Everyday Living (kitchen gadgets)
FMV (For Maximum Value)
HD Design (upscale kitchen gadgets)
Moto Tech (automotive)
Naturally Preferred (premium quality natural and organic brand)
Office Works (office and school supplies)
Private Selection (premium quality brand)
Splash Spa (body and bath)
Splash Sport (body and bath)

COMPETITORS

7-Eleven	NBTY
99 Cents Only	Publix
A&P	Raley's
Ahold U.S.A.	Randall's
Albertsons	Rite Aid
CVS	SUPERVALU
Chevron	Safeway
Costco Wholesale	Save Mart
Delhaize America	Stater Bros.
Dollar General	Sterling Jewelers
Exxon Mobil	Target Corporation
Family Dollar Stores	Tesco
GNC	Valero Energy
Giant Eagle	Vitamin Shoppe
H-E-B	Wal-Mart
Hy-Vee	Walgreen
IGA	Wegmans
Kmart	Whole Foods
Marsh Supermarkets	Winn-Dixie
Meijer	Zale

Income Statement
FYE: January 31

	REVENUE ($ mil.)	NET INCOME ($ mil.)	NET PROFIT MARGIN	EMPLOYEES
01/15*	108,465	1,728	1.6%	400,000
02/14	98,375	1,519	1.5%	375,000
02/13	96,751	1,497	1.5%	343,000
01/12	90,374	602	0.7%	339,000
01/11	82,189	1,116	1.4%	338,000
Annual Growth	7.2%	11.6%	—	4.3%

*Fiscal year change

2015 Year-End Financials

Debt ratio: 38.15%	No. of shares (mil.): 974
Return on equity: 32.10%	Dividends
Cash ($ mil.): 268	Yield: 0.0%
Current ratio: 0.78	Payout: 19.7%
Long-term debt ($ mil.): 9,771	Market value ($ mil.): 67,255

	STOCK PRICE ($) FY Close	P/E High/Low	PER SHARE ($) Earnings	Dividends	Book Value
01/15*	69.05	40 20	1.72	0.34	5.56
02/14	36.10	30 19	1.45	0.31	5.30
02/13	27.89	20 15	1.39	0.25	4.09
01/12	24.30	51 42	0.51	0.22	3.55
01/11	21.29	27 22	0.87	0.20	4.27
Annual Growth 34.2%		— —	18.6%	14.9%	6.8%

*Fiscal year change

L Brands, Inc

L Brands (formerly Limited Brands) is as much of a shopping-mall mainstay as food courts and teenagers. The company operates nearly 3000 specialty stores in North America and the UK primarily under the Victoria's Secret Bath & Body Works (BBW) and La Senza (in Canada) banners as well as corresponding websites and catalogs. Originally focused on apparel L Brands sold its ailing Limited and Express chains –leaving the company free to focus on two core businesses: Victoria's Secret and BBW. L Brands also owns apparel importer MAST Industries accessories boutique operator Henri Bendel apothecary C.O. Bigelow and The White Barn Candle Co. Founded in 1963 the company changed its name to L Brands in 2013.

Change in Company Name

The company belatedly changed its name from Limited Brands to L Brands to distance itself from the Limited Stores which it jettisoned in 2007.

Operations

In conjunction with the name change the company also realigned its reportable segments into Victoria's Secret Bath & Body Works (BBW) and Victoria's Secret and Bath and Body Works International. About 60% of sales come from domestic Victoria's Secret stores driven by its eponymous and PINK brands. Nearly a third of sales come from the BBW segment which also includes White Barn Candle and C.O. Bigelow brands.

MAST Industries (dba Mast Global Fashions) is the company's production sourcing and logistics arm - it accounts for the rest of sales. Mast is one of the world's largest contract manufacturers importers and distributors of apparel. Mast has manufacturing operations and joint ventures in more than a dozen countries including China Israel Mexico and Sri Lanka.

Geographic Reach

In addition to its 3000 US stores L Brands has about 650 retail stores in Canada the UK and the Middle East. International sales totaled $1.34 billion in fiscal 2015 (ended January) about 10% of L Brands' total. L Brands has a partnership with M.H. Alshaya (a popular franchise partner for many American retailers including American Eagle Outfitters and Pottery Barn) to operate stores in the Middle East.

Financial Performance

L Brands' revenue has been trending upward for several years. It saw its total net sales increase 6% to $11.4 billion in fiscal 2015 (ended January) versus the prior year as Victoria's Secret and BBW products sold well across all categories. After a dip in 2013 net income has been on an upward trajectory. It grew 15% to $1 billion due to the higher revenue. Cash from operations rose 43% from from $550 million to $1.7 billion on the strength of higher revenue and net income.

Strategy

The company's goal was for Victoria's Secret to blossom into a $10-billion brand but the global financial crisis decline in consumer confidence and poor performance of the La Senza business in Canada conspired to delay the growth strategy for the bra-and-panty business. The strategy at Victoria's Secret is to capture the teen and college-age female customer with its youth-oriented PINK brand with the hope that as she matures she will shop for sexier styles such as Angels and Very Sexy sold in Victoria's Secret stores. PINK is sold in freestanding stores as well as Victoria's Secret shops. While the retailer doesn't break out PINK sales the brand is meeting stiff competition from American Eagle's Aerie brand and Gilly Hicks by Abercrombie & Fitch. Both target the youth market. L Brands has been closing La Senza stores and repositioning the brand.

Going forward L Brands intends to continue international expansion but focus primarily on expanding stores and locations of Victoria's Secret and BBW in North America. It plans to increase the Victoria's Secret footprint by about 5% with 26 new stores and BBW by 3% with 24 new locations in fiscal 2015. Partners will open an additional 10 new Victoria's Secret stores (in the Middle East) and 50 new BBW stores in the Middle East Latin America Southeast Asia and Eastern Europe in 2015.

HISTORY

After a disagreement with his father in 1963 over the operation of the family store (Leslie's) Leslie Wexner then 26 opened the first Limited store in Columbus Ohio with $5000 borrowed from his aunt. The company was named from Wexner's desire to do one product line well –moderately priced fashionable attire for teenagers and young women.

When The Limited went public in 1969 it had only five stores but the rapid development of large covered malls spurred growth to 100 stores by 1976. Two years later The Limited acquired MAST Industries an international apparel purchasing and importing company. The company opened Express in 1980 to serve the teen market.

The Limited grew with acquisitions including the 1982 purchases of Lane Bryant (large sizes) and Victoria's Secret (lingerie). That year it formed the Brylane fashion catalog division and acquired Roaman's a bricks-and-mortar and catalog merchandiser of plus sizes.

Wexner bought The Lerner Stores (budget women's apparel) and Henri Bendel (high fashion) in 1985 sportswear retailer Abercrombie & Fitch (A&F) in 1988 and London-based perfumer Penhaligon's in 1990 (sold in 1997). The Limited introduced several in-store shops including Cacique (French lingerie) in 1988 and Limited Too (girls' fashions) which were later expanded into standalone stores. It also launched Structure (men's sportswear) in 1989 and Bath & Body Works shops in 1990. All of these stores were in malls often strategically clustered together.

The company closed many The Limited and Lerner stores in 1993 and sold 60% of its Brylane catalog unit to Freeman Spogli (Brylane went public in 1997). It opened four Bath & Body Works stores in the UK (its first non-US stores) to compete with British rival The Body Shop.

In 1994 The Limited bought Galyan's Trading Company a chain of sporting goods superstores. The company began spinning off its businesses while keeping controlling stakes; it spun off Intimate Brands (Victoria's Secret Cacique and Bath & Body Works) in 1995 and A&F in 1996. (The Limited sold its remaining 84% in A&F in 1998.)

The Limited closed more than 100 of its women's apparel stores in 1997 and Intimate Brands shuttered the Cacique chain; the next year The Limited closed nearly 300 more stores companywide (excluding the Intimate Brands chains) and the majority of its Henri Bendel stores.

In 1998 The Limited launched White Barn Candle Co. (candle and home fragrance stores). The following year the company spun off Limited Too its most successful chain as Too Inc. and reduced its interest in Galyan's to 40%. (Galyan's management and buyout firm Freeman Spogli bought the remaining 60% of the sporting goods chain.) The Limited (as well as Intimate Brands) declared a two-for-one stock split in 2000.

To boost profits in 2001 The Limited folded the Structure brand into the Express unit and spun off its Galyan's and Alliance Data Systems subsidiaries retaining 22% and 20% respectively. The Limited sold its Lane Bryant unit to Charming Shoppes for $335 million that year.

The Limited bought back the remaining shares of Intimate Brands it did not already own in March 2002 and over the course of the year phased it into a business segment. In May 2002 the company changed its name to Limited Brands from The Limited. Later that year Limited Brands sold off its remaining stake in Lerner New York and in late 2003 sold its Structure label (which it had rebranded as Express Men's) to Sears Roebuck and Co.

In 2007 Limited Brands completed its acquisition of lingerie maker and retailer La Senza based in Montreal for about $600 million. It also sold a 75% stake in its 251-store Limited Stores business to Sun Capital Partners taking a loss on the sale. In mid-2010 it sold the rest. Three years later in 2013 it finally changed the company name from The Limited to L Brands.

EXECUTIVES

EVP and CFO, Stuart B. Burgdoerfer, age 51, $824,000 total compensation
Chairman and CEO, Leslie H. Wexner, age 77, $1,924,000 total compensation
V Pres Database Mktg Dir Mail, William (Bill) Lepler
President and CEO Victoria's Secret, Sharen J. Turney, age 58, $1,442,000 total compensation
CIO, Steven M. Stone, age 54
COO, Charles C. (Charlie) McGuigan, age 58, $978,500 total compensation
CEO and President Bath & Body Works, Nicholas P.M. (Nick) Coe, age 52, $925,000 total compensation
Vice President Internal Audit, Bethmara Kessler
Executive Vice President Chief Financial Officer and Chief Administrative Officer, Martyn Redgrave
Auditors: Ernst & Young LLP

LOCATIONS

HQ: L Brands, Inc
Three Limited Parkway, Columbus, OH 43230
Phone: 614 415-7000
Web: www.lb.com

PRODUCTS/OPERATIONS

2015 Stores

	No.
Bath & Body Works U.S.	1,558
Victoria's Secret Stores U.S.	983
La Senza Canada	145
PINK U.S	115
Bath & Body Works Canada	88
Victoria's Secret Canada	31
ViHenri Bendel	29
PINK Canada	10
Victoria's Secret U.K.	8
PINK U.K.	2
Total	**2,969**

2015 Sales

	$ mil.	% of total
Victoria's Secret	7,207	63
Bath & Body Works	3,350	29
Victoria's Secret and Bath & Body Works International	336	3
Other	561	5
Total	**11,454**	**100**

Selected Retail Brands

Bath & Body Works
C.O. Bigelow
Henri Bendel
La Senza
Pink
The White Barn Candle Company
Victoria' s Secret

COMPETITORS

Abercrombie & Fitch	Macy' s
American Eagle	Mary Kay
Outfitters	Natori
Avon	Nordstrom
Body Shop	Revlon
CVS	Saks
Dillard' s	Sephora USA
Est©e Lauder	Shiseido Americas
Frederick' s of	Target Corporation
Hollywood	The Gap
Fruit of the Loom	Ulta
Hanesbrands	VF Corporation
J. C. Penney	Wal-Mart
Jockey International	Warnaco Group
Kiehl' s	

HISTORICAL FINANCIALS

Company Type: Public

Income Statement

FYE: January 31

	REVENUE ($ mil.)	NET INCOME ($ mil.)	NET PROFIT MARGIN	EMPLOYEES
01/15*	11,454	1,042	9.1%	80,100
02/14	10,773	903	8.4%	94,600
02/13	10,459	753	7.2%	99,400
01/12	10,364	850	8.2%	97,000
01/11	9,613	805	8.4%	96,500
Annual Growth	**4.5%**	**6.7%**	**—**	**(4.5%)**

*Fiscal year change

2015 Year-End Financials

Debt ratio: 63.16%	No. of shares (mil.): 292
Return on equity: —	Dividends
Cash ($ mil.): 1,681	Yield: 0.0%
Current ratio: 1.92	Payout: 67.4%
Long-term debt ($ mil.): 4,765	Market value ($ mil.): 24,712

	STOCK PRICE ($) FY Close	P/E High/Low	PER SHARE ($) Earnings	Dividends	Book Value
01/15*	84.63	24 14	3.50	2.36	0.06
02/14	52.36	21 14	3.05	1.20	(1.27)
02/13	47.25	20 16	2.54	5.00	(3.51)
01/12	41.46	16 10	2.70	3.80	0.46
01/11	28.92	14 8	2.42	4.60	4.60
Annual Growth **(66.0%)**	**30.8%**	**— —**		**9.7%**	**(15.4%)**

*Fiscal year change

L-3 Communications Holdings, Inc.

L-3's good defense is its best commercial offense. L-3 Communications Holdings provides products and services to the government based on Command Control Communications Intelligence Surveillance and Reconnaissance (C3ISR) including systems for satellite avionics (aircraft electronics) security and marine communications. It also provides aircraft maintenance and modernization. The US government primarily the Department of Defense (DoD) accounts for nearly 70% of its business but L-3 is expanding its commercial offerings. The company derives all of its income from operating subsidiary L-3 Communications Corporation (L-3).

Operations

L-3 operates through four main segments: Electronic Systems National Security Solutions (NSS) Communication Systems and Aerospace Systems. Its most lucrative segment is Electronic Systems which makes a variety of components subsystems and products and generates roughly 40% of its total sales each year. Aerospace Systems generates 35% and the rest account for the remainder.

Subsidiaries include L-3 Communications Integrated Systems L-3 Avionics Systems L-3 Communications Vertex Aerospace L-3 Communications Canada L-3 Insight Technology Interstate Electronics Corporation L-3 Global Communications Solutions and L-3 Fuzing & Ordnance Systems.

Geographic Reach

The company operates through nearly 400 locations in Australia Canada Europe and the US. Of this total it owns 35 locations and leases around 340. Almost 80% of total sales come from customers residing in the US.

Financial Performance

L-3 has seen its net sales and profits slowly diminish over the last four years. Revenues dipped by 4% from $12.6 billion in 2013 to $12.1 billion in 2014. Profits also dropped 15% from $778 million in 2013 to $664 million in 2014.

L-3's revenues have slowed due to the loss of contracts with the SOFSA Afghanistan Ministry of Defense (MoD) and Federal Aviation Administration (FAA) over the years. It also experienced lower sales related to linguist services training and logistics support projects for the US Army due to the drawdown of American military forces in Iraq.

Strategy

With such a major amount of business derived from the US government and DoD (the US Army and Air Force collectively account for about 70% of its total revenue) the company is vulnerable to the priorities of the Pentagon and other government agencies which have resulted in cuts in defense spending and additional troop withdrawals from the Middle East.

L-3 is using acquisitions as a means to benefit from changes in DoD and other government agency funding currently prioritized on high-tech electronics and systems over more traditional combat warfare equipment. The focus on security systems information technology (IT) and cyber security intelligence logistics unmanned aircraft systems (UAS) and reconnaissance vehicles bodes well for L-3 since these products are in its portfolio.

In addition to acquisitions the company enters into collaborative ventures with other businesses to develop new opportunities especially in the area of providing full-service rather than just products. Additionally L-3 has been transitioning from providing individual products and components to bundled products and services including logistics MRO (maintenance repair and overall) and supply chain management. Its revenues from services is now neck-and-neck with that of its products and L-3 plans to add additional services under existing programs.

Mergers and Acquisitions

In 2015 L-3 acquired UK-headquartered CTC Aviation Group (now known as L-3 CTC Ltd) for $220 million. L-3 CTC is a global airline pilot training and crew resourcing specialist catering to major airlines and retail customers globally. The acquisition expanded L-3's Commercial Aviation Training business.

In 2014 L-3 picked up Virginia-based Data Tactics Corporation —a specialized provider of Big Data analytics and cloud computing products serving the US DOD —for $57 million and renamed it L-3 Data Tactics.

HISTORY

In the early 1970s Frank Lanza caught defense giant Lockheed's eye by building Loral Corporation into an aerospace industry contender through acquisitions of smaller defense technology firms. Lockheed (now Lockheed Martin) eventually bought Loral in 1996 and made Lanza the head of defense electronics. Looking for more action Lanza formed L-3 Communications Holdings in 1997 by convincing Lockheed Martin's CEO to spin off a group of 10 communications technology units and put him at the helm. The operations were units from General Electric and Loral acquired by Lockheed Martin in 1993 and 1996 respectively.

In charge early on were two of the L's in the L-3 name: 20-year Loral executives Lanza (chairman and CEO by then old enough to retire) and Robert LaPenta (president and CFO). The third L stood for major backer Lehman Brothers. The company embarked on an acquisition binge (just as Loral had originally done) in 1997. L-3 targeted strapped independent companies and the potential noncore operations of large corporate mergers.

EXECUTIVES

SVP; President Communication Systems, John S. Mega, age 63
President and COO, Christopher E. Kubasik, age 54
Chairman and CEO, Michael T. Strianese, $1,350,000 total compensation
EVP Corporate Strategy and Development, Curtis Brunson, age 68, $643,173 total compensation
SVP and CFO, Ralph G. D'Ambrosio, age 48, $689,539 total compensation
SVP; President Electronic Systems, Steven (Steve) Kantor, age 71, $666,538 total compensation
SVP Washington Operations, Richard A. Cody, age 65

VP; President National Security Solutions, Les Rose, age 68
SVP and President Aerospace Systems, Mark Von Schwarz, age 55
VP and CIO, John Finegan
Vice President Mission Technology and Training, Patricia (Pat) Craig
Vice President And General Manager, Vance King
Auditors: PricewaterhouseCoopers LLP

LOCATIONS

HQ: L-3 Communications Holdings, Inc.
  600 Third Avenue, New York, NY 10016
Phone: 212 697-1111
Web: www.l-3com.com

2014 Sales

	$ mil.	% of total
US	9,172	76
UK	342	3
Canada	289	2
Australia	254	2
Germany	243	2
South Korea	226	2
Saudi Arabia	160	1
Japan	124	1
Other countries	1,314	11
Total	**12,124**	**100**

PRODUCTS/OPERATIONS

2014 Sales

	$ mil.	% of total
Electronic systems	4,714	38
Aerospace systems	4,326	35
Communication systems	2,040	17
National Security Solutions (NSS)	1,215	10
Eliminations	(171)	-
Total	**12,124**	**100**

2014 Sales

	$ mil.	% of total
Services	6,909	57
Products	5,215	43
Total	**12,124**	**100**

Selected Operations

Aircraft Modernization and Maintenance (AM&M)
  Aircraft engineering maintenance modification
  upgrades and logistics services
  Airborne traffic and collision avoidance systems
  Life cycle management services
  Ruggedization of displays computers and electronics
  Supply chain management
  Voice recorders flight data recorders and maritime
  hardened voyage recorders
Command Control and Communications and
  Intelligence Surveillance and Reconnaissance (C3ISR)
  Airborne space and surface data link terminals ground
  stations and transportable tactical SATCOM systems
  Communication systems for surface and undersea
  vessels and manned space flights
  Fleet management of special mission aircraft
  Ground-based satellite communications terminals and
  payloads
  Prime mission systems integration sensor
  development and operations and support
  Satellite command and control sustainment and
  support
  Satellite communication and tracking systems
  Secure communication terminals and equipment and
  secure network encryption products
  Shipboard communications
Electronic Systems
  Avionics and displays
  Electro-optic/infrared (EO/IR)
  Marine services
  Microwave
  Power and control systems
  Precision engagement
  Propulsion systems
  Security and detection
  Simulation and training
  Telemetry and advanced technology
  Undersea warfare
  Warrior systems

COMPETITORS

BAE SYSTEMS	ITT Corp.
CACI International	Lockheed Martin
CAE Inc.	Meggitt
Cubic Corp.	Northrop Grumman
DRS Technologies	Raytheon
DynCorp International	Rockwell Collins
FLYHT Aerospace	Sierra Nevada Corp
Solutions	Thales
General Dynamics	Trimble Navigation
Harris Corp.	United Technologies
Honeywell	telent
International	

HISTORICAL FINANCIALS

Company Type: Public

Income Statement

FYE: December 31

	REVENUE ($ mil.)	NET INCOME ($ mil.)	NET PROFIT MARGIN	EMPLOYEES
12/14	12,124	664	5.5%	45,000
12/13	12,629	778	6.2%	48,000
12/12	13,146	810	6.2%	51,000
12/11	15,169	956	6.3%	61,000
12/10	15,680	955	6.1%	63,000
Annual Growth	**(6.2%)**	**(8.7%)**	**—**	**(8.1%)**

2014 Year-End Financials

Debt ratio: 28.48%
Return on equity: 11.74%
Cash ($ mil.): 442
Current ratio: 1.88
Long-term debt ($ mil.): 3,940

No. of shares (mil.): 82
Dividends
  Yield: 1.9%
  Payout: 32.0%
Market value ($ mil.): 10,354

	STOCK PRICE ($) FY Close	P/E High/Low		PER SHARE ($) Earnings	Dividends	Book Value
12/14	126.21	16	13	7.56	2.40	64.42
12/13	106.86	12	9	8.54	2.20	70.17
12/12	76.62	9	8	8.30	2.00	60.41
12/11	66.68	10	6	9.03	1.80	67.03
12/10	70.49	12	8	8.25	1.60	62.27
Annual Growth	**15.7%**	**—**	**—**	**(2.2%)**	**10.7%**	**0.9%**

Laboratory Corporation of America Holdings

This company pricks and prods for profit. Laboratory Corporation of America (LabCorp) is a top provider of clinical laboratory services performing tests on more than 470000 patient specimens each day on behalf of managed care organizations hospitals doctors government agencies drug companies and employers. Its services range from routine urinalyses HIV tests and Pap smears to specialty testing for diagnostic genetics disease monitoring forensics identity clinical drug trials and allergies. Through Covance the company provides end-to-end drug development support. LabCorp operates more than 1700 service sites that collect specimens and some 40 primary labs where tests are performed.

Operations

In early 2015 LabCorp restructured its operations into two primary segments: LabCorp Diagnostics and Covance Drug Development. Many of the tests LabCorp Diagnostics performs each year are routine tests (including blood chemistry analyses blood cell counts and HIV tests) which account

for about 60% of annual revenues. Genomic and esoteric testing operations which includes LabCorp's Esoterix Monogram Biosciences and Integrated Genetics subsidiaries have grown to account for a larger percentage of sales (more than a third of total revenues) in recent years. Specialty testing units include Cellmark Forensics Dianon Pathology and MedTox Laboratories.

Covance Drug Development provides early drug development associated laboratory testing efficacy studies and clinical trial services to biopharmaceutical clients.

Geographic Reach

Most of LabCorp's operations are conducted through its extensive network of facilities throughout the US. The company also has joint ventures in Canada where it provides diagnostic testing services in several provinces and it has also established presences in China Japan Singapore the United Arab Emirates and the UK.

Covance has pre-clinical laboratories in Wisconsin Indiana Virginia Michigan and Indiana. It also operates labs in the UK (2) Germany China France and Singapore.

Altogether LabCorp operates in more than 60 countries.

Sales and Marketing

LabCorp uses a direct sales force to promote its products and services to customers including doctors hospitals clinical labs drugmakers managed care companies and government agencies. As payments from managed care entities (HMOs and PPOs) make up about half of LabCorp's net patient revenue gaining and maintaining contracts with these clients is a main thrust of the company's strategy. For instance LabCorp has a multi-year contract with UnitedHealth that makes LabCorp the insurer's exclusive national laboratory services provider.

Commercial clients are the company's second-largest source of earnings (35%) followed by Medicare and Medicaid (about 15%) and private patients.

Financial Performance

All of LabCorp's efforts towards expanding its offerings and geographic presence helped keep the company's finances healthy for several consecutive years with its revenue growing each year since 2008. In 2014 the group reported a 4% increase in sales to some $6.1 billion largely due to acquisitions in both of the company's segments along with growth in the company's managed care business and toxicology testing.

Although revenue increased slightly in 2013 profits fell 10% on increased cost of sales. This was primarily due to an increase in interest expense related to the issuance of some $700 million of senior notes.

Cash flow from operations has been declining slightly over the past four years. In 2014 operating cash flow decreased by 10% due to the decline in net income and changes in accounts payable.

Strategy

Over the past six years LabCorp has invested some $2.5 billion in strategic acquisitions. The company is focused on expanding its advanced testing capabilities especially in the areas of genetic and cancer testing. One particular area of interest for the company's product development efforts is the field of personalized medicine. It has introduced a number of "companion" diagnostic tests that determine whether a patient will react well or poorly to certain drugs. LabCorp is developing such tests internally as well as through partnerships with life science entities such as Duke University and Johns Hopkins University.

In 2014 the company installed its Propel robotic technology in a Florida laboratory; it plans to install the technology which is designed to increase automation in esoteric testing in other laboratories.

LabCorp strives to capitalize on its nationwide presence to strengthen managed care partnerships. In addition LabCorp looks to keep its physician customers happy with education tools and integrated information management systems including eLabCorp a Web-based tool that allows doctors to access testing services online and its electronic health record (EHR) solution. In 2013 the company introduced population analytics system LabCorp Beacon to physicians and hospitals; it also expanded its testing product line and introduced more than 150 new assays.

The company is also expanding consumer-focused tools such as its LabCorp Beacon patient portal. In 2014 it improved the user experience by enhancing the system's mobile and electronic medical record connectivity processes; it is working on adding new or improved self-service capabilities. Meanwhile LabCorp's specialty subsidiaries such as kidney stone analysis firm Litholink work to control costs for payers by focusing on providing patient-specific tools to manage chronic conditions.

In 2014 LabCorp launched Enlighten Health Genomics a new unit to utilize the diagnostic potential of next-generation sequencing technology.

Mergers and Acquisitions

In 2015 LabCorp bought the New Jersey-based Covance one of the world's largest contract research organizations and a leader in nutritional analysis for approximately $5.7 billion. The deal provided LabCorp with new revenue sources and a broader international presence which has long been a goal for the company. The company also completed the $85 million acquisition of diagnostic testing firm LipoScience; that move strengthened LabCorp's position in the cardiovascular and metabolic disorder testing market. LabCorp additionally purchased Bode Technology Group which provides specialized forensic DNA collection analysis and relationship testing.

EXECUTIVES

EVP CFO and Treasurer, Glenn A. Eisenberg, age 53, $338,542 total compensation
Chief Legal Officer and Secretary, F. Samuel Eberts, age 55, $436,085 total compensation
Chairman President and CEO, David P. (Dave) King, age 57, $1,013,000 total compensation
CEO Covance Drug Development, Deborah L. (Deb) Keller, age 52
EVP; CEO LabCorp Diagnostiics, James T. Boyle, age 58, $632,611 total compensation
SVP and CIO, Lance V. Berberian, age 52
Senior Vice President Research And Development And Science And Technology Labcorp, Marcia Eisenberg
Senior Vice President, Devin Lorsson
Auditors: PricewaterhouseCoopers LLP

LOCATIONS

HQ: Laboratory Corporation of America Holdings 358 South Main Street, Burlington, NC 27215
Phone: 336 229-1127
Web: www.labcorp.com

PRODUCTS/OPERATIONS

2014 Sales

	$ mil.	% of total
Core testing	3,656	61
Genomic & esoteric testing	2,025	34
Other	329	5
Total	**6,011**	**100**

2014 Sales by Payer

	% of total
Managed care	50
Commercial clients	35
Medicare and Medicaid	14
Private patients	1
Total	**100**

Selected Subsidiaries

DIANON Systems Inc. (pathology Connecticut)
Dynacare Laboratories Inc. (clinical labs; Tennessee Washington Wisconsin Canada)
Esoterix Inc. (esoteric testing Colorado)
Integrated Genetics (formerly Genzyme Genetics fertility testing labs across the US)
Integrated Oncology (formerly US Labs esoteric oncology tests US)
Litholink Corporation (kidney patient testing Illinois)
Monogram Biosciences Inc. (HIV resistance testing and personalized medicine California)
National Genetics Institute (NGI infection testing and blood screening California)
Viro-Med Laboratories Inc. (molecular microbial testing Minnesota)

Selected Acquisitions

COMPETITORS

Arup Laboratories
Bio-Reference Labs
Celera
CompuNet Clinical Laboratories
Covance
HedgePath
IDENTIGENE
Kroll Background America
Laboratory Sciences of Arizona
MEDTOX Laboratories
Medtox Scientific
Mid America Clinical Laboratories
NeoGenomics
Oncolab
Orchid Cellmark
Pathology Associates Medical Laboratories
Pharmaceutical Product Development
Psychemedics
Quest Diagnostics
Solstas
Sonic Healthcare
eScreen

HISTORICAL FINANCIALS

Company Type: Public

Income Statement

FYE: December 31

	REVENUE ($ mil.)	NET INCOME ($ mil.)	NET PROFIT MARGIN	EMPLOYEES
12/14	6,011	511	8.5%	36,000
12/13	5,808	573	9.9%	34,000
12/12	5,671	583	10.3%	34,000
12/11	5,542	519	9.4%	31,000
12/10	5,003	558	11.2%	31,000
Annual Growth	**4.7%**	**(2.2%)**	**—**	**3.8%**

2014 Year-End Financials

Debt ratio: 41.49%
Return on equity: 19.25%
Cash ($ mil.): 580
Current ratio: 1.73
Long-term debt ($ mil.): 2,682
No. of shares (mil.): 84
Dividends
Yield: —
Payout: —
Market value ($ mil.): 9,128

	STOCK PRICE ($) FY Close	P/E High/Low	PER SHARE ($) Earnings	Dividends	Book Value
12/14	107.90	18 15	5.91	0.00	33.34
12/13	91.37	17 14	6.25	0.00	29.07
12/12	86.62	16 14	5.99	0.00	29.06
12/11	85.97	19 15	5.11	0.00	25.60
12/10	87.92	16 13	5.29	0.00	24.08
Annual Growth	**5.3%**	**— —**	**2.8%**	**—**	**8.5%**

Lakeland Bancorp, Inc.

Lakeland Bancorp is shoring up in the Garden State. It's the holding company for Lakeland Bank which serves northern New Jersey from more than 50 branch offices. Targeting individuals and small to midsized businesses the bank offers standard retail products such as checking and savings accounts money market and NOW accounts and CDs. It also offers financial planning and advisory services for consumers. The bank's lending activities primarily consist of commercial loans and mortgages (more than half of the company's loan portfolio) and residential mortgages. Lakeland also offers commercial lease financing for office systems and heavy equipment. Lakeland Bancorp plans to acquire Somerset Hills Bancorp.

Geographic Reach

Lakeland serves customers located in New Jersey.

Operations

Lakeland boasts more than 50 banking offices across the New Jersey counties of Bergen Essex Morris Passaic Somerset Sussex Union and Warren.

Sales and Marketing

The financial institution serves a variety of customers from individuals to businesses to municipalities.

Mergers and Acquisitions

Lakeland acquired Bernardsville New Jersey-based Somerset Hills Bancorp which operates Somerset Hills Bank Sullivan Financial Services and Somerset Hills Investment Holdings and folding the company into its operations. The 2013 purchase allows Lakeland to extend its reach into Somerset Union and Morris counties.

Strategy

While the company is looking to expand its operations through strategic acquisitions Lakeland is also focused on providing its customers with less traditional banking delivery channels. To this end the company offers Internet banking mobile banking and cash management services.

Financial Services

Lakeland logged a 4% increase in revenue in fiscal 2013 to $135.2 million vs. 2012's $129.9 million. The financial institution attributes the bump to revenue rises in both interest and non-interest income. Its purchase of Somerset Hills and that company's $243.9 million in loans and leases at the time of acquisition provided Lakeland with a timely increase in average loans and leases. Non-interest income generated 17% of Lakeland's total 2013 revenue. Net income for the reporting period rose $3.23 million to $24.9 million. Thanks to an increase in net income and increase in the proceeds from the sale of loans Lakeland's 2013 cash flow from operations increased $2.14 million to $50.73 million.

Company Background

The company has been minimizing its exposure to commercial leases though as its leasing portfolio contributed to Lakeland's first reported annual loss in 2009. The company cut its leasing portfolio by about half —a move made to de-emphasize that line of business. Instead Lakeland has focused on strengthening its mortgage and commercial loan portfolios. In fact commercial loans have recently been the area of greatest growth for the bank.

EXECUTIVES

EVP and CFO, Joseph F. Hurley, age 64, $293,527 total compensation
President CEO and Director; CEO Lakeland Bank, Thomas J. Shara, age 57, $630,000 total compensation
EVP and Chief Retail Officer, Ronald E. (Ron) Schwarz, age 58, $258,731 total compensation
Regional President, Stewart E. McClure, age 61, $328,123 total compensation
COO and Regional President, Robert A. Vandenbergh, age 63, $350,173 total compensation
EVP Government and Business Services, Jeffrey J. Buonforte, age 63, $205,075 total compensation

SVP and Chief Credit Officer Lakeland Bank,
James R. Noonan, age 63
SVP and Chief Technology and Information Security Officer, Mary Kaye Nardone
EVP and Chief Lending Officer, David Yanagisawa, $220,000 total compensation
EVP General Counsel and Corporate Secretary, Timothy J. Matteson, age 45
Vice President, Steven Breeman
Vice President Commercial Lending, Bruce Bready
Vice President Of Information Technology, Marykaye Nardone
Vice President, Scott Heiman
Assistant Vice President, Eileen Diehl
Chairman Lakeland Bancorp and Lakeland Bank, Mary Ann Deacon, age 63
Auditors: KPMG LLP

LOCATIONS

HQ: Lakeland Bancorp, Inc.
250 Oak Ridge Road, Oak Ridge, NJ 07438
Phone: 973 697-2000
Web: www.lakelandbank.com

PRODUCTS/OPERATIONS

2013 Sales

	$ mil.	% of total
Interest		
Loans & fees	104	77
Investment securities	8	7
Other	1	-
Non-interest		
Service charges on deposit accounts	10	8
Commissions & fees	4	3
Net gains on debt extinguishment	1	1
Other	4	4
Total	**135**	**100**

COMPETITORS

Bank of America	PNC Financial
Bank of New York	Sovereign Bank
Mellon	Sussex Bancorp
Capital One	TD Bank USA
Clifton Bancorp	Valley National
Hudson City Bancorp	Bancorp
Investors Bancorp	Wells Fargo
JPMorgan Chase	
New York Community	
Bancorp	

HISTORICAL FINANCIALS

Company Type: Public

Income Statement

	ASSETS ($ mil.)	NET INCOME ($ mil.)	INCOME AS % OF ASSETS	EMPLOYEES
12/14	3,538	31	0.9%	566
12/13	3,317	24	0.8%	550
12/12	2,918	21	0.7%	522
12/11	2,825	19	0.7%	527
12/10	2,792	19	0.7%	529
Annual Growth	**6.1%**	**12.8%**	**—**	**1.7%**

FYE: December 31

2014 Year-End Financials

Debt ratio: 6.89%
Return on equity: 8.52%
Cash ($ mil.): 109
Current ratio: —
Long-term debt ($ mil.): —
No. of shares (mil.): 37
Dividends
　Yield: 2.5%
　Payout: 35.7%
Market value ($ mil.): 444

	STOCK PRICE ($) FY Close	P/E High/Low	PER SHARE ($) Earnings	Dividends	Book Value
12/14	11.70	15 12	0.82	0.29	10.01
12/13	12.37	18 13	0.71	0.27	9.28
12/12	10.18	15 12	0.72	0.24	9.00
12/11	8.62	18 12	0.63	0.22	9.22
12/10	10.97	21 11	0.54	0.18	9.34
Annual Growth	**1.6%**	**— —**	**10.8%**	**12.7%**	**1.7%**

Lakeland Financial Corp.

American dollars are preferred over Polish zloty in this Warsaw bank. Lakeland Financial is the holding company for Lake City Bank which servesÅarea business customers and individuals through more than 40 branches scattered across about a dozen northern Indiana counties. Founded in 1872 in Warsaw Indiana the bank offers such standard retail services as checking and savings accounts money market accounts and CDs. Commercial loans including agricultural loans and mortgagesÅmake upÅabout 80% of the bank's loan portfolio. Lake City Bank also offers investment products and services such as corporate and personal trust brokerage employee benefit plans and estate planning.

EXECUTIVES

Exec V Pres-general Counsel, Kristin L Pruitt
Chairman and CEO Lakeland Financial and Lake City Bank, Michael L. Kubacki, age 63, $453,841 total compensation
EVP Lakeland Financial and Lake City Bank, Charles D. Smith, age 71, $230,288 total compensation
EVP Retail Lakeland Financial and Lake City Bank, Kevin L. Deardorff, age 54, $189,077 total compensation
President CFO and Director; President and CFO Lake City Bank, David M. Findlay, age 53, $283,993 total compensation
Executive Vice President and Head Commercial Banking Department, Eric H. Ottinger, $168,247 total compensation
Vice President Controller, Teresa Bartman
Auditors: Crowe Horwath LLP

LOCATIONS

HQ: Lakeland Financial Corp.
202 East Center Street, P.O. Box 1387, Warsaw, IN 46581-1387
Phone: 574 267-6144
Web: www.lakecitybank.com

PRODUCTS/OPERATIONS

2014 Sales

	$ mil.	% of total
Interest		
Loans	105	72
Securities	11	8
Noninteresst		
Service charges on deposit accounts	9	6
Loan insurance and service fees	6	5
Wealth advisory fees	4	3
Investment brokerage fees	3	2
Other	6	4
Total	**147**	**100**

COMPETITORS

1st Source Corporation	PNC Financial
KeyCorp	
Northeast Indiana	
Bancorp	

HISTORICAL FINANCIALS

Company Type: Public

Income Statement

	ASSETS ($ mil.)	NET INCOME ($ mil.)	INCOME AS % OF ASSETS	EMPLOYEES
12/14	3,443	43	1.3%	496
12/13	3,175	38	1.2%	497
12/12	3,064	35	1.2%	493
12/11	2,889	30	1.1%	482
12/10	2,681	24	0.9%	467
Annual Growth	**6.4%**	**15.6%**	**—**	**1.5%**

FYE: December 31

2014 Year-End Financials

Debt ratio: 0.90%
Return on equity: 12.82%
Cash ($ mil.): 90
Current ratio: —
Long-term debt ($ mil.): —
No. of shares (mil.): 16
Dividends
　Yield: 1.8%
　Payout: 31.6%
Market value ($ mil.): 716

	STOCK PRICE ($) FY Close	P/E High/Low	PER SHARE ($) Earnings	Dividends	Book Value
12/14	43.47	16 13	2.61	0.82	21.94
12/13	39.00	17 10	2.33	0.74	19.65
12/12	25.84	13 11	2.15	0.84	18.28
12/11	25.87	14 10	1.88	0.62	16.92
12/10	21.46	17 13	1.32	0.62	15.36
Annual Growth	**19.3%**	**— —**	**18.6%**	**7.2%**	**9.3%**

Lam Research Corp

It's not uncommon for chip makers in need of critical manufacturing equipment to go on the Lam. Lam Research is a top maker of the equipment used to make semiconductors. The company's products address two key steps in the chip-making process. Its market-leading plasma etch machines are used to create tiny circuitry patterns on silicon wafers. Lam also makes cleaning equipment that keeps unwanted particles from contaminating processed wafers. The company's Customer Support Business Group provides products and services to maximize installed equipment performance. Lam's customers include many of the world's large chip makers; customers outside the US primarily in Asia represent the majority of sales. The company is buying KLA-Tencor for about $10.6 billion.

Geographic ReachKorea is California-based Lam's largest market accounting for nearly 26% of sales. Customers in Taiwan generate 21% of sales and the US contributes about 17%. Lam also does substantial business in Southeast Asia and China as well as in Europe. The company has manufacturing facilities in the US (Arizona Illinois and Ohio) and Rendsburg Germany.

Operations

The company has two wholly-owned subsidiaries: Silfex supplies high-purity custom silicon components and assemblies to the solar optics and semiconductor markets; Peter Wolters designs and manufactures high-precision grinding lapping polishing and deburring systems used in the automotive aerospace medical semiconductor manufacturing and other industries.

Sales and MarketingLam's top three customers - Samsung Electronics Micron Technology and Taiwan Semiconductor - together account for more than 30% of its revenue.

Financial Performance

In 2015 (ended June) sales increased 14% to $5.2 billion driven by customers investing in newer technology and adding manufacturing capacity. The strongest growth came from Korea up 25% and from the US where sales increased 25%. Sales were off 2% in Japan. Lam's profit increased 3.7% to $655 million in 2015 (from $633 million in 2014) propelled by higher sales partially offset by increased research and development expenses and selling general and administrative expenses.The company's cash from operating activities increased to $785 million in 2015 from $717 million in 2014 despite increase in accounts receivable and inventories. The company benefited from higher trade accounts payable and deferred profit of $86 million.

Strategy

The semiconductor business is notoriously cyclical rising and falling according to the strength of the overall economy. When the economy improves people buy more products with semiconductors in them. That's playing out at Lam where shipments in 2015 following a rise in 2014 on stronger customer demand for semiconductor equipment. Demand for chips for mobile and enterprise applications spurred higher shipments in 2015.

The high expense of semiconductor manufacturing equipment however has resulted in consolidation of manufacturers. Samsung and Intel are among the few companies left that make their own products. So far Lam has maintained a mix of sales to manufacturers such as Samsung and to contract chip makers such as Taiwan Semiconductor.

A heavy investor in innovation the company's R&D expenses during fiscal years 2015 2013 and 2012 were $825.2 million $716.7 million and $683.7 million respectively which includes spending on deposition etch single-wafer clean and other semiconductor manufacturing products.

In 2014 the company expanded its portfolio for atomic-scale processing with the addition of atomic layer etch to its portfolio of atomic layer deposition products.

Mergers and Acquisitions

The acquisition of KLA-Tencor which the companies agreed to in 2015 creates a company with complementary products and something of a one-stop shop for companies that make semiconductors. Lam makes the machines that make the chips and KLA-Tencor tests the finished chips. The company would serve 42% of the chip making market but it would still be susceptible to the booms and busts of the semiconductor business. Adding their revenue together ($7.8 billion) the company would edge closer to common competitor Applied Materials ($8 billion).

HISTORY

Early History

Chinese immigrant David Lam started Lam Research in 1980 to use plasma chemistry to improve processes for making semiconductors. The company introduced its first product AutoEtch in 1982 and went public in 1984. David Lam left the company in 1985. Roger Emerick became Lam Research's CEO in 1982 and continued in that post until 1997 presiding over the company's growth into an industry leader.

Lam Research introduced its Rainbow line of dry-etch equipment in 1987 and its Transformer Coupled Plasma technology in 1992. The company signed a development agreement in 1994 with the U.S. Display Consortium to develop equipment for making advanced circuits for flat-panel displays. Lam posted its first "gigabuck" year with annual revenues of $1.25 billion in fiscal 1996. Since then the company's revenues have yo-yoed up and down in response to cyclicality in the semiconductor equipment industry.

EXECUTIVES

EVP Global Products Group, Richard A. (Rick) Gottscho, age 64, $475,000 total compensation
SVP and CTO Corporate Technology Development, David J. (Dave) Hemker
President and CEO, Martin B. Anstice, age 48, $803,846 total compensation
EVP and CFO, Douglas R. (Doug) Bettinger, age 48, $494,231 total compensation
EVP and COO, Timothy M. (Tim) Archer, age 48, $580,769 total compensation
SVP Chief Legal Officer and Secretary, Sarah A. O'Dowd, age 65, $408,077 total compensation
SVP Strategic Development Corporate Marketing and Communications, Gary Bultman
Vice President Business Finance, Tina Correia
Vice President, Susan (Sue) Wilkerson
Group Vice President Global Sales and Corporate Marketing, Steven (Steve) Lindsay
Vice President Legal: Ethics and Compliance, Joy Cartun
Vice President and General Manager Dielectric Gapfill and Im PVD Ald Business Units, Kaihan Ashtiani
Vice President General Legal Affairs, Eric Janofsky
Corporate Vice President Business, Hwee Lim
Vice President Global Operations Lam Research Corporation, Abdi Hariri
Vice President of New Product Development Lam Research Corporation, Dave Hemker
Chairman, Stephen G. (Steve) Newberry, age 61
Auditors: Ernst & Young LLP

LOCATIONS

HQ: Lam Research Corp
   4650 Cushing Parkway, Fremont, CA 94538
Phone: 510 572-0200   **Fax:** 510 572-6454
Web: www.lamresearch.com

2015 Sales

	$ mil.	% of total
Asia/Pacific		
Korea	1,406	26
Taiwan	1,084	21
Japan	623	12
China	661	13
Other Countries	278	5
United States	890	17
Europe	314	6
Total	**5,259**	**100**

PRODUCTS/OPERATIONS

Selected Products

Plasma ("dry") wafer-etching equipment
Plasma-based bevel clean system
Single-wafer spin and linear clean products
Three-dimensional integrated circuit etch equipment
Transformer Coupled Plasma (TCP) silicon etch equipment

COMPETITORS

ASM International	Mattson Technology
Applied Materials	Plasma Etch
CollabRx	SCREEN Holdings
Ebara	Suss MicroTec
Hitachi	Tokyo Electron
High-Technologies	Veeco Instruments
Intevac	

HISTORICAL FINANCIALS

Company Type: Public

Income Statement

FYE: June 28

	REVENUE ($ mil.)	NET INCOME ($ mil.)	NET PROFIT MARGIN	EMPLOYEES
06/15	5,259	655	12.5%	7,300
06/14	4,607	632	13.7%	6,500
06/13	3,598	113	3.2%	6,600
06/12	2,665	168	6.3%	6,600
06/11	3,237	723	22.4%	3,700
Annual Growth	**12.9%**	**(2.4%)**	**—**	**18.5%**

2015 Year-End Financials

Debt ratio: 25.21%
Return on equity: 12.67%
Cash ($ mil.): 1,501
Current ratio: 2.38
Long-term debt ($ mil.): 1,001

No. of shares (mil.): 158
Dividends
   Yield: 0.0%
   Payout: 22.7%
Market value ($ mil.): 13,136

	STOCK PRICE ($) FY Close	P/E High/Low	Earnings	PER SHARE ($) Dividends	Book Value
06/15	82.86	21 16	3.70	0.84	33.72
06/14	66.95	18 12	3.62	0.18	30.98
06/13	44.34	72 47	0.66	0.00	27.56
06/12	37.95	33 26	1.35	0.00	27.49
06/11	43.22	10 6	5.79	0.00	19.99
Annual Growth	**17.7%**	**— —**	**(10.6%)**	**—**	**14.0%**

Land O' Lakes Inc

Best known for its #1 US butter brand Land O'Lakes looks to butter everyone's bread to boost its bottom line. One of the largest dairy co-ops in the nation it's owned by roughly 4400 dairy farmer/members and some 900 member associations. It markets dairy-based consumer food service and food ingredient items. The co-op makes more than 300 dairy products from the 12 billion pounds of milk that members supply annually. Land O'Lakes produces animal feed through Land O'Lakes Purina Feed. The co-op also offers members seed and crop protection products animal feed and agricultural assistance. It operates dairy facilities in the US and does business in all 50 states and 60-plus countries.

Operations

Land O'Lakes' operations span three segments: Dairy Foods (the co-op's largest business segment accounting for about a third of total sales) Crop Inputs and Feed. The Crop Inputs business Winfield Solutions is the leading crop inputs wholesaler in the US; its operations include development marketing and sales of seed (alfalfa corn soybeans) for an array of crops along with distributing a line of herbicides pesticides and other crop protection products. Land O'Lakes Purina Feed supplies livestock feed and animal milk replacers. Land O'Lakes sold its Layers (eggs) business conducted through MoArk in mid-2014.

Overall Land O'Lakes generated 34% of its total revenue in 2014 from Dairy Foods sales about 31% from Feed and 33% from Crop Inputs.

Geographic Reach

While Land O'Lakes' products are sold throughout the US and in 60 other countries the company does not break out its foreign sales. Growth markets for the co-op's products include China Mexico and Southeast Asia.Sales and MarketingBoasting 3200 direct producer-members and 1000 member cooperatives Land O'Lakes serves more than 30000 agricultural producers. Its dairy products are used by many of the nation's top food companies and manufacturers.Financial Performance

Land O'Lakes' revenues and profits have been trending higher over the past few years thanks to the cooperative's continued investments in growth initiatives. The co-op's net sales rose by 5% to $14.9 billion in 2014 mostly thanks to a double-digit growth in Dairy Foods sales as its branded-butter sales volumes strengthened. Crop Inputs sales also jumped 3% on stronger soybean volume driven by an increase in soybean acres and favorable product mix. Land O'Lakes' Feed sales shrank by 2% as commodity prices declined despite higher sales volumes in the lifestyle livestock and premix categories.Despite higher sales in 2014 the co-op's net income fell by 13% to $266.5 million as selling general and administrative expenses rose during the year. Land O'Lakes' operating cash nearly doubled to $786.6 million mostly thanks to added cashflows from its receivables inventories and prepaids and other current assets balances.

Strategy

Land O'Lakes' growth strategy is focused on developing and selling value-added branded products to major customers and high-growth markets at home and overseas. To that end the cooperative has pursued acquisitions joint ventures and alliances across its business segments. From 2012 through 2014 the cooperative spent $1 billion in growth initiatives which it has funded from cost savings through strict margin management.During 2014 for example the cooperative pursued several growth initiatives including product innovation facility improvements new technologies and extending the reach of its core brands to new customers. Also in 2014 it launched its international strategy and structure to move into new fast-growing economic regions such as Canada Mexico Africa and China through partnerships and acquisitions. Setting up operations in China Land O'Lakes worked to provide training and other services to Nestlé's Dairy Farming Institute a dairy training center in Shuangcheng. Land O'Lakes isn't opposed to selling off under-performing lines of business to free up resources for growth initiatives. In mid-2014 for example it sold its struggling Layers (egg) business (with operations in California and Missouri) to Opal Foods.Mergers and Acquisitions In February 2015 to boost its advertising effectiveness the coop purchased marketing communications and strategic consultant FLM+ which specialized in the agribusiness and rural community sector. In December 2013 Land O'Lakes purchased long-time supplier Geosys a satellite imaging and agricultural data provider to continue its quest to be a agribusiness leader.

In mid-2012 the company added to its dairy foods' business by buying out Kozy Shack Enterprises. The maker of chilled dairy desserts opened the door for Land O'Lakes to expand into the refrigerated desserts aisle –a new retail category for the company.

HISTORY

In the old days grocers sold butter from communal tubs and it often went bad. Widespread distribution of dairy products had to await the invention of fast reliable transportation. By 1921 the necessary transportation was available. That year about 320 dairy farmers in Minnesota formed the Minnesota Cooperative Creameries Association and launched a membership drive with $1375 mostly borrowed from the US Farm Bureau.

The co-op arranged joint shipments for members imposed strict hygiene and quality standards and aggressively marketed its sweet cream butter nationwide packaged for the first time in the familiar box of four quarter-pound sticks. A month after the co-op's New York sales office opened it was ordering 80 shipments a week.

Minnesota Cooperative Creameries as part of its promotional campaigns ran a contest in 1924 to name that butter. Two contestants offered the winning name –Land O'Lakes. The distinctive Indian Maiden logo first appeared about the same time and in 1926 the co-op changed its name to Land O'Lakes Creameries. By 1929 when it began supplying feed its market share approached 50%.

During WWII civilian consumption dropped but the co-op increased production of dried milk to provide food for soldiers and newly liberated concentration camp victims.

EXECUTIVES

President and CEO, Christopher J. (Chris) Policinski
EVP and CFO, Daniel E. (Dan) Knutson
EVP and COO Purina Animal Nutrition, David R. (Dave) Hoogmoed
Group EVP and Chief Supply Chain and Operations Officer Food and Feed, Beth E. Ford
EVP and COO Winfield Solutions, Mike Vande Logt
EVP Dairy Foods Businesses, Jerry Kaminski
VP and CIO, Mike Macrie
Executive Vice President Ag Businesses, Jim Fife
Vice President Human Resources, Karen Grabow
Vice President Finance, William Pieper
Executive Vice President and Chief Operating Officer Winfield Solutions, Mike Logt
National Sales Manager Dairy Ingredients, Susan (Sue) Grothe
Senior Vice President Corporate Marketing Strategy, Barry Wolfish
Vice President International Development Division, Jon Halverson
Vice President Manager Director, Daniel (Dan) Shin
Treasurer, Peter (Pete) Simonse
Auditors: KPMG LLP

LOCATIONS

HQ: Land O' Lakes Inc
   4001 Lexington Avenue North, Arden Hills, MN 55126
Phone: 651 481-2222
Web: www.landolakesinc.com

PRODUCTS/OPERATIONS

2014
$ mil %

Dairy Foods	5,098	34
Crop Inputs	4,917	33
Feed	4,688	31
Other/ Eliminations	261	3
Total	**14,965**	**100**

Selected Brands and Products
Crop Inputs
   AgriSolutions (seed)
   CROPLAN GENETICS (seed)
   Winfield Solutions (crop-protection products and seed)
Dairy Foods
   Retail Foods
   Butter/spreads
   LAND O' LAKES
   Cheese
   Alpine Lace
   LAND O' LAKES
   New Yorker
   Layers/eggs (MoArk LLC)
   Industrial foods
   Foodservice
   Ingredients
Feed (Purina Mills)
   Farm animal
   Beef cattle
   RangeLand

Dairy cattle
Propel
Equine
Equine Senior
Omolene
Poultry
Flock Raiser
Layena
Start & Grow
SunFresh
Swine
EcoCare
Pet
Exclusive
PMI Nutrition
Red Flannel
Zoo/exotic
Mazuri
Layers
   Eggs
   Eggland' s Best
   LAND O' LAKES All-Natural Farm Fresh Eggs

COMPETITORS

ADM	Kent Feeds
Agri-Mark	Latham Seed Company
Agrium	Mars Incorporated
Associated Milk	Mars Petcare
Producers	Michael Foods
Barkley Seed	Michael Foods Egg
Big Heart Pet Brands	Products
Blue Seal Feeds	Milk Specialties
Boulder Brands	Company
Breeder' s Choice	Mondelez International
Cal-Maine Foods	Monsanto Company
California Dairies	NC Hybrids
Inc.	National Dairy
Cargill	Nestl© Purina PetCare
ConAgra	Nestl© USA
Dairy Farmers of	Northwest Dairy
America	Pfister Hybrid Corn
Darigold Inc.	Pioneer Hi-Bred
Dean Foods	Prairie Farms Dairy
Fonterra	Rose Acre Farms
Foremost Farms	Royal Canin
Frontier Agriculture	Sakata Seed
HP Hood	Saputo
Harris Moran	Sargento
Hartz Mountain	Schreiber Foods
Hill' s Pet Nutrition	Syngenta Seeds
Iams	Unilever
Keller' s Creamery	Wilbur-Ellis

HISTORICAL FINANCIALS
Company Type: Public

Income Statement

	REVENUE ($ mil.)	NET INCOME ($ mil.)	NET PROFIT MARGIN	EMPLOYEES
				FYE: December 31
12/14	14,965	266	1.8%	—
12/13	14,236	305	2.1%	10,000
12/12	14,116	240	1.7%	—
12/11	12,849	182	1.4%	—
12/10	11,146	178	1.6%	—
Annual Growth	**7.6%**	**10.6%**	—	—

2014 Year-End Financials

Debt ratio: 16.35%	No. of shares (mil.): 0
Return on equity: 18.31%	Dividends
Cash ($ mil.): 592	Yield: —
Current ratio: 1.22	Payout: —
Long-term debt ($ mil.): 1,033	Market value ($ mil.): —

Las Vegas Sands Corp

Las Vegas Sands brings a touch of Venice to the US and China. Replete with gondoliers and a replica of the Rialto Bridge the company's Venetian Las Vegas Hotel Resort & Casino offers a 120000-sq.-ft. casino and a 4000-suite hotel as well as a shopping dining and entertainment complex. Through its majority-owned Sands China subsidiary the firm operates The Venetian Macau on the Cotai Strip (the Chinese equivalent of the Las Vegas Strip) as well as two other properties in Macao. Properties also include the Marina Bay Sands in Singapore and the partially-owned Sands Bethlehem in Bethlehem Pennsylvania.

Geographic Reach

The company's 70%-owned Sands China subsidiary consists of three casinos in Macao the only place in China where casinos are legal. These properties include the Sands Macau the Venetian Macau Resort Hotel Casino and the Four Seasons Macau. Elsewhere in Asia the company's Marina Bay Sands in Singapore opened in 2010 at a total cost of about $5.5 billion. In the US additional Las Vegas properties include The Palazzo Casino next door to the Venetian and the nearby Sands Expo Center trade show and convention center. Another US property is its Sands Casino Resort Bethlehem in Pennsylvania.

Sales and Marketing

The company advertises on television internet radio newspapers magazines and billboards. During fiscal 2014 it spent $140.4 million on advertising after spending $117.8 million in fiscal 2013 and $97.8 million in fiscal 2012.

Financial Performance

The company's revenue has enjoyed steady growth since 2010. During fiscal 2014 its revenue increased by 6% to $14.58 billion compared to $13.77 billion in fiscal 2013. The increase was primarily due to increased Casino revenues.

Las Vegas Sands' net income has been trending upward. In fiscal 2014 its net income increased by 23% to $2.84 billion compared to $2.31 billion in fiscal 2013. The spike was primarily due to a combination of higher gross annual revenue and decreased expenses.

The company's cash flow increased by 9% in fiscal 2014 to $4.83 billion compared to $4.44 billion the previous year. The increased cash on hand was primarily due to the increased net income and fewer accounts receivable.

Strategy

Las Vegas Sands is in the middle of a major international growth initiative with several projects in various stages of development. Despite the ambitious expansion plans abroad the company remains cautious in Las Vegas. Las Vegas Sands will explore opportunities to further expand its presence in Asia. The Parisian in Cotai will be Las Vegas Sands' next Macau resort.

EXECUTIVES

Senior Vice President Operations, Pusateri Paul
Chairman and CEO, Sheldon G. Adelson, age 81, $1,000,000 total compensation
President and COO, Robert G. (Rob) Goldstein, age 59, $1,500,000 total compensation
President Sands Bethlehem, Mark Juliano, age 60
EVP and Global General Counsel, Ira H. Raphaelson, age 61
President and CEO Marina Bay Sands, George Tanasijevich, age 54
SVP and CIO, Leslie (Les) Ottolenghi
President and COO The Venetian and The Palazzo, George Markantonis

Vice President Information Technology, Jeff Zabriskie
Vice President Of Marketing Operations, Scott Messinger
Vice President Of Finance, Kirk Godby
Vice President Human Resources, Dave Newton
Vice President Global Head Of Infrastructure And Operations, Edwin Grogan
Vice President Corporate Strategy, Patrick Dumont
Vice President Interior Design And Development Corporate Design And Development, Mark Signorio
Vice President Design Corporate Development, Michael (Mel) Dalton
Vice President Of Sales, Chandra Allison
Vice President And General Counsel, Frederick Kraus
Senior Vice President Chief Procurement and Sustainability Officer, Norbert Riezler
Senior Vice President General Counsel, J Gonzalez
Vice President Marketing, Rafael Larios
Vice President Government Relations, Andrew (Andy) Abboud
Senior Vice President Operations, Paul Pusateri
Vice President Marketing The Venetian The Palazzo, Rian Kirkman
Vice President Investor Relations, Alistair (Al) Scobie
Auditors: Deloitte & Touche LLP

LOCATIONS

HQ: Las Vegas Sands Corp
   3355 Las Vegas Boulevard South, Las Vegas, NV 89109
Phone: 702 414-1000
Web: www.lasvegassands.com

PRODUCTS/OPERATIONS

2014 Sales

	$ mil.	% of total
Casino	12,004	78
Rooms	1,540	10
Food & beverage	778	5
Mall	553	4
Convention retail & other	548	3
Promotional allowances	(841.9)	-
Total	**14,583**	**100**

2014 Sales

	% of total
Macao:	
The Venetian Macao	27
Sands Cotai Central	21
Four Seasons Macao	7
Sands Macao	8
Other Asia	2
Marina Bay Sands	22
United States	
las Vegas Operating Properties	10
Sands Bethlehem	3
Intersegment Eliminations	-
Total	**100**

Selected Properties

Las Vegas
   The Palazzo Resort Hotel Casino
   The Sands Expo and Convention Center
   The Venetian Resort Hotel Casino
China
   The Sands Macau (70%)
   The Venetian Macau (70%)
Singapore
   The Marina Bay Sands

COMPETITORS

Boyd Gaming	Penn National Gaming
Caesars Entertainment	Pinnacle Entertainment
Galaxy Entertainment	Rio All-Suite Hotel &
Genting Singapore	Casino
MGM Resorts	Tropicana
Melco Crown	Entertainment
Entertainment	Wynn Resorts

HISTORICAL FINANCIALS
Company Type: Public

Income Statement
FYE: December 31

	REVENUE ($ mil.)	NET INCOME ($ mil.)	NET PROFIT MARGIN	EMPLOYEES
12/14	14,583	2,840	19.5%	48,500
12/13	13,769	2,306	16.7%	48,500
12/12	11,131	1,524	13.7%	46,000
12/11	9,410	1,560	16.6%	40,000
12/10	6,853	599	8.7%	34,000
Annual Growth	**20.8%**	**47.5%**	**—**	**9.3%**

2014 Year-End Financials

Debt ratio: 44.69%
Return on equity: 38.18%
Cash ($ mil.): 3,506
Current ratio: 1.91
Long-term debt ($ mil.): 9,892

No. of shares (mil.): 798
Dividends
   Yield: 3.4%
   Payout: 60.4%
Market value ($ mil.): 46,427

	STOCK PRICE ($) FY Close	P/E High/Low	PER SHARE ($) Earnings	Dividends	Book Value
12/14	58.16	25 15	3.52	2.00	9.04
12/13	78.87	28 16	2.79	1.40	9.36
12/12	46.16	32 19	1.85	3.75	8.57
12/11	42.73	29 21	1.56	0.00	10.71
12/10	45.95	87 24	0.51	0.00	10.13
Annual Growth	**6.1%**	**— —**	**62.1%**	**—**	**(2.8%)**

Lauder (Estee) Cos., Inc. (The)

Auditors: KPMG LLP

LOCATIONS

HQ: Lauder (Estee) Cos., Inc. (The)
   767 Fifth Avenue, New York, NY 10153
Phone: 212 572-4200
Web: www.elcompanies.com

HISTORICAL FINANCIALS
Company Type: Public

Income Statement
FYE: June 30

	REVENUE ($ mil.)	NET INCOME ($ mil.)	NET PROFIT MARGIN	EMPLOYEES
06/15	10,780	1,088	10.1%	44,000
06/14	10,968	1,204	11.0%	42,400
06/13	10,181	1,019	10.0%	40,200
06/12	9,713	856	8.8%	38,500
06/11	8,810	700	8.0%	32,300
Annual Growth	**5.2%**	**11.6%**	**—**	**8.0%**

2015 Year-End Financials

Debt ratio: 19.87%
Return on equity: 29.04%
Cash ($ mil.): 1,021
Current ratio: 2.09
Long-term debt ($ mil.): 1,607

No. of shares (mil.): 374
Dividends
   Yield: 1.0%
   Payout: 29.7%
Market value ($ mil.): 32,487

	STOCK PRICE ($)	P/E	PER SHARE ($)		
	FY Close	High/Low	Earnings	Dividends	Book Value
06/15	86.66	31 25	2.82	0.92	9.72
06/14	74.26	25 21	3.06	0.78	10.07
06/13	65.77	27 19	2.58	1.08	8.47
06/12	54.12	54 24	2.16	0.53	7.03
06/11	105.19	59 31	1.74	0.38	6.66
Annual Growth	(4.7%)	— —	12.8%	25.2%	9.9%

Lear Corp.

Lear doesn't take a back seat to anyone when it comes to manufacturing automotive seats. The company's Seating business by far its most lucrative segment is a leader in the global market for manufacturing car seat systems and their components. The company's Electrical Power Management Systems (EPMS) segment produces automotive electronics including the manufacture of wire harnesses junction boxes terminals and connectors and body control modules. It operates from 219 facilities in 34 countries. Its largest customers include BMW Ford and General Motors Fiat and Volkswagen. Lear traces its history back to 1917 when it was founded in Detroit as American Metal Products.

HISTORY

Lear dates back to 1917 when American Metal Products began supplying seats to Detroit's fledgling car industry. The seat maker incorporated in 1928 and grew during the 1950s and 1960s by buying other auto parts makers.

Siegler Heating an industrial conglomerate with interests in the aerospace auto parts and manufacturing industries was founded in 1950 as a maker of climate-control equipment. Entrepreneur John Brooks and a group of associates bought the company (renamed Siegler Corporation) in 1954 and led it through a series of acquisitions including that of aerospace firm Lear in 1962. The company then became Lear Siegler.

Lear Siegler acquired American Metal Products in 1966. Beset by project delays the company's aerospace unit sputtered in the 1970s but the seat business did well. By 1985 metal seat frames had become Lear Siegler's major auto parts revenue producer. Spurred by growing competition with Japanese carmakers the company built a plant near a General Motors factory in Michigan to allow for swift delivery of its car seats.

In 1986 Forstmann Little bought the financially troubled Lear Siegler and began selling off the parts. Two years later the investment firm offered Lear Seating to its management (including Ken Way who had been with the company since 1966). Way took the company private in a $500 million LBO with the help of Kidder Peabody and the company's name was changed to Lear Seating. Kidder sold its stake in Lear Seating to Lehman Brothers in 1991.

Lear Seating bought a slice of Ford's North American automotive and trim operation and manufacturing factory in Ciudad Juárez Mexico in 1993. As a result of the purchase the company entered into a long-term supply agreement with Ford.

In another strategic buy of a customer's seat business Lear Seating acquired Fiat's seat operations in 1994. This purchase encompassed Sepi Poland Sepi S.p.A. (Italy) and a 35% stake in a Turkish joint venture giving Lear Seating a presence in those countries. The purchase also made the company Europe's largest seat maker and gave it access to Fiat's 5% of the global automotive market. That year Lear Seating went public.

In 1995 Lear Seating bought Automotive Industries and inked a contract to provide seats for Brazil's top-selling car the Volkswagen Gol. To reflect the broader scope of its business the company dropped "Seating" from its name and became Lear Corporation in 1996. That year the company acquired Pennsylvania-based Masland for $475 million and formed a joint venture with China's Jiangling Motors to make seats and interior trim for Ford and Isuzu vehicles.

Lear bought German manufacturer Keiper Car Seating in 1997 and BTR's Dunlop Cox which made a patented seat-adjusting system. It also bought ITT Industries' main North American seatmaking unit. In 1998 Lear purchased the automotive seating unit of GM's Delphi Automotive Systems subsidiary (now the independent Delphi) giving it a bigger chunk of GM's business as well as parts companies in the UK and Italy. To cut costs the company announced that it would shut down 18 plants and cut 2800 jobs in the US Europe and South America. Acquisitions continued however.

The company paid $2.3 billion for United Technologies' auto unit (but sold the electric motors unit to Johnson Electric Holdings for $310 million) to complete its instrument panel offerings in 1999. Lear also bought Hyundai Motor's seat business to boost Pacific Rim sales. The following year Lear sold its sealants and foam rubber business to GSC Industries' AcoustiSeal.

Early in 2002 Lear announced it would cut 6500 more jobs and close 21 manufacturing facilities. In light of the tightening automotive market Lear planned to shutter older plants and move work to more cost-efficient locations. In 2004 Lear acquired German automotive electronics maker Grote & Hartmann GmbH & Co. for $220 million.

In 2006 Lear sold $200 million in common stock to activist investor Carl Icahn whose funds already held 5% of the company. The sale gave Icahn a combined 16% stake in Lear. Early in 2007 Icahn offered to buy the entire company in a deal valued at $2.8 billion. Amid skepticism among shareholders Icahn raised his bid to $2.9 billion. However shareholders voted to reject the offer. Icahn then sold two-thirds of his Lear holdings in late 2008.

The company narrowed its product focus and sold its interior product lines (instrument panels door panels flooring acoustic systems and other interior products) in 2006. Before the year was out Lear struck a deal with Wilbur Ross whereby Lear contributed its North American interiors business and $25 million in cash to the International Automotive Components Group North America joint venture. The deal was completed in 2007. Lear got a 25% stake in the venture and warrants for an additional 7% equity interest.

In the midst of the Great Recession Lear filed for Chapter 11 bankruptcy emerging in late 2009. The company came out of bankruptcy with less than $1 billion in debt and $1.6 billion in cash. Lear received debtor-in-possession financing of about $500 million from secured lenders led by J.P. Morgan and Citigroup allowing it to continue its operations during reorganization.

EXECUTIVES

Vice President Corporate Controller, Wendy Foss
EVP and President Seating, Raymond E. (Ray) Scott, age 49, $828,223 total compensation
President and CEO, Matthew J. Simoncini, age 54, $1,290,000 total compensation
SVP and President Asia-Pacific Operations, Jay K. Kunkel, age 55
EVP Business Development and General Counsel, Terrence B. (Terry) Larkin, age 60, $828,223 total compensation
SVP and CFO, Jeffrey H. Vanneste, age 55, $708,268 total compensation
SVP; President Electrical, Frank C. Orsini, age 42, $683,073 total compensation
DVP Engineer, David (Dave) Jones
Vice President Global Health Safety And, Barbara (Barb) Boroughf
Vice President Finance Americas, Michael (Mel) Pape
Vice President Sales, Andrica Nuechterlein
Vice President Manufacturing Operations, Sven Damm
Vice President Finance, John Chittum
Vice President Marketing, Dale Lammers
Vice President Finance, Bernard Theisen
Vice President, Lisa Samartino
Vice President Information Technology Global Manufacturing Operations, Robert (Bob) Rinnan
Vice President, David Maxwell
Vice President, Srinivas Thota
Vice President, Mario Krug
Multi Cultural Vice President, Jolito Bustamante
Vice President, Javier Ramirez
Vice President Talent Acquisition, Dave McNulty
Vice President Metals, Christopher Eisenhart
Vice President Engineering, Stephen Rober
Vice President General Manager Truck Group, Dan Golles
Vice President Purchasing, Mandy Rice
Vice President Ford North America, Jeffrey S (Jeff) Edwards
Executivetive Assistant Senior Vice President Human Resources, Patricia (Pat) Krinock
Senior Vice President Human Resources, Thomas (Thom) DiDonato
Vice President Global Audit Services, Randy Kummer
Chairman, Henry D. G. Wallace, age 69
Vice Chairman, James Vandenberghe, age 66
Sec Treas, Jeff Mayer
Auditors: Ernst & Young LLP

LOCATIONS

HQ: Lear Corp.
21557 Telegraph Road, Southfield, MI 48033
Phone: 248 447-1500 **Fax:** 248 447-5250
Web: www.lear.com

2014 Sales

	$ mil.	% of total
US	3,708	21
Mexico	2,373	13
Germany	2,327	13
China	2,092	12
Other countries	7,224	41
Total	**17,727**	**100**

PRODUCTS/OPERATIONS

2014 Sales

	$ mil.	% of total
Seating	13,310	75
Electrical power management	4,416	25
Total	**17,727**	**100**

2014 Sales by Customer

	% of total
General Motors	22
Ford	21
BMW	11
Others	46
Total	**100**

Selected Products

Seating
  Adjusters
  Automotive seats
  Fabrics
  Head restraints
  Mechanisms
  Seat foam
  Structure systems
  Trim covers
Electrical power management
  Electrical distribution and power management
    systems
  Fuse boxes
  Junction boxes
  Terminals and connectors
  Wire harness assemblies
  High-power electrical systems
  Hybrid electrical systems
  Specialty electronics
  Audio sound systems
  In-vehicle television tuner module
  LED electronics (interior/exterior)
  Lighting control module
  Media console
  Radio amplifiers
  Wireless systems
  Keyless entry systems
  Passive entry systems
  Tire pressure monitoring systems

COMPETITORS

DENSO	Robert Bosch
Delphi Automotive	Stoneridge
Systems	Sumitomo
Faurecia	TS TECH CO
Johnson Controls	Toyota Boshoku
LEONI	Valeo
Magna International	Visteon
Methode Electronics	Yazaki
Mitsubishi Electric	ZF TRW Automotive

HISTORICAL FINANCIALS

Company Type: Public

Income Statement

FYE: December 31

	REVENUE ($ mil.)	NET INCOME ($ mil.)	NET PROFIT MARGIN	EMPLOYEES
12/15	18,211	745	4.1%	136,200
12/14	17,727	672	3.8%	125,200
12/13	16,234	431	2.7%	122,300
12/12	14,567	1,282	8.8%	113,400
12/11	14,156	540	3.8%	97,800
Annual Growth	6.5%	8.4%	—	8.6%

2015 Year-End Financials

Debt ratio: 20.78%
Return on equity: 25.33%
Cash ($ mil.): 1,196
Current ratio: 1.38
Long-term debt ($ mil.): 1,931

No. of shares (mil.): 74
Dividends
  Yield: 0.8%
  Payout: 10.2%
Market value ($ mil.): 9,146

	STOCK PRICE ($) FY Close	P/E High/Low		PER SHARE ($) Earnings	Dividends	Book Value
12/15	122.83	13	10	9.59	1.00	39.31
12/14	98.08	12	9	8.23	0.80	37.92
12/13	80.97	16	9	4.99	0.68	37.72
12/12	46.84	4	3	12.85	0.56	36.35
12/11	39.80	21	7	5.08	0.50	24.20
Annual Growth	32.5%	—	—	17.2%	18.9%	12.9%

LegacyTexas Financial Group Inc

With its eye on the Lone Star State Legacy-Texas Financial (formerly ViewPoint Financial) provides retail and commercial banking through its LegacyTexas Bank subsidiary which operates about 50 branches located mostly in the Dallas/Fort Worth area. LegacyTexas offers standard deposit products such as checking and savings accounts and CDs and uses deposit funds to originate primarily real estate loans: Commercial Real Estate loans account for nearly 50% of its lending portfolio while consumer real estate loans make up another nearly 20%. Non-real estate commercial loans make up almost 30% of its loan portfolio.

OperationsOutside of banking services the LegacyTexas offers brokerage services to buy and sell investments and insurance products through a third-party brokerage arrangement.About 82% of the company's total revenue came from loan interest (including fees) in 2014 and another 6% came from interest on its taxable and non-taxable securities. Most of LegacyTexas' remaining revenue came from service charges and fees on deposit accounts.Geographic ReachThe Plano-based company boasts 51 Texas branches with 48 of them located in the Dallas-Fort Worth Metroplex. Its two First National Bank of Jacksboro branches are in Jack in Wise counties in Texas. Sales and MarketingLegacyTexas' serves a diverse market of management professional and sales personnel office employees manufacturing and transportation workers service industry workers government employees and self-employed individuals. It spent $1.54 million on advertising in 2014 compared to $2.69 million and $1.75 million in 2013 and 2012 respectively.Financial PerformanceThe company has struggled to consistently grow its revenues and profits in recent years despite growing loan business mostly stemming from lost revenues from the sale of its mortgage-banking subsidiary in 2012.LegacyTexas' revenue rebounded by 7% to $31.3 million in 2014 primarily thanks to double-digit growth in its loan interest income driven by higher commercial loan volume. Despite higher revenue in 2014 the company's net income dipped by 1% to $31.3 million mostly due to higher loan loss provisions as commercial loan production picked up. LegacyTexas' operating cash levels fell by 21% to $52 million mostly from unfavorable changes in working capital related to its assets and liabilities. StrategyThe company formerly known as ViewPoint Financial significantly boosted its loan and deposit business and the size of its branch network through its early 2015 acquisition LegacyTexas Group. The deal made its branch network swell to 48 offices from just 31 before while adding some $1.63 billion in deposits and $1.4 billion in new loan business.The new LegacyTexas Group planned in 2015 to organically grow its loan portfolio focusing especially on making commercial real estate commercial and industrial and energy loans tied to high-quality assets. To cheaply raise funding for loans the bank plans to promote its non-interest-bearing demand deposit accounts especially in the commercial sector and using its treasury management services to provide a "catalyst for deposit growth."Mergers and Acquisitions

In January 2015 the former ViewPoint Financial acquired LegacyTexas Group in a $300 million deal to create one of the largest independent banks in Texas with assets of nearly $6 billion. The parent company then changed its name to LegacyTexas Financial and the bank changed its name to LegacyTexas Bank.Company BackgroundLegacyTexas Financial converted from a mutual holding company to a stock holding company in 2010. It sold its mortgage subsidiary VPM which operated a dozen loan production offices in Texas and Oklahoma in late 2012.

EXECUTIVES

EVP Chief Lending Officer, Thomas S. Swiley, age 65, $270,000 total compensation
EVP Chief Risk Officer and General Counsel, Scott A. Almy, $270,000 total compensation
EVP Chief Credit Officer, Mark Williamson
President and CEO, Kevin J. Hanigan, $535,000 total compensation
EVP Community Banking, Charles D. Eikenberg, $270,000 total compensation
Vice President Risk Officer, Dan Bailey
Senior Vice President Cao Int Chief Financial Officer Assistant Tre, Kari J Anderson
Executive Vice President Mortgage Operations, Pam Smithey
Vice President Community Banking Operations Manager, Nina Stork
Vice President Treasury Management Operations, Tracy Marshall
Chairman, Anthony J. LeVecchio, age 68
Vice Chairman, Gary D Basham, age 72
Auditors: Ernst & Young LLP

LOCATIONS

HQ: LegacyTexas Financial Group Inc
5851 Legacy Circle, Plano, TX 75024
Phone: 972 578-5000
Web: www.viewpointfinancialgroup.com

PRODUCTS/OPERATIONS

2014 Sales

	% of total
Interest and dividend income	88
Non interest income	12
Total	**100**

COMPETITORS

Amegy	PlainsCapital
BBVA Compass	SP Bancorp
Bancshares	Texas Capital
Bank of America	Bancshares
Cullen/Frost Bankers	Wells Fargo
North Dallas Bank	

HISTORICAL FINANCIALS

Company Type: Public

Income Statement

FYE: December 31

	ASSETS ($ mil.)	NET INCOME ($ mil.)	INCOME AS % OF ASSETS	EMPLOYEES
12/14	4,164	31	0.8%	530
12/13	3,525	31	0.9%	576
12/12	3,663	35	1.0%	572
12/11	3,180	26	0.8%	598
12/10	2,942	17	0.6%	613
Annual Growth	9.1%	15.1%	—	(3.6%)

2014 Year-End Financials

Debt ratio: —
Return on equity: 5.62%
Cash ($ mil.): 132
Current ratio: —
Long-term debt ($ mil.): —

No. of shares (mil.): 40
Dividends
  Yield: 2.0%
  Payout: 55.8%
Market value ($ mil.): 954

Leidos Holdings Inc

Leidos Holdings (formerly SAIC) provides a host of national security services to civil agencies of the US government all branches of the military and the intelligence community. Areas of expertise include cybersecurity; mission support; logistics; and intelligence surveillance and reconnaissance. It also operates one of the country's largest health system integrators and offers engineering services for energy (oil gas and electric) and industrial clients. In early 2016 Leidos agreed to a $5 billion combination with Lockheed Martin's Information Systems & Global Solutions segment to form a company focused on providing IT and intelligence services.

Change in Company Type

The combination with Lockheed's Information Systems & Global Solutions unit creates a $10 billion portfolio of products and services. Leidos said the combined company could serve more diverse markets with greater scale. Lockheed Martin will own 50.5% of the new operation. The transaction includes a special cash payment of approximately $1.8 billion to Lockheed Martin. The deal's overall value is about $5 billion based on Leidos' $55.22 5-day volume weighted average stock price. Shareholders and government regulators still need to sign off on the deal.

Leidos itself was formed in 2013 when Science Applications International Corp. spun out IT operations into a new company an called it Leidos (a name taken from the word kaleidoscope). The company still called Science Applications International Corporation handles government technical services. The company touted the split as expanding the addressable market for each entity by removing potential conflicts of interest within the organization as well as providing a more clearly defined growth strategy for each business.

Operations

The national security services Leidos supplies to government agencies generate 71% of its revenue. The rest comes from health and engineering services. The company's corporate business produces no revenue.

Geographic Reach

Leidos has more than 236 offices located in 40 states across the US as well as in more than a dozen international locations where it works with US customers.

Sales and Marketing

The company's major customers include US Government bodies including various intelligence agencies the US Army Navy and Air Force research agencies like the Defense Advanced Research Projects Agency the Department of Homeland Security NASA and others. In 2015 the US Government accounted for 79% of the total revenue (with the US Army contributing 16%).

Financial Performance

In 2015 (ended January) Leidos reported a 12% drop in revenue mainly due to a 13% decline in its National Security Solutions revenues attributable to the drawdown of overseas US military forces. Security revenue dropped 11% and health and engineering revenue was down 14%.

The posted posted a net loss of $323 million following a $164 million profit in 2014 despite lower costs of revenue and sales and general expenses. The sales decrease was exacerbated by goodwill impairment charges associated with the security and health and engineering businesses.

Leidos' cash flow from operating activities jumped to $396 million in 2015 from $195 million in 2014 with working capital increasing $217 million.

Strategy

From time to time the company divests non-strategic components of its business. During 2015 the company sold Cloudshield which was historically included in their National Security Solutions segment and primarily focused on producing a suite of cybersecurity hardware and associated software and services. It previously sold components of its operational test and evaluation services for US government customers which had been included in the Health and Engineering segment.

Mergers and Acquisitions

Leidos has a long history of expansion through acquisitions. Since 2009 it has completed 13 acquisitions. In 2014 it bought a special purpose limited liability company Plainfield Renewable Energy LLC (Plainfield) formed to create a renewable energy project. Acquisitions slowed in 2015 as Leidos concentrated on its new corporate make up.

HISTORY

Early History

Physicist Robert Beyster who worked at Los Alamos National Laboratory in the 1950s was hired by General Atomics in 1957 to establish and manage its traveling wave linear accelerator. When the company was sold to Gulf Oil in 1968 research priorities changed and Beyster left. He founded Science Applications Inc. (SAI) the following year and built his business from consulting contracts with Los Alamos and Brookhaven National Laboratory. During the first year Beyster instituted an employee-ownership plan that rewarded workers who brought on board new business with stock in SAI. Beyster's idea was to share the success of SAI and to raise capital.

In 1970 the company established an office in Washington DC to court government contracts. Despite a recession SAI continued to grow during the 1970s and by 1979 sales topped $100 million. The following year SAI restructured becoming a subsidiary of Science Applications International Corporation (SAIC) a new holding company.

During the 1980s defense buildup an emphasis on high-tech weaponry and SAIC's high-level Pentagon connections (directors have included former defense secretaries William Perry and Melvin Laird and former CIA director John Deutch) brought in contracts for submarine warfare systems and technical development for the Strategic Defense Initiative ("Star Wars"). As defense spending slowed with the end of the Cold War though SAIC began casting a wider net. By 1991 computer systems integration and consulting accounted for 25% of sales which surpassed the $1 billion mark.

EXECUTIVES

Chairman and CEO, Roger A. Krone, age 59, $493,269 total compensation
EVP and CFO, James C. (Jim) Reagan, age 56
EVP and Chief Human Resources Officer, Sarah K. Allen
President Health and Engineering, Jonathan W. Scholl

EVP and General Counsel, Vincent A. (Vince) Maffeo, $574,723 total compensation
CTO, S. Gulu Gambhir
SVP and CIO, Martin Miner
Vice President, Stephen (Steve) Patay
Vp Business Dev't Isg Group, James (Jamie) Bahel
Vice President Business Development, Karen Walton
Vice President Technology Applications SECTOR, Michael (Mel) Daniels
Assistant Vice President Project Manager, James Sauer
Vice President Senior Proposal Manager, Chris Overson
Vice President Division Manager, Nelson Johnson
Assistant Vice President Senior Program Manager Fo, Richard Deason
Senior Vice President Of Information Technology Services, Mike Cole
Assistant Vice President Senior Program Manager Fo, Richard Mitchell
Vice President Security Solutions, Jeffrey Murter
Vice President For Cybersecurity, Robert Pate
DHS Vice President, William (Bill) Carroll
Vice President Production, Paul Dickinson
Vice President Information Technology, Chris Russeau
Assistant Vice President, Philip Rabin
Vice President Lso Ssei Pm, Debbie Kerr
Vice President, Robert (Bob) Weidman
Vice President Director Of Communications, Melissa (Mel) Koskovich
Auditors: Deloitte & Touche LLP

LOCATIONS

HQ: Leidos Holdings Inc
11951 Freedom Drive, Reston, VA 20190
Phone: 571 526-6000
Web: www.leidos.com

PRODUCTS/OPERATIONS

2015 Sales

	$ mil.	% of total
National Security solutions	3,594	71
Health and engineering	1,485	29
Adjustments	(16)	-
Total	**5,063**	**100**

Selected Mergers and Acquisitions

FY2012
maxIT Healthcare (IT consulting to the health care industry)
FY2011
Vitalize Consulting Solutions (IT consulting to the health care industry)
FY2010
CloudShield (data security)
Reveal Imaging Technologies (detection equipment for airport baggage scanning)
R.W. Beck Group (consultancy)
Patrick Energy Services (power systems)
Science Engineering and Technology Associates Corporation (data analysis and surveillance systems)
Spectrum San Diego (x-ray security scanning systems)

COMPETITORS

Accenture
American Science and Engineering
BAE Systems Technology Solutions
Battelle Memorial
Booz Allen
CACI International
CH2M HILL
Computer Sciences Corp.
Exelis
General Dynamics
HP Enterprise Services
Honeywell Technology Solutions
IBM Global Services
KBR

KEYW
Kratos Defense & Security Solutions
L-3 Communications
Lockheed Martin Information Systems
ManTech
Northrop Grumman Info Systems
OSI Systems
Raytheon Intelligence Information and Services
Serco
Unisys

HISTORICAL FINANCIALS
Company Type: Public

Income Statement
FYE: January 30

	REVENUE ($ mil.)	NET INCOME ($ mil.)	NET PROFIT MARGIN	EMPLOYEES
01/15	5,063	(323)	—	19,000
01/14	5,772	164	2.8%	22,000
01/13	11,173	525	4.7%	40,000
01/12	10,587	59	0.6%	41,100
01/11	11,117	618	5.6%	43,400
Annual Growth	(17.9%)	—	—	(18.7%)

2015 Year-End Financials
Debt ratio: 35.54%
Return on equity: (-24.98%)
Cash ($ mil.): 443
Current ratio: 1.70
Long-term debt ($ mil.): 1,164

No. of shares (mil.): 74
Dividends
Yield: 3.0%
Payout: —
Market value ($ mil.): 3,064

	STOCK PRICE ($) FY Close	P/E High/Low		PER SHARE ($) Earnings	Dividends	Book Value
01/15	41.40	—	—	(4.36)	1.28	13.49
01/14	45.34	25	6	1.94	0.64	19.94
01/13	12.10	2	2	6.16	1.92	30.62
01/12	12.86	24	16	0.72	0.00	25.58
01/11	16.57	3	2	6.52	0.00	27.52
Annual Growth	25.7%	—	—	—	—	(16.3%)

Leidos, Inc.

EXECUTIVES

Chb-ceo, Roger A Krone
Vice President Human Resources, Clay Worley
Senior Vice President Treasurer, Marc Crown
Vice President Talent Management, Cheryl Getty
Vice President and Assistant Secretary Assistant General Counsel, Brian Liss
Vice President Director of Operations Contracts, Graeme Ritchie
Vice President, Brent Gerity
Vice President director communications, Melissa (Mel) Koskovich
Vice President of Finance, Michael (Mel) McCarthy
Senior Vice President Deputy General Counsel and Corporate Secretary, Ray Veldman
Vice President Sector Procurement Director, Will Jeffers
Vice President, Nelson Johnson
Executive Vice President Business Development Strategy, Michael (Mel) Leiter
Vice President and Director of Human Resources Shared Services, Gayle G Connatser
Executive Vice President, Julianne Miller
Division Manager Vice President, Jack Terry
Vice President Engineering And Design, Robert (Bob) Perry

Vice President International Business Development, Mike Monroe
Vice President Sector Director of Contracts, Stuart (Stu) Phillips
Vice President Division Manager, John (Jack) Macier
Vice President Chief Engineer, Derek Lewis
Vice President Regulatory Affairs, Samantha Segall
Vice President Marketing, Danielle Poblete
Senior Vice President Enterprise Shared Service Director, Chris Buffoni
Senior Vice President Mritime Systems Operation, Marty Occhi
Vice President Director of Business Development, Mike Cameron
Vice President Of Procurement, Tod Comin
Vice President Strategic Regulatory Finance, Joe Kozsurek
Vice President, Jonathan Michel
Vice President, Pamela Saunders
Vice President Miltary Health Operations, Pete Leroy
Vice President, Steve Schneider
Assistant Vice President And Deputy Division Manager And Prgm Manager, Paul Desantis
Senior Vice President Strategy, Leanne Hester
Vice President Director Of Finance Enterprise, Carl Honig
Vice President Sales Operations and Corporate Accounts, Jessica (Barnett) Campbell
Assistant Vice President Operations Pricing Manager, Stan Mikulski
Vice President Of Human Resources, Lisa Barkan
Vice President Procurement Director, Melissa (Mel) Cunkle
Senior Vice President Investor Relations, John (Jack) Sweeney
Vice President Division Manager, John (Jack) Winship
Senior Vice President Chief Human Resources Officer, Marjorie Bailey
Vice President Global Sales and Marketing, Chris Mann
Senior Vice President, Robert (Bob) Zitz
Senior Vice President CIO, Martin (Marti) Miner
Vice President Strategy and Business Development, Anne Herrera
Vice President Group Strategic Account D, Teresa Albo
Senior Vice President Corporate Controller and Chief Accounting Officer, Ken Sharp
Auditors: Deloitte & Touche LLP

LOCATIONS

HQ: Leidos, Inc.
11951 Freedom Drive, Reston, VA 20190
Phone: 571 526-6000
Web: www.leidos.com

HISTORICAL FINANCIALS
Company Type: Public

Income Statement
FYE: January 30

	REVENUE ($ mil.)	NET INCOME ($ mil.)	NET PROFIT MARGIN	EMPLOYEES
01/15	5,063	(317)	—	19,000
01/14	5,772	166	2.9%	22,000
01/13	11,173	526	4.7%	40,000
01/12	10,587	56	0.5%	41,000
01/11	10,921	611	5.6%	—
Annual Growth	(17.5%)	—	—	—

2015 Year-End Financials
Debt ratio: 26.32%
Return on equity: (-12.36%)
Cash ($ mil.): 473
Current ratio: 1.70
Long-term debt ($ mil.): 1,233

No. of shares (mil.): 0
Dividends
Yield: —
Payout: —
Market value ($ mil.): —

Lennar Corp.

Lennar is one of the largest homebuilding land-owning loan-making leviathans in the US along with D.R. Horton and Pulte Homes. The company builds single-family attached and detached homes in 18 states under brand names including Lennar Camelot NuHome and Greystone. Lennar targets first-time move-up and active adult buyers and markets its homes as "everything included." The company also provides financial services including mortgage financing title and closing services. During fiscal 2015 (ended November) Lennar delivered more than 24200 homes at an average price of $344000.

HISTORY

Lennar is the creation of Leonard Miller and Arnold Rosen and the name of the company is a combination of their given names. Rosen a Miami homebuilder formed F&R Builders in 1954. A year later Miller graduated from Harvard with no firm career plans. Having worked summers in Florida Miller decided it would be a good place to make his fortune and the 23-year-old began selling real estate there.

With $10000 earned from commissions Miller bought 42 lots and in 1956 entered a joint venture with Rosen to build homes on the lots. They worked well together and Miller soon joined F&R. The operation grew emphasizing marketing and concentrating on low- and medium-priced single-family homes for first-time buyers and retirees.

After expanding into commercial real estate in the late 1960s the duo folded F&R into a new company –Lennar Corporation –in 1971 and went public. During the 1970s and 1980s the company hawked Jacuzzi tubs and designer homes (such as the Calvin and the Liz) and promised customers "$10000 worth of extras" free at Midnight Madness shopping mall sales. Lennar also began expanding acquiring land and builders in the Phoenix area in 1973. Rosen retired in 1977.

Spurred by a recession Lennar began offering mortgage services nationwide in 1981 keeping the potentially lucrative servicing for itself and selling its mortgages to Fannie Mae Ginnie Mae and Freddie Mac among others. In 1984 it dissolved its construction operations and began subbing out its work (a practice that it continues today). Lennar was relatively unscathed by the recession of the late 1980s in part because Miller had foreseen a slump and had cut corporate debt and overhead. When other builders were overextending themselves by buying land in good times Miller had used profit to pay down debt so he would have the resources to buy land cheap when bad times arrived.

During the 1990s Lennar targeted other Sun Belt markets and began buying portfolios of distressed property in partnership with heavy hitters like Morgan Stanley. Although Miller had looked at Texas as a development site since 1987 it was not until 1991 that Lennar entered the state beginning in Dallas.

The company bought up the secured debt of Bramalea Homes in Southern California in 1995 and entered Northern California with its acquisition of Renaissance Homes. Lennar's acquisition of Village Homes and Exxon's Friendswood Development in 1996 made it Houston's top home builder and Lennar surpassed $1 billion in sales.

In 1997 Stuart Miller became president and CEO (Leonard his father remained chairman). That year Lennar also spun off its commercial real estate operations as LNR Property a separately traded public company and acquired Pacific Greystone a Los Angeles builder.

The following year the company strengthened its position in the western US acquiring three California homebuilders: Winncrest Homes (Sacramento) ColRich Communities (San Diego) and Polygon Communities (Southern California and Sacramento). Lennar also purchased North American Title an escrow and title services company operating in Arizona California and Colorado.

In 2000 Lennar bought fellow builder U.S. Home for about $1.1 billion in a deal that expanded its operations into 13 states. The company acquired the North and South Carolina operations of The Fortress Group in late 2001 giving Lennar the Don Galloway Homes and Sunstar Homes brands. Through its FG Acquisition Corporation subsidiary Lennar acquired 93% of The Fortress Group in 2002; it also added Maryland-based Patriot Homes and assets of California homebuilders Pacific Century Homes and Cambridge Homes to bring its homebuilding operations to 16 states.

In July 2002 Leonard Miller died of liver cancer. Stuart Miller continues to lead the company as its president and CEO. The company acquired nine homebuilders that year which expanded its operations into markets in Chicago (Concord Homes and Summit Homes) Baltimore the Carolinas and California's Central Valley; some of the acquisitions strengthened Lennar's position in its existing markets. Lennar subsidiary North American Title Group acquired The Sentinel Title Corporation with nine branches in Maryland Virginia and Washington DC.

Lennar continued to acquire in 2003 adding Seppala Homes and Coleman Homes (with a backlog of about 300 homes and 3000 owned or controlled homesites) expanding its positions respectively in South Carolina and the Central Valley of California. The company's North American Title Group Inc. subsidiary acquired Mid America Title Company (Waukegan Illinois) which strengthened Lennar's homebuilding operations in the Chicago market.

In mid-2003 an entity jointly owned by Lennar and LNR Property Corporation (real estate investment finance and management) agreed to acquire The Newhall Land and Farming Company (master-planned communities) for about $1 billion. The deal closed in January 2004 enabling LNR to buy existing income-producing commercial assets from the venture and Lennar to option certain current homesites. Also in 2004 Lennar's Texas operations grew with its cash purchase of San Antonio-based Connell-Barron Homes and the company expanded into Jacksonville Florida by acquiring Classic American Homes Inc. for an undisclosed cash price. Lennar closed out the year with increased revenues and earnings of 18% and 26% respectively over the previous year and a strong backlog of about 15550 homes valued at about $5 billion.

As the real estate market continued to thrive Lennar acquired regional builders mortgage operations and title and closing businesses. During 2005 Lennar entered the Boston New York City and Reno markets; it also expanded its Jacksonville operations by acquiring Admiral Homes. The condo and apartment buildings in New York and Boston were valued at more than $2 billion.

Along with the rest of the homebuilding industry Lennar started to see trouble in 2006 as interest rates rose and years of overbuilding began taking their toll. Fallout from the subprime mortgage crisis and global credit crunch further unraveled the market. Lennar's average price per home fell by $40000 and the number of homes delivered fell by approximately 40000 (in 2009 as compared with fiscal 2005).

In early 2007 Lennar and its spun-off investment unit LNR Properties reduced their stakes in LandSource a joint venture that invests in raw land (among the riskiest of real estate investments particularly vulnerable to market downturns). MW Housing Partners an investment vehicle of the California Public Employees' Retirement System bought 68% of LandSource for $900 million in cash and property; Lennar lowered its stake from 50% to 16%. The sale proved to be fortuitous for Lennar: Not only did it bring the company much-needed cash but it also reduced Lennar's exposure to the debt-laden LandSource which filed for Chapter 11 bankruptcy protection one year later. LandSource emerged from bankruptcy as the debt-free Newhall Land Development. In 2009 Lennar bought back a 15% stake in the reorganized company for $140.Lennar survived the economic downturn by shifting its focus and tightening its belt. As one of the larger builders Lennar weathered the downturn by exiting slower markets lowering prices and reducing staff. The company also bought fewer home sites and tightened its lending standards to reduce its exposure to loan defaults. The company also increased its focus on the first-time buyer and limited the number of home plans offered.

EXECUTIVES

Vice President and Treasurer, Diane J Bessette
Vice President Investor Relations, Marshall H Ames
Vice President Taxation, Michael Petrolino
VP and COO, Jonathan M. (Jon) Jaffe, age 55, $800,000 total compensation
VP and CFO, Bruce E. Gross, age 56, $650,000 total compensation
CEO, Stuart A. Miller, age 57, $1,000,000 total compensation
President, Richard (Rick) Beckwitt, age 55, $800,000 total compensation
CEO Rialto Capital Management, Jeffrey P. (Jeff) Krasnoff
President and CEO FivePoint Communities, Emile Haddad
Regional President Lennar Land and Homebuilding, Jeff Roos
Regional President Lennar Land and Homebuilding, Rob Hutton
President Lennar Ventures; CEO Sunstreet Energy Group, David J. Kaiserman
President North American Title Group, Thomas J. (Tom) Fischer
President Rialto Capital Management, Jay Mantz
President Universal American Mortgage and Eagle Home Mortgage, James T. (Jimmy) Timmons
President North American Title and North American Advantage Insurance, Emilio Fernandez
Regional President Lennar Land and Homebuilding, Fred Rothman
President Lennar Multifamily Communities, Todd Farrell
Regional President Lennar Multifamily Communities, Ed Easley
President Lennar Commercial, Eric Feder
Regional President Lennar Commercial, Mike Cohn
Regional President Lennar Commercial, Mike Parker
CTO, Stephen (Steve) Smith
CIO, Laura Lete
Regional President Lennar Homebuilding and Land, Greg McGuff
President Rialto Mortgage Finance, Brett Ersoff
CEO and Chief Investment Officer Rialto Mortgage Finance, Jon Herman
Division President, Bill Burgess
Vice President Sales And Marketing, Carlos Gonzalez
Regional Vice President Finance, Dustin Barker
Vice President Director, Lisa Galloway

Vice President, David (Dave) Baselice
Division President, Scott Johnson
Vice President Operations, Al Lee
Vice President, Ben Gainer
Division President, Mike Miller
Vice President Operations, David Jarvis
Vice President Marketing, Janice Hinshaw
Vice President Marketing and Sales, Sheryl McKibben
Vice President Marketing, John Liston
Vice President, Mike Southward
Senior Vice President Customer Management Services, Daris Horn
Vice President Of Operations, Frank Walker
Vice President Of Community Development, Jeff Clemens
Vice President, Russell Smith
Vice President Purchasing, Scott Handt
Division President, Brad Reisinger
Senior Vice President, Stuart Morkun
Division President, Craig Klingensmith
Vice President Community Developrnent, Greg Dooley
Vice President of Finance Operations Coastal Carolinas, Bob Mauch
Vice President Controller, Ryan Gatchalian
Division President, JJ Abraham
Vice President, Benjamin (Ben) Gainer
Assistant Treasurer Adm s, Kevin Cronin
Board Member, Janice Stucker
Assistant Treasurer, Jacqui Desouza
Auditors: DELOITTE & TOUCHE LLP

LOCATIONS

HQ: Lennar Corp.
700 Northwest 107th Avenue, Miami, FL 33172
Phone: 305 559-4000
Web: www.lennar.com

2013 Segment Sales

	% of total
Homebuilding East	31
Homebuilding West	20
Homebuilding Central	13
Homebuilding Houston	11
Homebuilding Other	8
Homebuilding Southeast Florida	8
Lennar Financial Services	7
Rialto Investments	2
Multifamily	-
Total	**100**

Selected Markets

Arizona
  Phoenix
  Tucson
California
  Bakersfield
  Fresno
  Los Angeles/Valencia
  Orange County
  Palm Springs
  Riverside County
  Sacramento
  San Bernardino
  San Diego
Colorado
  Denver
Florida
  Clermont
  Ft. Lauderdale
  Jacksonville
  Lakeland
  Miami
  Naples
  Orlando
  Sarasota
  Tampa
Illinois
  Chicago
Maryland
  Baltimore
  Maryland/DC Metro
New Jersey
  Edison Township

Mays Landing
Rockaway Township
North Carolina
  Charlotte
  Raleigh
South Carolina
  Charleston
  Greenville
  Myrtle Beach
Texas
  Austin
  Dallas/Fort Worth
  Houston
  San Antonio
Virginia
  Maryland/Virginia/Washington DC Metro
  Williamsburg

PRODUCTS/OPERATIONS

2015 Sales

	$ mil.	% of total
Homebuilding East	2,761	29
Homebuilding Central	1,213	13
Homebuilding West	2,365	25
Homebuilding Southeast Florida	801	8
Homebuilding Houston	730	8
Homebuilding Other	593	6
Lennar Financial Services	620	7
Rialto	221	2
Lennar Multifamily	164	2
Total	**9,473**	**100**

Selected Subsidiaries

360 Developers LLC
Camelot Ventures LLC
Eagle Bend Commercial LLC
Eagle Home Mortgage LLC
Heritage of Auburn Hills LLC
Lennar Associates Management LLC
Lennar Homes of California Inc.
Lennar Homes of Texas Sales and Marketing Ltd.
Lennar Ventures LLC
LH-EH Layton Lakes Estate LLC
Majestic Woods LLC
North American Title Company (MD)
Raintree Village L.L.C.
Savell Gulley Development LLC
Universal American Mortgage Company LLC
U.S. Home of Arizona Construction Co.

COMPETITORS

Beazer Homes	NVR
CalAtlantic	PulteGroup
D.R. Horton	Toll Brothers
Hovnanian Enterprises	Weyerhaeuser Real
KB Home	Estate
M.D.C.	

HISTORICAL FINANCIALS

Company Type: Public

Income Statement

FYE: November 30

	REVENUE ($ mil.)	NET INCOME ($ mil.)	NET PROFIT MARGIN	EMPLOYEES
11/15	9,474	802	8.5%	7,749
11/14	7,779	638	8.2%	6,825
11/13	5,935	479	8.1%	5,741
11/12	4,104	679	16.5%	4,722
11/11	3,095	92	3.0%	4,062
Annual Growth	**32.3%**	**71.8%**	**—**	**17.5%**

2015 Year-End Financials

Debt ratio: 34.85%
Return on equity: 15.33%
Cash ($ mil.): 1,173
Current ratio: 21.37
Long-term debt ($ mil.): 5,025
No. of shares (mil.): 211
Dividends
  Yield: 0.3%
  Payout: 4.8%
Market value ($ mil.): 10,813

	STOCK PRICE ($) FY Close	P/E High/Low		PER SHARE ($) Earnings	Dividends	Book Value
11/15	51.21	14	11	3.46	0.16	26.75
11/14	47.24	15	11	2.80	0.16	23.54
11/13	35.76	18	13	2.15	0.16	20.39
11/12	38.04	11	5	3.11	0.16	17.83
11/11	18.41	44	26	0.48	0.16	14.31
Annual Growth	**29.1%**	**—**	**—**	**63.9%**	**(0.0%)**	**16.9%**

Leucadia National Corp.

Holding company Leucadia National owns stakes in a variety of firms involved in manufacturing medical products gaming and beef processing. The investment firm typically seeks out troubled companies that it believes are undervalued. Some of its largest holdings include the National Beef Packaging Company; global securities and investment bank Jefferies Group; Leucadia Asset Management; HomeFed Corporation; a 50% stake in Berkadia Commercial Mortgage; Idaho Timber; Conwed Plastics; and Crimson Wine Group among others. It also has interests in gold and silver mining companies telecommunication services business in Italy and automobile dealerships.

Operations
Leucadia two reportable segments include Jefferies and National Beef which report the results of its investment banking and beef processing businesses respectively. All of Leucadia's other businesses and investments consist of Other Financial Services Businesses (including its asset management specialty finance commercial mortgage banking businesses and its 65% stake in real estate developer HomeFed) and Other Merchant Banking Businesses (including its manufacturing oil and gas exploration and production real estate and winery companies and its 23% stake in Harbinger). The company's National Beef Packing Company subsidiary one of the largest beef producers in the US brought in 68% of Leucadia's total revenue in 2014. The company processes packages and delivers fresh and frozen beef and beef by-products for sale to customers in the US and international markets. Its Jeffries subsidiary a securities and investment banking business brought in 26% of Leucadia's total revenue in 2014. Jefferies' capital markets business includes the firm's securities commodities futures and foreign exchange brokerage trading activities as well as investment banking consisting of underwriting and financial advisory activities. The subsidiary also provides the sales trading and origination support for various fixed income equity and advisory products and services. Jefferies also provides asset management services to investors in the US and overseas investment management services.As a diversified holding company Leucadia holds several other companies too. Idaho Timber remanufactures manufactures and distributes wood products. Conwed Plastics makes and markets lightweight plastic netting. The company also has a 50% stake in Berkadia Commercial Mortgage in a joint venture with Berkshire Hathaway. Other operations primarily consist of the company's wineries and energy projects.

Geographic Reach
The company owns and maintains facilities in Salt Lake City Utah devoted to corporate office space. Its subsidiaries own facilities in Georgia Virginia and Belgium that are used for plastics man-

ufacturing. Leucadia's wine-making operations boast both facilities and land in California Oregon and Washington. The firm's National Beef business leases corporate space in Kansas City Missouri. Its Idaho Timber unit has a presence in North Carolina Florida New Mexico and Texas.

Sales and Marketing
Through its various subsidiary companies Leucadia has a hand in several sectors such as beef processing real estate activities winery operations and manufacturing. Leucadia spent about $14.5 million on advertising expenses in 2014 compared to $14.6 million and $12.4 million in 2013 and 2012 respectively.

National Beef markets its products to national and regional retailers such as supermarket chains independent grocers club stores wholesalers and distributors foodservice providers and distributors other processors and the US military. National Beef exported products to more than 25 countries in 2014 with export sales representing 12% of revenue. The subsidiary lost its larger customer Wal-Mart which generated some 5% of National Beef's revenues when the retail giant stopped using them as a provider of its consumer-ready products in 2013.

Idaho Timber markets its products to local regional and national lumber retailers.

The company's plastics business sells products primarily through an employee sales force that's located in both the US and Europe.

Financial Performance
Leucadia's revenue has skyrocketed over the past few years ballooning from $1.32 billion in 2010 to $11.49 billion in 2014 thanks in large part to firm's prudent investments in Jefferies and National Beef. Its revenue jumped by 10% to $11.49 billion in 2014 mostly as its Jefferies subsidiary grew by 40% thanks to record investment banking income along with solid performance in the subsidiary's equity sales and trading business. Leucadia's National Beef revenue also rose by 5% for the year thanks to higher selling prices as fewer cattle were processed.Despite rising revenues Leucadia's profits have been declining for most of the past few years. The holding company's net income shrank by 45% to $199.03 million in 2014 mostly because of higher interest expenses from long-term debt and higher bad debt provisions most of which were related to a $52.3 million receivable from one of Jefferies' futures clients that declared bankruptcy during the year.Cash levels fell significantly in 2014 mostly as the company used $317.5 million toward acquiring its stake in Harbinger and used another $345.1 million toward further investments in its Leucadia asset management platform. It also spent more toward larger interest payments.

Strategy
Leucadia's investment strategy is to take a patient approach to create long-term value. To free capital for new investments the company regularly divests or shuts down holdings that aren't performing to expectations. In 2014 for example the company sold its gaming entertainment business Premier Entertainment Biloxi LLC which owned Hard Rock Hotel & Casino Biloxi for $250 million cash. Also that year the company sold all of its real estate properties and operations to HomeFed Corporation which had a plan to drive long-term growth for the properties. Leucadia's 65% stake in the real estate company ensured that it would share in the success of any such property growth. Since mid-2012 Leucadia has also sold mining energy real estate and gaming companies and shuttered medical products maker Sangart.

Mergers and Acquisitions
In March 2013 Leucadia acquired the shares of Jefferies Group it didn't already own in a deal val-

ued at $4 billion. The acquisition made Jefferies Group a subsidiary of Leucadia.

Prior to the Jefferies purchase the company's most transformational deal was the late 2011 acquisition of National Beef one of the largest meat processors in the US.

EXECUTIVES

Chief Executive Officer, Richard B. Handler,
$1,000,000 total compensation
President, Brian P. Friedman, age 59, $1,000,000
total compensation
EVP and General Counsel, Michael J. Sharp, age 59,
$1,000,000 total compensation
CFO, Teresa S. Gendron, $166,667 total compensation
Vice President, Joseph (Jo) OConnor
Vice President, Cullen Schaar
Vice President Treasurer, Rocco Nittoli
Executive Vice President, Thomas (Thom) Mara
Chairman, Joseph S. Steinberg, age 71
Treasurer Administrative Assistant, Andrea Galvez
Auditors: PricewaterhouseCoopers LLP

LOCATIONS

HQ: Leucadia National Corp.
520 Madison Avenue, New York, NY 10022
Phone: 212 460-1900   **Fax:** 212 598-4869
Web: www.leucadia.com

PRODUCTS/OPERATIONS

2014 Sales

	$ mil.	% of total
Beef Processing services	7,824	64
Investment banking	1,526	12
Interest income	1,052	9
Commissions	668	5
Principal transactions	662	5
Net realized security gains	30	-
Others	570	5
Total	**12,334**	**100**

COMPETITORS

Apollo Investment	H Group Holding
Berkshire Hathaway	Heico Companies
Berwind	Sun Capital
Blackstone Group	Veritas Capital
Castle Harlan	Wesco Financial

HISTORICAL FINANCIALS

Company Type: Public

Income Statement   FYE: December 31

	REVENUE ($ mil.)	NET INCOME ($ mil.)	NET PROFIT MARGIN	EMPLOYEES
12/14	11,486	199	1.7%	13,082
12/13	10,429	362	3.5%	14,647
12/12	9,193	854	9.3%	10,943
12/11	1,570	25	1.6%	11,711
12/10	1,320	1,939	146.9%	2,414
Annual Growth	**71.8%**	**(43.4%)**	**—**	**52.6%**

2014 Year-End Financials

Debt ratio: 17.57%	No. of shares (mil.): 367
Return on equity: 1.93%	Dividends
Cash ($ mil.): 11,648	Yield: 1.1%
Current ratio: 1.37	Payout: 44.6%
Long-term debt ($ mil.): 8,527	Market value ($ mil.): 8,239

	STOCK PRICE ($) FY Close	P/E High/Low		PER SHARE ($) Earnings	Dividends	Book Value
12/14	22.42	53	39	0.54	0.25	(0.24)
12/13	28.34	30	22	1.06	0.25	28.06
12/12	23.79	9	6	3.44	0.25	27.67
12/11	22.74	390	204	0.10	0.25	25.24
12/10	29.18	4	2	7.85	0.25	28.53
Annual Growth	**(6.4%)**	**—**	**—**	**(48.8%)**	**(0.0%)**	**—**

Level 3 Communications, Inc.

Level 3 Communications makes valuable connections through its networking efforts. Operator of one of the world's largest fiber-optic communications networks the firm connects customers in 60 countries. Its services include broadband Internet access wholesale voice origination and termination enterprise voice content distribution broadband transport and colocation. Wholesale customers include ISPs telecom carriers cable-TV operators wireless providers and the US government. The company markets its products and services directly to businesses state agencies and schools. Its content delivery unit targets video distributors Web portals online gaming and software companies and social networking sites.

HISTORY

Early History

Thoroughly modern Level 3 Communications was the brainchild of an Omaha Nebraska construction company that traces its roots to 1884 — the multinational Peter Kiewit Sons'. With cash to invest in the 1980s Kiewit acquired Metropolitan Fiber Systems which built fiber-optic networks for phone companies. In 1986 Kiewit executive James Crowe convinced CEO Walter Scott that Kiewit should build some phone circuits of its own and by 1987 Kiewit had created MFS Communications headed by Crowe to build networks in business districts. Kiewit slated $500 million for the project in 1989.

By 1995 MFS had gone public and was the biggest of the competitive local-exchange carriers (CLECs). That year Crowe and Scott heard Bill Gates speak on the power of the Internet to destroy traditional phone traffic. MFS launched "Project Silver" to decide how to respond. The answer: Buy UUNET. In 1996 MFS acquired the giant ISP and Internet backbone operator and in the process made itself an acquisition target. WorldCom bought MFS for $14 billion by year's end.

Within a month Crowe walked away from WorldCom (with several MFS execs in tow) to head Kiewit Diversified Group which had holdings in telecommunications technology and energy.

In 1998 Kiewit split into the Peter Kiewit Sons' construction group headed by Ken Stinson and a diversified company called Level 3 Communications headed by Crowe. Level 3 kept stakes in telecom companies RCN and C-TEC (now Commonwealth Telephone Enterprises). The Level 3 name came from the seven-layer Open Systems Interconnect (OSI) network model: The company saw its field of play in the bottom three levels —the physical plant data link and network layers.

Kiewit provided Crowe with a $2.5 billion grubstake; Level 3 went public and sold its oil interests and Michigan cable-TV operation. It retained its coal-mining and toll-road interests to help fund the buildout of a new fiber-optic network to be based on Internet protocol (IP) technology instead of the old circuit-switching system.

Level 3 secured rights-of-way from Burlington Northern and Union Pacific. The company found a new angel in Craig McCaw whose INTERNEXT agreed to plunge $700 million into the Level 3 network in return for capacity. By year's end the company had begun local networks in 25 US cities and had completed gateway sites in 17.

In 1999 Level 3 moved from Omaha to Broomfield Colorado deciding that it could grow faster in the Rockies. The company opened London and Frankfurt gateway sites after buying UK and German ISPs and it agreed to share construction costs on Western European routes with COLT . Level 3 hired Tyco International to develop an Atlantic undersea cable and agreed to participate in the building of the Japan-US Cable Network across the Pacific.

Fellow fiber baron Global Crossing agreed to buy a 50% interest in the transatlantic cable in 2000. By mid-year Level 3 had installed fiber across more than a third of its planned US intercity network. In early 2001 the company announced the completion of its network construction and said it would expand its European network to eight additional markets despite cutting about 6% of its workforce. Later that year Level 3 announced plans to buy McLeodUSA's wholesale dial-up Internet access assets for $55 million and in 2002 it completed the deal which enabled Level 3 to support dial-up Internet access in all 50 states.

For Level 3 as for many of its rivals demand for bandwidth capacity and services failed to reach expected levels and the company in 2001 scaled back its revenue estimates and cut almost 25% of its workforce. It also sold its Asian operations including its Tiger network and its capacity on a Japan-US submarine cable and backhaul network to Reach the wholesale carrier partnership of Telstra and PCCW.

However Level 3 received a shot in the arm in 2002 when an investment group that included Warren Buffett's Berkshire Hathaway invested $500 million in the company (it sold the stake in 2004). Level 3 acquired most of the assets of network services provider Genuity in a deal valued at $242 million. It later withdrew from Genuity's managed hosting business sending customers to CSC and sold the Midwest Fiber Optic Network a regional system acquired from Genuity to CenturyTel. The company had made an earlier unsuccessful bid to purchase Tulsa-based Williams Communications Group now WilTel Communications which later completed reorganization under bankruptcy protection.

Also in 2002 Level 3 acquired Massachusetts-based software distributor CorpSoft and Software Spectrum a business software distributor based in Texas. The companies were combined and Level 3 soon derived much of its revenues from software distribution which provided relief from the telecom sector's hard times. That year it sold its stake in Pennsylvania phone company Commonwealth Telephone Enterprises and its stake in RCN was written off following that company's bankruptcy.

In 2003 the company gained $46 million in cash and $139 million in reduced debt from its 65% interest in California Private Transportation Company following its sale of the SR-91 Toll Road to the Orange County (California) Transportation Authority. That year it teamed up with PanAmSat combining the two companies' network capabilities to form a hybrid fiber-optic and satellite delivery system for entertainment content and information to cable and TV broadcasters ISPs and others (PanAmSat was acquired in 2006 by Intelsat). In a separate deal Level 3 agreed to provide Internet access through its satellite platform to the 500000 Internet access customers of Hughes Electronics' DIRECTV unit.

The company acquired the managed modem business of ICG Communications in 2004.

Vyvx was acquired in 2005 when Level 3 bought WilTel Communications Group from Leucadia National. The company also sold its computer outsourcing services unit (i)Structure in 2005.

Level 3 made a number of acquisitions in 2006 including Progress Telecom TelCove metro transport services provider Looking Glass Networks and the rest of ICG Communications. It also sold its Software Spectrum subsidiary that year.

The company acquired Broadwing a provider of voice and data communications services for $254 million in early 2007. To diversify its services Level 3 also purchased SAVVIS's content delivery network services business for approximately $132 million and it bought online video management firm Servecast for $45 million.

Due to declining revenues from transport services for audio and video programming Level 3 sold the advertising portion of it Vyvx content distribution unit to DG FastChannel (now Digital Generation) for $129 million in 2008.

EXECUTIVES

Regional President North America and Asia Pacific (APAC), John T. Blount, age 56
CTO, John F. (Jack) Waters, age 51, $426,927 total compensation
President and CEO, Jeffrey K. (Jeff) Storey, age 55, $978,846 total compensation
EVP and CFO, Sunit S. Patel, age 53, $601,346 total compensation
Regional President EMEA and GAM, Andrew Crouch, age 44, $483,262 total compensation
EVP Chief Legal Officer and Secretary, John M. Ryan, age 52
Regional President Latin America, Hector R. Alonso, age 57, $427,125 total compensation
EVP and Chief Administrative Officer, Laurinda Y. Pang, age 45, $436,462 total compensation
Vice President Of Information Technology, Don Schank
Vice President Of Information Systems, Dan Cole
Vice President Of Information Technology, Jerry Cox
Vice President Of Information Systems, William Esperanza
Senior Vice President Marketing, Jeff Collins
Vice President of Information Systems, Fred Hartman
Vice President Of Technology, James Dwyer
Vice President, Mary Byrne
Vice President of Technology Systems, Mark Zhu
Vice President Treasury EMEA, Andy Gifford
Vice President Of Information Systems, Stephen Dunton
Vice President Of Information Systems, Ty Messerli
Vice President Of Technology, Andreas Onfermann
Vice President Of Technology, Jenny Bennett
Vice President Sales Operations Collaboration Svsc, Kim Kenney
Vice President Managing Corporate Counsel, Samantha Leapley
Vice President Finance, Peter McClure
Senior Vice President, Lisa Miller
Vice President Of Information Systems, Laurence Lipstone
Assistant Vice President Information Technology Audit Risk and Advisory Services, Dave Mueller

Vice President Of Information Systems, Earl Williams
Vice President Of Technology, Olen Perkins
Vice President Of Information Systems, Andrew Bates
Vice President of Information Systems, Randy Lussier
Vice President Of Information Systems, Jeff Hallman
Vice President Of Information Technology, Craig Burns
Vice President Of Technology, Alan Rudd
Vice President Of Information Technology, Sterling Snyder
Vice President Of Information Systems, Tara Farley
Vice President Sales, Caroline Witcomb
Vice President of Sales Collaboration, Carl Orleman
Vice President Of Technology Systems, Jason Tatarevich
Vice President Of Information Technology, William Singleton
Vice President Global Media Engineering, Greg Wallace
Vice President Sales, Julie Masino
Vice President Of Information Technology, Treva Belt
Vice President Of Information Technology, Bruce Carver
Vice President Total Rewards, Sarah Neill
Vice President Information Technology Operations, Jennifer Baker
Vice President Commercial Operations Information Technology, Elizabeth Lynch
National Account Manager, Dean Jones
Vice President of Data Center Product Management, Mike Benjamin
Svp Sales Europe Middle East And Africa (Emea), Andrew (Andy) Edison
National Account Manager, Marie Marshall
Vice President Of Technology, Jeremy Turff
Vice President Finance North America, John Merriman
Vice President of Sales and Services, Luis Guerrero
Vice President Business Development, Nigel Williams
Regional Vice President Sales, Christopher (Chris) Sikora
Regional Vice President, Jeff Lowney
Vice President General Manager, Michelle Preston
National Account Manager, David Franco
Vice President Global Information Technology Enterprise Architecture, Pete Caputo
Vice President Gm Memphis Little Rock, Joe Brooks
Vice President North America Network Planning, Mike McNamara
Senior Vice President Information Technology Chief Information Office, Deborah (Deb) Troudt
Vice President Managing Corporate Counsel, Nick Spence
Vice President Of Technology Systems, Michael Oconnell
Vice President Of Technology Systems, Hakan Sen
Vice President Sales, Brian Dolan
Vice President Of Information Systems, Joshua McKee
Vice President Information Technology Solutions Delievery, David Ward
Vice President Marketing, Michael Healy
Vice President, David Young
Vice President Information Technology Manager, Jennie Prins
Vice President Service Management Ip Services, John Treece
Area Vice President Business Development Public Sector, Stuart (Stu) Johnson
Vice President Supply Chain LatAm, Pablo Werner

Assistant Vice President Sales Information Technology, Rizwan Faruqui
Vice President of Sales, Marcos Malfatti
Vice President Of Technology Systems, Robert Fleary
Vice President, Dave Rosenberg
Vice President of Information Technology, Brianw Donnelly
Vice President Of Information Technology, Vickie Byrne
Senior Vice President Global Procurement and Supply Chain Operations, Ric Padilla
Vice President Offer Management Contents Mrkt Group, Billy Parker
Vice President Sistemas, Jose Arozamena
Senior Vice President of Sales North America West, Troy Knuckles
Vice President of Information Technology, Tony Nguyen
Vice President Sales, Sonia Ramsey
Vice President Sales, Tom Marx
Senior Vice President Field Operations, Fred Lawler
Chairman, James O. Ellis, age 67
Auditors: KPMG LLP

LOCATIONS

HQ: Level 3 Communications, Inc.
1025 Eldorado Blvd., Broomfield, CO 80021-8869
Phone: 720 888-1000
Web: www.level3.com

2014 Sales

	% of total
Core Network Services	
North America Enterprise Channel	41
North America Wholesale Channel	22
EMEA Enterprise Channel	8
EMEA Wholesale Channel	5
Latin America Enterprise Channel	9
Latin America Wholesale Channel	2
tw telecom-Eneterprice Channel	3
tw telecom-Wholesale Channel	1
Wholesale Voice Services & Other	9
Total	**100**

2014 Sales

	% of total
North America	71
EMEA	13
Latin America	12
tw telecom	4
Total	**100**

PRODUCTS/OPERATIONS

2014 Sales

	% of total
Core Network Services	91
Wholesale Voice Services & Other	9
Total	**100**

Selected Services

Communications services
  Transport and infrastructure
  Colocation
  Dark fiber (unconnected fiber)
  Metropolitan and intercity wavelengths
  Private line
  Professional services
  Transoceanic
  Voice
  Enterprise
  Wholesale voice origination and termination
  Wholesale VoIP component services
  IP and data
  ATM and frame relay
  Content delivery network (CDN) services
  Dedicated Internet access
  High-speed Internet access
  VPNs
  Managed IP (low-speed services primarily from Genuity acquisition)

Reciprocal compensation (interconnection agreements with carriers)
Vyvx (audio and video program broadcasting)
SBC contract services

COMPETITORS

AT&T	KPN
Akamai	Limelight
BT	Orange
COLT Group	Proximus
Cable & Wireless	SAVVIS
Communications	TCS America
CenturyLink	TeleCity
Cogent Communications	Telefnica
Deutsche Telekom	TeliaSonera
Equinix	Telmex
HP	Verizon Enterprise
IBM	Solutions
InterXion	XO Holdings
Internap	Zayo Group
Interoute	

HISTORICAL FINANCIALS

Company Type: Public

Income Statement

FYE: December 31

	REVENUE ($ mil.)	NET INCOME ($ mil.)	NET PROFIT MARGIN	EMPLOYEES
12/14	6,777	314	4.6%	13,500
12/13	6,313	(109)	—	10,000
12/12	6,376	(422)	—	10,800
12/11	4,333	(756)	—	10,900
12/10	3,651	(622)	—	5,500
Annual Growth	16.7%	—	—	25.2%

2014 Year-End Financials

Debt ratio: 54.10%	No. of shares (mil.): 341
Return on equity: 8.08%	Dividends
Cash ($ mil.): 580	Yield: —
Current ratio: 0.78	Payout: —
Long-term debt ($ mil.): 10,984	Market value ($ mil.): 16,856

	STOCK PRICE ($) FY Close	P/E High/Low		PER SHARE ($) Earnings	Dividends	Book Value
12/14	49.38	41	25	1.21	0.00	18.64
12/13	33.17	—	—	(0.49)	0.00	6.01
12/12	23.11	—	—	(1.96)	0.00	5.36
12/11	16.99	—	—	(5.51)	0.00	5.74
12/10	0.98	—	—	(5.55)	0.00	(1.41)
Annual Growth	166.4%			—	—	—

Liberty Interactive Corp

Liberty Interactive Corp. (formerly Liberty Media Corp.) stands by your right to shop at home and online. The company focuses on television and e-commerce sales through its QVC home-shopping subsidiary and numerous online businesses including CommerceHub Backcountry.com Bodybuilding.com and the online invitation site Evite. It also holds equity stakes in companies like Internet travel service Expedia HSN and LendingTree among others. Liberty Interactive Corp. was formed in 2011 when its predecessor restructured by merging and splitting off its Liberty Capital and Liberty Starz businesses under a newly-formed holding company also called Liberty Media.

Operations

Liberty Interactive operates through two main business divisions: QVC and Digital Commerce. QVC is the company's cash cow subsidiary ac-

counting for 84% of its total sales in 2014. The television brand broadcasts live shopping programs and sells merchandise online in the US and abroad. Home products made up 32% of QVC's sales in 2014 while beauty and apparel products generated 17% and 16% respectively. Jewelry accessories and electronic product sales each contributed more than 10% of QVC's total sales for the year.

Digital Commerce accounts for the remainder of Liberty's sales. Subsidiary companies under Liberty's online umbrella include outdoor gear e-tailer Backcountry.com; sports fitness and nutrition seller Bodybuilding.com which is one of the largest e-tailers in the supplement industry; Commerce-HUB a provider of Software-as-a-Service platforms for online retailers and their suppliers; Evite; and LMC Right Start. The company also has equity stakes in Expedia HSN Inc. FDT Companies Interval Leisure Group and LendingTree.

Geographic Reach

Liberty Interactive rings up about 70% of its sales in the US. Overseas Japan and Germany each account for about 10% of the company's total sales. QVC has shopping channels in Germany Japan Italy and the UK. The company also has a joint venture in China.Sales and MarketingFlagship subsidiary QVC distributes its television programs through satellite and optical fiber to cable and satellite system providers in the US Germany Japan the UK and neighboring countries. It also transmits programs via digital terrestrial broadcast television to viewers in Italy the UK and certain parts of the US and Germany. Additionally QVC offers a web-based catalog for retailers.Some of QVC's clients include: Comcast Time Warner Cable Cox Dish Network DirecTV Verizon and AT&T.Liberty Interactive spent $271 million on advertising expenses in 2014 up from $258 million and $247 million in 2013 and 2012 respectively.

Financial Performance

While Liberty Interactive's sales are back to their pre-recession levels thanks to an improved economy the company's profits are roughly one-tenth of what they were in 2009 (when Liberty's net income was $6.46 billion).Liberty's revenue shrank by nearly 7% to $10.50 billion in 2014 mostly because it lost a revenue source when it spun off its TripAdvisor subsidiary during the year. Outside of this transaction Liberty's revenue actually grew by 3% thanks to higher sales volumes from QVC and higher sales from its Digital Commerce businesses Backcountry Bodybuilding and CommerceHub.Despite revenue declines in 2014 Liberty's net income rose by 7% to $537 million thanks to a gain from the sale of its TripAdvisor subsidiary as well as a $75 million gain from the sale of its Provide Commerce floral and gifting business to FTD during the year. The company's cash from operations also spiked by 60% as its cash earnings grew and as it increased its accounts payable and other current liabilities balances.

Strategy

Liberty Interactive plans to grow its flagship QVC brand in 2015 by expanding the reach and depth of the brand internationally; showcasing products that offer unique quality and value; creating a differentiated customer experience through engaging content on its televised programming mobile and online formats; and leveraging its customer base to cross-sell its products through its multiple sales channels. Liberty Interactive has been focused on expanding QVC internationally and acquiring additional e-commerce businesses that complement and add to its holdings. In 2014 QVC entered France for the first time with plans to offer shoppers an immersive digital shopping experience through its e-commerce TV mobile and social channels by the summer of 2015. In July 2012 QVC entered into a joint venture in China taking a 49% interest in CNR Home Shopping a

distributor of live and recorded programming there.

The company has also sold off some of its holdings in recent years to free up resources and concentrate more on QVC. In 2014 it sold Provide Commerce it's second biggest money maker behind QVC to floral and gift retailing powerhouse FTD Companies. Also that year the company spun off TripAdvisor and the BuySeasons group to create a separate publicly-traded company called TripAdvisor Holdings.

Mergers and Acquisitions

In late 2013 to expand its presence in the growing European market subsidiary Backcountry bought Bergfreunde.de an e-commerce company that caters to outdoor enthusiasts in Germany Austria and Switzerland.In late 2012 Liberty Interactive bought a controlling interest in online travel company TripAdvisor from Diller and the Diller-von Furstenberg Family Foundation for $300 million. (Following the transaction Liberty owned 22% of the equity and 57% of the voting shares of TripAdvisor stock.) TripAdvisor's branded websites include tripadvisor.com in the US as well as local websites in 29 other countries including China under the brand daodao.com.Company BackgroundIn September 2011 Liberty Media Corp. changed its name to Liberty Interactive Corp. following the split-off of its Liberty Capital and Liberty Starz tracking stocks.

HISTORY

The man who would be king of cable programming got his start on the hardware end of the business. In 1970 John Malone became president of General Instrument's Jerrold Communications subsidiary which supplied equipment to the then-new cable TV industry. One of Jerrold's customers was Bob Magness a former Texas rancher who in the 1950s started the company that eventually became Denver-based cable operator Tele-Communications Inc. (TCI). In the early 1970s TCI struggled in need of leadership. In 1973 the 32-year-old Malone was named CEO of TCI.

Malone restructured TCI's debt in 1977 paving the way for expansion into bigger cable markets after deregulation in 1984. He also acquired programming buying stakes in Black Entertainment Television (33% 1979 sold to Viacom in 2001) the Discovery Channel (14% 1986) and American Movie Classics (50% 1986). In 1987 TCI helped save debt-plagued Turner Broadcasting and came away with 12% of Turner Broadcasting's stock.

Due in part to antitrust pressure from government regulators in 1991 TCI spun off much of its programming assets along with interests in 14 cable systems as Liberty Media. Malone became chairman and principal shareholder. In its first year the company launched Court TV in a joint venture and introduced film channel Encore. The next year it bought an interest in the Home Shopping Network (which became USA Networks in 1998 and later changed names to USA Interactive in 2002 InterActiveCorp in 2003 and finally IAC/InterActiveCorp in 2004).

In 1994 TCI reacquired Liberty Media; it issued a tracking stock the next year to reflect the value of Liberty's program assets. Also in 1995 Liberty Media and News Corp. joined forces to create FOX/Liberty Networks a national sports network designed to compete with Disney's ESPN.

EXECUTIVES

SVP and CFO, Christopher W. Shean, age 49, $392,109 total compensation
President and CEO, Gregory B. (Greg) Maffei, age 54, $765,769 total compensation

Vice President Of Publicity, Tamara Lantz
Vice President U.s. Neuroscience Business Unit Leader, Michael (Mel) Mason
Vice President Medical Affairs, Robert (Bob) Heine
Vice President Of Marketing, Christopher Konkoy
Vice President Government Affairs, Joe Kelley
Department Head, Scott Chapell
Vice President, Mike Burnham
Medical Director, Todd Durell
Executive Vice President Pharma Operations, Johnathan Schilling
Vice President Global Diversity, Patricia Martin
Vice President, David (Dave) Clifford
Vice President, Aarti Shah
Vice President Of Strategic Planning, Peter Johnson
Vice President and Treasurer, Thomas (Thom) Grein
Vice President, Julie Martin
First Vice President, Tim Jones
Vice President New Media, Paula Garrett
Vice President Marketing, Michael Stone
Vice President Marketing, Ponce Tidwell
Medical Director Alliance Products US, Oliver Bachmann
Medical Director, Anurita Majumdar
Vice President, Mark Pemberton
Senior Vice President Clinical and Regulatory Affairs, Robert (Bob) Bay
Vice President Global Quality, Carole Beer
Vice President Manufacturing, Myles Oneill
Vice President And Medical Director China, Li Wang
Chief Medical Officer Senior Vice President Drug Development Center of Excellence, Tim Garnett
Vice President, Jeff Emmick
Vice President Information Technology, Bryan Woodfork
Vice President Oncology Research, Greg Plowman
Vice President Global Medical Affairs, Robert W (Bob) Baker
Secretary, Tim Conrad
Secretary To The Livestock Marketing Department, Carine Maes
Board Member, Ed Parrish
Board Member, Mark Miklinski
Secretary, Meg Johnston
Secretary, Bill Dunn
Auditors: Ernst & Young LLP

LOCATIONS

HQ: Lilly (Eli) & Co.
Lilly Corporate Center, Indianapolis, IN 46285
Phone: 317 276-2000
Web: www.lilly.com

2014 Sales

	$ mil.	% of total
US	9,134	47
Europe	4,506	23
Japan	2,027	10
Other regions & countries	3,947	20
Total	**19,615**	**100**

PRODUCTS/OPERATIONS

2014 Sales

	$ mil.	% of total
Endocrinology	6,939	36
Neurosciences	3,596	18
Oncology	3,393	17
Cardiovascular	3,053	16
Other human pharmaceuticals	287	1
Animal health	2,346	2
Total	**19,615**	**100**

2014 Sales

	$ mil.	% of total
Human pharmaceuticals		
Alimta	2,792	14
Humalog	2,785	14
Cialis	2,291	12
Cymbalta	1,614	8
Humulin	1,400	7
Forteo	1,322	7
Zyprexa	1,037	5
Strattera	738	4
Effient	522	3
Evista	419	2
Other human pharmaceuticals	1,557	8
Animal health products	2,346	12
Collaboration & other	788	4
Total	**19,615**	**100**

Selected Products and Indications

Neuroscience
- Amyvid (florbetapir F 18 injection)
- Cymbalta (duloxetine hydrocholoride; depression anxiety pain; also for managing fibromyalgia and chronic musculoskeletal pain in the US)
- Prozac (fluoxetine hydrochloride; depression panic disorder obsessive-compulsive disorder and bulimia nervosa)
- Strattera (atomoxetine hydrochloride ADHD)
- Symbyax (olanzapine and fluoxetine hydrochloride bipolar and treatment-resistant depression)
- Zyprexa (olanzapine schizophrenia and bipolar)
- Zyprexa Relprevv (Zypadhera in the EU long-acting injectable Zyprexa)

Endocrinology (including diabetes)
- Actos (pioglitazone hydrochloride type 2 diabetes)
- Alimta (non-small cell lung cancer)
- Axiron (testosterone topical for testosterone deficiency)
- Erbitux (colorectal cancers head and neck cancers)
- Evista (raloxifene hydrochloride osteoporosis and breast cancer prevention in postmenopausal women)
- Forteo (osteoporosis)
- Gemzar (pancreatic cancer metastatic breast cancer non-small cell lung cancer; bladder cancer in the EU)
- Glucagon (injection rDNA origin)
- Humalog (insulin lispro injection rDNA origin; diabetes)
- Humalog Mix 75/25 (75% Insulin lispro protamine suspension 25% insulin lispro injection rDNA origin; diabetes)
- Humalog Mix 50/50 (50% Insulin lispro protamine suspension 50% insulin lispro injection rDNA origin; diabetes)
- Humalog Pen (insulin lispro rDNA origin; diabetes)
- Humatrope (somatropin for injection rDNA origin; growth disorders)
- Humulin (human insulin rDNA origin; diabetes)
- Humulin Pen (human insulin rDNA origin; diabetes)
- Tradjenta (type 2 diabetes)

Oncology (cancer)
- Alimta (pemetrexed non-small cell lung cancer and malignant pleural mesothelioma)
- Erbitux (colorectal head and neck cancers; from ImClone)
- Gemzar (gemcitabine hydrochloride; pancreatic breast lung bladder and ovarian cancers)

Cardiovascular
- Adcirca (pulmonary arterial hypertension)
- Cialis (tadalafil erectile dysfunction; benign prostatic hyperplasia in US)
- Efient/Effient (atherothrombotic events)
- Livalo (statin high cholesterol)
- ReoPro (percutaneous coronary intervention)

Animal Health (Elanco)
- Apralan (antibiotic to control enteric infections in calves and swine)
- Coban Monteban and Maxiban (anticoccidal for poultry)
- Comfortis (flea infestation prevention tablets for dogs)
- Micotil Pulmotil and Pulmotil AC (antibiotics for respiratory disease in cattle swine and poultry respectively)
- Paylean Optaflexx (leanness and performance enhancers for swine and cattle respectively)
- Posilac (protein supplement for enhanced milk productivity in cows)
- Reconcile (separation anxiety for dogs)
- Rumensin (feed additive)
- Surmax/Maxus (performance enhancer for swine and poultry)
- Trifexis (chewable tablet for dogs to prevent flea infestations and heartworm disease and control intestinal parasite infections)
- Tylan (antibiotic)

Other pharmaceuticals (including anti-infectives)
- Ceclor (bacterial infections)
- Vancocin (staphylococcal infections)

COMPETITORS

Abbott Labs	Mylan
Amgen	Myriad Genetics
AstraZeneca	Novartis
Baxter International	Novo Nordisk
Bayer AG	Pfizer
Boehringer Ingelheim	Ranbaxy Laboratories
Bristol-Myers Squibb	Roche Holding
Dr. Reddy' s	Sanofi
GlaxoSmithKline	Shire
Johnson & Johnson	Takeda Pharmaceutical
Merck	Teva
Merck KGaA	

HISTORICAL FINANCIALS

Company Type: Public

Income Statement

FYE: December 31

	REVENUE ($ mil.)	NET INCOME ($ mil.)	NET PROFIT MARGIN	EMPLOYEES
12/14	19,615	2,390	12.2%	39,135
12/13	23,113	4,684	20.3%	37,925
12/12	22,603	4,088	18.1%	38,350
12/11	24,286	4,347	17.9%	38,080
12/10	23,076	5,069	22.0%	38,350
Annual Growth	(4.0%)	(17.1%)	—	0.5%

2014 Year-End Financials

Debt ratio: 21.67%
Return on equity: 14.49%
Cash ($ mil.): 4,827
Current ratio: 1.09
Long-term debt ($ mil.): 5,367
No. of shares (mil.): 1,110
Dividends
Yield: 2.8%
Payout: 78.0%
Market value ($ mil.): 76,622

	STOCK PRICE ($) FY Close	P/E High/Low	PER SHARE ($) Earnings	Dividends	Book Value
12/14	68.99	33 23	2.23	1.96	13.84
12/13	51.00	13 11	4.32	1.96	15.79
12/12	49.32	15 10	3.66	1.96	12.91
12/11	41.56	11 9	3.90	1.96	11.70
12/10	35.04	8 7	4.58	1.96	10.78
Annual Growth	18.5%	— —	(16.5%)	(0.0%)	6.5%

Lincoln National Corp.

Who better to trust with your nest egg than the company that took its name from Honest Abe? Lincoln National which operates as Lincoln Financial Group provides retirement planning and life insurance to individuals and employers in the form of annuities 401k and savings plans and a variety of life dental and disability insurance products. It does business through such subsidiaries as Lincoln National Life Insurance and Lincoln Life & Annuity Company of New York. The company is also active in the investment management business offering individual and institutional clients such financial services as pension plans trusts and mutual funds through its subsidiaries.

Operations

Lincoln Financial serves about 91000 group insurance and retirement plan contracts which have a total of some 8.7 million participants. The group has a total of some $218 billion in assets under management. Its operations are divided into segments including annuities retirement plan services life insurance and group protection.

The largest segment life insurance (44% of sales in 2014) offers term products a linked benefit product and a critical illness rider. The annuities

President and CEO QVC Inc., Michael (Mike) George, age 53, $1,092,727 total compensation
SVP, Albert E. Rosenthaler, age 55, $346,444 total compensation
SVP and General Counsel, Richard N. (Rich) Baer, age 58, $424,875 total compensation
Vice President and Treasurer, Neal Dermer
Chairman, John C. Malone, age 74
Auditors: KPMG LLP

LOCATIONS

HQ: Liberty Interactive Corp
12300 Liberty Boulevard, Englewood, CO 80112
Phone: 720 875-5300
Web: www.libertyinteractive.com

2014 Sales

	$ mil.	% of total
US	7,617	72
Germany	1,003	10
Japan	912	9
Other countries	967	9
Total	**10,499**	**100**

PRODUCTS/OPERATIONS

2014 Sales

	$ mil.	% of total
QVC		
QVC	8,801	84
Digital Commerce	1,227	12
Ventures Group		
Digital Commerce	471	4
Total	**10,499**	**100**

Selected Subsidiaries and Investments

Backcountry.com Inc. (87% online backcountry gear)
Bodybuilding.com LLC (86% online bodybuilding products and equipment)
Celebrate Interactive Holdings LLC (100% online costume and party supply retail)
Evite Inc. (100% online party planning)
Expedia Inc. (25% online travel)
Gifts.com (100% online gifts)
HSN Inc. (37% online and TV shopping)
LMC Right Start (100% baby products)
LOCKERZ (38%)
Provide Commerce Inc. (100% e-commerce)
QVC (100% home shopping network)
TripAdvisor (57% online travel site)

COMPETITORS

Access TV	IAC
Amazon.com	Orbitz Worldwide
American Express	Priceline
EVINE Live	Travelocity
HSN	Wal-Mart

HISTORICAL FINANCIALS

Company Type: Public

Income Statement

FYE: December 31

	REVENUE ($ mil.)	NET INCOME ($ mil.)	NET PROFIT MARGIN	EMPLOYEES
12/14	10,499	537	5.1%	20,078
12/13	11,252	501	4.5%	23,079
12/12	10,054	1,530	15.2%	22,078
12/11	9,616	912	9.5%	22,077
12/10	10,982	1,892	17.2%	24,073
Annual Growth	(1.1%)	(27.0%)	—	(4.4%)

2014 Year-End Financials

Debt ratio: 43.19%
Return on equity: 8.52%
Cash ($ mil.): 2,306
Current ratio: 1.48
Long-term debt ($ mil.): 7,105
No. of shares (mil.): 617
Dividends
Yield: —
Payout: 74.2%
Market value ($ mil.): 18,177

	STOCK PRICE ($) FY Close	P/E High/Low	PER SHARE ($) Earnings	Dividends	Book Value
12/14	29.42	— —	(0.00)	0.00	9.18
12/13	29.35	— —	(0.00)	0.00	12.08
12/12	19.68	— —	(0.00)	0.00	12.23
12/11	16.22	— —	(0.00)	0.00	11.23
12/10	15.77	— —	(0.00)	0.00	15.41
Annual Growth	16.9%	— —	—	—	(12.1%)

LifePoint Health Inc

LifePoint Health (formerly LifePoint Hospitals) hopes that folks who get sick in the country won't head to the city to get well. The company operates about 65 hospitals located in non-urban areas. In most cases the hospitals (which house more than 8000 beds combined) are the only available acute care facilities in the region. LifePoint operates its hospitals in some 21 states through its subsidiaries with a concentration in the southeastern US. In many markets LifePoint also operates outpatient clinics that provide family care diagnostic surgical and therapeutic services. The company has 4100 physician partners.

Operations

Unlike major urban medical centers the hospitals that LifePoint operates don't usually engage in extensive medical research train legions of new doctors or perform complex surgeries. The facilities do provide a spectrum of health care services that include emergency care general surgery obstetrics oncology cardiology coronary care rehabilitation services pediatric services and diagnostic care.

The company has nearly 40 post-acute service providers and facilities as well as more than 30 outpatient centers. Its Duke LifePoint Healthcare partnership with Duke University Health System works to strengthen and improve the delivery of health care.

Geographic Reach

LifePoint has the heaviest concentration of facilities in Kentucky Tennessee Virginia New Mexico West Virginia Michigan Arizona and North Carolina.

Virginia accounted for 14% of revenue in 2014; Kentucky and Michigan accounted for 13% and 10% respectively.

Sales and Marketing

More than 40% of LifePoint's annual revenues come from private insurers (including HMO and PPO plans) while another 40% come from Medicare and Medicaid. More than 15% of revenues come from self-pay patients.

Financial Performance

LifePoint's revenues have been steadily rising over the past few years. In 2014 they rose 22% to $4.5 billion as same-hospital revenues rose on higher admissions. The company also felt a favorable impact from health care reform (in which more patients had coverage) and earned higher contracted rates from HMOs PPOs and other private insurers. Same-hospital admissions increased 2.7% primarily due to increases in surgeries and emergency department visits.

However net income has been falling for the past three years. It fell 2% to $126 million in 2014 as the company paid more in salaries and benefits and towards other expenses. Cash flow from operations rose 16% as LifePoint used less cash for accounts payable accrued salaries and other current liabilities.

Strategy

The company focuses on adding new service lines in its existing markets and investing in new technologies and on developing strategic partnerships with not-for-profit health care providers to achieve growth in new regions.

LifePoint maintains a competitive edge in many of its regional markets by being the sole provider of many of the health care services it offers. Even so LifePoint is working to increase the breadth of services provided by its hospitals in an effort to keep patients from having to travel outside the community for care especially in fields such as open-heart surgery psychiatric care and neurosurgery. Towards that end the company is improving methods of recruiting and retaining doctors; it is also working to control operating expenses while investing in system-wide capital improvement projects and technology upgrades.

One of its technology initiatives is to invest in electronic health record systems under federal health reform guidelines which aim to lower the cost of care through measures such as eliminating redundant procedures and lowering readmission rates. The company also manages procurement expenses by participating (and owning a 4% stake) in HealthTrust a group purchasing organization.

LifePoint struggles with containing expenses from serving charity care and self-pay customers that are part and parcel of running a health care system. To help offset losses related to caring for uninsured patients the company strives to negotiate favorable contracts with managed care and other private payers at each of its facilities.

To raise cash and save costs in 2014 the company agreed to sell certain assets of River Parishes Hospital and discontinue its operation. The following year it sold Lakeland Hospital Northwest Hospital and Russellville Medical Center in Alabama as well as the Putnam Community Medical Center in Florida.

LifePoint Hospitals changed its name to Life-Point Health in 2015 to reflect its growing focus on comprehensive health care including physician practices post-acute and outpatient services and wellness programs.

Mergers and Acquisitions

In addition to organic growth measures Life-Point also expands through regular acquisitions. The company targets small non-urban hospitals where it sees an opportunity for improved financial performance and LifePoint typically invests in facility upgrades once its purchases are complete. In 2015 through a joint venture with Norton Healthcare LifePoint added Indiana's 241-bed Clark Memorial Hospital; LifePoint also acquired the 52-bed Fleming County Hospital in Kentucky. Early the following year the company acquired South Carolina-based Providence Hospitals adding two hospitals 13 physician practices rehab centers sleep centers and a chest pain center.

Duke LifePoint Healthcare acquired Conemaugh Health System (operator of hospitals in west-central Pennsylvania) and North Carolina's Haywood Regional Medical Center and WestCare Health System in 2014; it also bought majority stakes in Rutherford Regional Hospital and Wilson Medical Center (both also in North Carolina). The following year LifePoint acquired Nason Hospital in Pennsylvania which became part of the Conemaugh Health System.

Company Background

LifePoint was born when hospital giant HCA spun off a group of about two dozen hospitals in 1999. It wasn't until its 2005 merger with Province Healthcare Company that LifePoint became the hulking presence it is today.

EXECUTIVES

Vice President, Dewitt Ezell
Chairman and CEO, William F. (Bill) Carpenter, age 60, $1,050,000 total compensation
President and COO, David M. Dill, age 46, $650,000 total compensation
President Central Group, R. Scott Raplee, age 50, $412,000 total compensation
Chief Medical Officer, Russell L. (Rusty) Holman, age 47
EVP and Chief Legal Officer, Paul D. Gilbert, age 49, $515,000 total compensation
EVP and Chief Administrative Officer, John P. Bumpus, age 55, $425,000 total compensation
SVP and CIO, Sean Tuley
EVP and CFO, Leif M. Murphy, age 47, $600,000 total compensation
President Western Group, Donald J. Bivacca, age 53
President Eastern Group, Jeffrey G. Seraphine, age 45
Senior Vice President Revenue Cycle Operations, Richard Flores
Vice President Reimbursement, William (Bill) Hoffman
Respiratory Therapy Director, Mark Mustard
Medical Director Sumner Regional Medical Center Emergency Department, Ray Pinkston
Vice President Human Resources, Marianne Freeman
Assistnat Vice President, Becky Janssen
Vice President Finance, Farely Reardon
Director Of Him, Charlotte Klaus
Clinical Director Meaningful Use, Kelly Lester
Clinical Director, Priscilla Snyder
Vice President Practice Management, Dan Sykes
Vice President Acquisition Integration And Transition Services, Sharon Marti
Senior Vice President UND, Peter (Pete) Radetich
Senior Vice President, Arthur Crumlish
Senior Vice President Chief Accounting Officer, Michael (Mel) Coggin
Vice President Practice Management, Tim Vaughn
Vice President and Associate General Counsel, Fabio Fallico
Clinical Director, Constance Berner
Senior Vice President Information Technology, Shawn Tuley
Radiology Director, Jay Cook
Vice President Clinical And Business Informatics, Brad Owens
Director Of Radiology, Rob Gaines
Vice President Capital Asset and Construction Management, Ed O'Dell
Vice President Risk Management, David (Dave) Fausett
Vice President Corporate Communications, Diane Huggins
Director of Nursing, Cindy Nichols
Board Member, John (Jack) Maupin
Board Member, Owen Shell
Auditors: Ernst & Young LLP

LOCATIONS

HQ: LifePoint Health Inc
330 Seven Springs Way, Brentwood, TN 37027
Phone: 615 920-7000
Web: www.lifepointhospitals.com

Selected Hospitals
Alabama
  Andalusia Regional Hospital
  Lakeland C
Northwest
  Russellville Hospital
  Vaughan Re
Arizona
  Havasu Regional Medical Center (Lake Havasu City)
  Valley Vie
Colorado
  Colorado P
Florida

Putnam Com
Georgia
  Rockdale M
Indiana
  Scott Memo
Kansas
  Western Pl
Kentucky
  Bluegrass
  Bourbon Co
  Clark Regi
    Georgetown Community Hospital
  Jackson Pu
  Lake Cumbe
  Logan Memo
  Meadowview
  Spring Vie
Louisiana
  Acadian Me
    Mercy Regional Medical Center (aka Ville Platte Medical Center)
    Minden Medical Center
  River Pari
  Teche Regi
Michigan
    Marquette General Health System
Mississippi
  Bolivar Me
Nevada
Northeaste
New Mexico
    Los Alamos Medical Center
    Memorial Medical Center of Las Cruces
North Carolina
    Maria Parham Medical Center (80% owned by Duke LifePoint Healthcare joint venture Henderson)
    Person Memorial Hospital (owned by Duke LifePoint Healthcare joint venture Roxboro)
Tennessee
    Athens Regional Medical Center
  Crockett H
  Emerald-Ho
    High Point Health System (formerly Sumner Regional Health Systems)
  Sumner Reg
  Hillside H
    Livingston Regional Hospital
  Riverview
  Southern T
  Trousdale
Texas
    Ennis Regional Medical Center
    Palestine Regional Medical Center
  Parkview R
Utah
  Ashley Reg
  Castleview
Virginia
  Clinch Val
    Danville Regional Medical Center
  Fauquier H
  Memorial H
    Twin County Regional Healthcare (owned by Duke LifePoint Healthcare joint venture)
  Twin Count
  Wythe Coun
West Virginia
    Logan Regional Medical Center
  Raleigh Ge
Wyoming
    Lander Regional Hospital
    Riverton Memorial Hospital

PRODUCTS/OPERATIONS

2014 Sales

	$ mil.	% of total
HMOs PPOs & other private insurers	2,476	47
Medicare	1,361	25
Self-pay	744	14
Medicaid	619	12
Other	98	2
Provisions for doubtful accounts	(817.8)	-
Total	**4,483**	**100**

COMPETITORS

Ascension Health	Mercy Health (OH)
CHRISTUS Health	Methodist Healthcare
Catholic Health	Sisters of Charity of

Initiatives
Community Health Systems
Covenant Health
HCA
Intermountain Health Care
Kaiser Foundation Hospitals
Mercy Health

Leavenworth
SunLink Health Systems
Tenet Healthcare
Tennova Healthcare
Universal Health Services
Wellmont Health System
West Tennessee Healthcare

HISTORICAL FINANCIALS

Company Type: Public

Income Statement   FYE: December 31

	REVENUE ($ mil.)	NET INCOME ($ mil.)	NET PROFIT MARGIN	EMPLOYEES
12/15	5,214	181	3.5%	40,000
12/14	4,483	126	2.8%	38,000
12/13	3,678	128	3.5%	31,000
12/12	3,391	151	4.5%	28,000
12/11	3,026	162	5.4%	23,000
Annual Growth	**14.6%**	**2.8%**	**—**	**14.8%**

2015 Year-End Financials

Debt ratio: 44.50%	No. of shares (mil.): 43	
Return on equity: 8.23%	Dividends	
Cash ($ mil.): 284	Yield: —	
Current ratio: 2.05	Payout: —	
Long-term debt ($ mil.): 2,643	Market value ($ mil.): 3,166	

	STOCK PRICE ($) FY Close	P/E High/Low		Earnings	PER SHARE ($) Dividends	Book Value
12/15	73.40	21	15	3.95	0.00	52.49
12/14	71.91	27	18	2.69	0.00	48.34
12/13	52.84	19	14	2.69	0.00	46.88
12/12	37.75	13	11	3.14	0.00	43.69
12/11	37.15	13	9	3.22	0.00	40.27
Annual Growth	**18.6%**		**—**	**5.2%**	**—**	**6.8%**

Lilly (Eli) & Co.

Healthwise Eli Lilly hopes everything will come up roses for you. Best known for its neuroscience products the pharmaceutical company also makes endocrinology oncology and cardiovascular care medicines. Its top-selling drugs include Cymbalta for depression and pain Alimta for lung cancer Humalog and Humulin insulin for diabetes and Cialis for erectile dysfunction. Lilly also makes medications to treat schizophrenia and bipolar disorder (Zyprexa) osteoporosis (Evista and Forteo) heart conditions (Effient) and ADHD (Strattera) as well as anti-infective agents and a growing line of animal health products.

HISTORY

Colonel Eli Lilly pharmacist and Union officer in the Civil War started Eli Lilly and Company in 1876 with $1300. His process of gelatin-coating pills led to sales of nearly $82000 in 1881. Later the company made gelatin capsules which it still sells. Lilly died in 1898 and his son and two grandsons ran the business until 1953.

Eli Lilly began extracting insulin from the pancreases of hogs and cattle in 1923; 6000 cattle glands or 24000 hog glands made one ounce of the substance. Other products created in the 1920s and 1930s included antiseptic Merthiolate sedative Seconal and treatments for pernicious anemia and heart disease. In 1947 the company began selling diethylstilbestrol (DES) a drug to prevent miscarriages. Eli Lilly researchers isolated the antibiotic erythromycin from a species of mold found in the Philippines in 1952. Lilly was also the major supplier of Salk polio vaccine.

The company enjoyed a 70% share of the DES market by 1971 when researchers noticed that a rare form of cervical cancer afflicted many of the daughters of women who had taken the drug. The FDA restricted the drug's use and Lilly found itself on the receiving (and frequently losing) end of a number of trailblazing product-liability suits that stretched into the 1990s.

The firm diversified in the 1970s buying Elizabeth Arden (cosmetics 1971; sold 1987) and IVAC (medical instruments 1977). It launched such products as analgesic Darvon and antibiotic Ceclor.

Lilly's 1982 launch of Humulin a synthetic insulin developed by Genentech made it the first company to market a genetically engineered product. In 1986 the company introduced Prozac; that year it also bought biotech firm Hybritech for $300 million (sold in 1995 for less than $10 million). In 1988 Lilly introduced anti-ulcerative Axid. It founded pesticides and herbicides maker DowElanco with Dow Chemical in 1989.

Trying to find a new product outlet the firm bought pharmacy benefit management company PCS Health Systems from what is now McKesson in 1994. But an FTC mandate to offer rival drugs and a lack of mail-order sales contributed to poor results which ultimately led Lilly to sell PCS to Rite Aid and exit this arena completely in 1998.

Eli Lilly in 1995 bought medical communications network developer Integrated Medical Systems. That year the firm and developer Centocor introduced ReoPro a blood-clot inhibitor used in angioplasties. The next year it launched antipsychotic Zyprexa Humalog and Gemzar and Prozac was approved to treat bulimia nervosa.

In 1997 the firm sold its DowElanco stake to Dow. In 1998 the Lilly Endowment passed the Ford Foundation as the US's largest charity largely due to Prozac (it has since been passed by the Bill & Melinda Gates Foundation). That year Lilly began trying to stop Chinese drugmakers from infringing on its patents for Prozac's active ingredient.

In 1999 a US federal judge found the firm illegally promoted osteoporosis drug Evista as a breast cancer preventative similar to AstraZeneca's Nolvadex. Lilly halted tests on its variation of heart drug Moxonidine after 53 patients died. Also that year Zyprexa was approved to treat bipolar disorder.

In 2000 the firm began marketing Prozac under the Sarafem name for severe premenstrual syndrome. A federal appeals court knocked more than two years off Prozac's patent reducing the expected 2003 expiration date to 2001 creating a negative impact on Lilly's annual sales (Prozac had accounted for 30% of revenues). Lilly suffered another blow when a potential successor to Prozac failed in clinical trials and became embroiled in legal maneuverings with generics maker Barr Pharmaceuticals.

While the firm fretted over Prozac and its patents it continued work to find its next blockbuster. In 2000 Lilly and partner ICOS announced favorable results from a study of erectile dysfunction treatment Cialis which was approved in Europe in 2002 and in the US in 2004. (Several years later Lilly acquired ICOS and with it full ownership of the Cialis franchise.)

In 2001 Lilly bought a minority stake in Isis Pharmaceuticals a developer of antisense drugs and licensed from it an antisense lung cancer drug. Also that year the firm launched Lilly BioVentures a venture fund aimed at private biotech startup companies. In 2002 the company settled with eight states in an infringement-of-privacy case involving the company's accidental disclosure of e-mail addresses for more than 600 Prozac patients.

In late 2004 the druggernaut was one of several pharmas hit by bad news about drug side effects. Lilly announced its attention-deficit disorder drug Strattera had been linked to rare liver problems. The company agreed to add warning labels about the potential side effects to the drug's packaging and advertisements. The company also began facing trouble over Zyprexa as consumer lawsuits claiming diabetes and high blood pressure began pouring in. The majority of suits were settled in 2005 and 2007 for some $1.2 billion.

Generalized anxiety disorder drug Cymbalta was approved by the FDA and released in 2006 and osteoporosis drug Evista was approved for an expanded indication as a breast cancer preventative for postmenopausal women in 2007.

Also in 2007 the company acquired and absorbed development partner ICOS for $2.1 billion; the deal gave Lilly full ownership of Viagra-competitor Cialis. Lilly dropped a joint-development effort with another partner Alkermes for an inhaled insulin device in 2008.

The company gradually reduced its workforce by more than 10% between 2003 and 2008 to fight off the effects of generic competition and other challenges. Other restructuring measures included an employee attrition plan announced in 2007 a management restructuring in 2008 and a manufacturing consolidation program launched in 2008.

After a lengthy lawsuit regarding its patents for its top seller Zyprexa a federal judge ruled in Lilly's favor in 2008 against generic manufacturers IVAX Dr. Reddy's Laboratories and Teva Pharmaceutical Industries. Federal courts ruled that the drug's patents would remain valid until October 2011.

To fuel growth in the biopharmaceuticals market the firm completed a $1 billion biotech research facility in Indianapolis in 2008. It further expanded through the 2008 acquisition of biotech firm ImClone for about $6.5 billion; ImClone began operating as a research subsidiary of Lilly following the transaction. ImClone already had one approved blockbuster therapy Erbitux for colorectal and head/neck cancers and was developing numerous other cancer therapy candidates. Lilly also expanded its biotech oncology program earlier that year by purchasing development partner SGX Pharmaceuticals for $64 million. SGX was absorbed into Lilly's research operations.

The company agreed in 2009 to pay $1.4 billion in government fines to settle allegations over its marketing tactics for Zyprexa.

The firm received FDA approval in 2009 on a top pipeline candidate blood thinner Effient (developed with Daiichi Sankyo) although the drug carried heavy warning labels due to fatal bleeding risks. Effient held great potential however with better efficacy than Plavix (made by Bristol-Myers Squibb and Sanofi-Aventis) which dominated the $8 billion market. Also in 2009 Adcirca for pulmonary arterial hypertension was approved by the FDA. New indications include 2009 approval of Zyprexa Relprevv a long-acting injectable version of Zyprexa and bipolar therapy Symbyax was expanded for treatment-resistant depression indications. It has also extended indications of Cialis for treating benign prostatic hyperplasia

Lilly also launched a major restructuring program in 2009 to reduce expenses. The program resulted in the sale of its Indiana pharmaceutical ingredients plant to Evonik Industries in early 2010. Lilly further reduced costs by contracting out the related manufacturing functions to Evonik. The company also increased outsourcing efforts by forming partnerships with several contract research organizations (CROs) including fir as Quintiles and Covance.

One development candidate awaiting proval was Bydureon a once-a-week versio isting diabetes treatment Byetta that Lilly developing with Amylin and Alkermes. I Lilly exited the partnership in 2011 after objected to Lilly's entering into a similar partnership with Boehringer Ingelheim. I sold Amylin back its co-marketing rights to

To bolster its endocrinology efforts and e enzyme replacement therapy market in 2(acquired Alnara Pharmaceuticals in a dea up to $390 million. The privately-held bio ogy company is focused on developing therapies to treat metabolic diseases. Alnar product is a pancreatic enzyme replaceme apy called liprotamase. Another acquisitio that year brought the company an imagir pound candidate when Lilly paid $290 mi front (plus another $550 million in milesto ments) to buy Avid Radiopharmaceuticals florbetapir is in development as a means for ing amyloid plaque in the brain a key indi Alzheimer's disease.

Its Elanco Animal Health unit purchase ropean portfolio of animal health produc Pfizer in 2010; the deal included marketing to certain vaccines parasiticides and feed a for pets and livestock.

EXECUTIVES

Chairman President and CEO, John C. Lechl age 60, $1,500,000 total compensation
EVP Science and Technology; President Lil Research Laboratories, Jan M. Lundberg, age $1,007,855 total compensation
EVP Global Services and CFO, Derica W. Ric 50, $1,019,700 total compensation
SVP and President Elanco Animal Health, J N. (Jeff) Simmons, age 48
SVP and President Diabetes Business Unit, Enrique A. Conterno, age 48, $682,890 total compensation
President Manufacturing Operations, Maria (age 55
SVP and President Emerging Markets, Alfon (Chito) Zulueta
SVP and President Lilly Oncology, Susan (Su Mahony, age 50
SVP and President Lilly Bio-Medicines, David Ricks, age 47
SVP Enterprise Risk Management and Chief Ethics and Compliance Officer, Melissa Staple Barnes
SVP and General Counsel, Michael J. Harringto $765,000 total compensation
Vice President for Global Market Research, To Ezell
National Account Manager, Max Gild
Senior Vice President Corporate Affairs And Communications, Alex M Azar
Vice President Corporate Development and Strategic Planning, Mitch Silverstein
Senior Management (Senior Vice President General Manager Director), Kent Supancik
Chief Marketing Officer Vice President Global Medi, Timothy Garnett
Vice President Sales and Marketing, Carrie Cout
Vice President Human Resources Emerging Markets Business Unit, Raymond Muller
Executive Vice President, Kelly Collett
Senior Vice President Research and Developme Kathryn Gilmore
Medical Director, Albert (Al) Allen
Medical Director, Murali Venugopalan
Department Head Space Planning, Brent Blancha
Senior Vice President Human Resources, Sonya Johnson

502

segment (28% of sales) offers fixed and variable annuities. Group protection offers non-medical policies primarily term life dental and disability products to the employer market. Retirement plan services (8% of sales) provides employers with plans and services primarily in the defined contribution retirement plan marketplace.

Sales and Marketing

Lincoln Financial Network distributes the company's products through a network of some 8500 agents while Lincoln Financial Distributors is the company's wholesale distributor serving brokers planners agents third-party administrators financial advisors and other intermediaries.

The company also markets its products through online and television advertising.

Lincoln Financial serves more than 17 million customers.

Financial Analysis

Lincoln Financial has seen revenue growth over the past five years. In 2014 revenue grew 13% to $13.5 billion due to growth in life insurance an annuities which saw increased premiums fee income and net investment income. As a result profits rose 22% to $1.5 billion that year.

Cash flow from operations more than tripled to $2.5 billion in 2014 as a result of successful trading securities purchases net sales and maturities and other factors.

Historically Lincoln Financial's investment income has accounted for more of its revenues than its insurance premiums or fees. This can be pretty sweet when the market is high but when investments lost their luster during the recession Lincoln Financial's net income suffered. Also fees tied to the value of variable accounts dropped down during that time further weakening the company's income. As the market improved Lincoln Financial's investments perked up variable accounts revived and so did the company's net income.

Strategy

To meet the challenges of difficult economic times in the market Lincoln Financial has adopted a strategy to strengthen its business that includes investing in high-quality corporate securities to reduce asset risk; escalating share repurchases and debt repayment; repricing life and annuity products to guarantee new business that is profitable; and making significant investments in businesses to increase its future earning power.

The company leverages its powerful distribution network to enter new markets while maintaining its position in existing markets. It targets the fastest-growing industry segments while steering away from long-term guarantee products.

Going forward Lincoln Financial will explore additional financial strategies to address the statutory reserve strain that comes with its term and universal life products that contain secondary guarantees. It will shift its business to focus on products with shorter duration liabilities and more limited liabilities. The company also plans to invest in technology and distribution to increase margins.

Recent new products introduced by Lincoln Financial include hybrid benefit riders Lincoln Lifetime Income Advantage 2.0 and Lincoln Lifetime Income Advantage 2.0 (Managed Risk) and its Lincoln LifeReserve Indexed universal life offering all of which it launched in 2014.

The company sold its Lincoln Financial Media subsidiary which included 15 radio stations to Entercom Communications in 2015. The media arm was a legacy from its acquisition of Jefferson-Pilot but Lincoln exited the industry to focus on insurance.

Normal 0   false false false   EN-US
X-NONE X-NONE

HISTORY

Wilbur Wynant a sort of Johnny Appleseed of shady fraternal benefits societies arrived in Fort Wayne Indiana in 1902. He persuaded several respected businessmen and professionals to help him found the Fraternal Assurance Society of America an assessable mutual organization in which surviving members contributed to the death benefits of deceased members. Wynant absconded within a couple of years and the local organizers restructured the society's remains as a stock company in 1905. To clean up the organization's reputation they obtained permission from Abraham Lincoln's son Robert to use his father's name and image.

In 1905 when the company wrote its first policy it had three agents including its leading executive Arthur Hall. By 1911 the company had 106 agents. Careful risk assessment was an early hallmark of the company and allowed it to accept business that other companies rejected based on more superficial analysis.

From a very early period the company grew through acquisitions. WWI increased claims but not as much as the global flu epidemic that followed the war. Organic growth continued in the 1920s.

Death and disability claims increased abnormally during the Depression and the company's underwriting became more stringent. Lincoln National used the financial turmoil of the period to buy other troubled insurers. Reinsurance became the firm's primary line until after WWII.

The company bought up other firms in the 1950s and 1960s and in 1968 it formed holding company Lincoln National. Soon it began diversifying buying Chicago Title and Trust (1969; sold 1985) as well as more life and reinsurance companies. Lincoln National also went into the health benefits business setting up its own HMO and investing in EMPHESYS (which it took public in 1994 divesting the remainder of its stock in 1995).

The collapse of the real estate market in many areas nicked results in the late 1980s and in 1990 the company accepted an infusion of cash from Dai-Ichi Mutual Life Insurance. Property/casualty results were hurt in the early 1990s by an unprecedented string of natural disasters.

With the growth of retirement savings from baby boomers hitting their 50s the company shifted gears into wealth management. In 1995 Lincoln National expanded its investment management capacities by purchasing Delaware Management Holdings and Laurentian Financial Group. The next year it bought the group tax-qualified annuity business of disability insurer UNUM (now UNUMProvident) and in 1997 bought Voyageur Fund Managers a tax-free-bond fund business. The company also took a 49% stake in a Mexican insurance company owned by Grupo Financiero Santander Serfin (sold in 2000). It sold its 83% interest in property/casualty firm American States Financial in 1996.

Lincoln National bought CIGNA's annuity and individual life insurance business and Aetna's US individual life insurance operations in 1998. It reorganized that year to help it absorb these businesses causing earnings to take a substantial hit.

In 1999 after nearly a century in the heartland Lincoln National moved its headquarters to Philadelphia. Other transformations included the sale of its individual disability income business in 1999. In 2001 it sold its reinsurance operations to Swiss Re to re-focus on wealth and asset accumulation products and services. The reshaping continued in 2002 when the company acquired employee benefits record-keeping firm The Administrative Management Group.

Lincoln National completed a merger/acquisition of Jefferson-Pilot in early 2006. The $7.5 billion deal combined the Lincoln Financial Group with the Jefferson Pilot Financial group (the operating brand for Jefferson-Pilot Corporation) and created a new company operating as Lincoln Financial Group. Led by management from both former organizations the new group expanded insurance and financial products offerings and national retail and wholesale distribution platforms.

EXECUTIVES

President Insurance and Retirement Solutions, Mark E. Konen, age 55, $625,250 total compensation

President CEO Director and President Lincoln Financial Group, Dennis R. Glass, age 65, $1,135,000 total compensation

EVP Chief Human Resources Officer and Enterprise Communications, Lisa M. Buckingham, age 49

President Annuity Solutions Lincoln Financial Distributors and Lincoln Financial Network, Wilford H. (Will) Fuller, age 44, $644,008 total compensation

EVP and CFO, Randal J. Freitag, age 52, $575,384 total compensation

EVP and Chief Investment Officer, Ellen Cooper, age 50

EVP and General Counsel, Adam G. Ciongoli, age 46, $353,077 total compensation

Vice President Of Sales, Robert Risk

Vice President Managing Director Portfolio Management Analytic, Paul Narayanan

Vice President Communications, Lujean Smith

Vice President Internet Business and Technology, Ann Colony

Assistant Vice President Income Product Market Development, Daniel (Dan) Herr

Assistant Vice President and Director, Linda Fairbanks

Assistant Vice President, Marlene Hammond

Senior Vice President Associate General Counsel And Litigation, Kelley Grady

Assistant Vice President, James Gasparotto

Assistant Vice President Information Technology Shared Services, Dave Vachon

Vice President, Roberta (Bobbi) Tielinen

Second Vice President Infrastructure Operations, Ricklin Nelson

Assistant Vice President Enterprise Information Technology Project Management Office, Patricia (Pat) Wells

Associate Vice President Enrollment Services, Joe Mitchell

Vice President Managing Director Tactical Strategies Fixed Inc, Jayson Bronchetti

Assistant Vice President Senior Employee Relations, Mary Carruth

Assistant Vice President Health, Audrey Im

Assistant Vice President Data Research and Analytics, Crystal Tucker

Vice President and Associate Actuary, Kris Kattmann

Assistant Vice President Facilities Management, Bryon Cooper

Senior Vice President Human Resources, George Murphy

Senior Vice President Markets And Invest, Andrew (Andy) Yorks

Assistant Vice President And Valuation Actuary, William (Bill) Panyard

Vp-mktg & Comm Of Insurance, Diane Russell

Assistant Vice President, Mike Link

National Account Manager, Matt Jasa

National Account Manager, Jeff Piccolo

Regional Vice President, Laura Degnon

Assistant Vice President Recruiter And Human Resources Business Partner, Karen Bradbury

Assistant Vice President Customer Service, Jim Rooney

Assistant Vice President Financial Reporting And Expense Controls, Kathy Tibke
Associate Vice President, Michael Selden
Vice President Of Sales, Marie Cochrane
Vice President Of Application Development, Srinivas Jonnada
Assistant Vice President Treasury, Brad Jeffrey
Assistant Vice President, Brian Gardner
Vice President and Branch Manager, Melissa (Mel) Hidalgo
Vice President Systems Development, Rebecca Trump
Assistant Vice President Corporate Digital Strategy, Brian Moody
Assistant Vice President, Loraine Bernard
Vice President, Brian Jenkins
Assistant Vice President Business Strategy, Barbara (Barb) Rayll
Vice President Marketing, Garethe Rich
Vice President, Nancy Smith
Vice President Operations, Emma Ladd
Assistant Vice President Senior Product Manager, Brian Wilson
Assistant Vice President Product Solutions Strategist, Andrew (Andy) Eldredge
Assistant Vice President Digital, James Tierney
Assistant Vice President, Teresa Norris-Phillips
Senior Vice President Of National Sales, Michael Hall
Vice President And Chief Counsel Annuities, Lawrence A Samplatsky
Assistant Vice President Senior Human Resources Business Partner, Kelly Pippett
Assistant Vice President, Laurie Scotti
Assistant Vice President Continuous Improvement, Keith Wagoner
Vice President Product Compliance, Pamela (Pam) Telfer
Assistant Vice President, Miko Pickett
Vice President Asset Liability Management, Nathan Hardiman
Assistant Vice President Business Intelligence Finance, Elizabeth (Beth) Keller
Second Vice President Corporate Actuary, Mike Antrobus
Assistant Vice President Underwriting And New Business Account Executive, Sandy Pope
Vice President Digital Strategy And Planning, Philip Bossy
Assistant Vice President Market Intelligence, Jamie Ranicar
Assistant Vice President Internal Audit, Wanda Pritchett
Vice President of Information Technology, Stephen (Steve) Hamilton
Vice President Talent Management, Nancy Rogers
Vice President, Nicole Delimitros
Vice President It, Scott Hardin
Senior Counsel And Assistant Vice President, Wayne Mcclain
Vice President Retirement Strategic Planning and Governance, Lisa Kinniry
Assistant Vice President Life and Annuity Strategy, Thomas (Thom) Goas
Assistant Vice President Corporate Actuary and ERM Lead, John (Jack) Martin
Assistant Vice President Meetings And Incentives, Richard (Dick) Gladson
Vice President, Kristi Harkenrider
Vice President Finance, John (Jack) Luviano
Vice President Absence Management Integrated Health Strat, Katie Dunnington
Vice President Sales, Ryan D Lommel
Assistant Vice President Digital Application Management, Mary Yates
Assistant Vice President, Frank Asplund
Assistant Vice President, Marc Tomlinson
Vice President And Managing Director Inv, Patrick (Paddy) McAllister
Chairman, William H. Cunningham, age 71

Board Member, Betty Nugent
Board Member, Fred Parmesano
Board Member, Marilyn Ondecker
Treasurer, Michael (Mel) Conte
Board Member, David McDunn
Auditors: Ernst & Young LLP

LOCATIONS

HQ: Lincoln National Corp.
150 N. Radnor Chester Road, Suite A305, Radnor, PA 19087
Phone: 484 583-1400
Web: www.lfg.com

PRODUCTS/OPERATIONS

2014 Revenues

	$ mil.	% of total
Insurance		
Life insurance	6,003	44
Group protection	2,445	18
Retirement		
Annuities	3,746	27
Retirement plan services	1,090	8
Other operations	435	3
Realized losses	(135)	-
Total	**13,554**	**100**

Selected Subsidiaries

First Penn-Pacific Life Insurance Company
Hampshire Funding Inc.
Jefferson-Pilot Investments Inc.
Lincoln Financial Investment Services Corporation
Lincoln Financial Securities Corporation
Lincoln Insurance Services Limited
Lincoln Investment Management Company
The Lincoln National Life Insurance Company
Lincoln National Management Corporation
Lincoln National Reinsurance Company (Barbados) Limited
Lincoln Reinsurance Company of Bermuda Limited

COMPETITORS

AEGON
AIG
AXA Financial
American Equity Investment Life Holding Company
Guardian Life
ING
John Hancock Financial Services
MassMutual
MetLife
Nationwide Financial
New York Life
Northwestern Mutual
Pacific Mutual
Principal Financial
Prudential
TIAA-CREF
The Hartford
Torchmark
Unum Group

HISTORICAL FINANCIALS

Company Type: Public

Income Statement

FYE: December 31

	ASSETS ($ mil.)	NET INCOME ($ mil.)	INCOME AS % OF ASSETS	EMPLOYEES
12/14	253,377	1,515	0.6%	11,046
12/13	236,945	1,244	0.5%	10,539
12/12	218,869	1,313	0.6%	9,742
12/11	202,906	294	0.1%	9,723
12/10	193,824	980	0.5%	9,500
Annual Growth	**6.9%**	**11.5%**	**—**	**3.8%**

2014 Year-End Financials

Debt ratio: 2.18%
Return on equity: 10.38%
Cash ($ mil.): 3,919
Current ratio: —
Long-term debt ($ mil.): —
No. of shares (mil.): 256
Dividends
Yield: 1.1%
Payout: 11.3%
Market value ($ mil.): 14,795

	STOCK PRICE ($) FY Close	P/E High/Low		PER SHARE ($) Earnings	Dividends	Book Value
12/14	57.67	10	8	5.67	0.64	61.35
12/13	51.62	11	6	4.52	0.48	51.17
12/12	25.90	6	4	4.56	0.32	55.17
12/11	19.42	34	15	0.92	0.20	48.62
12/10	27.81	13	8	2.54	0.04	40.56
Annual Growth	**20.0%**	**—**	**—**	**22.2%**	**100.0%**	**10.9%**

Linn Energy LLC

It's a Linn-Linn situation. Founder and chairman Michael Linn's namesake company Linn Energy has successfully drilled for oil and natural gas across the US although in recent years the company has narrowed its focus to exploiting assets in the Mid-Continent California and the Permian Basin. In 2012 the company reported proved reserves of 4.8 trillion cu. ft. of natural gas equivalent. The company operates about 70% of its more than 15800 gross productive wells. In addition to its core oil and gas activities Linn Energy pursues an aggressive hedging strategy to reduce the effects of oil price volatility on its annual income.

IPO
Looking for a new way to raise additional equity capital in 2012 the company formed Linn Co. LLC and launched an initial public offering which raised $1.1 billion. Linn Co. LLC was formed to buy shares in Linn Energy and expand its investor base. Linn Co. LLC used its IPO proceeds to help fund Linn Energy's acquisition strategy.

Geographic Reach
The company's oil and gas properties are located primarily in the Mid-Continent the Permian Basin Michigan California and the Williston Basin.

Sales and Marketing
In 2012 oil natural gas and NGL sales to Enbridge Energy Partners and DCP Midstream Partners accounted for 24% and 13% respectively of Linn Energy's total production volumes or 37% of the aggregate.

Financial Performance
Linn Energy's revenues increased by 9% in 2012 primarily due to higher marketing revenues and revenues generated from the newly acquired Jayhawk natural gas processing plant. Oil natural gas and NGL sales grew by 38% to $1.6 billion thanks to higher production volumes partially offset by lower commodity prices.

In 2012 the company posted a net loss in $386.6 million in 2012 (compared to net income of $438 million in 2011) due to higher operating expenses.

Strategy
Linn Energy has pursued a strategy of buying mature properties and extending the life of these natural gas fields by workovers and improved field operations including the use of additional production equipment and drilling activities.

To raise cash in 2015 the company sold its remaining position in Howard County in the Permian Basin for a contract price of $281 million.

In 2012 the company teamed up with an Anadarko Petroleum affiliate forming a $400 million joint venture to develop a carbon dioxide enhanced oil recovery project in the Salt Creek field in the Powder River Basin.

Mergers and Acquisitions

Dramatically growing its asset base in 2013 the company bought Berry Petroleum for $4.3 billion. The deal increased Linn Energy's estimated proved reserves and production by approximately 34% and 30% respectively.

In 2013 Linn Energy acquired oil and natural gas properties located in the Permian Basin for $525 million.

In 2012 Linn Energy acquired BP's Hugoton properties in Kansas for $1.2 billion and properties in East Texas from a separate company for $175 million. Later that year it agreed to another purchase from BP this time 12500 acres in Wyoming's Jonah Field. Linn paid more than $1 billion for the property which includes 750 producing wells and more than 730 billion cu. ft. of natural gas equivalent.

In 2011 the company bought additional assets in the Bakken shale and the Permian Basin (including the Cleveland play) for $434 million.

EXECUTIVES

Chairman President and CEO, Mark E. Ellis, age 59, $900,000 total compensation

EVP and COO, Arden L. Walker, age 56, $500,000 total compensation

EVP and CFO LINN Energy and Linnco LLC, David B. Rottino, age 49, $470,000 total compensation

SVP Houston Division Operations, Jamin B. McNeil, age 49, $375,000 total compensation

Vice President Marketing, Mark Cahill

Senior Vice President, Charlene Ripley

Vice President, Yancey Bishop

Vice President Investor Relations, Clay Jeansonne

Senior Vice President, Tanya Smith

Secretary Treasurer, Steven Sellers

Auditors: KPMG LLP

LOCATIONS

HQ: Linn Energy LLC
600 Travis, Suite 5100, Houston, TX 77002
Phone: 281 840-4000
Web: www.linnenergy.com

PRODUCTS/OPERATIONS

2012 Sales

	$ mil.	% of total
Oil natural gas & NGLs	1,601	90
Gains on derivatives	124	7
Marketing	37	2
Other	10	1
Total	**1,774**	**100**

COMPETITORS

Abraxas Petroleum	PDC Energy
Anadarko Petroleum	Pioneer Natural
Cimarex	Resources
Concho	SandRidge Energy
Energen	

HISTORICAL FINANCIALS

Company Type: Public

Income Statement

FYE: December 31

	REVENUE ($ mil.)	NET INCOME ($ mil.)	NET PROFIT MARGIN	EMPLOYEES
12/14	4,983	(451)	—	1,800
12/13	2,331	(691)	—	1,645
12/12	1,774	(386)	—	1,136
12/11	1,622	438	27.0%	824
12/10	772	(114)	—	700
Annual Growth	**59.4%**	**—**	**—**	**26.6%**

2014 Year-End Financials

Debt ratio: 62.69%	No. of shares (mil.): 331
Return on equity: (-8.66%)	Dividends
Cash ($ mil.): 1	Yield: 28.6%
Current ratio: 1.74	Payout: —
Long-term debt ($ mil.): 10,295	Market value ($ mil.): 3,363

	STOCK PRICE ($) FY Close	P/E High/Low	PER SHARE ($) Earnings	Dividends	Book Value
12/14	10.13	— —	(1.40)	2.90	13.69
12/13	30.79	— —	(2.94)	2.90	17.87
12/12	35.24	— —	(1.92)	2.87	18.88
12/11	37.91	16 13	2.51	2.70	19.33
12/10	37.49	— —	(0.80)	2.55	17.53
Annual Growth (27.9%)		— —	—	3.3%	(6.0%)

Lithia Motors, Inc.

Acquisitive Lithia Motors is a big hungry fish among US auto retailers. The company operates about 130 stores in select markets in more than a dozen states. The firm sells 30 brands of new domestic and imported vehicles and all brands of used cars and trucks through its stores and online. Chrysler (Dodge Jeep) and GM (Chevrolet Cadillac Saab) are the top sellers. Lithia Motors also offers financing and replacement parts and operates about 18 collision-repair centers. Unlike most consolidators it prefers to pay cash (rather than stock) for dealerships in smaller markets. Chairman Sidney DeBoer through Lithia Holding Co. controls Lithia Motors which was founded in 1946 by his father Walt.

Geographic Reach

Lithia sells 31 brands of new vehicles and all brands of used vehicles at 130 stores in 14 US states. Its dealerships are primarily located in the West and Midwest including more than a half a dozen dealerships in Alaska and nearly two dozen in Oregon. Texas is Lithia's biggest market accounting for 21% of the company's total sales.

Operations

The company has three segments: Domestic Import and Luxury.The Domestic segment is comprised of retail automotive franchises that sell new vehicles manufactured by Chrysler General Motors and Ford. The Import segment covers retail automotive franchises that sell new vehicles made by Honda Toyota Subaru Nissan and Volkswagen. The Luxury segment sells new vehicles manufactured made by BMW Mercedes-Benz and Lexus. The franchises in each segment also sell used vehicles parts and automotive services and automotive finance and insurance products.

Sales and Marketing

The company's advertising expense was $46.7 million in 2014 $39.6 million in 2013 and $31.9 million in 2012.Lithia sells through its stores and online website. It also maintains mobile versions of its websites and a mobile application in anticipation of greater adoption of mobile technology.It posts its inventory on major new and used vehicle listing services (cars.com autotrader.com kbb.com edmunds.com eBay craigslist etc.) to reach online shoppers. It also employs search engine optimization search engine marketing and online display advertising (including re-targeting) to reach more online prospects.

Financial Performance

The company's net sales have seen a consistent upward trend since 2010.In 2014 Lithia's net sales increased by 35% to increased sales from new ve-

hicle and used vehicle retail and finance and insurance.New vehicle sales improved due to volume growth. In 2014 each of Lithia's stores sold 56 retail used vehicle units per month compared to 53 retail used vehicle units per store per month in 2013 thanks to a larger number of late model vehicles being available in the marketplace.The increases in finance and insurance sales in 2014 were driven by higher vehicle sales volumes and prices.Lithia's net income has also been trending upward in recent years.In 2014 net income increased by 31% due to higher sales and income from discontinued operations partially offset by increased selling general and administrative expenses.That year the company's net cash provided by the operating activities decreased by $1.7 million (from $32.1 million in 2013) primarily due to change in trade payables accrued liabilities and other assets.

Strategy

Lithia Motors relies on acquisitions to increase its revenue and diversify its brand portfolio. Indeed the company has completed more than 100 acquisitions since it went public in 1996. Historically the auto dealer has bought about 10 franchises a year expanding mostly in its western base. However an acquisition in 2014 has extended Lithia's reach eastward to New York and New Jersey. Also in 2014 the company acquired a Ford store and opened a new Chrysler Jeep Dodge store in Wasilla Alaska.

The auto dealer relies heavily on GM and Chrysler brand models which combined accounted for nearly 50% of 2013 sales. The deep recession and turmoil among domestic automakers especially GM and Chrysler caused Lithia to revise its strategy by reducing its dependence on domestic manufacturers. However with the US economy and auto industry much improved Lithia is once again in the market for domestic dealerships. The auto dealer targets mid-sized regional markets for domestic and import franchises and metropolitan markets for its luxury dealerships. Lithia is also looking to body shops for growth. Currently the company operates 18 collision repair centers five of which are in Texas five in Oregon two in Idaho and one each in Alaska Washington Montana Iowa Nevada and New Jersey.The company strives for diversification in its products services brands and geographic locations to insulate us from market risk and to maintain profitability. It has developed a centralized support structure to reduce store level administrative functions. This allows store personnel to focus on providing a positive customer experience.Lithia's near-term goal for used vehicles is to retail an average of 75 units per store per month. In 2014 its stores sold an average of 56 retail used units per month. It believes used vehicles represent a significant area for organic growth.

Mergers and Acquisitions

In 2015 Lithia acquired Bitterroot Ford in Missoula Montana its first Ford store in the state.

In 2014 Lithia acquired DCH Auto Group one of the nation's largest dealer groups with about $2.3 billion in annualized revenue for $364 million. The purchase of DCH added 27 stores in Southern California New Jersey and New York and transformed Lithia into a national player.Other acquisitions in 2014 included Island Honda in Kahului Hawaii; Honolulu Buick GMC Cadillac and Honolulu Volkswagen in Honolulu Hawaii; Stockton Volkswagen in Stockton California; Corpus Christi Ford in Corpus Christi Texas; Beaverton GMC Buick and Portland Cadillac in Portland Oregon; Bellingham GMC Buick in Bellingham Washington; and Harris Nissan in Clovis California.

Company Background

In 2012 the company acquired Jerry Chambers Chevrolet Cadillac in Bellingham Washington and also bought Bitterroot Toyota in Missoula Montana. In 2011 Lithia bought Fresno Subaru and BMW Mini and Mercedes stores in Portland Oregon.

Lithia Motors was founded in 1946 by Walt De-Boer as a Chrysler-Plymouth-Dodge dealership in Ashland Oregon. Walt's son Sidney is its chairman and grandson Bryan is president and CEO of the growing auto dealer.

EXECUTIVES

President and CEO, Bryan B. DeBoer, age 48, $840,000 total compensation
SVP and CFO, Christopher (Chris) Holzshu, age 41, $420,000 total compensation
SVP Retail Operations, Scott Hillier, age 52, $420,000 total compensation
VP Information Technology and CIO, Mark Smith
Regional Manager Vice President, Ken Wright
Vice President Finance, Jd Spruill
Chairman, Sidney B. (Sid) DeBoer, age 71
Vice Chairman, M. L. (Dick) Heimann, age 71
Auditors: KPMG LLP

LOCATIONS

HQ: Lithia Motors, Inc.
  150 N. Bartlett Street, Medford, OR 97501
Phone: 541 776-6401
Web: www.lithia.com

2014 Stores

	No.
Oregon	24
California	30
Texas	17
New Jersey	10
Alaska	9
Montana	8
Washington	7
Idaho	5
Iowa	5
Nevada	4
North Dakota	3
New York	3
Hawaii	3
New Mexico	2
Total	**130**

PRODUCTS/OPERATIONS

2014 Sales

	$ mil.	% of total
Domestic	2,569	48
Import	1,889	35
Luxury	926	17
Corporate and other	4	-
Total	**5,390**	**100**

2014 Sales

	$ mil.	% of total
New vehicles	3,077	57
Used vehicle retail	1,362	25
Service body & parts	512	9
Used vehicle wholesale	195	4
Finance & insurance	190	4
Fleet & other	52	1
Total	**5,390**	**100**

COMPETITORS

Ancira
AutoNation
Autobytel
CarMax
David McDavid Auto
  Group
Gillman Companies
Group 1 Automotive
Internet Brands
McCombs Enterprises
Penske Automotive
  Group
Sonic Automotive

HISTORICAL FINANCIALS

Company Type: Public

Income Statement

FYE: December 31

	REVENUE ($ mil.)	NET INCOME ($ mil.)	NET PROFIT MARGIN	EMPLOYEES
12/14	5,390	138	2.6%	8,827
12/13	4,005	106	2.6%	5,700
12/12	3,316	80	2.4%	5,403
12/11	2,699	58	2.2%	4,397
12/10	2,131	13	0.6%	4,039
Annual Growth	**26.1%**	**78.3%**	**—**	**21.6%**

2014 Year-End Financials

Debt ratio: 63.16%
Return on equity: 22.97%
Cash ($ mil.): 29
Current ratio: 1.12
Long-term debt ($ mil.): 609
No. of shares (mil.): 26
Dividends
  Yield: 0.7%
  Payout: 12.8%
Market value ($ mil.): 2,274

	STOCK PRICE ($) FY Close	P/E High/Low	Earnings	Dividends	Book Value
12/14	86.69	18 10	5.26	0.61	25.66
12/13	69.42	18 9	4.05	0.49	20.65
12/12	37.42	12 7	3.07	0.47	16.67
12/11	21.86	11 6	2.21	0.26	14.14
12/10	14.29	27 10	0.52	0.15	12.18
Annual Growth	**56.9%**	**— —**	**78.3%**	**42.0%**	**20.5%**

Live Nation Entertainment, Inc.

Live Nation Entertainment holds center stage as the world's largest ticket seller and promoter of live entertainment. The company significantly expanded its ticketing services with the purchase of Ticketmaster Entertainment. The 2010 deal worth some $889 million created a powerful live-music conglomerate. The firm owns or operates about 160 venues in North America and Europe. Annually about 520 million people attend some 250000 Live Nation events. Live Nation also owns House of Blues venues through HOB Entertainment and dozens of prestigious concert halls. In addition Live Nation owns a stake in about 280 artists' music including albums tours and merchandise.

Geographic Reach

Live Nation owns operates or leases about 160 venues located throughout the world. The company generated about 65% of revenue from domestic operations during fiscal 2014.

Operations

Live Nation's reportable segments are Concerts Ticketing Artist Nation and Sponsorship & Advertising. In fiscal 2014 about 90% of its revenue came from its Concerts and Ticketing segments.

Its Concerts segment involves global promotion of live music events in its owned and operated venues and in rented third-party venues the operation and management of music venues and the production of music festivals across the world.

The Ticketing segment is primarily an agency business that sells tickets for events on behalf of its clients and retains a convenience charge and order processing fee for its services.

The company's Artist Nation segment provides management services to music artists in exchange for a commission on the earnings of these artists.

Its Sponsorship & Advertising segment employs a sales force that creates and maintains relationships with sponsors that allow businesses to reach customers through Live Nation's concert venue artist relationship and ticketing assets including advertising on its websites.

Sales and Marketing

Live Nation promotes its events and sells tickets through websites (www.livenation.com and www.ticketmaster.com). The company spent about $243 million on advertising and promotions during fiscal 2014. That was an increase compared to the $224 million Live Nation spent on advertising during 2013.

Financial Performance

The company's revenue increased by 6% to about $6.8 billion in fiscal 2014 up from $6.4 billion in fiscal 2013. The overall increase in revenue was primarily due to increases in its Concerts and Ticketing segments. The increase in Concerts revenue resulted from strategic priorities to grow owned and operated amphitheater and European festival profitability expand its portfolio of electronic dance music and other new festivals and expand into new geographic markets.

Despite the increase in revenue Live Nation recorded a net loss in fiscal 2014 due to direct operating expenses selling general and administrative expenses depreciation and amortization and income tax expenses.

Strategy

Live Nation has used joint ventures to expand its operations. The company continues to strengthen its core operations further expanding into additional global markets and optimizing cost structure. Its strategy is to expand its concert platform by adding artists and venues drive conversion of ticket sales through social and mobile channels and work to grow its sponsorship and advertising revenue.

Mergers and Acquisitions

The company has also used acquisitions to fuel its growth. In 2014 Live Nation's Ticketmaster acquired mobile-based Do-It-Yourself ticketing platform Eventjoy. Ticketmaster also acquired Brussels-based Belgian ticketing company Sherpa.be during 2014. In early 2015 Live Nation Sweden acquired SPG Live.

Ownership

Media conglomerate Liberty Media currently owns about 27% of Live Nation but hopes to eventually increase its share to about 35%.

HISTORY

Robert Sillerman began his career teaching advertisers how to reach young consumers. He started investing in radio and TV stations and founded SFX Broadcasting (named for a scrambling of his initials) in 1992. In early 1997 the firm entered the live entertainment field with the formation of SFX Concerts and the purchase of concert promoter Delsener/Slater.

When SFX Broadcasting agreed to be bought in 1997 by Capstar Broadcasting 87% controlled by investment firm Hicks Muse Tate & Furst (now HM Capital) SFX Entertainment was formed to house the live entertainment operations (it was spun off in 1998). In 1998 the company continued its rapid acquisition rate with the purchases of sports marketing and management team FAME New England concert promoter Don Law and national concert producer PACE Entertainment.

In 1999 the company bought concert promoter The Cellar Door Companies (which almost doubled SFX's size) sports marketing firm Integrated Sports International sporting event management company The Marquee Group sports talent agency Hendricks Management 50% of urban-music producer A.H. Enterprises and troubled theatrical producer Livent. SFX also made its first foray abroad through its purchase of Apollo Leisure a UK-based live entertainment firm. The company rolled all of its sports talent and marketing businesses into a new division SFX Sports Group that year.

In 2000 SFX jumped on the other side of the acquisition train when it was bought by radio station owner Clear Channel Communications for about $4 billion. Sillerman stepped down as chairman and CEO and was replaced by Clear Channel EVP Brian Becker. Later that year SFX acquired Philadelphia-based concert promoter and venue operator Electric Factory Concerts; Core Audience Entertainment Canada's second-largest concert promoter and events marketer; and the Cotter Group a North Carolina-based motorsports marketing agency.

In 2001 SFX acquired a majority interest in the International Hot Rod Association. It also bought professional golf talent agency Signature Sports Group. Later that year the company changed its name to Clear Channel Entertainment. It also continued expansion into Europe with the acquisition of Trident Agency and Milano Concerti music promotion businesses in Italy.

While operating as Clear Channel Entertainment Live Nation spent nearly $2 billion on acquisitions (Pace Entertainment Livent) almost single-handedly consolidating the live entertainment industry.

Before being spun off in December 2005 the company changed its name to CCE Spinco then Live Nation. Also that year Randall Mays became chairman and Michael Rapino replaced Becker as CEO. As part of the Clear Channel spinoff the company relocated from Houston to headquarters in tony Beverly Hills. It trimmed the fat by shutting down operating divisions such as museum exhibitions and music publishing (and laying off about 400 employees in the process) in order to focus on its core businesses of live music concerts venue management and website brand development.

In 2006 the company acquired rival HOB Entertainment for $354 million. Live Nation used the acquisition to expand its presence in the midsized venue business and fill in geographic gaps in its existing amphitheater network. As part of the deal Live Nation gained high-profile House of Blues-branded music venues such as San Francisco's Fillmore Auditorium Jones Beach in New York and London's Apollo Theatre and Wembley Arena. The company subsequently began rebranding many of its midsize clubs "Fillmore" after the San Francisco venue.

The company had in 2005 formed Delirium Concert LP a joint venture with Cirque du Soleil. The Delirium tour began in 2006. The following year Live Nation signed a $120 million deal with pop icon Madonna. Through its North American Music segment in 2007 Live Nation promoted or produced some 10000 live music events including tours for Van Halen Dave Matthews Band and Kenny Chesney. International Music operations for the year included Cirque De Soleil's Delirium as well as UK's Reading Festival. Also in 2007 the company produced global tours for legends such as The Police The Rolling Stones Genesis and The Who and presented some 5000 theatrical performances such as the UK touring production of Chicago through its Global Theater operations.

In 2008 the company divested itself of its North American theatrical assets. Later that year the company signed pacts with U2 and Jay-Z. Michael Cohl chairman and Live Nation Artists chief who spearheaded the deals later resigned over conflicts with CEO Rapino. Also in 2008 the company sold its motor sports operations. In early 2010 the company acquired Ticketmaster Entertainment and

Live Nation changed its name to Live Nation Entertainment.

EXECUTIVES

President House of Blues Entertainment, Ronald (Ron) Bension
EVP General Counsel and Secretary, Michael G. Rowles, age 50, $750,000 total compensation
Co-President North America Concerts, Mark Campana
CEO Music - Europe, Michael (Mike) Rapino, age 50, $2,300,000 total compensation
Chairman Global Music; President Global Touring, Arthur Fogel, age 62
COO, Joe Berchtold, $1,100,000 total compensation
President International and Emerging Markets, Alan Ridgeway, age 48, $730,025 total compensation
CFO, Kathy Willard, age 49, $850,000 total compensation
President Media and Sponsorship, Russell Wallach
President Live Nation Europe - Concerts, John Reid
EVP Mergers and Acquisitions and Strategic Finance, John Hopmans, age 56
President Ticketmaster North America, Jared Smith
Co-President North America Concerts, Bob Roux
President Ticketmaster International, Mark Yovich, age 40
CIO, David Huckabay
Senior Vice President Venue Sponsorships, Marc Abend
Vice President National Sales, Craig Hoover
Vice President Booking, Todd Miller
Vice President Strategic Alliances, Jeff Shaw
Vice President Finance, Katherine Porter
Senior Vice President Investor Relations, Maili Bergman
Vice President, John Loken
Vice President Customer And Member Services, Dan Houghtaling
Vice President Marketing, Beth Cosimi
Senior Vice President Software Engineering, Cameron Murdock
Senior Vice President Digital Media, Erin Yasgar
Vice President of Retail, Allison Meyerson
Vice President Strategic Alliances Live Nation Entertainment, Christopher (Chris) Swope
Vice President Finance, Reuben Sanchez
Vice President Marketing, Danielle Engel
Vice President Regional Sales, Jeff Wallace
Regional Vice President, Larry Wethers
Vice President Corporate Financial Planning, Brian Parisi
Vice President Marketing, Holli Mattison
Vice President, Brad Wavra
Senior Vice President Booking, Emily Simonitsch
Vice President Strategic Alliances, Libby Biason
Vice President Legal Affairs, Ellie Schwimmer
Vice President Brand Marketing, Dave Fortin
Senior Vice President Social Media, Ryan Okum
Vice President Business Development and Strategic Planning, Jon Glickstein
Senior Vice President Of Human Resources, Tracy Wagner
Vice President Operations Manager Oreilly Thunder Jam, Jim Marchyshyn
Executive Vice President Of North American Venues, Ned Collett
Vice President Marketing Solutions, Lisa Lugo
Executive Vice President, Wilson Rogers
Executive Vice President National Alliances, Darin Wolf
Vice President Legal And Business Affairs, Chris Laffoon
Senior Vice President Relationship and Loyalty Marketing, Phil Seward
Vice President Marketing, David Fortin
Vice President Tour Operations, Craig Evans

Vice President M and A Strategic Finance, Edward (Ed) Lee
Vice President Booking, Adam Cohen
Vice President, Joseph (Jo) Ventura
Senior Vice President Information Technology Systems, Jon Greenwood
Vice President Of Business Development, Frank Gutierrez
Vice President Marketing, Jim Bozzi
Vice President Finance, Carolyn Specht
Vice President Production, Craig Goetsch
Vice President Sales, Joel Wolinsky
Regional Vice President, Michael Myers
Senior Vice President, Richard Levy
Regional Vice President Premium Seat Sales, Kate Walsh
Senior Vice President, Darren Mcinnes
Vice President Media Director National Marketing, Julia Heiser
Vice President Purchasing, Gene Surh
Vice President Latin Programming Touring, Manuel Moran
Vice President Planning, George Duran
Senior Vice President, Eric Thorson
Regional Vice President, Danny Eaton
Vice President Digital Sales East, Jeremy Levine
Vice President Sponsorship Sales, Tobias Ekman
Vice President and Controller, Bill Janney
Vice President Finance, Frank Brayer
Senior Vice President Marketing, Joey Scoleri
Vice President Finance National Tourin, Lisa Howe
Vice President User Experience, Jacki Remus
Vice President Production, Leslie Holland
Vice President Risk Management, Jan Berger
Vice President Legal Affairs, Sheila Small
Vice President Special Events, Nickole Bruner
Senior Vice President Human Resources, Laura Morton-rowe
Vice President Booking, Marcel Thimot
Vice President Marketing, Brad Locker
Vice President, Ted Mankin
Senior Vice President Of Government Relations, Becky Relic
Vice President Accounting, Darrick McFarlin
Executive Vice President, Felix Mussenden
Vice President Of Engineering, Dennis Harvey
Vice President Touring, Craig Sneiderman
Senior Vice President, Stacey Harper
Executive Vice President Business Development North American Concerts, Chris Adelmann
Senior Vice President, Bill Lowe
Senior Vice President Marketing, Jackie Wilgar
Vice President Sales, Jill Jacob
Vice President Information Technology, Dave Gerardi
Senior Vice President and Treasurer, William (Bill) Lowe
Vice President Sales, Aj Silverman
Vice President Systems Engineering, Shakeel Sorathia
Vice President Information Services, James (Jamie) Cheung
Vice President of Marketing, Dave Niedbalski
Chairman, Gregory B. (Greg) Maffei, age 54
Auditors: Ernst & Young LLP

LOCATIONS

HQ: Live Nation Entertainment, Inc.
9348 Civic Center Drive, Beverly Hills, CA 90210
Phone: 310 867-7000
Web: www.livenationentertainment.com

2014 Sales

	$ mil.	% of total
Domestic operations	4,503	66
UK operations	772	11
Other operations	1,592	23
Total	**6,867**	**100**

PRODUCTS/OPERATIONS

2014 Sales

	$ mil.	% of total
Concerts	4,726	68
Ticketing	1,557	22
Artist Nation	389	6
Sponsorship & advertising	300	4
Other revenue	3	0
Eliminations	(110)	-
Total	**6,867**	**100**

COMPETITORS

Brillstein
CAA
Dodger Properties
Feld Entertainment
IMG
International Creative Management
Jujamcyn Theaters
Madison Square Garden
Nederlander Producing Company
Octagon
On Stage Entertainment
Palace Sports & Entertainment
Ryman
SMG Management
Shubert Organization
TBA Global
United Talent
Universal Music Group
Warner Music
WestwoodOne
William Morris Endeavor Entertainment

HISTORICAL FINANCIALS

Company Type: Public

Income Statement

FYE: December 31

	REVENUE ($ mil.)	NET INCOME ($ mil.)	NET PROFIT MARGIN	EMPLOYEES
12/14	6,866	(90)	—	14,000
12/13	6,478	(43)	—	7,400
12/12	5,819	(163)	—	7,100
12/11	5,384	(83)	—	6,600
12/10	5,063	(228)	—	6,500
Annual Growth	**7.9%**	—	—	**21.1%**

2014 Year-End Financials

Debt ratio: 34.46%
Return on equity: (-6.71%)
Cash ($ mil.): 1,382
Current ratio: 1.13
Long-term debt ($ mil.): 2,015

No. of shares (mil.): 201
Dividends
  Yield: —
  Payout: —
Market value ($ mil.): 5,253

	STOCK PRICE ($) FY Close	P/E High/Low	PER SHARE ($) Earnings	PER SHARE ($) Dividends	PER SHARE ($) Book Value
12/14	26.11	— —	(0.49)	0.00	6.45
12/13	19.76	— —	(0.22)	0.00	7.06
12/12	9.31	— —	(0.87)	0.00	7.10
12/11	8.31	— —	(0.46)	0.00	7.73
12/10	11.42	— —	(1.39)	0.00	7.83
Annual Growth	**23.0%**	— —	—	—	**(4.8%)**

LKQ Corp

Not just any part will do for LKQ. The company specifically distributes replacement parts and components needed to repair passenger cars and trucks. It's one of the leading aftermarket parts suppliers in the US through subsidiary Keystone Automotive (acquired in 2007). LKQ also offers reconditioned remanufactured and refurbished parts including wheels bumpers mirrors and engines as well as recycled parts that are reclaimed from salvage vehicles. Customers include collision repair and mechanical repair shops. Additionally LKQ operates self-service retail yards that allow customers to come in search through and buy recycled auto parts. To diversify acquisitive LKQ is expanding internationally.

Operations

LKQ operates through three business segments: North America with 61% of revenue; Europe 27% of revenue and Specialty 12% of revenue. The specialty category was formed after the 2014 acquisition of Keystone Specialty. In terms of products aftermarket and other new and refurbished parts made up more than two-thirds of the company's revenue. About 22% comes from recycling remanufactured and related products and services. The Other category was 10%.

The firm's self-service retail operation consists of about 70 auto parts yards in the US and Canada where customers can pay an admission fee to find parts for their vehicles on more than 1000 American and imported cars and light trucks. LKQ's yards also try to play an environmental role by buying unwanted vehicles and recycling and disposing of all fluids and materials. The heavy truck division consists of a dozen locations in North America that sell used trucks and new used and remanufactured heavy truck parts.

Geographic Reach

LKQ generates 70% of its sales in North America. The firm's newest market the UK accounts for nearly 20% of sales with the remainder coming from other countries (Taiwan the Netherlands Belgium France Guatemala Scandinavia Australia and Costa Rica). The company's operations in Mexico include an engine manufacturer and a bumper refurbishing business. LKQ sources most of its aftermarket inventory from auto parts manufacturers and distributors in the US Taiwan and China.

Financial Performance

Fast-growing LKQ's sales have posted double-digit gains in recent years and profits have followed suit. In 2014 sales reached $6.7 billion an increase of 33% versus 2013 while net income climbed 22% to $381.5 million. Sales grew in the US and Europe. Much of the increase came from acquisitions while 7% of the growth was organic. Cash flow from operations dropped to $371 million in 2014 from $428 million the year before partly as a result of more inventory in aftermarket products.

Strategy

Key to the company's growth strategy is acquisitions. Indeed LKQ has completed around 200 acquisitions in the US and abroad since its founding in 1998.

LKQ's geographic diversification strategy appears to be a smashing success. Indeed sales in the UK have increased by about 800% since 2011 making the company less reliant on the US market which now accounts for 68% of sales (vs. 90% in 2011). LKQ is also extending its business to include complementary products such as cooling products and paint.

The company has also worked on its supply chain expanding its network of parts warehouses and dismantling plants in major metros and operating a distribution system that allows for order fulfillment from regional warehouses located across the U.S. and Canada. It also is expanding its branch network in the UK.

Mergers and Acquisitions

In January 2014 the company bought Keystone Automotive Holdings (aka Keystone Specialty) for $455.4 million. Keystone Specialty is a distributor and marketer of specialty aftermarket equipment and accessories in North America that serves six product segments including truck and off-road recreational vehicle and towing. Overall in 2014 LKQ made 22 acquisitions including nine wholesale businesses in North America nine wholesale businesses in Europe two self-service retail operations and two specialty vehicle aftermarket businesses.

In addition to LKQ's purchase of Sator the company made 19 acquisitions in 2013 including 10 wholesale businesses in North America seven wholesale businesses in Europe and two self-service operations.

The firm expects to continue its acquisitive ways in the US and overseas in 2015 and beyond.

EXECUTIVES

CEO and Managing Director European Operations, John S. Quinn, age 56, $500,000 total compensation
President and CEO, Robert L. Wagman, age 51, $800,000 total compensation
EVP and CFO, Dominick P. (Nick) Zarcone
SVP Operations, Steven Greenspan, age 53, $350,000 total compensation
Vice President Finance and Chief Accounting Officer, Michael (Mel) Clark
Senior Vice President, Victor Casini
Vice President Finance And Chief Accounting Officer, Michael S Clark
Vice President of Engineering, Brandon Gee
Chairman, Joseph M. Holsten, age 62
Auditors: Deloitte & Touche LLP

LOCATIONS

HQ: LKQ Corp
  500 West Madison Street, Suite 2800, Chicago, IL 60661
Phone: 312 621-1950
Web: www.lkqcorp.com

2014 Sales

	$ mil.	% of total
US	4,499	67
UK	1,321	19
Other	918	14
Total	**6,740**	**100**

PRODUCTS/OPERATIONS

2014 Sales

	$ mil.	% of total
Aftermarket other new & refurbished products	4,613	68
Recycled remanufactured & related products & services	1,473	22
Other	653	10
Total	**6,740**	**100**

2014 Sales

	$ mil. % of total
North America	61
Europe	27
Specialty	12
Eliminations	-
Total	**100**

Selected Products & Services

Products
  Heavy truck and equipment parts
  New aftermarket replacement parts
  Paint and body shop supplies and equipment
  Rebuilt original equipment replacement parts
  Reconditioned original equipment replacement parts
  Recycled original equipment auto and truck parts
  Remanufactured engines and transmissions
Services
  Bulk sales
  Fleet services
  Insurer services
  National part purchase programs
  Salvage vehicle disposal
  Tire recycling

President and CEO QVC Inc., Michael (Mike) George, age 53, $1,092,727 total compensation
SVP, Albert E. Rosenthaler, age 55, $346,444 total compensation
SVP and General Counsel, Richard N. (Rich) Baer, age 58, $424,875 total compensation
Vice President and Treasurer, Neal Dermer
Chairman, John C. Malone, age 74
Auditors: KPMG LLP

LOCATIONS

HQ: Liberty Interactive Corp
12300 Liberty Boulevard, Englewood, CO 80112
Phone: 720 875-5300
Web: www.libertyinteractive.com

2014 Sales

	$ mil.	% of total
US	7,617	72
Germany	1,003	10
Japan	912	9
Other countries	967	9
Total	**10,499**	**100**

PRODUCTS/OPERATIONS

2014 Sales

	$ mil.	% of total
QVC		
QVC	8,801	84
Digital Commerce	1,227	12
Ventures Group		
Digital Commerce	471	4
Total	**10,499**	**100**

Selected Subsidiaries and Investments

Backcountry.com Inc. (87% online backcountry gear)
Bodybuilding.com LLC (86% online bodybuilding products and equipment)
Celebrate Interactive Holdings LLC (100% online costume and party supply retail)
Evite Inc. (100% online party planning)
Expedia Inc. (25% online travel)
Gifts.com (100% online gifts)
HSN Inc. (37% online and TV shopping)
LMC Right Start (100% baby products)
LOCKERZ (38%)
Provide Commerce Inc. (100% e-commerce)
QVC (100% home shopping network)
TripAdvisor (57% online travel site)

COMPETITORS

Access TV	IAC
Amazon.com	Orbitz Worldwide
American Express	Priceline
EVINE Live	Travelocity
HSN	Wal-Mart

HISTORICAL FINANCIALS

Company Type: Public

Income Statement

FYE: December 31

	REVENUE ($ mil.)	NET INCOME ($ mil.)	NET PROFIT MARGIN	EMPLOYEES
12/14	10,499	537	5.1%	20,078
12/13	11,252	501	4.5%	23,079
12/12	10,054	1,530	15.2%	22,078
12/11	9,616	912	9.5%	22,077
12/10	10,982	1,892	17.2%	24,073
Annual Growth	**(1.1%)**	**(27.0%)**	**—**	**(4.4%)**

2014 Year-End Financials

Debt ratio: 43.19%
Return on equity: 8.52%
Cash ($ mil.): 2,306
Current ratio: 1.48
Long-term debt ($ mil.): 7,105
No. of shares (mil.): 617
Dividends
  Yield: —
  Payout: 74.2%
Market value ($ mil.): 18,177

	STOCK PRICE ($) FY Close	P/E High/Low	PER SHARE ($) Earnings	Dividends	Book Value
12/14	29.42	— —	(0.00)	0.00	9.18
12/13	29.35	— —	(0.00)	0.00	12.08
12/12	19.68	— —	(0.00)	0.00	12.23
12/11	16.22	— —	(0.00)	0.00	11.23
12/10	15.77	— —	(0.00)	0.00	15.41
Annual Growth	**16.9%**	**— —**	**—**		**—(12.1%)**

LifePoint Health Inc

LifePoint Health (formerly LifePoint Hospitals) hopes that folks who get sick in the country won't head to the city to get well. The company operates about 65 hospitals located in non-urban areas. In most cases the hospitals (which house more than 8000 beds combined) are the only available acute care facilities in the region. LifePoint operates its hospitals in some 21 states through its subsidiaries with a concentration in the southeastern US. In many markets LifePoint also operates outpatient clinics that provide family care diagnostic surgical and therapeutic services. The company has 4100 physician partners.

Operations

Unlike major urban medical centers the hospitals that LifePoint operates don't usually engage in extensive medical research train legions of new doctors or perform complex surgeries. The facilities do provide a spectrum of health care services that include emergency care general surgery obstetrics oncology cardiology coronary care rehabilitation services pediatric services and diagnostic care.

The company has nearly 40 post-acute service providers and facilities as well as more than 30 outpatient centers. Its Duke LifePoint Healthcare partnership with Duke University Health System works to strengthen and improve the delivery of health care.

Geographic Reach

LifePoint has the heaviest concentration of facilities in Kentucky Tennessee Virginia New Mexico West Virginia Michigan Arizona and North Carolina.

Virginia accounted for 14% of revenue in 2014; Kentucky and Michigan accounted for 13% and 10% respectively.

Sales and Marketing

More than 40% of LifePoint's annual revenues come from private insurers (including HMO and PPO plans) while another 40% come from Medicare and Medicaid. More than 15% of revenues come from self-pay patients.

Financial Performance

LifePoint's revenues have been steadily rising over the past few years. In 2014 they rose 22% to $4.5 billion as same-hospital revenues rose on higher admissions. The company also felt a favorable impact from health care reform (in which more patients had coverage) and earned higher contracted rates from HMOs PPOs and other private insurers. Same-hospital admissions increased 2.7% primarily due to increases in surgeries and emergency department visits.

However net income has been falling for the past three years. It fell 2% to $126 million in 2014 as the company paid more in salaries and benefits and towards other expenses. Cash flow from operations rose 16% as LifePoint used less cash for

accounts payable accrued salaries and other current liabilities.

Strategy

The company focuses on adding new service lines in its existing markets and investing in new technologies and on developing strategic partnerships with not-for-profit health care providers to achieve growth in new regions.

LifePoint maintains a competitive edge in many of its regional markets by being the sole provider of many of the health care services it offers. Even so LifePoint is working to increase the breadth of services provided by its hospitals in an effort to keep patients from having to travel outside the community for care especially in fields such as open-heart surgery psychiatric care and neurosurgery. Towards that end the company is improving methods of recruiting and retaining doctors; it is also working to control operating expenses while investing in system-wide capital improvement projects and technology upgrades.

One of its technology initiatives is to invest in electronic health record systems under federal health reform guidelines which aim to lower the cost of care through measures such as eliminating redundant procedures and lowering readmission rates. The company also manages procurement expenses by participating (and owning a 4% stake) in HealthTrust a group purchasing organization.

LifePoint struggles with containing expenses from serving charity care and self-pay customers that are part and parcel of running a health care system. To help offset losses related to caring for uninsured patients the company strives to negotiate favorable contracts with managed care and other private payers at each of its facilities.

To raise cash and save costs in 2014 the company agreed to sell certain assets of River Parishes Hospital and discontinue its operation. The following year it sold Lakeland Hospital Northwest Hospital and Russellville Medical Center in Alabama as well as the Putnam Community Medical Center in Florida.

LifePoint Hospitals changed its name to LifePoint Health in 2015 to reflect its growing focus on comprehensive health care including physician practices post-acute and outpatient services and wellness programs.

Mergers and Acquisitions

In addition to organic growth measures LifePoint also expands through regular acquisitions. The company targets small non-urban hospitals where it sees an opportunity for improved financial performance and LifePoint typically invests in facility upgrades once its purchases are complete. In 2015 through a joint venture with Norton Healthcare LifePoint added Indiana's 241-bed Clark Memorial Hospital; LifePoint also acquired the 52-bed Fleming County Hospital in Kentucky. Early the following year the company acquired South Carolina-based Providence Hospitals adding two hospitals 13 physician practices rehab centers sleep centers and a chest pain center.

Duke LifePoint Healthcare acquired Conemaugh Health System (operator of hospitals in west-central Pennsylvania) and North Carolina's Haywood Regional Medical Center and WestCare Health System in 2014; it also bought majority stakes in Rutherford Regional Hospital and Wilson Medical Center (both also in North Carolina). The following year LifePoint acquired Nason Hospital in Pennsylvania which became part of the Conemaugh Health System.

Company Background

LifePoint was born when hospital giant HCA spun off a group of about two dozen hospitals in 1999. It wasn't until its 2005 merger with Province Healthcare Company that LifePoint became the hulking presence it is today.

EXECUTIVES

Vice President, Dewitt Ezell
Chairman and CEO, William F. (Bill) Carpenter, age 60, $1,050,000 total compensation
President and COO, David M. Dill, age 46, $650,000 total compensation
President Central Group, R. Scott Raplee, age 50, $412,000 total compensation
Chief Medical Officer, Russell L. (Rusty) Holman, age 47
EVP and Chief Legal Officer, Paul D. Gilbert, age 49, $515,000 total compensation
EVP and Chief Administrative Officer, John P. Bumpus, age 55, $425,000 total compensation
SVP and CIO, Sean Tuley
EVP and CFO, Leif M. Murphy, age 47, $600,000 total compensation
President Western Group, Donald J. Bivacca, age 53
President Eastern Group, Jeffrey G. Seraphine, age 45
Senior Vice President Revenue Cycle Operations, Richard Flores
Vice President Reimbursement, William (Bill) Hoffman
Respiratory Therapy Director, Mark Mustard
Medical Director Sumner Regional Medical Center Emergency Department, Ray Pinkston
Vice President Human Resources, Marianne Freeman
Assistnat Vice President, Becky Janssen
Vice President Finance, Farely Reardon
Director Of Him, Charlotte Klaus
Clinical Director Meaningful Use, Kelly Lester
Clinical Director, Priscilla Snyder
Vice President Practice Management, Dan Sykes
Vice President Acquisition Integration And Transition Services, Sharon Marti
Senior Vice President UND, Peter (Pete) Radetich
Senior Vice President, Arthur Crumlish
Senior Vice President Chief Accounting Officer, Michael (Mel) Coggin
Vice President Practice Management, Tim Vaughn
Vice President and Associate General Counsel, Fabio Fallico
Clinical Director, Constance Berner
Senior Vice President Information Technology, Shawn Tuley
Radiology Director, Jay Cook
Vice President Clinical And Business Informatics, Brad Owens
Director Of Radiology, Rob Gaines
Vice President Capital Asset and Construction Management, Ed O'Dell
Vice President Risk Management, David (Dave) Fausett
Vice President Corporate Communications, Diane Huggins
Director of Nursing, Cindy Nichols
Board Member, John (Jack) Maupin
Board Member, Owen Shell
Auditors: Ernst & Young LLP

LOCATIONS

HQ: LifePoint Health Inc
330 Seven Springs Way, Brentwood, TN 37027
Phone: 615 920-7000
Web: www.lifepointhospitals.com

Selected Hospitals
Alabama
  Andalusia Regional Hospital
  Lakeland C
  Northwest
   Russellville Hospital
  Vaughan Re
Arizona
  Havasu Regional Medical Center (Lake Havasu City)
  Valley Vie
Colorado
  Colorado P
Florida

Putnam Com
Georgia
  Rockdale M
Indiana
  Scott Memo
Kansas
  Western Pl
Kentucky
  Bluegrass
  Bourbon Co
  Clark Regi
   Georgetown Community Hospital
  Jackson Pu
  Lake Cumbe
  Logan Memo
  Meadowview
  Spring Vie
Louisiana
  Acadian Me
   Mercy Regional Medical Center (aka Ville Platte Medical Center)
   Minden Medical Center
  River Pari
  Teche Regi
Michigan
   Marquette General Health System
Mississippi
  Bolivar Me
Nevada
  Northeaste
New Mexico
  Los Alamos Medical Center
  Memorial Medical Center of Las Cruces
North Carolina
  Maria Parham Medical Center (80% owned by Duke LifePoint Healthcare joint venture Henderson)
  Person Memorial Hospital (owned by Duke LifePoint Healthcare joint venture Roxboro)
Tennessee
  Athens Regional Medical Center
  Crockett H
  Emerald-Ho
   High Point Health System (formerly Sumner Regional Health Systems)
  Sumner Reg
  Hillside H
   Livingston Regional Hospital
  Riverview
  Southern T
  Trousdale
Texas
  Ennis Regional Medical Center
  Palestine Regional Medical Center
  Parkview R
Utah
  Ashley Reg
  Castleview
Virginia
  Clinch Val
   Danville Regional Medical Center
  Fauquier H
  Memorial H
   Twin County Regional Healthcare (owned by Duke LifePoint Healthcare joint venture)
  Twin Count
  Wythe Coun
West Virginia
  Logan Regional Medical Center
  Raleigh Ge
Wyoming
  Lander Regional Hospital
  Riverton Memorial Hospital

PRODUCTS/OPERATIONS

2014 Sales

	$ mil.	% of total
HMOs PPOs & other private insurers	2,476	47
Medicare	1,361	25
Self-pay	744	14
Medicaid	619	12
Other	98	2
Provisions for doubtful accounts	(817.8)	-
Total	**4,483**	**100**

COMPETITORS

Ascension Health	Mercy Health (OH)
CHRISTUS Health	Methodist Healthcare
Catholic Health	Sisters of Charity of
Initiatives	Leavenworth
Community Health Systems	SunLink Health Systems
Covenant Health	Tenet Healthcare
HCA	Tennova Healthcare
Intermountain Health Care	Universal Health Services
Kaiser Foundation Hospitals	Wellmont Health System
Mercy Health	West Tennessee Healthcare

HISTORICAL FINANCIALS

Company Type: Public

Income Statement
FYE: December 31

	REVENUE ($ mil.)	NET INCOME ($ mil.)	NET PROFIT MARGIN	EMPLOYEES
12/15	5,214	181	3.5%	40,000
12/14	4,483	126	2.8%	38,000
12/13	3,678	128	3.5%	31,000
12/12	3,391	151	4.5%	28,000
12/11	3,026	162	5.4%	23,000
Annual Growth	**14.6%**	**2.8%**	**—**	**14.8%**

2015 Year-End Financials

Debt ratio: 44.50%
Return on equity: 8.23%
Cash ($ mil.): 284
Current ratio: 2.05
Long-term debt ($ mil.): 2,643
No. of shares (mil.): 43
Dividends
  Yield: —
  Payout: —
Market value ($ mil.): 3,166

	STOCK PRICE ($) FY Close	P/E High/Low	Earnings	Dividends	Book Value
12/15	73.40	21 15	3.95	0.00	52.49
12/14	71.91	27 18	2.69	0.00	48.34
12/13	52.84	19 14	2.69	0.00	46.88
12/12	37.75	13 11	3.14	0.00	43.69
12/11	37.15	13 9	3.22	0.00	40.27
Annual Growth	**18.6%**	**— —**	**5.2%**	**—**	**6.8%**

Lilly (Eli) & Co.

Healthwise Eli Lilly hopes everything will come up roses for you. Best known for its neuroscience products the pharmaceutical company also makes endocrinology oncology and cardiovascular care medicines. Its top-selling drugs include Cymbalta for depression and pain Alimta for lung cancer Humalog and Humulin insulin for diabetes and Cialis for erectile dysfunction. Lilly also makes medications to treat schizophrenia and bipolar disorder (Zyprexa) osteoporosis (Evista and Forteo) heart conditions (Effient) and ADHD (Strattera) as well as anti-infective agents and a growing line of animal health products.

HISTORY

Colonel Eli Lilly pharmacist and Union officer in the Civil War started Eli Lilly and Company in 1876 with $1300. His process of gelatin-coating pills led to sales of nearly $82000 in 1881. Later the company made gelatin capsules which it still sells. Lilly died in 1898 and his son and two grandsons ran the business until 1953.

Eli Lilly began extracting insulin from the pancreases of hogs and cattle in 1923; 6000 cattle glands or 24000 hog glands made one ounce of the substance. Other products created in the 1920s and 1930s included antiseptic Merthiolate sedative Seconal and treatments for pernicious anemia and heart disease. In 1947 the company began selling diethylstilbestrol (DES) a drug to prevent miscarriages. Eli Lilly researchers isolated the antibiotic erythromycin from a species of mold found in the Philippines in 1952. Lilly was also the major supplier of Salk polio vaccine.

The company enjoyed a 70% share of the DES market by 1971 when researchers noticed that a rare form of cervical cancer afflicted many of the daughters of women who had taken the drug. The FDA restricted the drug's use and Lilly found itself on the receiving (and frequently losing) end of a number of trailblazing product-liability suits that stretched into the 1990s.

The firm diversified in the 1970s buying Elizabeth Arden (cosmetics 1971; sold 1987) and IVAC (medical instruments 1977). It launched such products as analgesic Darvon and antibiotic Ceclor.

Lilly's 1982 launch of Humulin a synthetic insulin developed by Genentech made it the first company to market a genetically engineered product. In 1986 the company introduced Prozac; that year it also bought biotech firm Hybritech for $300 million (sold in 1995 for less than $10 million). In 1988 Lilly introduced anti-ulcerative Axid. It founded pesticides and herbicides maker DowElanco with Dow Chemical in 1989.

Trying to find a new product outlet the firm bought pharmacy benefit management company PCS Health Systems from what is now McKesson in 1994. But an FTC mandate to offer rival drugs and a lack of mail-order sales contributed to poor results which ultimately led Lilly to sell PCS to Rite Aid and exit this arena completely in 1998.

Eli Lilly in 1995 bought medical communications network developer Integrated Medical Systems. That year the firm and developer Centocor introduced ReoPro a blood-clot inhibitor used in angioplasties. The next year it launched antipsychotic Zyprexa Humalog and Gemzar and Prozac was approved to treat bulimia nervosa.

In 1997 the firm sold its DowElanco stake to Dow. In 1998 the Lilly Endowment passed the Ford Foundation as the US's largest charity largely due to Prozac (it has since been passed by the Bill & Melinda Gates Foundation). That year Lilly began trying to stop Chinese drugmakers from infringing on its patents for Prozac's active ingredient.

In 1999 a US federal judge found the firm illegally promoted osteoporosis drug Evista as a breast cancer preventative similar to AstraZeneca's Nolvadex. Lilly halted tests on its variation of heart drug Moxonidine after 53 patients died. Also that year Zyprexa was approved to treat bipolar disorder.

In 2000 the firm began marketing Prozac under the Sarafem name for severe premenstrual syndrome. A federal appeals court knocked more than two years off Prozac's patent reducing the expected 2003 expiration date to 2001 creating a negative impact on Lilly's annual sales (Prozac had accounted for 30% of revenues). Lilly suffered another blow when a potential successor to Prozac failed in clinical trials and became embroiled in legal maneuverings with generics maker Barr Pharmaceuticals.

While the firm fretted over Prozac and its patents it continued work to find its next blockbuster. In 2000 Lilly and partner ICOS announced favorable results from a study of erectile dysfunction treatment Cialis which was approved in Europe in 2002 and in the US in 2004. (Several years later Lilly acquired ICOS and with it full ownership of the Cialis franchise.)

In 2001 Lilly bought a minority stake in Isis Pharmaceuticals a developer of antisense drugs and licensed from it an antisense lung cancer drug. Also that year the firm launched Lilly BioVentures a venture fund aimed at private biotech startup companies. In 2002 the company settled with eight states in an infringement-of-privacy case involving the company's accidental disclosure of e-mail addresses for more than 600 Prozac patients.

In late 2004 the druggernaut was one of several pharmas hit by bad news about drug side effects. Lilly announced its attention-deficit disorder drug Strattera had been linked to rare liver problems. The company agreed to add warning labels about the potential side effects to the drug's packaging and advertisements. The company also began facing trouble over Zyprexa as consumer lawsuits claiming diabetes and high blood pressure began pouring in. The majority of suits were settled in 2005 and 2007 for some $1.2 billion.

Generalized anxiety disorder drug Cymbalta was approved by the FDA and released in 2006 and osteoporosis drug Evista was approved for an expanded indication as a breast cancer preventative for postmenopausal women in 2007.

Also in 2007 the company acquired and absorbed development partner ICOS for $2.1 billion; the deal gave Lilly full ownership of Viagra-competitor Cialis. Lilly dropped a joint-development effort with another partner Alkermes for an inhaled insulin device in 2008.

The company gradually reduced its workforce by more than 10% between 2003 and 2008 to fight off the effects of generic competition and other challenges. Other restructuring measures included an employee attrition plan announced in 2007 a management restructuring in 2008 and a manufacturing consolidation program launched in 2008.

After a lengthy lawsuit regarding its patents for its top seller Zyprexa a federal judge ruled in Lilly's favor in 2008 against generic manufacturers IVAX Dr. Reddy's Laboratories and Teva Pharmaceutical Industries. Federal courts ruled that the drug's patents would remain valid until October 2011.

To fuel growth in the biopharmaceuticals market the firm completed a $1 billion biotech research facility in Indianapolis in 2008. It further expanded through the 2008 acquisition of biotech firm ImClone for about $6.5 billion; ImClone began operating as a research subsidiary of Lilly following the transaction. ImClone already had one approved blockbuster therapy Erbitux for colorectal and head/neck cancers and was developing numerous other cancer therapy candidates. Lilly also expanded its biotech oncology program earlier that year by purchasing development partner SGX Pharmaceuticals for $64 million. SGX was absorbed into Lilly's research operations.

The company agreed in 2009 to pay $1.4 billion in government fines to settle allegations over its marketing tactics for Zyprexa.

The firm received FDA approval in 2009 on a top pipeline candidate blood thinner Effient (developed with Daiichi Sankyo) although the drug carried heavy warning labels due to fatal bleeding risks. Effient held great potential however with better efficacy than Plavix (made by Bristol-Myers Squibb and Sanofi-Aventis) which dominated the $8 billion market. Also in 2009 Adcirca for pulmonary arterial hypertension was approved by the FDA. New indications include 2009 approval of Zyprexa Relprevv a long-acting injectable version of Zyprexa and bipolar therapy Symbyax was expanded for treatment-resistant depression indications. It has also extended indications of Cialis for treating benign prostatic hyperplasia

Lilly also launched a major restructuring program in 2009 to reduce expenses. The program resulted in the sale of its Indiana pharmaceutical ingredients plant to Evonik Industries in early 2010. Lilly further reduced costs by contracting out the related manufacturing functions to Evonik. The company also increased outsourcing efforts by forming partnerships with several contract research organizations (CROs) including firms such as Quintiles and Covance.

One development candidate awaiting FDA approval was Bydureon a once-a-week version of existing diabetes treatment Byetta that Lilly was co-developing with Amylin and Alkermes. However Lilly exited the partnership in 2011 after Amylin objected to Lilly's entering into a similar diabetes partnership with Boehringer Ingelheim. Lilly also sold Amylin back its co-marketing rights to Byetta.

To bolster its endocrinology efforts and enter the enzyme replacement therapy market in 2010 Lilly acquired Alnara Pharmaceuticals in a deal worth up to $390 million. The privately-held biotechnology company is focused on developing protein therapies to treat metabolic diseases. Alnara's lead product is a pancreatic enzyme replacement therapy called liprotamase. Another acquisition later that year brought the company an imaging compound candidate when Lilly paid $290 million up front (plus another $550 million in milestone payments) to buy Avid Radiopharmaceuticals. Avid's florbetapir is in development as a means for detecting amyloid plaque in the brain a key indicator of Alzheimer's disease.

Its Elanco Animal Health unit purchased a European portfolio of animal health products from Pfizer in 2010; the deal included marketing rights to certain vaccines parasiticides and feed additives for pets and livestock.

EXECUTIVES

Chairman President and CEO, John C. Lechleiter, age 60, $1,500,000 total compensation

EVP Science and Technology; President Lilly Research Laboratories, Jan M. Lundberg, age 61, $1,007,855 total compensation

EVP Global Services and CFO, Derica W. Rice, age 50, $1,019,700 total compensation

SVP and President Elanco Animal Health, Jeffrey N. (Jeff) Simmons, age 48

SVP and President Diabetes Business Unit, Enrique A. Conterno, age 48, $682,890 total compensation

President Manufacturing Operations, Maria Crowe, age 55

SVP and President Emerging Markets, Alfonso G. (Chito) Zulueta

SVP and President Lilly Oncology, Susan (Sue) Mahony, age 50

SVP and President Lilly Bio-Medicines, David A. Ricks, age 47

SVP Enterprise Risk Management and Chief Ethics and Compliance Officer, Melissa Stapleton Barnes

SVP and General Counsel, Michael J. Harrington, $765,000 total compensation

Vice President for Global Market Research, Tony Ezell

National Account Manager, Max Gild

Senior Vice President Corporate Affairs And Communications, Alex M Azar

Vice President Corporate Development and Strategic Planning, Mitch Silverstein

Senior Management (Senior Vice President General Manager Director), Kent Supancik

Chief Marketing Officer Vice President Global Medi, Timothy Garnett

Vice President Sales and Marketing, Carrie Coutant

Vice President Human Resources Emerging Markets Business Unit, Raymond Muller

Executive Vice President, Kelly Collett

Senior Vice President Research and Development, Kathryn Gilmore

Medical Director, Albert (Al) Allen

Medical Director, Murali Venugopalan

Department Head Space Planning, Brent Blanchard

Senior Vice President Human Resources, Sonya Johnson

Vice President Of Publicity, Tamara Lantz
Vice President U.s. Neuroscience Business Unit Leader, Michael (Mel) Mason
Vice President Medical Affiars, Robert (Bob) Heine
Vice President Of Marketing, Christopher Konkoy
Vice President Government Affairs, Joe Kelley
Department Head, Scott Chapell
Vice President, Mike Burnham
Medical Director, Todd Durell
Executive Vice President Pharma Operations, Johnathan Schilling
Vice President Global Diversity, Patricia Martin
Vice President, David (Dave) Clifford
Vice President, Aarti Shah
Vice President Of Strategic Planning, Peter Johnson
Vice President and Treasurer, Thomas (Thom) Grein
Vice President, Julie Martin
First Vice President, Tim Jones
Vice President New Media, Paula Garrett
Vice President Marketing, Michael Stone
Vice President Marketing, Ponce Tidwell
Medical Director Alliance Products US, Oliver Bachmann
Medical Director, Anurita Majumdar
Vice President, Mark Pemberton
Senior Vice President Clinical and Regulatory Affairs, Robert (Bob) Bay
Vice President Global Quality, Carole Beer
Vice President Manufacturing, Myles Oneill
Vice President And Medical Director China, Li Wang
Chief Medical Officer Senior Vice President Drug Development Center of Excellence, Tim Garnett
Vice President, Jeff Emmick
Vice President Information Technology, Bryan Woodfork
Vice President Oncology Research, Greg Plowman
Vice President Global Medical Affairs, Robert W (Bob) Baker
Secretary, Tim Conrad
Secretary To The Livestock Marketing Department, Carine Maes
Board Member, Ed Parrish
Board Member, Mark Miklinski
Secretary, Meg Johnston
Secretary, Bill Dunn
Auditors: Ernst & Young LLP

LOCATIONS

HQ: Lilly (Eli) & Co.
Lilly Corporate Center, Indianapolis, IN 46285
Phone: 317 276-2000
Web: www.lilly.com

2014 Sales

	$ mil.	% of total
US	9,134	47
Europe	4,506	23
Japan	2,027	10
Other regions & countries	3,947	20
Total	19,615	100

PRODUCTS/OPERATIONS

2014 Sales

	$ mil.	% of total
Endocrinology	6,939	36
Neurosciences	3,596	18
Oncology	3,393	17
Cardiovascular	3,053	16
Other human pharmaceuticals	287	1
Animal health	2,346	2
Total	19,615	100

2014 Sales

	$ mil.	% of total
Human pharmaceuticals		
Alimta	2,792	14
Humalog	2,785	14
Cialis	2,291	12

Cymbalta	1,614	8
Humulin	1,400	7
Forteo	1,322	7
Zyprexa	1,037	5
Strattera	738	4
Effient	522	3
Evista	419	2
Other human pharmaceuticals	1,557	8
Animal health products	2,346	12
Collaboration & other	788	4
Total	19,615	100

Selected Products and Indications

Neuroscience
  Amyvid (florbetapir F 18 injection)
  Cymbalta (duloxetine duchloronide; depression anxiety pain; also for managing fibromyalgia and chronic musculoskeletal pain in the US)
  Prozac (fluoxetine hydrochloride; depression panic disorder obsessive-compulsive disorder and bulimia nervosa)
  Strattera (atomoxetine hydrochloride ADHD)
  Symbyax (olanzapine and fluoxetine hydrochloride bipolar and treatment-resistant depression)
  Zyprexa (olanzapine schizophrenia and bipolar)
  Zyprexa Relprevv (Zypadhera in the EU long-acting injectable Zyprexa)
Endocrinology (including diabetes)
  Actos (pioglitazone hydrochloride type 2 diabetes)
  Alimta (non-small cell lung cancer)
  Axiron (testosterone topical for testosterone deficiency)
  Erbitux (colorectal cancers head and neck cancers)
  Evista (raloxifene hydrochloride osteoporosis and breast cancer prevention in postmenopausal women)
  Forteo (osteoporosis)
  Gemzar (pancreatic cancer metastatic breast cancer non-small cell lung cancer; bladder cancer in the EU)
  Glucagon (injection rDNA origin)
  Humalog (insulin lispro injection rDNA origin; diabetes)
  Humalog Mix 75/25 (75% Insulin lispro protamine suspension 25% insulin lispro injection rDNA origin; diabetes)
  Humalog Mix 50/50 (50% Insulin lispro protamine suspension 50% insulin lispro injection rDNA origin; diabetes)
  Humalog Pen (insulin lispro rDNA origin; diabetes)
  Humatrope (somatropin for injection rDNA origin; growth disorders)
  Humulin (human insulin rDNA origin; diabetes)
  Humulin Pen (human insulin rDNA origin; diabetes)
  Tradjenta (type 2 diabetes)
Oncology (cancer)
  Alimta (pemetrexed non-small cell lung cancer and malignant pleural mesothelioma)
  Erbitux (colorectal head and neck cancers; from ImClone)
  Gemzar (gemcitabine hydrochloride; pancreatic breast lung bladder and ovarian cancers)
Cardiovascular
  Adcirca (pulmonary arterial hypertension)
  Cialis (tadalafil erectile dysfunction; benign prostatic hyperplasia in US)
  Efient/Effient (atherothrombotic events)
  Livalo (statin high cholesterol)
  ReoPro (percutaneous coronary intervention)
Animal Health (Elanco)
  Apralan (antibiotic to control enteric infections in calves and swine)
  Coban Monteban and Maxiban (anticoccidial for poultry)
  Comfortis (flea infestation prevention tablets for dogs)
  Micotil Pulmotil and Pulmotil AC (antibiotics for respiratory disease in cattle swine and poultry respectively)
  Paylean Optaflexx (leanness and performance enhancers for swine and cattle respectively)
  Posilac (protein supplement for enhanced milk productivity in cows)
  Reconcile (separation anxiety for dogs)
  Rumensin (feed additive)
  Surmax/Maxus (performance enhancer for swine and poultry)
  Trifexis (chewable tablet for dogs to prevent flea infestations and heartworm disease and control intestinal parasite infections)
  Tylan (antibiotic)
Other pharmaceuticals (including anti-infectives)
  Ceclor (bacterial infections)
  Vancocin (staphylococcal infections)

COMPETITORS

Abbott Labs	Mylan
Amgen	Myriad Genetics
AstraZeneca	Novartis
Baxter International	Novo Nordisk
Bayer AG	Pfizer
Boehringer Ingelheim	Ranbaxy Laboratories
Bristol-Myers Squibb	Roche Holding
Dr. Reddy' s	Sanofi
GlaxoSmithKline	Shire
Johnson & Johnson	Takeda Pharmaceutical
Merck	Teva
Merck KGaA	

HISTORICAL FINANCIALS

Company Type: Public

Income Statement

FYE: December 31

	REVENUE ($ mil.)	NET INCOME ($ mil.)	NET PROFIT MARGIN	EMPLOYEES
12/14	19,615	2,390	12.2%	39,135
12/13	23,113	4,684	20.3%	37,925
12/12	22,603	4,088	18.1%	38,350
12/11	24,286	4,347	17.9%	38,080
12/10	23,076	5,069	22.0%	38,350
Annual Growth	(4.0%)	(17.1%)	—	0.5%

2014 Year-End Financials

Debt ratio: 21.67%
Return on equity: 14.49%
Cash ($ mil.): 4,827
Current ratio: 1.09
Long-term debt ($ mil.): 5,367

No. of shares (mil.): 1,110
Dividends
  Yield: 2.8%
  Payout: 78.0%
Market value ($ mil.): 76,622

	STOCK PRICE ($) FY Close	P/E High/Low		PER SHARE ($) Earnings	Dividends	Book Value
12/14	68.99	33	23	2.23	1.96	13.84
12/13	51.00	13	11	4.32	1.96	15.79
12/12	49.32	15	10	3.66	1.96	12.91
12/11	41.56	11	9	3.90	1.96	11.70
12/10	35.04	8	7	4.58	1.96	10.78
Annual Growth	18.5%	—	—	(16.5%)	(0.0%)	6.5%

Lincoln National Corp.

Who better to trust with your nest egg than the company that took its name from Honest Abe? Lincoln National which operates as Lincoln Financial Group provides retirement planning and life insurance to individuals and employers in the form of annuities 401k and savings plans and a variety of life dental and disability insurance products. It does business through such subsidiaries as Lincoln National Life Insurance and Lincoln Life & Annuity Company of New York. The company is also active in the investment management business offering individual and institutional clients such financial services as pension plans trusts and mutual funds through its subsidiaries.

Operations

Lincoln Financial serves about 91000 group insurance and retirement plan contracts which have a total of some 8.7 million participants. The group has a total of some $218 billion in assets under management. Its operations are divided into segments including annuities retirement plan services life insurance and group protection.

The largest segment life insurance (44% of sales in 2014) offers term products a linked benefit product and a critical illness rider. The annuities segment (28% of sales) offers fixed and variable annuities. Group protection offers non-medical policies primarily term life dental and disability products to the employer market. Retirement plan services (8% of sales) provides employers with plans and services primarily in the defined contribution retirement plan marketplace.

Sales and Marketing

Lincoln Financial Network distributes the company's products through a network of some 8500 agents while Lincoln Financial Distributors is the company's wholesale distributor serving brokers planners agents third-party administrators financial advisors and other intermediaries.

The company also markets its products through online and television advertising.

Lincoln Financial serves more than 17 million customers.

Financial Analysis

Lincoln Financial has seen revenue growth over the past five years. In 2014 revenue grew 13% to $13.5 billion due to growth in life insurance an annuities which saw increased premiums fee income and net investment income. As a result profits rose 22% to $1.5 billion that year.

Cash flow from operations more than tripled to $2.5 billion in 2014 as a result of successful trading securities purchases net sales and maturities and other factors.

Historically Lincoln Financial's investment income has accounted for more of its revenues than its insurance premiums or fees. This can be pretty sweet when the market is high but when investments lost their luster during the recession Lincoln Financial's net income suffered. Also fees tied to the value of variable accounts dropped down during that time further weakening the company's income. As the market improved Lincoln Financial's investments perked up variable accounts revived and so did the company's net income.

Strategy

To meet the challenges of difficult economic times in the market Lincoln Financial has adopted a strategy to strengthen its business that includes investing in high-quality corporate securities to reduce asset risk; escalating share repurchases and debt repayment; repricing life and annuity products to guarantee new business that is profitable; and making significant investments in businesses to increase its future earning power.

The company leverages its powerful distribution network to enter new markets while maintaining its position in existing markets. It targets the fastest-growing industry segments while steering away from long-term guarantee products.

Going forward Lincoln Financial will explore additional financial strategies to address the statutory reserve strain that comes with its term and universal life products that contain secondary guarantees. It will shift its business to focus on products with shorter duration liabilities and more limited liabilities. The company also plans to invest in technology and distribution to increase margins.

Recent new products introduced by Lincoln Financial include hybrid benefit riders Lincoln Lifetime Income Advantage 2.0 and Lincoln Lifetime Income Advantage 2.0 (Managed Risk) and its Lincoln LifeReserve Indexed universal life offering all of which it launched in 2014.

The company sold its Lincoln Financial Media subsidiary which included 15 radio stations to Entercom Communications in 2015. The media arm was a legacy from its acquisition of Jefferson-Pilot but Lincoln exited the industry to focus on insurance.

Normal 0   false false false   EN-US
X-NONE X-NONE

HISTORY

Wilbur Wynant a sort of Johnny Appleseed of shady fraternal benefits societies arrived in Fort Wayne Indiana in 1902. He persuaded several respected businessmen and professionals to help him found the Fraternal Assurance Society of America an assessable mutual organization in which surviving members contributed to the death benefits of deceased members. Wynant absconded within a couple of years and the local organizers restructured the society's remains as a stock company in 1905. To clean up the organization's reputation they obtained permission from Abraham Lincoln's son Robert to use his father's name and image.

In 1905 when the company wrote its first policy it had three agents including its leading executive Arthur Hall. By 1911 the company had 106 agents. Careful risk assessment was an early hallmark of the company and allowed it to accept business that other companies rejected based on more superficial analysis.

From a very early period the company grew through acquisitions. WWI increased claims but not as much as the global flu epidemic that followed the war. Organic growth continued in the 1920s.

Death and disability claims increased abnormally during the Depression and the company's underwriting became more stringent. Lincoln National used the financial turmoil of the period to buy other troubled insurers. Reinsurance became the firm's primary line until after WWII.

The company bought up other firms in the 1950s and 1960s and in 1968 it formed holding company Lincoln National. Soon it began diversifying buying Chicago Title and Trust (1969; sold 1985) as well as more life and reinsurance companies. Lincoln National also went into the health benefits business setting up its own HMO and investing in EMPHESYS (which it took public in 1994 divesting the remainder of its stock in 1995).

The collapse of the real estate market in many areas nicked results in the late 1980s and in 1990 the company accepted an infusion of cash from Dai-Ichi Mutual Life Insurance. Property/casualty results were hurt in the early 1990s by an unprecedented string of natural disasters.

With the growth of retirement savings from baby boomers hitting their 50s the company shifted gears into wealth management. In 1995 Lincoln National expanded its investment management capacities by purchasing Delaware Management Holdings and Laurentian Financial Group. The next year it bought the group tax-qualified annuity business of disability insurer UNUM (now UNUMProvident) and in 1997 bought Voyageur Fund Managers a tax-free-bond fund business. The company also took a 49% stake in a Mexican insurance company owned by Grupo Financiero Santander Serfin (sold in 2000). It sold its 83% interest in property/casualty firm American States Financial in 1996.

Lincoln National bought CIGNA's annuity and individual life insurance business and Aetna's US individual life insurance operations in 1998. It reorganized that year to help it absorb these businesses causing earnings to take a substantial hit.

In 1999 after nearly a century in the heartland Lincoln National moved its headquarters to Philadelphia. Other transformations included the sale of its individual disability income business in 1999. In 2001 it sold its reinsurance operations to Swiss Re to re-focus on wealth and asset accumulation products and services. The reshaping continued in 2002 when the company acquired employee benefits record-keeping firm The Administrative Management Group.

Lincoln National completed a merger/acquisition of Jefferson-Pilot in early 2006. The $7.5 billion deal combined the Lincoln Financial Group with the Jefferson Pilot Financial group (the operating brand for Jefferson-Pilot Corporation) and created a new company operating as Lincoln Financial Group. Led by management from both former organizations the new group expanded insurance and financial products offerings and national retail and wholesale distribution platforms.

EXECUTIVES

President Insurance and Retirement Solutions, Mark E. Konen, age 55, $625,250 total compensation

President CEO Director and President Lincoln Financial Group, Dennis R. Glass, age 65, $1,135,000 total compensation

EVP Chief Human Resources Officer and Enterprise Communications, Lisa M. Buckingham, age 49

President Annuity Solutions Lincoln Financial Distributors and Lincoln Financial Network, Wilford H. (Will) Fuller, age 44, $644,008 total compensation

EVP and CFO, Randal J. Freitag, age 52, $575,384 total compensation

EVP and Chief Investment Officer, Ellen Cooper, age 50

EVP and General Counsel, Adam G. Ciongoli, age 46, $353,077 total compensation

Vice President Of Sales, Robert Risk

Vice President Managing Director Portfolio Management Analytic, Paul Narayanan

Vice President Communications, Lujean Smith

Vice President Internet Business and Technology, Ann Colony

Assistant Vice President Income Product Market Development, Daniel (Dan) Herr

Assistant Vice President and Director, Linda Fairbanks

Assistant Vice President, Marlene Hammond

Senior Vice President Associate General Counsel And Litigation, Kelley Grady

Assistant Vice President, James Gasparotto

Assistant Vice President Information Technology Shared Services, Dave Vachon

Vice President, Roberta (Bobbi) Tielinen

Second Vice President Infrastructure Operations, Ricklin Nelson

Assistant Vice President Enterprise Information Technology Project Management Office, Patricia (Pat) Wells

Associate Vice President Enrollment Services, Joe Mitchell

Vice President Managing Director Tactical Strategies Fixed Inc, Jayson Bronchetti

Assistant Vice President Senior Employee Relations, Mary Carruth

Assistant Vice President Health, Audrey Im

Assistant Vice President Data Research and Analytics, Crystal Tucker

Vice President and Associate Actuary, Kris Kattmann

Assistant Vice President Facilities Management, Bryon Cooper

Senior Vice President Human Resources, George Murphy

Senior Vice President Markets And Invest, Andrew (Andy) Yorks

Assistant Vice President And Valuation Actuary, William (Bill) Panyard

Vp-mktg & Comm Of Insurance, Diane Russell

Assistant Vice President, Mike Link

National Account Manager, Matt Jasa

National Account Manager, Jeff Piccolo

Regional Vice President, Laura Degnon

Assistant Vice President Recruiter And Human Resources Business Partner, Karen Bradbury

Assistant Vice President Customer Service, Jim Rooney

Assistant Vice President Financial Reporting And Expense Controls, Kathy Tibke
Associate Vice President, Michael Selden
Vice President Of Sales, Marie Cochrane
Vice President Of Application Development, Srinivas Jonnada
Assistant Vice President Treasury, Brad Jeffrey
Assistant Vice President, Brian Gardner
Vice President and Branch Manager, Melissa (Mel) Hidalgo
Vice President Systems Development, Rebecca Trump
Assistant Vice President Corporate Digital Strategy, Brian Moody
Assistant Vice President, Loraine Bernard
Vice President, Brian Jenkins
Assistant Vice President Business Strategy, Barbara (Barb) Rayll
Vice President Marketing, Garethe Rich
Vice President, Nancy Smith
Vice President Operations, Emma Ladd
Assistant Vice President Senior Product Manager, Brian Wilson
Assistant Vice President Product Solutions Strategist, Andrew (Andy) Eldredge
Assistant Vice President Digital, James Tierney
Assistant Vice President, Teresa Norris-Phillips
Senior Vice President Of National Sales, Michael Hall
Vice President And Chief Counsel Annuities, Lawrence A Samplatsky
Assistant Vice President Senior Human Resources Business Partner, Kelly Pippett
Assistant Vice President, Laurie Scotti
Assistant Vice President Continuous Improvement, Keith Wagoner
Vice President Product Compliance, Pamela (Pam) Telfer
Assistant Vice President, Miko Pickett
Vice President Asset Liability Management, Nathan Hardiman
Assistant Vice President Business Intelligence Finance, Elizabeth (Beth) Keller
Second Vice President Corporate Actuary, Mike Antrobus
Assistant Vice President Underwriting And New Business Account Executive, Sandy Pope
Vice President Digital Strategy And Planning, Philip Bossy
Assistant Vice President Market Intelligence, Jamie Ranicar
Assistant Vice President Internal Audit, Wanda Pritchett
Vice President of Information Technology, Stephen (Steve) Hamilton
Vice President Talent Management, Nancy Rogers
Vice President, Nicole Delimitros
Vice President It, Scott Hardin
Senior Counsel And Assistant Vice President, Wayne Mcclain
Vice President Retirement Strategic Planning and Governance, Lisa Kinniry
Assistant Vice President Life and Annuity Strategy, Thomas (Thom) Goas
Assistant Vice President Corporate Actuary and ERM Lead, John (Jack) Martin
Assistant Vice President Meetings And Incentives, Richard (Dick) Gladson
Vice President, Kristi Harkenrider
Vice President Finance, John (Jack) Luviano
Vice President Absence Management Integrated Health Strat, Katie Dunnington
Vice President Sales, Ryan D Lommel
Assistant Vice President Digital Application Management, Mary Yates
Assistant Vice President, Frank Asplund
Assistant Vice President, Marc Tomlinson
Vice President And Managing Director Inv, Patrick (Paddy) McAllister
Chairman, William H. Cunningham, age 71

Board Member, Betty Nugent
Board Member, Fred Parmesano
Board Member, Marilyn Ondecker
Treasurer, Michael (Mel) Conte
Board Member, David McDunn
Auditors: Ernst & Young LLP

LOCATIONS

HQ: Lincoln National Corp.
150 N. Radnor Chester Road, Suite A305, Radnor, PA 19087
Phone: 484 583-1400
Web: www.lfg.com

PRODUCTS/OPERATIONS

2014 Revenues

	$ mil.	% of total
Insurance		
Life insurance	6,003	44
Group protection	2,445	18
Retirement		
Annuities	3,746	27
Retirement plan services	1,090	8
Other operations	435	3
Realized losses	(135)	-
Total	13,554	100

Selected Subsidiaries

First Penn-Pacific Life Insurance Company
Hampshire Funding Inc.
Jefferson-Pilot Investments Inc.
Lincoln Financial Investment Services Corporation
Lincoln Financial Securities Corporation
Lincoln Insurance Services Limited
Lincoln Investment Management Company
The Lincoln National Life Insurance Company
Lincoln National Management Corporation
Lincoln National Reinsurance Company (Barbados) Limited
Lincoln Reinsurance Company of Bermuda Limited

COMPETITORS

AEGON
AIG
AXA Financial
American Equity Investment Life Holding Company
Guardian Life
ING
John Hancock Financial Services
MassMutual
MetLife
Nationwide Financial
New York Life
Northwestern Mutual
Pacific Mutual
Principal Financial
Prudential
TIAA-CREF
The Hartford
Torchmark
Unum Group

HISTORICAL FINANCIALS

Company Type: Public

Income Statement

FYE: December 31

	ASSETS ($ mil.)	NET INCOME ($ mil.)	INCOME AS % OF ASSETS	EMPLOYEES
12/14	253,377	1,515	0.6%	11,046
12/13	236,945	1,244	0.5%	10,539
12/12	218,869	1,313	0.6%	9,742
12/11	202,906	294	0.1%	9,723
12/10	193,824	980	0.5%	9,500
Annual Growth	6.9%	11.5%	—	3.8%

2014 Year-End Financials

Debt ratio: 2.18%
Return on equity: 10.38%
Cash ($ mil.): 3,919
Current ratio: —
Long-term debt ($ mil.): —

No. of shares (mil.): 256
Dividends
Yield: 1.1%
Payout: 11.3%
Market value ($ mil.): 14,795

	STOCK PRICE ($) FY Close	P/E High/Low		PER SHARE ($) Earnings	Dividends	Book Value
12/14	57.67	10	8	5.67	0.64	61.35
12/13	51.62	11	6	4.52	0.48	51.17
12/12	25.90	6	4	4.56	0.32	55.17
12/11	19.42	34	15	0.92	0.20	48.62
12/10	27.81	13	8	2.54	0.04	40.56
Annual Growth	20.0%	—	—	22.2%	100.0%	10.9%

Linn Energy LLC

It's a Linn-Linn situation. Founder and chairman Michael Linn's namesake company Linn Energy has successfully drilled for oil and natural gas across the US although in recent years the company has narrowed its focus to exploiting assets in the Mid-Continent California and the Permian Basin. In 2012 the company reported proved reserves of 4.8 trillion cu. ft. of natural gas equivalent. The company operates about 70% of its more than 15800 gross productive wells. In addition to its core oil and gas activities Linn Energy pursues an aggressive hedging strategy to reduce the effects of oil price volatility on its annual income.

IPO

Looking for a new way to raise additional equity capital in 2012 the company formed Linn Co. LLC and launched an initial public offering which raised $1.1 billion. Linn Co. LLC was formed to buy shares in Linn Energy and expand its investor base. Linn Co. LLC used its IPO proceeds to help fund Linn Energy's acquisition strategy.

Geographic Reach

The company's oil and gas properties are located primarily in the Mid-Continent the Permian Basin Michigan California and the Williston Basin.

Sales and Marketing

In 2012 oil natural gas and NGL sales to Enbridge Energy Partners and DCP Midstream Partners accounted for 24% and 13% respectively of Linn Energy's total production volumes or 37% of the aggregate.

Financial Performance

Linn Energy's revenues increased by 9% in 2012 primarily due to higher marketing revenues and revenues generated from the newly acquired Jayhawk natural gas processing plant. Oil natural gas and NGL sales grew by 38% to $1.6 billion thanks to higher production volumes partially offset by lower commodity prices.

In 2012 the company posted a net loss in $386.6 million in 2012 (compared to net income of $438 million in 2011) due to higher operating expenses.

Strategy

Linn Energy has pursued a strategy of buying mature properties and extending the life of these natural gas fields by workovers and improved field operations including the use of additional production equipment and drilling activities.

To raise cash in 2015 the company sold its remaining position in Howard County in the Permian Basin for a contract price of $281 million.

In 2012 the company teamed up with an Anadarko Petroleum affiliate forming a $400 million joint venture to develop a carbon dioxide enhanced oil recovery project in the Salt Creek field in the Powder River Basin.

Mergers and Acquisitions

Dramatically growing its asset base in 2013 the company bought Berry Petroleum for $4.3 billion. The deal increased Linn Energy's estimated proved reserves and production by approximately 34% and 30% respectively.

In 2013 Linn Energy acquired oil and natural gas properties located in the Permian Basin for $525 million.

In 2012 Linn Energy acquired BP's Hugoton properties in Kansas for $1.2 billion and properties in East Texas from a separate company for $175 million. Later that year it agreed to another purchase from BP this time 12500 acres in Wyoming's Jonah Field. Linn paid more than $1 billion for the property which includes 750 producing wells and more than 730 billion cu. ft. of natural gas equivalent.

In 2011 the company bought additional assets in the Bakken shale and the Permian Basin (including the Cleveland play) for $434 million.

EXECUTIVES

Chairman President and CEO, Mark E. Ellis, age 59, $900,000 total compensation

EVP and COO, Arden L. Walker, age 56, $500,000 total compensation

EVP and CFO LINN Energy and Linnco LLC, David B. Rottino, age 49, $470,000 total compensation

SVP Houston Division Operations, Jamin B. McNeil, age 49, $375,000 total compensation

Vice President Marketing, Mark Cahill

Senior Vice President, Charlene Ripley

Vice President, Yancey Bishop

Vice President Investor Relations, Clay Jeansonne

Senior Vice President, Tanya Smith

Secretary Treasurer, Steven Sellers

Auditors: KPMG LLP

LOCATIONS

HQ: Linn Energy LLC
600 Travis, Suite 5100, Houston, TX 77002
Phone: 281 840-4000
Web: www.linnenergy.com

PRODUCTS/OPERATIONS

2012 Sales

	$ mil.	% of total
Oil natural gas & NGLs	1,601	90
Gains on derivatives	124	7
Marketing	37	2
Other	10	1
Total	**1,774**	**100**

COMPETITORS

Abraxas Petroleum	PDC Energy
Anadarko Petroleum	Pioneer Natural
Cimarex	Resources
Concho	SandRidge Energy
Energen	

HISTORICAL FINANCIALS

Company Type: Public

Income Statement

FYE: December 31

	REVENUE ($ mil.)	NET INCOME ($ mil.)	NET PROFIT MARGIN	EMPLOYEES
12/14	4,983	(451)	—	1,800
12/13	2,331	(691)	—	1,645
12/12	1,774	(386)	—	1,136
12/11	1,622	438	27.0%	824
12/10	772	(114)	—	700
Annual Growth	**59.4%**	**—**	**—**	**26.6%**

2014 Year-End Financials

Debt ratio: 62.69%	No. of shares (mil.): 331
Return on equity: (-8.66%)	Dividends
Cash ($ mil.): 1	Yield: 28.6%
Current ratio: 1.74	Payout: —
Long-term debt ($ mil.): 10,295	Market value ($ mil.): 3,363

	STOCK PRICE ($) FY Close	P/E High/Low		PER SHARE ($) Earnings	Dividends	Book Value
12/14	10.13	—	—	(1.40)	2.90	13.69
12/13	30.79	—	—	(2.94)	2.90	17.87
12/12	35.24	—	—	(1.92)	2.87	18.88
12/11	37.91	16	13	2.51	2.70	19.33
12/10	37.49	—	—	(0.80)	2.55	17.53
Annual Growth	**(27.9%)**	**—**	**—**	**—**	**3.3%**	**(6.0%)**

Lithia Motors, Inc.

Acquisitive Lithia Motors is a big hungry fish among US auto retailers. The company operates about 130 stores in select markets in more than a dozen states. The firm sells 30 brands of new domestic and imported vehicles and all brands of used cars and trucks through its stores and online. Chrysler (Dodge Jeep) and GM (Chevrolet Cadillac Saab) are the top sellers. Lithia Motors also offers financing and replacement parts and operates about 18 collision-repair centers. Unlike most consolidators it prefers to pay cash (rather than stock) for dealerships in smaller markets. Chairman Sidney DeBoer through Lithia Holding Co. controls Lithia Motors which was founded in 1946 by his father Walt.

Geographic Reach

Lithia sells 31 brands of new vehicles and all brands of used vehicles at 130 stores in 14 US states. Its dealerships are primarily located in the West and Midwest including more than a half a dozen dealerships in Alaska and nearly two dozen in Oregon. Texas is Lithia's biggest market accounting for 21% of the company's total sales.

Operations

The company has three segments: Domestic Import and Luxury.The Domestic segment is comprised of retail automotive franchises that sell new vehicles manufactured by Chrysler General Motors and Ford. The Import segment covers retail automotive franchises that sell new vehicles made by Honda Toyota Subaru Nissan and Volkswagen. The Luxury segment sells new vehicles manufactured made by BMW Mercedes-Benz and Lexus. The franchises in each segment also sell used vehicles parts and automotive services and automotive finance and insurance products.

Sales and Marketing

The company's advertising expense was $46.7 million in 2014 $39.6 million in 2013 and $31.9 million in 2012.Lithia sells through its stores and online website. It also maintains mobile versions of its websites and a mobile application in anticipation of greater adoption of mobile technology.It posts its inventory on major new and used vehicle listing services (cars.com autotrader.com kbb.com edmunds.com eBay craigslist etc.) to reach online shoppers. It also employs search engine optimization search engine marketing and online display advertising (including re-targeting) to reach more online prospects.

Financial Performance

The company's net sales have seen a consistent upward trend since 2010.In 2014 Lithia's net sales increased by 35% to increased sales from new ve-

hicle and used vehicle retail and finance and insurance.New vehicle sales improved due to volume growth. In 2014 each of Lithia's stores sold 56 retail used vehicle units per month compared to 53 retail used vehicle units per store per month in 2013 thanks to a larger number of late model vehicles being available in the marketplace.The increases in finance and insurance sales in 2014 were driven by higher vehicle sales volumes and prices.Lithia's net income has also been trending upward in recent years.In 2014 net income increased by 31% due to higher sales and income from discontinued operations partially offset by increased selling general and administrative expenses.That year the company's net cash provided by the operating activities decreased by $1.7 million (from $32.1 million in 2013) primarily due to change in trade payables accrued liabilities and other assets.

Strategy

Lithia Motors relies on acquisitions to increase its revenue and diversify its brand portfolio. Indeed the company has completed more than 100 acquisitions since it went public in 1996. Historically the auto dealer has bought about 10 franchises a year expanding mostly in its western base. However an acquisition in 2014 has extended Lithia's reach eastward to New York and New Jersey. Also in 2014 the company acquired a Ford store and opened a new Chrysler Jeep Dodge store in Wasilla Alaska.

The auto dealer relies heavily on GM and Chrysler brand models which combined accounted for nearly 50% of 2013 sales. The deep recession and turmoil among domestic automakers especially GM and Chrysler caused Lithia to revise its strategy by reducing its dependence on domestic manufacturers. However with the US economy and auto industry much improved Lithia is once again in the market for domestic dealerships. The auto dealer targets mid-sized regional markets for domestic and import franchises and metropolitan markets for its luxury dealerships. Lithia is also looking to body shops for growth. Currently the company operates 18 collision repair centers five of which are in Texas five in Oregon two in Idaho and one each in Alaska Washington Montana Iowa Nevada and New Jersey.The company strives for diversification in its products services brands and geographic locations to insulate us from market risk and to maintain profitability. It has developed a centralized support structure to reduce store level administrative functions. This allows store personnel to focus on providing a positive customer experience.Lithia's near-term goal for used vehicles is to retail an average of 75 units per store per month. In 2014 its stores sold an average of 56 retail used units per month. It believes used vehicles represent a significant area for organic growth.

Mergers and Acquisitions

In 2015 Lithia acquired Bitterroot Ford in Missoula Montana its first Ford store in the state.

In 2014 Lithia acquired DCH Auto Group one of the nation's largest dealer groups with about $2.3 billion in annualized revenue for $364 million. The purchase of DCH added 27 stores in Southern California New Jersey and New York and transformed Lithia into a national player.Other acquisitions in 2014 included Island Honda in Kahului Hawaii; Honolulu Buick GMC Cadillac and Honolulu Volkswagen in Honolulu Hawaii; Stockton Volkswagen in Stockton California; Corpus Christi Ford in Corpus Christi Texas; Beaverton GMC Buick and Portland Cadillac in Portland Oregon; Bellingham GMC Buick in Bellingham Washington; and Harris Nissan in Clovis California.

Company Background

In 2012 the company acquired Jerry Chambers Chevrolet Cadillac in Bellingham Washington and also bought Bitterroot Toyota in Missoula Montana. In 2011 Lithia bought Fresno Subaru and BMW Mini and Mercedes stores in Portland Oregon.

Lithia Motors was founded in 1946 by Walt DeBoer as a Chrysler-Plymouth-Dodge dealership in Ashland Oregon. Walt's son Sidney is its chairman and grandson Bryan is president and CEO of the growing auto dealer.

EXECUTIVES

President and CEO, Bryan B. DeBoer, age 48, $840,000 total compensation
SVP and CFO, Christopher (Chris) Holzshu, age 41, $420,000 total compensation
SVP Retail Operations, Scott Hillier, age 52, $420,000 total compensation
VP Information Technology and CIO, Mark Smith
Regional Manager Vice President, Ken Wright
Vice President Finance, Jd Spruill
Chairman, Sidney B. (Sid) DeBoer, age 71
Vice Chairman, M. L. (Dick) Heimann, age 71
Auditors: KPMG LLP

LOCATIONS

HQ: Lithia Motors, Inc.
150 N. Bartlett Street, Medford, OR 97501
Phone: 541 776-6401
Web: www.lithia.com

2014 Stores

	No.
Oregon	24
California	30
Texas	17
New Jersey	10
Alaska	9
Montana	8
Washington	7
Idaho	5
Iowa	5
Nevada	4
North Dakota	3
New York	3
Hawaii	3
New Mexico	2
Total	**130**

PRODUCTS/OPERATIONS

2014 Sales

	$ mil.	% of total
Domestic	2,569	48
Import	1,889	35
Luxury	926	17
Corporate and other	4	-
Total	**5,390**	**100**

2014 Sales

	$ mil.	% of total
New vehicles	3,077	57
Used vehicle retail	1,362	25
Service body & parts	512	9
Used vehicle wholesale	195	4
Finance & insurance	190	4
Fleet & other	52	1
Total	**5,390**	**100**

COMPETITORS

Ancira	Group 1 Automotive
AutoNation	Internet Brands
Autobytel	McCombs Enterprises
CarMax	Penske Automotive
David McDavid Auto Group	Group
Gillman Companies	Sonic Automotive

HISTORICAL FINANCIALS

Company Type: Public

Income Statement

FYE: December 31

	REVENUE ($ mil.)	NET INCOME ($ mil.)	NET PROFIT MARGIN	EMPLOYEES
12/14	5,390	138	2.6%	8,827
12/13	4,005	106	2.6%	5,700
12/12	3,316	80	2.4%	5,403
12/11	2,699	58	2.2%	4,397
12/10	2,131	13	0.6%	4,039
Annual Growth	**26.1%**	**78.3%**	**—**	**21.6%**

2014 Year-End Financials

Debt ratio: 63.16%	No. of shares (mil.): 26
Return on equity: 22.97%	Dividends
Cash ($ mil.): 29	Yield: 0.7%
Current ratio: 1.12	Payout: 12.8%
Long-term debt ($ mil.): 609	Market value ($ mil.): 2,274

	STOCK PRICE ($) FY Close	P/E High/Low		PER SHARE ($) Earnings	Dividends	Book Value
12/14	86.69	18	10	5.26	0.61	25.66
12/13	69.42	18	10	4.05	0.49	20.65
12/12	37.42	12	7	3.07	0.47	16.67
12/11	21.86	11	6	2.21	0.26	14.14
12/10	14.29	27	10	0.52	0.15	12.18
Annual Growth	**56.9%**		**—**	**78.3%**	**42.0%**	**20.5%**

Live Nation Entertainment, Inc.

Live Nation Entertainment holds center stage as the world's largest ticket seller and promoter of live entertainment. The company significantly expanded its ticketing services with the purchase of Ticketmaster Entertainment. The 2010 deal worth some $889 million created a powerful live-music conglomerate. The firm owns or operates about 160 venues in North America and Europe. Annually about 520 million people attend some 250000 Live Nation events. Live Nation also owns House of Blues venues through HOB Entertainment and dozens of prestigious concert halls. In addition Live Nation owns a stake in about 280 artists' music including albums tours and merchandise.

Geographic Reach

Live Nation owns operates or leases about 160 venues located throughout the world. The company generated about 65% of revenue from domestic operations during fiscal 2014.

Operations

Live Nation's reportable segments are Concerts Ticketing Artist Nation and Sponsorship & Advertising. In fiscal 2014 about 90% of its revenue came from its Concerts and Ticketing segments.

Its Concerts segment involves global promotion of live music events in its owned and operated venues and in rented third-party venues the operation and management of music venues and the production of music festivals across the world.

The Ticketing segment is primarily an agency business that sells tickets for events on behalf of its clients and retains a convenience charge and order processing fee for its services.

The company's Artist Nation segment provides management services to music artists in exchange for a commission on the earnings of these artists.

Its Sponsorship & Advertising segment employs a sales force that creates and maintains relationships with sponsors that allow businesses to reach customers through Live Nation's concert venue artist relationship and ticketing assets including advertising on its websites.

Sales and Marketing

Live Nation promotes its events and sells tickets through websites (www.livenation.com and www.ticketmaster.com). The company spent about $243 million on advertising and promotions during fiscal 2014. That was an increase compared to the $224 million Live Nation spent on advertising during 2013.

Financial Performance

The company's revenue increased by 6% to about $6.8 billion in fiscal 2014 up from $6.4 billion in fiscal 2013. The overall increase in revenue was primarily due to increases in its Concerts and Ticketing segments. The increase in Concerts revenue resulted from strategic priorities to grow owned and operated amphitheater and European festival profitability expand its portfolio of electronic dance music and other new festivals and expand into new geographic markets.

Despite the increase in revenue Live Nation recorded a net loss in fiscal 2014 due to direct operating expenses selling general and administrative expenses depreciation and amortization and income tax expenses.

Strategy

Live Nation has used joint ventures to expand its operations. The company continues to strengthen its core operations further expanding into additional global markets and optimizing cost structure. Its strategy is to expand its concert platform by adding artists and venues drive conversion of ticket sales through social and mobile channels and work to grow its sponsorship and advertising revenue.

Mergers and Acquisitions

The company has also used acquisitions to fuel its growth. In 2014 Live Nation's Ticketmaster acquired mobile-based Do-It-Yourself ticketing platform Eventjoy. Ticketmaster also acquired Brussels-based Belgian ticketing company Sherpa.be during 2014. In early 2015 Live Nation Sweden acquired SPG Live.

Ownership

Media conglomerate Liberty Media currently owns about 27% of Live Nation but hopes to eventually increase its share to about 35%.

HISTORY

Robert Sillerman began his career teaching advertisers how to reach young consumers. He started investing in radio and TV stations and founded SFX Broadcasting (named for a scrambling of his initials) in 1992. In early 1997 the firm entered the live entertainment field with the formation of SFX Concerts and the purchase of concert promoter Delsener/Slater.

When SFX Broadcasting agreed to be bought in 1997 by Capstar Broadcasting 87% controlled by investment firm Hicks Muse Tate & Furst (now HM Capital) SFX Entertainment was formed to house the live entertainment operations (it was spun off in 1998). In 1998 the company continued its rapid acquisition spree with the purchases of sports marketing and management team FAME New England concert promoter Don Law and national concert producer PACE Entertainment.

In 1999 the company bought concert promoter The Cellar Door Companies (which almost doubled SFX's size) sports marketing firm Integrated Sports International sporting event management company The Marquee Group sports talent agency Hendricks Management 50% of urban-music producer A.H. Enterprises and troubled theatrical producer Livent. SFX also made its first foray abroad through its purchase of Apollo Leisure a UK-based live entertainment firm. The company rolled all of its sports talent and marketing businesses into a new division SFX Sports Group that year.

In 2000 SFX jumped on the other side of the acquisition train when it was bought by radio station owner Clear Channel Communications for about $4 billion. Sillerman stepped down as chairman and CEO and was replaced by Clear Channel EVP Brian Becker. Later that year SFX acquired Philadelphia-based concert promoter and venue operator Electric Factory Concerts; Core Audience Entertainment Canada's second-largest concert promoter and events marketer; and the Cotter Group a North Carolina-based motorsports marketing agency.

In 2001 SFX acquired a majority interest in the International Hot Rod Association. It also bought professional golf talent agency Signature Sports Group. Later that year the company changed its name to Clear Channel Entertainment. It also continued expansion into Europe with the acquisition of Trident Agency and Milano Concerti music promotion businesses in Italy.

While operating as Clear Channel Entertainment Live Nation spent nearly $2 billion on acquisitions (Pace Entertainment Livent) almost single-handedly consolidating the live entertainment industry.

Before being spun off in December 2005 the company changed its name to CCE Spinco then Live Nation. Also that year Randall Mays became chairman and Michael Rapino replaced Becker as CEO. As part of the Clear Channel spinoff the company relocated from Houston to headquarters in tony Beverly Hills. It trimmed the fat by shutting down operating divisions such as museum exhibitions and music publishing (and laying off about 400 employees in the process) in order to focus on its core businesses of live music concerts venue management and website brand development.

In 2006 the company acquired rival HOB Entertainment for $354 million. Live Nation used the acquisition to expand its presence in the midsized venue business and fill in geographic gaps in its existing amphitheater network. As part of the deal Live Nation gained high-profile House of Blues-branded music venues such as San Francisco's Fillmore Auditorium Jones Beach in New York and London's Apollo Theatre and Wembley Arena. The company subsequently began re-branding many of its midsize clubs "Fillmore" after the San Francisco venue.

The company had in 2005 formed Delirium Concert LP a joint venture with Cirque du Soleil. The Delirium tour began in 2006. The following year Live Nation signed a $120 million deal with pop icon Madonna. Through its North American Music segment in 2007 Live Nation promoted or produced some 10000 live music events including tours for Van Halen Dave Matthews Band and Kenny Chesney. International Music operations for the year included Cirque De Soleil's Delirium as well as UK's Reading Festival. Also in 2007 the company produced global tours for legends such as The Police The Rolling Stones Genesis and The Who and presented some 5000 theatrical performances such as the UK touring production of Chicago through its Global Theater operations.

In 2008 the company divested itself of its North American theatrical assets. Later that year the company signed pacts with U2 and Jay-Z. Michael Cohl chairman and Live Nation Artists chief who spearheaded the deals later resigned over conflicts with CEO Rapino. Also in 2008 the company sold its motor sports operations. In early 2010 the company acquired Ticketmaster Entertainment and

Live Nation changed its name to Live Nation Entertainment.

EXECUTIVES

President House of Blues Entertainment, Ronald (Ron) Bension
EVP General Counsel and Secretary, Michael G. Rowles, age 50, $750,000 total compensation
Co-President North America Concerts, Mark Campana
CEO Music - Europe, Michael (Mike) Rapino, age 50, $2,300,000 total compensation
Chairman Global Music; President Global Touring, Arthur Fogel, age 62
COO, Joe Berchtold, $1,100,000 total compensation
President International and Emerging Markets, Alan Ridgeway, age 48, $730,025 total compensation
CFO, Kathy Willard, age 49, $850,000 total compensation
President Media and Sponsorship, Russell Wallach
President Live Nation Europe - Concerts, John Reid
EVP Mergers and Acquisitions and Strategic Finance, John Hopmans, age 56
President Ticketmaster North America, Jared Smith
Co-President North America Concerts, Bob Roux
President Ticketmaster International, Mark Yovich, age 40
CIO, David Huckabay
Senior Vice President Venue Sponsorships, Marc Abend
Vice President National Sales, Craig Hoover
Vice President Booking, Todd Miller
Vice President Strategic Alliances, Jeff Shaw
Vice President Finance, Katherine Porter
Senior Vice President Investor Relations, Maili Bergman
Vice President, John Loken
Vice President Customer And Member Services, Dan Houghtaling
Vice President Marketing, Beth Cosimi
Senior Vice President Software Engineering, Cameron Murdock
Senior Vice President Digital Media, Erin Yasgar
Vice President of Retail, Allison Meyerson
Vice President Strategic Alliances Live Nation Entertainment, Christopher (Chris) Swope
Vice President Finance, Reuben Sanchez
Vice President Marketing, Danielle Engel
Vice President Regional Sales, Jeff Wallace
Regional Vice President, Larry Wethers
Vice President Corporate Financial Planning, Brian Parisi
Vice President Marketing, Holli Mattison
Vice President, Brad Wavra
Senior Vice President Booking, Emily Simonitsch
Vice President Strategic Alliances, Libby Biason
Vice President Legal Affairs, Ellie Schwimmer
Vice President Brand Marketing, Dave Fortin
Senior Vice President Social Media, Ryan Okum
Vice President Business Development and Strategic Planning, Jon Glickstein
Senior Vice President Of Human Resources, Tracy Wagner
Vice President Operations Manager Oreilly Thunder Jam, Jim Marchyshyn
Executive Vice President Of North American Venues, Ned Collett
Vice President Marketing Solutions, Lisa Lugo
Executive Vice President, Wilson Rogers
Executive Vice President National Alliances, Darin Wolf
Vice President Legal And Business Affairs, Chris Laffoon
Senior Vice President Relationship and Loyalty Marketing, Phil Seward
Vice President Marketing, David Fortin
Vice President Tour Operations, Craig Evans

Vice President M and A Strategic Finance, Edward (Ed) Lee
Vice President Booking, Adam Cohen
Vice President, Joseph (Jo) Ventura
Senior Vice President Information Technology Systems, Jon Greenwood
Vice President Of Business Development, Frank Gutierrez
Vice President Marketing, Jim Bozzi
Vice President Finance, Carolyn Specht
Vice President Production, Craig Goetsch
Vice President Sales, Joel Wolinsky
Regional Vice President, Michael Myers
Senior Vice President, Richard Levy
Regional Vice President Premium Seat Sales, Kate Walsh
Senior Vice President, Darren Mcinnes
Vice President Media Director National Marketing, Julia Heiser
Vice President Purchasing, Gene Surh
Vice President Latin Programming Touring, Manuel Moran
Vice President Planning, George Duran
Senior Vice President, Eric Thorson
Regional Vice President, Danny Eaton
Vice President Digital Sales East, Jeremy Levine
Vice President Sponsorship Sales, Tobias Ekman
Vice President and Controller, Bill Janney
Vice President Finance, Frank Brayer
Senior Vice President Marketing, Joey Scoleri
Vice President Finance National Tourin, Lisa Howe
Vice President User Experience, Jacki Remus
Vice President Production, Leslie Holland
Vice President Risk Management, Jan Berger
Vice President Legal Affairs, Sheila Small
Vice President Special Events, Nickole Bruner
Senior Vice President Human Resources, Laura Morton-rowe
Vice President Booking, Marcel Thimot
Vice President Marketing, Brad Locker
Vice President, Ted Mankin
Senior Vice President Of Government Relations, Becky Relic
Vice President Accounting, Darrick McFarlin
Executive Vice President, Felix Mussenden
Vice President Of Engineering, Dennis Harvey
Vice President Touring, Craig Sneiderman
Senior Vice President, Stacey Harper
Executive Vice President Business Development North American Concerts, Chris Adelmann
Senior Vice President, Bill Lowe
Senior Vice President Marketing, Jackie Wilgar
Vice President Sales, Jill Jacob
Vice President Information Technology, Dave Gerardi
Senior Vice President and Treasurer, William (Bill) Lowe
Vice President Sales, Aj Silverman
Vice President Systems Engineering, Shakeel Sorathia
Vice President Information Services, James (Jamie) Cheung
Vice President of Marketing, Dave Niedbalski
Chairman, Gregory B. (Greg) Maffei, age 54
Auditors: Ernst & Young LLP

LOCATIONS

HQ: Live Nation Entertainment, Inc.
9348 Civic Center Drive, Beverly Hills, CA 90210
Phone: 310 867-7000
Web: www.livenationentertainment.com

2014 Sales

	$ mil.	% of total
Domestic operations	4,503	66
UK operations	772	11
Other operations	1,592	23
Total	**6,867**	**100**

PRODUCTS/OPERATIONS

2014 Sales

	$ mil.	% of total
Concerts	4,726	68
Ticketing	1,557	22
Artist Nation	389	6
Sponsorship & advertising	300	4
Other revenue	3	0
Elminations	(110)	-
Total	**6,867**	**100**

COMPETITORS

Brillstein
CAA
Dodger Properties
Feld Entertainment
IMG
International Creative Management
Jujamcyn Theaters
Madison Square Garden
Nederlander Producing Company
Octagon
On Stage Entertainment
Palace Sports & Entertainment
Ryman
SMG Management
Shubert Organization
TBA Global
United Talent
Universal Music Group
Warner Music
WestwoodOne
William Morris Endeavor Entertainment

HISTORICAL FINANCIALS

Company Type: Public

Income Statement

FYE: December 31

	REVENUE ($ mil.)	NET INCOME ($ mil.)	NET PROFIT MARGIN	EMPLOYEES
12/14	6,866	(90)	—	14,000
12/13	6,478	(43)	—	7,400
12/12	5,819	(163)	—	7,100
12/11	5,384	(83)	—	6,600
12/10	5,063	(228)	—	6,500
Annual Growth	7.9%	—	—	21.1%

2014 Year-End Financials

Debt ratio: 34.46%
Return on equity: (-6.71%)
Cash ($ mil.): 1,382
Current ratio: 1.13
Long-term debt ($ mil.): 2,015

No. of shares (mil.): 201
Dividends
Yield: —
Payout: —
Market value ($ mil.): 5,253

	STOCK PRICE ($) FY Close	P/E High/Low	PER SHARE ($) Earnings	Dividends	Book Value
12/14	26.11	— —	(0.49)	0.00	6.45
12/13	19.76	— —	(0.22)	0.00	7.06
12/12	9.31	— —	(0.87)	0.00	7.10
12/11	8.31	— —	(0.46)	0.00	7.73
12/10	11.42	— —	(1.39)	0.00	7.83
Annual Growth	23.0%	— —	—	—	(4.8%)

LKQ Corp

Not just any part will do for LKQ. The company specifically distributes replacement parts and components needed to repair passenger cars and trucks. It's one of the leading aftermarket parts suppliers in the US through subsidiary Keystone Automotive (acquired in 2007). LKQ also offers reconditioned remanufactured and refurbished parts including wheels bumpers mirrors and engines as well as recycled parts that are reclaimed from salvage vehicles. Customers include collision repair and mechanical repair shops. Additionally LKQ operates self-service retail yards that allow customers to come in search through and buy recycled auto parts. To diversifyacquisitive LKQ is expanding internationally.

Operations

LKQ operates through three business segments: North America with 61% of revenue; Europe 27% of revenue and Specialty 12% of revenue. The specialty category was formed after the 2014 acquisition of Keystone Specialty. In terms of products aftermarket and other new and refurbished parts made up more than two-thirds of the company's revenue. About 22% comes from recycling remanufactured and related products and services. The Other category was 10%.

The firm's self-service retail operation consists of about 70 auto parts yards in the US and Canada where customers can pay an admission fee to find parts for their vehicles on more than 1000 American and imported cars and light trucks. LKQ's yards also try to play an environmental role by buying unwanted vehicles and recycling and disposing of all fluids and materials. The heavy truck division consists of a dozen locations in North America that sell used trucks and new used and remanufactured heavy truck parts.

Geographic Reach

LKQ generates 70% of its sales in North America. The firm's newest market the UK accounts for nearly 20% of sales with the remainder coming from other countries (Taiwan the Netherlands Belgium France Guatemala Scandinavia Australia and Costa Rica). The company's operations in Mexico include an engine manufacturer and a bumper refurbishing business. LKQ sources most of its aftermarket inventory from auto parts manufacturers and distributors in the US Taiwan and China.

Financial Performance

Fast-growing LKQ's sales have posted double-digit gains in recent years and profits have followed suit. In 2014 sales reached $6.7 billion an increase of 33% versus 2013 while net income climbed 22% to $381.5 million. Sales grew in the US and Europe. Much of the increase came from acquisitions while 7% of the growth was organic. Cash flow from operations dropped to $371 million in 2014 from $428 million the year before partly as a result of more inventory in aftermarket products.

Strategy

Key to the company's growth strategy is acquisitions. Indeed LKQ has completed around 200 acquisitions in the US and abroad since its founding in 1998.

LKQ's geographic diversification strategy appears to be a smashing success. Indeed sales in the UK have increased by about 800% since 2011 making the company less reliant on the US market which now accounts for 68% of sales (vs. 90% in 2011). LKQ is also extending its business to include complementary products such as cooling products and paint.

The company has also worked on its supply chain expanding its network of parts warehouses and dismantling plants in major metros and operating a distribution system that allows for order fulfillment from regional warehouses located across the U.S. and Canada. It also is expanding its branch network in the UK.

Mergers and Acquisitions

In January 2014 the company bought Keystone Automotive Holdings (aka Keystone Specialty) for $455.4 million. Keystone Specialty is a distributor and marketer of specialty aftermarket equipment and accessories in North America that serves six product segments including truck and off-road recreational vehicle and towing. Overall in 2014 LKQ made 22 acquisitions including nine wholesale businesses in North America nine wholesale businesses in Europe two self-service retail operations and two specialty vehicle aftermarket businesses.

In addition to LKQ's purchase of Sator the company made 19 acquisitions in 2013 including 10 wholesale businesses in North America seven wholesale businesses in Europe and two self-service operations.

The firm expects to continue its acquisitive ways in the US and overseas in 2015 and beyond.

EXECUTIVES

CEO and Managing Director European Operations, John S. Quinn, age 56, $500,000 total compensation
President and CEO, Robert L. Wagman, age 51, $800,000 total compensation
EVP and CFO, Dominick P. (Nick) Zarcone
SVP Operations, Steven Greenspan, age 53, $350,000 total compensation
Vice President Finance and Chief Accounting Officer, Michael (Mel) Clark
Senior Vice President, Victor Casini
Vice President Finance And Chief Accounting Officer, Michael S Clark
Vice President of Engineering, Brandon Gee
Chairman, Joseph M. Holsten, age 62
Auditors: Deloitte & Touche LLP

LOCATIONS

HQ: LKQ Corp
500 West Madison Street, Suite 2800, Chicago, IL 60661
Phone: 312 621-1950
Web: www.lkqcorp.com

2014 Sales

	$ mil.	% of total
US	4,499	67
UK	1,321	19
Other	918	14
Total	**6,740**	**100**

PRODUCTS/OPERATIONS

2014 Sales

	$ mil.	% of total
Aftermarket other new & refurbished products	4,613	68
Recycled remanufactured & related products & services	1,473	22
Other	653	10
Total	**6,740**	**100**

2014 Sales

	$ mil % of total
North America	61
Europe	27
Specialty	12
Eliminations	-
Total	**100**

Selected Products & Services

Products
Heavy truck and equipment parts
New aftermarket replacement parts
Paint and body shop supplies and equipment
Rebuilt original equipment replacement parts
Reconditioned original equipment replacement parts
Recycled original equipment auto and truck parts
Remanufactured engines and transmissions
Services
Bulk sales
Fleet services
Insurer services
National part purchase programs
Salvage vehicle disposal
Tire recycling

COMPETITORS

Cardone Industries	Halfords
Delphi Automotive	Jasper Engines
Systems	Kirk' s Automotive
Federal-Mogul	Titan International
Fred Jones Enterprises	U.S. Auto Parts
Hahn Automotive	Valeo

HISTORICAL FINANCIALS

Company Type: Public

Income Statement

FYE: December 31

	REVENUE ($ mil.)	NET INCOME ($ mil.)	NET PROFIT MARGIN	EMPLOYEES
12/14	6,740	381	5.7%	29,500
12/13	5,062	311	6.2%	23,800
12/12	4,122	261	6.3%	20,300
12/11	3,269	210	6.4%	17,900
12/10	2,469	169	6.8%	12,000
Annual Growth	28.5%	22.6%	—	25.2%

2014 Year-End Financials

Debt ratio: 33.45%
Return on equity: 15.05%
Cash ($ mil.): 114
Current ratio: 3.09
Long-term debt ($ mil.): 1,801

No. of shares (mil.): 303
Dividends
  Yield: —
  Payout: —
Market value ($ mil.): 8,533

	STOCK PRICE ($) FY Close	P/E High/Low		PER SHARE ($) Earnings	Dividends	Book Value
12/14	28.12	26	20	1.25	0.00	8.97
12/13	32.90	33	19	1.02	0.00	7.81
12/12	21.10	45	21	0.87	0.00	6.60
12/11	30.08	42	29	0.71	0.00	5.59
12/10	22.72	39	30	0.58	0.00	4.86
Annual Growth	5.5%	—	—	21.2%	—	16.5%

Lockheed Martin Corp.

Auditors: Ernst & Young LLP

LOCATIONS

HQ: Lockheed Martin Corp.
  6801 Rockledge Drive, Bethesda, MD 20817
Phone: 301 897-6000
Web: www.lockheedmartin.com

HISTORICAL FINANCIALS

Company Type: Public

Income Statement

FYE: December 31

	REVENUE ($ mil.)	NET INCOME ($ mil.)	NET PROFIT MARGIN	EMPLOYEES
12/14	45,600	3,614	7.9%	112,000
12/13	45,358	2,981	6.6%	115,000
12/12	47,182	2,745	5.8%	120,000
12/11	46,499	2,655	5.7%	123,000
12/10	45,803	2,926	6.4%	132,000
Annual Growth	(0.1%)	5.4%	—	(4.0%)

2014 Year-End Financials

Debt ratio: 16.64%
Return on equity: 86.90%
Cash ($ mil.): 1,446
Current ratio: 1.11
Long-term debt ($ mil.): 6,169

No. of shares (mil.): 314
Dividends
  Yield: 2.8%
  Payout: 55.5%
Market value ($ mil.): 60,467

	STOCK PRICE ($) FY Close	P/E High/Low		PER SHARE ($) Earnings	Dividends	Book Value
12/14	192.57	17	13	11.21	5.49	10.83
12/13	148.66	16	9	9.13	4.78	15.42
12/12	92.29	11	9	8.36	4.15	0.12
12/11	80.90	10	8	7.81	3.25	3.12
12/10	69.91	11	8	7.94	2.64	10.72
Annual Growth	28.8%	—	—	9.0%	20.1%	0.3%

Loews Corp.

When it comes to diversification Loews definitely has the low-down. The holding company's main interest is insurance through publicly traded subsidiary CNA Financial which offers commercial property/casualty coverage. Other wholly owned and partially owned holdings include hotels in the US and Canada through its Loews Hotels subsidiary. Its energy holdings include contract oil-drilling operator Diamond Offshore Drilling (which operates roughly 35 offshore oil rigs) and interstate natural gas transmission pipeline systems operator Boardwalk Pipeline. Loews is controlled and run by the Tisch family including co-chairmen and cousins Andrew and Jonathan.

HISTORY

In 1946 Larry Tisch who earned a business degree from New York University at age 18 dropped out of Harvard Law to run his parents' New Jersey resort. Younger brother Bob joined him in creating a new entity Tisch Hotels. The company bought two Atlantic City hotels in 1952 quickly making them profitable. Later Tisch purchased such illustrious hotels as the Mark Hopkins The Drake the Belmont Plaza and the Regency.

Moving beyond hotels the brothers bought money-losing companies with poor management. Discarding the management along with underperforming divisions they tightened operational control and eliminated such frills as fancy offices company planes and even memos.

In 1960 Tisch Hotels gained control of MGM's ailing Loew's Theaters to take advantage of their desirable city locations. The company then began demolishing more than 50 stately movie palaces and selling the land to developers. In 1968 the company bought Lorillard the oldest US tobacco company; it shed Lorillard's unprofitable pet food and candy operations and reversed its slipping tobacco market share.

Taking the Loews name in 1971 the company bought CNA Financial in 1974. The Tisch method turned losses of more than $200 million to profits of more than $100 million the very next year. It bought Bulova Watch in 1979 and guided by Larry's son Andrew it gradually returned to profitability.

In the early 1980s Loews entered the energy business by investing in oil supertankers. The company sold its last movie theaters in 1985. Then in 1987 Loews helped CBS fend off a takeover attempt by Ted Turner and ended up with about 25% of the company. Larry became president of the broadcaster.

In 1989 Loews acquired Diamond M Offshore a Texas drilling company and with the acquisition of Odeco Drilling in 1992 the company amassed the world's largest fleet of offshore rigs. The next year Loews grouped its drilling interests as Diamond Offshore Drilling.

In 1994 CNA expanded its insurance empire buying The Continental Corp. The next year Loews sold its interest in CBS and the following year Diamond Offshore Drilling merged with Arethusa (Off-Shore) Limited.

As deft as the Tisch brothers had been in accumulating their riches Larry's bearish investment strategy (short-selling stocks) cost Loews in the late 1990s (more than $900 million alone during 1997's bull market). Larry and Bob retired as co-CEOs at the end of 1998; Larry's son James already president and COO became CEO.

That year Lorillard signed on to the 46-state tobacco lawsuit settlement; the first payment cost the company $325 million (payments continue until 2025). Facing a softened insurance market CNA sold unprofitable lines to focus on commercial insurance; in 1999 it transferred its auto and homeowners lines to Allstate (it continues writing and renewing these policies) and put its life and life reinsurance units up for sale in 2000. Also that year Lorillard was hit with $16 billion of a record-breaking $144 billion punitive damage award in a smokers' class-action suit in Florida. CNA Financial paid out over $450 million in 2001-02 for claims related to the attacks on the World Trade Center.

In 2004 the company continued to expand its natural resource offerings when its subsidiary Boardwalk Pipelines (formerly known as TGT Pipeline) acquired Gulf South Pipeline which operates natural gas pipeline and gathering systems in Texas Louisiana Mississippi Alabama and Florida including several major supply hubs. Loews had acquired gas pipeline operator Texas Gas Transmission in 2003. Texas Gas operates natural gas pipeline systems reaching from the Louisiana Gulf Coast and East Texas north through Louisiana Arkansas Mississippi Tennessee Kentucky Indiana and into Ohio and Illinois.

Tobacco had long been a staple in Loews' portfolio until the company kicked the habit. Prior to quitting the company kept its 62% ownership of Lorillard rolled up as Carolina Group and traded it as a tracking subsidiary. Lorillard which included the Kent Newport and True cigarette brands in the US accounted for more than 20% of Loews' revenues. However after a steady stream of tobacco-related litigation the company spun Lorillard off into an independent public company in 2008 eliminating the Carolina Group and exiting the industry. Additionally while accessories make the outfit in 2008 Loews slipped its Bulova subsidiary off of its wrist and handed it to competitor Citizen Watch for $250 million.

Larry Tisch died at the age of 80 in 2003. Chairman Bob Tisch died of cancer in late 2005. Tisch also was co-owner of the New York Giants of the National Football League.

In keeping with the Loews strategy of acquiring what can be turned around letting go of what can't and the wisdom to know the difference the company spent $4 billion to acquire oil and gas exploration operator HighMount Exploration & Production and disposed of its tobacco interests and Bulova subsidiary in 2008.

EXECUTIVES

Senior Vice President Secretary And General Counsel, Jonathan D Kantor
Chairman and CEO CNA Financial Corporation, Thomas F. (Tom) Motamed
Co-Chairman; Chairman Loews Hotels, Jonathan M. Tisch, age 61, $975,000 total compensation
President and CEO, James S. Tisch, age 63, $975,000 total compensation

Vice Chairman Loews Hotels and Resorts, Paul W. Whetsell, age 64

SVP and CFO, David B. Edelson, age 55, $975,000 total compensation

President and CEO Diamond Offshore Drilling Inc., Marc Edwards

SVP and Chief Investment Officer, Richard W. Scott, age 61

SVP, Kenneth I. Siegel, age 58, $975,000 total compensation

VP and CIO, Robert D. Fields

President CEO and Director Boardwalk Pipeline Partners LP, Stanley Horton

President and CEO Loews Hotels and Resorts, S. Kirk Kinsell

Vice President Investor Public Relations, Mary Skafidas

Vice President Marketing, Elizabeth (Beth) Harlow

Vice President Real Estate, Debbie Walker

Vice President Real Estate, Jason Boxer

Vice President Loews Cna Holdings Investments, Winifred Harrison

Regional Vice President of Sales and Marketing, David (Dave) Wiener

Senior Vice President eCommerce and Distribution, Jimmy Suh

Senior Vice President, Marc Shapiro

Vice President, Ramu Venkatachalam

Co-Chairman, Andrew H. Tisch, age 66

Treasurer, Andrew Stegen

Auditors: Deloitte & Touche LLP

LOCATIONS

HQ: Loews Corp.
667 Madison Avenue, New York, NY 10065-8087
Phone: 212 521-2000
Web: www.loews.com

PRODUCTS/OPERATIONS

2014 Revenues

	$ mil.	% of total
Insurance premiums	7,212	50
Contract drilling revenues	2,737	19
Net investment income	2,163	16
Other	2,159	15
Investment gains	54	-
Total	14,325	100

2014 Revenues

	$ mil.	% of total
CNA Financial		
Specialty	3,708	26
Commercial	3,683	26
International	973	7
Other non-core	1,328	9
Diamond Offshore	2,825	20
Boardwalk Pipeline	1,236	8
Loews Hotels	475	3
Corporate & other	97	1
Total	14,325	100

Selected Subsidiaries

Boardwalk Pipeline Partners LP (53%)
CNA Financial Corporation (90%)
Diamond Offshore Drilling Inc. (53%)
Loews Hotels Holding Corporation (100%)

COMPETITORS

AIG	Marriott
American Financial Group	Noble
Apache	Range Resources
Berkshire Hathaway	Spectra Energy
Cabot Oil & Gas	Starwood Hotels & Resorts
Chubb Limited	Statoil
Cincinnati Financial	The Hartford
Energy Transfer	Transocean
Ensco	Travelers Companies
Four Seasons Hotels	W. R. Berkley
Hilton Worldwide	Wyndham Worldwide

Hyatt
Kinder Morgan Energy Partners

HISTORICAL FINANCIALS

Company Type: Public

Income Statement

FYE: December 31

	ASSETS ($ mil.)	NET INCOME ($ mil.)	INCOME AS % OF ASSETS	EMPLOYEES
12/14	78,367	591	0.8%	17,510
12/13	79,939	595	0.7%	18,175
12/12	80,021	568	0.7%	18,300
12/11	75,375	1,064	1.4%	18,250
12/10	76,277	1,288	1.7%	18,400
Annual Growth	0.7%	(17.7%)	—	(1.2%)

2014 Year-End Financials

Debt ratio: 13.19%	No. of shares (mil.): 372
Return on equity: 3.05%	Dividends
Cash ($ mil.): 364	Yield: 0.6%
Current ratio: —	Payout: 50.0%
Long-term debt ($ mil.): —	Market value ($ mil.): 15,671

	STOCK PRICE ($) FY Close	P/E High/Low	PER SHARE ($) Earnings	Dividends	Book Value
12/14	42.02	31 25	1.55	0.25	51.70
12/13	48.24	32 27	1.53	0.25	50.28
12/12	40.75	30 26	1.43	0.25	49.66
12/11	37.65	17 13	2.63	0.25	47.54
12/10	38.91	13 10	3.07	0.25	44.51
Annual Growth	1.9%	— —	(15.7%)	(0.0%)	3.8%

Lowe's Companies Inc

No longer a low-profile company Lowe's Companies has evolved from a regional hardware store operator into a nationwide chain of home improvement superstores bent on international expansion. The #2 US home improvement chain (after The Home Depot) Lowe's operates nearly 1800 stores in the US along with some 40 stores in Canada 10 stores in Mexico and an e-commerce site. Its stores sell roughly 36000 products for do-it-yourselfers and professionals for home improvement and repair projects such as lumber paint plumbing and electrical supplies tools and gardening products as well as appliances lighting and furniture. Lowe's is also the second-largest US home appliance retailer after Sears.

HISTORY

Company BackgroundLowe's Companies was founded in 1921 as Mr. L. S. Lowe's North Wilkesboro Hardware in North Wilkesboro North Carolina. A family operation by 1945 Mr. Lowe's store (which also sold groceries snuff and harnesses) was run by his son Jim and his son-in-law H. Carl Buchan. Buchan bought Lowe's share of the company in 1956 and incorporated as Lowe's North Wilkesboro Hardware; he wanted Lowe's as part of the company name because he liked the slogan "Lowe's Low Prices." The chain expanded from North Carolina into Tennessee Virginia and West Virginia. By 1960 Buchan had 15 stores and sales of $31 million —up $4 million from a decade before.

Buchan planned to create a profit-sharing plan for Lowe's employees but in 1960 he died of a heart attack at age 44. In 1961 Lowe's management and the executors of Buchan's estate established the Lowe's Employees Profit Sharing and Trust which bought Buchan's 89% of the company (later renamed Lowe's Companies). That year they financed the transaction through a public offering which diluted the employees' stock. Lowe's was listed on the NYSE in 1979.

Robert Strickland who had joined the company in 1957 became chairman in 1978. Revenues increased from $170 million in 1971 to more than $900 million with a net income of $25 million in 1979. Traditionally the majority of Lowe's business was in sales to professional homebuilders but in 1980 housing starts fell and company profits dropped. Concurrently The Home Depot introduced its low-price warehouse concept. Instead of building warehouse stores of its own Strickland changed the stores' layouts and by 1982 had redesigned half of the 229 stores to be more oriented toward do-it-yourself (DIY) consumers. The new designs featured softer lighting and displays of entire room layouts to appeal to women who made up over half of all DIY customers. In 1982 Lowe's made more than half of its sales to consumers for the first time in its history.

Although Lowe's had more than 300 stores by 1988 its outlets were only about 20000 sq. ft. (one-fifth the size of Home Depot's warehouse stores). By 1989 Lowe's which had continued to target contractors as well as DIYers was overtaken by Home Depot as the US's #1 home retail chain.

Since 1989 the company has focused on building larger stores taking a charge of $71 million in 1991 to phase out smaller stores and build warehouse outlets. In 1993 Lowe's opened 57 large stores (half were replacements for existing stores) almost doubling its total floor space.

The retailer opened 29 new stores in 1995. During 1996 Lowe's added a net of 37 stores and in 1997 it opened 42 stores in new markets. Also that year president and CEO Leonard Herring retired and was replaced by former COO Robert Tillman who also took the post of chairman when Strickland stepped down in 1998.

Also in 1998 the company entered a joint venture to sell an exclusive line of Kobalt-brand professional mechanics' tools produced by Snap-on and to better serve commercial customers began allowing them to special order items not stocked in stores. In addition Lowe's announced it would spend $1.5 billion over the next several years on a 100-store push into the western US. Lowe's westward expansion was fueled when it purchased Washington-based 38-store Eagle Hardware & Garden in 1999 in a stock swap deal worth $1.3 billion. The company gradually converted the Eagle stores into Lowe's.

In 2001 the company earmarked $2.4 billion of its $2.7 billion capital budget for store expansions and new distribution centers.

Robert Niblock was promoted from CFO to president in March 2003. Lowe's sold its some 30 outlets operating as The Contractor Yard to The Strober Organization in February 2004. In April 2004 the company opened its first predominantly urban-oriented store suited to the needs of city dwellers and building superintendents in Brooklyn.

Chairman and CEO Robert Tillman retired in January 2005. He was succeeded by president Robert Niblock.

Lowe's entered the Canadian market in 2007.

The home improvement chain expanded its distribution footprint in 2008 opening a regional distribution center in Pittston Pennsylvania and a flatbed distribution center in Purvis Mississippi.

During 2010 Lowe's opened its first location in Mexico (in Monterrey). In 2011 the company made a rare acquisition: online home-improvement retailer ATG Stores based in Kirkland Washington.

EXECUTIVES

Chief Human Resources Officer, Maureen K. Ausura, age 60, $527,000 total compensation
EVP and CFO, Robert A. Niblock, age 52, $1,280,000 total compensation
Senior Vice President Store Operations South Central, Dennis Knowles
Senior Vice President, John (Jack) Manna
Vice President, Melissa Birdsong
Chief Customer Officer, Michael A. Jones, age 52, $583,791 total compensation
CFO, Robert F. (Bob) Hull, age 51, $726,000 total compensation
COO, Rick D. Damron, age 52, $780,000 total compensation
Chief Supply Chain Officer, Stephen J. Szilagyi
Chief Development Officer and President International, Richard D. Maltsbarger, age 39
Chief Merchandising Officer, Michael P. McDermott
CIO, Paul D. Ramsay, age 50
Vice President Corporate Communications, Chris Ahearn
Senior Vice President Operations North Central Division, Brent Kirby
Svp-store Planning & Environme, Ronnie Damron
Senior Vice President GMM Seasonal, Troy Dally
Senior Vice President Store Operations, Kevin Measel
Senior Vice President, Michael (Mel) Tummillo
Vice President eCommerce and Mobility, Stephen (Steve) Carvelli
Senior Vice President and General Merchandising Manager Hardlines, Clinton T Davis
Vice President Store Operations, Jeff Blocker
Vice President Risk Management, Valerie Franco
Vice President Of Employer Relations, Gary Whitman
Vice President Market and Consumer Insight, John (Jack) Whitaker
Vice President, Darren Welborn
Vice President Innovation and Enterprise Architecture, James (Jamie) Brandt
Vice President of Merchandising, Macedonio Garza
Vice President Assistant General Counsel, Jeff Gray
Vice President Corporate Controller, Staci Dennis
Vice President of Client Services, Marian Craig
National Accounts Manager, Bill McGee
Vice President Corporate Communications, Clarissa Felts
Vice President Learning and Development, Lisa Doyle
Vice President Sales, Carolyn Bender
Vice President Merchandising And Store Support, Stephen (Steve) Taylor
Legal Secretary, Donna Foster
Vice President Assistant General Counsel, Kimberly Wells
Vice President Logistics Planning and Forecasting, Robin Bornkamp
Vice President Credit Project And Event Sales, Terry Johnson
Regional Vice President Of Stores, Jeffrey (Jeff) Sain
Senior Vice President, Belinda Rumple
Vice President Business Development, Harvey Hall
Regional Vice President Distribution, Calvin (Cal) Adams
Vice President Merchandising Home Environment, Angie Shore
Vice President Merchandising, Clint Davis
Vice President Rdc Operations, Gregory Powell
Senior Vice President Corporate Communications, Brian Peace
Vice President International Merchandising, Benedetto Mauceri
Merchandising Vice President, Dean Kochalka
Vice President Store Operations, David Rowland
Vice President Of Store Operations, Stacey Ryan

Vice President New Business Development, Jay Rebello
Vice President And General Manager Biological Systems Division, Garry Burke
Vice President Merchandising, Sean Macdonald
Regional Vice President West Region, Fred Sampson
Vice President Training, Greg Nell
Vice President Strategy And Alignment, Erin Sellman
Executive Vice President, Douglas Evans
Vice President Human Resources, Wanda Walkden
Vice President Vendor Service Management, Ron Lutz
Vice President And General Manager, Kevin Meagher
Vice President Corporate Communication, Tracey Ahearn
Merchandising Vice President Flooring Division, Joseph (Jo) Thomas
Vice President Human Resources Stores, Scott Purvis
Vice President Corporate Payables, Linda Coffey
Vice President Product Accounting, Kevin O'Brien
Vice President And Assistant General Counsel, Robert Oneale
Vice President Corporate Facilities, Troy Saunders
MVP Rough Electrical, Michael (Mel) Scott
Executive Vice President Logistics and D, Joseph M Mike (Jo) Mabry
Senior Vice President Deputy General Counsel, M Lee Reeves
Senior Vice President and Chief Accounting Officer, Matthew (Matt) Hollifield
Legal Secretary, Cindy Castine
Svp Corp Finance-treasurer, Tiffany L Mason
Vice President and Treasurer, David (Dave) Green
Assistant Treasurer Cash Management, Cindy Reins
Treasurer, Judy Davis
Board Member, Shannon Efird
Auditors: Deloitte & Touche LLP

LOCATIONS

HQ: Lowe's Companies Inc
1000 Lowe's Blvd., Mooresville, NC 28117
Phone: 704 758-1000
Web: www.lowes.com

2015 Stores

	No.
United States	1,793
Canada	37
Mexico	10
Total	**1,840**

PRODUCTS/OPERATIONS

2015 Sales

	$ mil.	% of total
Kitchens & appliances	8,007	14
Lumber & buildings materials	6,884	12
Tools & hardware	6,263	11
Fashion fixtures	5,591	10
Rough plumbing & electrical	4,928	9
Lawn & garden	4,639	8
Seasonal living	3,717	7
Paint	3,614	6
Home fashions storage & cleaning	3,263	6
Flooring	3,219	6
Millwork	3,135	6
Outdoor power equipment	2,339	4
Others	624	1
Total	**56,223**	**100**

Selected Proprietary Brands

allen+roth
Aquasource
Garden Treasures
Harbor Breeze
Kobalt
Portfolio

Reliabilt
Top Choice
Utilitech

Selected Subsidiaries

Lowe's Home Centers Inc.
Lowe's HIW Inc.

COMPETITORS

84 Lumber	Menard
Abbey Carpet	Northern Tool
Ace Hardware	RONA
Best Buy	Sears
CCA Global	Sherwin-Williams
Canadian Tire	Sutherland Lumber
Do it Best	True Value
HD Supply	Wal-Mart
Home Depot	Wolseley
McCoy Corp.	

HISTORICAL FINANCIALS

Company Type: Public

Income Statement

FYE: January 30

	REVENUE ($ mil.)	NET INCOME ($ mil.)	NET PROFIT MARGIN	EMPLOYEES
01/15	56,223	2,698	4.8%	266,000
01/14*	53,417	2,286	4.3%	262,000
02/13	50,521	1,959	3.9%	245,000
02/12	50,208	1,839	3.7%	248,000
01/11	48,815	2,010	4.1%	234,000
Annual Growth	**3.6%**	**7.6%**	**—**	**3.3%**

*Fiscal year change

2015 Year-End Financials

Debt ratio: 35.71%	No. of shares (mil.): 960
Return on equity: 24.80%	Dividends
Cash ($ mil.): 466	Yield: 1.2%
Current ratio: 1.08	Payout: 34.2%
Long-term debt ($ mil.): 10,815	Market value ($ mil.): 65,050

	STOCK PRICE ($) FY Close	P/E High/Low	PER SHARE ($) Earnings	Dividends	Book Value
01/15	67.76	26 16	2.71	0.87	10.38
01/14*	46.29	24 17	2.14	0.70	11.51
02/13	38.56	23 15	1.69	0.62	12.48
02/12	27.20	19 13	1.43	0.53	13.32
01/11	25.25	20 14	1.42	0.42	13.38
Annual Growth	**28.0%**	**— —**	**17.5%**	**20.0%**	**(6.1%)**

*Fiscal year change

M & T Bank Corp

M&T Bank Corporation is making a splash in the mid-Atlantic region. It is the holding company of M&T Bank which offers deposit loan trust investment brokerage and insurance services to more than two million individuals and small- and mid-sized businesses. With about $97 billion in total assets and $74 billion in deposits the bank operates more than 700 branches and 1500 ATMs in New York Pennsylvania and other eastern states and Washington DC in addition to Canada and the Cayman Islands. Its residential mortgage origination unit spans more than a dozen states in the South and West. The firm also manages a proprietary line of mutual funds the Wilmington Funds.
Operations

The bank holding company has two wholly-owned bank subsidiaries: M&T Bank and Wilmington Trust N.A. (M&T Bank represents 99% of the company's consolidated assets.) M&T Bank operates through six reportable segments: Retail Banking Commercial Banking Commercial Real Estate Residential Mortgage Banking Business Banking and Discretionary Portfolio.The Retail Banking segment which generates nearly 25% of total revenue offers a variety of services to consumers through several delivery channels that include banking offices ATMs telephone banking and Internet banking. The Commercial Banking segment brings in nearly 25% of revenue and offers a variety of credit products and banking services to middle-market and large commercial customers primarily within the markets it already serves. M&T Bank's Commercial Real Estate segment generates another 15% of revenue and provides credit services which are secured by several types of multifamily residential and commercial real estate and deposit services to its customers. Its Residential Mortgage Banking unit makes up 10% of revenue and originates and services residential mortgage loans for consumers and sells substantially all of the loans in the secondary market to investors or to the Discretionary Portfolio segment. The Business Banking segment brings in another 10% of revenue and provides deposit lending cash management and other financial services to small businesses and professionals through its banking office network and other delivery channels including business banking centers telephone banking Internet banking and ATMs. The Discretionary Portfolio segment focuses on securities residential mortgage loans and other assets; short-term and long-term borrowed funds; brokered certificates of deposit and interest rate swap agreements; and Cayman Islands branch deposits. The segment also provides customers with foreign exchange services.

Geographic Reach

Buffalo-based M&T Bank operates in New York Pennsylvania Maryland Delaware New Jersey Virginia West Virginia and the District of Columbia. It also boasts a full-service commercial banking office in Ontario Canada and an office in George Town Cayman Islands. Its regional headquarters is in Albany.

Sales and Marketing

The bank caters to customers through multiple channels such as its business banking centers telephone banking Internet banking and ATMs. It serves individuals and small- and mid-sized business customers. Gains in

M&T Bank did not spend money on advertising and promotion in 2014 but spent $56.6 million in 2013 and $59.6 million in 2012. However it did in 2014 secure a 10-year $60 million extension with the Baltimore Ravens to keep the naming rights to the M&T Bank Stadium along with an array of community focused programs all through the year 2027.

Financial Performance

Following several years of growth M&T Bank's revenue in 2014 declined by nearly 2% to $4.74 billion mostly as it collected less in interest income as yields on loans and leases federal funds sold and trading accounts fell in the low-interest environment. The company also collected less in service charges on deposit and trading accounts and generated fewer foreign exchange gains as the dollar strengthened.Net income in 2014 also fell by 6% to $1.07 billion after several years of growth mostly because of lower earnings. In addition M&T paid more toward salary and employee benefits equipment and net occupancy and other operating costs —which were all driven by increased spending to ensure that the bank's practices were compliant with the Bank Secrecy Act and anti-money-laundering laws.Despite lower earnings cash levels continued to rise in 2014 with operations providing $1.1 billion primarily because the bank used less cash toward originating loans for sale.

Strategy

M&T has faced headwinds for profit growth in recent years as concerns over lax anti-money laundering procedures led the Federal Reserve to order M&T to improve its systems. Indeed the bank spent heavily in 2014 to fix the problem causing it to take a loss. Also the bank is being squeezed by the slowdown in mortgage refinancing and rising regulatory costs.

But that hasn't stopped its office expansion plans. In 2014 the bank opened a commercial banking office in Cherry Hill to provide commercial lending residential mortgage wealth advisory and other non-deposit retail banking services to clients in southern New Jersey. In 2012 as part of M&T Bank's $10 million investment initiative in the Hudson Valley it opened retail branches in Newburgh. It also opened a branch in Georgetown and began building another retail branch in the Hamilton Square shopping center in Guilderland.To grow relationships with existing customers M&T Bank routinely expands its service offerings and products for its commercial and individual clients. In 2014 for example the bank sought to increase its market share in the commercial credit card market by expanding its commercial credit card line-up adding security chip technology a new card aimed at business executives and a new rewards program. In 2013 it partnered with SurePayroll Inc. to provide its small business customers with online payroll processing services. In 2012 M&T Bank launched a new commercial online platform enhancement for its Web Info-PLU$ system and introduced Mobile Banking for Business.

Mergers and Acquisitions

M&T Bank has often purchased smaller banks to expand its reach or strengthen its presence in existing markets. In November 2015 the bank acquired New Jersey's Hudson City Bancorp for $3.7 billion after originally announcing its intentions to buy the bank back in August 2012. The Hudson City acquisition would add some $19 billion in new loans and bring in 135 branches in the New York City metropolitan area while greatly expanding M&T Bank's presence in New Jersey.

Company Background

M&T Bank traces its roots to the founding of Manufacturers and Traders Bank in Buffalo New York. M&T Bank reorganized under a bank holding company in 1969 called First Empire State Corp. The name was changed in 1998 to M&T Bank Corporation.

EXECUTIVES

Chairman and CEO, Robert G. (Bob) Wilmers, age 80, $950,000 total compensation
EVP Wealth and Institutional Services Division, William J. (Bill) Farrell, age 57
EVP, Atwood Collins, age 69, $283,846 total compensation
President, Mark J. Czarnecki, age 59, $900,000 total compensation
EVP, Brian E. Hickey, age 63, $299,231 total compensation
EVP, Kevin J. Pearson, age 54, $625,000 total compensation
Regional President Central and Southern Virginia, Cecilia A. Hodges
EVP Human Resources, Stephen J. Braunscheidel, age 58
SVP and Deputy Credit Officer, Robert J. Bojdak, age 60
EVP and CIO, Michele D. Trolli, age 54
Regional President New Jersey Westchester County NY Rockland County and Connecticut, Paula Mandell

SVP and Manager Financial Performance Measurement Department, Ren G. Jones, age 51, $625,000 total compensation
EVP and Chief Risk Officer, Richard S. Gold, age 55, $650,000 total compensation
EVP and Treasurer, D. Scott N. Warman, age 49
EVP, Darren J. King
EVP M&T Bank Corporation and M&T Bank, Gino A. Martocci, age 49
Regional President New Jersey, Tom Comiskey
Regional President Westchester County NY Rockland County NY and Connecticut Region, Frank Micalizzi
Assistant Vice President Business Relationship Manager, Steve Steele
Vice President Operations Manager, Jackie Breeden
Vice President Reverse Mortgage Loan Officer, Sonja Hotaling
Vice President Business and Professional Banking, Giovanni Mazzei
Vice President Business Banking Relationship Manager, Steven (Steve) Bank
Assistant Vice President, Tianya McMillan
Vice President Group Manager, John (Jack) Cooper
Vice President, Karen Cullen
Assistant Vice President Branch Manager, Susan (Sue) Bell
Vice President Human Resources Data Analytics and Systems, Jennifer Shirk (Jen) Warner
Vice President, Amy Plante
Vice President Compliance Officer, Lori Kunzelman
Vice President Senior Counsel, Donna Suchan
Deputy Compliance Testing Officer Vice President, Stephen (Steve) Nalawadi
Assistant Vice President Marketing and Sales Support Coordinator, Amy Jablonski
Vice President EE Benefits, Liz Wilhelm
Vice President Commercial Real Estate, Jason Bishop
Vice President Business and Planning Manager, Melissa (Mel) Prohaska
Vice President Human Resources Business Partner, Amy Walker
Vice President EDW Program Management and Administration, Heather Brodbeck
Vice President Credit Analyst, Eric Swoboda
Vice President Business and Planning Manager, Patricia (Pat) Pizzicato
Vice President Credit Manager, Jeff Stachura
Vice President Senior Space Planner, Amy Stacey
Vice President Operations Manager, Stacey Kranz
Assistant Vice President; Business and Planning Analyst IV, Jane (Ginny) Antonovsky
Ast. Vice President: Merchant Services and Commercial Payment Solutions, Peter (Pete) Geiskopf
Business Banking Underwriter III Assistant Vice President, Adam Douglas
Vice President Business Banking, Pat Ponzo
Vice President and Business Banking Team Leader, Matthew (Matt) Cohen
Assistant Vice President Construction Administration, Gavin Musynske
Vice President Business and Professional Banking, Craig Gajewski
Assistant Vice President Instructional Designer Training Consultant, Mike Wolf
Assistant Vice President Business and Professional Banking Center Manager, Filomena Carfagno
Vice President and Business Banking Team Leader, Tristan Wright
Vice President Business and Professional Banking, Laurie Kaminsky
Assistant Vice President Business and Planning Manager, Sara Foore
Assistant Vice President Business and Planning Manager II, Jean Biondo-Rine
Vice President Relationship Manager in Business Banking, Andy Guckert

Commercial Product Manager Assistant Vice
 President, Jill MacDonald
Vice President Business and Professional
 Banking, Denise Myers Mlynarick
Vice President Business and Professional
 Banking, Tony DelVecchio
Vice President Business and Professional
 Banking, Jim Minniti
Vice President Business Banking Relationship
 Manager, Gary Jones
Business Banking Relationship Manager Vice
 President, Donna Davies
Vice President Business Banking Relationship
 Manager, Erin Way
Assistant Vice President Senior Training
 Specialist, Nancy Dispenza
Assistant Vice President Business Banking
 Relationship Manager, Cody Carbaugh
Assistant Vice President Senior Compliance
 Officer, Meghan Chadsey
Vice President Real Estate, Tom Daly
Assistant Vice President Human Resources
 Business Partner, Kristyn Berger
Vice Chairman M&T Bank, Jorge G. Pereira, age 81
Auditors: PricewaterhouseCoopers LLP

LOCATIONS

HQ: M & T Bank Corp
 One M & T Plaza, Buffalo, NY 14203
Phone: 716 635-4000
Web: www.mtb.com

PRODUCTS/OPERATIONS

Selected Subsidiaries
M&T Life Insurance Company
M&T Insurance Agency Inc
M&T Mortgage Reinsurance Company Inc.
M&T Real Estate Trust
M&T Realty Capital Corporation
M&T Securities Inc.
Wilmington Trust Company
Wilmington Trust Investment Advisors Inc.
Wilmington Funds Management Corporation
Wilmington Trust Investment Management LLC

2014 Sales

	$mil.
% of total	
Interst income	
Loans and leases	55
Others	7
Non interst income	
Trust income	11
Service charges on deposit accounts	9
Mortgage banking revenue	8
Brokerage services income	1
Others	9
Adjustments	.
Total	**100**

2014 Sales

	% of total
Retail Banking	24
Commercial Banking	23
Commercial Real Estate	15
Residential Mortgage Banking	9
Busienss Banking	9
Discretionary Portfolio	2
All others	17
Total	**100**

COMPETITORS

Citigroup	JPMorgan Chase
Citizens Financial	KeyCorp
Group	Northwest Bancshares
First Niagara	PNC Financial
Financial	Sovereign Bank
Fulton Financial	SunTrust
HSBC USA	TriState Capital

HISTORICAL FINANCIALS
Company Type: Public

Income Statement
FYE: December 31

	ASSETS ($ mil.)	NET INCOME ($ mil.)	INCOME AS % OF ASSETS	EMPLOYEES
12/14	96,685	1,066	1.1%	15,782
12/13	85,162	1,138	1.3%	15,893
12/12	83,008	1,029	1.2%	14,943
12/11	77,924	859	1.1%	15,666
12/10	68,021	736	1.1%	13,365
Annual Growth	**9.2%**	**9.7%**	**—**	**4.2%**

2014 Year-End Financials

Debt ratio: 8.11%
Return on equity: 9.02%
Cash ($ mil.): 8,069
Current ratio: —
Long-term debt ($ mil.): —

No. of shares (mil.): 132
Dividends
 Yield: 2.2%
 Payout: 37.7%
Market value ($ mil.): 16,621

	STOCK PRICE ($) FY Close	P/E High/Low	PER SHARE ($) Earnings	Dividends	Book Value
12/14	125.62	17 15	7.42	2.80	93.23
12/13	116.42	14 12	8.20	2.80	86.62
12/12	98.47	14 10	7.54	2.80	79.60
12/11	76.34	14 11	6.35	2.80	73.77
12/10	87.05	17 12	5.69	2.80	69.82
Annual Growth	**9.6%**	**— —**	**6.9%**	**(0.0%)**	**7.5%**

MACK-CALI REALTY L. P.

LOCATIONS

HQ: MACK-CALI REALTY L. P.
 4 BECKER FARM RD STE 104, ROSELAND, NJ
 070681734
Phone: 9735772472
Web: WWW.MACK-CALI.COM

HISTORICAL FINANCIALS
Company Type: Private

Income Statement
FYE: December 31

	ASSETS ($ mil.)	NET INCOME ($ mil.)	INCOME AS % OF ASSETS	EMPLOYEES
12/14	4,192	31	0.7%	2
12/13	4,515	(19)	—	—
12/12	4,526	46	1.0%	—
12/11	4,295	0	—	—
Annual Growth	**(0.8%)**	**—**	**—**	**—**

2014 Year-End Financials

Debt ratio: —
Return on equity: 4.90%
Cash ($ mil.): 29
Current ratio: —
Long-term debt ($ mil.): —

Dividends
 Yield: —
 Payout: —
Market value ($ mil.): —

Macy's Inc

LOCATIONS

HQ: Macy' s Inc
 151 West 34th Street, New York, NY 10001
Phone: 212 494-1602   **Fax:** 212 494-1838
Web: www.macys.com

HISTORICAL FINANCIALS
Company Type: Public

Income Statement
FYE: January 31

	REVENUE ($ mil.)	NET INCOME ($ mil.)	NET PROFIT MARGIN	EMPLOYEES
01/15*	28,105	1,526	5.4%	166,900
02/14	27,931	1,486	5.3%	172,500
02/13	27,686	1,335	4.8%	175,700
01/12	26,405	1,256	4.8%	171,000
01/11	25,003	847	3.4%	166,000
Annual Growth	**3.0%**	**15.9%**	**—**	**0.1%**
*Fiscal year change

2015 Year-End Financials

Debt ratio: 34.21%
Return on equity: 26.32%
Cash ($ mil.): 2,246
Current ratio: 1.57
Long-term debt ($ mil.): 7,265

No. of shares (mil.): 340
Dividends
 Yield: 0.0%
 Payout: 28.1%
Market value ($ mil.): 21,756

	STOCK PRICE ($) FY Close	P/E High/Low	PER SHARE ($) Earnings	Dividends	Book Value
01/15*	63.88	16 12	4.22	1.19	15.79
02/14	53.20	14 10	3.86	0.95	17.12
02/13	39.51	13 10	3.24	0.80	15.61
01/12	33.82	12 7	2.92	0.35	14.32
01/11	22.99	13 8	1.98	0.20	13.06
Annual Growth	**29.1%**	**— —**	**20.8%**	**56.1%**	**4.9%**
*Fiscal year change

MainSource Financial Group Inc

MainSource Financial wants to be the main source of financial services for residents and businesses in Indiana and beyond. It is the holding company of MainSource Bank which operates about 80 branches in the Hoosier State as well as neighboring portions of Ohio Illinois and Kentucky. The bank offers standard deposit and lending products in addition to trust and insurance services. Real estate loans account for the majority of MainSource Financial's lending portfolio which also includes other commercial and consumer loans. Through MainSource Insurance the company provides annuities and credit life insurance.

OperationsMainSource generated 53% of its total revenue from interest income on loans (including fees) in 2014 while another 17% of revenue came from interest income on the company's investment securities. The bank's service charges on deposit accounts contributed 14% to total revenue during the year while its mortgage banking income and trust and investment product fees made up 5% and 3% respectively.Geographic ReachMainSource Bank boasts around 80 branches across Iowa Ohio Illinois and Kentucky. Its branches span 31 counties in Indiana three counties in Illinois three counties in Ohio and five counties in Kentucky.Sales and MarketingMainSource Financial spent $3.19 million on marketing in 2014 compared to $3.66 million and $4.40 million in 2013 and 2012 respectively.Financial PerformanceAfter several years of revenue declines MainSource Financial's revenue rebounded by 1% to $146.10 million in 2014 mostly thanks to higher interest income from loan business growth but also thanks to higher service charges on deposit accounts.Higher revenue and lower loan loss provisions from a more credit-worthy loan portfolio in 2014 drove the bank's net income higher by 10% to a record $29.00 million for the year. Longer term the bank's annual profits have trended higher over the years as the bank's loan portfolio continues to improve its credit-quality amidst the strengthening economy.Despite higher earnings during the year MainSource's operating cash fell by 28% to $43.36 million as the bank collected less in net proceeds from the sale of its loans-held-for-sale. StrategyMainSource Financial has continued to selectively expand its branch network in recent years acquiring new branches from other banks in target markets while closing under-performing branches in other regions. Its 2015 branch purchases from Old National Bank and its full acquisition of MBT Bancorp in late 2014 added more than 10 branches to MainSource's network in Indiana and Ohio and added millions in new deposits and loan assets. Meanwhile in mid-2014 the bank closed two of its branches in Indiana (in Linton and Griffith) and an additional branch in Frankfurt Kentucky. In April 2013 MainSource closed eight of its branches –or roughly 10% of its total branch network –in seven locations in Indiana (Redkey Fortville Cambridge City Fountain City Trafalgar East Enterprise and Covington) as well as in Troy Ohio.Mergers and AcquisitionsIn January 2015 MainSource Financial agreed to purchase Old National Bank branches located in Union City Ohio as well as in Portland Richmond Brownstown and Batesville Indiana from Old National Bank which would add a total of $120 million in deposits and $30 million in loans to MainSource's books.In October 2014 the company completed its full acquisition of all shares of MBT Bancorp for a total of $13.9 million. The deal added MBT's bank subsidiary The Merchant Bank and Trust Company and extended MainSource's market presence in southeastern Indiana and the greater Cincinnati markets with six new branches. Company BackgroundThe company has made several acquisitions over the years including National City Corporation's Madison Bank & Trust Union Community Bancorp Peoples Ohio Financial and 1st Independence Financial Group.

EXECUTIVES

SVP CFO and Secretary, James M. (Jamie) Anderson, age 41, $227,726 total compensation
Chairman President and CEO, Archie M. Brown, age 54, $388,470 total compensation
President Indianapolis Region MainSource Bank, Daniel Cobb
Vice President Membership, Kevin Koehne
Secretary, Lisa McNealy
Auditors: Crowe Horwath LLP

LOCATIONS

HQ: MainSource Financial Group Inc
2105 North State Road 3 Bypass, Greensburg, IN 47240
Phone: 812 663-6734   **Fax:** 812 663-4812
Web: www.mainsourcebank.com

PRODUCTS/OPERATIONS

2011 Sales

	$ mil.	% of total
Interest		
Loans including fees	92	55
Investment securities	28	17
Other	0	-
Noninterest		
Service charges on deposit accounts	18	11
Net realized gains on securities	11	7
Interchange income	6	3
Mortgage banking	5	3
Other	6	4
Adjustments	(2.7)	-
Total	**166**	**100**

COMPETITORS

1st Source Corporation	KeyCorp
Bank of America	Old National Bancorp
Fifth Third	U.S. Bancorp
First Merchants	
German American Bancorp	

HISTORICAL FINANCIALS

Company Type: Public

Income Statement

FYE: December 31

	ASSETS ($ mil.)	NET INCOME ($ mil.)	INCOME AS % OF ASSETS	EMPLOYEES
12/14	3,122	29	0.9%	801
12/13	2,859	26	0.9%	772
12/12	2,769	27	1.0%	808
12/11	2,754	23	0.9%	805
12/10	2,769	14	0.5%	926
Annual Growth	3.0%	18.3%	—	(3.6%)

2014 Year-End Financials

Debt ratio: 1.32%
Return on equity: 8.71%
Cash ($ mil.): 64
Current ratio: —
Long-term debt ($ mil.): —
No. of shares (mil.): 21
Dividends
  Yield: 2.0%
  Payout: 28.9%
Market value ($ mil.): 454

	STOCK PRICE ($) FY Close	P/E High/Low	PER SHARE ($) Earnings	Dividends	Book Value
12/14	20.92	15 11	1.39	0.42	16.63
12/13	18.03	14 10	1.26	0.28	14.96
12/12	12.67	10 7	1.30	0.08	15.94
12/11	8.83	10 7	1.03	0.04	16.66
12/10	10.41	19 8	0.58	0.04	15.03
Annual Growth	19.1%	— —	24.4%	80.0%	2.6%

MAKE CORPORATION

Auditors: KUTCHINS ROBBINS & DIAMOND LT

LOCATIONS

HQ: MAKE CORPORATION
1 S 450 SMMIT AVE STE 165, OAKBROOK TERRACE, IL 60181
Phone: 6303760646
Web: WWW.MAKECOR.COM

HISTORICAL FINANCIALS

Company Type: Private

Income Statement

FYE: December 31

	REVENUE ($ mil.)	NET INCOME ($ mil.)	NET PROFIT MARGIN	EMPLOYEES
12/13	22,724	1,399	6.2%	192
12/12	20,101	851	4.2%	—
Annual Growth	13.1%	64.4%	—	—

ManpowerGroup

Millions of men (and women) have helped power this firm to the upper echelon of the staffing industry. ManpowerGroup is one of the world's largest providers of temporary employees connecting more than 6 million people in office industrial and professional positions every year. It offers services through different brands including ManpowerGroup Solutions Manpower Experis (accounting finance health and engineering positions) Manpower UK and Right Management which provides management consulting services focused on leadership development and assessment. ManpowerGroup has some 3000 owned or franchised offices in 80 countries and territories and assists more than 400000 clients.
Geographic Reach
Europe is ManpowerGroup's largest market accounting for almost 65% of the company's total sales in fiscal 2014. The Americas follow (generating more than 20%) while Asia/Pacific and the Middle East contribute nearly 11%.
Operations
Supplying temporary employees to businesses on an as-needed basis accounts for the bulk of the company's business with most of its sales coming from office and light-industrial placements.
ManpowerGroup's operating segments are primarily aligned by geography. They include the Americas Southern Europe Northern Europe APME (Asia Pacific and the Middle East) and Right Management.
Sales and Marketing
The company's total advertising expenses for fiscal 2014 was about $26 million. Its client mix consists of both small and medium-sized businesses and large national multinational clients. Large businesses accounted for about 57% of the company's revenues during fiscal 2014.
Financial Performance
ManpowerGroup's revenue spiked by 3% from $20.3 billion in 2013 to %20.8 billion in 2014. Profits also surged 49% from $288 million to $423 million over that same time period due to a decrease in selling and administrative expenses coupled with zero restructuring costs (compared to $89 million in 2013). ManpowerGroup's cash inflow from operations increased by $22 million to $89.5 million in fiscal 2013. However it dipped by 23% during 2014.
The revenue growth for 2014 was driven by a 4% rise in services in several markets in Southern Europe and Northern Europe. The company was particularly helped by increased demand form larger markets in France along with improving demand in Italy. ManpowerGroup was also helped by a revenue spike within the US driven by growth in larger national accounts and in the small/medium-sized business sectors.
Strategy
Apart from growing its services and geographic footprint through acquisitions ManpowerGroup focuses on diversifying its revenues beyond its core staffing and employment services by building its consulting and leadership training services.
Mergers and Acquisitions
In 2013 ManpowerGroup acquired Norwegian staffing specialist Workshop Holding. The purchase strengthened ManpowerGroup's recruitment operations in the building and construction markets. The year before ManpowerGroup obtained Damilo Group a French IT design specialist for $28 million.

HISTORY

Milwaukee lawyers Elmer Winter and Aaron Scheinfeld founded Manpower in 1948. It originally concentrated on supplying temporary help to industry during the first few years of the postwar boom. In the next few years the company expanded and in 1956 it began franchising. During the 1960s Manpower opened franchises in Europe Asia and South America. Unlike many of its competitors however it continued to emphasize blue-collar placements.

EXECUTIVES

EVP Global Strategy and Talent, Mara E. Swan, age 55, $560,000 total compensation
SEVP, Michael J. Van Handel, age 55, $660,000 total compensation
President, Darryl E. Green, age 54, $750,000 total compensation
Chairman and CEO, Jonas Prising, age 55, $950,000 total compensation
SVP Operational Excellence and IT; President Asia/Pacific and Middle East, Sriram (Ram) Chandrashekar, age 48
President Northern Europe, Jilko Andringa
EVP and CFO, John T. (Jack) McGinnis, age 48
Vice President Global Human Resources, Lisa Banner
Senior Vice President North America, Kip Wright
Vice President, Sheldon Schur
Auditors: Deloitte & Touche LLP

LOCATIONS

HQ: ManpowerGroup
100 Manpower Place, Milwaukee, WI 53212
Phone: 414 961-1000   **Fax:** 414 332-0796
Web: www.manpower.com

2014 Sales

	$ mil.	% of total
Southern Europe	7,510	36
Northern Europe	6,048	29
Americas	4,584	22
Asia Pacific & Middle East	2,327	11
Right Management	294	2
Total	**20,763**	**100**

PRODUCTS/OPERATIONS

Selected Services
Staffing
Industrial trades
Manpower Professional
  Engineering
  Finance
  Information technology
  Telecommunications
Office and clerical

COMPETITORS

Adecco	Randstad Holding
Kelly Services	Robert Half
Korn/Ferry	TrueBlue
Michael Page	Volt Information

HISTORICAL FINANCIALS

Company Type: Public

Income Statement

FYE: December 31

	REVENUE ($ mil.)	NET INCOME ($ mil.)	NET PROFIT MARGIN	EMPLOYEES
12/14	20,762	427	2.1%	26,000
12/13	20,250	288	1.4%	25,000
12/12	20,678	197	1.0%	28,000
12/11	22,006	251	1.1%	31,000
12/10	18,866	(263)	—	30,000
Annual Growth	**2.4%**	**—**	**—**	**(3.5%)**

2014 Year-End Financials

Debt ratio: 6.53%
Return on equity: 14.60%
Cash ($ mil.): 699
Current ratio: 1.49
Long-term debt ($ mil.): 423

No. of shares (mil.): 78
Dividends
  Yield: 1.4%
  Payout: 19.2%
Market value ($ mil.): 5,325

	STOCK PRICE ($) FY Close	P/E High/Low	PER SHARE ($) Earnings	Dividends	Book Value
12/14	68.17	16 11	5.30	0.98	37.68
12/13	85.86	23 12	3.62	0.92	36.72
12/12	42.44	19 13	2.47	0.86	32.63
12/11	35.75	23 11	3.04	0.80	31.08
12/10	62.76	— —	(3.26)	0.74	29.32
Annual Growth	**2.1%**	**— —**	**—**	**7.3%**	**6.5%**

Marathon Oil Corp.

In the long-running competition for profits in the oil and gas industry Marathon Oil is keeping up a steady pace. The company explores for oil and gas primarily in Canada Equatorial Guinea Iraq Libya Poland the UK and the US. In 2014 it reported proved reserves of more than 2.2 billion barrels of oil equivalent including 644 million barrels of synthetic oil derived from oil sands mining. Its major areas of production include Europe (the UK); Africa (Equatorial Guinea and Libya); and Canada (the Athabasca Oil Sands Project). In the US the company's core production assets are in Colorado the Gulf of Mexico Louisiana Oklahoma Texas and Wyoming.

HISTORY

Marathon Oil was founded in 1887 in Lima Ohio as The Ohio Oil Company by 14 independent oil producers to compete with Standard Oil. Within two years Ohio Oil was the largest producer in the state. This success did not go unnoticed by Standard Oil which proceeded to buy Ohio Oil in 1889. In 1905 the company moved to Findlay Ohio where it remained until it relocated to Houston in 1990.

When the US Supreme Court broke up Standard Oil in 1911 Ohio Oil became independent once again and expanded its exploration activities to Kansas Louisiana Texas and Wyoming.

In a 1924 attempt to drill three wells west of the Pecos River in Texas Ohio Oil mistakenly drilled three dry holes to the east. The company was on the verge of abandoning the project until a geologist reported the error. Ohio Oil drilled in the right area and the wells flowed. That year the company bought Lincoln Oil Refining —its first venture outside crude oil production.

Ohio Oil continued its expansion into refining and marketing operations in 1927. Following

WWII the company began international exploration. Through Conorada Petroleum (later Oasis) a partnership with Continental Oil (later Conoco and then ConocoPhillips) and Amerada Hess the company explored in Africa and South and Central America. Conorada's biggest overseas deal came in 1955 when it acquired concessions on more than 60 million acres in Libya.

In 1962 the company acquired Plymouth Oil and changed its name to Marathon Oil Company; it had been using the Marathon name in its marketing activities since the late 1930s. Marathon added a 200000-barrel-a-day refinery in Louisiana to its operations in 1976 when it acquired ECOL Ltd.

After a battle with Mobil U.S. Steel acquired Marathon in 1982 for $6.5 billion. U.S. Steel changed its name to USX in 1986 and acquired Texas Oil & Gas. That year the US government introduced economic sanctions against Libya putting Marathon's Libyan holdings in suspension.

USX consolidated Texas Oil and Marathon in 1990. After a protracted struggle with corporate raider Carl Icahn USX split Marathon and U.S. Steel into two separate stock classes in 1991. A third offering USX-Delhi Group (the pipeline operator division) followed the next year. (Koch Industries bought USX-Delhi in 1997.)

A consortium led by USX-Marathon signed an agreement with the Russian government in 1994 to develop oil and gas fields off Sakhalin Island (although USX-Marathon sold its stake in the project in 2000). In 1996 Marathon formed a venture ElectroGen International with East Coast utility DQE to develop power generation projects in the Asia/Pacific region.

In 1998 Marathon and Ashland merged their refining and retail operations creating Marathon Ashland Petroleum (MAP) with Marathon owning 62%. That year Marathon in a deal that boosted its reserves by 18% acquired Calgary-based Tarragon Oil and Gas.

As part of a restructuring drive in 1999 MAP sold its crude oil gathering business Scurlock Permian to Plains All American Pipeline. With oil prices rebounding Marathon ramped up its oil exploration in 2000 buying more deepwater leases in the Gulf of Mexico and acquiring an interest in an oil and gas play offshore the Republic of Congo.

The company bought Pennaco Energy a Colorado-based producer of coalbed methane gas for about $500 million in 2001 and it agreed to buy CMS Energy's Equatorial Guinea (West Africa) oil and gas assets in a $993 million deal that was completed in 2002. At the end of 2001 USX spun off U.S. Steel and changed the name of the remaining company to Marathon Oil Corporation. In 2002 Marathon acquired Globex Energy a privately held exploration and production company with assets in West Africa for $155 million.

In 2005 Ashland sold its 38% stake in Marathon Ashland to Marathon Oil for about $3.7 billion.

In addition to acquiring MAP Marathon Oil also obtained Ashland's maleic anhydride business a share of its Valvoline Instant Oil Change business in Michigan and Ohio and other assets.

In 2006 the company sold its oil and gas assets in the Khanty-Mansiysk autonomous region of western Siberia to LUKOIL for $787 million. That year Marathon Oil announced a plan to spend $3.2 billion to expand the crude oil refining capacity of its refinery in Garyville Louisiana.

As a way to expand its hydrocarbon asset base the company has been investing heavily in non-conventional exploration and production areas. In 2006 as part of a five-year $1.5 billion investment the company announced plans to drill as many as 225 new wells in western North Dakota in the Bakken Oil Formation (tight shale layers) over a five-year period. The following year Marathon Oil expanded into the Canadian oil sands market through the acquisition of Western Oil Sands for about $5.8 billion.

Seeking stronger financial returns in 2011 Marathon Oil (formerly a holding company with both upstream and downstream operations) spun off its downstream unit Marathon Petroleum (which had accounted for the bulk of its revenues) and became a pure-play exploration and production company.

On the acquisition side Marathon Oil has made significant investments in the South Texas Eagle Ford resource play. In 2011 it bought $3.5 billion of Eagle Ford assets from KKR and Hilcorp Energy. In 2012 it acquired 25000 net acres in the Eagle Ford shale play. The largest deals were the acquisitions of Paloma Partners II LLC for $768 million and an separate acquisition of proved and unproved properties for $232 million.

EXECUTIVES

EVP and CFO, John R. (J.R.) Sult, age 57, $600,000 total compensation
EVP General Counsel and Secretary, Sylvia J. Kerrigan, age 50, $575,000 total compensation
VP North America Production Operations, Lance W. Robertson, $458,019 total compensation
VP International and Offshore Production Operations, T. Mitchell (Mitch) Little, $423,558 total compensation
President and CEO, Lee M. Tillman, $1,036,346 total compensation
VP and CIO, Bruce A. McCullough
Vp Business Development, Steven (Steve) Guidry
Vice President Business Development, Felix Taubman
Senior Vice President Refining Marathon Oil, Jerry Welch
Vice President Geophysical It, Trevor Chargois
Vice President, Robert (Bob) Sovine
Executive Vice President, George Tranos
Vice President Human Resources, Deanna Jones
Vice President and Manager and Director, Ellen Norton
Vice President Accounting and Controller, Michael (Mel) Stewart
Vice President International, T Little
Chairman, Dennis H. Reilley, age 62
Auditors: PricewaterhouseCoopers LLP

LOCATIONS

HQ: Marathon Oil Corp.
    5555 San Felipe Street, Houston, TX 77056-2723
Phone: 713 629-6600
Web: www.marathonoil.com

PRODUCTS/OPERATIONS

2014 Sales

	% of total
North American E&P	70
International E&P	15
OSM	15
Total	**100**

2014 Sales

	% of total
Crude oil and condensate	76
Synthetic crude oil	14
Natural Gas	6
Natural Gas liquids	3
Other	1
Total	**100**

2014 Sales

	% of total
United States	70
Canada	15
Other International	13
Libya	2
Total	**100**

COMPETITORS

BP	Occidental Petroleum
Chevron	PEMEX
ConocoPhillips	Petrleos de
Exxon Mobil	Venezuela
Hess Corporation	Royal Dutch Shell
Koch Industries Inc.	

HISTORICAL FINANCIALS

Company Type: Public

Income Statement

FYE: December 31

	REVENUE ($ mil.)	NET INCOME ($ mil.)	NET PROFIT MARGIN	EMPLOYEES
12/14	11,258	3,046	27.1%	3,330
12/13	14,959	1,753	11.7%	3,359
12/12	16,221	1,582	9.8%	3,367
12/11	15,282	2,946	19.3%	3,322
12/10	73,621	2,568	3.5%	29,677
Annual Growth	**(37.5%)**	**4.4%**	**—**	**(42.1%)**

2014 Year-End Financials

Debt ratio: 17.75%
Return on equity: 15.09%
Cash ($ mil.): 2,398
Current ratio: 1.05
Long-term debt ($ mil.): 5,323
No. of shares (mil.): 675
Dividends
  Yield: 2.8%
  Payout: 1.05
Market value ($ mil.): 19,096

	STOCK PRICE ($) FY Close	P/E High/Low		PER SHARE ($) Earnings	Dividends	Book Value
12/14	28.29	9	6	4.46	0.80	31.14
12/13	35.30	15	12	2.47	0.72	27.75
12/12	30.66	16	10	2.23	0.68	25.86
12/11	29.27	13	5	4.13	0.80	24.36
12/10	37.03	10	8	3.61	0.99	33.48
Annual Growth	**(6.5%)**	**—**	**—**	**5.4%**	**(5.2%)**	**(1.8%)**

Marathon Petroleum Corp.

Marathon Petroleum has a long running commitment to fuel its customers. The former refining and marketing unit of Marathon Oil Corporation operates seven refineries with the capacity to process about 1.7 million barrels of crude oil a day. Marathon Petroleum sells refined products through a nationwide network of branded gas stations. It also holds stakes in pipelines and is one of the largest asphalt and light oil product terminal operators in the US. The company distributes petroleum products wholesale to private-brand marketers and to large commercial and industrial consumers as well as to the spot market.

Geographic Reach

Marathon Petroleum sells refined products at some 5500 Marathon-branded gas stations in 19 US states and through retail subsidiary Speedway SuperAmerica's 2760 outlets in 22 states. It also holds stakes in 8300 miles of pipeline (MPLX LP) and is one of the largest asphalt and light oil product terminal operators in the US (81 terminals in 2014). In addition the company has a large US private inland product fleet that includes 19 inland towboats and 200 barges.

Operations

The company's operations consist of three business segments: Refining & Marketing (which refines crude oil and other feedstocks at seven re-

fineries in the US Gulf Coast and Midwest regions purchases ethanol and refined products for resale and distributes refined products). It sells refined products to wholesale marketing customers buyers on the spot market its Speedway business segment and to independent entrepreneurs who operate Marathon retail outlets;

Speedway which sells transportation fuels and convenience products in the retail market in the Midwest primarily through Speedway convenience stores; and

Pipeline Transportation which transports crude oil and other feedstocks to Marathon Petroleum's refineries and other locations delivers refined products to wholesale and retail markets and affiliated pipeline assets and investments.

Sales and Marketing

Marathon Petroleum sells to wholesale suppliers of gasoline and distillates to resellers and consumers. Customers include independent retailers wholesale customers their Marathon brand jobbers and Speedway brand convenience stores airlines transportation companies and utilities. It also sells gasoline distillates and asphalt for export primarily out of their Garyville and Galveston Bay refineries.

The company sold 55% of its gasoline sales volumes and 89% of its distillates sales volumes on a wholesale or spot market basis in 2014. It also sells via retail outlets primarily in Florida Mississippi Tennessee and Alabama and branded lessee dealer marketing contract assignments primarily in Connecticut Maryland and New York. In 2014 Marathon had outstanding retail marketing contract assignments for 590 retail outlets.

Financial Performance

The company recorded fluctuation in net revenues in the last five years. In 2014 Marathon Petroleum's net revenues decreased by 2% due to lower refined product sales prices partially offset by an increase in refined product sales volumes and higher merchandise sales for its Speedway segment attributable to the convenience stores acquired from Hess. The Refining & Marketing segment revenues decline was primarily due to lower refined product sales prices partially offset by an increase in refined product sales volumes. Speedway revenues grew thanks to increases in gasoline and distillate sales (primarily due to increases in the number of convenience stores) and increases in merchandise sales partially offset by decreases in gasoline and distillate selling prices.

Pipeline Transportation revenues increased due to volume deficiency credits and higher average tariffs received on crude oil and refined products shipped partially offset by lower refined products and crude oil pipeline throughput volumes. Marathon Petroleum's net income increased by 20% due to higher Refining & Marketing income as the result of more favorable net product price realizations and higher US Gulf Coast and Chicago crack spreads partially offset by narrower crude oil differentials and higher turnaround and other direct operating costs. In addition net gain on disposal of assets increased as the result of the sale of two terminals and terminal assets and higher other income. In 2014 cash from operating activities decreased by 9% due to the changes in inventories and current accounts payable and accrued liabilities partially offset by an increase in net income and non-cash income adjustments.

Strategy

Marathon Petroleum is looking to expand its refining midstream logistics and retail businesses through acquisitions and organic growth.

The most significant achievement was completing the acquisition of Hess' retail operations. This transaction was truly transformative for Speedway increasing its store count to approximately 2750 and expanding its retail presence from nine Midwestern states to 22 states throughout the Midwest East Coast and Southeast. By the end of 2014 the company had converted 60 stores to the Speedway brand and is aiming to convert of all Hess stores by the end of 2016.

Mergers and Acquisitions

Boosting its midstream footprint in 2015 Marathon Petroleum and MXLP (the midstream master limited partnership sponsored by Marathon) signed a definitive merger agreement with MarkWest Energy Partners whereby MarkWest would become a wholly owned subsidiary of MPLX. The merger (which has an enterprise value for MarkWest of $20 billion) transforms MPLX into a large-cap diversified master limited partnership.

Growing its retail network in 2014 Marathon Petroleum bought Hess' gasoline stations for $2.8 billion. The move expanded Speedway's retail presence to 22 states throughout the East Coast and Southeast.

That year it also purchased a facility in Cincinnati Ohio from Felda Iffco Sdn Bhd Malaysia. The plant currently produces several products including biodiesel and glycerin.

To expand its refining capacity in 2013 Marathon Petroleum bought BP's 451000 barrels-of-oil-per-day refinery in Texas City in Galveston Bay for about $2.5 billion. (The base purchase price was $598 million plus inventories valued at $1.1 billion. The agreement also contains an earnout provision under which Marathon Petroleum might pay up to an additional $700 million over six years subject to certain conditions).

That year the company also acquired interests in three ethanol companies from Mitsui & Co. (U.S.A.) Inc. for $75 million.

Company Background

Growing its retail network in 2012 Marathon Petroleum's Speedway America unit bought 87 gas stations in Indiana and Ohio from GasAmerica Services. It purchased 23 in Illinois and Indiana in 2011.

In early 2012 Marathon Petroleum formed a tax-exempt limited partnership (MPLX) to take over some of its midstream operations. MPLX has an indirect 51% stake in about 2800 miles of pipeline across nine states in the Midwest and Gulf Coast as well as a Mississippi River barge dock and tank farms. (Marathon Petroleum retains the other 49% stake.) MPLX filed a $365 million initial public offering in July 2012 and went public in October 2012. Marathon Petroleum intends for MPLX to be the primary growth vehicle for its midstream business by transferring even more assets to the tax-exempt entity.

With an improving economy in 2011 Marathon Oil Corporation spun off Marathon Petroleum to improve shareholder returns by having two publicly traded companies —an exploration and production entity and a refining and marketing company.

To free up cash and to help it meet expansion costs in 2010 the company sold its Minnesota downstream assets (including a refinery and more than 230 gas stations/convenience stores) to investment firms TPG Capital and ACON Investments for about $900 million.

The company has invested $3.3 billion in a conventional refinery expansion at its Garyville Louisiana plant (completed in 2009) and put up $2.2 billion to upgrade its heavy oil processing unit in Detroit (completed in 2012).

Marathon Petroleum traces it roots to the formation of the Ohio Oil Company in 1887.

EXECUTIVES

President and CEO, Gary R. Heminger, age 61, $1,537,500 total compensation
President Speedway, Anthony R. (Tony) Kenney, age 62, $568,750 total compensation
SVP CFO and Treasurer, Timothy T. Griffith, age 45
SVP Supply Distribution and Planning, C. Michael Palmer, age 61, $537,500 total compensation
EVP and President MPLX, Donald C. (Don) Templin, age 51, $687,500 total compensation
SVP Refining, Richard D. Bedell, age 60, $587,500 total compensation
SVP Transportation and Logistics, George P. Shaffner, age 56
VP and CIO, Donald W. Wehrly, age 55
Sr V Pres, Pamela (Pam) Beall
Senior Vice President of Marketing, Thomas (Thom) Kelley
Vice President Business Development And Finance, Danna Garrett-Winn
Chairman, Thomas J. Usher, age 73
Assistant Treasurer Corporate Finance and Banking, Peter (Pete) Gilgen
Auditors: PricewaterhouseCoopers LLP

LOCATIONS

HQ: Marathon Petroleum Corp.
539 South Main Street, Findlay, OH 45840-3229
Phone: 419 422-2121
Web: www.marathonpetroleum.com

PRODUCTS/OPERATIONS

2014 Sales

	% of total
Refined products	93
Merchandise	4
Crude oil & refinery feedstocks	3
Transportation & other	0
Total	**100**

2014 Sales

	% of total
Refining & marketing	84
Speedway	15
Pipeline transportation	1
Total	**100**

Selected Products

Asphalt
Branded Distillates
Branded Gasoline
Branded Lubricants
Heavy Oil
Petroleum Coke
Specialty Products
Wholesale Light Products

COMPETITORS

BP	Koch Industries Inc.
CITGO	Motiva Enterprises
Chevron	Murphy Oil
ConocoPhillips	Shell Oil Products
Exxon Mobil	Sunoco
Hess Corporation	Tesoro
HollyFrontier	Valero Energy

HISTORICAL FINANCIALS

Company Type: Public

Income Statement

FYE: December 31

	REVENUE ($ mil.)	NET INCOME ($ mil.)	NET PROFIT MARGIN	EMPLOYEES
12/14	98,102	2,524	2.6%	45,340
12/13	100,254	2,112	2.1%	29,865
12/12	82,492	3,389	4.1%	25,985
12/11	78,759	2,389	3.0%	24,210
12/10	62,605	623	1.0%	25,803
Annual Growth	11.9%	41.9%	—	15.1%

2014 Year-End Financials

Debt ratio: 21.79%
Return on equity: 23.29%
Cash ($ mil.): 1,494
Current ratio: 1.32
Long-term debt ($ mil.): 6,610

No. of shares (mil.): 548
Dividends
  Yield: 4.0%
  Payout: 41.9%
Market value ($ mil.): 49,462

	STOCK PRICE ($) FY Close	P/E High/Low		PER SHARE ($) Earnings	Dividends	Book Value
12/14	90.26	22	17	4.39	1.84	19.62
12/13	91.73	27	18	3.32	1.54	18.38
12/12	63.00	13	6	4.95	1.20	17.56
12/11	33.29	13	8	3.34	0.23	13.31
Annual Growth	28.3%	—	—	7.1%	69.1%	10.2%

Markel Corp (Holding Co)

Have you ever thought about who insures the manicurist or an antique motorcycle? Specialty insurer Markel takes on the risks other insurers won't touch from amusement parks to thoroughbred horses to summer camps. Coverage is also available for one-time events such as golf tournaments and auto races. The company provides customized direct and facultative placements in the US and abroad as well as treaty reinsurance. Markel International provides specialty insurance internationally from its base in the UK and Alterra handles specialty insurance and reinsurance in the US and parts of Europe and Latin America. Meanwhile subsidiary Markel Ventures invests in noninsurance companies.OperationsThe company operates through three primary segments: US Insurance (more than half of all sale) International Insurance and Reinsurance.US Insurance writes commercial risks primarily excess and surplus lines which are distributed through a network of wholesale brokers. It also writes specialty coverage for niche markets. Excess insurance kicks in when a company's regular insurance fizzles out. For example a regular policy might pay up to $100000 on claims but the excess policy could then pay any amounts over $100000 and up to $1 million. Surplus insurance is coverage that no regular insurance company can offer and typically comes with a higher level of risk and higher-priced premiums.The specialty admitted business segment serves clients that engage in highly specialized activities requiring niche insurance coverage typically not offered by standard insurers. Underwriting entities include Thompson Insurance Enterprises (THOMCO) unit for medical child care and fitness facilities and FirstComp Insurance for workers' compensation as well as the Markel Insurance and Markel American Insurance units. The company's Alterra unit includes property/casualty reinsurance and specialty insurance covering things like medical malpractice and workers' compensation.Markel International based in London writes business worldwide including its syndicate at Lloyd's of London. It also offers global reinsurance products as does the Reinsurance segment.The remainder of revenues comes from private equity unit Markel Ventures —which invests in entities ranging from food equipment makers to medical providers —and from investment income.Geographic ReachMarkel primarily operates in the US market which accounts for about 75% of premiums. Its UK unit Markel International writes policies for UK clients as well as for on a global basis through the Lloyd's of London market. Markel has about 30 locations in North America 13 in Europe (including 10 in the UK) three in South America and six in the Asia/Pacific region.Sales and MarketingThe company distributes its products through independent agents and brokers.Financial PerformanceMarkel's revenues have increased each year over the last five years as the company has expanded through strategic acquisitions. Increased revenues in 2014 (growing 19% to some $5.1 billion) were attributed to higher earned premiums in all three operating segments and from the recent acquisition of Alterra.Net income which has been rising for the past three years increased 14% to $321 million in 2014 due to the higher revenue. However a decline in cash provided by receivables led to a 4% decline in cash flow from operations which slipped to $717 million that year.StrategyMarkel's strategy for growth is to leverage its expertise and specialized market knowledge of niche markets to differentiate its business from competitors. It is also looking to diversify into new specialty insurance markets as well as to make profitable venture capital investments through its private equity unit. Financially the company's aim is to generate consistent underwriting and operating profits and produce superior returns on its investments to increase its value for shareholders.The company is also focused on expanding international operations in the UK Europe the Asia/Pacific region and South America.Mergers and AcquisitionsIn 2013 Markel struck a larger-than-usual deal when it acquired Bermuda-based Alterra Capital Holdings for some $3.3 billion. Alterra provides property/casualty reinsurance and insurance operations in niche markets including medical malpractice and workers' compensation. In addition to expanding its specialty operations the purchase diversified Markel's operations into the reinsurance and large accounts businesses.Markel acquired Abbey Protection a London-based integrated specialty insurance and consultancy for $190.7 million in 2014.Recent non-insurance investments include the 2014 acquisition of car hauler equipment maker Cottrell as well as the purchase of several manufactured housing communities.

HISTORY

In the 1920s Sam Markel formed a mutual insurance company for "jitneys" (passenger cars refurbished as public transportation buses). In 1930 he founded Markel Service to expand nationally. To keep up with industry growth the company revamped itself as a managing general agent and independent claims service organization in the late 1950s. In 1978 Markel began covering taverns restaurants and vacant buildings. It created excess and surplus lines underwriter Essex Insurance in 1980.

Markel went public in 1986. The next year it invested in Shand Morahan and Evanston Insurance (specialty coverage including architects engineers

and lawyers professional liability; officers and directors insurance; errors and omissions; and medical malpractice). It bought summer camp insurer Rhulen Agency in 1989.

In the 1990s Markel began buying insurers with their own offbeat niches. In 1990 it bought the rest of Shand Morahan and Evanston Insurance. In 1995 it bought Lincoln Insurance (excess and surplus lines) from media giant Thomson (now Thomson Reuters). The next year the company bought Investors Insurance Holding (excess and surplus lines). Markel which already owned nearly 10% of Gryphon Holdings (commercial property/casualty) bought the rest in 1999.

Expanding internationally Markel bought Bermuda-based Terra Nova Holdings a reinsurer and a Lloyd's managing agency in 2000. The company experienced heavy losses in 2001 not only related to the events of September 11 but also to its slumping international business (the company took a $100 million charge).Unlike standard insurers (whose rates are generally regulated) specialty insurers can charge the rates they consider reasonable. To that end after taking significant losses from the 2005 hurricane season (Katrina Rita Wilma) and additional hits from the 2008 season (Gustav Ike) the company decided to raise the rates on its catastrophe-exposed businesses.

EXECUTIVES

Chairman and CEO, Alan I. Kirshner, age 79, $900,000 total compensation
President and Chief Investment Officer, Thomas S. Gayner, age 53, $750,000 total compensation
President and Co-COO, Richard R. Whitt, age 51, $750,000 total compensation
President and Co-COO, F. Michael Crowley, age 63, $750,000 total compensation
EVP and Chief Underwriting Officer, Gerard Albanese, age 62, $558,333 total compensation
EVP and CFO, Anne G. Waleski, age 48, $468,750 total compensation
EVP and Chief Actuarial Officer, Bradley J. Kiscaden, age 52
CIO, Mike Scyphers
Vice President, Chuck Kyte
Associate Vice President, Kathleen Olear
Vice President Investor, Mike Kotlowski
Vice President Marketing, Cara Bowen
Vice Chairman, Anthony F. Markel, age 73
Vice Chairman, Steven A. Markel, age 66
Auditors: KPMG LLP

LOCATIONS

HQ: Markel Corp (Holding Co)
   4521 Highwoods Parkway, Glen Allen, VA 23060-6148
Phone: 804 747-0136
Web: www.markelcorp.com

2014 Gross Written Premiums

	% of total
US	73
UK	9
Canada	3
Other countries	15
Total	**100**

PRODUCTS/OPERATIONS

2014 Revenues

	$ mil.	% of total
Earned premiums		
US insurance	2,022	39
International insurance	909	18
Reinsurance	908	18
Net investment income	363	7
Net realized investment gains	46	1
Other revenues	883	17
Total	**5,133**	**100**

COMPETITORS

Assurant
CNA Financial
Great American Insurance Company
HCC Insurance
Liberty International Underwriters
Meadowbrook Insurance
Medical Liability Mutual Insurance
National Indemnity Company
Nationwide
Penn-America
Philadelphia Insurance Companies
ProSight Specialty Insurance Group
RLI
Travelers Companies
United States Liability Insurance Group
XL Group plc

HISTORICAL FINANCIALS

Company Type: Public

Income Statement

FYE: December 31

	ASSETS ($ mil.)	NET INCOME ($ mil.)	INCOME AS % OF ASSETS	EMPLOYEES
12/14	25,200	323	1.3%	8,600
12/13	23,955	283	1.2%	7,200
12/12	12,556	258	2.1%	6,400
12/11	11,532	148	1.3%	5,400
12/10	10,825	267	2.5%	4,800
Annual Growth	**23.5%**	**4.9%**	**—**	**15.7%**

2014 Year-End Financials

Debt ratio: 8.94%
Return on equity: 4.54%
Cash ($ mil.): 1,960
Current ratio: —
Long-term debt ($ mil.): —

No. of shares (mil.): 13
Dividends
   Yield: —
   Payout: —
Market value ($ mil.): 9,534

	STOCK PRICE ($) FY Close	P/E High/Low	PER SHARE ($) Earnings	Dividends	Book Value
12/14	682.84	31 24	22.27	0.00	543.98
12/13	580.35	26 19	22.48	0.00	477.17
12/12	433.42	19 15	25.89	0.00	403.84
12/11	414.67	29 24	14.60	0.00	352.10
12/10	378.13	14 12	27.27	0.00	326.36
Annual Growth	**15.9%**	**— —**	**(4.9%)**	**—**	**13.6%**

Marriott International, Inc.

Marriott International signs in at the top of the lodging industry. The company is one of the world's leading hoteliers with some 4300 operated or franchised properties worldwide. Its hotels include such full-service brands as Renaissance Hotels and its flagship Marriott Hotels & Resorts as well as select-service and extended-stay brands Courtyard and Fairfield Inn. It also owns the Ritz-Carlton luxury chain and resort and manages about 45 golf courses. The Marriott family including J. W. Marriott Jr. owns about 30% of Marriott International.

Geographic Reach

While the bulk of its hotels are located in the US about 15% of its properties are international. Marriott has operations in more than 80 countries in the Americas the UK and Ireland the Middle East and Africa Asia Australia and Continental Europe.

Financial Performance

The company reported $13.8 billion in revenue for fiscal 2014. That was an increase of 8% compared to the prior fiscal period. Marriott's net income was $753 million in fiscal 2014 which was an increase of $127 million compared to fiscal 2013.

The company's cash from operations increased by $84 million in fiscal 2014 compared to the prior fiscal year and Marriott ended the year with a comfortable $1.2 in cash on hand.

Strategy

Marriott's business model focuses on managing and franchising hotels rather than owning them. More than 50% of its hotel rooms are operated by franchisees that pay the company fees and royalties as well as a percentage of their food and beverage revenue.

Mergers and Acquisitions

In 2015 Marriott agreed to acquire Starwood Hotels & Resorts Worldwide in a deal worth $12.2 billion. The merger will create the world's biggest hotel company with more than 5500 hotels and about 1.1 million rooms in some 100 countries worldwide. The deal which is expected to close in mid-2016 will also give Marriott more hotel properties in Asia Europe and Latin America.

HISTORY

The company began in 1927 as a Washington DC root beer stand operated by John and Alice Marriott. Later they added hot food and named their business the Hot Shoppe. In 1929 the couple incorporated and began building a regional chain.

Hot Shoppes opened its first hotel the Twin Bridges Marriott Motor Hotel in Arlington Virginia in 1957. When the Marriotts' son Bill became president in 1964 (CEO in 1972 chairman in 1985) he focused on expanding the hotel business. The company changed its name to Marriott Corp. in 1967. With the rise in airline travel Marriott built several airport hotels during the 1970s. By 1977 sales had topped $1 billion.

Marriott became the #1 operator of airport food beverage and merchandise facilities in the US with its 1982 acquisition of Host International and it introduced moderately priced Courtyard hotels in 1983. Acquisitions in the 1980s included a time-share business foodservice companies and competitor Howard Johnson. (Marriott later sold the hotels but kept the restaurants and turnpike units.)

The company entered three new market segments in 1987: Marriott Suites (full-service suites) Residence Inn (moderately priced suites) and Fairfield Inn (economy hotels). It also began developing "life-care" communities which provide apartments meals and limited nursing care to the elderly in 1988.

Marriott split its operations into two companies in 1993: Host Marriott to own hotels and Marriott International primarily to manage them. However Marriott International still owned some of the properties and in 1995 it bought 49% of the Ritz-Carlton luxury hotel group.

In 1996 Marriott purchased the Forum Group (assisted living communities and health care services) and merged it into Marriott Senior Living Services.

Marriott introduced its Marriott Executive Residences in 1997. Also that year the firm expanded overseas operations with its purchase of the 150-unit Hong Kong-based Renaissance Hotel Group

a deal that included branding rights to the Ramada chain.

In 1998 after the division of its lodging and food distribution services the new Marriott International then began trading as a separate company. That year Marriott also acquired the rest of Ritz-Carlton and established SpringHill Suites by Marriott.

Marriott entered the corporate housing business in 1999 through its acquisition of ExecuStay Corporation (renamed ExecuStay by Marriott) which provided fully furnished and accessorized apartments for stays of 30 days or more. The following year it joined Italy's Bulgari the world's #3 jeweler in a $140 million venture of luxury hotels sporting the Bulgari name.

Marriott refocused its operations on the lodging market in 2003 when it exited both the senior living and distribution services businesses. It sold Marriott Distribution Services (food and beverage distribution) to Services Group of America and sold Marriott Senior Living Services to Sunrise Assisted Living (the management business) and CNL Retirement Properties (nine communities). The following year Marriott sold the international branding rights to the Ramada and Days Inn chains to Cendant (now Avis Budget Group) for about $200 million.

In 2005 Marriott acquired about 30 properties from CTF Holdings (an affiliate of Hong Kong-based New World Development) for nearly $1.5 billion. It sold 14 properties immediately to Sunstone Hotel Investors and Walton Street Capital. The deal put an end to an ongoing legal battle between Marriott and CTF Holdings which had alleged that the hotelier had pocketed kickbacks and fees from outside vendors.

Marriott invested about $200 million in 2005 to upgrade its hotel beds with higher thread-count sheets and triple-sheeted tops and it renovated and upgraded many of its Courtyard and Residence Inn locations during 2006. A difficult 2009 called for the elimination of more than 1000 jobs. Also that year the company cut costs by modifying menus and restaurant hours adjusting room amenities and relaxing some brand standards.

In 2010 Marriott introduced two new hotel brands into the market: Edtion (a boutique luxury chain) and Autograph Collection (independent luxury properties that each have their own unique identity). The firm spun off its time-share business Marriott Vacations Worldwide in 2011.

EXECUTIVES

Executive Vice President Blobal Business Finance, Kevin Kimball
President and CEO, Arne M. Sorenson, age 56, $1,236,000 total compensation
EVP Finance and Global Treasurer, Carolyn B. Handlon
President and Managing Director Asia Pacific, Simon F. Cooper, age 69
Group President, David J. Grissen, age 58, $700,003 total compensation
EVP Lodging Human Resources, David A. Rodriguez, age 56
EVP and General Counsel, Edward A. (Ed) Ryan, age 61
President and Managing Director Europe, Amy C. McPherson, age 53
EVP and Global Chief Development Officer, Anthony G. (Tony) Capuano, age 49, $663,062 total compensation
EVP CFRST Brand Management and Operations, Tim Sheldon
EVP and Chief Marketing and Commercial Officer, Stephanie C. Linnartz
President and Managing Director Middle East and Africa, Alex Kyriakidis
CFO, Leeny K. Oberg, age 55

Vice President Engineering And Technical Services, Terry Smith
V Pres, Joseph (Jo) Ryan
Vice President Of Enterprise Operations, Ed Goldman
Senior Vice President Finance And Treasurer, Raymond G Murphy
Vice President Human Resources Policy Strategy and Compliance, Melissa (Mel) Milton
Assistant Vice President, Karina Barney
Vice President International Compensation And Benefits, Ken Feast
Vice President Development Planning And Feasibility, Christopher Froome
Vice President Information Technology, Jim Abramson
Vice President Estimating, Allan Smeaton
Vice President Information Technology, Kevin Reiners
Vice President Sales and Marketing, Chris Greenleaf
Senior Vice President Application Development and Enterprise Architecture, Eric Tagliere
Vice President, Cindy Braak
Vice President, Elaine Engle
Vice President Interior Design Global Services Architecture And Construction, Lionel Sussman
Market Vice President, Kevin Schwab
Vice President Of Application Architecture, Douglas (Doug) Wurtzel
Vice President, Gina Masterson
Regional Vice President, Mike Taylor
Area Vice President, Dan Kelleher
Vice President, Jeff Spilman
Vice President Sales, Dennis Edwards
Vice President Property Systems Servic, Laura Bouvier
Vice President Sales and Marketing, Kimberly West
Senior Vice President, Wolfgang Lindlbauer
Senior Vice President Lodging Development, Jim Fisher
Vice President Brand Operations Designanddevelop, Mark Sahler
Vice President Telecommunications, Robert (Bob) Galovic
Vice President Franchising, Steve Stamas
Vice President User Experience eCommerce Group, Mariana Calvacanti
Vice President Finance, Alberto Morales
Regional Vice President Sales And Marketing Asia Pacific, Kent Maury
Vice President And Senior Counsel, Taisha Urland
Senior Vice President Lodging Development, Christopher Rose
Senior Vice President Finance Department, Gary Rosenthal
Vice President, Jennie Benzon
Vice President And Senior Counsel, Linda Miller
Senior Vice President Human Resources, Tammy Smith
Vice President Of Operations, Bill Smith
Vice President Finance, Mark Gaber
Senior Vice President Brand Strategy And Innovation, Julie Moll
Vice President Development Caribbean And Latin America, Rodolfo Guillioli
Vice President Owner and Franchise Services, Paul Puzzanghero
Vice President Architecture and Application Development, Hurkan Balkir
Vice President Information Resources Americas, Welch Patricia
Vice President Operations, Kate Gruell
Senior Vice President And General Counsel, Myron Walker
Senior Vice President Global Asset Management, Catherine Young
Vice President, William Holmes
Vice President Marketing, Daniel Vihn
Vice President, Jim O'Hern

Marsh & McLennan Companies Inc.

Vice President, Chad O'neil
Vice President North American Development, Dan Mahoney
Vice President And General Counsel, Shea Gottshall
Senior Vice President Of Human Resources, Lynda Dubay
Senior Vice President, Janis Milham
Vice President Finance and Accounting, Robert (Bob) Kalchik
Vice President Operations, Christoph Roshardt
Vice President Health And Welfare, Judy Fennimore
Vice President Of Human Resources, Debbie Wilson
Vice President Information Resources, Mohammad Vaziri
Vice President Operations Officer, Chip Shewbridge
Regional Vice President Of Operations For Operator, Roger Goldesberry
Vice President IR Business Partnrshipandplan, Charles (Chas) Keppler
Vice President Leisure Business Development, Warren Ruello
Vice President Service Fulfillment, Denis Looney
Vice President Jw Marriott Hotels And Resorts Marriott Hotels And Resorts, Michael Darne
Communications Vice President, Leigh Brummerhoff
Solution Marketing Vice President, Kelly Keith
Vice President, Hannah Jeon
Vice President Sales And Marketing Support, Beth Jones
Vice President, Matt Fuller
Vice President, Anne Gunsteens
Executive Vice President Architecture And Construction, Susan Levenson
Executive Vice President Mergers Acquisitions and Business Development, Richard S (Dick) Hoffman
Senior Vice President Associate Genera, W David Mann
Vice President Global Operations Services, Peggy Roe
Vice President And Senior Counsel, C Carnot Evans
Vice President And Senior Counsel, Lisa Greenlees
Senior Vice President Owner And Franchise Services, John (Jack) Moore
Vice President, Stephen (Steve) Maselko
Senior Vice President Mergers and Acquisition, Richard (Dick) HoffmanmarriotCom
Vice President Owner and Franchise Services Initiatives Communication and Support, Roslyn Winegrad
Chairman, J. W. (Bill) Marriott, age 83
Treasurer, Lauren Webb
Board Of Directors And Committee Member, Lori Adair
Board Member, Johanna Glatz
Board Member, Ron Couget
Director And Chairman Emeritus, Jessica Cuba
Auditors: Ernst & Young LLP

LOCATIONS

HQ: Marriott International, Inc.
10400 Fernwood Road, Bethesda, MD 20817
Phone: 301 380-3000
Web: www.marriott.com

2014 Locations

	No.
Americas	3,539
Europe	
UK & Ireland	66
Continental Europe	237
Asia	170
Middle East & Africa	157
Australia	6
Total	**4,175**

PRODUCTS/OPERATIONS

2014 Sales

	$ mil.	% of total
North American full-service	8,323	61
North American limited-service	2,962	21
International Segment	2,255	16
Other Unallocated corporate	256	2
Total	**13,796**	**100**

Selected Operations and Brands

International lodging
  Courtyard by Marriott
  Fairfield Inn by Marriott
  JW Marriott Hotels & Resorts
  Marriott Executive Apartments
  Marriott Hotels & Resorts
  Ramada International
  Renaissance Hotels & Resorts
  Residence Inn by Marriott
Luxury hotels
  Bulgari Hotels & Resorts
  The Ritz-Carlton
North American full-service hotels
  JW Marriott Hotels & Resorts
  Marriott Conference Centers
  Marriott Hotels & Resorts
  Renaissance ClubSport
  Renaissance Hotels & Resorts
North American limited-service hotels
  Courtyard by Marriott
  Fairfield Inn by Marriott
  Marriott ExecuStay
  Residence Inn by Marriott
  SpringHill Suites by Marriott
  TownePlace Suites by Marriott

Selected Mergers and Acquisitions

FY2012
Gaylord Entertainment ($210 million; Nashville TN; hotel management company)

COMPETITORS

Accor	Four Seasons Hotels
Best Western	Hilton Worldwide
Carlson Hotels	Hyatt
Choice Hotels	InterContinental
Club Med	Hotels
Extended Stay America Inc.	LXR Luxury Resorts
	Loews Hotels
FRHI Hotels and Resorts	Starwood Hotels & Resorts

HISTORICAL FINANCIALS

Company Type: Public

Income Statement

FYE: December 31

	REVENUE ($ mil.)	NET INCOME ($ mil.)	NET PROFIT MARGIN	EMPLOYEES
12/14	13,796	753	5.5%	123,500
12/13	12,784	626	4.9%	123,000
12/12	11,814	571	4.8%	127,000
12/11	12,317	198	1.6%	120,000
12/10	11,691	458	3.9%	129,000
Annual Growth	**4.2%**	**13.2%**	—	**(1.1%)**

2014 Year-End Financials

Debt ratio: 55.08%
Return on equity: —
Cash ($ mil.): 104
Current ratio: 0.63
Long-term debt ($ mil.): 3,457
No. of shares (mil.): 279
Dividends
  Yield: 0.9%
  Payout: 32.7%
Market value ($ mil.): 21,841

	STOCK PRICE ($) FY Close	P/E High/Low	PER SHARE ($) Earnings	Dividends	Book Value
12/14	78.03	30 18	2.54	0.77	(7.86)
12/13	49.35	24 18	2.00	0.64	(4.75)
12/12	36.48	24 16	1.72	0.49	(4.13)
12/11	29.17	75 47	0.55	0.39	(2.35)
12/10	41.54	34 20	1.21	0.21	4.32
Annual Growth	**17.1%**	— —	**20.4%**	**38.8%**	—

Marsh & McLennan Companies Inc.

Marsh & McLennan Companies (MMC) is the ultimate insurance middleman. The company is one of the world's largest insurance brokers. Through core subsidiary Marsh the company provides a broad array of insurance-related brokerage consulting and risk management services to clients in more than 130 countries including large and small companies government entities and not-for-profit organizations. Its global reinsurance brokerage business is handled by subsidiary Guy Carpenter. MMC also owns Mercer which provides human resources and financial consulting services to customers in 40 nations worldwide and Oliver Wyman which provides management consulting services.

Geographic Reach

MMC provides services in the Americas the Asia/Pacific region and the EMEA (Europe Middle East and Africa) region. The US contributes about 45% of annual revenues.

Operations

Citing the rise of economic difficulties natural disasters such as tsunamis and hurricanes international terrorism and other hazards for businesses MMC has been working to expand its role as a risk consultant. The company's operations are split into two groups —the Risk and Insurance Services (RIS) division (Marsh and Guy Carpenter) and the Consulting division (Mercer and Oliver Wyman) — both of which help clients assess risks in their businesses and ascertain whether those risks are insurable.

The company's Marsh insurance subsidiary accounts for about 45% of annual revenues. The Mercer human resources business is MMC's second largest subsidiary accounting for more than a third of sales.

MMC's consulting segment accounted for 46% of the company's total revenue in 2014.

Sales and Marketing

MMC's business customers include small midsized and multinational corporations. Its consulting division serves entities engaged in industries including transportation communication technology energy retail and finance.

Financial Performance

The company has seen steady revenue growth over the last few years. Revenues rose by 6% in 2014 on 5% higher sales from the risk and insurance services segment thanks to organic and acquisitive growth offset by currency exchange translations. Sales increased across all its geographic segments in the Marsh business and in international markets in the Carpenter business. Consulting revenues also grew 6% in 2014 thanks to higher sales from the health retirement and investments business offset by currency exchange losses. MMC's net income rose 8% in 2014 on higher revenues and an increase in interest income. Operating cash flow grew by 57% in 2014 due to drop in cash used in net receivables and contributions to pension and other benefit plans in excess of 2014 expense/credit and cash generated from accrued compensation and employee benefits.

Strategy

MMC's Marsh subsidiary has been steadily branching out from its straight brokerage operations. It has expanded its offerings of risk and insurance-related services including benefits management international risk placement and consumer programs for executives employees and high-net-worth individuals.

Nonetheless like its leading US competitors Marsh's most basic strategy for growth through the years has been to buy up regional brokerages large and small. It has kept up a steady pace of acquisitions of regional commercial brokerage firms especially in the midsized business market. The Mercer business has also been expanding through acquisitions in recent years especially in the growing field of data solutions. Mercer is also seeking to expand its investment consulting operations.

In 2015 Mercer expanded its relationship with Benefitfocus including a strategic equity investment in that company.

While continuing to pursue an aggressive acquisition strategy —the firm acquired 65 businesses from 2008 through 2013 —MMC has also been working to de-risk its own operations by enacting some cost-cutting measures in recent years. Restructuring measures including layoffs and organizational changes aim to overcome the impact of historical regulatory and litigation issues as well as economic and competitive conditions on its bottom line.

Mergers and Acquisitions

Acquisitions in the Marsh (RIS) segment include the 2013-14 purchases of Smith Group Barney & Barney Torrent Technologies and Great Lakes Employee Benefits Services. International expansion efforts include the 2014 purchase of Peruvian insurance adviser Rehder y Asociados Group Quebec-based Kocisko Insurance Brokers and the 2015 acquisition of Belgium-based credit insurer Trade Insure.

In 2015 adding to its existing aviation and aerospace technical advisory expertise Oliver Wyman acquired TeamSAI a US-based leader in the maintenance repair and overhaul space. In 2015 the company also acquired The Benefit Planning Group Inc. a Durham North Carolina-based employee benefit consulting firm.

The Mercer (consulting) division expanded internationally through the 2014 purchase of UK management consultancy firm Corven.

HISTORY

Marsh & McLennan Companies dates back to the Dan H. Bomar Company founded in 1871 after the Great Chicago Fire. In 1885 a plucky Harvard dropout named Henry Marsh joined the company then known as R.A. Waller and Company. When Robert Waller died in 1889 Marsh and fellow employee Herbert Ulmann bought a controlling stake and renamed the company Marsh Ulmann & Co. Marsh pioneered insurance brokering and in 1901 set up U.S. Steel's self-insurance program.

In 1904 different directors at Burlington Northern Railroad promised their account to Marsh Ulmann as well as Manley-McLennan of Duluth (railroad insurance) and D.W. Burrows (a small Chicago-based railroad insurance firm). Rather than fight over it the firms joined forces to form the world's largest insurance brokerage. When Burrows retired in 1906 the firm became Marsh & McLennan.

In the early 20th century Marsh won AT&T's business and McLennan landed the account of Armour Meat Packing.

In 1923 Marsh & McLennan became a closely held corporation. Marsh sold out to McLennan in 1935. The company weathered the Depression without major layoffs by cutting pay and branching into life insurance and employee-benefits consulting after passage of the Social Security Act (1935).

The firm grew through acquisitions in the 1950s went public in 1962 and in 1969 formed a holding company that became Marsh & McLennan Companies. In the 1970s it diversified into investment management employee-benefits consulting

and geographically into the UK with C.T. Bowring Reinsurance. As the insurance business slowed in the 1980s the financial and consulting fields grew through acquisitions and organic growth.

With offices in the World Trade Center the company lost some 300 employees in the September 11 terrorist attacks. Following the attacks on the World Trade Center Marsh & McLennan launched a new subsidiary (AXIS Specialty) to deal with the capacity shortage in the insurance industry.

Two major Marsh & McLennan units came under legal fire in probes of the mutual fund and insurance brokerage industries respectively in the early 2000s. In 2003 Putnam agreed to settle securities fraud charges with the SEC and reimburse investors; many of Putnam's top officers were replaced and its compliance procedures were restructured.

The following year Marsh found itself at the center of a price-fixing investigation that involved several insurance companies including AIG and Chubb Limited. At least nine employees of Marsh and AIG pled guilty to criminal charges. Jeffery Greenberg the son of outspoken AIG chairman and CEO Maurice Greenberg who had served as Marsh & McLennan's chairman and CEO since 1999 resigned in 2004 as a result of the price-fixing allegations.

EXECUTIVES

Senior Vice President, Sandy Codding
President and CEO Mercer, Julio A. Portalatin, age 57, $887,500 total compensation
Chairman and CEO Marsh and McLennan Agency, David L. Eslick
President and CEO Guy Carpenter; Chairman Marsh & McLennan Companies International, Alexander S. (Alex) Moczarski, age 60, $800,000 total compensation
CFO, Mark C. McGivney
President and CEO, Daniel S. (Dan) Glaser, age 54, $1,400,000 total compensation
EVP and General Counsel, Peter J. Beshar, age 54, $800,000 total compensation
CIO, E. Scott Gilbert, age 60
President and CEO Marsh; Chairman Risk and Insurance Services, Peter Zaffino, age 49, $975,000 total compensation
President and CEO Oliver Wyman Group, Scott McDonald, age 49
Senior Vice President, Wendy S Rosler
Vice President, Lee Maness
Vice President, Nenita Rozzi
Senior Vice President Global Information Technology Operations, Michael Sheehan
Vice President Security Architecture and Engineering, Jeff Lund
Vice President Of Client Operations, William Walker
Senior Vice President, Lisa Kremer
Vice President Corperate Finance and interim Chief Financial Officer, Michael (Mel) Bischoff
Assistant Vice President Global Information Technology Finance, Eric Berman
Senior Vice President, James (Jamie) Paddon
Assistant Vice President, Frances (Fran) Epps
Assistant Vice President Marsh USA Inc., Cynthia Rufen-Blanchette
Senior Vice President, Jim Beatty
Senior Vice President, Damian Smith
Vice President Marsh USA Inc., Benjamin (Ben) Laurenzi
Senior Vice President Marsh Finpro, Peter (Pete) Stagias
Vice President Marsh Risk Consulting, Belinda Berwick
Vice President, Robert (Bob) Planos
Vice President Talent Acquisition, Cris Castillo
Senior Vice President, Michelle (Mitch) Pingor

Vice President Marsh Risk and Insurance Services, Tricia Biro
Assistant Vice President At Marsh, Alessandra Richmond
Vice President, Danielle Fields
Vice President Head Of Continuous Improvement And Strategy Qualified Solutions Group, Brian Scullin
Senior Vice President, Jennifer (Jen) Rogich
Vice President Risk Consultant, Edward (Ed) Guzy
Senior Vice President At Marsh, Robert (Bob) Schuhriemen
Vice President Marsh USA Inc., George Schiff
Senior Vice President, John (Jack) Samuels
Vice President Global Technology Services, Antonio Pollan
Vice President Operations, Jim Halkins
Vice President Employee Benefits Services, Charles Rosson
Vice President Finance, Geoffry Rosenthal
Assistant Vice President, Camellia Baker
Senior Vice President Risk Advisory and Business D, Susan (Sue) Friedman
Assistant Vice President, Faye White
Senior Vice President Surety Compliance Leader, Pamela (Pam) Beelman
Vice President Investor Relations, Keith Walsh
Vice President Managing Private Client Services Ac, Mary K Provaznik
Senior Vice President Portal, Carol Sigler
Assistant Vice President, Sebastian Aguayo
Vice President, Katherine (Kate) O'Leary
Assistant Vice President, Julia Yu
Vice President, Sakurako Yagi
Vice President, Ruth Erickson
Vice President of Marketing, Gloria Chin
Assistant Vice President, Kathi Cavanagh
Vice President Global Energy, Arthur (Art) Cooke
Vice President Claims Management, Paul Heidish
Senior Vice President Casualty Claims, Timothy (Tim) Emmerson
Senior Vice President in Financial Institutions Practice, Siobhan O'Brien
Vice President Marketing and Communications, Julie Chu
Vice President, Meredith Ryan-Reid
Senior Vice President, Dave Vasterling
Vice President Sales Manager, Dan Romero
Senior Vice President, Ronald Reinartz
Gerente Consultoria Senior Vice President, Mara Escobar
Senior Vice President Global Information Technology, Scott Francis
Senior Vice President Senior Financial Officer, Darlene Merino
Senior Vice President, Andrea Lieberman
Senior Vice President Finance, Joseph (Jo) Hury
Vice President, Jimmy Evans
Assustant Vice President, John (Jack) Raymond
Vice President Forensic Accounting and Claims Services Latin America, Katie Sulkowski
Vice President, Frank McKain
Senior Vice President Marsh Marine Practice, Raymond Komorowski
Senior Vice President Strategic Liability, Jeffrey (Jeff) Arm
Assistant Vice President Corporate Financial Planning and Analysis, Brent Donnelly
Senior Vice President, Thomas (Thom) Edridge
Vice President, Conan Dolce
Vice President Global Broking Specialties, Dan Carlson
Vice President National Brokerage Client Development, Bryan Levy
Vice President, Sandra Minidis
Vice President, Eric Harley
Senior Vice President, Kristen Stokes
Assistant Vice President, Anne Fitzgerald
Senior Vice President Information Technology and Operations, John G (Jack) Doran

Vice President, Sonya Pal
Assistant Vice President, Donna Duraku
Vice President, Jeffrey (Jeff) Ferrand
Systems Director Vice President Information Techn, Michele Leyvi
Senior Vice President, Agneta Jernbeck-Baker
Assistant Vice President Client Manager, Martin Goh
Senior Vice President, Eileen Quenell
Assistant Vice President, Heather Razo
Senior Vice President, Donna Filippi
Assistant Vice President Sales And Business Development, Pepper Periquet
Senior Vice President Retail Industry Practice, Linda Brown
Vice President Strategy, Robert (Bob) Jones
Senior Vice President, Jerome Kovach
Vice President, Joan Spiegel
Vice President, Patricia Robinson
Senior Vice President Corporate Finance, John Mollica
Senior Vice President, Joseph Asmar
Senior Vice President, John McGuire
Senior Vice President Southeast Communications Media and Technology (CMT) Practice Leader, Ted Young
Senior Vice President, Robert Curtis
Senior Vice President National Education Practice Transaction Specialist, Mark Turkalo
Assistant Vice President President, Louise Wallner
Senior Vice President Marsh Usa Inc, Wendy Rosler, age 53
Assistant Vice President, Gurgen Verdian
Vice President, Brian Rath
Senior Vice President, Randy Dickman
Vice President, James Sallada
Vice President Business Development, Hallie Beddes
Vice President, Michael (Mel) Price
Cpcu Senior Vice President Marsh Usa Inc, Maureen Biehl
Vice President Knowledge Manager, Karen Coffey
Senior Vice President Insurer Consulting Leader, Kevin Rabinowitz
Vice President, Romaneo Adams
Vice President In Marsh Risk Consulting's Reputational Risk And Crisis Management Practice Based, Susan Morton
Vice President, Virginia Del Lago
Assistant Vice President, Felix Chung
Vice President Of Marketing, Erica Jones
Vice President, Catherine Ricia
Senior Vice President, Dawn Buelow
Vice President, Lawrence Abernathy
Vice President, Jessica Hatch
Assistant Vice President, Thadd Northam
Vice President Environmental Practice, Jack Palis
Senior Vice President Oracle Applications Marsh Inc, Gursharanjit Sant
Assistant Vice President, Sonya Watson
Senior Vice President, Mark Alderman
Senior Vice President Global Program Manager, Lori Suske
Vice President, Raegan Buckley
Senior Vice President, Jeralyn Sorensen
Senior Vice President, Stanley Zimmerman
Senior Vice President, Eugene Charney
Assistant Vice President, Edward Mitchell
Executive Vice President Of Information Technology, Jennifer Adams
Vice President, Louise Casazza
Senior Vice President, Marcy Waterfall
Senior Vice President U S Marine And Energy, John Pallasch
Dip Fs (Gen Ins) Qpib Cipvice President Head Of Businessdevelopment Singapore, Andrew Paul
Vice President Human Resources Manager, Sarah Randall
Assistant Vice President, Kristin Will
Senior Vice President, Janis Thornton

Senior Vice President, Rita Patullo
Vice President, Michael Hargis
Senior Vice President Advanced Risk Solutions, Scott Sanderson
Senior Vice President, Ben Hetzer
Auditors: Deloitte & Touche LLP

LOCATIONS

HQ: Marsh & McLennan Companies Inc.
1166 Avenue Of The Americas, New York, NY 10036
Phone: 212 345-5000   Fax: 212 345-4809
Web: www.mmc.com

2014 Sales

	$ mil.	% of total
US	5,865	45
UK	2,111	16
Continental Europe	2,077	16
Asia/Pacific	1,420	11
Other regions & countries	1,517	12
Adjustments	(39)	-
Total	12,951	100

PRODUCTS/OPERATIONS

2014 Sales

	$ mil.	% of total
Risk & insurance services		
Marsh	5,774	45
Guy Carpenter	1,157	9
Consulting		
Mercer	4,350	34
Oliver Wyman Group	1,709	12
Adjustments	(39)	-
Total	12,951	100

Selected Acquisitions

COMPETITORS

Accenture
Anthony Clark International Insurance Brokers
Aon
BB&T
Bain & Company
Bollinger Inc.
Booz Allen
Brown & Brown
FTI Consulting
Fortegra Financial
Gallagher
Hub International
ING
Jardine Lloyd
McKinsey & Company
National Financial Partners
THB Group
USI
Wells Fargo Insurance Services
Willis Towers Watson

HISTORICAL FINANCIALS

Company Type: Public

Income Statement

FYE: December 31

	REVENUE ($ mil.)	NET INCOME ($ mil.)	NET PROFIT MARGIN	EMPLOYEES
12/14	12,951	1,465	11.3%	57,000
12/13	12,261	1,357	11.1%	55,000
12/12	11,924	1,176	9.9%	54,000
12/11	11,526	993	8.6%	52,400
12/10	10,550	855	8.1%	51,000
Annual Growth	5.3%	14.4%	—	2.8%

2014 Year-End Financials

Debt ratio: 18.99%
Return on equity: 19.59%
Cash ($ mil.): 1,958
Current ratio: 1.63
Long-term debt ($ mil.): 3,376

No. of shares (mil.): 540
Dividends
  Yield: 1.8%
  Payout: 40.0%
Market value ($ mil.): 30,918

	STOCK PRICE ($) FY Close	P/E High/Low		PER SHARE ($)		
			Earnings	Dividends	Book Value
12/14	57.24	22 17	2.65	1.06	13.06
12/13	48.36	20 14	2.43	0.96	14.46
12/12	34.47	17 14	2.13	0.90	11.99
12/11	31.62	18 14	1.79	0.86	10.91
12/10	27.34	18 13	1.55	0.81	11.78
Annual Growth	20.3%	— —	14.3%	7.0%	2.6%

Masco Corp.

Masco's ideal customer is a home improvement junkie with a thing for cabinets –and an obsession with hand-washing. It is a leading manufacturer of a variety of home improvement and building products with cabinet and plumbing products accounting for more than half of its sales. Cabinet brands include KraftMaid Quality Cabinets and Merillat in the US and The Moores Group and Tvilum-Scanbirk in Europe. Faucets and bath and shower accessories are sold under the Delta and Peerless brands in the US and as Hansgrohe in Europe. Masco also makes BEHR paints and stains windows doors staple guns locksets and HVAC products. It spun off its installation services business as TopBuild in 2015.

HISTORY

Masco founder Alex Manoogian moved to the US at age 19 in 1920. He wound up in Detroit and with partners Harry Adjemian and Charles Saunders he started Masco (the first letters of their last names plus "co" for "company") Screw Products Company eight days before the crash of 1929. Manoogian's partners left within the year.

Largely reliant on Detroit's auto industry Masco grew slowly during the Depression making custom parts for Chrysler Ford and others. With sales of $200000 by 1937 it went public on the Detroit Stock Exchange. During WWII Masco focused on defense and in 1942 sales passed $1 million. A new plant opened in 1948 in Dearborn Michigan as Masco resumed peacetime business mainly in the auto industry.

In 1954 Masco began selling Manoogian's one-handle kitchen faucet (Delta). Sales of faucets passed $1 million by 1958 and Masco opened a new faucet factory in Indiana.

Under Manoogian's son Richard –whose dinner was often delayed while his father used the stove to test the heat tolerance of new faucet parts — Masco Corporation (so renamed in 1961) diversified. From 1964 to 1980 it bought more than 50 companies concentrating on tool and metal casting energy exploration and air compressors. In 1984 the firm split. Masco Corporation pursued the course set by its successful faucet sales expanding its interests in home improvement and furnishings. The industrial products business was spun off as Masco Industries a separate public corporation (later Metaldyne) in which Masco maintained a sizable stake.

Masco Corporation became the #1 US furniture maker in the late 1980s by buying Lexington Furniture (1987) and Universal Furniture (1989) both of North Carolina. In 1990 Masco acquired KraftMaid cabinets.

Two years later the company sold its interests in Mechanical Technology Payless Cashways and Emco Limited of Canada (Masco bought back 40%

of Emco in 1997). Masco reduced its stake in Metaldyne from 47% to 35% in 1993.

Masco sought to establish itself in Europe and in 1994 it bought a German cabinetmaker and a UK producer of handheld showers. In 1996 founder Manoogian died but the company flowed on. It added a UK cabinetmaker a German shower manufacturer and a German insulation firm. That year Masco sold its troubled furniture unit to a group of investors and executives (who renamed the unit LifeStyle Furnishings International) for about $1 billion and further reduced its stake in Metaldyne to less than 20% (and later sold it all).

Acquisitions in 1997 included cabinetmakers Texwood Industries of Texas and Liberty Hardware Manufacturing of Florida. The next year it bought Vasco (heating systems and equipment Belgium) and Brugman (building and home-improvement products the Netherlands). It sold its Thermador unit (ovens and ranges) to US joint venture Bosch-Siemens Hausgerate.

Masco made 13 acquisitions from 1999 through early 2000 including Heritage Bathrooms (bathroom equipment UK) Faucet Queens (plumbing and hardware supply) GMU Group (kitchen cabinets Spain) Avocet Hardware (locks and hardware UK) BEHR Process (coatings) and Mill's Pride (cabinets). Boosting its services in 1999 it acquired The Cary Group an installer of fiberglass insulation.

To increase its geographic reach Masco bought Tvilum-Scanbirk (ready-to-assemble furniture Denmark) Masterchem Industries (specialty paint products) and Glass Idromassaggio (bathroom equipment Italy) in 2000. In late 2000 and early 2001 it acquired two US-based installation services companies Davenport Insulation Group and BSI Holdings respectively. Also in 2001 Masco acquired Milgard Manufacturing a vinyl window and patio door maker.

During 2002 Masco acquired home improvement products and service companies that included Bristan Ltd. (kitchen and bath faucets and shower and bath accessories) Brasstech Inc. (faucets plumbing specialties and bath accessories; California) Cambrian Windows Ltd. (vinyl window frames) Duraflex Ltd. (extruded vinyl frame components) Premier Manufacturing Ltd. (vinyl window and door frames) SCE Unlimited (siding shutters gutters; Illinois) IDI Group (fireplaces garage doors shower enclosures; Atlanta) Service Partners LLC (insulation and other building products Virginia) several small installation and other service companies and Diversified Cabinet Distributors (cabinets and countertops Atlanta). Masco also increased its interest in Hansgrohe AG (kitchen and bath faucets hand-held and fixed showerheads luxury shower systems and steam showers; Germany) to 64%. The company sold its StarMark Cabinetry business for about $15 million.

In 2003 Masco increased its ownership interest in Hansgrohe AG (kitchen and bath faucets hand-held and fixed showerheads luxury shower systems and steam showers; Germany) to 64% from 27%. The company established Color Solutions Centers in more than 1500 Home Depot stores throughout the US. Masco sold its Baldwin Hardware and Weiser Lock businesses (builders' hardware and locksets) to Black & Decker (now Stanley Black & Decker) and The Marvel Group a provider specialty products such as office work stations and machine stands to members of Marvel's management team (led by president John Dellamore) for $289 million in total. Acquisitions in 2003 included PowerShot Tool Company Inc. (fastening products New Jersey) and several small installation service companies for a combined $63 million.

The next year Masco sold its Jung Pumpen (pumps) The Alvic Group (kitchen cabinets) Alma

Kuchen (kitchen cabinets) E. Missel (acoustic insulation) and SKS Group (shutters and ventilation systems) businesses for $199 million. Masco continued its business review in 2005 selling two operating companies that made and distributed cabinets vanities medicine cabinets shower rods and bath accessories.

After reorganizing its European business operations Masco sold off several of its operating units including Gebhardt Consolidated (HVAC) The Heating Group (radiators) and GMU Group (cabinets). The company also disposed of North American businesses that were not core to its long-term growth strategy which included Computerized Security Systems (CSS) and Zenith Products (bathroom storage).

In 2008 the company merged its Mill's Price brand with KraftMaid to form the Masco Retail Cabinet Group. It also merged Merillat and Quality Cabinets to form Masco Builder Cabinet Group.

In addition to cutting costs through divestitures Masco has streamlined its operating structure to trim spending. In 2011 the company merged its wholesale and retail cabinet units to form Masco Cabinetry. It also decided to stop making ready-to-assemble cabinets a non-core offering.

Looking toward a growth market in 2012 Masco entered into the fast-growing Indian bathroom and kitchen faucet sector by launching its line of residential and commercial products in that country. The company sees India as an integral part of the global expansion plan for the Delta Faucet Company.

EXECUTIVES

VP CFO and Treasurer, John G. Sznewajs, age 48, $618,269 total compensation

President and CEO, Keith J. Allman, $842,788 total compensation

VP and Controller, John P. Lindow, age 51, $260,000 total compensation

Group President Global Plumbing, Richard O'Reagan, $405,492 total compensation

Vice President Business Development, Ham Schirmer

Vice President Finance, Liz Bryant

Vice President General Counsel Secretary, Gregory Wittrock

Vice President, John (Jack) Leekley

Chairman, J. Michael (Mike) Losh, age 69

Auditors: PricewaterhouseCoopers LLP

LOCATIONS

HQ: Masco Corp.
  21001 Van Born Road, Taylor, MI 48180
Phone: 313 274-7400
Web: www.masco.com

2013 Sales

	$ mil.	% of total
North America	6,634	81
Europe & other regions	1,539	19
Total	**8,173**	**100**

PRODUCTS/OPERATIONS

2013 Sales

	$ mil.	% of total
Plumbing products	3,183	39
Decorative architectural products	1,927	24
Installation & other services	1,412	17
Cabinets & related products	1,014	12
Other specialty products	637	8
Total	**8,173**	**100**

Selected Brand Names

Plumbing products
  Alsons
  American Shower & Bath

Aqua Glass
Axor
BrassCraft
Brasstech
Breuer
Bristan
Brizo
Caldera
Damixa
Delta
Glass
Hansgrohe
Heritage
Hot Spring
HÜPPE
BrassCraft
Mirolin
Newport Brass
Peerless
Pharo
Plumb Shop
Cabinets and related products
  KraftMaid
  Merillat
  Moores
  Quality Cabinets
  Tvilum-Scanbirk
  Woodgate
Decorative architectural products
  BEHR
  Decor Bathware
  Expressions
  Franklin Brass
  Kilz
  Liberty
Other specialty products
  Arrow
  Brugman
  Cambrian
  Duraflex
  Griffin
  Milgard Windows
  Powershot
  Premier
  Superia
  Thermic
  Vasco

COMPETITORS

Akzo Nobel Paints	MasterBrand Cabinets
Armstrong World Industries	Moen
Benjamin Moore	Norcraft Companies Inc.
Columbia Pipe	PPG Industries
Elkay Manufacturing	Pfister
Gerber Plumbing Fixtures	Republic National Cabinet
Grohe	Sherwin-Williams
Jacuzzi Brands	Waxman
Kohler	

HISTORICAL FINANCIALS

Company Type: Public

Income Statement

FYE: December 31

	REVENUE ($ mil.)	NET INCOME ($ mil.)	NET PROFIT MARGIN	EMPLOYEES
12/15	7,142	355	5.0%	25,000
12/14	8,521	856	10.0%	32,000
12/13	8,173	272	3.3%	32,000
12/12	7,745	(114)	—	30,000
12/11	7,467	(575)	—	31,000
Annual Growth	(1.1%)	—	—	(5.2%)

2015 Year-End Financials

Debt ratio: 60.26%	No. of shares (mil.): 330
Return on equity: 89.99%	Dividends
Cash ($ mil.): 1,716	Yield: 1.2%
Current ratio: 1.33	Payout: 33.8%
Long-term debt ($ mil.): 2,418	Market value ($ mil.): 9,353

STOCK PRICE ($)		P/E		PER SHARE ($)		
	FY Close	High/Low		Earnings	Dividends	Book Value
12/15	28.30	30	22	1.02	0.37	(0.41)
12/14	25.20	11	8	2.38	0.33	2.68
12/13	22.77	30	22	0.76	0.30	1.53
12/12	16.66	—	—	(0.33)	0.30	0.92
12/11	10.48	—	—	(1.66)	0.30	1.51
Annual Growth	28.2%	—	—	—	5.0%	—

MasterCard Inc

Surpassing Visa in market share —now that would be priceless. Serving approximately 22000 member financial institutions worldwide Master-Card is the #2 payment system in the US. The company does not issue credit or its namesake cards; rather it markets the MasterCard (credit debit and prepaid cards) and Maestro (debit and prepaid cards mainly in Europe) brands provides a transaction authorization network establishes guidelines for use and collects fees from members. The company provides its services in more than 210 countries and territories and its cards are accepted at more than 35 million locations around the globe. MasterCard also operates the Cirrus ATM network.

HISTORY

Company BackgroundA group of bankers formed The Interbank Card Association (ICA) in 1966 to establish authorization clearing and settlement procedures for bank credit card transactions. This was particularly important to banks left out of the rapidly growing BankAmericard (later Visa) network sponsored by Bank of America.

By 1969 ICA was issuing the Master Charge card throughout the US and had formed alliances in Europe and Japan. In the mid-1970s ICA modernized its system replacing telephone transaction authorization with a computerized magnetic strip system. ICA had members in Africa Australia and Europe by 1979. That year the organization changed its name (and the card's) to MasterCard.

In 1980 Russell Hogg became president when John Reynolds resigned after disagreeing with the board over company performance and direction. Hogg made major organizational changes and consolidated data processing in St. Louis. MasterCard began offering debit cards in 1980 and traveler's checks in 1981.

MasterCard issued the first credit cards in China in 1987. The next year it bought Cirrus then the world's largest ATM network. It also secured a pact with Belgium-based card company Eurocard (which later became Europay) to supervise Master-Card's European operations and help build the brand.

Hogg resigned in 1988 after disagreements with the board and was succeeded by Alex Hart. In 1991 the Maestro debit card was unveiled.

The 1990s were marked by trouble in Europe: The pact with Europay hadn't resulted in the boom MasterCard had hoped for customer service was below par and competition was keen. Alex Hart retired in 1994 and was succeeded by Eugene Lockhart who tackled the European woes. Lockhart considered ending the relationship but eventually worked things out with Europay. By the end of the decade Europay was locked in a vicious battle to undercut Visa's market share through lower fees.

MasterCard in 1995 invested in UK-based Mondex International maker of electronic set-value refillable smart cards. But US consumer resistance to cash cards and competition in the more advanced European market delayed growth in this area.

In October 1996 a group of merchants including Wal-Mart and Sears filed class-action lawsuits against both MasterCard and Visa challenging the "honor all cards" rule. Because usage fees are higher merchants balked at accepting consumers' MasterCard- or Visa-branded off-line or signature-based debit cards and claimed the card issuers violated antitrust laws by tying acceptance of debit to that of credit. In a dramatic twist minutes before the trial was set to begin in 2003 MasterCard announced a settlement (the card issuer was required to pay $125 million in 2003 and $100 million annually from 2004 through 2012).

Just months later armed with the lawsuit's settlement which also freed merchants to pick which credit and debit card services they use Wal-Mart (along with a handful of others) stopped accepting signature debit cards issued by MasterCard.

Lockhart resigned in 1997 and was succeeded by former head of overseas operations Robert Selander. Yet another management upheaval began in 1999 as the company moved to streamline its organizational structure and shift away from geographical divisions. It also said member banks could boost visibility by putting their logos on card fronts and moving MasterCard's logo to the back.

In 2002 MasterCard merged with Europay with which it already had close ties. As part of the transaction holding company MasterCard Incorporated was formed; MasterCard International become the company's main subsidiary and MasterCard Europe (formerly Europay) became its European subsidiary.

After some 40 years as a private entity Master-Card went public in 2006 in one of the largest IPOs of its time. Following the offering the approximately 1400 financial institutions that wholly owned MasterCard before the offering retained a stake of more than 40%. Two of the top three US banks (Citigroup and JPMorgan Chase) remained among MasterCard's largest shareholders.

Some of the proceeds from the company's IPO were used to fight antitrust lawsuits from such rivals as American Express and Discover as well as other payment processors. In 2008 the company agreed to a $1.8 billion settlement with American Express which had claimed that MasterCard and others tried to stop financial institutions from issuing its AmEx cards. Later that year MasterCard settled the Discover lawsuit agreeing to pay $862.5 million.

Also in 2008 MasterCard bought Ireland-based software provider Orbiscom. The acquired company's technology was used to create MasterCard inControl a platform for making secure Internet and telephone purchases.

MasterCard promoted president and COO Ajay Banga to CEO in 2010. He succeeded Robert Selander who stepped down after more than a dozen years at the helm.

EXECUTIVES

President UK and Ireland MasterCard Europe, Mark Barnett

Vice President Stategic, Michael (Mel) Fiore

CFO, Martina Hund-Mejean, age 54, $600,000 total compensation

President and CEO, Ajaypal S. (Ajay) Banga, age 55, $1,058,333 total compensation

President Global Products and Solutions, Gary J. Flood, age 57, $600,000 total compensation

President International Markets MasterCard Incorporated and MasterCard Worldwide, Ann Cairns, age 58, $619,778 total compensation

President MasterCard Technologies and Operations, Robert (Rob) Reeg, age 59

Chief Product Officer, Michael Miebach

Head of Digital Payments and MasterCard Labs, Garry Lyons

CIO, Ed McLaughlin

CEO ElectraCard Services, Ram Chari

President MasterCard Canada, Brian Lang

President North America Markets, Craig Vosburg, age 48

President Middle East and Africa, Raghu Malhotra

Senior Vice President Chief Admin Officer, Joy Thoma

Vice President Marketing, Mark Hearne

Vice President Product Development Authentication and Security Technologies, Ashfaq Kamal

Vice President US Prepaid Products, Ed Wang

Vice President and Senior Counsel, Joseph (Jo) Halprin

Vice President Team Lead, Candace Debarger

Senior Vice President and Group Head Digital Channel Engagement, Sherri Haymond

Vice President, Peter Berardino

Vice President Communications Mea, Sami Lahoud

Vice President Business Leader, Cheryl Castro

Vice President of Global Learning, Christine Schulte

Vice President Project Management Office, Fred Branca

Senior Business Lead Vice President IBCU Strategic Partnerships, Kevin Rowland

Vice President Sales and Client Management Strategic Partnerships Group, Patrick (Paddy) McKay

Vice President Of Merchant Fraud Control, John J (Jack) Brady

Vice President, Julie Schanzer

Vice President Technology Account Management, John (Jack) Scariot

Executive Vice President Chief Information Security Officer, Ron Green

Vice President National Merchant Sales, Nick Pifani

Vice President Technology Account Management, Timothy (Tim) Ware

Vice President Performance Analysis, John (Jack) Tullo

Account Vice President, Steffen Frey

Senior Vice President Business Development Finance, Rich Mascali

Vice President, Matthew (Matt) Sordi

Vice President Senior Account Manager, David (Dave) McPherson

Vice President Public Sector Payment Solutions Member Relations, Dan Ragheb

Vice President, Lars Scofield

Vice President Senior Business Leader, Josh Knopp

Vice President Senior Human Resources Business Partner, Meri Wax

Vice President, Andrew (Andy) Gillen

Vice President, Diane Cook

Vice President Business Leader, Will Hawkins

Senior Executive Vice President, Trish Preston

Vice President Mobile Alliances, Jeffrey Allen

Vice President Global Interactive Marketing, Elena D'andrea

Vice President Retail And Luxury Markets, Vivienne Conatser

Vice President of Sales and Marketing, Liz Birenbaum

Vice President Performance Management, Lois Miller

Vice President and Business Leader US Regional Accounts, Sharie Hunziker

Vice President, Thalia Comninellis

Vice President Business Leader Global Prepaid Solutions, Henry (Hal) Gewirtz

Vice President Corporate Communications, Marcus Molina

Vice President Acquirer Relations, Doug Whitehead

Vice President Human Resources, Mimi Wood

Vice President Franchise Development, Scott Gibney

Vice President. Debit Operations, James (Jamie) Froehlich

Senior Vice President And Assistant General Counsel, Colin Dobbyn

Vice President and Senior Counsel, Renee Pirone

Executive Vice President Mobile Solutions, Felix Marx

Vice President Market Development Acquirer and Merchant Relations, Andres Gonzalez

Vice President and Senior Counsel, Michael (Mel) Timko

North America Finance Senior Vice President, Larry Miller

Vice President Financial Analysis, Frank Barbuto

Corporate Level Senior Management Vice President Manager, Kelly Morehead

Vice President Senior Business Leader, Mark Lerner

Vice President Strategic Alliances, LouAnn LoRiggio

Senior Vice President Mobile Product Development, James (Jamie) Anderson

Vice President and Senior Business Leader Enterprise Development, Purnima Pattanayak

Vice President Senior Account Manager North America, Ferenc Tshibangu

Vice President And Senior Business Lea, Gidget Hall

Senior Vice President Travel Payments Solutions, Luis Yofe

Vice President Brand Strategy and Development, Charles (Chas) Silvestro

Vice President Engineering and Support, Mark Wootten

Vice President Us Media, Sharon Hamilton

Vice President Marketing Head, Guillermo Morrone

Vice President Global Commerce Development, David (Dave) Grossman

Vice President Executive Intelligence And Planning, Stacy Styles

Senior Vice President Investor Relations, Catherine (Cathy) Murchie

Vice President Operations and Support Emerging Payments Technology, Rick Davis

Senior Vice President Mergers and Acquisitions, Deepak Mahbubani

Senior Vice President Group Head, Ben Colvin

Vice President Systems Development, Bob Reany

Vice President Global PayPass Product Development, Mike Shadmani

Vice President Global Products and Solutions, Thomas (Thom) Cronin

Vice President Product Development and Management Mobile Payments, Venu Appana

Senior Vice President Core Consumer Products and Loyalty Solutions LAC, Miriam Olivera

Vice President President Direct Interactive Marketing, Jeff White

Vice President, Amy Winders

Vice President, Rick Allen

Vice President Corporate Card Product, Sandy Gennrich

Vice President Retail, Kerry Distefano

Vice President, Mike Pillatsch

Vice President Global Key Accounts Wil, Miles Blunt

Senior Vice President, Pilar S Ramos

Vice President _ Law and Franchise Integrity Regional Integration and Process Excellence, Peter (Pete) Lampasona

Vice President And Senior Business Leader, Salman Syed

Vice President, Mercedes Degarcia

Senior Business Leader (Vice President) Enterprise Architecture, Andrew (Andy) Barnes

Vice President Senior Business Leader, Craig Driver

Vice President Senior Business Leader, Kimberly Simon

Vice President Global Learning, Leigh Bochicchio

Vice President Network and Operations, David (Dave) Williams

Senior Vice President Managing Counsel, Cheryl Givner

Chairman, Richard N. Haythornthwaite, age 59

Vice Chairman, Walt W. Macnee, age 60

Auditors: PricewaterhouseCoopers LLP

LOCATIONS

HQ: MasterCard Inc
   2000 Purchase Street, Purchase, NY 10577
Phone: 914 249-2000
Web: www.mastercard.com

2012 Revenue

	% of total
US	39
International	61
Total	**100**

PRODUCTS/OPERATIONS

2013 Sales

	$ mil.	% of total
Domestic assessments	3,805	34
Transaction processing fees	3	30
Cross-border volume fees	2,793	24
Other	1,331	12
Adjustments	(2942)	-
Total	**8,346**	**100**

COMPETITORS

Alibaba.com	JCB International
Amazon.com	NYCE Payments Network
American Express	PULSE Network
China UnionPay	PayPal
Discover	Total System Services
Fifth Third	Visa Inc
First Data	Visa International

HISTORICAL FINANCIALS

Company Type: Public

Income Statement

FYE: December 31

	REVENUE ($ mil.)	NET INCOME ($ mil.)	NET PROFIT MARGIN	EMPLOYEES
12/15	9,667	3,808	39.4%	11,300
12/14	9,473	3,617	38.2%	10,300
12/13	8,346	3,116	37.3%	8,200
12/12	7,391	2,759	37.3%	7,500
12/11	6,714	1,906	28.4%	6,700
Annual Growth	9.5%	18.9%	—	14.0%

2015 Year-End Financials

Debt ratio: 20.20%
Return on equity: 59.42%
Cash ($ mil.): 5,747
Current ratio: 1.75
Long-term debt ($ mil.): 3,287

No. of shares (mil.): 1,116
Dividends
   Yield: 0.6%
   Payout: 19.6%
Market value ($ mil.): 108,654

	STOCK PRICE ($) FY Close	P/E High/Low	PER SHARE ($) Earnings	Dividends	Book Value
12/15	97.36	30 24	3.35	0.64	5.40
12/14	86.16	271 22	3.10	0.44	5.89
12/13	835.46	324191	2.56	0.21	6.27
12/12	491.28	226154	2.19	0.11	5.61
12/11	372.82	256148	1.49	0.06	4.63
Annual Growth	(28.5%)	— —	22.6%	80.7%	4.0%

Mattel Inc

Barbie is the platinum blonde in power at Mattel the #1 toy maker in the world. Its products include Barbie and Polly Pocket dolls Fisher-Price toys Hot Wheels and Matchbox cars American Girl dolls and books and various Barney Ferrari and other licensed items. Mattel also sells action figures and toys based on Walt Disney and Warner Bros. movies. To satisfy techie kids Mattel has accessorized Barbie with interactive games software and a line of MP3 players. The company has even licensed the Barbie name for eyewear. It also sells games (UNO) and puzzles. Mattel is trying to reduce its reliance on its biggest customers —Wal-Mart Toys 'R' Us and Target –through its own catalog and Internet sales.

Operations

Prior to fiscal 2013 Mattel operated its business through geographic segments: domestic and international. It now uses North America International and American Girl.

The North American segment (which generates 45% of sales) markets and sells toys in the US and Canada as its name suggests through the Mattel Girls & Boys Brands and Fisher-Price Brands categories. In the Mattel Girls & Boys Brands category Barbie includes brands such as Barbie fashion dolls and accessories with the Polly Pocket Little Mommy Disney Classics and Monster High lumped into the Other Girls Brands. Wheels include Hot Wheels Matchbox and Tyco R/C vehicles and play sets. Entertainment includes CARS Radica Toy Story Max Steel WWE Wrestling Batman and Superman as well as games and puzzles. The Fisher-Price Brands category includes Fisher-Price Little People BabyGear Imaginext Dora the Explorer Bubble Guppies Thomas & Friends Mike The Knight Octonauts Mickey Mouse Clubhouse Disney's Jake and the Never Land Pirates and Power Wheels.Products marketed by the International segment (45% of sales)are generally the same as those developed and marketed by the North America segment although some are developed or adapted for particular international markets. Mattel's products are sold directly to retailers and wholesalers in most European Latin American and Asian countries and in Australia and New Zealand and through agents and distributors in those countries where Mattel has no direct presence. The American Girl segment generates nearly 10% of sales and is a direct marketer children's publisher and retailer known for its flagship line of historical dolls books and accessories as well as the My American Girl and Bitty Baby brands. American Girl also publishes best-selling Advice & Activity books and the award-winning American Girl magazine. American Girl products are sold primarily in the US.

Geographic Reach

El Segundo California-based Mattel fills toy chests worldwide. The toymaker sells products in more than 150 nations across North America Europe Latin America and Asia Pacific. North America accounts for about 55% of revenue. Europe is the company's largest international market generating roughly 25% of Mattel's total sales. Latin America generates another nearly 15% of sales while Asia brings in the remainder.

Sales and Marketing

Mattel capitalizes on major events such as movie releases by focusing on product tie-ins. In total in 2014 the toymaker spent nearly $733.2 million (about 12% of net sales) on ads and promotion down 2% from the $750 million spent in 2013 and up 2% from the $718 million spent in 2012. Mattel also promotes its toys and characters through online and broadcast media. Looking at its brands the Mattel Girl's and Boy's brand products generate nearly 60% of all sales while the Fisher-Price brand products generate more than 30%. The company's American Girl brand brings in 10% of sales. The Construction and Arts & Crafts brand products bring in the remainder of revenue.

Mattel sells its products through its own retailers and wholesalers in most of the world and through agents and distributors in those countries where it has no direct presence. American Girl products are sold directly to consumers. Mattel supports its product lines with extensive advertising and consumer promotions. Advertising takes place at varying levels throughout the year and peaks during the traditional holiday season. Advertising includes television and radio commercials magazine newspaper and internet advertisements and social media. Promotions include in-store displays sweepstakes merchandising materials and major events focusing on products and tie-ins with various consumer products companies.

Wal-Mart Stores ($1.1 billion) Toys "R" Us ($600 million) and Target ($500 million) are the company's three largest customers altogether accounting for 35% of its worldwide sales. That total is beginning to decline as Mattel works to reduce its reliance on big retailers by selling more products directly.

Financial Performance

While the world's largest toy maker had seen its sales and profits rise steadily in recent years the company's fortunes reversed course in 2014. Mattel's revenue fell by 7% to $6.02 billion mostly as from a decline in Entertainment Fisher-Price Friends Barbie and core Fisher-Price product sales. With the exception of the Asia Pacific region where sales grew by 8% product sales from North America Europe and particularly Latin America declined by five to 10% —mostly due to lower sales of Entertainment and Barbie brand products.Net income dropped by 45% to $498.87 million mostly from the revenue declines but also because Mattel spent more on other selling and administrative expenses which involved design and development identifiable intangible asset amortization (mostly related to trade names and existing product lines) and bad debt expense costs.Despite lower earnings cash from operations jumped by 27% to $888.56 million mostly as the company paid significantly less toward toward its accounts payable accrued liabilities and income taxes payable obligations and because the company sold off more of its inventory.

Strategy

Mattel has looked to capitalize on global growth opportunities (such as with the Ever After High line) innovate for growth in its key brands (Barbie American Girl and Hot Wheels) expand its girls portfolio invest in international markets improve efficiencies in its supply chain operations and build its online and brick and mortar retail presence.

The company carried out the girls and international parts of its strategy in 2014 when it partnered with high-end Mexican retailer El Palacio de Hierro to offer American Girl merchandise in its stores. In early 2015 Mattel's popular American Girl division partnered with Fashion Angels a designer of tween girls' fashion-focused lifestyle and activity products to have the designer make craft kits and fashion sketchbooks for girls to create fashion accessories for themselves and their American Girl dolls.As part of its retail expansion strategy the company in early 2015 announced plans to open its own retail stores in Nashville Tennessee and Scottsdale Arizona.To cut its operating costs the company in 2015 launched its Funding Our Future cost-savings program designed to simplify global operations by making its supply-chains

more efficient and by making structural and process improvements.

Mergers and Acquisitions

With an eye on taking on LEGO Mattel acquired Canada's MEGA Brands the maker of Mega Bloks construction blocks in April 2014. Mattel paid $460 million in cash to acquire the company LEGO's biggest competitor.

HISTORY

A small California toy manufacturer began operating out of a converted garage in 1945 producing dollhouse furniture. Harold Matson and Elliot Handler named their new company Mattel using letters from their last and first names. Matson soon sold his share to Handler and his wife Ruth who incorporated the business in 1948.

The company's toy line had expanded by 1952 to include burp guns and musical toys and sales exceeded $5 million. Sponsorship of Walt Disney's Mickey Mouse Club (debuted 1955) a first in toy advertising was a shrewd marketing step for Mattel providing direct year-round access to millions of young potential customers.

In 1959 Mattel introduced the Barbie doll named after the Handlers' daughter Barbara and later introduced Ken named after their son. Barbie with her fashionable wardrobe and extensive line of accessories was an instant hit and eventually became the most successful brand-name toy ever sold.

Mattel went public in 1960 and within two years sales had jumped from $25 million to $75 million. It launched the popular Hot Wheels miniature cars line in 1968.

The Handlers were ousted from management in 1974 after an investigation by the SEC found irregularities in reports of the company's profits. The new management moved into non-toy businesses adding Western Publishing (Golden Books) and the Ringling Brothers-Barnum & Bailey Combined Shows circus in 1979.

Mattel and two former employees agreed in 2002 to pay $477000 in fines for making political donations in other people's names the third-largest fine ever imposed by the Federal Election Commission. Also that year the company closed its Kentucky manufacturing and distribution facilities and in early 2003 consolidated two of its manufacturing facilities in Mexico.

In a stinging defeat for Mattel in April 2011 a federal jury sided with MGA Entertainment in the long-running legal battle over ownership of the billion-dollar Bratz doll franchise. (MGA and Mattel started their catfight a decade ago.) The jury rejected Mattel's copyright infringement claims. Instead it found that Mattel has stolen trade secrets from MGA and said it owed the company $88.5 million. The decision reversed a 2008 ruling in which a jury sided with Mattel.

EXECUTIVES

CFO, Kevin M. Farr, age 57, $750,000 total compensation
EVP Chief Legal Officer and Secretary, Robert (Bob) Normile, age 56, $580,000 total compensation
Director, Christopher A. Sinclair, age 64
SVP and CIO, Paul Rasmusson
EVP Global Operations and Chief Supply Chain Officer, Peter D. Gibbons, age 54
President and COO, Richard Dickson, $455,096 total compensation
GM Senior Vice President Consumer Products, Jessica Dunne
Vice President Human Resources, Huey Wilson
Senior Vice President Creative Global Girls' And Games Brands, Evelyn Mazzocco
Vice President Marketing, Lori Pantel
VVMC Vice President, Jeff Verges

Vice President, Sibylle Addotta
Vice President Games, Mike Fulkerson
Vice President Human Resource, Kim GiordanellaGraham
Vice President Finance International, Jim Ward
Vice President Marketing, Carole Levine
Vice President Product Planning, Thomas Zeiler
Vice President Finance and Strategic Planning for Mattel Brands, Eric Chan
Executive Vice President, Jean McKenzie
Marketing Vice President, Nick Karamanos
Vice President International Finance, David (Dave) Traughber
Vice President Finance Logistics, William (Bill) McAleer
Senior Vice President, Gregg Stefanick
Vice President Product Development, Scott Goodman
Vice President Of Facilities, Frank Maranto
National Account Manager, Julia Lyrintzis
Vice President Of Mgpa, Kevin Lam
Global Senior Vice President, Ed Gawronski
Vice President General Counsel, Jamie Peters
Vice President Global Procurement At Mattel, Linda Theisen
Vice President Brand Marketing, Kathy Monetti
Vice President Girls Marketing, Clara Crowder
Vice President Sales and Marketing, Theresa Chatt
Vice President Internal Audit, Beverly Lively
Vice President Global Softlines Consumer Products, Aaron Duncan
Vice President Global Marketing Fisher Price Baby, Melissa Kustell
Senior Vice President Marketing and Design Girls, Tim Kilpin
Vice President, Alfred Chan
Design Vice President, Evelyn Viohl
Senior Vice President Strategic Planning and Finance, Mandana Sadigh
Vice President Supply Chain Strategy and Lean, Angela (Angie) Lam
Vice President Online Sales Marketing and Divisional Strategy, Justin Moser
Vice President Marketing, Jim Alley
Executive Vice President Bus Planning, Bryan Stockton
Board Member, Alicia Quintana
Board Member, Kim Raiford
Auditors: PricewaterhouseCoopers LLP

LOCATIONS

HQ: Mattel Inc
333 Continental Blvd., El Segundo, CA 90245-5012
Phone: 310 252-2000
Web: www.mattel.com

PRODUCTS/OPERATIONS

2014 Sales

	$ mil.	% of total
Mattel Girls & Boys Brands	3,897	65
Fisher-Price Brands	1,842	31
American Girl Brands	620	10
Construction and Arts & Crafts Brands	314	5
Other	43	1
Eliminations (694.6) -12		
Total	**6,023**	**100**

2014 Sales

	$ mil.	% of total
North America	3,011	50
International	3,061	51
American Girl	655	11
Eliminations (694.6) -12		
Total	**6,023**	**100**

Selected Brands

Boys
  Batman
  DC Universe
  Fireman Sam

Hot Wheels
Kung Fu Panda
Magic 8 Ball
Masters of the Universe
Matchbox
Mattel
Max Steel
MEGA BLOKS
Nickelodeon Rugrats
Radica
Scrabble (International)
Speed Racer
Tyco Radio Control
Yu-Gi-Oh!
Girls
American Girl
Angelina Ballerina
Barbie
Bitty Baby
Boom-O
Cabbage Patch Kids
Coconut
Disney
Diva Starz
ello
Fashion Avenue
Flavas
High School Musical
Just Like You
Little Mommy
Polly Pocket!
Infant and preschool
BabyGear
Barney
Blue' s Clues
Bob the Builder
Disney
Dora the Explorer
Fisher-Price
Geo Trax
Go-Diego-Go!
Little People
Matchbox Kids
Mickey Mouse
Pixter
Power Wheels
See ' n Say
Thomas & Friends
UNO
View-Master
Winnie the Pooh

COMPETITORS

Electronic Arts	Playmobil
Hasbro	Radio Flyer
JAKKS Pacific	Sanrio
LEGO	Simba Dickie Group
LeapFrog	Spin Master
MGA Entertainment	TakaraTomy
Marvel Entertainment	Toy Quest
Motorsports Authentics	Ty
Namco Bandai	VTech Holdings
Ohio Art	

HISTORICAL FINANCIALS

Company Type: Public

Income Statement

FYE: December 31

	REVENUE ($ mil.)	NET INCOME ($ mil.)	NET PROFIT MARGIN	EMPLOYEES
12/14	6,023	498	8.3%	31,000
12/13	6,484	903	13.9%	29,000
12/12	6,420	776	12.1%	28,000
12/11	6,266	768	12.3%	28,000
12/10	5,856	684	11.7%	31,000
Annual Growth	0.7%	(7.6%)	—	0.0%

2014 Year-End Financials

Debt ratio: 31.24%
Return on equity: 16.09%
Cash ($ mil.): 971
Current ratio: 2.93
Long-term debt ($ mil.): 2,100

No. of shares (mil.): 338
Dividends
  Yield: 4.9%
  Payout: 73.0%
Market value ($ mil.): 10,463

	STOCK PRICE ($) FY Close	P/E High/Low	PER SHARE ($) Earnings	Dividends	Book Value
12/14	30.95	33 20	1.45	1.52	8.72
12/13	47.58	18 14	2.58	1.44	9.58
12/12	36.62	17 12	2.22	1.24	8.96
12/11	27.76	13 10	2.18	0.92	7.75
12/10	25.43	14 10	1.86	0.83	7.53
Annual Growth	5.0%	— —	(6.0%)	16.3%	3.7%

MB Financial Inc

The "MB" in MB Financial doesn't stand for "Midsized Businesses" though that's its target market. The holding company owns MB Financial Bank which has about 85 branches in the Chicago area and one in Philadelphia. Commercial-related credits including mortgages operating loans lease financing and construction loans make up nearly 80% of the bank's loan portfolio. In addition to serving small and middle-market businesses MB Financial provides retail banking and lending to consumers. The company also offers wealth management and trust services through its Cedar Hill Associates subsidiary and brokerage through Vision Investment Services. LaSalle Systems leases technology-related equipment to corporations.

Sales and Marketing

MB Financial Bank primarily targets small and middle market businesses and individuals. In 2013 the firm spent $8.3 million on advertising compared to $8.2 million in 2012.

Financial Performance

MB Financial reported revenue of $452.3 million in 2013 an increase of 1% versus 2012 on an increase in non-interest income. Net income rose 9% over the same period to $98.5 million on falling expenses. Cash flow from operations increased by nearly $11 million primarily on rising net income.

Strategy

Taking advantage of the dozens of bank failures in 2009 MB Financial acquired Heritage Community Bank InBank Corus Bank and Benchmark Bank in separate FDIC-assisted transactions. In 2010 it acquired failed Chicago-area institutions Broadway Bank and New Century Bank in similar deals. Gains on these acquisitions helped the company's revenues (and profits) grow in 2010. Although the company didn't have the benefit of gains on acquisitions in 2011 (and revenues fell 20% to $493.7 million) profits continued to climb that year growing 89% to $38.7 million largely due to a lowered provision for loan losses. Also that year the bank got millions of dollars of non-performing loans off of its books via a sale to Colony Capital.

The company has said it will continue to acquire failed banks with FDIC assistance if the opportunity arises. It believes such transactions are more profitable because they usually include loss-share agreements with the regulator and often afford the acquirer more flexibility than traditional takeovers. Other strategies for growth include expanding its private banking and asset managements operations as well as its fee-based business services including treasury management and leasing.

Mergers and Acquisitions

In November 2015 Chicago-based MB Financial agreed to buy American Chartered Bancorp — along with its 15 American Chartered Bank branches in the Chicago-area $2.8 billion in assets and $2.2 billion in deposits —in a deal valued at $449 million.In August 2014 MB Financial completed its acquisition of Rosemont Illinois-based Taylor Capital Group the holding company for Cole Taylor Bank (CTB). With $5.7 billion in assets and some 10 branches in the Chicago metro area CTB was merged with MB Financial Bank. Like its acquirer CTB is a commercial bank focused on the middle market.

EXECUTIVES

President and CEO, Mitchell S. Feiger, age 56, $775,000 total compensation
EVP Wealth Management and Commercial Banking, Mark A. Heckler, $293,077 total compensation
EVP Commercial Banking Specialty, Edward F. Milefchik
EVP and Chief Credit Officer, Michael J. Morton
President and CEO MB Financial Bank, Mark A. Hoppe
VP and CFO, Jill E. York, $430,461 total compensation
VP MB Financial Inc. and EVP Administration MB Financial Bank, Rosemarie Bouman, $287,846 total compensation
EVP Commercial Banking, Lawrence G. Ryan
EVP and COO, Randall T. Conte
EVP and Chief Retail Banking Officer, Susan G. Peterson
EVP Risk Management, Brian J. Wildman, $292,846 total compensation
President MB Business Capital, John A. Curtis
Vice President, Michael Scarsella
Vice President Operations, Linda Ray
Vice President Trust Operations Manager, Abimbola Okubanjo
First Vice President, Mike Markovitz
Assistant Vice President Compliance Officer, Nora Reyes
Senior Vice President Of Commercial Banking, Timothy Broccolo
Vice President, Kathy Grele
Vice President Merchant Risk Operations Manager, Jennifer (Jen) Gallus
Senior Vice President and Division Manager Commercial Banking, Scott Mier
First Vice President, Terese Krafcheck
Vice President, John Bell
Executive Vice President, Matthew Robertson
First Vice President, Michael (Mel) Lynch
Vice President Projects and Business Intelligence Coordinator, Kristin Ulewicz
Assistant Vice President Information Technology, Sean Metoyer
Assistant Vice President Banking Center Manager, Pawel Mikolajczyk
Vice President, Michael Nylen
Vice President Commercial Banking, Michael Salvador
Vice President Specialized Finance, Sean McGuire
Vice President Business Intelligence, George Ostendorf
First Vice President, Carolyn Gergits
Assistant Vice President, Joe Wolsfeld
Senior Vice President Product Management, Judy Hill
Senior Vice President of Commerical Banking, Carl Anfenson
Vice President, Virginia Buschman
Executive Vice President and President MB Business Capital, Michael (Mel) Sharkey
Senior Vice President, Bernard Bartilad
Assistant Vice President Of Loan Review, Charles Jackson
Vice President International Banking Operations Manager and Business Deveopment, Paul Warfield
Assistant Vice President Asset Manager, Brian Nagorsky

First Vice President Business Developmnt, Jerry Kallio
Vice President, Rick J Chang
Assistant Vice President Employee Relations Office, Katie Drinan Allberry
Executive Vice President Coml And Indust Lending H, William (Bill) McGowan
Vice President, Jim Campobello
Vice President Mortgage Lending, Cindie Sedlacek
Assistant Vice President Account Analysis, Marcy Alfrejd
Vice President Collateral Manager, Lisette Alamo
Vice President, Anthony Gattuso
Assistant Vice President Banking Center Manager, James Slowik
Senior Vice President Finance Reporting Budgeting, John Francoeur
Regional President, Mark Rubert
Senior Vice President, Jennifer Brogan
Vice President Business Banking, Robert Baitler
Vice President Business Banking, Jim Marshall
First Vice President, Kenneth Engemann
Assistant Vice President Marketing Communications Manager, Diane Shaughnessy
Senior Vice President, Greg Urban
Vice President Treasury Management Sales, Eloy Hodges
First Vice President, Sandra Biske
Vice President Business Banking, Steve Grabavoy
Vice President Quality Assurance Manager, Chris Hicks
Assistant Vice President Compensation, Cindy Katsikas
Vice President Business Banking, Sam Elhaj
Assistant Vice President Banking Center Manager, Galina Veksler
Assistant Vice President Branch Manager, John Crouse
Vice President Marketing Manager, Megan (Meg) Garr
Assistant Vice President, Brenda Allen
Senior Vice President Underwriting, Cindy Jamroziak
Vice President, Stephanie Taverna
Vice President, Cindy Voda
Assistant Vice President Quality Control, Margie Acevedo
Vice President, Dion Haintz
First Vice President Chief Appraiser, Mitchell Zaveduk
Assistant Vice President Bsa Aml Loss Prevention Management, Michelle Mercer
First Vice President Retail Divisional Manager, Seth Heape
Vice President Lease Banking, Denise Ference
Senior Vice President Bsa Aml Officer, Carole Micheletto
Assistant Vice President Compensation And Benefits, Catherine Nacpil
Vice President Of Managed Assets, Mike Pindak
Assistant Vice President Marketing And Crm Administrator, Cari Dam
Senior Vice President Division Head, Thomas (Thom) Moran
Senior Vice President Lease Banking, Dennis Roesslein
First Vice President Regional Division M, Deborah (Deb) Wheeler
Senior Vice President Lease Banking, Stewart Kapnick
Vice President Senior Product Manager, Joseph (Jo) Vitale
Vice President and Counsel, Adriana Quick
Senior Vice President, Mitch Morgenstern
Vice President Commercial Banking, Michelle (Mitch) Christens
Senior Vice President Operations, Pete Steger
Vice President Senior Treasury Analyst Alm, Dale Saari

Senior Vice President Overseeing Credit, Jennifer (Jen) Rosenberg
Chairman, Thomas H. Harvey, age 54
Board Member, Christina Aguinaga
Vice Chairman, James N Hallene, age 55
Executive Board Member, Matt Weberling
Auditors: McGladrey LLP

LOCATIONS

HQ: MB Financial Inc
   800 West Madison Street, Chicago, IL 60607
Phone: 888 422-6562
Web: www.mbfinancial.com

PRODUCTS/OPERATIONS

2013 Sales

	$ mil.	% of total
Interest		
Loans	238	53
Investment securities	58	13
Other	0	-
Noninterest		
Lease financing net	61	15
Commercial deposit and treasury management fees	24	5
Trust and Asset management	19	4
Consumer and other deposit service fees	14	3
Card fees	11	2
Loan service fees	5	1
Others	18	4
Total	**452**	**100**

Selected Subsidiaries

MB Financial Bank N.A.
   Ashland Management Agency Inc.
   Cedar Hill Associates LLC (80%)
   LaSalle Systems Leasing Inc.
   LaSalle Business Solutions LLC
   Melrose Equipment Company LLC
   MB Deferred Exchange Corporation
   MB Financial Center LLC
   MB Financial Center Land Owner LLC
   MB Financial Community Development Corporation
   Vision Investment Services Inc.
   Vision Insurance Services Inc.7

COMPETITORS

Bank of America	Northern Trust
Citigroup	PNC Financial
Fifth Third	PrivateBancorp
Harris	U.S. Bancorp
JPMorgan Chase	Wintrust Financial

HISTORICAL FINANCIALS

Company Type: Public

Income Statement

FYE: December 31

	ASSETS ($ mil.)	NET INCOME ($ mil.)	INCOME AS % OF ASSETS	EMPLOYEES
12/14	14,602	86	0.6%	2,839
12/13	9,641	98	1.0%	1,775
12/12	9,571	90	0.9%	1,758
12/11	9,833	38	0.4%	1,684
12/10	10,320	20	0.2%	1,703
Annual Growth	**9.1%**	**43.1%**	**—**	**13.6%**

2014 Year-End Financials

Debt ratio: 1.84%	No. of shares (mil.): 74
Return on equity: 5.14%	Dividends
Cash ($ mil.): 312	Yield: 1.5%
Current ratio: —	Payout: 40.3%
Long-term debt ($ mil.): —	Market value ($ mil.): 2,457

	STOCK PRICE ($) FY Close	P/E High/Low	PER SHARE ($) Earnings	Dividends	Book Value
12/14	32.86	25 20	1.31	0.52	27.11
12/13	32.06	18 11	1.79	0.44	24.11
12/12	19.75	14 11	1.60	0.13	23.26
12/11	17.10	42 27	0.52	0.04	25.44
12/10	17.32	140 75	0.19	0.04	24.66
Annual Growth	**17.4%**	**— —**	**62.0%**	**89.9%**	**2.4%**

MBIA Inc.

MBIA will make sure that bonds get paid no matter what. The holding company's independent subsidiary National Public Finance Guarantee Corporation is a leading provider of insurance for municipal bonds and stable corporate bonds (such as utility bonds) in the US. Separately its MBIA Insurance Corporation provides global structured finance products and non-US public financial guarantees. MBIA's Cutwater business manages assets for public-sector clients. Other lines of business include tax compliance and risk management services along with buying and servicing municipal real estate tax liens.

Operations

The company conducts most of its business through three subsidiaries. Cutwater Asset Management handles asset management and has $23 billion in assets under management. MBIA Insurance Corporation issues structured finance and international insurance from six offices around the globe. National Public Finance Guarantee offers US public finance insurance. Formed after the economic collapse in 2008 National hasn't written any new business since 2009.

Geographic Reach

MBIA is headquartered in New York with several offices in the state along with operations in California and Colorado. Internationally the company has one office each in the UK Spain France and Mexico.

Financial Performance

The company reported a 50% drop in revenue for 2013 after showing growth the previous year. A decreased in premiums earned along with increased losses and other settlements caused the drop. Net income was affected and fell 80%. Cash from operations was the bright spot however as it rose nearly $3 billion after as it settled legal claims and saw reduced payments for some expenses.

Strategy

After years of work to stabilize its financial position and deal with the massive fallout from the subprime mortgage-backed security implosion that lead to the housing collapse and the Great Recession MBIA seems to be on more solid ground. In 2013 it settled the last of the subprime-related lawsuits with Bank of America Flagstar Bank and ResCap (it is still pursuing claims against Credit Suisse). It also resolved pending litigation and government investigations reduced its workforce saw the first dividend payment from National to the parent late in the year.

Company Background

That MBIA is still standing is remarkable. As one of the largest providers of insurance to asset- and mortgage-based securities MBIA was among the most vulnerable companies when the US housing market imploded in 2007. The company posted losses of $2.3 billion the last quarter of 2007 a result of its investments in subprime mortgage-backed securities.

MBIA split apart its public structured and asset management businesses to separate the stable from the unstable in early 2009: MBIA split its municipal bond insurance business off into an independent subsidiary named National Public Finance Guarantee Corporation. It receives a credit rating separate from the rest of MBIA's riskier structured-finance businesses.

Following the split some 20 banks grew prickly and sued MBIA with one hand while steadily collecting claims with the other. However by mid-2011 banks began dropping out of the lawsuit; the company settled with the final three in 2013.

HISTORY

In 1974 such insurers as Aetna CIGNA Fireman's Fund (now part of Allianz) and Continental (now part of CNA) formed consortium Municipal Bond Insurance Association. The insurance was intended to reduce investor risk and to boost ratings and cut costs for bond issuers. Holding company MBIA was incorporated and went public in 1986. Three years later it absorbed rival Bond Investors Group.

As bond insurance gained wide acceptance MBIA moved into coverage of investment-grade corporate bonds and asset- and mortgage-backed bonds. It also began offering institutional brokerage services and money market funds to municipal customers. But with acceptance came competition forcing MBIA to take on riskier bond issues. It joined forces with Ambac Indemnity in 1995 to offer bond insurance abroad; the decision pricked MBIA three years later when a Thai company defaulted.

It began investing in real estate tax lien and tax compliance companies in 1996 and picked up asset-backed bond insurer CapMAC Holdings in 1998 despite that company's exposure in Asia. The same year MBIA formed an alliance with Japan's Mitsui Marine & Fire (now Mitsui Sumitomo Insurance) and bought 1838 Investment Advisors which oversees assets of $6 billion.

The following year the company inked a deal to be the exclusive insurer of municipal bonds on Trading Edge's BondLink trading service. MBIA also sold its bond administration and consulting firm MBIA MuniFinancial saying it no longer fit with company strategy.

In 2000 MBIA's venture with Trading Edge opened for online business. That year the company exited its alliance with Mitsui Sumitomo Insurance.

Due to its decision to discontinue equity advisory services operations MBIA sold subsidiary 1838 Investment Advisors to that company's management in 2004; MBIA then focused its advisory services on fixed-income asset management.

EXECUTIVES

CEO and Chairman MBIA Insurance Corporation, Joseph W. (Jay) Brown, age 66, $1,000,000 total compensation

EVP General Counsel and Secretary, Ram D. Wertheim, age 61, $500,000 total compensation

President CFO and Chief Administrative Officer MBIA Inc. and Optinuity and CFO MBIA Insurance Corporation, C. Edward (Chuck) Chaplin, age 58, $750,000 total compensation

Managing Director and Chief Investment Officer; President MBIA Asset Management and MBIA Capital Management Corp., Clifford D. Corso, age 53, $641,667 total compensation

President COO MBIA Inc. and MBIA Insurance Corporation and President and CEO National, William C. (Bill) Fallon, age 55, $750,000 total compensation

EVP and Chief Portfolio Officer, Anthony McKiernan, age 45, $500,000 total compensation
Vice President, Timothy Keefe
Vice President Risk Management and Portfolio Reporting, Laura DeLena
Vice President, Matthew (Matt) Lagana
Assistant Vice President, Joel Turner
Assistant Vice President Of Operations, Stephanie Ciavarello
Assistant Vice President, Jackie Perez
Assistant Vice President, Joseph (Jo) Beattie
Vice President Tax, Steve Sutcliffe
Vice President Financial Guarantee Applications, Lynn Jacobs
Assistant Vice President Investor Relations, Jacquelyn Cruz
Assistant Vice President, Emily Johnson
Vice President Assistant General Counsel, Patrick (Paddy) Diamond
Vice President Corporate Marketing, Jude Westerfield
Assistant Vice President, John (Jack) Lucas
Assistant Vice President Investment Operations, Angelique Allen
Chairman, Daniel P. Kearney, age 75
Auditors: PricewaterhouseCoopers LLP

LOCATIONS

HQ: MBIA Inc.
1 Manhattanville Road, Suite 301, Purchase, NY 10577
Phone: 914 273-4545
Web: www.mbia.com

Selected Locations
US
  Armonk NY
  Denver
  New York
  San Francisco
International
  London
  Madrid
  Mexico City
  Paris

COMPETITORS

Ambac	Primus Guaranty
Assured Guaranty	Radian Group
FGIC	Syncora Holdings

HISTORICAL FINANCIALS

Company Type: Public

Income Statement

FYE: December 31

	ASSETS ($ mil.)	NET INCOME ($ mil.)	INCOME AS % OF ASSETS	EMPLOYEES
12/14	16,284	569	3.5%	252
12/13	16,953	250	1.5%	277
12/12	21,724	1,234	5.7%	352
12/11	26,873	(1,319)	—	382
12/10	32,279	52	0.2%	392
Annual Growth	(15.7%)	81.4%	—	(10.5%)

2014 Year-End Financials

Debt ratio: 47.99%	No. of shares (mil.): 191
Return on equity: 15.79%	Dividends
Cash ($ mil.): 782	Yield: —
Current ratio: —	Payout: —
Long-term debt ($ mil.): —	Market value ($ mil.): 1,831

	STOCK PRICE ($) FY Close	P/E High/Low		PER SHARE ($) Earnings	Dividends	Book Value
12/14	9.54	5	3	2.76	0.00	20.47
12/13	11.94	12	6	1.29	0.00	17.05
12/12	7.85	2	1	6.33	0.00	16.22
12/11	11.59	—	—	(6.69)	0.00	8.80
12/10	11.99	50	15	0.26	0.00	14.18
Annual Growth	(5.6%)	—	—	80.5%	—	9.6%

McDonald's Corp

Serving billions of hamburgers has put a shine on these arches. McDonald's has more than 36000 restaurants serving burgers and fries in about 120 countries. (There are more than 14250 Golden Arches locations in the US.) The popular chain is well-known for its Big Macs Quarter Pounders and Chicken McNuggets. Most of the outlets are free-standing units offering dine-in and drive-through service but McDonald's also has many eateries located in airports retail areas and other high-traffic locations. About 80% of the restaurants are run by franchisees or affiliates.

HISTORY

The first McDonald's opened in 1948 in San Bernardino California. In 1954 owners Dick and Mac McDonald signed a franchise agreement with 52-year-old Ray Kroc (a malt machine salesman) and a year later Kroc opened his first restaurant in Des Plaines Illinois. By 1957 Kroc was operating 14 McDonald's restaurants in Illinois Indiana and California. In 1961 Kroc bought out the McDonald brothers for $2.7 million.

In 1962 the now-ubiquitous Golden Arches appeared for the first time and the company sold its billionth burger. Ronald McDonald made his debut the following year and the company introduced its first new menu item —the Filet-O-Fish. Two years later McDonald's went public and ran its first TV ads. The company opened its first stores outside the US (in Canada) in 1967 and the next year it added the Big Mac to the menu and opened its 1000th restaurant.

During the 1970s McDonald's grew at the rate of about 500 restaurants per year and the first Ronald McDonald House (a temporary residence for families of hospitalized children) opened in 1974. The drive-through window appeared in 1975.

McDonald's introduced Chicken McNuggets in 1983. Kroc who had become senior chairman in the 1970s died the next year. Growing competition slowed the company's US sales growth to about 5% per year at the end of the 1980s. In response McDonald's added specially priced "value menu" items.

In 1990 the company made history and headlines when it opened the first McDonald's in Moscow. Two years later the Golden Arches expanded into China. The company stumbled with the pricey Arch Deluxe hamburger in 1996 and its Campaign 55 discount promotion the next year. However the giveaway of Teenie Beanie Babies in 1997 was its most successful promotion ever. McDonald's decentralized US operations that year to bring decision-making closer to local franchises. US division CEO Edward Rensi retired and was replaced by division chairman Jack Greenberg.

The next year Greenberg launched the Made For You food preparation system designed to reduce waste and produce a better tasting burger. He was named CEO later that year. McDonald's also made its first investment in another restaurant concept in 1998 when it bought a stake in Chipotle Mexican Grill a Denver-based chain of Mexican food restaurants. That same year saw the death of co-founder Dick McDonald who died at age 89.

During Greenberg's first year he slowed US expansion and stepped up international growth. In 1999 McDonald's added a third brand to its family when it acquired the Ohio-based Donatos Pizzeria chain. The company's biggest deal though came in 2000 when it purchased the Boston Market chain from struggling Boston Chicken for about $175 million.

Early in 2001 McDonald's unveiled its New Tastes Menu in which local markets could feature up to four regional or seasonal foods out of a 40-item national selection. The company continued its move toward diversification and international expansion purchasing a 33% stake in the UK limited-service sandwich chain Pret A Manger for $40 million. It also spun off its Japanese unit to the public retaining a 50% ownership stake.

But even with all its size and power McDonald's found out it was not immune to economic trouble and corporate blunders. The company suffered from ill-thought product changes less-than-successful marketing plans and the growing public preference for lighter fast-food options such as sub sandwiches and salads. Following three quarters of declining profits in 2001 McDonald's announced a major restructuring of its US operations. It cut about 700 corporate jobs hired five new managers and consolidated its service regions.

Business failed to improve however and in 2002 it laid off approximately 600 corporate employees and closed about 175 underperforming units. At the end of 2002 after the company posted its first quarterly loss in history vice chairman and president Jim Cantalupo a veteran of McDonald's international operation replaced Jack Greenberg as chairman and CEO.

McDonald's business began to improve during 2003 with the introduction of healthier menu fare. Late that year the company sold Donatos Pizza back to its founder Jim Grote and closed all Boston Market locations outside the US in order to focus more attention on its core chains. The company ended a joint venture with Seed Restaurant Group that would have led to the development of new Fazoli's locations. Japan however remained a particularly rough market: McDonald's Holdings (Japan) posted losses for both 2002 and 2003. It also gave up on efforts to establish the Pret A Manger sandwich shops in Japan.

Putting its advertising dollars to work McDonald's introduced a global branding campaign in 2003 to help change its image. Called 'I'm Lovin' It' the campaign attempted to up the restaurant chain's hip factor and draw young customers. These efforts showed positive results: McDonald's posted steady sales increases through most of 2003 and into early 2004 and investors were encouraged by the progress.

Cantalupo died in 2004. Director Andrew McKenna was named chairman and president. Charlie Bell became CEO. Diagnosed with cancer and undergoing surgery a month later Bell curtailed his workload but returned to his job full-time later that month. He underwent a second surgery procedure later that year again cancer-related and eventually stepped down near the end of 2004 in order to devote all his time to fighting cancer. (Bell died early the next year.) Vice chairman Jim Skinner assumed the mantle of CEO becoming the company's third chief executive in seven months. Mike Roberts the CEO of McDonald's USA assumed the additional titles of president and COO.

In a David and Goliath scenario the Venezuelan government ordered all 80 of the country's McDonald's restaurants closed for three days in 2005 as punishment for not following the country's tax laws. McDonald's sold a 35% stake in Chipotle through an IPO in 2006 and disposed of its remaining holdings later that year. It sold Boston Market to private equity firm Sun Capital Partners for $250 million the following year and in 2008 McDonald's cashed out its stake in Pret A Manger as part of a $670 million buyout by private equity firm Bridgepoint Capital.

In 2011 McDonald's sold its 50% stake in Hardcastle Restaurants one of two joint ventures operating McDonald's restaurants in India and converted it to a franchisee operation.

EXECUTIVES

President McDonald's USA, Michael D. (Mike) Andres, age 57
EVP General Counsel and Secretary, Gloria Santona, age 64
EVP Worldwide Supply Chain Development and Franchising, Jose Armario, age 55
EVP and Global Chief Marketing Officer, Silvia Lagnado
President McDonald's Europe, Douglas M. (Doug) Goare, age 62, $570,000 total compensation
EVP Strategy Business Development and Innovation, Chris (Chris K) Kempczinski, age 46
EVP and Chief People Officer, David Fairhurst, age 47
Chief Administrative Officer, Peter J. (Pete) Bensen, age 52, $858,333 total compensation
Corporate EVP and CFO, Kevin M. Ozan, age 52
President Asia/Pacific Middle East and Africa, David L. (Dave) Hoffmann, age 47, $533,333 total compensation
President CEO and Director, Stephen J. (Steve) Easterbrook, age 47, $633,333 total compensation
President Latin America, Edgardo Navarro
Corporate EVP Operations and Technology Systems, Jim Sappington, age 56
Managing Director McDonald's UK, Paul Pomroy
EVP and Global Chief Communications Officer, Robert Gibbs
EVP Marketing McDonaldÂ's Korea, Melanie Joh
Vice President and Chief Creative Officer, Marlena Peleo-Lazar
Vice President, Gerald Newman
Vice President Quality Assurance, Jeff Wilfong
Corporate Vice President, Francesca Debiase
Vice President Of Operations, Marcy Amble
Exec Vp Restaurant Sol Group, Jeff Stratton
Vice President U S Controller, Teresa Olson
Chairman, Andrew J. (Andy) McKenna
Auditors: Ernst & Young LLP

LOCATIONS

HQ: McDonald's Corp
One McDonald's Plaza, Oak Brook, IL 60523
Phone: 630 623-3000
Web: www.mcdonalds.com

2014 Sales

	$ mil.	% of total
Europe	11,078	40
US	8,651	32
Asia/Pacific Middle East & Africa	6,324	23
Other regions	1,388	5
Total	**27,441**	**100**

2014 Locations

	No.
US	14,358
Asia/Pacific Middle East & Africa	10,345
Europe	7,855
Other regions	3,708
Total	**36,258**

PRODUCTS/OPERATIONS

2014 Locations

	No.
Franchised	29,554
Company-owned	6,714
Total	**36,258**

Selected Products
Big Mac
Chicken McNuggets
Egg McMuffin
Filet-O-Fish
Happy Meal
Mac Snack Wrap
McCafe
McChicken
McDouble
McFlurry
McGriddle
McRib
Quarter Pounder

COMPETITORS

Burger King	Quiznos
CKE Restaurants	Sonic Corp.
Chick-fil-A	Starbucks
Church's Chicken	Subway
Dairy Queen	Tim Hortons
Jack in the Box	Wendy's
Panda Restaurant Group	YUM!
Popeyes	

HISTORICAL FINANCIALS
Company Type: Public

Income Statement
FYE: December 31

	REVENUE ($ mil.)	NET INCOME ($ mil.)	NET PROFIT MARGIN	EMPLOYEES
12/14	27,441	4,757	17.3%	420,000
12/13	28,105	5,585	19.9%	440,000
12/12	27,567	5,464	19.8%	440,000
12/11	27,006	5,503	20.4%	420,000
12/10	24,074	4,946	20.5%	400,000
Annual Growth	3.3%	(1.0%)	—	1.2%

2014 Year-End Financials

Debt ratio: 43.73%	No. of shares (mil.): 962
Return on equity: 32.97%	Dividends
Cash ($ mil.): 2,077	Yield: 3.5%
Current ratio: 1.52	Payout: 64.4%
Long-term debt ($ mil.): 14,989	Market value ($ mil.): 90,224

	STOCK PRICE ($) FY Close	P/E High/Low		PER SHARE ($) Earnings	Dividends	Book Value
12/14	93.70	21	18	4.82	3.28	13.35
12/13	97.03	19	16	5.55	3.12	16.16
12/12	88.21	19	16	5.36	2.87	15.25
12/11	100.33	19	14	5.27	2.53	14.09
12/10	76.76	17	13	4.58	2.26	13.89
Annual Growth	5.1%	—	—	1.3%	9.8%	(1.0%)

McGraw Hill Financial, Inc.

McGraw-Hill Financial (formerly The McGraw-Hill Companies) is now a provider of credit ratings benchmarks and analytics for the global capital and commodity markets. The company was a leading publisher of textbooks tests and related materials serving the elementary secondary and higher education markets through McGraw-Hill Education (MHE) before it spun that business off in 2013. Other businesses include S&P Ratings (indexes and credit ratings); S&P Capital IQ and S&P Indices (financial and business information); and Commodities and Commercial (Platts J.D. Power and Associates McGraw-Hill Construction and Aviation Week).Geographic ReachMcGraw-Hill Financial operates in 30 countries around the world. The company has more than 90 office locations with about 30 in the US. The US accounted for 60% of the company's revenue in fiscal 2014 while Europe brought in roughly 25% and Asia accounted for 10% of revenue.Sales and MarketingThe company spends millions per year on advertising and promotional costs. It spent $35 million on advertising in fiscal 2014 after spending $41 million in 2013 and $31 million in fiscal 2012.Financial PerformanceIn fiscal 2014 McGraw-Hill Financial's revenue was $5 billion. That was an increase of 4% compared to fiscal 2013. The spike was the result of growth from all of the company's segments. Even with the increased revenue McGraw-Hill Financial slumped to a net loss of $115 million because of high operating expenses.StrategyThe company spun off its education business in response to decreased spending on elementary and high school textbooks. Its financial business which provides global financial information research and analytics tools to investment advisors wealth managers and institutional investors has fared better.

EXECUTIVES

President J.D. Power and Associates, Finbarr J. (Fin) O'Neill, age 63
Vice President Technology, Rosalin Danner
Vice President Business Development Publications, Dale Johnson
President and CEO, Douglas L. (Doug) Peterson, age 56, $900,000 total compensation
Chief Global Economist and Head of Global Economics and Research, Paul Sheard, age 61
President Standard & Poor's Ratings Services, John L. Berisford, age 51, $550,000 total compensation
EVP and CFO, Jack F. Callahan, age 56, $750,000 total compensation
CEO S&P Dow Jones Indices, Alexander J. (Alex) Matturri, age 56
President Platts, Imogen Dillon Hatcher, age 52, $282,006 total compensation
EVP and General Counsel, Lucy Fato, age 48
Head Enterprise Risk Management; Vice Chairman Risk Policy Committee, Donald R. (Don) Howard
EVP Public Affairs, Courtney Geduldig
President S&P Capital IQ/SNL Financial, Mike Chinn
Acting EVP Human Resources, France Gingras
Vice President Product Development, Kathryn Cassino
Vice President Of Marketing, Connie Howard
Vice President International Affairs, Cynthia Baraddon
Vice President Of Compliance, John Dipoto
Vice President, Maryann Johnston
Vice President Sales, Jim Richardson
Vice President Solutions Engineering and Sourcing, Anand Deshpande
Senior Vice President And Publisher North America Businessweek, Geoffrey Dodge
Vice President Client Services, James (Jamie) Notarianni
Vice President Finance and Operations, J Garrett Henn
Chairman, Charles E. (Ed) Haldeman, age 66
Auditors: Ernst & Young LLP

LOCATIONS

HQ: McGraw Hill Financial, Inc.
  55 Water Street, New York, NY 10041
Phone: 212 438-1000
Web: www.mhfi.com

2014 Sales

	$ mil.	% of total
US	2,911	58
Europe	1,316	26
Asia	528	10
Other regions	296	6
Total	**5,051**	**100**

PRODUCTS/OPERATIONS

2014 Sales

	$ mil.	% of total
S&P Ratings	2,455	48
S&P Capital IQ	1,237	24
Commodities & Commercial	893	17
S&P DJ Indices	552	11
Adjustments	(86)	-
Total	**5,051**	**100**

COMPETITORS

A.M. Best	Interactive Data
Bloomberg L.P.	MSCI
D&B	Moody's
DBRS	Morningstar
Fair Isaac	Thomson Reuters
Fitch Ratings Inc.	

HISTORICAL FINANCIALS

Company Type: Public

Income Statement				FYE: December 31
	REVENUE ($ mil.)	NET INCOME ($ mil.)	NET PROFIT MARGIN	EMPLOYEES
12/15	5,313	1,156	21.8%	20,400
12/14	5,051	(115)	—	17,000
12/13	4,875	1,376	28.2%	17,000
12/12	4,450	437	9.8%	21,687
12/11	6,246	911	14.6%	22,660
Annual Growth	**(4.0%)**	**6.1%**	**—**	**(2.6%)**

2015 Year-End Financials

Debt ratio: 44.13%
Return on equity: 339.00%
Cash ($ mil.): 1,481
Current ratio: 1.13
Long-term debt ($ mil.): 3,468
No. of shares (mil.): 265
Dividends
  Yield: 1.3%
  Payout: 550.0%
Market value ($ mil.): 26,143

	STOCK PRICE ($) FY Close	P/E High/Low		PER SHARE ($) Earnings	Dividends	Book Value
12/15	98.58	25	20	4.21	1.32	0.73
12/14	88.98	—	—	(0.42)	1.20	1.79
12/13	78.20	15	9	4.91	3.62	4.80
12/12	54.67	36	27	1.53	3.52	2.75
12/11	44.97	15	12	3.00	1.00	5.46
Annual Growth	**21.7%**	—	—	**8.8%**	**7.2%**	**(39.5%)**

McKesson Corp.

McKesson moves medicine. As a top pharmaceuticals distributor in North America McKesson delivers prescription and generic drugs as well as health and beauty care products to more than 40000 retail and institutional pharmacies throughout the US. The company is also a major medical supplies wholesaler providing medical and surgical equipment to alternate health care sites such as doctors' offices surgery centers and long-term care facilities. In addition to distribution services McKesson offers software and technical services that help pharmacies health care providers and insurers manage supply chain clinical administrative and financial operations. The company was found in 1883.

HISTORY

John McKesson opened a Manhattan drugstore in 1833 and Daniel Robbins joined him as a partner in 1840. McKesson-Robbins soon expanded into chemical and drug production and the enterprise grew steadily. In 1926 after differences arose between the McKesson and Robbins heirs the company was sold to Donald Coster.

Coster was actually convicted felon Philip Musica who purchased McKesson-Robbins with fraudulently obtained bank loans. For more than a decade his real identity remained secret from all but one blackmailer. By 1930 McKesson-Robbins had wholesale drug operations in 33 states. The company appeared to be growing but a treasurer discovered a Musica-orchestrated accounting scam and a cash shortfall of $3 million. Faced with exposure Musica killed himself in 1939; company bankruptcy followed. McKesson-Robbins emerged from bankruptcy in 1941.

In a hostile takeover in 1967 San Francisco-based Foremost Dairies bought McKesson-Robbins to form Foremost-McKesson. Over the next 20 years the company bought liquor chemical and software wholesalers as well as several bottled-water companies. It sold Foremost Dairies in 1983 to focus on distribution changed its name to McKesson the next year and continued to build its drug wholesaling business through acquisitions. By 1985 it was the US's largest distributor of drugs and medical equipment wine and liquor bottled water and car waxes and polishes.

In 1986 McKesson narrowed its focus to the health industry by selling its liquor and chemical distributors. It acquired Canadian drug distributor Medis by halves in 1990 and 1991 and a 23% stake in Mexican drug distributor Nadro in 1993.

McKesson sold PCS the US's #1 prescription claims processor (acquired in 1970) to Eli Lilly in 1994. In 1996 the firm bought bankrupt distributor FoxMeyer Drug and sold its stake in Armor All (auto and home cleaning products) to Clorox.

In 1997 the company purchased General Medical the US's largest distributor of medical surgical supplies for about $775 million. McKesson began to focus on health care selling its Millbrook Distribution Services unit (health and beauty products general merchandise and specialty foods).

Under new CEO Mark Pulido it agreed to buy drug wholesaler AmeriSource Health (now AmerisourceBergen) but withdrew the offer in 1998 facing FTC opposition. Instead McKesson moved into information systems paying $14 billion for health care information top dog HBO & Company and forming McKesson HBOC. HBO a high-flyer in the high-growth health information systems segment balanced its rather dowdy drug and medical distribution operations.

But just months after the deal closed accounting inconsistencies at HBO prompted McKesson to restate fourth-quarter results for fiscal 1999 twice triggering shareholder lawsuits and a housecleaning of top brass. Five ex-HBO executives including McKesson HBOC chairman Charlie McCall (who was later indicted for securities fraud) were canned for using improper accounting methods. McKesson's veteran CEO Pulido and CFO Richard Hawkins were forced to resign for not seeing the problems coming.

The company changed its name to McKesson Corporation in 2001. The National Health Services Information Authority entered into an agreement with McKesson to develop a human resources and payroll system for use at the more than 600 NHS locations throughout the UK.

To catch then #1 pharmaceutical distributor Cardinal Health McKesson built up its core areas in 2003 and 2004 while trimming away some of the dead weight (Abaton.com Amysis Managed Care Systems and ProDental Corp.). The company bought PMO a specialty mail-order prescription business. It also acquired Canadian firm A.L.I.

Technologies which provided systems for managing medical images.

In 2007 McKesson acquired Oncology Therapeutics Network a specialty pharmaceuticals distributor for $519 million. McKesson launched a new Plasma and BioLogics division in 2008 to deliver plasma and plasma-related products to hospital pharmacies and it expanded its regional drug distribution network through the purchase of Midwest pharmacy distributor McQueary Brothers for $190 million.

EXECUTIVES

Vice President Of It, Terry Pfab
Chairman President and CEO, John H. Hammergren, age 56, $1,680,000 total compensation
EVP Human Resources, Jorge L. Figueredo, age 54, $610,000 total compensation
EVP and CFO, James A. Beer, age 54, $800,000 total compensation
EVP and Group President Domestic and International Distribution Solutions, Paul C. Julian, age 59, $1,065,000 total compensation
EVP CIO and CTO, Kathleen (Kathy) McElligott
EVP General Counsel and Chief Compliance Officer, Lori A. Schechter, age 53
EVP; Group President Technology Solutions, Patrick J. (Pat) Blake, age 51, $684,000 total compensation
EVP Corporate Strategy and Business Development, Bansi Nagji, age 50
Vice President Of Network Operations, Gary Roach
Vice President, Jeff Bowman
Vice President, Sam Mayercik
Vice President, Rich McKeon
Vice President, Vince Tighe
Director of Surgery Centers Northeast, Keith Slattery
Vice President of Sales primary Care South, Steve Tonnesen
Vice President Sales, Steve Williamson
Vice President Strategic Marketing, Stacey Irving
Vice President Care Management Solutions, Rose Higgins
Vice President of Professional Affairs, Buck Buckland
Vice President Strategic Partnerships and Business Development, Ted Boyle
Vice President Investor Relations, Ana Schrank
Vice President Financial Representative, Joanne Hunt
Assistant Vice President Product Development, Beth Kuzmak
Vice President Retail Sales, Perry Anderson
Vice President Retail Sales, David (Dave) Kelly
Vice President, Pete Pasquale
Vice President Product Management, Anupriyo Chakravarti
Vice President Financial Operations, Kevin Carroll
Senior Vice President Operations, Eddie Miller
National Vice President Business Development and Account Management, Sandra Warren
Vice President Operations, Tom Butterick
Vice President Global Sourcing Medical, James (Jamie) Hodges
Vice President Human Resources, Jeff Sauers
Vice President Corporate Strategy and Business Development, Al Linggi
Vice President Human Resources, Elaine Lemke
Vice President Of Corporate Tax, Paul Smith
Vice President Operations, Greg Tenbarge
Vice President Business Development, Devon Dickey
Vice President, Paula Adkison
Vice President GPO Services (Unity), Tim Boozan
Vice President Of Medical Affairs, Gene Simpson
Vice President Program Management, Scott Roosa
Vice President of Risk Management, Sharen Bond

Territory Vice President Revenue Management Solutions McKesson Provider Technologies, Brian Baughman
Director of Health Systems and Corporate Accounts, Heath Richardson
Vice President And General Manager, Andrew Moore
Territory Vice President, Robin Allen
Senior Vice President Information Technology Operations, Mike Kelly
Vice President Credit, Jenifer Schineller
Vice President Manager Director, Sunitha Jois
Enterprise Vice President, Kendall Echols
Associate Vice President, Lynn Garbee
Vice President High School National Accounts McKesson HBOC, Sharon Longwell
Vice President of Executive Talent, Katie Kaiser
Vice President Marketing, Chi Nguyen
Vice President National Accounts, Mike Ferguson
Vice President Inside Sales, Jackie Tucker
Vice President Pharmacy Optimization, Dave Ehlert
Vice President Of Internal Controls, Jill Robinson
Vice President, Mike Cesarz
Senior Vice President And General Manager Managed Services, Richard (Dick) Schickler
Vice President Client Management Emr, Bill Simpson
Vice President Indirect Sourcing And Procurement, Scott Wilkerson
Medical Director, Peter (Pete) Rosenberg
Regional Vice President Sales Western Region, David (Dave) Clark
Vice President of Operations Southwest Region, Josh Horton
Vice President Business Development, John (Jack) Steely
Vice President of Sales and Operations, Mauricio Chavez
Vice President, Stephanie Brooks
Vice President, Todd Philbrick
Vice President Automation Sales North, David (Dave) DiDomenico
Area Vice President, Keith Andelman
National Sales Director (TVP), Andrew (Andy) Dartnell
Assistant Vice President Software Development McKesson Corporation, Karen Erickson
Vice President of Marketing, Andy Burtis
Area Vice President, Mark Cox
Vice President Sales, Anne Curwin
Vice President Supplier Strategy, Claudia R Sacino
Vice President Sales Operations, Julie Clements
Senior Vice President General Manager, Derek Smith
Vice President Human Resources, Tiffany Owens
Senior Vice President Compensation and Benefits, Jerry Warren
Vice President Sales, Ashley Petit
Vice President Sales, Scott Spackman
Medical Director Physician Development, Robert (Bob) Roth
Vice President of Sales Health Systems, Rick Rothwell
Vice President Strategy and BD MHS, Megan (Meg) Callahan
Vice President Strategic Client Solutions, Cindy Criner
Senior Vice President Distribution Systems, Ronald (Ron) Bone
Vice President, Christopher (Chris) Corso
Regional Vice President of Sales, Ed Selleck
Vice President Business Development, Deann Cushman
Vice President Supply Chain Management, Chris Alverson
Vice President Of Sales, Michel Madeira
Vice President Medical Affairs, Summerpal Kahlon
Vice President, Michelle Freed
Assistant Vice President, Stephen Ayers

Vice President Sales, Vaughn Sutherland
Medical Director Business Development, Dan Dragolin
Vice President Of Sales, Deborah Smith
Vice President Of Distribution Center Operations, David Marriott
Assistant Vice President Gov and New Sales, Gary E Girvin
Vice President Of Operations, Steve Tarantino
Vice President Sales, Rod Nicholls
Vice President, Thierry Guyader
Senior Vice President, Michael Jordan
Division Vice President Customer Success, Bruce Christensen
Vice President Sales, Dylan Ross
Assistant Vice President Quality Assurance, Kathleen Reid
Vice President Fpanda, Jason Shook
Vice President of Sales McKesson Medical Surgical, Ronnie Simpson
Vice President Software Development Products, Bennie Jones
Vice President Of Sales, Casey Antonson
Vice President Of Finance, Ben Hext
Specialty Vice President, Randal Sanderson
National Vice President Sales Strategic Intelligence, Conrad Coopersmith
Vice President Strategy And Business Development, Janet Cutcliff
Vice President Office Product Sales, Kevin Boyle
Vice President Operations, Mark Turner
Vice President Corporate Strategy and BD, Kevin Kettler
Vice President Marketing And Sales Program, David Brown
Director of Radiology Coding, Dee Fulenwider
Vice President and General Manager, Derek Rago
Vice President Laboratory Account Sales, Jerry Morrow
Vice President Software Engineering, Jason Warner
Vice President of Sales Operations, Billy Callans
Vice President Of Customer Operations, Kathy McGrath
Regional Vice President, Greg Dover
Vice President Compensation Reports To Warren, John (Jack) Andrews
Vice President Channel Manager ERP Solutions, Mary Ellis
Vice President and General Manager, Andrew (Andy) Moore
Vice President McKesson Provider Technologies, Gerald (Jerry) Wilborn
Vice President Of Sales and Marketing, Rick Seiger
Vice President Senior Research Analyst Health Care, Bob Kanaga
Compliance President Vice President, Joe Lineberry
Vice President Marketing, Gina Bello-Holmes
National Vice President Of Sales, Kevin Sheilds
Vice President sales health Systems, Sidney (Sid) Mallory
National Vice President Consulting, Jeffrey (Jeff) Wescott
Vice President And Solution Line Manager Of Physician And Pharmacy Solutions, Bill Christopher
Vice President Hosting Strategy and Services, Davind Maharaj
Vice President, Andrewl Wilson
Senior Vice President Global Sourcing Medical, Andy Birken
Vice President General Manager of Outpatient Segment, Emilie Ray
Senior Vice President Distribution Operations, Don Walker
Vice President and General Manager, Lee Miller
Vice President Level, Vice president-sales Kim Diemand
Senior Vice President Chief, Robert (Bob) Pocica
Auditors: Deloitte & Touche LLP

LOCATIONS

HQ: McKesson Corp.
 One Post Street, San Francisco, CA 94104
Phone: 415 983-8300
Web: www.mckesson.com

2015 Sales

	% of total
US	80
International	20
Total	**100**

PRODUCTS/OPERATIONS

2015 Sales

	$ mil.	% of total
Distribution Solutions		
North America pharmaceutical distribution	143,711	80
International pharmaceutical distribution & services	26,358	15
Medical-surgical distribution & services	5,907	3
Technology Solutions	3,069	2
Total	**179,045**	**100**

Selected Operations and Services

Distribution Solutions (North America)
  McKesson Canada (drug distribution pharmacy and provider services)
  McKesson Medical-Surgical (includes ZEE Medical and Moore Medical supplies and equipment distribution)
  McKesson Patient Relationship Solutions (consumer adherence coaching outreach discount/trial programs)
  McKesson Pharmaceutical (drug health and beauty care products distribution)
  Institutional pharmacy services (consulting inventory management cost control SKY Packaging)
  Retail pharmacy services (Health Mart franchising consulting data and claims management cost control inventory management value brands redistribution repackaging refilling software)
  McKesson Pharmacy Systems (EnterpriseRx and PharmacyRx software financial operational and clinical solutions for retail and institutional pharmacies)
  McKesson Plasma and BioLogics (plasma-derivative products for hospitals)
  McKesson Specialty Health (solutions for specialty drug manufacturers and specialist care providers includes iKnowMed EHR)
  The US Oncology Network (cancer drug distribution)
  Nadro S.A. de C.V. (49% drug distribution Mexico)
  Parata Systems LLC (39% automated pharmacy and supply management systems and services)
Technology Solutions (North America Europe Israel)
  McKesson Automation (hospital dispensing and inventory management InterQual claims payment)
  McKesson Health Solutions (disease and case management claims management)
  McKesson Provider Technologies (clinical automation and physician practice management hospital inventory management and dispensing electronic health records software enterprise imaging revenue cycle outsourcing)
  RelayHealth (connectivity vendor neutral health information exchange)

Selected Acquisitions

COMPETITORS

Allscripts	Henry Schein
AmerisourceBergen	Imperial Distributors
Apothecary Products	Kinray
BioScrip	Medline Industries
Cardinal Health	Omnicare
Cerner	Owens & Minor
CuraScript	PharMerica
Emdeon	Quality King
FFF Enterprises	Quality Systems
Franz Haniel	Siemens Healthcare
GE Healthcare	Surgical Express
Grifols	The Harvard Drug Group
H. D. Smith Wholesale Drug	athenahealth

HISTORICAL FINANCIALS

Company Type: Public

Income Statement

FYE: March 31

	REVENUE ($ mil.)	NET INCOME ($ mil.)	NET PROFIT MARGIN	EMPLOYEES
03/15	179,045	1,476	0.8%	70,400
03/14	137,609	1,263	0.9%	42,800
03/13	122,455	1,338	1.1%	43,500
03/12	122,734	1,403	1.1%	37,700
03/11	112,084	1,202	1.1%	36,400
Annual Growth	**12.4%**	**5.3%**	**—**	**17.9%**

2015 Year-End Financials

Debt ratio: 18.27%	No. of shares (mil.): 232
Return on equity: 17.87%	Dividends
Cash ($ mil.): 5,341	Yield: 0.4%
Current ratio: 1.09	Payout: 13.1%
Long-term debt ($ mil.): 8,180	Market value ($ mil.): 52,478

	STOCK PRICE ($) FY Close	P/E High/Low		PER SHARE ($) Earnings	Dividends	Book Value
03/15	226.20	36	26	6.27	0.96	34.49
03/14	176.57	34	19	5.41	0.92	36.89
03/13	107.96	19	15	5.59	0.80	31.15
03/12	87.77	16	12	5.59	0.80	29.07
03/11	79.05	17	12	4.57	0.72	28.65
Annual Growth	**30.1%**	**—**	**—**	**8.2%**	**7.5%**	**4.7%**

Mercantile Bank Corp.

Mercantile Bank Corporation is the holding company for Mercantile Bank of Michigan (formerly Mercantile Bank of West Michigan) which boasts assets of nearly $3 billion and operates more than 50 branches in central and western Michigan around Grand Rapids Holland and Lansing. The bank targets local consumers and businesses offering standard deposit services such as checking and savings accounts CDs IRAs and health savings accounts. Commercial loans make up more than three-fourths of the bank's loan portfolio. Outside of banking subsidiary Mercantile Insurance Center sells insurance products.

OperationsMercantile Bank Corp. generated 82% of its total revenue from loan interest (including fees) in 2014 with securities interest contributing another 8% to total revenue. Service charges on deposit and sweep accounts and credit and debit card fees made up another 5% of Mercantile's total revenue while its mortgage banking income generated another 2%.Sales and MarketingMercantile provides its banking services to businesses individuals and government organizations. Its commercial banking services mostly cater to small- to medium-sized businesses. The company spent $1.315 million on advertising in 2014 compared to $1.113 million and $1.167 million in 2013 and 2012 respectively.Financial PerformanceMercantile Bank Corp's revenues had been declining for a number of years as its loan business withered while profits have remained mostly flat. The company had a breakout year in 2014 however after its historic acquisition of FirstBank Corp. The bank's revenue skyrocketed by 53% to $99.15 million (the highest level since 2009) mostly as the acquisition nearly doubled its loan assets and boosted its interest income on loans and securities by significant amounts. The bank's non-interest income also grew by 46% thanks to higher fee in-

come across the board also resulting from the recent acquisition. Higher revenue and a $3.2 million reduction in loan loss provisions with a stronger credit portfolio in 2014 also pushed the company's net income up by 2% to $17.33 million for the year. Mercantile's operating cash declined by 50% to $14.41 million due to changes in accrued interest and other liabilities during the year.StrategyMercantile Bank Corporation has been growing its loan business and branch network reach through strategic acquisitions of smaller banks and bank branches. Its mid-2014 acquisition of Firstbank Corporation was perhaps the most effective to date as the purchase doubled its assets and boosted the size of its branch network nearly seven-fold from seven branches to a whopping 53.Mergers and AcquisitionsIn June 2014 Mercantile Bank Corp. purchased Firstbank Corp of Alma Michigan for a total purchase price of $173 million adding 46 branches and $1.3 billion in assets. The deal which made Mercantile the third-largest bank based in the state also expanded the bank's service offerings diversified its loan portfolio boosted its loan origination capacity and significantly extended its geographic footprint into Michigan's lower peninsula.

EXECUTIVES

Chairman President and CEO; Chairman and CEO Mercantile Bank, Michael H. Price, age 58, $490,000 total compensation
SVP CFO and Treasurer Mercantile Bank Corporation and SVP and CFO Mercantile Bank of Michigan, Charles E. (Chuck) Christmas, age 49, $263,000 total compensation
EVP COO Secretary and DirectorMercantile Bank Corporation and President COO and Secretary Mercantile Bank of Michigan, Robert B. Kaminski, age 53, $315,000 total compensation
EVP Corporate Finance and Strategic Planning Mercantile Bank Corporation and Mercantile Bank of Michigan, Samuel G. Stone, age 70, $159,833 total compensation
Vice President Internal Auditor, Sandy Jager
Assistant Vice President Loan Review Assistant Manager, Glenda Stursma
Senior Vice President Commercial Lending, Kevin Paul
Vice President Security, Paul Wegener
Assistant Vice President Human Resources Specialist, Tina Van Valkenburg
Vice President Treasury Management, Joe Allen
Senior Vice President Business Development Officer, Brian Talbot
Vice President Commercial Loan Officer, Jeff Hicks
Branch Manager Vice President, Andrea Spagnuolo
Vice President, Teresa Rupert
Vice President Treasury Sales, Kimberly Labadie
Senior Vice President Commercial Lending, David Deboer
Assistant Vice President Assistant Man, Jennifer (Jen) Harris
Senior Vice President, Valicevic Joseph
Vice President, Craig Oosterhouse
Senior Vice President Corporate Banking, Matt Zimmerman
Senior Vice President Information Systems Manager, Allen (Al) Smith
Auditors: BDO USA, LLP

LOCATIONS

HQ: Mercantile Bank Corp.
  310 Leonard Street N.W., Grand Rapids, MI 49504
Phone: 616 406-3000

PRODUCTS/OPERATIONS

2014 Sales

	$ mil.	% of total
Interest income		
Loans and leases including fees	80	82
Securities taxable	6	6
Securities tax-exempt	1	2
Other	0	-
Noninterest income		
Service charges on accounts	2	3
Credit and debit card fees	2	2
Mortgage banking activities	1	2
Other	3	3
Total	**99**	**100**

COMPETITORS

Chemical Financial	Flagstar Bancorp
ChoiceOne Financial	Huntington Bancshares
Services	Independent Bank (MI)
Comerica	Macatawa Bank
Fifth Third	United Bancorp (MI)

HISTORICAL FINANCIALS

Company Type: Public

Income Statement

FYE: December 31

	ASSETS ($ mil.)	NET INCOME ($ mil.)	INCOME AS % OF ASSETS	EMPLOYEES
12/14	2,893	17	0.6%	731
12/13	1,426	17	1.2%	268
12/12	1,422	12	0.9%	264
12/11	1,433	37	2.6%	261
12/10	1,632	(13)	—	277
Annual Growth	**15.4%**	**—**	**—**	**27.5%**

2014 Year-End Financials

Debt ratio: 1.88%
Return on equity: 7.20%
Cash ($ mil.): 161
Current ratio: —
Long-term debt ($ mil.): —

No. of shares (mil.): 16
Dividends
  Yield: 11.8%
  Payout: 167.5%
Market value ($ mil.): 357

	STOCK PRICE ($) FY Close	P/E High/Low	PER SHARE ($) Earnings	Dividends	Book Value
12/14	21.02	19 15	1.28	2.48	19.33
12/13	21.58	11 8	1.95	0.45	17.54
12/12	16.50	14 7	1.33	0.09	16.84
12/11	9.75	2 2	4.07	0.00	19.17
12/10	8.20	— —	(1.72)	0.03	14.65
Annual Growth	**26.5%**	**— —**	**—**	**—201.5%**	**7.2%**

Merck & Co., Inc

Merck makes medicines for a number of maladies from stuffy noses and asthma to hypertension and arthritis. The pharmaceutical giant's top prescription drugs include diabetes drugs Januvia and Janumet anti-inflammatory Remicade cholesterol combatants Vytorin and Zetia and hypertension fighters Cozaar and Hyzaar. In addition Merck makes childhood and adult vaccines for such diseases as measles mumps pneumonia and shingles as well as veterinary pharmaceuticals through Merck Animal Health. The company sold its OTC drug and personal care offerings including Claritin allergy pills and Dr. Scholl's foot care products to Bayer AG in 2014.

HISTORY

Merck traces its roots to the formation of Schering-Plough in 1851 and the founding of the original Merck entity in 1887. (The two companies merged in 2009.)

Schering-Plough dates back to 1851 when Berlin chemist Ernst Schering began to sell chemicals to apothecary shops. By 1880 Schering's business (which eventually became Bayer Schering Pharma) was exporting pharmaceuticals to the US where a subsidiary (the predecessor to Schering-Plough) was established in 1928.

At the outbreak of WWII the US government seized the US Schering subsidiary severing links with its German parent. The company went on to develop such new drugs as Chlor-Trimeton one of the first antihistamines and the cold medicine Coricidin. The US government sold Schering in 1952 to Merrill Lynch which took it public. Schering bought White Labs (which made Coppertone sunscreen) in 1957. In the 1960s the company introduced Garamycin (antibiotic 1964) Tinactin (antifungal 1965) and Afrin (decongestant 1967).

Schering's 1971 merger with Memphis-based Plough expanded the product line to include such cosmetics and consumer items as Coppertone and Di-Gel. Plough's founder Abe Plough had borrowed $125 from his father to found the company in 1908. Abe remained chairman at Schering-Plough until 1976. Schering-Plough introduced many products after the merger including Lotrimin AF (antifungal 1975) antibiotic Netromycin (1980) and Drixoral (a cold remedy made nonprescription in 1982).

The company was one of the first drug giants to make significant investments in biotechnology: It bought DNAX Research Institute of Palo Alto California in 1982. Acquisitions in the late 1970s and 1980s included Scholl (foot care 1979) Key Pharmaceuticals (cardiovascular drugs 1986) and Cooper Companies (eye care 1988).

In 1993 Schering-Plough began marketing its non-sedating antihistamine Claritin in the US. (Claritin became an OTC drug in 2002.) The next year it gained FDA approval to market the first colored disposable contact lenses only to sell its contact lens business later in the year. In 1996 Schering-Plough bought Canji to strengthen its gene therapy research program. It strengthened its veterinary medicine segment in 1997 when it bought Mallinckrodt's animal health operations.

The firm bought the marketing rights to Centocor's treatment for Crohn's disease in 1998. In 1999 the FDA approved the company's Temodar a chemotherapy treatment for brain tumors and it bought the US rights to Pfizer's Bain de Soleil sun care product line. In 2000 Schering-Plough formed its first collaboration with Merck. In 2002 the company paid a $500 million fine to the FDA over manufacturing concerns.

As Schering-Plough's revenues started to decline in 2003 the company brought in several executives from Pharmacia including CEO Fred Hassan (who retired following the 2009 merger with Plough) to help streamline its operations and expand its R&D programs and product offerings. The firm gave itself a major boost by acquiring Akzo Nobel's Organon unit in 2007 growing in the areas of women's health care neurology vaccines animal health (Intervet) and third-party biologics manufacturing (through Diosynth).

The original Merck was started in 1887 when German chemist Theodore Weicker came to the US to set up a branch of German firm E. Merck AG (which was founded in 1668 and later became Merck KGaA). George Merck (grandson of the German company's founder) came in 1889 and formed a partnership with Weicker and eventually bought out Weicker's shares. At first the firm imported and sold drugs and chemicals from Germany but in 1903 it began manufacturing its own products. During WWI Merck gave the US government the 80% of the US Merck unit's stock owned by the family in Germany (George kept his shares). After the war the stock was sold to the public.

The firm acquired Powers-Weightman-Rosengarten of Philadelphia (a producer of antimalarial quinine) in 1927. Merck opened its first research lab in 1933; Merck scientists there developed the first steroid cortisone in 1944. Five Merck scientists received Nobel Prizes in the 1940s and 1950s. In 1953 Merck bought drugmaker Sharp & Dohme of Philadelphia which brought with it a strong sales force.

The 1958 introduction of Diuril (antihypertensive) and several other drugs (including the first measles vaccine) in the early 1960s was followed by a dry spell. In the 1970s an accelerated R&D organization created new products including Clinoril (antiarthritic) Flexeril (muscle relaxant) and Timoptic (for glaucoma). Merck introduced 10 major new drugs in the 1980s including Mevacor (high cholesterol) and Vasotec (high blood pressure).

In 1990 the company bought the nonprescription drug segment of ICI Americas; products from the purchase were contributed to a Consumer Pharmaceuticals joint venture with Johnson & Johnson. Merck bought pharmacy benefits manager Medco Containment Services in 1993. New drug launches in 1995 and 1996 included Cozaar (for reducing hypertension) and Pepcid AC (antacid). Also in 1996 Merck expanded its pharmacy benefit management operations with the purchase of Systemed.

In 1997 Merck and Rhône-Poulenc (now part of Sanofi-Aventis) merged their animal health units to form Merial. Merck also sold its insecticide and fungicide business to Novartis that year. In 1998 DuPont bought out Merck's 50% stake in a drug-marketing joint venture formed by the two firms in 1991. In 1999 the FDA approved Merck's preservative-free hepatitis B vaccine Recombivax HB.

In 2001 Merck acquired biotech firm Rosetta Inpharmatics. The company spun off its highly successful Medco Health Solutions drug distribution subsidiary in 2003.

In 2004 Merck pulled its blockbuster pain medication Vioxx off the market after studies linked the drug to increased risks of strokes and heart attacks. (Merck settled thousands of class-action and personal-injury lawsuits related to Vioxx in 2007 for $4.85 billion.) The Vioxx safety scandal along with the pending loss of patent protection on some of its biggest sellers like Zocor (which began facing competition in 2006) sent the company into recovery mode. Merck announced restructuring plans to make the company's operations leaner and more cost-effective in 2005 under new CEO Richard (Dick) Clark a longtime Merck executive. Between 2005 and 2008 the company eliminated more than 10000 jobs and closed a handful of manufacturing plants.

From 2006 to 2009 Merck worked aggressively to expand its biotech operations through the acquisition of companies including GlycoFi (biologic drug molecules) Abmaxis (monoclonal antibodies) Sirna Therapeutics (RNA interference or RNAi) and NovaCardia (cardiology drugs) as well as the follow-on (generic) biologic assets of Insmed. New drug launches included HIV drug Isentress and diabetes therapy Janumet in 2007 and blockbuster HPV vaccine Gardasil the world's first anti-cancer vaccine which was approved by the FDA in 2006.

In 2008 Merck sold off the assets of its Rosetta Inpharmatics subsidiary to Covance (gene expression laboratory assets) and Microsoft (expression analysis software assets). It also sold another research lab to PPD and contracted out certain lab functions to the buyer. Merck launched a new product Emend for chemotherapy side-effects that year. New drug launches in 2009 included Saphris a treatment for schizophrenia and bipolar disorder and Simponi the next-generation version of top-selling drug Remicade.

Cholesterol drug Vytorin —a combination of Schering-Plough's Zetia and Merck's Zocor — began facing controversy in 2008 when study results were released questioning the drug's effectiveness compared to Merck's older medication Zocor. Controversy over Vytorin along with some other pipeline setbacks (including the FDA's rejection of a Merck/Schering-Plough combo asthma drug and Merck's Cordaptive cholesterol candidate) led both predecessors Merck and Schering-Plough to announce layoffs and restructuring measures in 2008. Each company reduced its workforce by around 10% that year with their respective US sales teams bearing the brunt of the cuts. The companies' troubles with Vytorin came to a head in 2009 when they agreed to pay about $42 million to settle class-action lawsuits filed by consumers and health plans over Vytorin's efficacy.

Later that year Merck and Schering-Plough decided to merge taking the logical step of marriage to strengthen their defenses against future troubles (especially in light of increasing competitive challenges in the market) as well as to create cost savings opportunities and expanded avenues for revenue growth. The $41 billion transaction was conducted through a reverse-merger transaction in which the legacy Schering-Plough entity acquired the legacy Merck entity and took on the Merck name.

Following the merger Merck began simplifying its global branding under the Merck and MSD names gradually phasing out the Schering-Plough moniker. The purchase expanded Merck's offerings in areas including inflammation allergy and cancer treatment as well as biotech drugs. The acquisition also greatly expanded Merck's operations in the animal health and consumer health arenas.

However to gain Schering-Plough's animal health unit Intervet (later renamed Merck Animal Health) Merck had to sell its stake in veterinary joint venture Merial to partner Sanofi-Aventis for about $4 billion later that year to avoid anti-trust issues. (Merck and Sanofi-Aventis later explored options to strike a fresh veterinary medicine joint venture by combining Merial with Intervet; however after a year of planning the two companies called off the deal in 2011 due to concerns over further anti-trust issues.)

The company experienced a sharp gain in profits in 2009 (reporting net income of $12.9 billion) due to gains on the sale of the Merial stake and on recognized equity from assets previously owned jointly with Schering-Plough.

When the Merck/Schering-Plough merger closed the existing Merck CEO Dick Clark took the helm at the new Merck. Once the dust from the merger settled however Clark retired from the CEO post at the end of 2010 while remaining as chairman. President Kenneth Frazier stepped into the CEO role.

EXECUTIVES

Chairman President and CEO, Kenneth C. (Ken) Frazier, age 60, $1,500,000 total compensation
EVP and Chief Medical Officer, Michael Rosenblatt, age 67
EVP Strategic Communications Global Public Policy and Population Health, Julie L. Gerberding, age 60
EVP and CFO, Robert M. Davis, age 48, $650,384 total compensation
EVP; President Merck Manufacturing, Willie A. Deese, age 60
EVP; President Merck Research Laboratories, Roger M. Perlmutter, $1,000,000 total compensation
EVP; President Global Human Health, Adam H. Schechter, age 51, $962,388 total compensation
EVP Human Resources, Mirian M. Graddick-Weir, age 61
EVP; President Merck Animal Health, Richard R. DeLuca, age 52
EVP and General Counsel, Michael J. Holston
EVP and CIO, Clark Golestani
Vice President, Kevin Ravaioli
Associate Vice President Supply Chain, Julio Feliciano
Vice President Sales and Service, Peter (Pete) Basile
National Sales Manager, Ron McDaniel
Vice President Operations, Keith Gordon
Vice President Representative, Christina Fillinger
Vice President of Marketing, Lisa Zavis
Vice President, Raul Lacson
Senior Vice President Representative, Imtiaz Alam
Vice President, Denise Williams
Vice President Human Resources, Hao Wang
Vice President, Bill Jon
Vice President Health Economic Statistics, John (Jack) Cook
Associate Vice President, Ben Thorner
Vice President Biotechnology Development, Stephen Farrand
Vice President Manufacturing Division Strategy And Integration, Richard Hofmann
Medical Director Product Leader, Deborah (Deb) Rudin
Vice President Business Development and Licensing, Ji Li
Vice President Global Integrated Livestock Bu, Fabio Paganini
Vice President Global Compensation And Benefits, Jeff Geller
Vice President Finance Global Supply Chain, Joe Sukola
Vice President Global Engineering Services, Arthur Burson
Associate Medical Director, Lana Garafola
Pharm D, Afsaneh Akhtari
Vice President Global Research Quality Spri, Jacqueline Elbonne
Legal Pa For Uk Director And Also Pa To The Assistant Vice President For Europe And Canada, Michele Creamer
Vice President Of Information Technology, James Ciriello
Senior Vice President, Dorthe Mikkelsen
National Sales Manager, Jason Grafham
Assistant Vice President Global Communications, Mary Blake
National Sales Manager (TURKEY), Alper Alptekin
Senior Vice President Managing Director, Pierluigi Antonelli
Executive Vice President Process Solutions, Andrew Bulpin
Assistant Vice President Managing Director, Andras Bolcskei
Senior Vice President Strategy And Business Development, Galeota James
Associate Vice President Sterile Operations, David (Dave) Zisa
Assistant Vice President Merck, Brandon Brega
National Sales Manager Ruminants, Rui Nobrega
National Sales Manager (Ruminants): MSD Animal Health AUS, Michael (Mel) Schildkraut
Associate Vice President Emerging Markets, Steven (Steve) Cianciosi
Vice President And Therapeutic Area Biology Head, Mark Erion
Senior Vice President Finance Global Con, John (Jack) Canan
National Account Manager, Jason Osburn
Vice President And Assistant General Counsel, James (Jamie) Grasty
Group Vice President Global New Ventures and Strategic Commercial Development, Nancy Miller-Rich
Associate Vice President, Kirke Weaver
Associate Vice President of Operations and General Manager MSD Oss, Cees Mens
Secretary, Janet Karll
Auditors: PricewaterhouseCoopers LLP

LOCATIONS

HQ: Merck & Co., Inc
   2000 Galloping Hill Road, Keniworth, NJ 07033
Phone: 908 740-4000   **Fax:** 908 735-1500
Web: www.merck.com

2014 Sales

	$ mil.	% of total
US	17,071	41
Europe Middle East & Africa	13,174	31
Asia Pacific	3,951	9
Japan	3,471	8
Latin America	3,151	8
Other regions	1,419	3
Total	**42,237**	**100**

PRODUCTS/OPERATIONS

2014 Sales

	$ mil.	% of total
Pharmaceuticals - Primary care & women's health		
Diabetes	6,002	14
Cardiovascular	4,166	10
General medicine & Women's health	2,097	6
Pharmaceuticals - Hospital & specialty		
Immunology	3,061	7
Acute care	2,281	5
HIV	1,673	4
Hepatitis	534	1
Other hospital & specialty	257	1
Pharmaceuticals - Oncology	958	2
Pharmaceuticals - Diversified brands	4,933	12
Pharmaceuticals - Vaccines	5,302	13
Other pharmaceuticals	4,778	11
Animal health consumer care & other revenue	6,195	14
Total	**42,237**	**100**

Selected Products

Pharmaceuticals —Primary care and women's health
   Respiratory
      Asmanex (asthma)
      Clarinex/Aerius (allergies)
      Dulera (asthma)
      Nasonex (allergies)
      Proventil (asthma)
      Singulair (asthma and allergic rhinitis)
   Diabetes and Obesity
      Janumet (diabetes)
      Januvia (diabetes)
      Juvisync (diabetes)
   Cardiovascular
      Vytorin (combination Zetia and Zocor cholesterol)
      Zetia/Ezetrol (cholesterol)
   Women's Health and Endocrine
      Cerazette (contraceptive)
      Follistim/Puregon (fertility)
      Fosamax/Fosavance (osteoporosis)
      Implanon (contraceptive)
      NuvaRing (contraceptive)
      Zoely (contraceptive)
   Other Primary care and women's health
      Arcoxia (arthritis and pain)
      Avelox (antibiotic with Bayer)
      Maxalt (migraine)
Pharmaceuticals —Hospital and specialty
   Infectious Disease
      Cancidas (antifungal)
      Invanz (antibacterial)
      Isentress (antifungal HIV)
      Noxafil (antifungal)

PegIntron (hepatitis C)
Primaxin (antibiotic)
Immunology
Remicade (rheumatoid arthritis and Crohn' s disease)
Simponi (rheumatoid arthritis)
Oncology
Emend (chemotherapy-induced nausea and vomiting)
Intron A (melanoma)
Temodar/Temodal (brain tumors)
Other Hospital and specialty
Integrilin (injectable for acute coronary syndrome)
Saphris (schizophrenia bipolar)
Zioptan/Saflutan (glaucoma)
Vaccines
Gardasil (cervical cancer caused by HPV virus)
M-M-R II (measles mumps and rubella)
Pneumovax (pneumococcal disease)
ProQuad (measles mumps rubella varicella)
RotaTeq (rotavirus gastroenteritis)
Varivax (chicken pox)
Zostavax (shingles)
Diversified Brands (non-patent protected products)
Cozaar/Hyzaar (hypertension)
Propecia (male pattern hair loss)
Proscar (benign prostate enlargement)
Remeron (antidepressant)
Vasotec/Vaseretic (hypertension/heart failure)
Zocor (elevated cholesterol)
Animal Health (Intervet)
Aquaflor (antibiotic for farm-raised fish)
Banamine (nonsteroid anti-inflammatory)
Coccivac (poultry vaccine)
Exspot/Scalibor (canine topical insecticide)
M+PAC (swine pneumonia vaccine)
Nuflor (antimicrobial)
Otomax (canine otitis)
Paracox (poultry vaccine)

Selected Acquisitions

COMPETITORS

Abbott Labs	Heska
Alcon	Johnson & Johnson
Allergan	Meda Pharmaceuticals
Allergan plc	Merck KGaA
Amgen	Mylan
AstraZeneca	Novartis
Bausch & Lomb	Perrigo
Baxter International	Pfizer
Bayer AG	Roche Holding
Biogen	Sandoz International
Boehringer Ingelheim	GmbH
Bristol-Myers Squibb	Sanofi
Eli Lilly	Shire
Enanta	Teva
Gilead Sciences	Virbac Corporation
GlaxoSmithKline	Warner Chilcott

HISTORICAL FINANCIALS
Company Type: Public

Income Statement
FYE: December 31

	REVENUE ($ mil.)	NET INCOME ($ mil.)	NET PROFIT MARGIN	EMPLOYEES
12/14	42,237	11,920	28.2%	70,000
12/13	44,033	4,404	10.0%	76,000
12/12	47,267	6,168	13.0%	83,000
12/11	48,047	6,272	13.1%	86,000
12/10	45,987	861	1.9%	94,000
Annual Growth	(2.1%)	92.9%	—	(7.1%)

2014 Year-End Financials
Debt ratio: 21.77%—
Return on equity: 24.22%
Cash ($ mil.): 7,441
Current ratio: 1.77
Long-term debt ($ mil.): 18,699

Dividends
Yield: 3.1%
Payout: 96.7%
Market value ($ mil.): —

	STOCK PRICE ($) FY Close	P/E High/Low		PER SHARE ($) Earnings	Dividends	Book Value
12/14	56.79	15	12	4.07	1.77	17.14
12/13	50.05	34	27	1.47	1.73	17.00
12/12	40.94	24	18	2.00	1.69	17.52
12/11	37.70	19	15	2.02	1.56	17.93
12/10	36.04	147	114	0.28	1.52	17.64
Annual Growth	12.0%	—	—	95.3%	3.9%	(0.7%)

Mercury General Corp.

Named after the Roman god of commerce and travel Mercury General hopes to combine the two and become the ultimate auto insurance provider. The company is the parent of a group of insurers including Mercury Casualty Company that write automobile insurance for all risk classifications in more than a dozen states. Plain old private auto insurance accounts for about 80% of premiums written. However Mercury General also sells commercial vehicle insurance and a bit of homeowners mechanical breakdown umbrella and fire insurance. The company is a leader in the California auto market and has significant operations in Florida.

Operations

Mercury General offers automobile insurance products including comprehensive collision property damage body injury personal injury protection underinsured/uninsured motorist and other coverage. It also provides homeowners' coverage including dwelling liability personal property fire and other products.

Geographic Reach

While Mercury General has ventured out of its California comfort zone the state still accounts for more than 80% of total premiums. The company operated solely in its home state until 1990; it now underwrites auto insurance in more than a dozen other states including Arizona Florida Georgia Illinois Michigan Nevada New Jersey New York Oklahoma Pennsylvania Texas and Virginia.

Sales and Marketing

Mercury General sells policies through 8800 independent agents with approximately 1800 in California and another 1400 in Florida.

During 2014 the company spent a net $23.1 million on advertising which included television radio newspaper direct mail and online campaigns. It launched a national advertising campaign in 2015 which it expects to cost up to $48 million.

Financial Performance

After years of flat revenue Mercury General did report a slight 1% uptick in 2013 up $38 million to $2.8 billion. Revenue grew a further 7% to $3 billion in 2014 due mainly to rate increases in the California private passenger automobile and homeowners' businesses. Net income rose 59% to $178 that year as a result of the increased revenue.

Cash flow from operations also rose growing 18% to $247 as collected premiums increased and paid losses decreased. This was partially offset by a rise in paid expenses and income taxes.

StrategyCore to its strategy for growth is managing rates to achieve the right balance between attracting customers through lower rates and remaining competitive. The company places value in its agent relationships and underwriting processes to achieve favorable margins. To encourage policy growth and broaden its customer base Mercury General offers multi-policy discounts to those who

bundle their home and car insurance together. It also employs marketing initiatives to build brand recognition and generate leads. Mercury General is also focusing on gradually widening its operations by expanding into new states while being mindful of the risks of establishing new divisions. To that end the company has agreed to buy Workmen's Auto Insurance (which primarily sells nonstandard auto policies) for $8 million. Mercury General also maintains a conservative investment strategy by maximizing long-term performance opportunities.Technology is another key aspect it uses to build the business. In 2013 the company launched its online platform allowing customers to purchase a policy through the Internet.

EXECUTIVES
Interim Vice President South East Region, John (Jack) Sutton
VP and Chief Underwriting Officer, Kenneth G. Kitzmiller, age 68
President and CEO, Gabriel Tirador, age 50, $888,805 total compensation
SVP and CFO, Theodore R. Stalick, age 51, $553,643 total compensation
VP and Chief Investment Officer, Christopher Graves, age 49, $381,679 total compensation
VP and Chief Actuary, Charles Toney, age 53
SVP and CIO, Allan Lubitz, age 57, $419,284 total compensation
VP and Chief Product Officer, Robert Houlihan, age 58, $379,052 total compensation
VP Marketing, Brandt N. Minnich, age 48
Vice President Of Information Technology, Anderson Larry
Vice President Corporate Controller, David (Dave) Yeager
Legal Secretary, Stephanie Sonnier
Chairman, George Joseph, age 93
Auditors: KPMG LLP

LOCATIONS
HQ: Mercury General Corp.
4484 Wilshire Boulevard, Los Angeles, CA 90010
Phone: 323 937-1060   **Fax:** 323 857-7116
Web: www.mercuryinsurance.com

PRODUCTS/OPERATIONS

2014 Sales

	$ mil.	% of total
Net premium earned	2,796	93
Net investment income	125	4
Net realized investment	81	3
Other	8	
Total	**3,011**	**100**

Selected Products
Auto
  Commercial auto
  Mechanical breakdown (extended warranty coverage)
  Niche commercial
  Personal auto
Condo
  Contents coverage
  Guest medical protection and liability
  Personal liability protection
  Personal property
Homeowners
  Apartments
  Condominiums
  Single-family homes
Personal umbrella
Renter
  Liability protection
  Personal property

Selected Operating Brands and Divisions
AIS Management
American Mercury Insurance
American Mercury Lloyds Insurance

American Mercury MGA
Auto Insurance Specialists
California Automobile Insurance
California General Underwriters Insurance
Concord Insurance Services
Mercury Casualty
Mercury County Mutual Insurance
Mercury Group
Mercury Indemnity
Mercury Insurance
Mercury National Insurance
Mercury Select Management
PoliSeek AIS Insurance Solutions

COMPETITORS

21st Century Insurance	Farmers Group
Allstate	GEICO
Auto Club of Southern California	State Farm
Covanta Holding	USAA

HISTORICAL FINANCIALS

Company Type: Public

Income Statement

FYE: December 31

	ASSETS ($ mil.)	NET INCOME ($ mil.)	INCOME AS % OF ASSETS	EMPLOYEES
12/15	4,628	74	1.6%	4,300
12/14	4,600	177	3.9%	4,400
12/13	4,315	112	2.6%	4,500
12/12	4,189	116	2.8%	4,600
12/11	4,070	191	4.7%	4,500
Annual Growth	3.3%	(21.0%)	—	(1.1%)

2015 Year-End Financials

Debt ratio: 6.27%
Return on equity: 4.03%
Cash ($ mil.): 264
Current ratio: —
Long-term debt ($ mil.): —

No. of shares (mil.): 55
Dividends
Yield: 5.3%
Payout: 466.5%
Market value ($ mil.): 2,569

	STOCK PRICE ($) FY Close	P/E High/Low		PER SHARE ($) Earnings	Dividends	Book Value
12/15	46.57	45	34	1.35	2.47	33.01
12/14	56.67	18	13	3.23	2.46	34.02
12/13	49.71	25	18	2.04	2.45	33.15
12/12	39.69	21	17	2.13	2.44	33.55
12/11	45.62	13	10	3.49	2.41	33.86
Annual Growth	0.5%	—	—	(21.1%)	0.6%	(0.6%)

Meridian Bancorp Inc

Meridian Bancorp is the holding company of East Boston Savings Bank which provides standard deposit and lending services to individuals and businesses in the greater Boston area. The bank writes single-family commercial and multi-family mortgages as well as construction and business loans and consumer loans. East Boston Savings operates about 30 branches in eastern Massachusetts. Mutual holding company Meridian Financial Services owns 59% of Meridian Bancorp.

Geographic Reach

Meridian Bancorp operates across the greater Boston metropolitan area in Essex Middlesex and Suffolk counties.

Operations

The bank has about $2.7 billion in assets; commercial real estate loans comprise 45% of its loan portfolio.

Meridian owns a 40% stake in Hampshire First Bank a New Hampshire-chartered bank established in 2006.

Sales and Marketing

Meridian has devoted more dollars to advertising in recent years. It spent $2.95 million in fiscal 2013 on advertising up from $2.54 million in 2012 and $2.45 million in 2011.

Financial Performance

Like many small banks that survived the Great Recession Meridian has grown steadily the last few years. In 2013 it reported an 8% increase in revenue from $106 million to $115 million due to increased loan payments as interest rates recovered. Net income grew 24% from $12 million to $15 million on the strength of higher revenue and changes in the company's bookkeeping. Cash from operations jumped to $28 million after the company sold some of its loans.

Strategy

As part of its growth strategy the bank has bolstered its commercial real estate and business loans as well as its construction loans. Previously residential mortgages represent the company's largest loan segment.

The bank also intends to grow through the opening of new branches and pursuing branch acquisitions. It has opened 14 new branches in upscale Boston neighborhoods in the last two years and acquired another six.

To further enable growth Meridian in 2014 announced that it will convert from a mutual company to a public corporation.

EXECUTIVES

CFO and Treasurer, Mark L. Abbate, age 60
SVP Consumer and Business Banking, Keith D. Armstrong
Chairman President and CEO Meridian Interstate Bancorp and East Boston Savings Bank, Richard J. Gavegnano, age 67, $311,400 total compensation
EVP Corporate Banking, Frank Romano
EVP Lending, John Migliozzi
EVP and COO, John A. Carroll
SVP Electronic Banking, Mary Hagen
SVP Retail Banking, James Morgan
SVP Residential Lending, Joseph Nash
Auditors: Wolf & Company, P.C.

LOCATIONS

HQ: Meridian Bancorp Inc
67 Prospect Street, Peabody, MA 01960
Phone: 617 567-1500

Selected Locations
Allpoint Locator
Allston
Belmont
Cambridge
Danvers
Dorchester
East Boston
Everett
Jamaica Plain
Lynn
Medford
Melrose
Peabody
Revere
Saugus
Somerville
South Boston
South End
Wakefield
West Roxbury
Winthrop

PRODUCTS/OPERATIONS

2013 Sales

	$ mil.	% of total
Interest & dividend income		
Interest & fees on loans	89	78
Interest & debt securities	4	4
Dividends on equity securities	1	1
Non-interest income		
Gain on sale of securities	9	8
Customer service fees	7	6
Income from bank-owned life insurance	1	1
Mortgage banking gains	0	1
Loan fees & other income	0	1
Total	**114**	**100**

Selected Products & Services

Personal
  Deposit Rates
  Investments
  Personal Checking
  Personal Lending
  Personal Online Banking
  Retirement Services
  Savings & CDs
Business
  Business Checking
  Business Lending
  Business Online Banking
  Business Retirement Services
  Business Savings
  Deposit Rates
  Institutional Banking
  Merchant Services
Commercial
  Cash Management
  Commercial Lending
  Corporate Banking
  Deposit Rates

COMPETITORS

Bank of America	Middlesex Savings
Cambridge Financial	Peoples Federal
Citizens Financial Group	Bancshares Inc.
Eastern Bank	Sovereign Bank
	TD Bank USA

HISTORICAL FINANCIALS

Company Type: Public

Income Statement

FYE: December 31

	ASSETS ($ mil.)	NET INCOME ($ mil.)	INCOME AS % OF ASSETS	EMPLOYEES
12/14	3,278	22	0.7%	466
12/13	2,682	15	0.6%	455
12/12	2,278	12	0.5%	433
12/11	1,974	11	0.6%	392
12/10	1,835	13	0.7%	360
Annual Growth	15.6%	13.7%	—	6.7%

2014 Year-End Financials

Debt ratio: 5.24%
Return on equity: 5.40%
Cash ($ mil.): 290
Current ratio: —
Long-term debt ($ mil.): —

No. of shares (mil.): 54
Dividends
Yield: —
Payout: —
Market value ($ mil.): 614

	STOCK PRICE ($) FY Close	P/E High/Low		PER SHARE ($) Earnings	Dividends	Book Value
12/14	11.22	27	24	0.42	0.00	10.56
Annual Growth	—	—	—	—	—	—

Merrill Lynch Life Insurance Co.

EXECUTIVES
Pres, Marilyn Carp
Auditors: PricewaterhouseCoopers LLP

LOCATIONS
HQ: Merrill Lynch Life Insurance Co.
4333 Edgewood Road NE, Cedar Rapids, IA 52499-0001
Phone: 800 346-3677
Web: www.transamerica.com

HISTORICAL FINANCIALS
Company Type: Public

Income Statement
FYE: December 31

	ASSETS ($ mil.)	NET INCOME ($ mil.)	INCOME AS % OF ASSETS	EMPLOYEES
12/14	10,108	33	0.3%	—
12/13	10,555	(254)	—	—
12/12	10,535	165	1.6%	—
12/11	10,516	18	0.2%	—
12/10	11,491	137	1.2%	—
Annual Growth	(3.2%)	(29.8%)	—	—

2014 Year-End Financials
Debt ratio: —
Return on equity: 2.68%
Cash ($ mil.): 235
Current ratio: —
Long-term debt ($ mil.): —

No. of shares (mil.): 0
Dividends
  Yield: —
  Payout: 298.2%
Market value ($ mil.): —

Meta Financial Group Inc

Don't worry the money is real. Meta Financial Group is the holding company for MetaBank a thrift with about a dozen branches in Iowa and South Dakota. MetaBank offers standard deposit products and services including checking and savings accounts. Its lending and investment activities are weighted towards real estate and real estate-related assets; commercial and multifamily residential mortgages comprise more than half of the bank's loan portfolio. It also writes single-family residential mortgages and business loans. Meta Financial's bread and butter however is the bank'sÅMeta Payment Systems (MPS) division which provides prepaid cards consumer creditÅandÅATM sponsorship servicesÅnationwide.

The company has invested in MPS' growth by marketing new products and programs such asÅprepaid debit cards for tax refunds eco-friendlyÅrecycled or recyclable cardsÅand lines of credit on prepaid cards. The initiatives have paid off as MPS-related card fees account bring in the lion's share of Meta Financial's revenues and helped the company return to profitability in 2010.

In 2011 MetaBank received a ceaseÅand desist order from the Office of Thrift Supervision after the regulator determined that the bank engaged in unfair lending practices. It directed the company to discontinue its iAdvance subprime consumer lending program and suspend its tax loan and refund transfer operations.

Meta Financial sold trust services provider Meta Trust Company in 2010 and sold its MetaBank West Central commercial banking subsidiary to Anita Bancorporation in 2008. TheÅmoves allowed the company to focus on its stronger retail and payment services activities.

Directors and executive officers of Meta Financial own nearly 25% of the company's stock. Institutional investors own more than a quarter.

EXECUTIVES
EVP and COO Meta Financial Group and MetaBank, Troy Moore, age 47, $189,999 total compensation
EVP Secretary Treasurer and CFO, David W. Leedom, age 61, $215,000 total compensation
EVP and Director; EVP MetaBank; Division President Meta Payment Systems, Bradley C. (Brad) Hanson, age 51, $329,615 total compensation
EVP Meta Payment Systems, Scott Galit, age 45, $235,000 total compensation
Chairman of the Board President CEO of MFG and MetaBank, J. Tyler Haahr, age 52
Auditors: KPMG LLP

LOCATIONS
HQ: Meta Financial Group Inc
5501 South Broadband Lane, Sioux Falls, SD 57108
Phone: 605 782-1767
Web: www.metabank.com

PRODUCTS/OPERATIONS

2010 Sales

	$ mil.	% of total
Noninterest		
Card fees	93	68
Gain on sale of securities	2	2
Other	2	2
Interest		
Loans receivable including fees	24	18
Mortgage-backed securities	13	10
Other investments	0	-
Total	**136**	**100**

COMPETITORS
Bank of America	Green Dot
Blackhawk Network	HF Financial
Citi Prepaid Services	U.S. Bancorp
First National of Nebraska	West Bancorporation
Great Western Bancorp	nFinanSe

HISTORICAL FINANCIALS
Company Type: Public

Income Statement
FYE: September 30

	ASSETS ($ mil.)	NET INCOME ($ mil.)	INCOME AS % OF ASSETS	EMPLOYEES
09/15	2,529	18	0.7%	638
09/14	2,054	15	0.8%	453
09/13	1,691	13	0.8%	432
09/12	1,648	17	1.0%	410
09/11	1,275	4	0.4%	389
Annual Growth	18.7%	40.4%	—	13.2%

2015 Year-End Financials
Debt ratio: 0.49%
Return on equity: 8.09%
Cash ($ mil.): 27
Current ratio: —
Long-term debt ($ mil.): —

No. of shares (mil.): 8
Dividends
  Yield: 1.2%
  Payout: 20.3%
Market value ($ mil.): 341

	STOCK PRICE ($) FY Close	P/E High/Low		PER SHARE ($) Earnings	Dividends	Book Value
09/15	41.77	20	12	2.66	0.52	33.24
09/14	35.26	18	14	2.53	0.52	28.33
09/13	38.00	16	9	2.38	0.52	23.55
09/12	24.25	5	3	4.92	0.52	26.79
09/11	18.88	22	8	1.49	0.52	25.61
Annual Growth	22.0%	—	—	15.6%	(0.0%)	6.7%

MetLife Inc

While its name evolved from "metropolitan" MetLife's policies are found in villages towns and huge cities around the world. Operating through its Metropolitan Life Insurance subsidiary MetLife is the largest life insurer in the US. Its Insurance Products segment includes all of its group and individual life insurance and non-medical health insurance products (dental disability illness). Its Retirement Products segment includes annuity products. MetLife's Auto & Home segment works through subsidiary Metropolitan Property and Casualty. MetLife is a big player in Japan and growing in more than 50 other countries especially in Latin America. MetLife plans to split off much of its US life business.

Operations

MetLife is organized into six segments: Retail; Group Voluntary & Worksite Benefits; Corporate Benefit Funding; Latin America (the Americas); Asia; and Europe the Middle East and Africa (EMEA). Certain results are also reported in the operations of the Corporate & Other segment including MetLife Home Loans.

In the US MetLife provides a range of insurance and financial services offerings including life property/casualty disability dental guaranteed interest and annuities. These are distributed through both in-house and independent retail channels and in the workplace. Internationally the company provides life accident medical dental and other insurance as well as annuities and other retirement and savings products to individuals and groups.

The company's Retail segment is organized into two businesses: life and other (variable life products universal life products term life products whole life products disability products property & casualty); and annuities (variable annuities and fixed annuities). In 2014 retail sales accounted for 30% of total revenue.The Group Voluntary & Worksite Benefits segment is organized into Group and Voluntary and Worksite. Group insurance products and services include life dental group short- and long-term disability and accidental death and dismemberment coverages. That segment accounted for 26% of revenue in 2014.

The Corporate Benefit Funding segment handles investment management for large employers that offer retirement benefits including pension closeouts and specialized life insurance products used to fund such benefit plans. Corporate Benefit Funding accounted for 12% of revenue in 2014.

The company also services a number of long-term care insurance policies.

Geographic Reach

The company operates in the Americas and Asia and in Europe the Middle East and Africa (EMEA). In Latin America it operates in Argentina Brazil Chile Colombia Ecuador Mexico and Uruguay (which the bulk of regional revenues coming from Mexico Chile and Argentina).

The company operates in 10 countries in Asia with its largest operations in Japan and Korea. It also does business in Australia Bangladesh Hong Kong and Nepal and through a joint venture in China Malaysia and Vietnam. MetLife operates in about 30 countries across EMEA. The segment's biggest operations are in Poland the Persian Gulf and Russia.

While the US remains its largest overall market international sales accounted for about 30% of MetLife's revenues.

Sales and Marketing

Policies and other products are sold through a vast network of targeted marketing and sales forces financial advisors consultants agency distribution groups independent agents affiliated broker-dealers and direct marketing (including direct response television web-based lead generation telemarketing as well as through third parties and e-commerce). In addition MetLife sells some products through affinity groups and through employers.

At the end of 2014 the Group Voluntary & Worksite Benefits segment had more than 300 marketing representatives.

Financial Performance

After a small decline in 2012 revenue held steady in 2013 at about $68 billion but grew 8% to $73.3 billion in 2014. That growth was due to higher premiums and net derivative gains. The higher revenue contributed to an 87% jump in net income to $6.3 billion which in turn led to a 2% rise in operating cash flow (to $16 billion).

Strategy

In early 2016 MetLife announced plans to separate its US retail operations. Its MetLife Insurance Company USA General American Life Insurance Company Metropolitan Tower Life Insurance Company and several other units will be included in the transaction whether that be in the form of an initial public offering a spin-off or a sale. Together those units have represented about 20% of MetLife's total earnings. (US retail businesses that will not be divested include the closed-block life insurance property/casualty and Metropolitan Life Insurance Company's life and annuity operations.)

The move to divest part of its core operations comes in the wake of the financial crisis and subsequent changes in the regulatory landscape. According to US regulators MetLife is one of four non-bank entities to be deemed a systemically important financial institution which means it poses a risk to the economy if it should collapse. MetLife is fighting the designation but the pending separation of its US life insurance business should calm any unrest over the group's size. The newly created company will also benefit from having a lower capital and compliance burden.

This is not the first major shuffling of MetLife's operations in recent years. It is exiting the bulk of its banking operations to avoid the increased scrutiny of banks under Dodd-Frank financial regulations. The company is working to surrender its status as a bank holding company. In 2013 the company sold its MetLife Bank depository operations to General Electric's finance division. Previously MetLife Bank also offered residential mortgages but in 2012 stopped writing both new mortgages and reverse mortgages. MetLife retained the residential home loan portion of the business.

Going forward MetLife plans to focus on pension and retirement products insurance sold to employers and non-US life insurance. The company has pinned much of its growth efforts on emerging markets by increasing its already strong presence in the Asia/Pacific region and in Latin America through acquisitions and new product introductions. To support this growth the company has organized its operations along geographic lines: The

Americas; Europe the Middle East and Africa (EMEA); and Asia.

Some of the individual and group products MetLife sells overseas include life insurance accident and health insurance credit insurance and annuities and retirement products. It has also created a global employee benefits business to reach into new markets.

To focus on core international businesses Metlife has been selling off select foreign assets. In 2014 it sold its UK annuity business to Goldman Sachs Group company Rothesay Life Ltd. for $5 billion. The assurance covers benefits for more than 20000 individuals in the UK and Ireland.

MetLife is focused on growing its annuity business through a range of products. One example is its new guaranteed minimum withdrawal benefit VA FlexChoice.

In 2014 the company launched its MetLife SecureFlex Universal Life product.

MetLife has been working to cuts its expenses and is on track to meet its goal of achieving $1 billion in gross expense savings.

Mergers and Acquisitions

Expanding its presence in South America in 2013 MetLife acquired AFP Provida S.A. (a private pension fund administrator in Chile) from BBVA for $2 billion. The deal also includes a small asset management business in Ecuador. The purchase is part of the company's strategy of growth through acquisitions in emerging markets.

HISTORY

New York merchant Simeon Draper tried to form National Union Life and Limb Insurance to cover Union soldiers in the Civil War but investors were scared away by heavy casualties. After several reorganizations and name changes the enterprise emerged in 1868 as Metropolitan Life Insurance (MetLife) a stock company.

Sustained at first by business from mutual assistance societies for German immigrants MetLife went into industrial insurance with workers' burial policies. The firm was known for its aggressive sales methods. Agents combed working-class neighborhoods collecting small premiums. If a worker missed one payment the company could cancel the policy and keep all premiums paid a practice outlawed in 1900.

MetLife became a mutual company (owned by its policyholders) in 1915 and began offering group insurance two years later.

After a period of conservative management under the Eckers family from 1929 to 1963 MetLife began to change dropping industrial insurance in 1964. It started offering auto and homeowners insurance in 1974.

To diversify the company bought State Street Research & Management (1983) Century 21 Real Estate (1985 sold 1995) London-based Albany Life Assurance (1985) and Allstate's group life and health business (1988). In 1987 it took over the annuities segment of the failed Baldwin United Co. and expanded into Spain and Taiwan in 1988. During the early 1990s MetLife reemphasized insurance adding such new products as long-term-care insurance.

EXECUTIVES

Svp And Cio Corporate Systems, Georgette A Piligian, age 50

President Asia, Christopher G. Townsend, age 65, $537,532 total compensation

EVP and Global Chief Marketing Officer, Esther Lee

President Americas, William J. (Bill) Wheeler, age 53

EVP and Chief Human Resources Officer, Frans Hijkoop

Chairman President and CEO, Steven A. (Steve) Kandarian, age 63, $1,325,000 total compensation

EVP and CFO, John C. R. Hele, age 57, $625,000 total compensation

EVP Global Employee Benefits, Maria R. Morris, age 52, $525,000 total compensation

CEO Vietnam Business Segment, B. Dustin Ball

EVP and General Counsel, Ricardo A. Anzaldua

EVP and Chief Investment Officer, Steven J. Goulart, age 56, $539,167 total compensation

President Europe the Middle East and Africa, Michel Khalaf, $476,313 total compensation

EVP Global Technology and Operations, Martin J. (Marty) Lippert, $625,000 total compensation

CEO MetLife Australia, Deanne Stewart

Chairman MetLife Korea, Jong Kim

CEO MetLife Korea, Damien Green

CEO Malaysia, Ramzi Toubassy

Vice President Actuary, George Kalb

Assistant Vice President Accounting Technical Services, David Chamberlin

Vice President Learning and Development, John (Jack) Wiltshire

Executive Vice President Human Resources, Kathleen Henkel

Senior Vice President, Stuart Baritz

Regional Sales Vice President, Jordan Teel

Executive Vice President Senior Vice President Vice President, Benjamin Alcid

Regional Vice President Northeast Region, Joe Heaney

Vice President Information Technology, Maryann Prudente

Vice President Human Resources, Doris Jackson

Vice President Product Managment Indiv, Lynn Dumais

Assistant Vice President Global Reporting And Development, Jim Ebner

Assistant Vice President Human Resources Business Partner, Amy Berg

Assistant Vice President Global Operations Controller, Jay Dyer

Assistant Vice President Derivative Analytics, William Hayes

Vice President Sales and Global Strategies, Maximo Saravi

Vice President, Andrew (Andy) Aoyama

Assistant Vice President Actuary Traditional Life Valuation, Enid Reichert

Assistant Vice President Product Management, Kevin Finneran

Senior Vice President Employee Benefit Sales, Michael (Mel) Malouf

Senior Vice President, Craig Samples

Vice President, Stephanie Miller

Vice President, Michele Brooks

Divisional Vice President, Lance Carlson

Executive Vice President National Accounts, Glenn Petersen

Vice President Human Resources, Brenda Murphy

Vice President Human Resources, Don Otto

Vice President Of Sales, Lewis Robyn

Regional Sales Vice President Annuity Product Wholesaling Sales Desk, Anne Daley

Assistant Vice President, Linda Wintner

Vice President Investments Information Technology, Linda McCormick

Vice President Information Technology Institutiona, Joseph Carroll

Assistant Vice President, Michael Hudock

Vice President Multinational Solutions, Rudy Bethea

Assistant Vice President Talent Acquisition, Joann Butler

Vice President, Bob Broseker

Vice President Operations, Patty Treis

Vice President, Ilia Castellano

Assistant Vice President, Joseph Reo

Regional Vice President, Steve Noonan

Vice President Actuary, Marian Zeldin

Assistant Vice President Benefits, Jim Pabst
Regional Sales Vice President, Matlock Mike
Vice President Advanced Sales, Brian McKenna
Vice President of Sales and Marketing, Scott Beck
Vice President And Actuary, Sebastian Janssen
Vice President, Randy Stram
Assistant Vice President And Actuary, Jonathan Trend
Vice President MetLife Dental Products, Alan (Al) Hirschberg
Medical Director, Charles Arnold
Assistant Vice President Sec Reporting, Lynne Liberatore
Regional Sales Vice President, Leslie Quinn
Assistant Vice President And Actuary Asset Liability Management, Scott Yan
Vice President Ed, Bonnie Sullivan
Assistant Vice President Corporate Risk Management, Dion Rumsey
Vice President of Operations MetLife Broker Dealer, Bob Begun
Senior Vice President, Sean McNamara
Assistant Vice President, Rose Wolf
Assistant Vice President, Jennifer Frank
Senior Vice President, Robert Wright
Vice President, Joe Perillo
Vice President And Actuary, James (Jamie) Reilly
Assistant Vice President, Gladys Rosetta
Vice President, Jodi Conley
Vice President, Jan Eckert
Senior Vice President Global Head Of Alm, Bryan Boudreau
Vice President, Paul Hegg
Vice President Solution Delivery, Christopher Morbelli
Vice President, Michael (Mel) Nardone
Assistant Vice President Client Relationship And Bus, Patricia (Pat) Wessel
Vice President, Rahul Magan
Assistant Vice President, Evelyn Stark
Vice President, Harry Xiao
Assistant Vice President, Patricia Reile
Assistant Vice President, Ian Connor
Assistant Vice President, Tonya Richardson
Assistant Vice President, Robert (Bob) Bean
Assistant Vice President, John (Jack) Genovese
Assistant Vice President, Jeffrey (Jeff) Archer
Assistant Vice President Information Technology Solutions Delivery, Derek Hess
Assistant Vice President Planning And Business Development, Alfredo Risi
Assistant Vice President Sponsorship and Promotions, Dan Pincus
Assistant Vice President, William Devito
Assistant Vice President Global Workforce Reporting And Analytics, Laura Shubert
Vice President Information Technology Infrastructu, Gail Weimer
Assistant Vice President Marketing P, Denis Dwyer
Assistant Vice President International Benefits, Francesca Pulis
Vice President Human Resources, Tim Braswell
Vice President product Reporting and Analysis, Ray Digiovanni
Assistant Vice President, Jeffrey Hollander
Assistant Vice President Call Center Sales, Bill Messer
Assistant Vice President, Lisa Pang
Vice President, David (Dave) Rupper
Assistant Vice President, Kathy Eng
Vice President Global Talent Processes, Rachel Lee
Assistant Vice President and Actuary, Anthony Borelli
Regional Sales Vice President, Robert (Bob) Hall
Vice President Strategy, Sharon Rodriguez
Assistant Vice President, Chuck Arbo
Regional Sales Vice President, Brandon Fisk
Assistant Vice President and Actuary, Rachel D'Anna

Assistant Vice President And Cre Relationship Manager Global Corporate Services, Betty Dubuisson
Vice President Group Life Products, Graham Cox
Vice President, Don Anderson
Senior Vice President Global Strategy And Sales, Mike Malouf
Assistant Vice President Customer Centricity Metrics and Analytics at MetLife, John (Jack) Zazyczny
Vice President, Michele Zachensky
Executive Vice President U S Business MetLife Inc, Todd Katz
Senior Vice President and CIO Enterprise Application Development, Tom Wolf
Vice President, Ignazio Greco
Assistant Vice President, Cindy Pace
Assistant Vice President Advisor Teaming Field Implementation, Michael (Mel) O'brien
Vice President Of Strategy Enterprise Application Development, Alexander (Al) Hall
Vice President Associate And Workplace Security, Edward (Ed) Levy
Vice President Of Advanced Markets Team, Lori Epstein
Assistant Vice President, Dean Vescera
Assistant Vice President, George Tang
Vice President Auto And Home, Ralph Spontak
Assistant Vice President, Sarah Mellish
Assistant Vice President, Joe Gatt
Vice President Network Services, Laura Sokolski
Vice President Information Technology, Denise Anderson
Vice President Actuary, Laura Vazquez
Vice President, Geri Trout
Regional Sales Vice President, Ed Wustefeld
Vice President Of External Communications, Randolph Clerihue
Vice President, Rob Dill
Regional Sales Vice President, Ruth Larson
Assistant Vice President, Amie Donahue
Assistant Vice President, Lisa Vahdat
Vice President International H R, Marilee Casale
Executive Vice President Sales And Marketing, Tim Mitchell
Vice President, David Waldman
Assistant Vice President Enterprise Strategy Group, Kevin Chean
Auditors: Deloitte & Touche LLP

LOCATIONS

HQ: MetLife Inc
200 Park Avenue, New York, NY 10166-0188
Phone: 212 578-2211
Web: www.metlife.com

2014 Sales

	$ mil.	% of total
Americas		
Retail	21,843	30
Group Voluntary & Worksite Benefits	19,278	26
Corporate Benefit Funding	9,016	12
Latin America	5,598	8
Asia	12,583	17
EMEA	4,307	6
Corporate & other	691	1
Total	73,316	100

PRODUCTS/OPERATIONS

Selected Subsidiaries and Affiliates

American L
General American Life Insurance Company
Hyatt Legal Plans Inc. (prepaid legal plans)
MetLife Insurance Company USA
MetLife In
Metropolitan Property and Casualty Insurance Company
New England Life Insurance Company
Walnut Street Securities Inc. (mutual funds securities)

COMPETITORS

AEGON USA	Lincoln Financial
AIG	Group
AXA	MassMutual
Aetna	Meiji Yasuda Life
Aflac	Mutual of Omaha
Allianz	Nationwide
Allstate	New York Life
American General	Nippon Life Insurance
Aon	Northwestern Mutual
CIGNA	Pacific Mutual
COUNTRY Financial	Principal Financial
Genworth Financial	Prudential
Guardian Life	State Farm
ING	TIAA-CREF
John Hancock Financial	The Hartford
Services	USAA
Liberty Mutual	Zurich Insurance Group

HISTORICAL FINANCIALS

Company Type: Public

Income Statement

FYE: December 31

	ASSETS ($ mil.)	NET INCOME ($ mil.)	INCOME AS % OF ASSETS	EMPLOYEES
12/14	902,337	6,309	0.7%	68,000
12/13	885,296	3,368	0.4%	65,000
12/12	836,781	1,324	0.2%	64,000
12/11	799,625	6,981	0.9%	67,000
12/10	730,906	2,790	0.4%	66,000
Annual Growth	5.4%	22.6%	—	0.7%

2014 Year-End Financials

Debt ratio: 2.62%
Return on equity: 9.38%
Cash ($ mil.): 10,808
Current ratio: —
Long-term debt ($ mil.): —

No. of shares (mil.): 1,131
Dividends
Yield: 2.4%
Payout: 27.1%
Market value ($ mil.): 61,226

	STOCK PRICE ($) FY Close	P/E High/Low		Earnings	Dividends	Book Value
12/14	54.09	10	9	5.42	1.33	63.74
12/13	53.92	18	11	2.91	1.01	55.65
12/12	32.94	35	25	1.12	0.74	59.15
12/11	31.18	8	4	6.29	0.74	56.62
12/10	44.44	16	11	3.00	0.74	49.44
Annual Growth	5.0%	—	—	15.9%	15.7%	6.6%

MetLife Insurance Company of Connecticut

LOCATIONS

HQ: MetLife Insurance Company of Connecticut
11225 North Community House Road, Charlotte, NC 28277
Phone: 212 578-9500
Web: www.metlife.com

Company Type: Public

FYE: December 31

	ASSETS ($ mil.)	NET INCOME ($ mil.)	INCOME AS % OF ASSETS	EMPLOYEES
12/14	205,863	295	0.1%	—
12/13	188,039	720	0.4%	—
12/12	184,796	1,223	0.7%	—
12/11	171,771	1,240	0.7%	—
12/10	154,885	757	0.5%	—
Annual Growth	7.4%	(21.0%)	—	—

2014 Year-End Financials

Debt ratio: 0.45%	No. of shares (mil.): 0
Return on equity: 2.84%	Dividends
Cash ($ mil.): 1,206	Yield: —
Current ratio: —	Payout: —
Long-term debt ($ mil.): —	Market value ($ mil.): —

MGIC Investment Corp. (WI)

Since a pinkie-promise isn't good enough for most lenders there's MGIC Investment's mortgage insurance to protect lenders from homebuyers who don't hold up their end of the bargain. MGIC owns Mortgage Guaranty Insurance Corporation (MGIC) the largest provider of private mortgage insurance in the US. Such coverage allows otherwise-qualified buyers who aren't able to scrape up the standard 20% down payment to get mortgages. MGIC writes primary insurance on individual loans. The company's customers include banks mortgage brokers credit unions and other residential mortgage lenders. In 2014 MGIC had $159.3 billion primary insurance in force covering 1 million mortgages.Geographic Reach

MGIC operates in every US state Washington DC Puerto Rico and Guam.

Operations

MGIC's businesses include a range of investment subsidiaries reinsurance subsidiaries and assurance corporations. The company also offers some online products: eMagic.com a web portal where mortgage providers can shop for a variety of loan origination tools and Myers Internet a web hosting provider and lead generator.

Primary insurance provides mortgage default protection on individual loans and covers unpaid loan principal delinquent interest and certain expenses associated with the default and subsequent foreclosure or sale approved by MGIC. Pool insurance is generally used as an additional credit enhancement for certain secondary market mortgage transactions. It generally covers the excess of the loss on a defaulted mortgage loan which exceeds the claim payment under the primary coverage if primary insurance is required on that mortgage loan as well as the total loss on a defaulted mortgage loan which did not require primary insurance.Sales and Marketing

The company's customers include savings institutions commercial banks mortgage brokers credit unions mortgage bankers and other lenders.

Financial Performance

Still recovering from the US mortgage loan crisis of the late 2000s MGIC has reported a steady annual decline in its revenues since 2009. In 2013 its revenues dropped by 25% due to a decrease in net premium earned as the result of lower average insurance in force as well as an increase in premi-

ums ceded under risk sharing arrangements and lower investment income driven by the realized gains taken in prior years. The company saw a huge decline in realized losses and other-than-temporary impairments in 2013 due to lower sales of fixed income investments.Since inception the company has reported annual net losses. However MFIC saw a improvement in net loss in 2013 ($50 million compared to $927 million in 2012) due to a decrease in the number of new default notices received as well as a decrease in the estimated claim rate on recently reported delinquencies. Underwriting and other expenses for 2013 decreased primarily reflecting a reduction in headcount lower contract underwriting remedy costs and an increase in ceding commission related to risk sharing arrangements.After reaching its minimum point of $1.8 billion operating cash outflow in 2011 the company recovered over next two years. In 2013 operating cash outflow decreased by $597 million to $971 million due to decline in net loss and cash generated from deferred insurance policy acquisition costs and unearned premiums.

Strategy

The company saw home price appreciation continue as well as modest improvements in the employment picture throughout 2013. These conditions allowed MGIC to see an increase in new insurance policies issued while new delinquent notices delinquent inventory and claim payments declined.

Despite the company's careful pruning MGIC Investment's capital reserves are still vulnerable and have dipped below some regional regulatory requirements. To operate in markets where it doesn't meet minimum capital requirements the company created MGIC Indemnity Corporation (MIC) in 2010 and gave it a tidy pile of capital reserves and nice fresh books with no murky liabilities.

As the entire private mortgage insurance industry nervously gauges its future government-sponsored enterprises Freddie Mac and Fannie Mae have taken over a huge share of the business during the past few years. To gain customers MGIC has lowered its rates based upon borrower's credit scores.

Company Background

Before the mortgage mess unfolded in the US MGIC had marked its entry into the global market by opening offices in Toronto and in Sydney Australia. In less than two years however MGIC closed its Canadian office stopped issuing new policies abroad and began searching for a buyer for its Australian operations (which it records as immaterial) in order to focus on its domestic operations.

HISTORY

Milwaukee lawyer Max Karl founded MGIC in 1957 reinventing private mortgage guaranty insurance which had gone out of favor in the Depression. MGIC went public in 1961 suffered in the stagflated 1970s and entered the 1980s ready to expand. But poorly underwritten loans in such trouble spots as Texas and Oklahoma slammed MGIC.

Piano builder Baldwin United made a fruitless foray into financial services in 1982 paying too much for MGIC and going bankrupt in 1983. Northwestern Mutual bankrolled a management LBO in 1985. Surviving the weak real estate market of the 1980s MGIC went public again in 1991.

In 1995 MGIC debuted professional liability insurance products for lenders. Two years later it began selling homeowners extended warranties for appliances.

In the late 1990s changes in Fannie Mae and Freddie Mac mortgage insurance requirements hit MGIC hard. News reports that some insurers and lenders failed to inform homeowners when they

could cancel their mortgage insurance also gave the industry a black eye.

In 1998 MGIC began insuring second mortgages and joined with Enhance Financial Services Group (now owned by Radian Group) to form C-BASS to buy and securitize nonperforming mortgages. Meanwhile MGIC was busy buffing up its in-house appraisal default and prepayment prediction tools and bundling them with a variety of mortgage origination services that it began offering over its eMAGIC website in 1999. In 2000 the decision by Illinois to allow insurance of 100% home loans meant that MGIC could begin to insure such loans nationwide.

With low interest rates high employment rates and some key legislative pushes to encourage home ownership lenders and homebuilders enjoyed a heyday from 2001 to late-2006. These were also good years for MGIC which wrote up a storm of mortgage insurance on all of those home purchases.The subprime mortgage loan crisis that began in 2007 was brutal on MGIC and its competitors. MGIC responded by yanking hard on its own leash and tightening its underwriting standards to reduce its losses. The company stopped writing insurance on riskier loans and the blocks of pooled insurance sold on the secondary market curbed its coverage in states hardest hit by the resulting housing slump and raised its premium rates.During its headier days MGIC had set up two joint ventures with Radian Group: debt collections firm Sherman Financial and Credit-Based Asset Servicing and Securitization LLC (C-BASS) which invested in riskier mortgage assets. Both ventures were among the first to feel pain from the collapse of the subprime mortgage market and credit freezes. To cut its losses MGIC sold its 25% interest in Sherman Financial Group to Sherman in 2008 for about $125 million in cash and an $85 million promissory note. Around that same C-BASS of which MGIC held less than a 50% interest ceased operations but only after costing MGIC roughly the value of its entire equity in the venture. (By late 2010 C-BASS filed for Chapter 11 bankruptcy protection.)Faced with a pipeline full of pending claims investigations MGIC also turned to rescinding policies (known as rescissions) to help offset its losses. The company managed to shave $1 billion off its substantial 2009 losses by dropping policies with looming claims.

EXECUTIVES

Vice President Human Resources, Kurt Thomas
President and COO, Patrick Sinks, age 58, $524,423 total compensation
EVP General Counsel and Secretary, Jeffrey H. Lane, age 65, $415,385 total compensation
EVP Risk Management, Lawrence J. Pierzchalski, age 62, $449,654 total compensation
Chairman and CEO, Curt S. Culver, age 62, $898,269 total compensation
EVP and CFO, Timothy Mattke
Vice President Chief Compliance Officer, Dan Stilwell
Vice President Sales And Inf, Jerry Wormmeester
Vice President National Underwriting Operations, Claudia Koehler
Vice President Risk Management, Bernie Verhoeven
Vice President, Anita Mcclain
Assistant Vice President Regulatory Relations, Chris Burns
Vice President Managing Director Center, Robin Mallory
Vice President Regulatory Relations an, Heidi Heyrmann
Vice President, John (Jack) Schroeder
Vice President Managing Director, Todd Pittman
Assistant Treasurer, Paul Spiroff
Auditors: PricewaterhouseCoopers LLP

LOCATIONS

HQ: MGIC Investment Corp. (WI)
250 E. Kilbourn Avenue, Milwaukee, WI 53202
Phone: 414 347-6480
Web: www.mgic.com

PRODUCTS/OPERATIONS

2013 Sales

	$ mil.	% of total
Net premiums earned	943	91
Investment income	80	7
Realized investment gains	5	1
Other revenue	9	1
Total	1,039	100

Selected Direct and Indirect Subsidiaries

eMagic.com LLC
MGIC Assurance Corporation
MGIC Australia Pty Limited
MGIC Credit Assurance Corporation
MGIC Indemnity Corporation
MGIC Insurance Services Corporation
MGIC Investor Services Corporation
MGIC Mortgage and Consumer Asset I LLC
MGIC Mortgage and Consumer Asset II LLC
MGIC Mortgage Reinsurance Corporation
MGIC Mortgage Services LLC
MGIC Reinsurance Corporation
MGIC Reinsurance Corporation of Vermont
MGIC Reinsurance Corporation of Wisconsin
MGIC Residential Reinsurance Corporation
MGICA Pty Limited
MIC Reinsurance Corporation
MIC Reinsurance Corporation of Wisconsin
Mortgage Guaranty Insurance Corporation

COMPETITORS

Allied Home Mortgage	Radian Group
Essent Guaranty	Regions Mortgage
Freddie Mac	United Guaranty
GMAC Mortgage	VBA
Genworth Mortgage	Wells Fargo Home
Insurance	Mortgage
National Mortgage	
Insurance	

HISTORICAL FINANCIALS

Company Type: Public

Income Statement

FYE: December 31

	ASSETS ($ mil.)	NET INCOME ($ mil.)	INCOME AS % OF ASSETS	EMPLOYEES
12/14	5,266	251	4.8%	800
12/13	5,601	(49)	—	819
12/12	5,574	(927)	—	877
12/11	7,216	(485)	—	920
12/10	9,333	(363)	—	1,010
Annual Growth	(13.3%)	—	—	(5.7%)

2014 Year-End Financials

Debt ratio: 24.62%
Return on equity: 28.29%
Cash ($ mil.): 197
Current ratio: —
Long-term debt ($ mil.): —

No. of shares (mil.): 338
Dividends
Yield: —
Payout: —
Market value ($ mil.): 3,155

	STOCK PRICE ($) FY Close	P/E High/Low	Earnings	Dividends	Book Value
12/14	9.32	13 10	0.64	0.00	3.06
12/13	8.44	— —	(0.16)	0.00	2.20
12/12	2.66	— —	(4.59)	0.00	0.97
12/11	3.73	— —	(2.42)	0.00	5.95
12/10	10.19	— —	(2.06)	0.00	8.33
Annual Growth	(2.2%)	— —	—	—	(22.1%)

MGM Resorts International

It's not your imagination —MGM Resorts International (formerly MGM MIRAGE) is one of the world's largest gaming firms. The company's more than 15 partially or wholly owned properties include some of the biggest names on the Las Vegas Strip including MGM Grand The Mirage and the Monte Carlo as well as Luxor Bellagio and Mandalay Bay. MGM Resorts also owns or has a stake in other casinos in Nevada as well as in Michigan (MGM Grand Detroit) and Mississippi (Beau Rivage). Internationally it operates in China and Dubai. The company changed its name from MGM MIRAGE in 2010 to better reflect its family of hotel brands and its expanding global presence.

HISTORY

Billionaire Kirk Kerkorian purchased a stake in famed movie studio Metro-Goldwyn-Mayer (MGM; formed 1924) for just over $80 million in 1970. Around the same time he began acquiring property in Las Vegas and started construction on the city's largest hotel.

Financial difficulties led Kerkorian to sell his new hotel as well as many of MGM's assets in the early 1970s. But he kept the MGM name and used it for MGM Grand hotels in Las Vegas and Reno Nevada. In 1986 Kerkorian sold MGM Grand Hotels to Bally but he retained the rights to the MGM Grand name and logo. That year Kerkorian founded MGM Grand Inc. and took the company public in 1987. He set about snapping up Las Vegas property in the late 1980s and early 1990s.

In 1993 Kerkorian and company unveiled Las Vegas' MGM Grand a $1.1 billion complex featuring a 33-acre theme park and at the time the largest casino on the planet (171500 sq. ft.). The project was a success ($742 million in revenues its first year) and spawned plans for expansion.

The 1990s proved a challenge for MGM Grand however as attendance figures at the theme park dropped off and the company struggled to maintain profitability. In 1996 MGM Grand began planning for an Atlantic City casino and signed on as developer and manager for gaming company Tsogo Sun which was opening casinos in South Africa. The following year through its joint venture with Primadonna Resorts it opened the 2035-room hotel and casino New York-New York. In 1998 MGM Grand narrowly won its bid to become one of three groups to build casinos in Detroit. (The MGM Grand Detroit the following year and pulled in $4.8 million in its first three days.)

In 1999 the company bought Primadonna Resorts which gave MGM Grand complete ownership of New York-New York and three casino properties in Primm Nevada. (It sold the Primm properties in 2007.) The company appointed co-CEOs John Redmond and Daniel Wade to their posts in late 1999. (Redmond and Wade moved to other positions in the company when Terrence Lanni became CEO in 2001.)

In a landmark deal MGM Grand bought rival Mirage Resorts for $6.4 billion (including $2 billion in debt) in 2000 and became one of the top gaming companies in the world. (Mirage Resorts' newer casinos had posted less-than-exciting financial results and the company had become an attractive acquisition target.)

The purchase of Mirage Resorts allowed MGM Grand to add a string of opulent casinos to its collection. Among the casinos the deal brought to the

MGM Grand fold were Las Vegas strip properties Bellagio a luxurious European-style casino and The Mirage a tropical-themed casino. The Mirage Resorts acquisition also put Las Vegas' Treasure Island the Golden Nugget and Monte Carlo (50%-owned with Mandalay Resort Group) under the MGM Grand umbrella. Mirage Resorts' Beau Rivage in Biloxi Mississippi and the Golden Nugget in Laughlin Nevada also became MGM Grand properties.

Steven Wynn who had propelled Mirage Resorts from a single casino (the Golden Nugget) to its spot as one of the world's leading gaming companies opted not to join the merged firm. Later in 2000 MGM Grand changed its name to MGM MIRAGE. MGM MIRAGE laid off more than 6700 employees due to declining guest numbers in the wake of the September 11th terrorist attacks. In 2002 the company withdrew its $615 million bid for Chicago's Emerald Casino after the Illinois legislature passed a bill to increase gaming taxes by as much as 50%. Also that year the company ended its operations in South Africa where it managed four casinos.

In 2003 MGM MIRAGE closed its online casino citing an absence of sound regulatory policies regarding Internet gambling. The following year the company sold its Golden Nugget properties in Las Vegas and Laughlin to a private investment firm for $215 million. Also in 2004 MGM MIRAGE sold its MGM Grand Hotel and Casino in Darwin Australia.

The following year MGM MIRAGE purchased rival Mandalay Resort Group for about $7.9 billion briefly creating the world's largest gaming company. (It was surpassed later in 2005 when Harrah's bought Caesars.) In 2006 MGM Mirage and Boyd Gaming debuted a $200 million expansion of its Borgata casino.

Kerkorian's Tracinda Corp. entered into talks with MGM Mirage in 2007 to purchase the Bellagio and CityCenter properties. However it later scrapped those plans reportedly in part because Tracinda disagreed with the valuation of a separate development deal between MGM MIRAGE and Kerzner International.

Also in 2007 the company opened MGM Grand Macau a hotel that operates through MGM Resorts' majority-owned MGM China. The following year Lana resigned as chairman and CEO. He was replaced by James Murren. In 2009 the company opened CityCenter an $8 billion-plus mixed-use development on the Las Vegas Strip a joint venture with Dubai World. In order to lighten its debt in 2009 it sold Treasure Island Hotel & Casino on the Las Vegas Strip to Ruffin Acquisition LLC for $775 million.

The following year MGM MIRAGE changed its name to MGM Resorts International to emphasize the brand's scope. In 2011 MGM China filed an IPO.

EXECUTIVES

COO, Corey I. Sanders, age 51, $1,069,605 total compensation
President and Chief Marketing Officer, William J. Hornbuckle, age 57, $1,228,462 total compensation
Chairman and CEO, James J. Murren, age 53, $2,000,000 total compensation
Chief Design and Construction Officer and Director, Robert H. Baldwin, age 64, $1,650,000 total compensation
EVP Special Counsel Litigation and Chief Diversity Officer, Phyllis A. James, age 62
EVP CFO and Treasurer, Daniel J. D'Arrigo, age 46, $834,890 total compensation
EVP and Chief Accounting Officer, Robert C. Selwood, age 59, $439,286 total compensation
CEO MGM China Holdings Limited, Grant R. Bowie, age 57

President and COO MGM Springfield Development, Michael Mathis
EVP General Counsel and Secretary, John M. McManus, age 47
CEO MGM Growth Properties LLC (MGP), James C. Stewart, age 49
President and COO Circus Circus Las Vegas, Don Thrasher
EVP Corporate Strategy and Special Counsel and Senior Resident Executive for Greater China and Executive Director and General Manager of Diaoyutai MGM Hospitality Ltd., William M. Scott, age 54, $152,528 total compensation
EVP Operations and EVP and CFO CityCenter, Christopher Nordling, age 54
Vice President Of Strategic Sourcing, Mark Stolarczyk
Vice President, Cynthia Jones
Vice President Treasury, Pat Murphy
Vice President Chief Financial Officer Corporate Benefits, Jeff Ellis
Vice President Finance Shared Services Center, Diane Gonzales
Senior Vice President Marketing Mid East, Magdy Gayed
Vice President Contact Center Operations, Rick McGough
Vice President Information Management, Gerry Tuffy
Senior Vice President Marketing Europe Mid East, Marika Cardellino-Jensen
Executive Vice President Marketing, Chuck Bowling
Vice President Digital Design, Christopher (Chris) Hume
Vice President Of Marketing, Kevin Turra
Senior Vice President, Emily Lew
Vice President of Public Affairs Eastern Region, Kelley L Tucky
Vice President Investor Relations, Sarah Rogers
Vice President, Tom C Tuchschmidt
Vice President Compliance, Peggy Jacobs
Vice President Deputy General Counsel, Ed Mulholland
Assistant Vice President, Joyce Chester
Vice President Of Multimedia Mgm Mirage, Randy Dearborn
Vice President Planning and Development, Barrie Borovsky
Assistant Vice President, Hassan Dadkhah
Vice President, Bob Rosati
Vice President Human Resources, Michelle Ditondo
Vice President Of Player Development, Pete Brascia
Vice President Gaming Operations, Todd Haushalter
Vice President Information Technology Operations, Gregg Lowe
Vice President Of Facility Operations, Bill Ham
Vice President Of Labor Relations, Wendy Nutt
Senior Vice President Public Affairs, Alan (Al) Feldman
Senior Vice President Customer Development, Larry Altschul
Corporate Vice President Talent And Organizational Effec, Christopher Henry
Vice President, Paul Sinowitz
Assistant Vice President Taxes, Michael (Mel) McBeath
Vice President Retail Financial, Doreen Kaz
A. Vice Presidente Latin Marketing, Jorge Melatti
Vice President Of Finance, Yvette Harris
Vice President Of Arena Booking, Sid Greenfeig
Executive Vice President, Paul Berry
Vice President Environmental Compliance, Chris Brophy
Assistant Vice President Marketing (Aria), Alberto Reyes
Assistant Vice President Marketing Japanese, Iris Alpert

Senior Vice President Capital Markets And Strategy, Jim Freeman
Senior Vice President Europe and Middle East Marketing, Marika Jensen
Assistant Vice President Finance and Treasury, Bernard Efendi
Senior Vice President Customer Development, Casino Mgm
Treasurer, Emily Wang
Auditors: Deloitte & Touche LLP

LOCATIONS

HQ: MGM Resorts International
3600 Las Vegas Boulevard South, Las Vegas, NV 89109
Phone: 702 693-7120
Web: www.mgmresorts.com

2014 Sales

	$ mil.	% of total
Wholly owned domestic resorts	6,342	62
MGM China	3,282	33
Corporate & other	457	5
Total	10,082	100

PRODUCTS/OPERATIONS

2014 Sales

	$ mil.	% of total
Casino	5,878	54
Non-casino		
Rooms	1	16
Food & beverage	1,558	14
Entertainment retail & other	1,642	16
Adjustments	(766.3)	-
Total	10,082	100

Selected Properties

Nevada
  Las Vegas
  Bellagio
  Circus Circus
  CityCenter (50%)
  Excalibur
  Luxor
  Mandalay Bay Resort & Casino
  MGM Grand
  The Mirage
  Monte Carlo
  New York-New York
  Reno
  Circus Circus Reno
  Silver Legacy (50%; Reno NV)
  Other
  Railroad Pass (Henderson)
  Gold Strike (Jean)
Other US
  Beau Rivage (Biloxi MS)
  Gold Strike (Tunica County MS)
  MGM Grand Detroit
China
  MGM Grand Macau (51%; Macau)

COMPETITORS

Boyd Gaming	Sands China
Caesars Entertainment	Star City
Galaxy Entertainment	Station Casinos
Las Vegas Sands	Stratosphere
Pinnacle Entertainment	Tropicana
Rio All-Suite Hotel & Casino	Entertainment
Riviera Holdings	Trump Resorts
SJM	Wynn Resorts

HISTORICAL FINANCIALS

Company Type: Public

Income Statement

FYE: December 31

	REVENUE ($ mil.)	NET INCOME ($ mil.)	NET PROFIT MARGIN	EMPLOYEES
12/14	10,081	(149)	—	68,100
12/13	9,809	(156)	—	67,800
12/12	9,160	(1,767)	—	66,650
12/11	7,849	3,114	39.7%	66,800
12/10	6,019	(1,437)	—	61,000
Annual Growth	13.8%	—	—	2.8%

2014 Year-End Financials

Debt ratio: 53.03%
Return on equity: (-3.60%)
Cash ($ mil.): 2,283
Current ratio: 0.89
Long-term debt ($ mil.): 12,913
No. of shares (mil.): 491
Dividends
  Yield: —
  Payout: —
Market value ($ mil.): 10,504

	STOCK PRICE ($) FY Close	P/E High/Low		PER SHARE ($) Earnings	Dividends	Book Value
12/14	21.38	—	—	(0.31)	0.00	8.33
12/13	23.52	—	—	(0.32)	0.00	8.63
12/12	11.64	—	—	(3.62)	0.00	8.92
12/11	10.43	3	1	5.62	0.00	12.45
12/10	14.85	—	—	(3.19)	0.00	6.14
Annual Growth	9.5%	—	—	—	—	7.9%

Micron Technology Inc.

Micron Technology is one of the largest memory chip makers in the world. It makes DRAM (Dynamic Random Access Memory) NAND Flash and NOR Flash memory and other memory technologies. The company sells to customers in networking and storage consumer electronics solid-state drives and mobile telecommunications but its largest concentration (nearly a third of sales) is the computer market. Micron's products are offered under the Micron Lexar Crucial SpecTek and Elpida brands as well as private labels. The company generates about 84% of sales outside the US.

HISTORY

Micron Technology was founded in 1978 by twins Joe and Ward Parkinson and colleague Doug Pitman in the basement of a dentist's office. They started it as a semiconductor design firm but dreamed of manufacturing their own chips. In 1980 they persuaded several local businessmen including J. R. Simplot and Allen Noble to provide financial backing. They built their own production facility and in 1982 sold their first DRAM products.

Micron went public in 1984. The following year Japanese chip makers began dumping chips on the US market to capture market share causing huge losses for US DRAM makers. Micron filed an antidumping petition with the International Trade Commission and in 1986 the US and Japan agreed to a semiconductor trade pact to curb dumping.

By 1988 a shortage of memory chips had developed and Micron cashed in. The company began to diversify into SRAM (static random-access memory) chips and other add-in memory products for PCs. (The company wound down its SRAM product line in 2003 in the face of a dire industry slump.)

In the 1990s Micron expanded into PC manufacturing in part to soften the impact of the volatile cycles of the memory chip industry. It bought PC manufacturer ZEOS in 1995 merging it with two other Micron units to form Micron Electronics (later Interland and then Web.com prior to its 2007 acquisition by Website Pros) which it took public that year.

Also in 1995 Micron CEO and co-founder Joe Parkinson left the company after a clash with Simplot. Steve Appleton who had started as a production operator in 1983 became the new CEO. In early 1996 an internal power struggle triggered by longtime director Noble resulted in Appleton's ouster. But within a few days as several executives loyal to Appleton threatened to revolt Simplot wooed the CEO back. Noble resigned.

In 1998 Micron bought the memory chip business of Texas Instruments (TI) including plants in Texas Italy and Singapore. The complex deal made TI Micron's largest shareholder —it owned 15% of the company at the time —until TI sold off its remaining shares in Micron late in 2003.

In 1999 Micron sold its display division to flat-panel display maker PixTech; it received a 30% stake in PixTech (which folded in 2002). Later in 1999 Micron announced deals making it the primary supplier of memory chips for PC makers Compaq and Gateway. Also that year it acquired Rendition a designer of graphics chips as a part of its strategy to enter the logic chip business. The initial flagship project based on Rendition's technology was phased out in 2000 though Micron went ahead with development of other embedded chipsets —designed for use with AMD's Athlon microprocessor —using Rendition designs.

In 2001 the company acquired full ownership of Japan-based DRAM maker KMT Semiconductor when it bought out joint venture partner Kobe Steel for about $350 million. (KMT was subsequently renamed Micron Japan Ltd.)

Later in 2001 subsidiary Micron Electronics underwent a major overhaul when it sold its MicronPC business (now MPC Computers) to Gores Technology Group (now The Gores Group) and its SpecTek DRAM reselling business to parent Micron Technology. Micron Electronics then acquired Web hosting company Interland and took its name. The deal reduced Micron Technology's stake in the company from 61% to about 40% —a stake that Micron later gave to the not-for-profit Micron Technology Foundation. (Micron also gave up its two seats on Interland's board.)

Also that year the company acquired Photobit a small developer of CMOS image sensors an image-capturing chip that would become widely used in camera phones and digital still cameras among other uses. The acquisition launched Micron into a new semiconductor business line that would help the company withstand the volatile cycles of the memory chip business.

At the end of 2001 Micron struck a surprise deal with Toshiba to acquire the Japanese giant's Dominion Semiconductor unit in Virginia. (The deal was closed in 2002; Micron paid about $300 million in cash and stock for Dominion.)

In late 2001 and early 2002 Micron and rival Hynix Semiconductor engaged in round after round of negotiations about Micron's possible acquisition of some or all of Hynix's chip lines. In April 2002 the companies finally announced a complex provisional agreement for Micron to acquire Hynix's memory operations and invest in its other lines; a week later though Hynix's board of directors canceled the deal.

The company used a strong balance sheet to grow capacity during the steep industry swoon of the early 21st century but also stumbled a bit with slow product introductions. Micron surprised the industry in 2002 by announcing an agreement to buy the DRAM operations of Toshiba. The Toshiba purchase which cost Micron about $300 million in cash and stock saddled Micron with too much production capacity in the midst of an especially soft DRAM market. Micron rose on improved industry conditions after the chip industry slump ended in 2003 and returned to black ink by 2004.

In 2004 Intel made a $450 million investment in Micron giving the chip giant rights to a 5% ownership stake in the company.

In early 2006 Micron merged its mobile memory and systems memory business units into one memory products group responsible for NAND flash memory DRAM and specialty memory devices. The company also paid nearly $5 million to acquire a wafer fabrication facility in Nampa Idaho from ZiLOG. Micron planned to use the fab to make image sensor chips for camera phones digital still cameras and machine vision equipment among other applications.

In mid-2006 Micron acquired flash memory maker Lexar Media for about $850 million. The Lexar acquisition bolstered Micron's position in NAND flash memory the type of memory found in many MP3 players (such as the iPod nano and the iPod shuffle) digital still cameras and other portable electronics.

Also that year Photronics formed a joint venture with Micron Technology called MP Mask Technology Center. The memory chip manufacturer took ownership of slightly more than half of MP Mask. The JV would operate Micron's mask shop in Boise Idaho. The two companies built a facility called US NanoFab in Boise to conduct R&D on advanced technology in photomasks with Photronics contributing between $100 million and $150 million toward construction and equipping of the facility.

In late 2006 Micron bolstered its product portfolio in CMOS image sensors chips that are used in camera phones digital still cameras and other applications by acquiring the imaging sensor business of Broadcom Limited. The company paid around $53 million and hired about 90 employees from Broadcom as part of the transaction.

Micron moved into the market for solid-state drives based on NAND flash memory with the roll-out of its RealSSD product line in late 2007. The line was aimed at data storage applications in notebook computers enterprise computer servers and data networks. Its embedded USB drives can store from 1GB to 8GB while its 1.8-inch and 2.5-inch SSDs can hold from 8GB to 64GB. The introduction of RealSSD moved Micron into competition with manufacturers of hard-disk drives such as Hitachi Global Storage Seagate Technology and Western Digital. While HDDs were generally cheaper than SSDs the continually falling price of NAND flash made SSDs more price-competitive.

After months of speculation that the company would spin off its CMOS image sensor business Micron in 2008 launched a separate identity for the business as a division called Aptina Imaging. Image sensors were used in camera phones digital still cameras and high-definition video cameras among other applications. Micron was the leading supplier of CMOS image sensors in the world; the product line accounted for 11% of its sales (the rest was memory chips).

The volatile semiconductor market hit a cyclical downturn in 2008 and a global economic downturn followed in 2009 making the year particularly painful for chip makers. Responding to rapidly falling prices for DRAMs and NAND flash memory devices due to oversupply in the global market and declining customer demand Micron reduced its workforce by about 20% and phased out production of 200mm wafers at its Boise plant. The company also cut executive salaries by 20% and suspended its performance-based bonus plan for officers. Micron CEO Steve Appleton who is known to fly stunt jets for fun has steered Micron through the wild cycles of the memory chip market with an intense focus on cost control. Appleton took an additional 10% reduction in his base salary for 2009.

Furthering its non-memory ambitions in 2009 Micron entered the microdisplay market through its acquisition of Displaytech a designer of display panels and modules based on ferroelectric liquid crystal on silicon technology which is manufactured with a CMOS process on a single chip. The microdisplays marketed by Micron can be used in head-mounted display products or embedded in mobile phones to work as small projectors. The company has touted the integrated approach taken with the product which doesn't require any companion devices as digital micromirror devices do.

The company has also ventured into the solar market since photovoltaic production processes are similar to semiconductor production. In late 2009 Micron and Australia-based Origin Energy established a joint venture that develops and manufactures photovoltaic solar panels.

Also in 2009 Micron sold a 65% interest in its Aptina Imaging (imaging sensors) business to Riverwood Capital and TPG Capital for about $35 million; Micron retained a 35% equity stake in Aptina. The transaction allows Aptina and Micron to focus on their respective core businesses while retaining their ties in manufacturing marketing and product development. A portion of the buyers' 65% stake was in convertible preferred shares with a liquidation preference over common shares which resulted in Micron's ownership in Aptina's common stock to climb to 64% in 2011.

Longtime CEO Steve Appleton died unexpectedly in February 2012. He was replaced by president and COO Mark Durcan who was also named a director. Robert Switz a director since 2006 was named chairman. Sales VP Mark Adams was appointed president of the company.

EXECUTIVES

Vice President IS, Mahoney James
Vice President Operations, Jay Hawkins
CEO and Director, D. Mark Durcan, age 54, $1,005,289 total compensation
VP Worldwide Operations, Brian J. Shields, age 54, $417,116 total compensation
VP Memory Technology and Solutions, Brian M. Shirley, age 46, $581,708 total compensation
VP Worldwide Sales and Corporate Marketing, Steven L (Steve) Thorsen, age 50, $471,596 total compensation
VP Embedded Solutions, Thomas T. (Tom) Eby
VP Wireless Solutions, Michael J. (Mike) Rayfield, $384,770 total compensation
VP Finance and CFO, Ernie Maddock, age 57
CIO, Trevor Schulze
Vice President of Legal General Counsel and Corporate Secretary, Joel Poppen
Vice President Of Is, Ed Mahoney
Vice President, Matt Elzie
Vice President, Nathan Burt
Vice President Embedded Solutions, Tom Eby
National Account Manager, Mary Smith
Vice President Of World Wide Sales, Brad Anderson
Vice President Of Software Engineering, Steve Moyer
Vice President Wsg Marketing, Reynette Au
Vice President General Manager Micron Computer Services, Scott Bower
Vice President and General Manager Lexar Group, Wes Brewer
Vice President Memory System Development, Dean A Klein
Vice President World Wide Sales and Marketing, Michael (Mel) Sadler
Vice President Of System Solutions, Tom Snodgrass
Chairman, Robert E. (Bob) Switz, age 68

Vice President of Finance and Treasurer, Ken Rizvi
Assistant Treasurer, Gregory Routin
Treasurer, Dennis Parry
Auditors: PricewaterhouseCoopers LLP

LOCATIONS

HQ: Micron Technology Inc.
8000 S. Federal Way, Boise, ID 83716-9632
Phone: 208 368-4000
Web: www.micron.com

2015 Sales

	$ mil.	% of total
Asia/Pacific		
China	6,658	41
Taiwan	2,241	14
Japan	1,026	6
Other countries	2,037	12
US	2,565	16
Europe	1,248	8
Other	417	3
Total	**16,192**	**100**

PRODUCTS/OPERATIONS

2015 Sales

	$ mil.	% of total
Compute and Networking Business Unit	6,725	41
Mobile Business Unit	3,692	23
Storage Business Unit	3,687	23
Embedded Business Unit	1,999	12
Other	89	1
Total	**16,192**	**100**

2015 Sales

	$ mil.	% of total
DRAM	10,339	64
Non-volatile memory	5,274	32
Other	579	4
Total	**16,192**	**100**

Semiconductor Products
Dynamic ra
Direct Ram
Synchronou
Double dat
Flash memory devices
Memory modules
Photomasks

COMPETITORS

Atmel	SMART Modular
Cypress Semiconductor	Technologies
Integrated Device	Samsung Electronics
Technology	SanDisk
Kingston Technology	Seagate Technology
Mosel Vitelic	Sharp Corp.
Nanya	Toshiba Semiconductor
PNY Technologies	& Storage Products
Quantum Corporation	Viking Modular
Rambus	Solutions
SK Hynix	Western Digital

HISTORICAL FINANCIALS

Company Type: Public

Income Statement

FYE: September 3

	REVENUE ($ mil.)	NET INCOME ($ mil.)	NET PROFIT MARGIN	EMPLOYEES
09/15*	16,192	2,899	17.9%	31,800
08/14	16,358	3,045	18.6%	30,400
08/13	9,073	1,190	13.1%	30,900
08/12	8,234	(1,032)	—	27,400
09/11	8,788	167	1.9%	26,100
Annual Growth	**16.5%**	**104.1%**	**—**	**5.1%**

*Fiscal year change

2015 Year-End Financials

Debt ratio: 30.41%
Return on equity: 24.72%
Cash ($ mil.): 2,287
Current ratio: 2.20
Long-term debt ($ mil.): 6,252

No. of shares (mil.): 1,084
Dividends
Yield: —
Payout: —
Market value ($ mil.): 17,984

	STOCK PRICE ($) FY Close	P/E High/Low		PER SHARE ($) Earnings	Dividends	Book Value
09/15*	16.59	13	5	2.47	0.00	11.35
08/14	32.81	12	5	2.54	0.00	10.04
08/13	13.57	13	4	1.13	0.00	8.75
08/12	6.18	—	—	(1.04)	0.00	7.57
09/11	5.74	69	31	0.17	0.00	8.61
Annual Growth	**30.4%**	**—**	**—**	**95.2%**	**—**	**7.2%**

*Fiscal year change

Microsoft Corporation

Microsoft's ambitions to put a computer on every desk have evolved to put a computing device just about anywhere and connect it to the cloud rather than anchor it to a desk. Besides the Windows operating system and Office suite of productivity programs Microsoft makes tablets (Surface) game consoles (Xbox) and smartphones (Lumia). It even introduced its first laptop computer in 2015. Still software —for consumers and businesses —is Microsoft's biggest source of revenue. Much of Microsoft's software is sold through PC makers such as Acer Lenovo Dell Hewlett-Packard and Toshiba who pre-install the software on devices. Microsoft also sells directly online and through resellers. Other products include enterprise applications (Microsoft Dynamics) and server and storage software. Its Bing search engine is a (distant) No. 2 to Google. Azure the company's cloud computing business competes with Amazon Google and IBM.

Operations

Microsoft operates through six business segments: Devices and Consumer Device and Consumer Licensing Computing and Gaming Hardware Phone Hardware Device and Consumer Other Commercial Licensing and Commercial Other.

Accounting for 44% of the company's revenue the Commercial Licensing segment's products include Windows Server Microsoft SQL Server volume licensing of the Windows operating system Microsoft Office for business SharePoint Skype for Business and Microsoft Dynamics.

While it's unlikely to warrant changing Microsoft's name hardware accounts for an increasing amount of revenue for the company. As the company has release more computing devices hardware now generates nearly 20% of its revenue. That could increase with Microsoft's new Surface Pro notebook computer.

Geographic Reach Microsoft operates through subsidiaries in more than 100 countries and international sales account for 54% of revenue. The US generates the rest.

Sales and Marketing

Microsoft sells its products and services online and through OEMs distributors and resellers. The company does spend some money promoting its products and services —it reported advertising expenses of around $1.9 billion in 2015 (ended June) a bit of a reduction from $2.3 billion in 2014 and $2.6 billion in 2013. Financial Performance The company's revenue increased about 8% in 2015

(ended June) but net income plunged 44% compared with 2014. A 60% increase in hardware sales which included a full year of phone hardware helped boost revenue. Commercial revenue rose 5% with help from the commercial cloud and growth from Azure.

The drop of net income from $22 billion in 2014 to $12 billion in 2015 came from higher costs for impairment integration and restructuring and research and development. Impairment integration and restructuring expenses were $10 billion reflecting goodwill and asset impairment charges of $7.5 billion related to its Phone Hardware business. Another $2.5 billion went to integration and restructuring activities related to restructuring. Strategy Microsoft isn't just on the desktop anymore. From its Azure cloud computing operations to its Surface tablets (and now Surface Book notebook computer) the company is planting its flag in the cloud and mobile.

The company's cloud products and services for businesses are a growing part of its strategy. Customers are attracted by the stability of Microsoft products (and the company itself) as well as the industries —such as health care —that Microsoft's customers are in.

On the user end Microsoft bought the Devices & Services business of Finland's Nokia in a $7.2 billion all-cash deal that closed in 2014. Microsoft is committed to the smartphone market despite failure to gain much traction. In 2015 the company released new and update versions of its line of smartphones. In response to the lack of traction Microsoft has started to restructure the phone hardware business eliminating up to 7800 jobs in 2016.

Microsoft also have moved to make its software available for devices other than those that run Windows. It has developed Office products for the iPad and for Android devices. For Microsoft customers the company changed some policies reducing Windows upgrade costs. It offered free upgrades for the Windows 10 OS that it released in July. The Office 365 software is a cloud-based version of its Office productivity suite.

The company continues to depend on PC makers such as Dell and Lenovo to load its software on their computers. That means not only the operating system but Office as well. Microsoft's notebook computer is a direct competitor with similar products of its customers. The hope within Microsoft is that the computer will inject energy into the slumping PC market improving the environment for other PC makers as well.

Mergers and Acquisitions

In 2014 Microsoft made a highly publicized agreement to acquire Swedish gaming firm Mojang AB which created the hugely popular cult videogame Minecraft. The deal valued at $2.5 billion and anticipated to close by the end of the year will provide Microsoft with a hot mobile and cross-platform property that it hopes will spur growth for its own mobile offerings and attract a younger generation of consumers to its products.

HISTORY

Early History

Bill Gates and Paul Allen founded Microsoft (originally named Micro-soft) in 1975 after Gates dropped out of Harvard at age 19 to sell a version of the programming language BASIC. While Gates was at Harvard the pair wrote the language for Altair the first commercial microcomputer. The company was born in Albuquerque New Mexico and grew by modifying BASIC for other computers.

Gates and Allen moved Microsoft to their native Seattle in 1979 and began developing software that let others write programs. The modern PC era dawned in 1980 when IBM chose Microsoft to write the operating system for its new machines. Although hesitant at first Gates bought QDOS short for "quick and dirty operating system" for $50000 from a Seattle programmer renaming it the Microsoft Disk Operating System (MS-DOS).

Allen fell ill with Hodgkin's disease and left Microsoft in 1983. In the mid-1980s Microsoft introduced Windows a graphics-based version of MS-DOS that borrowed from rival Apple's Macintosh system. The company went public in 1986 and Gates became the industry's first billionaire a year later. Microsoft introduced Windows NT in 1993 to compete with the UNIX operating system popular on mainframes and large networks.

The early 1990s brought monopoly charges from inside and outside the industry. In 1995 antitrust concerns scotched a $1.5 billion acquisition of personal finance software maker Intuit.

EXECUTIVES

COO, B. Kevin Turner, age 50, $796,667 total compensation
CEO, Satya Nadella, age 47, $918,917 total compensation
EVP Corporate Strategy and Planning, Kurt DelBene, age 55, $638,333 total compensation
EVP and General Counsel, Bradford L. (Brad) Smith, age 56, $641,667 total compensation
EVP and Chief Marketing Officer, Christopher C. (Chris) Capossela, age 45
EVP Applications and Services, Qi Lu
Corporate VP and Chairman Microsoft Japan, Yasuyuki Higuchi, age 57
EVP Technology and Research, Harry Shum, $573,939 total compensation
EVP Human Resources, Kathleen T. Hogan, age 49
EVP Microsoft Cloud and Enterprise Group, Scott Guthrie
President Microsoft Asia Pacific, Cesar Cernuda
EVP Windows and Devices Group, Terry Myerson
EVP and CFO, Amy E. Hood, age 43, $603,333 total compensation
General Manager Africa and the Middle East, Mteto Nyati
General Manager Bahrain and Oman, Sherif Tawfik
EVP Business Development, Margaret (Peggy) Johnson, age 53
VP Microsoft Japan, Takuya Hirano
Vice President, Cindy Bates
Vice President, Kevin Funk
Vice President, Mary Smith
Vice President Market Data Information Technology, Alexis Castanares
Vice President, Kelly Rollin
Vice President Manufacturing, Alfred Ojukwu
Vice President of Sales MSNBC, Kyoo Kim
Vice President, Ilan Spillinger
Corporate Vice President Dynamics CRM, Robert (Bob) Stutz
Non Information Technology Director Vice President, Ward Ralston
Vice President of Marketing and Strategy, Ken Hite
CVP Oss Development, Rajesh Jha
Executive Vice President Networking CAM and Managed Services, Michael (Mel) Mccarter
Vice President Marketing, Cheryl Ricketts
Vice President, Mike McDuffie
Vice President, Bharat Shah
Senior MVP Lead, Tom Archer
Asp.net MVP, Javier Lozano
Vice President Of Marketing, John (Jack) Chase
Executive Vice President Human Resources, Lisa Brummel
Vice President Windows Live Experience Program Management, Chris Jones
Human Resources Director Or Vice President Of Human Resources, Rupert Bader
Vice President Engineering, Ed Clark
Assistant Vice President, Patrick Dengler

Vice President Entertainment And Devices Division Microsoft Canada Co, Greg Barber
Vice President Of Finance, Ashish Popli
Vice President Of Technology, Markus Kohler
Vice President Human Resources, Scott Yih
Vice President Marketing (North America Mobile Devices), Valerie (Val) Buckingham
CVP Cloud Infrastructure and Operations, Suresh Kumar
Corporate Vice President Strategy Planning And Analysis, Uhlaner Robert
Latam Assistant Vice President Communication Manager, Jennifer (Jen) Brooks
Svp Microsoft Services And It, Richard R Devenuti, age 58
National Sales Manager Unified Communications, Kristi Bannatyne
Business Dvpt Manager, Tracye Foy
Vice President BD Insurance Solutions Group Global, David (Dave) Lochridge
Corporate Vice President Microsoft Online, Ron Markezich
Vice President IT Operations and Applications Engineering, Neil Leslie
Vice President Of Server Development, James Holt
Corporate Vice President Outlook + Outlook.com + Exchange Program Management, Harvinder Bhela
Corporate Vice President Windows Marketing, Tony Prophet
Cvp Engineering, Richard (Dick) Qian
General Manager Global and Multinational Enterprise Accounts Vice President of Sales, Hein Hellemons
Vice President Americas Consulting, Robert Jorgenson
Vice President Eu Affairs, John (Jack) Vassallo
Corporate Vice President Program Management, Darryn Dieken
Vice President Data And Analytics, Paul Haverstock
Corporate Vice President Small And Midmarket Solutions And Partners Microsoft Corporation, Eduardo Rosini
Senior Vice President Product Strategy (Xbox Entertainment Studios), Randy Ahn
Executive Vice President Operating, Terry Ramsey
Vice President Global Enterprise Sales, Hayden Stafford
Senior Vice President President of EMEA, Neil Holloway
Corporate Vice President Deputy General, Mary Snapp
Vice President WW Industry and Global Accounts, Alberto Arciniega
Vice President Technical Computing, Tony Hey
CVP WW Tax, Bill Sample
Vice President, Ilya Balakleyevskiy
Vice President Performance Management, Carrie Viser
Vice President Dynamics Partner Sales And, Victor Morales
Vice President Product, Ya-Qin Zhang
Vice President And Deputy General Coun, David (Dave) Heiner
Vice President Strategic Emerging Business Development, Dan'l Lewin
Vice President WW Industry Sales Epg, Tito Arciniega
Vice President Product, David (Dave) Deloraine
Chairman, John W. Thompson, age 65
Auditors: Deloitte & Touche LLP

LOCATIONS

HQ: Microsoft Corporation
One Microsoft Way, Redmond, WA 98052-6399
Phone: 425 882-8080
Web: www.microsoft.com

2015 Sales

	$ mil.	% of total
US	42,941	46
Other countries	50,639	54
Total	**93,580**	**100**

PRODUCTS/OPERATIONS

2015 Sales

	$ mil.	% of total
Devices and consumers		
Hardware	17,707	19
Licensing	14,969	16
Other	8,825	9
Commercial		
Licensing	41,039	44
Other	10,836	12
Corporate and other	204	-
Total	**93,580**	**100**

Selected Products

Consumer software services and devices
　Xbox (video game console)
Desktop applications
　Access (relational database management)
　Excel (integrated spreadsheet)
　FrontPage (website publishing)
　MS Office (business productivity software suite)
　Outlook (messaging and collaboration)
　PowerPoint (presentation graphics)
　Project (project scheduling and resource allocation)
　Word (word processing)
Enterprise software
　BackOffice (server software suite)
　Content Management Server (content management)
　Exchange Server (messaging server)
　Proxy Server (Internet gateway)
　Site Server (website management)
　SQL Server (database and data analysis management)
　Systems Management Server (centralized management)
　Visio (visualization and diagramming suite)

Selected Acquisitions

COMPETITORS

Adobe Systems	Nintendo
Amazon.com	Nokia
Apple Inc.	Novell
CA Inc.	Opera Software
EMC	Oracle
Google	Red Hat
HP	SAP
IBM	Sony
Logitech	Yahoo!
Mozilla	salesforce.com

HISTORICAL FINANCIALS

Company Type: Public

Income Statement

FYE: June 30

	REVENUE ($ mil.)	NET INCOME ($ mil.)	NET PROFIT MARGIN	EMPLOYEES
06/15	93,580	12,193	13.0%	118,000
06/14	86,833	22,074	25.4%	128,000
06/13	77,849	21,863	28.1%	99,000
06/12	73,723	16,978	23.0%	94,000
06/11	69,943	23,150	33.1%	90,000
Annual Growth	**7.5%**	**(14.8%)**	**—**	**7.0%**

2015 Year-End Financials

Debt ratio: 20.03%—
Return on equity: 14.36%
Cash ($ mil.): 5,595
Current ratio: 2.50
Long-term debt ($ mil.): 27,808

Dividends
　Yield: 2.7%
　Payout: 50.2%
Market value ($ mil.): —

	STOCK PRICE ($) FY Close	P/E High/Low	PER SHARE ($) Earnings	Dividends	Book Value
06/15	44.15	33 27	1.48	1.21	9.98
06/14	41.70	16 12	2.63	1.07	10.90
06/13	34.55	14 10	2.58	0.89	9.48
06/12	30.59	16 12	2.00	0.76	7.92
06/11	26.00	11 8	2.69	0.61	6.82
Annual Growth	14.2%	— —	(13.9%)	18.7%	10.0%

	STOCK PRICE ($) FY Close	P/E High/Low	PER SHARE ($) Earnings	Dividends	Book Value
12/14	13.68	18 9	1.39	1.14	40.47
12/13	19.60	29 25	0.68	0.00	34.01
Annual Growth	(8.6%)	— —	19.6%	—	4.4%

Midcoast Energy Partners LP

Midcoast Energy Partners was formed by Enbridge Energy Partners in 2013 as an investment vehicle to own and grow its natural gas and NGL midstream business. It has minority stakes in Enbridge's network of natural gas and natural gas liquids (NGLs) gathering and transportation systems natural gas processing and treating facilities and NGL fractionation plants in Texas and Oklahoma. Organized as a limited partnership Midcoast Energy Partners is exempt from paying income tax as long as it distributes quarterly dividends to shareholders. It went public in 2013 raising $333 million. All proceeds went to Enbridge Energy Partners.

EXECUTIVES

Vp Finance, Stephen J (Steve) Neyland
Vp Natural Gas Marketing, Janet Coy
Auditors: PricewaterhouseCoopers LLP

LOCATIONS

HQ: Midcoast Energy Partners LP
1100 Louisiana Street, Suite 3300, Houston, TX 77002
Phone: 713 821-2000
Web: www.midcoastpartners.com

COMPETITORS

Buckeye Partners	Martin Midstream
DCP Midstream Partners	Partners
Duke Energy	ONEOK
Dynegy	Sunoco Logistics
Koch Industries Inc.	TransCanada
Magellan Midstream	Williams Companies

HISTORICAL FINANCIALS

Company Type: Public

Income Statement

FYE: December 31

	REVENUE ($ mil.)	NET INCOME ($ mil.)	NET PROFIT MARGIN	EMPLOYEES
12/14	5,894	144	2.4%	—
12/13	5,593	53	1.0%	—
12/12	5,357	167	3.1%	—
12/11	7,828	219	2.8%	—
12/10	6,654	157	2.4%	—
Annual Growth	(3.0%)	(2.1%)	—	—

2014 Year-End Financials

Debt ratio: 13.21%
Return on equity: —
Cash ($ mil.): 42
Current ratio: 1.07
Long-term debt ($ mil.): 760
No. of shares (mil.): 46
Dividends
 Yield: 8.3%
 Payout: 82.1%
Market value ($ mil.): 631

Mohawk Industries, Inc.

Mohawk Industries doesn't mind being trampled under foot. The company is one of the largest makers of commercial and residential carpets rugs and other floor coverings in the US (competing with rival Shaw Industries) and one of the largest carpet makers in the world. It produces a range of broadloom carpets and rugs under such names as Mohawk Aladdin Durkan Karastan Lees and Bigelow. Mohawk's Dal-Tile International division is a giant maker of ceramic tile and stone flooring. Unilin's laminate and wood flooring and other wood products round out Mohawk's operations. The company sells its wares to carpet retailers home centers mass merchandisers department stores and dealers.

Geographic Reach

Mohawk generates around 71% of its revenues in North America. It has manufacturing facilities located in Australia Brazil Canada China Europe India Malaysia Mexico Russia and the US.

Operations

Mohawk works through three main business segments: Carpet (38% of total sales); Ceramic (38%); and Laminate and Wood (24%). Once focused exclusively on carpets and rugs Mohawk has evolved adapting itself to changing customer tastes and spending habits. The company now offers popular alternatives to carpet such as hardwood laminate and ceramic tile. It has also reached outside of its premium-priced portfolio by rolling out a do-it-yourself flooring line that mimics the elegant look of materials like marble or limestone without the coldness chipping or costly installation of real stone.

Its breadth of operations is matched by its depth; Mohawk maintains a strong distribution and wide customer base (in addition to residential customers it serves government healthcare and educational institutions as well as corporate retail and public venues) which creates strong brand recognition.

Sales and Marketing

The company's top 10 customers accounted for nearly 20% of its total sales in 2013. It sells its products to more than 24000 customers which include independent floor covering retailers home centers and mass merchandisers department stores commercial dealers and end users.

Financial Performance

Mohawk has experienced four straight years of steady growth. Its revenues were up by 6% from $7.4 billion in 2013 to peak at $7.8 billion its highest total in at least seven years. Profits also jumped 52% from $349 million in 2013 to $532 million in 2014 due to an absence of loss from discontinued operations.

The growth for 2014 was fueled by a 13% surge in both tile and ceramic sales. Mohawk was also helped by strong residential channel growth and continued improvement in the commercial channel.

The company's operating cash flow has fluctuated over the last five years. After experiencing a sharp decline of $62 million in 2013 the company reported an operating cash flow increase of 26% to in 2014.

Mergers and Acquisitions

The company is looking to extend its international reach and augment its product portfolio through acquisitions. In 2013 it bought Spano Invest NV a panel board manufacturer based in Belgium for $168 million. Mohawk is combining Spano with its Unilin segment to become a leader in the chipboard industry. It also picked up Pergo a prominent maker of premium laminate flooring for $150 million. With a brand name that has become almost synonymous with laminate flooring in Europe Pergo makes a variety of flooring products with the look of hardwoods tile stone and other materials.

In a much larger transaction the company purchased the Marazzi Group for $1.5 billion a few months later. One of Europe's leading ceramic tile producers Marazzi makes and distributes tile and other flooring and ceramic bathroom products to more than 100 countries around the world.

Strategy

In addition to acquisitions the company grows its business in other ways. In 2013 it invested $367 million in capital projects including fiber innovation ceramic capacity an insulation board facility in Europe and it worked to make significant improvements to the productivity and efficiency of its newly acquired businesses. Throughout 2014 the company planned to invest an additional $500 million to enhance its capacity efficiency and productivity.

HISTORY

Mohawk traces its origins to the Shuttleworth family who founded the company in Amsterdam New York in 1878 setting up their business with 14 second-hand looms imported from England. The company was incorporated as Shuttleworth Brothers in 1902. It introduced the popular Karnak carpet design in 1908.

EXECUTIVES

Chairman and CEO, Jeffrey S. Lorberbaum, age 60, $1,082,144 total compensation
President and COO, W. Christopher (Chris) Wellborn, age 59, $935,056 total compensation
President Ceramic North America, John C. Turner, age 46
President Carpet, Brian M. Carson, age 50, $499,047 total compensation
VP Finance CFO and Assistant Secretary, Frank H. Boykin, age 59, $583,097 total compensation
President Laminate and Wood, Bernard P. Thiers, age 59, $661,699 total compensation
Vice President Finance, David B Toney
Senior Vice President Manufacturing, Joey Faircloth
Vice President Information Technology Project Manager, Brian Rosenbluh
Vice President Of Brand Management, Kent Clauson
Mohawk Residential Sales Flooring Residential Sales RVP Mid, Jeff Derusha
Vice President Manufacturing, Jeff Bruggs
Vice President Quality, Ed Richardson
Vice President Sales Bigelow and Mohawk Commercial Brands, Jeff Davis
Vice President Internal Audit, Carley Ferguson
Vice President of Sales Northern Ca NV, Gary Jones
Senior Vice President Commercial Resilient Business, David (Dave) Thoresen
Vice President of Flooring Production, Willy Chandler
Mohawk Hard Surfaces Hard Surface RVP Northeast District, Ron Connolly
Vice President Of Credit, Scott Harkins

Mohawk Commercial Sales Flooring Commercial
RVP Southeast Ac, Kathy Ogden
Senior Vice President Residental Sales, Jeff
Meadows
Mohawk Commercial Sales Flooring Commercial
RVP North Central, Kent Odefey
Vice President Of Sourcing, Jim Mason
Senior Vice President Sales, Randy Gardner
RVP Sales Central, Greg Tant
Vice President, Russell (Russ) Ence
Mohawk Commercial Sales Flooring Commercial
RVP Midwest Acco, Kristen Komis
Senior Vice President Prod Management, Bobby
Berrier
Vice President Commercial Product Development
and Design, Jackie Dettmar
Vice President Specialty Sales Mohawk Home,
Brandon Culpepper
Mohawk Residential Sales Flooring Residential
Sales RVP MID, Kevin Reilly
Vice President and Treasurer, Shailesh Bettadapur
Vice President Sales, Ken Duning
Regional Vice President, Jeffrey (Jeff) Wilson
Vice President Of Creative Services, Elise
Demboski
Vice President, Frank Endrenyi
Vice President Industry Relations, Allen Parker
Senior Vice President Customer Support, Dennis
Mitchell
Mohawk Commercial Sales Flooring Commercial
RVP Northeast Ac, Gary Graus
Vice President Finance, Christy Thomas
Vice President Sales, Tom Merriman
Vice President Marketing Sls, Bill Storey
Vice President of Northeastern Sales for the H,
Bob Nichols
Vice President Marketing and Sales, David (Dave)
Moyer
Vice President Internationalernational Sales,
Michael (Mel) Kephart
Vice President, Barry Kelley
Vice President Regional Manager, Detric Goss
Vice President Of Residential Carpet Product
Development, Jamie Welborn
National Sales Manager Builder, Doug Davis
Mohawk Commercial Sales Flooring Commercial
RVP Mountain West, Ralph Holland
Vice President Audit, Carly Ferguson
Vice President of Sales, Kelly Moore
Board Member, Mark Ruppert
Auditors: KPMG LLP

LOCATIONS

HQ: Mohawk Industries, Inc.
160 S. Industrial Blvd., Calhoun, GA 30701
Phone: 706 629-7721
Web: www.mohawkind.com

2014 Sales

	$ mil.	% of total
North America	5,547	71
Other regions	2,255	29
Total	7,803	100

PRODUCTS/OPERATIONS

2014 Sales

	$ mil.	% of total
Carpet	3,013	38
Ceramic	3,015	38
Laminate and wood	1,890	24
Inter-segment sales	(116.4)	-
Total	7,803	100

2014 Sales

	$ mil.	% of total
Tile	2,764	40
Soft Surface	3,087	35
Laminate and wood	1,951	25
Total	7,803	100
Products Selected

Residential Carpet
Commercial Carpet
Bath Rugs Area Rugs and Mats
Ceramic Ti
Laminate Flooring
Hardwood Flooring
Luxury Vin

Selected OperationsBath rugsBlanketsCarpet
padCarpetsCeramic tileCeramic tileDecorative
throws and pillowsDoormatsGlazed and unglazed
ceramic mosaic tileGlazed floor tileGlazed wall
tileHardwood flooringHardwood flooringInsulation
panelsLaminate flooring

COMPETITORS

Armstrong World
Industries
Beaulieu of America
Couristan
Dixie Group
Formica
Guilford Mills
Hollander Home
Fashions

Interface Inc.
Mannington Mills
Perstorp
Shaw Industries
Tarkett Inc.
Wilsonart
International

HISTORICAL FINANCIALS

Company Type: Public

Income Statement

FYE: December 31

	REVENUE ($ mil.)	NET INCOME ($ mil.)	NET PROFIT MARGIN	EMPLOYEES
12/14	7,803	531	6.8%	32,300
12/13	7,348	348	4.7%	32,100
12/12	5,787	250	4.3%	25,100
12/11	5,642	173	3.1%	26,200
12/10	5,319	185	3.5%	26,900
Annual Growth	10.1%	30.1%	—	4.7%

2014 Year-End Financials

Debt ratio: 27.20%
Return on equity: 11.98%
Cash ($ mil.): 97
Current ratio: 1.60
Long-term debt ($ mil.): 1,402

No. of shares (mil.): 72
Dividends
Yield: —
Payout: —
Market value ($ mil.): 11,328

	STOCK PRICE ($) FY Close	P/E High/Low	PER SHARE ($) Earnings	Dividends	Book Value
12/14	155.36	22 17	7.25	0.00	60.59
12/13	148.90	30 19	4.82	0.00	61.37
12/12	90.47	25 16	3.61	0.00	53.79
12/11	59.85	27 16	2.52	0.00	49.66
12/10	56.76	24 16	2.65	0.00	47.67
Annual Growth	28.6%	— —	28.6%	—	6.2%

Molina Healthcare Inc

Navigating the murky waters of federal health care plans is no easy feat but Molina Healthcare's mission is to help Medicaid and Medicare members find their way to health care. Its Health Plan segment arranges for the delivery of health services to some 3.5 million people who receive their care through Medicaid Medicare and other government-funded programs in 11 states. Its Medicaid Solutions segment provides business process outsourcing (BPO) solutions to Medicaid agencies in five states for their Medicaid Management Information Systems (MMIS) the tool used to support administration of state health care entitlement programs.

The family of founder C. David Molina controls the company through holdings and trusts.

Operations

Altogether Molina's operations provide plans or services to 3.5 million individuals in a dozen states. Molina's health plans segment accounts for a majority (98% in 2014) of revenues. The company's health plans provide medical services through state networks of contracted hospitals and physicians that accept Molina health plan coverage.

Geographic Reach

Molina's health plans primarily operate in Washington California South Carolina Texas Ohio and Michigan as well as in New Mexico Utah Florida and Wisconsin. The Medicaid Solutions business provides IT services in Idaho Louisiana Maine New Jersey West Virginia and the US Virgin Islands; it also administers a drug rebate program in Florida.

A third component of the company referred to as the direct delivery line of business (reported within the health plans segment) consists of about 25 primary care community clinics in California Florida New Mexico and Washington.

Molina's health plans segment leases 70 facilities while the Medicaid solutions segment leases a dozen facilities.

Financial Performance

Molina has reported steady revenue increases over the last few years; in 2014 revenue rose 27% to $9.7 billion on growth across both segments. The health plans segment saw a 28% rise in membership (due to Medicaid expansion as a result of the Affordable Care Act) as well as an 18% increase in monthly revenue per member. The Molina Medicaid solutions segment also saw growth in 2014 on higher Medicaid transaction volumes.

After two years in declines net income has rebounded in 2013 and 2014. Revenue increases drove profits up 18% to $62 million in 2014. Cash flow from operations spiked 458% to $1.1 billion that year as more cash was generated by medical claims and other accounts payable.

Strategy

Molina grows in its existing markets by increasing services and adding physicians to its provider networks. It also looks to add new members by increasing its brand awareness through marketing and advertising campaigns. In addition Molina enters new markets through both organic measures and through acquisitions targeting entry into large markets with competitive provider communities. In 2013 it added new members in New Mexico and South Carolina by purchasing other plans' contracts. In 2014 Molina acquired two Medicaid contracts in Florida adding some 73000 new members. Later that year it secured a contract to administer Puerto Rico's Medicaid program in a couple of regions adding some 350000 new members.

Molina's growth strategy also consists of opening additional primary care clinics in existing and new territories. The addition of more clinics helps Molina diversify its operations by expanding its involvement in the direct delivery of primary care. About 20% of Molina's California health plan membership is being served by its primary care clinics there.

Growing the direct delivery component of its business also helps Molina prepare for health care reform changes. Components of the health care reform bill call for increased health insurance coverage and changes to the way government health plans are reimbursed which could impact the company's financial returns on health plan operations. In addition Molina sees opportunities in the Affordable Care Act's provisions to expand state Medicaid programs as well as by participating in dual eligibility programs designed to improve the coor-

dination of care for members that are eligible for coverage under Medicaid and Medicare plans.

Mergers and Acquisitions

In 2015 Molina Healthcare of Michigan agreed to buy certain assets of HealthPlus of Michigan expanding its operations in the state. The deal will include assets of HealthPlus' Medicaid and MIChild (for uninsured children) businesses. Later that year Molina Healthcare of Florida agreed to buy assets of Preferred Medical Plan's Medicaid business in Florida while Molina Healthcare of Illinois planned to enter the Chicago market with the acquisition of certain assets of Accountable Care Chicago (aka MyCare Chicago). The Illinois unit also plans to buy certain Cook County-based Medicaid assets of accountable care entity Better Health Network.

Another deal was the acquisition of Providence Human Services (which provides behavioral and mental health services in more than 20 states) and Providence Community Services from The Providence Service Corporation for some $200 million. Those companies will now operate under the Pathways brand.

Company Background

Founded in 1980 Molina Healthcare is headed by founder C. David Molina's sons: Dr. J. Mario Molina who serves as chairman and CEO and John C. Molina who is a director and the company's CFO.

EXECUTIVES

Chief Accounting Officer, Joseph W. White, age 56, $515,000 total compensation

Chairman President and CEO, J. Mario Molina, age 56, $1,050,000 total compensation

CFO, John C. Molina, age 50, $878,000 total compensation

EVP Research and Development, Martha Molina Bernadett, $357,000 total compensation

COO, Terry P. Bayer, age 64, $644,000 total compensation

SVP General Counsel and Secretary, Jeff D. Barlow, age 52, $475,000 total compensation

CIO, Rick Hopfer

Associate Vice President for the Office of the Chief Information Officer, Debbie Simkins

Vice President of Clinic Operations, Gloria Calderon

Vice President Operations, Len Gillespie

Vice President Of Healthcare Services, Kim English

Vice President Network Management and Operations, Ami Cole

Mhi Associate Vice President Program Management, Kristine MacRae

Regional Vice President, Zarina Sparling

Assistant Vice President Mhi Enrollment Accounting, Becky Gutierrez

Assistant Vice President Information Technology, Ashwini Hassija

Regional Vice President, Kathie Mancini

Vice President Finance and Analytics, Richard (Dick) Rosenberg

Regional Vice President At Molina Healthcare, Del Bell

Assistant Vice President Rating, Ben Lynam

Vice President Network Management and Operations, Brandon Hendrickson

Vice President Of Pharmacy Services, Angelo Giambrone

Vice President Of Quality, Kevin Park

Vice President Government Contracts, Carl Kidd

Vice President Health Insurance, Janet Fosdick

Assistant Vice President Clinic Operations, Diane Sanchez

MHI Associate Vice President Proposal Responses, Phyllis Simon

Medical Director, Maria Diaz

MHU Associate Vice President Government Contracts, Douglas (Doug) Springmeyer

Associate Medical Director, Dave Donigian

Vice President, Mohit Ghose

Director Of Pharmacy, John Vu

Corporate Associate Vice President, Nancy G Neslen

Vice President Of Finance, Jane Dawson

Mhi Associate Vice President Corporate Oprs, Andrea Orleans

Vice President Sales, Ryan Boe

Vice President, Gwen Williams

Medical Director, Delores Baker

Vice President, Tom Standring

Vice President Of Call Centre, Randall Fillmore

Associate Vice President Health Plan Operations, Virginia Fuentes-rivera

Mhi Associate Vice President State Affairs, Cameron Smyth

Vice President Of Compliance, Joann Zarza-Garrido

Medical Director, Jeffrey Hunter

Vice President Information Technology, Michael Mayers

Medical Librarian, Phillip Garcia

Legal Secretary, Wendy Jones

Medical Director, Raymond Zastrow

Assistant Vice President Medicare Pharmacy Services, Erin Gordon

Vice President, Douglas Rodgers

Associate Medical Director, Ron Tomas

Medical Director, Jean Glossa

MHC Vice President Healthcare Services Um #119062, Deborah (Deb) Miller

Vice President Tax, George Figueroa

Medical Director of Behavioral Health, Ayo Afejuku

Associate Vice President of Government Contracts, David (Dave) Vinkler

Associate Vice President of Medicare Sales, Britt Travis

Vice President of Consolidated Plan Solutions, Marianne Czapla

Vice President Procurement, Bryce Berg

Executive Vice President Finance, Stephen (Steve) Harris

Executive Vice President Research and Innovation, Mmartha Bernadett

Regional Vice President Health Plan Operations, Zarina Shockley-Sparling

Vice President Network Strategy And Services, Kim Sweers

Auditors: Ernst & Young LLP

LOCATIONS

HQ: Molina Healthcare Inc
200 Oceangate, Suite 100, Long Beach, CA 90802
Phone: 562 435-3666   **Fax:** 562 437-1335
Web: www.molinahealthcare.com

2014 Membership by Health Plan

	% of total
California	22
Washington	19
Ohio	13
Texas	9
Michigan	9
New Mexico	8
Florida	6
North Carolina	4
Illinois	4
Wisconsin	3
Utah	3
Total	**100**

PRODUCTS/OPERATIONS

2014 Revenues

	$ mil.	% of total
Premiums	9,022	94
Services	210	2
Premium tax revenue	294	3
Health insurer fee	119	1
Investments	8	-
Other	12	-
Total	**9,666**	**100**

2014 Revenues

	$ mil.	% of total
Health Plans	9,456	98
Medicaid Solutions	210	3
Total	**9,666**	**100**

Selected Plans

Abria Health Plan
Molina Healthcare Plans by individual state subsidiaries
Molina Medicare Options (Medicare plan with prescription drug benefit)
Molina Medicare Options Plus (Medicare plan for dual-eligible individuals)

COMPETITORS

AMERIGROUP	HCSC
Aetna	HP Enterprise Group
Anthem	Health Net
Blue Cross Blue Shield	Humana
of Michigan	Kaiser Foundation
CIGNA	Health Plan
CNSI	L. A. Care Health Plan
Cambia Health	Premera Blue Cross
Solutions	Priority Health
Centene	Total Health Care
Community Health Group	UnitedHealth Group
Computer Sciences	WellCare Health Plans
Corp.	Xerox
Coventry Health Care	

HISTORICAL FINANCIALS

Company Type: Public

Income Statement

FYE: December 31

	REVENUE ($ mil.)	NET INCOME ($ mil.)	NET PROFIT MARGIN	EMPLOYEES
12/14	9,666	62	0.6%	10,500
12/13	6,588	52	0.8%	8,200
12/12	6,028	9	0.2%	5,800
12/11	4,769	20	0.4%	5,200
12/10	4,085	54	1.3%	4,200
Annual Growth	**24.0%**	**3.1%**	**—**	**25.7%**

2014 Year-End Financials

Debt ratio: 20.22%
Return on equity: 6.54%
Cash ($ mil.): 1,539
Current ratio: 1.49
Long-term debt ($ mil.): 905

No. of shares (mil.): 49
Dividends
  Yield: —
  Payout: —
Market value ($ mil.): 2,662

	STOCK PRICE ($) FY Close	P/E High/Low		PER SHARE ($) Earnings	Dividends	Book Value
12/14	53.53	41	25	1.29	0.00	20.32
12/13	34.75	35	22	1.13	0.00	19.47
12/12	27.06	175	85	0.21	0.00	16.73
12/11	22.33	96	32	0.45	0.00	16.48
12/10	27.85	24	15	1.32	0.00	15.82
Annual Growth	**17.7%**	**—**	**—**	**(0.6%)**	**—**	**6.5%**

Mondelez International Inc

Mondelez International (formerly Kraft Foods Inc.) makes what it takes to survive a global snack attack. The company's pantry of billion-dollar brands includes: Cadbury and Milka chocolates; LU Nabisco and Oreo biscuits; Trident gum; Tang powdered beverages; and Jacobs coffees. Mondelez International comprises the global snacking and

food brands of the former Kraft Foods whose North American operations were spun off to form Kraft Foods Group in 2012. Mondelez with about $35 billion in annual sales operations in more than 80 countries and sale in about 165 countries is the larger of the two businesses.

HISTORY

The Kraft tale began in 1903 when James L. Kraft began delivering cheese to Chicago grocers. His four brothers joined in forming the J.L. Kraft & Bros. Company in 1909. By 1914 the company had opened a cheese factory and was selling cheese across the US. Kraft developed its first blended pasteurized cheese the following year.

Kraft went public in 1924; four years later it merged with Philadelphia cream-cheese maker Phoenix and also created Velveeta cheese spread. In 1930 Kraft was bought by National Dairy but its operations were kept separate. New and notable products included Miracle Whip salad dressing (1933) macaroni and cheese dinners (1937) and Parkay margarine (1940). In the decades that followed Kraft expanded into foreign markets.

National Dairy became Kraftco in 1969 and Kraft in 1976 hoping to benefit from its internationally known trademark. To diversify Kraft merged with Dart Industries in 1980; Dart's subsidiaries (including Duracell batteries) and Kraft kept separate operations. With non-food sales sagging Dart & Kraft split up in 1986. Kraft kept its original lines and added Duracell (sold 1988); the rest became Premark International. Tobacco giant Philip Morris Companies bought Kraft in 1988 for $12.9 billion. The next year Philip Morris joined Kraft with another unit General Foods.

General Foods began when Charles Post who marketed a wheat/bran health beverage established the Postum Cereal Co. in 1896; he expanded the firm with such cereals as Grape-Nuts and Post Toasties. The company went public in 1922. Postum bought the makers of Jell-O (1925) Baker's chocolate (1927) Log Cabin syrup (1927) and Maxwell House coffee (1928) and in 1929 it acquired control of General Foods (owned by frozen vegetable pioneer Clarence Birdseye) and changed its own name to General Foods.

Its later purchases included Perkins Products (Kool-Aid 1953) and Kohner Brothers (toys 1970). Most of its non-food lines proved unsuccessful and were sold throughout the years. General Foods bought Oscar Mayer the US's #1 hot dog maker in 1981. Philip Morris bought General Foods for $5.6 billion in 1985.

The 1989 combination of Kraft and General Foods (the units still ran independently) created the largest US food maker Kraft General Foods. In the 1990s Kraft General Foods lost market share in areas such as frozen vegetables and processed meat. It introduced "light" meat products and stopped making nearly 300 food items. In 1993 it bought RJR Nabisco's cold cereal business (Shredded Wheat) and sold its Breyers ice-cream business to Unilever.

To streamline management Philip Morris integrated Kraft and General Foods in 1995. Newly named Kraft Foods sold off lower-margin businesses including its bakery unit and its North American table spreads business. Kraft bought Del Monte's shelf-stable pudding business (1995) and Taco Bell's grocery line (1996). It also sold its Lender's bagels (1996) and Log Cabin (1997) lines.

Deciding to eat healthy in early 2000 Kraft bought Boca Burger (soy products) for about $100 million and Balance Bar (meal-replacement snack bars drink mixes and beverages) for $268 million.

In 2000 parent Philip Morris (which renamed itself the Altria Group in 2003) outbid Danone and Cadbury Schweppes (later Cadbury) and agreed to buy Nabisco Holdings. It completed the deal that December for $18.9 billion (including $4 billion in debt) and began integrating those operations into Kraft Foods and Kraft Foods International. Then Philip Morris created a holding company for the newly combined food operations under the Kraft Foods Inc. name in 2001. The original Kraft Foods was renamed Kraft Foods North America.

Kraft Foods International CEO Roger Deromedi was appointed co-CEO of the new holding company along with Betsy Holden. Kraft Foods Inc. was spun off by Altria in 2001 in what was the US's second-largest IPO ever at the time (behind AT&T Wireless now AT&T Mobility).

Kraft cut 7500 jobs in 2002 as a result of the integration of Nabisco operations paying out $373 million in cash for severance and related costs. That year Kraft was also part of a $9 million settlement of a federal lawsuit regarding the use of genetically modified corn in its taco shells.

A strategy to shed brands that do not fit with the rest of the company's portfolio led Kraft to sell Farley's and Sathers in 2002 to FS Partners which renamed the company Farley's & Sathers Candy Company. Later that year Kraft sold some of its candy brands (Now and Later Intense Fruit Chews and Mity Bite) to FS Partners.

In a move to combat the population's growing obesity problem Kraft said in 2003 that it intended to reduce the fat and sugar content and cut the portion sizes of its food products as well as cease marketing in schools.

Deromedi shared the CEO slot with co-CEO Betsy Holden until 2003 at which time Deromedi was named sole CEO. (Holden was demoted to a marketing slot in the company and eventually left Kraft in 2005.) During his tenure as CEO Deromide was dogged by Kraft's looming spinoff from Altria and struggled to improve company profits by selling off underperforming and non-core brands.

The company in 2004 formed an alliance with Dr. Arthur Agatston of low-carb South Beach Diet fame to use the South Beach Diet trademark on some of its products including cereal meal replacements cereal bars refrigerated sandwich wraps and frozen entrees and pizza.

As part of Deromedi's plan to refashion Kraft's product lineup in 2005 the company sold its Altoids breath mints LifeSavers and CremeSavers candies brands whose combined sales were at the time estimated to be about $660 million a year. Wm. Wrigley Jr. Company paid about $1.4 billion for the popular brands.

Despite his best efforts to improve the bottom line Deromedi was shown the door in 2006. He was replaced by Frito-Lay's CEO Irene Rosenfeld (a former top Kraft executive who was instrumental in the company's acquisition and integration of Nabisco). She returned to Kraft after being head of Pepsico's Frito-Lay from 2004 to 2006.

Kraft extricated itself from the haze of second-hand tobacco smoke when it was spun off from Altria in 2007. Having edged toward splitting from its former parent for years the separation relieved the food maker of many headaches. It freed Kraft from any tobacco-related liability that Altria may be found guilty of post-spinoff. It also eliminated a significant layer of management which made it easier for Kraft to improve its sluggish sales.Focusing on sharpening its brand portfolio Kraft sold off its hot cereals business in 2007. The $200 million sale to B&G Foods included two old favorites Cream of Wheat and Cream of Rice. It also sold its Fruit2O and Veryfine juice brands and operations to Sunny Delight Beverages.

As part of its plan to offer new product categories Kraft entered the lucrative and popular pre-made salad market in 2007 with the introduction of South Beach Living brand chicken-salad kits.

Adding more on the expansion front Kraft bought the Spanish and Portuguese operations of United Biscuits that year; the deal returned to Kraft the rights to Nabisco trademarks such as Oreo Ritz and Chips Ahoy! in Europe the Middle East and Africa.

Kraft further expanded its foreign operations with its 2007 purchase of the cookie/biscuit business of Groupe Danone for some $7.6 billion. The purchase gave the company brands such as LU Petit Ecolier and Crème Roulée and made biscuits (cookies to us Yanks) the company's largest global business. It also added the Tiger and Prince brands to its Egyptian portfolio.

Billionaire Warren Buffett acquired a small percentage of Kraft in 2007 (less than 5% at the time) joining the also famously rich and famous-on-Wall Street corporate raiders Nelson Peltz (whose estimated Kraft holdings are 3%) and Carl Icahn (who owns about 3%) in ownership of the Velveeta vendor. Peltz and Ichan are typically activist investors making suggestions regarding company operations. Peltz has suggested that Kraft concentrate on its core brands as well as undertake divestitures to fund overseas expansion.

Kraft acquiesced to Peltz on one front agreeing with his investment operations collectively known as Trian Partners by adding two directors (selected by the company and supported by Trian) to its board in 2007. Kraft also signed a "standstill" agreement with Trian agreeing to support the board's full list of nominees at Kraft's next two annual meetings.

Late in 2007 Kraft announced the re-rebranding of its South Beach products from South Beach Diet to South Beach Living saying that it wanted to capture a more positive image for the products. That year the company also sold its Veryfine juice and Fruit2O water brands and operations to Sunny Delight company.

Kraft's 2008 sale of its slow-growing Post (Shredded Wheat Raisin Bran Honeycomb Grape-Nuts Pebbles and others) to Ralcorp a maker of private-label cereals and other foods is part of Kraft's strategy to pare down its brand offerings and concentrate on high-yield products. Ralcorp paid some $1.6 billion in stock for the acquisition. Post is the #3 US cereal maker by sales after General Mills and Kellogg. Post brought in more than $1 billion for Kraft in both 2006 and 2007.

In February 2010 Kraft acquired Cadbury for about $19 billion of which 60% was cash and 40% was stock. A majority of Cadbury's shareholders (almost 72% according to Kraft) accepted the offer effectively making Cadbury part of Kraft.

In October 2012 Kraft Foods split into two companies: a global snacks business Mondelez International and Kraft Foods Group (formerly Kraft Foods North America).

EXECUTIVES

Chairman and CEO, Irene B. Rosenfeld, age 61, $1,600,000 total compensation

EVP Human Resources, Karen J. May, age 57

EVP and CFO, Brian T. Gladden, age 50, $197,260 total compensation

EVP and President Latin America, Gustavo H. Abelenda, age 54, $650,000 total compensation

EVP Strategic Initiatives, David A. (Dave) Brearton, age 55, $750,000 total compensation

President Chocolate Asia-Pacific, Manu Anand

EVP and President Eastern Europe Middle East and Africa (EEMEA), Lawrence MacDougall, age 58

EVP Integrated Supply Chain, Daniel Myers, age 60

EVP and President Asia Pacific Eastern Europe Middle East and Africa (EEMEA), Timothy P. (Tim) Cofer, age 46, $815,068 total compensation

Chief Growth Officer, Mark Clouse, $746,589 total compensation

EVP Strategy, Tracey Belcourt
EVP and President Europe, Hubert Weber
Managing Director India, Chandramouli (Mouli) Venkatesan
EVP and General Counsel, Gerhard (Gerd) Pleuhs
President US Sales, Valerie Oswalt
EVP and President North America, Roberto Marques, age 50
President International Client Carat, Navaneeta Das
Managing Director Gulf and Pakistan, Alan Smith
President Cheese Grocery and Beverages Eastern Europe Middle East and Africa, Vishal Tikku
Managing Director Saudi Arabia, Jose Esteve
Managing Director Growth Markets EEMEA, Vanya Panayotova
Managing Director Pakistan, Usman Muneer
Senior Vice President Marketing Strategy And Comm, Dana Anderson
Executive Vice President; President Cheese and Dairy, Howard Friedman
Customer Vice President Sales Planning and Insights Central Area, Michael (Mel) Culver
Vice President Marketing Kraft Singles Natural Cheese And Velveeta, Mary Sagritanti
Vice President Human Resources Sales Commercial and Corporate, John (Jack) Markham
Senior Vice President Finance, Luca Zaramella
Vice President Sales Cheese and Dairy Business Unit, Dave Cichocki
Vice President ZBB Cost Leadership and Value Realization, Joher Akolawala
Senior Vice President Human Resources, Andrew (Andy) Gibson
Vice President and Corporate Controller, Melinda Whittington
Vice President Of Corporate Marketing Development, Ken Freeman
Vice President Operations CandD, James (Jamie) Durkin
Vice President Finance Sales Foodservice and Growth Channels, Conrad Wiederhold
Division Vice President Sales, Doug Skeoch
Senior Vice President And Corporate Controller, Kim Jones
Vice President Information Technology, Connie Frick
Vice President Marketing, Nina Barton
Vice President Customer Service and Logistics, Sandra Evett
Vice President Finance Integrated Supply Chain, Cheryl Duffy-Geiger
Vice Presiofent Human Resources, Gregory Lawless
Customer Vice President, Gregg Sappenfield
Vice President Broker Sales, Mario Miller
Senior Vice President Cis, Nick Sorvillo
Vice President Sales Drugs, Walt Zola
Vice President Human Resources Grocery Bu And Kraft University Relations, Ginny Packer
National Account Manager, Howard Gasser
Vice President and Treasurer, Matt West
National Sales Manager, Kathy Romine
Senior Vice President Cheese and Dairy Marketing, Matthew (Matt) Wohl
Customer Vice President Industry Development, Mike Ridenour
Vice President Sales Value, Modestino Mele
Executive Vice President RDQ and I, Chuck Davis
Vice President of Media Data and Customer Relationship Managment, Bob Rupczynski
Vice President Marketing Oscar Mayer Brands, Mike Donohoe
Executive Vice President Research Development Quality and Innovation, Charles (Chas) Davis
Group Vice President Kraft Foods Inc President Kraft Canada, Irene Rosenfield
Executive Vice President and Chief Marketing Officer, Mary West
Vice President, W Vernon

Vice President Foodservice Enhancers and Snack Nuts Integrated Supply Chain, Joe Metzger
Executive Vice President Global Supply Chain, Franz-Josef Vogelsang
Vice President Customer Target, David (Dave) Cichocki
Corporate Vice President of Human Resources, Karen May2
Executive Vice President Corporate Legal Affairs, Kim Rucker
Auditors: PRICEWATERHOUSECOOPERS LLP

LOCATIONS

HQ: Mondelez International Inc
   Three Parkway North, Deerfield, IL 60015
Phone: 847 943-4000
Web: www.mondelezinternational.com

2014 Sales

	$ mil.	% of total
US	6,143	18
International	28,101	82
Total	**34,244**	**100**

PRODUCTS/OPERATIONS

2014 Sales

	$ mil.	% of total
Biscuits	11,509	34
Chocolate	9,381	26
Beverages	5,678	17
Gum & Candy	4,660	14
Cheese & grocery	3,016	9
Total	**34,244**	**100**

Selected Products and Brands

Biscuits
  Barni
  BelVita
  Chips Ahoy
  Club Social
  Oreo
  Tuc
Chocolate
  Cadbury
  Lacta
  Milka
  Toblerone
Gum & Candy
  Chicklets
  Halls
  Stride
  Trident
Other
  Philadelphia (cream cheese)

COMPETITORS

Associated British Foods	Lindt & Sprngli
Clif Bar	Maple Leaf Foods
Community Coffee	Mars Incorporated
Dairy Crest	Michael Foods
Dairy Farmers of America	Mott' s
Dr Pepper Snapple Group	Mrs. Fields
Fehr Foods	Naked Juice
Frito-Lay	Nestl©
Fromageries Bel	Newman' s Own
Galaxy Nutritional Foods	Otis Spunkmeyer
General Mills	Parmalat Canada
Hershey	Pepperidge Farm
Kellogg	PowerBar
Kellogg U.S. Snacks	Russell Hobbs
Kerry Group	Smucker
Keurig Green Mountain	Snapple
	Snyder' s-Lance
	Unilever
	Voortman Cookies
	WhiteWave

HISTORICAL FINANCIALS

Company Type: Public

Income Statement

FYE: December 31

	REVENUE ($ mil.)	NET INCOME ($ mil.)	NET PROFIT MARGIN	EMPLOYEES
12/14	34,244	2,184	6.4%	104,000
12/13	35,299	3,915	11.1%	107,000
12/12	35,015	3,028	8.6%	110,000
12/11	54,365	3,527	6.5%	126,000
12/10	49,207	4,114	8.4%	127,000
Annual Growth	**(8.7%)**	**(14.6%)**	**—**	**(4.9%)**

2014 Year-End Financials

Debt ratio: 24.99%
Return on equity: 7.27%
Cash ($ mil.): 1,631
Current ratio: 0.84
Long-term debt ($ mil.): 13,865

No. of shares (mil.): 1,663
Dividends
   Yield: 1.6%
   Payout: 29.9%
Market value ($ mil.): 60,432

	STOCK PRICE ($) FY Close	P/E High/Low	PER SHARE ($)		
			Earnings	Dividends	Book Value
12/14	36.33	30 25	1.28	0.58	16.68
12/13	35.30	16 12	2.19	0.54	18.98
12/12	25.45	25 15	1.69	1.00	18.12
12/11	37.36	19 15	1.99	1.16	19.92
12/10	31.51	14 11	2.39	1.16	20.50
Annual Growth	**3.6%**	**— —**	**(14.5%)**	**(15.9%)**	**(5.0%)**

Monsanto Co.

An ear of corn the size of a Trident missile? Not quite but Monsanto is all about bioengineered crops. The company helps farmers grow more crops like corn cotton oilseeds and vegetables by applying biotechnology and genomics to seeds and herbicides. It produces genetically altered seeds that tolerate Roundup (its flagship product and the world's #1 herbicide) and resist bugs. The company also produces Asgrow DEKALB Deltapine and Seminis seeds. During the past decade Monsanto re-made itself into a seed and biotech company as opposed to one focused on agrochemicals a transition that was sped up with the acquisition of Delta and Pine Land.

HISTORY

Realizing he had only a German source for saccharin and foreseeing growing US demand for the product in 1901 drug firm buyer John Queeny spent $5000 to found Monsanto Chemical Works (using his wife's maiden name) to make saccharin in St. Louis. Monsanto soon added caffeine vanillin antiseptic phenol and aspirin; it went public in 1927.

Queeny's son Edgar became president in 1928. He branched out into rubber additives and plastics through acquisitions. In 1943 Monsanto began making styrene monomer used to produce the US Army's first synthetic rubber tires.

Monsanto and American Viscose joined forces to form synthetic-fiber firm Chemstrand in 1949 (Monsanto bought it in 1961). Chemstrand also developed Acrilan fibers (1952) and the synthetic surface AstroTurf (first used commercially in Houston's Astrodome 1966). In 1954 Monsanto and Bayer formed a joint venture to develop urethane foams (sold to Bayer 1967). Monsanto debuted the herbicides Lasso (1969) and Roundup (1973) and stopped making saccharin in 1972.

Monsanto bought drugmaker G. D. Searle (founded 1868) in 1985 inheriting lawsuits relating to its Copper-7 contraceptive IUD. It also got the rights to artificial sweetener aspartame (NutraSweet). In 1993 Monsanto bought Chevron's Ortho lawn and garden business for $416 million. It launched its first biotech product (to increase milk yields) the next year.

Searle's Robert Shapiro became CEO in 1995 and set out to create genetically altered foods. That year Monsanto bought Merck's specialty chemicals unit Syntex (birth-control pills) and 50% of biotech firm Calgene (it bought the rest in 1997).

In 1996 Monsanto bought a stake in DEKALB Genetics (it bought the rest in 1998) and introduced a Roundup-tolerant soybean. It bought Holden's Foundation Seeds (corn seed) in 1997 and spun off chemicals unit Solutia. Purchases in 1998 included the seed business of Cargill and the wheat-breeding business of Unilever (UK). It also said it would buy #1 cottonseed producer Delta and Pine Land but that deal was delayed by regulators and dropped altogether in 1999.

After calling off a $35 million merger with drugmaker American Home Products in 1998 Monsanto laid off workers and sold Ortho to The Scotts Company (now Scotts Miracle-Gro).

In 1999 Monsanto launched Celebrex an arthritis drug that set new prescription records. Meanwhile concerns about genetically modified foods prompted bans in the UK and Brazil (and later in other countries). Negative public reaction led Monsanto to stop developing seeds with a terminator gene that rendered them sterile.

To pay for acquisitions Monsanto sold its pharmaceutical intermediates business to Great Lakes Chemical (now Chemtura) and its algins (derived from algae) food ingredients business to International Specialty Products. Late in 1999 activists stepped up protests over bioengineered crops and lawyers filed a class-action suit alleging inadequate testing and unfair price influence.

Monsanto merged with Pharmacia & Upjohn in 2000 and the new entity Pharmacia Corporation (with Monsanto now a wholly owned subsidiary) set about restructuring selling Monsanto's NutraSweet Equal and Canderel sweeteners (in part to a group led by Michael Dell) as well as its biogums (food texturing and processing) business. The "new" Monsanto is focused solely on using advanced technology to grow better crops –the pharmaceutical and other operations of the old Monsanto have been assumed by Pharmacia. Consumer apprehension over so-called "Frankenfoods" and the like prompted Pharmacia to spin off about 15% of Monsanto to the public in 2000; the company spun off the remainder as a dividend to shareholders in 2002.

After two disappointing years of results in December 2002 CEO Hendrik Verfaillie resigned and chairman Frank AtLee assumed the position. In late May 2003 COO Hugh Grant was named president and CEO with AtLee returning to chair the board of directors. Less than a month later Grant initiated a reorganization of Monsanto placing focus on growing the company's seed business and redefining its goals and strategies for public acceptance of biotechnology. The company elected Grant chairman at its annual meeting in October of that year with AtLee staying on the board as a director.

The company formed American Seeds Inc. in 2004 as a holding company that would acquire and build up regional seed businesses. First on its plate was Indiana seed company Channel Bio Corp. which Monsanto bought for $120 million. Channel has three main lines of seed –Crow's Hybrid Corn Company Midwest Genetics Seed Genetics Inc. and Wilson Seeds –and 2% of the US corn seed market. Monsanto already had 14% of that

market. It added Nebraskan corn-seed producer NC Hybrids in 2005 at a price of $40 million.

In a more significant move Monsanto announced in the spring of 2005 that it had acquired fruit and vegetable seed maker Seminis for about $1.4 billion in cash and assumed debt. Seminis is among the world's largest fruit and vegetable seed producers with about 3500 varieties of seed sold in more than 150 countries. It continues as a wholly owned subsidiary of Monsanto with its own management remaining in place. The deal furthered the company's recent emphasis on growing its seeds business and changing its focus from agricultural chemicals.

Many analysts saw the move for Seminis as an indication Monsanto was trying to broaden its seed portfolio to give the company something to balance out its biotech business. Perhaps but Monsanto isn't content with the size of its GM seed business either. Later in 2005 the company purchased the cotton business of Emergent Genetics for $300 million. That business gives Monsanto a foothold in the cotton seed business similar to its existing corn and soybean product lines. Emergent ranked among the top three cotton seed companies with 12% of the market.

In 2010 Monsanto completed the purchase of the Chesterfield Village Research Center located in Chesterfield Missouri from Pfizer. In 2011 the company acquired Beeologics a start-up company engaged in the R&D of biological tools to provide targeted pest and disease control (with a focus on bee health).

In January 2013 Monsanto acquired select assets of privately-held Agradis a California firm focused on developing and commercializing products to improve crop production using new scientific and technology advances in genomics.

EXECUTIVES

EVP and CTO, Robert T. Fraley, age 62, $646,372 total compensation
Chairman and CEO, Hugh Grant, age 56, $1,506,269 total compensation
EVP Human Resources, Steven C. Mizell, age 55
President and COO, Brett D. Begemann, age 54, $761,404 total compensation
EVP Global Strategy, Kerry J. Preete, age 55
EVP Secretary and General Counsel, David F. Snively, age 61, $593,077 total compensation
SVP and CFO, Pierre Courduroux, age 50, $593,077 total compensation
VP International Row Crops and Vegetables, Michael J. Frank, age 50
VP Americas Row Crops, Michael K. Stern, age 53
President Monsanto European Row Crops, Leticia Gon alves
VP and CEO Climate Corporation, David A. Friedberg, age 34
Vice President Of Global Technology Transfer, Stefan Bledig
Vice-president Finance, Susie Cyr
Vice President Of Commercial Operations, Lisa Safarian
Vice President Information Technology Enterprise Services, Aldo Noseda
Medical Director, Craig Weitbrecht
Executive Vice President, Michael (Mel) Scallan
Vice President Product Management, Jim Bowman
Vice President And Chief Intellectual Property Pro, Scott Baucum
National Account Manager, Marty Krebs
Vice President, Greg Herman
Reg Vice President Finance Bh, Mike Edgerton
Vice President Programs and President Elect, Jeffrey G (Jeff) Mudd
National Accounts Manager, Kathy Peterson
Vice President Controller, Nicole Ringerberg
Vice President Finance, Mike Demarco

Vice President Global Marketing, Kathryn Olson
Vice President, Natalie Dinicola
Vice President President, Michael Horak
Vice President of External Affairs, Jerry Glover
Vice President Operations, Domenico Maturana
Vice President, Francisco Diaz
Vice President of Seeds and Traits Manufacturing, Mark Martino
Senior Vice President, Reed Herzig
Vice President Of Research, William Hugie
Vice President Information Technology, Harry Wiegert
Vice President Human Resources, Nancy Wolfe
Vice President Marketing, Tom Wilson
Vice President Technology, Ganesh Kishore
Vice President Global Talent Acquisit, Melissa Bharper
Vice President Global Talent Management Hrit Analytics And Benefits, Ray Kleeman
Vice President Global Integrated Farming Systems and Precision Planting Co., John (Jack) Raines
Vice President International Business, Atul Sharma
Senior Vice President Secretary General Counsel, R William Ide
Vice President Science Policy, Jerry J Hjelle
Secretary, Layne Prescott
Abm, Kevin Leak
Board Member, Joni Barron
Auditors: DELOITTE & TOUCHE LLP

LOCATIONS

HQ: Monsanto Co.
  800 North Lindbergh Blvd., St. Louis, MO 63167
Phone: 314 694-1000   **Fax:** 314 694-1057
Web: www.monsanto.com

2015 Sales

	$ mil.	% of total
US	8,612	57
Europe & Africa	1,834	12
Brazil	1,725	11
Argentina	871	6
Asia/Pacific	686	5
Canada	601	4
Mexico	537	4
Other	135	1
Total	**15,001**	**100**

PRODUCTS/OPERATIONS

2015 Sales

	$ mil.	% of total
Seeds & genomics		
Corn seed & traits	5,953	40
Soybean seed & traits	2,276	15
Vegetable seeds	816	5
Cotton seed & traits	523	3
Other crop seed & traits	675	5
Agricultural productivity	4,758	32
Total	**15,001**	**100**

Selected Brands

Crop protection
  Bullet
  Degree Brands
  Field Master
  Harness Brands
  INTRRO
  Landmaster II
  Lariat
  Maverick
  Micro-Tech
  PARRLAY
  Roundup PowerMAX
  Roundup WeatherMAX
  Roundup with CROPSHIELD Formulas
  RT 3
Industrial turf and ornamental
  AquaMaster
  Campaign
  Certainty Turf Herbicide

Outrider
QuikPRO
Roundup Original MAX
Roundup Pro
Roundup ProConcentrate
Roundup ProDry
Input traits
  Bollgard II
  Bollgard II Cotton with Roundup Ready Flex
  Roundup Ready Canola
  Roundup Ready Corn 2
  Roundup Ready Flex Cotton
  Roundup Ready Soybeans
  YieldGard Corn Borer
  YieldGard Plus
  YieldGard Plus with Roundup Ready Corn 2
  YieldGard Rootworm
  YieldGard Rootworm with Roundup Ready Corn 2
  YieldGard VT
Output traits
  Processor Preferred
  High Extractable Corn
  I-85 Program
  Vistive
Seed
  Asgrow
  DEKALB
  Interstate Seed
  Deltapine
  NC Hybrid

Selected Subsidiaries

Alellyx S.A.
American Seeds LLC
Asgrow Seed Company LLC
CanaVialis S.A. (Brazil)
Corn States LLC
Seminis Vegetable Seeds Inc.
WestBred LLC

COMPETITORS

ADM	Nippon Soda
BASF SE	Origin Agritech
Bayer CropScience	Pfister Hybrid Corn
Dow AgroSciences	Pioneer Hi-Bred
DuPont Agriculture	Sakata Seed
FMC	Scotts Miracle-Gro
GROWMARK	Syngenta
NC Hybrids	Syngenta Seeds

HISTORICAL FINANCIALS

Company Type: Public

Income Statement

FYE: August 31

	REVENUE ($ mil.)	NET INCOME ($ mil.)	NET PROFIT MARGIN	EMPLOYEES
08/15	15,001	2,314	15.4%	25,500
08/14	15,855	2,740	17.3%	27,000
08/13	14,861	2,482	16.7%	26,200
08/12	13,504	2,045	15.1%	26,000
08/11	11,822	1,607	13.6%	26,100
Annual Growth	6.1%	9.5%	—	(0.6%)

2015 Year-End Financials

Debt ratio: 41.26%
Return on equity: 31.13%
Cash ($ mil.): 3,701
Current ratio: 2.05
Long-term debt ($ mil.): 8,429

No. of shares (mil.): 467
Dividends
  Yield: 2.0%
  Payout: 35.1%
Market value ($ mil.): 45,691

	STOCK PRICE ($) FY Close	P/E High/Low	PER SHARE ($) Earnings	Dividends	Book Value
08/15	97.65	26 18	4.81	1.96	14.94
08/14	115.65	24 19	5.22	1.72	16.23
08/13	97.89	23 18	4.60	1.50	23.74
08/12	87.11	23 16	3.79	1.20	22.14
08/11	68.93	25 16	2.96	1.12	21.57
Annual Growth	9.1%	— —	12.9%	15.0%	(8.8%)

Morgan Stanley

One of the world's top investment banks Morgan Stanley serves up a smorgasbord of financial services. The company operates in three primary business segments: institutional securities (capital raising corporate lending financial advisory services for corporate and institutional investors); wealth management group (brokerage and investment advisory services financial planning for individual investors and businesses); and investment management (services and products including alternative investments equity fixed income; merchant banking; investment activities). Morgan Stanley has a presence in more than 40 nations serving corporate institutional government and individual clients.

HISTORY

In 1934 the Glass-Steagall Act required the J. P. Morgan bank (now part of JPMorgan Chase & Co.) to sell its securities-related activities. The next year Henry Morgan Harold Stanley and others established Morgan Stanley as an investment bank. Capitalizing on old ties to major corporations the firm handled $1 billion in issues its first year. By 1941 when it joined the NYSE it had managed 25% of all bond issues underwritten since Glass-Steagall took effect.

In the 1950s Morgan Stanley was known for handling large issues alone. Clients included General Motors U.S. Steel General Electric and DuPont. The firm avoided the merger wave of the 1960s but in the early 1970s it formed Wall Street's first mergers and acquisitions (M&A) department. In 1974 Morgan Stanley handled its first hostile takeover International Nickel's (now Vale Inco) buy of ESB the world's #1 battery maker.

Morgan Stanley went public in 1986. It escaped the carnage of the 1987 crash but a lawsuit arising from investor dissatisfaction with its M&A and LBO activities during that period lasted well into the 1990s.

By 1994 it was talking to possible merger mates including Dean Witter and finally merged with Dean Witter Discover in 1997 creating Morgan Stanley Dean Witter & Co. The San Francisco brokerage founded by Dean Witter in 1924 had remained regional for 40 years serving wealthy customers. In 1977 the firm merged with Reynolds Securities another regional retail brokerage started by Richard Reynolds Jr. the son of the founder of Reynolds Metals (now part of Alcoa) and grandnephew of the founder of R.J. Reynolds Tobacco. The new company Dean Witter Reynolds became the #2 US brokerage after Merrill Lynch and one of the top 10 US underwriters.

Dean Witter needed capital in the early 1980s and sold itself to Sears which hoped to turn it into a financial Allstate. Sears put in a retail-oriented management team and tried to shoehorn Dean Witter into in-store brokerages. Sears' indifference to the investment side hobbled operations.

The Discover card introduced by Sears and Dean Witter in 1986 was a hit but by the late 1980s it was obvious Sears would never be a financial giant. The retailer spun off Allstate Insurance and the newly renamed Dean Witter Discover in 1993.

Amazingly all but six of Morgan Stanley's 3700 World Trade Center employees survived the September 11 2001 terrorist attack on the towers. Hoping to capitalize on deregulations and privatizations in Europe as well as the rise of the individual investor Morgan Stanley acquired UK-based private bank Quilter & Co. in 2001 (then later sold

it to Citigroup in 2006). Also that year the firm dropped the public use of "Dean Witter" in 2001 for promotional purposes and then dropped it completely in 2002.

When regulatory scrutiny fell on the mutual fund industry Morgan Stanley was charged with failing to adequately disclose the incentives its brokers and managers received for selling certain funds. In 2003 the firm agreed to pay a $50 million fine and adopt a "plain English" approach to informing investors about its product fees and broker compensation.

In mid-2004 the firm agreed to pay $54 million to settle a sex discrimination lawsuit filed on behalf of more than 300 female employees who claimed they were denied promotions and salary raises.

Unhappy with the firm's performance eight former Morgan Stanley executives (dubbed the Group of Eight) publicly called for the ouster of chairman and CEO Philip Purcell in 2005; Purcell was replaced by John Mack. That same year a jury ordered Morgan Stanley to pay more than $1.5 billion to Ronald Perelman now the chairman of cosmetics giant Revlon. (Morgan Stanley in 2003 rejected an offer from Perelman to settle the dispute for $20 million.) Perelman contended that Morgan Stanley withheld knowledge of massive accounting fraud at appliance maker Sunbeam when he sold his camping gear firm Coleman to that company for some $1.5 billion in cash and stock in 1998; a Florida appeals court overturned the verdict in 2007.

In 2006 the firm agreed to pay a $15 million fine to settle charges that it was uncooperative and did not produce documents during investigations performed by the Securities and Exchange Commission (SEC). In addition the company settled charges (while not pleading guilty) that it falsely claimed to arbitration claimants and regulators that it lost e-mails on September 11 2001; it agreed to pay $12.5 million in 2007.

Morgan Stanley had been one of the largest credit card issuers through Discover Financial Services. However it spun those operations off in 2007. Discover was the last remnant of the company's merger with the venerable Dean Witter at the end of the previous century.

After the company wrote down more than $9 billion in mortgage-related investments in 2007 it was compelled to sell part of itself to an investment arm of the Chinese government China Investment Corp. for some $5 billion in order to raise capital. The equity units included in the deal could be converted to a nearly 10% stake in Morgan Stanley.

As its traditional investment banking business faced hard times Morgan Stanley increasingly focused on private equity investing. In 2008 the company's Infrastructure unit teamed up with Ontario Teachers' Pension Plan to acquire electrical services provider SAESA the Chilean subsidiary of Public Service Enterprise Group. In 2007 Morgan Stanley teamed up with Apax Partners Worldwide to buy insurance brokerage Hub International. The previous year Morgan Stanley acquired TransMontaigne a Denver-based oil and gas transportation company (sold in 2014) and Heidmar Group a Connecticut-based marine transportation and logistics firm (it later sold Heidmar's lightering business).

In order to shore up the big banks during the financial crisis the US government invested $250 billion in healthy banks to help them jumpstart their operations; Morgan Stanley received about $10 billion of that. The cash —part of the $700 billion taxpayer-fueled bailout in 2008 —came with several stipulations including restrictions on executive pay and the order to use the funds not hoard them. Deciding it didn't need the money that badly Morgan Stanley repaid the $10 billion in 2009. The company announced in late 2008 that it would cut its staff by 10% in an effort to reduce costs.

Also in 2008 the Federal Reserve mandated that Morgan Stanley and Goldman Sachs (the other remaining independent bulge-bracket US investment bank) convert to a bank holding company structure. The structure subjected them to tighter scrutiny but enabled them to acquire a commercial bank to shore up their balance sheets if need be. The move came after rivals Bear Stearns Merrill Lynch and Lehman Brothers were either acquired or went bankrupt.

In 2009 Morgan Stanley sold its remaining stake in investment analysis and market index firm MSCI to raise capital. The deal brought the company some $625 million.

Morgan Stanley also shook up its top leadership. John Mack stepped down as CEO in early 2010; he remained chairman but stepped down at the end of 2011. James Gorman the firm's co-president succeeded Mack at the helm of the company and as chairman. The change marked a significant shift for Morgan Stanley as it scaled back its operations in riskier proprietary trading.

Morgan Stanley's Asian operations got a boost in 2011 when regulators in China gave the go-ahead for the company to begin establishing operations there. It launched a joint securities venture with China Fortune Securities later that year; Morgan Stanley owns a third of the business the maximum stake allowed. China is a strategic market for growth for the company as are the emerging economies of Brazil and India.

The company in 2012 sold its Quilter wealth management division which serves the UK's mass-wealth market to private equity firm Bridgepoint Capital to focus on its wealthiest clients and institutional investors.

EXECUTIVES

Chairman and CEO, James P. Gorman, age 57, $1,500,000 total compensation
EVP and COO, James A. (Jim) Rosenthal, age 61, $1,000,000 total compensation
Global Co-Head Investment Banking, Franck Petitgas
President, Colm Kelleher, age 58, $6,795,386 total compensation
Co-Chief Operating Officer of Institutional Securities, Andy Saperstein
Global Head of Sales and Trading, Ted Pick
EVP and CFO, Jonathan Pruzan, age 47
Co-head Global Healthcare Banking, Michele Colocci
Head of Consulting Group, James J. (Jim) Tracy
EVP and Chief Risk Officer, Keishi Hotsuki, age 52
Global Co-Head of Investment Banking, Mark Eichorn
Global Co-Head of Fixed Income, Michael Heaney
Global Co-Head of Fixed Income, Robert Rooney
Co-Chief Operating Officer of Institutional Securities, Clare Woodman
Head Morgan Stanley Private Wealth Management, Vince Lumia
Head Capital Markets, Elizabeth Dennis
Global Operations Officer Investment Banking Division, John Collins
Chairman Investment Banking, Clint Gartin
First Vice President, Brian Peter
Senior Vice President Wealth Management, Shawn Landau
Vice President, Joel Thompson
Vice President Head of Risk and Control Product Group, Michael (Mel) Tessler
Senior Vice President investments, Howard Perkins
Vice President, Vinay Prabhu
First Vice President, Eric Gottlieb
Vice President Digital Strategy and Customer Innovation, Richard (Dick) Vong

Vice President Financial Planning Specialist, David (Dave) Yost
Assoc Vice President Financial Advisor, Ted Tenney
Portfolio Management Director Vice President Wealth Management, Martin (Marti) Pawelec
Vice President Wealth Management, Kevin Giddens
First Vice President Financial Advisor, Maurice Altshuler
Assistant Vice President Repurchase Management, Ranju Rahil
Senior Vice President Portfolio Management Director, Michael (Mel) Warr
Vice President Financial Advisor, Stuart (Stu) Munro
Vice President, Kevin Barry
First Vice President Branch Manager, Todd Emily
Senior Vice President and Family Wealth Director, Randy Levitt
Product Controller Vice President, Diana Lau
Senior Vice President Wealth Management, Jorey Bernstein
Vice President, LI Xiao
Senior Vice President, Spencer Larson
Associate Vice President, Christopher M (Chris) Lucero
Vice President, Sergio Lazzara
Senior Vice President, Al Haddad
Vice President Wealth Management Resident Mana, Timothy (Tim) Ely
Second Vice President Wealth Management Morgan, John (Jack) Ayers
Vice President Financial Advisor, Michael (Mel) Souza
Senior Vice President Wealth Management Financial Advisor Financial Planning Specialist, Branko Gegich
Vice President Of Learning and Development, Theresa Dinh
Vice President, Michael (Mel) Wong
Vice President In Senior Relationship Management, Tiffany Fung
Vice President Financial Advisor Retirement Planni, Bruce Donaghy
Vice President, Tracy Solley
Vice President, Lesley (Les) Matthews
Vice President Property Trading, Asif Khan
Vice President, Desiree Ally
Senior Vice President Investments; Financial Advisor, Douglas (Doug) Ruby
Wealth Advisor Associate Vice President, Paul Urbanek
Vice President Morgan Stanley Smith Barney, Richard Zinman
Vice President Of Technology, Lawrence Soohoo
Vice President Morgan Stanley Operations Risk And, Michelle (Mitch) Cuilla
Senior Vice President And Senior Financial Advisor, Lee Corey
First Vice President Wealth Advisor, Robyn Redfield
Vice President Senior Investment Management Cons, Anthony David
Vice President Director Of Community Affairs, Joan Steinberg
Senior Vice President Greater Pittsburgh Complex Manager, Robert (Bob) Meredith
Senior Vice President Of Client Services Nationa, Richard (Dick) French
First Vice President, David Bartoli
Senior Vice President Financial Advisor, Ralph Colo
Vice President And Financial Advisor, Charles (Chas) Walz
Vice President, Andrew (Andy) Earls
Vice President of Morgan Stanley and is based in New York, Adam Shaw
Senior Vice President For Investments, David Napolitano
Senior Vice President, Ted Hart

Senior Vice President Financial Advisor, Herman Bates
Vice President Morgan Stanley Japan, Rolands Vilums
Senior Vice President Of The Ledoux Greer Group, Bruce Ledoux
Vice President, Daniel (Dan) Nito
Vice President, Antonio Musumeci
Vice President Wired Infrastructure, Joaquin David
Vice President Global Wealth Management Group (GWMG), Reginald (Reg) Garner
First Vice President Financial Advisor, Dick Breining
Vice President Strategic Investments Group, Jorge Lopez-Aranda
Senior Vice President Portfolio Manager Wealth Advisor, Frank Corrigan
Vice President IT, Diane Kennelly
Vice President IT, Suzanne Burke
Vice President, Charles Friedman
Vice President Enterprise Data and Services, Jose Pimentel
Vice President, Geoffrey Burke
Vice President, Brian Saltzman
Vice President, Ruben Badar
Vice President, Duncan Fudge
Vice President Senior Portfolio Manager Financial Advisor, Roger Johnson
Vice President Private Banking, Todd Allen
Vice President Talent Management Information Technology, Mary Ellen Keller
Vice President, Andy Jaglall
Vice President Information Technology, Hernan Martinez
Vice President Controller And Principal Account Off, Roberto Nunez
National Account Manager, Rosie Bailey
Vice President Wealth Management, John Park
Senior Vice President, Bill Elliot
Vice President Unix And Storage Operations, Peter Hollaubek
Senior Vice President, Wes Gates
Vice President Operations, Richard Linkens
Vice President Securities Reference Data Production Management, Shirish Naik
First Vice President, Daniel Kreer
Vice President Information Technology, Anne Egan
Vice President Of Operations, Kuen Doo
Senior Vice President, John Zitzmann
Vice President, Jason Drumheller
Senior Vice President, David Norton
Vice President Investment Advisor Research, Brian Glanz
Vice President Enterprise Web Operations, Nicholas Romanelli
Vice President Information Technology, David Kempster
Vice President Head of Strategy for Human Resources and Corporate Technology, Priya Shah
Vice President Assistant Complex Manager Financi, Frank Ro
First Vice President, Thomas Niles
Vice President Strategic Infrastructure Team, Tina Shah
First Vice President, Ladonna Giachino
Fixed Income Technology Vice President, Adam Anderson
Vice President Commodities Operations, Brent Masucci
Vice President Of Operations, Ehab Aziz
Vice President, Kate Alleyn
Second Vice President Wealth Management, Mark Roycroft
Vice President Corporate and Post Trade Technology, Mohan Longia
Headquarters Assistant Vice President, George Faas
Vice President Corporate Technology, David (Dave) Daniels

Vice President Enterprise Infrastructure Cost Transparency Business Analyst, Cindy Lam

First Vice President Financial Advisor, James (Jamie) Ritchie

First Vice President, Matthew Koch

Senior Vice President And Financial Advisor, Anthony Brock

Senior Vice President Financial Advanced, Stan Alpert

Vice President Private Banker, John Feeney

First Vice President, Thomas Tazza

Senior Vice President Financial Advisor, Michael Gates

Senior Vice President, Eric Boory

Vice President Wealth Advisor, Vitia Kozielski

Senior Vice President, David Sonnenschein

Vice President Technology and Data Management, Wayne Westervelt

Senior Vice President, Chet Ringeisen

Senior Vice President Senior Portfolio Manager, Bradley Forman

Vice President Db2 Database Architect, Jack Rajpurohit

Second Vice President Financial Advisor, Timothy Owings

Senior Vice President Wealth Advisor, Dan Anderson

Vice President Information Technology Department, Francis Rial

Vice President Employment Tax Compliance, Ionel Raducanu

First Vice President, William (Bill) Dredge

Senior Vice President Wealth Advisor, Rick Hughes

Vice President Operations, Andrew Becker

Associate Vice President, Harrison Hill

Senior Vice President for Global Wealth Management, Chris Corona

Auditors: Deloitte & Touche LLP

LOCATIONS

HQ: Morgan Stanley
1585 Broadway, New York, NY 10036
Phone: 212 761-4000
Web: www.morganstanley.com

2014 Sales

	% of total
Americas	73
EMEA	14
Asia-Pacific	13
Total	**100**

PRODUCTS/OPERATIONS

2014 Sales

	$ mil.	% of total
Interest income	5,413	14
Non-interest income		
Asset management distribution and administration fees	10,570	28
Trading	9	25
Investment banking	5,948	16
Commission and fees	4,713	12
Investments	836	2
Others	1,096	3
Total	**37,953**	**100**

2014 Sales

	% of total
Institutional Securities	49
Wealth Management	43
Investment Management	8
Eliminations	-
Total	**100**

COMPETITORS

Brown Brothers Harriman	MF Global
CIBC	Marsh & McLennan
Charles Schwab	Merrill Lynch
Citigroup	Nomura Securities
	Oppenheimer Holdings

Citigroup Global Markets
Deutsche Bank
FMR
Franklin Templeton
Goldman Sachs
JPMorgan Chase
Lehman Brothers
Raymond James Financial
State Street
T. Rowe Price
TD Bank
UBS
Wells Fargo Securities

HISTORICAL FINANCIALS

Company Type: Public

Income Statement

FYE: December 31

	ASSETS ($ mil.)	NET INCOME ($ mil.)	INCOME AS % OF ASSETS	EMPLOYEES
12/14	801,510	3,467	0.4%	55,802
12/13	832,702	2,932	0.4%	55,794
12/12	780,960	68	0.0%	57,061
12/11	749,898	4,110	0.5%	61,899
12/10	807,698	4,703	0.6%	62,542
Annual Growth	**(0.2%)**	**(7.3%)**	**—**	**(2.8%)**

2014 Year-End Financials

Debt ratio: 19.06%
Return on equity: 5.07%
Cash ($ mil.): 87,591
Current ratio: —
Long-term debt ($ mil.): —
No. of shares (mil.): 1,950
Dividends
  Yield: 0.9%
  Payout: 13.9%
Market value ($ mil.): 75,698

	STOCK PRICE ($) FY Close	P/E High/Low		PER SHARE ($) Earnings	Dividends	Book Value
12/14	38.80	24	17	1.60	0.35	36.34
12/13	31.36	23	14	1.36	0.20	33.89
12/12	19.12	—	—	(0.02)	0.20	31.46
12/11	15.13	25	10	1.23	0.20	32.20
12/10	27.21	12	9	2.63	0.20	37.84
Annual Growth	**9.3%**		**—**	**(11.7%)**	**15.0%**	**(1.0%)**

Mosaic Co (The)

Lots of little pieces have joined together to form The Mosaic Company's big picture. The company ranks as one of the world's largest makers of phosphate and potash crop nutrients. Mosaic's potash operations position the company at the top of the industry along with Uralkali and PotashCorp. Mosaic ranks as the second-largest potash fertilizer company in North America (behind PotashCorp). Mosaic's potash mines are located in Canada and the US. The company does more than 50% of its business outside North America where India and Brazil are its biggest markets.

Geographic Reach

The company serves customers in 40 countries. It mines phosphate rock in Florida and processes rock into finished phosphate products at facilities in Florida and Louisiana. It mines potash in Saskatchewan New Mexico and Michigan.

Mosaic owns port facilities in Savage Minnesota as well as warehouse distribution facilities in Pekin Illinois; Henderson Kentucky; Melbourne Kentucky; and Houston Texas. Its distribution operations also include leased distribution space or contractual throughput agreements in other key geographical areas such as California Florida Illinois Indiana Iowa Kentucky Louisiana Maryland Minnesota Nebraska New York North Dakota Pennsylvania and Texas.

Its Canadian customers include independent dealers and national accounts. Mosaic also leases

and owns warehouses in Manitoba Ontario Quebec and Saskatchewan.

Its distribution activities include sales offices port terminals and warehouses in the US Canada and several other countries. In addition Mosaic's international distribution activities include blending bagging and production facilities in Argentina Brazil Chile China and India.

Operations

In fiscal 2014 the company produced 9.3 million tons of phosphate nutrients.

The Phosphates Segment produced 8.7 million tons of concentrated phosphate crop nutrients during 2014. Both its phosphates and potash production account for approximately 14% of world annual output and 71% of North American annual production.

Sales and Marketing

The company sells phosphate-based crop nutrients and animal feed ingredients throughout North America and internationally. Its distribution activities include sales offices port terminals and warehouses in the US Canada and several other key international countries. In addition international distribution activities include blending bagging or production facilities in Brazil China India and Paraguay. Outside of the US and Canada they market their Phosphates segments products through our own international distribution activities as well as a sales force focused on geographies outside of North America.Potash Segment sell potash throughout North America and internationally principally as fertilizer but also for use in industrial applications and to a lesser degree as animal feed ingredients.

Mosaic markets its Canadian potash outside of the US and Canada through Canpotex Limited an export association. It also markets much of its phosphates through the Phosphate Chemicals Export Association (PhosChem). During fiscal 2014 PhosChem marketed about 67% of Mosaic's phosphate export sales volume.

Financial Performance

In fiscal 2014 Mosaic's net revenues declined by 9% led by and 18% drop in potash sales due to lower prices.That year the company's net income dropped by 46% as the result of lower revenues.Mosaic's cash from operating activities increased 22% due to a change in accounts payable accrued liabilities and other current assets ans non-current assets.

Strategy

The company is looking to continue to expand its potash production facilities in line with its view of the long-term fundamentals of increasing global demand in that business. Mosaic's plans to increase annual operational capacity for finished product of 5 million tons.

Following a 2014 deal with Saudi Arabian Mining Company and Saudi Basic Industries Corporation to form a joint venture the company announced plans to further expand its MicroEssentials capacity (its premium micronutrient product) through an integrated phosphate production facility in Saudi Arabia. Global demand for MicroEssentials continues to grow and exceed their current production capacity. When the current expansion is complete it will have capacity to produce 3.5 million tonnes of the product. Mosaic owns 25% of the joint venture and markets 25% of its production. The joint venture offers an additional source of phosphate crop nutrients and facilitate access to key customers in India and elsewhere in Asia.The potash expansion projects in Saskatchewan Canada are proceeding toward completion with highly successful capacity proving runs completed at Esterhazy and Colonsay and with the K3 mine shafts at Esterhazy nearing their final depth.In 2014 Mosaic took steps to optimize itr business portfolio by exiting the fertilizer distribution business in Chile and Argentina and stopped muriate of potash production at the Carlsbad New Mexico mine. That year the company sold its salt operations at the Hersey Michigan mine for $55 million. It also closed its low producing potash operations at Hersey allowing the company to focus on higher producing potash mines.

Mergers and Acquisitions

In 2013 the company acquired the phosphate business of CF Industries for $1.2 billion in cash plus $200 million to fund CF Industries' asset retirement obligation escrow. Ad part of the deal Mosaic gained the 22000-acre South Pasture phosphate mine and beneficiation plant in Hardee County Florida a phosphate manufacturing plant in Plant City Florida and an ammonia terminal and finished product warehouse facilities in Tampa. The CF Industries' facilities produce 1.8 million tonnes of phosphate fertilizer per year.

Company Background

In 2012 the company was seeking to take advantage of global growth in middle classes in emerging markets where higher per-capita incomes are driving the demand for more meat and dairy and the grain needed to produce them. It invested nearly $900 million in capital spending for potash expansions in 2012.

Mosaic also made gains in its phosphates business in 2011. It sold some of its operations in Brazil which helped fund an investment of another phosphates source in Peru that Mosaic believes will bolster the company's position as one of the world's leading integrated phosphate producers. Mosaic bought a 35% interest in a joint venture with Vale and Mitsui & Co. in the Miski Mayo mine in Peru for $385 million. Production of phosphate rock estimated at 4 million tons per year began that year.

Mosaic was originally created through the merger of IMC Global and Cargill's former crop nutrition unit in 2004. In 2011 Cargill divested its 64% of Mosaic shares to its shareholders and debtholders in a $24 billion transaction splitting off Mosaic and ending its status as a majority-owned company.

EXECUTIVES

EVP and CFO, Richard L. (Rich) Mack, age 47, $579,167 total compensation

SVP Phosphate Operations, Gary (Bo) Davis, age 62, $450,000 total compensation

President and CEO, James (Joc) O'Rourke, age 54, $730,000 total compensation

SVP Potash Operations, Walter F. (Walt) Precourt, age 50

Assistant Vice President Business Development, Courtney Mattson

Vice President of Phosphate Concentrate Operations, Joe Kline

Vice President Reseller Sales, Bill Moulin

Vice President Of Human Resources, Katherine (Kate) Hoien

Executive Vice President Business Development and Strategy, Lawrence Stranghoener

Vice President, Jack Murphy

Vice President Client Services, Angie Damron-Beene

Vice President of Human Resources Solutions, Kelli Jorgensen

Senior Vice President Human Resources, Corrine Ricard

Senior Vice President Human Resources, Sue Loerts

Chairman, Robert L. Lumpkins, age 71

Auditors: KPMG LLP

LOCATIONS

HQ: Mosaic Co (The)
3033 Campus Drive, Suite E490, Plymouth, MN 55441
Phone: 800 918-8270   **Fax:** 763 577-2990
Web: www.mosaicco.com

2013 Sales

	% of total
United States	38
Brazil	21
Canpotex	12
Canada	7
India	5
Argentina	3
Japan	2
Australia	2
China	2
Others	8
Total	**100**

PRODUCTS/OPERATIONS

2013 Sales

	$ mil.	% of total
Phosphates	6,494	65
Potash	3,529	35
Corporate & other	(49.8)	-
Total	**9,974**	**100**

2013 Sales

	% of total
Phosphate Crop Nutrients	41
Potash Crop Nutrients	34
Crop Nutrient Blends	15
Other	10
Total	**100**

Premium Crop Nutrients
MicroEssentials® SZ™
MicroEssentials® S15™
MicroEssentials® S10™
K-Mag® Granular
K-Mag® Premium
K-Mag® Special Standard
K-Mag® Standard
Pegasus® Fine
Pegasus® Granular
Potash
  White Stan
  Red Granul
  Red Standa
  Crystal Gr
Crystal Turf 150
Phosphates
Diammonium Phosphate (DAP) 18-46-0
Monoammonium Phosphate (MAP) 11-52-0
Powdered MAP
Feed Ingredients
Biofos®
Dyna-K®
Dynamate®
Dyna-K White®
Nexfos®
Industrial Products
FSA Products
Hydrofluorosilicic Acid (FSA or HFS)
Potash Products
  White Fine
  White Gran
White Industrial High Quality
White Industrial Special
  Red Standa

COMPETITORS

Agrium	K+S
Arab Potash	Potash Corp
CF Industries	Sinofert
Israel Chemicals	Uralkali

HISTORICAL FINANCIALS

Company Type: Public

Income Statement

FYE: December 31

	REVENUE ($ mil.)	NET INCOME ($ mil.)	NET PROFIT MARGIN	EMPLOYEES
12/14	9,055	1,028	11.4%	9,100
12/13*	4,765	340	7.1%	8,200
05/13	9,974	1,888	18.9%	8,400
05/12	11,107	1,930	17.4%	8,000
05/11	9,937	2,514	25.3%	7,700
Annual Growth	(2.3%)	(20.0%)	—	4.3%

*Fiscal year change

2014 Year-End Financials

Debt ratio: 20.96%
Return on equity: 9.35%
Cash ($ mil.): 2,374
Current ratio: 3.35
Long-term debt ($ mil.): 3,778

No. of shares (mil.): 367
Dividends
  Yield: 2.1%
  Payout: 37.3%
Market value ($ mil.): 16,778

	STOCK PRICE ($) FY Close	P/E High/Low	PER SHARE ($) Earnings	Dividends	Book Value
12/14	45.65	19 15	2.68	1.00	29.12
12/13*	47.27	80 51	0.80	1.00	26.53
05/13	60.82	14 10	4.42	1.00	31.53
05/12	47.68	16 10	4.42	0.28	28.16
05/11	70.85	16 7	5.62	0.20	26.07
Annual Growth	(10.4%)	— —	(16.9%)	49.5%	2.8%

*Fiscal year change

Motorola Solutions Inc.

Motorola has returned to its roots of providing communications equipment for public safety. The company sold its enterprise unit which provided rugged mobile computers rugged mobile computers tablets and barcode scanners in 2014 and will focus on its public safety and commercial customers. The enterprise sale came three years after Motorola got out of the mobile phone business. Now the company designs and makes two-way radios and wireless broadband products used in private voice and data networks and public safety communications systems. More than half of sales come from customers in the US. The company traces its roots to the 1930s when it made radios for police cars.

Operations

Motorola's Products segment offers an extensive portfolio of infrastructure devices accessories and software and account for 65% of sales. Its primary customers are government public safety and first-responder agencies municipalities and commercial and industrial customers who operate private communications networks and manage a mobile work force.

The Services segment accounting for the remaining 35% of sales provides a range of services for Motorola customers.

Geographic Reach

The company has a presence in the Americas Europe the Middle East Africa and the Asia/Pacific. Motorola posted higher sales in North America Latin America and Europe in 2013 but they dropped in the Asia Pacific and Middle East region. The US is the company's biggest market accounting for about 54% of its sales. It operates four major facilities for manufacturing and distribution in the US Malaysia Mexico and Germany. Motorola outsources about a third of its manufacturing to third-parties outside the US.

Sales and Marketing

The US government is Motorola's biggest customer with multiple agencies making up 8% of company revenue. Other major customer groups include education health care hospitality human services manufacturing petrochemical transportation and logistics and utilities. Advertising spending dropped by about a third to $61 million in 2014.

Financial Performance

Motorola restated earnings to take into account the sale of its enterprise business. In 2014 revenue fell 32% to $5.8 billion from 2013 with a decrease in the Products segment on lower devices and system sales in the Americas. Profit jumped 18% to $1.3 billion in 2014 from 2013 buoyed by a $2 billion gain from the discontinued enterprise operations. Cash flow from operations turned negative in 2014 at $685 million from a positive cash flow of $944 million in 2013.

Strategy

Motorola narrowed its focus to communications for public safety and commercial users when it sold its enterprise business to Zebra Technologies. The move cut Motorola's revenue to about $6 billion. The company wants to expand the product it sells for first-responders police and fire departments and public safety-oriented other government functions to other markets with similar communications needs. Markets include hospitality mining classified communications military transportation education and utility.

The company has made strategic investments in several companies to extend its technologies into new areas. The companies include CyPhy Works a developer of advanced unmanned aerial vehicles (UAVs) also known as drones. The investment is part of Motorola's strategy to connect its with real-time data and intelligence. Other companies in which Motorola has invested are VocalZoom a developer of sensors for speech enhancement and SceneDoc maker of mobile investigative software.

Motorola expanded its line to include digital radio platforms that offer multi-site coverage. With its $36 million acquisition of Twisted Pair Solutions in 2013 the company extended its MOTOTRBO radio to commercial users of smartphones internationally. Moving a portion of the 40 million radios in the global market still running on analog technology to digital technology is in the company's plans.

In services the company has expanded lifecycle management contracts which enable customers to receive software updates and provide continuing revenue to Motorola.

Motorola is investing in public safety broadband networks based on the LTE standard. After delays as standards were finalized the company expects to see higher public safety LTE revenues in 2015 with international customers leading the way.

Motorola received a $1 billion infusion in summer 2015 with an investment by Silver Lake Partners a private equity firm.

Mergers and Acquisitions

In 2015 Motorola expanded its cloud computing offerings with its acquisition of PublicEngines a privately held provider of cloud-based crime analysis predictive policing and citizen engagement capabilities. Also in 2015. Motorola bought Emergency CallWorks a privately held provider of Next-Generation 9-1-1 (NG9-1-1) call-taking software for public safety. Emergency CallWorks' product includes multimedia information into a 911 call.

HISTORY

Motorola got its start in 1928 when Paul Galvin then 33 founded Galvin Manufacturing in Chicago to make battery eliminators so early radios could run on household current instead of batteries. The following year Galvin began making car radio receivers and trying to develop a mobile radio for the police. In 1940 the company developed the first handheld two-way radio for the US Army.

In 1947 Galvin renamed the company Motorola after its car radios. In the late 1950s Motorola started making integrated circuits and microprocessors stepping outside its auto industry mainstay. When Galvin died in 1959 his son Robert became CEO. The company's purchase that year of a hospital communications systems maker led it to produce some of the first pagers.

Over the years the company has expanded and contracted evening launching a satellite system to handle its communications.m An early leader in cell phones the company failed to make the transition to smart phone. Eventually the company divested parts of the business to again focus on communications oriented toward public safety applications.

EXECUTIVES

Chairman and CEO, Gregory Q. (Greg) Brown, age 56, $1,287,500 total compensation
SVP and Chief Innovation Officer, Eduardo Conrado, age 48, $424,346 total compensation
SVP Global Solutions and Services, Bruce Brda, age 54
EVP and President Sales and Marketing, Mark F. Moon, age 51, $669,712 total compensation
SVP and CTO, Paul Steinberg, age 54
EVP and CFO, Gino A. Bonanotte, age 51, $615,481 total compensation
EVP General Counsel and Chief Administrative Officer, Mark S. Hacker, $488,942 total compensation
Executive Vice President President Global Custo, Joseph M (Jo) Guglielmi
Vice President Global Government Affairs And Country Management, George Spas
Corporate Vice President Finance, Gary Tatje
Vice President Human Resources, Marty Rogers
MSSSI Vice President, Patrick (Paddy) Glennon
Vice President and Director, Ken Notter
Vice President Legal and Government Affairs, Luisa Gamboa
Vice President Motorola Solutions Credit Company, David (Dave) Kliefoth
Vice President Global Services and Portfolio Management, Mike Cost
Vice President Global Services and Solutions, Greg Billings
MSSI Vice President North America Vertex Standard Brands, Michael (Mel) Gray
Appointed Vice President, Debora Courtright
Vice President Stategic Accounts, William Murphy
Vice President Operations Services and Solutions, Clint Quanstrom
Senior Vice President Sales NA, Jack Molloy
Territory Vice President, Mark Schmidl
Vice President Sales Operations and Learning, Chris Lonnett
Mssi Vice President Director of Sales, Derek Phipps
Territory Vice President, John Willett
Corp. Vice President, Kelly Kirwan
Vice President, Bob Wartmann
Vice President, Dan Delaney
Vice President of Marketing South East, Michael (Mel) Roth
Vice President Engineering, Ted Kozlowski
Vice President Of Environment Health And Safety, Jodi Shapiro
Vice President And Director Of Sales Nyc, James Munro
Corporate Vice President Assistant General Counse, Jonathan Meyer

National Account Manager and Corporate Sales Manager, Stuart (Stu) Jackson
Vice President, John Otten
Vice President Purchasing, Sheetal Shah
Vice President Of Sales, Edward Fuerst
Vice President Mssi, Mike Devente
Vice President Business Development, Robert Bixler
Vice President MSSI, Rishi Bhaskar
Senior Vice President Publishing and Media Relations, Jeffrey D (Jeff) Madsen
Vice President Supply Chain, Mike Fleming
Executive Vice President Director of Human Resources, Glenn A Gienko
Vice President Motorola Solutions Sales Services Inc., Bill Jacob
Vice President Psion Sales, Frederic Bismuth
Manager Global Government Relations and Treasurer Motorola Solutions Political Action Committee, Paul Newman
Secretary To Vice President of Human Resources, Laura Davis
Auditors: KPMG LLP

LOCATIONS

HQ: Motorola Solutions Inc.
  1303 East Algonquin Road, Schaumburg, IL 60196
Phone: 847 576-5000   **Fax:** 847 576-3477
Web: www.motorolasolutions.com

2014 Sales

	$ mil.	% of total
US	3,354	57
China	160	3
UK	128	2
Israel	95	2
Other countries	2,144	36
Total	**5,881**	**100**

PRODUCTS/OPERATIONS

2014 Sales

	$ mil.	% of total
Products	3,807	65
Services	2,074	35
Total	**5,881**	**100**

Selected Products and Services

Devices
  Mobile computers
  Mobile-to-mobile wireless modules
  Public safety LTE infrastructure devices and services (handheld USB modem vehicle modem)
  Radio-frequency identification products (RFID) and accessories
  Two-way radios and pagers
  Two-way radio accessories
Networks
  Mobile broadband (public safety LTE)
  Private broadband networks
  Wireless broadband networks
Services
  Enterprise
  Enterprise video solutions
  Integrated enterprise communications
  Managed network infrastructure
  Managed security and compliance
  Supply chain visibility solutions
  Government and Public Safety
  Advanced video security systems
  Complex network design and integration
  Interoperability and unified communications
  Next-generation command and control
  Public safety managed services
Software
  Application development framework
  Mobility software
  Network design software
  Public sector applications
  Support and help desk applications
Systems
  Dispatch systems
  Enterprise voice systems
  SCADA Systems (real-time facilities monitoring and control)

HISTORICAL FINANCIALS

Company Type: Public

Income Statement

FYE: December 31

	REVENUE ($ mil.)	NET INCOME ($ mil.)	NET PROFIT MARGIN	EMPLOYEES
12/14	5,881	1,299	22.1%	15,000
12/13	8,696	1,099	12.6%	21,000
12/12	8,698	881	10.1%	22,000
12/11	8,203	1,158	14.1%	23,000
12/10	19,282	633	3.3%	51,000
Annual Growth	(25.7%)	19.7%	—	(26.4%)

2014 Year-End Financials

Debt ratio: 32.62%
Return on equity: 40.63%
Cash ($ mil.): 3,954
Current ratio: 3.06
Long-term debt ($ mil.): 3,396

No. of shares (mil.): 219
Dividends
Yield: 1.9%
Payout: 23.2%
Market value ($ mil.): 14,744

	STOCK PRICE ($) FY Close	P/E High/Low	PER SHARE ($) Earnings	Dividends	Book Value
12/14	67.08	13 11	5.29	1.30	12.44
12/13	67.50	16 13	4.06	1.14	14.38
12/12	55.68	18 15	2.96	0.96	11.83
12/11	46.29	14 3	3.41	0.44	16.36
12/10	9.07	5 3	1.87	0.00	32.37
Annual Growth	64.9%	— —	29.7%	—	(21.3%)

MRC Global Inc

MRC Global (formerly McJunkin Red Man) is one of the world's largest suppliers of parts and supplies used by energy and industrial customers. Operating from 400-plus locations predominantly in North America the company distributes more than 200000 pipe valves and fittings (PVF) as well as general and specialty products. A major slice of MRC Global's sales comes from maintenance repair and operations (MRO) contracts including procurement warehousing and inventory management. Core customers are oil and gas exploration and production giants as well as transmission and storage oil refining and petrochemical processing companies such as BP Exxon Mobil and Valero.

Geographic Reach

The company serves more than 18000 customers through more than 400 service locations throughout North America Europe Asia and Australia. Its US network is made up of 150 branches and eight distribution centers.

In 2014 the US accounted for 76% of the company's total revenues.

Operations

MRC Global provides pipe valves fittings and related products and services to the energy and industrial sectors across each of the upstream (exploration production and extraction of underground oil and gas) midstream (gathering and transmission of oil and gas gas utilities and the storage and distribution of oil and gas) and downstream (crude oil refining and petrochemical pro-

cessing) markets through their distribution operations located throughout the world.

The company has three geographical operating segments: US Canada and International. The US segment maintains distribution operations throughout the country with concentrations in the most active oil and natural gas producing regions. The network is comprised of 134 branch locations 9 distribution centers 13 valve automation service centers and 102 third-party pipe yards. This segment accounted for 74% of MRC Global's revenues in 2014.The Canadian segment has distribution operations throughout western Canada with concentrations in Alberta and western Saskatchewan. It has 40 branch locations 1 distribution center 1 valve automation service center and 21 third-party pipe yards. This segment represented 11% of the company's total revenues in 2014.The International segment (15% of revenues) includes 61 branch locations located throughout Europe Asia Australasia and the Middle East with 7 distribution centers in the UK Norway Singapore the Netherlands the UAE and Australia. It also maintains 20 valve automation service centers in Europe Asia and Australia.

MRC Global has set its sights on becoming the world's largest distributor of PVF and related products. To this end MRC Global promotes itself as a one-stop shop for PVF purchases. Its operations couple sole-source supply agreements with MRO contracts throughout all phases of work in oil and gas and other process industries.

Sales and Marketing

The company distributes products to a wide variety of end-users. It has operations in 20 countries and direct sales activities in 90. Their broad distribution network and customer base allow them to capitalize on their extensive inventory offering. MRC Global also sells its products via its inside sales force. They also have regional sales teams based in their core geographic regions.Its principal customers are companies active in the upstream midstream and downstream sectors of the oil and gas industry as well as in other industrial and energy sectors.It directly sells in 45 countries. In 2014 MRC Global's 25 largest customers represented 47% of total sales.

Financial Performance

In 2014 MRC Global's net revenues increased by 3%.Revenues from US sales grew thanks to organic growth across major product lines and sectors with the emphasis being in valves and line pipe in the upstream and midstream sectors responsive to growth in customer capital spending increases in rig count and well completions as well as market share gains.   Canadian sales decreased due to the divestiture of the company's progressive cavity pump distribution business and the decline of the Canadian dollar relative to the U. dollar.Revenues from international sales increased primarily as the result of the acquisitions of Stream Flangefitt Stainless Ltd. MSD and Hypteck which collectively added $320.2 million in revenues in2014.In 2014 MRC Global net income decreased by 5% due to higher selling general and administrative expenses (including an increase in expenses related to severance and related costs and charges related to the cancellation of executive employment agreements) and other expenses.Other expenses increased due to a charge related to the divestiture of their Canadian PCP business $4.1 million related to the disposition of the rolled and welded pipe business $2.5 million of foreign currency losses and $1.1 million in expense related to the change in the fair value of derivatives.

In 2014 cash from operating activities decreased by 133% due to the changes in accounts receivable inventories and accounts payable excluding the impact of acquisitions.MRC Global experienced a significant increase in accounts receivable dur-

ing 2014 due to a growth in business activity throughout the year combined with the impact of the timing of payments from various large customers.

Strategy

MRC Global emerged from 2014 with a much stronger geographic diversification and is continuing to focus on organic growth and timely execution of its international strategy. To support its customers in producing regions the company continues to extend the reach and efficiency of hub-and-spoke system of Regional Distribution Centers in 2015 extending its operations in Pittsburgh and opening new centers in Rotterdam and in the UAE. Activity in US shale plays is expected to continue to drive midstream business although at a slower pace. The downstream market gives the company the potential for more than $100 billion in projects for planned expansion and new build-out of petrochemical facilities. MRC Global's one-stop shop strategy is underpinned both by efforts to augment its customer base including penetration of new geographies neighboring markets (such as crude oil refining and petrochemical processing) and acquisitions that complement the company's core activities.In 2014 the company divested its Canadian PCP business to Europump which Halliburton subsequently purchased.

Mergers and Acquisitions

As part of its strategy to expand globally in key markets and be the world's leading PVF distributor in 2014 the company acquired Norway-based Stream AS for $260 million. Stream is the leading PVF distributor and provider of flow control products solutions and services to the offshore oil and gas industry on the Norwegian Continental Shelf. That year a subsidiary also acquired Hypteck is a Norwegian provider of instrumentation and process control products to the offshore marine and onshore industries with a focus on the Norwegian Continental Shelf.In 2014 MRC Global's Singapore subsidiary MRC Transmark Pte. Ltd. bought MSD Engineering (Pte) Limited a major distributor and regional service provider of valve and valve automation solutions to customers in Singapore Brunei China Malaysia Indonesia Thailand Vietnam and Taiwan. MSD Engineering had 2013 sales of $26 million and now operates as MRC MSD Engineering.To support our customers' growth in a major oil US producing region in 2013 the company acquired Texas-based Dan H. Brown Inc. D/B/A Flow Control Products (Flow Control). Founded in 1981 Flow Control is a leading provider of pneumatic electric and electro-hydraulic valve automation packages and related field support to the Permian Basin energy industry. To boost its position in the Permian Basin in 2013 the company also bought Production Specialty Services which has service 18 locations.

Company Background

In a major deal in 2012 the company signed five-year deal to supply Royal Dutch Shell with valves and automation services. The contract covers Shell's upstream midstream and downstream project and maintenance repair and operations requirements in North America Europe Asia Australia the Middle East and Africa. It also covers carbon steel stainless and alloy pipe fittings and flanges in the US and stainless steel and alloy pipe fittings and flanges in Canada.

The company acquired Sydney-based OneSteel Piping Systems a division of OneSteel Limited's distribution business in 2012 for about $67.7 million. OPS now operates as MRC Piping Systems Australia. The unit is a top PVF supplier and distributor to oil and gas mining and mineral processing markets throughout Australia.

In 2011 MRC Global acquired the majority of the operating assets of Cherokee Oklahoma based Chaparral Supply LLC a wholly owned subsidiary of SandRidge Energy Inc. Chaparral Supply provides pipe valve and fitting products and oilfield supplies to its parent.

In 2011 the company acquired Stainless Pipe and Fittings Australia the largest distributor of stainless steel piping products in the southern hemisphere. The buy extends MRC Global's holdings in premier pipe fittings and flange operations and complements its 2009 purchase of Transmark the leading valve distributor in the eastern hemisphere.

MRC Global went public in 2012. Its IPO raised $477.3 million which the company used to pay down debt.

MRC Global evolved from a merger financed by Goldman Sachs through PVF Holdings in 2007; the deal brought together industrial and oilfield pipe suppliers McJunkin Corporation of Charleston West Virginia and Red Man Pipe & Supply of Tulsa Oklahoma.

EXECUTIVES

SVP Energy Tubular Products, James E. (Jim) Dionisio, age 64
Chairman President and CEO, Andrew R. (Andy) Lane, age 56, $850,000 total compensation
SVP Business Development, Rory M. Isaac, age 65, $406,115 total compensation
EVP Corporate Affairs General Counsel and Corporate Secretary, Daniel J. (Dan) Churay, age 53, $396,538 total compensation
SVP Valves Fittings Flanges Alloys and Oilfield Supply, Gary A. Ittner, age 63, $397,500 total compensation
EVP and CFO, James E. (Jim) Braun, age 55, $471,538 total compensation
SVP and CIO, Nasser A. Farshchian
SVP Europe Region, Steiner Aasland
SVP Asia Pacific and Middle East Region, John Bowhay
Senior Vice President Business Developer, Dave Dillon
Vice President Human Resources, Jason Graves
Corporate Vice President, Tommy Bruns
Vice President Investor Relations, Cinda Bowling
Corporate Vice President, Stuart Spears
Vice President Business Development, Joe Barnes
Auditors: Ernst & Young LLP

LOCATIONS

HQ: MRC Global Inc
2 Houston Center, 909 Fannin Street, Suite 3100, Houston, TX 77010
Phone: 877 294-7574
Web: www.mrcglobal.com

2014 Sales

	% of total
US	74
Canada	11
International	15
Total	**100**

PRODUCTS/OPERATIONS

2014 Sales

	% of total
Valves fittings flanges & other products	
Valves & specialty products	32
Carbon steel fittings and flanges and stainless steel and alloy pipe and fittings	21
Other	18
Energy carbon steel tubular products	
Line pipe	19
Oil country tubular goods	10
Total	**100**

2014 Sales

	$ mil.	% of total
Upstream	2,806	47
Midstream	1,654	28
Downstream and other industries	1,472	25
Total	**5,993**	**100**

Selected Products

General Products
  Bolted couplings
  Compression couplings
  Cut gaskets
  Grooved piping systems
  Machine bolts
  Pipe hangers and supports
  Pressfit systems
  Repair clamps
  Sheet packing
  Spiral wound gaskets
  Stud bolts and hex nuts
Instrumentation
  Diaphragm seals
  Pressure gauges
  RTD' s (resistance temperature detectors) and thermocouples
  Thermometers
  Thermowells
Oilfield products
  API (American Petroleum Institute) couplings
  Belts
  Chokes
  Clamps
  Hubs
  Liners
  Packing
  Polished rods
  Pony rods
  Pump units
  Pup joints
  Rod couplings
  Sheaves
  Stuffing boxes
  Sucker rods
  Well heads
Pipe Fittings and Flanges
  Fittings and flanges
  Butt weld fittings
  Cast fittings and flanges
  Forged fittings and flanges
  High yield fittings and flanges
  Outlet fittings
  Pipe and swaged nipples
  Sweat fittings
  Tube fittings and valves
  Pipe and tubing
  API line pipe
  Continuous weld pipe
  DSAW (double submerged arc welded)
  ERW (electric resistance welded)
  Exchanger tubing
  Flareweld pipe
  Instrumentation tubing
  Pressure tubing
  Seamless pipe
  Plastic lined products
  Kynar lined pipe and fittings
  Polypropylene lined pipe and fittings
  Teflon lined pipe and fittings
Steam Products
  Accessories
  Condensate pumps
  Controls and regulators
  Engineered products
  Eye wash stations
  Gauges and instrumentation
  Pre-insulated tubing
  Safety showers
  Steam traps
  Strainers
  Temperature measurement
  Valves
Valves and Automation
  Automation
  Electric multi-turn
  Electric quarter-turn
  High pressure gas actuation systems
  Hydraulic actuators
  Limit switches/position indicators
  Low pressure gas actuation systems
  Pneumatic multi-turn
  Pneumatic quarter-turn valves
  Positions
  Pressure switches
  Solenoid valves
  Ball valves
  Floating
  Metal seated
  Plastic lined
  Top Entry
  Trunnion
  "V" Port
  Butterfly valves
  High performance
  Plastic lined
  Triple offset
  Multi-turn valves
  Bellowseal valves
  Cryogenic valves
  Diaphragm valves
  HF acid valves
  Knife gate valves
  Needle valves
  Pressure seal valves
  Stop wafer and ANSI (American National Standards Institute) check
  Plug valves
  Lubricated
  Non-lubricated
  Plastic lined
  Quarter-turn valves

Selected Brands

MRC Mcjunkin Red Man Corporation
MRC Transmark
MRC SPC
MRC Piping Systems Australia

Selected Mergers and Acquisitions

COMPETITORS

Applied Industrial Technologies	National Oilwell Varco
Blue Tee	Piping & Equipment
Cameron International	W.W. Grainger
Ferguson Enterprises	Wilson
HD Supply	WinWholesale
Industrial Distribution Group	Wolseley
	Wrth Group

HISTORICAL FINANCIALS

Company Type: Public

Income Statement

FYE: December 31

	REVENUE ($ mil.)	NET INCOME ($ mil.)	NET PROFIT MARGIN	EMPLOYEES
12/14	5,933	144	2.4%	4,900
12/13	5,230	152	2.9%	5,150
12/12	5,570	117	2.1%	4,780
12/11	4,832	28	0.6%	4,100
12/10	3,845	(51)	—	—
Annual Growth	**11.5%**	—	—	—

2014 Year-End Financials

Debt ratio: 37.52%
Return on equity: 10.54%
Cash ($ mil.): 25
Current ratio: 2.83
Long-term debt ($ mil.): 1,445
No. of shares (mil.): 102
Dividends
  Yield: —
  Payout: —
Market value ($ mil.): 1,547

	STOCK PRICE ($) FY Close	P/E High/Low	PER SHARE ($) Earnings	Dividends	Book Value
12/14	15.15	23 10	1.40	0.00	13.69
12/13	32.26	22 16	1.48	0.00	13.13
12/12	27.78	23 16	1.22	0.00	11.68
Annual Growth	**(14.1%)**	— —	**3.5%**	—	**4.0%**

Murphy Oil Corp

Murphy's Law? Turn that oil into money. Newly minted as a pure-play upstream company Murphy Oil explores for and produces oil and gas —primarily in the US but also in Canada Malaysia and the UK. In 2014 the company reported undeveloped proved reserves of 336.2 million barrels of oil 105.6 million barrels of synthetic crude oil and 1.7 trillion cubic feet of natural gas. In 2013 Murphy Oil completed the separation of its US retail marketing operations with the spin-off of Murphy USA Inc. as a stand-alone company. It also began to sell its UK marketing and refining assets in 2014 in order to become an exploration and production player.

Geographic Reach

Murphy Oil has exploration and operations in Canada Malaysia Republic of the Congo the UK the US and a handful of other countries.

The company's exploration and production activities are subdivided into four geographic segments.US: The Eagle Ford Shale area of South Texas and in the deepwater Gulf of Mexico.Canada: Three significant non-operated asset (the Hibernia and Terra Nova field's offshore Newfoundland in the Jeanne d' Arc Basin and Syncrude Canada in northern Alberta; and interests in one wholly-owned heavy oil area and two wholly-owned significant natural gas areas in the Western Canadian Sedimentary Basin). Malaysia: Majority interests in eight separate production sharing contracts.All other countries: Australia Indonesia Vietnam Namibia and the Republic of the Congo.

Murphy Oil's more than 400 UK gas stations operated primarily under the MURCO brand. It also owned a refinery in Milford Haven Wales. The company's UK assets were in the process of being sold in 2014.

Operations

On the exploration and production side of the business the company has more than 16732 net acres of developed and undeveloped properties in 13 countries. In 2014 the company reported proved developed reserves of 218.5 million barrels of oil 105.6 million barrels of synthetic crude oil and 812.1 billion cubic feet of natural gas. Murphy Oil's 5% stake in Syncrude Canada helps diversify the company's oil holdings. Syncrude is the world's #1 producer of light sweet crude oil; the synthetic blend is refined into gasoline and various kinds of fuel as well as chemical feedstocks.

Financial Performance

In 2014 the company's net revenues increased by 2% due to higher oil and natural gas sales volumes partially offset by weaker crude oil sales prices.

Murphy Oil's net income decreased by 19% in 2014 due to the presence of other expenses primarily related to write-down in value of materials inventory associated with its Malaysia operations.The company's cash inflow decreased by 5% in 2014 due to changes in working capital.

Strategy

In a major strategic move to focus on oil and gas exploration and production Murphy Oil spun off Murphy USA in 2013 and exited its UK downstream operations in 2014. It sold its 400 MURCO branded gas stations in the UK and in 2015 was looking to sell its 130000 barrel-a-day refinery in Milford Haven Wales.

Company Background

As part of a strategic restructuring focused on exiting the refining business and to raise cash to pay down debt and to invest in its other core activities in 2011 the company sold its Superior Wisconsin refinery to Calumet Specialty Products Partners for $434 million. It also sold its refinery in Meraux Louisiana to Valero Energy for $585 million.

Boosting its exploration and production profile in 2011 the company acquired 156000 net acres of mineral rights in the northeastern British Columbia Montney area including Tupper and Tup-

per West and also acquired 146000 net acres of land in Southern Alberta that is prospective for light oil. That year it also signed a production sharing contract with Suriname's state oil company Staatsolie Maatschappij Suriname N.V. giving it 100% working interest and operatorship of Block 48 offshore Suriname.

Murphy Oil was incorporated in Louisiana in 1950 as Murphy Corporation.

EXECUTIVES

EVP and CFO, John W. Eckart, age 56, $447,367 total compensation

EVP and General Counsel, Walter K. Compton, age 52, $538,108 total compensation

President and CEO, Roger W. Jenkins, age 53, $1,295,833 total compensation

Vice President Corp Insurance, John (Jack) Dumas

Vice President World Wide Refining, Stephen (Steve) Hunkus

V Pres-treas, John (Jack) Gardner

Vice President Human Resources and Administration, Maria Martinez

Vice President, Bill Stobaugh

Vice President Manager Director, Connie Singleton

Vice President Planning and Services, Todd Montgomery

Chairman, Claiborne P. Deming, age 61

Secretary to Steven Cosse GC, Lydia Bates

Auditors: KPMG LLP

LOCATIONS

HQ: Murphy Oil Corp
200 Peach Street, P.O. Box 7000, El Dorado, AR 71730-7000
Phone: 870 862-6411   **Fax:** 870 864-3673
Web: www.murphyoilcorp.com

2013 Sales

	$ mil.	% of total
Malaysia	2,337	43
United States	1,798	33
Canada	1,150	21
Republic of the Congo	83	2
Others	20	1
Total	**5,390**	**100**

COMPETITORS

Apache	Nexen
BP	Noble Energy
Canadian Natural	Repsol
Chevron	Royal Dutch Shell
Encana	Suncor
Exxon Mobil	

HISTORICAL FINANCIALS

Company Type: Public

Income Statement

FYE: December 31

	REVENUE ($ mil.)	NET INCOME ($ mil.)	NET PROFIT MARGIN	EMPLOYEES
12/14	5,476	905	16.5%	1,712
12/13	5,390	1,123	20.8%	1,875
12/12	28,626	970	3.4%	9,185
12/11	27,745	872	3.1%	8,610
12/10	23,345	798	3.4%	8,994
Annual Growth	(30.4%)	3.2%	—	(33.9%)

2014 Year-End Financials

Debt ratio: 17.93%	No. of shares (mil.): 177
Return on equity: 10.55%	Dividends
Cash ($ mil.): 1,193	Yield: 2.6%
Current ratio: 1.04	Payout: 39.3%
Long-term debt ($ mil.): 2,536	Market value ($ mil.): 8,967

	STOCK PRICE ($) FY Close	P/E High/Low		PER SHARE ($) Earnings	Dividends	Book Value
12/14	50.52	13	9	5.03	1.33	48.30
12/13	64.88	12	10	5.94	1.25	46.87
12/12	59.55	13	9	4.99	3.68	46.91
12/11	55.74	17	9	4.49	1.10	45.31
12/10	74.55	18	12	4.13	1.05	42.52
Annual Growth	(9.3%)	—	—	5.1%	6.0%	3.2%

Murphy USA Inc

It may not be the biggest but Murphy USA (ticker symbol MUSA) is no mouse in the gas station market. Murphy USA markets refined products through its network of branded gasoline stations and convenience stores customers and unbranded wholesale customers in 23 southern and midwestern US states. The company's more than 1200 retail gas stations (more than 1000 of which are in Wal-Mart Supercenter parking lots) sell gas under the Murphy USA brand. The company owns the land underlying about 900 of the more than 1000 gas stations located in Wal-Mart lots and rented the rest. Formerly a wholly owned subsidiary of Murphy Oil it was spun off in 2013.

Change in Company Type

In 2013 Murphy Oil completed the spin-off of its US retail marketing business into an independent public company –Murphy USA Inc. The spin-off was achieved through the distribution to Murphy Oil's shareholders of one share of Murphy USA common stock for every four shares of Murphy Oil stock. It holds through its subsidiaries the US retail marketing business that was separated from its former parent company plus certain ethanol production facilities and other assets and liabilities of Murphy Oil that supported the activities of the US retail marketing operations.

Geographic Reach

Murphy USA has retail stations in 23 US states (primarily in the Southeast in Florida and Tennessee) as well as in the Southwest and the Midwest.

Operations

The company markets retail motor fuel products and convenience merchandise through its own chain of retail stations almost all of which are in close proximity to Wal-Mart stores. Its business also includes product supply and wholesale assets such as product distribution terminals and pipelines. The remainder of the parent's former ethanol segment (including an ethanol production facility in Hereford Texas is accounted for under "Corporate and other assets."Petroleum product sales accounted for 86% of the company's total revenues in 2013; Merchandise sales 12%; and Ethanol sales and other 2%.

Sales and Marketing

The sells gasoline under the Murphy USA and Murphy Express brands.

Financial Performance

Murphy USA's revenues declined by 6% in 2013 due to lower petroleum product sales due to lower retail fuel prices; partially offset by increased Merchandise sales and Ethanol sales and other. The decline in retail volumes (3% down on 2012) was due to significantly less price volatility year over year a decrease in the duration of the Wal-Mart discount program year over year and overall weaker consumer demand.However net income increased by more than 100% in 2013 thanks to a decrease in the purchase price of motor fuel for both the retail and wholesale locations; the absence of an impairment charge; increased gain on sale of its North Dakota crude supply assets; and increased income related to a gain on sale of the Hankinson ethanol facility.

Strategy

The company is looking to build additional retail gas stations at Wal-Mart Supercenters and other standalone locations. In 2013 the company opened its 1200th store in front of a Wal-Mart in the company's headquarters hometown of El Dorado Arkansas.

In 2012 it signed an agreement that allows the company to build 200 new sites at Wal-Mart locations over the next few years and paid $42 million in 2013 as a first installment on these land purchases. It continues to work with Walmart on the implementation and improvement of the fuel discount program as it believes it is an effective promotional tool for maximizing fuel volumes and investment returns.Murphy USA is also evaluating its kiosk strategy in an effort to maximize its site economics and return on investment. As part of that strategy it is refining its new 1200 sq. ft. format design to create a foundation to increase its higher-margin non-tobacco sales and diversify its merchandise offerings.It also focuses on improving its infrastructure to lower overhead costs and on long-term investment. It plans to continue to focus its product supply and wholesale efforts on activities that enhance its ability to be a low-price retail fuel leader by optimizing its fuel supply contracts to capitalize on market dynamics whenever possible and minimizing physical product supply and wholesale asset ownership.In an effort to exit non-core businesses in the fall of 2013 the company sold underperforming subsidiary Hankinson Renewable Energy LLC (which owns and operates the Hankinson North Dakota ethanol plant) to Guardian Hankinson LLC for $173 million.

Company Background

Boosting its customer offerings in 2010 the company teamed up with Western Union signing a deal to offer online money transfer services at its Murphy USA gas stations and Murphy Express convenience stores across the country.

As part of its former parent's decision to exit the refining business in 2011 MUSA sold its Superior Wisconsin refinery to Calumet Specialty Products Partners for $475 million. It also sold its refinery in Meraux Louisiana to Valero Energy for $625 million. The divestitures transformed MUSA into a pure gas station/convenience store company.

EXECUTIVES

VP and Treasurer, Mindy K. West, age 46

SVP Field Operations, Marn K. Cheng, age 49, $323,292 total compensation

SVP Retail Operations, Jeffrey A. (Jeff) Goodwin, age 56, $331,458 total compensation

President and CEO, R. Andrew Clyde, age 51, $818,750 total compensation

SVP General Counsel and Secretary, John A. Moore, age 47, $382,417 total compensation

Vice President And Controller, Donnie Smith

Chairman, R. Madison Murphy, age 57

Secretary, Tami Hendricks

Auditors: KPMG LLP

LOCATIONS

HQ: Murphy USA Inc
 200 Peach Street, El Dorado, AR 71730-5836
Phone: 870 875-7600
Web: www.murphyusa.com

PRODUCTS/OPERATIONS

2013 Sales

	$ mil.	% of total
Petroleum product sales	15,560	86
Merchandise sales	2,159	12
Ethanol sales & other	363	2
Total	**18,083**	**100**

2013 Stores

States	no. of stores
Texas	253
Florida	112
Tennessee	82
Georgia	81
North Carolina	75
Alabama	68
Arkansas	61
Lousiana	61
South Carolina	52
Oklahoma	50
Mississippi	50
Missouri	46
Ohio	42
Kentucky	39
Indiana	32
Illinois	26
Michigan	23
Iowa	21
New Mexico	9
Minnesota	7
Colorado	6
Virginia	6
Kansas	1
Total	**0**	**1,203**

COMPETITORS

7-Eleven	Hess Corporation
Alon Brands	QuikTrip
Chevron	Racetrac Petroleum
ConocoPhillips	Royal Dutch Shell
Couche-Tard	Valero Energy
Exxon Mobil	

HISTORICAL FINANCIALS

Company Type: Public

Income Statement

FYE: December 31

	REVENUE ($ mil.)	NET INCOME ($ mil.)	NET PROFIT MARGIN	EMPLOYEES
12/14	17,209	243	1.4%	9,450
12/13	18,083	235	1.3%	8,250
12/12	19,655	83	0.4%	7,900
12/11	19,273	324	1.7%	—
12/10	15,592	157	1.0%	—
Annual Growth	**2.5%**	**11.6%**	**—**	**—**

2014 Year-End Financials

Debt ratio: 25.46%	No. of shares (mil.): 45
Return on equity: 32.19%	Dividends
Cash ($ mil.): 328	Yield: —
Current ratio: 1.61	Payout: —
Long-term debt ($ mil.): 492	Market value ($ mil.): 3,148

	STOCK PRICE ($) FY Close	P/E High/Low		PER SHARE ($) Earnings	Dividends	Book Value
12/14	68.86	13	7	5.26	0.00	18.79
12/13	41.56	9	7	5.02	0.00	14.04
Annual Growth	**13.5%**	**—**	**—**	**1.2%**	**—**	**7.5%**

National Bank Holdings Corp

As seems only rational National Bank Holdings is the holding company for NBH which has more than 140 branches that operate as Bank Midwest in Kansas and Missouri under the Community Banks of Colorado and Bank of Choice banners in Colorado under the Community Banks of California banner in that state and as Hillcrest Bank in Texas and Colorado. Targeting small to medium-sized businesses and consumers the banks offer traditional checking and savings accounts as well as commercial and residential mortgages agricultural loans and commercial loans.

Geographic Reach

National Bank Holdings serves clients through a network of 97 banking centerswith the majority of those banking centers located in the greater Kansas City area and Colorado.

The bank serves small- to medium-sized businesses and consumers via its network of banking locations and through online and mobile banking products.

Operations

The company's primary operations are conducted through NBH Bank which provides a variety of banking products to both commercial and consumer clients. For 2013 it reported $4.9 billion in assets $1.9 billion in loans $3.8 billion in deposits and $897.8 million in shareholders' equity. Covered loans comprised 16.7% of the total loan portfolio compared to 33.2% in 2012.

Sales and Marketing

In 2013 National Bank Holdings posted $5.3 million for advertisements compared to $5.5 million in 2012.

Financial Performance

The company has reported a decline in revenues over the past few years. In 2013 revenues decreased by 20% due to lower interest and dividend income and non-interest income as the result of lower purchased loan balances coupled with lower yields earned on the non 310-30 loan portfolio and on the investment portfolio. Noninterest income decreased due to higher amortization of its FDIC indemnification asset.After experiencing net loss in 2012 due to huge increase in the non interest expenses as a result of increased salaries and benefits of the employees and real estate owned expenses in 2013 National Bank Holdings posted net income of $6.93 million(compared to net loss of $0.5 million in 2012). This was primarily due to a decrease in the provision for loan losses due to lower impairment charges on the ASC 310-30 loan pools thanks to gross cash flow improvements resulting from the company's re-measurement of expected future cash flows on those underlying pools coupled with improved credit quality metrics in the non 310-30 portfolio.In 2013 National Bank Holdings reported a cash outflow of $25.6 million (compared to cash outflow of $130.8 million in 2012) primarily due to increased income tax paid and increased depreciation and amortization.

Strategy

In 2013 the company announced that it will streamline its focus on serving its clients through full-service banking centers across its core geography of Colorado Kansas Missouri and Texas as well as through online and mobile banking channels. The move will result in the integration of its limited-service retirement center locations into its full-service banking center network as well as the exit of its limited presence in California.

Company Background

Formed in 2009 National Bank Holdings went public in 2012.

The company intends to use a portion of the proceeds from its IPO (more than $135 million) to acquire distressed banks and for general corporate purposes. Since 2009 National Bank Holdings has grown its presence in the central US through acquisitions of banks including those seized by the FDIC during the financial crisis in 2008. The company continues to look to its existing and new markets for acquisition opportunities.

Prior to its filing National Bank Holdings was minority-owned by a number of private shareholders and corporate entities including Taconic Capital Advisors Wellington Management and Paulson & Co.

EXECUTIVES

Chairman President and CEO, G. Timothy (Tim) Laney, age 55, $500,000 total compensation
Chief of Enterprise Technology & Integration and NBH Bank N.A. Midwest/ Texas Division President, Thomas M. (Tom) Metzger, $300,000 total compensation
Chief Financial Officer, Brian F. Lilly, age 56, $295,705 total compensation
Chief Risk Officer, Richard U. Newfield, age 54, $300,000 total compensation
Auditors: KPMG LLP

LOCATIONS

HQ: National Bank Holdings Corp
7800 East Orchard Road, Suite 300, Greenwood Village, CO 80111
Phone: 720 529-3336

PRODUCTS/OPERATIONS

2013 Sales

	$ mil.	% of total
Interest and dividend income		
Fees and loans	139	59
Investment securities	54	23
Others	2	1
Non-interest income		
Service charges	16	7
Bank card fees	10	4
OREO related write-up and others	4	2
FDIC loss sharing	2	1
Others	5	3
Adjustments	(19.0)	-
Total	**215**	**100**

COMPETITORS

BBVA Compass Bancshares
Bank of America
Bank of the West
Capitol Federal Financial
Central Bancompany
Commerce Bancshares
Enterprise Financial Services
FirstBank Holding Company
JPMorgan Chase
KeyCorp
U.S. Bancorp
UMB Financial
Wells Fargo
Zions Bancorporation

HISTORICAL FINANCIALS

Company Type: Public

Income Statement

FYE: December 31

	ASSETS ($ mil.)	NET INCOME ($ mil.)	INCOME AS % OF ASSETS	EMPLOYEES
12/14	4,819	9	0.2%	1,056
12/13	4,914	6	0.1%	1,108
12/12	5,410	(0)	—	1,205
12/11	6,352	41	0.7%	
12/10	0	6	—	
Annual Growth	—	11.0%	—	—

2014 Year-End Financials

Debt ratio: —
Return on equity: 1.08%
Cash ($ mil.): 256
Current ratio: —
Long-term debt ($ mil.): —
No. of shares (mil.): 38
Dividends
  Yield: 1.0%
  Payout: 105.2%
Market value ($ mil.): 755

	STOCK PRICE ($) FY Close	P/E High/Low		PER SHARE ($) Earnings	Dividends	Book Value
12/14	19.41	97	84	0.22	0.20	20.43
12/13	21.40	155	126	0.14	0.20	19.99
12/12	18.99	—	—	(0.01)	0.05	20.84
Annual Growth	0.5%	—	—	—	41.4%	(0.5%)

National General Holdings Corp

Auditors: BDO USA, LLP

LOCATIONS

HQ: National General Holdings Corp
59 Maiden Lane, 38th Floor, New York, NY 10038
Phone: 212 380-9500
Web: www.nationalgeneral.com

HISTORICAL FINANCIALS

Company Type: Public

Income Statement

FYE: December 31

	ASSETS ($ mil.)	NET INCOME ($ mil.)	INCOME AS % OF ASSETS	EMPLOYEES
12/14	4,439	102	2.3%	2,980
12/13	2,837	42	1.5%	2,029
12/12	2,718	32	1.2%	2,101
12/11	2,524	44	1.7%	
12/10	0	102	—	
Annual Growth	—	0.0%	—	—

2014 Year-End Financials

Debt ratio: 6.85%
Return on equity: 12.01%
Cash ($ mil.): 132
Current ratio: —
Long-term debt ($ mil.): —
No. of shares (mil.): 93
Dividends
  Yield: 0.2%
  Payout: 4.6%
Market value ($ mil.): 1,739

	STOCK PRICE ($) FY Close	P/E High/Low		PER SHARE ($) Earnings	Dividends	Book Value
12/14	18.61	18	12	1.07	0.05	11.34
Annual Growth	—	—	—	—	—	

National Oilwell Varco Inc

National Oilwell Varco has the equipment and skills that big energy companies need. It provides goods and services to exploration and production companies operating in oil patches around the world as well to infrastructure clients. It operating segments are Rig Systems Rig Aftermarket Wellbore Technologies and Completion & Production Solutions. The company makes distributes and services oil and gas drilling equipment for land and offshore drilling rigs. Its mechanical components include drawworks mud pumps cranes jacking systems automated pipehandling tools top drives and traveling equipment. Other products include masts derricks substructures and cranes.

Geographic Reach

National Oilwell Varco has significant non-US operations in Canada Europe the Far East the Middle East Africa Southeast Asia Latin America. It operates 900 locations on six continents including a network of 420 distribution service centers and 320 repair and manufacturing facilities to serve its oil and gas company customers. It has major facilities in Denmark France the Netherlands Norway Canada UK and US and a presence in Singapore Mexico Malaysia Brazil South Korea and the UAE. The company got more than 70% of its total revenues in 2014 from operations outside of the US.

Operations

Rig Systems (National Oilwell Varco's largest segment) designs makes and sells land rigs offshore drilling equipment packages and drilling rig components. Equipment and technologies include substructures derricks and masts; cranes; pipe lifting racking rotating and assembly systems; fluid transfer technologies such as mud pumps; pressure control equipment (including blowout preventers; power transmission systems including drives and generators; and rig instrumentation and control systems. The segment supports land and offshore drillers.The company's Rig Aftermarket segment provides comprehensive aftermarket products and services to support land rigs and offshore rigs and drilling rig components manufactured by the Rig Systems segment. It provides spare parts repair and rentals as well as technical support field service and first well support field engineering and customer training through a network of aftermarket service and repair facilities strategically located in major areas of drilling operations.

National Oilwell Varco's Wellbore Technologies segment provides equipment and technologies used to perform drilling operations and offers services that optimize their performance including solids control and waste management equipment and services drilling fluids premium drill pipe wired pipe tubular inspection and coating services instrumentation downhole tools and drill bits.The Completion & Production Solutions segment designs manufactures and sells equipment and technologies needed for hydraulic fracture stimulation (including pressure pumping trucks and pumps blenders sanders hydration units injection units flowline manifolds and wellheads); well intervention (coiled tubing units coiled tubing and wireline units and tools); onshore production (composite pipe surface transfer and progressive cavity pumps and artificial lift systems); and offshore production (floating production systems and subsea production technologies).

Sales and Marketing

Substantially all of Rig Systems' capital equipment and Rig Aftermarket's spare parts sales and a large portion of their smaller pumps and parts sales are made through the company's direct sales force and distribution service centers. Sales to foreign oil companies are often made with or through agent or representative arrangements.

The company's Rig Systems and Rig Aftermarket segments' customers include drilling contractors shipyards and other rig fabricators well servicing companies pressure pumpers national oil companies major and independent oil and gas companies supply stores and pipe-running service providers. Rig Systems sells directly to drilling contractors rig fabricators well servicing companies pressure pumping companies national oil companies major and independent oil and gas companies and also through distribution companies.

Products within Wellbore Technologies and Completion & Production Solutions are rented and sold worldwide through National Oilwell Varco's own sales force and through commissioned representatives. Wellbore Technologies' customers are mainly oil and gas companies drilling contractors oilfield service companies and oilfield rental companies. Completion & Production Solutions' customers are predominantly service companies and oil and gas companies.

Financial Performance

In 2014 National Oilwell Varco's net revenues decreased by 6% due to the spin-off of its distribution business in 2014. Net income increased by 8% due to higher sales. The company's cash from operating activities decreased by 18% due to inventories and billings in excess of costs driven by increased market activities.

Strategy

The oil services provider has aggressively expanded and grown its businesses over the last few years through acquisitions and investment in organic growth. Acquisitions play a big part in National Oilwell Varco's strategy of increasing its market share. The company completed 10 acquisitions during the year for an aggregate price of $291 million. The company's Rig Systems group will continue to focus on designing and manufacturing discrete drilling equipment components as well as building complete integrated drilling equipment packages for both land and offshore applications. The Completion & Production Solutions segment is focusing on improving wellbore completions while the Wellbore Technologies segment is directing its attention to enhancing drilling performance through offering a superior range of downhole tools bits premium drill pipe waste management services solids control drilling fluids instrumentation tubular inspection and tubular coating services. To focus on its core manufacturing and services businesses in 2014 National Oilwell Varco spun-off of its distribution business as an independent public company named NOW Inc.

Mergers and Acquisitions

In 2013 it acquired Robbins & Myers a provider of services and equipment to the upstream oil and gas industry in an all-cash transaction for $2.5 billion. Robbins & Myers' complementary products include downhole tools pumps and valves. This was the company's second-largest acquisition since it bought Grant Prideco for about $7.2 billion in 2008. That year it also bought Canadian equipment distributor CE Franklin for about $240 million.

Company Background

In 2012 National Oilwell Varco bought parts and supplies provider Wilson International from Schlumberger. Wilson has an extensive supply chain portfolio with which National Oilwell Varco expects to take advantage of new market opportunities. It also bought Denmark-based flexible pipe maker NKT Flexibles (a joint venture between NKT Holding and Subsea 7) for $670 million.

National Oilwell Varco bought 17 companies for $2.9 billion in 2012 and 10 companies for more than $1 billion in 2011. Significant acquisitions included that of oilfield equipment maker and services provider Ameron in a $777 million deal a move that helped to expand National Oilwell Varco's Fiberglass & Composite Tubulars business.

National Oilwell Varco took its current form when National Oilwell and Varco International merged in 2005.

EXECUTIVES

Chairman President and CEO, Clay C. Williams, age 52, $871,154 total compensation
CFO, Jose A. Bayardo, age 43
VP and CTO, Hege Kverneland
President Wellbore Technologies, Fadi (Mike) Matta
President Rig Systems and Rig Aftermarket, Joseph W. (Joe) Rovig, age 54, $482,692 total compensation
President Completion and Production Solutions, Kirk Shelton
President NOV Ameron, Toby Zyroll
CIO, Alex Philips
Vice President Information Technology And Chief Information Officer, Debra Dobbins
Vice President Sales, Bradley Long
Vice President Global Corporate Accounts, Tab Tettleton
Senior Vice President Strategy and Shared Services, Michelle (Mitch) Lewis
Executive Vice President Of Information Technology, Wendy Ho-schnell
Vice President Manufacturing, Jeff Stolasz
Vice President Sales, Bob Lepera
Vice President Chief Compliance Officer, Keith Hennessee
Vice President of Sales and Operations, Todd Lee
Senior Vice President, Jaehwa Park
Vice President Operations China, Lynn White
Senior Vice President, Sungwoo Lee
Vice President Manufacturing and Supply, Larry Engel
Vice President Research and Development and Quality Assurance, David W (Dave) Granderson
Vice President Information Systems, Mark Davies
Vice President Business Development, Bobby Chance
Vice President Finance, David Keener
Vice President Application Engineering, Randy Lucas
Vice President Sales Operations Latin America, Jim Stephen
Operations Vice President, Carlton Roy
Vice President Finance, Jim Lock
Vice President Drill Bits, Mark Tooley
Vice President Engineering npd, David (Dave) Cardellini
Vice President Finance, Lisa Jones
Vice President Corporate Controller And Chief Accounting Officer, Bob Blanchard
Vice President Regional Sales Asia Pacific, Jason Major
Group Vice President Latin America Wel, Ronn Tips
Auditors: Ernst & Young LLP

LOCATIONS

HQ: National Oilwell Varco Inc
7909 Parkwood Circle Drive, Houston, TX 77036-6565
Phone: 713 346-7500
Web: www.natoil.com

2014 Sales

	$ mil.	% of total
US	6,097	28
South Korea	3,472	16
china	1,905	9
Brazil	1,299	6
Singapore	1,157	5
Norway	881	4
UK	715	4
Canada	645	3
Other countries	5,269	25
Total	**21,440**	**100**

PRODUCTS/OPERATIONS

2014 Sales

	$ mil.	% of total
Rig System	9,848	42
Rig After market	3,222	14
Wellbore Technologies	5,722	24
Completion and Production	4,645	20
Eliminations (1997) (9)		
Total	**21,440**	**100**

Selected Products and Services

Automation systems
Computer control systems
Derricks
Drawworks
Drilling motors
Electrical power systems
Masts
Mud pumps
Specialized downhole tools (including fishing tools drilling jars shock tools)
Substructures
Supply chain management
Top drives
Well drilling and servicing (drill stem technology)
Technology Solutions
Coiled Tubing Equipment
Coiled Tubing Equipment Services
Coiled Tubing Instrumentation
Coiled Tubing Pressure Control
Coiled Tubing Products and Service
Coiled Tubing Pumping Support
Coiled Tubing Software
CT Equipment Repair Center
Well Service and Completion
All Terrain Vehicles
Cementing
Completion Fluids and Services
Flowline Equipment
Fluid End Expandables
Frac Sand Handling Equipment
Multipurpose Pumps
Nitrogen Equipment
Rigs
Snubbing Equipment
Stimulation Equipment
TCP Products
Wireline
Workover
Tubular and Corrosion Control
Coiled Tubing Products and Service
Conductors and Casing
Corrosion Control
Drill Pipe Services
Drilling Tubulars
Fiber Glass Pipe
Inspection Services
Line Pipe Services
Machining Services
New Pipe Services
Specialty Inspection Services
Sucker Rod Services
Surveillance Services
Tubular Leak Detection
Used Pipe Services
Supply Chain
Artificial Lift
Electrical Products
Integrated Supply
Oilfield Supply
RigPAC
RigStore
ValveAutomation
Production
Artificial Lift

Floating Production Solutions
Fluid King Pump Expendables
Multipurpose Pumps
Process Equipment
Production Pressure Control
Lifting and Handling
AHTS Equipment Packages
Cabelay Systems
Cranes
Marine Vessel Equipment
Mooring Systems
Pipelay Systems
Winches
Industrial
Construction Supply
Fiber Glass Pipe
Fluid End Expendables
Monoflo - Mono
Multipurpose Pumps
Nitrogen Equipment
Power Systems
Protective Lining Products
Solids Control
Water Transmission
Engineering and Project Management
New Technology Development
Project Specific Solutions
Successful Project Execution
Drilling
Aftermarket Services
Control and Advisory Systems
Drill Bits
Drilling Business Solutions
Drilling Expendables Databook
Drilling Fluids
Drilling Fluid Equipment
Drilling Pressure Control
Drilling Tubulars
Flowline Equipment
Fluid End Expendables
Fluid End Modules and Accessories
Fluid Transfer Systems
Handling Tools
Hoisting
Instrumentation Data Acquisition
Iron Roughnecks
Jacking and Skidding
Mining and Minerals
Motion Compensation
Multipurpose Pumps
Pipe Handling
Power Systems
Rigs
Rotating Equipment
Specialty Inspection Services
Structures
Top Drive Systems
Waste Management
Downhole
Advanced Drilling Solutions
Borehole Enlargement
Coring Services
Directional Tools
Downhole Motors
Drill Bits
Drilling Tools
Fishing Tools
Intervention and Completion Tools
Service Equipment
Telemetry Drill Strings

Selected Brands
AmClyde
Ameron
Baylor
Bear Pumps
Best Flow Products
BlackMax - BlackStar
Bowen
Brandt
Continental Emsco
CTES
Fiber Glass Systems
Gaso
HSI
Hydrastab
IntelliServ
Quality Tubing
ReedHycalog
Rolligon
Texas Oil Tools

Wheatley
Wheatley Gaso
XL Systems

Selected Mergers and Acquisitions

COMPETITORS

Aker Solutions
Baker Hughes
Bechtel
Cameron International
FMC Technologies
Forum Energy
GE Oil
Halliburton
McDermott
Nabors Industries

Schlumberger
Siemens AG
Sparrows Offshore
  Services
Stewart & Stevenson
  LLC
Superior Energy
Technip
Weatherford
  International

HISTORICAL FINANCIALS
Company Type: Public

Income Statement
FYE: December 31

	REVENUE ($ mil.)	NET INCOME ($ mil.)	NET PROFIT MARGIN	EMPLOYEES
12/14	21,440	2,502	11.7%	63,642
12/13	22,869	2,327	10.2%	63,779
12/12	20,041	2,491	12.4%	60,235
12/11	14,658	1,994	13.6%	49,475
12/10	12,156	1,667	13.7%	41,027
Annual Growth	15.2%	10.7%	—	11.6%

2014 Year-End Financials
Debt ratio: 9.43%
Return on equity: 11.66%
Cash ($ mil.): 3,536
Current ratio: 2.19
Long-term debt ($ mil.): 3,014
No. of shares (mil.): 418
Dividends
  Yield: 2.5%
  Payout: 27.4%
Market value ($ mil.): 27,456

	STOCK PRICE ($) FY Close	P/E High/Low	PER SHARE ($) Earnings	Dividends	Book Value
12/14	65.53	15 11	5.82	1.64	49.39
12/13	79.53	15 12	5.44	0.91	51.89
12/12	68.35	15 10	5.83	0.49	47.41
12/11	67.99	18 11	4.70	0.45	41.56
12/10	67.25	17 8	3.98	0.41	37.39
Annual Growth	(0.6%)	— —	10.0%	41.4%	7.2%

National Penn Bancshares Inc (Boyertown, Penn.)

LOCATIONS
HQ: National Penn Bancshares Inc (Boyertown, Penn.)
  645 Hamilton Street, Suite 1100, Allentown, PA 18101
Phone: 800 822-3321

HISTORICAL FINANCIALS
Company Type: Public

Income Statement
FYE: December 31

	ASSETS ($ mil.)	NET INCOME ($ mil.)	INCOME AS % OF ASSETS	EMPLOYEES
12/14	9,750	98	1.0%	1,771
12/13	8,591	53	0.6%	1,737
12/12	8,529	98	1.2%	1,772
12/11	8,486	87	1.0%	1,791
12/10	8,844	21	0.2%	1,843
Annual Growth	2.5%	46.7%	—	(1.0%)

2014 Year-End Financials
Debt ratio: 2.07%
Return on equity: 8.51%
Cash ($ mil.): 413
Current ratio: —
Long-term debt ($ mil.): —
No. of shares (mil.): 147
Dividends
  Yield: 3.9%
  Payout: 60.2%
Market value ($ mil.): 1,549

	STOCK PRICE ($) FY Close	P/E High/Low	PER SHARE ($) Earnings	Dividends	Book Value
12/14	10.53	16 13	0.70	0.41	8.08
12/13	11.33	31 25	0.37	0.40	7.76
12/12	9.32	15 13	0.66	0.41	8.00
12/11	8.44	16 11	0.56	0.09	7.77
12/10	8.03	85 56	0.10	0.04	8.32
Annual Growth	7.0%	— —	62.7%	78.9%	(0.7%)

Navient Corp

LOCATIONS
HQ: Navient Corp
  123 Justison Street, Wilmington, DE 19801
Phone: 302 283-8000
Web: www.navient.com

HISTORICAL FINANCIALS
Company Type: Public

Income Statement
FYE: December 31

	ASSETS ($ mil.)	NET INCOME ($ mil.)	INCOME AS % OF ASSETS	EMPLOYEES
12/14	146,352	1,149	0.8%	6,200
12/13	159,543	1,418	0.9%	—
12/12	0	939	—	—
Annual Growth	—	10.6%	—	—

2014 Year-End Financials
Debt ratio: 93.52%
Return on equity: 23.37%
Cash ($ mil.): 1,443
Current ratio: —
Long-term debt ($ mil.): —
No. of shares (mil.): 401
Dividends
  Yield: 2.0%
  Payout: 16.7%
Market value ($ mil.): 8,681

	STOCK PRICE ($) FY Close	P/E High/Low	PER SHARE ($) Earnings	Dividends	Book Value
12/14	21.61	8 6	2.69	0.45	10.45
12/13	0.00	— —	3.12	0.60	13.14
12/12	0.00	— —	1.90	0.50	(0.00)
Annual Growth	—	— —	19.0%	(5.1%)	—

Navigators Group, Inc. (The)

The Navigators Group writes specialty lines of insurance and reinsurance to clients whom it hopes are good navigators themselves. The company's various subsidiaries write marine liability and other lines of business primarily in the US and the UK. Its Navigators Insurance and Navigators Underwriting Agency (NUA) units specialize in ocean marine insurance including hull energy and cargo insurance as well as property insurance for inland marine and onshore energy concerns. Navigators Specialty primarily provides excess and surplus (high risk) lines. The firm's subsidiaries are also involved in professional liability especially directors' and officers' coverage as well as general liability for contractors.

Operations In early 2015 Navigator realigned its reporting structure creating four primary segments that align with the types of coverage it writes: US Insurance International Insurance Global Reinsurance and Corporate.Navigators' global product lines are distributed through a network of retail and wholesale brokers. In addition to its specialty property/casualty insurance and reinsurance policies the company and its subsidiaries provide catastrophe risk management services.In the International Insurance segment NUA serves as a Lloyd's of London underwriting agency managing Lloyd's Syndicate 1221. The unit primarily underwrites marine and related lines of business along with offshore energy professional liability insurance and construction coverage for onshore energy businesses.

Geographic Reach

Outside its core markets of the US and the UK Navigators has operations in several European nations such as Belgium Denmark and Sweden mainly through NUA's activity on the European Lloyd's of London insurance exchange (via Lloyd's Syndicate 1221). The firm has also established offices in emerging markets such as Brazil and China.

Financial Performance

Revenue which has largely been on the rise for the past five years rose 12% to $1 billion in 2014 on higher net written premiums and investment income. Net written premiums increased 12.6% that year due to higher retention rates in the reinsurance business as well as growth in gross written property/casualty premiums.

Net income on the other hand has been more erratic than revenue. In 2014 it grew 50% to $95 million thanks primarily to Navigator's higher revenue. Cash flow from operations has been growing every year and in 2014 it rose 63% to $222 million.

Strategy

The company is focused on strengthening and controlling costs within its existing operations. At the same time Navigators is looking for opportunities to expand into new niche coverage areas and regions aiming for underserved commercial markets with high-value assets and low-frequency loss levels.

As such in 2014 principal underwriting agency subsidiary Navigators Management Company launched NAVSecure a new cyber liability privacy and date breach coverage product. It also added to its specialty professional liability offerings with the new Allied Healthcare Errors & Omissions product.

To boost operations abroad European underwriting management subsidiary Navigators Underwriting opened new offices in Paris; Milan Italy; and Rotterdam The Netherlands in 2014.

EXECUTIVES

President CEO and Director; Chair Navigators Insurance and Navigators Management, Stanley A. (Stan) Galanski, age 56, $725,000 total compensation
SVP Chief Underwriting Officer and Chief Risk Officer, H. Clay Bassett, age 49, $416,667 total compensation
President Navigators Technical Risk, Stephen R. Coward, age 61, $319,950 total compensation
President and CEO Navigators Management Company Inc., Vincent C. Tizzio, $252,083 total compensation
Managing Director Navigators Underwriting Agency Ltd. & Navigators Insurance Company (UK), Paul V. Hennessy, age 67
President Inland Marine, Edward J. Helfers
President Navigators Specialty, Jeff L. Saunders
SVP and CFO, Ciro M. DeFalco, $380,000 total compensation
President Navigators Commercial, Adrien T. Robinson
President US Management Liability, Steven R. Kuuskvere
President Marine, Michael J. McKenna
President navigators Pro (Europe), Carl L. Bach
President Navigators Underwriting Ltd., Printhan Sothinathan
Vice President Cargo, Tod Sklens
Assistant Vice President Environmental Practice, Brett Schoech
Assistant Vice President, Suzanne Gough
Vice President, Robert Hatcher
East Coast Zonal Vice President Environmental Division, Paul Dastis
Senior Vice President, Steven Carabases
Senior Vice President and Chief Administrative Officer, R Eisdorfer
Senior Vice President Human resources, Denise Lowsley
Chairman, Terence N. Deeks, age 75
Vice President And Corporate Treasurer, Ellen Dion
Auditors: KPMG LLP

LOCATIONS

HQ: Navigators Group, Inc. (The)
400 Atlantic Street, Stamford, CT 06901
Phone: 203 905-6090
Web: www.navg.com

PRODUCTS/OPERATIONS

2014 Gross Written premiums

	% of total
Insurance companies	75
Lloyd's Operations	25
Total	**100**

2014 Sales

	$ mil % of total
Net earned premiums	91
Net investment income	7
Net realized gains	1
Others	1
Total	**100**

Selected Subsidiaries

Millennium Underwriting Ltd. (UK)
Navigators A/S (Denmark)
Navigators Corporate Underwriters Ltd. (UK)
Navigators Holdings (UK) Ltd.
Navigators Insurance Company
Navigators Management Company Inc.
Navigators Management (UK) Limited
Navigators NV (Belgium)
Navigators Specialty Insurance Company
Navigators Underwriting Agency Ltd. (UK)
Navigators Underwriting Limited (UK)
NUAL AB (Sweden)

Selected Products and Services:Commercial Surety

Standard Transactional
Non Standard Transactional
Account
Program
Energy and Engineering
Onshore Energy
Offshore Energy
Construction
Operational Engineering
Excess Casualty
Umbrella & Excess (Wholesale Brokerage)
Umbrella & Excess (Retail Agency)
Environmental Casualty
Contractors Pollution Liability
Site Pollution Legal Liability
NP3 sm General & Environmental Liability (Mfg. & Distributors)
NP4 sm General Environmental & Professional Liability (Env' l Consultants)
Environmental Excess
Inland Marine
Commercial Output Policy
Construction
Specialty
Transportation
Management Liability
Directors & Officers Liability
Employment Practices Liability
Fiduciary Liability
Crime Liability
Nonprofit D & O Liability
Marine
Bluewater Hull
Brownwater Hull
Cargo
Specie
Transportation
Marine & Energy Liability
War
Protection & Indemnity
Primary Casualty
General Liability
NAVIGATORS RE
Accident & Health
Agriculture
Latin American & Caribbean
Professional Liability Reinsurance
Property & Casualty
Life Sciences
Global Package Solutions
Commercial Auto
Professional Liability
Lawyers Professional Liability
Accountants Professional Liability
Miscellaneous Professional Liability
Insurance Agents & Brokers E&O
Technology Media & Cyber Liability
Design Professionals Liability
Real Estate Professionals E&O

COMPETITORS

AIG
AXA Corporate Solutions
Allianz
Amica Mutual
Arch Insurance Group
Aspen Insurance
Berkshire Hathaway
CNA Financial
Global Indemnity
ProSight Specialty Insurance Group
RLI
Safeco
Specialty Underwriters' Alliance
Travelers Companies
White Mountains Insurance Group
XL Group plc
Zurich American

Income Statement

FYE: December 31

	ASSETS ($ mil.)	NET INCOME ($ mil.)	INCOME AS % OF ASSETS	EMPLOYEES
12/14	4,464	95	2.1%	651
12/13	4,169	63	1.5%	596
12/12	4,007	63	1.6%	567
12/11	3,670	25	0.7%	522
12/10	3,531	69	2.0%	494
Annual Growth	6.0%	8.2%	—	7.1%

2014 Year-End Financials

Debt ratio: 5.90%	No. of shares (mil.): 14
Return on equity: 9.88%	Dividends
Cash ($ mil.): 90	Yield: —
Current ratio: —	Payout: —
Long-term debt ($ mil.): —	Market value ($ mil.): 1,047

	STOCK PRICE ($) FY Close	P/E High/Low		PER SHARE ($) Earnings	Dividends	Book Value
12/14	73.34	11	8	6.51	0.00	71.93
12/13	63.16	15	11	4.42	0.00	63.54
12/12	51.07	12	10	4.45	0.00	62.61
12/11	47.68	32	23	1.69	0.00	57.57
12/10	50.35	12	9	4.24	0.00	52.68
Annual Growth	9.9%	—	—	11.3%	—	8.1%

Navistar International Corp.

Navistar's gonna roll its truckin' convoy 'cross the USA and beyond. The company makes its products under brand names International (commercial trucks and military/defense vehicles) MaxxForce (diesel engines) and IC Bus (school and commercial buses). It makes diesel engines for the pickup truck van and SUV markets. Navistar's parts group supplies engine parts and its financial sector offers sales and lease financing for dealers and customers. Navistar which operates production plants in Argentina Brazil Canada Mexico and the US derives most of its sales from North America.

Geographic Reach

Navistar's main product development and engineering facilities reside in Lisle and Melrose Park Illinois; Madison Heights Michigan; and Columbia South Carolina. In North America the company has 12 manufacturing and assembly facilities. The US accounts for roughly 70% of its revenues while other major markets include Brazil (8%) Canada (7%) and Mexico (6%).

Operations

Navistar operates in four industry segments: North America Truck North America Parts Global Manufacturing Operations and Financial Services which consists of NFC and foreign finance operations. The Truck division which is the company's largest segment has manufacturing operations in Canada Mexico South Africa and the US.

Parts has manufacturing operations located in the US Brazil and Argentina and sells to OEMs in North and South America. Engine brands include MaxxForce and MWM International. The Parts segment supports large fleet and other customers with a wide selection of truck trailer and engine

parts. It distributes to North America and the rest of the world through its 11 regional parts distribution centers or by direct shipment.

The Operations segment's revenue comes from outside the North America markets and primarily consists of its Brazilian subsidiary and its truck and parts export businesses under the International and IC brands. Operations also has engine manufacturing units in Argentina. The Financial Services segment provides retail wholesale and lease financing of products which are sold by the truck segment and its dealers within the US and Mexico.

Sales and Marketing

The company sell sits products through its independent dealer network in North America. It has about 760 distribution and service network retail outlets in the US and Canada about 85 in Mexico and 360 international locations.

Financial Performance

Navistar's revenues dropped 6% from $10.8 billion in 2014 to $10.1 billion in 2015. The decline was fueled by a 46% drop in Global Operations sales due to lower volumes and unfavorable foreign currency exchange rates in its South American engine operations driven by an economic downturn in Brazil.

The company has also suffered four straight years of net losses: $3 billion $898 million $619 million and $184 million for 2012 2013 2014 and 2015 respectively. Over the years the company has suffered from high income tax expenses and restructuring charges among other costs.

Over the last five years Navistar's cash flow has nosedived falling significantly each year from $1.11 billion in 2010 to a negative cash flow of $336 million in 2014. It bounced back however posting $46 million in positive cash flow during 2015.

Strategy

Part of the company's game plan is acquisitions alliances joint ventures and divestitures to expand its market share domestically and internationally and to focus on its core truck operations. Navistar capitalizes on the synergies between itself and the companies it purchases. It continues to pursue complementary relationships with other global truck and bus businesses as well as defense businesses.

In 2015 Navistar sold foundry operations in Waukesha Wisconsin and closed a foundry in Indianapolis Indiana. In 2014 it sold the E-Z Pack and Continental Mixer businesses and consolidated its engine manufacturing footprint moving engine production in Huntsville Alabama; to Melrose Park Illinois.

For the China market the company has found a partner in Anhui Jianghuai Automobile (JAC) and the two have signed a joint venture agreement to manufacture diesel engines for that country's market. The company is continuing to explore South Central and North America with a primary focus on Brazil for manufacturing expansion opportunities.

HISTORY

Virginia-born inventor Cyrus McCormick perfected the reaper in 1831 and moved west to open a factory in Chicago in 1846. Before his death in 1884 McCormick had implemented such innovations as installment plans written guarantees and factory-trained repairmen. In 1902 with help from banker J. P. Morgan the company merged with Deering Harvester (agricultural machinery) and several smaller companies to form International Harvester (IH); it soon controlled 85% of US harvester production.

IH set up its first overseas plant in 1905 in Sweden. It entered the tractor industry in 1906 and in 1907 it began making the forerunner of the truck —the Auto Buggy. By 1910 IH was making 1300

trucks and 1400 tractors annually and had exceeded $100 million in sales. After several decades the company was renamed Navistar International in 1986.

EXECUTIVES

EVP and CFO, Walter G. Borst, age 54, $700,000 total compensation
SVP and General Counsel, Steven K. (Steve) Covey, age 65, $575,000 total compensation
President North American Truck and Parts, William R. (Bill) Kozek, age 53
SVP and CIO, Terry S. Kline, age 53
President and CEO, Troy A. Clarke, age 59, $900,000 total compensation
President Operations, Persio Lisboa, age 50
Vice President National Marketing, Marty Gottner
Senior Vice President Global Manufacturing and Quality, William (Bill) Osborne
National Account Manager, Gary Marracino
Vice President Product Development, David Majors
Vice President Supply Chain, Joe Kory
Vice President, Jan Allman
Vice President Tax, Carol Garnant
Vice President Representative Clients Customers, Michael Scribner
Senior Vice President And General Manager Parts Division, Phyllis Cochran
National Account Manager, Katie Sundra
Vice President Business Development North America Truck, Mike Sandfort
National Account Manager, Kyle Bailey
Vice President Dealer Sales, Bob Mann
Vice President Global Op, Bernardo Valenzuela
Chairman, James H. (Jim) Keyes, age 75
Treasurer, Stephen (Steve) Gilligan
Auditors: KPMG LLP

LOCATIONS

HQ: Navistar International Corp.
2701 Navistar Drive, Lisle, IL 60532
Phone: 331 332-5000
Web: www.navistar.com

2014 Sales

	$ mil.	% of total
US	7,760	72
Brazil	833	8
Canada	749	7
Mexico	657	6
Other	807	7
Total	**10,806**	**100**

PRODUCTS/OPERATIONS

2014 Sales

	$ mil.	% of total
North America Truck	7,080	62
North America Parts	2,517	22
Global Operations	1,557	14
Financial services	232	2
Adjustments	(580)	-
Total	**10,806**	**100**

Selected Brands Products and Services

Engines
  MaxxForce
  MWM International
Services
  Navistar Electronics
  Navistar Financial
  Navistar Parts
Vehicles
  IC Bus
  International Trucks
  Navistar Defense

COMPETITORS

All American Group	Hino Motors
BAE SYSTEMS	Isuzu

Blue Bird	Leyland Trucks
Cummins	Mercedes-Benz U.S.
Daimler	International
Deere	Mitsubishi Motors
Detroit Diesel	North America
Fiat Chrysler	Oshkosh Truck
Force Protection	PACCAR
Ford Motor	Scania
Forest River	Spartan Motors
Freightliner Custom	Thor Industries
Chassis	Tiffin Motorhomes
General Dynamics	Toyota
General Dynamics Land	UD Trucks
Systems	Volvo
General Motors	Winnebago

HISTORICAL FINANCIALS
Company Type: Public

Income Statement
FYE: October 31

	REVENUE ($ mil.)	NET INCOME ($ mil.)	NET PROFIT MARGIN	EMPLOYEES
10/15	10,140	(184)	—	13,200
10/14	10,806	(619)	—	14,200
10/13	10,775	(898)	—	14,800
10/12	12,948	(3,010)	—	16,900
10/11	13,958	1,723	12.3%	19,000
Annual Growth	(7.7%)	—	—	(8.7%)

2015 Year-End Financials

Debt ratio: 79.17%	No. of shares (mil.): 81
Return on equity: —	Dividends
Cash ($ mil.): 1,071	Yield: —
Current ratio: 1.22	Payout: —
Long-term debt ($ mil.): 4,188	Market value ($ mil.): 1,002

	STOCK PRICE ($) FY Close	P/E High/Low		PER SHARE ($) Earnings	Dividends	Book Value
10/15	12.30	—	—	(2.25)	0.00	(63.40)
10/14	35.37	—	—	(7.60)	0.00	(57.15)
10/13	36.16	—	—	(11.17)	0.00	(45.28)
10/12	18.75	—	—	(43.56)	0.00	(41.73)
10/11	42.07	3	1	22.64	0.00	(0.31)
Annual Growth (26.5%)		—	—	—	—	—

NBT Bancorp. Inc.

NBT Bancorp is the holding company for NBT Bank and its Pennstar Bank and Hampshire First Bank divisions which together operate about 155 branches mainly in suburban and rural areas of central and northern New York northeastern Pennsylvania western Massachusetts southern New Hampshire and northwestern Vermont. The banks offer services such as checking and savings accounts CDs and trust services. Its loan portfolio is dominated by business and commercial real estate loans. Its EPIC Advisors unit administers retirement plans while Mang Insurance Agency sells personal and commercial coverage. NBT Capital provides venture funding to growing area businesses. In 2013 the company acquired Alliance Financial.

Strategy
New York-based NBT Bancorp is moving into neighboring states and building its presence in existing markets through acquisitions.

In 2013 the company had assets of $7.7 billion and stockholders' equity of $816.6 million. Some 44% of NBT Bancorp's loan portfolio comprises commercial and industrial agricultural commercial construction and commercial real estate loans.

Sales and Marketing
NBT Bancorp serves individuals businesses and municipalities. To get its name in front of existing and potential customers the company spent $3.2 million on advertising in 2013 vs. $2.9 million in 2012. 2011's ad spending came in at $3.5 million.

Mergers and Acquisitions
Valued at $233 million NBT's purchase of Alliance Financial which closed in 2013 has bolstered its presence in central New York by adding 26 branches in Onondaga Cortland Madison Oneida and Oswego counties. The purchase added $1.4 billion in assets including $920 million in net loans held for investment and $1.1 billion in deposits.

Previously it purchased Hampshire First Bank in 2012 adding its first five branches in New Hampshire. The company made a foray into Massachusetts through the 2011 purchase of four branches in Berkshire County that were divested by Berkshire Hills Bancorp to satisfy antitrust concerns regarding its takeover of Legacy Bancorp. It opened a fifth branch in the state in 2012.

Financial Performance
Revenue rose for NBT Bancorp in 2013 by $45.2 million to $371.9 million vs. 2012's $326.7 million. The firm points to both interest and non-interest income for the gains. Acquisitions such as its purchase of Alliance Financial in 2013 are working to bolster its business. A decrease in interest expenses and increase in revenue spurred net income to increase some 13% in 2013 to $61.7 million from $54.6 million in 2012. In general cash from operations has run parallel with revenue. Indeed the firm's operating cash flow saw a $119.3 million boost in 2013 from $88.9 million in 2012.

Company Background
NBT Bancorp remained profitable through the recession that began in 2008 even as real estate values fell and the number of non-performing loans in its portfolio grew. In response the company increased its loan collection efforts and focused on selling conforming real estate mortgages. It also stopped originating auto leases.

NBT Bancorp was founded in 1986. However NBT Bank traces its roots to 1856.

EXECUTIVES

President and CEO NBT Bancorp and NBT Bank, Martin A. Dietrich, age 59, $675,000 total compensation

SEVP and CFO, Michael J. Chewens, age 53, $433,600 total compensation

EVP and President Retail Banking; President Pennsylvania, David E. Raven, age 52, $413,100 total compensation

EVP and President Commercial Banking, Jeffrey M. Levy, age 53, $423,300 total compensation

EVP and CIO, Joseph R. Stagliano

EVP and Director Human Resources, Catherine M. Scarlett

EVP and President Wealth Management, Timothy L. Brenner, age 58, $321,400 total compensation

EVP General Counsel and Corporate Secretary, F. Sheldon Prentice

EVP Strategic Support, Jack H. Webb

Vice President, Ed Mitchell

Assistant Vice President Information Technology Officer Security Officer, Heidi Fisher

Vice President Marketing, Jenni Bliven

Senior Vice President Information Processing Division, Robert (Bob) Roselli

Regional President, Stephen Lubelczyk

Vice President Sales, Marc Malnati

Vice President Product Manager, Sharon Horning

Vice President Information Processing, Robert (Bob) Keller

Vice President, John (Jack) Keshavan

Vice President And Retail North Division Manager, Ishmael McGhee

Vice President Corporate Tax, James (Jamie) Vooys

Assistant Vice President And Branch Manager, Linda Kelsey

Chairman NBT Bancorp, Daryl R. Forsythe, age 72

Auditors: KPMG LLP

LOCATIONS
HQ: NBT Bancorp. Inc.
52 South Broad Street, Norwich, NY 13815
Phone: 607 337-2265   **Fax:** 607 336-7538
Web: www.nbtbancorp.com

PRODUCTS/OPERATIONS

2013 Sales

	$ mil.	% of total
Interest		
Loans & leases	238	64
Securities available for sale	28	7
Other	1	1
Non-interest		
Insurance and other financial services revenue	24	8
Service charges on deposit accounts	19	5
Trust	16	4
ATM & debit card fees	15	4
Retirement plan administration fees	11	3
Bank-owned life insurance income	3	1
Other	11	3
Total	**371**	**100**

Selected Subsidiaries
Broad Street Property Associates Inc.
CNB Realty Trust
Colonial Finance Services Inc.
EPIC Advisors Inc.
FNB Financial Services Inc.
Hathaway Agency Inc.
LA Lease Inc.
Mang Insurance Agency LLC
NBT Bank National Association
NBT Capital Corp.
NBT Financial Services Inc.
NBT Holdings Inc.
NBT Services Inc.
Pennstar Bank Services Company
Pennstar Financial Services Inc.

COMPETITORS

Astoria Financial	KeyCorp
Community Bank System	M&T Bank
First Niagara Financial	Oneida Financial
HSBC USA	Sovereign Bank
	TrustCo Bank Corp NY

HISTORICAL FINANCIALS
Company Type: Public

Income Statement
FYE: December 31

	ASSETS ($ mil.)	NET INCOME ($ mil.)	INCOME AS % OF ASSETS	EMPLOYEES
12/14	7,797	75	1.0%	1,840
12/13	7,652	61	0.8%	1,742
12/12	6,042	54	0.9%	1,581
12/11	5,598	57	1.0%	1,565
12/10	5,338	57	1.1%	1,499
Annual Growth	9.9%	6.9%	—	5.3%

2014 Year-End Financials

Debt ratio: 2.98%	No. of shares (mil.): 43
Return on equity: 8.93%	Dividends
Cash ($ mil.): 146	Yield: 3.2%
Current ratio: —	Payout: 49.7%
Long-term debt ($ mil.): —	Market value ($ mil.): 1,153

	STOCK PRICE ($)	P/E		PER SHARE ($)	
	FY Close	High/Low	Earnings	Dividends	Book Value
12/14	26.27	16 13	1.69	0.84	19.69
12/13	25.90	18 13	1.46	0.81	18.77
12/12	20.27	15 12	1.62	0.80	17.24
12/11	22.13	14 10	1.71	0.80	16.23
12/10	24.15	16 12	1.66	0.80	15.46
Annual Growth	2.1%	— —	0.4%	1.2%	6.2%

NCR Corp.

You can still find NCR at the nexus of people and money. Born during the waning days of the Wild West as National Cash Register NCR is a leading maker of ATMs. The company also makes point-of-sale (POS) terminals bar code scanners and related printer consumables. Other retail and financial systems offerings include check image processing systems and self-service kiosks for hospitality retail and travel applications. NCR's services segment provides maintenance and support as well as professional services such as systems integration and managed services. NCR which facilitates more than 550 million transactions daily does business in more than 180 countries. About 60% of its sales are generated outside the US.

OperationsThe company's largest segment financial services represents about 50% of sales and includes ATMs and payment processing hardware and software. Its retail solutions segment accounts for about a third of total sales and includes POS terminals and bar-code scanners. The hospitality and emerging industries segments –which include POS hardware and software for restaurants and sports/entertainment venues and products and services for the manufacturing travel and gaming industries respectively –bring in the remaining revenue.

Geographic ReachThe US is NCR's largest market accounting for 41% of sales with the Americas as a whole contributing about 50%. Europe and the AMEA (Asia Middle East and Africa) region each account for about a quarter of revenue. The company saw growth across all regions except the Americas outside the US. The US market grew 14%.NCR has manufacturing facilities in Australia Austria Brazil China Hungary India and the US.

Sales and MarketingThe company's products and services are marketed primarily through a direct sales force although it does to a lesser degree tap a network of distributors and resellers.

Financial PerformanceNCR reported revenue of about $6.6 billion in 2014 an 8% increase from the prior year marking the fifth consecutive year of rising sales for the company. Despite the rise in sales net income fell 57% over the same period to $191 million on higher expenses. The rise in revenue was driven by double-digit growth in NCR's financial services and upticks in the hospitality and emerging industries segments. Retail solutions revenue ticked 1% lower. The company continued to operate as its own ATM in 2014 generating 86% more cash ($524 million) than it did in 2013.

StrategyIn a major strategic move NCR in 2014 expanded in China via a partnership with Shanghai Anmao Information Technology Co. to put point-of-sale technology in retail outlets across the country. China along with Brazil India and Russia and key emerging markets for NCR.

In 2014 NCR formalized the shift of its business toward software-based consumer transaction technologies. It began a restructuring designed reallocate resources to reorient its focus on businesses with opportunities for higher growth and bigger margins. It is rationalizing its product portfolio and phasing out older commodity product lines. The company spent $104 million in 2014 on the restructuring plan which continued in 2014.

In 2015 NCR rolled out its cloud-based ATM software called Kalpana. While the ATM still dispenses hard currency its running on software residing in an NCR data center. Moving ATM operations to the cloud is to reduce costs by 40% speed up new services offerings and reduce the impact of malware.

Mergers Acquisitions and Divestments
Focusing on financial services the company acquired Digital Insight Corp. a leader in online and mobile banking software for $1.65 billion in early 2014. It also recently acquired Alaric Systems Ltd. a London-based software firm that provides secure transaction switching and fraud prevention for about $84 million. Together the Digital Insight and Alaric purchases extend NCR's existing capabilities in the banking industry to form a complete enterprise software platform that will deliver across all digital and physical channels - mobile online branch and ATM.

In February 2013 NCR bought the Israeli retail software provider Retalix Ltd. for $791 million. In December 2013 it acquired Alaric Systems Ltd. for about $84 million. Alaric makes secure transaction switching and fraud prevention software. In January 2014 NCR purchased California-based Digital Insight Corp. a provider of online and mobile banking products for $1.65 billion.

HISTORY

Early History
John Patterson bought control of a Dayton Ohio cash register factory in 1882 and founded National Cash Register (NCR). Colonel Edward Deeds (who later became chairman) joined NCR in 1889 and hired inventor Charles Kettering in 1904 to develop an electric cash register. (The duo also developed an electric car ignition system and left NCR to start Dayton Engineering Laboratories Co. or Delco.)

By the 1920s NCR controlled 90% of the cash register market. That decade NCR introduced accounting machines which became almost as important to the company as cash registers. NCR's stock dropped from $154 to $6.87 in the crash of 1929 but by 1936 the company had fully recovered.

Responding to the commercialization of computers following WWII NCR bought computer developer Computer Research in 1952. During the 1960s the company introduced mainframe computers opened data processing centers established microelectronics research facilities and introduced disk-based computers. However NCR failed to automate its primary products –cash registers and accounting machines. In 1969 the company had record profits of $50 million; by 1971 they had plunged to $2 million.

William Anderson who became president in 1972 is credited with saving NCR. He slashed its Dayton workforce by 75% and focused the company on computing with an emphasis on retail scanners and ATMs.

EXECUTIVES

Senior Vice President WCS, Chris Wallace
SVP and President NCR Financial Services, Andrew S. (Andy) Heyman, age 51, $504,039 total compensation
Chairman CEO and President, William R. (Bill) Nuti, age 51, $1,000,000 total compensation
SVP CFO and Chief Accounting Officer, Robert P. (Bob) Fishman, age 51, $538,502 total compensation
SVP and President Retail Solutions Division, Michael B. Bayer, age 51, $214,662 total compensation
CIO, William T. (Bill) VanCuren
EVP Services Hardware Solutions and Enterprise Quality, Frederick J. (Rick) Marquardt, age 56, $499,038 total compensation
Vice President, David (Dave) Lewis
Vice President Americas, Tad Phelps
Vice President Telecommunication and Technology Markets and Managing Director NCR Belgium vof, Luc Brusselaers
Vice President Field Services Worldwide Customer Service, Leo Boyle
Assistant Law Vice President, Ellen Samuels
Vice President And General Manager Fld Service Cntr, Kent Mahlke
National Sales Manager, Matt Wheat
Vice President and General Manager Systems Management, Vincent Pugliese
Vice President Human Resources, Joyce Hoyle
Law Vice President, John (Jack) Ackermann
Global Vice President Software Engineering Research and Development, Eli Rosner
Vice President, Ken Fabian
Assistant Vice President, Carl Cirillo
Vice President Global Services, Mark Vigoroso
Executive Vice President, Jon Wulf
Exec V Pres, Rick Marquardt
Vice President Strategic Accounts and Business Development North America Retail, Danny Westheimer
Vice President Operations Petroleum and Convenience Retail, Eric Stecker
Vice President Financial Solutions Division Manufacturing Operations Solutions Delivery, Ernest Miller
North American Sales Vice President, Tom Bond
Vice President Fp And A, Adam Mallah
Vice President Americas Sales, Tony Tamburrano
Global Vice President Financial Services Sales, Mark Davies
Vice President Sales Petroleum and Convenience Retail, Douglas (Doug) Henderson
Vice President Strategy and Marketing, Michelle (Mitch) Fischer
Sol Sales Manager Vice President, Mark Leinenkugel
Vice President And General Manager, Rand Schenck
Vice President Of Global Manufacturing, Rob Visintainer
Vice President Global Sales Enterprise Merchandising and Supply Chain Systems, Rik Schrader
Vice President Services, Peter Christie
Vice President Business Development Managed Services, Mike Keogh
Vice President, Burbank Herndon
Senior Vice President, Steve Oleksyn
Accounting Vice President, Kitty Reed
Senior Vice President, Garth Richard
Vice President of Services Wal Mart, Phillip (Phil) Pack
Vice President Of Solution Sales, Susan Boyme
Vice President Of Sales, Jeffrey Sanders
Vice President Marketing, Dick Arnold
Vice President Sales, John Carter
Vice President Communications, Anthony Piniella
Vice President Product Development, Gordon Brooks
Vice President, Michael Chandler
National Account Manager, Wayne Miller
Vice President, Richard Arnold
Vice President (Special Projects), Arun Kochhar
Vice President Retail Marketing Retail Solutions Group, Daniel Bogen

Global Vice President For Operational Excellence
A, George Patterson
Vice President (Marketing), Vijay Nagarajan
National Account Manager, Greg O'Brien
Vice President Telecommunications And
Technology Americas, Troy Behrends
Vice President Information Technology, Trudy
Reiser
Vice President US Regional Financial Accounts,
Adams Jerry
Vice President Sales Operations Americas, Rick
Holt
Treasurer, John (Jack) Boudreau
Auditors: PricewaterhouseCoopers LLP

LOCATIONS

HQ: NCR Corp.
3097 Satellite Boulevard, Duluth, GA 30096
Phone: 937 445-5000
Web: www.ncr.com

2014 Sales

	$ mil.	% of total
Americas		
US	2,723	41
Other	634	10
Asia Middle East & Africa	1,640	25
Europe	1,594	24
Total	**6,591**	**100**

PRODUCTS/OPERATIONS

2014 Sales

	$ mil.	% of total
Product	2,892	44
Service		
Support services	1,989	30
Professional and installation services	1,710	26
Total	**6,591**	**100**

2014 Sales

	$ mil.	% of total
Financial services	3,561	54
Retail solutions	2,008	30
Hospitality	659	10
Emerging industries	363	6
Total	**6,591**	**100**

Selected Acquisitions

COMPETITORS

ACI Worldwide	Ingenico
Acxiom	MICROS Systems
BancTec	Motorola Solutions
Cummins-Allison	Netflix
Datalogic Scanning	Oki Electric
De La Rue	Optimal Group
Dell	Oracle
Diebold	Outerwall
Fidelity National	PAR Technology
Information Services	Retalix
Fiserv	SANYO
Fujitsu	SITA
Gilbarco	Toshiba TEC
HP	Triton Systems
Honeywell	Unisys
International	VeriFone
Hyosung	Wincor Nixdorf
IBM	

HISTORICAL FINANCIALS

Company Type: Public

Income Statement

FYE: December 31

	REVENUE ($ mil.)	NET INCOME ($ mil.)	NET PROFIT MARGIN	EMPLOYEES
12/14	6,591	191	2.9%	30,200
12/13	6,123	443	7.2%	29,300
12/12	5,730	146	2.5%	25,700
12/11	5,443	53	1.0%	23,500
12/10	4,819	134	2.8%	21,000
Annual Growth	**8.1%**	**9.3%**	**—**	**9.5%**

2014 Year-End Financials

Debt ratio: 42.51%
Return on equity: 10.49%
Cash ($ mil.): 511
Current ratio: 1.49
Long-term debt ($ mil.): 3,472

No. of shares (mil.): 168
Dividends
Yield: —
Payout: —
Market value ($ mil.): 4,913

	STOCK PRICE ($) FY Close	P/E High/Low	PER SHARE ($) Earnings	Dividends	Book Value
12/14	29.14	33 21	1.12	0.00	11.10
12/13	34.06	16 10	2.62	0.00	10.62
12/12	25.48	28 18	0.89	0.00	7.66
12/11	16.46	61 45	0.33	0.00	5.07
12/10	15.37	19 13	0.83	0.00	5.53
Annual Growth	**17.3%**	**— —**	**7.8%**	**—**	**19.0%**

Nelnet Inc

Got Ivy League tastes on a community college budget? Nelnet may be able to help. The education planning and financing company helps students and parents plan and pay for college educations. Nelnet is mostly known for servicing federal student loans. The firm manages about $76 billion in student loan assets most of which are government loans. However in light of regulatory changes to the student lending market Nelnet is increasingly expanding its fee-based education services. It serves the K-12 and higher education marketplace providing long-term payment plans college enrollment services and software and technology services. The firm is part of financial holding company Farmers & Merchants Investment.

Geographic Reach
The company has offices in the US and Canada.
Operations
Nelnet provides innovative educational services in loan servicing payment processing education planning and asset management for families and educational institutions. The Company's four operating segments offer a broad range of services designed to simplify education planning and financing for students and families and the administrative and financial processes for schools and financial institutions.

The largest is Asset Generation and Management which acquires and manages Nelnet's student loan holdings. The portfolio includes Nelnet's existing loans originated under the now-defunct Federal Family Education Loan Program (FFELP). However in efforts to diversify its fee-based business and lessen its dependence on student loans the company is focused on developing new products and growing in areas such as tuition payment processing and lead generation products and services such as enrollment management and test prep services.

The three fee-based segments include Student Loan and Guaranty Servicing which services FFELP and other third-party loans writes and services private student loans and provides loan servicing software. (Nelnet is one of four companies providing servicing for the Department of Education.) Tuition Payment Processing and Campus Commerce serves the K-12 market as well as higher education providing financing for families and processing services for schools. Enrollment Services works to connect students with schools by providing marketing for schools and publishing school directories and test preparation study guides for potential students.

Sales and Marketing
The company's customers include students and families colleges and universities specifically financial aid business and admissions offices K-12 schools lenders state agencies and government entities.

Financial Performance
Nelnet has seen steady growth in revenues in the last few years. In 2013 the company's revenue increased to $1.14 billion (compared to $923.7 million in 2012) primarily due to an increase in Student Loan and Guaranty Servicing (as the result of growth in servicing volume under the company's contract with the Department of Education) and an increase in collection revenues from defaulted FFELP loan assets on behalf of guaranty agencies. Tuition Payment Processing and Campus Commerce revenues grew due to a higher number of managed tuition payment plans as a result of providing more plans at existing schools and obtaining new school customers.Net income increased to $302.7 million in 2013 (from $117.8 million in 2012) due to higher revenues and lower operating costs (the result of a decrease in depreciation and amortization costs). In 2013 Nelnet's operating cash flow increased to $387.2 million (compared to $299.3 million in 2012) due to higher net income and proceeds from the termination of one of the company's cross-currency interest rate swaps. The increase in cash provided by operating activities was partially offset by the impacts of changes in non-cash fair value adjustments for derivatives.

Strategy
The company grows organically and through acquisitions.

Mergers and Acquisitions
To strengthen its student loans business Nelnet in 2014 acquired CIT's student lending business for $1.1 billion. The deal included all of CIT's government-guaranteed student loans assets and servicing rights.

In 2014 FACTS Management brand a part of Nelnet's Tuition Payment Processing and Campus Commerce segment and the leader in payment plan services for K-12 schools acquired RenWeb School Management Software one of the leading school information systems for private and faith-based schools. RenWeb currently helps over 3000 schools automate administrative processes like admissions scheduling student billing attendance and grade book management. By automating these tasks RenWeb gives teachers more time to shape the lives of students while saving money and resources. FACTS helps over 6500 schools with tuition management billing and financial aid assessment services.

Company Background
Nelnet has been through a turbulent few years as student loan reform and the financial crisis disrupted business and sent revenues down. The company's ability to adapt to the economic pressures and policy changes have helped it land face-up following the recession. Measures taken including laying off staff and tightening lending practices helped boost profits despite lower revenues. Al-

though non-FFELP servicing income and payment processing revenues grew in 2011 FFELP servicing revenues declined as the portfolio further shrunk and school marketing sales decreased as schools cut back on spending. As a result revenues fell that year by 8% to $979 million. Net income increased 8% (to $204 million) in 2011 compared to 2010 when the company had expenses related to restructuring. Also in 2010 Nelnet paid the US government $55 million to settle a lawsuit claiming it had made false statements to receive extra subsidies.

In a blow to the student lending industry President Barack Obama eliminated the FFELP and prohibited private lenders from making federal student loans in 2010. All new federal student loans began going directly through the Department of Education's Direct Loan Program. As a result Nelnet no longer originates new FFELP loans.

But the change didn't put an end to Nelnet. The company was awarded a five-year servicing contract for federally owned student loans including existing FFELP loans. Nelnet also began servicing new loans generated directly under the Federal Direct Loan Program. The contract was a major win for the company. Nelnet expects that its fee-based revenue will increase as the servicing volume for these loans increases (while the FFELP portfolio declines). The company is also focusing on improving its customer service to increase the allotted percentage of new government loans it services.

CEO Michael Dunlap controls the company holding 68% of the voting power for Nelnet. Dunlap and his family also own Farmers & Merchants Investment.

EXECUTIVES

COO, Terry J. Heimes, age 51, $550,000 total compensation
CEO, Jeffrey R. (Jeff) Noordhoek, age 49, $550,000 total compensation
President, Timothy A. (Tim) Tewes, age 56, $375,000 total compensation
CFO, James D. (Jim) Kruger, $375,000 total compensation
Executive Vice President Chief Credit Officer, Jennifer (Jen) Termaat
Vice President Consumer Relations, Marc Vernon
SP Senior Vice President, Dana D Kelly
Vice President Technical Integration, Amit Mittal
Executive Chairman, Michael S. (Mike) Dunlap, age 52
Vice Chairman, Stephen F. (Steve) Butterfield, age 63
Auditors: KPMG LLP

LOCATIONS

HQ: Nelnet Inc
121 South 13th Street, Suite 100, Lincoln, NE 68508
Phone: 402 458-2370
Web: www.nelnet.com

PRODUCTS/OPERATIONS

2013 Sales

	$ mil.	% of total
Interest		
Loans	638	56
Investments	6	-
Noninterest		
Loan & guaranty servicing	243	21
Enrollment services	98	9
Tuition payment processing & campus commerce revenue	80	7
Gains on sale of loans & debt repurchases net	11	1
Other	65	6
Total	**1,144**	**100**

COMPETITORS

American Student Assistance
Bank of America
Brazos Higher Education Service Corp.
College Loan Corporation
First Marblehead
Great Lakes Higher Education
JPMorgan Chase
Pennsylvania Higher Education Assistance Agency
Sallie Mae
Texas Guaranteed
Wells Fargo

HISTORICAL FINANCIALS

Company Type: Public

Income Statement

	ASSETS ($ mil.)	NET INCOME ($ mil.)	INCOME AS % OF ASSETS	EMPLOYEES
				FYE: December 31
12/14	30,098	307	1.0%	3,100
12/13	27,770	302	1.1%	2,800
12/12	26,607	178	0.7%	2,500
12/11	25,852	204	0.8%	2,400
12/10	25,893	189	0.7%	2,200
Annual Growth	**3.8%**	**12.9%**	**—**	**9.0%**

2014 Year-End Financials

Debt ratio: 93.12%
Return on equity: 19.41%
Cash ($ mil.): 130
Current ratio: —
Long-term debt ($ mil.): —

No. of shares (mil.): 46
Dividends
 Yield: 0.8%
 Payout: 6.1%
Market value ($ mil.): 2,142

	STOCK PRICE ($) FY Close	P/E High/Low		PER SHARE ($) Earnings	Dividends	Book Value
12/14	46.33	7	5	6.62	0.40	37.31
12/13	42.14	7	4	6.50	0.40	31.13
12/12	29.79	8	6	3.74	1.40	25.00
12/11	24.47	6	4	4.23	0.37	22.62
12/10	23.69	6	4	3.81	0.70	18.75
Annual Growth	**18.3%**	**—**	**—**	**14.8%**	**(13.1%)**	**18.8%**

NetApp, Inc.

NetApp knows storage backwards and forwards and on premise and in the cloud. The company makes data storage systems used by businesses for archiving and backup. It's moving much of its hardware and software to cloud-based storage applications. It offers products for hybrid cloud storage extending customers' IT infrastructure to the cloud environments of Amazon Google and Microsoft. NetApp enables customers' use of flash storage another relatively new market for the company. The company's FlexPod product developed with Cisco Systems is designed to helped customers manage applications from Oracle SAP and Citrix. The company mainly sells to the energy financial services government health care and IT sectors through distributors. It makes about a quarter of its revenues from direct sales.

Operations

About 60% of NetApp's revenue comes from its product segment whiles hardware maintenance and other services bring in about 25% with software maintenance accounting for the rest. The company outsources its manufacturing to third parties in the US Europe and Asia.

Geographic Reach

The US is the company's largest market representing around 56% of its sales. Europe the Middle East and Africa account for nearly 30% while the Asia/Pacific generates 14% of sales.

Sales and Marketing

NetAPP has field sales offices in 50 countries. It employs a multichannel distribution strategy selling products and services to end users and service providers through a direct sales force and through channel partners including value-added resellers system integrators OEMs and distributors. During 2013 sales from indirect channels represented 82% of its net revenues. NetApp's major customers include Arrow Electronics (23% of total sales) and Avnet (16%).

Financial Performance

NetAPP's revenue declined for the second year in a row down 3.2% to $6.12 billion in 2015 (ended April). Sales were off 7% in products its biggest segment on lower sales of its line of Fabric-Attached Storage (FAS) systems. The company had lower sales across its geographic segments.

The company's net income fell 12% in 2015 to $560 million which was attributed to lower sales and higher sales and marketing costs and taxes. Cash flow from operations also fell to $1.27 billion in 2015 from $1.35 billion in 2014.

Strategy

A large part of NetApp's strategy to help its customers move their storage to the cloud computing environment. And a large part of the company's cloud strategy is hybrid cloud which combines premise storage and external cloud storage. The company's research and development spending increased almost 11% from 2014 to 2015.

Instead of competing with cloud providers like Amazon's Amazon Web Services IBM SoftLayer and Microsoft's Azure it wants to make it easier for customers to use those services. In 2015 NetApp released products to help customers extend their IT infrastructure including data management and data protection to Azure and AWS.

Customers have shown a preference for NetApp's newer FAS mid-range and high-end systems and its E-series systems as they shift from the company's entry level FAS systems. Discounts of systems resulted in lower average selling prices overall of its configured systems.

To help develop new cloud and other product offerings NetApp operates a research and development lab in Research Triangle Park North Carolina. The lab provides shared-services infrastructure for testing its hardware and software against conditions found in enterprise data centers and cloud environments.

In 2015 NetApp initiated a restructuring to reduce costs. The company expected to reduce headcount by about 500 which would cost between $25 million and $35 million. The company plans to direct savings toward the parts of its business bringing higher returns.

Mergers and Acquisitions

NetApp continues to use acquisitions to add functionality to its product line to enter new markets and to adapt to evolving technology. In 2014 the company purchased Riverbed Technology's SteelStore product line for $80 million. SteelStore products support backup applications and cloud providers that give customers choices in how they extend their existing data protection infrastructure into the cloud. In 2013 NetApp snapped up mobile device software provider ionGrid for $17 million and storage technology provider CacheIQ for $91 million.

HISTORY

Early History
David Hitz and James Lau along with Michael Malcolm founded Network Appliance in 1992. The

trio saw a market for file servers hardware that takes the storage duties out of high-performance UNIX-based computers and speeds data flow.

Donald Valentine of Sequoia Capital invested in Network Appliance in 1994 and was named chairman. He promptly brought on board as CEO Daniel Warmenhoven the top executive of telecommunications company Network Equipment Technologies. (It was the return of a favor —Warmenhoven had given Valentine a tip on investing in a late-1980s fledgling named Cisco Systems.) Warmenhoven ditched the company's network of resellers and built an in-house sales and marketing unit. Network Appliance went public in 1995.

The company in 1996 forged a deal with Microsoft to let Network Appliance's file servers support the software giant's Internet-based network file storage standard. The beefed-up sales emphasis helped the company turn its first profit in fiscal 1996. The next year it bought online caching software specialist IMC. Acquisition costs dropped earnings for fiscal 1997.

EXECUTIVES

Senior Vice President And Chief Information Office, Marine Levanson
Vice President Operations, Tom Gerstenberger
SVP and CIO, Cynthia A. (Cindy) Stoddard
EVP, David Hitz, age 52, $322,500 total compensation
EVP, James K. Lau, age 56, $236,154 total compensation
President and Head Go-To-Market Operations, Robert E. (Rob) Salmon, age 55, $613,942 total compensation
EVP Human Resources, Gwendolyn (Gwen) McDonald
Chief Technology Officer, Mark F. Bregman, age 58
CEO, George Kurian, age 48, $428,000 total compensation
SVP; General Manager Technology Enablement and Solutions Organization, Rich Clifton
EVP Finance and Operations and CFO, Nicholas R. (Nick) Noviello, age 46, $504,327 total compensation
Senior Vice President, Jay Kidd
Chief Strategy Officer Senior Vice President, Jonathan (Jon) Kissane
Vice President Systems Engineering, Roger Anderson
Vice President Internal Audit, Mark Gosling
Vice President Supply Chain Technical Services, Kim Weller
Vice President Information technology Midwest Region, Richard (Dick) Scheffenegger
Vice President of FPandA, Bob Parker
Vice President Product Management Data Ontap Group, John (Jack) Frederiksen
Vice President Sales Information technology Logistics and Fulfillment, Karthik Balakrishnan
Vice President World Wide Legal Commer, Tim OLeary
Vice President Product Operations, Julie Estko
Vice President, George Shaheen
Vice President of Human Resources Operations, Nancy Saunders
Vice President Engineering Data Protection Group, Octavian Tanase
Vice President Worldwide Sales Operations, Stacey Cornelius
Vice President Strategic Merchandising, Cherie Farris
Vice President Manager Director, Phuong Nguyen
Vice President Technology, Roberto Miller
Vice President Supply Chain, Michael Wais
Vice President Services Product Management, Steffen Low
Vice President corporate Controller, Mark Valentine
Senior Vice President Human Resources, Gary Bencomo
Vice President Manager Director, Gary Moreali

Senior Vice President Global Sales, Ed Deenihan
Vice President Quality and Customer Advocacy, Dick Pocock
Vice President Sales, Ron Salmon
Executive Vice President Finance and Chief Financial Officer, Nick Noviello
Vice President Of International Sales, Tim Pitcher
Vice President, Maya Palem
Vice President Of Sales, David (Dave) Paulus
Senior Vice President Sales, Rob Salmon
Vice President Information Technology, Valery Loiseau
Vice President Worldwide Sales Operations, Jane Vaillancourt
Executive Vice President Product Operations, Manesh Goel
Vice President Of Human Resources, Sven Kinden
Vice President And General Manager, Jon Mellon
Vice President Americas Channel Sales, Todd Palmer
Vice President Corporate Development, Steve Mitzenmacher
Vice President and General Manager NAS and V Series Business Units, Brendon Howe
Vice President, Randy Blatt
Vice President Of Human Resources, Derek Bomar
Vice President Protocols Engineering, Greg Germain
Vice President General Manager, Maltide Miramda
Vice President, Greg Adas
Vice President Quality And Customer Advocacy, Fred Pocock
Senior Vice President Fas Systems Group, David Mason
Vice President Customer Experience, Steve Blaz
Vice President Legal and Tax General Counsel and Secretary, Andrew (Andy) Kryder
Vice President Information Technology, Mike Fitzner
Senior Vice President Engineering and, Steven (Steve) Kleiman
Vice President Corporate Development, J Ahn
Vice President Global System Integrators, W Thomas Stanley
Senior Vice President Operations, Bill Berg
Chairman, T. Michael (Mike) Nevens, age 66
Vice Chairman, Tom Mendoza
Assistant Treasurer, Maura Campbell
Member Board Of Directors, Robert (Bob) Wall
Treasurer Sergeant, Dan Chilton
Board Member, Gerald Coon
Executive Board Member, Romil Shah
Auditors: Deloitte & Touche LLP

LOCATIONS

HQ: NetApp, Inc.
  495 East Java Drive, Sunnyvale, CA 94089
Phone: 408 822-6000
Web: www.netapp.com

2015 Sales

	$ mil.	% of total
Americas	3,446	56
Europe Middle East & Africa	1,857	30
Asia Pacific	818	14
Total	**6,122**	**100**

PRODUCTS/OPERATIONS

2015 Sales

	$ mil.	% of total
Product	3,654	60
Service	1,569	25
Software entitlements & maintenance	898	15
Total	**6,122**	**100**

Selected Products

Object Storage Software
OnCommand Management Software
Platform OS

Protection Software
Protocols
Storage Security Systems
Storage Systems
Data OnTap storage operating system.

COMPETITORS

Dell	Microsoft
Dot Hill	Oracle
EMC	Quantum Corporation
HP	XIO
Hitachi Data Systems	Xyratex
IBM	

HISTORICAL FINANCIALS

Company Type: Public

Income Statement

FYE: April 24

	REVENUE ($ mil.)	NET INCOME ($ mil.)	NET PROFIT MARGIN	EMPLOYEES
04/15	6,122	559	9.1%	12,810
04/14	6,325	637	10.1%	12,490
04/13	6,332	505	8.0%	13,060
04/12	6,233	605	9.7%	12,149
04/11	5,122	673	13.1%	10,212
Annual Growth	**4.6%**	**(4.5%)**	**—**	**5.8%**

2015 Year-End Financials

Debt ratio: 15.82%
Return on equity: 15.59%
Cash ($ mil.): 1,921
Current ratio: 2.50
Long-term debt ($ mil.): 1,487

No. of shares (mil.): 306
Dividends
  Yield: 1.8%
  Payout: 34.7%
Market value ($ mil.): 11,056

	STOCK PRICE ($) FY Close	P/E High/Low	PER SHARE ($) Earnings	Dividends	Book Value
04/15	36.12	25 19	1.75	0.66	11.15
04/14	35.00	25 18	1.83	0.60	11.67
04/13	34.87	29 19	1.37	0.00	13.23
04/12	39.03	33 20	1.58	0.00	11.78
04/11	52.11	32 17	1.71	0.00	10.11
Annual Growth	**(8.8%)**	**— —**	**0.6%**	**—**	**2.5%**

Netflix Inc.

Tapping technologies from multiple eras Netflix steers couch potatoes away from the video store to the mailbox or Internet. The company's more than 57 million subscribers in 50 countries can download movies or rent DVDs for a monthly fee through Netflix.com. Movies are delivered via the US Postal Service from distribution centers located in major US cities or streamed to some 1000 devices including PCs and TVs. Netflix ships millions of discs daily in the US and does not charge late fees or have due dates; its service employs user ratings to predict preferences and make recommendations. Netflix is focused on shifting its focus away from DVD rental to its fast-growing steaming service particularly overseas.

Geographic Reach

The Netflix business has moved beyond the borders of the US to Canada Latin America Europe the UK and the Nordics. The company is relying on these international markets for long-term growth opportunities. Currently Netflix rings up about 16% of its sales overseas and has subscribers in more than 50 countries.

Operations

Netflix allows members to enjoy more than 2 billion hours of TV shows and movies per month including original series documentaries and feature films on any internet connected scree anytime anywhere as much as they want.

The company has organized its business into three operating segments: domestic streaming international streaming and domestic DVD. Its two streaming segments generate nearly $3.5 billion in revenue through monthly subscriptions for streaming content accessed through a growing number of devices and account for about 80% of its net revenue. Netflix also maintains its legacy domestic DVD business (20%) through the segment that sells monthly subscriptions for DVDs by mail.

Average paid international streaming memberships accounted for 27% of the company's total average paid streaming memberships in 2014 compared to 20% in 2013.

Sales and Marketing

In 2014 the company spent $533.1 million for advertising (compared to $404 million in 2013 and $351 million 2012).

Financial Performance

Netflix has achieved significant growth over the last several years. In 2014 revenue of the company increased by 26% due to growth in both international and domestic streaming memberships as well as increases in average revenue per paying member resulting from the introduction of higher priced plans.

The revenue growth from streaming in the US was due to the 22% growth in the average number of paid memberships as well as to the 2% increase in average monthly revenue per paying member resulting from price increases. The increase in international revenues was primarily due to the 82% growth in paid international memberships as well as the 1% increase in average monthly revenue per paying member resulting from price increases offset partially by the impact of exchange rate fluctuations.

The Domestic DVD segment revenues dropped due to a 16% decrease in the average number of paid memberships.Netflix's net income increased by 137% in 2014 due to higher revenues and the absence of a loss on extinguishment of debt that was present in 2013.Cash provided by operating activities decreased by $81.3 million primarily due to a 32% increase in payments for content other than DVD library as well as increased payments associated with higher operating expenses. The higher use of cash was partially offset by higher revenues.

Strategy

To grow overseas Netflix must contend with rivals that offer DVD rentals in Europe and online downloads of movies. Today more than 1000 devices have the capacity to stream from Netflix. Through strategic agreements with others Netflix has expanded its library of available selections to satisfy the growing appetites of its customers. During the past few years it has added content from CBS Disney MTV Networks and Sony and continues to explore agreements with pay TV channels and networks such as HBO as it invests aggressively in streaming content. In 2015 it planned to invest $500 million on technology development to improve its services (and more than $3 billion on conten).

Looking to new markets for growth Netflix is focusing on expanding its streaming subscription business (launched in 2007) domestically and globally. In 2015 the company launched its movie and TV streaming service in Cuba and announced plans to launch video streaming service in Japan.

The company introduced its streaming services in Germany Austria Switzerland France Belgium and Luxembourg in 2014. It launched its streaming service in the UK the Netherlands Ireland and Nordic countries in 2013.

Company Background

Netflix logged its first full year of international sales in Latin America in 2012.

EXECUTIVES

Chairman President and CEO, Reed Hastings, age 55, $2,961,539 total compensation
Chief Product Officer, Neil Hunt, age 54, $1,750,000 total compensation
Chief Content Officer, Ted Sarandos, age 51, $2,776,923 total compensation
Chief Streaming and Partnerships and International Development Officer, Greg Peters, age 44, $999,431 total compensation
VP Financial Planning and Analysis, David Wells, age 43, $943,077 total compensation
Vice President Business Development, Bill Holmes
Vice President Finance, David (Dave) Burt
Vice President Of Marketing, Jerret West
Vice President Business and Legal Affairs, Heather Mccauley
Vice President Aquisitions, Larry Tanz
Vice President Business and Legal Affairs, Bryony Gagan
Vice President Partner Product Development, Gregory Peters
Vice President Finance and Controller, JC Berger
Board Director, Rich Barton
Auditors: Ernst & Young LLP

LOCATIONS

HQ: Netflix Inc.
100 Winchester Circle, Los Gatos, CA 95032
Phone: 408 540-3700
Web: www.netflix.com

PRODUCTS/OPERATIONS

2014 Sales

	% of total
Domestic Streaming	62
International Streaming	24
Domestic DVD	14
Total	**100**

Selected Netflix Streaming Devices

Apple iPhone
Apple iPad
Apple iPod touch
Apple TV
Blu-ray disc players
Digital video recorders
Google TV
Internet video players
Internet-connected TVs
Home theatre systems
Microsoft Xbox 360 console
Nintendo Wii console
Sony PS3 console

COMPETITORS

AT&T	Google
Amazon.com	HBO
Apple Inc.	Hastings Entertainment
Best Buy	Hulu
Charter Communications	Kroger
Columbia House	Redbox
Comcast	Showtime Networks
Cox Communications	Target Corporation
DIRECTV	Time Warner Cable
DISH Network	Verizon
EchoStar	Wal-Mart

HISTORICAL FINANCIALS

Company Type: Public

Income Statement

FYE: December 31

	REVENUE ($ mil.)	NET INCOME ($ mil.)	NET PROFIT MARGIN	EMPLOYEES
12/15	6,779	122	1.8%	3,700
12/14	5,504	266	4.8%	2,450
12/13	4,374	112	2.6%	2,327
12/12	3,609	17	0.5%	2,429
12/11	3,204	226	7.1%	2,927
Annual Growth	20.6%	(14.2%)	—	6.0%

2015 Year-End Financials

Debt ratio: 23.24%
Return on equity: 6.01%
Cash ($ mil.): 1,809
Current ratio: 1.54
Long-term debt ($ mil.): 2,371
No. of shares (mil.): 427
Dividends
  Yield: —
  Payout: —
Market value ($ mil.): 48,948

	STOCK PRICE ($) FY Close	P/E High/Low	PER SHARE ($) Earnings	Dividends	Book Value
12/15	114.38	2440327	0.28	0.00	5.20
12/14	341.61	764495	0.62	0.00	4.39
12/13	368.17	1380334	0.26	0.00	3.20
12/12	92.59	29181214	0.04	0.00	1.91
12/11	69.29	489104	0.59	0.00	1.66
Annual Growth	13.3%	— —(17.2%)	—	33.1%

New York Community Bancorp Inc.

It's big banking in the Big Apple and beyond. New York Community Bancorp is the holding company for one of the largest thrifts in the US New York Community Bank as well as New York Commercial Bank (also dba Atlantic Bank) and seven other banking divisions. In its home state New York Community Bank operates through Queens County Savings Bank Richmond County Savings Bank Roosevelt Savings Bank and Roslyn Savings Bank. It serves customers in New Jersey through its Garden State Community Bank division. New York Community Bank also does business as AmTrust Bank which operates in Arizona and Florida and Ohio Savings Bank. Altogether New York Community Bancorp has about 275 bank branches in five states.

Geographic Reach

Westbury New York-based New York Community Bancorp has branches in five states: New York home to about 155 community and commercial bank branches; New Jersey with about 50 locations; Ohio and Florida with some 25 branches each; and Arizona with more than a dozen locations.

Operations

Serving both consumers and business customers the banks provide standard services such as checking and savings accounts CDs IRAs credit cards mortgages and loans. They offer life and long-term care insurance through an agreement with third-party provider LPL Financial. New York Community Bancorp typically does not open new stand-alone branches but has been increasing its presence in its market areas by adding locations inside grocery stores and extending business hours. Its commercial arm New York Commercial

Bank has 30 branches in Manhattan Queens Brooklyn Westchester County and Long Island including 18 that operate under the name Atlantic Bank. New York Community Bancorp also owns investment advisory firm Peter B. Cannell & Co.

Multifamily mortgage loans (with an emphasis on rent-regulated apartment buildings) are the company's key assets making up more than 70% of its loan book. New York Community Bancorp prefers rent-regulated properties because they tend to have lower-than-average tenant turnover and can often be expected to bring in steady income during economic downturns. The company also focuses on loans secured by commercial real estate in New York and New Jersey.

Financial Performance

The company has seen a slow decline in its revenues since 2010. In 2014 New York Community Bancorp's revenues decreased by 2% due to a drop in interest and non-interest income. Interest income decreased due to the effect of the continued low-rate environment which reduced loan yields on mortgage and other loans. Non-interest income declined due to a drop in mortgage banking income as the result of a large decrease in loan origination income.New York Community Bancorp's net income increased by 2% due to benefits from its provision for loan losses and a decline in non-interest expenses.The company's operating cash inflow decreased by 47% in 2014 due to a change in working capital as a result of a decrease in other liabilities and lower proceeds from the sale of loans originated for sale.

Strategy

New York Community Bancorp has grown its deposit and loan business as well as its branch network through acquisitions of other banks.Mergers and AcquisitionsIn October 2015 New York Community Bancorp agreed to acquire Astoria Financial Corporation which holds Astoria Bank —one of New York's largest thrifts. The deal would boost the size of New York Community Bancorp's branch network —as well as its deposit assets —by about one-third after adding around 85 new branches and nearly $10 billion in deposit business.

Company Background

In 2012 it acquired some $2.2 billion in deposits mainly short-term CDs but also money market accounts from Aurora Bank.

New York Community Bank was founded in 1859. New York Community Bancorp was incorporated in 1993.

EXECUTIVES

Vice President Investor Relations, Ilene Angarola
Senior Vice President Human Resources, Bernard Terlizzi
SEVP and COO, Robert Wann, age 60, $950,000 total compensation
President and CEO, Joseph R. Ficalora, age 68, $1,350,000 total compensation
SEVP and CFO, Thomas R. (Tom) Cangemi, age 46, $750,000 total compensation
EVP and Corporate Secretary, R. Patrick Quinn
SEVP and Chief Lending Officer, James J. Carpenter, age 54, $675,000 total compensation
EVP and Chief Accounting Officer, John J. Pinto, age 44, $510,000 total compensation
EVP and CIO, Robert Brown
Senior Vice President and Controller, James (Jamie) Speranza
Assistant Vice President Regional Human Resources Director, Patricia (Pat) King
Assistant Vice President Development and Training, Ann Nunez
Executive Vice President and Chief Credit Officer, Shannon Mashburn
Executive Vice President, Barbara Tosi-renna

Second Vice President Staff Attorney, Laura Coleman
Senior Vice President Mortgage, Charles Baker
Senior Vice President, Michael Frain
Vice President BSA AML Administrator Fraud, Dina Gaballa
Executive Vice President, Andrew Kaplan
Second Vice President, Boris Gadol
Assistant Vice President Branch Manager, Shoby Isaac
Vice President And Assistant Counsel, Candace Carter
Vice President, Catherine Bifulco
Senior Vice President, Bob Angarola
Assistant Vice President Procurement, Susan (Sue) Pace-Burke
Senior Vice President, Robert Dufort
Senior Vice President Director of External Reporting, Stephen (Steve) Zahn
Vice President Sarbanes Oxley Project Manager Executive Oversight Group, Janet Shand
Assistant Vice President Of Retail Sales, Edward Day
Application Development Manager First Vice President, Sharon Michitsch
Edandt Training Manager Vice President, Susan Weaver
Second Vice President Compliance And Loan Admin. Officer, Matilda Economou
Vice President Commercial Lending, John Adams
First Vice President, Georgiana Reese
Assistant Vice President Manager Of Loan Admin Customer Service, Ken Hsiung
Assistant Vice President Procurment Services Manager Operations Support Group, John (Jack) Butler
Senior Vice President Development And Reporting Specialist, Artie Gyftopoulos
Vice President And Commercial Loan Officer, Linda Orth
Quality Assurance Manager Assistant Vice President, Julie Dubeansky
Executive Vice President Chief Corporate Governance Officer and Corporate Secretary, R Quinn
Vice President, John (Jack) Langton
Chairman, Dominick Ciampa, age 82
Auditors: KPMG LLP

LOCATIONS

HQ: New York Community Bancorp Inc.
615 Merrick Avenue, Westbury, NY 11590
Phone: 516 683-4100
Web: www.mynycb.com

2014 Locations

	No.
New York Community Bank	
New York	121
New Jersey	51
Ohio	28
Florida	26
Arizona	14
New York Commercial Bank	35
Total	**275**

PRODUCTS/OPERATIONS

2014 Sales

	$ mil.	% of total
Interest		
Mortgage & other loans	1,414	74
Securities & money market investments	268	14
Noninterest		
Mortgage banking income	63	3
Fee income	36	2
Bank-owned life insurance	27	1
Net gain on sales of securities	14	1
Other	75	5
FDIC indemnification expenses	(14.9)	—
Total	**1,884**	**100**

Selected Operations

AmTrust Bank (Arizona Florida)
Atlantic Bank (New York commercial bank)
Garden State Community Bank (New Jersey)
Ohio Savings Bank (Ohio)
Queens County Savings Bank (Queens NY)
Richmond County Savings Bank (Staten Island NY)
Roosevelt Savings Bank (Brooklyn NY)
Roslyn Savings Bank (Long Island NY)

COMPETITORS

Apple Bank for Savings	Provident Financial
Astoria Financial	Services
Bank of America	Ridgewood Savings Bank
Citigroup	Safra Bank
Emigrant Bank	TD Bank USA
Flushing Financial	Valley National
HSBC USA	Bancorp
Investors Bancorp	Wells Fargo
JPMorgan Chase	

HISTORICAL FINANCIALS

Company Type: Public

Income Statement

FYE: December 31

	ASSETS ($ mil.)	NET INCOME ($ mil.)	INCOME AS % OF ASSETS	EMPLOYEES
12/14	48,559	485	1.0%	3,416
12/13	46,688	475	1.0%	3,381
12/12	44,145	501	1.1%	3,458
12/11	42,024	480	1.1%	3,348
12/10	41,190	541	1.3%	3,883
Annual Growth	**4.2%**	**(2.7%)**	**—**	**(3.2%)**

2014 Year-End Financials

Debt ratio: 0.74%	No. of shares (mil.): 442
Return on equity: 8.43%	Dividends
Cash ($ mil.): 564	Yield: 6.2%
Current ratio: —	Payout: 92.5%
Long-term debt ($ mil.): —	Market value ($ mil.): 7,081

	STOCK PRICE ($) FY Close	P/E High/Low	PER SHARE ($) Earnings	PER SHARE ($) Dividends	PER SHARE ($) Book Value
12/14	16.00	16 14	1.09	1.00	13.06
12/13	16.85	16 12	1.08	1.00	13.01
12/12	13.10	13 10	1.13	1.00	12.88
12/11	12.37	17 10	1.09	1.00	12.73
12/10	18.85	16 12	1.24	1.00	12.69
Annual Growth	**(4.0%)**	**— —**	**(3.2%)**	**(0.0%)**	**0.7%**

NewBridge Bancorp

Bridging the gap between its community banks and North Carolinians NewBridge Bancorp is the holding company that owns NewBridge Bank which operates about 40 branches plus a handful of loan production offices located primarily in the state's Piedmont Triad Region. Boasting more than $2.5 billion in total assets the community bank offers personal and business banking products and services including checking and savings accounts and loans as well as wealth management services including investment and asset management and estate planning. Real estate-secured loans make up nearly 90% of the bank's $1.6 billion loan portfolio. Raleigh-based Yadkin Bank agreed to buy NewBridge in late 2015.

OperationsNewBridge generated nearly 70% of its total revenue from interest income on fees and loans in 2014 while another 14% came from interest on its investment securities. About 10% of revenues came from its Retail Banking fees while its Wealth Management and Mortgage Banking services generated 3% and 2% of total revenue during the year respectively. The bank's two subsidiaries include LSB Properties and Henry Properties which together own the bank's acquired real estate. NewBridge also owns FNB Financial Services Capital Trust I a statutory trust that facilitates the issuance of trust preferred securities.Geographic ReachNewBridge operates around 40 branch offices and eight loan production offices in North Carolina's four largest markets —Charlotte Raleigh the Cape Fear Region and the Piedmont Triad region. Its loan production offices are in Winston-Salem Asheboro Morganton and Raleigh in North Carolina as well as in Charleston and Greenville in South Carolina.Sales and MarketingNewBridge spent $1.78 million on advertising in 2014 compared to $1.58 million and $1.51 million in 2013 and 2012 respectively.Financial PerformanceNewBridge's revenue has been rising in recent years thanks to commercial loan business growth and strategic bank acquisitions. The bank's revenue jumped by 19% to $102.53 million in 2014 mostly as the bank's loan assets grew by 27% during the year yielding more interest income. The bank's Retail Banking fees and Wealth Management services revenue also rose by 2% and 14% in 2014 respectively.Despite higher revenue in 2014 the bank's net income dove 33% to $13.98 million mostly as the bank incurred $2.9 million more in acquisition-related expenses during the year. The bank also spent more toward personnel expenses resulting from new bank acquisitions as well as from hiring its new middle-market banking group and expanding its commercial banking team.NewBridge's operating cash also fell by 23% to $17.39 million during the year mostly due to lower cash earnings.StrategyNewBridge Bancorp grows both organically and through acquisitions of smaller banks. In 2014 and early 2015 through its strategic acquisitions of Premier Commercial Bank and Capstone Bank NewBridge greatly expanded its branch reach into new markets in the Carolinas bolstered its commercial and mortgage banking business capabilities and added millions of dollars in new loan and deposit business. It's also been growing its internal operations with an eye toward building its commercial banking business. To this end throughout 2014 the bank added a middle-market banking team designed to serve companies with revenues between $25 million and $250 million. It also spent 2014 expanding its small business banking services broadening its treasury services and enhancing its wealth management business. NewBridge emphasized in 2015 that it would also work on integrating and gaining efficiencies from growth initiatives and become more productive at all levels of operations. While it will look for the right partnership opportunities most of its efforts will focus on leveraging its assets more efficiently and profitably. Mergers and AcquisitionsIn February 2015 the bank purchased the Premier Commercial Bank which held $169 million in total assets expanding NewBridge's reach and commercial banking operations in the Piedmont Triad area of North Carolina (one of its four key markets) while bolstering its retail mortgage banking capabilities in multiple markets.In 2014 NewBridge Bank purchased CapStone Bank of Raleigh North Carolina expanding its banking presence in four of the top metro markets in North Carolina. Newbridge would continue to operate CapStone's four branches under the Capstone Bank name until a systems conversion.Company Background

In the aftermath of the financial crisis NewBridge participated in the Troubled Asset Relief Program/Capital Purchase Program and as a result the government controlled a nearly 15% stake in the company.

EXECUTIVES

President and Chief Executive, Pressley A. Ridgill, age 63, $349,594 total compensation
EVP and CFO, Ramsey K. Hamadi, age 45
EVP and Chief Banking Officer, David P. Barksdale, age 51, $187,500 total compensation
EVP and Chief Credit Officer, William W. (Wes) Budd, age 52, $185,417 total compensation
EVP and Chief Resource Officer, Robin S. Hager, age 52, $181,250 total compensation
Vice Chairman, Barry Z. Dodson, age 65
Chairman NewBridge Bancorp and NewBridge Bank, Michael S. Albert, age 60
Auditors: Dixon Hughes Goodman LLP

LOCATIONS

HQ: NewBridge Bancorp
1501 Highwoods Boulevard, Suite 400, Greensboro, NC 27410
Phone: 336 369-0900
Web: www.newbridgebank.com

PRODUCTS/OPERATIONS

2014 Sales

	$ mil.	% of total
Interest		
Loans including fees	71	70
Securities & other	14	14
Noninterest		
Retail banking	10	10
Wealth management services	2	3
Other	3	3
Total	**102**	**100**

Select Subsidiaries

FNB Financial Services Capital Trust I
NewBridge Bank
  LSB Properties Inc.
  Henry Properties LLC
  Prince George Court Holdings Inc.
  Peoples Finance Company of Lexington Inc.

COMPETITORS

BB&T	First Bancorp (NC)
BNC Bancorp	Piedmont Federal
Bank of America	Southern Community
Citizens South	Financial
CommunityOne Bancorp	SunTrust

HISTORICAL FINANCIALS

Company Type: Public

Income Statement

FYE: December 31

	ASSETS ($ mil.)	NET INCOME ($ mil.)	INCOME AS % OF ASSETS	EMPLOYEES
12/14	2,520	13	0.6%	487
12/13	1,965	20	1.1%	449
12/12	1,708	(25)	—	442
12/11	1,734	4	0.3%	442
12/10	1,807	3	0.2%	497
Annual Growth	**8.7%**	**42.6%**	**—**	**(0.5%)**

2014 Year-End Financials

Debt ratio: 3.64%
Return on equity: 7.02%
Cash ($ mil.): 34
Current ratio: —
Long-term debt ($ mil.): —
No. of shares (mil.): 37
Dividends
  Yield: —
  Payout: —
Market value ($ mil.): 324

	STOCK PRICE ($) FY Close	P/E High/Low	PER SHARE ($) Earnings	Dividends	Book Value
12/14	8.71	23 17	0.38	0.00	6.22
12/13	7.43	12 6	0.65	0.00	5.86
12/12	4.63	— —	(1.80)	0.00	12.52
12/11	3.87	49 30	0.11	0.00	10.44
12/10	4.70	170 72	0.03	0.00	10.42
Annual Growth	**16.7%**	**— —**	**88.7%**		**—(12.1%)**

Newell Rubbermaid, Inc.

Newell Rubbermaid wants to get its products into your drawers your kitchen cabinets and your workbench. The go-to company for men women and children makes housewares (Rubbermaid plastic products Calphalon cookware) home furnishings (Levolor blinds) juvenile products (Graco) hair products (Goody) and office items (DYMO Sanford Sharpie). Newell Rubbermaid sells its items to mass retailers (Target) and home and office supply stores (Staples). Past Gillette executive Michael Cowhig is chairman while Michael Polk took over as president and CEO in 2011. Contrary to popular belief the company's home solutions products are not its largest business; it actually brings in more from its office supply sales.
Operations

Newell Rubbermaid operates its business through five core business segments: Home Solutions Writing Tools Commercial Products and Baby & Parenting. (The company sold its hardware business in 2013.)

The Home Solutions segment which brings in nearly 30% of total sales makes and distributes a wide range of consumer products - tubs bins containers and other storage tools - under multiple brand names. It primarily targets the female head of household. Its indoor/outdoor organization items and food and home storage products are primarily sold under the Rubbermaid Roughneck and TakeAlongs names.

Newell Rubbermaid's Writing business which generates 30% of revenue makes writing instruments for use in business and at home. It markets its products directly to mass merchants warehouse clubs grocery/drug stores office superstores office supply stores contract stationers and travel retail and other retailers.

The Tools segment makes up 15% of sales and includes hand tools and power tool accessories industrial bandsaw blades cutting tools for pipes and HVAC systems and industrial labeling solutions.

Commercial Products brings in another 15% of sales and covers cleaning and refuse products hygiene systems material handling solutions and medical and computer carts.

Newell Rubbermaid's Baby & Parenting segment the smallest with just over 10% of sales makes infant and juvenile products (such as swings highchairs car seats strollers and play yards) sold under the Graco Baby Jogger Aprica and Teutonia names.
Geographic Reach

Newell Rubbermaid boasts a global operation. The company operates in more than 100 countries in the Americas Europe the Middle East Africa and the Asia Pacific region. About 70% of the company's business comes from the US while Europe Middle East and Africa (EMEA) region generates just over 10% of sales. Latin America and the Asia Pacific region split nearly 15% of revenue while Canada brings in the remainder of total sales.

Sales and Marketing

The office products maker sells its products in more than 100 countries through large mass merchandisers such as discount stores home centers warehouse clubs office superstores commercial distributors and e-commerce companies.

Newell Rubbermaid relies on the largest retailer in the world to help it peddle its products. Sales to Wal-Mart and its subsidiaries which include Sam's Club have slipped a bit in recent years. In 2014 the behemoth retailer generated 11% of consolidated net sales. The company's other top customers that year included Bed Bath & Beyond Lowe's Office Depot Amazon Staples Target The Home Depot Toys 'R' Us and Essendant.The company has been boosting its marketing spend in recent years particularly in the Americas. The company spent $136.3 million on cooperative advertising with customers in 2014 up from $117.7 million and $117.6 million in 2013 and 2012 respectively. It also spent $188.5 million on advertising and promotion costs in 2014 or 26% more than in 2013 and 35% more than it spent in 2012.

Financial Performance

Sales have been mostly flat for the mature company over the past few years. Revenue grew by less than 1% to $5.73 billion in 2014 thanks to modest growth in all segments save for its Baby & Parenting business which declined by nearly 5%. Most of the company's growth came from its Writing division which benefited from positive pricing and advertising and merchandising support in the Americas Asia and the EMEA region. The Commercial Products and Tools divisions also grew thanks to higher sales driven by new pricing and distribution efforts.Despite higher sales net income dipped by 20% to $377.8 million mostly because the company spent more on SG&A expenses related to increased advertising and restructuring-related spending and also because it paid $65.4 million for pension settlement charges involving a voluntary offer to certain pension plan participants. Between 2009 and 2013 Newell Rubbermaid's annual profit has ranged from a low of $125.2 million (2011) to a high of $474.6 million (2013).Cash levels continued to remain mostly flat with operations providing $634.1 million in 2014 or 5% less cash than in 2013 mostly because of lower earnings.

Strategy

Newell Rubbermaid has been making strategic cuts to dispose of under-performing brand and business lines. In 2014 the company discontinued its Endicia and Culinary electrics and retail businesses which were part of its Writing division. Also in 2014 in effort to simplify its operations in the EMEA region it closed a manufacturing and a distribution center exited certain markets and product lines (including its baby and parenting products in nearly 20 EMEA countries) and ended its direct sales channels in more than 50 of the 120 countries in the region. The company has also been pursuing strategic acquisitions to expand its product lines. In late 2014 it acquired Ignite Holdings' Contigo and Avex beverage container brands with the purchase aimed at transforming Newell Rubbermaid into a larger faster growing more global and more profitable company. That year it also acquired Baby Jogger Holdings to expand its line of activity strollers and accessories. The following year the company said it would purchase Elmer's Products and its well-known Elmer's Krazy Glue and X-Acto brands for $600 million. Newell Rubbermaid has been aggressively ramping up its marketing strategy in recent years to market innovation and new product launches and

in building its existing brands particularly in the Americas. In addition in early 2015 the company created its global e-commerce hub in New York City in an effort to expand its online revenue worldwide.

Late in 2015 a year of mega-mergers the company announced it would pay about $13 billion for consumer products company Jarden. The move will bring to Newell Rubbermaid Sunbeam and Oster appliances Coleman outdoor gear First Alert home safety products Ball canning jars Diamond matches and plastic cutlery Loew-Cornell art supplies K2 snowboards and Bee and Bicycle brand playing cards.

Mergers and Acquisitions

In early 2014 Newell Rubbermaid leaped into the durable beverage container market (think travel mugs and reusable water bottles) when it purchased Ignite Holdings maker of the Contigo and Avex brands for about $125 million. Later the same year it paid $83 million to strengthen the group with the purchase of bubba brands maker of the 52-ounce Bubba Mug and 128-ounce Bubba Jug from Zone Holdings.Also in 2014 the company purchased Baby Jogger Holdings which designs and markets premium infant activity strollers and accessories for $206.5 million to expand its product offerings from its Baby & Parenting business.

HISTORY

Businessmen in Ogdensburg New York advanced curtain rod maker W.F. Linton Co. $1000 to relocate from Rhode Island in the early 1900s. Local wholesaler Edgar Newell signed off on the loan; when the company went bankrupt in 1903 he was forced to take over. The company renamed Newell Manufacturing set up plants in Canada and Freeport Illinois to ease shipping costs and speed delivery.

Production expanded into towel racks ice picks and other items; Woolworth's decision to carry Newell's products turned the company into a national supplier. Edgar Newell died in 1920. The company made its first acquisition in 1938 buying window treatment specialist Drapery Hardware.

The Newell companies were consolidated in the mid-1960s into a single corporation. Daniel Ferguson was named president in 1965 and served alongside his CEO father Leonard one of Newell's original employees. During his tenure Daniel hitched the company's future to the growing dominance of large discount stores. Newell went from a $14 million family business to a global multi-line conglomerate by acquiring products that it distributed to these big buyers. The company went public in 1972.

As for Rubbermaid it was originally a balloon maker in the 1920s called Wooster Rubber. By the mid-1930s Ohio's Wooster Rubber had acquired the Rubbermaid product line of rubber housewares. It went public in 1955 and two years later changed its name to Rubbermaid. During the 1980s the company enjoyed a decade of phenomenal growth. Newell's $6 billion purchase of Rubbermaid in 1999 sealed its biggest deal yet and resulted in a name change: Newell Rubbermaid.

EXECUTIVES

President CEO and Director, Michael B. (Mike) Polk, age 54, $1,200,000 total compensation
EVP and CFO, John K. Stipancich, age 46, $535,000 total compensation
EVP and Chief Human Resources Officer, Paula S. Larson, $525,000 total compensation
EVP and COO, Joseph A. Arcuri, age 51
SVP Information Technology and CIO, Dan Gustafson
President Tools, Jeff Hohler

Vice President of Human Resources Intercraft, Brian Stull
Vice President of Marketing, John (Jack) Travers
Vice President of Finance, Michael (Mel) Stark
Vice President Finance, Brian Fought
Vice President Legal Affairs home Sol. Director Government Aff, Mark Johnson
Global Vice President Finance, Matt Miller
Vice President of Integration Corporate Development, Alan (Al) Cranston
Vice President Engineering, Chuck Jones
Vice President Research and Development, Daily Gist
Chairman, Michael T. Cowhig, age 68
Auditors: Ernst & Young LLP

LOCATIONS

HQ: Newell Rubbermaid, Inc.
Three Glenlake Parkway, Atlanta, GA 30328
Phone: 770 418-7000
Web: www.newellrubbermaid.com

2014 North America Sales

	% of total
US	93
Canada	7
Total	**100**

2014 International Sales

	% of total
Europe Middle East & Africa	46
Latin America	27
Asia Pacific	27
Total	**100**

PRODUCTS/OPERATIONS

2014 Sales

	% of total
Writing	30
Home Solutions	28
Tools	15
Commercial Products	15
Baby & Parenting	12
Total	**100**

2014 Sales

	$ mil.	% of total
Writing - Writing Instruments	1,451	25
Writing - Technology Solutions	257	4
Home Solutions - Rubbermaid Consumer	867	15
Home Solutions - Decor	315	6
Home Solutions - Other	392	7
Tools	852	15
Commercial Products	837	15
Baby & Parenting	753	13
Total	**5,727**	**100**

Selected Brands & Trade Names

Cleaning organization and decor
  Brute
  Kirsch
  Levolor
  Roughneck
  Rubbermaid
  TakeAlongs
  TC
Office products
  Accent
  Berol
  DYMO
  Eberhard Farber
  Expo
  Liquid Paper
  Paper Mate
  Parker
  rotring
  Sharpie
  Uni-Ball (under license)
  Vis-à-vis
  Waterman
Home and family
  Ace
  Aprica
  Avex

Calphalon
Calphalon One
Contigo
Cooking with Calphalon
Goody
Graco
Katana
Kitchen Essentials
Solano
Teutonia

COMPETITORS

ACCO Brands	Knape & Vogt
Acme United	Lancaster Colony
Alticor	Libbey
Avery Dennison	Lifetime Brands
BIC	Myers Industries
Bridgestone	Owens-Illinois
Coleman	Springs Global US
Crayola	Sterilite
Decorator Industries	Tupperware Brands
Dixon Ticonderoga	Uniek
Faber-Castell	WKI Holding
Home Products	Wilton Brands
International	ZAG Industries
Katy Industries	

HISTORICAL FINANCIALS

Company Type: Public

Income Statement

FYE: December 31

	REVENUE ($ mil.)	NET INCOME ($ mil.)	NET PROFIT MARGIN	EMPLOYEES
12/14	5,727	377	6.6%	17,400
12/13	5,692	474	8.3%	18,300
12/12	5,902	401	6.8%	18,300
12/11	5,864	125	2.1%	19,900
12/10	5,759	292	5.1%	19,400
Annual Growth	(0.1%)	6.6%	—	(2.7%)

2014 Year-End Financials

Debt ratio: 37.15%	No. of shares (mil.): 269
Return on equity: 19.26%	Dividends
Cash ($ mil.): 199	Yield: 1.7%
Current ratio: 1.28	Payout: 41.7%
Long-term debt ($ mil.): 2,084	Market value ($ mil.): 10,254

	STOCK PRICE ($) FY Close	P/E High/Low		PER SHARE ($) Earnings	Dividends	Book Value
12/14	38.09	28	21	1.35	0.66	6.88
12/13	32.41	20	13	1.63	0.60	7.44
12/12	22.27	16	12	1.37	0.43	6.96
12/11	16.15	47	26	0.42	0.29	6.41
12/10	18.18	18	13	0.96	0.20	6.55
Annual Growth	20.3%	—	—	8.9%	34.8%	1.2%

Newmont Mining Corp. (Holding Co.)

Newmont Mining goes for the gold. Once the clear #1 gold producing company in the world Newmont now ranks #2 behind Barrick. Newmont produces about 5.6 million ounces of gold annually and has proved and probable reserves of 82.2 million ounces of gold and 7.9 million pounds of copper. It has significant assets in the US mining in Nevada since 1965. It also has assets in Australia Canada Ghana Indonesia Mexico Peru and New Zealand. Newmont mines copper mostly through

its Batu Hijau project in Indonesia and Boddington project in Australia. The company produced about 144 million pounds of copper in 2014. Operations in North America and South America account for more than half of Newmont's gold production.

HISTORY

The company was founded in 1921 and began publicly trading in 1925. BlackRock Inc. owns 13% of Newmont.

Colonel William Boyce Thompson a flamboyant trader founded the Newmont Co. in 1916 to trade his various oil and mining stocks. The Newmont name was a combination of New York and Montana where Thompson grew up. The company was renamed Newmont Corporation in 1921 and Newmont Mining Corporation in 1925 when it went public. Thompson died five years later. During its first 10 years Newmont focused on investing and trading stocks in promising mineral properties including US copper and gold mines.

Newmont's gold mines bolstered the company throughout the Depression. During the 1940s its focus shifted to copper and Africa. It bought Idarado Mining in 1943 and Newmont Oil in 1944 (sold 1988). The company grew during the 1950s by acquiring stakes in North American companies involved in offshore oil drilling nickel mining and uranium oxide production. It also bought stakes in copper mines in South Africa and South America.

Newmont started producing gold from the Carlin Trend in Nevada in the mid-1960s. It bought a one-third stake in Foote Mineral (iron alloys and lithium) in 1967; by 1974 it controlled 83% of the company (sold 1987). In 1969 Newmont merged with Magma Copper one of the US's largest copper companies. A Newmont-led consortium bought Peabody Coal the US's largest coal producer from Kennecott Copper in 1977 (sold 1990).

After its 1980 discovery of one of the century's most important gold stakes Gold Quarry in the Carlin Trend Newmont spent a decade fending off takeover attempts. The company began selling off noncore operations to focus on gold. Magma Copper was spun off to stockholders in 1988.

A proposed merger with American Barrick Resources a major stockholder collapsed in 1991. Former Freeport-McMoRan VP Ronald Cambre became CEO in 1993 and that year the company began mining in Peru. A 1994 action by the French government one of Newmont's partners in Peru's Yanacocha Mine kicked off a protracted battle over the property's ownership. The claim was upheld in 1998 raising Newmont's stake to more than 50%. Reflecting its increasing interest in Indonesia in 1996 Newmont and Japan's Sumitomo formed a joint venture to exploit gold reserves on Sumbawa Island. In 1997 the company increased its gold reserves and territory by acquiring Santa Fe Pacific Gold for about $2.1 billion.

For years Newmont and Barrick Gold Corporation operated interlocked mining claims in Nevada's Carlin Trend which prevented optimal exploitation by either company. In 1999 both companies agreed to a mutually advantageous land swap in the region.

In 2000 an Indonesian court ordered the closure of the Minahasa mine over a local tax dispute; the company's joint venture agreed to pay a $500000 penalty to settle the matter. Newmont was fined $500000 after a mercury spill at its Yanacocha mine. That year Newmont settled the lingering ownership dispute over the Yanacocha.

Company president Wayne Murdy became CEO early in 2001 (he replaced Cambre as chairman in 2002). Newmont acquired Battle Mountain Gold in 2001 for nearly $600 million. Late that year Newmont moved to acquire Australia's top gold pro-

ducer Normandy Mining (setting off a bidding war with AngloGold) as well as Canadian gold miner France-Nevada Mining Corp. AngloGold bowed out of the "battle for Normandy" in early 2002 but later completed a three-way deal in which it acquired Normandy and Franco-Nevada.

In 2003 Newmont reduced its stake in Kinross Gold from 14% to 5% and it considered selling off the Ghanaian interests it had gained in the Normandy merger. However in 2004 Newmont literally discovered a gold mine in Ghana –a major district with some 16 million equity ounces of gold.

Murdy retired in 2007; taking the helm was former CEO Richard O'Brien. In 2007 Newmont spun off its royalty assets acquired in 2002 as Franco-Nevada Corporation. Those assets then operated as Newmont Mining Corporation of Canada now a subsidiary of Newmont.

In 2008 Newmont bought Canadian gold producer Miramar Mining which controls the Hope Bay project for about $1.5 billion. It also acquired in 2009 a 33% stake in Boddington from Anglo-Gold Ashanti for about $1 billion giving Newmont 100% of the Boddington project.

In 2011 Newmont acquired Fronteer Gold a Canadian company with properties in the US Turkey and Peru for $2.3 billion. The deal significantly expands Newmont's holdings in Nevada.

EXECUTIVES

HQ: Newmont Mining Corp. (Holding Co.)
6363 South Fiddler' s Green Circle, Greenwood Village, CO 80111
Phone: 303 863-7414   **Fax:** 303 837-5837
Web: www.newmont.com

2014 Sales

	% of sales
United Kingdom	76
Philippines	4
Japan	4
Korea	4
Germany	3
Indonesia	3
Mexico	2
Others	4
Total	**100**

PRODUCTS/OPERATIONS

2014 Sales

	$ mil.	% of total
Gold	6,592	90
Copper	700	10
Total	**7,292**	**100**

COMPETITORS

AngloGold Ashanti	Harmony Gold
Barrick Gold	Inmet Mining
Freeport-McMoRan	Kinross Gold
Gold Fields	Newcrest Mining
Goldcorp	

HISTORICAL FINANCIALS

Company Type: Public

Income Statement   FYE: December 31

	REVENUE ($ mil.)	NET INCOME ($ mil.)	NET PROFIT MARGIN	EMPLOYEES
12/14	7,292	508	7.0%	13,700
12/13	8,322	(2,462)	—	15,085
12/12	9,868	1,809	18.3%	16,400
12/11	10,358	366	3.5%	17,100
12/10	9,540	2,277	23.9%	15,500
Annual Growth	(6.5%)	(31.3%)	—	(3.0%)

2014 Year-End Financials

Debt ratio: 26.67%
Return on equity: 4.98%
Cash ($ mil.): 2,403
Current ratio: 2.47
Long-term debt ($ mil.): 6,480
No. of shares (mil.): 498
Dividends
Yield: 1.1%
Payout: 22.0%
Market value ($ mil.): 9,425

	STOCK PRICE ($) FY Close	P/E High/Low		PER SHARE ($) Earnings	Dividends	Book Value
12/14	18.90	27	17	1.02	0.23	20.60
12/13	23.03	—	—	(4.94)	1.23	20.58
12/12	46.44	18	12	3.63	1.40	27.73
12/11	60.01	97	68	0.73	1.00	26.07
12/10	61.43	14	9	4.55	0.50	27.08
Annual Growth	(25.5%)	—	—	(31.2%)	(18.1%)	(6.6%)

News Corp (New)

They say no news is good news but the new News Corp. is making headlines. In mid-2013 media mogul Rupert Murdoch split his print media and broadcast media holdings into separate companies. News Corp. now consists of newspapers (The Wall Street Journal New York Post Australia's Herald Sun and The Sun and The Times in the UK) information services (Dow Jones and Factiva) and book publishing (HarperCollins). It also owns FOX SPORTS Australia a stake in Australian real estate web portal REA Group and a 50% share of Australian pay-TV provider FOXTEL. Murdoch's US-based TV and film holdings are now organized into Twenty-First Century Fox which includes networks FOX and FOX News.

Geographic Reach

The company's subsidiaries are located in Australia the UK and the US. In addition book publisher HarperCollins has a warehouse in Scotland and Dow Jones runs an office in Hong Kong. North America accounts for more than 40% of sales.

Operations

News Corp. divides its operations into six segments –- news and information services book publishing cable network programming digital real estate services digital education and other. (Its 50% stake in FOXTEL is treated as an equity investment.) The print and digital media publications (news and information services book publishing) account for the majority of revenues.

The news and information services segment also includes News America Marketing Group (NAMG) a publisher and distributor of coupons in newspapers and on the SmartSource.com website. NAMG's customers include many of the largest consumer packaged-goods advertisers in the US and Canada. It reaches 74 million households for its freestanding coupon inserts and about 56000 retail outlets for its in-store advertising.

The digital education segment consists of Amplify the brand for News Corp.'s digital education business.

During the split Murdoch moved the Australian TV operations to News Corp. in order to allow the US TV operations to grow as a stand-alone division.

Sales and Marketing

The company spent about $534 million on advertising and promotional expenses during fiscal 2015.

Financial Performance

News Corp.'s revenue has been flat across the past five fiscal years. It reported revenue of $8.63 billion for fiscal 2015 which was a slight increase compared to the prior year.

The company suffered a net loss of $147 million in fiscal 2015 primarily because of impairment and restructuring charges. Despite the net loss and a slight drop in cash on hand News Corp's cash flow remains strong. The company had $831 billion in cash on hand at the end of fiscal 2015.

Strategy

Splitting the business into separate publishing and entertainment companies allows each company to pursue uninhibited industry-specific opportunities benefit from greater financial and operational flexibility and provide investors with a more targeted investment opportunity.

Mergers and Acquisitions

In September 2013 News Corp. exited the small-town local newspaper business when it sold its Dow Jones Local Media Group with 33 publications to an affiliate of Fortress Investment Group to be managed by GateHouse Media. The Dow Jones Local Media Group daily newspapers included the Cape Cod Times (Hyannis Massachusetts) and The Record (Stockton California). In addition to daily and weekly newspapers it also operated the papers' websites as well as news and advertising niche publications.

Ownership

Chairman Rupert Murdoch with an estimated net worth of $11 billion owns almost 40% of the company's voting stock.

EXECUTIVES

CEO Amplify, Joel T. Klein, age 68
CEO Harper Collins, Brian Murray, age 48
Chairman and CEO News America Marketing, Martin (Marty) Garofalo
CEO News UK, Rebekah Brooks, age 47
Chief Executive, Robert Thomson, age 55, $992,308 total compensation
CTO, Paul Cheesbrough
CFO, Bedi A. Singh, $655,769 total compensation
CEO News Corp Australia, Julian Clarke
CEO The New York Post, Jesse Angelo
CEO Dow Jones & Company, William (Will) Lewis
CEO Storyful, Rahul Chopra
CEO Move Inc., Ryan OÁHara
EVP and Chief Communications Officer of News Corp.Mr. James E. Kennedy
Senior Executive Vice President, Gerson Zweifach
Vice President, Linden Slaugh
Senior Vice President Treasurer, Rakesh Jobanputra
Senior Vice President Corporate Audit, Neil Aaron
Associate General Counsel and Vice President, Audrey Susanin
Senior Vice President Technology Business Operations, Aashish Chandarana
Vice President Telecommunications, Guy Wheaton
Vice President Strategic Sourcing Procurement, Tracey Williamson
Vice President Of Technology, Dan Gould
Vice President Marketing Services At News America Marketing, Marissa Bishop
Vice President Tax Operations, Scott Lindstrom
Senior Vice President, Paula Wardynski, age 58
Senior Vice President Physical Production, Thomas Imperato
Vice President Sales And Marketing, Brian Turchin
Vice President Information Technology, Cindy Schwan
Senior Vice President Media Relations, Lou Ermilio
Vice President Of Information Technology, Gianluca Daniello
Senior Vice President Strategy And Corporate Development European Television, Marc Heller
Vice President Manager Director, Trista Reiser
Senior Vice President Corporate Affairs, Jim Platt
Vice President Global Transfer Pricing, Kathrin Zoeller
Vice President, Robert Ennis
Executive Vice President Office Of The Chairman, Jeremy Phillips
Co-Chairman News Corp and 21st Century Fox, Lachlan K. Murdoch, age 42
Executive Chairman, K. Rupert Murdoch, age 84
Assistant Treasurer, Stanley Pauzer
Auditors: Ernst & Young LLP

LOCATIONS

HQ: News Corp (New)
1211 Avenue of the Americas, New York, NY 10036
Phone: 212 416-3400
Web: www.newscorp.com

2015 Sales

	$ mil.	% of total
US & Canada	3,917	45
Europe	1,982	23
Australia and others	2,734	32
Total	**8,633**	**100**

PRODUCTS/OPERATIONS

2015 Sales by Business Segment

	$ mil.	% of total
News & information services	5,731	66
Book publishing	1,667	20
Digital real estate services	625	7
Cable Network programming	500	6
Digital education	109	1
Other	1	0
Total	**8,633**	**100**

2015 Sales

	$ mil.	% of total
Advertising	3,835	44
Circulation & subscription	2,654	31
Consumer	1,594	18
Other	550	6
Total	**8,633**	**100**

List of Items
Newspapers
Dow Jones
  Barron's (
Dow Jones Licensing Services
Dow Jones Newswires
Factiva (online news and business research)
The Wall Street Journal
The Wall Street Journal Digital Network
All Things Digital
BigCharts (stock market information)
FINS (financial services employment listings)
MarketWatch
WSJ.com
New York Post
  News Inter
The Sun
The Sunday Times
The Times
  News Limit
The Advert
The Austra
The Courie
The Daily
Herald Sun
The Mercur
Northern T
Sunday Her
Sunday Mai
The Sunday
Sunday Tas
The Sunday
The Sunday
Book publishing
HarperCollins Publishers
Cable network programming
FOX SPORTS Australia
Digital real estate services
  REA (61.6%)
Other
  Amplify (d
  Foxtel (50

COMPETITORS

Bloomberg L.P.	LexisNexis
Crain Communications	New York Times
Financial Times	Pearson plc
Forbes	Simon & Schuster
Graham Holdings	Thomson Reuters
Hachette Book Group	Valassis
Hearst Corporation	

HISTORICAL FINANCIALS

Company Type: Public

Income Statement

FYE: June 30

	REVENUE ($ mil.)	NET INCOME ($ mil.)	NET PROFIT MARGIN	EMPLOYEES
06/15	8,633	(147)	—	25,000
06/14	8,574	239	2.8%	22,000
06/13	8,891	506	5.7%	24,000
06/12	8,654	(2,075)	—	24,000
06/11	9,095	678	7.5%	—
Annual Growth	**(1.3%)**	**—**	**—**	**—**

2015 Year-End Financials

Debt ratio: —
Return on equity: (-1.17%)
Cash ($ mil.): 1,951
Current ratio: 1.84
Long-term debt ($ mil.): —
No. of shares (mil.): 581
Dividends
  Yield: —
  Payout: —
Market value ($ mil.): 8,485

	STOCK PRICE ($) FY Close	P/E High/Low	PER SHARE ($) Earnings	Dividends	Book Value
06/15	14.59	— —	(0.26)	0.00	20.57
06/14	17.94	45 36	0.41	0.00	22.91
Annual Growth	**(5.0%)**	**— —**	**—**	**—**	**(2.6%)**

NewStar Financial Inc

No hot air here: NewStar Financial is in the business of providing middle-market companies with the capital they need to create a spark. The commercial financier provides a variety of loans (primarily secured senior debt) for refinancing acquisitions consolidations and commercial real estate and equipment purchases to clients in the retail and consumer health care media and information and energy industries among others. Its loans typically range from $10 million to $50 million. Newstar also offers investment advisory and asset management services to institutional investors through managed credit funds that invest in its originated loans.

OperationsNewStar operates an asset management unit and four specialized lending groups including: Leveraged Finance (which generated 81% of the firm's 2014 revenue) which provides senior secured cash flow loans as well as second lien and unitranche loans; Real Estate (11% of revenue) which offers first mortgage debt mostly to finance acquisitions of commercial real estate properties; Business Credit (4% of revenue) which provides senior secured asset-based loans mostly to fund working capital needs of mid-sized companies; and Equipment Finance (4% of revenue) which offers leases loans and lease lines to finance equipment and other capital purchases. Overall more than 90% of NewStar's revenue comes from interest income while less than 5% comes from fee and asset management income.Geographic ReachThe Boston-based firm has offices in Atlanta; Chicago; Dallas; Darien Connecticut; Los Angeles; New York; Portland; and San Francisco. Sales and MarketingNewStar targets its marketing and services toward private equity firms mid-sized companies corporate executives banks real estate investors and other financial intermediaries. It serves clients in industries including retail and consumer products health care media and information and energy. Its clients have included DZ Bank Wells Fargo Natixis Capital Markets TIDI Products Centerplate and Media Storm.Financial PerformanceNewStar's revenues and profits have been on the rise in recent years thanks to growing loan business and declining loan loss provisions as its loan portfolio's credit quality has improved with higher property valuations in the strengthened economy.The firm's revenue rose by 7% to $135.9 million in 2014 thanks to higher interest income from continued growth in its loan business particularly driven by its Leveraged Finance and Real Estate financing arms.Despite higher revenue in 2014 NewStar's net income dove by 57% to $10.6 million mostly as credit loss provisions nearly tripled during the year as it had to cover for more of its impaired loans. Its cash levels declined sharply with operations using $110.8 million in 2014 (compared to providing $56.8 million in 2013) after adjusting its earnings for non-cash items mostly related to net proceeds from the sale of its loans held-for-sale.StrategyNewStar Financial continues to add to its lines of specialty financing lines to grow its business. It may also partner with other financial firms to bolster its financial lending capacity.

Toward these ends in 2015 it formed its NewStar Warehouse Funding subsidiary which entered a $175 million revolving warehouse arrangement with Citibank to partially fund eligible loans originated by its Leveraged Finance Group. In late 2014 NewStar partnered with GSO Capital (the credit division of Blackstone) and Franklin Square Capital Partners (the largest manager of business development companies) to expand its lending and asset management platforms.Mergers and AcquisitionsIn October 2015 NewStar continued to add to its specialty financing lineup after purchasing private alternative asset manager Feingold O'Keeffe Capital for $19.3 million (net of acquired cash). The deal nearly added $2.3 billion in new assets under management growing NewStar's total AUM by nearly 50% to $6.4 billion.

EXECUTIVES

Managing Director and Head of Equipment Finance, Stephen J. (Steve) O'Leary
Chairman President and CEO, Timothy J. Conway, age 60, $475,000 total compensation
Managing Director and Head of Strategy and Corporate Development, Robert K. Brown
Chief Investment Officer, Peter A. Schmidt-Fellner, age 58, $400,000 total compensation
CFO, John K. Bray, age 58, $350,000 total compensation
Managing Director and Head of Commercial Real Estate, J. Daniel (Dan) Adkinson, age 59
Managing Director and Head of Treasury and Asset Management, John J. Frishkopf, age 51
Managing Director and Head of Asset-Based Lending, Michael D. Haddad
Chief Credit Officer, Daniel D. (Dan) McCready, age 58, $269,230 total compensation
Managing Director and Head of Leveraged Finance Origination, Patrick F. McAuliffe, age 57, $300,000 total compensation
Head of Leverage Financed Capital Markets, Mark R. du Four
Vice President Of Information Technology, Jenifer Mulboom
Assistant Vice President, Renee Cedorchuk
Auditors: KPMG LLP

LOCATIONS

HQ: NewStar Financial Inc
  500 Boylston Street, Suite 1250, Boston, MA 02116
Phone: 617 848-2500
Web: www.newstarfin.com

PRODUCTS/OPERATIONS

2014 Lending Portfolio

	% of total
Leveraged finance	81
Real estate	11
Business credit	4
Equipment finance	4
Total	**100**

2014 Sales

	$ mil.	% of total
Interest	136	92
Fee income	2	2
Asset management income	1	1
Gain on derivatives & other	(0.2)	-
Other income	7	5
Total	**147**	**100**

COMPETITORS

Ally Commercial Finance	JPMorgan Chase
	MicroFinancial

Bank of America
Bank of the West
CIT Group
Citigroup

ORIX USA
People' s United
Equipment Finance

HISTORICAL FINANCIALS

Company Type: Public

Income Statement

FYE: December 31

	ASSETS ($ mil.)	NET INCOME ($ mil.)	INCOME AS % OF ASSETS	EMPLOYEES
12/14	2,811	10	0.4%	98
12/13	2,606	24	0.9%	101
12/12	2,157	23	1.1%	104
12/11	1,946	14	0.7%	88
12/10	1,974	10	0.5%	82
Annual Growth	9.2%	0.9%	—	4.6%

2014 Year-End Financials

Debt ratio: 31.42%
Return on equity: 1.69%
Cash ($ mil.): 33
Current ratio: —
Long-term debt ($ mil.): —

No. of shares (mil.): 46
Dividends
  Yield: —
  Payout: —
Market value ($ mil.): 597

	STOCK PRICE ($) FY Close	P/E High/Low		PER SHARE ($) Earnings	Dividends	Book Value
12/14	12.80	81	47	0.21	0.00	13.75
12/13	17.77	37	23	0.46	0.00	12.65
12/12	14.01	27	18	0.45	0.00	12.06
12/11	10.17	42	28	0.27	0.00	11.42
12/10	10.57	50	19	0.19	0.00	10.96
Annual Growth	4.9%	—	—	2.5%	—	5.8%

NextEra Energy Inc

For a Florida company without any oranges NextEra Energy produces a lot of juice. Its operations across the US and Canada include an independent power production business but most of its revenues come from utility Florida Power & Light (FPL). The unit distributes electricity to 4.7 million customers. Subsidiary FPL Group Capital owns nonutility businesses including NextEra Energy Resources an independent power producer and energy marketer. Overall NextEra Energy has more than 44900 MW of generating capacity. Subsidiary FPL FiberNet leases wholesale fiber-optic capacity to telephone cable and Internet providers; it operates a 9050 mile network.

HISTORY

During Florida's land boom of the early 1920s new homes and businesses were going up fast. But electric utilities were sparse and no transmission lines linked systems.

In 1925 American Power & Light Company (AP&L) which operated utilities throughout the Americas set up Florida Power & Light (FPL) to consolidate the state's electric assets. AP&L built transmission lines linking 58 communities from Miami to Stuart on the Atlantic Coast and from Arcadia to Punta Gorda on the Gulf.

FPL accumulated many holdings including a limestone quarry streetcars phone companies and water utilities and purchases in 1926 and 1927 nearly doubled its electric properties. In 1927 the company used an electric pump to demonstrate how swamplands could be drained and cultivated.

During the 1940s and 1950s FPL sold its non-electric properties. The Public Utility Holding Company Act of 1935 forced AP&L to spin off FPL in 1950. The company was listed on the NYSE that year.

FPL grew with Florida's booming population. In 1972 its first nuclear plant (Turkey Point south of Miami) went on line. In the 1980s it began to diversify with the purchase of real estate firm W. Flagler Investment in 1981 and FPL Group was created in 1984 as a holding company. It subsequently acquired Telesat Cablevision (1985) Colonial Penn Group (1985 insurance) and Turner Foods (1988 citrus groves). FPL Group formed ESI Energy in 1985 to develop nonutility energy projects.

Diversification efforts didn't pan out and in 1990 the firm wrote off about $750 million. That year sticking to electricity the utility snagged its first out-of-state power plant in Georgia acquiring a 76% stake (over five years). FPL Group sold its ailing Colonial Penn unit in 1991; two years later it sold its real estate holdings and some of its cable TV businesses.

The utility gave environmentalists cause to complain in 1995. First the St. Lucie nuclear plant was fined by the Nuclear Regulatory Commission for a series of problems. FPL also wanted to burn orimulsion a cheap tar-like fuel. (Barred by the governor the utility gave up the plan in 1998.)

In 1997 FPL Group created FPL Energy an independent power producer (IPP) out of its ESI Energy and international operations; FPL Energy teamed up with Belgium-based Tractebel the next year to buy two gas-fired plants in Boston and Newark New Jersey.

FPL Energy built wind-power facilities in Iowa in 1998 and in Wisconsin and Texas in 1999; it also bought 35 generating plants in Maine in 1999. That year FPL Group sold its Turner Foods citrus unit and the rest of its cable TV holdings. By 2000 FPL Energy owned interests in plants in 12 states.

Out of its fiber-optic operations FPL Group in 2000 created subsidiary FPL FiberNet to market wholesale capacity. That year talks of Spanish utility giant Iberdrola purchasing FPL Group ended when Iberdrola's shareholders objected; in 2001 plans to merge with New Orleans-based Entergy fell through after a series of disagreements. The deal would have created one of the US's largest power companies.

In 2002 FPL Group purchased an 88% interest in the Seabrook Nuclear Generating Station in New Hampshire for $837 million from a consortium of US utilities including Northeast Utilities (since renamed Eversource Energy) and BayCorp Holdings. In 2005 FPL Group acquired Gexa Corp. a Houston-based electric utility.

Late in 2005 FPL agreed to buy rival power concern Constellation Energy Group Inc. in an $11 billion stock deal. However the companies called the deal off in 2006 citing uncertainty about regulatory approvals.

FPL Energy had agreed to purchase British Energy's 50% stake in nuclear power generation firm AmerGen Energy in 2003; however Exelon which owns the other half of AmerGen exercised its right of first refusal and purchased the remainder of AmerGen.

The company purchased the Point Beach Nuclear Plant in Two Rivers from WEC Energy for $924 million in 2007.

In 2009 the company acquired three wind power developments in South Dakota Texas and Wisconsin from Babcock & Brown for about $350 million.

In 2010 NextEra Energy acquired four small solar photovoltaic projects located in Ontario from First Solar.

In 2009 its Lone Star Transmission subsidiary was allocated $565 million of a $4.9 billion transmission grid improvement program to deliver wind power to West Texas and the Texas Panhandle. Lone Star will build and operate 250 miles of the 2300-MW project.

In 2010 the company changed its corporate name from FPL Energy to NextEra Energy in order to better reflect its strategic focus on green energy and to differentiate it from subsidiary Florida Power & Light.In 2012 this unit bought the 165-MW Cimarron I Wind Energy Center from CPV Renewable Energy Company. The addition of the Cimarron Wind Energy Center is consistent with the company's strategy to add fully-contracted clean energy projects to its portfolio.In 2011 NextEra Energy Resources sold its ownership interest in the approximately 583-MW Rhode Island State Energy Center to subsidiaries of Entergy for $346 million.That year the company signed nearly 2200 MW of long-term wind and solar contracts. Growing its solar portfolio it acquired the 550 MW Desert Sunlight Solar Farm near Desert Center California from First Solar in 2011.

EXECUTIVES

Chairman and CEO, James L. (Jim) Robo, age 53, $1,215,000 total compensation

Vice Chairman and CFO, Moray P. Dewhurst, age 60, $703,100 total compensation

EVP and General Counsel, Charles E. Sieving, age 42, $689,000 total compensation

President and CEO NextEra Energy Resources, Armando Pimentel, age 53, $745,900 total compensation

President and CEO Florida Power & Light, Eric E. Silagy

EVP Human Resources and Corporate Sevices, Deborah H. Caplan

CFO, John Ketchum

Vice President Engineering and Construction Division, Craig Arcari

Vice President, Michael (Mel) Broker

Vice President, Ron Reagan

Vice President Midstream U S. Gas Assets, Ajey Chandra

Executive Vice President Federal Regulatory Affairs, Joe Kelliher

Vice President And Chief Litigation Counsel, Robert (Bob) Sendler

Treas, Peter D (Pete) Boylan

Assistant Treasurer Corporate Finance, Nicholas Vlisides

Auditors: Deloitte & Touche LLP

LOCATIONS

HQ: NextEra Energy Inc
700 Universe Boulevard, Juno Beach, FL 33408
Phone: 561 694-4000   **Fax:** 561 694-4620
Web: www.nexteraenergy.com

PRODUCTS/OPERATIONS

2014 Sales

	$ mil.	% of total
Florida Power & Light	11,421	67
NextEra Energy Resources	5,191	30
Corporate & other	409	3
Total	**17,021**	**100**

Selected Subsidiaries and Divisions

Florida Power & Light Company
  Energy Marketing and Trading
FPL Group Capital Inc.
  NextEra Energy Resources LLC
  FPL FiberNet LLC
  New Hampshire Transmission LLC
  Lone Star Transmission

AES	Florida Public
Bangor Hydro-Electric	Utilities
Berkshire Hathaway	JEA
Energy	Oglethorpe Power
CMS Energy	Progress Energy
Calpine	Public Service
Chesapeake Utilities	Enterprise Group
Delmarva Power	SCANA
Duke Energy	Seminole Electric
Edison International	Sempra Energy
Entergy	Southern Company
Exelon	TECO Energy

HISTORICAL FINANCIALS

Company Type: Public

Income Statement
FYE: December 31

	REVENUE ($ mil.)	NET INCOME ($ mil.)	NET PROFIT MARGIN	EMPLOYEES
12/14	17,021	2,469	14.5%	13,800
12/13	15,136	1,908	12.6%	13,400
12/12	14,256	1,911	13.4%	14,400
12/11	15,341	1,923	12.5%	14,800
12/10	15,317	1,957	12.8%	15,000
Annual Growth	2.7%	6.0%	—	(2.1%)

2014 Year-End Financials

Debt ratio: 38.74%
Return on equity: 13.01%
Cash ($ mil.): 577
Current ratio: 0.72
Long-term debt ($ mil.): 24,367

No. of shares (mil.): 443
Dividends
  Yield: 2.7%
  Payout: 66.6%
Market value ($ mil.): 47,086

	STOCK PRICE ($) FY Close	P/E High/Low	PER SHARE ($) Earnings	Dividends	Book Value
12/14	106.29	19 15	5.60	2.90	44.96
12/13	85.62	20 15	4.47	2.64	41.47
12/12	69.19	16 13	4.56	2.40	37.90
12/11	60.88	13 11	4.59	2.20	35.92
12/10	51.99	12 10	4.74	2.00	34.36
Annual Growth	19.6%	— —	4.3%	9.7%	7.0%

NGL Energy Partners LP

NGL Energy Partners' is devoted to natural gas liquids (NGL) logistics crude oil logistics water services and retail propane. Its crude oil logistics segment (its largest) buys crude oil from producers and transports it for resale at pipeline injection points storage terminals barge loading facilities rail facilities refineries and other trade hubs. It also retails wholesales and stores propane and other natural gas liquids. Wholesale operations deliver propane to third-party storage and transportation facilities. Retail operations include leasing propane tanks and other equipment and propane delivery. The retail propane segment has a propane storage capacity of 10.8 million gallons.

Geographic Reach

The company's Crude oil logistics segment's operations are located near areas of high crude oil production such as the Bakken Shale Basin in North Dakota the Niobrara Shale Basin in Colorado the Mississippi Lime Basin in Oklahoma the Permian Basin in Texas and New Mexico and the Eagle Ford Basin in Texas. It Water Services' facilities are near fields with high levels of oil and natural gas production such as the Pinedale Anticline Basin in Wyoming the DJ Basin in Colorado and

the Permian and Eagle Ford Basins in Texas. The natural gas liquids logistics segment's terminals are in Jefferson City Missouri East St. Louis Illinois and in St. Catherines Ontario Canada.

Operations

The company's crude oil logistics segment purchases crude oil from producers and transports it for resale at pipeline injection points storage terminals barge loading facilities rail facilities refineries and other trade hubs. In 2013 it owned 300 trucks 270 trailers 463 leased rail cars and 4 towboats and 10 barges. In addition it also owned 42 pipeline injection facilities in Kansas Oklahoma North Dakota New Mexico Texas and Montana and leased 12 rail transload facilities in Colorado Kansas North Dakota Oklahoma and Texas. Its crude oil logistics business operates under the High Sierra Transportation High Sierra Crude Oil Marketing & Transportation Pecos Andrews Oil Buyers Striker and Third Coast Towing brands.NGL Energy Partners' water services segment revenues are derived from the gathering transportation treatment and disposal of wastewater generated from oil and natural gas production operations and from the sale of recycled water and recovered hydrocarbons. It operates 90 trucks and 70 frac tanks.The NGL logistics segment purchases propane butane and other NGLs from refiners processing plants producers and other parties and sells the product to retailers refiners and other participants in the wholesale markets. It owns 17 terminals leases underground storage capacity and operates a fleet of leased rail cars.The company's retail propane business (retail marketing and the sale and distribution of propane and distillates propane tanks equipment and supplies) serves more than 270000 residential agricultural commercial and industrial customers. It owns or leases 86 customer service locations and 94 satellite distribution locations. In addition it owns 420 bulk storage tanks with capacities ranging from 5000 to 90000 gallons; and has about 296000 stationary customer storage tanks with capacities ranging from 7 to 30000 gallons.NGL Energy Partners owns two major operating subsidiaries: High Sierra Energy LP; and NGL Energy Operating LLC.

Financial Performance

The company saw a huge increase in revenues in 2013 to $4 billion (from $1 billion in 2012) primarily due to increased revenues in the crude oil logistics and retail propane segments.The acquisition of High Sierra allowed the company to form a crude oil segment from which it derived increased sales of $2 billion in 2013 from crude oil sales and $16 million of revenues from the transportation of crude oil owned by other parties. That year the spread between crude oil prices in the mid-continent region and crude oil prices in south Texas widened gave NGL Energy Partners the opportunity to for generate favorable margins by transporting crude from one region to the other.The retail propane segment's revenues grew by more than 100% thanks to higher volumes fueled by acquisitions despite oa decline in pricesThe natural gas lquids logistics segment's revenues increased due to increased contributions derived from High Sierra from propane sales; and as well as increased volume sold due primarily to the 2011 SemStream acquisition.The company's net income jumped to $48 million in 2013 from $8 million in 2012 primarily due to higher reveneus partially offset by increased interest and other expenses.

Strategy

Take advantage of its vertical integration the company is looking enhance its ability to transport crude oil from the wellhead to refiners wastewater from the wellhead to treatment for disposal recycle or discharge and transport natural gas liquids from processing plants to end users including re-

tail propane customers. It plans to achieve organic growth by investing in new assets that increase volumes and pursue acquisitions that add scale to its crude oil logistics platform and enhance the geographic diversity of its water services segment.

To raise cash in 2016 NGL Energy Partners sold TransMontaigne GP LLC (a general management services company and general partner of Denver-based fuel-terminal owner TransMontaigne Partners L.P.) to ArcLight Capital for $350 million.

Mergers and Acquisitions

Growing its water services businesses in 2014 NGL Energy Partners acquired the water disposal and hauling business of Oilfield Water Lines LP (a partnership between High Roller Wells and the Mark Cuban Companies) for $168 million. The deal gave it strategically located oil and gas water disposal facilities to its portfolio of water treatment and gathering infrastructure. The acquisition brings 90000 barrels per day of additional disposal capacity in the growing Eagle Ford Shale in South Texas.

Expanding its midstream business in 2013 NGL Energy Partners acquired diversified midstream energy company Gavilon LLC for $890 million. (The deal follows the company's 2011 purchase of SemGroup's SemStream unit for about $282 million).

In 2013 the company completed six business combination transactions to acquire retail propane and distillate operations primarily in the northeastern and southeastern US (for $71 million) and During four acquisitions to expand the assets and operations of its crude oil logistics and water services businesses (for about $53 million).In the fall of 2013 NGL Energy Partners' wholly-owned subsidiary NGL Supply Terminal Company LLC acquired the natural gas liquid assets from Keyera Energy Inc. a Delaware corporation for $43 million in cash; which consists of four rail to truck propane terminal facilities and related assets located in Albuquerque NM Superior MT Shelton and Vancouver WA.

In 2012 it acquired Downeast Energy's Maine and New Hampshire distribution assets (50000 customers and annual deliveries of 12 million gallons of retail propane and 28 million gallons of distillate.)

That year the company continued its buying spree with the acquisition of Denver-based High Sierra Energy LP and its general partner High Sierra Energy GP LLC for about $693 million. High Sierra Energy has crude oil gathering water treatment and natural gas liquids (NGL) operations.

In 2012 NGL Energy Partners completed the contribution of Pacer Propane assets to NGL Energy Partners in exchange for about $31 million in cash plus net working capital and 1.5 million NGL Energy Partners common units. The acquisition of Pacer Propane expanded the company's geographic footprint into the western US and added 17 million gallons of annual volume.

Company Background

NGL Energy Partners went public in 2011. The company use the $72 million proceeds from the IPO to repay debt from acquisitions and purchase additional propane and midstream assets or businesses.

NGL Energy Partners is part of NGL Energy Holdings which is owned by company management and NGL Holdings. Silverthorne Operating holds the company's operating subsidiaries. The multi-layer structure is common among energy companies. NGL Holdings owned about 27% of the company pre-IPO. Brothers and co-presidents Shawn and Todd Coady together owned 38% through Hicks Oil & Hicksgas Incorporated.

Formed in 2010 by several investors NGL Energy Partners acquired and combined the assets and operations of NGL Supply a wholesale propane and terminalling business founded in 1967 and Hicksgas a retail propane business founded in 1940.

EXECUTIVES

Vice President Wholesale, Stan Bugh
CEO, H. Michael Krimbill, age 61, $292,500 total compensation
President Retail Division, Shawn W. Coady, age 53, $311,250 total compensation
SVP Finance and Treasurer, Atanas H. Atanasov, $287,500 total compensation
EVP, David C. Kehoe, $323,731 total compensation
President Eastern Retail Operations, Vincent J. Osterman, $250,000 total compensation
President; President and CEO High Sierra Energy, James J. (Jim) Burke, $381,750 total compensation
EVP NGL Crude Logistics, Don Robinson
EVP NGL Liquids, Jack Eberhardt
EVP Operations (Refined Products), Gregory J. (Greg) Pound
Executive Vice President Midstream Division, David (Dave) Eastin
Senior Vice President Legal, Bill Laughlin
Vice President Of Business Development, Bradley Atkinson
Senior Vice President Accounting, Patrice Armbruster
Senior Vice President Refined Fuels, Donald Jensen
Vice President Finance and Controller, Sharra Straight
Vice President supply, Mark McGinty
Auditors: Grant Thornton LLP

LOCATIONS

HQ: NGL Energy Partners LP
6120 South Yale Avenue, Suite 805, Tulsa, OK 74136
Phone: 918 481-1119
Web: www.nglenergypartners.com

PRODUCTS/OPERATIONS

2015 Sales

	% of total
Crude oil logistics	39
Refined products and renewables	
Refined products sales	39
Renewables sales & other	3
Liquids	
Propane	8
Other	7
Retail propane	3
Water services	1
Total	**100**

COMPETITORS

AmeriGas Partners	Equistar Chemicals
Crestwood Midstream Partners LP	Exxon Mobil
	Ferrellgas Partners
Duke Energy	Huntsman International
Dynegy	Occidental Petroleum
Energy Transfer	Spectra Energy
Enterprise Products	Williams Companies

HISTORICAL FINANCIALS

Company Type: Public

Income Statement

	REVENUE ($ mil.)	NET INCOME ($ mil.)	NET PROFIT MARGIN	EMPLOYEES
03/15	16,802	29	0.2%	3,100
03/14	9,699	48	0.5%	2,500
03/13	4,417	48	1.1%	1,970
03/12	1,310	7	0.6%	890
03/11	622	12	2.0%	353
Annual Growth	**128.0%**	**23.9%**	**—**	**72.1%**

FYE: March 31

2015 Year-End Financials

Debt ratio: 42.00%
Return on equity: —
Cash ($ mil.): 41
Current ratio: 1.48
Long-term debt ($ mil.): 2,745

No. of shares (mil.): 103
Dividends
Yield: 9.0%
Payout: —
Market value ($ mil.): 2,725

	STOCK PRICE ($) FY Close	P/E High/Low		PER SHARE ($) Earnings	Dividends	Book Value
03/15	26.23	—	—	(0.29)	2.37	20.46
03/14	37.53	74	52	0.51	2.01	19.22
03/13	26.90	28	21	0.96	1.69	16.46
03/12	20.61	72	58	0.32	0.85	13.85
Annual Growth	**6.2%**	**—**	**—**	**—**	**29.0%**	**10.3%**

NIKE Inc

Fleet-of-footwear NIKE named for the Greek goddess of victory is the world's #1 shoe and apparel company. NIKE designs develops and sells a variety of products and services to help in playing basketball and soccer (football) as well as in running men's and women's training and other action sports. Under its namesake brand NIKE also markets sports-inspired products for children and various competitive and recreational activities such as golf tennis and walking and sportswear by Converse and Hurley. NIKE sells through more than 930-owned retail stores worldwide an e-commerce site and to thousands of retail accounts independent distributors and licensees.

Geographic Reach

NIKE is based near Beaverton Oregon; it has a 394-acre site with 44 buildings. In fiscal 2015 (May year end) North America accounted for 45% of sales) Western Europe (19%) Emerging Markets (13%) Greater China (10%) Central & Eastern Europe (5%) and Japan (2%). Other operations account for the rest of its revenues.

In the US NIKE owns a full product line distribution center in Memphis Tennessee and four other distribution centers three of which are leased also in Memphis. NIKE Brand apparel and equipment are also shipped from its Foothill Ranch California distribution center which the company leases. The company also owns or leases distribution and customer service facilities outside the United States. The most significant are the distribution facilities located in Laakdal Belgium; Taicang China; Tomisato Japan and Incheon Korea all of which the company owns.The company has branch offices and subsidiaries in Argentina Australia Austria Belgium Bermuda Brazil Canada Chile China Croatia Cyprus the Czech Republic Denmark Finland France Germany Greece Hong Kong Hungary India Indonesia Ireland Israel Italy Japan Korea Malaysia Mexico New Zealand

the Netherlands Norway Panama the Philippines Poland Portugal Russia Singapore Slovakia Slovenia South Africa Spain Sri Lanka Sweden Switzerland Taiwan Thailand Turkey the UAE the UK the US Uruguay and Vietnam.

Operations

NIKE operates in six geographic segments: North America Western Europe Central & Eastern Europe Greater China Japan and Emerging Markets. Almost all of the company's branded footwear and apparel is made by third-party manufacturers outside of the US mainly in Vietnam China and Indonesia. Its equipment products are made both in the US and abroad.

In fiscal 2015 sales in the US (including sales of its Other Businesses unit) accounted for about 45% of total revenues. Converse and Hurley its affiliate brands and NIKE Golf comprise NIKE's Other Businesses. NIKE sells to thousands of US retail accounts which include a mix of footwear stores; sporting goods stores; athletic specialty stores; department stores; skate tennis and golf shops; and other retail accounts. During 2015 NIKE's three largest customers accounted for more than 25% of US sales. Non-US sales for the behemoth brand generated roughly 55% of total revenues. NIKE sells its products to retail accounts through its own Direct to Consumer (DTC) operations and through a mix of independent distributors licensees and sales representatives worldwide. The company sells to thousands of retail accounts and operates 45 distribution centers overseas.

Footwear accounted for 60% of the company's revenues in 2015.

Sales and Marketing

Worldwide NIKE sells its products to retail accounts through NIKE-owned retail stores and Internet websites and through a mix of independent distributors and licensees. NIKE also sells its products to wholesale customers and directly to consumers through its Direct to Consumer operations. It also enters into licensing agreements that permit unaffiliated parties to make and sell certain apparel digital devices and applications and other equipment designed for sports activities.

The company sells to thousands of retail accounts and ships products from 45 distribution centers outside of the US.

NIKE markets its footwear and other products globally through diverse advertising and promotional programs and campaigns including print social media online advertising and endorsement contracts with celebrity athletes. In fiscal 2015 the company spent more than $3.03 billion on advertising and promotions up from about $2.75 billion the prior year.

During fiscal 2015 NIKE's three largest customers helped to bring in 26% of US sales. During the same reporting period the company's three largest customers outside of the US accounted for some 6% of total non-US sales.

Financial Performance

During the past decade NIKE's sales and earnings per share have grown 10% and 13% respectively on an annual compounded basis. Its return on invested capital has increased from 23% to 28% and its expanded gross margins by about 150 basis points.

The company saw strong growth in revenues over the last five years. In 2015 NIKE's revenues increased by 10% due to sales increases across a number of markets including North America (12%) Western Europe (15%) Central and Eastern Europe (2%) and Converse (18%).

The increase in NIKE Brand footwear revenues for fiscal 2015 was driven by strong performance in its Sportswear Basketball Running and Football (Soccer) categories. Footwear unit sales increased by 9%; the higher selling price per pair contributed approximately 8% points of footwear revenue growth. The increase in average selling price per pair was driven by a shift to higher-priced products and the favorable impact of growth in NIKE's higher-priced DTC business. NIKE Brand apparel revenues for fiscal 2015 was driven by growth in most key categories led by Sportswear Running and Women's Training.The company's net income has followed the revenue trend over the last five years. In 2015 net income increased by 21% due to higher revenues.

NIKE's operating cash flow in fiscal 2015 increased by 55%.

Strategy

NIKE e-commerce revenues grew by 55% in fiscal 2015 to more than $1 billion fueled by an expansion to new countries and supported by infrastructure investments.

In addition to brand strength NIKE has fueled momentum by launching a stream of new products including the NIKE Fuelband a digital device to track daily activity and the Flyknit a technology designed to lighten footwear weight and improve fit. In anticipation of replacing rival Reebok as the maker of NFL-branded apparel and uniforms NIKE also expanded its offerings with new high-performance uniforms for all 32 NFL teams.

The company continues to diversify one of its apparel technologies Dri-FIT which is the adaptive foundation of everything from shirts to socks. Key Dri-FIT performance products introduced in 2015 included NIKE Pro Hyperwarm Running Dri-FIT Knit and the NIKE Pro Bra Collection.

HISTORY

Phil Knight a good miler and Bill Bowerman a track coach who tinkered with shoe designs met at the University of Oregon in 1957. The two men formed Blue Ribbon Sports in 1962 in an effort to make quality American running shoes. The next year they began selling Tiger shoes manufactured by Japanese shoe manufacturer Onitsuka Tiger. They sold the running shoes out of cars at track meets.

The company rebranded as NIKE in 1972 named for the Greek goddess of victory. The NIKE "Swoosh" logo was designed by a graduate student named Carolyn Davidson who was paid $35. The same year NIKE broke with Onitsuka in a dispute over distribution rights.

NIKE re-evaluated its long-term growth strategy in fiscal 2012 and as a result divested its Cole Haan and Umbro businesses in February 2013 and November 2012 respectively. NIKE sold Umbro to Iconix Brand Group for $225 million. The company sold Cole Haan to London-based private equity firm Apax Partners for $570 million.

EXECUTIVES

Vice President and General Manager NIKE USA, Craig Cheek
Vice President Global Brand Design, Greg Hoffman
Vice President and General Manager Asia Pacific, Roland P Wolfram
Vice President US Brand, Ken Dice
Vice President Aparrel US, Joe Serino
Vp Global Apparel, Jan Singer, age 52
President and CEO, Mark G. Parker, age 59, $1,550,000 total compensation
President Product and Merchandising, Jeanne P. Jackson, age 63, $885,000 total compensation
COO, Eric D. Sprunk, age 51, $935,000 total compensation
President NIKE Brand, Trevor A. Edwards, age 52, $935,000 total compensation
VP and General Manager Global Footwear, Michael Spillane, age 52

EVP Chief Administrative Officer and General Counsel, Hilary K. Krane, age 51
EVP Global Sports Marketing, John F. Slusher, age 46
EVP Global Human Resources, David J. Ayre, age 55
VP and General Manager Emerging Markets, Tom Peddie
VP and General Manager Global Women's Division, Heidi OÅNeill
VP and GM Nike UK and Ireland, Marc van Pappelendam
President Nike Golf, Daric Ashford
VP and GM NIKE WomenÅ's, Amy Montagne
EVP and CFO, Andrew (Andy) Campion
VP and General Manager Greater China, Angela Dong
CIO, Jim Scholefield
CEO Nike Korea, Wook-hwan (David) Song
Vice President and General Manager US Running, Amy White
Vice President BRAND Human Resources, Steve Conroy
Vice President and General Manager Central and Eastern Europe, Michaela Stitz
Vice President Logistics and Geography Operations, Gerry Rogers
Vice President Director Manager, Teresa Mains
Vice President Director Manager, Trish Young
Vice President Director Manager, Steve Dilley
Vice President Creative Director Apparel, Thomas Walker
Vice President USA Footwear, Dan Jones
Vice President and Chief Administrative Officer, Ronald (Ron) McCray
Vice President Information Technology, Matt Farrer
Vice President Design Creative Director, Keith Crawford
Vice President Human Resources Business Partner Europe, Susy Bobenrieth
Vice President General Manager Global Womens Training, Heidi ONeill
Vice President Creative Director Golf, Kurt Parker
Vice President, Ryan Reid
Vice President GOVERNMENT and PUBLIC AFFAIRS, Sean B O'Hollaren
Vice President Corporate Strategy and Development, Alicia Erdman
Executive Vice President of Meth Production, Jim Ford
Vice President Global Category Wome, Heidi O'Neill
Event Vice President, Leroy Ebanks
Assistant To Hans George Vice President North America Merchandising, Heather Oakes
Vice President General Manager Womens TRNG Emerging MKTS., Jinky Panganiban
Vice President Director Of Operations, Rene Frei
Vice President Global Apparel and Equipment Materials Nike, Susi Proudman
Vice President Marketing, Kevin Smith
Vice President E Commerce, Lisa Lynham
Vice President Of Corporate Operations, David Taylor
Vice President Creative Director Athletic Training, Janett Nichol
Vice President Global Entertainment Marketing, Pamela McConnell
Vp Commerce Affiliates, Clare L Hamill, age 61
Clinic Director, Craig Davis
Vice President Creative Director Apparel, Charlie Holmes
Vice President Director Manager, Nick Athanasakos
Vice President Treasure, Bob Woodruff
Vice President Global Product And Merchandising Human Resources, Ellen Foley
Associate Vice President of Information technology and Sales, James (Jamie) Johnson
Vice President, Ron Chan

Inp: Vice President and General Manager Northern Europe, Ulrike Koehler
Vice President Apparel Sports Categ, John (Jack) Notar
Vice President Sales Emerging Markets, Mike Best
Vice President Direct To Consumer Technology, Steven Dee
Vice President And General Manager, Mark Anderson
Vice President North America Human Resources, Monique Matheson
Vice President Principal Accounting Officer Corporate Controller, Bernard F Pliska
Vice President Director of Technology, Scott Marien
Vice President Footwear Sportswear NIKE Inc., Andrea Correani
Vice President and President NIKE Golf NIKE Inc., Cindy Davis
Vice President Global Basketball Sports Marketing, Lynn Merritt
Vice President Western Europe Marketing, Dirk-Jan van Hameren
Vice President Global Planning and Development, Chris Clipper
Vice President Global Operations and Technology, Hans Vanalebeek
Vice President It, Ralph Dilorio
Vice President Chief Operating Officer Direct to Consumer, Christiana Shi
Vice President Creative Design, Tinker Hatfield
Vice President and General Manager France, Eric Cuenot
Executive Vice President Creative Director, Cole Haan
Vice President Footwear Sportswear, Greg Thompson
Vice President North America Athletic Training, Mark Riley
Vice President of International Business and Government Relations, Joseph (Jo) Ha
Vice President Footwear Design, John (Jack) Hoke
Chairman, Philip H. Knight, age 77
Assistant Secretary Nike Inc, Peter H Koehler
Secretary, John (Jack) Coburn
Advisory Board Member, Mario Lafortune
Auditors: PricewaterhouseCoopers LLP

LOCATIONS

HQ: NIKE Inc
One Bowerman Drive, Beaverton, OR 97005-6453
Phone: 503 671-6453
Web: www.nike.com

2015 Sales

	% of total
North America	45
Western Europe	19
Emerging Markets	13
Greater China	10
Central & Eastern Europe	5
Japan	2
Global Brand Divisions	-
Converse	6
Corporate —	
Total	**100**

PRODUCTS/OPERATIONS

2015 Sales

	% of total
NIKE Brand	
Footwear	60
Apparel	28
Equipment	6
Global Brand Divisions	-
Converse	6
Corporate —	
Total	**100**

Selected Products

Athletic Shoes
Aquatic
Auto racing
Baseball
Basketball
Bicycling
Cheerleading
Cross-training
Fitness
Football
Golf
Running
Soccer
Tennis
Volleyball
Wrestling

Athletic Wear and Equipment
Accessories
Athletic bags
Bats
Caps
Digital devices
Eyewear
Fitness wear
Gloves
Golf clubs
Headwear
Jackets
Pants
Protective equipment
Running clothes
Shirts
Shorts
Skirts
Snowboards and snowboard apparel
Socks
Sport balls
Timepieces
Uniforms

COMPETITORS

ASICS	Quiksilver
Acushnet	R. Griggs
Amer Sports	Ralph Lauren
Callaway Golf	Rawlings Sporting
Columbia Sportswear	Goods
Deckers Outdoor	Rollerblade
FUBU	Russell Brands
Fila Korea	Saucony
Fruit of the Loom	Skechers U.S.A.
Hanesbrands	Steven Madden
Iconix Brand Group	Timberland
Juicy Couture	Timex
K-Swiss	Tommy Hilfiger
Levi Strauss	Under Armour
Li Ning	VF Corporation
Mizuno	Victoria's Secret
New Balance	Stores
Oakley	Wolverine World Wide
PUMA SE	adidas

HISTORICAL FINANCIALS

Company Type: Public

Income Statement

FYE: May 31

	REVENUE ($ mil.)	NET INCOME ($ mil.)	NET PROFIT MARGIN	EMPLOYEES
05/15	30,601	3,273	10.7%	62,600
05/14	27,799	2,693	9.7%	56,500
05/13	25,313	2,485	9.8%	48,000
05/12	24,128	2,223	9.2%	44,000
05/11	20,862	2,133	10.2%	38,000
Annual Growth	10.1%	11.3%	—	13.3%

2015 Year-End Financials

Debt ratio: 5.83%
Return on equity: 27.82%
Cash ($ mil.): 3,852
Current ratio: 2.52
Long-term debt ($ mil.): 1,079

No. of shares (mil.): 1,714
Dividends
  Yield: 0.0%
  Payout: 29.1%
Market value ($ mil.): 174,262

	STOCK PRICE ($) FY Close	P/E High/Low	PER SHARE ($) Earnings	Dividends	Book Value
05/15	101.67	55 39	1.85	0.54	7.41
05/14	76.91	52 39	1.49	0.47	6.22
05/13	61.66	78 37	1.36	0.41	6.24
05/12	108.18	95 65	1.18	0.35	5.67
05/11	84.45	82 60	1.10	0.29	5.26
Annual Growth	4.7%	— —	13.9%	16.8%	9.0%

NiSource Inc. (Holding Co.)

NiSource is the main energy source for resourceful Americans living in the Midwest the South and New England. The company's utility subsidiaries distribute natural gas to about 3.8 million customers in seven states. NiSource also generates transmits and distributes power to some 460000 customers in 20 counties in its home state through its largest subsidiary Northern Indiana Public Service Company (NIPSCO). NiSource owned one of the largest natural gas transmission and underground storage systems in the US including a more than 15000-mile interstate pipeline system. However to become a pure play utility group it spun off this business in 2015.

Geographic Reach

Through subsidiary Columbia Energy NiSource owns and operates five distribution subsidiaries that provide natural gas to 2.2 million residential commercial and industrial customers in Ohio Pennsylvania Virginia Kentucky and Maryland. NiSource also distributes natural gas in Indiana through NIPSCO. Columbia Gas of Massachusetts distributes natural gas to end users in Massachusetts.

Operations

The energy holding company operates in two major business areas: gas distribution; and electric generation transmission and distribution.

The company's gas distribution operations segment owns and operates 58414 miles of pipelines and related facilities.

Sales and Marketing

The company's utility subsidiaries distribute natural gas to about 3.8 million customers in seven states within a corridor that runs from the US Gulf Coast through the Midwest to New England.

Financial Performance

In 2014 the company's net revenue increased by 14% due to higher gas distribution sales as the result of an increase of $93.4 million for regulatory and service programs; an increase in large customer revenues of $6.5 million; higher revenues of $5.9 million due to customer growth and an increase in off-system sales of $5.6 million. In addition NiSource reported higher revenues from the recovery of storage inventory costs of $3.8 million and a settlement of $3.2 million at Columbia of Massachusetts.

In 2014 NiSource's net income decreased by 0.4% due to an increase in operation and maintenance costs and depreciation and amortization.The company's cash inflow decreased by 8% due lower net income and changes in working capital as a result of changes in inventories and exchange gas receivable/payable.

Strategy

NiSource believes that its long-term success lies in developing a portfolio that balances creating more efficiencies in its regulated utility operations while expanding its higher-growth gas transmission and storage businesses.In 2015 NiSource spun off its pipelines into a separately traded public company. The new company Columbia Pipeline Group includes 15000 miles of natural gas pipeline and 300 billion cu. ft. of storage plus other midstream assets in the Marcellus and Utica shales.

The company's Columbia Transmission's operations were located in Delaware Kentucky Maryland New Jersey New York North Carolina Ohio Pennsylvania Virginia and West Virginia and Columbia Gulf's operations are located in Kentucky Louisiana Mississippi Tennessee Texas and Wyoming. In recent years NiSource has also sold other non-core businesses. In 2013 Lake Erie Land a wholly-owned subsidiary of NiSource was pursuing the sale of the real estate assets it owns. NDC Douglas Properties a subsidiary of NiSource Development Company was in the process of exiting its low income housing investments. In addition to raise cash the company sold certain retail services business assets (warranty protection solutions and energy efficiency leasing solutions for residential and small business utility customers) to AGL Resources in 2013. The deal includes 500000 existing customer plans in Indiana Massachusetts Ohio Pennsylvania and Kentucky. The company exited these business lines in 2013. It also sold the commercial and industrial natural gas portfolio of its unregulated natural gas marketing business that year.

HISTORY

NiSource's earliest ancestor was the South Bend (Indiana) Gas Light Company founded in 1868 by the Studebaker brothers (of later auto fame) to supply gas. In 1886 a natural-gas discovery near Kokomo Indiana led to a boom in northern Indiana's use of the fuel. By 1900 steel plants and other industries had set up shop along Lake Michigan in northwestern Indiana and in Illinois.

Another NiSource ancestor was formed in 1901 as Hammond Illuminating but it changed its name to South Shore Gas and Electric. In 1909 Northern Indiana Gas and Electric was founded by merging South Shore with other regional utilities. The next year Northern Indiana acquired South Bend.

A third NiSource predecessor Calumet Electric (founded in 1912) had acquired several utilities by the early 1920s when utility magnate Samuel Insull bought it to add to his huge Midland Utilities holding company. In 1923 Insull bought Northern Indiana Gas and Electric which merged three years later with Calumet to form Northern Indiana Public Service Company (NIPSCO). NIPSCO acquired its current service territory in 1930 when it swapped some areas with another Midland subsidiary.

The Public Utility Holding Company Act of 1935 beginning the regulation of regional monopolies forced Midland to divest NIPSCO in 1947. In the 1950s and 1960s NIPSCO built two power plants and tripled its natural gas supply through a contract with a Houston gas company.

Responding to rising demand NIPSCO in 1970 applied to build a nuclear unit at its Bailly plant estimated to cost $180 million. In 1981 the nuke was abandoned after its cost rose to $2.1 billion. Reorganizing in 1987 NIPSCO became part of holding company NIPSCO Industries.

The Energy Policy Act of 1992 ushered in wholesale-power competition. That year NIPSCO acquired Kokomo Gas and Fuel and in 1993 it picked up Northern Indiana Fuel and Light and Crossroads Pipeline.

To prepare for oncoming retail competition NIP-SCO in 1993 divided the electric and gas utilities into competing units and increased NIPSCO's marketing force. In 1997 NIPSCO branched out buying water utility holding company IWC Resources and the next year it began a customer choice program for its natural gas customers (all gas was delivered through its distribution lines however).

The company changed its name to NiSource in 1999 but did not alter its acquisition strategy. NiSource entered the US Northeast's gas market where deregulation plans were under way by purchasing New England utility Bay State Gas. A unit of Bay State Gas EnergyUSA bought natural gas marketer TPC and NiSource began integrating its nonregulated operations into EnergyUSA.

After launching a hostile takeover which it later withdrew NiSource purchased natural gas giant Columbia Energy Group for $6 billion in 2000. NiSource then sold its salt cavern gas storage and pipeline construction subsidiaries as well as certain Columbia electric generation and LNG facilities. In 2001 NiSource sold its Columbia Propane unit to AmeriGas Partners; it also agreed to sell water company IWC Resources (and its utility subsidiary Indianapolis Water) to the City of Indianapolis (the sale was completed in 2002).

In 2002 NiSource teamed up with the merchant services unit of Aquila (formerly UtiliCorp) to form an energy marketing and trading joint venture; however NiSource later backed out of the partnership due to instability in the energy trading industry. It also shut down its coal-fired Mitchell Generating Station and sold its SM&P Utility Resources subsidiary to The Laclede Group.

The following year NiSource sold its Columbia Transmission Communications (Transcom) subsidiary to Neon Communications (which itself was acquired by Globix in 2005).To pay down debt and focus on its core operations in 2008 NiSource sold Northern Utilities and Granite State Gas Transmission to Unitil for about $202 million. It also sold its Whiting Clean Energy facility to BP Alternative Energy North America for $217 million.In 2010 the company initiated three separate projects (for a total of $80 million) in the Majorsville Pennsylvania area to aggregate Marcellus Shale gas production for downstream transmission.

To boost its gas transmission and storage assets and take advantage of the burgeoning shale gas market in 2012 the company formed joint ventures with Hilcorp Energy to develop gas production and midstream infrastructure in the Utica shale in Northeastern Ohio and Western Pennsylvania.

EXECUTIVES

President Columbia Gas of Massachusetts, Stephen H. (Steve) Bryant
EVP and Chief Legal Officer, Carrie J. Hightman, age 57, $483,750 total compensation
President and CEO, Joseph (Joe) Hamrock, age 52, $487,500 total compensation
EVP NIPSCO, Violet G. Sistovaris
President Columbia Gas of Maryland and Columbia Gas of Pennsylvania, Mark Kempic
EVP Corporate Affairs and Human Resources, Robert D. (Rob) Campbell, age 55, $270,000 total compensation
EVP; Group CEO Northern Indiana Public Service Co. (NIPSCO), Jim L. Stanley, age 60
President Columbia Gas of Kentucky, Herbert A. (Herb) Miller
President Columbia Gas of Ohio, Dan Creekmur, age 35
EVP CFO and Treasurer, DOnald Brown
President Columbia Gas of Virginia, Brent Archer
Vice President Information Technology Manager, Dick James

Vice President Technical And Support Services, Monica Nguyen
Vice President Service Delivery, Stuart Stern
Vice President of IT Service Performance, Cassandra Pullin
Vice President Of Finance, Joe Mulpas
Vice President, Michael Alverson
Vice President, Barbara McKay
Vice President Audit, Larry Francisco
Vice President Marketing Services, Dale Williams
Vice President of Information Technology, Julie McElmurry
Vice President, Joel Hoelzer
Vice President Marketing And Regulatory Strategy, Carl Levander
Vice President Marketing And Volume Management, Peter (Pete) Kinsella
Executive Vice President and Group Chief Executive Officer Columbia Pipeline Group (CPG), Glen Kettering
Vice President Human Resources, Rob Campbell
Vice President Controller, Jeffrey (Jeff) Grossman
Vice President Distribution, K P Foley
Senior Vice President Field Operations, Keith Wooldridge
Chairman, Richard L. (Rich) Thompson, age 75
Vice President Deputy General Counsel and Assistant Secretary, Robert (Bob) Smith
Assistant Treasurer, Mark Downing
Auditors: DELOITTE & TOUCHE LLP

LOCATIONS

HQ: NiSource Inc. (Holding Co.)
  801 East 86th Avenue, Merrillville, IN 46410
Phone: 877 647-5990
Web: www.nisource.com

PRODUCTS/OPERATIONS

2014 Sales

	$ mil.	% of total
Gas distribution	2,597	40
Gas transmission & storage	1,872	29
Electric	1,672	26
Other	328	5
Total	**6,470**	**100**

Selected Subsidiaries

Utility operations
  Bay State Gas Company (natural gas utility)
  Colombia Gas of Kentucky Inc. (natural gas utility)
  Columbia Gas of Maryland Inc. (natural gas utility)
  Columbia Gas of Ohio Inc. (natural gas utility)
  Columbia Gas of Pennsylvania Inc. (natural gas utility)
  Columbia Gas of Virginia Inc. (natural gas utility)
  Kokomo Gas and Fuel Company (natural gas utility)
  Northern Indiana Fuel and Light Company Inc. (NIFL natural gas utility)
  Northern Indiana Public Service Company (NIPSCO electric and natural gas utility electric generation)
Gas transmission and storage operations
  Columbia Gas Transmission Corporation
  Columbia Gulf Transmission Company
  Crossroads Pipeline Company
Other operations
  CNS Microwave (telecommunications infrastructure)
  EnergyUSA-TPC (energy marketing and asset management)
  NiSource Energy Technologies (distributed power generation technologies)

COMPETITORS

AEP	FirstEnergy
Atmos Energy	IPALCO Enterprises
Baltimore Gas and Electric	NSTAR
Constellation Energy Group	National Grid USA
Dominion Resources	New Jersey Resources
Duke Energy	Nicor Gas
EQT Corporation	RGC Resources
Eversource Energy	Southern Union
	Unitil
	Vectren

HISTORICAL FINANCIALS

Company Type: Public

Income Statement

FYE: December 31

	REVENUE ($ mil.)	NET INCOME ($ mil.)	NET PROFIT MARGIN	EMPLOYEES
12/14	6,470	530	8.2%	8,982
12/13	5,657	532	9.4%	8,477
12/12	5,061	416	8.2%	8,286
12/11	6,019	299	5.0%	7,957
12/10	6,422	292	4.5%	7,604
Annual Growth	**0.2%**	**16.1%**	**—**	**4.3%**

2014 Year-End Financials

Debt ratio: 40.21%	No. of shares (mil.): 316
Return on equity: 8.79%	Dividends
Cash ($ mil.): 25	Yield: 6.1%
Current ratio: 0.62	Payout: 155.4%
Long-term debt ($ mil.): 8,155	Market value ($ mil.): 13,406

	STOCK PRICE ($) FY Close	P/E High/Low		PER SHARE ($) Earnings	Dividends	Book Value
12/14	42.42	26	19	1.67	1.02	19.54
12/13	32.88	19	15	1.70	0.98	18.77
12/12	24.89	18	16	1.39	0.94	17.90
12/11	23.81	23	17	1.03	0.92	17.73
12/10	17.62	17	14	1.04	0.92	17.66
Annual Growth	**24.6%**	**—**	**—**	**12.6%**	**2.6%**	**2.6%**

Noble Energy, Inc.

Noble Energy prizes petroleum and has the reserves to prove it. Noble looks for oil and natural gas and produces and markets them in the US and internationally. US operations are focused on the Denver-Julesberg Basin and Marcellus Shale and the Gulf of Mexico. The company's international operations include onshore and offshore activities in the the Asia/Pacific region the Middle East the Mediterranean West Africa and the North Sea. In 2014 Noble reported proved reserves of about 1.4 billion barrels of oil equivalent. The company markets natural gas NGLs and oil.

Geographic Reach

Noble's five core areas are the Denver-Julesberg (DJ) Basin (onshore US); the Marcellus Shale (onshore US); the deepwater Gulf of Mexico (offshore US); offshore West Africa; and offshore Eastern Mediterranean. Outside of the US it has offices in Cameroon China Cyprus Equatorial Guinea Israel Nicaragua and the UK.

The US accounts for 62% of the company's 2014 revenues; West Africa 26%; Eastern Mediterranean 10%; and other countries 2%.

Operations

The company is a leading independent energy company engaged in worldwide oil and gas exploration and production. Its 2014 proved reserves mix included 31% global liquids (crude oil and NGLs) 36% international natural gas and 33% US natural gas. International operations accounted for 39% of its total sales volumes in 2014 and 86% natural gas and 14% crude oil and condensate.

Sales and Marketing

Crude oil natural gas condensate and NGLs produced in the US are sold under short-term and long-term contracts at market-based prices adjusted for location and quality. Crude oil and condensate are distributed through pipelines and by trucks and rail cars to gatherers transportation companies and refineries.

Deepwater Gulf of Mexico production is sold under short-term and long-term contracts at market-based prices. Onshore production of crude oil and condensate are distributed through pipelines and by trucks and rail cars to gatherers transportation companies and refineries. Gulf of Mexico production is distributed through pipelines.

In Israel Noble sells natural gas from the Mari-B Noa and Pinnacles fields and have contracted to sell natural gas from the Tamar field under long-term contracts.

The company's UK North Sea crude oil production is transported by tanker and sold on the spot market. In China it sells crude oil into the local market through pipelines under a long-term contract at market-based prices.

Sales to Glencore Energy accounted for 22% of 2014 total oil gas and NGL sales. Shell Trading (US) Company and Shell International Trading and Shipping Limited accounted for 10% of 2014 total oil gas and NGL sales or 15% of crude oil sales.

Financial Performance

In 2014 Noble's net revenues increase by 2% due to higher natural gas (25%) and NGL (26%) sales offset by lower crude oil and condensate revenues due to lower oil prices. Natural gas sales increased due to higher sales volumes in the Marcellus Shale and Eastern Mediterranean offset by lower sales volumes due to non-core onshore US property divestures in 2013. NGL revenues were up due to higher sales volumes in the DJ Basin and Marcellus Shale offset by lower NGL prices linked to crude oil price declines. In 2014 Noble's net income increased by 24% due to a commodity derivative instrument gain from crude oil. That year cash from operating activities increased by 19%.

Strategy

Noble focuses on organic growth from exploration and development drilling and augments that with a periodic opportunistic new business development (mergers and acquisitions). The company is continuing its program to drilling higher value extended-reach laterals in both the DJ Basin and the Marcellus drilling. To manage the portfolio for superior returns and to ensure geographic portfolio diversification it periodically sells non-core assets. Noble signed a gas sales deal with Arab Potash and Jordan Bromine (both of which are located in Amman Jordan) in 2014 to supply them (beginning with 2016) with gas from the Tamar field offshore Israel.

In 2014 the company spun off CONE Midstream Partners in 2014 with net proceeds of $200 million to Noble. CONE Midstream Partners should provide an efficient vehicle for future development of the midstream infrastructure needed to support Marcellus development. Both Noble and CONSOL Energy retained 32% stakes in the partnership.

Mergers and Acquisitions

Boosting its shale oil and gas assets in 2015 Noble acquired Rosetta Resources in an all-stock transaction valued at $2.1 billion plus the assumption of Rosetta's net debt of $1.8 billion. Rosetta's liquids-rich asset base includes 50000 net acres in the Eagle Ford Shale and 56000 net acres in the Permian (46000 acres in the Delaware Basin and 10000 acres in the Midland Basin).

Growing its Gulf of Mexico portfolio in 2014 the company acquired working interests in 17 deepwater exploration leases in the Atwater Valley protraction area deepwater Gulf of Mexico. It bought a 50% working interest in 13 leases and an average 26% working interest in four leases.

HISTORY

The company was founded by Lloyd Noble in 1932.

In 2009 Noble made its largest exploration discovery to date an estimated 6 trillion cu. ft. gas find at Tamar an offshore Israel field. It also made a major find in the Galapagos oil development in the Gulf of Mexico.

Following the moratorium on deepwater drilling in the Gulf of Mexico in the wake of the BP rig disaster in 2010 in 2011 Noble Energy was the first company to be awarded a permit to resume drilling in the Gulf.

Further boosting its US shale holdings in 2011 Noble Energy teamed up with CONSOL Energy to jointly develop CONSOL's 663350 Marcellus Shale acres in Pennsylvania and West Virginia. It agreed to pay CONSOL $3.4 billion over several years for its 50% stake.

To raise cash in 2012 Noble sold three onshore US properties in Kansas western Oklahoma western Texas and the Texas Panhandle for $1 billion. The properties included interests in about 1400 producing wells on approximately 109000 net acres.

EXECUTIVES

Vice President, Gerald (Jerry) Stevenson
EVP and CFO, Kenneth M. (Ken) Fisher, age 53, $590,096 total compensation
EVP Exploration New Ventures Frontier EHSR and Business Innovation, Susan M. Cunningham, age 60, $538,366 total compensation
Chairman President and CEO, David L. Stover, age 58, $763,943 total compensation
SVP General Counsel and Secretary, Arnold J. Johnson, age 60, $449,712 total compensation
SVP Eastern Mediterranean, J. Keith Elliott, age 71
SVP and Advisor to CEO, Ted D. Brown, $480,000 total compensation
VP and CIO, Gary Birdwell
SVP US Onshore, Charles J. (Chip) Rimer
EVP Operations, Gary W. Willingham
Country Manager Noble Energy Israel, Binyamin Zomer
Senior Vice President, Alan Bullington
Vice President Investor Relations, David R (Dave) Larson
Vice President, Colin Sinclair
Vice President for the Eastern Mediterranean, Lawson Freeman
Vice President Strategic Planning and Environmental Analysis, Garry Willingham
Senior Vice President Eastern Mediterranean, Keith Elliott
Vice President Human Resources, Lee Robison
Vice President Communications And Government Relations, Ben Dillon
Auditors: KPMG LLP

LOCATIONS

HQ: Noble Energy, Inc.
  1001 Noble Energy Way, Houston, TX 77070
Phone: 281 872-3100   **Fax:** 281 872-3111
Web: www.nobleenergyinc.com

2014 Sales

	$ mil.	% of total
US	3,184	62
West Africa	1,338	26
Eastern Mediterranean	479	10
Other international & corporate	100	2
Total	5,101	100

PRODUCTS/OPERATIONS

2014 Sales

	$ mil.	% of total
Oil Gas & NGLs	4,931	97
Income from Equity Method Investees	170	3
Total	5,101	100

Selected Subsidiaries

Energy Development Corporation (China) Inc.
Energy Development Corporation (HIPS) Inc.
Gasdel Pipeline System Incorporated
HGC Inc.
Noble Energy Marketing Inc.
Producers Service Inc.

COMPETITORS

Abraxas Petroleum	Exxon Mobil
Anadarko Petroleum	Helmerich & Payne
Apache	Hercules Offshore
BP	Hess Corporation
Black Hills	Murphy Oil
Bonanza Creek	Pioneer Natural
Cabot Oil & Gas	Resources
Chevron	Range Resources
Clayton Williams	Repsol
Energy	Royal Dutch Shell
Dominion Resources	Stone Energy
EOG	TOTAL

HISTORICAL FINANCIALS

Company Type: Public

Income Statement

FYE: December 31

	REVENUE ($ mil.)	NET INCOME ($ mil.)	NET PROFIT MARGIN	EMPLOYEES
12/14	5,101	1,214	23.8%	2,735
12/13	5,015	978	19.5%	2,527
12/12	4,223	1,027	24.3%	2,190
12/11	3,763	453	12.0%	1,876
12/10	3,022	725	24.0%	1,772
Annual Growth	14.0%	13.8%	—	11.5%

2014 Year-End Financials

Debt ratio: 27.36%	No. of shares (mil.): 364
Return on equity: 12.45%	Dividends
Cash ($ mil.): 1,183	Yield: 1.4%
Current ratio: 1.22	Payout: 20.8%
Long-term debt ($ mil.): 6,103	Market value ($ mil.): 17,297

	STOCK PRICE ($) FY Close	P/E High/Low	PER SHARE ($) Earnings	Dividends	Book Value
12/14	47.43	24 13	3.27	0.68	28.31
12/13	68.11	45 21	2.69	0.55	25.52
12/12	101.74	36 27	2.86	0.46	23.07
12/11	94.39	78 53	1.27	0.40	20.41
12/10	86.08	42 27	2.05	0.36	19.45
Annual Growth	(13.8%)	— —	12.4%	17.2%	9.8%

Nordstrom, Inc.

Service with a smile is a part of Nordstrom's corporate culture. One of the nation's largest upscale apparel and shoe retailers Nordstrom sells clothes shoes and accessories through more than 115 Nordstrom department stores and over 165 off-price outlet stores (Nordstrom Rack) in nearly 40 states and online. It also operates a pair of Jeffrey luxury boutiques a "Last Chance" clearance store online private sale site HauteLook and personalized clothing service Trunk Club. With its easy-return policy and touches such as thank-you notes from employees Nordstrom has earned a reputation for top-notch customer service. Nordstrom family members who own about 25% of the retailer's stock closely supervise the chain.

HISTORY

Company Background In 1901 John Nordstrom a lumberjack and successful gold miner used his Alaska Gold Rush money to open Wallin & Nordstrom shoe store in Seattle with shoemaker Carl Wallin. Nordstrom retired in 1928 and sold his half of the business which included a second store to his sons Everett and Elmer. Wallin sold his share to the brothers after retiring the following year. A third Nordstrom son Lloyd joined in 1933. The shoe chain thrived and incorporated as Nordstrom's in 1946.

By 1963 Nordstrom's was the largest independent shoe chain in the country. The company diversified by acquiring Best Apparel's stores in Seattle and Portland Oregon. Three years later Nordstrom's bought Portland's Nicholas Ungar a fashion retailer and merged it with one of its shoe stores in Portland under the name Nordstrom Best.

Renaming itself Nordstrom Best in 1966 the company went public in 1971 and changed its name again in 1973 to Nordstrom. The retailer grew steadily throughout the 1970s opening new stores boosting sales in existing stores and diversifying. In 1976 Nordstrom started Place Two featuring apparel and shoes in smaller stores than its traditional department layouts. It moved into Southern California (Orange County) two years later. Buoyed by almost $300 million in new sales Nordstrom executives planned an aggressive expansion.

Nordstrom opened its first store on the East Coast in 1988 in Virginia. The chain continued to expand opening stores in Northern California and in the affluent Washington DC suburbs.

The 1989 San Francisco earthquake along with a national downturn hurt retail sales significantly. Nordstrom's much-touted focus on customer service had a downside: The company was investigated in 1990 for not paying employees for customer services they performed including delivery of merchandise on their own time. (Three years later Nordstrom set aside $15 million to pay back wages to employees who had performed off-the-clock services.)

The company continued to expand in the East and Midwest opening its first store in the New York City area in 1991. In 1993 the retailer opened a men's boutique in New York (Façonnable). Looking for new ways to attract customers Nordstrom introduced a mail-order catalog the next year.

Following the family's business tradition six members of Nordstrom's fourth generation began running the company in 1995. Third-generation members James Nordstrom John Nordstrom Bruce Nordstrom and Jack McMillan retired as co-chairmen and were replaced by non-family members Ray Johnson and John Whitacre. (Johnson retired in 1996.)

Nordstrom created Nordstrom.com a partnership with Benchmark Capital and Madrona Investment Group in 1999 to consolidate its catalog and Internet operations.

In early 2000 amid slumping sales the company dissolved the co-presidency. Less than a year later however the Nordstroms were back in charge. Chairman and CEO Whitacre resigned and Blake Nordstrom took over running the company as president. His father Bruce came out of retirement to take the chairman's role. Later the company bought the French design company Façonnable which supplies the products for its Façonnable boutiques.

In May 2002 the company bought out Benchmark's and Madrona's minority stake in Nordstrom.com.

Nordstrom bought a majority interest in August 2005 in luxury specialty stores Jeffrey New York and Jeffrey Atlanta. Terms of the agreement were not disclosed. The Jeffrey stores had about $35 million in sales in 2004. Also in 2005 the company opened stores in Atlanta; Dallas; Irvine California; and San Antonio.

In late 2007 Nordstrom sold its four US Façonnable boutiques and 37 European locations to Lebanon-based M1 Group for about $210 million. Overall in 2007 Nordstrom opened three full-line department stores and a single Rack store.

Nordstrom opened its first full-line department store in Hawaii in early 2008. That October amid economic gloom the retailer opened a store in Pittsburgh. Overall the retailer opened eight new Nordstrom stores and half a dozen Rack outlets in 2008. In 2009 it added three full-line Nordstrom locations and 13 Rack outlets.

Nordstrom acquired e-tailer HauteLook for $180 million in stock in March 2011. Based in Los Angeles HauteLook is a leader in online private sales.

EXECUTIVES

CEO and Co-President, Blake W. Nordstrom, age 54, $722,986 total compensation
Exec V Pres-pres Credit Group, Kevin Knight
EVP and CFO, Michael G. Koppel, age 58, $742,000 total compensation
EVP and Co-President; President Merchandising, Peter E. (Pete) Nordstrom, age 53, $722,986 total compensation
EVP and Co-President; President Nordstrom.com, Erik B. Nordstrom, age 53, $722,986 total compensation
EVP General Counsel and Secretary, Robert B. Sari, age 58
EVP and Regional Manager Southern California, Robert J. Middlemas, age 58
EVP and President Nordstrom Rack, Geevy S. K. Thomas, age 50
EVP and CIO, Daniel F. (Dan) Little, age 54, $552,806 total compensation
EVP and President Stores, James F. (Jamie) Nordstrom, age 42
EVP and Chief Marketing Officer, Brian K. Dennehy, age 50
EVP and General Merchandise Manager MenÂ's Apparel, David M. Witman, age 56
EVP and General Merchandise Manager Accessories and Women's Specialized Divisions, Margaret Myers, age 68
EVP and General Merchandise Manager Designer Women's and Kids Apparel, Tricia D. Smith, age 44
EVP and General Merchandise Manager Shoe Division, Scott A. Meden, age 52
EVP Finance and Treasurer, James A. Howell, age 50
EVP and General Merchandise Manager Nordstrom Rack, Paige L. Thomas, age 44
EVP and President Nordstrom Product Group, Mark J. Tritton, age 51
EVP Strategy and Development, Kenneth J. (Ken) Worzel, age 50, $535,889 total compensation
EVP Nordstrom Merchandising Group, Teri Bariquit, age 49
EVP and General Merchandise Manager Cosmetics Division, Gemma Lionello, age 50
EVP; Chairman and CEO Nordstrom fsb; President Nordstrom Credit, Steven C. Mattics, age 46
EVP Supply Chain, Michael Sato
EVP Online Merchandising, Kirk Beardsley
EVP and President Nordstromrack.com and HauteLook, Terence Boyle
EVP Human Resources, Chrstine Deputy
EVP IT, Samuel J. Hogenson
EVP User Experience and Optimization, Brian Saltzman
Vice President Finance, Michelle Buzzoni
Vice President Consumer Insights, Lynda Firey-oldroyd
Vice President, John (Jack) Hall
Vice President Internal Audit and Financial Controls, Dominique Vincenti
Vice President, Tacey Powers
Vice President Information Systems, Mark Peterson
Vice President and Director Supply Chain Strategy, Sherene Huntzinger
Vice President of Procurement, Steve Kesinger
Vice President Information Technology, Don Swis
Vice President Diversity, Amelia Letcher
Executive Vice President Supply Chain, Mike Sato
Executive Vice President Strategy and Development, Ken Worzel
Vice President Finance, Jim Howell
Chairman, Enrique (Rick) Hernandez, age 60
Auditors: Deloitte & Touche LLP

LOCATIONS

HQ: Nordstrom, Inc.
1617 Sixth Avenue, Seattle, WA 98101
Phone: 206 628-2111
Web: www.nordstrom.com

2014

Stores	Count
California	70
Texas	23
Florida	21
Illinois	15
Washington	14
New York	12
Virginia	10
Arizona	9
Massachusetts	9
Ohio	9
Oregon	9
Georgia	8
Maryland	8
New Jersey	8
Colorado	7
Michigan	7
Pennsylvania	5
Utah	5
Missouri	4
North Carolina	4
Minnesota	3
Nevada	3
Washington D.C.	3
Connecticut	2
Hawaii	2
Indiana	2
Kansas	2
Oklahoma	2
Rhode Island	2
South Carolina	2
Tennessee	2
Wisconsin	2
Alabama	1
Alaska	1
Alberta	1
Delaware	1
Idaho	1
Iowa	1
Kentucky	1
Maine	1
Total	**292**

PRODUCTS/OPERATIONS

PRODUCTS OFFERED: Selected

Dresses
Tops
Jeans
Sweaters
Coats
Jackets
Pants
Suits
Skirts
 Swimsuits
 Active Yog
 Bras Panti
Shapewear

Sleep Loun
Hosiery Le
Plus-Size Clothing
Petite-Size Clothing
Maternity Clothing
Shoes
  Handbags &
Watches
Jewelry
Fine Jewelry
Optical Frames & Reading Glasses
Sunglasses
  Scarves & Hats & Hair Accessories
Winter Accessories
Gloves
Belts
  Luggage &
  Tech Acces
  Hosiery &

2014 Stores

	No.
Nordstrom full-line stores - U.S.	116
Nordstrom Rack	167
Other	9
Total	**292**

2014 Sales

	$ mil.	% of total
Retail	13,110	97
Credit card	396	3
Total	**13,506**	**100**

Selected Retail Operations

HauteLook (private-sale website for apparel and home
  decor)
Jeffrey (boutiques)
Last Chance (clearance store)
Nordstrom (specialty stores selling apparel shoes and
  accessories for women men and children)
Nordstrom Direct (catalogs and online ordering)
Nordstrom Rack (outlets selling merchandise from
  Nordstrom specialty stores and manufacturers)

COMPETITORS

Ann Taylor	J. Crew
Astor & Black	Lands' End
Barneys	Macy' s
Benetton	Men' s Wearhouse
Bloomingdale' s	Neiman Marcus
Bluefly	Nine West
Brooks Brothers	Saks Fifth Avenue
Cach©	Talbots
Caleres	The Gap
Dillard' s	Tiffany & Co.
Donna Karan	Von Maur
Eddie Bauer LLC	Wayfair
J. C. Penney	

HISTORICAL FINANCIALS

Company Type: Public

Income Statement

FYE: January 31

	REVENUE ($ mil.)	NET INCOME ($ mil.)	NET PROFIT MARGIN	EMPLOYEES
01/15*	13,506	720	5.3%	67,000
02/14	12,540	734	5.9%	62,500
02/13	12,148	735	6.1%	61,000
01/12	10,877	683	6.3%	56,500
01/11	9,700	613	6.3%	52,000
Annual Growth	**8.6%**	**4.1%**	—	**6.5%**

*Fiscal year change

2015 Year-End Financials

Debt ratio: 33.87%	No. of shares (mil.): 190
Return on equity: 31.95%	Dividends
Cash ($ mil.): 827	Yield: 0.0%
Current ratio: 1.87	Payout: 35.4%
Long-term debt ($ mil.): 3,123	Market value ($ mil.): 14,486

	STOCK PRICE ($) FY Close	P/E High/Low	PER SHARE ($) Earnings	Dividends	Book Value
01/15*	76.20	21 15	3.72	1.32	12.84
02/14	57.45	17 14	3.71	1.20	10.88
02/13	55.12	16 13	3.56	1.08	9.71
01/12	48.55	16 12	3.14	0.92	9.42
01/11	40.91	16 10	2.75	0.76	9.27
Annual Growth	**16.8%**	— —	**7.8%**	**14.8%**	**8.5%**

*Fiscal year change

Norfolk Southern Corp.

Transportation titan Norfolk Southern is the one big train that could. Its main subsidiary Norfolk Southern Railway transports freight over a network consisting of about 20000 route miles in 20-plus states in the eastern southeastern and Midwestern US and in Ontario and Quebec. The rail system is made up of more than 15000 route miles owned by Norfolk Southern and nearly 5000 route miles of trackage rights which allow the company to use tracks owned by other railroads. Norfolk Southern transports coal and general merchandise including automotive products and chemicals. In late 2015 the company rejected an unsolicited takeover by Canadian Pacific in a deal worth $37.8 billion.

Geographic Reach

The company operates in 22 US states and Washington DC and transport overseas freight via several Atlantic and Gulf Coast ports.

Operations

Norfolk Southern reports through three segments: General Merchandise Coal and Intermodal. General Merchandise accounts for 60% of the company's revenues. The segment is subdivided into five commodity groups: Agriculture/Consumer/Government (such commodities and products as soybeans wheat beverages canned goods ethanol and military items); Chemicals (sulfur petroleum products plastics among others —major customers include DuPont and Sunbelt Chlor Alkai Partnership); Metals/Construction (steel aluminum cement bricks etc); Automotive (finished vehicles from and auto parts for such auto OEMs as Ford General Motors and Toyota); and Paper/Clay/Forest (lumber and wood products pulp board and paper products wood fibers wood pulp scrap paper and clay). The General Merchandise segment carried about 124 million tons on more than 2.5 million railroad carloads in 2014.

It also offers intermodal services (freight transportation by a combination of train and truck) through its Triple Crown Services unit.

In 2014 the company operated more than 4260 locomotives and more than 71300 freight cars.

Coal is Norfolk Southern's single largest commodity group accounting for 20% of revenues. The company carried about 142 million tons of coal in 2014 originating from major coal basins and destined for more than 80 coal generation plants as well as export metallurgical and industrial facilities. Operating in the eastern US Intermodal carried about 4 million units in 2014 for such clients as intermodal marketing companies international steamship lines and truckers.

Financial Performance

In 2014 Norfolk Southern's revenues increased by 3% due to higher volumes partially offset by lower average revenue per unit (the effects of lower rates and changes in the mix of business more than offset higher fuel surcharges). General Merchandise (58% of 2014 revenues) grew due to growth in increased volumes and improvement in revenue per unit; followed by an increase in Intermodal (20%) which benefited from growth in volume through new intermodal terminals and new service lanes. However Coal (22%) saw its revenues decline due to a decrease in carload volume and revenues per unit.In 2014 income increased by 5% thanks to higher revenues and income from railway operations along with lower fuel expenses partially offset by increase in purchased services and higher taxes.The company's operating cash flow decreased by 7% in 2014 due to increased tax payments and reduced current maturities of long-term debt. The cash flow was also affected by the higher accounts receivables.

Strategy

Looking ahead Norfolk Southern expects domestic metallurgical coal to struggle with less demand. Industrial coal shipments are expected to rise over the years to meet demand from new business. Demand for utility coal will decrease as a mild winter and low natural gas prices divert need for it. Agriculture/Consumer/Government's revenues will rise in response to more demand for ethanol and animal feed.

Chemicals are expected to enjoy a healthy next few years thanks to more shipments of crude oil from the Midwest to Eastern refineries and more demand for liquefied petroleum. Metals/Construction is forecast to respond to growth in the natural gas drilling market and higher metal-related traffic volumes. Automotive is also expected to respond to higher production of light vehicles in North America.

The company's focus is on safety service levels cost control productivity operational efficiency and a market-based approach to pricing.

Streamlining its operations in 2015 Norfolk Southern announced plans to close its Roanoke office building and relocate its functions currently to Atlanta or Norfolk. In 2014 the company opened a new Thoroughbred Bulk Transfer terminal in Chesapeake which allows customers to transfer a large array of commodities between rail cars and trucks. With its close proximity to nearby container terminals the terminal will serve Hampton Roads-served markets as well as overseas markets.Upgrading its locomotive fleet in 2014 the company launched the new GoRail locomotive which entered into the company's regular freight service.

Thanks in part to $267 million of capital funding from several states and the federal government Norfolk Southern continues to work on the Crescent Corridor an intermodal route spanning 11 states from New Jersey to Louisiana. Norfolk Southern is heralding the railroad as a solution to highway congestion relief. In 2013 Norfolk Southern opened its third Crescent Corridor intermodal facility a new $97 million terminal in South Central Pennsylvania that advances its multi-state rail infrastructure initiative connecting the Southeast and the Northeast.

Mergers and Acquisitions

In 2014 the company announced plans to acquire 282.55 miles of rail line between Sunbury Pennsylvania and Schenectady New York from the Delaware & Hudson Railway (D&H) a subsidiary of Canadian Pacific Railway. The deal allows the company to connect businesses in central Pennsylvania to upstate New York and New England and gives the company single-line routes from Chicago and the southeastern US to Albany New York and its recently built Mechanicville New York intermodal terminal.Additionally the company agreed to buy D&H's car shop in Binghamton along with other facilities along the corridor.

HISTORY

Norfolk Southern Corporation resulted from the 1982 merger of two US rail giants —Norfolk & Western Railway Company (N&W) and Southern Railway Company —which had emerged from more than 200 and 150 previous mergers respectively.

N&W dates to 1838 when one track connected Petersburg Virginia to City Point (now Hopewell). This eight-miler became part of the Atlantic Mississippi & Ohio (AM&O) which was created by consolidating three Virginia railways in 1870.

In 1881 Philadelphia banker E.W. Clark bought the AM&O and renamed it the Norfolk & Western. N&W rolled into Ohio by purchasing two other railroads (1892 1901).

The company took over the Virginian Railway a coal carrier with track paralleling much of its own in 1959. In 1964 N&W became a key railroad in the Midwest by acquiring the New York Chicago & St. Louis Railroad and the Pennsylvania Railroad's line between Columbus and Sandusky Ohio. It also leased the Wabash Railroad with lines from Detroit and Chicago to Kansas City and St. Louis.

Southern Railway can be traced back to the South Carolina Canal & Rail Road a nine-mile line chartered in 1827 and built by Horatio Allen to win trade for Charleston's port. It began operating the US's first regularly scheduled passenger train in 1830 and became the world's longest railway when it opened a 136-mile line to Hamburg South Carolina (1833).

Soon other railroads sprang up in the South including the Richmond & Danville (Virginia 1847) and the East Tennessee Virginia & Georgia (1869) which were combined to form the Southern Railway System in 1894. Southern eventually controlled more than 100 railroads forging a system from Washington DC to St. Louis and New Orleans.

The 1982 merger of Southern and N&W created an extensive rail system throughout the East South and Midwest. Norfolk Southern (a holding company created for the two railroads) also bought North American Van Lines in 1985. Triple Crown Services the company's intermodal subsidiary was started in 1986. The company also made a failed attempt to take over Piedmont Aviation the next year.

Norfolk Southern revived North American Van Lines by selling its refrigerator truck operation Tran-star (1993) and suspending its commercial trucking line. But it later sold the rest of the motor carrier (1998) to focus on rail operations.

When CSX announced its plans to buy Conrail in 1997 Norfolk Southern's counteroffer led to a split of the former Northeastern monopoly between Norfolk Southern (58%) and CSX (42%). Problems with integrating Conrail's assets hurt Norfolk Southern's results. But by 2000 it had regained some of the traffic it had lost to service problems and its intermodal shipping business also gained speed. In 2004 Norfolk Southern and CSX reorganized Conrail to give each parent company direct ownership of the portion of Conrail's assets that it operates. Conrail still operates switching facilities and terminals used by both Norfolk Southern and CSX.

Norfolk Southern got hit in the wallet in 2001: The company agreed to pay $28 million to settle a racial discrimination lawsuit brought by black employees in 1993. Norfolk Southern began rounds of layoffs and closed redundant depots and facilities in 2001.

In 2005 nine people died in South Carolina when chlorine gas leaked from a ruptured car on a Norfolk Southern freight train. The car was breached when the train crashed into a company-owned locomotive and two train cars that were parked on a siding.

The company opened the Heartland Corridor in 2010 between Chicago and Norfolk Virginia.

EXECUTIVES

Vice President, Henry C Wolf
SVP Administration, James A. (Jim) Hixon, age 61, $600,000 total compensation
VP Information Technology, Cindy C. Earhart
VP Intermodal Marketing, Michael R. (Mike) McClellan
President and CEO, James A. (Jim) Squires, age 53, $750,000 total compensation
VP Transportation, Terry N. Evans
EVP Finance and CFO, Marta R. Stewart, age 57, $500,000 total compensation
VP Information Technology, Fredric M. Ehlers
VP Network and Service Management, Jerry W. Hall
EVP and Chief Marketing Officer, Alan H. Shaw
Vp Business, Robert (Bob) Martinez
Assistant Vice President Human Resource, Gloria Dana
Assistant Vice President, Frank Brown
National Account Manager, Rick Lentz
Assistant Vice President Budget Planning and Operations, Donald (Don) Glenum
Group Vice President Paper Clay and Forest Products, Scott McGregor
Associate Medical Director, Paula Lina
Vice President Chief Engineer Design, Dave Becker
AVP Accounting Operations, Stacia Minton
Assistant Vice President Finance, Trevor Pardee
National Account Manager, Brady Daniels
Vice President Sales And Technical Support, Calvin (Cal) Roberts
Group Vice President Domestic Intermodal, James (Jamie) Bolander
Vice President Government Relations, Elizabeth (Beth) Lawlor
National Account Manager, Tom Landrum
National Account Manager, Bill Flanagan
Assistant Vice President Real Estate, Patti Carroll
Assistant Vice President Sourcing, Ben Chapman
Vice President Marketing and Sales Industrial Products, David (Dave) Lawson
Assistant Vice President Mechanical, Donald (Don) Graab
Vice President, F Wimbush
Assistant Vice President Information Technology Operations, Mark Wolf
Vice President Taxation, Robert (Bob) Kesler
Chairman, Charles W. (Wick) Moorman, age 63
Board Member, Thomas Bell
Board Member, Burton Joyce
Assis Vice Chairman, C Carbaugh
Auditors: KPMG LLP

LOCATIONS

HQ: Norfolk Southern Corp.
Three Commercial Place, Norfolk, VA 23510-2191
Phone: 757 629-2680
Web: www.nscorp.com

PRODUCTS/OPERATIONS

2014 Sales

	$ mil.	% of total
Coal	2,382	20
Intermodal	2,562	22
Chemicals	1,863	16
Agriculture consumer government	1,498	13
Metals & construction	1,521	13
Automotive	1,004	9
Paper clay and forest	794	7
Total	**11,624**	**100**

Selected Facilities Served

Active coal-loading facilities
Auto assembly plants
Auto distribution facilities
Bulk transfer facilities
Coal and iron ore transload facilities
General warehouses/distribution centers
Intermodal terminals
Just-in-time rail auto parts center
Lumber reload centers
Metals distribution centers
Paper distribution centers
Paper mills
Power generation plants served
Steel mills and processing facilities
Triple Crown Service terminals
Vehicle mixing centers

COMPETITORS

APL Logistics	Kansas City Southern
American Commercial Lines	Kirby Corporation
Burlington Northern Santa Fe	Landstar System
CSX	PVH
Canadian National Railway	Piedmont Natural Gas
Canadian Pacific Railway	Pier 1 Imports
Genesee & Wyoming	Pilgrim' s Pride
Hub Group	Pinnacle West
Ingram Industries	Pitney Bowes
J.B. Hunt	Plum Creek Timber
	Schneider National
	Union Pacific
	Werner Enterprises

HISTORICAL FINANCIALS

Company Type: Public

Income Statement

FYE: December 31

	REVENUE ($ mil.)	NET INCOME ($ mil.)	NET PROFIT MARGIN	EMPLOYEES
12/15	10,511	1,556	14.8%	30,456
12/14	11,624	2,000	17.2%	29,482
12/13	11,245	1,910	17.0%	30,103
12/12	11,040	1,749	15.8%	30,943
12/11	11,172	1,916	17.2%	30,329
Annual Growth	(1.5%)	(5.1%)	—	0.1%

2015 Year-End Financials

Debt ratio: 29.46%
Return on equity: 12.65%
Cash ($ mil.): 1,101
Current ratio: 1.18
Long-term debt ($ mil.): 9,393

No. of shares (mil.): 297
Dividends
  Yield: 2.7%
  Payout: 42.6%
Market value ($ mil.): 25,190

	STOCK PRICE ($) FY Close	P/E High/Low	PER SHARE ($) Earnings	Dividends	Book Value
12/15	84.59	22 14	5.10	2.36	40.93
12/14	109.61	18 14	6.39	2.22	40.25
12/13	92.83	15 10	6.04	2.04	36.55
12/12	61.84	14 10	5.37	1.94	31.08
12/11	72.86	14 11	5.45	1.66	30.00
Annual Growth	3.8%	— —	(1.6%)	9.2%	8.1%

Northern Tier Energy LP

Northern Tier Energy makes gasoline and sells it too. The company owns one of only two oil refineries in Minnesota and more than 260 SuperAmerica gas stations across Minnesota and Wisconsin. Its oil refinery produces 97800 barrels per day of gasoline diesel jet fuel and asphalt. The company also owns storage and transportation assets including terminals storage tanks rail loading and unloading facilities and a dock on the Mississippi River. In addition Northern Tier Energy owns a 17% stake in the 300-mile Minnesota Pipeline (Koch Industries owns the rest) that transports crude oil to its refinery.

Change in Company Type

In 2013 the company's controlling stockholders (ACON Investments and TPG Capital) sold their ownership in Northern Tier Energy to Western Refining for $775 million. As a result Western Refining owns 100% of the general partner or 38.7% of Northern Tier Energy.

Geographic Reach

The company has operations in Minnesota South Dakota and Wisconsin. Northern Tier also operates convenience stores and franchises convenience stores primarily in Minnesota and Wisconsin under the SuperAmerica trademark and owns a bakery and commissary under the Super-Mom's brand.

Operations

Northern Tier Energy splits its operations into the refinery and retail businesses. Energy marketer J.P. Morgan Commodities Canada Corporation supplies the Minnesota refinery with crude oil under an agreement through 2015. Besides its SuperAmerica gas stations the refinery also supplies gas and diesel fuel to 90 Marathon-branded gas stations located in its marketing area.

The retail segment is made up of 165 company-owned SuperAmerica gas stations and 95 franchised stores (organized under SuperAmerica Franchising LLC) mostly located in Minnesota and Wisconsin but it does have two stores in South Dakota. The stores are supplied with general merchandise (tobacco and grocery items) by wholesaler Eby-Brown and with baked goods and other prepared food by its own SuperMom's Bakery.

Sales and Marketing

The company's refinery supplies almost all of the gasoline and diesel sold in company-operated and franchised convenience stores and in independently-owned and operated Marathon branded stores within its distribution area. Its retail customers primarily include retail end-users motorists and commercial drivers.

Asphalt and heavy fuel oil are sold to a broad customer base including asphalt paving contractors government entities (including states counties cities and townships) and to asphalt roofing shingle manufacturers.

Financial Performance

Northern Tier Energy's revenues have grown steadily since 2010. It grew by 7% by 11% in 2014 due to tincreased revenue from the refining segment offset by lower retail revenues. Refining revenues increased by 12% due to higher sales volumes of crude and refined products thanks to refinery capacity expansion completed in 2013 less unplanned maintenance at the St. Paul Park Refinery in the 2014. Retail revenues declined due to lower fuel prices. Northern Tier Energy's net income increased by 4% due to higher revenues lower turnaround and related costs and the absence of a loss from derivative activities and losses from early extinguishment of debt. In 2014 net cash provided by operating activities decreased by $10 million as a result of an increase in inventories a loss from from the change in fair value of outstanding derivatives and a loss from the lower cost of market inventory adjustment.

Strategy

The company's strategy is to grow its SuperAmerica branded retail business (to which it can supply transportation fuels from its refinery) by expanding its SuperAmerica franchise business. On the refining side it plans to continue its efforts to benefit from its access to cost-advantaged crude oil and increase refinery use with high-return capital

projects that also improves yield of light products. A component of the company's growth strategy is to selectively consider accretive acquisitions within the refining industry and retail market which give it access to advantageous crude oil supplies distribution and logistics infrastructure and potential operating synergies.

Company Background

Northern Tier Energy went public with a $230 million IPO in 2012.

Following the IPO TPG and ACON Investments owned the majority of its voting power; each company also retained two seats on Northern Tier Energy's board of directors. Northern Tier Energy used the proceeds from its IPO to pay off Marathon Petroleum and its two investors.

Northern Tier Energy might be new but its properties are not. The company was formed by private investment firms TPG Capital and ACON Investments which bought the Minnesota oil refinery and SuperAmerica gas stations from Marathon for $608 million in October 2010. (Marathon Petroleum sold the properties in order to focus on the lower Midwest and Southeast.)

Without suspending operations TPG Capital and ACON Investments established Northern Tier Energy and its subsidiaries (Northern Tier Investments SuperMom's Bakery and SuperAmerica Franchising LLC) to own and manage the refinery and supply the gas stations.

EXECUTIVES

President CEO and Director, David L. (Dave) Lamp, $670,192 total compensation
VP Retail, Jack A. Helmick
EVP General Counsel and Secretary, Melissa M. Buhrig, $218,203 total compensation
VP Logistics, Jason Akey
VP St. Paul Park Refinery, Rick Hastings
SVP and Chief Commercial Officer, Scott L. Stevens, $169,231 total compensation
EVP and CFO, Karen Davis
Chairman, Paul L. Foster, age 57
Auditors: Deloitte & Touche LLP

LOCATIONS

HQ: Northern Tier Energy LP
1250 W. Washington Street, Suite 300, Tempe, AZ 85281
Phone: 602 302-5450
Web: www.ntenergy.com

PRODUCTS/OPERATIONS

2014 Sales

	$ mil.	% of total
Refining	5,097	79
Retail	1,390	21
Other	(932.1)	-
Total	**5,556**	**100**

COMPETITORS

7-Eleven	Holiday Companies
7-Eleven	Holiday Companies
BP	Kwik Trip
BP	Kwik Trip
CITGO	Marathon Petroleum
CITGO	Marathon Petroleum
Chevron	Shell Oil Products
Chevron	Shell Oil Products
ConocoPhillips	Sunoco
ConocoPhillips	Sunoco
Exxon Mobil	Tesoro
Exxon Mobil	Tesoro
Flint Hills	Valero Energy
Flint Hills	Valero Energy

HISTORICAL FINANCIALS

Company Type: Public

Income Statement

FYE: December 31

	REVENUE ($ mil.)	NET INCOME ($ mil.)	NET PROFIT MARGIN	EMPLOYEES
12/14	5,556	241	4.3%	2,950
12/13	4,979	231	4.6%	2,896
12/12	4,653	197	4.2%	2,893
12/11	4,280	28	0.7%	2,667
12/10	344	24	7.2%	—
Annual Growth	100.3%	76.7%	—	—

2014 Year-End Financials

Debt ratio: 30.74%
Return on equity: —
Cash ($ mil.): 87
Current ratio: 1.53
Long-term debt ($ mil.): 362

No. of shares (mil.): 92
Dividends
  Yield: 12.2%
  Payout: 102.2%
Market value ($ mil.): 2,053

	STOCK PRICE ($) FY Close	P/E High/Low		PER SHARE ($) Earnings	Dividends	Book Value
12/14	22.14	11	8	2.61	2.71	4.35
12/13	24.60	13	7	2.51	3.49	4.36
12/12	25.44	—	—	(0.00)	1.48	5.26
Annual Growth	(3.4%)	—	—	—	16.3%	(4.6%)

NORTHERN TIER ENERGY LP

Northern Tier Energy makes gasoline and sells it too. The company owns one of only two oil refineries in Minnesota and more than 260 SuperAmerica gas stations across Minnesota and Wisconsin. Its oil refinery produces 97800 barrels per day of gasoline diesel jet fuel and asphalt. The company also owns storage and transportation assets including terminals storage tanks rail loading and unloading facilities and a dock on the Mississippi River. In addition Northern Tier Energy owns a 17% stake in the 300-mile Minnesota Pipeline (Koch Industries owns the rest) that transports crude oil to its refinery.

Change in Company Type

In 2013 the company's controlling stockholders (ACON Investments and TPG Capital) sold their ownership in Northern Tier Energy to Western Refining for $775 million. As a result Western Refining owns 100% of the general partner or 38.7% of Northern Tier Energy.

Geographic Reach

The company has operations in Minnesota South Dakota and Wisconsin. Northern Tier also operates convenience stores and franchises convenience stores primarily in Minnesota and Wisconsin under the SuperAmerica trademark and owns a bakery and commissary under the Super-Mom's brand.

Operations

Northern Tier Energy splits its operations into the refinery and retail businesses. Energy marketer J.P. Morgan Commodities Canada Corporation supplies the Minnesota refinery with crude oil under an agreement through 2015. Besides its SuperAmerica gas stations the refinery also supplies gas and diesel fuel to 90 Marathon-branded gas stations located in its marketing area.

The retail segment is made up of 165 company-owned SuperAmerica gas stations and 95 franchised stores (organized under SuperAmerica Franchising LLC) mostly located in Minnesota and Wisconsin but it does have two stores in South Dakota. The stores are supplied with general merchandise (tobacco and grocery items) by wholesaler Eby-Brown and with baked goods and other prepared food by its own SuperMom's Bakery.

Sales and Marketing

The company's refinery supplies almost all of the gasoline and diesel sold in company-operated and franchised convenience stores and in independently-owned and operated Marathon branded stores within its distribution area. Its retail customers primarily include retail end-users motorists and commercial drivers.

Asphalt and heavy fuel oil are sold to a broad customer base including asphalt paving contractors government entities (including states counties cities and townships) and to asphalt roofing shingle manufacturers.

Financial Performance

Northern Tier Energy's revenues have grown steadily since 2010. It grew by 7% by 11% in 2014 due to tincreased revenue from the refining segment offset by lower retail revenues. Refining revenues increased by 12% due to higher sales volumes of crude and refined products thanks to refinery capacity expansion completed in 2013 less unplanned maintenance at the St. Paul Park Refinery in the 2014.Retail revenues declined due to lower fuel prices.Northern Tier Energy's net income increased by 4% due to higher revenues lower turnaround and related costs and the absence of a loss from derivative activities and losses from early extinguishment of debt. In 2014 net cash provided by operating activities decreased by $10 million as a result of an increase in inventories a loss from from the change in fair value of outstanding derivatives and a loss from the lower cost of market inventory adjustment.

Strategy

The company's strategy is to grow its SuperAmerica branded retail business (to which it can supply transportation fuels from its refinery) by expanding its SuperAmerica franchise business. On the refining side it plans to continue its efforts to benefit from its access to cost-advantaged crude oil and increase refinery use with high-return capital projects that also improves yield of light products.A component of the company's growth strategy is to selectively consider accretive acquisitions within the refining industry and retail market which give it access to advantageous crude oil supplies distribution and logistics infrastructure and potential operating synergies.

Company Background

Northern Tier Energy went public with a $230 million IPO in 2012.

Following the IPO TPG and ACON Investments owned the majority of its voting power; each company also retained two seats on Northern Tier Energy's board of directors. Northern Tier Energy used the proceeds from its IPO to pay off Marathon Petroleum and its two investors.

Northern Tier Energy might be new but its properties are not. The company was formed by private investment firms TPG Capital and ACON Investments which bought the Minnesota oil refinery and SuperAmerica gas stations from Marathon for $608 million in October 2010. (Marathon Petroleum sold the properties in order to focus on the lower Midwest and Southeast.)

Without suspending operations TPG Capital and ACON Investments established Northern Tier Energy and its subsidiaries (Northern Tier Investments SuperMom's Bakery and SuperAmerica Franchising LLC) to own and manage the refinery and supply the gas stations.

EXECUTIVES

President CEO and Director, David L. (Dave) Lamp, $670,192 total compensation
VP Retail, Jack A. Helmick
EVP General Counsel and Secretary, Melissa M. Buhrig, $218,203 total compensation
VP Logistics, Jason Akey
VP St. Paul Park Refinery, Rick Hastings
SVP and Chief Commercial Officer, Scott L. Stevens, $169,231 total compensation
EVP and CFO, Karen Davis
Chairman, Paul L. Foster, age 57
Auditors: PRICEWATERHOUSECOOPERS LLP HO

LOCATIONS

HQ: NORTHERN TIER ENERGY LP
  38C GROVE ST STE 1, RIDGEFIELD, CT 068774667
Phone: 2032446550
Web: WWW.NTENERGY.COM

PRODUCTS/OPERATIONS

2014 Sales

	$ mil.	% of total
Refining	5,097	79
Retail	1,390	21
Other	(932.1)	-
Total	**5,556**	**100**

COMPETITORS

7-Eleven	Holiday Companies
7-Eleven	Holiday Companies
BP	Kwik Trip
BP	Kwik Trip
CITGO	Marathon Petroleum
CITGO	Marathon Petroleum
Chevron	Shell Oil Products
Chevron	Shell Oil Products
ConocoPhillips	Sunoco
ConocoPhillips	Sunoco
Exxon Mobil	Tesoro
Exxon Mobil	Tesoro
Flint Hills	Valero Energy
Flint Hills	Valero Energy

HISTORICAL FINANCIALS

Company Type: Private

Income Statement

FYE: December 31

	REVENUE ($ mil.)	NET INCOME ($ mil.)	NET PROFIT MARGIN	EMPLOYEES
12/14	5,556	241	4.3%	642
12/13	4,979	231	4.6%	—
12/12	4,653	197	4.2%	—
Annual Growth	**9.3%**	**10.6%**		

2014 Year-End Financials

Debt ratio: ——		Dividends	
Return on equity: 4.30%		Yield: —	
Cash ($ mil.): 87		Payout: —	
Current ratio: 0.80		Market value ($ mil.): —	
Long-term debt ($ mil.): —			

Northern Trust Corp.

Northern Trust Corporation works to keep its clients' trust. Founded in 1889 flagship subsidiary The Northern Trust Company and other units bearing the Northern Trust name offer banking and trust services brokerage asset servicing securities lending and proprietary mutual funds (the Northern Funds). The firm provides its services to institutional clients and affluent individuals from more than 90 offices in nearly 20 states and more than 15 countries. Operating through two main segments —Corporate and Institutional Services (C&IS) and Wealth Management —Northern Trust has more than $6 trillion of assets under custody and some $960 billion under management.

Operations

Northern Trust made 64% of its total revenue from trust investment and similar servicing fees in 2014 while it made another 16% from interest income on loans and leases. It also made 6% of total revenue from interest income on securities and another 5% from foreign exchange trading income.The firm operates through two segments: Corporate and Institutional Services (C&IS) and Wealth Management. A third business unit Asset Management provides asset management and related services to both the C&IS and Wealth Management businesses.

The C&IS division provides global master trust and custody services trade settlement and reporting fund administration banking and brokerage as well as investment operations outsourcing and analysis asset management and servicing brokerage and banking services. Clients include retirement funds fund managers foundations and endowments insurance companies and government entities. The company added hedge fund services to its activities through the 2011 purchase of fund administrator Omnium (now Northern Trust Hedge Fund Services) from Citadel in a deal that added more than $70 billion in assets under administration. The C&IS business unit's client relationships are supported from international locations in North America Europe the Middle East and the Asia Pacific region. C&IS also executes related foreign exchange transactions from offices located in the US the UK and Singapore.

Northern Trust's Wealth Management segment offers trust and investment management custody philanthropic consulting estate administration private banking and brokerage services to individuals and families that have more than $200 million of assets.

Geographic Reach

Based in Chicago Northern Trust has a presence in the US across 18 states and Washington DC and internationally in Europe the Middle East and the Asia Pacific region where it has offices in China Hong Kong India Japan and Singapore.Sales and MarketingThe firm serves corporations institutions and affluent families and individuals.

Financial Performance

Northern Trust has enjoyed revenue and profit growth over the past few years as its assets under custody and management continue to grow with new business and appreciating equity markets. Still the company has yet to return to its revenue high mark of $5.68 billion (reached in 2008) and its profit high of $864.2 million (reached in 2009).The firm's revenue rose by 5% to $4.51 billion in 2014 thanks again to growing trust investment and other servicing fees driven by new business rising equity markets and favorable foreign exchange rate movements. Northern Trust's assets under custody (AUC) grew by 7% to $5.6 trillion for the year (including $3.5 trillion in global custody assets) while its assets under management (AUM) rose by 6% to $934.1 billion. The company also enjoyed rising interest income from its securities and its Federal Reserve Deposits as it increased its average earning asset base by double digits. Higher revenue in 2014 and strong cost controls drove Northern Trust's net income up by 11% to $811.80 million. Segment wise the C&IS division's net income grew by 14% while the Wealth Management division grew by 3%; both stemming from

AUM and AUC growth. Northern Trust's cash levels also continued rising with cash from operations rising by double digits to $936.0 million in 2014.Strategy

Northern Trust looks to expand its geographic footprint across the world grow its client base and strategically partner with other firms to seek opportunities in growing marketplaces. Toward its international growth expansion plans the company in 2015 established an asset management sales and client servicing team in Melbourne Australia to provide its asset management products and services to institutional investors across Australia and New Zealand. Also in 2015 to support its Asia Pacific growth strategy and its "local business" strategy to support clients as close to their local markets as possible Northern Trust opened its Seoul representative office in fast-growing South Korea. In 2014 the company added its third Asia Pacific office for the year with the opening of its Manila office in the Philippines. In 2013 Northern Trust put down roots in the Middle East by opening a new office in Saudi Arabia.As an example of its partnership growth strategy Northern Trust partnered with the Bank of Taiwan in 2015 to provide institutional and governmental clients in Taiwan with a combination of the bank's local expertise and Northern Trust's global custody and asset servicing capabilities.Mergers and AcquisitionsIn December 2015 Northern Trust agreed to buy UK-based institutional brokerage firm Aviate Global to bolster its global brokerage business and expand its reach in Europe the Middle East and the Asia-Pacific regions.Company BackgroundAs part of its international growth plan Northern Trust expanded in Europe with the 2011 purchase of Bank of Ireland's fund administration investment operations outsourcing and custody business. The acquisition was combined with Northern Trust's existing operations in Ireland which is a European hub for cross-border fund administration. The company worked to support European fund managers by expanding its depositary services across multiple fund types asset classes fund locations and investment strategies as well as by implementing the Alternative Investment Fund Managers Directive (AIFMD).In 2010 Northern Trust expanded its Wealth Management business with the acquisition of Los Angeles-based investment advisory Waterline Partners.

HISTORY

Company BackgroundWhen banker Byron Smith took time off to handle family concerns in 1885 friends turned to him for advice on trust and estate matters. It occurred to him that there was a market for such services within a banking framework.

Smith tested new Illinois banking and trust laws by arranging for state banking authorities to reject his charter application for Northern Trust. As Smith had hoped the charter was upheld by the Illinois Supreme Court.

Northern Trust opened in 1889 in one of Chicago's new skyscrapers the Rookery. With $1 million in capital —about 40% from Smith and the rest from the likes of Marshall Field (retailing) Martin Ryerson (steel) and Philip Armour (meatpacking) —the bank attracted $138000 in deposits its first day.

By 1896 the bank was firmly established; Smith began taking a salary and the company issued its first dividend. Ten years later the firm built its solid granite edifice the "Gray Lady of LaSalle Street" where it still resides.

The bank began buying commercial paper in 1912 joined the Federal Reserve System in 1917 and became a custodian for expropriated German assets during WWI. Byron Smith died in 1914 and was succeeded by his son Solomon.

Northern Trust rejected the get-rich-quick ethos of the 1920s. It was so strong during the Depression that after the 1933 bank holiday people actually clamored to make deposits and the bank administered the Depression-era scholarship fund that helped Ronald Reagan attend college. By 1941 almost half of Northern Trust's commercial deposits originated outside the Chicago area. The bank kept growing during and after WWII.

Solomon Smith retired in 1963; his son Edward took over and launched the company's expansion overseas (Northern Trust International was formed in 1968) and out of state (Florida in 1971 Arizona in 1974). The firm's business was helped by the 1974 passage by Congress of ERISA which required company retirement plans to be overseen by an outside custodian. Edward retired in 1979.

Northern Trust expanded locally when Illinois legalized intrastate branch banking in 1981. In 1987 the company lost money due in part to defaults on loans made to developing countries. It moved into California in 1988 and Texas in 1989.

Northern Trust navigated the early 1990s recession expanded geographically in the mid-1990s and added services through acquisitions. In 1995 the company became the first foreign trust company to operate throughout Canada. That year it bought investment management service RCB International (now Northern Trust Global Advisors). It expanded in the Sun Belt with such acquisitions as Dallas' Metroplex Bancshares and was made first custodian for the Teacher Retirement System of Texas (1997).

In 1998 the company expanded into Michigan and broke into the Cleveland and Seattle markets in 1999. Northern Trust entered cyberspace as well launching a website for its mutual funds. In 2000 the company opened locations in Nevada and Missouri and bought Florida-based investment adviser Carl Domino Associates (renamed Northern Trust Value Investors). Also that year the bank bought Ireland's Ulster Bank Investment Services.

In 2004 Northern Trust bought the fund management custody and trust operations of Baring Asset Management from Amsterdam-based ING Groep.

EXECUTIVES

Executive Vice President Marketing, Cheryl Dodge

Executive Vice President and Managing Director North America Sales and Servicing, Lyle Logan

Executive Vice President Worldwide Operations and Technology The Northern Trust Company, Brian Ovaert

Executive Vice President, James (Jamie) Rauh

London Ex Vice President, Teresa A Parker

Vice President Of Loans, Jean Sheridan

Vice President, Lloyd Wennlund

Executive Vice President Corporate and Institutional Services Northern Trust Company, Wilson Leech

Vice President, Donald Berk

Senior Vice President and Senior Portfolio Manager for Northern Trust Global Inv, George Maris

Senior Vice President, Michael A (Mel) Vardas

Senior Vice President CandIS Consulting Division Global Product and Strategy, Griff Ehrenstrom

Vice President, Wayne Johnson, age 64

President, William L. (Bill) Morrison, age 64, $800,000 total compensation

EVP and President Wealth Management, Steven L. (Steve) Fradkin, age 53, $600,000 total compensation

Chairman and CEO Northern Trust Corporation and Northern Trust Company, Frederick H. (Rick) Waddell, age 61, $975,000 total compensation

EVP and Chief Risk Officer, Jeffery D. Cohodes, age 54

EVP and COO, Jana R. Schreuder, age 56, $600,000 total compensation

EVP and President Asset Management, Stephen N. Potter, age 58, $587,500 total compensation

EVP and President Enterprise Shared Operations Services, Joyce St. Clair, age 55

EVP and Head Global Fund Services, Peter B. Cherecwich, age 50

EVP and CFO, Stephen B. (Biff) Bowman, age 51, $493,750 total compensation

EVP and Chief Investment Officer, Robert P. (Bob) Browne, age 50

EVP and Head Asia Pacific Region, William Mak

EVP and President Corporate and Institutional Services, Michael G. O'Grady, age 49, $600,000 total compensation

EVP and General Counsel, Susan C. Levy, age 57

EVP Human Resources, S. Gillian Pembleton, age 56

Vice President Of Corporate Real Estate, Richard Saulig

Vice President, Ken Bell

Senior Vice President Enterprise Architect, Ravi Gundimeda

Senior Vice President, Paul D'Ouville

Vice President Worldwide Technology, Maureen Shaughnessy-mikulski

Senior Vice President, John (Jack) O'Connell

Senior Vice President, Barbara A O'Connell, age 65

Ex Vice Pres, John (Jack) Grube

Senior Vice President Mainframe And Network Services, William (Bill) Jarrett

Senior Vice President Human Resources, Robert (Bob) Chapelle

Second Vice President Worldwide Techn, Tracy Nguyen

Vice President Global Compliance Information Technology, Ted Sausen

Vice President, Anne Gulotta

Vice President Marketing, Mychelle Peterson

Senior Vice Presidentinvestment Operations Outsourcing, Daniel Houlihan

Senior Vice President Regional Fiduciary Director, Thomas (Thom) Iskalis

Vice President Of Information Technology, Jeffrey Blust

Senior Vice President Managing Director, Brayton Alley

Vice President Information Technology, Ken Le Breux

Vice President, James (Jamie) Lange

Vice President, Thomas Smith

Executive Vice President and Head Corporate Risk Management, Joyce St Clair

Vice President, Corinne McClintic

Vice President C and Information Systems Strategic Product Development, Robert (Bob) Potsic

Senior Vice President Corporate Business Development, Eric Strickland

Vice President Of Technology, Thomas (Thom) Jaeggin

Senior Vice President, Elizabeth V (Beth) White

Vice President Community Lending Unit, Karen Daley

Vice President Portfolio Manager, Chris Fronk

Vice President Us Sales, Paul McDonough

Senior Vice President Managing Director, Scott Roads

Vice President Integrated Risk Management, Carolyn M Schiffels

Vice President private Banker, Brenda Distler

Vice President, Rich Michaels

Senior Vice President, Timothy (Tim) Geraghty

Senior Vice President Public Finance, Allan Ambrose

Second Vice President, James Shanel

Second Vice President Fund ADM, Barbara (Barb) Malinowski

Vice President of Marketing, Mark Welch
Senior Vice President Global Procurement, John Freel
Senior Vice President, David (Dave) Llewellyn
Vice President Trust Real Estate, Kenneth Hutson
Vice President Public Funds, Frank Fauser
Vice President Portfolio Manager, Michael Chico
Vice President Enterprise Architecture, Vivek Kinra
Vice President of Investment Risk and Analytical Services, Mark Warner
Senior Vice President Compliance, Debra Brzoska
Senior Vice President private Banker, Jeff White
Vice President, Greg Werra
Senior Vice President And Medical Doctor Wealth Advisory Services, Linda Nolan
Vice President Architecture and Innovation, Chris Butwell
Senior Vice President Mainframe And Network Services, Rick Kellemen
Vice President, Peggy O'Leary
Vice President of Marketing, Andrew (Andy) Rakowski
Vice President Finance, David (Dave) Sullivan
Second Vice President, Bradley Blackwell
Vice President, Matt Adams
Vice President Marketing and Communications, Melissa (Mel) Hulver
Vice President, Chuck Needham
Senior Vice President, Cathy Jennings
Senior Vice President Managing Director Private Client Services, Deb Finnegan
Vice President, Sharon Fine
Vice President, Kristin Missil
Vice President Human Resources, Denyse Reese
Senior Vice President, Trip Moore
Executive Vice President, Jennifer Driscoll
Senior Vice President Chief Banking Officer PFS Central Region, Paul Theiss
Vice President, Andrew Glick
Senior Vice President worldwide Technologies, John (Jack) Burke
Senior Vice President, Joseph Fedacsek
Vice President, Kristina Jakstys
Vice President Corporate Actions, Marcia Banks
Vice President Operations and Technology, Manan Mehta
Vice President Strategic Sourcing, Angela (Angie) Quates
Senior Vice President Information Technology, Jim Pecyna
Vice President Risk Analyst, Paul Loeffel
Vice President Wealth Management, Al Combs
Vice President, Bernie Doerr
Senior Vice President, Nina Staley
Vice President Corporate Re Western Division, Jennifer (Jen) Dryden
Vice President Risk Management, Scott Winkates
Vice President, Steven Santiccioli
Vice President Worldwide Technology, Mike Morena
Vice President, Grace Murphy
Vice President Alt Inv Performance Consultant, Chris Gilbert
Second Vice President Real Estate Division, Gewndolyn Warren
Vice President Solutions Architect, Siddhesh Sawant
Vice President, Katy Elsey
Vice President, Jeff Mathews
Vice President Corporate Banking, Daniel (Dan) Hintzen
Vice President Private Banking, Matthew (Matt) Riegel
Senior Vice President, Mary Prado
Vice President, Anita Nikolov
Second Vice President Private Business Group, Rick Eddington
Vice President and Portfolio Manager, Jason A Lawit
Second Vice President, Bryan Rose

Second Vice President, Len Soderblom
Vice President Enterprise Banking, Sandy Wiles
Vice President Senior Product Marketing Manager Investments, Julie Mccoy
Vice President Information Security, Kate Plattenberger
Second Vice President Vmware Infrastruct, Tim McCartney
Senior Vice President, Thomas James
Vice President Senior Business Development Officer, Nancy Lyon
Vice President Private Banking, Dick Resseguie
Vice President Operations Risk, Monica Steeg
Vice President Personal Financial Services, Nora Garvey
Vice President Estate Settlement Services, George Metzler
Senior Vice President Foundation and Institutional, Dave Cyganiak
Vice President Wealth Management, Christine Fleming
Vice President Information Technology, Bob Schroeder
Vice President Information Technology, Larry Wells
Senior Vice President PFS Client Servicing Solutions, Julie Sausen
Senior Vice President, Michael Furey
Vice President Of Human Resources, Mae Jones
Senior Vice President, Mark Hardtke
Senior Vice President, Thomas Kim
Vice President Food and Bev, Robert (Bob) Lugo
Vice President, Chris Price
Senior Vice President, Phil Maughan
Senior Management (Senior Vice President General Manager Director), Brad Biales
Vice President Software And Application Development, Ganesh Hariharan
Vice President, Ann Schroeder
Vice President Of It Operations, Parag Chheda
Second Vice President Senior Recruiter Staffing Consultant, Bill Kaminsky
Auditors: KPMG LLP

LOCATIONS

HQ: Northern Trust Corp.
50 South LaSalle Street, Chicago, IL 60603
Phone: 312 630-6000
Web: www.northerntrust.com

Selected Operations

US
Arizona
California
Colorado
Connecticut
Delaware
Florida
Georgia
Illinois
Massachusetts
Michigan
Minnesota
Missouri
Nevada
New York
Ohio
Texas
Washington
Wisconsin
International
Africa
Australia
Canada
China
Hong Kong
India
Ireland
Japan
Luxembourg
Middle East
The Netherlands
New Zealand
Saudi Arabia

Singapore
Sweden
UK

PRODUCTS/OPERATIONS

2014 Sales

	% of total
Trust Investment & Other Servicing Fees	64
Interest Income	26
Foreign Exchange Trading Income	5
Security Commissions & Trading Income	1
Treasury Management Fees	1
Other Operating Income	3
Total	**100**

Selected Subsidiaries

Northern Investment Corporation
Northern Investment Management Company
Northern Trust Bank FSB
The Northern Trust Company
  MFC Company Inc.
  Norlease Inc.
  The Northern Trust Company Canada
  Northern Trust Holdings Limited (UK)
  Northern Trust Global Services Limited (UK)
  The Northern Trust International Banking Corporation
  Northern Trust Cayman International Ltd. (Cayman Islands)
  The Northern Trust Company of Hong Kong Limited
  Northern Trust Fund Managers (Ireland) Limited
  Northern Trust (Ireland) Limited
  Northern Trust Custodial Services (Ireland) Limited
  Northern Trust Fund Services (Ireland) Limited
  Northern Trust Investor Services (Ireland) Limited
  Northern Trust Property Services (Ireland) Limited
  Northern Trust Management Services Limited (UK)
  Northern Trust Partners Scotland Limited (UK)
  Northern Trust Scottish Limited Partnership (99% UK)
  Northern Trust Luxembourg Capital S.A.R.L.
  Northern Trust Investments Inc.
  NTG Services LLC
  NT Mortgage Holdings LLC
The Northern Trust Company of Delaware
The Northern Trust Company of New York
Northern Trust Global Advisors Inc.
  The Northern Trust Company of Connecticut
  NT Global Advisors Inc. (Canada)
Northern Trust Global Investments Japan K.K.
Northern Trust Holdings L.L.C.
Northern Trust NA
  Northern Annuity Sales Inc.
  Realnor Properties Inc.
  Waterline Partners LLC
Northern Trust Securities Inc.
Northern Trust Services Inc.
Nortrust Holding Corporation
  Northern Trust Bank N.A.
Nortrust Realty Management Inc.

COMPETITORS

Bank of America	Deutsche Bank
Bank of New York	FMR
Mellon	Fifth Third
Barclays	Harris
Bessemer Trust	JPMorgan Chase
Brown Brothers	Morgan Stanley
Harriman	State Street
Citigroup	Wells Fargo

HISTORICAL FINANCIALS

Company Type: Public

Income Statement

FYE: December 31

	ASSETS ($ mil.)	NET INCOME ($ mil.)	INCOME AS % OF ASSETS	EMPLOYEES
12/14	109,946	811	0.7%	15,400
12/13	102,947	731	0.7%	14,800
12/12	97,463	687	0.7%	14,200
12/11	100,223	603	0.6%	14,100
12/10	83,843	669	0.8%	12,800
Annual Growth	7.0%	4.9%	—	4.7%

2014 Year-End Financials

Debt ratio: 3.08%
Return on equity: 9.92%
Cash ($ mil.): 35,365
Current ratio: —
Long-term debt ($ mil.): —

No. of shares (mil.): 233
Dividends
  Yield: 1.9%
  Payout: 42.7%
Market value ($ mil.): 15,731

	STOCK PRICE ($) FY Close	P/E High/Low	PER SHARE ($) Earnings	Dividends	Book Value
12/14	67.40	21 17	3.32	1.30	36.20
12/13	61.89	21 17	2.99	1.23	33.34
12/12	50.16	18 14	2.81	1.18	31.50
12/11	39.66	23 14	2.47	1.12	29.53
12/10	55.41	22 17	2.74	1.12	28.19
Annual Growth	5.0%	— —	4.9%	3.8%	6.4%

Northfield Bancorp Inc (DE)

Auditors: KPMG LLP

LOCATIONS

HQ: Northfield Bancorp Inc (DE)
  581 Main Street, Woodbridge, NJ 07095
Phone: 732 499-7200
Web: www.eNorthfield.com

HISTORICAL FINANCIALS

Company Type: Public

Income Statement

FYE: December 31

	ASSETS ($ mil.)	NET INCOME ($ mil.)	INCOME AS % OF ASSETS	EMPLOYEES
12/14	3,020	20	0.7%	321
12/13	2,702	19	0.7%	326
12/12	2,813	16	0.6%	330
12/11	2,376	16	0.7%	267
12/10	2,247	13	0.6%	—
Annual Growth	7.7%	10.1%	—	—

2014 Year-End Financials

Debt ratio: —
Return on equity: 3.09%
Cash ($ mil.): 76
Current ratio: —
Long-term debt ($ mil.): —

No. of shares (mil.): 48
Dividends
  Yield: 1.7%
  Payout: 63.4%
Market value ($ mil.): 716

	STOCK PRICE ($) FY Close	P/E High/Low	PER SHARE ($) Earnings	Dividends	Book Value
12/14	14.80	36 30	0.41	0.26	12.27
12/13	13.20	45 32	0.34	0.49	12.36
12/12	15.25	55 43	0.29	0.09	10.00
12/11	14.16	35 28	0.42	0.23	9.44
12/10	13.32	46 32	0.33	0.19	9.16
Annual Growth	2.7%	— —	5.6%	8.2%	7.6%

Northrop Grumman Corp

Northrop Grumman defends its high place in the defense sector. As one of the world's top military contractors (behind Lockheed Martin and Boeing) the company operates through four business sectors: Aerospace Systems (aircraft spacecraft laser systems electronic subsystems); Electronic Systems (radar sensors chemical detection countermeasure systems); Information Systems (C4ISR or command control communications computers intelligence surveillance reconnaissance); and Technical Services (systems support training and simulation). The US government represents most of Northrop Grumman's sales.

HISTORY

Huntington Ingalls Industries Jack Northrop co-founded Lockheed Aircraft in 1927 and designed its record-setting Vega monoplane. He founded two more companies —Avion Corporation (formed in 1928 and bought by United Aircraft and Transportation) and Northrop Corporation (formed in 1932 with Douglas Aircraft which absorbed it in 1938) —before founding Northrop Aircraft in California in 1939.

During WWII Northrop produced the P-61 fighter and the famous Flying Wing bomber which failed to win a production contract. In the 1950s Northrop depended heavily on F-89 fighter and Snark missile sales. When Thomas Jones succeeded Jack Northrop as president (1959) he moved the company away from risky prime contracts in favor of numerous subcontracts and bought Page Communications Engineers (telecommunications 1959) and Hallicrafters (electronics 1966) to reduce its dependence on government contracts.

In the early 1970s Northrop was hit with a bribery scandal and the disclosure of illegal payments to Richard Nixon's 1972 campaign fund; Jones was eventually fined for an illegal contribution. As a result a shareholder lawsuit forced Jones to resign as president (he was allowed to remain as chairman). In 1981 the company won the B-2 bomber contract. Jones retired as chairman in late 1990 and under the leadership of Kent Kresa (who became CEO in early 1990 and chairman when Jones retired) Northrop pleaded guilty to 34 counts related to fudging test results on some government projects; it was fined $17 million. In a related shareholders' suit Northrop paid $18 million in damages in 1991.

Northrop and The Carlyle Group bought LTV's Vought Aircraft Industries (now named Triumph Aerostructures - Vought Aircraft Division) in 1992. In 1994 it paid $2.1 billion for Grumman Corporation a premier electronic systems firm and man-

ufacturer of fighter aircraft for the US Navy and changed its name to Northrop Grumman.

In 1929 Roy Grumman Jake Swirbul and Bill Schwendler founded Grumman; within three months it had a contract to design a Navy fighter. Grumman completed its first commercial aircraft (the Grumman Goose) in 1937 and went public in 1938. It soared during WWII on the wings of its Wildcat and Hellcat fighter planes.

Grumman built its first corporate jet (Gulfstream) in 1958 and began work on the Lunar Module for the Apollo space program in 1963. It was near bankruptcy during the 1970s due to costs related to its F-14 Tomcat fighter. Grumman rebuilt its military business in the 1980s and achieved its greatest success in electronic systems.

The UK Ministry of Defence awarded a $279 million contract to Northrop Grumman in 1995 to develop and produce a system to counter infrared missiles. In 1997 Northrop Grumman bought Logicon (information and battle-management systems). It then agreed to an $11.6 billion purchase by Lockheed Martin but the US government citing concerns about increased lack of competition in the defense industry blocked the deal in 1998. As a result Northrop Grumman began a restructuring that cut 10500 defense and aircraft jobs and added 2500 positions to its Logicon subsidiary.

In 1999 Northrop Grumman bought the information systems division of California Microwave for $93 million and Allegheny Teledyne's Ryan Aeronautical (aerial drones) for $140 million. The next year Northrop Grumman sold its underperforming commercial aerostructures business to The Carlyle Group in a $1.2 billion transaction in order to focus on its growing defense electronics and information technology segments. Later in 2000 Northrop Grumman acquired Comptek Research and bought Federal Data (information systems for the US government) from Carlyle in a transaction valued at $302 million. Pension income that year accounted for more than $500 million (about 55%) of the company's pretax profit.

In 2001 the company completed the deal to acquire Litton Industries for $3.8 billion plus $1.3 billion in debt. In the fall Northrop Grumman acquired the electronics and information unit of Aerojet-General Corp. a subsidiary of GenCorp (later renamed Aerojet Rocketdyne) for about $300 million (it became Grumman's Space Systems Division). While its wallet was open the company agreed to match the $2.6 billion that General Dynamics had agreed to pay for submarine and aircraft carrier builder Newport News —a move that the US Defense Department endorsed. In December Honeywell agreed to pay Northrop Grumman $440 million to settle an antitrust and patent infringement lawsuit that Litton had filed against Honeywell in 1990.

The deal to buy Newport News was completed in early 2002. Northrop Grumman then made a hostile $6 billion bid for conglomerate TRW when TRW's stock plunged following the sudden departure of its CEO David Cote to Honeywell. In the wake of Northrop Grumman's spurned initial bid Raytheon General Dynamics and BAE SYSTEMS made offers for TRW's aerospace and defense assets. Finally though TRW accepted a sweetened $7.8 billion offer from Northrop Grumman in July 2002.

The acquisition fortified Northrop Grumman's position in military satellites missile systems and systems integration. In fact Northrop signed a consent decree with the US Justice Department in which the company agreed (under pain of fines) that it wouldn't take unfair advantage of its exclusive position when selling certain components — such as satellite sensors —to competitors.

TRW's Systems unit became Northrop Grumman Mission Systems; TRW's Space and Electronics unit was later known as Northrop Grumman Space Technology. As for TRW's car parts business Northrop sold all but 19.6% of the unit to Blackstone Group for about $4.7 billion to pay down debt; by early 2005 Northrop reduced its stake to 9.9%.

In April 2003 Kresa stepped down as president and CEO and Ronald Sugar took over those roles; Sugar added the chairmanship to his title when Kresa retired in October.

Among Northrop's 2004 contracts were $1.04 billion for X-47B Joint Unmanned Combat Air Systems $1.2 billion (preferred bidder) for E-3D AWACS contract support and $1.4 billion for the CVN 21 generation aircraft carrier. The company also split an $8.4 billion submarine contract with General Dynamics.

Early in 2005 Northrop sold 7.2 million shares of its TRW Automotive stake raising more than $142 million and reducing its stake to 9.9%. It also acquired Integic Corporation an IT company that specialized in business process management and enterprise health applications.

In 2006 Northrop Grumman established Northrop Grumman Technical Services (NGTS) as a separate sector; it was tasked with consolidating Northrop's logistics operations across its various sectors.

Late that same year Northrop Grumman agreed to buy Essex Corporation —a provider of signal image and information processing for defense and intelligence customers in the US. The deal was valued at about $580 million including the assumption of debt. The deal was completed early in 2007 and Essex became a part of Northrop Grumman Mission Systems (now Northrop Grumman Information Systems).

In 2008 the company shed its Electro-Optical Systems business (night vision and applied optics products) to L-3 Communications for $175 million.

In 2009 Northrop Grumman sold its Advisory Services Division comprising subsidiary TASC (engineering and consulting services to the US military and state governments) to private equities General Atlantic LLC and KKR for $1.65 billion. The sale brings Northrop Grumman into compliance with a new federal law that strengthens conflict of interest rules for defense contractors that both sell to and provide consulting for the US military.

Expanding its aerospace and information capabilities the company purchased Sonoma Photonics and assets from Swift Engineering's Killer Bee Unmanned Air Systems lineup for its Aerospace Systems sector (2009). The deal followed its acquisition of 3001 International for $92 million (a nearly three times larger investment) in 2008. The Virginia-based geospatial data collection and analysis provider not only bolstered Northrop Grumman's military offerings but it also reeled in a host of new civilian customers.

Also in 2009 Northrop Grumman settled two decade-old lawsuits with the US government. It agreed to pay $325 million to resolve allegations that it provided defective military satellite parts to the National Reconnaissance Office. The second lawsuit was filed by Northrop Grumman against the US government for uncompensated costs incurred as a result of the cancellation of the Tri-Service Standoff Attack Missile program.

To concentrate more on its core areas Northrop Grumman spun off its shipbuilding business under former subsidiary Huntington Ingalls Industries in 2011. Despite modest increases in year-over-year revenues the shipbuilding sector had struggled to regain profitability after suffering a loss in 2008 attributable to absorbing most of the company's goodwill impairment charge. Also in 2011 the company reduced operations in other segments. It sold its Viper Strike laser-guided bomb operations

in Alabama to European consortium MBDA for an undisclosed amount. And it lowered its participation in the National Security Technologies joint venture that manages and operates the Nevada National Security Site.

Focusing on increasing its presence in the Asia/Pacific in 2012 Northrop Grumman purchased M5 Network Security a provider of cyber security and secure mobile communications technology based in Australia.

EXECUTIVES

Corporate VP, James F. (Jim) Palmer, $866,154 total compensation
Chairman President and CEO, Wesley G. (Wes) Bush, $1,524,231 total compensation
VP and President Aerospace Systems, Thomas E. (Tom) Vice, $762,115 total compensation
VP and CTO, Patrick M. Antkowiak
COO, Gloria A. Flach, $762,115 total compensation
VP and President Technical Services, Christopher T. Jones
VP; President Mission Systems, Kathy Warden
VP; President Enterprise Services and Chief Strategy Officer, Mark A. Caylor
VP Command and Control Systems Information Systems, Jack Dorsett
VP Government Relations, Sid Ashworth
VP and CFO, Kenneth L. Beddingfield
Vice President Deputy General Counsel, Kathryn Simpson
Vice President Human Resources, Heidi Hendrix
Vp Oper Cyber Division, Skip Magness
Vice President Of International Operations, Jock Scharfen
Vice President Intelligence, Scott White
Vice President, Judy McFarland
Vice President Compensation, Daniel Hickey
Vp Corporate Supply Chain, Jaime Bohnke
Vice President Business Development, Diane Reineke
Vice President Basic Research, Tom Pieronek
Senior Vice President, Monty Frahm
Vice President, Gerald Davis
Vice President Of Unmanned Systems, Gene Fraser
Vice President Manufacturing, Ingrid Vaughan
Vice President, Anne Szemborski
Vice President Engineering And Manufacturing, Michael (Mel) Hinkey
Vice President Business Development Northrop Grumman Space Technology, Jeffrey Grant
Vice President Business Management Chief Financial Officer Integrated Systems Eastern Region, Richard (Dick) Leo
Vice President, Kelly Whalen
Vice President and General Manager, Greg Schmidt
Vice President corporate Lead Executive Huntsville, Kevin Campbell
Secretary Treasurer, Precious Haines
Auditors: DELOITTE & TOUCHE LLP

LOCATIONS

HQ: Northrop Grumman Corp
2980 Fairview Park Drive, Falls Church, VA 22042
Phone: 703 280-2900
Web: www.northropgrumman.com

PRODUCTS/OPERATIONS

2014 Sales

	$ mil.	% of total
Aerospace Systems	9,997	38
Electronic Systems	6,951	27
Information Systems	6,222	24
Technical Services	2,799	11
Intersegment eliminations	(1990)	-
Total	**23,979**	**100**

2014 Sales by Customer

	% of total
US government	84
Other customers	16
Total	**100**

2014 Sales

	$ mil.	% of total
Product sales	14,015	58
Service sales	9,964	42
Total	**23,979**	**100**

COMPETITORS

3M
Aerojet Rocketdyne
Airbus Group
BAE SYSTEMS
Boeing
Caterpillar
Cubic Corp.
Elbit Systems
Emerson Electric
Exelis
Finmeccanica
GE
General Dynamics
Hanjin Heavy Industries & Construction
Honeywell Aerospace
ITT Corp.
Johnson Controls
Leidos
Lockheed Martin
Meggitt
Raytheon
Rockwell Collins
ThalesRaytheonSystems
United Technologies

HISTORICAL FINANCIALS

Company Type: Public

Income Statement

FYE: December 31

	REVENUE ($ mil.)	NET INCOME ($ mil.)	NET PROFIT MARGIN	EMPLOYEES
12/15	23,526	1,990	8.5%	65,000
12/14	23,979	2,069	8.6%	64,300
12/13	24,661	1,952	7.9%	65,300
12/12	25,218	1,978	7.8%	68,100
12/11	26,412	2,118	8.0%	72,500
Annual Growth	(2.9%)	(1.5%)	—	(2.7%)

2015 Year-End Financials

Debt ratio: 26.24%
Return on equity: 31.20%
Cash ($ mil.): 2,319
Current ratio: 1.16
Long-term debt ($ mil.): 6,416

No. of shares (mil.): 181
Dividends
  Yield: 1.6%
  Payout: 29.8%
Market value ($ mil.): 34,232

	STOCK PRICE ($) FY Close	P/E High/Low		PER SHARE ($) Earnings	Dividends	Book Value
12/15	188.81	18	14	10.39	3.10	30.46
12/14	147.39	15	11	9.75	2.71	36.37
12/13	114.61	14	8	8.35	2.38	48.81
12/12	67.58	9	7	7.81	2.15	39.77
12/11	58.48	9	6	7.52	1.97	40.71
Annual Growth	34.0%	—	—	8.4%	12.0%	(7.0%)

Northwest Bancshares, Inc. (MD)

Northwest Bancshares is the holding company for Northwest Bank which boasts $9 billion in assets and operates about 180 branches in mostly in Pennsylvania but also in northern Maryland western New York and eastern Ohio. Founded in 1896 the bank offers checking and savings accounts CDs credit cards and trust and investment management services. It mainly uses funds from deposits to write a variety of loans and to invest in mortgage-backed securities and municipal bonds. Residential mortgages and home equity loans make up nearly 60% of the company's loan portfolio while commercial real estate loans make up almost 30%. Consumer and business loans make up the remainder.

OperationsNorthwest Bancshares operates two business segments: Community Banking which makes up around 95% of the company's overall revenue and includes the business activities of its savings bank subsidiary Northwest Bank; and the Community Finance segment which offers personal installment loans for consumer and real estate products through its Northwest Consumer Discount Company subsidiary. Other subsidiaries offer title insurance retail brokerage services and employee benefits consulting. About 75% of the company's total revenue came from loan interest (including fees) in 2014 while another 6% came from interest on its mortgage-backed taxable and tax-exempt investment securities. The rest of its revenue came from service charges and fees (10%) trust and financial services income (3%) insurance commission income (2%) and other miscellaneous income sources. The bank had a staff of more than 2200 employees at the end of 2014.Geographic ReachAbout 75% of Northwest's loan assets are secured in Pennsylvania while 15% are secured in New York state. The company's Northwest Consumer Discount Company subsidiary operates more than 50 consumer finance offices in Pennsylvania.Financial PerformanceNorthwest Bancshares has struggled to consistently grow its revenues and profits in recent years due to shrinking interest margins on its loans and amidst the low-interest environment combined with stubborn levels of loan loss provisions stemming from its nonperforming loans.The company's revenue dipped by around 1% to $376.1 million in 2014 mostly as its interest income declined with shrinking loan and investment assets and lower interest margins. Its non-interest income grew by 9% however thanks to growth in its trust and financial services income.Revenue declines and a $3.8 million hike in compensation and employee benefit costs from merit increases and restructuring-related severance pay caused Northwest's profits to fall by 7% to $61.9 million in 2014. Its operating cash levels plummeted by nearly 30% to $90.5 million mostly after adjusting its earnings for non-cash items related to its net proceeds from its loans held for sale.Strategy

Northwest Bancshares' strategy reiterated in 2015 is to grow its higher-yielding consumer and commercial loan portfolio faster than the rate of its fixed-rate residential mortgage loans which have dominated its loan portfolio in years past. Another key component of its business strategy is to "rely on its reputation for customer service and knowledge of local markets" to seize new business opportunities within the communities it serves.The company has historically grown its loan and deposit business as well as its geographic reach through acquisitions of banks branches and other financial services providers in or around its target markets.Mergers and AcquisitionsIn August 2015 Northwest Bancshares acquired LNB Bancorp along with its Lorain National Bank subsidiary for $179 million adding 21 offices in Lorain Cuyahoga and Summit counties in Ohio to its branch network.

HISTORY

Company BackgroundIn 2007 the company bought Penn Laurel Financial the holding company for CSB Bank broadening its presence in central Pennsylvania. Two years later it acquired the single-branch Keystone State Savings Bank north of Pittsburgh.

The company reorganized in late 2009 by switching from a two-tier mutual holding company to a stock holding company. Under the plan mutual holding company Northwest Bancorp MHC which had owned about two-thirds of Northwest Bancorp was merged into Northwest Savings Bank and its shares were retired. Northwest Bancorp was renamed Northwest Bancshares.

In 2010 Northwest Bancshares arranged to acquire NexTier bank which would have been its largest purchase ever. However the proposed deal was called off after it became apparent that Northwest Bancshares would not receive regulatory approval for the deal. (Without elaborating the company said that the FDIC had criticized the bank's consumer compliance program.)

EXECUTIVES

Chairman President and CEO Northwest Bancshares Inc. and Northwest Bank, William J. Wagner, age 61, $634,921 total compensation
SVP Marketing and Operations and Chief Marketing Officer Northwest Bancorp and Northwest Savings Bank, David E. Westerburg, $205,306 total compensation
Ohio Region President Northwest Bancshares Inc. and Northwest Bank, Kevin W. Nelson, age 50
SEVP and Chief Revenue Officer Northwest Bancshares Inc. and Northwest Bank, Steven G. Fisher, age 58, $313,378 total compensation
SEVP and CFO Northwest Bancshares Inc. and Northwest Bank, William W. Harvey, age 48, $313,378 total compensation
EVP and Chief Risk Officer Northwest Bancshares Inc. and Northwest Savings Bank, Thomas J. Townsend
EVP Finance and Controller Northwest Bancshares Inc. and Northwest Savings Bank, Gerald J. Ritzert, age 46
SVP and CIO Northwest Bancorp and Northwest Savings Bank, Andrew C. (Drew) Young
SVP Human Resourcs Northwest Bancorp and Northwest Savings Bank, Julia W. McTavish
EVP and Chief Credit Officer Northwest Savings Bank, Michael G. Smelko, $206,875 total compensation
EVP Chief Counsel Corporate Secretary and CMS Enterprise Oversight Officer, Richard K. Laws
Auditors: KPMG LLP

LOCATIONS

HQ: Northwest Bancshares, Inc. (MD)
100 Liberty Street, Warren, PA 16365
Phone: 814 726-2140
Web: www.northwestsavingsbank.com

PRODUCTS/OPERATIONS

2014

	$ mil.	% of total
Community Banking	352	94
Consumer Finance	20	5
All Other	3	1
Total	**376**	**100**

2014 Sales

	$ mil.	% of total
Interest		
Loans receivable	282	75
Mortgage-backed securities	10	3
Taxable Investment securities	4	1
Tax-free Investment securities	6	2
Interest-earning deposits	0	0
Noninterest		
Service charges & fees	36	10
Trust & other financial services	12	3
Insurance commissions	8	2
Income from bank owned life insurance	4	1
Gain on sale of investments net	4	1
Net impairment losses	0	0
Loss on real estate owned net	(0.1)	0
Mortgage banking income	1	0
Other operating income	5	2
Total	**376**	**100**

Selected Subsidiaries

Northwest Savings Bank
  Allegheny Services Inc. (investment holdings)
  Boetger and Associates Inc. (actuarial and employee benefits services)
  Great Northwest Corporation (investment holdings)
  Northwest Capital Group Inc. (investment holdings)
  Northwest Consumer Discount Company Inc. (consumer finance)
  Northwest Financial Services Inc. (retail brokerage)
  Northwest Settlement Agency LLC (title insurance)
  Veracity Benefit Designs Inc.

COMPETITORS

Allegheny Valley Bancorp	Fidelity Bancorp (PA)
AmeriServ Financial	First Commonwealth Financial
Citizens Financial Group	First Niagara Financial
Dollar Bank	M&T Bank
Emclaire Financial	PNC Financial
F.N.B. (PA)	S&T Bancorp

HISTORICAL FINANCIALS

Company Type: Public

Income Statement

FYE: December 31

	ASSETS ($ mil.)	NET INCOME ($ mil.)	INCOME AS % OF ASSETS	EMPLOYEES
12/14	7,775	61	0.8%	2,220
12/13	7,881	66	0.8%	2,231
12/12	7,942	63	0.8%	2,220
12/11	7,957	64	0.8%	2,121
12/10	8,148	57	0.7%	2,040
Annual Growth	(1.2%)	1.9%	—	2.1%

2014 Year-End Financials

Debt ratio: 10.66%
Return on equity: 5.58%
Cash ($ mil.): 240
Current ratio: —
Long-term debt ($ mil.): —
No. of shares (mil.): 94
Dividends
  Yield: 12.9%
  Payout: 241.7%
Market value ($ mil.): 1,187

	STOCK PRICE ($) FY Close	P/E High/Low	PER SHARE ($) Earnings	Dividends	Book Value
12/14	12.53	22 18	0.67	1.62	11.22
12/13	14.78	20 16	0.73	0.62	12.27
12/12	12.14	19 16	0.68	0.60	12.05
12/11	12.44	21 17	0.64	0.43	11.85
12/10	11.78	24 19	0.53	0.40	11.85
Annual Growth	1.6%	— —	6.0%	41.9%	(1.4%)

NORTHWEST FARM CREDIT SERVICES ACA

Customer-owned financial cooperative Northwest Farm Credit Services is an agricultural lender that provides financial services to farmers ranchers agribusinesses commercial fishermen timber producers and rural home owners in Alaska Idaho Montana Oregon and Washington. The company has a network of around 45 branches and offers a broad range of flexible loan programs to meet the needs of people in the agriculture business. Northwest Farm Credit also provides leasing services appraisal services and life mortgage disability and crop insurance as well as legal advocacy and assistance to customers in need. It is part of the Farm Credit System a network of lenders serving the US agriculture industry.

Geographic Reach

Northwest Farm Credit serves customers through 45 branch offices located throughout the US Northwest and in Alaska.Operations

- The credit union provides financing and related services to farmers ranchers agribusinesses commercial fishermen timber producers rural homeowners and crop insurance customers. Northwest Farm Credit provides $12 billion in loans. Farm Credit System a nationwide network of borrower-owned lending institutions of which it is part provides $205 billion in loans to rural America.Sales and Marketing

Northwest Farm Credit finances farmers ranchers agribusinesses commercial fishermen timber producers and rural homeowners as well as farm-related businesses agricultural cooperatives and rural utilities.

Financial Performance

The company has seen a slow decline in its revenues over the past few years. In 2013 Northwest Farm Credit's revenues dropped by 5% due to lower interest and noninterest income. Interest income declined as a result of a decrease in loan spread caused in part by greater prepayment expense competitive pressures and an increase in the average loan volume in lower spread lines of business. Noninterest income declined due to a refund received in 2012 from the Farm Credit System Insurance Corporation related to the Farm Credit Insurance Fund.However the company's net income increased by 27% in 2013 due to a benefit from the provision for credit losses and a decline in interest expenses. In 2013 Northwest Farm Credit's operating cash inflow decreased to $200.79 million (from $238.41 million in 2012) due to a change in the company's current assets and liabilities.

Mergers and Acquisitions

In 2014 the company expanded its operations in Montana by buying Culbertson State Agency's crop insurance portfolio.

Company Background

The US Congress created the Farm Credit System in 1916 to meet the financial needs of farmers ranchers and cooperatives who invest as well as borrow from the institutions within the system. All Farm Credit System members are regulated by the Farm Credit Administration.

EXECUTIVES

EVP Financial Services, Fred (Fred) DePell
EVP and General Counsel, Thomas (Tom) Tracy
EVP Corporate Administration and Secretary, Joan E. Haynes
EVP CFO and CIO, Tom Nakano

Vice President, Marnie Vandenberg
Assistant Vice President country Home Lending, Matt Koch
Branch Manager Assistant Vice President, Jeffrey Rodenbaugh
Relationship Manager II Assistant Vice President, Natasha Jungers
Retiredf Vice President Credit, Val Warehime
Relationship Manager Vice President, Steve Smith
Assistant Vice President Operations, Jessi Dressen
Vice President Credit, Brandon Stacey
Vice President Credit Officer, Richard Harris
Assistant Vice President Loan Accounting, Sophie Conley
Regional Vice President, Lance Zollinger
Credit Manager And Assistant Vice President, Rick Guenther
Credit Officer And Assistant Vice President, Eric Gray
Vice President Agribusiness, Rich Fehringer
Relationship Manager And Assistant Vice President, Michael Mills
Relationship Manager Vice President Agribusiness, Tom Howard
Chairman, Drew Eggers
Vice Chairman, Kevin Riel

LOCATIONS

HQ: NORTHWEST FARM CREDIT SERVICES ACA
1700 S ASSEMBLY ST # 102, SPOKANE, WA 992242116
Phone: 5098382429

COMPETITORS

Bank of America	U.S. Bancorp
First Interstate	Wells Fargo
Idaho Independent Bank	Zions Bancorporation
KeyCorp	
Northwest Bancorporation	

HISTORICAL FINANCIALS

Company Type: Private

Income Statement

FYE: December 31

	ASSETS ($ mil.)	NET INCOME ($ mil.)	INCOME AS % OF ASSETS	EMPLOYEES
12/13	9,604	236	2.5%	500
12/12	9,471	187	2.0%	—
12/11	8,696	159	1.8%	—
12/10	8,705	0	—	—
Annual Growth	3.3%	—	—	—

2013 Year-End Financials

Debt ratio: ——
Return on equity: 51.50%
Cash ($ mil.): 39
Current ratio: —
Long-term debt ($ mil.): —

Dividends
Yield: —
Payout: —
Market value ($ mil.): —

NRG Energy Inc

A company with twice the energy in its name is doubling its efforts to deliver power. NRG Energy a leading power producer with a generating capacity of about 52000 MW (including 1186 MW of solar power assets) is getting greener as it invests in wind and solar power. The vast majority of NRG's power plants are in North America but it also has one in Australia. Its portfolio includes more than 190 generation units at about 100 power plants. It also markets natural gas oil and other commodities NRG's retail units (including Reliant Energy and Green Mountain Energy) distribute power to about 3 million customers across the US. In 2015 it announced plans to spin off its renewables businesses to pay down debt.

Geographic Reach

NRG has generation assets in the US and Australia. Its retail and thermal subsidiaries serve customers in 16 US states. Its NGR Thermal unit provides third-party steam to downtown heating and cooling systems in cities such as Pittsburgh San Diego San Francisco and Harrisburg Pennsylvania.

Operations

The company's major operations comprise of retail businesses (Reliant Energy Green Mountain Energy and Energy Plus) conventional power generation assets and alternative energy businesses. Other activities include international businesses a thermal and chilled water business and maintenance services.

Sales and Marketing

NRG's retail electricity divisions serve nearly 3 million residential business commercial and industrial customers in 47 US states.

Financial Performance

The company's net revenues grew a steadily between 2010 and 2014 except for a slight decrease in 2012. In 2014 NRG's revenues increased by 40% due to higher energy capacity and retail revenues as a result of increased demand for electricity and fuel price volatility. NRG posted net income of $134 million in 2014 (compared to net loss of $386 million in 2013) due to higher net revenues a decline in impairment losses a gain on sale of equity-method investment and the absence of impairment losses on investments.In 2014 the company's cash inflow increased by 19% to $1.51 billion (compared to $1.27 billion a year earlier) due to higher net income and changes in working capital as a result of accounts receivable/trade.

Strategy

NRG has pulled back on international exposure looking to grow its position in the fragmented but less risky North American market. It is also pushing green energy and energy conservation.

The company has reorganized its businesses and personnel on the basis of key target customer segments. Its new structure includes NRG Business NRG Home and NRG Renew. NRG Carbon 360 and NRG eVgo are two other distinct businesses.

In 2015 NRG Home expanded its US operations into North Carolina. The company is offering solar solutions in the state providing homeowners with the opportunity to install solar through financing options that require zero-money down

In 2014 NRG and Unilever United States Inc. formed a strategic partnership to support the Unilever Sustainable Living Plan which is Unilever's global blueprint for sustainable growth that aims to double the size of Unilever's business while reducing the company's environmental footprint and increasing its positive social impact.

That year NRG Home Solar one of the country's leading residential solar companies expanded its US operations to Connecticut. As part of the expansion the company opened the new Connecticut headquarters in Middletown where it offers fully integrated solar solutions throughout the state. In 2014 NRG eVgo further expanded access to the company's electric vehicle (EV) charging network by partnering with BMW on its new ChargeNow DC Fast program. As a result BMW i3 drivers in California can enjoy unlimited no cost 30 minute DC fast charging at eVgo Freedom Station sites equipped with DC Combo Fast Charging through 2015. In 2014 NRG Home announced the opening of two new California offices in Merced and San Diego to further build on the company's comprehensive energy operations around the state.In

2013 NRG launched NRG Residential Solutions a retail energy business that offers consumers choice in their energy options by allowing them to customize their electricity plans based on what is important to them.

Expanding its cleaner-burning natural gas power plant assets in 2013 the company opened its El Segundo Energy Center a 550 MW natural gas–fueled combined-cycle generating plant near Los Angeles.

Mergers and Acquisitions

In 2014 the company acquired Pure Energies Group (a residential solar industry leader in the critical area of web-based customer acquisition) and Goal Zero (which offers personal solar devices).

Expanding its US generation capacity in 2014 the company acquired most of the assets of Edison Mission Energy for $2.6 billion. It also bought the competitive retail electricity business of Dominion Resources for $165 million. Dominion serves more than 600000 customer accounts in Connecticut Illinois Maryland Massachusetts New Jersey New York Ohio and Pennsylvania and through its Cirro Energy brand in Texas

In 2013 NRG bought the 399 MW Gregory cogeneration plant in Corpus Christi Texas from a consortium of affiliates of Atlantic Power Corporation John Hancock Life Insurance Company (U.S.A.) and Rockland Capital LLC for $245 million.

Company Background

In 2012 the company bought GenOn Energy in a $1.7 billion stock deal. The deal creates the largest competitive generator in the US with generating capacity in the East Gulf Coast and West and an enterprise value of $18 billion. The parties hope that synergies balance sheet efficiencies increased economies of scale and geographic diversity will save the expanded company $300 million a year in free cash flow.

Responding to government demands for utilities to increase their use of renewables in 2011 it bought the 290-MW Agua Caliente solar project in Arizona from First Solar. (To secure financial support in 2012 NRG sold a 49% stake in the project to MidAmerican Energy). When completed in 2014 it will be the largest operational photovoltaic site in the world producing enough energy to power more than 225000 homes. Its electricity will be sold to Pacific Gas and Electric in California through 2039.

Expanding its retail presence in the US Northeast in 2011 the company bought Philadelphia-based electricity and natural gas provider Energy Plus Holdings for $190 million.

In 2011 it began to create the US's first privately funded network of electric vehicle charging stations. Based in Houston the chain opened its first charging station that year and plans to open about 60 more under the eVgo brand.

In 2010 NRG also acquired alternative energy provider Northwind Phoenix which operates a district cooling system providing chilled water to commercial buildings in the central business district of Phoenix.

That year NRG agreed to acquire about 3900 MW of generating power in a deal with the Blackstone Group which had planned to buy Dynegy for some $4.7 billion. However the Dynegy deal fell through prompting NRG to restrategize. (It subsequently acquired 1300 MW plant in East Texas for $525 million from the Kelson Limited Partnership in a move to fill in some of the gaps in its combined-cycle gas portfolio).

T. Rowe Price Associates owns 12% of NRG.

EXECUTIVES

EVP and President Alternative Energy Services, Denise M. Wilson, age 52, $588,466 total compensation
EVP and President Gulf Coast Region and President and CEO NRG Carbon 360, John W. Ragan, age 52, $588,466 total compensation
EVP and Regional President East, Lee Davis
President NRG Distributed Generation, Thomas D. Gros
President and CEO, Mauricio Gutierrez, age 41, $623,977 total compensation
President and CEO NRG Renew, Thomas P. (Tom) Doyle
EVP and CFO, Kirkland B. Andrews, age 44, $623,977 total compensation
SVP NRG Business Solutions, Robert J. Gaudette, age 42
SVP and President NRG Retail, Elizabeth Killinger
SVP and Regional President West, John Chillemi
EVP and General Counsel, David R. Hill, $479,039 total compensation
SVP and Chief Marketing Officer, Sicily Dickenson
President and CEO NRG Home, Steve McBee
President NRG Home Solar, Kelcy Pegler
Vice President Of Investor Relations, Chad Plotkin
Vice President, Gaetan Frotte
Executive Vice President Strategy, Jonathan (Jon) Baliff
Vice President, Bruce Chung
Vice President, Chris Moser
Vice President, Steve Rose
Vice President Assistant Controller, Mary Stillwell
Vice President, Chris Haas
Vice President, Albert Scerbo
Vice President of Operations, Mitchell (Mitch) Samuelian
Vice President, Chris Phillips
Senior Vice President, Ben Trammell
Senior Vice President Sustainability Policy And, Steve Corneli
Vice President, Jonathan (Jon) Milley
Vice President Channel Marketing, Morgan Smith
Senior Vice President Trading and Marketing, Paul Weiss
Senior Vice President, Nahla Azmy
Executive Vice President President Northeast Regio, Curtis Morgan
Senior Vice President Asset Management And Development, Howard Taylor
Vice President Tax, Raymond Salort
Vice President Assistant Controller, Mary-lee Stillwell
Senior Vice President Operations, Fran Sullivan
Vice President Business Development, Edouard Macguffie
Vice President Wholesale Information Technology, Robert D (Bob) Thibeault
Vice President, Christopher (Chris) Sotos
Vice President Engineering and Project Services, Robert (Bob) Patrick
Executive Vice President and Chief Administrative, Patti Heifer
Vice President Development Generation, David (Dave) Greeson
Vice President Operations Midwest, Don Claybaugh
Chairman, Howard E. Cosgrove, age 68
Vice Chairman, Edward R. Muller, age 63
Auditors: KPMG LLP

LOCATIONS

HQ: NRG Energy Inc
211 Carnegie Center, Princeton, NJ 08540
Phone: 609 524-4500
Web: www.nrgenergy.com

PRODUCTS/OPERATIONS

2014 Sales

	$ mil.	% of total
Retail	7,385	42
Energy	7,130	40
Capacity	2,109	12
Other	556	3
Mark-to-market activities	541	3
Contract Amortization	(13)	-
Adjustments	(1840)	-
Total	**15,868**	**100**

Selected Subsidiaries

Energy Plus
Green Mountain Energy Company (retail power)
NEO Corporation (distributed generation; landfill gas hydroelectric and other renewable generation)
NRG Power Marketing Inc. (power sales)
NRG Resource Recovery (waste-to-energy facilities)
NRG Texas LLC (power generation)
NRG Thermal Corporation (district heating and cooling combined heat and power facilities)
Reliant Energy Texas Retail LLC
Texas Genco LP (power generation)
West Coast Power LLC (power generation)

Selected Mergers and Acquisitions

COMPETITORS

AEP	Entergy
AES	FirstEnergy
Accent Energy	Gexa Energy
Alliant Energy	Integrys Energy
Avista	Services
Berkshire Hathaway	Nicor Gas
Energy	PG&E Corporation
Calpine	PPL Corporation
Cogentrix Energy	PSEG Power
Community Energy	Preferred Energy
Direct Energy	Services
Duke Energy	SCANA
Dynegy	Sempra Generation
Edison International	Tenaska
Energy Future	

HISTORICAL FINANCIALS

Company Type: Public

Income Statement

FYE: December 31

	REVENUE ($ mil.)	NET INCOME ($ mil.)	NET PROFIT MARGIN	EMPLOYEES
12/14	15,868	134	0.8%	9,806
12/13	11,295	(386)	—	7,786
12/12	8,422	559	6.6%	8,792
12/11	9,079	197	2.2%	5,193
12/10	8,849	477	5.4%	4,964
Annual Growth	**15.7%**	**(27.2%)**	**—**	**18.6%**

2014 Year-End Financials

Debt ratio: 50.10%
Return on equity: 1.35%
Cash ($ mil.): 2,188
Current ratio: 1.77
Long-term debt ($ mil.): 19,900
No. of shares (mil.): 336
Dividends
Yield: 2.0%
Payout: 234.7%
Market value ($ mil.): 9,073

	STOCK PRICE ($) FY Close	P/E High/Low		PER SHARE ($) Earnings	Dividends	Book Value
12/14	26.95	164	112	0.23	0.54	29.86
12/13	28.72	—	—	(1.22)	0.45	30.43
12/12	22.99	10	6	2.35	0.18	31.82
12/11	18.12	33	23	0.78	0.00	34.00
12/10	19.54	14	10	1.84	0.00	33.59
Annual Growth	**8.4%**	**—**	**—**	**(40.5%)**	**—**	**(2.9%)**

Nucor Corp.

Nucor takes a "minimillist" approach to succeeding in the steel industry. At its minimills Nucor produces hot- and cold-rolled steel steel joists and metal buildings. It has the capacity to produce more than 26 million tons of steel per year. North America's largest recycler of scrap metal it produces steel by melting scrap in electric arc furnaces. Most products are sold to steel service centers manufacturers and fabricators. Subsidiary Harris Steel fabricates rebar for highways and bridges and other construction projects. Its David J. Joseph Company unit processes and brokers metals pig iron hot briquetted iron and direct reduced iron (DRI). In 2014 Nucor recycled 19 million tons of scrap steel.

HISTORY

Nucor started as the second carmaking venture of Ransom Olds who built his first gasoline-powered car in 1897. Two years later Samuel Smith a Detroit copper and lumber magnate put up $199600 to finance Olds Motor Works. A fire destroyed the company's Detroit plant in 1901 so Olds moved production to Lansing Michigan where he built America's first mass-produced car —the Oldsmobile. In 1904 Olds left Olds Motor Works which was bought by General Motors (GM) in 1908 and formed Reo Car Company (renamed Reo Motor Car in 1906). In addition to cars it eventually made trucks and buses.

By the end of the Depression Ford GM and Chrysler commanded over 85% of the US passenger car market. Reo stopped making cars in 1936 and sold its truck manufacturing operations in 1957. Meanwhile it had formed Reo Holding which in 1955 merged with Nuclear Consultants to form Nuclear Corporation of America. The new company offered services such as radiation studies and made nuclear instruments and electronics.

In 1962 Nuclear bought steel joist maker Vulcraft and gained the services of Kenneth Iverson. The diverse company was unprofitable losing $2 million on $22 million in sales in 1965. That year Iverson took over as CEO moved headquarters to Charlotte North Carolina and shut down or sold about half of the company's businesses. By focusing on its profitable steel joist operations the firm ended 1966 in the black. Because the company depended on imports for 80% of its steel needs Iverson decided to move into steel production. Nuclear Corporation built its first minimill in 1969.

The company was renamed Nucor in 1972. It started making steel deck (1977) and cold-finished steel bars (1979). Production tripled and sales more than doubled between 1974 and 1979.

Nucor began to diversify adding grinding balls (used in the mining industry to process ores 1981); steel bolts steel bearings and machined steel parts (1986); and metal buildings and components (1987). Nucor and Japanese steelmaker Yamato Kogyo formed Nucor-Yamato and built a mill in 1988 to produce wide-flange beams (for heavy construction). The following year Nucor opened a state-of-the-art mill in Crawfordsville Indiana and another mill near Hickman Arkansas in 1992.

Iverson turned over his CEO duties to company veteran John Correnti in 1996. The next year Nucor began building a steel beam mill in South Carolina and added a galvanizing facility to its Hickman mill.

In 1998 Nucor announced plans to build its first steel plate mill which became operational in 2000. The company slashed prices twice in 1998 to compete against low-cost imports from Russia Japan

and Brazil. Both sales and earnings declined that year due to low metal prices reduced shipments and start-up costs for new plants. The company raised its prices in 1999 and continued its expansion plans. Differences with the board prompted Correnti to resign in 1999; chairman David Aycock assumed his duties. In September 2000 Aycock resigned from the company and Daniel DiMicco formerly an EVP moved up to the rank of CEO.

Nucor along with Australia's Broken Hill Proprietary Corporation and Japan's Ishikawajima-Harima Heavy Industries began a joint venture in 2000 for its technology strip casting. The new technology allows steel production in smaller cheaper plants. In 2001 Nucor purchased a significant amount of assets of Auburn Steel a producer of merchant steel bar for $115 million.

In 2002 Nucor teamed up with Companhia Vale do Rio Doce (Vale) a Brazilian producer and exporter of iron-ore pellets to develop low-cost iron based products. That year Nucor purchased Alabama-based Trico Steel a steel sheet producer for approximately $116 million. In late 2002 Nucor bought financially troubled Birmingham Steel for $615 million in cash and debt.

Nucor Steel Kingman LLC a subsidiary of Nucor Corporation purchased the Kingman Arizona rebar and wire rod rolling unit of North Star Steel for around $35 million in 2003.

Its Vulcraft unit saw an increase in non-residential building construction in 2004 which boosted sales of joist girders steel deck and steel joists. Nucor bought Nucor Tuscaloosa in mid-2004 a producer of coiled plate with an annual capacity of around 700000 tons. The following year saw the company purchase Ohio's Marion Steel for approximately $110 million. The mill was added to Nucor's bar products line.

Record high prices in the industry (led by high demand throughout the world) led to record high sales in 2004. As a matter of fact Nucor's first half of the year outpaced previous annual highs and the company achieved that feat again in the second half.

The company named CEO DiMicco chairman in 2006.

In the latter half of the last decade it started a program of rapid external growth. It acquired the former Connecticut Steel Verco Manufacturing and Canadian steel products maker Harris Steel which like Connecticut Steel had been a customer and partner of Nucor for years. Harris itself made an acquisition in 2008 when it bought rebar fabricator and distributor Ambassador Steel. Nucor also expanded its downstream operations with the 2007 acquisition of building systems maker MAGNATRAX for $280 million. Its largest acquisition was that of the David J. Joseph Company a scrap metal broker that had supplied Nucor's minimills for 40 years.

The company has always operated primarily in the US but in 2008 it moved into the international market with the formation of a European joint venture with Duferco. The JV produces steel beams and merchant bar products from manufacturing locations in Italy and serves the European and North African markets. Nucor put about $650 million into the new venture called Nucor S.r.l. Duferdofin.

That year it also expanded considerably in the US by spending $1 billion to buy ferrous and nonferrous metals group The David J. Joseph Company.

In 2010 Nucor formed a US-based joint venture with Mitsui & Co. Nucor paid $225 million for its half of the venture named Steel Technologies.

In 2012 Nucor acquired New Jersey-based Skyline Steel and its subsidiaries from ArcelorMittal for about $605 million. Skyline which has served as a distributor of Nucor's products for more than 20 years accelerated Nucor's growth in steel pil-

ing and foundation products. Steel sheet piles are long structural sections having a vertical interlocking system that creates a wall. Skyline's flagship products include hot-rolled and cold-formed sheet piles and pipe piling. A steel foundation distributor in North America Skyline serves industries that include marine construction bridge and highway construction heavy civil construction and underground commercial parking.

In 2011 Nucor sold its NuPro Steel subsidiary to Steel Technologies its joint venture with Mitsui & Co. NuPro produces flat-rolled steel at its plant in Crawfordsville Indiana. Nucor also announced that Steel Technologies would build a steel processing plant in Mexico to serve Japanese electronics and auto companies moving into the region.

In early 2011 Nucor and joint venture partners Rio Tinto Group Mitsubishi and Shougang Corp. permanently closed the high-intensity smelt (hismelt) steel plant in Kwinana Western Australia. Nucor had a 25% stake in the joint venture that was terminated.

EXECUTIVES

EVP Flat-Rolled Products, Ladd R. Hall, $442,900 total compensation
Chairman President and CEO, John J. Ferriola, $950,000 total compensation
Vice President General Manager Vulcraft Division St Joe Indiana, Shannon Phillips
VP; General Manager Bar Mill Division (Jewett Texas), James R. Darsey, $400,400 total compensation
EVP, R. Joseph Stratman, $442,900 total compensation
EVP CFO and Treasurer, James D. (Jim) Frias, $426,500 total compensation
EVP Fabricated Construction Products, Raymond S. Napolitan
EVP Beam and Plate Products, D. Chad Utermark, age 47
EVP Engineered Bar Products, David A. Sumoaski
Vice President, Tammy Willis
Assistant Vice President, Anna Ehrich
Vice President, Paige Okelley
Vice President General Manager Nucor Steel Auburn Inc Auburn New York, David (Dave) Smith
Evp Engineered Bar Products, Dave Sumoski
Vice President; President Vulcraft And Verco Group, James (Jamie) Dasey
Vice President International Development, Bill Abbey
Vice President Manufacturing, Bob McKee
Vice President Of Marketing, Allen Behr
Vice President Of Marketing, Drew Wilcox
Executive Vice President Beam Plate Products, Chad Utermark
Secretary, A Rae Eagle
Auditors: PricewaterhouseCoopers LLP

LOCATIONS

HQ: Nucor Corp.
1915 Rexford Road, Charlotte, NC 28211
Phone: 704 366-7000   **Fax:** 704 362-4208
Web: www.nucor.com

PRODUCTS/OPERATIONS

2014 Sales

	$ mil.	% of total
Steel Mills	14,723	70
Steel Products	4,032	19
Raw Materials	2,349	11
Total	**21,105**	**100**

Selected Products

Alloy steel
Cold-drawn steel bars

Finished hex caps
Hex-head cap screws
Locknuts
Structural bolts and nuts
Carbon steel
  Angles
  Beams
  Channels
  Cold-drawn steel bars
  Finished hex nuts
  Flats
  Floor plate
  Galvanized sheet
  Grinding balls
  Hexagons
  Hot-rolled sheet
  Reinforcing bars
  Structural bolts and nuts
  Wide-range beams
Engineered products
  Composite floor joists
  Floor deck
  Joists
  Joist girders
  Pre-engineered metal buildings
  Roof deck
  Special-profile steel trusses
Stainless steel
  Cold-rolled steel
  Hot-rolled steel
  Pickled sheet

Selected Subsidiaries

Harris Steel Inc.
Harris Steel ULC (Canada)
The David J. Joseph Company
Magnatrax Corporation
Nucor Castrip Arkansas LLC
Nucor Energy Holdings Inc.
Nucor-Yamato Steel Company

2014 Sales by Product

	% of total
Sheet	28
Bar	19
Steel products	19
Structural	13
Raw materials	11
Plate	10
Total	**100**

COMPETITORS

AK Steel Holding Corporation	Harsco
Alcoa	Illinois Tool Works
ArcelorMittal USA	Johnson Controls
BlueScope Steel	Renco
Commercial Metals	Schnitzer Steel
Cummins	Steel Dynamics
Dow Chemical	Tata Europe
Gerdau Ameristeel	United States Steel

HISTORICAL FINANCIALS

Company Type: Public

Income Statement

FYE: December 31

	REVENUE ($ mil.)	NET INCOME ($ mil.)	NET PROFIT MARGIN	EMPLOYEES
12/14	21,105	713	3.4%	23,600
12/13	19,052	488	2.6%	22,300
12/12	19,429	504	2.6%	22,200
12/11	20,023	778	3.9%	20,800
12/10	15,844	134	0.8%	20,500
Annual Growth	7.4%	51.9%	—	3.6%

2014 Year-End Financials

Debt ratio: 29.36%	No. of shares (mil.): 319
Return on equity: 9.26%	Dividends
Cash ($ mil.): 1,024	Yield: 3.0%
Current ratio: 3.07	Payout: 70.6%
Long-term debt ($ mil.): 4,360	Market value ($ mil.): 15,649

	STOCK PRICE ($) FY Close	P/E High/Low	PER SHARE ($) Earnings	Dividends	Book Value
12/14	49.05	26 21	2.22	1.48	24.36
12/13	53.38	36 28	1.52	1.47	24.02
12/12	43.16	29 22	1.58	1.46	24.06
12/11	39.57	20 13	2.45	1.45	23.60
12/10	43.82	119 87	0.42	1.44	22.55
Annual Growth	2.9%	— —	51.6%	0.7%	2.0%

O'Reilly Automotive, Inc.

No need to jump O'Reilly Automotive's battery. The fast-growing company sells automotive after-market parts (both new and remanufactured) maintenance supplies professional service equipment tools and accessories through some 4400 stores in 40-plus states and online. Many O'Reilly Automotive stores also offer customers a range of services including oil and battery recycling battery testing paint mixing and tool rental. The company wheels and deals with automotive professionals as well as do-it-yourself customers. Founded in 1957 by Charles F. O'Reilly and his son "Chub" O'Reilly Automotive is still family run.

Operations

Do-it-yourself customers account for about 58% of the chain's sales with the other 42% of sales coming from professional services provider customers.

The company's stores carry about 23000 SKUs and average 7200 total square feet. The stores receive inventory five nights a week from O'Reilly's distribution centers.

Geographic Reach

Missouri-based O'Reilly Automotive has stores in 43 states including Alaska and Hawaii. Texas and California are its largest markets with more than 600 stores and more than 500 stores respectively.

Sales and Marketing

Advertising expenses in 2014 amounted to $79 million up from about $78 million spent on advertising in 2013.

To attract do-it-yourself customers O'Reilly Automotive leverages an integrated marketing program which includes television radio direct mail and newspaper distribution in-store and online promotions and sports and event sponsorships. The company also participates in cooperative advertising with its vendors. Its combination of brand and product/price messaging drives retail traffic and purchases which frequently coincide with key sales events. To stimulate sales among racing enthusiasts O'Reilly Automotive sponsors multiple nationally-televised races and more than 1300 grassroots local and regional motorsports events throughout 42 states. It was also the title sponsor for two National Association for Stock Car Racing the national series events in Texas and five National Hot Rod Association races from California to North Carolina.As part of its First Call program O'Reilly Automotive maintains a full-time sales staff of 700 that is strategically located across its market areas. Each sales representative is dedicated to calling upon selling to and servicing its professional service provider customers. Targeted marketing materials such as flyers quick reference guides and catalogs are produced and distributed

on a regular basis to professional service providers paint and body shops and fleet customers. Also the company sells automotive products directly to independently-owned parts stores (called jobber stores) throughout its trade areas.

Financial Performance

O'Reilly Automotive's revenue has increased since 2003 and performed well during the recession. The company's growth streak continued in 2014 with sales up 8.5% to $7.2 billion and net income rising 16% to $778 million. Driving the increase in sales were the addition of 200 net new stores and an increase in same-store sales. The company credits its best-in-class customer service superior inventory availability a broader selection of products offered in most stores a targeted promotional and advertising effort through a variety of media and localized promotional events continued improvement in merchandising and store layouts compensation programs for all store team members (that provide incentives for performance) and its continued focus on serving both do-it-yourself and professional service provider customers for its continuing success. Indeed both DIY and professional customers spent more at O'Reilly stores in fiscal 2014 although DIY customers made fewer trips.

Strategy

O'Reilly Automotive adheres to a "dual market" strategy by appealing to both do-it-yourself (DIY) and professional service providers. (In 2014 about 58% of O'Reilly's sales were to DIY customers with the rest to professionals.) The company believes that its tiered distribution model provides industry-leading parts availability and store in-stock positions while lowering its inventory carrying costs and controlling inventory. To this end the auto parts chain has made significant capital investments in its distribution center network allowing it to efficiently service new stores that are planned to open in contiguous market areas as well as servicing its existing stores network. O'Reilly Automotive is aiming for a total growth capacity of more than 800 stores in its distribution center network.

As part of its continuing efforts to enhance its distribution network in 2014 it's implementing a voice-picking technology in additional distribution centers; rolling out enhanced routing software to enhance logistics efficiencies; launching additional labor management software to improve distribution center productivity and overall operating efficiency; developing further automated paperless-picking processes; improving proof of delivery systems to boost the accuracy of product movement to stores; continuing to define and implement best practices in all distribution centers; and making proven return-on-investment-based capital enhancements to material handling equipment in distribution centers including conveyor systems picking modules and lift equipment.

O'Reilly also seeks to attract customers to its auto parts stores by offering enhanced services and programs such as used oil oil filter and battery recycling a loaner tool program machine shops and drum and rotor resurfacing to name a few.

The company is expanding its nationwide presence by opening stores at a rapid rate. After opening about 200 net new stores in 2014 the chain plans to add about 205 new stores in 2014.

O'Reilly Automotive operates about 300 strategically placed hub stores which average 10000 sq. ft. and carry an average of 41000 SKUs. In addition to serving do-it-yourself and professional service provider customers in their markets hub stores offer access to an expanded selection of SKUs on a same-day basis.

Mergers and Acquisitions

In October 2014 O'Reilly purchased a 4900-square foot auto repair shop Punta Gorda Florida for $575000.

In 2012 the company expanded its capabilities by acquiring the auto-parts-related assets of VIP Parts Tires & Service a large privately-held automotive parts tires and service chain in New England. The asset purchase included 56 stores located throughout Maine New Hampshire and Massachusetts as well as a distribution center located in Lewiston Maine.

EXECUTIVES

Vice President Eastern Division, Brad Beckham
Vp Western Division, Larry Ellis
EVP Expansion, Ted F. Wise, age 64, $402,692 total compensation
President and CEO, Gregory L. (Greg) Henslee, age 54, $1,087,500 total compensation
EVP Store Operations and Sales, Jeff M. Shaw, age 52, $340,385 total compensation
EVP Finance and CFO, Thomas G. (Tom) McFall, age 44, $633,269 total compensation
EVP Supply Chain, Gregory D. (Greg) Johnson, age 49
SVP Information Systems, Jeff Lauro
Vice President Sales and Marketing, Vernon (Vern) Schnautz
Svp Inventory Management, Randy Johnson
Vice President Northern Division, Kenny Martin
Senior Vice President Merchandise And Marketing, Mike Swearengin
Co-Chairman and COO, Lawrence P. (Larry) O'Reilly, age 68
Chairman, David E. O'Reilly, age 66
Auditors: Ernst & Young LLP

LOCATIONS

HQ: O' Reilly Automotive, Inc.
233 South Patterson Avenue, Springfield, MO 65802
Phone: 417 862-6708
Web: www.oreillyauto.com

2014 Locations

	No.
Texas	615
California	512
Missouri	190
Georgia	178
Illinois	167
Tennessee	153
Washington	151
Ohio	148
North Carolina	141
Michigan	134
Arizona	133
Florida	118
Oklahoma	116
Minnesota	115
Alabama	114
Indiana	109
Arkansas	104
Wisconsin	104
Louisiana	100
Colorado	90
South Carolina	84
Kansas	76
Mississippi	73
Iowa	70
Kentucky	67
Utah	59
Oregon	58
Virginia	54
Nevada	85
New Mexico	45
Idaho	36
Maine	35
Nebraska	35
Montana	27
New Hampshire	18
Wyoming	18
North Dakota	15
Alaska	14
Hawaii	12
South Dakota	12
Massachusetts	7
West Virginia	6
Pennsylvania	1
Total	**4,366**

PRODUCTS/OPERATIONS

Selected Products

Accessorie
Accessorie
Air Conditioning
Battery &
Belts & Ho
Body & Tri
Brakes
Charging &
Cooling &
Engine Par
Exhaust
Filters & PCV Valves
Fuel & Emi
Hardware &
Ignition &
Lighting &
Oil Fluids
Performance
Suspension
Tire & Whe
Tools & Eq
Transmissi
Truck & To
Waxes & Wa
Wipers

COMPETITORS

Acheeve Inc.	Target Corporation
Advance Auto Parts	U.S. Auto Parts
AutoZone	VIP
CARQUEST	Wal-Mart
Genuine Parts	Whitney Automotive
Pep Boys	Group
Sears	

HISTORICAL FINANCIALS

Company Type: Public

Income Statement

FYE: December 31

	REVENUE ($ mil.)	NET INCOME ($ mil.)	NET PROFIT MARGIN	EMPLOYEES
12/14	7,216	778	10.8%	67,926
12/13	6,649	670	10.1%	62,533
12/12	6,182	585	9.5%	53,615
12/11	5,788	507	8.8%	49,148
12/10	5,397	419	7.8%	47,142
Annual Growth	7.5%	16.7%	—	9.6%

2014 Year-End Financials

Debt ratio: 21.35%
Return on equity: 39.06%
Cash ($ mil.): 250
Current ratio: 1.08
Long-term debt ($ mil.): 1,396
No. of shares (mil.): 101
Dividends
  Yield: —
  Payout: —
Market value ($ mil.): 19,571

	STOCK PRICE ($) FY Close	P/E High/Low	PER SHARE ($) Earnings	Dividends	Book Value
12/14	192.62	26 17	7.34	0.00	19.87
12/13	128.71	22 14	6.03	0.00	18.56
12/12	89.42	22 16	4.75	0.00	18.66
12/11	79.95	22 14	3.71	0.00	22.37
12/10	60.42	21 12	2.95	0.00	22.76
Annual Growth	33.6%	— —	25.6%	—	(3.3%)

Occidental Petroleum Corp

Harnessing its heritage of Western technical know-how Occidental Petroleum engages in oil and gas exploration and production and makes basic chemicals plastics and petrochemicals. In 2014 it reported proved reserves of 2.8 billion barrels of oil equivalent primarily from assets in the US the Middle East North Africa and Latin America. Subsidiary Occidental Chemical (OxyChem) produces acids chlorine and specialty products and owns Oxy Vinyls the #1 maker of polyvinyl chloride (PVC) resin in North America. Occidental Petroleum's midstream and marketing units gather treat process transport store trade and market crude oil natural gas NGLs condensate and CO_2 and generate and market power.

HISTORY

Founded in 1920 Occidental Petroleum struggled until 1956 when billionaire industrialist Dr. Armand Hammer sank $100000 into the company then worth $34000. It drilled two wells and both came in. Hammer eventually gained control of the company.

Occidental's discovery of California's second-largest gas field (1959) was followed by a concession from Libya's King Idris (1966) and the discovery of a billion-barrel Libyan oil field. In 1968 Occidental bought Signal Oil's European refining and marketing business as an outlet for the Libyan oil. It also diversified buying Island Creek Coal and Hooker Chemical.

In 1969 Occidental sold 51% of its Libyan production to the Libyan government under duress after Idris was ousted. (It suspended operations there in 1986). It soon began oil exploration in Latin America (1971) and in the North Sea (1972-73) where it discovered the lucrative Piper field. Other projects included a 20-year fertilizer-for-ammonia deal with the USSR (1974) and a coal joint venture with China (1985).

During the 1980s Occidental sold some foreign assets and bought US natural gas pipeline firm MidCon (1986). It also bought Iowa Beef Processors (IBP) for stock worth $750 million (1981) and then spun off 49% of it in 1987 for $960 million.

In 1983 Hammer hired Ray Irani to revive Occidental's ailing chemicals business (losses that year: $38 million). Irani integrated operations to ensure higher margins during industry downturns and purchased Diamond Shamrock Chemicals (1986) Shell's vinyl chloride monomer unit (1987) a DuPont chloralkali facility (1987) and Cain Chemical (1988). OxyChem's profits reached almost $1.1 billion by 1989.

Hammer died in 1990 and Irani became CEO. In 1991 to reduce debt Occidental exited the Chinese coal business and sold the North Sea oil properties. Occidental also spun off IBP the largest US red-meat producer to its shareholders.

Occidental paid Irani $95 million in 1997 to buy out his employment contract; instead his compensation (a minimum of $1.2 million a year) was tied to the company's fortunes. That year Occidental's $3.65 billion bid won the US government's auction of its 78% stake in California's Elk Hills petroleum reserve one of the largest in the continental US.

To help pay for Elk Hills the company sold MidCon to K N Energy for $3.1 billion in 1998. Occidental traded its petrochemical operations to Equistar Chemicals a partnership between Lyondell (now LyondellBasell) and Millennium Chemicals for $425 million and a 29.5% stake.

In a venture with The Geon Company Occidental in 1999 formed Oxy Vinyls the #1 producer of polyvinyl chloride (PVC) resin in North America. That year also brought a windfall: Chevron agreed to pay Occidental $775 million to settle a lawsuit stemming from the 1982 withdrawal by Gulf (later acquired by Chevron) of an offer to buy Cities Service (later acquired by Occidental).

In 2000 Occidental sold its 29% stake in Canadian Occidental back to the company for $828 million to help fund the purchase of oil and gas producer Altura Energy a partnership of BP and Shell Oil for $3.6 billion. Later that year the company sold some Gulf of Mexico properties to Apache for $385 million.

Occidental acquired a new exploration block in Yemen in 2001. The next year it sold its 30% of Equistar Chemicals to Lyondell in exchange for a 21% stake in Lyondell. In 2005 it acquired a stake in a gas and oil production site located in Texas' Permian Basin from ExxonMobil for a reported $972 million. Occidental closed the acquisition of Vintage Petroleum for a reported $3.8 billion in early 2006.

The government of Ecuador seized Occidental Petroleum's Ecuadorian assets in 2006 as part of a nationalization drive. That year Plains Exploration and Production sold non-core oil and gas properties to Occidental for $865 million.

Also in 2006 Occidental reduced its stake in Lyondell from 12% to 8%. The following year Occidental sold its remaining Lyondell shares on the open market.

In North America in 2008 the company bought a 15% stake in the Joslyn Oil Sands project for nearly $500 million. That project is based in Alberta Canada and is operated by Total.

The company re-entered Libya in 2008.

Beefing up its investment vehicles in 2009 the company purchased Citigroup's commodities trading unit (Philbro LLC).

To raise cash to pay down debt in 2011 the company sold its Argentina-based assets to China Petrochemical for $2.45 billion. The deal helped cover some of the costs of Occidental's $3.4 billion acquisition (in late 2010 and early 2011) of safer US-based assets —oil and gas properties in South Texas and North Dakota.

In the US in 2012 Occidental paid $2.3 billion for oil and gas properties in the Permian Basin Williston Basin South Texas and California.That year Occidental and Magellan Midstream Partners L.P. formed BridgeTex Pipeline Company LLC (BridgeTex) to build the 450-mile-long BridgeTex Pipeline to transport 300000 barrels per day of crude oil between the Permian region and the Gulf Coast refinery markets.

EXECUTIVES

CEO and Director, Stephen I. (Steve) Chazen, age 68, $1,500,000 total compensation
Vice President, Jean Hall
EVP President OXY Oil and Gas International, Edward A. (Sandy) Lowe, age 63, $625,000 total compensation
EVP Strategy and Development, Cynthia L. Walker, age 39, $600,000 total compensation
EVP Operations, Willie C.W. Chiang, age 54, $625,000 total compensation
President and COO, Vicki A. Hollub, age 55, $519,697 total compensation
EVP and CFO, Christopher G. (Chris) Stavros, age 51, $507,860 total compensation
VP and CIO, Ioannis A. Charalambous
Vice President Marketing and Asset Optimization, Shawn McGovern

Senior Vice President Trading, Greg Hood
Vice President Health Environment Safety And Security, Wesley Scott
Vice President Sales and Marketing, James (Jamie) Clarken
Executive Vice President Business Support, James (Jamie) Lienert
Chairman, Eugene L. (Gene) Batchelder, age 67
Vice Chairman, Spencer Abraham, age 62
Auditors: KPMG LLP

LOCATIONS

HQ: Occidental Petroleum Corp
5 Greenway Plaza, Suite 110, Houston, TX 77046
Phone: 713 215-7000
Web: www.oxy.com

2014 Sales

	% of total
US	62
Qatar	14
Oman	13
Colombia	5
Other countries	6
Total	**100**

PRODUCTS/OPERATIONS

2014 Sales

	$ mil.	% of total
Oil & gas	13,887	69
Chemicals	4,817	24
Midstream marketing & other	1,373	7
Adjustments	(765)	-
Total	**19,312**	**100**

Selected Subsidiaries

Occidental Chemical Corp. (OxyChem; chemicals polymers and plastics)
  Oxy Vinyls LP (76% polyvinyl chloride)
Occidental Energy Marketing Inc. (energy marketing)
Occidental Exploration and Production Company (exploration and production)
Phibro (international commodities trading)

COMPETITORS

Apache	Huntsman International
Ashland Inc.	Imperial Oil
BP	J.M. Huber
ConocoPhillips	Koch Industries Inc.
Devon Energy	Marathon Oil
Dow Chemical	Olin
DuPont	PEMEX
Eastman Chemical	Royal Dutch Shell
Exxon Mobil	Sunoco
Hess Corporation	TOTAL

HISTORICAL FINANCIALS

Company Type: Public

Income Statement

FYE: December 31

	REVENUE ($ mil.)	NET INCOME ($ mil.)	NET PROFIT MARGIN	EMPLOYEES
12/14	21,947	616	2.8%	11,700
12/13	25,736	5,903	22.9%	12,900
12/12	24,253	4,598	19.0%	12,300
12/11	24,119	6,771	28.1%	11,300
12/10	19,157	4,530	23.6%	11,000
Annual Growth	**3.5%**	**(39.3%)**	**—**	**1.6%**

2014 Year-End Financials

Debt ratio: 12.15%
Return on equity: 1.58%
Cash ($ mil.): 3,789
Current ratio: 1.68
Long-term debt ($ mil.): 6,838
No. of shares (mil.): 890
Dividends
  Yield: 3.5%
  Payout: 41.9%
Market value ($ mil.): 71,788

	STOCK PRICE ($)	P/E		PER SHARE ($)		
	FY Close	High/Low	Earnings	Dividends	Book Value
12/14	80.61	133 93	0.79	2.88	39.26
12/13	95.10	14 10	7.32	2.56	48.46
12/12	76.61	19 13	5.67	2.16	49.68
12/11	93.70	14 8	8.32	1.84	46.39
12/10	98.10	18 13	5.56	1.47	39.97
Annual Growth	**(4.8%)**	**— —**	**(38.6%)**	**18.3%**	**(0.4%)**

Office Depot, Inc.

Paper and paper clips add up to big money for Office Depot. The world's #2 office supply chain (behind Staples) Office Depot sells office supplies through some 2000 retail stores in about 60 countries following its merger with OfficeMax. The big-box retail stores sell to both consumers and small and medium-sized businesses. In addition to general office supplies (about two-thirds of sales) its stores offer computer hardware and software furniture art and school supplies and printing and copying services. Office Depot also sells goods through catalogs and call centers the Internet and a contract sales force. Faced with declining organic sales in 2015 the company agreed to be acquired by Staples.

HISTORY

Pat Scher Stephen Dougherty and Jack Kopkin opened the first Office Depot one of the first office supply superstores in Lauderdale Lakes Florida in 1986. Scher was selected as chairman. By the end of the year the fledgling company had opened two more stores (both in Florida).

Office Depot opened seven more stores in 1987. When Scher died of leukemia that year the company recruited David Fuente former president of Sherwin-Williams' Paint Store Division as chairman and CEO. Office Depot continued its breakneck expansion under Fuente. In 1988 —the year the company went public —it opened 16 stores and broke into new markets in four states.

The chain stepped up its pace and by 1990 it had expanded into several other areas including the South and Midwest. Office Depot also added computers and peripherals and opened its first delivery center.

In 1991 the company became North America's #1 office products retailer and expanded its presence in the West through the acquisition of Office Club another warehouse-type office supply chain with 59 stores (most in California). Fuente remained chairman and CEO while former Office Club CEO Mark Begelman became president and COO. (Begelman who left in 1995 and eventually formed the MARS music chain had founded the first Office Club in 1987 in Concord California; he took it public in 1989.)

The company entered the international market with its 1992 purchase of Canada's H. Q. Office International and through licensing agreements in 1993 (in Colombia and Israel). Office Depot created its business services division by acquiring various contract stationers including Eastman Office Products (the West Coast's #1 contract office supplier) in the mid-1990s and added locations in Mexico and Poland; it established a joint venture in France with retailer Carrefour in 1996.

Also in 1996 Office Depot announced a $3.4 billion agreement to be acquired by Staples which would have created a company with more than 1100 stores. However the government blocked the purchase on antitrust grounds in 1997 and the agreement dissolved. Unfettered by merger distractions Office Depot resumed opening stores at a rapid pace including two in Thailand and took its catalog and delivery services online. It then established a joint venture with Japanese retailer Deo Deo.

In 1998 Office Depot acquired Viking Office Products in a $2.7 billion deal. With more than 60% of its sales coming from outside the US Viking augmented Office Depot's already strong delivery network and international expansion. Office Depot acquired the remaining 50% of its French operations from Carrefour in 1998 and the remaining 50% of its Japanese operations from Deo Deo in 1999.

Office Depot started putting Internet kiosks in its US stores in 2000 allowing customers to browse and shop company Web sites. In July 2000 Bruce Nelson CEO of Viking replaced Fuente as CEO of Office Depot. Citing weak computer sales and high warehouse prices the company closed about 70 stores and cut its workforce. In early 2002 Nelson was named chairman as well as CEO after Fuente stepped down.

Office Depot sold its Australian operations to Officeworks a unit of Coles Myer in January 2003. Office Depot used the proceeds to expand its faster-growing European operations. Also that year the company acquired the retail operations of French office supplier Guilbert from Pinault-Printemps-Redoute a move that doubled the company's business in Europe. (Staples had acquired Guilbert's mail-order business the previous year.)

In 2004 the company acquired about 125 retail locations from troubled toy seller Toys "R" Us converting 50 of those into Office Depot locations and selling off the remainder.

Nelson left the company and Neil Austrian served as interim head. Office Depot named AutoZone leader Steve Odland as CEO and chairman in 2005. That year the company shuttered its Viking Office Products brand in the US consolidating its catalog sales under the Office Depot banner. (It still markets products through Viking in international markets.) The business services division also sells technology products through Tech Depot (formerly 4SURE.com).

The company acquired privately held Allied Office Products (AOP) the largest independent dealer of office products and services in the US in 2006. AOP became part of Office Depot's North American Business Solutions Division.

Office Depot opened 70 new stores in 2007 (vs. 115 the previous year).

In mid-2008 the company acquired 13 stores in Sweden through the acquisition of AGE Kontor & Data AB a contract and retail office supply company operating there.

In 2009 the company closed about 125 stores in North America and exited the Japanese market.

CEO Steve Odland resigned in November 2010. In late 2010 Israeli department store operator New Hamashbir Lazarchan acquired Office Depot's operations in Israel for $50 million. New Hamashbir Lazarchan also agreed to pay royalties on revenues generated by Office Depot Israel which has about 45 stores.

Office Depot appointed new leadership in mid-2011 naming interim leader Neil Austrian as the company's permanent replacement for chief executive and chairman. Austrian has served as a director at Office Depot since 1998. He stepped in to lead the office products retailer on a temporary basis following the resignation of Steve Odland in late 2010. Odland's resignation came soon after Office Depot settled Securities and Exchange Commission charges that the company selectively in-

formed analysts and institutional investors that its earnings would fall short of estimates. Office Depot agreed to pay $1 million while Odland and the firm's former CFO agreed to pay $50000.

EXECUTIVES

EVP and President International, Steven M. (Steve) Schmidt, age 61, $675,000 total compensation
Chairman and CEO, Roland C. Smith, age 60, $1,400,000 total compensation
EVP and CFO, Stephen E. Hare, age 61, $750,000 total compensation
President North America, Mark S. Cosby, age 56, $375,962 total compensation
EVP and Chief Strategy Officer, Juliet Johansson, age 45
EVP and Chief Legal Officer, Elisa D. Garcia C., age 58, $575,000 total compensation
EVP Retail, Troy Rice
EVP Contract Sales, Steve Calkins
EVP Merchandising, Ronald Lalla
EVP and Chief People Officer, Michael Allison, age 57, $525,000 total compensation
SVP and Global CIO, Todd Hale
EVP E-Commerce, Mike Kirschner
EVP Marketing, Tim Rea
SVP Supply Chain, Tim Beauchamp
Senior Vice President for Information Technology, Andy Parry
Vp-investor Relations, Michael (Mel) Steele
Vice President Bsd, John Nixon
Vice President Finance, Diana Davis
National Account Manager, Jacqueline Mancilla
Vice President Ecommerce Technology, Carl Brisco
Regional Vice President, Marc Ehle
Vice President Of Construction, Frank Betancourt
National Account Manager, Chris Austin
Vice President Enterprise Account Management, Steve Dvorchak
Regional Vice President, Kristen Driscoll
Vice President Transformation Delivery, Sharon McGregor
National Account Manager, Chris Bombela
Vice President, Alex Jaime
National Account Manager, Ashley Stuhr
Senior Vice President General Merchandise Manager Office Supplies and Furniture, Petter Knutrud
Senior Vice President Integration, Deb O'Connor
Auditors: Deloitte & Touche LLP

LOCATIONS

HQ: Office Depot, Inc.
6600 North Military Trail, Boca Raton, FL 33496
Phone: 561 438-4800   **Fax:** 561 265-4406
Web: www.officedepot.com

2014

	$ mil.	% of total
US	12,132	75
International	3,964	25
Total	**16,096**	**100**

PRODUCTS/OPERATIONS

2014 Sales

	$ mil.	% of total
North American Retail	6,528	41
North American Business Solutions	6,013	37
International	3,400	21
Other	155	1
Total	**16,096**	**100**

Selected Products

Office supplies
  Basic supplies and labels
  Binders and accessories
  Breakroom and janitorial supplies
  Business cases
  Calendars and planners

Desk accessories
Executive gifts
Filing and storage
Paper and envelopes
Pens pencils and markers
School supplies
Technology products
  Audio-visual equipment and supplies
  Cameras
  Computers and related accessories (including monitors and printers)
  Copiers
  Data storage supplies
  Fax machines
  Networking supplies
  PDAs
  Software
Office furniture
  Armoires
  Bookcases
  Carts and stands
  Chair mats and floor mats
  Chairs
  Desks
  Filing cabinets
  Lamps and light bulbs
  Office furnishings
  Panel systems
  Tables
  Workstations

COMPETITORS

Amazon.com	Lyreco
Apple Inc.	RadioShack
BJ's Wholesale Club	Ricoh USA
Best Buy	School Specialty
CDW	Staples
Costco Wholesale	Systemax
Essendant	Target Corporation
FedEx Office	The UPS Store
Fry's Electronics	Wal-Mart
Insight Enterprises	

HISTORICAL FINANCIALS

Company Type: Public

Income Statement

FYE: December 27

	REVENUE ($ mil.)	NET INCOME ($ mil.)	NET PROFIT MARGIN	EMPLOYEES
12/14	16,096	(354)	—	56,000
12/13	11,242	(20)	—	64,000
12/12	10,695	(77)	—	38,000
12/11	11,489	95	0.8%	39,000
12/10	11,633	34	0.3%	40,000
Annual Growth	**8.5%**	**—**	**—**	**8.8%**

2014 Year-End Financials

Debt ratio: 10.32%
Return on equity: (-19.27%)
Cash ($ mil.): 1,071
Current ratio: 1.46
Long-term debt ($ mil.): 674

No. of shares (mil.): 545
Dividends
  Yield: —
  Payout: —
Market value ($ mil.): 4,819

	STOCK PRICE ($) FY Close	P/E High/Low	PER SHARE ($) Earnings	Dividends	Book Value
12/14	8.84	— —	(0.66)	0.00	2.97
12/13	5.19	— —	(0.29)	0.00	3.89
12/12	3.27	— —	(0.39)	0.00	3.67
12/11	2.15	28 8	0.22	0.00	3.85
12/10	5.45	— —	(0.01)	0.00	4.09
Annual Growth	**12.9%**	**— —**	**—**	**—**	**(7.7%)**

Old National Bancorp (Evansville, IN)

Old National Bank is old but it's not quite national. Founded in 1834 the main subsidiary of Old National Bancorp operates about 200 bank centers across Indiana Kentucky Michigan and Illinois. The bank serves consumers and business customers offering standard checking and savings accounts credit cards and loans. Its treasury segment manages investments for bank and commercial clients. Business loans commercial and residential mortgages and consumer loans account for most of Old National's lending activity. The company also sells insurance manages wealth for high-net-worth clients and offers investment and retirement services through third-party provider LPL Financial.

OperationsOld National Bancorp operates two main segments: Banking which generates the bulk of Old National's revenue and provides traditional loan and deposit products as well as wealth management services; and Insurance which provides commercial property and casualty surety loss control services employee benefits consulting and administration as well as personal insurance.The bank generated 51% of its revenue from loan interest (including fees) in 2014 while another 14% came from interest on investment securities. Insurance premiums and commissions contributed 7% to the company's total revenues that year while wealth management fees made up another 5%.Geographic Reach

The bank's nearly 200 banking centers are located across four Midwestern states and Kentucky. Most are in the central northern and southern parts of Indiana; while others are in central Illinois; Western Kentucky and Louisville; Grand Rapids Southeastern and Southwestern Michigan; and Ohio. Sales and MarketingOld National has identified metropolitan areas within its market including Indianapolis; Louisville Kentucky; and Lafayette Indiana for growth within its core community banking segment.The company spent $9.59 million on marketing in 2014 up from $7.21 million and $7.45 million in 2013 and 2012 respectively.

Financial Performance

Old National Bancorp's revenues and profits have been on the uptrend for the past several years thanks to new loan business from a series of bank acquisitions and declining loan loss provisions as its loan portfolio's credit quality has improved with the strengthened economy. The company's revenue rose by 5% to $554.86 million in 2014 mostly thanks to new loan business stemming from the bank's acquisitions of Tower Financial United Bancorp and LSB Financial during the year along with organic loan growth. Higher revenue in 2014 coupled with strong cost controls lower interest on deposits and a continued decline in loan loss provisions drove Old National's net income higher by 3% to $103.62 million for the year.Old National's operating cash fell by 21% to $199.72 million after adjusting its earnings for non-cash items related to its net sales proceeds from the sale of its residential real estate loans held-for-sale.

Strategy

Old National continues to seek out additional branch and whole bank acquisitions to grow its loan business and expand its geographic reach. Its acquisition of United Bancorp in mid-2014 for example added nearly $1 billion in new loan business and $869 million in wealth management assets under management while doubling Old National's presence in Michigan to 36 total branches.The

company is also pursuing growth by increasing its focus on commercial banking and cross-selling its insurance and wealth management offerings. To this end Old National in 2014 bought the insurance accounts (consisting of mostly commercial property/casualty accounts) serviced by the Evansville branch office of Wells Fargo Insurance.Meanwhile it is also selectively exiting markets that haven't been profitable. In early 2015 as part of its ongoing efficiency improvement efforts the bank announced that it would sell 17 of its banking centers including all twelve of its branches in Southern Illinois and close or consolidate another 19 branches in other states over the following months.Mergers and AcquisitionsIn December 2014 Old National agreed to acquire Founders Financial Corporation along with its Founders Bank & Trust subsidiary in Grand Rapids Michigan for $91.7 million which would add nearly $460 million in total assets and four branches in Kent County.In November 2014 the company purchased LSB Financial and its Lafayette Savings Bank subsidiary for $51.8 million adding five branches near Lafayette Indiana.In July 2014 the company acquired Ann Arbor-based United Bancorp along with United Bank & Trust for a total of $122 million adding 18 branches in Michigan nearly $919 million in total assets a $963 million loan servicing portfolio and $688 million in trust assets under management.In April 2014 Old National purchased Indiana-based Tower Financial along with its Tower Bank & Trust subsidiary adding seven new branches and some $556 million in trust assets under management.In 2013 the bank bolstered its presence in Michigan after acquiring two dozen Bank of America branches in northern Indiana and southwest Michigan. The previous year the bank purchased Indiana Community Bancorp which added 17 branches in the southeastern part of the state. The transaction was valued at nearly $80 million.

EXECUTIVES

President CEO and Director, Robert G. (Bob) Jones, age 58, $650,000 total compensation
EVP and Chief Legal Counsel, Jeffrey L. (Jeff) Knight, age 55, $271,731 total compensation
EVP and Chief Credit Officer, Daryl D. Moore, age 57, $299,059 total compensation
EVP and Chief Client Services Officer, Annette W. Hudgions, age 57, $250,016 total compensation
Executive Vice President, Caroline J. Ellspermann, age 47
Eastern Regional CEO, Dennis P. Heishman
SEVP and CFO, Christopher A. (Chris) Wolking, age 55, $313,770 total compensation
President and CEO Old National Insurance, Thomas A. (Tom) Flynn
Executive Vice President Community Relations and Social Responsibility Officer, Kathy Schoettlin
Region CEO Old National Bank, Randall (Randy) Reichmann
EVP and Chief Risk Officer, Candice J. Rickard, age 51
Regional CEO Southern, James Sandgren
Northern Regional CEO, Dan L. Doan
EVP and Director Corporate Strategy, James C. Ryan, age 43
EVP and CIO, John R. Kamin
EVP and Chief Human Resources Officer, Kendra L. Vanzo
Vice President Technology Services Manager, Janet Wandling
Senior Vice President, Gary McDowell
Assistant Vice President, Sherry Beck
Executive Vice President Senior Vice President Vice President Risk privacy compliance, Stephanie White
Assistant Vice President, Julie Grubb

Vice President Loss Share Team Leader And Corporate Oreo Manager, Wade Alexa
Vice President, Brian Henning
Vice President Associate Counsel, Tom Washburne
Assistant Vice President Director Of Corporate Training, Julie Falls
Physical Security Manager Vice President, Donna Harlow
Assistant Vice President Special Assets, Scott Servoss
Vice President International Banking Manager, Kim Humphrey
Senior Vice President of Marketing, Scott Adams
Vice President Bank Controller, Brendon Falconer
Assistant Vice President, Ed Armantrout
Vice President Financial Planning, Toni Wander
Assistant Vice President, Chad Smith
Vice President, Kevin Murphy
Assistant Vice President, Sandy Keen
Assistant Vice President, Gidget Rowe
Vice President Finance, Alan Orear
Vice President Sarbanes Oxley Analyst, Denise Rexing
Vice President, Randy Lilly
Assistant Vice President, Jenny Clark
Assistant Vice President Mortgage Loan Officer, Debra Fulkerson
Assistant Vice President, Greg Allaben
Vice President Business Banking, Glen Jacobs
Executive Vice President Marketing, Denise Ramond
Vice President, Jeff Sims
Vice President, Roger Ferguson
Vice President Manager, Sabrina Mancuso
Assistant Vice President Commercial Lender, Mike Devoy
Retail Center Manager Vice President, Stacy Fuqua
Chairman, Larry E. Dunigan, age 72
Auditors: Crowe Horwath LLP

LOCATIONS

HQ: Old National Bancorp (Evansville, IN)
One Main Street, Evansville, IN 47708
Phone: 812 464-1294
Web: www.oldnational.com

PRODUCTS/OPERATIONS

2014 Sales

	$ mil.	% of total
Interest		
Loans including fees	306	51
Investment securities	83	14
Noninterest		
Service charges on deposit accounts	47	8
Insurance premiums & commissions	41	7
Wealth management fees	28	5
ATM Fees	25	4
Investment product fees	17	3
Mortgage banking revenue	6	1
Other	41	7
Adjustments	(43.3)	-
Total	**554**	**100**

COMPETITORS

Fifth Third	JPMorgan Chase
First Financial (IN)	MainSource Financial
German American Bancorp	PNC Financial
Huntington Bancshares	Peoples Bancorp (IN)
	U.S. Bancorp

HISTORICAL FINANCIALS

Company Type: Public

Income Statement
FYE: December 31

	ASSETS ($ mil.)	NET INCOME ($ mil.)	INCOME AS % OF ASSETS	EMPLOYEES
12/14	11,647	103	0.9%	2,938
12/13	9,581	100	1.1%	2,608
12/12	9,543	91	1.0%	2,684
12/11	8,609	72	0.8%	2,551
12/10	7,263	38	0.5%	2,491
Annual Growth	12.5%	28.3%	—	4.2%

2014 Year-End Financials

Debt ratio: 2.32%
Return on equity: 7.89%
Cash ($ mil.): 239
Current ratio: —
Long-term debt ($ mil.): —

No. of shares (mil.): 116
Dividends
  Yield: 2.9%
  Payout: 46.3%
Market value ($ mil.): 1,739

	STOCK PRICE ($) FY Close	P/E High/Low		PER SHARE ($) Earnings	Dividends	Book Value
12/14	14.88	16	13	0.95	0.44	12.54
12/13	15.37	16	13	1.00	0.40	11.64
12/12	24.06	—	—	0.95	0.36	11.81
12/11	24.06	—	—	0.76	0.28	10.92
12/10	24.06	—	—	0.44	0.28	10.08
Annual Growth	(11.3%)	—	—	21.2%	12.0%	5.6%

Old Republic International Corp.

Old Republic International keeps pace with changing financial times. With more than 100 subsidiaries across North America Old Republic International's primary operations are conducted through the Old Republic General Insurance division which offers commercial liability and property/casualty insurance (mostly commercial trucking workers' compensation and general liability policies). In addition the company's Title Insurance group specializes in naturally issuing title insurance to property owners and lenders. Its Old Republic National Title subsidiary is one of the US's oldest and largest title insurance companies with offices throughout the US.

Operations

Commercial property/casualty policies issued by the general insurance segment account for more than half of the company's sales. Meanwhile the title insurance segment accounts for some 30% of revenues while the company's Republic Financial Indemnity Group (RFIG comprising mortgage guaranty and consumer credit indemnity runoff operations) brings in about 5% of sales. The company also maintains a small life and health insurance business.

In 2014 about three-fourths of the company's consolidated title premium and fee income came from independent title agents and underwritten title companies. The rest stemmed from direct operations including branches of its title insurance businesses and wholly owned agency and service subsidiaries.

Geographic Reach

Through its subsidiaries Old Republic is licensed to do business throughout the US including de-

pendent territories as well as in all Canadian provinces.

Sales and Marketing

While Old Republic does sell some of its property/casualty and specialty products directly it relies on independent agencies brokers and financial institutions to distribute the majority. The company focuses on certain sectors especially transportation commercial construction health care education forest products energy manufacturing and financial services.

Title insurance and related settlement products are sold through some 270 company offices and through agencies and underwritten title companies throughout the US.

Financial Performance

After years of seeing strong growth revenue rose a marginal 2% to $5.5 billion in 2014. General insurance operations grew 9% that year thanks to new business higher premiums on rate improvements and customer retention rates but the title insurance and RFIG runoff operations saw declines.

Net income which has been in fluctuation fell 8% to $410 million in 2014 as a result of higher benefits claims and settlement expenses. Cash flow from operations peaked in 2013 at $687 million but as higher amounts of cash were used towards claims and prepaid federal income taxes Old Republic reported a cash outflow of $181 million.

Revenue roller coasters and net income fluctuations don't bother Old Republic as its public filings clearly state that it looks at its business in five-to-10-year intervals and therefore isn't bothered by the ups and downs in shorter cycles. The health of its general insurance business and the fact that it carries very little debt make it easier to take that view.

Strategy

In response to troubles in the real estate market over the past few years Old Republic has increased its focus on its commercial liability and property/casualty operations. The firm is focused on long-term returns on its underwriting operations. As such it spreads its risk over diversified operations and assets to reduce liability exposures. Growth efforts include a mix of internal growth initiatives the establishment of new subsidiaries to serve new sectors and the streamlining of operations through mergers.

EXECUTIVES

Chairman and CEO, Aldo C. (Al) Zucaro, age 76, $855,000 total compensation
President and COO, R. Scott Rager, age 66, $490,000 total compensation
SVP Title Insurance; President Old Republic National Title Insurance, Rande K. Yeager, age 66, $485,000 total compensation
SVP and CFO, Karl W. Mueller, age 55, $445,000 total compensation
President and COO Old Republic General Insurance Group Inc. (ORGIG), Craig R. Smiddy, age 51
President Old Republic Risk Management Inc., Steve Oberst, age 48
Vice President Director Financial Reporting, Stephanie Richards
Senior Vice President Secretary, Spencer LeRoy
Vice President Human Resources, Chester Cedars
Executive Vice Chairman, James A. (Jim) Kellogg, age 63
Auditors: KPMG LLP

LOCATIONS

HQ: Old Republic International Corp.
  307 North Michigan Avenue, Chicago, IL 60601
Phone: 312 346-8100
Web: www.oldrepublic.com

PRODUCTS/OPERATIONS

2014 Sales

	$ mil.	% of total
General insurance	3,113	57
Title insurance	1,791	32
Runoff (RFIG)	282	5
Consolidated realized investment gains	272	5
Other	70	1
Total	**5,530**	**100**

COMPETITORS

AEGON	Investors Title
AIG	Kingsway
AXA	PMI Group
Allianz	Progressive
Berkshire Hathaway	Corporation
CNA Financial	Radian Group
Chubb Limited	Stewart Information
Farmers Group	Services
Fidelity National	The Hartford
Financial	Travelers Companies
First American	Unum Group
ING	W. R. Berkley

HISTORICAL FINANCIALS

Company Type: Public

Income Statement
FYE: December 31

	ASSETS ($ mil.)	NET INCOME ($ mil.)	INCOME AS % OF ASSETS	EMPLOYEES
12/14	16,988	409	2.4%	8,000
12/13	16,534	447	2.7%	7,900
12/12	16,226	(68)	—	7,800
12/11	16,050	(140)	—	7,900
12/10	15,882	30	0.2%	8,000
Annual Growth	1.7%	92.1%	—	0.0%

2014 Year-End Financials

Debt ratio: 5.68%
Return on equity: 10.64%
Cash ($ mil.): 136
Current ratio: —
Long-term debt ($ mil.): —

No. of shares (mil.): 260
Dividends
  Yield: 4.9%
  Payout: 42.6%
Market value ($ mil.): 3,818

	STOCK PRICE ($) FY Close	P/E High/Low		PER SHARE ($) Earnings	Dividends	Book Value
12/14	14.63	11	9	1.44	0.73	15.04
12/13	17.27	10	6	1.74	0.72	14.49
12/12	10.65	—	—	(0.27)	0.71	13.86
12/11	9.27	—	—	(0.55)	0.70	14.55
12/10	13.63	118	77	0.13	0.69	15.90
Annual Growth	1.8%	—	—	82.4%	1.4%	(1.4%)

Omnicom Group, Inc.

It might not be omnipotent but Omnicom Group creates advertising that is omnipresent. The company ranks as the world's #1 corporate media services conglomerate with advertising marketing and public relations operations. It serves global advertising clients through its agency networks BBDO Worldwide DDB Worldwide and TBWA Worldwide while such firms as GSD&M's Idea City

Merkley + Partners and Zimmerman Advertising provide services for regional and national clients. Its Diversified Agency Services division including Fleishman-Hillard Integer and Rapp provides public relations and other marketing services.

Geographic Reach

Omnicom has US offices in New York Connecticut and Florida while it has international offices in London Shanghai and Singapore. The group's network of agencies serves some 5000 clients in more than 100 countries. In fiscal 2014 about 60% of the company's revenue came from the Americas while Europe contributed about 30% and the remaining 10% came from the Asia Pacific region.

Sales and Marketing

As a leading global advertising marketing and corporate communications company Omnicom has a large and diverse client base. Its largest client accounted for 2.6% of fiscal 2014 revenue. Its top 100 clients accounted for approximately 50% of fiscal 2014 revenue.

Financial Performance

The company's revenue has been trending upward over the last five years. In fiscal 2014 it reported $15.3 billion in revenue an increase compared to the previous fiscal year's revenue of $14.5 billion. The growth was primarily organic.

Strategy

Omnicom's fortunes have been buoyed in part by its agency networks and their consistently strong creative work (traditional media advertising accounts for almost half of its revenue) but the bulk of its growth has traditionally come from such areas as customer relationship management (CRM) and specialty communications.

Omnicom sees continued growth being tied to its ability to provide an ever-expanding menu of services to its largest clients especially in the digital and social media arenas. The company has also been focused on expanding its media planning and buying operations.

HISTORY

Omnicom Group was created in 1986 to combine three leading ad agencies into a single group capable of competing in the worldwide market. BBDO Worldwide founded in New York in 1928 as Batten Barton Durstine & Osborn had a huge PepsiCo account and developed the Pepsi Generation campaign. Doyle Dane Bernbach Group (DDB) which had created the fahrvergnügen ads for Volkswagen had strong ties in Europe. And Needham Harper Worldwide which had served up the "You Deserve a Break Today" commercials for McDonald's had connections in Asia. BBDO remained separate but DDB and Needham Harper were merged to form DDB Needham Worldwide. The business services units (public relations firms and direct marketers) of each of these companies were tucked under the Diversified Agency Services (DAS) umbrella.

Bruce Crawford a previous chairman of BBDO who had just finished a stint running New York's Metropolitan Opera became chairman and CEO in 1989. He transformed DAS from a chaotic group of shops into an integrated marketing giant and ran Omnicom as a holding company of independent operating units working together through cross-referrals. By keeping costs low especially interest expenses Omnicom survived the 1990-91 recession with little pain. The company acquired Goodby Berlin & Silverstein (now Goodby Silverstein & Partners) in 1992. The next year TBWA Advertising (founded in Paris in 1970 by American Bill Tragos) was added to Omnicom's roster.

The merger spree continued in 1994 when Omnicom purchased WWAV Group the largest direct-marketing agency in the UK. In 1995 Omnicom fused TBWA with Chiat/Day (founded in 1968 by Jay Chiat and Guy Day) to form TBWA International Network. Omnicom also acquired Michigan-based Ross Roy Communications (later Interone Marketing Group). In 1997 DDB Needham won back its McDonald's account after a 15-year hiatus. That year Crawford stepped down as CEO (though he remained chairman) and John Wren took control of Omnicom.

In 1998 the company acquired PR firm Fleishman-Hillard adding to the PR clout it established with the acquisition of Ketchum Communications (now Ketchum) in 1996. Omnicom also acquired GGT Group of London for $235 million. (GGT's New York office Wells BDDP had lost a large Procter & Gamble account that year.) It merged GGT's BDDP Worldwide with BBDP to form TBWA Worldwide. BBDO landed a $200 million account with PepsiCo's Frito-Lay that year.

Omnicom's position in Europe was boosted in 1999 when it bought the Abbot Mead Vickers (now Abbot Mead Vickers BBDO) shares it didn't already own. That year TBWA founder William Tragos retired from the company (replaced by Lee Clow) and DDB Needham changed its moniker to DDB Worldwide Communications Group. Omnicom also bought market research firm M/A/R/C for about $95 million and invested $20 million in pharmaceutical clinical trials company SCIREX. In 2000 BBDO scored a major coup over rival FCB Worldwide (now part of Interpublic) by landing the $1.8 billion DaimlerChrysler account. The next year it formed Seneca Investments to hold its stakes in several i-services shops including Agency.com and Organic. (Omnicom acquired the interactive agencies outright in 2003.)

After years of acquisitions and fine-tuning its operating structure Omnicom encountered the effects of the global recession in late 2008. Like most players in the media communications and advertising industries Omnicom experienced declines in revenue and net income at the end of 2009. It attributed the crisis within the automotive industry and declines in the demand for its sports and event marketing services as major reasons for the drops.

In 2010 the company acquired seven companies including Sales Power an in-store promotion company catering to South China and Maslov PR a public relations firm based in Moscow. Among the twelve companies it acquired in 2011 was Nancy Bailey & Associates a corporate licensing and consulting firm.

EXECUTIVES

EVP and CFO, Philip J. Angelastro, age 51, $513,542 total compensation
President and CEO, John D. Wren, age 63, $1,000,000 total compensation
President and CEO FleishmanHillard, John Saunders, age 57
Vice Chairman; Chairman Asia Pacific, Serge Dumont
EVP, Asit Mehra
EVP and Dean Omnicom University, Janet Riccio
EVP, Rita E. Rodriguez
EVP, Peter Sherman
CEO Omnicom Digital, Jonathan B. Nelson, $770,833 total compensation
SVP General Counsel and Secretary, Michael J. O'Brien, $700,000 total compensation
Vice President of Finance DAS Division, Fred Canoro
Senior Vice President Operations, Min Chang
Senior Vice President Finance Contrller, Peter (Pete) Swiecicki
Senior Vice President Business Development, Elizabeth Neill
Senior Vice President, Kenneth (Ken) Corriveau
Executive Vice President, Thomas Carey

Vice President Development, Jacqueline Indelicato
Vice President Human Resources, Leslie Chiocco
Vice President Strategy and Corporate Development, Ankur Manglik
Vice President, Robert (Bob) Miller
Vice President of Finance Operations, Brian Sullivan
Chairman, Bruce Crawford, age 87
Treasurer, Shelly Laskin
Board Of Directors, Gary Roubos
Treasurer, Angie Hickman
Auditors: KPMG LLP

LOCATIONS

HQ: Omnicom Group, Inc.
437 Madison Avenue, New York, NY 10022
Phone: 212 415-3600   **Fax:** 212 415-3393
Web: www.omnicomgroup.com

2014 Sales

	$ mil.	% of total
US	9,121	60
EMEA	4,594	30
Asia Pacific	1,602	10
Total	**15,317**	**100**

PRODUCTS/OPERATIONS

2014 Sales

	$ mil.	% of total
Advertising	7,593	50
Customer relationship management	5,254	34
Public relations	1,393	9
Specialty communications	1,076	7
Total	**15,317**	**100**

Selected Operations

Global advertising networks
  BBDO Worldwide
  DDB Worldwide
  TBWA Worldwide
National advertising agencies
  Goodby Silverstein & Partners (San Francisco)
  GSD&M' s Idea City (Austin TX)
  Martin|Williams (Minneapolis)
  Merkley + Partners (New York City)
  Zimmerman Partners Advertising (Fort Lauderdale FL)
Marketing and consulting agencies
Direct response
  Interbrand (brand identity)
  M/A/R/C Research (market research)
  Rapp (direct marketing)
  Targetbase (direct marketing)
Promotional marketing
  The Beanstalk Group (brand licensing and consulting)
  CPM (field marketing)
  The Integer Group (retail marketing)
  Kaleidoscope (sports and event marketing)
  Millsport (sports and event marketing)
Public relations
  Clark & Weinstock
  Cone
  Fleishman-Hillard
  Gavin Anderson & Company
  GPC International
  Ketchum
  Porter Novelli International
  Smythe Dorward Lambert
Specialty communications
  Adelphi Group (health care)
  Corbett Accel Healthcare (health care)
  Dieste (multicultural marketing)
  Doremus (business-to-business advertising)
  SafirRosetti (security and intelligence)
Media services
  Icon International
  Novus Print Media
  OMD Worldwide
  PHD Network

COMPETITORS

Dentsu	Interpublic Group
Dentsu Aegis	Publicis Groupe
Hakuhodo	WPP
Havas	

HISTORICAL FINANCIALS

Company Type: Public

Income Statement
FYE: December 31

	REVENUE ($ mil.)	NET INCOME ($ mil.)	NET PROFIT MARGIN	EMPLOYEES
12/15	15,134	1,093	7.2%	74,900
12/14	15,317	1,104	7.2%	74,000
12/13	14,584	991	6.8%	71,800
12/12	14,219	998	7.0%	71,000
12/11	13,872	952	6.9%	70,600
Annual Growth	2.2%	3.5%	—	1.5%

2015 Year-End Financials

Debt ratio: 20.67%	No. of shares (mil.): 239
Return on equity: 41.26%	Dividends
Cash ($ mil.): 2,605	Yield: 2.6%
Current ratio: 0.84	Payout: 45.9%
Long-term debt ($ mil.): 3,564	Market value ($ mil.): 18,136

	STOCK PRICE ($) FY Close	P/E High/Low		PER SHARE ($) Earnings	Dividends	Book Value
12/15	75.66	18	15	4.41	2.00	10.23
12/14	77.47	18	15	4.24	1.90	11.55
12/13	74.37	20	13	3.71	1.60	13.91
12/12	49.96	15	12	3.61	1.20	13.21
12/11	44.58	15	11	3.33	1.00	12.82
Annual Growth	14.1%	—	—	7.3%	18.9%	(5.5%)

Oneok Inc.

ONEOK ("one oak") is OK with its singled-minded pursuit of profits from natural gas activities. Through its 37.6%-owned ONEOK Partners (of which it is the general partner) it operates 11300 miles of gas-gathering pipeline and 7400 miles of transportation pipeline as well as gas processing plants and storage facilities. The unit also owns one of the US's top natural gas liquids (NGL) systems. ONEOK's energy services unit focuses on marketing natural gas across the US. To focus on its core pipeline businesses in 2014 ONEOK spun off its regulated utilities (Oklahoma Natural Gas Kansas Gas Service and Texas Gas Service which distribute natural gas to more than 2.1 million customers) as ONE Gas.

HISTORY

In 1906 Oklahoma Natural Gas (ONG) was founded to pipe natural gas from northeastern Oklahoma to Oklahoma City. A 100-mile pipeline was completed the next year. In 1921 ONG created two oil companies to pump out the oil it found as a result of its natural gas exploration.

ONG changed hands many times in the 1920s ending up with utility financier G. L. Ohrstrom and Company which milked it dry by brokering acquisitions (purchasing gas properties and then selling them to ONG) and collecting fees. Stock sales drove revenues inflating the stock's price and the inflated price triggered more stock sales. The bubble burst on October 29 1929. A series of leadership changes ensued and in 1932 the company was dissolved and reincorporated. Under president Joseph Bowes ONG recovered wooing back dissatisfied customers and upgrading its pipelines.

In the late 1930s the company pioneered a type of underground storage that injected gas into depleted gas reservoirs in the summer and withdrew it during winter's peak use times.

The 1950s and 1960s saw the company expand. In 1962 it created its first subsidiary Oklahoma Natural Gas Gathering Company selling gas out of state and therefore subject to federal regulation.

ONG was not affected in the lean 1970s by federal laws that kept wellhead prices low for gas transported across state lines because its main operations were confined to Oklahoma. Congress deregulated wellhead prices in 1978 spurring exploration but causing great price fluctuations in the 1980s. In 1980 ONG changed its name to ONEOK.

In the 1980s ONEOK signed take-or-pay contracts which forced it to pay for gas offered by its suppliers even if it had no customers. When recession in the 1980s caused demand to drop ONEOK had to pay for high-priced natural gas it couldn't sell. In 1988 the company was ordered to pay some $50 million to supplier Forest Oil of Denver. A year later ONEOK was sued for allegedly failing to tell stockholders about the take-or-pay agreements (settled in 1993 for $5.5 million). It later sold more than half of its oil and gas reserves to Mustang Energy for $52 million to finance the Forest Oil court award. The company was still settling lawsuits over the agreements into the 1990s; it settled the last of the claims by 1998.

ONEOK began buying gas transmission and production facilities in Oklahoma and creating drilling alliances in the 1990s. In 1997 ONEOK bought the natural gas assets of Westar Energy formerly Western Resources for $660 million and ONEOK stock worth $800 million. The acquisition doubled the number of ONEOK's customers and increased its gas marketing gathering and transmission operations.

The company also acquired Southern Union's Texas natural gas distribution business (540000 customers) as well as Southern Union's stake in a Mexican gas utility and its propane distribution gas marketing and gas transmission operations in the southwestern US for $420 million.

ONEOK acquired Northern Plains Natural Gas a general partner of pipeline operator Northern Border Partners (later renamed ONEOK Partners) from CCE Holdings (a joint venture of Southern Union and GE Commercial Finance) for $175 million in 2004. The transaction followed CCE Holdings' acquisition of Enron's CrossCountry Energy unit.

Also in 2004 ONEOK changed the name of its wholesale energy unit from ONEOK Energy Marketing and Trading to ONEOK Energy Services.

The company bought Koch Industries' natural gas liquids assets in 2005 for $1.35 billion.

EXECUTIVES

Vice President, David (Dave) Roth
EVP and Chief Administrative Officer, Robert F. (Rob) Martinovich, age 57, $500,000 total compensation
VP Gas Supply and Project Development Energy Division, Terry K. Spencer, age 56, $700,000 total compensation
SVP Operations, Wesley J. Christensen, age 61, $400,000 total compensation
SVP CFO and Treasurer, Derek S. Reiners, age 44, $375,000 total compensation
VP Natural Gas Gathering and Processing, Kevin L. Burdick, age 50
VP and CIO, Brien H. Brown
VP Natural Gas Pipelines, J. Phillip (Phill) May
EVP Strategic Planning and Corporate Affairs, Walter S. Hulse
SVP Natural Gas Liquids ONEOK Partners, Sheridan C. Swords
Vice President Commercial G And P, Michael A Fitzgibbons

Vice President Natural Gas Pipeline Operations, Craig A Forsander
Vice President Manufacturing, Lane Fisher
Director Media Relations, Brad Borror
Vice President of Procurement, Gwen Bayhylle
Vice President Asset Management and Engineering Natural Gas Distribution, Ronald (Ron) Bridgewater
Vice President Financial Controller, Michael D (Mel) Clark
Vice President Information Technology, Charles Andrews
Vice President Technology fixed Income, Jackie Mitchell
Vice President Commercial Intrastate Natural Gas Pipelines, Wesley Dunbar
Vice President Marketing Oneok Energy Resources, George Drake
Vice President Workforce Development, Rhonda Hartley
Vice President and Associate General Counsel, Stephen B (Steve) Allen
Vice President Chief Accounting Officer, Mike Miers
Vice President, John (Jack) Sommer
Vice President Operations Oklahoma Natural Gas, W Kent Shortridge
Senior Vice President General Counsel Assistant Secretary, Stephen (Steve) Lake
Vice President Natural Gas Liquids Optimization, John (Jack) O'Dell
Vice President Marketing Services, S Walker
Vice President Rates and Regulatory Affairs, Ron Mucci
Vice President western Region, Dan Walker
Vice President Natural Gas Liquids Optimization, John D (Jack) Odell
Chairman ONEOK ONEOK Partners and ONE Gas, John W. Gibson, age 62
Auditors: PricewaterhouseCoopers LLP

LOCATIONS

HQ: Oneok Inc.
 100 West Fifth Street, Tulsa, OK 74103
Phone: 918 588-7000   **Fax:** 918 588-7273
Web: www.oneok.com

PRODUCTS/OPERATIONS

2014 Sales

	$ mil.	% of total
Natural Gas Liquids	10,545	76
Natural Gas Gathering and Processing	2,967	21
Natural Gas Pipeline	350	3
Other and Eliminations	(1668.3)	-
Total	**12,195**	**100**

COMPETITORS

Adams Resources	Energen
BP	Energy Future
CMS Energy	Enterprise Products
Dynegy	Exxon Mobil
EQT Corporation	National Fuel Gas
Enable Midstream Partners	Southwest Gas
	Williams Companies

HISTORICAL FINANCIALS

Company Type: Public

Income Statement
FYE: December 31

	REVENUE ($ mil.)	NET INCOME ($ mil.)	NET PROFIT MARGIN	EMPLOYEES
12/14	12,195	314	2.6%	2,269
12/13	14,602	266	1.8%	1,927
12/12	12,632	360	2.9%	4,859
12/11	14,805	360	2.4%	4,795
12/10	13,030	334	2.6%	4,839
Annual Growth	(1.6%)	(1.6%)	—	(17.2%)

2014 Year-End Financials

Debt ratio: 47.07%
Return on equity: 21.44%
Cash ($ mil.): 172
Current ratio: 0.55
Long-term debt ($ mil.): 7,192

No. of shares (mil.): 208
Dividends
 Yield: 4.2%
 Payout: 143.5%
Market value ($ mil.): 10,372

	STOCK PRICE ($) FY Close	P/E High/Low	PER SHARE ($) Earnings	Dividends	Book Value
12/14	49.79	47 30	1.49	2.13	2.84
12/13	62.18	48 31	1.27	1.48	11.31
12/12	42.75	51 23	1.71	1.27	10.39
12/11	86.69	50 32	1.68	1.08	10.84
12/10	55.47	35 26	1.55	0.91	11.46
Annual Growth	(2.7%)	— —	(1.0%)	23.6%	(29.4%)

ONEOK Partners LP

For ONEOK Partners it's OK to have three businesses: natural gas pipelines; gas gathering and processing; and natural gas liquids (NGLs). Its pipelines include Midwestern Gas Transmission Guardian Pipeline Viking Gas Transmission and OkTex Pipeline. The ONEOK affiliate operates 17100 miles of gas-gathering pipeline and 7600 miles of transportation pipeline as well as gas processing plants and storage facilities (with 52 billion cu. ft. of capacity). It also owns one of the US's top natural NGL systems (more than 7200 miles of pipeline).OperationsONEOK Partners operates in three business segments: natural gas gathering and processing; natural gas pipelines; and natural gas liquids.Geographic ReachThe company gathers and processes natural gas in the Mid-Continent region which includes the NGL-rich Cana-Woodford Shale and Granite Wash formations the Mississippian Lime formation of Oklahoma and Kansas and the Hugoton and Central Kansas Uplift Basins of Kansas.The Natural Gas Pipelines segment owns and operates regulated natural gas transmission pipelines natural gas storage facilities and natural gas gathering systems for non-processed gas. It also provide interstate natural gas transportation and storage service. The company's interstate natural gas pipeline assets transport natural gas through pipelines in North Dakota Minnesota Wisconsin Illinois Indiana Kentucky Tennessee Oklahoma Texas and New Mexico.Its Natural gas liquids assets provide nondiscretionary services to producers that consist of facilities that gather fractionate and treat NGLs and store NGL products primarily in Oklahoma Kansas and Texas. It also owns or has stakes in natural gas liquids gathering and distribution pipelines in Oklahoma Kansas Texas Wyoming and Colorado and terminal and storage facilities in Missouri Nebraska Iowa and Illinois. In addition it owns natural gas liquids distribution and refined petroleum products pipelines in Kansas Missouri Nebraska Iowa Illinois and Indiana that connect the company's Mid-Continent assets with Midwest markets including Chicago.

Financial Performance

Revenues decreased by 10% in 2012 due to lower net realized natural gas and NGL product prices offset partially by higher natural gas and NGL sales volumes from completed capital projects. The increase in natural gas supply resulting from the development of nonconventional resource areas in North America and a warmer than normal winter caused natural gas prices to drop. NGL prices particularly ethane and propane also decreased in 2012 due primarily to increased NGL production and an increase in available supply. Propane prices also were affected by a warmer than normal winter.

ONEOK Partners' net income grew by 7% in 2012 thanks to lower costs of sales and fuels and lower interest expenses.

Strategy

The company pursues a strategy of building up its fee-based earnings coupled with organic growth and complementary acquisitions in both conventional oil and gas and unconventional (shale plays).

It is looking to increase NGL volumes gathered and fractionated in its NGL segment and natural gas volumes processed in its natural gas gathering and processing segment as producers continue to develop NGL-rich resource plays in the Mid-Continent and Rocky Mountain areas.

In 2012 ONEOK Partners announced plans to invest up to $360 million to grow its projects in the Woodford Shale formation.

Ownership

Energy services company ONEOK holds a 42% stake in ONEOK Partners and 100% of its general partner.

Company Background

ONEOK Partners was formed in 2006 when ONEOK spun off its gathering and processing NGLs pipelines and storage businesses for $3 billion following that company's acquisition of Northern Border Partners (which was founded in 1993). Building out its assets in 2007 the company acquired an interstate pipeline system from Kinder Morgan Energy Partners for $300 million.

EXECUTIVES

Evp Operations, Robert F Martinovich, age 58
Senior Vice President Natural Gas Liquids, Sheridan Swords
Vice President Natural Gas Gathering And Processing, Kevin Burdick
Senior Vice President Chief Financial Officer Treasurer, Derek Reiners
V Pres Commercial, Michael A Fitzgibbons
Vice President Natural Gas Pipeline Operations, Craig A Forsander
Auditors: PricewaterhouseCoopers LLP

LOCATIONS

HQ: ONEOK Partners LP
100 West Fifth Street, Tulsa, OK 74103
Phone: 918 588-7000
Web: www.oneokpartners.com

PRODUCTS/OPERATIONS

Natural Gas Pipelines
Midwestern Gas Transmission Company
Viking Gas Transmission Company
Guardian Pipeline
OkTex Pipeline Company
ONEOK Gas Transportation
ONEOK Gas Gathering
ONEOK Gas Storage

ONEOK WesTex Transmission
ONEOK Texas Gas Storage
Mid Continent Market Center
ONEOK Transmission Company
 Natural Ga
Crestone Energy Ventures
ONEOK Field Services
ONEOK Rockies Midstream

COMPETITORS

Dynegy
Enbridge
Kinder Morgan Energy
 Partners

Panhandle Eastern Pipe
 Line
TransCanada

HISTORICAL FINANCIALS

Company Type: Public

Income Statement
FYE: December 31

	REVENUE ($ mil.)	NET INCOME ($ mil.)	NET PROFIT MARGIN	EMPLOYEES
12/14	12,191	910	7.5%	—
12/13	11,869	803	6.8%	—
12/12	10,182	887	8.7%	—
12/11	11,322	830	7.3%	—
12/10	8,675	472	5.4%	—
Annual Growth	8.9%	17.8%	—	—

2014 Year-End Financials

Debt ratio: 48.52%
Return on equity: —
Cash ($ mil.): 42
Current ratio: 0.46
Long-term debt ($ mil.): 6,038

No. of shares (mil.): 253
Dividends
 Yield: 7.6%
 Payout: 128.6%
Market value ($ mil.): 10,059

	STOCK PRICE ($) FY Close	P/E High/Low	PER SHARE ($) Earnings	Dividends	Book Value
12/14	39.63	26 16	2.33	3.01	23.45
12/13	52.65	26 20	2.35	2.87	21.53
12/12	53.99	20 17	3.04	2.59	20.28
12/11	57.74	26 11	3.35	2.33	16.88
12/10	79.50	47 32	1.75	2.23	16.05
Annual Growth	(16.0%)	— —	7.4%	7.8%	9.9%

Opus Bank Irvine (CA)

LOCATIONS

HQ: Opus Bank Irvine (CA)
19900 MacArthur Blvd., 12th Floor, Irvine, CA 92612
Phone: 949 250-9800
Web: www.opusbank.com

HISTORICAL FINANCIALS

Company Type: Public

Income Statement
FYE: December 31

	ASSETS ($ mil.)	NET INCOME ($ mil.)	INCOME AS % OF ASSETS	EMPLOYEES
12/14	5,084	43	0.9%	585
12/13	3,738	143	3.8%	550
12/12	2,860	22	0.8%	—
12/11	0	(22)	—	—
Annual Growth	—	—	—	—

2014 Year-End Financials

Debt ratio: —
Return on equity: 5.97%
Cash ($ mil.): 316
Current ratio: —
Long-term debt ($ mil.): —

No. of shares (mil.): 28
Dividends
Yield: —
Payout: —
Market value ($ mil.): 799

	STOCK PRICE ($) FY Close	P/E High/Low	PER SHARE ($) Earnings	Dividends	Book Value
12/14	28.37	22 18	1.38	0.00	28.41
12/13	0.00	— —	4.96	0.00	28.95
Annual Growth	—	— —	(34.7%)	—	(0.6%)

Oracle Corp.

Oracle can't foretell the future but it helps its customers better manage their way into the future by supporting their business operations. The leader in enterprise software (about 76% of its sales) it also provides hardware and services to help companies improve their processes. Best known for its focus on databases it offers aid in areas such as managing business data collaboration and application development customer relationship management and supply chain management. In recent years the company has aggressively used acquisitions to expand such as its entry into the hardware business with the purchase of Sun Microsystems.

HISTORY

Larry Ellison Robert Miner Bruce Scott and Edward Oates founded System Development Laboratories in 1977 to create a database management system according to theoretical specifications published by IBM. Ellison had studied physics at the University of Chicago but dropped out in the 1960s to seek his fortune in Silicon Valley. He was part of the team that developed the first IBM-compatible mainframe. Miner an experienced programmer was the main developer of Oracle's database manager which was able to run on many computer brands and was introduced in 1979. The company also changed its name that year to Relational Software.

In 1983 the company changed its name again this time to Oracle in order to more closely align itself with its primary product. Oracle went public in 1986 and within two years had a 36% share of Uncle Sam's PC database market. It also added financial management graphics and human resource management software.

Oracle's rapid growth came at a great cost. It gained notoriety as a leader in vaporware —that is announced products that actually had not yet been developed. When the company's software was released it was sometimes bug-ridden and lacked promised features. Duplicate billings and the booking of unconsummated sales inflated revenues.

Oracle recorded a loss for fiscal 1991 accompanied by a downward restatement of earnings for past years. Its stock nosedived. The company laid off 400 employees and revised its growth estimates. Ellison stabilized the company with $80 million in financing from Nippon Steel.

Thanks to Oracle7 (launched in 1992) the company within two years became the #1 database management software maker. Sales for fiscal 1994 hit $2 billion. Ellison by that time had developed a reputation as an extravagant adventurer (his hobbies included yacht racing and piloting disarmed fighter planes).

Oracle formed affiliate Network Computer Inc. in 1997 to market Internet appliances (with no disk drive and local memory) that Ellison envisioned would strip Microsoft of its operating system ubiquity. Oracle and Netscape (now owned by Time Warner) merged joint venture Navio Communications one year later into Network Computer (renamed Liberate Technologies) redesigned around interactive software and spun off in 1999.

Also in 1999 the company bought three niche front-office software specialists and took its Oracle Japan subsidiary public. The next year it partnered with rival Commerce One to provide software and support for a giant online venture merging the Web-based procurement exchanges of General Motors Ford Motor and Daimler.

Oracle continued to expand its portfolio of business applications in 2001 introducing warehouse supply chain and customer relationship management software as well as software suites targeted at small businesses.

The company launched a hostile takeover bid for PeopleSoft in 2003 just days after the rival software maker had disclosed plans to acquire J.D. Edwards. PeopleSoft's board unanimously rejected the initial all-cash offer of $5.1 billion deeming the unsolicited bid inadequate and citing antitrust concerns. After bitter negotiations that included a number of rejected bids Oracle finally reached an agreement to acquire PeopleSoft for $10.3 billion in late 2004; the deal closed in early 2005.

Soon after the PeopleSoft deal closed Oracle again pursued a takeover. Rival SAP had announced plans to acquire retail software developer Retek for about $500 million. After a brief bidding war Oracle purchased Retek for about $670 million. The company followed that acquisition with a host of smaller deals in 2005 including identity management software developer Oblix; data management software maker TimesTen; retail inventory management software developer ProfitLogic; and logistics software provider Global Logistics Technologies.

Not content to rest on its acquisitive laurels Oracle initiated another blockbuster deal in 2006 purchasing Siebel Systems for $5.85 billion. The company also added Portal Software to its fold in 2006. The following year Oracle bought business intelligence software provider Hyperion Solutions for about $3.3 billion and Agile Software for about $495 million.

In 2008 Oracle completed another big deal the purchase of application server software and middleware maker BEA Systems in a transaction valued at $8.5 billion. An offer of a mere $6.7 billion in late 2007 was rejected by BEA which was formed by veterans of Sun Microsystems to address the need to adapt mainframe systems to a network computing platform.

Oracle next set its sights on what would become one of its most ambitious acquisitions to date. In 2009 it announced plans to buy Sun Microsystems for about $7.4 billion. The deal which was Oracle's first significant entry into the market for hardware and chips was completed in early 2010. The company used the Sun purchase it made in 2010 to extend its software expertise to Sun's servers Solaris operating system and SPARC chips enabling it to offer customers integrated hardware and software systems (much like rivals IBM and Hewlett-Packard). The company also bought Passlogix a provider of single sign-on products for the enterprise market late in 2010.

Since then Oracle has continued to make acquisitions to strengthen its products offerings in cloud computing and data as a service. It also kept in-house development of new products going at full tilt.

The company made its most significant personnel change in decades when founder Larry Ellison gave up the CEO seat while remaining chairman of the board. Assuming a co-CEO arrangement were longtime Oracle executive Safra Catz and Mark Hurd who joined the company in 2010. He had been at Hewlett-Packard and NCR.

EXECUTIVES

Executive Chairman and CTO, Lawrence J. (Larry) Ellison, age 71, $1 total compensation
EVP Oracle Customer Support Services, Charles A. (Chuck) Rozwat, age 67, $600,000 total compensation
CEO, Mark V. Hurd, age 58, $950,000 total compensation
EVP Global Business Units, Robert K. (Bob) Weiler, age 65
SVP Oracle Cloud Go-To-Market and Product Business Groups, Shawn Price
SVP and President and CEO Oracle Japan, Hiroshige (Hiro) Sugihara, age 55
CEO, Safra A. Catz, age 53, $950,000 total compensation
President Oracle Product Development, Thomas Kurian, age 48, $800,000 total compensation
SVP and General Manager Oracle Marketing Cloud, Kevin Akeroyd, age 43
EVP Microelectronics Group, Michael E. (Mike) Splain, age 59
EVP Oracle Latin America, Luiz Meisler, age 62
SVP and CIO, Mark E. Sunday, age 60
EVP Systems, John F. Fowler, age 54, $700,000 total compensation
EVP General Counsel and Secretary, Dorian E. Daley, age 56
EVP and President Oracle EMEA and Asia Pacific, Lo c le Guisquet, age 53
Group VP Product Technology Business Group, Robert G. Shimp
SVP Worldwide Operations, Cindy Reese
SVP Industries Business Unit, Sonny Singh
EVP Chief of Staff and Head of Corporate Development, Douglas Kehring
SVP North American Technology Division, Rich Geraffo
SVP Cloud Development, Peter S. Magnusson
EVP Corporate Controller and Chief Accounting Officer, William C. West, age 53
Consulting RVP, George Thomas
Senior Vice President, Andy Bailey
Senior Vice President Alliances And Channels Asia Pacific, Mark Lewis
Vice President Remote Technology Center, Doug Rhoades
Vice President, Brian S Higgins
Senior Vice President And General Manager, Rodger Smith
Vice President, Brent Grech
Group Vice President Partner Enablement And Communications, Joel Borellis
Vice President, Kate To
Vice President Global HRMS Product Development, Rob Watson
Group Vice President, Greg Calhoun
Vice President Of Software Development, Markus Flierl
Vice President of ZFS Storage Engineering, Scott Tracy
Vice President Customer Loyalty, Joan Smeal
Vice President, Michael (Mel) Brewer
Vice President, Terrance Wampler
Vice President EBS Practice, Robert (Bob) Allen
Vice President Product Development Information Technology, Campbell Webb
Vice President Product Eloqua, John (Jack) Stetic
Vice President Engineering, Eric Tran Le
Regional Vice President ??? Consulting, Vishal Singh
National Account Manager, Rod Corbin

Regional Vice President, David (Dave) Greiff
Area Vice President Sales, Steve Sybert
Vice President Global Business Delivery, Mark Rabne
Vice President Marketing, Peter Utzschneider
Vice President Investor Relations, Ken Bond
Regional Vice President, Jeff Keplar
Consulting Vice President JD Edwards, Steven (Steve) Reeter
Senior Vice President, Ian Smith
Vice President Product Development, Ilan Bensimhon
Vice President, Julie Barton
Consulting Vice President, Ellen Lapriore
Vice President, John Emery
Vice President Release Management, Jesus Ortiz
National Account Manager, Magnus Larsson
Regional Vice President, Michael Placido
Vice President, Patrick Cook
Vice President, Matt Fox
Group Vice President, Paolo Juvara
Vice President, Thomas Hildebrand
Regional Vice President, Lupe Noguera
Vice President Sales, Prashant Lele
Vice President Global Practices, Ellen Eder
Vice President Of Alliances And Channels, Kapi Attawar
Vice President Of Software Development, Omri Traub
Group Vice President And Global Head Of Product Consulting, Kishore Kapoor
Executive Vice President, Iman Refaei
Group Vice President, Brendan Logan
Business Development Vice President, James (Jamie) Decker
Senior Vice President Of Engineering, Douglas Doedens
Vice President Epm Applications, Matthew Bradley
Vice President, Sally Piao
Vice President Strategy and Product Marketing, Yasser Mahmud
Senior Vice President, Joanne Olsen
Executive Vice President, Rex Wang
Vice President Enterprise Solutions, Benoit Chaffanjon
National Account Manager, Chris Marshburn
Area Vice President, Mark Goldman
Regional Vice President, Kirby Rouser
Regional Vice President, David Memmolo
Vice President, Carol Adams
Vice President Technology Solutions And Channels, Alan Hartwell
Vice President Applications Development, Manish Srivastava
Senior Vice President Of Global Practices And Risk Management, Richard Allison
National Account Manager, Daniel Carey
Vice President Sales, Jan Zeman
Group Vice President, Jim Standard
Vice President Sales Operations, Martyn Langley
Group Vice President Oracle Applications Development, David (Dave) Vap
Vice President, Steve Cox
Vice President Applications Bu Eastern Europe And Cis, Vasilis Dimopoulos
Vice President Delivery, Bill Weber
Vice President Sales, William (Bill) Bagshaw
Vice President, Marta Kowalska
Area Vice President, Ryan Feaver
Vice President Of Epm And Bi Marketing, Rich Clayton
Group Vice President Sales and Bus Development (saas), Mike Hogan
Vice President Professional Services Emea Oracle Utilities Global Business Unit, Brad Kitchin
Vice President Product Strategy, Stephen (Steve) Johnston
Vice President Standard High Volume (SHV) Systems Division, Douglas (Doug) Kennedy

Vice President Customer Experience Strategy and Design, Brian Curran
Vice President of Global Marketing, David (Dave) Boyce
Vice President Customer Services Emea Major Accounts, Nick Harber
Regional Vice President Americas, Mike Bressanelli
Senior Vice President, Ramana Valluri
Vice President, Penelope Lie
Regiondl Vice President, Jeff Fleetwood
Vice President Of Product Support, Paul Martin
National Account Manager, Justin Garza
Senior Vice President Of Marketing, Mary Jones
Vice President, Steve Mollenkamp
Senior Vice President, Arvind Kumar
Vice President Operations Tech and System Suppor, Paul Williamson
Vice President of Drug Product Operations, Rajesh Banerjee
Vice President, Chuck Jones
Sales Vice President Bi Analytics And Epm Latin America, Marvio Portela
Vice President World Wide Consulting Tel, John Dempsey
Senior Vice President Oracle Epm, Alain Blanc
Retail Vice President, William O'Brien
Vice President Finance Europe North, Oliver Schlemper
Senior Vice President Oracle Database Server Techn, Andrew Mendelsohn
Vice President Product Management and Project Portfolio Management (PPM), Hirak Kayal
Vice President Software Development, Tom Chwojko-frank
Vice President Consulting, Heather Graham
Regional Vice President, Brook Crichton
Regional Vice President Higher Education, Lynn Derrick
Vice President Of Bd, Giovanna Sangiorgi
Group Vice President, Mandar Borkar
Vice President Central Europe, Pawel Piwowar
Senior Vice President, Prakash Ramamurthy
Regional Vice President, Timothy Tarkinton
Vice President Accounts, Jason Lerman
Vice President, Maha Muzumdar
Vice President Software Development, Ryan Carroll
Vice President Of Product Management And Product Development, Amit Zavery
Vice President Sales Manufacturing Industry, Junichi Iijima
Area Vice President, Jack Davis
Vice President Of Business Operations, Mitch Codkind
Vice President Sales Operations, Cynthia Kuzemkan
Vice President Technology Consulting Services, Ashok Rajan
Area Vice President Public Sector Sales, Tommie Fern
Vice President Linux And Infrastructure, Van Okamura
Vice President Sales Applications, Tibor Beles
Senior Vice President Oracle Managed Cloud Services, Steve McMillan
Vice President Applications Business Unit, Scott Dawes
Senior Vice President North America Support Services, John (Jack) Jones
Vice President Lad Support And Ondemand, Daniel (Dan) Barmat
Vice President Of Sales For The Americas, Ed Coke
Auditors: Ernst & Young LLP

LOCATIONS

HQ: Oracle Corp.
500 Oracle Parkway, Redwood City, CA 94065
Phone: 650 506-7000
Web: www.oracle.com

2014 Sales

	$ mil.	% of total
US	16,809	44
UK	2,309	6
Japan	1,558	4
Germany	1,483	4
Canada	1,190	3
France	1,148	3
Australia	994	3
Other countries	12,784	33
Total	**38,275**	**100**

Selected Acquisitions

FY 2013
Responsys (marketing automation software)
Nimbula (private cloud infrastructure management software)
Tekelec (data management)
Acme Packet (data management)
FY 2012
Collective Intellect (social media monitoring software)
Vitrue (social media software)
Eloqua (marketing automation software)
Skire (project management software)
SelectMinds (human resources software)
Xsigo Systems (networking technology)

PRODUCTS/OPERATIONS

2014 Sales

	$ mil.	% of total
Software		
License updates and product support	18,206	47
New licenses	9,416	25
Others	1,577	4
Hardware systems		
Products	2,976	8
Support	2,396	6
Services	3,704	10
Total	**38,275**	**100**

Selected Products

Software
  Business applications
  Business intelligence
  Customer experience
  Customer relationship
  Enterprise content
  Financial
  Governance risk & compliance
  Human capital
  Supply chain
  Databases
  Enterprise application integration
  Middleware
Services
  Consulting
  Cloud computing
  Enterprise architecture
  Systems integration
  Education/training
Hardware
  Servers (SPARC servers x86 servers)
  Solaris operating system (hardware-related software)
  Storage & tape

COMPETITORS

ADP	JDA Software
Accenture	JasperSoft
Akana	Manhattan Associates
BMC Software	MicroStrategy
CA Inc.	Microsoft
CDC Software	NCR
Ceridian	Novell
Cisco Systems	Open Text
Courion	Pegasystems
Dell Software	Progress Software
EMC	Red Hat
Fujitsu Technology Solutions	SAP
HP	SAS Institute
HP Autonomy	Sage Group
Hitachi	Software AG
IBM	SuccessFactors
Infor Global	TIBCO Software
Informatica	Teradata
Intel	Workday Inc.
	salesforce.com

HISTORICAL FINANCIALS
Company Type: Public

Income Statement
FYE: May 31

	REVENUE ($ mil.)	NET INCOME ($ mil.)	NET PROFIT MARGIN	EMPLOYEES
05/15	38,226	9,938	26.0%	132,000
05/14	38,275	10,955	28.6%	122,000
05/13	37,180	10,925	29.4%	120,000
05/12	37,121	9,981	26.9%	115,000
05/11	35,622	8,547	24.0%	108,000
Annual Growth	1.8%	3.8%	—	5.1%

2015 Year-End Financials
Debt ratio: 37.83%—
Return on equity: 20.80%
Cash ($ mil.): 21,716
Current ratio: 4.13
Long-term debt ($ mil.): 39,959

Dividends
Yield: 0.0%
Payout: 23.0%
Market value ($ mil.): —

	STOCK PRICE ($) FY Close	P/E High/Low	PER SHARE ($) Earnings	Dividends	Book Value
05/15	43.49	20 17	2.21	0.51	11.20
05/14	42.02	17 12	2.38	0.48	10.50
05/13	33.78	16 11	2.26	0.42	9.61
05/12	26.47	17 12	1.96	0.24	8.91
05/11	34.22	22 13	1.67	0.21	7.85
Annual Growth	6.2%	— —	7.3%	24.8%	9.3%

Oritani Financial Corp (DE)

Oritani Financial could give an oratory on local banking in New Jersey. The holding company owns Oritani Bank which offers retail and commercial deposit and loan banking services from about 25 locations in several Garden State counties. Oritani Financial specializes in multi-family and commercial real estate lending which make up more than half of its loan portfolio. Oritani Financial also writes one- to four-family and second mortgages as well as equity and construction loans. It invests in real property through its Hampshire Financial Oritani LLC and Ormon divisions; Oritani Asset is a real estate investment trust (REIT). Century-old Oritani Bank has more than $2 billion in assets.

Geographic Reach

Oritani Bank has 25 full-service branches in Bergen Essex Hudson and Passaic counties in New Jersey.

Financial Performance

The bank's 2012 (ends June) revenue increased 4% vs. the prior year and net income grew by 11% over the same period. The revenue increase was due to a 4% jump in interest income. partially offset by a nearly 1% drop in non-interest income. Fiscal 2012 marked Oritani Bank's eighth consecutive year of increasing revenue although growth has slowed somewhat. The increase in net income in 2012 was primarily due to a higher net interest spread and a larger asset base.

Strategy

Oritani Bank is expanding its branch network. It recently opened new branches in Ramsey Upper Montclair and Clifton New Jersey.

EXECUTIVES

EVP and COO, Michael A. DeBernardi, age 61, $263,846 total compensation
Svp And Chief Compliance Officer, Rosanne Buscemi
Vice President, Paul Cordero
Chairman; President and CEO, Kevin J. Lynch, age 68, $550,750 total compensation
EVP and CFO, John M. Fields, age 52, $211,077 total compensation
EVP and Chief Lending Officer, Thomas G. Guinan, age 51, $211,077 total compensation
Vice President, John Pagano
Vice President, Bing Luh
Vice President Business Development, Jack Anastasi
Vice President Commercial Lending, Noah Littell
Senior Vice President and Secretary, Philip Wyks
Auditors: KPMG LLP

LOCATIONS

HQ: Oritani Financial Corp (DE)
370 Pascack Road, Township of Washington, NJ 07676
Phone: 201 664-5400
Web: www.oritani.com

PRODUCTS/OPERATIONS

2012 Sales

	$ mil.	% of total
Interest		
Mortgage loans	108	85
Interest on securities available for sale	11	9
Interest on securities held & dividends	2	2
Federal funds sold & short-term investments	0	-
Noninterest		
Bank-owned life insurance	1	1
Real estate operations	1	1
Service charges	1	1
Other	1	1
Total	**127**	**100**

COMPETITORS

1st Colonial Bancorp	Sun Bancorp (NJ)
Hudson City Bancorp	Valley National
OceanFirst Financial	Bancorp
Provident Financial Services	

HISTORICAL FINANCIALS
Company Type: Public

Income Statement
FYE: June 30

	ASSETS ($ mil.)	NET INCOME ($ mil.)	INCOME AS % OF ASSETS	EMPLOYEES
06/15	3,353	46	1.4%	235
06/14	3,140	41	1.3%	233
06/13	2,831	39	1.4%	212
06/12	2,700	31	1.2%	217
06/11	2,587	28	1.1%	206
Annual Growth	6.7%	13.3%	—	3.3%

2015 Year-End Financials
Debt ratio: 23.75%
Return on equity: 8.99%
Cash ($ mil.): 11
Current ratio: —
Long-term debt ($ mil.): —

No. of shares (mil.): 44
Dividends
Yield: 5.9%
Payout: 97.9%
Market value ($ mil.): 706

	STOCK PRICE ($) FY Close	P/E High/Low	PER SHARE ($) Earnings	Dividends	Book Value
06/15	16.05	14 12	1.10	0.95	11.76
06/14	15.39	17 15	0.94	0.95	11.57
06/13	15.68	17 15	0.92	1.03	11.43
06/12	14.39	21 16	0.71	0.50	11.30
06/11	12.79	24 17	0.54	0.38	11.63
Annual Growth	5.8%	— —	19.5%	26.2%	0.3%

Oshkosh Corp (New)

Need to plow through Sahara sands or Buffalo snow? Oshkosh has your ride. The company makes and sells heavy-duty vehicles and vehicle bodies for commercial access fire and emergency and defense work. Commercial and access lines include concrete batch plants refuse vehicle bodies (McNeilus brand) tow trucks (Jerr-Dan) and aerial work platforms (JLG). Its emergency offerings range from snow blowers to aircraft rescue and firefighting vehicles (Pierce). More than 30 plants build the lineup. Vehicles are sold via dealers to global airport institutional construction and municipal markets. Oshkosh also makes tactical trucks for the Department of Defense.

Geographic Reach

Oshkosh has manufacturing locations in eight US states and in Australia Belgium Canada China France and Romania. It also has joint ventures in Brazil and Mexico. The US accounts for nearly 80% of its net sales.

Operations

Oshkosh divides its operations across four segments. The access equipment segment —consisting of JLG and Jerr-Dan —generates 56% of sales and makes aerial work platforms tow trucks and telehandlers used by rental companies construction contractors manufacturing companies home improvement stores and the military.

Commercial (16%) makes rear- and front-discharge concrete mixers refuse collection vehicles portable and stationary concrete batch plants for ready-mix companies and waste haulers.

The defense segment (15% of total sales) supplies the US and foreign militaries as well as law-enforcement agencies with military tactical wheeled vehicles.

The fire and emergency segment (13%) supplies commercial and custom firefighting vehicles and equipment vehicles for aircraft rescue snow removal and broadcasting ambulances and mobile medical trailers.

Sales and Marketing

JLG sells its products through 3500 locations spanning six continents. Oshkosh markets its Jeff-Dan carrier and wreckers through a network of 60 independent distributors.

The US government represents about 15% of the company's sales. It spent $22.1 million on advertising in 2015 and $20.4 million in 2014.

Financial Performance

Oshkosh is attempting to recover altitude since it posted record-setting revenues of $9.8 billion during 2010. Revenues have declined the last two years falling 11% from $7.7 billion in 2013 to $6.8 billion in 2014. Net sales decreased by $710.1 million in fiscal 2015 (September year end) due to lower defense sales partially offset by higher commercial sales.

The decrease in defense segment sales was primarily due to an expected decline in sales to the

DoD and lower international sales of M-ATVs. The increase in commercial segment sales was due to higher refuse collection vehicle unit volume an increase in sales of higher content units with both chassis and bodies and improved aftermarket parts and service sales.

Net income decreased by $79.8 million compared to 2014 due to lower sales selling general and administrative expenses as the result of lower incentive compensation expenses. Oshkosh's net cash provided by operating activities decreased by $87.9 million in fiscal 2015.

Strategy

Challenged by customer markets that have been down variously from 40% to 90% and especially by a lower US defense budget Oshkosh has been implementing a lean strategy of cutting non-value added labor that has included reducing its manufacturing operations by 20% and unifying its purchasing operations into a single global unit. In 2014 the company announced it was eliminating 250 to 300 hourly positions and 70 salaried positions from its defense segment. These measures are included under a plan called MOVE.

The company intends to continue to pursue the MOVE strategy in fiscal 2016 and beyond with the belief that this strategy will continue to drive actions that will position the Oshkosh to deliver strong shareholder value in the coming years.

Other prongs in the strategy include using new technologies to expand the functions of its products and developing business in the emerging markets of Asia Eastern Europe the Middle East and Latin America. Expanding international operations and sales is a significant part of the company's growth strategy for fiscal 2016.

HISTORY

Bernhard Mosling and William Besserdich founded Oshkosh Truck in 1917 attracting investors with Old Betsy a four-wheel-drive 3000-pound truck. Over the next few decades the company developed a range of heavy-duty vehicles. Sales took off when the US Army gave truck contracts to Oshkosh during WWII. Commercial sales increased after the war the result of demand from mining and plantation companies. Oshkosh Truck went public in 1985. To reflect its more diverse operations Oshkosh changed its name from Oshkosh Truck Corporation to Oshkosh Corporation in 2008.

EXECUTIVES

EVP General Counsel and Secretary, Bryan J. Blankfield, age 53, $457,744 total compensation
VP and Managing Director Oshkosh Capital, Kevin S. Ramsburg
EVP Government Operations and Industry Relations, Joseph H. (Jay) Kimmitt, age 64, $390,886 total compensation
CEO, Wilson R. Jones, age 53, $629,232 total compensation
EVP and CFO, David M. Sagehorn, age 51, $609,237 total compensation
EVP and Chief Procurement Officer, Gregory L. (Greg) Fredericksen, age 53
EVP and President Access Equipment, Frank R. Nerenhausen, age 50, $408,770 total compensation
EVP and President Fire and Emergency, James W. (Jim) Johnson, age 50
SVP Corporate Engineering and Technology, Gary W. Schmiedel, age 53
EVP and President Defense, John M. Urias, age 61, $447,348 total compensation
VP and CIO, Dave Schecklman
SVP and President Commercial, Bradley M. (Brad) Nelson

EVP and Chief Human Resources Officer, Janet L. Hogan, age 50, $134,039 total compensation
Vice President Human Resources, Jodie Larsen
Vice President Of Engineering, Tom Quigley
Assistant Vice President Digital Marketing, Steve Tighe
Vice President Ethics and Compliance, Robin Schroeder
Executive Vice President Information Technology, Gary Schaniedel
Vice President Materials Management, Tim Jones
Vice President Finance, Chris Leary
Chairman, Richard M. Donnelly, age 71
Auditors: DELOITTE & TOUCHE LLP

LOCATIONS

HQ: Oshkosh Corp (New)
P.O. Box 2566, Oshkosh, WI 54903-2566
Phone: 920 235-9151
Web: www.oshkoshcorporation.com

2015 Sales

	$ mil.	% of total
North America		
US	4,789	79
Other North America	302	5
Europe Africa & the Middle East	564	9
Rest of the world	441	7
Total	**6,098**	**100**

PRODUCTS/OPERATIONS

2015 Sales

	$ mil.	% of total
Access equipment	3,400	56
Defense	939	15
Commercial	978	16
Fire & emergency	815	13
Adjustments	(35.4)	-
Total	**6,098**	**100**

BRANDS
JLG Industries
Oshkosh Defense
Pierce
McNeilus
IMT
Frontline Communications
CON-E-CO
London Machinery
Jerr-Dan
Oshkosh Airport Products

Selected Products

Access equipment
  Aerial work platforms
  Boom lifts
  Scissor lifts
  Stock pickers
  Telehandlers
  Towing & recovery equipment
  Trailers
  Vertical mast lifts
Commercial
  All-make parts
  Automated mobile & stationary compactors
  Concrete batch plants
  Container handling equipment
  Demountable containers
  Rear- & front-discharge mixers
  Rear front & side loaders
  Refuse collection vehicle bodies
  Revolution® mixer drums
Defense
  Armored wheeled vehicles
  Heavy equipment transporters (HET)
  Heavy expanded mobility tactical trucks (HEMTT)
  High-mobility trailers
  Logistic vehicle system replacements (LVSR)
  Medium tactical trucks (MTT)
  Medium tactical vehicle replacements (MTVR)
  Off road tractor/trailers
  Palletized load system (PLS) trucks & trailers
  Urban assault vehicles
Fire & emergency
  Aircraft rescue & fire fighting (ARFF) vehicles
  Ambulances

Custom & commercial fire apparatus
Rescue & homeland security apparatus
Snow blowers & plow trucks

COMPETITORS

AM General	J C Bamford Excavators
BAE Systems Land & Armaments	L-3 Communications
Collins Industries	Leyland Trucks
Daimler	MAN
Daimler Trucks North America	MANITOU BF
Dover Corp.	Mack Trucks
E-ONE	Miller Industries
Federal Signal	Navistar
Force Protection	Navistar International
General Dynamics Land Systems	PACCAR
Haulotte	Skyjack
Heil Environmental	Spartan Motors
Hyundai Motor	Terex
Iveco S.p.A.	Trinity Industries
	UD Trucks
	Volvo

HISTORICAL FINANCIALS

Company Type: Public

Income Statement

FYE: September 30

	REVENUE ($ mil.)	NET INCOME ($ mil.)	NET PROFIT MARGIN	EMPLOYEES
09/15	6,098	229	3.8%	13,300
09/14	6,808	309	4.5%	12,000
09/13	7,665	318	4.1%	11,900
09/12	8,180	230	2.8%	13,200
09/11	7,584	273	3.6%	13,100
Annual Growth	**(5.3%)**	**(4.3%)**	—	**0.4%**

2015 Year-End Financials

Debt ratio: 20.34%
Return on equity: 11.78%
Cash ($ mil.): 42
Current ratio: 1.67
Long-term debt ($ mil.): 855
No. of shares (mil.): 75
Dividends
  Yield: 1.8%
  Payout: 21.3%
Market value ($ mil.): 2,741

	STOCK PRICE ($) FY Close	P/E High/Low		PER SHARE ($) Earnings	Dividends	Book Value
09/15	36.33	19	12	2.90	0.68	25.33
09/14	44.15	16	12	3.61	0.15	24.86
09/13	48.98	14	7	3.55	0.00	24.36
09/12	27.43	12	6	2.51	0.00	20.24
09/11	15.74	13	5	2.99	0.00	17.48
Annual Growth	**23.3%**	—	—	**(0.8%)**	—	**9.7%**

Owens & Minor, Inc.

Owens & Minor (O&M) makes sure surgeons aren't left empty handed after shouting "Scalpel stat!" A leading distributor of medical and surgical supplies the company carries more than 220000 products from about 1300 manufacturers. Products distributed by O&M include surgical dressings endoscopic and intravenous products needles syringes sterile procedure trays gowns gloves and sutures. The firm also offers software consulting and other services to help customers manage their supplies. O&M's customers are primarily hospitals and health systems and the purchasing organizations that serve them. It delivers products to roughly 4500 health care providers from about 55 distribution centers across the US. Operations O&M operates in two segments: Domestic and International. In the US it provides distribution packaging and logistics services; the International operations comprise its European third-party logistics and packaging businesses.About 95% of O&M's sales come from the distribution of medical supplies. The company's major product suppliers include Covidien and Johnson & Johnson whose products account for almost 15% and 10% of O&M's revenues respectively. In addition to delivering products made by its supply partners the distributor sells some 2900 value products under its own MediChoice label. To support its distribution operations O&M offers training programs for health professionals on topics ranging from equipment use supply management leadership and safety.O&M's supply chain management services include third-party logistics services for medical device and pharmaceutical firms. Such services are provided by subsidiaries OM HealthCare Logistics (in the US) and Movianto (in Europe).Geographic ReachThough US operations account for most of O&M's sales (95% of revenue in 2014) the company is working to branch out into international medical distribution markets including Europe. Its Movianto unit operates more than 25 logistics centers in about a dozen European countries including Belgium the Czech Republic Denmark France Germany the Netherlands Portugal Slovakia Spain Switzerland and the UK.Sales and MarketingMost of O&M's sales are attributed to contracts with acute-care hospitals which are often represented by group purchasing organizations (GPOs) or integrated healthcare networks (IHNs). GPO Novation is the largest client accounting for around 35% of the company's earnings with GPOs MedAssets (including its Broadlane unit) accounting for about 25% of sales Premier accounting for more than 20% and HealthTrust Purchasing Group accounting for more than 10%. The company also has an ongoing exclusive supplier agreement with the US Department of Defense. Additional clients include other government agencies and alternate health care locations such as physician clinics nursing homes and surgery centers. In addition O&M provides outsourced distribution services to suppliers of surgical and medical products.Financial PerformanceO&M's sales have seen slow growth over the past five years. Revenue increased 4% to $9.4 billion in 2014 due to growth in its Domestic segment; this was largely due to growth in its larger customer accounts. (Sales to smaller customers declined that year.) Increases in the International segment were a result of new buy/sell contracts and growth in the fee-for-service business (which represents some two-thirds of the segment's net revenue).Despite the revenue growth net income fell 40% to $66 million as expenses rose. O&M also reported a cash outflow of $3.7 million in 2014 versus an inflow the previous year due to change in accounts payable and an increase in cash used in inventories.StrategyAs the health care industry has consolidated so have the industries that serve it and O&M works to remain competitive by providing supply chain management tools and services in addition to supplies to help its customers control costs. Its OMSolutions business unit provides outsourcing and resource management services to acute care providers including fee-based one-on-one consultations and physical inventory reviews as well as inventory tracking and purchasing software. It is also working to improve its information technology and infrastructure resources many of which are managed by third party Dell Perot Systems the IT outsourcing unit of Dell.While the company experiences a successful level of revenue and income growth from greater product and service sales to existing customers as well as the addition of new clients O&M doesn't shy away from partnerships and acquisitions as other ways to help boost sales and services. For example O&M holds a seven-year lease and technology services deal val-

ued at $68 million with Penske Truck Leasing and its Penske Logistics unit to consolidate its delivery fleet with one vendor. That partnership is slated to last at least until 2017.The company completed a three-year $54 million upgrade to its IT infrastructure in the US in 2014. The investment was designed to increase operational and data management efficiencies improve customer experience and cut costs.Mergers & AcquisitionsIn 2014 the firm acquired one of its suppliers Medical Action Industries a provider of custom procedure trays and minor procedure kits for about $208 million. (About 45% of Medical Action's nearly $288 million in revenue comes from O&M.)Also that year O&M acquired Irish surgical kitting company ArcRoyal for some $50 million further bolstering its capabilities in the European market.

HISTORY

George Gilmer Minor Jr.'s great-grandfather was an apothecary and surgeon in colonial Williamsburg Virginia. His grandfather was Thomas Jefferson's personal physician. Minor himself worked as a wholesale drug salesman in Richmond after the Civil War. In 1882 he and rival wholesaler Otho Owens partnered to form the Owens & Minor Drug Company. The company was both a retail and wholesale business with a storefront that filled prescriptions and sold sundries paints oils and window glass. When Owens died in 1906 Minor became the company's president.

During the 1920s the Owens family sold their stake in the firm. George Gilmer Minor III served briefly as the company's president in the early 1940s; his son George Gilmer Minor IV (called Mr. Minor Jr. to differentiate him from his father) became president in 1947.

In 1954 Owens & Minor installed its first computerized order fulfillment system. The following year the firm became Owens Minor & Bodeker when it bought the Bodeker Drug Company which was both older and larger than Owens & Minor.

After 84 years in the drug wholesale business the company entered the medical and surgical distribution business after buying A&J Hospital Supply in 1966 and Powers & Anderson in 1968. In 1971 Owens Minor & Bodeker went public. By the end of the decade the company had operations in 10 states.

The fourth Minor to run the firm G. Gilmer Minor III (Mr. Minor Jr.'s son) was named president in 1981 (he became CEO in 1984). Under his direction Owens Minor & Bodeker would complete the transition from a drug wholesaler to a medical supplies distributor. In 1981 it purchased the Will Ross subsidiary of G.D. Searle (then the country's #2 medical and surgical supplies distributor).

The company reverted to its original name on its 100th anniversary in 1982. By 1984 medical supplies supplanted wholesale drugs as its primary source of income. In 1988 Owens & Minor listed on the NYSE.

The company passed the $1 billion revenue mark in 1990 and later sold its wholesale drug business. It extended its reach with the purchase of Lyons Physician Supply in 1993 and Stuart Medical (the #3 national distributor) in 1994.

EXECUTIVES

SVP Administration and Operations, Erika T. Davis, age 52, $520,972 total compensation
SVP Strategic Relationships, Charles C. Colpo, age 58, $448,734 total compensation
President and CEO, James L. (Jim) Bierman, age 62, $781,157 total compensation
Vice President Technology, Charles Eismamn

EVP and CFO, Richard A. (Randy) Meier, age 55, $605,157 total compensation
SVP General Counsel and Corporate Secretary, Grace R. den Hartog, age 63, $452,562 total compensation
SVP and CIO, Richard W. (Rick) Mears, age 55
Vice President Corporate Development, Robert K Snead
Vice President Supply Chain Performance, Scott Watkins
Vice President And Manager For Alaska Operations, Marina Ammann
Vice President Global Tax, Chris McGowan
Executive Chairman, Craig R. Smith, age 64
Board Of Director, Theresa Chamberlain
Auditors: KPMG LLP

LOCATIONS

HQ: Owens & Minor, Inc.
9120 Lockwood Boulevard, Mechanicsville, VA 23116
Phone: 804 723-7000   **Fax:** 804 723-7100
Web: www.owens-minor.com

2014 Sales

	$ mil.	% of total
US	8,951	95
UK	253	2
France	54	1
Germany	47	1
Other European countries	132	1
Total	**9,440**	**100**

PRODUCTS/OPERATIONS

2014 Sales

	% of total
Domestic	95
International	5
Total	**100**

Selected Products and Services

Clinical Supply Solutions (inventory and contract management service)
Implant Purchase Manager (utilization contract compliance and billing)
OMDirect (Internet order fulfillment)
OMSolutions (resource management and consulting)
PANDAC system (helps track and control operating room inventories)
QSight (clinical inventory management system)
SurgiTrack (customizable surgical supply service)
WISDOM Gold (allows customers to track inventory usage and other information to keep costs down)

COMPETITORS

AmerisourceBergen	McKesson
Buffalo Supply	Medline Industries
Cardinal Health	Metro Medical Supply
DHL	PSS World Medical
FedEx	Patterson Companies
Henry Schein	SourceOne
Invacare Supply Group	Surgical Express
Johnson and Johnson	Tri-anim
Health Care Systems	UPS
Kerma Medical Products	

HISTORICAL FINANCIALS

Company Type: Public

Income Statement

FYE: December 31

	REVENUE ($ mil.)	NET INCOME ($ mil.)	NET PROFIT MARGIN	EMPLOYEES
12/14	9,440	66	0.7%	5,700
12/13	9,071	110	1.2%	6,700
12/12	8,908	109	1.2%	4,800
12/11	8,627	115	1.3%	4,800
12/10	8,123	110	1.4%	4,800
Annual Growth	3.8%	(11.9%)	—	4.4%

2014 Year-End Financials

Debt ratio: 22.25%
Return on equity: 6.60%
Cash ($ mil.): 56
Current ratio: 1.86
Long-term debt ($ mil.): 608
No. of shares (mil.): 63
Dividends
Yield: 2.8%
Payout: 77.5%
Market value ($ mil.): 2,214

	STOCK PRICE ($) FY Close	P/E High/Low		PER SHARE ($) Earnings	Dividends	Book Value
12/14	35.11	35	30	1.06	1.00	15.71
12/13	36.56	22	16	1.76	0.96	16.23
12/12	28.51	18	16	1.72	0.88	15.37
12/11	27.79	19	15	1.81	0.80	14.47
12/10	29.43	27	15	1.75	0.71	13.52
Annual Growth	4.5%	—	—	(11.8%)	9.0%	3.8%

Owens Corning

Owens Corning (OC) operates in the PINK. Famous for its Pink Panther mascot and its trademarked PINK glass fiber insulation the company is a top global maker of building and composite material systems. The building materials company makes insulation roofing fiber-based glass reinforcements and other materials for the residential and commercial markets. Its composite products business makes glass fiber reinforcement materials for the transportation industrial infrastructure marine wind energy and consumer markets. Owens Corning traces its historical roots to 1938.

HISTORY

Company BackgroundIn the 1930s Corning Glass Works and Owens-Illinois Glass independently found that glass fiber has special resilience and strength. Realizing the potential market they formed joint venture Owens-Corning Fiberglas in 1938. The companies expanded rapidly in the 1940s and 1950s establishing several US plants and one in Canada. Their products included fine fibers thermal wool textiles and continuous filaments.

A US antitrust decree in 1949 denied the two founding firms any control over Owens-Corning. Each retained one-third ownership when the company went public in 1952. During the 1950s Owens-Corning developed new uses for fiberglass in automobile bodies shingles and insulation. In the 1960s the company expanded overseas. Fiberglass uses multiplied as applications developed in aerospace tires and underground tanks.

By 1980 the company had invested more than $700 million in acquisitions and made the Pink Panther its mascot. Owens-Corning introduced a rolled insulation in 1982.

The company successfully fended off a takeover attempt by Wickes Companies in 1986 but the effort left Owens-Corning with $2.6 billion in debt. It sold 10 businesses halved its research budget and laid off or lost to divestitures 46% of its workforce.

The company bought Fiberglas Canada that country's largest fiberglass-insulation maker in 1989. To expand globally Owens-Corning formed alliances in 1990 with BASF Lucky-Goldstar and Siam Cement.

Owens-Corning spent $65 million in 1991 on restructuring and took an $800 million charge to cover its liability to asbestos-exposure lawsuits (the company stopped making asbestos in 1972). That year it exchanged its commercial roofing business

for the residential roofing business of Schuller International.

In 1994 Owens-Corning acquired UC Industries a maker of foam board insulation and bought Pilkington's insulation and industrial supply business. It also formed joint venture Alpha/Owens-Corning the largest producer of polyester resin in North America.

The company bought Western Fiberglass Group in 1995. That year Owens-Corning Fiberglas changed its name to Owens Corning and recouped part of its asbestos-related charge when it received a $330 million arbitration settlement from one of its insurers. Owens Corning formed a joint venture in India in 1995. Asbestos-litigation charges led to another loss in 1996.

In 1997 Owens Corning made several acquisitions including vinyl-siding maker Fibreboard and Amerimark Building Products a maker of vinyl and aluminum materials. In 1998 falling insulation prices led the company to announce layoffs and a restructuring plan that included plant closures. To pay off debt the company sold its half of Alpha/Owens-Corning to Alpha Corporation marking its exit from polyester-resin manufacturing. The company also agreed to take $550 million in a deal with France's Groupe Porcher Industries to form a joint venture for its fiberglass yarns and specialty materials businesses.

Seeking to end a liability issue that had dogged the company for a quarter of a century Owens Corning agreed in 1998 to pay out $1.2 billion to settle 176000 asbestos-related lawsuits. However the deal dissolved in 1999 when the US Supreme Court disallowed the settlement. Owens Corning then set up a $2.6 billion reserve fund to settle the claims. Also that year the company formed a joint venture (Decillion) with Geon to make fiberglass and PVC composites. In 2000 Owens Corning added to its acoustic panel business with the acquisition of Conwed Designscape. Still dogged by lawsuits that could eventually cost the company billions the company filed for bankruptcy protection late in 2000.

In 2001 Owens Corning sold its engineered pipe systems business to joint venture partner Saudi Arabian Amiantit Company. Seeking a foothold in the growing acoustic ceiling market the restructured company bought Wall Technology later that year.

Owens Corning increased its loose fill and thermacube insulation products line and capacity in 2002 in response to growing demand. It also acquired Woodbridge Virginia-based Certified Basements a basement finishing systems franchise and strengthened its position in Europe through a distribution contract with an Ashland Inc. subsidiary Ashland Finland OY to distribute its composite products through Ashland Specialty Chemical Company. Also that year Owens Corning's HOMExperts Home Repair and Improvements business expanded its service to Los Angeles San Francisco and Sacramento by acquiring assets of California-based Home Finishes LLC. (HOMExperts also operates in Atlanta Boston Chicago Denver Indianapolis Minneapolis/St. Paul and Washington DC.)

Following a period of falling stock prices for the company the New York Stock Exchange suspended its trading in December 2002. In early 2003 the company filed a bankruptcy reorganization plan to settle asbestos litigation. Under the plan Owens Corning provided partial payments to its creditors (mainly through distributing common stock and notes of the new reorganized company) and its existing common stock was canceled.

In 2004 Owens Corning Automotive (UK) Ltd. acquired the automotive assets of long-time customer Lancaster Fibre Technology Ltd. (UK). Lancaster Fibre Technology bases its automotive so-

lutions on Owens Corning's Silentex Noise Control automotive silencer technology. It also purchased full ownership of Vitro Fibras (Mexico) a venture it had begun with Vitro (glass products Mexico) in 1957 to make light-density fiberglass products; molded pipe; board; and composite reinforcements. Owens Corning paid $71.5 million for Vitro's 60% stake.

The company emerged from bankruptcy in 2006. As part of the bankruptcy reorganization the company's paid some $5 billion in asbestos claims along with an additional $2.4 billion earmarked for debt holders.

After shedding the ponderous weight of bankruptcy the company didn't stand still. Owens Corning strengthened its composite operations in late 2007 when it acquired the reinforcements and composite fabrics business of materials giant Saint-Gobain.

While the company focused growth on its composites business it began trimming off other operations. Saint-Gobain acquired Owens Corning's vinyl siding business Norandex in 2007. Also that year it sold its continuous filament mat business to AGY and its Fabwel composite panels business to Crane.

In June 2013 Owens Corning acquired Thermafiber Inc. a manufacturer of mineral wool commercial and industrial insulation products. The purchase included a 145000 square-foot manufacturing plant in Wabash Indiana.

EXECUTIVES

Chairman President and CEO, Michael H. (Mike) Thaman, age 51, $1,104,167 total compensation
Group President Composite Solutions, Arnaud P. Genis, age 50, $557,500 total compensation
SVP and CFO, Michael C. McMurray, age 50, $500,000 total compensation
Vice President and Managing Director Asia Pacific Building Materials, Daniel (Dan) Zhang
Senior Vice President Organization and Administration, Dan Smith
Vice President Human Resources CSB, Paula Russell
Vice President Human Resources, Robert (Bob) Paxton
Vice President Government Affairs, John (Jack) Libonati
Auditors: PricewaterhouseCoopers LLP

LOCATIONS

HQ: Owens Corning
One Owens Corning Parkway, Toledo, OH 43659
Phone: 419 248-8000
Web: www.owenscorning.com

2014 Sales

	$ mil.	% of total
US	3,557	67
Asia/Pacific	636	12
Europe	575	11
Canada & other	508	10
Total	**5,276**	**100**

PRODUCTS/OPERATIONS

2014 Sales

	$ mil.	% of total
Composites	1	36
Roofing	1,748	32
Insulation	1,746	32
Corporate eliminations	(153)	-
Total	**5,276**	**100**

COMPETITORS

Associated Materials	Masco
Ball Corp.	Mohawk Industries

CertainTeed
Champion Window
China Fiberglass Co.
  Ltd.
Deceuninck
Dow Chemical
GAF Materials
Johns Manville
Knauf Insulation
Lennox
Louisiana-Pacific

Owens-Illinois
PPG Industries
SIG plc
Saint-Gobain
Sherwin-Williams
Stanley Black and
  Decker
TAMKO
USG
Valspar

HISTORICAL FINANCIALS

Company Type: Public

Income Statement

FYE: December 31

	REVENUE ($ mil.)	NET INCOME ($ mil.)	NET PROFIT MARGIN	EMPLOYEES
12/15	5,350	330	6.2%	15,000
12/14	5,276	226	4.3%	14,000
12/13	5,295	204	3.9%	15,000
12/12	5,172	(19)	—	15,000
12/11	5,335	276	5.2%	15,000
Annual Growth	0.1%	4.6%	—	0.0%

2015 Year-End Financials

Debt ratio: 25.35%
Return on equity: 8.88%
Cash ($ mil.): 96
Current ratio: 1.38
Long-term debt ($ mil.): 1,702

No. of shares (mil.): 115
Dividends
  Yield: 1.4%
  Payout: 31.6%
Market value ($ mil.): 5,451

	STOCK PRICE ($) FY Close	P/E High/Low		PER SHARE ($) Earnings	Dividends	Book Value
12/15	47.03	17	12	2.79	0.68	32.26
12/14	35.81	24	15	1.91	0.64	31.34
12/13	40.72	26	21	1.71	0.00	32.20
12/12	36.99	—	—	(0.16)	0.00	29.91
12/11	28.72	17	9	2.23	0.00	30.61
Annual Growth	13.1%	—	—	5.8%	—	1.3%

Owens-Illinois, Inc.

Owens-Illinois (O-I) is involved in more toasts than party-goers on New Year's Eve. The world's largest maker of glass containers touts a leading market presence with 49000 customers in 85 countries around the world. O-I offers more than 10000 types of glass containers such as bottles in a wide range of shapes sizes and colors used to hold beer wine liquor as well as soft drinks juice and other beverages. It also makes glass containers for foods such as soups salad dressings and dairy products and for pharmaceuticals. Some of its products are made using recycled glass. Major customers have included such heavy hitters as Anheuser-Busch InBev Coca-Cola Diageo H.J. Heinz and Nestle.

Geographic Reach

Altogether O-I operates almost 80 manufacturing plants in 23 countries. It has joint ventures in China Malaysia the US and Vietnam. In addition the company operates machine shops that rebuild and repair its glass forming machines as well as a mold shop to make molded shapes. Engineering support sites for its glass manufacturing operations are located Australia Columbia Poland Peru and the US.

The company divides its operations across four reportable segments based on geography: Europe

(40% of total sales) North America (29%) South America (17%) and Asia/Pacific (14%).

Sales and Marketing

O-I sells most of its glass container products directly to customers under yearly or multi-year supply agreements however some of its products are sold through distributors. Customers range from large multinationals to small local breweries and wineries.

Financial Performance

The company's overall revenues have gradually declined the last three years falling 3% from $6.97 billion in 2013 to $6.78 billion in 2014. Its profits also plunged 59% from $184 million to $75 million over that same time period due to higher selling and administrative expenses.

The declines for 2014 was primarily driven by a 18% drop in Asia/Pacific revenues and a 2% decline from South America. Glass container shipments were down 20% largely due to planned plant closures in China as well as lower shipments in Australia due to weaker demand in the domestic beer and export wine markets.

Strategy

O-I grows through acquisitions and joint ventures. In 2013 it formed a joint venture Glass to Glass LLC with California-based eCullet. The new venture supplies glass sorting equipment used to make more high-quality recycled glass available for use in O-I plants. The JV opened its first recycled glass processing center Portland Oregon in late 2013.

It also looks to product development to grow its business. In mid-2014 it opened an Innovation Center a combined R&D and pilot plant at its global headquarters in Ohio. At the Innovation Center employees will research new concepts in glass production and qualify emerging technologies to improve the glass-making process.

Simultaneously O-I is placing a priority on winning over customers that have shied away from glass packaging as well as encouraging existing ones to use more. To this end its marketing efforts piggyback on the wave toward sustainable packaging. Along with developing a variety of container features and functions the company highlights the benefits of glass recyclability.

Mergers and Acquisitions

In a historic transaction O-I in 2015 acquired the food and beverage glass container business from Vitro S.A.B. de C.V. for $2.15 billion. Vitro is the largest supplier of glass containers in Mexico. The deal included Vitro's five food and beverage glass container plants in Mexico a plant in Bolivia and the food and beverage business of Vitro Packaging its North American distribution business based in Plano Texas. The transaction cemented O-I with a competitive position in the attractive glass segment within the packaging market in Mexico

HISTORY

The Owens Bottle Machine Corp. was incorporated in Toledo Ohio in 1907 as the successor to a four-year-old New Jersey company of the same name. It initially grew by acquiring small glass companies. In 1929 Owens bought the Illinois Glass Co. (medical and pharmaceutical glass) and became Owens-Illinois Glass.

The company bought Libbey Glass (tableware) in 1935. Three years later Owens-Illinois and Corning Glass which were both studying uses for glass fiber began Owens-Corning Fiberglass a joint venture with a virtual industry monopoly.

After WWII Owens-Illinois (O-I) started to diversify beyond glass. The company went public in 1952. In 1956 it bought National Container (cardboard boxes). It also created a semi-rigid plastic container that was adopted by bleach and detergent companies.

EXECUTIVES

V Pres, James W Baehren
President Latin America, Andr ©L pez, $425,833
  total compensation
VP and Chief Process Improvement Officer, Ron White
VP and CTO, Giancarlo Currarino
President O-I North America, Sergio Galindo
SVP and CFO, Jan A. Bertsch
CEO, Andres Lopez
Managing Director O-I Europe, Vitaliano Torno
President O-I South America, Miguel Alvarez
President O-I Asia Pacific, Timothy Connors
Vice President Internet Marketing, Benjamin Hagan
Vice President New Business Development, Oscar Enriquez
Vice President Of Quality, Steve Jenkins
Vice President Global People Operations, Randy Miller
Vice President Sales and Marketing North America, Shawn Welch
Vice President and Associate General Counsel, Joseph J (Jo) O'Hara
Vice President Supply Chain, Jim Nordmeyer
Senior Vice President Chief Administrative Officer and General Counsel, James (Jamie) Baehren
Senior Vice President Chief Human Resources Officer, Paul Jarrell
Chairman and CEO, Albert P. L. (Al) Stroucken
Auditors: Ernst & Young LLP

LOCATIONS

HQ: Owens-Illinois, Inc.
One Michael Owens Way, Perrysburg, OH 43551
Phone: 567 336-5000
Web: www.o-i.com

2014 Sales

	$ mil.	% of total
Europe	2,794	41
North America	2,003	29
South America	1,159	17
Asia/Pacific	793	12
Other	35	1
Total	**6,784**	**100**

PRODUCTS/OPERATIONS

Selected Subsidiaries

Owens-Illinois Group Inc.
OI General Finance Inc.
OI General FTS Inc.
OI Castalia STS Inc.
OI Levis Park STS Inc.
Owens-Illinois General Inc.
Owens Insurance Ltd.
Universal Materials Inc.
OI Advisors Inc.
OI Securities Inc.
OI Transfer Inc.
Maumee Air Associates Inc.
OI Australia Inc.
Continental PET Holdings Pty. Ltd.
ACI America Holdings Inc.
ACI Ventures Inc.
Owens-Brockway Packaging Inc.
Owens-Brockway Glass Container Inc.
OI Andover Group Inc.
The Andover Group Inc.
Brockway Realty Corporation
NHW Auburn LLC
OI Auburn Inc.
SeaGate Inc.
SeaGate II Inc.

COMPETITORS

Alcoa
Amcor
Anchor Glass
AptarGroup
BWAY

Rexam
Reynolds Group
  Holdings Limited
Saint-Gobain
Saint-Gobain

Ball Corp.	Containers
Bemis	Sealed Air Corp.
Berry Plastics	Silgan
Consolidated Container	Sonoco Products
Crown Holdings	Tetra Pak
Graham Packaging	Tupperware Brands
Jarden	Vidrala
Newell Rubbermaid	Vitro
Plastipak	

HISTORICAL FINANCIALS

Company Type: Public

Income Statement

FYE: December 31

	REVENUE ($ mil.)	NET INCOME ($ mil.)	NET PROFIT MARGIN	EMPLOYEES
12/15	6,156	(74)	—	27,000
12/14	6,784	75	1.1%	21,100
12/13	6,967	184	2.6%	22,500
12/12	7,000	184	2.6%	22,500
12/11	7,358	(510)	—	24,000
Annual Growth	(4.4%)	—	—	3.0%

2015 Year-End Financials

Debt ratio: 59.16%	No. of shares (mil.): 160
Return on equity: (-9.11%)	Dividends
Cash ($ mil.): 399	Yield: —
Current ratio: 1.10	Payout: —
Long-term debt ($ mil.): 5,345	Market value ($ mil.): 2,804

	STOCK PRICE ($) FY Close	P/E High/Low	PER SHARE ($) Earnings	Dividends	Book Value
12/15	17.42	— —	(0.47)	0.00	2.90
12/14	26.99	78 51	0.45	0.00	7.05
12/13	35.78	32 19	1.11	0.00	8.84
12/12	21.27	22 15	1.11	0.00	5.37
12/11	19.38	— —	(3.11)	0.00	5.10
Annual Growth	(2.6%)	— —	—	—	—(13.2%)

PACCAR Inc.

Old PACCARs never die they just get a new Peterbilt. PACCAR is one of the world's largest designers and manufacturers of big rig diesel trucks. Its lineup of light- medium- and heavy-duty trucks includes the Kenworth Peterbilt and DAF nameplates. The company also manufactures and distributes aftermarket truck parts for these brands. PACCAR's other products include Braden Carco and Gearmatic industrial winches. With the exception of a few company-owned branches PACCAR's trucks and parts are sold through independent dealers. Its PACCAR Financial Services and PacLease subsidiaries offer financing and truck leasing respectively.Geographic ReachThe company owns manufacturing plants in five US states three countries in Europe and a facility in each of Australia Canada South America and Mexico. PACCAR Financial Services operates through three continr nts spanning around 20 countries.In the European light/medium market PACCAR competes with DAF cab-over-engine trucks assembled in the UK by Leyland. About 50% of PACCAR's revenues are generated outside the US with nearly 25% coming from Europe.Sales and Marketing

PACCAR delivers its products and services to customers worldwide through its dealer network of nearly 2000 locations. PACCAR International sells the company's products in more than 100 countries.

Operations

The company's truck segment generates roughly 77% of total sales while parts accounts for 16%. The remainder comes from its financial services and other segment.Financial PerformancePACCAR's balance sheet has made a milestone comeback after the painful effects of the recession. From 2013 to 2014 total revenue increased by 11% topping out at roughly $19 billion the highest in the company's history. Net income also surged 5% from $1.2 billion to a record-setting $1.4 billion during that same time period.The historic growth in 2014 was primarily due to 12% growth in truck sales and 9% growth in parts sales. Sales from the US also surged by 24% during the year. The growth in truck revenue was due to higher truck deliveries in the US and Canada and higher price realization in Europe related to higher content Euro 6 emission vehicles. Parts sales in 2014 jumped due to higher aftermarket demand across all markets.PACCAR experienced a large surge in operating cash flow in 2013; however cash flow in 2014 declined by 11% to $2.1 billion due to higher wholesale receivables on new trucks receivables and inventories.StrategyPACCAR continues to examine business opportunities in Asia with a primary focus on Brazil China and India. It completed construction of a 300000 square-foot DAF truck assembly facility in Ponta Grossa Brasil in late 2013 and began assembling the DAF XF for Brasil and other South American markets. Its new DAF CF vehicle will launch in Brazil in 2015.

HISTORY

William Pigott founded the Seattle Car Manufacturing Company in 1905 to produce railroad cars for timber transport. Finding immediate success Pigott began to make other kinds of railcars in 1906. When the Seattle plant burned the next year the company moved near Renton Washington. In 1911 Pigott renamed the company Seattle Car & Foundry.

In 1917 Seattle Car merged with the Twohy Brothers of Portland. The new company Pacific Car & Foundry was sold to American Car & Foundry in 1924. Pacific Car then diversified into bus manufacturing structural steel fabrications and metal technology.

Pacific Car was in decline by 1934 when William's son Paul bought it; since then the company has remained under family management. Paul Pigott added Hofius Steel and Equipment and Tricoach a bus manufacturer in 1936. The company entered the truck-making business with the 1945 purchase of Seattle-based Kenworth.

In the 1950s Pacific Car became the industry leader in mechanical refrigerator car production. It began producing off-road heavy trucks and acquired Peterbilt Trucks of Oakland (1958). To augment its winch business Pacific Car bought Canada's Gearmatic in 1963.

The company moved its headquarters to Bellevue Washington in 1969 and changed its name to PACCAR in 1971.

EXECUTIVES

Vice President Human Resources, Jack Levier
President and CFO, Robert J. (Bob) Christensen, age 59, $691,634 total compensation
President, Ronald E. (Ron) Armstrong, age 59, $972,115 total compensation
EVP, Daniel D. (Dan) Sobic, age 62, $609,903 total compensation
SVP and CIO, T. Kyle Quinn, age 54, $421,538 total compensation
VP and President DAF Trucks, Harrie C.A.M. Schippers, age 53, $396,022 total compensation
SVP Financial Services, Robert A. Bengston, age 59, $396,538 total compensation

Senior Vice President, Gary Moore
Vice President Procurement, Martin Schuebel
National Account Manager, Neil Dunn
Vice President Finance, Mike Headley
Vice President Education, Tara Brown
Vice President of Finance, Val O Leary
Vice President Corporate Development, Ken Hastings
Vice President, Thomas (Thom) Lundahl
Vice President, David (Dave) Anderson
Vice President Of Marketing, Michele Conrad
Executive Vice President, Dan Sobic
Vice President and Controller, Michael (Mel) Barkley
Vice President, James (Jamie) Cardillo
Vice President Human Resources, Cheryl Nishimoto
Vice President Human Resources, Lauriegone Baker
Vice President E Commerce, Peter (Pete) Danes
Vice President, Art Clemencia
Purchasing Vice President, Tom Lundahl
General Manager and PACCAR Vice President, William (Bill) Jackson
Vice President, Bob Bengston
Chairman and CEO, Mark C. Pigott, age 62
Auditors: Ernst & Young LLP

LOCATIONS

HQ: PACCAR Inc.
777 - 106th Ave. N.E., Bellevue, WA 98004
Phone: 425 468-7400
Web: www.paccar.com

2014 Sales

	$ mil.	% of total
US	10,106	53
Europe	4,835	26
Other regions	4,055	21
Total	18,997	100

PRODUCTS/OPERATIONS

2014 Sales

	$ mil.	% of total
Truck	14,594	77
Parts	3,077	16
Financial services	1,204	6
Other	121	1
Total	18,997	100

Selected Divisions and Subsidiaries

DAF Trucks N.V. (The Netherlands)
Dynacraft (battery cables hose assemblies and air conditioning hardlines)
Kenworth
Kenworth Mexicana S.A. de C.V.
Leyland Trucks Limited (UK)
PACCAR Australia Pty. Ltd.
PACCAR Engines
PACCAR Financial Corp.
PACCAR Mexico S.A. de C.V.
PACCAR of Canada Ltd.
Canadian Kenworth Co.
Peterbilt of Canada
PACCAR Parts
PACCAR Sales North America Inc.
PACCAR Winch
Braden Winches & Hoists
Carco Winches
Gearmatic Winches

COMPETITORS

AGCO	Iveco S.p.A.
Caterpillar	MAN
Cummins	Mack Trucks
Daimler	Meritor
Dana Holding	Morris Material
Deere	Handling
Eaton	Navistar International
Fiat Chrysler	Oshkosh Truck
Ford Motor	Scania
General Motors	UD Trucks
Hino Motors	Volvo
Isuzu	

Income Statement
FYE: December 31

	REVENUE ($ mil.)	NET INCOME ($ mil.)	NET PROFIT MARGIN	EMPLOYEES
12/15	19,115	1,604	8.4%	23,000
12/14	18,997	1,358	7.2%	23,300
12/13	17,123	1,171	6.8%	21,800
12/12	17,050	1,111	6.5%	21,800
12/11	16,355	1,042	6.4%	23,400
Annual Growth	4.0%	11.4%	—	(0.4%)

2015 Year-End Financials

Debt ratio: 40.70%	No. of shares (mil.): 351
Return on equity: 23.43%	Dividends
Cash ($ mil.): 2,016	Yield: 4.8%
Current ratio: 1.84	Payout: 50.0%
Long-term debt ($ mil.): 8,591	Market value ($ mil.): 16,652

	STOCK PRICE ($) FY Close	P/E High/Low	PER SHARE ($) Earnings	Dividends	Book Value
12/15	47.40	15 10	4.51	2.32	19.76
12/14	68.01	18 14	3.82	1.86	19.05
12/13	59.17	18 14	3.30	1.70	18.73
12/12	45.21	15 11	3.12	1.58	16.54
12/11	37.47	20 11	2.86	1.30	15.03
Annual Growth	6.1%	— —	12.1%	15.6%	7.1%

Pacific Mutual Holding Co.

Life insurance is "alive and whale" at Pacific Mutual Holding. The company's primary operating subsidiary Pacific Life Insurance (whose logo is a breaching whale) is a top California-based life insurer. Lines of business include a variety of life insurance products for individuals and businesses; annuities and mutual funds geared to individuals and small businesses; management of stable value funds fixed income investments and other investments for institutional clients and pension plans; and real estate investing. Additionally its Aviation Capital Group subsidiary provides commercial jet aircraft leasing. The company is owned by its Pacific Life shareholders.

Aside from Pacific Life the company's other major operating subsidiary is Pacific Life & Annuity which provides life insurance annuities and other investment products for individuals and businesses.

Pacific Mutual's operating strategy is to focus and strengthen its core line-up of products of life insurance annuities and mutual funds by investing in its subsidiaries and in turn their operating subsidiaries growing successful business segments. In recent years it has added on reinsurance and life retrocession through acquisitions. In 2012 the company sold its College Savings Bank subsidiary to a syndicate of investors to focus on its core products.

Like most in the market Pacific Mutual suffered steep investment losses in 2008. However as the market has slowly crawled back to life the company's investments have revived. More significantly like many other insurers in the past few years revenues from policy fees and premiums have boomed as risk-averse investors sought the stabil-

ity of life insurance products. In 2011 Pacific Mutual achieved revenues of $5.9 billion an increase of about 5% from 2010 and its net income soared 42% to $679 million.

Pacific Mutual Holding was created in 1997 following a conversion to a mutual holding company structure. Pacific LifeCorp is the intermediate stockholding company which owns 100% of Pacific Life and can take on outside capital funding (though it has not done so).

HISTORY

The Pacific Mutual Life Insurance began business in 1868 in Sacramento California as a stock company. Its board was dominated by California business and political leaders including three of the "Big Four" who created the Central Pacific Railroad (Charles Crocker Mark Hopkins and Leland Stanford) and three former governors (Stanford Newton Booth and Henry Huntley Haight). Stanford (founder of Stanford University) was the company's first president and policyholder.

By 1870 Pacific Mutual Life was selling life insurance throughout most of the western US. Expansion continued in the early 1870s into Colorado Kentucky Nebraska New York Ohio and Texas. The company ventured into Mexico in 1873 but sold few policies. It had better luck in China accepting its first risk there in 1875 and in Hawaii where it started business two years later. In 1881 Pacific Mutual Life moved to San Francisco.

Leland Stanford died in 1893. The eponymous university and Stanford's widow though rich in assets found themselves struggling through a US economic depression. The benefit from Stanford's policy kept the university open until the estate was settled.

In 1905 Conservative Life bought the firm. The Pacific Mutual Life name survived the acquisition just as its records survived the fire that ravaged San Francisco after the 1906 earthquake. Pacific Mutual Life then relocated to Los Angeles.

The company squeaked through the Depression after a flood of claims on its noncancellable disability income policies forced Pacific Mutual Life into a reorganization plan initiated by the California insurance commissioner (1936). After WWII Pacific Mutual Life entered the group insurance and pension markets.

After 83 years as a stock company and an eight-year stock purchasing program Pacific Mutual Life became a true mutual in 1959.

Pacific Mutual Life relocated to Newport Beach in 1972. During the 1980s it built up its financial services operations including its Pacific Investment Management Co. (PIMCO founded 1971). The company was in trouble even before the stock crash of 1987 because of health care costs and over-investment in real estate. That year it brought in CEO Thomas Sutton who sold off real estate and emphasized HMOs and fee-based financial services.

In the 1990s the firm cut costs and increased its fee income. PIMCO Advisors L.P. was formed in 1994 when PIMCO merged with Thomson Advisory Group. The merger gave Pacific Mutual Life a retail market for its fixed-income products a stake in the resulting public company and sales that offset interest-rate variations and changes in the health care system.

In 1997 the company assumed the corporate-owned life insurance business of failed Confederation Life Insurance; it also merged insolvent First Capital Life into Pacific Life as Pacific Corinthian Life. That year Pacific Mutual Life which became Pacific Mutual Holding became the first top-10 US mutual to convert to a mutual holding company thus allowing it the option of issuing stock to fund acquisitions. Because the firm remained partially

mutual however policyholders retained ownership but got no shares of Pacific LifeCorp its new intermediate stockholding company.

To compete with such one-stop financial service behemoths as Citigroup Pacific Mutual began selling annuities through a Compass Bank subsidiary in 1998. The next year it bought controlling interests in broker-dealer M.L. Stern and investment adviser Tower Asset Management. In 2000 the world's #2 insurer Allianz bought all of PIMCO Advisors (now Allianz Global Investors of America) other than the interest retained by Pacific Mutual when it spun off the investment manager. (Pacific Mutual gradually sold its holdings in the firm and thus its stake in Pacific Investment Management Company through sales to Allianz.)

Pacific Mutual Holding sharpened its focus on individuals and small businesses in 2001 with the sale of its reinsurance unit to what is now Scottish Re.

With its focus so firmly on life insurance Pacific Life sold its group health insurance business (which included medical dental and life policies) to PacifiCare in 2005.

Pacific Mutual rearranged some of its investment arm in 2007 when it formed Pacific Asset Management to act as a third-party manager for structured credit transactions. It then shed some of its broker/dealer businesses and sold its minority stake in Pacific Investment Management Company (PIMCO) to majority-owner insurance giant Allianz for $288 million. It had already sold smaller chunks of its PIMCO stake to Allianz in previous years.

EXECUTIVES

Assistant Vice President Of Portfolio And Product Merchandising Life Insurance Division, Jose Miscolta

Auditors: Deloitte & Touche LLP

LOCATIONS

HQ: Pacific Mutual Holding Co.
700 Newport Center Drive, Newport Beach, CA 92660-6397
Phone: 949 219-3011
Web: www.pacificmutual.com

COMPETITORS

AIG	MassMutual
AXA Financial	MetLife
Boeing Capital	Mutual of Omaha
CIT Transportation	Nationwide
Finance	New York Life
Great-West Life	Northwestern Mutual
Assurance	Penn Mutual
Guardian Life	Principal Financial
John Hancock Financial	Prudential
Services	StanCorp Financial
Lincoln Financial	Group
Group	

HISTORICAL FINANCIALS
Company Type: Public

Income Statement
FYE: December 31

	ASSETS ($ mil.)	NET INCOME ($ mil.)	INCOME AS % OF ASSETS	EMPLOYEES
12/14	137,048	540	0.4%	—
12/13	129,921	720	0.6%	—
12/12	123,697	460	0.4%	—
12/11	116,811	679	0.6%	—
12/10	115,992	480	0.4%	—
Annual Growth	4.3%	3.0%	—	—

Debt ratio: 6.49%—
Return on equity: 5.66%
Cash ($ mil.): 3,656
Current ratio: —
Long-term debt ($ mil.): —

Dividends
Yield: —
Payout: —
Market value ($ mil.): —

PacifiCorp

PacifiCorp has refocused on its core businesses: regulated utilities Pacific Power and Rocky Mountain Power which together provide electricity to 1.8 million customers in six western states. The subsidiaries operate 16300 miles of transmission lines and 62800 miles of distribution lines. PacifiCorp owns or has stakes in almost 75 thermal hydroelectric and renewable generation facilities that supply its utilities with about 10600 MW of net capacity. Its PacifiCorp Energy unit purchases power from other generators and it sells excess power to wholesale customers in the western US. The company is a unit of Berkshire Hathaway's MidAmerican Energy Holdings.

OperationsPacifiCorp consists of three business units: PacifiCorp Energy (electric generation commercial energy trading and coal mining) Pacific Power (electricity distribution to customers in Oregon Washington and California) and Rocky Mountain Power (power distribution to customers in Utah Wyoming and Idaho). Geographic ReachPacifiCorp is headquartered in Oregon and serves customers in California Idaho Oregon Utah Washington and Wyoming. Financial AnalysisPacifiCorp's 2013 revenues followed a years long trend and rose by about 5% to $5.14 billion from $4.88 billion in 2012 due to higher energy prices. Net income also increased by 27% to $682 million from $537 million the prior year due to some unusual items which lead to lower after tax charges. Exclusive of those net income rose 11%. Cash from operations on the other hand decreased about 5% from $1.62 billion to $1.55 billion as the company used cash to pay income taxes.

Strategy

As part of its plan to continuously expand it generating capacity PacifiCorp through Rocky Mountain Power began building a 9000-panel solar farm in Utah that will provide power for about 500 homes.

HISTORY

Utility holding company Electric Bond and Share bought several small West Coast utilities and formed Pacific Power & Light (PP&L) in 1910 then expanded its service area through acquisitions and by building transmission lines. The Public Utility Holding Company Act of 1935 forced Electric Bond and Share to unload PP&L in 1950. Uncertainty over government power contracts spurred PP&L to build its own hydroelectric dams. In 1953 PP&L merged with Mountain States Power (which had two small phone companies) expanding into Idaho Montana and Wyoming.

In 1961 the utility merged with California Oregon Power and began operating coal-fired plants and acquiring some 1.5 billion tons of Montana and Wyoming coal reserves.

PP&L acquired Telephone Utilities (Washington) and long-distance company Alascom (Alaska) in the 1970s. It also formed the Northern Energy Resources Company (NERCO) to manage its coalmining units.

The firm reorganized in 1982 becoming PacifiCorp. PP&L became a subsidiary and the phone services were renamed Pacific Telecom. In the mid-1980s PacifiCorp bought a financial service firm and explored for oil and gas through NERCO. In 1987 PacifiCorp merged with Utah Power and opened its grid to independent power producers.

By the early 1990s PacifiCorp was dropping poor performers. It entered wholesale power marketing in 1994 the year Fred Buckman became CEO. Under Buckman PacifiCorp bought Australian utility company Powercor in 1995 split Pacific Telecom into a separate subsidiary sold Alascom to AT&T and split its utility operations into generation transmission and retail sales units.

PacifiCorp bought natural gas marketer TPC in 1997 but sold TPC's gas pipeline to El Paso Natural Gas (now El Paso Energy). That year PacifiCorp agreed to buy the UK's Energy Group for about $9.6 billion including debt and sold Pacific Telecom to Century Telephone (now CenturyTel) and Pacific Generation an independent power producer to NRG Energy.

But in 1998 Buckman's plans began to unravel. Rival suitor Texas Utilities (which became TXU which in turn became Energy Future Holdings) for example cost the company $67 million by outbidding it for Energy Group. And PacifiCorp's power trading arm lost $151 million when its suppliers couldn't meet the energy demands of a sweltering hot summer in the western US. Buckman resigned replaced by chairman Keith McKennon and PacifiCorp was forced to reorganize. Later it agreed to be bought by UK-based Scottish Power.

In 1999 PacifiCorp sold TPC to NIPSCO (now called NiSource) for $132.5 million. It also sold its Montana service area to Flathead Electric Cooperative and exited most of its power-trading operations.

Scottish Power completed its purchase of PacifiCorp in 1999 and Alan Richardson replaced McKennon as CEO. The next year PacifiCorp sold its Centralia Washington coal-fired power plant and an adjacent coal mine to Canada's TransAlta for $554 million and it sold Powercor for $2.14 billion to Cheung Kong Infrastructure.

PacifiCorp experienced an unscheduled outage at one of its Utah power plants for about six months in 2000-01 which coupled with unusually high-priced wholesale electricity in the region caused losses for the company and led it to request rate increases for its service territories in 2001. That year PacifiCorp's interest in PacifiCorp Power Marketing (now PPM Energy) its remaining energy trading unit was transferred to another Scottish Power unit.

Growing its national market share MidAmerican Energy Holdings acquired PacifiCorp in 2006 from Scottish Power for a reported $5.1 billion.

EXECUTIVES

Chairman and CEO, Gregory E. (Greg) Abel, age 52
President and CEO Pacific Power, Stefan A. Bird, age 45
President PacifiCorp Transmission, R. Patrick (Pat) Reiten, age 54, $320,000 total compensation
SVP and CFO, Douglas K. (Doug) Stuver, age 52, $252,000 total compensation
President and CEO Rocky Mountain Power, Cindy A. Crane, age 53, $224,538 total compensation
SVP Transmission and System Operations, Natalie L. Hocken, age 45
President and CEO PacifiCorp Energy, Michael G. Dunn, age 50, $320,000 total compensation
Vice President Manager Director, Esther Giezendanner
Vice President, Chris Moore
Vp And Chief Environmental Counsel, Cathy Woollums

Vice President Resource Development and Construction, Chad Teply
Vice President, Chris Turner
Vice President Customer Service, Matt Feist
Vice President Customer Service, Paula Broussard
Vice President Services, Loren Morse
Vice President, Willie Apodaca
Vice President Finance, Stan Jensen
Vice President Community And Government Relations, Scott Bolton
Board Member, Brent Gale
Board Member, Mark Stenberg
Secretary, Katie Mandzij
Auditors: Deloitte & Touche LLP

LOCATIONS

HQ: Pacificorp
825 N.E. Multnomah Street, Portland, OR 97232
Phone: 503 813-5645
Web: www.pacificorp.com

PRODUCTS/OPERATIONS

2013 Customers

	No.
Residential	1,522
Commercial	208
Industrial and irrigation	34
OThers	3
Total	**1,767**

Selected Subsidiaries

PacifiCorp Energy
Pacific Power
Rocky Mountain Power

COMPETITORS

AES Wind Generation
Avista
Bonneville Power
Cascade Natural Gas
Chelan County PUD
Edison International
First Wind Holdings
IDACORP
Idaho Power
NV Energy
NW Natural
PG&E Corporation
PPL Montana
Pacific Gas and Electric
Pinnacle West
Portland General Electric
Public Utility District No. 1 of Clark County
Puget Energy
Questar
Questar Gas
Riverside Electric Utility
San Diego Gas & Electric
Seattle City Light
Sempra Energy
Sierra Pacific Power

HISTORICAL FINANCIALS

Company Type: Public

Income Statement

FYE: December 31

	REVENUE ($ mil.)	NET INCOME ($ mil.)	NET PROFIT MARGIN	EMPLOYEES
12/14	5,252	698	13.3%	5,900
12/13	5,147	682	13.3%	6,000
12/12	4,882	537	11.0%	6,300
12/11	4,586	555	12.1%	6,400
12/10	4,432	566	12.8%	6,300
Annual Growth	**4.3%**	**5.4%**	**—**	**(1.6%)**

2014 Year-End Financials

Debt ratio: 31.76%
Return on equity: 8.98%
Cash ($ mil.): 23
Current ratio: 1.36
Long-term debt ($ mil.): 6,919

No. of shares (mil.): 357
Dividends
 Yield: 0.0%
 Payout: 103.8%
Market value ($ mil.): 41,412

	STOCK PRICE ($) FY Close	P/E High/Low		PER SHARE ($) Earnings	Dividends	Book Value
12/14	116.00	—	—	(0.00)	7.00	21.73
12/13	114.79	—	—	(0.00)	7.00	21.81
12/12	116.00	—	—	(0.00)	7.00	21.41
12/11	105.00	—	—	(0.00)	7.00	20.48
12/10	125.00	—	—	(0.00)	7.00	20.48
Annual Growth	(1.9%)	—	—	—	(0.0%)	1.5%

Packaging Corp of America

Every day is Boxing Day at Packaging Corporation of America (PCA) one of the largest containerboard manufacturers in the US. It produces about 3.5 million tons of containerboard a year most of which is converted into corrugated boxes and ships about 48.2 billion square feet of corrugated products. PCA's mills also churn out about 2.25 million tons of kraft linerboard and about a million tons of semi-chemical corrugating medium. The company sells to a diverse group of industries. Its corrugated packaging includes shipping containers for manufactured goods retail boxes and displays and wax-coated boxes and meat boxes for agricultural use.

Operations

The company operates in three segments: packaging paper and corporate and other. Packaging which accounts for 78% of sales produces a variety of corrugated packaging products. The paper segment 20% of sales makes and sells a range of papers including communication papers and pressure sensitive papers (collectively white papers) and market pulp. PCA's Paper segment operates under the trade name Boise Paper. Corporate and other includes support staff services and related assets and liabilities transportation assets and activity related to other ancillary support operations.

Nationwide the corrugated products industry consists of 535 companies and 1200 plants. Plants generally serve a market radius of around 150 miles. At PCA more than 80% of the containerboard produced at its plants are used by its corrugated products locations. Remaining output is used by external customers. Along with containerboard corrugated containers retail packaging storage supplies and heavy-duty packaging products the company provides services including graphics design technical support value improvement branding and e-commerce support.

Geographic Reach

PCA operates eight containerboard mills (five containerboard mills and three paper mills) and about 100 corrugated products plants in more than 30 US states. The company's substantial manufacturing footprint is enhanced by a technical and development hub half a dozen regional graphic design centers and several printing and distribution sites. PCA also leases cutting rights on 88000 acres of timberland and has supply agreements on an additional 281000 acres –most neighboring its Counce Tennessee and Valdosta Geor-

gia mills. The company operates also has some converting operations in Europe Mexico and Canada.

Sales and Marketing

PCA promotes its products through a direct sales and marketing force as well as independent brokers and distribution partners. It employs a sales manager and sales representatives at most of its corrugated product manufacturing locations. The company serves 19000 customers in more than 30000 locations. About three-quarters of sales of corrugated products go to local and regional accounts (located near a single PCA plant); remaining sales come from national accounts (customers who have widespread locations and are served by several PCA plants). Products are distributed by rail or truck. Rail shipments account for 65% of the tons shipped; truck shipments 35%. PCA's largest paper segment customer has been Office Depot.

Financial Performance

Over the last five years PCA's revenue has steadily grown with a strong burst in 2014. Revenue increased 60% to $5.8 billion in 2014 over 2013. PCA benefited from having a full year of operations of late-2013 acquisition Boise on its books and higher sales volumes and higher prices from the company's normal operations. The packaging segment grew with the full year acquisition results of Boise and half year results of Crockett Packaging which was acquired in 2014. The paper segment sales increased also due to high sales volumes.

PCA might turn out a lot of paper but that doesn't mean it's rolling out big profits. Net income dropped 11% to about $390 million in 2014 because of an increase in overall operating expenses in the paper segment. But the company cited its 2014 tax rate of 36% as the major reason for the profit decrease. In 2013 the company had an income tax benefit from the reversal of the reserve for unrecognized tax benefits from alternative energy tax credits.Over the last five years the company has maintained a steady increase in operating cash flows. In 2014 PCA's operating cash flow increased 21% to $736 million due to higher inventories levels and lower accounts payable due to the timing of payments; offset to a decrease in federal and state income taxes receivable.

Strategy

The company grows through internal expansions and acquisitions.

PCA's mills use both wood and recycled fiber (the primary raw material) offering PCA a competitive flexibility for mitigating the ups and downs of fiber prices. The proximity of PCA's US customers helps minimize freight costs.

Mergers and Acquisitions

In 2014 the company acquired Crockett Packaging a corrugated products manufacturer for $21.2 million.

In 2013 in a major move PCA acquired Boise (a large maker of packaging and white paper products) for $2.1 billion. The acquisition expanded PCA's corrugated products geographic reach and offerings provided low-cost lightweight containerboard capacity for continued growth in the packaging business and provided meaningful opportunities in the white paper business.

Company Background

In 2011 PCA acquired a specialty sheet plant in Chicago (Field Packaging) a sheet plant in Huntsville Alabama (Packaging Materials Company) and a full-line combining plant in Denver (Colorado Container Corporation).

To expand its manufacturing capacity PCA opened a new full-line converting plant in Reading Pennsylvania in 2011. It also acquired several packaging businesses that year.

The company has also enacted some cost containment measures at existing plants in recent years including implementing energy efficiency programs during 2010. It also underwent management reorganization in 2010 following shareholder pressure. To overcome effects of the economic recession which crushed US demand for corrugated packaging and containerboard PCA reduced operating capacity levels at its mills during 2009.

PCA was formed by Madison Dearborn in 1999 in order to acquire the containerboard and corrugated product operations of Pactiv. PCA blossomed five years later when it purchased the assets of Acorn Corrugated Box Company a maker of graphics packaging and displays.

EXECUTIVES

Chairman and CEO, Mark W. Kowlzan, age 60, $1,024,002 total compensation
SVP Paper, Judith M. (Judy) Lassa, age 57
EVP Corrugated Products, Thomas A. (Tom) Hassfurther, age 59, $804,438 total compensation
SVP General Counsel and Corporate Secretary, Kent A. Pflederer, age 44, $412,008 total compensation
SVP Sales and Marketing Corrugated Products, Thomas W. H. (Tom) Walton, age 55, $338,000 total compensation
SVP Mill Operations, Charles J. (Jack) Carter, age 56, $412,008 total compensation
SVP and CFO, Robert P. (Bob) Mundy
Vice President, Dwight Haley
Vice President Environmental Health Safety and Operations, Bruce Ridley
Vice President Engineering, Nam Shin
Vice President Containerboard Mill Operations, Jack Carter
Vice President Corporate Technology And Engineering, Ray Shirley
Vice President And General Manager, Donald (Don) Haag
Vice President, Rachel Knott
Vice President Human Resources, Harry Well
Vice President Engineering, Anil Sethy
Vice President Technology Development, Al Forbes
Vice President Operation Services, Bryan Sorensen
Vice President Containerboard Sales, Gerald Greeter
Vice President, Kevin Hart
Board Member, Eric Walters
Auditors: KPMG LLP

LOCATIONS

HQ: Packaging Corp of America
1955 West Field Court, Lake Forest, IL 60045
Phone: 847 482-3000
Web: www.packagingcorp.com

PRODUCTS/OPERATIONS

2013 Sales

	% of total
Packaging	94
Paper	6
Corporate and other	-
Total	**100**

Selected Products

Containerboard
Corrugated containers
Heavy-duty packaging
 BulkMaster
 ExportPack
 Grid-Lok
Produce packaging
 BulkMaster
 Field-to-Retail
Record storage boxes
Retail packaging and displays
 Point-of-purchase displays
 Point-of-sale packaging
 Shelf shipper-displays

COMPETITORS

Amcor	Kapstone Paper and
Atlas Container	Packaging
Bio Pappel	Norampac
Georgia-Pacific	Pratt Industries USA
Graphic Packaging	Sonoco Products
Holding	Southern Container
Greif	corp
International Paper	WestRock

HISTORICAL FINANCIALS

Company Type: Public

Income Statement
FYE: December 31

	REVENUE ($ mil.)	NET INCOME ($ mil.)	NET PROFIT MARGIN	EMPLOYEES
12/14	5,852	392	6.7%	14,000
12/13	3,665	436	11.9%	13,600
12/12	2,843	163	5.8%	8,600
12/11	2,620	158	6.0%	8,300
12/10	2,435	205	8.4%	8,100
Annual Growth	24.5%	17.6%	—	14.7%

2014 Year-End Financials

Debt ratio: 44.49%	No. of shares (mil.): 98
Return on equity: 27.70%	Dividends
Cash ($ mil.): 124	Yield: 2.0%
Current ratio: 2.58	Payout: 30.1%
Long-term debt ($ mil.): 2,371	Market value ($ mil.): 7,678

	STOCK PRICE ($) FY Close	P/E High/Low	PER SHARE ($) Earnings	Dividends	Book Value
12/14	78.05	20 15	3.99	1.60	15.47
12/13	63.28	14 9	4.47	1.51	13.37
12/12	38.47	23 15	1.68	1.00	9.88
12/11	25.24	19 13	1.57	0.80	9.45
12/10	25.84	13 10	2.00	0.60	9.86
Annual Growth	31.8%	— —	18.8%	27.8%	11.9%

PacWest Bancorp

PacWest Bancorp is the holding company for Pacific Western Bank which operates about 65 branches in Southern California plus three in the San Francisco Bay Area. The bank caters to small and midsized businesses and their owners and employees offering traditional deposit and loan products and services. Commercial real estate mortgages business loans (including Small Business Administration loans) and construction loans account for most of the bank's lending activities. It also originates residential mortgage consumer and other loans. The bank offers investment services and international banking through agreements with correspondent banks.

Geographic Reach

PWB's branches are located throughout California in Los Angeles Orange Riverside San Bernardino Santa Barbara San Diego San Francisco San Luis Obispo San Mateo and Ventura Counties.

Operations

The company's BFI Business Finance subsidiary and Financial Pacific Western division provides asset-based lending and factoring of accounts receivable to small businesses in Arizona California and the Pacific Northwest. PacWest added to its commercial lending operations with the acquisition of Utah-based Marquette Equipment Finance (renamed Pacific Western Equipment Finance) in early 2012. The unit has lease receivables in 45 states.

Strategy

PacWest has grown through acquisitions of California community banks and other companies. It has made more than 20 acquisitions since 1999. During the economic downturn PacWest took advantage of a rash of bank failures through FDIC-assisted transactions. The acquired institutions were merged into Pacific Western Bank. Under the loss-sharing deals the FDIC agreed to reimburse PacWest for future losses tied to the acquisitions.

Mergers and Acquisitions

PacWest acquired First California Financial Group operator of First California Bank in May 2013. The $237 million purchase added six branches (after consolidation) and approximately $1.7 billion in assets to PacWest. (First California Bank has branches in Los Angeles Orange Riverside San Bernardino San Diego San Luis Obispo and Venture counties.) Previously in a 2012 non-FDIC-assisted deal PacWest bought American Perspective Bank adding two branches and a loan office in the Central Coast area.

Later in 2012 PacWest sold 10 branches to Opus Bank an Irvine California-based bank. The sale is part of PacWest's ongoing effort to improve efficiency and profitability. Cutting loose the 10 branches will save the company about $2 million each year.

EXECUTIVES

EVP and Director the Company and Pacific Western Bank, Daniel B. Platt, age 68, $52,500 total compensation

EVP and Chief Risk Officer, Suzanne R. Brennan, age 64, $165,000 total compensation

CEO, Matthew P. (Matt) Wagner, age 58, $754,167 total compensation

EVP and CFO Pacific Western Bank, Patrick J. (Pat) Rusnak, age 51

EVP and Chief Accounting Officer, Lynn M. Hopkins, age 47

EVP; Director Human Resources, Christopher D. Blake, age 55, $298,958 total compensation

EVP and Chief Credit Officer, Bryan M. Corsini, age 53, $375,624 total compensation

EVP; President CapitalSource, James J. (Jim) Pieczynski, age 52, $554,539 total compensation

EVP Operations and Systems, Mark Christian

EVP General Counsel and Corporate Secretary, Kori L. Ogrosky

Executive Vice President Chief Credit Officer, Robert (Bob) Dyck

Chairman, John M. Eggemeyer, age 69

Auditors: KPMG LLP

LOCATIONS

HQ: PacWest Bancorp
10250 Constellation Blvd., Suite 1640, Los Angeles, CA 90067
Phone: 310 286-1144
Web: www.pacwestbancorp.com

PRODUCTS/OPERATIONS

Selected Mergers & Acquisitions

COMPETITORS

Bank of America	Rabobank America
CVB Financial	San Diego County
California Bank &	Credit Union
Trust	U.S. Bancorp
City National	Wells Fargo
JPMorgan Chase	Westamerica
MUFG Americas Holdings	

HISTORICAL FINANCIALS

Company Type: Public

Income Statement
FYE: December 31

	ASSETS ($ mil.)	NET INCOME ($ mil.)	INCOME AS % OF ASSETS	EMPLOYEES
12/14	16,234	168	1.0%	1,443
12/13	6,533	45	0.7%	1,110
12/12	5,463	56	1.0%	991
12/11	5,528	50	0.9%	982
12/10	5,529	(62)	—	929
Annual Growth	30.9%	—	—	11.6%

2014 Year-End Financials

Debt ratio: 5.03%	No. of shares (mil.): 103
Return on equity: 7.83%	Dividends
Cash ($ mil.): 313	Yield: 2.7%
Current ratio: —	Payout: 65.1%
Long-term debt ($ mil.): —	Market value ($ mil.): 4,683

	STOCK PRICE ($) FY Close	P/E High/Low	PER SHARE ($) Earnings	Dividends	Book Value
12/14	45.46	25 20	1.92	1.25	34.04
12/13	42.22	40 23	1.08	1.00	17.66
12/12	24.77	16 13	1.54	0.79	15.74
12/11	18.95	17 10	1.37	0.21	14.66
12/10	21.38	— —	(1.77)	0.04	13.06
Annual Growth	20.8%	— —	—	136.4%	27.1%

Park National Corp. (Newark, OH)

Customers can park their money with Park National. The holding company owns Park National Bank which operates more than 120 branches in Ohio and northern Kentucky through 11 community banking divisions. The banks provide an array of consumer and business banking services including traditional savings and checking accounts and CDs. Business loans including commercial leases and mortgages operating loans and agricultural loans account for about 35% of Park National's loan portfolio. The banks also originate consumer residential real estate and construction loans. Park National's nonbank units include consumer finance outfit Guardian Finance Scope Aircraft Finance and Park Title Agency.

Geographic Reach

Park National Corporation and its subsidiaries operate in Ohio and northern Kentucky.

Operations

Each of Park National Corporation's bank affiliates specialize in serving specific geographic locations. It's bank divisions include: Century National Bank; Fairfield National Bank; Farmers Bank; First-Knox National Bank; Park National Bank; Richland Bank; Security National Bank; Second National Bank; Unity National Bank; and United Bank.

Financial Performance

The company's revenue decreased in fiscal 2013 compared to the previous year. It reported $336.2 million in revenue for fiscal 2013 down from $378.1 million in fiscal 2012.

The company's net income dropped slightly in fiscal 2013 compared to the prior period as well. It reported a net income of $77 million in fiscal

2013 after netting a little more than $78 million the prior year.

Park National Corporation's cash on hand increased by almost $10 million in fiscal 2013 compared to fiscal 2012 levels.

EXECUTIVES

President and CEO, David L. Trautman, age 53, $775,000 total compensation
CFO Treasurer and Secretary; SVP and CFO Park National Bank, Brady T. Burt, age 40, $325,000 total compensation
Chairman, C. Daniel (Dan) DeLawder, age 65
Auditors: Crowe Horwath LLP

LOCATIONS

HQ: Park National Corp. (Newark, OH)
50 North Third Street, Newark, OH 43055
Phone: 740 349-8451
Web: www.parknationalcorp.com

PRODUCTS/OPERATIONS

Selected Affiliates
Century National Bank
Fairfield National Bank
Farmers Bank
First-Knox National Bank
Guardian Finance Company
Park National Bank
Richland Bank
Scope Aircraft Finance
Second National Bank
Security National Bank
United bank
Unity National Bank

COMPETITORS

Bank of America	PNC Financial
Fifth Third	U.S. Bancorp
First Place Bank	Wayne Savings
FirstMerit	Bancshares
Huntington Bancshares	Wells Fargo
JPMorgan Chase	

HISTORICAL FINANCIALS

Company Type: Public

Income Statement

FYE: December 31

	ASSETS ($ mil.)	NET INCOME ($ mil.)	INCOME AS % OF ASSETS	EMPLOYEES
12/14	7,003	84	1.2%	1,801
12/13	6,638	77	1.2%	1,836
12/12	6,642	78	1.2%	1,826
12/11	6,972	82	1.2%	1,920
12/10	7,298	74	1.0%	1,969
Annual Growth	(1.0%)	3.2%	—	(2.2%)

2014 Year-End Financials

Debt ratio: 4.67%
Return on equity: 12.45%
Cash ($ mil.): 237
Current ratio: —
Long-term debt ($ mil.): —
No. of shares (mil.): 15
Dividends
Yield: 4.2%
Payout: 68.8%
Market value ($ mil.): 1,362

	STOCK PRICE ($) FY Close	P/E High/Low	PER SHARE ($) Earnings	Dividends	Book Value
12/14	88.48	16 13	5.46	3.76	45.39
12/13	85.07	17 13	5.01	3.76	42.29
12/12	64.63	15 13	4.88	3.76	42.20
12/11	65.06	15 10	4.95	3.76	48.19
12/10	72.67	16 12	4.51	3.76	48.43
Annual Growth	5.0%	— —	4.9%	(0.0%)	(1.6%)

Parker Hannifin Corp.

Parker-Hannifin operates on a big scale (its motion control equipment helped sink a replica of the Titanic in the Academy Award-winning film.) Operating through two business segments —Diversified Industrial and Aerospace —Parker-Hannifin is a leading global manufacturer of motion and control technologies including fluid power systems for the manufacturing and processing industries; hydraulic fuel pneumatic and electromechanical systems and components for the aerospace/defense industry; and motion and control systems for the heating ventilation air conditioning and refrigeration (HVACR) and transportation industries. The company traces its historical roots back to 1918.

Geographic Reach

Parker-Hannifin operates 320 manufacturing plants and nearly 100 distribution centers and 150 sales and administrative offices in 40 states and in roughly 50 other countries worldwide. North America accounts for roughly 60% of its sales.

Operations

Parker-Hannifin is a leading worldwide diversified manufacturer of motion and control technologies and systems. It provides precision engineered technologies products and services for a wide variety of mobile industrial and aerospace markets.

Its largest division the Industrial segment is made up of the Automation Filtration Fluid Connectors Hydraulics Instrumentation and Seal groups. Sales of Industrial products in North American and international markets are made primarily to original equipment manufacturers (OEMs) and their replacement markets in various sectors within the manufacturing processing and transportation industries. They include agriculture alternative energy chemical processing construction machinery factory automation food production life sciences material handling paper robotics and water among many others.

Sales of Aerospace segment products are sold mainly to commercial and military customers in the OEM and maintenance repair and overhaul end user markets. They are used in aircraft engines missiles unmanned aerial vehicles and in power generation applications.

Financial Performance

Parker-Hannifin enjoyed a banner year in 2014 as revenues reached more than $13.2 billion a company milestone. However revenues fell 4% to $12.7 billion in 2015. The slight dip in revenues was driven by a 10% drop in international sales mostly due to unfavorable currency rate changes reflecting the strengthening of the US dollar against most currencies.

Parker-Hannifin's profits remained flat —hovering around the $1 billion mark from 2014 to 2015 —due to the decreased sales losses on disposal of assets and increased interest expenses. In addition the company's operating cash flow has fluctuated over the last five years.

Strategy

The company seeks to enhance its operations and profitability through a strategy of identifying and acquiring businesses with complementary products and services and by divesting businesses that are not considered to be a good long-term fit. It also focuses on building up its operations around targeted regions technologies and markets through acquisitions and organic growth.

Mergers and Acquisitions

Growing its global footprint the company completed four acquisitions in 2015 whose aggregate sales for their most recent fiscal year prior to acquisition were approximately $27 million. Parker-Hannifiny made three acquisitions in 2014 for a total price of $19 million and eight acquisitions throughout 2013 for a total price of $621 million in cash. Highlighted purchases during 2013 included PGI International a maker of flow control components and systems to be integrated into its Instrumentation segment and Velcon Filters a filtration systems business with annual sales of around $115 million.

HISTORY

Entrepreneurial engineer Arthur Parker founded the Parker Appliance Company in 1918 to make pneumatic brake boosters. Its products were designed to help trucks and buses stop more easily. Unfortunately Parker's own truck slid off an icy road and over a cliff in 1919 destroying the company's inventory and ending that line of business.

Undeterred Parker started a hydraulics and pneumatic components business in 1924 to serve automotive and industrial clients. In 1927 the fuel-linkage system the company developed for the Spirit of St. Louis helped Lindbergh cross the Atlantic. The company prospered during the Depression; sales reached $2 million in 1934. Two of Parker's long-term clients were Douglas Aircraft and Lockheed.

The company went public in 1938. It employed 5000 defense workers during WWII. After Parker died in 1945 his wife Helen hired new management to focus on the automation market. The firm bought cylinder maker Hannifin in 1957 and became Parker-Hannifin.

In 1960 Parker-Hannifin formed an international unit in Amsterdam and it set up a German subsidiary in 1962. Overseas acquisitions and increased demand from the space program and the aviation market spurred growth in the 1960s. Patrick Parker the founder's son became president in 1968 and chairman in 1977. Parker-Hannifin expanded its aerospace business in 1978 with the purchase of Bertea (electrohydraulic flight controls). Patrick Parker continued as CEO until 1983 and as chairman until 1999.

EXECUTIVES

VP and President Fluid Connectors Group, Robert W. (Bob) Bond, age 57, $517,200 total compensation
President and COO, Lee C. Banks, age 52, $720,000 total compensation
VP and CIO, William G. (Bill) Eline, age 59
VP and President Instrumentation Group, John R. Greco, age 61
VP and Chief Technology and Innovation Officer, M. Craig Maxwell, age 57
VP and President Aerospace Group, Roger S. Sherrard, age 49
EVP Human Resources, Daniel S. (Dan) Serbin, age 61
Chairman and CEO, Thomas L. (Tom) Williams, age 56, $720,000 total compensation
VP Global Supply Chain and Procurement, John G. Dedinsky, age 58
EVP Finance and Administration and CFO, Jon P. Marten, age 59, $611,310 total compensation
VP and President Automation Group, Yoon (Michael) Chung, age 52
VP and President Asia Pacific Group, Kurt A. Keller, age 57
VP; President Engineered Materials Group, Andrew D. Ross
VP; President Latin America Group, Candido Lima
VP and President Filtration Group, Robert Malone
VP; President Europe Middle East and Africa Group, Joachim Guhe
Vice President Business Development, Jeff Vangundy
National Sales Manager Fluid Connectors, Frans Wessels

PBF Energy Inc

Oil refiners meet the new kid on the block. Less than a decade old PBF Energy's three oil refineries (formerly owned by Valero and Sunoco) and located in Delaware New Jersey and Ohio have a combined production capacity of about 540000 barrels per day. The refineries produce gasoline ultra-low-sulfur diesel heating oil jet fuel lubricants petrochemicals and asphalt for the Midwestern and Northeastern US. The company indirectly owns the general partner and approximately 52.1% of the limited partnership interest of PBF Logistics LP. PBF Energy is majority-owned by investment firms The Blackstone Group and First Reserve.

Geographic Reach

The company operates refineries in Paulsboro Toledo and Delaware City sells its products in the Northeast and Midwest US and elsewhere in Canada and the US.

Operations

PBF Energy operates two reportable business segments: Refining (which accounted for all of its 2014 revenues) and Logistics (through PBF Logistics). In 2014 the total throughput rates in the East Coast (Delaware City and Paulsboro) and Mid-Continent (Toledo) refineries averaged 325300 barrels per day (bpd) and 127800 bpd respectively. The total refined product barrels sold at East Coast and Mid-Continent refineries averaged 350800 bpd and 144100 bpd respectively.

Sales and Marketing

The company has product offtake agreements for a large portion of its product sales. The remainder of its refined products are sold through short-term contracts or on the spot market.

Financial Performance

In 2014 PBF Energy's revenues increased by 4% due to higher throughput rates in the East Coast and Mid-Continent refineries as the result of higher run rates favorable economics and planned downtime at Delaware City refinery. That year the company posted a net loss of $38.24 million (compared to net income of $39.54 million in 2013) due to higher costs and expenses as a result of changes in cost of sales; higher operating expenses (attributable to an increase of $42.7 million in energy and utilities costs driven by higher natural gas prices); an increase of $16.1 million related to employee compensation; and $1.9 million of higher outside engineering and consulting fees (related to refinery maintenance projects); and general and administrative expenses. In 2014 PBF Energy's cash inflow increased by 57% due to changes in working capital as a result of changes in accounts receivable inventories and accounts payable.

Strategy

To expand the logistics assets supporting its business PBF Energy spun off its logistics segment as PBF Logistics in 2014. PBF Logistics plans to grow by acquiring additional logistics assets for PBF Energy and from third parties. In 2014 PBF Logistics LP announced plans acquire the Toledo Storage Facility (its second asset drop-

down acquisition) from a subsidiary of PBF Energy for $150 million.

Expanding its operations in 2013 the company completed a second crude unloading facility at the Delaware City refinery that increased its rail crude unloading capacity from 40000 barrels per day to 110000. That year PBF Energy announced plans to add an additional 40000 barrels per day of heavy crude rail unloading capability at the refinery. It invested about $416 million in construction costs to make good on the announcement.

In 2013 PBF Energy signed a deal with Continental Resources for the oil company to supply PBF Energy with Bakken crude oil. The deal marks a shift for the East Coast refinery market – a market that has historically relied on imports of foreign oil.

The company has also inked long-term deals with Statoil as the only supplier for crude oil at the Delaware and New Jersey refineries while Morgan Stanley Capital Group (a commodities-based subsidiary of Morgan Stanley) supplies all of the crude to the Ohio plant. In addition Morgan Stanley Capital Group buys most of the clean products and intermediates produced at the Delaware and New Jersey refineries. PBF Energy is not anticipating any shortage in demand since most oil refineries in the US are located in California Texas or the South.

Company Background

PBF Energy was created in 2008 by Swiss oil refiner Petroplus to help it establish a foothold in the US. Petroplus and The Blackstone Group each invested $667 million to begin buying oil refineries at the height of the global economic recession when larger companies were looking to sell off assets to drum up cash. PBF first bought the Delaware refinery from Valero in 2010 for $220 million. (The low price tag came because the refinery had been shut down since 2009.) Next came the New Jersey refinery again purchased from Valero for $358 million.

In 2011 PBF Energy bought an Ohio refinery from Sunoco for $400 million.

PBF Energy went public in 2012 with an IPO that raised $429 million. The IPO came as a quick turnaround before PBF Energy was able to recognize any significant revenue and the company used the $613 million in proceeds to pay back its principal investors Blackstone and First Reserve.

EXECUTIVES

National Sales Manager Base Oils, Scott Carter Scott Carter
CEO, Thomas J. Nimbley, age 63, $850,000 total compensation
SVP and Co-Head of Commercial, Thomas L. O'Connor, age 42
President, Matthew C. Lucey, age 41, $533,333 total compensation
SVP and CFO, C. Erik Young, age 39, $366,667 total compensation
SVP; President PBF Logistics, Todd OÂMalley, age 42, $341,667 total compensation
SVP Refining, Herman Seedorf, age 63
VP and Co-Head of Commercial, Paul Davis, age 52, $325,000 total compensation
CIO, Richard Loew
Executive Chairman, Thomas D. OÂMalley, age 73
Auditors: Deloitte & Touche LLP

LOCATIONS

HQ: PBF Energy Inc
One Sylvan Way, Second Floor, Parsippany, NJ 07054
Phone: 973 455-7500
Web: www.pbfenergy.com

PRODUCTS/OPERATIONS

2014 Sales

	% of total
Gasoline & distillates	85
Feedstocks and other	5
Chemicals	4
Asphalt and blackoils	4
Lubricants	2
Total	**100**

COMPETITORS

Alon USA Energy	Placid Refining
CITGO Refining and Chemicals	San Joaquin Refining
	Shell Oil Products
Chevron	Sunoco
ConocoPhillips	Tauber Oil
Exxon Mobil	Tesoro Refining and Marketing
Flint Hills	
HollyFrontier	United Refining
Marathon Petroleum	Valero Energy
Motiva Enterprises	Western Refining Inc.
Paramount Petroleum	

HISTORICAL FINANCIALS

Company Type: Public

Income Statement

FYE: December 31

	REVENUE ($ mil.)	NET INCOME ($ mil.)	NET PROFIT MARGIN	EMPLOYEES
12/14	19,828	(38)	—	1,714
12/13	19,151	39	0.2%	1,735
12/12	20,138	1	0.0%	1,612
Annual Growth	(0.8%)	—	—	3.1%

2014 Year-End Financials

Debt ratio: 24.25%	No. of shares (mil.): 81
Return on equity: (-4.08%)	Dividends
Cash ($ mil.): 397	Yield: 4.5%
Current ratio: 1.52	Payout: 28.3%
Long-term debt ($ mil.): 1,260	Market value ($ mil.): 2,184

	STOCK PRICE ($)	P/E	PER SHARE ($)		
	FY Close	High/Low	Earnings	Dividends	Book Value
12/14	26.64	— —	(0.51)	1.20	14.86
12/13	31.46	34 17	1.20	1.20	16.49
12/12	29.05	354328	0.08	0.00	17.81
/0.00	—	—(0.00)	0.00	(0.00)	
/0.00	—	—(0.00)	0.00	(0.00)	
Annual Growth	—	— —	—	—	—

Peabody Energy Corp

In a time in which people still get most of their power from coal-fired plants Peabody Energy is king. The world's largest private-sector coal producer Peabody owns stakes in 26 mines (25 majority owned) and processing facilities in the US and Australia. It sells about 249 million tons of coal annually and maintains 7.6 billion tons of proved and probable reserves. US customers primarily power companies account for most of Peabody's sales and its coal fuels almost 50% of US power. Its operations include coal trading and brokering coalbed methane production transportation-related services and development of coal-based generating plants. The company has also begun investing in carbon capture technology.

Geographic Reach

Vice President strategic Pricing, Dick Braun
Vice President Sales and Marketing, Dan Hartnett
Vice President Information Technology Seal Group, Terry Koch
Vice President Human Resources, Kevin Ruffer
Vice President Business Development Au, Paul Horvac
Vice President Human Resources, Linda Smith
Vice President Supply Chain, Jim Brady
Vice President of Technology and Innovation, Brian Lane
Senior Vice President Marketing and Product Development, Nina Razvan
Vice President Of Operations, Jim Rowell
Vice President Facilities, Barbara Blair
Vice President Ethics And Integrity, Peter (Pete) Rea
G Vice President Human Resources, Mc Fraser
Vice President of Human Resources Europe, Malcolm Lewis
Vice President Tax, Guy Fabe
Vice President Business Development Mergers and Acquisitions Seal Group Parker Hannifin Corp., Achilleas Dorotheou
Vice President Human Resources, Nathaniel Jackson
Aerospace Vice President of Asia, Pui Ho
Vice President Human Resources Mexico and Latin America, Rachel Morales
Vice President Sales and Marketing, Robert (Bob) Mitchell
Area Vice President Human Resourcesautomation and Fluid Connectors Groups, R Crump
Board Member, Glenn Crame
Board Member, Grace Monserrate
Auditors: Deloitte & Touche LLP

LOCATIONS

HQ: Parker Hannifin Corp.
   6035 Parkland Boulevard, Cleveland, OH 44124-4141
Phone: 216 896-3000
Web: www.parker.com

2015 Sales

	$ mil.	% of total
North America	7,891	62
International	4,820	38
Total	12,711	100

PRODUCTS/OPERATIONS

2015 Sales

	$ mil.	% of total
Industrial		
North America	5,715	45
International	4,741	37
Aerospace	2,254	18
Total	12,711	100

Selected Brand Names

Atlas Cylinders
Balston
Bayside
Bellows
Cabett
Calzoni
Chelsea
Chomerics
Compumotor
croloop
CTC
Ermeto
Fluid Power
Gold Ring
Greer
Gresen
Hiross
IPS
Jet-Pipe
Lucifer
Miller
Ross
Schrader
Sempress
Skinner
Sporlan
STC

Operating Groups and Selected Products
Aerospace
   Aircraft wheels and brakes
   Flight control components
   Fuel systems
   Pneumatic pumps and valves
Climate and industrial controls
   Expansion valves
   Filter-dryers
   Hose assemblies
   Pressure regulators
   Solenoid valves
Industrial
   Automation
   Air preparation units
   Electric actuators
   Human/machine interface hardware and software
   Indexers
   Multi-axis positioning tables
   Pneumatic valves
   Stepper and servo drives
   Structural extrusions
   Vacuum products
   Filtration
   Cabin air filters
   Compressed-air and gas-purification filters
   Fuel conditioning filters
   Fuel filters/water separators
   Gas generators
   Gas generators
   Hydraulic lubrication and coolant filters
   Lube oil and fuel filters
   Monitoring devices
   Nitrogen and hydrogen generators
   Process chemical and microfiltration filters
   Water desalinization and purification
   Fluid Connectors
   Couplers
   Diagnostic equipment
   Hoses and hose fittings
   Tube fittings
   Valves
   Hydraulics
   Accumulators
   Cylinders
   Electrohydraulic systems
   Hydrostatic steering units
   Metering pumps
   Motors and pumps
   Power units
   Rotary actuators
   Sensors
   Valves
   Instrumentation
   Ball plug and needle valves
   Cylinder connections
   Fluoropolymer fittings
   Miniature solenoid valves
   Multi-solenoid manifolds
   Packless ultra-high-purity valves
   Quick connects
   Regulators
   Spray guns
   Transducers
   Tubing
   Ultra-high-purity tube fittings
   Seals
   Gaskets and packings
   Metal and plastic composite seals
   Medical devices seals and instruments
   O-rings
   O-seals
   Thermal management products

COMPETITORS

Actuant	Meggitt (North Hollywood)
Applied Industrial Technologies	Moog
Atlas Copco	Numatics
Bosch Rexroth	Pall Corporation
Colfax	Roper Technologies
Crane Co.	SMC Corp.
Curtiss-Wright	SPX
Danfoss	Senior plc
Dayco Products	Swagelok

Donaldson Company	TI Automotive
Eaton	TSI Incorporated
Emerson Electric	Tyco
Festo	United Technologies
Freudenberg-NOK	Visteon
GE Aviation	Watts Water Technologies
Honeywell International	Woodward Governor
IMI plc	Zodiac Aerospace
ITT Corp.	

HISTORICAL FINANCIALS
Company Type: Public

Income Statement

	REVENUE ($ mil.)	NET INCOME ($ mil.)	NET PROFIT MARGIN	EMI
06/15	12,711	1,012	8.0%	
06/14	13,215	1,041	7.9%	
06/13	13,015	948	7.3%	
06/12	13,145	1,155	8.8%	
06/11	12,345	1,057	8.6%	
Annual Growth	0.7%	(1.1%)	—	

2015 Year-End Financials

Debt ratio: 23.97%
Return on equity: 17.21%
Cash ($ mil.): 1,180
Current ratio: 2.38
Long-term debt ($ mil.): 2,723

No. of shares (mil.): 138
Dividends
Yield: 2.0%
Payout: 30.9%
Market value ($ mil.): 16,119

	STOCK PRICE ($) FY Close	P/E High/Low		PER SHAR Earnings	Dividen
06/15	116.33	19	15	6.97	2.37
06/14	125.73	19	14	6.87	1.86
06/13	95.40	16	11	6.26	1.70
06/12	76.88	12	8	7.45	1.54
06/11	89.74	15	8	6.37	1.25
Annual Growth	6.7%	—	—	2.3%	17.3%

PayPal Holdings Inc

LOCATIONS

HQ: PayPal Holdings Inc
   2211 North First Street, San Jose, CA 95131
Phone: 408 967-1000
Web: www.paypal.com

HISTORICAL FINANCIALS
Company Type: Public

Income Statement
FYE: Dec

	REVENUE ($ mil.)	NET INCOME ($ mil.)	NET PROFIT MARGIN	EMPL
12/15	9,248	1,228	13.3%	1
12/14	8,025	419	5.2%	1
12/13	6,727	955	14.2%	
12/12	5,662	778	13.7%	
Annual Growth	17.8%	16.4%	—	

2015 Year-End Financials

Debt ratio: —
Return on equity: 11.16%
Cash ($ mil.): 1,393
Current ratio: 1.52
Long-term debt ($ mil.): —

No. of shares (mil.): 1,224
Dividends
Yield: —
Payout: —
Market value ($ mil.): 44,309

Peabody has offices in Australia China Germany India Indonesia Singapore the UK and the US. In addition to its coal mines in Australia and the US the company owns a noncontrolling interest in a mining operation in Venezuela.

The company got about 59% of its revenues from the US in 2014.

Operations

In 2014 Peabody operated five mining segments (Powder River Basin Mining Midwestern US Mining Western US Mining Australian Metallurgical Mining and Australian Thermal Mining) and a Trading and Brokerage segment. A sixth segment Corporate and Other includes mining and export/transportation joint ventures energy-related commercial activities as well as the management of coal reserve and real estate holdings.

The company's Western US Mining segment is comprised of Powder River Basin Southwest and Colorado mining operations; the Midwestern US Mining segment includes active mining operations in Illinois and Indiana and are a mix of surface and underground mining extraction processes and coal with a high sulfur content; and the Australian Mining segment (mines in Queensland and New South Wales). Peabody's Trading and Brokerage segment engages in the direct and brokered trading of coal and freight-related contracts in Australia China Germany India Indonesia Singapore the UK and the US.

The Corporate and Other Segment includes selling and administrative items joint venture activities resource management past mining obligations and other energy-related commercial activities.

In 2014 Peabody produced and sold 227.2 million and 249.8 million tons of coal respectively from its continuing operations.

Sales and Marketing

Coal brokering is conducted both as principal and agent in support of various coal production-related activities that may involve coal produced from their mines coal sourcing arrangements with third-party mining companies or offtake agreements with other coal producers. In fiscal 2014 the company derived 25% of its total revenues from its five largest customers.

In 2014 75% of Peabody's total sales (by volume) was to US electricity generators 23% to customers outside the US and 2% to the U.S. industrial sector. Some 83% of its worldwide sales (by volume) was delivered under long-term contracts.

Financial Performance

Peabody's net revenues decreased by 3% in 2014 due to a decline in Midwestern US Mining Trading and Brokerage and Australian Mining revenues. The decline in Trading and Brokerage segment revenues reflected lower pass-through charges for transportation costs due to a decrease in physical volumes partially offset by an improvement in net realized contract margins. Revenues from the Midwestern US Mining segment were adversely impacted by lower coal prices and an unfavorable volume and mix variance (reflecting the first quarter 2014 exhaustion of coal reserves at its Viking-Corning Pit Mine). The increase in Western US Mining segment revenues was largely driven by a rise in sales volumes. That growth reflected the impacts on customer demand of higher natural gas prices lower customer coal stockpile levels and an increase in heating-degree days during the winter months tempered by the adverse effect of poor rail performance in the US Powder River Basin and lower cooling-degree days in the summer months. The segment also benefited in 2014 from higher realized coal prices due to additional contract revenues from finalized pricing under one of the company's sales agreements and a favorable customer mix.

The decrease in Australian Mining segment was primarily driven by lower coal prices partially off-

set by the favorable impact of changes in volume and mix. In 2014 the company's net loss increased by 52% due to a decrease in sales higher losses from equity affiliates and changes in income tax provisions. Cash from operating activities decreased by 53% due to changes in accounts receivable changes in receivable from the accounts receivable securitization program inventories and net assets from coal trading activities.

Strategy

While strong supplies and declining seaborne coal prices have tempered near-term expectations the company's long-term outlook for international coal market segments is positive based on anticipated growth in Asia. Peabody expects global coal demand to rise by 700 million tonnes between 2013 and 2016 led by urbanization and industrialization trends in China and India and the new global coal-fueled generation that will be built during that time. Peabody also estimates that seaborne metallurgical coal demand will grow by up to 15% during this period. In the US coal is projected to fuel 40% of electricity demand in 2017. Thermal coal consumption from the low-cost US regions (Southern Powder River and Illinois basins) is expected to increase by 50 to 70 million tons by 2017 as natural gas prices recover demand from other regions is displaced and expected coal plant retirements are offset by higher plant utilization rates.

Peabody is committed to enhance safety expand productivity reduce costs and contain capital to respond to the prolonged market downturn and shape a stronger more competitive company. It focuses on organic growth projects in Australia and the US including expanding and extending existing mines and developing new ones. It is also working to grow its global Trading and Brokerage platform including sourcing coal from third-parties via purchases and joint venture arrangements and expanding its presence in the Asia-Pacific region through strategic partnerships and joint ventures.

In 2014 the company agreed to establish a 50/50 joint venture with Glencore combining the existing operations of the Peabody's Wambo Open-Cut Mine in Australia with the adjacent coal reserves of Glencore's United Mine.

To raise cash to pay down debt in 2015 the company agreed to sell its New Mexico and Colorado coal assets to Bowie Resource Partners LLC for $358 million. In 2014 it sold a non-strategic exploration tenement asset in Australia for $62.6 million and non-strategic coal reserves in Kentucky for $29.6 million.

In 2013 Peabody and China's Shenhua Group signed a deal to create Sino-Pacific Coal Trading Corporation Pte. Ltd. a Singapore-based joint-venture company to supply Shenhua's growing coal import demand with thermal coal from Peabody's global production and coal trading platform.

That year Peabody closed its underperforming Wilkie Creek Mine in Queensland's Surat Basin.

Company Background

As part of this geographic expansion in 2012 Peabody opened an office in Balikpapan Indonesia a seaport city in the East Kalimantan province (Indonesia is the fastest-growing supplier of thermal coal to both China and India).

For better returns in 2012 the company converted its Wilpinjong and Millennium mines in Australia from contract mining to owner-operated sites. To meet safety standards and cut costs that year Peabody closed its Willow Lake Mine in Illinois and its Air Quality Mine in Indiana.

In 2011 Peabody joined with the world's largest steel producer ArcelorMittal to make an offer to jointly acquire Macarthur Coal and its extensive holdings in Australia's Bowen Basin (270 million tons of coal reserves and mines that produced about 4 million metric tons in 2010). Under terms of the deal Peabody was to hold a 60% stake in

Macarthur and ArcelorMittal 40%. Their joint venture was called PEAMCoal. Macarthur's largest shareholder China-based Citic Resources which owned 25% agreed to an offer of A$16 a share. Shortly after PEAMCoal took a majority stake in Macarthur ArcelorMittal backed out of the deal and sold its stake in the joint venture back to Peabody. Through its subsidiary PEAMCOAL Peabody acquired full control of Macarthur at a cost of about $5 billion.

Peabody was founded in 1883 as a coal supplier but began coal mining in earnest in 1926.

EXECUTIVES

Vice President Engineering, John (Jack) Rusnak
Vice President Environmental, Mark R Yingling
President Australia, Charles F. Meintjes, age 52, $550,000 total compensation
President Americas, Kemal Williamson, age 55, $500,000 total compensation
EVP Technical Services, Jeane L. Hull, age 60, $447,292 total compensation
EVP and CFO, Amy B. Schwetz
President and CEO, Glenn L. Kellow, age 47, $800,000 total compensation
EVP and Chief Human Resources Officer, Andrew P. (Andy) Slentz, age 53
EVP Chief Legal Officer Government Affairs and Corporate Secretary, A. Verona Dorch
Group Executive Strategy and Development, Christopher J. (Chris) Hagedorn, age 42
Senior Vice President Midwest Operations, Marc Hathhorn
Vice President Human Resources, Carolyn Sheppard
Vice President Human Resources, Geofrey Woodcroft
Vice President Of Information Technology, Michael Bailey
National Corporate Vice President Human Resources, Steve Callahan
Vice President and Treasurer, James (Jamie) Tichenor
Vice President Public Sector and Defense, Summer Belden
Vice President and General Manager of Colorado Operations, Pat Sollars
Executive Vice President CAO, Sharon Fiehler
Vice President of Benefits, Julie Nadolyn
Chairman, Robert A. (Bob) Malone, age 63
Board Member, Heather Wilson
Auditors: Ernst & Young LLP

LOCATIONS

HQ: Peabody Energy Corp
701 Market Street, St. Louis, MO 63101-1826
Phone: 314 342-3400
Web: www.peabodyenergy.com

PRODUCTS/OPERATIONS

2014 Sales

	$ mil.	% of total
US Mining		
Western	2,825	41
Midwestern	1,198	18
Australian	2,671	39
Trading & Brokerage	58	1
Corporate & other	38	1
Total	6,792	100

Selected Mergers and Acquisitions

COMPETITORS

Alliance Resource	CONSOL Energy
Alpha Natural	China Coal Energy
Resources	Cloud Peak Energy
Anglo American	Glencore

Arch Coal   North American Coal
BHP Billiton   RAG AG

HISTORICAL FINANCIALS
Company Type: Public

Income Statement
FYE: December 31

	REVENUE ($ mil.)	NET INCOME ($ mil.)	NET PROFIT MARGIN	EMPLOYEES
12/14	6,792	(777)	—	8,300
12/13	7,013	(512)	—	8,300
12/12	8,077	(575)	—	8,200
12/11	7,974	946	11.9%	8,300
12/10	6,860	802	11.7%	7,200
Annual Growth	(0.2%)	—	—	3.6%

2014 Year-End Financials

Debt ratio: 45.39%	No. of shares (mil.): 18
Return on equity: (-23.44%)	Dividends
Cash ($ mil.): 298	Yield: 0.3%
Current ratio: 0.92	Payout: —
Long-term debt ($ mil.): 5,965	Market value ($ mil.): 140

	STOCK PRICE ($) FY Close	P/E High/Low	PER SHARE ($) Earnings	PER SHARE ($) Dividends	PER SHARE ($) Book Value
12/14	7.74	— —	(44.10)	5.10	150.43
12/13	19.53	— —	(29.55)	5.10	217.07
12/12	26.61	— —	(32.85)	5.10	273.91
12/11	33.11	1 1	52.80	5.10	303.49
12/10	63.98	1 1	42.75	4.43	258.70
Annual Growth	(41.0%)	— —	—	3.6%	(12.7%)

Peapack-Gladstone Financial Corp.

Peapack-Gladstone Financial hopes its customers are happy as peas in a pod. The company is the parent of Peapack-Gladstone Bank which operates more than 20 branches serving New Jersey's Hunterdon Morris Somerset and Union counties. Founded in 1921 the bank serves area individuals and small businesses by providing such traditional services as checking savings and money market accounts; CDs; IRAs; and credit cards. It offers trust and investment management services through its PGB Trust and Investments unit. Mortgages secured by residential properties represent about half of the company's loan portfolio. The bank also originates commercial real estate construction consumer and business loans

Operations

PGB Trust and Investments which accounts for some 15% of the company's revenues has approximately $2 billion in assets under administration.

Financial Performance

The company reported revenue of $77.6 million for fiscal 2013 up slightly from the $77.4 million it reported for revenue in fiscal 2012. Its net income declined from $9.7 million in fiscal 2012 down to fiscal $9.26 million in fiscal 2013. Despite the decline in net income the company's cash on hand actually increased by about $60 million in fiscal 2013 compared to fiscal 2012 levels.

EXECUTIVES
EVP and CFO Peapack-Gladstone Financial and Peapack-Gladstone Bank, Jeffrey J. Carfora, age 57

CEO and Director, Douglas L. Kennedy, age 56
President Trust and Investments, Craig C. Spengeman, age 59, $250,000 total compensation
SVP Retail Lending, Michael J. Giacobello
SVP and General Counsel Peapack-Gladstone Bank, Finn M.W. Casperson, age 45
SVP and Branch Administrator, Robert A. Buckley
SVP and Senior Commercial Lender Peapack-Gladstone Bank, Vincent A. Spero
SVP and Chief Risk Officer, Karen A. Rockoff
Vice President Corporate Trainer, Doreen Macchiarola
Chairman, Frank A. Kissel, age 64
Auditors: Crowe Horwath LLP

LOCATIONS
HQ: Peapack-Gladstone Financial Corp.
500 Hills Drive, Suite 300, Bedminster, NJ 07921-1538
Phone: 908 234-0700
Web: www.pgbank.com

COMPETITORS

Bank of America	PNC Financial
Hudson City Bancorp	TD Bank USA
JPMorgan Chase	Valley National Bancorp
MSB Financial	

HISTORICAL FINANCIALS
Company Type: Public

Income Statement
FYE: December 31

	ASSETS ($ mil.)	NET INCOME ($ mil.)	INCOME AS % OF ASSETS	EMPLOYEES
12/14	2,702	14	0.6%	306
12/13	1,966	9	0.5%	326
12/12	1,667	9	0.6%	292
12/11	1,600	12	0.8%	295
12/10	1,505	7	0.5%	284
Annual Growth	15.8%	18.1%	—	1.9%

2014 Year-End Financials

Debt ratio: 0.40%	No. of shares (mil.): 15
Return on equity: 7.21%	Dividends
Cash ($ mil.): 31	Yield: 1.0%
Current ratio: —	Payout: 17.3%
Long-term debt ($ mil.): —	Market value ($ mil.): 281

	STOCK PRICE ($) FY Close	P/E High/Low	PER SHARE ($) Earnings	PER SHARE ($) Dividends	PER SHARE ($) Book Value
12/14	18.56	18 14	1.22	0.20	15.99
12/13	19.10	20 14	1.01	0.20	14.48
12/12	14.08	16 10	1.05	0.20	13.69
12/11	10.75	11 8	1.25	0.20	13.92
12/10	13.05	23 16	0.68	0.20	13.39
Annual Growth	9.2%	— —	15.7%	(0.0%)	4.5%

Penney (J.C.) Co.,Inc. (Holding Co.)

J. C. Penney Company is a holding company for struggling department store operator J. C. Penney Corp. One of the largest department store and e-commerce retailers in the US J. C. Penney Corp. operates some 1000 JCPenney department stores in 49 states and Puerto Rico. In a bid to revive the aging chain Penney hired —and has since fired — former Apple stores chief Ron Johnson as CEO.

Following a disastrous decline in the business ex-CEO Myron Ullman returned to lead the company. He was succeeded by former Home Depot executive Marvin Ellison in mid-2015.

Geographic Reach J. C. Penney Company's operating business J. C. Penney Corp. has a presence throughout the continental US Alaska and Puerto Rico. Its supply chain network operates 14 facilities in the US. OperationsJ. C. Penney Corp. is one of the nation's largest apparel and home furnishing retailers. It has about 1020 stores where customers can discover a broad assortment of national private and exclusive brands to fit all shapes sizes occasions and budgets.

Sales and Marketing

The operating company sells merchandise and services to consumers through its department stores and its website (jcpenney.com). The company fulfills online customer purchases by direct shipment to the customer from its distribution facilities and stores or from its suppliers' warehouses and by in-store customer pick up.

EXECUTIVES
EVP and Chief Customer and Marketing Officer, Mary Beth West, age 52
EVP and CFO, Edward J. (Ed) Record, age 45, $642,045 total compensation
EVP and Chief Merchant, Elizabeth H. (Liz) Sweney, age 61
EVP Stores, Joseph (Joe) McFarland, age 47
SVP and GMM Fine Jewelry and Accessories, Pam Mortensen, age 60
SVP and General Merchandise Manager Women's Accessories, Jan Hodges
SVP and GMM Men's Apparel, John J. Tighe, age 46
EVP Product Development Design and Sourcing, Ken Mangone, age 56
SVP and GMM Women's Apparel and JCP Salon, Siiri Dougherty
EVP Human Resources, Brynn L. Evanson, age 45, $487,500 total compensation
SVP and GMM Children's Apparel, Lesa Nelson
EVP and CIO, Therace Risch
SVP and GMM Footwear Handbags and Intimate Apparel, Jodie Johnson
President and CEO, Marvin R. Ellison, age 50, $325,000 total compensation
EVP and General Counsel, Janet Link
EVP Omnichannel, Mike Rodgers
Executive Vice President JCPenney Stores, Tony Bartlett
Senior Vice President Marketing, Debra Berman
Senior Vice President Sourcing, Ron Shulman
Vice President Supply Chain Operations, Ron Harper
Svp And Controller, Dennis P Miller, age 63
Vice President Customer Care At JC Penney, Jane (Ginny) Sanford
Vice President, Eric Blackwood
Legal Secretary, Jo Nolte
Vice President Of Global Product Services, Michael Hannaford
Vice President eCommerce and Digital Operations, Josh Friedman
Vice President Director of Loss Prevention, Stan Welch
Senior Vice President Merchandise and Marketing Integration, Katheryn Burchett
Division Vice President Finance, Kathleen Mertz
Vice President, Laura Sandall
Chairman, Thomas J. (Tom) Engibous, age 62
Auditors: KPMG LLP

LOCATIONS
HQ: Penney (J.C.) Co.,Inc. (Holding Co.)
6501 Legacy Drive, Plano, TX 75024-3698
Phone: 972 431-1000
Web: www.jcpenney.com

PRODUCTS/OPERATIONS

BRANDS

The JCPenney
JCP
Liz Claiborne
Claiborne
Okie Dokie
Worthington
a.n.a
St. John's Bay
The Original Arizona Jean Company
Ambrielle
Decree
Stafford
J. Ferrar
Xersion

2015 Sales

	% of total
Women's apparel	24
Men's apparel and accessories	22
Home	12
Women's accessories including Sephora	12
Children's apparel	10
Family footwear	8
Fine jewelry	7
Services and other	5
Total	**100**

COMPETITORS

Ascena Retail	Kohl's
Bed Bath & Beyond	Macy's
Belk	Men's Wearhouse
Bon-Ton Stores	Nordstrom
Caleres	Ross Stores
Costco Wholesale	Sears
Destination XL Group	Stage Stores
Dillard's	TJX Companies
Eddie Bauer LLC	Target Corporation
Foot Locker	The Gap
J. Crew	Wal-Mart
Kmart	Zale

HISTORICAL FINANCIALS

Company Type: Public

Income Statement

FYE: January 31

	REVENUE ($ mil.)	NET INCOME ($ mil.)	NET PROFIT MARGIN	EMPLOYEES
01/15*	12,257	(771)	—	114,000
02/14	11,859	(1,388)	—	117,000
02/13	12,985	(985)	—	116,000
01/12	17,260	(152)	—	159,000
01/11	17,759	389	2.2%	156,000
Annual Growth	(8.9%)	—	—	(7.5%)

*Fiscal year change

2015 Year-End Financials

Debt ratio: 52.06%
Return on equity: (-30.92%)
Cash ($ mil.): 1,318
Current ratio: 1.93
Long-term debt ($ mil.): 5,360

No. of shares (mil.): 304
Dividends
  Yield: —
  Payout: —
Market value ($ mil.): 2,217

	STOCK PRICE ($) FY Close	P/E High/Low	PER SHARE ($) Earnings	Dividends	Book Value
01/15*	7.27	— —	(2.53)	0.00	6.28
02/14	5.92	— —	(5.57)	0.00	10.13
02/13	19.88	— —	(4.49)	0.20	14.46
01/12	41.42	— —	(0.70)	0.80	18.57
01/11	32.29	21 12	1.63	0.80	23.04
Annual Growth	(31.1%)	— —	—	—	(27.8%)

*Fiscal year change

Penske Automotive Group Inc

Penske Automotive Group (PAG) has lots of lots. The US' #2 publicly traded auto dealer behind AutoNation PAG operates about 180 auto franchises from California to New York and Puerto Rico and another 150 franchises abroad mainly in the UK. It sells more than 40 car brands. Non-US brands including AUDI BMW and Honda generate roughly 70% of sales. PAG also sells used vehicles provides financing and runs about 30 collision repair centers. UK subsidiary Sytner Group operates more than 100 franchises selling 20 brands of mostly high-end models. Additionally PAG holds a 9% stake in Penske Truck Leasing (PTL) known for commercial leasing rental and contract maintenance. Chairman Roger Penske leads PAG.

Operations

As part of its business PAG operates through three reportable segments: Retail Retail Commercial Truck and Other. The company's Retail segment consists of its automotive retail operations while PAG's Other segment focuses on its recently acquired commercial vehicle business Hertz rental business and investments in non-automotive retail operations. The newest segment Retail Commercial Truck was established after PAG acquired heavy-duty truck dealership Around the Clock Freightliner Group (since renamed Premier Truck Group) in 2014.

In 2014 the company sold more than 398000 new and used vehicles.

Geographic Reach

Michigan-based Penske Automotive Group (PAG) rings up some 60% of its sales in the US and Puerto Rico. The remainder comes from its overseas franchises which are predominantly found in the UK but also in Germany and Italy. The company also has operations in Australia and New Zealand.

Sales and Marketing

PAG's advertising expense totaled $93.3 in 2014 versus $82.9 million in 2013. The company conducts its advertising and marketing at the local level as it works to build its retail operations. In recent years it has concentrated on Internet and other digital media including its own websites such as www.PenskeCars.com and www.sytner.co.uk. In many markets it also taps traditional marketing vehicles including newspaper direct mail magazine television and radio advertising. Automobile manufacturers supplement its local and regional advertising through large advertising campaigns that promote their brands and offer attractive financing packages and other incentive programs.

The auto retailer and wholesaler offers nearly 40 vehicle brands with about 70% of its total retail revenue in 2014 generated from brands of non-US-based manufacturers and 70% generated from premium brands such as Audi BMW Mercedes-Benz and Porsche. To its benefit BMW/MINI franchises brought in 27% of PAG's total revenue in 2014 while Audi/Volkswagen/Porsche/Bentley franchises accounted for 22% of revenue. Franchises for Toyota/Lexus/Scion generated 15% of revenue followed by Mercedes-Benz/Sprinter/smart at 11%.

Financial Performance

With the economic recovery heating up in the US and the UK and pent-up demand for new vehicles on the rise the auto dealer has seen its sales and profits climb in recent years. In 2014 PAG reported sales of $17.2 billion an increase of 17% versus 2013. The company sold more than 398000 new and used vehicles in 2014 —around 32000 more than in 2013. Same-store new vehicle sales rose 6% while same-store sales of used vehicles increased by 15%. (Sales of new vehicles accounted for 50% of the revenue mix in 2014 while used vehicles represented 29%.)

Net income rose 17% over the same reporting period to $287 million driven by the higher sales. Cash flow from operations which has been fluctuating over the past few years rose 22% to $366 million.

Strategy

PAG's long-term strategy focuses on offering a mix of mainly premium-brand vehicles and related services.

Considered to be a well-capitalized dealership group with expertise in identifying acquiring and integrating dealerships PAG works to grow its business through regular purchases within the fragmented automotive retail market. To this end the company bought a 50% stake in a group of eight BMW and MINI franchises in Barcelona a new market for PAG. It also acquired locations in Knoxville and Chattanooga Tennessee that year. In 2013 it entered Australia and New Zealand with the purchase of a commercial vehicle business there.

PAG acquired an engine power systems and other spare parts distributor active in the Asia/Pacific region especially Australia and New Zealand in 2015. That purchase was aimed to enhance its commercial vehicle distribution operations.

The company has also completed some divestitures as of late. In 2015 it sold its car rental operations which included Hertz franchises in Tennessee and Indiana. PAG also divested seven franchises including four in Germany.

Mergers and Acquisitions

Growth is further targeted through acquisitions and alliances. The company acquired BMW of Greenwich a dealership in Greenwich Connecticut with about $190 million in annual sales in 2013 expanding its stable of luxury dealerships. In 2014 it acquired franchises in Connecticut and the UK.

On the commercial side of the business in 2013 PAG acquired Western Star Trucks Australia the exclusive importer and distributor of Western Star heavy-duty trucks (a Daimler brand) MAN heavy- and medium-duty trucks and buses (a VW group brand) and Dennis Eagle refuse collection trucks together with associated parts across Australia New Zealand and parts of Southeast Asia. Expanding its commercial truck retail division in late 2014 PAG acquired a majority stake in The Around the Clock Freightliner Group (ATC since renamed Premier Truck Group) a heavy-duty truck dealership with more than a dozen locations in Texas Oklahoma and New Mexico that sell Freightliner Western Star and Sprinter branded trucks. Penske now owns 91% of Premier Truck Group.

Also in 2014 PAG acquired MTU-DDA which distributes diesel and gas engines and power systems.

EXECUTIVES

Chairman and CEO, Roger S. Penske, age 78, $1,200,000 total compensation
President, Robert H. Kurnick, age 53, $700,000 total compensation
Chairman Sytner Group, Gerard Nieuwenhuys, age 54
EVP Investor Relations and Corporate Development, Anthony R. (Tony) Pordon, age 51
Managing Director Sytner Group, Darren Edwards
EVP West Operations, Bernie Wolfe, age 59
EVP Strategic Development, George Brochick, age 67
EVP Central Operations and Financial Services, R. Whitfield Ramonat, age 54

EVP General Counsel and Secretary, Shane M.
  Spradlin, age 45, $474,327 total compensation
EVP East Operations, John Cragg
President Penske Commercial Vehicles US,
  Richard Shearing, age 41
SVP and Corporate Controller, J.D. Carlson, age 45
Vice President Finance, Terry Speer
Vice President Manufacturer Relations, Jason
  Hoover
Vice President Corporate Information Technology
  Security, William Megary
Vice President Marketing and Communications,
  Bud Denker
Executive Vice President Marketing Assistant,
  Cindy Wells
Executive Vice President And General Counsel,
  Walter P Czarnecki, age 72
Vice President Of Information Technology,
  Richard Hook
Vice President Finance, James Harris
Vice President, Jerry Byrd
Assistant Vice President Business Process
  Improvement, Matt Gaor
Senior Vice President Human Resources, Tim
  Roop
Executive Vice President Human Resources, Hiro
  Ishikawa
Area Vice President, Chris Bunch
Senior Vice President, Michael Famiglietti
Area Vice President, Bruce Heath
Senior Vice President Penske Automotive Group,
  Tony Pordon
Vice President of Finance, Jd Carlson
Auditors: Deloitte & Touche LLP

LOCATIONS

HQ: Penske Automotive Group Inc
  2555 Telegraph Road, Bloomfield Hills, MI 48302-0954
Phone: 248 648-2500   Fax: 248 648-2525
Web: www.penskeautomotive.com

2014 Sales

	$ mil.	% of total
US	10,435	61
International	6,741	39
Total	17,177	100

2014 Stores

	No.
US	179
UK	133
Germany	6
Italy	9
Total	327

PRODUCTS/OPERATIONS

2014 Sales

	$ mil.	% of total
New vehicles	8,672	50
Used vehicles	4,947	29
Service & parts	1,712	10
Fleet & wholesale	834	5
Finance & insurance	435	3
Commercial vehicle & car rental	574	3
Total	17,177	100

COMPETITORS

Asbury Automotive	JM Family Enterprises
AutoNation	Jordan Automotive
Autobytel	Larry H. Miller Group
Avis Budget	Lithia Motors
CarMax	Lookers
Ed Morse Auto	Microsoft
Enterprise Group	National Car Rental
Fletcher Jones	Pendragon
Group 1 Automotive	Potamkin Automotive
Hendrick Automotive	Serra Automotive
Holman Enterprises	Sonic Automotive

HISTORICAL FINANCIALS
Company Type: Public

Income Statement
FYE: December 31

	REVENUE ($ mil.)	NET INCOME ($ mil.)	NET PROFIT MARGIN	EMPLOYEES
12/14	17,177	286	1.7%	22,100
12/13	14,705	244	1.7%	18,000
12/12	13,163	185	1.4%	16,700
12/11	11,556	176	1.5%	15,600
12/10	10,713	108	1.0%	14,800
Annual Growth	12.5%	27.6%	—	10.5%

2014 Year-End Financials

Debt ratio: 56.52%	No. of shares (mil.): 90
Return on equity: 18.16%	Dividends
Cash ($ mil.): 36	Yield: 1.5%
Current ratio: 1.07	Payout: 25.6%
Long-term debt ($ mil.): 1,316	Market value ($ mil.): 4,428

	STOCK PRICE ($) FY Close	P/E High/Low		PER SHARE ($) Earnings	Dividends	Book Value
12/14	49.07	16	12	3.17	0.78	18.31
12/13	47.16	17	10	2.70	0.62	16.67
12/12	30.09	16	9	2.05	0.46	14.44
12/11	19.25	12	8	1.94	0.24	12.58
12/10	17.42	15	9	1.18	0.00	11.31
Annual Growth	29.6%	—	—	28.0%	—	12.8%

People's United Financial, Inc.

People's United Financial is the holding company for People's United Bank (formerly People's Bank) which boasts more than 400 traditional branches supermarket branches commercial banking offices investment and brokerage offices and equipment leasing offices across New England and eastern New York. In addition to retail and commercial banking services the bank offers trust wealth management brokerage and insurance services. Its lending activities consist mainly of commercial mortgages (more than a third of its loan portfolio) commercial and industrial loans (more than a quarter) residential mortgages equipment financing and home equity loans. Founded in 1842 the bank has $36 billion in assets.

OperationsPeople's United operates two core business segments Retail Banking and Commercial Banking which both share duties of the bank's now-defunct Wealth Management division. The bank also has a non-core Treasury division that manages the company's securities portfolio and other investments.Commercial Banking which makes up more than half of the company's total revenue provides business loans equipment financing (through People's Capital and Leasing Corp. or PCLC and People's United Equipment Finance Corp or PUEFC) and municipal banking as well as trust services for corporations and institutions and private banking services for wealthy individuals. Retail Banking which makes up around 20% of total revenues provides deposit services residential mortgages and home equity loans financial advisory and investment management services as well as life insurance through People's United Insurance Agency. Overall the bank generated 68% of its total revenue from loan interest in 2014 and 7%

from interest on securities. About 10% of total revenues came from bank service charges while investment management fees commercial banking lending fees insurance revenue and brokerage commissions each made up less than 3% of overall revenue for the year.Geographic ReachPeople's United has more than 400 branches across Connecticut southeastern New York Massachusetts Vermont New Hampshire and Maine. Connecticut is its largest lending market with 27% of the bank's loan portfolio being extended to consumers and businesses in the region in 2014. New York and Massachusetts are the bank's next largest markets with a 19% and 18% share of its loan portfolio.Sales and MarketingThe bank sells its products and services through investment and brokerage offices commercial branches online banking and investment trading and through its 24-hour telephone banking service. The company's PCLC and PUEFC affiliates have a sales presence in 16 states to support equipment financing operations throughout the US.People's United spent $13 million on advertising in 2014 compared to $15.4 million and $17.7 million in 2013 and 2012 respectively.Financial PerformancePeople's United has struggled to meaningfully grow its revenue in recent years though profits have been rising as the bank has taken fewer loan losses as its loan portfolio has become more credit-worthy amidst the improving econor. The bank's revenue inched up by less than 1% to $1.35 billion in 2014 mostly thanks to residential mortgage business growth as well as growth among the bank's other loan types. Driving higher interest income People's United grew its loan assets by $2.6 billion while interest-earning securities assets grew by $201 million for the year. Higher revenue coupled with a decline in loan loss provisions in 2014 drove the bank's net income higher by 8% to $251.7 million. The company's operating cash slipped by 8% to $350 million for the year after adjusting its earnings for non-cash items.StrategyPeople's United emphasizes cross-selling financial products by developing client relationships and has increasingly tied employee compensation to this ability. The company is particularly focused on building its small business lending wealth management and insurance business. It also continues to open new branches and seeks acquisition targets for further growth.One other key element of its strategy involves boosting its deposit assets through its expanded convenient store reach. In early 2015 the company boasted nearly 150 full-service branches in Stop & Shop supermarkets across Connecticut and southeastern New York which comprised 36% of the bank's total branch network and held 14% of its total deposits. Much of this is attributed to a key acquisition in 2012 when the company purchased nearly 60 branches (many within Stop & Shop supermarkets) in the New York metro area from RBS Citizens. People's United already had more than 80 Stop & Shop branches in Connecticut so the deal strengthened its relationship with the retailer and expanded its presence in the New York market.Company background

One of the main goals of People's United has been to build its presence in the two largest metropolitan areas in its market New York City and Boston. One of the largest in the Boston area Danvers Bancorp added some 30 branches and carried a price tag of approximately $493 million. People's United also acquired LSB Corporation and Butler Bank the latter in an FDIC-assisted transaction that included a loss-sharing agreement with the regulator covering all acquired loans and foreclosed real estate of the failed bank bringing in another 10 branches in the Boston area. In 2010 People's United bought Bank of Smithtown which had about 30 branches primarily on Long Island in New York.

People's United Financial acquired commercial lender Financial Federal Corporation in 2010 (now People's United Equipment Finance) which provides financing and leasing to small and midsized business nationwide.

People's United Financial underwent significant transformation in past years. The company demutualized and converted to a stock holding company in 2007 and early the following year acquired multibank holding company Chittenden Corporation. The deal added some 140 branches doubling People's United Bank's branch network and expanding its reach beyond Connecticut and New York and into the rest of New England.

EXECUTIVES

Vice President Corporate Communications, Valerie (Val) Carlson

Vice President, Susan Stanley

President and CEO, John P. (Jack) Barnes, age 59, $890,384 total compensation

SEVP Corporate Development and Strategic Planning, Kirk W. Walters, age 60, $468,461 total compensation

SVP and President Merrill Bank, William P. (Bill) Lucy, age 56

Chief Financial Officer, R. David Rosato, age 53

EVP Marketing and Regional Banking People's United Bank, Robert R. (Bob) D'Amore, age 62, $429,323 total compensation

SVP and President Chittenden Bank, Michael L. Seaver

SEVP Wealth Management, Louise T. Sandberg, age 63

SVP and President The Bank of Western Massachusetts and Flagship Bank, Timothy P. Crimmins

Market Leader New York, Sara M. Longobardi

President Northern Connecticut, Michael J. Casparino

SEVP Human Resources, David K. Norton, age 60, $411,231 total compensation

SEVP Commercial Banking, Jeffrey J. (Jeff) Tengel, age 52, $408,654 total compensation

President Southern Connecticut, Armando F. Goncalves

SEVP and General Counsel, Robert E. Trautmann, age 61

SEVP and Chief Administrative Officer, Lee C. Powlus

SVP; President Ocean Bank Division, Dianne M. Mercier

President Southern Maine, Daniel P. (Dan) Thornton

Vice President Information Technology, Carol Anderson

Divisional Vice President, Ellen Kritemeyer

Senior Executive Vice President; Chief Risk Officer, Chantal Simon

Vice President Human Resources, Ginger Roper

Vice President, Robert (Bob) Massaro

Vice President Information Technology, Albert Sanna

Vice President Financial Services Manager, Cheryl Nickerson

Senior Vice President Treasurer, David Rosato

Divisional Vice President, Walter Kaercher

Senior Vice President Risk Management, Scott Gyllensten

Vice President, Virginia (Ginny) Magnuson

Vice President Of Sales, Jeffrey Morrison

Vice President Market Research, Craig Noble

Executive Vice President Chief Credit Officer, David (Dave) Bodor

Vice President Regional Banking Operational Risk, Sara Smith

Vice President Asset Recovery, Kevin Bowler

Vice President Human Resources, Michelle McNeil

Vice President, Joann Keller

Vice President, Michael Harkins

Vice President, Kathleen Zembrzuski

Vice President, Peter Martinez

Vice President Fairfie D Market Manager, Bryan Kelsey

Assistant Vice President, Deanna Wilson

Vice President, Jon Handwerk

Vice President, Amy York

Vice President Loan Resolution, Matthew Carter

Senior Vice President, Sonja Fuller

Vice President Customer Experience, Michele Gasco

Senior Vice President Regional Manager, Kenneth (Ken) Nuzzolo

Vice President, David Weber

Financial Services Manager Assistant Vice President, Brad Croteau

Divisional Vice President, Peter (Pete) Brestovan

Assistant Vice President, Patrick Talcott

Vice President Market Manager, Jonathan (Jon) Cretella

Vice President Capital Markets, Russ Hardy

Senior Executive Vice President Wealth, Galan Daukas

Vice President, Kasi L White

Vice President, Ken Nuzzolo

Vice President New Haven Regional Manager., James (Jamie) Macdonald

Vice President Information Techonlogy Control and Assurance, Sue Bascom-Erazmus

Vice President Director of Tax, Kathleen Jones

Vice President Market Manager, Keara Piscitelli

Market Manager Assistant Vice President, Alice Baird

Senior Vice President And Director Marketing, Kathleen Schirling

Vice President, Fabrizio Anthony

Vice President Treasury Sales, Denise Lemay

Vice President, Arne Hammarlund

Vice President Customer Service Manager, Joan Foster

Executive Vice President Chief Credit Officer, Dave Berey

Vice President Deposit Operations, Dee Lemnah

Vice President, Kathleen Appellof

Senior Vice President Commercial Services, Kathy Neumann

Vice President, Robert (Bob) Bursey

Assistant Vice President Senior Fiduciary Services Specialist, Eulalie Paris

Assistant Vice President, Read Breeland

Vice President, Robert (Bob) Maquat

Vice President, Kevin Noyes

Vice President, Daniel Reilly

Vice President and Portfolio Manager, Michael (Mel) Lufkin

Vice President Customer Service Manager, Magda Wachel-Florczyk

Vice President Commercial Banking, Richard Iovanne

Vice President Market Manager, Thomas Burden

Senior Vice President, Sarah Slatter

Vice President, Louis Paffumi

Vice President Of Finance, Shelley Colvin

Assistant Vice President Customer Service, Ana Saraiva

Vice President, Alfred Tanguay

Financials Services Manager Assistant Vice President, Andrea Kantaros

Assistant Vice President, Kasey Franzoni

Vice President, Steve Beecher

Vice President Of Knowledge Management, Christine Loxsom

Senior Vice President, Kathleen Lepak

Vice President Real Estate Administration And Business Continuity, Rosemary H Kennedy

Vice President Financial Analyst, Rita Rivers

Vice President Finance, Brian Connery

Vice President Purchasing, Theresa Knies

Vice President, Donna Frate

Senior Vice President Commercial Relationship Manager, Stephanie Pierce

Vice President Corporate Security, Gary Dagan

Senior Vice President Commercial, Lisa Cook

Assistant Vice President, David Schalk

Assistant Vice President Customer Service Manager, Derek Scialdone

Senior Vice President Senior Portfolio, Michael Williams

Senior Vice President, Michael Gingras

Senior Vice President Government, Maura Kelly

Vice President, Mark Judge

Financial Services Mananger Assistant Vice President, Amy Pasquarelli

Vice President Nh Loan Resolution, Alan Byrne

Senior Vice President, Jeffery Paz

Assistant Vice President, Tuyen Le

Assistant Vice President, Bryan Hebert

Vice President Financial Services Manager, Ashley Rice

First Vice President, John Bundschuh

Vice President Treasury Management Sales, Maureen Larivee

Assistant Vice President, Kurtis Denison

Vice President, Bethany Dubuque

Vice President, Lisa Rollins

Senior Vice President, Jody Cole

Manager Asset Management Group Senior Vice President, Russell (Russ) Caffry

Vice President Market Manager, David Cavanaugh

Senior Vice President, Roz Rubin

Senior Vice President Commercial Lending, Tom Wolcott

Vice President, Steven Wurtz

Vice President, Rose Morgan

Vice President And Senior Counsel, Paul Benoit

Vice President Wholesale Lending, William Simics

Assistant Vice President Business Services Officer, Andrea Relkin

Senior Vice President Senior Commercial Real Estate Lender, Suzanne Wakeen

Vice President Trust And Investment Management, Gray Horn

Vice President Commercial Lending, Debbie Boyle

Senior Vice President, Gregory Batsevitsky

Vice President Financial Officer, Paul Feldhaus

Assistant Vice President Financial Services Manager, Jennifer Lynch

First Vice President Senior Credit Officer, Dave Sherrill

Vice President Technology, Mk Mokel

Vice President of Loans, Cynthia P Belak

Region Manager Senior Vice President Commercial Real Estate Finance, Kathleen Hayes

Vice President Alm, Jessie Li

Senior Vice President, Sylvia Mackinnon

Vice President, Darrin Fodor

Vice President, Angela (Angie) Gallagher

Senior Vice President Commercial RE Finance, Linda Tremblay

Market Manager Vice President, Sheldon Berg

Vice President, Timothy B (Tim) Hodges

Vice President Financial Services Manager, Wadie Boutros

Vice President, Michael (Mel) Rispoli

Vice President Retail Market Manager, Matthew (Matt) Wildman

Senior Vice President, Mark Leonardi

Vice President Corporate Finance, Raymond Leonzi

Senior Vice President Wealth Management, David (Dave) Dixon

Financial Services Manager Assistant Vice President, Cheryl Hagmann

Financial Services Manager Assistant Vice President, Alex Slootskiy

Auditors: KPMG LLP

LOCATIONS

HQ: People's United Financial, Inc.
850 Main Street, Bridgeport, CT 06604
Phone: 203 338-7171   **Fax:** 203 338-2545
Web: www.peoples.com

PRODUCTS/OPERATIONS

2014 Sales

	$ mil.	% of total
Interest & dividends		
Loans		
Commercial real estate	354	26
Commercial	351	26
Residential mortgage	153	12
Consumer	73	5
Securities	96	7
Other	1	.
Noninterest		
Bank service charges	128	10
Investment management fees	41	3
Operating lease income	41	3
Commercial banking lending fees	33	2
Insurance revenue	29	2
Other	76	4
Adjustment	(0.9)	.
Total	**1,381**	**100**

COMPETITORS

Bank of America	KeyCorp
Citibank	Liberty Bank
Citizens Financial	Sovereign Bank
Group	TD Bank USA
Fairfield County Bank	Webster Financial

HISTORICAL FINANCIALS

Company Type: Public

Income Statement

FYE: December 31

	ASSETS ($ mil.)	NET INCOME ($ mil.)	INCOME AS % OF ASSETS	EMPLOYEES
12/14	35,997	251	0.7%	5,397
12/13	33,213	232	0.7%	5,429
12/12	30,324	245	0.8%	5,442
12/11	27,567	198	0.7%	5,477
12/10	25,037	85	0.3%	5,198
Annual Growth	**9.5%**	**30.9%**	**—**	**0.9%**

2014 Year-End Financials

Debt ratio: 2.87%	No. of shares (mil.): 307
Return on equity: 5.47%	Dividends
Cash ($ mil.): 971	Yield: 4.3%
Current ratio: —	Payout: 80.1%
Long-term debt ($ mil.): —	Market value ($ mil.): 4,672

	STOCK PRICE ($) FY Close	P/E High/Low		PER SHARE ($) Earnings	Dividends	Book Value
12/14	15.18	19	16	0.84	0.66	15.05
12/13	15.12	21	16	0.74	0.65	14.88
12/12	12.09	19	16	0.72	0.64	14.84
12/11	12.85	25	19	0.57	0.63	14.62
12/10	14.01	71	51	0.24	0.62	14.53
Annual Growth	**2.0%**	**—**	**—**	**36.8%**	**1.6%**	**0.9%**

Peoples Bancorp, Inc. (Marietta, OH)

Peoples Bancorp offers banking for the people by the people and of the people. The holding company owns Peoples Bank which has about 50 branches in rural and small urban markets in Ohio Kentucky and West Virginia. The bank offers traditional services such as checking and savings accounts CDs loans and trust services. Commercial and agricultural loans including those secured by commercial real estate account for the majority of the bank's lending activities. Its Peoples Financial Advisors division offers investment management services while Peoples Insurance sells life health and property/casualty coverage.

Operations

Credit cards and brokerage services are offered through third-party providers.

Financial Performance

The company's revenue increased from $103.7 million in fiscal 2012 up to $104.6 million for fiscal 2013. However despite the slight spike in annual revenue Peoples Bancorp's net income decreased from $29.9 million in fiscal 2012 down to $29 million for fiscal 2013.

The company's cash on hand decreased by about $1 million in fiscal 2013 compared to fiscal 2012 levels.

Strategy

Peoples Bancorp is looking to increase its revenue from service changes and other fees and commissions particularly from insurance and wealth management which are not reliant on fluctuating interest rate margins.

The company is also looking to strengthen its brand and build deeper relationships with its clients.

EXECUTIVES

EVP and Chief Administrative Officer, Carol A. Schneeberger, age 58, $215,000 total compensation
EVP and Chief Commercial Lending Officer, Daniel K. (Dan) McGill, $234,000 total compensation
EVP Retail Banking, Richard W. Stafford, age 49, $161,654 total compensation
EVP and Chief Credit Officer, Timothy Kirtley, $210,000 total compensation
President CEO and Director, Charles Sulerzyski, $450,000 total compensation
EVP CFO and Treasurer Peoples Bancorp and Peoples Bank N.A., John C. Rogers, age 55
Vice President, Rose Nardi
Senior Vice President, Matthew (Matt) Evans
Vice President Sales and Marketing, Thomas E (Thom) Betz
Executive Vice President Human Resources, Michael W (Mel) Hager
Vice President Of Marketing, Brenda Sparks
Vice President Finance, Joseph P (Jo) Flinn
Senior Vice President, Doug Ankrom
Vice President Director Of Risk Management, Ann Helmick
Vice President Commercial Lending, Greg Ullman
Vice President Commercial Lender, Teresa Flinn
Vice President, Steven (Steve) Nulter
Senior Vice President, Michael (Mel) Belville
Senior Vice President, David (Dave) Reitzel
Senior Vice President Chief Financial Officer, Amanda Bryan
Senior Vice President And Corporate Counsel, Ryan Kirkham
Vice President Controller, Kathryn Bailey
Executive Vice President Chief Credit Officer, Charlie Guildner
Vice President Commercial Loan Officer, Adam Rustad
Vice President Chief Credit Officer, Alan (Al) Larsen
Senior Vice President Sales And Professional Development Manager, Roxanne Bilski
Chairman, Richard Ferguson, age 68
Auditors: Ernst & Young LLP

LOCATIONS

HQ: Peoples Bancorp, Inc. (Marietta, OH)
138 Putnam Street, P.O. Box 738, Marietta, OH 45750
Phone: 740 373-3155
Web: www.peoplesbancorp.com

COMPETITORS

1st West Virginia	Huntington Bancshares
Bancorp	Ohio Valley Banc
BB&T	U.S. Bancorp
Fifth Third	United Bankshares
FirstMerit	

HISTORICAL FINANCIALS

Company Type: Public

Income Statement

FYE: December 31

	ASSETS ($ mil.)	NET INCOME ($ mil.)	INCOME AS % OF ASSETS	EMPLOYEES
12/14	2,567	16	0.6%	699
12/13	2,059	17	0.9%	546
12/12	1,918	20	1.1%	494
12/11	1,794	12	0.7%	513
12/10	1,837	5	0.3%	534
Annual Growth	**8.7%**	**31.5%**	**—**	**7.0%**

2014 Year-End Financials

Debt ratio: 2.12%	No. of shares (mil.): 14
Return on equity: 5.94%	Dividends
Cash ($ mil.): 61	Yield: 2.3%
Current ratio: —	Payout: 38.4%
Long-term debt ($ mil.): —	Market value ($ mil.): 385

	STOCK PRICE ($) FY Close	P/E High/Low		PER SHARE ($) Earnings	Dividends	Book Value
12/14	25.93	20	15	1.36	0.60	22.92
12/13	22.51	15	12	1.63	0.54	20.89
12/12	20.43	12	8	1.92	0.45	21.02
12/11	14.81	15	9	1.07	0.30	19.67
12/10	15.65	55	28	0.34	0.40	22.06
Annual Growth	**13.5%**	**—**	**—**	**41.4%**	**10.7%**	**1.0%**

PepsiCo Inc.

The PepsiCo challenge (to archrival Coca-Cola) never loses its fizz for the world's #2 carbonated soft drink maker. Its soft drink brands include Pepsi Mountain Dew and their diet alternatives. Cola is not the company's only beverage: Pepsi sells Tropicana orange juice Gatorade sports drink SoBe tea and Aquafina water. The company also owns Frito-Lay the world's #1 snack maker with offerings such as Lay's Ruffles Doritos and Cheetos. The Quaker Foods unit makes breakfast cereals (Life Quaker oatmeal) Rice-A-Roni rice and Near East side dishes. Pepsi products are available in 200-plus countries; the US generates 50% of sales. The company operates its own bottling plants and distribution facilities.

Operations

PepsiCo's success is founded upon a broad portfolio of mega brands each of which generates more than $1 billion in annual sales. Business is supported by nearly 700 manufacturing facilities worldwide. Operations are organized into six business units: consisting of Frito-Lay North America (FLNA); Quaker Foods North America (QFNA); its Latin American food and snack businesses (LAF) including the Sabritas and Gamesa businesses in

Mexico and snacks maker Mabel in Brazil; PepsiCo Americas Beverages (PAB) which includes bottling and distribution in North America and Latin America and the Gatorade and Tropicana brands; PepsiCo Europe which houses all the beverage food and snack businesses in Europe; and finally PepsiCo Asia Middle East and Africa (AMEA) which includes all the beverage food and snack businesses in that region.PepsiCo's PAB division generates more than 30% of revenue for the company while the FLNA and PepsiCo Europe divisions each bring in around 20%. The company's LAF and AMEA divisions each make up 10% of revenue. The remainder of revenue comes from QFNA.

Geographic Reach

PepsiCo rings up more than 50% of its sales in the US. Important international markets for the company include Russia Mexico Canada and the UK. PepsiCo is also active in emerging and developing markets particularly Brazil China India Africa and the Middle East.

Sales and Marketing

To promote its products PepsiCo uses a combination of sales incentives discounts advertising and other marketing activities. The company spent $3.9 billion on advertising and other marketing activities in 2014 the same as it spent in 2013 and about 20% more than it spent in 2012.

PepsiCo's customers include wholesale distributors as well as grocery and convenience stores mass merchandisers membership stores authorized independent bottlers and food service distributors including hotels and restaurants. The company's snacks beverages and other products are brought to market through direct-store-delivery (DSD) customer warehouse and distributor networks. Wal-Mart is its largest customer accounting for 12% of its 2014 sales; the retail giant accounts for about 20% of PepsiCo's North American business.

Financial Performance

PepsiCo's revenue has remained flat for the past few years growing by less than 1% to $66.68 billion in 2014. The company reported that most of its growth was thanks to higher sales volume from its FLNA business in North and Latin America driven by higher Doritos and double-digit growth in variety pack products; and growth from its AMEA business in the Asia and Middle East region. Revenue from the company's European division declined by $462 million (or 3%) due to unfavorable foreign exchange rates which caused significant headwinds to the company's top-line growth.Profits have also been mostly flat in recent years with net income dipping by 3% to $6.51 billion in 2014 mostly as the company spent more on SG&A expenses mostly related to a combination of higher shipping and handling research and development and restructuring expenses.Cash from operations however jumped by 8% to $10.5 billion mostly as the company didn't have to pay as much in cash tax payments as it did in 2013.

Strategy

Key to PepsiCo's growth strategy is to drive sales for its retail customers by introducing new products and enhancing existing products through more focus on global research and development. To this end in early 2015 the company introduced two new flavors of its Moutain Dew Kickstart brand and a new Quaker Instant Oats Caldo porridge product line across the Philippines. In 2014 the company boosted its research and development spending by 8% to $718 million; indeed product innovations accounted for 9% of its net revenue that year (up from 8% in 2012). Reflecting some success that year the company was reportedly the largest contributor to US retail sales among the largest 30 food and beverage manufacturers.It's also been driving its snack brands to new markets

as it bolts on new and more nutritious foods categories through small acquisitions and alliances. In 2013 Muller Quaker Dairy a joint venture between PepsiCo and Theo Muller Group (a Germany-based privately held dairy holding company) opened of its new yogurt manufacturing facility in Batavia New York. It serves as the national production and distribution center for a premium lineup of Müller brand yogurts to US supermarket and club retailers.

The company continues to expand its marketing efforts to grow more internationally. In 2014 the company launched its largest-ever global campaign for Pepsi and Lay's cross-promoting the two brands in 28 markets around the world. Also that year leading global football (soccer) club Manchester United Football Club and PepsiCo agreed to work together in a multi-year regional sponsorship agreement in Asia-Pacific. In 2013 PepsiCo announced plans to invest $5.5 billion in India by 2020 and $5 billion in Mexico to spread brand awareness in those regions.To improve its profitability over the long term the company also continues to focus on improving productivity by lowering overhead costs utilizing its global scale getting rid of duplication and implementing new cost-saving technologies. In 2014 it managed to save $1 billion in productivity costs and plans to do the same each year until 2019. The company plans to do this through increased automation in operations using more share services restructuring its global manufacturing operations to optimize its assets and resources and restructuring its distribution network among other measures.

HISTORY

Pharmacist Caleb Bradham invented Pepsi in 1898 in New Bern North Carolina. He named his new drink Pepsi-Cola (claiming it cured dyspepsia or indigestion) and registered the trademark in 1903. Following The Coca-Cola Company's example Bradham developed a bottling franchise system. By WWI 300 bottlers had signed up. After the war Bradham stockpiled sugar to safeguard against rising costs but in 1920 sugar prices plunged forcing him into bankruptcy in 1923.

Pepsi existed on the brink of ruin under various owners until Loft Candy bought it in 1931. Its fortunes improved in 1933 when in the midst of the Depression it doubled the size of its bottles to 12 ounces without raising the five-cent price. In 1939 Pepsi introduced the world's first radio jingle. Two years later Loft Candy merged with its Pepsi subsidiary and became The Pepsi-Cola Company.

Donald Kendall who became Pepsi-Cola's president in 1963 turned the firm's attention to young people ("The Pepsi Generation"). It acquired Mountain Dew in 1964 and became PepsiCo in 1965 when it acquired Frito-Lay.

In 1972 PepsiCo agreed to distribute Stolichnaya vodka in the US in exchange for being the only Western firm allowed to bottle soft drinks in the USSR. With the purchases of Pizza Hut (1977) Taco Bell (1978) and Kentucky Fried Chicken (1986) it became a major force in the fast-food industry.

When Coca-Cola changed its formula in 1985 Pepsi had a short-lived victory in the cola wars (until the return of Coca-Cola classic the new formula having been a dismal failure). The rivalry was extended to ready-to-drink tea in 1991 when in response to Coca-Cola's Nestea venture with Nestlé PepsiCo teamed up with Lipton.

Between 1991 and 1996 PepsiCo aggressively expanded its overseas bottling operations. However its efforts contrasted markedly with Coca-Cola's well-oiled international distribution machine. The firm then shifted its attention to the

organization of its overseas network. Roger Enrico became CEO in 1996.

A year later PepsiCo spun off its $10 billion fast-food unit as TRICON Global Restaurants (now known as YUM! Brands Inc.) putting itself in a better position to sell its soft drinks at other restaurants. Also in 1997 it bought Borden's Cracker Jack snack and Smith's snacks from the UK's United Biscuits.

In 1998 it bought Seagram's market-leading Tropicana juices (rival of Coca-Cola's Minute Maid) for $3.3 billion. The firm sold a 65% stake in its new Pepsi Bottling Group to the public in 1999.

Its more than $13 billion purchase of The Quaker Oats Company in 2001 added the dominant Gatorade sports drink brand to its lineup. To make room for Gatorade PepsiCo sold its competing All Sport energy drink to The Monarch Beverage Company an Atlanta-based soda company later that year.

PepsiCo began a major restructuring of its PepsiCo Beverages & Foods division in 2003. The restructuring resulted in four company divisions: PepsiCo International PepsiCo Beverages North America Frito-Lay North America and Quaker Foods North America.

In 2004 PepsiCo approached juice maker Ocean Spray about a joint venture but was turned away by the cranberry farmers who own the juice manufacturer. The company bought General Mills' stake of their joint venture Snack Ventures Europe (SVE) in 2005 for $750 million. The deal gave Pepsi control of Europe's largest snack food company.

EXECUTIVES

CEO PepsiCo Americas Beverages, Albert P. (Al) Carey, age 63, $860,000 total compensation

Chairman and CEO, Indra K. Nooyi, age 59, $1,600,000 total compensation

Senior Vice President Sales, Randolph W Melville, age 57

Senior Vice President Human Resources, Michele Thatcher

EVP Human Resources and Chief Human Resources Officer, Cynthia M. Trudell, age 62

EVP Global Research and Development and Chief Scientific Officer, Mehmood Khan, age 56, $700,000 total compensation

President Frito-Lay North America, Thomas R. (Tom) Greco

President PepsiCo West Europe and South Africa, Richard D. Evans

Vice Chairman and CFO, Hugh F. Johnston, age 54, $845,000 total compensation

President Global Beverages Group, Brad Jakeman

President PepsiCo Mexico, Pedro Padierna

President South America Caribbean and Central American Foods, Olivier Weber

President Latin America Beverages, Luis Montoya

SVP and CIO, Robert L. Dixon

EVP Global Categories and Operations, Enderson Guimaraes, age 55, $746,154 total compensation

CEO Asia Middle East and Africa, Sanjeev Chadha, $675,000 total compensation

CEO PepsiCo Europe, Ramon Laguarta

Chairman PepsiCo Greater China Region, Katty Lam

EVP Global Categories and Franchise Management, Eugene Willemsen

EVP Communications, Jon Banner

President PepsiCo North America Nutrition, Oswald Barckhahn

SVP Global Supply Chain Operations, Rich Beck

SVP and Chief Procurement Officer, Grace Puma Whiteford

CEO PepsiCo Latin America Foods, Laxman Narasimhan

EVP Government Affairs General Counsel and Corporate Secretary, Tony West
EVP Global Operations, Brian Newman
Vice President of Product Development, Noel Anderson
Vice President Information Technology, Thad Lents
Marketing Vice President, Haston Lewis
Vice President Marketing, Curt Fast
Vice President Information Technology, Darrell Harvey
National Account Manager Sales, Aaron Parker
Senior Vice President Strategic Communications, Nancy T Lintner
Vice President of Bottler Relations, Denis Sacks
Vice President Human Resources, Mike Gilligan
Vice President, Bill Woolston
Vice President Human Resources, Janine Waclawski
Vice President Engineering Anheuser busch Inc, Chris VanHorn
Senior Vice President Operations, Richard Delaney
Vice President Global Beverage Design, Moira Cullen
Finance Senior Vice President Paf Controller, Kathy Nittolo
Vice President Of Operations, Gary Murtha
Region Vice President Assistant, Valerie (Val) Matthews
Senior Vice President, Jessica Burt
Vice President Manager Director, Terry Cobelli
Vice President Marketing, Jim Foderaro
National Sales Manager, Jill Griffith
Executive Vice President Flna, David C (Dave) Rader
Gov Affairs Vice President, Diego T Ruiz
Vice President Corporate Communications, Tiffany Novinger
Executive Vice President, Eric Forrest
Customer Management Vice President Walmart, Deanna Jurgens
Finance Vice President, Simon Walton
Executive Vice President Marketing, Mike Minnehan
Senior Vice President Sales, Mario Mercurio
Sc Vice President, Tony Mattei
Executive Vice President Sales West, Vijaysekhar Badde
Vice President Engineering, Piper Thornton
Vice President Of Human Resources, Linda Reddy
Vice President Business Development, Bryan Morrow
Vice President Enterprise Systems, George Legge
Vice President, Sheri Mungai
Vice President Corporate and Commercial Planning Europe, Claire Stone
Vice President, Chris Lansing
Vice President, Stefania Gvillo
Shop Insights Vice President, Scott Finlow
Vice President, Shridhar Kulkarni
Vice President Finance, Eric Brown
Vice President Of Restaurant Strategy, Byron Brooks
Vice President Government Affairs, Phil Swink
Vice President, Kevin Davis
Finance Vice President Bus Cntrl, Joan Horgan
Insights Senior Vice President, Sara LaPorta
Finance Senior Vice President, Paul Ruh
Senior Vice President Finance North America, Cynthia Swanson
Food Service Presell Representative, Ken Serbenta
Senior Vice President Finance, Nick Dalessandro
Vice President Marketing Nbd Snacks, Ruchira Jain
Sc Vice President, Carl Pfleger
Marketing Vice President, Greg Lyons
Vice President Sales, Greg Kerl
Vice President Business Operations, Charles Wright
Vice President Marketing GAMESA, Roberto Martinez

Vice President Of Sales Information Technology, Herb Jarvis
Vice President Equipment, Christine Sisler
Vice President Human Resources, Jessica Tolle
Vice President, Pat Riley
Legal Vice President, Joseph (Jo) Ferretti
Marketing Fin Vice President, Christy A Jacoby
Vice President Of Sales, Bobbie Fetter
Sc Vice President, Tim Purtell
Legal Vice President, Cynthia Shereda
Vice President Field Sales, Richard Tompkins
Vice President Sales, Joel Condra
Sc Vice President North Bu, Craig Eberly
Senior Vice President Strategy and Platform Portfolio Management, Christine Cioffe
National Account Manager Sales, Patrick (Paddy) Golden
Vice President Global Nutrition, Richard Black
Vice President Supply Chain Sales, Mike Schonberg
Vice President Sales, Mike Herman
Sales Vice President, Craig Musgrove
Vice President Sales And Marketing, Michael (Mel) Carey
Vice President and Assistant Controller Financial Reporting, Kevin Gould
Sc Senior Vice President, Myra Franke
Vice President Business Development North America, Hugh Roth
Vice President Labor Relations, Carolyn Fisher
Vice President Global Snacks Innovation, Alison Payne
Vice President Of Finance, Siobahn Milholm
Vice President Global Design, Minda Gralnek
Vice President Finance I, Lisa F Miller
Senior Vice President of Sales, Robertop Martinez
Vice President Sales East Region, Eric Harrison
Vice President Head of Global Brand Design, Richard (Dick) Bates
Executive Vice President Marketing, Craig Denney
Vice President Purchase, Ashish Karanjkar
National Account Manager, Laura Blakey
Vice President Technical Operations, Mary Good
Medical Director Cardiovascular, Maria Afonso
Vice President Human Resources, Bhavna Bhaskar
National Sales Manager Modern Trade, Ismail Sabry
Vice President Of Procurement, Art Schick
National Account Manager, Erin Morrison
Vice President Projects, Bhaskar Choudhury
Vice President Marketing CEE, Dean Robson
Vice President, Carla De Quintal
Vice President Consumer Strategy, Tekla Back
Sales Vice President, Gary Stubbings
National Sales Manager, Tony Huerta
Vice President Multicultural Marketing Pepsi Cola North America, Frank Cooper
Vice President Foodservice Division, Kathryn Matheson
Vice President, Olga Nuti
Rvp Assistant, Linda Sullivan
Vice President Marketing, Suzette Johnson
Vice President Strategic Insights, Laura Jones
Vice President Pepsico Canada, Robert (Bob) Foy
Vice President Human Resources, Clair Niver
Senior Vice President Operations, Joseph Zakaria
Vice President and General Manager of Philadelphia Market Unit, Dave Fitts
Vice President of Manufacturing and Warehouse Operations, Tyrone A Sapenter
Vice President, Tarkan Gurkan
Vice President of Yum Brands, Mike Valdron
Vice President Of Marketing For Atlantic Business Unit, Tammy Sumpter
National Account Manager, Tony Bailey
Sales Fin Vice President, Jim Hathaway
Vice President Procurement, Satyajit Talluri
Vice President, Tom Winters
Vice President Of Engineering, Rashid Mehmood
Vice President Corporate Communications, Jay Cooney
Auditors: KPMG LLP

LOCATIONS

HQ: PepsiCo Inc.
  700 Anderson Hill Road, Purchase, NY 10577
Phone: 914 253-2000
Web: www.pepsico.com

2013 Sales

	$ mil.	% of total
US	33,626	50
Russia	4,908	7
Mexico	4,347	7
Canada	3,195	5
UK	2,115	3
Brazil	1,835	3
Other countries	16,389	25
Total	**66,415**	**100**

2014 Sales

	$ mil.	% of total
US	34,219	51
Russia	4,414	7
Mexico	4,113	6
Canada	3,022	5
UK	2,174	3
Brazil	1,790	3
Other countries	16,951	25
Total	**66,683**	**100**

PRODUCTS/OPERATIONS

2014 Sales

	$ mil.	% of total
PepsiCo Americas Beverages	21,154	31
Frito-Lay North America	14,502	22
Europe	13,290	20
Latin America Foods	8,442	13
Asia Middle East & Africa	6,727	10
Quaker Foods North America	2,568	4
Total	**66,683**	**100**

Selected Brands

Asia Middle East and Africa
  7UP
  Aquafina
  Cheetos
  Chipsy
  Doritos
  Kurkure
  Lay' s
  Mirinda
  Mountain Dew
  Pepsi
  Quaker
  Smith' s
  Tropicana
Europe
  7UP
  Cheetos
  Chudo
  Diet Pepsi
  Doritos
  Lay' s
  Pepsi
  Pepsi Max
  Quaker
  Ruffles
  Tropicana
  Walkers
Frito-Lay North America
  Cheetos
  Doritos
  Fritos
  Lay' s
  Ruffles
  Sabra (joint venture)
  Santitas
  SunChips
  Tostitos
Latin America Foods
  Cheetos
  Doritos
  Marias Gamesa
  Quaker
  Ruffles
  Saladitas
PepsiCo Americas Beverages
  7UP and Diet 7UP (outside the US)
  Aquafina

Diet Mountain Dew
Diet Pepsi
Gatorade
Mirinda
Mountain Dew
Pepsi
Sierra Mist
Tropicana Pure Premium
Quaker Foods North America
Aunt Jemima
Cap' n Crunch
Life
Near East
Pasta Roni
Quaker
Quaker Chewy
Rice-A-Roni

COMPETITORS

American Beverage	Jones Soda
Anadolu Efes	Kellogg
Arla Foods	Kraft Foods Group Inc.
Asahi Breweries	Lactalis
Big Red	Merisant
Bongrain	Monarch Beverage
Britvic	Monarch Beverage (GA)
Campbell Soup	Mondelez International
Carolina Beverage	Monster Beverage
Celestial Seasonings	Mountain Valley
Chiquita Brands	National Beverage
Clearly Canadian	National Grape
Coca-Cola	Cooperative
Coca-Cola FEMSA	Nestl©
ConAgra	New Leaf
Cott	Odwalla
DS Services	Parmalat
Danone Water	Polar Beverages
Diamond Foods	Princes Limited
Dr Pepper Snapple	Procter & Gamble
Group	Red Bull
Energy Brands	Reed' s
Fraser & Neave	Snapple
FrieslandCampina	Snyder' s-Lance
General Mills	Sunny Delight
Golden Enterprises	Tree Top
Grupo Bimbo	True Drinks
Hawaiian Springs	Weaver Popcorn Company
Inventure foods	Wet Planet Beverages

HISTORICAL FINANCIALS

Company Type: Public

Income Statement

FYE: December 26

	REVENUE ($ mil.)	NET INCOME ($ mil.)	NET PROFIT MARGIN	EMPLOYEES
12/15	63,056	5,452	8.6%	263,000
12/14	66,683	6,513	9.8%	271,000
12/13	66,415	6,740	10.1%	274,000
12/12	65,492	6,178	9.4%	278,000
12/11	66,504	6,443	9.7%	297,000
Annual Growth	(1.3%)	(4.1%)	—	(3.0%)

2015 Year-End Financials

Debt ratio: 47.78%
Return on equity: 37.24%
Cash ($ mil.): 9,096
Current ratio: 1.31
Long-term debt ($ mil.): 29,213

No. of shares (mil.): 1,448
Dividends
Yield: 0.0%
Payout: 75.2%
Market value ($ mil.): 145,582

	STOCK PRICE ($) FY Close	P/E High/Low		PER SHARE ($) Earnings	Dividends	Book Value
12/15	100.54	28	24	3.67	2.76	8.23
12/14	97.05	23	18	4.27	2.53	11.72
12/13	82.71	20	16	4.32	2.24	15.88
12/12	68.02	19	16	3.92	2.13	14.44
12/11	66.35	18	15	4.03	2.03	13.16
Annual Growth	10.9%	—	—	(2.3%)	8.1%	(11.1%)

Performance Food Group Co

LOCATIONS

HQ: Performance Food Group Co
12500 West Creek Parkway, Richmond, VA 23238
Phone: 804 484-7700
Web: www.pfgc.com.

HISTORICAL FINANCIALS

Company Type: Public

Income Statement

FYE: June 27

	REVENUE ($ mil.)	NET INCOME ($ mil.)	NET PROFIT MARGIN	EMPLOYEES
06/15	15,270	56	0.4%	12,000
06/14	13,685	15	0.1%	—
06/13	12,826	8	0.1%	—
Annual Growth	9.1%	159.3%	—	—

2015 Year-End Financials

Debt ratio: 42.54%
Return on equity: 12.22%
Cash ($ mil.): 9
Current ratio: 1.49
Long-term debt ($ mil.): 1,429

No. of shares (mil.): 86
Dividends
Yield: —
Payout: —
Market value ($ mil.): —

	STOCK PRICE ($) FY Close	P/E High/Low		PER SHARE ($) Earnings	Dividends	Book Value
06/15	0.00	—	—	0.64	0.00	5.68
06/14	0.00	—	—	0.18	0.00	5.00
Annual Growth	—	—	—	88.6%	—	6.6%

Pfizer Inc

Pfizer pfabricates pfarmaceuticals pfor quite a pfew inpfirmities. The company is one of the world's largest research-based pharmaceuticals firms producing medicines for ailments in fields including cardiovascular health metabolism oncology immunology and neurology. Its top prescription products include cholesterol-lowering Lipitor pain management drugs Celebrex and Lyrica pneumonia vaccine Prevnar and erectile dysfunction treatment Viagra as well as arthritis drug Enbrel antibiotic Zyvox and high-blood-pressure therapy Norvasc. Consumer health products include such leading brands as Advil Centrum and Robitussin. Pfizer is merging with Allergan in a $160 billion deal —the largest health care merger to date.

HISTORY

Charles Pfizer and his cousin confectioner Charles Erhart began making chemicals in Brooklyn in 1849. Products included camphor citric acid and santonin (an early antiparasitic). The company incorporated in 1900 as Chas. Pfizer & Co. was propelled into the modern drug business when it was asked to mass-produce penicillin for the war effort in 1941.

Pfizer discovered Terramycin and introduced it in 1950. Three years later it bought drugmaker Roerig its first major acquisition. In the 1950s the company opened branches in Belgium Canada Cuba Mexico and the UK and began manufacturing in Asia Europe and South America. By the mid-1960s Pfizer had worldwide sales of more than $200 million.

Beginning in the late 1950s Pfizer made Salk and Sabin polio vaccines and added new drugs such as Diabinese (antidiabetic 1958) and Vibramycin (antibiotic 1967). It moved into consumer products in the early 1960s buying BenGay Desitin and cosmetics maker Coty (sold 1992). It bought hospital products company Howmedica in 1972 (sold 1998) and heart-valve maker Shiley in 1979.

When growth slowed in the 1970s new chairman Edmund Pratt increased R&D expenditures resulting in Minipress (antihypertensive 1975) Feldene (arthritis pain reliever 1980) and Glucotrol (antidiabetic 1984). Licensing agreements with foreign companies let Pfizer sell antihypertensive Procardia XL and antibiotic Cefobid. In the 1980s Pfizer expanded its hospital products division buying 18 product lines and companies.

Lawsuits over the failure of about 500 heart valves and the alleged falsification of records led Pfizer to divest most of Shiley's operations in 1992. Drugs released that year included antidepressant Zoloft antibiotic Zithromax and cardiovascular agent Norvasc.

In 1995 Pfizer bought SmithKline Beecham's animal health business and Procter & Gamble's Bain de Soleil skin care line (sold 1999).

In 1997 Pfizer began promoting Lipitor the cholesterol-lowering drug discovered by partner Warner-Lambert; it grabbed nearly 13% of the market in its first four months. Pfizer also launched Aricept Eisai's treatment for Alzheimer's disease.

Pfizer made headlines (and lots of men happy) when the company won FDA approval for Viagra in 1998. The little blue pill became a pop icon and made the company a household name.

When Warner-Lambert said in 1999 that it would merge with American Home Products (now Wyeth) Pfizer sued to prevent the union and eventually succeeded with its own hostile bid. The merger with Warner-Lambert was completed and CEO William Steere retired. Pfizer also sold its animal feed additive business.

Pfizer IBM and Microsoft in 2001 formed a joint venture to sell software to automate prescription writing and other administrative procedures in physicians' offices. Determined to narrow its focus on pharmaceuticals the company in 2002 sold its Tetra fish care then sold its Adams confectionery and Schick-Wilkinson Sword shaving products businesses in 2003.

That year Pfizer purchased rival Pharmacia for $54 billion making it the world's largest research-based pharmaceutical company. Following its two giant acquisitions the company trimmed some 20000 people. In 2004 Pfizer acquired the research divisions of QuoreX which develops antibacterial drugs targeting hospital infections. It also purchased Esperion Therapeutics a developer of cholesterol drugs headed by Lipitor discoverer Roger Newton for $1.2 billion. (Pfizer eventually spun Esperion back off into a private independent entity in 2008 after its development drugs didn't pan out as planned although Pfizer retained some assets and a minority stake in the spinoff.)

In the wake of revelations that Merck's Vioxx increased the risk for cardiovascular diseases in 2004 Pfizer reviewed its own COX-2 pain medication Celebrex. Preliminary studies showed Celebrex increased the risk of heart attack; Pfizer didn't pull Celebrex off the market but did add a "black box" warning of possible cardiovascular and gastrointestinal risks. (In 2008 Pfizer reached an agreement in principle to settle for $894 million most of its pending patient lawsuits alleging that Celebrex caused heart attacks and strokes.)

Acquisitions in 2005 included the purchase of Angiosyn a private biotech working on an anti-angiogenesis therapy for macular degeneration (which can lead to blindness) and Idun Pharmaceuticals which was developing apoptosis (programmed cell death) inhibitors to treat liver disease cancer and other diseases.

That year the company scooped up research partner Vicuron Pharmaceuticals which had two anti-infective (anidulafungin and dalbavancin) drugs under review by the FDA and Bioren which has developed a technology that helps drugs last longer through antibody optimization. (Pfizer divested Vicuron as part of its cost-cutting efforts in 2009.)

While acquiring new holdings on the pharmaceutical front Pfizer trimmed its non-pharmaceutical businesses between 2003 and 2005 including operations it acquired with Pharmacia and its European generics portfolio. The company's animal health division sold off its diagnostics products division (which manufactured tests for bovine tuberculosis and paratuberculosis) to Swiss firm Prionics.

On the consumer health care front the population's increased germaphobia translated into high dollars for Pfizer following the acquisition of Purell. However Pfizer later unloaded its consumer unit altogether refocusing efforts onto its core pharmaceutical business. Johnson & Johnson in 2006 acquired the whole consumer caboodle including such brands as Benadryl Listerine Nicorette Rolaids and Sudafed for $16.6 billion. To comply with regulatory requirements for the deal the companies sold Zantac marketing rights in the US to Boehringer Ingelheim for $510 million; they sold the Cortizone Kaopectate and Unisom brands to Chattem.

As part of its ongoing acquisition strategy Pfizer bought biotech firm Rinat Neuroscience which was developing drugs for pain Alzheimer's disease and other neurological disorders in 2006. Pfizer also acquired vaccine technology firm PowderMed that year and it spent $1.4 billion acquiring Sanofi's joint rights to inhaled insulin drug Exubera. (Pfizer dropped Exubera from its product list in late 2007 however due to lukewarm response from physicians and patients. The company took a $2.8 billion charge as a result.)

EXECUTIVES

EVP Corporate Affairs, Sally Susman, age 54
Senior Vice President Finance And Strategic Management, Bill Roche
Regional President U S for the Oncology Business Unit, Elizabeth (Beth) Barrett
Vice President Worldwide Therapeutic Area Head Cardiovascular Clinical Development, Neville Jackson
EVP Business Operations and CFO, Frank A. D'Amelio, age 57, $1,268,750 total compensation
Chairman and CEO, Ian C. Read, age 62, $1,815,000 total compensation
Group President Global Innovative Pharma Business, Geno J. Germano, age 55, $1,150,000 total compensation
EVP and Chief Medical Officer, Freda C. Lewis-Hall, age 59, $800,000 total compensation
President Worldwide Research and Development, Mikael Dolsten, age 56, $1,177,500 total compensation
EVP and General Counsel, Douglas M. (Doug) Lankler, age 49
EVP Worldwide Human Resources, Charles H. (Chuck) Hill, age 59

Group President Global Established Pharma Business, John Young, $1,040,000 total compensation
EVP Strategy Portfolio and Commercial Operations, Laurie J. Olson
EVP; President Pfizer Global Supply, Anthony J. Maddaluna
Group President Vaccines Oncology and Consumer Healthcare Business, Albert Bourla
EVP and Chief Compliance and Risk Officer, Rady Johnson
Medical Director; Medical Director Primary Care, Warachal Faison
Vice President Manufacturing, Kevin Nepveux
Vice President Wss Specialty Care, Christopher Wohlberg
Vice President International Tax, Andre B Petrunoff
Medical Director, Michael Wajnrajch
Medical Director, Hernan Valdez
Vice President Human Resources, Mario Antonelli
Vice President, Ann Kerrigan-amaral
Executive Vice President, Neil Clayton
Senior Vice President Of Product, Chris Hillebrecht
Medical Director of Drug Safety and Risk Management, Ami Nagarajan
Vice President Medical Affairs, Ivan Levinson
Vice President Tumor Strategy, Maria T Koehler
Medical Director, Jean Chow
Vice President Of Medical Affairs And, Paul Mensah
Vice President Of Global Security, Matthew (Matt) Bassiur
Vice President WorldwideHeadCl, Barbara (Barb) Tardiff
Headquarters Senior Vice President, Gary Taglialatela
Vice President Head of Norht America Clinical Operations, Christopher (Chris) Yardley
Vice President External Affairs and Worldwide Communications, Elizabeth (Beth) Golden
National Sales Manager, Ka-hyun Kim
Senior Vice President, Richard Korsmeyer
Vice President, Leigh Savary
Pharmd, John Ostrosky
Vice President Global Head Strategy and Innovation Primary Care BU, Frederik Bay
Vice President Finance Onc and SC, Peter S (Pete) McGuigan
Vice President Finance Establ Products, Kevin Sullivan
Vice President Operations Speciality and Bio, Simon Orchard
Medical Director, George Sands
National Account Manager, Teri Kittredge
Executive Vice President Development, Shaileen English
Vice President Consumer Healthcare Qo, Moira Griffiths
Associate Medical Director, Nadia Sapozhnicov
Vice President, James Kupiec
Commercial Vice President, Nanette Cocero
Assistant Vice President Clinical Affairs, Sheila Ronkin
Medical Director, Charles (Chas) Tressler
Senior Vice President, Timothy Dunne
Clinical Director, Peter Park
Vice President, Hubert Pouleur
Corporate Communications Vice President, Russell P (Russ) Orrico
Vice President, Jim Hageman
Medical Director, Younos Abdulsattar
Vice President Portfolio And Decision An, Julie Schiffman
Vice President Global Procurement and Operations Manufacturing, Ron Perry
National Account Manager, Mark Desantis
Vice President, John Clark
Vice President of Clinical Supply Chain, Michael (Mel) Ku

Vice President Transferpricing, Barbara (Barb) Gallagher
Vice President Worldwide Technology, Jim Cullen
Assistant Vice President Chem Tech, Will Somers
National Account Manager, Alan J (Al) Hemler
Vice President, Beth Lawry
Vice President Of Investor Relations, Jim Gardner
Senior Vice President Global Regulatory Affairs, Peter Honig
Vice President, Domenica Askeland
Senior Vice President, Carol Carino
Senior Vice President, Kostas Giamouridis
Vice President, Ian Mills
Vice President, Lynne Handanyan
Medical Director, Moh Ong
Vice President, John Watson
Vice President, Lisa Housianitis
Vice President, Bruno Cluzel
Assistant Vice President Marketing New Bus, Beth White
Vice President, Thomas Petry
Senior Vice President, Jaume Pons
Vice President Marketing and New Product Development Japan and Asia, Koenraad Bostoen
Senior Vice President Chief Sales Officer Orphan and Genetic Diseases Research and Development, Kevin Lee
Vice President Sales and Marketing, Simon Hawcutt
Senior Vice President, Kathrin U Jansen
Vice President Of Experimental Medicine, John Lin
Vice President, Tommy Dolan
First Vice President, Megan McMahon
Vice President Global Therapeutics Franchise, Don Kerrigan
Vice President Learning, David (Dave) Davis
Past President Vice President Education Instructor, Micheal Manchester
Executive Vice President Of Sales, Li-ping Chang
Vice President Human Resources, Sander de Beer
Assistant Vice President Glbl Business Development, Kevin Higgins
Senior Vice President, Charlie Hewes
Vice President, Reema Dogra
Associate Medical Director, Silvina Gallo
Vice President, Myra Flanagan
Vice President Leadership, Julian Thompson
Vice President Of Worldwide Business Development, Doug Giordano
Vice President Discovery Research Groton, Tim Rolph
Vice President, Linda Baltz
Medical Director Pcbu Medical Lead, Won-sik Lee
Medical Director, Sonal Bhatia
Medical Director, Wen-Yi Shau
Medical Director Medical Team Leader Primary Care, Katrijn Houbracken
Vice President Human Resources Voc, Kimberly Zerrenner
Senior Vice President Human Resources Gep And Compliance, Don Stewart
National Sales Manager, Samir Botros
Medical Director, Jack Bukowski
Vice President Emerging Markets, Ana Luque
Vice President Tax, William Carapezzi
Vice President, Theresa Oxley
Senior Vice President Ww Safety Strategy, Patrizia Cavazzoni
Vice President, Pamela (Pam) Schwartz
Vice President For Global Regulatory A, David McGavin
Vice President Tax Planning, Joseph Gruber
Vice President, John Harms
Senior Vice President Wrd Development And Strategic Operations, Evan Loh
Vice President, Regina Rantz
Executive Vice President, Karine Gravel
Medical Director Psychiatry and Neurology, Brian Klee

Vice President Bioprocess Research and
Development, David (Dave) Brunner
Medical Director, Marina Brodsky
Vice President, Chewah Lee
National Sales Manager, Gary Ellis
Vice President Manufacturing Finance, Jack
Justiniano
Senior Vice President Of Worldwide Strategy And
Innovation, Kristin Peck
Vice President, Raymond Kerins
National Account Manager, John Bartholme
Vice President Global Procurement, Samuel Dowell
Vice President Scottsdale Operations, Beatrice
Colombo
Vice President Strategic Research Partnerships,
Ronald C (Ron) Newbold
Vice President Womens Health Urology Primary
Care Business Unit, Susan (Sue) O'Connor
National Sales Manager Immun, Simon Goodger
Vice President Marketing, Neil Failes
Vice President Of Marketing, Martina Porru
Vice President Payer and Channel Customers,
David (Dave) Gans
Vice President Corporate and Government
Customers Group, David (Dave) Moules
Vice President Eucan Afme Medical And
Regulatory Pfizer Global Pharmaceuticals, Jack
Watters
Regional President Emea Pch, Tarek Youssef
Medical Director US Medical, Vaibhav Katkade
Pharmacy Manager, Dirk Potgieter
Associate Medical Director, David Witcombe
Medical Director, Jun Musa
National Sales Manager, Beatriz Sanchez
Vice President Finance, Serge Roussel
Vice President, John Hutchison
Associate Medical Director, Krishan Thiru
Auditors: KPMG LLP

LOCATIONS

HQ: Pfizer Inc
235 East 42nd Street, New York, NY 10017
Phone: 212 733-2323
Web: www.pfizer.com

2014 Sales

	$ mil.	% of total
US	19,073	38
Developed Europe	11,719	24
Emerging markets	11,499	23
Other developed regions	7,314	15
Total	51,584	100

PRODUCTS/OPERATIONS

2014 Sales

	% of total
Biopharmaceuticals	92
Consumer healthcare	7
Other	1
Total	100

2014 Sales

	$ mil
% of total	
Global established pharmaceutical	51
Global innovative pharmaceutical	28
Global vaccines oncology & consumer healthcare	20
Other	1
Total	100

Selected Products

Pharmaceuticals
Aricept (Alzheimer' s disease)
Aromasin (breast cancer)
+Arthrotec (osteoarthritis and rheumatoid arthritis)
BeneFIX (hemophilia)
BMP2 (bone and cartilage development)
Caduet (high cholesterol and blood pressure dual
therapy)
Camptosar (colorectal cancer)
Cardura (hypertension and enlarged prostate disease)

Celebrex (arthritis pain)
Chantix/Champix (smoking cessation)
Dalacin/Cleocin (antibiotic for bacterial infections)
Detrol/Detrol LA (overactive bladder)
Diflucan (antifungal)
Effexor (antidepressant and anxiety disorder
treatment)
Enbrel (arthritis treatment)
Fragmin (anticoagulant)
Genotropin (growth hormone deficiency)
Geodon/Zeldox (schizophrenia and bipolar disorder)
Inspra (high blood pressure)
Lipitor (cholesterol)
Lyrica (nerve pain)
Medrol (inflammation)
Methotrexate (severe psoriasis)
Neurontin (epilepsy)
Norvasc (hypertension)
Premarin (hormone replacement therapy)
Prevnar (pneumococcus vaccine)
Pristiq (antidepressant)
Protonix (protein pump inhibitor)
Quillivant XR (ADHD)
Rapamune (organ rejection preventative)
Rebif (multiple sclerosis)
ReFacto AF/Xyntha (hemophilia)
Relpax (migraines)
Revatio (hypertension)
Selzentry (HIV)
Skelaxin (muscle relaxant)
Somavert (acromegaly)
Spiriva (chronic obstructive pulmonary disease)
Sulperazon (antibiotic)
Sutent (carcinoma and tumors)
Toviaz (overactive bladder)
Tygacil (anti-infective)
Unasyn (injectable antibacterial)
Vfend (fungal infections)
Viagra (impotence)
Xalatan/Xalacom (glaucoma)
Xanax XR (anti-anxiety treatment)
Zithromax/Zmax (antibiotic)
Zoloft (depression)
Zosyn/Tazocin (anti-infective)
Zyvox (antibiotic)
Animal Health
Cerenia (nausia treatment for canines)
Convenia (canine and feline antibiotics)
Draxxin (cattle antibiotic)
Excede (cattle antibiotic)
Improvac (swine vaccine for boar taint)
Palladia (dog cancer treatment)
Revolution/Stronghold (antiparasitic for dogs and cats)
Rimadyl (canine osteoarthritis treatment)
Suvaxyn (swine vaccine)
Consumer Health
Advil (analgesic)
Anbesol (oral pain relief)
Caltrate (nutritional supplement)
Centrum (vitamins)
ChapStick (lip care)
Dimetapp (cough/cold remedy)
Emergen-C (vitamin C supplement)
FiberCon (laxative)
Nexium (acid reflux)
Preparation H (hemorrhoid treatment)
Robitussin (cough/cold remedy)
ThermaCare (aches and pains)

Selected Mergers & Acquisitions

COMPETITORS

AbbVie	GlaxoSmithKline
Abbott Labs	Johnson & Johnson
Allergan plc	Merck
Amgen	Merck KGaA
Apotex	Mylan
Astellas	Novartis
AstraZeneca	Novo Nordisk
Baxter International	Perrigo
Bayer AG	Prestige Brands
Biogen	Procter & Gamble
Boehringer Ingelheim	Ranbaxy Laboratories
Bristol-Myers Squibb	Roche Holding
Carma Laboratories	Sanofi
Chattem	Sun Pharmaceutical
Crucell	Teva
Eli Lilly	

HISTORICAL FINANCIALS

Company Type: Public

Income Statement

FYE: December 31

	REVENUE ($ mil.)	NET INCOME ($ mil.)	NET PROFIT MARGIN	EMPLOYEES
12/14	49,605	9,135	18.4%	78,300
12/13	51,584	22,003	42.7%	77,700
12/12	58,986	14,570	24.7%	91,500
12/11	67,425	10,009	14.8%	103,700
12/10	67,809	8,257	12.2%	110,600
Annual Growth	(7.5%)	2.6%	—	(8.3%)

2014 Year-End Financials

Debt ratio: 21.67%
Return on equity: 12.38%
Cash ($ mil.): 3,343
Current ratio: 2.67
Long-term debt ($ mil.): 31,541

Dividends
Yield: 3.3%
Payout: 73.2%
Market value ($ mil.): —

	STOCK PRICE ($) FY Close	P/E High/Low	PER SHARE ($) Earnings	Dividends	Book Value
12/14	31.15	23 19	1.42	1.04	11.33
12/13	30.63	10 8	3.19	0.96	11.92
12/12	25.08	13 11	1.94	0.88	11.17
12/11	21.64	17 13	1.27	0.80	10.85
12/10	17.51	19 14	1.02	0.72	10.96
Annual Growth	15.5%	— —	8.6%	9.6%	0.8%

PG&E Corp. (Holding Co.)

Pacific Gas and Electric is specific about its services. The utility distributes electricity to almost 5.2 million residential commercial and industrial customers and natural gas to approximately 4.3 million customers in Central and Northern California. Pacific Gas and Electric has interests in power plants with a total of 7414 MW of generating capacity. It is also engaged in electricity procurement and transmission and natural gas procurement transportation and storage. Pacific Gas and Electric is the major subsidiary of holding company PG&E Corporation.

Operations

Electricity accounts for about 80% of Pacific Gas and Electric's revenue.

In a major setback in September 2010 one of Pacific Gas and Electric's natural gas lines ruptured in San Bruno near San Francisco's international airport. The resulting explosion and a major fire caused several deaths and the razing of more than 50 homes and damage to another 120. The incident resulted in the parent company taking a third quarter 2010 charge of $238 million. By early 2012 it was also facing more than 100 lawsuits over the accident.

Financial Performance

The company's revenue increased 1% in 2012 as electricity income rose 4% but natural gas dipped 10% due to lower prices. Net income dipped as the company spent more on operating costs.

Strategy

To help meet California's long-term carbon emission requirements and to help meet the ambitious state target of utilities producing 33% of power from renewable sources by 2020 Pacific Gas and Electric is pursuing energy efficiency and breaking ground on new projects. The company is the first US utility that has committed to purchasing wave-generated power. In terms of solar power it has signed deals with Topaz Solar Farms a subsidiary of OptiSolar and High Plains Ranch II a subsidiary of SunPower Corporation to develop 750 MW of high-efficiency PV solar energy. It agreed to buy electricity generated from Arizona's Agua Caliente solar plant from NRG Energy when the plant is completed in 2014. It is also looking to develop wind farms with IBERDROLA RENEWABLES.

EXECUTIVES

Vice President Information Technology Operations, Desmond A Bell
Vice President and Controller, Stephen (Steve) Cairns
Auditors: Deloitte & Touche LLP

LOCATIONS

HQ: PG&E Corp. (Holding Co.)
77 Beale Street, P.O. Box 770000, San Francisco, CA 94177
Phone: 415 973-1000   **Fax:** 415 267-7265
Web: www.pgecorp.com

PRODUCTS/OPERATIONS

2012 Sales

	$ mil.	% of total
Electric	12,014	80
Natural gas	3,021	20
Total	**15,035**	**100**

COMPETITORS

AEP	PacifiCorp
AES	Portland General
APX	Electric
Avista	Riverside Electric
Bonneville Power	Utility
Calpine	Sacramento Municipal
Constellation Energy	Utility
Group	San Diego Gas &
Duke Energy	Electric
Edison International	Sempra Energy
Entergy	SoCalGas
Exelon	Southern California
FirstEnergy	Edison
Modesto Irrigation	Southern Company
District	Tractebel Engineering
NV Energy	Turlock Irrigation
NW Natural	District
North Baja Pipeline	Western Area Power
Northern California	Administration
Power Agency	

HISTORICAL FINANCIALS

Company Type: Public

Income Statement

FYE: December 31

	REVENUE ($ mil.)	NET INCOME ($ mil.)	NET PROFIT MARGIN	EMPLOYEES
12/14	17,090	1,450	8.5%	22,581
12/13	15,598	828	5.3%	21,166
12/12	15,040	830	5.5%	20,593
12/11	14,956	858	5.7%	19,274
12/10	13,841	1,113	8.0%	19,424
Annual Growth	**5.4%**	**6.8%**	**—**	**3.8%**

2014 Year-End Financials

Debt ratio: 26.08%	No. of shares (mil.): 475
Return on equity: 9.64%	Dividends
Cash ($ mil.): 449	Yield: 3.4%
Current ratio: 1.08	Payout: 61.6%
Long-term debt ($ mil.): 15,050	Market value ($ mil.): 25,338

	STOCK PRICE ($) FY Close	P/E High/Low	PER SHARE ($) Earnings	Dividends	Book Value
12/14	53.24	18 13	3.06	1.82	33.09
12/13	40.28	26 22	1.83	1.82	31.41
12/12	40.18	24 21	1.92	1.82	30.35
12/11	41.22	23 18	2.10	1.82	29.35
12/10	47.84	17 14	2.82	1.82	28.55
Annual Growth	**2.7%**	**— —**	**2.1%**	**(0.0%)**	**3.8%**

Philip Morris International Inc

Philip Morris International (PMI) knows how to light up a room. The company makes seven of the world's top 15 tobacco brands laying claim to at least 15% of the international cigarette market outside the US. The company's brands by sales volume are Marlboro (the world's #1-selling cigarette) L&M Bond Street Philip Morris Chesterfield and Parliament. (Marlboro accounts for about a third of PMI's total shipment volume.) Top local brands include Fortune Morven Gold and Dji Sam Soe. PMI's portfolio spans the price spectrum with premium mid-priced and value-priced products. Formerly part of Altria PMI has grown through acquisitions and alliances with cigarette and smokeless tobacco makers.

OperationsThe company operates four segments according to the company's top geographic markets. PMI's European Union segment generates more than 35% of revenue while the Eastern Europe Middle East & Africa (EMEA) segment makes up another nearly 30%. Asia makes up nearly 25% of revenue while Canada brings in the remainder.PMI's other tobacco products (OTP) primarily include tobacco for roll-your-own and make-your-own cigarettes pipe tobacco cigars and cigarillos. Geographic Reach

New York-based PMI's products are sold in more than 180 markets worldwide. The European Union and the EMEA region are its largest markets together accounting for more than 60% of sales. PMI operates more than 50 manufacturing facilities located in Africa Asia Canada Europe Latin America the Middle East.Sales and MarketingPMI products are marketed and promoted through several channels including: point of sale communications brand events access-restricted Web sites print and direct communication to verified adult smokers (via mail e-mail and other electronic communication tools). The company spent $439 million on advertising in 2014 up from $435 million in 2013 and down from $483 million spent in 2012.PMI distributes its products directly to retailers single independent distributors Zonified distribution and national or regional wholesalers. The company also directly supplies key accounts which include gas stations retail chains and supermarkets.PMI's largest factories are based in Philippines Turkey Germany Poland Indonesia Argentina Ukraine Mexico and Russia. It also maintains contract manufacturing relationships with 23 third-party manufacturers across 23 markets. In addition the company manufactures its hand-rolled cigarettes through 38 third-party operators in Indonesia. In 2014 25 of PMI's facilities each manufactured more than 10 billion cigarettes while six produced more than 30 billion units.The company's international brands made up 72% of

its shipment volume during 2014 while the Marlboro brand made up 33%.

Financial Performance

Revenue in 2014 inched up by less than 1% to $80.1 billion mostly thanks to price increases and the impact of the company's recent acquisitions. Its cigarette shipments however continued a steady decline overall despite market share growth in the European Union EEMA and Latin American & Canada regions and slightly higher shipments in the European Union. While worldwide Marlboro brand shipments declined by nearly 3% the company's Parliament brand shipments grew by more than 5% across all regions (especially in Turkey). Profit declined for a second straight year with net income falling by 12% to $7.49 billion in 2014 mostly due to unfavorable currency impacts on operating income and higher interest expenses from increased average debt levels.Cash from operations fell by 24% to $7.74 billion in 2014 mostly due to a combination of lower cash earnings higher cash payments related to exit costs and because the company had to use more cash for accrued liabilities and other assets largely due to the timing of payments for excise taxes.

Strategy

With traditional cigarette sales being threatened as the world becomes more health conscious Philip Morris International has partnered with its former parent Altria Group to transition its product commercialization toward more reduced-risk products such as e-cigarettes. In 2014 for example the company agreed to market Altria's e-vapor products internationally through a strategic licensing and distribution agreement. In exchange Altria agreed to market two of PMI's heated tobacco products in the US. In mid-2014 PMI acquired the UK-based Nicocigs Limited to help expand its e-cig product line further.Meanwhile PMI competes for smokers' loyalty with the international tobacco giants British American Tobacco Imperial Tobacco and Japan Tobacco several regional and local tobacco companies and also state-owned companies in Algeria Egypt and several Asian countries by offering a range of premium mid-price and low-price brands. Its American blend cigarettes Marlboro L&M and Chesterfield are its most popular brands with the Marlboro brand alone making up 33% of the company's 2014 shipment volume. Indeed by the end of 2014 PMI boasted at least 15% market share in 103 of its markets including Australia Canada Germany Japan Korea Mexico Russia and Thailand among others.To turn around its slowly declining profit situation the company has also pursued a number of cost cutting measures in recent years to streamline operations and boost margins. During 2014 the company spent roughly $300 million on productivity and cost savings initiatives designed to enhance production processes harmonize tobacco blends streamline product specifications and brand variants provide supply chain improvements and improve spending efficiency. To this end in 2014 the company made several production-boosting moves including: changing its buying model and purchasing tobacco directly through contracts with US growers through two suppliers (Alliance One International and Universal Corporation) which created better supply chain efficiency; restructuring its business in Egypt to enhance profitability and growth in North African and Middle Eastern markets; ceasing and transitioning its costly cigarette manufacturing operations in Australia to an affiliate in Korea; and closing a factory in Canada.Mergers and AcquisitionsIn June 2014 PMI purchased UK-based e-vapor company Nicocigs Limited for $103 million.

Company Background

PMI is a result of a spinoff from Altria in 2008. The separation positioned PMI as an independent publicly traded company free from its US branch Philip Morris USA. Altria simultaneously avoided an entanglement in various US legal and regulatory issues.PMI has made a number of acquisitions to enhance its brand-rich portfolio and geographic presence. In mid-2011 PMI took over a cigarette manufacturer in Jordan. The purchase followed PMI's acquisition of a cigar business comprising trademarks in Australia and New Zealand. During 2011 PMI also revised its joint venture with Vietnam National Tobacco Corp. (Vinataba) in Vietnam opening the door to licensing the Marlboro label as PMI established a local branch to build its brands.

In 2009 PMI acquired the South African tobacco branch of Swedish Match for 1.93 billion ZAR (about $256 million) giving PMI a leg up in producing smokeless tobacco products and builds upon a joint venture between PMI and Swedish Match to market Swedish style snus and other smokeless tobacco lines outside of Scandinavia and the US. (Altria moved to dominate the rapidly rising niche by taking over UST a leader in the US market for smokeless products including the Copenhagen Husky and Skoal brands.) In the same month PMI purchased the Petterøes tobacco business for $209 million pocketing fine-cut brands popular in Sweden and Norway.

EXECUTIVES

CEO, Andr ⒸCalantzopoulos, age 57, $1,615,871 total compensation
President Asia Region, Martin G. King, age 51, $904,627 total compensation
President Reduced-Risk Products, Miroslaw Zielinski, age 54, $1,013,852 total compensation
CFO, Jacek Olczak, age 50, $1,045,532 total compensation
SVP and CIO, Patrick Brunel, age 49
President European Union Region, Frederic de Wilde, age 47
President Eastern Europe Middle East Africa Region and PMI Duty Free, Drago Azinovic, age 52
SVP Operations, Antonio Marques, age 59
President Philip Morris Fortune Tobacco Corp. (PMFTC), Roman Militsyn
President Latin America and Canada Region, Jeanne Poll ̈s, age 50
Vice President Treasury Planning, Peter (Pete) Luongo
Vice President Information Technology Support Cent, Terry Coates
Vice President Supply Chain, Hafed Belhadj
Vice President Finance, Andreas Kurali
Vice President Contributions and External Labor Policy, Jennifer (Jen) Goodale
Vice President Global Government Affairs, John Scruggs
Vice President And Associate General Counsel, Steven Rissman
Senior Vice President Corporate Affairs, Jeanne Polles
Chairman, Louis C. Camilleri, age 60
Board Member, Werner Geissler
Auditors: PricewaterhouseCoopers SA

LOCATIONS

HQ: Philip Morris International Inc
120 Park Avenue, New York, NY 10017
Phone: 917 663-2000 **Fax:** 917 663-5372
Web: www.pmi.com

PRODUCTS/OPERATIONS

Selected Brands
Local brands
Apollo-Soyuz (Russia)
Assos (Greece)
Belmont (Canada)
Best (Serbia)
Boston (Colombia)
Canadian Classics (Canada)
Champion (Philippines)
Classic (Serbia)
Delicados (Mexico)
Diana (Italy)
Dji Sam Soe (Indonesia)
f6 (Germany)
Fortune (Philippines)
Hope (Philippines)
Morven Gold (Pakistan)
Number 7 (Canada)
Optima (Russia)
Petra (Czech Republic and Slovakia)
Sampoema A (Indonesia)
Sampoema Kretek (Indonesia)
Mid-price brands
L&M
Chesterfield
Other international brands
Benson & Hedges
Bond Street
Lark
Muratti
Next
Philip Morris
Red & White
Premium-price
Marlboro
Merit
Parliament
Virginia Slims
Other tobacco products
Interval (France)
Petter?es (Norway and Sweden)
Swedish Match snus smokefree tobacco

2014 Shipment Volumes

	% of total
International brands	72
Local brands	28
Total	**100**

COMPETITORS

British American Tobacco	Japan Tobacco
Gudang Garam	Reemtsma Cigarettenfabriken
Imperial Tobacco	

HISTORICAL FINANCIALS
Company Type: Public

Income Statement
FYE: December 31

	REVENUE ($ mil.)	NET INCOME ($ mil.)	NET PROFIT MARGIN	EMPLOYEES
12/14	80,106	7,493	9.4%	82,500
12/13	80,029	8,576	10.7%	91,100
12/12	77,393	8,800	11.4%	87,100
12/11	76,346	8,591	11.3%	78,100
12/10	67,713	7,259	10.7%	78,300
Annual Growth	**4.3%**	**0.8%**	**—**	**1.3%**

2014 Year-End Financials

Debt ratio: 83.71%	No. of shares (mil.): 1,546
Return on equity: —	Dividends
Cash ($ mil.): 1,682	Yield: 4.7%
Current ratio: 1.02	Payout: 78.0%
Long-term debt ($ mil.): 26,929	Market value ($ mil.): 125,995

	STOCK PRICE ($) FY Close	P/E High/Low	PER SHARE ($) Earnings	Dividends	Book Value
12/14	81.45	19 16	4.76	3.88	(8.16)
12/13	87.13	18 16	5.26	3.58	(4.89)
12/12	83.64	18 14	5.17	3.24	(2.10)
12/11	78.48	16 12	4.85	2.82	0.13
12/10	58.53	15 11	3.92	2.44	1.95
Annual Growth	**8.6%**	**— —**	**5.0%**	**12.3%**	**—**

Phillips 66

Phillips 66 is one of the largest independent refiners in the US and the world by sales (though rival Valero Energy leads it by capacity). The company has global refining and marketing midstream and chemical operations. It has a crude processing capacity of more than 3.6 million barrels per day and it sells fuel at about 8600 retail outlets in the US and Europe under such brands as 76 Conoco JET and Phillips 66. Its midstream business handles natural gas gathering and processing partly through DCP Midstream a joint venture with Spectra Energy. Phillips 66's chemicals business is conducted through CPChem a joint venture with Chevron.

Geographic Reach

Phillips 66 operates primarily in the US but also in Europe (UK and Germany) and Asia. In 2014 the company got about 69% of its revenues from the US and 18% from Europe.

CPChem has manufacturing plants in Belgium China Colombia Qatar Saudi Arabia Singapore South Korea and the US.

Sales and Marketing

The company markets gasoline diesel and aviation fuel through 8600 marketer-owned or -supplied outlets in 48 US states. Its wholesales through a network of marketers operating 7000 outlets on both a branded and unbranded basis. Most of its branded marketing sales are made in the Midcontinent Rockies and West Coast regions where its wholesale marketing operations can efficiently access its refineries. It also sells aviation gasoline and jet fuel at about 900 Phillips 66-branded locations in the US.

It has marketing operations (primarily owned leased or joint venture retail sites) in five European countries. It markets retail and wholesale products in Austria Germany and the UK under the JET brand. A joint venture markets products in Switzerland under the Coop brand name. Phillips 66 also markets aviation fuels LPG heating oil's transportation fuels marine bunker fuels bitumen and fuel coke specialty products to commercial customers and into the bulk or spot market in Austria Germany Ireland Switzerland and the UK.

The company has held brand-licensing agreements with 700 sites. Its refined products are marketed on both a branded and unbranded basis.

The advertisement expenses in the year 2014 2013 and 2012 are $70 $68 and $57 respectively.

Financial Performance

In 2014 Phillips 66's net sales decreased by 6% due to lower crude oil and petroleum product prices. The chemical segment revenue decreased by 22% due to lower ethylene and polyethylene sales volumes and increased costs related to the a fire at its Port Arthur facility.Midstream segment revenues dropped by 9% due to lower DCP Midstream sales stemming from a decrease in NGL and crude prices. Net income increased rose by almost 28% in 2014 due to lower expenses of purchased crude oil and products (because of lower prices) and income from discontinued operations offset by selling general and administrative expenses. Income from discontinued operations increased by $645 million due to the completion of Phillips Specialty Products Inc. deal (sold to Berkshire Hathaway) share exchange. Selling general and administrative expenses increased due to additional fees under marketing consignment fuels agreements as well as costs associated with acquisitions.In 2014 Phillips 66's net cash provided by operating activities decreased by 41% due to an increase in inventories change in accounts and notes receivable and accounts payable.

Strategy

Though the company's refining capacity is huge it may be looking long term to reduce its business in that area. The higher margin pipeline and chemicals businesses are being groomed for growth while the company has closed and sold several refining plants. It has announced plans to more than double what it spends on chemicals and pipelines. Wall Street valuates pipeline companies at eight times earnings (before interest tax depreciation and amortization) while refiners get 3% below. Global demand for chemicals is expected to increase and the industry is benefiting from lower prices for natural gas.

In the short term Phillips 66 is focusing on four strategic areas: Improving refinery output; Improving its lower cost crude runs in its refineries by expanding its truck rail rack and marine capability to deliver such crude to its refineries; Controlling costs and expenses; and Funding growth to bring in better returns.

In 2014 it teamed up with Energy Transfer Partners to form two joint ventures to develop the Dakota Access Pipeline and Energy Transfer Crude Oil Pipeline projects. The projects will allow Phillips 66 to increase its access to North American crude oil assets and build momentum in its midstream business are expected to begin commercial operations in 2016.

In 2013 the company formed Phillips 66 Partners a master limited partnership to own operate develop and acquire primarily fee-based crude oil refined petroleum product and NGL pipelines and terminals as well as other transportation and midstream assets.

As part of a push to secure a greater supply of lower cost crude for it refineries in 2013 Phillips 66 signed a five-year contract with Global Partners under which Global will use its rail transloading logistics and transportation system to deliver crude oil from the Bakken region of North Dakota to the Phillips 66 Bayway refinery in New Jersey.

As part of a reorganization in 2013 the company sold Phillips Specialty Products Inc. (a flow improver business) to Berkshire Hathaway.

Company Background

ConocoPhillips one of the largest oil companies in the US completed the spinoff of its refineries pipelines and chemicals division into a new company called Phillip 66 in May 2012. Phillips 66 became the newest heavyweight in independent US refining —similar in size to Valero Energy and roughly twice the size of Marathon Petroleum.

In 2012 it invested $459 million to acquire from DCP Midstream a one-third ownership in DCP Sand Hills Pipeline LLC and DCP Southern Hills Pipeline LLC. To raise cash to pay down debt in 2012 ConocoPhillips sold its refinery in Trainer Pennsylvania for $229 million. In 2011 it also sold its refinery in Wilhelmshaven Germany its Seaway Products Pipeline Company to DCP Midstream and its Colonial Pipeline Company and Seaway Crude Pipeline Company.

EXECUTIVES

EVP Finance and CFO, Greg G. Maxwell, age 58, $714,286 total compensation
Chairman and CEO, Greg C. Garland, age 58, $1,510,427 total compensation
EVP Refining, Lawrence M. (Larry) Ziemba, $674,396 total compensation
EVP Midstream, Robert A. (Bob) Herman, age 57
VP Technology, Merl R. Lindstrom
President, Tim G. Taylor, age 61, $888,188 total compensation
EVP Legal General Counsel and Corporate Secretary, Paula A. Johnson, $596,676 total compensation

EVP Investor Relations Strategy Corporate and Government Affairs, C.Clayton (C.C.) Reasor
Vice President Communications and Public Affairs, Ann Oglesby
Senior Vice President Hse Projects and Procurement, Deborah (Deb) Adams
Employee Excellence VPP Coordinator, Jerry Manning
VPP Coordinator, Ivory Broussard
VPP Maintenance Coordinator, Joe Garcia
VPP Maintenance Coordinator, Crystal Stewart
Vice President Global Trading Commercial, Maria Hooper
Vice President Strategic Development, Ben Hur
Senior Vice President Investor Relations Strategy And Corporate Relations, Clayton Reasor
Senior Vice President Commercial, W John
Vice President Treasurer, Brian Wenzel
Auditors: Ernst & Young LLP

LOCATIONS

HQ: Phillips 66
  3010 Briarpark Drive, Houston, TX 77042
Phone: 281 293-6600
Web: www.Phillips66.com

2014 Sales

	% of total
US	69
UK	12
Germany	6
Other countries	13
Total	**100**

PRODUCTS/OPERATIONS

2014 Sales

	$ mil.	% of total
Marketing and Specialities	108,992	66
Refining	47,063	29
Midstream	5,118	3
Chemicals	7	-
Corporate and Other	32	-
Equity in earnings of affiliates	2,466	2
Net gains of dispositions	295	-
Other income	120	-
Total	**164,093**	**100**

Selected Brands

76
Conoco
Coop
Copylene
CPreme
E-Gas
JET
Kendall
Liquid Power
Phillips 66

COMPETITORS

ADM	Motiva Enterprises
Aventine	National Cooperative
BP	Refinery Association
CITGO	Shell Oil Products
Chevron	Sinclair Oil
Exxon Mobil	Sunoco
Green Brick Partners	TOTAL
Hess Corporation	Tesoro
HollyFrontier	Valero Energy
Marathon Petroleum	

HISTORICAL FINANCIALS

Company Type: Public

Income Statement

FYE: December 31

	REVENUE ($ mil.)	NET INCOME ($ mil.)	NET PROFIT MARGIN	EMPLOYEES
12/14	164,093	4,762	2.9%	14,000
12/13	174,809	3,726	2.1%	13,500
12/12	182,922	4,124	2.3%	13,500
12/11	200,614	4,775	2.4%	12,400
12/10	148,656	735	0.5%	—
Annual Growth	**2.5%**	**59.5%**	**—**	**—**

2014 Year-End Financials

Debt ratio: 17.82%
Return on equity: 21.87%
Cash ($ mil.): 5,207
Current ratio: 1.50
Long-term debt ($ mil.): 7,842

No. of shares (mil.): 546
Dividends
  Yield: 2.6%
  Payout: 24.7%
Market value ($ mil.): 39,176

	STOCK PRICE ($) FY Close	P/E High/Low		PER SHARE ($) Earnings	Dividends	Book Value
12/14	71.70	10	8	8.33	1.89	39.51
12/13	77.13	12	8	6.02	1.33	37.19
12/12	53.10	8	4	6.48	0.45	33.32
Annual Growth	**7.8%**	**—**	**—**	**6.5%**	**43.2%**	**4.4%**

Phoenix Companies, Inc. (The)

Fiscal firestorms might reduce assets to ashes but The Phoenix Companies gives its customers a chance to rise again. The holding company's primary subsidiary Phoenix Life Insurance offers life insurance annuities and a hybrid of the two it calls "alternative retirement solutions." Historically the company targeted wealthy individuals and institutions but it is newly focused on the merely secure. The Phoenix Companies' distribution arm Saybrus Partners wholesales its products which are sold through third-party agents brokers and financial planning firms. Phoenix has about $5.5 billion in funds under management.

Operations

The company operates through two business segments - Life and Annuity and Saybrus. Life and Annuity includes its eponymous segments as well as the the company's closed block of business that's in run-off. Saybrus offers life insurance and consulting to Phoenix's partner's financial advisors at bankers brokers and insurance retailers. The segment also supports the company's independent distribution organizations.

Geographic Reach

Like many insurance companies Phoenix has its headquarters in Hartford Connecticut; key subsidiary Phoenix Life Insurance offices in East Greenbush New York.

Sales and Marketing

Phoenix targets customers who are age 50 or older with investable assets of $500000 or more.

The company uses independent agents to sell its products.Financial PerformancePhoenix has reported several years of declining revenue including 2013 when it dropped another 4% from $1.8 billion to $1.7 billion as premiums declined due to fewer policies in force. After a 2012 drop in net income the company reported an increase that took the company from net loss to net income. The $5.1 million net income was from a decline in policy benefits. Company BackgroundAfter a hundred years as a mutual company Phoenix demutualized and went public in 2001. Marketing partner State Farm holds 5% of the company's shares but has suspended sales of Phoenix products.

EXECUTIVES

Vice President Information Technology, Terry Davis
Vice President Corporate Finance, Allison Gomes
Second Vp-life Annuity, Nancy Turner
Evp And Chief Administrative Officer, Jody A Beresin
Vp-enterprises Services, Joleen Speight
Vice President Investor Relations, Naomi Kleinman
Assistant Vice President And Senior Compliance Off, Doreen Bonner
Managing Director Institutional Business Development Phoenix Investment Partners, James V (Jamie) Hilger
Vice President, Paula Kern
Vice President, Abbey Mcdermott
Auditors: KPMG LLP

LOCATIONS

HQ: Phoenix Companies, Inc. (The)
One American Row, Hartford, CT 06102-5056
Phone: 860 403-5000
Web: www.phoenixwm.com

PRODUCTS/OPERATIONS

2013 Revenues

	$ mil.	% of total
Net investment income	787	46
Fee income	551	32
Premiums	351	21
Investment gain	21	1
Total	**1,711**	**100**

Selected ProductsAnnuitiesFixed AnnuitiesSingle Premium Immediate AnnuitiesVariable AnnuitiesLife InsuranceWhole LifeUniversal LifeIndexed Universal LifeVariable Universal Life

COMPETITORS

AEGON USA	MassMutual
AXA Financial	MetLife
Allstate	Nationwide
CNA Financial	New York Life
Great American Financial Resources	Northwestern Mutual Principal Financial
John Hancock Financial Services	Prudential The Hartford

HISTORICAL FINANCIALS

Company Type: Public

Income Statement

FYE: December 31

	ASSETS ($ mil.)	NET INCOME ($ mil.)	INCOME AS % OF ASSETS	EMPLOYEES
12/14	21,745	(213)	—	640
12/13	21,624	5	0.0%	620
12/12	21,629	(168)	—	600
12/11	21,439	8	0.0%	600
12/10	21,076	(12)	—	625
Annual Growth	**0.8%**	**—**		**0.6%**

2014 Year-End Financials

Debt ratio: 1.74%
Return on equity: (-47.40%)
Cash ($ mil.): 450
Current ratio: —
Long-term debt ($ mil.): —
No. of shares (mil.): 5
Dividends
 Yield: —
 Payout: —
Market value ($ mil.): 399

	STOCK PRICE ($) FY Close	P/E High/Low		PER SHARE ($) Earnings	Dividends	Book Value
12/14	68.87	—	—	(37.09)	0.00	56.31
12/13	61.40	68	28	0.88	0.00	100.53
12/12	24.73	—	—	(29.20)	0.00	88.39
12/11	1.68	2	1	1.40	0.00	193.67
12/10	2.54	—	—	(2.20)	0.00	199.05
Annual Growth	**128.2%**	**—**	**—**	**—**		**—(27.1%)**

Pilgrims Pride Corp.

Pilgrim's Pride couldn't be blamed if it spread its tail feathers and did a barnyard strut. As one of the world's top chicken processors it boasts operations in the US Mexico and Puerto Rico in breeding hatching raising processing and distributing chicken. The company sells prepared poultry products under the Pilgrim's Pride and EatWellStayHealthy labels to retail food outlets distributors and food service operators. It sells fresh frozen value-added prepared chicken and deli products. In addition to producing 10.2 billion pounds of live chicken annually Pilgrim's Pride also produces table eggs and chicken by-products for use as animal feed. The company is majority owned by Brazil's JBS.

Operations

The company operates its business in a dozen US states Mexico and Puerto Rico. (For reporting purposes Pilgrim's Pride rolls its sales from Puerto Rico into its US business segment.) The poultry producer operates 27 fresh processing plants eight prepared foods cook plants five fresh processing plant in Puerto Rico three processing plants in Mexico and distribution centers inlcuding 13 in Mexico and one in Puerto Rico.

Pilgrim's Pride generates approximately 90% of its sales by processing 6.9 billion pounds of dressed chicken. The chicken processor operates 28 feed mills 36 hatcheries processing plants and distribution centers in more than a dozen states in the US as well as in Puerto Rico and Mexico. It also owns a small pork-raising operation acquired during the Gold Kist acquisition.

Geographic Reach

Colorado-based Pilgrim's Pride rings up about 80% of its sales in the US. Mexico is next with 13%. The company exports its products to about 100 countries worldwide; its key foreign export markets include Eastern Europe (including Russia) the Far East (including China) and Mexico. It is the #2 poultry company in Mexico (behind Bochco).

Sales and Marketing

Pilgrim's Pride which exports its products to customers in some 95countries (including Mexico) It's two biggest customers accounted for about 15% of sales. The company targets the food service industry primarily chain restaurants and food processors such as YUM! Brands Burger King Wendy's and Chick-fil-A as well as retail customers the likes of grocery store chains Wal-Mart Kroger and Publix and wholesale clubs Costco and Sam's Club.

Financial Performance

Net sales for Pilgrim's Pride rose 2% in 2014 versus 2013 to $8.58 billion while net income jumped 29% to $711 million over the same period. It was the third consecutive year of steeply increasing profits after Pilgrim's posted a loss of nearly $500 million in 2011. Cash flow from operations has soared along with growth in net income.

The rise in 2014 revenue was attributed to higher sales in the US and Mexico Pilgrim's two core markets. Higher poultry prices and continued strong demand for chicken products in combination with constrained supply boosted sales by 2% in the US. The cost of sales for US segment decreased because of lower feed costs and a decrease in wages and benefits. In Mexico sales increased by 2.8% due to favorable foreign currency translation and an increase in prices.

Strategy

In June 2014 Pilgrim's Pride lost a bidding war to acquire Hillshire Brands (the maker of Jimmy Dean Sausages) to meat giant Tyson Foods. Tyson acquired Hillshire for $63 per share topping Pilgrim's $55 bid. The battle for Hillshire emphasizes how badly large commodity meat companies want to acquire popular and more profitable brands. As a consolation prize or sorts Pilgrim's Pride in July agreed to buy Tyson's poultry business in Mexico (Tyson de México) in a deal valued at $400 million. Indeed the poultry provider is working to expand into additional international markets to reduce its reliance on the US. In Mexico for instance it is expanding distribution of dark meat chicken products. It also identifies the Commonwealth of Independent States (CIS) including Russia and Asia Pacific as regions with promising growth potential.

Additionally the company's strategy focuses on improving its product mix and reducing selling general and administrative expenses through employee layoffs and supply chain and margin improvements. It is also reviewing more drastic options for streamlining operations including restructuring selling assets consolidating operations and relocating employees.

Company Background

JBS acquired its stake after Pilgrim's Pride emerged from Chapter 11 bankruptcy in 2009. Since its initial investment the beef and pork producer has increased its share in Pilgrim's Pride to about 75% gained through subsidiary JBS USA's acquisition of nearly 19 million shares from Lonnie "Bo" Pilgrim in 2012. Pilgrim's Pride has used the money from the stock sale to pay off creditors and fund its struggling operations. Taking over Pilgrim's Pride opened the door for JBS into the US poultry market. As part of the acquisition Pilgrim's Pride was integrated into JBS USA which itself is controlled by the Batista family (specifically Wesley Batista and his brother Joesley Batista). The chicken processor's longtime headquarters in East Texas and a satellite corporate office in Atlanta were shuttered and its corporate and administrative functions relocated to JBS's US headquarters in Greeley Colorado.

HISTORY

Early History

Aubrey Pilgrim formed Pilgrim's Pride as Farmer's Feed and Seed Co. in 1946 with $1000 in cash and a $2500 note. Aubrey and brother Lonnie "Bo" Pilgrim (who joined the business in 1947) sold their first chicken from a pen behind their farm supply store and began to give away 100 baby chicks with each feed sack purchase. The Pilgrims bought back some of the grown birds to resell at a profit.

As demand for chickens grew Farmer's Feed and Seed took its first steps toward creating a vertically integrated chicken company. It opened its first processing plant in 1957 and entered the distribution business three years later delivering chicken to restaurants and grocery stores in northeastern Texas. Bo took over the business when Aubrey died of a heart attack in 1966.

The company was renamed Pilgrim's Industries in 1968 (and Pilgrim's Pride in 1985). Eggs became part of the product mix in 1969. That year Pilgrim's acquired Market Produce Co. a food distributor with facilities in Arlington Odessa and El Paso Texas. By 1979 the company was selling 1 million birds every week.

In the 1970s and 1980s Pilgrim grew through acquisitions and by using TV advertising to build a national brand. Its first TV commercial "The President Speaks" was a humorous 1983 spot featuring Bo in a wide-brimmed pilgrim's hat addressing his TV audience. To offset the wide swings in prices and profits in the highly cyclical commodity chicken industry Pilgrim moved into prepared foods in 1986 the year it went public. The firm expanded into the Mexican consumer market in 1988 through the purchase of several chicken producers there.

EXECUTIVES

EVP Operations - Technical Services and Engineering, Walter F. Shafer
CEO, Don Jackson, age 64
SVP Commodity Risk Management Feed Ingredient Purchasing and Export Sales, Charles Von Der Heyde
CFO, Fabio Sandri, age 43, $375,000 total compensation
EVP Sales and Operations, Jayson Penn
EVP Sales and Operations - Prepared Foods, Kevin Miller
Senior Vice President Human Resources, Doug Schult
Vice President, Roger Austin
Executive Vice President Finance, Brenda Carr
Vice President Sales, John (Jack) Curran
Senior Vice President Of Research and Development, Phil Hurwitz
Vice President Operations Acctng, Mark Glover
Senior Vice President Commodity Risk Management, Charles Von Heyde
Vice President Of Sales, Greg Nyhus
Senior Vice President Operations Case Ready and Retail Operations, Larry Higdem
Vice President International and Head Of E, Alexander (Al) Ivannikov
Senior Vice President Prepared Foods Regional Operations, Ronald (Ron) Morris
Chairman, Wesley Mendon 9 Batista
Auditors: KPMG LLP

LOCATIONS

HQ: Pilgrims Pride Corp.
1770 Promontory Circle, Greeley, CO 80634-9038
Phone: 970 506-8000
Web: www.pilgrims.com

2014 Sales

	% of total
US	89
Mexico	11
Total	**100**

PRODUCTS/OPERATIONS

2014 Sales

	% of total
US chicken	
Fresh chicken	55
Prepared chicken	21
Export & other chicken by-products	7
Mexico chicken	11
Other products	
US	6
Mexico —	
Total	**100**

BRANDS

Pilgrim' s
Pierce Chicken

Gold Kist Farms
Country Pride
Savoro
Products
Fresh chicken
Fully cooked
Ready to cook
Individually frozen

COMPETITORS

Allen Family Foods	Hormel
American Foods	Jobbers Meat Packing
Bachoco	Keystone Foods
Cargill Meat Solutions	Perdue Incorporated
Clougherty Packing	Rose Acre Farms
Coleman Natural Foods	Sanderson Farms
Cooper Farms	Smithfield Foods
Eberly Poultry	Tecumseh Poultry
Farmer' s Pride	Tyson Fresh Meats
Harvest Meat Company	

HISTORICAL FINANCIALS

Company Type: Public

Income Statement

FYE: December 28

	REVENUE ($ mil.)	NET INCOME ($ mil.)	NET PROFIT MARGIN	EMPLOYEES
12/14	8,583	711	8.3%	35,000
12/13	8,411	549	6.5%	36,700
12/12	8,121	174	2.1%	33,000
12/11	7,535	(496)	—	39,500
12/10	6,881	87	1.3%	89,100
Annual Growth	**5.7%**	**69.0%**	**—**	**(20.8%)**

2014 Year-End Financials

Debt ratio: 0.14%	No. of shares (mil.): 259
Return on equity: 38.74%	Dividends
Cash ($ mil.): 576	Yield: —
Current ratio: 2.53	Payout: —
Long-term debt ($ mil.): 3	Market value ($ mil.): 8,825

	STOCK PRICE ($) FY Close	P/E High/Low		PER SHARE ($) Earnings	Dividends	Book Value
12/14	34.07	14	6	2.74	0.00	8.47
12/13	16.47	9	3	2.12	0.00	5.75
12/12	7.19	12	6	0.70	0.00	3.50
12/11	5.99	—	—	(2.32)	0.00	2.59
12/10	7.12	31	14	0.41	0.00	5.01
Annual Growth	**47.9%**			**60.8%**	**—**	**14.1%**

Pinnacle Financial Partners Inc.

Pinnacle Financial Partners works to be at the top of the community banking mountain in central Tennessee. It's the holding company for Tennessee-based Pinnacle Bank which has grown to nearly 35 branches in the Nashville and Knoxville areas since its founding in 2000. Serving consumers and small- to mid-sized business the $6 billion financial institution provides standard services such as checking and savings accounts CDs credit cards and loans and mortgages. The company also offers investment and trust services through Pinnacle Asset Management while its insurance brokerage subsidiary Miller Loughry Beach specializes in property/casualty policies.
Operations

Pinnacle Financial Partners' commercial and industrial loans and commercial real estate loans account for nearly 40% and 20% respectively of its total portfolio of loans.

As part of its primary services to both individual and commercial clients Tennessee-based subsidiary Pinnacle Bank provides core deposits including savings checking interest-bearing checking money market and certificate of deposit accounts.

The bank's lending products include commercial real estate and consumer loans to individuals and small- to medium-sized businesses and professional entities. Pinnacle Bank Partners also offers auto dealer finance services to certain automobile dealers and their customers. Additionally it offers Pinnacle-branded consumer credit cards to select clients.Its convenience-centered products and services include 24-hour telephone and Internet banking debit and credit cards direct deposit and cash management services.
Geographic Reach

Based in Tennessee Pinnacle Financial Partners has become the second-largest bank holding company in the state with nearly 35 offices in eight Middle Tennessee counties and four Knoxville offices. It boasts locations in Nashville Knoxville Murfreesboro Dickson Ashland City Mt. Juliet Lebanon Franklin Brentwood Hendersonville Goodlettsville Smyrna and Shelbyville.
Sales and Marketing

Pinnacle Bank traditionally has obtained its deposits through personal solicitation by its officers and directors although it has used media advertising more in recent years due to its advertising and banking sponsorship with the Tennessee Titans NFL Football team. While it would prefer its customers to bank in person the institution allows customers to bank remotely.

Its marketing and other business development costs have risen in recent years: $4.13 million $3.639 million and $3.636 million in 2014 2013 and 2012 respectively.
Financial Performance

Pinnacle Financial Partners has enjoyed steady revenue and profit growth for the past several years thanks to positive loan growth. Revenue in 2014 rose by 9% to a record $258.77 million mostly to thanks to 9% growth in interest income from loans as the bank's loan assets grew by double digits. Pinnacle also saw double-digit growth in its fee income from service charges on deposit accounts as deposit balances grew and double-digit growth in its investment services income and trust fees as brokerage and trust account balances grew.

Higher revenue drove net income up by 22% to a record $70.47 million. Operations provided $95.06 million or 25% less cash than in 2013 primarily because the bank collected roughly $30 million less in proceeds from its mortgage loans held for sale than it did the year before.
Strategy

Pinnacle Financial Partners been looking to diversify its revenue streams through strategic investments in recent years. In early 2015 for example Tennessee-based subsidiary Pinnacle Bank purchased a 30% membership interest in Bankers Healthcare Group LLC which makes term loans to healthcare professionals and practices for $75 million.Primarily serving small- to medium-sized businesses in the Nashville and Knoxville areas the company in 2013 began extending its reach in its primary markets by opening its fourth full-service banking location in the Knoxville market in the Cedar Bluff area.

EXECUTIVES

President and CEO, M. Terry Turner, age 59, $784,700 total compensation

EVP and Chief Administrative Officer, Hugh M. Queener, age 59, $376,700 total compensation
EVP and Senior Lending Officer; Manager Client Advisory Group Nashville, J. Edward (Ed) White, age 65, $145,000 total compensation
EVP and Director Assocaite and Client Experience, Joanne B. Jackson, age 58, $117,000 total compensation
CFO, Harold R. Carpenter, age 56, $376,700 total compensation
SVP and Manager Trust and Investment Advisory, Robert Newman
President Pinnacle Knoxville, Mike DiStefano
Chief Credit Officer; President Pinnacle Knoxville, J. Harvey White, $283,800 total compensation
EVP and Manager Pinnacle Asset Management, Gary Collier
SVP and Senior Credit Officer Real Estate, Mike Hendren
SVP and Senior Credit Officer, Tim Huestis
SVP and CIO, Randy Withrow
President and CEO PNFP Capital Markets, Roger Osborne
SVP and Manager Residential Mortgage Services, Ross Kinney
EVP and Area Executive Rutherford County, Bill Jones
Chief Investment Officer, Mac Johnston
SVP Small Business Banking, Chip Higgins
EVP and Financial Advisor, Jerry Hampton
President Pinnacle Memphis, Damon Bell
Senior Vice President, Buddy Cutsinger
Senior Vice President Financial Advisor, Vickie Manning
Senior Vice President And Financial Advisor, Brande Thomas
Mortgage Advisor Senior Vice President, Jeff Mayfield
Senior Vice President and Financial Advisor, Eric Kruse
Senior Vice President, Larry Trabue
Senior Vice President, Mary Smith
Senior Vice President Mortgage Advisor, Chris Maultsby
Vice President, Dave Rowe
Vice President Mortgage Advisor, John (Jack) Pope
Vice President Underwriter, Ron Kloak
Senior Vice President, Ken Warren
Vice President, Luciano Scala
Senior Vice President, Todd Carter
Senior Vice President, Deon Ducey
Senior Vice President And Office Leader, Sherrie Hicks
Senior Vice President, Brock Kidd
Vice President Compliance And Community Development, Carla Jarrell
Senior Vice President Business Banking Financial Advisor, Dennis Mitchell
Executive Vice President And Chief Financial Officerand#8230, Alan Haefele
Vice President Mortgage Advisor, Sandra Austin
Senior Vice President, Sherry McHaffie
Senior Vice President And Mortgage Advisor, Keith Cole
Senior Vice President Lending, Roger Leitner
Senior Vice President, Donna Taylor
Vice President Finance, Mike Hammontree
Vice Chairman, Ed C. Loughry, age 72
Chairman, Robert A. (Rob) McCabe, age 64
Auditors: KPMG LLP

LOCATIONS

HQ: Pinnacle Financial Partners Inc.
150 Third Avenue South, Suite 900, Nashville, TN 37201
Phone: 615 744-3700
Web: www.pnfp.com

PRODUCTS/OPERATIONS

2014 Revenue

	% of total
Interest Income	80
Non-interest Income	20
Total	**100**

Selected Subsidiaries

Pinnacle Advisory Services Inc.
Pinnacle Credit Enhancement Holdings Inc.
Pinnacle National Bank
  Miller & Loughry Inc. (dba Miller Loughry Beach)
  PFP Title Company
  Pinnacle Community Development Corporation
  Pinnacle Nashville Real Estate Inc.
  Pinnacle Rutherford Real Estate Inc.
  Pinnacle Rutherford Towers Inc.
  Pinnacle Service Company Inc.
PNFP Insurance Inc.

COMPETITORS

BB&T	Regions Financial
Bank of America	SunTrust
Fifth Third	U.S. Bancorp
First Horizon	

HISTORICAL FINANCIALS

Company Type: Public

Income Statement

FYE: December 31

	ASSETS ($ mil.)	NET INCOME ($ mil.)	INCOME AS % OF ASSETS	EMPLOYEES
12/14	6,018	70	1.2%	767
12/13	5,563	57	1.0%	748
12/12	5,040	41	0.8%	726
12/11	4,863	43	0.9%	743
12/10	4,909	(24)	—	764
Annual Growth	**5.2%**	—	—	**0.1%**

2014 Year-End Financials

Debt ratio: 1.60%
Return on equity: 9.23%
Cash ($ mil.): 187
Current ratio: —
Long-term debt ($ mil.): —

No. of shares (mil.): 35
Dividends
  Yield: 0.8%
  Payout: 15.9%
Market value ($ mil.): 1,413

	STOCK PRICE ($) FY Close	P/E High/Low	PER SHARE ($) Earnings	Dividends	Book Value
12/14	39.54	20 15	2.01	0.32	22.46
12/13	32.53	20 11	1.67	0.08	20.55
12/12	18.84	18 14	1.10	0.00	19.57
12/11	16.15	15 9	1.09	0.00	20.67
12/10	13.58	— —	(0.93)	0.00	20.00
Annual Growth	**30.6%**	— —	—	—	**2.9%**

Pioneer Natural Resources Co

Oil and gas explorer Pioneer Natural Resources' frontier is not in the Western prairies but below them and below the Rocky Mountains the Midcontinent West Texas South Texas and elsewhere. The large independent exploration and production company reported proved reserves of about 799.5 million barrels of oil equivalent in 2014. The vast majority of the company's reserves are found within the US (including in Alaska where the company was the first independent explorer to produce

from a North Slope oilfield). Its main assets are in Texas. It has stakes in more than 10710 net producing wells.

Geographic Reach
The company maintains offices in Anchorage Alaska; Denver Colorado; and Midland Texas. In Texas it has operations in the liquid-rich Eagle Ford Shale Hugoton and West Panhandle fields; and the Raton gas field; and the Spraberry oil field.

Operations
The company has only one reportable operating segment —oil and gas exploration and production. In 2014 Pioneer Natural Resources drilled 1423 gross (1242 net) development wells 99% of which were successfully completed as productive wells (for a total drilling cost of $4.9 billion).

Sales and Marketing
In 2014 Plains Marketing accounted for 24% of Pioneer Natural Resources' revenues; Occidental Energy Marketing 13%; and Enterprise Products Partners 11%.

Financial Performance
The company's revenues have grown steadily since 2010.In 2014 Pioneer Natural Resources' revenues increased by 36% due to higher sales of purchased oil and gas and net derivative gains. The increase in net derivatives was primarily as a result of changes in forward commodity prices and changes in the company's portfolio of derivatives. That year the net income of the company increased by 211% thanks to the absence of impairment of oil and gas properties charges and about $1 billion of income from continuing operations before income taxes.

Net cash provided by the operating activities increased by 10% in 2014 due to higher net income and a change in income tax receivables.

Strategy
Pioneer Natural Resources' revenues come from its US operations where the oil firm focuses on exploiting low-risk long-lived basins. The strategies employed to achieve this mission are predicated on maintaining financial flexibility capital allocation discipline and enhancing net asset value through accretive drilling programs joint ventures and acquisitions. It also pursues derivative arrangements covering a portion of its oil NGL and gas production.

The company is also selling non-core properties to pay down debt.

Securing funding to expand its drilling program and to pay down debt in 2014 the company sold its Hugoton field assets in Kansas to Linn Energy for $340 million. That year Pioneer Natural Resources also sold its Alaska subsidiary to Caelus Energy Alaska LLC for $300 million.

In 2014 the company completed the sale of its majority interest in Sendero Drilling for $31 million and sold proved and unproved properties in Gaines and Dawson counties in the Spraberry field in West Texas for $72 million. It also sold its interest in unproved oil and gas properties adjacent to the company's West Panhandle field operations for $38 million. In 2013 it sold its Barnett Shale assets in North Texas to an undisclosed private party for cash proceeds of $155 million.

In 2013 Pioneer Natural Resources sold a 40% stake in 207000 net acres leased in Wolfcamp Shale play (Permian Basin) in the southern portion of the Spraberry Trend Area Field to Sinochem for $1.7 billion.

During 2014 2013 and 2012 Pioneer Natural Resources sold other proved and unproved properties inventory and other property and equipment and recorded net gains of $4 million $5 million and $3 million respectively.

Mergers and Acquisitions
In 2013 Pioneer Natural Resources Company acquired 52%-owned Pioneer Southwest Energy Partners L.P. which then became a wholly-owned

subsidiary of Pioneer Natural Resources USA through a stock-for-unit exchange.

HISTORY

The 1997 merger of MESA and Parker & Parsley moved quickly to pull itself out of the dry hole created by its own debt and the industry's late-1990s dropoff. Parker & Parsley began in 1962 as a partnership between geologist Howard Parker and engineer Joe Parsley. In 1977 it began drilling wells in West Texas. Southmark a Dallas real estate firm bought the company in 1984; in 1989 management purchased it from Southmark. The company went public in 1991.

T. Boone Pickens founded Petroleum Exploration in 1956. In 1964 Petroleum Exploration and Pickens' Canadian holding Altair Oil and Gas merged as MESA and went public. With gas prices declining in the 1990s MESA began selling assets. Pickens resigned as CEO in 1996.

Richard Rainwater took control of MESA and then merged the firm into Parker & Parsley which became Pioneer Natural Resources. The company moved into Argentina when it paid $1.2 billion for Calgary-based Chauvco Resources in 1997.

To streamline operations and reduce debt Pioneer cut its workforce and in 1999 it sold 400 US properties to Prize Energy.

Pioneer sold oil and gas properties in Texas and Canada in 1999 and moved to consolidate its Permian Basin operations by offering to buy out limited partners. It also drilled its first deepwater well in the Gulf of Mexico and acquired additional properties in Argentina.

In 2000 the company disposed of noncore natural gas assets in Louisiana New Mexico and Oklahoma. At the same time it boosted its deepwater holdings in the Gulf of Mexico. The next year the company announced successful test drilling in its prospects in Argentina and South Africa.

Pioneer also announced an oil discovery in 2001 on its Ozona Deep prospect in the Gulf of Mexico indicating another deepwater production asset for the company. In 2003 Pioneer teamed up with Woodside Energy to conduct a joint exploration program in the shallow-water Texas Shelf region of the Gulf of Mexico.

In 2005 Pioneer sold the Martin Creek Conroy Black and Lookout Butte oil and gas properties in Canada to Ketch Resources for $199 million. That year it acquired oil and gas assets in the Permian Basin and South Texas for a total of $177 million.

Realigning its exploration portfolio the company sold all of its operations in Argentina in 2006 to Apache for $675 million. That year Pioneer sold the bulk of its Gulf of Mexico oil and gas assets to Marubeni Offshore Production for $1.3 billion. In 2007 the company sold its Canadian subsidiary to Abu Dhabi National Energy Company PJSC for $540 million.

In 2009 the company reported a sharp dip in revenues as the result of global recession's impact on lowering commodity prices and weakening demand for oil and gas. Although Pioneer made about $89 million of property acquisitions (primarily in its South Texas shale) in 2009 financial conditions prompted the company to sell non-core assets to pay down debt. It sold its assets in the Spraberry field in West Texas to a subsidiary Pioneer Southwest Energy Partners for $168.2 million. It also sold its Mississippi and shelf properties in the Gulf of Mexico for about $24 million.

To gain capital to develop its US shale properties in 2010 Pioneer entered a joint venture selling a 45% stake in its southern Texas gas field Eagle Ford Shale to the USA subsidiary of India's Reliance Industries for $1.15 billion.

It has exited higher risk foreign ventures. To raise cash and to focus on its core North Ameri-

can assets in 2011 the company sold its Tunisia-based exploration and production units to OMV for $866 million. It also sold its South African business in 2012 for $38 million.

Securing an industrial sands business to support its hydraulic fracturing drilling activities in the Wolfcamp Shale and Barnett Shale plays in Texas in 2012 Pioneer acquired Carmeuse Industrial Sands for $297 million.

EXECUTIVES

EVP Corporate and Operations, Mark S. Berg, age 56, $407,692 total compensation
President and COO, Timothy L. (Tim) Dove, age 58, $626,539 total compensation
Chairman and CEO, Scott D. Sheffield, age 62, $984,769 total compensation
EVP and CFO, Richard P. (Rich) Dealy, age 49, $481,385 total compensation
EVP Business Development and Technology, Chris J. Cheatwood, age 54, $420,385 total compensation
VP Marketing, John C. Distaso
EVP Permian Operations, J. D. Hall, age 49
EVP STAT WAT and Corporate Engineering, Kenneth H. Sheffield, age 54
VP and CIO, Stephanie D. Stewart
Vp Marketing, Scott Sapaugh
Executive Vice President Operations, J D Hall
Exececutive Vice President Domestic Operations, Jay Still
Vice President Of Engineering And Deve, Denny Bullard
Vice President, Jim Thornton
Vice President Hes, William Knight
Vice President Information Technology, Glen Paris
Auditors: Ernst & Young LLP

LOCATIONS

HQ: Pioneer Natural Resources Co
5205 N. O' Connor Blvd., Suite 200, Irving, TX 75039
Phone: 972 444-9001 **Fax:** 972 969-3587
Web: www.pxd.com

PRODUCTS/OPERATIONS

2014 Sales

	% of total
Oil & gas	71
Sales of purchased oil & gas	14
Derivative gains	14
Interest & other	1
Gain from disposition of assets	0
Total	**100**

COMPETITORS

Anadarko Petroleum	Matador Resources
Apache	Newfield Exploration
BP	Noble Energy
Bonanza Creek	Petrohawk Energy
Carrizo Oil & Gas	Royal Dutch Shell
Chesapeake Energy	SM Energy
Exxon Mobil	Swift Energy
Hess Corporation	TOTAL
Marathon Oil	YPF

HISTORICAL FINANCIALS

Company Type: Public

Income Statement

FYE: December 31

	REVENUE ($ mil.)	NET INCOME ($ mil.)	NET PROFIT MARGIN	EMPLOYEES
12/14	5,055	930	18.4%	4,075
12/13	3,719	(838)	—	4,203
12/12	3,228	192	6.0%	3,667
12/11	2,786	834	29.9%	3,304
12/10	2,471	605	24.5%	2,248
Annual Growth	19.6%	11.3%	—	16.0%

2014 Year-End Financials

Debt ratio: 17.85%
Return on equity: 12.25%
Cash ($ mil.): 1,025
Current ratio: 1.49
Long-term debt ($ mil.): 2,665
No. of shares (mil.): 149
Dividends
  Yield: 0.0%
  Payout: 1.2%
Market value ($ mil.): 22,179

	STOCK PRICE ($) FY Close	P/E High/Low		PER SHARE ($) Earnings	Dividends	Book Value
12/14	148.85	36	20	6.38	0.08	57.59
12/13	184.07	—	—	(6.16)	0.08	46.29
12/12	106.59	75	51	1.50	0.08	46.12
12/11	89.48	15	9	6.88	0.08	45.04
12/10	86.82	17	8	5.08	0.08	35.74
Annual Growth	14.4%	—	—	5.9%	(0.0%)	12.7%

PLACID HOLDING COMPANY

Auditors: HEIN & ASSOCIATES LLP DALLAS

LOCATIONS

HQ: PLACID HOLDING COMPANY
1601 ELM ST STE 3900, DALLAS, TX 752014708
Phone: 2148808479

HISTORICAL FINANCIALS

Company Type: Private

Income Statement

FYE: December 31

	REVENUE ($ mil.)	NET INCOME ($ mil.)	NET PROFIT MARGIN	EMPLOYEES
12/13	4,929	47	1.0%	2
12/02	532	3	0.6%	—
12/01	579	18	3.1%	—
12/00	564	0	—	—
Annual Growth	18.1%	—	—	—

2013 Year-End Financials

Debt ratio: ——
Return on equity: 1.00%
Cash ($ mil.): 51
Current ratio: 1.10
Long-term debt ($ mil.): —
Dividends
  Yield: —
  Payout: —
Market value ($ mil.): —

PLACID REFINING COMPANY LLC

A calm presence in the volatile oil and gas industry Placid Refining owns and operates the Port Allen refinery in Louisiana which converts crude oil into a number of petroleum products including diesel ethanol gasoline liquid petroleum gas jet fuel and fuel oils. Placid Refining's refinery has the capacity to process 80000 barrels of crude oil per day. The company is one of the largest employers and taxpayers in West Baton Rouge Parish. Placid Refining which is controlled by Petro-Hunt distribute fuels across a dozen states in the southeastern US from Texas to Virginia and is a major supplier of jet fuel to the US military.

Placid Refining's refinery (purchased in 1975) is strategically located on a 80-plus acre lot near the Mississippi River and about two miles from Interstate Highway 10 and about 10 minutes by car from downtown Baton Rouge.

To meet growing demand the Placid Refining invested $300 million in the late 2000s to expand the Port Allen refinery's throughput capacity from 55000 barrels per day to 80000 barrels per day. As part of this process in 2009 the company completed a 20000 barrels per day fluidized catalytic cracker gasoline hydrotreater.

In 2011 Placid Refining agreed to reduce the nitrogen oxide and sulfur dioxide emissions from its Port Allen refinery and agreed to pay $675000 to the State of Louisiana to settle previous emission violations.

EXECUTIVES

V Pres, Ron Hurst
Treasurer, Barry Joffrion
Auditors: HEIN & ASSOCIATES LLP DALLAS

LOCATIONS

HQ: PLACID REFINING COMPANY LLC
1601 ELM ST STE 3400, DALLAS, TX 752017201
Phone: 2148808479
Web: WWW.PLACIDREFINING.COM

COMPETITORS

CITGO Refining and
Chemicals
NuStar Energy

United Refining
Valero Energy

HISTORICAL FINANCIALS

Company Type: Private

Income Statement

FYE: December 31

	REVENUE ($ mil.)	NET INCOME ($ mil.)	NET PROFIT MARGIN	EMPLOYEES
12/13	4,929	47	1.0%	200
12/11	4,699	4	0.1%	—
12/10	3,686	39	1.1%	—
12/06	2,925	0	—	—
Annual Growth	7.7%	—	—	—

2013 Year-End Financials

Debt ratio: ——
Return on equity: 1.00%
Cash ($ mil.): 42
Current ratio: 1.10
Long-term debt ($ mil.): —

Dividends
  Yield: —
  Payout: —
  Market value ($ mil.): —

Plains All American Pipeline, L.P.

The term "All American" includes Canada for Plains All American Pipeline which has pipeline operations in the US and north of the border. The limited partnership is engaged in the transportation storage terminalling and marketing of crude oil refined products natural gas liquids (NGL) and liquefied petroleum gas (LPG) and owns extensive gathering terminal and storage facilities in across the US and in Canada. At the end of 2014 Plains All American Pipeline owned 17800 miles of gathering crude oil NGL and refined product pipelines throughout the US and Canada operated a fleet of 800 trailers 150 barges and 72 transport tugs and owned 29 million barrels of storage capacity.

HISTORY

Goodyear Tire & Rubber subsidiary Celeron began designing the All American Pipeline in 1983 to bring heavy crude from California to the less-regulated refineries of Texas. It was completed in 1987 at a cost of $1.6 billion but by 1991 only a trickle of oil was dribbling through. The pipeline did not post a profit until 1994.

Prospects began to look up in the mid-1990s when Chevron Texaco and Exxon signed contracts to use the pipeline beginning in 1996. Plains Resources bought the pipeline in 1998 for $400 million; the company created Plains All American Pipeline to acquire and operate the pipeline then sold off a 43% stake in an IPO that raised $260 million. The next year Plains All American bought Scurlock Permian (2300 miles of pipeline) from Marathon Ashland Petroleum for $141 million and the West Texas Gathering System from Chevron (450 miles) for $36 million.

Shareholders sued Plains All American in 1999 after it reported that an employee's unauthorized crude-oil trading would cost the company about $160 million. (In 2000 the company agreed to pay $29.5 million plus interest to settle the cases.)

Plains All American announced plans to mothball all but the California section of the All American Pipeline in 1999. The next year El Paso Energy bought the 1088-mile section of the pipeline that was to be deactivated plus the right to run fiber-optic cable over the entire pipeline for $129 million.

Targeting Canada as part of its expansion strategy in 2001 Plains All American bought about 450 miles of oil pipeline and other midstream assets from Murphy Oil and acquired crude oil and LPG marketing firm CANPET Energy. Also that year Plains Resources reduced its stake in Plains All American from 44% to 29%.

In 2002 the company acquired the Wapella Pipeline System located in southeastern Saskatchewan and southwestern Manitoba. It also bought Shell Pipeline's West Texas crude oil pipeline assets for $315 million. Plains All American Pipeline continued its acquisition streak in 2003 with the acquisitions of the South Saskatchewan pipeline system in Canada and the ArkLaTex pipeline system originating in Sabine Texas.

In 2004 Plains All American continued its expansion with the acquisition of interests in the Capline and Capwood pipeline systems from Shell Pipeline Company for about $158 million. It also acquired the crude oil and pipeline operations of Link Energy for about $330 million and the Cal Ven pipeline system from Unocal Canada for about

$19 million. Later that year the company continued its system expansion by acquiring the Schaefferstown propane storage facility from Koch Hydrocarbon for about $32 million.

In 2006 the company acquired Andrews Petroleum and Lone Star Trucking for $205 million. It also acquired stakes in a number of Gulf Coast crude oil pipeline systems from BP Oil Pipeline Company for $133.5 million. That year in a major deal the company acquired Pacific Energy Partners for $2.4 billion moving the company beyond crude oil and into the refined products and barging businesses.

In 2007 Plains All American Pipeline acquired LPG storage facilities in Arizona and South Carolina.

In 2008 Occidental Petroleum acquired 10% of the company's general partner boosting the amount of new capital available for Plains All American Pipeline to pay down debt and make further acquisitions. It also boosted its Canadian midstream assets with the acquisition of Rainbow Pipeline (crude oil gathering and pipelines).

In 2012 to boost its midstream assets the company bought BP's Canadian NGL operations for $1.7 billion.

EXECUTIVES

Svp, John R (Jack) Keffer
President and COO, Harry N. Pefanis, $300,000 total compensation
EVP, Phillip D. (Phil) Kramer, $250,000 total compensation
Chairman and CEO, Greg L. Armstrong, $375,000 total compensation
EVP Operations and Business Development, Mark J. Gorman
EVP General Counsel and Secretary, Richard K. McGee
SVP Technology Process and Risk Management, Alfred A. (Al) Lindseth
EVP and CFO, Al Swanson, $250,000 total compensation
President Plains Midstream Canada, W. David (Dave) Duckett, $276,666 total compensation
EVP Commercial Activities, John P. von Berg, $250,000 total compensation
EVP, John R. Rutherford, $62,500 total compensation
President PNGS, Dean Liollio, age 57
Executive Vice President Commercial Activities, John V Berg
Vice President, David Wright
Vice President Director, James Capra
Vice President Pipeline Business Development, Samuel (Sam) Brown
Senior Vice President Technology Process Risk Management, Al Lindseth
Vice President and Treasurer, Charles (Chas) Kingswell-smith
Vice President, Patrick Diamond
Vice President Engineering, Daniel (Dan) Nerbonne
Vice President Treasurer, Sharon Spurlin
Vice President Marketing, John (Jack) Reid
Senior Vice President Commercial Activities, JohnVon Berg
Assistant Treasurer, Michael (Mel) McLaughlin
Auditors: PricewaterhouseCoopers LLP

LOCATIONS

HQ: Plains All American Pipeline, L.P.
333 Clay Street, Suite 1600, Houston, TX 77002
Phone: 713 646-4100
Web: www.plainsallamerican.com

2014 Sales

	$ mil.	% of total
US	34,860	80
Canada	8,604	20
Total	**43,464**	**100**

2014 Sales

	$ mil.	% of total
Supply and logistics	42,114	97
Transportation	774	2
Facilities	576	1
Total	**43,464**	**100**

COMPETITORS

Buckeye Partners	ONEOK
Enbridge	Sunoco Logistics
Enterprise Products	TransMontaigne
NGL Energy Partners	

HISTORICAL FINANCIALS
Company Type: Public

Income Statement
FYE: December 31

	REVENUE ($ mil.)	NET INCOME ($ mil.)	NET PROFIT MARGIN	EMPLOYEES
12/14	43,464	1,384	3.2%	5,300
12/13	42,249	1,361	3.2%	4,900
12/12	37,797	1,094	2.9%	4,700
12/11	34,275	966	2.8%	3,800
12/10	25,893	505	2.0%	3,500
Annual Growth	**13.8%**	**28.7%**	**—**	**10.9%**

2014 Year-End Financials

Debt ratio: 45.15%	No. of shares (mil.): 375
Return on equity: —	Dividends
Cash ($ mil.): 403	Yield: 4.9%
Current ratio: 0.88	Payout: 111.8%
Long-term debt ($ mil.): 8,762	Market value ($ mil.): 19,251

	STOCK PRICE ($) FY Close	P/E High/Low	Earnings	PER SHARE ($) Dividends	Book Value
12/14	51.32	25 19	2.38	2.55	21.68
12/13	51.77	21 16	2.80	2.33	21.28
12/12	45.24	38 18	2.40	2.11	19.80
12/11	73.45	30 23	2.44	1.95	17.54
12/10	62.79	54 43	1.20	1.88	15.38
Annual Growth	**(4.9%)**	**— —**	**18.7%**	**8.0%**	**9.0%**

Plains GP Holdings, L.P

Auditors: PricewaterhouseCoopers LLP

LOCATIONS

HQ: Plains GP Holdings, L.P
333 Clay Street, Suite 1600, Houston, TX 77002
Phone: 713 646-4100
Web: www.plainsallamerican.com

HISTORICAL FINANCIALS
Company Type: Public

Income Statement
FYE: December 31

	REVENUE ($ mil.)	NET INCOME ($ mil.)	NET PROFIT MARGIN	EMPLOYEES
12/14	43,464	70	0.2%	5,300
12/13	42,249	15	0.0%	4,900
12/12	37,797	3	0.0%	—
12/11	34,275	2	0.0%	—
12/10	25,893	2	0.0%	—
Annual Growth	**13.8%**	**143.2%**	**—**	**—**

2014 Year-End Financials

Debt ratio: 44.14%	No. of shares (mil.): 606
Return on equity: 5.20%	Dividends
Cash ($ mil.): 404	Yield: 2.6%
Current ratio: 0.88	Payout: 142.5%
Long-term debt ($ mil.): 9,298	Market value ($ mil.): 15,563

	STOCK PRICE ($) FY Close	P/E High/Low	Earnings	PER SHARE ($) Dividends	Book Value
12/14	25.68	67 48	0.47	0.67	2.73
12/13	26.77	267 215	0.10	0.00	1.71
Annual Growth	**(1.0%)**	**— —**	**47.2%**	**—**	**12.5%**

PNC Financial Services Group (The)

PNC Financial Services has returned to its traditional banking roots but it also offers a wide range of other financial services. Its flagship PNC Bank subsidiary operates nearly 2700 branches in more than a dozen states in the mid-Atlantic the Midwest and Florida. In addition to retail and corporate banking the company offers insurance investments personal and institutional asset management and capital markets products and services. Boasting total assets of roughly $345 billion and total deposits exceeding $230 billion the firm also owns boutique investment bank Harris Williams and about a quarter of money management giant BlackRock.

Operations

The diversified financial services organization provides a wide range of services retail and business banking; residential mortgage banking; specialized services for corporations and government bodies (corporate banking real estate finance asset-based lending and other). It also offers wealth management and asset management services.PNC Financial Services operates five core business segments based on these activities. It generated nearly 40% of its total revenue from its Retail Banking business 35% from its Corporate & Institutional Banking business 7% from its Asset Management Group and 10% from a combination of its Residential Mortgage Banking business and its BlackRock investment (it owns a 25% stake in BlackRock the world's largest publicly traded asset management firm).Broken down further the firm generated 58% of its total revenue from interest income (mostly from loans) in 2014 while most of the rest came from a combination of asset management fees (9%) Corporate services fees (9%) consumer services fees (7%) residential mortgage fees (4%) and service charges on deposits (4%).

Geographic Reach

PNC's major geographic markets located in Alabama Delaware Florida Georgia Kentucky Illinois Indiana Ohio Maryland Michigan Missouri New Jersey North Carolina Ohio Pennsylvania South Carolina Washington D.C. Wisconsin and Virginia. It also provides some products and services internationally.Sales and MarketingPNC spent $253 million on advertising in 2014 compared to $246 million and $279 million in 2013 and 2012 respectively.

Financial Performance

PNC has struggled to grow its revenue above the $17 billion mark in recent years (it hasn't exceeded the mark since 2010). The company's revenue dipped by nearly 4% to $16.28 billion in 2014 mostly because its net interest income on its loans and investment securities dropped from lower interest yields in the continued low-rate environment and lower investment securities balances. Despite its Residential Mortgage business shrinking by 30% due to lower origination volumes PNC managed to keep its non-interest income stable thanks to double-digit asset management revenue growth from its BlackRock investment as well stronger average equity markets and positive net inflows from its investor clients. Despite revenue declines in 2014 PNC managed to keep its profit mostly stable at $4.21 billion. This was mostly thanks to a reduction in provision for credit losses as the credit quality of the bank's loan portfolio improved in the strengthening economy; and also thanks to a 2% decline in non-interest expenses driven by lower headcount and benefits costs as part of its long-term cost-savings initiative. Cash from operations also remained flat in 2014 at $5.56 billion.

Strategy

PNC has recommitted itself to its core retail corporate and mortgage banking activities in recent years. The company has been focused on growing in under-penetrated markets via acquisitions customer retention and acquiring new customers. In 2014 for example PNC expanded its commercial banking services across Canada to take advantage of the country's cross-border financing and banking needs for both Canadian companies and US companies doing business in the region.The financial company has also been following its "Continuous Improvement Program" to cut costs to fund its investments in infrastructure including those related to cybersecurity and the company's datacenters as well as investments in its diversified businesses including its Retail Banking transformation. In 2014 the company exceeded its annual improvement goal of $500 million in cost savings which helped its profit remain stable for the year despite a 4% dip in revenue. In 2015 the company expected to save $400 million more through its cost-cutting measures to help fund its business and technology investments.PNC is also looking to add new clients through building relationships with employers and universities. Along these lines in 2014 it announced the opening of a financial services center on Clemson University's campus to serve more than 26000 students faculty and staff. It would be the first PNC university banking branch in North or South Carolina.Shifting toward digital banking the company enabled its credit and debit cards to be Apple Pay compatible in late 2014.

Mergers and Acquisitions

PNC acquired RBC Bank (USA) from Royal Bank of Canada in 2012. The nearly $3.5 billion acquisition extended PNC's retail banking franchise in the Southeast and cemented its place among the five largest banks in the US.

HISTORY

First National Bank of Pittsburgh opened in 1863. In 1913 the bank consolidated with Second National Bank of Pittsburgh and in 1921 it bought Peoples National. The company changed its name to Pittsburgh National after a long expansion following the Depression and WWII. In 1983 Pittsburgh National merged with Provident National of Philadelphia (founded by Quakers in 1865) to form PNC Corp. The union combined Pittsburgh National's corporate lending strength with Provident's money management and trust operations.

EXECUTIVES

President and CEO PNC Mortgage, Joseph C. (Joe) Guyaux, age 64, $620,000 total compensation
EVP and Chief Credit Officer, Michael J. Hannon, age 58

Chairman President and CEO, William S. (Bill) Demchak, age 52, $1,089,615 total compensation
EVP and Head Retail Banking, Neil F. Hall, age 66
EVP Chief Investment Officer and Treasurer, E. William (Bill) Parsley, age 49, $500,000 total compensation
EVP and CFO, Robert Q. (Rob) Reilly, age 50, $500,000 total compensation
EVP and Head Corporate and Institutional Banking, Michael P. Lyons, age 44, $700,000 total compensation
EVP and Head Technology and Operations, Steven C. (Steve) Van Wyk, age 56, $490,385 total compensation
EVP and Head Asset Management Group, Orlando C. Esposito, age 56
EVP and Chief Customer Officer, Karen L. Larrimer, age 52
EVP and Chief Risk Officer, Joseph E. Rockey, age 50
EVP General Counsel and Head Regulatory and Government Affairs, Gregory B. Jordan
EVP and General Auditor, Stacy M. Juchno, age 39
Senior Vice President And General Manager Consumer Loan Operations, Neal Heiss
Vice President Marketing, Richard (Dick) Kopchinski
Senior Vice President, Linda Morris
Senior Vice President Public Finance, George Whitmer
Vice President Marketing Research and Competitive Analysis, Maritza Mercader-Hughes
Vice President Chief Enterprise Architect, Eric Meredith
Senior Vice President, John (Jack) Wilden
Executive Vice President, Frederick (Fred) Frank
Vice President Planned Giving Services, Chip Giese
Vice President, Charles A (Chas) Steck
Vice President, Glen Siniawski
Senior Data Analyst Assistant Vice President, Katherine (Kate) Novak
Assistant Vice President Database Department, Tom Bucko
Vice President Strategic Accounts, Jim Foley
Assistant Vice President and Manager Online Product, Roy Hess
Senior Vice President and Assistant General Auditor, Tom Burch
Senior Vice President treasury Management, Richard (Dick) Wessels
Vice President National Sales Manager, Jason E VanSickle
Vice President Network Services, Thomas Gooch
Senior Vice President, Alan (Al) McCrum
Vice President, Keith Moellering
Vice President Information Marketing Systems, John Demarchis
Senior Vice President, Helen Anne Miles
Senior Vice President and Retail Banking Manager, Mary A Koch
Executive Vice President Marketing, Bradley Penn
Vice President Media Rels, Jonathan (Jon) Williams
Vice President, Amy March
Vice President, Frank Freda
Vice President Director Corporate Marketing, Traci Mitchell
Senior Vice President Of Marketing, Michael Ball
Vice President Technology, Roberta Kunz
Vice President, Tom Majeski
Vice President Information Technology, Eric Lyninger
Vice President Special Assets, Andrew (Andy) Schmidt
Senior Vice President, Bruce Colbourn
Vice President, Jon Randall
Vice President, Michael (Mel) Zacherl
Vice President, Jim Noble
Senior Vice President And Credit Card Manager Business Banking, Jim Atteberry
Executive Vice President, Fallon William
Executive Vice President Marketing, Carolyn King

Senior Vice President Group Manager, William (Bill) Smith
Business Analyst III Assistant Vice President, Alette Pauly
Vice President of Data Networking, Mike Stull
Executive Vice President Operations, Harry Klein
Assistant Vice President Campus Recruiting Manager, Dana Feinstein
Vice President, Melissa Kwiatkowski
Vice President retail Lending, John (Jack) Holcomb
Assistant Vice President, Barbara (Barb) Jones
Vice President, Paul Trozzo
Executive Vice President Marketing, Dave Rico
Vice President, Dan Gaffney
Vice President Corporate Banking, Fran Kilroy
Executive Vice President Marketing, Cesar Rivas
Talent Acquistion Assistant Vice President, Lori Taylor
Vice President Management Information Systems, Tom Dzara
Vice President, Barbara (Barb) Roehm
Vice President Manager Loan Closing and FulFillment Consumer Loan Services, Kerry Stith
Vice President, Carolyn Schwarz
Vice President, Peter Dine
Vice President, Nick Camino
Vice President Group Manager Corporate Marketing, Barbara (Barb) Martocci
Vice President, Connie Genco
Vice President, Kirsten Bowie
Vice President, David Caster
Vice President Senior Manager, Wei Cheng
Senior Vice President, Beth Dorsey
Vice President, Ted Toothman
Vice President Business Development, Dave Panneton
Vice President, Michael Picard
Senior Vice President Director of New Branch Investment, Patrick (Paddy) Martin
Vice President Senior Organizational Devel, Vicki Brown
Ex Senior Vice President Marketing and Public Relations, John (Jack) Alden
Branch Manager Vice President, Michael Joy
Vice President Technology, Rita Cook
Vice President Account Development, Louise Perchinsky
Vice President Of Information Technology, Matt Dekman
Vice President Information Technology, Jean Matter
Senior Vice President Information Technology, Dave Shaw
Vice President Of Marketing, Darren Meyers
Vice President Marketing Research and Competitive Analysis, Candace Skiles
Vice President Health Business Banking Division, Rusty Benfield
Assistant Vice President And Sales Officer, Kellie McClung
Senior Vice President, Daniel Pavlick
Senior Vice President, Marva Harris
Assistant Vice President Management Information Systems Marketing, Alan Palguta
Vice President Direct Marketing, Laura Watson
Vice President Consumer Lending Technology Pnc Financial Services, Mia Ruppert
Vice President, Roderick Hirsch
Vice President Management Information Systems, Jacqueline Hudson
Senior Vice President, Daniel Stella
Vice President Card Services, Al Moeller
Vice President Product Development, Mark Vizza
Senior Vice President Receivables Management Network Manager, Philip Ahwesh
Senior Vice President Management Information Systems Technology, David (Dave) Lee
Vice President, Davie Huddleston
Vice President, Richard Seymour

Assistant Vice President Customer Service Manager, Elizabeth (Beth) Ponder
Vice President, Salvatore Patti
Vice President Finance, Roxanne Larson
Vice President Finance, Jeff Manganello
Senior Vice President Online Banking, Leah Rubenstein
Vice President Relationship Manager Dealer Finance, Charles (Chas) Dougherty
Vice President Operations, Cindy Magdinec
Vice President Finance, James Steffy
Vice President Project Director, Sherrie Young
Assistant Vice President, John Florio
Vice President Sales and Marketing, Cheryl Kraft
Regional Manager Senior Vice President, Alisa Winslow
Vice President Finance, John McCool
Vice President, Deborah Rowett
Vice President And Senior Business Banker, Jackie Velesz
Business Banker Ii Assistant Vice President, Carl Witkowski
Vice President Community Development Banking Consultant, Maria Thompson
Senior Vice President Product Manager, Janet Hoyt
Vice President Assistant Secretary And Director, Michael Setzenfand
Vice President Nfsc Compliance Manager, Carol Meyer
Senior Vice President, Charles Garoklanian
Vice President Master Black Belt, Mary Chrobak
Vice President, Frank Sajer
Senior Vice President Market Manager, Charles Rhodes
Vice President, Adam Barone
Vice President, Deborah (Deb) Madigan
Senior Vice President Treasury Management, Lynn Nettleton
Senior Vice President Strategic Planning, Thomas (Thom) Kunz
Application Systems Development Manager Vice President, John (Jack) Mayberry
Senior Vice President And Regional Manager, Alan B (Al) Trivilino
Vice President and Manager Corporate Marketing, Ray Appleton
Vice President, Michael (Mel) Anselmo
Vice President, Timothy (Tim) Hunter
Assistant Vice President Senior Product Manager, Paula Rowe
Vice President, Laura Schuster
Resource Storage Vice President, Jane (Ginny) Messmer
Vice President Customer Service, Christina Borror
Auditors: PricewaterhouseCoopers LLP

LOCATIONS

HQ: PNC Financial Services Group (The)
One PNC Plaza, 249 Fifth Avenue, Pittsburgh, PA 15222-2707
Phone: 412 762-2000   **Fax:** 412 762-5798
Web: www.pnc.com

Selected Banking Markets
Delaware
Florida
Georgia
Illinois
Indiana
Kentucky
Maryland
Michigan
Missouri
New Jersey
Ohio
Pennsylvania
Virginia
Washington DC
West Virginia
Wisconsin

2014 Sales

Interest	$ mil.	% of total
Loans	7,427	46
Investment securities	1,624	10
Other	380	2
Noninterest		
Asset management	1,513	9
Corporate services	1,415	9
Consumer services	1,254	7
Service charges on deposits	662	4
Residential mortgage	618	4
Other	1,399	9
Adjustments	(11)	-
Total	**16,281**	**100**

2014 Sales

	% of total
Retail Banking	39
Corporate and Institutional Banking	35
Asset Managment group	7
Residential Mortgage Banking	5
BlackRock	5
Non-Strategic Asset Portfolio	4
Others	5
Total	**100**

Selected Subsidiaries

PNC Bancorp Inc.
 PNC Bank National Association
 PNC Bank Capital Securities LLC
 PNC Capital Leasing LLC
 PNC Preferred Funding LLC
 PNC REIT Corp.
PNC Holding LLC
 PNC Funding Corp
 PNC Investment Corp.
 PNC Venture LLC

COMPETITORS

Bank of America	JPMorgan Chase
Capital One	KeyCorp
Citigroup	M&T Bank
Citizens Financial	Sovereign Bank
Group	TD Bank USA
Fifth Third	U.S. Bancorp
Harris	Wells Fargo
Huntington Bancshares	

HISTORICAL FINANCIALS

Company Type: Public

Income Statement
FYE: December 31

	ASSETS ($ mil.)	NET INCOME ($ mil.)	INCOME AS % OF ASSETS	EMPLOYEES
12/14	345,072	4,207	1.2%	53,587
12/13	320,296	4,227	1.3%	54,433
12/12	305,107	3,001	1.0%	56,285
12/11	271,205	3,071	1.1%	51,891
12/10	264,284	3,397	1.3%	50,769
Annual Growth	6.9%	5.5%	—	1.4%

2014 Year-End Financials

Debt ratio: 8.19%
Return on equity: 9.68%
Cash ($ mil.): 36,139
Current ratio: —
Long-term debt ($ mil.): —

No. of shares (mil.): 523
Dividends
 Yield: 2.0%
 Payout: 25.7%
Market value ($ mil.): 47,713

	STOCK PRICE ($) FY Close	P/E High/Low		PER SHARE ($)	
			Earnings	Dividends	Book Value
12/14	91.23	12 10	7.30	1.88	85.18
12/13	77.58	10 8	7.39	1.72	79.56
12/12	58.31	13 10	5.30	1.55	73.87
12/11	57.67	11 8	5.64	0.00	64.62
12/10	60.72	12 9	5.74	0.40	57.49
Annual Growth	10.7%	— —	6.2%	47.2%	10.3%

Popular Inc.

Popular is popular and not just in Puerto Rico. Founded in 1893 Popular is the holding company for Banco Popular de Puerto Rico (BPPR) the largest bank on the island with approximately 175 branches. In addition to offering commercial and retail banking BPPR owns subsidiaries that specialize in vehicle financing and leasing (Popular Auto) insurance (Popular Insurance) financial advisory and brokerage services (Popular Securities) and mortgages (Popular Mortgage). Popular also owns Banco Popular North America (BPNA) which targets the US Hispanic population from about 100 branches across five major US states.

Geographic Reach

Popular operates in the two primary markets of Puerto Rico and the US. It targets the Hispanic population in the US from about 100 branches in California Florida Illinois New Jersey and New York.

Operations

Popular's other financial services include the insurance agency and reinsurance businesses of Popular Insurance Popular Insurance V.I. Popular Risk Services and Popular Life Re. BPNA also owns E-LOAN Popular Equipment Finance and Popular Insurance Agency USA. E-LOAN's sole purpose is to provide an online platform to raise deposits for BPNA.

Financial Performance

Popular has suffered revenue declines over the last two years. Revenues dropped 9% from $2.5 billion in 2011 to nearly $2.3 billion in 2012. However the company's profits surged 62% from $151 million in 2011 to $255 million in 2012.

The fall in revenue was due to a decrease in interest income driven by declines in investment securities and trading account securities. Non-interest income also dropped in 2012 mainly due to a $56 million expense it paid on a FDIC loss share. (This was the result of a lower provision for loan losses on covered loans and higher amortization of the loss share asset due to a decrease in expected losses.)

The rise in profits was due to an income tax benefit of $73 million and a tax benefit of $27 million it earned from the Puerto Rico Department of Treasury during 2012.

Strategy

As a result of the company's losses Popular exited some lines of business such as its small consumer loan unit Popular Finance and the assets of the US-based Popular Equipment Finance. Indeed most of the company's reductions were made in the US. Popular cut some 40% of its workforce there decreased its branch network from nearly 140 to about 100 and exited Texas. It also sold some $1.2 million in loans and servicing assets of its US mortgage subsidiary Popular Financial Holdings to affiliates of Goldman Sachs. That deal provided Popular with more than $700 million in additional liquidity and Popular has continued to seek other sale opportunities.

To broaden its target audience beyond the Hispanic community Popular rebranded itself in the US switching its name from "Banco Popular" to "Popular Community Bank". The change which was initially begun in pilot markets in 2010 was completed officially in 2012 when the company changed its name in New York City.

EXECUTIVES

Chairman President and CEO, Richard L. Carri n, age 62, $1,400,000 total compensation

EVP Financial and Insurance Services, Juan O. Guerrero, age 55, $375,000 total compensation
EVP Administration, Eduardo J. Negr n, age 50, $385,000 total compensation
EVP Retail Banking and Operations Group, N ctor O. Rivera, age 68, $375,000 total compensation
EVP and CFO, Carlos J. V zquez, age 56, $650,000 total compensation
EVP Corporate Risk Management, Lidio V. Soriano, age 46
President and COO, Ignacio lvarez, age 56, $615,000 total compensation
EVP Commercial Credit, Eli Sep lveda, age 52, $420,000 total compensation
EVP Individual Credit Group, Gilberto Monz n, age 55
EVP General Counsel Chief Legal Officer and Secretary, Javier D. Ferrer, age 53
EVP Commercial Credit Administration Group, Ileana Gonzalez
Senior Vice President, Adnan Assad
Vice President, Clifton Tufts
Executive Vice President General Counsel, Ignacio Alvarez
Vice President, Carlos Payan
Auditors: PricewaterhouseCoopers LLP

LOCATIONS

HQ: Popular Inc.
 Popular Center Building, 209 Munoz Rivera Avenue, Hato Rey, San Juan 00918
Phone: (787) 765 9800
Web: www.popular.com

PRODUCTS/OPERATIONS

2014 Sales

	% of total
Interest income	75
Non interest income	25
Total	**100**

Selected Subsidiaries and Affiliates

Banco Popular de Puerto Rico
 BP Sirenusa International LLC (US)
 Popular Auto Inc.
 Popular Mortgage Inc.
Popular Capital Trust I (US)
Popular Insurance Inc.
Popular International Bank Inc.
 Banco Popular North America (US)
 E-LOAN Inc.
 Equity One Inc.
 Popular Insurance V.I. Inc. (US Virgin Islands)
Popular Life RE
Popular Securities Inc.

COMPETITORS

Bank of America	JPMorgan Chase
Bolivar Banco	OFG Bancorp
Venezuela	RBC Financial Group
Citigroup	Santander BanCorp
First BanCorp (Puerto Rico)	Scotiabank

HISTORICAL FINANCIALS

Company Type: Public

Income Statement
FYE: December 31

	ASSETS ($ mil.)	NET INCOME ($ mil.)	INCOME AS % OF ASSETS	EMPLOYEES
12/14	33,096	(313)	—	7,752
12/13	35,749	599	1.7%	8,059
12/12	36,507	245	0.7%	8,072
12/11	37,348	151	0.4%	8,329
12/10	38,722	137	0.4%	8,277
Annual Growth	(3.8%)	—	—	(1.6%)

2014 Year-End Financials

Debt ratio: 2.75%	No. of shares (mil.): 103
Return on equity: (-7.05%)	Dividends
Cash ($ mil.): 7,506	Yield: —
Current ratio: —	Payout: —
Long-term debt ($ mil.): —	Market value ($ mil.): 3,523

	STOCK PRICE ($) FY Close	P/E High/Low		PER SHARE ($) Earnings	Dividends	Book Value
12/14	34.05	—	—	(3.08)	0.00	41.24
12/13	28.73	6	4	5.78	0.00	44.44
12/12	20.79	9	1	2.35	0.00	39.84
12/11	1.39	3	1	1.40	0.00	38.20
12/10	3.14	—	—	(0.60)	0.00	37.16
Annual Growth	81.5%	—	—	—	—	2.6%

PowerShares DB Commodity Index Tracking Fund

Auditors: PricewaterhouseCoopers LLP

LOCATIONS

HQ: PowerShares DB Commodity Index Tracking Fund
c/o Invesco PowerShares Capital Management LLC,
3500 Lacey Road, Suite 700, Downers Grove, IL 60515
Phone: 800 983-0903
Web: www.dbfunds.db.com

HISTORICAL FINANCIALS

Company Type: Public

Income Statement

FYE: December 31

	ASSETS ($ mil.)	NET INCOME ($ mil.)	INCOME AS % OF ASSETS	EMPLOYEES
12/14	4,948	(45)	—	—
12/13	6,799	(53)	—	—
12/12	6,614	(50)	—	—
12/11	5,471	(47)	—	—
12/10	5,110	(34)	—	—
Annual Growth	(0.8%)	—	—	—

2014 Year-End Financials

Debt ratio: —	No. of shares (mil.): 219
Return on equity: (-0.93%)	Dividends
Cash ($ mil.): 745	Yield: —
Current ratio: —	Payout: —
Long-term debt ($ mil.): —	Market value ($ mil.): 4,048

	STOCK PRICE ($) FY Close	P/E High/Low		PER SHARE ($) Earnings	Dividends	Book Value
12/14	18.45	—	—	(0.21)	0.00	18.40
12/13	25.66	—	—	(0.21)	0.00	25.61
12/12	27.78	—	—	(0.22)	0.00	27.72
12/11	26.84	—	—	(0.00)	0.00	26.83
12/10	27.55	—	—	(0.00)	0.00	27.57
Annual Growth	(9.5%)	—	—	—	—	(9.6%)

PPG Industries, Inc.

Thanks to its range of product offerings you won't catch PPG Industries painting itself into a corner. Performance and industrial coatings –such as paints (Pittsburgh Paints Lucite and Monarch) stains (Olympic) and sealants –account for most of its sales; the remainder comes from glass materials. PPG's glass offerings include flat glass for buildings fabricated glass and continuous-strand fiberglass used in aircraft and buildings. The company has sold its chemical commodities and optical products businesses in order to focus on its core coating and glass segments.

HISTORY

After the failure of his first two plate-glass manufacturing plants John Ford persuaded former railroad superintendent John Pitcairn to invest $200000 in a third factory in 1883 in Creighton Pennsylvania. The enterprise Pittsburgh Plate Glass (PPG) became the first commercially successful US plate-glass factory.

Ford left in 1896 after Pitcairn established a company distribution system replacing glass jobbers. Ford went on to found a predecessor of competitor Libbey-Owens-Ford (now owned by glassmaker Pilkington).

Pitcairn built a soda ash plant in 1899 bought a Milwaukee paint company the following year and began producing window glass in 1908. Pitcairn died in 1916 leaving his stock to his sons.

Strong automobile and construction markets in the early 20th century increased demand for the company's products. In 1924 PPG revolutionized glass production with the introduction of a straight-line conveyor manufacturing method. In the 1930s and 1940s PPG successfully promoted structural glass for use in the commercial construction industry.

PPG was listed on the NYSE in 1945. In 1952 it started making fiberglass and in 1968 the company adopted its present name.

Vincent Sarni (CEO 1984-93) recognized that 85% of the company's sales were to the maturing construction and automobile industries. Sarni decided to move the company into growing industries such as electronics.

In 1986 PPG spent $154 million on acquisitions including the medical electronics units of Litton Industries and Honeywell. It acquired the medical technology business of Allegheny International in 1987 and bought Casco Nobel a coatings distributor and the Olympic and Lucite paint lines from Clorox in 1989.

The company which owned one-third of Dutch fiberglass producer Silenka BV acquired the rest in 1991. In 1992 PPG acquired a silica plant in the Netherlands its first in Europe. Two years later it acquired the European automotive coatings business of Netherlands-based Akzo Nobel.

In the 1990s PPG backed away from Sarni's earlier strategies for greater diversification and unloaded a number of high-tech businesses. The firm refocused on its core coatings glass and chemicals operations. PPG acquired Matthews Paints a leading maker of paints for outdoor signs and the refinish coating business of Lilly Industries in 1995.

The company bolstered its chemical operations in 1997 with the addition of France's Sipsy Chime Fine. That same year President and COO Raymond LeBoeuf took over as CEO. In 1998 PPG sold its European flat and automotive glass business to Belgium-based Glaverbel. Acquisitions that year included Australia-based Orica's technical coatings unit and the US paint operations (Porter Paints) of Akzo Nobel.

In 1999 PPG expanded its European coatings business with the purchase of Belgium-based Sigma Coatings' commercial transport coatings unit and Akzo Nobel's aircraft coatings and sealants company PRC-DeSoto International. That year PPG also bought Imperial Chemical Industries' Germany-based coatings business for large commercial vehicles and its US-based auto refinish and industrial coatings businesses. PPG's acquisition spree continued in 2000 with architectural coating maker Monarch Paint.

Early in the new decade PPG suffered from flat or declining earnings from existing operations. Amid falling sales and lower prices for chemicals and glass PPG began to cut jobs and closed some facilities. Still the company recorded its first loss in more than 10 years in 2002 and its second straight year of declining sales.

Like many manufacturers in its industry PPG has been exposed to potentially costly asbestos litigation mainly because of its 50% stake in the bankrupt Pittsburgh Corning a joint venture with Corning that made insulation with asbestos. In 2002 PPG and its insurers agreed to pay roughly $2.7 billion to settle its asbestos claims.

LeBoeuf retired in 2005. He was replaced by president and COO Charles Bunch who had joined the company in 1979 and worked up through the ranks of first the finance department and then the coatings operations.

In 2008 PPG acquired SigmaKalon for $3 billion. SigmaKalon was among the top 10 paint manufacturers in the world and did business almost entirely outside the US. The company now operates as PPG's Architectural Coatings segment. That same year PPG sold its auto glass business to private equity group Kohlberg & Company which set the unit up as a stand-alone company called Pittsburgh Glass Works. PPG received $330 million plus a 40% interest in the company.

In 2011 PPG acquired Equa-Chlor a producer of chlorine caustic soda and muriatic acid for $27 million. Equa-Chlor produces about 220 tons of chlorine per day. In addition to its products PPG also bought Equa-Chlor's distribution system which includes a railcar fleet it integrated into its own. The deal for the Washington state-based company bolsters PPG's chlor-alkali business in the Northwest US and expands its overall supply chain.

As part of its push to expand in emerging markets in 2011 PPG formed a joint venture with an India-based company Harsha Exito Engineering Private to produce fiber glass reinforcement products.

It made two foreign acquisitions to expand its international operations in 2011. First it bought the business assets of Ducol Coatings South Africa Ltd. which had served as an importer and distributor of PPG's automotive refinish products in South Africa since 2003. PPG also expanded its joint venture with India-based Asian Paints (India's largest coatings company) and created a second 50-50 JV in 2012. The deals boosts PPG's position in the Chinese and Asian packaging coatings industry part of its global strategy to expand into emerging regions.

During 2012 the company made four acquisitions related to its coatings business for a total of $288 million including US-based Spraylat Corp. Denmark based Dyrup A/S and the coatings business of Ecuador-based Colpisa Colombiana de Pinturas.

EXECUTIVES

Chairman and CEO, Charles E. Bunch, $1,393,333 total compensation

President and COO, Michael H. McGarry, $614,583 total compensation
VP Information Technology, Werner Baer
EVP and CFO, Frank S. Sklarsky, $666,733 total compensation
VP Research and Development Coatings and CTO, Charles F. Kahle
EVP, Viktoras R. Sekmakas, $575,000 total compensation
President PPG EMEA and VP Automotive Coatings EMEA, Jean-Marie Greindl
VP Science and Technology and CTO-elect, David S. Bem
President PPG Asia Pacific and VP Protective and Marine Coatings Asia Pacific, Michael Horton
VP Industrial Coatings, Shelley J. Bausch
VP PPG Architectural Coatings Mexico and CEO PPG Comex, Marcos Achar Levy
Vice President Strategic Planning, Aziz Giga
Auditors: PricewaterhouseCoopers LLP

LOCATIONS

HQ: PPG Industries, Inc.
  One PPG Place, Pittsburgh, PA 15272
Phone: 412 434-3131
Web: www.ppg.com

2014 Sales

	$ mil.	% of total
The Americas		
US	6,323	42
Other countries	1,718	11
Europe/Middle East/Africa	4,802	31
Asia/Pacific	2,517	16
Total	**15,360**	**100**

PRODUCTS/OPERATIONS

2014 Sales

	$ mil.	% of total
Performance Coatings	8,698	57
Industrial Coatings	5,553	36
Glass	1,111	7
Adjustments	(2)	-
Total	**15,360**	**100**

Selected Products

Performance Coatings
  Aerospace coatings
  Architectural coatings (Lucite paints Olympic stains)
  Refinish
Industrial Coatings
  Automotive coatings chemicals adhesives and sealants
  Industrial coatings
  Packaging coatings (food and beverage containers)
Commodity Chemicals
  Calcium hypochlorite
  Caustic soda
  Chlorine
  Chlorine derivatives
  Phosgene derivatives
Optical and Specialty Materials
  Optical products (Transitions variable-tint lenses)
  Silica products
Glass
  Aircraft transparencies
  Coated glass
  Continuous-strand fiberglass
  Flat glass

COMPETITORS

3M	Ferro
Akzo Nobel	Kelly-Moore
Axalta Coating Systems	Nippon Paint
BASF Coatings AG	Nippon Sheet Glass
BEHR	Pilkington Group
Benjamin Moore	RPM International
Dow Chemical	Sherwin-Williams

HISTORICAL FINANCIALS

Company Type: Public

Income Statement

FYE: December 31

	REVENUE ($ mil.)	NET INCOME ($ mil.)	NET PROFIT MARGIN	EMPLOYEES
12/14	15,360	2,102	13.7%	44,400
12/13	15,108	3,231	21.4%	41,400
12/12	15,200	941	6.2%	39,200
12/11	14,885	1,095	7.4%	38,400
12/10	13,423	769	5.7%	38,300
Annual Growth	**3.4%**	**28.6%**	**—**	**3.8%**

2014 Year-End Financials

Debt ratio: 22.89%	No. of shares (mil.): 271
Return on equity: 41.57%	Dividends
Cash ($ mil.): 686	Yield: 2.2%
Current ratio: 1.40	Payout: 34.8%
Long-term debt ($ mil.): 3,544	Market value ($ mil.): 62,865

	STOCK PRICE ($) FY Close	P/E High/Low	PER SHARE ($) Earnings	Dividends	Book Value
12/14	231.15	31 23	7.52	2.62	19.05
12/13	189.66	17 12	11.14	2.42	17.79
12/12	135.35	44 28	3.03	2.34	13.23
12/11	83.49	28 20	3.44	1.13	10.70
12/10	84.07	36 25	2.32	2.18	11.34
Annual Growth	**28.8%**	**— —**	**34.2%**	**4.7%**	**13.8%**

PPL Corp

PPL packs a powerful punch in Kentucky Pennsylvania Tennessee Virginia and the UK. It distributes electricity to 10 million customers through regulated subsidiaries PPL Electric Utilities two utilities in Kentucky and Western Power Distribution Holdings in the UK. The company has 19000 MW of generating capacity and also sells energy wholesale in key US markets. Western Power Distribution operates four of the 15 distribution networks providing electricity service in the UK though WPD (South West) and WPD (South Wales). In 2015 PPL sold its competitive energy operations in order to focus on its regulated utility businesses.

HISTORY

PPL's wires reach back to Lehigh Coal & Navigation which was formed in 1822 to mine Pennsylvania coal and build a canal to deliver it to Philadelphia. Heavy industry and steel mills flourished in the Lehigh Valley and Thomas Edison formed small electric companies to serve the area in the early 1880s. Rivals soon followed and by 1900 there were 64 companies in what would become PPL's territory.

Lehigh formed Lehigh Navigation Electric in 1912 to provide power to its coal mines only to lose control of the company to conglomerate Electric Bond & Share in 1917. S. Z. Mitchell Electric Bond & Share's president merged the renamed Lehigh Valley Light & Power with six other utilities to form Pennsylvania Power & Light (PP&L) in Allentown in 1920. The next year PP&L became a subsidiary of National Power & Light.

PP&L bought more than 60 neighboring utilities in a decade and by 1930 industrial customers accounted for 70% of power sales. The company also built a 220000-volt transmission interconnection line with neighbors Philadelphia Electric (now

PECO Energy a unit of Exelon) and Public Service Electric and Gas of New Jersey (now part of Public Service Enterprise Group). During the Depression the company offset falling industrial sales with residential sales.

The Public Utility Holding Company Act of 1935 forced large utility holding companies to streamline their businesses and by 1948 National Power & Light had unloaded PP&L.

To keep up with postwar demand PP&L built several coal-fired power plants. By 1964 industry still accounted for about a third of sales but suburbs assumed greater importance. PP&L began operating coal mines in the early 1970s and started building the Susquehanna nuclear plant.

Although its proprietary coal supply helped PP&L weather skyrocketing fuel costs in the 1970s huge construction delays endemic to nukes hit the utility for $4 billion by the time Susquehanna was completed in 1982. Flat sales in the late 1980s led to 2000 job cuts and to a reorganization by CEO William Hecht.

In 1992 the federal Energy Policy Act signaled the end of the monopoly era by promoting wholesale competition. PP&L formed Power Markets Development (now PPL Global) in 1994 to make energy investments worldwide. The next year it created holding company PP&L Resources to house both regulated and non-regulated businesses.

The Customer Choice Act was passed in Pennsylvania in 1996 ushering in competition and the utility formed its non-regulated retail power sales arm PP&L EnergyPlus. PP&L also bought 25% of Chile's Empresas Emel in 1997 (upped to 67% 1999). Fellow US utility Southern Company which bought UK utility SWEB in 1995 had turned over a 51% stake in SWEB to PP&L Resources by 1998.

PP&L Resources began buying mechanical contracting firms in 1998 to complement its electric business and it purchased natural gas and propane distributor Penn Fuel Gas.

In 1999 the company bought generating facilities with a total capacity of 1315 MW from Montana Power. Also that year PP&L Resources and Southern sold SWEB's supply business and the SWEB brand name to London Electricity a unit of Electricité de France. PP&L Resources and Southern retained their stakes in SWEB's distribution network which was renamed Western Power Distribution (later changed to WPD Holdings UK after it acquired British utility Hyder in 2000).

PP&L Resources changed its name to PPL Corporation in 2000 and reorganized into four major operating subsidiaries: PPL Utilities PPL EnergyPlus PPL Generation and PPL Global. PPL's restructuring efforts separated its regulated distribution operations from its non-regulated generation supply and services operations.

In 2002 PPL's Brazilian utility Companhia Energética do Maranhão (Cemar) filed for bankruptcy protection and fell under the control of the Brazilian government. (PPL divested its interest in Cemar in 2004.) Also in 2002 PPL purchased the remaining 49% stake in WPD Holdings UK (now Western Power Distribution Holdings) from Mirant (now GenOn Energy) for $235 million.

In 2007 the company sold its Latin American companies as well as its domestic telecommunications and synthetic fuels businesses.

In 2008 PPL sold its US propane and gas distribution unit.

Buoyed by a rebounding economy in 2010 PPL acquired E.ON U.S. the owner of Kentucky's two major utilities Louisville Gas & Electric and Kentucky Utilities for $7.6 billion. The utilities serve 1.2 million customers primarily in Kentucky. The deal

HOOVER'S HANDBOOK OF AMERICAN BUSINESS 2016

made PPL stronger (with 19000 MW of generating capacity) and more geographically diverse.

Expanding its regulated power operations in 2011 the company acquired the UK's #2 electric distribution business WPD Midlands Holdings (formerly Central Networks) for $5.7 billion. The deal gave the company greater market share in the UK and added to 2011 earnings and cash flow. In 2012 and 2013 PPL invested in several projects to upgrade the UK distribution system.

In 2011 to raise cash PPL sold its stakes in some non-core generating stations in the US to an affiliate of LS Power Equity for $381 million. The company was also pursuing further rate increases across its service areas in order to defray costs.

Growing its US power capacity in 2012 PPL acquired AES Ironwood and AES Prescott which together own and operate the 705 MW AES Ironwood natural gas-fired power plant in Lebanon Pennsylvania from a unit of AES Corporation for $302 million.

EXECUTIVES

Chairman President and CEO LG&E and KU Energy, Victor A. Staffieri, $811,220 total compensation
EVP General Counsel and Secretary, Robert J. Grey, $563,253 total compensation
CEO Western Power Distribution, Robert A. Symons, $872,710 total compensation
Chairman President and CEO, William H. Spence, $1,126,760 total compensation
President PPL Electric Utilities, Gregory N. Dudkin
President PPL Global and PPL Energy Services, Rick L. Klingensmith
SVP and CFO, Vincent (Vince) Sorgi, age 43, $398,404 total compensation
Vice President Production, Stephanie Raymond
Vice President Marketing and Economic Development, Raymond Suhocki
Executive Vice President Business Development And Strategy, Mark Smith
Vice President Finance, James Wagner
Vice President Business Development, Joseph (Jo) Clifford
Vice President, Michael (Mel) Kroboth
Senior Vice President Operations, Greg Dudkin
Board Member, Joe Macieunas
Treasurer, Sidney Richard
Treasurer, Mark Wilten
Auditors: Deloitte & Touche LLP

LOCATIONS

HQ: PPL Corp
Two North Ninth Street, Allentown, PA 18101-1179
Phone: 610 774-5151   **Fax:** 610 774-5106
Web: www.pplweb.com

2014 Sales

	$ mil.	% of total
US	8,878	77
UK	2,621	23
Total	**11,499**	**100**

PRODUCTS/OPERATIONS

2014 Sales

	$ mil.	% of total
Utility	7,782	67
Wholesale energy marketing	1,808	16
Unregulated retail Energy	1,239	11
Energy-related businesses	670	6
Total	**11,499**	**100**

Selected Subsidiaries

PPL Development Corporation (acquisition and divestiture activities)
PPL Electric Utilities Corporation (electricity distribution)

PPL Energy Supply (nonregulated operations)
PPL EnergyPlus LLC (wholesale and retail energy marketing)
PPL Generation LLC (electricity generation)
PPL Montana LLC (electricity generation)
PPL Global LLC (international utility operations)
Western Power Distribution Holdings Limited (formerly WPD Holdings UK electricity distribution)
PPL Services Corporation (shared services for PPL Corp. and other subsidiaries)

Selected Mergers & Acquisitions

COMPETITORS

ABB	Green Mountain Energy
AEP	HC Energa
Avangrid	Maine & Maritimes
Canadian Utilities	Midwest Generation
Centrica	Ontario Power
Con Edison	Generation
Constellation Energy	Orange & Rockland
Group	Utilities
Covanta	Pepco Holdings
Delmarva Power	Public Service
Dominion Resources	Enterprise Group
Duke Energy	Scottish and Southern
Duquesne Light	Energy
Holdings	South Jersey
EnergySolve	Industries
Exelon	Southern Company
FirstEnergy	TransAlta

HISTORICAL FINANCIALS

Company Type: Public

Income Statement

FYE: December 31

	REVENUE ($ mil.)	NET INCOME ($ mil.)	NET PROFIT MARGIN	EMPLOYEES
12/14	11,499	1,737	15.1%	17,391
12/13	11,860	1,130	9.5%	18,108
12/12	12,286	1,526	12.4%	17,729
12/11	12,737	1,495	11.7%	17,722
12/10	8,521	938	11.0%	14,000
Annual Growth	**7.8%**	**16.7%**	**—**	**5.6%**

2014 Year-End Financials

Debt ratio: 44.73%
Return on equity: 13.31%
Cash ($ mil.): 1,751
Current ratio: 0.83
Long-term debt ($ mil.): 18,856

No. of shares (mil.): 665
Dividends
  Yield: 4.4%
  Payout: 61.5%
Market value ($ mil.): 24,190

	STOCK PRICE ($) FY Close	P/E High/Low	Earnings	Dividends	Book Value
12/14	36.33	14 11	2.61	1.49	20.47
12/13	30.09	18 15	1.76	1.47	19.78
12/12	28.63	12 10	2.60	1.44	18.01
12/11	29.42	11 9	2.70	1.40	18.72
12/10	26.32	15 11	2.17	1.40	16.98
Annual Growth	**8.4%**	**— —**	**4.7%**	**1.6%**	**4.8%**

Praxair, Inc.

Praxair makes lighter than air and heavier than air gases available for practical applications. The largest North American industrial gas supplier it produces and sells atmospheric gases (oxygen nitrogen argon and rare gases) as well as process and specialty gases (CO2 helium and hydrogen) for the chemicals food and beverage semiconductor and healthcare industries worldwide. It serves 25 diverse industries across more than 50 countries.

Its Praxair Surface Technologies unit supplies high-temperature and corrosion-resistant metallic ceramic and powder coatings mainly to the aircraft plastics and primary metals markets. Praxair builds on-site gas plants and also provides gases by the cylinder.

HISTORY

The origins of Praxair date to the work of Karl von Linde a professor of mechanical engineering at the College of Technology in Munich Germany in the late 1800s. In 1895 he created the cryogenic air liquefier. Von Linde built his first oxygen-production plant in 1902 and a nitrogen plant in 1904 and in the first decade of the 20th century he built a number of air-separation plants throughout Europe.

By 1907 von Linde had moved to the US and founded Linde Air Products in Cleveland to extract oxygen from air. Linde Air Products joined rival Union Carbide in 1911 in experimenting with the production of acetylene; it became a unit of Union Carbide in 1917. America's war effort and economic expansion in the 1920s spurred the development of new uses for industrial gases. Union Carbide's Linde unit also contributed to the development of the atomic bomb in the 1940s when its scientists perfected a process for refining uranium.

As Union Carbide expanded worldwide over the next two decades Linde became America's #1 producer of industrial gases. In the 1960s Linde expanded into oxygen-fired furnaces for steel production and the use of nitrogen in refrigerators. By the early 1980s Linde accounted for 11% of Union Carbide's annual sales.

The disastrous 1984 chemical accident at Union Carbide's plant in Bhopal India coupled with heavy debt and falling sales forced Union Carbide to reorganize. In 1992 Linde was spun off as Praxair. William Lichtenberger former president of Union Carbide headed the new company and pushed global expansion. Two years later Praxair set up China's first helium transfill plants for medical magnetic resonance imaging. In 1995 the company began operations in India and Peru.

In 1996 Praxair Surface Technologies bought Miller Thermal (thermal spray coatings) and Maxima Air Separation Center (industrial and specialty gases Israel). Also that year the company picked up $60 million when it sold the Linde name and trademark to Linde a German engineering and industrial gas company. Praxair purchased and then spun off Chicago Bridge & Iron. The company kept only its Liquid Carbonic division the world's leading supplier of carbon dioxide for processing. The move opened up a new market in carbonated beverages for Praxair.

In 1997 and 1998 Praxair constructed plants and to control its own delivery systems acquired 20 packaged-gases distributors in the US and one in Germany. The company also formed a joint venture in China to produce high-purity nitrogen and other specialty gases for electronics and then teamed up with rival L'Air Liquide in a production joint venture.

Praxair supplied an argon-based protection system for the Shroud of Turin's public display in Italy in 1998. It also installed the industry's first small on-site hydrogen-generating system at an Indiana powdered-metals plant. In 1999 the company formed a global alliance with German pharmaceutical and chemicals company Merck KGaA to provide gases and chemicals to the semiconductor industry. The same year Praxair acquired Materials Research Corporation a maker of thin-film deposition materials for semiconductors and the TAFA Group which makes thermal-spray equipment and related products.

In 2001 Praxair underwent a restructuring that included layoffs in its surface technologies unit (hurt by the decline in jet orders) and Brazilian operations. The next year the company started work on a new plant to serve Singapore's high-tech industry. Praxair boosted its health care segment with the acquisition of Alpine Medicine.

In 2004 Praxair Healthcare Services bought Home Care Supply for $245 million. With Home Care Supply joining the company's existing operations the combined Healthcare Services unit grew its sales to $750 million worldwide slightly more than 10% of Praxair's total annual sales. The home care market became more important for Praxair as the company saw high growth potential in it (and high margins) and wanted to be able to compete with rivals L'Air Liquide and Air Products and Chemicals.

The company bought some of L'Air Liquide's German assets for about $650 million later that year. Due to antitrust requirements the French company needed to dispose of the businesses after buying much of Messer Group earlier in the year. The acquisition put Praxair's European sales over $1 billion annually.

In 2006 Praxair sold the aviation repair business of the Surface Technologies unit to Gridiron Capital and Skyview Capital. The firms created a new company called PAS Technologies to house operations that serve both the commercial and military sectors with the repair of aviation engine and airframe parts and the application of protective coatings to those parts. Also that year Praxair's distribution unit acquired Medical Gas of Illinois and Withrow Oxygen Service of California.

Praxair expanded its presence in the Middle East in 2010 by acquiring a 49% stake in the ROC Group's operations in Kuwait United Arab Emirates and Qatar.

In 2011 Praxair sold its US homecare business to Apria Healthcare. The former Praxair segment provided home respiratory services home medical equipment and nutrition therapies through a network of more than 80 branches across the country. The transaction allowed Praxair to focus on expanding its institutional healthcare business worldwide although it maintains some of its homecare units outside of the US.

In 2011 the company spent $294 million on acquisitions primarily for industrial and specialty packaged gas distributors in the US. It also invested in a joint venture in the Middle East and gained a larger ownership stake in its Scandinavian joint venture (Yara Praxair).

That year Praxair also agreed to develop and market a new process technology with Midrex Technologies (a subsidiary of Kobe Steel) to produce direct reduced iron (DRI) using a variety of fuels including coke oven gas. The company hopes to find new markets for the production of DRI which is usually made from a gas produced from natural gas or coal.

Subsidiary Praxair Distribution also expanded in 2011 acquiring Houston-based National Alloy and Equipment which supplies technical support to makers of high-pressure control packages and drilling risers for oil and energy companies and American Gas Group one of the largest independent specialty gas producers in North America.

Building on its presence in Russia Praxair agreed to acquire the industrial and packaged gases operations of Russian tire company SIBUR - Russian Tyres in 2012. With four major projects in Russia having a total production capacity of more than 3500 tons of gases per day under its belt the company hopes to become the leading industrial gas manufacturer throughout southern Russia.

In 2012 it signed a 15-year agreement with Honeywell Resins & Chemicals to buy carbon dioxide for Praxair's new plant at the Honeywell site.

That year the company's Shanghai-based Praxair China unit started up a new air separation plant in Nanjing for Meishan Iron and Steel Co. a subsidiary of giant steel manufacturer Baosteel Group.

In 2012 Praxair Canada acquired Canadian Cylinder & Gases Inc. an independent distributor of industrial and specialty gases and welding equipment. It also acquired five Airgas branch locations in western Canada including Calgary Red Deer and Edmonton Alberta and Regina and Saskatoon Saskatchewan. This acquisition supports its growth strategy in western Canada to better serve existing customers and home oxygen clients in Alberta and Saskatchewan.

In 2012 Praxair Distribution acquired Harlingen Texas-based Acetylene Oxygen Company a distributor of Praxair industrial gases. Praxair Distribution also acquired Welders Industrial Supply LLC an independent distributor of industrial and specialty gases welding equipment supplies and related services to customers in the greater Houston area.

EXECUTIVES

Chairman President and CEO, Stephen F. (Steve) Angel, $1,287,500 total compensation
SVP; President White Martins Gases Industriais and Praxair South America, Domingos H. G. Bulus
EVP, Eduardo F. Menezes, $552,500 total compensation
President Praxair Europe, Daniel H. (Dan) Yankowski
President Praxair Distribution, Scott W. Kaltrider
President Praxair Asia, John M. Panikar
EVP, Scott E. Telesz, $575,000 total compensation
SVP and CFO, Matthew J. (Matt) White, $500,000 total compensation
VP and CIO, Marc A. Franciosa
CTO, Todd A. Skare
President Praxair Canada, Sean Durbin
President Praxair Mexico, Benjamin (Ben) Glazer
President Global Hydrogen, Samir J. Serhan
Vice President Sales, Andy Kurelek
Vice President Operations Praxair Healthcare Services, Jeff Barnhard
Vice President And General Manager Us Praxair Distribution, Randall Brittingham
Vice President and Controller, Mathew White
Vice President Sales, Ed Haversang
Auditors: PricewaterhouseCoopersLLP

LOCATIONS

HQ: Praxair, Inc.
39 Old Ridgebury Road, Danbury, CT 06810-5113
Phone: 203 837-2000
Web: www.praxair.com

2014 Sales

	% of total
North America	52
South America	16
Europe	13
Asia	13
Surface technologies	6
Total	**100**

PRODUCTS/OPERATIONS

2014 Sales by Distribution Method

	% of total
On-site (includes noncryogenics)	29
Merchant(delivered liquids)	34
Packaged gases (cylinders)	28
Other	9
Total	**100**

2014 Sales by End Market

	% of total
Manufacturing	24
Metals	17
Energy	14
Chemicals	10
Electronics	7
Healthcare	8
Food & Beverage	8
Aerospace	3
Other	9
Total	**100**

Selected Mergers and Acquisitions

COMPETITORS

Air Products	L' Air Liquide
Airgas	Teleflex
Balchem	The Linde Group
Chromalloy Gas Turbine	
GKN Aerospace	
Chem-tronics	

HISTORICAL FINANCIALS

Company Type: Public

Income Statement

	REVENUE ($ mil.)	NET INCOME ($ mil.)	NET PROFIT MARGIN	FYE: December 31 EMPLOYEES
12/14	12,273	1,694	13.8%	27,780
12/13	11,925	1,755	14.7%	27,560
12/12	11,224	1,692	15.1%	26,539
12/11	11,252	1,672	14.9%	26,184
12/10	10,116	1,195	11.8%	26,261
Annual Growth	**5.0%**	**9.1%**	**—**	**1.4%**

2014 Year-End Financials

Debt ratio: 46.75%	No. of shares (mil.): 289
Return on equity: 27.70%	Dividends
Cash ($ mil.): 126	Yield: 2.0%
Current ratio: 1.14	Payout: 41.2%
Long-term debt ($ mil.): 8,669	Market value ($ mil.): 37,477

	STOCK PRICE ($) FY Close	P/E High/Low	PER SHARE ($) Earnings	Dividends	Book Value
12/14	129.56	23 21	5.73	2.60	19.44
12/13	130.03	22 18	5.87	2.40	22.47
12/12	109.45	21 18	5.61	2.20	20.47
12/11	106.90	20 16	5.45	2.00	18.38
12/10	95.47	25 19	3.84	1.80	19.05
Annual Growth	**7.9%**	**— —**	**10.5%**	**9.6%**	**0.5%**

Priceline Group Inc. (The)

The Priceline Group (formerly priceline.com) would like to name itself the king of online travel. At website priceline.com buyers can "name their own price" for airline tickets hotel rooms rental cars cruises and vacation packages. Customers can also choose set-price options. With its patented business model Priceline generates most of its sales from travel-related services. In the case of airline tickets and hotel reservations it generates sales on the margin keeping the difference between the price paid by the individual and what it shelled out for the ticket or hotel room. Founded in 1997 it operates six primary brands: Booking.com priceline.com Agoda.com KAYAK and rentalcars.com and OpenTable.

Geographic Reach

The Connecticut-based global online travel giant generates about three-quarters of its revenue outside the US. The Netherlands now accounts for 60% of Priceline Group's total revenue.

Sales and Marketing

The travel company aggressively promotes its brands online. In recent years Priceline has extended its reach to offline campaigns as well to add depth to its brands.

The Priceline Group which spent about $1.8 billion in 2013 on its total online advertising relies on Internet search engine keyword purchases referrals from meta-search sites and travel research websites affiliate programs banner and pop-up advertisements and email campaigns to boost its bottom line. It has also invested some $127.5 million in Priceline-branded offline advertising in the US. Indeed in fall 2014 the company launched its first national brand campaign in Canada to enhance its growing presence there.

Operations

Priceline operates an online global travel services network. It works to connect customers looking to make travel reservations with providers of travel services worldwide including more than 295000 hotels and accommodations. Hotel reservation services are conducted primarily under the Booking.com priceline.com and Agoda.com brands.

In the US the company offers reservations via its namesake priceline.com brand for rental cars airline tickets vacations packages destination services and cruises. Internationally the company offers a retail price-disclosed hotel and accommodation reservation service through global brands Booking.com (the world's largest online hotel and accommodation website) and Agoda.com (an online hotel reservation service with operations primarily in Asia). Booking.com partners with more than 275000 properties in 180-plus countries and territories to offer its customers hotel and accommodation reservations on various websites and in more than 40 languages. Extending its reach to online restaurant reservations Priceline Group acquired OpenTable in mid-2014.

Financial Performance

As the online travel category has grown so have Priceline Group's sales and profits. In 2013 the company's sales grew 29% versus 2012 to a record $6.8 billion. Net income increased 33% over the same period to $1.9 billion. Indeed over the past decade Priceline Group's sales have grown by nearly 800% and profits have risen in each of the last seven years.

The company attributes the growth to an increase in agency merchant and other revenues. The Booking.com business spurred growth among agency revenues. Growth in the Priceline retail rental-car business and the integration of hotels from the Booking.com extranet on the priceline.com website both contributed toward increasing US agency revenues. Merchant revenues rose as well in 2013 as compared to 2012 due to increases in its Agoda.com hotel business rentalcars.com rental car business and priceline.com merchant price-disclosed hotel business.

Strategy

Partnering with other travel giants has helped Priceline expand its business and provide a more diverse revenue stream. In 2013 Priceline entered a long-term agreement with United Airlines to implement the United Technology Application as the primary connectivity between the pair. As part of the alliance Priceline and United Airlines plan to develop ancillary products and services to be delivered to customers through the United Technology Application. In 2014 it partnered with General Motors to roll out a priceline.com powered hotel booking service through the new ChevroletApp-Shop.

Priceline Group has also made frequent use of acquisitions to bolster its stable of online brands including the online travel comparison site KAYAK and restaurant booking service OpenTable.

Mergers and Acquisitions

In its biggest purchase to date Priceline Group in July 2014 acquired the online restaurant reservation service OpenTable for $2.6 billion in cash. The online travel giant is looking to extend its reach to restaurant reservations.

In June 2014 Priceline Group acquired Buuteeq Inc. a digital cloud-based marketing platform for hotels worldwide.

Adding to its operations Priceline acquired its smaller rival Kayak Software for $1.8 billion in cash and stock in May 2013. The deal was the largest in Priceline's history and could provide a new source of revenue (advertising) for the company. Kayak Software is an online travel comparison and booking site that makes most of its money from referrals and advertising. Post sale subsidiary Kayak operates as an independent brand within The Priceline Group.

Company Background

In April 2014 the company changed its name from Priceline.com to The Priceline Group to better reflect the growth of its business and all of its subsidiaries and brands including Booking.com priceline.com KAYAK OpenTable and others.

HISTORY

Priceline founder Jay Walker launched a string of ventures before making the leap into e-commerce. In 1994 he founded Walker Digital an entrepreneurial think tank formed to develop business models that could germinate into new companies.

In 1996 Walker Digital found the impetus that would drive Priceline: Each day major airlines have more than 500000 empty seats. Walker's team reasoned that if the airlines were offered even a discounted price for these empty seats they'd jump at the chance to cut their losses. Based on that premise Walker Digital developed a "name your price" system and founded Priceline in 1997.

The company launched its airfare service in 1998 and obtained financing from General Atlantic Partners and Paul Allen's Vulcan Ventures (now called Vulcan Northwest). That year it expanded into hotel reservations and added a car-buying service. Richard Braddock became chairman and CEO in 1998.

Priceline added home financing services to its offerings in 1999. The company went public with a chart-busting IPO later that year. Priceline also launched a rental car service. Branching into the retail arena it licensed its technology to WebHouse Club for use in selling grocery products. The company sued Microsoft in 1999 claiming that company's Expedia unit's name-your-own-price hotel reservation service violated Priceline's patent.

In 2000 the company licensed its business model to several international ventures including General Atlantic Partners' Priceline.com Europe (headed by Dennis Malamatinas former Burger King CEO) SOFTBANK's Priceline.com Japan (a deal that was later cancelled) MyPrice in Australia and New Zealand (also cancelled) and Asian conglomerate Hutchinson Whampoa. In collaboration with Alliance Capital (now AllianceBernstein) Priceline created subsidiary pricelinemortgage to act as mortgage broker.

Daniel Schulman became CEO later that year. Jay Walker resigned as vice chairman at the end of 2000 after taking on the role of CEO at Walker Digital. After deciding it would probably never be profitable WebHouse Club shut down ending Priceline's foray into grocery sales. Known for its splashy ads Priceline dumped pop icon William Shatner as its TV spokesperson in favor of Sex and the City star Sarah Jessica Parker. (Shatner returned in 2002.) Later that year the company fired Schulman and reappointed Braddock as CEO.

In 2002 the company joined with National Leisure Group to offer cruises from its website. Later that year Priceline purchased the assets of discount travel site Lowestfare.com. It also announced plans to sell cars under a marketing agreement with Autobytel. In late 2002 Braddock passed his CEO responsibilities to president Jeffery Boyd. (Braddock remained as chairman.)

A handful of new international destinations (Australia Japan Indonesia Malaysia South Korea Taiwan) was added in 2003 to Priceline's hotel reservation service. In April 2004 chairman Richard Braddock (former president of Citicorp and one of the last remaining high-profile board members) resigned from the company. Director Ralph Bahna was then named chairman. The following month Priceline acquired most of Travelweb.com. That September it bought Active Hotels of Britain for about $161 million in cash. In December 2004 Priceline acquired the remaining stake in Travelweb for about $4 million.

EXECUTIVES

Vice President Of Financial Planning, Matt Tynan

Chairman priceline.com, Christopher L. (Chris) Soder, age 55, $360,000 total compensation

SVP Technology, Michael P. Diliberto

CEO OpenTable, Matthew (Matt) Roberts, age 46

SVP and General Counsel, Peter J. Millones, age 45, $330,000 total compensation

EVP Corporate Development and Head Worldwide Strategy and Planning, Glenn D. Fogel, age 53, $315,000 total compensation

SVP CFO and Chief Accounting Officer, Daniel J. Finnegan, age 53, $315,000 total compensation

CEO priceline.com, Paul J. Hennessy

CEO agoda.com, Robert Rosenstein, age 48

President and CEO Priceline Group and CEO Booking.com B.V., Darren R. Huston, age 49, $750,000 total compensation

CEO rentalcars.com, Greg Wills

CEO KAYAK, Steve Hafner

EVP Global Operations, Maelle Gavet

President and COO Booking.com, Gillian Tans, age 44

Senior Vice President Of Corporate Development, Todd Henrich

Vice President: Marketing Planning and Analysis, Ben Harrell

Senior Vice President Information Technology Operations, Ken Jones

Vice President Of Operations, Caser Viera

Vice President Air Suppliers, Brigit Zimmerman

Vice President Business Analysis Hotels, Michael (Mel) Banks

Vice President Engineering, Giri Nathan

Vice President Tax, Gerald Lambert

Senior Vice President Rental Cars, William Jose

Vice President, Patricia Stevenson

Vice President Hotel Revenue Management, Chris Winter

Vice President Controller Us Operations, Matthew Dewald

Vice President Associate General Counsel, Brian Macdonald

Vice President Of Public Relations, Brian Ek

Senior Vice President Global Infrastructure, Glen Dalgleish

Vice President Media Group, Greg Slattery

Senior Vice President Finance and Investor Relations, Matthew N (Matt) Tynan

Vice President Internal Audit, Shahzad Khawaja

Chairman, Jeffery H. (Jeff) Boyd, age 58
Auditors: DELOITTE & TOUCHE LLP

LOCATIONS

HQ: Priceline Group Inc. (The)
800 Connecticut Avenue, Norwalk, CT 06854
Phone: 203 299-8000 **Fax:** 203 595-0160
Web: www.pricelinegroup.com

2014 Sales

	$ mil.	% of total
The Netherlands	5,519	66
US	1,798	21
Other	1,124	13
Total	**8,442**	**100**

PRODUCTS/OPERATIONS

2014 Sales

	$ mil.	% of total
Agency	5,845	69
Merchant	2,186	26
Advertising and other	410	5
Total	**8,442**	**100**

Selected Products

Airline tickets
Cruises
Hotel rooms
Rental cars
Restaurant reservations
Vacation packages

Selected Brands

agoda.com
Booking.com
KAYAK
OpenTable
priceline.com
rentalcars.com

COMPETITORS

Alibaba Group	Internet Brands
Amadeus IT	Intuit
Amazon.com	Microsoft
American Express	Orbitz Worldwide
Apple Inc.	Prestige Travel
AutoNation	Restaurant.com
AutoTrader	Sabre
Autobytel	SavvyDiner.com
BCD Travel	Travelocity
Carlson Wagonlit	Travelport
Expedia	Travelzoo
Facebook	TripAdvisor
GetThere	Yahoo!
Google	Yelp
Groupon	

HISTORICAL FINANCIALS

Company Type: Public

Income Statement

FYE: December 31

	REVENUE ($ mil.)	NET INCOME ($ mil.)	NET PROFIT MARGIN	EMPLOYEES
12/15	9,223	2,551	27.7%	15,500
12/14	8,441	2,421	28.7%	12,700
12/13	6,793	1,892	27.9%	9,500
12/12	5,260	1,424	27.1%	7,000
12/11	4,355	1,059	24.3%	5,000
Annual Growth	**20.6%**	**24.6%**	**—**	**32.7%**

2015 Year-End Financials

Debt ratio: 35.35%	No. of shares (mil.): 49
Return on equity: 29.39%	Dividends
Cash ($ mil.): 1,477	Yield: —
Current ratio: 2.47	Payout: —
Long-term debt ($ mil.): 6,158	Market value ($ mil.): 63,252

	STOCK PRICE ($) FY Close	P/E High/Low	PER SHARE ($) Earnings	Dividends	Book Value
12/15	1,274.95	29 20	49.45	0.00	177.29
12/14	1,140.21	30 22	45.67	0.00	164.96
12/13	1,162.40	32 17	36.11	0.00	132.86
12/12	620.39	27 17	27.66	0.00	78.14
12/11	467.71	26 19	20.63	0.00	51.69
Annual Growth	**28.5%**	**— —**	**24.4%**	**—**	**36.1%**

Primerica Inc.

Primerica primarily offers insurance and asset management services. The company offers term life insurance coverage written by affiliate Primerica Life Insurance to more than 4 million customers in the US and Canada. It also offers serves as a broker of debt consolidation loans investment and savings products and long-term care insurance through other underwriters. Taking pages from franchise and multi-level marketing playbooks it markets its products to middle-income customers through a network of contracted independent sales representatives.

Geographic Reach

The company's US operations account for more than 80% of revenues with the remainder of sales coming from Canadian markets.

Operations

Sales of term life insurance account for more than half of Primerica's annual revenues. The life insurance segment covers some 4.3 million lives and has some $670 billion in life insurance policies in force.

In addition the company serves 1.9 million customers from its investment and savings segment (35% of sales) which handles assets valued at some $37 billion. The actual investment products (including mutual funds and variable annuities) are supplied by such firms as Invesco Legg Mason and MetLife.

Primerica also distributes a handful of specialty products including individual long-term care insurance prepaid legal services and referrals for other insurance products.

Sales and Marketing

Primerica has structured its insurance distribution model to attract part-time professionals and entrepreneurial types who are willing to build up face-to-face relationship with clients. They can also earn higher commissions as they recruit and supervise more part-time sales representatives. New recruits pay the company a fee for their training and then must work to secure their license to sell insurance in their state or province.

The company has built up a network of some 92500 sales representatives who target middle income consumers (those with annual household incomes of between $30000 and $100000). Its investment and savings products are distributed by its broker-dealer subsidiaries (PFS Investments and PFSL Investments Canada) and some 22000 of its independent representatives.

Financial Performance

Primerica experienced an 8% increase in revenues to some $1.2 billion in 2012 marking a turnaround after two years of declining sales. The 2012 results were attributed to premium and policy growth in the life insurance segment; increased commissions and fees from the investment and savings segment; and net investment gains. Growth achievements were slightly offset by a de-

cline in the corporate and other distributed products segment.

Net income continued on a downward trend though the 3% decline to $174 million was an improvement over sharper declines in 2011 and 2010. The company's finances suffered from asset transfers and reinsurance agreements that were part of its separation process from former parent Citigroup which was itself suffering from heavy financial losses following the mortgage and credit crisis of 2008.

Strategy

The company is focused on streamlining operations and strengthening its finances. It opened a new headquarters location in 2013 to consolidate functions to one location and strengthen sales support and service capabilities. Primerica is working to improve its capital position by conducting share repurchase transactions with stockholder Warburg Pincus.

In addition the company is working to launch new product lines that can be issued faster with lower face values and the company is seeing modest sales growth through these efforts. In 2013 Primerica expanded its retirement solutions when it launched a new annuity product through its distribution agreement with Lincoln Financial. The company also looks to increase sales by attracting new insurance distribution recruits which has been a challenge for Primerica during years of rough economic conditions.

Ownership

Warburg Pincus owned an 11% stake in Primerica as of December 2012 (down from 25% in 2010) while Wellington Management owned a 9% stake.

The company was a subsidiary of Citigroup until it was spun off in a $320 million IPO in 2010. All proceeds from Primerica's IPO went to Citigroup which retained about a 40% stake in Primerica. Citigroup divested the remaining shares by 2011 in a gradual process. The spin-off was part of Citigroup's strategy to focus on its banking operations and strengthen its finances.

EXECUTIVES

Chairman - Primerica Distribution; Co-Chief Executive Officer; Director, John A. Addison Jr., age 57
Chairman of the Board; Co-Chief Executive Officer, D. Richard (Rick) Williams, age 58
EVP Corporate Relations, Mark Supic
Regional VP, Margarita Vazquez
CIO, David Wade
EVP General Counsel Chief Administrative Officer and Corporate Secretary, Peter W. Schneider, age 58
Chief Financial Officer; Executive Vice President, Alison S. Rand, age 46
Investor Relations, Kathryn Kieser
Chief Operating Officer; Executive Vice President, Gregory C. Pitts
REGIONAL Vice President Registered Re, Beth Lambert
SENIOR Vice President Registered Re, Carter Poole
SENIOR NATIONAL SALES Director Registered Re, Jann Marque
Executive Vice President; Chief Marketing Officer, Chess Britt
President of Primerica Life Insurance Co., Jeffrey Fendler
Executive Vice President and Chief Business Technology Officer, Michael Adams
President of PFS Investments, William Kelly
Regional Vice President from Houston agrees, Todd Greer
Director, Robert F. McCullough, age 72

LOCATIONS

HQ: Primerica Inc.
 1 Primerica Parkway, Duluth, GA 30099
Phone: 770 381-1000
Web: www.primerica.com

HISTORICAL FINANCIALS

Company Type: Public

Income Statement

FYE: December 31

	ASSETS ($ mil.)	NET INCOME ($ mil.)	INCOME AS % OF ASSETS	EMPLOYEES
12/14	10,738	181	1.7%	2,579
12/13	10,329	162	1.6%	2,605
12/12	10,337	173	1.7%	2,547
12/11	9,998	178	1.8%	2,537
12/10	9,884	257	2.6%	2,510
Annual Growth	2.1%	(8.4%)	—	0.7%

2014 Year-End Financials

Debt ratio: 5.54%	No. of shares (mil.): 52
Return on equity: 14.71%	Dividends
Cash ($ mil.): 192	Yield: 0.8%
Current ratio: —	Payout: 15.3%
Long-term debt ($ mil.): —	Market value ($ mil.): 2,831

	STOCK PRICE ($) FY Close	P/E High/Low		PER SHARE ($) Earnings	Dividends	Book Value
12/14	54.26	17	12	3.29	0.48	23.87
12/13	42.91	15	10	2.83	0.44	22.29
12/12	30.01	11	8	2.71	0.24	22.62
12/11	23.24	11	8	2.36	0.10	21.93
12/10	24.25	7	6	3.40	0.02	19.65
Annual Growth	22.3%	—	—	(0.8%)	121.3%	5.0%

Principal Financial Group, Inc.

For a child in elementary school avoiding the principal is paramount. But for folks looking toward retirement seeking The Principal may be wise. Founded in 1879 Principal Financial Group (or The Principal) is a top administrator of employer-sponsored retirement plans offering pension products and services as well as mutual funds annuities asset management trust services and investment advice. Its insurance segment provides group and individual life and disability insurance and group dental and vision coverage. To compete with banks encroaching on the company's territory and to maximize customer asset retention subsidiary Principal Bank offers online banking.

Operations

PFG boasts nearly 20 million customers and some $519 billion of assets under management. PFG offers its financial products and services through four main segments: Retirement and Investor Services Principal Global Investors Principal

International and U.S. Insurance Solutions. The Retirement and Investor Services which generates roughly 50% of total revenue provides retirement and other financial products and services mostly to businesses (and their employees) and other individuals. The U.S. Insurance Solutions segment brings in another 30% of total sales and provides individual life insurance and specialty benefits insurance which includes group dental and vision individual and group disability and group life insurance along with non-medical fee-for-service claims administration services. The Principal International segment generates more than 10% of total sales and does business in countries with large middle classes and growing long-term savings. The business currently operates in Brazil Chile China Hong Kong Special Administrative Region India Mexico and Southeast Asia. The remainder of revenue comes from the Principal Global Investors segment which offers asset management services to the company's internal asset accumulation business insurance operations and the Corporate segment along with third-party clients. Sales and MarketingPFG's serves individuals businesses and institutional investors through a network of about 14500 independent brokers consultants and agents as well as through its own sales force at more than 40 offices nationwide. Principal Bank focuses on small and medium-sized businesses offering services by telephone mail and the Internet. Geographic Reach

PFG's international arm Principal International has operations in Brazil Chile China Hong Kong India Mexico and Southeast Asia. The firm focuses on countries with large middle classes and favorable demographics. Principal Global Investors has offices in about a dozen countries including Australia China Japan the United Arab Emirates the US and the UK.

Financial Performance

PFG has experienced three straight years of revenue growth with revenue jumping by 13% to $10.48 billion in 2014. The growth for 2014 was fueled by higher premium revenue from the company's payout annuity unit of business and from higher fees stemming from an uptick in average account values from new investor business and strong stock market performance. PFG was also helped by additional net investment income from its Chilean investments.

Higher revenue also pushed net income up by 26% to $1.18 billion in 2014 marking the company's sixth straight year of profit growth. Operations provided $3.10 billion or 40% more cash than in 2013 thanks in part to higher earnings but mostly because PFG sold some of its real estate assets and had favorable fluctuations in payables and receivables assocated with the timing of settlements.

Strategy

PFG aims to become a global player in retirement services targeting countries in Asia and Latin America that rely on private-sector defined-contribution pension plans to accommodate their growing number of retirees. The company typically builds its international business through startups acquisitions and joint ventures. PFG has exited underperforming businesses such as medical insurance to focus on asset management at home and abroad.

In the US PFGI courts firms with fewer than 1000 employees for its insurance and pension products; that market is primed for growth as a relatively low percentage of small to midsized businesses currently offer these products. Its strategy for growth also includes targeting large institutional clients for its asset management operations which include Principal Global Investors. The company serves approximately 650 institutional investors.

Mergers Acquisitions and Divestments

PFG in 2014 acquired AXA's Mandatory Provident Fund (MPF) and Occupational Retirement Schemes Ordinance (ORSO) pension business in Hong Kong for approximately $335 million. The deal ehanced PFG's position within the key market of Hong Kong.

In 2013 PFG acquired Chilean pension management firm AFP Cuprum S.A. for $1.5 billion. The company was lured by the attractive emerging retirement and long-term savings markets such as Chile Mexico and Brazil that AFP Cuprum serves. Also in 2013 to grow its assets PFG acquired a 55% interest in Liongate Capital Management LLP and Liongate Limited —a global alternative investment boutique and hedge fund investor with $1.4 billion in assets under management —for a transaction price of $44 million.

In October 2012 PFG scooped up First Dental Health a California-based preferred provider organization (PPO) with more than 11000 dentists operating in Arizona California and Nevada. The acquisition bolstered PFG's specialty benefits insurance business.

HISTORY

Principal Financial was founded as the Bankers Life Association in 1879 by Edward Temple a Civil War veteran and banker. Life insurance became popular after the war but some dishonest insurers canceled customers' policies before they had to pay out benefits. Bankers Life an assessable association (members shared the cost of death benefits as the claims arose) was intended to provide low-cost protection to bankers and their families. The company soon began offering life insurance to nonbankers but it refused to insure women because of the high mortality rate among mothers during childbirth.

EXECUTIVES

Vice President Network Development, Lance Marshall
Vice President Sales, Joseph Martin
Vice President Sales, Rob Elwood
Vice President Sourcing, Brent Fritz
Vice President Tax, Rich Wireman
Vice President Investor Relations, John Egan
Senior Vice President, Cindy Dicks
Vice President Of Sales, Ron Altbaum
Vice President Of Human Resources, Mindy Moss
Vice President, Renee Schaaf
Senior Vice President Risk Management, Lou Flori
Regional Vice President, Peter Seltz
Vice President Sales, David Sandstead
Assistant Vice President, Diane Howe
Regional Vice President Life, Jeff Warkenthien
Vice President, Jill Szambelan
Life Regional Vice President, Dave House
Senior Vice President Retirement Distrib, Timothy Minard
Disability Income Regional Vice President (DI RVP) covering the states of Indiana, Dianne Crouse
Vice President Life, Don Cooper
Vice President of Annuity Distribution, Steven (Steve) Becker
Vice President Marketing and Sales Desk Individual Life and Specialty Benefits, Joleen Workman
Chairman, Larry D. Zimpleman, age 64
Auditors: Ernst & Young LLP

LOCATIONS

HQ: Principal Financial Group, Inc.
  711 High Street, Des Moines, IA 50392
Phone: 515 247-5111
Web: www.principal.com

Selected Operations
Australia
Brazil
Chile
China
Hong Kong
India
Indonesia
Japan
Malaysia
Mexico
Singapore
Thailand
UK
US

PRODUCTS/OPERATIONS

2014 Sales

	% of total
Fees & other revenues	35
Premiums & other considerations	33
Net investment income	31
Net realized capital gains	1
Total	**100**

2014 Sales by Segment

	$ mil.	% of total
Retirement & Investor Services	5,523	51
US Insurance Solutions	3,262	30
Principal International	1,275	12
Principal Global Investors	725	7
Corporate	(232.4)	-
Adjustments	(77.2)	-
Total	**10,477**	**100**

COMPETITORS

AIG
AXA
Aetna
Allianz
BlackRock
FMR
ING

JPMorgan Chase
John Hancock Financial Services
Lincoln Financial Group
MassMutual
MetLife
Morgan Stanley Investment Management
PIMCO
T. Rowe Price
The Vanguard Group
Unum Group

HISTORICAL FINANCIALS

Company Type: Public

Income Statement

	ASSETS ($ mil.)	NET INCOME ($ mil.)	INCOME AS % OF ASSETS	EMPLOYEES
12/15	218,685	1,234	0.6%	14,895
12/14	219,087	1,144	0.5%	14,873
12/13	208,191	912	0.4%	14,792
12/12	161,926	805	0.5%	13,373
12/11	148,298	715	0.5%	13,527
Annual Growth	**10.2%**	**14.6%**	**—**	**2.4%**

FYE: December 31

2015 Year-End Financials

Debt ratio: 1.50%
Return on equity: 12.66%
Cash ($ mil.): 2,564
Current ratio: —
Long-term debt ($ mil.): —
No. of shares (mil.): 291
Dividends
  Yield: 3.3%
  Payout: 36.5%
Market value ($ mil.): 13,107

	STOCK PRICE ($) FY Close	P/E High/Low	PER SHARE ($) Earnings	Dividends	Book Value
12/15	44.98	14 11	4.06	1.50	31.95
12/14	51.94	15 11	3.65	1.28	34.65
12/13	49.31	17 10	2.95	0.98	32.81
12/12	28.52	12 9	2.57	0.78	33.20
12/11	24.60	16 10	2.15	0.70	32.01
Annual Growth	**16.3%**	**— —**	**17.2%**	**21.0%**	**(0.0%)**

PrivateBancorp, Inc.

It's your private banker a banker for money and any old teller won't do. PrivateBancorp is the holding company for The PrivateBank and Trust Co which provides commercial and community banking real estate lending investments and money management services to middle-market companies commercial real estate professionals small business owners executives and wealthy individuals and their families. The bank boasts over $15.6 billion in assets around 25 branches in the Chicago area and 10 branches across Atlanta Cleveland Denver Des Moines Detroit Milwaukee Minneapolis Kansas City and St. Louis. Specializing in mid-market business lending commercial loans make up 66% of its loan portfolio.

Operations

PrivateBancorp operates two main segments: Banking which generates nearly 99% of its total revenue and makes up 89% of its assets; and Asset Management (formerly Trust and Investments) which provides investment management personal trust and estate administration custodial and escrow retirement account administration and brokerage services. The company's Lodestar Investment Counsel subsidiary provides trust and investment management services to families foundations and high-net-worth individuals with more than $500000 to invest. The company which had a staff of 1168 employees generated 72% of its

total revenue from loan interest (including fees) in 2014 and another 10% from interest on taxable and tax-exempt investment securities. The remainder of revenue came from fee-based income from treasury management (4%) asset management (3%) capital markets products (3%) deposit service charges (1%) and various other fees.Geographic ReachIn addition to its 34 branches in the Midwest PrivateBancorp has mid-market business development offices in Colorado Connecticut Georgia Iowa Michigan Minnesota Missouri and Ohio.Financial PerformancePrivateBancorp's revenues and profits have been rising thanks to steady growth in loan business (particularly commercial and industrial loan growth) added fee revenues and declining loan loss provisions as its loan portfolio's credit quality has improved with higher property valuations in the strengthened economy.The bank's revenue rose by 6% to a record $642 million in 2014 mostly driven by continued loan business growth as loan asset balances grew by $972 million over the year. The bank's non-interest income grew by 3% on higher treasury management loan letter of credit and commitment fees and syndication fees also helping to grow its top line.Higher revenue and continued declines in interest expenses and loan loss provisions in 2014 drove PrivateBancorp's net income higher by 25% to a record $153.1 million. The bank's operating income fell by more than half to $94.6 million after adjusting its earnings for non-cash items mostly related to its net proceeds from the sale of its loans held-for-sale.

Strategy

Privatebancorp's long-term goal reiterated in 2015 is "to be the bank of choice in the Midwest for middle market companies." As part of its effort to court mid-sized businesses PrivateBank has specialty banking groups devoted to the architecture construction and engineering health care and security alarm financing sectors. Targeting firms with $50 million to $2 billion in annual revenues the bank has expanded its fee-based activities such as treasury management and capital markets services. PrivateBancorp also utilizes its variety of service offerings to cross-sell its wealth management services to executives who have commercial banking relationships with the company.In addition to introducing new lines of business to organically grow its revenues the bank said in 2015 that it would "consider selective acquisitions" of retail banks to build its core deposit base gain market share in its target markets and/or bolster its product offerings.Company BackgroundPrivateBancorp changed its focus to court mid-market businesses originally in 2007. Formerly modeled after a traditional European private bank PrivateBancorp launched a strategic plan in late 2007 in response to Bank of America's acquisition of Chicago-based LaSalle Bank hoping to capitalize on area consumers and middle-market firms alienated by the sale. Former LaSalle Bank CEO Larry Richman was named president and CEO of PrivateBancorp and PrivateBank that year. PrivateBancorp also recruited several other LaSalle executives. The new management team's goal was to transform the organization into a leading middle market commercial bank. To that end over the next four years the bank added nearly 1000 client relationships and shifted the composition of its loan portfolio toward commercial and industrial loans.

Chicago-based investment firm GTCR Golder Rauner owns about 13.5% of PrivateBancorp.

EXECUTIVES

President CEO PrivateBancorp, Larry D. Richman, age 62, $2,250,000 total compensation

Executive Managing Director; President Commercial Real Estate, Karen B. Case, age 56, $56,435 total compensation

Executive Managing Director; President National Commercial Banking, Bruce R. Hague, age 60, $462,083 total compensation

Executive Managing Director; President Illinois Commercial and Specialty Banking, Bruce S. Lubin, age 61, $945,000 total compensation

Managing Director and CFO, Kevin M. Killips, age 59, $1,040,833 total compensation

Managing Director; President Personal Client Services, C. Brant Ahrens, age 44, $358,333 total compensation

CTO, James (Chip) Bennett

Senior Vice President, Evelyn Smith

Vice President, Robert Frentzel

Chairman, James M. (Jim) Guyette

Board Member, William R Rybak

Auditors: Ernst & Young LLP

LOCATIONS

HQ: PrivateBancorp, Inc.
120 South LaSalle Street, Chicago, IL 60603
Phone: 312 564-2000
Web: www.pvtb.com

PRODUCTS/OPERATIONS

2011 Sales

	$ mil.	% of total
Interest		
Loans including fees	413	72
Taxable securities	61	11
Other	6	1
Noninterest		
Loan and credit-related fees	22	4
Treasury management	19	3
Capital markets products	19	3
Trust and investments	17	3
Mortgage banking	6	1
Net securities gains	5	1
Other	6	1
Total	**579**	**100**

Selected Subsidiaries

The PrivateBank and Trust Company
  BBH Financial Advisors Inc.
  Lodestar Investment Counsel LLC
  PB Real Estate LLC
  PBTC & Company LLC
  PRIVATESTAR LLC
  TPB Title Agency LLC

COMPETITORS

Bank of America	Northern Trust
First Midwest Bancorp	Park Bancorp
Harris	Wintrust Financial
MB Financial	

HISTORICAL FINANCIALS

Company Type: Public

Income Statement

FYE: December 31

	ASSETS ($ mil.)	NET INCOME ($ mil.)	INCOME AS % OF ASSETS	EMPLOYEES
12/14	15,603	153	1.0%	1,168
12/13	14,085	122	0.9%	1,116
12/12	14,057	77	0.6%	1,105
12/11	12,416	44	0.4%	1,045
12/10	12,465	1	0.0%	1,060
Annual Growth	**5.8%**	**216.9%**	**—**	**2.5%**

2014 Year-End Financials

Debt ratio: 1.89%
Return on equity: 11.00%
Cash ($ mil.): 424
Current ratio: —
Long-term debt ($ mil.): —
No. of shares (mil.): 78
Dividends
  Yield: 0.1%
  Payout: 2.1%
Market value ($ mil.): 2,611

	STOCK PRICE ($) FY Close	P/E High/Low	PER SHARE ($) Earnings	Dividends	Book Value
12/14	33.40	17 13	1.94	0.04	18.95
12/13	28.93	19 10	1.57	0.04	16.75
12/12	15.32	20 13	0.88	0.04	15.65
12/11	10.98	38 16	0.43	0.04	18.07
12/10	14.38	— —	(0.17)	0.04	17.21
Annual Growth	**23.5%**	**— —**	**—**	**(0.0%)**	**2.4%**

ProAssurance Corp.

ProAssurance protects professional health associates –the doctors dentists and nurses of the US. One of the largest medical liability insurance providers in the nation ProAssurance is the holding company for ProAssurance Indemnity ProAssurance Casualty and other subsidiaries that sell liability coverage for health care providers primarily in the South and Midwest. Its customers include individual doctors in private practice as well as large physician groups clinics and hospitals. Its ProAssurance Specialty Insurance subsidiary writes excess and surplus (higher risk) lines of medical professional liability insurance. ProAssurance Casualty also provides some coverage for legal professionals.

Operations

ProAssurance operates through four primary segments: Specialty Property and Casualty (more than half of all sales) Workers' Compensation (about a quarter of sales) Lloyd's Syndicate and Corporate.

Physician policies make up ProAssurance's largest business accounting for about 80% of annual insurance premiums. Other key product groups include policies covering other health professionals medical facilities and legal professionals. Medmarc Casualty Insurance and Noetic Specialty Insurance write products liability coverage for medical technology and life sciences while Eastern Alliance Insurance provides workers' compensation. ProAssurance is also the majority capital provider to Lloyd's of London Syndicate 1729 which began writing business in 2014.

Geographic Reach

Although the company is licensed throughout the US its operations are concentrated in select states in the southern and midwestern US. Its largest markets –Alabama Pennsylanvia and Texas –together account for about a third of the company's premiums.

The company owns office facilities in Alabama Michigan Nevada Tennessee and Wisconsin.

Sales and Marketing

ProAssurance employs an internal sales force to write its health care professional liability policies. It also utilizes independent agencies and brokerages.

Customers include physicians dentists specialists (including podiatrists) allied health care professionals medical facilities lawyers life science and medical technology entities.

Financial Performance

ProAssurance is able to sustain financial stability during turbulent market conditions through disciplined underwriting prudent pricing and loss reserve practices and conservative investment strategies. Revenue rose 15% to $852 million in 2014 largely due to the recent addition of workers' compensation business acquired with Eastern Alliance Insurance. The group's participation in

the new Lloyd's Syndicate 1729 also drove up earnings. These increases were partially offset by a decline in net premiums for the Specialty Property and Casualty segment.

Net income has been somewhat turbulent over the past five years. It dropped 34% to $196 million in 2014 largely as a result of higher expenses related to the acquisition of Eastern Alliance Insurance and the investment in Lloyd's Syndicate 1729.

Cash flow from operations was on the decline until 2014 when it rebounded by 149% to $96 million. That turnaround was attributed to an increase in cash generated by receivables from reinsurers and a change in unearned premiums.

Strategy

ProAssurance's plans for long-term growth are based on the controlled expansion of its existing operations and by acquiring other specialty insurance companies or books of business. The company looks to expand in both existing and new territories and product lines. For instance the firm is working to grow in fields outside of the medical professional customer base partly due to increasing competition in the physician coverage market.

The company's aggressive acquisitions are part of its strategy to better compete against larger property/casualty insurance firms as well as smaller niche providers. ProAssurance works to provide local services that cater to the liability climates of its core geographies; it also focuses on targeted customer segments (medical and legal) to allow for a deep understanding of the industries' needs. In addition to acquisitions ProAssurance expands through organic growth efforts including new product launches as well as by forming partnerships with professional associations. As part of its strategy to expand geographically its Eastern Alliance Insurance unit opened a new office in Michigan in 2014.

In late 2013 the company became a corporate member of Lloyd's of London becoming the majority capital provider to the new Syndicate 1729. The move provided ProAssurance and its subsidiaries with more direct access to international professional liability opportunities in the health care sector.

Mergers and Acquisitions

In 2013 the company expanded through the purchase of Medmarc Insurance Group a liability underwriter for medical technology and life science policies in a $154 million transaction. The purchase also added some legal professional coverage operations.

EXECUTIVES

Chairman President and CEO, W. Stancil (Stan) Starnes, age 66, $854,100 total compensation

President Healthcare Professional Liability Group Chief Underwriting Officer and Chief Actuary, Howard H. Friedman, age 56, $476,325 total compensation

EVP and CFO, Edward L. (Ned) Rand, age 48, $443,475 total compensation

SVP and Chief Marketing Officer Professional Liability Group, Jeffrey L. Bowlby

President Eastern Insurance, Michael L. Boguski, age 52

EVP Corporate Secretary and General Counsel, Jeffrey P. Lisenby, age 46

SVP and Chief Medical Officer, Hayes V. Whiteside

Group Technology Officer Information Systems, Michael Stoeckert

President and Chief Medical Officer Podiatric Insurance Company of America (PICA), Ross E. Taubman

Vice President And General Manager, Charles (Chas) Francis

Assistant Vice President External Reporting, Dianne Baldwin
Regional Vice President Risk Management, Lizabeth Brott
Regional Vice President Claims, Richard (Dick) Walter
Vice President, Randy Chaffinch
Vice President, Tyler Campbell
Vice President dental Program, Michael (Mel) Peterman
Vice President Operations, Duncan Manley
Vice President of Corporate Investments, Larry Cochran
Vice President Health Care Facilities Underwriting, Jerry Chiarella
Vice President underwriting, Karen Carlile
Regional Vice President Claims, Hal Mcclelland
Vice President sales, Greg Wood
Vice President, David (Dave) Goss
Vice President, Vicky Gould
Vice President of Operations, Sally Gilmore
Board Member, Julie Kus
Auditors: Ernst & Young, LLP

LOCATIONS

HQ: ProAssurance Corp.
100 Brookwood Place, Birmingham, AL 35209
Phone: 205 877-4400 **Fax:** 205 802-4799
Web: www.proassurance.com

PRODUCTS/OPERATIONS

2014 Sales by Segment

	% of total
Specialty Property and Casualty	58
Workers' Compensation	23
Corporate	17
Lloyd's Syndicate	2
Eliminations	-
Total	**100**

2014 Sales

	$ mil
% of total	
Net premium earned	82
Net investment	15
Net realized investment gains	2
Other income	1
Total	**100**

COMPETITORS

Berkshire Hathaway	NCMIC
CNA Financial	Physicians' Reciprocal
COPIC	Insurers
Coverys	Princeton Insurance
Dentists Insurance	Company
Company	State Volunteer Mutual
EDIC	Insurance
Markel	The Doctors Company
Medical Liability	Travelers Companies
Mutual Insurance	White Mountains
Monitor Liability	Insurance Group
Managers Inc.	

HISTORICAL FINANCIALS

Company Type: Public

Income Statement

FYE: December 31

	ASSETS ($ mil.)	NET INCOME ($ mil.)	INCOME AS % OF ASSETS	EMPLOYEES
12/14	5,169	196	3.8%	967
12/13	5,150	297	5.8%	962
12/12	4,876	275	5.6%	690
12/11	4,998	287	5.7%	652
12/10	4,875	231	4.8%	739
Annual Growth	1.5%	(4.0%)	—	7.0%

2014 Year-End Financials

Debt ratio: 4.84%	No. of shares (mil.): 56
Return on equity: 8.64%	Dividends
Cash ($ mil.): 197	Yield: 8.5%
Current ratio: —	Payout: 115.5%
Long-term debt ($ mil.): —	Market value ($ mil.): 2,553

	STOCK PRICE ($) FY Close	P/E High/Low		PER SHARE ($) Earnings	Dividends	Book Value
12/14	45.15	15	13	3.30	3.86	38.17
12/13	48.48	11	9	4.80	1.05	39.13
12/12	42.19	21	9	4.46	3.13	36.85
12/11	79.82	17	12	4.66	0.25	35.42
12/10	60.60	17	13	3.60	0.00	30.17
Annual Growth	(7.1%)	—	—	(2.2%)	—	6.1%

Procter & Gamble Co.

The Procter & Gamble Company (P&G) boasts dozens of billion-dollar brands for home hair and health. The world's largest maker of consumer packaged goods divides its business into five global segments. The company also makes pet food water filters and over-the-counter acid-reflux medication. About two dozen of P&G's brands are billion-dollar sellers including Always Braun Crest Fusion Gillette Head & Shoulders Mach3 Olay Oral-B Pantene and Wella in the beauty and grooming segment as well as Bounty Charmin Dawn Downy Duracell Gain Pampers and Tide in the household care segment. P&G's hundreds of brands are available in more than 180 countries.

HISTORY

Candle maker William Procter and soap maker James Gamble merged their small Cincinnati businesses in 1837 creating The Procter & Gamble Company (P&G) which incorporated in 1890. By 1859 P&G had become one of the largest companies in Cincinnati with sales of $1 million. It introduced Ivory a floating soap in 1879 and Crisco shortening in 1911.

The Ivory campaign was one of the first to advertise directly to the consumer. Other advertising innovations included sponsorship of daytime radio dramas in 1932. P&G's first TV commercial for Ivory aired in 1939.

Family members headed the company until 1930 when William Deupree became president. In the 29 years that Deupree served as president and then chairman P&G became the largest US seller of packaged goods.

After years of researching cleansers for use in hard water P&G introduced Tide detergent in 1947. It began a string of acquisitions when it picked up Spic and Span (1945; sold 2001) Duncan Hines (1956; sold 1998) Charmin Paper Mills (1957) and Folgers Coffee (1963 sold 2008). P&G launched Crest toothpaste in 1955 and Head & Shoulders shampoo and Pampers disposable diapers in 1961.

Rely tampons were pulled from shelves in 1980 when investigators linked them to toxic shock syndrome. In 1985 P&G moved into health care when it purchased Richardson-Vicks (NyQuil Vicks) and G.D. Searle's nonprescription drug division (Metamucil). The acquisitions of Noxell (1989; CoverGirl Noxzema) and Max Factor (1991) made it a top cosmetics company in the US. (It sold Noxzema in 2008.)

P&G began a major restructuring in 1993 cutting 13000 jobs and closing 30 plants. The firm acquired Eagle Snacks from Anheuser-Busch in 1996 and sued rival Amway over rumors connecting P&G and its moon-and-stars logo to Satanism. (The suit was dismissed in 1999.) Also in 1996 the FDA approved the use of olestra a controversial fat substitute developed by P&G.

In 1997 it acquired Tambrands (Tampax tampons) making P&G #1 in feminine sanitary protection. Impatient with progress on its sales goals in 1998 P&G began restructuring to focus on global business units rather than geographic regions. Chairman John Pepper handed over his chairman and CEO title in 1999 to president Durk Jager who promised five new products a year and a shakeup of the corporate culture.

In 1999 the company announced further reorganization plans including 15000 job cuts worldwide by 2005. That same year P&G bought The Iams Company (maker of Eukanuba- and Iams-brand dog and cat foods).

With earnings flat Jager resigned in 2000. P&G insider Alan G. Lafley immediately assumed the president and CEO duties and Pepper returned to succeed Jager as chairman.

In 2001 P&G announced job cuts for 9600 employees to further reduce costs. It also sold its Comet cleaner business. That year P&G completed its purchase of the Clairol hair care company from Bristol-Myers Squibb for nearly $5 billion.

In 2002 P&G closed three Clairol plants one warehouse and one distribution center —eliminating about 750 jobs. Production of Clairol products was moved to existing P&G plants. It also sold its olestra plant in Cincinnati to Twin Rivers Technologies but retained ownership of the Olean brand and technology. Additionally it sold its Jif peanut butter and Crisco shortening brands to J.M. Smucker and several personal care brands (including Sea Breeze and Vitalis) to Helen of Troy.

In 2002 P&G branched out in a joint venture with Clorox to help it improve the Glad-brand plastic bags and wraps. P&G held a 10% stake in the Glad venture until late 2004 when the company invested another $133 million to boost its stake to 20% the limit allowed by the agreement.

Also that year Lafley announced that P&G had completed its multiyear restructuring and would stop reporting two sets of results (one with restructuring charges and one without).

Further expanding its hair care segment and building on its successes with Clairol P&G purchased the first of several stakes in Wella in 2003 (it now owns the entire company). That year P&G also entered the premium pet food market with its purchase of The Iams Company for $2.3 billion. And to secure its foothold in China P&G bought the remaining 20% stake in its joint venture with partner Hutchison Whampoa China Ltd. in 2004 for $1.8 billion.

P&G bought four brands to sell in Southeast Asia in its effort to erode market share from Unilever. In 2005 P&G purchased Fab Trojan Dynamo and Paic laundry brands sold in Hong Kong Singapore Thailand and Malaysia from Colgate-Palmolive.

The company reached its lofty spot as the world's largest consumer products company in 2005 through one of its boldest moves —buying Boston-based The Gillette Company for about $57 billion. Overnight the ambitious deal gave P&G the golden ticket to leapfrog over former #1 supplier Unilever. P&G's purchase of Gillette added well-known complementary brands to its already vast portfolio such as Gillette razors and blades Duracell batteries Oral-B oral care items and Braun appliances.

In 2006 P&G paired up with ARYx Therapeutics to develop that company's gastrointestinal disorder treatment.

In 2007 P&G paired its marketing savvy with the diagnostics expertise of Inverness Medical Innovations to form a joint venture company called SPD Swiss Precision Diagnostics. The joint venture makes and markets in-home diagnostic products including pregnancy tests and ovulation/fertility monitoring products under the Clearblue PERSONA Accu-Clear and other names. P&G paid $325 million for its 50% stake in the venture.

EXECUTIVES

Group President Global Grooming, Charles E. Pierce, age 59
Group President Global Sustainability, Martin Riant, age 57, $936,667 total compensation
Group President Global Beauty, Patrice J. L. Louvet, age 51
President and CEO, David S. Taylor, age 57, $945,000 total compensation
Group President North America Selling and Market Operations, Carolyn Tastad, age 52
Group President Global Health Care, Steven D. (Steve) Bishop, age 51
Group President Global Fabric and Hone Care, Giovanni Ciserani, age 53, $796,667 total compensation
Group President Global Family Care, Mary L. Ferguson-McHugh, age 56
President Global Personal Health Care, Thomas M. Finn, age 53
CFO, Jon R. Moeller, age 51, $850,000 total compensation
Global Design Officer, Philip J Duncan, age 50
CIO, Linda W. Clement-Holmes, age 53
Global Product Supply Officer, Yannis Skoufalos, age 57
President Beauty Specialty Businesses, Colleen E. Jay, age 53
President, Hatsunori Kiriyama, age 53
President Europe Selling & Market Operations, Gary Coombe
CTO, Kathleen B. (Kathy) Fish
President India Middle East and Africa Selling and Market Operations, Mohamed Samir
President Global Home Care and P&G Professional, George Tsourapas, age 55
President Global Fabric Care and Brand Building Organization Global Fabric and Home Care, Shailesh G. Jejurikar
President Global Skin and Personal Care, R. Alexandra Keith
President Global Business Services, Julio Nemeth
President Latin America Selling and Market Operations, Juan F. Posada
President Greater China Selling and Market Operations, Matthew S. Price
President Asia/Pacific Selling and Market Operations, Magesvaran Suranjan
Vice President; Managing Director UK and Ireland, Irwin Lee
Vice President Of Global Sustainability, Len Sauers
Vice President Of Education, Fabio Sementilli
Vice President of Residential Mortgages, Dave Musolino
Vice President and General Manager, Jeff Davis
Vice President Finance Global Business Units, Luis Felipe Visoso
Vice President Global Oral Care, Bonnie Curtis
Vice President Marketing, Michelle (Mitch) Stacy
Vice President Marketing and Brand Strategy, Fuyuo Tanaka
Senior Vice President, Bob Goebel
Vice President and General Counsel, Steven (Steve) Miller
Vice President Of Communications, Lisa Bartz

Vice President, Dicky Kho
Vice President Consumer Market Knowledge, Delaine Hampton
Vice President, Nayantara Bali
Vice President Customer Business Development, Dominick Gigante
Vice President Of Franchising, Thomas F (Thom) Flaherty
Vice President Marketing, Berenike Ullmann
Vice President Sales, Frank Craft
Vice President Finance and Accounting Global Household Care, Winston Griffin
Vice President CMK Western Europe, Anne Doberstein
Vice President, Patrick Conklin
Vice President, Norm Hill
Vice President, Gale Beckett
Vice President Technology and Environmental Sustainability, Glenn Bochner
Vice President Operations, Dawn Seiler
Vice President Technology, Subramanian Arasakesari
Call Center customer Service Director Vice President, Ron Chisholm
Director Managed Care, Debbie Burge
Vice President Director of Facilities, Frank Patterson
National Account Manager, Pam Crewdson
Vice President Of Quality Management, April Cielica
National Sales Manager Canada, David (Dave) Roberts
Vice President Retail Development, Glenn Renegar
Associate Medical Director, Paul Nicholson
Vice President Product Supply Baby Care, Eric Hagemeister
National Account Manager, Oliver Seaman
Vice President And General Manager Research And Development, Petra Hanke-baier
National Accounts Manager, Alexandra Petrenko
Vice President Corporate Solutions, Bob Martindale
Vice President Wella Germany Austria Switzerland, Ralf Billharz
Vice President And General Manager Central Europe, Marek Kapuscinski
National Account Manager, Sarah Fish
Senior Vice President Marketing, Jenny Vaughn
National Sales Manager Health Care, Mike Mccracken
National Account Manager, Shelagh Clark
Vice President Female Beauty Latin America, Gerardo Rios
Vice President Management Systems, Frank Caccamo
Vice President Finance and Accounting Gillette, Samy Zekhout
Vice President Global Male Shave Care, Mang Jm
Vice President New Business Creation, J Brad Lang
Vice President and Global Brand Franchise Leader Pantene and Herbal Essences, Burkhard Pieroth
Sr V Pres-comptroller-treas, Valarie Sheppard
Chairman, Alan G. (A. G.) Lafley, age 67
Treasurer, Ltanya Cole
SHS Band Booster Treasurer, Lisa Hennessy
Secretary, Maryann Meyer
Secretary, Fatima Correa
Board Member, Bo Passey
Secretary, Jenny Tan
Abm, Christina Morazzani
Abm, Lana Baaklini
Abm, Jenny Lundie
Board Member, Janusz Dziurzynski
Board Member, Mike Kowal
Auditors: Deloitte & Touche LLP

LOCATIONS

HQ: Procter & Gamble Co.
One Procter & Gamble Plaza, Cincinnati, OH 45202
Phone: 513 983-1100
Web: www.pg.com

2014 Sales

	% of total
North America	39
Asia	18
Western Europe	18
Central & Eastern Europe Middle East & Africa	15
Latin America	10
Total	**100**

PRODUCTS/OPERATIONS

2014 Sales

	% of total
Fabric Care and Home Care	32
Baby Care and Family Care	25
Beauty	23
Health Care	9
Grooming	10
Corporate	1
Total	**100**

Selected Mergers & Acquisitions

FY2010
Natura Pet Products (California holistic and natural pet foods)
Sara Lee European air-freshener business ($470 million plug-in and stand-by air fresheners aerosol sprays and toilet cleaners)
FY2009
The Art of Shaving (high-end men's shaving and skin care products)
FY2005
The Gillette Company ($57 billion Boston maker of razors blades batteries and oral care items)

Selected Divestitures

FY2012
Pringles ($2.7 billion to Kellogg Company)
FY2011
PUR water purification business (to Helen of Troy)
Zest (to High Ridge Brands P&G retaining the rights to sell Zest in the Philippines the Middle East and Latin America)
FY2009
Prescription drug unit ($3 billion to Warner Chilcott)
FY2008
Folger Coffee Company ($3 billion to The J. M. Smucker Company)
Infusium 23 (to Helen of Troy)
Noxzema (to Alberto-Culver P&G retaining business in parts of Western Europe)
FY2006
SpinBrush ($75 million to Church & Dwight)

Selected Segments & Their Billion Dollar Brands

Fabric Care & Home Care
 Ace
 Ariel
 Dawn
 Downy
 Duracell
 Febreze
 Gain
 Iams
 Tide
Beauty
 Head & Shoulders
 Olay
 Pantene
 SK-II
 Wella
Baby Care & Family Care
 Bounty
 Charmin
 Pampers
Health Care
 Always
 Crest
 Oral-B
 Vicks
Grooming
 Braun

Fusion
Gillette
Mach3

COMPETITORS

Alticor	Mary Kay
Amway	Meda Pharmaceuticals
Avon	Nestl©
BIC	Pfizer
Bath & Body Works	Philips Electronics
Baxter of California	Revlon
Body Shop	Russell Hobbs
Bristol-Myers Squibb	S.C. Johnson
Church & Dwight	SANYO
Clorox	SEB
Colgate-Palmolive	Sanofi
Discus Dental	Scott' s Liquid Gold
Dr. Bronner' s	Shiseido
Edgewell Personal Care	Spectrum Brands
Est©e Lauder	Tom' s of Maine
Henkel	Turtle Wax
Johnson & Johnson	Unilever
Kimberly-Clark	VIVUS
L' Or©al	

HISTORICAL FINANCIALS

Company Type: Public

Income Statement
FYE: June 30

	REVENUE ($ mil.)	NET INCOME ($ mil.)	NET PROFIT MARGIN	EMPLOYEES
06/15	76,279	7,036	9.2%	110,000
06/14	83,062	11,643	14.0%	118,000
06/13	84,167	11,312	13.4%	121,000
06/12	83,680	10,756	12.9%	126,000
06/11	82,559	11,797	14.3%	129,000
Annual Growth	(2.0%)	(12.1%)	—	(3.9%)

2015 Year-End Financials

Debt ratio: 23.44%—
Return on equity: 10.69%
Cash ($ mil.): 6,845
Current ratio: 1.00
Long-term debt ($ mil.): 18,329

Dividends
Yield: 3.3%
Payout: 82.3%
Market value ($ mil.): —

	STOCK PRICE ($) FY Close	P/E High/Low		PER SHARE ($) Earnings	Dividends	Book Value
06/15	78.24	37	31	2.44	2.59	22.99
06/14	78.59	20	18	4.01	2.45	25.53
06/13	76.99	20	15	3.86	2.29	24.82
06/12	61.25	18	15	3.66	2.14	23.09
06/11	63.57	16	14	3.93	1.97	24.46
Annual Growth	5.3%	—	—	(11.2%)	7.1%	(1.5%)

Progressive Corp. (OH)

It's risky business and Progressive loves it. Long a leader in nonstandard high-risk personal auto insurance Progressive has motored beyond its traditional business into standard-risk and preferred auto insurance as well as other personal-use vehicle coverage (motorcycles RVs and snowmobiles) through carriers including majority-owned American Strategic Insurance. Progressive also offers commercial policies for heavy trucks vans and lighter trucks. It writes a bit of professional liability insurance for directors and officers as well. The company markets directly to consumers online and by phone and through more than 35000 independent agents who account for the majority of its business.

Operations

Personal insurance accounted for 85% of the company's 2014 revenues while commercial auto represented 9%. Other indemnity and service business accounts for less than 1% of the company's revenues while fees and other revenues account for 2%. Progressive offers coverage to auto insurance customers underwritten by third-party insurance carriers. Progressive also offers personal umbrella insurance that provides coverage for the extras in life such as personal injury and legal defense. The company had 13.8 million policies in force at the end of 2014.

Progressive has more than 50 subsidiaries one mutual insurance affiliate and a limited partnership investment affiliate.

Geographic Reach

Progressive operates throughout the US and sells personal auto insurance on via Internet in Australia.

In addition to its headquarters additional offices and call center operations in Mayfield Village Ohio the company owns locations in Colorado Springs Colorado; Tampa Florida; and Tempe Arizona.

Sales and MarketingIts US customer service group (which support policy servicing agency distribution claims and direct sales operations) are located at call centers in Mayfield Village Ohio; Austin Texas; Tampa Florida; Sacramento California; Tempe Arizona; and Colorado Springs Colorado.

Total advertising costs in 2014 were $681.8 million up from $619.8 million in 2013.

Financial Performance

Organic growth has lifted the company's revenues every year since 2008. They grew by 7% in 2014 on growth in the personal lines of business as rates increased and customers bought higher premium policies. Commercial product rate increases also led to an overall premium increase. The company has been working on providing its customers with new insurance options (as well as increasingly investing in marketing efforts) which has paid off in higher revenues.

Net income increased 10% in 2014 to $1.3 billion thanks to the higher revenue. Despite that growth cash flow from operations slid 9% to $1.7 billion as more cash was used in premiums receivable and less cash was provided by loss and loss adjustment expense reserves.

Strategy

Unlike some insurers who in fat markets earn more from their investments than their premiums more than 90% of Progressive's revenues have historically come from policy premiums.

The company's actual insurance operations have remained profitable and grown as it has entered into new geographic markets and expanded distribution of its personal auto products online. Already among the leading US auto insurers based on premiums (just behind State Farm and Allstate) Progressive is aiming to be on top.

Because it is fairly easy for customers to switch auto insurers Progressive competes on price and accessibility. To attract new customers the company's television ads featuring its perky spokesperson "Flo" have shot up the company's brand recognition. Operating on the premise that a few drivers are responsible for the majority of claims and that previous risk models were incomplete Progressive is now also offering rates that are tied to actual usage.

To retain customers Progressive is promoting its non-auto personal products through bundled packages with lower auto rates. Once a customer has bought a bundled package of home/auto/umbrella coverage they are also much less likely to switch insurance providers.

In 2014 the company introduced its agency auto product in Massachusetts; with this launch Progressive now offers Agency and Direct auto insurance in every US state.

Mergers and Acquisitions

In 2015 Progressive acquired a majority stake (67%) of ARX Holding a homeowners' insurance carrier for $875 million. That deal expanded its product portfolio; Progressive intends to acquire the rest of the firm it doesn't already own by the year 2021.

HISTORY

Attorneys Jack Green and Joseph Lewis founded Progressive Mutual Insurance in Cleveland in 1937. Initially offering standard auto insurance the company attracted customers through such innovations as installment plans for premiums (a payment method popularized during the Depression) and drive-in claims services (the company was headquartered in a garage). Progressive's early years were uncertain —at one point the founders were even advised to go out of business —but the advent of WWII bolstered business: Car and insurance purchases were up but accidents were down as gas rationing limited driving.

Then came the suburbs and cars of the 1950s. While most competitors sought low-risk drivers Progressive exploited the high-risk niche through careful underwriting and statistical analysis. Subsidiary Progressive Casualty was founded in 1956 (the year after Joseph Lewis died) to insure the best of the worst. Lewis' son Peter joined the company in 1955 and helped engineer its early-1960s expansion outside Ohio. After Green retired in 1965 Peter gained control of the company through a leveraged buyout and renamed it The Progressive Corporation. Six years later Lewis took it public and formed subsidiary Progressive American in Florida.

In the mid-1970s the industry went into a funk as it was hit by a wave of consolidations and rising interest rates. Lewis set a goal for the company to always earn an underwriting profit instead of depending on investments to make a profit. Progressive achieved stellar results during the 1970s especially after states began requiring drivers to be insured and other insurers began weeding out higher risks.

Competition in nonstandard insurance grew in the 1980s as major insurers such as Allstate and State Farm joined the fray with their larger sales forces and deeper pockets. In 1988 California's Proposition 103 retroactively reduced rates; Progressive fought California's demand for refunds but set aside reserves to pay them.

That year Lewis hired Cleveland financier Alfred Lerner to guide company investments. Lerner invested $75 million in Progressive via a convertible debenture; five years later he converted it to stock half of which he sold for $122 million. Soon after he was asked to resign. In 1993 Progressive settled with California for $51 million and applied to earnings the remaining $100 million in refund reserves. (Company soul-searching related to Proposition 103 led to the launch of Progressive's now-famous "Immediate Response" vehicles which provide 24-hour claims service at accident sites.)

In 1995 Progressive's practice of using consumer credit information to make underwriting decisions drew the attention of Arkansas and Vermont insurance regulators who said the company might be discriminating against people who didn't have the credit cards Progressive used to evaluate creditworthiness. In 1996 insurance regulators in Alaska Maryland and Texas also began probing Progressive's credit information practices.

In 1997 Progressive bought nonstandard auto insurer Midland Financial Group. As competition grew in 1999 the company cut rates and said it would write no new policies in Canada. In 2000 —

with underwriting margins dropping industrywide –the company continued advertising aggressively. Progressive stopped writing new homeowners insurance in 2002 instead concentrating on its core operations. In 2006 the company began offering personal umbrella coverage.

The company took a bold international expansion measure in 2009: Launching personal auto insurance online in Australia. International expansion has not been a key strategy for Progressive but apparently the time was right for such growth. And apparently the company is prepared to give the new operation time to grow which is good considering that it has not yet made significant contributions to overall revenues.

EXECUTIVES

Vice President Chief Accounting Officer, Jeffrey (Jeff) Basch

Chairman President and CEO, Glenn M. Renwick, age 60, $750,000 total compensation

Chief Legal Officer, Charles E. (Chuck) Jarrett, age 58, $463,269 total compensation

Chief Investment Officer, William M. (Bill) Cody, age 53, $417,692 total compensation

COO Personal Lines, Susan Patricia (Tricia) Griffith, age 51, $487,115 total compensation

President Commercial Lines Group, John A. Barbagallo, age 56

CFO, John P. Sauerland, age 51, $487,115 total compensation

President Personal Lines, Pat Callahan

President Claims, Michael (Mike) Sieger

CIO, Steve Broz

Medical Director, Crystal Kastberg

Assistant Vice President Human Resources Director Business, Patricia (Pat) Bemer

Vice President Information Technology, Edward Fowler

Vice President Information Technology, Paul Wilson

Vice President and Treasurer The Progressive Corporation, Thomas (Thom) King

Auditors: PricewaterhouseCoopers LLP

LOCATIONS

HQ: Progressive Corp. (OH)
6300 Wilson Mills Road, Mayfield Village, OH 44143
Phone: 440 461-5000   **Fax:** 440 446-7168
Web: www.progressive.com

PRODUCTS/OPERATIONS

2014 Sales

	% of total
Personal Lines	85
Commercial Auto	9
Investments	3
Fees & other revenues	2
Other	1
Total	**100**
Insurance Options	
Auto Insurance	
Local Car Insurance	
Motorcycle Insurance	
Boat Insurance	
RV Insurance	
Commercial Auto Insurance	
Truck Insurance	
Homeowners Insurance	
Renters Insurance	
Business Insurance	
Life Insurance	
Health Insurance	
Umbrella Insurance	

COMPETITORS

21st Century Insurance	Nationwide
Allstate	Ohio Casualty
American Family Insurance	Old Republic
Cincinnati Financial	State Auto Financial
Farmers Group	State Farm
GEICO	Travelers Companies
Infinity Property & Casualty	USAA
Liberty Mutual	White Mountains Insurance Group

HISTORICAL FINANCIALS

Company Type: Public

Income Statement

FYE; December 31

	ASSETS ($ mil.)	NET INCOME ($ mil.)	INCOME AS % OF ASSETS	EMPLOYEES
12/14	25,787	1,281	5.0%	26,501
12/13	24,408	1,165	4.8%	26,145
12/12	22,694	902	4.0%	25,889
12/11	21,844	1,015	4.6%	25,007
12/10	21,150	1,068	5.1%	24,638
Annual Growth	**5.1%**	**4.6%**	**—**	**1.8%**

2014 Year-End Financials

Debt ratio: 8.39%	No. of shares (mil.): 587
Return on equity: 19.53%	Dividends
Cash ($ mil.): 108	Yield: 5.5%
Current ratio: —	Payout: 73.5%
Long-term debt ($ mil.): —	Market value ($ mil.): 15,865

	STOCK PRICE ($) FY Close	P/E High/Low		PER SHARE ($) Earnings	Dividends	Book Value
12/14	26.99	13	10	2.15	1.49	11.79
12/13	27.27	14	11	1.93	1.28	10.39
12/12	21.10	16	13	1.48	1.41	9.94
12/11	19.51	14	11	1.59	0.40	9.47
12/10	19.87	14	10	1.61	1.16	9.13
Annual Growth	**8.0%**	**—**	**—**	**7.5%**	**6.5%**	**6.6%**

Prospect Capital Corporation

Prospect Capital is a closed-end investment fund with holdings in the consumer food health care and manufacturing sectors among others. The company targets privately held middle-market firms with annual revenues of less than $750 million; it also considers thinly traded public companies or turnaround situations. Prospect's portfolio includes interests in more than 100 companies mainly through senior loans and mezzanine debt. The company also makes equity and secured debt investments. Typically investing from $5 million to $250 million per transaction Prospect is a long-term investor that maintains regular contact with its portfolio company's management and participates in their board meetings.

Geographic Reach

New York-based Prospect Capital invests primarily in US companies but also in Canada the Cayman Islands and Ireland. About 80% of the firm's investment portfolio is in the US.

Operations

Prospect has elected to be regulated as a business development company (BDC) a status which affords the firm certain tax benefits. Although it initially targeted on industrial and energy investments the company has broadened its focus in the past few years and minimized its holdings in the energy sector.

Financial Performance

Prospect Capital reported revenue of $576.3 million in fiscal 2013 (ended June) an 80% increase over the year earlier period. Net income rose 16% over the same period to nearly $221 million. Prospect's financial prospects have brightened considerably in recent years with revenue up more than 500% since fiscal 2009 and steeply rising profits. The 80% increase in fiscal 2013 revenue was primarily due to 98% increase in interest income as a result of interest earned on the mezzanine loan. Dividend income rose as well.

Strategy

Prospect Capital pursues a diversified investment strategy investing in 124 long-term portfolio investments and CLOs (collateralized loan obligations) and to a lesser extent money market funds. In fiscal 2013 (ended June) the firm originated $3.1 million of new investments. Prospect's origination efforts are focused primarily on secured lending to reduce portfolio risk investing primarily in first lien loans and subordinated notes in CLOs though it also engages in select junior debt and equity investments. First lien loans represent about 55% of its investment portfolio with second lien loans representing about 25%. Diversified financial services is the firm's single largest industry sector for investment followed by consumer finance durable consumer products consumer services and software and computer services. Together these five industries constitute more than half of Prospect's investment portfolio.

In 2013 the firm invested $144.5 million in four new transactions encompassing 19 rent-producing multifamily residential properties totaling 5652 rental units. Combined with its prior investments Prospect has a invested a total of $288.3 million in 10 separate transactions encompassing 25 multifamily residential properties with more than 9100 rental units.

Mergers and Acquisitions

In 2013 Prospect acquired A 94% stake in Nationwide Acceptance LLC a Chicago based consumer finance company.

EXECUTIVES

Vice President, Seb Cervinka

Managing Director Portfolio Management, Frank V Saracino

Vice President Capital Markets, Nishil Mehta

Vice President Investments and Portfolio Management and Vice President Legal, Ian Shainbrown

Vice President Tax, David Wong

Senior Vice President and Deputy General Counsel, Justin Wertman

Vice President Legal, Adam Burton

Board Member, Andrew C (Andy) Cooper

Auditors: BDO USA, LLP

LOCATIONS

HQ: Prospect Capital Corporation
10 East 40th Street, 42nd Floor, New York, NY 10016
Phone: 212 448-0702
Web: www.prospectstreet.com

PRODUCTS/OPERATIONS

Selected Current Investments

AIRMALL US
Ajax Rolle
AWCNC (mac
Blue Coat Systems Inc. (software computer service)
Borga Inc.
Boxercraft (textiles and leather)
Broder Bro
Crossman C
Focus Prod
Grocery Ou

Harley Mar
Injured Wo
Nationwide
National B
NMMB (advertising media buying)
NRG Manufacturing Inc. (drilling rig components)
R-V Indust
Wind River Resources (oil and gas production)

COMPETITORS

ACI Capital	OHA Investment
Apollo Investment	Stephens Group
First Reserve	TPG
GFI Energy Ventures	Venrock
Katalyst	

HISTORICAL FINANCIALS

Company Type: Public

Income Statement   FYE: June 30

	ASSETS ($ mil.)	NET INCOME ($ mil.)	INCOME AS % OF ASSETS	EMPLOYEES
06/15	6,798	362	5.3%	—
06/14	6,477	357	5.5%	—
06/13	4,448	324	7.3%	—
06/12	2,255	186	8.3%	—
06/11	1,549	94	6.1%	—
Annual Growth	44.7%	40.1%	—	—

2015 Year-End Financials

Debt ratio: 38.47%	No. of shares (mil.): 359
Return on equity: 9.91%	Dividends
Cash ($ mil.): —	Yield: 16.1%
Current ratio: —	Payout: 110.2%
Long-term debt ($ mil.): —	Market value ($ mil.): 2,646

	STOCK PRICE ($) FY Close	P/E High/Low		PER SHARE ($) Earnings	Dividends	Book Value
06/15	7.37	11	7	1.03	1.19	10.31
06/14	10.63	10	8	1.19	1.32	10.56
06/13	10.80	8	6	1.57	1.28	10.72
06/12	11.39	7	5	1.63	1.22	10.83
06/11	10.11	11	8	1.10	1.21	10.36
Annual Growth	(7.6%)	—	—	(1.6%)	(0.4%)	(0.1%)

Prosperity Bancshares Inc.

Prosperity Bancshares reaches banking customers across the Lone Star State. The holding company for Prosperity Bank operates about 230 branches across Texas and about 15 more in Oklahoma. Serving consumers and small to midsized businesses the bank offers traditional deposit and loan services in addition to wealth management retail brokerage and mortgage banking investment services. Prosperity Bank focuses on real estate lending: Commercial mortgages make up the largest segment of the company's loan portfolio (33%) followed by residential mortgages (24%). Credit cards business auto consumer home equity loans round out its lending activities.

OperationsAbout 63% of Prosperity's total revenue came from loan interest (including fees) in 2014 while another 22% came from interest on its investment securities. The rest of its revenue came from non-sufficient fund fees (4%) credit and debit card income (3%) deposit account service charges

(2%) trust income (1%) mortgage income (1%) and brokerage income (1%). Geographic Reach

Prosperity Bancshares operates 230 Texas banking locations across Houston South Texas the Dallas/Fort Worth metroplex East Texas Bryan/College Station Central Texas and West Texas. It also has 15 branch locations in Oklahoma (including Tulsa).Sales and MarketingThe bank mainly targets consumers and small and medium-sized businesses and tailors its products to the specific needs of a given market.Financial PerformanceProsperity's revenues and profits have been prospering thanks to loan and deposit business growth from acquisitions and declining loan loss provisions as its loan portfolio's credit quality has improved with higher property valuations in a strengthened economy. The company's revenue jumped by 32% to $837.7 million in 2014 mostly as its loan interest income swelled by 40% on loan asset growth from its F&M acquisition. The bank's non-interest income rose by 29% as well from new deposit account service fees from the acquisition and additional income from its newly added brokerage and trust business. Higher revenue and strong operating cost controls in 2014 drove Prosperity's net income higher by 34% to $297.4 million while its operating cash levels rose by 13% to $348.3 million on higher cash earnings.

Strategy

Prosperity Bancshares bases its growth strategy on three key elements: Internal loan and deposit business growth through "individualized customer service" and service line expansion opportunities; cost controls to maximize profitability; and acquisitions.Toward its internal business growth initiatives Prosperity spent 2012 and 2013 launching its new trust brokerage mortgage lending and credit card products and services to customers for the first time. With cost-controls in mind the bank tracks its branches "as separate profit centers" noting each branch's interest income efficiency ratio deposit growth loan growth and overall profitability. That way it can reward individual branch managers and presidents accordingly by merit rather than giving higher compensation across the board.The acquisitive Prosperity Bancshares has been buying up small banks in Texas —and now Oklahoma —as it hopes to hit a sweet spot in the market between the national giants that dominate the Texas banking scene and smaller community banks.

Mergers and Acquisitions

In January 2016 furthering its presence in the Houston market Prosperity Bancshares purchased Tradition Bancshares along with its seven branches in the Houston Area (Bellaire Katy and the Woodlands) $540 million in assets $239 million in loans and $483.8 million in deposits. In April 2014 toward expansion in the Oklahoma and Dallas markets Prosperity purchased Tulsa-based F&M Bancorporation and its subsidiary The F&M Bank & Trust Company. The deal added 13 branches including nine in Tulsa and surrounding areas three in Dallas and a loan production office in Oklahoma City. In April 2013 it acquired Coppermark Bank one of Oklahoma City's largest banks with six branches in Oklahoma City and three locations in North Dallas for $194 million. The deal also added the credit card and agent bank merchant processing business from its subsidiary Bankers Credit Card Services.In January 2013 the company boosted its market share in East Texas after buying East Texas Financial Services and its four First Federal Bank Texas branch locations including three branches in Tyler and one in Gilmer.Company Background

In early 2012 Prosperity acquired Texas Bankers a three-branch Austin bank with some $72 million in assets. The merger increased Prosperity's number of Central Texas branches to 34

banking locations. It followed that deal with the purchase of The Bank Arlington a single-branch bank operating in the Dallas/Ft. Worth area. It acquired single-branch Community National Bank of Bellaire Texas in late 2012.

Also in 2012 Prosperity expanded into West Texas after it merged American State Financial Corporation and its American State Bank subsidiary into its operations. The deal added $3 billion in assets and 37 West Texas banking offices in Lubbock Midland/Odessa and Abilene.

EXECUTIVES

Executive Vice President Cashier Prosperity Bank, Michael (Mel) Harris
Executive Vice President and Chief Risk Officer Prosperity Bank, Theresa Hollaway
EVP Cashier Prosperity Bank, Mike Harris
Senior Chairman and CEO, David Zalman, age 58, $851,567 total compensation
CFO; EVP and CFO Prosperity Bank, David Hollaway, age 59, $425,000 total compensation
Vice Chairman; Chairman and COO Prosperity Bank, H. E. (Tim) Timanus, age 71, $452,400 total compensation
Vice Chairman and Area Chairman Central Texas, Edward Z. (Eddie) Safady
EVP Regulatory and Compliance Prosperity Bank, Rhonda L. Carroll
Chief Lending Officer Prosperity Bank, Randy D. Hester, $325,000 total compensation
SEVP Financial Operations and Administration Prosperity Bank, Mike Epps, $327,625 total compensation
EVP and CIO Prosperity Bank, Gisela Riggan
Chief Risk Oficer, Jennifer Willcoxon
Chief Credit Officer Prosperity Bank, Merle Karnes
President Prosperity Bank, Bob Benter
EVP Prosperity Bancshares and Prosperity Bank, Robert (Bob) Dowdell
Chairman Wealth Management, Russell Marshall
Exec V Pres-general Counsel, Charlotte Rasche
Seniorvice President, Keith Page
Executive Vice President Prosperity Bancshares and Prosperity Bank, Bob Dowdell
Assistant Vice President Marketing Specialist, Amber McCloud
Vice President, Brent Adams
Auditors: Deloitte & Touche LLP

LOCATIONS

HQ: Prosperity Bancshares Inc.
Prosperity Bank Plaza, 4295 San Felipe, Houston, TX 77027
Phone: 713 693-9300
Web: www.prosperitybankusa.com

PRODUCTS/OPERATIONS

2014 Sales

	$ mil.	% of total
Interest		
Loans including fees	525	63
Securities	188	22
Federal funds sold	0	-
Noninterest		
Non-sufficient funds fees	37	4
Debit card and ATM card income	22	3
Service charges on deposit accounts	16	2
Trust income	8	1
Brokerage income	5	1
Mortgage income	4	1
Other	28	3
Total	**837**	**100**

COMPETITORS

Amegy	JPMorgan Chase
BBVA Compass	North Dallas Bank
Bancshares	Texas Capital

Bank of America Bancshares
Citibank Wells Fargo
Comerica Woodforest Financial
Cullen/Frost Bankers

HISTORICAL FINANCIALS

Company Type: Public

Income Statement

FYE: December 31

	ASSETS ($ mil.)	NET INCOME ($ mil.)	INCOME AS % OF ASSETS	EMPLOYEES
12/14	21,507	297	1.4%	3,096
12/13	18,642	221	1.2%	2,995
12/12	14,583	167	1.2%	2,266
12/11	9,822	141	1.4%	1,664
12/10	9,476	127	1.3%	1,708
Annual Growth	22.7%	23.5%	—	16.0%

2014 Year-End Financials

Debt ratio: 0.82%
Return on equity: 9.86%
Cash ($ mil.): 677
Current ratio: —
Long-term debt ($ mil.): —

No. of shares (mil.): 69
Dividends
  Yield: 1.7%
  Payout: 23.8%
Market value ($ mil.): 3,863

	STOCK PRICE ($) FY Close	P/E High/Low	PER SHARE ($) Earnings	Dividends	Book Value
12/14	55.36	16 12	4.32	0.99	46.50
12/13	63.39	18 11	3.65	0.89	42.19
12/12	42.00	15 12	3.23	0.80	37.01
12/11	40.35	15 10	3.01	0.72	33.41
12/10	39.28	16 10	2.73	0.64	31.11
Annual Growth	9.0%	— —	12.2%	11.6%	10.6%

Protective Life Insurance Co

Need protection in New York? Hire a body guard. Need to protect your assets? Protective Life & Annuity Insurance would like to help. Protective Life and Annuity Insurance markets and sells financial security in the form of term and universal life insurance policies and fixed and variable annuity products. Although the company is based in Alabama and licensed to sell insurance throughout the US it exclusively serves clients in New York. Protective Life and Annuity Insurance is a subsidiary of Protective Life Insurance Company which is part of Protective Life Corporation.

Operations

Every state has unique requirements that insurance companies must meet in order to gain permission to operate there. New York's insurance code has the stiffest requirements and many small companies simply choose not to operate in that market. However the market is so large and tempting that other companies opt to maintain separate subsidiaries that exclusively serve New York. In this instance parent company Protective Life Insurance Company serves the rest of the US while Protective Life & Annuity is strictly focused on New York.

Sales and Marketing

The company sells coverage through independent agents broker-dealers and financial institutions as well as through partnerships with employer groups and through its own sales division.

EXECUTIVES

Chairman and CEO, John D. Johns
Chief Investment Officer, Carl S. Thigpen
Vice Chairman and Chief Financial Officer, Richard Bielen
Chief Risk Officer, Michael G. Temple
Vice President Of Marketing, Teri Schultz
Investments Second Vice President, Steve Clikas
Vice President Cash Management, Patty Cobb
Auditors: PricewaterhouseCoopers LLP

LOCATIONS

HQ: Protective Life Insurance Co
  2801 Highway 280 South, Birmingham, AL 35223
Phone: 205 268-1000
Web: www.protective.com

COMPETITORS

Guardian Insurance and Penn Mutual
  Annuity Prudential
MetLife The Hartford
New York Life

HISTORICAL FINANCIALS

Company Type: Public

Income Statement

FYE: December 31

	ASSETS ($ mil.)	NET INCOME ($ mil.)	INCOME AS % OF ASSETS	EMPLOYEES
12/14	69,992	491	0.7%	2,457
12/13	68,296	291	0.4%	2,415
12/12	57,157	308	0.5%	2,284
12/11	52,791	347	0.7%	2,058
12/10	47,476	258	0.5%	1,840
Annual Growth	10.2%	17.5%	—	7.5%

2014 Year-End Financials

Debt ratio: 2.25%
Return on equity: 9.35%
Cash ($ mil.): 268
Current ratio: —
Long-term debt ($ mil.): —

No. of shares (mil.): 5
Dividends
  Yield: —
  Payout: 60.9%
Market value ($ mil.): —

Provident Financial Services Inc

Provident wants to be a prominent force in the New Jersey banking scene. Provident Financial Services owns The Provident Bank which serves individuals businesses and families from 85 branches across more than 10 northern and central New Jersey counties. Founded in 1839 the $8.5 billion-bank offers traditional deposit and lending products as well as wealth management and trust services. About 50% of its revenue comes from real estate loan interest while another 25% comes from interest on commercial and consumer loans. Construction loans round out its lending activities. The company's Provident Investment Services subsidiary sells life and health insurance and investment products.

Operations Provident which staffed more than 1020 employees boasted some $8.5 billion in total assets loans of $6.1 billion and deposits of $5.8 billion at the end of 2014. Mortgages loans made up 70% of its total loan portfolio that year. Geographic ReachThe bank's 86 branches are located in northern and central New Jersey as well as in

Pennsylvania (in the Bucks Lehigh and Northampton counties). Its administrative offices are in Iselin New Jersey while its satellite loan production offices are in Covent Station Flemington Paramus Princeton and West Orange in New Jersey; and in Bethleham and Newtown Pennsylvania.Sales and MarketingProvident targets individuals families and businesses in its primary market areas in New Jersey (which covered a population of 6.9 million or 78% of the state's population) and Pennsylvania (where the bank's primary market covered 10% of that state's population. Provident's primary markets include a mix of urban and suburban communities. It serves companies in a variety of industries including pharmaceutical and other manufacturing companies network communications insurance and financial services healthcare and retail businesses. Financial PerformanceProvident has struggled to consistently grow its revenues in recent years due to shrinking interest margins on loans amidst the low-interest environment. Its profits however have been rising thanks to declining loan loss provisions as its loan portfolio's credit quality has improved with higher property valuations in a strengthened economy.The bank's revenue rose by 8% to $320.5 million in 2014 mostly thanks to added interest income from loan asset growth –including a 9% rise in real estate secured loan business and a 24% rise in commercial loan business –stemming from its acquisition of Team Capital Bank.Higher revenue and a continued decline in loan loss provisions in 2014 drove Provident's net income higher by 4% to $73.6 million. Its operating cash levels dipped by 3% to $96.4 million after adjusting its earnings for non-cash items mostly related to an increase in other assets.StrategyProvident Financial continues to look for strategic acquisition opportunities of banks and other financial services providers to grow its loan and deposit business and extend its branch network into more of its primary market areas.The company also remains focused on its conservative lending practices and is seeking to diversify its portfolio and reduce risk by placing more emphasis on commercial real estate multifamily residential and business loans.Mergers and AcquisitionsIn May 2014 Provident Financial Services purchased Team Capital Bank for $115.1 million effectively extending its reach into Eastern Pennsylvania and the affluent counties of Hunterdon and Somerset. The deal also added $964 million in total assets $631 million in loan assets and $770 million in deposits. Company Background

In 2011 the company acquired Beacon Trust Company an asset manager for individuals municipalities corporations pension funds and not-for-profit organizations. The deal significantly expanded its wealth management business and boosted its assets under management to some $1.5 billion.

EXECUTIVES

Chairman President and CEO, Christopher P. Martin, age 59, $608,846 total compensation
EVP and CFO, Thomas M. Lyons, age 51, $349,308 total compensation
EVP and Director Retail Banking The Provident Bank, Michael A. Raimonde, age 63, $238,370 total compensation
EVP General Counsel and Corporate Secretary The Provident Bank, John F. Kuntz, age 60, $312,700 total compensation
EVP and Chief Lending Officer The Provident Bank, Donald W. Blum, age 59, $314,562 total compensation
EVP and CIO The Provident Bank, Jack Novielli, age 56
EVP and and Chief Human Resources Officer The Provident Bank, Janet D. Krasowski, age 62

EVP and Chief Credit Officer The Provident Bank, Brian Giovinazzi, age 61, $161,138 total compensation
EVP and Chief Wealth Officer The Provident Bank, James D. Nesci, age 43, $274,423 total compensation
SVP and Chief Risk Officer The Provident Bank, James Christy
Vice President Of Central Region Business Banking Team, Brown Small
Board Member, Craig Marsh
Auditors: KPMG LLP

LOCATIONS

HQ: Provident Financial Services Inc
239 Washington Street, Jersey City, NJ 07302
Phone: 732 590-9200
Web: www.providentnj.com

PRODUCTS/OPERATIONS

2014 Sales

	$ mil.	% of total
Interest		
Real estate secured loans	166	52
Commercial loans	50	16
Consumer loans	23	7
Securities & other	38	12
Non-interest		
Fees	31	10
Other	9	3
Total	**320**	**100**

COMPETITORS

Bank of America	PNC Financial
Capital One	TD Bank USA
Citibank	Valley National
Hudson City Bancorp	Bancorp
JPMorgan Chase	
New York Community	
Bancorp	

HISTORICAL FINANCIALS

Company Type: Public

Income Statement
FYE: December 31

	ASSETS ($ mil.)	NET INCOME ($ mil.)	INCOME AS % OF ASSETS	EMPLOYEES
12/14	8,523	73	0.9%	1,021
12/13	7,487	70	0.9%	942
12/12	7,283	67	0.9%	941
12/11	7,097	57	0.8%	963
12/10	6,824	49	0.7%	957
Annual Growth	**5.7%**	**10.3%**	**—**	**1.6%**

2014 Year-End Financials

Debt ratio: 3.75%
Return on equity: 6.83%
Cash ($ mil.): 103
Current ratio: —
Long-term debt ($ mil.): —
No. of shares (mil.): 64
Dividends
Yield: 3.3%
Payout: 50.8%
Market value ($ mil.): 1,172

	STOCK PRICE ($) FY Close	P/E High/Low	PER SHARE ($) Earnings	Dividends	Book Value
12/14	18.06	16 13	1.22	0.60	17.63
12/13	19.32	16 12	1.23	0.76	16.87
12/12	14.92	14 11	1.18	0.71	16.37
12/11	13.39	15 10	1.01	0.47	15.88
12/10	15.13	18 12	0.88	0.44	15.38
Annual Growth	**4.5%**	**— —**	**8.5%**	**8.1%**	**3.5%**

Prudential Annuities Life Assurance Corp

Prudential Annuities Life Assurance has a name that fits —the company is the annuities business unit of life insurance giant Prudential Financial. It offers variable and fixed annuities and other retirement and long-term investment products and services. Prudential Annuities Life Assurance's products are distributed through independent financial planners brokers and banks. It holds the lead position in the US variable annuities market; its variable annuities are distributed by Prudential Annuities Distributors. The company which is part of Prudential Financial's US Retirement Solutions and Investment Management Division targets US residents with a household income level of above $100000.

Prudential Annuities aims to grow its customer base by offering innovative new products to potential and existing clients as well as by using a broad distribution network.

Parent company Prudential Financial carefully built up its annuities business through a series of acquisitions. Formerly known as American Skandia Life Assurance the business was acquired in 2003 by Prudential Financial from the Swedish insurance company Skandia Insurance Company. The company's name was changed to Prudential Annuities Life Assurance in early 2008. In 2006 Prudential acquired the variable annuity operations of Allstate for $635 million. The annuities business was rolled into Prudential Annuities Life Assurance while Prudential Annuities Distributors gained exclusive access to market annuities through Allstate's sales force.
Auditors: PricewaterhouseCoopers LLP

LOCATIONS

HQ: Prudential Annuities Life Assurance Corp
One Corporate Drive, Shelton, CT 06484
Phone: 203 926-1888
Web: www.investor.prudential.com

COMPETITORS

American Equity Investment Life Holding Company
Genworth Financial
Great American Financial Resources
John Hancock Financial Services
Kansas City Life
Lincoln Financial Group
MassMutual
MetLife
National Western
Northwestern Mutual
Presidential Life

HISTORICAL FINANCIALS

Company Type: Public

Income Statement
FYE: December 31

	ASSETS ($ mil.)	NET INCOME ($ mil.)	INCOME AS % OF ASSETS	EMPLOYEES
12/14	52,472	250	0.5%	—
12/13	53,521	848	1.6%	—
12/12	52,855	634	1.2%	—
12/11	52,313	(212)	—	—
12/10	57,266	421	0.7%	—
Annual Growth	**(2.2%)**	**(12.2%)**	**—**	**—**

2014 Year-End Financials

Debt ratio: —
Return on equity: 14.74%
Cash ($ mil.): 63
Current ratio: —
Long-term debt ($ mil.): —
No. of shares (mil.): 0
Dividends
Yield: —
Payout: 136.3%
Market value ($ mil.): —

Prudential Financial, Inc.

Prudential Financial wants to make sure its position near the top of the life insurance summit is set in stone. Prudential known for its Rock of Gibraltar logo is one of the top US life insurers and also one of the largest life insurance companies worldwide. The firm is perhaps best known for its individual life insurance though it also sells group life and disability insurance as well as annuities. Prudential also offers investment products and services including asset management services mutual funds and retirement planning. In Asia the company operates through its Gibraltar Life Insurance unit. Prudential has some $1.2 trillion in assets under management.

Operations

Prudential Financial earns a majority of revenues from premiums and fees on insurance policies and retirement products. Overall the company has some $3.5 trillion in gross life insurance policies in force around the globe as well as more than $1 trillion in assets under management.

The company's domestic operations are conducted through two divisions: US Retirement Solutions and Investment Management (individual and group annuities retirement and asset management) and US Individual Life and Group Insurance (personal and commercial insurance). US Retirement Solutions and Investment Management accounted for 34% of revenues in 2014 while US Individual Life and Group Insurance accounted for 19% of revenues.

Prudential's International Insurance business offers individual life insurance policies through Tokyo-based Gibraltar Life Insurance to affluent and middle income customers in Asia. Elsewhere it maintains a smaller presence in other parts of Europe and Latin America. International Insurance accounted for 35% of revenues in 2014.

For accounting purposes Prudential has separated any dividend-producing policies issued prior to its demutualization in 2001. That segment known as its Closed Block business segment accounts for about 10% of the company's revenues.

Geographic Reach

Prudential's US operations account for two-thirds of sales. The company also offers international products in more than 40 countries in regions including Asia Latin America and Europe.

The International Insurance segment owns offices in Argentina Brazil Japan Korea Malaysia and Taiwan; and leases offices in Italy Mexico and Poland. The Asset Management segment which includes international investment operations leases offices in India Japan and Taiwan.

Sales and Marketing

Prudential distributes its insurance and annuity products through independent brokers and agencies as well as through Allstate and Prudential's own force of some 2600 internal agents. The company's investment products are marketed through an in-house sales force while its retirement products are primarily sold through third-party financial advisors benefit consultants and brokers.

Individual life products are offered through third-party channels including independent brokers banks general agencies and producer groups.

Gibraltar Life distributes its products through affinity groups banks and from an in-house fleet of Life Planners who target affluent customers and small businesses.

Financial Performance

Revenue for Prudential has grown over the last five years including a 73% jump in 2012 to some $84.8 billion primarily due to a legal settlement in the retirement segment. So it wasn't surprising when revenue fell 51% to $41.5 billion as the company had closed several transactions at the end of 2012. Revenue recovered by 30% to $54 billion in 2014 as the company saw growth in its US Retirement Solutions and Investment Management and Asset Management divisions. US Individual Life and Group Insurance also grew but international operations declined that year.

Higher revenues helped the company return to black as it reported profits of $1.4 billion (versus a loss of $667 million in 2013). Cash flow from operations more than doubled to $19.2 billion as net income and cash generated from future policy benefits and other insurance liabilities rose.

Strategy

The company pursues growth in its current business lines both organically as well as through acquisitions joint ventures and investments.

Prudential has pursued intensive international growth in recent years with a focus on expanding its insurance and retirement operations in emerging markets. It is concentrating on deepening its presence in markets where it already operates such as Japan. To reach that objective the company has spent about a decade building up its holdings in Japan through a series of acquisitions. To expand in China Prudential is also carefully working on a 50/50 joint venture with a unit of the Chinese conglomerate Fosun Group. The company has already established a joint venture in India which it also considers a high-growth market. Expanding in Europe Prudential opened a new office in Milan in 2015.

In the US market Prudential seeks to provide wealth protection products to individual and group customers. It is expanding both its US insurance and its US retirement and investment management divisions through increased distribution and marketing efforts as well as through occasional acquisitions. In 2015 the group's mutual fund business Prudential Investment launched the Prudential Core Bond Fund a fixed-income platform investing in such assets as US government securities mortgage-related securities and corporate debt.

Mergers and Acquisitions

In 2014 the company agreed to buy an indirect ownership stake of between 34% and 40% in Adminisradora de Fondos de Pensions Habitat (AFP Habitat) which provides retirement services in Chile. It also acquired UniAsia Life Assurance in Malaysia (since renamed Gibraltar BSN Life) expanding its presence in Southeast Asia.

Giving some attention to its domestic operations in early 2013 Prudential completed the acquisition of the individual life insurance operations of The Hartford for some $615 million. The purchase added some 700000 policies to Prudential's roster and broadened its distribution network and product offerings in the US market.

In 2015 Prudential Real Estate Investors bought a 49-story Class A office building in Chicago on behalf of institutional investors.

HISTORY

In 1873 John Dryden founded the Widows and Orphans Friendly Society in New Jersey to sell workers industrial insurance (low-face-value weekly premium life insurance). In 1875 it became The Prudential Friendly Society taking the name from England's Prudential Assurance Co. The next year Dryden visited the English company and copied some of its methods such as recruiting agents from its targeted neighborhoods.

Prudential added ordinary whole life insurance in 1886. By 1900 the firm was selling more than 2000 such policies annually and had 3000 agents in eight states. In 1896 the J. Walter Thompson advertising agency (now the WPP Group) designed Prudential's Rock of Gibraltar logo.

The firm issued its first group life policy in 1916 (Prudential became a major group life insurer in the 1940s). In 1928 it introduced an Accidental Death Benefit which cost it an extra $3 million in benefits the next year alone (death claims rose drastically early in the Depression).

In 1943 Prudential mutualized. The company began decentralizing operations in the 1940s. Later it introduced a Property Investment Separate Account (PRISA) which gave pension plans a real estate investment option. By 1974 the firm was the US's group pension leader.

The insurer bought securities brokerage The Bache Group to form Pru Bache (now Prudential Securities) in 1981. Bache's forte was retail investments an area expected to blend well with Prudential's insurance business. Under George Ball Pru Bache tried to become a major investment banker —but failed. In 1991 Ball resigned leaving losses of almost $260 million and numerous lawsuits involving real estate limited partnerships.

Despite the 1992 settlement of the real estate partnership suits Prudential remained under scrutiny by several states because of "churning" a process in which agents generated commissions by inducing policyholders to trade up to more expensive policies. In 1995 new management led by former Chase Manhattanite Arthur Ryan brought sales under control sold such units as reinsurance and mortgage servicing and put its $6 billion real estate portfolio on the block. (In 1997 it sold its property management unit and Canadian commercial real estate unit; in 1998 it sold its landmark Prudential Center complex in Boston.)

In 1996 regulators from 30 states found that Prudential knew about the churning earlier than it had admitted had not stopped the perpetrators and had even promoted them. A 1997 settlement called for the company to pay restitution but the more than $2 billion estimated cost was thought to be less than the losses customers had suffered.

As the financial services industry continued to restructure Prudential in 1998 announced plans to demutualize. To focus on life insurance the company sold its health care unit to Aetna in 1999. The same year Prudential paid $62 million to resolve more churning claims revamped itself into international institutional and retail divisions and trimmed jobs. Ending its attempts to originate business the company cut 75% of its investment banking staff in 2000.

Demutualized Prudential Financial's 2001 IPO —one of the largest ever in the insurance industry —raised more than $3 billion. Prudential Financial became the holding company name for all operations making Prudential Insurance (the company's former name) a subsidiary and pure life insurer.

EXECUTIVES

Senior Vice President Europe and Latin America, William (Bill) Ray

Vice President Chief Governance Officer Secretary, Margaret (Peg) Foran

Chairman and CEO, John R. Strangfeld, age 61, $1,400,000 total compensation

Vice President And Corporate Counsel, C White

Executive Vice President Prudential Financial and Prudential Institution, Jean Hamilton

EVP and COO International, Charles F. (Charlie) Lowrey, age 57, $770,000 total compensation

SVP and CIO, Barbara G. Koster, age 60

EVP and COO US Businesses, Stephen (Steve) Pelletier, $632,962 total compensation

EVP and General Counsel, Susan L. Blount, age 58

EVP and CFO, Robert M. Falzon, $650,000 total compensation

SVP and Chief Investment Officer, Scott G. Sleyster

CEO Prudential Group Insurance, Lori Dickerson Fouch ©

CEO DHFL Pramerica Life Insurance (DPLI), Anoop Pabby

SVP and Chief Risk Officer, Nick Silitch

SVP and Chief Actuary, Richard Lambert

President Prudential Group Insurance, Andrew Sullivan

Vice President Of Information Technology, Kelly Nicholson

Vice President Information Technology, Robert Bastian

Vice President, Kathy Callahan

Vice President Information Technology, Michael Falzon

Vice President Information Technology, Jim Tonno

Vice President Individual Life Insurance Technology, Steven (Steve) Leitman

Vice President Information Technology, Diana D'Amore

Senior Vice President Treasurer, Bernard Jacob

Vice President Human Resources, Dawn Gammon

Vice President Human Resources, Suzy Domenick

Vice President Human Resources, Suzy Burnham

Vice President Human Resources, Kevin Prue

Vice President Information Systems, John Huetz

Vice President Information Systems, Scott Neely

Vice President Information Technology Shared Services, Chris Donahue

Medical Director, Myrtho Montes

Vice President Information Systems, Charles Sevola

Vice President Information Technology, Elaine Forsyth

Vice President Finance, Kenneth Tanji

Vice President Marketing, June Amori

Vice President, Robert Davis

Vice President, Dave Jungk, age 70

Vice President Corporate Counselor, Lisa Chow

Sr V Pres-cro, Nicholas Silitch

Senior Vice President Strategy and Chief Marketing Officer, Michelle (Mitch) Crecca

Vice President Information Systems, Patrick Busby

Vice President Human Resources, Kim Baldesweiler

Regional Vice President, Chuck Brousseau

Vice President Human Resources, Susan (Sue) Chegwidden

Vice President Distribution, Anthony Fontano

Vice President Governmental Affairs Southeast Region, Michael (Mel) Jennings

Senior Vice President Investments, Moya Chew-Lai

Vice President Human Resources, Deborah Hopper

Vice President, Nigel Nunoo

Vice President Strategy and Development, Bryan Comite

Vice President Regional Consultant, Jason Church

Vice President Corporate Counsel, Kelley Butler

Vice President Compliance, Ellen Koke

Senior Vice President Investment Risk Management, Craig Gardner

Vice President Marketing Management, Gregg Cromeans

Vice President Information Systems, Matt Schuette

Vice President, Peter Cody

Vice President Information Systems, Dele Oladapo
Vice President Financial Systems, John Toner
Vice President Accounting Information Services, Donna Harris
Regional Sales Coordinator Vice President, Scott Wilson
Vice President Internal Audit, John (Jack) Koskoski
Vice President Corporate Counsel (1998), Todd Moffett
Vice President Underwriting Policy And Shared Services, Barbara (Barb) Hastie
Vice President Financial Planning And Analysis, Dennis Kane
Vice President, Anthony Coletta
Vice President Business Development, Barbara (Barb) Germann
Vice President Regional Consultant, Laura Nardone
Vice President, Noah Krieger
Vice President Emerging Markets, David Masse
Vice President, Alice Pena
Vice President Process Management, Greg Steffe
Vice President, Eileen Schlegel
Vice President, Juzer Mohammedshah
Vice President, Joanne Accurso-Soto
Vice President Institutional Investment Products Group, John (Jack) Bradley
Vice President Technology, Dawn Johnson
Vice President Underwriting, Michael Farrell
Vice President of Annuities Information Technology, Dawn Davis
Vice President Information Systems, Michael Boatwright
Divisional Vice President Life Sales, Doug Peterson
Vice President Information Systems, Venkata Natarajan
Vice President Financial Reporting, Rita Lombardi
Vice President, Rich Martin
Vice President Marketing Metrics, Bob Conover
Vice President Information Systems, Chris Huydic
Vice President Corporate Counsel (1997), William Bulmer
Vice President Accounting and Finance, Patrick (Paddy) Jones
Vice President Information Technology, Nicholas Defeis
Vice President, Wonhee Kang
Vice President Sales, Maryellen Reardon
Vice President Program Management Office, Annemarie Bowman
Vice President In The San Francisco Corporate Finance Office, David Nguyen
Vice President Learning, Mary McCabe
Vice President Finance, Christine Knight
Vice President Regional Sales Coordinator, David (Dave) Sherlock
Vice President Leadership Dev Intl, Barbara (Barb) Fuchs
Vice President Business Development, Jane (Ginny) Devereaux
Vice President, Amy McCarthy
Vice President Information Technology, Ray Slider
Vice President Of Financial Reporting, Stanley Lezon
Vice President, John Kinghorn
Vice President Finance total Retirement Solutions, William (Bill) Auger
Vice President Of Project Management, Aimara Toledo
Vice President Client Management, Robert Moore
Senior Vice President, Stephen (Steve) Collins
Vice President And Corporate Counsel, Christine Parsadaian
Vice President Counsel, Lisa Wolmart
Vice President, Marcus Berry
Vice President Information Systems, Tom Large
Vice President, Steven Bloom
Vice President, Usha Archer
Vice President Asset and Portfolio Management Single Client Accounts, Christopher (Chris) Silva

Vice President Information Technology, Ann Delmedico
Vice President Regional Sales Manager, Chris Sheckley
Vice President, Sally Finning
Vice President Audit, Jack Lipari
Vice President, Ron Doughty
Vice President Business Finance, Stephen Durocher
Vice President, David Winans
Vice President Marketing Research and Analysis, Scott Halpern
Vice President Field Technology, Anthony Melchione
Vice President, Malcolm Dalrymple
Vice President Strategy Planning and Communications, Sean McLaughlin
Investment Vice President, Anna Totdahl
Vice President, Devang Gambhirwala
Vice President Life Financial Strategy, Caroline Zhang
Vice President of Medical Underwriting, Elaine Schwartz
Vice President, Surangi Patel
Vice President Operational Risk Management, Robert Tyndall
Vice President Marketing Management, Diane Velona
Vice President Corporate Compensation, Haroon Saeed
Vice President Business Analysis, Paul Parseghian
Vice President, Catherine Marcus
Vice President, Frank Papasavas
Vice President and Chief Diversity Officer, Michele Meyer-Shipp
Senior Vice President Strategic Relationships, Harry Delassio
Vice President Regional Sales Manager, Kinga Gawron
Vice President Asset Liability Management Finance, Thomas Brennan
Functional Vice President Human Resources, Louise Sheppard
Vice President Information Systems, Susan Alfano
Vice President Information Systems, Bill Devine
Vice President Regional Sales Manager, Matthew (Matt) Craig
Regional Sales Vice President, Lawrence Slabosz
Vice President Middle Market Segment, Robert Love
Regional Vice President, Robert Carvalho
Vice President Human Resources, Annmarie Jackiewicz
Vice President National Accounts, Trish Dedolce
Vice President Compliance Training, Alan Greatorex
Auditors: PricewaterhouseCoopers LLP

LOCATIONS

HQ: Prudential Financial, Inc.
  751 Broad Street, Newark, NJ 07102
Phone: 973 802-6000
Web: www.investor.prudential.com

2014 Sales

	$ mil.	% of total
US	35,793	66
Other countries	18,312	34
Total	54,105	100

PRODUCTS/OPERATIONS

2014 Revenues

	$ mil.	% of total
International insurance	20,066	35
US Retirement solutions & investment management	19,627	34
US Individual Life & group insurance	10,583	19
Closed block business	6,906	12
Corporate & adjustments	(3077)	-
Total	54,105	100

COMPETITORS

AEGON	Great-West Lifeco
AIG	ING
AXA	John Hancock Financial
Aetna	Services
Aflac	MassMutual
Allianz	Meiji Yasuda Life
American Financial	Merrill Lynch
Group	MetLife
American Life	Nationwide Life
Insurance	Insurance
Aviva	Nippon Life Insurance
Berkshire Hathaway	Northwestern Mutual
COUNTRY Financial	Principal Financial
Charles Schwab	Prudential plc
Citigroup	The Hartford
Dai-ichi Life	The Vanguard Group
FMR	Zurich Insurance Group

HISTORICAL FINANCIALS

Company Type: Public

Income Statement

	ASSETS ($ mil.)	NET INCOME ($ mil.)	INCOME AS % OF ASSETS	EMPLOYEES
12/14	766,655	1,381	0.2%	48,331
12/13	731,781	(667)	—	47,355
12/12	709,298	469	0.1%	48,498
12/11	624,521	3,666	0.6%	50,104
12/10	539,854	3,195	0.6%	41,044
Annual Growth	9.2%	(18.9%)	—	4.2%

FYE: December 31

2014 Year-End Financials

Debt ratio: 3.81%
Return on equity: 3.58%
Cash ($ mil.): 14,918
Current ratio: —
Long-term debt ($ mil.): —
No. of shares (mil.): 454
Dividends
  Yield: 2.4%
  Payout: 45.0%
Market value ($ mil.): 41,144

	STOCK PRICE ($) FY Close	P/E High/Low		Earnings	Dividends	Book Value
12/14	90.46	29	24	3.23	2.17	91.84
12/13	92.22	—	—	(1.55)	1.73	76.19
12/12	53.33	68	47	0.94	1.60	82.95
12/11	50.12	9	6	7.22	1.45	79.19
12/10	58.71	11	8	5.75	1.15	66.73
Annual Growth	11.4%	—	—	(13.4%)	17.2%	8.3%

PSEG Power LLC

Power player PSEG Power does not play with power it markets it for profit. The company is the independent power production and energy marketing subsidiary of Public Service Enterprise Group (PSEG). The unit owns and/or manages about 25 power stations in Connecticut New Jersey New York and Pennsylvania. It oversees PSEG Nuclear LLC (which operates the Salem and Hope Creek generating stations in New Jersey and owns 50% of the Peach Bottom plant in Pennsylvania) and PSEG Fossil LLC (which has gas oil coal and natural gas power plants). PSEG Power has installed capacity of more than 13466 MW. Its PSEG Energy Resources and Trade unit buys and sells wholesale power natural gas and other energy commodities.

Geographic Reach

PSEG Power operates in Connecticut New Jersey New York and Pennsylvania.

Operations

The company oversees the operations of 25 power stations. It operates through three principal direct wholly owned subsidiaries: PSEG Nuclear LLCPSEG Fossil LLC and PSEG Energy Resources and Trade.

PSEG Power sells energy capacity and ancillary services on a wholesale basis under contract to power marketers and to load serving entities and by bidding energy capacity and ancillary services into the markets for these products. It also has contracts for energy capacity financial transmission rights gas emission allowances and other energy-related contracts to optimize the value of its portfolio of generating assets and its electric and gas supply obligations.

Financial Performance

In 2013 the company's revenues increased by 4% to $5.1 billion primarily due to changes in generation and supply revenues. Generation revenues increased as the result of higher capacity revenues flowing from higher average auction prices and an increase in operating reserve revenues in PJM and higher net revenues of $36 million from an increase in generation sold in the PJM and NE regions These increases were partly offset by higher mark-to-market losses in 2013 lower volumes of electricity sold under basic generation service contracts and lower average pricing and a net decrease of $120 million due to lower volumes on wholesale load contracts).PSEG Power's net income decreased by 3% in 2013 as the result of higher operation and maintenance costs due to an increase in planned outage and maintenance costs (at its gas-fired Bethlehem Energy Centerplant in New York Bergen gas-fired plant in New Jersey Linden gas-fired plant in New Jersey and 23%-owned Conemaugh coal-fired plant in Pennsylvania) and higher outage costs at its nuclear generating plants.That year the company's operating cash inflow decreased to $1.3 billion (from $1.4 billion in 2012) primarily due to lower earnings and higher tax payments partially offset by a drop in margin deposit and employee benefit plan funding.

Strategy

PSEG Power integrates its generating assets and gas supply business with its wholesale energy fuel supply energy trading and marketing and risk management operations. PSEG redistributes properties between its units as a way to pay down debt and streamline operations.

Company Background

In 2011 PSEG Power sold generating assets (two 1000 MW gas-fired plants) in Texas in two separate transactions in order to raise $686 million. The company closed the sale of the Guadalupe plant for $351 million in March 2011 and the Odessa plant for $335 million in July 2011. The proceeds from the sale of the facilities in West Texas and South Texas were used for general corporate purposes.

(In 2009 PSEG transferred to PSEG Power some 2000 MW of traditional generating capacity in Texas from PSEG Energy Holdings as part of a reorganization to focus the latter company on renewable energy development).

EXECUTIVES

Chief Financial Officer; Executive Vice President, Caroline Dorsa, age 55
VP and Controller, Derek M. Di Risio, age 50
Chairman of the Board; President; Chief Executive Officer, Ralph Izzo, age 57
President and Chief Operating Officer of PSEG Power LLC, William (Bill) Levis, age 58
President, Richard P. Lopriore, age 65
President and Chief Nuclear Officer, Thomas P. Joyce, age 61
SVP PSEG Nuclear, Robert C. Braun

VP Finance Power PSEG Services, Daniel J. (Dan) Cregg
VP Power Operations and Asset Management PSEG Energy Resources and Trade, Raymond V. DePillo
Manager External Affairs, Neil Brown
VP Salem Generating Station PSEG Nuclear, Carl J. Fricker
Media Relations Fossil, Nancy Tucker-Datrio
Media Relations Fossil, Michael Jennings
Media Relations Fossil and Nuclear, Joseph (Skip) Sindoni
Media Relations, Jennifer (Jenn) Kramer
VP-Ops Support, Paul J. Davison
VP Hope Creek PSEG Nuclear, John F. Perry
VP-Gas Supply, John P. Scarlata
EVP CFO and Director, Caroline Dorsa, age 54
Director, Eileen A. Moran, age 58
President and Chief Operating Officer of PSEG Power LLC, William (Bill) Levis, age 58
Auditors: Deloitte & Touche LLP

LOCATIONS

HQ: PSEG Power LLC
 80 Park PlazaaT25, Newark, NJ 07102-4194
Phone: 973 430-7000
Web: www.pseg.com

PRODUCTS/OPERATIONS

Subsidiaries
PSEG Energ
PSEG Fossil LLC (gas oil and coal-fired power plants)
PSEG Nuclear LLC (nuclear power plants)

COMPETITORS

AEP	Exelon Energy
AES	InterGen
Calpine	International Power
Duke Energy	NRG Energy
Exelon	Sempra Generation

HISTORICAL FINANCIALS
Company Type: Public

Income Statement
FYE: December 31

	REVENUE ($ mil.)	NET INCOME ($ mil.)	NET PROFIT MARGIN	EMPLOYEES
12/14	5,434	760	14.0%	2,973
12/13	5,063	644	12.7%	2,633
12/12	4,865	647	13.3%	2,614
12/11	6,143	1,098	17.9%	2,699
12/10	6,558	1,143	17.4%	2,803
Annual Growth	(4.6%)	(9.7%)	—	1.5%

2014 Year-End Financials
Debt ratio: 21.11%—
Return on equity: 13.31%
Cash ($ mil.): 9
Current ratio: 1.99
Long-term debt ($ mil.): 2,243

Dividends
 Yield: —
 Payout: 117.7%
Market value ($ mil.): —

Public Service Enterprise Group Inc.

In the Garden State Public Service Enterprise Group's (PSEG) diversified business model has it smelling like a rose. Regulated subsidiary Public Service Electric and Gas (PSE&G) transmits and distributes electricity to 2.2 million customers and natural gas to 1.8 million customers in New Jersey. Nonregulated subsidiary PSEG Power operates PSEG's generating plants. PSEG Power's 13146-MW generating capacity comes mostly from nuclear and fossil-fueled plants in the US Northeast and Mid-Atlantic regions. The company's total generating output in 2014 was 54000 GWh. Other operations (under PSEG Energy Holdings) include energy infrastructure investments solar and other renewable plant development.

Geographic Reach

Once a major global power player PSEG has sold most of its overseas independent power plant interests in order to focus on its core North American power businesses primarily in Northeastern and Mid-Atlantic states.

Operations

PSEG operates three businesses: PSEG Power PSE&G and Energy Holdings. The Power unit is a wholesale energy supply company that integrates its generating asset operations with wholesale energy fuel supply energy trading and marketing and risk management activities. PSEG Power sells wholesale natural gas primarily through a full requirement basic gas supply service contract with PSE&G to meet the gas supply requirements of PSE&G's customers.

In addition to its nuclear and fossil generation fleet Power owns and operates 109 MW of photovoltaic solar generation facilities and holds 50% of an oil-fired generation facility in Hawaii. Some 13146 MW of capacity is nuclear and fossil generated and located in the US Northeast and Mid-Atlantic.

Utility PSE&G provides transmission and distribution of electric energy and gas in New Jersey. Energy Holdings owns and manages lease investments and solar generation projects.

PSEG Energy Holdings earns its revenues primarily from its portfolio of lease investments. PSEG Earns revenues from its regulated rate tariffs under which it provides electric transmission and electric and gas distribution to residential commercial and industrial customers in its service territory. Power earns revenues by selling energy capacity and ancillary services on a wholesale.

Sales and Marketing

The company distributes 58% of its electricity to commercial customers 32% to residential and 10% to industrial. Some 60% of its gas sales is to residential customers.Power also sells wholesale natural gas primarily through a full-requirements BGSS contract with PSE&G to meet the gas supply requirements of PSE&G's customers.

Financial Performance

In 2014 PSEG's net revenues increased by 9.2% due to higher revenues from Power. The majority of Power's revenues relate to bilateral contracts which are accounted for on the accrual basis as the energy is delivered and also include changes in the value of non-trading energy derivative contracts. PSE&G's sales also improved.Net income increased by 22% due primarily to higher transmission revenues at PSE&G and mark-to-market gains in 2014 (compared to losses in 2013 and higher volumes of gas sales under the BGSS contract and to third party customers at Power). The increase was also due to lower operations and maintenance costs at PSE&G and Power partially offset by lower volumes of electricity sold under the BGS contract and higher fuel costs incurred to generate electricity at Power.

PSEG's operating cash flow increased by $2 million primarily due to net changes subsidiaries and tax payments.

Strategy

The company is seeking to maintain a strong operational and financial performance in a difficult economy and a strict regulatory environment.

In 2014 it invested $765 million solar generation. It also invested $1.2 billion in the Energy Strong program which will modernize and strengthen PSE&G's distribution systems to better withstand severe weather like Superstorm Sandy. It also proposed investing an additional $1.6 billion by 2020 to modernize PSE&G's gas systems.The company completed North Central Reliability project and continued to execute four major regional transmission projects.In 2014 it commenced operating Long Island Power Authority's transmission and distribution infrastructure with an opportunity to extend for an additional eight years.

In 2014 PSEG Power announced that it will become a member of the PennEast Pipeline Company LLC which is developing a 100-mile pipeline that will bring lower cost natural gas to New Jersey homes and businesses. The PennEast Pipeline will begin in Luzerne County in northeastern Pennsylvania and end at Transco's Trenton-Woodbury interconnection in New Jersey.

Mergers and Acquisitions

Growing its green energy portfolio in 2014 PSEG's subsidiary PSEG Solar Source announced that it will acquire the ERWR Whitcomb Farm Solar project from juwi solar. The facility renamed as the PSEG Essex Solar Energy Center is located 4 miles northeast of Burlington Vermont and has a nameplate capacity of 3.6 MW. The acquisition will increase PSEG's Solar Source portfolio to 110 MW.

In 2013 PSEG Solar Source announced that it purchased two utility-scale solar power plants totaling 4.4 MW from Canadian Solar Inc. The solar installations are the largest in Shasta county California built at more than 3300 feet in elevation.

HISTORY

Tragedy struck Newark New Jersey in 1903 when a trolley slid down an icy hill and collided with a train killing more than 30 people. While investigating the accident state attorney general Thomas McCarter discovered the mismanagement of the trolley company and many of New Jersey's other transportation gas and electric companies. Planning to buy and consolidate these companies McCarter resigned and established the Public Service Corporation in 1903 with several colleagues.

The company formed divisions for gas utilities electric utilities and transportation companies. The trolley company generated almost half of Public Service's sales during its first year.

In 1924 the gas and electric companies consolidated as Public Service Electric and Gas (PSE&G). A new company was formed that year to operate buses and in 1928 it merged with the trolley company to form Public Service Coordinated Transport (later Transport of New Jersey). PSE&G signed interconnection agreements with two Pennsylvania electric companies in 1928 to form the first integrated power pool —later known as the Pennsylvania-New Jersey-Maryland Interconnection. The Public Utility Holding Company Act of 1935 ushered in the era of regulated regional monopolies ensuring PSE&G a captive market.

During the 1960s PSE&G joined Philadelphia Electric to build its first nuclear plant at Peach Bottom Pennsylvania. The company completed a second nuke in 1977 at Salem New Jersey. Its third one went on line at Hope Creek New Jersey. However plant mismanagement earned PSE&G a slew of fines in the 1980s and 1990s.

The company sold its transportation system to the State of New Jersey in 1980. Five years later PSE&G formed holding company Public Service Enterprise Group (PSEG) to move into nonutility enterprises and created Community Energy Alternatives (CEA now PSEG Global) to invest in independent power projects. In 1989 Enterprise Diversified Holdings (now PSEG Energy Holdings) was formed to handle activities ranging from real estate to oil and gas production.

CEA and three partners acquired a Buenos Aires power plant in 1993. Taking advantage of overseas privatization in the late 1990s it expanded into Asia and with AES purchased two Argentine electric companies.

PSE&G's nuclear problems resurfaced when the Salem plant was shut down in 1995 to rectify equipment breakdowns. In 1997 PSEG paid Salem partners Delmarva Power & Light and PECO Energy $82 million to settle their lawsuits charging mismanagement of Salem; both units were back on line by 1998.

Continuing to diversify in the late 1990s PSEG formed PSEG Energy Technologies in 1997 to market power and acquired five mechanical services companies in 1998 and 1999.

In 1999 PSEG Global teamed up with Panda Energy International to build three merchant plants in Texas (to be completed by 2001). It also planned plants in India and Venezuela and joined Sempra Energy to buy 90% of Chilquinta Energía an energy distributor in Chile and Peru. In 2000 it bought 90% of a distributor serving Argentina and Brazil.

New Jersey's electricity markets were deregulated in 1999; a year later the company transferred PSE&G's generation assets to nonregulated unit PSEG Power. PSEG Power also took charge of PSEG Global's plants under development in Illinois Indiana and Ohio; announced plans for new plants in New Jersey; and acquired an Albany New York plant from Niagara Mohawk.

PSEG Global completed a power plant in Texas in 2001. It also bought 94% of generator and distributor Saesa from Chile's largest conglomerate Copec for $460 million; it later acquired the rest of Saesa through a tender offer. It also purchased a Peruvian generation firm ElectroAndes for $227 million.

In 2002 PSEG Power acquired two Connecticut plants from WEC Energy for approximately $270 million.

PSEG had agreed to be acquired by Exelon but both New Jersey and Pennsylvania opposed the merger and the deal fell through in 2006.

In 2006 PSEG Global sold its 32% stake in RGE a Brazilian electric distribution company with approximately 1.1 million customers to Companhia Paulista de Força e Luz. In 2008 it sold the SAESA Group of Companies (a power distribution group) in southern Chile to a consortium formed by Morgan Stanley Infrastructure and the Ontario Teachers' Pension Plan for $887 million.

EXECUTIVES

EVP and CFO, Caroline Dorsa, age 55, $673,006 total compensation

VP Electric Delivery PSE&G, Ralph A. LaRossa, age 51, $640,866 total compensation

Chairman President and CEO, Ralph Izzo, age 57, $1,142,307 total compensation

President PSEG Energy Resources & Trade, Shahid Malik

President and COO PSEG Power, William (Bill) Levis, age 58, $669,540 total compensation

President PSEG Fossil, Richard P. Lopriore

President and Chief Nuclear Officer PSEG Nuclear, Robert C. Braun

VP Regulatory PSEG Services, Tamara L. Linde, $397,010 total compensation

VP Asset Management and Centralized Services PSE&G, David M. Daly

President PSEG Services Corporation, Derek M. Di Risio, age 50

President PSEG Power Ventures and PSEG Solar Source, Diana L. Drysdale

Vice President Corporate Communications, Kathleen Fitzgerald

Vice President Risk Management Chief Risk Officer, Laurent Pommier

Vice President of Employee Benefits Health and Safety, John (Jack) Tiberi

Vice President Manager Director, Donald (Don) Staudt

Department Head, Carlo Ruggiero

Vice President Of Customer Information Technology, Thomas Flaherty

Senior Vice President, Kenneth Brown

Vice President Financ, Rose Chernick

Vice President Hope Creek PSEG Nuclear, John (Jack) Perry

Treasurer, Bradford Huntington

Board Member, Michael Percarpio

Secretary Treasurer, John Povich

Assistant Treasurer, Benjamin Zoe

Auditors: Deloitte & Touche LLP

LOCATIONS

HQ: Public Service Enterprise Group Inc.
80 Park Plaza, P.O. Box 1171, Newark, NJ 07101-1171
Phone: 973 430-7000
Web: www.pseg.com

PRODUCTS/OPERATIONS

2014 Sales

	$ mil.	% of total
PSE&G	6,766	53
Power	5,434	43
Others	455	4
Adjustments	(1769)	-
Total	**10,886**	**100**

Selected Subsidiaries

PSEG Energy Holdings Inc. (nonutility companies)
 PSEG Global Inc. (solar plants and other alternative energy investments)
 PSEG Resources Inc. (energy infrastructure investments)
PSEG Power LLC
 PSEG Fossil LLC (operator of PSEG' s fossil fuel plants)
 PSEG Nuclear LLC (operator of PSEG' s nuclear plants)
 PSEG Energy Resources and Trade LLC (energy marketing)
PSEG Services Corporation (management and administrative services for PSEG)
Public Service Electric and Gas Company (PSE&G distribution of electricity and gas)

COMPETITORS

AEP	NRG Energy
AES	National Grid USA
CenterPoint Energy	New Jersey Resources
Con Edison	NextEra Energy
Constellation Energy Group	NiSource
Delmarva Power	PPL Corporation
Eversource Energy	Sempra Energy
Exelon	South Jersey Industries
FirstEnergy	Tractebel Engineering

HISTORICAL FINANCIALS

Company Type: Public

Income Statement

FYE: December 31

	REVENUE ($ mil.)	NET INCOME ($ mil.)	NET PROFIT MARGIN	EMPLOYEES
12/14	10,886	1,518	13.9%	12,689
12/13	9,968	1,243	12.5%	9,887
12/12	9,781	1,275	13.0%	9,798
12/11	11,079	1,503	13.6%	9,784
12/10	11,793	1,564	13.3%	9,965
Annual Growth	(2.0%)	(0.7%)	—	6.2%

2014 Year-End Financials

Debt ratio: 25.88%
Return on equity: 12.76%
Cash ($ mil.): 402
Current ratio: 1.18
Long-term debt ($ mil.): 8,261

No. of shares (mil.): 505
Dividends
Yield: 3.5%
Payout: 60.4%
Market value ($ mil.): 20,947

	STOCK PRICE ($) FY Close	P/E High/Low	PER SHARE ($) Earnings	Dividends	Book Value
12/14	41.41	15 10	2.99	1.48	24.09
12/13	32.04	15 12	2.45	1.44	22.95
12/12	30.60	13 12	2.51	1.42	21.31
12/11	33.01	12 10	2.96	1.37	20.30
12/10	31.81	11 9	3.08	1.37	19.04
Annual Growth	6.8%	— —	(0.7%)	1.9%	6.1%

Publix Super Markets, Inc.

Publix Super Markets tops the list of privately owned grocery operators in the US. By emphasizing service and a family-friendly image over price Publix has outgrown and outperformed its regional rivals. More than two-thirds of its 1095 stores are in Florida but it also operates in Alabama Georgia South Carolina Tennessee and North Carolina (a new market for the company). Publix makes some of its own bakery deli dairy goods and fresh prepared foods at its own manufacturing plants in Florida and Georgia. Also many stores house pharmacies and banks. Founder George Jenkins began offering stock to Publix employees in 1930. Employees own about 31% of Publix which is still run by the Jenkins family.

Operations

In addition to more than 1000 supermarkets Publix operates eight distribution centers in Florida and one in Georgia. The company also operates two bakeries (Atlanta and Lakeland Florida) three dairies (Deerfield Beach and Lakeland Florida and Lawrenceville Georgia) three fresh foods processing plants (Deerfield Beach Jacksonville and Lakeland Florida) and a printing services plant in Lakeland.

Geographic Reach

Publix has supermarkets located in Florida Georgia Alabama South Carolina Tennessee and North Carolina.

It restocks store shelves from seven distribution centers in Florida and one in Georgia.

Sales and Marketing

Publix spent $ 232.5 million and $217.5 million on advertising in 2014 and 2013 respectively.

Financial Performance

Publix reported retail sales of $30.8 billion in 2014 an increase of 6% over the prior year. The sales gain part of a four-year trend was driven by a rise in same-store sales. Food price inflation and increased customer traffic helped drive same-store sales and reflects the improving economic climate in the regional supermarket operator's markets.

Net income has also been trending up and finished 2014 at $1.7 billion a 5% increase over the previous year due to higher revenue. Cash from operations also rose by $209.9 million to $2.7 billion.

Strategy

Publix opened 32 supermarkets in 2014 including some in new markets like North Carolina. The supermarket operator doubled its presence in the Charlotte North Carolina area with the purchase of seven stores there from BI-LO. It opened its first new store in Charlotte in 2014. It also opened new stores in South Carolina in 2013.

Publix is facing increased competition from BI-LO Holding which swallowed Winn-Dixie in 2012 and Sweetbay Supermarket in 2014. It's also squaring off against Harris-Teeter now owned by Kroger and supercenter giant Wal-Mart Stores in North Carolina. Kroger acquired Harris-Teeter to increase its presence in the Southeast Publix's market.

To better focus on its core supermarket business Publix sold its 14-store PIX convenience store chain to Circle K (owned by Canada's Couche-Tard) in late 2013.

Mergers and Acquisitions

Publix is buying up shopping centers that house its supermarkets. In October 2014 it acquired seven of the 18 shopping centers it anchors in the Tampa Bay area and southwest Florida. It purchased six more by mid-2015 and had $1.3 billion set aside to buy more in the back half of the year. It will also use some of that money to build and renovate stores.

Ownership

The grocery chain's employees own about 31% of Publix Super Markets' stock through the Employee Stock Ownership Plan.

HISTORY

George Jenkins age 22 resigned as manager of the Piggly Wiggly grocery in Winter Haven Florida in 1930. With money he had saved to buy a car he opened his own grocery store Publix next door to his old employer. The small store (named after a chain of movie theaters) prospered despite the Depression and in 1935 Jenkins opened another Publix in the same town.

Five years later after the supermarket format had become popular Jenkins closed his two smaller locations and opened a new more modern Publix Market. With pastel colors and electric-eye doors it was also the first US store to feature air conditioning.

Publix Super Markets bought the All-American chain of Lakeland Florida (19 stores) in 1944 and moved its corporate headquarters to that city. The company began offering S&H Green Stamps in 1953 and in 1956 it replaced its original supermarket with a mall featuring an enlarged Publix and a Green Stamp redemption center. Publix expanded into South Florida in the late 1950s.

As Florida's population grew Publix continued to expand opening its 100th store in 1964. Publix was the first grocery chain in the state to use barcode scanners; all its stores had the technology by 1981. The company beat Florida banks in providing ATMs and during the 1980s opened debit card stations.

Publix continued to grow in the 1980s safe from takeover attempts because of its employee ownership. In 1988 it installed the first automated check-out systems in South Florida giving patrons an always-open checkout lane.

The chain stopped offering Green Stamps in 1989 and most of the $19 million decrease in Publix advertising expenditures was attributed to the end of the 36-year promotion. That year after almost six decades "Mr. George" —as founder Jenkins was known —stepped down as chairman in favor of his son Howard. (George died in 1996.)

In 1991 Publix opened its first store outside Florida in Georgia as part of its plan to become a major player in the Southeast. Publix entered South Carolina in 1993 with one supermarket; it also tripled its presence in Georgia to 15 stores.

The United Food and Commercial Workers Union began a campaign in 1994 against alleged gender and racial discrimination in Publix's hiring promotion and compensation policies.

Publix opened its first store in Alabama in 1996. That year a federal judge allowed about 150000 women to join a class-action suit filed in 1995 by 12 women who had sued Publix charging that the company consistently channeled female employees into low-paying jobs with little chance for good promotions. The case which at the time was said to be the biggest sex discrimination lawsuit ever was set to go to trial but in 1997 the company paid $82.5 million to settle and another $3.5 million to settle a complaint of discrimination against black applicants and employees.

Publix promised to change its promotion policies but two more lawsuits alleging discrimination against women and blacks were filed in 1997 and 1998. The suit filed on behalf of the women was denied class-action status in 2000. Later that year the company settled the racial discrimination lawsuit for $10.5 million. Howard Jenkins stepped down as CEO in mid-2001; his cousin Charlie Jenkins took the helm.

Publix introduced the Hispanic-themed Sabor format in 2005 in Kissimmee Florida.

In 2007 the chain began offering seven popular antibiotics free at some 685 Publix Pharmacies. The drugs account for almost 50% of the generic pediatric prescriptions filled at Publix. Also in 2007 the company launched a new store format called GreenWise Market (the name Publix has already given to its store-within-a-store natural/organic sections and private-label line of specialty foods) to court more health-conscious consumers and compete with national organic chains such as Whole Foods.

CEO Charlie Jenkins retired in 2008 and was succeeded by his cousin and Publix president Ed Crenshaw. The company completed the roughly $500 million acquisition of 49 Albertsons stores in Florida the same year.

In May 2011 Publix sold its 36 Crispers restaurants in Florida (acquired in 2007) to Healthy Food Concepts LLC an affiliate of a Florida-based investment group thereby exiting the restaurant business.

Publix entered North Carolina in 2014 with a 56000-square-foot store in the Ballantyne Town Center in Charlotte.

EXECUTIVES

CFO and Treasurer, David P. Phillips, age 55, $845,430 total compensation

President and Director, William E. (Ed) Crenshaw, age 64, $920,430 total compensation

General Counsel and Secretary, John A. Attaway, age 56, $581,300 total compensation

Chairman and President Publix Super Markets Charities, Carol Jenkins Barnett, age 59

President, Randall T. (Todd) Jones, age 52, $861,010 total compensation

SVP and CIO, Laurie Z. Douglas, age 51, $716,125 total compensation

LOCATIONS

HQ: Publix Super Markets, Inc.
  3300 Publix Corporate Parkway, Lakeland, FL 33811
Phone: 863 688-1188
Web: www.publix.com

2014 Supermarkets

	No.
Florida	760
Georgia	182
Alabama	58
South Carolina	51
Tennessee	38
North Carolina	6
Total	**1,095**

PRODUCTS/OPERATIONS

2014 Sales

	% of total
Grocery	85
Other	15
Total	**100**

Selected Supermarket Departments

Bakery
Banking
Dairy
Deli
Ethnic foods
Floral
Groceries
Health and beauty care
Housewares
Meat
Pharmacy
Photo processing
Produce
Seafood
Foods Processed
Baked goods
Dairy products
Deli items

COMPETITORS

ALDI	Rite Aid
CVS	Sedano' s
Costco Wholesale	Southeastern Grocers
Food Lion	The Pantry
IGA	Wal-Mart
Ingles Markets	Walgreen
Kmart	Whole Foods
Kroger	

HISTORICAL FINANCIALS

Company Type: Public

Income Statement

FYE: December 27

	REVENUE ($ mil.)	NET INCOME ($ mil.)	NET PROFIT MARGIN	EMPLOYEES
12/14	30,802	1,735	5.6%	175,000
12/13	29,147	1,653	5.7%	166,000
12/12	27,706	1,552	5.6%	158,000
12/11	27,178	1,491	5.5%	152,000
12/10	25,328	1,338	5.3%	148,000
Annual Growth	**5.0%**	**6.7%**	**—**	**4.3%**

2014 Year-End Financials

Debt ratio: 1.44%	No. of shares (mil.): 774
Return on equity: 21.07%	Dividends
Cash ($ mil.): 407	Yield: 0.0%
Current ratio: 1.38	Payout: 33.1%
Long-term debt ($ mil.): 192	Market value ($ mil.): 11,423

	STOCK PRICE ($) FY Close	P/E High/Low		PER SHARE ($) Earnings	Dividends	Book Value
12/14	14.75	7	7	2.23	0.74	11.13
12/13	15.50	—	—	2.12	0.70	10.16
12/12	15.50	—	—	1.98	0.89	8.77
12/11	15.50	—	—	1.90	0.53	7.90
12/10	15.50	15	9	1.70	0.46	9.30
Annual Growth	**(1.2%)**	—	—	**7.0%**	**12.6%**	**4.6%**

PulteGroup, Inc.

PulteGroup pulls its weight in providing homes for American families. PulteGroup targets a cross-section of home buyers nationwide by buying land to build single-family houses duplexes townhouses and condominiums. Its Centex brand is marketed to entry-level buyers while Pulte Homes aims to capture customers looking to trade up. PulteGroup also builds Del Webb retiree communities mostly in Sun Belt locales for the growing number of buyers in the 55-plus age range. The company sells its homes in some 50 markets across more than 25 states. In 2014 its homes sold for an average price of $329000. The company became one of the top homebuilders in the US when it merged with rival Centex Homes in 2009.

HISTORY

Company BackgroundWilliam Pulte built his first home in Detroit in 1950 and incorporated his business in 1956 as William J. Pulte Inc.

In 1961 the company built its first subdivision in Detroit. During that decade Pulte moved into Washington DC (1964) Chicago (1966) and Atlanta (1968). In 1969 Pulte merged with Colorado's American Builders to form the Pulte Home Corporation a publicly traded company.

Originally a builder of high-priced single-family homes Pulte began expanding into affordable and midrange housing markets. To lower costs it pioneered modular designs and prebuilt components. Pulte architects designed the Quadrominium a large structure with four separate two-bedroom units each with its own entrance and garage (priced at a mere $20000 per unit in the 1970s).

Pulte formed Intercontinental Mortgage (later renamed ICM Mortgage) and began making home loans in 1972. The company ran into trouble in 1988 when it was accused of forcing Pulte homebuyers in Baltimore to use ICM financing instead of cheaper loans from the county. Pulte settled by repaying the difference in loan costs.

By the mid-1980s Pulte was one of the US's largest on-site homebuilders. PHM Corporation was created in 1987 as a holding company for the Pulte group of companies. That year PHM entered the thrift business by assisting the Federal Savings and Loan Insurance Corp.'s S&L bailout. It acquired five Texas S&Ls (with assets of $1.3 billion) for $45 million and eventually combined them to form First Heights (finally discontinuing the business in 1994).

Pulte Homes' Quality Leadership customer satisfaction program introduced in the early 1990s paid off in 1991 as Pulte enjoyed record sales despite a depressed home market. Renamed Pulte Corporation in 1993 the company soon faced rising interest rates which dampened the US housing market and affected the Mexican peso. Pulte recorded a $2 million foreign-currency loss on an

affordable-housing venture in Mexico in 1994. Nonetheless it began a second joint venture in that country in 1995 and helped form mortgage bank Su Casita with nine Mexican homebuilders to finance home construction on its border. That year it also started developing retirement communities when it bought the Ponds at Clearbrook in New Jersey.

In 1996 its Mexican joint venture Condake-Pulte began building thousands of affordable homes for General Motors and Sony employees in maquiladora residential areas near the US-Mexico border. The company also bought Rhode Island's top homebuilder LeBlanc.

Pulte restructured in 1997 and a year later shed its manufactured housing and building supply business. It also acquired DiVosta one of Florida's largest homebuilders and Tennessee-based Radnor Homes.

The company's 1988 foray into S&Ls came back to haunt it in 1998: The Federal Deposit Insurance Corp. won a lawsuit that accused the builder of abusing tax benefits associated with the S&Ls. (Pulte settled the case in 2001 by paying $41.5 million.) In 1999 Pulte bought the interest held by investment firm Blackstone Group its partner in active-adult homebuilding.

The next year Pulte joined other builders in an Internet-based building materials cooperative. Also in 2000 the company began dealings to expand its homebuilding operations into Argentina.

The company changed its name to Pulte Homes in 2001. That year Mark O'Brien became the company's CEO. He directed Pulte through the major acquisition of retirement community developer Del Webb for about $800 million in stock and $950 million in assumed debt. The combined company became the largest US homebuilder. In 2002 Pulte reorganized the structure of its operations in Mexico and created Pulte Mexico S. de R.L. de C.V. one of the largest builders in that country.

Adding to its portfolio of accolades Pulte was named 2002 "Builder of the Year" by Professional Builder magazine and in 2003 Pulte ranked 19th among the "Top 50 Best-Performing Companies" in Business Week's performance rankings of the Standard & Poor's 500-stock index.

Pulte expanded its operations in the fast-growing San Diego area in 2003 by purchasing assets of ColRich Communities which included about 500 entitled lots in five communities in the South Bay and Coastal North areas of San Diego. It boosted its presence in the Albuquerque Phoenix and Tucson markets by acquiring Sivage-Thomas Homes (Albuquerque) with about 7000 lots in the region and Del Webb entered the Reno Nevada market with its Sierra Canyon active adult community. O'Brien left the company in June 2003 after having served in senior management positions for six years (and 21 total years) within the company. EVP and COO Richard Dugas stepped up to become the company's president and CEO at that time.

In September 2003 the US Court of Federal Claims awarded Pulte and related parties $48.7 million as a result of a breach of contract by the US government related to Pulte's acquisition of five savings and loans in 1988.

J.D. Power and Associates recognized Pulte as a top performer for its fifth consecutive year in its "2004 New Home Builder Customer Satisfaction Study." Out of the 25 markets it surveyed Pulte ranked highest in 14 markets #2 in nine markets and #3 in six markets.

At the close of 2004 Pulte sold some operations in Argentina to real estate developer Grupo Farallon. The next year it sold its Mexican and remaining Argentine homebuilding enterprises to focus exclusively on US operations.The downturn in the US housing market —due to a toxic cocktail of higher home prices increased foreclosures high unemployment and constraints on mortgage lending —led to weakened demand for new homes and higher cancellation rates. For Pulte this trend meant decreased profitability and a decline in homebuilding activity. Pulte responded to the downturn and adjusted its operations by cutting jobs and shuttering plants to meet lower demand levels.

The company bought rival Centex in 2009. The acquisition made Pulte the largest homebuilder in the US and also strengthened Pulte's offerings in the lower-priced home segment.

A year following the Centex merger founder William Pulte retired from the company and from its board of directors. He was named chairman emeritus.

EXECUTIVES

Chairman President and CEO, Richard J. Dugas, age 50, $1,200,000 total compensation
Area President Southeast Area, Peter J. Keane, age 50
EVP Field Operations, Harmon D. Smith, age 51, $625,000 total compensation
VP and CIO, Joseph L. Drouin
President and CEO Pulte Financial Services, Debra W. (Deb) Still
EVP Human Resources, James R. (Jim) Ellinghausen, age 57, $525,000 total compensation
EVP and CFO, Robert T. (Bob) O'Shaughnessy, age 49, $700,000 total compensation
Area President Midwest Area, Anthony W. (Tony) Barbee
Area President East Area, Stephen P. (Steve) Schlageter, age 44
Area President West Area, John J. Chadwick, age 53
EVP Homebuilding Operations, Ryan R. Marshall, age 40, $482,308 total compensation
VP and Chief Marketing Officer, Manish M. Shrivastava
VP Sales and Operations North Florida Division, Sean Strickler
Area President Texas Area, Stephen V. Teodecki
Auditors: Ernst & Young LLP

LOCATIONS

HQ: PulteGroup, Inc.
   3350 Peachtree Road NE, Suite 150, Atlanta, GA 30326
Phone: 404 978-6400
Web: www.pultegroupinc.com

Selected Homebuilding Regions
Florida
North (IL IN MI MN MO Northern CA OH OR WA)
Northeast (CT DE MD MA NJ NY PA RI VA)
Southeast (GA NC SC TN)
Southwest (AZ CO HI NV NM Southern CA)
Texas

PRODUCTS/OPERATIONS

2014 Sales

	% of total
North	25
Southeast	16
Florida	16
Texas	15
Southwest	14
Northeast	12
Financial Services	2
Total	**100**

2014 Sales

	$ mil.	% of total
Home building		
Home Sales	5662.3	97
Land Sales	34.5	1
Financial Serives	125	2
Total	**5,822**	**100**

Selected Brands
Centex (entry-level buyers)
Del Webb (active-adult buyers)
DiVosta (Florida)
Pulte Homes (move-up buyers)

COMPETITORS

Beazer Homes	M.D.C.
CalAtlantic	Meritage Homes
D.R. Horton	NVR
Hovnanian Enterprises	Pardee Homes
KB Home	Toll Brothers
Lennar	

HISTORICAL FINANCIALS
Company Type: Public

Income Statement
FYE: December 31

	REVENUE ($ mil.)	NET INCOME ($ mil.)	NET PROFIT MARGIN	EMPLOYEES
12/15	5,981	494	8.3%	4,542
12/14	5,822	474	8.1%	4,149
12/13	5,679	2,620	46.1%	3,843
12/12	4,820	206	4.3%	3,634
12/11	4,136	(210)	—	3,579
Annual Growth	**9.7%**	**—**	**—**	**6.1%**

2015 Year-End Financials

Debt ratio: 26.63%	No. of shares (mil.): 349
Return on equity: 10.33%	Dividends
Cash ($ mil.): 754	Yield: 1.8%
Current ratio: 9.70	Payout: 25.0%
Long-term debt ($ mil.): 2,387	Market value ($ mil.): 6,222

	STOCK PRICE ($) FY Close	P/E High/Low		PER SHARE ($) Earnings	Dividends	Book Value
12/15	17.82	17	12	1.36	0.33	13.63
12/14	21.46	17	13	1.26	0.23	13.01
12/13	20.37	4	2	6.72	0.15	12.19
12/12	18.16	34	12	0.54	0.00	5.66
12/11	6.31	—	—	(0.55)	0.00	5.07
Annual Growth	**29.6%**	**—**	**—**	**—**	**—**	**28.1%**

PVH Corp

PVH has the buttoned-up look covered. A top global apparel player it is the world's largest dress shirt and neckwear company. PVH owns and globally markets lifestyle brands Calvin Klein and Tommy Hilfiger. Its closet also overflows with clothing accessories and footwear for men women and children. PVH owns Heritage Brands which include Van Heusen IZOD ARROW and Bass. Private-label and licensed brands such as DKNY Kenneth Cole New York and MICHAEL Michael Kors round out its wardrobe. PVH generates sales from multiple channels: more than 1900 company-operated retail stores retailers licensees franchisees distributors who resell and royalty and advertising fees.

Operations
PVH organizes its business into three main areas. Generating more than half of PVH's revenue Tommy Hilfiger consists of North America and International segments. Calvin Klein consists of the Calvin Klein Licensing and Other (Calvin Klein Apparel) segments comprising Calvin Klein dress furnishings sportswear and outlet retail divisions in North America. Finally Heritage Brands consists of the Heritage Brand Dress Furnishings

(men's dress shirts and neckwear) Wholesale Sportswear and Retail segments.

In addition to the more than 1900 retail stores that it operates PVH maintains wholesale and retail warehousing and distribution centers in the US Canada Japan and the Netherlands that inspect sort pack and ship goods to customers.

Sales and Marketing
PVH's Calvin Klein Tommy Hilfiger and Heritage Brands businesses all distribute products through multiple channels including retail wholesale and licensing to third parties. Within the retail channel each business has its own network of company-operated stores (those in the US and Canada tend to be located in outlet malls) specialty stores and company-operated e-commerce sites. On the wholesale side Calvin Klein and Tommy Hilfiger products are sold to distributors for resale stores operated by licensees and franchisees and department stores like Macy's (PVH's top customer) and Dillard's. Tommy Hilfiger products are also sold through joint ventures in such emerging markets as Brazil China and India.

Heritage Brands products are distributed wholesale to the likes of Bon-Ton Stores J. C. Penney Kohl's and Sears. Each of the Calvin Klein Tommy Hilfiger and Heritage Brands businesses have a number of licensing partners domestically and abroad who have the right to manufacture and wholesale specified products under one or more brands or are granted the right to open retail stores under the licensed brand name.

PVH targets the marketing of its brands at distinct consumer demographics. The company advertises its brands through digital media (including its e-commerce and social media sites) national print media television outdoor signage special events promotions and store locations. It also advertises through product tie-ins and sport sponsorships (Calvin Klein/basketball Van Heusen/football and IZOD/golf). The Tommy Hilfiger marketing team also coordinates appearances by the designer himself Tommy Hilfiger at runway shows special events and flagship store openings.

Strategy
PVH's strength lies in the fact that it maintains a strong diversified brand portfolio that is growing through acquisitions and supported by a model that offers multiple brands and product types globally at different price points and across a range of distribution channels —from retail to licensing —allowing PVH to reach a broad range of consumers in various geographic regions thus reducing reliance on any one demographic.

HISTORY

Moses Phillips came to America from Poland in 1881. While living in a one-room apartment in Pottsville Pennsylvania he sold flannel shirts (which his wife sewed) to coal miners from a pushcart. He soon brought the rest of his family to the US and upgraded the pushcart to a horse and buggy. Business continued to grow and the Phillips-Jones Corporation was formed in 1907.

The company moved to New York in 1914 and control passed from father to son for four generations. Isaac followed Moses then Seymour took over in 1941 until he handed the reins to Lawrence who joined the company in 1948 and became president and CEO in 1969. Ads in the 1950s featured such actors as Anthony Quinn Burt Lancaster and Ronald Reagan in Van Heusen shirts. In 1957 the company received its new name Phillips-Van Heusen (PVH). It grew via acquisitions throughout the 1970s and began selling its merchandise at its own outlet stores in 1979 but it didn't want its products sold at the off-price outlets that became popular in the early 1980s. The company stopped doing business with stores and distributors that allowed PVH merchandise to reach cut-price vendors.

In 1987 PVH bought back more than 5 million shares of stock in order to fend off an acquisition bid by the Hunt family of Texas. Lawrence stepped down in 1993 ending the unbroken chain of Phillipses at the helm. In 1995 the Phillips family sold its stake in the business. In June 2011 the company renamed itself PVH Corp. officially dropping the Phillips-Van Heusen moniker to emphasize its diversified portfolio of brands.

EXECUTIVES

President Geoffrey Beene Retail, Margaret P. (Meg) Lachance
Chairman and CEO, Emanuel (Manny) Chirico, age 58, $1,350,000 total compensation
President Izod Wholesale and Retail, Molly Yearick
EVP Chief Operating and Financial Officer, Michael A. (Mike) Shaffer, age 53, $833,333 total compensation
CEO Heritage Brands and North America Wholesale, Francis K. (Ken) Duane, age 59, $1,041,667 total compensation
President Swimwear Speedo, Jim Gerson
President Licensing, Kenneth L. (Ken) Wyse
CEO Tommy Hilfiger PVH Europe, Daniel Grieder, $928,169 total compensation
EVP Marketing Group, Michael (Mike) Kelly
CEO Tommy Hilfiger Americas, Gary Sheinbaum
CEO Calvin Klein, Steven B. (Steve) Shiffman, age 57, $808,333 total compensation
President National Brand Sportswear, Geoffrey (Geoff) Barrett
EVP Logistics Services, Kevin J. Urban
President Calvin Klein Men's Sportswear and Jeanswear, Alexander (Alex) Cannon
SVP and Chief Risk Officer, Melanie Steiner
President Dress Shirts, David Sirkin
President Core Intimates, Leslie (Les) Hall
President Global Calvin Klein Underwear, Cheryl Abel-Hodges
President Calvin Klein Retail, Nicholas (Nick) Strange
President Calvin Klein Asia Pacific, Frank Cancelloni
EVP General Counsel and Secretary, Mark D. Fischer
EVP Human Resources, David F. (Dave) Kozel
EVP and CIO, Eileen Mahoney
Chief Supply Chain Officer, William (Bill) McRaith
EVP Wholesale Canada, Richard Deck
Country Manager Mexico, Marcela Wartenbergh
Vice President National Sales Manager, Lex Israel
Group Vice President Womens Sourcing, Susan (Sue) Parson
National Sales Manager, Orest Kostecki
Vice President Design, Karen Fischer
Vice President Purchasing, Jason Zuckerman
Group Vice President Human Resources, Danielle Korins
Vice President of Mens Design Van Heusen Retail, Jeanne Clarke
Vice President Of Sales, Mike Sousa
Vice President Regional Sales Manager, John Karwacki
Vice President Brand Manager, Jim Beckman
Senior Vice President Finance And Controller, John (Jack) Hayes
Senior Vice President Design, John Crocco
Vice President Design Technology, Matt Mandracchia
Vice President Human Resources, Danielle Bernier
Vice President Of Information Technology, Arne Tjalma
Vice President Distribution, Richard Vuich
Vice President of Marketing Intimate Apparel Underwear, Erin Lynn
Vice President Sales and Planning, Milena Schaefer

Executive Vice President Global Supply Chain, Jeff Sluder
Vice President Human Rights, Roopa Nair
Senior Vice President, Jillian Zino
Vice President Of Design For Timberland Apparel, Michael Flynn
Vice President Retail And Human Resources Admin, Carla David
Senior Vice President Business Development, Matt McCullough
Vice President Finance Global Supply Chain, John (Jack) Benz
Vice President Of Technical Design, Kelley Robinson
Vice President Advertising, Michael Delellis
Vice President Finance And Operations, Guilford Robinson
Vice President Advertising and Integrated Media (Tommy Hilfiger), Eric Lichtmess
Group Vice President Corporate Operations, Dom Zino
Vice President Real Estate, Lauren Kinder
National Sales Manager, Keith Roberson
Senior Vice President Tax, Elizabeth Maguire
Vice President Dmm Vh Men's Sportswear Dress, Donna Williams
Vice President Of Planning Calvin Klein, Jodi Haag
Vice President Wholesale Demand Planning, Stefanie Pagovich
National Sales Manager Calvin Klein, Eric Anderson
Senior Vice President Of Communications, Tiffin Jernstedt
Vice President Of Finance And Administration, Harry MA
Vice President Of Merchandising And Design Speedo Softgoods, Giorgi Duvall
Vice President, Abhishek Nawani
Vice President Construction X 6306, Susan Pierce
Group Vice President Corporate Applications, Matt Skinner
Senior Vice President Sales And Marketing The Underwear Group, Larry Meltzer
Vice Chairman and Executive Chairman Tommy Hilfiger, Fred Gehring, age 60
Treasurer, Eric Reliford
Board Member, Jared Eberly
Auditors: Ernst & Young LLP

LOCATIONS

HQ: PVH Corp
200 Madison Avenue, New York, NY 10016
Phone: 212 381-3500
Web: www.pvh.com

2015 Sales

	$ mil.	% of total
US	4,404	53
Europe	2,304	28
Asia	779	10
Canada	468	6
Other foreign	283	3
Total	**8,186**	**100**

PRODUCTS/OPERATIONS

2015 Sales

	$ mil.	% of total
Tommy Hilfiger International	1,946	24
Tommy Hilfiger North America	1,635	20
Calvin Klein North America	1,550	19
Heritage Brand Wholesale	1,445	17
Calvin Klein International	1,308	16
Heritage Brand Retail	355	4
Total	**8,186**	**100**

Selected Brands

Owned
ARROW
Bass
Calvin Klein

Eagle
IZOD
Tommy Hilfiger
Van Heusen
Licensed
Axcess
Chaps
Claiborne
Donald J. Trump Signature Collection
DKNY
Elie Tahari
Geoffrey Beene
Ike Behar
J. Garcia
JOE Joseph Abboud
John Varvatos
Jones New York
Kenneth Cole New York
Kenneth Cole Reaction
MICHAEL Michael Kors
Michael Kors Collection
Nautica
Robert Graham
Sean John
Ted Baker
U.S. POLO ASSN.

COMPETITORS

Allen-Edmonds	Kellwood
Armani	Kenneth Cole
Caleres	Levi Strauss
Capital Mercury	Nine West
Apparel	Oxford Industries
Donna Karan	Perry Ellis
Eddie Bauer LLC	International
Genesco	Prada
Gucci	Ralph Lauren
Haggar	Reebok
Hugo Boss	The Gap
J. Crew	Timberland
Kate Spade	VF Corporation

HISTORICAL FINANCIALS

Company Type: Public

Income Statement

FYE: February 1

	REVENUE ($ mil.)	NET INCOME ($ mil.)	NET PROFIT MARGIN	EMPLOYEES
02/15	8,241	439	5.3%	34,100
02/14	8,186	143	1.8%	33,200
02/13*	6,043	433	7.2%	28,700
01/12	5,890	317	5.4%	25,700
01/11	4,636	53	1.2%	22,700
Annual Growth	**15.5%**	**69.0%**	**—**	**10.7%**

*Fiscal year change

2015 Year-End Financials

Debt ratio: 32.44%	No. of shares (mil.): 82
Return on equity: 10.12%	Dividends
Cash ($ mil.): 479	Yield: 0.0%
Current ratio: 2.03	Payout: 2.8%
Long-term debt ($ mil.): 3,438	Market value ($ mil.): 9,098

	STOCK PRICE ($) FY Close	P/E High/Low		PER SHARE ($) Earnings	Dividends	Book Value
02/15	110.26	25	20	5.27	0.15	52.89
02/14	120.87	78	59	1.74	0.15	52.76
02/13*	116.26	20	12	5.87	0.15	44.61
01/12	76.70	17	12	4.36	0.15	39.90
01/11	58.05	87	47	0.80	0.15	36.42
Annual Growth	**17.4%**	**—**	**—**	**60.2%**	**(0.0%)**	**9.8%**

*Fiscal year change

QCR Holdings Inc

Quad City is muscling in on the community banking scene in the Midwest. QCR Holdings is the holding company for Quad City Bank and Trust Cedar Rapids Bank and Trust Rockford Bank and Trust and First Wisconsin Bank and Trust. Together the banks have about 10 offices serving the Quad City area of Illinois and Iowa as well as the communities of Cedar Rapids Iowa; Rockford Illinois; and Milwaukee. The banks offer traditional deposit products and services and concentrate their lending activities on local businesses: Commercial real estate loans make up nearly half of the loan portfolio; commercial loans and leases make up another third.QCR Holdings' Bancard subsidiary provides credit card processing services; its majority-owned M2 Lease Funds leases machinery and equipment to commercial and industrial businesses.QCR Holdings has grown by launching operations in new geographic markets and then building upon them. In 2007 the company acquired its fourth bank charter (First Wisconsin Bank & Trust) and began operating in the Milwaukee metropolitan area but announced plans to sell the bank to Iowa-based National Bancshares Inc. the following year.

Company executives and board members collectively own 12% of QCR Holdings; bank investor Jeffrey Gendell owns 7% through Tontine Financial Partners.

EXECUTIVES

EVP Funds Management, Victor J. Quinn
Director; Chief Lending Officer; President and CEO Cedar Rapids Bank & Trust, Larry J. Helling, age 59, $202,500 total compensation
EVP and Chief Credit Officer, William M. Tank
Director; Chairman Quad City Bank & Trust, Mark C. Kilmer, age 56
President and CEO Rockford Bank and Trust, Thomas Budd
President and CEO Quad City Bank and Trust, John H. Anderson
EVP Deposit Operations and Informational Services, John A. Rodriguez
VP and CTO, Michael J. Wyffels
President; Chief Executive Officer of the Company and the Bank and Director of the Company, Daniel Blanton
Chief Financial Officer; Group Vice President of the Company and the Bank, Darrell Rains
Vice President Controller, Jeri Vandervinne
Vice President And Controller, Nick Anderson
Executive Vice President And Chief Operations Officer And Cashier, John McEvoy
Assistant Vice President Compliance, Thomas (Thom) King
Chairman of the Board of the Company and Vice Chairman of the Bank, Robert Pollard
Auditors: McGladrey LLP

LOCATIONS

HQ: QCR Holdings Inc
3551 7th Street, Moline, IL 61265
Phone: 309 743-7724
Web: www.qcbt.com

COMPETITORS

Bank of America	First National of
Blackhawk Bancorp	Nebraska
First Business	MidWestOne
Financial	U.S. Bancorp
First Midwest Bancorp	

HISTORICAL FINANCIALS
Company Type: Public

Income Statement
FYE: December 31

	ASSETS ($ mil.)	NET INCOME ($ mil.)	INCOME AS % OF ASSETS	EMPLOYEES
12/14	2,524	14	0.6%	409
12/13	2,394	14	0.6%	400
12/12	2,093	12	0.6%	356
12/11	1,966	9	0.5%	355
12/10	1,836	6	0.4%	350
Annual Growth	8.3%	22.7%	—	4.0%

2014 Year-End Financials

Debt ratio: 7.55%	No. of shares (mil.): 7
Return on equity: 10.25%	Dividends
Cash ($ mil.): 73	Yield: 0.4%
Current ratio: —	Payout: 4.3%
Long-term debt ($ mil.): —	Market value ($ mil.): 142

	STOCK PRICE ($) FY Close	P/E High/Low	Earnings	PER SHARE ($) Dividends	Book Value
12/14	17.86	10 10	1.72	0.08	18.12
12/13	17.03	8 6	2.08	0.08	18.72
12/12	13.22	8 5	1.85	0.08	28.55
12/11	9.10	11 8	0.92	0.08	29.92
12/10	7.14	25 13	0.53	0.08	28.39
Annual Growth	25.8% (10.6%)	— —	34.2%	(0.0%)	

Qualcomm, Inc.

Cell phone makers wireless carriers and governments worldwide call on QUALCOMM to engineer a quality conversation. The company pioneered the commercialization of the code-division multiple access (CDMA) technology used in digital wireless communications equipment and satellite ground stations mainly in North America. It generates most of its sales through the development and marketing of semiconductor chips and system software based on CDMA and other technologies. QUALCOMM also licenses technology rights from its large intellectual property portfolio (patents copyrights trade secrets). Smaller segments are focused on wireless communications products and strategic investments in start-ups and other firms.

HISTORY

Professors Irwin Mark Jacobs and Andrew Viterbi founded digital signal processing equipment company Linkabit in 1968. M/A-COM acquired the company in 1980. Led by Jacobs Viterbi and five other executives left M/A-COM Linkabit in 1985 to start engineer-focused QUALCOMM (for "quality communications") to provide contract R&D services. The company's first home was located above a strip mall pizza parlor in San Diego. CEO Jacobs dreamed of modifying code-division multiple access (CDMA) —a secure wireless transmission system developed during WWII —for commercial use.

In 1988 QUALCOMM introduced OmniTRACS a satellite-based system that tracks the location of long-haul truckers. By 1989 when QUALCOMM unveiled its version of CDMA the company was working on military contracts worth $15 million.

In 1990 the company interrupted the Cellular Telecommunications Industry Association's (CTIA) plans to adopt a rival technology called time-division multiple access when communications service providers NYNEX (now part of Verizon) and Ameritech (later part of SBC Communications and now part of AT&T) adopted QUALCOMM's maverick technology. QUALCOMM initiated a CDMA public relations blitz and by 1991 Motorola AT&T Clarion and Nokia had signed product development and testing agreements.

The company went public in 1991 and introduced the Eudora e-mail software program (named for "Why I Live at the P.O." author Eudora Welty) which it licensed from the University of Illinois. That year QUALCOMM and Loral Corporation unveiled plans for Globalstar a satellite telecommunications system similar to the Iridium system. The CTIA adopted CDMA as a North American standard for wireless communications in 1993.

In 1996 most of the major US cellular carriers upgraded to CDMA. However QUALCOMM's earnings fell due to manufacturing startup expenses and R&D and marketing costs. Earnings bounced back the next year and the company signed a contract to supply wireless ground stations for Globalstar. Also in 1997 Russia charged a QUALCOMM technician with espionage but allowed him to return to the US.

The company spun off its wireless phone service operations in 1998 as Leap Wireless International. It also formed Wireless Knowledge a joint venture with Microsoft to develop software and services for Internet access from portable computing devices.

In 1999 QUALCOMM and rival Ericsson settled a bitter dispute over the use of CDMA as an industry standard when they signed a cross-licensing deal. QUALCOMM sold its cell phone operations to Kyocera in 2000. The company also bought SnapTrack (cell phone location software) and signed a potentially huge deal with China Unicom. The latter was a step forward for Chinese carriers and equipment makers itching to use CDMA in a region where the Global System for Mobile Communication (GSM) rules.

Later that year rivals Nokia and Motorola teamed up to push for the standardization of Motorola's 1Xtreme technology over QUALCOMM's high-data-rate (HDR) format for 3G networks. (However 1Xtreme is based on QUALCOMM's CDMA patents.) By mid-2000 the company made plans to spin off its semiconductor subsidiary to the public. QUALCOMM cancelled the IPO a year later.

In 2001 the Chinese government after years of balking at CDMA in favor of 3G granted QUALCOMM and China Unicom permission to install a CDMA-based network. That year Microsoft sold its stake in Wireless Knowledge; the joint venture became a subsidiary of QUALCOMM.

In 2003 the company shut down Wireless Knowledge and absorbed its operations. It also augmented its OmniTRACS offerings by acquiring fleet management operations from a subsidiary of Alcatel (now Alcatel-Lucent). The following year QUALCOMM bought UK-based user interface designer Trigenix.

QUALCOMM purchased content delivery software specialist Elata in 2005. EVP Paul Jacobs son of co-founder Irwin Mark Jacobs took over as CEO in mid-2005; his father remained chairman of the company. Early the following year QUALCOMM acquired semiconductor designer Berkäna Wireless for about $56 million in cash. It also closed on its acquisition of Flarion Technologies a developer of a proprietary version of OFDM (orthogonal frequency-division multiplexing) technology called FLASH-OFDM. An alternative to WiMAX FLASH-OFDM is a cellular broadband technology used to connect mobile devices to networks. QUALCOMM paid about $600 million in cash and stock for Flarion and the deal included milestone incentives that could add another $205 million to the price.

In 2006 QUALCOMM paid a $1.8 million fine to the federal government for exercising operational control over Flarion before actually closing the transaction to acquire the chipset company. The fine was part of an agreement with the US Department of Justice; QUALCOMM officially denied any wrongdoing saying it disagreed with the Justice Department that its acquisition agreement with Flarion violated any federal laws or regulations.

In late 2006 QUALCOMM acquired Airgo Networks which specialized in Wi-Fi networking gear and paid $39 million for the Bluetooth assets of RF Micro Devices.

The Eudora e-mail program became an open-source product in May 2007 with QUALCOMM ceasing commercial sales of the product. In late 2006 the company released the final commercial versions of Eudora for Macintosh and Windows computers and cut the price to less than $20. Future versions of Eudora were to be based on the Thunderbird e-mail software platform developed by The Mozilla Foundation.

At the end of 2007 QUALCOMM acquired Firethorn Holdings for about $210 million in cash. Firethorn previously a unit of ITC Holding is a developer of software for mobile banking services on cell phones and other wireless devices. Its products are implemented by such financial institutions as Regions Financial SunTrust Banks and Wachovia and by wireless services providers like AT&T Mobility and Verizon Wireless.

Taking a leaf from such competitors as Intel and Nokia with their corporate venture capital operations (Intel Capital and BlueRun Ventures respectively) QUALCOMM put $500 million into QUALCOMM Ventures to make equity investments in a variety of start-up ventures. Portfolio companies include A123 Systems (rechargeable batteries for portable devices) AirPlay (interactive games for cell phones) Airvana (radio access network infrastructure) Bitfone (mobile device management software) Obopay (mobile payment service) and China Techfaith Wireless Communication Technology (mobile design house).

In 2007 QUALCOMM Ventures said it would invest €100 million in European companies developing mobile application or platform software handset components network infrastructure and core technologies for 3G (WCDMA) wireless communications. Its first investment went to Paris-based Streamezzo a developer of rich-media software platforms and services for mobile communications.

QUALCOMM and rival Broadcom have been embroiled in patent battles for over two years. The International Trade Commission (ITC) ruled in 2007 that new mobile phones being imported into the US with certain QUALCOMM chipsets were barred from sale because they infringed on a Broadcom patent. QUALCOMM appealed the ruling to no avail. Three months later a federal appeals judge stayed the import ban and in 2008 the US Court of Appeals for the Federal Circuit vacated the ITC ban and asked it to reconsider the case. The following year Broadcom and QUALCOMM reached a legal settlement dismissing all patent claims against each other and granting each certain rights under their patent portfolios. The company agreed to pay Broadcom $891 million in cash over four years under the settlement with $200 million due in mid-2009.

Perhaps piling on in the wake of the ITC ruling against QUALCOMM Nokia not only filed a patent infringement claim against the company but it also joined with other vendors to nudge the European Commission the European Union's antitrust regulator to upgrade its investigation into QUALCOMM's royalty practices. The two companies reached a legal settlement on patents in 2008 agreeing to dismiss all litigation. Nokia also agreed to withdraw its complaint with the European Commission. The settlement called for Nokia to assign certain patents related to the GSM OFDMA and WCDMA wireless standards to QUALCOMM and for the handset giant to pay a lump sum and royalties to QUALCOMM under a 15-year licensing agreement. Nokia later reported the lump-sum payment made before the end of 2008 totaled €1.7 billion (about $2.5 billion). In November 2009 the European Commission closed the formal antitrust case against the company based on the inability to draw any conclusions; all complaints were withdrawn.

In early 2009 QUALCOMM acquired graphics and multimedia assets from Advanced Micro Devices (AMD) for $65 million in cash. The company previously licensed graphics cores from AMD's handheld business. QUALCOMM hired about 170 engineers from AMD's handheld business in connection with the deal.

In 2010 the Qualcomm Innovation Center subsidiary bought San Francisco-based iSkoot a provider of service that enable cell phone makers to include social networking features on their smartphones.

EXECUTIVES

Executive Vice President Human Resources Executive, Daniel L (Dan) Sullivan
Senior Vice President and General Manager, Neville Meijers
EVP and CFO, George S. Davis, age 58, $724,043 total compensation
Co-President Qualcomm CDMA Technologies, Venkata S. M. (Murthy) Renduchintala, age 50, $659,808 total compensation
Chairman Qualcomm China, Frank Meng
EVP General Counsel and Corporate Secretary, Donald J. Rosenberg, age 64, $675,002 total compensation
CEO, Steven M. (Steve) Mollenkopf, age 46, $1,069,239 total compensation
President, Derek K. Aberle, age 45, $772,734 total compensation
CTO, Matthew S. (Matt) Grob, age 48
Co-President Qualcomm CDMA Technologies, Cristiano R. Amon, age 45, $474,048 total compensation
EVP Human Resources, Michelle Sterling
Vice President Location Products And Technology, Cormac Conroy
Vice President Engineering, Michael (Mel) Ellison
Medical Director, Ilene J Klein
Vice President Technology, Eric Lekven
Vice President, Eduardo Esteves
Vice President Business Operations, Liz Gasser
Vice President Business Development, Moon Park
Vice President Regulatory Engineering, Paul Guckian
Senior Vice President Chief Ip Strategist, Roger Martin
Vice President Operations and Supply Chain, Jim Seto
Senior Vice President Marketinq and Product MQMT., Johan Lodenius
Senior Vice President of Business Development, Laurie Yoler
Senior Vice President Principal Accounting Officer, John M (Jack) Miller
Vice President Global Marketing Public Relations And Communications, Dan Novak
Vice President Technology, Kent Walker
Vice President Of Engineering, Kevin Cadieux
Vice President Strategic Development, Ed Charbonneau
Vice President Collections, Donovan Ash

Vice President Cheif Patent Counsel, Philip Wadsworth
Vice President Corporate Strategy and Treasurer, Vern Rodenberg
Vice President Engineering Adreno Gpu Software, Jon Thomason
Vice President Technologies, Farrukh Usmani
Senior Vice President, Magnus Felke
Vice President Finance and Assistant General Manager, Steve Dhanens
Senior Vice President And General Manager, Eric Reifschneider
Vice President of Partner Relations, Michael (Mel) Wallace
Vice President Marketing, Don MacDonald
Vice President Patent Counsel, Mark E Wadrzyk
Vice President Engineering, Chienchung Chang
Vice President and Legal Counsel, David (Dave) Marr
Senior Vice President of Global Operation, Roawen Chen
Vice President%2c+suupply+chain+operations, Rick Vingerelli
Senior Vice President Finance And Direct Invest, Paul Fiskness
Senior Vice President Engineering, Steve Sprigg
Vice President Technical Publications, Kristie McCue
Senior Vice President Government Affairs, Nate Tibbits
Vice President Of IS, Norm Halvin
Vice President Engineering, Krishna Murti
Vice President Engineering, Iain Finlay
Vice President, Brian Mcgee
Vice President Of Product Management Mpq, Ji Park
Vice President, Nagraj Kashyap
National Account Manager, Leslie Perretti
Vice President Marketing, Melissa (Mel) Hayes
Vice President And Counsel Government Affairs, Laurie C Self
Vice President Internal Audit, Mark Dunham
Senior Vice President Engineering, Susie Armstrong
Vice President Business Development, Vikas Jain
Senior Management (Senior Vice President General Manager Director), Kerri Graham
Vice President Portfolio and Program Management, Malcolm Spencer
Vice President Technology, John (Jack) Ketchum
Senior Vice President Technology, Peter (Pete) Black
Vice President (Engineering), Sudarshan Keshava
Vice President Technology, Robert Kimball
Vice President Operations, Malcangio Frank
Vice President Engineering, Jack Steenstra
Vice President, Wei Wang
Vice President Of Corporate Security, Steve Davis
Vice President of Government Affairs, Dean Brenner
Vice President Information Technology, Tom Fisher
Vice President Of Technology, Sherman Gregory
Vice President and Treasurer, Dick Grannis
Vice President and Legal Counsel, Joshua (Josh) Walker
Vice President Strategy And Analysis, Yiwan Wong
Vice President Of Finance, Warren Kneeshaw
Vice President, Mark Jerger
Vice President, Lee Wilson
Vice President, Yan Chenwei
Vice President of Engineering, Eric Demers
Vice President Engineering, Yenamandra Rao
Vice President Learning And Development, Tamar Elkeles
Vice President Product Management, James Wilson
Vice President Engineering, Brian Harms
Vice President Of Product Management, Nakul Duggal

Executive Vice President Asia Pacific and Middle East and Africa, Jing Wang
Senior Vice President Strategy and Corporate Developmentvp Strategy QCT, Andy Oberst
Vice President and Legal Counsel, Roy Hoffinger
Vice President Engineering AMS Design, Gene McAllister
Senior Vice President Legal Counsel, Carol Lam
Executive Vice President of the Americas and India, Peggy L Johnson
Vice President Engineering, Steve Locicero
Vice President Programming FLO TV Incorporated QUALCOMM Incorporated, Mike Bailey
Vice President Software Strategy QUALCOMM Incorporated, Rob Chandhok
Executive Vice President General Counsel, Lou Lupin
Senior Vice President Enterprise Architecture, Rob Gilmore
Vice President Product Management, Jim Tran
Vice President Sales, Kun Qian
Vice President Information Technology, Robert (Bob) Gentile
Vice President Qualcomm Korea, Te-Won Lee
Vice President Government Affairs, Steve Crout
Vice President of Business Development, Jay Wright
Vice President, Steve Molloy
Senior Vice President Business Development, Larry Hartigan
Vice President Technology, Vk Jones
Vice President Business Development Wireless Health, Rick Valencia
Vice President Engineering, Greg Burns
Senior Vice President Business Development and Engineering, Ed Knapp
Vice President Engineering, Nish Abrol
Vice President Patent Counsel, Timothy (Tim) Loomis
Vice President Technology, Naga Bhushan
Senior Vice President Government Affairs, Bill Bold
Vice President Technology, Michael (Mel) Luby
Executive Vice President European Innovation Devel, Andrew (Andy) Gilbert
Vice President Finance, David (Dave) Cianflone
Executive Vice President and President QUALCOMM Technology Licensing, Steven (Steve) Altman
Vice President Employee Relations, Jane (Ginny) Baker
Executive Vice President and Chief Tec, Robert (Bob) Podavani
QCT Senior Vice President Engineering, Jim Thompson
Vice President Product Management, Christiano Amon
Vice President Wireless Connectivity, Barry Matsumori
Vice President Operations, Greg Cisewski
Senior Executive Assistant to Senior Vice President, Cheryl Girardot
Senior Vice President For Engineering, Ed Tiedemann
Vice President, Clarence Chui
Vice President of Government Affairs, Alice Tornquist
Vice President Engineering, Andrew (Andy) Hunter
Senior Vice President Of Engineering, Anthony Schwarz
Vice President Technology, Je Woo Kim
Senior Vice President Technology, Klein Gilhousen
Senior Vice President Of Salesandmarketing, Matt Milne
Vice President Strategic Development, Chris Borroni Bird
Vice President Of Technology, Geoffrey Yeap
Vice President of Commercialization and Operations, Nayeem Islam

Executive Chairman, Paul E. Jacobs, age 53
Secretary, Maria Terris
Secretary Executive, Anna Ford
Secretary, Beth Flanagan
Secretary Executive, Laurie Mee
Secretary Executive, Cynthia Almazan
Secretary Senior, Louise East
Secretary Senior, Pat Stewart
Secretary Executive, Sue Rogness
Secretary Executive, Wendy Walsh
Treasurer, David Vargas
Assistant Treasurer, Michael Spitzmiller
Secretary Senior, Sally Thompson
Board Member and Advocate, Dave Hanson
Secretary Senior, Judi Poler
Treasurer, Akash Palkhiwala
Secretary Senior, Katy Martin
Auditors: PricewaterhouseCoopers LLP

LOCATIONS

HQ: Qualcomm, Inc.
5775 Morehouse Dr., San Diego, CA 92121-1714
Phone: 858 587-1121
Web: www.qualcomm.com

2013 Sales

	$ mil.	% of total
China	12,288	49
South Korea	4,983	20
Taiwan	2,683	11
US	805	3
Other Countries	4,107	17
Total	**24,866**	**100**

PRODUCTS/OPERATIONS

2013 Sales

	$ mil.	% of total
QCT (Qualcomm CDMA Technologies)	16,715	67
QTL (Qualcomm Technology Licensing)	7,554	30
QWI (Qualcomm Wireless & Internet)	613	3
Adjustments	(16)	-
Total	**24,866**	**100**

2013 Sales

	$ mil.	% of total
Equipment & services	16,988	68
Licensing	7,878	32
Total	**24,866**	**100**

Selected Operations and Products

Code-Division Multiple Access (CDMA) Technologies Group
  Integrated circuits
  Baseband
  Intermediate-frequency
  Power management
  Radio-frequency
  Systems software
Engineering Services Group
Enterprise Services
Firethorn Holdings
Flarion Technologies
Government Technologies
Innovation Center
Internet Services
MediaFLO Technologies
MEMS Technologies
Qualcomm Ventures
Strategic Initiatives
Technology Licensing Group
  CDMA technologies and patents (cdmaOne CDMA2000 WCDMA TD-SCDMA)
  Royalties from products incorporating CDMA technology
Wireless and Internet Group
  Digital Media
  Digital motion picture delivery systems (under development)
  Government systems (development and analysis services; wireless base stations and phones)
  Internet Services
  Applications development software for wireless devices (BREW)
  Wireless Systems

Low-Earth-orbit satellite-based telecommunications system (Globalstar)

COMPETITORS

Apple Inc.	NAVTEQ
CSR plc	NEC
Fujitsu	NVIDIA
IBM Microelectronics	NXP Semiconductors
Infineon Technologies	Nokia
Intel	Panasonic Corp
InterDigital	Renesas Electronics
Marvell Technology	STMicroelectronics
Maxim Integrated Products	Samsung Electronics
	Spreadtrum
MediaTek	Texas Instruments
Motorola Mobility	Trimble Navigation

HISTORICAL FINANCIALS

Company Type: Public

Income Statement

FYE: September 27

	REVENUE ($ mil.)	NET INCOME ($ mil.)	NET PROFIT MARGIN	EMPLOYEES
09/15	25,281	5,271	20.8%	33,000
09/14	26,487	7,967	30.1%	31,300
09/13	24,866	6,853	27.6%	31,000
09/12	19,121	6,109	31.9%	26,600
09/11	14,957	4,260	28.5%	21,200
Annual Growth	14.0%	5.5%	—	11.7%

2015 Year-End Financials

Debt ratio: 21.59%	No. of shares (mil.): 1,524
Return on equity: 14.98%	Dividends
Cash ($ mil.): 7,560	Yield: 0.0%
Current ratio: 3.62	Payout: 55.9%
Long-term debt ($ mil.): 9,969	Market value ($ mil.): 81,107

	STOCK PRICE ($) FY Close	P/E High/Low		PER SHARE ($) Earnings	Dividends	Book Value
09/15	53.22	24	16	3.22	1.80	20.62
09/14	75.06	17	14	4.65	1.54	23.47
09/13	67.38	18	14	3.91	1.20	21.42
09/12	62.47	19	13	3.51	0.93	19.65
09/11	50.29	23	17	2.52	0.81	16.03
Annual Growth	1.4%	—	—	6.3%	22.1%	6.5%

Quanta Services, Inc.

To quickly quantify Quanta's services: This specialty contractor designs installs repairs and maintains network infrastructure across North America and abroad. The company serves the electric power and the oil and natural gas pipeline industries mainly in the US Canada and Australia. Quanta's other services include outsource management and other specialty work such as installing traffic and light rail control systems directional drilling and constructing wind and solar power facilities. Founded in 1997 more than two-thirds of the company's revenues now come from its Electric Power Infrastructure segment.

Operations

Quanta operates through two primary segments: Electric Power Infrastructure which made up 67% of revenue in 2014; and Oil & Gas Infrastructure (31% of revenue). The company sold Quanta Fiber Networks in 2015 thus shedding its Fiber Optic Licensing segment which made up just 2% of 2014 revenues.

Geographic Reach

Houston-based Quanta Services generates around 75% of its revenue in the US. Its next largest market is in Canada which makes up another 20% of its business followed by Australia. Other international offices are in South Africa India and Latin America (Chile Colombia Costa Rica Ecuador Guatemala Mexico Panama and Peru).

Sales and Marketing

The company mostly serves companies in the electric power and oil & gas markets though it also serves commercial industrial and governmental organizations. Quanta's 10 largest customers accounted for about a third of its total revenue in 2014; its largest customer 6%. Clients include American Electric Power Australia Pacific Duke Energy Google PG&E Corp. and TransCanada Corp among many others.

Financial Performance

Quanta's annual revenues and profits have nearly doubled since 2010 mostly thanks to new business from acquisitions and higher demand for its power and energy infrastructure services with the strengthened economy. Quanta's revenue jumped by 20% to $7.85 billion in 2014 thanks to continued growth in its Oil & Gas Infrastructure services business which increased its income by 31% on pipeline projects related to shale development in North America and thanks to 17% growth in its Electric Power Infrastructure business stemmed by acquisitions in the US Canada and Australia (mostly transmission-related) and increased capital spending by customers (mostly related to distribution).Despite higher revenue in 2014 Quanta's net income fell by 26% to $297 million mostly as it suffered more than $100 million worth of non-recurring long-term contract receivable provisions related to an electric power infrastructure services project completed in 2012. The company also paid some $68 million toward incremental general and administrative costs associated with its acquired companies and incurred nearly $39 million in expenses that stemmed from an adverse arbitration decision regarding a contract dispute with the National Gas Company of Trinidad and Tobago (NGC) on a 2010 directional drilling project. Quanta's operating cash also plummeted by 30% to $310 million mostly as cash earnings declined.

Strategy

Quanta reiterated in 2015 its main strategy to grow by acquiring companies that complement its business broaden its portfolio of service offerings and/or extend its geographic footprint in its three main markets of the US Canada and Australia. A larger service portfolio also allows the company to boost sales with existing customers through cross-selling.Several trends in the market place present Quanta with opportunities to grow. As demand for electricity in North America continues to increase and the electric power grid system is aging Quanta is well positioned to take advantage of increased demand for its services. Renewable energy such as wind and solar also present opportunities for Quanta to provide transmission line installation and project management services. Indeed some recent notable projects it's secured include the 1100 km-Labrador Island Link HVdc Transmission Project in Newfoundland and the 500 kV Transmission Project in Alberta (both awarded in 2014) —two of the largest electric transmission projects ever undertaken in North America.

Quanta also sees potential for growth in the natural gas segment as development of gas shale formations in North America have provided more supply of natural gas —and thus expectations of more demand for natural gas-fired power plants and pipelines over the next two decades. Already in 2015 Quanta Services nabbed an engineering procurement and construction services project for Rockies Express Pipeline's REX Zone Three Capacity Enhancement Project.

The company has retreated from a few business lines over the past few years to free up resources and better focus on its main energy infrastructure operations. In 2015 for example it sold its Fiber Optic Leasing business to Crown Castle International for $1 billion. In 2012 it exited its telecommunications infrastructure services business after it sold substantially all of its domestic telecommunications infrastructure services operations to Dycom Industries for $265 million.

Mergers and Acquisitions

In 2014 Quanta acquired nine companies for a total price of $284.3 million in cash all of which enhanced its electric power and oil & gas infrastructure service offerings in the US and Canada and bolstered its expertise in Australia to include electric power infrastructure offerings. The acquisitions included four Canada-based electric power infrastructure services companies; two Canada-based oil and gas infrastructure services businesses; an Australia-based electric power infrastructure services company; an American general engineering and construction company specializing in hydrant fueling waterfront and utility construction for the US Department of Defense (an Oil and Gas Infrastructure Services activity); and a US-based geotechnical and geological engineering services company (included in its Electric Power Infrastructure Services segment).In 2013 the company acquired six businesses which included electric power infrastructure services companies and oil and gas infrastructure services companies in the US Canada and Australia. The company paid a total of $341.1 million in cash and about 3.5 million shares of Quanta common stock valued at about $88.9 million. The purchases enabled Quanta to further enhance its electric power infrastructure service and oil and gas infrastructure operations at home and abroad.

Also in 2013 the company sold its ownership interest in Howard Midstream Energy Partners LLC (acquired in 2011) for approximately $220.9 million in cash. resulting in a pre-tax gain of about $112.7 million. Howard owns operates and constructs midstream oil and gas plant and pipeline facilities. The acquisition was made in order to position Quanta for more opportunities in the development of the Texas Eagle Ford shale region.

EXECUTIVES

CFO, Derrick A. Jensen, age 44, $537,500 total compensation
COO, Earl C. (Duke) Austin, age 45, $781,250 total compensation
EVP Corporate Development, Jesse E. Morris, age 47, $429,931 total compensation
EVP and General Counsel, Steven J. Kemps, age 51, $126,346 total compensation
President and CEO, James F. O'Neil, age 56, $987,500 total compensation
Vice President Of Operations, Joseph Tortomase
Treasurer, Nick Grindstaff
Chairman, Bruce E. Ranck
Treasurer, Jeff Walker
Auditors: PricewaterhouseCoopers LLP

LOCATIONS

HQ: Quanta Services, Inc.
2800 Post Oak Boulevard, Suite 2600, Houston, TX 77056
Phone: 713 629-7600
Web: www.quantaservices.com

PRODUCTS/OPERATIONS

2014 Sales

	$ mil.	% of total
Electric power services	5,238	67
Oil and gas infrastructure	2,444	31
Fiber optic licensing & other	168	2
Total	**7,851**	**100**

COMPETITORS

Cable Com	MDU Construction
Comm-Works	Services
Dycom	MYR Group
EMCOR	MasTec
Goldfield	Mass Electric
Henkels & McCoy	Pike Corporation
Integrated Electrical	Tetra Tech
Services	

HISTORICAL FINANCIALS

Company Type: Public

Income Statement

FYE: December 31

	REVENUE ($ mil.)	NET INCOME ($ mil.)	NET PROFIT MARGIN	EMPLOYEES
12/14	7,851	296	3.8%	24,600
12/13	6,522	401	6.2%	20,900
12/12	5,920	306	5.2%	17,800
12/11	4,623	132	2.9%	17,500
12/10	3,931	153	3.9%	13,751
Annual Growth	18.9%	18.0%		15.7%

2014 Year-End Financials

Debt ratio: 1.29%
Return on equity: 6.78%
Cash ($ mil.): 190
Current ratio: 2.25
Long-term debt ($ mil.): 72
No. of shares (mil.): 218
Dividends
  Yield: —
  Payout: —
Market value ($ mil.): 6,193

	STOCK PRICE ($) FY Close	P/E High/Low		PER SHARE ($) Earnings	Dividends	Book Value
12/14	28.39	28	19	1.35	0.00	20.69
12/13	31.56	17	14	1.87	0.00	19.56
12/12	27.29	19	14	1.44	0.00	17.67
12/11	21.54	39	25	0.62	0.00	16.10
12/10	19.92	32	23	0.72	0.00	15.62
Annual Growth	9.3%	—	—	17.0%	—	7.3%

Quest Diagnostics, Inc.

Quest Diagnostics is testing its ability to be the world's leading clinical lab. The company performs diagnostics on some 156 million specimens each year including routine clinical tests such as cholesterol checks Pap smears and HIV screenings. Quest Diagnostics also performs esoteric testing (such as genetic screening) and anatomic pathology testing (such as tissue biopsies for cancer testing). In all the company serves half of the physicians and hospitals in the US as well as government agencies and other clinical labs. Quest Diagnostics has more than 2200 patient service centers where samples are collected and the Quest Diagnostic Nichols Institute where new diagnostics are developed.

Operations

More than 90% of Quest's revenue comes from its diagnostic information services (DIS) segment which includes its routine clinical anatomic pathology gene-based esoteric and drugs-of-abuse testing businesses. In the realm of diagnostic testing Quest strives to make itself ubiquitous with a comprehensive menu of tests (more than 3000) and a network of labs and collection sites that blanket the US. In addition to its more than 2200 patient service centers where samples are collected the company maintains a staff of 4000 field phlebotomists who collect blood samples in physicians' offices. It also provides pathology testing services and staffing within hospitals. Other workers include the contracted paramedical examiners who conduct examinations for life insurance applicants.

The company also offers a number of other products and services through its diagnostic solutions segment. Its online data management system the Care360 physician portal lets doctors order diagnostic tests review results prescribe medication and manage patient files while its Care360EHR is an electronic health record (EHR) product. Quest also offers software that helps patients schedule tests and assess their results. A small portion of sales comes from providing testing services to drug companies' clinical trials. Additionally Quest provides global testing and risk assessment services for the life insurance industry.

Quest's logistics capabilities include approximately 3000 courier vehicles and 20 aircraft that combined make tens of thousands of stops daily.

Geographic Reach

The company's products and services are used by customers in more than 130 countries. While more than 95% of sales come from the US market Quest aims for its international operations to eventually account for more than 10% of revenues. The firm is especially focused on expanding in the developing world where the diagnostic testing market is more fragmented. Key growth markets outside the US include India Ireland Mexico Puerto Rico Sweden and the UK. The company operates clinical laboratories in India England Mexico and Puerto Rico.

In addition to its patient service centers located across the US Quest has a dozen major laboratory facilities in California Florida Georgia Illinois Maryland New Jersey Pennsylvania Texas and Virginia.

Sales and Marketing

Quest's customers include commercial laboratories employers government agencies health plans life insurers not-for-profit organizations pain clinics physicians and EHR vendors.

Financial Performance

As a result of asset divestitures connected with a strategic realignment program as well as lower sales volume Quest reported revenue declines in fiscal years 2012 and 2013. However revenue increased 4% to $7.4 billion in fiscal 2014 led by growth in the DIS segment which saw a boost from the acquisitions of Solstas Summit Health and Steward as well as six new professional lab services agreements executed in 2013 and 2014. Net income fell 34% to $556 million due to increases in cost of services primarily driven by additional operating costs associated with its recent acquisitions.

Cash flow from operations which has fluctuated over the past five years grew 44% to $938 million in fiscal 2014 largely due to a decline in income tax payments from the previous year.

Strategy

Despite its lofty position in the clinical testing market Quest has been conducting cost-cutting measures to keep its competitive edge. The company has been aiming to refocus on its core testing product lines simplify its organization and return to growth. Recent initiatives have included included the divestiture of the HemoCue point-of-care testing business to Radiometer Medical for some $300 million as well as sale of the rights to a pharmaceutical product ibrutinib to Royalty Pharma for $485 million both in 2013.

The strategic program also includes capital spending to further growth initiatives including potential acquisitions. Quest's expansion programs are especially focused on widening its product lines in the growing esoteric and gene-based testing markets with a focus on areas such as cancer cardiovascular and neurological diagnostics as well as personalized medicine products (genetic tests to determine a patient's most effective medication regimen). The company also hopes to profit from the growing number of laboratories integrating clinical information systems into their practices.

Quest is collaborating with the Centers for Disease Control and Prevention to identify trends in screening diagnosis and treatment of four strains of viral hepatitis in the US based on analysis of the firm's national testing database.

Mergers and Acquisitions

Quest has traditionally looked to grow its reach by acquiring firms with complementary locations or testing capabilities. Towards that end the company has made a number of acquisitions that have increased its presence in specific testing categories such as cancer biopsy tests. In 2014 it acquired Solstas Lab Partners Group a North Carolina-based commercial laboratory with operations in nine states in the Southeast for $572 million. It also acquired Summit Health a provider of onsite prevention and wellness programs for $152 million; and it completed the acquisition of Steward's outreach laboratory service operations for $34 million.

HISTORY

Quest Diagnostics began as one man's quest to make clinical tests more affordable. Pathologist Paul Brown started Metropolitan Pathological Laboratory (MetPath) in his Manhattan apartment in 1967. To help his business take off in 1969 he bought two $55000 blood analyzers that could automatically perform a dozen common tests; the machines allowed him to charge patients $5.50 while hospitals and other labs were charging upwards of $40. Investments in emerging lab technology helped MetPath continue to beat competitors' prices and grow its business. It made its first profit in 1971 and eventually attracted the attention of Corning Glass Works which bought 10% of the company in 1973.

MetPath's growth was due in part to investments in technology. The company built a state-of-the-art central lab in New Jersey in 1978 that could process some 30000 specimens daily; it also went on an acquisition spree to expand across the US. These investments left the firm swamped with debt and Corning bought the company in 1982.

An autonomous unit of Corning MetPath continued to grow as Medicare reimbursement for lab tests went up and more doctors ordered more tests to catch and prevent disease before it happened. To cut costs in the mid-1980s the company reorganized its facilities to create a regional lab network. A reorganization in 1990 at its parent placed MetPath in the Corning Lab Services subsidiary.

Corning Lab Services strengthened its operations in the early 1990s by buying labs from regional operators. In 1994 MetPath became Corning Clinical Laboratories. Around the same time the company found itself besieged with demands from HMOs and other managed care providers to lower its costs. Also during this time the company settled a handful of federal suits accusing it of fraudulent Medicare billing. In the face of increasing pressure parent Corning spun off its lab testing business to the public as Quest Diagnostics in 1996.

On its own Quest aimed to grow through acquisitions. In 1999 it bought rival SmithKline Beecham Clinical Laboratories from GlaxoSmithKline. (GSK gained a minority stake in Quest

through the deal; it gradually sold off all shares in Quest by 2011.) Continuing its growth strategy in the 21st century it bought American Medical Laboratories to expand its esoteric testing operations in 2002. The company was finally able to close its acquisition of Unilab in early 2003 after the deal ran into delays with the FTC. Quest sold some labs and service contracts in northern California to LabCorp to appease FTC regulators.

To expand internationally the company began providing testing services in India in 2008 including esoteric testing for hospitals tests for the life insurance industry and diagnostics for global clinical trials.

EXECUTIVES

President and CEO, Stephen H. (Steve) Rusckowski, age 57, $1,050,000 total compensation
Vice President Tax, Stephen A Calamari
SVP Chief Medical Officer and Group Executive - Diagnostic Solutions Businesses, Jon R. Cohen, age 60, $573,900 total compensation
SVP and Group Executive -Clinical Franchise Solutions, Catherine T. Doherty, age 52, $534,615 total compensation
SVP Commercial, Everett V. Cunningham, age 48
SVP and CFO, Mark J. Guinan, age 53, $550,000 total compensation
SVP Operations, James E. Davis, age 52, $536,539 total compensation
SVP and CIO, Lidia Fonseca
Medical Director, Harvey Kaufman
Regional Vice President, Sally Elliott
Vice President Clinical Trials, Christopher Fikry
Vice President Health And Wellness Services, Steven (Steve) Burton
Senior Vice President Science Innovation, Jay Wohlgemuth
Vice President Procurement, William Burg
Chairman, Daniel C. (Dan) Stanzione, age 69
Assistant Treasurer, Tracy Cinco-Abela
Assistant General Counsel and Secretary, William (Bill) O'Shaughnessy
Board Member, Maya Patel
Treasurer, Dee Boyd
Auditors: PricewaterhouseCoopers LLP

LOCATIONS

HQ: Quest Diagnostics, Inc.
Three Giralda Farms, Madison, NJ 07940
Phone: 973 520-2700
Web: www.QuestDiagnostics.com

PRODUCTS/OPERATIONS

2014 Revenues

	$ mil.	% of total
Diagnostic information services	6,873	92
Other	562	8
Total	**7,435**	**100**

2014 Revenues

	% of total
Clinical testing	
Routine clinical testing	55
Gene-based & esoteric testing	34
Forensic drugs-of-abuse testing services	3
Healthcare IT clinical trials testing insurance services & diagnostic products	8
Total	**100**

COMPETITORS

Alere	Oncolab
Arup Laboratories	Pathology Associates
Bio-Reference Labs	Medical Laboratories
Genomic Health	Psychemedics
LabCorp	Solstas
Medtox Scientific	Sonic Healthcare

HISTORICAL FINANCIALS

Company Type: Public

Income Statement

FYE: December 31

	REVENUE ($ mil.)	NET INCOME ($ mil.)	NET PROFIT MARGIN	EMPLOYEES
12/14	7,435	556	7.5%	45,000
12/13	7,146	849	11.9%	41,000
12/12	7,382	555	7.5%	41,000
12/11	7,510	470	6.3%	42,000
12/10	7,368	720	9.8%	42,000
Annual Growth	0.2%	(6.3%)	—	1.7%

2014 Year-End Financials

Debt ratio: 38.09%	No. of shares (mil.): 144
Return on equity: 13.48%	Dividends
Cash ($ mil.): 192	Yield: 1.9%
Current ratio: 0.94	Payout: 36.8%
Long-term debt ($ mil.): 3,244	Market value ($ mil.): 9,657

	STOCK PRICE ($) FY Close	P/E High/Low	PER SHARE ($) Earnings	Dividends	Book Value
12/14	67.06	18 13	3.81	1.29	29.87
12/13	53.54	11 9	5.54	1.20	27.42
12/12	58.27	19 16	3.46	0.68	26.29
12/11	58.06	21 16	2.92	0.40	23.46
12/10	53.97	15 11	4.05	0.40	23.63
Annual Growth	5.6%	— —	(1.5%)	34.0%	6.0%

Quintiles Transnational Holdings Inc

Quintiles Transnational has plenty to CRO about. One of the world's largest contract research organizations (CROs) it helps pharmaceutical biotechnology and medical device companies develop and sell their products. The firm provides a comprehensive range of clinical trials management services including patient recruitment data analysis laboratory testing and regulatory filing assistance. Its consulting unit offers strategic advice at every stage of drug discovery and development and its capital and commercial divisions assist with project funding and sales and marketing efforts. Quintiles which had been a private company since 2003 went public again in 2013.

IPO

The company sought up to $600 million but managed to raise almost $950 million. It used a portion of the proceeds to pay off a loan; the remainder was set aside for general corporate purposes such as supporting its strategic growth initiatives. Quintiles which was founded in 1982 was a public company from 1994 until 2003.

Operations

Quintiles Transnational provides consulting on product development and commercialization services for drugs that are ready to go to market. Services include conducting late phase clinical trials on drugs after they've been released (post-marketing research) and setting up the information technology a drug maker needs to support a marketed drug. Additionally the company provides financing and partnering support which invests in client companies (either through cash or services) in return for royalties on sales of approved products.

Its operations are divided into two segments Product Development and Integrated Healthcare

Services. Product Development serves biopharmaceutical customers with research and development activities such as clinical research and clinical trial services. It accounted for about 60% of sales in 2014. The other sales comes from Integrated Healthcare Services which offers sales and marketing services to both pharmaceutical customers and the broader health care market. Offerings include real-world research market access and consulting and analytics and technology consulting.

Geographic Reach

The company has operations in about 100 countries in the Americas Europe Africa and the Asia/Pacific region. In recent years it has been focusing on international expansion especially in Asia. It has a presence in all major biopharmaceutical markets including the US Japan and Europe as well as Brazil Russia India and China (the BRIC countries). In 2015 it opened a regional headquarters in China to better serve customers in the area.

Quintiles Transnational has Product Development offices in the US (3) England Scotland South Africa Japan India and Singapore. It has Integrated Healthcare Services locations in the US Germany England and Japan. The company owns facilities in Japan and Spain that serve both segments.

The Americas accounts for about a third of all revenues.

Sales and Marketing

The company serves large multinational and regional/domestic biopharmaceutical firms in the US Europe Asia Japan Canada and Latin America.

Advertising expenses in 2014 reached $16 million up from $14.8 million in 2013 and $14.5 million in 2012.

Financial Performance

Revenue grew 7% in 2014 boosted by a 14% increase in new business and the acquisitions of clinical research company Novella and electronic health records firm Encore. The Product Development segment's net new business rose 16% while new business in the Integrated Healthcare Services segment rose 9%.

Additionally overall net income rose 57% to $356 million in 2014 on higher revenues and a decline in interest expenses. Cash flow from operations rose 10% to $432 million that year.

Strategy

Demand for outsourced clinical development services has been growing as belt-tightening pharma and biotech companies look to trim costs even as they are desperate to find and develop new products. Quintiles Transnational has focused efforts on developing services that help its clients reduce risk and time-to-market. For instance its Cenduit subsidiary a joint venture with Thermo Fisher Scientific helps control clinical trials costs by automating delivery of supplies among other things. In 2015 it partnered with Quest Diagnostics to launch Q2 Solutions a clinical trials lab services provider. And in 2014 the company launched specialized services for emerging biopharmaceutical customers.

Quintiles Therapeutics is focused on oncology cardiovascular the central nervous system diabetes and internal medicine. These five areas represented more than 70% of its total biopharmaceutical product pipeline in 2014.

Additionally the company is investing in quality data and electronic health records. It has acquired data analytics products and services as well as personnel and created a proprietary data integration tool to manage data from multiple sources.

As part of its restructuring efforts which were approved in 2015 the company plans to close certain facilities and lay off personnel (less than 10% of its total workforce).

Normal 0   false false false   EN-US X-NONE X-NONE

Mergers and Acquisitions

In 2013 Quintiles Therapeutics acquired Novella Clinical for some $146.6 million. The clinical research organization which specializes in oncology medical devices and diagnostics primarily operates in the US and Europe. The purchase added to the company's Product Development segment.

On the other hand the firm boosted its Integrated Healthcare Services segment when it acquired Encore Health Resources for approximately $91.5 million in 2014. Encore provides health information analytics and technology services including strategic and advisory consulting.

HISTORY

Quintiles was founded by Dennis Gillings a British biostatistician who had worked with Hoechst (later part of Sanofi) on data analysis in the 1970s. Gillings set up Quintiles (Quantitative Information Technology In The Life and Economic Sciences) in 1982 at the University of North Carolina where he was then teaching. The company grew as drug companies began outsourcing some of the more irksome tasks of drug development. Quintiles went public in 1994.

The company used the proceeds of the IPO to expand its health economics segment with the purchases of Benefit International (1995) and Lewin Group (1996). These purchases introduced it to such new clients as governments and HMOs. Quintiles' 1996 purchase of Innovex (unrelated to the computer hardware maker of the same name) made it the world's largest CRO. The buying spree continued in 1997 and 1998. Among the purchases were some intended to strengthen Quintiles' marketing services (Data Analysis Systems Inc. Q.E.D. International and France-based Serval). The firm also formed new collaborations with such academic research organizations as Johns Hopkins Medicine.

In 1999 Quintiles expanded its marketing arm with the purchase of Pharmaceutical Marketing Services (parent of the leading pharmaceuticals industry research company Scott-Levin) and jumped headlong into data mining with its purchase of ENVOY —which processed insurance claims. Quintiles found the core business uninspiring and sold it to Healtheon (now Emdeon formerly WebMD) the next year. But it kept rights to ENVOY's stream of treatment outcome and insurance data gleaned from health care providers hospitals payers and pharmacies —a treasure house of information useful to salespeople and health providers.

The company continued in 2000 to add offices in Europe Asia and Latin America. It also opened additional offices in the US and Europe to help Japanese pharmaceutical companies market their products in those regions. Late in the year Quintiles bought the clinical development unit of Pharmacia.

In 2001 Quintiles became embroiled in a legal dispute with WebMD involving the availability of data associated with ENVOY; the company challenged WebMD's efforts to withhold such data. The two companies settled the squabble later that year and agreed to sever all ties. Also in 2001 Quintiles streamlined operations and cut about 5% of its workforce.

The future structure of the CRO came into question at the end of 2002. Gillings presented the company with a buyout offer; he planned to take the company private so he could pursue a new growth strategy Wall Street would surely find risky. The board rejected that offer in October 2002 but it opened up an auction. Some leading equity firms reportedly made offers but Gillings —with backing from Blackstone Group and BANK ONE's One Equity Partners (later part of JPMorgan Chase) — placed another offer for Quintiles and won the prize in April 2003. Some five months later Quintiles went private.

EXECUTIVES

EVP and CFO, Kevin K. Gordon, age 52, $580,000 total compensation

President Real-World and Late Phase Research, Cynthia L. Verst-Brasch

President Consulting, Jay D. Norman, age 57

EVP Chief Customer and Governance Officer, Derek M. Winstanly, age 69, $500,000 total compensation

SVP and Head Asia Markets, Anand Tharmaratnam

President Clinical Development, Paula Brown Stafford

CEO and Director, Thomas H. (Tom) Pike, age 56, $1,040,000 total compensation

EVP General Counsel and Secretary, James H. (Jim) Erlinger, age 57, $434,375 total compensation

President Payer & Provider Solutions, Brian Kelly

Chief Medical and Scientific Officer, Jeffrey A. Spaeder

President Technology and Solutions, Richard Thomas

Chief Compliance Officer, Dipti Amin

President Integrated Commercial Services and Solutions, W. Scott Evangelista

President Advisory Services, Elgar Peerschke

President Global Delivery Network, Kris Wadia

Vice President Safety Knowledge and Reporting, Matt McKeever

Chairman, Dennis B. Gillings, age 71

Auditors: PricewaterhouseCoopers LLP

LOCATIONS

HQ: Quintiles Transnational Holdings Inc
4820 Emperor Blvd., Durham, NC 27703
Phone: 919 998-2000
Web: www.quintiles.com

2014 Sales

	$ mil.	% of total
Americas		
US	1,589	38
Other	194	5
Europe & Africa		
UK	402	10
Other	1,121	27
Asia/Pacific		
Japan	471	11
Other	386	9
Reimbursed expenses	1,294	-
Total	**5,460**	**100**

PRODUCTS/OPERATIONS

2014 Sales

	$ mil.	% of total
Product development	3,097	57
Integrated healthcare services	1,068	19
Reimbursed expenses	1,294	24
Total	**5,460**	**100**

Selected Products and Services

Capital services
  Funding assistance
  Managed partnerships
Clinical Services
  Biostatistics
  Central laboratory services
  Lifecycle safety monitoring
  Medical writing
  Pharmacokinetic studies
  Patient recruitment
  Phase I-III clinical trial design
Commercial Services
  Post-approval programs
  Regulatory services
  Safety monitoring

Selected Therapeutic Specialties

Cardiovascular

Central nervous system
Endocrinology
Infectious diseases
Internal medicine
Oncology
Pediatrics
Public health government services
Women's health

COMPETITORS

Albany Molecular Research	PRA Health Sciences
Charles River Laboratories	PharmaNet Development Group
Covance	Pharmaceutical Product Development
GlaxoSmithKline R & D	Premier Research Group
ICON	Quest Diagnostics
INC Research	UDG Healthcare
Nordion	WuXi PharmaTech
PAREXEL	inVentiv Health
PDI Inc.	

HISTORICAL FINANCIALS

Company Type: Public

Income Statement

FYE: December 31

	REVENUE ($ mil.)	NET INCOME ($ mil.)	NET PROFIT MARGIN	EMPLOYEES
12/15	5,737	387	6.7%	36,100
12/14	5,460	356	6.5%	32,600
12/13	5,099	226	4.4%	28,200
12/12	4,865	177	3.6%	—
12/11	4,327	241	5.6%	—
Annual Growth	**7.3%**	**12.5%**	—	—

2015 Year-End Financials

Debt ratio: 62.85%
Return on equity: —
Cash ($ mil.): 979
Current ratio: 1.51
Long-term debt ($ mil.): 2,419

No. of shares (mil.): 119
Dividends
  Yield: —
  Payout: —
Market value ($ mil.): 8,196

	STOCK PRICE ($) FY Close	P/E High/Low	Earnings	Dividends	Book Value
12/15	68.66	25 18	3.08	0.00	(4.73)
12/14	58.87	22 16	2.72	0.00	(5.67)
12/13	46.34	25 23	1.77	0.00	(5.15)
Annual Growth	**10.3%**	— —	**14.9%**	—	—

Qwest Corp

EXECUTIVES

Exec V Pres-cao-contrl, David D Cole
Auditors: KPMG LLP

LOCATIONS

HQ: Qwest Corp
100 CenturyLink Drive, Monroe, LA 71203
Phone: 318 388-9000
Web: www.centurylink.com

HISTORICAL FINANCIALS

Company Type: Public

Income Statement

FYE: December 31

	REVENUE ($ mil.)	NET INCOME ($ mil.)	NET PROFIT MARGIN	EMPLOYEES
12/14	8,838	970	11.0%	23,000
12/13	8,753	964	11.0%	22,800
12/12	8,848	849	9.6%	21,400
12/11*	6,635	543	8.2%	25,000
03/11	2,268	299	13.2%	—
Annual Growth	**40.5%**	**34.2%**	—	—

*Fiscal year change

2014 Year-End Financials

Debt ratio: 36.40%
Return on equity: 10.32%
Cash ($ mil.): 6
Current ratio: 0.82
Long-term debt ($ mil.): 7,262

No. of shares (mil.): 0
Dividends
  Yield: 0.0%
  Payout: 144.3%
Market value ($ mil.): 0

	STOCK PRICE ($) FY Close	P/E High/Low	Earnings	Dividends	Book Value
12/14	26.80	— —	(0.00)	1.84	
12/13	23.13	— —	(0.00)	1.84	
12/12	26.81	— —	(0.00)	1.84	
12/11*	26.54	— —	(0.00)	0.89	
Annual Growth	**0.2%**	— —	—	**20.1%**	**(1.8%)**

*Fiscal year change

Radian Group, Inc.

Radian Group is glowing from a conflagration of private mortgage insurance claims. Through subsidiaries Radian Guaranty Radian Mortgage Assurance and Radian Insurance Radian Group provides traditional private mortgage insurance coverage to protect lenders from defaults by borrowers who put down a deposit of less than 20% when buying a home. Such coverage provides protection on individual loans and covers unpaid loan principal and delinquent interest. Its pool insurance covers limited exposure on groups of loans. Radian still insures municipal bonds written before 2008 through its financial guaranty business. Radian Group's customers include mortgage bankers commercial banks and savings institutions.

Operations

The company operates in two segments: The mortgage insurance division offers credit-related insurance coverage primarily private mortgage insurance as well as risk services for lending agencies. These operations are primarily conducted through the Radian Guaranty subsidiary.

Meanwhile the financial guaranty segment –handled by the Radian Asset Assurance unit –insures a runoff portfolio of public finance and structured finance credits. The unit which no longer actively markets policies historically offered direct insurance or reinsurance for credit based risks as well as credit protection through default swaps and financial guaranty transactions.

During headier days the government encouraged lenders to turn more Americans into homeowners and Radian made a steady diet of insuring subprime mortgages. However that strategy meant that it was among the first to be hit and hit hard when the housing market imploded and mortgage defaults piled up.

Financial Performance

While Radian's net premiums earned from mortgage insurance have remained fairly steady the company's revenues plummeted in 2010 due to the ongoing degradation of the credit default swaps in its financial guaranty segment. Some $537.5 million in losses were pinned on financial guaranty in 2010.

While stabilized markets caused the segment to return more than $1 billion in revenues in 2011 (causing overall Radian revenues to jump 79% to $1.9 billion) credit default swaps triggered another negative earnings figure (some $45.5 million in losses) for the financial guaranty operations in 2012. This caused an overall 58% decline in revenue to some $825.4 million in 2012.

Net income soared to $302 million in 2011 an 83% increase from its net loss in 2010 of $1.8 billion but then fell into the red again in 2012 as Radian reported a net loss of $451.5 million.

Strategy

As the credit environment slowly stabilizes the company is working to capture more high-quality mortgage insurance business and diversify its customer base. Towards this end in 2012 the company expanded its eligibility criteria under the federal Home Affordable Refinance Program (HARP). It is also focused on reducing risk exposure in the financial guaranty segment; managing losses in the legacy financial guaranty and mortgage insurance portfolios; and improving liquidity and capital positions.

Radian hopes its future will brighten as the economy improves. Stabilized job and real estate market will go a long way to reducing the number of mortgage defaults the company might cover. In the meantime it does have a back-up plan: If its primary operating subsidiary Radian Guaranty's risk-to-capital ratio gets too far out of whack sister subsidiary Radian Mortgage Assurance is being groomed to take over writing new business.

Mergers and Acquisitions

In 2015 real estate consulting subsidiary Clayton Holdings acquired Pittsburgh-based title agency ValuAmerica. Through that purchase Clayton gained ValuAmerica's technology platform which streamlines supply chains and workflows for mortgage lenders.

HISTORY

Radian Group was born from the ashes of the 1987 stock crash and the rubble of the natural disasters of the early 1990s. Parent insurance company Reliance Group was deep in debt and desperately in need of cash. To raise money Reliance separated CMAC Investment (and operating subsidiary Commonwealth Mortgage Assurance) from subsidiary Commonwealth Land Title and took the company public in 1992.

In 1994 after two years of lackluster stock performance the board promoted CFO Frank Filipps (an American International Group veteran) to CEO. Filipps limited commissions to new policies rather than retained business. The pokey stock nosed up with some help from low interest rates and high numbers of new mortgage loans. Despite a raise in interest rates in 1995 the company continued to expand its market share.

In 1996 the company launched Prophet Score a new risk-assessment model that allowed CMAC to expand its coverage to include subprime loans. These measures jump-started sales to new highs in 1997 and 1998. Nevertheless CMAC (and its competitors) suffered in the market because of negative publicity: private mortgage (PMI) insurers were slammed for keeping quiet when borrowers' equity rose to 20% the point when PMI is usually considered unnecessary. In 1999 CMAC bought former rival Amerin and changed the name of the combined company to Radian Group.

Radian diversified its operations through the 2001 acquisition of credit-based insurance and financial services provider Enhance Financial (renamed Radian Reinsurance and later merged into Radian Asset Assurance Inc.) In 2002 Radian sold off the Enhance Consumer Services subsidiary.

In 2005 Filipps departed to join Clayton Holdings. Sanford Ibrahim was then named CEO.

The company expanded into Asia in 2005 through a partnership with Standard Chartered Bank (Hong Kong) with Radian as the exclusive provider of residential mortgage insurance to the lender. However the deal did not take root and Standard Chartered Bank yanked their contract in early 2008.

As the credit markets went into meltdown that year the company began pulling back on the riskiest of bonds (such as second-liens) by mid-2007 but by early 2008 its ratings had been lowered.

In response to the market troubles Radian stopped insuring certain types of higher-risk home loans and began working with existing mortgage services to help distressed borrowers modify their loan terms. The company's Radian Asset Assurance operations in the US and UK also stopped accepting new business as part of its general hunkering down to ride out the storm and in 2010 it put the UK unit into liquidation.

EXECUTIVES

EVP Finance, C. Robert (Bob) Quint, age 55, $400,000 total compensation
President Radian Guaranty Inc, Teresa A. Bryce Bazemore, age 55, $500,000 total compensation
EVP and CFO, J. Franklin (Frank) Hall, age 47
President Radian Asset Assurance Inc, David J. (Dave) Beidler
CEO, Sanford A. Ibrahim, age 63, $900,000 total compensation
SVP and CIO Radian Group and Radian Guaranty, Lawrence C. DelGatto, $300,000 total compensation
EVP and Chief Risk Officer, Derek Brummer, $373,077 total compensation
President Clayton Holdings LLC, Joseph D'Urso
Senior Vice President Capital Markets, Christopher (Chris) Curran
Vice President Operations Strategy and Analysis, Maria Mast
Vice President Enterprise Risk Management, Art Boyle
Vice President Risk Analytics, Larry Cordell
Vice President Financial Planning and Analysis, Robert (Bob) Schrof
Senior Vice President Head of Risk Analytics, Mark Beardsell
Assistant Vice President, Manish Kumar
Vice President Director Of Administration, Colleen Teears
Vice President of Communications Financial Advisor, Christine LoStracco
Assistant Vice President Investment Accounting, Kelley Dougherty-Cahill
Assistant Vice President Corporate Accounting, Abigail Rodriguez
Vice President Internal Audit Manager, Jeff John
Vice President Information Technology Gl Vice President Information Technology Global Operations, Marty Nebel
Assistant Vice President Operations Strategy and Analysis, Lin Fang
Assistant Vice President Treasury, Eugene Cichanowsky
Vice President National Account Manager, Lora Wasson
Vice President Purchasing, John (Jack) Morozin
Vice President Pricing, Eric Calaman
Vice President Regional Manager, Patrick (Paddy) Ballog
Vice President Operations Planning and Delivery, Brian Giardino
Director, Herbert Wender, age 78
Auditors: PricewaterhouseCoopers LLP

LOCATIONS

HQ: Radian Group, Inc.
1601 Market Street, Philadelphia, PA 19103
Phone: 215 231-1000
Web: www.radian.biz

PRODUCTS/OPERATIONS

2012 Revenues

	$ mil.	% of total
Mortgage insurance	870	100
Financial guaranty	(45.5)	-
Total	**825**	**100**

COMPETITORS

Assured Guaranty	Old Republic
Essent Guaranty	Triad Guaranty
Genworth Financial	US Department of
MGIC Investment	Veterans Affairs
National Mortgage	United Guaranty
Insurance	

HISTORICAL FINANCIALS

Company Type: Public

Income Statement

FYE: December 31

	ASSETS ($ mil.)	NET INCOME ($ mil.)	INCOME AS % OF ASSETS	EMPLOYEES
12/14	6,859	959	14.0%	1,702
12/13	5,621	(196)	—	782
12/12	5,903	(451)	—	696
12/11	6,656	302	4.5%	650
12/10	7,620	(1,805)	—	767
Annual Growth	(2.6%)	—	—	22.1%

2014 Year-End Financials

Debt ratio: 17.64%	No. of shares (mil.): 191
Return on equity: 61.68%	Dividends
Cash ($ mil.): 30	Yield: 0.0%
Current ratio: —	Payout: 0.3%
Long-term debt ($ mil.): —	Market value ($ mil.): 3,194

	STOCK PRICE ($) FY Close	P/E High/Low		PER SHARE ($) Earnings	Dividends	Book Value
12/14	16.72	3	2	4.16	0.01	11.37
12/13	14.12	—	—	(1.18)	0.01	5.43
12/12	6.11	—	—	(3.41)	0.01	5.51
12/11	2.34	4	1	2.26	0.01	8.88
12/10	8.07	—	—	(15.74)	0.01	6.46
Annual Growth	20.0%	—	—	—	(0.0%)	15.2%

Ralph Lauren Corp

Ralph Lauren Corporation is galloping at a faster clip than when its namesake founder first entered the arena over 45 years ago. With golden mallet brands such as Polo by Ralph Lauren Chaps RRL Club Monaco and RLX Ralph Lauren the company designs and markets apparel and accessories home furnishings and fragrances. Its collections are available at nearly 13000 retail locations worldwide including many upscale and mid-tier department stores (Macy's contributes 12% of RL's wholesale revenue). It operates 460-plus Ralph Lauren and Club Monaco retail stores worldwide as well as 540 concession-based shops-within-shops and 10 e-commerce sites. American style icon and founder Lauren is stepping down as CEO.

HISTORY

Company BackgroundRalph Lauren a suave Manhattanite was actually born Ralph Lifschitz in the Bronx New York. It is said that his father Frank an immigrant Russian housepainter and muralist informally changed the family's name to Lauren and inspired his son to recreate himself in the image of a mythic upper class.

After high school Ralph who formally changed his name to Lauren became a salesman at Brooks Brothers and then a sales representative for Rivetz a Boston tie maker. In 1967 he landed a job as a tie designer for Beau Brummel of New York. The company gave him his own style division which he named Polo because of the sport's refined image. The next year Lauren started Polo Fashions to make tailored menswear. Partner Peter Strom teamed up with Lauren in the early 1970s. Although its designs received critical acclaim Polo Fashions had a bumpy start as Lauren adjusted to the business aspect of his fashion label.

Lauren's profile rose in the 1970s when he won three Coty Awards for design and produced costumes for the movie The Great Gatsby. In 1971 Lauren adopted his polo-player-on-a-horse logo and introduced a line for women. That year the first licensed Polo store opened (on Rodeo Drive in Beverly Hills) along with his first in-store boutique (at Bloomingdale's in New York City). He added shoes to the lineup in 1972 licensed his womenswear line the next year and launched a licensed fragrance line in 1978.

By 1980 Polo Fashions had become Polo Ralph Lauren. Encouraged by the success of the licensed products Lauren led the designer charge into home furnishings introducing his Home Collection in 1983. He opened his flagship store in New York City three years later. The company expanded upmarket with its Purple Label and downmarket with Polo Jeans denims and a line of paints in 1996.

Following the stampede of fashion-house IPOs Polo went public in 1997. The next year moving to reduce expenses the company restructured its divisions. In 1999 Polo paid $85 million for hip Canadian retailer Club Monaco to compete in the burgeoning youth market. It also opened RL a fine-dining restaurant adjacent to its retail outlet in Chicago's famed shopping district.

In early 2000 Polo purchased its European licensee Poloco for $230 million giving the company greater control of its brand. Then in a 50-50 joint venture with NBC and its affiliates Polo formed Ralph Lauren Media Company to sell its products via the Internet as well as broadcast cable and print media. Also that year the company closed 11 underperforming Club Monaco locations and announced plans to shut down all of its jeans stores. To extend its European reach even further Polo bought its Italian licensee PRL Fashions of Europe in 2001.

Polo Ralph Lauren inked one of the most significant licensing deals in company history —and what it considers to be a great match to boot —in 2005. The firm paired with the United States Tennis Association (USTA) to form a four-year global partnership and was designated the official apparel sponsor of the US Open through 2008. The agreement involved among other things an official shirt designed by Lauren for on-court officials co-branded US Open/Polo Ralph Lauren merchandise and joint marketing programs. In 2006 the company entered a licensing agreement with Luxottica valued at more than $1.75 billion over a 10-year period.

The company's agreement with the USTA gave it the momentum to seal a deal with The All England Club and Wimbledon in 2006 that extends through 2010. Polo Ralph Lauren as part of the agreement became the exclusive outfitter of Wimbledon —the first official designer in the 129-history of the games. Polo Ralph Lauren creates and outfits on-court officials and sells its Wimbledon collection at its freestanding stores as well as through select retailers and Polo.com.

Initiatives for 2007 included the launch of a new group named Global Brand Concepts formed to develop lifestyle brands for specialty and department stores including J.C. Penney's American Living Collection. The group designs and markets new products including accessories home decor and women's men's and children's apparel.

That year Polo Ralph Lauren purchased the remaining 50% stake in Polo.com from both Ralph Lauren Media a unit of NBCUniversal and ValueVisions Media for about $175 million. The move gave Polo full control over its plans to develop its online presence domestically and abroad.

The company brought its East Coast lifestyle brand to Asia when it opened its first freestanding flagship store in Tokyo in 2006. The next year Polo Ralph Lauren secured a foothold in the Japanese apparel and accessories market by purchasing the 50% balance of Polo Ralph Lauren Japan for some $23 million and making it a wholly owned subsidiary. The company also increased its stake in Impact 21 Co. a Japanese sub-licensee from 20% to 97% in. Impact 21 operates the company's men's women's and jeans apparel and accessories business in Japan.

Founder Ralph Lauren stepped down as CEO in November 2015 but remained involved with the company as chairman and chief creative officer.

EXECUTIVES

EVP and Chief Administrative Officer, Mitchell A. Kosh, age 66, $850,000 total compensation

SVP Finance, Robert L. Madore

President Luxury Collections, Val @e Hermann, age 48, $882,692 total compensation

CEO, Stefan Larsson, age 40

President Global Brands, Christopher H. Peterson, age 48, $900,000 total compensation

Vice President Of Ecommerce Technology, Sharon French

Vice President, Robert Westreich

Vice President of Customs, Maureen Gray

Vice President of Manufacturing and Operations, Janet Monaco

Vice President Of Merchandising Blue Label, Brooke Allinson

Vice President Benefits and Human Resources Administration, Helene Pliner

Senior Vice President Interactive Technology, David (Dave) Adams

Vice President Denim Design, Mary Bruno

Vice President Planning And Allocation Factory Store Concept, Bradley Eckhart

Vice President Information Technology, Elizabeth (Beth) Block

Vice President Technical Manufacturing, Paul Haffner

Vice President Information Technology Infrastructure, Jonathan Zwang

Vice President Energy Management, Nicole Cunningham

Senior Vice President Legal Department, Avery Fischer

Vice President Concepts And Golf, Charles (Chas) Schaefer

Vice President Of Design, Callery McGee

Vice President Marketing And Communications, Adrian Kahan

Vice President Blue Label, Ruth Perretti

Executive Vice President Manufacturing, Richard Bangs

Senior Vice President Global Manufacturing, John Cox

Vice President sales and Retail Development collection and Black Label, Alicynne Sher

Vice President Product Management, Mike Cottell

Vice President Finance, Paul Wickman

Senior Vice President Supply Chain Logistics And Operations, Russ G Locurto

Vice President, Patricia (Pat) Faz

Senior Vice President of Global Sourcing, Sandy Gundersen

Zone Vice President, Jane (Ginny) Wicks

Vice President Of Design Women's Footwear, Nancy Boas

Vice President Platform Engineering, Atif Khan

Vice President Of Licensed Business, Meegan Colgan

Vice President Business Planning Store Planning and Analytics, Michele Tezer

Vice President Creative Director, Amir Mohammady

Vice President Menswear Design, Matthew White

Vice President Rlx Design And Development, Sasha Kelly

Vice President, Calvin Churchman

Vice President Global Manufacturing And Sourcing, Sanjeev Dua

Vice President Global Marketing, Tom Jarrold

Vice President Chief Information Security and Privacy Officer, Scott Lancaster

Executive Assistant To The Senior Vice President Of Interactive Technology, Erika Keller

Vice President Advertising And Design, Marcy Barrett

Vice President Retail Marketing, Debra Kanabis

Vice President Men`s Rugby Designer, Lee Norwood

Vice President Production and Sourcing, Hannah (Hanna) Bradford

Senior Vice President Creative Services, Karen Elliott

Vice President Real Estate Counsel, Smita Butala

Vice President Internal Audit, Amy Cheema

Vice President Architecture And Strategy, David (Dave) Horner

Vice President Finance Europe, Christoffer Lund

Vice President advertising operations, Sonya Summerfield

Vice President, Doreen Bollhofer

Vice President Product Presentation, Greg Bishop

Vice President Human Resources, Andrea Carter

Vice President Distribution, Steve Wuebker

Vice President Marketing And Creative Direction, Amy Jasse

Vice President Information Technology Europe, Chris Butcher

Senior Vice President Global Merchandising, Heather Cerbone

Vice President Merchandising, Angela (Angie) Cohen

Vice President Specialty Sales Home, Wendy Hare

Vice President Facilities Energy Engineering, Lj Mohan

Senior Vice President Marketing and Licensing, Nancy Vignola

Senior Vice President Global Manufacturing, Don Baum

Vice President Retail Development, George Rakotci

Vice President Human Resources, Karen Omara

Executive Vice President Global Creati, Alfredo Paredes

Vice President Creative Services, Sarah O%27REILLY

Vice President Product Development, Rebecca Handler

Senior Vice President Real Estate, Steve Yalof

Vice President Digital Operations Planning, George Koveos

Vice President Product Presentation and Training Polo Retail Group, Baldo LaRussa

Vice President Of Product Development And Production, Ian Nash

Chairman and Chief Creative Officer, Ralph Lauren, age 75

Secretary, Lisa Washington

Auditors: Ernst & Young LLP

LOCATIONS

HQ: Ralph Lauren Corp
650 Madison Avenue, New York, NY 10022
Phone: 212 318-7000
Web: www.RalphLauren.com

2015 Sales

	% of total
Americas	67
Europe	21
Asia	12
Total	**100**

PRODUCTS/OPERATIONS

2015 Sales

	% of total
Retail	52
Wholesale	46
Licensing	2
Total	**100**

Selected Brand Names & Licenses
Wholesale

Lauren by Ralph Lauren
Pink Pony
Polo Ralph Lauren
Ralph by Ralph Lauren
Ralph Lauren Black Label
Ralph Lauren Blue Label
Ralph Lauren Purple Label
Ralph Lauren Polo Sport
Retail
Club Monaco
Ralph Lauren
Polo Ralph Lauren
Polo Sport
Licensing Partners
Fitz and Floyd Inc.
Hanesbrands
Kohl' s Department Stores Inc.
L' Oréal S.A.
Luxottica Group
Peerless Inc.
The Warnaco Group
WestPoint Home Inc.

COMPETITORS

Abercrombie & Fitch	Jos. A. Bank
American Eagle	Kate Spade
Outfitters	Kenneth Cole
Ann Taylor	Kering
Armani	L.L. Bean
Benetton	LVMH
Brand Matter	Lands' End
Burberry	Laura Ashley
Calvin Klein	Levi Strauss
Christian Dior	Martha Stewart Living
Coach Inc.	Michael Kors Holdings
Donna Karan	Nautica Apparel
Ermenegildo Zegna	Nine West
Escada	PVH
Est©e Lauder	Perry Ellis
Gianni Versace	International
Gucci	Richemont
Guess?	St. John Knits
H&M	The Gap
Haggar	Tiffany & Co.
Herm's	Tommy Bahama
Hugo Boss	Tommy Hilfiger
J. Crew	

HISTORICAL FINANCIALS

Company Type: Public

Income Statement

FYE: March 28

	REVENUE ($ mil.)	NET INCOME ($ mil.)	NET PROFIT MARGIN	EMPLOYEES
03/15	7,620	702	9.2%	25,000
03/14	7,450	776	10.4%	23,000
03/13	6,944	750	10.8%	23,000
03/12*	6,859	681	9.9%	25,000
04/11	5,660	567	10.0%	24,000
Annual Growth	**7.7%**	**5.5%**	**—**	**1.0%**

*Fiscal year change

2015 Year-End Financials

Debt ratio: 12.92%
Return on equity: 17.76%
Cash ($ mil.): 500
Current ratio: 2.80
Long-term debt ($ mil.): 536

No. of shares (mil.): 86
Dividends
Yield: 0.0%
Payout: 23.4%
Market value ($ mil.): 11,324

	STOCK PRICE ($) FY Close	P/E High/Low	PER SHARE ($) Earnings	Dividends	Book Value
03/15	131.22	23 16	7.88	1.85	45.09
03/14	158.24	22 17	8.43	1.70	45.48
03/13	169.31	22 17	8.00	1.60	41.63
03/12*	174.33	24 16	7.13	0.80	39.40
04/11	126.63	22 12	5.75	0.50	34.97
Annual Growth	**0.9%**	**— —**	**8.2%**	**38.7%**	**6.6%**

*Fiscal year change

Raymond James Financial, Inc.

Call it Ray or Ray Jay. Raymond James Financial doesn't mind as long as it's getting calls from customers. The diversified financial services company offers investment and financial planning services primarily through subsidiary Raymond James & Associates (RJA) which provides securities brokerage investment banking and financial advisory services in North America and Europe. Its Raymond James Financial Services offers financial planning and brokerage services via independent financial advisors as well as through alliances with community banks. Other units provide asset management trust and banking services. The firm has more than 2500 branches offices and independent contractor branches.

Operations

The company's business is divided into a handful of segments. Its total client assets equal some $486 billion.

The Private Client Group is the largest segment accounting for some 65% of the company's revenue. It provides retail brokerage and financial planning services to nearly 2 million customers located mainly in the US Canada and the UK. The segment's client assets under administration amounts to some $451 billion.The company's Capital Markets segment generates another 20% of revenue and handles investment banking and equity research services.

The Asset Management segment which makes up less than 10% of revenue and oversees some $40 billion on behalf of clients includes Eagle Asset Management Eagle Boston Investment Management Eagle Fund Distributors Raymond James

Trust and investment advisory programs through agreements with other asset managers.Geographic Reach

Florida-based Raymond James Financial generates about 90% of its revenue from its business in the US. Canadian customers produce a little less than 10% of revenue and European customers made up the remainder.

Sales and Marketing

Through three broker/dealer subsidiaries and its combined 6200 financial advisors Raymond James Financial serves about 2.5 million accounts through its 2500-plus locations.

Financial Performance

Raymond James Financial has been on the upswing with fiscal 2014 marking a fifth straight year of revenue growth and an all-time high. Revenue jumped by 8% to $4.97 billion in fiscal 2014 with across the board segment growth as more people invested and client assets under administration swelled by 12% to $475 billion. The bulk of this revenue growth came from securities commissions and fees from increased investment transactions but a significant amount also was generated through investment advisory fees and account and service fees.The company's net income also grew for its fifth year in a row climbing by 31% to a record high of $480.3 million in fiscal 2014. The jump in profit was mostly thanks to higher revenues but also because the bank didn't incur acquisition expenses as it did in 2013.Operations provided $507.6 million in fiscal 2014 or roughly 23% less cash than in 2013 mostly because the company experienced a net decrease in client cash deposits in brokerage accounts compared to the year before.Mergers and Acquisitions

Raymond James Financial aims to be a "serial niche acquirer" of brokerages boutique investment banks and asset managers.

It has been building its Capital Markets business through acquisitions. In one of its largest purchases to date in any segment the company in 2012 bought the investment banking and brokerage business of Morgan Keegan from Regions Financial for $1.2 billion and integrated the Morgan Keegan platform into its RJ&A platform. Raymond James Financial previously purchased boutique investment bank Lane Berry & Co. International in Boston in 2009 and Chicago-based investment bank and brokerage Howe Barnes Hoefer & Arnett in 2011.

To boost its large-cap investments the firm in 2012 acquired a 45% interest in ClariVest Asset Management.

RJ Bank acquired the Canadian operations of Allied Irish Banks in 2012 adding a portfolio of approximately $430 million in loan commitments. In conjunction with the deal RJ Bank launched a new finance company in Canada which will help the company grow its corporate and real estate banking business. It's part of Raymond James Financial's strategy of expanding its corporate lending business to additional markets.

HISTORY

Robert James often called the "founder of financial planning" first started a construction business in Ohio after his WWII service in the US Navy and then began a Florida home-building company. He got into the financial services business in 1954 with Florida Mutual Fund a company he and Gerard Jobin formed that eventually became American National Growth Fund. But when most companies were selling just stocks or mutual funds James saw a need for a more comprehensive approach to investing. He decided to focus on helping individual clients learning about their financial needs and goals and then working with them on everything from investments to taxes. To that end he began offering seminars for retirees.In 1960 those seminars had turned into a new company James and Associates which two years later became Robert A. James Investments. In 1964 James acquired Raymond and Associates a firm started by Edward Raymond in 1962; the newly merged firm was renamed Raymond James & Associates (RJA).James' son Thomas joined the firm in 1966 the year the company's revenues first surpassed $1 million. Over the next several years the company expanded its investment offerings and set up new divisions. It added Investment Management & Research as an affiliate broker/dealer in 1967 and Planning Corporation of America as a general insurance agency in 1968.Raymond James Financial incorporated as a holding company in 1969 and Thomas James became CEO the next year. RJA formed Eagle Asset Management in 1975 RJ Oil & Gas (subsidiary for oil and gas limited partnerships) in 1977 securities and real estate subsidiaries in 1980 (Robert Thomas Securities and RJ Properties respectively) and an equipment leasing subsidiary (RJ Leasing) in 1982.Raymond James Financial went public in 1983 the year Robert James died. Two years later the company organized its Heritage Family of Funds. RJA became an international company in the late 1980s opening an office in Paris in 1987 and in Geneva the next year. It also began offering a cash management program in 1988 and began its Stock Loan Department. Trust and banking subsidiaries were begun in 1992 and 1994 respectively followed by the creation of Equity Capital Markets Group in 1996.In 2000 Raymond James Financial crossed the billion-dollar-mark hitting $1.7 billion in sales. That year it acquired Canadian investment firm Goepel McDermid (renamed Raymond James Ltd.) to offer individual and institutional investment services to the Canadian market and it launched Raymond James Killik a UK joint venture that became Raymond James Investment Services in 2002.In 2006 Raymond James Financial reduced front-end commissions with variations of variable annuity products; the next year it kicked off its Wealth Solutions department a unit designed to help high-net-worth clients and their advisors. Also that year Raymond James Financial extended its deal to attach its name to the home stadium of the NFL's Tampa Bay Buccaneers through 2015.

EXECUTIVES

Vice President Of Information Technology, Bruce Philipoom

President Global Equities and Investment Banking Raymond James & Associates, Jeffrey E. (Jeff) Trocin, $303,750 total compensation

EVP Finance CFO and Treasurer, Jeffrey P. Julien, $270,000 total compensation

COO and CEO Raymond James & Associates, Dennis W. Zank, $327,500 total compensation

President Raymond James Financial; President Fixed Income and Capital Markets, John C. Carson, $300,000 total compensation

President Raymond James Financial Services, Scott A. Curtis

CEO, Paul C. Reilly, age 60, $445,000 total compensation

President and CEO Raymond James Bank, Steven M. Raney

Chairman and CEO Raymond James Ltd., Paul D. Allison

President Raymond James & Associates Private Client Group, Tash Elwyn

EVP Technology and Operations, Bella L. Allaire

EVP Asset Management Group, Jeff Dowdle

Vice President, Bert Berkwich

Vice President Software Engineering, Mark Abbott

Vice President of Financial Services, Howard Sachs

Vice President Managing Director of Acquisitions, Kevin Kilbane

Vice President, Charlie Williams

Vice President Private Wealth And Retirement Plan Advisor, Nathaniel Hester

Branch Manager Senior Vice President investments, George J Garro

Executive Vice President, Charles (Chas) Bauder

Vice President Information Technology, Genie Blanton

Executive Vice President, William H (Bill) Dietz

Vice President marketing Director of Corporate Ser, Lisa Turley

Senior Vice President Investments, Jeffrey Weiss

Vice President, Mark Matheson

First Vice President, Jennifer Simmons

Vice President Director Of Acquisitions, Robert Long

Senior Vice President Chief Architect, Sateesh Prabakaran

Executive Vice President, Ed Cashman

Vice President Deposit Operations, Barbara Shore

Senior Vice President Investments, Dennis Lindeman

Associate Vice President, Peter Delaney

Vice President Business Development Financial Institutions Division, Will MacKey

Vice President Fixed Income Department, Robert (Bob) Howley

Vice President Investments, Scott Thompson

Vice President Consulting Services, Nicholas Lacy

Senior Vice President, Bob Blain

Senior Vice President, Bill Specht

Vice President, Scott Brinner

Senior Vice President Head Of Healthcare Real Estate, Laca Wonghammond

First Vice President Investments, Rachel Gammerman

Vice President Investments, Sandy Russell

Senior Vice President In The Real Estate Investmen, Jamie Graff

Senior Vice President Business Development Group, Ken Grider

Senior Vice President Investments, John Reuter

Assistant Vice President Personal Banker, Valerie Pratt

Senior Vice President, Jeff Factor

Vice President Information Technology, Frank Bugh

Vice President Finance, Alexandra Band

Senior Vice President, Chris Choate

Senior Vice President Equity Research Real Estate, William A (Bill) Crow

Vice President Of Investments, James Heinen

Vice President, Terry McCormick

Vice President Marketing Strategy and Client Experience, Tim Killgoar

Assistant Vice President Of Information Technology, Brian Miller

Vice President Operations And Corporate Technology, Meri-Ellen Cain

Vice President, Ann Hensler

Senior Vice President Wealth Management Technology, Juergen Dittgen

Senior Vice President Of Operations, Denise Samson

Vice President Investments, Sonya Choeff

Vice President Equity Trading, Terrie Stewart

First Vice President Investments, Kenneth (Ken) Lampos

Vice President Investments, Ladd Bednar

Vice President, Vasanta Pundarika

Vice President Equity Syndicate, Bill Cosper

Vice President Investments, Pai Charasika

Senior Vice President Investments, Dave Barber

Vice President Equity linked Securities, Claude Lawrence

Vice President structured Credit Trading, Brian Linde

Senior Vice President, Dianne Klaiss

Associate Vice President Investments, Beverly Ainsley

Senior Vice President, Sharon Ioannidis

Vice President Of Information Technology, Greg Etchison

Senior Vice President Equity Research Infrastruct, Michael (Mel) Turits

Assistant Vice President Capital Access, Karen Fry

Vice President, Daniel Fairweather

Senior Vice President Institute Equity Sales Trader, Mike Christian

Senior Vice President Mortgage Banking Operations, Jennifer (Jen) Abele

Senior Vice President Investments, Brian Randall

Senior Vice President, Maria Palermo

Vice President Marketing Manager, Stephanie Brown

Vice President Assistant Treasurer, Ron Whitaker

CFP Vice President Of Investments, Kevin Tierney

Vice President Institutional Equity Sales, Joe Campo

Associate Vice President Investments, Elizabeth Aulick (Beth) Robertson

Vice President Investments, Angie Conley

Vice President, Justin Roman

Senior Vice President Head of Agency and Treasury Trading, Joe Larizza

Senior Vice President, Hal Greer

Vice President Investments, Trey Haydon

Senior Vice President Fi Trading, Randall Hawkins

Vice President Investments, Mark Mazman

Senior Vice President, Fred Coble

Senior Vice President, Tom Donegan

Cfa Vice President, John (Jack) Freeman

Vice President Fi Trading, Chad Runnels

Senior Vice President Investments, Doug Cooper

Vice President Investments, Jeffrey Miley

Vice President Investments, Gregory Majors

Vice President Investments, Tim Kelley

First Vice President Fi Administration, Dee Cook

Vice President Investments, Bruce Haltinner

Vice President International Financial Consultant, Vita Barrio

First Vice President Investments, John (Jack) Chesney

Vice President Corporate And Executive Services, Jeanna Bryan

Senior Vice President Investments, Jeff Harring

Senior Vice President Operations, Joe Barkley

First Vice President Investments, Tom Mahoney

Vice President Inv Banking, Scott Green

Senior Vice President High Net Worth, Ted Ruddock

Vice President Trading And Project Management, AL Caudullo

Vice President Banks and Thrifts, Andrew (Andy) Ross

Senior Vice President Chief Lending Officer, Tom Macina

Vice President, Scott Englehardt

Vice President Vice President, Jerry Willenborg

Assistant Vice President Freedom Product Specialist, Ivana Goyette

Assistant Vice President Development Services, Don Carlton

Vice President Of Investments, Paul Rampolla

Assistant Vice President Human Resources Partner, Andrea Grayson

Vice President Tax and Financial Reporting, Bradley Allen

Senior Vice President financial advisor, Chip Lee

Vice President Investments, Sean Fitzpatrick

Senior Vice President Branch Manager, Rick Hadrava

Senior Vice President Investments, Shelly Church

Senior Vice President Investments, Tom Ross

Senior Vice President, Steven (Steve) Shapiro

Vice President, Chris Cowing

Vice President, Salit Nagy-todd

Associate Vice President Investments, Michael (Mel) Lowe
Senior Vice President Investments Branch Manager, Matt Quigley
Vice President Of Correspondent Services, Linda Oosting
Vice President Tax, Brad Bond
Vice President Compliance, Brad Cole
First Vice President of Investments, Douglas (Doug) Clark
Vice President, Stephen Christenson
Senior Vice President, Mark Ranney
Senior Vice President Fixed Income Sales, Geoffrey Waters
Senior Vice President Investments, Mark Teed
Assistant Vice President, Roberta (Bobbi) Green
Vice President Investments, Matt McCurry
Vice President Chief Underwriter Raymond James Tax, Rick Cargo
Senior Vice President Of Investments, Todd Tindall
Vice President Public Finance, Ogden Kniffin
Vice President, Jozsi Popper
Assistant Vice President Of Financial Reporting, Julie Rambo
Vice President, Holly Hayes
Vice President Investments, Anthony Morrison
First Vice President Investments, Charles (Chas) Robinton
Vice President Finance and Investor Relations, Paul Shoukry
Assistant Vice President, Robin Ernst
Vice President National Sales Manager, Dan Mallard
Auditors: KPMG LLP

LOCATIONS

HQ: Raymond James Financial, Inc.
880 Carillon Parkway, St. Petersburg, FL 33716
Phone: 727 567-1000
Web: www.raymondjames.com

2013 Sales

	$ mil.	% of total
US	4,177	91
Canada	310	7
Europe	83	2
Other	23	—
Total	**4,595**	**100**

PRODUCTS/OPERATIONS

2013 Sales By Segment

	$ mil.	% of total
Private Client Group	2,930	63
Capital Markets	945	20
RJ Bank	356	8
Asset Management	292	6
Other	126	3
Total	**4,595**	**100**

2013 Sales

	$ mil.	% of total
Securities commissions & fees	3,007	66
Interest	473	10
Account & service fees	363	8
Investment banking	288	6
Investment advisory fees	282	6
Net trading profits	34	1
Other	145	3
Total	**4,595**	**100**

Selected Subsidiaries

Eagle Asset Management Inc.
Eagle Boston Investment Management Inc.
Eagle Fund Distributors Inc.
Howe Barnes Hoefer & Arnett Inc.
Lane Berry & Co. International
Planning Corporation of America
Raymond James & Associates
Raymond James Argentina Sociedad De Bolsa S.A.
Raymond James Asset Management International S.A. (France)

Raymond James Bank FSB (dba RJ Bank)
Raymond James Brasil S.A.
Raymond James Canada LLC
Raymond James Capital Partners L.P.
Raymond James European Holdings Inc.
Raymond James Financial Services Inc.
Raymond James Investment Services Limited (UK 75%)
Raymond James Ltd. (Canada)
Raymond James Tax Credit Funds Inc.
Raymond James Trust N.A.
RJ Delta Fund Management S.A. (Argentina)

COMPETITORS

Charles Schwab	National Financial
E*TRADE Financial	Partners
Edward Jones	Piper Jaffray
FMR	Principal Financial
LPL Financial	TD Ameritrade
Legg Mason	Wells Fargo Advisors
Merrill Lynch	

HISTORICAL FINANCIALS

Company Type: Public

Income Statement

FYE: September 30

	REVENUE ($ mil.)	NET INCOME ($ mil.)	NET PROFIT MARGIN	EMPLOYEES
09/15	5,308	502	9.5%	14,850
09/14	4,965	480	9.7%	13,900
09/13	4,595	367	8.0%	13,650
09/12	3,897	295	7.6%	13,900
09/11	3,399	278	8.2%	11,300
Annual Growth	**11.8%**	**15.9%**	**—**	**7.1%**

2015 Year-End Financials

Debt ratio: 7.09%	No. of shares (mil.): 142
Return on equity: 11.59%	Dividends
Cash ($ mil.): 5,506	Yield: 1.4%
Current ratio: 0.47	Payout: 20.6%
Long-term debt ($ mil.): 1,762	Market value ($ mil.): 7,093

	STOCK PRICE ($) FY Close	P/E High/Low	PER SHARE ($) Earnings	Dividends	Book Value
09/15	49.63	17 14	3.43	0.72	31.64
09/14	53.58	16 12	3.32	0.64	29.33
09/13	41.67	18 14	2.58	0.56	26.25
09/12	36.65	17 11	2.20	0.52	23.73
09/11	25.96	18 11	2.19	0.52	20.47
Annual Growth	**17.6%**	**— —**	**11.9%**	**8.5%**	**11.5%**

Raytheon Co.

Raytheon ("light of the gods") shines in the upper pantheon of US military contractors; the company regularly places among the Pentagon's top 10 prime contractors. Its air/land/sea/space/cyber defense offerings include reconnaissance targeting and navigation systems as well as missile systems (Patriot Sidewinder and Tomahawk) unmanned ground and aerial systems sensing technologies and radars. Additionally Raytheon makes systems for communications (satellite) and intelligence radios cybersecurity and air traffic control. It also offers commercial electronics products and services as well as food safety processing technologies. The US government accounts for a large portion of sales.

Geographic Reach

Raytheon maintains offices in nearly 20 countries and has established global companies to serve customers Australia Spain France Germany Canada and the UK. The company sells products and services to customers in 80 nations although the US accounts for about three-fourths of sales (with the Asia-Pacific and Middle East and North Africa regions each bringing in an additional 10%).

Sales and Marketing

The US government accounted for 70% of Raytheon's sales in 2014. While it consistently counts among its customers the US Department of Defense (DoD) the Federal Bureau of Investigation (FBI) and NASA as well as members of the US military and US intelligence communities Raytheon also has some key international customers. The company has contracts with South Korea to provide air and missile defense systems with Japan for training Saudi Arabia for surveillance systems and Australia for joint standoff weapons. Other main global clients include Finland Germany Taiwan and the United Arab Emirates.

Operations

To support its customers worldwide Raytheon serves defense and intelligence markets via four business segments: Integrated Defense Systems (IDS) Intelligence Information and Services (ISS) Missile Systems (MS) and Space and Airborne Systems (SAS). Previously the company operated in six segments but it restructured in April 2013. Its former segments included Network Centric Systems (NCS) and Technical Services (TS).

Having patented the first microwave more than 65 years ago Raytheon is still developing and designing futuristic realities. The product that stands out most in the company's portfolio is the missile however. As the world's #1 missile maker Raytheon is a key player in US efforts to construct a comprehensive missile defense system. Such systems need intercept vehicles sensors command and control systems and systems integration expertise. Raytheon's precision engagement offerings include the company's missiles as well as radars data links targeting and warning systems and lasers. In recent years the company has released an air and missile defense systems product line which includes the Standard Missile-3 the Exoatmospheric Kill Vehicle (EKV) and branded development programs.

Financial Performance

Raytheon's revenues have been gradually declining the last four years with revenues dipping 4% from $23.7 billion in 2013 to $22.8 billion in 2014. Profits however jumped 12% from $2 billion in 2013 to $2.2 billion in 2014 due to a decrease in operation expenses. Raytheon's operating cash flow in 2014 decreased by 19% to $2.18 billion due to cash outflows in pension and other post-retirement benefit plans.

The decline in revenue for 2014 was fueled by a drop in IDS sales due to the scheduled completion of certain production phases on various Patriot programs for international customers. It was also hurt by lower net sales on a close combat tactical radar program and on a missile defense radar program for an international customer. MS sales also dipped due to declines in production within the US Army budget.

Strategy

Raytheon's business is contingent to a great extent on the federal defense budget. With the US budget deficit hitting an all-time high in recent years the present administration is struggling to prioritize among such spending initiatives as defense homeland security health care reform and alternative energy development.

Raytheon's diverse product lineup puts it in a better position to weather budget cuts than some of its competitors that handle a limited number of defense products and services. The company's offerings run the gamut from kill vehicles (ballistic missile interceptors) to pasteurization technology and GPS satellites.

Mergers and Acquisitions

The company's cybersecurity business has been getting a lot of attention of late primarily through multiple acquisitions which reflect Raytheon's general strategy for building its operations and growing its customer base. In 2014 Raytheon acquired Virginia-based Blackbird Technologies a provider of persistent surveillance secure tactical communications and cybersecurity products to the intelligence and special operations market for $420 million. Blackbird became part of the company's IIS business.

In 2015 Raytheon augmented its MS segment when it acquired Sensintel a privately held provider of unmanned aircraft systems products to the intelligence and special operations markets.

HISTORY

In 1922 Laurence Marshall and several others founded American Appliance Company to produce home refrigerators. When their invention failed Marshall began making Raytheon (meaning "light of/from the gods") radio tubes. Raytheon was adopted as the company's name in 1925. It bought the radio division of Chicago's Q. R. S. Company in 1928 and formed Raytheon Production Company with National Carbon Company (makers of the Eveready battery) to market Eveready Raytheon tubes in 1929.

EXECUTIVES

Vice President Communications and Corporate Affairs, Pamela (Pam) Wickham
Vice President, Walter F Doran
VP; President Raytheon Intelligence Information and Services (IIS), David C. Wajsgras, age 56, $929,694 total compensation
President Global Business Services, Rebecca B. Rhoads, age 57
VP Business Development; CEO Raytheon International Inc., John D. Harris, age 53
VP Contracts and Supply Chain, David Wilkins
VP; President Space and Airborne Systems (SAS), Richard R. (Rick) Yuse, age 64, $678,268 total compensation
Chairman and CEO, Thomas A. (Tom) Kennedy, age 60, $1,057,698 total compensation
VP; President Missile Systems, Taylor W. Lawrence, age 52, $383,237 total compensation
CIO, Kevin T. Neifert
President Raytheon International, Thomas A. Vecchiolla
VP and CFO, Anthony F. O'Brien
President Integrated Defense Systems, Wesley D. Kremer, age 50
President Raytheon International Inc. Canada, Mark Nicol
Vice President, Roger W Anderson
Senior Vice President General Counsel Secretary, Jay B Stephens
Vp Legal, Mark D Nielsen
Vice President Membership, Catherine (Cathy) Dixon
Vice President Human Resources, Randall Fort
Vice President Internal Controls and Accounting, Kathy Slate
Vice President Business Development, Ira Allen
Assistant Vice President Risk, Diane Murphy
V Pres Hr & Global Security, Randa Newsome
Vice President Emerging Technologies, Chris Bencal
Vice President Global Talent Development And Learning, Beth Carlson
Vice President Human Resources, Tim Harris
Vice President Sales and Marketing, Judy Durkin
Vice President, Jon Sastri
Vice President; Program Management Excellence, Larry Briggs
Business Development Vice President, David Scott

Vice President Finance, Tom Wied
Vice President Information Technology, Bob Boulton
RTSC Vice President, John Balaguer
Vice President, Greg Provisor
Vice President Engineering Technology and Field Operations, Todd Probert
Senior Vice President Worldwide Sales, Stephen Pace
Vice President Investor Relations, Todd Ernst
Vice President of Integrated Communications Systems, David (Dave) Farnsworth
Vice President Subcontracts Espx, John (Jack) Norton
Vice President, James (Jamie) Wade
Vice President, Scott Henderson
Assistant Vice President, Luis A Cabrera
Auditors: PricewaterhouseCoopers LLP

LOCATIONS

HQ: Raytheon Co.
870 Winter Street, Waltham, MA 02451
Phone: 781 522-3000
Web: www.raytheon.com

2013 Sales

	$ mil.	% of total
US	17,260	73
Asia/Pacific	2,590	11
Middle East & North Africa	2,396	10
Europe & other regions	1,460	6
Total	**23,706**	**100**

PRODUCTS/OPERATIONS

2013 Sales

	$ mil.	% of total
Missile Systems	6,599	26
Integrated Defense Systems	6,489	25
Space & Airborne Systems	6,371	25
Intelligence & Information Systems	6,045	24
Adjustments	(1798)	-
Total	**23,706**	**100**

Selected Products

Integrated Defense Systems (IDS)
  Aegis Weapon Systems radar equipment
  AN/AQS Minehunting Sonar System
  Joint Land Attack Cruise Missile Defense Elevated Netted Sensor (JLENS)
  Landing Platform Dock Amphibious Ship LPD-17
  Patriot Air and Missile Defense System
  Sea-Based X-Band Radar (SBX)
  Ship Self-Defense System (SSDS)
  Surface-Launched AMRAAM (SLAMRAAM)
  Terminal High Altitude Area Defense (THAAD) Radar
Intelligence and Information Systems (IIS)
  Army Research Lab
  Communications systems
  Department of Education programs
  Distributed Common Ground System
  Emergency Patient Tracking System
  Global Broadcast Service
  Global Hawk Ground Segment
  Information solutions programs
  Managed data storage solutions
  Mobile Very Small Aperture Satellite Terminal
  National Polar-Orbiting Operational Environmental Satellite System Program
  RedWolf telecommunications surveillance
  Signal and imagery intelligence programs
  Supercomputing
  U-2 (field support)
  UAV systems and ground stations
Missile Systems (MS)
  Advanced Medium-Range Air-to-Air missile (AMRAAM)
  AIM-9X Sidewinder
  Evolved SeaSparrow (ESSM)
  Excalibur long-range artillery system
  Exoatmospheric Kill Vehicle
  Extended Range Guided Munition (ERGM)
  High-Speed Anti-Radiation Missile Targeting System
  Paveway laser-guided bombs
  Maverick AGM-65 missiles
  Tomahawk and Tactical Tomahawk cruise missiles

TOW Javelin Phalanx Standard and SeaRAM missiles
Network Centric Systems (NCS)
  Airspace management and homeland security
  Command and control systems
  Combat systems
  Integrated communications systems
  Precision technologies and components
Space and Airborne Systems (SAS)
  Active electronically scanned array radars
  Airborne radars and processors
  Electronic warfare systems
  Electro-optic/infrared sensors
  Intelligence surveillance and reconnaissance systems
  Space and missile defense technology
Technical Services (TS)
  Base operations
  Logistics support
  Maintenance support
  Professional services
  Treaty compliance monitoring
  Weapons security and destruction

Selected Markets

Command Control Communication and Intelligence (C3I)
  Systems provide integrated real-time support for on- and off-battlefield and transform raw data into actionable intelligence
Cybersecurity
  Provides cyber capabilities to the Intelligence DoD and DHS markets as well as embedding cybersecurity in Raytheon's products and IT infrastructure
Effects
  Achieves specific military actions or outcomes from force protection to theater/national missile defense
Homeland Security
  Domestic and international homeland security markets especially transportation security immigration control/identity management critical infrastructure protection maritime security energy security intelligence program support law enforcement solutions a
Mission Support
  Provides total life-cycle and training system engineering logistics and maintenance support to customer
Sensing
  Acquires precise situational data across air space ground and underwater domains and generates information needed for effective battlespace decisions

COMPETITORS

BAE Systems Inc.	Honeywell Aerospace
Boeing	Interstate Electronics
Crane Aerospace &	L-3 Avionics
Electronics	Lockheed Martin
DRS Technologies	MBDA
Emerson Electric	Meggitt-USA
Exelis	Northrop Grumman
Fluor	Rockwell Collins
GE	Saab AB
Harris Corp.	Sierra Nevada Corp

HISTORICAL FINANCIALS

Company Type: Public

Income Statement

FYE: December 31

	REVENUE ($ mil.)	NET INCOME ($ mil.)	NET PROFIT MARGIN	EMPLOYEES
12/15	23,247	2,074	8.9%	61,000
12/14	22,826	2,244	9.8%	61,000
12/13	23,706	1,996	8.4%	63,000
12/12	24,414	1,888	7.7%	67,800
12/11	24,857	1,866	7.5%	71,000
Annual Growth	(1.7%)	2.7%	—	(3.7%)

2015 Year-End Financials

Debt ratio: 18.20%	No. of shares (mil.): 299
Return on equity: 21.11%	Dividends
Cash ($ mil.): 2,328	Yield: 2.1%
Current ratio: 1.60	Payout: 38.5%
Long-term debt ($ mil.): 5,330	Market value ($ mil.): 37,234

	STOCK PRICE ($) FY Close	P/E High/Low	PER SHARE ($) Earnings	Dividends	Book Value
12/15	124.53	19 14	6.80	2.62	33.87
12/14	108.17	15 12	7.18	2.37	31.03
12/13	90.70	15 9	6.16	2.20	35.03
12/12	57.56	10 8	5.65	2.00	24.47
12/11	48.38	10 7	5.28	2.10	24.13
Annual Growth	26.7%	— —	6.5%	5.7%	8.8%

Realogy Group LLC

LOCATIONS

HQ: Realogy Group LLC
175 Park Avenue, Madison, NJ 07940
Phone: 973 407-2000
Web: www.realogy.com

HISTORICAL FINANCIALS

Company Type: Public

Income Statement

FYE: December 31

	REVENUE ($ mil.)	NET INCOME ($ mil.)	NET PROFIT MARGIN	EMPLOYEES
12/14	5,328	143	2.7%	10,700
12/13	5,289	438	8.3%	10,800
12/12	4,672	(543)	—	10,800
12/11	4,093	(441)	—	10,400
12/10	4,090	(99)	—	10,500
Annual Growth	6.8%	—	—	0.5%

2014 Year-End Financials

Debt ratio: 55.44%
Return on equity: 6.83%
Cash ($ mil.): 313
Current ratio: 1.17
Long-term debt ($ mil.): 3,891

No. of shares (mil.): 146
Dividends
  Yield: —
  Payout: —
Market value ($ mil.): —

Realogy Holdings Corp

Realogy Holdings (formerly Domus Holdings) has the goods for domestic bliss for a lot of people. It is the largest franchisor of residential real estate offices in the world with about 13500 offices in more than 100 countries. Its brands include Century 21 Coldwell Banker ERA Better Homes and Gardens Real Estate and Sotheby's. In addition to franchising the company owns and operates about 700 offices under the already mentioned brands along with the Corcoran Group and Citi Habitats labels. It also provides relocation title and settlement services and mortgages. The residential real estate giant changed its name and went public in late 2012.

Operations

Realogy boasts the world's largest residential real estate brokerage business (under its subsidiary NRT LLC) and the world's largest residential real estate brokerage franchising business (under RFG) offering a large portfolio of well-known brands. Its company-owned brokerage operates under the Coldwell Banker Corcoran Group Sotheby's International Realty ZipRealty and Citi Habitats brand names. Its franchise brands include: Century

21 Coldwell Banker Coldwell Banker Commercial ERA Sotheby's International Realty and Better Homes and Gardens Real Estate.The company generated nearly 75% of its total revenue from its company-owned real estate brokerage services in 2014 while 13% came from its real estate franchise services and 7% came from title and settlement services under the company's Title Resource Group subsidiary. In addition to its company-owned and franchised real estate brokerages Realogy is a leading provider of employee relocation services in the US and internationally serving nearly two-thirds of the Fortune 50 companies. The company's relocation services business Cartus generated 7% of all revenue in 2014.

Geographic Reach

The US accounts for 98% of New Jersey-based Realogy's revenue. The company's relocation services business is active in the US Canada Europe and Asia.Sales and MarketingThe company's Title and Settlement Services provide closing and escrow services to customers and real estate companies including the company-owned real estate brokerage and relocation services businesses as well as a targeted list of large financial institution clients including PHH Corporation.Realogy's company-owned brokerage offices staffed some 45000 independent sales agents in more than 45 of the 100 largest US metropolitan areas in 2014. It spent about $188 million on advertising during the year up from $174 million in 2013.

Financial Performance

Realogy's business has been steadily growing in tandem with the strengthening US housing market for the past several years. Revenue in 2014 inched about 1% higher to $5.33 billion thanks mostly to a 5%-plus increase in the average home-sale price through both its Company-Owned Real Estate Brokerage and Real Estate Franchise Services divisions. Lower refinancing volume through its Title and Settlement Services segment along with 2% to 3% lower home sale transaction volume however offset some of Realogy's top-line gains.The company's profits reversed course in 2014 with net income plummeting by 67% to $143 million as it incurred $87 million worth of income tax provisions with an effective tax rate of 37%. In 2013 by comparison the company received a non-recurring income tax benefit of $242 million which allowed profit to skyrocket for the year. Cash levels in 2014 also declined as cash earnings shrank.StrategyWith the housing market improving in recent years Realogy is growing its real estate brokerage operations through strategic acquisitions. Less than a year after purchasing ZipRealty in mid-2014 the company announced that it would begin rolling out ZipRealty's tech-savvy platforms to certain franchisees as well as their independent sales associates and their customers. Realogy believes the new tools offer tremendous value proposition to customers and should boost sales in the years ahead. Beyond large company acquisitions Realogy likes to purchase local real estate brokerages to expand its reach into communities. In 2014 for example one of its NRT subsidiaries bought the Harrisburg Pennsylvania-based multi-office residential brokerage and property management firm Realty Select (doing business as Coldwell Banker Select Professionals Select Property & Association Management and Select Partners) to expand its business in the region. In 2013 the firm's NRT subsidiary spent $32 million to acquire 15 similar real estate brokerage operations.

Mergers and Acquisitions

In 2014 Realogy Holdings acquired California-based ZipRealty a national real estate brokerage and provider of technology and comprehensive online marketing tools to the residential real estate brokerage industry for $6.75 per share in an all-cash deal valued at $166 million. ZipRealty oper-

ates 23 offices in 19 markets across the US.Company BackgroundRealogy in October 2012 raised $1 billion in its IPO a vote of confidence of sorts in the recovery of the residential real estate market in the US. Realogy used the IPO proceeds to reduce its more than $7 billion in debt. Despite losing $540 million in the two years prior to its IPO the firm believed the real estate market was poised for recovery. Its strategy included growing all segments of its business though it offered no specifics on that front.

EXECUTIVES

EVP General Counsel and Corporate Secretary, Marilyn J. Wasser, age 59
Chairman President and CEO, Richard A. Smith, age 61, $1,000,000 total compensation
President and CEO Realogy Franchise Group, Alexander E. (Alex) Perriello, age 67, $550,000 total compensation
President and CEO NRT, Bruce G. Zipf, age 58, $575,000 total compensation
President and CEO Cartus, Kevin J. Kelleher, age 60, $475,000 total compensation
EVP and Chief Human Resources Officer, Sunita Holzer
EVP CFO and Treasurer, Anthony E. (Tony) Hull, age 56, $600,000 total compensation
President and CEO Title Resource Group, Donald J. (Don) Casey, age 53
SVP and CIO, Stephen Fraser
Board Of Directors, Fiona Dias
Auditors: PricewaterhouseCoopers LLP

LOCATIONS

HQ: Realogy Holdings Corp
175 Park Avenue, Madison, NJ 07940
Phone: 973 407-2000
Web: www.realogy.com

2014 Sales

	$ mil.	% of total
United States	5,201	98
All other countries	127	2
Total	**5,328**	**100**

PRODUCTS/OPERATIONS

2014 Sales

	$ mil.	% of total
Company-owned real estate brokerage services	4,078	73
Real estate franchise services	716	13
Relocation services	419	7
Title and settlement services	398	7
Corporate and other	(283)	-
Total	**5,328**	**100**

Selected Brands

Better Homes and Gardens Real Estate
Century 21
Coldwell Banker
Coldwell Banker Commercial
ERA
Sotheby's International Realty

COMPETITORS

Baird & Warner	HomeServices
Brookfield Global Relocation	HomeVestors of America
	Investors Title
Brookfield Residential Properties	Jones Lang LaSalle
	Keller Williams
CBRE Group	Move Inc.
Corky McMillin	NRT LLC
Counselor Realty	New Valley
Cushman & Wakefield	Old Republic Title
Draper and Kramer	RE/MAX
Ebby Halliday Realtors	SIRVA
First American	Stewart Title
Fortune International Realty	Weichert Realtors

Income Statement

FYE: December 31

	REVENUE ($ mil.)	NET INCOME ($ mil.)	NET PROFIT MARGIN	EMPLOYEES
12/14	5,328	143	2.7%	10,700
12/13	5,289	438	8.3%	10,800
12/12	4,672	(543)	—	10,800
12/11	4,093	(441)	—	10,400
12/10	4,090	(99)	—	13,500
Annual Growth	6.8%	—	—	(5.6%)

2014 Year-End Financials

Debt ratio: 55.44%
Return on equity: 6.83%
Cash ($ mil.): 313
Current ratio: 1.17
Long-term debt ($ mil.): 3,891

No. of shares (mil.): 146
Dividends
  Yield: —
  Payout: —
Market value ($ mil.): 6,513

	STOCK PRICE ($) FY Close	P/E High/Low	PER SHARE ($) Earnings	Dividends	Book Value
12/14	44.49	51 35	0.97	0.00	14.89
12/13	49.47	18 14	2.99	0.00	13.76
12/12	41.96	— —	(14.41)	0.00	10.43
Annual Growth	1.5%	— —	—	—	9.3%

Regions Financial Corp

Regions Financial ain't just whistling Dixie anymore. The holding company for Regions Bank which sprouted in the US South has grown by acquiring other financial services firms over the years. Boasting nearly $120 billion in total assets the bank has more than 1600 branches and 2000 ATMs across 16 states stretching from the Southeast and Texas northward through the Mississippi River Valley. In addition to providing standard banking services such as deposit accounts loans and mortgages and credit cards to retail customers and small businesses Regions Financial also serves larger corporations and boasts wealth management division for affluent individuals.

Operations

Since reorganizing its management structure in late 2014 Regions Financial operates three main segments: Corporate Bank Consumer Bank and Wealth Management. The Consumer Bank serves mainly retail and small business customers while the Corporate Bank serves middle-market and large commercial clients. Region's Wealth Management division provides trust and investment services to affluent individuals.Broadly speaking roughly 55% of Regions Financial's total revenue came from loan interest (including fees) in 2014 while 11% came from interest on taxable securities. Another 14% total revenue came from deposit account service charges while card and ATM fees and mortgage banking income made up 6% and 3% of total revenue for the year respectively. About 30% of the bank's total loan portfolio was made up of consumer residential real estate loans in 2014.

Regions Insurance Group a subsidiary of Regions Financial provides insurance products to bank customers.

Geographic Reach

Regions Financial boasts 1650 banking offices and 2000 ATMs across 16 states. About 50% of its branches are in Florida Tennessee and Alabama while about 20% are in Mississippi Georgia and Louisiana. The rest are in Arkansas Illinois Indiana Iowa Kentucky Missouri North Carolina South Carolina Texas and Virginia.

Sales and Marketing

Regions Financial serves some four million households throughout the South Midwest and Texas. It sells and markets its products directly through its branches and through other channels such as the Internet and mobile banking. Its Wealth Management customers are affluent individuals while its business customers include corporate middle market small business and commercial real estate developers and investors.Regions spent $95 million on marketing in 2014 compared to $98 million and $87 million in 2013 and 2012 respectively.

Financial PerformanceRegions Financial has experienced declining revenue over the past few years but has also enjoyed mostly rising annual profit as the credit quality of its loan portfolio has led to lower loan loss provision charges. The bank's revenue slipped by 5% to $5.41 billion in 2014 mostly as its mortgage banking income declined from a lack of residential mortgage demand (and thus mortgage originations) amidst rising loan rates. Interest income from loans also fell by 2% as the low-rate environment continued to lead to lower interest margins on loans.Despite revenue declines in 2014 Region Financial's profit continued its upward trend with net income rising by 3% to $1.16 billion. Helping to pad its bottom line the bank paid $69 million less in loan loss provisions (about half as much as in 2013) as its loan portfolio's credit quality continued to improve. It also paid less interest expense on deposits for the year.Even with higher earnings cash from operations fell sharply for the year mostly as the bank collected less in net proceeds from its sales of loans held for sale.

Strategy

Regions Financial remains optimistic about its long-term prospects in its home markets in the Southeast which are predicted to outpace average growth in the next several years. The company in 2015 reaffirmed that it would focus its future investments on markets with significant population growth deposits and business activity particularly in Atlanta New Orleans St. Louis Houston Tampa Austin Dallas Miami Orlando and Indianapolis.

With the goal of diversifying its income streams Regions has also been busy expanding its insurance business into more markets. In 2014 as part of its strategy to expand its coverage and product offerings throughout the Southeast and Texas Regions opened new insurance offices in Athens Georgia and Dallas Texas to provide property casualty insurance and other insurance brokerage services to companies and individuals located in the promising markets. In 2013 Regions Insurance also opened an office in Columbia South Carolina.

HISTORY

Regions Financial was created out of three venerable Alabama banks. The oldest First National Bank of Huntsville was founded in 1855. When 10 years later the bank was besieged by Union troops a loyal cashier hid securities in the chimney and refused to tell the soldiers where they were. A few years later it was robbed by Jesse James (for years the bank kept in its vaults a gun purported to belong to a James gang member). First National Bank of Montgomery was founded in 1871 and Exchange Security Bank in 1928.

Banking veteran Frank Plummer consolidated the three banks to form Alabama's first multibank holding company First Alabama Bancshares in 1971. The combined firm then became the bank that ate Alabama. But even as it gobbled up other banks its diet remained bland: Its lending programs were modest and focused on a narrow range of business.

The bank's growth in the 1980s was solid if unexciting as it picked up community banks in Alabama (Anniston National Bank and South Baldwin Bank among others) and Georgia (Georgia Co. a mortgage subsidiary of Columbus Bank and Trust). Before he died in 1987 Plummer brought in Willard Hurley as chairman. Hurley put the brakes on acquisitions when they overloaded the bank's data-processing systems. He also put the company up for sale igniting its stock price for a while but there were no serious suitors.

When Hurley passed the baton to Stanley Mackin in 1990 the bank was still rumored to be for sale. But Mackin had other ideas. He put the bank back on its acquisition track and raised the bar on profitability expectations for each department. In 1993 Mackin orchestrated First Alabama's purchase of Secor a failed New Orleans thrift outbidding rival AmSouth Bancorporation. The Secor purchase raised eyebrows but First Alabama sold some branches and folded other operations into its organization.

In 1994 First Alabama changed its name to Regions Financial in order to reflect its out-of-state operations. The next year Regions rolled into Georgia in a big way leaping from a few banks to holdings with approximately $4 billion in assets. Rumors of a merger with either Wachovia or SunTrust Banks popped up in 1996 but the bank continued on its independent course. The next year the company's tank-like progress was halted when it was outbid for Mississippi's Deposit Guaranty Corp. by First American.

By way of consolation Regions in 1998 bought First Commercial Corp. of Little Rock paying a premium price for its 26 banks mortgage company and investment company. Regions also acquired 13 other companies that year and began a major overhaul of its systems concurrently with the assimilation of these operations. This effort included the consolidation of the back-office aspects of its retail and indirect lending operations.

Mackin retired in 1998 and banking veteran Carl Jones Jr. became CEO. Under his direction the bank continued its geographic infill strategy with acquisitions of banks and branches in Arkansas Florida Louisiana Tennessee and Texas in 1999 and 2000. The company also sold its credit card portfolio to MBNA (since acquired by Bank of America) and in 2001 acquired Memphis-based investment bank Morgan Keegan.

Regions Financial has looked for acquisitions in order to grow geographically and diversify its product and services mix. It fortified its foothold in the South and expanded into the Midwest with its blockbuster merger with Union Planters in 2004. Roughly two years later the company acquired fellow Birmingham-based bank AmSouth for nearly $10 billion in stock. The latter deal created one of the 10 largest banks in the US and helped Regions Financial keep pace with other megabanks in its markets such as Bank of America and SunTrust. The deals also helped entrench the company in states such as Alabama Arkansas Mississippi and Tennessee where it is a market leader.

EXECUTIVES

Executive Vice President Commercial Real Estate,
Rex Bradley
Chairman President and CEO, O. B. Grayson Hall,
$993,750 total compensation
SEVP and Head Corporate Banking Group, John
M. Turner, age 55
SEVP and Head General Bank, John B. Owen,
$641,500 total compensation

SEVP General Counsel and Corporate Secretary, Fournier J. (Boots) Gale, $555,000 total compensation

SEVP and President Mid-America Region, Ronald G. (Ronnie) Smith

SEVP and President South Region, William E. (Bill) Horton

SEVP and Strategic Planning and Execution, C. Keith Herron

SEVP; President East Region, Brett D. Couch

SEVP and Head Consumer Services Group, Scott M. Peters

SEVP and Head Wealth Management Group, William D. (Bill) Ritter

SEVP and CFO, David J. Turner, $627,250 total compensation

SEVP Operations and Technology, Cynthia M. (Cindy) Rogers

SEVP and Director Human Resources, David R. (Dave) Keenan

SEVP and Chief Credit Officer, Barbara (Barb) Godin

SEVP and Chief Risk Officer, C. Matthew Lusco, $550,000 total compensation

SEVP and CFO Business Operations and Support, Ellen Jones

Executive Vice President Business and Community Banking, Lynetta Steed

Senior Vice President Director of Operational and Information Risk, John (Jack) Haley

Vice President Finance, Dusty Rhodes

Senior Vice President Senior Credit Officer Commercial Real Estate, Aubrey Martin

Senior Vice President Of Infrastructure, James Pryor

Vice President, Amanda Morris

Vice President Business Banking, Nina Merchant

Vice President, Glena Dameron

Senior Vice President, Mary Hughes

Vice President Mortgage Production Manager, Daniel Brennan

Vice President Private Wealth Management, Paul Mitchell

Senior Vice President Business Banking Group, Pat O'Beirne

Vice President Finance, Diane Greenhaw

Senior Vice President Direct Marketing Manager, Jim Screws

Senior Vice President Risk Management, Tommy Tynes

Senior Vice President, Tom Simpson

Assistant Vice President Trust Operations, Chuck Pack

Branch Manager Vice President, Justin Powell

Vice President, Evin Lumsden

Vice President, Ed Cox

Senior Vice President, Bucky Croom

Vice President Mortgage Banker, Tiffany Davis

Senior Vice President Manager, Brenda Landers

Vice President Business Banking Workout, Terrell Barkley

Senior Vice President Asset Manager, Philip Cooper

Vice President Operations, Jane Sebeck

Vice President Business Development Support, Indira Hiremath

Vice President Corporate Accounting Close Out, Barbara (Barb) Glenn

Vice President, John Eubank

Assistant Vice President, Brian Wykle

Senior Vice President, Kim Bradley

Assistant Vice President Accounting Operations Manager, Janice Ray

Assistant Vice President, Lori Chambers

Vice President, Lyn Cone

Vice President Business Banking Sales Support, Ginger Blake

Vice President Branch Manager, Simone Small

Senior Vice President Applications and Core Systems, Dana Schneider

Executive Vice President Treasury Management Services, James Hicks

Vice President Private Banking, Joe Petriccione

Vice President Of Applications Development, Adam Senn

Vice President For Corporate Security, Amos Frazier

Vice President Treasury Management, Connie Livingston

Vice President bsa aml Compliance, Amy Wehner

Assistant Vice President Mortgage Loan Officer, Elizabeth Hickman

Senior Vice President, John (Jack) Boston

Senior Vice President, David (Dave) Neely

Assistant Vice President Branch Manager, Mitch Markus

Senior Vice President, Kevin Collins

Senior Vice President Human Resources, Hinton Taylor

Vice President, Lisa Law

Vice President, Paul Carruthers

Senior Vice President, Doug Kittrell

Senior Vice President Assistant General Counsel, Janine Smith

Senior Vice President, Susan Baker

Senior Vice President Commercial Banking, Bill Hinrichs

Branch Manager Vice President, Jennifer (Jen) de Conti

Vice President, McKenzie Shappley

Vice President, Melissa Rosado

Assistant Vice President Branch Relationship Manager, Josh Allen

Senior Vice President Relationship Marketing, Brooks Hubbard

Vice President, Stephanie Slade

Vice President Manager, Steve Rueve

Executive Vice President, Brandy Werner

Vice President, Scott Sarrat

Vice President Manager Leasing And Equipment Finan, Scott McClain

Financial Sales Director Vice President, Theresa Zeringue

Vice President Senior Recruiter Audit Compliance Finance and Risk, Sharon Chandler

Assistant Vice President BSA Aml Analyst, Heidi Holland

Vice President Site Manager, Vikki Kelley

Executive Vice President, Markel Wyatt

Senior Vice President Performance Management Integration, Brenda Brazil

Assistant Vice President Database Marketing Administrator, Quentin Carter

Senior Vice President Information Technology Compliance and Operational Risk, Abe DeLeon

Vice President Mortgage Operations, Keli Myers

Senior Vice President Relationship Manager, Christopher Sullivan

Vice President Issues Management, Chris Scribner

Vice President Responsible Lending Policy Officer, Janice Hovey

Assistant Vice President Corp Security For Ge, Michael (Mel) Cosper

Vice President Sbic Funds Manager, Kirk Mobley

Vice President Consumer Helpdesk, Gaynor Scogin

Vice President Area Sales Manager, Edward (Ed) Midyett

Vice President Business Development Officer, Thomas (Thom) Habel

Senior Vice President Database Marketing and Reporting, David (Dave) Bailey

Vice President Institutional Services, Scott Nailen

Executive Vice President Compensation and Benefits, Jill Shelton

Second Vice President, Frank Caley

Executive Vice President, Dave Smith

Vice President, Suzie Leatherbury

Vice President Commercial Real Estate, Todd Harris

Senior Vice President Consumer Sales Manager, Ken Knapp

Senior Vice President Director of Enterprise Risk, Chad Webb

Assistant Vice President Assistant Manager Interna, Angel Odom

Vice President Application Development Manager, Richard Weaver

Assistant Vice President, Valencia Jackson

Senior Vice President Manager Of Decision Sciences, Keith Harrah

Vice President, Jared Hall

Senior Vice President, Shelby Mackey

Vice President Associate and Risk Network Communications Officer, Susan (Sue) Anderson

Vice President Business Relationship Manager, Lacey Furr

Vice President Client Services Officer, Stuart White

Vice President, Jan Walton

Senior Vice President Risk Management Audit, Chad Fooshee

Assistant Vice President Senior Operations Auditor, Tammy Guthrie

Assistant Vice President Branch Manager, Mandy Kitzmiller

Vice President, Angela Whisenant

Senior Vice President, Donald Sinclair

Senior Vice President, Dave Hackney

Senior Vice President Senior Credit Officer, Peter Hull

Senior Vice President, Douglas Croker

Vice President Audit Manager internal Audit, Anna Hatcher Barnes

Vice President Area Human Resources Manager, Kristi Crossland

Senior Vice President Senior Commercial Portfolio Manager, Michael (Mel) Murphey

Vice President Senior Compliance and Operational Risk Auditor, Rusk Feltman

Executive Vice President Director of Emerging Credit Risk, Mark Jarema

Senior Vice President, John Gerety

Executive Vice President, Randall Shepard

Assistant Vice President Business Continuity, Kyle Puchta

Assistant Vice President Sba Underwriter, Lenzy Tipton

Vice President Branch Sales, Harold Putnam

Vice President, John Ziannis

Assistant Vice President, Contina Woods

Vice President, Pamela Thompson

Senior Vice President Risk Special Assets, Lynn Johnston

Vice President Operational Risk, Walt Autrey

Senior Vice President Senior Credit Officer, William Bateman

Vice President, Angela McKenzie

Vice President Customer Communications, Bret Pippen

Senior Vice President of Mortgage Systems, Ginger Ricchetti

Senior Vice President, Harry Waugh

Vice President Business Intelligence Analys, Robert (Bob) Butterfield

Senior Vice President, Dale Johnson

Vice President, Dana Allison

Vice President Organization and Leadership Development, David (Dave) Lyons

Vice President Corporate Banking, Dan Goller

Auditors: Ernst & Young LLP

LOCATIONS

HQ: Regions Financial Corp
1900 Fifth Avenue North, Birmingham, AL 35203
Phone: 205 581-7890
Web: www.regions.com

2014 Branch Locations

	No.
Florida	361
Tennessee	249

Alabama		239
Missippi		139
Georgia		136
Louisiana		109
Arkansas		96
Texas		81
Missouri		66
Indiana		63
Illinois		61
South Carolina		30
Kentucky		15
Iowa		13
North Carolina		6
Virginia		2
Total		**1,666**

PRODUCTS/OPERATIONS

2014 Sales

	$ mil.	% of total
Interest income		
Loans	2,941	55
Securities	615	11
Others	32	-
Non-interest income		
Service charges on deposits	695	14
Card and ATM fees	334	6
Mortgage income	149	3
Others	643	11
Total	**5,409**	**100**

Selected Products

Banking
  Checking
  Money Market
  Savings
  CDs
  Regions Visa CheckCard
  Business Checking
  Business Savings
  Merchant Services
  Treasury Management
  Payroll
  Audit Confirmations
Commercial Banking
  Deposit Services
  Treasury Management
  Online Services
  Merchant Services
  Global Trade Finance
  Corporate Trust
Private Wealth Management
  Solutions for Individuals
  Credit and Risk Management
  Wealth Management
  Solutions for Professionals

COMPETITORS

Arvest Bank	First Horizon
BB&T	First NBC Bank
BBVA Compass	Investar
Bancshares	JPMorgan Chase
Bank of America	SunTrust
Capital One	Synovus
Citigroup	Trustmark
First Citizens	Wells Fargo
BancShares	Woodforest Financial

HISTORICAL FINANCIALS

Company Type: Public

Income Statement

FYE: December 31

	ASSETS ($ mil.)	NET INCOME ($ mil.)	INCOME AS % OF ASSETS	EMPLOYEES
12/15	126,050	1,062	0.8%	23,916
12/14	119,679	1,155	1.0%	23,723
12/13	117,396	1,122	1.0%	24,255
12/12	121,347	1,120	0.9%	23,427
12/11	127,050	(215)	—	26,813
Annual Growth	**(0.2%)**	**—**	**—**	**(2.8%)**

2015 Year-End Financials

Debt ratio: 2.45%		No. of shares (mil.): 1,297
Return on equity: 6.28%		Dividends
Cash ($ mil.): 5,314		Yield: 2.4%
Current ratio: —		Payout: 31.5%
Long-term debt ($ mil.): —		Market value ($ mil.): 12,454

	STOCK PRICE ($) FY Close	P/E High/Low		Earnings	PER SHARE ($) Dividends	Book Value
12/15	9.60	14	12	0.75	0.23	12.98
12/14	10.56	14	11	0.80	0.18	12.55
12/13	9.89	13	9	0.77	0.10	11.44
12/12	7.13	11	6	0.71	0.04	10.97
12/11	4.30	—	—	(0.34)	0.04	13.11
Annual Growth	**22.2%**	**—**	**—**	**—**	**54.9%**	**(0.2%)**

Reinsurance Group of America, Inc.

Just what is reinsurance? Here hold this pile of insurance risk while we explain that holding company Reinsurance Group of America (RGA) is one of the largest life reinsurers in the US. RGA provides insurance companies with reinsurance on the risks they've taken on allowing them to reduce their liability and increase their business volume. Its operations are organized into three large groups: Global Mortality which covers individual life insurance policies; Global Group Health and Long-Term Care including critical illness coverage; and Global Financial Markets for annuities and financial coverage. RGA operates in about 30 countries in North America the Asia/Pacific Europe and South Africa.

Operations

The company's US operating unit RGA Reinsurance provides both traditional life reinsurance and reinsurance on investment assets such as annuities and corporate-owned life insurance policies. Its customers are generally large US-based life insurance companies. In addition to its traditional mortality-risk and asset reinsurance the US operations also offer financial reinsurance to help its customers meet regulatory requirements. Its Global Financial Solutions unit consists of three businesses: asset-intensive reinsurance financial reinsurance and longevity risk transfer.

The company also provides e-underwriting solutions to help customers write policies better and more quickly.

At the close of 2014 RGA had life reinsurance in force valued at about $3 trillion and about $45 billion in consolidated assets.

Geographic Reach

The US and Latin America accounted for 55% of its revenue in 2014.

The company is expanding internationally particularly in such emerging markets as China India Mexico and the Middle East. It has offices in Australia Barbados Bermuda Canada China France Germany Hong Kong India Ireland Italy Japan Malaysia Mexico the Netherlands New Zealand Poland Singapore South Africa South Korea Spain Taiwan Turkey the United Arab Emirates the UK and the US. Normal 0 false false false EN-US X-NONE X-NONE

Sales and Marketing

RGA's top five customers generate some $1.9 billion representing about one-fifth of its gross premiums.

Financial Performance

The company has seen revenue growth over the past five years. In 2014 revenue grew 6% to $10.9 billion mainly due to more life reinsurance in force and higher investment income (up 1%). Net income also rose 6% climbing to $684 million thanks to the increased revenue. Cash flow from operations which has been on a roller coaster rose 35% to $2.3 billion as a result of the higher net income a decline in cash used in accrued investment income and an increase in cash provided by deferred policy acquisition costs.

Strategy

RGA's strategy for growth has positioned the company well for harsh economic times and industry challenges. To achieve profitable results the company relies on its strong underwriting capabilities and disciplined pricing as well as geographic expansion and diversification in the products and services it offers. It is especially widening its mortality offerings in North America including facultative automatic and in-force block reinsurance. It also looks to leverage existing client relationships. In addition the company is looking to profit from the aging US population of baby boomers which is concerned with retirement income and estate planning.

As part of its efforts to diversify RGA has been seeking new longevity risk contracts. (Longevity risk refers to the risk of having to make payments to a retiree for a longer period than planned for if the person lives longer than expected.) Subsidiary RGA Canada signed an agreement in 2015 through which it will participate in a syndicated reinsurance transaction led by Sun Life Assurance Company of Canada. Through the transaction it will reinsure the longevity risks associated with pension obligations held by Canadian communications company BCE.

To help strengthen its underwriting capabilities RGA in 2014 selected Innodata subsidiary Synodex's data computing to assess life insurance risk and investigate claims. By using Synodex data RGA should improve its bottom line by cutting costs and by underwriting more quickly and consistently.

In recent years RGA has opened new offices in Turkey and China to expand its global presence. It is also constructing a new US headquarters building to meet future growth needs.

Mergers and Acquisitions

In 2013 RGA purchased Dutch life insurer Leidsche Verzekeringen Maatschappij for $12.5 million.

The following year it acquired Aurora National Life Assurance from Swiss Re; that business includes some 82000 policies in force (roughly two-thirds annuities and one-third life products). Then in 2015 RGA agreed to buy some $22 billion in term life reinsurance policies (approximately 290000 policies) from Ireland-based XL Group.

EXECUTIVES

SEVP and Head of EMEA Markets, Paul A. Schuster, $547,865 total compensation

SEVP and CFO, Jack B. Lay, $598,104 total compensation

President CEO and Director, A. Greig Woodring, $1,056,154 total compensation

EVP General Counsel and Secretary, William L. Hutton

EVP and Chief Risk Officer, Todd C. Larson, age 52

EVP and Chief of Staff, Robert M. Musen

EVP Global Financial Solutions and President RGA Financial Group L.L.C., John P. Laughlin

SEVP and COO, Donna H. Kinnaird, $535,750 total compensation

EVP and CIO, Mark E. Showers

EVP and Chief Human Resources Officer, Gay Burns
President, Anna Manning
EVP and Head Asia Markets, Allan E. O'Bryant, $463,631 total compensation
EVP Global Acquisitions, Scott D. Cochran
SEVP Global Life and Health Markets, Alain P. N @meh
EVP and Chief Investment Officer, Timothy (Tim) Matson
Senior Vice President And Chief Actuary, Doug Knowling
Vice President Deputy Compliance Counsel, Robert (Bob) Jett
Vice President And Senior Actuary Global Financial Solutions, Michael (Mel) Frings
Regional Vice President, Joseph Klimchak
Vice President Information Management And Analytics Services, Mike Foster
Senior Vice President Public Relations, Yuko Oshima
Vice President Business Development, Andr Dreyer
Vice President Actuary, Julie Decker
Vice President And Chief Actuary Latin America, Manuel Santos
Senior Vice President Operations, Jeffrey (Jeff) Birkholz
Senior Vice President, Brian Haynes
Vice President Finance, John (Jack) Hayden
Vice President, James Kellett
Vice President Investment Accounting, Sylvia Scheuler
Vice President Life Product Services, David (Dave) Burgoon
Vice President Regional Manager, Jeff Deters
Sales Vice President U S Individual Health, Winona Berdine
Vice President Information Technology Asia Pacific, Penny Snell
Vice President, Wendy Swanson
Senior Vice President Of The Latin American Division, Jaime Correa
Vice President Underwriting Operations, David Wheeler
Vice President, Donna Megregian
Senior Vice President Global Research And Development, Tim Rozar
Vice President Valuation And Financial Analysis, Chris Murphy
Vice President of Sales, Eric Riley
Vice President, Jeff Hopson
Vice President, David Vnenchak
Vice President, Brill John
Vice President Actuary, Brian Sibley
Vice President And Actuary, Dustin Hetzler
Information Technology Director Vice President, Matt Empey
Senior Vice President Heathcare, Steven Abood
Vice President Business Process and It, Carol Mahassek
Vice President Corporate Underwriting Auditor, Pat Bradley
Senior Vice President, Dave Fischer
Vice President Business Planning, Abraham Gootzeit
Vice President Credit Research And Risk Management, Scott Stone
Vice President Global Financial Solutions, Keith Politte
Vice President And Marketing Actuary, William Boyd
Vice President, Curt Zepeda
Vice President Information Technology Finance And Investment Solutions, Susan Nieman
Vice President Audit and Underwriting, Pamela M (Pam) Berger
Vice President Information Technology, Craig Smyth
Senior Vice President and Associate Gc, Dana Wiele

Vice President Information Technology Operations, Keith Smyth
Senior Vice President Corporate Actuary And Chief Risk Officer, Fsa Cochran
Senior Vice President Operations and Technology, Leonard (Len) Arokium
Chairman, J. Cliff Eason
Assistant Treasurer, Jeffrey Boyer
Auditors: Deloitte & Touche LLP

LOCATIONS

HQ: Reinsurance Group of America, Inc.
16600 Swingley Ridge Road, Chesterfield, MO 63017
Phone: 636 736-7000
Web: www.rgare.com

2014 Revenues

	$ mil.	% of total
US and Latin America	6,297	58
Asia/Pacific	1,756	16
Europe Middle East and Africa	1,557	14
Canada	1,181	11
Corporate & other	110	1
Total	**10,904**	**100**

Selected Countries of Operation

Australia
Barbados
Bermuda
Canada
China
France
Germany
Hong Kong
India
Ireland
Italy
Japan
Malaysia
Mexico
Netherlands
New Zealand
Poland
Singapore
South Africa
South Korea
Spain
Taiwan
Turkey
United Arab Emirates
UK
US

PRODUCTS/OPERATIONS

2014 Revenues

	$ mil.	% of total
Net premiums	8,669	79
Investment income	1,713	16
Investment gains	186	2
Other revenues	334	3
Total	**10,904**	**100**

Selected Products and Services

e-Underwriting solutions
Facultative and underwriting expertise
Financial solutions
Group reinsurance
Individual life reinsurance
Individual living benefits reinsurance
Product development

Selected Subsidiaries

Reinsurance Company of Missouri Incorporated (RCM)
RGA Americas Reinsurance Company Ltd. (RGA Americas)
RGA Atlantic Reinsurance Company Ltd. (RGA Atlantic)
RGA International Reinsurance Company (RGA International)
RGA Life Reinsurance Company of Canada (RGA Canada)
RGA Reinsurance Company (Barbados) Ltd. (RGA Barbados)
RGA Reinsurance Company (RGA Reinsurance)
RGA Reinsurance Company of Australia Limited (RGA Australia)

COMPETITORS

AEGON USA	Munich Re America
Berkshire Hathaway	Munich Re Group
General Re	SCOR Reinsurance
Generali	Swiss Re
Hannover Re	

HISTORICAL FINANCIALS

Company Type: Public

Income Statement

FYE: December 31

	ASSETS ($ mil.)	NET INCOME ($ mil.)	INCOME AS % OF ASSETS	EMPLOYEES
12/14	44,679	684	1.5%	2,070
12/13	39,674	418	1.1%	1,890
12/12	40,360	631	1.6%	1,766
12/11	32,104	599	1.9%	1,655
12/10	29,081	574	2.0%	1,535
Annual Growth	**11.3%**	**4.5%**	**—**	**7.8%**

2014 Year-End Financials

Debt ratio: 6.93%
Return on equity: 10.56%
Cash ($ mil.): 1,645
Current ratio: —
Long-term debt ($ mil.): —
No. of shares (mil.): 68
Dividends
  Yield: 1.4%
  Payout: 13.9%
Market value ($ mil.): 6,026

	STOCK PRICE ($) FY Close	P/E High/Low		PER SHARE ($) Earnings	Dividends	Book Value
12/14	87.62	9	7	9.78	1.26	102.13
12/13	77.41	13	9	5.78	1.08	83.87
12/12	53.52	7	6	8.52	0.84	93.47
12/11	52.25	8	6	8.09	0.60	83.65
12/10	53.71	7	6	7.69	0.48	68.71
Annual Growth	**13.0%**	**—**	**—**	**6.2%**	**27.3%**	**10.4%**

Reliance Steel & Aluminum Co.

Reliance Steel & Aluminum shows its mettle as North America's largest metals service center company. Through a network of 300-plus service and distribution centers (many dealing only in specialty metals) in 39 US states it processes and distributes more than 100000 metal products worldwide to more than 125000 customers in a broad range of industries. Reliance markets carbon alloy stainless steel and specialty steel products as well as aluminum brass copper and titanium products. Markets include the aerospace construction manufacturing semiconductor and electronics and transportation industries.

Geographic Reach

Reliance operates in 39 US states and in Australia Belgium Canada China Malaysia Mexico Singapore South Korea the UAE and the UK.

Operations

The company purchases a variety of metals from primary producers and sell these products in small quantities based on its customers' needs. It performed metals processing services or first-stage processing (45% of sales orders in 2014) before delivering the products to customers through a network of metals service centers. Carbon steel accounted for 54% of Reliance's revenues in 2014.

Sales and Marketing

Reliance has 2180 sales personnel in 44 US states and 12 other countries that provide marketing services. It also operates a fleet of 1780 trucks to service its smaller customers. It serves 125000 customers in a broad range of industries.

In February 2015 the metals service center industry it is estimated that there were approximately 10600 metal wholesale locations in the United States operated by approximately 7500 companies in 2014. The four largest U.S. metals service center companies represented less than 10% of the estimated $221.6 billion industry total in 2014. Based on this estimate their U.S. revenues of $9.80 billion in 2014 accounted for approximately 4.4% of the entire U.S. market. In 2014 approximately 97% of their orders were from repeat customers.

Financial Performance

The company recorded a steady increase in net revenues over the last five years.In 2014 revenues increased by 13% due to the acquisition of Metals USA in 2013 and a 6.1% growth in same-store tons sold.End markets that continued to perform well in 2014 were auto (primarily through the toll processing businesses in the US and Mexico) and aerospace. Manufacturing also performed reasonably well but sales began to decline in late 2014 as oil prices dropped rapidly and customers reduced spending. Non-residential construction its largest end market continued to improve modestly.

Reliance's net income increased by 16% due to higher net sales and the absence of impairment of intangible assets.Net cash provided by operating activities decreased by 44% due to a larger working capital (primarily accounts receivable and inventories) investment in 2014 as the result of an improved demand environment and increases in metal pricing.

Strategy

The company seeks to improve its operating results through organic growth activities and strategic acquisitions to enhance products add customers and increase its geographic diversification. Reliance believes that this strategy makes the company less vulnerable to regional or industry-specific economic volatility. Its internal growth activities includes opening new plants and adding to its processing capabilities or relocating centers to new facilities. It also continues to expand the types of metals it sells and the processing services it offers.Reliance focuses on improving the operating performance at acquired locations by integrating them into its operational model and providing it access to capital and other resources to promote growth and efficiencies. It also believes that its focus on servicing customers with small order sizes and quick turnaround along with its growth and diversification strategy have been instrumental in the company's ability to produce industry-leading operating results among publicly traded metals service center companies in North America. The company continues to pursue internal growth by opening new facilities building or expanding existing facilities and adding processing equipment.

Since its IPO in 1994 Reliance has been on something of a spending binge buying up a number of smaller rivals. The company has grown significantly over the years through a series of acquisitions both large and small. It has successfully purchased 59 businesses including three acquisitions in 2014.

Mergers and Acquisitions

In 2014 Reliance acquired Aluminium Services UK Limited the holding company parent of All Metal Services the world's largest independent raw material service provider to the aerospace and defense industries supporting customers in more than 40 countries worldwide.

That year it also bought Fox Metals and Alloys (a Houston Texas-based steel distributor specializing in alloy carbon and stainless steel bar and plate products primarily servicing OEMs and ma-

chine shops that serve the oil gas and petrochemical industries) and Northern Illinois Steel Supply (a value-added distributor and fabricator of a variety of steel and non-ferrous metal products primarily structural steel components and parts for the energy and petrochemical sectors).

The company bought Metals USA in 2013 for $786 million. Metals USA makes a wide range of products and services in the heavy carbon steel flat-rolled steel non-ferrous metals and building products markets. The acquisition adds 48 service centers across the US to Reliance's existing operations and complements its existing customer base product mix and geographic footprint.

That year it also acquired Travel Main Holdings LLC a real estate holding company with a portfolio of 18 real estate properties all of which are leased by certain of its subsidiaries. The $78.9 million deal included the assumption of $43.8 million of debt.

Company Background

In 2012 the company acquired through subsidiary Feralloy Corporation Alabama-based GH Metal Solutions for an undisclosed price. GH Metal is a carbon steel products processor and fabricator with about $44 million in annual sales.

That year it moved to expand its operations in Tennessee again when subsidiary Precision Strip acquired the Worthington Steel Vonore plant part of Worthington Industries for an undisclosed price. The plant processes and distributes carbon steel aluminum and stainless steel products on a toll basis (processing the metal for a fee without taking ownership of it).

A key addition for serving energy companies came in 2011 when Reliance acquired Houston-based Continental Alloys & Services for about $200 million. Continental is a materials management company that supplies steel and alloy pipe tube and bar products and manufactures various tools designed for energy service companies. It has 12 locations in seven countries.

The company was founded in 1939.

EXECUTIVES

President Valex, Daniel A. Mangan
President CCC Steel, Brian M. Tenenbaum
SEVP and CFO, Karla R. Lewis, age 50, $532,500 total compensation
EVP Operations, William K. Sales, age 58, $482,000 total compensation
President and CEO, Gregg J. Mollins, age 60, $712,500 total compensation
Co-Managing Director All Metal Services, David L. Potts
President AMI Metals, Scott A. Smith
EVP Operations, James D. Hoffman, age 56, $482,000 total compensation
Managing Director Metalweb, Bruce Maggs
President and CEO Metals USA, Robert C. McPherson, age 51
President Allegheny Steel Distributors, Bernie J. Herrmann
President Precision Strip, Joseph B. Wolf
President Pacific Metal, John S. Nosler
President Toma Metals, Daniel T. Yunetz
President Infra-Metals, Mark A Haight, age 56
President Earle M. Jorgensen Co., James Desmond
SVP Operations, Stephen P. (Steve) Koch, age 48, $417,000 total compensation
President Siskin Steel & Supply, Paul J. Loftin
President Yarde Metals, Matthew L. (Matt) Smith
President Sugar Steel, Robert J. Sugar
President Chapel Steel, Stanley J. (Stan) Altman
President Clayton Metals, Brian K. Cleveland
CIO, Susan C. Borchers, age 54
President Feralloy Corp., Carlos Rodriguez-Borjas
President American Metals, Nicole Heater
President Crest Steel, Kristofer M. Farris

President Delta Steel, Eric J. Offenberger
President Diamond Manufacturing, David L. Simpson
SVP Operations, Michael P. Shanley
President National Specialty Alloys, Mark Russ
President Precision Flamecutting and Steel, John D. Murray
President Service Steel Aerospace, Douglas Nesbitt
President Sunbelt Steel Texas, Michael Kowalski
President Viking Materials, Michael Allen
President Chatham Steel, Jerome Rooney
President Precision Strip, Joseph P. Wolf
President Continental Alloys & Services, Randall C. (Randy) Zajicek
Co-Managing Director All Metal Services, Ronald T. Stocker
President Liebovich Bros. Inc., David Corirossi
President Northern Illinois Steel Supply Company, Michael J. Ruth
President and COO PDM Steel Service Centers Inc., Sean Mollins
President Phoenix Metals Company, Barry L. Epps
Vice President General Counsel & Corporate Secretary, William (Bill) Smith
Vice President, Donald Prebola
Vice President Purchasing and Operations, John (Jack) Inglis
Chairman, David H. (Dave) Hannah, age 64
Auditors: KPMG LLP

LOCATIONS

HQ: Reliance Steel & Aluminum Co.
350 South Grand Avenue, Suite 5100, Los Angeles, CA 90071
Phone: 213 687-7700
Web: www.rsac.com

2014 Sales by Region

	% of total
US	
Midwest	30
Southeast	18
West/Southwest	17
California	9
Mid-Atlantic	7
Northeast	6
Pacific Northwest	4
Mountain	3
Other countries	6
Total	**100**

PRODUCTS/OPERATIONS

2014 Sales by Commodity

	% of total
Carbon Steel	54
Aluminum	15
Stainless Steel	14
Alloy	9
Toll Processing	2
Other	6
Total	**100**

Selected Processing Services

Bending
Blanking
Cutting-to-length
Electropolishing
Fabricating
Pipe Threading
Precision plate sawing
Shape cutting/burning
Skin milling
Slitting
Tee splitting and straightening
Welding

COMPETITORS

A. M. Castle	Ryerson
Balli	Steel Technologies
O' Neal Steel	Ternium Mexico
Olympic Steel	Worthington Industries
Russel Metals	

HISTORICAL FINANCIALS
Company Type: Public

Income Statement
FYE: December 31

	REVENUE ($ mil.)	NET INCOME ($ mil.)	NET PROFIT MARGIN	EMPLOYEES
12/14	10,451	371	3.6%	14,900
12/13	9,223	321	3.5%	14,000
12/12	8,442	403	4.8%	11,600
12/11	8,134	343	4.2%	10,650
12/10	6,312	194	3.1%	9,610
Annual Growth	13.4%	17.6%	—	11.6%

2014 Year-End Financials

Debt ratio: 29.56%
Return on equity: 9.32%
Cash ($ mil.): 106
Current ratio: 4.71
Long-term debt ($ mil.): 2,222

No. of shares (mil.): 77
Dividends
  Yield: 2.2%
  Payout: 32.3%
Market value ($ mil.): 4,738

	STOCK PRICE ($) FY Close	P/E High/Low		PER SHARE ($) Earnings	Dividends	Book Value
12/14	61.27	16	12	4.73	1.40	53.00
12/13	75.84	18	15	4.14	1.26	50.00
12/12	62.10	12	8	5.33	0.80	46.79
12/11	48.69	13	7	4.58	0.48	41.91
12/10	51.10	21	13	2.61	0.40	37.83
Annual Growth	4.6%	—	—	16.0%	36.8%	8.8%

Renasant Corp

Those who are cognizant of their finances may want to do business with Renasant Corporation. The holding company owns Renasant Bank which serves consumers and local business through about 80 locations in Alabama Georgia Mississippi and Tennessee. The bank offers standard products such as checking and savings accounts CDs credit cards and loans and mortgages as well as trust retail brokerage and retirement plan services. Its loan portfolio is dominated by residential and commercial real estate loans. The bank also offers agricultural business construction and consumer loans and lease financing. Subsidiary Renasant Insurance sells personal and business coverage.

Financial Performance
The company's revenue increased in fiscal 2013 compared to the prior year. It reported revenue of $252.6 million for fiscal 2013 up from $228 million in revenue for fiscal 2012.

Renasant's net income also went up in fiscal 2013 compared to the previous fiscal period. It reported net income of about $33.5 million for fiscal 2013 up from net income of $26.6 million in fiscal 2012.

The company's cash on hand decreased by about $24 million in fiscal 2013 compared to fiscal 2012 levels.

Strategy
Renasant has looked to diversify its loan portfolio. The bank has reduced its amount of loans for construction and land development —a sector that has been hit particularly hard —by tightening its underwriting standards.It's also been growing through acquistions. In late 2014 for example Renasant purchased Heritage Financial Group in an all stock merger deal that amounted to $258 million. The move added $1.9 billion in assets $1.2 billion in loan assets and $1.3 billion in deposit assets to Renasant's collection. In addition the move

significantly expanded the bank's geographic reach adding 48 banking mortgage and investment offices in Alabama Florida and Georgia. All told the deal made Renasant one of the largest community banks in the Southeast region of the United States.

EXECUTIVES

Chairman and CEO, E. Robinson (Robin) McGraw, age 68, $600,000 total compensation
President and COO Renasant Corporation and Renasant Bank, C. Mitchell (Mitch) Waycaster, age 57, $320,000 total compensation
EVP; President Northern Division, R. Rick Hart, age 67, $433,300 total compensation
EVP, Michael D. Ross, age 51, $320,000 total compensation
CFO and EVP, Kevin D. Chapman, $280,000 total compensation
Executive Vice President and Chief Operating Officer, John (Jack) Gregory
Vice President Information Technology, Barbara (Barb) Daniels
Senior Vice President, Gregory Goldberg
First Vice President, Lisa Fite
Auditors: HORNE LLP

LOCATIONS

HQ: Renasant Corp
  209 Troy Street, Tupelo, MS 38804-4827
Phone: 662 680-1001
Web: www.renasant.com

COMPETITORS

BBVA Compass Bancshares	First Horizon
BancorpSouth	Hancock Holding
Citizens Holding	Regions Financial
Citizens National Bank of Meridian	Trustmark

HISTORICAL FINANCIALS
Company Type: Public

Income Statement
FYE: December 31

	ASSETS ($ mil.)	NET INCOME ($ mil.)	INCOME AS % OF ASSETS	EMPLOYEES
12/14	5,805	59	1.0%	1,471
12/13	5,746	33	0.6%	1,483
12/12	4,178	26	0.6%	1,096
12/11	4,202	25	0.6%	1,030
12/10	4,297	31	0.7%	996
Annual Growth	7.8%	17.1%	—	10.2%

2014 Year-End Financials

Debt ratio: 1.63%
Return on equity: 8.65%
Cash ($ mil.): 161
Current ratio: —
Long-term debt ($ mil.): —

No. of shares (mil.): 31
Dividends
  Yield: 2.3%
  Payout: 36.1%
Market value ($ mil.): 913

	STOCK PRICE ($) FY Close	P/E High/Low		PER SHARE ($) Earnings	Dividends	Book Value
12/14	28.93	17	14	1.88	0.68	22.56
12/13	31.46	26	15	1.22	0.68	21.21
12/12	19.14	19	14	1.06	0.68	19.80
12/11	15.00	17	12	1.02	0.68	19.44
12/10	16.91	13	9	1.38	0.68	18.75
Annual Growth	14.4%	—	—	8.0%	(0.0%)	4.7%

Republic Bancorp, Inc. (KY)

The second-largest bank holding company based in Kentucky Republic Bancorp is the parent of Republic Bank & Trust whichÂhasÂabout 40 branches inÂcentral Kentucky and southern Indiana. It also owns Republic Bank a thrift with a handful of branches in metropolitan TampaÂand a single location in the Cincinnati area.ÂIn 2012 Republic Bancorp entered the Nashville and Minneapolis marketÂthrough theÂFDIC-assisted acquisitions of the failedÂ Tennessee Commerce BankÂ and FirstÂ Commercial Bank respectively.ÂThe company's banksÂoffer deposit accounts loans and mortgages credit cards private banking and trust services.

Republic Bancorp's lendingÂactivities mainly consistÂof residential mortgages and commercial real estate loans which together account for some three-fourths of the company's loan book. The companyÂalso offered loans secured by income tax refunds throughout the US. The segment provided refund anticipation loans to more than 3 million customers in 2010 but came under fire from regulators. That year theÂInternal Revenue Service announced it would stop supplying Debt Indicator information (used to determineÂwhether aÂtaxpayer is creditworthy) to institutions that issue such loans. As a result theÂFDIC in 2011 announced that Republic Bank & Trust's origination of refund anticipation loans withoutÂDebt Indication information was unsafe and issued a cease-and-desist order; the tax season of 2012 was the final season the company offered the loans.

Income tax refund loans are typically offered to unbanked and underbanked customers. Republic Bancorp hopes to otherwise tap into that market which includes some 30 million US households by offering nontraditional banking products. To that end the company is also offering prepaid cards. In addition Republic also offers electronic refund checks and deposits which carry no risk to the company.

In 2011 the company entered the warehouse lending business through which it offers short-term credit facilities secured by single-family residences to mortgage bankers nationwide. The move follows somewhat of a trend of community banks adding to their commercial loan operations by offering warehouse lending. Within a year Republic had committed lines of credit totaling some $108 million.

Republic Bancorp's revenues grew 12% in 2011 from $281 million in 2010 to $314 million. Profits grew even more from $65 million in 2010 to $94 million in 2011 (an increase of 45%). The growth was largely driven by an increase in net interest and noninterest income in the company's tax refund solutions segment. Republic also decreased its provision for loan losses in 2011. To offset declines in net interest income from its traditional banking segment the company has tweaked its investment strategy as well as boosted its loan portfolio through acquisitions. Republic has also cut its operating expenses.

The Trager family including the estate of founder Bernard his son Steven (chairman and CEO) and nephew Scott (president) controls a majority of Republic Bancorp.

EXECUTIVES

Vice Chairman; President Republic Bank & Trust,
  A. Scott Trager, age 62, $350,000 total compensation

President and CEO; CEO Republic Bank & Trust, Steven E. (Steve) Trager, age 54, $353,000 total compensation

EVP CFO and Chief Accounting Officer Republic Bancorp and Republic Bank & Trust, Kevin Sipes, age 43, $281,500 total compensation

Vice President Director of Prepaid, David (Dave) Jenkins

Senior Vice President, Nancy Presnell

Assistant Vice President Systems Administrator Pro, Sandro Luis Fajardo

Vice President and Director Processing, Gerard Mattingly

Senior Vice President, Lisa Butcher

Assistant Vice President Technology Services Managerand#8230; Scott Estes

Assistant Vice President Finance Project Manager, Tim Wheatley

Vice President Accounting, Peggy Wakefield

Vice President Project Services Manager, Michelle (Mitch) Cunningham

Vice President Technology Services, Sean Omahoney

Assistant Vice President Assistant Fin, Lara Recktenwald

Vice President, John (Jack) Rippy

Senior Vice President, Barbara (Barb) Trager

Vice President and Controller, Mike Newton

Senior Vice President Chief Marketing Officer, Michael (Mel) Sadofsky

Assistant Vice President Banking Center Supervisor, Robin Verenna

Chairman, Bernard M. Trager, age 86

Auditors: Crowe Horwath LLP

LOCATIONS

HQ: Republic Bancorp, Inc. (KY)
601 West Market Street, Louisville, KY 40202
Phone: 502 584-3600
Web: www.republicbank.com

PRODUCTS/OPERATIONS

2011 Sales

	$ mil.	% of total
Interest		
Loans including fees	177	56
Taxable investment securities	15	5
Other	2	1
Noninterest		
Electronic refund check fees	88	28
Service charges on deposit accounts	14	4
Debit card interchange fees	5	2
Mortgage banking	3	1
Gain on sale of banking center & other	7	3
Adjustments	(0.3)	-
Total	**314**	**100**

COMPETITORS

BB&T	Home Federal
Bank of America	KeyCorp
Citizens First	PNC Financial
Community Trust	Stock Yards Bancorp
Farmers Capital Bank	U.S. Bancorp
Fifth Third	

HISTORICAL FINANCIALS

Company Type: Public

Income Statement

FYE: December 31

	ASSETS ($ mil.)	NET INCOME ($ mil.)	INCOME AS % OF ASSETS	EMPLOYEES
12/14	3,747	28	0.8%	735
12/13	3,371	25	0.8%	750
12/12	3,394	119	3.5%	820
12/11	3,419	94	2.8%	728
12/10	3,622	64	1.8%	766
Annual Growth	0.8%	(18.3%)	—	(1.0%)

2014 Year-End Financials

Debt ratio: 1.10%	No. of shares (mil.): 20
Return on equity: 5.23%	Dividends
Cash ($ mil.): 72	Yield: 2.9%
Current ratio: —	Payout: 53.4%
Long-term debt ($ mil.): —	Market value ($ mil.): 515

	STOCK PRICE ($) FY Close	P/E High/Low		PER SHARE ($) Earnings	Dividends	Book Value
12/14	24.72	18	16	1.38	0.74	26.80
12/13	24.54	23	17	1.22	0.69	26.09
12/12	21.13	5	3	5.69	1.75	25.60
12/11	22.90	5	4	4.49	0.61	21.59
12/10	23.75	8	5	3.10	0.56	17.74
Annual Growth	1.0%	—	—	(18.3%)	7.1%	10.9%

Republic Services, Inc.

Homeowners and businesses across the US and in Puerto Rico pledge allegiance to Republic Services and the trash collection for which it stands. The company is the second-largest nonhazardous waste management provider in the US behind leader Waste Management in terms of revenues and geographic coverage. Republic provides waste disposal services for commercial industrial municipal and residential customers through its network of 340 collection companies. The company owns or operates 189 solid waste landfills 198 transfer stations and 60 recycling centers. It also has 72 landfill-to-gas and a handful of other renewable energy projects.

HISTORY

Republic Services began in 1980 as Republic Resources an oil exploration and production company. In 1989 after a stockholder group tried to force Republic into liquidation Browning-Ferris (BFI) founder Thomas Fatjo stepped in gained control of Republic Resources and refocused it on a field he knew well –solid waste. Renamed Republic Waste the company began making acquisitions.

In 1990 Michael DeGroote founder of BFI competitor Laidlaw bought into Republic Waste. In 1995 Wayne Huizenga –who co-founded Waste Management in 1971 and was beginning to develop a national auto sales organization in the mid-1990s after his tenure as chairman and CEO of Blockbuster Entertainment –approached DeGroote about a deal. They rejected an immediate merger of the waste and auto businesses because the latter was not well-enough developed and would drag down Republic's numbers. Instead they agreed to merge Republic and the Hudson Companies (a trash business owned by Huizenga's brother-in-law Harris Hudson) to sell Huizenga a large interest in Republic through a private offering and to

give him control of the board (in 1995). The company became Republic Industries.

Huizenga's investment brought a flood of new investors. With new resources Republic Industries became a driving force in the garbage industry's consolidation binge and the company bought more than 100 smaller waste haulers between 1995 and 1998. Republic Industries spun off about 30% of its waste business as Republic Services in 1998; the IPO raised $1.3 billion. Republic's acquisition trend continued as it agreed to buy 16 landfills 136 commercial collection routes and 11 transfer stations from Waste Management for $500 million. Later that year Waste Management veteran James O'Connor succeeded Huizenga as CEO although Huizenga continued as chairman.

Investors filed class-action lawsuits against Republic in 1999 claiming the Waste Management purchases held far more integration problems than the company admitted. In 2000 Republic swapped nine of its solid-waste operations for eight Allied Waste businesses which Allied needed to divest in order to gain federal approval for its merger with BFI.

While many firms in the industry were selling off assets in 2001 Republic was expanding its operations in the Northern California market by acquiring Richmond Sanitary Services. Huizenga retired as chairman at the end of 2002 and was once again succeeded by O'Connor. Huizenga stayed on the board as a director until May 2004.

In 2007 the company sold Living Earth Technology Company (a noncore stand-alone business in Texas) for about $37 million. In 2008 prior to its megadeal with Allied Waste Republic rebuffed a takeover bid by industry leader Waste Management.

In late 2008 Republic Services the once #3 industry player acquired #2 company Allied Waste for $6 billion to place it closer to industry leader Waste Management in terms of revenues and geographic coverage. Following the acquisition Republic divested assets in seven markets (six municipal solid waste landfills six collection businesses and three transfer stations) in order to meet US antitrust regulations.

During 2012 the company invested $76 million on five recycling centers and plans to continue to look for opportunities to expand its recycling capabilities.

EXECUTIVES

President and CEO, Donald W. (Don) Slager, $1,000,000 total compensation

Vice President Business Development, Marc Scott

EVP and Chief Development Officer, Brian A. Bales

EVP and COO, Robert (Rob) Maruster, age 43, $247,692 total compensation

Region President Central Region, Justin C. Boswell

EVP Human Resources, Jeffrey A. (Jeff) Hughes, $428,400 total compensation

EVP General Counsel and Corporate Secretary, Michael P. (Mike) Rissman, $408,000 total compensation

EVP Customer Development, Jon Vander Ark

Region President East Region, Tim Stuart

SVP and CIO, Bill Halnon

EVP and CFO, Charles F. (Chuck) Serianni, age 53, $343,823 total compensation

Region President West Region, Nathan Cabbil

Senior Vice President Treasurer, Edward A Lang

Vice President Engineering and Environmental Services, Joe Benco

Vice President Information Systems, Richard (Dick) Simon

Senior Vice President Finance And Administration, Fred Hays

Vice President, Andrea Sohnly

Vice President Purchasing, Nick Stefkovich

LOCATIONS

HQ: Republic Services, Inc.
  18500 North Allied Way, Phoenix, AZ 85054
Phone: 480 627-2700
Web: www.republicservices.com

2014 Sales

	$ mil.	% of total
West	3,489	40
Central	2,622	30
East	2,498	28
Corporate Entities	178	2
Total	**8,788**	**100**

PRODUCTS/OPERATIONS

2014 Sales

	$ mil.	% of total
Collection		
Commercial	2,723	31
Residential	2,193	25
Industrial	1,784	20
Other	37	1
Landfill Operations		
Landfill	1,086	12
Transfer net	408	5
Set of recycled Commodities	390	4
Other Non-core	164	2
Total	**8,788**	**100**

COMPETITORS

Casella Waste Systems	WCA Waste
Progressive Waste	Waste Connections
Recology	Waste Industries USA
Rumpke	Waste Management
Safety-Kleen	

HISTORICAL FINANCIALS

Company Type: Public

Income Statement

FYE: December 31

	REVENUE ($ mil.)	NET INCOME ($ mil.)	NET PROFIT MARGIN	EMPLOYEES
12/15	9,115	749	8.2%	33,000
12/14	8,788	547	6.2%	31,000
12/13	8,417	588	7.0%	31,000
12/12	8,118	571	7.0%	30,000
12/11	8,192	589	7.2%	30,000
Annual Growth	**2.7%**	**6.2%**	**—**	**2.4%**

2015 Year-End Financials

Debt ratio: 36.81%	No. of shares (mil.): 345
Return on equity: 9.66%	Dividends
Cash ($ mil.): 32	Yield: 2.6%
Current ratio: 0.67	Payout: 65.1%
Long-term debt ($ mil.): 7,568	Market value ($ mil.): 15,203

	STOCK PRICE ($) FY Close	P/E High/Low	PER SHARE ($) Earnings	Dividends	Book Value
12/15	43.99	21 18	2.13	1.16	22.49
12/14	40.25	27 20	1.53	1.08	21.96
12/13	33.20	22 18	1.62	0.99	21.93
12/12	29.33	20 16	1.55	0.91	21.33
12/11	27.55	21 16	1.56	0.84	20.77
Annual Growth	**12.4%**	**— —**	**8.1%**	**8.4%**	**2.0%**

Reynolds American Inc

Hot does not begin to describe Reynolds American Inc. (RAI). The holding company holds the #2 spot among US makers of cigarettes and smokeless tobacco through RJR Tobacco (smokeless) and American Snuff. RJR Tobacco produces many of the top-selling cigarette brands: Camel Doral Kool Pall Mall Newport Salem and Winston. It also makes and markets smoke-free Camel tobacco products. American Snuff offers moist snuff under the value-priced Grizzly and premium Kodiak brands. RAI businesses include cigarette makers Santa Fe Natural Tobacco and Lorillard and nicotine gum maker Niconovum. RAI is the result of a merger of R.J. Reynolds Tobacco and Brown & Williamson a subsidiary of British American Tobacco that owns 42% of RAI.

Operations

Reynolds American (RAI) operates through the R. J. Reynolds Tobacco Company (aka RJR Tobacco) which accounts for more than 80% of its total sales and ranks as the second-largest cigarette maker in the US. Its familiar brands include Camel Pall Mall Winston Cool Doral and Salem. RAI's smokeless tobacco business American Snuff represents 9% of sales while Santa Fe Natural Tobacco (8% of sales) manufactures and sells cigarettes and other tobacco products under the Natural American Spirit brand. Santa Fe products are made from all natural additive-free tobacco. RAI's Niconovum USA subsidiary (acquired in 2009) makes nicotine replacement gum mouth spray and pouches under the Zonnic brand name in Sweden. R.J. Reynolds Vapor Company makes electronic cigarettes under the VUSE name for limited distribution.

The company's Lorillard subsidiary (pocketed in 2015) makes Newport Kent Old Gold and True cigarette brands as well as SKYCIG e-cigarettes.

Geographic Reach

RJR Tobacco's manufacturing plants are in the Winston-Salem North Carolina area while American Snuff's facilities are in Memphis Tennessee; Clarksville Tennessee; and Winston-Salem North Carolina. Santa Fe's manufacturing plant is in Oxford North Carolina and Lorillard produces cigarettes in Greensboro North Carolina.

Sales and Marketing

RJR Tobacco distributes its cigarettes primarily through a combination of direct wholesale deliveries from a local distribution center and public warehouses throughout the US. Its largest customer is McLane Company one of the nation's largest distributors of grocery and tobacco products. McLane accounted for 31% of the tobacco products maker's revenue in 2014 while sale to distributor Core-Mark accounted for about 11%.

RAI reported advertising costs of $140 million $110 million and $72 million for 2014 2013 and 2012 respectively.

Financial Performance

RAI has struggled to grow sales in its core business amid the decline in cigarette smoking in the US. However in 2014 the company reported a 3% increase in revenues thanks to a 1% growth in RJR Tobacco due to higher net pricing; a 5% growth in American Snuff due to higher pricing and an increase in moist snuff volume.Net income increased by 14% in 2014 due to higher selling general and administrative expenses and the cost of products sold.

RAI's operating cash flow increased by 24% in 2014 due to cash generated from pension and postretirement.

Strategy

Sales and profits in the US cigarette industry and RJR Tobacco are under assault from falling consumption increases in state excise taxes and governmental regulations and restrictions such as marketing limitations public smoking bans and more. In response RAI is seeking to transition its customers from cigarettes to the use of its smokeless tobacco products such as Camel Snus (small pouches filled with tobacco that users stick between the cheek and gum). Indeed in contrast to the declining US cigarette market US moist snuff volumes grew about 2% in 2014. Profit margins on these smokeless products are generally higher than of cigarettes.

RJR Tobacco's marketing approach uses a retail pricing strategy including discounting at retail to defend certain brands' shares of market against competitive pricing pressure.

In 2014 the company sold Reynolds Building to a partnership consisting of PMC Property Group and Kimpton Hotels & Restaurants for $7.8 million.

After paying just $340 million for Sante Fe Natural Tobacco in 2002 RAI sold the brand's overseas rights to Japanese Tobacco in 2015 for $5 billion. It retained the US rights where the brand has been growing quickly while letting a company with an established global distribution apparatus take over international sales.

Mergers and Acquisitions

In mid-2015 RJR Tobacco completed its acquisition of Lorillard Inc. the maker of Newport brand cigarettes for a total of $27.4 billion. The combination of two of the nation's oldest and biggest tobacco companies created a formidable #2 to rival Altria Group Inc. owner of Philip Morris USA. The companies sold the Kool Salem Winston Maverick and blu eCig brands to Imperial Tobacco Group for $7.1 billion to ease regulatory concerns about competition.

HISTORY

R. J. Reynolds formed the R.J. Reynolds Tobacco Company in 1875 in Winston North Carolina to produce chewing tobacco. In the late 1890s Reynolds lost two-thirds of the company to the American Tobacco Trust but he regained control in 1911 after the trust was dismantled by the government. Two years later the company introduced Camel.

After Reynolds died in 1918 leadership passed to Bowman Gray whose family ran the company for the next 50 years. Camel held the #1 or #2 cigarette position throughout the 1930s and 1940s and Reynolds became the largest domestic cigarette company. In response to growing health concerns in the 1950s the company introduced its filtered Winston (1954) and Salem (1956) brands.

In response to growing antismoking sentiment Reynolds Tobacco began diversifying into foods and other nontobacco businesses beginning in the 1960s. Acquisitions included Chun King Patio Foods American Independent Oil Del Monte Inglenook wines Smirnoff vodka Kentucky Fried Chicken Sunkist beverages and Canada Dry all of which it had sold by 1991. In September 1985 Reynolds acquired Nabisco Brands (Newtons Oreo Planters nuts) for $4.9 billion. In 1986 the parent company was re-named RJR Nabisco Inc.

In November 1988 RJR Nabisco agreed to be acquired by Kohlberg Kravis Roberts (KKR). The deal valued in excess of $25 billion closed in April 1989. After being privately held for a period KKR took RJR Nabisco Holdings public in 1991. In early 1995 KKR divested its remaining holdings in RJR Nabisco. Also that year Andrew Schindler was promoted to CEO of the firm.

Prior to 1999 RJR was a subsidiary of RJR Nabisco Holdings Corp. (RJRN). In 1999 following the sale of the company's international tobacco business to Japan Tobacco for $8 billion the remaining tobacco and food businesses were separated and RJRN was renamed Nabisco Group Holdings Corp. (NGH). In June the former parent company RJRN was renamed RJ Reynolds Tobacco Holdings Inc. and became an independent publicly traded company again with RJ Reynolds Tobacco Company as its wholly owned subsidiary. (The separation was accomplished through a spinoff of the domestic tobacco business to RJR Nabisco stockholders.)

In January 2002 RJRT acquired the Santa Fe Natural Tobacco Company maker of the Natural American Spirit additive-free cigarette brand for $340 million in cash.

In September 2003 the company said it would focus marketing activities on its Camel and Salem brands. It also launched a two-year plan to cut costs by $1 billion which included cutting jobs by 40%. By the end of 2003 RJRT had cut 1400 jobs. Shortly thereafter the company announced merger plans with Brown & Williamson.

Before combining with RJRT to create Reynolds American in July 2004 Brown & Williamson had been ordered to cut back on promoting its Kool brand which was associated with hip-hop music. The issue carried over to Reynolds American which agreed in October 2004 to settle several related lawsuits in New York Illinois and Maryland by paying $1.5 million toward antismoking campaigns and severely restricting Kool promotions that critics said targeted Black youth.

EXECUTIVES

President Niconovum AB and Niconovum USA, Tommy J. Payne, age 58, $399,275 total compensation
President Santa Fe Natural Tobacco, Michael A. (Mike) Little, age 55
EVP Operations and Chief Scientific Officer R.J. Reynolds Tobacco Company, Jeffery S. (Jeff) Gentry, age 58, $490,850 total compensation
EVP and Chief Human Resources Officer Reynolds American and RAI Services, Lisa J. Caldwell, age 56
EVP and CFO, Andrew D. Gilchrist, age 42, $628,575 total compensation
SVP General Counsel and Secretary Reynolds American and RAI Services Company, Martin L. (Mark) Holton, age 57, $568,225 total compensation
EVP Public Affairs Reynolds American R.J. Reynolds Tobacco R.J. Reynolds Vapor Company and RAI Services, Robert H. (Rob) Dunham, age 48
President American Snuff Company, Randall M. (Mick) Spach, age 56
President and COO R.J. Reynolds Tobacco, Debra A. Crew, age 44, $155,000 total compensation
President and CEO; President RAI Services, Susan M. Cameron, age 56
President R.J. Reynolds Vapor Company, Frederic P. (Fred) Ampolini, age 50
Vice President Investor Relations, Ken Whitehurst
Vice President Media Relations, Maura T Payne

Vice President And Internal Auditor, Susan (Sue) Wilson
Chairman, Thomas C. (Tom) Wajnert, age 71
Senior Vice President Treasurer, Daniel A (Dan) Fawley
Auditors: KPMG LLP

LOCATIONS

HQ: Reynolds American Inc
401 North Main Street, Winston-Salem, NC 27101
Phone: 336 741-2000   **Fax:** 336 728-8888
Web: www.reynoldsamerican.com

PRODUCTS/OPERATIONS

2014 Sales

	$ mil.	% of total
RJR Tobacco	6,767	80
American Snuff	783	9
Santa Fe	658	8
Other	263	3
Total	**8,417**	**100**

Selected Brands
American Snuff (smokeless tobacco)
  Grizzly
  Kodiak
Lorillard
  Kent
  Newport
  Old Gold
  True
  SKYCIG (e-cigarettes)
RJR Tobacco (cigarettes)
  Camel
  Camel Dissolvables (smoke-free tobacco)
  Orbs
  Sticks
  Strips
  Camel Snus (smoke-free pouch)
  Capri
  Misty
  Pall Mall
  State Express 555 (RJR' s super-premium cigarette licensed from British American Tobacco)
  VUSE (e-cigarettes)
Santa Fe Natural Tobacco
  Natural American Spirit
Other
  Niconovum (nicotine replacement therapies)

COMPETITORS

Auri	Rock Creek
Commonwealth Brands	Pharmaceuticals
GSK Italy	Smokin Joes
JT International	Swisher International
Nat Sherman	UST llc
Philip Morris USA	Vector Group

HISTORICAL FINANCIALS
Company Type: Public

Income Statement
FYE: December 31

	REVENUE ($ mil.)	NET INCOME ($ mil.)	NET PROFIT MARGIN	EMPLOYEES
12/15	10,675	3,253	30.5%	5,700
12/14	8,471	1,470	17.4%	5,400
12/13	8,236	1,718	20.9%	5,290
12/12	8,304	1,272	15.3%	5,050
12/11	8,541	1,406	16.5%	5,450
Annual Growth	**5.7%**	**23.3%**	**—**	**1.1%**

2015 Year-End Financials
Debt ratio: 32.78%
Return on equity: 28.57%
Cash ($ mil.): 2,567
Current ratio: 1.17
Long-term debt ($ mil.): 16,941
No. of shares (mil.): 1,427
Dividends
  Yield: 3.0%
  Payout: 52.2%
Market value ($ mil.): 65,872

	STOCK PRICE ($) FY Close	P/E High/Low		PER SHARE ($)		
			Earnings	Dividends	Book Value
12/15	46.15	34 16	2.57	1.39	12.79
12/14	64.27	49 34	1.38	1.34	4.26
12/13	49.99	34 26	1.57	1.24	4.80
12/12	41.43	41 35	1.12	1.17	4.75
12/11	41.42	35 26	1.20	1.08	5.42
Annual Growth	**2.7%**	**— —**	**21.0%**	**6.6%**	**23.9%**

Rite Aid Corp.

Rite Aid ranks a distant third (behind Walgreen and CVS) in the US retail drugstore business with nearly 4600 drugstores in some 30 states and the District of Columbia. Rite Aid stores generate roughly 70% of their sales from filling prescriptions while the rest comes from selling health and beauty aids convenience foods greeting cards and more including some 3500 Rite Aid brand private-label products. More than 60% of all Rite Aid stores are freestanding and over half have drive-through pharmacies. The company was founded in 1962 and is being purchased by pharmacy leader Walgreens Boots Alliance.

HISTORY

Company BackgroundWholesale grocer Alex Grass founded Rack Rite Distributors in Harrisburg Pennsylvania in 1958 to provide health and beauty aids and other sundries to grocery stores. He offered the same products at his first discount drugstore Thrif D Discount Center opened in 1962 in Scranton Pennsylvania. Four years later the company began placing pharmacies in its 36 stores. Rite Aid went public and adopted its current name in 1968 and the next year it made the first of many diverse acquisitions: Daw Drug Blue Ridge Nursing Homes and plasma suppliers Immuno Serums and Sero Genics.

Purchases in the 1970s included Sera-Tec Biologicals of New Jersey (blood plasma) and nearly 300 stores. By 1981 Rite Aid was the #3 drugstore chain and sales exceeded $1 billion. In 1984 it bought the American Discount Auto Parts chain and Encore Books chain and spun off its wholesale grocery operation in 1984 as Super Rite retaining a 47% stake (sold 1989).

Acquisitions added almost 900 stores during the 1980s. Expansion costs eroded Rite Aid's profit margins and the company focused on integrating its buys in 1990.

As part of a major restructuring in 1994 the company began selling its non-drugstore assets. Also in 1994 Rite Aid acquired Pharmacy Card and Intell-Rx and merged the two to form Eagle Managed Care.

Martin Grass took Rite Aid's reins from his dad in 1995. That year the company agreed to buy Revco at the time the #2 drugstore operator but the deal was derailed by FTC and Department of Justice objections in 1996. Rite Aid bounced back and acquired Thrifty PayLess (with more than 1000 stores) for about $2.3 billion in 1996. The deal gave the company more than 3600 stores and a presence in the western US. Also in 1996 Rite Aid exited several markets. In 1998 it closed many smaller stores and bought PCS Health Systems (the #1 US pharmacy benefits manager) from drug maker Eli Lilly and merged its Eagle Managed Care division into PCS.

In 1999 after a Wall Street Journal investigation Rite Aid revealed that Martin Grass Alex Grass and other family members held stakes in several suppliers and real estate interests doing business with the company. That year Rite Aid partnered with General Nutrition Companies Inc. (GNC) and took a 25% stake in the Internet retailer drugstore.com. Later in 1999 Rite Aid began slashing its $5.1 billion debt by cutting corporate staff and selling off some stores in California and the Pacific Northwest. CEO Martin Grass resigned and a team of former Fred Meyer officers —led by Robert Miller —took over.

In 2000 the company secured $1 billion from Citibank to reduce debt and provide capital. In July 2000 the company announced it would restate profits that over the past two years had been inflated in excess of $1 billion. Later that year Rite Aid sold PCS Health Systems to pharmacy benefits manager Advance Paradigm for more than $1 billion (about $500 million less than what Rite Aid originally paid for it). Rite Aid announced plans in 2001 to expand GNC concessions to additional stores.

To raise cash Rite Aid sold large blocks of its drugstore.com stock trimming its original 25% stake to less than 10% by April 2002. Former chairman and CEO Martin Grass former general counsel and vice chairman Franklin Brown and former CFO Frank Bergonzi among others were indicted in June 2002 for allegedly falsifying Rite Aid's books.

In April 2003 former chairman and CEO Martin Grass agreed to pay nearly $1.5 million to settle a lawsuit in which shareholders alleged that Rite Aid's books were falsified inflating the stock's value. In June Grass and former CFO Franklyn Bergonzi both pleaded guilty to conspiracy to defraud shareholders. Eric Sorkin Rite Aid's former VP of pharmacy services pleaded guilty to conspiring to obstruct justice. The following month Rite Aid began mailing checks totaling nearly $140 million to thousands of its current and former shareholders damaged by the accounting scandal at the company. In October former chief counsel Franklin Brown was convicted of conspiracy and lying to the Securities and Exchange Commission among other charges.

Despite its high debt load Rite Aid reportedly made a $4 billion cash-and-stock offer for struggling rival Eckerd but lost out to CVS and Canada's Jean Coutu Group who divvied up Eckerd in mid-2004.

In May 2004 Grass whose father founded Rite Aid struck a plea deal with prosecutors under which he was sentenced to eight years in prison. Also in May several other former company executives including Sorkin and ex-CFO Frank Bergonzi were sentenced in the accounting scandal. In June Rite Aid agreed to pay the US government $5.6 million (plus another $1.4 million to more than 20 states) to settle a federal lawsuit alleging the drugstore chain submitted false prescription claims to government insurance programs. In October former vice chairman Brown was sentenced to 10 years in prison the longest sentence of six Rite Aid officials charged in the accounting scandal.

CFO John Standley resigned in 2005 to join supermarket operator Pathmark Stores as its CEO. Standley joined Rite Aid as its CFO in 1999.

In April 2007 the company agreed to a store swap with California-based Longs Drug Stores. Under the terms of the agreement Rite Aid acquired six Longs stores in Northern California Oregon and Washington in exchange for giving Longs six of its stores in Nevada.

In its first major deal since its brush with bankruptcy in 1999 Rite Aid acquired more than 1850 Brooks and Eckerd drugstores and six distribution centers from Canada's Jean Coutu Group in a cash-and-stock deal valued at about $4 billion in June 2007.

Rite Aid exited the Las Vegas market in 2008 saying it was not a core market and had not contributed to overall results. It sold 27 of its Las Vegas stores to Walgreens. It March 2009 Rite Aid made a similar disposal of all seven of its stores in San Francisco and five locations in eastern Idaho when it sold them to Walgreen. Rite Aid said the stores were in areas with too light a store presence to operate efficiently. In July Rite Aid agreed to pay $500000 in consumer refunds to settle charges by the FTC that the company falsely advertised its Germ Defense line of cold-and-flu remedies as preventing illness or reducing the severity and duration of symptoms. The FTC said Rite Aid did not have evidence to support its Germ Defense product claims. Rite Aid founder Alex Grass died in August 2009 at the age of 82.

President and CEO John Standley added the title of chairman in mid-2012.

EXECUTIVES

Chairman and CEO, John T. Standley, age 52, $1,035,000 total compensation
SVP NY Metro Division, Mark Kramer, age 65
SEVP CFO and Chief Administrative Officer, Darren W. Karst, age 55
EVP Merchandising and Distribution, Enio A. (Tony) Montini, age 63
SVP Marketing, John Learish, age 49
EVP Store Operations, Bryan Everett, age 46
President Rite Aid Corporation and CEO Rite Aid Stores, Kenneth A. (Ken) Martindale, age 55, $878,250 total compensation
SVP Mid-Atlantic Division, Scott Bernard
SVP Western Division, Bill Romine
SVP Northeast Division, Derek Griffith
EVP and Chief Human Resources Officer, Dedra N. Castle, age 49
SVP and CIO, Steve Rempel
EVP Pharmacy, Jocelyn Konrad
SVP Southern Division, Bill Jackson
Vice President Store Operations, Francis Spirk
Vice President General Merchandise Seasonal and Garden, Steve Koch
Pharmacy Manager, John Stanbrough
Pharmacy Manager, Rita Naoum
Pharmacy Manager, Kathlynn Chu
Pharmacy Manager, Elizabeth Robertson
Rph, Rajesh Kumar
Pharmacy Manager, Joan Rimkunas
Pharmacy Manager, Shannon Casta
Pharmacy Manager, Pavan Rambhatla
Pharmacy Manager, Kevin Reed
Pharmacy Manager, Deepika Duggineni
Pharmacy Manager, Subodha Lingayat
Pharmacist Manager, Glenda Parks
Pharmacy Manager, Erin Martinez
Pharmacy Manager, Malou Solomon
Pharmacy Manager, Shaun Mallam
Pharmacy Manager, Noune Soukiasian
Pharmacy Manager, Jessica Troyano
Pharmacy Manager, Sherri Wiswell
Pharmacy Manager, Gregory Sellwood
Pharmacy Manager, Ryan Coyle
Pharmacy Manager, Kari McCabe
Pharmacy Manager, Katee Tiballi
Pharmacy Manager, Karin Ryan
Pharmacy Manager, Ngozi Onumonu
Pharmacy Manager, Derek J Colston
Regional Vice President, Sri Pinninti
Vice President Health, Bill Bergin
Vice President Generic Pharmaceutical Purchasing And Clinical Services, Owen Mcmahon
Vice President Group Finance, William Karper
Pharmacy Manager, Heloise Swanepoel
Rph, Mohammed Mohiuddin
Pharmacy Manager, Tracy Gay
Pharmacist Manager, Mandy Hoysan
Pharmacy Manager, Pape Ndiaye
Pharmacy Manager, Anthony Chappell
Divisional Vice President, Alison Sredanovich
Regional Vice President, Dave Ricketts
Pharmacy Manager, Debbie Butz
Pharmacy Manager, Haley Ondecko
Pharmacy Manager, Marieta Nisperos
Regional Vice President Operations, David (Dave) Thomas
Regional Pharmacy Vice President, Bill Cropper
Pharmacy Manager, Stefani Horton
Pharmacy Manager, April Gary
RVP, Don Kinney
Pharmacy Manager, Aaron Speak
Regional Pharmacy Vice President, Jodi L Smith
Vice President, Tim Nixon
Pharmacy Manager, Laura Kirk
Pharmacy Manager, Hunter Goode
Senior Vice President, Daniel (Dan) Miller
Senior Vice President Human Resources, Steve Vitatoe
Vice President Pharmacy Operations, Dennis Yoney
Regional Vice President, Jeffery Ellison
Vice President, Jessica Espinal
Pharmacy Manager, Nikki Henderson
Pharmacy Manager, Jessica Reising
Senior Vice President Category Management, Enioanthony Montini
Pharmacy Manager, Nagakishore Edupuganti
Pharmacy Manager, Donald Brensinger
Pharmacy Manager, Liza Miller
Pharmacy Manager, Sandra Cohn
Regional Vice President, Ken Jordan
Vice President Pharmacy, Gregg Montgomery
Pharmacy Manager, Melanie C Weitz
Vice President Of Information Systems Development, Robert Krostosky
Senior Vice President, Todd McCarty
Regional Vice President, David Mahan
Regional Vice President, Bob Silsby
Rph, Fady Soliman
Pharmacy Manager, Nagaraju Gajawada
Executive Vice President Store Operations, Robert K (Bob) Thompson
Pharmacist Manager, Louis Andriko
Pharmacy Manager, Mansi Mehta
Pharmacy Manager, Wendy Brody
Senior Vice President International Assurance and Chief Comp Officer, Anthony Bellezza
Pharmacy Manager, A Somaini
Executive Vice President, Tony Montini
Pharmacy Manager, Wael Baramawi
Pharmacy Manager, Khatchatur Sarafian
Treasurer, Ken Skill
Board Member, Michael (Mel) Regan
Auditors: Deloitte & Touche LLP

LOCATIONS

HQ: Rite Aid Corp.
  30 Hunter Lane, Camp Hill, PA 17011
Phone: 717 761-2633   **Fax:** 717 975-5905
Web: www.riteaid.com

2015 Stores

	No.
New York	607
California	577
Pennsylvania	537
Michigan	276
New Jersey	257
North Carolina	224
Ohio	224
Virginia	192
Georgia	181
Massachusetts	146
Maryland	142
Washington	139
Kentucky	116
West Virginia	104
South Carolina	95
Alabama	93

Tennessee	81
Maine	79
Connecticut	77
Oregon	72
New Hampshire	68
Louisiana	62
Rhode Island	43
Delaware	42
Vermont	37
Mississippi	26
Utah	22
Colorado	20
Idaho	13
Indiana	10
District of Columbia	7
Nevada	1
Total	**4,570**

PRODUCTS/OPERATIONS

2015 Sales

	$ mil.	% of total
Pharmacy	18,114	68
Front-end	8,232	31
Other	181	1
Total	**26,528**	**100**

2015 Sales

	% of total
Prescription drugs	69
General merchandise & other	17
Over-the-counter medications & personal care	9
Health & beauty aids	5
Total	**100**

Selected Merchandise and Services

Beverages
Convenience foods
Cosmetics
Designer fragrances
Greeting cards
Health and personal care products
Household items
Over-the-counter drugs
Photo processing
Prescription drugs
Private-label products
Seasonal merchandise
Vitamins and minerals

COMPETITORS

A&P	Kroger
Ahold U.S.A.	Marc Glassman
BJ's Wholesale Club	Medicine Shoppe
CVS	Publix
Costco Wholesale	Safeway
Dollar General	Target Corporation
Family Dollar Stores	Wal-Mart
Kinney Drugs Inc.	Walgreen
Kmart	

HISTORICAL FINANCIALS

Company Type: Public

Income Statement

FYE: February 28

	REVENUE ($ mil.)	NET INCOME ($ mil.)	NET PROFIT MARGIN	EMPLOYEES
02/15*	26,528	2,109	8.0%	89,000
03/14	25,526	249	1.0%	89,000
03/13	25,392	118	0.5%	89,000
03/12	26,121	(368)	—	90,000
02/11	25,214	(555)	—	91,800
Annual Growth	1.3%	—	—	(0.8%)

*Fiscal year change

2015 Year-End Financials

Debt ratio: 63.69%
Return on equity: —
Cash ($ mil.): 115
Current ratio: 1.70
Long-term debt ($ mil.): 5,544

No. of shares (mil.): 988
Dividends
  Yield: —
  Payout: —
Market value ($ mil.): 7,889

STOCK PRICE ($)	P/E		PER SHARE ($)		
FY Close	High/Low		Earnings	Dividends	Book Value
02/15* 7.98	4	2	2.08	0.00	0.06
03/14 6.59	29	7	0.23	0.00	(2.18)
03/13 1.68	17	8	0.12	0.00	(2.72)
03/12 1.67	—	—	(0.43)	0.00	(2.88)
02/11 1.28	—	—	(0.64)	0.00	(2.48)
Annual Growth 58.0%	—	—	—	—	—

*Fiscal year change

RiverSource Life Insurance Co

Life insurance nsk

EXECUTIVES

Chb-pres, John R Worner
Regional Vice President, Mark Keeling
Auditors: PricewaterhouseCoopers LLP

LOCATIONS

HQ: RiverSource Life Insurance Co
1099 Ameriprise Financial Center, Minneapolis, MN 55474
Phone: 612 671-3131

HISTORICAL FINANCIALS

Company Type: Public

Income Statement

FYE: December 31

	ASSETS ($ mil.)	NET INCOME ($ mil.)	INCOME AS % OF ASSETS	EMPLOYEES
12/14	118,136	965	0.8%	—
12/13	117,004	842	0.7%	—
12/12	109,748	650	0.6%	—
12/11	105,380	779	0.7%	—
12/10	102,626	796	0.8%	—
Annual Growth	3.6%	4.9%	—	—

2014 Year-End Financials

Debt ratio: —
Return on equity: 22.81%
Cash ($ mil.): 307
Current ratio: —
Long-term debt ($ mil.): —

No. of shares (mil.): 0
Dividends
  Yield: —
  Payout: 93.2%
Market value ($ mil.): —

RLI Corp.

You might wonder what folks in Illinois know about earthquake insurance but as a specialty property/casualty insurer Peoria-based RLI knows how to write such policies. Through its subsidiaries the company mainly offers coverage for US niche markets —risks that are hard to place in the standard market and are otherwise underserved. It focuses on public and private companies as well as non-profit organizations. RLI's commercial property/casualty lines include products liability property damage marine cargo directors and officers liability medical malpractice and general liability. It

also writes commercial surety bonds and a smattering of specialty personal insurance.

Operations

RLI's specialty commercial property/casualty operations are conducted through its RLI Insurance Mt. Hawley Insurance Contractors Bonding and Insurance Company and RLI Indemnity subsidiaries. Personal offerings account for small portion of RLI's revenues and include homeowners insurance in Hawaii home business coverage pet insurance and personal umbrella (supplemental property/casualty) policies.

Geographic Reach

While the company operates in all 50 US states the District of Columbia and Puerto Rico California is RLI's largest market accounting for about 20% of the company's premiums.

Sales and Marketing

RLI markets its products to brokers and independent agents through branch offices scattered across the US.

Financial Analysis

Like many insurers RLI's finances took a negative hit from the economic turmoil of 2008 and 2009. The company improved its returns as of 2010 and hasn't looked back. In 2013 it reported a 7% increase in revenue from $661 million to $706 million due to increased net premiums especially in the casualty segment. New products also made strong contributions. Net income grew 33% from $103 million to $126 million on increased revenue and decline in losses. Cash from operations a category that has fluctuated for RLI improved by $99 million due to investments.

Strategy

The company has gradually expanded its range of products with an emphasis on property insurance. In 2012 RLI entered the recreational vehicle (RV) insurance market by forming an underwriting partnership with Recreation Insurance Specialists. In 2013 it saw growth in its casualty business in transportation professional liability umbrella and admitted package businesses.

Mergers and Acquisitions

In 2014 the company purchased 20% of Prime Holdings Insurance Services for $5.3 million. The Utah-based company sells excess and surplus lines insurance in 49 states through a network of brokers; it specializes in hard-to-place risks (underwater hotels English Channel swims bungee jumps from helicopters).

In 2012 RLI moved into the field of medical malpractice coverage through the acquisition of Rockbridge Underwriting Agency. Two years later it launched RLI Healthcare a healthcare liability division serving hospital systems long-term and outpatient care facilities and clinical research providers with surplus lines in all 50 states.

Company Background

Gerald Stephens founded the company in 1961 and served as its chairman from 2001 until his retirement in 2011.

EXECUTIVES

Vice President Vice President Personnel, Jeffrerey Fick
Vpres-chief Claim Officer, Don Driscoll
President and COO RLI Insurance and Mt. Hawley Insurance Companies, Michael J. (Mike) Stone, age 66, $515,000 total compensation
Chairman and CEO, Jonathan E. Michael, age 61, $750,000 total compensation
EVP Operations, Craig W. Kliethermes, age 50, $385,692 total compensation
VP and Chief Investment Officer; Treasurer, Aaron P. Diefenthaler
VP and CFO, Thomas L. Brown, $373,731 total compensation
VP Information Technology, Murali Natarajan

Vice President RLI Transportation, Dan Meyer
Assistant Vice President Specialty Markets, Paul Harris
Assistant Vice President, Carol Rawls Smith
Assistant Vice President Executive Products Group, David (Dave) Shanosky
Assistant Vice President fidelity Group, Thomas (Thom) Huber
Vice President Public Transportation, Tim Hathy
Vice President, Marty Marion
Assistant Vice President Risk Services, Timothy C (Tim) O'Bryan
Assistant Vice President, Terry Driggs
Assistant Vice President Information Technology Governance, Dallas Pettingill
Vice President General Counsel Corporate Secretary, Aniel O Kennedy
Vice President Human Resources, Jeffrey (Jeff) Fick
Assistant Vice President Controller, Jeff Myers
Vice President Miscellaneous Professional Liability, Brian Flynn
Vice President Internal Audit And Compliance, Robert Nichols
Specialty Products Assistant Vice President Channel Management, David (Dave) Willett
Vice President Operations, Richard (Dick) Quehl
Vice President Controller, Todd W Bryant
Vice President, Donald (Don) Driscoll
Vice President General Counsel, Dan Kennedy
Assistant Vice President, Mary Kostyk
Treasurer, John Robison
Treasurer, Robert Ogle, age 57
Board Director and Member of the Finance and Executive Resources Committee, Jordan Graham
Auditors: KPMG LLP

LOCATIONS

HQ: RLI Corp.
9025 North Lindbergh Drive, Peoria, IL 61615
Phone: 309 692-1000   Fax: 309 692-1068
Web: www.rlicorp.com

PRODUCTS/OPERATIONS

2013 Revenues

	$ mil.	% of total
Net premiums earned		
Casualty	324	46
Property	200	28
Surety	106	15
Net investment income	52	8
Net realized gains	22	3
Total	**705**	**100**

Selected Products

Commercial
Casualty
Contractors bonding and insurance
Executive products liability
Marine
Professional services
Property
Reinsurance
Specialty programs
Transportation
Personal
Homeowners (Hawaii)
Home business owners
Personal umbrella
Surety Bonds

COMPETITORS

Arch Insurance Group
Baldwin & Lyons
CNA Financial
Chubb Limited
Crum & Forster
Endurance Specialty
Great American Insurance Company
Great West Casualty
HCC Insurance

James River Group
Lancer Insurance
Lexington Insurance
Markel
Meadowbrook Insurance
Navigators
Philadelphia Insurance Companies
Safeco
The Hartford
Travelers Companies
United States Liability Insurance Group

HISTORICAL FINANCIALS

Company Type: Public

Income Statement

FYE: December 31

	ASSETS ($ mil.)	NET INCOME ($ mil.)	INCOME AS % OF ASSETS	EMPLOYEES
12/14	2,775	135	4.9%	882
12/13	2,740	126	4.6%	870
12/12	2,644	103	3.9%	897
12/11	2,695	130	4.8%	862
12/10	2,514	127	5.1%	734
Annual Growth	**2.5%**	**1.5%**	**—**	**4.7%**

2014 Year-End Financials

Debt ratio: 5.39%
Return on equity: 16.18%
Cash ($ mil.): 30
Current ratio: —
Long-term debt ($ mil.): —

No. of shares (mil.): 43
Dividends
Yield: 7.5%
Payout: 123.2%
Market value ($ mil.): 2,129

	STOCK PRICE ($) FY Close	P/E High/Low	PER SHARE ($) Earnings	Dividends	Book Value
12/14	49.40	31 13	3.09	3.71	19.61
12/13	97.38	35 22	2.90	4.34	19.29
12/12	64.66	31 25	2.40	6.26	18.73
12/11	72.86	24 16	3.05	3.10	19.35
12/10	52.57	20 16	3.00	8.15	18.87
Annual Growth	**(1.5%)**	**— —**	**0.7%**	**(17.9%)**	**1.0%**

Robinson (C.H.) Worldwide, Inc.

C.H. Robinson Worldwide (CHRW) keeps merchandise moving. A third-party logistics (3PL) provider the company arranges freight transportation using trucks trains ships and airplanes belonging to other companies. It contracts with some 66000 carriers. CHRW handles about 14.3 million shipments per year for its 46000-plus customers that include companies in the food and beverage manufacturing and retail industries. Besides transportation the company also offers logistics for supply chain management services through some 280 offices. In addition CHRW buys sells and transports fresh produce throughout the US.

HISTORY

In the early 1900s Charles H. Robinson began a produce brokerage in Grand Forks North Dakota. Robinson entered a partnership in 1905 with Nash Brothers the leading wholesaler in North Dakota and the company C.H. Robinson was born.

Robinson became president but soon relinquished control under mysterious circumstances (rumor had it he ran off with Annie Oakley). H. B.

Finch took charge and by 1913 a new company Nash Finch became C.H. Robinson's sole owner.

As a subsidiary C.H. Robinson primarily procured produce for Nash Finch which helped it expand into Illinois Minnesota Texas and Wisconsin. To avoid FTC scrutiny over preferential treatment Nash Finch split CHR in two: C.H. Robinson Co. owned by C.H. Robinson employees which sold produce to Nash Finch warehouses; and C.H. Robinson Inc. owned by Nash Finch.

After WWII the interstate highway system and refrigerated trucks changed the industry. No longer dependent on railroads C.H. Robinson began charging for truck brokerage of perishables. The two companies formed by the 1940s split reunited under the C.H. Robinson name in the mid-1960s; Nash Finch kept a 25% stake in the company and sold the rest to employees. Not surprisingly Nash Finch wanted to divert C.H. Robinson profits to its other businesses so in 1976 C.H. Robinson employees bought out Nash Finch.

The next year D. R. "Sid" Verdoorn was named president and Looe Baker became chairman. They focused on increasing C.H. Robinson's data-processing capability and adding branch offices. In 1980 the Motor Carrier Act deregulated the transportation industry and C.H. Robinson entered the freight-contracting business acting as a middleman for all types of goods. The company grew rapidly from about 30 offices in 1980 to more than 60 in 1990.

As part of its overall effort to become a full-service provider C.H. Robinson formed its Intermodal Division (more than one mode of transport) in 1988. It also established an information services division (1991) and bought fruit juice concentrate distributor Daystar International (1993). By this time the company was working with more than 14000 shippers and moving more than 500000 shipments a year.

Meanwhile C.H. Robinson had ventured overseas with the launch of its international division in 1989. It entered Mexico in 1990 and added air-freight operations and international freight forwarding through the 1992 purchase of C.S. Green International. In 1993 C.H. Robinson picked up a 30% stake in French motor carrier Transeco (acquiring the rest later) and opened offices in Mexico Chile and Venezuela.

The company went public in 1997 and became C.H. Robinson Worldwide (CHRW). The next year Verdoorn who was CEO assumed the additional role of chairman. The following year the company acquired Argentina's Comexter transportation group to gain market share in South America and it expanded its European operation in 1999 through the purchase of Norminter a French third-party logistics provider. Much closer to home CHRW bought Eden Prairie-based Preferred Translocation Systems a logistics provider to LTL carriers and Chicago-based transportation provider American Backhaulers.

In 2000 CHRW partnered with PaperExchange.com Inc. the global e-business marketplace for the pulp and paper industry to provide an exclusive logistics service to PaperExchange.com members. CHRW continued to expand in 2002 with the purchase of Miami-based Smith Terminal Transportation Services. Verdoorn stepped down as CEO that year and company president John Wiehoff was promoted to replace him. Verdoorn retired at the end of 2006 and Wiehoff succeeded him as chairman.

The company acquired three US-based produce sourcing and marketing companies —FoodSource Inc. FoodSource Procurement and Epic Roots —in 2004 for a reported $270 million. That year CHRW added seven offices in China by acquiring a Dalian-based freight forwarder and in 2005 it gained operations in Germany Italy and the US by buying two freight forwarding companies Hirdes Group Worldwide and Bussini Transport. Also in 2005 CHRW bought US-based freight broker Payne Lynch & Associates as well as an India-based freight forwarder Triune. The following year (2006) the company acquired US-based LXSI Services a specialist in domestic airfreight and expedited ground transportation management that had gross revenue of about $25 million.

In mid-2008 CHRW acquired Transera International Holdings a project forwarding business based in Canada. Transera has office locations in Canada Dubai Singapore and the US and has annual revenues of about $125 million.

In 2009 the company purchased London-based Walker Logistics Overseas an international freight forwarder serving primarily the electronics telecommunications medical sporting goods and military industries. The acquisition expanded its capabilities in Asia-to-Europe trade and brought two key distribution gateways —London and Amsterdam. CHRW then expanded its produce distribution business even further in 2009 by opening a European-based produce sourcing company in France which will focus on bringing fresh produce from France Italy and Spain to North and South America Europe Asia and Middle Eastern countries. That same year CHRW acquired certain assets of International Trade & Commerce (ITC) a US customs brokerage company that specializes in warehousing distribution and services between the US and Mexico. Also in 2009 the company bought Rosemont Farms as well as Quality Logistics which provides logistics for produce transportation; both companies are based in Florida.

In 2010 CHRW expanded its transportation management services to India by building a new facility and control tower operations. The India-based facility was established to serve customers in South and Southeast Asia as well as in Pakistan and the Middle East.

CHRW divested its former payment services segment T-Chek (only 1% of total sales in 2012) in October 2012 to Electronic Funds Source LLC for $303 million in cash. The T-Chek unit provided such services as funds transfer and fuel purchasing management and CHRW made the deal to focus on its core transportation and logistics services.

In late 2012 CHRW acquired Phoenix International a provider of international ocean air and customs brokerage freight forwarding services. CHRW bought Phoenix for nearly $572 million in cash and roughly $63.5 million in newly-issued CHRW stock in a deal that sizably enhanced its international freight forwarding capabilities.

During that same time period CHRW swallowed up Apreo Logistics S.A. a freight forwarding firm based in Poland. The acquisition strengthened the company's toehold in Europe and further diversified its modal offering.

EXECUTIVES

SVP and CIO, Chad M. Lindbloom, age 51, $270,000 total compensation
Chairman President and CEO, John P. Wiehoff, age 53, $410,000 total compensation
CFO, Andrew C. Clarke, age 44
President Robinson Fresh, James P. (Jim) Lemke, age 48, $210,000 total compensation
Chief Commercial Officer, Christopher J. (Chris) O'Brien, age 47
President Europe, Bryan D. Foe, age 47
VP Global Forwarding North America, Mike Short
VP Management Services, Jordan T. Kass, age 42
President North American Surface Transportation, Robert Biesterfeld
National Account Manager, Randy Roth

Senior Vice President and Chief Credit Officer Commercial Banking, Mike Fong
National Account Manager, Jean Boesch
Vice President Global Forwarding Sales, Matt McInerney
National Account Manager, Zach Deloache
National Account Manager, Andy Hutson
National Account Manager, Michael Samstad
Cash Application Assistant Vice President, Sarah Carlson
Vice President Finance EAi, Sarah Wagner
National Account Manager, Jen Theisen
Vice President, Brendan Keane
National Account Manager, Tiffany Popovici
National Account Manager, Ryan Ballein
National Account Manager, Kayla Simons
National Accounts Manager, Jose Molina
National Account Manager, Jason Calhoun
Vice President Global Transportation, Timothy Manning
National Account Manager, Santiago Correa
Assistant Vice President, Raymon Sez
National Account Manager, Gina Myers
National Account Manager, Marissa Roge
Vice President Information Technology, Steve Enberg
National Account Manager, Matt Lapolice
Vice President, Pat Nolan
National Account Manager, Michelle (Mitch) Clayton
National Account Manager, Channel Wilson
Treasurer, Troy A Renner, age 50
Board Member, Sergio Cordon
Board Member, Kevin Grossi
Board Member, Brian Short
Board Member, Jodee Kozlak
Board Member, James (Jamie) Stake
Auditors: Deloitte & Touche LLP

LOCATIONS

HQ: Robinson (C.H.) Worldwide, Inc.
14701 Charlson Road, Eden Prairie, MN 55347-5088
Phone: 952 937-8500   **Fax:** 952 937-6714
Web: www.chrobinson.com

2014 Sales

	$ mil.	% of total
US	11,800	88
Other countries	1,669	12
Total	**13,470**	**100**

PRODUCTS/OPERATIONS

2014 Sales

	$ mil.	% of total
Transportation	11,922	89
Sourcing	1,533	11
Payment services	14	-
Total	**13,470**	**100**

Selected Services
Air
Intermodal
Less-than-truckload
Logistics
  Customs brokerage
  Transportation management services
  Warehousing services
Ocean
Truckload

COMPETITORS

ALC	Hub Group
APL Logistics	J.B. Hunt
BNSF Logistics	Kuehne + Nagel
CEVA Logistics	International
Cass Information	Landstar Inway
Systems	MIQ Logistics
Chiquita Brands	Menlo Worldwide
Comdata	Panalpina
CorTrans Logistics	Penske Truck Leasing

DHL	Ryder System
Dole Food	Schneider Logistics
Exel	TLC
Expeditors	Transplace
FedEx Trade Networks	UPS Supply Chain
Fresh Del Monte	Solutions
Produce	

HISTORICAL FINANCIALS
Company Type: Public

Income Statement

FYE: December 31

	REVENUE ($ mil.)	NET INCOME ($ mil.)	NET PROFIT MARGIN	EMPLOYEES
12/14	13,470	449	3.3%	11,521
12/13	12,752	415	3.3%	11,676
12/12	11,359	593	5.2%	10,929
12/11	10,336	431	4.2%	8,353
12/10	9,274	387	4.2%	7,628
Annual Growth	**9.8%**	**3.8%**	**—**	**10.9%**

2014 Year-End Financials

Debt ratio: 15.56%   No. of shares (mil.): 146
Return on equity: 45.27%   Dividends
Cash ($ mil.): 128   Yield: 1.9%
Current ratio: 1.34   Payout: 49.3%
Long-term debt ($ mil.): 500   Market value ($ mil.): 10,968

	STOCK PRICE ($) FY Close	P/E High/Low	PER SHARE ($) Earnings	Dividends	Book Value
12/14	74.89	25 17	3.05	1.43	7.15
12/13	58.35	26 21	2.65	1.40	6.26
12/12	63.22	19 14	3.67	1.34	9.32
12/11	69.78	31 24	2.62	1.20	7.64
12/10	80.19	34 22	2.33	1.04	7.25
Annual Growth	**(1.7%)**	**— —**	**7.0%**	**8.3%**	**(0.4%)**

Rockwell Automation, Inc.

Rockwell Automation only rocks to the scintillating sounds of its control products. The company is one of the world's largest industrial automation companies serving automotive food and beverage (including dairy) personal care life sciences oil and gas mining and paper and pulp markets. Rockwell's control products & solutions unit makes industrial automation products such as motor starters and contractors relays timers signaling devices and variable-speed drives. To complement its automation product offerings its architecture & software unit offers factory management software and motion control sensors and machine safety components.

Geographic Reach

Rockwell has operations in Belgium Brazil Canada China Hong Kong Mexico Poland Singapore Switzerland and the US. Its control products segment is headquartered in Milwaukee while architecture & software is stationed in Mayfield Heights Ohio.

Half its sales come from the US but Rockwell also maintains a presence in the international markets of Brazil Canada China Germany Italy Mexico and the UK.

Operations

The company holds a solid global market share in process control technology which includes PAC systems (programmable automation controller) that use sensors computers and software. Rockwell's branded PlantPAx Process Automation System competes effectively with the more traditional distributed control system (DCS) which are larger and more costly.

Control products is the larger of Rockwell's two units representing 56% of total sales. This segment manufactures intelligent motor and industrial control products under the ICS Triplex brand. The company's architecture & software unit markets products such as hardware software and communication components needed to control industrial processes and communicate the results to the manufacturer. Brand names for this segment include Rockwell Software and FactoryTalk. Both segments market products and services under the Rockwell Automation Allen-Bradley and A-B brand names.

Sales and Marketing

Independent distributors account for about 70% of worldwide sales and 90% of sales in North America. The company also markets its products through a direct sales force.

Financial Performance

After posting record-setting revenues of $6.6 billion in 2015 Rockwell saw its revenues decline 5% to $6.3 billion in 2015. Its profits remained flat hovering around the $827 million mark for both 2014 and 2015.

The revenue decline for 2015 was fueled by a 6% drop in control products sales and a 3% dip in architecture & software sales. It was also affected by revenue declines in Canada (16%) and the Middle East & Africa (EMEA; 13%) region.

The company's operating cash flow has steadily risen the last few years climbing 15% from 2014 to 2015 due to changes in receivables and accounts payable.

Strategy

Leveraging strong growth in emerging markets Rockwell Automation has devised a strategy of globalizing by localizing adapting products services and operations to be closer to customers. The company's long-term strategy for broader growth includes innovations to attract more industries to its customer base increasing its partner network acquisitions to obtain complementary technology and expand geographically. The strategy that includes these goals and others is intended to reach revenue growth of 6-8% and increase the percentage of sales outside the US to 60%.

Mergers and Acquisitions

Acquisitions are key to the company's growth. In early 2014 the company acquired Jacobs Automation an expert in intelligent track motion control technology. Jacobs provides customers with new technology to enhance performance and flexibility so they can quickly respond to changing market demands. Months later Rockwell picked up ESC Services a global hazardous energy control provider of lockout-tagout services. That deal will enable Rockwell Automation customers to increase their asset utilization and strengthen their enterprise risk management offerings.

HISTORY

Rockwell Automation is the legacy of two early-20th-century entrepreneurs: Willard Rockwell and Clement Melville Keys. Rockwell gained control in 1919 of Wisconsin Parts Company an Oshkosh Wisconsin maker of automotive axles. He went on to buy a number of industrial manufacturers merging them in 1953 to create Rockwell Spring & Axle. Renamed Rockwell-Standard in 1958 it led the world in the production of mechanical automotive parts by 1967.

In 1928 Keys founded North American Aviation (NAA) as a holding company for his aviation interests. General Motors bought NAA in 1934 and named James Kindelberger as its president. The company moved in 1935 from Maryland to Inglewood California where it built military training planes. NAA merged with Rockwell-Standard creating North American Rockwell in 1967. The company adopted the Rockwell International name in 1973. It wasn't until the beginning of the new century when the company changed its name to Rockwell Automation.

EXECUTIVES

Chairman and CEO, Keith D. Nosbusch, age 64, $1,182,414 total compensation

SVP General Counsel and Secretary, Douglas M. (Doug) Hagerman, age 54, $573,852 total compensation

SVP Global Sales and Marketing, John P. McDermott, age 57, $436,699 total compensation

SVP and CFO, Theodore D. (Ted) Crandall, age 60, $617,423 total compensation

SVP and CTO, Sujeet Chand, age 57

SVP Operations and Engineering Services, Martin (Marty) Thomas, age 57

SVP Control Products and Solutions, Blake D. Moret, age 52, $566,092 total compensation

SVP Architecture and Software, Frank C. Kulaszewicz, age 51, $566,092 total compensation

President Asia/Pacific, Tom O'Reilly

President Latin America, Joe Sousa

Regional VP. Canada, Thomas Denato

Vice President Ind. Components, Robert (Bob) Lennon

Vice President Casualty Broker, Linda Ferrell

Vice President Of Strategic Technologies, James Hull

Vice President Logistics, David Kenney

Vice President Manufacturing, Dominic Coletta

Vice President Engineering Rockwell Automation Inc., John (Jack) Floresta

Vice President Global OEM Solutions, Christopher (Chris) Zei

Vice President Channel Sales, Dave Stormo

Vice President Business Development, Keith A Harpenau

Vice President Supply Chain Rockwell Automation Inc., Mike Irwin

Senior Vice President, Michelle (Mitch) Love

Legal Secretary, Alexander Vinciczky

Vice President of Sales and Marketing, Joe Kann

Vice President Manufacturing, Terry Gebert

Vice President Information Technology Rockwell Automation Inc., Jerome Fox

Senior Vice President Operations, Jeff Moore

Vice President Professional Services (RA Incuity), Andrew (Andy) Ellis

Vice President Sales, John Sousa

National Accounts Manager, Lisa Kilgas

Vice President, David Dorgan

Auditors: DELOITTE & TOUCHE LLP

LOCATIONS

HQ: Rockwell Automation, Inc.
1201 South Second Street, Milwaukee, WI 53204
Phone: 414 382-2000
Web: www.rockwellautomation.com

2015 sales

	$ mil.	% of total
United States	3,446	55
Europe Middle East and Africa	1,174	18
Asia Pacific	834	13
Latin America	486	8
Canada	366	6
Total	**6,307**	**100**

PRODUCTS/OPERATIONS

2015 Sales

	$ mil.	% of total
Control products & solutions	3,558	56
Architecture & software	2,750	44
Total	**6,308**	**100**

COMPETITORS

ABB	OMRON
Danaher	Schneider Electric
Dematic SARL	Select Business
Emerson Electric	Solutions
FANUC	Siemens AG
Hitachi	Toshiba
Honeywell ACS	Weiss Instrument
Metso	Wonderware
Mitsubishi Corp.	Yokogawa Electric

HISTORICAL FINANCIALS

Company Type: Public

Income Statement

FYE: September 30

	REVENUE ($ mil.)	NET INCOME ($ mil.)	NET PROFIT MARGIN	EMPLOYEES
09/15	6,307	827	13.1%	22,500
09/14	6,623	826	12.5%	22,500
09/13	6,351	756	11.9%	22,000
09/12	6,259	737	11.8%	22,000
09/11	6,000	697	11.6%	21,000
Annual Growth	1.3%	4.4%	—	1.7%

2015 Year-End Financials

Debt ratio: 23.43%	No. of shares (mil.): 132
Return on equity: 33.68%	Dividends
Cash ($ mil.): 1,427	Yield: 2.5%
Current ratio: 3.05	Payout: 40.7%
Long-term debt ($ mil.): 1,500	Market value ($ mil.): 13,435

	STOCK PRICE ($) FY Close	P/E High/Low		PER SHARE ($) Earnings	Dividends	Book Value
09/15	101.47	21	16	6.09	2.60	17.05
09/14	109.88	21	17	5.91	2.32	19.44
09/13	106.94	20	13	5.36	1.98	18.61
09/12	69.55	16	10	5.13	1.75	13.25
09/11	56.00	20	11	4.80	1.48	12.32
Annual Growth	16.0%	—	—	6.1%	15.2%	8.5%

Rockwell Collins, Inc.

Rockwell Collins a spin-off of Rockwell Automation makes aviation electronics and communication equipment for commercial and military aircraft. The company boasts that nearly every commercial cockpit contains something made by Rockwell Collins. It also provides flight simulation and training MRO services navigation and surveillance systems. The company has three primary segments: commercial systems (avionics and inflight entertainment systems for commercial aircraft); government systems (airborne/ground/shipboard communication systems with military applications and overhaul services); and information management services business (communications systems integration and security solutions).

Geographic Reach

Rockwell Collins operates through 60 locations in some 25 countries including France Canada Germany Japan Australia China India Italy Spain

Singapore Brazil the United Arab Emirates Saudi Arabia the UK and the US. Rockwell Collins makes about 60% of its sales in the US.

Operations

The government systems segment (44% of total sales) provides products for a variety of uses but they all have the common theme of design for use under rugged conditions constrained by challenges in relation to size weight and power. These products include satellite communications systems handheld navigation devices flight controls helmet-mounted displays and training systems.

The company's commercial systems segment (46%) provides systems and products for the original manufacturing retrofitting and upgrading of aircraft. Products include the Pro Line Fusion integrated avionics system cabin management systems head-up guidance systems primary actuation systems and simulators for crew training. The segment serves a range of customers from the biggest aircraft makers in the world to owners of individual aircraft. Aftermarket products are sold through distributors and to regional airline operators.

Sales and Marketing

Rockwell Collins markets its systems products and services directly to government systems and commercial systems customers through an internal marketing and sales force. The company also utilizes a worldwide dealer network to distribute its products and international sales representatives to assist with international sales and marketing.

The US government accounts for 30% of sales. Customers include the Department of Defense US Coast Guard civil agencies defense contractors foreign ministries commercial air support manufacturers and airlines.

Financial Performance

In 2015 Rockwell Collins' revenue increased by 5% to peak at roughly $5.2 billion a new company milestone. The historic growth for 2015 was fueled by additional revenue from acquisitions and a surge in sales within its information management services segment. Rockwell Collins' profits also surged 14% to peak at a record-setting $686 million in 2015. In addition the company's operating cash flow hs steadily risen the last four years.

Strategy

Joint ventures are an important element of the company's strategy for growth. It maintains 50-50 JVs with BAE Systems for Data Link Solutions (serving the worldwide data link market); Elbit Systems for Vision Systems International (helmet-mounted cueing systems for the military fixed-wing market); Honeywell International for Integrated Guidance Systems (weapons guidance and navigation products); and Quadrant Group for Quest Flight Training (aircrew training for the UK Ministry of Defense). Throughout 2012 it established additional joint ventures with airlines and research institutes in the important country of China.

Rockwell Collins continues to execute its strategy to reshape its government systems portfolio to align with the changing dynamics of the defense environment. During 2014 Rockwell Collins divested two businesses: DataPath and KOSI. The decision was part of an overall strategy to reshape its government systems segment to focus on growing markets for the company's core products and services.Mergers and Acquisitions

Rockwell Collins in both 2014 and 2015 achieved revenue milestones with the aid of a key acquisition. In 2013 it purchased ARINC a global provider of air-to-ground data and voice communication service for $1.4 billion. Combining ARINC's communication networks and services with the company's onboard aircraft

In 2015 the company acquired International Communications Group (ICG) which provides satellite-based global voice and data communication products and services for the aviation industry for $50 million. The deal broadened the company's flight deck and connectivity portfolio.Previously in 2015 Rockwell Collins acquired Pacific Avionics Pty. Limited which provides technologies used for wireless information distribution. It made the purchase for $24 million as the acquisition further enhanced its cabin products and information management services portfolios.

EXECUTIVES

Vice President Treasuer, Douglas (Doug) Stenske
EVP and COO Commercial Systems, Kent L. Statler, age 50, $602,454 total compensation
SVP and CFO, Patrick E. Allen, age 51, $600,600 total compensation
SVP Operations, Bruce M. King, age 54
SVP Engineering and Technology, Nan Mattai, age 63
SVP Human Resources, Martha L. May, age 48, $367,500 total compensation
SVP International and Service Solutions, Colin Mahoney, age 50
VP Commercial Sales Marketing and Customer Support, Scott R. Gunnufson
VP and Managing Director Europe Middle East and Africa International and Service Solutions, Claude Alber
EVP and COO Government Systems, Philip J. (Phil) Jasper, age 47, $474,231 total compensation
Chairman President and CEO, Roberf K. (Kelly) Ortberg, age 55, $955,769 total compensation
VP and Managing Director Asia Pac, Jim Walker
SVP Information Management Services, Jeff Standerski
Vice President and General Manager Cabin Systems, Glen T Dodson
Vice President Of Logistics, Dan Schleder
Vice President Business Development, Mike Myers
Vice President, Diane Hudson
Vp-mergers & Acquisitions, Rick Schmidt
Vice President Compensation and Benefits, Melodee Webb
Vice President Engineering, Steve Nieuwsma
Vice President manufacturing Operations, Rose Donnelly
Vice President and General Manager Mobility and Rotary Wing Solutions Government Systems, Phil J Jasper
Vice President, John Chapin
Vice President, Tom Lemke
Vice President Market Development And Regulatory Affairs, Billie Platner
Vice President Client Services, Dan Doyle
Vice President Operations, Mark Correll
Sr V Pres-gen Counsel-sec, Robert J Perna
Vice President, Stephanie Bails
Vice President Strategy Development, Bryan Vester
Vice President Government Systems Strategy Business Development, David (Dave) Nieuwsma
Vice President Advanced Technology Center, John (Jack) Borghese
Vice President of Kaiser Aerospace, JW Borghese
Vice President Internal Audit, Amy McDonald
Vice President Enterprise Quality, Paul ENye
Vice President and General Manager Business and Regional Systems, Craig Olson
Treasurer, Heather Stansberry
Treasurer, Stefanie Wiese
Treasurer, Chad Van Dorston
Treasurer, Cheri Martens
Board Member, Craig Goudie
Secretary, Tippett Cindi
Auditors: DELOITTE & TOUCHE LLP

LOCATIONS

HQ: Rockwell Collins, Inc.
400 Collins Road N.E., Cedar Rapids, IA 52498
Phone: 319 295-1000
Web: www.rockwellcollins.com

2015 Sales

	$ mil.	% of total
US	3,174	61
Europe	915	17
Asia/Pacific	503	10
Canada	369	7
Africa/Middle East	155	3
Latin America	128	2
Total	**5,244**	**100**

PRODUCTS/OPERATIONS

2015 Sales

	$ mil.	% of total
Government systems		
Avionics	1,390	26
Communication products	401	8
Surface solutions	200	4
Navigation products	196	4
Commercial systems		
Air transport aviation electronics	1,385	26
Business & regional aviation electronics	1,049	20
Information management services	623	12
Total	**5,244**	**100**

Selected Products and Services

Government/Defense (airborne and surface)
  Cockpit display
  Communications
  Engineering services
  Flight deck subsystems
  Maintenance repair parts and after-sales support
  Military data link
  Navigation (including radio navigation)
  Simulation and training
Commercial (air transport aviation electronics and business and regional aviation electronics)
  Communications
  Electro-mechanical
  Information management
  Integrated avionics (Pro Line Fusion)
  Integrated cabin electronics
  Maintenance repair parts and after-sales support services
  Navigation
  Simulation and training
  Surveillance

COMPETITORS

BAE SYSTEMS	L-3 Communications
Ball Corp.	Meggitt
Boeing	Northrop Grumman
CAE Inc.	Panasonic Avionics
Chemring	Radiall
DRS Technologies	Raytheon
Esterline	Smiths Group
Exelis	Thales
General Dynamics	Trimble Navigation
Harris Corp.	ViaSat
Honeywell Aerospace	

HISTORICAL FINANCIALS

Company Type: Public

Income Statement

FYE: September 30

	REVENUE ($ mil.)	NET INCOME ($ mil.)	NET PROFIT MARGIN	EMPLOYEES
09/15	5,244	686	13.1%	19,500
09/14	4,979	604	12.1%	20,000
09/13	4,610	632	13.7%	18,300
09/12	4,726	609	12.9%	19,000
09/11	4,806	634	13.2%	20,500
Annual Growth	**2.2%**	**2.0%**	**—**	**(1.2%)**

2015 Year-End Financials

Debt ratio: 28.80%	No. of shares (mil.): 131
Return on equity: 36.50%	Dividends
Cash ($ mil.): 252	Yield: 1.5%
Current ratio: 1.51	Payout: 25.3%
Long-term debt ($ mil.): 1,680	Market value ($ mil.): 10,795

	STOCK PRICE ($) FY Close	P/E High/Low		PER SHARE ($) Earnings	Dividends	Book Value
09/15	81.84	19	14	5.13	1.26	14.22
09/14	78.50	19	15	4.42	1.20	14.06
09/13	67.86	16	11	4.58	1.20	11.98
09/12	53.64	14	11	4.15	1.08	8.85
09/11	52.76	16	11	4.06	0.96	9.93
Annual Growth	11.6%	—	—	6.0%	7.0%	9.4%

Ross Stores, Inc.

Ross wants to let you dress (and lots more) for less. A leading off-price apparel retailer (behind TJX Cos. and Kohl's) Ross operates more than 1300 Ross Dress for Less and dd's DISCOUNTS stores that sell closeout merchandise including men's women's and children's clothing at prices well below those of department and specialty stores. While apparel accounts for more than half of sales it also sells small furnishings toys and games luggage and jewelry. Featuring the Ross "Dress for Less" trademark the chain targets 18- to 54-year-old white-collar shoppers from primarily middle-income households. Ross and dd's stores are located in strip malls in more than 30 states mostly in the western US and Guam.

Geographic Reach

With its headquarters in California Ross has more than a quarter of its 1210 stores in 33 states (including Florida Texas Arizona and Georgia) the District of Columbia and Guam. The company's distribution centers and warehouses are in Pennsylvania South Carolina and California.

Operations

Ross Stores operates two brands of off-price retail apparel and home fashion stores: Ross Dress for Less and dd's DISCOUNTS. Ross is the largest off-price apparel and home fashion chain offering first-quality in-season name-brand and designer apparel as well as accessories footwear and home decor at between 20%-70% off department and specialty store regular prices. Launched in 2004 dd's DISCOUNTS serves one of the fastest-growing demographic markets in the US. The ultra-low-price spinoff which offers brand-name apparel at a 20%-70% discount has grown to more than 150 locations in about 15 states including big ones such as California Florida and Texas. The stores which average 26100 square feet are located in strip shopping centers in urban and suburban neighborhoods.

The retailer operates five distribution processing facilities: two each in California and South Carolina and one in Pennsylvania. These distribution centers are the sole source of its stores merchandise. By the end of 2015 Ross Stores anticipates investing in two new distribution centers. (A distribution center in Shafter California was under construction in 2014.)

Additionally the discounter owns two and leases three other warehouse facilities for packaway storage. To distribute merchandise to stores on a regular basis Ross Stores enlists the help of third-party cross docks. Shipments are made by contract carriers to stores between three and six times per week depending on the location.

Sales and Marketing

Ross Stores which spent $72 million on advertising in fiscal 2015 relies primarily on television as a medium to share the Ross Dress for Less value proposition with its current and potential customers. The company believes that television advertising is the most efficient and cost-effective medium while it continues to use additional channels to build brand awareness. However advertising for its dd's DISCOUNTS stores is focused on new store grand openings and local grass roots initiatives.

Financial Performance

Ross Stores has seen its sales jump to $11 billion in fiscal 2015 from $5.9 billion in fiscal 2008. The fast-growing chain saw its fiscal 2015 (ends January) revenues grow by 8% mostly due to contributions from 86 new stores and a slight increase in sales at existing stores. The revenue uptick lifted net income by 10% that year.

The company's operating cash flow grew by 34% in fiscal 2015 due to due to higher net earnings and an increase in accounts payable leverage (defined as accounts payable divided by merchandise inventory). Changes in accounts payable leverage are primarily driven by the levels and timing of inventory receipts and payments.

Strategy

The company's expansion strategy is to open additional stores based on market penetration local demographic characteristics competition expected store profitability and the ability to leverage overhead expenses.

Ross Stores' off-price business model appears to be just the right fit for both during and after the recession. Amid strong sales the retailer is adding stores. Over the past four years the company has added about 235 new locations including many dd's DISCOUNTS shops. New markets for the retailer include Illinois and the District of Columbia. In fiscal 2015 the company opened 73 new Ross stores and 22 new dd's Discounts.

Going forward the company plans to continue adding stores in existing markets while opening Ross and dd's stores in new markets. To boost its relationships with suppliers Ross does not require them to provide markdown/promotional allowances or return privileges. This combined with opportunistic purchases (closeouts such as manufacturer overruns and canceled orders) allows the company to obtain large discounts on merchandise. As a result Ross Stores' customers typically pay 20% to 60% less than department and specialty store prices. Ross holds down costs by offering minimal service and few frills inside its stores.

HISTORY

In 1957 the Ross family founded Ross Stores and opened its first junior department store; by 1982 there were six of the stores in the San Francisco area. That year two retailing veterans Stuart Moldaw (founder of Country Casuals and The Athletic Shoe Factory) and Donald Rowlett (creator of Woolworth's off-price subsidiary J. Brannam) led the acquisition of the company. Moldaw (chairman) and Rowlett (president) wanted to create an off-price chain in California where —despite the success such endeavors were having in the rest of the country —such stores were largely absent. The duo intended to establish a foothold by saturating California markets before competitors muddied the waters.

They restocked the stores with brand-name men's women's and children's apparel shoes accessories and domestics merchandise at reduced prices. Before the end of 1982 they opened two more Ross "Dress for Less" stores; the next year 18 more were added including the chain's first non-California store in Reno Nevada (much of the chain's expansion came through the acquisition of existing strip mall stores). Another 40 stores were added in 1984.

The company went public in 1985 to help fund its expansion and extended its reach to include Colorado Florida Georgia New Mexico and Oregon; that year it opened 41 stores.

In August 2004 Ross opened its first three dd's DISCOUNTS stores in Vallejo San Leandro and Fresno California. The retailer moved its headquarters from Newark California to Pleasanton in mid-2004 and then sold the Newark property for about $17 million.

EXECUTIVES

President and Chief Development Officer, James S. Fassio, age 60, $925,550 total compensation
CEO, Barbara Rentler, age 57, $1,182,723 total compensation
President and COO, Michael B. O'Sullivan, age 51, $1,039,192 total compensation
SVP and CFO, Michael J. Hartshorn, $558,971 total compensation
Senior Vice President, Michael (Mel) Hamilton
Executive Vice President Merchandising, Robert (Bob) Bernard
Executive Vice President Strategy Marketing and Human Resources, Ken Caruana
Vice President Property Management, John Fox
Vice President of Field Human Resources, Jack Bellotti
Senior Vice President Human Resources, Deon Riley
Group Vice President Corporate Real Estate, Jerry Bernie
Chairman, Michael A. Balmuth, age 65
Auditors: Deloitte & Touche LLP

LOCATIONS

HQ: Ross Stores, Inc.
  5130 Hacienda Drive, Dublin, CA 94568-7579
Phone: 925 965-4400
Web: www.rossstores.com

2015 Stores

	No.
California	335
Texas	197
Florida	166
Arizona	68
Georgia	51
Illinois	49
Pennsylvania	43
Washington	40
North Carolina	38
Virginia	34
Colorado	29
Nevada	31
Oregon	31
Tennessee	29
Maryland	23
South Carolina	21
Oklahoma	20
Alabama	19
Hawaii	17
Utah	16
Missouri	16
Louisiana	14
New Jersey	13
Idaho	10
New Mexico	10
Mississippi	8
Arkansas	6
Kansas	6
Montana	6
Indiana	5
Kentucky	5
Wyoming	2
Delaware	1
District of Columbia	1
Guam	1
Total	**1,362**

PRODUCTS/OPERATIONS

2015 Sales

	% of total
Women's apparel	29

Home accents bed & bath	24
Accessories lingerie fine jewelry & fragrances	13
Men's apparel	13
Shoes	13
Children's apparel	8
Total	**100**

2015 Stores

	No.
Ross Dress for Less	1,210
dd's DISCOUNTS	152
Total	**1,362**

Selected Merchandise

Bed and bath
Children's apparel
Cookware
Educational toys
Fine jewelry
Fragrances
Gourmet foods
Home accents
Ladies' apparel
  Accessories
  Dresses
  Junior
  Lingerie
  Maternity
  Misses sportswear
  Petites
  Women's World
Luggage
Men's apparel
  Traditional men's
  Young men's
Shoes
Small electronics
Small furnishings
Sporting goods and exercise equipment

COMPETITORS

Ascena Retail	J. C. Penney
Big Lots	Kmart
Burlington Coat	Kohl's
Factory	Men's Wearhouse
Cato	Sears
Charming Shoppes	TJX Companies
Family Dollar Stores	Target Corporation
Fred's	Wal-Mart

HISTORICAL FINANCIALS

Company Type: Public

Income Statement

FYE: January 31

	REVENUE ($ mil.)	NET INCOME ($ mil.)	NET PROFIT MARGIN	EMPLOYEES
01/15*	11,041	924	8.4%	71,400
02/14	10,230	837	8.2%	66,300
02/13	9,721	786	8.1%	57,500
01/12	8,608	657	7.6%	53,900
01/11	7,866	554	7.1%	49,500
Annual Growth	**8.8%**	**13.6%**	**—**	**9.6%**

*Fiscal year change

2015 Year-End Financials

Debt ratio: 8.47%	No. of shares (mil.): 414
Return on equity: 43.26%	Dividends
Cash ($ mil.): 696	Yield: 0.0%
Current ratio: 1.36	Payout: 18.1%
Long-term debt ($ mil.): 398	Market value ($ mil.): 38,054

	STOCK PRICE ($) FY Close	P/E High/Low		PER SHARE ($) Earnings	Dividends	Book Value
01/15*	91.71	43	28	2.21	0.40	5.49
02/14	67.91	42	28	1.94	0.34	4.70
02/13	59.43	39	29	1.77	0.28	4.00
01/12	51.09	64	32	1.43	0.22	3.29
01/11	65.46	57	38	1.16	0.16	2.82
Annual Growth	**8.8%**	**—**	**—**	**17.5%**	**25.7%**	**18.1%**

*Fiscal year change

Ryder System, Inc.

When it comes to commercial vehicles and distribution Ryder System wants to be the designated driver. The company's Fleet Management Solutions (FMS) segment acquires manages maintains and disposes of fleet vehicles for commercial customers. Similarly the Supply Chain Solutions (SCS) segment provides logistics and supply chain services from industrial start (raw material supply) to finish (product distribution). SCS also offers dedicated contract carriage service by supplying trucks drivers and management and administrative services to customers on a contract basis. Ryder's worldwide fleet of more than 207000 vehicles ranges from tractor-trailers to light-duty trucks.

Operations

Ryder System operates through two main divisions: Fleet Management Solutions (FMS —full service leasing contract maintenance contract-related maintenance and commercial rental of trucks tractors and trailers in North America and the UK) and Supply Chain Solutions (SCS —supply chain solutions including distribution and transportation services in North America and Asia). FMS generates 65% of its total sales; SCS 35%.

Sales and Marketing

Its FMS customers in the US range from small businesses to large national enterprises operating in a wide variety of industries the most significant of which are food and beverage transportation and warehousing housing business and personal services and industrial. The company's customers include Associated Grocers Bendix Cisco Clark and Reid and CVS/Caremark.

Geographic Reach

The company operates in North America (Canada Mexico and the US) Europe (Germany and the UK) and Asia (China and Singapore). The US accounted for 85% of its total revenues in 2014.

Financial Performance

Ryder has enjoyed several consecutive years of sizable growth. Revenues jumped 3% from $6.42 billion in 2013 to $6.64 billion in 2014. After experiencing profit increases for several straight years Ryder saw its profits dip 8% from $238 million to $213 million over that same period.

The growth in 2014 was fueled by an increase in lease and rental revenues primarily driven by higher prices on full service lease vehicles. It was also helped by higher commercial rental revenue due to an improvement in rental pricing. Services revenue increased primarily due to new business and higher volumes within its SCS business segment. In addition Ryder was aided by a 8% boost in sales from Europe and a 59% surge from Asia.

The erosion of profits for 2014 was driven by a spike in selling general and administrative expenses due to increased pension settlement charges. Ryder's operating cash flow has followed its revenue trend over the last five years increasing 12% to $1.37 billion in 2014 primarily due to favorable timing within accounts payable.

Strategy

Ryder continues to grow primarily through FMS-related acquisitions. In 2014 Ryder purchased Bullwell Trailer Solutions a UK-based trailer repair and maintenance company for a purchase price of approximately $15 million. The acquisition complemented the FMS business segment and enabled the company to enhance its strong market proposition in trailers.

The FMS business provides full service leasing contract maintenance and commercial rental to small businesses as well as large national enterprises engaged in a diverse range of activities including transportation grocery lumber and wood products food service and home furnishings. This segment maintains about 600 locations in the US Puerto Rico and Canada along with about 175 on-site maintenance facilities.

Another way the company remains competitive is to be prepared for the unpredictability of supply chain logistics due in part to higher fuel prices and increased regional labor costs. To achieve this the company creates partnerships with third-party logistics (3PL) providers. Such alliances enable the company to keep its networks flexible and efficient. This strategy and others like it come subsequent to the global economic downturn that forced Ryder to discontinue certain of its SCS operations in South America and Europe to focus on serving the US Canada Mexico UK and Asia markets.

In 2015 Ryder opened a new service facility in Canada as Ryder continues to see growth and expansion in Newfoundland as businesses look to outsource fleet management and maintenance within the region.

HISTORY

Ryder Truck Rental founded in Miami by Jim Ryder in 1933 was the first truck leasing company in the US. It rented trucks in four southern states until 1952 when it bought Great Southern Trucking (renamed Ryder Truck Lines) doubling its size. In 1955 the year it went public as Ryder System Ryder bought Carolina Fleets (a South Carolina trucking company) and Yellow Rental (a northeastern leasing service). More purchases over the next decade extended its truck rental business across the US and into Canada. Ryder Truck Lines was sold to International Utilities in 1965.

EXECUTIVES

EVP and CFO, Art A. Garcia, age 53, $432,150 total compensation
Chairman President and CEO, Robert E. Sanchez, age 49, $753,750 total compensation
EVP and Chief Adminsitrative Officer, Gregory F. Greene, age 55
EVP and Chief Marketing Officer, Karen M. Jones, age 52
EVP Chief Legal Officer and Secretary, Robert D. Fatovic, age 49, $375,000 total compensation
President Global Fleet Management Solutions, Dennis C. Cooke, age 50, $522,600 total compensation
EVP and Chief Sales Officer, John J. Gleason, age 59
President Ryder Dedicated Transport Solutions, John J. Diez
President Global Supply Chain Solutions (SCS), J. Steven (Steve) Sensing
CIO, Melvin (Mel) Kirk
Vice President Shared Services Center, Jeanette Mccarty
Vice President Sales, James Moore
Vice President Of Information Technology Infrastructure Dcc, Michael (Mel) Pivowar
Vice President Audit Services, Clifford (Cliff) Zoller
Vice President Investor Relations and Public Affairs, Robert (Bob) Brunn
SP First Vice President, Sylvia Andis
Vpof Sales, Mike Thompson
First Vice President, Tammy Megowan
Vice President Business Development, Jason Sonnbichler
Vice President Of National Sales (West), Scott Anderson
Vice President Business Development, Mark Swenson
Vice President Talent Management, Amparo Bravo
Vice President Of Operations, Sobeida Alvarez

Vice President Business Development, Ron Mullowney

Vice President Of Risk Management, Amy Wagner

Vice President, Elizabeth Carey

Vice President Of Tax, Ben Schmoyer

Senior Vice President Chief Marketing Officer, Karen Joness

Vice President Of Sales, Alex Madrinkian

Vice President, Rodney (Rod) Morris

Vice President Information Technology, Mike Parvor

Vice President Business Development, Tim Sweeney

Senior Vice President And Chief Information Officer Ryder System Inc, Kevin Bott

Vice President National Sales, Richard Cibos

Vice President Manager Director, Tom Knutilla

Vice President Information Technology, Stephen Hitchings

Vice President Corporate Tax, Joaquin Alonso

Vice President Automotive, Dick Jennings

Vice President Technology Services and Operations, Mike Pivowar

Senior Vice President Human Resources, Greg Greene

Senior Vice President of Sales, John (Jack) Deris

Vice President Compliance, Robert (Bob) Johnston

Vice President Compensation and Benefits, Charles R (Chas) Patton

Senior Vice President and General Manager, Tom Pettit

Vice President International Supply Chain Solutions, Eugenio Sevilla-sacasa

Vice President Supply Chain Excellence, Gary Allen

Vice President Information Technology, Mel Kirk

National Account Manager, Dale Kubala

Senior Vice President Finance and Treasurer, Dan Susik

Assistant Treasurer, Steve Goel

Auditors: PricewaterhouseCoopers LLP

LOCATIONS

HQ: Ryder System, Inc.
  11690 N.W. 105th Street, Miami, FL 33178
Phone: 305 500-3726
Web: www.ryder.com

2014 Sales

	$ mil.	% of total
US	5,614	85
Canada	435	7
Europe	400	6
Mexico	158	2
Asia	30	-
Total	6,638	100

PRODUCTS/OPERATIONS

2014 Sales

	$ mil.	% of total
Fleet management solutions	4,655	65
Supply chain solutions	2,461	35
Adjustments	(478.1)	-
Total	6,638	100

Selected Services

Fleet Management Solutions
  Commercial rental
  Contract maintenance
  Full service leasing
  Used vehicles
Supply Chain Solutions
  Distribution management
  Transportation management
Dedicated Contract Carriage

COMPETITORS

ArcBest
Barloworld Handling
Penske Truck Leasing
Schenker Inc.

C.H. Robinson Worldwide
FedEx
J.B. Hunt
Landstar System
Schneider National
UPS
UniGroup
YRC Worldwide

HISTORICAL FINANCIALS

Company Type: Public

Income Statement

FYE: December 31

	REVENUE ($ mil.)	NET INCOME ($ mil.)	NET PROFIT MARGIN	EMPLOYEES
12/15	6,571	304	4.6%	33,100
12/14	6,638	218	3.3%	30,600
12/13	6,419	237	3.7%	28,900
12/12	6,256	209	3.4%	27,700
12/11	6,050	169	2.8%	27,500
Annual Growth	2.1%	15.8%	—	4.7%

2015 Year-End Financials

Debt ratio: 50.31%
Return on equity: 16.01%
Cash ($ mil.): 60
Current ratio: 0.65
Long-term debt ($ mil.): 4,883

No. of shares (mil.): 53
Dividends
  Yield: 2.7%
  Payout: 34.7%
Market value ($ mil.): 3,040

	STOCK PRICE ($) FY Close	P/E High/Low		PER SHARE ($) Earnings	Dividends	Book Value
12/15	56.83	17	9	5.71	1.56	37.15
12/14	92.85	23	17	4.11	1.42	34.30
12/13	73.78	16	11	4.53	1.30	35.56
12/12	49.93	14	8	4.09	1.20	28.57
12/11	53.14	18	11	3.28	1.12	25.77
Annual Growth	1.7%	—	—	14.9%	8.6%	9.6%

S & T Bancorp Inc (Indiana, PA)

S&T Bancorp is the bank holding company for S&T Bank which boasts nearly $5 billion in assets and serves customers from some 60 branch offices in western Pennsylvania. Targeting individuals and local businesses the bank offers such standard retail products as checking savings and money market accounts CDs and credit cards. Business loans including commercial mortgages make up more than 80% of the company's loan portfolio. The bank also originates residential mortgages construction loans and consumer loans. Through subsidiaries S&T Bank sells life disability and commercial property/casualty insurance provides investment management services and advises the Stewart Capital Mid Cap Fund.

OperationsS&T Bancorp operates through three main business segments: Community Banking which offers traditional banking services and commercial and consumer loans; Wealth Management which boasts $2 billion in assets under management and administration and provides brokerage services trust and custodial services and investment advisory for affluent individuals and institutions; and Insurance which offers commercial property and casualty insurance group life and health coverage employee benefit services and personal insurance products through S&T Insurance Group LLC.Its S&T Bancholding subsidiary provides investment services in the Wealth Management segment while its Stewart Capital Advisors

subsidiary provides investment advisory services in the segment.Overall S&T Bancorp generated 72% of its total revenue from loan interest (including fees) in 2014 plus another 6% from interest on its investment securities. About 10% of its total revenue came from debit and credit card fees and deposit account service charges while wealth management fees and insurance fees made up 6% and 3% of total revenue that year respectively. Geographic ReachHeadquartered in Indiana Pennsylvania S&T Bancorp boasts branches in a dozen counties in the state including: Allegheny Armstrong Blair Butler Cambria Centre Clarion Clearfield Indiana Jefferson Washington and Westmoreland counties. It also has loan production offices in northeast and central Ohio and in western New York.Sales and MarketingTargeting both individuals and local businesses S&T Bancorp spent $3.32 million on marketing in 2014 up from the $2.93 million and $3.21 million it spent in 2013 and 2012 respectively.Financial PerformanceS&T Bancorp's revenue has slowly declined in recent years due to shrinking interest margins on loans amidst the low-interest environment. The firm's profits however have been rising thanks to declining loan loss provisions as its loan portfolio's credit quality has improved with the strengthened economy. Following several years of top-line declines the bank's revenue inched up by nearly 1% to $206.86 million in 2014. The rise was mostly thanks to higher interest income as overall earning-asset balances grew by nearly 7% during the year reflecting the bank's growing loan business and increased investment securities assets. Wealth Management fees also continued to grow rising by 6% during the year. Higher revenue coupled with lower interest expenses on deposits and a $6.6 million reduction in loan loss provisions in 2014 drove S&T Bancorp's net income higher by 15% to $57.91 million. S&T's operating cash levels fell by 9% to $78.1 million for the year after adjusting its earnings for non-cash items mostly related to its net proceeds from sales of its mortgage loans originated-for-sale.

Strategy

S&T Bancorp reiterated in 2015 that its growth strategy is centered around organic growth in existing and new markets and growth through strategic acquisitions that introduce new lines of business. Its 2015 acquisition of Integrity Bancshares for example expanded S&T's footprint eastward across four counties in Pennsylvania and added millions of dollars worth of new loan business. Also that year the bank entered the western part of New York for the first time with the opening of a new loan production office in the region.

In late 2012 the bank extended its operations into its neighbor Ohio when it opened a handful of branches in Akron. That same year the bank acquired Mainline Bancorp and Gateway Bank of Pennsylvania bolstering its presence in its core western Pennsylvania market.

Mergers and Acquisitions

In March 2015 S&T Bancorp purchased Camp Hill-based Integrity Bancshares for $155 million adding $860 million in assets and eight branches expanding S&T's geographic footprint eastward into Cumberland Dauphin Lancaster and York counties in Pennsylvania. S&T added that the acquisition positioned the bank in high-growth markets within the state and added experienced members to the bank's loan team.In 2012 the bank acquired Mainline Bancorp and Gateway Bank of Pennsylvania. Both transactions served to expand S&T's presence in western Pennsylvania.

EXECUTIVES

SEVP and COO, David P. Ruddock, age 53, $265,000 total compensation

President and CEO S&T and S&T Bank, Todd D. Brice, age 52, $525,000 total compensation

Manager Branch Administration, Richard A. (Rich) Fiscus

SEVP and CFO, Mark Kochvar, age 54, $278,000 total compensation

EVP Commercial Lending, David G. Antolik, age 48, $302,000 total compensation

EVP and Chief Investment Officer Wealth Management, Malcolm E. Polley, age 52

SEVP Chief Risk Officer and Secretary, Ernest J. Draganza

EVP and Deputy Chief Credit Officer, William (Bill) Kametz

SEVP and Chief Credit Officer, Patrick Haberfield

SEVP and Chief Banking Officer, Rebecca Stapleton

EVP and Commercial Loan Officer, Steve Drahnak

EVP and Chief Audit Executive, LaDawn D. Yesho

EVP, David Richards

EVP Marketing Division Manager, Rob Jorgenson

EVP and CIO, Jim Mill

EVP and Manager, Robert Jogrenson

SEVP and Market Executive, Thomas J. Sposito

Vice President Mortgage Underwriting Manager, Christine Rumbaugh

Vice President Relationship Manager Ii, Ron Barner

Vice President Network Operations Manager, Ron Todd

Vice President Community Banking, Tammy Czyz

Vice President Sales and Marketing Financial Advisor, Bonnie Confer

Chairman S&T and S&T Bank, Charles G. Urtin

Vice Chairman S&T and S&T Bank, Christine J. Toretti, age 58

Auditors: KPMG LLP

LOCATIONS

HQ: S & T Bancorp Inc (Indiana, PA)
800 Philadelphia Street, Indiana, PA 15701
Phone: 800 325-2265
Web: www.stbancorp.com

PRODUCTS/OPERATIONS

2014 Sales

	% of total
Interest	
Loans including fees	72
Investment securities & other	6
Noninterest	
Wealth management fees	6
Debit and credit card fees	5
Service charges on deposit accounts	5
Insurance fees	3
Others	3
Total	100

Selected Subsidiaries

9th Street Holdings Inc.
Commonwealth Trust Credit Life Insurance Company (50%)
S&T Bank
S&T Insurance Group LLC
S&T-Evergreen Insurance LLC
S&T Bancholdings Inc.
S&T Professional Resources Group LLC
S&T Settlement Services LLC
Stewart Capital Advisors LLC

COMPETITORS

AmeriServ Financial
Citizens Financial Group
F.N.B. (PA)
Fidelity Bancorp (PA)
First Commonwealth Financial
Northwest Bancshares
PNC Financial

HISTORICAL FINANCIALS

Company Type: Public

Income Statement

FYE: December 31

	ASSETS ($ mil.)	NET INCOME ($ mil.)	INCOME AS % OF ASSETS	EMPLOYEES
12/14	4,964	57	1.2%	945
12/13	4,533	50	1.1%	948
12/12	4,526	34	0.8%	1,027
12/11	4,119	47	1.1%	909
12/10	4,114	43	1.1%	936
Annual Growth	4.8%	7.4%	—	0.2%

2014 Year-End Financials

Debt ratio: 0.92%
Return on equity: 9.82%
Cash ($ mil.): 109
Current ratio: —
Long-term debt ($ mil.): —
No. of shares (mil.): 29
Dividends
Yield: 2.2%
Payout: 36.7%
Market value ($ mil.): 888

	STOCK PRICE ($) FY Close	P/E High/Low	Earnings	PER SHARE ($) Dividends	Book Value
12/14	29.81	16 11	1.95	0.68	20.42
12/13	25.31	15 10	1.70	0.61	19.21
12/12	18.07	20 13	1.18	0.60	18.08
12/11	19.55	17 11	1.41	0.60	17.44
12/10	22.59	19 12	1.34	0.60	20.70
Annual Growth	7.2%	— —	9.8%	3.2%	(0.3%)

Salesforce.Com Inc

Salesforce.com champions the power of the social enterprise. The company offers Internet-based applications that manage employee collaboration as well as customer information for sales (Salesforce Sales Cloud) marketing (Salesforce Marketing Cloud) and customer support (Salesforce Service Cloud) providing clients with a rapidly deployable alternative to traditional more time-consuming and user-maintained software installations. Salesforce counts more than 100000 users of its customer relationship management (CRM) software and its customers come from a variety of industries including financial services telecommunications manufacturing and entertainment. It generates most of its revenues from the US.

Operations

The company also offers Force.com part of its vision to not only be the leader in enterprise-targeted social applications but also a platform for developing and offering such applications for its customers. Force.com provides the tools for application creation customization integration deployment (through its AppExchange marketplace) and integration.

Geographic Reach

The geographic spread of Salesforce's revenue has remained fairly consistent in recent years with 72% coming from customers in the Americas about 18% from European customers and those in the Asia/Pacific region accounting for about 10%.

Sales and Marketing

Salesforce counts more than 100000 customers in all shapes and sizes from small businesses with one subscription to large enterprises with hundreds of thousands. With such a large customer base no one counts for more than 5% of sales.

The company uses a direct sales force made up of telephone sales reps based in regional hubs and field sales reps in territories close to their customers. Just over 50% of revenue goes to sales and marketing a level the company expects to maintain as it seeks more customers and build awareness. Salesforce has cranked up advertising spending in the past few years. Its advertising expense was $203 million in 2015 (ended January) $156 million in 2014 and $110 million in 2013.

Financial Performance

As a pioneer in demonstrating the sales potential and scalability of the Software-as-a-Service (SaaS) business model Salesforce's revenues have grown substantially every year. Sales grew a healthy 32% in 2015 (ended January) to reach almost $5.4 billion. The company added new customers and existing customers upgraded accounts and added subscriptions to boost revenue. Salesforce also counted full-year revenue from its July 2013 acquisition of Exact Target. As it has since 2012 Salesforce posted a net loss which reached $262 million in 2015 compared to $232 million in 2014. Operating expenses increased almost across the board – in R&D marketing and sales general and administrative – as the company concentrated on developing its products and adding customers. R&D spending increased 21%. Cash flow from operations increased to $1.17 billion in 2015 from $875 million in 2014.

Strategy

Acquisitions and partnerships help drive growth but Salesforce also relies on internal development. The company expanded its social networking and collaboration capabilities with Chatter which began as an enterprise instant messaging-style application for sharing updates and data within organizations on people projects groups and documents.

In 2015 Salesforce added an analytics cloud service to its product portfolio with Salesforce Marketing Cloud Predictive Decisions. The application enables companies to quickly deploy sales service marketing and custom analytics apps using any data source. Customers' employees can examine business data uncover connections and take action on their mobile device

While its largest market is the US the company is looking to Europe for growth. (Sales there grew 33% in 2015). In response it opened a data center in the UK with NTT Europe a subsidiary of Japan's Nippon Telegraph and Telephone Corporation. It is Salesforce.com's sixth data center worldwide. Saleforce also opened a data center in France with Interxion as the service provider. Salesforce.com has two more data centers in its plans for Europe.

Mergers and Acquisitions

In 2014 Salesforce paid $390 million for RelateIQ a Palo Alto California start-up with a CRM product that automates sales priorities.

In 2013 Salesforce acquired in a $2.5 billion transaction cloud marketing platform ExactTarget. The deal expands its CRM capabilities adding marketing expertise to its sales service and cloud platforms. Also that year it entered into a nine-year partnership with Oracle through which the enterprise software giant will integrate some of its programs with Salesforce products; Salesforce will also increase its use of Oracle products.

EXECUTIVES

Chairman and CEO, Marc Benioff, age 50, $1,440,000 total compensation

Co-Founder, Parker Harris, age 48, $650,000 total compensation

President Products, Alex Dayon, $650,000 total compensation

Vice Chairman President and COO, Keith G. Block, age 54, $1,000,000 total compensation

EVP Salesforce Industries, John Wookey, age 54

President Global Enterprise Sales, Anthony Fernicola

President Sales and Customer Success, Maria Martinez, age 57

CEO ExactTarget Marketing Cloud, Scott S. McCorkle, age 49

EVP and CFO, Mark J. Hawkins, age 54, $325,000 total compensation

Chief Marketing Officer, George Hu, age 40, $600,000 total compensation

EVP and Chief Legal Officer, Burke F. Norton, age 48, $650,000 total compensation

President Global Commercial Sales, Brian Millham

Chairman and CEO Japan, Shinichi Koide

EVP and Chief Marketing Officer, Lynn Vojvodich

CIO, Ross Meyercord

EVP Worldwide Alliances and Channels, Tyler Prince

Enterprise Corporate Sales Vice President, Will Anastas

Vice President Technology and Alliance, Ryuji Enoki

Regional Vice President, Adam Gilberd

Vice President Platform Developer Marketing, Adam Seligman

Senior Vice President Corporate Development and Strategy, John (Jack) Somorjai

Area Vice President, Robert Zimmermann

Vice President Corporate Communications, Jane (Ginny) Hynes

Vice President Corporate Sales, Phil Bradley

Vice President Enterprise Sales, Paul Seminara

Vice President Sales, Patrick (Paddy) Blair

Vice President Service Cloud Product Marketing, Fergus Griffin

Executive Vice President Operations And Mobility, Todd Pierce

Vice President Global Operations Salesforce University, Shane Anastasi

Regional Vice President, Stephen Harrison

Regional Vice President Corporate Sales, Evans Killeen

Auditors: Ernst & Young LLP

LOCATIONS

HQ: Salesforce.Com Inc
The Landmark @ One Market, Suite 300, San Francisco, CA 94105

Phone: 415 901-7000

Web: www.salesforce.com

2015 Sales

	$ mil.	% of total
Americas	3,868	72
Europe	984	18
Asia/Pacific	520	10
Total	**5,373**	**100**

Selected Mergers and Acquisitions

FY2013
ExactTarget ($2.5 billion email marketing software)

FY2012
Buddy Media ($690 million social media marketing software)
GoInstant ($50 million collaboration software)
Jigsaw ($140 million business contact data provider)

FY2011
Assistly ($58 million customer service software)
Dimdim (collaboration software)
Heroku ($210 million app development platform)
Manymoon ($13 million social productivity app)
Radian6 ($320 million social networking software)
Model Metrics ($66 million consultancy)
Rypple (social performance management software)

PRODUCTS/OPERATIONS

2015 Sales

	$ mil.	% of total
Subscription & support	5,013	93
Professional services & other	359	7
Total	**5,373**	**100**

COMPETITORS

CDC Software	NetSuite
Google	Oracle
IBM	SAP
Infor Global	Sage Software
KANA	SugarCRM
Microsoft Dynamics	

HISTORICAL FINANCIALS

Company Type: Public

Income Statement

FYE: January 31

	REVENUE ($ mil.)	NET INCOME ($ mil.)	NET PROFIT MARGIN	EMPLOYEES
01/15	5,373	(262)	—	16,000
01/14	4,071	(232)	—	13,300
01/13	3,050	(270)	—	9,800
01/12	2,266	(11)	—	7,785
01/11	1,657	64	3.9%	5,306
Annual Growth	**34.2%**	**—**	**—**	**31.8%**

2015 Year-End Financials

Debt ratio: 12.82%	No. of shares (mil.): 650
Return on equity: (-7.46%)	Dividends
Cash ($ mil.): 908	Yield: —
Current ratio: 0.81	Payout: —
Long-term debt ($ mil.): 1,370	Market value ($ mil.): 36,726

	STOCK PRICE ($) FY Close	P/E High/Low	PER SHARE ($) Earnings	Dividends	Book Value
01/15	56.45	— —	(0.42)	0.00	6.11
01/14	60.53	— —	(0.39)	0.00	5.02
01/13	172.13	— —	(0.48)	0.00	4.05
01/12	116.80	— —	(0.02)	0.00	3.04
01/11	129.14	1205497	0.12	0.00	2.40
Annual Growth	**(18.7%)**	**— —**	**—**	**—**	**26.3%**

SanDisk Corp.

SanDisk is a top producer of data storage products based on flash memory which retains data even when power is interrupted. Its products — which are sold to four primary end-markets (mobile consumer electronics computing and enterprise and hyperscale data centers) —include removable and embedded memory cards used in digital cameras mobile phones digital audio/video players GPS devices tablets and other electronic gear as well as USB flash drives and solid-state drives (SSDs). It also licenses technologies from its portfolio of some 4700 US and international patents. SanDisk serves consumers and enterprises worldwide with most of its sales coming from outside the US. In 3Q 2015 SanDisk agreed to be bought by Western Digital the leading maker of disk drives. The value of the cash-and-stock transaction was set at $19 billion.

OperationsSanDisk outsources all of its controller component manufacturing and much of its assembly and test operations to foundries (contract semiconductor manufacturers). Its flash memory wafers primarily come from manufacturing joint ventures with Toshiba which produce finished wafers in Japan that are sold to SanDisk and Toshiba. SanDisk also has in-house assembly and test operations in China.

The company's commercial channel two-thirds of its total revenues in 2013 while retail sales accounted for the remaining third.

Geographic ReachThe company has locations across the Americas the Asia-Pacific region and Europe. Some 68% of its 2014 sales came from the Asia/Pacific region including 31% from China. The US accounted for 17% and the EMEA (Europe Middle East and Africa) region 12%.

Sales and MarketingThe company's products are distributed primarily by retailers and original equipment manufacturers (OEMs). Its retail channel includes electronics stores office superstores and mass merchandisers among other locations. SanDisk sells products directly to OEMs for use in mobile phones tablets gaming consoles and other computer devices.The company's top 10 customers and licensees represent more than 45% of sales; Apple is its largest single customer accounting for nearly 20% of 2014 sales.

SanDisk boosted its spending on advertising in 2014 with about $28 million compared to $19.6 million in 2013 and $16.2 million in 2012.

Financial Performance

The company's revenues rose by 7% in 2014 to $6.63 billion thanks to a 36% increase in the number of gigabytes sold (with no change in the average selling price per gigabyte) and an increase in commercial revenues related to higher sales of client and enterprise SSD products although sales of embedded memory products declined.SanDisk followed a 150% in 2014 with a 3% drop in 2014. Revenue dipped to $1.01 billion in 2014 because of higher operating costs related to the company's mid-2014 acquisition of Fusion-io.

In 2014 the company reported cash provided by operating activities of $1.7 billion down from $1.86 billion in 2013 on the lower profit and higher accounts receivables.

Strategy

While SanDisk has been the riding the wave of rising popularity for flash memory it also had to watch out for the wave of consolidation that has cresting in memory and semiconductor companies. The company joined the consolidation wave with its agreement to be bought by Western Digital. The deal combines the leading hard disk drive (HDD) maker (Western Digital) and a leading flash maker (SanDisk). Memory users are increasingly turning to flash for applications such as data centers but there's still a sizable market for HDDs. The deal should enable the company to approach the market from a position of strength but competition is intense as HDD companies fight for market share and the flash battle is just beginning.

Even with the acquisition SanDisk's strategy for growth is focused on increasing overall revenue by lowering the cost of the NAND flash memory that powers its technology and by working with other companies to develop new NAND applications and products. To cushion itself against possible limits to the development of NAND SanDisk also invests in alternative technologies including bit-cost scalable 3-dimensional NAND (BiCS) and 3-dimensional resistive RAM (3D ReRAM).

During 2014 SanDisk partnered with Giga-Spaces Technologies a provider of in-memory computing and cloud orchestration technologies to deliver a new product that enables customers to obtain the full performance scalability and cost benefits of flash storage. In the same year company also partnered with Arrow Electronics a leading global technology distributor under which Arrow will offer a wide variety of SanDisk commercial flash storage products to its more than 100000 customers worldwide. Also in 2014 SanDisk and Toshiba agreed to work together in building and operating a chip plant that will convert to 3D NAND from 2D NAND.

In new products SanDisk released in 2015 an all-flash storage platform called InfiniFlash storage system that delivers large capacity performance and reliability to for big data and hyperscale workloads while reducing data center complexity and costs.

In 2014 SanDisk opened its newest research and development facility in Marlborough Massachusetts.

In early 2013 SanDisk joined with NVIDIA to launch a flash drive optimized for use with NVIDIA's Tegra 4 which the company bills as the world's fastest mobile processor.

Mergers and Acquisitions

In mid-2014 the company announced a major acquisition offering $1.1 billion in cash for Fusion-io a maker of flash memory products. The deal will help SanDisk accelerate efforts to create a flash-transformed data center for customers while Fusion-io will benefit from SanDisk's vertical integration.

Following the acquisition SanDisk spun out the ioControl that had been a part of Fusion-io. The new entity will be known as NexGen Storage the name it held before it was acquired by Fusion-io. Hybrid systems incorporating hard-disk drives are not part of SanDisk's strategic focus.

HISTORY

SanDisk was co-founded as SunDisk in 1988 by Eli Harari an expert on nonvolatile memory technology. SunDisk's first product based on a four-megabit flash chip was developed with AT&T Bell Labs and released in 1991. In 1992 the company formed a development partnership with disk drive maker Seagate Technology; as part of the pact Seagate acquired 25% of SunDisk.

Because SunDisk was being confused with Sun Microsystems in 1995 the company changed its name to SanDisk. It went public that year and introduced the industry's smallest Type II (a PC card slot size designation) flash storage card –the CompactFlash. Sales increased by nearly 80% in 1995 SanDisk's first profitable year. The next year SanDisk and Matsushita (now Panasonic) developed double-density flash a breakthrough technology that doubled the capacity of flash storage products.

EXECUTIVES

President and CEO, Sanjay Mehrotra, age 56, $1,028,846 total compensation

EVP Administration and CFO, Judy Bruner, $639,135 total compensation

SVP and General Manager Mobile and Connected Solutions, Drew Henry

EVP Memory Technology, Siva Sivaram, $245,769 total compensation

EVP and Chief Strategy Officer, Sumit Sadana, $532,000 total compensation

SVP Technology and Fab Operations; President SanDisk Japan, Atsuyoshi Koike

SVP and CIO, Ravi Naik

SVP Worldwide Operations, Manish Bhatia

SVP and General Manager Client Storage Solutions, Kevin Conley

SVP Global Manufacturing and Supply Chain Operations, Gursharan Singh

SVP IP Licensing and Chief Legal Officer, Mark Brazeal

Senior Vice President Solid StateDrives, Thomas (Thom) Rampone

Vice President Embedded Mobile Engineer, Lisa Kho

Vice President OEM Business Development and Strategic Initiatives, Erez Schwartz

Vice President Product and Test Engineering, David (Dave) Duffin

Senior Vice President Of Human Resourc, Tom Baker

Sales Vice President, Doug Hauck

General Vice President Manager, Alper Ilkbahar

Senior Vice President And General Manager Enterprise Storage Solutions, John (Jack) Scaramuzzo

Vice President Americas Commercial Sales And Support, Richard Hegberg

Vice President Engineering Systems And Software Solu, Kirk Law

National Sales Manager, David (Dave) Moser

Vice President Quality and RELIABILITY, Sharo McAfee-Hunter

Chairman, Michael E. Marks, age 64

A Treasurer, John (Jack) Joy

Auditors: Ernst & Young LLP

LOCATIONS

HQ: SanDisk Corp.
951 SanDisk Drive, Milpitas, CA 95035
Phone: 408 801-1000   **Fax:** 408 542-0503
Web: www.sandisk.com

2014 Sales

	$ mil.	% of total
Asia/Pacific		
China	2,026	31
Taiwan	864	13
Other countries	1,464	22
US	1,136	17
Europe Middle East & Africa	814	12
Other regions	321	5
Total	**6,627**	**100**

PRODUCTS/OPERATIONS

2014 Sales

	$ mil.	% of total
Commerical	4,454	67
Retail	2,172	33
Total	**6,627**	**100**

Selected Products

Embedded data storage devices (FlashDrive)
MP3 music players (Sansa)
Portable storage devices (Cruzer)
Removable storage cards (used in cellular phones digital cameras digital music players digital voice recorders and personal digital assistants)
  CompactFlash
  Memory Stick
  MultiMedia
  Secure Digital
  SmartMedia

COMPETITORS

Apple Inc.	SK Hynix
Atmel	SMART Modular
Creative Technology	Technologies
Fusion-io	STMicroelectronics
Imation	Samsung Electronics
Intel	Seagate Technology
Iriver	Silicon Motion
Kingston Technology	Sony
Lexar	Toshiba Semiconductor
Macronix International	& Storage Products
Micron Technology	Verbatim Corp.
Microsoft	Viking Modular
PNY Technologies	Solutions
Philips Electronics	Western Digital

HISTORICAL FINANCIALS

Company Type: Public

Income Statement

FYE: January 3

	REVENUE ($ mil.)	NET INCOME ($ mil.)	NET PROFIT MARGIN	EMPLOYEES
01/16*	5,564	388	7.0%	8,790
12/14	6,627	1,007	15.2%	8,696
12/13	6,170	1,042	16.9%	5,459
12/12	5,052	417	8.3%	4,636
01/12	5,662	986	17.4%	3,939
Annual Growth	**(0.4%)**	**(20.8%)**	**—**	**22.2%**

*Fiscal year change

2016 Year-End Financials

Debt ratio: 23.30%
Return on equity: 6.23%
Cash ($ mil.): 1,478
Current ratio: 2.82
Long-term debt ($ mil.): 1,237
No. of shares (mil.): 200
Dividends
  Yield: 0.0%
  Payout: 49.4%
Market value ($ mil.): 15,272

	STOCK PRICE ($) FY Close	P/E High/Low	PER SHARE ($) Earnings	Dividends	Book Value
01/16*	75.99	52 24	1.82	0.90	28.56
12/14	101.31	24 15	4.23	1.05	30.26
12/13	70.24	16 10	4.34	0.45	30.93
12/12	42.68	31 18	1.70	0.00	30.09
01/12	49.21	13 8	4.04	0.00	29.13
Annual Growth	**11.5%**	**— —**	**(18.1%)**	**—**	**(0.5%)**

*Fiscal year change

Sandy Spring Bancorp Inc

Sandy Spring Bancorp is the holding company for Sandy Spring Bank which operates around 50 branches in the Baltimore and Washington DC metropolitan areas. Founded in 1868 the bank is one of the largest and oldest headquartered in Maryland. It provides standard deposit services including checking and savings accounts money market accounts and CDs. Commercial and residential real estate loans account for nearly three-quarters of the company's loan portfolio; the remainder is a mix of consumer loans business loans and equipment leases. The company also offers personal investing services wealth management trust services insurance and retirement planning.

Operations

Sandy Spring Bancorp's nonbank subsidiaries include money manager West Financial Services and Sandy Spring Insurance which sells annuities and operates insurance agencies Chesapeake Insurance Group and Neff & Associates.

Financial Performance

The company's revenue increased in fiscal 2013 compared to the previous year. It reported $196.9 million in revenue for fiscal 2013 after bringing in revenue of $190.8 million in fiscal 2012.

The company's net income also went up in fiscal 2013 compared to the prior period. It claimed a profit of about $44 million in fiscal 2013 after netting a little more than $36 million in fiscal 2012.

Sandy Spring Bancorp's cash on hand increased by about $43 million in fiscal 2013 compared to fiscal 2012 levels.

Mergers and Acquisitions

In 2012 Sandy Spring Bancorp acquired CommerceFirst Bancorp a small Maryland bank with a strong Small Business Administration lending practice. The $25.4 million transaction added five branches to Sandy Spring Bank's network.

EXECUTIVES

Senior Vice President, Dennis Neville
EVP General Counsel and Secretary, Ronald E. Kuykendall, age 62, $250,173 total compensation
EVP Wealth Management Insurance Mortgage, R. Louis (Lou) Caceres, age 52, $299,135 total compensation
President and CEO Bancorp and Bank, Daniel J. (Dan) Schrider, age 50, $508,192 total compensation
EVP and CFO Bancorp and Bank, Philip J. Mantua, age 56, $295,962 total compensation
EVP and CIO, John D. Sadowski, age 51
EVP Commercial and Retail Banking, Joseph O'Brien, $320,962 total compensation
EVP and Chief Credit Officer, Ronda M. McDowell
Vice President, John Paparello
Senior Vice President, Brian Schott
Senior Vice President Mortgage Division Manager, Lynne Pulford
Senior Vice President Credit Administration, Peter (Pete) Hickling
Vice President Regional Operations Manager, Marsha Maloney
Vice President, Christopher (Chris) Huang
Senior Vice President, Todd Ellis
Senior Business Analyst Assistant Vice President, Stephen (Steve) Marsico
Vice President Marketing Communications Manager, Jennifer (Jen) Schell
Senior Vice President, Bill Hill
Vice President Commercial Portfolio, Michael Irwin
Vice President, Denise Kratz
Vice President HRIS Project Administrator, Patti Boyle
Vice President, Bill Howland
Vice President Commercial Lending, Heather Burke
Assistant Vice President Public Relations Specialist, Amanda Walsh
Vice President, Sandra Workman
Vice President, Sima Kowkabi
Vice President, Bill Brock
Senior Vice President Assistant Controller, Louise Basore
Vice President, Brita Jones
Senior Vice President, Scott Sims
Senior Vice President Director of Corporate Security And Contigency Planning, Rob Turano
Vice President Sba Officer, David (Dave) Steinhoff
Assistant Vice President Bsa Aml Administrator, Susan (Sue) Booth
Mortgage Banker Assistant Vice President Mortgage Lender Loan Officer Construction Loans Conventional And Fha Financin, Karen Gouker
Vice President And Treasury Sales Officer, Michelle (Mitch) Coates
Vice President and Director Corporate Communications, Sharon Murphy
Assistant Vice President Trust Administrator, Mardelle Channon
Chairman, Robert L. Orndorff, age 59
Abm, Shan Vengada
Auditors: Ernst & Young LLP

LOCATIONS

HQ: Sandy Spring Bancorp Inc
17801 Georgia Avenue, Olney, MD 20832
Phone: 301 774-6400
Web: www.sandyspringbank.com

PRODUCTS/OPERATIONS

COMPETITORS

BB&T	Fulton Financial
Bank of America	OBA Financial Services
Bay Bancorp	PNC Financial
Capital One	SunTrust

HISTORICAL FINANCIALS

Company Type: Public

Income Statement

FYE: December 31

	ASSETS ($ mil.)	NET INCOME ($ mil.)	INCOME AS % OF ASSETS	EMPLOYEES
12/14	4,397	38	0.9%	727
12/13	4,106	44	1.1%	725
12/12	3,955	36	0.9%	707
12/11	3,711	34	0.9%	713
12/10	3,519	23	0.7%	711
Annual Growth	5.7%	12.9%	—	0.6%

2014 Year-End Financials

Debt ratio: 0.80%	No. of shares (mil.): 25
Return on equity: 7.48%	Dividends
Cash ($ mil.): 95	Yield: 2.9%
Current ratio: —	Payout: 49.6%
Long-term debt ($ mil.): —	Market value ($ mil.): 653

	STOCK PRICE ($) FY Close	P/E High/Low	PER SHARE ($) Earnings	Dividends	Book Value
12/14	26.08	18 15	1.52	0.76	20.83
12/13	28.19	16 11	1.77	0.64	19.98
12/12	19.42	13 11	1.48	0.48	19.41
12/11	17.55	14 10	1.41	0.34	18.52
12/10	18.43	18 8	1.05	0.05	16.95
Annual Growth	9.1%	— —	9.7%	97.5%	5.3%

Sanmina Corp

Sanmina means to be a top contract manufacturer of sophisticated electronic components. It designs and makes printed circuit boards and board assemblies backplanes and backplane assemblies enclosures cable assemblies optical components and modules and memory modules. In addition the company provides services such as design and engineering materials management order fulfillment and in-circuit testing. It serves OEMs in the health care defense medical aerospace telecommunications and technology industries among others. Because its customers have production facilities in lower-cost regions some 84% of sales come from outside the US.

Operations
Sanmina's Integrated Manufacturing Solutions unit (78% of 2015 (ended October) sales) makes printed circuit board assembly and test optical and radio frequency modules. The Components Products and Services unit (22% of sales) makes interconnect systems and mechanical systems components in addition to memory and storage products and other services.

Geographic ReachSanmina has 75 facilities in 25 countries on six continents. Mexico is the company's largest geographic segment with 31% of revenue. It moved passed China 22% of revenue as Sanmina's biggest market two years ago. US customers account for 16% of revenue.

Sales and Marketing

The company supplies OEMs primarily in the communications networks defense and aerospace industrial and semiconductor systems medical multimedia computing and storage automotive and clean technology sectors. Two markets —Industrial Medical and Defense and Communications Network —each accounted for about 40% of revenue in 2015. Sanmina's top 10 customers together generate half of sales.

Sanmina sells through its direct sales force as well as representative sales firms.

Financial Performance
Sanmina posted its second straight year of sales growth in 2015 (ended October) with a 3% increase to $6.37 billion. Efforts to reach new customers paid with a 5% increase in the IMS segment but CPS sales dropped 7%.

Net income grew a bit in 2015 —some 91% —coming it at $377 million from $197 million in 2014. Tax accountants might get some credit since much of the gain came from an income tax benefit.

StrategyOperating in a highly cyclical industry the company is continually restructuring in order to provide more cost-efficient products to its customers.

Its strategy includes extending its technology capabilities; building customer partnerships; moving into diverse end markets; pursuing strategic transactions; and cutting costs. The company is emphasizing growth in its CPS segment and it made improvements in its backplane technologies a key element of CPS.

In order to reduce costs and exert greater control over production the company follows suit with its customers locating its components plants in lower-cost regions while its final system assembly plants sit near customers and their end-markets. It continues to eye regions such as Latin America Eastern Europe China Southeast Asia and India for opportunities to keep its manufacturing costs down. In May 2014 the company bought a manufacturing facility in Mexico from Motorola Solutions.

Mergers and Acquisitions
In 2015 Sanmina bought a privately-held company that designs and manufactures equipment for the oil and gas industry. The acquisition adds to Sanmina's oil and gas capabilities. It is part of its CPS segment.

HISTORY

Early History
Bosnian immigrants Jure Sola (chairman and CEO) and Milan Mandaric founded Sanmina in 1980 to provide just-in-time manufacturing of printed circuit boards (PCBs). The name Sanmina comes from the names of Mandaric's children.

During the late 1980s and early 1990s Sanmina shifted production to higher-margin components such as backplane assemblies and subassemblies. Mandaric an entrepreneur with other interests left in 1989. The company went public in 1993.

Like other contract manufacturers Sanmina began bolstering its operations through acquisitions. The company bought manufacturing plants from Comptronix (1994) Assembly Solutions (1995) Golden Eagle Systems (1996) and Lucent Technologies (1996). In 1997 the company bought contract electronics maker Elexsys International which was headed by Milan Mandaric. Sanmina also opened a plant in Ireland.

EXECUTIVES

Chairman and CEO, Jure Sola, age 64, $896,538 total compensation
EVP and CFO, Robert K. (Bob) Eulau, age 53, $510,000 total compensation

EVP Europe and Asia Sales, Dennis R. Young, age 64, $350,000 total compensation
SVP and CIO, Manesh Patel
EVP Global Human Resources, Alan M. Reid, age 52, $290,000 total compensation
EVP and Chief Business Officer, Charles F. Kostalnick, age 50, $398,846 total compensation
Executive Vice President Human Resour, David L (Dave) Pulatie
Vice President Business Development, Randy Thomas
Executive Vice President and Chief Business Officer, Chuck Kostalnick
Vice President Human Resources, Lindsey Tullett
Sales Vice President, Dan Mulhern
Vice President Business Development, James Murphy
Vice President And General Manager, Joe Wong
Executive Vice President, Bob Cusick
Vice President Global Supply Management, Troy Hiner
Vice President, Rick Chang
Vice President EHandS, Khalid Ruhullah
Vice President Manufacturing Engineering, John (Jack) Jamieson
Vice President Technical Resources EMS and Optical Technology Greater China Region, Bernard Leung
Vice President Global Commodities, Mark Tan
Vice President Legal Counsel, Ed Attanasio
Vice President Finance And Controller, Michelle (Mitch) Dang
Senior Vice President of Global Manufacturing Medical Operations, Gary Switzer
Vice President Corporate Development, George Chen
Vice President Quality Assurance And Ra, Tim McGinnis
Vice President And Assistant General Counsel, Chris Sadeghian
Vice President, Ash Sharma
Senior Vice President Mechanical Systems Division, Patrick (Paddy) Macdonald
Vice President Customer Supply Chains, Tom Pendergrass
Vice President, Joe Banavige
Vice President Business Development, Thomas (Thom) Mosier
Senior Vice President Finance And Corporate Controller, Todd Schull
Senior Vice President Business Develo, Greg White
Senior Vice President Corporate Devel, Robin Walker
Vice President, Carl Boklund
Vice President Global Supply Chain Management (Indirect Procurement And Global Logistics), Kelli Fahey
Vice President, John (Jack) Dullea
Vice President Of Operations, William Adams
Vice President of Marketing, Daniel (Dan) Liddle
Vice President Finance Tcg, Ted Wilson
Vice President Finance, James Moylan
Executive Vice President, Eugene McCabe
Senior Vice President, Vahid Ghassemian
Senior Vice President Business Development, Brad Kolb
Senior Vice President Operations, Sushil Dhiman
Vice President Internal Audit, Wendy Phillips
Vice President Business Development, Henrik Oja
Senior Vice President Strategic Marketing, Carl Gustin
Vice President, Michael (Mel) Sparacino
Executive Vice President Human Resources, Robert Alberico
Senior Vice President Customer Experience And Strategy, Erik Swennumson
Executive Vice President of Communications, David (Dave) Dutkowsky

Vice President (Information Technology) And Managing Director, Rajeev Gollarahalli
Senior Vice President Of Chief Quality O, Anca Thompson
Vice President Of Operations, Mike Keri
Vice President Sales Backplane Division, Robert (Bob) Voskian
Senior Vice President Sales And Marketing Optical And Micro Electronics, Nat Mani
Vice President Internal Audit, Aroon Gudibande
Vice President Aircraft Systems, Bob Kloote
Vice President Engineering, Drew Doblar
Senior Vice President Interconnect Technology Systems, Hegarty Barry
Vice President, James (Jamie) Griffin
Executive Vice President Chief Financial Officer, Bob Eulau
Vice President Information Technology, Steve Bruton
Senior Vice President global Human Resources, Andy Reid
Vice President Of Global Compensation An, X Xpon
Executive Vice President Global Human Resources, Dave Pulatie
Senior Vice President, Joe Rauschmayer
Senior Vice President Of Operations, Michael (Mel) Doty
Executive Vice President and Chief Operating Officer Asia EMEA and Global Services, Michael (Mel) Landy
Executive Vice President Operations EMEA, Dietmar Guenther
Vice President Technology, Steven (Steve) Dedlock
Senior Vice President Sales, Ken Haney
Vice President Sales, Hardie Harris
Vice President, Rick Laponzina
Senior Vice President, Digel Oliver
Vice President and Corporate Treasurer, Walter Boileau
Board Member, Wayne Shortridge
Board Of Directors, Gene Sapp
Auditors: PricewaterhouseCoopers LLP

LOCATIONS

HQ: Sanmina Corp
2700 N. First St., San Jose, CA 95134
Phone: 408 964-3500
Web: www.sanmina.com

2015 Sales

	$ mil.	% of total
Mexico	1,979	31
China	1,510	24
US	1,029	16
Other countries	1,855	29
Total	**6,374**	**100**

PRODUCTS/OPERATIONS

2015 Sales

	$ mil.	% of total
Industrial defense & medical	2,528	40
Communications	2,482	39
Embedded computing & storage	1,363	21
Total	**6,374**	**100**

2015 Sales

	% of total
IMS	78
CPS	22
Total	**100**

Selected Services

Backplane assembly
Cable assembly
Circuit assembly
Circuit fabrication
Configuration
Distribution
Enclosures

Engineering
Forward logistics
In-circuit testing
Inventory management
Materials management
Order fulfillment
Printed circuit board design
Reverse engineering
Sustaining engineering
System assembly and testing

COMPETITORS

AMD	NCR
Benchmark Electronics	Nam Tai
CTS Corp.	Plexus
Celestica	SMTC Corp.
Flextronics	SYNNEX
Hon Hai	Seagate Technology
IBM Canada	TTM Technologies
Inventec	Universal Scientific
Jabil	Venture Corp.
Lexmark	Western Digital
Molex	Wistron
Multi-Fineline Electronix	

HISTORICAL FINANCIALS

Company Type: Public

Income Statement

FYE: October 3

	REVENUE ($ mil.)	NET INCOME ($ mil.)	NET PROFIT MARGIN	EMPLOYEES
10/15*	6,374	377	5.9%	43,854
09/14	6,215	197	3.2%	43,101
09/13	5,917	79	1.3%	40,909
09/12	6,093	180	3.0%	44,879
10/11	6,602	68	1.0%	45,505
Annual Growth	**(0.9%)**	**53.0%**	**—**	**(0.9%)**

*Fiscal year change

2015 Year-End Financials

Debt ratio: 15.38%	No. of shares (mil.): 78
Return on equity: 26.83%	Dividends
Cash ($ mil.): 412	Yield: —
Current ratio: 1.74	Payout: —
Long-term debt ($ mil.): 423	Market value ($ mil.): 1,668

	STOCK PRICE ($) FY Close	P/E High/Low		PER SHARE ($) Earnings	Dividends	Book Value
10/15*	21.37	6	4	4.41	0.00	19.48
09/14	21.60	10	6	2.27	0.00	15.18
09/13	17.54	19	8	0.93	0.00	12.97
09/12	8.51	6	3	2.16	0.00	11.81
10/11	6.68	20	8	0.83	0.00	9.54
Annual Growth	**33.7%**	**—**	**—**	**51.8%**	**—**	**19.5%**

*Fiscal year change

Santander Consumer USA Holdings Inc

This auto finance company aims to put credit-impaired car buyers in the driver's seat. Santander Consumer USA (SCUSA) makes subprime new and used vehicle loans to buyers at more than 14000 Chrysler Ford GM and Toyota dealerships throughout the US. The technology-driven company also originates loans through independent dealers such as CarMax banks and its direct-to-consumer website Roadloans.com. SCUSA also provides refinancing and cash-back refinancing services. While subprime loans make up more than 80% of its loan portfolio the company is looking to increase its prime loan business. Founded in 1995 SCUSA is owned by Spanish banking giant Banco Santander SA. The company went public in 2014.

IPO

Santander Consumer USA (SCUSA) went public in January 2014 with an offering valued at $1.5 billion. The IPO capitalizes on the rebound in auto sales as credit-impaired borrowers return to the car market. Post IPO Banco Santander owns 61% of SCUSA.

Financial Performance

The auto lender reported more than $2.9 billion in finance and other interest income in 2012 a 14% increase versus 2011.

Strategy

SCUSA is looking to expand its portfolio of prime loans through partnerships with automakers. To that end in February 2013 SCUSA entered into a 10-year agreement with Chrysler whereby it originates private-label loans and leases under the Chrysler Capital brand. The company relies on third-party banks and parent company Banco Santander for approximately $12 billion and $5 billion respectively in committed financing. It also has agreements with Bank of America and Sovereign to fund the Chrysler Capital business.

Company Background

In 2006 Banco Santander acquired a 90% stake in Drive Financial from HBOS and the company's founding partners for $651 million. Drive changed its name to Santander Consumer USA in 2008.

Auditors: Deloitte & Touche LLP

LOCATIONS

HQ: Santander Consumer USA Holdings Inc
1601 Elm Street, Suite 800, Dallas, TX 75201
Phone: 214 634-1110
Web: www.santanderconsumerusa.com

COMPETITORS

Ally Bank	Credit Acceptance
Bank of America	Ford Motor Credit
Capital One Auto	GM Financial
Finance	Toyota Motor Credit

HISTORICAL FINANCIALS

Company Type: Public

Income Statement

	REVENUE ($ mil.)	NET INCOME ($ mil.)	NET PROFIT MARGIN	EMPLOYEES
12/14	6,127	766	12.5%	4,400
12/13	4,245	697	16.4%	4,100
12/12	3,244	715	22.0%	3,900
12/11	3,047	768	25.2%	—
12/10	2,325	438	18.8%	—
Annual Growth	27.4%	15.0%	—	—

FYE: December 31

2014 Year-End Financials

Debt ratio: 85.99%	No. of shares (mil.): 348
Return on equity: 24.54%	Dividends
Cash ($ mil.): 33	Yield: 0.7%
Current ratio: 6.80	Payout: 8.4%
Long-term debt ($ mil.): 27,811	Market value ($ mil.): 6,843

	STOCK PRICE ($) FY Close	P/E High/Low		PER SHARE ($) Earnings	Dividends	Book Value
12/14	19.61	12	8	2.15	0.15	10.20
Annual Growth	—	—	—	—	—	—

Santander Holdings USA Inc.

Santander Holdings USA is the parent company of Sovereign Bank which reigns in the Northeast with more than 700 branch locations. TheÂbankÂcaters to individuals and small to mid-sized businesses offeringÂdeposits creditÂcards insurance and investmentsÂas well as commercial loans and mortgages (which together account for nearlyÂhalf of its total portfolio) and residential mortgages and home equity loansÂ(more than a quarter).ÂSantander Holdings also owns a majority of Santander Consumer USA which purchases and services subprime car loans made byÂauto dealerships and other companies.ÂSpain-based banking giant Banco Santander acquired the rest of Sovereign BancorpÂit didn't already own in 2009.Founded in 1902 Sovereign Bank has grown by making some 30 acquisitions since 1990. Its acquisitive ways have brought the company new markets and sometimes new headaches. For example its 2006 purchase of Independence Community Bank and its 125 branches gave the bank a foothold in the New York metro area and linked the bank's mid-Atlantic and New England operations. The deal was fraught with difficulties including shareholder concern over where power of the company would end up if the company sold shares to fund the acquisition. In the ensuing tumultous years three CEOs were replaced as Sovereign tried to overcome its exposure to bad loans.Streamlining back-office operations were among the cost-cutting efforts utilized to stop the company's losses. The bank transferred its loan servicing operations to Santander Consumer USA and stopped originating indirect auto loans in the Southeast and Southwest after that business performed poorly.Santander Holdings returned to profitability in 2009 after Sovereign Bancorp suffered more than $3 billion in (mainly investment- and credit-related) losses in 2007 and 2008 combined as the company ramped up its focus on risk management and collections. It continued its momentum into 2010 and 2011 as the economy showed signs of improvement. In 2011 the company reported revenue growth of 23% (some $7.2 billion) and net income growth of some 19% (some $1.3 billion) as both interest and noninterest earnings increased. Santander Holdings has stabilized the credit quality of its loan portfolio and experienced fewer net charge-offs and lowered its provisions for loan losses. Improved performance from investments an uptick in net interest margins and acquisitions by Santander Consumer helped the company's results as well.As Santander Holdings continues to keep a close eye on credit quality its strategies for growth include courting large corporate clients and strengthening its core retail business by adding new products. In early 2012 Sovereign Bank changed its charter from a thrift to a national commercial bank which provides it with more flexibility to target corporate clients in particular. The company is also focused on specialized business lines such as lending for multifamily housing in Brooklyn New York.In 2011 the company sold a 35% stake in Santander Consumer to an investment group and its management team. The deal brought Santander nearly $1 billion enough to account for its biggest noninterest earnings of the year.

HISTORY

Sovereign which had built itself into a regional powerhouse appealed to the Spanish bank as it pursued growth in the US. Santander acquired its initial stake in the company of about 20% in 2006 later upped that to about 25% then bought the restÂfor nearlyÂ$2 billion in early 2009.The deal was fraught with difficulties though. Sovereign planned to fund the acquisition by selling an additional stake to Santander a move that was opposed by some shareholders concerned about control of the company. Sovereign and theÂopposing shareholders launched a volley of lawsuits and countersuits. Ultimately the disputes were settled with Sovereign adding independent directors (including one from lead shareholder Relational Investors) to its board and with Relational Investors agreeing to back Sovereign's board nominees for a number of years.There was more turmoil to come though.ÂLater inÂ2006 Sovereign's longtime CEO Jay Sidhu was forced to resign under criticism over the company's stock price and performance. AÂfew weeks later the presidentÂand COO of the bank resigned after being passed over for Sidhu's position which went to former vice chairman Joe Campanelli.Campanelli consolidated senior leadership in his home base of Boston (instead of in theÂPhiladelphia headquarters) and centralized the company's decision-making process to address inefficiencies in the organization. The bank's new leadership closed branches cut jobs andÂceased its wholesale mortgage business in order to concentrate onÂits coreÂretail banking operations.However turmoil in the financial industry affected banks throughout the world including smaller banks that didn't receive government support. Sovereign stock value fell more than 70% in 2008 and the board elected to replace Campanelli as CEO. (His strategy of expanding into new loan areas beyond the Northeast was called into question for increasing the bank's exposure to risk.) Paul Perrault formerly CEO ofÂChittenden CorporationÂtook the helm of the company in early 2009 but wasÂreplaced afterÂless thanÂa month on the job by Gabriel Jaramillo when Santander completed its acquisition of Sovereign.After the deal was complete Santander implemented its own cost-saving efforts such as streamlining its back-office operations.ÂThe bank transferred itsÂloan servicing operations to Santander Consumer USA and stopped originating indirect auto loans in the Southeast and Southwest after that business performed poorly.

EXECUTIVES

Evp And Chief Accounting Officer, Thomas D (Thom) Cestare
Evp-govt Affairs & Public Poli, Jesse O Villarreal
Senior Vice President Strategic Marketing, Cathleen Ingersoll
Vice President, Michael Jones
Vice President Community Development Inv, George Demoulias
Executive Vice President Head, Manuel Baldasano
Auditors: Deloitte & Touche LLP

LOCATIONS

HQ: Santander Holdings USA Inc.
75 State Street, Boston, MA 02109
Phone: 617 346-7200
Web: www.sovereignbank.com

Selected Locations

Connecticut
Delaware
Maryland
Massachusetts
New Hampshire

New Jersey
New York
Pennsylvania
Rhode Island

PRODUCTS/OPERATIONS

2013 Sales

	$ mil.	% of total
Interest		
Loans	1,958	58
Investment securities	330	10
Deposits	6	.
Noninterest		
Equity method investment	426	12
Consumer banking fees	228	7
Commercial banking fees	199	6
Mortgage bankin revenue	122	4
Bank owned life insurance	57	3
Others	54	.
Total	**3,384**	**100**

COMPETITORS

Bank of America	M&T Bank
Citibank	PNC Financial
Citizens Financial	People' s United
Group	Financial
Fulton Financial	TD Bank USA
HSBC USA	Webster Financial
JPMorgan Chase	Wells Fargo
KeyCorp	

HISTORICAL FINANCIALS

Company Type: Public

Income Statement

FYE: December 31

	REVENUE ($ mil.)	NET INCOME ($ mil.)	NET PROFIT MARGIN	EMPLOYEES
12/14	11,919	2,335	19.6%	14,000
12/13	3,383	628	18.6%	9,100
12/12	3,687	561	15.2%	8,920
12/11	7,249	1,172	16.2%	8,557
12/10	5,813	1,022	17.6%	11,714
Annual Growth	**19.7%**	**22.9%**	**—**	**4.6%**

2014 Year-End Financials

Debt ratio: 33.52%	No. of shares (mil.): 530
Return on equity: 14.55%	Dividends
Cash ($ mil.): 3,068	Yield: 7.1%
Current ratio: 0.11	Payout: —
Long-term debt ($ mil.): 39,709	Market value ($ mil.): 13,541

	STOCK PRICE ($) FY Close	P/E High/Low	PER SHARE ($) Earnings	Dividends	Book Value
12/14	25.53	— —	(0.00)	1.83	34.96
12/13	25.39	— —	(0.00)	1.83	26.03
12/12	25.17	— —	(0.00)	1.83	25.45
12/11	25.00	— —	(0.00)	1.83	24.21
12/10	25.15	— —	(0.00)	1.83	21.73
Annual Growth	**0.4%**	**— —**	**—**	**(0.0%)**	**12.6%**

SCANA Corp

SCANA (from "South CAroliNA") is cooking with natural gas and electricity in South Carolina North Carolina and Georgia. The holding company serves 692000 electricity customers and 342000 gas customers through utilities South Carolina Electric & Gas (SCE&G) Public Service Company of North Carolina and SCANA Energy (in Georgia).

SCANA has an electric generating capacity of about 5240 MW derived from fossil-fueled power plants and hydroelectric and nuclear generation facilities. Unregulated operations include retail and wholesale energy marketing and trading gas transportation power plant management and appliance and HVAC maintenance.

Geographic Reach

The company has operations in Georgia North Carolina and South Carolina. In South Carolina SCANA's electric service area covers 24 counties throughout South Carolina.

Operations

SCANA's has two utilities: SCE&G generates transmits distributes and sells electricity to retail and wholesale customers (and it also purchases sells and transports natural gas to retail customers) while Public Service Company of North Carolina (PSNC) purchases sells and transports natural gas to retail customers. PSNC serves approximately 521000 residential commercial and industrial customers.SCE&G's resale customers include municipalities electric cooperatives other investor-owned utilities registered marketers and federal and state electric agencies.

South Carolina Fuel Company Inc. (which manages nuclear fuel certain fossil fuels and emission and other environmental allowances);

SCANA Energy Marketing Inc. (which markets natural gas);

SCANA Energy (which markets natural gas in Georgia's retail market);

ServiceCare Inc. (which provides service contracts on home appliances and HVAC units); and

SCANA Services Inc. (which provides administrative management and other services to SCANA's business units).

Sales and Marketing

Through a wholly-owned nonregulated subsidiary SCANA markets natural gas to retail customers in Georgia and to wholesale customers across the Southeast.

The local distribution operations of SCE&G purchases transports and sells natural gas to retail customers in portions of South Carolina.Financial Performance

In 2014 SCANA's net revenues increased by 10% due to sales growth in its reportable segments.Revenues grew driven by higher electricity gas retail gas marketing and energy marketing retail sales volumes primarily due to the effects of weather and customer growth and rate increases. SCANA also reported higher industrial sales in volumes in energy marketing and a grow in demand in retail gas marketingThe company has reported strong net income growth over the last five years. In 2014 SCANA's net income increased by 14% due to the effects of weather customer growth and rate increases. Higher electric and gas margins were partially offset by an increase in operating and maintenance expenses and higher depreciation expense property taxes and interest expenses.In 2014 SCANA's cash from operating activities decreased by 30% due to the changes in prepayment regulatory assets and liabilities and derivative financial instruments.

Strategy

To raise cash to pay down debt in 2015 the company sold Carolina Gas Transmission Corporation and SCANA Communications (to Dominion Resources) and Spirit Communications in deals valued at $650 million.

SCAN is looking for an improving economy and increase in industrial activities in its service area to life the demand for the company's services. The Port of Charleston continues to see increased traffic residential and commercial customer growth rates in SCANA's regulated businesses also were positive in 2014 and regional unemployment rates also showed signs of improvement.

In 2014 SCE&G experienced a net increase of approximately 10000 electric customers (growth rate of 1.4%). For the period 2015-2017 the SCANA and SCE&G's total consolidated regulated natural gas customer base is projected to increase annually 2.4% and 2.3% respectively.

Ownership

SCANA Corporation Stock Purchase Savings Plan owns 10% of SCANA.

HISTORY

SCANA's earliest ancestors include Charleston Gas Light Company (1846) and Columbia Gas Light Company (1852) formed to light those cities' streets. After barely surviving the Civil War the companies rebuilt only to face the greater challenge posed by Thomas Edison's lightbulb in 1879.

Electric utilities such as Charleston Electric Light Company (1886) began to emerge and they also introduced electric trolleys which were commonly operated by electric utilities to boost power consumption. After a series of mergers among utilities in South Carolina the Columbia Electric Street Railway Light and Power Company (1892) and Charleston Consolidated Railway Gas and Electric Company (1897) were formed to handle energy and transit needs in their respective cities.

The 1920s brought another wave of utility mergers and consolidation in South Carolina. Columbia Electric Street Railway became part of the Broad River Power Company in 1925 and Charleston Consolidated Railway became a part of South Carolina Power Company the next year. In 1937 Broad River was renamed South Carolina Electric & Gas (SCE&G).

SCE&G went public in 1948. After a two-year fight with the South Carolina Public Service Authority SCE&G finally gained approval to purchase South Carolina Power Company in 1950. During the 1950s it built several power plants and natural gas distribution lines and joined other utilities to build the Southeast's first nuclear plant prototype in 1959.

A dozen years later SCE&G and the South Carolina Public Service Authority began building a nuke near the pilot plant. Because of delays related to the Three Mile Island accident and stricter regulations the plant cost $1.3 billion by the time it was completed in 1984.

SCE&G and Carolina Energies merged in 1982 under the SCE&G name. SCANA Corporation was formed two years later to allow the company to separate its utility business from nonregulated activities. The company formed an energy marketing subsidiary in 1988.

EXECUTIVES

Vice President Marketing and Communications, Cathy Love

Chairman President and CEO, Kevin B. Marsh, age 60, $1,107,287 total compensation

EVP; President Generation and Transmission and COO South Carolina Electric & Gas Company, Stephen A. Byrne, age 56, $574,254 total compensation

EVP and CFO; President SCANA Energy Georgia and SCANA Energy Marketing, James E. (Jimmy) Addison, age 55, $574,254 total compensation

SVP; President and COO PSNC Energy; President South Carolina Electric & Gas, D. Russell (Rusty) Harris, age 50

CIO, Randal M. (Randy) Senn

SVP and Chief Nuclear Officer South Carolina Electric & Gas, Jeffrey B. (Jeff) Archie, age 57

SVP and General Counsel, Ronald T. (Ron) Lindsay, age 64, $425,131 total compensation

SVP; President Retail Operations South Carolina Electric & Gas, W. Keller Kissam, age 48
Senior Vice President; President and Chief Operating Officer Carolina Gas Transmission, Paul Fant
Vice President Of Information Technology, Philip Kleckley
Auditors: Deloitte & Touche LLP

LOCATIONS

HQ: SCANA Corp
100 SCANA Parkway, Cayce, SC 29033
Phone: 803 217-9000
Web: www.scana.com

PRODUCTS/OPERATIONS

2014 Sales

	% of total
Electric Operation	53
Gas-nonregulated	26
Gas regulated	21
Total	**100**

2014 Sales

	% of total
Electric Operation	53
Gas Distribution	20
Energy Marketing	16
Retail Gas & Marketing	10
Other	1
Total	**100**

Selected Operations

Carolina Gas Transmission Corp. (gas transportation and natural gas purchase transmission and sale; LNG liquefaction storage and regasification plants)
Public Service Company of North Carolina Incorporated (dba PSNC Energy natural gas distribution)
SCANA Communications Inc. (fiber-optic telecommunications tower construction and investments)
SCANA Energy Marketing Inc. (electricity and natural gas marketing)
SCANA Energy (retail natural gas marketing)
SCANA Services Inc. (support services)
ServiceCare Inc. (maintenance for home appliances)
South Carolina Electric & Gas Company (SCE&G electric and gas utility)
South Carolina Fuel Company Inc. (financing for SCE&G's nuclear fuel fossil fuel and sulfur dioxide emission allowances)
South Carolina Generating Company Inc. (GENCO owns and operates Williams power plant and sells electricity to SCE&G)

COMPETITORS

AEP	North Carolina
AGL Resources	Electric Membership
CenterPoint Energy	PS Energy
Dominion Resources	Piedmont Natural Gas
Duke Energy	Progress Energy
Dynegy	Santee Cooper
Entergy	Sempra Energy
Green Mountain Energy	Southern Company
Laclede Group	TVA
NextEra Energy	

HISTORICAL FINANCIALS

Company Type: Public

Income Statement
FYE: December 31

	REVENUE ($ mil.)	NET INCOME ($ mil.)	NET PROFIT MARGIN	EMPLOYEES
12/14	4,951	538	10.9%	5,886
12/13	4,495	471	10.5%	5,989
12/12	4,176	420	10.1%	5,842
12/11	4,409	387	8.8%	5,889
12/10	4,601	376	8.2%	5,877
Annual Growth	**1.8%**	**9.4%**	**—**	**0.0%**

2014 Year-End Financials

Debt ratio: 39.25%		No. of shares (mil.): 142	
Return on equity: 11.15%		Dividends	
Cash ($ mil.): 137		Yield: 3.4%	
Current ratio: 0.85		Payout: 55.4%	
Long-term debt ($ mil.): 5,531		Market value ($ mil.): 8,619	

	STOCK PRICE ($) FY Close	P/E High/Low	PER SHARE ($) Earnings	Dividends	Book Value
12/14	60.40	17 12	3.79	2.10	34.95
12/13	46.93	16 13	3.39	2.03	33.08
12/12	45.64	16 14	3.15	1.98	31.47
12/11	45.06	15 12	2.97	1.94	29.92
12/10	40.60	14 12	2.98	1.90	29.15
Annual Growth	**10.4%**	**— —**	**6.2%**	**2.5%**	**4.6%**

Schein (Henry), Inc.

From Poughkeepsie to Prague Henry Schein outfits dental offices around the world with everything they need. The company is a leading global distributor of dental supplies equipment and pharmaceuticals. Henry Schein provides everything from the delicate hand held tools up to the X-ray equipment and patient chairs as well as office supplies and anesthetics. But the company isn't only interested in teeth: It also supplies doctors' offices veterinarians and other office-based health care providers with diagnostic kits surgical tools drugs vaccines and animal health products. Other offerings include practice management software repair services and financing.

HISTORY

For more than 50 years Henry Schein distributed drugs made by Schein Pharmaceuticals. In 1992 management spun off the drug business and led by former accountant Stanley Bergman began acquiring other dental supply companies at a terrific rate: 34 between 1994 and 1996 alone.

The company went public in 1995 and bought more than a dozen businesses. These purchases which included product marketer Vertex Corporation's distribution unit moved Henry Schein into the medical and veterinary supply fields. The purchase of Schein Dental Equipment (founded by Marvin Schein) boosted per-customer sales by adding big-ticket merchandise to the product mix.

Acquisitions continued hot and heavy as the company boosted operations abroad. The purchases hit the bottom line; Schein avoided bloat by restructuring operations closing facilities and developing new systems. The company consolidated 13 distribution centers into five in 1997. The following year the firm expanded into Canada and bought a controlling stake in UK direct marketer Porter Nash.

To boost profits the company announced in 2000 that it would cut 5% of its workforce. It also shut down some facilities and sold its software development business as part of its overall restructuring plan. In 2001 the firm resumed its acquisitions when it bought the dental supply business of drug maker Zila. Over the next few years it expanded internationally when it bought up firms in the Czech Republic Germany Italy New Zealand and the UK.

Choosing to focus on supplying office-based health care practitioners in 2006 it sold its hospital supply business for $36.5 million. Other dispositions have included the sale of its oncology and specialty pharmaceutical businesses (2007) and a dental products wholesaler (2009). In 2009 Henry Schein acquired a majority stake in Butler Animal Health tripling the size of its domestic animal health operations; the unit was renamed Butler Schein Animal Health following the deal. (The company increased its stake in Butler Schein Animal Health to about 72% in 2012.)

Henry Schein expanded its health care technology segment in 2010 through the acquisition of majority ownership of ImproMed and McAllister Software Systems both developers of veterinary practice management systems in the US. In 2011 the company entered the veterinary market in Australia and New Zealand with the $92 million buy of Provet Holdings. The purchase helped Henry Schein cement its strategy to expand its international health care distribution unit which grew from some $2.5 billion in sales in 2010 to some $3 billion in sales in 2011.

EXECUTIVES

Vice President and General Manager Medical Sales, Brad Connett
EVP Chief Strategic Officer and Director, Mark E. Mlotek, age 59, $521,231 total compensation
EVP and Chief Administrative Officer, Gerald A. Benjamin, age 62, $521,231 total compensation
President Henry Schein Inc. CEO Global Dental Group and Director, James P. Breslawski, age 61, $661,426 total compensation
EVP CFO and Director, Steven Paladino, age 58, $521,231 total compensation
Chairman and CEO, Stanley M. Bergman, age 66, $1,268,846 total compensation
SVP and Chief Merchandising Officer, Michael Racioppi, age 60, $340,275 total compensation
President International Dental Group, Robert (Bob) Minowitz, age 56
President Medical Group, David C. (Dave) McKinley, age 62
SVP and CTO, James A. (Jim) Harding, age 59
CEO Global Strategic Portfolio Group, Lonnie Shoff, age 56
President Global Animal Health Group, Peter McCarthy
SVP Global Supply Chain, Paul Rose, age 57
Vice President Corporate Finance, Ronald (Ron) South
Vice President Finance, Charles Crawford
Vice President, Howard S Stapler
Vice President Treasurer, Ferdinand Jahnel
Vice President Audit And Compliance, Thomas Adamcewicz
Senior Vice President Administration and Finance, Scott Becker
Vice President Product Merchandising, Marguerite Walsh
Vice President Global Distribution, David Kagey
Vice President Finance, Eileen Rosenbaum
Senior Vice President Administration, Rich Miranda
Vice President Schein Creative, Bob Possenriede
National Sales Manager, Doug Statham
Vice President Marketing, Peg Olin-Lederman
Senior Vice President Corporate and Legal Affairs Secretary, Michael (Mel) Ettinger
Vice President Marketing, Peter (Pete) Jugoon
Vice President, Lynne McHugh
Vice President Business Development And Strategic Relationships, David (Dave) Chen
Vice President Marketing, Michael Allsop
Vice President Sales Operations, Charlie Crawford
Vice President and General Manager, Ann Marie Schneider
Vice President, Angela Mancuso
Vice President Of Sales, Michael (Mel) Stone
Vice President Corporate Brand Development, Napoleon Monroe

Vice President and Senior Counsel Litigation, Marjorie Han

Vice President Business Development, Edward L (Ed) Mohr

Vice President of Infrastructure Administration, Peter (Pete) Dellacroce

National Sales Manager, Deanna Evans

National Account Manager, Jeremy Belloit

Vice President Information Technology, Gail Gregory

Vice President National Telesales Operations, Jim Loiacono

Vice President and Treasurer, Graham Stanley

Vice President Of Loans, Steve Steinbrunner

Vice President, Peter (Pete) Hoag

Vice President Claims Information Technology, Pat Gunning

Senior Management (Senior Vice President General Manager Director), Debbie Bua

Vice President, Jesse Garringer

Vice President, Don Cohen

Vice President, Leonard (Len) David

Global Security Vice President, Chris Berry

Senior Vice President Corporate Business Development Group and Director, Jim Harding

Vice President Business Development, Rick Miranda

Vice President of Advertising, Bob Possenreid

Vice President Customer Service and Facilities, Jim Mullins

Executive Vice President And Chief ADM, Jerry Benjamin

Vice President of Product Management, Stephen (Steve) Roberts

Member Board Of Directors, Alperin Barry

Auditors: BDO USA, LLP

LOCATIONS

HQ: Schein (Henry), Inc.
135 Duryea Road, Melville, NY 11747
Phone: 631 843-5500
Web: www.henryschein.com

2014 Sales

	$ mil.	% of total
US	6,247	60
Other countries	4,124	40
Total	**10,371**	**100**

PRODUCTS/OPERATIONS

2014 Sales

	$ mil.	% of total
Health care distribution		
Dental	5,381	52
Animal health	2,898	28
Medical	1,742	17
Technology & value-added services	348	3
Total	**10,371**	**100**

COMPETITORS

Allscripts	McKesson
Benco Dental	NextGen
Burkhart Dental	Omega Pharma
Cardinal Health	PSS World Medical
Carestream Health	Patterson Companies
Darby Dental	Sybron Dental
IDEXX Labs	athenahealth
MWI Veterinary Supply	eClinicalWorks

HISTORICAL FINANCIALS

Company Type: Public

Income Statement

FYE: December 26

	REVENUE ($ mil.)	NET INCOME ($ mil.)	NET PROFIT MARGIN	EMPLOYEES
12/15	10,629	479	4.5%	19,000
12/14	10,371	466	4.5%	17,500
12/13	9,560	431	4.5%	16,000
12/12	8,939	388	4.3%	15,000
12/11	8,530	367	4.3%	15,000
Annual Growth	**5.7%**	**6.8%**	**—**	**6.1%**

2015 Year-End Financials

Debt ratio: 12.45%
Return on equity: 16.86%
Cash ($ mil.): 72
Current ratio: 1.50
Long-term debt ($ mil.): 463

No. of shares (mil.): 82
Dividends
  Yield: —
  Payout: —
Market value ($ mil.): 12,947

	STOCK PRICE ($) FY Close	P/E High/Low	PER SHARE ($) Earnings	Dividends	Book Value
12/15	157.09	28 22	5.69	0.00	35.00
12/14	137.39	25 20	5.44	0.00	33.49
12/13	114.43	23 16	4.93	0.00	32.53
12/12	79.96	19 15	4.32	0.00	29.75
12/11	64.43	18 15	3.97	0.00	27.05
Annual Growth	**25.0%**	**— —**	**9.4%**	**—**	**6.7%**

Schwab (Charles) Corp.

The once-rebellious Charles Schwab is all grown up as the discount broker now offers the same traditional brokerage services it shunned some three decades ago. Schwab manages about $2.5 trillion in assets for nearly 11 million individual investors and institutional clients. Traders can access its services via telephone wireless device the Internet and through more than 325 offices in some 45 states plus London and Hong Kong. Besides discount brokerage the firm offers financial research advice and planning; investment management; retirement and employee compensation plans; and about 70 proprietary Schwab and Laudus mutual funds. Chairman Charles Schwab owns more than 13% of his namesake firm.

Operations

The financial services and brokerage firm operates through two business segments: its Investor Services segment which offers retail brokerage and banking services to individual investors retirement plan services and corporate brokerage services; and its Advisor Services (formerly Institutional Services) segment which provides custodial trading and support services to institutional investors.More than 40% of the company's revenue comes from asset management and administration fees which are made up of mostly mutual fund service fees advice solutions fees and other fees. Another nearly 40% of revenue comes from interest income on cash investment securities brokerage-related receivables and loans to banking clients. Trading revenue makes up another 15% of total revenue and consists of commission and principal transaction income. Through its Charles Schwab Bank (CSB) subsidiary which provides mortgages CDs and other banking products the company remains in step with the industry-wide movement toward one-stop shopping for financial services. This strategy as well as its ongoing pur-

suit of technological innovations and product expansion helps the company meet the evolving financial services needs of its diverse client base. CSB has more than 980000 banking accounts.

The company's OneSource service offers investors access to more than 2000 no-load funds. Schwab also provides access to nearly 28000 bonds bond funds and other fixed income investment products from more than 300 dealers. Additional services include futures and commodities trading access to IPOs and educational investment materials including ratings of more than 3000 stocks. Schwab provides trading and support services to independent investment advisors as well.

Geographic Reach

San Francisco-based Schwab has more than 325 branch offices in 45 US states as well as offices in London Hong Kong and Puerto Rico.Sales and MarketingThe company provides financial services to both individuals and institutional clients. Its Advisor Services segment provides custodial trading and support services to independent investment advisors and retirement business services to independent retirement plan advisors and record keepers with assets plans held at Schwab Bank.In 2014 the company had $2.46 trillion in client assets across 9.4 million active brokerage accounts more than 980000 banking accounts and 1.5 million corporate retirement plan participants.

Financial Performance

Thanks to the rising US stock market —which has led to higher management fee income from higher assets under management balances and new business — Charles Schwab has enjoyed healthy revenue and profit growth over the past several years. Schwab's revenue in 2014 jumped by more than 11% to $6.06 billion thanks primarily to higher asset management and administration fees as total client assets grew by 10% to $2.46 trillion over the year which reflected $124.8 billion worth of net new client assets and one million new brokerage accounts combined with healthy stock market growth. Mutual fund services fee revenue also grew thanks to market appreciation and growth in clients assets invested in the firm's OneSource mutual funds and equity and bond funds. Advice solutions fees increased due to growth in client assets enrolled in advisory and managed account programs.Higher revenue in 2014 pushed net income up by 23% to $1.32 billion. Operations provided $2.35 billion or 42% more cash than in 2013 thanks mostly to higher earnings but also because the bank suffered less of a drop in brokerage deposit balances than in 2013.

Mergers and Acquisitions

Charles Schwab continues to grow via acquisitions. To that end it purchased Massachusetts-based ThomasPartners a dividend income-focused asset management firm with some $2.3 billion in assets under management for $85 million in cash in December 2012. Company BackgroundPreviously in 2011 Charles Schwab acquired retail brokerage optionsXpress. The $1 billion deal expanded its client base and online equity options and futures trading business and it has already boosted the company's trading revenues. In another 2011 transaction Charles Schwab acquired Compliance11 which allowed the company to offer compliance monitoring and reporting services.

HISTORY

During the 1960s Stanford graduate Charles Schwab founded First Commander Corp. which managed investments and published a newsletter. But he failed to properly register with the SEC and after a hiatus he returned to the business under the name Charles Schwab & Co. in 1971. Initially a full-service broker Schwab moved into discount brokerage after the SEC outlawed fixed commissions in 1975. While most brokers defiantly raised commissions Schwab cut its rates steeply.

From 1977 to 1983 Schwab's client list increased thirtyfold and revenues grew from $4.6 million to $126.5 million enabling the firm to automate its operations and develop cash-management account systems. To gain capital Charles sold the company to BankAmerica (now Bank of America) in 1983. Schwab grew but federal regulations prevented expansion into such services as mutual funds and telephone trading. Charles bought his company back in 1987 and took it public. When the stock market crashed later that year trading volume fell by nearly half from 17900 per day. Stung Schwab diversified further offering new fee-based services. Commission revenues fell from 64% of sales in 1987 to 39% in 1990 but by 1995 the long bull market had pushed commissions to more than 50%.

In 1989 Schwab introduced TeleBroker a 24-hour Touch-Tone telephone trading service available in English Spanish Mandarin or Cantonese.

Schwab continued to diversify courting independent financial advisors. Other buys included Mayer & Schweitzer (1991 now Schwab Capital Markets) an OTC market maker that accounted for about 7% of all NASDAQ trades. In 1993 the firm opened its first overseas office in London but traded only in dollar-denominated stocks until it bought Share-Link (later Charles Schwab Europe) the UK's largest discount brokerage in 1995. It subsequently sold the British pound sterling brokerage business to Barclays PLC although it has maintained its US dollar business in the UK.

During the next year Schwab made a concerted effort to build its retirement services by creating a 401(k) administration and investment services unit. In 1997 Schwab allied with J.P. Morgan Hambrecht & Quist and Credit Suisse First Boston (CSFB) to give its customers access to IPOs; the next year the relationship with CSFB deepened to give Schwab access to debt offerings. In late 1997 and early 1998 Schwab reorganized to reflect its new business lines. The firm also began recruiting talent rather than promoting from within.

Expansion was key at the turn of the century. In 1999 Schwab moved toward more broker-advised investing: It inked a deal (geared toward its retirement products customers) with online financial advice firm Financial Engines and introduced Velocity a desktop system designed to make trading easier for fiscally endowed investors. In 2000 Schwab bought online broker CyBerCorp (later CyberTrader) as well as U.S. Trust which markets to affluent clients.

While Schwab's World Trade Center offices were destroyed by the September 11 terrorist attacks the company did not lose any of its New York staff.

To pare expenses Schwab reduced its workforce by about 35% between 2000 and 2003. Founder and chairman Charles Schwab relinquished his role of co-CEO in early 2003 only to move back into the driver's seat in mid-2004 when former CEO David Pottruck was asked to step down by the company's board.

One of Schwab's first orders of business was to reexamine the company's 2004 acquisition of SoundView Technology Group which was combined with its Capital Markets operations to form Schwab SoundView Capital Markets. While the purchase was intended to help the company beef up its services for institutional investors Schwab said that SoundView lacked "synergy" with the company's tradition of supporting the individual investor and sold the business to Swiss bank UBS.

Schwab acquired The 401(k) Companies from Nationwide Financial Services in 2007. The addition became part of the company's existing Charles

Schwab Trust subsidiary which serves as a trustee for employee benefit plans. Also that year Schwab sold U.S. Trust to Bank of America for some $3.3 billion in cash and shut down its CyberTrader day trading arm merging the direct-access brokerage's business with its own.

EXECUTIVES

President and CEO, Walter W. (Walt) Bettinger, age 54, $1,000,000 total compensation

President and CEO Charles Schwab Bank, Paul V. Woolway

EVP Investment Management Services, G. Andrew (Andy) Gill, age 52

EVP and CFO, Joseph R. Martinetto, age 53, $575,000 total compensation

EVP Client Solutions, James D. McCool, age 56, $550,000 total compensation

President and CEO Charles Schwab Investment Management, Marie A. Chandoha

EVP International Services and Special Business Development, Lisa Kidd Hunt

EVP Human Resources, Martha Tuma

EVP and Head Advisor Services, Bernard J. Clark, age 56, $500,000 total compensation

EVP Operational Services, Ron Carter

EVP and Chief Marketing Officer, Jonathan M. Craig

EVP Corporate Risk, Nigel J. Murtagh

EVP Internal Audit, Leona Tang

EVP Retirement Plan Services, Steven H. (Steve) Anderson

EVP and CIO, Jim McGuire

EVP General Counsel and Corporate Secretary, David R. Garfield

EVP Investor Services Segments and Platforms, Naureen Hassan

EVP Investor Services, Terri R. Kallsen

Vice President Financial Consultant, Rich Munneke

Vice President BM, Greg Locker

Vice President Financial Consultant, Greg Czarnecky

Vice President Financial Consultant, Mike Gula

Vice President Information Technology Strategy And Infrastructure, David (Dave) Russakov

Vice President Financial Consultant Menlo Park Branch, Tracy Zhang

Vice President Risk Management, Paul Mallett

Vice President Retirement Plan Sales, Luis Arellano

Vice President, Fred Webster

Vice President Information Technology, Ed Fulkerson

Vice President Financial Consultant, Ming Chen

Vice President Financial Consultant, Joseph (Jo) Craig

Vice President Sales And Marketing, Cheryl Carone

Vice President Financial Consultant Charles Schwab and Co. Inc., Jesus Arroyo

Financial Consultant Vice President, Travis Gularte

Vice President Financial Consultant, David (Dave) Mattox

Vice President Financial Consultant Charles Schwab and Co. Inc., Jeff Brendle

Vice President Financial Consultant, John (Jack) Curren

Vice President Financial Consultant, Matthew (Matt) Lamb

Vice President, Don Bakhaus

Vice President Financial Consultant, Martin (Marti) Dunn

Vice President, Kurt Leneis

Vice President Regulatory Affairs, Irene Gilbert

Vice President Financial Consultant, Jeffrey (Jeff) Anderson

Vice President Financial Consultant, Mario Giannetta

Vice President, Andrew (Andy) Mason

Vice President, Brian Burke

Vice President Financial Consultant Paramus NJ. Branch, Jeffrey (Jeff) Wogel

Vice President, Glenn Kennedy

Vice President, Troy Davis

Vice President Financial Consultant, Stephen (Steve) Cetrulo

Vice President Financial Consultant, Jane (Ginny) Gudgel

Vice President Financial Consultant, Chuck Kallgren

Vice President Financial Consultant, Paul Kidder

Vice President, William Matthews

Vice President Financial Consultant Anaheim Branch, Edward (Ed) LeBeau

Vice President Financial Consultant, Robert (Bob) Kay

Vice President Financial Consultant, Kristen Yost

Vice President Financial Consultant Houston Town and Country TX Isc, Edward (Ed) Rossi

Vice President and Branch Manager, Gregory Matthews

Vice President Financial Consultant, Tatum Schuler

Vice President Financial, James Riefe

Vice President Model Risk Management, Marc Bourzutschky

Vice President, James Westbay

Vice President, Jeff Borges

Vice President Financial Consultant, Ron Sperry

Vice President, John Gutierrez

Vice President Financial Consultant, David (Dave) Burchfield

Vice President, Joan Wong

Vice President, William Parrott

Vice President Financial Consultant, Selene Argao

Vice President Financial Consultant, James (Jamie) Beyersdorf

Vice President, Brian Openshaw

Vice President, Dale Kalman

Vice President, Neil Campbell

Vice President Financial Consultant, Illya Bermant

Vice President, Jason Fay

Vice President Of Sales And Marketing, Daniel (Dan) Fiala

Vice President Financial Consultant, Brett Woodward

Vice President Financial Consultant Legacy Village Branch, Matthew (Matt) Heck

Vice President, Steven Brakman

Vice President Financial Consultant, Danny Jones

Vice President Financial Consultant, Christopher (Chris) Armstrong

Vice President Financial Consultant, Nona Wilgus

Vice President Client Experience, Dave Gray

Vice President, Michael Solomon

Vice President Sales Retirement Plan Services, Jen Papay

Vice President Of Sales, Aline Eliecagary

Vice President Financial Consultant, Mark Dorff

Vice President, Brian Cox

Vice President Of Corporate Public Relations, Susan Forman

Vice President Finance, Peter Pavlakis

Vice President Financial Consultant, Michael (Mel) Viselli

Vice President Financial Consultant, James (Jamie) O'Bryan

Vice President, Stephan Spangenberg

Vice President Senior Financial, James Schwarz

Vice President Treasury Capital Markets, Dennis Goldman

Regional Vice President, Scot Kobashigawa

Vice President Financial Consultant, Nicolas (Nick) Robatel

Vice President Financial Consultant, Stephen (Steve) Cless

Vice President, Dennis Mojares

Senior Vice President Corporate Development, Michael Hecht

Vice President Financial Consultant, Tristyn Eames

Vice President Financial Consultant, Jason Burke

Vice President Finance, Aubrey Thacker

Vice President Financial Consultant Schwab Private Client, Jess Ramos

Vice President financial Consultant, Donna Niemann

Vice President Financial Consultant, Philip Choi

Vice President Financial Consultant, Daphne Lawrence

Vice President Financial Consultant, Edward (Ed) Shupe

Vice President Financial Consultant, Jonathan (Jon) Geiger

Senior Vice President Financial Consultant, Michael Maniscalco

Vice President Financial Consultant, Thomas (Thom) Franz

Vice President Financial Consultant, Tiffany Le

Vice President Financial Consultant, Patrick (Paddy) Means

Vice President Financial Consultant, Michael (Mel) Spear

Vice President Financial Consultant, Teb Yu

Vice President Financial Consultant, Robert (Bob) Freddino

Vice President Financial Consultant, Thomas (Thom) Clooney

Vice President Financial Consultant, Shawn Jennings

Vice President Financial Consultant, Chris Landry

Vice President Financial Consultant, Steven (Steve) Jaksch

Vice President Financial Consultant, Ludgy Lilavois

Vice President Financial consultant, Renata Rodriguez

Vice President Of Participant Services, Catherine Golladay

Vice President Financial Consultant, Robert (Bob) Gannon

Vice President Financial Consultant, James (Jamie) Titus

Vice President Financial Consultant, Scott Sollars

Vice President Financial Consultant, Laura Strott

Vice President Financial Consultant, Brandon Lilley

Vice President Financial Consultant, Anthony Johnson

Vice President Financial Consultant, Tobias Dufek

Vice President Financial Consultant, German Ramirez

Vice President Financial Consultant, Adam Lewis

Vice President Regional Banking Manager, Eva Favila

Senior Vice President, Michael Loudermilk

Vice President Financial Consultant, Jeff Peterson

Senior Vice President Core Technology Services, Dennis Howard

Vice President Financial Consultant Ca Insurance License #0B27845, Cynthia Leal

Vice President Financial Consultant, Danny Bhavsar

Vice President financial Consultant, Elizabeth Mulcahy

Vice President Financial Consultant, Michael Mealy

Vice President Financial Consultant, Denise Patridge

Vice President Legislative And Regulatory Affairs, Scott Eckel

Vice President Financial Consultant, Chris Veale

Vice President ??? Financial Consultant, Kevin Maas

Vice President Financial Consultant Carlsbad Branch, Ron Scherdorf

Vice President Financial Consultant, Bruce Gruenberg

Vice President Financial Consultant, Bona Sun

Vice President Financial Consultant, James Ridley

Auditors: Deloitte & Touche LLP

LOCATIONS

HQ: Schwab (Charles) Corp.
211 Main Street, San Francisco, CA 94105
Phone: 415 667-7000   Fax: 415 627-8894
Web: www.aboutschwab.com

PRODUCTS/OPERATIONS

2013 Sales

	$ mil.	% of total
Asset management & administration fees		
Mutual funds	1,193	22
Advice solutions	718	13
Others	404	7
Interest	2,085	38
Trading revenue	913	16
Other	236	4
Net impairment losses on securities	(10)	-
Total	**5,539**	**100**

Selected Subsidiaries

Charles Schwab Bank
Charles Schwab Investment Management Inc. (mutual fund investment adviser)
Schwab Holdings Inc.
  Charles Schwab & Co. Inc. (securities broker-dealer)

COMPETITORS

Ameriprise	Morgan Stanley
Bank of America	Principal Financial
E*TRADE Financial	Raymond James
Edward Jones	Financial
FMR	Scottrade
Franklin Templeton	ShareBuilder
John Hancock Financial	T. Rowe Price
Services	TD Ameritrade
Legg Mason	The Vanguard Group

HISTORICAL FINANCIALS

Company Type: Public

Income Statement

FYE: December 31

	REVENUE ($ mil.)	NET INCOME ($ mil.)	NET PROFIT MARGIN	EMPLOYEES
12/14	6,058	1,321	21.8%	14,600
12/13	5,435	1,071	19.7%	13,800
12/12	4,883	928	19.0%	13,800
12/11	4,691	864	18.4%	14,100
12/10	4,248	454	10.7%	12,800
Annual Growth	**9.3%**	**30.6%**	**—**	**3.3%**

2014 Year-End Financials

Debt ratio: 1.23%
Return on equity: 11.91%
Cash ($ mil.): 11,363
Current ratio: 0.35
Long-term debt ($ mil.): 1,899

No. of shares (mil.): 1,310
Dividends
  Yield: 0.8%
  Payout: 25.5%
Market value ($ mil.): 39,571

	STOCK PRICE ($) FY Close	P/E High/Low		PER SHARE ($) Earnings	Dividends	Book Value
12/14	30.19	32	25	0.95	0.24	9.00
12/13	26.00	33	18	0.78	0.24	8.00
12/12	14.36	22	17	0.69	0.24	7.51
12/11	11.26	28	15	0.70	0.24	6.07
12/10	17.11	52	34	0.38	0.24	5.18
Annual Growth	**15.3%**	**—**	**—**	**25.7%**	**(0.0%)**	**14.8%**

Seaboard Corp.

With pork and turkey from the US flour from Haiti and sugar from Argentina Seaboard has a lot on its plate. The diversified agribusiness and transportation firm has operations in some 45 countries in the Americas the Caribbean and Africa. Seaboard sells its pork and poultry in the US and abroad. Overseas it trades grain (wheat soya) operates power plants and feed and flour mills and grows and refines sugar cane. Seaboard owns a shipping service for containerized cargo between the US the Caribbean and South America; it has shipping terminals in Miami and Houston and a fleet of about 20 vessels (two owned the rest chartered) and ships to ports worldwide. Seaboard is run by descendants of founder Otto Bresky.

Operations

Seaboard ranks as one of the nation's top five pork producers based on sows in production. It's also a top-10 pork processor based on daily processing capacity. In the US Seaboard is a leading producer and processor of pork with operations in Oklahoma Kansas Texas Colorado Utah and Montana. (It has the capacity to produce about 4 million hogs annually.) Despite what some consider to be an industry oversupply of pork Seaboard has significantly expanded its pork business with an emphasis on private-label preseasoned pork products. It markets some of its pork products under the Prairie Fresh (in the US) Seaboard Farms (international) and Daily's brands. The company has an agreement with Missouri-Based Triumph Foods to process and market all of Triumph's pork products.

Overseas the company operates mainly commodity merchandising grain processing sugar production and electric power generation (in the Dominican Republic). In addition to shipping and the trading of sugar pork and commodities Seaboard grows and processes citrus and sugar and has distillery operations in Argentina; it manufactures ethanol and has trucking transportation operations in the US. It also owns jalapeño farms in Texas and Honduras.

Geographic Reach

Kansas-based Seaboard is a global company that serves several segments such as agribusiness and ocean cargo transportation in about 45 countries specifically in the Americas the Caribbean and Africa. Its largest market is Central and South America and the Caribbean representing nearly 40% of annual sales.

Financial Performance

After several years of consistent sales growth Seaboard reported a slight dip 3% in 2014. Lower sales volume for the power generation marine cargo and sugar segments caused the hiccup. Net income however increased 78% on the sale of a 50% interest in one of its pork operations.

Strategy

Seaboard has been expanding its processing and delivery infrastructure at home and abroad to be as efficient as possible. It has also been moving into non-food related operations including fuel alcohol and electricity generation in Argentina and refined coal processing in the Oklahoma.

Mergers Acquisitions and Divestments

In September 2014 Seaboard's processed meats division sold a 50% stake in Daily's Premium Meats to its processing partner Triumph Foods for $72.5 million making Seaboard and Triumph co-owners of the business. The sale provided additional capital to expand production and geographic reach of the Daily's brand.

In July 2013 Seaboard acquired a 50% stake in a flour milling business in Gambia for about $9.1 million.

HISTORY

Otto Bresky founded his company as a flour broker in 1916. He acquired his first flour mill in Atchison Kansas in 1918 and the following year purchased the Imperial Brewery Co. in Kansas City and converted it to a flour mill. Over the next four decades Bresky ground out a series of acquisitions of milling companies. In 1928 he purchased Rodney Milling Co. and retained the name as the identity for the family business. The company then purchased Ismert-Hincke Milling Co. (1938) and the Consolidated Flour Mills Co. (1950). In 1959 Rodney Milling merged with publicly traded Hathaway Industries and changed its name to Seaboard Allied Milling Corp.

In the 1960s Seaboard Allied became one of the first millers to shift flour milling from the source of the raw materials (the wheat fields of the Great Plains) to the population centers in the Southeast and on the East Coast. In 1962 Seaboard Allied built a flour mill in Chattanooga Tennessee. It then purchased George Urban Milling Company in Buffalo New York (1965) and built a flour mill in Jacksonville Florida (1966). But Bresky's expansionist strategy did not stop at the Atlantic Seaboard. The company acquired a flour mill in Guayaquil Ecuador in 1966 (a joint venture with Continental Grain Co.) then constructed flour mills in Freetown Sierra Leone (1968) and Georgetown Guyana (1969).

Bresky retired in 1973 and was succeeded by his son Harry. A chip off the old block Harry acquired a flour mill in Cleveland Tennessee and built flour mills in Buchanan Liberia and in Sapele Nigeria that year. In 1978 Seaboard Allied acquired Mochasa Ecuador's leading producer of animal feed and launched Top Feeds a mixed-feed plant in Sapele.

Facing stiff competition in the mill business from agribusiness giants in 1982 Seaboard Allied sold all its US flour mills to Cargill. The company changed its name to Seaboard that year and began expanding outside the US. In 1983 the company formed Seaboard Marine a shipping business in Florida to serve its increasingly far-flung enterprises.

In addition to geographic diversification the company expanded into new agribusiness areas. Seaboard acquired Central Soya's poultry unit in 1984 and it bought the Elberton Poultry Company the next year. Seaboard commenced shrimp farming operations in Ecuador in 1986 and in Honduras in 1987. Two years later Transcontinental Capital Corporation (Bermuda) a subsidiary began supplying power from a floating power barge to the Dominican Republic.

Seaboard entered the hog business in 1990 by acquiring a pork-processing plant in Albert Lea Minnesota. It opened a hog-processing facility in Guymon Oklahoma in 1996 and closed the Minnesota plant. That year the company bought a stake in Ingenio y Refinerio San Martin del Tabacal an Argentina-based sugar cane and citrus company. It then acquired flour-mill pasta-plant and cookie operations in Beira Mozambique.

After serving as CEO for more than 30 years in 2006 Harry Bresky stepped down as CEO (but remained as chairman) and turned over the company's reins to his son Steven. Harry Bresky died in 2007.

In 2010 Seaboard acquired a 50% stake in Butterball LLC.

EXECUTIVES

Vice President Integrated Business Strategies, Gary Louis
Vice President, David M Becker
Vice President Taxation and Business Development, David (Dave) Oswalt
SVP Engineering, James L. (Jim) Gutsch
EVP and CFO, Robert L. Steer, age 56, $720,000 total compensation
Chairman President and CEO, Steven J. Bresky, age 62, $915,000 total compensation

CEO Pork, Terry J. Holton, $485,385 total compensation
CEO Marine, Edward A. (Eddie) Gonzalez, age 50, $445,000 total compensation
CEO Commodity Trading and Milling, David M. Dannov, age 54, $720,000 total compensation
CEO Sugar, Hugo Rossi
CEO Power, Armando G. Rodriguez
Vice President Live Operations, Stephen (Steve) Summerlin
Vice President Internet Marketing, Doug Ewing
Vice President Corporate Controller and Chief Accounting Officer, Michael (Mel) Trollinger
Vice President Of Human Resources, Kay Stinson
Auditors: KPMG LLP

LOCATIONS

HQ: Seaboard Corp.
9000 W. 67th Street, Shawnee Mission, KS 66202
Phone: 913 676-8800
Web: www.seaboardcorp.com

2014 Sales

	$ mil.	% of total
Caribbean Central & South America	2,414	37
Africa	1,661	26
US	1,396	22
Pacific Basin & Far East	424	7
Canada/Mexico	347	5
Eastern Mediterranean	156	2
Europe	72	1
Total	**6,473**	**100**

PRODUCTS/OPERATIONS

2014 Sales

	$ mil.	% of total
Products	5,372	83
Services	906	14
Other	194	3
Total	**6,473**	**100**

2014 Sales

	$ mil.	% of total
Commodity Trading & Milling	3,499	54
Pork	1,717	27
Marine	852	13
Power	189	3
Sugar	199	3
All other	15	—
Total	**6,473**	**100**

Selected Operations

Cargo shipping
Citrus production and processing
Commodity merchandising (wheat corn and soybean meal)
Domestic trucking transportation
Electric power generation
Flour maize and feed milling
Jalape?o pepper processing
Pork production and processing
Sugar production and refining

COMPETITORS

ADM	Imperial Sugar
APL	Jennie-O
American Crystal Sugar	Johnsonville Sausage
Bay State Milling	Louis Dreyfus Group
Bunge Limited	M. A. Patout
CGC	Makino
CHS	Mondelez International
CSX	NYK Line
Cargill	Neptune Orient
Carr' s Milling	Nicor Gas
Chelsea Milling	Nutreco
Chiquita Brands	Organic Milling
Colonial Group	Overseas Shipholding
Crowley Maritime	Group
Della Natura	Smithfield Foods
Commodities	Southern States
Dole Food	Star of the West
Evergreen Marine	Sunkist

Evergreen Mills	Sdzucker
Farmers Rice Milling	Tate & Lyle
Fresh Del Monte	Tyson Foods
Produce	U.S. Sugar
Genco Shipping and	Viterra Inc.
Trading	Western Sugar
Horizon Milling	Cooperative
Hormel	

HISTORICAL FINANCIALS

Company Type: Public

Income Statement

FYE: December 31

	REVENUE ($ mil.)	NET INCOME ($ mil.)	NET PROFIT MARGIN	EMPLOYEES
12/14	6,473	365	5.6%	10,778
12/13	6,670	205	3.1%	11,397
12/12	6,189	282	4.6%	11,295
12/11	5,746	345	6.0%	10,573
12/10	4,385	283	6.5%	10,865
Annual Growth	**10.2%**	**6.5%**	**—**	**(0.2%)**

2014 Year-End Financials

Debt ratio: 2.05%	No. of shares (mil.): 1
Return on equity: 14.07%	Dividends
Cash ($ mil.): 36	Yield: —
Current ratio: 3.23	Payout: —
Long-term debt ($ mil.): —	Market value ($ mil.): 4,914

	STOCK PRICE ($) FY Close	P/E High/Low		PER SHARE ($) Earnings	Dividends	Book Value
12/14	4,197.95	13	8	309.96	0.00	2,320
12/13	2,794.97	17	15	171.92	0.00	2,081
12/12	2,529.88	11	8	234.54	12.00	1,924
12/11	2,036.00	9	6	284.66	0.00	1,717
12/10	1,991.00	9	5	231.69	9.00	1,460
Annual Growth	**20.5%**	**—**	**—**	**7.5%**	**—**	**12.3%**

Seacoast Banking Corp. of Florida

Seacoast Banking Corporation is the holding company for Seacoast National Bank which has about 35 branches in Florida with a concentration on the state's southeastern coast. Serving individuals and areas businesses the bank offers a range of financial products and services including deposit accounts credit cards trust services and private banking. Commercial and residential real estate loans account for most of the bank's lending activities; to a lesser extent it also originates business and consumer loans. The bank also provides financial planning services as well as mutual funds and other investments.

Operations

A division of the bank Seacoast Marine Finance specializes in boat loans of $200000 and greater which it typically sells into the secondary market. It has an office in Florida and two in California.

Geographic Reach

Seacoast National Bank has 34 branches in 12 counties across Florida stretching from Broward County north through the Treasure Coast and into Orlando and west to Okeechobee and surrounding counties.

Financial Performance

Seacoast Banking has been a victim of the economic turmoil and a weak housing market in Florida posting declining revenues since 2008. In

2013 sales fell 6% to $95.5 million. However the bank recorded $51.9 million in profits due to a one-time income tax benefit. The downward trend in its profits have been fueled by significant losses on loan provisions and compounded by a lack of revenue growth. The bank has in recent years been consolidating and closing branches to cut its operating costs.

Strategy

During 2013 Seacoast National Bank significantly expanded its banking technology platform by introducing digital deposit capture on smartphones new mobile platforms for consumer and business customers a rebranding of its website and enhancing its ATM capabilities. About 40% of its online customers also use the mobile application.

Mergers and Acquisitions

In 2014 the bank announced plans for its first acquisition in years. Seacoast National agreed to buy The BANKshares Inc. a Winter Park Florida-based bank that operates 12 branches under the BankFIRST name. The BankFIRST branches will be rebranded as Seacoast National creating the sixth-largest Florida bank by total assets. Previous acquisitions were completed in 2002 and 2006.

EXECUTIVES

Chairman and CEO, Dennis S. (Denny) Hudson, age 58, $500,000 total compensation
EVP and CFO, William R. Hahl, age 66, $310,000 total compensation
EVP and Chief Credit Officer, David D. Houdeshell, age 55, $250,000 total compensation
Chief Risk Officer, Maria G. Frias, age 52, $175,000 total compensation
Vice President And General Auditor, David Kelso
Senior Executive Vice President; President and Chief Operating Officer First National Bank, O Strickland
Auditors: KPMG LLP

LOCATIONS

HQ: Seacoast Banking Corp. of Florida
815 Colorado Avenue, Stuart, FL 34994
Phone: 772 287-4000
Web: www.seacoastbanking.com

PRODUCTS/OPERATIONS

2013 Revenue

	% of total
Interest Income	
Interest and fees on loans	60
Interst on securities and others	14
Non-interest Income	26
Total	**100**

Selected Services

Commercial and retail banking
Mortgage services
Wealth management

COMPETITORS

Atlantic Coast Financial	CenterState Banks
	EverBank Financial
BB&T	PNC Financial
BBX Capital	Regions Financial
Bank of America	SunTrust
BankUnited	Wells Fargo

HISTORICAL FINANCIALS

Company Type: Public

Income Statement

FYE: December 31

	ASSETS ($ mil.)	NET INCOME ($ mil.)	INCOME AS % OF ASSETS	EMPLOYEES
12/14	3,093	5	0.2%	579
12/13	2,268	51	2.3%	519
12/12	2,173	(0)	—	508
12/11	2,137	6	0.3%	420
12/10	2,016	(33)	—	398
Annual Growth	**11.3%**	**—**	**—**	**9.8%**

2014 Year-End Financials

Debt ratio: 3.70%
Return on equity: 2.23%
Cash ($ mil.): 100
Current ratio: —
Long-term debt ($ mil.): —

No. of shares (mil.): 33
Dividends
Yield: 0.0%
Payout: —
Market value ($ mil.): 456

	STOCK PRICE ($) FY Close	P/E High/Low	PER SHARE ($) Earnings	Dividends	Book Value
12/14	13.75	68 48	0.21	0.00	9.44
12/13	12.20	5 1	2.44	0.00	8.40
12/12	1.61	— —	(0.25)	0.00	8.73
12/11	1.52	12 8	0.15	0.00	8.98
12/10	1.46	— —	(2.40)	0.00	8.89
Annual Growth	**75.2%**	**— —**	**—**	**—**	**1.5%**

Sealed Air Corp.

Pop-Pop-Pop sounds like cha-ching for Sealed Air. Best known as the company that created Bubble Wrap Sealed Air also makes Instapak foam Jiffy mailers and Fill-Air inflatable packaging systems through its Product Care segment. Its largest segment Food Care makes Cryovac bags trays and absorbent pads for use by food processors and supermarkets to protect meat and poultry. Other products include shrink packaging for consumer goods such as toys and CDs; medical packaging for pacemakers and IV fluid; and specialty packaging for fabricators and the manufacturing industry. Sealed Air serves customers in 175 countries and operates through three major subsidiaries: Sealed Air Cryovac and Diversey.

Geographic Reach

Geographically the company's subsidiaries own 114 manufacturing facilities worldwide with each facility tailoring the products it makes to the demands of the local market. In 2014 its operations generated approximately 65% of its revenue from outside the US.

Operations

Sealed Air in 2014 reorganized into three global business segments in order to efficiently integrate Diversey into its operations. It operates through Product Care (food and drink packaging; 21% of total sales) Diversey (representing Diversey's legacy business; almost 30%) and Food Care (new segment featuring the company's former protective packaging shrink packaging and specialty materials segments; 50%).

Sales and Marketing

Sealed Air sells its products through over 7100 sales marketing and customer service personnel throughout the world who sell and market products to and through a large number of distributors fabricators converters e-commerce and mail order

fulfillment firms and contract packaging firms as well as directly to customers.

It targets food and beverage processors business supply distributors consumer products manufacturers hotel operators retailers building contractors educational institutions and health care providers as customers.

Financial Performance

Sealed Air achieved unprecedented growth in 2014 with revenues increasing 1% from $7.7 billion in 2013 to peak at a record-setting $7.8 billion in 2014. The historic growth for 2014 was due to a rise in all its segments from favorable product price mixes constant currency sales increases and higher unit sales volumes.

Product Care sales jumped 3% in 2014 resulting from a favorable product price mix as the segment shifted its focus from general use towards high-performance packaging products and services. The segment also observed higher unit sales volumes from growth in the e-commerce and third-party logistics sectors across all regions.

Sealed Air's profits more than doubled from $124 million in 2013 to $258 million in 2014 due to lower interest expenses and a $21 million gain from a claims settlement. The company's operating cash flow however plummeted to a negative cash flow of $202 million in 2014 primarily due to cash paid on settlement agreements.

Strategy

In order to continue to develop and introduce new products Sealed Air has decided to outsource some of its technically less complex product lines such as foam and plastic trays to third-party manufacturers. The outsourcing requires less investment from the company in regard to capital expenditure and it frees up the company to develop more innovative products (the company has more than 4900 patents) which the company hopes will continue to improve its competitive advantage.

Mergers and AcquisitionsSealed Air often augments its product portfolio through the use of acquisitions. In 2015 it acquired Intellibot Robotics a US-based privately owned company that specializes in the development of robotic commercial floor cleaning machines. The business will be integrated into Sealed Air's Diversey division and its leading brand of TASKI floor cleaning machines.

HISTORY

In the late 1950s after US engineer Al Fielding and Swiss inventor Marc Chavannes found no takers for their plastic air-bubble-embossed wallpaper they came up with Bubble Wrap the first product of Sealed Air which they founded in 1960 and took public soon after. AirCap as the material was first known didn't just protect products from damage; it also reduced storage and shipping costs.

EXECUTIVES

Vice President Information Technology Sealed Air Corp., Ruth Roper
SVP and CFO, Carol P. Lowe, age 49, $540,313 total compensation
President and CEO, Jerome A. Peribere, age 59, $1,150,000 total compensation
VP Research and Development and CTO, Robert L. (Bob) Tatterson, age 50
President Food Care, Karl R. Deily, age 57, $470,500 total compensation
SVP and Chief Supply Chain Officer, Emile Z. Chammas, age 46, $477,480 total compensation
President Diversey Care, Ilham Kadri, $433,073 total compensation
President Product Care, Ken Chrisman
Vice President Corporate Communications and Sustainability, James (Jamie) Whaley

Vice President Of Transportation, John Husveth
Global Vice President of New Opportunities, Jim Mize
Vice President Global Engineering, Ram Ramesh
Vice President Technology and Innovation Institutional and Laundry Business Unit, Stephen (Steve) Dalton
Auditors: KPMG LLP

LOCATIONS

HQ: Sealed Air Corp.
8215 Forest Point Boulevard, Charlotte, NC 28273
Phone: 201 791-7600   **Fax:** 201 703-4205
Web: www.sealedair.com

2013 Sales

	$ mil.	% of total
US	2,729	35
Europe	2,447	32
Asia Middle East Africa & Turkey	846	11
Latin America	824	11
Japan Australia & New Zealand	565	7
Canada	277	4
Total	**7,690**	**100**

PRODUCTS/OPERATIONS

2013 Sales

	$ mil.	% of total
Food Care	3,811	50
Diversey care	2,160	28
Product care	1,608	21
Other	111	1
Total	**7,690**	**100**

Selected Brands

Bubble Wrap
CRYOVAC
Ethafoam
Fill-Air
Instapak
Jiffy Mailer
Korrvu
Shanklin

Selected Products

Food Packaging
  Absorbent pads and case liners
  Bulk packaging
  Foam trays
  Laminates
  Lidstock
  Pouches
  Rollstock
  Vacuum bags
Medical Packaging
  Cleanroom blisters
  Films (Nexcel and Nelipak brands)
  Lidding material
  Medical device packaging
  Sealing machines
Protective Packaging
  Air cushioning (Bubble Wrap)
  Cushioned mailing bags (Jiffy Mailer)
  Foam packaging (Instapak)
  Inflatable packaging and cushioning (Fill-Air and FillTeck)
  Paper cushioning (PackTiger)
  Paper packaging (Kushion Kraft and Custom Wrap)
  Polyethylene fabrication foam (Cellu-Cushion CelluPlank Stratocell)
  Polyethylene foam (Cell-Aire)
  Suspension and retention packaging (Korrvu)
Shrink Packaging
  Equipment
  Films
Specialty Materials
  Foams
  Solar pool heating
  TurboTag RF Temperature Monitoring system
  Vacuum insulated panels

COMPETITORS

3M	Packaging Dynamics
AEP Industries	Pactiv

Ashland Inc.
Avery Dennison
Ball Corp.
Bemis
Clorox
Crown Holding Company
Eastman Chemical
Ecolab
Huhtamᴏki
Intertape Polymer
Polyair Inter Pack
Praxair
Printpack
Procter & Gamble
Reynolds Food Packaging
Sonoco Products
Tekni-Plex
Winpak

HISTORICAL FINANCIALS

Company Type: Public

Income Statement

FYE: December 31

	REVENUE ($ mil.)	NET INCOME ($ mil.)	NET PROFIT MARGIN	EMPLOYEES
12/14	7,750	258	3.3%	24,000
12/13	7,690	124	1.6%	25,000
12/12	7,648	(1,410)	—	25,000
12/11	5,640	149	2.6%	26,300
12/10	4,490	255	5.7%	16,100
Annual Growth	**14.6%**	**0.2%**	**—**	**10.5%**

2014 Year-End Financials

Debt ratio: 54.89%
Return on equity: 20.23%
Cash ($ mil.): 322
Current ratio: 1.56
Long-term debt ($ mil.): 4,282

No. of shares (mil.): 210
Dividends
  Yield: 1.2%
  Payout: 43.3%
Market value ($ mil.): 8,933

	STOCK PRICE ($) FY Close	P/E High/Low	Earnings	PER SHARE ($) Dividends	Book Value
12/14	42.43	36 24	1.20	0.52	5.52
12/13	34.05	53 27	0.58	0.52	7.08
12/12	17.51	— —	(7.31)	0.52	7.42
12/11	17.21	32 18	0.80	0.52	15.40
12/10	25.45	16 12	1.44	0.50	15.09
Annual Growth	**13.6%**	**— —**	**(4.5%)**	**1.0%**	**(22.2%)**

Sears Holdings Corp

In the world of retail Sears Holdings is an appliance giant. In addition to home appliances the company is a leading retailer of tools as well as lawn and garden fitness and automotive repair equipment. With roughly 1700 retail stores across the US Sears Holdings operates through subsidiaries Sears Roebuck and Co. and Kmart offering proprietary Sears brands including Kenmore Craftsman and DieHard. Beyond retail Sears Holdings is the largest provider of home installation and product repair services in the US. In 2014 Sears Holdings spun off Lands' End and reduced its once majority stake in Sears Canada to just 12% as it sought to raise cash to overcome struggling store sales.

Operations

Sears Holdings operates two segments: Sears Domestic which boasts nearly 720 full-line stores that generated 55% of Sears Holdings' total sales in fiscal 2015 (ended January 1 2015); and Kmart which had around 980 Kmart stores that contributed another 39% to Sears Holdings' total sales. The firm de-consolidated its Sears Canada segment (which made up around 7% of annual sales) in late 2014.By product the retailer generated 44% of its total sales from hardline merchandise (electronics appliances tools etc.) and another 28% from apparel and soft home items. About 14% of sales came from food and drug sales while

service (installation and repair) made up another 8% of total sales during the year.

Outside of retail Sears Holdings has a real estate business unit called Sears Holdings Real Estate one of the largest corporate real estate organizations in the world. It offers for sale or lease closed Kmart and Sears stores. It also leases empty space inside and outside of the stores.

Geographic Reach

Sears Holdings subsidiary Sears Roebuck and Co. has Sears-branded and affiliated stores in all 50 states and Puerto Rico. Subsidiary Kmart boasts Kmart-branded stores in 49 states Guam Puerto Rico and the US Virgin Islands.Sales and MarketingThe retailer has been decreasing its advertising spend over the past few years as sales have declined. It spent $1.1 billion on advertising in FY2015 down from $1.5 billion and $1.6 billion in fiscal years 2014 and 2013.

Financial Performance

Declining store sales and mounting losses have plagued Sears Holdings for the past several years as the popularity of e-commerce and fierce competition from other big box retailers has been growing.The retailer's net sales fell 14% to $31.2 billion during fiscal 2015 (ended January 1 2015) with sales declines in both Sears and Kmart stores. Sears Domestic store sales declined 11% mostly due to its mid-2014 separation of Lands' End as well as store closings in the US and 2.1% drop in comparable store sales. Sears Canada store sales plummeted 45% mostly because of the de-consolidation of the Canada-based business but also because of an 8% drop in comparable store sales. Kmart sales also fell by 8% for the year due to store closings and as comparable store sales dipped 1.4%. Steep revenue declines caused Sears Holdings' losses to deepen to $1.6 billion despite a decrease in cost of sales and buying and occupancy costs. The retailer's operations used $1.3 billion or 25% more cash than in FY2014 as the company suffered deeper operating losses.

Strategy

Sears Holdings outlined three main objectives in 2015 to ensure its long-term success: restoring profitability; focusing on its best members (most loyal customers) best stores and best categories (home appliances home services and fitness equipment); and enhance its financial flexibility through sales of store assets and investor fundraising.The retailer has been trying to adapt to the rapid consumer change from brick-and-mortar stores toward e-commerce in recent years. In 2015 the company continued shifting from being product centric to becoming "member centric" catering to members' needs "wherever whenever and however they want to shop" as stated in the February 2015 Chairman's letter. The member-centric model is built on two platforms: Shop Your Way the loyalty membership platform; and Integrated Retail the technology platform that connects its "ecosystem" of retail channels to member "touchpoints" (i.e. online and through mobile apps). Facing years of losses Sears Holdings has been forced to to close dozens of stores cut thousands of jobs and sell real estate and other assets to turn its business around. In 2014 as Sears' business continued to deteriorate the company sold off most of its stake in its struggling Sears Canada business spun off its Lands' End retail business and considered doing the same for its Sears Auto Center business.

The pairing of Sears and Kmart was intended to leverage the strengths of both chains by making their products brands (Kenmore Craftsman DieHard) and services (including auto and appliance repair) available through more locations and distribution channels. That strategy failed to increase in sales for either retailer. Company BackgroundSears Holdings was created in 2005 as a result of the $11.9 billion mega-merger of Sears and struggling Kmart masterminded by chairman and CEO Edward Lampert.

Chairman Lampert added the CEO title in February 2013 when Louis D'Ambrosio stepped down due to health issues in his family. D'Ambrosio became the chief executive of Sears Holdings in February 2011.

EXECUTIVES

EVP and CFO, Robert A. (Rob) Schriesheim, age 55, $800,000 total compensation
President Hardlines, Lynn S. Pendergrass
EVP and CIO, Jeffrey A. (Jeff) Balagna, age 55, $750,000 total compensation
Chairman and CEO, Edward S. (Eddie) Lampert, age 51, $1 total compensation
SVP; President Automotive, Norman L. (Norm) Miller, age 53
President Home Services, Sean Skelley, age 48
President Kenmore Craftsman and DieHard, Tom Park
President And Chief Member Officer Sears Roebuck & Co, Joelle Maher
CEO Seritage Growth Properties, Benjamin Schall
President and Chief Member Officer Kmart, Alasdair James
SVP; President Pharmacy, Phil Keogh
President Fulfillment, Girish Lakshman
Information Technology Vice President, Margaret (Peg) Landreville
Senior Vice President President Kmart Pharmacy, Mark Panzer
Vice President Customer Experience Online, Donald (Don) Fotsch
DVP General Manager Appliance Builder District, Kristen Elder
Division Vice President of Operations, Paul Paluch
Senior Vice President Inventory Management, Robert (Bob) Phelan
DVP Sears Commercial, Geoffrey Baird
Vice President Craftsman, Kris Malkoski
Vice President And General Manager Retail Services Kmart, Michael (Mel) Mcnerney
Senior Vice President logistics, Patrick (Paddy) James
Vice President Real Estate, James Terrell
National Account Manager, Jeff Dollard
Division Vice President Marketing, Dan Marks
Divisional Vice President Sporting Goods Merchandising, Russell (Russ) Winstead
DVP Store Operations, Tyrone Schiele
Vice President GMM RTW Sears and Cosm. Frag, Charles (Chas) Jayson
Pharmacy Manager, Jason Neal
DVP Chief Financial Officer Consumer Electronics, Steve Ferrone
Vice President Inventory Management, Jeffrey Grant
Vice President Finance, Scott Caines
Vice President Abd and Operations Ha, Shawn Pauli
Vice President Of Finance, Tom Knapp
Regional Vice President, Dan Morris
Senior Vice President Shop Your Way, Eric Jaffe
Vice President Of Intimates, Kathy Thomas
Senior Vice President Finance, Jason Hollar
Vice President General Manager Retail Services Region, Anne Hand
Vice President Divisional Merchandise Manager, Kerry Hartman
Divisional Vice President Human Resources, Phillip (Phil) Etter
Vice President of Real Estate Development, Sam Judd
District Vice President for Store Initiatives, Norm Buchanan
Divisional Vice President, Carlos Fojo
Vice President Sales, Daniel (Dan) Horan
Divisional Vice President, John (Jack) Johnson

Divisional Vice President Global Sourcing, Maria Matos
Divisional Vice President Information Technology Enterprise Marketing and Pricing Systems, Ted Rudman
Vice President And General Manager Marketplace, Tony Chvala
Divisional Vice President Chief Marketing Officer Grocery And Drug, R Whitton
Vice President Supply Chain, William Johnson
Divisional Vice President Procurement, David (Dave) Acquaviva
Vice President Procurement, Hemant Porwal
Divisional Vice President Procurement, John (Jack) Petrie
Vice President Tax, Jim Misplon
Vice President And General Manager Retail Services Kmart, Dave Rodney
Dvp Kenmore Product Development, Tom Desalvo
Dvp, Gary Mitzner
Vice President Business Solutions, Dennis Estep
Vice President And General Manager Retail Services Kmart, Steven Debber
Divisional Vice President Home Services Online, Sandeep Patil
Chief Marketing Officer Of Home Appliances And Vice President Of, Kevin Brown
Div Vice President Ny Technical Design, Vanessa Allen
Vice President Space Management And Analytics, Amy Higgins
Vice President Ecommerce Program And Product Management, Christopher Kraft
Vice President Chief Financial Officer Grocery Drug And Rx, Jonathan Carpenter
Division Vice President Marketing Health and Well, Paula Rosentreter
Divisional Vice President and Chief Financial Officer Supply Chain, Gide Kouatchou
Division Vice President Digital Media Marketing, Adriana Kogelis
Dvp Human Resources Retail Services, Megan Van Pelt
Divisional Vice President Head Of Sears Retail Human Resources, Colleen Kozak
Vice President Media Services, Perianne Grignon
Vice President And Gmm Women's Apparel Kmart, Cathy Caligan
Vice President Information Technology, Marge Landreville
Vice President Inventory Management, Jeff Fuerst
Senior Vice President And President Supply Chain, William Hutchinson
Vice President Gmm Sears, Patty Warwick
Divisional Vice President Kmart Soft, Robert (Bob) Kim
Vice President integrated Business Intelligence, Robert (Bob) Raible
DVP Logistics, Brent Mckinney
Divisional Vice President Retail Systems And Techna, David (Dave) Broome
Vice President And Deputy GC, Mike Kier
Vice President Retail Operations, Steve Scharfl
Vice President Retail Operations SHC, David (Dave) Rich
Vice President Logistics and Operations, Trach Joan
Vice President Supply Chain Systems and Support, Brian Ferguson
Executive Vice President Of Retail Store Operation, William (Bill) White
Secretary To Executive, Heather Brown
Secretary To Executive, Ann Veldey
Secretary To Executive, Linda Gradisher
Secretary To Executive, Julie Negron
Secretary To Executive, Frances Jolivette
Secretary To Executive, Chiquita Coleman
Vice President And Corporate Treasurer, Scott Huckins
Auditors: Deloitte & Touche LLP

LOCATIONS

HQ: Sears Holdings Corp
3333 Beverly Road, Hoffman Estates, IL 60179
Phone: 847 286-2500
Web: www.sears.com

PRODUCTS/OPERATIONS

2015 Sales

	$ mil.	% of total
Sears Domestic	17,036	55
Kmart	12,074	39
Sears Canada	2,088	7
Total	**31,198**	**100**

2015

	$ mil.	% of total
Hardlines	13,608	44
Apparel and Soft Home	8,602	28
Food and Drug	4,338	14
Service	2,412	8
Other	2,238	6
Total	**31,198**	**100**

Selected Subsidiaries

Kmart Corporation
Kmart Holding Corporation
Sears Canada Inc.
Sears Home Improvement Products Inc.
Sears Outlet Stores LLC
Sears Roebuck Acceptance Corp.
Sears Roebuck and Co.
Sears Roebuck de Puerto Rico Inc.
SRC Real Estate Holdings (TX) LLC

COMPETITORS

Ace Hardware	Macy's
Amazon.com	Menard
AutoZone	Office Depot
Bed Bath & Beyond	Pep Boys
Best Buy	ServiceMaster
Dillard's	Target Corporation
Home Depot	The Gap
Hudson's Bay	Wal-Mart
J. C. Penney	Whirlpool
Kohl's	Zale
Lowe's	

HISTORICAL FINANCIALS

Company Type: Public

Income Statement

FYE: January 31

	REVENUE ($ mil.)	NET INCOME ($ mil.)	NET PROFIT MARGIN	EMPLOYEES
01/15*	31,198	(1,682)	—	196,000
02/14	36,188	(1,365)	—	249,000
02/13	39,854	(930)	—	246,000
01/12	41,567	(3,140)	—	293,000
01/11	43,326	133	0.3%	280,000
Annual Growth	**(7.9%)**	**—**	**—**	**(8.5%)**

*Fiscal year change

2015 Year-End Financials

Debt ratio: 28.77%	No. of shares (mil.): 107
Return on equity: (-428.08%)	Dividends
Cash ($ mil.): 250	Yield: —
Current ratio: 0.96	Payout: —
Long-term debt ($ mil.): 3,110	Market value ($ mil.): 3,407

	STOCK PRICE ($) FY Close	P/E High/Low	PER SHARE ($) Earnings	Dividends	Book Value
01/15*	31.84	— —	(15.82)	0.00	(8.89)
02/14	36.37	— —	(12.87)	0.00	16.41
02/13	47.55	— —	(8.78)	0.00	25.99
01/12	44.06	— —	(29.40)	0.00	40.39
01/11	76.08	104 51	1.19	0.00	78.08
Annual Growth	**(19.6%)**	**—**	**—**	**—**	**—**

*Fiscal year change

Selective Insurance Group Inc

Selective Insurance Group is trying to be more accepting –without becoming indiscriminate. Since the early 1990s the property/casualty insurance holding company has been expanding its service area beyond its native New Jersey to reach the entire eastern US seaboard and much of the Midwest. Commercial policies sold by its nine subsidiaries include workers' compensation and commercial automobile property and liability insurance. Personal lines include homeowners and automobile insurance. The company also offers federal flood insurance administration services and some excess and surplus (E&S nonstandard) insurance.

Operations

The company operates through four reportable segments: Standard Commercial Lines Standard Personal Lines E&S Lines and Investments.

The Standard Commercial Lines segment which serves business not-for-profit organizations and government agencies accounts for about three-fourths of Selective's net premiums written. Standard Personal Lines—including flood insurance coverage –follows representing about 15% of net premiums written. Finally E&S Lines which covers more unusual risks than standard insurance accounts for nearly 10% of net premiums written.

The company's flood insurance is sold to businesses and individuals through the National Flood Insurance Program.

Geographic Reach

Selective primarily writes commercial policies in 22 eastern and midwestern states plus Washington DC. It also offers flood and E&S insurance policies in all 50 states plus Washington DC.

While New Jersey still accounts for more than 20% of Selective's net written premiums the company intends to become a "super-regional" insurer. By doing business in a wider geographic range Selective hopes to spread out its catastrophic risk exposure. It maintains its headquarters in New Jersey and regional branch offices in six other states.

Sales and Marketing

Some 2000 independent agencies market Selective's standard insurance products with a focus on providing commercial policies to small and mid-sized businesses and government entities. Its nationwide flood protection products are sold by a network of some 5000 retail agents while E&S policies are sold through about 100 wholesale agencies.

Target clients include manufacturing and wholesale community and public services and mercantile and services customers.

Promotional efforts are conducted through radio television billboard and other advertising venues.

Financial Performance

Revenue which has been rising since 2010 grew another 7% to $2 billion in 2014. This was primarily driven by higher sales in both commercial and personal standard lines.

Profits have been recovering since 2011 when storms including Hurricane Irene brought catastrophe losses topping $118 million. In 2014 net income grew 33% to $141.8 million on higher sales and net realized gains (despite an increase in losses and loss expenses). Cash flow from operations dropped to $103.3 million largely due to a change in other assets and accrued salaries and benefits.

Strategy

Selective is building up its portfolio of personal and commercial E&S insurance products through organic and acquisitive strategies. It has been es-tablishing regional business teams with full underwriting authority in order to build up its presence in local markets; it also developed a more aggressive plan to drive up business. Additionally the company has invested in technology that speeds up the process of writing new commercial business policies to improve customer and agency services.

In late 2014 the company released The Selective EdgeSM adding coverage options such as towing and labor and accidental airbag deployment for personal lines customers.

EXECUTIVES

Assistant Vice President Information Architecture and Strategy, Eric Thiessen
Assistant Vice President Claims, John (Jack) Kollar
Assistant Vice President Pricing Special Projects, Jeffrey (Jeff) Roth
Chairman and CEO, Gregory E. Murphy, age 60, $900,000 total compensation
EVP and Chief Actuary, Ronald J. Zaleski, age 61, $437,692 total compensation
EVP General Counsel and Chief Compliance Officer, Michael H. Lanza, age 54, $496,923 total compensation
EVP and CFO, Dale A. Thatcher, age 54, $571,154 total compensation
President and COO, John J. Marchioni, age 45, $725,000 total compensation
EVP and Chief Human Resources Officer, Kimberly Burnett, age 57
EVP; Head Commercial Insurance, Douglas T. Eden
EVP and Chief Claims Officer, George A. Neale
EVP and CIO, Gordon J. Gaudet
Vice President, Dennis L Barger
Assistant Vice President, Robert (Bob) Mitchell
Assistant Vice President IT Selective Insurance Company of America, Cynthia Sanchez
Assistant Vice President Product Development Yardley Pa, Stephen (Steve) Wright
Assistant Vice President of Benefits, Donna Manzi
Assistant Vice President Reinsurance, Shadi Albert
Vice President Claims Workers Compensation, Christie Harris
Vice President regional manager, John (Jack) Anthony
Vice President, Stephanie Chase
Vice President, Melissa Littell
Assistant Vice President Reserving, Brad Rigotty
Vice President Asset Management, George Cherrie
Assistant Vice President, Peter (Pete) Veiga
Vice President, Jim Klotz
Vice President Personal Lines Pricing, Mindy Oosten
Senior Vice President Information Technology Services Infrastructure and Administrative Services, Kevin Jenkins
Assistant Vice President underwriting Manager selectives Heartland Region, Carol Ryan
Senior Vice President Of Claims, Doug Holbrook
Vice President, Amy Gauli
Assistant Vice President, Bob Montone
Assistant Vice President Northeast Regional Manager Claims, Vincent Disimone
Assistant Vice President Bond Underwriting Manager, Debra Paziora
Vice President Leadership and Professional Development Selective Insurance Company of Ameri, Maryanne Spatola
Vice President Controller, Tony D Harnett
Vice President Tax and Treasury, Sarita Chakravarthi
Assistant Vice President, Stephen D (Steve) Coward
Assistant Vice President Claims Service Center, Susan L (Sue) Brown
Assistant Vice President Flood Operations, Cassie Masone
Assistant Vice President, Vere Bryan
Vice President Bonds East Hanover NJ, Timothy (Tim) Marchio
Assistant Vice President Actuarial Pricing, Sean Ritson
Assistant Vice President And Field Operations Manager Of Northeast Region, Michael (Mel) Mazzarella
Vice President Underwriting Manager Middle Atlantic Region Office, Edith Aguila
Assistant Vice President, Zhikun Wu
Executive Vice President Chief Investment Officer, Kerry Guthrie
Senior Vice President Chief Investment Officer, Joseph (Jo) Eppers
Assistant Vice President Infrastructure Planning and Integration for ITS Department, Robert (Bob) McKenna
Vice President, Laurie Slader
Auditors: KPMG LLP

LOCATIONS

HQ: Selective Insurance Group Inc
40 Wantage Avenue, Branchville, NJ 07890
Phone: 973 948-3000 **Fax:** 973 948-0282
Web: www.selective.com

PRODUCTS/OPERATIONS

2014 Revenues

	$ mil.	% of total
Standard Commercial Lines	1,430	70
Standard Personal lines	298	15
E&S Lines	140	7
Investments	165	8
Other	0	-
Total	**2,034**	**100**

2014

	$ mil.	% of total
Net premiums earned	1,852	91
Net investment income earned	138	7
Net realized gains	26	1
Other income	17	1
Total	**2,034**	**100**

Selected Acquisitions

COMPETITORS

Cincinnati Financial	Progressive
GEICO	Corporation
Hanover Insurance	Scottsdale Insurance
Company	State Farm
Harleysville Group	The Hartford
Liberty Mutual	Travelers Companies
Markel	Zurich Insurance Group
NJM Insurance	

HISTORICAL FINANCIALS

Company Type: Public

Income Statement

FYE: December 31

	ASSETS ($ mil.)	NET INCOME ($ mil.)	INCOME AS % OF ASSETS	EMPLOYEES
12/14	6,581	141	2.2%	2,200
12/13	6,270	106	1.7%	2,100
12/12	6,794	37	0.6%	2,100
12/11	5,736	19	0.3%	2,000
12/10	5,231	65	1.3%	1,900
Annual Growth	5.9%	21.3%	—	3.7%

2014 Year-End Financials

Debt ratio: 5.76%	No. of shares (mil.): 56
Return on equity: 11.68%	Dividends
Cash ($ mil.): 23	Yield: 1.9%
Current ratio: —	Payout: 24.2%
Long-term debt ($ mil.): —	Market value ($ mil.): 1,538

	STOCK PRICE ($)	P/E	PER SHARE ($)		
	FY Close	High/Low	Earnings	Dividends	Book Value
12/14	27.17	11 9	2.47	0.53	22.54
12/13	27.06	15 10	1.87	0.52	20.63
12/12	19.27	29 24	0.68	0.52	19.77
12/11	17.73	51 33	0.36	0.52	20.39
12/10	18.15	15 12	1.20	0.52	19.95
Annual Growth	10.6%	— —	19.8%	0.5%	3.1%

Sempra Energy

Sempra Energy's takes a pragmatic approach to make money in utility and other energy markets in the US and around the world. In the US Sempra distributes natural gas to more than 7.2 million customer meters and electricity to 3.4 million customer meters through its Southern California Gas (SoCalGas) and San Diego Gas & Electric (SDG&E) utilities. Other reporting segments include Sempra US Gas & Power (natural gas and renewables) and Sempra International (Sempra Mexico and Sempra South American Utilities) which were formerly known as Sempra Global. Sempra Energy companies serve more than 31 million consumers worldwide.

HISTORY

Sempra Energy is the latest incarnation of some of California's leading lights. Formed by the $6.2 billion merger between Enova and Pacific Enterprises the company traces its roots back to the 1880s.

Enova began as San Diego Gas which lit its first gaslights in 1881 and added electricity in 1887 (when it became San Diego Gas & Electric Light). Massive utility holding company Standard Gas & Electric bought the company in 1905 and renamed it San Diego Consolidated Gas & Electric. Over the next few decades San Diego Consolidated expanded through acquisitions and even stayed profitable during the Depression. But the 1935 Public Utilities Holding Company Act forced Standard to divest many of its widespread utilities and in 1940 San Diego Consolidated went public as San Diego Gas & Electric (SDG&E).

SDG&E grew quickly until the 1970s when new environmental laws slowed plans to build more power plants and rates soared because the company had to purchase power. The company finally added more generating capacity in the 1980s and the state of California allowed SDG&E to diversify into real estate software and oil and gas distribution. In 1995 it created Enova to serve as its holding company.

Meanwhile up the coast in San Francisco Pacific Enterprises began as gas lamp rental firm Pacific Lighting in 1886; it quickly moved into gas distribution to defend its market against electricity. The firm bought three Los Angeles gas and electric utilities in 1889 and continued to grow through acquisitions; it consolidated all of its utilities in the 1920s. Pacific Lighting sold its electric properties to the city of Los Angeles in 1937 in exchange for a long-term gas franchise.

The company entered oil and gas exploration in 1960. A decade later it merged its gas utility operations into Southern California Gas (SoCalGas). Pacific Lighting continued to diversify in the 1980s buying two oil and gas companies and three drugstore chains. Renamed Pacific Enterprises in 1988

the company launched an unsuccessful diversification effort that cost it $88 million in 1991. Over the next two years it sold off noncore businesses to focus on SoCalGas and in the mid-1990s it began moving into South and Central America. This included a joint venture with Enova and Mexico's Proxima SA to build and operate Mexico's first private utility.

Pacific Enterprises and Enova agreed in 1997 to a $6.2 billion merger; Sempra Energy was born in 1998. That year California began deregulating its retail power market. In response Sempra sold SDG&E's non-nuclear power plants (1900 MW) in 1999. It used the proceeds to eliminate its competitive transition charge and in turn lowered its electric rates.

But under deregulation rates tripled by mid-2000; that summer the California Public Utilities Commission (CPUC) implemented a rate freeze for electric customers. Wholesale power prices soared and rolling blackouts occurred in 2000 and 2001 as a result of the state's inadequate energy supply. In 2001 the CPUC began allowing utilities to increase their rates and SDG&E agreed to sell its transmission assets to the state for about $1 billion.

Sempra sold its 72.5% share in power marketing firm Energy America to British energy company Centrica in 2001. In 2002 the company purchased bankrupt utility Enron's London-based metals trading unit for about $145 million; later that year it purchased Enron's metals concentrates and metals warehousing businesses.

The company restructured its competitive energy business units in 2005 renaming several divisions and dividing the former Sempra Energy Solutions operations (retail energy marketing and services for commercial and industrial customers) under the Commodities and Generation divisions. That year Sempra sold one of its gas storage units to Vulcan's investment company for a reported $250 million; Vulcan is headed up by Microsoft co-founder Paul Allen

In 2006 the company settled class-action litigation that claimed that two of its subsidiaries Southern California Gas and San Diego Gas & Electric had helped to create the 2000-2001 energy crises in California by restricting the supply of natural gas to the state.

In 2007 Sempra was awarded a $172 million settlement arising from a 2002 dispute over the company's minority stakes in two Argentine natural gas holding companies.

In 2008 Sempra Energy formed a commodities marketing joint venture with The Royal Bank of Scotland RBS Sempra Commodities.

In a move to expand its midstream and distribution assets in the southeastern US in 2008 the company acquired EnergySouth for $510 million.

The company reported a jump in its revenues in 2010 thanks to a recovering global economy that drove up energy demand along with higher oil and gas prices and increased rates. Losses related to winding down its commodities unit trimmed Sempra Energy's net income for the year.

Building its midstream portfolio in 2010 the company acquired El Paso's Mexico-based pipeline and compression assets for $300 million.

In 2010 and 2011 Sempra Energy exited the commodities trading business. (In 2008 Sempra Energy had formed a partnership with The Royal Bank of Scotland to operate RBS Sempra Commodities including Sempra Energy Trading which traded and markets wholesale energy commodities in Asia Europe and North America. However to refocus its operations around its more financially reliable North American businesses to pay down debt and to meet EU antitrust requirements in 2010 the company sold the European and Asian segments of this partnership to JP Morgan Chase for about

$1.6 billion. It also sold that unit's retail commodity operations to Noble Group for $318 million and eventually wound down its joint venture with The Royal Bank of Scotland).

In early 2012 the company consolidated Sempra Generation Sempra Pipelines & Storage and Sempra LNG (together formerly Sempra Global) into Sempra International and Sempra US Gas & Power to improve its management and pursue strategic initiatives. Sempra US Gas & Power includes natural gas and renewables while Sempra International includes subsidiaries Sempra Mexico and Sempra South American Utilities.

Taking advantage of abundant natural gas supply from US shale plays In 2013 Sempra Energy teamed up with GDF SUEZ Mitsubishi and Mitsui & Co. to design and build an LNG export facility at the Cameron LNG receipt terminal in Hackberry Louisiana capable of processing 13.5 million tons per year. To raise cash to fund its growth initiative the company sold one 625-MW block of Sempra U.S. Gas & Power's 1250-MW Mesquite Power natural gas-fired power plant to Salt River Project Agricultural Improvement and Power District for $371 million. In 2012 BP Wind Energy and Sempra U.S. Gas & Power expand their strategic relationship by agreeing to jointly develop the Mehoopany Wind Farm in Pennsylvania and the Flat Ridge 2 Wind Farm in Kansas (a combined investment of more than $1 billion).

Growing its natural gas footprint in the Southeast US in 2012 Sempra U.S. Gas & Power agreed to buy Hattiesburg Mississippi-based Willmut Gas & Oil Company a natural gas utility which provides service to about 20000 customers in Hattiesburg and the surrounding area.

EXECUTIVES

Vice President, Kevin Sagara
EVP and General Counsel, Martha B. Wyrsch, age 55, $550,000 total compensation
Chairman and CEO, Debra L. (Debbie) Reed, age 59, $1,124,600 total compensation
President and CEO Southern California Gas Company, Dennis V. Arriola, age 55
President, Mark A. Snell, age 59, $740,000 total compensation
EVP and CFO, Joseph A. (Joe) Householder, age 59, $618,000 total compensation
SVP and CIO San Diego Gas & Electric, J. Chris Baker
Chairman and CEO Infraestructura Energ ©tica Nova S.A. de C.V., Carlos Ruiz, age 65
President and CEO Sempra U.S. Gas & Power, Patricia K. (Patti) Wagner
EVP External Affairs and Corporate Strategy, Steven D. Davis, age 59
CEO San Diego Gas & Electric, Jeffrey W. Martin
Vice President Information Technology Web Application Development Rbs Sempra, Bob Anderson
Vice President Marketing, Beth Bellanca
Senior Vice President Corporate Development at Sempra Energy, James (Jamie) Lambright
Vice President Engineering And Construction, Farid Bogani
Vice President, Sam Perez
Vice President Regulatory Relations, Dan Skopec
Vice President Corporate Compliance, Randall B Peterson, age 58
Vice President Business Origination, Michael (Mel) Sliwowski
Senior Vice President, Gloria Rowland
Director Media Relations, Hanan Eisenman
Vice President, Chuck Manzuk
Vice President, Clay Faber
Vice President, Keith Polmanteer
Vice President, Monica Wiggins

Senior Vice President Regulatory And Finance,
Schavrien Lee
Vice President ?? Audit Services, Karen Sedgwick
Regional Vice President International Relations,
Tania Ortiz
Vice President Corporate Tax and Chief Tax
Counsel, Paul Yong
Vice President And Treasurer, Kathryn Frodermann
Vice President Communications, Randall Clark
Executive Vice President External Affairs, Jessie
Knight
Vice President, Patrick (Paddy) Lee
Secretary Compl Manager, Patrick (Paddy) Canney
Treasurer, Tim Ransdell
Director of Financial Analysis Assistant
Treasurer, Ken Deremer
Vice Chairman, Justice Urbas
Auditors: Deloitte & Touche LLP

LOCATIONS

HQ: Sempra Energy
488 8th Avenue, San Diego, CA 92101
Phone: 619 696-2000
Web: www.sempra.com

2014 Sales

	% of total
US	79
South America	14
Mexico	7
Total	100

PRODUCTS/OPERATIONS

2014 Sales

	$ mil.	% of total
SDG&E	4,329	37
SoCalGas	3,855	33
Sempra South American Utilities	1,534	13
Sempra Natural Gas	979	8
Sempra Mexico	818	8
Sempra Renewables	35	1
Adjustments	(512)	-
Elimination	(3)	-
Total	11,035	100

COMPETITORS

AEP	IBERDROLA
AES	Los Angeles Water and
AT&T	Power
Avista	NRG Energy
CMS Energy	NV Energy
Calpine	PG&E Corporation
CenterPoint Energy	PacifiCorp
Constellation Energy	Public Service
Group	Enterprise Group
Dominion Resources	Sacramento Municipal
Duke Energy	Utility
Edison International	Southern Company
Endesa S.A.	Southwest Gas
Entergy	Tenaska
Exelon Energy	Williams Companies
FirstEnergy	

HISTORICAL FINANCIALS

Company Type: Public

Income Statement

FYE: December 31

	REVENUE ($ mil.)	NET INCOME ($ mil.)	NET PROFIT MARGIN	EMPLOYEES
12/14	11,035	1,262	11.4%	17,046
12/13	10,557	1,088	10.3%	17,122
12/12	9,647	920	9.5%	16,893
12/11	10,036	1,407	14.0%	17,483
12/10	9,003	733	8.1%	13,504
Annual Growth	5.2%	14.5%	—	6.0%

2014 Year-End Financials

Debt ratio: 36.16%
Return on equity: 11.30%
Cash ($ mil.): 570
Current ratio: 0.83
Long-term debt ($ mil.): 12,167
No. of shares (mil.): 246
Dividends
Yield: 2.3%
Payout: 57.6%
Market value ($ mil.): 27,431

	STOCK PRICE ($) FY Close	P/E High/Low	PER SHARE ($) Earnings	Dividends	Book Value
12/14	111.36	25 19	4.63	2.64	46.06
12/13	89.76	22 17	4.01	2.52	45.11
12/12	70.94	20 15	3.48	2.40	42.51
12/11	55.00	10 8	5.62	1.92	41.09
12/10	52.48	19 15	2.98	1.56	37.96
Annual Growth	20.7%	— —	11.6%	14.1%	5.0%

ServisFirst Bancshares, Inc.

ServisFirst Bancshares is a bank holding company for ServisFirst Bank a regional commercial bank with about a dozen branches located in Alabama and the Florida panhandle. The bank also has a loan office in Nashville. ServisFirst Bank targets privately-held businesses with $2 million to $250 million in annual sales as well as professionals and affluent customers. The bank focuses on traditional commercial banking services including loan origination deposits and electronic banking services such as online and mobile banking. Founded in 2005 by its chairman and CEO Thomas Broughton III the bank went public in 2014 with an offering valued at nearly $57 million.

IPO

ServisFirst Bancshares sold 625000 shares priced at $91 per share. Proceeds from the May 2014 IPO will be used to support the bank's growth plans both in Alabama and in other states.

Geographic Reach

Birmingham-based ServisFirst Bank has branches in Birmingham Huntsville Montgomery Mobile Dothan Pensacola and Nashville.

Financial Performance

The bank reported net income of $41.2 million in 2013 compared with $34 million in 2012. The increase was primarily due to an increase in net interest income which rose nearly 20% to $112.5 million. Noninterest income increased 4% to $10 million in 2013.

As of March 2014 the bank had total assets of approximately $3.6 billion total loans of $2.9 billion and total deposits of about $3.0 billion.

EXECUTIVES

President and CEO ServisFirst Bancshares and ServisFirst Bank, Thomas A. (Tom) Broughton, age 59, $350,000 total compensation
EVP and COO ServisFirst Bancshares and ServisFirst Bank, Clarence C. Pouncey, age 58, $263,000 total compensation
EVP CFO Treasurer and Secretary ServisFirst Bancshares and ServisFirst Bank, William M. Foshee, age 60, $230,000 total compensation
EVP ServisFirst Bancshares and President and CEO ServisFirst Bank of Huntsville, Andrew N. (Andy) Kattos, age 45
President and CEO ServisFirst Bank of Mobile, William (Bibb) Lamar, age 71

EVP ServisFirst Bancshares and President and CEO ServisFirst Bank of Montgomery, G. Carlton (Carl) Barker, age 60
EVP ServisFirst Bancshares and President and CEO ServisFirst Bank of Pensacola, Rex D. McKinney, age 52
EVP Correspondent Banking ServisFirst Bancshares and ServisFirst Bank, Rodney E. Rushing, age 57, $245,000 total compensation
SVP and Chief Credit Officer ServisFirst Bancshares and ServisFirst Bank, Don G. Owens, age 63, $187,200 total compensation
President and CEO ServisFirst Bank of Atlanta, Ken Barber
EVP and Chief Lending Officer, Doug Rehm
CEO ServisFirst Bank Dothan, B. Harrison Morris, age 38
Assistant Vice President of Private Banking of ServisFirst Bank, Ron Morrison
Chairman ServisFirst Bancshares and ServisFirst Bank, Stanley M. (Skip) Brock, age 64
Auditors: Dixon Hughes Goodman, LLP

LOCATIONS

HQ: ServisFirst Bancshares, Inc.
850 Shades Creek Parkway, Birmingham, AL 35209
Phone: 205 949-0302
Web: www.servisfirstbank.com

2013 Branches

	No.
Alabama	10
Florida	2
Total	12

COMPETITORS

Bank of America	Wells Fargo
Bank of the Ozarks	

HISTORICAL FINANCIALS

Company Type: Public

Income Statement

FYE: December 31

	ASSETS ($ mil.)	NET INCOME ($ mil.)	INCOME AS % OF ASSETS	EMPLOYEES
12/14	4,098	52	1.3%	298
12/13	3,520	41	1.2%	262
12/12	2,906	34	1.2%	—
12/11	0	23	—	—
Annual Growth	—	30.7%	—	—

2014 Year-End Financials

Debt ratio: 0.49%
Return on equity: 14.88%
Cash ($ mil.): 296
Current ratio: —
Long-term debt ($ mil.): —
No. of shares (mil.): 24
Dividends
Yield: 0.9%
Payout: 15.6%
Market value ($ mil.): 817

	STOCK PRICE ($) FY Close	P/E High/Low	PER SHARE ($) Earnings	Dividends	Book Value
12/14	32.95	42 13	2.09	0.32	16.41
12/13	0.00	— —	1.90	0.17	13.48
Annual Growth	—	— —	3.3%	23.9%	6.8%

Sherwin-Williams Co.

No matter how you coat it Sherwin-Williams is one of the top paint manufacturers in the US and worldwide (along with Akzo-Nobel PPG Industries and Henkel). Sherwin-Williams' products include a variety of paints finishes coatings applicators and varnishes sold under brands such as Dutch Boy Krylon Sherwin-Williams Thompson's WaterSeal Ronseal Sayerlack and Minwax. The company operates more than 4000 paint stores worldwide. It sells automotive finishing and refinishing products through wholesale branches worldwide. Other outlets include mass merchandisers home centers independent dealers and automotive retailers. Employees own 13% of the company via an Employee Stock Purchase and Savings Plan.

HISTORY

In 1870 Henry Sherwin bought out paint materials distributor Truman Dunham and joined Edward Williams and A. T. Osborn to form Sherwin Williams & Company in Cleveland. The business began making paints in 1871 and became the industry leader after improving the paint-grinding mill in the mid-1870s patenting a reclosable can in 1877 and improving liquid paint in 1880.

In 1874 Sherwin-Williams introduced a special paint for carriages beginning the concept of specific-purpose paint. (By 1900 the company had paints for floors roofs barns metal bridges railroad cars and automobiles.) Sherwin-Williams incorporated in 1884 and opened a dealership in Massachusetts in 1891 that was the forerunner of its company-run retail stores. The company obtained its "Cover the Earth" trademark in 1895.

Before the Depression Sherwin-Williams bought a number of smaller paint makers: Detroit White Lead (1910) Martin-Senour (1917) Acme Quality Paints (1920) and The Lowe Brothers (1929). Responding to wartime restrictions the company developed a fast-drying and water-reducible paint called Kem-Tone and the forerunner of the paint roller the Roller-Koater.

Sales doubled during the 1960s as the company made acquisitions including Sprayon (aerosol paint 1966) but rising expenses kept earnings flat. In 1972 the company expanded its stores to include carpeting draperies and other decorating items. But long-term debt ballooned from $80 million in 1974 to $196 million by 1977 when the company lost $8.2 million and suspended dividends for the first time since 1885.

John Breen became CEO in 1979 reinstated the dividend purged over half of the top management positions and closed inefficient plants. He also focused stores on paint and wallpaper merchandise and purchased Dutch Boy (1980).

In 1990 Sherwin-Williams began selling Dutch Boy in Sears stores and Kem-Tone in Wal-Marts. Acquisitions that year included Borden's Krylon and Illinois Bronze aerosol operations and DeSoto's architectural coatings segment which made private-label paints for Sears and Home Depot. In 1991 Sherwin-Williams bought two coatings business units from Cook Paint and Varnish and the Cuprinol brand of coatings.

Sherwin-Williams purchased paint manufacturer Pratt & Lambert in 1996. That year it introduced several new products including Low Temp 35 a paint for low temperatures; Healthspec a low-odor paint; and Ralph Lauren designer paints. Prep-Rite do-it-yourself interior primers debuted in 1997. Also that year Sherwin-Williams bought Thompson Minwax (Thompson's Water Seal Minwax Wood Products) from Forstmann Little and Chile-based Marson Chilena a spray paint maker.

The company streamlined some of its business segments and trimmed jobs in 1998. Christopher Connor president of the Paint Stores group replaced Breen as CEO in 1999 and chairman in 2000. Also in 2000 Sherwin-Williams moved into the European automotive coatings market by acquiring Italy-based ScottWarren.

In late 2001 the company acquired Wisconsin-based Mautz Paint Company.

After a rough but still profitable 2001 the company grew revenues and profits for its consumer units (consumer paints and paint stores) in 2002 thanks largely to a healthy do-it-yourself market. Sales for its automotive finishes and international units however were down because of a slow collision-repair market and currency-exchange effects.

In 2010 Sherwin-Williams bought Arch Chemicals' Sayerlack a leading Italian wood care coating company and acquired Becker Acroma Industrial Wood Coatings a Swedish manufacturer of industrial wood coatings. It also acquired all shares of AlSher Titania (a joint venture with Altair Nanotechnologies) it did not already own giving it a 100% stake in the technology company. AlSher Titania is developing a promising titanium dioxide technology that Sherwin-Williams plans to commercialize.

That same year the company also acquired Pinturas Cóndor an Ecuadorian diversified coatings supplier with $60 million in annual sales bolstering its market share in architectural paint in Latin America.

Among its acquisitions in 2011 was UK-based Leighs Paints a leader in fire-protectant (intumescent) coatings. (Because the intumescent technology prolongs the structural integrity of steel and concrete in a catastrophic fire more people are able to evacuate.)

In 2012 Sherwin-Williams made a significant purchase in the buyout of Jiangsu Pulanna Coating Co. headquartered in Changzhou China. Pulanna is an automotive refinishes coatings manufacturer and the deal improved Sherwin-Williams' presence in the most populous country in the world.

Also in 2012 Sherwin-Williams picked up Geocel Holdings a maker of caulks sealants and adhesives serving construction and repair applications. Geocel has locations in the US and the UK and the deal strengthened Sherwin-Williams' Consumer Group segment.

In a major geographic expansion in late 2012 the company agreed to acquire Grupo Comex a leader in the paint and coatings market in Mexico for $2.34 billion. However Mexico's antitrust regulator blocked the deal in mid-2013 stating the new company could artificially set higher prices at its discretion. Sherwin-Williams subsequently terminated the proposed deal.

EXECUTIVES

CEO, John G. Morikis, age 52, $849,444 total compensation
Senior Vice President Human Resources, Thomas Hopkins
President and General Manager Canada Division The Americas Group, Paul R. Clifford
CIO, Thomas J. (Tom) Lucas
SVP Finance and CFO, Sean P. Hennessy, age 58, $640,666 total compensation
President The Americas Group, Robert J. Davisson, age 55, $524,612 total compensation
President and General Manager South Western Division The Americas Group, Monty J. Griffin, age 55
President and General Manager Diversified Brands Division Consumer Group, Cheri M. Phyfer, age 44
President and General Manager Automotive Division Global Finishes Group, Thomas C. Hablitzel, age 53
President and General Manager Global Supply Chain Division Consumer Group, Joel D. Baxter, age 55

President and General Manager Mid Western Division The Americas Group, Peter J. Ippolito, age 51
President and General Manager Protective and Marine Coatings Division Global Finishes Group, Ronald B. Rossetto
President Global Finishes Group, David B. Sewell
President Southeastern Division Paint Stores Group, Todd V. Wipf
President Eastern Division The Americas Group, Brian L. Gallagher
President and General Manager Latin America Division The Americas Group, Pablo Garcia-Casas
President and General Manager Product Finishes Division Global Finishes Group, Dennis H. Karnstein
Senior Vice President General Counsel An, Catherine (Cathy) Kilbane
Vice President Quality Engineering EHS and S North America, Theresa Siegrist
Vice President Sales, Brian Padden
Vice President, Edwin Molina
Vice President S. West Area, Donny Dean
Vice President Of Sales, Jim Sinko
Vice President Human Resources, Paul Reoli
National Account Manager, Timothy (Tim) Skufca
Executive Vice President Sales and Marketing, Jim Shepard
Vice President Sales, Pat Herman
Vice President Of Purchasing, Ray Pasicnyk
National Account Manager, Harvey Kulkin
Vice President of Sales, Bill Rauterkus
Vice President Human Resources for Diversified Brands Division, Paul Alvarez
Vice President of Sales and Marketing, Nate Shinsky
Senior Vice President Marketing Paint Stores, Karl Schmitt
Vice President National Accounts, Mark Henderson
Vice President And Director of Operation, Alfred Scott
Vice President Operations, George Young
Vice President Marketing Sherwin Williams Protective, Brad Rossetto
Vice President, Kerri Rodgers
Senior Vice President Woodcare Products, Dominick Pisciotta
National Sales Manager, Christopher Olden
SP Senior Vice President, Bill Landin
Vice President Human Resources Paint Stores Group, Tom Gilligan
Vice President of Sales and Business Development, Jennie S Gerardot
Vice President Engineering, Beth Egan
Vice President Human Resources, Scott Gradert
Senior Vice President, Ryan Rampton
Vice President Research and Development, Diana Strongosky
Vice President of Technology Global Finishes Group, Gale Murphy
Vice President Sales, Tom Meredith
Vp Corporate Audit And Loss Prevention, Bob Barauskas
Vice President Taxes And Assistant Secretary Sherwin Williams Company, Michael Cummins
Vice President, Bill Desantis
National Account Manager, Jeff Crayton
Vice President Of Sales, Keith Rosenzweig
Vice President Taxes and Assistant Secretary Sherwin Williams Company, Michael (Mel) Cummins
Vice President Corporate Controller, Allen (Al) Mistysyn
National Sales Manager, Tj Chizmar
Chairman, Christopher M. (Chris) Connor, age 59
Board Member, Gerry Miller
Treasurer, Narsi Bodapati
Assistant Treasurer, Jeffrey Miklich
Board Member, Joseph Banks
Auditors: Ernst & Young LLP

LOCATIONS

HQ: Sherwin-Williams Co.
101 West Prospect Avenue, Cleveland, OH 44115-1075
Phone: 216 566-2000   **Fax:** 216 566-3310
Web: www.sherwin.com

PRODUCTS/OPERATIONS

2014 Sales

	$ mil.	% of total
Paint Stores Group	6,851	61
Global Finishes Group	2,080	19
Consumer Group	1,420	13
Latin America Coatings Group	771	7
Administrative	4	-
Total	**11,129**	**100**

Operations
Paint Stores
  Products
    Architectural coatings
    Industrial maintenance
    Marine products
  Brands
    ArmorSeal
    Brod-Dugan
    Con-Lux
    FlexBon Paints
    Hi-Temp
    Kem
    Mautz
    Mercury
    Old Quaker
    Powdura
    Pro-Line
    SeaGuard
    Sherwin-Williams
Consumer
  Products
    Architectural paints
    Industrial maintenance
    Paints
    Private-label coatings
    Stains
    Wood finishings
    Varnishes
  Brands
    Cuprinol
    Dupli-color
    Dura Clad
    Dutch Boy
    EverLast
    Formby' s
    H&C
    Krylon
    Martin Senour
    Maxwood Latex Stains
    Minwax
    Plastic Kote
  Pratt & La
    Red Devil
    Rubberset
    Signature Select
    Thompson' s
    White Lightning
Automotive Finishes
  Products
    Finishing refinishing and touch-up products for motor
    vehicles
  Brands
    Baco
    Excelo
    Lazzuril
    Martin Senour
    ScottWarren
    Sherwin-Williams
    Western
International Coatings
  Products
    Architectural paints
    Industrial maintenance products
    Stains
    Varnishes
    Wood finishing products
  Brands
    Andina
    Colorgin
    Dutch Boy
    Globo

Kem-Tone
Krylon
Marson
Martin Senour
Minwax
Pratt & La
Pulverlack
Ronseal
Sherwin-Williams
Sumare

COMPETITORS

Akzo Nobel	Ferro
BASF SE	H.B. Fuller
BEHR	Home Depot
Benjamin Moore	Kelly-Moore
California Products	Lowe' s
Comex Group	PPG Industries
Coronado Paint	RPM International
Diamond Vogel Paint	True Value
DuPont	Valspar
Dunn-Edwards	Wal-Mart

HISTORICAL FINANCIALS

Company Type: Public

Income Statement

FYE: December 31

	REVENUE ($ mil.)	NET INCOME ($ mil.)	NET PROFIT MARGIN	EMPLOYEES
12/14	11,129	865	7.8%	39,674
12/13	10,185	752	7.4%	37,633
12/12	9,534	631	6.6%	34,154
12/11	8,765	441	5.0%	32,988
12/10	7,776	462	5.9%	32,228
Annual Growth	9.4%	17.0%	—	5.3%

2014 Year-End Financials

Debt ratio: 31.64%
Return on equity: 62.50%
Cash ($ mil.): 40
Current ratio: 0.96
Long-term debt ($ mil.): 1,122

No. of shares (mil.): 94
Dividends
  Yield: 0.8%
  Payout: 25.6%
Market value ($ mil.): 24,911

	STOCK PRICE ($) FY Close	P/E High/Low	PER SHARE ($) Earnings	Dividends	Book Value
12/14	263.04	30 20	8.78	2.20	10.52
12/13	183.50	26 21	7.26	2.00	17.72
12/12	153.82	26 15	6.02	1.56	17.35
12/11	89.27	21 16	4.14	1.46	14.61
12/10	83.75	20 14	4.21	1.44	15.04
Annual Growth	33.1%	— —	20.2%	11.2%	(8.5%)

SHI INTERNATIONAL CORP.

Businesses that need more than boxes of hardware and software can call SHI International. The company distributes scores of computer hardware and software products from suppliers such as Adobe Cisco HP Microsoft and McAfee. It resells PCs networking products data storage systems printers software and keyboards among other items. SHI offers a range of professional services including software licensing asset management managed desktop services systems integration and vocational training. The company serves corporate government and health care customers from more than 30 offices across the US Canada the UK

Germany France and Hong Kong. SHI was founded in 1989 by Chairman Koguan Leo.

Geographic Reach

Based in Somerset New Jersey SHI has a global reach through its 30-plus offices located across the US Canada the UK Germany France and Hong Kong. In the US the company operates primarily in Texas and California but also in Arizona Colorado Florida Georgia Illinois Indiana Kansas Massachusetts Michigan Minnesota Missouri New Jersey New York Pennsylvania Virginia and Washington. Specifically its cloud briefing center is housed in New York City and its corporate call center runs from Austin Texas. The company's 420000-sq.-ft. headquarters operates beside its 140000-sq.-ft. Integration Center in Somerset New Jersey.

Operations

SHI serves several sectors and verticals. The company specializes in software and hardware procurement deployment planning configuration data center optimization IT asset management and cloud computing as well as custom IT solutions.

Financial Performance

SHI International rang up $5 billion in sales in 2013 a 15% increase versus the prior year. SHI's public sector corporate and enterprise commercial sales divisions each surpassed $1 billion in sales for the first time in 2013. Combined the strategic enterprise and international divisions accounted for an additional $2 billion in revenue for the year.

The seller of IT products and services boasts a 99% annual customer retention rate.

Strategy

The company has transformed itself from a $1 million regional reseller of software to a $5 billion global provider of information technology products and services.To this end SHI has invested some $20 million in a new data center that provides cloud services specifically what the company terms infrastructure-as-a-service (IaaS). The data center is one of six in the US that houses virtual machines for IT professionals to provide services such as application deployment disaster recovery software-as-a-service (SaaS). It also offers on-demand burst computing services where customers use the additional bandwidth to handle peaks in demand. HP Networking provides the network infrastructure for the data center which became operational in 2011.

SHI's professional services unit already provides some cloud services and data center consulting. SHI sees IaaS as a logical extension of the software asset management (SAM) service it already provides. Under the SAM program SHI handles software deployment licensing compliance and inventories across a business.

SHI partners with Omaha Nebraska-based information security software specialist Solutionary to manage data security services using its ActiveGuard software product to block computer network security breaches as data center security is one of the biggest concerns for businesses in a cloud computing environment.

Awards and Recognition

SHI is the largest minority and women-owned Business Enterprise (MWBE) in the US. The company's ranked 17th on CRN's 2013 Solution Provider 500 list of the largest IT solution providers in North America.

EXECUTIVES

President and CEO, Thai Lee, age 58
VP Finance and Corporate Secretary, Paul Ng
VP and General Manager, Hal Jagger
Chief Technology Officer, Richard (Rich) Taggart
Vice President Material Handling Division, Pete Hackett
National Account Manager, Thomas Miner

Vice President Information Technology, Sam Mourad
Vice President COMMERCIAL and INDUSTRIAL PROPERTIES, Nehal Patel
Vice President New Business Development, Celeste Lee
Chairman, Koguan Leo
Auditors: COHN REZNICK LLP NEW YORK NE

LOCATIONS

HQ: SHI INTERNATIONAL CORP.
290 DAVIDSON AVE, SOMERSET, NJ 088734145
Phone: 7327648888
Web: WWW.SHI.COM

PRODUCTS/OPERATIONS

Selected Products
Accessories
Peripherals
Hardware
Memory
Software

Selected Services
Cloud services
Computer vocational training services
Data center services
Events
Hardware services
Networking
POLARIS Software asset management
Storage
Strategic consulting
Webinars

COMPETITORS

ASI Computer Technologies	Computacenter
Agilysys	Ingram Micro
Arrow Electronics	Insight Enterprises
Avnet	PC Mall
CDW	Softchoice
CompuCom	Tech Data

HISTORICAL FINANCIALS

Company Type: Private

Income Statement

FYE: December 31

	REVENUE ($ mil.)	NET INCOME ($ mil.)	NET PROFIT MARGIN	EMPLOYEES
12/13	5,003	74	1.5%	2,500
12/12	4,389	61	1.4%	—
12/11	3,757	35	1.0%	—
12/08	0	0		—
Annual Growth	—	—	—	—

2013 Year-End Financials

Debt ratio: ——
Return on equity: 1.50%
Cash ($ mil.): 96
Current ratio: 1.20
Long-term debt ($ mil.): —

Dividends
Yield: —
Payout: —
Market value ($ mil.): —

Signature Bank (New York, NY)

Signature Bank marks the spot where some professional New Yorkers bank. The institution provides customized banking and financial services to smaller private businesses their owners and their top executives through 30 branches across the New York metropolitan area including all five boroughs Long Island and affluent Westchester County. The bank's lending activities mainly entail real estate and business loans. Subsidiary Signature Securities offers wealth management financial planning brokerage services asset management and insurance while its Signature Financial subsidiary offers equipment financing and leasing. Founded in 2001 the bank now boasts assets of roughly $29 billion.

Operations

Mortgage loans including commercial real estate loans multifamily residential mortgages home loans and lines of credit and construction and land loans comprise the bulk of Signature Bank's loan portfolio (and much of its asset base as well). The bank which staffed some 1010 employees at the end of 2014 generated 68% of its revenue from interest on loans and leases that year while 20% came from interest on its securities available-for-sale and 7% came from securities held-to-maturity. The remainder of its revenue came from fees and service charges (2%) and various other miscellaneous sources.

Geographic Reach

The bank's nearly 30 branch offices are mostly in the New York metropolitan area which includes Manhattan Brooklyn Westchester Long Island Queens the Bronx Staten Island and Connecticut. Sales and Marketing

Signature Bank mostly serves privately-owned businesses their owners and senior managers (typically with a net worth between $500000 and $20 million).

Financial Performance

The company's revenues and profits have risen in recent years thanks to strong organic loan business growth and declining loan loss provisions as its loan portfolio's credit quality has improved with higher property valuations in the strengthened economy.

Signature's revenue jumped by 22% to a record $959.3 million in 2014 mostly as loan interest (on commercial loans mortgages and leases) and security interest income continued to grow as the bank built up its interest-earning assets during the year. Higher revenue and a continued decline and loan loss provisions in 2014 boosted the bank's net income by 30% to a record $296.7 million. Signature's operating cash levels more than doubled to $421 million on higher cash earnings.

Strategy

Signature Bank has long targeted privately-held businesses that have fewer than 1000 employees and revenues of less than $200 million. Some of its target clients include real estate owners/companies law firms accounting firms entertainment business managers medical professionals retail establishments money management firms and non-profit foundations. The bank continues to expand its service lines particularly focusing on specialty financing to grow its business organically. In 2015 it planned to offer direct commercial vehicle financing through a network of approved commercial vehicle dealerships in New York's Tri-State area with loans targeting small and mid-size business borrowers looking to acquire commercial vehicles and fleets. Also that year it formed its Maryland-based Signature Public Funding Corp subsidiary to provide municipal finance and tax-exempt lending and leasing products to local state and federal government agencies nationwide.

The bank's emphasis on personal service helped it to grow its deposit base and loan portfolio in 2011. During a time when many other banks struggled under the weight of bad loans in a bad economy Signature Bank achieved record earnings for the fourth consecutive year. Founded in 2001 as an alternative to mega-banks Signature Bank was spun off from Bank Hapoalim in 2004.

EXECUTIVES

President CEO and Director, Joseph J. DePaolo, $577,500 total compensation
SVP and CFO, Vito Susca
President CEO and Director, Michael G. O'Rourke
EVP, Kevin P. Bastuga
EVP, Bryan D. Duncan
VP Retail Operations Manager, Ella Riordan-Pacheco
Senior Vice President, Carl Gambino
Vice President, John C Spagnuolo
Senior Vice President Group Director, Gary Shulevich
Senior Vice President Group Director, Leon Kratsberg
Vice President Portfolio Manager, Robert (Bob) Wallace
Vice President, Phyllis Rosenfeld
Executive Vice President Marketing Sales, Kai Dare
Senior Vice President Group Director, Matthew Weltman
Vice President, Eugene Cartin
Vice President, Sal Trifiletti
Senior Vice President Group Director, James (Jamie) Buck
Senior Vice President Group Director, Richard (Dick) Murasso
Senior Vice President Funding Officer, Brant Ward
Vice President, John (Jack) Ricchezza
Vice President Private Banking, Sue Frick
Senior Vice President, Frank Sabalja
Senior Vice President Group Director, Robert (Bob) Bloch
President, Blake Tibbitts
Senior Vice President, Gary Sarro
Vice President, George Greene
Senior Vice President, David Berman
Vice President, Maria Vetrano
Vice President, Kerry Mach
Senior Vice President, Ronald Berkowitz
Executive Vice President, Joseph Fantauzzi
Senior Vice President Group Director, James (Jamie) Handal
Senior Vice President Group Director, Brian Hallinan
Vice President Director Of Operations, Richard Pelcher
Vice President, Barbara (Barb) Von Borstel
Senior Vice President, Peter (Pete) Marra
Chairman and Director, Leonard S. Caronia
Auditors: KPMG LLP

LOCATIONS

HQ: Signature Bank (New York, NY)
565 Fifth Avenue, New York, NY 10017
Phone: 646 822-1500
Web: www.signatureny.com

PRODUCTS/OPERATIONS

2014 Sales

	$ mil.	% of total
Interest		
Loans net	655	68
Securities available for sale	193	20
Securities held to maturity	69	7
Other	5	1
Noninterest		
Fees & service charges	19	2
Commissions	10	1
Net gains on sales of loans	5	1
Net gains on sales of securities	5	
Other	2	-
Adjustments	(7.8)	-
Total	**959**	**100**

COMPETITORS

Apple Bank for Savings	Herald National Bank
Astoria Financial	JPMorgan Chase
Bank Leumi USA	New York Community
Capital One	Bancorp
Citigroup	Safra Bank
HSBC USA	TD Bank USA

HISTORICAL FINANCIALS

Company Type: Public

Income Statement

FYE: December 31

	ASSETS ($ mil.)	NET INCOME ($ mil.)	INCOME AS % OF ASSETS	EMPLOYEES
12/14	27,318	296	1.1%	1,010
12/13	22,376	228	1.0%	945
12/12	17,456	185	1.1%	844
12/11	14,666	149	1.0%	720
12/10	11,673	102	0.9%	660
Annual Growth	23.7%	30.6%	—	11.2%

2014 Year-End Financials

Debt ratio: —	No. of shares (mil.): 50
Return on equity: 13.81%	Dividends
Cash ($ mil.): 299	Yield: —
Current ratio: —	Payout: —
Long-term debt ($ mil.): —	Market value ($ mil.): 6,338

	STOCK PRICE ($) FY Close	P/E High/Low	PER SHARE ($) Earnings	Dividends	Book Value
12/14	125.96	22 17	5.95	0.00	49.61
12/13	107.42	22 15	4.76	0.00	38.06
12/12	71.34	18 14	3.91	0.00	34.94
12/11	59.99	18 13	3.37	0.00	30.49
12/10	50.06	21 13	2.46	0.00	22.84
Annual Growth	25.9%	— —	24.7%	—	21.4%

Simmons First National Corp.

Simmons First National thinks it's only natural it should be one of the largest financial institutions in The Natural State. The holding company owns Simmons First National Bank and seven other community banks that bear the Simmons First Bank name and maintain local identities; together they operate around 90 branches throughout Arkansas and in Kansas and Missouri. Serving consumers and area businesses the banks offer standard deposit products like checking and savings accounts IRAs and CDs. Lending activities mainly consist of commercial real estate loans single-family mortgages and consumer loans such as credit card and student loans.

Operations

In addition to Simmons First National Bank the company owns Simmons First Bank of Jonesboro Simmons First Bank of South Arkansas Simmons First Bank of Northwest Arkansas Simmons First Bank of Russellville Simmons First Bank of Searcy Simmons First Bank of El Dorado and Simmons First Bank of Hot Springs. Simmons First Trust Company a subsidiary of Simmons First National Bank provides trust and fiduciary services; Simmons First Investment Group offers broker-dealer services.

Financial Performance

The company's revenue increased in fiscal 2013 compared to the previous fiscal year. It reported $183.7 million in revenue for fiscal 2013 up from $177.5 million in revenue for fiscal 2012.

Despite the increased revenue the company's net income decreased in fiscal 2013 compared to the prior year. It reported net income of $23 million in fiscal 2013 down from a net income of more than $27 million in fiscal 2012. Cash flow remained stable year-over-year even with the drop in net income.

Strategy

Simmons tries to differentiate itself from smaller competitors by offering a wider array of products while striving to provide more personalized service than larger regional banks.

EXECUTIVES

EVP Organizational Development, Stephen C. Massanelli, age 59
Chairman and CEO, George A. Makris, age 58, $502,500 total compensation
SEVP CFO and Treasurer, Robert A. Fehlman, age 50, $306,614 total compensation
EVP and Central and Northeast Arkansas Regional Chairman Simmons First National Bank, Barry K. Ledbetter
President and Chief Credit Officer Simmons First National Bank, N. Craig Hunt
EVP and South Arkansas Regional Chairman Simmons First National Bank, Freddie G. Black
EVP Corporate Strategy and Performance and Secretary, Susan F. Smith, age 53
President Chief Banking Officer and Director, David L. Bartlett, age 63, $376,142 total compensation
EVP, Marty D. Casteel, age 63, $304,180 total compensation
EVP Controller Chief Accounting Officer and Investment Relations Officer, David W. Garner, age 45
EVP Marketing, Robert C. Dill, age 72, $179,393 total compensation
EVP and Chief Risk Officer, Tina M. Groves, age 45
EVP Technology and Operations Simmons First National Bank, Lisa W. Hunter
SVP and Marketing Director Simmons First National Bank, Amy W. Johnson
President El Dorado Community Bank, Robert L. Robinson
Chairman Russellville Community Chairman, Ronald B. (Ron) Jackson
President Hot Springs Community Bank, Steven W. (Steve) Trusty
President Conway Community Bank, Jason Culpepper
EVP and General Counsel, Patrick A. Burrow, age 61
EVP Specialty Lending Simmons First National Bank, Larry L. Bates
EVP and Tennessee Regional Chairman Simmons First National Bank, John C. Clark
EVP and Kansas and Missouri Regional Chairman Simmons First National Bank, Gary E. Metsger
Vice President, Clint Parton
Assistant Vice President Trust Officer And Financial Advisor, Kevin Lacewell
Senior Vice President, Paul Baker Paul Baker
Senior Vice President, David Scruggs
Assistant Vice President Loans, Esther Chapman
Vice President Loan Review Manager, David Coleman
Executive Vice President Specialty Banking Group, Craig Hunt
Vice President Of Human Resources, Susan Robinson
Executive Vice President Operations, Glenda Tolson
Vice President Regional Manager, Zilpha Wilson

Vice President Marketing, Stephen Lasseigne
Vice President Financial Analysis Manager, Donna Renfro
Vice President, Kevin Archer
Vice President Market Manager, Dorvan Wiley
Auditors: BKD, LLP

LOCATIONS

HQ: Simmons First National Corp.
501 Main Street, Pine Bluff, AR 71601
Phone: 870 541-1000
Web: www.simmonsfirst.com

COMPETITORS

Arvest Bank	Bear State Financial
BOK Financial	Home BancShares
BancorpSouth	IBERIABANK
Bank of America	Regions Financial
Bank of the Ozarks	U.S. Bancorp

HISTORICAL FINANCIALS

Company Type: Public

Income Statement

FYE: December 31

	ASSETS ($ mil.)	NET INCOME ($ mil.)	INCOME AS % OF ASSETS	EMPLOYEES
12/14	4,643	35	0.8%	1,331
12/13	4,383	23	0.5%	1,306
12/12	3,527	27	0.8%	1,052
12/11	3,320	25	0.8%	1,075
12/10	3,316	37	1.1%	1,108
Annual Growth	8.8%	(1.0%)	—	4.7%

2014 Year-End Financials

Debt ratio: 2.91%	No. of shares (mil.): 18
Return on equity: 7.95%	Dividends
Cash ($ mil.): 335	Yield: 2.1%
Current ratio: —	Payout: 54.3%
Long-term debt ($ mil.): —	Market value ($ mil.): 734

	STOCK PRICE ($) FY Close	P/E High/Low	PER SHARE ($) Earnings	Dividends	Book Value
12/14	40.65	20 16	2.11	0.88	27.38
12/13	37.15	26 17	1.42	0.84	24.89
12/12	25.36	17 14	1.64	0.80	24.55
12/11	27.19	20 13	1.47	0.76	23.70
12/10	28.50	14 11	2.15	0.76	23.01
Annual Growth	9.3%	— —	(0.5%)	3.7%	4.4%

SLM Corp.

Those who graduated magna cum payments may not be familiar with SLM but they probably know its more common moniker Sallie Mae. Holding more than $8 billion in student loans SLM's main subsidiary Sallie Mae Bank is one of the nation's largest education loan providers and specializes in originating acquiring financing and servicing private student loans which are not guaranteed by the government. The company also earns fees for its processing and administrative offerings through various subsidiaries. SLM spun off its education loan management servicing and asset recovery business to form Navient Corporation in 2014.

HISTORY

The Student Loan Marketing Association was chartered in 1972 as a response to problems in the Guaranteed Student Loan Program of 1965. For years the GSL program had tinkered with rates to induce banks to make loans but servicing the small loans was expensive and troublesome. Sallie Mae began operations in 1973 buying loans from their originators; its size provided economies of scale in loan servicing.

Originally only institutions making educational or student loans were allowed to own stock in Sallie Mae. This was later changed so that anyone could buy nonvoting stock. In 1993 voting stock was listed on the NYSE.

Sallie Mae was always a political football altered again and again to reflect the education policies of the party in power. When it was founded during the Nixon administration its loans were restricted by a needs test which was repealed during the Carter years. The Reagan administration reimposed the needs test and at the same time sped up the schedule under which the company was to become self-supporting which it did by late 1981.

Forced to rely on its own resources Sallie Mae turned to creative financing. One of its traditional advantages was that its loan interest rates were linked to Treasury bills traditionally about 3% above the T-bill rate. The company became a master at riding the spread between its cost of funds and the interest rates it charged.

Between 1983 and 1992 Sallie Mae's assets swelled by more than 400% and its income rose by almost 500%. As the firm grew management became more visible with high pay and extravagant perks. Although salaries were not inconsistent with those of executives at comparable private corporations the remuneration level and perks irked Congress. But Sallie Mae kept growing —in 1992 it expanded its facilities and added 900 new staff members.

The 1993 Omnibus Budget Reconciliation Act with its transfer of the student loan program directly to the government and its surcharge on Sallie Mae began to adversely affect earnings in 1994. While awaiting permission to alter its charter the company stepped up its marketing efforts especially to school loan officers who advised students on loan options.

In 1995 then-COO Albert Lord led a group of stockholders in a push to cut operating expenses and repackage student loans as securities à la Freddie Mac and Fannie Mae. Lord and some of his supporters won seats on the board (as well as the enmity of Lawrence Hough who resigned as CEO in the midst of the melee). That year Sallie Mae bought HICA Holding one of two private insurers of education loans. In 1996 Congress passed legislation forcing Sallie Mae's privatization.

Despite SLM's rising stock shareholders were unhappy with chairman William Arceneaux's status quo business plan. Lord gained control in 1997.

In 1998 the organization became SLM Holding. Assets and earnings were muted that year when unfavorable market conditions prevented Sallie Mae from securitizing its loans.

The firm the next year expanded its lending operations by buying Nellie Mae. Also in 1999 Sallie Mae teamed with Answer Financial to sell insurance. Growth continued in 2000 when the company bought loan servicer Student Loan Funding Resources as well as the marketing student loan servicing and administrative operations of USA Group; the company changed its name to USA Education following the acquisition. The company also cut some 1700 jobs approximately 25% of its workforce.

The following year Sallie Mae teamed with Intuit allowing the financial software company access to Sallie Mae's 7 million customers. It also launched online recruiting service TrueCareers that year.

In 2002 it bought Pioneer Credit Recovery and General Revenue Corporation two of the nation's largest student loan collection agencies. It also reverted to the SLM moniker to reconnect with the name by which it has so long been known.

The privatization plan put into place in the mid-'90s (orchestrated in large part by then-CEO Lord) came to fruition nearly four years ahead of schedule when SLM transitioned to a private organization in December 2004.In 2007 SLM saw its stock values plummet to their lowest levels in about a decade. A number of industry-wide factors figured into the losses not the least of which was the downturn in the credit market. Also affecting the company was the signing into law of the College Cost Reduction and Access Act (CCRAA). Intended to reform student lending and cut costs for borrowers the act slashed subsidies for lenders participating in the Federal Family Education Loan Program (FFELP). The reform cut into the company's interest-earning operations. As a result SLM increased its focus on higher-yielding private education loans which carry a lower risk.Additionally SLM that year became ensnared in a student-lending industry probe led by New York attorney general Andrew Cuomo. The company agreed to a $2 million settlement and to abide by a code of conduct regarding its dealings with college employees.One of the most dramatic results of the troubles was the collapse of a planned acquisition by a consortium of investment firms. The planned $8.8 billion deal included buyers J.C. Flowers (which was to own about a half of SLM) Bank of America and JPMorgan Chase. In the midst of the industry probe J.C. Flowers sought a change in SLM's leadership in an effort to secure regulatory approval for the acquisition; Thomas J. (Tim) Fitzpatrick was ousted as CEO. Ultimately the buyers canceled the deal citing the reduced potential value of SLM. The student lender filed a lawsuit to challenge the termination but eventually dropped the suit. It later cut more than 10% of its workforce.

EXECUTIVES

Chairman and CEO, Raymond J. Quinlan, $600,000 total compensation
EVP and General Counsel, Laurent C. Lutz, $525,000 total compensation
EVP and CFO, Steven J. McGarry, $375,000 total compensation
SVP and Chief Risk Officer, Jeffery F. Dale, age 53, $400,000 total compensation
EVP and Chief Marketing Officer, Charles P. Rocha, $375,000 total compensation
Vice President Regional Sales and Marketing, Shannon Cross
Assistant Vice President Network Services, Peter Tropf
Vice President, Jonathan Boyles
Vice President Finance Other Credit, Doug Maurer
Senior Vice President Operations Administration, Sheila Ryan-Macie
Vice President And Associate General Counsel, Anne Milem
Auditors: KPMG LLP

LOCATIONS

HQ: SLM Corp.
300 Continental Drive, Newark, DE 19713
Phone: 302 451-0200
Web: www.salliemae.com

PRODUCTS/OPERATIONS

2014 Sales

	$ mil.	% of total
Interest		
Lons	660	79
Investments	8	1
Cash & cash equivalents	4	1
Non-Interest income		
Gain on sale of loans	121	14
Other	39	5
Adjustments	(4.0)	-
Total	**831**	**100**

Selected Subsidiaries

HICA Holding
Sallie Mae Bank
Sallie Mae Inc.
SLM Education Credit Finance Corporation
   Bull Run I LLC
   SLM Education Credit Funding LLC
SLM Investment Corporation
Southwest Student Services Corporation

COMPETITORS

Bank of America
Brazos Higher Education Service Corp.
Citizens Financial Group
Discover
Educational Funding of The South
First Marblehead
FirstCity Financial
Great Lakes Higher Education
KeyCorp
Mohela
Nelnet
PNC Financial
Pennsylvania Higher Education Assistance Agency
SunTrust
Texas Guaranteed

HISTORICAL FINANCIALS

Company Type: Public

Income Statement

FYE: December 31

	ASSETS ($ mil.)	NET INCOME ($ mil.)	INCOME AS % OF ASSETS	EMPLOYEES
12/14	12,972	194	1.5%	1,000
12/13	159,543	1,418	0.9%	7,200
12/12	181,260	939	0.5%	6,800
12/11	193,345	633	0.3%	6,600
12/10	205,307	530	0.3%	7,600
Annual Growth	(49.9%)	(22.2%)	—	(39.8%)

2014 Year-End Financials

Debt ratio: —	No. of shares (mil.): 423
Return on equity: 5.20%	Dividends
Cash ($ mil.): 2,359	Yield: 5.8%
Current ratio: —	Payout: 44.1%
Long-term debt ($ mil.): —	Market value ($ mil.): 4,315

	STOCK PRICE ($) FY Close	P/E High/Low		PER SHARE ($) Earnings	Dividends	Book Value
12/14	10.19	63	19	0.42	0.60	4.32
12/13	26.28	8	5	3.12	0.60	13.14
12/12	17.13	9	7	1.90	0.50	11.18
12/11	13.40	14	10	1.18	0.30	10.31
12/10	12.59	14	11	0.94	0.00	9.51
Annual Growth	(5.2%)	—	—	(18.2%)	—	(17.9%)

Smucker (J.M.) Co.

The J. M. Smucker Company gets its bread and butter from more than just making and marketing jelly. The company known for manufacturing its namesake Smucker's fruit spread and for selling the Jif peanut butter brand has expanded its product portfolio to include Folgers the #1-coffee brand in the US as well as market leaders in espresso (Café Bustelo) and premium java (Dunkin' Donuts licensed). Other top-shelf lines are Hungry Jack and Pillsbury baking mixes and frostings Eagle canned milk and Crisco shortening and oils among others. Smucker's brands are sold to consumers through retail outlets in the US and Canada with some products exported.

Operations

Smucker's operations are divided among four business segments: US Retail Coffee US Retail Pet Foods US Retail Consumer Foods and International Foodservice and Natural Foods. The US retail market segments are distinguished by product which combined account for more than 75% of the company's sales. (Consumer foods and coffee each contributed 37% of revenue in fiscal 2015.)

The International Foodservice and Natural Foods segment (22% of sales) comprises Smucker's portfolio of brands that are distributed both at home and abroad through retailers (grocery stores mass merchandisers club stores and drug stores) as well as through food service suppliers and operators such as restaurants educational and health care institutions and natural foods stores.

After acquiring Big Heart Smucker established its newest segment US Retail Pet Foods. That unit contributed 4% of revenue in 2015.

Smucker's long-term agreements include one with Dunkin' Donuts to manufacture and market its namesake coffee brand; the pact is effective until 2034. In the single-serve coffee market Smucker holds sway through a manufacturing and distribution deal with Keurig Green Mountain and Keurig. Smucker also totes royalty-free licensing agreements with General Mills National Dairy and Nestlé to make and sell respectively Pillsbury flour and baking mixes Borden canned milk and Carnation canned milk.

Geographic Reach

Smucker operates in the US where it generates more than 90% of its revenue. It has an international presence as well through its extended reach into Canada Mexico and China. The company has established a small customer base along with some manufacturing facilities in Canada and a limited export market.

Sales and Marketing

Products are sold through direct sales and brokers to a broad range of retailers. Wal-Mart and subsidiaries account for more than a quarter of sales. Indeed the company's top 10 customers generate some 60% of Smucker's revenue. The company's International Foodservice and Natural Foods business distributes Smucker's products through retailers and food service suppliers and operators both domestically and internationally.

In fiscal 2015 Smucker spent about $107 million on advertising down slightly from $125 million the prior year.

Financial Performance

The company saw revenue increased 1% to $5.6 billion in fiscal 2015 (ended April) largely due to the addition of the US Retail Pet Foods segment which offset lagging sales of coffee and consumer foods.

Net income which has been fluctuating over the past few years decreased by $220.3 million to

$344.9 million as Smucker saw selling distribution and administrative expenses go up. This was largely due to the acquisition of Big Heart. Cash flow from operations declined $122.8 million to $733.2 million primarily due to changes in assets and accrued liabilities.

Strategy

Smucker's strategy focuses on growth through owning and marketing the #1 brand name food products in North America with potential for worldwide appeal. Acquisitions and manufacturing and distribution agreements underpin these ends. As part of the company's long-term growth objectives it is working to increase sales by 6% and earnings per share by more than 8% annually on average. While the sales contribution from acquisitions will vary from year to year it expects organic growth including new products to add up to 4% per year and acquisitions to contribute the remainder over the long term. Products launched in 2015 included Café Bustelo K-Cup pods and Jif To Go Dippers; pipeline products range from Dunkin' Donuts K-Cup pods to Milk-Bone Good Morning dog vitamin treats.

In response to ongoing declines in the green coffee futures market Smucker lowered the prices of most of its US packaged coffee products (with the exception of its K-Cup pods) in 2015. It slashed prices by an average of 6%; the move was intended to bring coffee sales volumes back up.

With the 2015 acquisition of Big Heart Pet Brands the company instantly became a player in the growing pet food and snacks market. The company plans to pay down debt it took to finance that purchase over the next three to five years.

Mergers and Acquisitions

In early 2015 Smucker purchased Big Heart Pet Brands in a cash and stock transaction valued at $5.8 billion (including $2.6 billion of debt). Smucker gained a huge product portfolio with the deal adding such notable names as Mew Mix Milk-Bone Kibbles 'n Bits Natural Balance and Milo's Kitchen among others to its own list of brands.

In 2014 the company bought Sahale Snacks a maker of nut and fruit mixes. The Seattle-based company rings up an estimated $50 million in annual sales from warehouse clubs convenience stores and supermarkets. In 2013 Smucker purchased privately held $45 million-in-sales Enray to strengthen its natural foods business. Enray which is based in California is a supplier of organic grains beans and seeds.

HISTORY

Jerome Smucker began operating a steam-powered cider mill in 1897 for farmers in Orrville Ohio but he found that his biggest business was selling apple butter made using a secret Smucker family recipe. By the 1920s The J. M. Smucker Company had begun producing a full line of preserves and jellies and in 1935 it acquired its first fruit-processing operations.

Under Jerome's grandson Paul Smucker the company gained widespread national distribution by the mid-1960s. Tim Smucker succeeded his father Paul as president in 1981 then as chairman in 1987 when his brother Richard became president.

The company's growth has been enhanced through the development of its industrial fruit fillings business and acquisitions of domestic natural juice and peanut butter companies including Knudsen & Sons (1984) After the Fall (1994) and Laura Scudder's (from National Grape Co-op 1994). It has gradually expanded internationally through acquisitions. In 1993 it acquired the jam preserves and pie-filling unit of Canada's Culinar. In a 1998 deal Smucker purchased Australia's Allowrie jam and Lackersteens marmalade lines.

Smucker sold its flagging Mrs. Smith's frozen pie business to Flowers in 1997 less than two years after buying the unit from Kellogg. It bought Kraft's domestic fruit spread unit in 1997 and in 1999 purchased the northwestern Adams peanut butter business from Pro-Fac Cooperative. Smucker kept the Adams name but shifted packaging to its Pennsylvania peanut butter plant.

Spreading into retail the company opened a store in 1999 in its hometown of Orrville and then launched online and catalog sales. Also that year Smucker bought a fruit filling plant in Brazil from Groupe Danone a major customer. During 2000 the company's Henry Jones Foods subsidiary (Australia) purchased Taylor Foods (sauces marinades).

Smucker acquired International Flavors & Fragrances' formulated fruit and vegetable preparation businesses in 2001. Moving beyond its stronghold in natural peanut butter brands the next year Smucker purchased the Jif peanut butter and Crisco cooking oil and shortening brands from Procter & Gamble. The $670 million purchase price for Jif and Crisco included shifting 53% of Smucker stock into the hands of P&G shareholders.

A decision to concentrate on North America led to the $37 million sale of Australian subsidiary Henry Jones Foods in 2004. Also that year Smucker sold its operations in Brazil to Cargill and closed down two fruit processing plants in California and Oregon. Its purchase of International Multifoods that year added an array of US brands to the Smucker family including Pillsbury flour baking mixes and ready-to-spread frostings; Hungry Jack pancake mixes syrup and potato side dishes; Martha White baking mixes and ingredients; and PET evaporated milk brands. Canadian brands included Robin Hood flour and baking mixes Bick's pickles and condiments and Golden Temple flour and rice.

To further its strategy of concentrating on its core retail brands in 2005 Smucker sold its US foodservice and bakery business and the Canadian operations of Gourmet Baker (all part of its International Multifoods acquisition) to Value Creation Partners. The following year the company sold its Canadian grain-based foodservice operations and industrial businesses to Cargill and CHS Inc. The operations were integrated into leading US flour miller Horizon Milling (which is jointly owned by Cargill and CHS). Adding to its namebrand offerings in 2006 Smucker acquired the White Lily brand of flours baking mixes and frozen biscuits from C.H. Guenther.

The company extended its baking offerings with the 2007 acquisition of sweetened condensed and evaporated milk producer Eagle Family Foods Holdings. Smucker paid $133 million in cash and $115 million in assumed debt for it. Eagle is a good fit with Smucker's PET milk products. Given Smucker's size and subsequent bargaining power with food retailers (including Wal-Mart the giant in US food retailing) and Eagle's domination of the North American canned-milk sector (it is the largest producer of evaporated and sweetened condensed milk in the US and Canada) the pairing of the two companies was a sensible move for both.

EXECUTIVES

SVP and CFO, Mark R. Belgya, age 54, $475,000 total compensation
CEO, Richard K. Smucker, age 67, $980,000 total compensation
President Coffee and Foodservice, Steven T. Oakland, age 54, $526,000 total compensation
Vice President Marketing, Kelly Crouse
President Big Heart Pet Food and Snacks, David J. West, age 52, $101,260 total compensation

President International and Chief Administrative Officer, Barry C. Dunaway, age 52, $330,000 total compensation
President Consumer and Natural Foods and Director, Mark T. Smucker, age 46, $355,000 total compensation
VP and Managing Director Canada and International, David J. Lemmon
VP and General Manager Foodservice, Kevin G. Jackson
Vice President Of Marketing, Kent Wadsworth
Vice President of Finance and Accounting Canada Strategic Business Area, Aurelio Calabretta
Vice President Sales and Trade Marketing, Stephen (Steve) Kouri
Vice President Finance, Mark Draa
Vice President General Manager Natural and Specialty Foods, Danielle Barran
Vice President Food and Beverages, Jim O'Rourke
Vice President Coffee Product Development, Jim Trout
National Sales Manager, Mike Workman
National Account Manager, Jesse Thelen
Vice President, Brad Reber
Vice President, Bill Cortner
Vice President Logistics, Gary Baumstark
Vice President Market Research, Jill Boyce
Vice President Business Development, Michael (Mel) Mast
Vice President Industry And Government Affairs, Julia Sabin
Vice President Sales And Marketing, John (Jack) Hall
Vice President Marketing Consumer, Vince Byrd
Vice President U.S. Grocery Sales, Jim Brown
National Sales Manager, Greg Stiff
Vice President of Supply Chain and Operations, Todd Campbell
Vice Chairman, Vincent C. Byrd, age 60
Chairman, Timothy P. (Tim) Smucker, age 71
Auditors: Ernst & Young LLP

LOCATIONS

HQ: Smucker (J.M.) Co.
One Strawberry Lane, Orrville, OH 44667-0280
Phone: 330 682-3000
Web: www.jmsmucker.com

2015 Sales

	$ mil.	% of total
Domestic	5,189	91
International		
Canada	414	7
Other countries	90	2
Total	**5,693**	**100**

PRODUCTS/OPERATIONS

2015 Sales

	$ mil.	% of total
US retail coffee	2,076	37
US retail consumer foods	2,105	37
International foodservice & natural foods	1,273	22
US Retail Pet Foods	239	4
Total	**5,693**	**100**

Selected Products

Baking mixes and ready-to-spread frostings
Canned milk
Coffee
Flour and baking ingredients
Frozen sandwiches
Fruit spreads
Juices and beverages
Peanut butter
Pickles and condiments
Shortening and oils
Syrups
Toppings

Selected Brands by Segment

International foodservice and natural foods
Bick' s
Café Bustelo
Café Pilon
Carnation (under license)
Crisco
Crosse & Blackwell
Double Fruit
Five Roses
Folgers
Golden Temple
Jif
Plate Scapers
R.W. Knudsen
Recharge
Red River
Robin Hood
Santa Cruz Organic
Smucker' s
US retail coffee
Café Bustelo
Café Pilon
Folgers
Dunkin' Donuts (under license)
Millstone
US retail consumer foods
Adams
Borden and Elsie design (under license)
Crisco
Dickinson' s
Eagle Brand
Fungetti
Goober
Hungry Jack
Jif
Laura Scudder' s
Magic Shell
Magnolia
Martha White
Pillsbury (under license)
Smucker' s
Uncrustables
White Lily

COMPETITORS

B&G Foods	Hershey
Boyd Coffee	Hormel
Caribou Coffee	Keurig Green Mountain
Chiquita Brands	Mondelez International
Coca-Cola	Monster Beverage
Coca-Cola North America	National Grape Cooperative
Community Coffee	Nestl©
ConAgra	Ocean Spray
Cranberries Limited	PepsiCo
Darigold Inc.	Pinnacle Foods
Dean Foods	Spectrum Organic Products
Diamond Foods	Starbucks
Diedrich Coffee	Tata Global Beverages
Dole Food	Tree Top
E.D. Smith	Tropicana
General Mills	Unilever
Goya	Welch' s
H. J. Heinz Limited	

HISTORICAL FINANCIALS

Company Type: Public

Income Statement
FYE: April 30

	REVENUE ($ mil.)	NET INCOME ($ mil.)	NET PROFIT MARGIN	EMPLOYEES
04/15	5,692	344	6.1%	7,370
04/14	5,610	565	10.1%	4,775
04/13	5,897	544	9.2%	4,875
04/12	5,525	459	8.3%	4,850
04/11	4,825	479	9.9%	4,500
Annual Growth	**4.2%**	**(7.9%)**	**—**	**13.1%**

2015 Year-End Financials

Debt ratio: 36.55%
Return on equity: 5.69%
Cash ($ mil.): 125
Current ratio: 2.01
Long-term debt ($ mil.): 5,944

No. of shares (mil.): 119
Dividends
  Yield: 2.1%
  Payout: 45.8%
Market value ($ mil.): 13,861

	STOCK PRICE ($) FY Close	P/E High/Low	PER SHARE ($) Earnings	PER SHARE ($) Dividends	PER SHARE ($) Book Value
04/15	115.92	35 29	3.33	2.50	59.27
04/14	96.68	21 17	5.42	2.26	49.46
04/13	103.23	21 15	5.00	2.04	48.35
04/12	79.63	20 17	4.06	1.88	46.82
04/11	75.07	18 13	4.05	1.64	46.35
Annual Growth	**11.5%**	**— —**	**(4.8%)**	**11.1%**	**6.3%**

Sonic Automotive, Inc.

No stranger to speed O. Bruton Smith has raced Sonic Automotive to the front of the pack of US auto dealers behind larger rivals such as AutoNation and Penske Automotive. Founded with five dealerships in 1997 Sonic today owns more than 120 new- and used-vehicle dealerships and about 20 collision repair centers in major markets in more than a dozen states including Texas the Carolinas Alabama and Tennessee. The company sells some 25 brands of cars and light trucks and offers vehicle financing. Chairman Smith who runs Sonic Automotive with his son Scott is also the majority owner of Speedway Motorsports which operates more than half a dozen NASCAR auto racetracks.

Operations
The company sells new vehicles including luxury (BMW Lexus Land Rover and Volvo) mid-line import (Honda Nissan and Toyota) and domestic brands (Ford and General Motors). Luxury brands accounted for 56% of new vehicle sales in 2014; while the company's mid-line and domestic brands accounted for about 31% and 13% respectively.

Sonic divides its business into Franchised Dealerships and EchoPark which are stand-alone used car locations without services.

Geographic Reach
Houston is Sonic's #1 market accounting for more than 20% of sales in 2014. Alabama and Tennessee combined accounted for more than 10% of the auto dealer's total sales.

Sales and Marketing
Sonic's advertising expenses amounted to about $57.4 million in 2014 compared to about $56.6 million in 2013 and $50.3 million in 2012.

Financial Performance
Sonic has reported consistent revenue growth for the past five years. And its revenue was up again in 2014 by 4% to $9.2 billion due to increased new and used vehicle sales as well as all services. Toyota/Scion dealerships lead the pack with 4% increase in new vehicle sales.

Net income which has not been as consistent increased in 2014 by 19% to reach $97 million due to higher revenue.

Strategy
As part of the company's strategic plans Sonic is primarily focused in growing its operations in metropolitan markets in the Southeast Southwest Midwest and the West (California). The company's long-term growth strategy is to target luxury or mid-line import brands in regions where it already operates.

Delving deeper into the used-car market Sonic began opening stand-alone used-car dealerships — under the EchoPark name —in 2014. The brand challenges CarMax in used-car sales. The company will consider expanding its geographic footprint with acquisitions in its EchoPark segment.

Mergers and Acquisitions

In 2014 the company spent $50.9 in cash on two luxury franchises one mid-line import franchise and one domestic franchise. It also sold nine franchised dealerships.

In 2013 the company acquired two luxury franchise operations and underlying assets (including real estate) for a total of $88.2 million.

Company Background

The Smiths control the company through their ownership of about 40% of Sonic Automotive's voting stock.

EXECUTIVES

President and CEO, B. Scott Smith, age 47, $1,033,150 total compensation

EVP Operations, Frank J. (Jeff) Dyke, age 48, $922,500 total compensation

VP and Chief Marketing Officer, Rachel M. Richards

EVP and CFO, Heath R. Byrd, $642,708 total compensation

VP Information Technology, Christopher (Chris) Maritato

Executive Vice President Of Corporate Development, John Russ

Regional Vice President Tn Dc, Kevin Gaither

Vice President of Talent Management, Doug Bryant

Vice President Fixed Opps, Hugh Whiles

Vice President Of Talent Management, Edd Doug Bryant

Chairman, O. Bruton Smith, age 88

Vice Chairman, David B. Smith, age 40

Auditors: KPMG LLP

LOCATIONS

HQ: Sonic Automotive, Inc.
4401 Colwick Road, Charlotte, NC 28211
Phone: 704 566-2400   **Fax:** 704 536-5116
Web: www.sonicautomotive.com

2014 Dealerships

	No.
Houston	22
Southern California	15
Northern California	13
Alabama/Tennessee	12
North & South Carolina/Georgia	9
Florida	6
Mid-Atlantic	6
Dallas	5
Colorado	5
Ohio	3
Las Vegas	2
Disposed Franchises	2
Total	**100**

PRODUCTS/OPERATIONS

2014 Sales

	$ mil.	% of total
New vehicles	5,124	56
Used vehicles	2,310	25
Parts service & collision repair	1,296	14
Finance insurance & other	300	3
Wholesale vehicles	166	2
Total	**9,197**	**100**

COMPETITORS

Asbury Automotive	Enterprise Rent-A-Car
AutoNation	Group 1 Automotive
AutoTrader	Gunn Automotive
Autobytel	Internet Brands
CarMax	JM Family Enterprises
Darcars	Penske Automotive
David McDavid Auto Group	Group
	Sewell Automotive
DriveTime Automotive	

HISTORICAL FINANCIALS

Company Type: Public

Income Statement

FYE: December 31

	REVENUE ($ mil.)	NET INCOME ($ mil.)	NET PROFIT MARGIN	EMPLOYEES
12/14	9,197	97	1.1%	9,300
12/13	8,843	81	0.9%	9,100
12/12	8,365	89	1.1%	9,300
12/11	7,871	76	1.0%	9,200
12/10	6,880	89	1.3%	9,200
Annual Growth	**7.5%**	**2.0%**	**—**	**0.3%**

2014 Year-End Financials

Debt ratio: 63.97%
Return on equity: 15.19%
Cash ($ mil.): 4
Current ratio: 1.07
Long-term debt ($ mil.): 742

No. of shares (mil.): 50
Dividends
  Yield: 0.3%
  Payout: 5.3%
Market value ($ mil.): 1,377

	STOCK PRICE ($) FY Close	P/E High/Low	PER SHARE ($) Earnings	Dividends	Book Value
12/14	27.04	15 11	1.84	0.10	13.09
12/13	24.48	16 13	1.53	0.10	11.64
12/12	20.89	13 7	1.53	0.10	9.89
12/11	14.81	11 7	1.29	0.10	9.93
12/10	13.24	8 5	1.49	0.03	8.80
Annual Growth	**19.5%**	**— —**	**5.4%**	**41.4%**	**10.4%**

Sonoco Products Co.

Sonoco Products believes you can judge a container by its packaging. The company is one of the world's largest makers of industrial and consumer packaging used by the food consumer goods construction and automotive industries. Its consumer packaging segment produces round and shaped composite cans for snack foods powdered beverages pet food and more. Sonoco makes flexible and rigid packaging (paper and plastic) for food personal care items and chemicals and it produces paperboard tubes and cores too for industrial protective packaging. The company's end-to-end packaging services include co-packing and fulfillment supply chain management and point-of-purchase display design/assembly.

Geographic Reach

Sonoco operates more than 335 locations around the world in nearly 35 countries concentrated in Canada Europe and the US. Around 65% of its total sales are generated from the US each year. Sonoco's international sales are concentrated in Europe (17%) followed by Canada (6%).

Operations

The company divides its business structure into four chief business segments. Its two largest segments —Consumer Packaging and Paper and Industrial Converted Products —each represented around 40% of its total sales for 2014. Protective Solutions and Display and Packaging each generated roughly 10%.

Financial Performance

Sonoco has enjoyed exceptional growth over the last five years. Revenues increased 3% from almost $4.9 billion in 2013 to more than $5 billion a historic milestone for the company. Profits jumped 9% from $219 million in 2013 to peak at $239 million in 2014 due to the additional revenue coupled with a decrease in interest expenses.

The historic growth was due to a 6% spike in Display and Packaging sales as a result of increased organic sales with existing customers and higher volumes in US. Sonoco was also helped by a 4% jump in Consumer Packaging sales.

Sonoco experienced declines in operating cash flow untill 2011 but recovered during the next two years. In 2013 operating cash flow increased by $134 million due to the higher net income and non-cash pension and a decline in cash used for pension and post-retirement plan contributions. However cash flow decreased by $120 million to $418 million in 2014.

Strategy

The company's goal is to reach $5.5 billion to $6 billion in sales over the next three or four years. It plans to achieve this by growing its existing products and services portfolio by $300 million and new product sales by $350 million. It also expects future acquisitions to contribute an additional $500 million in annual sales. (It reached the $5 billion revenue milestone in 2014.)

Inherit to its strategy are the company's ongoing efforts to improve its operating structure and keep a lid on costs. In 2013 it closed a thermoforming packaging plant in Ireland due to shifting market conditions in Europe. Looking to launch offices in fast-growing markets Sonoco in 2014 opened its third manufacturing plant in Russia and announced plans to invest $20 million to build a new production facility in Kuala Lampur Malaysia.

Mergers and Acquisitions

Sonoco also looks to acquisitions as a means for growth. In 2015 the company acquired a two-thirds stake in Graffo Paranaense de Embalagens S/A (Graffo) a flexible packaging business located in Brazil. Sonoco made the deal in order to grow its presence in an important emerging market.

In 2014 the company obtained Weidenhammer Packaging Group a European provider of composite cans along with composite drums and rigid plastic containers for $360 million. The deal enhanced its rigid paper packaging operations and is expected to increase its net sales in Europe to approximately 21% of total sales. Also in 2014 Sonoco picked up Dalton Paper Products (DPP) in order to fortify its paper and industrial converted products business segment.

HISTORY

Sonoco Products originated during the South's industrial renewal after the Civil War. Major James Coker and son James Jr. (who had been badly wounded at the Battle of Chickamauga) founded the Carolina Fiber company in Hartsville South Carolina to make pulp and paper from pine trees. The business was based on a thesis James Jr. wrote in 1884 at Stevens Institute of Technology in Hoboken New Jersey. The essay explained how to make paper pulp using the sulfite process.

After failing to sell the pulp commercially the Cokers decided to use it to make paper cones for the textile industry which was seeing rapid growth in the southern US. In 1899 Major Coker and investor W. F. Smith formed the Southern Novelty Company. Major Coker's son Charles became president in 1918. As sales neared $1 million in 1923 the company changed its name to Sonoco.

EXECUTIVES

President CEO and Director, M. Jack Sanders, age 61, $915,507 total compensation

VP Protective Solutions, Vicki B. Arthur

Group VP Paper Tubes and Cores NA, Rodger D. Fuller, age 53, $370,425 total compensation

VP Primary Materials Group NA, Marty F. Pignone, age 58

VP and CFO, Barry L. Saunders, age 55, $498,156 total compensation

Group VP Global Rigid Paper and Plastics, R. Howard Coker, age 52, $443,338 total compensation

SVP Global Industrial Products and Protective Solution, John M. Colyer, age 54, $531,546 total compensation

SVP Global Consumer Packaging and Services, Robert C. (Rob) Tiede, age 53, $530,836 total compensation

VP Industrial Europe, Adam Wood

Div Pres-genmgr Sonoco Alloyd, Jeff Christensen

Div President Manufacturing Protective Solutions, Ron O'Neal

Vice President, Martin Ryan

Chairman, Harris E. DeLoach

Auditors: PricewaterhouseCoopers LLP

LOCATIONS

HQ: Sonoco Products Co.
1 North Second Street, Hartsville, SC 29550
Phone: 843 383-7000   **Fax:** 843 383-7008
Web: www.sonoco.com

2014 Sales

	$ mil.	% of total
US	3,285	65
Europe	841	17
Canada	292	6
Other	595	12
Total	**5,014**	**100**

PRODUCTS/OPERATIONS

2014 Sales

	$ mil.	% of total
Consumer Packaging	1,962	39
Paper & Industrial Converted Products	1,902	38
Display & Packaging	664	13
Protective Solutions	484	10
Total	**5,014**	**100**

Selected Products and Services

Paper and Industrial Converted Products
  Tubes and cores
  Concrete forms
  Molded plugs
  Pallets
  Pallet components
  Paperboard tubes cores
  Roll packaging
  Rotary die boards
  Void forms
  Paper
  Boxboard
  Chipboard
  Corrugating medium
  Lightweight corestock
  Linerboard
  Recovered paper
  Recycled paperboard
  Specialty grades
  Tubeboard
  Sonoco Recycling
  Collection processing and recycling of old corrugated containers paper plastic metal glass other recyclable materials
Consumer Packaging
  Ends and closures
  Aluminum steel and peelable membrane easy-open closures for composite metal and plastic containers
  Printed flexible packaging
  Thin-gauge rotogravure flexographic and combination printed film (laminations and rotogravure cylinder engraving brand artwork management)
  Thin-gauge packaging
  Rigid packaging - blow molded plastics
  Monolayer and multilayer bottles and jars
  Rigid packaging - paper
  Composite paperboard cans (round and shaped)
  Fiber cartridges
  Single-wrap paperboard packages
  Rigid packaging - thermoformed plastic
  Mono coated and barrier and non-barrier laminated tubs cups spools consumer and institutional trays

Packaging Services
  Paperboard specialties
  Rixie coasters
  Stancap glass covers
  Other paper amenities
  Point-of-purchase (P-O-P)
  Contract packaging co-packing and fulfillment services
  Designing manufacturing assembling packing and distributing temporary semi permanent and permanent P-O-P displays
  Service centers
  Packaging supply chain management (custom packing fulfillment primary package filling scalable service centers)
Protective Packaging
  Molded and extruded plastics (product design tool design and fabrication; manufacturing in both injection molding and extrusion technologies)
  Protective packaging
  Contract package testing
  Sonopost technology
  Sonobase carriers
  Sonopop systems

COMPETITORS

Amcor	Greif
AptarGroup	International Paper
Avery Dennison	Owens-Illinois
Ball Corp.	Pactiv
Bemis	Sealed Air Corp.
Caraustar	Silgan
Crown Holdings	The Newark Group
Graphic Packaging	WestRock
Holding	

HISTORICAL FINANCIALS

Company Type: Public

Income Statement

FYE: December 31

	REVENUE ($ mil.)	NET INCOME ($ mil.)	NET PROFIT MARGIN	EMPLOYEES
12/14	5,014	239	4.8%	20,800
12/13	4,848	219	4.5%	19,900
12/12	4,786	196	4.1%	19,900
12/11	4,498	217	4.8%	19,600
12/10	4,124	201	4.9%	17,300
Annual Growth	**5.0%**	**4.4%**	**—**	**4.7%**

2014 Year-End Financials

Debt ratio: 29.77%
Return on equity: 14.86%
Cash ($ mil.): 161
Current ratio: 1.54
Long-term debt ($ mil.): 1,200

No. of shares (mil.): 100
Dividends
  Yield: 2.9%
  Payout: 54.9%
Market value ($ mil.): 4,396

	STOCK PRICE ($) FY Close	P/E High/Low		PER SHARE ($) Earnings	Dividends	Book Value
12/14	43.70	19	16	2.32	1.27	14.98
12/13	41.72	19	14	2.12	1.23	16.75
12/12	29.73	18	15	1.91	1.19	14.76
12/11	32.96	17	13	2.13	1.15	14.09
12/10	33.67	18	14	1.96	1.11	14.84
Annual Growth	**6.7%**	**—**	**—**	**4.3%**	**3.4%**	**0.2%**

South State Corp

South State Corporation (formerly First Financial Holdings) is the holding company for South State Bank (formerly South Carolina Bank and Trust and South Carolina Bank and Trust of the Piedmont both known as SCBT). The bank operates branches throughout the Palmetto state as well as in select counties in Georgia and North Carolina. Serving retail and business customers the banks provide deposit accounts loans and mortgages as well as trust and investment planning services. More than half of the company's loan portfolio is devoted to commercial mortgages while consumer real estate loans make up more than a quarter. South State has assets of nearly $8 billion.

OperationsBeyond its retail and commercial banking mortgage lending consumer finance and trust and investment businesses the bank operates registered investment advisors Minis & Co. and First Southeast 401K Fiduciaries as well as limited-purpose broker-dealer First Southeast Investor Services.South State Corporation generated 70% of its total revenue from loan interest (including fees) in 2014 while another 4% came from interest income on investment securities. Service charges and Bankcard services income made up another 14% of total revenue while trust and investment services income and mortgage banking income each contributed roughly 4% during the year.Geographic ReachSouth State Corporation boasts nearly 130 branches across nearly 20 counties in South Carolina a handful of counties in North Carolina and about a dozen counties in the northeast and coastal regions of Georgia.Financial PerformanceSouth State Corporation's revenues and profits have been on the rise over the past few years mostly thanks to continued growth of its loan business and declining loan loss provisions as its loan portfolio's credit quality has improved with the strengthened economy.The company's revenue jumped by 28% to $436.72 million in 2014 which was mostly driven by 20% growth in its loan interest income as its average loan asset balances swelled by a similar percentage. South State's non-interest income also swelled by 76% thanks to higher deposit account service charge bankcard service trust and investment service and mortgage banking fees from overall growth in the business through acquisitions and organic initiatives. Higher revenue and controlled operating costs in 2014 drove the bank's net income higher by 53% to $75.44 million. South State's operating cash levels declined by 51% to $118.65 million for the year after adjusting its earnings for non-cash net sales proceeds from its mortgage loans held-for-sale and as the bank spent more cash toward its accrued income taxes.StrategyThough it does sometimes expand or relocate its existing branches to better position its locations for more growth South State Corporation has been mostly growing its loan business and branch network through strategic bank and branch acquisitions. Its 2015 acquisition of 13 branch locations from Bank of America for example extended South State's reach into six new markets and three existing markets while adding millions of dollars worth of new loan business.Mergers and AcquisitionsIn 2015 South State Corporation agreed to purchase 12 South Carolina branches and one Georgia branch from Bank of America expanding its reach into six new markets. The acquired branches were located in Hartwell Georgia; as well as Florence Greenwood Orangeburg Sumter Newberry Batesburg-Leesville Abbeville and Hartsville in South Carolina.Company BackgroundSouth State Corporation and South State Bank changed their names from First Financial Holdings and South Carolina Bank and Trust respectively in 2014. The change was designed to better promote the South State brand with customers.

EXECUTIVES

CEO, Robert R. Hill, age 48, $645,000 total compensation

CFO and COO, John C. Pollok, age 49, $442,000 total compensation
Chief Banking Officer, John F. Windley, age 63, $315,000 total compensation
Chief Credit Officer and Chief Risk Officer, Joseph Burns, $295,000 total compensation
President, R. Wayne Hall, $203,405 total compensation
EVP and Corporate Secretary, William C. Bochette
Senior Vice President, Leo A Smith
Senior Vice President And Commercial Consumer Lender, Jimmy Lindsey
Senior Vice President And Senior Relationship Manager, Bill Coker
Vice President, Reid Davis
Senior Vice President Technology, Ross Bagley
Senior Executive Vice President, Dane H Murray
Vice President, Kelley Morabito
Executive Vice President Chief Financial Officer, Donald (Don) Pickett
Senior Vice President Corporate Counsel, V Comer
Chairman, Robert R. Horger, age 64
Vice Chairman, Paula Harper Bethea
Auditors: Dixon Hughes Goodman LLP

LOCATIONS

HQ: South State Corp
520 Gervais Street, Columbia, SC 29201
Phone: 800 277-2175
Web: www.southstatebank.com

PRODUCTS/OPERATIONS

2011 Sales

	$ mil.	% of total
Interest		
Loans including fees	319	70
Investment securities	20	4
Other	1	-
Noninterest		
Service charges on deposit accounts	36	10
Bankcard services income	29	6
Trust and investment services income	18	4
Mortgage banking	16	4
Securities gains net -	0	
Amortization of FDIC indemnification asset	(21.9)	0
Other	16	4
Total	**436**	**100**

COMPETITORS

BB&T	Regions Financial
Bank of America	Security Federal
Bank of South Carolina	
First Citizens Bancorporation	

HISTORICAL FINANCIALS

Company Type: Public

Income Statement

FYE: December 31

	ASSETS ($ mil.)	NET INCOME ($ mil.)	INCOME AS % OF ASSETS	EMPLOYEES
12/14	7,826	75	1.0%	2,081
12/13	7,931	49	0.6%	2,106
12/12	5,136	30	0.6%	1,324
12/11	3,896	22	0.6%	1,071
12/10	3,594	51	1.4%	1,015
Annual Growth	**21.5%**	**9.8%**	**—**	**19.7%**

2014 Year-End Financials

Debt ratio: 1.29%	No. of shares (mil.): 24
Return on equity: 7.67%	Dividends
Cash ($ mil.): 237	Yield: 1.2%
Current ratio: —	Payout: 30.0%
Long-term debt ($ mil.): —	Market value ($ mil.): 1,620

	STOCK PRICE ($) FY Close	P/E High/Low	PER SHARE ($) Earnings	Dividends	Book Value
12/14	67.08	22 18	3.08	0.82	40.78
12/13	66.51	28 17	2.38	0.74	40.72
12/12	40.18	20 14	2.03	0.69	29.97
12/11	29.01	22 15	1.63	0.68	27.19
12/10	32.75	10 7	4.08	0.68	25.79
Annual Growth	**19.6%**	**— —**	**(6.8%)**	**4.8%**	**12.1%**

Southern California Edison Co.

One of the Golden State's largest utilities Southern California Edison (SCE) distributes power to a population of more than 14 million people (5 million customer accounts) in central coastal and southern California (excluding Los Angeles and some other cities). SCE has 6310 MW of net generating capacity from stakes in nuclear hydroelectric and fossil-fueled power plants (although it has sold a number of its fossil-fueled facilities in response to the state's deregulation legislation). The utility sells excess power to wholesale customers. SCE is a unit of utility and competitive power holding company Edison International.

Geographic Reach

SCE supplies and delivers electricity to a 50000 square-mile area of southern California. This service area contains a population of nearly 14 million people and SCE serves the population via about 5 million customer accounts.

Operations

The utility's system consists of about 12782 circuit miles of transmission lines and more than 90401 circuit miles of distribution lines and more than 700 distribution substations.

Financial Performance

The company reported stable revenue growth over the past few years. In 2013 its revenues grew by 6% due to higher state utility commission-related revenues to support rate base growth and an increase in FERC-related revenues related to higher rates.SCE has seen a slow decline in its net income since 2011. In 2013 the company's profits decreased by 40% due to higher operating costs and income tax.In 2013 the company's operating cash inflow declined to $3.28 billion (from $4.09 billion in 2012) due to a drop in net income and a change in current assets and liabilities.

Strategy

Parent Edison International has been addressing the changing industry environment by focusing SCE on investing in and strengthening its electric grid and driving operational and service excellence to improve system safety reliability and service while controlling costs and rates. At the same time Edison International is investing in competitive businesses to meet the electricity needs of commercial and industrial customers both inside and beyond SCE's service area.

In recent years the utility has been ramping up its green energy options in order to comply with the state of California's aggressive long term renewable energy goal. As part of its strategy to reduce its fossil-fuel power plant holdings in 2013 SCE sold its ownership interest in Units 4 and 5 of the Four Corners Generating Station a coal-fired electric generating facility in New Mexico to

the operator of the facility Arizona Public Service Company for $181 million.

SCE also offers power contract options designed to help smaller biomass generators and is installing up to 150 solar photovoltaic installations on Southern California commercial rooftops. The utility is also installing smart electric meters —digital two-way communication devices which allow customers and the utility to better manage energy use than the older mechanical meters can.

EXECUTIVES

Vice President, Barbara (Barb) Mathews
Executive Vice President And General Counsel Edison International, Robert L Adler
VP and CIO, Todd L. Inlander
VP Power Production, Enrique (Henry) Martinez
SVP Power Supply and Operational Services, Stuart R. Hemphill
VP Operational Services and Chief Procurement Officer, Douglas R. Bauder
SVP Transmission and Distribution, Peter T. Dietrich
SVP and CFO, Maria Rigatti, age 51
VP Distribution, Gregory M. Ferree
VP Transmission Substations and Operations, Paul J. Grigaux
VP Safety Security and Compliance, Dana Kracke
Chairman President and CEO, Ted Craver
Vice President, Russell C Swartz
Vice President And General Auditor Edison International, Megan Scott
Vice President Technology Business Development, Pedro J Pizarro
Vice President Engineering And Information Technology, Erica Darplee
Senior Vice President Customer Service, Kevin Payne
Vice President Investor Relations Edison International, Scott Cunningham
Vice President and Treasurer, Robert C (Bob) Boada
Vice President, George Couts
Vice President, Dan Tunnicliff
Vice President Business Customer Division, Lisa Cagnolatti
Vice President, Anthony Blakemore
Vice President, Debbie Rodgers
Senior Vice President And Chief Nuclear, Joe Sheppard
Executive Vice President Generation, Harold Ray
Vice President Tax Edison International, Jeff Barnett
Vice President and Controller, Mark C Clarke
Vice President Human Resources, Patricia (Pat) Miller
Senior Vice President Corporate Communications, Janet Clayton
Vice President Risk Management, David (Dave) Heller
Treasurer, John Butler
Auditors: PricewaterhouseCoopers LLP

LOCATIONS

HQ: Southern California Edison Co.
2244 Walnut Grove Avenue, P.O. Box 800, Rosemead, CA 91770
Phone: 626 302-1212

PRODUCTS/OPERATIONS

2013 Sales

	% of total
Commercial customers	42
Residential customers	40
Industrial customers	5
Public authorities	5
Resale sales	1
Agriculture & other customers	7
Total	**100**

2013 Fuel Sources

	% of total
Purchased power	79
SCE-owned generation	21
Total	**100**

COMPETITORS

American States Water	Portland General
Avista	Electric
Bonneville Power	Sacramento Municipal
Calpine	Utility
Imperial Irrigation	San Diego Gas &
District	Electric
NV Energy	SoCalGas
PacifiCorp	
Pacific Gas and	
Electric	

HISTORICAL FINANCIALS

Company Type: Public

Income Statement   FYE: December 31

	REVENUE ($ mil.)	NET INCOME ($ mil.)	NET PROFIT MARGIN	EMPLOYEES
12/14	13,380	1,565	11.7%	13,600
12/13	12,562	1,000	8.0%	13,599
12/12	11,851	1,660	14.0%	16,515
12/11	10,577	1,144	10.8%	18,069
12/10	9,983	1,092	10.9%	18,230
Annual Growth	7.6%	9.4%	—	(7.1%)

2014 Year-End Financials

Debt ratio: 21.42%	No. of shares (mil.): 434
Return on equity: 12.31%	Dividends
Cash ($ mil.): 38	Yield: 0.0%
Current ratio: 0.71	Payout: 36.1%
Long-term debt ($ mil.): 9,624	Market value ($ mil.): 9,785

	STOCK PRICE ($) FY Close	P/E High/Low		PER SHARE ($) Earnings	Dividends	Book Value
12/14	22.50	— —		(0.00)	1.08	30.54
12/13	20.58	— —		(0.00)	1.08	27.91
12/12	22.20	— —		(0.00)	1.08	27.00
12/11	22.60	— —		(0.00)	1.08	22.90
12/10	19.20	— —		(0.00)	1.08	21.17
Annual Growth	4.0%	— —		—	(0.0%)	9.6%

Southern Company (The)

Southern Power is responding to the power of the burgeoning population growth in the South. The company owns builds acquires and markets energy in the competitive wholesale supply business. It develops and operates independent power plants in the southeastern US. The company which is part of Southern Company's generation and energy marketing operations has more than 8800 MW of primarily fossil-fueled facilities generating capacity operating or under construction in Alabama California Florida Georgia Nevada North Carolina Texas and New Mexico. Southern Power's electricity output is marketed to wholesale customers in the region. It is also developing solar power facilities.

Geographic Reach

Southern Power has operations Alabama California Florida Georgia Nevada New Mexico North Carolina and Texas.

Operations

The company is a wholesale energy provider serving electricity needs of municipalities electric cooperatives and investor-owned utilities. Southern Power and its subsidiaries own and operate 17 facilities in eight states. Its renewable assets include biomass and solar. It has entered into long-term power sales agreements for 79% of its capacity through 2018 and 70% of its capacity through 2023.

Financial Performance

In 2013 the company's revenues increased by 8% primarily due to higher capacity revenues under power purchase agreements (PPAs) with non-affiliates (especially due to a new PPA served by Plant Nacogdoches which began in June 2012) and an increase in capacity amounts under existing PPAs. it also reported an $80.4 million increase in energy sales under PPAs with non-affiliates reflecting a 30% rise in energy prices and a $7.8 million increase related to new solar contracts (which began in 2013) served by Plants Campo Verde and Spectrum. This increase was partially offset by an $11.8 million decrease in energy sales under PPAs with affiliates reflecting a 48% slump in power sales due to lower demand partially offset by a 28.9% increase in energy prices. Southern Power's net income decreased by 6% in 2013 as a result of increased power purchases by affiliates and higher interest expenses. In 2013 the company's operating cash inflow increased to $604.36 million (from $573.13 million in 2012) due to an increase in cash received from investment tax credits.

Southern Power has seen revenue growth since 2009 except for a slight decrease in 2012 due to lower energy sales from PPAs reflecting a 25.8% drop in the average price of energy and a 1.3% decrease in KwH sales.

Strategy

The company is expanding its regional generation portfolio with the possibility of boosting overall generating capacity to almost 10000 MW.

In a move to diversify its operations parent Southern Company transferred its ownership of renewable generation unit Southern Renewable Energy (SRE) to Southern Power in 2011. Among other properties SRE and Turner Renewable Energy operate Plant Cimarron a 30 MW solar photovoltaic plant near Cimarron New Mexico.

In 2012 Southern Power completed building Units 1 through 4 of a combustion turbine natural gas generating plant in Cleveland County North Carolina. The plant has a capacity of 720 MW.

Mergers and Acquisitions

In 2014 Southern Power and Turner Renewable Energy acquired the largest solar facility in New Mexico the 50-MW Macho Springs Solar Facility. The Southern Power-Turner Renewable Energy partnership's seventh solar project and its second-largest overall the plant is expected to generate enough electricity to power more than 18000 homes.

In 2013 the partnership acquired the Campo Verde Solar Facility the fifth acquisition of solar plant by the renewable energy entity.

EXECUTIVES

Vice President and Senior Production Officer, Kimberly Flowers
Executive Vice President, Doug Jones
EVP and COO, Mark A. Crosswhite, age 53
VP and CFO, William C. (Bill) Grantham, age 45
Chairman President and CEO, Thomas A. Fanning
EVP Engineering and Construction Services, Penny Manuel

Vice President Information Technology, Jim Trupiano
Vice President, Fred Williams
Vice President Strategic Planning and Compliance, Bart Wood
Senior Vice President Human Resources, Marsha Johnson
Vice President Of Construction Support, Ashley Newton
Vice President Enterprise Direct Sales, Lisa Piotter
Vice President Fleet Operations Support, Bradley Adams
Senior Vice President Chief Environmental Off, Larry S Monroe
Executive Vice President Customer Services Georgia Power, Mickey A Brown
Senior Vice Presiden, Kim Greene
Vice President Communications, Carrie Kurlander
Vice President Customer Services, Louise Scott
Vice President Nuclear, Charlton Salter
Vice President, Brad Delcambre
Vice President And Senior Counsel, Stephen (Steve) Wakefield
Senior Vice President Finance and Treasurer, Kimberly Greene
Vice President Mobile Area, Mike Saxon
Vice President Nuclear Plant Site, Cheryl Gayheart
Executive Vice President; President and Chief Executive Officer Alabama Power, Charles (Chas) Mccrary
Exec Vice Pres, Andrew (Andy) Dearman
National Accounts Manager, Norman Collins
National Accounts Manager, Jeff Webster
Vice President Controller, Robert Morris
Site Vice President of Joseph M Farley Nuclear Plant, Thomas (Thom) Lynch
Senior Vice President Of New Media Sales, James Alexander
Vice President Of Human Resources, Judy Murphy
Vice President Public Relations, Bobbie Knight
Senior Vice President Compliance Officer, Thomas (Thom) Bishop
Assistant Vice President of Marketing and Sales, Stephen (Steve) Bennett
Vice President, Dave Altman
Senior Vice Presiden, James (Jamie) Miller
Vice President Customer Services, Myrna Pittman
Vice President, Pete Ivey
Board Member, Henry A Clark
Asst Treas, Todd Perkins
Secretary, Laura Patterson
Board Member, Jeff Orgeron
Vice Chairman, Michael Christie
Treasurer, Randy Derieux
Auditors: Deloitte & Touche LLP

LOCATIONS

HQ: Southern Company (The)
30 Ivan Allen Jr. Boulevard, N.W., Atlanta, GA 30308
Phone: 404 506-5000   **Fax:** 404 506-0455
Web: www.southerncompany.com

PRODUCTS/OPERATIONS

2013 Sales

	$ mil.	% of total
Wholesale		
Non-affiliates	922	72
Affiliates	345	27
Other	6	1
Total	**1,275**	**100**

COMPETITORS

AEP	Duke Energy
AEP	Duke Energy
AES	Entergy
AES	Entergy
Calpine	NextEra Energy
Calpine	NextEra Energy

Company Type: Public

Income Statement
FYE: December 31

	REVENUE ($ mil.)	NET INCOME ($ mil.)	NET PROFIT MARGIN	EMPLOYEES
12/14	18,467	2,031	11.0%	26,369
12/13	17,087	1,710	10.0%	26,300
12/12	16,537	2,415	14.6%	26,439
12/11	17,657	2,268	12.8%	26,377
12/10	17,456	2,040	11.7%	25,940
Annual Growth	1.4%	(0.1%)	—	0.4%

2014 Year-End Financials

Debt ratio: 34.08%
Return on equity: 9.79%
Cash ($ mil.): 710
Current ratio: 0.71
Long-term debt ($ mil.): 20,841

No. of shares (mil.): 907
Dividends
 Yield: 4.2%
 Payout: 89.0%
Market value ($ mil.): 44,581

	STOCK PRICE ($) FY Close	P/E High/Low		PER SHARE ($) Earnings	Dividends	Book Value
12/14	49.11	23	18	2.18	2.08	23.51
12/13	41.11	26	21	1.87	2.01	22.70
12/12	42.81	18	16	2.67	1.94	22.33
12/11	46.29	18	14	2.55	1.87	21.57
12/10	38.23	16	13	2.36	1.80	20.49
Annual Growth	6.5%	—	—	(2.0%)	3.7%	3.5%

Southern Copper Corp

Auditors: Galaz, Yamazaki, Ruiz Urquiza, S.C. (member of Deloitte Touche Tohmatsu Limited)

LOCATIONS

HQ: Southern Copper Corp
1440 East Missouri Avenue, Suite 160, Phoenix, AZ 85014
Phone: 602 264-1375   **Fax:** 602 264-1397
Web: www.southerncoppercorp.com

HISTORICAL FINANCIALS
Company Type: Public

Income Statement
FYE: December 31

	REVENUE ($ mil.)	NET INCOME ($ mil.)	NET PROFIT MARGIN	EMPLOYEES
12/14	5,787	1,332	23.0%	12,735
12/13	5,952	1,618	27.2%	12,665
12/12	6,669	1,934	29.0%	12,085
12/11	6,818	2,336	34.3%	12,145
12/10	5,149	1,554	30.2%	11,126
Annual Growth	3.0%	(3.8%)	—	3.4%

2014 Year-End Financials

Debt ratio: 36.41%
Return on equity: 23.51%
Cash ($ mil.): 363
Current ratio: 2.16
Long-term debt ($ mil.): 4,006

No. of shares (mil.): 806
Dividends
 Yield: 1.6%
 Payout: 27.7%
Market value ($ mil.): 22,749

	STOCK PRICE ($) FY Close	P/E High/Low		PER SHARE ($) Earnings	Dividends	Book Value
12/14	28.20	21	16	1.61	0.46	7.20
12/13	28.71	22	13	1.92	0.68	6.26
12/12	37.86	17	12	2.28	3.71	5.39
12/11	30.18	18	9	2.76	2.46	4.77
12/10	48.74	27	14	1.83	1.68	4.58
Annual Growth	(12.8%)	—	—	(3.2%)	(27.7%)	12.0%

Southside Bancshares, Inc.

Southside Bancshares is the holding company for Southside Bank which boasts nearly 65 branches across East North and Central Texas with many around the cities of Tyler and Longview. About one-third of its branches are located in supermarkets (including Albertsons and Brookshire stores) and 40% are motor bank facilities. The bank provides traditional services such as savings money market and checking accounts CDs and other deposit products as well as trust and wealth management services. Real estate loans primarily residential mortgages make up about half of the company's loan portfolio which also includes business consumer and municipal loans. The bank has total assets exceeding $4.8 billion.

OperationsSouthside generated 48% of its total revenue from loan interest in 2014 while interest income on taxable investment securities and mortgage-backed securities made up 16% and 19% respectively. About 9% of its revenue came from deposit service fees and another 2% came from trust income.Geographic ReachThe bank's branches are located in East North and Central Texas. Its main markets are in East Texas the greater Fort Worth area and the greater Austin area. It is also an affiliate with more than 55000 foreign ATMs worldwide.Sales and MarketingSouthside which staffed 813 employees at 2014's end serves individuals businesses municipal entities and non-profit organizations in local communities.Financial Performance

Southside Bancshares' revenues and profits have been falling over the past several years despite consistent growth in loan and investment interest income mostly because the bank's gains on securities held-for-sale have declined.The company's revenue dipped by 4% to $148.3 million in 2014 mostly due to a $5.6 million decline in gains on the sale of its AFS securities and a $2.8 million impairment of equity related to its investment in SFG Finance stemming from the sale of loans purchased by SFG and the repossessed assets. Lower revenue and an uptick in loan loss provisions in 2014 caused Southside's net income to tumble 49% to $20.8 million for the year while its operating cash levels dipped by 6% to $56 million on lower cash earnings.

Strategy

Southside looks to acquire financial institutions to grow its loan business and expand its geographic reach outside of its existing markets. Its 2014 acquisition of OmniAmerican Bank alone helped boost its loan assets by more than 60% to $2.17 billion while adding 14 branches in a new market (Dallas/Fort Worth).To grow its deposits and deepen its presence in the markets it serves the company has also been expanding its network of banking locations —both in-store and full-service branches.

Mergers and Acquisitions

In December 2014 the company acquired OmniAmerican Bank to boost its loan business and expand its footprint to the Dallas area. The deal added 14 full-service branches in the 12-county Dallas/Fort Worth metroplex and more than $763 million in new loan business.

EXECUTIVES

Senior Executive Vice President, Jeryl Story
President and CFO Southside Bancshares and Southside Bank, Lee R. Gibson, age 58, $416,392 total compensation
CEO and Director Southside Bancshares and Southside Bank, Sam Dawson, age 68, $486,524 total compensation
Regional President North Texas Southside Bank, Tim Carter, age 59
Regional President Central Texas Southside Bank, Peter M. Boyd, age 59, $369,766 total compensation
EVP and Chief Credit Officer Southside Bank, Earl W. (Bill) Clawater, age 61, $204,615 total compensation
EVP and Chief Analytics Officer Southside Bank and Company Secretary, Brian K. McCabe, age 54, $163,692 total compensation
Regional President East Texas Southside Bank, Tim Alexander, age 58
Vice President Information Technology, George Hall
Senior Vice President, Ken Kizer
Executive Vice President, Randall R Hendrix
Board Member, Alton Cade
Vice Chairman, John R. (Bob) Garrett, age 62
Chairman, W.D. (Joe) Norton, age 78
Board Member, Joe Norton, age 40
Board Member, Melvin B Lovelady, age 80
Board Member, Paul W Powell, age 83
Board Member, William Sheehy, age 75
Auditors: Ernst & Young LLP

LOCATIONS

HQ: Southside Bancshares, Inc.
1201 S. Beckham Avenue, Tyler, TX 75701
Phone: 903 531-7111
Web: www.southside.com

PRODUCTS/OPERATIONS

2014 Sales

	$ mil.	% of total
Interest		
Loans	70	48
Mortgage-backed & related securities	28	19
Investment securities	24	16
Other	0	-
Non-interest		
Deposit services	15	9
Gain on sale of securities	2	2
Trust income	3	2
Back owned life insurance income	1	1
Gain on sale of loans	0	-
Other	4	3
Adjustments	(2.8)	-
Total	148	100

COMPETITORS

Bank of America	Jacksonville Bancorp
Capital One	of Illinois
East Texas Financial	Regions Financial

HISTORICAL FINANCIALS

Company Type: Public

Income Statement

FYE: December 31

	ASSETS ($ mil.)	NET INCOME ($ mil.)	INCOME AS % OF ASSETS	EMPLOYEES
12/14	4,807	20	0.4%	813
12/13	3,445	41	1.2%	640
12/12	3,237	34	1.1%	574
12/11	3,303	39	1.2%	557
12/10	2,999	39	1.3%	578
Annual Growth	12.5%	(14.8%)	—	8.9%

2014 Year-End Financials

Debt ratio: 1.25%
Return on equity: 6.08%
Cash ($ mil.): 84
Current ratio: —
Long-term debt ($ mil.): —

No. of shares (mil.): 25
Dividends
  Yield: 3.0%
  Payout: 91.5%
Market value ($ mil.): 732

	STOCK PRICE ($) FY Close	P/E High/Low		PER SHARE ($) Earnings	Dividends	Book Value
12/14	28.91	33	24	1.04	0.95	16.80
12/13	27.34	14	10	2.09	0.86	13.14
12/12	21.06	13	12	1.73	1.00	13.05
12/11	21.66	12	9	1.96	0.73	12.92
12/10	21.07	11	9	1.97	0.69	10.74
Annual Growth	8.2%	—	—	(14.8%)	8.2%	11.8%

Southwest Airlines Co

Southwest Airlines will fly any plane (as long as it's a Boeing) and let passengers sit anywhere they like (as long as they get there first). Sticking with what has worked Southwest has expanded its low-cost no-frills no-reserved-seats approach to air travel throughout the US to serve nearly 90 destinations across North America. Now the largest carrier of US domestic passengers Southwest still stands as an inspiration for scrappy low-fare upstarts the world over. The carrier has enjoyed 41 straight profitable years amid the airline industry's ups and downs. Southwest's fleet numbers about 700 aircraft including 665 Boeing 737s.

Geographic Reach

Southwest serves more than 90 destinations in some 40 US states in addition to the District of Columbia Puerto Rico Mexico Jamaica The Bahamas Aruba and the Dominican Republic.

Operations

By adding AirTran to its hangar (AirTran was purchased in 2011) Southwest now has access to more airports in the eastern and southeastern US (including a coveted spot at Delta's home airport in Atlanta) as well as to international destinations in the Caribbean and Mexico.

Simplicity has been key to Southwest's success. Most of the carrier's flights are less than two hours and it usually lands at small airports to avoid congestion at competitors' larger hubs; in Dallas it's the big dog at little Love Field its birthplace and in Chicago it accounts for most of the traffic at Midway Airport. Southwest's (and AirTran's) fleet consists primarily of one type of aircraft –the Boeing 737 –to minimize training and maintenance costs.

Financial Performance

Southwest has achieved unprecedented growth over the last five years. Its revenues grew 5% from $17.7 billion in 2013 to $18.6 billion in 2014 a historic milestone. Profits also skyrocketed 51% from

$754 million in 2013 to a record-setting $1.1 billion in 2014 due to the higher revenue coupled with a steep decline in fuel and oil prices.

The historic growth for 2014 was driven by a bump in passenger revenues fueled by increased passenger yield increased fares and a marginal increase in capacity. Freight revenues for 2014 also rose primarily due to higher average rates charged as a result of fuel surcharges and an increase in other revenues.

Southwest's operating cash flow increased from $2.5 billion in 2013 to $2.9 billion in 2014 due to the higher profits in addition to cash generated from accounts payable and accrued liabilities and air traffic liability.

Strategy

Protective of its low-cost image Southwest has staunchly resisted charging passengers baggage fees. However it has seen the value of this strategy and has rolled out new fees that have included allowing passengers to bring small dogs or cats into the cabin for a one-way charge of $75 and charging a one-way $50 fee for unaccompanied minors.

A large part of Southwest's growth strategy has included the integration of AirTran Airways which it acquired in 2011 for about $3.2 billion. (It officially retired the AirTran brand in late 2014.) As a result of this integration Southwest in 2014 launched international services to Jamaica (Montego Bay) the Bahamas (Nassau) and Aruba (Oranjestad). The carrier currently provides its international services to five destinations in Mexico Jamaica The Bahamas Aruba and the Dominican Republic. Throughout 2015 Southwest plans to launch destinations in San Jose Costa Rica; Puerto Vallarta Mexico; and Belize City Belize.

Another major strategy to stay profitable includes fleet modernization. Southwest is replacing older Boeing 737 planes with the larger and more fuel-efficient Boeing 737-800 for expansion to locations of greater distance and it plans to begin using another new fuel-efficient model the Boeing 737 Max in 2017.

HISTORY

Texas businessman Rollin King and lawyer Herb Kelleher founded Air Southwest in 1967 as an intrastate airline linking Dallas Houston and San Antonio. The now-defunct Braniff and Texas International sued questioning whether the region needed another airline but the Texas Supreme Court ruled in Southwest's favor. In 1971 the company renamed Southwest Airlines made its first scheduled flight.

Operating from Love Field in Dallas Southwest adopted "love" as the theme of its early ad campaigns serving love potions (drinks) and love bites (peanuts). When other airlines moved to the new Dallas/Fort Worth International Airport (DFW) in 1974 Kelleher insisted on staying at Love Field gaining a virtual monopoly there.

EXECUTIVES

EVP and Chief Commercial Officer; President AirTran Airways, Robert E. (Bob) Jordan, age 55, $465,000 total compensation

Vice Chairman, Ron Ricks, age 66, $457,500 total compensation

Chairman President and CEO, Gary C. Kelly, age 59, $675,000 total compensation

EVP and CFO, Tammy Romo, age 52, $426,250 total compensation

EVP and COO, Michael G. (Mike) Van de Ven, age 53, $465,000 total compensation

VP Technology Operations and CTO, Craig Maccubbin, age 48

SVP and CIO, Randy Sloan

EVP Corporate Services and Aiport Affairs, Jeff Lamb, age 52

SVP General Counsel and Corporate Secretary, Mark Shaw

VP Marketing, Ryan Green

Managing Director Business Development, Dave Harvey

Managing Director Network Planning, Adam Decaire

Vp Operations Coordination Center, Jeff Martin

Auditors: Ernst & Young LLP

LOCATIONS

HQ: Southwest Airlines Co
P.O. Box 36611, Dallas, TX 75235-1611
Phone: 214 792-4000   Fax: 214 792-5015
Web: www.southwest.com

PRODUCTS/OPERATIONS

2014 Sales

	$ mil.	% of total
Passenger	17,658	95
Freight	175	1
Other	772	4
Total	18,605	100

COMPETITORS

Alaska Air	Frontier Airlines
American Airlines Group	JetBlue
	US Airways
Delta Air Lines	United Continental

HISTORICAL FINANCIALS

Company Type: Public

Income Statement

FYE: December 31

	REVENUE ($ mil.)	NET INCOME ($ mil.)	NET PROFIT MARGIN	EMPLOYEES
12/15	19,820	2,181	11.0%	49,583
12/14	18,605	1,136	6.1%	46,278
12/13	17,699	754	4.3%	44,831
12/12	17,088	421	2.5%	45,861
12/11	15,658	178	1.1%	45,392
Annual Growth	6.1%	87.1%	—	2.2%

2015 Year-End Financials

Debt ratio: 14.91%
Return on equity: 30.86%
Cash ($ mil.): 1,583
Current ratio: 0.54
Long-term debt ($ mil.): 2,541

No. of shares (mil.): 647
Dividends
  Yield: 0.6%
  Payout: 10.4%
Market value ($ mil.): 27,886

	STOCK PRICE ($) FY Close	P/E High/Low		PER SHARE ($) Earnings	Dividends	Book Value
12/15	43.06	15	10	3.27	0.29	11.36
12/14	42.32	26	11	1.64	0.20	10.03
12/13	18.84	18	10	1.05	0.13	10.47
12/12	10.24	19	14	0.56	0.03	9.57
12/11	8.56	58	32	0.23	0.02	8.90
Annual Growth	49.8%	—	—	94.2%	99.5%	6.3%

SpartanNash Co.

In the grocery and distribution wars Spartan-Nash (formerly Spartan Stores) is up for the fight. The grocery retailer and wholesaler operates 100 Michigan supermarkets under the Family Fare Supermarkets No Frills D&W Fresh Market VG's

Food and Pharmacy Sun Mart and more than a dozen other banners. Besides selling national brand-goods stores offer private-label items under the Spartan TopCare Valu Time and Full Circle names. SpartanNash is also a leading grocery wholesaler distributing more than 55000 food and merchandise items to 2100 independent supermarkets in Michigan Indiana and Ohio. Founded in 1917 as a cooperative grocery distributor Spartan Stores acquired Nash-Finch in 2013.

OperationsSpartanNash operates three main business segments. Food Distribution which makes up roughly 40% of the company's total revenue comprises 12 distribution centers that ship 55000 SKU's of food general merchandise floral pharmacy and health and beauty care products. Its Retail division (30% of revenue) sells items from its 160-plus company-owned retail stores operating under more than 15 banners (including Family Fare Supermarkets No Frills Bag ‘N Save Family Fresh Markets D&W Fresh Markets Sun Mart and Econo Foods). SpartanNash's Military segment (30% of revenue) contracts with manufacturers to distribute grocery products to US military commissaries and exchanges; it's the largest distributor to such US military properties in the world. By product SpartanNash generates more than 60% of its revenue from non-perishable items while another roughly 30% comes from the sale and distribution of perishable items. Just over 5% of its revenue comes from fuel and pharmacy sales.Geographic ReachGrand Rapids Michigan-based SpartanNash owns more than 160 stores in 10 states and distributes to more than 2000 independent grocers across 46 US states. Its military operations serve commissaries and exchanges in 27 US states the District of Columbia Europe Cuba Puerto Rico Bahrain and Egypt.Sales and MarketingSpartanNash spent $41.1 million on advertising in fiscal 2015 (ended January 3) up from $15.3 million and $13.6 million in FY2014 and FY2013 respectively.Financial PerformanceThe retailer and wholesaler has struggled to grow its revenues and profits over the past few years with sluggish economic growth in Michigan and surrounding Midwestern states.SpartanNash had a breakout year in fiscal 2015 (ended January 3) however with revenue spiking by 148% to a record $7.92 billion thanks mostly to added revenue across all segments from its recent merger with Nash-Finch Company. Incremental sales increases related to new Food Distribution customers along with two additional weeks added to the company's fiscal year also helped boost its top line. Its Retail segment's comparable store sales also grew by 1% despite the closure of 11 stores.Higher revenue in FY2015 boosted SpartanNash's net income to $58.6 million (compared to $741 thousand the prior year) while the company's operating cash levels more than doubled to $139 million thanks to higher cash earnings.

Strategy

To drive sales and foster customer loyalty SpartanNash has been renovating its stores (it completed 10 major remodels during 2014) and continues to develop its private-label brand and loyalty card programs across all of its banners.

Through SpartanNash's neighborhood market strategy the company endeavors to distinguish itself from other food retailers such as supercenters and limited-assortment stores by emphasizing convenient locations and offering demographically targeted merchandise high-quality fresh foods and value pricing. It's been expanding its product offerings in its stores adding more than 400 new items (including 250 exclusive corporate-brand products) during 2014 with plans to introduce 500 new items (including 300 new unique items) throughout 2015.Another part of its growth strat-

egy includes select acquisitions of retail grocery stores grocery store chains or distribution facilities.

Mergers and Acquisitions

In November 2013 in a strategic move that gave Spartan Stores an extended reach beyond its Midwestern stronghold and boosted its retail holdings the company purchased Minneapolis-based grocery distributor Nash-Finch. Valued at $1.3 billion the all-stock deal made Spartan Stores the largest food supplier to US military stores.

HISTORY

Company BackgroundMaking dinner in the early 1900s often required several shopping stops: the grocer for canned goods a butcher for meat and yet another place for produce. Eventually the big grocery chains began offering one-stop shopping not to mention better prices due to greater buying power. Worrying about how to compete in 1917 approximately 100 small grocers met in Grand Rapids Michigan to discuss organizing a cooperative; almost half of those formed the Grand Rapids Wholesale Grocery Co. The stores remained independent operating under different names but achieving economies of scale and volume buying through the co-op. They also began developing a variety of services for member stores. Sales topped $1 million in 1934.

Over the years the company expanded beyond its Grand Rapids origins. In 1950 it formed subsidiary United Wholesale which served independent grocers on a cash-and-carry basis. It acquired the Grand Rapids Coffee Company in 1953. The next year the co-op launched its first private-label item Spartan Coffee with a green Spartan logo reminiscent of the Michigan State University mascot. The company changed its name to Spartan Stores in 1957.

Spartan Stores entered retailing in the early 1970s when it bought 19 Harding's stores. It became a for-profit company in 1973 but continued to provide rebates to customers based on their purchases. Spartan Stores began offering insurance to its customers in 1979.

Concerned about the direction of the company customers named Patrick Quinn formerly a VP at a small chain of grocery stores as president and CEO in 1985. To focus on the wholesale business and to avoid any appearance of conflict of interest in both supplying member stores and operating competing stores Spartan Stores sold its 23 retail stores between 1987 and 1994 giving customer stores the first option on them. It entered the convenience store wholesale business with its 1987 acquisition of L&L/Jiroch. Two years later the co-op acquired Associated Grocers of Michigan (later known as Capistar closed in 1996).

Sales topped $2 billion in 1991. Spartan Stores expanded its convenience store operations in 1993 by buying wholesaler J.F. Walker. Despite record sales in 1996 a $46 million restructuring charge that included extensive technological improvements led to a $21.7 million loss the largest in the company's history. The following year Jim Meyer who had joined Spartan Stores in 1973 replaced the retiring Quinn as president and CEO. Also in 1997 the company stopped giving its customers rebates finally doing away with the last remnants of its co-op years.

To keep Michigan customers out of the clutches of its wholesaling rivals Spartan Stores re-entered retailing in 1999 by acquiring eight Ashcraft's Markets. It bought 13 Family Fare stores and 23 Glen's grocery stores that year. In early 2000 the company sold off its insurance business. Later that year Spartan Stores acquired food and drug chain Seaway Food Town (Michigan and Ohio) for about $180 million and began publicly trading.

In 2001 the company purchased longtime customer Prevo's Family Markets a supermarket chain with 10 stores in western Michigan. In an effort to reduce debt and improve profitability in mid-2002 the company announced plans to close its Food Town stores which suffered from competitors such as Meier Kroger and Farmer Jack's. (By mid-2003 Spartan had sold the last of its 26 Food Town stores. Spartan Stores' retail operations had accounted for about 40% of the company's sales.)

In 2003 Spartan Stores sold seven shopping centers in Michigan for $46 million as part of its strategy to sell noncore properties and focus on its retail and distributions businesses. That year James Meyer retired as president and CEO of Spartan Stores and was succeeded by Craig Sturken a former executive of the Great Atlantic & Pacific Tea Company. Later the company sold convenience store suppliers L&L/Jiroch and J.F. Walker to Knoxville Tennessee-based distributor H.T. Hackney Co.

Spartan Stores sold the assets of United Wholesale Grocery Co. a privately held firm in Michigan for about $10 million in 2004. The sale marked Spartan's exit from the convenience store distribution business. The company also closed or sold all of its Food Town stores for $42.1 million.

In 2005 the company opened three fuel centers in Michigan under the Family Fare Quick Stops and Glen's Quick Stop banners. The company acquired D&W Food Centers the following year and purchased about 20 stores from G&R Felpausch in 2007. Spartan Stores' retail expansion continued in 2008 when it acquired more than 15 stores from V.G.'s Food Center. Sturken stepped down as CEO that year and was replaced by Dennis Eidson. In early 2011 Sturken took a less responsible role as chairman and advisor as he looked to transition out of the business.

EXECUTIVES

General Counsel Secretary and Director, Alex J. DeYonker, age 65, $407,581 total compensation
VP Information Technology and CIO, David deS. (Dave) Couch, age 64, $205,920 total compensation
EVP COO and CFO, David M. (Dave) Staples, age 52, $509,138 total compensation
President and CEO, Dennis Eidson, age 61, $891,202 total compensation
EVP Retail Operations, Theodore C. (Ted) Adornato, age 61, $366,731 total compensation
President Wholesale and Distribution Operations, Derek R. Jones, age 46, $317,030 total compensation
EVP Merchandising and Marketing, Larry Pierce, age 60
EVP General Counsel and Secretary, Kathleen M. (Kathy) Mahoney, age 60
EVP and President MDV, Edward L. (Ed) Brunot, age 51, $419,923 total compensation
Vice President Fresh Merchandising, Brian Haaraoja
Divisional Vice President for Supermarket Operations, Mark Lamberies
Vice President Corporate Affairs, Jeanne Norcross
Vice President Finance, Tom Van Hall
Chairman, Craig C. Sturken, age 71
Auditors: Deloitte & Touche LLP

LOCATIONS

HQ: SpartanNash Co.
850 76th Street S.W., P.O. Box 8700, Grand Rapids, MI 49518
Phone: 616 878-2000

PRODUCTS/OPERATIONS

2014 Sales

	$ mil.	% of total
Retail	2,284	29
Food Distribution	3,356	42
Military	2,275	29
Total	**7,916**	**100**

2014 Sales

	$ mil.	% of total
Non-perishables	4,998	63
Perishables	2,449	31
Fuel	178	2
Pharmacy	289	4
Total	**7,916**	**100**

2014 Retail Stores

	No. of stores
Family Fare Supermarkets	68
No Frills	17
VG's Food and Pharmacy	11
D&W's Fresh Markets	11
Sum Mart	11
Bag N save	9
Econofoods	8
valu land	6
Family fresh market	6
Family thrift center	4
Supermercado Nuestra Familia	3
Other	8
Total	**0**	**162**

Selected Retail Brands
Full Circle
Spartan
Spartan Fresh Selections
Top Care
Valu Time

COMPETITORS

Alex Lee	IGA
Associated Wholesale Grocers	Kroger
	McLane
C&S Wholesale	Meijer
Coastal Pacific Food Distributors Inc.	Miner's
	S. Abraham & Sons
Core-Mark	SUPERVALU
Costco Wholesale	Wal-Mart

HISTORICAL FINANCIALS

Company Type: Public

Income Statement
FYE: January 3

	REVENUE ($ mil.)	NET INCOME ($ mil.)	NET PROFIT MARGIN	EMPLOYEES
01/15*	7,916	58	0.7%	16,100
12/13	2,597	0	0.0%	15,900
03/13	2,608	27	1.1%	8,650
03/12	2,634	31	1.2%	8,400
03/11	2,533	32	1.3%	8,600
Annual Growth	**33.0%**	**16.0%**	**—**	**17.0%**

*Fiscal year change

2015 Year-End Financials

Debt ratio: 29.51%	No. of shares (mil.): 37
Return on equity: 7.93%	Dividends
Cash ($ mil.): 6	Yield: 0.0%
Current ratio: 1.90	Payout: 30.9%
Long-term debt ($ mil.): 550	Market value ($ mil.): 969

	STOCK PRICE ($) FY Close	P/E High/Low	Earnings	PER SHARE ($) Dividends	Book Value
01/15*	25.82	17 12	1.55	0.48	19.91
12/13	23.73	810512	0.03	0.35	18.92
03/13	17.55	15 11	1.25	0.32	15.43
03/12	18.12	15 10	1.39	0.26	14.57
03/11	15.08	12 9	1.42	0.20	13.51
Annual Growth	**14.4%**	**— —**	**2.2%**	**24.5%**	**10.2%**

*Fiscal year change

SPDR Gold Trust

LOCATIONS

HQ: SPDR Gold Trust
c/o World Gold Trust Services, LLC, 685 Third Ave.
27th Floor, New York, NY 10017
Phone: 212 317-3800
Web: www.spdrgoldshares.com

HISTORICAL FINANCIALS

Company Type: Public

Income Statement
FYE: September 30

	ASSETS ($ mil.)	NET INCOME ($ mil.)	INCOME AS % OF ASSETS	EMPLOYEES
09/14	30,250	(230)	—	—
09/13	35,812	4,505	12.6%	—
09/12	50,726	2,407	4.7%	—
09/11	42,736	7,340	17.2%	—
09/10	37,991	1,208	3.2%	—
Annual Growth	**(5.5%)**	**—**	**—**	**—**

2014 Year-End Financials

Debt ratio: —	No. of shares (mil.): 257
Return on equity: (-0.70%)	Dividends
Cash ($ mil.): —	Yield: —
Current ratio: —	Payout: —
Long-term debt ($ mil.): —	Market value ($ mil.): 29,901

	STOCK PRICE ($) FY Close	P/E High/Low	Earnings	PER SHARE ($) Dividends	Book Value
09/14	116.21	— —	(0.85)	0.00	116.97
09/13	128.18	15 10	11.75	0.00	118.18
09/12	171.89	31 26	5.71	0.00	114.40
09/11	158.06	10 7	17.87	0.00	103.71
09/10	127.91	41 32	3.10	0.00	88.29
Annual Growth	**(2.4%)**	**— —**	**—**	**—**	**7.3%**

Spectra Energy Corp

Spectra Energy covers the spectrum of natural gas activities —gathering processing transmission storage and distribution. Spectra Energy operates more than 22000 miles of transmission pipeline and has 305 billion cu. ft. of storage capacity in the US and Canada. Units include U.S. Gas Transmission Texas Eastern Transmission Algonquin Gas Transmission BC Pipeline Division Natural Gas Liquids Division and Market Hub Partners. It also has stakes in DCP Midstream (a gas gathering and

NGL joint venture) Maritimes & Northeast Pipeline Gulfstream Natural Gas System Spectra Energy Income Fund and 61% of Spectra Energy Partners. Its Union Gas unit distributes gas to 1.4 million Ontario customers.

Geographic Reach

The company has four major segments: Spectra Energy Partners Distribution Western Canada Transmission & Processing and Field Services. Spectra Energy Partners operates in northeastern and southeastern United States and operates a crude oil pipeline system that connects Canadian and US producers to refineries in the Rocky Mountains and the Midwest. Distribution serves natural gas customers in Ontario Canada. Western Canada Transmission & Processing serves customers in western Canada and the northern US. Field Services gathers natural gas from the Mid-Continent Rocky Mountain East Texas-North Louisiana Barnett Shale Gulf Coast South Texas Central Texas Antrim Shale and Permian Basin.

All told Spectra Energy has more than 100 facilities across North America.

In 2014 Canada accounted for 63% of Spectra Energy's revenues.

Operations

In 2013 Spectra Energy reorganized and sold almost all of its US assets to Spectra Energy Partners. As a result of this transaction the company realigned their reportable segments structure. It currently manages its businesses in four reportable segments: Spectra Energy Partners Distribution Western Canada Transmission & Processing and Field Services.

Spectra Energy Partners provides transmission storage and gathering of natural gas for customers in various regions of the Midwestern northeastern and southeastern US and operates a crude oil pipeline system that connects Canadian and U.S. producers to refineries in the U.S. Rocky Mountain and Midwest regions. Spectra Energy Partners accounted for 37% of the company's total revenues in 2014.

Distribution provides retail natural gas distribution service (its Union Gas unit distributes gas to 1.4 million customers in 400 communities in Ontario). It also provides natural gas transportation and storage services to other utilities and energy market customers.

Western Canada Transmission & Processing (31% of 2014 revenues) provides its customers with transportation services to move natural gas natural gas gathering and processing services and NGL extraction fractionation transportation storage and marketing services.

Field Services gathers processes treats compresses transports and stores natural gas; it also fractionates transports gathers processes stores markets and trades NGLs. Its DCP Midstream joint venture is 50% owned by Phillips 66. DCP operates in 17 US states.

Transportation storage and processing of natural gas accounted for 56% of Spectra Energy's revenues in 2014.

Sales and Marketing

The company's customers (end-users) purchase gas directly from suppliers or marketers as well as through retail and wholesale outlets.

Financial Performance

Spectra Energy's revenues increased by 7% in 2014 due to following results. Spectra Energy Partners sales increased by 15% as the result of $168 million expansion projects (primarily at Texas Eastern) and $68 million due to acquisitions; Distribution revenues decreased by $5 million due to currency translations and lower storage prices; and Western Canada Transmission & Processing sales increased by $135 million due higher sales volumes and non-cash mark-to-market gains.In 2014 Spectra Energy's net income increased by 4% due to higher net sales which outpaced an rise in total operating expenses.Net cash provided by operating activities increased by $191 million in 2014 due to higher earnings and distribution from unconsolidated affiliates partially offset by changes in working capital.

Strategy

The company's strategy is to solidify its position as a premier natural gas infrastructure enterprise by developing new opportunities and projects while enhancing its core customer service reliability cost management and compliance skills.

In 2014 Spectra Energy announced details of the $3 billion Access Northeast project designed to reliably meet growing demand for natural gas in New England while providing environmental and economic benefits to the region. This project will expand natural gas pipeline capacity into the New England Market to meet critical demand for reliable electric power generation. These plans for expansion of the Algonquin and Maritimes pipeline systems are in response to the New England governors initiative on new energy infrastructure.

That year the company announced plans to continue earnings growth through capital efficient projects such as transportation and storage expansion to support a two-pronged “supply push”/“market pull” strategy as well as continued focus on optimizing the performance of the existing operations through organizational efficiencies and cost control.As a cost control move in 2014 Spectra Energy agreed to sell its two-thirds ownership interest in Main Pass Oil Gathering Company to American Midstream for $14 million.In 2013 the company completed its New Jersey – New York Expansion Project. The new pipeline an extension of Spectra Energy's Texas Eastern and Algonquin Gas systems is designed to supply customers in the region with 800 million cubic feet per day of natural gas.That year Sabal Trail Transmission LLC a joint venture of Spectra Energy and NextEra Energy won a 465-mile interstate natural gas pipeline contract from Florida Power & Light Company to construct a more than 1 billion cubic feet per day pipeline originating in Tallapoosa County Alabama extending through Georgia and ending at the Central Florida Hub near Orlando. In 2013 Spectra Energy also announced that the Sand Hills and Southern Hills natural gas liquids pipelines (each one-third owned by DCP Midstream Phillips 66 and Spectra Energy) has been brought into service. The 720-mile Sand Hills NGL Pipeline transporting NGLs from production in the Permian Basin and Eagle Ford Shale while the 800-mile Southern Hills NGL Pipeline ships NGLs from Mid-continent fields.

In a major restructuring to free up cash in 2013 Spectra Energy agreed to transfer its remaining US transmission storage and liquids assets to Spectra Energy Partners for $2.2 billion. In 2013 Spectra Energy also transferred its 50% stake in the Express-Platte crude oil pipeline system to Spectra Energy Partners for $410 million.

Mergers and Acquisitions

Expanding its role in the oil pipeline market in 2013 Spectra Energy bought the Express-Platte Pipeline System from Borealis Infrastructure the Ontario Teachers Pension Plan and Kinder Morgan Energy Partners for $1.5 billion. The Express-Platte System is one of just three major pipelines moving crude oil from Western Canada to the US Rockies and Midwest refineries and markets.

Company Background

In 2012 Spectra Energy acquired one-third of DCP Sand Hills Pipeline and DCP Southern Hills Pipeline (NGL pipelines) from DCP Midstream for $459 million.

In 2012 Spectra Energy opened a new natural gas processing plant in Dawson Creek British Co-

lumbia part of its $1.5 billion investment strategy in infrastructure. That year it also signed a deal with BG Group to develop a pipeline from northeast British Columbia to serve BG Group's potential LNG export facility in Prince Rupert on the northwest coast of the province.

To raise cash in 2012 it sold a 38.76% interest in Maritimes & Northeast Pipeline to Spectra Energy Partners for $375 million.

In a move to boost its Gulf Coast natural gas storage position in 2010 Spectra Energy acquired the Bobcat Gas Storage asset from Haddington Energy Partners and GE Energy Financial Service for about $540 million.

The company was founded in 2006.

EXECUTIVES

CFO, John Patrick (Pat) Reddy, $606,443 total compensation

Group Vp Us Regulatory Affairs; President And Ceo Spectra Energy Partners, Gregory Rizzo

Chief Administrative Officer, Dorothy M. Ables, $461,673 total compensation

Chairman President and CEO, Gregory L. (Greg) Ebel, $1,127,500 total compensation

President Spectra Energy Transmission West, R. Mark Fiedorek

President US Transmission and Storage, William T. (Bill) Yardley, $409,500 total compensation

President Canadian LNG, Douglas P. (Doug) Bloom

President Union Gas Limited, Stephen W. (Steve) Baker

General Counsel, Reginald D. (Reggie) Hedgebeth, $551,507 total compensation

Chief Development Officer, Guy G. Buckley

Vice President, Joe Martucci

Vice President Data Processing Executive Executive Officer, Stephen (Steve) Craft

Board Of Directors, Theopolis Holeman

Auditors: Deloitte & Touche LLP

LOCATIONS

HQ: Spectra Energy Corp
5400 Westheimer Court, Houston, TX 77056
Phone: 713 627-5400
Web: www.spectraenergy.com

2014 Sales

	% of total
Canada	63
U.S.	37
Total	**100**

PRODUCTS/OPERATIONS

Selected Mergers and Acquisitions

COMPETITORS

Dynegy	Koch Industries Inc.
Entergy	Piedmont Natural Gas
Enterprise Products	TransMontaigne
Kinder Morgan	Williams Companies

HISTORICAL FINANCIALS

Company Type: Public

Income Statement

FYE: December 31

	REVENUE ($ mil.)	NET INCOME ($ mil.)	NET PROFIT MARGIN	EMPLOYEES
12/14	5,903	1,082	18.3%	5,900
12/13	5,518	1,038	18.8%	5,800
12/12	5,075	940	18.5%	5,600
12/11	5,351	1,184	22.1%	5,700
12/10	4,945	1,049	21.2%	550
Annual Growth	**4.5%**	**0.8%**	**—**	**81.0%**

2014 Year-End Financials

Debt ratio: 43.12%
Return on equity: 12.99%
Cash ($ mil.): 215
Current ratio: 0.61
Long-term debt ($ mil.): 12,769

No. of shares (mil.): 671
Dividends
  Yield: 3.7%
  Payout: 92.2%
Market value ($ mil.): 24,357

	STOCK PRICE ($) FY Close	P/E High/Low	PER SHARE ($) Earnings	Dividends	Book Value
12/14	36.30	27 21	1.61	1.38	12.16
12/13	35.62	24 17	1.55	1.22	12.68
12/12	27.38	22 19	1.44	1.15	13.43
12/11	30.75	17 13	1.81	1.06	12.39
12/10	24.99	16 12	1.61	1.00	12.03
Annual Growth	**9.8%**	**— —**	**(0.0%)**	**8.3%**	**0.3%**

Spirit AeroSystems Holdings Inc

Unlike the Wright Brothers modern aerospace designers and manufacturers like Spirit AeroSystems Holdings operate with more resources than a wing and a prayer. The company makes commercial and military airplane components such as fuselages propulsion systems wings and underwing parts. It designs and builds aerostructures for every Boeing aircraft currently in production and provides components to Boeing's chief rival Airbus. Spirit AeroSystems claims to be the largest supplier of wing parts for Airbus' A320 aircraft and produces the majority of aerostructures for Boeing's 737. Spirit AeroSystems maintains operations in the US the UK and Asia.

Geographic Reach

The company has its headquarters in Wichita Kansas and other operations in China France Malaysia Ireland Russia and the UK. The US accounts for 87% of its total sales while the UK generates almost 10%.

Operations

Spirit AeroSystems' operations are divided among three segments. Fuselage Systems is its most lucrative generating almost 50% of total sales each year. Propulsion Systems and Wing Systems each earn nearly 25% of sales.

The Fuselage Systems segment develops produces and markets forward mid and rear fuselage sections and systems primarily to aircraft makers.The Propulsion Systems segment develops produces and markets struts/pylons nacelles (including thrust reversers) and related engine structural components primarily to aircraft or engine OEMs.The Wing Systems segment develops produces and markets wings and wing components (including flight control surfaces) and other miscellaneous structural parts primarily to aircraft OEMs.

All segments provide related spares and maintenance services.

Sales and Marketing

About 83% of Spirit AeroSystems' revenues comes from Boeing while Airbus accounts for 10%. This customer concentration risk gets offset by the fact that it's the only source for most of its products and its contracts give it supplier rights for the life of the aircraft program for most models. (Spirit AeroSystems began as an internal supplier for Boeing aircraft.) Other customers include Gulfstream and Sikorsky the US government and major defense contractors.

Financial Performance

Spirit AeroSystems' revenues has maintained a steady growth over the past few years. In 2014 the company's revenues grew by 14% due to higher production volume driven by strong customer demand across all segments and increased spares orders partially offset by lower deliveries of B747s and B767s.

The company's income has seen a decreasing trend over the last five years until fiscal 2014 when the income increased by about $1 billion (from a net loss of $621.4 million in 2013) due to higher revenues lower research and development expenses no expenses gained from natural catastrophes and major tax benefits affected by lower of tax rate. These were partially offset by higher selling general and administrative expenses due to the write-off of uncollectible accounts receivable and increases in incentive plan accruals and consulting costs.

In 2014 Spirit AeroSystems' operating cash flows increased by 39% due to increased net incomes and lower outflows in accounts receivables partially offset by a growth in outflows in inventories divestitures accounts payable and taxes.

Strategy

In 2015 the company's strategic plan includes improving performance and productivity reducing costs leveraging its investments in support of future aircraft rate increases and continuing its progress on the Airbus A350 airliner.It is reducing cost through cost saving initiatives and improving operational efficiency through centralization of functions and is investing in new technology to bring the most advanced techniques manufacturing and automation to Spirit AeroSystems' customers.Growing its sales network in 2014 Spirit AeroSystems opened a sales office at the Tinker Business and Industrial Park in Midwest City Oklahoma.

That year the company changed the name of its aftermarket business from Spirit Aftermarket Customer Support to Global Customer Support & Services to reflect the organization's focus on the customer.

Company Background

To keep production up to better serve its two main customers the company has been expanding its manufacturing capabilities with new facilities in North Carolina and abroad in Malaysia which is its first Asian facility and in France. The North Carolina facility which started operations in 2010 makes composite panels and wing components; the Malaysian plant (opened in 2009) performs the same operations. The French facility which began operations in 2011 assembles center fuselage sections.

The company was founded in 2005 when Boeing spun off its Wichita Division and Oklahoma operations as a new entity Spirit AeroSystems.

Investment firm Scopia Capital Management owns about 16% of the company.

EXECUTIVES

President and CEO, Larry Lawson, $688,463 total compensation
SVP Business Development and CTO, H. David Walker, age 64, $199,992 total compensation
SVP Defense and Contracts, Philip D. Anderson, age 50, $400,005 total compensation
SVP and General Manager Airbus and A350 XWB Program Management, John Pilla, age 55, $334,618 total compensation
EVP and General Manager Boeing Business and Regional Jet Programs, David M. Coleal, $508,080 total compensation
SVP Operations, Duane Hawkins
SVP Strategy M&A and Investor Relations, Heidi Wood

SVP and CFO, Sanjay Kapoor, $119,133 total compensation
SVP Global Customer Support and Services; General Manager Oklahoma Operations, Bill Brown
Senior Vice President Sales And Marketing, Dave Walker
Vice President Finance and Treasurer, Mark Suchinski
Senior Vice President Chief Administration Officer, Sam Marnick
Senior Vice President General Counsel Secretary, Jon Lammers
Senior Vice President Global Customer Support and Services; General Manager Oklahoma Operations, William (Bill) Brown
Auditors: Ernst & Young LLP

LOCATIONS

HQ: Spirit AeroSystems Holdings Inc
3801 South Oliver, Wichita, KS 67210
Phone: 316 526-9000
Web: www.spiritaero.com

2012 Sales

	$ mil.	% of total
US	4,612	85
UK	470	9
Other	315	6
Total	**5,397**	**100**

COMPETITORS

Airbus
Boeing
Bombardier
Dassault Aviation
Embraer
Finmeccanica
Fuji Heavy Industries
GKN
Gulfstream Aerospace
Kawasaki Heavy Industries
Lockheed Martin
Mitsubishi Heavy Industries
Northrop Grumman
Saab AB
Snecma
Textron
Triumph Aerostructures - Vought Aircraft Division
Triumph Group
United Technologies

HISTORICAL FINANCIALS

Company Type: Public

Income Statement

FYE: December 31

	REVENUE ($ mil.)	NET INCOME ($ mil.)	NET PROFIT MARGIN	EMPLOYEES
12/15	6,643	788	11.9%	15,200
12/14	6,799	358	5.3%	15,402
12/13	5,961	(621)	—	14,177
12/12	5,397	34	0.6%	14,623
12/11	4,863	192	4.0%	13,932
Annual Growth	**8.1%**	**42.3%**	**—**	**2.2%**

2015 Year-End Financials

Debt ratio: 19.61%
Return on equity: 42.17%
Cash ($ mil.): 957
Current ratio: 2.26
Long-term debt ($ mil.): 1,097

No. of shares (mil.): 125
Dividends
　Yield: —
　Payout: —
Market value ($ mil.): 6,305

	STOCK PRICE ($) FY Close	P/E High/Low		PER SHARE ($) Earnings	Dividends	Book Value
12/15	50.07	10	7	5.66	0.00	17.60
12/14	43.04	18	10	2.53	0.00	11.83
12/13	34.08	—	—	(4.40)	0.00	10.22
12/12	16.97	108	59	0.24	0.00	13.89
12/11	20.78	19	11	1.35	0.00	13.75
Annual Growth	**24.6%**	**—**	**—**	**43.1%**	**—**	**6.4%**

Sprague Resources LP

Venerable but spry Sprague Resources delivers when it comes energy delivery. The company founded in 1870 as a coal and oil supplier has grown into one of the largest fuel suppliers in the northeast. Sprague Resources' products include diesel gasoline home heating oil jet fuel and residual fuels. The company distributes about 50 billion cu. ft. of natural gas 1.3 billion gallons of petroleum products and 2.5 million tons of bulk materials each year. It also owns or operates 15 storage terminals that can hold more than 9 million barrels of refined products. In 2013 the company went public raising $153 million which it will use for working capital and to pay down debt.

Operations

Sprague Resources is a holding company organized as a limited partnership; all operations are conducted through its general partner Sprague Resources GP LLC. Sprague Resources GP LLC is ultimately owned by Axel Johnson. As a limited partnership Sprague Resources is exempt from paying federal income tax so long as it makes quarterly distributions to shareholders.

EXECUTIVES

President CEO and Director, David C. (Dave) Glendon, age 49, $350,000 total compensation
SVP COO CFO and Director, Gary A. Rinaldi, age 58, $350,000 total compensation
VP Refined Products, Thomas F. Flaherty, age 59, $251,960 total compensation
VP and Chief Risk Officer, Steven D. Scammon, age 53, $245,774 total compensation
VP and Business Development, Joseph S. Smith, age 58, $237,106 total compensation
VP and Chief Accounting Officer, John W. Moore, age 57, $245,457 total compensation
VP Materials Handling, James Therriault, age 54
VP Operations, Burton S. Russell, age 60
VP Natural Gas, Brian W. Weego, age 49
Chairman, Michael D. (Mike) Milligan, age 51
Auditors: Ernst & Young LLP

LOCATIONS

HQ: Sprague Resources LP
185 International Drive, Portsmouth, NH 03801
Phone: 800 225-1560
Web: www.spragueenergy.com

PRODUCTS/OPERATIONS

2012 Sales

	% of total
Refined products	93
Natural gas	6
Materials handling	1
Total	**100**

COMPETITORS

Cheshire Oil	Global Partners
Getty Petroleum Marketing	NSTAR
	World Fuel Services

HISTORICAL FINANCIALS

Company Type: Public

Income Statement

FYE: December 31

	REVENUE ($ mil.)	NET INCOME ($ mil.)	NET PROFIT MARGIN	EMPLOYEES
12/14	5,069	122	2.4%	580
12/13	4,600	(27)	—	—
12/12	4,043	(12)	—	400
12/11	3,797	29	0.8%	—
12/10	2,817	15	0.6%	—
Annual Growth	15.8%	67.2%	—	—

2014 Year-End Financials

Debt ratio: 61.45%
Return on equity: —
Cash ($ mil.): 4
Current ratio: 1.26
Long-term debt ($ mil.): 424

No. of shares (mil.): 20
Dividends
  Yield: 6.6%
  Payout: 26.8%
Market value ($ mil.): 490

	STOCK PRICE ($) FY Close	P/E High/Low		PER SHARE ($) Earnings	Dividends	Book Value
12/14	23.45	5	3	5.84	1.57	5.55
12/13	18.24	—	—	(1.50)	0.28	1.49
Annual Growth	6.5%	—	—	—	53.4%	39.0%

Sprint Corp (New)

Auditors: Deloitte & Touche LLP

LOCATIONS

HQ: Sprint Corp (New)
  6200 Sprint Parkway, Overland Park, KS 66251
Phone: 855 848-3280
Web: www.sprint.com

HISTORICAL FINANCIALS

Company Type: Public

Income Statement

FYE: March 31

	REVENUE ($ mil.)	NET INCOME ($ mil.)	NET PROFIT MARGIN	EMPLOYEES
03/15	34,532	(3,345)	—	31,000
03/14*	8,875	(151)	—	36,000
12/13	16,891	(1,860)	—	38,000
12/12	0	(27)	—	—
Annual Growth	—	—	—	—

*Fiscal year change

2015 Year-End Financials

Debt ratio: 40.75%—
Return on equity: (-14.23%)
Cash ($ mil.): 4,010
Current ratio: 0.89
Long-term debt ($ mil.): 32,531

Dividends
  Yield: —
  Payout: —
Market value ($ mil.): —

	STOCK PRICE ($) FY Close	P/E High/Low		PER SHARE ($) Earnings	Dividends	Book Value
03/15	4.74	—	—	(0.85)	0.00	5.47
03/14*	9.19	—	—	(0.04)	0.00	6.42
12/13	10.75	—	—	(0.54)	0.00	6.50
12/12	0.00	—	—	(0.00)	0.00	
	1,001.29					
Annual Growth	—	—	—	—	—	—(92.6%)

*Fiscal year change

St Jude Medical Inc

If your heart has trouble catching the beat St. Jude Medical's got rhythm to spare. The company is a global medical device manufacturer focused on improving the treatment of some of the world's most expensive epidemic diseases. St. Jude Medical operates in one segment producing six principal product categories: ICD (implantable cardiac defibrillator) Systems (the largest category representing 35% of total earnings) Pacemaker Systems Atrial Fibrillation Products Vascular Products Structural Heart Products and Neuromodulation Products. The company sells its products in more than 100 countries; the US is its largest market. St. Jude Medical was formed in 1976.

OperationsSt. Jude Medical started out making mechanical heart valves but half of its revenue these days comes from pacemakers and ICDs. ICDs correct for tachycardia or overly fast heartbeats. Pacemakers in contrast to ICDs are used to treat patients whose hearts beat too slowly. St. Jude developed one of the industry's first pacemakers with wireless telemetry —which in this case allows the patient to be monitored by his physician from a distance from the time of implantation all the way through to his follow-up.

The company's atrial fibrillation products include electrophysiology introducers and catheters; cardiac mapping navigation and recording systems; and ablation systems. The company also makes vascular products such as vascular closure products pressure management guidewires tomography imaging products vascular plugs heart failure monitoring devices and other accessories. Structural heart products include heart valve repair or replacement products and structural heart defect devices while neuromodulation products use spinal cord or brain stimulation to treat chronic pain or movement disorders.

During fiscal 2014 the company combined its former Implantable Electronic Systems and Cardiovascular and Ablation Technologies divisions into a single research and development organization consolidating manufacturing and distribution functions around the world. Further realignment efforts are intended to improve productivity and cut costs.

Geographic Reach

In addition to the US which accounts for about half of revenues St. Jude's largest markets include Europe and the Asia/Pacific region (especially Japan which accounts for more than 10% of revenues).

The company has US manufacturing facilities in California Minnesota Arizona South Carolina Texas New Jersey Oregon and Massachusetts. It has foreign manufacturing plants in Brazil Puerto Rico Costa Rica Sweden Malaysia and Thailand. The company also maintains sales and administrative offices at 33 US locations in 11 states as well as more than 100 locations in 35 countries.

Sales and Marketing

St. Jude's key geographic markets are the US Europe and the Asia/Pacific region (including Japan). It sells directly to health care professionals in the US Canada and Japan. It also has direct sales organizations in 20 countries in Europe five countries in Latin America and 10 countries in the Asia/Pacific region. The company uses a combination of direct sales and independent distributors in other markets.

Financial Performance

After seeing revenue decreases for two years the company posted a 2% revenue increase to $5.6 billion in fiscal 2015. This increase was driven by higher sales of atrial fibrillation products as well as earnings from the newly acquired CardioMEMS and NeuroTherm businesses. Structural heart products sales also rose that year.

Net income increased 39% to $1 billion in fiscal 2015 thanks to the higher revenue and lower expenses. Cash flow from operations rose 36% to $1.3 billion on the higher profits and changes in current assets and liabilities.StrategyThe company aggressively introduces new cardiac rhythm management (CRM) products in a bid to take market share from its main competitors in the field Medtronic and Boston Scientific. It invests more than 10% of its annual income in research and development of new products and also conducts vigorous marketing campaigns to boost sales of existing products.

Even as St. Jude has been busily introducing new CRM products it hasn't forgotten about its other lines. The company looks to strengthen all of its product groups through acquisitions and organic product development. In 2013 it launched new stent technologies navigation systems defibrillator devices and tissue valves in certain markets. The following year it launched two ablation catheters to strengthen its atrial fibrillation offerings.

The company has also been buying up other companies to access new technologies. In 2014 it bought CardioMEMS and NeuroTherm boosting its heart failure and chronic pain programs. The company is particularly excited about the potential of CardioMEMS HF system a heart failure monitor which has reduced hospitalizations.

St. Jude Medical like most other companies operating in the health care industry is still working out how new health care laws will impact its operations. The company faces legislative challenges including proposed new excise taxes on all US medical device sales and potential reimbursement changes through Medicare provisions aimed at improving quality and decreasing costs.

The company has also encountered challenges in the ICD market which is experiencing declining implant procedure volumes due to negative publicity over their use.

Mergers and Acquisitions

The company agreed to buy cardiac device maker Thoratec Corporation for $3.4 billion in 2015. The move will invigorate its pipeline of products helping it gain access to new technologies.

Also in 2015 St. Jude acquired Spinal Modulation developer of the Axium Neurostimulator System. That deal made St. Jude the only medical device maker to offer radiofrequency ablation dorsal root ganglion stimulation and spinal cord stimulation treatments for chronic pain.

In 2014 St. Jude purchased the 80% of CardioMEMSit didn't already own. The company makes a wireless implant that helps physicians remotely manage chronic cardiovascular diseases such as heart failure and aneurysms. The device was approved by the FDA in 2014. St. Jude had bought a 20% stake in CardioMEMS previously and exercised its option to buy the company outright when its implant was approved. That year it also acquired NeuroTherm a maker of pain management devices for approximately $200 million in cash.

In August 2013 St. Jude spent $171 million for Endosense for $171 million. This acquisition brought the company an irrigated ablation catheter approved for use in the EU. Later that year St. Jude acquired Nanostim for $121 million because the company had developed the first leadless pacemaker approved in the EU.

HISTORY

Manuel Villafana who started Cardiac Pacemakers in 1972 founded St. Jude Medical four years later to develop the bileaflet heart valve. In 1977 patient Helen Heikkinen received the first St. Jude heart valve. The firm also went public that year.

Villafana left in 1981 and established competitor Helix Biocore. St. Jude expanded into tissue valves with its purchase of BioImplant in 1986.

In the mid-1980s St. Jude gained market share when devices from Pfizer and Baxter International had problems. Concerns that the company hadn't diversified led to a joint venture in 1992 with Hancock Jaffe Laboratories to develop a bioprosthetic (constructed of animal tissue) heart valve. In 1994 it bought Siemens' pacemaker unit doubling revenues and tripling its sales force.

The firm continued diversifying buying Daig (cardiac catheters) in 1996 and Ventritex (cardiac defibrillators) in 1997. In 1997 the FDA approved St. Jude's Toronto SPV tissue valve marking its entry into that market. In 1999 St. Jude landed on CalPERS's list of worst-performing companies as it lagged behind rivals Guidant and Medtronic. A management shake-up followed and the firm strengthened its product lines buying Tyco International's Angio-Seal subsidiary (cardiac sealant) and Vascular Science (artery connectors). The next year the FDA stepped up its regulatory oversight after the company and its competitors recalled or issued warnings regarding defective or potentially defective devices.

In 2002 St. Jude bought Getz Bros. its largest distributor in Japan. The firm scooped up two other firms Irvine Biomedical and Epicor Medical in 2004.

EXECUTIVES

EVP, John C. Heinmiller, age 60, $768,500 total compensation

President CEO and Director, Michael T. Rousseau, age 60, $788,288 total compensation

Group President, Eric S. Fain, $708,462 total compensation

President International, Denis M. Gestin, age 52, $752,400 total compensation

VP Finance and CFO, Donald J. Zurbay, age 48, $468,846 total compensation

VP Global Clinical Affairs and Chief Medical Officer, Mark D. Carlson

President Americas Division, Joel D. Becker

VP Information Technology and CIO, Mark W. Murphy

VP Global Operations and Supply Chain, Scott P. Thome

Vice President Clinical Education And Training, Laurie Fischer

Vice President Systems Development, Alan Smythe

Vice President Of Area Sales, Michael T (Mel) Moore

Area Vice President, Ryan Walters

Vice President, Doug Nock

Area Vice President, Carlton Brock

Vice President Technical Services, Larry Selznick

Vice President Corporate And National Accounts, John (Jack) Knighten

Area Vice President, Rhett Harty

Area Vice President Sales, Terry Preston
Auditors: Ernst & Young LLP

LOCATIONS

HQ: St Jude Medical Inc
One St. Jude Medical Drive, St. Paul, MN 55117
Phone: 651 756-2000   **Fax:** 651 756-3301
Web: www.sjm.com

2015 Sales

	$ mil.	% of total
US	2,657	47
Japan	526	10
Other regions	2,439	43
Total	**5,622**	**100**

PRODUCTS/OPERATIONS

2015 Sales

	$ mil.	% of total
ICD Systems	1,746	31
Pacemaker Systems	1,047	19
Atrial Fibrillation products	1,044	18
Vascular Products	709	13
Structural Heart Products	639	11
Neuromodulation Products	437	8
Total	**5,622**	**100**

Selected Products and services

Cardiac Rhythm ManagementConnectivity and Remote Care

CRT DevicesHF Management SystemICD Devices

Implant Tools and Accessories

Leads

Pacemakers

EP Products

AccessDiagnostic

Intracardiac Imaging

Mapping and Visualization

NavigationRec

COMPETITORS

Abbott Labs	Empi
Bard	Johnson & Johnson
Biosense Webster	Medtronic
Boston Scientific	Terumo
Cyberonics	Volcano Corporation
Edwards Lifesciences	W.L. Gore

HISTORICAL FINANCIALS

Company Type: Public

Income Statement

FYE: January 3

	REVENUE ($ mil.)	NET INCOME ($ mil.)	NET PROFIT MARGIN	EMPLOYEES
01/15*	5,622	1,002	17.8%	16,000
12/13	5,501	723	13.1%	16,000
12/12	5,503	752	13.7%	15,000
12/11	5,611	825	14.7%	16,000
01/11	5,164	907	17.6%	15,000
Annual Growth	**2.1%**	**2.5%**	**—**	**1.6%**

*Fiscal year change

2015 Year-End Financials

Debt ratio: 37.88%
Return on equity: 23.39%
Cash ($ mil.): 1,442
Current ratio: 1.47
Long-term debt ($ mil.): 2,273

No. of shares (mil.): 286
Dividends
Yield: 0.0%
Payout: 31.2%
Market value ($ mil.): 18,616

	STOCK PRICE ($) FY Close	P/E High/Low	PER SHARE ($) Earnings	Dividends	Book Value
01/15*	64.94	20 16	3.46	1.08	14.65
12/13	62.25	25 14	2.49	1.00	14.63
12/12	35.47	19 13	2.39	0.92	13.85
12/11	34.30	21 13	2.52	0.84	14.00
01/11	42.75	16 13	2.75	0.00	13.29
Annual Growth	**11.0%**	**— —**	**5.9%**	**—**	**2.5%**

*Fiscal year change

ST. JOSEPH HEALTH SYSTEM

St. Joseph Health System has earned a medal for decades by caring for patients on the West Coast and more recently the South Plains. The health care network includes 16 acute care hospitals home health agencies hospice care outpatient services skilled nursing facilities community clinics and physician organizations throughout California and in eastern New Mexico and West Texas. In its primary market of California the health system has some 2900 beds at 10 hospitals. Its Covenant Health System unit operates in Texas and New Mexico with about 1200 beds in its network of some 50 primary care facilities. St. Joseph is merging with fellow not-for-profit Providence Health & Services.

Operations

In 2013 the system discharged more than 142000 patients and had more than 4 million outpatient and 513000 emergency department visits.

Geographic Reach

The network operates acute care hospitals home health agencies urgent care centers and other health care delivery organizations throughout California and in eastern New Mexico and West Texas. Based in Irvine St. Joseph serves 10 communities in its operating regions.

Sales and Marketing

Government payments accounted for 44% of net patient revenue in 2013 while private payers accounted for 42%.

Financial Performance

Revenue increased 14% to $5.6 million due to an increase in patient service earnings. Net income decreased 83% though to $353 million as salary and benefits expenses increased. Operating cash flow fell 38% to $327 million that year.

Strategy

Already one of the largest health systems on the West Coast St. Joseph continues to grow thanks principally to its proficient fundraising.

The system invests regularly in network and facility expansion efforts. In 2013 it formed an affiliation with Hoag Memorial Hospital Presbyterian which operates two hospitals in Orange County. The Hoag operations are being combined with five of St. Joseph's area hospitals to form a new network called Covenant Health Network. The affiliated facilities will provide comprehensive care in the region while retaining their respective identities and religious affiliations.

In 2014 St. Joseph entered a collaborative care initiative with Cigna to improve access to health care and enhance care coordination.

In 2015 the system agreed to merge with Providence Health & Services which operates more than 30 hospitals in five western states. The combination will create a larger provider network of hospitals physician groups and outpatient centers eliminating some overhead expenses in the process. Furthermore by creating economies of scale the new organization will be better positioned to negotiate with health plans.

Company Background

St. Joseph Health System traces its roots back to 1920 when St. Joseph Hospital in Eureka California was first established. The health care system was officially organized in 1982 as it expanded and took on additional health care facilities. The system is a ministry of The Sisters of St. Joseph of Orange which itself was organized in 1912.

EXECUTIVES

President and CEO Redwood Memorial Hospital and St. Joseph Hospital Eureka, Joe Mark
EVP Mission Integration, Marian Schubert
EVP West Texas and Southern New Mexico, Richard H. Parks
EVP Strategic Services, Annette M. Walker
EVP Northern California Region, Kevin Klockenga
Chief Financial Officer, Jo Escasa-Haigh
Vice President Performance Improvement, Mary Ann Vincent
Vice President Quality And Medical Affairs, Mark Montgomery
Assistant Vice President Executive Architect, Wesley Okamoto
Vice President Revenue Cycle, Kimberly Sullivan
Senior Vice President Governance, Suzanne Sassus
Director Of Medical Records, Daniel Pothen
Senior Vice President General Counsel, Shannon Dwyer
Information Technology Executive Vice President, Bill Murin
Medical Records Director, Sandy Barber
Assistant Vice President Of Information Technology Solutions Delivery, Jeff Allport
Vice President Shared Operations Revenue Cycle Se, Debbie Salas
Vice President Clinical Informatics, Joon Saddul
Vice President Mission Integration, John Perring-mulligan
Assistant Vice President, Kevin Murphy
Senior Vice President Of Human Resources, Ryan Faulkner
Vice President and General Manager, Karen Wilson
Assistant Vice President Risk Management, Lisa Ramthun
Assistant Vice President, Ronald Scott
Senior Vice President Ministry Integrity, Margaret Hambleton
Senior Vice President Operations, Toni Small
Vice President Human Resources, Stephen Eckberg
Vice President Of Strategic Services, Ned Laubacher
Vice President IS Strategy, Larry Stofko
Chairman, Walter W. (Bill) Noce
Controller And Treasurer, Darren Montalvo
Secretary, Denise Blanchard
Board of Directors, Kathleen Kelly
Auditors: ERNST & YOUNG LLP IRVINE CA

LOCATIONS

HQ: ST. JOSEPH HEALTH SYSTEM
3345 MICHELSON DR STE 100, IRVINE, CA 926120693
Phone: 9493814000
Web: WWW.STJHS.ORG

Selected Operations

Northern California
  Petaluma Valley Hospital
  Queen of t
  Redwood Me
  St. Joseph
  St. Joseph
  Santa Rosa Memorial Hospital

Southern California
  Mission Ho
    Mission Hospital Laguna Beach
  St. Joseph
  St. Jude M
  St. Mary M
West Texas/Eastern New Mexico
  Covenant Health System
  Artesia Ge
  Covenant H
  Covenant H
  Covenant M
  Nor-Lea Ge
  Roosevelt

PRODUCTS/OPERATIONS

2014 Sales

	% of total
Net patient service net of provision for doubtful accounts	76
Premium	20
Other	4
Total	**100**

COMPETITORS

Adventist Health
Arrowhead Medical Center
Banner Health
Catholic Health Initiatives
Cedars-Sinai Medical Center
Citrus Valley Health Partners
City of Hope
Dignity Health
HCA
Loma Linda University Medical Center

Los Angeles County Health Department
Memorial Health Services
Pasadena Hospital Association
Prospect Medical
Scripps health
Sutter Health
Tenet Healthcare
Western Medical Center - Santa Ana

HISTORICAL FINANCIALS

Company Type: Private

Income Statement

FYE: June 30

	REVENUE ($ mil.)	NET INCOME ($ mil.)	NET PROFIT MARGIN	EMPLOYEES
06/14	5,631	353	6.3%	21,500
06/13	4,955	2,082	42.0%	—
06/10	4,268	268	6.3%	—
06/08	3,943	0	—	—
Annual Growth	6.1%	—	—	—

2014 Year-End Financials

Debt ratio: ——
Return on equity: 6.30%
Cash ($ mil.): 269
Current ratio: 0.90
Long-term debt ($ mil.): —

Dividends
  Yield: —
  Payout: —
Market value ($ mil.): —

StanCorp Financial Group Inc

Providing insurance and related financial services is standard operating procedure at StanCorp Financial Group. Through Standard Insurance (aka The Standard) and other divisions the company offers a range of financial products nationwide including group and individual disability coverage life and accident insurance retirement plans and supplemental group benefit plans. The insurance services segment holds approximately 42000 group policies covering 6.1 million employees throughout the US. The company's asset management segment provides investment advisory retirement planning mortgage lending and other financial services. Meiji Yasuda Life Insurance is buying StanCorp for approximately $5 billion.

Operations

StanCorp's operating subsidiaries which fall under either Insurance Services or Asset Management include The Standard Standard Life Insurance of New York Standard Retirement Services StanCorp Mortgage Investors StanCorp Investment Advisers StanCorp Real Estate and StanCorp Equities. The Insurance Services business contains two product segments —Employee Benefits (including group disability group life and accidental death and dismemberment group dental group vision and absence management services) and Individual Disability.

The Insurance Services segment accounts for 85% of total revenues (Employee Benefits representing 76% and Individual Disability representing 9% of revenue).

StanCorp's Asset Management segment offers an array of retirement products including 401(k) 403(b) and 457 plans; defined benefit plans money purchase pension plans and individual annuities. The segment also provides investment advisory and management services. The company does a smidgen of commercial mortgage lending for small retail office and industrial properties.

Revenues from the Asset Management segment represent 15% of total revenue.

Geographic Reach

With its main offices in Portland Oregon StanCorp is licensed to sell insurance throughout the US including Washington DC and the dependent territories of Guam Puerto Rico and the Virgin Islands. The company has about 60 regional sales and policy processing offices across the country. More than 65% of its customers are located in western and central US states followed by customers in the Southeast and the Northeast.

Sales and Marketing

The company's insurance products are sold through its sales force and independent employee benefit brokerage and consulting firms. State and local government entities and educational organizations account for nearly half of group product sales; other group policies are sold to entities in sectors including health care manufacturing professional services and finance. About 35% of policies are sold to large groups (clients with more than 7500 employees) followed by small and mid-sized entities.

The asset management business sells products through affiliated broker dealers. It pitches its retirement plans at businesses that have between $1 million and $10 million in plan assets. Its annuities are targeted at conservative investors. Retirement plans are primarily targeted towards small to mid-sized businesses.

Financial Performance

After revenues peaked at $2.9 billion in 2012 StanCorp saw a couple of years of modest decline. In 2014 revenue decreased 3% to $2.8 billion as employee benefits sales dropped leading to a decrease in premiums. Net investment income also dipped that year. The decline in revenue led to a 4% dip in net income (to $219 million).

Cash flow from operations decreased 15% to $238.2 million in 2014 primarily as a result of changes in reserve requirements in employee benefits and other assets and other liabilities.

Strategy

The company engages in a conservative growth strategy with a focus on strengthening its core business lines and increasing market penetration in areas where it has a small presence. StanCorp also seeks to diversify earnings by pursuing market opportunities and adding new offerings to its asset management and insurance businesses.

In 2015 StanCorp agreed to be acquired by Tokyo-based Meiji Yasuda Life Insurance the oldest life insurance firm in Japan. The move will expand Meiji Yasuda's operations in the US; StanCorp will become its primary US unit.

EXECUTIVES

VP and Chief Investment Officer Standard Insurance Company, Scott A. Hibbs, age 53, $421,538 total compensation

SVP and CFO StanCorp Financial Group and Standard Insurance Company, Floyd F. Chadee, age 58, $529,369 total compensation

SVP Information Technology Standard Insurance Company, David M. O'Brien, age 58

VP Employee Benefits Standard Insurance Company, Daniel J. (Dan) McMillan, age 48, $488,462 total compensation

VP Individual Disability Insurance and Marketing and Communications, Katherine Durham, age 48

Chairman President and CEO StanCorp Financial Group and Standard Insurance Company, J. Greg Ness, age 57, $944,231 total compensation

Director Third Party Administrator (TPA) Relationships, Matthew (Matt) King

Assistant Vice President Information Technology So, Raghu Crowley

Assistant Vice President Information Technology Infrastructure, Sherri Borgmeyer

Assistant Vice President Information Technology In, Greg List

Second Vice President Corporate Communications, Cherri Roden

Assistant Vice President Controller, Rob Ericson

Assistant Vice President Shared Services, Dayna V Kirk

Auditors: Deloitte & Touche LLP

LOCATIONS

HQ: StanCorp Financial Group Inc
1100 SW Sixth Avenue, Portland, OR 97204
Phone: 971 321-7000
Web: www.stancorpfinancial.com

2014 Premiums by Customer Geography

	% of total
West	35
Central	31
Southeast	18
Northeast	16
Total	**100**

PRODUCTS/OPERATIONS

2014 Revenues

	$ mil.	% of total
Insurance Services		
Employee Benefits	2,106	76
Individual Disability	251	9
Asset Management	427	15
Adjustments	(15.2)	-
Total	**2,770**	**100**

2014 Premiums by Customer Industry

	% of total
Public	27
Education	24
Health care	10
Manufacturing	9
Professional	8
Finance	7
Transportation	2
Services	2
Utilities	1
Retail	1
Other	9
Total	**100**

Selected Subsidiaries

StanCorp Equities Inc.
StanCorp Investment Advisers Inc.
StanCorp Mortgage Investors LLC
StanCorp Real Estate LLC
Standard Retirement Services Inc.
Standard Insurance Company
The Standard Life Insurance Company of New York
Standard Management Inc.

COMPETITORS

Aetna	Guardian Life
Aflac	MassMutual
Ameritas	MetLife
Assurant Employee Benefits	Ohio National
	Pacific Mutual
CNA Financial	Principal Financial
Delphi Financial Group	Prudential
GatesMcDonald	Unum Group

HISTORICAL FINANCIALS
Company Type: Public

Income Statement
FYE: December 31

	ASSETS ($ mil.)	NET INCOME ($ mil.)	INCOME AS % OF ASSETS	EMPLOYEES
12/14	22,729	219	1.0%	2,803
12/13	21,393	228	1.1%	2,702
12/12	19,791	138	0.7%	2,875
12/11	18,433	139	0.8%	2,974
12/10	17,843	189	1.1%	3,091
Annual Growth	**6.2%**	**3.8%**	**—**	**(2.4%)**

2014 Year-End Financials

Debt ratio: 2.22%	No. of shares (mil.): 42
Return on equity: 10.14%	Dividends
Cash ($ mil.): 251	Yield: 1.8%
Current ratio: —	Payout: 25.0%
Long-term debt ($ mil.): —	Market value ($ mil.): 2,940

	STOCK PRICE ($) FY Close	P/E High/Low		PER SHARE ($) Earnings	Dividends	Book Value
12/14	69.86	14	11	5.05	1.30	51.61
12/13	66.25	13	7	5.13	1.10	48.79
12/12	36.67	13	9	3.12	0.93	48.83
12/11	36.75	16	8	3.09	0.89	45.42
12/10	45.14	12	9	4.02	0.86	41.42
Annual Growth	**11.5%**	**—**	**—**	**5.9%**	**10.9%**	**5.7%**

Stanley Black & Decker Inc

Stanley Black & Decker has the tools that neighbors envy. As a top US toolmaker it markets hand tools mechanics' tools power tools pneumatic tools and hydraulic tools. The company's tool shed is bulging with additional items such as garden tools plumbing products (Pfister) and cleaning items (Dustbuster) as well as security hardware (Kwikset) and door products. Besides the Stanley and Black & Decker brands it sells such brands as Bostitch Mac Tools and DEWALT. Stanley Black & Decker peddles its products through home centers and mass-merchant distributors as well as through third-party distributors. Founded in 1843 Stanley changed its name after merging with Black & Decker in 2010.

Operations

Stanley Black & Decker operates its business through three segments: Construction & Do-It-Yourself (which generates 50% of sales) Security (20%) and Industrial (30%).

The Construction & Do-It-Yourself segment comprises the Professional Power Tool and Accessories business and the Consumer Power Tool business which includes outdoor products and the Hand Tools Fasteners & Storage business. The Security segment houses the Convergent Security Solutions (CSS) and Mechanical Access Solutions (MAS) businesses. The Industrial segment consists of the Industrial and Automotive Repair (IAR) Engineered Fastening and Infrastructure businesses. The Infrastructure business consists of the Oil & Gas and the Hydraulics businesses.

Geographic Reach

Stanley Black & Decker boasts operations in the US Canada Europe and Asia. The US accounts for about 50% of revenue followed by Asia (10%) Canada (5%) France (5%) and the rest of Europe (25%).

Sales and Marketing

The Construction & Do-It-Yourself segment sells its products to professional end users distributors and retail consumers. The majority of sales are distributed through retailers including home centers mass merchants hardware stores and retail lumber yards.

Among the Security segment the CSS business sells to consumers retailers educational financial and healthcare institutions as well as commercial governmental and industrial customers. Products are sold predominantly on a direct sales basis. The MAS business sells and installs automatic doors commercial hardware locking mechanisms electronic keyless entry systems keying systems tubular and mortise door locksets. MAS sell to commercial customers primarily through direct and independent distribution channels.

The IAR business sells hand tools power tools and engineered storage solution products. The business sells to industrial customers in a wide variety of industries and geographies. The products are distributed through third party distributors as well as a direct sales force. The Engineered Fastening business primarily sells engineered fasteners designed for specific industrial applications.

Stanley Black & Decker spent $121.5 million on advertising in fiscal 2014 (ended January 2015) compared to $121.1 million and $121.4 million in FY2013 and 2012 respectively. Cooperative advertising costs with customers came in at $206.5 million in FY2014 compared to $172.4 million and $159.8 million in FY2013 and 2012 respectively.

Financial Performance

Stanley Black & Decker has achieved healthy revenue and profit growth over the years thanks to acquisitions and organic growth stemming from its newer business lines. The company's revenue rose by 4% to a record $11.3 billion in fiscal 2014 (ended January 2015) thanks to sales growth in its CDIY and Industrial businesses. CDIY drove most of the gains as its organic sales rose 7% in North America thanks to new product introductions expanded retail offerings and partnerships and an overall stronger tool market. CDIY's organic sales in Europe grew by nearly double digits thanks to new product launches and an expanding retail footprint despite facing headwinds in the region's struggling economy. In the emerging markets the company's tool business expanded by 4% thanks to more mid-price tool launches. Stanley Black & Decker's Industrial business sales rose by 7% driven by a combination of 5% organic sales growth and 3% acquisition growth primarily from its recent Infastech acquisition.

Stanley Black & Decker's net income rebounded by 55% to $760.9 million in FY2014 thanks mostly to higher revenue but also thanks much to lower restructuring charges and asset impairments as it wound down its recent acquisition integration processes. In FY2013 profits had fallen by 45% as the company incurred a $498 million loss from its discontinued operations related to two small businesses that were being held-for-sale within the Security and Industrial segments. The company's operating cash rebounded sharply as well in FY2014 thanks to higher cash earnings and lower one-time restructuring and related payments.

Strategy

Beyond tools Stanley Black & Decker has been diversifying into higher growth and higher profit businesses such as security and health care to lessen its reliance on big-box retailers.

The company stated in 2015 that its long-term financial objective of 4-6% organic annual revenue growth and double-digit total revenue growth could be achieved through a combination of: fostering growth in its newer engineered fastening infrastructure and security businesses; strengthening its presence in emerging markets; selectively choosing markets were its brand and value proposition is valuable and have room for growth; strategically acquiring companies that bolster or complement its services (mostly in the tool industry). Stanley Black & Decker also re-emphasized in 2015 its desire to foster a "true organic growth culture" by encouraging innovation and by becoming a more digitally enabled enterprise. To cut costs and drive efficiency throughout its supply chain Stanley Black & Decker continued in 2015 to employ its Stanley Fulfillment System (SFS). The SFS uses continuous improvement strategies that work in unison and include: sales and operations planning (S&OP) operational lean complexity reduction global supply management and order-to-cash excellence techniques.

Mergers and Acquisitions

In 2013 the company expanded its Engineered Fastening business and extended its reach into emerging markets with its $826-million acquisition of Hong Kong's Infastech a leading global manufacturer and distributor of specialty engineered fastening technologies. Stanley Black & Decker funded the acquisition by selling off its home and hardware improvement group to Spectrum Brands Holdings for $1.4 billion in cash.

To grow its international CDIY business in 2013 Stanley Black & Decker acquired a 60% controlling share in Jiangsu Guoqiang Tools Co. Ltd. (GQ) for a total purchase price of $49 million. GQ is a manufacturer and seller of power tools armatures and stators in both domestic and foreign markets.

In 2012 the company expanded its business segments by purchasing Tong Lung Metal Industry for nearly $103 million. The company makes and sells commercial and residential locksets. Stanley Black & Decker also acquired AeroScout for $238.8 million (to integrate into the Security and Industrial segments) Powers Fasteners for $220.5 million and Lista North America for $89.7 million.

Company Background

Stanley Black & Decker is the result of a $4.5 billion merger between Stanley Works and rival Black & Decker in 2010. The company traces its roots back to 1843 when Frederick Stanley opened a bolt shop in a converted early-19th-century armory in New Britain Connecticut. In 1852 he teamed with his brother and five friends to form The Stanley Works to cast form and manufacture various types of metal.

EXECUTIVES

Chairman and CEO, John F. Lundgren, age 63, $1,304,167 total compensation

President and COO, James M. (Jim) Loree, age 57, $810,000 total compensation

VP and CIO, Rhonda O. Gass, age 51

SVP and Group Executive Global Tools and Storage, Jeffery D. (Jeff) Ansell, age 48, $625,000 total compensation

President Emerging Markets Group, Bhupinder S. (Ben) Sihota, age 56

SVP and CFO, Donald (Don) Allan, age 50, $625,000 total compensation

President Latin America, Jaime A. Ramirez, age 48, $400,000 total compensation

President Sales and Marketing Global Tools and Storage, John H. A. Wyatt, age 57

President Power Tools, William S. (Bill) Taylor, age 59

President Vertical Markets Stanley Security, D. Brett Bontrager, age 53, $525,000 total compensation

President Advanced Industrial Solutions, Barbara Popoli

President Stanley Security North Americas and Emerging Markets, James J. Cannon, age 44

President Stanley Engineered Fastening, JoAnna L. Sohovich, age 43

President Global Hand Tools and Storage, Jon Michael Adinolfi

President Latin America, Govind Arora

President Stanley Security Europe, Aru Bala

President Stanley Oil and Gas, Pete Morris

President Asia, Yingli (Christine) Yan

Vice President Human Resources CDIY, Stephen (Steve) Subasic

National Sales Manager, Maria Ford

Vice President Of Manufacturing, Robert Schwartz

Vice President New Business, Rich Coulcher

Vice President Marketing, Allison Nicolaidis

Vice President Human Resources Global Emerging Markets, Matthew (Matt) Barkley

Vice President Measuring and Layout Business Unit, Kyle Dancho

Vice President of Information Technology, Bob St John

PAC Treasurer, Scott Bannell

Auditors: Ernst & Young LLP

LOCATIONS

HQ: Stanley Black & Decker Inc
1000 Stanley Drive, New Britain, CT 06053
Phone: 860 225-5111   **Fax:** 860 827-3895
Web: www.stanleyblackanddecker.com

2014 Sales

	% of total
North America	
US	48
Canada	5
Other Americas	7
Europe	
France	6
Other Europe	23
Asia	11
Total	**100**

PRODUCTS/OPERATIONS

2014 Sales

	% of total
Construction & Do-It-Yourself	49
Industrial	31
Security	20
Total	**100**

Selected Brand Names

Atro
Black & Decker
Blackhawk
Bostitch
DEWALT
Dustbuster
Facom
FatMax
Jensen
Kwikset
LaBounty
Mac Tools

Powerlock
Pfister
Proto
Scumbuster
SnakeLight
Stanley
Vidmar
Virax
ZAG

COMPETITORS

ASSA ABLOY	Klein Tools
Atlas Copco	Kohler
Beam Suntory	Makita
Bosch	Masco
Danaher	Panasonic Corp
Eastern Company	Robert Bosch
Edgewell Personal Care	Robert Bosch LLC
Electrolux	Royal Appliance
Emerson Electric	Sandvik
Hitachi	Snap-on
Illinois Tool Works	Textron
Ingersoll-Rand	Toro Company
Jacuzzi Brands	Trane Inc.

HISTORICAL FINANCIALS
Company Type: Public

Income Statement   FYE: January 3

	REVENUE ($ mil.)	NET INCOME ($ mil.)	NET PROFIT MARGIN	EMPLOYEES
01/15*	11,338	760	6.7%	50,400
12/13	11,001	490	4.5%	50,700
12/12	10,190	883	8.7%	45,327
12/11	10,376	674	6.5%	44,700
01/11	8,409	198	2.4%	36,700
Annual Growth	**7.8%**	**40.0%**	**—**	**8.3%**

*Fiscal year change

2015 Year-End Financials

Debt ratio: 24.27%
Return on equity: 11.32%
Cash ($ mil.): 496
Current ratio: 1.39
Long-term debt ($ mil.): 3,839

No. of shares (mil.): 157
Dividends
  Yield: 0.0%
  Payout: 42.8%
Market value ($ mil.): 15,087

	STOCK PRICE ($) FY Close	P/E High/Low	PER SHARE ($) Earnings	Dividends	Book Value
01/15*	96.02	20 16	4.76	2.04	40.92
12/13	81.01	29 23	3.09	1.98	43.73
12/12	72.06	15 11	5.30	1.80	41.68
12/11	67.60	19 12	3.97	1.64	41.43
01/11	66.87	50 37	1.32	1.34	42.18
Annual Growth	**9.5%**	**— —**	**37.8%**	**11.1%**	**(0.8%)**

*Fiscal year change

Staples Inc

Staples is clipping along as the #1 office supply superstore operator in the US and as a worldwide leader in the office category. It sells office products furniture computers and other supplies through more than 1900 Staples stores in the Americas Europe and Australia. In addition to its retail outlets Staples sells office products via the Internet and through its catalog and direct sales operations including subsidiary Quill Corp. The company also provides document management and copying services at its stores. Facing increasing competition from the merged Office Depot and OfficeMax Staples agreed to acquire the combined company in early 2015.

Operations

The office products giant's North American retail business (stores and online) contributes about 45% of sales. Its North American Commercial segment sells and delivers office products and services directly to business and accounts for about 35% of total sales. Staples' International arm runs stores and provides direct-to-consumer and direct-to-business delivery of office products in about two dozen countries.

Core office supplies ink and toner and business technology are Staples' largest product lines accounting for about 25% 20% and 15% respectively of total revenue.

Geographic Reach

Staples rings up more than two-thirds of its sales in the US. Canada is the chain's second-largest market accounting for more than 10% of sales. Staples has about 110 stores in the UK as well as a retail presence in about a half a dozen other countries in Europe and Australia and Argentina.

Sales & Marketing

The company targets customers through a variety of adverting and marketing formats including radio and television printed circulars online advertising mobile apps and social media. It spent about $495 million on advertising and marketing in fiscal 2015 down from nearly $500 million in 2014 and about $535 million in 2013.

Financial Performance

Staples' sales have declined for each of the past three years with sales in fiscal 2015 (ended January) falling 3% to $22.4 billion. The company blamed declining same-store sales (down 4%) in North America ongoing weakness abroad store closures and unfavorable foreign exchange rates partially offset by growth in its online and commercial businesses in North America. Declining sales of office supplies business machines and technology accessories ink and toner and computers were partially offset by growth in other product categories such as facilities and breakroom supplies furniture and copy and print services.

Profit has been fluctuating in recent years. After a loss of more than $200 million in 2013 net income rebounded to $620 million in 2014 but fell again to about $135 million in 2015 primarily because of the impact of inventory writedowns restructuring costs goodwill and long-lived asset impairment charges. Cash flow from operations continued its relatively steady decline. Indeed the $1 billion in cash generated from operations in fiscal 2015 is down about a third over the past four years.

Strategy

International expansion became a priority for Staples when sales in North America slowed as a result of the deep recession. To that end Staples focused on further expanding its operations in Europe where it had grown to about 320 retail locations. Amid weak European economies and the company's overall focus on cost-cutting Staples later shuttered some international locations bringing its number of European stores down to about 285. It continues to build a foundation for future growth however particularly in Asia and South America with delivery businesses in Argentina Brazil China and Taiwan as well as a franchise arrangement with a partner in India.

As consumers continue to migrate toward purchasing more merchandise and services online Staples is also closing retail stores in North America. Indeed the chain plans to close 225 stores in North America by the end of 2015. To help drive traffic to its retail stores Staples has added an in-store pickup option for purchases made online. Shoppers can also use an iPad app or new in-store touch screen kiosks to make purchases.

To counter the effects of its shrinking office supplies business Staples has expanded the number of its stores that sell tablets and mobile devices. It's also inking partnerships to expand its merchandise mix. In mid-2014 for example Staples began offering workplace furnishings from Steelcase on Staples.com and in certain US Staples stores. The company's future plans include an expansion of more service offerings such as copy and print and technology services.

Mergers and Acquisitions

Staples two main competitors in the US Office Depot and OfficeMax merged in late 2013 to create a combined company with about $17 billion in annual sales an amount that while impressive is still substantially below the $24 billion and change Staples rang up in fiscal 2013. Together they hoped to create a more formidable rival to Staples but in early 2015 Staples agreed to acquire the combined entity in a deal worth more than $6 billion. The deal is expected to close by the end of 2015 and will create an office supply behemoth with sales of nearly $40 billion.

In July 2014 Staples acquired Vancouver-based PNI Digital Media whose technology enables retailers to offer on-demand personalized products including business cards invitations and photo books for about $67 million. In October 2013 the company purchased San Mateo-based Runa a software company that helps online retailers increase sales by personalizing the shopping experience.

In a move that significantly enlarged its footprint in Europe Staples acquired Netherlands-based business supply wholesaler Corporate Express NV after a hard-fought deal valued at about $2.7 billion. Corporate Express is a major office products wholesaler with more than half of its sales generated in the US through Corporate Express US. The acquisition also established Staples's contract business in Canada.

HISTORY

A veteran of the supermarket industry (and the man who developed the idea for generic food) Thomas Stemberg was fired from his executive position with Connecticut supermarket Edwards-Finast in 1985. Stemberg began searching for a niche retail market —he found one in office supplies which he estimated at $100 billion.

While large companies could buy in bulk from dealers smaller businesses were served by mom-and-pop office supply stores that charged much higher prices. Applying the supermarket model to office supply Stemberg founded Staples in late 1985 with Leo Kahn a former competitor in the supermarket business. With money from Kahn and venture capital firms Staples opened its first store in a Boston suburb the next year.

In 1987 the retailer moved into the New York City area and continued to expand throughout the Northeast. By early 1989 —the year it went public —it had 23 stores. The company introduced a line of low-priced private-label products in 1989.

Aggressive expansion began the following year when Staples opened three stores in Southern California and introduced two new concepts: Staples Direct (delivery operations for midsized businesses) and Staples Express (downtown stores offering smaller merchandise selections). International growth included buying a stake in Canada's Business Depot (1991) and 48% of MAXI-Papier a European office supply store chain (1992). It also paired up with Kingfisher to establish stores in the UK (Kingfisher sold its interest to Staples in 1996).

EXECUTIVES

Exec V Pres Human Resources, Susan S Hoyt
Senior Vice President Fin North American Delive, Steven (Steve) Bussberg

Chairman and CEO, Ronald L. (Ron) Sargent, age 59, $1,249,208 total compensation
SVP and CFO, Christine T. Komola, age 47, $584,063 total compensation
President North American Operations, Shira D. Goodman, age 53
President North American Stores & Online, Demos Parneros, age 52, $693,050 total compensation
EVP General Counsel and Secretary, Michael Williams, age 61
President International Operations and Transformation, John Wilson, age 54, $668,000 total compensation
Vp-environmental Affairs, Mark Buckley
Vice President, Bernard Schachter
Senior Vice President Corporate Pricin, Donna Rosenberg
Vice President, Mark A Weiss
Vice President, Rick Gilbertson
Vice President Global Supply Chain, Roger Wil
Vice President General Auditor, Patrick (Paddy) Lacchia
Vice President Sales, Matt Thornley
Vice President Real Estate, David Schulman
Vice President Of Finance, Christopher Long
Vice President PT And Uk Retail And Online, Carlos Maia
Vice President Asset Protection, Robert (Bob) Mcgrath
Regional Vice President, Bob Wolfe
Vice President Product Development Sourcing and Quality, Brad Young
Senior Vice President Quill, Michael (Mel) Patriarca
Vice President Merchandise Planning An, Paul Mccarron
Vice President Design Facility Management And Energy, Andrew (Andy) Thorpe
Assistant Vice President Sps, Ralph Torres
Senior Vice President Operations Middle Atlantic and Southeast, Otis Pannell
Vice President Financial Plan and Analysis, Stephen (Steve) Stanton
Vice President Operations and Customer Satisfaction Us Retail, Catherine (Cathy) Demeo
Senior Vice Presiden, Andrew (Andy) Lewis
Senior Vice President Finance and Treasurer, Nicholas Hotchkin
Executive Vice President Human Resources, Shaira Goodman
Executive Vice President Global eCommerce and Chief Digital Officer, Faisal Masud
Vice Chairman, Joseph G. (Joe) Doody, age 62
Auditors: Ernst & Young LLP

LOCATIONS

HQ: Staples Inc
Five Hundred Staples Drive, Framingham, MA 01702
Phone: 508 253-5000   **Fax:** 508 370-8955
Web: www.staples.com

2015 Sales

	$ mil.	% of total
US	16,022	71
Canada	2,697	12
International	3,773	17
Total	**22,492**	**100**

2015 Stores

	No.
US	1,364
Canada	315
UK	112
Germany	59
Netherlands	41
Portugal	34
Norway	19
Sweden	12
Australia	11
Argentina	9
Finland	7
Total	**1,983**

PRODUCTS/OPERATIONS

2015 Sales

	$ mil.	% of total
North American stores & online	10,448	46
North American commercial	8,270	37
International	3,773	17
Total	**22,492**	**100**

2015 Sales

	% of total
Core office supplies	26
Ink and toner	20
Business technology	14
Facilities and breakroom	10
Paper	9
Services	9
Computers and mobility	6
Office furniture	6
Total	**100**

Selected Operations

Corporate Express (US Europe office products wholesale)
Office Centre (stores The Netherlands)
Quill Corporation (US catalog)
Staples (stores North America and Europe)
Staples Business Advantage (contract stationers for midsized to large businesses)
Staples Business Delivery
Staples Express (smaller-store format)
Staples National Advantage (contract stationers for large multiregional businesses)
Staples The Office Superstore (stores Canada)
Staples.com (Internet shopping site)

COMPETITORS

Amazon.com	Insight Enterprises
Apple Inc.	Lyreco
BJ's Wholesale Club	Office Depot
Best Buy	RadioShack
CDW	Ricoh USA
Costco Wholesale	S.P. Richards
Dell	Systemax
Essendant	Target Corporation
FedEx Office	Tesco
Fry's Electronics	The UPS Store
HP	Wal-Mart

HISTORICAL FINANCIALS

Company Type: Public

Income Statement

FYE: January 31

	REVENUE ($ mil.)	NET INCOME ($ mil.)	NET PROFIT MARGIN	EMPLOYEES
01/15*	22,492	134	0.6%	79,075
02/14	23,114	620	2.7%	83,008
02/13	24,380	(210)	—	85,087
01/12	25,022	984	3.9%	87,782
01/11	24,545	881	3.6%	89,019
Annual Growth	**(2.2%)**	**(37.5%)**	**—**	**(2.9%)**

*Fiscal year change

2015 Year-End Financials

Debt ratio: 10.82%
Return on equity: 2.36%
Cash ($ mil.): 627
Current ratio: 1.57
Long-term debt ($ mil.): 1,024

No. of shares (mil.): 640
Dividends
 Yield: 0.0%
 Payout: 228.5%
Market value ($ mil.): 10,917

	STOCK PRICE ($) FY Close	P/E High/Low		PER SHARE ($) Earnings	Dividends	Book Value
01/15*	17.05	86	51	0.21	0.48	8.29
02/14	13.16	18	13	0.94	0.48	9.39
02/13	13.51	—	—	(0.31)	0.44	9.16
01/12	16.01	16	9	1.40	0.40	10.08
01/11	22.32	21	14	1.21	0.36	9.63
Annual Growth	**(6.5%)**	—	—	**(35.5%)**	**7.5%**	**(3.7%)**

*Fiscal year change

Starbucks Corp.

Wake up and smell the coffee —Starbucks is everywhere. The world's #1 specialty coffee retailer Starbucks has more than 21000 coffee shops in about 60 countries. The outlets offer coffee drinks and food items as well as roasted beans coffee accessories and teas. Starbucks operates more than 10700 of its own shops which are located mostly in the US while licensees and franchisees operate roughly 10600 units worldwide (including many locations in shopping centers and airports). In addition Starbucks markets its coffee through grocery stores food service customers and licenses its brand for other food and beverage products.

HISTORY

Starbucks was founded in 1971 in Seattle by coffee aficionados Gordon Bowker Jerry Baldwin and Ziv Siegl who named the company for the coffee-loving first mate in Moby Dick and created its famous two-tailed siren logo. They aimed to sell the finest-quality whole bean and ground coffees. By 1982 Starbucks had five retail stores and was selling coffee to restaurants and espresso stands in Seattle. That year Howard Schultz joined Starbucks to manage retail sales and marketing. In 1983 Schultz traveled to Italy and was struck by the popularity of coffee bars. He convinced Starbucks' owners to open a downtown Seattle coffee bar in 1984. It was a success; Schultz left the company the following year to open his own coffee bar Il Giornale which served Starbucks coffee.

Frustrated by its inability to control quality Starbucks sold off its wholesale business in 1987. Later that year Il Giornale acquired Starbucks' retail operations for $4 million. (Starbucks' founders held on to their other coffee business Peet's Coffee & Tea.) Il Giornale changed its name to Starbucks Corporation prepared to expand nationally and opened locations in Chicago and Vancouver. In 1988 the company published its first mail-order catalog.

Starbucks lost money in the late 1980s as it focused on expansion (it tripled its number of stores to 55 between 1987 and 1989). Schultz brought in experienced managers to run Starbucks' stores. In 1991 it became the nation's first privately owned company to offer stock options to all employees.

In 1992 Starbucks went public and set up shops in Nordstrom's department stores. The following year it began operating cafes in Barnes & Noble bookstores. The company had nearly 275 locations by the end of 1993. Starbucks inked a deal in 1994 to provide coffee to ITT/Sheraton hotels (later acquired by Starwood Hotels & Resorts). The next year it capitalized on its popular in-house music selections by selling compact discs. Also in 1995 Starbucks joined with PepsiCo to develop a bottled coffee drink and agreed to produce a line of premium coffee ice cream with Dreyer's.

Starbucks expanded into Japan and Singapore in 1996. Also that year the company created Caffe Starbucks an online store located on AOL's marketplace. In 1997 Starbucks began testing sales of whole-bean and ground coffees in Chicago supermarkets.

In 1998 Starbucks expanded into the UK when it acquired that country's Seattle Coffee Company chain (founded in 1995) for about $86 million and converted its stores into Starbucks locations. It also announced plans to sell coffee in supermarkets nationwide through an agreement with Kraft Foods. In 1999 Starbucks bought Tazo an Oregon-based tea company as well as music retailer

Hear Music and opened its first store in China. Schultz toned down his Internet plans in late 1999 after investors and analysts voiced skepticism.

In 2000 Schultz ceded the CEO post to president Orin Smith remaining chairman but focusing primarily on the company's global strategy. Starbucks jumpstarted its worldwide expansion the next year opening about 1100 stores worldwide including locations in a handful of new European countries such as Austria and Switzerland. It also spun off its Japanese operations as a public company. The following year the company opened its first shop in Spain and went on to open Starbucks locations in Greece and Germany. Later in 2002 it announced large-scale expansion plans in Mexico and Latin America.

The next year Starbucks acquired Seattle Coffee Company (and its Seattle's Best Coffee brand) from Popeyes for $72 million. The deal gave Starbucks an additional 150 coffee shops (as if it needed them) but more importantly it gave the coffee giant the Seattle's Best Coffee brand and wholesale coffee business. It also got something new out of the deal: franchised locations.

Starbucks was one of the first national retailers to jump on the Wi-Fi bandwagon teaming with Hewlett-Packard and Deutsche Telekom's T-Mobile unit to offer high-speed wireless Internet access at 1200 of its locations in the US London and Berlin. In 2004 Starbucks and Hewlett-Packard unveiled their Hear Music service which allows Starbucks customers to create custom music CDs in some locations. It later premiered the Hear Music channel on XM Satellite Radio (later SIRIUS XM Radio) and launched a new Hear Music CD-burning media bar (co-developed with HP) in selected stores.

In 2005 the company began offering a hot chocolate in its US and Canada markets and in conjunction with Jim Beam Brands (now Beam) it introduced Starbucks Coffee Liqueur and Starbucks Cream Liqueur. That year Starbucks signed agreements with Suntory in Japan and Uni-President in Taiwan to sell its ready-to-drink coffees in those countries. Additionally Smith retired as president and CEO in 2005; he was replaced by Starbucks' North American president Jim Donald.

The company acquired full ownership of joint ventures Coffee Partners Hawaii and Cafe del Caribe (Puerto Rican outlets) in 2006. While Starbucks continued to dominate the coffee business traffic at its stores began to decline in 2007. The company brought Schultz back as CEO in 2008 replacing Donald.

Starbucks acquired fruit and vegetable juice maker Evolution Fresh in 2011 for $30 million in cash. In December 2012 the company purchased Teavana Holdings Inc. for $620 million in cash. Teavana operates some 300 Heaven of Tea retail stores.

EXECUTIVES

Senior Vice President Finance Global Business Operations, Troy Alstead
Chairman and CEO, Howard D. Schultz, age 62, $1,500,000 total compensation
CTO, Gerri Martin-Flickinger
President and COO, Kevin R. Johnson, age 54
President Evolution Fresh, Jeff Hansberry, age 50, $521,269 total compensation
Group President US Americas and Teavana, Clifford (Cliff) Burrows, age 56, $786,116 total compensation
Group President China and Asia Pacific Channel Development and Emerging Brands, John Culver, age 54, $625,205 total compensation
Chief Creative Officer and President Global Development and Evolution Fresh Retail, Arthur Rubinfeld, age 61, $484,058 total compensation

Executive Vice President General Counsel and Secretary, Lucy Lee Helm, $493,172 total compensation
EVP Public Affairs, Vivek Varma
Chief Community Officer, Blair H. Taylor
EVP and Chief Partner Resources Officer, Scott Pitasky
EVP and President Teavana, Annie Young-Scrivner, age 46, $514,885 total compensation
EVP and CFO, Scott H. Maw, $511,633 total compensation
EVP Global Coffee, Craig Russell
EVP Global Supply Chain, D. Deverl Maserang, age 51
President Starbucks Global Channel Development, Michael Conway
Chief Digital Officer, Adam Brotman
Global Chief Strategy Officer, Matthew Ryan
Vice President Information Strategies, Sherry Maple
Senior Vice President Store Development, Michael Malanga
Sr Vp And Pres Glbl Cnsmr Prd, Gerardo Lopez
Vice President Assistant General Counsel, Mark Aoki Fordham
Vice President Human Resources, Adrienne Gemperle
Regional Vice President Of Operations, Tom Ferguson
Vice President Technology, Doug Ebert
Vice President Human Resources, Angel Yu
Vice President Of Operations, Dino Tatangelo
Regional Vice President, Denise Nelsen
Vice President Information Management Services, Elizabeth (Beth) King
Vice President Sales, Kristi Brooks
Vice President Information Technology, Kristy Cameron
Senior Vice President Deputy General Counsel, Paul Mutty
Vice President Manager Director, Lesley Blyth
National Sales Manager Starbucks Coffee Company, Sharon Meehan
Senior Vice President Global Supply Chain Operations Manufacturing, Partha Kundu
Senior Vice President Total Pay, Chris Gann
Senior Vice President Design, Tony Gale
Vice President Global Operations Planning And Communications, Trudi Slater
Senior Vice President Gbl Design And Construction Execution, Bill Transue
Vice President Benefits, Ron Crawford
Vice President Global Research and Development, Mary Wagner
CPA CISA Vice President Puget Sound Chapter of ISACA, Mike Santos
Vice President Marketing, Tiffany Lee
Vice President Retail Sales, Mark Lauderdale
Vice President Finance, Rachel Ruggeri
Vice President andGM Foodservice Operations, Trish Lum
Regional Vice President, Nancy Bennett
Vice President Global Business Systems Development, Janet Landers
Vice President Zone Licensed Stores East, Lisa Compton
Senior Vice President Finance, David Chichester
Senior Vice President Western Pacific, Cosimo Laporta
Vice President Global Supply Chain, Sylvia Wilks
Regional Vice President Operations, Traci York
Vice President Global Talent Acquisition, John Phillips
Regional Vice President, Suzanne Dechant
Vice President Field Information Technology, Lisa Orchard
Vice President Research And Industry Information, Ben Heege
Vice President Of Operations, Mark Cromett

Senior Vice President Marketing and Category US and Americas, Bernard Acoca
Senior Vice President Deputy General Counsel International And Re, Michael Fink
Senior Vice President Partner Resources Us Retail, James Koster
Vice President Global Learning, Stephen Krempl
Vice President of Operations teavana, Nancy McLaughlin
National Sales Manager Foodservice, Jason Carter
Vice President Of It Support, Doug Wayles
Vice President Concept Development, Charles (Chas) Cain
Vice President Of Digital Strategy, David Alstadter
Regional Vice President, Ross Shadix
Senior Vice President Southeast Plains, Paul Twohig
Vice President Finance, Ryan Ziegelmann
Senior Vice President Finance, Charles (Chas) Jemley
Vice President Assistant General Counsel Litigation, Matt Swaya
Senior Vice President Northwest Mountain Division, Chris Carr
Senior Vice President Real Estate and Store Development Starbucks Coffee International, Mark Wesley
Vice President Business Intelligence, Mike Manzano
Vice President Global Communications and Public Affaris, Corey Dubrowa
Vice President Assistant General Counsel Corporate and Securities, Sophie Hume
Executive Assistant; Vice President Of E Commerce, Wendy Becklun
Senior Vice President Partner Resources U.S. and Americas, Marissa Andrada
Vice President design americas Global Development, Bill Smith
Board Member, Patrick K Coe
Auditors: DELOITTE & TOUCHE LLP

LOCATIONS

HQ: Starbucks Corp.
2401 Utah Avenue South, Seattle, WA 98134
Phone: 206 447-1575
Web: www.starbucks.com

PRODUCTS/OPERATIONS

2014 Sales

	$ mil.	% of total
Company-operated retail	12,977	79
Licensing	1,588	10
CPG foodservice & other	1,881	11
Total	**16,447**	**100**

2014 Sales

	% of total
Beverages	58
Food	15
Packaged and single serve coffees	14
Coffee-making equipment & other merchandise	13
Total	**100**

2014 Locations

	No.
Company-owned	10,713
Licensed	10,653
Total	**21,366**

COMPETITORS

Caff Nero	Keurig Green Mountain
Caribou Coffee	Lavazza
Celestial Seasonings	McDonald' s
Cinnabon	Nestl©
Community Coffee	Panera Bread
Dunkin	Republic of Tea
Einstein Noah Restaurant Group	The Coffee Bean
	Tim Hortons

Farmer Bros.	Whitbread
Greggs	Whole Foods
Jamba	illy

HISTORICAL FINANCIALS

Company Type: Public

Income Statement

FYE: September 27

	REVENUE ($ mil.)	NET INCOME ($ mil.)	NET PROFIT MARGIN	EMPLOYEES
09/15	19,162	2,757	14.4%	238,000
09/14	16,447	2,068	12.6%	191,000
09/13	14,892	8	0.1%	182,000
09/12*	13,299	1,383	10.4%	160,000
10/11	11,700	1,245	10.6%	149,000
Annual Growth	**13.1%**	**22.0%**	**—**	**12.4%**

*Fiscal year change

2015 Year-End Financials

Debt ratio: 18.86%
Return on equity: 49.86%
Cash ($ mil.): 1,530
Current ratio: 1.19
Long-term debt ($ mil.): 2,347

No. of shares (mil.): 1,485
Dividends
  Yield: 0.0%
  Payout: 35.1%
Market value ($ mil.): 86,121

	STOCK PRICE ($) FY Close	P/E High/Low		PER SHARE ($) Earnings	Dividends	Book Value
09/15	57.99	53	26	1.82	0.64	3.92
09/14	75.17	60	50	1.36	0.52	3.52
09/13	77.33	15466	8994	0.01	0.42	2.97
09/12*	50.71	67	40	0.90	0.34	3.41
10/11	37.29	50	31	0.81	0.26	2.94
Annual Growth	**11.7%**	**—**	**—**	**22.4%**	**25.3%**	**7.4%**

*Fiscal year change

Starwood Hotels & Resorts Worldwide Inc

Starwood Hotels & Resorts Worldwide knows how to shine a light on hospitality. One of the world's largest hotel companies it has about 1125 properties in about 100 countries. Starwood's hotel empire consists of upscale brands such as Sheraton and Westin. It operates about 100 luxury resorts and hotels through its St. Regis and Luxury Collection units while its 40 W Hotels offer ultra-modern style. Other brands include Four Points (value-oriented) Le Méridien (European-inspired) Aloft (select-service) and Element (extended stay). Starwood Vacation Ownership operates about 15 time-share resorts. In 2015 Marriott agreed to acquire Starwood for about $12.2 billion.

Geographic Reach

Starwood is focused on international expansion. The dramatic economic growth in Asia Europe Latin America the Middle East and Africa is fueling demand for Starwood's brands worldwide.

Operations

The company manages and operates hotel business in three separate hotel segments: the Americas; Europe Africa and the Middle East (EAME); and Asia Pacific.

Sales and Marketing

Starwood's loyalty program "Starwood Preferred Guest" is a frequent guest incentive marketing program allowing members to earn and redeem points for room stays room upgrades and flights. Starwood uses multi-media advertising campaigns including television radio internet and print advertisements to drive guests to its properties.

Financial Performance

Starwood's revenue decreased in fiscal 2014 compared to fiscal 2013. Starwood reported about $5.98 billion in revenue for fiscal 2014 compared to $6.1 billion in fiscal 2013. The company's profits also decreased in fiscal 2014 compared to the previous year. Starwood reported a net income of $633 million for fiscal 2014 after claiming a net income of $635 million for fiscal 2013.

Strategy

Starwood is focused on growth in Africa China Europe India South Asia and Latin America. The company expects to have 100 hotels under operation in the Asia Pacific region by 2015. Starwood also plans to increase its operating hotel footprint in Latin America by 50% during the next five years opening an average of seven new hotels per year in the region. Starwood continues to expand in Europe as well where it expects to open more than 60 new hotels and resorts across by 2020.

Mergers and Acquisitions

The merger with Marriott will create the world's biggest hotel company with more than 5500 hotels and about 1.1 million rooms in some 100 countries worldwide. The deal is expected to close in mid-2016.

HISTORY

Barry Sternlicht earned his MBA from Harvard in 1986 and joined the fast track at JMB Realty bringing the company a UK real estate deal involving Randsworth Trust in 1989. He left two years later to start Starwood Capital Group with backers including the wealthy Burden and Ziff families. (JMB and its pension fund partners meanwhile lost their shirts when Randsworth went belly-up during the recession of the early 1990s.) In 1995 Starwood Capital joined Goldman Sachs and Nomura Securities to buy Westin Hotel (renamed Westin Hotels & Resorts) from Japanese construction firm Aoki. Founded in Washington State in 1930 Westin was acquired by UAL (now United Continental) in 1970 then Aoki bought it in 1988 during a boom in Japanese investments in US real estate.

Also in 1995 Sternlicht bought Hotel Investors Trust (a hotel REIT) and Hotel Investors Corp. (hotel management) two struggling firms whose chief attraction was their rare paired-share status allowing management company profits to flow through the REIT to investors exempt from corporate income tax. (The structure was banned in 1984 but four such entities were grandfathered in under the law.) The companies were renamed Starwood Lodging Trust and Starwood Lodging Corp. (together Starwood Lodging). Through more acquisitions Starwood amassed a collection of about 110 hotels by 1997.

Starwood's industry standing took a quantum leap in early 1998 when it acquired the 50% of the Westin hotel chain that Starwood Capital didn't already own and bought lodging giant ITT the former telephone industry conglomerate and owner of the Sheraton hotel chain. ITT —with more than 400 hotels and gaming properties (Desert Inn Caesars) —fought off a hostile takeover bid from Hilton Hotels (now Hilton Worldwide) and accepted Starwood Lodging's $14.6 billion offer. (Starwood Capital made $22 million in advising fees on the deal.) Later that year the firm changed its name to Starwood Hotels & Resorts bought four former Ritz-Carlton hotels and sold eight all-suite hotels to FelCor Suite Hotels (now FelCor Lodging Trust). Sternlicht then chose Walt Disney executive and Harvard classmate Richard Nanula to take

the reins of Starwood's operating company. In late 1998 it launched W Hotels.

Before Congress closed the paired-share loophole for new acquisitions Starwood Hotels went on a shopping spree becoming a standard corporation in 1999. Nanula resigned that year apparently after repeated clashes with Sternlicht. The company bought time-share resort company Vistana —renamed Starwood Vacation Ownership (SVO) –and purchased the portion of European hotel operator Ciga (part of which Sheraton had acquired in 1994) that it didn't already own.

Gaming profits had begun to fall off in 1999 however as the Asian economic crisis stymied the flow of gambling-hungry tourists. The following year Starwood sold its Caesars unit to Park Place Entertainment for $3 billion and its Desert Inn hotel and casino to Mirage Resorts founder Steve Wynn for about $270 million. Tight economic conditions forced Starwood to cut costs and curtail discretionary spending. That year SVO began building new resorts in Arizona Colorado and Hawaii. Starwood saw its business begin to suffer following the September 11 2001 terrorist attacks which kept many potential travelers at home. As a result Starwood cut about 12000 jobs roughly 25% of its workforce.

To pay down its debt Starwood raised about $1.5 billion in capital by selling bonds (2002) and sold its Italian Ciga assets —including luxury hotels a golf club and other real estate interests —to Colony Capital (2003).

In 2004 Steven Heyer former president and COO of Coca-Cola was named CEO as Sternlicht began setting the stage for his retirement from the company. He stayed on for nearly another year as executive chairman however before leaving the company altogether. The company's expansion efforts in 2005 included the acquisition of the Le Meridien brand for $225 million. (In a separate agreement Lehman Brothers and Starwood Capital Group by then an unaffiliated fund managed by Sternlicht jointly acquired the real estate properties.) In 2006 Starwood sold some 30 properties to Host Hotels & Resorts for about $4 billion. Heyer resigned from the company in 2007. Later that year Frits van Paasschen was named CEO.

Before the company's financials began improving in 2010 the company divested its Bliss spa and product business in order to focus on its core hospitality business. Starwood sold Bliss to spa company Steiner Leisure Limited in 2010 after consumer demand for luxury services fell during the weak economy in 2009 and 2008. Starwood raised some much-needed cash from the deal which was worth about $100 million. It continued to offer Bliss spas and amenities however in W Hotels and St. Regis Hotels.

EXECUTIVES

SVP and CFO, Alan M. Schnaid
Co-President The Americas, Sergio D. Rivera, age 53, $732,830 total compensation
President Global Development, Simon M. Turner, age 54, $766,785 total compensation
EVP and Chief Human Resources Officer, Jeffrey M. (Jeff) Cava, age 64
SVP Global Brand Leader Westin and Le M ©ridien, Brian Povinelli
President Europe Africa and Middle East, Michael Wale
CEO, Thomas B. (Tom) Mangas
EVP and CIO, Martha Poulter, age 44
President Asia Pacific, Stephen Ho
Non-Executive Chairman Asia Pacific, Miguel Ko
Co-President The Americas, Osvaldo V. Librizzi
SVP Brands and Shared Services, John Peyton
SVP Global Brand Leader The Luxury Collection Hotels and Resorts, Hoyt H. Harper

SVP Global Brand Leader St. Regis Hotels and Resorts, Jim Petrius
SVP Specialty Select Brands Aloft Element Four Points by Sheraton, Brian McGuinness
Senior Vice President of Sales North America, Mary Casey
Vice President, Jessica N White
Information Technology Chief Architect Vice President, Christopher Clanton
Vice President Operations Mexico Central America Caribbean, Jean-Marc Janod
Vice President, Matthew Barry
Vice President Of Operations, Jose Ponte
Vice President Global Communications, Eve Dreher
Vice President Supply Chain, Adrian Oyekanmi
Chairman, Bruce W. Duncan, age 64
Board Member, Pat Siciliano
Auditors: Ernst & Young LLP

LOCATIONS

HQ: Starwood Hotels & Resorts Worldwide Inc
One StarPoint, Stamford, CT 06902
Phone: 203 964-6000
Web: www.starwoodhotels.com

PRODUCTS/OPERATIONS

Selected Brands
Aloft
Element
Four Points by Sheraton
Luxury Collection
Le Méridien
Sheraton
Westin

2014 Sales

% of total	$ mil
Americas	26
EAME	10
Asia Pacific	6
Vacation ownership and residential	11
Other revenues from managed and franchised hotels	45
Other corporate revenues — unallocated	2
Total	**100**

2014 Sales

% of total	$ mil
Owned Leased and Consolidated Joint Venture Hotels	26
Management Fees Franchise Fees and Other Income	18
Vacation Ownership and Residential	11
Other Revenues from Managed and Franchised Properties	45
Total	**100**

COMPETITORS

Accor	LXR Luxury Resorts
Bluegreen	Loews Hotels
Carlson Hotels	Marriott
Diamond Resorts	Millennium & Copthorne
FRHI Hotels and	Hotels
Resorts	Omni Hotels
Four Seasons Hotels	Silverleaf Resorts
Hilton Worldwide	Wyndham Worldwide
Hyatt	
InterContinental	
Hotels	

HISTORICAL FINANCIALS
Company Type: Public

Income Statement
FYE: December 31

	REVENUE ($ mil.)	NET INCOME ($ mil.)	NET PROFIT MARGIN	EMPLOYEES
12/14	5,983	633	10.6%	180,400
12/13	6,115	635	10.4%	181,400
12/12	6,321	562	8.9%	171,000
12/11	5,624	489	8.7%	154,000
12/10	5,071	477	9.4%	145,000
Annual Growth	4.2%	7.3%	—	5.6%

2014 Year-End Financials

Debt ratio: 34.00%
Return on equity: 25.92%
Cash ($ mil.): 935
Current ratio: 0.95
Long-term debt ($ mil.): 2,574

No. of shares (mil.): 172
Dividends
Yield: 4.9%
Payout: 143.8%
Market value ($ mil.): 14,000

	STOCK PRICE ($) FY Close	P/E High/Low		PER SHARE ($) Earnings	Dividends	Book Value
12/14	81.07	25	21	3.40	4.00	8.83
12/13	79.45	24	17	3.28	1.35	17.51
12/12	57.36	21	17	2.86	1.25	16.24
12/11	47.97	25	14	2.51	0.50	15.08
12/10	60.78	24	13	2.51	0.30	12.81
Annual Growth	7.5%	—	—	7.9%	91.1%	(8.9%)

State Auto Financial Corp.

Thanks to State Auto Financial the state of auto insurance is healthy in the Midwest. The company sells property/casualty policies through several subsidiaries writing personal commercial and specialty coverage including automobile homeowners multi-peril and workers' compensation insurance. It also participates in an insurance pool through its parent company State Auto Mutual Insurance which owns more than 60% of State Auto Financial and provides the offices for its headquarters. Subsidiary Stateco Financial Services manages the company's invested assets. State Auto Financial is the only part of State Auto Mutual that is publicly traded.

Operations

The company has four reportable segments: personal insurance business insurance specialty insurance and investment operations. The personal insurance segment provides primarily personal automobile and homeowners to the personal insurance market. The business insurance segment provides commercial automobile commercial multi-peril property data compromise and risk control insurance covering small-to-medium sized commercial exposures in the business insurance market. The specialty insurance segment provides commercial coverages including workers' compensation that require specialized product underwriting claims handling or risk management services through a distribution channel of retail agents and wholesale brokers which may include program administrators and other specialty sources. The investment operations segment managed by subsidiary Stateco provides investment services.

Geographic Reach

Through the mutual pool State Auto Financial and its sister companies known collectively as State Auto Group market products through independent insurance agencies in about 35 states. Ohio Kentucky and Texas are State Auto Financial's biggest markets accounting for almost 30% of its annual premiums. The company focuses its business insurance sales on small-to-medium-sized companies.

Financial Analysis

State Auto Financial's personal insurance products account for more than half of the company's revenues.

The company saw its revenues drop by 26% in 2012 thanks to an decrease in premiums earned driven changes to the way the company accounts for personal auto and homeowner lines of business. The changes were partially based on State Auto Financial's plan to focus less on the wind-damage prone Midwest and Southeast while expanding in other geographic regions. On the plus side net income rose to $10.7 million due to fewer catastrophic losses. Cash flow took a hit as the company used more funds for operating expenses.

Strategy

While its revenues have grown steadily with just personal and standard commercial products State Auto Financial has made moves to diversify its products. The company has begun offering data protection and other more modern coverage. It has also decided to move its geographic focus away from the tornado-prone Midwest and Southeast.

EXECUTIVES

SVP and Chief Risk Officer, Cynthia A. Powell, age 54
President and CEO, Michael E. (Mike) LaRocco, age 58
SVP and CFO, Steven E. English, age 54, $447,231 total compensation
VP and Director Operation Effectiveness, Lyle D. Rhodebeck, age 57
SVP Secretary and General Counsel, James A. (Jay) Yano, age 64, $357,692 total compensation
SVP Standard Lines, Joel E. Brown, age 57
SVP and Director Specialty Lines, Jessica E. Buss, age 43, $372,692 total compensation
SVP and Chief Claims Officer, Stephen P. Hunckler, age 56
Regional Vice President, Kevin Kelly
Regional Vice President and Branch Manager, Lester Brue
Vp State Auto Financial State Automobile Mutual Insurance State Auto Property And Casualty Insurance, Timothy (Tim) Reik
Western Region Vice President, Todd Richardson
Vice President, Rob Gritton
Vice President Chief Risk Officer, Bill Cody Bill Cody
RVP Personal Underwriting, Amy L Skaggs
Vice President Specialty Claims, Jay Carleton
Assistant Vice President Product Mangement, Rudy Palenik
Assistant Vice President Actuarial Department, Alp Can
Assistant Vice President Director of C, Gene Roberts
Vice President, Lee Holland
Chairman, Robert P. (Bob) Restrepo, age 64
Auditors: Ernst & Young LLP

LOCATIONS

HQ: State Auto Financial Corp.
518 East Broad Street, Columbus, OH 43215-3976
Phone: 614 464-5000

2012 Direct Written Premiums

	% of total
Ohio	12
Texas	9
Kentucky	7
Indiana	5
Tennessee	5
Minnesota	5
Pennsylvania	4
Illinois	4
Arkansas	3
Connecticut	3
Florida	3
Maryland	3
Michigan	3
West Virginia	3
Other states	31
Total	**100**

PRODUCTS/OPERATIONS

2012 Revenues

	$ mil.	% of total
Insurance premiums		
Personal insurance	1,042	61
Business insurance	327	19
Specialty insurance	245	14
Investment income & other	107	6
Total	**1,721**	**100**

COMPETITORS

AIG	Kentucky Employers' Mutual
Allstate	
American Family Insurance	Nationwide
American Southern	Progressive Corporation
COUNTRY Financial	State Farm
GEICO	The Hartford
GMAC Insurance	Travelers Companies

HISTORICAL FINANCIALS
Company Type: Public

Income Statement
FYE: December 31

	ASSETS ($ mil.)	NET INCOME ($ mil.)	INCOME AS % OF ASSETS	EMPLOYEES
12/14	2,766	107	3.9%	2,274
12/13	2,496	60	2.4%	2,384
12/12	2,477	10	0.4%	2,423
12/11	2,790	(146)	—	2,451
12/10	2,722	24	0.9%	2,483
Annual Growth	0.4%	44.7%	—	(2.2%)

2014 Year-End Financials

Debt ratio: 3.64%
Return on equity: 12.96%
Cash ($ mil.): 86
Current ratio: —
Long-term debt ($ mil.): —

No. of shares (mil.): 40
Dividends
Yield: 1.8%
Payout: 28.3%
Market value ($ mil.): 909

	STOCK PRICE ($) FY Close	P/E High/Low		PER SHARE ($) Earnings	Dividends	Book Value
12/14	22.22	9	7	2.60	0.40	21.34
12/13	21.24	15	9	1.49	0.40	19.29
12/12	14.94	64	47	0.27	0.55	18.20
12/11	13.59	—	—	(3.65)	0.60	18.82
12/10	17.42	33	22	0.62	0.60	21.24
Annual Growth	6.3%	—	—	43.1%	(9.6%)	0.1%

State Bank Financial Corp

State Bank Financial Corp. aspires to one dayÅliveÅin the center of central Georgia's banking world.ÅA holding company State Bank Financial operates through subsidiary State Bank and Trust Company a state-charted commercial bank that serves individuals and businesses throughout central Georgia and in the Atlanta metropolitan area. Through some two dozen branches the bank offers traditional checking and savings accounts as well as commercial and residential real estate mortgages construction and commercial loans and consumer loans. Formed in 2010 State Bank Financial holds more than $2.8 billion in assets.

The holding company was formed to acquire the assets of distressed banks many of which fell victim to the 2008 credit crisis and ensuing recession. With the assistance of the FDIC and proceeds raised in a private offering of common stock State Bank Financial acquired seven community banks between 2009 and 2011 and re-branded them as State Bank and Trust Co. The acquisitions expanded the bank's presence in its core central Georgia and metro Atlanta markets. State Bank Financial intends to continue leveraging such acquisitions to strengthen its presence in these markets.

EXECUTIVES

Chairman CEO State Bank Financial Corporation and Chairman State Bank, Joseph W. (Joe) Evans, age 65, $415,000 total compensation
General Counsel Secretary SBFC and Vice Chairman and Secretary State Bank, J. Daniel (Dan) Speight, age 58, $365,000 total compensation
Vice Chairman COO SBFC and CEO State Bank, J. Thomas Wiley, age 61, $365,000 total compensation
EVP SBFC and State Bank and Chief Credit Officer State Bank, David F. Black, age 39
EVP and CIO SBFC and State Bank, David W. Cline, age 54
EVP and Enterprise Risk Officer SBFC abd State Bank, Steven G. Deaton, age 52
EVP Chief Revenue and Chief Deposit Officer State Bank, Michael R. Fitzgerald, age 56
EVP and Senior Banking Officer State Bank, Michael S. Sims, age 51
EVP and Director Real Estate Banking State Bank, Bradford L. Watkins, age 48
EVP Corporate Development, David Brown
EVP and CFO, Sheila E. Ray, age 56
Vice Chairman and Executive Risk Officer SBFC and Chief Risk Officer State Bank, Kim M. Childers, age 55
Auditors: Dixon Hughes Goodman LLP

LOCATIONS

HQ: State Bank Financial Corp
3399 Peachtree Road N.E., Suite 1900, Atlanta, GA 30326
Phone: 404 475-6599

PRODUCTS/OPERATIONS

2013 Sales

	% of total
Interest and dividend income	
Loans receivable	87
Investment securities	4
Deposits in other banks and other	1
Noninterest income	
Service charges on deposit accounts	2
Payroll fee income	2
Others	4
Amortization of FDIC receivable for loss sharing agreements	
Total	**100**

COMPETITORS

BB&T	SunTrust
Bank of America	Synovus
Citizens Bancshares	Wells Fargo
Regions Financial	

HISTORICAL FINANCIALS

Company Type: Public

Income Statement

FYE: December 31

	ASSETS ($ mil.)	NET INCOME ($ mil.)	INCOME AS % OF ASSETS	EMPLOYEES
12/14	2,882	30	1.1%	566
12/13	2,600	12	0.5%	577
12/12	2,662	22	0.9%	605
12/11	2,746	43	1.6%	605
12/10	2,828	45	1.6%	495
Annual Growth	0.5%	(9.2%)	—	3.4%

2014 Year-End Financials

Debt ratio: 0.10%	No. of shares (mil.): 32
Return on equity: 6.86%	Dividends
Cash ($ mil.): 481	Yield: 0.7%
Current ratio: —	Payout: 15.4%
Long-term debt ($ mil.): —	Market value ($ mil.): 645

	STOCK PRICE ($) FY Close	P/E High/Low		PER SHARE ($) Earnings	Dividends	Book Value
12/14	19.98	21	16	0.92	0.15	14.38
12/13	18.19	46	36	0.38	0.12	13.62
12/12	15.88	25	20	0.69	0.06	13.48
12/11	15.11	13	9	1.32	0.00	12.52
12/10	14.50	11	10	1.40	0.00	11.37
Annual Growth	8.3%	—	—	(10.0%)	—	6.1%

State Street Corp.

Ol' Blue Eyes sang about the State Street in Chicago but investors may find Boston's State Street more melodious. Through its flagship State Street Bank and other subsidiaries the company provides investment management and servicing trading and research services. Its activities include trust and custody fund accounting foreign exchange shareholder services and other administrative services for institutional clients such as mutual and other investment funds pension plans insurance companies foundations endowments and investment managers. Founded in 1792 State Street has more than $28 trillion of assets under custody and administration in addition to more than $2.4 trillion under management.

HISTORY

Company BackgroundThe US's chaotic post-revolutionary era gave birth to the first ancestor of State Street Corporation. Union Bank was founded in 1792 by Boston businessmen breaking the eight-year monopoly held on Boston banking by Massachusetts Bank (a forerunner of FleetBoston which was acquired by Bank of America in 2004). Governor John Hancock's distinctive signature graced Union's charter; the bank set up shop at 40 State Street near the port and enjoyed the glory days of New England's shipping trade.

In the mid-19th century Boston's financial eminence faded as New York flexed its economic muscle. In 1865 the bank was nationally chartered and changed its name to National Union Bank of Boston. It got a new neighbor in 1891: Directors of Third National Bank set up State Street Deposit & Trust to engage in the newfangled business of trusts.

In 1925 National Union Bank merged with State Street and inherited its custodial business. The bank grew through the 1950s; acquisitions included the Second National Bank and the Rockland-Atlas National Bank.

In 1970 State Street converted to a holding company –the State Street Boston Financial Corp. (State Street Boston Corp. as of 1977). The company also went international that decade opening an office in Munich Germany.

Soaring inflation and the recession of the 1970s forced the company to radically rethink its mission. The 1974 passage of the Employee Retirement Income Security Act changed the laws governing the management of pension funds and created an opportunity. State Street was one of the first banks to move aggressively into high-tech information processing and affiliate Boston Financial Data Services began servicing pension assets in 1974.

Encouraged by that success in 1975 new CEO William Edgerly (who served until 1992) steered State Street away from branch banking and into investments trusts and securities processing. An early achievement was designing PepsiCo's retirement plan. Fee-based sales approached 50% of revenues; the company could now quit focusing on lending. In the 1980s and 1990s the company built its administration and investment management businesses overseas and moved into software.

Evolving in the late 1990s State Street left non-core businesses but expanded globally. In 1997 it formed European Direct Capital Management to invest in eastern and central Europe. State Street Global Advisors opened a London office in 1998 to serve wealthy individuals outside the US.

The company sold its commercial banking business to Royal Bank of Scotland in 1999 signaling an exit from that business and narrowing State Street's scope to the asset and investment management businesses. The company also bought Wachovia's custody and institutional trust business and teamed with Citigroup to sell 401(k) retirement products.

In 2000 State Street created FX Connect an electronic foreign exchange trading system. Also that year David Spina took over as CEO from the retiring Marshall Carter.

The firm bought Bel Air Investment Advisors and its broker/dealer affiliate Bel Air Securities in 2001 to cater to the ultrawealthy. In 2003 State Street sold its corporate trust business to U.S. Bancorp and its private asset management business to Charles Schwab's U.S. Trust. Spina retired in 2004; his protégé Ron Logue stepped in as chairman and CEO.

In 2007 State Street added bulk by acquiring another Boston-based fund accounting and servicing provider Investors Financial Services. The company boosted its foreign exchange offerings with the acquisition of Currenex. The following year State Street and Citigroup sold their CitiStreet retirement and pension plan management joint venture to ING Groep for some $900 million.

The US Treasury invested some $2 billion in the company in 2008 as part of a broader bailout plan to restore confidence and increase liquidity. State Street was among eight other top banks that received a combined $250 billion; the company repaid the full amount within months.

In the distressed economic climate State Street's servicing and management revenues declined due to lower equity market valuations and lending volumes and an increase in bankruptcies. The company hit its nadir in 2009 when it reported more than $2 billion in losses.

EXECUTIVES

CEO State Street Global Advisors, Ronald P. (Ron) O'Hanley, age 58

Executive Vice President, Maureen P Corcoran

EVP and CFO, Michael W. Bell, $800,000 total compensation

EVP and Global Head State Street Alternative Investment Solutions, George E. Sullivan

EVP and Global Cash Chief Investment Officer State Street Global Advisors, Steven Meier

Chairman President and CEO, Joseph L. (Jay) Hooley, age 58, $1,000,000 total compensation

EVP and Head of Regulatory Industry and Government Affairs, Stefan M. Gavell

EVP and Head Global Markets and Global Services Asia Pacific, Wai Kwong Seck

EVP and Chief Legal Officer, Jeffrey N. Carp, $550,000 total compensation

EVP, Gunjan Kedia

EVP and Global Head State Street Portfolio Solutions, Nicholas T. (Nick) Bonn

EVP and CIO, Christopher (Chris) Perretta

EVP and Chief Administrative Officer State Street Global Advisors, Marc P. Brown

EVP Corporate Advisory Services, James C. Caccivio

EVP, Jeff Conway

EVP and CTO, Albert J. (Jerry) Cristoforo

EVP, Sharon E. Donovan Hart

EVP and Head State Street Global Exchange, Lou Maiuri

EVP, Kristi Mitchem, age 44

EVP Chief Human Resources and Citizenship Officer, Alison A. Quirk

EVP and Head Global Operations, Robert Kaplan

President and COO, Michael F. (Mike) Rogers, age 58, $908,710 total compensation

EVP and Treasurer, David J. Gutschenritter

EVP and Head Sector Solutions Sales EMEA, Stefan Gmuer

EVP and Head Tax and Tax Advantaged Investments, Dennis E. Ross

EVP and Head Global Services EMEA, William Slattery

EVP and Head State Street Client Technology Services, Brian J. Walsh

EVP and COO State Street Global Human Resources, Kathryn M. (Kathy) Horgan

EVP, Richard G. Taggart, age 55

EVP and General Counsel, David C. Phelan

EVP Trading and Clearing, Martine Bond

EVP, Michael J. Wilson

EVP, Tracy Atkinson

EVP, Patrick D. Centanni

EVP and Chief Administrative Officer Corporate Audit Division, Denise DeAmore

EVP and Chief Investment Officer, Paul J. Selian

EVP and Chief Marketing Officer, Hannah Grove

EVP and General Counsel, Phillip S. Gillespie

EVP and Chief Risk Officer, Andrew Kuritzkes

EVP Alternative Asset Managers Solutions, Maria Cantillon

EVP and COO State Street Global Services EMEA, Anthony Carey

President State Street Global Advisors, Greg Ehret

Global Chief Investment Officer, Rick Lacaille

EVP and Chief Compliance Officer, Cuan Coulter

EVP, David Crawford

EVP and Head Application Development and Maintenance, Ali El Abboud

EVP and Head Specialized Products Group State Street Global Services Investment Services Americas, Brenda Lyons

EVP Head of Institutional Investor Services, Stephen F. (Steve) Nazzaro

EVP and International Chief Risk Officer, David Suetens

EVP and Chief Architect, Kevin Sullivan

EVP and Managing Director State Street Bank GmbH, Jorg Ambrosius

EVP and Global COO Alternative Investment Solutions, Thomas Bieber

EVP and Global Head Foreign Exchange, Anthony C. Bisegna

EVP State Street Global Advisors and CIO Global Equity Beta Solutions, Lynn S. Blake

EVP and Head State Street Global Services Ireland, Susan Dargan

EVP Chief Innovation Officer and Head Advisory and Information Solutions, Jessica Donohue

EVP State Street Global Services Asia Pacific, Andrew Erickson

EVP and Head Sector Solutions Americas and Global Alternatives, Scott R. FitzGerald

EVP and Head Global Total Rewards and HR State Street, Todd Gershkowitz

EVP and Head Derivatives Securities Valuation and Internal Recon Centers of Excellence, John Griffin

EVP Global Operations and Technology, James Hardy

EVP and Head EMEA State Street Global Advisors, Mike Karpik

EVP International Finance and Treasury, Mark R. Keating

EVP State Street Global Markets, Karen D. Keenan

EVP State Street Global Markets, Ian Martin

EVP, Ivan Matviak

EVP and General Auditor, Michael Richards

EVP SSGA and Global Head SPDR Exchange Traded Funds Business and Head Intermediary Distribution United States; Chairman SSgA Funds Management Inc., James E. (Jim) Ross

EVP and Head Global Markets EMEA, Rajen Shah

EVP and Head State Street Global Markets' Sales and Trading and Research, Mark J.A. Snyder

Senior Vice President, Martin (Marti) Sullivan

Vice President Global Markets Technology, Julee Sanderson

Information Technology Management Executive Vice President Senior Vice President, Peter (Pete) Hiotelis

Vice President Of Information Technology, Phil Pengeroth

Vice President Director Manager Of Finance Human Ra, Donald (Don) Carmichael

Vice President Information Technology, Chandra Busannagari

Vice President Product Manager For Risk And Analytical Solutions, Paul Sommers

Vice President Information Technology, Siddharth Jeevan

Assistant Vice President Institutional FX Sales, Dalia Debs

Vice President, Carlton Hood

Executive Vice President, John Serhant

Executive Vice President, Michael Williams

Vice President Global Markets Technology, Steve Lin

Vice President, Andy McDonald

Vice President State Street Investment Analytics, Jim Robbio

Assistant Vice President, Linda Donohue

Vice President Product Manager ETF Operations, Adam Hicks

Assistant Vice President Information Technology Investor Technical Services, Robert Hill

Vice President, Michelle (Mitch) Loranger

Vice President, Kevin McCormick

Vice President Marketing, Christopher Ward

Vice President, Iang Jeon

Vice President, Paul Ananth

Senior Vice President, Susan (Sue) Luo

Assistant Vice President, Pengbo Tang

Vice President of Creative, John (Jack) McClain

Senior Vice President Corporate Audit, John Roof

Vice President, Kishore Kottapalli

Vice President, Robert (Bob) Bagdasarian

Application Development Manager Vice President, Luis Veratudela

Vice President Head of Fixed Income and Global Cash Front Office Systems, David (Dave) Boatwright

Vice President Information Technology, Srihari Valiveti

Vice President Information Technology And Office Of Architecture, Jagadeeswara G Nagalamadaka

Assistant Vice President, Ed Alter

Vice President, Rebecca Hayes

Vice President Gre, Ross Connell

Vice President, Chris Mccarthy

Assistant Vice President, Alistair (Al) Roberts

Vice President State Street Investment Analytics, Scott Verrill

Vice President US Investment Services, George Skritakis

Vice President, Vikas Goel

Vice President Software Development, Vijay Addanki

Assistant Vice President, Yingying Chen

Vice President, Eric Larson

Vice President, Rick Federico

Vice President Technical Project Services, Linda Schwalje

Vice President Human Resources Business Partner, Tammy Chojnowski

Assistant Vice President, Brajendra Prasad

Vice President State Street Global Services, Jay Fulchino

Assistant Vice President Alternative Investment Solutions, Shane Schoenith

Assistant Vice President, Raquel Ellis

Assistant Vice President, Lofgren Jennifer

Assistant Vice President Information Technology, Scott Wheeler

Assistant Vice President, Joe Costa

Vice President Senior Relationship Manager, Linda Ng

Vice President, David Greenfield

Investor Relations Assistant Vice President, Kevin Brady

Vice President Senior Application Development, Harish Babbar

Senior Vice President, Marcy Barker

Vice President Securities Finance, Brian McLoone

Vice President, John Donohue

Vice President, Jeff Durkee

Vice President Compliance, Mark Leaden

Vice President, Rajeev Jain

Vice President, Brian O'Sullivan

Vice President Information Technology Architecture, Dushyant Ralhan

Vice President, Michelle Griffiths

Assistant Vice President At Private Edge Group, Jason Mao

Vice President Program and Project Manager, Jonathan (Jon) Nesbit

Vice President Systems Analyst, Michelle (Mitch) Hayward

Senior Vice President, Richard Young

Assistant Vice President, Todd Kroner

Assistant Vice President Network Architecture, Lokesh Aggarwal

Vice President, Yeng Butler

Senior Vice President Privacy Officer, Gerald Spada

Vice President Marketing Support, Laurence Bardsley

Assistant Vice President, Dennis Spaulding

Assistant Vice President Project Manager, Karen Rodeo

LOCATIONS

HQ: State Street Corp.
One Lincoln Street, Boston, MA 02111
Phone: 617 786-3000
Web: www.statestreet.com

2013 Assets Mix

	% of total
North America	75
Europe/Middle East/Africa	20
Asia/Pacific	5
Total	**100**

PRODUCTS/OPERATIONS

2014 Revenues

	% of total
Total Fee Revenue	75
Interest revenue	25
Total	**100**

2014 Service Revenues

	% of total
Servicing fees	48
Interest revenue	25
Management fees	11
Trading services	10
Securities finance	4
Processing fees & other	2
Total	**100**

COMPETITORS

Bank of New York	JPMorgan Chase
Mellon	Morgan Stanley
Citigroup	Northern Trust
Credit Suisse (USA)	Principal Financial
Deutsche Bank	SEI Investments
First Data	UBS Financial Services
Fiserv	

HISTORICAL FINANCIALS

Company Type: Public

Income Statement

FYE: December 31

	ASSETS ($ mil.)	NET INCOME ($ mil.)	INCOME AS % OF ASSETS	EMPLOYEES
12/14	274,119	2,037	0.7%	29,970
12/13	243,291	2,136	0.9%	29,430
12/12	222,582	2,061	0.9%	29,660
12/11	216,827	1,920	0.9%	29,740
12/10	160,505	1,556	1.0%	28,670
Annual Growth	**14.3%**	**7.0%**	**—**	**1.1%**

2014 Year-End Financials

Debt ratio: 3.66%
Return on equity: 9.73%
Cash ($ mil.): 96,302
Current ratio: —
Long-term debt ($ mil.): —

No. of shares (mil.): 415
Dividends
Yield: 1.4%
Payout: 24.8%
Market value ($ mil.): 32,593

	STOCK PRICE ($) FY Close	P/E High/Low	PER SHARE ($) Earnings	Dividends	Book Value
12/14	78.50	17 14	4.57	1.16	51.72
12/13	73.39	15 10	4.62	1.04	46.94
12/12	47.01	11 9	4.20	0.96	45.50
12/11	40.31	13 8	3.79	0.72	39.80
12/10	46.34	15 11	3.09	0.04	35.46
Annual Growth	**14.1%**	**— —**	**10.3%**	**132.1%**	**9.9%**

Steel Dynamics Inc.

Steel Dynamics may operate mini-mills but it produces big steel. Steel Dynamics operates electric arc furnace mini-mills steel scrap processing and metals recycling centers and steel fabrication facilities. The company sells to companies in the automotive construction and manufacturing industries as well as to steel processors and service centers primarily in the Midwestern and eastern US. Among its mini-mill output are beams rails and other products used in the construction industrial machinery and transportation industries. Steel Dynamics' annual steel shipping capacity is 11 million tons.

Geographic Reach

The company has operations in Indiana (Butler Columbia City Jeffersonville and Pittsboro) Mississippi (Columbus) Pennsylvania (Pittsburgh) Virginia (Roanoke) and West Virginia (Huntington). It also serves the Southern US and Mexico markets.

Operations

Steel Dynamics has three reporting segments: steel operations metals recycling and ferrous resources operations and steel fabrication operations. Its Steel operations has six electric-arc furnace mini-mills producing steel from steel scrap Its Flat Roll Division sheet steel products such as hot rolled cold rolled and coated steel products used by automakers and other industries which is Long Products Division sells structural steel beams and pilings for the construction industry and industrial quality grade rail for the railroad industry. In 2014 the company's steel operations accounted for 55% of net sales.

The Metals recycling and Ferrous Resources segment includes Steel Dynamic's metals recycling operations liquid pig iron production facility and Minnesota iron operations. The company's steel fabrication operations include six New Millennium Building Systems plants which fabricate steel joists trusses girders and decking used by the non-residential construction industry.

All told the company operates six steel mills eight steel processing facilities two iron production facilities more than 90 metals recycling locations and six steel fabrication plants.

Sales and Marketing

Steel Dynamics' primary customers for structural steel products are steel service centers steel fabricators and a range of other manufacturers including metal building firms general construction contractors developers brokers and governmental entities.

Financial Performance

In 2014 the company's revenues rose by 19% due to an increase in steel fabrication and steel offset by a drop in intra-company segment sales. Steel fabrication sales increased by 44% due to 31% higher shipments and a rise in selling prices. Steel operations' sales increased by 25% due to record shipments of 7.4 million tons (including both sheet products and long products).That year Steel Dynamics' net income decreased by $32.3 million due to higher impairment charges selling general and administrative expenses and other costs. Impairment charges of $260 million were related to its Minnesota ironmaking operations. The increase in selling general and administrative expenses of about $43 million were related to higher profit sharing incentive compensation and stock compensation expenses which grew due to increased profitability before impairment charges. The "other expense" increased by $22.3 million primarily due to $25.2 million in acquisition and finance costs associated with the acquisition of a Columbus mini-

mill.In 2014 net cash provided by the operating activities increased by 98% driven primarily by a change in inventories and accrued expenses offset by corresponding decreases in accounts payable.

Strategy

Steel Dynamics is seeking to maintain and enhance one of the lowest operating cost structures in the North American steel industry by optimizing the use of its equipment enhance productivity and explore new technologies to lower production costs. The company may seek to enter new markets in strategic geographic locations that offer attractive growth opportunities by acquiring new businesses or by entering joint ventures or alliances.

Mergers and Acquisitions

In 2014 Steel Dynamics acquired Mississippi-based Severstal Columbus LLC one of the newest and most technologically advanced mini-mills in North America for $1.6 billion. The acquisition expands and diversifies the company's steel operating base increasing Steel Dynamics' annual steel shipping capacity to 11 million tons a 40% increase.

Company Background

Growing its share of the rail market in 2012 Steel Dynamics announced plans to install a heat-treating system (capable of producing up to 350000 tons of standard strength and head hardened plain carbon steel rails for North America's railroad industry) at its Columbia City Indiana Structural and Rail Division.

Steel Dynamics entered a joint venture in 2011 with Spain's Lafarga Group to construct a $39 million facility which will produce copper wire rod from recycled copper. The operation to be named SDI LaFarga LLC will be built in Indiana and utilize a source of copper scrap that had previously been diverted for export to China. The plant is targeted to be operational in 2013.

Steel Dynamics was incorporated in 1993.

EXECUTIVES

Vice President Human Resources, Benjamin Eisbart
VP and General Manager Roanoke Bar Division, Thomas J. (Joe) Crawford, $262,083 total compensation
President and CEO, Mark D. Millett, $948,000 total compensation
EVP Metals Recycling; President and COO OmniSource, Russell B. Rinn, $266,667 total compensation
VP Sheet Products, Glenn Pushis
Manager Information Technology, Robert E. (Bob) Francis
EVP and CFO, Theresa E. Wagler, $495,000 total compensation
VP Bar Products, Barry Schneider
VP and President Steel of West Virginia, Timothy R. (Tim) Duke
VP and President New Millennium Building Systems, Christopher A. (Chris) Graham, $266,667 total compensation
EVP Steelmaking; President and COO Steel Operations, Richard P. Teets, $622,000 total compensation
VP and General Manager Structural and Rail Division, Rob Simon
COO New Millennium Building Systems, Jim Anderson
General Manager Sales and Marketing Long Products, Bill Brown
Vice President Treasurer and Risk Manager, Richard (Dick) Poinsatte
Vice President, Thomas (Thom) Hartman
Vice President and Treasurer, Rick Poinsatte
Vice President, William (Bill) Brown
Vice President Professional Liability, Patty Snyder
Vice President Finance, John Morris

Vice President Iron Resources, David (Dave) Bednarz
Vice President And General Manager, Glenn Pushin
Vice President Information Technology, Ricky Gillenwater
Vice President Of Ferrous Resources, Richard (Dick) Brady
Vice President and Corporate Controller, Theresa Waglr
Vice President and General Manager, Joe Crawford
Chairman, Keith E. Busse
Auditors: Ernst & Young LLP

LOCATIONS

HQ: Steel Dynamics Inc.
7575 West Jefferson Blvd, Fort Wayne, IN 46804
Phone: 260 969-3500
Web: www.steeldynamics.com

PRODUCTS/OPERATIONS

2014 Sales

	$ mil.	% of total
Steel	5,969	55
Metals recycling/ferrous resources	4,091	38
Steel fabrication	631	6
Other	123	1
Intra-Company (Adjustments)	(2059.5)	-
Total	8,756	100

Selected Products

Cold-rolled galvannealed
Cold-rolled hot-dipped galvanized
Direct reduced iron
Fully processed cold-rolled sheet
Hot-rolled galvannealed
Hot-rolled hot-dipped galvanized
Hot-rolled pickled and oiled
Liquid pig iron
Structural products (steel joists trusses)
Steel Operations
Sheet Products
  Hot rolled Products
  Cold Rolled Products
Long Products
  Structural
  Wide flange American Standard and miscellaneous beams
  H piling
  Channel sections
Rail Products
  Engineered Bar Products
  Merchant Bar Products
  Specialty Shapes
Metals Recycling   No. 2 shredded
  No. 1 bundles
  Plate and structural
  No. 1 busheling
  Turnings
  Heavy melt
  Briquettes
  Copper granules
  Stainless steel bundles
Steel Fabrication Operations   Joists
  Decking
  Castellated beams
  Cambered beams

COMPETITORS

AK Steel Holding Corporation
ArcelorMittal USA
Canam Steel Corporation
Commercial Metals
Evraz
Gerdau Ameristeel
Nucor
Timken
United States Steel
Wheeling Corrugating

HISTORICAL FINANCIALS

Company Type: Public

Income Statement

FYE: December 31

	REVENUE ($ mil.)	NET INCOME ($ mil.)	NET PROFIT MARGIN	EMPLOYEES
12/14	8,755	157	1.8%	7,780
12/13	7,372	189	2.6%	6,870
12/12	7,290	163	2.2%	6,670
12/11	7,997	278	3.5%	6,530
12/10	6,300	140	2.2%	6,180
Annual Growth	8.6%	2.8%	—	5.9%

2014 Year-End Financials

Debt ratio: 41.36%
Return on equity: 5.75%
Cash ($ mil.): 361
Current ratio: 3.50
Long-term debt ($ mil.): 2,977

No. of shares (mil.): 241
Dividends
  Yield: 2.3%
  Payout: 41.8%
Market value ($ mil.): 4,766

	STOCK PRICE ($) FY Close	P/E High/Low	PER SHARE ($) Earnings	Dividends	Book Value
12/14	19.74	37 23	0.67	0.46	12.06
12/13	19.54	23 16	0.83	0.44	11.43
12/12	13.73	22 14	0.73	0.40	10.96
12/11	13.15	16 7	1.22	0.40	10.58
12/10	18.30	31 20	0.64	0.30	9.62
Annual Growth	1.9%	— —	1.2%	11.3%	5.8%

Sterling Bancorp (DE)

Sterling Bancorp is the holding company for Sterling National Bank a community-based thrift operating dozens of offices in New York's Hudson Valley region and Greater New York City area. Founded in 1888 the bank attracts consumers and business clients by offering traditional deposit products such as checking and savings accounts and CDs. It uses funds from deposits to originate primarily real estate loans and mortgages. Sterling Bancorp which has assets of more than $7 billion was formerly Provident New York Bancorp; Provident acquired the former Sterling Bancorp in late 2013 and changed its name as well as the name of its banking subsidiary to Sterling.

Financial Performance

In fiscal 2013 Sterling Bancorp reported revenue of about $160 million up 9% from the prior year. The increase was primarily because of an 18% jump in loans that year (powered by commercial real estate and commercial and industrial loans) offset slightly by a decline in noninterest income.

Net income was also up in 2013 rising 27% to $25 million. Net cash from operations was down about 10% to $22.6 million.

Mergers and Acquisitions

Sterling is focused on expanding in the greater New York metropolitan region and increasing the importance of its commercial banking operations. To that end in late 2013 it acquired the former Sterling Bancorp and took its name. The acquisition added the former Sterling's varied commercial and consumer lending products as well as its presence in the New York City area.

EXECUTIVES

Senior Vice President And Director Of Support Services, John Fitzpatrick
Vice President, Rita Kokkoris

Executive Vice President Chief Risk Officer, Daniel Rothstein
Assistant Vice President Research And Database Marketing Manager, David Gerbino
Assistant Vice President Risk Management, Helen Runchey
Vice President, Kristen Santos
Vice President, John Willis
Vice President And Community Business Loan Officer, Frank Armstrong
Senior Vice President Director of Marketing, Suzanne Copeland
Vice President And Purchasing Manager, Vincent Mazzillo
Assistant Vice President Electronic Banking, Robert (Bob) Foster
Auditors: Crowe Horwath LLP

LOCATIONS

HQ: Sterling Bancorp (DE)
400 Rella Boulevard, Montebello, NY 10901
Phone: 845 369-8040
Web: www.sterlingbancorp.com

COMPETITORS

Capital One
Citibank
HSBC USA
JPMorgan Chase
KeyCorp
M&T Bank

HISTORICAL FINANCIALS

Company Type: Public

Income Statement

FYE: December 31

	ASSETS ($ mil.)	NET INCOME ($ mil.)	INCOME AS % OF ASSETS	EMPLOYEES
12/14*	7,424	17	0.2%	829
09/14	7,337	27	0.4%	836
09/13	4,049	25	0.6%	543
09/12	4,022	19	0.5%	522
09/11	3,137	11	0.4%	550
Annual Growth	33.3%	13.1%	—	14.7%

*Fiscal year change

2014 Year-End Financials

Debt ratio: 1.46%
Return on equity: 1.86%
Cash ($ mil.): 121
Current ratio: —
Long-term debt ($ mil.): —

No. of shares (mil.): 83
Dividends
  Yield: 1.9%
  Payout: 82.3%
Market value ($ mil.): 1,207

	STOCK PRICE ($) FY Close	P/E High/Low	PER SHARE ($) Earnings	Dividends	Book Value
12/14*	14.38	72 55	0.20	0.28	11.62
09/14	12.79	40 32	0.34	0.27	11.49
09/13	10.89	20 15	0.58	0.24	10.89
09/12	9.41	19 11	0.52	0.24	11.12
09/11	5.82	35 19	0.31	0.24	11.39
Annual Growth	35.2%	— —	(13.6%)	5.3%	0.7%

*Fiscal year change

Stifel Financial Corp.

Stifel Financial doesn't repress investors. Through subsidiaries Stifel Nicolaus (founded 1890) Thomas Weisel Century Securities Associates Stifel Bank & Trust and others the financial services holding company provides asset management financial advice and banking services for private individuals corporations municipal and institutional clients in the US. Stifel also offers brokerage and mergers and acquisitions advisory services for corporate clients underwrites debt and equity and provides research on more than 1000 US and European equities. The firm boasts nearly 370 US offices with a concentration in the Midwest and mid-Atlantic regions and additional offices in Canada and Europe.

OperationsStifel Financial operates two main business segments: Global Wealth Management and The Institutional Group. The Global Wealth Management segment consists of two businesses: Stifel Bank which provides traditional banking products and services and the Private Client Group which is made up of offices across the US that provide securities brokerage services and insurance products. The Institutional Group segment provides securities brokerage trading and research services to institutions and specializes in the sale of equity and fixed-income products.The firm generated 30% of its total revenue from commissions in 2014 while 26% and 18% of revenue came from investment banking fees and principal transactions respectively. The company's asset management and service fees brought in another 17% of total revenue while interest income made up 8% during the year.Geographic Reach

The company headquartered in Missouri with about 330 private client offices and 37 Institutional Group offices mostly across the US as well as in certain foreign locations in Canada and Europe.Sales and MarketingWith its 2800 financial advisors and 138 independent contractors Stifel serves individuals corporations municipalities and institutions. Its broker-dealer subsidiaries boast more than 1.5 million accounts from customers based in the US and Europe.

Financial Performance

Stifel's revenues and profits have been growing at a healthy clip in recent years with growth across all business lines as the financial markets have appreciated and demand for investor capital has strengthened. The firm's revenues jumped by 11% to a record $2.25 billion in 2014 mostly driven by its recent investment bank asset management and wealth management firm acquisitions (particularly De La Rosa Oriel and 1919 Investment Counsel) which led to more client assets more private client group offices and a larger financial advisor staff; and thus more commission and fee income. Investment banking revenue climbed by 26% during the year with higher collections of advisory fees and equity-capital raising revenue while the firm's asset management and service fees also rose by 26% thanks to larger numbers and higher asset values of fee-based accounts.Higher revenue and a $7.8 million decline in losses on discontinued operations in 2014 drove the firm's net income up by nearly 9% to a record $176.07 million. Stifel's operating cash fell by 64% to $250 million during the year after adjusting its earnings for non-cash items such as broker dealer and clearing organizations receivables. StrategyStifel has fortified its operations and extended its international footprint mainly through strategic acquisitions as well as through partnerships. In 2015 to extend its reach into Israel the firm's Stifel Nicolaus subsidiary signed an exclusive investment banking collaboration agreement with Leumi Partners the investment & merchant banking arm of Bank Leumi le-Israel (Israel's largest banking group). The deal allowed Stifel Nicolaus to work with the foreign firm to provide investment banking services to Israel-related companies with strategic advisory services or fundraising of debt or equity on public or private markets across North America and in other regions. In 2015 and 2014 the firm made a slew of acquisitions to broaden and bolster its service offerings and financial advisor staff and expand its Global

Wealth Management client assets by more than $250 billion.

Mergers and Acquisitions

In December 2015 Stifel purchased Barclays' Wealth and Investment Management Americas franchise in the US along with its 180 financial advisors managing some $56 billion in total client assets. Also looking to boost client assets and financial advisor count in 2015 Stifel acquired financial services firm Sterne Agee Group which boosted Stifel's Global Wealth Management team by 35% to more than 2800 financial advisors and independent representatives with $200 billion-plus in client assets. The deal also bolstered Stifel's fixed-income platform. Additionally in 2015 the firm acquired the California-based public finance investment banking boutique De La Rosa which strengthened Stifel's position in key underwriting markets in California. Similarly that year it acquired the Montgomery Alabama-based public finance investment banking firm Merchant which serves key markets in the Southeastern US.In 2014 it purchased Oriel Securities a London-based stockbroking and investment banking firm. Stifel made the deal to create a larger middle market investment banking group in London with broad research coverage across most sectors of the economy equity and debt sales and trading and investment banking services.

Also in 2014 Stifel bought 1919 Investment Counsel & Trust Company (formerly Legg Mason Investment Counsel & Trust Co.) from rival financial services firm Legg Mason. 1919 provides customized investment advisory and trust services on a discretionary basis to individuals families and institutions throughout the country. Its portfolio managers manage more than $9 billion in assets. 1919 is part of Stifel's Global Wealth Management segment and should be an ideal complement to its existing wealth management platform.

In mid-2013 Stifel obtained KCG Holdings' US institutional fixed income sales and trading business. Altogether Stifel's and KCG's combined teams boast some 90 sales and trading professionals across the US and Europe. The team covers high-yield and investment-grade corporate bonds asset-backed and mortgage-based securities loan trading and fixed income research in certain sectors and companies.

EXECUTIVES

Vice Chairman and SVP Investment Banking, Richard J. Himelfarb, age 74, $250,000 total compensation

Co-Chairman President and CEO, Ronald J. (Ron) Kruszewski, age 56, $200,000 total compensation

President and CFO, James M. Zemlyak, age 55, $175,000 total compensation

EVP; President and Co-Director Institutional Group, Thomas P. Mulroy, age 53, $250,000 total compensation

SVP; President and CEO Keefe Bruyette and Woods Inc. (KBW), Thomas B. (Tom) Michaud, age 51, $250,000 total compensation

EVP; President and Co-Director Institutional Group, Victor J. Nesi, age 55, $250,000 total compensation

SVP and Chief Risk Officer, James M. Marischen, age 35

Senior Vice President, David Sliney

Vice President Mortgage Banker, Dan Bayer

Vice Chairman and SVP, Ben A. Plotkin, age 59

Co-Chairman, Thomas W. (Thom) Weisel, age 74

Auditors: Ernst & Young LLP

LOCATIONS

HQ: Stifel Financial Corp.
501 N. Broadway, St. Louis, MO 63102-2188
Phone: 314 342-2000
Web: www.stifel.com

PRODUCTS/OPERATIONS

2014 Sales

	$ mil.	% of total
Commissions	674	30
Investment banking	578	26
Principal transactions	409	18
Asset management & service fees	386	17
Interest	186	8
Others	14	1
Total	**2,249**	**100**

Selected Subsidiaries

Broadway Air Corp.
Butler Wick & Co. Inc.
Century Securities Associates Inc.
    CSA Insurance Agency Incorporated
Choice Financial Partners Inc.
First Service Financial Company
    Stifel Bank & Trust
Hanifen Imhoff Inc.
Missouri Valley Partners
Stifel Asset Management Corp.
Stifel Nicolaus Limited (UK)
Stifel Nicolaus & Company Incorporated
    Ryan Beck Holdings LLC
    Stifel Nicolaus Insurance Agency Incorporated
Stifel Nicholas Limited (UK)
Thomas Weisel Partners Group Inc.

COMPETITORS

Bank of America	Morgan Stanley
Cowen Group	Oppenheimer Holdings
Edward Jones	Piper Jaffray
Goldman Sachs	Raymond James
JMP Group	Financial
Jefferies Group	Robert W. Baird & Co.
Lazard	Wells Fargo Advisors

HISTORICAL FINANCIALS

Company Type: Public

Income Statement

FYE: December 31

	ASSETS ($ mil.)	NET INCOME ($ mil.)	INCOME AS % OF ASSETS	EMPLOYEES
12/14	9,518	176	1.8%	6,200
12/13	9,008	162	1.8%	5,862
12/12	6,966	138	2.0%	5,343
12/11	4,951	84	1.7%	5,097
12/10	4,213	1	0.0%	4,906
Annual Growth	**22.6%**	**210.0%**	**—**	**6.0%**

2014 Year-End Financials

Debt ratio: 7.43%	No. of shares (mil.): 66
Return on equity: 8.04%	Dividends
Cash ($ mil.): 739	Yield: —
Current ratio: —	Payout: —
Long-term debt ($ mil.): —	Market value ($ mil.): 3,384

	STOCK PRICE ($) FY Close	P/E High/Low		PER SHARE ($) Earnings	Dividends	Book Value
12/14	51.02	20	16	2.31	0.00	35.00
12/13	47.92	19	12	2.20	0.00	32.30
12/12	31.97	15	11	2.20	0.00	27.23
12/11	32.05	46	15	1.33	0.00	25.15
12/10	62.04	1571	1080	0.03	0.00	24.79
Annual Growth	**(4.8%)**	**—**	**—**	**188.6%**	**—**	**9.0%**

Stock Yards Bancorp Inc

Stock Yards Bancorp is the holding company of Stock Yards Bank & Trust which operates about 35 branches primarily in and around Louisville Kentucky but also in Indianapolis and Cincinnati. Founded in 1904 the bank targets individuals and regional business customers offering standard retail services such as checking and savings accounts credit cards certificates of deposit and IRAs. Trust services are also available; brokerage and credit card services are offered through agreements with other banks. Real estate mortgages account for about 60% of the bank's loan portfolio which also includes commercial (27%) construction and consumer loans.

Geographic Reach

Kentucky-based Stock Yards Bancorp serves customers in the metropolitan areas of Louisville Indianapolis and Cincinnati.

Operations

With $2.29 billion in assets Stock Yards Bancorp operates through a pair of subsidiaries: Stock Yards Bank & Trust Company and S.Y. Bancorp Capital Trust II. Stock Yards Bank & Trust Company is a wholly owned subsidiary of Stock Yards Bancorp and boasts $2.2 billion in company assets.

Mergers and Acquisitions

The bank extended the reach of its operations into Oldham County in 2013 through its $19.9-million purchase of The Bancorp Inc. The acquisition boosted the bank's branch number by five to 35 locations.

Strategy

Aside from strategically adding to its branch locations by extending its geographic reach Stock Yards Bancorp is working to expand its loan categories to increase both the size and composition of its portfolio of loans. Additionally the financial institution is focused on better serving new and existing clients across its local markets by increasing its commercial and industrial and commercial real estate categories.

Financial Performance

Since the recession Stock Yards Bancorp has logged several years of organic growth. Thanks to those clients who took advantage of historically low interest rates by either refinancing their homes or buying one Stock Yards Bancorp logged a 5% revenue increase in fiscal 2012 as compared to 2011. Also contributing toward Stock Yards Bancorp's revenue was revenue from federal funds sold and mortgage loans held for sale. Comprising an average 40% of non-interest income income from investment management and trust services rose 3% during the reporting period due to higher asset values and a growing client base. Net income for Stock Yards Bancorp saw a 9% boost in 2012 vs. 2011 attributable to a drop in deposit expenses and decline in the provision for loan losses.

EXECUTIVES

SEVP, Kathy C. Thompson, age 53, $345,000 total compensation

Chairman and CEO, David P. Heintzman, age 55, $535,000 total compensation

EVP Secretary Treasurer and CFO, Nancy B. Davis, age 59, $232,000 total compensation

EVP and Chief Lending Officer, Philip S. Poindexter, age 49, $270,000 total compensation

President, James A. (Ja) Hillebrand, age 46, $375,000 total compensation

EVP and Chief Risk Officer, William M. Dishman, age 53

EVP and Chief Strategic Officer, Clay Stinnett

EVP Retail Banking Brokerage and Business Banking, Michael J. Croce

Auditors: KPMG LLP

LOCATIONS

HQ: Stock Yards Bancorp Inc
1040 East Main Street, Louisville, KY 40206
Phone: 502 582-2571

PRODUCTS/OPERATIONS

2012 Revenues by Category

	$ mil.	% of total
Interest income	86	69
Non-interest income	38	31
Total	**125**	**100**

Selected Products & Services

Personal Banking
  Banking
  Personal Lending
  Personal Investing & Wealth Management Services
Business Banking
  Credit Loans & Leasing
  Deposit Services
  Treasury Management
  Business Retirement Plans
Wealth Management Services
  Investment Management
  Financial Planning
  Trust & Estate Services
  Brokerage Service

COMPETITORS

Community Bank Shares of Indiana	PNC Financial
Fifth Third	Porter Bancorp
First Capital	Republic Bancorp
Home Federal	U.S. Bancorp

HISTORICAL FINANCIALS

Company Type: Public

Income Statement

FYE: December 31

	ASSETS ($ mil.)	NET INCOME ($ mil.)	INCOME AS % OF ASSETS	EMPLOYEES
12/14	2,563	34	1.4%	524
12/13	2,389	27	1.1%	519
12/12	2,148	25	1.2%	495
12/11	2,053	23	1.1%	480
12/10	1,902	22	1.2%	475
Annual Growth	**7.7%**	**11.0%**	**—**	**2.5%**

2014 Year-End Financials

Debt ratio: —
Return on equity: 14.23%
Cash ($ mil.): 74
Current ratio: —
Long-term debt ($ mil.): —

No. of shares (mil.): 14
Dividends
  Yield: 2.6%
  Payout: 40.0%
Market value ($ mil.): 492

	STOCK PRICE ($) FY Close	P/E High/Low	PER SHARE ($) Earnings	Dividends	Book Value
12/14	33.34	14 11	2.36	0.88	17.63
12/13	31.92	18 11	1.89	0.81	15.71
12/12	22.42	13 11	1.85	0.77	14.74
12/11	20.53	15 11	1.71	0.72	13.58
12/10	24.55	15 12	1.67	0.69	12.37
Annual Growth	**8.0%**	**— —**	**9.0%**	**6.3%**	**9.3%**

Stryker Corp.

Is this an operating room or Dad's workshop? Stryker's surgical products include such instruments as drills saws and even cement mixers. The company's Orthepaedic segment makes artificial hip and knee joints trauma implants bone cement and other orthopedic supplies. The MedSurg equipment segment houses microsurgery instruments endoscopy equipment and communications and patient handling tools. Stryker's neurotechnology and spine unit provides rods screws and artificial discs for spinal surgeries as well as coils and stents for cerebral vascular procedures. The firm's products are marketed globally to hospitals doctors and other health care facilities via direct sales personnel and distributors.

OperationsThe company's Orthopaedic (formerly reconstructive) segment makes up the largest portion of sales accounting for 43% of annual revenues in 2014. The division's leading products include the Triathlon and Scorpio knee implant systems Simplex bone cement the VariAx and Hoffman systems and the Oasys spinal implant.Stryker's MedSurg division is almost as large bringing in nearly $3.8 billion in sales (or 39% of total revenues). The MedSurg Equipment division includes surgical navigation systems endoscopic systems emergency medical equipment and other medical devices. Its biggest customers are hospitals and other care providers who have to invest a decent chunk of cash in order to upgrade their surgical equipment.The company's smallest segment —Neurotechnology & Spine —accounted for 18% of sales in 2014.Geographic ReachStryker operates about 30 manufacturing and R&D facilities worldwide primarily in the US Asia Africa the Middle East and Europe. While it markets its products in more than 100 countries and is looking to grow in international markets sales in the US continue to make up the majority (about 70%) of annual revenues.Sales and MarketingIn the US Stryker uses its own sales and marketing force maintaining separate dedicated sales teams for each of its core product lines to doctors hospitals and other care providers. By allowing for specialization each team can provide expertise and guidance directed specifically to customers in each of the medical specialties Stryker serves. In markets outside the US Stryker's products are sold through company-owned subsidiaries as well as third-party distributors and medical device dealers. Financial PerformanceStryker's revenues have increased steadily over the last five years. In 2014 it grew 7% to $9.7 billion led by 10% growth in the MedSurg segment and 5% growth in the Orthopaedics and Neurotechnology & Spine segments. Higher unit sales a shift in product mix and acquisitions all helped contribute to the segments' growth but were partially offset by the unfavorable impact of foreign currency exchange rates that year.Despite the higher revenues net income has fallen for the past three years. Higher R&D spending cost improvement efforts and increased operating expenses led profits to drop 49% to $515 million in 2014. Cash flow from operations slipped 5% to $1.8 billion as a result of the lower net income and an increase in inventories.StrategyStryker expands its operations through a balance of internal R&D programs partnerships and a steady stream of acquisitions. Focus areas of growth including widening its presence geographically and expanding its product offerings in core and complementary fields of medicine. Geographically the company targets Brazil Russia India and China through both its standard line of products and its lower cost Trauson brand.The company spends between 5% and 6.3%

of annual revenues on R&D programs each year; its R&D budget totaled some $614 million in 2014. In the Orthopaedics segment the company has followed the implant strategy of staying on top of the latest technology by consistently upgrading and introducing new versions of its popular brands. In 2013 for instance it launched the Tritanium Cementless Baseplate for its Triathlon Knee System and added the Secur-Fit Advanced Femoral Hip Stem to its Orthopaedics Modeling and Analytics system. In 2015 it received FDA clearance for its Mako total knee application. Also that year the company launched the LITe (less invasive technologies) ALIF Procedural Solutions and Aero-AL Anterior Lumbar Interbody and Fixation platforms adding to its growing portfolio of ALIF products.

Mergers and Acquisitions

Purchases in recent years have brought the company new software and manufacturing technologies and entered it into new lines of business such as minimally invasive devices for treatment of stroke and brain conditions. In 2014 Stryker's buying streak continued as it picked up four new companies: MedSurg company Patient Safety Technologies for $120 million small joint replacement manufacturer Small Bone Innovations for about $358 million operating room equipment maker Berchtold Holding AG for an undisclosed amount and hip arthroscopy product maker Pivot Medical. In 2015 the company acquired private Canadian firm CHG Hospital Beds which markets beds across Canada the US and the UK.In early 2016 Stryker announced plans to buy personal products maker Sage Products for $2.8 billion. Sage which specializes in items that prevent hospital-acquired conditions will become part of Stryker's MedSurg segment.

Company BackgroundStryker was founded in 1941 by Dr. Homer Stryker; members of the Stryker family still own a minority portion of the company's stock.

HISTORY

Stryker was founded in 1941 by Dr. Homer Stryker an orthopedic surgeon who had invented several orthopedic devices. It was incorporated in 1946 as a Michigan company. The company expanded through organic measures and occasional acquisitions over the following decades while the Stryker family kept a hand in its operations.

Beginning in 2009 Stryker set out to further diversify its operations through acquisitions. In 2010 Stryker purchased supportive surface maker (think: beds and tables) Gaymar Industries for approximately $150 million in cash. The two companies were already well-acquainted through a long-standing supply and sales agreement in the US.

Its $1.5 billion acquisition of Boston Scientific's neurovascular division in 2011 added minimally invasive devices (such as coils stents and balloon catheters) for the treatment of cerebral conditions such as brain aneurysms and hemorrhagic and ischemic strokes.

Stryker further boosted its neurovascular operations later that year when it acquired Concentric Medical a maker of clot removal products for use in ischemic stroke procedures for some $135 million. Following these acquisitions Stryker rearranged its operating structure from two divisions into three: Reconstructive MedSurg Equipment and Neurotechnology and Spine.

The company's OP-1 bone growth product was so successful that in 2011 the company sold the product franchise to Olympus for $60 million. During 2011 Stryker acquired synthetic bone graft material maker Orthovita for some $304 million in cash. It also spent $150 million to purchase France's Memometal Technologies for its in hand and foot device products.

EXECUTIVES

VP and CFO, William R. Jellison, age 57, $536,667 total compensation
Group President Orthopaedics, David K. Floyd, $513,333 total compensation
Chairman President and CEO, Kevin A. Lobo, $1,055,000 total compensation
Group President Global Quality and Operations, Lonny J. Carpenter, $407,361 total compensation
Group President MedSurg and Neurotechnology, Timothy J. Scannell, $568,500 total compensation
VP and CIO, Bijoy Sagar
Group President International, Ramesh Subrahmanian, $526,667 total compensation
VP Communications Public Affairs and Strategic Marketing, Yin C. Becker
Group CFO MedSurg & Neurotechnology (MSNT), Glenn Boehnlein
Vice President, Chris Schuckman
Vice President Sales and Marketing, Derick Elliott
Vice President Finance Business Strategy Neurovascular Division, Ghislain Gackiere
Vice President Business Development and Strategic Planning, Bill Roskopf
Assistant Vice President Assistand to Chief Information Officer, Karen Smit
Associate Vice President Marketing, MelindA Slaughter
Chairman Emeritus, John (Jack) Brown
Auditors: Ernst & Young LLP

LOCATIONS

HQ: Stryker Corp.
2825 Airview Boulevard, Kalamazoo, MI 49002
Phone: 269 385-2600   **Fax:** 269 385-1062
Web: www.stryker.com

2014 Sales

	$ mil.	% of total
US	6,558	68
EMEA (Europe Middle East & Africa)	1,371	14
Asia Pacific	1,368	14
Other countries	378	4
Total	**9,675**	**100**

PRODUCTS/OPERATIONS

2014 Sales

	$ mil.	% of total
Orthopaedics	4,153	43
MedSurg Equipment	3,781	39
Neurotechnology & Spine	1,741	18
Total	**9,675**	**100**

Selected Acquisitions

COMPETITORS

Arthrex	Midmark Corporation
B. Braun Melsungen	Olympus
CONMED Corporation	Orthofix
Corin Group	RTI Surgical
DJO Global	STERIS
DePuy	Smith & Nephew
DePuy Spine	Synthes
Genzyme Biosurgery	Tornier
Hill-Rom Holdings	Wright Medical Group
Kinetic Concepts	Zimmer Biomet
Medtronic	
Medtronic Sofamor Danek	

HISTORICAL FINANCIALS

Company Type: Public

Income Statement

FYE: December 31

	REVENUE ($ mil.)	NET INCOME ($ mil.)	NET PROFIT MARGIN	EMPLOYEES
12/15	9,946	1,439	14.5%	27,000
12/14	9,675	515	5.3%	26,000
12/13	9,021	1,006	11.2%	25,000
12/12	8,657	1,298	15.0%	22,010
12/11	8,307	1,345	16.2%	21,241
Annual Growth	**4.6%**	**1.7%**	**—**	**6.2%**

2015 Year-End Financials

Debt ratio: 24.76%	No. of shares (mil.): 373
Return on equity: 16.82%	Dividends
Cash ($ mil.): 3,379	Yield: 1.5%
Current ratio: 2.27	Payout: 46.0%
Long-term debt ($ mil.): 3,253	Market value ($ mil.): 34,667

	STOCK PRICE ($) FY Close	P/E High/Low		PER SHARE ($) Earnings	Dividends	Book Value
12/15	92.94	27	24	3.78	1.42	22.82
12/14	94.33	71	55	1.34	1.26	22.74
12/13	75.14	28	21	2.63	1.10	23.93
12/12	54.82	17	15	3.39	0.90	22.62
12/11	49.71	19	13	3.45	0.75	20.17
Annual Growth	**16.9%**	**—**	**—**	**2.3%**	**17.1%**	**3.1%**

Sun Bancorp Inc. (NJ)

Sun Bancorp revolves around New Jersey. Boasting nearly $3 billion in total assets the holding company for Sun National Bank targets individuals and local businesses in central and southern New Jersey through some 60 branch locations. Sun National Bank offers standard retail services including savings accounts CDs and IRAs. The company's primary lending focus is originating industrial and commercial loans (including Small Business Administration (SBA) loans and lines of credit) which account for some 75% of its portfolio. Sun National Bank stopped providing residential mortgage and home equity loans in the second half of 2014. It offers investment services through Prosperis Financial Solutions.

OperationsSun Bancorp generated 74% of its total revenue from interest income on loans in 2014 while interest on investment securities and service charges on deposit accounts each contributed 8% to total revenue during the year. About 2% of total revenue came from the bank's Mortgage Banking business.The bank changed its investment services arm's name from Sun Financial Solutions to Prosperis Financial Solutions in Summer 2015 as part of a broader rebranding effort.Geographic ReachSun Bancorp boasts more than 45 branches and 15 office locations mostly across New Jersey but also in the metropolitan New York City and Philadelphia Pennsylvania markets. Sun Bancorp also loan production offices in New York and Pennsylvania.Sales and MarketingThe bank offers its community banking services to consumers small businesses and mid-size companies. It spent $2.06 million on advertising in 2014 compared to $2.83 million and $2.81 million in 2013 and 2012 respectively.Financial PerformanceSun Bancorp has been slowing climbing its way out of the red over the past several years as it works to sell off some of its risky loan assets.

Fewer loan assets has led to declining revenue over the years but this has been in line with the bank's long-term de-risking strategy. The bank's revenue fell by 21% to $107.98 million in 2014 mostly due to a 14% decline in interest income as the bank collected lower yields on its loans investment securities and equity investments amidst the continued low-interest environment. Sun Bancorp's non-interest revenue also shrank by 44% after it exited its mortgage banking business and made fewer investment securities gains during the year. Sun Bancorp suffered its sixth consecutive year of losses with its net losses deepening in 2014 to $29.81 million (compared to a loss of $9.94 million in 2013). Most of this was driven by steep revenue declines but $14.6 million in additional loan loss provisions were also to blame as the company sold off more of its non-performing loans while also correspondingly reducing its allowance for loan losses during the year. The company's operating cash also fell sharply during the year to $14.04 million mostly due to lower cash earnings.

Strategy

With an overall strategy to grow its commercial loan business Sun Bancorp reiterated in 2015 that its focus is on expanding further into highly-dense markets in central and northern New Jersey as well as in Manhattan. Based on key demographic and economic indicators the bank believes these markets offer more business opportunities and growth potential than in southern New Jersey. Accordingly in 2015 it consolidated nine of its branches into nearby locations and sold a branch in Hammonton in southern New Jersey to Cape Bank (of Cape Bancorp) for more than $34 million. In 2014 Sun Bancorp sold six offices in Cape May County as well as an office in Atlantic county —all branches located in south New Jersey —to Sturdy Savings Bank. Sun Bancorp has been known to grow through acquisitions as well as through new branch openings. In 2012 Sun National Bank expanded its reach and opened a commercial lending office in Pennsylvania to serve the Philadelphia area. Company Background

To strengthen its balance sheet Sun Bancorp in the past sold loans to investors and offered common stock. In 2010 Chairman Bernard Brown and WL Ross & Co. invested $100 million in equity in the bank. As a result Brown and his family own about 10% of Sun Bancorp and director WL Ross owns about 25% of the company.

EXECUTIVES

Chairman & Interim President & CEO, Sidney R. (Sid) Brown, $178,200 total compensation
EVP and CFO, Thomas R. Brugger, age 48, $36,250 total compensation
EVP Consumer Banking Sun National Bank, Edward (Ed) Malandro, $237,850 total compensation
EVP and Director Wholesale Lending, Bradley (Brad) Fouss, $280,000 total compensation
President CEO and Director Sun Bancorp and Sun National Bank, Thomas X. Geisel, age 54, $550,000 total compensation
EVP and Chief Administrative Officer, Michele Estep, $250,000 total compensation
Executive Vice President and Chief Risk Officer, Albert J. Celini
Vice President Information Technology and Solutions Group, Jeff Wills
Auditors: Deloitte & Touche LLP

LOCATIONS

HQ: Sun Bancorp Inc. (NJ)
350 Fellowship Road, Suite 101, Mount Laurel, NJ 08054
Phone: 856 691-7700
Web: www.sunnb.com

PRODUCTS/OPERATIONS

2011 Sales

	$ mil.	% of total
Interest		
Loans	112	73
Securities & other	13	9
Noninterest		
Service charges on deposit accounts	11	7
Gain on Sale of loans	3	2
BOLI income	3	2
Investment products income	2	2
Net gain on sales of investment securities	1	1
Losses	(12.8)	-
Other	4	4
Total	**140**	**100**

Selected Subsidiaries

Sun National Bank
2020 Properties L.L.C.
Sun Financial Services L.L.C.
Sun Home Loans Inc.

COMPETITORS

1st Constitution Bancorp	Provident Financial Services
Bank of America	Republic First Bank
Cape Bancorp	Sovereign Bank
Citigroup	TF Financial
Fulton Financial	Valley National Bancorp
Ocean Shore	
PNC Financial	

HISTORICAL FINANCIALS

Company Type: Public

Income Statement

FYE: December 31

	ASSETS ($ mil.)	NET INCOME ($ mil.)	INCOME AS % OF ASSETS	EMPLOYEES
12/14	2,715	(29)	—	509
12/13	3,087	(9)	—	690
12/12	3,224	(50)	—	750
12/11	3,183	(67)	—	713
12/10	3,417	(185)	—	696
Annual Growth	**(5.6%)**	**—**	**—**	**(7.5%)**

2014 Year-End Financials

Debt ratio: 3.68%
Return on equity: (-12.15%)
Cash ($ mil.): 548
Current ratio: —
Long-term debt ($ mil.): —
No. of shares (mil.): 18
Dividends
  Yield: —
  Payout: —
Market value ($ mil.): 361

	STOCK PRICE ($) FY Close	P/E High/Low	PER SHARE ($) Earnings	PER SHARE ($) Dividends	PER SHARE ($) Book Value
12/14	19.40	— —	(1.67)	0.00	13.18
12/13	3.52	— —	(0.57)	0.00	13.47
12/12	3.54	— —	(2.81)	0.00	14.51
12/11	2.42	— —	(4.19)	0.00	17.17
12/10	4.64	— —	(31.24)	0.00	25.37
Annual Growth	**43.0%**	**— —**	**—**		**—(15.1%)**

Sunoco Logistics Partners L.P.

Sunoco Logistics Partners Âacquires owns and operates a large swath of midstream and downstream assets primarily in tandem with former parent and current affiliate ÂSunoco. This includes ownership of more than 7900 miles of crude oilÂrefined product and oil gathering pipelines and minority interests in four refined product pipelines (Explorer Pipeline Wolverine Pipe Line West Shore Pipe Line and Yellowstone Pipe Line) as well asÂmore than 40 terminals and other storage assets related to Sunoco's refining and marketing operations in the Midwest Gulf Coast and Eastern states. Sunoco Logistics Partners also purchases domestic crude and resells it toÂSunoco's refining and marketing unit.

Operations

Sunoco Logistics Partners operates inÂindustry segments including crude oil acquisition and marketing refined products pipelines terminal facilities and crude oil pipeline. The company's refined products pipelines segmentÂconsists of 2500 miles of petroleum products pipeline and serves customers primarily in the Northeast and Midwest regions of the US. Through its terminal facilities unit Sunoco Logistics Partners is capable of storing 42 million barrels of refined products and crude oil. TheÂcrude oilÂpipeline segment consisting of about 4900 miles of crude oil pipelines primarily serves customers in Oklahoma and Texas. It also has 500 miles of crude oil gathering lines that supply the trunk pipelines.

The company gets the bulk of its revenues from crude oil acquisition and marketing activities.

Financial Analysis

Higher oil and refined product prices helped to liftÂSunoco Logistics Partners' revenue by 39% inÂ2011 thanks to an increase in revenues from terminal facilities (up 52%) crude oil pipelines (44%) and crude oil acquisition and marketing (40%) segments. Net income dropped by 7% inÂ2011 due to an increase in operating expenses other interest costs and debt expense.

Except for a revenue slump in 2009 (caused by the drop in demand for oil and oil products as a result of the global recession) Sunoco Logistics PartnersÂsaw an upward trend in revenues from 2007 to 2011.

Strategy

The company pursues a strategy of growing its businesses organically and through complementary acquisitions (more than 20Âsince 2002).ÂExpanding its pipeline assets in 2011 the company acquiredÂcontrol ofÂInland Corp. (which has a 350-mile refined-products pipeline and related facilities) for $100 million. It also acquired the Eagle Point tank farm and related assets in Westville New Jersey fromÂSunocoÂfor $100 million.

That year Sunoco LogisticsÂPartners acquired a crude oil acquisition and marketing business fromÂTexon. The purchase consists of a lease crude business and gathering assets in 16 states primarily in the western US. (It had acquired the butane blending business of Texon in 2010 for $140 million plus inventory).

Ownership

In 2012ÂSunocoÂ(which formed Sunoco Logistics Partners in 2002 to operate a major portion of its midstream and downstream assets) controlled about 34% of the company including a 2%Âgeneral partner interest.

EXECUTIVES

Vp, David (Dave) Chalson
Vice President Business Development, Hank Alexander
Senior Vice President General Counsel Secretary of Sunoco Partners LLC, Kathleen Shea-Ballay
Auditors: Grant Thornton LLP

LOCATIONS

HQ: Sunoco Logistics Partners L.P.
3807 West Chester Pike, Newtown Square, PA 19073
Phone: 866 248-4344
Web: www.sunocologistics.com

PRODUCTS/OPERATIONS

2011 Sales

	% of total
Crude oil acquisition & marketing	92
Terminal facilities	4
Crude oil pipelines	3
Refined product pipelines	1
Total	**100**

COMPETITORS

Buckeye Partners	Magellan Midstream
CITGO	Marathon Petroleum
Enbridge Energy	Plains All American
Enterprise Products	Pipeline
Kinder Morgan Energy	RKA Petroleum
Partners	TransMontaigne
Kinder Morgan	TransMontaigne
Management	Partners

HISTORICAL FINANCIALS

Company Type: Public

Income Statement

FYE: December 31

	REVENUE ($ mil.)	NET INCOME ($ mil.)	NET PROFIT MARGIN	EMPLOYEES
12/14	18,088	291	1.6%	2,250
12/13	16,639	463	2.8%	2,000
12/12*	3,194	139	4.4%	1,700
10/12	9,950	381	3.8%	—
12/11	10,918	313	2.9%	1,500
Annual Growth	18.3%	(2.4%)	—	14.5%

*Fiscal year change

2014 Year-End Financials

Debt ratio: 31.22%	No. of shares (mil.): 226
Return on equity: —	Dividends
Cash ($ mil.): 101	Yield: 3.4%
Current ratio: 1.02	Payout: 84.9%
Long-term debt ($ mil.): 4,260	Market value ($ mil.): 9,445

	STOCK PRICE ($) FY Close	P/E High/Low		PER SHARE ($) Earnings	Dividends	Book Value
12/14	41.78	184	73	0.51	1.43	29.54
12/13	75.48	46	30	1.63	2.35	29.87
12/12*	49.73	94	59	0.55	1.84	29.26
10/12	49.49	67	21	1.57	1.73	(0.00)
12/11	39.40	83	27	1.27	0.81	5.30
Annual Growth	2.0%	—	—	(26.2%)	21.0%	77.3%

*Fiscal year change

SunTrust Banks, Inc.

Coca-Cola fast cars and SunTrust Banks —this Sun Belt company is southern to its core. Its flagship SunTrust Bank subsidiary operates about 1450 branches in about a dozen southeastern and mid-Atlantic states. With total assets of about $190 billion and total deposits of about $140 billion the bank offers standard retail and commercial services such as credit deposit and investment services. SunTrust also operates subsidiaries that offer mortgage wealth and investment management in-

surance investment banking equipment leasing and brokerage services. The official bank of Grand American Road Racing it was an underwriter for the IPO of icon Coca-Cola and was one of its largest shareholders.

HISTORY

Company BackgroundSunTrust was born from the union of old-money Georgia and new-money Florida. Founded in 1891 the Trust Company of Georgia (originally Commercial Traveler's Savings Bank) served Atlanta's oldest and richest institutions. It helped underwrite Coca-Cola's IPO in 1919; the bank's ownership stake in Coke stemmed from its early involvement with the beverage maker.

Beginning in 1933 Trust acquired controlling interests in five other Georgia banks. As regulation of multibank ownership relaxed in the 1970s Trust acquired the remaining interests in its original banks and bought 25 more. At the height of the Sun Belt boom in 1984 Trust was the most profitable bank in the nation. The next year it united with Sun Banks.

Sun Banks was formed in 1934 as the First National Bank at Orlando. It grew into a holding company in 1967 and in the early 1970s helped assemble the land for Walt Disney World. The Sun name was adopted in 1973.

Under president and CEO Joel Wells Sun Banks began an acquisition-fueled expansion within Florida. Between 1976 and 1984 Sun Banks' approximate asset growth was an astronomical 500% and branch count grew fivefold (51 to 274).

After a lingering courtship Sun and Trust formed a super holding company over the two organizations. When the marriage was consummated in 1985 Sun brought a dowry of $9.4 billion in assets and Trust contributed $6.2 billion. Trust's chairman Bob Strickland became chairman and CEO for the new Atlanta-based SunTrust and Wells became president.

In 1986 SunTrust bought Nashville Tennessee-based Third National Bank the #2 banking company in the Volunteer State. But problems with Tennessee real estate loans plagued SunTrust. In 1990 it increased the amount of loans it wrote off; the bank's ratings suffered because of nonperforming loans on properties in overbuilt Florida. While nonperforming assets decreased in Tennessee in 1991 they climbed in Florida and Georgia.

Strickland stepped down as chairman and CEO in 1990. Wells died in 1991 and James Williams a conservative banker who instilled strict fiscal management in the Trust banks became chairman and CEO. Under his direction the company reduced its nonperforming assets and began diversifying its business lines.

In 1993 the bank adopted accounting rules that caused it to revalue its Coca-Cola stock from its historic value of $110000 to almost $1.1 billion. The dividends from these holdings contributed substantially to revenues.

SunTrust continued developing its nonbanking financial services: It expanded its investment services outside its traditional southern US market and bought Equitable Securities (now SunTrust Equitable Securities) in 1998. That year president Phillip Humann succeeded Williams as chairman and CEO. SunTrust also nearly doubled its branch count when it bought Crestar Financial a banking powerhouse in the mid-Atlantic and Southeast.

In 1999 the company created a new trust business to serve high-net-worth clients and it consolidated its 27 banking charters in six states into one based in Georgia the following year. In 2001 SunTrust made an unsolicited offer for Wachovia which was on track to be acquired by First Union.

After a heated proxy campaign Wachovia's board of directors and shareholders voted down SunTrust's bid. Also that year the company bought the institutional business of investment bank Robinson-Humphrey a unit of Citigroup's Salomon Smith Barney.

SunTrust bought National Commerce Financial in 2004 for some $7 billion. The deal helped the bank expand in existing territories as well as provide entry into the growing North Carolina market where SunTrust had been conspicuously absent. The company divested its 49% stake in First Market Bank (Ukrop's Super Markets owns the rest) which it acquired in the National Commerce deal. SunTrust unloaded the unit in part because it has branches in Kroger Publix Safeway and Wal-Mart stores.

The company placed on administrative leave or dismissed several financial officers after it had to restate its earnings for the first two quarters of 2004 due to miscalculations of its loan loss reserves. (The SEC concluded an investigation into the matter in 2006 without recommending penalties.)

Former president and COO Jim Wells became CEO in 2007; Humann remained as chairman but stepped down the following year.

SunTrust bought GB&T Bancshares in 2008 adding about 20 branches in north and central Georgia.

To raise money and streamline operations SunTrust spun off several noncore operations in 2008. Like many of its peers SunTrust took part in the Federal Reserve's bailout in 2008 selling the government about $4.9 billion in preferred shares. The company repaid the government in 2011. That helped contribute to better earnings that year. SunTrust also reported higher net interest income and lower provision for credit losses.

The nationwide economic crisis impacted many of SunTrust's core markets in the Southeast particularly hard as credit markets froze and unemployment levels increased. The bank suffered some $1.6 billion in losses in 2009 alone mainly related to bad loans both on the consumer and commercial levels. By 2010 the company began to see improvements in charge-offs delinquencies and nonperforming loans but loan demand remained soft. In 2011 Sun Trust's financial performance improved and its loan portfolio grew by 6%. However the economic recovery was slow and spotty interest rates remained low and new federal regulations hit SunTrust's fee revenue streams.

EXECUTIVES

EVP and Chief Human Resources Officer, Kenneth J. (Ken) Carrig, age 58
Corporate EVP General Counsel and Corporate Secretary, Raymond D. Fortin, age 62
Chief Risk Officer, Jerome T. Lienhard, age 58
Chairman and CEO, William H. (Bill) Rogers, age 57, $925,000 total compensation
EVP and Wholesale Banking Executive, Mark A. Chancy, age 51, $625,000 total compensation
EVP and CFO, Aleem Gillani, age 52, $600,000 total compensation
Leader Consumer and Private Wealth Management Segment, Thomas E. (Tom) Freeman, age 64, $600,000 total compensation
Commercial and Business Banking Executive, Hugh S. (Beau) Cummins
President Virginia Division, John G. Stallings
EVP and Consumer Channels Sales and Service Executive, Rilla S. Delorier, age 48
President Carolinas Division, David Stevens
Leader Consumer Banking, Bradford R. (Brad) Dinsmore, age 52
EVP and CIO, Anil Cheriyan, age 57, $500,000 total compensation

President Winston-Salem Market, Hugh Roberts
EVP and Chief Marketing Officer, Susan S. Johnson
Co-Head of SunTrust Private Wealth
  Management, Allison Dukes
President Central Virginia, Phillip Avant
President Shenandoah Valley, Mary (Mac) Maclin
  Weems
President Charlotte Region, Jenna Kelly
Vice President, Michael Maguire
Vice President, Andy Tullis
Vice President Marine and Rv Finance, Michael
  (Mel) Zenker
Senior Vice President, Mark Flynn
Group Vice President, Karen Kinsey
Vice President Consumer Deposit Pricing Analyst,
  Brian Raack
Senior Vice President Human Resources, Stephen
  Glidden
Vice President, Dan Nichols
Assistant Vice President Customer Care Manager,
  Michelle Mathews
First Vice President, Greg Greer
Vice President Real Estate Valuation Services,
  Gary Craig
Vice President Portfolio Manager, Felicia Davis
Group Vice President Treasury Management
  Services, Janet Stingo
Vice President CRE Risk Officer Professional
  Development, Robin Dyer
Vice President, Jennifer (Jen) Sexton
Vice President, Carolyn Desislets
Vice President, Josh Pruitt
Senior Vice President, Charity Volman
Senior Vice President Commercial Banking,
  Reuben Clarson
Cl Credit Risk Management Vice President, Yue
  Lai
Assistant Vice President Commercial Special
  Assets, Keith Sturmer
Senior Vice President, Brian Lewis
Senior Vice President Commercial Real Estate,
  Anthony Fink
Senior Vice President Operational Risk
  Management, Beatriz Pagan
Vice President, Dave Hevner
Vice President, Richard Qka
Vice President, Gregory Downes
Vice President Wholesale Marketing Manager,
  Melanie Mitchell
Vice President marketing Information Analyst,
  Baker Belle
Vice President Corres Account Executive, Charles
  C (Chas) Dugger
Senior Vice President, Richard Appel
First Vice President, Robert (Bob) Mayo
Vice President Manager Risk, Steve Shaffer
Vice President Infrastructure Planning and
  Delivery Services Coordinator, David (Dave) Sims
Vice President Administration, David Crow
Vice President The Help Line Manager, Maureen
  Kelley
Vice President Information Technology
  Infrastructure, Richard Willman
Vice President Retirement Services, Brent Breedon
Vice President Risk Review, Kathy Gearing
First Vice President, Mona Parsons
Manager Assistant Vice President, Dev Bhandary
Vice President Real Estate, Mark Fryer
Vice President Information Technology, Nancy
  Kearney
Assistant Vice President Financial Services
  Representative, Babs Fedder
First Vice President, Joe Cosby
Vice President, Laura McNerney
First Vice President, Frank Anderson
Vice President and Branch Manager, Susan (Sue)
  Gist
Vice President, Craig Jackson
First Vice President, Edana Hough
Assistant Vice President Finance, Karen Helms

Vice President of Operation, Denise Principe
Vice President Marketing Analytics, Brian Peterson
Senior Vice President, Jill Wilkinson
First Vice President Market Research, Jason
  Archambault
Assistant Vice President Systems Management
  and Support, Mark Hallock
Assistant Vice President, William (Bill) Thomas
Vice President Of Sponsorship Marketing,
  Roderick Douthit
Assistant Vice President, Nadia Mahmoud
Developer Assistant Vice President, Susan (Sue)
  Darling
Vice President Client Advisot, Teresita Flores
Vice President, Jose Lopezisa
Vice President Client Advisor, Chris Pantano
Senior Vice President Credit Risk Management
  Executive, Hugh Kimbrough Hugh Kimbrough
Vice President Derivative And Calypso
  Information Technology, Daniel Mazeall
First Vice President Merchant Services, Oscar
  Nunez
Vice President Of Applications Development,
  Sanford Matthews
Vice President Finance Systems Operations, Gladu
  Andrew
Vice President Corporate Strategies, Jay Poole
First Vice President Risk Management Officer,
  Luke Maslow
Vice President Eis Workstream Manager, Josh
  Takis
First Vice President OREO Group, Christyne
  Albury
First Vice President, Paul Neal
Group Vice President Risk Management and Data
  Management, Stephanie Withers
Group Vice President Enterprise Execution
  Services, Ron Thomas
Vice President Operations, Tarra Sullivan
First Vice President Consumer Card Product
  Manager, David (Dave) Stroud
Vice President, Lory Liberty
First Vice President And Senior Counsel, Adam
  Humphreys
Assistant Vice President Corporate Security,
  Debbie Liguori
Vice+President, Amy Humphries
Senior Vice President Head Of Deposits And
  Payments, Shannon Johnson
Social Media Engagement Manager Assistant Vice
  President, Adelma Stanford
Assistant Vice President, Karen Davis
Vice President Commercial Relationship Manager,
  Evan Kaplan
Senior Vice President Institutional Real Estate,
  Ward Ebbert
Vice President, Diane Jorgensen
FVP and Senior Counsel, Susan (Sue) Craft
Vice President, Laura Fedor
Vice President Branch Manager, Marilyn Lavecchia
Senior Vice President Group Portfolio Manager,
  Deborah (Deb) Armstrong
Group Vice President, Bob Grosch
Group Vice President Stoli Integration Manager,
  Janet Solomon
Senior Vice President And Geography
  Relationship Manager Orlando WLS, Joe Borowski
Assistant Vice President, Rosana Liriano
Assistant Vice President, Jennifer (Jen) Fessia
GVP, Celia Mackenzie
Assistant Vice President, John Logan
Vice President And Branch Manager, Aileen Payne
First Vice President And Senior Counsel, Kimberly
  Pierro
Group Vice President, Ron Bier
Assistant Vice President, Joshua McCann
Group Vice President Deposit Profitability And
  Analytics Manager, Gina Farrell
Senior Vice President Corporate Compliance
  Manager, Nishant Desai

Assistant Vice President, David Massey
Vice President Diversified Commercial Division,
  Peter (Pete) Lee
Business Relationship Manager Vice President,
  Cassandra Naville
Vice President Commercial Relationship Manager,
  Sarah Daley
First Vice President, Julie Hwang
Vice President, Sharon Schiffer
Vice President At Suntrust Bank, Deborah Carter
Assistant Vice President, Kevin Seay
Vice President, Todd Dees
First Vice President, Jasmine Grant
Vice President, Barry Painter
Assistant Vice President Syndicated Deal
  Administrator, Tania Brown
Assistant Vice President Talent Acquisition, Doug
  Ledford
Senior Vice President, Mary Dearie-ruhlin
Assistant Vice President, Monique Lapierre
Vice President, Kevin Hart
Vice President Relationship Manager, Nicolas Peaa
Vice President Client Care Department Manager,
  Lavada Richards
Vice President, Donna Rinier
Vice President And Branch Manager, Elizabeth
  (Beth) Alfonso
Vice President Branch Manager Mirasol Office,
  Sharon Mollenhauer
Svp Auditing, David (Dave) Bilko
First Vice President Private Wealth Management
  Client Advisor Legal Specialty Group, David
  (Dave) Simmons
Senior Vice President SunTrust Insurance Group,
  David (Dave) McLaughlin
Vice President Client Advisor, Earle Simmons
Assistant Vice President Relationship Manager
  Commercial Banking, Hilliary Jones
Vice President Branch Manager 4, Deborah Hillman
Vice President, Michael (Mel) Dunleavey
Auditors: Ernst & Young LLP

LOCATIONS

HQ: SunTrust Banks, Inc.
  303 Peachtree Street, N.E., Atlanta, GA 30308
Phone: 800 786-8787
Web: www.suntrust.com

PRODUCTS/OPERATIONS

Selected Services
Auto & Home Insurance
Mobile Banking
Money Services
Online Banking
Personal Checking
Personal Credit Cards
Savings Mo

2014 Sales

	$ mil.	% of total
Interest income		
Interest and fees on loans	4,695	54
Interest and dividend on securities	613	7
Trading account interest and others	76	1
Non interest income		
Service charges on deposit accounts	645	8
Trust and investment management income	423	5
Investment banking income	404	5
Other charges and fees	368	4
Card fees	320	4
Retail investment services	297	3
Mortgage production related income	201	2
Trading income	182	2
Others	498	5
Adjustments	(15)	-
Total	**8,707**	**100**

COMPETITORS

BB&T	First Citizens
BBVA Compass	BancShares

Bancshares	First Horizon
BBX Capital	JPMorgan Chase
BancorpSouth	Regions Financial
Bank of America	Synovus
Citigroup	Wells Fargo

HISTORICAL FINANCIALS

Company Type: Public

Income Statement

FYE: December 31

	ASSETS ($ mil.)	NET INCOME ($ mil.)	INCOME AS % OF ASSETS	EMPLOYEES
12/14	190,328	1,774	0.9%	24,638
12/13	175,335	1,344	0.8%	26,281
12/12	173,442	1,958	1.1%	26,778
12/11	176,859	647	0.4%	29,182
12/10	172,874	189	0.1%	29,056
Annual Growth	2.4%	75.0%	—	(4.0%)

2014 Year-End Financials

Debt ratio: 7.51%
Return on equity: 7.99%
Cash ($ mil.): 7,069
Current ratio: —
Long-term debt ($ mil.): —

No. of shares (mil.): 524
Dividends
  Yield: 1.6%
  Payout: 21.3%
Market value ($ mil.): 21,978

	STOCK PRICE ($) FY Close	P/E High/Low	PER SHARE ($) Earnings	Dividends	Book Value
12/14	41.90	13 11	3.23	0.70	43.86
12/13	36.81	15 11	2.41	0.35	39.96
12/12	28.35	8 5	3.59	0.20	38.94
12/11	17.70	35 17	0.94	0.12	37.37
12/10	29.51	— —	(0.18)	0.04	46.22
Annual Growth	9.2%	— —	—	104.5%	(1.3%)

Supervalu Inc.

SUPERVALU understands the lure of a good deal. The company offers wholesale grocery distribution and logistics services to more than 2000 independent retailers and about 185 military commissaries in the US and overseas. It supplies brand-name and private-label goods in every price range. It also has more than 1330 owned and licensed Save-A-Lot grocery stores which hold the #1 spot (by revenue) in the extreme-value grocery category. SUPERVALU's retail operations include nearly 200 regional grocery stores under the Cub Foods Shoppers Food & Pharmacy Shop 'n Save Farm Fresh Hornbachers and Rainbow banners. All told the company covers about 40 states through nearly 20 distribution centers.

Operations

The company reports its operations as independent business retail food and Save-A-Lot. The largest segment accounting for 46% of revenue is the independent business group or the distribution and logistics operations. It serves more than 2000 retail customers in 41 states from 17 distribution centers. SUPERVALU's wholesale customers include conventional and upscale supermarkets combination food and drugstores supercenters convenience stores limited assortment stores and e-tailers. SUPERVALU offers its retailers private labels in every price range and in virtually every store category from the value-priced Shoppers Value brand to the premium Preferred Selection and organic Wild Harvest lines. SUPERVALU also offers retailers support services such as store design and construction.

Retail food or all the regional grocery stores includes nearly 200 stores and contributes about 27% of revenue. Save-A-Lot's 1330+ stores in nearly 40 states make up the rest.

Geographic Reach

SUPERVALU's headquarters is in Minnesota most Save-A-Lot stores are in the eastern and southeastern US and its distribution business serves most of the nation and military commissaries in the US Puerto Rico Spain Cuba Guam Korea and Japan.

Financial Performance

After the company overspent for underperforming assets sold them off and then reorganized revenue dropped drastically in 2013. But it has held steady since then and even gained 4% in fiscal 2015 (ended February) to finish at $17.82 billion due to new distribution accounts and higher sales in its other two divisions.

Net income has been up and down the last few years for SUPERVALU growing significantly in 2014 and then leveling off in 2015 to $192 million due to higher revenue and lower debt.

Strategy

SUPERVALU is putting its money behind its successful Save-A-Lot format by expanding the extreme-value chain's reach through new store development and growth of its licensee network. Also in 2014 the company streamlined its wholesale organization by consolidating three regions into two forming new East and West teams located in Virginia and Minnesota respectively.

Mergers and Acquisitions

After a year of divestments in 2013 SUPERVALU returned to acquisition mode in May 2014 with the purchase of 18 Rainbow Foods stores in the Twin Cities (Minnesota) area from rival Roundy's. SUPERVALU which was part of a consortium acquiring the stores will convert about 10 of them to its Cub Foods format.

HISTORY

SUPERVALU's predecessor was formed in Minneapolis in the 1870s –and again in 1926. In 1871 wholesalers Hugh Harrison George Newell and W. D. Washburn joined forces to create Newell and Harrison. Newell bought out his partners in 1874 and renamed the firm George R. Newell Co. Five years later Harrison formed his own operation H. G. Harrison Co. In 1926 the companies merged creating Winston & Newell Co. the largest grocery distributor to independent grocers in the Midwest.

The company was part of the Independent Grocers Alliance from 1928-1942 before adopting the name Super Valu Stores in 1954. It expanded by acquiring chains such as Piggly-Wiggly Midland (1958 Wisconsin) and a number of wholesale operations across the US.

Super Valu entered nonfood retailing in 1971 by acquiring ShopKo a discount department store chain. Two years later it founded clothing chain County Seat (sold 1983). Super Valu added a new format to its food operations by purchasing Cub Stores (warehouse-style groceries) in 1980; it later combined its Cub Stores and ShopKo formats. More acquisitions followed including Atlanta's Food Giant chain. Super Valu named Michael Wright CEO in 1981 and chairman in 1982.

Super Valu acquired Scott's an Indiana food store chain in 1991 and sold a 54% interest in ShopKo to the public. The company changed its name to SUPERVALU in 1992 and bought food wholesaler Wetterau making it the #1 independent food distributor in the US and giving it the Save-A-Lot franchise (launched in 1978).

Experiencing sluggish distribution growth SUPERVALU continued to expand its retail holdings. Acquisitions in 1994 included Sweet Life Foods (280 stores) and 30 Texas T Stores. In 1996 it ac-

quired six St. Louis Price Chopper warehouse stores and Fleming's Sav-U-Foods converting the 21 stores to Save-A-Lots and establishing a presence in California. SUPERVALU sold its remaining 46% stake in ShopKo the next year. In 1999 the company signed a deal to supply 1350 Kmart stores. SUPERVALU also acquired distributor and food retailer Richfood Holdings.

The company completed its acquisition of 1124 stores from Albertsons in June 2006. The new stores included Acme Markets Bristol Farms Jewel Shaw's Supermarkets Star Markets and Albertsons stores. Looking to take back sales lost to natural and organic grocery chains SUPERVALU launched its own natural foods division called Sunflower Market in 2006. (SUPERVALU originally had planned to open as many as 50 Sunflower Markets but in early 2008 announced it would close its five Sunflower Markets as they did not deliver expected results.)

Throughout 2009 as recession gripped the country SUPERVALU closed or sold more than 100 stores nationwide including about 40 Albertsons stores in Utah to grocery wholesaler Associated Food Stores. The closings were part of an effort by the company to scale back spending.

In 2010 SUPERVALU made several divestments. Early in the year it sold off its Payson Store Fixtures division which made fixtures millwork and decor items to DGS Retail. It sold its Bristol Farms chain of more than a dozen upscale supermarkets in California to local management and the West Coast investment firm Endeavour Capital for an undisclosed amount in October.

In September 2011 the company sold more than 100 fuel centers associated with its Albertsons Cub Foods Hornbacher's and Jewel-Osco banners to four different buyers. The sale was part of SUPERVALU's effort to raise cash by selling non-core assets.

In 2013 the company completed the sale of five retail banners — Albertsons Jewel Acme and Shaw's/Star Market –to an affiliate of a Cerberus Capital Management-led investor consortium for $3.3 billion.

EXECUTIVES

CEO, Mark Gross, age 51
EVP and COO, Bruce H. Besanko, age 57, $687,981 total compensation
EVP and CIO, Randy G. Burdick, age 57, $550,385 total compensation
CEO Save-A-Lot, Eric Claus, age 58
EVP Independent Business and Supply Chain, Mike Stigers
President Save-A-Lot, Ritchie Casteel, age 65, $458,654 total compensation
EVP Human Resources and Corporate Communications, Michele A. Murphy, age 61, $417,308 total compensation
EVP General Counsel and Corporate Secretary, Karla C. Robertson, age 44
EVP Merchandising Marketing and Retail, Mark Van Buskirk, age 57
EVP and Chief Strategy Officer, Rob Woseth, age 44
EVP and CFO, Susan Grafton
Executive Vice President, Michael (Mel) Moore
Vice President Finance, Carl McLean
Vice President Marketing Systems Retail Systems and Retail Field, Rick Collison
Pharmacy Manager, Jeff Ward
Vice President Finance, Tom Kujak
Vice President Logistics, Micheal Lech
Vice President corporate Compensation, Shannon Anglin
Vice President Center Store West Division, Donna Banks-Ficcio
Group Vice President Technology, Mark Bates

Vice President General Merchandise And Health And Beauty Care Merchandising, Tom Yeager
Senior Vice President Food Merchandising, Steve Fox
Vice President Dinner Solutions, Justin Time
Chairman, Gerald L. Storch, age 58
Auditors: KPMG LLP

LOCATIONS

HQ: Supervalu Inc.
11840 Valley View Road, Eden Prairie, MN 55344
Phone: 952 828-4000
Web: www.supervalu.com

PRODUCTS/OPERATIONS

2014 Sales

	% of total
Independent business	46
Retail food	27
Save-A-Lot	26
Corporate	1
Total	**100**

2014 Stores

	No.
Save-A-Lot	1,334
Regional grocery	194
Total	**1,528**

Selected Banners

Cub
Farm Fresh
Hornbacher's
Save-A-Lot (discount retail)
Shop ' N Save
Shoppers

Selected Services

Accounting
Category management
Consumer and market research
Financial assistance
Insurance
Merchandising assistance
Personnel training
Private-label program
Retail operations counseling
Site selection and purchasing or leasing assistance
Store design and construction
Store equipment
Store management assistance
Store planning
Strategic and business planning

Selected Private-Label Brands

Culinary Circle
essensia
equaline
Flavorite
HomeLife
Richfood
Shopper's Value
Wild Harvest

COMPETITORS

A&P	Krasdale Foods
ALDI	Kroger
Ahold U.S.A.	Marsh Supermarkets
Alex Lee	McLane
Arden Group	Meijer
Associated Wholesale Grocers	Piggly Wiggly Midwest
BJ's Wholesale Club	Rite Aid
Big Y Foods	Roundy's
Bozzuto's	Safeway
C&S Wholesale	Schnuck Markets
CVS	Sherwood Food
Costco Wholesale	SpartanNash
Delhaize America	Stater Bros.
Dierbergs Markets	Stop & Shop
Dollar General	Target Corporation
Dollar Tree	Wakefern Food
Family Dollar Stores	Wal-Mart
	Walgreen

Giant Eagle
Hannaford Bros.
Jetro Cash & Carry
Whole Foods
Winn-Dixie

HISTORICAL FINANCIALS

Company Type: Public

Income Statement

FYE: February 28

	REVENUE ($ mil.)	NET INCOME ($ mil.)	NET PROFIT MARGIN	EMPLOYEES
02/15	17,820	192	1.1%	38,500
02/14	17,155	182	1.1%	35,800
02/13	17,097	(1,466)	—	35,000
02/12	36,100	(1,040)	—	130,000
02/11	37,534	(1,510)	—	142,000
Annual Growth	**(17.0%)**	—	—	**(27.8%)**

2015 Year-End Financials

Debt ratio: 60.82%
Return on equity: —
Cash ($ mil.): 114
Current ratio: 1.11
Long-term debt ($ mil.): 2,693

No. of shares (mil.): 260
Dividends
  Yield: —
  Payout: —
Market value ($ mil.): 2,569

	STOCK PRICE ($) FY Close	P/E High/Low		PER SHARE ($) Earnings	Dividends	Book Value
02/15	9.88	14	9	0.73	0.00	(2.48)
02/14	6.10	12	5	0.70	0.00	(2.88)
02/13	3.85	—	—	(6.91)	0.18	(19.86)
02/12	6.65	—	—	(4.91)	0.26	(27.58)
02/11	8.55	—	—	(7.13)	0.35	(23.62)
Annual Growth	**3.7%**	—	—	—	—	—

SVB Financial Group

SVB Financial Group is the holding company for Silicon Valley Bank which serves emerging and established companies involved in technology life sciences and private equity and provides customized financing to entrepreneurs executives and investors in such industries. It also offers deposit accounts loans and international banking and plays matchmaker for young firms and private investors. SVB Financial also provides investment advisory brokerage and asset management services; and provides credit and banking services to wealthy individuals.

Operations

The company operates in three segments: Global Commercial Bank SVB Private Bank and SVB Capital.

Global Commercial Bank segment is comprised of Commercial Bank SVB Specialty Lending SVB Analytics and Debt Fund Investments. Commercial Bank serves commercial clients in the technology venture capital/private equity life science and cleantech industries. SVB Analytics provides equity valuation services to private companies and venture capital/private equity firms while Debt Fund Investments has investments in debt funds.

SVB Private Bank provides personal financial solutions for consumers while its capital arm SVB Capital focuses primarily on funds management.As part of its lending activities Silicon Valley Bank sometimes pursues warrants to purchase equity stakes in its clients. About 80% of the bank's loan portfolio is dedicated to commercial loans with about half of those going to software and internet companies and another 25% of commercial loans going toward private equity or venture capital

firms. Traditionally focused on up-and-coming firms the bank has implemented a strategy of courting larger later-stage clients.

Geographic Reach

SVB Financial has 28 offices in the US as well as seven branches in China India Israel and the UK.

Sales and Marketing

SVB Financial's clients are primarily venture capital and private equity professionals. Its customers include Active Power Coskata EnerNOC Joule and Solexant.

Financial Performance

SVB's revenue grew for its fifth straight year with revenue rising by 4% to $1.46 billion in 2014. Though nearly all income streams grew the main drivers of growth came from higher interest income from investment securities and loans as average deposit and loan balances grew respectively. A 130% boost in net gains on derivative instruments also contributed significantly to the company's top line.Despite higher revenue net income reversed course in 2014 and fell by 12% to $478.72 million. The drop was mostly because SVB paid higher compensation and benefits as it gave its employees market-adjusted raises and hired 146 new staff members to support its product development operational sales advisory and commercial banking operations and initiatives. Operations provided $255.52 million or 33% more cash than in 2013 mostly because more of its earnings were cash payments as opposed to 2013 when non-cash gains on investment securities made up a larger share of earnings. The company also enjoyed higher cash generation from foreign exchange spot contracts.

Strategy

SVB Financial Group has been focused on growing its loan business and assets to drive growth in recent years. Indeed in 2014 the company's loan assets grew by 32% to $14.4 billion while deposits grew 52% to $34.3 billion —both factors that led the company to record-high revenue by the end of the year.It's also been selectively expanding and divesting its overseas operations to focus resources on profitable segments. In early 2015 subsidiary SVB Bank agreed to sell all of its outstanding stock in its non-banking financial subsidiary SVP India Finance Private Limited to Singapore-based investment firm Temasek. In 2012 the company opened a banking branch in the UK and started a joint venture bank in China.

Company Background

Greg Becker who joined SVB Financial in 1993 was named the company's CEO in 2011. He succeeded Ken Wilcox who became chairman and is focused on the company's efforts to expand in China including a joint venture with Shanghai Pudong Development Bank.

HISTORY

Silicon Valley Bank was founded in 1983 by Roger Smith to provide banking services to tech startups in San Jose. The bank boomed along with tech companies during the 1980s lending to the likes of Cisco Systems.

In 1990 the bank spread east to Boston's burgeoning technology alley. It also expanded into residential and commercial real estate lending. The recession of 1989 to 1991 found Silicon Valley Bancshares with an overextended loan portfolio and in 1992 the bank booked a loss due to nonperforming loans; the next year it was put under federal supervision.

To rally stockholder confidence the company brought in new management and demoted Smith from chairman to vice chairman; he left the in 1995. The bank reduced its real estate lending and diversified into factoring foreign exchange and executive banking for venture capitalists and clients' upper management.

The 1995 IPO frenzy aided the company's turnaround. Silicon Valley cashed in on warrants it had taken as collateral from young companies. Regulatory supervision was lifted in 1996 and the bank soon opened offices in the Atlanta; Austin Texas; Boulder Colorado; Phoenix; and Seattle areas.

In 1999 Silicon Valley Bancshares created a website targeted at technology firms in need of financing employees office space and equipment. However nonperforming loans began to dog the bank once again affecting profits and bringing a regulatory request to boost capital reserves.

In 2000 despite being hammered by the high-tech stock selloff the company continued to expand opening offices in West Palm Beach Florida and North Carolina's Research Triangle and successfully capitalizing its first venture fund. The following year it bought tech-focused investment bank Alliant Partners (later renamed SVB Alliant) to broaden its service offerings.

Still licking its wounds from the tech bust the company ceased lending to the entertainment industry and to churches in 2002. Silicon Valley Bancshares changed its name to SVB Financial Services in 2005.

SVB Alliant struggled with losses for years and SVB Financial explored its options including spinning the unit off to management. It ultimately decided to shut down the division which ceased operations in 2008.

EXECUTIVES

Chief Strategy and Risk Officer, Marc J. Verissimo, age 60, $310,679 total compensation
President Asia, David A. Jones, age 57, $431,447 total compensation
COO and Principal Operating Officer, Bruce Wallace, $398,113 total compensation
President and CEO Silicon Valley Bank, Gregory W. (Greg) Becker, age 48, $835,613 total compensation
Head U.S. Banking, Joan Parsons, $399,780 total compensation
CFO, Michael (Mike) Descheneaux, age 48, $499,780 total compensation
Head Relationship Management, John D. China, $373,113 total compensation
Head EMEA and India; President UK Branch, Phil Cox
Chief Credit Officer Silicon Valley Bank, Marc Cadieux
CIO, Beth Devin
Vice President, Arman Zand
Vice President, Steven (Steve) Reel
Vice President, Jenny Moody
Senior Vice President, Dave Bhagat
Vice President, Christopher Leary
Vice President Relationship Manager, Anthony Raley
Vice President, Suzann Russell
Vice President Relationship Manager Corporate Technology, Phil Silvia
Vice President, Joe Werner
Vice President, Damarie Rodriguez
Vice President Of Information Technology, Derrick Ponugoti
Vice President Relationship Manager, Bret Turner
Vice President and Foreign Exchange Trader, Patrick (Paddy) Chin
Vice President, Lauren Cole
Vice President, Michael Kalicak
Vice President Private Equity Services, Amy Choi
Senior Vice President Sales Origination, Mark Gallagher
Vice President With the Private Bank, Michael (Mel) Conway

Vice President, Julian Nash
Vice President, Tim Barnes
Vice President Product Management, Susan (Sue) Merrill
Senior Vice President, Jim Hori
Senior Vice President, Laura Scott
Vice President Marketing, Jane Lodato
Vice President Founders Bank, Jigar Patel
Vice President of Global Sales, Michael (Mel) Quinn
Vice President, Jimmy Gan
Assistant Vice President letter Of Credit Consultant senior, John (Jack) Dossantos
Senior Vice President, Andy Tsao
Senior Vice President, Dale Kirkland
Vice President Operations, Julie Robertson
Vice President Relationship Manager, John Peck
Vice President, Benjermin Colombo
Vice President, Patrick Scheper
Assistant Vice President, Brian Harrison
Senior Vice President, Michael Tramack
Vice President Service Management, Roger Leon
Vice President, Carolyn Grant
Senior Vice President Senior Loan Workout Advisor, Brian Bell
Vice President, Josh Dorsey
Vice President, Dino Pillinini
Vice President Corporate Finance, Raj Morey
Senior Vice President and Senior Relationship Manager, Dan Aguilar
Vice President, Reisa Babic
Vice President, Alex Barry
Vice President Finance, Russell (Russ) Follansbee
Chairman, Roger F. Dunbar, age 69
Board Member, Eric A Benhamou
Board Member, Joel P Friedman, age 68
Board Member, Kate Mitchell, age 58
Board Of Directors, Eric Benhamou
Board Member, C Kramlich
Vice Chairman of the Board of the Bank Head Relationship Management, Harry Kellogg
Auditors: KPMG LLP

LOCATIONS

HQ: SVB Financial Group
3003 Tasman Drive, Santa Clara, CA 95054-1191
Phone: 408 654-7400
Web: www.svb.com

Selected Offices
US
Atlanta
Austin TX
Broomfield CO
Chicago
Dallas
Irvine CA
Menlo Park CA
Minnetonka MN
New York
Newton MA
Palo Alto CA
Philadelphia
Phoenix
Pleasanton CA
Portland OR
Raleigh NC
Salt Lake City
San Diego
San Francisco
Santa Rosa CA
Seattle
St. Helena CA
Tysons Corner VA
International
Bangalore India
Beijing
Herzliya Pituach Israel
London
Mumbai India
Shanghai

PRODUCTS/OPERATIONS

2014 Sales

	$ mil.	% of total
Interest		
Loans	610	42
Investment securities	274	19
Other	6	-
Noninterest		
Net gains on investment securities	267	17
Net gains on derivative instruments	96	7
Foreign exchange fees	71	5
Credit card fees	41	3
Deposit service charges	39	3
Lending related fees	25	2
Letters of credit	15	1
Client investment fees	14	1
Other	(1.3)	-
Total	**1,464**	**100**

Selected Subsidiaries and Affiliates
Silicon Valley Bank
SVB Analytics Inc.
SVB Asset Management
SVB Business Partners (Beijing) Co. Ltd.
SVB Business Partners (Shanghai) Co. Ltd.
SVB Global Financial Inc.
SVB Global Investors LLC
SVB Growth Investors LLC
SVB India Advisors Pvt. Ltd.
SVB Israel Advisors Ltd.
SVB Qualified Investors Fund LLC
SVB Real Estate Investment Trust
SVB Securities
SVB Strategic Investors LLC
SVB Strategic Investors Fund L.P.
Venture Investment Managers L.P.

COMPETITORS

BancWest	Comerica
Bank of America	Heritage Commerce
Citigroup	MUFG Americas Holdings
City National	U.S. Bancorp

HISTORICAL FINANCIALS
Company Type: Public

Income Statement
FYE: December 31

	ASSETS ($ mil.)	NET INCOME ($ mil.)	INCOME AS % OF ASSETS	EMPLOYEES
12/14	39,344	478	1.2%	1,914
12/13	26,417	546	2.1%	1,704
12/12	22,766	175	0.8%	1,615
12/11	19,968	171	0.9%	1,526
12/10	17,527	94	0.5%	1,357
Annual Growth	22.4%	49.8%	—	9.0%

2014 Year-End Financials
Debt ratio: 1.15%
Return on equity: 20.01%
Cash ($ mil.): 1,700
Current ratio: —
Long-term debt ($ mil.): —
No. of shares (mil.): 50
Dividends
  Yield: —
  Payout: —
Market value ($ mil.): 5,911

	STOCK PRICE ($) FY Close	P/E High/Low	PER SHARE ($) Earnings	Dividends	Book Value
12/14	116.07	25 18	5.31	0.00	55.33
12/13	104.86	22 12	4.70	0.00	42.93
12/12	55.97	17 12	3.91	0.00	41.02
12/11	47.69	16 9	3.94	0.00	36.07
12/10	53.05	24 16	2.24	0.00	30.15
Annual Growth	21.6%	— —	24.1%	—	16.4%

Symantec Corp.

Digital security isn't just a matter of semantics for Symantec. The company provides security storage and systems management software for businesses and consumers. Symantec's applications handle such functions as virus protection PC maintenance data backup and recovery intrusion detection data loss prevention spam control content filtering and remote server management. The company also provides managed services and training. Symantec is probably best known for its popular Norton consumer security software which the company markets to PC users worldwide. But with declining revenue the company agreed to sell its data storage business Veritas for $8 billion. This deal forestalls a move to break off Veritas into an independent public company. With the sale Symantec will focus on its security products.

Operations
Symantec's information management segment is its biggest business accounting for 39% of the company's revenue for 2015 (ended March). The segment provides backup and recovery archiving and eDiscovery and data storage.

Enterprise security brings in 32% of revenue. Its products are Secure Socket Layer (SSL) Certificates authentication mail and web security data center security data loss prevention information security services endpoint security and management encryption and mobile security software. The consumer security segment mainly Norton security software accounts for 29% of revenue.

Geographic Reach
The company's corporate headquarters are in Mountain View California. Symantec has operations in more than 50 countries throughout the Americas Europe the Middle East Africa Asia Pacific/Japan and Latin America. About 45% of sales come from outside the Americas.

Sales and Marketing
Symantec sells its products through a direct sales force as well as through distributors resellers/e-commerce computer manufacturers and systems integrators.

Financial Performance
For the second straight year Symantec experienced a dip in sales in 2015 (year-end March) to $6.5 billion from $6.67 billion in 2014. The consumer segment's sales were off 9% and enterprise security sales dropped 2%. Information management posted a 2% revenue gain for the year. The company's profit was off 2% dropping to $878 million in 2015. Cash flow from operations rose to $1.31 billion in 2015 from $1.38 billion in 2014.

Strategy
Symantec was ready to split its data storage unit into a business but in the end decided to sell it. In the deal expected to close in early 2016 the Carlyle Group will pay $8 billion for the Veritas unit. Minus expenses and a $1.5 billion stock buyback Symantec will have a good deal of cash to invest in its security business.

In 2015 Symantec streamlined its consumer security line by streamlining its products into a single Norton Security offering. Symantec also deepened its enterprise security offerings with a managed advanced threat protection service and a managed incident response service.

Mergers and Acquisitions
One thing the company didn't do in 2015 was make a significant acquisition.

Previously in 2014 it bought NitroDesk which makes a third-party email app TouchDown that allows businesses to set email security policies like authentication encryption and copy/paste restrictions.

HISTORY

Early History
Artificial intelligence expert Gary Hendrix founded Symantec in 1982. Gordon Eubanks a former student of the late industry pioneer Gary Kildall and founder of C&E Software was appointed CEO in 1983 and bought the company in 1984. Realizing that Symantec could not compete against Microsoft and Lotus Eubanks began buying niche-market software firms. In 1990 a year after going public Symantec merged with DOS utilities market leader Peter Norton Computing. It bought 13 companies between 1990 and 1994.

Symantec bought Delrina (maker of WinFax) in 1995 and then slowed its acquisition pace and concentrated on the growing Internet market. In 1996 it sold Delrina's electronic forms business to JetForm.

Symantec filed copyright-infringement charges against Network Associates (now McAfee) in 1997. The next year a suit was filed against Symantec on behalf of antivirus product users alleging that it ignored its warranty by charging to fix a year-2000 software glitch.

The company went on another acquisition binge buying the antivirus operations of both IBM and Intel in 1998 and acquiring rival Quarterdeck in 1999. When Eubanks left that year to head an enterprise software startup IBM exec John Thompson stepped in and became the first African-American CEO of a major software company.

In 2000 Symantec sold its Internet tools division to BEA Systems in a deal valued at about $75 million. It also acquired L-3 Communications' network security operations. Late that year it bought rival network security software maker AXENT Technologies in a $975 million deal.

EXECUTIVES

EVP and General Manager Information Management Business, John B. Gannon, age 68
President and CEO, Michael A. Brown, age 56, $36,364 total compensation
EVP and CFO, Thomas J. Seifert, age 49, $30,000 total compensation
EVP CTO and General Manager Emerging Endpoints, Amit Mital
EVP and General Manager Enterprise Security, Balaji Yelamanchili
EVP General Counsel and Secretary, Scott C. Taylor, age 50, $420,000 total compensation
EVP Norton Business Unit, Fran Rosch
SVP and CIO, Sheila Jordan
Senior Vice President North America, Brett Shirk
EVP and Chief Product Officer Veritas, Matt Cain
SVP and General Manager Trust Services, Roxane Divol
VP and General Manager Cyber Security Services, Samir Kapuria
Executive Vice President and Acting CFO Veritas, Don Rath
Vice President Product and Service Delivery, Tom Powledge
Vice President Sales, John (Jack) Gladish
Vice President, Steve Mann
Vice President Information Technology Service Delivery, John Hughes
Board Member, Geraldine Laybourne
Auditors: KPMG LLP

LOCATIONS

HQ: Symantec Corp.
350 Ellis Street, Mountain View, CA 94043
Phone: 650 527-8000
Web: www.symantec.com

2015 Sales

	$ mil.	% of total
Americas	3,586	55
EMEA	1,813	28
Asia/Pacific/Japan	1,109	17
Total	**6,508**	**100**

PRODUCTS/OPERATIONS

2015 Sales

	$ mil.	% of total
Information management	2,558	39
Enterprise security	2,063	32
Consumer security	1,887	29
Total	**6,508**	**100**

2015 Sales by Product

	% of total
Content subscriptions & maintenance	88
License	12
Total	**100**

Selected Products
Consumer products
  Backup
  Fraud detection service
  Identity protection authentication
  Internet security
  PC tune-up
Security and compliance
  Compliance and security management
  Messaging management
Services
  Maintenance and support
  Training
Storage and server management
  Data protection
  Endpoint security
  Storage and server management

Selected Acquisitions
NitroDesk (2014 email app)
Nukona (2012 mobile application management software)
Odyssey Software (2012 mobile device management software)
LiveOffice (2012 hosted archiving provider)
Clearwell Systems (2011 legal software)
Gideon Technologies (2010 public-sector security software and services)
PGP Corporation (2010 data protection services)
GuardianEdge Technologies (2010 data protection services)
MessageLabs (2008 email protection service)
PC Tools (2008 privacy and security software)
SwapDrive (2008 online storage and data backup services)
AppStream (2008 remote program deployment and management services)
Vontu (2007 data loss prevention services)
Altiris (2007 IT asset management software)
Company-i (2006 financial data-center services)
Revivio (2006 data protection software)
Relicore (2006 data center change and configuration management)
IMlogic (2006 enterprise instant messaging)
BindView Development (2006 IT security compliance software)
Sygate Technologies (2005 network-access control services)
WholeSecurity (2005 antivirus software)

COMPETITORS

Avocent	HP
CA Inc.	IBM
Carbonite	Kaspersky Lab
Check Point Software	LANDesk
Cisco Systems	McAfee
CommVault	Microsoft
Comodo	Novell
Courion	Oracle
DataCore	RSA Security
Dell Software	SecureWorks
EMC	Smith Micro
F-Secure	Sophos
F5 Networks	Trend Micro
FalconStor	Verizon
GoDaddy	Zone Labs
Google	

Income Statement

FYE: April 3

	REVENUE ($ mil.)	NET INCOME ($ mil.)	NET PROFIT MARGIN	EMPLOYEES
04/15*	6,508	878	13.5%	19,000
03/14	6,676	898	13.5%	20,800
03/13	6,906	765	11.1%	21,500
03/12	6,730	1,172	17.4%	20,500
04/11	6,190	597	9.6%	18,600
Annual Growth	1.3%	10.1%	—	0.5%

*Fiscal year change

2015 Year-End Financials

Debt ratio: 15.84%	No. of shares (mil.): 684
Return on equity: 14.73%	Dividends
Cash ($ mil.): 2,874	Yield: 0.0%
Current ratio: 1.22	Payout: 47.6%
Long-term debt ($ mil.): 1,746	Market value ($ mil.): 16,108

	STOCK PRICE ($) FY Close	P/E High/Low		PER SHARE ($) Earnings	Dividends	Book Value
04/15*	23.55	21	16	1.26	0.60	8.68
03/14	19.79	21	14	1.28	0.60	8.34
03/13	24.68	23	12	1.08	0.00	7.77
03/12	18.70	13	10	1.57	0.00	7.04
04/11	18.46	24	16	0.76	0.00	5.97
Annual Growth	6.3%	—	—	13.5%	—	9.8%

*Fiscal year change

Synchrony Financial

Auditors: KPMG LLP

LOCATIONS

HQ: Synchrony Financial
777 Long Ridge Road, Stamford, CT 06902
Phone: 203 585-2400
Web: www.synchronyfinancial.com

HISTORICAL FINANCIALS

Company Type: Public

Income Statement

FYE: December 31

	ASSETS ($ mil.)	NET INCOME ($ mil.)	INCOME AS % OF ASSETS	EMPLOYEES
12/14	75,707	2,109	2.8%	11,000
12/13	59,085	1,979	3.3%	9,333
12/12	53,462	2,119	4.0%	—
12/11	0	1,890	—	—
Annual Growth	—	3.7%	—	—

2014 Year-End Financials

Debt ratio: 36.27%	No. of shares (mil.): 833
Return on equity: 25.66%	Dividends
Cash ($ mil.): 11,828	Yield: —
Current ratio: —	Payout: —
Long-term debt ($ mil.): —	Market value ($ mil.): 24,804

	STOCK PRICE ($) FY Close	P/E High/Low		PER SHARE ($) Earnings	Dividends	Book Value
12/14	29.75	11	8	2.78	0.00	12.57
12/13	0.00	—	—	(0.00)	0.00	(0.00)
Annual Growth	—	—	—	—	—	—

Synnex Corp

SYNNEX connects technology sellers with buyers and helps with customer service after the sale. The company distributes PCs peripherals software and consumer electronics from manufacturers that include Dell Hewlett-Packard Panasonic Lenovo Seagate and Microsoft. SYNNEX also provides design and support services. Its Concentrix segment offers customer support services using phone chat Web e-mail and digital print. The company's online services include parts catalogs configuration and ordering. In addition the company offers contract design and assembly build-to-order and configure-to-order services for manufacturers and systems integrators.

Operations

SYNNEX operates through two segments: Distribution Services (DS) and Concentrix. The DS segment which accounts for 89% of the company's revenue distributes IT systems peripherals system components software networking equipment CE and complementary products. It also offers data center server and storage solutions. The Concentrix segment accounting for 11% of sales offers a range of business process outsourcing (BPO) services to customers such as those in technical support renewals management lead management direct sales customer service back office processing and information technology outsourcing (ITO).

Geographic Reach

Based in California SYNNEX has operations in Canada China Costa Rica Hungary India Japan Mexico Nicaragua the Philippines the UK and the US. The US is the company's largest market contributing 73% of sales in 2015 (ended November) followed by Canada with 11% and Japan with 8%.

The company has about 40 distribution and administrative facilities in the US Canada Japan and Mexico. It has warehouses in California Georgia Virginia Illinois Texas New Jersey Ohio Florida Mississippi and Oregon.

Concentrix operates about 90 delivery centers and administrative facilities in numerous countries throughout North America Europe and Asia Pacific.

Sales and Marketing

SYNNEX maintains a sales headquarters in Greenville South Carolina. A dedicated sales staff serves its large commercial government reseller and retail customers. SYNNEX also markets its products and services to smaller resellers and OEMs through dedicated regional sales teams. The company also employs dedicated product management and business development specialists who focus on selling and promoting the products and services of selected suppliers or for specific end-market verticals.

Hewlett-Packard had been Synnex's biggest OEM supplier providing 25% of revenue in 2014 and 2015. That might change with the breakup of HP into HP Inc. which sells PCs and printers and Hewlett-Packard Enterprise which sells servers and large systems.

Financial Performance

SYNNEX reported sales of $13.3 billion in 2015 (ended November) a 3.6% decrease from 2014. Sales in the DS unit fell 6% because a vendor that provided consumer electronics products was bought by a third party. The Concentrix business posted a 29% growth spurt as it continued to benefit from the acquisition of IBM's CRM operations.

Profit jumped 16% higher in 2015 to $208 million —a company high —as Synnex had lower cost of revenue in 2015 from 2014.

Synnex revved up cash flow in 2015 to $643 million compared to negative cash flow of $234 million in 2014.

Strategy

The tech products distributor pursues a decentralized regional strategy placing its distribution facilities near reseller customers and their end-users to benefit from lower shipping costs and shorter delivery times. SYNNEX looks to expand its business into areas primarily related to its core distribution business as well as other support logistics business process outsourcing and related value-added services. While the lion's share of the company's sales are rung up in North America and Japan the company is looking to grow in India. In 2015 the company opened a second Concentrix facility in Visakhapatnam.

Synnex also opened a service delivery center in Bogota Colombia to provide service to a banking clients. The center is the fifth Concentrix location in Latin America. A new delivery center in Porto Portugal is to help the company increase business from existing accounts and develop new accounts in Europe.

Mergers and Acquisitions

The 2014 acquisition of IBM's customer relationship management (CRM) business expanded SYNNEX's operations. As part of the Concentrix subsidiary it created a leading customer engagement services company in the CRM/BPO market.

Company Ownership

MiTAC International Corporation owns about 25% of SYNNEX with FMR holding another 13% stake.

EXECUTIVES

President and CEO, Kevin M. Murai, age 52, $608,654 total compensation
Senior Vice President HP Product Marketing, David (Dave) Dennis
Vice President Strategy Development, Pradip Madan
President Hyve Solutions, Stephen Ichinaga, age 54
President North American Distribution, Peter Larocque, age 54, $441,274 total compensation
President Broadline Division SYNNEX Canada, Mitchell P. Martin, age 52
SVP and CIO, Gary Gulmon, age 54
SVP Marketing North America, Robert L. (Bob) Stegner
COO, Dennis Polk, age 49, $441,274 total compensation
CFO, Marshall Witt, $414,423 total compensation
President New Age Electronics, Fred Towns
EVP; President Concentrix, Christopher (Chris) Caldwell, $405,291 total compensation
President and CEO SYNNEX Infotec, Yoshitake Matsumoto
Associate Vice President Information Systems, Kirt Minor
Associate Vice President of Information Systems, Bo Li
Vice President Sales, Dendy Wakefield
Assistant Vice President Inventory Procurement, Cynthia Su
Vice President Sales, Bruce Holappa
Senior Vice President Partner Advocacy, Michael R (Mel) Thomson
Vice President Sales, Matt Sturrock
Vice President Sales, Kyle Russell
Vice President Sales, John (Jack) Jandoc
Senior Vice President Information Technology, Robert Sturycz
Vice President Of Marketing, Mike Gazdic
Vice President Marketing, Laverne Davis
Vice President Sales, Nick Paul
Assistant Vice President Sales, Willa Flemate
Vice President Us Marketing, Jack Quinn
Vice President Human Resources, Debra Torette

Vice President Sales, Melanie Brown
Svp Sales, Scott Barker
Senior Vice President, Scott Shamlin
Vice President Sales, Mike Henson
Vice President Sales, Andrew Christiansen
Vice President HP Enterprise Sales, Peter (Pete)
Montana
Vice President Sales, Debbie Burnett
National Account Manager, Keith Cox
Assistant Vice President Commercial Sales Smb,
John Phillips
Vice President Of Retail Sales, Eric Kirkendall
Vice President Of Human Resources, Deborah
Laturette
Vice President Sales, Derek Alexander
Senior Vice President Systems Integration, Steve
Ichinaga
Vice President Of Software, Denna Mensch
Senior Vice President, James Stutts
Vice President Of Enterprise Products, Doug Bone
Vice President Mobility And Connected Solutions,
Tim Acker
Senior Vice President Operations, Tim Rush
Vice President for Sales, Don Lv
Board Member, Andrea M Zulberti
Chairman, Dwight Steffensen, age 72
Auditors: KPMG LLP

LOCATIONS

HQ: Synnex Corp
44201 Nobel Drive, Fremont, CA 94538
Phone: 510 656-3333
Web: www.synnex.com

2015 Sales

	$ mil.	% of total
United States	9,869	73
Canada	1,429	11
Japan	1,003	8
Other	1,035	8
Total	**13,338**	**100**

PRODUCTS/OPERATIONS

2015 Sales

	$ mil.	% of total
Technology solutions	11,936	89
Concentrix	1,416	11
Inter-segment	(14.9)	-
Total	**13,338**	**100**

Selected Subsidiaries

Concentrix Technologies Limited
ComputerLand Corporation
Concentrix Technologies (India) Private Limited
Concentrix Corporation
Concentrix Costa Rica S.A.
Concentrix Free Trade Zone S.A.
Concentrix HK Limited
Concentrix Nicaragua S.A
License Online Inc.
Sennex Enterprises Limited
SIT Funding Corporation
SYNNEX Canada Limited
SYNNEX GBS Limited
SYNNEX GBS Inc.
SYNNEX Information Technologies (Beijing) Ltd
SYNNEX Information Technologies (Chengdu) Ltd
SYNNEX Information Technologies (China) Ltd
SYNNEX Information Technologies (UK) Ltd
SYNNEX Infotec Corporation
SYNNEX Investment Holdings Corporation
SYNNEX Logistics Corporation
SYNNEX de México S.A. de C.V
SYNNEX New (BVI) Corporation
SYNNEX NewHK Limited
SYNNEX Software Technologies (HK) Limited
SYNNEX-Concentrix Corporation
SYNNEX-Concentrix UK Limited
Concentrix Europe Limited
Intelligent Outsourcing of Central America S.A
VisionMAX Limited

Selected Services

Distribution
  Contract assembly
  Distribution services
  Logistics services
Global Business Services
  Automated service renewals software
  Customer services
  Hosted renewals services software in Europe
  (RenewalsManager)
  Financing services
  Marketing services
  Outsourced back-office services
  Technical support services

COMPETITORS

Arrow Electronics	Premier Farnell
Avnet	Sanmina
Benchmark Electronics	ScanSource
Celestica	ServiceSource
Convergys	Tech Data
D & H Distributing	TeleTech
Flextronics	Teleperformance
Hon Hai	Westcon
Ingram Micro	Wistron
Jabil	Yosun
Plexus	

HISTORICAL FINANCIALS

Company Type: Public

Income Statement

FYE: November 30

	REVENUE ($ mil.)	NET INCOME ($ mil.)	NET PROFIT MARGIN	EMPLOYEES
11/15	13,338	208	1.6%	72,500
11/14	13,839	180	1.3%	64,000
11/13	10,845	152	1.4%	14,500
11/12	10,285	151	1.5%	11,615
11/11	10,409	150	1.4%	10,948
Annual Growth	**6.4%**	**8.5%**	**—**	**60.4%**

2015 Year-End Financials

Debt ratio: 16.45%
Return on equity: 12.08%
Cash ($ mil.): 336
Current ratio: 1.90
Long-term debt ($ mil.): 638

No. of shares (mil.): 39
Dividends
  Yield: 0.6%
  Payout: 11.3%
Market value ($ mil.): 3,694

	STOCK PRICE ($) FY Close	P/E High/Low		PER SHARE ($) Earnings	Dividends	Book Value
11/15	94.27	18	13	5.24	0.58	45.92
11/14	71.44	17	11	4.57	0.13	42.48
11/13	66.16	16	8	3.06	0.00	37.93
11/12	33.02	11	7	3.99	0.00	36.01
11/11	29.35	9	6	4.08	0.00	32.03
Annual Growth	**33.9%**	**—**	**—**	**6.5%**	**—**	**9.4%**

Synovus Financial Corp.

Synovus Financial has a nose for community banking. The holding company owns flagship subsidiary Synovus Bank and more than 25 locally-branded banking divisions that offer deposit accounts and consumer and business loans in Alabama Florida Georgia South Carolina and Tennessee. Through more than 280 branches the bank provides checking and savings accounts loans and mortgages and credit cards. Other divi-

sions offer insurance private banking wealth and asset management and other financial services. Nonbank subsidiaries include Synovus Mortgage Synovus Trust investment bank and brokerage Synovus Securities and GLOBALT which provides asset management and financial planning services.Geographic ReachGeorgia-based Synovus Financial has about 130 bank branches in Georgia. Florida is the bank's second largest market with nearly 50 branches while Alabama and South Carolina are home to more than 40 each.Financial PerformanceWhile the bank reported a 10% decline in revenue in 2013 versus 2012 to $1.18 billion and an 81% plunge in net income (to $159.4 million) it did make some progress on the long road to recovery. Significantly the bank redeemed its obligations under TARP (troubled asset relief program) in July 2013 funding more than two-thirds of the TARP redemption with internally available funds. The firm redeemed the remainder with proceeds from offerings of its common and preferred stock. Its loan portfolio grew by about $516 million up nearly 3% versus 2012. Credit quality also continued to improve while the bank lowered expenses.Synovus blamed its continuing revenue slide on lower interest and non-interest income in 2013 versus 2012. Interest income fell on lower income on loans and investment securities. Non-interest income suffered relative to 2012 when the bank experienced higher levels of investment securities gains and gains on private equity investments as well as a decline in income from mortgage banking.StrategySynovus has been cutting costs raising capital and improving efficiency in the aftermath of the residential and commercial real estate bust that hit the southeastern US particularly hard. During the dark days of the banking crisis (2008 to 2009) the company slashed about 10% of its workforce and it cut approximately 10% more in 2010 and 2011. It also closed nearly 40 branches and consolidated others.Also Synovus which has traditionally maintained separate charters and local boards of directors for its subsidiary banks consolidated all of its charters into one in 2010 in order to reduce complexity and improve efficiency. Synovus also consolidated by merging some of its banks in Georgia and Florida; two of its Florida banking subsidiaries (one de novo and the other formed in the merger of three subsidiaries' banking charters) have taken the Synovus Bank brand a new strategy for the company.The company returned to profitability in 2012 and remained profitable (although considerably less so) in 2013. To right itself Synovus has deemphasized commercial real estate lending and increased its focus on commercial and industrial banking including specialized services such as asset-based lending international banking and treasury management in an effort to increase revenue. The company is courting large corporate clients in the health care manufacturing distribution financial services natural resources and transportation sectors. Among smaller enterprises it targets professional practices such as physicians attorneys and accountants particularly for its private banking business.Mergers and AcquisitionsIn May 2013 Synovus assumed $56.8 million in deposits that belonged to failed Sunrise Bank from its receiver the FDIC. As part of the deal the bank acquired $492000 in loans.

HISTORY

In 1885 W. C. Bradley founded his eponymous company (today a manufacturing and development concern). Three years later he invested in a new bank that would eventually bear the name of its Georgia hometown: Columbus Bank and Trust. (Bradley's investment in Atlanta-based Coca-Cola today accounts for the lion's share of his family's wealth.) When Bradley died his son-in-law Abbott Turner joined the bank's board of directors followed by Turner's son William.

In 1958 the bank hired James Blanchard as president. The next year Columbus Bank and Trust became one of the first banks to issue credit cards. The company's credit processing business grew leading it to computerize the process in 1966 and train its own employees to operate the equipment. (It decided to go it alone after a failed joint-venture attempt with corporate cousin W.C. Bradley Co.)

In a little more than a decade Blanchard led the bank to triple its assets. When he died in 1969 the search for a new leader took the bank's directors in a surprising direction: They offered the position to Blanchard's son Jimmy a young attorney with no banking experience. The board pressed him to take the job which he did in 1971 after a brief apprenticeship.

From the start the younger Blanchard emphasized the company's financial services operations such as credit card processing. Taking advantage of new laws opening up the banking and financial services industry in the early 1970s the bank reorganized in 1972 incorporating CB&T Bancshares to serve as a holding company for Columbus Bank and Trust. In 1973 CB&T's financial services division finished a new software product called the Total System which allowed electronic access to account information. CB&T used the groundbreaking software to start processing other banks' paperwork including an ever-growing number of credit card accounts. In 1983 CB&T spun off financial services division Total System Services (TSYS) but retained a majority stake in the company.

Blanchard helped win passage of Georgia's multibank holding law and further deregulation in the early 1980s allowed the company to operate across state lines. It bought four banks in Florida and Georgia in 1983 and 1984 and snapped up six more (including an Alabama bank) in 1985. Meanwhile TSYS benefited from the trend to outsource credit card processing.

In 1989 CB&T changed its name to Synovus a combination of the words "synergy" and "novus" the latter word meaning (according to the company) "of superior quality and different from the others listed in the same category."

During the early 1990s Synovus swept up 20 banks in its market area after the bank bust. After 1993 acquisitions dropped off until 1998 when Synovus announced three acquisitions in two weeks. That year it also said it was planning to move further into Internet and investment banking as well as auto and life insurance. In 1999 the company bought banks in Georgia and Florida; it also moved into debt collection with its purchase of Wallace & de Mayo which was renamed Total System Services (TSYS). In 2007 Synovus spun off TSYS.

The company grew its retail investment operations with the acquisitions of Atlanta-area asset managers Creative Financial Group in 2001 and GLOBALT in 2002. Jimmy Blanchard who had ultimately become Synovus Financial's chairman retired as an executive in 2005 but remained on the board. The long-time executive stepped down from the board in 2012.Fred Green abruptly stepped down as president of Synovus in 2009. CEO Richard Anthony assumed his responsibilities until early 2010 when Kessel Stelling was named president and COO of the company. Stelling was named CEO later that year after Anthony who remained chairman took a medical leave of absence. Anthony retired from the board in 2012. Stelling then took on the additional roll of chairman.In May 2013 the bank acquired three branches of a failed Valdosta-based bank.

EXECUTIVES

EVP and CFO, Thomas J. Prescott, age 60, $526,792 total compensation
EVP and COO, Allen J. Gula, age 60, $524,192 total compensation
EVP and Chief Risk Officer, Mark G. Holladay, age 59, $428,454 total compensation
EVP and Chief Retail Banking Officer, D. Wayne Akins
President Synovus Trust Company, George G. Flowers
President GLOBALT Investments, William H. Roach
Chairman President and CEO, Kessel D. Stelling, age 59, $1,161,023 total compensation
EVP Financial Management Services, J. Barton Singleton, age 51
EVP and Chief Community Banking Officer, R. Dallis (Roy) Copeland, age 46, $321,554 total compensation
EVP and Chief Corporate Banking Officer, Curtis J. Perry
CIO, Renee S. Roth
President Commercial Banking at Citizens First, Mac McKnight
CTO, Santosh Kokate
Chief Digital Officer, Amyn Tajani
Vice President Regional Sales, Ron Ward
Vice President Commercial Lending Commercial Bank and Trust, Heath Schondelmayer
Assistant Vice President Project Management Synovus Financial Corp., Theresa Radney
Senior Vice President, Steven Evans
Vice President Commercial Banking, John Barry
Vice President Information Technology Audit Manager, Laurette Smith
Vice President Human Resources, Amy Goins
Vice President Product Management, Lynn White
Executive Vice President Retail Branches Columbus Band And Trust, Carolynn Obleton
Vice President Senior Manager Compliance, Angela Isaac
Vice President Corporate AML Officer, Sue Nelson
Senior Vice President And Chief Audit Executive, Stephen Sawyer
Senior Vice President And Director Of Compliance, Beth Burns
Director of Health and Welfare Benefits, Mary Stranger
Vice President Accounting Manager, Liz Gobbel
Vice President Cash Management Specialist, Margie Richard
Vice President And Portfolio Manager, Daniel Morgan
Vice President Tax Compliance Manager, Jim Buchs
Vice President Information Systems, Cathy Reilly
Senior Vice President, Robbie Jones
Senior Vice President Diversity And Career Resources, Audrey Hollingsworth
Vice President Information Systems, Catherine (Cathy) OReilly
Vice President Credit Risk Management, Brett Willis
Auditors: KPMG LLP

LOCATIONS

HQ: Synovus Financial Corp.
1111 Bay Avenue, Suite 500, Columbus, GA 31901
Phone: 706 649-2311
Web: www.synovus.com

2013 Bank Branches

	No.
Georgia	129
Florida	49
Alabama	43
South Carolina	42
Tennessee	18
Total	**281**

PRODUCTS/OPERATIONS

2013 Sales

	$ mil.	% of total
Interest		
Loans including fees	866	74
Investment securities available for sale	52	5
Other	10	-
Noninterest		
Service charges on deposit accounts	77	6
Fiduciary & asset management fees	43	4
Bankcard fees	30	3
Brokerage & investment banking	27	2
Mortgage banking income	22	2
Other fee income	22	2
Other	29	2
Total	**1,182**	**100**

Selected Subsidiaries and Divisions

AFB&T
Bank of Coweta
The Bank of Nashville
Bank of North Georgia
The Bank of Tuscaloosa
CB&T Bank of East Alabama
CB&T Bank of Middle Georgia
Citizens First Bank
The Coastal Bank of Georgia
Coastal Bank and Trust
Coastal Bank and Trust of Alabama
Cohutta Banking Company
Columbus Bank & Trust
Commercial Bank
Commercial Bank and Trust Company
Community Bank & Trust of Southeast Alabama
The First Bank of Jasper
First Coast Community Bank
First Commercial Bank
First Commercial Bank of Huntsville
First State Bank & Trust
Georgia Bank & Trust
GLOBALT Inc.
NBSC
SB&T
Sea Island Bank
Sterling Bank
Synovus Bank
Synovus Bank of Jacksonville
Synovus Bank of Florida
Synovus Mortgage Corp.
Synovus Securities Inc.
Synovus Trust Company N.A.
The Tallahassee State Bank
Trust One Bank

COMPETITORS

BB&T	First Citizens
BBVA Compass	BancShares
Bancshares	First Horizon
BBX Capital	Regions Financial
BancorpSouth	SunTrust
Bank of America	Trustmark
Citigroup	Wells Fargo
Fidelity Southern	

HISTORICAL FINANCIALS

Company Type: Public

Income Statement

FYE: December 31

	ASSETS ($ mil.)	NET INCOME ($ mil.)	INCOME AS % OF ASSETS	EMPLOYEES
12/14	27,051	195	0.7%	4,511
12/13	26,201	159	0.6%	4,696
12/12	26,760	830	3.1%	4,963
12/11	27,162	(60)	—	5,224
12/10	30,093	(790)	—	6,109
Annual Growth	**(2.6%)**	**—**	**—**	**(7.3%)**

2014 Year-End Financials

Debt ratio: 2.83%
Return on equity: 6.52%
Cash ($ mil.): 511
Current ratio: —
Long-term debt ($ mil.): —
No. of shares (mil.): 136
Dividends
  Yield: 0.8%
  Payout: 21.4%
Market value ($ mil.): 3,688

	STOCK PRICE ($) FY Close	P/E High/Low		PER SHARE ($) Earnings	Dividends	Book Value
12/14	27.09	21	2	1.33	0.24	22.34
12/13	3.60	4	3	0.91	0.28	21.23
12/12	2.45	0	0	5.95	0.28	31.77
12/11	1.41	—	—	(1.05)	0.00	25.20
12/10	2.64	—	—	(8.68)	0.28	26.72
Annual Growth	79.0%	—	—	—	(3.8%)	(4.4%)

Sysco Corp.

This company has the menu that people depend on. Sysco is the #1 food service supplier in North America serving more than 425000 customers with a fleet of 9400 delivery vehicles and 190 distribution centers in the US Bahamas Canada and Ireland. Its core broadline distribution business supplies food and non-food products to restaurants schools hotels health care institutions and other customers while its SYGMA Network focuses on supplying chain restaurants. Sysco distributes both nationally-branded products and its own private-label goods. In addition Sysco supplies customers with specialty produce and meat products and it distributes kitchen equipment and supplies for the hospitality industry.

Geographic Reach

The company is a global supplier of food and related products. Boasting a noteworthy footprint in the US and Canada as the #1 foodservice supplier in North America Sysco operates more than 190 facilities across the US Ireland Northern Ireland the Bahamas Puerto Rico and Canada.

Operations

Providing food and related products to the food service or food-away-from-home industry Sysco operates its business primarily through two reportable segments: Broadline (81% of sales) and SYGMA (13%). Its Broadline business focuses on distributing a full line of food products and a variety of non-food products directly to customers. SYGMA on the other hand distributes a full line of food products and non-food items to chain restaurant customers. The company's Other segment which brings in the remaining 6% of revenue includes its specialty produce and lodging industry products business the part of its business that distributes specialty imported products and a company that distributes to international customers.

Sales and Marketing

Sysco relies on restaurants. Customers in the restaurant industry account for 62% of sales with fast food giant The Wendy's Company helping to bring in nearly a quarter of Sysco's SYGMA business. Hospitals and nursing homes hotels and motels and schools and colleges bring in the rest of Sysco's revenue along with operations that don't fit neatly into these segments. Reported separately under the Other segment the company generates 20% of sales from specialty produce and lodging industry items and via a unit that distributes products to international customers. The wholesale food services distribution business is highly fragmented with a patchwork of regional and local suppliers as competitors.

On a national scale Sysco jockeys for customers with rivals U.S. Foods and Performance Food Group. The company claims to serve about 18% of the estimated $235 billion foodservice market.

Financial Performance

Sysco has achieved unprecedented revenue growth over the years with revenues climbing 5% from $44.4 billion in 2013 to peak at a record-setting $46.5 billion in 2014. Despite the historic revenue growth Sysco's profits slipped 6% in 2014 due to the rising cost of sales and operating expenses.

It attributed the 2014 revenue growth to a 4% sales surge from its Broadline segment and a 7% bump from SYGMA. The Broadline segment's gains came from product cost inflation and the resulting increase in selling prices sales from acquisitions that occurred within the past 12 months and improving case volumes. Strategy

Sysco is working to boost its core Broadline business in the US Canada and Ireland. It's also exploring opportunities to profitably grow its market share by expanding beyond its core business.

The company also continues to focus on its multi-year Business Transformation Project. The initiative consists of designing and deploying an Enterprise Resource Planning (ERP) system; implementing an operating cost transformation initiative; and rolling out a product cost reduction and category management initiative involved in using market data and customer insights to make changes to product pricing and product assortment.

Mergers and Acquisitions

In a sweeping move for the foodservice industry Sysco in late 2013 announced plans to acquire its rival U.S. Foods for $3.5 billion. The deal will boost its share of the US market to about 25% from about 18%. By combining Sysco and US Foods the company expects to achieve annual synergies of at least $600 million and estimated annual sales of approximately $65 billion. The deal has been pushed back due to delays in talks with anti-trust regulators and is expected to close in early 2015.

Sysco also aims to acquire smaller competitors who haven't fared quite as well during the downturn. Indeed in 2013 the company acquired foodservice operations in Nassau Bahamas; San Francisco California; San Jose California; Stockton California; Ontario Canada; Quebec Canada; Orlando Florida; Dublin Ireland; St. Cloud Minnesota; Co. Down Northern Ireland; Greenville Ohio; and Houston Texas. Its 2012 acquisition of European Imports Ltd. helped it expand into the specialty import products segment. Purchasing Crossgar a leading privately owned foodservice supplier in Northern Ireland strengthened Sysco's presence on the island and complemented its 2009 acquisition of Pallas Foods. Other 2012 conquests include Appert's Foodservice Buchy Food Service Central Seafood Company and Metro Richelieu's Distagro. Their combined annual revenues were about $520 million.

HISTORY

Sysco was founded in 1969 when John Baugh a Houston wholesale food distributor formed a national distribution company with the owners of eight other US wholesalers. Joining Baugh's Zero Foods of Houston to form Sysco were Frost-Pack Distributing (Grand Rapids Michigan) Louisville Grocery (Louisville Kentucky) Plantation Foods (Miami) Thomas Foods and its Justrite subsidiary (Cincinnati) Wicker (Dallas) Food Service Company (Houston) Global Frozen Foods (New York) and Texas Wholesale Grocery (Dallas). The company went public in 1970. Sysco which derives its name from Systems and Services Company benefited from Baugh's recognition of the trend toward dining out. Until Sysco was formed small independent operators almost exclusively provided food distribution to restaurants hotels and other non-grocers.

EXECUTIVES

Vice President Human Resources, Susan (Sue) Billiot
SVP Marketing, William W. (Bill) Goetz
Senior Vice President, Charles W (Chas) Staes
Senior Vice President Finance, Kirk Drummond
Vice President Merchandising and Supply Chain Manaagement, Neil G Theiss
Assistant Vice President Information Technology, John (Jack) Holzem
EVP Merchandising and Supply Chain, William B. (Bill) Day, age 58, $508,333 total compensation
SVP Distribution Services, R. Scott Charlton, age 56
President and CEO SYSCO Food Services of Charlotte, William J. (Bill) DeLaney, age 59, $1,194,583 total compensation
President and COO, Thomas L. (Tom) Ben Cage 52, $616,667 total compensation
EVP and CFO; Merger Integration Leader, Robert C. (Chris) Kreidler, age 51, $712,500 total compensation
EVP Corporate Affairs and Chief Legal Officer, Russell T. Libby, age 49
SVP; President Sysco Ventures, Brian C. Beach
EVP and CTO, Wayne Shurts, age 56, $585,000 total compensation
Vice President, Loren Gausman
Vice President Merchandising Sales and Sysco Brand Development, John T (Jack) McIntyre
Vice President Quality Assurance, Craig G Watson, age 64
Vice President of Finance and Chief Financial Officer Sysco Chicago, Joel Grade
Vice President Employee Benefits, Mark Wisnoski
Vice President Merchandising and Marketing, Brian Smith
Vice President, Dick Abbey
Senior Vice President General Counsel, Michael (Mel) Nichols
Vice President Territory Sales, Colby Morse
Vice President Marketing, Robbie Blake
Regional Vice President, Gardner Victoria
RegionalVice President, Justin Hiraki
Regional Vice President Multi Unit Accounts Western Region, Debbie Martin
Vice President Business Development, Dominick Launi
Vice President Of Human Resources, Tony Watson
Vice President, Bryan Allred
Assistant Vice President, Barry Robinson
Vice President Operations, Mike Turner
Vice President Systems, Kristin Lindsay
Executive Vice President South and West U.S. Foodservice Operations, Stephen (Steve) Smith
National Sales Manager, Donovan Mike
Executive Vice President, Mark Will
Director of Utilization Review and Risk Management, Mark Kleiman
Vice President Business Resources, Paul Hudson
Vice President Sales Technologies, Dennis Hernandez
Vice President Of Merchandising, Jeff Hartley
Vice President Merchandising, Kate B Kerg
Vice President Corporate Communications, Charley Wilson
Vice President Territory Sales, Chad Lostin
Vice President Financial Reporting, Scott Stone
Rocky Mountain Market Vice President of Merchandising, Tracy Lenhardt
Vice President Information Technology, Danny Byrd
Senior Vice President, Michael Morrison
Vice President Corporate Business Development, Greg Keller
Vice President Operations, Ron Shanks
Executive Vice President, Jay Holden
Regional Vice President New Business Development, Scott Nemelka

Vice President Of Information Technology, Valerie Walls
Vice President of Finance and Chief Financial Officer Sysco Las Vegas, Jim Sherman
Senior Vice President, Bene Tom
Vice President Product and Field Marketing, Rich Doggett
Vice President Merchandising And Marketing, Chris Flint
Senior Vice President Of Logistics, Raina Avalon
Vice President Of Sales, Clark Hincher
Vice President Marketing, Jason Hooter
Regional Vice President, Vincent E Purves
Vice President Sales, John (Jack) Roberts
Vice President Merchandising, Bill Tubb
National Sales Manager Sysco Brand Sales And Development, Greg Deboer
Vice President Distribution Services, Gary Cullen
Vice President Foodservice Operations So, Michael (Mel) Headrick
Vice President Sales, Ken Blasser
Vice President Merchandising, Chris O'Keefe
Vice President Sales, Ken Borglum
Vice President Of Marketing, Sharon Armentrout
Vice President Finance, John Roderigue
Vice President Of Information Technology, Lucas Wagner
Vice President, Andrew (Andy) Malcolm
Vice President Territory Sales, Danny Chen
Vice President Of Finance, Alma Vega
Vice President Territory Sales, Kelly Ferris
National Account Manager, Jennifer (Jen) Vance
Vice President, John A (Jack) Hall
Vice President, Daniel Gentry
National Account Manager, Amy Carman
Vice President Of Merchandising, Richard Weis
Regional Vice President, Nancy Brooks
Vice President Sales, Perry Rutledge
Vice President Of Sales, Ted Behen
Senior Vice President Sales and Marketing, Jim Hope
Vice President Merchandising and Marketing, Pam Bava
Assistant Vice President Of Marketing, Tracey Mills
Vice President Sourcing, Christopher Shepardson
Vice President Financial Planning and Analysis, Elton Evans
Vice President Of Information Systems, Rex Walters
Vice President Call Center, Alena Galsnte
Executive Vice President, Saul Adelsberg
Assistant Vice President Of Transportation, Billy Brodnax
Executive Vice President, Lisa Gough
Executive Vice President Buck Head Beef Northeast, Howard Horn
Vice President Merchandsiing, Joyce Carlin
Vice President Finance, Kristin Kotler
Vice President Operations, Arv Klein
Vice President Supply Chain Management, Masao Nishi
Vice President Sales, Matthew (Matt) Myers
Vice President Deputy General Counsel and Assistant Secretary, Thomas (Thom) Kurz
Vice President Operations, Gary Licho
Executive Vice President Hallsmith Sysco Food Services, Frederick (Fred) Casinelli
Vice President of Marketing Corporate, John (Jack) Miko
Vice President Finance, Mark Daubert
Senior Vice President Foodservice Operations (Western Region), James (Jamie) Lankford
Vice President Human Resources, Julia Gannon
Vice President Finance, Jim Amos
Vice President of Merchandising and Marketing, Bobbie McDonald
Vice President, Steve Bodden
Vice President Human Resources, Tim Cash
Senior Vice President Marketing, Bill Goetz
Vice President Merchandising, Brian R Todd

Vice President of Operations, Phil Sperling
Vice President of Sales, Steve Otis
Vice President Information Systems, Scott Bowling
Vice President Finance, Kirk Logeley
Vice President Information Technology, Dawnell Muecke
Senior Vice President Chief Communications and Government Relations Officer, Nehl Horton
Senior Vice President Distribution Services, Scott Charlton
Senior Vice President General Counsel, Adam Skorecki
Vice President Marketing, Randy Ruiter
Vice President Procurement, Eric Zeilor
Vice President Of Finance, Carlos Reyes
Vice President, Matt Whitney
Vice President Operations, Shawn Ressler
Senior Vice President Merchandising and Marketing, Debbie Morey
Chairman, Jacquelyn M. (Jackie) Ward, age 77
Secretary, Connie S Brooks
Secretary, Tim Davis
Treasurer, Alan (Al) Sachs
Secretary, Ellen Drumm
Assistant Treasurer, Marty Gauthier
Board Of Directors, James Owen
Board Member, Lee Gersch
Auditors: Ernst & Young LLP

LOCATIONS

HQ: Sysco Corp.
1390 Enclave Parkway, Houston, TX 77077-2099
Phone: 281 584-1390   Fax: 281 584-2880
Web: www.sysco.com

2014 Sales

	% of total
US	87
Canada	11
Other	2
Total	**100**

PRODUCTS/OPERATIONS

2014 Sales

	% of total
Broadline	81
SYGMA	13
Other	6
Total	**100**

2014 Sales

	% of total
Fresh & frozen meats	19
Canned & dry food	18
Frozen fruits vegetables bakery & other	13
Dairy products	11
Poultry	10
Fresh produce	8
Paper & disposables	7
Seafood	5
Beverage products	4
Janitorial products	2
Equipment & smallware	2
Medical supplies	1
Total	**100**

COMPETITORS

Ben E. Keith
Bunzl
Edward Don
Foodbuy
Golden State Foods
Gordon Food Service
MAINES
McLane Foodservice

Meadowbrook Meat Company
Performance Food Group
Reinhart FoodService
Shamrock Foods
US Foods
UniPro Foodservice

HISTORICAL FINANCIALS

Company Type: Public

Income Statement

FYE: June 27

	REVENUE ($ mil.)	NET INCOME ($ mil.)	NET PROFIT MARGIN	EMPLOYEES
06/15	48,680	686	1.4%	51,700
06/14	46,516	931	2.0%	50,300
06/13	44,411	992	2.2%	48,100
06/12*	42,380	1,121	2.6%	47,800
07/11	39,323	1,152	2.9%	46,000
Annual Growth	5.5%	(12.1%)	—	3.0%

*Fiscal year change

2015 Year-End Financials

Debt ratio: 40.31%
Return on equity: 13.08%
Cash ($ mil.): 5,130
Current ratio: 1.22
Long-term debt ($ mil.): 2,271

No. of shares (mil.): 594
Dividends
  Yield: 0.0%
  Payout: 102.6%
Market value ($ mil.): 22,804

	STOCK PRICE ($) FY Close	P/E High/Low	PER SHARE ($) Earnings	Dividends	Book Value
06/15	38.37	36 31	1.15	1.18	8.85
06/14	37.85	24 20	1.58	1.14	8.99
06/13	34.16	21 17	1.67	1.10	8.86
06/12*	29.81	17 13	1.90	0.80	8.00
07/11	31.39	17 14	1.96	1.03	7.95
Annual Growth	5.1%		— — (12.5%)	3.5%	2.7%

*Fiscal year change

T-Mobile US Inc

T-Mobile US is one of the largest providers of wireless voice and data communications services in the US. The company's 61 million T-Mobile and MetroPCS contract and prepaid consumer customers use its networks domestically and are able to connect to the compatible network of Deutsche Telekom when in Europe. It also offers low-cost no-contract mobile services through the GoSmart brand. In addition T-Mobile sells phones tablets PDAs and accessories from such vendors as Apple Nokia and Samsung. It has about 8000 T-Mobile and MetroPCS branded retail sites. In 2013 Deutsche Telekom acquired smaller rival MetroPCS via a reverse merger and combined it with T-Mobile; Deutsche Telekom owns about two-thirds of the combined company.

Sales and Marketing
T-Mobile markets its services and products via its own network of retail locations as well as through more than 60000 third-party retail locations and online. Its largest customer segment (about 70% of revenue) is postpaid subscribers. Prepaid customers account for about a quarter of revenue and wholesale clients roaming charges and other services generate the rest.

Financial Analysis In 2014 T-Mobile reported about $29 billion in revenue up 21% from the prior year. The growth was powered by a $2 billion increase in prepaid service revenues a $1 billion rise in postpaid service revenues and a $1.5 billion increase in equipment sales. The contributions of the Metro PCS network also contributed to revenue growth.

T-Mobile's profit zoomed more than 600% higher in 2014 to $247 million on the higher revenue. Cash flow from operations also rose in 2014 from 2013 to $4.15 billion from $3.5 billion.

Strategy The company has crafted a "Un-carrier" strategy to compete with the big boys such as Verizon Wireless and AT&T Mobility. It has offered a line of Simple Choice plans that eliminate annual contracts as well as caps and overage charges. T-Mobile has also introduced a simpler handset upgrade program and reduced some international calling rates and roaming fees when traveling outside the US. The company pays early termination fees for customers who leave another carrier for T-Mobile. Other carriers have followed the company's lead and done away with contracts.

Another key initiative of T-Mobile's strategy is heavy investment in network modernization to support its nationwide 4G LTE (long-term evolution) technology. Wideband LTE is available in 245 markets and is expected to be available in more than 260 markets by the end of 2015. Extended Range LTE covers nearly 175 million people and is on track to cover more than 350 markets by year-end 2015.

HISTORY

T-Mobile USA moved to strengthen its presence in the southern US in 2008 with the purchase of SunCom Wireless for $2.4 billion. The deal added over 1 million customers in the southern US and Caribbean region. Other areas where T-Mobile USA added services in 2008 included Birmingham Alabama where it spent $31 million to build out its network and Washington D.C.

EXECUTIVES

EVP and CIO, Gary A. King, age 57, $488,462 total compensation

President and CEO, John J. Legere, age 57, $1,250,000 total compensation

COO, G. Michael (Mike) Sievert, age 46, $550,000 total compensation

EVP and CFO, J. Braxton Carter, age 56, $650,000 total compensation

EVP Corporate Services, David R. (Dave) Carey, age 61

EVP General Counsel and Secretary, David A. (Dave) Miller, age 54

President T-Mobile Indirect Channels, Thomas C. Keys, age 57

SVP and Chief People Officer, Larry L. Myers, age 60

EVP Corporate Strategy, Peter A. Ewens, age 52

EVP and CTO, Neville R. Ray, age 52

EVP T-Mobile Retail and Direct Channels, Jon A. Freier

EVP and Chief Marketing Officer, J. Andrew Sherrard

National Account Manager, Vance Reyes

Senior Vice President Strategy, Peter (Pete) Ewans

Vice President Customer Service, Brian Brueckman

Vice President Business Development, Dirk Mosa

Vice President Customer Care, Femi Lakeru

Vice President Business Sales, Ty Trenary

Executive Assistant to Mike Ross Vice President o, Mauread Bray

Senior Inside Sales Vice President, Jim Gowan

Vice President Business Sales, Tricia Sihapanya

Vice President Of Enterprise Information Technology, Mike Ross

Vice President Corporate Strategy And Analysis, Seth Schuler

Senior Vice President Fin cao, Michael (Mel) Morgan

Vice President Risk Management, Alexander Stadler

Vice President Operations Sales Operations, John (Jack) Whittington

Vice President Engineering, David Gallacher

Vice President Risk, Michael Kinneman

Vice President Real Estate And Facilities, Sean Prasad

Vice President Real Estate Design Visual Merchandising, Robert (Bob) Hill

Executive Vice President Information Technology, Unmukt Gadkari

Vice President Business Sales, Amber Powers

Vice President Corporate Communications, Janice Kapner

National Account Manager, Shawn-Patrick Norris

Vice President Chief Compliance Officer, Steven (Steve) Cochran

Vice President Human Resources, Molly Luna

National Sales Manager, Richard Apgar

National Account Manager, John Barber

Vice President Federal Regulatory Affairs, Kathleen Ham

National Account Manager, Michael Brugger

Vice President Marketing, Ajay Singh

Vice President Business Sales, Amanda Owens

Senior Vice President Finance, Terri Smith

Vice President of Procurement and Supply Chain Strategy, Mike Lincoln

Vice President National Retail, James (Jamie) Kirby

Vice President Local Channel Management And Reporting, Savinay Dangi

Vice President Business Operations, Vickie Cahoon

Executive Assistant To Bala Subramanian Vice President of Enterprise Architecture, Jennifer (Jen) Jirsa

Vice President Sales, Marcus Almeida

Vice President Information Systems, Leanne Prince

Vice President Sales, Renee Williams

Vice President Finance and Planning, Stefan Gross

National Account Manager, Mark Moses

Vice President Enterprise Product Strategy, James Brody

Vp-new York Area, Terry Hayes

Senior Vice President Of Brand Communications, Peter Deluca

National Account Manager, Jon Ferrian

Vice President, Richard (Dick) Horton

Senior Inside Sales Vice President, Mike Davison

Vice President Business Sales, Jamie Rayeski

Vice President of Marketing and Product Public Relations, Elaine Devereux

Vice President Marketing, Karin Giffney

Vice President Of Customer Care, Karen Sullivan

Senior Vice President Risk Management, Simon Agyemang

Vice President Product Development, Warren McNeel

Sales Vice President, Brad Treese

Vice President Sales, Cynthia McClarnon

Vice President, Ronald Dickson

Vice President Sales, Kevin Glassman

Vice President Area Field Sales, Gabriel Torres

Assistant To Senior Vice President Engineering And Operations, Kelly Digregorio

Vice President Product Management, Andrew Morrison

Vice President Human Resources, Nicole Furuc

Vice President Corporate Governance and Securities, Marc Rome

Vice President Wlan Europe, Ilja Wagner

National Account Manager, Diego Andrade

Vice President Of Reverse Logistics, Scott Searls

Vice President Business Development, Jim Porter

National Account Manager RPS, Tracy Avanzo

National Account Manager, Hugh McNichol

Chairman, Timotheus (Tim) H łtges, age 53

Auditors: PricewaterhouseCoopers LLP

LOCATIONS

HQ: T-Mobile US Inc
12920 S.E. 38th Street, Bellevue, WA 98006-1350
Phone: 425 378-4000
Web: www.T-Mobile.com

PRODUCTS/OPERATIONS

2014 Sales

	$ mil.	% of total
Branded postpaid	14,392	48
Branded Prepaid	6,986	23
Equipment Sales	6,789	23
Wholesale	731	2
Roaming and other services	266	1
Other	319	1
Total	**29,564**	**100**

2014 Customers

	No. mil
Branded postpaid	27
Branded prepaid	16
Wholesale	11
Total	**55**

COMPETITORS

AT&T Mobility	TracFone
Boost Mobile	U.S. Cellular
CenturyLink	Verizon Wireless Inc.
Cricket	Virgin Mobile USA
Sprint Communications	

HISTORICAL FINANCIALS

Company Type: Public

Income Statement

FYE: December 31

	REVENUE ($ mil.)	NET INCOME ($ mil.)	NET PROFIT MARGIN	EMPLOYEES
12/14	29,564	247	0.8%	45,000
12/13	24,420	35	0.1%	40,000
12/12	19,719	(7,336)	—	—
12/11	20,618	(4,718)	—	—
Annual Growth	12.8%	—	—	—

2014 Year-End Financials

Debt ratio: 33.33%	No. of shares (mil.): 807
Return on equity: 1.65%	Dividends
Cash ($ mil.): 5,315	Yield: —
Current ratio: 1.59	Payout: —
Long-term debt ($ mil.): 18,794	Market value ($ mil.): 21,753

	STOCK PRICE ($) FY Close	P/E High/Low	PER SHARE ($) Earnings	Dividends	Book Value
12/14	26.94	112 79	0.30	0.00	19.40
12/13	33.64	666 187	0.05	0.00	17.76
12/12	9.94	— —	(13.70)	0.00	11.42
12/11	8.68	— —	(8.81)	0.00	(0.00)
/0.00	—		(0.00)	0.00	(0.00)
Annual Growth	—	—	—	—	—

Talmer Bancorp Inc

Talmer Bancorp is a bank holding company primarily serving states in the Midwest. It offers online banking and bill payment services online cash management safe deposit box rentals debit card and ATM card services. It supplies a variety of loans including loans for small and medium-sized businesses residential mortgages commercial real estate and a variety of commercial and consumer demand savings and time deposit products. The company owns three subsidiary banks: Talmer Bank and Trust a Michigan state-chartered bank; First Place Bank a federal savings association; and Talmer West Bank a Michigan state-chartered bank. Chemical Bank agreed to buy Talmer Bancorp for $1.1 billion in January 2016.

IPO

Talmer Bancorp went public in 2014 and raised more than $202 million in proceeds. It plans to use the proceeds to repay debt invest in organic growth and make acquisitions.

Operations

The company's three subsidiary banks include Talmer Bank and Trust First Place Bank and Talmer West Bank. It has total assets of about $4.7 billion total loans of nearly $3 billion and total deposits of $3.7 billion.Geographic ReachTalmer's banks operate through nearly 95 branches in Michigan Ohio Indiana Wisconsin Illinois Nevada and New Mexico and 13 lending offices located primarily in the Midwest.

Financial Performance

Talmer generated revenue of about $180 million for 2012; this was down from the $233 million it posted the previous year.

Strategy

Talmer intends to grow as a Midwest regional bank holding company by integrating and growing its existing operations. It aims to achieve this through organic growth and the acquisition of additional banking franchises including under-performing and under-capitalized banks and other complementary assets.

EXECUTIVES

COO and President Talmer Bank & Trust, Thomas C. (Tom) Shafer, age 56
Executive Managing Director and CIO Talmer Bancorp and Talmer Bank and COO First Place Bank, Gregory R. (Greg) Bixby, age 49
Vice Chairman Talmer Bancorp and Talmer Bank and President and CEO Talmer West Bank, Gary S. Collins, age 56
CFO and Executive Managing Director of Talmer Bancorp and Talmer Bank and CFO and Director First Place Bank, Dennis L. Klaeser, age 57, $361,539 total compensation
President CEO and Director Talmer Bancorp Inc. and Chairman President and CEO Talmer Bank and Trust, David T. Provost, age 61, $500,000 total compensation
Chairman, Gary H. Torgow, age 58
Auditors: Crowe Horwath LLP

LOCATIONS

HQ: Talmer Bancorp Inc
2301 West Big Beaver Rd., Suite 525, Troy, MI 48084
Phone: 248 498-2802
Web: www.talmerbank.com

PRODUCTS/OPERATIONS

2012 Sales

	$ mil.	% of total
Interest Income		
Interest & fees on loans	112	57
Interest on securities & other	9	5
FDIC indemnification asset	(19.2)	-
Non-interest income		
FDIC loss sharing income	22	11
Accelerated discount on acquired loans	18	10
Mortgage banking & other loan fees	17	9
Deposit fee income	8	4
Net gains on sales of securities	6	3
Other income	2	1
Total	179	100

COMPETITORS

First Financial (IN)	Independent Bank (MI)
First Merchants	Mercantile Bank
Firstbank	Old National Bancorp
Flagstar Bancorp	STAR Financial Group

HISTORICAL FINANCIALS

Company Type: Public

Income Statement
FYE: December 31

	ASSETS ($ mil.)	NET INCOME ($ mil.)	INCOME AS % OF ASSETS	EMPLOYEES
12/14	5,870	90	1.5%	1,408
12/13	4,547	98	2.2%	1,446
12/12	2,347	21	0.9%	1,550
12/11	2,123	33	1.6%	—
12/10	0	44	—	—
Annual Growth	—	19.4%	—	—

2014 Year-End Financials

Debt ratio: 1.14%
Return on equity: 13.18%
Cash ($ mil.): 182
Current ratio: —
Long-term debt ($ mil.): —

No. of shares (mil.): 70
Dividends
  Yield: 0.1%
  Payout: 1.7%
Market value ($ mil.): 990

	STOCK PRICE ($) FY Close	P/E High/Low	PER SHARE ($) Earnings	Dividends	Book Value
12/14	14.04	11 10	1.21	0.02	10.80
Annual Growth	—	— —	—	—	—

Targa Resources Corp

Targa Resources Corp. (formerly Targa Resources Investments) has targeted natural gas profits. It indirectly owns Targa Resources GP the general partner and 2% owner of Targa Resources Partners. Targa Resources Partners is a midstream natural gas and natural gas liquids (NGLs) company that gathers processes transports and sells natural gas and NGLs in the US. It owns or operates about 11400 miles of natural gas gathering pipelines moving gas from wells in Texas and the Louisiana coast and other Gulf of Mexico locations. The partnership also operates scores of processing plants and storage facilities primarily in the southwestern US.

Geographic Reach

The partnership owns or commercially manages terminal facilities in a number of states including Texas Louisiana Arizona Nevada California Florida Alabama Mississippi Tennessee Kentucky New Jersey. and Washington.Its natural gas gathering processing and treating assets are in North Texas West Texas New Mexico and the Louisiana Gulf Coast and NGL assets (fractionation transport storage and terminaling facilities low sulfur natural gasoline treating facilities pipeline transportation and distribution assets propane storage and truck terminals) are primarily located near Houston Texas and in Lake Charles Louisiana.

Operations

Targa Resources Corp. does not directly own any operating assets. It generates revenues from general and limited partner interests in its operating partner Targa Resources Partners a major US provider of midstream natural gas and NGL services.

The company is engaged in the business of gathering compressing treating processing and selling natural gas and storing fractionating treating transporting terminaling and selling NGLs and NGL products and gathering storing and terminaling crude oil and storing terminaling and selling refined petroleum products. Its two divisions are Gathering and Processing (Field Gathering and

Processing and Coastal Gathering and Processing); and Logistics and Marketing (Logistics Assets and Marketing and Distribution).

Its Gathering and Processing Division consists of gathering compressing dehydrating treating conditioning processing and marketing natural gas and gathering crude oil. Its Field Gathering and Processing segment's operations consist of Sand Hills Versado SAOU North Texas and Badlands. In 2013 the Field Gathering and Processing segment gathered and processed natural gas from the Permian Basin in West Texas and Southeast New Mexico the Fort Worth Basin including the Barnett Shale in North Texas and the Williston Basin in North Dakota. The Coastal Gathering and Processing segment assets are located in the onshore region of the Louisiana Gulf Coast accessing natural gas from the Gulf Coast and the Gulf of Mexico.Its Logistics Assets segment uses its platform of integrated assets to receive fractionate store treat transport and deliver NGLs typically under fee-based arrangements; its gathering and processing assets and are primarily located at Mont Belvieu and Galena Park near Houston Texas and in Lake Charles Louisiana. Its Marketing and Distribution segment transports distributes and markets NGLs via terminals and transportation assets across the U.S. The Partnership owns or commercially manages terminal facilities in a number of states including Texas Louisiana Arizona Nevada California Florida Alabama Mississippi Tennessee Kentucky New Jersey and Washington. Its transportation assets include 716 railcars 75 owned and leased transport tractors and 22 company-owned pressurized NGL barges. The Marketing and Distribution segment operates 14 terminals with a combined storage capacity of 307 million gallons and throughput capacity of 496 million gallons.

Sales and Marketing

The partnership markets its own NGL production and also buyscomponent NGL products from other NGL producers and marketers for resale. The Partnership also earns margins by purchasing and reselling NGL products in the spot and forward physical markets. To effectively serve its Distribution and Marketing customers the Partnership contracts for and uses many of the assets included in its Logistics Assets segment.

Targa Resources' wholesale propane marketing operations primarily sell propane and related logistics services to major multi-state retailers independent retailers and other end-users.The company also markets natural gas available to it from the Gathering and Processing segments purchases and resells natural gas in selected US markets.

Financial Performance

In 2014 Targa Resources' net sales increased by 31% due to a increase in NGL volumes higher fee-based and other revenues and an increase in natural gas commodity sales prices partially offset by lower NGL and condensate prices.Logistics and Marketing segments reported increased export activities and higher fractionation fees; Field Gathering and Processing throughput volumes increased as the result o system expansions and increased producer activity as well as higher natural gas prices. In 2014 Targa Resources' net income increased by 110% due to higher revenues as well as increased other income stemming from transaction costs related to the pending Atlas Mergers. This was partially offset by increased depreciation and amortization related to the planned amortization of the Badlands intangible assets and higher depreciation related to major organic investments placed in service including continuing development at Badlands the international export expansion project High Plains and Longhorn plants CBF Train 4 and other system expansions.The net cash provided by the operating activities increased by 99% in 2014 due to increased net income gain on sale or disposition of assets a change in working capital receivables and accounts payable and other liabilities.

Strategy

Through its operating partnership the company is focused on production from shale plays and by the deployment of shale exploration and production technologies in both liquids-rich natural gas and crude oil resource plays for driving its growth. It is actively pursuing natural gas gathering and processing and NGL fractionation opportunities associated with liquids-rich natural gas from shale and other resource plays such as portions of the Barnett Eagle Ford Utica and Marcellus Shales and with even richer casinghead gas opportunities from active crude oil resource plays such as the Wolfberry and the Bone Springs Avalon and Bakken Shale plays.

Targa Resources Corp and Targa Resources Partners have spent $5.3 billion in acquisitions and growth capital expenditures of which approximately $1.2 billion was for acquisitions from third-parties.Targa Resources Partners also continues to invest significant capital to expand through organic growth projects including $1 billion in 2013 out of which about 54% were distributed to Logistics and Marketing and 46% to Gathering and Processing. It planned to invest $650 million in both large and small organic growth projects in 2014.

In 2014 it completed constructing a new cryogenic processing plant and related gathering and compression facilities for North Texas to meet increasing production and continued producer activity in the area. In addition it is also constructing a cryogenic processing plant and related gathering and compression facilities for SAOU to meet increasing production and continued producer activity on the eastern side of the Permian Basin. The company planned to invest about $375 million for the plants and associated projects.

During 2013 it invested $250 million to expand its gathering and processing business in the Williston Basin North Dakota assets. With this it also added a natural gas processing plant and during 2014 it planned an investment of $180 million for further expansion of this business including an additional cryogenic processing plant.In an effort to expand fractionation capacity in Texas to support the Utica Marcellus Texas NGL Pipeline in 2013 Targa Resources Partners signed a letter of intent with Kinder Morgan Energy Partners to form a joint venture to construct NGL fractionation facilities at Mont Belvieu Texas.

Mergers and Acquisitions

In a major move to grow its midstream assets in 2015 Targa Resources Partners and Targa Resources Corp. acquired Atlas Pipeline Partners L.P. and Atlas Energy L.P respectively in a deal valued at about $7.7 billion. The Atlas companies have leadership positions in the Eagle Ford Mississippi Lime and Woodford/SCOOP areas.

In 2013 Targa Resources Partners acquired additional property on the Houston Ship Channel that provides expansion potential for both its Petroleum Logistics clean fuels business and its propane/butane export capabilities.

In 2012 the company acquired Saddle Butte Pipeline LLC's crude oil gathering pipeline and terminal system and natural gas gathering and processing operations for $976 million. The acquired business (renamed Targa Badlands) has a combined crude oil operational storage capacity of 70000 barrels including the Johnsons Corner Terminal (20000 barrels of storage capacity) and Alexander Terminal (30000 barrels).

Company Background

Warburg Pincus took Targa Resources Corp. public in 2010. In preparation for going public in 2010 Targa Resources Corp. sold its 77% stake in Venice Energy Services to Targa Resources Part-

ners for $175.6 million. The company realized no proceeds from the $300 million offering.

The company was formed in 2005.

EXECUTIVES

CEO, Joe Bob Perkins, age 54, $554,167 total compensation
President Finance and Administration, Jeffrey J. (Jeff) McParland, age 60, $463,333 total compensation
President and COO, Michael A. Heim, age 67, $526,667 total compensation
EVP General Counsel and Secretary, Paul W. Chung, age 54
SVP CFO and Treasurer, Mattthew J. (Matt) Meloy, age 37, $366,667 total compensation
Vice President Business Development, Brad D Reese
Vice President Finance, Howard M Tate
Vice President Of Petroleum Logistics, Vincent Dicosimo
Executive Chairman, James W. Whalen, age 74
Auditors: PricewaterhouseCoopers LLP

LOCATIONS

HQ: Targa Resources Corp
1000 Louisiana St., Suite 4300, Houston, TX 77002
Phone: 713 584-1000   **Fax:** 713 584-1100
Web: www.targaresources.com

PRODUCTS/OPERATIONS

2014 Sales

	$ mil.	% of total
Marketing & distribution	7,454	86
Logistics	392	5
Coastal gathering & processing	389	5
Field gathering & processing	387	4
Other	(8)	-
Corporate and Eliminations	0	-
TRC Non-Partnership	0	-
Total	**8,616**	**100**

COMPETITORS

BP	Enterprise Products
Chevron	Hiland Partners
DCP Midstream Partners	J-W Operating
Devon Energy	ONEOK Partners
Enbridge	

HISTORICAL FINANCIALS

Company Type: Public

Income Statement

FYE: December 31

	REVENUE ($ mil.)	NET INCOME ($ mil.)	NET PROFIT MARGIN	EMPLOYEES
12/14	8,616	423	4.9%	1,350
12/13	6,556	65	1.0%	1,277
12/12	5,885	38	0.6%	1,192
12/11	6,994	30	0.4%	1,096
12/10	5,469	(15)	—	1,020
Annual Growth	**12.0%**	**—**	**—**	**7.3%**

2014 Year-End Financials

Debt ratio: 47.54%
Return on equity: 265.54%
Cash ($ mil.): 81
Current ratio: 1.07
Long-term debt ($ mil.): 2,885

No. of shares (mil.): 42
Dividends
  Yield: 2.5%
  Payout: 110.1%
Market value ($ mil.): 4,469

	STOCK PRICE ($) FY Close	P/E High/Low	PER SHARE ($)		
			Earnings	Dividends	Book Value
12/14	106.05	62 35	2.43	2.68	4.03
12/13	88.17	57 34	1.55	2.06	3.53
12/12	52.84	56 43	0.91	1.52	3.41
12/11	40.69	55 36	0.74	0.93	3.73
12/10	26.81	— —	(30.94)	0.00	3.41
Annual Growth	**41.0%**	**— —**	**—**	**—**	**4.2%**

Target Corp

Purveyor of all that is cheap yet chic Target is the US's #2 discount chain (behind Wal-Mart). The fashion-forward discounter operates some 1795 Target and SuperTarget stores across North America as well as an online business at Target.com. Target and its larger grocery-carrying incarnation SuperTarget have carved out a niche by offering more upscale trend-driven merchandise than rivals Wal-Mart and Kmart. Target also issues its proprietary Target credit card good only at Target. The company is growing its grocery business and aggressively expanding stores. It entered the Canadian market in 2013 with 124 stores but pulled out in early 2015 after failing to win over Canadian shoppers.

HISTORY

The panic of 1873 left Joseph Hudson bankrupt. After he paid his debts at 60 cents on the dollar he saved enough to open a men's clothing store in Detroit in 1881. Among his innovations were merchandise-return privileges and price marking in place of bargaining. By 1891 Hudson's was the largest retailer of men's clothing in the US. Hudson repaid his creditors from 1873 in full with interest. When Hudson died in 1912 four nephews expanded the business.

Former banker George Dayton established a dry-goods store in 1902 in Minneapolis. Like Hudson he offered return privileges and liberal credit. His store grew to a 12-story full-line department store.

After WWII both companies saw that the future lay in the suburbs. In 1954 Hudson's built Northland in Detroit then the largest US shopping center. Dayton's built the world's first fully enclosed shopping mall in Edina a Minneapolis suburb in 1956. In 1962 Dayton's opened its first discount store in Roseville (naming the store Target to distinguish the discounter from its higher-end department stores).

Dayton's went public in 1966 the same year it began the B. Dalton bookstore chain. Three years later it merged with the family-owned Hudson's forming Dayton Hudson. Dayton Hudson purchased more malls and invested in such specialty areas as consumer electronics and hard goods. Target had 24 stores by 1970.

The Target chain became the company's top moneymaker in 1977. The next year Dayton Hudson bought California-based Mervyn's (later Mervyns). In the late 1970s and 1980s it sold nine regional malls and several other businesses including the 800-store B. Dalton chain to Barnes & Noble. The Target stores division purchased Indianapolis-based Ayr-Way (1980) and Southern California-based Fedmart stores (1983). In the late 1980s Dayton Hudson took Target to Los Angeles and the Northwest. Robert Ulrich who began with the company as a merchandise trainee in 1967 became president and CEO of the Target stores division in 1987 and chairman and CEO of Dayton Hudson in 1994.

Dayton Hudson opened the first Target Greatland store in 1990. By this time it had 420 Target stores. Also that year Dayton Hudson bought the Marshall Field's chain of 24 department stores from B.A.T Industries. Marshall Field's began as a dry-goods business that Marshall Field bought in 1865 and subsequently built into Chicago's premier upscale retailer.

SuperTarget stores were introduced in 1995. The Target stores division opened stores in the Mid-Atlantic and Northeast the next year while the department store division began selling off its Marshall Field's locations in Texas.

In 1998 Dayton Hudson boosted its Internet presence by purchasing direct-marketing company Rivertown Trading; it also bought apparel supplier Associated Merchandising that year. In 2000 Dayton Hudson renamed itself Target Corporation. In early 2001 the company renamed its Dayton's and Hudson's chains Marshall Field's. Also that year Target acquired the rights to 35 former Montgomery Wards stores from the bankrupt retailer.

The nation's #2 discounter was #1 when it came to corporate giving in 2001. Target topped the Forbes list of America's Most Philanthropic Companies that year donating 2.5% of its 2000 income (nearly $86 million). By comparison Wal-Mart gave away $116.5 million in 2001 less than 1% of its income in 2000.

In 2002 the company reopened 30 of the former Montgomery Ward stores as Target outlets. Net of closings 94 Target stores opened in 2002 while neither Mervyns nor Marshall Field's added to their store counts. In March 2003 three new SuperTarget stores opened in the Dallas/Fort Worth area.

2004 was a year of divestments for Target. In January the discounter announced it was exiting the catalog business. To that end in April Target sold its Signals and Wireless gifts catalogs to Universal Screen Arts for an undisclosed sum. In July Target sold its Marshall Field's business to The May Department Stores Co. for about $3.2 billion in cash. In September Target completed the sale of 257 Mervyns stores in 13 states to an investment group that includes Cerberus Capital Management Lubert-Adler/Klaff and Partners and Sun Capital Partners as well as its Mervyns credit card receivables to GE Consumer Finance for a combined sum of approximately $1.65 billion in cash. (Later Mervyns filed for bankruptcy and closed the last of its stores by the end of 2008.)

In October 2005 vice chairman Gerald Storch resigned unexpectedly after more than a dozen years with the company. No reason was given for his departure. In the largest mass opening in Target's history the retailer opened 60 new stores on October 9.

In July 2006 Target.com extended its partnership with Amazon Enterprise Solutions a unit of online retailer Amazon.com through August 2010. Amazon provides e-commerce technology to the discount chain.

In May 2008 Ulrich who served as chairman and CEO since 1994 handed his CEO title to president Gregg Steinhafel. (Steinhafel joined the retailer in 1979 and worked his way up the executive ranks.) Also in May Target closed on the sale of a 47% stake in its credit-card receivable to JP-Morgan Chase for $3.6 billion. The five-year deal allows Target to buy back the stake at the end of the term. In October the company opened a pair of stores in Alaska thereby expanding its retail presence to 48 states. In November Target said no thanks to a plan Ackman had proposed for Target to spin off its real estate holdings in a bid to increase shareholder value citing uncertainty about valuation assumptions and the potential reduction in financial flexibility as a result of spin off.

Ulrich retired from the board in January 2009 and Steinhafel added the chairman's title to his job description.

In April 2010 Target stopped offering new credit card applicants its co-branded Visa credit card.

Chairman president and CEO Steinhafel resigned in May 2014 five months after a massive data breach at the company. In July 2014 the company named retail veteran Brian Cornell as chairman and CEO. Cornell 55 joined Target from PepsiCo Americas Foods where he served as CEO and oversaw the global food business. Before joining PepsiCo Cornell served as president and CEO of Sam's Club a division of Wal-Mart Stores.

EXECUTIVES

Senior Vice President Real Estate, Scott Nelson

EVP Merchandising Apparel and Home, Patricia (Trish) Adams

EVP and Chief Marketing Officer, Jeffrey J. Jones, age 47, $700,000 total compensation

EVP Chief Legal Officer and Corporate Secretary, Timothy R. (Tim) Baer, age 54

EVP and Chief Corporate Social Responsibility Office, Laysha L. Ward, age 47

Chairman and CEO, Brian C. Cornell, age 56, $595,000 total compensation

President Target.com and Mobile, Jason Goldberger

EVP Global Supply Chain and Operations, Keri Jones

EVP and Chief Merchandising and Supply Chain Officer, Kathryn A. (Kathee) Tesija, age 52, $950,000 total compensation

EVP and Chief Stores Officer, Tina M. Tyler, age 49, $725,000 total compensation

EVP and Chief Human Resources Officer, Jodeen A. Kozlak, age 51

EVP and COO, John J. Mulligan, $919,231 total compensation

Chief Strategy and Innovation Officer, Casey Carl

SVP Merchandising Health and Beauty, Jose Barra

EVP and CIO, Mike McNamara

President and Managing Director Target India, Navneet Kapoor

President Target Financial and Retail Services, Scott Kennedy

EVP and CFO, Cathy R. Smith, age 51

CEO Target Canada; SVP Treasury and Tax, Aaron Alt

President Target Sourcing Services, Kelly Caruso

Vice President Law, Terri Simard

Pharmacy Manager, Jason Sheakoski

Pharmacy Manager, Mikel Gilbert

Pharmacy Manager, Kenne Currie

Pharmacy Manager, Manus Dolan

Pharmd, Haleh Campbell

Pharmacy Manager, Tricia Wurster

Vice President Administrative Assistant, Elizabeth (Beth) Carson

Pharmacy Manager, Melissa Fritz

Pharmacy Manager, Joseph Legrand

Pharmacy Manager, Scott Moore

Pharmacy Manager, Will Peck

Pharmacy Manager, Casey Rhea

VPMM Domestics, Andrea Kellick

Senior Vice President Brand and Category Marketing, Rick Gomez

Senior Vice President Region II, Robert (Bob) Thompson

Senior Vice President, Linda Staupe

Pharmacy Manager, Bernard Brown

Vice President Administrative Assistant, Leslie Marston

Vice President Administrative Assistant, Lisa Chaika

Executive Vice President Executive Assistant, Bridget Hicks

Senior Vice President, Stephen Brinkley

Vice President and General Manager, Steve Mattson

Vice President Administrative Assistant, Heather Bean

Vice President Assistant, Melissa Loth

Senior Vice President Assistant, Nicole Saucier

Vice President Administrative Assistant, Cara Thrane

Pharmacy Manager, Jessica Vaughn

Senior Vice President Administrative Assistant, Toni Mcmanus

Vice President Assistant, Jennifer Komarek

Vice President Assistant Merch, Nadean Mueller

Senior Vice President Administration Human Resources Support Lead, Kate Boegemann

Pharmacy Manager, Kristopher Tidwell

Pharmacy Manager, Jacqueline Jansen

Pharmacist Manager, Kristin Hillman

Pharmacy Manager, Allison Allbrooks

Vice President Merchandise Manager, Tim Curoe

Senior Vice President Chief Information Security Officer, Brad Maiorino

Vice President Administrative Assistant, Michelle (Mitch) Halverson

Pharmacy Manager, Farzad Tafazzoli

Vice President Of Communications, Dustee Jenkins

Vice President Administrative Assistant, Cindy Fernandes

Vice President Administrative Assistant, Vonnie Zuehlke

Vice President General Counsel Employee and Labor Relations, Jim Rowader

Pharmacy Manager, David Navarro

Pharmacy Manager, Angel Amaro

Pharmacy Manager, Thomas (Thom) Hubiack

Vice President Finance Operations, Patti Johnson

Vice President Assistant Corporate Financial Planning, Bethany Borucki

Senior Vice President Administrative Assistant Marketing, Jaime Samson

Pharmacy Manager, Carrie Kennett

Vice President General Merchandise Manager Ladies Apparel, Nina Barjesteh

Vpgmm Merchandising, Deb Bollom

Pharmacy Manager, Lisa Reilly

Vice President Assistant, Heidi Rockswold

Pharmacy Manager, Purvi Shah

Pharmacy Manager, Jeremy Mable

Vice President Administrative Assistant TTS, Amanda Clausen

Senior Group Vice President, Jim Hogan

Vice President Assistant, Julie Simanski

Pharmacy Manager, Martine Sav

Pharmacy Manager, David (Dave) Cathcart

Pharmacy Manager, Nicole Giampapa

Vice President GMM, Rachael Vegas

Vice President Administrative Assistant, Diane Manlove

Senior Vice President Administrative A, Patricia (Pat) Hilleman

Senior Vice President Of Sales, Desi Bellamy

Senior Vice President Of Merchandising, Mark Schindele

Vice President Sales and Marketing, Vickie Strange

Senior Vice President Media and Guest Engagement, Kristi Argyilan

Senior Vice President New Business Integration and Operations, Peter (Pete) Glusker

Executive Vice President Marketing, Michael (Mel) Francis

Pharmacy Manager, Sujeev Vhan

Vice President Assistant, Kristen Anderson

Vice President Multichannel Operations, Philip Mckoy

Group 297 Vice President Assistant, Trina Kennedy

Vice President Administrative Assistant, Tamara Sherrill

Vice President Assistant, Margie Chapman

TSS Global Vice President Finance, Elsa Louie

Senior Vice President Assistant, Jennifer Krinke
Vice President Of WFM, Daniel (Dan) Traczyk
Vice President Assistant, Tracy Robbinspierce
Senior Vice President Assistant, Milagros Hanson
Pharmacy Manager, Mulu Gizaw
Pharmacy Manager, Eileen Major
Vice President of Product Design, Julie Guggemos
Vice President Of Distribution Operations, Diane Closs
Pharmacy Manager, Matthew Lindauer
Executive Vice President Merchandising Apparel and Home, Trish Adams
Vice President Assistant, Rhonda Broyles
Senior Vice President GC Sec'y, TimothyR Baer
Senior Group Vice President, Bill Hall
Pharmacy Manager, Rosa Leung
Vice President Target, Nancy Whitesell
Pharmacy Manager, Rushi Shah
Vice President Assistant, Stacy Sassen
Vice President Assistant, Christina Hayes
Senior Vice President Assistant, Janell Joyner
Vice President Assistant, Pat Pacyga
Pharm D, Amber Ovide
Group Vice President Administrator, Laverne White
Pharmacy Manager, Luck Sinasa
Vice President Assistant Style Marketing, Martie Weiske
Group Vice President Assistant, Tammy Stephens
Pharmacy Manager, Amanda Lefler
Executive Vice President Chief Legal Officer and Corporate Secretary, Tim Baer
Pharmacy Manager, Kari Ratkevich
Pharmacy Manager, Jaime Tolbert
Pharmacy Manager, Manish Patel
Vice President Assistant, Katie Jones
Pharmacy Manager, Len Kolencik
Pharmacy Manager, Denise Spring
Pharmacy Manager, Maria Chinaka
Treasurer, Morgan Thomas
Assistant Treasurer, Sara Ross
Vice Chairman, Mollie McCarty
Auditors: Ernst & Young LLP

LOCATIONS

HQ: Target Corp
1000 Nicollet Mall, Minneapolis, MN 55403
Phone: 612 304-6073
Web: www.target.com

2015 US Locations

	No.
California	268
Texas	148
Florida	123
Illinois	88
Minnesota	75
New York	71
Pennsylvania	65
Ohio	63
Virginia	57
Michigan	56
Georgia	52
North Carolina	49
Arizona	47
New Jersey	44
Colorado	41
Wisconsin	39
Maryland	38
Massachusetts	37
Washington	37
Missouri	36
Indiana	32
Tennessee	31
Alabama	22
Iowa	21
Connecticut	20
Oregon	19
South Carolina	19
Kansas	18
Nevada	17
Louisiana	16
Oklahoma	16
Kentucky	14
Nebraska	14
Utah	13

	No.
New Mexico	10
New Hampshire	9
Arkansas	9
Montana	7
Idaho	6
Mississippi	6
West Virginia	6
Maine	5
South Dakota	5
Hawaii	4
North Dakota	4
Rhode Island	4
Alaska	3
Delaware	3
Wyoming	2
District of Columbia	1
Total	**1,790**

PRODUCTS/OPERATIONS

2015 Sales

	% of total
Household essentials	25
Food & pet supplies	21
Apparel & accessories	19
Hardlines	18
Home furnishings & décor	17
Total	**100**

2015 Stores

	No.
Expanded food assortment	1,292
SuperTarget	249
Target General merchandise stores	240
CityTarget stores	8
Targetexpress	1
Total	**1,790**

Selected Designer Private Labels

Amy Coe (children's bedding and accessories)
Liz Lange (maternity)
Michael Graves Design (housewares)
Mossimo (junior fashions)
Sonia Kashuk (cosmetics and fragrances)
Todd Oldham (bedding and furniture)

Selected Private Labels

Archer Farms (food)
Cherokee (apparel)
Choxie (candy)
Furio (housewares)
Honors (apparel)
In Due Time (maternity wear)
Market Pantry
Merona (apparel)
Nick & Nora (apparel)
Playwonder (toys)
Utility (apparel)
Xhilaration (apparel)

Selected Other Operations

Rivertown Trading (catalogs and e-commerce)
    Britannia (British video and gifts)
    I Love A Deal (apparel housewares and jewelry)
    Seasons (traditional)
Target Receivables Corp.

COMPETITORS

Amazon.com	L Brands
BJ's Wholesale Club	Loblaw
Bed Bath & Beyond	Lowe's
Best Buy	Macy's
CVS	PETCO
Container Store	Ross Stores
Costco Wholesale	SUPERVALU
Dillard's	Safeway
Dollar General	Sears Holdings
Euromarket Designs	TJX Companies
Foot Locker	The Gap
Hart Stores	Toys ''R'' Us
Home Depot	Wal-Mart
J. C. Penney Company	Walgreen
Kohl's	Williams-Sonoma
Kroger	eBay

HISTORICAL FINANCIALS

Company Type: Public

Income Statement

FYE: January 31

	REVENUE ($ mil.)	NET INCOME ($ mil.)	NET PROFIT MARGIN	EMPLOYEES
01/15*	72,618	(1,636)	—	347,000
02/14	72,596	1,971	2.7%	366,000
02/13	73,301	2,999	4.1%	361,000
01/12	69,865	2,929	4.2%	365,000
01/11	67,390	2,920	4.3%	355,000
Annual Growth	**1.9%**	**—**	**—**	**(0.6%)**

*Fiscal year change

2015 Year-End Financials

Debt ratio: 30.91%
Return on equity: (-10.85%)
Cash ($ mil.): 2,210
Current ratio: 1.20
Long-term debt ($ mil.): 12,705

No. of shares (mil.): 640
Dividends
    Yield: 0.0%
    Payout: —
Market value ($ mil.): 47,126

	STOCK PRICE ($) FY Close	P/E High/Low		PER SHARE ($) Earnings	Dividends	Book Value
01/15*	73.61	—	—	(2.56)	1.90	21.86
02/14	56.64	24	18	3.07	1.58	25.64
02/13	61.15	14	11	4.52	1.32	25.66
01/12	50.05	13	11	4.28	1.10	23.64
01/11	54.35	15	12	4.00	0.84	22.00
Annual Growth	**7.9%**	**—**	**—**	**—**	**22.6%**	**(0.2%)**

*Fiscal year change

TCF Financial Corp

TCF Financial is the holding company for TCF National Bank which offers retail and small-business services through more than 430 locations. TCF provides standard services such as checking and savings accounts CDs consumer and business loans mortgages and insurance and is a leading issuer of Visa debit cards. Residential mortgages account for nearly half of the company's loan and lease portfolio. TCF also offers specialized lending services such as commercial leasing equipment finance inventory finance and indirect auto loans across the US.

Geographic Reach

TCF has nearly 430 locations in Arizona (seven branches) Indiana (four) Illinois (194) Michigan (53) Minnesota (108) South Dakota (one) and Wisconsin (25).

Operations

TCF operates through three primary segments: lending (71% of total revenues) funding (28%) and support services (1%).

Campus banking is also an important part of the company's operations. TCF has exclusive marketing alliances with several colleges including the University of Illinois and University of Michigan and is a leading provider of campus cards that serve as ID library security and stored-value cards in addition to ATM cards. Also as a part of its effort to build brand recognition on college campuses the company paid $35 million for the naming rights to the University of Minnesota's football stadium which opened in 2009 for 25 years.

Financial Performance

TCF saw its revenues hover around the $1.4 billion mark in 2011 and 2012. However it suffered a net loss of $213 million in 2012 due to a 78% spike in noninterest expenses and provision for credit losses. Over the years the company has suffered from declines in interest income and revenues from its funding segment also declined by 13% during 2012.

Strategy

TCF aims to attract customers through convenience. To that end more than half its branches are inside supermarkets and many of its locations are open seven days a week. While many of the company's peers attempt to grow their branch networks through acquisitions TCF has expanded by opening up new branches —more than 100 since 2003.

In order to reduce its reliance on interest-based income such as loans and leases which are subject to interest rate fluctuations and other outside factors TCF is focusing on growing its income from fees and service charges from products like checking accounts and credit cards.

The company has also experienced growth in its specialty finance operations including TCF Equipment Finance TCF Inventory Finance and Winthrop Resources which leases computers servers and other technology equipment. TCF continued to grow the business in 2011 when it bought California-based Gateway One a provider of consumer loans mainly for used cars.

EXECUTIVES

Executive Vice President of Corporate Human Resources of TCF Bank, Barbara (Barb) Shaw
Chairman, William A. Cooper, age 72, $1,500,000 total compensation
CEO, Craig R. Dahl, age 60, $550,000 total compensation
EVP and CFO TCF Equipment Finance; EVP Winthrop Resources, Thomas F. (Tom) Jasper, age 47, $550,000 total compensation
EVP Consumer Banking, Michael S. Jones, age 47, $324,808 total compensation
EVP Wholesale Banking, William S. Henak, age 58
Chief Risk Officer, James M. Costa, age 46
Chief Credit Officer TCF Financial and TCF Bank, Mark A. Bagley, age 54
CIO, Tom Butterfield
CFO and Treasurer, Brian W. Maass, age 42
Vice President, Dan Delgadillo
Assistant Vice President Financial Plans Manager, Scott Johnson
Vice President, Faye Erickson
Vice President Information Technology Audit Manager, Benjamin Thomas
Atm Channel Manager Vice President, Erin Kolb
Assistant Vice President Corporate Information Technology, Steve Larock
Vice President Product Management And Retail Functional, Jan Patterson
Executive Vice President, Joseph Doyle
Vice President Environmental Risk Manager, Cpg De Vries
Auditors: KPMG LLP

LOCATIONS

HQ: TCF Financial Corp
200 Lake Street East, Mail Code EX0-03-A, Wayzata, MN 55391-1693
Phone: 952 745-2760
Web: www.tcfbank.com

PRODUCTS/OPERATIONS

2012 Sales

	$ mil.	% of total
Lending	981	71
Funding	380	28
Support Services	13	1
Total	**1,375**	**100**

2012 Sales

	$ mil.	% of total
Interest	884	64
Noninterest	490	36
Total	**1,375**	**100**

2012 Branches by Type

	No.
Supermarket branches	228
Traditional branches	192
Campus branches	8
Total	**428**

Selected Subsidiaries

Fidelity National Capital Inc. (also dba Winthrop Capital)
TCF Agency Inc.
TCF Agency Insurance Services Inc.
TCF Bank International Inc.
TCF Commercial Finance Canada Inc. (also dba Financement Commercial TCF Canada Inc.)
TCF Equipment Finance Inc. (also dba TCF Leasing Inc.)
TCF Insurance Agency Inc.
TCF Inventory Finance Inc.
TCF Investments Management Inc.
TCF National Bank
TCF Portfolio Services Inc.
Winthrop Resources Corporation (also dba TCF Small Business Lending)

COMPETITORS

Anchor BanCorp	Bremer Financial
Associated Banc-Corp	Northern Trust
Bank Mutual	U.S. Bancorp
Bank of America	Wells Fargo

HISTORICAL FINANCIALS
Company Type: Public

Income Statement

FYE: December 31

	ASSETS ($ mil.)	NET INCOME ($ mil.)	INCOME AS % OF ASSETS	EMPLOYEES
12/14	19,394	174	0.9%	7,023
12/13	18,379	151	0.8%	7,449
12/12	18,225	(212)	—	7,328
12/11	18,979	109	0.6%	7,143
12/10	18,465	146	0.8%	7,363
Annual Growth	**1.2%**	**4.4%**	**—**	**(1.2%)**

2014 Year-End Financials

Debt ratio: 1.47%
Return on equity: 8.55%
Cash ($ mil.): 1,115
Current ratio: —
Long-term debt ($ mil.): —
No. of shares (mil.): 167
Dividends
  Yield: 1.2%
  Payout: 19.2%
Market value ($ mil.): 2,661

	STOCK PRICE ($) FY Close	P/E High/Low	PER SHARE ($) Earnings	Dividends	Book Value
12/14	15.89	18 15	0.94	0.20	12.67
12/13	16.25	20 15	0.82	0.20	11.83
12/12	12.15	— —	(1.37)	0.20	11.40
12/11	10.32	24 12	0.71	0.20	11.65
12/10	14.81	18 12	1.05	0.20	10.30
Annual Growth	**1.8%**	**— —**	**(2.7%)**	**(0.0%)**	**5.3%**

Teachers Insurance & Annuity Assn. of America (N.Y.)

Life insurance nsk

EXECUTIVES

Chairman, Jeff Ross
Senior Vice President Information Technology, Bill Brucella
Executive Vice President And President, Robert (Bob) Leary
Second Vice President Corporate Facilities, Thomas Fjellman
Vice President Corporate Communications, Don Ferenci
Field Vice President M Marketing And Products, Michael (Mel) Barsky
Vice President Invest And Finance Reporting, Michelle Haines
Vice President Wealth Marketing Strategy, Lisa Whittaker
Vice President Marketing, Thomas White
Vice President Benefits And Human Resources Operations, Robert (Bob) Weinman
Second Vice President Benefits, Thomas Hartnett
Vice President Of In, John McGovern
Vice President M Marketing And Products, Liz Debenedictis
Rvp, Jim Viets
Vice President Of Education, Holland Nance
Vice President, Christina Estrada
Vice President and Head Wealth Management Marketing, Beth Goldstein
Vice President Information Technology Strategic Ar, Brooks Thomas
Senior Business Control Specialist Vice President, Sokya Lindsay
EVP and Chief Legal Officer, Brandon Becker
Auditors: PRICEWATERHOUSECOOPERS LLP

LOCATIONS

HQ: Teachers Insurance & Annuity Assn. of America (N.Y.)
730 Third Avenue, New York, NY 10017
Phone: 212 490-9000
Web: www.tiaa-cref.org

HISTORICAL FINANCIALS
Company Type: Public

Income Statement

FYE: December 31

	ASSETS ($ mil.)	NET INCOME ($ mil.)	INCOME AS % OF ASSETS	EMPLOYEES
12/14	262,634	984	0.4%	—
12/13	250,494	1,751	0.7%	—
12/12	0	2,042	—	—
12/11	225,932	2,359	1.0%	—
12/10	214,544	1,381	0.6%	—
Annual Growth	**5.2%**	**(8.1%)**	**—**	**—**

2014 Year-End Financials

Debt ratio: —
Return on equity: 3.04%
Cash ($ mil.): 1,542
Current ratio: —
Long-term debt ($ mil.): —
No. of shares (mil.): 0
Dividends
  Yield: —
  Payout: —
Market value ($ mil.): —

Tech Data Corp.

Tech Data is 100% committed to IT products distribution. One of the world's largest wholesale distributors of technology products Tech Data provides thousands of different items to more than 115000 resellers in 100-plus countries. Its catalog of products includes computer components (disk drives keyboards and video cards) networking equipment (routers and bridges) peripherals (printers modems and monitors) systems (PCs and servers) and software. Tech Data also provides technical support configuration integration financing electronic data interchange (EDI) and other logistics and product fulfillment services. More than 60% of Tech Data's revenues are generated outside the US.

Geographic Reach

Florida-based Tech Data sells to customers in more than 100 countries throughout North America South America Europe the Middle East and Africa. Europe is the company's largest market accounting for 62% of sales.

Operations

Tech Data operates as a distributor of technology products logistics management and other value-added services in the Americas (including North America and South America) and Europe.

Sales and Marketing

Tech Data is one of the world's largest technology distributors. It helps companies like Hewlett Packard Apple Cisco Microsoft and hundreds of others bring their products to market and it offers a wide range of technical and business support services. Its products are purchased directly from vendors in significant quantities.

Products purchased from Hewlett Packard account for 19% of Tech Data's net sales while Apple products represent for 15%.

The company's customers include approximately 115000 value-added resellers direct marketers retailers and corporate resellers who support the diverse technology needs of end users.Its sales team consists of field sales and inside telemarketing sales representatives. Customers typically call its inside sales teams on dedicated telephone numbers or contact it through various electronic methods to place orders. If the product is in stock and the customer has available credit customer orders are generally shipped the same day from the logistics center nearest the customer or the intended end-user.

Financial Performance

In fiscal 2015 net sales increased by 3% due to higher sales from both the Americas and Europe.The increase in net sales in the Americas came from stronger demand for broadline products particularly personal computer systems.The growth in net sales in Europe reflected stronger demand for broadline products particularly personal computer systems and mobility products.Tech Data's net income decreased by $4.7 million due to an increased provision for income taxes and lower LCD settlements partially offset by higher sales.The increase in the provision for income taxes was primarily due to the relative mix of earnings and losses within certain countries in which Tech Data operates and adjustments to income tax reserves and valuation allowances.The company had been a claimant in proceedings seeking damages from certain manufacturers of LCD flat panel displays. During fiscal 2015 and 2014 Tech Data reached settlement agreements with certain manufacturers in the amount of $5.1 million and $35.5 million net of attorney fees and expenses.In fiscal 2015 Tech Data's net cash provided by the operating activities decreased by $259.7 million due to a change in accounts payable.

Strategy

As manufacturers have promoted more direct relationships with their customers the need for middlemen in the industry has dwindled and many tech product distributors have gone under. Tech Data was spared this fate due to its size and scope but it continually looks to cut costs in order to survive in a business characterized by thin margins. The company has also expanded its service offerings which range from pre- and post-sale technical support to customized shipping documents and electronic commerce integration.

Tech Data's diversification strategy seeks to continuously remix its product and customer portfolios toward higher growth and higher return market segments through organic growth and acquisitions. The company is looking to capitalize on new market opportunities in specialty areas such as data center software mobility and consumer electronics.

The company's execution strategy is supported by its highly efficient infrastructure combined with its multiple service offerings to generate demand develop markets and provide supply chain services for its vendors and customers.The final tenet of the company's strategy is innovation. Its IT systems and e-business tools and programs have provided its business with the flexibility to effectively navigate fluctuations in market conditions structural changes in the technology industry as well as changes created by products it sells. The company's strategic focus categories include products in the areas of Broadline Data Center Software Mobility and Consumer Electronics.In 2015 Tech Data announced an expanded agreement with Hewlett Packard Enterprise to offer Aruba Networks; an expanded agreement with Brocade to offer the Virtual Application Delivery platform; a new agreement with Infinio Systems Inc. to offer data center solutions; and new Mitel solutions available from the Tech Data Cloud Solutions Store. That year the company introduced EmpowerMe a new online learning management system for HP authorized solution providers. EmpowerMe offers users exclusive incentives industry news information about products and services and in-depth training to enhance solution providers' businesses growth and profitability.In 2015 Tech Data also introduced an online one-stop mobile solutions portal that helps solution providers easily access new mobile services available through the company's Mobile Solutions & Retail division. Using the portal solution providers can now access device configuration application support deployment services product care renewals and carrier activations.

In order to cut costs and to focus on core regions in 2015 Tech Data agreed to sell its business operations in Chile Peru and Uruguay.

Mergers and Acquisitions

In 2015 Tech Data acquired certain assets of Signature Technology Group (STG a leading North American provider of data center and professional services). STG's services are offered through Tech Data's Advanced Infrastructure Solutions division the company's data center business in the Americas. The addition of STG strengthened the data center offerings further diversified the company's services portfolio and provided added value for its customers.

HISTORY

Tech Data grew out of an electronics distribution business founded by Edward Raymund a University of Southern California graduate who started out as a representative for electronics manufacturers. By the early 1960s he had established an industrial electronics distribution business in Florida.

In 1974 he incorporated that business as Tech Data.

In 1981 Raymund's 25-year-old son Steven who had earned master's degrees in economics and international politics from Georgetown University's School of Foreign Service joined Tech Data on a temporary basis to work on the company's catalog. At that time Tech Data sold diskettes and other computer supplies to local companies and had about $2 million in sales.

Steven Raymund's favored status at the company angered a group of managers. Shortly after he arrived at Tech Data they copied the company's client list and walked out. The defection nearly sank Tech Data but Steven Raymund stayed on when his father handed him two-thirds of the company.

With the PC industry beginning to take off Steven Raymund positioned Tech Data as a middleman between computer and peripheral manufacturers and resellers. Steven was named COO in 1984. He became CEO in 1986 the year the company went public.

Tech Data began to distribute software in 1992 and a year later the company signed up Microsoft and inked a distribution deal for IBM computer systems. In 1994 Tech Data purchased U.S. Software Resource a California-based distributor of more than 500 business and entertainment software titles thereby increasing its software list and gaining high-profile publishers such as Borland International (now Borland Software) and Corel as suppliers.

Also in 1994 Tech Data began a global expansion when it bought France's largest distributor of wholesale computer products Softmart International.

To further build its business in Europe Tech Data in late 2012 acquired several distribution companies owned by UK-based Specialist Distribution Group (SDG) in the UK France and the Netherlands. Combined the acquired businesses generate sales of about €1.4 billion ($1.75 billion). Previously Tech Data bought Triade Holding a Netherlands-based distributor of consumer electronics and IT products in 2010. The purchase strengthened Tech Data's IT business and accelerated its diversification into consumer electronics in the Netherlands Denmark and the Benelux region; it also supported operations across Europe by adding new specialty products vendors and customers. As part of the transaction Tech Data's joint venture with Brightstar Brightstar Europe (formed in 2007) acquired Triade subsidiary Mobile Communication Company (MCC) a mobility products distributor in Benelux. Total value of both deals was €83 million (about $123 million). (Later Tech Data in 2012 bought its joint venture partner Brightstar's 50% ownership in Brightstar Europe for more than $165 million as well as several distribution companies in the UK from the distribution arm of IT services company Specialist Computer Holdings.)

EXECUTIVES

President Europe, N Ctor Cano, age 50, $843,693 total compensation

Vice President Sales, Rich Pereira

CEO and Director, Robert M. Dutkowsky, age 60, $1,057,690 total compensation

President the Americas, Joseph H. Quaglia, age 50, $447,092 total compensation

EVP and CIO, John Tonnison, age 46, $427,680 total compensation

EVP and CFO, Charles V. (Chuck) Dannewitz

Vice President Supply Chain Systems In, Joanne Persinger

Vice President Of Information Technology, Scott Moore

Vice President E Business, Phil Filippelli
Senior Vice President Human Resources,
 Lawrence Hamilton
National Account Manager, Ralph Ignacio
Vice President Of Ecommerce, John Thomason
Vice President, Angela Norrie
National Account Manager, Terri Beckwith
Vice President Financial Accounting, Tracey Troina
Vice President Information Technology, David
 (Dave) Johnson
Vice President Marketing, John Miller
Vice President, Karen Wise
Senior Vice President and Corporate Controller,
 Joseph (Jo) Trepani
Vice President of Networking Marketing, Charles
 (Chas) Bartlett
Vice President Global Enterprise Architecture and
 Information Technology Security, Daniel (Dan)
 Lasher
Vice President Cisco Solutions Group, Angela
 (Angie) Beltz-Norrie
Vice President Manager Director, Cathy Clark
Vice President Cisco Solutions Group, Angie Beltz
Assistant Treasurer, Scott Walker
Treasurer, Gael Manzo
Auditors: Ernst & Young LLP

LOCATIONS

HQ: Tech Data Corp.
 5350 Tech Data Drive, Clearwater, FL 33760
Phone: 727 539-7429
Web: www.techdata.com

2015 Sales

	$ mil.	% of total
Europe	17,264	62
Americas	10,406	38
Total	27,670	100

PRODUCTS/OPERATIONS

2015 Sales

	% of total
Broadline	47
Data centers	22
Software	18
Mobility	10
Consumer electronics	3
Total	100

2015 Sales by Channel

	% of total
VARs (Value added resellers)	45
Direct marketers and retailers	30
Corporate resellers	25
Total	100

Solutions
Credit Services
Marketing Services
 Education
Technical Services
Products and services
 Logistics
Supply Chain Services
Technical Services
Marketing Services
Solutions Center

COMPETITORS

ASI Computer	MA Laboratories
Technologies	MicroAge
Agilysys	NTT Com Security
Arrow Electronics	New Age Electronics
Avnet	Ricoh USA
Black Box	SED International
Communications Supply	SHI International
CompuCom	SYNNEX
D & H Distributing	ScanSource
Dell	Softmart
Gigaset	UNICOM Government
IBM	Westcon
Ingram Micro	ZT Group

HISTORICAL FINANCIALS

Company Type: Public

Income Statement

FYE: January 31

	REVENUE ($ mil.)	NET INCOME ($ mil.)	NET PROFIT MARGIN	EMPLOYEES
01/15	27,670	175	0.6%	8,900
01/14	26,821	179	0.7%	9,100
01/13	25,358	176	0.7%	9,100
01/12	26,488	206	0.8%	8,300
01/11	24,375	214	0.9%	8,700
Annual Growth	3.2%	(4.9%)	—	0.6%

2015 Year-End Financials

Debt ratio: 5.97%
Return on equity: 8.63%
Cash ($ mil.): 543
Current ratio: 1.49
Long-term debt ($ mil.): 353

No. of shares (mil.): 37
Dividends
 Yield: —
 Payout: —
Market value ($ mil.): 2,134

	STOCK PRICE ($) FY Close	P/E High/Low	PER SHARE ($) Earnings	Dividends	Book Value
01/15	57.10	15 11	4.57	0.00	52.44
01/14	53.92	12 9	4.71	0.00	55.14
01/13	50.91	13 9	4.50	0.00	50.75
01/12	51.92	11 8	4.66	0.00	48.06
01/11	46.91	11 8	4.36	0.00	45.26
Annual Growth	5.0%	— —	1.2%	—	3.8%

Tegna Inc

This company spreads the word through websites and television broadcasts. TEGNA (formerly Gannett) has a large portfolio of media and digital businesses to deliver a wide range of content. Its television and digital businesses make the company one of the largest and most geographically diverse media companies in the US. TEGNA's two top digital properties are automotive-related site Cars.com and job site CareerBuilder. The company's media division includes more than 45 television stations making it the largest independent station group of major network affiliates in the top 25 markets. TEGNA was formed when Gannett spun off its newspaper publishing businesses including USA TODAY.

Geographic Reach

CareerBuilder is the largest online job site in North America measured both by traffic and revenue. The website has a presence in more than 60 markets worldwide.

TEGNA's media division reaches approximately one-third of all television households in the US and represents the #1 NBC affiliate group #1 CBS affiliate group and #4 ABC affiliate group (excluding owner-operators).

Operations

The company operates through two divisions: TEGNA Media and TEGNA Digital.

TEGNA Digital's Cars.com is a popular online destination for automotive consumers seeking objective information about cars. The site draws more than 30 million monthly visits. TEGNA Digital also operates G/O Digital a one-stop shop for small businesses looking to connect with consumers through digital marketing. G/O Digital partners with more than 5000 of the nation's top brands and retailers across more than 110 local markets.

The company's digital division also include Clipper a local advertising and marketing solutions provider.

Strategy

TEGNA was formed in 2015 through a spin-off transaction which separated Gannett's publishing and broadcasting operations. The idea was too optimize profitability for each part of the previously larger single company.

EXECUTIVES

President and CEO, Gracia C. Martore, age 64, $1,000,000 total compensation
Senior Vice President Human Resources, Roxanne Horning
SVP Diversified Business and Development Newspaper Division, John A. (Jack) Williams, age 65, $540,000 total compensation
President TEGNA Media, David T. (Dave) Lougee, age 57, $650,025 total compensation
EVP and CFO, Victoria D. Harker, age 50, $655,000 total compensation
Vice President Of Technology Gannett Broadcasting, Jeff Johnson
Vice President National Sales USCP, Howard Griffin
Vice President of Operations, Stacey Martin
Senior Vice President Labor Relations, Wendell J Van Lare
Vice President Strategy and Business Development, Joe Hurd
Vice President and Outside Sales, Charles (Chas) Loeher
Vice President and General Sales Manager, Kim Krause
Vice President of Advertising and Sales, Tom Baylerian
Vice President Investor Relations, Michael (Mel) Dickerson
Vice President Technology, Daniel (Dan) Babb
Vice President Corp Strategy, Saira Stahl
Vice President Human Resources, Keith Bulling
Regional Vice President Distribution And West, Steve Reed
Vice President and Strategy and Business Development, Raghav Mathur
Group Vice President Sales, Andy Lobred
Vice President and Product and Services, Tracey Bowyer
National Account Manager, Melissa (Mel) Bencomo
Vice President Sales CPG, Ramona Biliunas
National Sales Manager and WGRZ TV, Karen Vachon
Group Vice President Marketing and Strategy, Jim Weigert
Senior Vice President and Digital Sales, Richard (Dick) Knopke
Vice President and Agency Services, Khalil Dhouti
Vice President Audit, Jane (Ginny) Wimbush
Vice President and Treasurer, Michael (Mel) Hart
Vice President and Product Development and Desgn, Jeff Dionise
Senior Vice President, Brooke Spectorsky
Vice President and Senior News Executive, Rob Mennie
Vice President, Doug Wilson
Vice President Local Digital Sales, Maria Meadows
Senior Vice President General Counsel Secretary, Todd Mayman
Senior Vice President And Co head fixe, Nancy Angell
Chairman, Marjorie (Marge) Magner, age 65
Auditors: Ernst & Young LLP

LOCATIONS

HQ: Tegna Inc
7950 Jones Branch Drive, McLean, VA 22107-0150
Phone: 703 854-7000
Web: www.gannett.com

COMPETITORS

21st Century Fox	Media General
CBS	Raycom Media
E. W. Scripps	Sinclair Broadcast
Hearst Corporation	Group
Local TV	Tribune Media

HISTORICAL FINANCIALS

Company Type: Public

Income Statement

FYE: December 28

	REVENUE ($ mil.)	NET INCOME ($ mil.)	NET PROFIT MARGIN	EMPLOYEES
12/14	6,008	1,062	17.7%	31,250
12/13	5,161	388	7.5%	31,600
12/12	5,353	424	7.9%	30,700
12/11	5,239	458	8.8%	31,000
12/10	5,438	588	10.8%	32,600
Annual Growth	2.5%	15.9%	—	(1.1%)

2014 Year-End Financials

Debt ratio: 40.12%	No. of shares (mil.): 226
Return on equity: 35.81%	Dividends
Cash ($ mil.): 118	Yield: 0.0%
Current ratio: 1.31	Payout: 17.4%
Long-term debt ($ mil.): 4,488	Market value ($ mil.): 7,201

	STOCK PRICE ($) FY Close	P/E High/Low		PER SHARE ($) Earnings	Dividends	Book Value
12/14	31.76	7	6	4.58	0.80	14.36
12/13	29.22	17	11	1.66	0.80	11.83
12/12	17.61	10	7	1.79	0.80	10.22
12/11	13.55	9	4	1.89	0.24	9.82
12/10	15.43	8	5	2.43	0.16	9.03
Annual Growth	19.8%	—	—	17.2%	49.5%	12.3%

Telephone & Data Systems, Inc.

One of the top US phone companies that's not related to Ma Bell Telephone and Data Systems (TDS) has about 6 million local phone and wireless customers in 36 states. The company's core business unit U.S. Cellular serves about 4.8 million customers in 23 states; key markets are in the central and mid-Atlantic regions. The company also offers fixed-line and broadband Internet services in rural and suburban markets in 36 states through its TDS Telecom subsidiary which provides local service to 1.2 million access lines through more than 110 incumbent local-exchange carriers (ILEC). Data networking and hosted telecom services are provided to business clients through the TDS Business unit.

Operations

TDS is more telephone than data systems with more than 78% total revenue coming from wireless services sold by US Cellular. TDS owns 84% of US Cellular's stock. The company also owns 63% of Airadigm Communications a Wisconsin-based wireless provider operating independently from U.S. Cellular. The company's hosted and management services segment account for 5% of revenue. Those services are grouped under the OneNeck IT Services subsidiary.

Aside from its core telecom operations TDS has an 80% interest in commercial printing business Suttle-Straus which provides corporate communications direct mail advertising materials and distribution services to customers primarily in the Midwest.

Sales and Marketing

U.S. Cellular sells its services through distribution channels that include retail sales and service centers direct sales third-party national retailers independent agents and its website and telesales for customers seeking to contact U.S. Cellular through the Internet or by phone. TDS increased its advertising to $228 million in 2014 from $213 million in 2013. It however devoted more than $241 million to advertising in 2012.

Financial Performance

Net revenue inched up to $5.01 billion in 2014 from $4.49 billion in 2013 a 2.2% difference. The TDS cable unit drove the increase with higher residential and commercial revenues from from acquisitions. Revenue from HMS (service and equipment) increased also with help from acquisitions as well as growth in recurring services such as co-location dedicated hosting hosted application management. and cloud computing services. Revenue in the wireline segment fell about $10 million in 2014 from 2013 a 1% decline.

TDS posted a loss of $136.3 million in 2014 compared to a profit of some $142 million in 2013. Acquisitions increased the company's cost of equipment and products. TDS also determined that the carrying value of HMS goodwill exceeded its fair value of goodwill and it recognized an $84 million impairment loss.

Cash flow from operations was $395 million at the end of 2014 compared to $494 million the year before.

Strategy

The company continues to expand its presence in the business broadband market with high-speed dedicated broadband hosted and managed IP telephony point-to-point Ethernet and other hosted and managed services such as colocation dedicated hosting hosted application management and cloud computing services.

The company has stated that it plans to use 75% of its available resources to build its product and services portfolio particularly in hosted and managed services. Acquisitions are a big part of the plan but the company has no acquisition activity through 3Q 2015.

US Cellular expanded its sales locations in 2014 when Wal-Mart Sam's Club RadioShack and Dollar General began offering the carrier's products and services at some stores.

Mergers and Acquisitions

TDS uses acquisitions to expand its service area and diversify its selection of services. In fiscal 2014 its TDS Telecom subsidiary purchased BendBroadband a cable and broadband company headquartered in Bend Oregon for $261 million. The deal adds to TDS' cable television business and expands its footprint in the Pacific Northwest.

Further south in 2013 it bought Baja Broadband a cable company serving some 200000 homes in New Mexico for nearly $270 million. The acquisition furthers the company's strategy of expanding into adjacent businesses such as cable and managed services. In 2012 it purchased Des Moines Iowa-based IT services provider Vital Support Systems for $45 million to boost its hosted and managed services unit.

HISTORY

Early History

LeRoy Carlson Sr. learned the ins and outs of rural phone operators when he owned a small firm that supplied equipment and forms to independent phone companies. In the mid-1950s he began buying some of these small phone companies which he consolidated with a phone book publisher and his equipment company to form Telephones Inc. Carlson sold the company to Contel in 1966.

Carlson continued to buy and sell rural carriers allowing them to retain local management while he provided centralized purchasing and system upgrades. In 1969 he bought 10 rural providers in Wisconsin and consolidated all of his companies into Telephone and Data Systems (TDS).

Between 1970 and 1975 TDS acquired 32 rural phone companies. When smaller companies in its established regions became scarce TDS bought rural phone providers from large independents. As TDS diversified the wireline subsidiary became TDS Telecommunications.

The company began offering paging services in Wisconsin in 1972 and later created subsidiary American Paging (1981). In 1975 TDS moved into cable TV service eventually creating TDS Cable Communications (1984) but it sold the holdings in 1986.

Getting a head start on the big Bells in the cellular race TDS began seeking licenses in the early 1980s eventually winning a 5% stake in the Los Angeles market. Although buffeted by larger independents it placed a high priority on cellular operations and formed subsidiary United States Cellular Corporation in 1983. Two years later US Cellular launched services in Tennessee and Oklahoma.

EXECUTIVES

SVP Acquisitions and Corporate Development, Scott H. Williamson, age 64, $627,500 total compensation

SVP Finance and Treasurer, Peter L. Sereda, age 53

President and CEO, LeRoy T. (Ted) Carlson, $1,352,700 total compensation

SVP and CIO, Kurt B. Thaus

SVP Technology Services and Strategy, Joseph R. Hanley

SVP Finance and Chief Accounting Officer, Douglas D. Shuma, age 53, $377,950 total compensation

VP and Chief Information Security Officer, Theodore E. Wiessing

Vice President Internal Audit, Frieda Ireland

Vice President Corporate Devel, Kenneth (Ken) Kotylo

Vice President Corporate Relations, Jane (Ginny) McCahon

Assistant Treasurer, John Toomey

Chairman, Walter C. D. Carlson

Auditors: PricewaterhouseCoopers LLP

LOCATIONS

HQ: Telephone & Data Systems, Inc.
30 North LaSalle Street, Suite 4000, Chicago, IL 60602
Phone: 312 630-1900   **Fax:** 312 630-1908
Web: www.teldta.com

PRODUCTS/OPERATIONS

2014 Sales

	$ mil.	% of total
US Cellular	3,892	78
TDS Telecom	1,120	21
Other	28	1
Adjustments	- -	
Total	**5,009**	**100**

COMPETITORS

AT&T	Horry Telephone
Atlantic Tele-Network	NII Holdings
Cavalier Telephone	NTELOS
CenturyLink	Sprint Communications
Cincinnati Bell	Suddenlink

Cricket
FairPoint
  Communications Inc.
Farmers
  Telecommunications
HC2 Holdings

Communications
T-Mobile USA
Verizon
Verizon Wireless Inc.
XO Holdings

HISTORICAL FINANCIALS
Company Type: Public

Income Statement
FYE: December 31

	REVENUE ($ mil.)	NET INCOME ($ mil.)	NET PROFIT MARGIN	EMPLOYEES
12/14	5,009	(136)	—	10,600
12/13	4,901	141	2.9%	10,500
12/12	5,345	81	1.5%	12,100
12/11	5,180	200	3.9%	12,300
12/10	4,986	143	2.9%	12,400
Annual Growth	0.1%	—	—	(3.8%)

2014 Year-End Financials

Debt ratio: 22.39%
Return on equity: (-3.39%)
Cash ($ mil.): 471
Current ratio: 1.66
Long-term debt ($ mil.): 1,993

No. of shares (mil.): 107
Dividends
  Yield: 2.1%
  Payout: —
Market value ($ mil.): 2,724

	STOCK PRICE ($) FY Close	P/E High/Low	PER SHARE ($) Earnings	Dividends	Book Value
12/14	25.25	— —	(1.26)	0.54	36.40
12/13	25.78	24 16	1.29	0.51	37.87
12/12	22.14	39 26	0.75	0.49	37.14
12/11	23.81	17 10	1.83	0.47	36.54
12/10	31.52	23 18	1.36	0.45	36.70
Annual Growth	(5.4%)	— —	—	4.5%	(0.2%)

TENASKA MARKETING VENTURES

LOCATIONS

HQ: TENASKA MARKETING VENTURES
  14302 FNB PKWY, OMAHA, NE 681544446
Phone: 4027586100
Web: WWW.TENASKA.COM

HISTORICAL FINANCIALS
Company Type: Private

Income Statement
FYE: December 31

	REVENUE ($ mil.)	NET INCOME ($ mil.)	NET PROFIT MARGIN	EMPLOYEES
12/07	10,309	0	—	91
12/05	9,470	0	—	—
12/04	0	0	—	—
12/03	4,940	0	—	—
Annual Growth	20.2%	—	—	—

Tenet Healthcare Corp.

Tenet Healthcare is here to spread the doctrine of good health. The for-profit company operates 80 acute care hospitals with more than 20800 beds in 14 US states including California Florida and Texas. They range from small community facilities offering basic care to major hospitals such as the 650-bed Brookwood Medical Center in Birmingham Alabama. In addition to its acute care holdings Tenet also operates specialty hospitals skilled nursing facilities physician practices outpatient centers imaging centers health plans and other health care units that form regional networks around its main hospitals. It also operates Conifer Health Solutions a patient billing and communications company.

HISTORY

Hospital attorney Richard Eamer along with attorneys Leonard Cohen and John Bedrosian founded National Medical Enterprises (NME) in 1969. After its IPO NME bought 10 hospitals nursing homes an office building and land in California. Within six years the company owned operated and managed 23 hospitals and a home health care business. It sold medical equipment and bottled oxygen and provided vocational training for nurses.

In the 1970s NME expanded into hospital construction and bought five Florida hospitals. By 1981 NME was the #3 health care concern in the US owning or managing 193 hospitals and nursing homes. In the 1980s NME diversified further buying nursing homes and mental health centers. By the end of the decade the company's Specialty Hospital Group brought in more than 50% of revenues. NME was the second-largest publicly owned health care company in the US (after HCA) by 1985.

In 1990 NME reversed course spinning off most of its long-term-care businesses but kept 19 UK nursing facilities operated by its Westminster Health Care subsidiary (sold 1996). In 1992 the company acquired an Australian hospital management firm.

That year several insurance companies sued NME alleging fraudulent psychiatric claims; NME settled the suits in 1993. Federal agents later raided company headquarters seizing papers related to the suspected fraud. That year investment banker Jeff Barbakow took over as CEO forcing out Eamer and Cohen.

In 1993 and 1994 NME dumped most of its psychiatric and rehabilitation facilities using the proceeds to help pay penalties stemming from the federal investigation into alleged insurance fraud kickbacks and patient abuse at its psychiatric units. NME paid another $16 million in related state fines. (Related civil lawsuits were settled in 1997.)

The company's name change to Tenet Healthcare coincided with new purchases throughout the South in 1995 and 1996.

The next few years were mixed for Tenet. On the upside it bought OrNda HealthCorp which complemented Tenet's existing networks. Tenet and MedPartners (now Caremark Rx) then the #1 practice management firm formed a Southern California hospital-doctor network in 1997 that gave both companies heft in dealing with HMOs (the partnership crumbled in 1999 when MedPartners exited practice management to focus on pharmacy benefits management and ceased operations in California). Merger discussions began with embattled market leader Columbia/HCA (now HCA) but fizzled.

In 1998 Tenet bought eight Philadelphia hospitals owned by the bankrupt Allegheny Health Education & Research Foundation. The company was dogged by another investigation this time by the Health and Human Services Inspector General's office over allegations the company paid more than fair market value for a physician practice in return for kickbacks. Tenet in 2004 agreed to pay about $31 million to settle two lawsuits stemming from these allegations.

Like many companies in the industry in 1999 Tenet began feeling the effects of the Balanced Budget Act of 1997 which mandated more scrutiny of Medicare expenditures to health care providers. In response the company began divesting some of its hospitals; it also shed its practice management business and reorganized its corporate structure.

Tenet rebounded and acquired hospitals in 2001 and 2002 but the next year proved not so kind. Federal investigations into the company's billing practices particularly those related to Medicare began late in 2002. In 2003 the company settled claims brought by the Department of Justice that doctors performed unnecessary cardiac surgeries at its Redding Medical Center (now Shasta Regional Medical Center) in California; the settlement cost Tenet $54 million (plus millions more to settle patients' claims). Tenet sold the facility in 2004 and also disposed of more than a dozen other facilities cutting its holdings from 115 to 100.

An even larger sell-off began in 2004 and included nearly 20 hospitals in California and others in Louisiana Massachusetts (all three were sold to Vanguard Health Systems in early 2005) Missouri and Texas. The company also exited the Nevada market when it sold Lake Mead Hospital Medical Center in Las Vegas in early 2004. Additionally the company ended some operating leases and joint ventures primarily in California; sold its Barcelona Spain hospital; and sold about a dozen home health agencies and hospice providers to Amedisys.

Tenet Healthcare moved its headquarters from Santa Barbara California to Dallas in 2005. The move was intended to streamline operations and save money.

Tenet saw some hard times in 2005 and spent years struggling to emerge from several subsequent years of investigations lawsuits and bad publicity. Its New Orleans and Mississippi facilities were hit hard by Hurricane Katrina in 2005 and its Memorial Medical Hospital in New Orleans became a symbol of the city's devastation after several dozen bodies were found there in the aftermath of the storm. The company has since sold both locations.

In 2006 it resolved multiple federal investigations regarding its billing practices by agreeing to a $900 million deal with the Justice Department. Its sale of hospitals post-Katrina was part of a larger plan announced in 2006 to sell off about a dozen facilities ridding itself of some low-performing operations partly to pay its $900 million bill to government investigators and partly so it could invest in equipment upgrades at its remaining hospitals. (The sales followed a larger-scale divestiture of about 25 facilities begun earlier.) In 2009 Tenet sold the USC University Hospital and Kenneth Norris Jr. Cancer Hospital to the University of Southern California for $275 million.

In 2010 Tenet sold its stake in supply chain and clinical workforce management firm Broadlane to MedAssets for some $159 million.

In late 2010 fellow hospital operator and rival Community Health Systems(CHS) made an unsolicited bid to acquire Tenet in a deal worth some $7.3 billion ($3.3 billion in cash and stock plus the assumption of $4 billion in debt). Tenet responded with a resounding "thanks but no thanks" saying the bid undervalued the company. CHS remained persistent despite a "poison pill" plan Tenet adopted and a volley of lawsuits. After Tenet's board rejected a plumped up offer of $4.1 billion in cash CHS formally withdrew all offers in 2011.

EXECUTIVES

Vice President Operations, Ricky Johnston
Chairman and CEO, Trevor Fetter, age 55, $1,250,000 total compensation
CEO Northeast Region, Erik G. Wexler
CEO Western Region, Jeffrey (Jeff) Koury
President Conifer Health Solutions, Stephen M. (Steve) Mooney
SVP Chief Managed Care Officer, Clint Hailey
CFO, Daniel J. (Dan) Cancelmi, age 52, $565,923 total compensation
SVP and General Counsel, Audrey T. Andrews, age 47, $459,616 total compensation
CEO Southern Region, Garry Gause
SVP Physician Resources, Gary K. Ruff, $400,000 total compensation
President Hospital Operations, Britt T. Reynolds, age 49, $690,616 total compensation
SVP Clinical Operations and Chief Clinical Officer, Kelvin A. Baggett
Chief Medical Officer, Mark R. Montoney
CEO San Antonio Market, Graham Reeve
SVP Operations Florida, Marsha Powers
CEO Texas Region, Eric Evans
SVP Applied Clinical Informatics and CIO, Paul T. Browne
CEO Detroit Market, Joseph (Joe) Mullany
CEO South Texas Market, Manuel R. (Manny) Vela
CEO Placentia-Linda Hospital, Audrey Gregory
Executive Chairman Aspen Healthcare, Mark Kopser
CEO United Surgical Partners International, Bill Wilcox
CEO El Paso Market, Sally Deitch
CEO Aspen Healthcare, Des Shields
CEO Chicago Market, Anthony Tedeschi
Vice President Taxes, Douglas (Doug) Rabe
Assistant Vice President Mgd Care Finance, Amy Thomason
Regional Vice President Chief Financial Officer, Bill Durham
Assistant Vice President National Contracting and Strategic Planning, Adele Paulett
Vice President Regional Finance Information technology, Wesley O James
Senior Vice President Acquisitions And D, Harold Pilgrim
Vice President Consumer Applications, Brian Barnes
Assistant Vice President Managed Care, John (Jack) Widdel
Director Physician Recruitment And Onboarding, Christina Rivera
Director Of Pharmacy, Alfred Ochlak
Vice President Finance Acquisitions and Development, Mark Peacock
Vice President Corporate Financial Planning, Stephen Diaz
Director Of Pharmacy Operations, Matt Moss
Director Of Radiology Services, Anthony Davis
Vice President, Stephen Preston
Vice President Human Resources Hospital Operations, Lisa Whaley
Vice President Chief Financial Officer Central Region At Tenet Healthcare, Kathryn Engstrom
Physical Therapy, Martin Roque
Vice President Physicians Relations, Lane Cooley
Assistant Vice President Finance Accountable Care, Rick Watson
Vice President For Human Resources, Don Currier
Director Of Radiology, David Fuller
Vice President Marketing, Elizabeth Miller
Director Managed Care, Amy Dozier
Director Managed Care, Annette Rooney

Vice President Finance, Rod Reasoner
Vice President Operations Finance Tenet Healthcare Southern States Region, Wes James
Senior Vice President Marketing Government Relatns, Marilynn Robinson
Vice President Corporate Sourcing, Richard (Dick) Yonker
Director of Radiology, Jim Morrell
Vice President and Regional Chief Information Officer, Mary Garrido
Vice President Financial Information Systems, Michael (Mel) Hongola
Vice President, Janie Patterson
Vice President and Assistant General Counsel Legal Operations, Sue Monaco
Vice President Assistant General Counsel (2002), John (Jack) Tilly
Vice President Government Programs, Craig Armin
Executive Vice President Human Resources, David L (Dave) Archer
Vice Chairman, Keith B. Pitts, age 57
Secretary executive, Vickie Jackson
Auditors: Deloitte & Touche LLP

LOCATIONS

HQ: Tenet Healthcare Corp.
    1445 Ross Avenue, Suite 1400, Dallas, TX 75202
Phone: 469 893-2200
Web: www.tenethealth.com

Selected Hospitals

Alabama
    Brookwood Medical Center (Birmingham)
California
    Desert Regional Medical Center (Palm Springs)
    Doctors Hospital of Manteca
    Doctors Medical Center (Modesto)
    Fountain Valley Regional Hospital and Medical Center
    John F. Kennedy Memorial Hospital (Indio)
    Lakewood Regional Medical Center
    Los Alamitos Medical Center
    Placentia Linda Hospital
    San Ramon Regional Medical Center
    Sierra Vista Regional Medical Center (San Luis Obispo)
    Twin Cities Community Hospital (Templeton)
Florida
    Coral Gables Hospital
    Delray Medical Center (Delray Beach)
    Good Samaritan Hospital (West Palm Beach)
    Hialeah Hospital
    North Shore Medical Center (Miami)
    North Shore Medical Center - FMC Campus (Lauderdale Lakes)
    Palm Beach Gardens Medical Center
    Palmetto General Hospital (Hialeah)
    Saint Mary' s Medical Center (West Palm Beach)
    West Boca Medical Center (Boca Raton)
Georgia
    Atlanta Medical Center
    North Fulton Regional Hospital (Roswell)
    South Fulton Medical Center (East Point)
    Spalding Regional Medical Center (Griffin)
    Sylvan Grove Hospital (Jackson)
Missouri
    Des Peres Hospital (St. Louis)
    Saint Louis University Hospital
North Carolina
    Central Carolina Hospital (Sanford)
    Frye Regional Medical Center (Hickory)
Pennsylvania
    Hahnemann University Hospital (Philadelphia)
    St. Christopher' s Hospital for Children (Philadelphia)
South Carolina
    Coastal Carolina Hospital (Hardeeville)
    East Cooper Regional Medical Center (Mt. Pleasant)
    Hilton Head Hospital
    Piedmont Medical Center (Rock Hill)
Tennessee
    Saint Francis Hospital (Memphis)
    Saint Francis Hospital-Bartlett
Texas
    Centennial Medical Center (Frisco)
    Cypress Fairbanks Medical Center (Houston)
    Doctors Hospital at White Rock Lake (Dallas)
    Houston Northwest Medical Center

Lake Pointe Medical Center (Rowlett)
Nacogdoches Medical Center
Park Plaza Hospital (Houston)
Providence Memorial Hospital (El Paso)
Sierra Medical Center (El Paso)
Sierra Providence East Medical Center (El Paso)

PRODUCTS/OPERATIONS

2014 Revenues

	$ mil.	% of total
General hospitals	16,013	93
Conifer	1,193	7
Adjustments	(591)	-
Total	**16,615**	**100**

2014 Patient Revenues

	% of total
Managed care	59
Medicare	22
Medicaid	9
Indemnity self-pay & other	10
Total	**100**

COMPETITORS

Adventist Health System Sunbelt Healthcare
Ascension Health
Banner Health
CHRISTUS Health
Carolinas HealthCare System
Catholic Health Initiatives
Community Health Systems
Dignity Health
HCA
HealthSouth
LifePoint Health
Memorial Health Services
Mercy Health
SSM Health Care
Sutter Health
Texas Health Resources
United Surgical Partners
Universal Health Services
University Health Services
WellStar Health System

HISTORICAL FINANCIALS

Company Type: Public

Income Statement

FYE: December 31

	REVENUE ($ mil.)	NET INCOME ($ mil.)	NET PROFIT MARGIN	EMPLOYEES
12/14	16,615	76	0.5%	108,989
12/13	11,102	(104)	—	103,711
12/12	9,119	133	1.5%	59,164
12/11	8,854	94	1.1%	57,705
12/10	9,205	1,152	12.5%	56,605
Annual Growth	**15.9%**	**(49.3%)**	**—**	**17.8%**

2014 Year-End Financials

Debt ratio: 65.08%
Return on equity: 10.81%
Cash ($ mil.): 193
Current ratio: 1.32
Long-term debt ($ mil.): 11,695
No. of shares (mil.): 98
Dividends
    Yield: —
    Payout: —
Market value ($ mil.): 4,985

	STOCK PRICE ($) FY Close	P/E High/Low		PER SHARE ($) Earnings	Dividends	Book Value
12/14	50.67	527	323	0.12	0.00	6.62
12/13	42.12	—	—	(1.32)	0.00	7.79
12/12	32.47	25	3	1.30	0.00	10.92
12/11	5.13	16	7	0.48	0.00	13.71
12/10	6.69	1	0	8.16	0.00	14.54
Annual Growth	**65.9%**	**—**	**—**	**(65.2%)**	**—**	**(17.9%)**

Tenneco Inc

Tenneco ensures vehicles are riding steady without exhausting a lot of smoke. The auto parts maker designs and distributes ride-control equipment (including shock absorbers struts and suspensions) under the Monroe brand and emissions-control systems (catalytic converters exhaust pipes and mufflers) under the Walker brand. It also makes Clevite elastomer products (bushings mounts and springs) for vibration control in cars and heavy trucks. It supplies both OEMs and aftermarket wholesalers and retailers. Major customers include GM Ford Advance Auto Parts and Uni-Select. Tenneco operates on six continents and is growing its presence in key Asia/Pacific markets.

Geographic Reach

In addition to key alliances and joint ventures Tenneco operates 90 manufacturing facilities on six continents throughout the world. Most recently the company has opened manufacturing facilities in India China and Thailand. North America represented almost 50% of its total sales in 2014; Europe and South America (plus India) collectively accounted for 36%; and the Asia/Pacific region accounted for the remainder.

Operations

Tenneco divides its operations across six segments. These are structured geographically and are managed along its two major product lines of emission control and ride control. These segments are: North America Clean Air North America Ride Performance Europe South and India Clean Air Europe South and India Ride Performance Asia Pacific Clean Air and Asia Pacific Ride Performance. Emission control accounted for about 70% of the company's revenue in 2014.

As stricter environmental standards are enacted Tenneco finds itself well positioned as a supplier of emission control systems. The company has developed diesel particulate filters (DPFs) for passenger cars and medium-duty trucks both in Europe and North America. The filters when used with converters can reduce emissions of particulates by as much as 90% and nitrogen oxide by up to 85%. Tenneco also produces selective catalytic reduction (SCR) systems.

Another trend in the automotive industry that is building Tenneco's business is OEMs endeavoring to simplify their assembly process thus reducing costs and development times. To achieve this the OEMs are outsourcing more of the design and manufacturing of vehicle parts as well as fully-integrated systems that support emission control anti-lock braking roll-control and powertrains. This trend has given rise to Tier 1 systems integrators in addition to Tier 1 suppliers —Tenneco fits the bill for both roles. To boost its position even further the company offers just-in-time (JIT) systems for its emission control operations and has built JIT facilities close to a customer's plant for quick delivery of product components.

Sales and Marketing

Tenneco has separate sales and marketing efforts underway for its OE and aftermarket businesses. For OE sales the company's sales and marketing team is an integrated group of professionals including engineers and program managers who are organized by customer and product type (ride control and emission control). In 2014 the company served more than 70 different OEMs and commercial truck and off-highway engine manufacturers worldwide.

For aftermarket sales however the sale force covers multiple product lines and sells aftermarket products through four primary channels of distri-bution: The traditional three-step distribution system of full-line warehouse distributors jobbers and installers; the two-step distribution system of full-line warehouse distributors that carry only specified automotive product groups and installers; direct sales to retailers; and direct sales to installer chains. The company also serves locomotive agricultural construction and commercial truck and off-highway markets.

Its customers have included National Auto Parts Association Advance Auto Parts Uni-Select O'Reilly Automotive Aftermarket Auto Parts Alliance and AutoZone in North America Temot Autoteile GmbH Autodistribution International Group Auto Union Auto Teile Ring and AP United in Europe and Rede Presidente in South America. GM accounted for 15% of 2014 revenues; Ford 13%.

Tenneco spent $53 million on advertising and promotion expenses in 2013 and $57 million in 2014.

Financial Performance

Tenneco has enjoyed unprecedented growth over the last five years. From 2013 to 2014 its total sales increased by 6% to peak at a record-setting $8.4 billion. Tenneco's net income also climbed by 24% during that same time period.

The historic growth for 2014 was due to higher global light vehicle volumes the launching of new light vehicle platforms and a growing commercial truck and off-highway and aftermarket businesses in its all the regions.

In 2014 Tenneco's operating cash flow decreased by 32% to $341 million due to changes in inventories and prepayments and lower cash inflows.

Strategy

The company focuses on growth through increasing production volumes launching new technology and geographic expansion both organically and via strategic acquisitions and alliances. Tenneco is also eying adjacent markets to expand its portfolio of products and systems. Not limiting itself to passenger cars or medium-size trucks the company is positioning its emissions and ride control systems for heavy-duty trucks buses and agricultural and construction equipment.

On 2013 Tenneco increased its investment in Tenneco Tongtai Exhaust Company Limited (located in Dalian China) from 80% to 100%. That year it introduced its Scalable Architecture concept (for advanced electronic suspension technologies) which uses intelligent actuator constructions to scale semi-active suspension systems up to advanced and fully-active applications.Mergers and Acquisitions

In 2014 Tenneco acquired exclusive rights to the digital valve technology (previously licensed from Sturman) used in Tenneco's DRiV suspension products. DRiV is a suspension system designed by Tenneco featuring electronically controlled dampers with hydraulic valves for use in automotive light and heavy-duty trucks off-road equipment locomotives and other vehicle damping applications.

HISTORY

Tennessee Gas and Transmission began in 1943 as a division of the Chicago Corporation headed by Gardiner Symonds and authorized to build a pipeline from West Virginia to the Gulf of Mexico. With the US facing WWII fuel shortages the group finished the project in 11 months.

After WWII Tennessee Gas went public with Symonds as president. It merged its oil and gas exploration interests into Tennessee Production Company (1954) which with Bay Petroleum (bought 1955) became Tenneco Oil in 1961. Symonds acquired complementary firms and en-tered the chemical industry by buying 50% of Petro-Tex Chemical in 1955.

Tenneco Oil moved its headquarters to Houston in 1963 to better ship natural gas from the Texas Gulf Coast. Symonds bought Packaging Corporation of America a maker of shipping containers pulp and paperboard products in 1965. A year later the company which had become a conglomerate adopted the Tenneco name.

2013 Sales

	$ mil.	% of total
North America	3,913	50
Europe South America India	2,980	37
Asia/Pacific	1,071	13
Total	**7,964**	**100**

PRODUCTS/OPERATIONS

2013 Sales

	$ mil.	% of total
Emission-control systems & products		
OEM	5,117	64
Aftermarket	327	4
Ride-control systems & products		
OEM	1,567	20
Aftermarket	953	12
Total	**7,964**	**100**

Selected Brands and Products

Emission control systems (DNX DynoMax Fonos Gillet Thrush and Walker)
Aftertreatment control units
Burner systems
Catalytic converters and diesel oxidation catalysts
Diesel particulate filters (DPFs)
Exhaust manifolds
Hangers and isolators
High-frequency turbo decoupler
Hydrocarbon vaporizers and injectors
Lean NOx traps
Mufflers
Pipes
Resonators
Selective catalytic reduction (SCR)
Ride control systems (DNX Fric-Rot Kinetic Monroe and Rancho)
Coil and leaf springs
Computerized electronic suspension (CES)
Corner and full axle modules
Heavy duty truck and train shocks
Kinetic suspension technology
Shock absorbers and struts
Suspension systems
Top mounts
Vibration control components (Clevite Elastomers)
Engine and body mounts
Exhaust isolators
Leaf and coil springs
Spring seats
Suspension control arm link and stabilizer bar bushings

COMPETITORS

Benteler Automotive	Kolbenschmidt Pierburg
Cooper-Standard Automotive	Letts Industries
Edelbrock	Meritor
Faurecia Exhaust Systems	Metaldyne
	Wescast Industries
	ZF Group NAO

HISTORICAL FINANCIALS

Company Type: Public

Income Statement

FYE: December 31

	REVENUE ($ mil.)	NET INCOME ($ mil.)	NET PROFIT MARGIN	EMPLOYEES
12/14	8,420	226	2.7%	29,000
12/13	7,964	183	2.3%	26,000
12/12	7,363	275	3.7%	25,000
12/11	7,205	157	2.2%	24,000
12/10	5,937	39	0.7%	22,000
Annual Growth	**9.1%**	**55.2%**	**—**	**7.2%**

2014 Year-End Financials

Debt ratio: 28.15%
Return on equity: 48.60%
Cash ($ mil.): 282
Current ratio: 1.35
Long-term debt ($ mil.): 1,069

No. of shares (mil.): 61
Dividends
  Yield: —
  Payout: —
Market value ($ mil.): 3,465

	STOCK PRICE ($) FY Close	P/E High/Low	PER SHARE ($) Earnings	Dividends	Book Value
12/14	56.61	18 13	3.66	0.00	8.12
12/13	56.57	19 11	2.97	0.00	7.11
12/12	35.11	9 5	4.50	0.00	4.07
12/11	29.78	18 9	2.55	0.00	(0.00)
12/10	41.16	66 27	0.63	0.00	(0.07)
Annual Growth	**8.3%**	**— —**	**55.3%**	**—**	**—**

Tennessee Valley Authority

Tennessee Valley Authority (TVA) may not be an expert on state attractions like Dollywood and the Grand Ole Opry but it is an authority on power generation. A US government-owned corporation TVA is the largest public power producer in the country. It sells wholesale electricity to more than 150 municipal and cooperative power distributors which serve some 9 million people in Tennessee and parts of Alabama Georgia Kentucky Mississippi North Carolina and Virginia. It also sells power directly to large industries and federal agencies. In addition TVA provides flood control and land management for the Tennessee River system and assists utilities and state and local governments with economic development.

Geographic Reach

The Authority serves 170 counties in Alabama Georgia Kentucky Mississippi North Carolina Tennessee and Virginia. Tennessee accounts for 65% of the entity's revenues.

Operations

TVA operates 11 fossil plants 3 nuclear plants and 29 hydro plants. TVA provides electric power through a network of about 16000 miles of transmission line. Most of its power comes from traditional generation sources. Its facilities include fossil fuel-powered hydroelectric nuclear combustion turbine and combined-cycle plants. TVA has an agreement to produce tritium a radioactive gas that boosts the power of nuclear weapons for the US Department of Energy at its Watts Bar nuclear plant.

Sales and Marketing

In fiscal 2014 TVA provided electricity to 52 large industrial customers six federal agency customers and 155 local power company (LPC) customers that serve more than nine million people in parts of seven southeastern states. The United States Enrichment Corporation a subsidiary of USEC is TVA's largest directly served industrial customer. Two of the largest LPCs served by TVA are the Memphis Light Gas and Water Division (9% of TVA's fiscal 2014 revenues) and Nashville Electric Service 8%.

Financial Performance

In fiscal 2014 TVA's revenues grew by 2% due to higher sales volume to LPCs and a non-fuel base rate increase; offset by a lower fuel cost recovery from sales to industries directly served due to the reduction in demand by USEC. Industrial power sales decreased due to a drop in demand from industries directly served.That year the company's net income increased by 73% due to higher revenues and a decrease in expenses (especially in fuel expenses caused by timing of the fuel cost recovery mechanism and a reduction in sales volume) offset by an increase in power purchases.Over the last five years the company's has maintained a growth in its operating cash flows. In fiscal 2014 the operating cash flow increased by 15% (due to higher net income recovery of insurance proceeds related to the 2008 Kingston ash spill) offset by increased outflow in accounts receivable and increased pension contributions.

Strategy

The company plans to add three more nuclear plants by 2020 and is working with the DOE to reprocess waste from its existing plants.

It is also expanding its renewable energy portfolio and operates 16 solar energy sites and and one wind energy site. TVA is working toward obtaining 50% of its power supply from low- or zero-carbon-emitting or renewable sources by 2020. It also announced plans to replace its older and less efficient coal units with cleaner sources of power.

The company is also looking to cut operating and maintenance costs by $500 million by the end of 2015 through a high-level realignment of its strategic business units.In 2014 TVA began construction on a new hatchery and aquatic center along the Cumberland River with an investment of almost $1.5 million led by its $1 billion clean-air project at Gallatin Fossil Plant. That year it also approved replacing the Allen Fossil Plant in Memphis with a $975 million cleaner-burning natural gas plant that will help ensure continued low-cost electricity for the greater Memphis area. As part of its partnership with DuPont in 2014 TVA agreed on a plan to convert an existing limited-use combustion turbine at Johnsonville into a highly efficient combined heat and power plant.

HISTORY

TVA was established by Congress in 1933 primarily to reduce flood damage improve navigation on the Tennessee River and promote agricultural and industrial development in the region. In 1999 government appropriations for the authority ceased.

In 1924 the Army Corps of Engineers finished building the Wilson Dam on the Tennessee River in Alabama to provide power for two WWI-era nitrate plants. With the war over the question of what to do with the plants became a political football.

An act of Congress created the Tennessee Valley Authority (TVA) in 1933 to manage the plants and Tennessee Valley waterways. New Dealers saw TVA as a way to revitalize the local economy through improved navigation and power generation. Power companies claimed the agency was unconstitutional but by 1939 when a federal court ruled against them TVA had five operating hydroelectric plants and five under construction.

During the 1940s TVA supplied power for the war effort including the Manhattan Project in Tennessee. During the postwar boom between 1945 and 1950 power usage in the Tennessee Valley nearly doubled. Despite adding dams TVA couldn't keep up with demand so in 1949 it began building a coal-fired unit. Because coal-fired plants weren't part of TVA's original mission in 1955 a Congressional panel recommended the authority be dissolved.

Though TVA survived its funding was cut. In 1959 it was allowed to sell bonds but it no longer received direct government appropriations for power operations. In addition it had to pay back the government for past appropriations.

TVA began to build the first unit of an ambitious 17-plant nuclear power program in Alabama in 1967. However skyrocketing costs forced it to raise rates and cut maintenance on its coal-fired plants which led to breakdowns. In 1985 five reactors had to be shut down because of safety concerns.

In 1988 former auto industry executive Marvin Runyon was appointed chairman of the agency. "Carvin' Marvin" cut management sold three airplanes and got rid of peripheral businesses saving $400 million a year. In 1992 Runyon left to go to the postal service and was replaced by Craven Crowell who began preparing TVA for competition in the retail power market.

TVA ended its nuclear construction program in 1996 after bringing two nuclear units on line within three months a first for a US utility. The next year it raised rates for the first time in 10 years planning to reduce its debt. In response to a lawsuit filed by neighboring utilities it agreed to stop "laundering" power by using third parties to sell outside the agency's legally authorized area.

In 1999 the authority finished installing almost $2 billion in scrubbers and other equipment at its coal-fired plants so that it could buy Kentucky coal along with cleaner Wyoming coal. That year however the EPA charged TVA with violating the Clean Air Act by making major overhauls on some of its older coal-fired plants without getting permits or installing updated pollution-control equipment. It ordered TVA to bring most of its coal-fired plants into compliance with more current pollution standards. The next year TVA contested the order in court stating compliance would jack up electricity rates.

TVA was fined by the US Nuclear Regulatory Commission in 2000 for laying off a nuclear plant whistleblower.

In 2008 a holding pond at TVA's coal-burning Kingston Fossil Plant failed and dumped some 5.4 million cu. yd. of fly ash over 400 acres in eastern Tennessee's Roane County. The slide knocked down utility poles and trees and damaged at least a dozen homes (some beyond repair). Although no one was hurt some residents were cut off by the spill prompting officials to build a new road. The flooding was the pond's third reported incident in six years. The cleanup will likely cost more than $1 billion. Some 14 lawsuits were filed against the TVA as a result of the incident.

William D. Johnson former chairman president and CEO of Progress Energy was named president and CEO of TVA in 2013.

EXECUTIVES

EVP and CFO, John M. Thomas, age 52, $520,000 total compensation

EVP and Chief Nuclear Officer, Joseph P. (Joe) Grimes

EVP Customer Resources, Kenneth R. Breeden, age 67

EVP and COO, Charles G. (Chip) Pardee, age 55

EVP and Chief External Relations Officer, Robin E. (Rob) Manning, age 59

EVP External Relations, Van M. Wardlaw, age 55

CIO, Daniel A. (Dan) Traynor, age 58

EVP and General Counsel, Ralph E. Rodgers, age 60, $401,539 total compensation

President and CEO, William D. (Bill) Johnson, $712,500 total compensation

Vice President, James Cowart

Vice President Supply Chain, Russ Steward

Vice President Risk Management, Randy Petty

Vice President Nuclear Oversight, Steven Douglas

Senior Vice President Communications Government And Valley Relations, Emily Reynolds

Senior Vice President Watts Bar Operation and Construction, Mike Skaggs

Executive Vice President and Chief Nuclear Officer, Joe Grimes

Chairman, Joe Ritch

Board Member, William (Bill) Jenkins

Board Member, Robert (Bob) Campbell

Auditors: Ernst & Young LLP

LOCATIONS

HQ: Tennessee Valley Authority
400 W. Summit Hill Drive, Knoxville, TN 37902
Phone: 865 632-2101
Web: www.tva.gov

2012 Sales

	$ mil.	% of total
Electricity sales		
Tennessee	6,889	60
Alabama	1,556	14
Kentucky	1,230	11
Mississippi	1,038	9
Georgia	234	2
North Carolina	69	1
Virginia	49	1
Other revenues	155	2
Total	**11,220**	**100**

PRODUCTS/OPERATIONS

2012 Sales

	$ mil.	% of total
Electricity sales		
Municipalities & cooperatives	9,506	85
Industries directly served	1,442	13
Federal agencies & other	138	1
Other revenues	134	1
Total	**11,220**	**100**

HISTORICAL FINANCIALS

Company Type: Public

Income Statement — FYE: September 30

	REVENUE ($ mil.)	NET INCOME ($ mil.)	NET PROFIT MARGIN	EMPLOYEES
09/15	11,003	1,111	10.1%	10,918
09/14	11,137	469	4.2%	11,542
09/13	10,956	271	2.5%	12,612
09/12	11,220	60	0.5%	12,762
09/11	11,841	162	1.4%	12,893
Annual Growth	**(1.8%)**	**61.8%**	**—**	**(4.1%)**

2015 Year-End Financials

Debt ratio: 51.26%—
Return on equity: 16.70%
Cash ($ mil.): 300
Current ratio: 0.89
Long-term debt ($ mil.): 23,930

Dividends
Yield: 3.9%
Payout: —
Market value ($ mil.): —

	STOCK PRICE ($) FY Close	P/E High/Low	PER SHARE ($) Earnings	Dividends	Book Value
09/15	24.65	— —	(0.00)	0.95	(0.00)
09/14	23.91	— —	(0.00)	0.99	(0.00)
09/13	22.23	— —	(0.00)	1.03	(0.00)
09/12	26.90	— —	(0.00)	1.18	(0.00)
09/11	26.35	— —	(0.00)	1.13	(0.00)
Annual Growth	**(1.7%)**	**— —**	**—**	**(4.1%)**	**—**

Terex Corp.

Terex is a "T-Rex" when it comes to making a variety of cranes aerial platforms and construction and materials processing equipment. Its construction business makes compaction equipment such as compact track loaders and excavators as well as road building products. Another arm makes aerial lifts from articulating to telescopic booms used in industrial and construction overhead jobs. Terex products are sold in more than 100 countries around the globe to the construction forestry

and recycling shipping and utility industries under brands Terex Genie and Powerscreen. In mid-2015 Terex agreed to acquire and merge with Finnish rival Konecranes in an all-stock deal.

Change in Company Type

Terex agreed in mid-2015 to merge with Finnish rival Konecranes in an all-stock deal that creates a company with a combined $10 billion in 2014 revenue. The new company will be called Konecranes Terex PLC. Terex shareholders will own about 60% of the combined company; Konecranes stockholders 40%.

Geographic Reach

Terex sells its machinery products through around 15 owned and leased facilities spanning the states of Connecticut Indiana Iowa Michigan Minnesota Mississippi Ohio Oklahoma South Carolina South Dakota and Washington. Internationally it owns and leases almost 50 facilities in Austria Brazil China France Germany India Italy Switzerland South Africa the UK and the Asia/Pacific.

Operations

The company makes and sells its construction and materials processing equipment across five operating segments. Aerial Work Platforms (AWP) generated about 30% of total revenues in 2014. The company's newest segment Material Handling & Port Solutions (MHPS) accounted for 24% of total sales. MHPS makes industrial cranes and industrial crane components under the Demag and Gottwald brand names. The Cranes segment generated 24% of revenues while Construction earned 11% and Materials Processing brings in 9%.

Terex offers financial products and services to assist in the acquisition of Terex equipment through Terex Financial Services.

Sales and Marketing

Terex sells its products through a worldwide network of dealers rental companies independent distributors major accounts and direct sales to clients.

The company's broad range of equipment is used by various industries including the construction infrastructure manufacturing shipping transportation refining energy utility quarrying and mining industries.

Financial Performance

After declining in 2013 Terex's revenues increased 3% to $7.3 billion in 2014. Its net income has shown significant growth over the years jumping 41% to $319 million in 2014. The company's operating cash flow in 2014 increased due to the higher revenue and a gain on the disposition of discontinued operations.

The growth for 2014 was fueled by an 11% increase in AWP due to growth from the North American rental channels continued replacement demand in Europe and Asia Pacific and growing demand in China. Terex also experienced a 5% bump in MHPS sales due to higher port automation technology demand within Western Europe.

Strategy

Terex's growth plan involves targeting developing markets with a slew of specialty machinery and industrial equipment using acquisitions and joint ventures. It has a joint venture in Russia partnering with Russian Machines a seller of road construction machinery operating in 14 regions throughout the country. Terex also has a 65% stake in Jinan China-based boom crawler-maker Shandong Topower Heavy Machinery. Other forays into China include launching the Terex Port Equipment facility in Xiamen and the Aerial Work Platforms (Genie brand) factory in Changzhou.

It is also looking to address complexity reduction in our company through Portfolio Management (streamlining product portfolios) Simplification (process and system optimization) and Financial Efficiency (working capital capital structure and tax efficiency).

In mid-2014 the company sold its trucking business to Volvo Construction Equipment Corporation for $160 million. The business manufactured and sold off-highway rigid and articulated haul trucks. Included in the deal was a manufacturing facility in Motherwell Scotland.

HISTORY

Real estate entrepreneur Randolph Lenz moved into heavy equipment manufacturing with the purchase of bankrupt snowplow maker FWD Corporation in 1981. That was followed the same year with the acquisition of Northwest Engineering a maker of construction equipment started in the 1920s.

In 1986 the company acquired Terex USA the North American distributor of parts for off-highway Terex trucks from General Motors and later Terex Equipment the UK-based truck maker. The company changed its corporate name to Terex Corporation in 1987. That year Terex entered the mobile-crane market with the purchase of Koehring Cranes. Terex acquired mining-truck maker Unit Rig in 1988 and trailer maker Fruehauf in 1989. It moved into aerial work platforms in 1991 with the acquisition of Mark Industries and picked up the forklift business of Clark Equipment the following year. (Clark invented the forklift truck in 1928.)

EXECUTIVES

Vice President Finance, Tom Haitz
President and CEO, John L. Garrison
President Terex Material Handling & Port Solutions, Stoyan (Steve) Filipov, age 46, $565,353 total compensation
President Terex Materials Processing and Terex Fuchs, Kieran Hegarty, age 48
President Terex Construction, George Ellis, age 54, $369,000 total compensation
SVP and CFO, Kevin Bradley, age 52, $574,625 total compensation
President Terex Cranes and China and Latin America, Kenneth D. Lousberg, age 47, $365,666 total compensation
President Terex Aerial Work Platforms, Matthew (Matt) Fearon, age 53
VP Terex Services North America, Scott Hensel
President Terex Financial Services, CJ Johnson
Vice President Info Research, Kevin O'Reilly
Vice President Services, Mariusz Maciejewski
Senior Vice President Finance and Business Development, Brian Henry
Vice President Business Processes, Sheila Ellis
Vice President Caterpillar National Accounts, David (Dave) Hubbell
National Account Manager, Michael Liberto
Group Vice President Human Resources, Eileen Mulry
Vice President Ne Region Terex Awp Genie Industries, Adrian Max
Vice President Human Resources, Sridhar Sukumaran
Vice President, Owen Jervis
Vice President Strategic Accounts, Joe Krider
Vice President Strategic Accounts Western Region, David (Dave) Roembke
Vice President Finance and Information Services AWP EMEAR, Matthias Jung
Group Vice President Finance Cranes Segment, Brian Daly
Vice President Strategic Accounts, Wayne Norris
Vice President Finance, Ian Lundie
Vice President Of Sales For Europe Middle East Africa, Phil Graysmark
Vice President, Roger Brown
Vice President, Tommy Nix
Vice President Finance China, Angel Tian
Vice President, Parimal Parima

Vice President Finance Developing Markets at Terex Corporation, Gilberto Carvalho
Vice President North America Operations and Global Manufacturing Strategy, Dean Wisler
Vice President Of Human Resources Mining, Peter Rall
Vice President Sales and Marketing, Jim Lohan
Senior Vice President Secretary and General Counsel, Eric Cohen
Vice President Talent Development Diversity and Inclusion, Amy George
Vice President Terex Construction, Tom Sparks
Vice President of Operations, Greg Kryshtalowych
Chairman, David A. Sachs, age 55
Auditors: PricewaterhouseCoopers LLP

LOCATIONS

HQ: Terex Corp.
200 Nyala Farm Road, Westport, CT 06880
Phone: 203 222-7170   **Fax:** 203 222-7976
Web: www.terex.com

2014 Sales

	$ mil.	% of total
US	2,746	38
Europe		
Germany	642	9
UK	401	5
Other European countries	1,480	20
Other regions	2,037	28
Total	**7,308**	**100**

PRODUCTS/OPERATIONS

2014 Sales

	$ mil.	% of total
Aerial Work Platforms (AWP)	2,369	32
Cranes	1,791	24
Material Handling & Port Solutions (MHPS)	1,783	24
Construction	836	11
Materials Processing (MP)	653	9
Adjustments	(125.0)	-
Total	**7,308**	**100**

Selected Products

Cranes
  Lattice boom crawler cranes
  Lattice boom truck cranes
  Mobile telescopic cranes
  Specialized port and rail equipment
  Gantry cranes
  Lift trucks and forklifts
  Mobile harbor cranes
  Reach stackers
  Replacement parts and components
  Ship-to-shore cranes
  Straddle and sprinter carriers
  Tower cranes
  Truck-mounted cranes (boom trucks)
Aerial Work Platforms
  Aerial work platform equipment
  Light towers
  Material lifts
  Portable aerial work platforms
  Replacement parts
  Scissor lifts
  Self-propelled articulating and telescopic booms
  Telehandlers
  Trailer-mounted articulated booms
  Trailer-mounted light towers
  Utility equipment
Construction
  Compact construction equipment
  Compact track loaders
  Crawler conversion parts for skid steer loaders and aerial work platforms
  Loader backhoes
  Mini and midi excavators
  Site dumpers
  Skid steer loaders
  Tunneling equipment
  Wheel loaders
  Heavy construction equipment
  Material handlers
  Scrapers

Roadbuilding equipment
Asphalt and concrete equipment (pavers transfer devices plants mixers reclaimers/stabilizers placers and cold planers)
Bridge inspection equipment
Landfill compactors
Materials processing
  Apron feeders
  Components and replacement parts
  Crushers (mobile base)
  Screens (mobile base)
  Washing systems
Material Handling and Port Solutions
  Crane components and equipment
  Process cranes
  Rope and chain hoists
  Standard cranes

COMPETITORS

Altec Industries	JLG Industries
Astec Industries	Kobelco Construction
Atlas Copco	Machinery America
Blount International	Komatsu
Caterpillar	Konecranes
Charles Machine Works	Legris Industries
Deere	Group
Doosan Heavy	MANITOU BF
Industries	Manitowoc
Dynapac	Marmon Group
Fontaine Trailer	Metso
Furukawa	Multiquip
Gehl	Oshkosh Truck
Haulotte	Sandvik
Hitachi Construction	Skyjack
Machinery	Sumitomo
Hyundai Heavy	Textron
Industries	Trail King Industries
Instant UpRight	Volvo
J C Bamford Excavators	Wacker Neuson

HISTORICAL FINANCIALS

Company Type: Public

Income Statement

FYE: December 31

	REVENUE ($ mil.)	NET INCOME ($ mil.)	NET PROFIT MARGIN	EMPLOYEES
12/14	7,308	319	4.4%	20,400
12/13	7,084	226	3.2%	20,500
12/12	7,348	105	1.4%	21,300
12/11	6,504	45	0.7%	22,600
12/10	4,418	358	8.1%	16,300
Annual Growth	**13.4%**	**(2.9%)**	**—**	**5.8%**

2014 Year-End Financials

Debt ratio: 30.18%
Return on equity: 15.20%
Cash ($ mil.): 478
Current ratio: 2.04
Long-term debt ($ mil.): 1,636

No. of shares (mil.): 105
Dividends
  Yield: 0.9%
  Payout: 8.9%
Market value ($ mil.): 2,939

	STOCK PRICE ($) FY Close	P/E High/Low		PER SHARE ($) Earnings	Dividends	Book Value
12/14	27.88	15	9	2.79	0.25	19.03
12/13	41.99	21	13	1.93	0.05	19.93
12/12	28.11	28	15	0.93	0.00	18.27
12/11	13.51	93	23	0.41	0.00	17.52
12/10	31.04	9	5	3.30	0.00	19.27
Annual Growth	**(2.6%)**	**—**	**—**	**(4.1%)**	**—**	**(0.3%)**

Tesoro Corporation

Once a player in the exploration and production field Tesoro Corporation (formerly Tesoro Petroleum) has been enjoying a more refined existence in recent years as a downstream operator. The independent oil refiner and marketer operates six US refineries —in Alaska California (three) North Dakota Utah and Washington —with a combined capacity of 850000 barrels per day. It produces gasoline jet fuel diesel fuel fuel oil liquid asphalt and other fuel products. Tesoro markets fuel to more than 2200 branded retail gas stations (including 595 company-operated stations under the Tesoro Shell and USA Gasoline brands) primarily in Alaska and the Western US. It owns 36% of Tesoro Logistics LP.

Geographic Reach

Tesoro serves customers in Alaska and 17 states in the Western US. The company has refineries in Alaska California North Dakota Utah and Washington. Its supply and distribution operations include bulk terminals in Anchorage Alaska; Boise Idaho Burley Idaho; Port Angeles Washington; Salt Lake City Utah; Stockton California; Vancouver Washington; as well as six locations in Hawaii.

Operations

The company has three operating segments: Refining retail and oil and gas. It operates six petroleum refineries which manufacture gasoline and gasoline blendstocks jet fuel diesel fuel residual fuel oil and other refined petroleum products. Tesoro's refining segment (75% of Tesoro's 2014 revenues) also sells refined products to unbranded marketers and to markets outside of the US.

Tesoro's retail-marketing system includes more than 2200 branded retail gas stations.

Tesoro Logistics (36%-owned by Tesoro) has crude oil and natural gas gathering assets natural gas processing and crude oil and refined products terminalling transportation and storage assets acquired from Tesoro and third parties. Tesoro Logistics' gathering segment consists of crude oil natural gas and produced water gathering systems in the North Dakota Williston Basin/Bakken Shale area and the Uinta Vermillion and greater Green River basins

Financial Performance

Tesoro has reported strong revenue growth over the last five years.In 2014 net revenues increased by 8% due to growth across all of its segments.Revenues from the sales of refined products increased by 9% due to increased refined product sales volumes as a result of the Los Angeles acquisition (BP's regional refining and marketing assets) partially offset by a decrease in the average product sales price.Revenue from terminalling and transportation throughput volumes increased driven by acquisitions of the Northwest Products System and the logistics assets that were part of its Los Angeles acquisition. Pipeline gathering throughput volume also increase due to continued expansion of Tesoro Logistics' crude oil gathering assets and acquisition of the Rockies natural gas business. Total revenues increased thanks to higher throughput volumes in terminalling and transportation from Tesoro Logistics' 2013 acquisitions. The Rockies natural gas business acquisition contributed $23 million in natural gas processing revenue in 2014.The company recorded net income in the last four years after a loss in 2010.

In 2014 Tesoro reported an increase of 104.6% due to stronger net revenues driven by acquisitions which more than offset higher operating expenses.Tesoro's cash from operating activities increased by 59% in 2014.

Strategy

The company's strategy is to improve operational efficiency and effectiveness by focusing on safety and reliability system improvements and cost leadership drive commercial excellence by strengthening the supply trading and optimization activities to provide additional value to the business. It is also focusing on its ogistics assets growing its marketing business and other strategic opportunities accretive to shareholder value.

A key part of Tesoro's strategy is to step up business in the Mid-Continent and West Coast regions of the US. The company will continue to invest in ongoing initiatives around synergy and business improvement objectives and planned to invest additional $550 to $670 million of annual improvements during 2015 for West Coast improvements capturing margin improvements and growing logistics operations.In 2015 Tesoro upgraded its crude oil fleet with the addition of 210 enhanced tank cars.

In 2014 the company announced plans to gather intermediate feedstock primarily reformate from its West Coast refining system for xylene extraction at Anacortes Washington. The $400 million initial investment is designed to recover up to 15000 barrels per day of mixed xylene (used to make polyester fibers and films for clothing food packaging and beverage containers) which will mainly be exported to Asia.

To raise cash to invest in US mainland businesses in 2013 Tesoro completed the sale of Tesoro Hawaii for $539 million.

Mergers and Acquisitions

Growing its logistics portfolio in 2014 affiliate Tesoro Logistics agreed to buy QEP Resources' wholly owned natural gas gathering and processing business QEP Field Services LLC including its 58% partnership interests in QEP Midstream Partners LP.

In 2014 Tesoro and Tesoro Logistics completed the acquisition of certain terminalling and pipeline assets owned by Tesoro and certain of its subsidiaries. Tesoro Logistics acquired Tesoro Alaska Pipeline Company LLC which owns a refined products pipeline located in Alaska for $28.6 million.

In 2013 Tesoro bought BP's Southern California refining and marketing assets including the 266000 barrels-per-day Carson refinery and 800 dealer-operated gas stations for more than $2.5 billion.

HISTORY

Founded by Robert West in 1964 as a spinoff of petroleum producer Texstar Petroleum was hamstrung by debt from the get-go. In 1968 West merged Tesoro with Intex Oil and Sioux Oil to invigorate its financial standing.

Reborn the company constructed an Alaska refinery and began a 10-year stretch of petroleum-related acquisitions usually at bargain prices including almost half of the oil operations of British Petroleum (BP) in Trinidad which became Trinidad-Tesoro Petroleum. By 1973 earnings had quintupled.

In 1975 Tesoro paid $83 million for about a third of Commonwealth Oil Refining Company (Corco) a troubled Puerto Rican oil refiner one-and-a-half times its size. Debt soon was troubling Tesoro again and the company divested many of its holdings including refineries in Montana and Wyoming. Corco declared bankruptcy in 1978. That year Tesoro was hit with tax penalties and revealed it had bribed officials in foreign countries.

The company fought takeover attempts and bankruptcy in the 1980s and sold its half of Trinidad-Tesoro in 1985. In the 1990s it expanded its natural gas operations and returned to profitability.

In 1998 Tesoro bought a refinery and 32 retail outlets in Hawaii from an affiliate of BHP and a refinery in Washington from an affiliate of Shell. To concentrate on its downstream businesses the company in 1999 sold its exploration and production operations in the US (to EEX for $215 million) and in Bolivia (to BG for about $100 million).

EXECUTIVES

EVP and CFO, Steven M. (Steve) Sterin, age 44, $263,846 total compensation
EVP General Counsel and Secretary, Charles S. (Chuck) Parrish, age 57, $558,474 total compensation
President Tesoro Logistics GP, Phillip M. Anderson
SVP Marketing, Claude P. Moreau
Chairman President and CEO, Gregory J. (Greg) Goff, age 58, $1,495,000 total compensation
SVP Refining, Brian Coffman
EVP Strategy and Business Development, Cynthia (CJ) Warner, age 56, $139,327 total compensation
EVP Operations, Keith M. Casey, age 48, $549,415 total compensation
Auditors: Ernst & Young LLP

LOCATIONS

HQ: Tesoro Corporation
 19100 Ridgewood Pkwy, San Antonio, TX 78259-1828
Phone: 210 626-6000
Web: www.tsocorp.com

PRODUCTS/OPERATIONS

2014 Sales

	$ mil.	% of total
Refining		
Refined products	38,112	72
Crude oil resales & other	1,456	3
Tesoro Logistics LP		
Gathering	137	-
Processing	23	-
Terminalling and transportation	442	1
Retail		
Fuel	12,518	24
Merchandise & other	240	0
Adjustments	(12295)	0
Total	**40,633**	**100**

COMPETITORS

Arctic Slope Regional Corporation	Northern Tier Energy
Big West Oil	Petro Star
Chemoil	Phillips 66
Chevron U.S.A	Shell Oil Products
Gas Depot	Tauber Oil
Gibson Energy	Valero Energy
HollyFrontier	Western Refining Inc.
National Cooperative Refinery Association	

HISTORICAL FINANCIALS

Company Type: Public

Income Statement

FYE: December 31

	REVENUE ($ mil.)	NET INCOME ($ mil.)	NET PROFIT MARGIN	EMPLOYEES
12/14	40,633	843	2.1%	5,600
12/13	37,601	412	1.1%	7,000
12/12	32,974	743	2.3%	5,700
12/11	30,303	546	1.8%	5,400
12/10	20,583	(29)	—	5,300
Annual Growth	**18.5%**	**—**	**—**	**1.4%**

2014 Year-End Financials

Debt ratio: 25.69%	No. of shares (mil.): 124
Return on equity: 19.26%	Dividends
Cash ($ mil.): 1,000	Yield: 1.4%
Current ratio: 1.46	Payout: 20.7%
Long-term debt ($ mil.): 4,254	Market value ($ mil.): 9,291

	STOCK PRICE ($) FY Close	P/E High/Low	PER SHARE ($) Earnings	Dividends	Book Value
12/14	74.35	12 7	6.44	1.10	35.64
12/13	58.50	21 13	3.00	0.90	32.64
12/12	44.05	8 4	5.25	0.27	30.77
12/11	23.36	8 5	3.81	0.00	26.21
12/10	18.54	— —	(0.21)	0.25	22.45
Annual Growth	41.5%	— —	—	44.8%	12.2%

Texas Capital Bancshares Inc

Texas Capital Bancshares is the parent company of Texas Capital Bank with more than 10 branches in Austin Dallas Fort Worth Houston and San Antonio. The bank targets high-net-worth individuals and Texas-based businesses with more than $5 million in annual revenue with a focus on the real estate financial services transportation communications petrochemicals and mining sectors. Striving for personalized services for its clients the bank offers deposit accounts Visa credit cards commercial loans and mortgages equipment leasing wealth management and trust services. Its BankDirect division provides online banking services. Founded in 1998 Texas Capital Bancshares has about $11.7 billion in assets.

Financial Performance

The bank reported $488.6 million in revenue in 2013 an nearly 11% increase versus 2012. Net income was flat at about $121 million after posting three consecutive years of gains. Cash flow from operations continued its steep three year decline. The bank's total assets increased 11% from about $10.5 billion in 2012 to $11.7 billion in 2013. Total deposits increased 24% year over year to about $9.3 billion.

Strategy

Headquartered in Dallas Texas Capital Bank (TCB) believes that its Texas roots give it a competitive advantage over larger competitors that are headquartered out of state. Indeed TCB is gaining market share and is expanding by hiring experienced bankers and support staff. The bank is looking to grow within its main metropolitan markets but has also branched out beyond the borders of its home state. The bank has an Cayman Islands branch to offer offshore cash management and deposit products to it core clientele.

EXECUTIVES

President CEO and Director, George F. Jones, age 71, $585,000 total compensation
President and CEO Texas Capital Bancshares Inc. President and CEO Texas Capital Bank, C. Keith Cargill, age 62, $346,667 total compensation
EVP and Chief Lending Officer Dallas Region, Vince A. Ackerson, $297,500 total compensation
Regional President Texas Capital Bank Austin, Kerry L. Hall
Regional President Texas Capital Bank Dallas, Russell Hartsfield
CFO and COO Texas Capital Bancshares; COO Texas Capital Bank, Peter B. Bartholow, age 66, $361,667 total compensation
Chief Risk Officer and Chief Credit Officer Texas Capital Bank, John D. Hudgens, $316,667 total compensation

EVP and COO Texas Capital Bank, James C. (Jim) White
Regional President Texas Capital Bank Fort Worth, Jeff Moten
Regional President Texas Capital Bank San Antonio, David Pope
Regional President Texas Capital Bank Houston, John Sarvadi
Vice President Manager Credit Underwriting, Anthony Violi
Senior Vice President Compensation Director, Chris Gullo
Senior Vice President Director of In, Paul Bowler
Vice President in Commercial Banking Group, Guy Miller
Vice President Of Information Technology Infrastructure, Randy Tiegs
Senior Vice President In The Southwest Corporate Banking Division, Paul Howell
Senior Vice President Risk Management Officer, Terry King
Vice President Fraud Investigator, Jamie Burud
Vice President Security, Neal Baker
Senior Vice President, Don Rosics
Vice President, Jimmie Schellinger
Executive Vice President, Brent Johnston
Executive Vice President, Ronald (Ron) Baker
Executive Vice President Human Resources and LD, Cara McDaniel
Vice President Product Development Manager, Andrew (Andy) Milburn
Senior Vice President Energy Banking Texas Capital Bank, Jonathan (Jon) Gregory
Chairman, Larry L. Helm, age 67
Auditors: Ernst & Young LLP

LOCATIONS

HQ: Texas Capital Bancshares Inc
2000 McKinney Avenue, Suite 700, Dallas, TX 75201
Phone: 214 932-6600
Web: www.texascapitalbank.com

COMPETITORS

Amegy	Comerica
BBVA Compass Bancshares	Cullen/Frost Bankers
	JPMorgan Chase
BOK Financial	Prosperity Bancshares
Bank of America	Wells Fargo

HISTORICAL FINANCIALS

Company Type: Public

Income Statement

	ASSETS ($ mil.)	NET INCOME ($ mil.)	INCOME AS % OF ASSETS	EMPLOYEES	FYE: December 31
12/14	15,899	136	0.9%	1,142	
12/13	11,714	121	1.0%	1,016	
12/12	10,540	120	1.1%	881	
12/11	8,137	75	0.9%	786	
12/10	6,446	37	0.6%	699	
Annual Growth	25.3%	38.4%	—	13.1%	

2014 Year-End Financials

Debt ratio: 9.43%
Return on equity: 10.57%
Cash ($ mil.): 1,330
Current ratio: —
Long-term debt ($ mil.): —
No. of shares (mil.): 45
Dividends
  Yield: —
  Payout: —
Market value ($ mil.): 2,485

	STOCK PRICE ($) FY Close	P/E High/Low	PER SHARE ($) Earnings	Dividends	Book Value
12/14	54.33	23 17	2.88	0.00	32.45
12/13	62.20	22 14	2.72	0.00	26.72
12/12	44.82	17 10	3.00	0.00	20.53
12/11	30.61	15 10	1.98	0.00	16.36
12/10	21.34	22 13	1.00	0.00	14.30
Annual Growth	26.3%	— —	30.3%	—	22.7%

TEXAS COUNTY AND DISTRICT RETIREMENT SYSTEM

LOCATIONS

HQ: TEXAS COUNTY AND DISTRICT RETIREMENT SYSTEM
901 S MO PAC EXPY IV500, AUSTIN, TX 787465776
Phone: 5123288889
Web: WWW.TCDRS.ORG

HISTORICAL FINANCIALS

Company Type: Private

Income Statement

	ASSETS ($ mil.)	NET INCOME ($ mil.)	INCOME AS % OF ASSETS	EMPLOYEES	FYE: December 31
12/11	17,828	(101)	—	108	
12/10	18,116	2,178	12.0%	—	
12/09	16,287	3,503	21.5%	—	
12/08	12,833	0	—	—	
Annual Growth	11.6%	—	—	—	

2011 Year-End Financials

Debt ratio: —
Return on equity: (-14.10%)
Cash ($ mil.): 15
Current ratio: —
Long-term debt ($ mil.): —
Dividends
  Yield: —
  Payout: —
Market value ($ mil.): —

Texas Instruments Inc.

One of the world's oldest and largest semiconductor makers Texas Instruments (TI) offers more than 100000 products. Its largest segment is analog semiconductors which change real-world signals (such as sound and images) into the digital data streams. Analog product are used to manage power in all electronic devices; TI sells these products to customers in the consumer electronics and industrial markets among others. The company also makes embedded processors which can process data from analog chips and handle specific tasks in electronic devices. TI's other products include digital light processing (DLP) chips used in high-definition projectors custom semiconductors and calculators. It generates most of its sales from the Asia/Pacific region.

Operations The company operates through three segments: analog embedded processing and other. The analog business which accounts for about 62% of sales includes high-volume analog and logic products power management semiconductors and catalog analog products such as amplifiers and data converters. The embedded processing segment which includes digital signal processors (DSPs) and microcontrollers generates about 21% of sales. The remaining 17% of sales comes from smaller products lines such as calculators and application-specific integrated circuits (ASICs).

Geographic Reach TI has design manufacturing or sales operations in some three dozen countries across Asia Europe and North America. The Asia-Pacific region (including Japan) is its leading market accounting for more than two-thirds of revenue; Europe accounts for 18% of revenue and the US for about 12%.

Sales and Marketing The company markets its products through a direct sales force as well as via distributors and third-party sales representatives. Distributors generate about 60% of sales.

Financial Analysis

The bar chart of TI's sales for the past five years goes from peak to valley and back up to peak. Sales for 2014 were $13 million a 7% increase from 2013 and closer to the $13.9 billion in sales the company posted in 2010. In 2014 the analog and embedded processing segments grew a healthy 13% and 12% respectively. However sales of the segment of other products (mainly legacy wireless chips) slipped 14% lower. Power products led the analog growth and microcontrollers and processors paced the embedded segment.

The company followed higher revenue with a 30% increase in net income which hit $2.82 billion in 2014. (The 2010 number was $3.2 billion). Besides the increased revenue TI's bottom line benefited from lower restructuring charges.

TI closed 2014 with nearly $3.9 billion in cash flow from operations compared to $3.38 billion in 2013.

Strategy TI's strategy is to focus on its analog and embedded processing businesses which the company expects to account for 90% of revenue in the next few years (up from 44% in 2006). To that end the company wound down its wireless business moving away from products for mobile devices and toward embedded markets which the company sees as more suitable for growth. The company's R&D spending was lower in 2014 but that reflected the exit from wireless.

The company is also working to expand its customer base including attracting more small customers. In 2013 its largest customer accounted for just 7% of revenue compared to nearly a quarter of revenue in 2009.

HISTORY

Early History

Clarence "Doc" Karcher and Eugene McDermott founded Geophysical Service Inc. (GSI) in Newark New Jersey in 1930 to develop reflective seismology a new technology for oil and gas exploration. In 1934 GSI moved to Dallas. The company produced military electronics during WWII including submarine detectors for the US Navy. GSI changed its name to Texas Instruments (TI) in 1951.

TI began making transistors in 1952 after buying a license from Western Electric. The company went public on the New York Stock Exchange in 1953. In 1954 it introduced the Regency Radio the first pocket-sized transistor radio. (That year TI also produced the first commercial silicon transistor.) Impressed by the radio IBM president Thomas Watson made TI a major supplier to IBM in 1957.

That year the company opened a plant in the UK —its first foreign operation.

TI engineer Jack Kilby invented the integrated circuit (IC) in 1958. (Working independently Intel co-founder Robert Noyce developed an IC at the same time while working at Fairchild Semiconductor; the two men are credited as co-inventors. In 2000 Kilby was awarded the Nobel Prize in Physics for his work; Noyce could not be awarded the prize since he had died 10 years earlier.)

Other breakthroughs included terrain-following airborne radar (1958) handheld calculators (1967) and single-chip microcomputers (1971). During the 1970s TI introduced innovative calculators digital watches home computers and educational toys such as the popular Speak & Spell —the first TI product to use digital signal processors (DSPs) which decades later would become a major driver of TI's growth.

EXECUTIVES

Senior Vice President High Performance Analog, Arthur (Art) George
Chairman President and CEO, Richard K. (Rich) Templeton, age 56, $1,107,083 total compensation
SVP and General Manager Analog Business, Stephen A. (Steve) Anderson, age 53, $508,750 total compensation
SVP Technology and Manufacturing, Kevin J. Ritchie, age 59, $647,917 total compensation
SVP and CFO, Kevin P. March, age 58, $628,333 total compensation
SVP; General Manager Embedded Processing, R. Gregory (Greg) Delagi, age 52, $622,917 total compensation
EVP Business Operations, Brian Crutcher, age 42, $739,583 total compensation
VP and CIO, Ellen Barker
SVP Worldwide Sales and Applications, Bing Xie
SENIOR VICE PRESIDENT MGR, Terri West
Vice President WW Facilities, David (Dave) Thomas
Vice President, Eftechios Lambouses
Senior Vice President General Counsel and Secretary, Allan Campbell
Vice President Investor Relations, Ron Slaymaker
Vice President Sales, Hosam Galal
Vice President Digital Signal Processing Systems Semiconductor Group, Niels Anderskouv
Senior Vice President Channel Marketing, Sami Kiriaki
Vice President Sales Administration, Tom Springmeier
Auditors: Ernst & Young LLP

LOCATIONS

HQ: Texas Instruments Inc.
12500 TI Boulevard, Dallas, TX 75243
Phone: 214 479-3773
Web: www.ti.com

2014 Sales

	$ mil.	% of total
Asia/Pacific		
Japan	1,032	8
Other countries	7,915	61
Europe	2,293	18
US	1,625	12
Other regions	180	1
Total	**13,045**	**100**

PRODUCTS/OPERATIONS

2014 Sales

	$ mil.	% of total
Analog	8,104	62
Embedded processing	2,740	21
Other	2,201	17
Total	**13,045**	**100**

2014 Sales by Market

	% of total
Industrial	31
Personal electronics	29
Communications equipment	17
Automotive	13
Enterprise sytems	6
Calculators	4
Total	**100**

Selected Products

Semiconductors
  Analog and mixed-signal
  Amplifiers and comparators
  Clocks and timers
  Data converters
  Power management chips
  Radio-frequency (RF) chips
  Application-specific integrated circuits (ASICs)
  Digital light processors (DLPs micro-mirror-based devices for video displays)
  Digital signal processors (DSPs)
  Microcontrollers
  Microprocessors
  Standard logic
Educational Technology
  Calculators (including graphing handheld and printing models)

COMPETITORS

Analog Devices	Maxim Integrated
Atmel	Products
CASIO COMPUTER	Microchip Technology
CSR plc	NVIDIA
Canon	NXP Semiconductors
Fairchild	ON Semiconductor
Semiconductor	QUALCOMM
HP	Renesas Electronics
Infineon Technologies	Richtek Technology
Intel	Corp.
Intersil	STMicroelectronics
Linear Technology	Samsung Electronics
Marvell Technology	

HISTORICAL FINANCIALS

Company Type: Public

Income Statement

FYE: December 31

	REVENUE ($ mil.)	NET INCOME ($ mil.)	NET PROFIT MARGIN	EMPLOYEES
12/14	13,045	2,821	21.6%	31,003
12/13	12,205	2,162	17.7%	32,209
12/12	12,825	1,759	13.7%	34,151
12/11	13,735	2,236	16.3%	34,759
12/10	13,966	3,228	23.1%	28,412
Annual Growth	**(1.7%)**	**(3.3%)**	**—**	**2.2%**

2014 Year-End Financials

Debt ratio: 26.19%	No. of shares (mil.): 1,046
Return on equity: 26.62%	Dividends
Cash ($ mil.): 1,199	Yield: 2.3%
Current ratio: 2.92	Payout: 54.3%
Long-term debt ($ mil.): 3,641	Market value ($ mil.): 55,958

	STOCK PRICE ($) FY Close	P/E High/Low	PER SHARE ($) Earnings	Dividends	Book Value
12/14	53.47	21 16	2.57	1.24	9.93
12/13	43.91	23 16	1.91	1.07	9.98
12/12	30.89	22 17	1.51	0.72	9.89
12/11	29.11	19 13	1.88	0.56	9.61
12/10	32.50	13 8	2.62	0.49	8.94
Annual Growth	**13.3%**	**— —**	**(0.5%)**	**26.1%**	**2.7%**

Textron Inc.

Officers corporate and military really take to Textron. The company's E-Z-GO golf carts enrich their golfing jaunts while its Cessna and Beechcraft airplanes and Bell helicopters whisk them around the world. In addition its auto parts keep their cars running and its Financial subsidiary provides loans. Besides golf carts and car parts Textron's industrial segment makes power tools electrical and fiber optic assemblies and turf maintenance equipment. The Textron systems segment sells land and marine systems sensors and unmanned aerial vehicles to the Defense Department. Various US government entities account for about one-third of Textron's sales.

Geographic Reach

The company operates about 60 plants in the US and about 50 outside the US. The US accounted for 62% of its total sales in 2014. Other major markets include Europe (13%) and Latin America and Mexico (9%).

Operations

In 2014 the company's recent acquisition of Beechcraft was integrated into its former Cessna segment to create the Textron Aviation segment. This segment generated 33% of net sales in 2014 and produces the Citation jet Caravan single-engine utility turboprop T-6 AT-6 military and CitationAir single-engine piston aircraft which are distributed through a direct sales force and independent sales representatives.

Bell Helicopter supplies the US military with the V-22 tilt rotor aircraft which can operate with the features of both a fixed-wing craft and a helicopter and the H-1 helicopter. Through service sites co-located with Cessna and some 100 independent dealers Bell Helicopter provides repair and overhaul and customizing services for an installed base of 13000 helicopters. The segment represents 31% of sales.

Textron Systems 12% of sales serves markets that include aerospace defense general aviation and homeland security. Besides the US military the segment sells to foreign militaries approved by the US government. Textron systems' Overwatch business supplies intelligence software for the defense intelligence and law enforcement markets.

Industrial 25% of sales operates through subsidiaries Kautex (blow-molded plastic fuel systems for cars light trucks all-terrain vehicles); Greenlee (powered equipment electrical test and measurement instruments and other products under the Greenlee Klauke Paladin Tools and Tempo brand names); E-Z-GO (golf carts and off-road utility vehicles under the E-Z-Go and Cushman brands); and Jacobsen (professional turf-maintenance equipment and specialized turf-care vehicles). Finance 2% of sales includes Textron Financial Corporation and offers financing for new Cessna aircraft Bell helicopters E-Z-GO golf carts and Jacobsen turf-care equipment.

Financial Performance

Textron enjoyed significant growth for 2014 mainly due to acquisitions. Revenues climbed 15% to peak at $13.9 billion in 2014 while net income climbed 20% to $600 million. In 2014 its operating cash flows increased by 49% to $1.2 billion due to the increase in net income followed by cash inflows from accrued liabilities and accounts receivable largely at Bell.

The growth for 2014 was driven by increases in the Textron Aviation and Industrial segments offset by lower revenues in the Bell Textron Systems and Finance segments. Textron Aviation sales skyrocketed 64% primarily from its Beechcraft acquisition and an increase in volumes shipped largely related to Citation jets. The Industrial segment rose by 11% due to higher sales volumes of fuel systems and functional components.

Mergers and Acquisitions

The company occasionally beefs up its segments through acquisitions. In March 2014 Textron expanded rapidly through the $1.4 billion purchase of plane maker Beechcraft. It combined Beechcraft and Cessna into its newest segment: Textron Aviation. The deal added significantly to Textron's revenues during 2014.

HISTORY

Pioneer conglomerate builder Royal Little founded Special Yarns Corporation a Boston textile business in 1923 and merged it with the Franklin Rayon Dyeing Company in 1928. The result Franklin Rayon Corporation moved its headquarters to Providence Rhode Island in 1930 and changed its name to Atlantic Rayon in 1938.

The company expanded during WWII to make parachutes and in 1944 adopted the name Textron to reflect the use of synthetics in its textiles. Between 1953 and 1960 Textron bought more than 40 businesses including Bell Helicopter before banker Rupe Thompson took over in 1960.

Thompson sold weak businesses such as Amerotron Textron's last textile business (1963) but also bought 20 companies between 1960 and 1965. By 1968 when former Wall Street attorney William Miller replaced Thompson as CEO Textron made products ranging from chain saws to watchbands. Miller sold several companies and bought Jacobsen Manufacturers (lawn care equipment 1978) before leaving Textron in 1978 to head the Federal Reserve and become treasury secretary under President Jimmy Carter.

EXECUTIVES

VP and CIO, Diane K. Schwarz
Chairman President and CEO, Scott C. Donnelly, age 53, $1,080,000 total compensation
EVP General Counsel Secretary and Chief Compliance Officer, E. Robert Lupone, age 55, $646,154 total compensation
President and CEO Textron Aviation, Scott A. Ernest
EVP Human Resources, Cheryl H. Johnson, age 54, $340,385 total compensation
President Industrial Segment and Textron Tools and Test Division, J. Scott Hall
President Textron Specialized Vehicles, Kevin P. Holleran
President and CEO Textron Systems Corporation, Ellen Lord
EVP and CFO, Frank T. Connor, age 55, $840,385 total compensation
President and CEO Kautex, Vicente Perez
President Jacobsen, David Withers
President and CEO TRU Simulation + Training Inc., James Takats
President and CEO Textron Financial Corporation, R. Danny Maldonado
President and CEO Bell Helicopter, Mitch Snyder
Senior Vice President Finance, Eric Salander
Vice President Integrated Supply Chain, David (Dave) Higgins
Vice President Security, Ronnie Stone
Vice President Business Development, Donald (Don) Wilbourn
Senior Vice President International Finance, Tracy Cassil
Vice President Integrated Supply Chain, Michael Kieran
Vice President, Paul Rerick
Vice President Of Human Resources And Compliance, David Green
Vice President and Treasurer, Mary F Lovejoy
Vice President Information Technology, Jeff Rose
Senior Vice President General Manager, Jeff Bell
Vice President Intelligent Battlefield Systems, Dave O'Brien
Auditors: Ernst & Young LLP

LOCATIONS

HQ: Textron Inc.
40 Westminster Street, Providence, RI 02903
Phone: 401 421-2800
Web: www.textron.com

2013 Sales

	$ mil.	% of total
US	7,512	62
Europe	1,535	13
Asia & Australia	1,111	9
Latin America & Mexico	878	7
Middle East & Africa	693	6
Canada	375	3
Total	**12,104**	**100**

PRODUCTS/OPERATIONS

2013 Sales

	$ mil.	% of total
Bell	4,511	37
Industrial	3,012	25
Cessna	2,784	23
Textron Systems	1,665	14
Finance	132	1
Total	**12,104**	**100**

2013 Sales

	$ mil.	% of total
Rotor aircraft	4,511	37
Fixed-wing aircraft	2,784	23
Fuel systems & functional components	1,853	15
Unmanned aircraft systems armored security vehicles precision weapons & other	1,665	14
Gold turf-care & light transportation vehicles	713	6
Powered tools testing & measurement equipment	446	4
Finance	132	1
Total	**12,104**	**100**

Selected Products

Cessna
 Business jets
 Overnight express package carrier aircraft
 Single engine piston aircraft
 Single engine turboprops
Bell
 Commercial helicopters
 Military helicopters
 Tiltrotor aircraft
Industrial
 Kautex
 Blow-molded fuel tank systems
 Headlamp washer systems
 Engine camshafts
 Plastic bottles and containers
 Selective satalytic reduction systems
 Windshield washer systems
 E-Z-GO
 Golf carts
 Multipurpose utility vehicles
 Off-road utility vehicles
 Greenlee
 Electrical connectors
 Electrical test instruments
 Fiber optic assemblies
 Hand tools
 Hydraulic power tools
 Measurement instruments
 Powered equipment
 Jacobsen
 Turf-maintenance equipment
 Specialized turf-care vehicles
Textron Systems
 Advanced marine craft
 Airborne surveillance
 Armored security vehicles
 Countersniper devices
 Ground-based surveillance
 Intelligence software
 Precision weapons
 Situational awareness software

Simulation systems
Training systems
Unmanned aircraft systems
Finance (captive commercial finance for new aircraft
helicopter golf and turf-care equipment)

COMPETITORS

AgustaWestland	Kaman
Airbus Group	Lockheed Martin
Boeing	Magna International
Bombardier	Moog
Claverham	Northrop Grumman
Deere	Northstar Aerospace
Embraer	Piper Aircraft
GE	Raytheon
General Dynamics	Rolls-Royce
Honda	Spirit AeroSystems
Honeywell	Sun Hydraulics
International	Terex
Illinois Tool Works	Toro Company
Ingersoll-Rand	United Technologies
Johnson Controls	ZF TRW Automotive

HISTORICAL FINANCIALS

Company Type: Public

Income Statement

FYE: January 3

	REVENUE ($ mil.)	NET INCOME ($ mil.)	NET PROFIT MARGIN	EMPLOYEES
01/15*	13,878	600	4.3%	34,000
12/13	12,104	498	4.1%	32,000
12/12	12,237	589	4.8%	33,000
12/11	11,275	242	2.1%	32,000
01/11	10,525	86	0.8%	32,000
Annual Growth	7.2%	62.5%	—	1.5%

*Fiscal year change

2015 Year-End Financials

Debt ratio: 26.53%
Return on equity: 13.64%
Cash ($ mil.): 731
Current ratio: 1.72
Long-term debt ($ mil.): 3,866

No. of shares (mil.): 276
Dividends
  Yield: 0.0%
  Payout: 3.7%
Market value ($ mil.): 11,663

	STOCK PRICE ($) FY Close	P/E High/Low		PER SHARE ($) Earnings	Dividends	Book Value
01/15*	42.17	21	15	2.13	0.08	15.45
12/13	36.61	21	14	1.75	0.08	15.54
12/12	24.12	14	9	2.00	0.08	11.03
12/11	18.49	33	17	0.79	0.08	9.84
01/11	23.64	79	52	0.28	0.08	10.78
Annual Growth	15.6%	—	—	66.1%	(0.0%)	9.4%

*Fiscal year change

TFS Financial Corp

TFS Financial is the holding company for Third Federal Savings and Loan a thrift with some 45 branches and loan production offices in Ohio and southern Florida. The bank offers such deposit products as checking savings and retirement accounts and CDs. It uses funds from deposits to originate a variety of consumer loans primarily residential mortgages. Third Federal also offers IRAs annuities and mutual funds as well as retirement and college savings plans. TFS subsidiary Third Capital owns stakes in commercial real estate private equity funds and other investments. Mutual holding company Third Federal Savings and Loan Association of Cleveland owns nearly three-quarters of TFS Financial.

Residential mortgages and home equity loans account for nearly all of TFS Financial's loan portfolio. The bank operates in battered housing-market areas in Florida and Ohio where it is one of the largest home mortgage lenders in the Cleveland metropolitan area. It has traditionally targeted low-income buyers seeking to buy affordable housing particularly through its erstwhile Home Today loan program.

The bank didn't categorize the Home Today loans as subprime mortgages but nevertheless tightened its underwriting standards in 2009 in the wake of the subprime mortgage crisis. It also stopped issuing high loan-to-value ratio loans in 2008 and interest-only loans in 2009. It curtailed its home equity lending activity in 2010 after entering into a memorandum of understanding with regulators regarding that portion of its portfolio.

Like the banking industry overall TFS Financial has seen elevated levels of loan defaults and foreclosures as the economy reeled. Nonetheless the company has still been able to turn a profit.

EXECUTIVES

V Pres, Meredith S Weil
Auditors: Deloitte & Touche LLP

LOCATIONS

HQ: TFS Financial Corp
  7007 Broadway Avenue, Cleveland, OH 44105
Phone: 216 441-6000
Web: www.thirdfederal.com

COMPETITORS

Bank of America	JPMorgan Chase
Citigroup	KeyCorp
Fifth Third	PNC Financial
FirstMerit	U.S. Bancorp
Huntington Bancshares	Wells Fargo

HISTORICAL FINANCIALS

Company Type: Public

Income Statement

FYE: September 30

	ASSETS ($ mil.)	NET INCOME ($ mil.)	INCOME AS % OF ASSETS	EMPLOYEES
09/15	12,368	72	0.6%	—
09/14	11,803	65	0.6%	—
09/13	11,269	55	0.5%	—
09/12	11,518	11	0.1%	—
09/11	10,892	9	0.1%	—
Annual Growth	3.2%	67.0%	—	—

2015 Year-End Financials

Debt ratio: —
Return on equity: 4.07%
Cash ($ mil.): 155
Current ratio: —
Long-term debt ($ mil.): —

No. of shares (mil.): 290
Dividends
  Yield: 1.8%
  Payout: 40.7%
Market value ($ mil.): 5,018

	STOCK PRICE ($) FY Close	P/E High/Low		PER SHARE ($) Earnings	Dividends	Book Value
09/15	17.25	71	55	0.25	0.31	5.95
09/14	14.32	66	52	0.22	0.07	6.10
09/13	11.97	68	45	0.18	0.00	6.05
09/12	9.07	249	201	0.04	0.00	5.85
09/11	8.13	363	260	0.03	0.00	5.74
Annual Growth	20.7%	—	—	69.9%	—	0.9%

The Bancorp, Inc.

The Bancorp is —what else? —Åthe holding company for The Bancorp Bank which provides financial services in the virtual world. On its home turf of the Philadelphia and Wilmington DelawareÅmetropolitan areas The Bancorp Bank offers deposit lending andÅrelated services targeting wealthy individuals and small to midsized businesses it believes are underserved by larger banks in the market. Nationally The Bancorp provides private-label online banking services for some 300 affinity groups issues prepaid debit cardsÅprocesses merchant credit card transactions and acts as a custodian for health savings accounts (HSAs).As an online bankÅthe companyÅhas no branches; however it does operate three loan production offices in the PhiladelphiaÅarea. The companyÅalso operates vehicleÅfleet leasing businessesÅJefferson Leasing and Mears Motor Leasing which are active in about 40 states. Commercial and constructin loans and commercial mortgages dominate The Bancorp's loan portfolio.ÅThe company's strategies for growth include generating deposits through its prepaid card community banking merchant processing and wealth management operations the funds of which it will expand its lending operations. It also hopes to market its offerings to customers of its affinity groups and generally drive up business in its home region. The Bancorp has also explored the possibility of establishing a new savings bank in southern New Jersey adjacent to its primary market area; the move would add a thrift charter to help accelerate the bank's nationwide expansion.The Bancorp's earnings have been growing since the company lost money in 2008. Revenues in 2011 grew 15% to $119 million while profits grew 70% to $8.9 million. The increases were buoyed by higher prepaid card fees resulting from higher transaction volumes. Additionally prepaid card wealth management health care and merchant processing deposits all grew that year. However the company increased its provision for loan losses in both 2010 and 2011 allowing for challenges in the economic climate.

EXECUTIVES

EVP Strategy CFO and Secretary, Paul Frenkiel, age 63, $310,805 total compensation
President CEO and COO, Frank M. Mastrangelo, age 47, $509,508 total compensation
EVP and Chief Credit Officer The Bancorp Inc. and The Bancorp Bank, Donald F. (Don) McGraw, age 58, $257,115 total compensation
EVP and Chief Lending Officer, Scott R. Megargee, age 63, $202,541 total compensation
EVP Commercial Lending, Arthur M. Birenbaum, age 58, $423,207 total compensation
EVP and CIO, Peter (Pete) Chiccino
SVP Healthcare Solutions and Affinity Banking, Jill E. Kelly
SVP Loan Administration, Sandra C. Reel
SVP and Chief Risk Officer, James D. (Jim) Hilty
SVP and Managing Director Payment Solutions Group, Jeremy Kuiper
EVP Commercial and Construction Real Estate Lending, Dan Sacho
Vice President Information Security Officer, Joe Curcio
Vice President 1031 Exchange Services, Christine Cataldi
Vice President Private Client Services, Jeanne Fields
Vice President Platform Sales Private Client Services, Erin Allard

Chairman The Bancorp Inc. and The Bancorp Bank, Daniel G. Cohen, age 45
Auditors: Grant Thornton LLP

LOCATIONS

HQ: The Bancorp, Inc.
409 Silverside Road, Wilmington, DE 19809
Phone: 302 385-5000
Web: www.thebancorp.com

PRODUCTS/OPERATIONS

2011 Sales

	$ mil.	% of total
Interest		
Loans including fees	74	63
Securities	12	10
Other	1	1
Noninterest		
Prepaid fees	18	16
Service fees on deposit accounts	2	2
Other	9	8
Adjustments	(0.1)	
Total	**119**	**100**

COMPETITORS

Citizens Financial Group	Royal Bancshares
E*TRADE Bank	Sovereign Bank
M&T Bank	Sun Bancorp (NJ)
PNC Financial	TD Bank USA
Republic First Bank	WSFS Financial

HISTORICAL FINANCIALS

Company Type: Public

Income Statement

FYE: December 31

	ASSETS ($ mil.)	NET INCOME ($ mil.)	INCOME AS % OF ASSETS	EMPLOYEES
12/14	4,986	57	1.1%	684
12/13	4,706	25	0.5%	624
12/12	3,699	16	0.4%	532
12/11	3,010	8	0.3%	428
12/10	2,395	5	0.2%	373
Annual Growth	**20.1%**	**81.9%**	**—**	**16.4%**

2014 Year-End Financials

Debt ratio: 0.27%	No. of shares (mil.): 37
Return on equity: 16.83%	Dividends
Cash ($ mil.): 1,067	Yield: —
Current ratio: —	Payout: —
Long-term debt ($ mil.): —	Market value ($ mil.): 411

	STOCK PRICE ($) FY Close	P/E High/Low	PER SHARE ($) Earnings	Dividends	Book Value
12/14	10.89	13 5	1.49	0.00	8.46
12/13	17.91	28 16	0.66	0.00	9.56
12/12	10.97	25 15	0.50	0.00	9.06
12/11	7.23	38 23	0.28	0.00	8.20
12/10	10.17	— —	(0.04)	0.00	7.60
Annual Growth	**1.7%**	**— —**	**—**	**—**	**2.7%**

The Gap, Inc.

The ubiquitous clothing retailer Gap has been filling closets with jeans and khakis T-shirts and poplin since the Woodstock era. The firm which operates about 3400 stores worldwide built its iconic casual brand on basics for men women and children but over the years has expanded through the urban chic chain Banana Republic family budgeteer Old Navy online-only retailer Piperlime and Athleta a purveyor of activewear. Other brand extensions include GapBody GapKids and babyGap; each also has its own online incarnation. All Gap clothing is private-label merchandise made exclusively for the company. From the design board to store displays Gap controls all aspects of its trademark casual look.

HISTORY

Donald Fisher and his wife Doris opened a small store in 1969 near what is now San Francisco State University. The couple named their store The Gap (after "the generation gap") and concentrated on selling Levi's jeans. The couple opened a second store in San Jose California eight months later and by the end of 1970 there were six Gap stores. The Gap went public six years later.

In the beginning the Fishers catered almost exclusively to teenagers but in the 1970s they expanded into activewear that would appeal to a larger spectrum of customers. Nevertheless by the early 1980s The Gap —which had grown to about 500 stores —was still dependent upon its largely teenage customer base. However it was less dependent on Levi's (about 35% of sales) thanks to its growing stable of private labels.

In a 1983 effort to revamp the company's image Donald hired Mickey Drexler a former president of AnnTaylor with a spotless apparel industry track record as The Gap's new president. Drexler immediately overhauled the motley clothing lines to concentrate on sturdy brightly colored cotton clothing. He also consolidated the stores' many private clothing labels into the Gap brand. As a final touch Drexler replaced circular clothing racks with white shelving so clothes could be neatly stacked and displayed.

Also in 1983 The Gap bought Banana Republic a unique chain of jungle-themed stores that sold safari clothing. The company expanded the chain which enjoyed tremendous success in the mid-1980s but slumped after the novelty of the stores wore off late in the decade. In response Drexler introduced a broader range of clothes (including higher-priced leather items) and dumped the safari lines in 1988. By 1990 Banana Republic was again profitable.

The first GapKids opened in 1985 after Drexler couldn't find clothing that he liked for his son. During the late 1980s and early 1990s the company grew rapidly opening its first stores in Canada and the UK. In 1990 it introduced babyGap in 25 GapKids stores featuring miniature versions of its GapKids line. The Gap announced in 1991 it would no longer sell Levi's (which had fallen to less than 2% of total sales) and would sell nothing but private-label items.

Earnings fell in fiscal 1993 because of Gap division losses brought on by low margins and high rents. The company shuffled management positions and titles as part of a streamlining effort. It rebounded in 1994 by concentrating on improving profit margins rather than sales and by launching Old Navy Clothing Co. named after a bar Drexler saw in Paris. Banana Republic opened its first two stores outside the US both in Canada in 1995.

Robert Fisher (the founders' son) became the new president of the Gap division (including babyGap and GapKids) in 1997 and was charged with reversing the segment's sales decline. The company refocused its Gap chain on basics (jeans T-shirts and khakis) and helped boost its performance with a high-profile advertising campaign focusing on those wares. Later in 1997 the Gap opened an online Gap store. In 1998 it began opening Torpedo Joe submarine-themed shops in select Old Navy flagships.

Also in 1998 the retailer opened its first Gap-Body stores and introduced its only catalog (for Banana Republic). In late 1999 amid sluggish Gap division sales Robert Fisher resigned and Drexler took over his duties. Gap misjudged fashion trends in 2000 which resulted in two years of disappointing earnings. After a 10% reduction in its workforce the company returned to a more conservative fashion approach.

The company split Gap and Gap International into two separate units in early 2002 to improve performance in the flagship brand. In September Drexler retired and was replaced by Paul Pressler a veteran of The Walt Disney Company.

Gap sold its 10 stores in Germany to Swedish retailer H&M in 2004 taking a $14 million writedown related to the sale.

The next year the retailer launched Forth & Towne its first new chain in a decade with the new stores catering to women over the age of 35. Also Gap dipped its toes into personal care products by signing an agreement with Inter Parfums in mid-2005. As part of the deal Inter Parfums develops formulates manufactures and packages the products which are branded under the Gap and Banana Republic names. The Gap markets and sells them in its GapBody stores.

In January 2006 Gap entered into a 10-year non-exclusive services agreement with International Business Machines valued at $1.1 billion. As a result IBM took over certain information technology functions from the retailer; up to 400 Gap employees joined IBM as a result of the deal. Gap Direct launched an online footwear business called Piperlime in November.

CEO Pressler left the company and the board in January 2007 after four years in the top job. He was succeeded as CEO on an interim basis by Robert Fisher previously the non-executive chairman of the retailer. In June the company shut down its Forth & Towne retail format after less than two years in business. In July Gap named a new chairman and CEO Glenn Murphy. Murphy joined the company from Canadian drugstore chain Shoppers Drug Mart where he had retired as chairman and CEO in March. Stung by allegations in the British press of forced child labor in India being used in the manufacture of apparel for its Gap Kids chain Gap in November announced a package of measures intended to strengthen its commitment to eradicating the exploitation of children in the garment industry. Actions include a $200000 grant to improve working conditions and an upcoming conference dedicated to finding solutions to issues related to child labor.

In October 2008 Gap acquired Athleta a direct-marketer of women's active wear for about $150 million. Gap purchased Athleta as part of its strategy to diversify its brand offerings. The company also opened its first Banana Republic and Gap brand factory stores in Canada in late October extending its outlet busuiness launched in 1994 to Canada. The retailer opened 101 new stores and shuttered 119 locations in 2008.

Don Fisher Gap co-founder died in September 2009 at the age of 81. Also in 2009 Gap began opening stores inside Mexico's leading department store chain Distribuidora Liverpool via a franchise agreement.

In November 2010 Gap entered Italy with a store in Milan.

EXECUTIVES

EVP and CFO, Sabrina L. Simmons, age 51, $825,000 total compensation
President and General Manager Athleta, Nancy Green, age 53

President Growth Innovation and Digital, Arthur (Art) Peck, age 59, $943,269 total compensation
EVP Global Product Old Navy, Jill Stanton, age 53
President and General Manager Intermix, Jyothi Rao
EVP General Counsel Chief Compliance Officer and Secretary, Michelle Banks, age 51
EVP Global Supply Chain, Sonia Syngal, age 45
SVP Global Responsibility; President Gap Foundation, Bobbi Silten
Global President Gap, Jeff Kirwan, age 49
Head of Gap Outlet, Andi Owen, age 50
EVP Digital and Customer Experience, Solomon (Sol) Goldfarb, age 50
Vice President finance europe, Mark Webb
Vice President Social and Environmental Responsibility, Kindley Lawlor
Vice President Merchandising, Ceri Williams
Vice President Ocm, Rita Martell
Vice President Finance, John Moyer
Vice President Talent Strategy And Services, Tanya Hurwitz
Vice President And Deputy General Coun, Tom Lima
Vice President of Stores Old Navy, Lynn Albright
Vice President Store Development North America and Europe, Anthony Maldonado
Vice President Human Resources and Communications, Sudarshana Rangachary
Vice President Human Resources China Retail, Chris Baer
Vice President Omnichannel Customer Experience, Sarah Hammond
Vice President Real Estate and Store Development Asia, Scott Martin
Vice President North American Transportation and Europe Logistics, Shawn Curran
Vice President Old Navy Store Strategies and Business Solutions, Amy Solliday
Vice President General Manager Banana Republic Online (Global), Chris Phillips
Senior Vice President and General Manager, Jodi Bricker
Senior Vice President Corporate Finance and Treasurer, Roger Chelemedos
Vice President of Stores East Territory, Sheri Cabrera
Vice President Global Web General Manager Old Navy Online, Kevin Durrance
Vice President Global Talent Management and Organization Effectiveness, Pablo Gaito
Vice President and General Manager Piperlime, Lexi Tawes
Vice President Merchandising Gap International, Michael (Mel) Richardson
Vice President Boys and Toddler Boys Global Design, Cheryl Pagano
Senior Vice President Global Real Estate Store Development and Franchise Services, Ray Miolla
Senior Vice President and General Manager Global Gap Outlet, Aimee Lapic
Vice President Brand Exposure and Promotions, Kristin Peterson
Executive Vice President Corp STRG Bus Development, Art Peck
Executive Vice President Global Product Operations Gap Inc., John (Jack) Keiser
Executive Vice President Chief Information Officer, Tom Keiser
Chairman, Robert J. (Bob) Fisher, age 60
Auditors: Deloitte & Touche LLP

LOCATIONS

HQ: The Gap, Inc.
Two Folsom Street, San Francisco, CA 94105
Phone: 415 427-0100
Web: www.gapinc.com

2014 Sales

	$ mil.	% of total
US	12,672	77
Asia	1,502	9
Canada	1,137	7
Europe	917	6
Other regions	207	1
Total	**16,435**	**100**

2014 Stores (excluding franchise)

	No.
North America	2,671
Asia	289
Europe	204
Total	**3,164**

PRODUCTS/OPERATIONS

2014 Sales

	$ mil.	% of total
Old Navy global	6,619	40
Gap	6,165	38
Banana Republic global	2,922	18
Other	729	4
Total	**16,435**	**100**

2014 Stores

	No.
Company-operated	
Gap	1,389
Old Navy	1,022
Banana Republic	650
Athleta	65
Intermix	37
Piperlime	1
Franchise	375
Total	**3,539**

Selected Stores and Brands

Athleta (women' s activewear)
babyGap (clothing for infants and toddlers)
Banana Republic (upscale clothing and accessories)
Gap (casual and active clothing and body care products)
GapBody (intimate apparel)
GapKids (clothing for children)
Old Navy (lower-priced family clothing)
Piperlime (online shoes)

COMPETITORS

Abercrombie & Fitch	J. Crew
Amazon.com	Juicy Couture
American Eagle Outfitters	Kohl' s
Ann Taylor	L.L. Bean
Arcadia	Lands' End
A©ropostale	Levi Strauss
Babies " R" Us	Macy' s
Benetton	Marks & Spencer
Bleach Group	NIKE
Calvin Klein	Nautica Apparel
Children' s Place	Nordstrom
Dillard' s	OshKosh B' Gosh
Express	PVH
Fast Retailing	REI
Foot Locker	Ralph Lauren
Fruit of the Loom	Reebok
Guess?	Ross Stores
Gymboree	Sears
H&M	TJX Companies
HSN	Talbots
Inditex	Target Corporation
J. C. Penney	VF Corporation
	Wal-Mart

HISTORICAL FINANCIALS

Company Type: Public

Income Statement

FYE: January 31

	REVENUE ($ mil.)	NET INCOME ($ mil.)	NET PROFIT MARGIN	EMPLOYEES
01/15*	16,435	1,262	7.7%	141,000
02/14	16,148	1,280	7.9%	137,000
02/13	15,651	1,135	7.3%	136,000
01/12	14,549	833	5.7%	132,000
01/11	14,664	1,204	8.2%	134,000
Annual Growth	2.9%	1.2%	—	1.3%

*Fiscal year change

2015 Year-End Financials

Debt ratio: 17.59%
Return on equity: 41.87%
Cash ($ mil.): 1,515
Current ratio: 1.93
Long-term debt ($ mil.): 1,332
No. of shares (mil.): 421
Dividends
  Yield: 0.0%
  Payout: 30.6%
Market value ($ mil.): 17,341

	STOCK PRICE ($) FY Close	P/E High/Low		PER SHARE ($) Earnings	Dividends	Book Value
01/15*	41.19	16	12	2.87	0.88	7.09
02/14	38.08	17	11	2.74	0.70	6.87
02/13	32.97	16	9	2.33	0.50	6.25
01/12	18.93	15	10	1.56	0.45	5.68
01/11	19.20	14	9	1.88	0.40	6.94
Annual Growth	21.0%	—	—	11.2%	21.8%	0.5%

*Fiscal year change

THE PRIDDY FOUNDATION

LOCATIONS

HQ: THE PRIDDY FOUNDATION
807 8TH ST STE 1010, WICHITA FALLS, TX 763013310
Phone: 9407238720
Web: WWW.PRIDDYFDN.ORG

HISTORICAL FINANCIALS

Company Type: Private

Income Statement

FYE: December 31

	REVENUE ($ mil.)	NET INCOME ($ mil.)	NET PROFIT MARGIN	EMPLOYEES
12/13	8,791	3	0.0%	4
12/12	3	(4)	—	—
12/10	32	27	86.7%	—
12/09	0	0	—	—
Annual Growth	—	—	—	—

2013 Year-End Financials

Debt ratio: ——
Return on equity: —
Cash ($ mil.): 14
Current ratio: —
Long-term debt ($ mil.): —
Dividends
  Yield: —
  Payout: —
Market value ($ mil.): —

Thermo Fisher Scientific Inc

Whether for research analysis discovery or diagnostics Thermo Fisher Scientific gets the laboratory ready to assist mankind. The company makes and distributes analytical instruments equipment and other laboratory supplies —from chromatographs and spectrometers to Erlenmeyer flasks and fume hoods. It also provides specialty diagnostic testing products as well as clinical analytical tools. Thermo Fisher serves more than 40000 customers worldwide in its key markets of health care and diagnostics biotech and pharmaceutical academic research institutions and government and industrial and applied settings including environmental quality and process control.

Operations

Laboratory Services which provides just about everything needed to run a lab generate 38% of Thermo Fisher's revenue. With about a quarter of revenue is the Life Sciences Solutions segment which provides reagents instruments and consumables used in biological and medical research drug discovery and production and for vaccines and diagnosis. Analytical Instruments and Specialty Diagnostics account for 19% of revenue each.

Geographic Reach

Thermo Fisher gets about half of its sales in the US. With no country outside the US representing a double-digit percentage of sales Thermo Fisher sees lots of room to grow internationally and is aiming for a quarter of sales to come from emerging markets by 2016. Key countries include China (currently 7% of sales) India South Korea Brazil and Russia. Supporting its global expansion efforts in 2012 it opened a demonstration lab and training center in Seoul as well as a manufacturing facility in China.

Sales and Marketing

Pitching Thermo Fisher's offerings is a team of direct sales personnel. The company also uses e-commerce third-party distributors and other channels. It ramped up marketing efforts in 2014 with a big increase in advertising spending. It spent $47.7 million in 2014 up from $33.2 million in 2013.

Financial Performance

Thermo Fisher reported robust increases in revenue and net income in 2014. Revenue jumped 29% higher to $16.9 billion in 2014 from $13.1 billion in 2013. The big revenue leap was in life sciences as the acquisition of Life Technologies fueled a sales increase of 489%. Sales in Laboratory Services rose 3.2%. Net income rose with the higher revenue. Cash flow from operation was 30% higher in 2014 rising to $2.62 billion from $2.0 billion in 2013. The increase was attributed to the increase in net income and changes in working capital.

Strategy

While acquisitions continue to be a strong component in Thermo Fisher's growth strategy the company also uses divestitures to keep its business focused. In 2014 it sold its cell culture gene modulation and magnetic beads businesses to GE Healthcare for $1 billion. Later that year it sold Cole-Parmer Instrument Company to private equity firm GTCR for $480 million. Cole-Parmer makes laboratory equipment under the brands Masterflex Oakton and Digi-Sense.

Thermo Fisher increased its investment in research and development in 2014 spending about $691 million compared to $396 million in 2013.

The company's customers are susceptible to market forces that might reduce their R&D spending. Pharmaceutical research could be affected by mergers and academic research could be affected by reduced federal spending for basic research.

Mergers and Acquisitions

In early 2014 Thermo Fisher finalized a huge deal that will move it to the head of the pack in life sciences tools particularly the growing field of genetic testing. It bought California-based Life Technologies for about $13.6 billion plus the assumption of debt. Life Technologies develops tools and systems for gene cloning expression and analysis.

The cash from making bread-and-butter laboratory equipment (beakers microscope slides) is used to buy small innovative companies that can benefit from Thermo Fisher's resources and drive the company's steady growth especially in emerging markets.

In 2015 Thermo Fisher bought Alfa Aesar a manufacturer of research chemicals for $405 million in cash. The acquisition adds to Thermo Fisher's portfolio of chemicals solvents and reagents. Also in 2015 Thermo Fisher bought Advanced Scientifics Inc. a provider of single-use technologies for customized bio-processing for $300 million in cash. ASI's product line helps Thermo Fisher meet customer demand in the bio-processing market. Both Alfa Aesar and ASI operate internationally which helps Thermo Fisher's drive to increase overseas sales.

HISTORY

Early History

Predating the acquiring company Thermo Electron Fisher Scientific dates back to 1902 when 20-year-old Chester Fisher bought the stockroom of Pittsburgh Testing Laboratories (established 1884) and formed Scientific Materials Co. The company's earliest products supplied from Europe included simple tools such as microscopes balances and calorimeters. It published its first catalog in 1904.

When the outbreak of WWI disrupted supplies from Europe Scientific Materials established its own R&D and manufacturing facilities. It acquired Montreal-based Scientific Supplies in 1925 and the following year changed its name to Fisher Scientific Company. By 1935 Fisher had doubled its size adding glass-blowing operations and an instrument shop.

During the German occupation of Greece in WWII George Hatsopoulos part of a well-to-do family packed with politicians and engineering professors made radios for the Greek resistance. After the war he came to the US and became a professor of mechanical engineering at MIT. With a $50000 loan Hatsopoulos founded Thermo Electron in 1956 to identify emerging technology needs and create solutions for them.

In 2006 Thermo Electron merged with Fisher Scientific International in a stock-swap transaction valued at nearly $11 billion. (

EXECUTIVES

Vice President Of Information Technology, Kevin McEvoy

EVP and Chief Administrative Officer, Peter M. (Pete) Wilver, age 55, $673,962 total compensation

President and CEO, Marc N. Casper, age 47, $1,254,808 total compensation

EVP; President Life Sciences Solutions, Mark P. Stevenson, age 52, $723,077 total compensation

EVP; President Laboratory Products and Services, Alan J. Malus, age 55, $716,153 total compensation

SVP and CFO, Stephen Williamson

SVP; President Analytical Instruments, Thomas W. (Tom) Loewald, age 51, $56,812 total compensation

SVP; President Specialty Diagnostics, Andrew J. (Andy) Thomson, age 50

President Asia-Pacific and Emerging Markets, Syed A. Jafry

SVP; President Customer Channels, Gregory J. (Greg) Herrema

SVP; President Laboratory Products, Frederick M. (Fred) Lowery

SVP and CIO, Joseph C. Beery

Vice President Strategic Marketing, Steven (Steve) Silverman

Vice President, Mark P Zacur

Vice President Corporate Counsel, Peter (Pete) Brennan

Vice President, Denny Cannon

National Sales Manager Industrial, Kyle Rehberg

Vice President and General Manager, Michael (Mel) Shafer

Vice President Human Resources, Art Wood

Vice President Information Technology, Randy Carter

Vice President Finance and Admin, Nicholas Pezzuolo

Vice President General Manager RNA Technologies, Mitchell (Mitch) Kennedy

Vice President Of Marketing and Product Development, David (Dave) Malinas

Vice President, Neeraja Putta

Vice President Operations, Lisa Robillard

Vice President, Gisele Vlietstra

Vice President of Finance, Gregory Siuciak

Vice President Information Technology, Krish Kumar

Vice President, Gary Galluzzi

Vice President Human Resources, Keith Tucker

Vice President of Engineering, Jerry Welch

Vice President Global Real Estate and Construction, Dave Waldron

Vice President Inside Sales, Sarah Frey

Vice President Information Technology, Jeff Wilks

Vice President Human Resources, Karen Kinsley

Vice President Information Technology, Abdalla Doleh

Vice President and General Manager, Mitch Kennedy

Vice President And Director Of Finance, Marisa Shim

Vice President Finance, Matt Richards

Vice President World Wide Finance, Andy Long

Vice President Operations Speciality Gla, Wes Lollar

Vice President Inside Sales, Kimberly Brown

Vice President CORPORATE FINANCIAL PLANNING and ANALYSIS, James (Jamie) Lane

Senior Vice President of Commercial Real Estate Sales, Karen Edwards

Vice President of Human Resources at Thermo Fisher Scientific, Valerie (Val) Mulhern

Vice President Marketing Mass Spectrometry, Ken Miller

Regional Vice President, Christian Andasse

Vice President and General Counsel Fisher Healthcare, Leslie Ann Goldman

Vice President Clinical Services North America and Facility Network, Leon Wyszkowski

Vice President Information Technology, Liberino Martino

Regional Sales Vice President, Anne Porter

Vice President and Chief Employment Counsel, Peter (Pete) Kim

Vice President Consulting, Anita Sakaria

Vice President Sales Support, Markus Kellmann

Vice President Global Marketing and Customer Experience, Rich Oprison

Vice President of Strategy Portfolio and Business Development, Lalit Dhir

Vice President Human Resources Biosciences,
Fiona Walker
Vice President Corporate Marketing and CMD
Japan, Keiko Hattori
Vice President Investor Relations and Treasurer,
Ken Apicerno
Vice President Deputy General Counsel (2006),
Jonathan C (Jon) Wilk
Executive Vice President Marketing, Tony Smith
Senior Vice President Sales, Keith Katzgrau
Vice President Human Resources, Susan G (Sue)
Rice
Vice President Finance, Gregg Siuciak
Vice President Marketing, Lynda Thomas
Vice President Of Finance, James (Jamie) Chopas
Vice President Asia Service Operations, Michael
(Mel) Kinderman
Chairman, Jim P. Manzi, age 63
Assistant Treasurer, Maura Spellman
Board Member, Benoit J Limon
Treasurer Membership Chairman, Amber Diamond
Board Member, Nelson Romero
Board Member, Cheryl L Buckley
Board Member, Jukka Kalliokoski
Board Member, Paul Webster
Auditors: PricewaterhouseCoopers LLP

LOCATIONS

HQ: Thermo Fisher Scientific Inc
   81 Wyman Street, Waltham, MA 02451
Phone: 781 622-1000   Fax: 781 933-4476
Web: www.thermofisher.com

2012 Sales

	$ mil.	% of total
US	6,424	51
China	735	6
Germany	681	6
UK	507	4
Other countries	4,161	33
Total	**12,509**	**100**

2014 Sales

	$ mil.	% of total
US	8,147	49
China	1,223	7
Germany	1,005	6
UK	754	4
Other countries	5,758	34
Total	**16,889**	**100**

PRODUCTS/OPERATIONS

2014 Sales

	$ mil.	% of total
Laboratory Products & Services	6,601	38
Life Sciences Solutions	4,195	24
Specialty Diagnostics	3,343	19
Analytical Instruments	3,252	19
Adjustments	(503.4)	-
Total	**16,889**	**100**

2014 Sales

	$ mil.	% of total
Products	14,715	87
Services	2,174	13
Total	**16,889**	**100**
Services		
Custom Services		
Instrument & Qualification Services		
Out-Licensing and OEM Sales		
Most Popular Products		
TaqMan Real-Time PCR Assays		
Oligos Pri		
Lipofectamine Reagents		
TRIzol Reagents		
SuperScript Reverse Transcriptase		
eSolutions		
eProcurement		
Supply Center		
Instrument Management		

Selected Products

Analytical Instruments

Automation and Robotics
Life Science Research consumables
Chemicals
Consumables
Custom Products
Diagnostics
Equipment
Furniture
Software

Selected Brands

ABgene
Barnant
Barnstead
BioImage
Cellomics
Dharmacon
Dionex
Electrothermal Engineering
Erie Scientific
Fisher Diagnostics
Gerhard Menzel
HyClone
Lab Vision/NeoMarkers
Matrix
Microgenics
Milwaukee Nucleic Acid Technologies
NERL
Owl Separation Systems Inc.
Pierce
Richard-Allan Scientific
Seradyn
TC Tech
Unity Lab Services

Selected Acquisitions

COMPETITORS

Abbott Labs	Life Technologies
Agilent Technologies	Corporation
Beckman Coulter	Mettler-Toledo
Becton Dickinson	Newport Corp.
Bio-Rad Labs	Nordion
Bruker	PerkinElmer
Corning	QIAGEN
Danaher	Roche Diagnostics
Emerson Electric	Roper Technologies
Halma	Shimadzu
Harvard Bioscience	Sigma-Aldrich
Hitachi	Tektronix
Honeywell	VWR
International	Waters Corp.
IDEXX Labs	Yokogawa Electric
Johnson & Johnson	

HISTORICAL FINANCIALS

Company Type: Public

Income Statement

FYE: December 31

	REVENUE ($ mil.)	NET INCOME ($ mil.)	NET PROFIT MARGIN	EMPLOYEES
12/14	16,889	1,894	11.2%	51,000
12/13	13,090	1,273	9.7%	50,000
12/12	12,509	1,177	9.4%	38,900
12/11	11,725	1,329	11.3%	39,300
12/10	10,788	1,035	9.6%	37,200
Annual Growth	**11.9%**	**16.3%**	**—**	**8.2%**

2014 Year-End Financials

Debt ratio: 33.99%	No. of shares (mil.): 400
Return on equity: 10.13%	Dividends
Cash ($ mil.): 1,343	Yield: 0.4%
Current ratio: 1.22	Payout: 14.4%
Long-term debt ($ mil.): 12,351	Market value ($ mil.): 50,175

	STOCK PRICE ($) FY Close	P/E High/Low	PER SHARE ($) Earnings	Dividends	Book Value
12/14	125.29	27 23	4.71	0.60	51.31
12/13	111.35	31 18	3.48	0.60	46.57
12/12	63.78	20 14	3.21	0.54	43.26
12/11	44.97	19 12	3.46	0.00	40.49
12/10	55.36	22 16	2.53	0.00	39.25
Annual Growth	**22.7%**	**— —**	**16.8%**	**—**	**6.9%**

Time Warner Cable Inc

Time Warner Cable (TWC) makes coaxial quiver. The company is the #2 US cable company after Comcast with operations in more than two dozen states across the country. It serves more than 15.2 million mostly residential customers (about 625000 business customers) with video high-speed data (primarily through ISP brand Road Runner) and voice offerings as well as security and home management. In addition to video voice and data other business services include networking and transport outsourced IT and cloud computing. In April 2015 rival Comcast dropped its $45 billion bid to acquire TWC because of regulatory hurdles. A month after that door closed another one opened. TWC accepted a $55 billion offer from Charter Communications.

OperationsTWC also operates local news broadcasting stations in New York (including New York City) North Carolina and Texas regional sports networks as well as a news sports and entertainment online portal.

The company generates more than 80% of revenue from its residential services; business services and advertising account for about 15% and 5% respectively.

Geographic Reach
Its core service areas are in New York the Midwest Texas the Carolinas and southern California.

Sales and MarketingTWC markets its products and services via a host of direct channels (online telemarketing e-mail marketing door-to-door sales) as well as through third-party partners and retailers. In 2014 TWC served approximately 10.8 million residential video subscribers 11.7 million residential high-speed data subscribers 5.3 million residential voice subscribers and 85000 Intelligent Home customers. The Company spent about $684 million on advertising in 2014 compared to $676 million in 2013.

Financial AnalysisThe company has seen strong revenue growth over the last decade. Sales in 2014 rose 3% to $22.81 billion on higher business service revenue from the inclusion of revenue from DukeNet (an acquisition) as well as and growth in high-speed data and voice subscribers. Election year advertising drove advertising revenue higher. The residential services segment saw an increase in high-speed data revenue which was partly offset by decreases in video and voice revenue.The higher revenue translated into a 4% rise in net income to $2.03 billion in 2014. Cash flow from operations has been steady over the past several years; in 2014 it rose $597 million to $6.3 billion.

Strategy
Growth in TWC's residential operations has slowed in recent years as it operates in mature competitive markets. The company seeks to extend its services to mobile devices and to non-TV devices to help it retain and gain customers. In a deal with Microsoft TWC will make its TV app available

for the Xbox One video game and entertainment system. Consumers with an Xbox Live account will have access to free and subscription On Demand titles. TWC teamed up with Boingo to provide Passpoint roaming access to their subscribers. Qualified TWC Internet customers and Boingo subscribers can connect to secure WiFi networks at thousands of locations including 25 high traffic airports in the U.S.

Expanding options for its customers us important as alternatives to cable and satellite TV profilerate. While TWC carries nascent competitors such as Netflix and Hulu via its ISP such services could eat into TWC's more profitable cable business. Another potential problem for TWC is the Federal Communications Commission's vote to regulate the Internet like a utility. That could prevent TWC and its competitors (or eventual partner Comcast) from finding sources of revenue in different tiers of service.

The company is focused on improving the quality and reliability of its residential products and offering distinguished customer service. TWC expects to see continued strong growth in its business services segment; it predicts revenue of more than $5 billion from those offerings by 2018.

Mergers and AcquisitionsAcquisitions have played their part in TWC's strategy. In 2014 the company closed its acquisition of DukeNet Communications. The $600 million purchase bolstered TWC's business services wholesale transport offerings by adding some 8700 route miles in the southeastern US to the company's fiber optic network.

EXECUTIVES

EVP and Chief Communications Officer, Ellen M. East, age 53

Chairman and CEO, Robert D. (Rob) Marcus, age 49, $1,500,000 total compensation

EVP General Counsel and Secretary, Marc Lawrence-Apfelbaum, age 59, $650,000 total compensation

COO, Dinesh C. (Dinni) Jain, age 49, $1,000,000 total compensation

EVP Chief Video Officer and COO Time Warner Cable Networks, Melinda C. Witmer, age 53

EVP and Chief Product People and Strategy Officer, Peter C. Stern, age 44, $625,000 total compensation

EVP and CTO, Hamid R. Heidary, age 57

EVP and COO Media Services, Joan H. Gillman

SVP Controller Chief Accounting Officer and Co-CFO, William F. Osbourne

EVP and Chief Government Relations Officer, Gail G. MacKinnon, age 53

EVP and COO Business Services, Philip G. Meeks, $332,308 total compensation

EVP and COO Residential Services, John Keib

SVP Treasurer and Co-CFO, Matthew Siegel

Vice President For Government Affairs, Ed Kozelek

Svp Business Services Product, Greg King

Area Vice President of Operations, Steve Dvoskin

Vice President Of Communications, Bobby Amirshahi

Vice President, Matt Haines

National Account Manager, Frank Wersan

Senior Vice President Human Resources, Paul Gilles

Vice President Prod Development Business Services, Joseph (Jo) DeLotto

National Account Manager, Bob Lawson

GVP Communications and Change Management, Sherri Johnson

Vice President Marketing, Sanjay Chatterjee

Vice President Of Operations And Engineer, Joe Truncale

Vice President Of Consumer Marketing, Jose Perez

Vice President Research, Marshall Jacobowitz

Regional Vice President of Sales, Lisa Meier

Vice President Marketing And Media, Scott Christiansen

Vice President Marketing, Darrel Hegar

Vice President Human Resources Operations, Mark Imhoff

Vice President Human Resources National Division Denver, Linda Williams

Vice President Sales, Louis Brazzoni

Vice President Finance East Region Time Warner Cable Media, John (Jack) Osmanski

Vice President In Communications West, Milinda Martin

Vice President Government and Community Relations (Programming), Ann Hall

Senior Vice President Government Relations, Steven (Steve) Teplitz

Senior Vice President, Dan Finnerty

Senior Vice President and Chief Sales Officer, Jeffrey (Jeff) Painting

Auditors: Ernst & Young LLP

LOCATIONS

HQ: Time Warner Cable Inc
60 Columbus Circle, New York, NY 10023
Phone: 212 364-8200
Web: www.timewarnercable.com

PRODUCTS/OPERATIONS

2014 Sales

	$ mil.	% of total
Residential		
Video	10,002	43
High-speed data	6,428	28
Voice	1,932	8
Other	84	-
Business services		
High-speed data	1,341	6
Voice	511	2
Wholesale transport	415	2
Video	365	2
Other	206	1
Advertising	1,127	5
Other	645	3
Eliminations	(244)	-
Total	**22,812**	**100**

COMPETITORS

AT&T	Level 3 Communications
Apple Inc.	Netflix
Cablevision Systems	RCN Corporation
Charter Communications	ReaLLinx
Cincinnati Bell	Skype
Comcast	Sprint Communications
Cox Communications	Suddenlink
DIRECTV	Communications
DISH Network	T-Mobile USA
Frontier	Verizon
Communications	Vonage
Grande Communications	YouTube
Hulu	

HISTORICAL FINANCIALS

Company Type: Public

Income Statement

FYE: December 31

	REVENUE ($ mil.)	NET INCOME ($ mil.)	NET PROFIT MARGIN	EMPLOYEES
12/15	23,697	1,844	7.8%	56,600
12/14	22,812	2,031	8.9%	55,170
12/13	22,120	1,954	8.8%	51,600
12/12	21,386	2,155	10.1%	51,000
12/11	19,675	1,665	8.5%	48,500
Annual Growth	**4.8%**	**2.6%**	**—**	**3.9%**

2015 Year-End Financials

Debt ratio: 45.66%	No. of shares (mil.): 283
Return on equity: 21.68%	Dividends
Cash ($ mil.): 1,170	Yield: 2.0%
Current ratio: 0.62	Payout: 56.0%
Long-term debt ($ mil.): 22,497	Market value ($ mil.): 52,578

	STOCK PRICE ($) FY Close	P/E High/Low		PER SHARE ($) Earnings	Dividends	Book Value
12/15	185.59	30	21	6.44	3.75	31.75
12/14	152.06	21	18	7.17	3.00	28.54
12/13	135.50	20	13	6.70	2.60	24.98
12/12	97.19	14	9	6.90	2.24	24.45
12/11	63.57	16	11	4.97	1.92	23.90
Annual Growth	**30.7%**	**—**	**—**	**6.7%**	**18.2%**	**7.4%**

Time Warner Inc

Even among media titans this company is a giant. Time Warner is one of the world's largest media conglomerate behind Walt Disney and News Corporation with operations spanning television and film. Through subsidiary Turner Broadcasting the company runs a portfolio of popular cable TV networks including CNN TBS and TNT. Time Warner also operates pay-TV channels HBO and Cinemax. Its Warner Bros. Entertainment meanwhile includes films studios (Warner Bros. Pictures New Line Cinema) TV production units (Warner Bros. Television Group) and comic book publisher DC Entertainment. In 2014 the company spun off its print publishing operations.

HISTORY

Though formed in 2001 AOL Time Warner was the result of decades of advancement in the media industry. An elder statesman compared to relative newcomer America Online Time Warner's roots extend back to 1922 —the year that Henry Luce and Briton Hadden founded publisher Time Inc. and brothers Harry Abe Jack and Sam Warner established the origins of Warner Bros. which later became Warner Communications.

America Online's ancestry stretches back to the early 1980s when Stephen Case joined the management of a company called Control Video. Later renamed Quantum Computer Services the company created the online service that would become America Online in 1985. Quantum Computer Services changed its name to America Online in 1991. It went public the next year.

As America Online was germinating Time Inc. and Warner Communications were eyeing each other. The two companies merged in 1990 to form Time Warner. Gerald Levin was appointed CEO in 1992. To shave off debt Time Warner grouped several of its properties into Time Warner Entertainment in 1992 in which U S West (which later became MediaOne Group) bought a 25% interest.

Time Warner's 1996 acquisition of Ted Turner's Turner Broadcasting System further elevated Time Warner's profile on the media stage. For America Online 1996 marked the first year the company began charging its subscribers a flat rate vastly increasing the amount of time they spent online.

America Online grew through acquisitions of CompuServe in 1998 and Netscape Communications in 1999. Meanwhile Time Warner had created Time Warner Telecom and taken it public. After AT&T's announcement that it would acquire

MediaOne MediaOne gave up its 50% management control of Time Warner Entertainment but retained its 25% ownership interest. AT&T's acquisition of MediaOne was completed in 2000 thus giving AT&T 25% of Time Warner Entertainment. (AT&T later boosted its stake to 27%.)

America Online announced that it would acquire Time Warner in early 2000. To please European regulators Time Warner subsequently abandoned its plans to combine the Warner Music Group with EMI Group's music operations. After a lengthy review by regulatory bodies America Online acquired Time Warner for $106 billion and formed AOL Time Warner in 2001. Case became chairman and Levin was appointed CEO. The newly formed company soon began streamlining cutting more than 2400 jobs in the process. (It cut another 1700 jobs at America Online later that year.) Also that year America Online invested about $100 million in Amazon.com.

Levin retired from the company in 2002 and was replaced by co-COO Richard Parsons. The following year AOL Time Warner finally succeeded in buying Comcast's stake in Time Warner Entertainment (Comcast gained its share of TWE when it bought the cable assets of AT&T in 2002). The following year Case and Turner both resigned their executive positions with the company but remained on the board of directors. (Case left the board in 2005.) And in a move to distance itself from the struggling online unit the company dropped AOL from its moniker and returned to being known as Time Warner Inc.

Time Warner started off 2004 by ridding itself of Warner Music Group which it sold for $2.6 billion to a group led by former Seagram executive Edgar Bronfman Jr. and investment firm Thomas H. Lee Partners. It also sold the NBA's Atlanta Hawks and the NHL's Atlanta Thrashers for $250 million to a private investment group called Atlanta Spirit.

The company's flagship Internet service officially shortened its name to simply AOL in early 2006. Also that year Time Warner sold its book publishing unit Time Warner Book Group to French media firm Lagardère. Time Warner Cable joined with Comcast to acquire Adelphia Communications for $17.6 billion in cash and stock; as part of the deal Adelphia shareholders sold part of their newly acquired stake in TWC through an IPO in 2007. Later that year Time Warner sold its Atlanta Braves baseball team (once owned by former vice chairman Ted Turner) to Liberty Media in a deal that valued the team at $460 million.

Parsons retired as CEO at the beginning of 2008 and was replaced by Jeffrey Bewkes who previously oversaw the company's entertainment divisions. Bewkes replaced Parsons as Time Warner chairman as well at the end of that year.

Never able to achieve significant synergies between the online media and traditional film and TV content arms despite several restructuring attempts Time Warner was burdened with debt and suffering losses. This ultimately led the company to spin off AOL as a separate publicly traded company in 2009. The separation valued AOL at less than $3 billion far less than the $124 billion valuation of the original AOL-Time Warner merger. In another high-profile disposal during 2009 Time Warner spun off its remaining stake in Time Warner Cable.

In 2011 the company's Filmed Entertainment unit released the final film in the immensely popular Harry Potter series. Harry Potter and the Deathly Hallows: Part 2 was the year's top film in terms of ticket sales pulling in a colossal $1.3 billion in 2011.

In 2014 Time Warner spun off its print publishing operations.

EXECUTIVES

EVP Global Public Policy, Carol A. Melton, age 61
EVP Corporate Marketing and Communications, Gary L. Ginsberg, age 53, $872,740 total compensation
President Warner Bros. Consumer Products, Brad Globe
Chairman and CEO, Jeffrey L. (Jeff) Bewkes, age 63, $2,000,000 total compensation
EVP and General Counsel, Paul T. Cappuccio, age 54, $1,341,315 total compensation
CEO Warner Bros. Entertainment, Kevin Tsujihara
President Warner Bros. Unscripted and Alternative Television, Mike Darnell
EVP International and Corporate Strategy, Olaf J. Olafsson, age 52, $902,411 total compensation
Chairman and CEO Home Box Office, Richard L. Plepler
President and COO New Line Cinema, Toby Emmerich
President and Chief Content Officer Warner Bros. Television Group and President Warner Bros. Television Warner Horizon Television and Animation, Peter Roth
President Creative Development and Worldwide Production Warner Bros. Pictures, Greg Silverman
Chairman and CEO Turner Broadcasting System Inc., John Martin, age 47, $1,600,000 total compensation
President DC Entertainment and President and Chief Content Officer Warner Bros. Interactive Entertainment, Diane Nelson
President Domestic Distribution Warner Bros. Pictures, Dan Fellman
President Warner Bros. Studio Facilities, Jon Gilbert
President Worldwide Marketing and International Distribution Warner Bros. Pictures, Sue Kroll
President International Distribution Warner Bros. Pictures, Veronika Kwan Vandenberg
President Warner Bros. International Television Distribution, Jeffrey R. Schlesinger
President HBO Programming, Michael Lombardo
President HBO Documentary Films, Sheila Nevins, age 76
President Worldwide Physical Production Warner Bros. Pictures, Steve Papazian
President Warner Bros. Worldwide Home Entertainment Distribution, Ronald J. Sanders
President Turner Broadcasting System International, Gerhard Zeiler, age 58
President The CW Television Network, Mark Pedowitz
President Business and Strategy Warner Bros. Television Group, Craig Hunegs
EVP and CFO, Howard M. Averill, age 51, $1,200,000 total compensation
President HBO Miniseries, Kary Antholis
EVP and Chief Human Resources Officer, Karen Magee, age 54
President Warner Bros. Domestic Television Distribution, Kenneth (Ken) Werner, age 61
President Worldwide Business Affairs Warner Bros. Pictures, Steven S. Spira
CIO, Mitchell (Mitch) Klaif
President Programming Sales, Charles Schreger
President HBO Films, Len Amato
President CNN Worldwide, Jeff Zucker
President Music Warner Bros. Pictures, Paul Broucek
EVP and General Manager Warner Bros. Interactive Entertainment, David Haddad
President Turner Broadcasting System Inc., David Levy
President HBO Sports, Ken Hershman
President Animation Digital Production and Visual Effects Warner Bros. Pictures, Chris DeFaria
President and GM Cartoon Network Adult Swim and Boomerang, Christina Miller
President Global Distribution, Tom Woodbury
President Warner Bros. Animation and Warner Digital Series, Sam Register
Vice Chairman Warner Bros. Entertainment, Ed Romano
Vice President Project Management, Joel Brenner
Senior Vice President And Deputy Controller, Doug Horne
Senior Vice President Marketing and Digital (TruTV), Puja Vohra
Vice President Global Information Technology Workforce Management, Ashish Malhotra
Vice President Employee Benefits, Brian Mullin
Senior Vice President, Rachel Lam
Vice President International Tax, John (Jack) Petito
Vice President Finance, Amos Smith
Vice President Finance, Saroosh Ahmed
Vice President Finance, Ken Shelton
Resource Development Director and Vice President, Roy Spence
Senior Vice President Marketing, Russel Arons
Vice Presidentand Assistant Controller, John (Jack) Talamo
Executive Vice President And Chief Finan, Robert (Bob) Roth
Vice President Corporate Responsibility, Lisa Quiroz
Vice President Public Policy, Josh Hurvitz
Auditors: Ernst & Young LLP

LOCATIONS

HQ: Time Warner Inc
One Time Warner Center, New York, NY 10019-8016
Phone: 212 484-8000   **Fax:** 212 489-6183
Web: www.timewarner.com

2014 Sales

	$ mil.	% of total
US and Canada	19,102	70
Europe	4,684	17
Asia / Pacific Rim	1,711	6
Latin America	1,575	6
All other regions	287	1
Total	**27,359**	**100**

PRODUCTS/OPERATIONS

2014 Sales

	$ mil.	% of total
Content	12,350	46
Subscriptions	9,945	36
Advertising	4,502	16
Other	562	2
Total	**27,359**	**100**

2014 Sales

	$ mil.	% of total
Warner Bros	12,526	44
Turner	10,396	37
Home Box office	5,398	19
Intersegment eliminations	(961)	-
Total	**27,359**	**100**

COMPETITORS

21st Century Fox	Lagard˜re Active
Bertelsmann	Liberty Interactive
CBS Corp	Meredith Corporation
Discovery	NBCUniversal
Communications	Sony Pictures
Disney	Entertainment
Hearst Corporation	Viacom

HISTORICAL FINANCIALS

Company Type: Public

Income Statement

FYE: December 31

	REVENUE ($ mil.)	NET INCOME ($ mil.)	NET PROFIT MARGIN	EMPLOYEES
12/14	27,359	3,827	14.0%	25,600
12/13	29,795	3,691	12.4%	34,000
12/12	28,729	3,019	10.5%	34,000
12/11	28,974	2,886	10.0%	34,000
12/10	26,888	2,578	9.6%	31,000
Annual Growth	0.4%	10.4%	—	(4.7%)

2014 Year-End Financials

Debt ratio: 35.56%
Return on equity: 14.08%
Cash ($ mil.): 2,618
Current ratio: 1.43
Long-term debt ($ mil.): 21,376

No. of shares (mil.): 832
Dividends
　Yield: 1.4%
　Payout: 27.9%
Market value ($ mil.): 71,069

	STOCK PRICE ($) FY Close	P/E High/Low		PER SHARE ($) Earnings	Dividends	Book Value
12/14	85.42	20	14	4.34	1.27	29.42
12/13	69.72	18	12	3.92	1.15	33.41
12/12	47.83	15	11	3.09	1.04	32.06
12/11	36.14	14	10	2.71	0.94	30.76
12/10	32.17	15	12	2.25	0.85	29.97
Annual Growth	27.7%	—	—	17.8%	10.6%	(0.5%)

TJX Companies, Inc.

Rifling through the racks is an art at TJX stores. The TJX Companies operates nearly 3400 stores worldwide under half a dozen retail brand names including the two largest off-price clothing retailers in the US: T.J. Maxx and Marshalls which operate 2000-plus stores nationwide. T.J. Maxx sells brand-name family apparel accessories shoes domestics giftware and jewelry at discount prices while Marshalls offers similar items plus a broader selection of shoes and menswear through nearly 1000 stores. Its HomeGoods chain of 500-plus US stores focuses exclusively on home furnishings. T.K. Maxx is the company's European retail arm with 400-plus stores in the UK Ireland Germany and Poland.

HISTORY

Cousins Stanley and Sumner Feldberg opened the first Zayre (Yiddish for "very good") store in Hyannis Massachusetts in 1956. During the next 15 years the number of stores grew to nearly 200.

Zayre purchased the Hit or Miss chain which sold upscale women's clothing at discounted prices in 1969. When the recession of the early 1970s hit superb results at Hit or Miss prompted Zayre to look for further opportunities in the off-price apparel marketplace. Zayre hired Ben Cammarata to create a new store concept and in March 1977 he opened the first T.J. Maxx in Auburn Massachusetts to market discounted upscale family clothing. Six years later Zayre formed the catalog retailer Chadwick's of Boston to sell Hit or Miss apparel by mail.

The company came to rely increasingly on its specialty operations to provide consistent sales and income as its flagship general merchandise stores often struggled. By 1983 the specialty chains were producing almost half of Zayre's sales.

In the second half of the 1980s Zayre's upscale (yet still off-priced) retailers' sales rose while its general merchandise stores (targeting lower-income customers) dropped. To keep its specialty stores unhindered by its flagging Zayre stores it established The TJX Companies as a public company in 1987. Zayre sold about 17% of its new subsidiary to the public with Cammarata as CEO.

Zayre sold its 400 general merchandise stores in 1988 to Ames for about $430 million in cash $140 million in Ames stock and a receivable note. The next year the company spun off its warehouse club operations as Waban (the warehouse component eventually became BJ's Wholesale) and merged with its subsidiary The TJX Companies taking that name.

TJX acquired Winners Apparel a Toronto-based five-store apparel chain in 1990. That year in the same month that Ames declared bankruptcy TJX established a $185 million reserve against losses it might suffer through its ownership of Ames' stock. Ames emerged from bankruptcy two years later and TJX was left with 4% of Ames' voting shares and over 100 empty Ames stores. TJX sold or leased most of them.

Also in 1992 TJX opened HomeGoods gift and houseware outlets in three of its remaining Ames stores and closed about 70 Hit or Miss stores. That year the company paid off about $128 million of its long-term debt. Encouraged by the success of its off-price operations in Canada in 1994 TJX opened five T.K. Maxx stores (similar to T.J. Maxx and Winners Apparel) in the UK.

A year later TJX paid $550 million for Melville's ailing chain of 450 Marshalls clothing stores. In addition the company sold its Hit or Miss apparel chain.

To help pay for Marshalls TJX sold the Chadwick's of Boston catalog in 1996 to retailer Brylane for about $325 million. Two years later the company opened two T.K. Maxx stores in the Netherlands and said it planned to have 75 stores in Europe in three years. It also debuted the A.J. Wright discount chain in New England in 1998.

In 1999 TJX elected Cammarata to the additional post of chairman and elevated Ted English to president and COO. In 2000 Cammarata relinquished his CEO post to English but remained chairman. Citing the successes of its new stores the company announced in early 2001 it expected to increase its total number of stores 12% annually for the next several years. Also that year the company shuttered its T.K. Maxx stores in the Netherlands. Seven TJX employees perished on September 11 2001 when their flight bound for Los Angeles crashed into the World Trade Center during the worst terrorist attack in US history.

In 2002 the company opened HomeSense a new Canadian home furnishings chain fashioned after its US counterpart HomeGoods. In December 2003 TJX finalized its acquisition of Bob's Stores a Connecticut-based discount retail chain with 31 stores in the Northeast.

In September 2005 English resigned abruptly after five years as the company's CEO. In October the company closed down its tjmaxx.com and homegoods.com Web sites citing poor sales.

In March 2006 TJX cut about 250 jobs in its corporate and divisional offices and reduced the salaries of a dozen senior executives including its chairman and acting CEO and its president by 10% in an effort to increase profits.

A year after the abrupt resignation of CEO Edmond English in September 2005 TJX named company president Carol Meyrowitz to the post effective January 2007. (Cammarata had been acting CEO of the company in the interim.) Also in January 34 A.J. Wright stores were closed.

In November 2007 TJX reached a settlement with Visa and Fifth Third Bancorp stemming from a breach of its computer systems in which customer data was stolen. Under the terms of the agreement TJX will fund up to $40.9 million for recovery payments for US Visa issuers. Also in the fall of 2007 the retailer's European arm T.K. Maxx entered the German market with five stores there.

In 2008 TJX sold money-losing Bob's Stores which has about 35 locations in the Northeast to the private equity firms Versa Capital Management and Crystal Capital for an undisclosed amount.

EXECUTIVES

Vice President, Jeffrey Naylor, age 56
President CEO and Director, Ernie Herrman, age 54, $1,327,693 total compensation
SEVP and Group President, Nan Stutz, age 57
SEVP and Group President, Richard Sherr, age 57, $812,309 total compensation
SEVP Finance and CFO, Scott Goldenberg, age 61, $663,463 total compensation
CIO, Peter Lindenmeyer
SEVP and Group President, Ken Canestrari, age 54
President The Marmaxx Group, Michael MacMillan, age 58, $962,308 total compensation
CTO, John Reichelt
Assistant Vice President, John Forbes
Area Vice President Director, Gina Adamo
Vice President Product Development, Christine Bourget
Asstant Vice President RE Research Finance andv Systems, Sean Anderson
Assistant Vice President Merchandise Manager, David (Dave) Macdonald
Vice President, Lisa Schwartz
Vice President merchandising, Paula Bingham
Vice President Supply Chain Systems, Mark Holmes
Assistant Vice President, Brett Amosson
Assistant Vice President Of Planning, Sarah Ziemba
Assistant Vice President Finance and General Accounting, Kevin Foley
Assistant Vice President Merchandise Planning, Debra Duprez
Vice President General Merchandise Manager, Shade Jennifer
Assistant Vice President Merchandise Manager Sheets Deco, Corina Roth
Vice President Human Resources, Kelli McNary
Vice President Merchandising, Brian Francione
Senior Vice President Ecommerce, Elaine Boltz
DVP Merchandise Manager, Paul Bibbo
Assistant Vice President, Laura Hollister
Vice President Finance, Peter Daniels
Assistant Vice President Corporate Benefits Director, Lauren Mullin
Avpd Enterprise Process Improvement, Mark Rosen
Assistant Vice President General Manager, Tim Linton
Vice President End User Services, Sandra Rossetsky
Vice President Gmm Mens, Ken Shuler
Assistant Vice President Loss Prevention, Kate Hughes
Assistant Vice President Merchandise Planning, Nancy Atchue
Assistant Vice President Planning eCommerce, Katie Fink
Assistant Vice President Loss Prevention, Kevin Taparausky
Vice President Gmm, Marla Minns
Assistant Vice President Store Planning, Jon Nelson
Senior Vice President Merchandising, Norm Cantin
Assistant Vice President, Lisa Pratico
Vice President Global Compensation, Julio Mantilla
Assistant Vice President Director Loss Prevention, Frederick L (Fred) Mullen

Vice President Of Merchandising, Tim Miner
Vice President Gmm, Nancy Carpenter
Regional Vice President, Guy Reda
Assistant Vice President Human Resources Administration, Julie Dawson
Assistant Vice President Of Application Development, Joe Walsh
Vice President Supply Chain Applications, Dave Spooner
Vice President Information Technology Supply Chain Business Solutions, James (Jamie) Joyce
Assistant Vice President, Joanne Wolfe
Vice President Office Services Director, Mike Brogan
VPLP, Peter (Pete) Betrovski
DVP Merchandise Manager, Michael (Mel) Neel
Vice President Finance, John Klinger
Assistant Vice President International Tax, Barbara (Barb) House
DVP DMM E Commerce, Inna Leipzig
Assistant Vice President Director Of Business Planning And Analysis, Mark Lussier
Cio Chief Technology Officer Vice President Information Technology, Gary Tiesenga
Divisional Vice President Merchandise Manager Ecommerce, Lisa Pena
Vice President Store Systems, Laura Keith Mulcahy
Vice President, David Federico
Vice President Store Systems Director, Martin (Marti) Whitmore
Assistant Vice President Corporate Communications, Colleen Beauregard
Senior Vice President GMM, Pam Pretzer
Senior Regional Vice President, Mike Jacobson
Assistant Vice President, Steve Dellazoppa
Senior Vice President Store Operations A J Wright, Mike McGrath
Assistant Vice President Construction, John Cox
Assistant Vice President Human Resources Business Partner, Sandi Anderson
Avpd Information Technology Security Architecture, Reed Augliere
Vice President Loss Prevention Director, Richard Peck
Assistant Vice President Merchandise Manager Home Accent, Marni Jones
Assistant Vice President Merchandise Planning, Mark Corcoran
DVP Merchandise Manager, Pat Kelly
Vice President, Cheryl Oldfield
Senior Vice President Global Sourcing and Procurement, Marc A Boesch
Assistant Vice President of Financial Planning and Analysis, Robert (Bob) Borek
Vice President The Marmaxx Group, Charlotte Arnold
Vice President Of Loss Prevention Marmaxx Group, Robert (Bob) Maclea
Vice President HomeGoods, Stephen (Steve) Mastrangelo
Vice President The Marmaxx Group, Nancy Mendis
Assistant Vice President Store Operations Home Goods, Mike Farrell
Senior Vice President and Director Brand Development TJX Companies, Barry Zelman
Assistant Vice President International Tax Director, David (Dave) Averill
Senior Vice President Global Talent Management, Lynn Jack
Assistant Vice President Loss Prevention, Kevin Kurtz
Vice President Of Global Talent Development, Carolyn Fischer
Assistant Vice President Merchandise Manager, Lynn Samuels
Vice President, Lou Luciano
Assistant Vice President Supply Chain Business Services, Richard (Dick) Oppenheimer
Assistant Vice President Merchandise Manager, Sally Reilly

Vice President of Corporate Communications, Doreen Thompson
Assistant Vice President Compensation, April Fontaine
Assistant Vice President Product Development, Kathy Batson
Assistant Vice President Product Development, Paul Lyle
Vice President, Bob Cooke
Assistant Vice President Planning Marshalls, Jacqui Hebden
Assistant Vice President Sweaters and Knits Merchandise Manager Marmax Tjx and Marshalls, Patti Piesco
Assistant Vice President Merchandise Manager, Mark Lisnow
Vice President Director Of Real Estate, Denise Downing
Senior Vice President Treasurer, Mary Reynolds
Vice President End User Services, Sandy Rossetsky
Assistant Vice President Retirement Benefits Director, Colin Hamilton
Chairman, Carol M. Meyrowitz, age 61
Assistant Treasurer, Nancy Hendrickson
Board Member, Mike McDonnell
Auditors: PricewaterhouseCoopers LLP

LOCATIONS

HQ: TJX Companies, Inc.
 770 Cochituate Road, Framingham, MA 01701
Phone: 508 390-1000   Fax: 508 390-2091
Web: www.tjx.com

2015 Stores

	No.
United States	2,581
Canada	368
Europe	440
Total	**3,389**

2015 Sales

	$ mil.	% of total
US		
Marmaxx	18,687	64
HomeGoods	3,414	12
Europe		
T.K. Maxx/HomeSense	4,092	14
Canada		
Winners/HomeSense	2,883	10
Total	**29,078**	**100**

PRODUCTS/OPERATIONS

Selected Stores

HomeGoods (off-price home fashion chain)
HomeSense (off-price home fashion chain Canada and UK)
Marshalls (off-price retailer of apparel shoes home fashions)
Marshalls Mega-Stores (combination Marshalls and HomeGoods stores)
Sierra Trading Post (off-price online retailer of outdoor gear and apparel)
T.J. Maxx (off-price retailer of apparel shoes home fashions)
T.J. Maxx ' N More (combination T.J. Maxx and HomeGoods stores)
T.K. Maxx (off-price retailer of apparel shoes home fashions Europe)
Winners Apparel (off-price family apparel chain Canada)

2015 Sales

	% of total
Clothing & footwear	57
Home fashions	29
Jewelry & accessories	14
Total	**100**

COMPETITORS

ASDA	Kmart
Amazon.com	Kohl' s
Bed Bath & Beyond	Liberty Interactive

Belk	Macy' s
Big Lots	Men' s Wearhouse
Burlington Coat Factory	Primark
Caleres	Ross Stores
Cato	Sears
Charming Shoppes	Shopko Stores
Children' s Place	Sports Authority
Claire' s Stores	Stage Stores
Dillard' s	Stein Mart
Dollar General	Target Corporation
Eddie Bauer LLC	Tesco
Foot Locker	The Gap
Inditex	Tuesday Morning Corporation
J. C. Penney	Wal-Mart

HISTORICAL FINANCIALS

Company Type: Public

Income Statement

FYE: January 31

	REVENUE ($ mil.)	NET INCOME ($ mil.)	NET PROFIT MARGIN	EMPLOYEES
01/15*	29,078	2,215	7.6%	198,000
02/14	27,422	2,137	7.8%	191,000
02/13	25,878	1,906	7.4%	179,000
01/12	23,191	1,496	6.5%	168,000
01/11	21,942	1,343	6.1%	166,000
Annual Growth	**7.3%**	**13.3%**	**—**	**4.5%**

*Fiscal year change

2015 Year-End Financials

Debt ratio: 15.14%
Return on equity: 52.30%
Cash ($ mil.): 2,493
Current ratio: 1.71
Long-term debt ($ mil.): 1,684

No. of shares (mil.): 684
Dividends
 Yield: 0.0%
 Payout: 21.2%
Market value ($ mil.): 45,151

	STOCK PRICE ($) FY Close	P/E High/Low		PER SHARE ($) Earnings	Dividends	Book Value
01/15*	65.94	21	16	3.15	0.67	6.23
02/14	57.36	21	15	2.94	0.55	6.00
02/13	45.30	26	13	2.55	0.44	5.06
01/12	67.37	34	24	1.93	0.36	4.30
01/11	47.71	29	22	1.65	0.29	3.98
Annual Growth	**8.4%**	**—**	**—**	**17.5%**	**23.8%**	**11.9%**

*Fiscal year change

Tompkins Financial Corp

Tompkins Financial is the holding company for Tompkins Trust Company The Bank of Castile and Mahopac Bank which offer traditional banking services through some 45 offices in upstate New York. It also owns the 20-branch Pennsylvania-based VIST Bank. Funds from deposit products such as checking savings and money market accounts are mainly used to originate real estate loans and mortgages as well as commercial and consumer loans. Tompkins also offers trust and estate financial and tax planning and investment management services through Tompkins Financial Advisors. Tompkins Insurance Agencies sells property/casualty coverage in central and western New York and Pennsylvania.

Operations

Tompkins Financial operates in three segments: banking insurance and wealth management. Banking represents most of its revenue —more than

80%. About 70% of the banks' loan portfolios is made up of commercial and commercial real estate loans.Tompkins' Insurance and Wealth Management divisions operate through subsidiaries and make up roughly 10% and 5% of sales respectively. Its subsidiary Tompkins Insurance Agencies Inc. offers property and casualty insurance services and employee benefit consulting services. The firm's trust company Tompkins Financial Advisors offers trust financial planning and wealth management services.Geographic ReachBetween its four bank subsidiaries the Tompkins operates 66 branches in the US with more than two thirds of the branches in New York and around 20 branches in Pennsylvania.Sales and MarketingThe company's banks target individual and small business customers for its financial services. Tompkins spent $4.94 million on its marketing expenses in 2014 or slightly less than the $4.96 million spent in 2013 but 22% more than what it spent in 2012.

Financial Performance

Tompkin's revenue rose for a second straight year growing by less than 1% to $255.26 million in 2014 most thanks to growth in the company's non-interest fee income from an increase in deposit account service charges card services income and growth in personal health and benefit insurance sales.The company's net income ended higher for a second year as well thanks to higher revenue lower interest expense on deposits and lower provisions for loan losses as its loan portfolio's credit improved. Operations provided $77.36 million or 8% less cash than in 2013 mostly because in 2013 the company was able to use more funds from its prepaid accounts to pay for FDIC insurance.

Strategy

The company's strategy for growth includes making inroads into new markets and new business areas through acquisitions. It entered the southeastern Pennsylvania market with its 2012 acquisition of VIST Financial parent of VIST Bank (which continues to operate under a separate charter under existing management) VIST Insurance and VIST Capital Management. The deal added about 20 branches to Tompkins' network along with $889 million in new loan business and $1.2 billion in new deposits.Mergers and AcquisitionsIn August 2012 Tompkins Financial purchased VIST Financial Corp in an all stock transaction valued at $86 million. The deal added all 20 VIST Bank branches (and VIST Bank's assets) in Pennsylvania the VIST Capital Management business and the VIST Insurance business which doubled Tompkin's annual insurance revenue; all of which were folded into Tompkins' banking operations Tompkins Financial Advisors and Tompkins Insurance Agencies operations respectively.

EXECUTIVES

EVP President and CEO VIST Bank, Robert D. (Bob) Davis, age 67
Director; Vice Chairman Tompkins Insurance Agencies, James R. Hardie, age 71
Executive Vice President Chief Operations Officer Chief Financial Officer & Treasurer, Francis M. Fetsko, age 50, $281,877 total compensation
President CEO and Director, Stephen S. Romaine, age 51, $474,898 total compensation
Executive Vice President, David S. Boyce, age 48, $185,000 total compensation
VP Tompkins Investment Services Tompkins Trust, Gregory J. Hartz, age 54, $237,107 total compensation
Executive Vice-President, Gerald J. Klein, age 56, $238,369 total compensation
Executive Vice President; President & COO of VIST Bank, Scott L. Gruber, age 59
EVP Corporate Marketing, Susan M. Valenti
SVP - Chief Technology Officer, Bradley G. James

Executive Vice President Director of Human Resources, Rosemary Hyland
Vice President Retail Sales Manager Bank Of Castile, Robert (Bob) Bennett
Vice President Finance, Kevin Harty
Vice President Learning And Development, Laura Geary
Vice President Corporate Risk Management, Greg Smith
Vice President Information Systems, Terry Barber
Vice President Corporate Risk Management, Randy Lovell
Vice President, Nancy Phayre
Vice President Tompkins Investment Ser, Samuel (Sam) Brewer
Assistant Vice President Telecommunicati, Charles (Chas) Brown
Chairman Tompkins Financial Corporation and Tompkins Trust Company, James J. Byrnes, age 72
Vice Chairman, James W. (Jim) Fulmer, age 63
Auditors: KPMG LLP

LOCATIONS

HQ: Tompkins Financial Corp
The Commons, P.O. Box 460, Ithaca, NY 14851
Phone: 888 503-5753
Web: www.tompkinsfinancial.com

PRODUCTS/OPERATIONS

2014 Sales

	$ mil.	% of total
Interest		
Loans	151	60
Available-for-sale securities	31	12
Other	2	-
Noninterest		
Insurance commissions & fees	28	11
Investment services	15	6
Service charges on deposit accounts	9	4
Card services income	7	3
Other	9	4
Adjustments	(0.3)	-
Total	**255**	**100**

2014 Sales

	$mil.
% of total	
Banking	83
Insurance	11
Wealth Management	6
Others	-
Total	**100**

COMPETITORS

Bank of America	Elmira Savings Bank
Chemung Financial	First Niagara
Citigroup	Financial
Citizens Financial	HSBC USA
Group	JPMorgan Chase
Community Bank System	M&T Bank

HISTORICAL FINANCIALS

Company Type: Public

Income Statement

FYE: December 31

	ASSETS ($ mil.)	NET INCOME ($ mil.)	INCOME AS % OF ASSETS	EMPLOYEES
12/14	5,269	52	1.0%	1,037
12/13	5,003	50	1.0%	989
12/12	4,837	31	0.6%	939
12/11	3,400	35	1.0%	743
12/10	3,260	33	1.0%	766
Annual Growth	**12.8%**	**11.4%**	**—**	**7.9%**

2014 Year-End Financials

Debt ratio: 0.96%		No. of shares (mil.): 14	
Return on equity: 11.02%		Dividends	
Cash ($ mil.): 56		Yield: 2.9%	
Current ratio: —		Payout: 45.1%	
Long-term debt ($ mil.): —		Market value ($ mil.): 820	

	STOCK PRICE ($) FY Close	P/E High/Low	PER SHARE ($) Earnings	Dividends	Book Value
12/14	55.30	16 13	3.48	1.62	32.94
12/13	51.39	15 11	3.46	1.54	31.10
12/12	39.64	17 15	2.43	1.46	30.71
12/11	38.51	13 11	3.20	1.40	26.91
12/10	39.16	14 11	3.11	1.33	25.08
Annual Growth	**9.0%**	**— —**	**2.9%**	**5.1%**	**7.0%**

Torchmark Corp.

Torchmark aims to be a beacon in the world of insurance. It is the holding company for a family of firms; its member companies specialize in lower-end individual life insurance and supplemental health insurance. Torchmark subsidiaries which include flagship Liberty National Life offer whole and term life insurance supplemental health insurance accidental death insurance Medicare supplements and long-term care health policies for the elderly. Its American Income Life sells life insurance policies to labor union and credit union members in the US Canada and New Zealand. Torchmark sells its products through direct marketing as well as a network of exclusive and independent agents.

OperationsAt the beginning of 2014 Torchmark reorganized its segments to separate its Medicare Part D business as a standalone unit. (It was previously included in the health segment.) The group's core operations are the marketing and underwriting of insurance –divided into the life health annuity and Medicare Part D segments –and the management of its investments. Life insurance products include traditional and interest-sensitive whole life coverage as well as term life insurance. Health products include Medicare Supplement cancer accident long-term care and limited-benefit hospital and surgical coverages. Medicare Part D provides prescription drug coverage for Medicare beneficiaries while annuities includes fixed-benefit contracts.Targeting middle-income citizens Torchmark's Liberty National Life provides life and supplemental health policies primarily in the southeastern US. Torchmark's United American Insurance subsidiary writes supplemental health coverage and Medicare supplemental insurance. A smaller subsidiary Globe Life and Accident offers life insurance and supplemental health products direct to consumers through print online and television ads. Life insurance is the company's largest segment and delivers about 50% of revenue. It has more than $60 million dollars of life insurance in force.Geographic Reach

Torchmark's operations are based in Oklahoma and Texas although its services extend to customers across the US and in New Zealand and Canada.Sales and MarketingTorchmark markets its products through a variety of methods including direct mail insert media inbound calls and the Internet. The company's main Liberty National Life subsidiary uses a direct sales force to sell its products. The subsidiary has about 1500 producing agents and about 65 branch offices across the US.Direct response advertising costs charged to earnings totaled $8 million in 2014 up from $6 million in 2013 but down from $16 million in 2012. Capitalized advertising costs totaled $1.15 billion in 2014 versus $1.09 billion in 2013.Financial PerformanceTorchmark has reported several years of revenue growth including 2014 when it rose another 5% from $3.8 billion to $3.9 billion on strong gains in health insurance and life insurance growth. Growth in net investment income also contributed to the revenue growth.After several years of flat net income the company saw a 2% dip from $528 million to $527 million as it paid out more to policyholders in 2013. This was followed by another 2% decline to $542 million in 2014 caused by higher life policyholder benefits paid and increases in commissions premium taxes and acquisition costs. Cash flow from operations decreased 23% in 2014 to $864 million.StrategyTorchmark's insurance strategy is centered on selling life and health products to middle-income households. In recent years the company has especially been focused on young families with children.It has also been focused on expanding its distribution channels. Although labor union membership has been on the decline over the past decade the number of agents producing for American Income has more than tripled in that same time span.The company's investment segment invests almost exclusively in long-range fixed maturities that meet certain quality and yield objectives. Unlike many other life insurers Torchmark makes the bulk of its revenues from its premiums and relatively little (about 20%) from its investments. This allows it to ride out the economic downturns more smoothly while other life insurers take significant revenue hits when their investments fizzle.

HISTORY

It began as a scam plain and simple. In 1900 the Heralds of Liberty was founded as a fraternal organization —but its real reason for existence was to funnel money to its founders according to Frank Samford Torchmark's CEO from 1967 to 1985; Samford was also the great-grandson of the governor who signed the group's charter and the son of the state insurance commissioner who oversaw the Heralds of Liberty's rehabilitation into a real insurance company.

The Heralds offered a joint life distribution plan under which policyholders were divided by age; when a person died his or her beneficiary was paid along with the holder of the lowest-numbered insurance certificate in the class (if they were paid at all; the Heralds were not scrupulous about that). Postal authorities called this plan a lottery and it was illegal in many states. But the Heralds' fraternal order status allowed it to circumvent Alabama insurance laws until 1921 when its infractions could no longer be ignored.

The organization operated under state supervision until 1929 when it was recapitalized as stock company Liberty National. By 1934 despite the Depression the company was financially sound.

In 1944 Liberty National merged with funeral insurance company Brown-Service whose large sales force began selling Liberty National's policies. The added sales helped the company grow and make acquisitions from the 1950s through the 1970s. Even after it discontinued funeral insurance the company still paid out benefits. (As late as 1985 half of all Alabamans who died had the policies.)

Liberty National reorganized itself as a holding company in 1980 to accommodate the purchase of Globe Life And Accident. In 1981 it acquired Continental Investment Corp. which owned United Investors Life Insurance Waddell & Reed (financial services) and United American Insurance. In 1982 the holding company became Torchmark. Throughout its growth spurt it refrained from of-

fering high-yield financial products and thus escaped the worst effects of the economic disruptions of the late 1980s. Its 1990 acquisition of Family Service Life Insurance put it back in the funeral insurance business (it exited again in 1995 and sold the unit in 1998).

Sales in the 1990s were affected by a decline in cash-value life insurance and Medicare supplements. Slack sales forced the company to stop having agents collect premiums personally and by 1996 all accounts were handled by mail.

In 1998 the company sought to sell its 28% stake in property insurer Vesta Insurance Group after that company became the target of numerous lawsuits. Torchmark was only able to reduce its stake to 24% on the open market but in 2000 Vesta bought out Torchmark's holdings.

Torchmark was haunted in 2000 by its own version of the undead —burial policies. An investigation by Alabama regulators was sparked by a Florida court order forcing the company to stop collecting premiums on old burial policies for which African-Americans had been charged higher premiums. In 2001 and 2002 Torchmark was hit by another dozen lawsuits including allegations of overcharging.

EXECUTIVES

Co-Chairman and Co-CEO, Larry M. Hutchison, age 61, $821,058 total compensation
Co-Chairman and Co-CEO, Gary L. Coleman, age 62, $821,058 total compensation
CEO American Income Life and Liberty National Life, Roger C. Smith, age 62, $569,693 total compensation
EVP and Chief Marketing Officer, Glenn D. Williams, age 55
EVP and Chief Administrative Officer and CEO United American, Vern D. Herbel, age 57, $509,923 total compensation
EVP and CFO, Frank M. Svoboda, age 53, $449,768 total compensation
EVP and Chief Investment Officer, W. Michael Pressley, age 63, $459,847 total compensation
EVP and Chief Actuary, Ben W. Lutek, age 56
President Liberty National Life Insurance Co., Steven J. (Steve) DiChiaro, age 48
SVP and General Counsel, R. Brian Mitchell, age 51
President Global Life and Accident Insurance Co., Bill E. Leavell, age 52
President Family Heritage Life Insurance Company of America, Kenneth J. (Ken) Matson
President United America Insurance Company; President First United American Insurance Company, Michael C. Majors
EVP and CIO, James (Bo) McPartland
EVP Innovations and Business Development, J. Matthew Darden
Vice President Internal Audit, Saumil Patel
Assistant Vice President, Donita Jacobs
Vice President, Terri Slinkard
Assistant Vice President Of Information Technology, Jeff Poole
Vice President Actuary, Peter (Pete) Hendee
Senior Vice President Facilities, Douglas Gockel
Vice President Accounting, Ed Smith
Assistant Vice President, Karim Charaniya
Assistant Vice President And Senior Project Manager United American, Greg Bouska
Vice President Information Technology American Income Life, Greg Bozonelos
Vice President Information Technology, Elliott Scott
Auditors: Deloitte & Touche LLP

LOCATIONS

HQ: Torchmark Corp.
3700 South Stonebridge Drive, McKinney, TX 75070
Phone: 972 569-4000
Web: www.torchmarkcorp.com

PRODUCTS/OPERATIONS

2014 Revenues

	$ mil.	% of total
Insurance		
Life	1,966	50
Health	1,242	31
Other insurance	0	.
Investment income	729	18
Realized investment gains	23	1
Other income	2	.
Total	**3,964**	**100**

Selected Subsidiaries

American Income Life Insurance Company
Family Heritage Life Insurance Company of America
First United American Life Insurance Company
Globe Life And Accident Insurance Company
Liberty National Life Insurance Company
United American Insurance Company

COMPETITORS

Aflac	Monumental Life
Allstate	Northwestern Mutual
Amalgamated Life	Penn Treaty
Gerber Life	Prudential
Guardian Life	State Farm
Lincoln Financial	Texas Life
Group	USAA
MassMutual	Unum Group
MetLife	

HISTORICAL FINANCIALS

Company Type: Public

Income Statement

FYE: December 31

	ASSETS ($ mil.)	NET INCOME ($ mil.)	INCOME AS % OF ASSETS	EMPLOYEES
12/14	20,214	542	2.7%	2,980
12/13	18,191	528	2.9%	2,890
12/12	18,776	529	2.8%	3,042
12/11	17,156	517	3.0%	3,187
12/10	16,159	517	3.2%	3,291
Annual Growth	**5.8%**	**1.2%**	**—**	**(2.5%)**

2014 Year-End Financials

Debt ratio: 4.91%	No. of shares (mil.): 127
Return on equity: 12.81%	Dividends
Cash ($ mil.): 66	Yield: 0.9%
Current ratio: —	Payout: 12.6%
Long-term debt ($ mil.): —	Market value ($ mil.): 6,930

	STOCK PRICE ($) FY Close	P/E High/Low	PER SHARE ($) Earnings	Dividends	Book Value
12/14	54.17	20 12	4.09	0.51	36.72
12/13	78.15	20 13	3.79	0.68	28.13
12/12	51.67	14 12	3.61	0.57	30.86
12/11	43.39	21 10	3.15	0.30	28.03
12/10	59.74	22 16	2.80	0.41	22.53
Annual Growth	**(2.4%)**	**— —**	**9.9%**	**5.7%**	**13.0%**

TowneBank

LOCATIONS

HQ: TowneBank
5716 High Street, Portsmouth, VA 23703
Phone: 757 638-7500
Web: www.townebank.com

HISTORICAL FINANCIALS

Company Type: Public

Income Statement

FYE: December 31

	ASSETS ($ mil.)	NET INCOME ($ mil.)	INCOME AS % OF ASSETS	EMPLOYEES
12/14	4,982	42	0.8%	1,737
12/13	4,673	41	0.9%	1,741
12/12	4,405	37	0.9%	1,599
12/11	4,081	33	0.8%	1,540
12/10	3,871	30	0.8%	1,512
Annual Growth	6.5%	8.6%	—	3.5%

2014 Year-End Financials

Debt ratio: 0.64%
Return on equity: 7.12%
Cash ($ mil.): 214
Current ratio: —
Long-term debt ($ mil.): —

No. of shares (mil.): 35
Dividends
 Yield: 2.8%
 Payout: 36.4%
Market value ($ mil.): 532

	STOCK PRICE ($) FY Close	P/E High/Low	PER SHARE ($) Earnings	Dividends	Book Value
12/14	15.12	14 11	1.18	0.43	17.32
12/13	15.39	15 12	1.14	0.38	16.59
12/12	15.49	15 12	1.03	0.41	17.57
12/11	12.24	22 14	0.77	0.31	17.13
12/10	15.89	24 15	0.71	0.31	16.54
Annual Growth	(1.2%)	— —	13.6%	8.5%	1.2%

Toyota Motor Credit Corp.

Toyota Motor Credit (TMCC) is the US financing arm of Toyota Financial Services which is a subsidiary of Toyota Motor Corporation the world's largest carmaker. TMCC provides retail leasing retail and wholesale sales financing and other financial services to Toyota and Lexus dealers and their customers for the purchase of new and used cars and trucks. It offers similar services to Toyota industrial equipment dealers. TMCC which underwrites and services the finance contracts operates three regional customer service centers and some 30 dealer sales and service branches across the US and Puerto Rico.

OperationsTMCC organizes its business around two product categories: Finance and Insurance.Its Finance segment which generates more than 90% of the company's total sales acquires a variety of retail finance products such as consumer and commercial installment sales contracts in the US and Puerto Rico as well as leasing contracts –either direct finance leases or operating leases from US vehicle or industrial equipment dealers. The segment also provides dealer financing (including wholesale financing revolving credit lines and working capi-

tal loans) and real estate financing for vehicle and industrial equipment dealers in the US and Puerto Rico.The Insurance division operates through subsidiary Toyota Motor Insurance Services which underwrites and sells insurance products such as extended service coverage total loss protection and prepaid maintenance protection. It also provides marketing and claims administration services related to covering select risks of vehicle dealers and their customers in the US. Broken down TMCC generated 67% of its total revenue from operating leases in fiscal 2015 (ended March) and another 20% from retail financing income. Its Insurance premium and contract revenue brought in 7% of total revenue while dealer financing revenue (4%) and investment income (2%) brought in the rest.Geographic ReachThe California-based company serves dealers and their customers across the US. About 21% of TMCC's vehicle retail and lease contracts were based in California in fiscal 2015 while 10% were from Texas 8% were from New York and 6% came from New Jersey.Financial PerformanceTMCC has seen its revenues and profits trend downward for most of the past several years. However the company's revenue has been recovering since 2014.TMCC's revenue inched up by more than 1% to $8.10 billion in fiscal 2015 (ended March) mostly as its Operating Lease business grew by 21% thanks to higher average outstanding earning asset balances as Toyota Motor Sales USA (the primary US distributor of Toyota Lexus and Scion vehicles) focused more on pushing lease subvention during the year. The company's Insurance business also grew thanks to higher premiums and contract revenues resulting from an increase in the average number of agreements in force during the year.Higher revenue in fiscal 2015 allowed TMCC's profit to rebound sharply with net income jumping by 40% to $1.20 billion. Cash from operations declined by 23% to $3.77 billion as the company collected less in cash earnings after foreign exchange currency adjustments.

EXECUTIVES

Vice President Human Resources, Julia Wada
Auditors: PricewaterhouseCoopers LLP

LOCATIONS

HQ: Toyota Motor Credit Corp.
 19001 S. Western Avenue, Torrance, CA 90501
Phone: 310 468-1310
Web: www.toyotafinancial.com

PRODUCTS/OPERATIONS

2015 Sales

	$ mil.	% of total
Financing		
Operating leases	6,113	67
Retail	1,797	20
Dealer	400	4
Insurance premiums earned & contract revenues	638	7
Investment & other	194	2
Total	**9,142**	**100**

COMPETITORS

Ally Financial	Ford Motor Credit
American Honda Finance	GM Financial
AutoNation	Mercedes-Benz Credit
Capital One Auto Finance	Volkswagen Financial Services
Daimler Financial Services	Volvo Car Finance

HISTORICAL FINANCIALS

Company Type: Public

Income Statement

FYE: March 31

	REVENUE ($ mil.)	NET INCOME ($ mil.)	NET PROFIT MARGIN	EMPLOYEES
03/15	9,142	1,197	13.1%	3,251
03/14	8,099	857	10.6%	3,210
03/13	7,988	1,331	16.7%	3,210
03/12	8,146	1,486	18.2%	3,220
03/11	8,843	1,853	21.0%	3,170
Annual Growth	0.8%	(10.3%)	—	0.6%

2015 Year-End Financials

Debt ratio: 82.31%
Return on equity: 14.73%
Cash ($ mil.): 2,407
Current ratio: 0.09
Long-term debt ($ mil.): 63,225

No. of shares (mil.): 0
Dividends
 Yield: —
 Payout: —
Market value ($ mil.): —

Tractor Supply Co.

Farmers and ranchers can gear up for more than just a tractor pull at Tractor Supply Company (TSC). Besides providing agricultural machine parts the farm and ranch supply retailer offers animal feeds fencing power tools riding mowers and work clothing as well as tools for gardening irrigation welding and towing. TSC offers both name-brand merchandise and its own stable of private-label goods. It operates about 1382 stores in some 49 US states under the Tractor Supply Company and Del's Farm Supply banners. Stores are concentrated in rural areas and near large cities to cater to full- and part-time farmers ranchers and contractors. TSC also operates a growing online business.

Geographic Reach

TSC operates stores in 49 US states. Its largest market is Texas home to 145-plus stores followed by Ohio (with more than 85) Michigan (77) Pennsylvania (74) and New York (more than 70).

Operations

The farm and ranch supplies retailer operates stores under the Tractor Supply and Del's Feed and Farm Supply banners. It also sells products online. Livestock and pet products account for more than 44% of sales.

Sales and Marketing

The company's advertising expenses for 2014 2013 and 2012 were $70.4 million $65.6 million and $62.6 million respectively.

TSC's products are sourced through both US and international vendors. It purchases its products from a group of 800 vendors.The company operates a distribution network for supplying stores with merchandise and in2014 its stores received 70% of its merchandise through this network while the remaining merchandise was shipped directly to the stores from its vendors.To drive store traffic and position ourselves as a destination store TSC promotes broad selections of merchandise with newspaper circulars customer targeted direct mail and email and internet offerings.

Financial Performance

TSC has seen an upward trend in its net sales since 2010.In 2014 net sales increased by 11% due to a high contribution from Livestock and Pet sales. Comparable store transaction count increased while comparable store average ticket increased 0.6% that year driven by continued strong results in key consumable usable edible products and an increase in traffic counts.Net income has followed the similar trend that of its revenues.In 2014 TSC's net income increased by 13% due to increased sales partially offset by higher selling general and administrative expenses. The increase in selling general and administrative expenses primarily reflects new store growth and variable costs associated with its comparable store sales growth.Net cash provided by the operating activities increased by 23% that year.

Strategy

TSC's strategy is to expand its US market presence through opening new retail stores; enhancing financial performance through comparable store sales growth achieved through targeted merchandising and marketing programs supported by strong customer service; growing product margin through strategic sourcing inventory and markdown management product pricing and transportation costs; leveraging operating costs by focusing on the elimination of waste in all of its processes; expanding market opportunities via e-commerce and internet-supported sales; and growing through selective acquisitions to complement its organic growth.

The company's target customers are home land pet and livestock owners who generally have above average income and below average cost of living. It seeks to serve a customer base that primarily lives in towns outlying major metropolitan markets and in rural communities.

Already the largest farm and ranch supply chain in the nation TSC has rapidly expanded its retail footprint in recent years and will continue to do so in the future.

In 2015 the company announced the expansion of its Purina feed offering and its position as the first nationally authorized Purina feed retailer in the US. It began offering an extended assortment of select Purina brand feeds including Ultium horse feed Wind and Rain minerals and Honor Show Chow show feed in its stores nationwide.In 2015 TSC opened its 1400th store.

In 2014 the chain added 107 stores including their first stores in Arizona Nevada and Wyoming. In 2014 company planned to continue its expansion into these new markets.

TSC has identified more than 800 new markets for potential stores and is open to acquisition opportunities. Meanwhile TSC has stemmed the growth of Del's Farm Supply while working to refine its retail concept. With only about 25 Del's stores in the Pacific Northwest and Hawaii TSC opted not to add any new locations in recent years.

In 2014 it continued to invest in its omni-channel platform and expanded capabilities related to fulfillment options product information and site research. It also introduced an optimized mobile and tablet experience improved the site response time and added additional product offerings for vendor direct to customer drop shipments. It also opened two HomeTown Pet stores that year. Its strategy also seeks to reduce or mitigate the effects of purchase price volatility by taking advantage of vendor incentive programs economies of scale from increased volume of purchases adjusting retail prices and selectively buying from the most competitive vendors.

Company Background

TSC was founded in 1938.

EXECUTIVES

SVP General Counsel and Corporate Secretary, Benjamin F. (Ben) Parrish, age 59, $376,461 total compensation

EVP CFO and Treasurer, Anthony F. (Tony) Crudele, age 59, $482,692 total compensation

President and CEO, Gregory A. (Greg) Sandfort, age 60, $934,615 total compensation

EVP Operations and Real Estate, Lee J. Downing, age 43, $392,308 total compensation

EVP and Chief Merchandising Officer, Steve K. Barbarick, age 47, $416,231 total compensation

SVP and Chief Information Officer, Robert D. Mills, age 42, $305,962 total compensation

CMO Executive Vice President, Craig Sanford

Vice President E Commerce Sourcing, Karen Howard

Vice President Store Administration, John (Jack) Gardner

Vice President Information Technology, George Argodale

Controller and Treasurer, Alexander (Al) Stanton

Chairman, Cynthia T. Jamison, age 55

Auditors: Ernst & Young LLP

LOCATIONS

HQ: Tractor Supply Co.
5401 Virginia Way, Brentwood, TN 37027
Phone: 615 440-4000
Web: www.tractorsupply.com

2014 Locations

	No.
Texas	145
Ohio	85
Michigan	77
Pennsylvania	74
New York	73
Tennessee	71
North Carolina	66
Georgia	54
Florida	51
Kentucky	47
Virginia	48
Indiana	45
Alabama	45
Oklahoma	33
South Carolina	32
California	36
Louisiana	28
Mississippi	25
West Virginia	24
Arizona	22
Arkansas	21
Maine	19
Missouri	18
Washington	18
New Hampshire	17
Illinois	16
Wisconsin	16
Kansas	15
Massachusetts	16
New Mexico	17
Maryland	18
Nebraska	12
New Jersey	12
Connecticut	11
Minnesota	10
Colorado	14
North Dakota	11
Iowa	7
Vermont	7
South Dakota	6
Delaware	4
Montana	3
Wyoming	3
Oregon	2
Hawaii	2
Rhode Island	2
Nevada	2
Idaho	1
Utah	1
Total	**1,382**

2013 Locations

	No.
Texas	138
Ohio	81
Michigan	72
New York	71
Pennsylvania	68
Tennessee	66
North Carolina	61
Georgia	51
Florida	49
Kentucky	47
Virginia	46
Indiana	45
Alabama	43
Oklahoma	31
South Carolina	29
California	25
Louisiana	25
Mississippi	25
West Virginia	24
Arkansas	20
Maine	19
Missouri	18
Washington	18
New Hampshire	17
Illinois	16
Wisconsin	15
Kansas	14
Massachusetts	14
New Mexico	14
Maryland	13
Nebraska	12
New Jersey	11
Connecticut	10
Minnesota	10
Arizona	8
Colorado	8
Iowa	7
North Dakota	7
Vermont	7
South Dakota	6
Delaware	4
Montana	3
Hawaii	2
Oregon	2
Idaho	1
Rhode Island	1
Nevada	1
Wyoming	1
Total	**1,276**

PRODUCTS/OPERATIONS

2014 Sales

	% of total
Livestock & pet	44
Hardware tools truck& towing	22
Seasonal gift & toy	20
Clothing & footwear	9
Agriculture	5
Total	**100**

Selected Private Label Brands

4health (pet food)
Bit & Bridle (apparel)
C.E. Schmidt (apparel and footwear)
Countyline (livestock farm and ranch equipment)
Dumor (livestock feed)
Groundwork (lawn and garden supplies)
Huskee (outdoor power equipment)
JobSmart (hardware and tools)
Masterhand (tools and tool chests)
Milepost (equine products)
Producers Pride (livestock feed)
Paws ' n Claws (pet food)
Red Shed (gifts and collectibles)
Retriever (pet food)
Royal Wing (bird feeding supplies)
Traveller (truck and automotive products)

COMPETITORS

Ace Hardware	Sears
Agrium	Southern States
Farm King	Tennessee Farmers
Home Depot	Co-op
Lowe' s	True Value
Miles Enterprises	Wal-Mart
Northern Tool	Wilbur-Ellis

HISTORICAL FINANCIALS
Company Type: Public

Income Statement
FYE: December 27

	REVENUE ($ mil.)	NET INCOME ($ mil.)	NET PROFIT MARGIN	EMPLOYEES
12/14	5,711	370	6.5%	21,100
12/13	5,164	328	6.4%	19,200
12/12	4,664	276	5.9%	17,300
12/11	4,232	222	5.3%	16,400
12/10	3,638	167	4.6%	14,700
Annual Growth	11.9%	21.9%	—	9.5%

2014 Year-End Financials

Debt ratio: 0.25%
Return on equity: 29.28%
Cash ($ mil.): 51
Current ratio: 2.11
Long-term debt ($ mil.): 4

No. of shares (mil.): 136
Dividends
Yield: 0.0%
Payout: 22.9%
Market value ($ mil.): 10,627

	STOCK PRICE ($) FY Close	P/E High/Low	PER SHARE ($) Earnings	Dividends	Book Value
12/14	77.92	29 21	2.66	0.61	9.48
12/13	75.54	56 28	2.32	0.49	8.93
12/12	87.47	53 36	1.90	0.36	7.37
12/11	70.15	49 30	1.51	0.22	7.07
12/10	48.40	62 31	1.13	0.14	6.41
Annual Growth	12.6%	— —	24.0%	44.5%	10.3%

TRAMMO INC.

Fertilizers liquefied petroleum gas (LPG) and petrochemicals are the "ammo" which international trader Trammo (formerly Transammonia) uses in its battle with competitors. The company trades distributes and transports these commodities around the world. Trammo's fertilizer business includes ammonia phosphates and urea. Its Sea-3 subsidiary imports and distributes propane to residential commercial and industrial customers in the northeastern US and Florida. The Trammochem unit trades in petrochemicals specializing in aromatics methanol methyltertiary butyl ether (MTBE) benzene and olefins. Its Trammo Gas trades LPG and propane as well as ethane butane and natural gas in the US.

Geographic Reach

Trammo has expanded its reach into the global market establishing merchandising and trading offices in Singapore China and the United Arab Emirates. Those offices complement its other global operations in Africa Asia Europe the Middle East and South America. It has major representative offices in Amman Beijing Cairo Dubai Hong Kong and Shanghai.

Its Fertilizers and Commodities Division's regional hubs are in Zurich Tampa Dubai Shanghai and Singapore; the Ammonia Division has hubs in Tampa and Dubai. The Chemicals Division maintains regional hubs in Zurich Darien (Connecticut) Dubai Shanghai and Singapore; while the Gas Division maintains hubs in Houston Tampa and Newington (New Hampshire).

Trammo has more than 30 offices worldwide.

Operations

The company operates three divisions: Chemicals Commodities and Gas. The Chemicals Division's annual sales volumes increased to 4.7 million metric tons in 2013. It key products include aromatics olefins and oxygenates. The Commodi-

ties Division accounted for two thirds of the Trammo Group's sales volumes and for 41% of its revenues; it's worldwide traded volume reached 27.7 million metric tons in 2013. The Gas Division's business areas include LPG business Trammo Gas and Petrochemicals Ltd and Sea-3 Inc. Trammo's international traded ammonia volume was more than 2.8 million metric tons in 2013.

Sea-3 is the largest importer and distributor of liquefied propane in the Northeastern US. It also supplies propane to the western and central portions of Florida. It moves 200000 metric tones of product per year.

Trammochem merchandises and trades in petrochemicals around the world.

Trammo Gas markets and trades LPG (primarily propane) in the US. Trammo Gas International Inc. operates two gas carriers which transport LPG worldwide for third parties. In 2013 the gas division traded 8 million metric tons of products.

Financial Performance

In 2013 Trammo had revenues of $12.5 billion.

Strategy

In 2015 the company's Ammonia Division and Fertilizers and Commodities Division merged into a new division —Commodities. The merger will allow Trammo to increase operational synergies use its global infrastructure to provide a larger portfolio of products and to more clearly present itself as a single company with different products.

Trammo opened offices in Ivory Coast and Dar Es Salaam in 2014 to strengthens its presence in the emerging African market.

In 2013 Transammonia changed its name to Trammo to more accurately represent the broad spectrum of products and services it provides.

Company Background

In 2010 the company's bulk carriers division entered the commodity shipping business. TA Bulk Carriers operates a fleet of 15 to 20 vessels which trade worldwide but focus on the handysize market (25000-35000 metric tons deadweight) in the Atlantic basin. In 2010 it transported about 2.9 million metric tons of cargo primarily fertilizers and grains.

Trammo is owned by founder Ronald Stanton who founded the company in 1965 as an international ammonia trader. It branched into fertilizer merchandising and trading in 1967 LPG trading in 1978 and petrochemicals trading in 1987.

EXECUTIVES

EVP and CFO, Edward G. Weiner
EVP and General Counsel, Fred Lowenfels
CEO Fertilizers & Commodities Division, Christian Wendel
CEO Chemicals Division, Ashok Kishore
CEO Ammonia Division, Jeffrey Minnis
CEO Gas Division, Dave Smothermon
President and CEO, Henk Dalfsen
Vice President Information Technology, Dudley Cox
Senior Vice President Ammonia Division, Bernard Rock
Assistant Vice President, Donald Madden
Vice President, Todd Matthes
Board Member, Oliver K Stanton, age 52
Auditors: DELOITTE & TOUCHE LLP NEW YOR

LOCATIONS

HQ: TRAMMO INC.
320 PARK AVE RM 1001, NEW YORK, NY 100226987
Phone: 2122233200
Web: WWW.GUIDE8480.GUIDECHEM.COM

PRODUCTS/OPERATIONS

Major SubsidiariesSea-3 (liquefied propane)Trammo Gas (LPG)Trammo Gas International Inc. (LPG transportation for third parties.Trammo Petroleum (crude oil and oil products)Trammochem (petrochemicals)Fertilizers and CommoditiesNitrogen BasedAnhydrous Ammo

COMPETITORS

Agrium	Dynegy
BASF SE	HELM
CF Industries	Koch Industries Inc.
Cargill	Magellan Midstream
ConAgra	Yara

HISTORICAL FINANCIALS
Company Type: Private

Income Statement
FYE: December 31

	REVENUE ($ mil.)	NET INCOME ($ mil.)	NET PROFIT MARGIN	EMPLOYEES
12/13	11,315	(11)	—	440
12/12	12,152	35	0.3%	—
12/11	11,303	31	0.3%	—
12/10	8,414	0	—	—
Annual Growth	10.4%	—	—	—

2013 Year-End Financials

Debt ratio: ——
Return on equity: (-0.10%)
Cash ($ mil.): 221
Current ratio: 1.00
Long-term debt ($ mil.): ——

Dividends
Yield: —
Payout: —
Market value ($ mil.): —

TravelCenters of America LLC

TravelCenters of America (TCA) is in the fuel food and relaxation business for the long haul. The company's network of more than 280 interstate highway travel centers in more than 45 US states and Ontario Canada is one of the largest of its kind in North America. Its TCA and Petro locations provide fuel fast-food and sit-down restaurants (Country Pride Buckhorn Family) convenience stores and lodging. With professional truck drivers as its main customers some outlets also offer "trucker-only" services such as laundry and shower facilities TV rooms and truck repair. TCA leases 184 of its locations from Hospitality Properties Trust (HPT) its largest shareholder.

Operations

As part of its business TCA operates and franchises travel centers under two brands: TravelCenters of America with more than 170 locations and Petro Stopping Centers (acquired in 2007) with more than 75 locations about 60 of which are company-operated. TCA also operates "Road-Squad" the largest nationwide emergency roadside service network with more than 430 heavy-duty emergency vehicles.

While TCA offers food to fuel truck drivers and motorists about 79% of the company's revenue comes from the sale of fuel for vehicles. The rest comes from human food and other items sold in it stores.

Sales and Marketing

TCA caters to professional truck drivers and travelers who rely on gas stations and convenience stores while on the road. Customers include trucking fleets and their drivers independent truck drivers and motorists. The company's advertising costs were $22.7 million in 2013 $20.5 million in 2012 and $18.8 million in 2011.

Financial Performance

TCA's revenue slipped lower for the second year in a row dropping 2% in 2014 to $7.7 billion from 2013. On the flip side the company's profit reached a new high $60.9 million in 2014. The company has now posted four years of profit after a five-year streak of losses.

Revenue is dependent on fuel prices and when fuel prices drop so does TCA's revenue. Fuel revenue was off 5% in 2014 while nonfuel revenue rose 11%. The market forces that depressed revenue unleashed the company's profit to a 93% gain as the company paid less for the fuel that it sold. The company buys fuel at daily market rates and works with multiple suppliers at most locations.

The company's cash from operating activities increased to $161 million in 2014 from $71 million due to changes in inventories and accounts payable.

Strategy

The company is building its cross-country network of travel centers through acquisitions (by opportunistically buying up smaller competitors) and by opening new locations.

In 2015 TCA opened a new TA Truck Service facility in Columbia South Carolina and a Popeyes Louisiana Kitchens restaurant in Lincoln and Tuscaloosa Alabama and Coachella California.

With fuel accounting for such a large portion of its total sales (79% in 2014) TCA is vulnerable to wild swings in prices. (About 90% of TCA's historical fuel sales are diesel while 10% are gasoline. The company sells biodiesel at some locations and to offer liquified natural gas (LNG) at an expanded number of locations in 2015.)

Mergers and Acquisition

TCA in 2015 agreed to acquire Quaker Steak & Lube casual dining restaurants and other assets including existing restaurant operations restaurant franchise program and bottled sauces for retail sale business for $25 million. Quaker Steak & Lube has more than 50 locations most of them franchised in 16 states mostly in Pennsylvania and Ohio. TCA plans to convert some of its full service restaurants to the Quaker Steak & Lube brand and expand the number of franchises and the number of stand-alone company restaurants.

EXECUTIVES

Vice President Human Resources, Bruce Sebera
Vice President Marketing and Public Relations, Tom Liutkus
Managing Director President and CEO, Thomas M. O'Brien, age 49, $300,000 total compensation
SVP Truck Service Marketing and Operations, Skip McGary
EVP Sales, Michael J. Lombardi, age 64, $339,000 total compensation
EVP CFO and Treasurer, Andrew J. Rebholz, age 51, $300,000 total compensation
EVP and General Counsel, Mark R. Young, age 52, $300,000 total compensation
EVP Operations, Barry A. Richards, age 62, $267,000 total compensation
SVP Construction Maintenance and Environmental, Peter P. Ward
Senior Vice President Retail Marketing and Operations, John (Jack) McGary
Senior Vice President MKTNG, Szima Joe
Vice President Reporting and Treasury, Gary Townsend

Vice President Information Systems, Micheal Rowe
Executive Vice President, Ara Bagdasarian
Senior Vice President Construction, Pete Ward
Senior Vice President, Randy Graham
Auditors: McGladrey LLP

LOCATIONS

HQ: TravelCenters of America LLC
24601 Center Ridge Road, Suite 200, Westlake, OH 44145-5639
Phone: 440 808-9100
Web: www.tatravelcenters.com

PRODUCTS/OPERATIONS

2013 Sales

	$ mil.	% of total
Fuel	6,481	82
Non-fuel	1,450	18
Rent & royalties from franchisees	12	-
Total	**7,944**	**100**

2013 Locations

	No.
TravelCenters of America	172
Petro Stopping Centers	75
Travel centers and others	34
Total	**281**

COMPETITORS

Bowlin Travel Centers	Pilot Flying J
Chevron	Royal Dutch Shell
Exxon Mobil	Sapp Bros Travel
Love's Country Stores	Centers
Marathon Petroleum	Stuckey's

HISTORICAL FINANCIALS
Company Type: Public

Income Statement
FYE: December 31

	REVENUE ($ mil.)	NET INCOME ($ mil.)	NET PROFIT MARGIN	EMPLOYEES
12/14	7,778	60	0.8%	22,330
12/13	7,944	31	0.4%	20,670
12/12	7,995	32	0.4%	17,750
12/11	7,888	23	0.3%	16,000
12/10	5,962	(65)	—	15,170
Annual Growth	**6.9%**	—		**10.1%**

2014 Year-End Financials

Debt ratio: 39.50%	No. of shares (mil.): 38
Return on equity: 12.54%	Dividends
Cash ($ mil.): 224	Yield: —
Current ratio: 2.11	Payout: —
Long-term debt ($ mil.): 562	Market value ($ mil.): 484

	STOCK PRICE ($) FY Close	P/E High/Low		PER SHARE ($) Earnings	Dividends	Book Value
12/14	12.62	8	4	1.62	0.00	13.53
12/13	9.74	12	4	1.06	0.00	12.06
12/12	4.70	6	4	1.12	0.00	11.97
12/11	4.25	13	3	0.98	0.00	11.07
12/10	3.77	—	—	(3.78)	0.00	13.95
Annual Growth	**35.3%**	—	—	—	—	**(0.8%)**

Travelers Companies Inc (The)

Running a business is a risk The Travelers Companies will insure. While it does offer personal auto and homeowners insurance the company's largest segment is commercial property/casualty insurance to businesses big and small. It is one of the largest business insurers in the US providing commercial auto property workers' compensation marine and general and financial liability coverage to companies in North America (the largest percentage of business) and the UK. The company also offers surety and fidelity bonds as well as professional and management liability coverage for commercial operations.

Operations

Travelers' business insurance segment serving all sizes of businesses has traditionally accounted for more than half of the company's annual premiums earned. In 2014 the company realigned its reporting segments combining its international and business units into the Business and International Insurance segment. The segment offers property/casualty insurance and related services to clients primarily in the US as well as in the UK Canada Ireland and throughout other parts of the world as a corporate member of Lloyd's. In 2014 Business and International Insurance accounted for more than 40% of net earned premiums.

As part of the structural reorganization the bond and financial products group joined with specialty coverages to form the Bond & Specialty Insurance segment. It writes fidelity and surety general liability and property workers' compensation commercial automobile and commercial multi-peril lines. The segment accounted for more than 15% of net earned premiums in 2014.

Personal insurance which was unchanged by the realignment accounts for a third of the company's premiums. It is slowly growing through geographic expansion. Offerings include homeowners auto flood and umbrella policies.

Travelers also offers reinsurance.

Geographic Reach

While the vast majority (about 95%) of the company's business is in the US it does have a presence in the UK where it operates through two arms: Travelers Insurance Company and Travelers Syndicate Management within Lloyd's of London. The two businesses offer commercial property/casualty and risk management services. Travelers also has modest operations in Canada Brazil and Ireland. It's looking to expand in Latin America as well as in India and China.

The company employs field claim management teams in 21 centers and 53 satellite and specialty-only offices in 45 states.

Sales and Marketing

Customers include commercial businesses government agencies associations and individuals.

Travelers' offerings are distributed through about 13000 independent agents and brokers across the US. In business and international some 11400 agents are supported by three customer service centers and more than 130 field offices.

The personal products are distributed through some 11000 independent agents employee and affinity groups and direct marketing. Meanwhile the bond & specialty insurance segment distributes products through more than 6000 independent agents and brokers.

Financial Performance

Despite general market turmoil Travelers' revenues have maintained a slow-but-steady growth rate in recent years —a sign that the company has spread itself smoothly across industries and took no significant hits to its premiums. In 2014 the company reported a 4% increase in revenues to some $27.2 billion due to higher premiums earned in the business and international insurance segment (primarily due to the acquisition of Dominion) and growth in the bond & specialty segment (reflecting the impact of lower reinsurance costs). Fee income also grew 10% due to higher serviced premium volume in workers' compensation residual market pools and higher claims in the large deductible business. Those gains were partially offset by a decline in the personal insurance business.

Net income levels have been more volatile for the company. Investment income recovered from stock market woes just in time for an uptick of catastrophe claims in 2010 and 2011 due to harsh weather events and Travelers' net income dropped both years following common share repurchases. In 2012 net income returned to growth rising some 73% to nearly $2.5 billion in 2012 and 49% to $3.7 billion in 2013. The increases were attributed to decreased claims from catastrophe losses. In 2014 net income grew marginally (by less than 1%) due to higher revenues but partially offset by increases in operating expenses.

Cash from operations decreased by $123 million to $3.7 billion due to higher levels of claims and claims adjustment expenses general and administrative expenses commission expenses and higher income tax payments.

Strategy

The company launched a restructuring program in 2013 to reduce operating expenses in the personal insurance division. The program aims to improve Travelers' competitive position in the private passenger auto insurance market. The program which aims to cut $140 million in annual expenses by 2015 includes a workforce reduction of about 450 jobs (less than 2% of total employees) and facility consolidation efforts.

Though Travelers has reduced its international holdings in recent years the company is pursuing opportunities in emerging markets such as Brazil. For example in 2015 it bought a 95% stake in the property/casualty operations of its J. Malucelli joint venture in that country (which now operates under the Travelers brand). The firm is also considering expansion in high-growth countries such as India and China.

The company's claims management strategy is focused on segmentation of claims and appropriate technical specialization to drive effective claim resolution practices.

Mergers and Acquisitions

Travelers expanded in North America through the $1.1 billion purchase of The Dominion of Canada General Insurance from E-L Financial in late 2013. The move improves Travelers position with brokers and customers across Canada; the acquired business is being combined with existing Canadian operations (Travelers Canada) headquartered in Toronto.

HISTORY

St. Paul Minnesota was a boomtown in 1852 thanks to traffic on the Mississippi. Settlers knew fire insurance was a must in their wooden town but there were no local insurers. Buying policies from eastern companies and getting claims processed was difficult —especially in the winter when river traffic stopped.

In 1853 a group of local investors led by George and John Farrington and Alexander Wilkin formed St. Paul Mutual Insurance a mixed stock and mutual company (mutual members shared in the firm's profits and losses while stockholders could

benefit by selling if the company's value rose). St. Paul Mutual sold its first policy the following year.

The company changed its name in 1865 to St. Paul Fire and Marine Insurance stopped offering mutual policies and expanded throughout the Midwest. Claims from the Chicago Fire in 1871 nearly sank the company which assessed its shareholders $15 for each share of stock but prompt and full payment of claims resulted in more business. By the turn of the century St. Paul Fire and Marine was operating nationwide.

Although the company was hard hit by shipping losses in WWI it continued expanding joining other US insurers in the American Foreign Insurance Association to market insurance in Europe.

In 1926 St. Paul Fire and Marine organized its first subsidiary St. Paul Mercury Indemnity to write liability insurance policies. Other additions included coverage for automobiles aircraft burglary and robbery and in 1940 turkey farming.

During WWII St. Paul Fire and Marine joined the War Damage Corp. a government-financed consortium that paid claims for war damage. The St. Paul Companies was formed in 1968 as the umbrella organization for the various subsidiaries and the firm grew through purchases.

Lines of business blossomed during the 1970s including life and title insurance leasing a mail-order consumer finance company oil and gas and real estate. Many of these were sold during the 1980s but one The John Nuveen Co. (1974) became the nucleus of St. Paul's financial services operations.

EXECUTIVES

EVP and Chief Administrative Officer, Andy F. Bessette, age 62

EVP and Chief Investment Officer, William H. (Bill) Heyman, age 67, $750,000 total compensation

President and COO, Brian W. MacLean, age 62, $925,000 total compensation

Vice Chairman and CFO, Jay S. Benet, age 63, $750,000 total compensation

EVP Human Resources, John P. Clifford, age 59

EVP Strategic Development and Corporate Treasurer, Maria Olivo, age 50

Vice Chairman and CEO Personal Insurance and Bond & Specialty Insurance, Doreen Spadorcia, age 58

EVP and General Counsel, Kenneth F. (Ken) Spence, age 60

EVP and Chief Marketing and Communications Officer, Lisa M. Caputo, age 51

Vice Chairman Travelers Canada, Brigid Murphy

EVP Enterprise Risk Management; CFO Business and International Insurance, Fred R. Donner, age 58

CEO and Director, Alan D. Schnitzer, age 50, $750,000 total compensation

EVP Field Management; COO Business Insurance, Patrick J Kinney

EVP and Co-President Business Insurance, Michael F. Klein

EVP Public Policy and President Travelers Institute, Joan Kois Woodward

EVP and President Bond and Specialty Insurance, Thomas M. (Tom) Kunkel

EVP; President Personal Insurance, Greg C Toczydlowski

EP and Co-President Business Insurance, Marc E Schmittlein

EVP and President International, Kevin C. Smith

EVP and CIO, Madelyn Lankton

EVP Claim Services, Robert C. (Bob) Brody

EVP and Chief Underwriting Officer, Marlyss J. Gage

EVP Enterprise Risk Management and Chief Risk Officer, Bruce R Jones

EVP Operations Enterprise Business Intelligence and Analytics and eBusiness, Julie Trowbridge-Dillman

EVP and Co-President Business Insurance, William C Malugen

CEO Travelers Europe, Matthew Wilson

CEO Travelers Canada, Duane Sanders

Vice President, Lucille Mulroy

Vice President Of Information Technology Operations, Kevin Reilly

Vice President Of Human Resource, Donna Grici

Claim Center Vice President, Claude Howard

Vice President Platform Office, William Devine

Regional Vice President, Mark Boragno

Second Vice President Corporate Procurement, Harry Captain

Assistant Vice President Financial Controls Accounting Operations, Paul Munson

Regional Vice President, Kevin Cahill

Vice President Business Analytics, Nathan Lacombe

Vice President Strategic Development Mergers and Acquisitions, David (Dave) Belany

Legal Secretary, Georgette Mcdermott

Vice President Claims, James Ostrowski

Vice President, Michael Toner

Vice President, Greg Michels

2Vp E Business, Rob Johnson

Zone Vice President Public Sector, David (Dave) Hyde

Vice President International, Richard Smith

Vice President Middle Market Strategy And Chief Administrative Officer, Lisa Morgan

Vice President Business Intelligence and Data Analytics, Joe Vellaiparambil

Regional Vice President, Steven Ringler

Executive Vice President, Gail Deangelis

Vice President Direct, Teri Deehan

Agribusiness Regional Vice Presidentthe Travelers Companies, Carl Miller

Second Vice President Information Systems, Edward (Ed) Finkle

Legal Secretary, Yolanda Ratliff

Regional Vice President Select Group, Sean Ramalho

Legal Secretary, Lucy Lopez

Regional Vice President, Doug Dooren

Second Vice President Crime And Fi Bond Claim Bond And Financial Products, Robert (Bob) Flowers

Vice President, John Komidar

2Vp Human Resources, Karen Marchetti

Vice President Finance, Jeffrey Longo

2Vp Operating Model Platform Strategy Business Insurance, Dianna Wallquist

Executive Vice President Sales and Marketing, Gary Ross

Legal Secretary, Joanne Ferrandina

2Vp Of Underwriting, Yllon Herron

Legal Secretary, Paula Laware

2Vp Bi Shared Finance Expense Management, Tom Soisson

Vice President Pm1 Central Southeast Region, Joseph (Jo) Meisinger

Regional President Upper Midwest, Rick Smith

Regional Vice President, Dave York

Second Vice President, Pamela Latty

2Vp Information Technology Operations, Bryant H Lewis

National Account Manager, Fred Putorti

Second Vice President, Marci Freida

Vice President, Bala Thiru

Vice President Premium Audit, Katie Hunlock

Second Vice President, Glenn Serrano

Vice President, Thomas Robison

Underwriting Vice President, Rebecca Glenn

2VP Human Resources, Lorrie Higgins

Legal Secretary, Maria Eilola

Vice President, Ken Chapman

Vice President Strategy, Stewart Murchie

Vice President Field Services, Robert Wullner
Vice President Operations and Systems, Steve Howard
Division President, Maureen Bass
2Vp Finance Corporate Services and Legal, Erin Wait
Regional Vice President, Michael Verdin
Second Vice President Reinsurance Travelers Insurance C, Sharon Timins
2VP Middle Market Operations, Brad Warne
Second Vice President Program Manager, John (Jack) Dabney
Second Vice President Practice Leader Cargo, William (Bill) Markham
Vice President Chief Underwriting Office, Robin Udhwan
2VP Business Analysis Operating Model, Jay Coon
Rvp Select Accounts, Lisa Pechan
RVP Oil and Gas, Peggy Genet
Second Vice President Complex Claim, David (Dave) Millam
Executive Vice President Chief Operations Office, Brian McLean
Vice Chairman, Irwin R. Ettinger, age 77
Chairman, Jay S. Fishman, age 62
Treasurer, Jim Strupp
Executive Board Member, Sue McKinney
Board Member, Alexis Cruz
Auditors: KPMG LLP

LOCATIONS

HQ: Travelers Companies Inc (The)
485 Lexington Avenue, New York, NY 10017
Phone: 917 778-6000
Web: www.travelers.com

2014 Revenues

	$ mil.	% of total
US	25,091	93
Canada	1,474	5
Other countries	597	2
Total	**27,162**	**100**

PRODUCTS/OPERATIONS

2014 Revenues

	$ mil.	% of total
Premiums		
Business insurance	14,512	53
Personal insurance	7,125	26
Bond & specialty insurance	2,076	8
Net investment income	2,787	10
Fee income	438	2
Investment gains	79	-
Other revenues	145	1
Total	**27,162**	**100**

List of Items
Business
Commercial Automobile
Commercial Multi-Peril
Commercial Property
General Liability
Workers' Compensation
Individual
Affinity Auto and Home Program
Auto Insurance
Boat and Yacht Insurance
Condo Insurance
Flood Insurance
Homeowners Insurance
Identity Fraud Protection
Renters Insurance
Umbrella Insurance
Valuable Items Coverage
Wedding and Private Events Insurance

Selected Subsidiaries and Divisions

J. Malucelli Participacoes em Seguros e Resseguros S.A. (49.5% Brazil)
St. Paul Fire and Marine Insurance Company
Travelers Property Casualty Corp.
  The Standard Fire Insurance Company
  Travelers Casualty and Surety Company
  Travelers Casualty and Surety Company of America

The Travelers Indemnity Company
  First Floridian Auto and Home Insurance Company
  First Trenton Indemnity Company (Travelers of New Jersey)
The Premier Insurance Co. of Massachusetts
Travelers Insurance Company Limited (UK)
Travelers Syndicate Management Limited (UK)

COMPETITORS

AIG	Chubb Limited
AXA	Liberty Mutual Agency
Allianz	Markel
Allstate	Nationwide
American Financial Group	The Hartford
	W. R. Berkley
CNA Financial	Zurich Insurance Group

HISTORICAL FINANCIALS

Company Type: Public

Income Statement

FYE: December 31

	ASSETS ($ mil.)	NET INCOME ($ mil.)	INCOME AS % OF ASSETS	EMPLOYEES
12/15	100,184	3,439	3.4%	30,900
12/14	103,078	3,692	3.6%	30,200
12/13	103,812	3,673	3.5%	30,800
12/12	104,938	2,473	2.4%	30,500
12/11	104,602	1,426	1.4%	30,600
Annual Growth	(1.1%)	24.6%	—	0.2%

2015 Year-End Financials

Debt ratio: 6.23%
Return on equity: 14.20%
Cash ($ mil.): 380
Current ratio: —
Long-term debt ($ mil.): —

No. of shares (mil.): 295
Dividends
  Yield: 2.1%
  Payout: 21.3%
Market value ($ mil.): 33,395

	STOCK PRICE ($) FY Close	P/E High/Low		PER SHARE ($) Earnings	Dividends	Book Value
12/15	112.86	11	9	10.88	2.38	79.75
12/14	105.85	10	7	10.70	2.15	77.08
12/13	90.54	9	7	9.74	1.96	70.14
12/12	71.82	12	9	6.30	1.79	67.32
12/11	59.17	19	14	3.36	1.59	62.31
Annual Growth	17.5%	—	—	34.1%	10.6%	6.4%

TriCo Bancshares (Chico, CA)

People looking for a community bank in California's Sacramento Valley can try TriCo. TriCo Bancshares is the holding company for Tri Counties Bank which serves customers through some 65 traditional and in-store branches in 23 counties in Northern and Central California. Founded in 1974 Tri Counties Bank provides a variety of deposit services including checking and savings accounts money market accounts and CDs. Most patrons are retail customers and small to midsized businesses. The bank primarily originates real estate mortgages which account for about 65% of its loan portfolio; consumer loans contribute about 25%. TriCo has agreed to acquire rival North Valley Bancorp.

Mergers and Acquisitions

TriCo in January 2014 announced plans to buy its rival in Northern California North Valley Bancorp (NVB) for about $178.4 million. NVB is the parent company of North Valley Bank which had about $918 million in assets and 22 commercial banking offices across eight Northern California counties at the end of 2013. At closing which is expected in the second or third quarter of 2014 NVB will be merged into Tri Counties Bank. The combined bank would have about $3.6 billion in assets.

Geographic Reach

Based in Chico California Tri Counties Bank operates 66 branches (41 traditional branches and 25 in-store branches) in 23 counties in Northern and central California including Fresno Kern Mendocino Napa Sacramento and Yuba counties.

Operations

In addition to its retail banking products and services the company provides wholesale banking and investment services; TriCo offers brokerage services through an arrangement with Raymond James Financial. The company does not provide trust or international banking services.

Financial Performance

In 2013 net interest income the company's primary source of revenue rose 0.6% compared with 2012 to $102.2 million. The slight increase in net interest income was mainly due to a decrease in average balance of other borrowings a shift in deposit balances from relatively high interest rate earning time deposits to noninterest-earning demand and savings deposits an increase in the average balance of investments securities and an increase in the average balance of loans; all of which were substantially offset by a decrease in the average yield on loans.

Strategy

The bank's growth has been fueled by acquisitions and the opening of new branches; it frequently opens branches within grocery stores or other retailers including Wal-Mart. TriCo in 2010 acquired the three branches of Granite Community Bank which had been seized by regulators. The transaction which also included most of the failed bank's assets and deposits was facilitated by the FDIC and includes a loss-sharing agreement with the agency. The following year TriCo acquired Citizens Bank of Northern California. The FDIC-assisted deal included seven branches. The acquisitions are part of TriCo's strategy of adding new customers.

EXECUTIVES

EVP and CFO TriCo Bancshares and Tri Counties Bank, Thomas J. (Tom) Reddish, age 55, $309,601 total compensation
EVP and Chief Credit Officer, Craig Carney, age 56, $269,217 total compensation
EVP Wholesale Banking, Richard O'Sullivan, age 58, $256,094 total compensation
President CEO and Director, Richard P. Smith, age 57, $526,234 total compensation
EVP and Chief Retail Banking Officer, Daniel K. (Dan) Bailey, age 46, $263,074 total compensation
EVP and COO, Carol Ward
SVP and CIO, Bruce Barnett
Vice President Facilities Expansion MA, Chimene Sonsteng
Regional Vice President Northern San Joaquin Region, David (Dave) Allumbaugh
Vice President, Mark Hammer
Executive Vice President and Chief Retail Banking Officer, Dan Bailey
Chairman, William J. Casey, age 70
Vice Chairman, Michael W. Koehnen, age 54
Auditors: Crowe Horwath LLP

LOCATIONS

HQ: TriCo Bancshares (Chico, CA)
  63 Constitution Drive, Chico, CA 95973
Phone: 530 898-0300   **Fax:** 530 898-0310
Web: www.tcbk.com

PRODUCTS/OPERATIONS

2013 Sales

	$ mil.	% of total
Interest		
Loans including fees	97	68
Debt securities	6	5
Dividends	0	-
Other	1	1
Noninterest		
Service charges & fees	25	18
Commissions	3	2
Gain on sale of loans	5	4
Other	3	2
Total	**143**	**100**

COMPETITORS

Bank of America	MUFG Americas Holdings
Bank of the West	PremierWest
Central Valley	Wells Fargo
Community Bancorp	Westamerica

HISTORICAL FINANCIALS

Company Type: Public

Income Statement

FYE: December 31

	ASSETS ($ mil.)	NET INCOME ($ mil.)	INCOME AS % OF ASSETS	EMPLOYEES
12/14	3,916	26	0.7%	1,009
12/13	2,744	27	1.0%	794
12/12	2,609	18	0.7%	831
12/11	2,555	18	0.7%	799
12/10	2,189	6	0.3%	749
Annual Growth	**15.6%**	**44.4%**	**—**	**7.7%**

2014 Year-End Financials

Debt ratio: 1.67%	No. of shares (mil.): 22
Return on equity: 7.80%	Dividends
Cash ($ mil.): 610	Yield: 1.7%
Current ratio: —	Payout: 28.0%
Long-term debt ($ mil.): —	Market value ($ mil.): 561

	STOCK PRICE ($) FY Close	P/E High/Low	PER SHARE ($) Earnings	Dividends	Book Value
12/14	24.70	19 15	1.46	0.44	18.41
12/13	28.37	17 9	1.69	0.42	15.61
12/12	16.75	15 12	1.18	0.36	14.33
12/11	14.22	14 10	1.16	0.36	13.55
12/10	16.15	61 35	0.37	0.40	12.64
Annual Growth	**11.2%**	**—**	**40.9%**	**2.4%**	**9.9%**

Trinity Industries, Inc.

If Trinity Industries had a theme song it would be sung by Boxcar Willie. The company manufactures auto carriers box cars gondola cars hopper cars intermodal cars and tank cars —in short railcars for hauling everything from coal to corn syrup. Trinity also leases and manages railcar fleets. Its Inland Barge unit builds barges used to transport coal grain and other commodities. In addition to transportation other Trinity businesses provide products and services to the industrial energy (structural towers for wind turbines metal contain-

ers for liquefied petroleum gas and fertilizer) and construction (concrete aggregates highway guardrails) sectors.Geographic ReachAbout 90% of the company's business is US-generated. The rest of the company's business is generated in Mexico where company tanks are manufactured under the brand name TATSA. Throughout North America Trinity serves its customers from five business groups: Rail Construction Products Railcar Leasing Inland Barge and Energy Equipment. The divisions conduct business through subsidiaries.

OperationsTrinity Rail Group in 2014 shipped about 30255 railcars –44% market share (by shipment) —of the North American railcar industry. The division manufactures freight railcars that transport liquids gases and dry cargo. The company's Construction Products Group produces concrete aggregates and asphalt; it manufactures highway products which include beams and girders used in highway bridge construction. Other highway products include guardrails cable barrier systems and crash cushions which are sold in the US and over 60 countries worldwide. Trinity's Railcar and Leasing Management Services Group operates primarily through Trinity Industries Leasing Company (TILC) as well as other subsidiaries and markets its services under the TrinityRail brand name. It provides leasing options to companies involved in petroleum chemical agricultural and energy industries among others.Inland Barge Group makes dry cargo barges (flat-deck and hopper) which transport products such as grain coal and aggregates. Tank barges carry petroleum fertilizer chemicals and other liquid cargoes. This business makes fiberglass barge covers and deck hardware (brand name Nabrico) including hatches castings and winches for other watercraft and dock facilities. Primary customers are commercial marine transportation companies.Trinity's Energy Equipment Group makes tank containers and tank heads for pressure vessels propane tanks and structural wind towers. Trinity Industries de Mexico (brand name TATSA) manufactures containers for liquefied petroleum gas. It also manufactures containers for fertilizers comestibles and ammonia.Sales and Marketing

Trinity sells its products and services through its own sales personnel operating in Canada Mexico Singapore Sweden the UK and the US.Financial PerformanceTrinity has enjoyed significant growth over the last few years. From 2013 to 2014 its net revenues jumped 41% from $4.4 billion to peak at a record-setting $6.2 billion. The company's profits soared by 81% from $376 million in 2013 to $678 million in 2014 another company milestone. The historic growth for 2014 was attributed to a 73% surge in Railcar and Leasing Management Services Group sales and a 49% spike in Energy Equipment Group sales resulting primarily from increased demand for storage container vessels and other product lines. The rise in profits for 2014 was fueled by the additional revenue coupled with increased gains on the disposition of property plant and equipment. Trinity's cash flow has also increased the last several years climbing from $662 million in 2013 to $819 million in 2014.Strategy-One way Trinity has achieved milestone revenue growth is through acquisitions. Overall the company invested $720 million for acquisitions in 2014. That year it acquired the assets of WesMor Cryogenic Companies which specialized in the manufacturing repair and rehabilitation of cryogenic containers that store and transport LNG.Trinity also obtained Alloy Custom Products an Indiana-based manufacturer and repairer of cryogenic transportation products including cryogenic tanks and semitrailers that store and transport LNG and other industrial gases. The transaction expanded Trinity's product offerings and geographic footprint in the cryogenics containers

market within its Energy Equipment Group.In addition in 2014 Trinity bought Meyer Steel Structures a provider of tubular steel structures for electricity transmission and distribution and the utility steel structures for approximately $600 million. Meyer was integrated into the Energy Equipment Group. The acquisition enhanced Trinity's presence in the energy and infrastructure markets. In 2013 the company strengthened its Construction Products Group through the purchase of assets owned by Texas Industries. It bought aggregates operations located in California Colorado and Texas and inherited Texas Industries' DiamondPro product line. Also in 2013 it acquired the assets of Forjas Metálicas S.A. de C.V for $23 million. Formet is located in Monterrey Mexico and it designs manufactures and sells galvanized and corrugated steel products for the electricity transmission and highway products markets.

HISTORY

Trinity Industries resulted from the 1958 merger of Trinity Steel a maker of metal products for the petroleum industry and Dallas Tank Co. The enterprise was headed by Ray Wallace a Trinity Steel veteran since the 1940s. The company took the name Trinity Industries in 1966.

EXECUTIVES

Vice President Information Technology, Theis Rice
Vice President, Andrea F Cowan
Vice President Information Technology, Madhuri Andrews
Vice President Finance, David (Dave) Laroche
Chairman President and CEO, Timothy R. Wallace, age 62, $1,000,000 total compensation
SVP; Group President Construction Products and Inland Barge, William A. (Bill) McWhirter, age 50, $575,000 total compensation
SVP and Chief Legal Officer, S. Theis Rice, age 65, $416,000 total compensation
SVP and Group President TrinityRail, D. Stephen (Steve) Menzies, age 60, $615,000 total compensation
Treasurer, James E. Perry, age 44, $500,000 total compensation
VP Information Technology, Tammy D. Gilbert, age 54
VP and CTO, Stephen W. Smith, age 65
SVP and Chief Administrative Officer, Melendy E. Lovett
V Pres-gen Coun-trinityrail, Jared Richardson
Vice President Trinity Structural Towers Operations, Dennis Knudson
Vice President, Terry Goodwin
Vice President Engineering Manager, Rich Bacsi
Vice President Of Finance, Terry Winham
Vice President Sales and Marketing, George Craton
Vice President Human Resources, Katherine Collins
Senior Vice President Business Development, Bob Hulick
Vice President Sales and Marketing, Brad Jones
Vice President Corporate Strategic Planning, Scott Beasley
Vice President Business Development, Jay Tulimieri
Vice President Government Relations, Linda Sickels
Vice President of Business Systems, Lynne Storey
Vice President Railcar Division, Dale Hill
Vice President, Eric Marchetto
Vice President Human Resources, Natascha Anderson
Vice President U.S. Eastern Region and Canada, John (Jack) Gallaher
Vice President Leasing Trinity Industries Leasing, Robert Wright
Vice President, Bob Pennington
Vice President Operations MExico, Rogelio Garcia

Vice President Finance and Accounting, Georgia Papageorge
Vice President, Joe Morreale
Vice President Quality Assurance, Lee Verhey
Vice President Materials Management, Rick Kemp
Senior Vice President Supply Chain Management, John Guarino
Senior Vice President Logistics, Gary Holt
Vice President Information Technology, David (Dave) Akeena
Vice President Human Resources, Gail Peck
Division President, Tom Faherty
Vice President TANK Car Engineer, Tom Dalrymple
Vice President, Jim Ivy
Vice President And Controller Trinityrail, Mark Howell
Vice President Chief Legal Officer, S Rice
Assistant Treasurer, Peggy Bernard
Treasurer, Neil Shoop
Auditors: Ernst & Young LLP

LOCATIONS

HQ: Trinity Industries, Inc.
2525 N. Stemmons Freeway, Dallas, TX 75207-2401
Phone: 214 631-4420   **Fax:** 214 589-8501
Web: www.trin.net

PRODUCTS/OPERATIONS

2013 Sales

	$ mil.	% of total
Rail Group	2,093	48
Railcar Leasing & Management Services Group	645	15
Inland Barge Group	576	13
Energy Equipment Group	536	12
Construction Products Group	508	12
Other	4	-
Total	**4,365**	**100**

2013 Sales

	$ mil.	% of total
Manufacturing	3,719	85
Leasing	645	15
Total	**4,365**	**100**

Selected Products and Services

Construction products
  Aggregates
  Anti-icing systems for bridges
  Beams
  Flexible post delineators
  Girders
  Highway crash cushions
  Highway guardrails
  Highway safety devices
  Ready-mix concrete
  Truck-mounted attenuators
Energy equipment
  Container heads
  Fertilizer containers
  Liquefied petroleum gas containers
  Wind towers
Inland barge
  Deck barges
  Fiberglass barge covers
  Hopper barges
  Tank barges
Rail
  Box cars
  Freight cars
  Gondola cars
  Hopper cars
  Intermodal cars
  Tank cars
Railcar leasing and management services
  Railcar leasing repair and management

COMPETITORS

ALSTOM	FreightCar America
American Railcar	GATX
Industries	GE Rail Services
Amsted Industries	Greenbrier Companies
Blue Tee	Lafarge North America

CEMEX	LafargeHolcim
Clipper Windpower	Nippon Sharyo
Conrad Industries	Vulcan Materials

HISTORICAL FINANCIALS
Company Type: Public

Income Statement
FYE: December 31

	REVENUE ($ mil.)	NET INCOME ($ mil.)	NET PROFIT MARGIN	EMPLOYEES
12/14	6,170	678	11.0%	21,950
12/13	4,365	375	8.6%	18,460
12/12	3,811	255	6.7%	15,490
12/11	3,075	142	4.6%	13,390
12/10	2,189	67	3.1%	9,270
Annual Growth	**29.6%**	**78.1%**	**—**	**24.0%**

2014 Year-End Financials

Debt ratio: 40.68%	No. of shares (mil.): 155
Return on equity: 25.13%	Dividends
Cash ($ mil.): 887	Yield: 1.2%
Current ratio: 2.48	Payout: 8.6%
Long-term debt ($ mil.): 3,553	Market value ($ mil.): 4,358

	STOCK PRICE ($) FY Close	P/E High/Low		PER SHARE ($) Earnings	Dividends	Book Value
12/14	28.01	20	6	4.19	0.35	19.25
12/13	54.52	24	15	2.38	0.50	15.52
12/12	35.82	23	14	1.60	0.40	12.98
12/11	30.06	43	23	0.89	0.17	11.62
12/10	26.61	63	36	0.43	0.32	11.06
Annual Growth	**1.3%**	**—**	**—**	**77.2%**	**2.3%**	**14.9%**

TriState Capital Holdings, Inc.

TriState Capital Holdings has found its niche right in the middle of the banking industry. The holding company owns TriState Capital Bank a regional business bank that caters to midsized businesses or those annually earning between $5 million and $300 million. TriState Capital also offers private banking services nationally to high-networth individuals. Its loan portfolio consists of about 50% commercial loans 30% commercial real estate loans and 20% private banking-personal loans. The bank serves clients from branches in Cleveland; New Jersey; New York City Philadelphia and Pittsburgh. Altogether it has some $2 billion in assets. TriState Capital went public in mid-2013.
IPO

The company does not have any specific plans outlined for its proceeds but will likely use it for general corporate purposes which might include maintaining liquidity at the holding company providing equity capital to the bank to fund balance sheet growth and possibly investing in or acquiring wealth management businesses.
Company Background

TriState Capital was founded in 2007 by two banking industry executives —chairman and CEO James Getz who spent 20 years at Federated Investors and vice chairman William Schenck the former secretary of banking for Pennsylvania.
Strategy

The company's founders saw an opportunity in serving what they perceived was an underserved

market —midsized businesses. Consolidation had left major national banks catering to individuals and large businesses while community banks served individuals and small businesses.
Ownership

Prior to the offering investment firm Lovell Minnick Partners held a 20% stake in TriState Capital Holdings in exchange for its $50 million investment in 2012.

EXECUTIVES

Chairman President and CEO, James F. (Jim) Getz, $1,500,000 total compensation
President Commercial Banking, David A. Molnar
Vice Chairman and CFO, Mark L. Sullivan, $425,000 total compensation
Regional President New Jersey, Kenneth R. Orchard
Regional President New York, Thomas N. Gilmartin
Regional President Ohio, John D. Barrett
Regional President Eastern Pennsylvania, Joseph M. Finley
Regional President Western Pennsylvania, Vince Locher
President Private Bank Team, Charles C. Fawcett
Senior Vice President Relationship Manager, Michael Blasko
Senior Vice President Relationship Manager, Michael (Mel) Blasko
Vice Chairman, A. William (Bill) Schenck
Auditors: KPMG LLP

LOCATIONS

HQ: TriState Capital Holdings, Inc.
One Oxford Centre, 301 Grant Street, Suite 2700, Pittsburgh, PA 15219
Phone: 412 304-0304

COMPETITORS

Bank of America	HSBC Private Bank
Bank of New York	Herald National Bank
Mellon	JPMorgan Private Bank
Boston Private	Julius Baer
Brown Brothers	Lakeland Bancorp
Harriman	M&T Bank
Citigroup	Safra Bank
Citigroup Private Bank	U.S. Trust
First Republic (CA)	

HISTORICAL FINANCIALS
Company Type: Public

Income Statement
FYE: December 31

	ASSETS ($ mil.)	NET INCOME ($ mil.)	INCOME AS % OF ASSETS	EMPLOYEES
12/14	2,846	15	0.6%	182
12/13	2,290	12	0.6%	129
12/12	2,073	10	0.5%	119
12/11	1,833	7	0.4%	—
12/10	0	15	—	—
Annual Growth	**—**	**1.1%**	**—**	**—**

2014 Year-End Financials

Debt ratio: —	No. of shares (mil.): 28
Return on equity: 5.32%	Dividends
Cash ($ mil.): 99	Yield: —
Current ratio: —	Payout: —
Long-term debt ($ mil.): —	Market value ($ mil.): 287

	STOCK PRICE ($) FY Close	P/E High/Low		PER SHARE ($) Earnings	Dividends	Book Value
12/14	10.24	26	16	0.55	0.00	10.88
12/13	11.86	29	24	0.49	0.00	10.25
Annual Growth	**(3.6%)**	**—**	**—**	**2.9%**	**—**	**1.5%**

Trustco Bank Corp. (N.Y.)

In Banking They Trust. TrustCo Bank Corp is the holding company for Trustco Bank which boasts more than 140 branches across eastern New York central and western Florida and parts of Vermont Massachusetts and New Jersey. The bank offers personal and business customers a variety of deposit products loans and mortgages and trust and investment services. It primarily originates residential and commercial mortgages which account for more than three-quarters of its loan portfolio. It also writes business construction and installment loans and home equity lines of credit.

OperationsTrustCo Bank Corp generated 77% of its total revenue from interest and fees on loans in 2014 while interest on its securities available for sale (which were mostly residential mortgage-backed securities and collateralized mortgage obligations but also its GSE SBA-backed securities) made up another 16% of the bank's revenue. Customer service fees and Trustco Financial Services income made up 6% and 3% of total revenue in 2014 respectively.Sales and MarketingTrustco provides personal and business banking services to individuals partnerships and corporations among other kinds of business and organizations. It spent $2.49 million on advertising in 2014 compared to $2.83 million and $3.84 million in 2013 and 2012 respectively.Financial PerformanceTrustco has struggled to grow its revenue in recent years though its profits have been rising at a healthy clip mostly because its loan loss provisions have dissipated with an improving credit portfolio amidst the strengthening economy. TrustCo's revenue rose by nearly 4% to $176.85 million in 2014 mostly as new branch openings during the year added nearly double-digit loan business growth. The bank also collected more interest income from its securities as it invested more and made a gain on the sale of its Florida regional headquarters property.Higher revenue and a decline in interest expense on deposits in the low-interest environment also drove the bank's net income up by 11% to $4.38 million. A continuing decline in loan loss provisions buoyed by improving economic conditions (especially in Florida) also helped boost the bank's bottom line.Despite higher earnings in 2014 TrustCo's operating cash fell by 21% to $49.54 million during the year as it spent more toward acquiring additional assets.StrategyTrustCo has focused on building its loan business through new branch additions as well as through growth from its existing offices in recent years. Using this strategy in 2014 the bank added five new branches and successfully boosted its deposit business by 2.7% to $4.03 billion while loan balances swelled by 8.6% to $3.16 billion as the bank aggressively pushed its loan business during the year.The bank underwent a major branch expansion from 2002 through 2009 and more than doubled its branch network in New York and Florida by opening new locations (more than 75 of them). It continues to open new branches albeit not as rapidly.

EXECUTIVES

President and CEO, Robert J. McCormick, age 52, $880,000 total compensation
Administrative VP Branch Administration/Marketing Trustco Bank, Scot R. Salvador, age 49, $510,000 total compensation
EVP, Robert M. Leonard, age 53, $260,000 total compensation

Treasurer TrustCo and SVP Trustco Bank, Eric W. Schreck, age 48, $255,000 total compensation
SVP and CFO TrustCo Bank Corp NY and Trustco Bank, Michael M. Ozimek, $142,500 total compensation
Chairman, Thomas O. Maggs, age 71
Auditors: Crowe Horwath LLP

LOCATIONS

HQ: Trustco Bank Corp. (N.Y.)
5 Sarnowski Drive, Glenville, NY 12302
Phone: 518 377-3311   **Fax:** 518 381-3668
Web: www.trustcobank.com

PRODUCTS/OPERATIONS

2011 Sales

	$ mil.	% of total
Interest		
Loans including fees	129	73
Securities	30	17
Other	1	1
Noninterest		
Fees for services to customers	8	5
Trustco Financial Services	5	3
Other	2	1
Total	**177**	**100**

COMPETITORS

Arrow Financial	HSBC USA
Ballston Spa Bancorp	Hudson Valley FCU
Bank of America	KeyCorp
Citizens Financial Group	M&T Bank
First Niagara Financial	NBT Bancorp

HISTORICAL FINANCIALS

Company Type: Public

Income Statement

FYE: December 31

	ASSETS ($ mil.)	NET INCOME ($ mil.)	INCOME AS % OF ASSETS	EMPLOYEES
12/14	4,644	44	1.0%	737
12/13	4,521	39	0.9%	708
12/12	4,346	37	0.9%	759
12/11	4,243	33	0.8%	726
12/10	3,954	29	0.7%	738
Annual Growth	**4.1%**	**10.8%**	**—**	**(0.0%)**

2014 Year-End Financials

Debt ratio: —	No. of shares (mil.): 94
Return on equity: 11.70%	Dividends
Cash ($ mil.): 671	Yield: 3.6%
Current ratio: —	Payout: 55.8%
Long-term debt ($ mil.): —	Market value ($ mil.): 689

	STOCK PRICE ($) FY Close	P/E High/Low	PER SHARE ($) Earnings	Dividends	Book Value
12/14	7.26	16 13	0.47	0.26	4.15
12/13	7.18	18 12	0.42	0.26	3.83
12/12	5.28	15 13	0.40	0.26	3.82
12/11	5.61	17 10	0.39	0.26	3.62
12/10	6.34	19 14	0.38	0.26	3.31
Annual Growth	**3.4%**	**— —**	**5.2%**	**0.6%**	**5.8%**

Trustmark Corp.

Trustmark Corporation is the holding company for Trustmark National Bank which has 208 locations mainly in Mississippi but also in East Texas the Florida panhandle and Tennessee where it also operates its Somerville Bank & Trust subsidiary in the Memphis area. Focusing on individuals and small businesses Trustmark offers a range of financial products and services such as checking and savings accounts certificates of deposit credit cards insurance investments and trust services. The diversified financial services firm has about $11.7 billion in assets.Geographic Reach

Mississippi by far is Trustmark's largest market accounting for 63% of 2013 revenues. Tennessee Texas and Florida contributed about 9% 7% and 10% respectively.

Operations

Trustmark operates through three operating segments: General Banking Insurance and Wealth Management. The General Banking Division is responsible for all traditional banking products and services including a full range of commercial and consumer banking services such as checking accounts savings programs overdraft facilities commercial installment and real estate loans home equity loans and lines of credit drive-in and night deposit services and safe deposit facilities offered through 208 offices in Alabama Florida Mississippi Tennessee and Texas. The Wealth Management Division serve Trustmark's customers as a financial partner providing reliable guidance and sound practical advice for accumulating preserving and transferring wealth.Trustmark's Insurance Division provides a full range of retail insurance products including commercial risk management products bonding group benefits and personal lines coverage through Trustmark National Bank subsidiary FBBI a Mississippi corporation.

Subsidiary Fisher Brown Bottrell sells insurance while Trustmark Investment Advisors provides wealth management products and services including the proprietary Performance Fund family of mutual funds. The latter unit has approximately $9 billion of assets under management.

Financial Performance

After experiencing a revenue dip in 2012 due to decrease in interest income in 2013 Trustmark's revenues increased by 8% thanks to an increase in the net interest income due to a significant increase in interest and fees on acquired loans related to the BancTrust acquisition as well as modest declines in the cost of interest-bearing deposits. These gains were partially offset by downward repricing of loans and securities. After experiencing sizable growth over the last few years in 2013 Trustmark's net income decreased to $117.1 million (from $117.2 million in 2012) due to an increase in the noninterest expenses as a result of BancTrust non-routine merger expenses and increases in salaries and employee benefits services and fees and ORE/foreclosure expenses.In 2013 the company's operating cash inflow increased to $155.4 million (compared to $92.1 million in 2012) was due to a major increase in net assets and liabilities and a decline in purchases and originations of loans held for sale.

Strategy

Trustmark is growing its branch network by opening or acquiring new offices with a focus on the Houston and Memphis markets.

In 2013 Trustmark opened a new 12000-sq.-ft. office location on the first and second floors of the Nexen Building in Bunker Hill. Trustmark operates 15 locations in the Houston market with loans outstanding of approximately $835 million and deposits of approximately $425 million.

Mergers and Acquisitions

In 2013 the company purchased two branches in Oxford Mississippi from SOUTHBank F.S.B. That year it also bought Mobile Alabama-based BancTrust Financial Group for $55 million providing Trustmark entry into more than 15 markets in Alabama and enhancing the Trustmark franchise in the Florida Panhandle.

Company Background

Trustmark grew in 2011 with the FDIC-assisted acquisition of Heritage Banking Group. It took over the failed bank's assets and deposits after the institution was closed by regulators. The transaction added four bank branches in Mississippi (four other locations were consolidated due to their proximity to existing Trustmark branches).

BlackRock Inc. owns more than 11% of Trustmark Corp's. shares.

Trustmark National Bank traces its roots to 1889 when it was first chartered in Mississippi.

EXECUTIVES

President; Chief Executive Officer; Director of the Company and the Bank, Gerard R. (Jerry) Host, age 60, $244,167 total compensation

Treasurer and Principal Financial Officer; EVP and CFO Trustmark National Bank, Louis E. Greer, age 60, $244,167 total compensation

Vice President RECOVERY Department, Terry Collins

Vice President Systems Support, Shane Breland

First Vice President Management Information Systems, Walt James

First Vice President Audit, George Shirley

Senior Vice President, Robert Hardison

Vice President And Trust Officer In The Trust Department, Agnes Tribble

Chairman, Daniel A. (Dan) Grafton, age 68

Auditors: Crowe Horwath LLP

LOCATIONS

HQ: Trustmark Corp.
248 East Capitol Street, Jackson, MS 39201
Phone: 601 208-5111 **Fax:** 601 354-5053
Web: www.trustmark.com

2011 Revenue

	$ mil.	% of total
Mississippi	406	80
Tennessee	39	8
Florida	25	5
Texas	37	7
Total	**551**	**100**

PRODUCTS/OPERATIONS

2013 Sales

	$ mil.	% of total
Interest		
Loans including fees	334	57
Taxable securities	78	13
Other	1	-
Noninterest		
Service charges on deposit accounts	51	8
Bank card & other fees	36	6
Mortgage banking	33	6
Insurance commissions	30	5
Wealth management	29	5
Other	(7.5)	-
Total	**588**	**100**

Selected Subsidiaries

F. S. Corporation
First Building Corporation
Somerville Bank & Trust Company
Trustmark National Bank
  Fisher Brown Bottrell Insurance Inc.
  Trustmark Investment Advisors Inc.
  Trustmark Securities Inc.

COMPETITORS

BancorpSouth	Hancock Holding
Capital One	Regions Financial
Citizens Holding	Renasant
First Horizon	Wells Fargo
Great Southern Bancorp	

HISTORICAL FINANCIALS

Company Type: Public

Income Statement

FYE: December 31

	ASSETS ($ mil.)	NET INCOME ($ mil.)	INCOME AS % OF ASSETS	EMPLOYEES
12/14	12,250	123	1.0%	3,060
12/13	11,790	117	1.0%	3,110
12/12	9,828	117	1.2%	2,666
12/11	9,727	106	1.1%	2,537
12/10	9,553	100	1.1%	2,490
Annual Growth	**6.4%**	**5.3%**	**—**	**5.3%**

2014 Year-End Financials

Debt ratio: 0.91%	No. of shares (mil.): 67
Return on equity: 8.91%	Dividends
Cash ($ mil.): 315	Yield: 3.7%
Current ratio: —	Payout: 50.0%
Long-term debt ($ mil.): —	Market value ($ mil.): 1,656

	STOCK PRICE ($) FY Close	P/E High/Low	PER SHARE ($) Earnings	Dividends	Book Value
12/14	24.54	15 12	1.83	0.92	21.04
12/13	26.84	16 13	1.75	0.92	20.11
12/12	22.46	14 12	1.81	0.92	19.86
12/11	24.29	16 10	1.66	0.92	18.94
12/10	24.84	17 12	1.57	0.92	17.98
Annual Growth	**(0.3%)**	**— —**	**3.9%**	**(0.0%)**	**4.0%**

Twenty-First Century Fox Inc

This media company is crazy like a fox. Twenty-First Century Fox (formerly known as News Corporation) owns and operates a portfolio of cable broadcast film pay television and satellite assets spanning the globe. The company's massive portfolio of cable and broadcasting networks and properties includes FOX FX Fox News Fox Business Network Fox Sports National Geographic Channels Fox Pan America Sports MundoFox STAR and 28 local television stations; film studio Twentieth Century Fox Film; and television production studios Twentieth Century Fox Television and Shine Group.

HISTORY

In 1952 Rupert Murdoch inherited two Adelaide Australia newspapers from his father. After launching the Australian the country's first national daily in 1964 Murdoch moved into the UK market. He bought tabloid News of the World a London Sunday paper in 1968 and London's Sun the next year. In 1973 Murdoch hit the US buying the San Antonio Express-News and founding the Star tabloid. He followed this up in 1976 by buying the New York Post. Murdoch formed News Corporation in Australia in 1979.

Moving upmarket in 1981 Murdoch bought the London Times and 40% of Collins Publishers a

London book publisher. After buying the Chicago Sun-Times in 1983 (sold 1986) Murdoch bought 13 US travel hotel and aviation trade magazines from Ziff-Davis as well as film studio Twentieth Century Fox in 1985. In 1986 Murdoch bought six Metromedia stations and launched FOX Broadcasting the first new US TV network since 1948.

Print was not forgotten however and in the late 1980s News Corp. picked up US book publisher Harper & Row as well as Triangle Publications (TV Guide and other magazines). It also bought textbook publisher Scott Foresman and the rest of Collins Publishers. (Harper & Row was later merged with Collins to form HarperCollins.)

In 1996 Murdoch launched the FOX News Channel an all-news cable channel. The next year News Corp.'s FOX Kids joint venture bought Pat Robertson's International Family Entertainment.

In 1998 the company bought the Los Angeles Dodgers and stakes in the new Los Angeles-area Staples Center sports arena. (It sold its stake in the Staples Center in 2004.) Also that year News Corp. spun off part of Fox Entertainment in one of America's largest IPOs raising $2.7 billion.

That year News Corp. sold TV Guide to Tele-Communications Inc.'s United Video Satellite Group (now Gemstar-TV Guide International) for $800 million in cash and a 21% stake. The company also bought the 50% of FOX/Liberty Networks (now FOX Sports Net) it didn't own and transferred ownership to Fox Entertainment. The deal gave John Malone's Liberty Media holding company an 8% stake (later 19%) in News Corp.

In 1999 News Corp. purchased a 10% stake of wireless ISP OmniSky. The following year Sky acquired nearly 25% of Kirch PayTV the German pay-TV operation of KirchGruppe. Murdoch placed all of the company's satellite holdings into a new entity Sky Global Networks. (News Corp. folded Sky Global back into its operations in 2002 when it failed in its initial bid to buy DIRECTV.) Also that year News Corp. bought a stake in China's state-owned telecom operator Netcom.

In 2001 along with partner Haim Saban News Corp. sold the Fox Family Channel to Disney for about $5.2 billion. That year the FCC approved the company's $4.8 billion purchase of TV station group Chris-Craft. The deal gave News Corp. an additional 10 TV stations.

News Corp. in 2003 finally realized its dream of owning a chunk of DIRECTV when it bought 34% of Hughes Electronics the satellite television company's parent from General Motors. News Corp. transferred its interest in Hughes (which changed its name to The DIRECTV Group) to its Fox Entertainment subsidiary. The following year in an effort to make its stock more attractive to US investors News Corp. shifted its incorporation from Australia to the US. It also purchased the rest of Fox Entertainment that it didn't already own for $6.2 billion.

In 2005 News Corp. made its push into online and digital entertainment. Anchoring the new operations it acquired MySpace.com operator Intermix Media for about $580 million. (Other assets owned by Intermix were later sold to Demand Media.) The deal was an about-face for a company that eschewed the World Wide Web during the dotcom boom of the 1990s.

The company made another splash in the television industry when it launched MyNetworkTV in 2006. The startup network was established in response to rivals WB and UPN merging to form The CW Television Network.

The following year News Corp. expanded its holdings significantly when it acquired newspaper giant Dow Jones along with its flagship paper The Wall Street Journal for $5.6 billion. A newspaper man at heart Murdoch doggedly pursued Dow Jones and its controlling Bancroft family through a lengthy —and at times contested —negotiation process primarily to get his hands on the flagship title.

In 2008 the company exchanged its 40% stake in DIRECTV along with some regional sports networks and $625 million in cash for Liberty Media's 19% stake in News Corp.

Looking to still expand its interests in television broadcasting in 2011 News Corp acquired UK TV production company Shine Group in a stock swap deal valued at $670 million. Shine which was founded and is managed by Elisabeth Murdoch the daughter of Rupert has operations in 10 territories. The deal gave News Corp. a stronger presence in the increasingly crucial international TV production market.

In 2011 the company finally decided that its Myspace investment failed to pay off as growth in online ad revenue significantly slowed and the social network site decisively lost the battle to attract users against the reigning social media champion Facebook. As a result News Corp. sold Myspace to digital advertising network provider Specific Media for a paltry $35 million. (It also obtained a minority equity stake in Specific Media.)

Also during this time News Corp. was faced with troubles at its News International UK newspaper unit when it became embroiled in scandal. In the summer of 2011 its News of the World was accused of hiring private investigators to hack into citizens' and public officials' voice mails. The paper was eventually shut down after 168 years of publication. In addition several senior executives resigned and the company dropped plans to acquire the remaining 61% of Sky that it didn't already own for about £7.8 billion ($12.5 billion.)

In 2013 News Corp. split itself into two companies. Entertainment assets like Fox News formed a new company called Twenty-First Century Fox while publishing units including The Wall Street Journal The New York Post and HarperCollins formed a company called News Corporation.

EXECUTIVES

CEO, James R. Murdoch, age 42, $3,000,000 total compensation

SEVP and Chairman National Geographic Channels U.S., David Hill, $1,750,000 total compensation

Vice Chairman, Chase Carey, age 61, $4,050,000 total compensation

Chairman and CEO Twentieth Century Fox Film, James N. (Jim) Gianopulos, $1,741,000 total compensation

SEVP and CFO, John P. Nallen, $2,000,000 total compensation

Chairman and CEO Fox Television Group, Gary Newman

Chairman and CEO Fox Television Group, Dana Walden

President Fox Searchlight Pictures, Peter Rice, age 49

EVP Government Affairs, Michael Regan

Chairman and CEO FOX News and Fox Television Stations, Roger Ailes, age 75, $5,000,000 total compensation

EVP and Chief Communications Officer, Julie Henderson

President Digital Fox Networks Group, Brian Sullivan, age 53

EVP and Deputy Group General Counsel, Janet Nova

SEVP Group General Counsel and Chief Compliance Officer, Gerson A. Zweifach, age 62, $3,000,000 total compensation

CEO Star India, Uday Shankar

Vice President Technology and Operations, Marc Cacciola

Vice President Sales And Marketing, Brian Turchin

Group Vice President Digital Media, Ron Stitt
Vice President Fox One Integrated Global Sales And Marketing, Karolina Cuprys
Vice President Product Development and Digital Operations, John (Jack) Fiedler
Co-Chairman, Lachlan K. Murdoch, age 42
Co-Chairman, K. Rupert Murdoch, age 84
Auditors: Ernst & Young LLP

LOCATIONS

HQ: Twenty-First Century Fox Inc
  1211 Avenue of the Americas, New York, NY 10036
Phone: 212 852-7000
Web: www.21cf.com

Sales 2014

	$ mil.	% of total
U.S. and Canada	18,563	64
Europe	5,724	20
Other	4,700	16
Total	**28,987**	**100**

PRODUCTS/OPERATIONS

Sales 2014

	$ mil.	% of total
Cable Network Programming	13,773	46
Filmed Entertainment	9,525	31
Television	4,895	16
Direct Broadcast Satellite Television	2,112	7
Other Corporate and Eliminations	(1318)	-
Total	**28,987**	**100**

Sales 2014

	$ mil.	% of total
Affiliate fees	10,353	36
Content	8,677	30
Advertising	7,609	26
Subscription	1,964	7
Other	384	1
Total	**28,987**	**100**

Selected Operations

Filmed entertainment
  Feature film production and distribution
  Fox Filmed Entertainment
  Fox 2000
  Fox Atomic
  Fox Searchlight Pictures
  Twentieth Century Fox
  Twentieth Century Fox Animation
  Twentieth Century Fox Home Entertainment
  Television production and distribution
  Fox Television Studios
  Twentieth Century Fox Television
  Twentieth Television
Cable network programming
  Big Ten Network (49%)
  Fox Business Network
  Fox College Sports
  Fox International Channels
  LAPTV (32% Latin American pay television)
  Fox Movie Channel
  Fox News Channel
  Fox Pan American Sports (33%)
  Fox Sports en Espa?ol
  Fox Sports Latin America
  Fox Reality
  Fox Soccer Channel
  Fox Sports Net
  FUEL TV
  FX
  National Geographic Channel (67% cable channel)
  NGC Network Latin America (67% National Geographic Channel)
  NGC Network International (75% National Geographic Channel International)
  SPEED
Television
  FOX Broadcasting
  Fox Television Stations
  KCOP (MyNetworkTV Los Angeles)
  KDFI (MyNetworkTV Dallas)
  KDFW (FOX Dallas)
  KMSP (FOX Minneapolis)
  KRIV (FOX Houston)
  KSAZ (FOX Phoenix)

KTBC (FOX; Austin TX)
KTTV (FOX Los Angeles)
KTXH (MyNetworkTV Houston)
KUTP (MyNetworkTV Phoenix)
WAGA (FOX Atlanta)
WDCA (MyNetworkTV; Washington DC)
WFLD (FOX Chicago)
WFTC (MyNetworkTV Minneapolis)
WFXT (FOX Boston)
WHBQ (FOX Memphis)
WJBK (FOX Detroit)
WNYW (FOX New York City)
WOFL (FOX; Orlando FL)
WOGX (FOX; Gainesville FL)
WPWR (MyNetworkTV Chicago)
WTTG (FOX; Washington DC)
WTVT (FOX Tampa)
WTXF (FOX Philadelphia)
WUTB (MyNetworkTV Baltimore)
WWOR (MyNetworkTV New York City)
MyNetworkTV
Shine Ltd. (television production UK)
Star Group (international television broadcasting Asia)
Direct broadcast satellite
  British Sky Broadcasting (39% UK)
  Sky Deutschland (45% Germany)
  SKY Italia

COMPETITORS

CBS Corp	Sony Pictures
Disney	Entertainment
MGM	Time Warner
NBCUniversal	Viacom

HISTORICAL FINANCIALS

Company Type: Public

Income Statement

FYE: June 30

	REVENUE ($ mil.)	NET INCOME ($ mil.)	NET PROFIT MARGIN	EMPLOYEES
06/15	28,987	8,306	28.7%	20,500
06/14	31,867	4,514	14.2%	27,000
06/13	27,675	7,097	25.6%	25,600
06/12	33,706	1,179	3.5%	48,000
06/11	33,405	2,739	8.2%	51,000
Annual Growth	(3.5%)	32.0%	—	(20.4%)

2015 Year-End Financials

Debt ratio: 38.04%
Return on equity: 47.96%
Cash ($ mil.): 8,428
Current ratio: 2.39
Long-term debt ($ mil.): 18,795

No. of shares (mil.): 2,038
Dividends
  Yield: 0.8%
  Payout: 7.0%
Market value ($ mil.): 66,343

	STOCK PRICE ($) FY Close	P/E High/Low		PER SHARE ($) Earnings	Dividends	Book Value
06/15	32.55	10	8	3.90	0.28	8.45
06/14	35.15	18	15	1.99	0.25	7.89
06/13	32.58	11	7	3.03	0.17	7.34
06/12	22.29	47	29	0.47	0.18	10.36
06/11	17.70	18	11	1.04	0.15	11.23
Annual Growth	16.4%	—	—	39.2%	16.4%	(6.9%)

Tyson Foods, Inc.

Tyson is more than simply chicken. One of the largest US chicken producers Tyson's Fresh Meats division makes it a giant in the beef and pork sectors as well. The company also offers value-added processed and pre-cooked meats and refrigerated and frozen prepared foods. Its chicken operations are vertically integrated —the company hatches the eggs supplies contract growers with the chicks and feed and brings them back for processing when ready. Tyson's brands include Tyson Jimmy Dean Hillshire Farm Sara Lee Ball Park Wright Aidells and State Fair. Its customers include retail wholesale and food service customers worldwide.

HISTORY

During the Great Depression Arkansas poultry farmer John Tyson supported his family by selling vegetables and poultry. In 1935 after developing a method for transporting live poultry (he installed a food-and-water trough and nailed small feed cups on a trailer) he bought 500 chickens in Arkansas and sold them in Chicago.

For the next decade Tyson bought sold and transported chickens. By 1947 the year he incorporated the company as Tyson Feed & Hatchery he was raising the chickens himself. He emphasized chicken production opening his first processing plant in 1958 in Springdale where he implemented an ice-packing system that allowed the company to send its products greater distances.

John's son Don took over as manager in 1960 and in 1963 it went public as Tyson Foods. Tyson Country Fresh Chicken (packaged chicken that would become the company's mainstay) was introduced in 1967.

Rapid expansion included a new egg-processing building (1970) a new plant and computerized feed mill (1971) and the acquisitions of Prospect Farms (1969 precooked chicken) and the Ocoma Foods Division (1972 poultry) as well as hog operations.

Health-conscious consumers increasingly turned from red meats to poultry during the 1980s. Tyson became the industry leader with several key acquisitions of poultry operations including the Tastybird division of Valmac (1985) Lane Processing (1986) and Heritage Valley (1986). Its 1989 purchase of Holly Farms added beef and pork processing.

Don Tyson relinquished the CEO position to Leland Tollett in 1991. The company increased its presence in Mexico the next year through a joint venture with poultry producer Trasgo. Also in 1992 the firm plunged into seafood with the purchase of Arctic Alaska Fisheries and Louis Kemp Seafood.

Tyson bought Culinary Foods (frozen foods) and Trasgo in 1994 and the seafood division of International Multifoods in 1995. High feed costs and an oversupply of chickens brought down company earnings the next year. In 1997 the company pleaded guilty to charges that it illegally gave former Agriculture Secretary Mike Espy thousands of dollars' worth of gifts; the settlement included $6 million in fines and fees.

Tyson bought embattled Hudson Foods' poultry operations in 1998. The company said it would take a charge that year of $196 million to restructure. It also sold turkey processor Willow Brook Foods (now part of Cargill Meat Solutions) to Willow Brook management in 1998. That year John H. Tyson grandson of the founder was elected chairman.

In 1999 Tyson sold its seafood business for about $180 million in a two-part transaction to International Home Foods and Trident Seafoods. John Tyson became CEO in 2000.

As the winner in a bidding war with Smithfield Foods in 2001 Tyson agreed to buy IBP Inc. the #1 beef processor and #2 pork processor in the US for nearly $3.2 billion. Tyson tried to back away from the table after accounting irregularities were discovered at an IBP subsidiary but a Delaware judge ordered Tyson to sit down and finish dinner. The deal was made final in September and Tyson changed the beef processor's name to IBP Fresh Meats.

In late 2001 Tyson Foods and six managers were indicted for conspiring to smuggle illegal immigrants from Mexico and Central America to work for lower than legal wages in 15 of its US poultry processing plants. Two managers made plea bargains and testified for the government; another manager committed suicide. Tyson and the remaining three managers were acquitted of the conspiracy charges in 2003.

Suffering from mild indigestion after the merger in 2002 Tyson announced a restructuring to trim some fat from its fresh pork operations and agreed to sell its Specialty Brands (frozen foods) subsidiary. In early 2003 sold off its frozen appetizer business DFG Foods.

Following the discovery of bird flu on a Texas chicken farm in 2004 and the subsequent banning of the importation of US chicken products by other countries Tyson consolidated and automated its poultry operations resulting in hundreds of layoffs at the company.

Tyson announced in 2004 it was being formally investigated by the SEC regarding perquisites given to executives including retired senior chairman Don Tyson and then-current chairman and CEO John Tyson. By August the SEC recommended civil action against the company for its failure to disclose $1.7 million in corporate perks given to Don Tyson without authorization from Tyson's compensation committee. Although Don Tyson had already reimbursed the company $1.53 million for then-unspecified benefits the SEC also announced plans to recommend civil action be taken against him. With neither the company nor Tyson admitting any guilt the case was settled in 2005 with Tyson paying the SEC $700000 in fines and the company $1.5 million. Many of the perks were not disclosed because Don Tyson did not fill out SEC-required questionnaires; however disclosed perks included having the company pay for his housekeeping and lawn maintenance and routine non-business use of the corporate jet by his family and friends.

In 2005 the company opened its largest case-ready meat plant in Sherman Texas. However that January and February it suspended operations at four of its other beef plants and cut back at a fifth due to a shortage of cattle and the loss of beef exports due to the US's 2003 case of BSE (Bovine spongiform encephalopathy or "mad cow" disease).

Growing concern over the role of trans-fatty acids (from hydrogenated vegetable oils) in diet and health led Tyson to begin removing them from its processed foods such as breaded chicken nuggets and chicken tenders. The company announced the removal of trans-fats from all its retail poultry and school foodservice products in 2005.

Recognizing the growing market for alternative and renewable fuels and recognizing its unending supply of meat by-products (in this case such lovelies as fat tallow lard and grease) Tyson decided to get into the alternative fuel market in 2007 with the formation of a 50-50 joint venture with fuel refiner Syntroleum called Dynamic Fuels. The joint venture was set up to explore the possibility of producing synthetic fuel from Tyson's waste products for the diesel- jet- and military-fuel markets. In conjunction with this joint venture Tyson created a new business unit Tyson Renewable Products.

EXECUTIVES

EVP and General Counsel, David L. Van Bebber, age 59

EVP and CFO, Dennis Leatherby, age 55, $600,333 total compensation

President and CEO, Donnie Smith, age 56, $1,092,107 total compensation

EVP and Chief Human Resources Officer, Mary A. Oleksiuk, age 53

SVP Fresh Meats Sales and Marketing, Noel White, age 57, $711,114 total compensation

President North American Operations, Donnie D. King, age 54, $784,046 total compensation

SVP and CIO, Gary Cooper

EVP Corporate Affairs, Sara Lilygren

President Retail Packaged Brands, Andy Callahan

President International and Chief Global Growth Officer, Sally Grimes

EVP Strategy and New Ventures, Hal Carper

EVP Operation Services, Mike Roetzel

CTO, Devin Graham

Executive Vice President Business Process and Continuous Improvement, Russell (Russ) Tooley

Vice President and General Manager Engineered Materials, Jeff Sandorf

Vice President Recruitment Retention And Education, Larry Hopkins

Vice President Foodservice Sales, Joel Sappenfield

Sales National Account Vice President, Devin Cole

National Sales Manager, Scott Rea

Vice President Of Direct Materials, Lindsay Piepho

Vice President Indirect Purchasing Corporate Purchasing, Melanie Russell

Vice President Customer Development East, Bill Creighton

Vice President of Business Development, Lori Simco

Vice President, Les Kimbrough

Division Vice President Case ready Meats Poultry, Bernie Adcock

Vice President Pet Products, William (Bill) Mayer

Vice President Marketing, Bill Welsh

National Sales Manager Grocery Channel, Peter (Pete) Chesna

Operations Vice President, Eddie Chancellor

Vice President, Russell (Russ) Nugent

Vice Presidentof Sales, Mike Brown

Vice President Distribution Sales, Donnie Ganoung

Vice President Of Human Resources Operations, Hector Gonzalez

Vice President Marketing Services, Susan (Sue) Quillin

Tyson CVP, Todd McCool

Vice President, Chad Vacha

Vice President Engineering and Maintenance, David (Dave) Gladbach

Vice President, Thomas (Thom) Dykhouse

Senior Vice President Foodservice Marketing, Kim M Cupelli

Vice President Marketing (Ready to Eat Products and New Ventures), Tom Mertensotto

RSM West Coast CVP, Kristopher Duckworth

Vice President Operations, Bo Watson

Vice President Consumer Prod Customer Development, David (Dave) Bray

Vice President Federal Governmental Relations, Chuck Penry

Vice President Operations Accounting, Rodney (Rod) Edwards

Vice President Sales Productivity, Eric Stadler

Vice President Diversity, Cathy Clark

Vice President Of Business Development, Chris Benson

Vice President And General Manager, Darwin Gore

Vice President Fresh Meats Foodservice, Glenn Strickholm

Vice President Information Technology, Nancy Higginbotham

Vice President, Bob Kooyman

Sls Deli Vice President, Brent Schmiegelow

Vice President Food Service Sales East, Mike Curtin

Senior Vice President Corporate Marketing And Communications, Charlie Young

Senior Vice President Business Development Natural Fds, Joseph (Jo) Depippo

Vice President Internal Audit, April Gage

Vice President General Manager, Bernard F Leonard
Assistant Vice President Credit Finance, Larry Alsip
Vice President Channel and Customer Business Development, Mark Elser
Vice President Marketing, Eric LeBlanc
Senior Vice President and Marketing Manager, Jeff Sandore
Vice President Food Service Operations, Doug Ramsey
Senior Vice President Chief Accounting Officer And Controller, Craig Hart
Vice President and General Manager the Pork Group Inc, John (Jack) Thomas
Vice President, Robert (Bob) Shuey
Vice President, Bill Mayer
Vice President Of Pork Procurement, Gary Machan
Vice President International Finance And Accountin, Hubert Mendonca
Chairman, John H. Tyson, age 62
Treasurer, Michelle Brown
Secretary, R Hudson
Auditors: PricewaterhouseCoopers LLP

LOCATIONS

HQ: Tyson Foods, Inc.
 2200 West Don Tyson Parkway, Springdale, AR 72762-6999
Phone: 479 290-4000   **Fax:** 479 290-7984
Web: www.tyson.com

PRODUCTS/OPERATIONS

2015 Sales

	% of total
Beef	41
Chicken	27
Prepared foods	18
Pork	12
Other	2
Total	**100**

Selected Products and Brands

Meats fresh
 Certified Angus Beef
 Chairman' s Reserve (beef)
 Golden Trophy Steaks (beef)
 Open Prairie Angus Beef
 Star Ranch Angus Beef
 Supreme Tender (pork)
 Tyson (beef chicken Cornish game hens pork)
 Tyson Holly Farms (chicken)
Meats processed
 Bonici (foodservice; chicken wings pizza toppings)
 Chicken Twists (foodservice)
 Premium Chunk (canned chicken)
 Right Size (foodservice; beef patties chicken patties)
 Tyson (bacon beef chicken pork)
 Wright (bacon)
Prepared foods
 Any' Tizers (chicken snacks)
 Doskocil (value-added meats for pizza industry)
 Heat ' N Eat Entrees (beef chicken pork)
 Lady Aster (entrees)
 Mexican Original (flour and corn tortilla products)
 Skillet Creations (beef and chicken meal kits)

COMPETITORS

Big Heart Pet Brands	Kraft Foods Group Inc.
Buckhead Beef	Laura' s Lean Beef Co.
CGC	Mars Incorporated
Cargill	Mondelez International
Casa de Oro Foods	National Beef Packing
Clougherty Packing	New Market Poultry
Coleman Natural Foods	Perdue Incorporated
ConAgra	Petaluma Poultry
Cooper Farms	Pilgrim' s Pride
Eberly Poultry	Plainville Farms
Empire Kosher Poultry	Raeford Farms
Foster Farms	Rosen' s Diversified
Freedman Meats	Sanderson Farms
Gruma	Shelton' s

H. J. Heinz Limited
Hormel
JBS
Koch Foods

Smithfield Foods
Tecumseh Poultry
U.S. Premium Beef

HISTORICAL FINANCIALS

Company Type: Public

Income Statement

FYE: October 3

	REVENUE ($ mil.)	NET INCOME ($ mil.)	NET PROFIT MARGIN	EMPLOYEES
10/15*	41,373	1,220	2.9%	113,000
09/14	37,580	864	2.3%	124,000
09/13	34,374	778	2.3%	115,000
09/12	33,278	583	1.8%	115,000
10/11	32,266	750	2.3%	115,000
Annual Growth	**6.4%**	**12.9%**	**—**	**(0.4%)**

*Fiscal year change

2015 Year-End Financials

Debt ratio: 29.23%
Return on equity: 12.92%
Cash ($ mil.): 688
Current ratio: 1.52
Long-term debt ($ mil.): 6,010

No. of shares (mil.): 369
Dividends
 Yield: 0.0%
 Payout: 13.5%
Market value ($ mil.): 16,380

	STOCK PRICE ($) FY Close	P/E High/Low		PER SHARE ($) Earnings	Dividends	Book Value
10/15*	44.39	15	12	2.95	0.40	26.26
09/14	37.74	18	11	2.37	0.30	23.64
09/13	28.60	14	7	2.12	0.30	18.03
09/12	16.02	13	9	1.58	0.16	16.75
10/11	17.36	10	7	1.97	0.16	15.29
Annual Growth	**26.5%**	—	—	**10.6%**	**25.7%**	**14.5%**

*Fiscal year change

U.S. Bancorp (DE)

Not quite a bank for the entire US U.S. Bancorp is nonetheless one of the largest bank holding companies in the nation with $403 billion in assets. It owns U.S. Bank (the US' 5th largest commercial bank) and other subsidiaries that provide consumer and commercial loans deposits and credit cards as well as merchant processing mortgage banking trust and investment management brokerage services insurance and corporate payments. The bank has more than 3000 branches and 5000 ATMs in 25 states in the Midwest and West including one of the most extensive networks of branches inside grocery stores. Commercial loans account for roughly 30% of its total loan portfolio; commercial real estate loans 17%.

Operations
The bank holding company's major lines of business are wholesale banking and commercial real estate; consumer and small business banking; wealth management and securities services; payment services; and treasury and corporate support. The company is also one of the largest providers of corporate credit cards and payment services to the US government. Its largest fee-gathering subsidiary is Elavon a leading processor of merchant credit card transactions in the US Canada Latin America and Europe.

Geographic Reach
U.S. Bancorp provide services through a network of more than 3175 banking offices in 25 US states and more than 5025 ATMs principally in the Midwest and West. California is its largest

market.Sales and MarketingThe bank spent $382 million on marketing and business development expenses in 2014 or about 7% more than in 2013 and about 2% less than it spent in 2012.

Financial Performance
U.S. Bancorp's revenue rebounded by more than 1% to $21.39 billion in 2014 mostly thanks to higher fee-related income including 10% growth in its trust and investment fees as a result of account growth stronger market conditions and business expansion. Adding some headwinds against growth the bank's mortgage banking revenue declined by 26% as it originated and sold fewer of its mortgage loans held for sale. Profit rose for a fifth-straight year with net income inching up by less than 1% to $5.85 billion in 2014. Profit grew thanks to a combination of higher revenue lower interest expenses as the bank paid lower interest on deposits and other debt and lower credit loss provisions as credit quality in the company's loan portfolio improved.Operations provided $5.33 billion or 53% less cash than in 2013 mostly as the bank earned less in proceeds from its sales on loans-held-for-sale.

Strategy
U.S. Bancorp has been growing its business through acquisitions sometimes expanding its operations internationally. Since the Great Recession the bank has found success in purchasing troubled banks for cheap but generally pursues acquisitions to expand service offerings add branches and extend its reach pad its interest-earning loan assets and add customer deposits to fuel future loan business. U.S. Bancorp has also been expanding its fee-based services such as treasury management corporate trust institutional custody merchant processing and freight payment services. Indeed in 2014 fee-related income added more than $270 million to the bank's revenue and greatly offset the heavy losses in mortgage banking income that year as the bank originated and sold fewer held-for-sale mortgage loans.

The bank has also been dabbling in technology to retain and grow its customer base. In 2014 it piloted software that lets customers speak a simple pass phrase such as “my voice is my password” to access a credit card account on a mobile device. In addition as a complement to Access Online the bank's exclusive data-management and reporting tool the company launched a new app that provides bank customers with real-time access to essential account information from virtually anywhere. Also that year U.S. Bank and Viewpost North America teamed up to offer a co-branded microsite. Hosted on the U.S. Bank website small business customers can easily connect their bank accounts to the Viewpost network where they can also connect to their trading partners to exchange electronic invoices and payments.

Mergers and AcquisitionsIn 2014 U.S. Bancorp Fund Services agreed to acquire Quintillion Limited (Quintillion) an Ireland-based full-service hedge fund administrator to expand its alternative investment servicing network and support the European investment community.

Also in 2014 the company acquired Chicago-area Charter One branch from Citizens Financial Group giving U.S. Bank more than 160 branches in the Chicagoland area and nearly doubles U.S. Bank's deposit market share in the Chicago area.Growing its corporate trust services business that year the company agreed to buy the document custodian business of Ally Bank. As a document custodian U.S. Bank stores and safeguards a wide array of collateral loan files including commercial and residential mortgages equipment leases home equity and improvement loans and vehicle loans and leases. In 2013 Bancorp entered into a definitive agreement to buy the municipal bond trustee business of Deutsche Bank. The deal will add $57 billion to the more than $3 trillion in assets under administration within U.S. Bank's corporate trust division. U.S. Bank has approximately 125000 trust and agency contracts. The Deutsche Bank transaction will add another 1100 contracts.

Also in 2013 U.S. Bancorp's Elavon subsidiary acquired Toronto-based Collective Point of Sale Solutions Ltd. The deal expanded Elavon's presence and distribution network in Canada.

HISTORY

When Farmers and Millers Bank was founded in 1853 it operated out of a strongbox in a rented storefront. After surviving a panic in the 1850s the bank became part of the national banking system in 1863 as First National Bank of Milwaukee. The bank grew and in 1894 it merged with Merchants Exchange Bank (founded 1870).

In 1919 the bank merged again with Wisconsin National Bank (founded 1892) to form First Wisconsin National Bank of Milwaukee a leading financial institution in the area from the 1920s on.

First Wisconsin grew through purchases over the next decade though the number of banks fell after the 1929 stock market crash; by the end of WWII it had 11 banks. State and federal legislation particularly the 1956 Bank Holding Company Act (which proscribed acquisitions and branching) constrained postwar growth. In the 1970s Wisconsin eased restrictions on intrastate branching and the bank began to grow again.

Growth accelerated in the late 1980s after Wisconsin and surrounding states legalized interstate banking in adjoining states in 1987. That year First Wisconsin bought seven Minnesota banks and then moved into Illinois. The company focused on strong well-run institutions. Also that year it sold its headquarters and used the proceeds to fund more buys. In 1988 in its first foray outside the Midwest the company bought Metro Bancorp in Phoenix targeting midwestern retirees moving to Arizona.

In 1989 First Wisconsin changed its name to Firstar. The early 1990s saw the company move into Iowa (Banks of Iowa 1990) buy in-state rivals (Federated Bank Geneva Capital Corporation 1992) and roll into Illinois (DSB Corporation 1993). The next year it bought First Southeast Banking Corp. (of Wisconsin) and merged it along with Firstar Bank Racine and Firstar Bank Milwaukee into one bank.

To strengthen its position against larger competitors Firstar continued its buying spree in 1995 (Chicago bank First Colonial Bankshares and Investors Bank Corp. of Minneapolis/St. Paul) and 1996 (Jacob Schmidt Company). The acquisitions left the company bloated: In 1996 Firstar began a restructuring designed to cut costs and increase margins. The restructuring project ended in 1997 but by then its performance lagged behind other midwestern banks considerably. In an effort to diversify it allied with EVEREN Securities to offer debt underwriting and sales fixed income products and public finance advisory services. But it was too little too late; under pressure from major stockholders to seek a partner Firstar began looking for a buyer.

It found Star Banc. Established in 1863 as The First National Bank of Cincinnati under a bank charter signed by Abraham Lincoln Star Banc over the years added branches and bought other banks. The company renamed all of its subsidiary banks Star Bank in 1988 and took the name Star Banc in 1989.

In 1998 Star Banc chairman Jerry Grundhofer approached Firstar about a combination. Negotiations proceeded quickly and a new Firstar was born.

The next year Firstar bought Mercantile Bancorporation. The purchase enabled the bank to expand its international banking services into such markets as Kansas Nebraska and Missouri. In 2000 the company made arrangements to buy U.S. Bancorp a Minneapolis-based bank with roots dating back to 1929. Under the terms of the acquisition Firstar would shed its own name in favor of the more appropriate U.S. Bancorp moniker. U.S. Bancorp completed the conversion of Firstar Bank branches to the U.S. Bank moniker during 2002.

EXECUTIVES

Vice Chairman Wealth Management and Securities Services, Terrance R. (Terry) Dolan, age 53

Vice President Media Relations, Teri Charest

Vice Chairman Payment Services; Chairman and CEO Elavon, Pamela A. (Pam) Joseph, age 55, $675,000 total compensation

EVP Human Resources, Jennie P. Carlson, age 54

Chairman President and CEO, Richard K. Davis, age 57, $1,200,000 total compensation

President and COO, Andrew Cecere, age 54, $725,000 total compensation

EVP General Counsel and Corporate Secretary, James L. Chosy, age 51

Vice Chairman Wholesale Banking, Richard B. (Dick) Payne, age 67, $500,000 total compensation

EVP, John R. Elmore, age 59

Vice Chairman and Chief Risk Officer, P. William (Bill) Parker, age 58, $550,000 total compensation

Vice Chairman Technology and Operations Services, Jeffry H. (Jeff) von Gillern, age 49

Vice Chairman Consumer Banking Sales and Support, Kent V. Stone, age 57

EVP and Chief Credit Officer, Mark G. Runkel, age 39

Vice Chairman and CFO, Kathleen A. (Kathy) Rogers, age 49

Vice Chairman Payment Services, Shailesh M. Kotwal, age 50

EVP Strategy and Corporate Affairs, Katherine B. Quinn, age 50

President Retail Payment Solutions (RPS), John Steward

Vice President And Trust Manager, Terri L Dowell

Assistant Vice President Communications, Bill Brady

Vice President Consumer Credit Products, David (Dave) Herpers

Senior Vice President Small Business, Alan (Al) Ellison

Vice President of Information Technology Security, Coni Pasch

Senior Vice President Dealer Services Regional Manager North Central Region, Dave Donarski

Vice President Fraud Data Analytics, Jill McFarling

Senior Vice President Risk Infrastructure, Jim Putman

Assistant Vice President Application Consultant Commercial Leasing, Krishna Devarajulu

Vice President Procurement Operations Manager, Michael Lori

Vice President, Jill Gomez

Senior Vice President Customer Solutions, Mary Carney

Vice President US Bancorp Investments and Insurance, John (Jack) Falk

Executive Vice President, Ross Carey

Vice President Ultra High Net Worth And Private Client Reserves, Amy Satterlund

Senior Vice President Prepaid Card Services, Johnnie Carroll

Vice President Retail Payments Innovation, Kenneth (Ken) Beirne

Vice President, Scott Miller

Senior Vice President Risk Analytics, Jacob Seljan

Vice President Mergers and Technology Integration, James (Jamie) McVey

Vice President Senior Financial Consultant, John Leos

Senior Vice President Collections Control, James (Jamie) Blyskal

Senior Vice President Operational Risk Management, Andrew Dell

Vice President, Michael (Mel) Dorn

Vice President Credit Risk Assessment, Jennifer (Jen) Briglia

Vice President Treasury Management Consultant, Paul Kozar

Vice President, Scott Farrell

Assistant Vice President Operations, Donnette Reid

Executive Vice President Chief Financial Officer Cascade Financial And Cascade Bank; Treas, Roberto Salinas

Vice President corporate Credit Risk Manager, Brian Richter

Vice President Credit Approval Commercial Real Esate and Community Banks, Kyle Schmidt

Vice President of Market Information and Research, Jill Enabnit

Vice President Chicago West District Manager, Mike Fasshauer

Vice President Correspondent Banking, Mark Sowinski

Vice President Information Technology Service Managment, Jim Berghs

Vice President Ultra High Net Worth And Private Client Reserves, Christine Hansen

Vice President And Relationship Manager, Terry Neal

Senior Vice President, Mehrasa Raygani

Senior Vice President Risk Manager, Kirt Bolte

Vice President Technology Finance Group, Gregory Giannone

Vice President Senior Property Manager, Andrew (Andy) McGlenon

Assistant Vice President Operations Manager, Kari Schlotfeldt

Vice President Treasury Management Consultant, Joan Pearce

Vice President, Anthony Ziman

Senior Vice President Insurance Services Division, Frank Ahlborn

Vice President, Kelly Matsuoka

Vice President, Zenaida Maniates

Vice President, Michael Lamarche Michael (Mel) Lamarche

Vice President And Manager Commercial Operations, Victor Kapusinski

Vice President BCM, Geno Pandolfi

Vice President, Cory Patrick

Assistant Vice President, Dhiren Patel

Vice President, Steve Kramer

Senior Vice President risk Management L Retail Pay, Marcia Palmer

Technology Compliance Manager And Vice President, Paul Betz

Assistant Vice President, Darrell Hirsch

Executive Vice President, Eric Milos

Vice President Information Technology, Anita Beltran

Senior Vice President, Terry Neher

Vice President Corporate Banking Portfolio Manager, Daniel (Dan) Yu

Senior Vice President, Wendy Waldron

Assistant Vice President, Maureen Splettstaszer

Vice President Business Development, Chris Venhoff

Vice President of Operation, Sean Skaggs

Vice President Enterprise Network and Telephony Services, Brian Vik

Senlor Vice President National Corporate Banklng, Barry Litwin

Vice President Portfolio Manager, Magnus McDowell

Senior Vice President Treasury, David (Dave) Hill

Vice President Commercial Banking, Beth Eaton

Vice President Foreign Exchange, Andy Rindels

Vice President, Roger Gross
Senior Vice President Director Internal Risk, Patricia (Pat) Ryan
Senior Vice President, Christopher (Chris) Schaaf
Vice President, Lisa Gutierrez
Assistant Vice President Commercial and Business Banking Officer, Sara Le
Vice President, Howard Goldberg
Executive Vice President Managing Director Europe Elavon, Simon Haslam
Senior Vice President Treasury Management Product Management, Mary Burchette
Vice President, Suzanne Bedros
Vice President, Kevin Penders
Vice President and Credit Manager, Melanie Rossetta
Senior of Vice President, David (Dave) Albanesi
Senior Vice President, Carol Gilstrap
Vice President Corporate Credit Risk Management, Gregory Gay
Vice President Loan Administration, Cheryl Dingess
Vice President, John Pearson
Regional President Community Banking, Scott Powell
Senior Vice President of Asset Management, Steve Brigger
Vice President of Credit Administration, Scott Kohls
Vice President, Betty Kinoshita
Senior Vice President Group Head National Corporate and Institutional Banking, Joseph (Jo) Murphy
Assistant Vice President Operations Manager, Jocelyn Kilpatrick
Vice President Information Technology, Breck Rumley
Vice President Quality Management, Richard McCarthy
Senior Vice President Of Finance, Kurt Swiecichowski
Vice President, Anthony Messina
Vice President Technology, Michele Nestel
Vice President Regional Sales Manager International Banking Group, Brian Cobb
Vice President and Account Manager, Patricia (Pat) Welling
Vice President Operations, Mark Sutherland
Vice President, Joseph (Jo) Bree
Assistant Vice President, Rita Halbur
Vice President, Philip Koski
Senior Vice President Risk Management Strategy Execution, Michael (Mel) Leary
Assistant Vice President Voice Implementation Projects, Joy Abts
Vice President Information Technology, Alfonso Gonzalez
Senior Vice President Quality Assurance, AnnMarie Janke
Vice President Area Manager, John Cronen
Senior Vice President And Senior Investment Strategist, Rob Haworth
Assistant Vice President, Ashley Johnson
Vice President Sales, Richard Struck
Vice President and Director, Suzanne Galvin
Vice President Loan Capital Markets, Dipti Goel
Senior Vice President, Frederick (Fred) Body
Senior Vice President Regional Credit Officer, Randall Borchardt
Vice President Foreign Exchange Trading, Peter Azzinaro
Senior Financial Advisor Vice President Private Client Reserve, Joel Schwartz
Senior Vice President And Business Infor, Mark Sauceman
Vice President Portfolio Manager, Matt Scullin
Vice President Comercial Team Lead, Corey Hansen
Vice President, George Deer
Vice President Business Banking Manager, Brent Blume

Senior Vice President commercial Real Estate relationship Manager, Curt Steiner
Assistant Vice President, Becky Burton
Senior Vice President Sales, Doug Ichiuji
Assistant Vice President, Melody Scott
Assistant Vice President Account Manager, Lisa Moorehead
Asst.Vice President Technology Services, Laura Rumrey
Vice President commercial Banking portfolio Manager, Alain Kamdem
Assistant Vice President, Jodi Shireman
Vice President commercial Banking portfolio Manager, Jason (rodney) Winters
Vice President Program and Project Management, Bernie White
Vice President, Riky Wahyu
Senior Vice President, Kevin Miller
Auditors: Ernst & Young LLP

LOCATIONS

HQ: U.S. Bancorp (DE)
800 Nicollet Mall, Minneapolis, MN 55402
Phone: 651 466-3000
Web: www.usbank.com

Selected Locations
Arizona
Arkansas
California
Colorado
Idaho
Illinois
Indiana
Iowa
Kansas
Kentucky
Minnesota
Missouri
Montana
Nebraska
Nevada
New Mexico
North Dakota
Ohio
Oregon
South Dakota
Tennessee
Utah
Washington
Wisconsin
Wyoming

PRODUCTS/OPERATIONS

2014 Revenue

	$ mil.	% of total
Interest		
Loans	10,113	46
Investment securities	1,866	9
Loans held for sale	128	1
Other	121	1
Noninterest		
Merchant processing services	1,511	6
Trust & investment management fees	1,252	6
Credit & debit card revenue	1,021	5
Mortgage banking	1,009	5
Commercial products	854	4
Corporate payment products	724	3
Deposit service charges	693	3
Treasury management fees	545	3
ATM processing services	321	2
Investment products fees & commissions	191	1
Other	1,043	5
Total	**21,392**	**100**

Selected Subsidiaries
111 Tower Investors Inc. (Minnesota)
Access Mortgage Solutions LLC (Delaware)
AIS Europe Limited (UK)
AIS Fund Administration Ltd. (Cayman Islands)
CF Title Co. (Delaware)
Daimler Title Co. (Delaware)
DSL Service Company (California)
Eclipse Funding LLC (Delaware)
Elan Life Insurance Company Inc. (Arizona)

COMPETITORS

BancWest	Huntington Bancshares
Bank of America	JPMorgan Chase
Capital One	KeyCorp
Citigroup	MUFG Americas Holdings
Fifth Third	TCF Financial
First National of Nebraska	Wells Fargo
Great Western Bancorp	Zions Bancorporation

HISTORICAL FINANCIALS

Company Type: Public

Income Statement

FYE: December 31

	ASSETS ($ mil.)	NET INCOME ($ mil.)	INCOME AS % OF ASSETS	EMPLOYEES
12/14	402,529	5,851	1.5%	66,750
12/13	364,021	5,836	1.6%	65,565
12/12	353,855	5,647	1.6%	64,486
12/11	340,122	4,872	1.4%	62,529
12/10	307,786	3,317	1.1%	60,584
Annual Growth	**6.9%**	**15.2%**	**—**	**2.5%**

2014 Year-End Financials

Debt ratio: 6.19%	No. of shares (mil.): 1,785
Return on equity: 13.83%	Dividends
Cash ($ mil.): 10,654	Yield: 2.1%
Current ratio: —	Payout: 31.3%
Long-term debt ($ mil.): —	Market value ($ mil.): 80,275

	STOCK PRICE ($) FY Close	P/E High/Low	PER SHARE ($) Earnings	Dividends	Book Value
12/14	44.95	15 13	3.08	0.97	24.35
12/13	40.40	13 11	3.00	0.89	22.53
12/12	31.94	12 10	2.84	0.78	20.86
12/11	27.05	12 8	2.46	0.50	17.79
12/10	26.97	16 12	1.73	0.20	15.37
Annual Growth	**13.6%**	**— —**	**15.5%**	**48.2%**	**12.2%**

U.S. VENTURE INC.

Smitten with the love of oil distribution the founding Schmidt family owns and operates U.S. Venture (formerly U.S. Oil). The company's U.S. Oil division (formerly U.S. Petroleum Operations) supplies refined oil products to residents in the Midwest and does a lot more. In addition to the wholesale distribution of oil products (its largest revenue generator) the company operates gas stations and installs gas pumps tanks and other petroleum-related equipment. U.S. Venture also provides plumbing and HVAC services (Design Air) collects used waste oil to be processed into burner fuel and has a metal custom manufacturing unit.

Geographic Reach

Under its U.S. AutoForce brand U.S. Oil also operates about a dozen warehouses in Illinois Minnesota Missouri Nebraska Iowa South Dakota and Wisconsin offering auto parts (for brakes exhausts and suspensions) and tires. U.S. Venture operates 12 refined products terminals across the Midwest (with a total storage capacity of about 127 million gallons at its bulk fuel storage tanks) including the Cheboygan 164000 barrels facility.

Operations

U.S. Venture's operating divisions are:

Design Air (serving commercial and residential HVAC contractors throughout Wisconsin and Upper Michigan);

Express Convenience Centers (gas stations and convenience stores throughout Wisconsin);

U.S. AutoForce (tires automotive parts and lubricants);

U.S. Custom Manufacturing (forming and supplying metal tubing for the automotive furniture and lawn and garden and other industries; it also makes frame components handles and rails);

U.S. Lubricants (lubricants for trucking industrial and commercial customers in the Upper Midwest);

U.S. Oil (bulk storage terminals wholesale and branded distribution of petroleum products multiple-brand C-store Jobbership and gas station-related real estate activities); and

U.S. Petroleum Equipment (tanks pumps and related equipment for petroleum-based products and vehicle lift equipment; it also offers installation and lighting services throughout Wisconsin and Upper Michigan).Strategy

The company has grown its geographic presence through complementary acquisitions.

Mergers and Acquisitions

Expanding its green fuel options in 2013 U.S. Oil bought six compressed natural gas fueling stations from We Energies (two in Milwaukee and one each in Appleton Franklin Racine and Waukesha) bring U.S. Oil's total to nine in Wisconsin. U.S. Oil plans to add a minimum of 50 additional GAIN Clean Fueling sites by 2018.

Growing is presence in North Central Wisconsin and the Upper Peninsula of Michigan in 2012 the bought Draeger Oil Company's branded dealer division. Under the terms of the deal U.S. Oil provides fuel supply to more than 50 retail gas stations while Draeger retained the transportation portion.

U.S. Ventures (U.S. Oil) also expanded its petroleum products distribution presence in Indiana in 2012 through the purchase of Farmersburg-based Trueblood Oil's branded wholesale fuel supply business.

Company Background

U.S. Oil was established in the 1950s as Schmidt Oil by the sons of local fuel distributor Albert Schmidt who landed his first job in the oil business in 1923. The company changed its name to U.S. Venture in 2010 to reflect the company's increasingly diverse portfolio of entrepreneurial businesses.

EXECUTIVES

Vice President Sales and Marketing, Paul Kubic
Vice President Human Resources, Lori Hoersch
Secretary and Treasurer, Ray Schmidt
Auditors: DELOITTE & TOUCHE LLP MILWAU

LOCATIONS

HQ: U.S. VENTURE INC.
425 BETTER WAY, APPLETON, WI 549156192
Phone: 9207396101
Web: WWW.USVENTURE.COM

PRODUCTS/OPERATIONS

Selected Operations

Design Air (heating and air conditioning equipment)
Express Convenience Centers (gas stations and car washes)
U.S. AutoForce (exhaust pipe manufacturing and autoparts distribution)
U.S. Custom Manufacturing (tube bending and fabrication)
U.S. Lubricants (motor oil and related products)
U.S. Oil (gasoline fuel oil and natural gas)
U.S. Petroleum Equipment (petroleum-related equipment installation)

COMPETITORS

7-Eleven	Quality State Oil
Apex Oil	Company
Marathon Oil	QuikTrip
Motiva Enterprises	Sunoco

HISTORICAL FINANCIALS

Company Type: Private

Income Statement

FYE: July 31

	REVENUE ($ mil.)	NET INCOME ($ mil.)	NET PROFIT MARGIN	EMPLOYEES
07/14	9,088	49	0.5%	1,000
07/13	7,346	47	0.6%	—
07/12	5,906	60	1.0%	—
07/11	4,847	0	—	—
Annual Growth	23.3%	—	—	—

2014 Year-End Financials

Debt ratio: ——
Return on equity: 0.50%
Cash ($ mil.): 5
Current ratio: 0.90
Long-term debt ($ mil.): —

Dividends
Yield: —
Payout: —
Market value ($ mil.): —

UGI Corp.

UGI (derived from its original name United Gas Improvement) is a leading energy services marketing and distribution company and distributes propane across the US and internationally. The company is led by its 26%-owned propane distributor AmeriGas Partners the largest source of the holding company's sales and a leading US propane marketer. It also has utility operations: Its UGI Utilities subsidiary distributes electricity to 62000 customers and gas to about 617000 customers in Pennsylvania. The company's other operations include energy marketing in the mid-Atlantic region propane distribution in Asia and Europe and electricity generation and energy services.

Geographic Reach

Internationally UGI has interests in propane distributors in Austria China the Czech Republic Denmark Finland France Hungary Norway Poland Romania Slovakia Sweden and Switzerland primarily through its Antargaz and Flaga subsidiaries. France-based Antargaz annually sells more than 156 million retail gallons of propane; Flaga 326 million gallons. AvantiGas operates in the UK.

Operations

The company's segments comprise of AmeriGas Propane; an international LPG segment comprising UGI France; an international LPG segment principally comprising Flaga and AvantiGas; Gas Utility; Energy Services; and Electric Generation. The company refers to both international segments together as UGI International; and Energy Services and Electric Generation together as Midstream & Marketing. UGI's largest segment AmeriGas (42% of fiscal 2015 sales) sells propane to more than 2 million retail and wholesale customers a year in 50 US states. AmeriGas also offers propane-related products and services and provides propane storage services. UGI subsidiary UGI Enterprises which operates the company's midstream and marketing division markets natural gas and electricity and offers HVAC (heating ventilation and air-conditioning) and energy management services to more than 150000 (unable to verify) customers in the mid-Atlantic region of the US. Another subsidiary

UGI Development is involved in power generation ventures in Pennsylvania. Its natural gas distribution utility business (Gas Utility) is conducted through its wholly owned subsidiary UGI Utilities and its subsidiaries UGI Penn Natural Gas and UGI Central Penn.

Sales and Marketing

UGI's US propane distribution business is conducted through AmeriGas Partners. AmeriGas Propane is responsible for managing the Partnership which serves customers from 2000 propane distribution locations. It sells propane primarily to residential commercial/industrial motor fuel agricultural and wholesale customers. Commercial users include hotels restaurants churches warehouses and retail stores. The Partnership operates as an interstate carrier in 48 states throughout the continental United States. It is also licensed as a carrier in the Canadian Provinces of Ontario British Columbia and Quebec. In fiscal 2015 AmeriGas Partners distributed more than 1.2 billion gallons. Some 96% of the Partnership's 2015 sales (based on gallons sold) were to retail accounts and 4% were to wholesale and supply customers.

It supplies power to customers through the use of the transmission and distribution facilities of 20 utility systems.

Financial Performance

UGI's revenues saw a 19% decline to $6.7 billion in fiscal 2015. AmeriGas Propane's revenues decreased by 22% due to a decline in retail propane revenues as a result of lower average retail selling prices principally the result of lower propane product costs and lower retail volumes sold. Also wholesale propane revenues decreased due to lower wholesale volumes sold and lower wholesale selling prices. The decline was also due to dip in revenue from UGI International as a result of the combined impact on revenues of the significantly weaker euro and to a lesser extent the British pound sterling and the effects of lower average LPG sales prices at each of its European LPG businesses. Midstream & Marketing's revenues also declined during fiscal 2015 due to lower natural gas retail power peaking and Electric Generation revenues. The lower retail power revenues reflected decreased sales volumes and lower prices. The 5% decline in gas utility also contributed to the decline. UGI's net income decreased by 17% in fiscal 2015 due to a decline in revenues. Despite lower net income the company's operating cash flow increased by 16% in fiscal 2015 due to a change in inventories and an increase in cash provided by accounts receivable and accrued utility revenues. The increase in cash flow from changes in operating working capital reflected the impact on such cash flows from a major decline in energy commodity costs.

Strategy

UGI is focused on expanding its core natural gas electric and propane operations. It is also seeking complementary acquisition opportunities to continue its growth in the US and abroad.

During fiscal 2015 the company completed a number of transactions in pursuit of this strategy and made progress on larger internally generated capital projects including infrastructure projects to further support the development of natural gas in the Marcellus Shale region of Pennsylvania. The company also seeks to grow its midstream asset business by constructing new pipelines and gathering systems. That year UGI's Energy Services unit commenced service on the Union Dale Lateral pipeline to transport locally produced natural gas to PNG and completed its Temple LNG project that increased the liquefaction capacity of its natural gas liquefaction storage and vaporization facility in Temple Pennsylvania. In addition Energy Services made progress on its participation in the PennEast Pipeline project to develop an approximately 118-mile pipeline from Pennsylvania to New Jersey.

Mergers and Acquisitions

In 2015 the company's French subsidiary France SAS (formerly UGI Bordeaux Holding) acquired TOTAL's LPG distribution business in France for €423 million. The Totalgaz Acquisition nearly doubles UGI's retail LPG distribution business in France. That year Flaga acquired Total's LPG distribution business in Hungary.

In 2014 Energy Services acquired a retail natural gas marketing business located principally in western Pennsylvania from EQT Energy LLC an affiliate of EQT Corporation.

HISTORY

United Gas Improvement was set up in 1882 by Philadelphia industrialist Thomas Dolan and other investors to acquire a gasworks and a new coalgas manufacturing process. The firm also bought electric utilities and street railways across the US and moved into construction. The 1935 Public Utility Holding Company Act led to United Gas Improvement's restructuring when the SEC ordered the divestiture of many of its operations in 1941. The company converted to natural gas in the 1950s and entered the liquefied petroleum gas (LPG) business in 1959. It became UGI Corporation in 1968.

UGI shifted its emphasis to propane in the late 1980s buying Petrolane in 1995 and combining it with AmeriGas Propane to create AmeriGas Partners which then went public. Overseas UGI launched a joint venture in 1996 to build an LPG import project in Romania. The next year it signed a deal to distribute propane in China.

In 1999 UGI moved into consumer products by opening its first Hearth USA retail store in Rockville Maryland which offered hearth items spas grills and patio accessories. It ventured into a growing European market by purchasing FLAGA GmbH a leading gas distributor in Austria and the Czech Republic.

That year a 1997 Pennsylvania law kicked in restructuring the state's electricity industry and enabling customers to choose their electricity provider. In response UGI separated its distribution and power generation operations and in 2000 contributed the bulk of its generation assets to a partnership with Allegheny Energy that sells power to UGI Utilities and other distributors.

In 2001 UGI Enterprises purchased a 20% interest in French propane distributor Antargaz. Also that year the company closed its Hearth USA retail stores. Through its UGI Energy Services subsidiary UGI completed the acquisition of TXU Energy in 2003.

UGI acquired the remaining 80% interest in Antargaz in 2004 expanding its operations in France. Later that year the company continued its European expansion through the acquisition of BP's retail propane distribution business in the Czech Republic.

In 2006 the company acquired the natural gas utility assets of PG Energy for about $580 million. During the next year its Gas Utility unit purchased approximately 79 billion cu. ft. of natural gas for sale to retail core market and off-system sales customers.

To expand its base of gas customers in Pennsylvania in 2008 UGI Utilities acquired PPL Gas Utilities for $32 million. It soon changed that company's name to UGI Central Penn Gas.

In 2010 UGI took advantage of BP's need to raise cash due to its oil spill problems and acquired the liquefied petroleum gas distribution business of BP in Denmark. It also picked up Shell's LPG operations in Poland. Both deals expanded UGI's footprint in the European LPG market.

In fiscal year 2012 the company acquired some of Shell's LPG distribution operations in Europe. The terms of the deal were not disclosed but included the businesses in Belgium Denmark Finland Luxembourg the Netherlands Norway Sweden and the UK adding to the UGI's European market growth with an estimated 300 million gallons of LPG.

That year AmeriGas Partners acquired Energy Transfer Partners' propane distribution business (Heritage Propane). The acquired business conducted propane operations in 41 US states through HOLP and Titan Propane LLC.

In 2013 UGI subsidiary Flaga acquired BP's LPG distribution business in Poland. BP's Polish LPG business distributes more than 150 million gallons of LPG a year.

EXECUTIVES

Vice President Accounting and Financial Control and Chief Risk Officer, Davinder Athwal
VP New Business Development; President UGI Enterprises and UGI Energy Services, Bradley C. Hall, age 62, $420,007 total compensation
President and CEO, John L. Walsh, age 60, $1,027,169 total compensation
CFO, Kirk R. Oliver, age 57, $522,552 total compensation
VP General Counsel and Secretary, Monica M. Gaudiosi, age 53, $420,007 total compensation
President and CEO UGI Utilities, Robert F. (Bob) Beard, age 49
CEO Antargaz, Eric Naddeo
President and CEO AmeriGas, Jerry E. Sheridan, age 49, $506,018 total compensation
CEO FLAGA Group, Reinhard Sch illbauer
Managing Director AvantiGas, Neil Murphy
President UGI International, Roger Perreault
Legal Secretary, Sue Linkenhoker
Vice President Engineering, Chuck Hurchalla
Vice President Engineering, Hans Bell
Legal Secretary, Tracie Roberts
Regional Vice President, Steve Quagliana
Vice President of Human Resources, Jim Budd
Vice President Government Affairs, J Love
Treasurer, Robert (Bob) Knauss
Chairman, Lon R. Greenberg, age 65
Assistant Secretary, Jessica Milner
Treasurer, Daniel J (Dan) Platt
Auditors: Ernst & Young LLP

LOCATIONS

HQ: UGI Corp.
460 North Gulph Road, King of Prussia, PA 19406
Phone: 610 337-1000
Web: www.ugicorp.com

PRODUCTS/OPERATIONS

2015 Sales

	$ mil.	% of total
AmeriGas propane	2,885	42
UGI International		
UGI France	1,122	16
Flaga & other	686	10
Midstream & marketing		
Energy Services	1,041	15
Electric generation	75	1
Gas utility	933	13
Corporate	179	3
Adjustments	(232.6)	-
Total	**6,691**	**100**

Selected Subsidiaries and Affiliates

AmeriGas Inc.
AmeriGas Propane Inc.
  AmeriGas Partners L.P. (26%)
  AmeriGas Propane L.P.
  AmeriGas Technology Group Inc.
  Petrolane Incorporated

Four Flags Drilling Company Inc.
Ashtola Production Company
  UGI Ethanol Development Corporation
Newbury Holding Company
UGI Enterprises Inc. (energy marketing and services)
  CFN Enterprises Inc.
  Eastfield International Holdings Inc.
  FLAGA GmbH (propane distribution; Austria the Czech Republic and Slovakia)
  Eurogas Holdings Inc.
  McHugh Service Company
  UGI Energy Services Inc.
  GASMARK (gas marketing)
  POWERMARK (electricity marketing)
  UGI International Enterprises Inc.
  UGI Europe Inc.
  Antargaz (propane distribution France)
  FLAGA GmbH (propane distribution Austria)
UGI Properties Inc.
UGI Utilities Inc. (natural gas and electric utility)
United Valley Insurance Company

COMPETITORS

Chesapeake Utilities	Ferrellgas Partners
Dominion Resources	National Fuel Gas
Duquesne Light	NorthWestern
Holdings	PPL Corporation
Energy Transfer	Suburban Propane
Exelon	

HISTORICAL FINANCIALS

Company Type: Public

Income Statement

FYE: September 30

	REVENUE ($ mil.)	NET INCOME ($ mil.)	NET PROFIT MARGIN	EMPLOYEES
09/15	6,691	281	4.2%	13,570
09/14	8,277	337	4.1%	12,800
09/13	7,194	278	3.9%	12,800
09/12	6,519	199	3.1%	9,200
09/11	6,091	232	3.8%	9,750
Annual Growth	**2.4%**	**4.8%**	**—**	**8.6%**

2015 Year-End Financials

Debt ratio: 36.88%	No. of shares (mil.): 172
Return on equity: 10.50%	Dividends
Cash ($ mil.): 369	Yield: 2.5%
Current ratio: 0.87	Payout: 58.5%
Long-term debt ($ mil.): 3,441	Market value ($ mil.): 6,003

	STOCK PRICE ($) FY Close	P/E High/Low	PER SHARE ($) Earnings	Dividends	Book Value
09/15	34.82	24 20	1.60	0.89	15.62
09/14	34.09	28 17	1.92	1.08	15.44
09/13	39.13	26 19	1.61	1.11	14.52
09/12	31.75	27 21	1.17	0.71	13.22
09/11	26.27	24 19	1.37	1.02	11.79
Annual Growth	**7.3%**	**— —**	**3.9%**	**(3.4%)**	**7.3%**

UMB Financial Corp

UMB Financial is the holding company for four UMB-branded commercial banks serving Arizona Colorado Illinois Kansas Nebraska Oklahoma and Missouri. Through some 110 branches the banks offer standard services such as checking and savings accounts credit and debit cards and trust and investment services. Commercial loans account for more than 50% of UMB's loan portfolio. Beyond its banking business it offers insurance brokerage services leasing treasury management health savings accounts and proprietary mutual funds through its more than 20 subsidiaries. Founded in 1913 the bank ranks first in the Kansas City market (based on deposits).OperationsIt operates through four business segments: Bank Payment Solutions Institutional Investment Management and Asset Servicing. Its Bank segment focuses on traditional commercial and consumer banking treasury management leasing foreign exchange merchant bankcards wealth management brokerage insurance capital markets investment banking corporate trust and correspondent banking. The Payment Solutions segment offers consumer and commercial credit and debit cards prepaid debit card solutions healthcare services and institutional cash management. UMB Financial's Institutional Investment Management segment serves the intermediary and institutional markets through mutual funds traditional separate accounts and sub-advisory relationships using private equity and fixed income investment strategies. The Asset Servicing segment caters to the asset management industry and supports investment products such as mutual funds alternative investments and managed accounts.Geographic ReachUMB Financial's four commercial banks are located in Arizona Colorado Kansas and Missouri. Its principal subsidiary bank Missouri-based UMB Bank n.a. also has branches in Illinois Kansas Nebraska and Oklahoma. In Texas the firm operates a loan production office.Sales and MarketingUMB Financial serves commercial retail government and correspondent bank customers through its branch locations call center Internet banking and network of ATMs.The company spent $24.15 million toward marketing and business development expenses in 2014; up from $22.7 million in 2013 but down from the $24.6 million it spent in 2012.Financial PerformanceUMB Financial has enjoyed rising revenue and profit in recent years thanks to loan asset growth and . Revenue in 2014 grew by more than 2% to $862.56 million thanks to 8% growth in trust and securities processing fee income and thanks to higher loan interest income from another year of double-digit growth in average loan balances.Following several years of profit growth net income in 2014 fell by 10% to $120.66 million mostly because the bank spent more toward salary raises and incurred higher benefit costs but also because it spent more on equipment and a contingency reserve it established in 2014 related to a settlement agreement involving the sellers and employees of PCM. Cash from operations fell by 21% to $243.78 million partially from lower cash earnings but also because it adjusted for fewer non-cash items such as accrued expenses and taxes than it did in 2013.The company's loan assets grew by 14% to $7.47 billion in 2014 while its total deposits increased slightly to $13.62 billion.StrategyUMB Financial is focused on four main strategies for growth. The first is to grow its fee-based business through acquisitions or organically as fee-based services are typically non-credit related and are not generally affected by fluctuations in interest rates. Accordingly the bank has boosted its non-interest income by 20% over the past three years from $414 million in 2011 to $498.7 million in 2014. In mid-2014 to add fuel to this growth UMB Bank purchased the Oklahoma Corporate Trust Business from RCB Bank to be incorporated into its own business in the region expanding the company's reach into the Oklahoma Corporate Trust Market. The second strategy is to focus on net interest income through loan and deposit growth. In 2014 for example the bank grew its loan assets by a whopping 14% adding $16.8 million in net interest income (5% more than in 2013) to the bank's top line. Thirdly UMB Financial aims to improve operating efficiencies by offering more services through its existing branch network which helped it grow its loan and deposit business greatly

in 2014. Fourth the firm is focused on managing its capital to promote investor confidence and acquisition opportunities.Mergers and AcquisitionsIn late 2014 UMB agreed to buy commercial finance firm Marquette Financial from longtime owners the Pohlad family for $182 million. The acquisition would increase UMB's presence in key growth markets Arizona and Texas —where Marquette operated Meridian Bank. As part of the deal the Pohlad family gained a 7% stake in UMB (the second-largest stake behind chairman Mariner Kemper who holds 12%).Company BackgroundTo grow its fee-based business and diversify its business model UMB has made several acquisitions in its past. The company built up its investment advisory and corporate trust business through several 2009 purchases. In 2010 UMB made 10 acquisitions including Prairie Capital Management and Indiana-based Reams Asset Management. The deals more than doubled UMB's Scout Investment Advisors' assets under management to more than $27 billion.

EXECUTIVES

CEO UMB Healthcare Services, Dennis L. Triplett, age 62
EVP and Chief Risk Officer, David D. Kling, age 68, $245,028 total compensation
Chairman and CEO, J. Mariner Kemper, age 42, $847,373 total compensation
EVP Sales Marketing and Communication, Heather K. Miller
Vice Chairman; President and CEO UMB Bank, Michael D. (Mike) Hagedorn, age 49, $420,953 total compensation
President Commercial Banking, Craig L. Anderson, age 55, $370,154 total compensation
President Private Wealth Management, Dana Abraham
CEO Scout Investments, Andrew J. (Andy) Iseman, age 51, $415,000 total compensation
EVP Operations and Technology Group and Chief Administrative Officer, Daryl S. Hunt, age 59
EVP Organizational Effectiveness and Chief Human Resources Officer, Lawrence G. (Larry) Smith, age 68
EVP Consumer Services, Christine Pierson, age 52
EVP CFO and Chief Accounting Officer, Brian J. Walker, age 43
President UMB Fund Services Inc., Anthony J. (Tony) Fischer, age 56
President Institutional Asset Management, Todd Duncan
Managing Director Prairie Capital Management, Brian Kaufman
EVP and General Counsel, Scott Stengel
President Insitutional Banking and Investor Services, Jim Cornelius
EVP and Chief Credit Officer, Chris Swett
Chief Lending Officer, Tom Terry
CIO, Jig Patel
Executive Vice President, Stephen M Kitts
Senior Vice President Investment Division, Raleigh Trovillion
Senior Vice President Corporate Counsel, Brian Boland
Vice President Senior Loan Review Officer, Christopher Nelson
Senior Vice President Employee Services, Jim Rawlings
Executive Vice President Of Marketing Communications, Steve Warta
Vice President Banking Services Compliance Directo, Stephanie Boryla
Vice President Information Technology, Kris Loveless
Senior Vice President U.S. Corporate Banking, Shawn Thomas

Vice President Senior Loan Review Officer, Dawn Dolliver
Vice President Senior Loan Review Officer, Sue Hart
Vice President Investment Banking, Bill Patterson
Vice President, Jeff Grasser
Vice President Senior Loan Review, James (Jamie) Engelhart
Vice President Commercial Banking, Jess Adams
Assistant Vice President Enterprise Application Supoort, Brad Shultz
Senior Vice President Loan Operations, Linda Gallagher
Vice President Commercial Banking Officer, Glen Beussink
Vice President, Jackie Comfort
Vice President Correspondent Banking, Jackie Wise
Vice President Financial Consultant, Tony Beach
Vice President And Senior Loan Review, Larene Jackson
Assistant Vice President Commercial, Shannon Eigenberger
Vice President, Jack Misiewicz
Vice President New Business Development, Scott Reeves
Senior Vice President, Brian Denvir
Assistant Vice President, Matthew (Matt) Smith
Vice President Regional Sales Manager, David (Dave) Youngstrom
Vice President Business Development Healthcare Services, Jeff Costello
Vice President Loss Mitigation, Curtis Lynch
Vice President Director Of Interactiv, Terry Kincheloe
Vice President, Rebecca Larason
Vice President Commercial Banking, Joseph Driscoll
Vice President Private Banking Client Manager, Matthew (Matt) Scholfield
Vice President, Christopher (Chris) Cox
Vice President Commercial Loan Officer CFS Sales, Cory Miller
Assistant Vice President Financial Center Manager, Erika Miller
Financial Center Manager Vice President, Sarah Antrobus
Senior Vice President, Deloss McKnight
Senior Vice President Wealth Advisor, Rob Oltjen
Vice President Commercial Banking, Matt Sanders
Vice President Commercial Lending, Ryan Ward
Vice President, Kohl Karen
Senior Vice President, Kathryn Anastasio
Assistant Vice President Business Banking, Edin Salkic
Vice President Senior Business Banking R, David (Dave) Lemmon
Vice President Ag Loan Officer, Tony Geiger
Vice President, Mark Volkmer
Senior Vice President Credit Risk Director, James (Jamie) Canilglia
Vice President Fraud, Debbie Phillips
Vice President Commercial Lending, Clarence Nichols
Senior Vice President, Blake Smith
Vice President Corporate Trust, Laura Roberson
Vice President Corporate Trust, Brian Krippner
Senior Vice President Cashier, Ann Porter
Senior Vice President Retail Banking, Eric Craine
Assistant Vice President Digital, Melanie Woods
Vice President And Program Operations Management Lssbb, Renee Taylor
Vice President Ultranetwork, James Braddock
Vice President Management Information Systems Quality, Annie Schroeder
Vice President Treasury, Brendan Morse
Vice President Product Development and Marketing, Bruce Parker
Vice President Senior Loan Review, James Engelhart

Vice President Of Commercial Underwriting, Rebecca Lang

Executive Vice President Trust Investments, James Moffett

Senior Vice President Chief Lending Officer Arizona, Robert Faver

Senior Vice President Director Of Managed Account Solutions, Scot Knight

Banking Center Manager II and Assistant Vice President, Jessica Ranger

Vice President Commercial Banking, Allen Chaffee

Trust Advisor Assistant Vice President, Josh Hahn

Vice President and Trust Advisor, Rhonda Murray

Vice President Loss Mitigation Manager, Sean Murphy

Vice President Finance, Debbie Johnson

Assistant Vice President and Unit Finance Manager, Eric Wheeler

Vice President, Lee Speir

Vice President Commercial Banking, William (Bill) Thomasjr

Executive Vice President, Steve Kitts

Finance: Vice President, Benjamin (Ben) Black

Vice President Middle Office Manager, Maggie Bowen

Assistant Vice President Trust Advisor, Karin Behnk

Vice President Banking Center Manager, Tammy Price

Vice President Finance, Jon Henderson

Senior Vice President, Ron Sager

Vice President Assistant Controller, Nicole Van Denabeele

Vice President Director FDIC Sweep, Doug Pagliaro

Assistant Vice President Financial Center Manager, Paul Bischmann

Senior Vice President Commercial Real Estate, Cydney Gurgens

Vice President, Victor Zarrilli

Senior Vice President, Charles (Chas) Wolf

Executive Vice President and Chro, Larry Smith

Vice President, Ann Maurer

Vice President Process Engineering, John (Jack) Wilson

Vice President Card Services, Leslie Lagan

Senior Vice President, Shelly Nischbach

Assistant Vice President Information Technology, Michael (Mel) Rattenne

Assistant Vice President, Marni Sorrick

Vice President Commercial Card Sales Officer, Peter (Pete) Swenson

Assistant Vice President and Assistant Treasurer, Maria Pfeifer

Vice President and Assistant Treasurer, David (Dave) Daly

Auditors: KPMG LLP

LOCATIONS

HQ: UMB Financial Corp
1010 Grand Boulevard, Kansas City, MO 64106
Phone: 816 860-7000   Fax: 816 860-7143
Web: www.umb.com

PRODUCTS/OPERATIONS

2014 Sales

	$ mil.	% of total
Interest income		
Loans	245	29
Securities	115	13
Others	3	-
Non-interest income		
Trust and securities processing	288	34
Service charges on deposit accounts	85	11
Bankcard fees	67	8
Trading and investment banking	19	2
Brokerage fees	10	1
Others	27	2
Total	862	100

Selected Subsidiaries & Affiliates

Grand Distribution Services LLC
J.D. Clark & Company
Kansas City Financial Corporation
Kansas City Realty Company
Prairie Capital Management LLC
Scout Distributors LLC
Scout Investment Advisors Inc.
UMB Banc Leasing Corp.
UMB Bank and Trust n.a.
UMB Bank Arizona n.a.
UMB Bank Colorado n.a.
UMB Capital Corporation
UMB Community Development Corporation
UMB Distribution Services LLC
UMB Financial Services Inc.
UMB Fund Services Inc.
UMB Insurance Inc.
UMB National Bank of America
UMB Realty Company LLC
UMB Redevelopment Corporation
UMB Trust Company of South Dakota
United Missouri Insurance Company

COMPETITORS

BOK Financial
Bank of America
Capitol Federal Financial
Commerce Bancshares
Dickinson Financial
First National of Nebraska

Great Southern Bancorp
Guaranty Bancorp
TCF Financial
U.S. Bancorp
Zions Bancorporation

HISTORICAL FINANCIALS

Company Type: Public

Income Statement

FYE: December 31

	ASSETS ($ mil.)	NET INCOME ($ mil.)	INCOME AS % OF ASSETS	EMPLOYEES
12/14	17,500	120	0.7%	3,592
12/13	16,911	133	0.8%	3,498
12/12	14,927	122	0.8%	3,448
12/11	13,541	106	0.8%	3,448
12/10	12,404	91	0.7%	3,355
Annual Growth	9.0%	7.3%	—	1.7%

2014 Year-End Financials

Debt ratio: 0.05%
Return on equity: 7.66%
Cash ($ mil.): 2,010
Current ratio: —
Long-term debt ($ mil.): —

No. of shares (mil.): 45
Dividends
  Yield: 1.6%
  Payout: 32.2%
Market value ($ mil.): 2,590

	STOCK PRICE ($) FY Close	P/E High/Low		PER SHARE ($) Earnings	Dividends	Book Value
12/14	56.89	25	20	2.65	0.91	36.10
12/13	64.28	20	13	3.20	0.87	33.30
12/12	43.82	17	12	3.04	0.83	31.71
12/11	37.25	17	12	2.64	0.79	29.46
12/10	41.44	20	14	2.26	0.75	26.24
Annual Growth	8.2%	—	—	4.1%	5.0%	8.3%

Umpqua Holdings Corp

Umpqua Holdings thinks of itself not so much as a bank but rather a retailer that sells financial products. Consequently many of the company's 395 Umpqua Bank "stores" in northern California northern Nevada Oregon and Washington feature coffee bars and computer cafes. While customers sip Umpqua-branded coffee pay bills online attend a financial seminar catch a poetry reading or check out wares from local merchants staff members pitch deposit accounts mortgages loans life insurance investments and more. Subsidiary Umpqua Investments (formerly Strand Atkinson Williams & York) provides retail brokerage services through more than a dozen locations; most are inside Umpqua Bank branches.

Geographic Reach

Oregon-based Umpqua Bank has branches in Idaho Washington Oregon California and Northern Nevada. Umpqua Investments has offices in Portland Lake Oswego and Medford Oregon as well as Santa Rosa California.

Operations

In addition to its Umpqua Investments and Umpqua Bank subsidiaries Umpqua Bank has a wholly-owned subsidiary Financial Pacific Leasing a commercial equipment leasing company. Umpqua Private Bank caters to high net worth individuals and nonprofit organizations.

Financial Performance

Umpqua Holdings reported revenue of $564.3 million in 2013 a 5% decline versus 2012 on lower interest and non-interest income. Net interest income fell as a result of lower assets primarily covered loans investment securities and a decrease in net interest margin partially offset by a rise in non-covered loans and leases and a decrease in interest-bearing liabilities. Non-interest income decrease due to a huge decline in the gain on investment securities.

After three consecutive years of rising profits net income declined by 3% in 2013 versus 2012 to $98.4 million.

Strategy

Umpqua Bank is expanding beyond its traditional market along the Interstate 5 corridor from Seattle to Sacramento. Indeed since 2000 Umpqua has acquired and integrated about a dozen financial institutions. In April 2014 Umpqua Bank acquired $10-billion-in-assets Sterling Financial Corp. headquartered in Spokane Washington. The merger created the West Coast's largest community bank with some $22 billion in assets and 394 stores across five states. Sterling branches are being rebranded as part of the $1.9 billion deal.

Umpqua Bank differentiates itself by encouraging clients to come into its stores instead of using impersonal interfaces like ATMs and electronic banking more cost-effective methods preferred by many of its competitors. The bank's "Next Generation" stores feature interactive touch-screen walls fresh fruit and cold drinks. It hopes the touchy-feely environment will inspire customers to make impulse purchases like home equity loans or investments.

Mainly consumer focused Umpqua Bank established a business banking division in 2011 to court small and mid-sized business clients. It is pursuing deposit growth assembling new lending teams and adding new stores in key metropolitan areas like Portland Oregon; Seattle; San Francisco; and California's Silicon Valley. It continues to look for other acquisition opportunities as well including those beyond its usual stomping grounds.

Umpqua Holdings has also focused on expanding its private banking operations targeting customers with more than $1 million to invest. The company established a wealth management division in 2009 and launched a trust services group the following year. It provides asset management services through an agreement with independent firm Ferguson Wellman Capital Management.

EXECUTIVES

SEVP and COO Umpqua Holdings and Umpqua Bank, Brad F. Copeland, age 67, $504,167 total compensation

President CEO and Director, Raymond P. (Ray) Davis, age 66, $873,333 total compensation

EVP Cultural Enhancement Umpqua, Barbara J. Baker, age 66, $147,477 total compensation

EVP Corporate Secretary and General Counsel Umpqua Holdings and Umpqua Bank, Steven L. Philpott, age 64

Chief Financial Officer; Executive Vice President of the Company and the Bank, Ronald L. (Ron) Farnsworth, age 45, $290,000 total compensation

EVP Treasurer and Principal Accounting Officer Umpqua Holdings and Umpqua Bank, Neal T. McLaughlin, age 47

EVP Wealth Management Umpqua Holdings and Umpqua Bank, Kelly J. Johnson, age 54, $300,000 total compensation

EVP and Commercial Region Manager Washington State Umpqua Bank, Danielle Burd

EVP Commercial Banking Umpqua Bank, Cort OÅHaver, $293,589 total compensation

EVP of Commerical Banking of the Company and the Bank, Cort OHaver

Executive Vice President and Chief Credit Officer of the Company and the Bank, Mark Wardlow

EVP of Community Banking of the Company and the Bank, Ulderico Calero

EVP of Commerical Banking of the Company and the Bank, Cort O'Haver

Senior Vice President Corporate Communications, Eve Callahan

Vice President Of Benefits, Jennifer Hollenbeck

Senior Vice President Data Processing, Bo Harrison

Senior Vice President and Manager Private Banking Division, Donna Huntsman

Vice President Business Development Officer, Susan (Sue) Jensen

Senior Vice President Credit Administrator Credit Quality Administration, Paul Jelle

Vice President Vice President Sales and Marketing Sales Staff Manager Retail, Marie Fidler

Senior Vice President and Manager, David (Dave) Brown

Auditors: Moss Adams LLP

LOCATIONS

HQ: Umpqua Holdings Corp
One SW Columbia Street, Suite 1200, Portland, OR 97258
Phone: 503 727-4100
Web: www.umpquaholdingscorp.com

PRODUCTS/OPERATIONS

2013 Sales

	$ mil.	% of total
Interest		
Loans including fees	398	67
Taxable investment securities	43	8
Other	1	-
Noninterest		
Mortgage banking	78	14
Service charges on deposit accounts	31	5
Brokerage commissions & fees	14	2
Adjustments	(3.1)	4
Total	**564**	**100**

2013 Sales

	$ mil.	% of total
Community Banking	432	77
Home Lending	101	18
Wealth Management	30	5
Total	**564**	**100**

COMPETITORS

Bank of America	KeyCorp
Bank of the West	U.S. Bancorp
Banner Corp	Washington Federal
Cascade Bancorp	Wells Fargo
Columbia Banking	

HISTORICAL FINANCIALS

Company Type: Public

Income Statement

FYE: December 31

	ASSETS ($ mil.)	NET INCOME ($ mil.)	INCOME AS % OF ASSETS	EMPLOYEES
12/14	22,613	147	0.7%	4,569
12/13	11,636	98	0.8%	2,490
12/12	11,795	101	0.9%	2,376
12/11	11,563	74	0.6%	2,255
12/10	11,668	28	0.2%	2,185
Annual Growth	**18.0%**	**51.1%**	—	**20.3%**

2014 Year-End Financials

Debt ratio: 6.00%
Return on equity: 5.36%
Cash ($ mil.): 1,605
Current ratio: —
Long-term debt ($ mil.): —

No. of shares (mil.): 220
Dividends
  Yield: 3.5%
  Payout: 80.0%
Market value ($ mil.): 3,745

	STOCK PRICE ($) FY Close	P/E High/Low	PER SHARE ($)		
			Earnings	Dividends	Book Value
12/14	17.01	24 20	0.78	0.60	17.17
12/13	19.14	22 14	0.87	0.60	15.43
12/12	11.79	15 13	0.90	0.34	15.41
12/11	12.39	20 12	0.65	0.24	14.91
12/10	12.18	105 69	0.15	0.20	14.34
Annual Growth	**8.7%**	— —	**51.0%**	**31.6%**	**4.6%**

UNION BANK AND TRUST COMPANY

Union Bank & Trust a subsidiary of financial services holding company Farmers & Merchants Investment operates more than 35 branches throughout Nebraska and in Kansas. As Nebraska's third-largest privately-owned bank it offers traditional deposit and trust services as well as insurance equipment finance and investment management services. Consumer loans account for the largest portion of the bank's portfolio followed by commercial real estate and farmland loans. Union Bank also originates business loans and residential mortgages. Affiliate company Union Investment Advisors manages the Stratus family of mutual funds. Another Farmers & Merchants unit Nelnet Capital offers brokerage services.

Geographic Reach

Union Bank operates mostly in Nebraska but also in Kansas.

Sales and Marketing

The bank primarily serves customers in Lincoln and Omaha as well as the Kansas City metropolitan area.

Operations

Union Bank has grown to become one of Nebraska's largest privately-owned banks. As of mid-2013 it boasted bank assets of $2.6 billion and trust assets of $11.8 billion.

Aside from its branches in Nebraska and Kansas Union Bank offers banking products and services through its online mobile and electronic banking services.

Strategy

Union Bank continues to expand its footprint in existing markets. The financial institution will have added three new Nebraska branches to its portfolio by 2014.

Company Background

The bank was originally founded in 1917 as Farmer's State Bank. It took on the Union Bank name in 1935 and became Union Bank & Trust in 1959.

Company Ownership

The company has been controlled by the Dunlap family since 1965.

EXECUTIVES

Vice President And Business Development Officer, Michael (Mel) Kulas

LOCATIONS

HQ: UNION BANK AND TRUST COMPANY
3643 S 48TH ST, LINCOLN, NE 685064390
Phone: 4024880941
Web: WWW.UBT.COM

PRODUCTS/OPERATIONS

Selected Services

Business banking
  Investment
Personal banking
Wealth management

Selected Affiliates

InfoVisa
Nelnet Capital LLC
Nelnet Inc.
Union Agency Inc.
Union Equipment Finance LLC
Union Investment Advisors
Union Title Company LLC
Zelle

COMPETITORS

Bank of America	Great Western Bancorp
Bank of the West	JPMorgan Chase
Citigroup	Pinnacle Bancorp
First National of Nebraska	U.S. Bancorp
	Wells Fargo

HISTORICAL FINANCIALS

Company Type: Private

Income Statement

FYE: December 31

	ASSETS ($ mil.)	NET INCOME ($ mil.)	INCOME AS % OF ASSETS	EMPLOYEES
12/13	2,862	35	1.3%	800
12/08	2,437	16	0.7%	—
12/06	1,518	18	1.2%	—
Annual Growth	**9.5%**	**10.0%**		

2013 Year-End Financials

Debt ratio: —
Return on equity: 22.60%
Cash ($ mil.): 49
Current ratio: —
Long-term debt ($ mil.): —

Dividends
  Yield: —
  Payout: —
Market value ($ mil.): —

Union Bankshares Corp (New)

Union Bankshares (formerly Union First Market Bankshares) is the holding company for Union Bank & Trust which operates approximately 100 branches in central northern and coastal portions of Virginia. The bank offers standard services such as checking and savings accounts credit cards and certificates of deposit. Union Bank & Trust maintains a loan portfolio heavily weighted towards real estate: Commercial real estate loans make up more than 30% while one- to four-family residential mortgages and construction loans account for approximately 15% and 20% respectively. The bank also originates personal and business loans.Other financial services are provided through subsidiaries Union Investment Services (brokerage and investment advisory services through an arrangement with Raymond James Financial) Union Insurance Group (long-term care and business owner coverage) and Union Mortgage Group which provides mortgage brokerage services from about 15 offices.Union Bankshares primarily operates in Virginia. Its Union Mortgage Group provides mortgage brokerage services from offices in Virginia Maryland and the Carolinas. Union Mortgage is additionally licensed to operate in states in the Mid-Atlantic the Southeast and in Washington DC.The company's profits have risen dramatically due to the 2010 acquisition of First Market Bank. In 2010 profits nearly tripled (to $22.9 million from the 2009 earnings of $8.4 million) while in 2011 they rose a further 33% to $30.5 million. The acquisition led to an increase in net interest income a primary contributor to the company's growth. Also in 2011 Union Bankshares lowered its provision for loan losses as its loan portfolio continued to improve post-recession. Expenses that year were lower than in 2010 when the acquisition closed. Slightly offsetting the improvements mortgage earnings fell by nearly half in 2011 due to the stagnant residential mortgage market. Although profits have risen revenues have remained relatively flat falling 2% in 2011 to $232.9 million.Union Bankshares' strategy for growth includes buying other banks as well as opening new branches of its own. Then named Union Bank and Trust the company acquired First Market Bank in 2010 to nearly double its branch total. (The holding company then also added "First Market" to its name and moved its headquarters to Richmond.) The company has also grown through de novo branching and through purchases of branches and related companies. It acquired an existing branch in Harrisonburg plus some $74 million in loan assets from NewBridge Bank in 2011.Also that year the bank opened up seven new locations inside Martin's grocery stores where it already had more than 20 in-store branches. In the past couple of years the company has consolidated its bank subsidiaries creating operating efficiencies as well as a stronger unified brand.Virginia-based specialty insurer Markel Corporation owns 14% of Union Bankshares.

EXECUTIVES

President CEO and Director, G. William (Billy) Beale, age 65, $679,021 total compensation
EVP Union Bankshares and President Union Bank and Trust Company, John C. Neal, age 65, $349,986 total compensation
EVP Union Bankshares and Chief Retail Officer Union Bank & Trust, Elizabeth M. Bentley, age 54, $263,011 total compensation
EVP and Director Operations and Information Technology, Rex A. Hockemeyer, age 61, $160,000 total compensation
EVP and Chief Risk Officer, David G. (Dave) Bilko, age 55
EVP and CFO, Robert M. (Rob) Gorman, age 56, $344,000 total compensation
EVP Union Bankshares and Chief Banking Officer Union Bank & Trust, D. Anthony (Tony) Peay, age 55, $303,983 total compensation

Executive Vice President General Counsel Corporate Secretary, Janis Orfe
Vice President Commerical Cash Management, Robbin Muldoon
Senior Vice President Commercial Banker, Morfit Debra
Senior Vice President Chief Information Officer, Joe Brown
Vice President, Paul Barrett
Vice President, Matt Meduna
Vice President, Nathan Jantzi
Assistant Vice President In House Counsel, Christine Wilcox
Vice President, Sean Link
Vice President Talent Acquisition, Cynda Berger
Auditors: Ernst & Young LLP

LOCATIONS

HQ: Union Bankshares Corp (New)
1051 East Cary Street, Suite 1200, Richmond, VA 23219
Phone: 804 633-5031
Web: www.bankatunion.com

PRODUCTS/OPERATIONS

2011 Sales

	$ mil.	% of total
Interest		
Loans including fees	168	72
Securities including dividends	20	9
Other	0	-
Noninterest		
Gains on sales of loans	19	8
Service charges on deposit accounts	8	4
Other service charges commissions & fees	12	5
Other	4	2
Adjustments	(2.5)	-
Total	**232**	**100**

Selected Mergers and Acquisitions

COMPETITORS

BB&T	PNC Financial
Bank of America	Regions Financial
C&F Financial	SunTrust
Eastern Virginia Bankshares	TowneBank
JPMorgan Chase	Wells Fargo

HISTORICAL FINANCIALS

Company Type: Public

Income Statement

FYE: December 31

	ASSETS ($ mil.)	NET INCOME ($ mil.)	INCOME AS % OF ASSETS	EMPLOYEES
12/14	7,359	52	0.7%	1,471
12/13	4,176	34	0.8%	1,025
12/12	4,095	35	0.9%	1,044
12/11	3,907	30	0.8%	1,045
12/10	3,837	22	0.6%	1,005
Annual Growth	**17.7%**	**23.1%**	**—**	**10.0%**

2014 Year-End Financials

Debt ratio: 4.07%	No. of shares (mil.): 45
Return on equity: 7.43%	Dividends
Cash ($ mil.): 132	Yield: 2.4%
Current ratio: —	Payout: 50.8%
Long-term debt ($ mil.): —	Market value ($ mil.): 1,088

STOCK PRICE ($) FY Close	P/E High/Low	PER SHARE ($) Earnings	Dividends	Book Value
12/14	24.08	23 19	1.14	0.58	21.66
12/13	24.81	19 11	1.38	0.54	17.55
12/12	15.77	12 10	1.37	0.37	17.25
12/11	13.29	14 9	1.07	0.28	16.13
12/10	14.78	22 14	0.83	0.25	16.46
Annual Growth	**13.0%**	**— —**	**8.3%**	**23.4%**	**7.1%**

Union Pacific Corp

Venerable Union Pacific Railroad (UP) has been chugging down the track since the 19th century. Owned by Union Pacific Corporation (UPC) UP is one of the nation's leading rail carriers operating more than 66000 freight cars and about 8500 locomotives. UP transports automobiles; chemicals; energy (fuel); and industrial agricultural and other bulk freight over a system of some 32000 rail miles in 23 states in the western two-thirds of the US. UPC owns more than 26000 route miles of its rail network; leases and trackage rights which allow it to use other railroads' tracks account for the rest. UP's customers have included automakers General Motors and Toyota as well as retail outlet Lowe's.

HISTORY

In 1862 the US Congress chartered the Union Pacific Railroad (UP) to build part of the first transcontinental railway. The driving of the Golden Spike at Promontory Utah in 1869 marked the linking of the East and West coasts as UP's rails met those of Central Pacific Railroad (predecessor of Southern Pacific or SP) which had been built east from Sacramento California.

In 1872 the New York Sun revealed the Credit Mobilier scandal: UP officials had pocketed excess profits during the railroad's construction. Debt and lingering effects of the scandal forced UP into bankruptcy in 1893.

A syndicate headed by E. H. Harriman bought UP in 1897. After reacquiring the Oregon branches it lost in the bankruptcy UP gained control of SP (1901) and Chicago & Alton (1904). The Supreme Court ordered UP to sell its SP holdings in 1913 on antitrust grounds. In the 1930s UP diversified into trucking and in the 1970s and 1980s it moved into oil and gas production.

UP bought trucking firm Overnite Transportation in 1986. During the 1980s UP also built up its rail operations acquiring the Missouri Pacific and Western Pacific railroads in 1982 and the Missouri-Kansas-Texas Railroad in 1988. It joined Chicago and North Western (CNW) Railway managers in an investment group led by Blackstone Capital Partners that bought CNW in 1989.

CNW traced its roots to the Galena & Chicago Union Railroad which was founded by Chicago's first mayor W. B. Ogden in 1836 and merged with CNW in 1864. By 1925 the North Western (as it was then known) had tracks throughout the Midwest. In 1995 UP completed its purchase of CNW and made a bid for SP.

SP was founded in 1865 but its history dates to 1861 when four Sacramento merchants founded Central Pacific. By building new track and buying other railroads (including SP in 1868) Central Pacific had expanded throughout California Texas and Oregon by 1887. The two railroads merged in

1885 under the SP name. In 1983 SP was sold to a holding company controlled by Philip Anschutz which in 1995 agreed to sell the company to UP.

UP completed its SP acquisition in 1996 but assimilation of the purchase led to widespread rail traffic jams. UP also sold its remaining interest in Union Pacific Resources an oil company it had spun off the year before. In 1997 UP moved from Bethlehem Pennsylvania to Dallas and joined a consortium led by mining company Grupo México that won a bid to run two major Mexican rail lines. In the US however fatal collisions led to a federal review of UP which found a breakdown in rail safety such as overworked employees and widespread train defects. Meanwhile regulators seeking to resolve UP's massive freight backlog ordered the railroad to open its Houston lines to competitors.

The company decentralized its management into three regions (north south and west) in 1998 to improve traffic flow. It also hired more workers added new trains and realigned routes while selling Skyway Freight Systems its logistics services unit.

In 1999 UP moved its headquarters from Dallas to Omaha Nebraska where Union Pacific Railroad offices already were located. In 2000 it formed Fenix a holding company charged with developing and expanding the company's telecommunications and technology assets. (By 2003 however UP had reabsorbed Fenix and scaled back its support for its remaining technology subsidiaries.)

The company expanded its less-than-truckload operations into the western US in 2001 by buying Motor Cargo Industries. Also that year it completed the integration of Southern Pacific's operations.

UP sold its trucking unit Overnite Corporation (a holding company for Overnite Transportation and Motor Cargo Industries) in an IPO in 2003. (Overnite Corporation was acquired by United Parcel Service in 2005 and renamed UPS Freight the next year.) UP sold its Timera subsidiary (workforce management software) in 2004.

Traffic congestion in the UP system brought on by a shortage of train crews caused some freight from UPS and other customers to be rerouted onto trucks in 2004. The crew shortage was attributed in part to a greater-than-expected number of retirements in 2003. UP accelerated its hiring and training efforts but the company still had to restrict freight volume in an effort to minimize bottlenecks.

In 2006 Union Pacific Railroad reorganized its operating structure going from four regions to three: northern southern and western. Service units of the company's central region were reassigned to the northern and southern regions. The company added 45 miles of double track to its Sunset Corridor in 2008.

In the midst of the Great Recession UPC's 2009 freight volumes decreased 16% from 2008's numbers. The company was forced to raise its rates by about 6%; it also parked approximately 26% of its locomotives 18% of its freight car stock and furloughed about 3000 employees.

As the nation slowly recovered economically UPC realized a 13% increase in volume in 2010 over 2009 with automotive intermodal and industrial product shipments showing the strongest growth. Even with 2010 fuel prices more than 30% higher than 2009 the company's freight revenues increased 20% in 2010. UPC cited economic improvement across the majority of its market sectors as the reason for the recovery.

In mid-2012 UPC subsidiary PS Technology (PST) acquired the Yard Control Systems division of Ansaldo STS USA. The acquisition boosted PST's enterprise management capabilities by adding rail yard process control and automation technology.

EXECUTIVES

Assistant Vice President Commercial Strategic Analysis and Integration, Roland Fortner

EVP and CFO Union Pacific Corporation and Union Pacific Railroad, Robert M. Knight, age 58, $519,500 total compensation

SVP and CIO Union Pacific Corporation and Union Pacific Railroad, Lynden L. Tennison

Chairman President and CEO, Lance M. Fritz, age 52, $629,643 total compensation

EVP Marketing and Sales, Eric L. Butler, age 54, $435,333 total compensation

EVP and Corporate Secretary, Diane K. Duren, age 55, $453,333 total compensation

EVP Operations, Cameron Scott

Asst V Pres-gen Mgr Upds, Kate Betsworth

Assistant Vice President Dispatching, Mark Payne

Vice President Public Affairs, Brenda Mainwaring

National Account Manager, William Billner

Assistant Vice President Chemicals, Shawntell Kroese

Assistant Vice President Labor Relations, Terry Olin

Senior Vice President Construction, Steven Griffin

Vice President Mexico, Bernardo Ayala

Vice President Supply, Lynn Kelly

Assistant Vice President Intermodal Sales, Matthew (Matt) Gloeb

National Accounts Manager, Tim Morgan

Vice President, Scott Clark

Assistant Vice President Sales Ind Products, Randy Evans

Assistant Vice President Public Affairs, Juan Carreon

Assistant Vice President Intermodal Marketing, Paul Borseth

Vice President and GM Ag Products, Jason Hess

Assistant Vice President Investor Relns, Michelle (Mitch) Gerhardt

Vice President Human Resources, Sherrye Hutcherson

Vice President Marketing Industrial Development, Jim Lombard

Assistant Vice President Information Technology, Ashok Fichadia

Assistant Treasurer, Steve Oiness

Auditors: DELOITTE & TOUCHE LLP

LOCATIONS

HQ: Union Pacific Corp
1400 Douglas Street, Omaha, NE 68179
Phone: 402 544-5000
Web: www.up.com

PRODUCTS/OPERATIONS

2014 Sales

	$ mil.	% of total
Freight		
Intermodal	4,489	19
Coal	4,127	17
Industrial products	4,400	18
Chemicals	3,664	15
Agricultural	3,777	16
Automotive	2,103	9
Other	1,428	6
Total	23,988	100

COMPETITORS

American Commercial Lines
Burlington Northern Santa Fe
CSX
Canadian National Railway
Canadian Pacific Railway

Ingram Industries
J.B. Hunt
Kansas City Southern
Kirby Corporation
Landstar System
Norfolk Southern
Schneider National
Werner Enterprises

HISTORICAL FINANCIALS

Company Type: Public

Income Statement

FYE: December 31

	REVENUE ($ mil.)	NET INCOME ($ mil.)	NET PROFIT MARGIN	EMPLOYEES
12/15	21,813	4,772	21.9%	47,457
12/14	23,988	5,180	21.6%	47,201
12/13	21,963	4,388	20.0%	46,445
12/12	20,926	3,943	18.8%	45,928
12/11	19,557	3,292	16.8%	44,861
Annual Growth	2.8%	9.7%	—	1.4%

2015 Year-End Financials

Debt ratio: 26.01%
Return on equity: 22.78%
Cash ($ mil.): 1,391
Current ratio: 1.29
Long-term debt ($ mil.): 13,607

No. of shares (mil.): 849
Dividends
  Yield: 2.8%
  Payout: 38.0%
Market value ($ mil.): 66,408

	STOCK PRICE ($) FY Close	P/E High/Low	PER SHARE ($)		
			Earnings	Dividends	Book Value
12/15	78.20	22 14	5.49	2.20	24.38
12/14	119.13	35 17	5.75	1.91	23.99
12/13	168.00	35 27	4.71	2.96	23.27
12/12	125.72	31 25	4.14	2.49	21.17
12/11	105.94	31 24	3.36	0.97	19.35
Annual Growth	(7.3%)	— —	13.1%	22.9%	5.9%

United Bankshares, Inc.

United Bankshares (no relation to Ohio's United Bancshares) keeps it together as the holding company for two subsidiaries doing business as United Bank (WV) and United Bank (VA). Combined the banks boast some $12 billion in assets and operate roughly 130 branches that serve West Virginia Virginia and Washington DC as well as nearby portions of Maryland Pennsylvania and Ohio. The branches offer traditional deposit trust and lending services with a focus on residential mortgages and commercial loans. United Bankshares also owns United Brokerage Services which provides investments asset management and financial planning in addition to brokerage services.

Operations

The company's loan portfolio is made up of commercial and construction commercial and residential real estate and consumer loans (including credit card and home equity loans).United Bankshares generated 75% of its total revenue from interest and fees on loans in 2014 plus an additional 7% from interest and dividends on its investment securities. The company generated about 9% of its total revenue from deposit services fees and another 4% from trust and brokerage services fees.Geographic ReachUnited Bankshares boasts some 130 full-service branches including more than 55 across the state of West Virginia nearly 70 in the Shenendoah Valley region of Virginia and the Northern Virginia Maryland and Washington DC metro area and a handful of branches split between southwestern Pennsylvania and southeastern Ohio.Sales and MarketingThe company spent $4.76 million on advertising in 2014 up from $3.78 million and $4.27 million spent in 2013 and 2012 respectively.Financial PerformanceUnited Bankshares' revenues and profits have trended higher over the past few years thanks to growth in its loan business from acquisitions increased trust and brokerage services fee income and declining interest expense on deposits amidst the low-interest environment.The company's revenue jumped by nearly 34% to a record $499.50 million in 2014 mostly as its interest income spiked by 37% after its Virginia Commerce acquisition added new interest-earning assets and increased the average yields on its loans investments and security assets. United Bankshare's non-interest income also swelled by 22% thanks to higher income from fees from trust and brokerage services bankcard fees and merchant discounts and net gains on investment securities.Higher revenue in 2014 boosted the company's profits by 52% to a record $129.89 million while the company's operating cash grew by 2% thanks to higher cash earnings.

Strategy

United Bankshares has historically expanded through small bank and branch acquisitions closing nearly 30 bank purchases in the past quarter-century. Its growth strategy has mainly been focused in on the Washington DC/suburban Maryland/northern Virginia market though its also expanded into Pennsylvania in recent years as well. In 2014 for example the company extended its reach into Washington DC while boosting its loan business by $2 billion after completing its largest-ever acquisition of Virginia Commerce Bancorp.Mergers and AcquisitionsIn January 2014 United Bankshares acquired Arlington-based Virginia Commerce Bancorp for a total cost of $585.53 million. The deal expanded United's reach into the Washington DC metropolitan area and added $2.07 billion in new loan business and $2.02 billion in deposits. Company BackgroundThe 2011 acquisition of West Virginia-based Centra Financial Holdings gave United Bankshares its first branches in Pennsylvania and entry into the Pittsburgh market.

EXECUTIVES

EVP the Company and United Bank and WV, James B. Hayhurst, age 69, $225,000 total compensation

President, Richard M. Adams, age 47, $328,846 total compensation

COO, James J. Consagra, age 55, $334,462 total compensation

EVP and COO United Bank (VA), Craige L. Smith, age 63, $243,750 total compensation

EVP and CFO, W. Mark Tatterson, age 40

EVP, Darren K. Williams

Vice President Credit Administration, Troy Lemasters

Vice President, Kerry Casto

Vice President Director Of Institutional Sales, Bill Vyskocil

Vice President and Chairman Equity Strategies Committee, Steve Sears

Assistant Vice President, Susan Ingram

Assistant Vice President Information Technology Adand#8230, Andrew (Andy) Dawson

Vice President Bankcards, Cristina Smith

Senior Vice President Loan Administration, Stephen Robinson

Vice President, Donna Sellers

Operations Senior Vice President, Ken Greear

Assistant Vice President Information Technology Audit Manager, Jason Moore

Assistant Vice President Technical Services, Keith Brill

Board Member, Louise Hamrick

Auditors: Ernst & Young LLP

LOCATIONS

HQ: United Bankshares, Inc.
300 United Center, 500 Virginia Street, East, Charleston, WV 25301
Phone: 304 424-8716
Web: www.ubsi-inc.com

PRODUCTS/OPERATIONS

2014 Sales

	$ mil.	% of total
Interest		
Loans including fees	383	75
Interest and dividends on securities	33	7
Other	0	-
Noninterest		
Fees from deposit services	42	9
Fees from trust & brokerage services	18	4
Other	28	5
Adjustment (losses)	(8.4)	-
Total	**499**	**100**

COMPETITORS

BB&T	JPMorgan Chase
Bank of America	M&T Bank
Burke & Herbert Bank	PNC Financial
Cardinal Financial	SunTrust
City Holding	United Bancorp
Fifth Third	Virginia Commerce
Fulton Financial	Bancorp
Huntington Bancshares	WesBanco

HISTORICAL FINANCIALS

Company Type: Public

Income Statement

FYE: December 31

	ASSETS ($ mil.)	NET INCOME ($ mil.)	INCOME AS % OF ASSETS	EMPLOYEES
12/14	12,328	129	1.1%	1,703
12/13	8,735	85	1.0%	1,528
12/12	8,420	82	1.0%	1,529
12/11	8,451	75	0.9%	1,619
12/10	7,155	71	1.0%	1,451
Annual Growth	**14.6%**	**15.9%**	**—**	**4.1%**

2014 Year-End Financials

Debt ratio: 1.81%	No. of shares (mil.): 69
Return on equity: 9.63%	Dividends
Cash ($ mil.): 752	Yield: 3.4%
Current ratio: —	Payout: 69.9%
Long-term debt ($ mil.): —	Market value ($ mil.): 2,595

	STOCK PRICE ($) FY Close	P/E High/Low	PER SHARE ($) Earnings	Dividends	Book Value
12/14	37.45	20 15	1.92	1.28	23.90
12/13	31.45	19 14	1.70	1.25	20.66
12/12	24.34	19 14	1.64	1.24	19.74
12/11	28.27	19 12	1.61	1.21	19.29
12/10	29.20	19 12	1.65	1.20	18.18
Annual Growth	**6.4%**	**— —**	**3.9%**	**1.6%**	**7.1%**

United Community Banks, Inc. (Blairsville, GA)

United Community Banks is the holding company for United Community Bank (UCB) which provides consumer and business banking products and services through nearly 105 branches across Georgia North Carolina Tennessee and South Carolina. Commercial loans including construction loans and mortgages account for the largest portion of UCB's loan portfolio (more than 50%); residential mortgages make up 30%. The company which boasts roughly $8 billion in assets also has a mortgage lending division and provides insurance through its United Community Insurance Services subsidiary (aka United Community Advisory Services).

Operations

The bank's retail mortgage lending division United Community Mortgage Services (UCMS) sells and services mortgages for Fannie Mae and Freddie Mac and provides fixed and adjustable-rate home mortgages. It also offers retail brokerage services through an affiliation with a third-party broker/dealer.About 65% of UCB's total revenue came from loan interest (including fees) in 2014 while another 16% came from taxable investments. The rest of its revenue came from service charges and fees (10%) mortgage loan fees (2%) and brokerage fees (2%) among other sources.Geographic ReachUCB's nearly 105 branches are located in Georgia (in the north the Atlanta-Sandy Springs-Roswell metro area Gainsville metro area and coastal areas); western North Carolina; eastern and central Tennessee; and South Carolina (in the Greenville-Anderson-Mauldin metro area).Sales and MarketingThe bank provides community banking services for individuals small businesses and corporations.Financial PerformanceUCB has struggled to consistently grow its revenues in recent years due to shrinking interest margins on loans amidst the low-interest environment. Its profits however have been rising thanks to declining loan loss provisions as its loan portfolio's credit quality has improved with higher property valuations in the strengthened economy.The bank's revenue inched higher by 1% to $304 million in 2014 thanks to an increase in interest income stemming from strategic business growth initiatives designed to add new business lines and expand into new markets as well as balance sheet management and restructuring actions taken in the second quarter of the year. Despite higher revenue in 2014 UCB's net income dove 75% to $67.6 million mostly because in 2013 it had received a non-recurring income tax benefit of $238 million stemming from reversal of a deferred tax valuation allowance. Not counting this item however the bank's profit before taxes nearly tripled during the year. UCB's operating cash levels dropped by 47% to $101.9 million in 2014 due to lower cash earnings.StrategyUCB has been concentrating on growing its small business lending business in recent years. In 2014 it made "significant investments" in its SBA business after acquiring Business Carolina which specialized in SBA and USDA lending.It also continues to pursue bank acquisitions to expand its reach in its existing core markets and boost its loan and deposit business. Its acquisitions in 2015 and 2014 alone have added over $1 billion in new loan business and $1.3 billion in new deposits.Mergers and AcquisitionsIn May 2015 UCB bought Tennessee-based MoneyTree Corporation and its 10 First National Bank branches in east Tennessee. The deal added $425 million in assets $354 million in deposits and $253 million in new loan business to UCB's books.In September 2014 the company purchased Palmetto Bancshares and its Palmetto Bank branches expanding its footprint into "major" southeastern metro markets in Greenville and the Upstate South Carolina area. The deal also added $1.2 billion in assets $832 million in loans and $967 million in deposits.In June 2014 UCB purchased Columbia-based Business Carolina a commercial lender that specialized in SBA and USDA loans for $31.3 million in cash. The deal included $25 million in loans $6 million in other assets and substantially all of the company's employees.

EXECUTIVES

Chairman and CEO, Jimmy C. Tallent, age 62, $600,000 total compensation

EVP and CFO, Rex S. Schuette, age 63, $375,000 total compensation

President Community Banking, William M. (Bill) Gilbert, age 59, $275,000 total compensation

President CEO Southern National, Steven L. Holcomb

President and COO, H. Lynn Harton, $475,000 total compensation

EVP General Counsel and Chief Risk Officer, Bradley J. (Brad) Miller

EVP and Chief Credit Officer, Robert A. (Rob) Edwards

Senior Vice President, Debbie Williams

Vice President Special Assets, Marla Kephart

Assistant Vice President, Kathy Christiansen

Senior Vice President Retail Credit Administration, Chuck Valerio

Assistant Vice President Incentive Marketing Manager, Diana White

Vice President Security, Bill Poitevint

Assistant Vice President, Wendy Cawthon

Vice President Mortgage Banker, Angie Abston

Assistant Vice President Technology Support Manager, Karl Krauss

Assistant Vice President, Shelia Partin

Vice President, Sandy Worley

Senior Vice President Real Estate Lending, Rick Ellis

Vice President Of Business Development And Marketing, Elaine Bell

Senior Vice President, Steve Feld

Assistant Vice President, Erick Housch

Senior Vice President, Donald Harris

Vice President Commercial Lending, Ray Civitts

Senior Vice President Corporate Services Support, Jeanette Garrett

Assistant Vice President, Donna Schmidt

Assistant Vice President, Deborah Wright

Vice President, Todd Johnson

Senior Vice President, Matt McHugh

Assistant Vice President Controller, Jason Boskey

Vice President, Kathy Arwood

Senior Vice President, Zachary Welch

Vice President and Branch Manager, Vicky Helton

Assis Vice President Branch Manager, David (Dave) Sherrod

Vice President, Jane Callihan

Assistant Vice President Business Banking Underwriting, Eric Rivenbark

Vice President, Nick Harty

Senior Vice President Commercial Banking, Ben Walker

Vice President, Judy Levine

Senior Vice President, Phil Beaudette

Assistant Vice President, Rob Andrews

Executive Vice President Commercial lender, Bud Turner

Executive Vice President, Wayne Lowrey

Senior Vice President, Alan Kumler

Senior Vice President Builder Finance, Scott Ernest

Senior Vice President, Benjamin Walker

Senior Vice President, Gaye Reese

Vice President Business Development, Angie Chastain

Treasurer, Katrina Johnson

Assistant Treasurer, Mitchell Bleske

Treasurer, Michael (Mel) Burke

Auditors: PricewaterhouseCoopers LLP

LOCATIONS

HQ: United Community Banks, Inc. (Blairsville, GA)
125 Highway 515 East, Blairsville, GA 30512
Phone: 706 781-2265
Web: www.ucbi.com

PRODUCTS/OPERATIONS

2011 Sales

	$ mil.	% of total
Interest		
Loans including fees	239	69
Taxable investment securities	55	16
Other	3	1
Noninterest		
Service charges & fees	29	8
Mortgage loans & related fees	5	2
Brokerage fees	3	1
Net securities gains	0	—
Other	12	3
Adjustment	(0.7)	-
Total	**347**	**100**

COMPETITORS

Atlantic Coast Financial	Peoples Bancorp (NC)
BB&T	Regions Financial
Bank of America	Southeastern Bank Financial
Bank of Oak Ridge	Southeastern Banking
Fidelity Southern	SunTrust
First Citizens BancShares	Synovus
Georgia Bancshares	WGNB
Georgia-Carolina Bancshares	

HISTORICAL FINANCIALS

Company Type: Public

Income Statement

FYE: December 31

	ASSETS ($ mil.)	NET INCOME ($ mil.)	INCOME AS % OF ASSETS	EMPLOYEES
12/14	7,566	67	0.9%	1,506
12/13	7,425	273	3.7%	1,472
12/12	6,802	33	0.5%	1,553
12/11	6,983	(226)	—	1,706
12/10	7,443	(345)	—	1,763
Annual Growth	0.4%	—	—	(3.9%)

2014 Year-End Financials

Debt ratio: 1.72%
Return on equity: 8.81%
Cash ($ mil.): 192
Current ratio: —
Long-term debt ($ mil.): —

No. of shares (mil.): 60
Dividends
  Yield: 0.5%
  Payout: 10.8%
Market value ($ mil.): 1,141

	STOCK PRICE ($) FY Close	P/E High/Low	PER SHARE ($) Earnings	Dividends	Book Value
12/14	18.94	18 14	1.11	0.11	12.27
12/13	17.75	4 2	4.44	0.00	13.39
12/12	9.44	27 17	0.38	0.00	10.07
12/11	6.99	— —	(5.97)	0.00	10.00
12/10	1.95	— —	(18.80)	0.00	33.56
Annual Growth	76.5%	— —	—	—	(22.2%)

United Continental Holdings Inc

United Continental Holdings (UAL) unites cities around the globe through its primary United Air Lines subsidiary. While United Air Lines is its main line the company also has regional operations which are operated under contract by United Express. Combined the company handles an average of roughly 5050 flights a day to more than 370 domestic and international destinations from hubs that include Chicago Denver Houston Los Angeles San Francisco and Washington DC. Like most airlines the company sells the majority of its seat inventory through travel agencies and global distribution systems in addition to its main website.

Operations

UAL operates more than 1257 aircraft including aircraft operated by regional carriers on its behalf. It generates its revenues across four segments: passenger mainline (69% of total sales) passenger regional (18%) cargo (2%) and other (11%).

The company is a member of the Star Alliance network which offers more than 18000 daily flights to 193 countries worldwide and includes 27 member airlines.

Financial Performance

UAL achieved unprecedented growth in 2014 as revenues climbed 2% from $38.3 billion in 2013 to peak at a record-setting $38.9 billion in 2014. Profits also skyrocketed by nearly 100% from $571 million to $1.1 billion during that same time period due to a decrease in expenses related to aircraft fuel in addition to reduced aircraft rents affected by lease expirations.

The historic growth for 2014 was attributed to an uptick in the average fare per passenger and an increase in capacity and traffics causing an increase in passenger revenue. The fare increase for 2014 was due in part to a strong domestic demand environment and a number of new long-haul routes that generated higher fares than the system average. Cargo revenue also spiked 6% primarily due to higher freight volumes and an improvement in mail revenue.

UAL's operating cash flow increased 82% from $1.44 billion in 2013 to $2.63 billion in 2014 due to increased incomes along with a surge in cash from advance ticket sales and receivables.

Strategy

UAL has ordered a number of fuel-efficient Airbus and Boeing aircraft to replace the older fleet. In mid-2013 UAL was one of the first North American carriers to take delivery and fly the Boeing 787 Dreamliner aircraft. It has 50 Dreamliners scheduled for delivery between 2013 and 2020. The 787 anticipated to be "a game changer" for the company and for the airline industry will allow both United Air Lines and Continental to enter new long-haul markets and to replace older less efficient widebody aircraft.

In 2015 UAL plans to take delivery of 23 Boeing 737-900ER aircraft 11 Boeing 787-9 aircraft 11 Embraer E175 aircraft and two used Boeing 737-700 aircraft.

HISTORY

In 1929 aircraft designer Bill Boeing and engine designer Fred Rentschler of Pratt & Whitney joined forces to form United Aircraft and Transport. Renamed United Air Lines in 1931 the New York-based company offered one of the first coast-to-coast airline services. In 1934 United's manufacturing and transportation divisions split. Former banker Bill Patterson became president of the latter United Air Lines and moved it to the Chicago area. In 1969 UAL Corp. was formed as a holding company.

A subsidiary of UAL Corporation merged with and into Continental in October 2010 with Continental surviving as a wholly-owned subsidiary of UAL. Upon closing of the merger UAL became the parent company of both Continental and United Air Lines and UAL Corporation's name was changed to United Continental Holdings. The transaction created the world's largest airline. In 2013 United Air Lines Inc. was merged into Continental to form one legal entity and Continental's name and brand was changed to United Airlines Inc.

EXECUTIVES

SVP Finance and Acting CFO, Gerald (Gerry) Laderman
President and CEO, Oscar Munoz, age 58
EVP and CIO, Linda P. Jojo, age 49
Interim CEO, Brett J. Hart, age 46
EVP and COO, Gregory L. (Greg) Hart, age 49, $766,859 total compensation
EVP Human Resources and Labor Relations, Michael P. (Mike) Bonds, age 53
SVP and Chief Marketing Officer, Thomas F. (Tom) O'Toole
Vice President corporate Real Estate, Kate Gebo
Chairman, Henry L. Meyer, age 65
Vice Chairman and Chief Revenue Officer, James E. (Jim) Compton, age 59
Auditors: Ernst & Young LLP

LOCATIONS

HQ: United Continental Holdings Inc
233 South Wacker Drive, Chicago, IL 60606
Phone: 872 825-4000
Web: www.unitedcontinentalholdings.com

2013 Sales

	$ mil.	% of total
Domestic (US & Canada)	22,092	58
Atlantic	7,132	19
Pacific	5,794	15
Latin America	3,261	8
Total	**38,279**	**100**

PRODUCTS/OPERATIONS

2013 Sales

	$ mil.	% of total
Passenger		
Main line	25,997	68
Regional	7,125	19
Cargo	882	2
Other	4,275	11
Total	**38,279**	**100**

COMPETITORS

Air France-KLM	Japan Airlines
AirTran Airways	JetBlue
Alaska Air	Mesa Air
Alitalia	Qantas
American Airlines Group	SkyWest
	Southwest Airlines
British Airways	UPS
Delta Air Lines	US Airways
FedEx	Virgin Atlantic
Frontier Airlines	Airways

HISTORICAL FINANCIALS

Company Type: Public

Income Statement

FYE: December 31

	REVENUE ($ mil.)	NET INCOME ($ mil.)	NET PROFIT MARGIN	EMPLOYEES
12/14	38,901	1,132	2.9%	84,000
12/13	38,279	571	1.5%	87,000
12/12	37,152	(723)	—	88,000
12/11	37,110	840	2.3%	8,700
12/10	23,229	253	1.1%	86,000
Annual Growth	**13.8%**	**45.4%**	**—**	**(0.6%)**

2014 Year-End Financials

Debt ratio: 32.43%
Return on equity: 42.08%
Cash ($ mil.): 4,384
Current ratio: 0.65
Long-term debt ($ mil.): 10,692

No. of shares (mil.): 374
Dividends
Yield: —
Payout: —
Market value ($ mil.): 25,052

	STOCK PRICE ($) FY Close	P/E High/Low		PER SHARE ($) Earnings	Dividends	Book Value
12/14	66.89	22	12	2.93	0.00	6.40
12/13	37.83	24	14	1.53	0.00	8.24
12/12	23.38	—	—	(2.18)	0.00	1.45
12/11	18.87	11	6	2.26	0.00	5.46
12/10	23.82	24	10	1.08	0.00	5.27
Annual Growth	**29.5%**			**28.3%**	**—**	**5.0%**

United Financial Bancorp Inc (New)

EXECUTIVES

Secretary Rockville Financial and Rockville Bank, Judy L. Keppner, age 55
SVP Human Resources and Organizational Development Rockville Bank, Richard J. Trachimowicz, age 59, $138,531 total compensation
SVP and CFO Rockville Financial SVP and CFO Rockville Bank, John T. Lund, age 43
President and CEO; President and CEO Rockville Bank, William H. W. Crawford IV
Senior Vice President Investor Relations, Marliese Shaw
Director, William J. (Bill) McGurk, age 72
Director, Michael A. Bars, age 58
Director, C. Perry Chilberg, age 65
Director, David A. Engelson, age 70
Director, Raymond H. Lefurge Jr., age 64
Director, Stuart E. Magdefrau, age 59
Director, Rosemarie Novello Papa, age 69
Director, Richard M. Tkacz, age 61
Auditors: Wolf & Company, P.C.

LOCATIONS

HQ: United Financial Bancorp Inc (New)
45 Glastonbury Boulevard, Glastonbury, CT 06033
Phone: 860 291-3600
Web: www.bankatunited.com

COMPETITORS

Bank of America	RBS Citizens Financial Group
Citibank	
Liberty Bank	SI Financial
Naugatuck Valley Financial	Sovereign Bank
	TD Bank USA

New England Bancshares	United Financial Bancorp
PSB Holdings Inc.	
People's United Financial	Webster Financial
	Westfield Financial

HISTORICAL FINANCIALS

Company Type: Public

Income Statement

FYE: December 31

	ASSETS ($ mil.)	NET INCOME ($ mil.)	INCOME AS % OF ASSETS	EMPLOYEES
12/14	5,476	6	0.1%	725
12/13	2,301	14	0.6%	358
12/12	1,998	15	0.8%	346
12/11	1,749	7	0.4%	281
12/10	1,678	12	0.7%	236
Annual Growth	**34.4%**	**(13.7%)**	**—**	**32.4%**

2014 Year-End Financials

Debt ratio: 3.82%
Return on equity: 1.50%
Cash ($ mil.): 86
Current ratio: —
Long-term debt ($ mil.): —

No. of shares (mil.): 49
Dividends
Yield: 2.7%
Payout: 235.2%
Market value ($ mil.): 711

	STOCK PRICE ($) FY Close	P/E High/Low		PER SHARE ($) Earnings	Dividends	Book Value
12/14	14.36	91	76	0.16	0.40	12.16
12/13	14.21	28	23	0.54	0.40	11.53
12/12	12.90	24	18	0.56	0.52	11.39
12/11	10.36	43	36	0.25	0.21	11.30
Annual Growth	**8.5%**		**(10.6%)**	**18.2%**		**1.9%**

United Fire Group, Inc.

The United Fire Group companies join together to offer a unified range of property/casualty and life insurance products. The group operates through its United Fire & Casualty subsidiary which in turn holds entities that carry a variety of property/casualty offerings including fidelity and surety bonds and fire auto employee liability homeowners and workers' compensation lines. More than 1300 independent agencies in some 45 states sell its property/casualty products to businesses and individuals. The United Life division of United Fire & Casualty sells life annuity and credit life products to individuals and groups through some 950 independent agents in more than 30 states.

Geographic Reach

The company markets its products from its headquarters in Iowa and from four regional offices in California Colorado New Jersey and Texas and it operates primarily in adjacent areas of the midwestern southern and western US.

Operations

United Fire's property/casualty insurance offerings account for more than 90% of its annual insurance premiums with a majority of those policies being written to commercial group customers. The company also offers certain personal policies to individual customers.

Sales and Marketing

In order to increase policy placement in its existing markets United Fire offers profit-sharing and commission programs to its independent agents. It also seeks to provide modern technological tools to best serve both its agents and its policyholders.

Financial Performance

The company's revenue has been growing year-over-year. It reported revenue of $877 million in fiscal 2013 up from $813.2 million in revenue for fiscal 2012.

Net income also increased in fiscal 2013 compared to the prior year. The company netted $76 million in fiscal 2013 after reporting net income of $40 million in fiscal 2012.

United Fire's cash flow decreased by about $11 million in fiscal 2013 compared to the previous fiscal period.

Strategy

United Fire looks to expand into new markets to reduce the risk potential in its concentrated areas of operation.

EXECUTIVES

VP General Counsel and Secretary, Neal R. Scharmer, age 59, $250,000 total compensation

COO, Michael T. Wilkins, age 52, $388,600 total compensation

VP and Chief Investment Officer, Barrie W. Ernst, age 61, $305,000 total compensation

President and CEO, Randy A. Ramlo, age 54, $595,000 total compensation

VP and Chief Claims Officer, David E. Conner, age 57

CFO, Dawn M. Jaffray, age 50

VP Information Services, Scott A. Minkel, age 54

VP Corporate Marketing, Colleen R. Sova, age 62

Assistant Vice President Midwest Regional Office, Corey J. Ruehle

VP and COO United Life Insurance Company, Michael J. Sheeley

CTO, Brian Frese

Assistant Vice President Personal Lines, Victoria Hefel

Assistant Vice President Commercial Lines, Michael Hart

Vice President Of Accounting, Sue Haupert

Vice President, Al Schons

Vice President, Douglas Penn

Vice President Human Resources, Timothy Spain

Vice President, Debbie Johnstone

Assistant Vice President West Coast Regional Claims Manager, Mary Bianco

Vice Chairman, John A. Rife, age 73

Chairman, Jack B. Evans, age 67

Auditors: Ernst & Young LLP

LOCATIONS

HQ: United Fire Group, Inc.
118 Second Avenue S.E., Cedar Rapids, IA 52401
Phone: 319 399-5700
Web: www.unitedfiregroup.com

PRODUCTS/OPERATIONS

Selected Subsidiaries

United Fire & Casualty Company
Addison Insurance Company
American Indemnity Financial Corporation
Texas General Indemnity Company
Lafayette Insurance Company
Mercer Insurance Group Inc.
Financial Pacific Insurance Company
Mercer Insurance Company
Franklin Insurance Company
Mercer Insurance Company of New Jersey Inc.
United Fire & Indemnity Company
United Fire Lloyds
United Life Insurance Company

COMPETITORS

AIG	Hanover Insurance
Allstate	John Hancock Financial
American Family Insurance	Services
American Financial	Liberty Mutual
	MassMutual

Group	Progressive
Arrowpoint Capital	Corporation
Corp.	Prudential
CNA Surety	State Farm
Chubb Limited	The Hartford
Erie Indemnity	Travelers Companies
Farmers Group	White Mountains
GEICO	Insurance Group

HISTORICAL FINANCIALS

Company Type: Public

Income Statement

FYE: December 31

	ASSETS ($ mil.)	NET INCOME ($ mil.)	INCOME AS % OF ASSETS	EMPLOYEES
12/14	3,856	59	1.5%	981
12/13	3,720	76	2.0%	943
12/12	3,694	40	1.1%	909
12/11	3,618	0	0.0%	894
12/10	3,007	47	1.6%	654
Annual Growth	6.4%	5.6%	—	10.7%

2014 Year-End Financials

Debt ratio: —	No. of shares (mil.): 25
Return on equity: 7.39%	Dividends
Cash ($ mil.): 90	Yield: 2.6%
Current ratio: —	Payout: 39.2%
Long-term debt ($ mil.): —	Market value ($ mil.): 744

	STOCK PRICE ($) FY Close	P/E High/Low	PER SHARE ($) Earnings	Dividends	Book Value
12/14	29.73	14 10	2.32	0.78	32.67
12/13	28.66	11 7	2.98	0.69	30.87
12/12	21.84	17 10	1.58	0.60	28.90
12/11	20.18	— —	(0.00)	0.60	27.29
12/10	22.32	13 9	1.80	0.60	27.35
Annual Growth	7.4%	— —	6.6%	6.8%	4.5%

United Natural Foods Inc.

Distribution is second nature for United Natural Foods Inc. (UNFI). The company is one of the top wholesale distributors of natural organic and specialty foods in the US and Canada. It owns more than 30 distribution centers that supply 85000-plus items to 40000 customers including independently-owned retailers supernatural chain Whole Foods (its #1 customer) and traditional supermarkets. The company offers groceries supplements produce frozen foods and ethnic and kosher food products. UNFI also operates about a dozen natural-products retail stores under the Earth Origins banner and it produces roasted nuts dried fruits and other snack items through subsidiary Woodstock Farms.

Operations

UNFI's wholesale division (97% of sales) is augmented by specialty products units such as subsidiary Albert's Organics which supplies more than 5000 customers with fruits vegetables and other perishable items. The division also distributes vitamins through Select Nutrition and ethnic food items and related products through its UNFI Specialty business. The company has built up its own food brands through subsidiary Blue Marble Brands. The unit offers more than 650 products marketed under 15 brand names directly to retailers as well as third party distributors.

UNFI's retail arm Earth Origins operates a dozen natural products stores primarily in Florida but also in Maryland and Massachusetts. The company also has a retail store in Vancouver British Columbia that does business as Drive Organics.

Geographic Reach

Through its acquisition of SunOpta Distribution Group the company's wholly-owned subsidiary UNFI Canada became the largest distributor of natural organic and specialty foods including kosher fare in Canada. UNFI has five distribution centers in Canada. UNFI Canada contributes about 5% of UNFI's sales.

Sales and Marketing

Whole Foods Market is UNFI's largest wholesale customer representing about 35% of its net sales. It's the only customer that accounts for more than 10% of sales. Conventional supermarkets including Kroger Publix and Wegman's and mass market chains account for about 25% of sales.

Financial Performance

UNFI has seen strong growth over the past decade with revenue in fiscal 2015 (ended July) up 20% to $8.2 billion. The rise is a result of organic growth (both meanings of organic) as natural and organic products continue to appeal to customers and gain share in the market. The company's wholesale operations saw double-digit sales increases across all customer markets.

Net income has been rising right along with revenue and hit nearly $140 million in fiscal 2015 up 11%. Cash flow from operations has been up and down in recent years amid changes in inventories among other items. In fiscal 2015 cash flow from operations fell 22% to about $49 million as the company reported an increase in inventories as a result of stocking new facilities.

Strategy

UNFI has succeeded at taking market share away from its competition thanks to demand for its slate of premium services coupled with its expanding distribution capacity and targeted acquisitions. Indeed the company has invested more than $415 million in its distribution network and infrastructure during the past five years. In 2014 it opened a new distribution in Wisconsin (Racine) and the following year opened new locations in New York (Hudson Valley) and Wisconsin (Prescott). Plans in 2016 call for a new facility in Gilroy California.

UNFI enjoys long-standing relationships with some of the industry's largest customers including Whole Foods where it enjoys primary supplier status. Nonetheless competition in the industry is fierce; UNFI goes head-to-head with Kehe Food which acquired another rival Tree of Life from Dutch food giant Wessanen in 2010. The company also contends with traditional grocery wholesalers such as C & S Wholesale and SpartanNash (formerly Nash-Finch) which distribute a growing number of organic food items.

Mergers and Acquisitions

The company's UNFI West purchased perishable foods distributor Tony's based in West Sacramento California in 2014 for about $206 million. The company which continues to operate as Tony's Fine Foods serves the western US as well as Alaska and Hawaii.

In 2013 the company acquired Minnesota-based Trudeau Foods from owner Arbor Investments. Trudeau Foods is a distributor of natural organic and specialty foods that serves more than 600 customers across Minnesota North Dakota Wisconsin and Michigan's Upper Peninsula.

HISTORY

Rhode Island retailer Norman Cloutier founded Cornucopia Natural Foods in 1978 and soon focused on distribution. During the 1980s Cornucopia grew by acquiring other natural foods distributors. It bought suppliers Natural Food Systems (seafood) and BGS Distributing (vitamins) in 1987 and 1990 respectively. Cornucopia expanded into the Southeast in 1991 when it opened a distribution center in Georgia.

Reviving its interest in retailing Cornucopia formed Natural Retail Group in 1993 to buy and run natural foods stores. During the next two years it acquired several retailers. The company expanded its distribution operations in the West in 1995 adding Denver-based Rainbow Distributors.

In 1996 Cornucopia merged with the leading natural foods distributor in the western US Sacramento-based Mountain People's which Michael Funk had founded 20 years earlier. The combined company became United Natural Foods with Cloutier as chairman and CEO and Funk as president and vice chairman; it went public later that year.

United Natural Foods became the largest natural foods distributor when it bought New Hampshire-based Stow Mills in 1997. The next year it added Hershey Imports an importer and processor of nuts seeds and snacks and Albert's a distributor of organic produce. With the purchase of Mother Earth Markets in 1998 the company's retailing operations had grown to 16 stores but by mid-1999 it had sold four stores. That year United Natural Foods' East Coast consolidation problems became so profound that top customer Whole Foods announced it was finding backup distribution sources.

Funk replaced Cloutier as CEO and the company handed the chairman's post to board member Thomas Simone in 1999. In 2000 after the resignation of Cloutier from the board of directors United Natural Foods adopted a poison-pill plan to block potential takeovers. The company leased a distribution center in the Los Angeles area in 2001 to increase market share in the Southwest. It also acquired Florida's Palm Harbor Natural Foods.

In mid-2002 United Natural Foods lost one of its two largest customers —Wild Oats Markets — when that company defected to rival specialty foods distributor Tree of Life. However United Natural Foods soon won that business back. In October the company completed the acquisition of privately held Blooming Prairie Cooperative for approximately $31 million. In late 2002 the company merged with Northeast Cooperatives a natural foods distributor in the Midwest and Northeast.

That year United Natural Foods discontinued the management sales and support operations at its Hershey Imports subsidiary but continued to manufacture and distribute products from the Edison New Jersey plant.

In 2004 the company renewed its distribution agreement with Wild Oats with a five-year pact. United Natural Foods later announced a new three-year distribution agreement with Whole Foods which it renewed in 2006. Whole Foods later acquired Wild Oats in 2007. That year United Natural Foods acquired ethnic and specialty food distributor Millbrook Distribution Services for about $85 million.

CEO Funk stepped down in 2008 and was replaced by former Performance Food Group chief Steven Spinner.

EXECUTIVES

President and CEO, Steven L. (Steve) Spinner, age 56, $872,300 total compensation

COO, Sean F. Griffin, age 55, $440,300 total compensation

SVP General Counsel Chief Compliance Officer and Corporate Secretary, Joseph J. (Joe) Traficanti, age 64, $367,150 total compensation

SVP National Sales and Service; President East Region, Craig H. Smith, age 55, $366,100 total compensation

SVP and CIO, Eric A. Dorne, age 53

President Woodstock Farms Manufacturing and Blue Marble Brands, Christopher P. Testa, age 44

SVP National Supply Chain and Strategy; President West Region, Donald P. McIntyre, age 59

SVP CFO and Treasurer, Michael P. Zechmeister

Vice President Of Field Sales, Jack Murphy

National Information Technology Vice President UNFI Fresh, Mark Geery

Vice President Of Distribution Central Region, John (Jack) Hummel

National Vice President Supplier Relationship Management, Marc R Ghidotti

Chairman, Michael S. Funk, age 61

Auditors: KPMG LLP

LOCATIONS

HQ: United Natural Foods Inc.
313 Iron Horse Way, Providence, RI 02908
Phone: 401 528-8634
Web: www.unfi.com

PRODUCTS/OPERATIONS

2015 Sales by Customer Type

	$ mil.	% of total
Supernatural chains	2,822	35
Independently-owned natural products retailers	2,650	32
Conventional supermarkets	2,132	26
Other	581	7
Total	**8,185**	**100**

2015 Sales

	$ mil.	% of total
Wholesale	8,099	97
Other	225	3
Adjustments	(140.4)	-
Total	**8,185**	**100**

Selected Acquisitions

Fiscal 2012
B.K. Sethi Distribution Ltd. ($3 million; Ontario Canada; specialty food distribution)
Fiscal 2011
SunOpta Distribution Group ($66 million; Ontario Canada; specialty food distribution)

Selected Operations

Manufacturing division
Woodstock Farms (import roasting packaging and distribution of nuts dried fruit seeds trail mixes granola natural and organic snack items and confections and Blue Marble Brands products)
Retail division
Earth Origins (natural products retail stores in Florida Maryland Massachusetts)
Wholesale division
Albert' s Organics (distributor of organically grown produce and perishable items)
Select Nutrition (distributor of vitamins minerals and supplements)
UNIFI Canada (natural organic and specialty business in Canada)
UNFI Specialty (specialty distributor in the Eastern and Midwestern portions of the US)

COMPETITORS

Associated Wholesale Grocers	KeHE Distributors
C&S Wholesale	SUPERVALU
DPI Specialty Foods	SpartanNash
	Wal-Mart

HISTORICAL FINANCIALS

Company Type: Public

Income Statement

FYE: August 1

	REVENUE ($ mil.)	NET INCOME ($ mil.)	NET PROFIT MARGIN	EMPLOYEES
08/15	8,184	138	1.7%	8,700
08/14	6,794	125	1.8%	8,700
08/13*	6,064	107	1.8%	7,300
07/12	5,236	91	1.7%	7,000
07/11	4,530	76	1.7%	6,900
Annual Growth	**15.9%**	**16.0%**	**—**	**6.0%**

*Fiscal year change

2015 Year-End Financials

Debt ratio: 21.54%
Return on equity: 10.58%
Cash ($ mil.): 17
Current ratio: 2.93
Long-term debt ($ mil.): 537
No. of shares (mil.): 50
Dividends
Yield: —
Payout: —
Market value ($ mil.): 2,281

	STOCK PRICE ($) FY Close	P/E High/Low	PER SHARE ($) Earnings	Dividends	Book Value
08/15	45.53	30 16	2.76	0.00	27.66
08/14	58.71	30 23	2.52	0.00	24.98
08/13*	60.31	28 22	2.18	0.00	22.28
07/12	54.62	30 18	1.86	0.00	19.97
07/11	41.75	28 20	1.60	0.00	17.93
Annual Growth	**2.2%**	**— —**	**14.6%**	**—**	**11.4%**

*Fiscal year change

UNITED NETWORK FOR ORGAN SHARING

LOCATIONS

HQ: UNITED NETWORK FOR ORGAN SHARING
700 N 4TH ST, RICHMOND, VA 232191414
Phone: 8047824800
Web: WWW.TRANSPLANTLIVING.ORG

HISTORICAL FINANCIALS

Company Type: Private

Income Statement

FYE: September 30

	REVENUE ($ mil.)	NET INCOME ($ mil.)	NET PROFIT MARGIN	EMPLOYEES
09/09	35,111	340	1.0%	300
09/08	35	0	0.2%	—
Annual Growth	**98509.7%**	**568121.7%**	**—**	**—**

2009 Year-End Financials

Debt ratio: ——
Return on equity: 1.00%
Cash ($ mil.): 4
Current ratio: 1.30
Long-term debt ($ mil.): —
Dividends
Yield: —
Payout: —
Market value ($ mil.): —

United Parcel Service Inc

The ubiquitous Brown is more than chocolate-colored trucks or a plain-vanilla delivery business. United Parcel Service (UPS) is the world's largest package delivery company transporting about 18 million packages and documents per business day throughout the US and to 220-plus countries. Its delivery operations use a fleet of more than 106000 motor vehicles and 600-plus aircraft. In addition to package delivery the company offers services such as logistics and freight forwarding through UPS Supply Chain Solutions and less-than-truckload (LTL) and truckload (TL) freight transportation through UPS Freight.

Geographic Reach

The company's international scope is immensely vast; it serves customers in more than 220 countries worldwide. However the US generates 75% of its total revenue while other countries account for the remaining 25%. It has more than 2300 operating facilities.

Operations

Domestic package delivery is the company's largest business segment accounting for about 60% of sales. International package delivery is its second largest segment representing roughly 20% of UPS' total sales. Along with logistics and trucking the company's supply chain and freight segment which generates the remainder of sales includes mail expediting (UPS Mail Innovations) and financial services (UPS Capital) businesses as well as postal and business services store franchiser Mail Boxes Etc. which maintains UPS Store and Mail Boxes Etc. locations in the US and overseas.

Sales and Marketing

UPS delivers packages each business day for 1.6 million shipping customers to 8.2 million receivers (consignees). It targets industries such as health care government retail automotive industrial manufacturing and aerospace.

Financial Performance

UPS has enjoyed four years of steady revenue growth with revenues rising 5% from $55.4 billion in 2013 to peak at a record-setting $58.2 billion in 2014. The historic growth for 2014 was fueled by increases from its domestic (4%) and international (5%) package segments. The increase was also attributed to a 7% bump in deferred domestic package sales and a 6% jump in ground domestic sales.

Unlike its revenues UPS' profits have fluctuated over the years. After surging in 2013 profits decreased 31% to $3 billion in 2014 due to a significant spike in operating expenses especially compensation and benefits. The income was also affected by an uptick in other expenses including repairs and maintenance and purchased transportation.

UPS' operating cash flow remained steady from 2011 to 2013 but dropped by 22% to $5.7 billion in 2014 due to the decrease in income along with a decrease in inflows from accrued wages and withholdings.

Strategy

UPS' extensive global reach is a selling point for its supply chain management offerings which are tailored to customers in industries such as consumer goods and retail health care and technology. The company is seeing a growing trend among businesses outsourcing supply chain management viewing it as a strategic advantage to have effective management of their supply chains.

Package delivery revenue is increasing overseas where UPS continues to expand through infrastructure investments and selected acquisitions. The company has completed a $200 million 70% expansion of its European air hub in Cologne Germany.

Mergers and Acquisitions

Over the years UPS has enhanced its operations through the use of acquisitions. The company in mid-2015 made industry headlines through the $1.8 billion purchase of Coyote Logistics a Chicago-based third party logistics (3PL) company that offers truckload less-than-truckload (LTL) and intermodal air land and ocean transportation services in North America and Europe. Through the deal UPS expects to benefit from synergies in purchased transportation backhaul utilization cross-selling to customers in addition to technology systems and industry best practices.

In 2014 UPS purchased Poltraf Sp. z o.o. a pharmaceutical logistics company from Poland. Also in 2014 UPS picked up UK-based Polar Speed a provider of temperature-sensitive pharmaceutical supply chain products and services.

In 2013 the company acquired Hungary-based pharmaceutical logistics company CEMELOG Zrt in a move that enhanced its health care reach and expertise in the increasingly important markets of Central and Eastern Europe. All these deals strengthened UPS' health care expertise and network in Europe.

HISTORY

Seattle teens Jim Casey and Claude Ryan started American Messenger Company a delivery and errand service in 1907. They were soon making small-parcel deliveries for local department stores and in 1913 changed the company's name to Merchants Parcel Delivery. Casey who led the company for 50 years established a policy of manager ownership best service and lowest rates. In 1916 new employee Charlie Soderstrom chose the brown paint still used on the company's vehicles. Service expanded outside Seattle in 1919 when Merchants Parcel bought Oakland California-based Motor Parcel Delivery later changing its name to United Parcel Service (UPS).

EXECUTIVES

Vice President Cargo, Don Herbert
President UPS International, James J. (Jim) Barber
EVP and Chief Commercial Officer, Alan Gershenhorn, age 57, $494,338 total compensation
Chairman and CEO, David P. Abney, age 60, $674,546 total compensation
CIO and Global Business Services Officer, David A. (Dave) Barnes, age 60, $454,347 total compensation
President US Operations, Myron A. Gray, age 58, $472,149 total compensation
CFO, Richard Peretz
SVP Engineering, Mark Wallace
President U.S. Western Region, George Willis
Vice President International Marketing, Derek Woodward
Vice President West Los Angeles District, Timothy (Tim) Robinson
Vice President Technology and Architecture, Mark Hilbush
Vice President Finance, Rich Peretz
Vice President International E Commerce Technology and Trade Direct, Carl Strenger
Upper Management Vice President, Wayne Herring
Regional Vice President West Region Mail Boxes Etc Inc, Duane Furukawa
Vice President, Scott Wicker
Vice President Information Services, John (Jack) Nallin

National Account Manager, Rick Wolf
Vice President CRM Technology, Tina Latuga
National Accounts Manager, Dwain Evans
Vice President Revenue Management and Pricing, Ken Burroughs
Vice President Healthcare Sales, Lisa Lafave
Vice President Of Public Affairs, Amgad Shehata
Vice President Applications, Nick Gray
Senior Management Senior Vice President General Manager, Randi Turner
Vice President Human Resources, Kevin Foley
Vice President Security Isrg Asia Pacific Pacific Region, Kevin Greene
Vice President, Bill Kendall
Vice President of Operations, Cindy Miller
Vice President Midmarket Sales, Glenn Mason
Vice President Global Accounts Sales, Kathy Fantauzzi
Corporate Vice President Global Accounts, Jim Darcy
Vice President Sales High Tech Sector, David (Dave) O'Leary
Vice President CSC Strategy, Frank Zipp
Vice President, Thomas (Thom) Gebhard
Vice President Global Sales, Michael (Mel) Mulholland
Vice President Symposiums, Bill Norris
Vice President, Ted Payne
Vice President; Sales And Marketing, Joe Racanelli
Vice President International Marketing, John (Jack) Miltenis
Vice President Sales West Region, Rusty Tebo
Vice President Of Transportation Services, Ed Gueren
Vice President Of Industrial Engineering, Chuck Holland
East Region Vice President Of Sales, Camille Kielty
Vice President Business Development, Cornell Howard
Vice President, Jerry McDonough
Vice President of Business Development, Grady Hopper
Vice President of Customer Technology Marketing, Stu Marcus
Vice President, Adam Feinberg
Vice President, Joe Vanderbeck
Vice President Swenson Hardware, Jerry Dvorak
Vice President, Robert (Bob) Marsh
Vice President Gta Toronto Facilities, Mike Pope
Senior Vice President Marketing and Sales, James (Jamie) Thome
Vice President Sales, Ken O'Connell
Vice President, Chuck Altimari
Vice President Public Relations, Steven (Steve) Gaut
Vice President Finance, Carlos Cubias
National Accounts Manager, Ruby E Brunelle
Senior Vice President, Lisa Martin
National Account Manager, Thomas Anonsen
Vice President, Paul White
Vice President Of Marketing, Alan Hall
Vice President Sales and Marketing, Robert (Bob) Debatto
National Account Manager, Joe Bradley
Vice President of Cach, Bob Latchford
Vice President Corporate Public Affairs, Rich McArdle
Senior Vice President;Manager, Burt White
Vice President Customer Care Americas, Patty Cheek
Svp Of Sales, Paul Hoelting
Vice President Fleet Maintenance Us Operations, Larry Cook
Executive Vice President of Service parts logistics, Scott Collins
Vice President, Dominic Culotta
Vice President, Jose Garcia
Vice President, Donna Martinez
Senior Vice President Strategy, John (Jack) Duffy
Vice President Fleet Planning, Ken Cook

Vice President Engineering, Cheri Fulginiti
Vice President Strategic Accounts, Todd Schindler
Vice President, Peter (Pete) Walsh
National Account Manager, Alicia Ziegler
Vice President Finance, David Minton
Vice President, Albert (Al) Wright
Vice President Shared Services, Jim Madeiros
Vice President New Product Concepts Competitive Inte, Paul Vassallo
Vice President, James (Jamie) Owens
Senior Vice President General Counsel Secretary, Lesley T (Les) Knight
Vice President, Charles (Chas) Brown
Vice President East Central Region, Joseph Zito
Vice President National Accounts Worldwide Services, Steven Harmon
National Account Manager, Robert Musca
Vice President Airline Ground Support, William Jacob
Vice President Sales Global Accounts, Jerry Felton
Vice President South Florida District, William Smith
Vice President Information Technology e Ventures, Walid El-Kadi
Vice President Finance, Craig Partridge
Vice President Inside Sales, Ralph Trujillo
Vice President Sales, Steve Fuller
Vice President SAG and Program Management, Ron Jordan
Vice President Enterprise Sales, Bill Washington
Vice President Air District, Steve Mockus
Vice President Corporate Public Affairs, Nicole Clifton
Vice President Strategic Account Sales, Tim Gombac
Vice President Sales, Keith Cox
Vice President Of Human Resources, Nikki Edwards
Vice President Strategic Accounts Retail Sales, Costello Art
Senior Vice President Strategy Ups Freight, Kevin Hartman
Vice President Customer Service, Betty Schmitz
Vice President, Michael Plourde
Vice Prespident Of Sales Americas, Pedro Anaya
National Account Manager, Lynn Caldwell
Vice President Sales, Brian Fosse
Vice President of Healthcare Strategic Accounts, Angela (Angie) Watson
Vice President Corporate Transportation Services, Kenneth (Ken) Buenker
Vice President Enterprise Sales, Sheila Dunn
Vice President, Keith Hall
National Account Manager, Nick Colson
Vice President Information technology Eastern US, Stephen (Steve) Hydrick
Vice President of Revenue Management Marketing, Jon Steppe
Vice President, Tom Cox
National Accounts Manager, Laura Loughner
Senior Vice President Blue Water Hull, Anita Moran
Vice President of Operations South America, Oscar de la Fuente
National Account Manager, Timothy (Tim) Binkis
Vice President Sales, Jeff Baumblatt
National Account Manager, Michelle (Mitch) Verhelle
Regional Vice President of Finance, Jay Bowers
National Accounts Manager, Brian F mcQuade
Vice President Organizational Development, Stephen (Steve) Campbell
Vice President Sales, Steve Evans
Vice President Legal Department, Matthew (Matt) Capozzoli
Vice President Marketing, Kurt Kuehn
Senior Vice President Human Resources And Manager Public Affairs Group, Allen (Al) Hill
Vice President, Mark Sobolewski
Vice President, Donna Atkins
Vice President Training, Heather Moseley

Vice President of Worldwide Sales, Yuki Takai
Vice President International E Commerce, Michael (Mel) Ryan
Vice President West Region Sales, Mike Turner
Vice President Information Systems, Roger Dingus
Vice President Sales, James (Jamie) Owen
Senior Vice President Human Resources, Lytana Kids
National Account Manager, Lynn Caldwell-Denny
Vice President Human Resources, Joseph (Jo) Schneider
Vice President, Kay Townsend
National Account Manager, Robin Tidwell
Vice President, James (Jamie) Bruce
Vice President Operations Metro Jersey District, Mark Kemper
Vice President Finance, Andrew (Andy) Dolny
Vice President Labor Relations, Chuck Martorana
Auditors: Deloitte & Touche LLP

LOCATIONS

HQ: United Parcel Service Inc
55 Glenlake Parkway, N.E. Atlanta, GA 30328
Phone: 404 828-6000
Web: www.ups.com

PRODUCTS/OPERATIONS

2013 Sales

	$ mil.	% of total
US domestic package		
Ground	24,194	44
Next day air	6,443	12
Deferred	3,437	6
International package		
Export	9,166	16
Domestic	2,667	5
Cargo	596	1
Supply chain & freight		
Forwarding & logistics	5,492	10
Freight	2,882	5
Other	561	1
Total	55,438	100

COMPETITORS

American Airlines Group	Nippon Express
Canada Post	Panalpina
Deutsche Post	Royal Mail
FedEx	Ryder System
Japan Post	TNT Express
La Poste	US Postal Service
Lufthansa	United Continental
	YRC Worldwide

HISTORICAL FINANCIALS

Company Type: Public

Income Statement

FYE: December 31

	REVENUE ($ mil.)	NET INCOME ($ mil.)	NET PROFIT MARGIN	EMPLOYEES
12/14	58,232	3,032	5.2%	435,000
12/13	55,438	4,372	7.9%	395,000
12/12	54,127	807	1.5%	399,000
12/11	53,105	3,804	7.2%	398,000
12/10	49,545	3,488	7.0%	400,600
Annual Growth	4.1%	(3.4%)	—	2.1%

2014 Year-End Financials

Debt ratio: 30.41%
Return on equity: 70.39%
Cash ($ mil.): 2,291
Current ratio: 1.37
Long-term debt ($ mil.): 9,864
No. of shares (mil.): 905
Dividends
Yield: 2.4%
Payout: 66.5%
Market value ($ mil.): 100,609

	STOCK PRICE ($) FY Close	P/E High/Low	PER SHARE ($) Earnings	Dividends	Book Value
12/14	111.17	34 28	3.28	2.68	2.37
12/13	105.08	23 16	4.61	2.48	7.01
12/12	73.73	97 83	0.83	2.28	4.88
12/11	73.19	20 16	3.84	2.08	7.31
12/10	72.58	21 16	3.48	1.88	8.05
Annual Growth	11.2%	— —	(1.5%)	9.3%	(26.4%)

United Rentals, Inc.

No cash to buy a bulldozer? No worries —just lease one from United Rentals. The company considers itself the #1 commercial and construction equipment renter in the world serving customers in the commercial infrastructure industrial and residential sectors. It operates through a network of more than 880 locations in the US and Canada and provides about 3300 equipment items —everything from general to heavy construction and industrial equipment to hand tools special-event items (such as aerial towers) power (diesel generators) and HVAC equipment and trench-safety equipment. It also sells new and used equipment as well as rental-related and contractor supplies and parts.

Geographic Reach

The largest equipment rental company in the world operates rental locations in 49 US states and 10 Canadian provinces with a majority in Texas (120 locations). The US accounts for 87% of its net sales.

Operations

United Rentals' general rentals accounted for 88% of its 2014 revenues; trench safety power and HVAC equipment rentals 12%.

Sales and Marketing

The company markets its products and services through its Sales Force (sales staff at the company's branches and customer care centers); National Account Program (managers dedicated to large customer accounts); E-Rentals portal (online e-commerce site) and advertising (trade publications yellow pages the Internet radio and direct mail).

Financial Performance

United Rentals achieved unprecedented growth in 2014 with revenues surging 15% from almost $5 billion in 2013 to a record-setting $5.7 billion in 2014. The historic growth for 2014 was fueled by additional revenue provided by an acquisition along with an increase in equipment rentals. The growth in rental equipment sales was primarily due to a 10% spike in the volume of original equipment cost on rent a 5% rental rate increase and changes in the company's rental mix.

The company's profits surged 40% from $387 million in 2013 to $540 million a company milestone. The profit growth was attributed to the increase in revenue coupled with a decrease in restructuring costs. United Rentals also experienced a more than 100% increase in operating cash flow in 2013 due to the higher profits and additional cash generated from prepaid expenses and other assets and accounts payable. Operating cash flow jumped 16% to peak at $1.8 billion in 2014.

Strategy

Because of its size United Rentals rallies more resources over smaller businesses. Competitive advantages include more purchasing leverage a wider range of equipment and services and the more convenient movement of assets between locations.

United Rentals enhances its operating efficiencies by ramping up through consolidation of functions including payroll and accounts payable.

In order to manage the age composition and size of its fleet the company routinely sells used rental equipment and invests in new equipment. United Rentals acts as a dealer of new equipment for many leading equipment makers such as Genie Industries Skyjack (aerial lifts) Sullair (compressors) and Terex (telehandlers). At most branches United Rentals sells various supplies and merchandise and offers repair and maintenance services.

It expands its specialty branch network by opening new locations. Throughout 2015 the company plans to open at least 16 specialty rental branches/tool hubs. In 2014 it launched seven branches in the US and one in Canada. The year before it opened 18 branches in the US and Canada. United Rentals also grows through acquisitions.

Mergers and Acquisitions

In 2014 United Rentals enhanced its specialty pump segment through the $780 million purchase of National Pump. National Pump produces specialty pumps through a total of 35 branches including four branches in western Canada.

Also that year United Rentals acquired the power and HVAC assets of Blue-Stream Services a provider of equipment rental services. The acquisition expanded the footprint of the company's power and HVAC specialty rental operations in the Gulf and provided a significant cross-selling opportunity to the company's network.

HISTORY

Bradley Jacobs had made a fortune in the garbage business having used United Waste Systems as a roll-up company to buy small trash-hauling firms in that fragmented industry. Flush with cash after he sold United Waste Systems in 1997 to USA Waste Services (now Waste Management) Jacobs launched the same roll-up strategy to consolidate the equipment-rental industry. He and his management team bought six leasing companies and started United Rentals. The company which went public in 1997 had acquired 38 rental companies in 20 states by mid-1998.

EXECUTIVES

Vice President Business Development, Ned Graham
Vice President Strategy And Planning, Kenneth (Ken) Mettel
Region Vice President, Mark Tapia
EVP and CFO, William B. Plummer, age 56, $551,221 total compensation
President and CEO, Michael J. Kneeland, age 61, $950,000 total compensation
EVP and COO, Matthew J. Flannery, age 50, $548,668 total compensation
SVP Business Services and CIO, Dale A. Asplund, age 47, $479,343 total compensation
SVP General Counsel and Corporate Secretary, Jonathan M. Gottsegen, age 48, $411,631 total compensation
SVP Sales and Marketing, Juan P. Corsillo
Executive Vice President, Anthony Leopold
Regional Vice President, Chad Matter
National Account Manager Oil And Gas, John (Jack) Bebout
Region Vice President, Pat Lowry
Vice President Environmental Health And Safety, James (Jamie) Dorris
Vice President Controller, John (Jack) Fahey
National Account Manager, Jeff Johnson
National Account Manager, Klay Kaminski
National Account Manager, Curt Mellett

Vice President of Corporate Communications, Fred Bratman
Executive Vice President Corporate Services, Kurtis Barker
Vice President Human Resources, Craig Pintoff
Vice President Managed Services, Gordon McDonald
Regional Vice President, Randal Hajner
Vice President Business Process, Loretta Foley
Vice President Internal Audit, Helge Jacobsen
Senior Vice President Operations, David Ledlow
National Accounts Manager, William Sheffield
Senior Vice President, Paul McDonnell
National Account Manager, David (Dave) Capps
National Account Manager, Jeremy Epps
Senior Vice President Human Resources, Linda Luman
National Account Manager, Christopher Cox
National Accounts Manager, Gina Rollins
Vice President, Scott Gorton
National Account Manager, Brian Knauer
Vice President Sales and Operations, Gregg Christensen
National Account Manager Oil and Gas, Brian Nagel
Chairman, Jenne K. Britell, age 72
Assistant Treasurer, Colin Fox
Auditors: Ernst & Young LLP

LOCATIONS

HQ: United Rentals, Inc.
100 First Stamford Place, Suite 700, Stamford, CT 06902
Phone: 203 622-3131
Web: www.unitedrentals.com

2014 Sales

	$ mil.	% of total
Domestic	4,962	87
Foreign	723	13
Total	**5,685**	**100**

PRODUCTS/OPERATIONS

2014 Sales

	$ mil.	% of total
General Rental	5,002	88
The trench safety power and HVAC and pump solutions	683	12
Total	**5,685**	**100**

2014 Sales

	$ mil.	% of total
Equipment rentals	4,819	85
Sales of rental equipment	544	10
Sales of new equipment	149	3
Contractor supplies sales	85	1
Service & other revenues	88	1
Total	**5,685**	**100**

Selected Products

Aerial lifts
Backhoes
Barricades
Compressors
Cones
Contractor supplies
Ditching equipment
Earth-moving equipment
Forklifts
Generators
Hand tools
Heaters
Light towers
Material-handling equipment
Message boards
Pavement-marking systems
Portable power units
Power washers
Pumps
Skid-steer loaders
Trench shields
Warning lights
Water pumps

COMPETITORS

AMECO
Atlas Lift Truck Rentals
Case Power & Equipment
Hertz
Maxim Crane Works
NES Rentals
Neff
RDO Equipment
Sunbelt Rentals
Ziegler inc

HISTORICAL FINANCIALS

Company Type: Public

Income Statement

FYE: December 31

	REVENUE ($ mil.)	NET INCOME ($ mil.)	NET PROFIT MARGIN	EMPLOYEES
12/15	5,817	585	10.1%	12,700
12/14	5,685	540	9.5%	12,500
12/13	4,955	387	7.8%	11,850
12/12	4,117	75	1.8%	11,300
12/11	2,611	101	3.9%	7,500
Annual Growth	22.2%	55.1%	—	14.1%

2015 Year-End Financials

Debt ratio: 67.55%
Return on equity: 35.74%
Cash ($ mil.): 179
Current ratio: 1.05
Long-term debt ($ mil.): 7,555

No. of shares (mil.): 91
Dividends
Yield: —
Payout: —
Market value ($ mil.): 6,657

	STOCK PRICE ($) FY Close	P/E High/Low		PER SHARE ($) Earnings	Dividends	Book Value
12/15	72.54	17	10	6.07	0.00	16.08
12/14	102.01	21	13	5.15	0.00	18.37
12/13	77.95	19	11	3.64	0.00	19.81
12/12	45.52	51	30	0.79	0.00	16.93
12/11	29.55	21	8	1.38	0.00	1.64
Annual Growth	25.2%	—	—	44.8%	—	77.0%

United States Steel Corp.

Steel crazy after all these years United States Steel (U.S. Steel) is North America's largest integrated steelmaker. The company operates mills throughout the Midwest in the US; in Ontario Canada; and in Slovakia. U.S. Steel makes a wide range of flat-rolled and tubular steel products and its annual production capacity is 24.4 million net tons of raw steel. Its customers are primarily in the automotive appliance construction oil and gas and petrochemical industries. In addition U.S. Steel mines iron ore and procures coke which provide the primary raw materials used in steelmaking. It is also engaged in railroad and barge operations and real estate.

HISTORY

U.S. Steel was conceived through a 1901 merger of 10 steel companies that combined their furnaces ore deposits railroad companies and shipping lines. The deal involved industrial pioneers Andrew Carnegie Charles Schwab Elbert Gary and J. P. Morgan.

Morgan had helped organize the Federal Steel Company in 1898 and he then wanted to create a centralized trust to dominate the soaring steel market. Carnegie owned the largest US steel company at the time Carnegie Steel but wanted to retire.

In 1900 Schwab Carnegie Steel's president outlined the idea of the steel trust based on a merger of the Carnegie and Federal steel companies. Morgan asked Schwab to persuade Carnegie to sell his steel mills and name his price. Morgan didn't haggle when Carnegie responded that he would sell for almost half a billion dollars.

The Carnegie-Morgan combination created the world's first billion-dollar company. It produced 67% of the country's steel in its first year (its steel complex and the Indiana town where it was located were named after Gary who was CEO until 1927).

The company boomed during WWI and WWII. But its market share fell to about 30% by the 1950s although it set new profit records in 1955. During the 1970s prospects for long-term growth in steel became dismal in light of rising costs foreign competition and competitive pricing.

In 1982 U.S. Steel doubled its size when it bought Marathon Oil a major integrated energy company with huge oil and gas reserves in the US and abroad. It continued to cut back its steelmaking capacity laying off 100000 employees closing steel mills and selling off assets.

The company bought Texas Oil & Gas in 1986 and renamed itself USX Corporation to reflect the decreasing role of steel in its business. Also that year corporate raider Carl Icahn USX's largest single shareholder unsuccessfully tried to get the company to sell its steel operations. In 1988 USX bought 49% of Transtar a group of rail and water transport providers. (It purchased the remaining stake in 2001 making Transtar a wholly owned subsidiary.)

Stockholders in 1991 approved splitting the company into two separate entities under the USX umbrella: U.S. Steel and Marathon. During the 1990s U.S. Steel continued to close steelmaking facilities. In 1992 USX joined five other leading US steel producers in a suit against subsidized foreign steelmakers. The next year the company formed two joint ventures with Japan's Kobe Steel.

In 1994 U.S. Steel teamed up with rival Nucor to explore a new technology that would reduce much of the cost and pollution of the steelmaking process. The company agreed to pay $106 million in fines and improvements in 1996 to settle charges of air pollution violations involving its Indiana plant. That year blast furnace outages at two U.S. Steel plants cost the company more than $100 million.

U.S. Steel began upgrading several of its facilities in 1997 and 1998 and entered into a number of domestic and foreign joint ventures including one in Slovakia and another in Mexico. Seeing prices drop in 1998 and 1999 the company cut production and joined other US steelmakers in charging rivals in Brazil Japan and Russia with unlawfully dumping low-priced steel in the US.

In 2000 U.S. Steel acquired the core activities of leading central European steelmaker VSZ. The $495 million (excluding investments) deal —U.S. Steel's first major foray into Europe —included an agreement to invest some $700 million in VSZ's facilities.

Early in 2001 USX spun off its steel operations as United States Steel Corporation; the remaining energy businesses began operating as Marathon Oil Corporation. Also that year USX-U.S. Steel and Bethlehem Steel announced they were in talks about possibly merging the two companies. Subsequently USX-U.S. Steel and National Steel (U.S. subsidiary of NKK) began talks of merging its businesses. In order for the deal to close National Steel would have to restructure its debt and the Bush administration would have to implement its plan to curtail steel imports. At the end of 2001 due to shareholder pressure USX-U.S. Steel split apart from its holding company USX Corporation and the steel operations unit went back to trading under its original name United States Steel Corporation. The breakup left the company with over $1.3 billion in debt (Marathon Oil assumed $900 million of the company's debt).

U.S. Steel signed an option agreement to purchase the remaining 53% of National Steel in 2002. That year U.S. Steel sold its stake in VSZ.

In its pursuit to consolidate U.S. Steel along with other US steelmakers received concessions (40% import tariffs and assistance with its huge retiree health-care costs) from the Bush administration. In March 2002 the Bush administration on recommendations of the International Trade Commission imposed tariffs of 8%-30% providing temporary relief to U.S. Steel and the US steel industry. The administration rejected any retiree bailout plan and in December 2003 ended the tariffs 16 months ahead of schedule.

In 2003 U.S. Steel made the monumental move to purchase National Steel for roughly $1.1 billion in cash including liabilities. AK Steel which had an offer of roughly $1.1 billion vehemently challenged U.S. Steel but the deal fell through after labor negotiations with United Steelworkers of America proved unsuccessful. With the combined manufacturing capabilities of National Steel and U.S. Steel the company's raw steel production came in at around 20 million tons of steel annually both domestically and internationally which made it the nation's largest steel producer until the formation of Mittal Steel USA in 2005. The year 2003 also saw the expansion of U.S. Steel's European businesses with the acquisition of Sartid.

U.S. Steel again jumped into the industrywide consolidation game in 2007 when it spent a combined $3.3 billion to buy tubular goods maker Lone Star Technologies and the former Stelco in separate deals. Lone Star Technologies was among the nation's largest makers of welded steel tubes for use in the oilfield. The acquired business complemented U.S. Steel's own product line for the energy industry which consisted largely of seamless tubes. The Stelco deal on the other hand added to the company's core business. Focusing on slab products used in the flat-rolled market Stelco raised U.S. Steel's production capacity to more than 30 million tons a year. Upon closing of the deal U.S. Steel changed Stelco's name to U.S. Steel Canada.

Although U.S. Steel agreed to maintain certain production and employment levels at the plants in Canada it stopped operations in 2009 when demand weakened in response to the global economic slump. The Canadian government responded by taking the company to court in 2009 and a later settlement of the dispute led U.S. Steel to agree to invest $50 million in its two Canadian plants by 2015.

U.S. Steel Canada sold its Bar Mill and Bloom and Billet Mill at its Ontario operations to Max Aicher (North America) in 2010. Also in 2010 U.S. Steel sold the assets of its Mobile River Terminal Company and of Warrior and Gulf Navigation.

In 2011 the company sold Oklahoma-based subsidiary Steel Coil Services to Macsteel Service Centers USA.

In 2012 it exited its Serbia business (U.S. Steel Serbia) after the European economy slid significantly and weak demand caused the company to lose more than $200 million from its Serbian operations in 2011. U.S. Steel sold the segment to the Serbian government for only $1. U.S. Steel Serbia was part of the company's U.S. Steel Europe business.

In 2012 U.S. Steel also sold the non-core assets of Birmingham Southern Railroad Company and the Port Birmingham Terminal and recognized a pretax gain of $89 million.

EXECUTIVES

SVP and CTO, David L. Britten, age 56
VP Industrial Solutions, Joseph R. (Joe) Scherrbaum, age 58
EVP and CFO, David B. (Dave) Burritt, age 59, $1,186,250 total compensation
SVP Consumer Solutions, Sara A. Greenstein
SVP and Chief Risk Officer, Larry T. Brockway, age 53
VP and General Director U.S. Steel Serbia, Douglas R. Matthews, age 50, $518,750 total compensation
SVP Tubular Business, David J. Rintoul, age 58
VP European Solutions and President US Steel Ko·Šice, Scott D. Buckiso, age 48
President and CEO, Mario Longhi, $1,186,250 total compensation
VP and CIO, Charles G. Balawajder, age 59
VP Service Center Solutions, Geoff M. Turk
General Manager Minnesota Ore Operations, Lawrence W. (Larry) Sutherland
SVP Government Affairs General Counsel and Chief Compliance Officer, Suzanne R. Folsom, $506,775 total compensation
SVP Automotive Solutions, James E. Bruno
Senior Vice President Of Development, Emmett Beever
Chairman, David S. (Dave) Sutherland, age 66
Secretary Safety and Ih, Lori Banziger
Auditors: PricewaterhouseCoopers LLP

LOCATIONS

HQ: United States Steel Corp.
  600 Grant Street, Pittsburgh, PA 15219-2800
Phone: 412 433-1121   **Fax:** 412 433-4818
Web: www.ussteel.com

2014 Sales

	$ mil.	% of total
North America	14,616	83
Europe	2,891	17
Total	**17,507**	**100**

PRODUCTS/OPERATIONS

Selected Subsidiaries

Acero Prime S. R. L de CV (44% steel processing and warehousing)
Delray Con
Double Eagle Steel Coating Company (50% with Severstal; steel processing)
PRO-TEC Coating Co. (50% with Kobe Steel; steel processing)
Transtar I
U. S. Stee
USS-POSCO Industries (50% with Pohang Iron & Steel; steel processing)
Worthington Specialty Processing (50% with Worthington Industries; steel processing)

2014 Sales

	$ mil.	% of total
Flat-rolled	12,895	68
US Steel Europe	2,936	16
Tubular products	2,774	15
Other	269	1
Adjustments	(1367)	-
Total	**17,507**	**100**

COMPETITORS

AK Steel Holding Corporation
Allegheny Technologies
ArcelorMittal
Baosteel
BlueScope Steel
B= HLER-UDDEHOLM
Carpenter Technology
Gerdau Ameristeel
JFE Holdings
Kobe Steel
Nippon Steel & Sumitomo Metal Corporation

Nucor
POSCO
SSAB North America
SSAB Svenskt
Salzgitter
Simec
Steel Dynamics
Tata Steel
Ternium
ThyssenKrupp Steel
Wuhan Iron & Steel

HISTORICAL FINANCIALS

Company Type: Public

Income Statement

FYE: December 31

	REVENUE ($ mil.)	NET INCOME ($ mil.)	NET PROFIT MARGIN	EMPLOYEES
12/14	17,507	102	0.6%	23,000
12/13	17,424	(1,672)	—	38,500
12/12	19,328	(124)	—	39,000
12/11	19,884	(53)	—	43,000
12/10	17,374	(482)	—	42,000
Annual Growth	0.2%	—	—	(14.0%)

2014 Year-End Financials

Debt ratio: 28.41%
Return on equity: 2.85%
Cash ($ mil.): 1,354
Current ratio: 1.80
Long-term debt ($ mil.): 3,120

No. of shares (mil.): 145
Dividends
  Yield: 0.7%
  Payout: 29.4%
Market value ($ mil.): 3,895

	STOCK PRICE ($) FY Close	P/E High/Low		PER SHARE ($) Earnings	Dividends	Book Value
12/14	26.74	65	32	0.69	0.20	26.08
12/13	29.50	—	—	(11.56)	0.20	23.14
12/12	23.85	—	—	(0.86)	0.20	24.10
12/11	26.46	—	—	(0.37)	0.20	24.30
12/10	58.42	—	—	(3.36)	0.20	26.80
Annual Growth	(17.7%)	—	—	—	(0.0%)	(0.7%)

United Technologies Corp

United Technologies (UTC) has the worldwide industrial expertise to lift you up and cool you down. Its Otis UTC Climate Controls & Security Pratt & Whitney and Sikorsky segments develop technologies systems and services for the aerospace construction and security industries. Climate Controls & Security makes alarms monitoring equipment surveillance and access control systems and fire and hazard detection products. Otis is the world's largest elevator and escalator manufacturing company. Pratt & Whitney makes commercial and military engines while Sikorsky makes helicopters. UTC Aerospace Systems produces engine controls and flight systems for military and commercial clients.

Geographic Reach

UTC operates through 4000 locations in more than 70 countries. The US generates around 60% of its total sales; Europe and the Asia/Pacific follow contributing 20% and 15% respectively.

Operations

After a wave of massive acquisitions and divestitures over the last few years UTC has realigned under five well-diversified business segments. UTC's core Climate Controls & Security segment makes security products and firefighting equip-

ment for commercial governmental and residential applications. This segment represented nearly 25% of UTC's total sales for 2014.

The other remaining segments include Pratt & Whitney (22% of sales) Otis (20%) UTC Aerospace Systems (22%) and Sikorsky (11%).

Sales and Marketing

The company serves customers residing in the commercial and industrial (contributing 45% revenue) commercial aerospace (35%) and military aerospace and space (20%) sectors. The US government contributed 15%.

Financial Performance

UTC achieved historic growth in 2014 with revenues peaking at $65.1 billion a company milestone. Profits also surged 9% from $5.7 billion in 2013 to a record-setting $6.2 billion in 2014 due to the higher revenue and lower selling general and administrative costs driven by lower pension expenses. Its cash flow from operations in 2014 decreased by 2% to $7.34 billion due to reductions in accounts receivable in its aerospace businesses fueled by accelerated customer collections.

The historic growth for 2014 was fueled by increases in UTC Aerospace Systems (7%) and Otis (4%) along with more significant growth from Sikorsky (19%). Sikorsky was helped by an uptick in international military and commercial craft sales. The growth for 2014 also reflected increased demand for residential heating ventilation and air conditioning (HVAC) equipment in the North American markets for UTC Climate Controls & Security along with growth in commercial aftermarket volumes for Pratt & Whitney.

Strategy

UTC strives to maintain a balance between its private and military sectors its commercial and aerospace operations and its original equipment (OE) and aftermarket products and services. It also juggles fluctuations in the market that may impact one or more of its businesses. These fluctuations include changing fuel costs and contracts from the US Department of Defense (DoD) which are subject to policies set by the White House and Congress.

This strategy of product balance is combined with geographic balance which has the company investing in emerging markets that show great growth potential such as Argentina Brazil China Mexico the Middle East Russia and South Africa. UTC is champing at the bit to acquire aerospace and commercial companies with operations in India looking to achieve $2.5 billion in revenues from the country by 2015.

As it focuses on its core aerospace and building systems operations UTC in early 2013 sold its UTC Power unit to Oregon-based ClearEdge Power. In late 2015 it also sold its former Sikorsky helicopter subsidiary to Lockheed Martin for $9 billion.

HISTORY

In 1925 Frederick Rentschler and George Mead founded Pratt & Whitney Aircraft (P&W) to develop aircraft engines. P&W merged with Seattle-based Boeing Airplane Company and Chance Vought Corporation in 1929 to form United Aircraft & Transport. United Aircraft soon bought aviation companies Hamilton Aero Standard Steel Propeller and Sikorsky.

After congressional investigations led to new antitrust laws United Aircraft split in 1934 into three independent entities: United Airlines Boeing Airplane Company and United Aircraft. United Aircraft retained P&W and several other manufacturing interests.

A design flaw in engines produced for Boeing 747s sent P&W on an expensive trip back to the drawing board in the late 1960s. A concerned board of directors appointed Harry Gray a 17-year

veteran of Litton Industries as president in 1971. Gray transformed the company into a conglomerate; it adopted its present name in 1975.

The company entered into a new stage of development with the milestone 2012 acquisitions of Goodrich and Rolls-Royce's share in the International Aero Engines (IAE) joint venture. The $16.5 billion acquisition of Goodrich an aircraft components manufacturer was one of UTC's largest. Through the transaction UTC absorbed $1.9 billion in assumed debt but it also sizably boosted its services to the commercial aerospace/defense industry and increased its revenues. Goodrich was combined with the former Hamilton Sundstrand operations and now form its UTC Aerospace Systems segment.

EXECUTIVES

President Large Commercial Engines Pratt & Whitney; EVP and COO Pratt & Whitney, Robert F. Leduc, age 59
President UTC Climate Controls and Security (CCS), Robert J. (Bob) McDonough
SVP Science and Technology, J. Michael McQuade
President CEO and Director, Gregory J. Hayes, age 54, $949,583 total compensation
SVP Government Relations, Timothy J. McBride, age 53
SVP and General Counsel, Charles D. Gill, age 51, $676,250 total compensation
SVP Strategic Planning, Michael R. (Mike) Dumais, age 48
COO Intercontinental Operations UTC Building and Industrial Systems, Philippe Delpech
President UTC Aerospace Systems, David L. Gitlin
VP and CIO, Nancy M. Davis
SVP Strategic Projects, Michael B. (Mick) Maurer
SVP and CFO, Akhil Johri, age 54
SVP Aerospace Business Develpment, David P. Hess
Vice President, Greg Deldicque
Vice President and Counsel, Ginny Kim
Vice President Engineering And Technology Hamilton Sundstrand, Dave Carter
Chairman, Edward A. Kangas, age 55
Auditors: PricewaterhouseCoopers LLP

LOCATIONS

HQ: United Technologies Corp
  10 Farm Springs Road, Farmington, CT 06032
Phone: 860 728-7000   Fax: 860 728-7028
Web: www.utc.com

2014 Sales

	$ mil.	% of total
US	38,155	59
Europe	12,630	19
Asia/Pacific	8,795	14
Other	5,513	8
Eliminations	7	
Total	65,100	100

PRODUCTS/OPERATIONS

2014 Sales

	$ mil.	% of total
UTC Climate Controls & Security	16,823	25
Pratt & Whitney	14,508	22
UTC Aerospace Systems	14,215	22
Otis	12,982	20
Sikorsky	7,451	11
Eliminations	(879)	-
Total	65,100	100

2014 Sales by Market

	% of total
Commercial & industrial	45
Commercial aerospace	35
Military aerospace & space	20
Total	100

2014 Sales

	$ mil.	% of total
Product sales	47,632	73
Service sales	17,468	27
Total	**65,100**	**100**

Selected Operations

Otis (elevators escalators moving walkways and service)

Pratt & Whitney (commercial military business jet and general aviation aircraft engines auxiliary power units and parts and services)

UTC Aerospace Systems (aerospace products and aftermarket services)

UTC Climate Controls & Security (heating ventilating air conditioning and refrigeration systems and security systems)

COMPETITORS

AAR Corp.	Lennox
Aerojet Rocketdyne	Lockheed Martin
AgustaWestland	Mitsubishi Electric
BAE SYSTEMS	Northrop Grumman
Boeing	Parker-Hannifin
DynCorp International	Precision Castparts
Emerson Electric	Raytheon
GE	Rolls-Royce
General Dynamics	SAFRAN
Hitachi	SPX
Honeywell	Siemens AG
International	ThyssenKrupp
IDEX	Trane Inc.
Kaman	Tyco
L-3 Communications	

HISTORICAL FINANCIALS

Company Type: Public

Income Statement

FYE: December 31

	REVENUE ($ mil.)	NET INCOME ($ mil.)	NET PROFIT MARGIN	EMPLOYEES
12/15	56,098	7,608	13.6%	197,200
12/14	65,100	6,220	9.6%	211,500
12/13	62,626	5,721	9.1%	212,400
12/12	57,708	5,130	8.9%	218,000
12/11	58,190	4,979	8.6%	199,900
Annual Growth	(0.9%)	11.2%	—	(0.3%)

2015 Year-End Financials

Debt ratio: 23.35%
Return on equity: 25.98%
Cash ($ mil.): 7,075
Current ratio: 1.18
Long-term debt ($ mil.): 19,320

No. of shares (mil.): 838
Dividends
 Yield: 2.6%
 Payout: 39.5%
Market value ($ mil.): 80,540

	STOCK PRICE ($) FY Close	P/E High/Low	PER SHARE ($) Earnings	Dividends	Book Value
12/15	96.07	14 10	8.61	2.56	32.63
12/14	115.00	17 14	6.82	2.36	34.32
12/13	113.80	18 13	6.25	2.20	34.76
12/12	82.01	15 12	5.66	2.03	28.20
12/11	73.09	16 12	5.49	1.87	24.12
Annual Growth	7.1%	— —	11.9%	8.2%	7.9%

UnitedHealth Group Inc

UnitedHealth unites its health plans with consumers across the US. As a leading health insurer it offers a variety of plans and services to group and individual customers nationwide. Its UnitedHealthcare health benefits segment manages HMO PPO and POS plans as well as Medicare Medicaid state-funded and supplemental vision and dental op-

tions. Together the UnitedHealthcare businesses serve more than 40 million members. In addition UnitedHealth's Optum health services units —OptumHealth OptumInsight and OptumRx —provide wellness and care management programs financial services information technology solutions and pharmacy benefit management (PBM) services to an additional 45 million.

HISTORY

Dr. Paul Ellwood became known as the "Father of the HMO" for his role as an early champion of the health care concept. As a neurology student in the 1950s Ellwood recognized that applying business principles to medicine could minimize costs and make health care more affordable. Although the HMO was considered a radical approach to health care reform Ellwood got Congress and the Nixon administration to approve his HMO model in 1970; the next year he hired Richard Burke to put the model into action. Burke established United HealthCare (UHC) in 1974 to manage the not-for-profit Physicians Health Plan of Minnesota (PHP). UHC incorporated in 1977.

The company bought HMOs and began managing others operating 11 HMOs in 10 states by 1984 the year it went public. Its expansion continued with the purchases of HMOs Share Development (1985) and Peak Health Care (1986). Unfortunately acquisitions and startups began to eat away at UHC's financial health. Meanwhile Burke CEO of both UHC and PHP was accused by PHP doctors of having a conflict of interest after a change in the HMO's Medicare policy threatened to cut off patients from some member hospitals. Burke resigned in 1987 and was replaced by Kennett Simmons formerly president of Peak.

That year investment firm Warburg Pincus bought nearly 40% of UHC providing it with much-needed cash. UHC lost nearly $16 million in 1987 largely from a restructuring that axed the company's Phoenix HMO as well as startups in six other markets. The next year UHC sold its share of Peak Health Care.

In the late 1980s UHC adopted a new strategy of acquiring specialty companies that provided fee income. It also continued building its HMO network through acquisitions hoping to gain critical mass in such varied markets as the Midwest and New England.

Physician William (Bill) McGuire another former Peak president was named UHC's chairman and CEO in 1991. That year PHP and Share merged into Medica. Warburg Pincus distributed its UHC shares to several pension funds and financial institutions.

The company's expansion accelerated in the 1990s with a string of purchases in the Midwest but there were also divestitures. In 1994 UHC sold subsidiary Diversified Pharmaceutical Services providing cash for still more purchases including GenCare (St. Louis) Group Sales and Service of Puerto Rico and MetraHealth a former joint venture of Travelers Group and Metropolitan Life. UHC's interest in fee-based businesses continued with the 1997 purchase of Medicode a major provider of health care information products.

In 1998 the firm planned to buy rival Humana. However bloated UHC decided it should slim down to prepare to consummate the agreement; when UHC announced that it would charge $900 million in costs against earnings its plummeting stock price devalued the primary currency of the deal which quickly collapsed. That year it began offering MediGap and other supplements to AARP members.

The company changed its name to UnitedHealth Group in 2000. It also added UK-based contract research organization ClinPharm International to In-

genix that year and it announced it would let doctors —not administrators —choose what treatment patients would get partially because it was spending more on care scrutiny than the practice saved. Nevertheless many doctors claimed the process was still restrictive.

In 2000 the American Medical Association (AMA) and other parties sued the company claiming it used faulty Ingenix data to reduce payments to member doctors. (UnitedHealth settled the AMA lawsuit in 2009 for $350 million without admitting any wrongdoing as well as some state lawsuits related to the database.)

UnitedHealth's strategy for expansion in the early 21st century concentrated on acquisitions and joint ventures. To expand its Medicaid services business the firm bought AmeriChoice in 2002. The company also bought Mid Atlantic Medical Services because its HMOs and specialty health care operations complemented UnitedHealth's core operations. Golden Rule was acquired in late 2003 so UnitedHealth could enter the individual health insurance market by providing medical savings accounts. UnitedHealth also bought individual health care reimbursement account provider Definity Health in late 2004 for the same purpose. To increase its market share in the northeastern US the company bought Oxford Health Plans that year.

UnitedHealth spent $8.8 billion to acquire and integrate PacifiCare in 2005. Adding 3 million customers the acquisition gave UnitedHealth a leading position in the California and West Coast markets but it also prompted a landslide of complaints from customers alleging mishandled claims. The California Insurance Commissioner and other state agencies sought fines of more than $1 billion. While PacifiCare continued to exist as a health plan brand of UnitedHealth the PacifiCare administrative operations were integrated into other UnitedHealth units including UnitedHealthcare. The PacifiCare Prescription Benefits unit became separate operating division of UnitedHealth.

Chairman and CEO McGuire became the focus of inquiry in 2006 over a scandal involving the back-dating of stock options awarded to him and other company executives. Following a board inquiry McGuire was shown the door and was replaced by Stephen Hemsley formerly the company's president and COO. The back-dating brouhaha continued to be a distraction for UnitedHealth and in 2008 it opted to settle several related shareholder lawsuits by agreeing to pay more than $900 million.

Continuing the acquisitive strategy it laid out after the turn of the millennium the company in 2006 bought Deere & Company's employee health plan as well as Student Resources the student insurance division of HealthMarkets' MEGA Life subsidiary.

The company changed the name of its supplemental health division from Specialized Care Service to OptumHealth in 2007. As part of the restructuring a number of other UnitedHealth businesses were merged into OptumHealth including ACN Group United Resources Networks United Behavioral Health PacifiCare Behavioral Health Exante Bank and Exante Financial Services.

UnitedHealth completed several large acquisitions in 2008 spending $730 million to purchase Fiserv's health-related businesses including Fiserv Health (benefits administration for 2 million members) Avidyn Health (care facilitation) Fiserv Health Specialty Solutions (administration) and Innoviant Pharmacy Benefits Management. UnitedHealth also paid $980 million to acquire Unison Health Plans and used it to expand its AmeriChoice unit.

UnitedHealth completed its controversial purchase of Nevada insurance provider Sierra Health Services for approximately $2.6 billion in 2008 gaining some 600000 health plan members in the state and boosting its position in the growing Southwest market. The acquisition took nearly a year to receive approval from the Department of Justice due to competition concerns. Approval was finally gained on the contingency that UnitedHealth sell its Las Vegas Medicare Advantage program representing some 27000 customers to Humana for $185 million. Sierra Health's operating units including Health Plan of Nevada and Sierra Health and Life became part the UnitedHealthcare Nevada division following the acquisition.

EXECUTIVES

EVP, William A. Munsell, $700,000 total compensation
CEO and Director, Stephen J. Hemsley, $1,300,000 total compensation
EVP, Jeannine M. Rivet, $465,000 total compensation
Vice President Of Training, Christopher Carlson
EVP and Chief Enterprise Operations, Dirk C. McMahon
EVP, Anthony Welters, $750,000 total compensation
Vice Chairman and CEO Optum, Larry C. Renfro, age 61, $900,000 total compensation
EVP Medical Affairs and Chief Medical Officer, Richard Migliori
President and CFO, David S. Wichmann, age 53, $900,000 total compensation
EVP Human Capital, D. Ellen Wilson
EVP and Chief Legal Officer, Marianne D. Short, $750,000 total compensation
Director UnitedHealth Group and CEO Amil, Edson Bueno
EVP External Affairs, Cory B. Alexander
SVP Marketing and Brand, Terry Clark
Vice President Application Development, Patrick Langan
Vice President, Mark Dicello
Regional Sales Vice President, Shawn Mobley
Senior Vice President Client Development, Bruce Mead
Vice President Sales and Account Management, John (Jack) Norton
Vice President New Product Strategy, Patsy Piazza
Vice President e Solutions, John (Jack) O'Neil
Account Vice President, Rapalyea Sarah
Vice President Marketing Ovations, Ellen Sexton
Senior Vice President, Anne Gavel
Vice President Dental Provider Operations, Edward (Ed) Sverdlin
Senior Vice President, Jim Thomas
Vice President Of Marketing, Randy Blum
Vice President Sales, Philip Brun
Vice President, Lori Cleary
Senior Vice President Human Capital, Chris Coleman
Senior Vice President, Mark Duhaime
Vice President Network Services, Jim Gasper
Vice President Consumer Marketing, Diane Slayton
Senior Vice President Center for Nursing Advancement, Dawn Bazarko
Director Of Health, Christopher Reuter
Vice President of Network Management For Wa Or and Ak, Dustin Taylor
Vice President Operations and Planning, Steven (Steve) Mueller
Vice President Of Key Account Sales, Robert (Bob) Benkert
Vice President Customer Service, Paul Shamansky
Vice President Marketing, Jason Gitman
Vice President Center For Health Reform, Deborah Sundal
Vice President Finance, Troy Salley
Vice President Of Sales, Bryan Palmer
PS North America Vice President Sales Business Development, Craig Condon
Vice President Finance Systems Data Management, Cami Whitt
Vice President Of Sales, Dave Milich
Regional Vice President, Jake Logan

Vice President Capital Reporting Group Finance and Capital Controller, Michael (Mel) Burkhardt
Senior Vice President Corporate Commo, Bruce Jasurda
Vice President Sales, Munira Mohamed
Vice President, Judd Frahm
Vice President Retulatory Affairs, Joy Higa
Vice President Aso Marketing, Steven (Steve) Beecy
Vice President New Market Development, Marilyn Levi-baumgarten
Vice President Product Management, Monty Page
Vice President Sales And Account Management, Charles (Chas) Carter
Vice President Key Account Sales Northern CA, Jeff Dooley
Senior Vice President Member Services Cs, Vivian Lindsay
Vice President Operations Advocacy, Mary Higgins
Vice President Information Technology, Marsha Rauenhorst
Vice President, Susan Yates
Assistant Vice President Underwriting, Karl Hibbs
Vice President Client Relations, Alison Richards
Vice President of Sales and Account Management Key Accounts, Cory Foreman
Health Services Director, Marguerite Mauradian
Vice President Information Technology, Donna McCart
Medical Director, Morris Jutcovich
Vice President Product Management, Todd Spaulding
Vice President Marketing and Business Development, Marc Salinas
Vice President Strategy, Matthew Horton
Senior Vice President Development Management, Dave Pelner
Senior Vice President Evercare, John (Jack) Enderle
Vice President Accounting Policy, Amy Shaw
Vice President Operations, Nancy Burghardt
Executive Vice President, Chris Ritchie
Vice President Oxford, Randall Weinstock
Regional Vice President, Matt Guisinger
Vice President Global Health, David (Dave) Powell
Regional Vice President Account Manager, Kelli Lowery
Vice President Partnership Marketing Unitedhealthcare Medicare And Retirement, Nancy Oliker
Vice President Human Resources Operations, Christine Anderson
Vice President Business Development, Eugene Jasper
Vice President Marketing, Heidi Svendsen
Vice President Finance and Controller Optum Collaborative Care, Victoria Stenslie
National Vice President, Jennifer (Jen) Kuhn
Vice President, Cris Dubord
Vice President Sales and Account Management, Paul Marden
Medical Director, Denise Callari
Medical Director UnitedHealthcare of Pennsylvania, Philip Benditt
Vice President Information Technology, Kevin Kantola
Senior Vice President, Diane Thomas
Vice President Finance, Kevin Carlson
Vice President Exante Group, Jim Koji
Vice President, Rothschild Lori
Sales Vice President National Accounts, Jessica Bass
Vice President Of Clinical Pharmacy Services, Mike Sanderson
Vice President Clinical Product Development, Michael Weitzner
Vice President Of Finance, Heather Catlin
Vice President Information Technology, Ken Washuta
Vice President Sales, Danielle Peacock
Executive Vice President, Jeffery Verney
National Vice President, Eric Meier

Vice President, Claire Verity
Medical Director, Tony Sun
Vice President Business Development, Mary Beeson
Vice President Application Development, Alison Nelson
Vice President Technology Strategy, Jess Lewis
Senior Account Vice President, Kim Mccurdy
Vice President Compliance, Sharon Schmid
Vice President Public Sector Sales, Ray Devault
Vice President International Planning, Mark Kuck
Vice President Sales, John Elliott
Vice President Information Technology, Oren Hermel
Vice President Healthcare Economics, Vince Zuccarello
Vice President Customer Care, Susan Edberg
Vice President Risk Management, Randy Jacob
Vice President Small Business, Doug Metzger
Vice President Information Technology, Deb McQuade
Vice President Integration Services, Brooke Kreitler
Vice President Business Development, Neal Heyman
Vice President Information Technology, John Turnbull
Vice President Finance, Paul Runice
Vice President Marketing, Brad Hunt
Director of Pharmacy Management, Susan Maddux
National Vice President Consulting Relations, Michael Finn
Vice President, Judith Perlman
Senior Vice President Public Affairs, Mike Tuffin
Vice President Clinical Strategy, Karen Keown
Director Of Pharmacy, Louis Cutcliffe
Vice President Sales, Jack Shuff
Vice President, Robert King
Vice President Sales, Kim Lewis
Vice President Of Consumer Insights, Michelle Legros
Vice President Network Management State Of Texas, Ellen Damato
Vice President And Actuary, Dewayne Ullsperger
Vice President Sales, Geoff Buro
Vice President National Alliances, Randy Spicer
Vice President Of Strategic Initiatives, Brett Edelson
Vice President Business Development, Matthew Aaefedt
Medical Director Central Region Clinical, Larry Weisel
Vice President Quality Solutions, Peter (Pete) Naumann
Senior Vice President Global Health, Molly Joseph
Vice President Corporate Real Estate, Restor Johnson
Senior Vice President Public Relations, Robert (Bob) Oberrender
Vice President, Erin Carnish
Vice President Consultant Relations National Accounts, Brian Bellows
Vice President Innovation And Research and Development, Chuck Officer
Vice President of Sales and Account Management, H Timothy
Executive Vice President Human Capital, D Wilson
Vice President E Business Small Group, Cindi Middaugh
Vice President Information Technology, Martin (Marti) Toomb
Auditors: DELOITTE & TOUCHE LLP

LOCATIONS

HQ: UnitedHealth Group Inc
UnitedHealth Group Center, 9900 Bren Road East, Minnetonka, MN 55343
Phone: 952 936-1300
Web: www.unitedhealthgroup.com

PRODUCTS/OPERATIONS

2014 Sales

	$ mil.	% of total
UnitedHealthcare	119,798	71
Optum		
OptumRx	31,976	19
OptumHealth	11,032	7
OptumInsight	5,227	3
Adjustments	(37559)	-
Total	**130,474**	**100**

Selected Operations

Optum (Health Services division)
  OptumHealth (specialty benefits)
  OptumInsight (formerly Ingenix information
  technology and consulting services)
  OptumRx (formerly Prescription Solutions pharmacy
  benefit management)
UnitedHealthcare (Health Plans division)
  UnitedHealthcare Community & State (former
  operations of AmeriChoice public-sector programs)
  UnitedHealthcare Employer & Individual (health plans
  for individuals businesses employers)
  UnitedHealthcare International (expatriate coverage
  for global accounts)
  UnitedHealthcare Medicare & Retirement (former
  operations of Ovations benefits for people age 50 and
  older)
  UnitedHealthcare Military & Veterans (TRICARE West
  Region contract)

COMPETITORS

AMERIGROUP	HCSC
APS Healthcare	Health Net
ActiveHealth	Healthways Inc.
Management	Humana
Aetna	IMS Health
Anthem	Kaiser Foundation
CIGNA	Health Plan
CVS	Magellan Health
Centene	MetLife
Coventry Health Care	Molina Healthcare
Delta Dental Plans	Prudential
Dental Health Alliance	Qmedtrix Systems
Express Scripts	WellCare Health Plans

HISTORICAL FINANCIALS
Company Type: Public

Income Statement
FYE: December 31

	REVENUE ($ mil.)	NET INCOME ($ mil.)	NET PROFIT MARGIN	EMPLOYEES
12/15	157,107	5,813	3.7%	200,000
12/14	130,474	5,619	4.3%	170,000
12/13	122,489	5,625	4.6%	156,000
12/12	110,618	5,526	5.0%	133,000
12/11	101,862	5,142	5.0%	99,000
Annual Growth	**11.4%**	**3.1%**	**—**	**19.2%**

2015 Year-End Financials

Debt ratio: 28.81%
Return on equity: 17.54%
Cash ($ mil.): 10,923
Current ratio: 0.74
Long-term debt ($ mil.): 25,460

No. of shares (mil.): 953
Dividends
  Yield: 1.5%
  Payout: 29.7%
Market value ($ mil.): 112,111

	STOCK PRICE ($) FY Close	P/E High/Low	PER SHARE ($) Earnings	Dividends	Book Value
12/15	117.64	21 16	6.01	1.88	35.50
12/14	101.09	18 12	5.70	1.41	34.02
12/13	75.30	13 9	5.50	1.05	32.54
12/12	54.24	11 9	5.28	0.80	30.60
12/11	50.68	11 8	4.73	0.61	27.23
Annual Growth	**23.4%**	**— —**	**6.2%**	**32.3%**	**6.9%**

Univar Inc

Auditors: Ernst & Young LLP

LOCATIONS

HQ: Univar Inc
  3075 Highland Parkway, Suite 200, Downers Grove, IL
  60515
Phone: 331 777-6000
Web: www.univar.com

HISTORICAL FINANCIALS
Company Type: Public

Income Statement
FYE: December 31

	REVENUE ($ mil.)	NET INCOME ($ mil.)	NET PROFIT MARGIN	EMPLOYEES
12/14	10,373	(20)	—	8,900
12/13	10,324	(82)	—	—
12/12	9,747	(197)	—	—
Annual Growth	**3.2%**	**—**	**—**	**—**

2014 Year-End Financials

Debt ratio: 62.87%
Return on equity: (-6.39%)
Cash ($ mil.): 206
Current ratio: 1.73
Long-term debt ($ mil.): 3,739

No. of shares (mil.): 100
Dividends
  Yield: —
  Payout: —
Market value ($ mil.): —

	STOCK PRICE ($) FY Close	P/E High/Low	PER SHARE ($) Earnings	Dividends	Book Value
12/14	0.00	— —	(0.20)	0.00	2.48
12/13	0.00	— —	(0.83)	0.00	3.81
Annual Growth	**—**	**— —**	**—**	**—**	**—(19.4%)**

Universal Health Services, Inc.

With dozens of health care facilities in nearly every state Universal Health Services (UHS) isn't quite ubiquitous but it's working on it. One of the nation's largest for-profit hospital operators UHS owns or leases about 25 acute care hospitals with a total of some 5800 beds primarily in rural and suburban communities. It also operates outpatient surgery centers and radiation treatment facilities most of which are located near its acute care hospitals. In addition UHS' behavioral health division operates more than 200 psychiatric and substance abuse hospitals with a combined capacity of more than 20000 beds; its UK-based Cygnet unit operates another 19 facilities. UHS is controlled by founder and CEO Alan Miller.

Operations

UHS receives about half of its annual revenues from its acute care segment which includes medical hospitals surgical outpatient facilities and radiation oncology centers. The remainder of the company's revenue comes from its portfolio of behavioral health hospitals which includes residential facilities for teens adult psychiatric hospitals substance abuse facilities and special education schools for students with emotional problems.

The company's behavioral health business accounted for 49% of total revenue in 2014. Net revenues from its acute care hospitals surgical hospitals surgery centers and radiation oncology centers accounted for the other 51%.

UHS provides central resources to its network of facilities including purchasing information services finance facilities planning administrative personnel marketing public relations and physician recruitment.

Geographic Reach

UHS' acute care facilities are located in more than half a dozen states and are situated mostly in smaller towns and cities with limited competition though the division does have facilities in a few larger markets (such as Las Vegas and Washington DC). UHS' behavioral health hospitals are scattered across about 40 US states as well as Puerto Rico the US Virgin Islands and the UK The company's biggest markets for both segments are California Nevada and Texas which together account for about 45% of the company's revenue.

Sales and Marketing

Both of UHS' operating segments (acute care hospitals and behavioral health hospitals) earn between 40% and 50% of revenues from managed care providers (HMOs PPOs) with the remainder of sales coming from traditional Medicare and Medicaid plans and other sources.

Financial Performance

UHS' growth strategies helped it to steadily increase sales over the past decade; in 2014 revenue increased 11% to $8.1 billion (versus $7.3 billion in 2013) as net revenues generated at its facilities rose. Acquisitions made during the year (including its UK unit Cynet a Nevada commercial health insurer and a 124-bed behavioral care facility in Washington DC) also contributed to the growth.

Net income grew 7% to $545 million in 2014 as a result of the higher revenue and a decline in interest expense. Cash flow from operations rose 17% to $1 billion that year due to a change in working capital accounts.

Strategy

While the company's growth strategy is to build or purchase new facilities in rapidly growing areas —it has grown both of its units through selective acquisitions and construction efforts over the years —UHS also has no qualms about ridding itself of operations that just don't quite fit anymore. In 2013 the company sold Peak Behavioral Health Services which operates a facility near El Paso Texas; that divestiture was in accordance with FTC requirements after UHS acquired Ascend Health Corporation in 2012.

By focusing its operations on high-growth regions UHS also works towards its goal of increasing hospital utilization rates (which is often a key indicator of the financial health of a hospital). To further draw more patients and high-quality physicians to its existing facilities the company invests in new technology makes capital improvements and increases the breadth of services it offers. Initiatives include upgrades to surgical equipment and billing systems as well as the implementation of electronic health record (EHR) systems to improve patient care coordination. UHS is especially expanding its outpatient service capabilities as payers put pressure on hospitals to control inpatient care costs.

Mergers and Acquisitions

The company is focused on acquiring hospitals to expand operations. In 2014 it purchased a 124-bed behavioral health care facility and outpatient treatment center in Washington DC. It also bought a commercial health insurance company headquartered in Reno Nevada.

In 2014 UHS made its first acquisition outside of the Americas when it purchased Cygnet Health Care for some $335 million. Cygnet provides acute psychiatric services from about 20 facilities in the UK. It followed that deal up with the 2015 purchases of the 46-bed Orchard Portman House Hospital (now named Cygnet Hospital-Taunton) and the four-hospital system Alpha Hospitals both in the UK.

EXECUTIVES

Vp And Controller, Charles F (Chas) Boyle
Vice President and General Counsel, Matthew (Matt) Klein
SVP CFO and Secretary, Steve G. Filton, age 57, $546,321 total compensation
Chairman and CEO, Alan B. Miller, age 77, $1,537,560 total compensation
SVP; President Behavioral Health Care, Debra K. Osteen, age 59, $601,023 total compensation
SVP; President Acute Care, Marvin G. Pember, age 61, $581,823 total compensation
President and Director, Marc D. Miller, age 44, $666,692 total compensation
VP Information Services, Michael S. Nelson
Vice President and Director, Mia Simms-Bullock
Executive Vice President General Counsel and Secretary, Kim Lederer
Vice President And Director, Brenda Simons
Vice President Center Applications, Lorraine Castro
Vice President And Director Of Environmental Laboratory, Pat Tyrrell
Vice President tax, Teresita Beuschlein
Senior Vice President Arc Information Systems, Cathy Terlescki
Vice President and Director, Russann Jeantet
Vice President and Director, Carrie Kelleher
Vice President Of Sales Operations, Mike Kaminskas
Regional Vice President, Adam Konkoly-thege
Executive Vice President, Beatriz Hadley
Vice President and Director, Christina Romero
Senior Vice President Business Development, Brad Balon
Vice President Of Sales Operations, Will Decuyper
Vice President and Director, Timothy (Tim) Powell
Executive Legal Secretary, Alice Mcrae
Senior Vice President President Acute Care, Michael (Mel) Marquez
Vice President, Thomas Marchozzi
Vice President of Admissions Services, Tasha Hoffmann
Vice President Performance Process Improvement, Chuck Debusk
Vice President And Director, Jerilin Cummings
Vice President and Director, Brandy Albright
Director Of Radiology Services, Jeff Otto
Director Patient Care nursing, Diane Quick
Assistant Vice President Hospital Finance, J P Christen
Vice President And Director, Frank Pizzuto
Director Of Clinical Services, Brian Bill
Vice President Acute Care Div, Frank Lopez
Vice President Chief Compliance Officer and Privacy Officer, Jim Caponi
Executive Vice President Of Finance, Andy Belen
Director Of Pharmacy, Kristen Palasthy
Senior Vice President Marketing And Sales, Stephanie Stephenson
Vice President Sales and Marketing, Glen Padula
Vice President and Director, Shawna Edmundson
Division Vice President, Roz Hudson
Director Of Clinical Services, John Russum
Executive Vice President Of Finance, Stephanie Hill
Vice President Practice Development, Deidre Taylor
Vice President Human Resources, Geraldine Geckle
Vice President Financial Operations, Chris Recon
Executive Vice President Sales and Mar, Joseph (Jo) Granger
Director of Nursing, Ashley Fisher
Sales Vice President, Steve Alonge
Secretary Treasurer, Martha Syms
Auditors: PricewaterhouseCoopers LLP

LOCATIONS

HQ: Universal Health Services, Inc.
Universal Corporate Center, 367 South Gulph Road, King of Prussia, PA 19406
Phone: 610 768-3300
Web: www.uhsinc.com

Selected Acute Care Hospitals and Specialty Centers
California
  Corona Reg
  Palmdale R
  Southwest
  Southwest
  Temecula V
Florida
  Lakewood R
  Manatee Me
    Palms Westside Clinic ASC (50% Royal Palm Beach)
    Wellington Regional Medical Center (West Palm Beach)
Nevada
  Centennial
    Desert Springs Hospital (72% Las Vegas)
  Northern N
    Spring Valley Hospital Medical Center (72% Las Vegas)
    Summerlin Hospital Medical Center (72% Las Vegas)
    Valley Hospital Medical Center (72% Las Vegas)
South Carolina
  Aiken Regi
  Aurora Pav
  Cancer Car
Oklahoma
  St. Mary's
Puerto Rico
  OJOS/Eye S
Texas
  Cornerston
  Doctors' H
  Fort Dunca
  Northwest
    Northwest Texas Surgery Center (majority owned Amarillo)
  The Pavili
  South Texa
  Edinburg R
  Edinburg C
  McAllen Me
  McAllen He
  South Texa
  Texoma Med
  TMC Behavi
Washington D.C.
  The George

PRODUCTS/OPERATIONS

2014 Sales

	$ mil.	% of total
Acute care hospital services	4,105	51
Behavioral health services	3,945	49
Other	14	1
Total	**8,065**	**100**

2014 Sales

	% of total
Managed care (HMOs PPOs & managed Medicare/Medicaid)	50
Medicare	21
Medicaid	15
Other	14
Total	**100**

COMPETITORS

Adventist Health
Adventist Health System Sunbelt Healthcare
AmSurg
Ascension Health
Banner Health
CHRISTUS Health
CRC Health
Community Health Systems
Devereux Foundation
HCA
Hazelden Betty Ford
LifePoint Health
Mercy Health
Northwestern Human Services
Sutter Health

Tenet Healthcare
Texas Health Resources
UBH
United Surgical Partners

HISTORICAL FINANCIALS
Company Type: Public

Income Statement
FYE: December 31

	REVENUE ($ mil.)	NET INCOME ($ mil.)	NET PROFIT MARGIN	EMPLOYEES
12/14	8,065	545	6.8%	68,700
12/13	7,283	510	7.0%	66,100
12/12	6,961	443	6.4%	65,100
12/11	7,500	398	5.3%	65,400
12/10	5,568	230	4.1%	65,100
Annual Growth	**9.7%**	**24.1%**	**—**	**1.4%**

2014 Year-End Financials
Debt ratio: 36.53%
Return on equity: 15.61%
Cash ($ mil.): 32
Current ratio: 1.37
Long-term debt ($ mil.): 3,210
No. of shares (mil.): 98
Dividends
  Yield: 0.2%
  Payout: 6.0%
Market value ($ mil.): 10,983

	STOCK PRICE ($) FY Close	P/E High/Low		PER SHARE ($) Earnings	Dividends	Book Value
12/14	111.26	21	13	5.42	0.30	37.85
12/13	81.26	16	9	5.14	0.20	33.06
12/12	48.35	11	8	4.53	0.60	27.80
12/11	38.86	14	8	4.04	0.20	23.77
12/10	43.42	18	12	2.34	0.20	20.31
Annual Growth	**26.5%**	**—**		**23.4%**	**10.7%**	**16.8%**

Unum Group

Through injury or illness Unum works to keep employees employed. A top disability insurer in the US and the UK it offers short-term and long-term disability insurance as well as life and accidental death and dismemberment insurance to individuals and groups in a workplace benefits setting. Specialty coverage offerings include cancer dental and travel insurance. US subsidiaries include Unum Life Insurance Company of America Provident Life and Accident First Unum Life Colonial Life & Accident Insurance and The Paul Revere Life Insurance Company. It operates as Unum Limited in the UK. Unum's products are sold through field sales agents and independent brokers. In 2014 Unum paid out $6 billion in benefits.

Operations

Around 60% of Unum's annual premiums come from the Unum US segment which offers group disability life and accident policies as well as supplemental and voluntary policies under the Unum America and Provident Brands and sold in the workplace setting. The Colonial Life segment — which offers accident sickness disability and life products sold at the workplace —accounted for 12% of sales in 2014 while the Unum UK segment represented some 6% of sales. Unum also generates revenue from its closed block business which services policies in the runoff segments (long-term care non-workplace individual disability) where the company no longer issues new policies.

The company covers 20 million people worldwide and counts 175000 businesses in the US among its customers (including a third of the Fortune 500). In 2014 the group's disability business alone helped more than 230000 people return to work.

Geographic Reach

The US market contributes about two-thirds of annual revenues. Unum runs four primary operating centers (in Tennessee Maine Massachusetts and South Carolina) and about 35 sales offices scattered across the US market. Its Unum Limited office is the headquarters for the smaller Unum UK operations.

Sales and Marketing

The company strives to maintain close relationships with its sales force as well as with its independent agents and brokers as it relies on these representatives to market its products to employers.

Unum advertises through print media (in such publications as Bloomberg Businessweek The New Yorker Forbes and HR Magazine) and through online videos on sites such as CNBC.com WebMD and Hulu.

Financial Performance

While its overall revenue growth has been slow as of late —which Unum primarily attributes to economic impacts on US employment levels —the company believes its strategic restructuring measures will provide for an increase in future sales levels. In 2014 revenue rose a marginal 1.5% to $10.5 billion on premium growth in all business segments. Increased sales and premium rate increases helped promote growth; realized investment gains also rose but were partially offset by a decline in net investment income.

Net income has fluctuated over the past few years including taking a major dip in 2011. In 2014 it fell 52% to $413 million as commissions and other expenses increased. Cash flow from operations increased 19% to $1.2 billion due to lower cash used in receivables and income tax as well as an increase of cash coming in from insurance reserves and liabilities.

Strategy

Unum seeks to achieve a competitive edge by providing group individual and voluntary workplace products that can be combined with other coverage to better integrate benefits for customers. The insurer has stayed ahead of the game in the disability market by sticking to conservative investment and growth strategies primarily seeking to expand its group product offerings and its geographic presence through organic measures.

The company has especially seen growth in its voluntary benefits products which allow employees to purchase individual coverage products on a supplemental basis. Such options are increasingly important as economic difficulties put pressure on low and middle-income workers. Unum has also expanded its offering of services to help employers and government agencies manage costs such as its leave management program flexible corporate contribution programs and wellness initiatives.

While expanding in areas where the greatest market needs are seen the firm also occasionally exits (or places into runoff) certain businesses where demand has slowed.

The company is focused on its infrastructure and employees with an aim towards simplifying products and processes. It hopes to expand into new markets and deepen coverage offerings while broadening employer relationships.

In 2013 Unum launched a new dental product that is now available nationwide. Through the United Concordia Alliance Network its dental customers have access to an extensive PPO network.

Unum introduced a new disability offering allowing employers to choose between financial protection plans in 2015.

HISTORY

Coal was discovered in eastern Tennessee in the 1870s; in 1887 several Chattanooga professional men formed the Provident Life & Accident Insurance Co. to provide medical insurance to miners. But it was a case of the inexperienced serving the uninsurable and by 1892 the company was on the brink of ruin. The founders sold half the company for $1000 to Thomas Maclellan and John McMaster two Scotsmen who had failed at banking in Canada.

While Maclellan handled the business end McMaster scoured the coalfields for customers. He even went into the mines pitching to individual miners and bringing along someone to dig coal for them so they wouldn't lose money by stopping work to listen.

The partners bought the rest of the company in 1895. Provident grew thanks to the cooperation of mining companies which deducted premiums from miners' pay. Provident added sickness and industrial insurance (low-benefit life policies). In 1900 after a period of strained relations Maclellan bought out McMaster.

After 1905 northern insurers began moving into the industrializing South. To meet the competition Provident reorganized and added capital and its stepped-up sales efforts brought in such lucrative business as railroad accounts. Provident added life insurance in 1917. The first policy was bought by Robert Maclellan who became president when his father died in 1916.

Provident acquired the Southern Surety Co. in 1931. During and after WWII group sales exploded as employee benefit packages proliferated. Provident which by then operated nationally entered Canada in 1948. Four years later R. L. Maclellan succeeded his father as president (R. L. stepped down in 1971). Provident's growth in the 1970s stemmed from its life units but it also developed a large health insurance operation.

The health care operations were hammered by rising medical costs in the 1980s so the company moved into managed care. But the combination of increased health care costs and a real estate crash gave the company a one-two punch in the late 1980s and early 1990s. An accounting change in 1993 further hit profits. In 1994 new president Harold Chandler initiated a reevaluation of Provident's operations and future which resulted in Provident's exit from the health care business beginning in 1995.

Provident began a major move into disability insurance in 1997. It bought 83% of rival disability insurer The Paul Revere Corporation from Textron. About 10000 Paul Revere insurance brokers later filed suit alleging they were denied millions of dollars in commissions. In exchange for its $300 million aid in the purchase Switzerland's Zurich Insurance (now Zurich Financial Services) received about 15% of Provident. The company also acquired GENEX Services (vocational rehabilitation and related services) and sold its dental insurance business to Ameritas Life Insurance. In 1998 Provident sold its annuity business to American General (now a subsidiary of AIG).

In 1998 with both Provident and Unum Corporation looking for ways to enhance business the companies commenced merger negotiations and completed the transaction the next year. But the merger was more expensive than anticipated and problems in integrating the companies' sales forces slowed policy sales.

Company operations began melding more smoothly and UnumProvident began addressing the problems with its sales force as well as adding customer service staff in 2000. It pulled money out of reserves by reinsuring several blocks of acquisition-related businesses and sold an inactive shell subsidiary licensed to sell annuities in most states to Allstate. In 2001 the company sold its Provident National Assurance subsidiary to Allstate. UnumProvident faced accusations that the company denied valid disability claims in 2002. These accusations resulted in legal actions in a number of states.

UnumProvident acquired Sun Life Financial's UK life insurance group in 2003 in a move designed to expand the company's operations in the UK. UnumProvident sold its Unum Japan Accident Insurance subsidiary to Hitachi Capital Corporation (Hitachi) in 2004.

As part of a rebranding effort following years of corporate restructuring to focus on core operations the company changed its name from UnumProvident to Unum Group in 2007.

In 2007 the company divested its GENEX Services unit a provider of disability management and workers' compensation services. GENEX's specialty services no longer fit into Unum's strategy to focus on its primary disability insurance operations. In 2009 it stopped offering new individual long-term care policies as part of its strategy to focus on core offerings in the workplace setting. In 2011 the company decided to exit the group long-term care insurance business as well after deeming the product line as non-core.

EXECUTIVES

EVP and General Counsel, Lisa G. Iglesias
Vice President The Benefits Center, Rob Hecker
SVP Corporate Marketing and Public Relations, Joseph R. (Joe) Foley
President CEO and Director, Richard P. (Rick) McKenney, age 47, $712,404 total compensation
President and CEO Unum US, Michael Q. Simonds, $512,019 total compensation
CFO, John F. (Jack) McGarry, age 57
EVP Global Services, Chris J. Jerome
EVP and Chief Investment Officer, Breege A. Farrell, $433,786 total compensation
President and CEO Colonial Life, Tim Arnold
President and CEO Unum UK, Peter G O'Donnell
SVP and CIO, Kate Miller
Assistant Vice President and Chief Information Security Officer, Lynda Fleury
Assistant Vice President Actuarial Business Analyst, Joyce Whaley
Senior Vice President, Pamela (Pam) Davis
National Account Manager, Jim Zelenka
Vice President, Lorrie Spaulding
Assistant Vice President, Wilson Haizlip
Assistant Vice President Contact Center, Charlene Jackson
National Account Manager, Melana C Kipp
Assistant Vice President, Stephen (Steve) Reed
Vice President Internal Controls, Rick Patton
Senior Vice President Chief Risk Officer, Steven Zabel
National Account Manager, Preston Cox
National Account Manager, Tanja Savage
Vice President, Vince Servizzi
Vice President, John (Jack) Leeming
Vice President Uk Fixed Income, Bob Brant
Assistant Vice President, Tony Bombassi
Assistant Vice President, Ken Barber
Assistant Vice President Broker Compensation And Contact Center Operations, Wes Hilliard
Vice President, Jim Plourde
Vice President Of Customer Services, Rhonda Lindsay Muller
Vice President, Stephen Carden
National Account Manager, Evan Howe
Assistant Vice President Actuary, Paul Lavallee
Assistant Vice President, Tom Simmons
Assistant Vice President, Jay Barriss
Assistant Vice President, Glenda Wilson
Vice President, Philip Sharp

Vice President, Greg Breter
Assistant Vice President, Chris Castleberry
Vice President, Marianne Justin
Assistant Vice President Digital Marketing,
Bethany Branon
Assistant Vice President LTD Benefit Operations,
Bob Berry
Assistant Vice President And Managing Counsel,
Pamela J%2E (Pam) Castrucci
Assistant Vice President Corporate Treasury, Tyler
Siira
National Account Manager, Douglas Burnip
Assistant Vice President Finance, Paul Foster
Vice President Core Group And Ncg Finance, Scott
Carter
Vice President, Zachary Nelson
National Account Manager, Maria Ferguson
Assistant Vice President, Maureen Welch
Assistant Vice President Global Information And
Records Management, Don Duffy
Assistant Vice President, Denise Houser
Vice President, Andrea Gordon
Vice President, Stephanie Dyhrberg
Vice President Asset Liability Management And
Investment Strategy, Rob Hensley
Vice President, Jim Harris
Assistant Vice President Human Resources
Senior Business Partner, Debbie Plager
Assistant Vice President Of Hispanic Initiative,
Bilda Acuna
Assistant Vice President Senior Human Re, Laura
Coleman
Vice President Distribution Channel Expansion,
Christopher Quinn
Assistant Vice President And Senior Counsel
Employment Law, Ellen McCann
Vice President Op And Sales Tech, Brent Rogers
Assistant Vice President Corporate Development,
Andrew (Andy) Sharp
National Account Manager, Kathryn Wells
Vice President Individual Acquisitions, Randy
Robinson
Vice President Compensation Human Resources,
Rhonda Rigsby
Assistant Vice President Contact Center, Cj
Jackson
Assistant Vice President Strategic Block
Development, Frank Clu
Assistant Vice President, Dennis Hersom
Vice President, Rhonda Lindsay-Muller
Vice President Communications Services, Randy
Chapman
Vice President Individual Disability Insurance
Operations and Market Development, Leston
Welsh
Chairman, Thomas R. (Tom) Watjen, age 60
Assistant Vice President and Assistant Treasurer,
Linda Bessman
Vice President and Corporate Treasurer, Kevin
McMahon
Auditors: Ernst & Young LLP

LOCATIONS

HQ: Unum Group
1 Fountain Square, Chattanooga, TN 37402
Phone: 423 294-1011
Web: www.unum.com

PRODUCTS/OPERATIONS

2013 Sales

	$ mil.	% of total
Unum US	4,517	44
Closed block (individual disability & long-term care)	1,318	13
Colonial Life	1,232	12
Unum UK	556	5
Net investment income	2,492	24
Investment gain	6	-
Other	230	2
Total	**10,353**	**100**

Selected Products and Services
Accidental death and dismemberment
Dental insurance
Disability (long-term and short-term)
Life insurance
Supplemental health
Voluntary benefits

Selected Subsidiaries and Brands
Colonial Life & Accident Insurance
Duncanson & Holt (US and UK)
  Trafalgar Underwriting Agencies (UK)
First Unum Life Insurance
Provident Investment Management
Provident Life and Accident Insurance
Provident Life and Casualty Insurance
The Paul Revere Life Insurance
The Paul Revere Variable Annuity Insurance
Unum Life Insurance Company of America
Unum Limited (UK)
UnumProvident International (Bermuda)

COMPETITORS

AEGON	Liberty Mutual
AXA Financial	Lincoln Financial
Aflac	Group
Allianz	MassMutual
American General	MetLife
Assurant	Mutual of Omaha
CIGNA	Northwestern Mutual
CNA Financial	Principal Financial
GatesMcDonald	Prudential
Guardian Life	Torchmark
John Hancock Financial	
Services	

HISTORICAL FINANCIALS
Company Type: Public

Income Statement

FYE: December 31

	ASSETS ($ mil.)	NET INCOME ($ mil.)	INCOME AS % OF ASSETS	EMPLOYEES
12/14	62,497	413	0.7%	9,500
12/13	59,403	858	1.4%	9,200
12/12	62,236	894	1.4%	9,100
12/11	60,179	235	0.4%	9,400
12/10	57,307	886	1.5%	9,500
Annual Growth	**2.2%**	**(17.4%)**	**—**	**0.0%**

2014 Year-End Financials

Debt ratio: 4.21%	No. of shares (mil.): 252
Return on equity: 4.80%	Dividends
Cash ($ mil.): 102	Yield: 1.7%
Current ratio: —	Payout: 17.5%
Long-term debt ($ mil.): —	Market value ($ mil.): 8,801

	STOCK PRICE ($) FY Close	P/E High/Low		PER SHARE ($) Earnings	Dividends	Book Value
12/14	34.88	23	19	1.61	0.62	33.90
12/13	35.08	11	6	3.23	0.55	33.30
12/12	20.82	8	6	3.17	0.47	31.87
12/11	21.07	34	26	0.78	0.40	29.30
12/10	24.22	10	7	2.71	0.35	28.25
Annual Growth	**9.5%**	**—**	**—**	**(12.2%)**	**15.4%**	**4.7%**

Valero Energy Corp.

Valero Energy was not only named after a mission (the Mission San Antonio de Valero) it is on a mission to be the largest independent refiner in the US. Valero churns out about 2.9 million barrels per day refining low-cost residual oil and heavy crude into cleaner-burning higher-margin products including low-sulfur diesels. It operates 15 refineries in the US Canada the UK and Aruba. It also has 11 ethanol plants with a combined production capacity of about 1.3 billion gallons per year. Once a more diversified company Valero has exited the retail business in order to focus on its oil refining and ethanol operations.

HISTORY

Valero Energy was created as a result of the sins of its father Houston-based Coastal States Gas Corporation. Led by flamboyant entrepreneur Oscar Wyatt energy giant Coastal had established Lo-Vaca Gathering Company as a gas marketing subsidiary. Bound by long-term contracts to several Texas cities Coastal was not able to meet its contractual obligations when gas prices rose in the early 1970s and major litigation against the company resulted. The Texas Railroad Commission (the energy-regulating authority) ordered Coastal to refund customers $1.6 billion.

To meet the requirements 55% of Lo-Vaca was spun off to disgruntled former customers as Valero Energy at the end of 1979. The new company was born fully grown –as the largest intrastate pipeline in Texas –with accountant-cum-CEO Bill Greehey the court-appointed chief of Lo-Vaca at its head. Greehey relocated the company to San Antonio where it took its Valero name (from the Alamo or Mission San Antonio de Valero) and put some distance between itself and its discredited former parent. Under Greehey's direction Valero developed a squeaky-clean image by giving to charities stressing a dress code and keeping facilities clean.

Greehey diversified the company into refining unleaded gasoline. Valero bought residual fuel oil from Saudi Arabian refiners and in 1981 built a refinery in Corpus Christi Texas which went on line two years later. But in 1984 a glut of unleaded gasoline on the US market from European refiners undercut Valero's profits. To stay afloat Valero sold pipeline assets including 50% of its West Texas Pipeline in 1985 and 51% of its major pipeline operations in 1987. Refining margins finally began to improve in 1988. With one of the most modern refineries in the US Valero did not have to spend a bundle to upgrade its refining processes to meet the tougher EPA requirements of the 1990s.

In 1992 Valero expanded its refinery's production capacity and acquired two gas processing plants and several hundred miles of gas pipelines from struggling oil firm Oryx Energy (acquired by Kerr-McGee in 1999). That year Valero became the first non-Mexican business engaged in Mexican gasoline production when it signed a deal with state oil company Petróleos Mexicanos S.A. to build a gasoline additive plant there.

To expand its natural gas business substantially in 1994 Valero bought back the 51% of Valero Natural Gas Partners it didn't own. Valero also teamed up with regional oil company Swift Energy in a transportation marketing and processing agreement. As part of that arrangement Valero agreed to build a pipeline linking Swift's Texas gas field with a Valero plant.

In 1997 the company sold Valero Natural Gas to California electric utility PG&E gaining $1.5 billion for expansion. It then purchased Salomon's oil refining unit Basis Petroleum (two refineries in Texas and one in Louisiana) and the next year picked up Mobil's refinery in Paulsboro New Jersey.

With low crude oil prices hurting its bottom line in 1999 Valero explored partnerships with other refiners as a way to cut operating costs. In 2000 the company bought Exxon Mobil's 130000-barrel-per-day Benicia California refinery along with 340 retail outlets for about $1 billion.

In 2001 Valero gained two small refineries when it bought Huntway Refining a leading supplier of asphalt in California. Dwarfing that deal Valero also bought Ultramar Diamond Shamrock for $4 billion in cash and stock (it assumed about $2.1 billion of debt in the deal). As part of the deal and to comply with the demands of regulators in 2002 Valero sold the Golden Eagle (San Francisco-area) refinery and 70 retail service stations in Northern California to Tesoro for $945 million.

In 2003 the company acquired Orion Refining's Louisiana refinery for about $530 million and the next year it acquired an Aruba refinery from asset-shedding El Paso Corp. for $640 million. Suncor Energy bought a Colorado-based refinery from Valero for a reported $30 million in 2005.

The 2005 acquisition of Premcor made Valero the largest independent refiner on the Gulf Coast a major national player.

Greehey turned over the leadership reins to another company veteran Bill Klesse in early 2006. The following year the company sold its Lima Ohio refinery to Husky Energy.

In 2008 the company sold its Krotz Springs Louisiana refinery to Alon USA Energy for $333 million.

In 2009 Valero had an opportunity for international refinery expansion and a foothold in Europe when it agreed to acquire Dow Chemical's 45% interest in Dutch refinery Total Raffinaderij Nederland N.V. However the deal fell through and the stake was sold to LUKOIL.

That year it bought seven ethanol production facilities from VeraSun Energy for $475 million.

To cut costs in 2010 it sold its Delaware City refinery. It also sold its Paulsboro New Jersey refinery that year to PBF Holding for $340 million. It also sold its 50% stake in a pipeline that brings deepwater crude oil from the Gulf of Mexico to the US to Genesis Energy for $330 million.

Expanding its global footprint in 2011 Valero bought Chevron's Pembroke refinery and marketing and logistics assets across the UK for $1.7 billion. It also boosted its US assets that year buying Murphy Oil's refinery outside New Orleans for $585 million to complement its St. Charles facility. Valero also bought Chevron USA Inc.'s Louisville and Lexington Kentucky product terminals expanding its wholesale marketing presence in eastern Kentucky with product supplied primarily from the Valero Memphis Refinery.

It made its first foray into ethanol production in 2009 buying seven ethanol production facilities from VeraSun Energy which was operating under Chapter 11 bankruptcy protection. Valero paid about $475 million for the facilities.

EXECUTIVES

EVP and General Counsel, Jay D. Browning, $541,667 total compensation
Senior Vice President Project Execution, Anthony Jones
SVP Wholesale Marketing, Gary L. Arthur
VP and CIO, Cheryl Thomas
EVP and CFO, Michael S. (Mike) Ciskowski, $810,000 total compensation
VP Transportation, Ken Applegate
EVP and Chief Administrative Officer, R. Michael (Mike) Crownover, $516,667 total compensation
VP Europe, Eric Fisher
Chairman President and CEO, Joseph W. (Joe) Gorder, $1,150,000 total compensation
EVP Refining Operations and Engineering, Lane Riggs, $558,333 total compensation
VP Alternative Fuels, Martin Parrish
SVP Supply International Operations and Systems Optimization, Gary Simmons

Vice President Marketing, Maratea Joe
Senior Vice President And Deputy General Counsel, Jason W Fraser
Vice President Sales, Linda Ellis
Vice President Market Anlysis, Richard (Dick) Grissom
Vice President Crude Oil Feedstock Trading, Kerry O'Brien
Vice President of Sales and Marketing, Richard (Dick) Garrett
Vice President Of Marketing, Curt Lundquist
Vice President Of Regional Operations, Rodney Reese
Vice President Refinery Accounting, Jeffrey L (Jeff) Jones
Vice President Of Public Relations, Robbie Schaefer
Vice President Membership, Shawna Krepps
Vice President Corporate Development International, Francois Trudelle
Vice President, Dora Bazan
Vice President, James Greenwood
Vice President Marketing Lacros, David (Dave) Hernandez
Vice President event Marketing, John (Jack) Hill
Vice President Sales, Brett Nellis
Vice President International Brands Group, Tammy Dullnig
Vice President Event Marketing, John Hill
Vice President Sales, Allan Simpson
Vice President Corporate Communications, Julia Rendon
Vice President Of Production, Tim Dwyer
Vice President, Ashley Smith
Vice President Risk Management, Joe Van Horn
Executive Vice President exploration and production Americas, Steve Bain
Vice President, Donna Titzman
Vice President Corporate Development, Richard (Dick) Lashway
Vice President Sales, Mike Whyte
Vice President Project Execution, Tony Jones
Vice President Tax At Valero Energy Corporation, Stephanie Davis
Board Member, Randy Saenz
Board Member, Tira Anderson
Treasurer, Dan Stanush
Board of Director and Vice President, Leslie Sullivan
Board Of Director And Vice President, Alisa Lomas
Board Of Director And Vice President, Randy Stier
Board Of Director And Vice President, John (Jack) Marrow
Board Member, Thomas Tave
Board Member, Pearl Adams
Board Member, Ramon Riojas
Auditors: KPMG LLP

LOCATIONS

HQ: Valero Energy Corp.
One Valero Way, San Antonio, TX 78249
Phone: 210 345-2000 Fax: 210 246-2646
Web: www.valero.com

2014 Sales

		$ mil.	% of total
US		91,499	70
UK 14 182	11		
Canada		10,410	8
Other countries		14,753	11
Total		**130,844**	**100**

PRODUCTS/OPERATIONS

2014 Sales

	$ mil.	% of total
Refining	126,004	96
Ethanol	4,840	4
Retail -	0	
Total	**130,844**	**100**

Selected Products

Asphalt
Bunker oils
CARB Phase II gasoline
Clean-burning oxygenates
Conventional gasoline
Crude mineral spirits
Customized clean-burning gasoline blends for export markets
Ethanol
Gasoline blendstocks
Home heating oil
Jet fuel
Kerosene
Low-sulfur diesel
Lube oils
Petrochemical feedstocks
Petroleum coke
Premium reformulated and conventional gasolines
Reformulated gasoline
Sulfur

COMPETITORS

ADM	Motiva Enterprises
Aventine	National Cooperative
BP	Refinery Association
CITGO	Phillips 66
CVR	Sinclair Oil
Chevron	Sunoco
Exxon Mobil	TOTAL
Green Brick Partners	TPC Group
HollyFrontier	Tesoro
Marathon Petroleum	Western Refining Inc.

HISTORICAL FINANCIALS

Company Type: Public

Income Statement

FYE: December 31

	REVENUE ($ mil.)	NET INCOME ($ mil.)	NET PROFIT MARGIN	EMPLOYEES
12/14	130,844	3,630	2.8%	10,065
12/13	138,074	2,720	2.0%	10,007
12/12	139,250	2,083	1.5%	21,671
12/11	125,987	2,090	1.7%	21,942
12/10	82,233	324	0.4%	20,313
Annual Growth	12.3%	83.0%	—	(16.1%)

2014 Year-End Financials

Debt ratio: 14.02%
Return on equity: 18.09%
Cash ($ mil.): 3,689
Current ratio: 1.66
Long-term debt ($ mil.): 5,780
No. of shares (mil.): 514
Dividends
  Yield: 2.1%
  Payout: 15.0%
Market value ($ mil.): 25,458

	STOCK PRICE ($) FY Close	P/E High/Low		PER SHARE ($) Earnings	Dividends	Book Value
12/14	49.50	9	6	6.85	1.05	40.20
12/13	50.40	10	7	4.97	0.85	36.34
12/12	34.12	9	5	3.75	0.65	32.66
12/11	21.05	8	5	3.68	0.30	29.49
12/10	23.12	41	27	0.57	0.20	26.43
Annual Growth	21.0%	—	—	86.2%	51.4%	11.1%

Valley National Bancorp

Valley National Bancorp is high on New Jersey and New York. The holding company owns Valley National Bank which serves commercial and retail clients through more than 200 branches in northern and central New Jersey and in the New York City boroughs of Manhattan Brooklyn and Queens as well as on Long Island. The bank provides standard services like checking and savings accounts loans and mortgages credit cards and trust services. Subsidiaries offer asset management mortgage and auto loan servicing title insurance asset-based lending and property/casualty life and health insurance. Founded as The Passaic Park Trust Company in 1927 Valley National is looking to expand in Florida.

Operations

In addition to its commercial and retail banking operations Valley National Bancorp through its subsidiaries operates: an all-line insurance agency that offers property and casualty life and health insurance; a wealth management advisory business; title insurance agencies in New York and New Jersey. It also specializes in general aviation financing commercial equipment leasing and custom financing for health care professionals and law firms.

Financial Performance

Valley National reported revenue of $744.7 million in 2013 a decline of 6% versus 2012 on lower interest income caused by lower yields on average interest earning assets as a result of low long-term market interest rates. Net income fell 8% over the same period to about $132 million on lower revenue and an increase in non-interest expenses.

Strategy

One of the leading commercial banks in the New York and New Jersey metro areas Valley National has set its sights on Florida with its proposed acquisition of Boca Raton-based 1st United Bankcorp the largest commercial bank in Palm Beach County. The deal which is valued at $312 million would add a 21 branch network covering urban banking markets in Florida and approximately $1.7 billion in assets. Combined the two companies will have about $18.1 billion in assets nearly $13 billion in loans and $12.7 billion in deposits. The deal is expected to close in late 2014.

Commercial real estate and construction loans account for the largest portion of Valley's loan portfolio (47%). However the bank has ramped up its residential lending and has been actively marketing its home loan refinancing products amid continued low interest rates.

Mergers and Acquisitions

Valley National completed its approximately $222 million acquisition of New York-based bank holding company State Bancorp at the beginning of 2012. The deal which brought in 17 branches is part of Valley's overall strategy to expand its presence throughout New York City metropolitan area. It marked the company's first foray in Long Island and added locations in Manhattan and Queens as well. It also provides an opportunity to build retail relationships in new markets as State Bancorp focused more on commercial clients. Valley typically targets consumers disillusioned with larger banks.

In 2010 the company acquired the branches and most of the assets and deposits of failed Manhattan-based financial institutions LibertyPointe Bank and Park Avenue Bank in FDIC-assisted transactions. It also opened a loan production office in Bethlehem Pennsylvania to offer residential mortgages and title insurance. Valley continues to look for additional expansion opportunities.

EXECUTIVES

EVP and President VNB New York LLC, James G. Lawrence, age 72, $408,890 total compensation
EVP and Chief Administrative Officer, Robert J. Mulligan, age 68
SEVP and COO, Peter Crocitto, age 58, $545,750 total compensation
EVP and Chief Commercial Lending Officer, Robert M. (Rob) Meyer, age 69, $465,000 total compensation
SEVP and CFO, Alan D. Eskow, age 67, $545,750 total compensation
Chairman President and CEO, Gerald H. Lipkin, age 75, $1,123,500 total compensation
EVP and Chief Retail Lending Officer, Albert L. Engel, age 67, $440,000 total compensation
EVP and Director of Sales, Dianne M. Grenz
EVP and Director of Marketing, Bernadette M. Mueller, age 56
EVP and Treasurer, Ira Robbins, age 40
EVP and Director of Retail Operations, Andrea Onorato
Assistant Vice President Commercial Loans, John Kenny
Vice President, Peter Alvarez
Assistant Vice President, Tony Dibenedetto
Vice President commercial Loans, John (Jack) Falcone
Vice President commercial Loans, Mark Gomberg
Senior Vice President, John (Jack) Prol
First Vice President Senior Attorney, Harold Steinberg
Vice President, Dave Denoya
Senior Vice President, Carlo Alibrandi
Vice President, Timothy Tierney
Assistant Vice President Branch Sales Manager, Marie Castro
Vice President Business Development, Floyd Wilmoth
Vice President, Claudia Orourke
Assistant Vice President Business Development Commercial Loans, Kristen Upadek
Assistant Vice President Branch Sales Manager, Anthony Deniro
Vice President Sales Manager, Veronica Valentine
Senior Vice President Commercial Lending, John Murphy
Vice President Retail Training, Mary Black
Senior Vice President, Chip Woodbury
Vice President, Karen Conway
Assistant Vice President Branch Manager, Debra Simpson
Assistant Vice President, Paul Cronen
Auditors: KPMG LLP

LOCATIONS

HQ: Valley National Bancorp
1455 Valley Road, Wayne, NJ 07470
Phone: 973 305-8800
Web: www.valleynationalbank.com

PRODUCTS/OPERATIONS

2013 Sales

	$ mil.	% of total
Interest		
Loans including fees	537	72
Investment securities	78	10
Other	0	-
Noninterest		
Net gains on sale of loans	33	5
Service charges on deposit accounts	24	3
Insurance commissions	15	2
Gain on securities transaction	14	2
Gain on sale of assets	10	1
Trust & investment services	8	1
Other	20	4
Total	**744**	**100**

COMPETITORS

Bank of America	JPMorgan Chase
Capital One	New York Community
Citigroup	Bancorp
Dime Community	PNC Financial
Bancshares	TD Bank USA
Hudson City Bancorp	Wells Fargo

HISTORICAL FINANCIALS

Company Type: Public

Income Statement

FYE: December 31

	ASSETS ($ mil.)	NET INCOME ($ mil.)	INCOME AS % OF ASSETS	EMPLOYEES
12/14	18,793	116	0.6%	2,907
12/13	16,156	131	0.8%	2,908
12/12	16,012	143	0.9%	2,910
12/11	14,244	133	0.9%	2,754
12/10	14,143	131	0.9%	2,720
Annual Growth	7.4%	(3.0%)	—	1.7%

2014 Year-End Financials

Debt ratio: 3.91%
Return on equity: 6.83%
Cash ($ mil.): 830
Current ratio: —
Long-term debt ($ mil.): —

No. of shares (mil.): 232
Dividends
  Yield: 4.5%
  Payout: 78.5%
Market value ($ mil.): 2,254

	STOCK PRICE ($) FY Close	P/E High/Low	PER SHARE ($) Earnings	Dividends	Book Value
12/14	9.71	19 16	0.56	0.44	8.03
12/13	10.12	16 13	0.66	0.60	7.72
12/12	9.30	18 12	0.73	0.65	7.57
12/11	12.37	20 13	0.75	0.66	7.09
12/10	14.30	23 17	0.73	0.65	7.28
Annual Growth	(9.2%)	— —	(6.6%)	(9.4%)	2.5%

VENTURE ELECTRICAL CONTRACTORS INC.

LOCATIONS

HQ: VENTURE ELECTRICAL CONTRACTORS INC.
2110 PEWAUKEE RD STE 110, WAUKESHA, WI 531882482
Phone: 2625422727
Web: WWW.VENTURE-ELECTRIC.COM

HISTORICAL FINANCIALS

Company Type: Private

Income Statement

FYE: December 31

	REVENUE ($ mil.)	NET INCOME ($ mil.)	NET PROFIT MARGIN	EMPLOYEES
12/13	16,837	68	0.4%	100
12/12*	16	181	1080.0%	—
06/10	4	0	7.4%	—
Annual Growth	668.5%	272.2%	—	—

*Fiscal year change

2013 Year-End Financials

Debt ratio: ——
Return on equity: 0.40%
Cash ($ mil.): 518
Current ratio: 1.20
Long-term debt ($ mil.): ——

Dividends
  Yield: —
  Payout: —
Market value ($ mil.): —

Veritiv Corp

LOCATIONS

HQ: Veritiv Corp
1000 Abernathy Road NE, Building 400, Suite 1700, Atlanta, GA 30328
Phone: 770 391-8200

HISTORICAL FINANCIALS

Company Type: Public

Income Statement

FYE: December 31

	REVENUE ($ mil.)	NET INCOME ($ mil.)	NET PROFIT MARGIN	EMPLOYEES
12/14	7,406	(19)	—	8,900
12/13	4,089	242	5.9%	—
12/12	4,123	5	0.1%	—
12/11	4,327	(27)	—	—
Annual Growth	19.6%	—	—	—

2014 Year-End Financials

Debt ratio: 42.14%
Return on equity: (-4.30%)
Cash ($ mil.): 57
Current ratio: 2.30
Long-term debt ($ mil.): 1,067

No. of shares (mil.): 16
Dividends
  Yield: —
  Payout: —
Market value ($ mil.): 830

	STOCK PRICE ($) FY Close	P/E High/Low	PER SHARE ($) Earnings	Dividends	Book Value
12/14	51.87	— —	(1.62)	0.00	32.03
12/13	0.00	— —	(0.00)	0.00	15.48
Annual Growth	—	— —	—	—	27.4%

Verizon Communications Inc

Verizon is the #1 wireless phone service in the US (ahead of rival AT&T Mobility) and the #2 US telecom services provider overall (after AT&T). The company's core mobile business Verizon Wireless serves about 137 million total customers. (Verizon Wireless was a joint venture with Vodafone until 2014 when Verizon bought out Vodafone's stake for $130 billion.) Verizon's wireline unit with more than 19 million voice connections (end of 2014) provides local telephone long-distance Internet access and digital TV services to residential and wholesale customers. In addition Verizon offers a wide range of telecom managed network and IT services to commercial and government clients in more than 150 countries. Verizon moved to expand its video and advertising capabilities with the acquisition of AOL for $4.4 billion in mid-2015.

Operations

The company's Verizon Wireless segment account for 69% of revenue. It operates one of the most extensive wireless networks in the US and the largest fourth-generation LTE and third-generation Evolution—Data Optimized (EV-DO) networks. The 4G LTE network covers more than 98% of the US population.

The Wireline segment 30% of revenue provides voice data and video communications products and enhanced services including broadband video and data corporate networking services data center and cloud services security and managed network services and local and long distance voice services.

Geographic Reach

Verizon is all over the horizon with offices in 150 countries. It operates two R&D centers in San Francisco and Waltham Massachusetts.

Sales and Marketing

Verizon sells its prepaid and postpaid wireless phone services through its website its own stores and national retailers such as Best Buy Costco Target and Wal-Mart. It also has a dedicated telemarketing sales force. In 2014 its average account paid $159.80 a month a 4% increase from 2013's average of $154.

The company is also a major advertiser with a coordinated program of TV print radio outdoor signage Internet and point-of-sale media promotions.

Financial Performance

The company reported 2014 revenue of $127 billion up5% from 2013. Its growing wireless business (up 8.2% for 2014) outpaced the receding wireline business (down 0.5%). Mobile sales again grew in response to higher subscriber numbers (5 million new customers) and growing use of data services as well as a smartphone-driven increase in equipment sales. The key culprit in the decline of the wireline segment was traditional voice revenues falling in the global wholesale and enterprise businesses. However those wireline decreases were offset by higher sales (up 3.8%) of its FiOS digital cable service.

Profits on the other hand fell by $1.8 billion to $9.6 billion in 2014 from 2013 which was a record high net income. Verizon had higher operating expenses in 2014 from increases in severance pension and benefits charges.

Cash flow also dropped in 2014 to $30 billion from $39 billion because of higher tax payments.

Strategy

Verizon increased its focus on the wireless world when it bought the 45% stake in Verizon Wireless that it didn't own from Vodafone in 2014 for $130 billion. Under the deal Verizon paid $58.9 billion in cash $60.2 billion in stock and an additional $11 billion from smaller transactions to the UK-based carrier. The split was part of an effort by Vodafone to exit joint ventures and partnerships that it doesn't control in order to expand in other areas. Verizon already had operational control of the company and with full ownership now has access to full profits and can better position itself against the fierce competition in the US mobile market.

In early 2015 the company sold wireline operations (including FiOS lines) in Texas California and Florida to Frontier Communications for about $10.5 billion. The deal sent 1.2 million FiOS Internet subscribers and 1.5 million FiOS video subscribers as wells as landline subscribers to Frontier. The operations had generated more than $5 billion in revenue for Verizon.

With a competitive eye toward the convergence of wireline communications and digital broadcasting services Verizon has been building out its fiber-to-the-premises (FTTP) network which powers FiOS at a cost of $18 billion to improve digital video transmission services and gain an edge on leading cable operators like Comcast and Time Warner Cable. The upgraded network infrastructure replaces traditional copper network connections with fiber optics in order to increase broadband capacity.

The company bid more than $10 billion to win 181 spectrum licenses in a Federal Communications Commission auction.Verizon is looking for every opportunity to make FiOS services available to customers. FiOS can be accessed through Verizon wireless services and devices and is also available on devices from industry-leading partners such as Microsoft's Xbox home video game console. Verizon also sees FiOS as key to expanding its offerings such as enabling users to remotely monitor and control their home's lights locks thermostats and appliances.

The company's venture with video kiosk firm Redbox to launch a streaming video service shut down in late 2014. The service Redbox Instant by Verizon ended when Redbox withdrew.

Mergers and AcquisitionsVerizon has used the acquisition of regional mobile phone companies to transform itself from a purely wireline telephone company into a leading US wireless carrier and telecom services provider. It has responded to the migration of callers to cell phone and digital phone accounts (such as those offered by cable companies) by downsizing its consumer landline business and investing in enterprise customers. The landscape of today's Verizon is dominated by wireless FiOS broadband and global strategic services.

Verizon's acquisition of AOL provides the carrier with boosts in traffic for mobile and video as well as a strong presence in programmatic advertising. AOL's ad technologies are to enable Verizon to more precisely place ads in front of willing buyers. AOL also brought several high-profile content sites including the Huffington Post TechCrunch and Engadget.

In 2014 it sold spectrum licenses to T-Mobile for $2.3 billion while at the same time picking up licenses on a different spectrum to add capacity to its 4G LTE (long-term evolution) network. In 2012 it paid $4 billion for spectrum licenses from Advanced Wireless Service to facilitate its 4G LTE network.

HISTORY

Verizon Communications (the name is a combination of veritas the Latin word for truth and horizon) was born in 2000 when Bell Atlantic bought GTE but the company's roots are as old as the telephone. What is now Verizon began as one of the 1870s-era phone companies that evolved into AT&T Corp. and its Bell System of regional telephone operations.

AT&T lived happily as a regulated monopoly until a US government antitrust suit led to its breakup in 1984. Seven regional Bell operating companies (RBOCs or Baby Bells) emerged in 1984 including Bell Atlantic. The new company based in Philadelphia received local phone service rights in six states and Washington DC; cellular company Bell Atlantic Mobile Systems; and one-seventh of Bellcore the R&D subsidiary (now Telcordia).

After an era of deconsolidation phone companies started to come back together in different firms amid the growing shift from landlines to mobile phones. Bell Atlantic and Vodafone AirTouch (which became Vodafone Group) combined their US wireless operations including PrimeCo to form Verizon Wireless in 2000. Regulators later that year approved Bell Atlantic's acquisition of GTE and Verizon Communications was formed.

The company went through several phases of mergers and divestitures and arrived in 2015 as the second largest wireless carrier in the US behind AT&T.

EXECUTIVES

EVP and Chief Strategy Officer, Roy H. Chestnutt, age 56
Chairman and CEO, Lowell C. McAdam, age 61, $1,580,769 total compensation
EVP Wireless Operations Verizon Wireless, David Small

EVP and Chief Information and Technology Architect, Roger Gurnani, age 54
EVP and Chief Administrative Officer, Marc C. Reed, age 56
EVP; President Strategic Initiatives, Daniel S. (Dan) Mead, age 62, $940,385 total compensation
SVP and Global President Verizon Enterprise Solutions, Christopher M. (Chris) Formant, age 63
EVP; President Operations, John G. Stratton, age 54, $785,577 total compensation
EVP; President Product Innovation and New Businesses, Marni Walden
EVP and CFO, Francis J. (Fran) Shammo, age 55, $815,385 total compensation
EVP and President Verizon Wireline Network Operations, W. Robert (Bob) Mudge, age 55
EVP Public Policy and General Counsel, Craig Silliman
SVP and Group President Consumer and Mass Business (CMB) Sales and Service, Tami Erwin
Vice President, Brian Lane
Vice President Finance, Susan Kim
Senior Vice President Investor Relations, John Doherty
Senior Vice President, Holyce Groos
Area Vice President Customer Service, Cara White
Senior Vice President Verizon Telecommunications, Quintin Lew
Vice President, Christopher Kimm
Vice President Supply Chain Financial Advisor, Stephanie Webster
National Account Manager, Fran Morris
Senior Vice President Human Resources, Lawrence Marcus
Vice President Sales and Marketing, Rocco Tricarico
Vice President Of Software Engineering, Kim Voegele
Area Sales Vice President Enterprise Sales, Alan (Al) McMillan
Vice President, Paul L Mattiola
National Account Manager, Chuck Keeler
Vice President Marketing Communications, Jay Jaffin
Vice President Finance Transformation, Jose Piazza
Vice President Technology, Michelle Michel
National Account Manager, John (Jack) Welker
Vice President hrbp, Lisa Damask
Vice President Sales, Sheryl Tolbert-johnson
National Account Manager, Richard (Dick) Mullin
Vice President of Wireless Policy Development, Charla Rath
Vice President, Joseph Russo
Vice President Digital Meda Services, Kurt Smith
Area Vice President, Charlie Burns
Area Vice President, Gordon Littley
Vice President And Associate General Counsel, David Kauffman
Vice President, Tamara Preiss
Area Vice President, Albert Lao
Vice President, Michele Dupre
Vice President Customer Care, Anne Bishop
Regional Vice President Public Policy, Karen Campbell
Vice President Human Resources Business Partner, Claudia Healy
Senior Vice President Business Development, Steven (Steve) Smith
Executive Director Network Operations Vps, Sam Luxton
Senior Vice President, Gurudutt Pai
Vice President, Roland Hicks
Vice President Of Marketing And Sales For Middle Atlantic Region, Mary Yarbrough
Vice President Of Engineering, Joseph Cook
Area Sales Vice President Enterprise Sales, Nicholas Fotos
Vice President of Marketing, Bob Gilbride
Vice President, Pam Nelson

Group Vice President Sales, Dan Feldman
Vice President Regulatory Affairs, Ava-marie Madeam
Group Vice President, Scott Eason
Regional Vice President, Jim Tinson
National Account Manager, Rob Parker
Senior Vice President, Mark Keam
Vice President Of Video Solutions, Shawn Strickland
Vice President Of Marketing, Marcela Zamora
Vice President Of Finance, Carrie Hughes
Vice President Global Customer Care, Karen Maguire
Senior Vice President Of Human Resourc, Connia Nelson
Legal Secretary, Dawn Cooper
Area Sales Vice President Enterprise Sales, Chris Parady
Vice President Government, Ulises Diaz
Vice President Finance, Sara Orr
Vice President Of Sales, Philip Burroughs
Vice President Business Solutions Development, Jack Waters
Vice President, John (Jack) Edmunds
Vice President Fleet Operations, Kenneth Jack
Vice President Business Process Excellence and Innovation, Sisir Padhy
Vice President Operations, Michelle Swittenberg
Vice President Of Product Development, Michael Palmer
Senior Vice President Global Real Estate, John Vazquez
Vice President, Shelly Ashwill
National Account Manager, Shirley Bily
Senior Vice President National Operations Support, Thomas (Thom) Maguire
Manager Vps Marketing And Sales, Janice Crandall
National Account Manager, Carolyn Jussaume
Vice President of Sales Western Region, Scott Martin
Vice President, Paul Mattiola
Vice President, Robert (Bob) Fisher
Senior Vice President of Sales, Richard (Dick) Black
Executive Vice President; President Strategic Initiatives, Dan Mead
Vice President Marketing, Khris Stillman
Vice President Marketing, Bob Smith
Vice President of Fleet, Ken Jack
Board Member, Bob Tomaso
Secretary Manager Network Operations, Emmanuel Kostakis
Secretary Manager Network Operations, Paul Mcguire
Board Member, Thomas Bolger
Board Member, Beryl Thompson
Board Member, Robert Connolly
Secretary Manager Network Operations, Derek White
Auditors: Ernst & Young LLP

LOCATIONS

HQ: Verizon Communications Inc
1095 Avenue of the Americas, New York, NY 10036
Phone: 212 395-1000
Web: www.verizon.com

PRODUCTS/OPERATIONS

Selected Acquisitions
CloudSwitch (2011 cloud computing software)
Terremark Worldwide (2011 IT infrastructure services)
Alltel (2009 wireless telecommunications services)
Rural Cellular (2009 wireless telecommunications)
Cybertrust (2007 data security services)

2014 Sales

	$ mil.	% of total
Wireless		
Service	72,630	57
Equipment & other	15,016	12

Wireline		
Mass markets	18,047	14
Global enterprise	13,684	11
Global wholesale	6,222	5
Other	476	-
Corporate eliminations and Other	1,004	1
Total	**127,079**	**100**

COMPETITORS

360networks	Level 3 Communications
AT&T	Sprint Communications
CenturyLink	T-Mobile USA
Charter Communications	Time Warner Cable
Comcast	U.S. Cellular
Cox Communications	XO Holdings
Cricket	Yellowbook

HISTORICAL FINANCIALS
Company Type: Public

Income Statement
FYE: December 31

	REVENUE ($ mil.)	NET INCOME ($ mil.)	NET PROFIT MARGIN	EMPLOYEES
12/14	127,079	9,625	7.6%	177,300
12/13	120,550	11,497	9.5%	176,800
12/12	115,846	875	0.8%	183,400
12/11	110,875	2,404	2.2%	193,900
12/10	106,565	2,549	2.4%	194,400
Annual Growth	4.5%	39.4%	—	(2.3%)

2014 Year-End Financials
Debt ratio: 48.68%—
Return on equity: 37.65%
Cash ($ mil.): 10,598
Current ratio: 1.06
Long-term debt ($ mil.): 110,536
Dividends
Yield: 4.5%
Payout: 88.4%
Market value ($ mil.): —

	STOCK PRICE ($) FY Close	P/E High/Low	PER SHARE ($) Earnings	Dividends	Book Value
12/14	46.78	21 19	2.42	2.14	2.96
12/13	49.14	13 10	4.00	2.08	13.57
12/12	43.27	152119	0.31	2.02	11.60
12/11	40.12	47 39	0.85	1.96	12.69
12/10	35.78	40 29	0.90	1.91	13.64
Annual Growth	6.9%	— —	28.1%	2.8%	(31.8%)

VF Corp.

V.F. Corporation is the name behind the labels. Among the world's top jeans makers it owns a bevy of denim brands: Lee Riders Wrangler and Rock & Republic. Other holdings include JanSport and Eastpak (backpacks) North Face and Eagle Creek (outdoor gear) Red Kap and Bulwark (work clothes) Nautica (sportswear) lucy (women's athletic apparel) 7 For All Mankind (premium denim casual wear) and Vans (footwear). V.F.'s Majestic label offers licensed MLB NFL and NBA apparel. Direct sales to consumers are rung up through Internet sites and more than 1400 VF-operated retail stores worldwide. About 60% of V.F. products are sold through department and specialty stores mass merchants and discounters.

Operations

V.F.'s fast-growing Outdoor & Action Sports business has grown to account for more than 50% of the company's sales. V.F.'s stable of popular outdoor brands include The North Face Jansport Vans Kipling SmartWool and recently-acquired Timberland a maker of adventure-oriented footwear and apparel. Its Jeanswear business which generates about 25% of sales includes the Lee Riders Rustler and Wrangler brands as well as the fashion denim and sportwear brand Rock & Republic. Imagewear which includes licensed athletic apparel and occupational clothing accounts for 10% of sales.

The company's direct-to-consumer operations include full-price stores outlet stores and e-commerce. V.F. operates more than 1400 stores most of which are single-brand shops such as The North Face Timberland Vans and 7 For All Mankind among others. It also runs about 85 VF Outlet stores in the US that sell a broad range of excess quantities of VF-branded products. On the wholesale side of the business VF distributes apparel to specialty stores department stores national chains and mass merchants.

Geographic Reach

V.F. Corp. rings up more than 60% of its sales in the US while the remainder comes primarily from Europe and Asia but also from Canada Mexico and Latin America. The apparel maker has manufacturing plants in the US Mexico Central and South America the Caribbean Europe and the Middle East.

Sales and Marketing

The company generates most of its sales through other retail chains. V.F. Corporation's 10 largest customers accounted for 20% of total revenues in 2014. Retail-giant Wal-Mart Stores is V.F.'s largest customer accounting for 8% of its total sales in 2014 and a major buyer of its jeanswear.V.F. also sells products on a direct-to-consumer basis through VF-operated stores and e-commerce sites which accounted for 26% of total revenues in 2014. The apparel maker buys ads in trade publications and on radio and television. Its digital initiatives include social media mobile platforms and the Internet. The company spent nearly $714 million (almost 6% of net sales) on advertising and promotion in 2014 up from $671 million in 2013.

Financial Performance

V.F. Corporation has enjoyed revenue and profit growth for much of the past several years as it continues its worldwide expansion. Continued strong demand for its outdoor and action sports brands propelled V.F.'s sales to a record $12.28 billion in fiscal 2015 (ended January) an increase of 8% over the prior fiscal year. Its Outdoor & Action Sports line grew by 13% during the year thanks to double-digit global sales growth for The North Face Vans and Timberland brands. The company's direct-to-consumer revenue grew by 22% thanks to double-digit growth for The North Face and Vans brands while international sales in the Americas European and Asia Pacific regions grew 14% 9% and 17% respectively.Despite higher revenue net income reversed course in 2014 falling by 13% to $1.05 billion mostly because of higher goodwill impairment and intangible asset expenses. Cash from operations in 2014 grew by 13% to $1.7 billion primarily thanks to higher cash earnings.

Strategy

V.F. Corp. takes a two-track approach to growth: both organic and through acquisitions. The company already established an aggressive revenue target of $17.3 billion by 2017 (up from $12.28 billion in 2014) expecting annual growth of 10% (8% from organic growth and 2% from anticipated acquisitions). To this end V.F. Corp. opened 188 stores worldwide in 2014 after opening 164 stores in 2013 focusing on brands with high retail-growth potential such as Vans The North Face Timberland Kipling and Splendid. Beyond its brick-and-mortar stores the company expects its direct-to-consumer business via e-commerce sites for countries around the world will grow at a faster pace the overall growth of the company. In late 2014 the company continued to roll out country-specific brand sites in Europe and Asia enhancing its ability to deliver a superior localized consumer experience. Also in 2014 V.F. opened a new distribution center in fast-growing China to enhance its responsiveness and grow sales in the emerging region.

V.F. Corp. is not afraid to cut brands that aren't profitable to free up resources. In 2012 for example it sold its majority stake in upscale men's designer brand John Varvatos to private equity Lion Capital.Company Background

The gear-and-apparel maker has invested heavily in acquisitions to further build its outdoor and action sports business which has grown to account for more than 50% of sales. V.F. in September 2011 acquired global footwear maker Timberland for $2 billion. Marking the biggest acquisition in the company's history V.F. was enticed by Timberland's overseas presence and its strong growth during the past decade. A year earlier on the wholesaling side V.F. took control of its Vans-branded products marketing venture in Mexico. The roughly $30 million purchase also put V.F. in charge of Vans retail stores. V.F. Corp. was hoping to boost its outdoor business and its bottom line further through its 2013 bid to take over Australia's boardwear maker Billabong but the Aussie company wanted more than the 526.8 million Australian dollars (US $556 million) V.F. was willing to pay.

V.F. founded in 1899 is controlled in part by trusts established by its late founder John Barbey.

HISTORY

In 1899 six partners including banker John Barbey started the Reading Glove and Mitten Manufacturing Company. Barbey bought out his five partners in 1911 and changed the name of the Reading Pennsylvania company to Schuylkill Silk Mills in 1913. Barbey expanded the mills' production to include underwear and changed the mills' name to Vanity Fair Silk Mills (after a contest with a $25 prize in 1919).

Barbey (who banned the word "underwear") and his son J. E. led their lingerie company to national prominence. The mills made only silk garments until the 1920s when synthetics were developed. In response to the US embargo on silk in 1941 Vanity Fair changed to rayon finally converting to the new wonder fabric nylon tricot in 1948. Vanity Fair was then manufacturing all stages of its nylon products from filament to finished garment. It won awards for its innovative advertising with photographs of live models in Vanity Fair lingerie.

J. E. owned all of Vanity Fair's stock until 1951 when he sold one-third of his holdings to the public. In 1966 the stock previously traded over the counter was listed on the NYSE.

EXECUTIVES

Vice President Americas Sourcing, John (Jack) Strasburger
Vice President Human Resources, Susan (Sue) Williams
Chairman and CEO, Eric C. Wiseman, $1,300,000 total compensation
VP; Group President International, Karl H. Salzburger, $896,738 total compensation
VP; Group President Jeanswear Imagewear and South America, Scott H. Baxter, $800,000 total compensation
VP and CFO, Scott A. Roe, age 50
VP Mergers and Acquisitions, Franklin L. (Frank) Terkelsen
VP and CIO, Martin Schneider
VP; President Supply Chain, Thomas A. Glaser
SVP Americas, Steven E. (Steve) Rendle, age 55, $706,154 total compensation
VP Direct-to-Consumer, Brendan Sullivan
Vice President eBus, Joe Plaster
Vice President of Marketing Communications Western, Allen (Al) Montgomery
Vice President Information Technology, Joan Stogner
Senior Vice President Risk Management, Bill Clodfelter
Vice President Engineering and Technical Services, Kishore Patwa
Vice President Customer Service, Amanda Ballard
Vice President Of Information Technology Service, Ray Harris
Vice President Of Retail, Kurt Kleespies
Vice President of Marketing Nautica U, Nina FloodCampo
Vice President Global Innovation Center, Sudhakar Puvvada
Vice President, Madison Heid
Vice President RDD, Paula Bacheller
Vice President, Jim Sinor
Vice President Sales, Steve Morton
Vice President, Lou Wall
Vice President, Tracy Hairston
Vice President, Raquel Kaiser
Vice President Us Mnnufincm Ring, Aaron Ledet
Vice President Corporate Taxes, Richard Lipinski
Vice President, Giuliano Sartori
Vice President Sales, Ken Wood
Vice President Human Resources Supply Chain, Rod Hewitt
Vice President Customer Teams, Steve Hager
Vice President Internal Audit, Scott Moree
Vice President Gmm, Bill Lynch
Vice President Of Human Resources Abo, Wendy Thomas
Vice President Design Research And Development, Paul Herron
Vice President Stores Nautica, Kevin Tennant
Vice President Operations Supply Chain Sportswear Coalition, Karen Smith
Vice President of Product Merchandising Design Product Development, Peggi Jones
Vice President, Anita Graham
Vice President of Sales, Eden Richman
Senior Vice President Americas, Steve Rendle
Vice President Strategy, Chris Holcombe
Vice President, Mark Dimuro
Vice President Sales, Rico Pasqualini
Vice President Human Resources, Susan (Sue) McDonald
Vice President Global Consumer And Shopper Insight, Karyn Peterson
National Account Manager, Dennis Feldmann
Vice President mens Sales Division General Manager wrangler, Kathy Welch
Board Member, Garrett Chapman
Board Member, Brandi Cosper
Assistant Treasurer, Linda Matthews
Assistant Treasurer, Dave Kovach
Auditors: PricewaterhouseCoopers LLP

LOCATIONS

HQ: VF Corp.
105 Corporate Center Boulevard, Greensboro, NC 27408
Phone: 336 424-6000
Web: www.vfc.com

2013 Sales

	$ mil.	% of total
US	7,124	62
Foreign primarily Europe	4,294	38
Total	11,419	100

PRODUCTS/OPERATIONS

2013 Sales

	$ mil.	% of total
Outdoor & action sports	6,379	56
Jeanswear	2,811	25
Imagewear	1,066	9
Sportswear	624	5
Contemporary brands	415	4
Other	123	1
Total	**11,419**	**100**

2013 Sales

	$ mil.	% of total
Net sales	11,302	99
Royalty income	117	1
Total	**11,419**	**100**

Selected Brands

Contemporary brands
  7 For All Mankind
  Ella Moss
  Splendid
Imagewear
  Bulwark
  Chef Designs
  Horace Small
  Majestic
  Red Kap
Jeanswear
  Lee
  Riders
  Rock & Republic
  Rustler
  Timber Creek by Wrangler
  Wrangler
Sportswear
  Kipling
  Nautica
Outdoor and action sports
  Eagle Creek
  Eastpak
  JanSport
  Kipling
  lucy
  Napapijri
  Reef
  SmartWool
  The North Face
  Timberland
  Vans

Selected Licenses

Harley-Davidson Motor Company
Major League Baseball
MLB Players Association
National Basketball Association
National Football League
National Hockey League

Selected major colleges and universities

COMPETITORS

Abercrombie & Fitch	L.L. Bean
American Eagle	Levi Strauss
Outfitters	OshKosh B' Gosh
Calvin Klein	Patagonia Inc.
Columbia Sportswear	REI
Diesel SpA	Reebok
Guess?	Rocky Brands
J. C. Penney	Russell Brands
Joe' s Jeans	Sears Holdings
Johnson Outdoors	The Gap
Kate Spade	Tommy Hilfiger
Kellwood	True Religion Apparel
Koos Manufacturing	Williamson-Dickie
L Brands	Manufacturing

HISTORICAL FINANCIALS

Company Type: Public

Income Statement

FYE: January 3

	REVENUE ($ mil.)	NET INCOME ($ mil.)	NET PROFIT MARGIN	EMPLOYEES
01/15*	12,282	1,047	8.5%	59,000
12/13	11,419	1,210	10.6%	59,000
12/12	10,879	1,086	10.0%	57,000
12/11	9,459	888	9.4%	58,000
12/10	7,702	571	7.4%	47,000
Annual Growth	12.4%	16.4%	—	5.8%

*Fiscal year change

2015 Year-End Financials

Debt ratio: 14.52%
Return on equity: 17.60%
Cash ($ mil.): 971
Current ratio: 2.58
Long-term debt ($ mil.): 1,423

No. of shares (mil.): 432
Dividends
  Yield: 0.0%
  Payout: 46.5%
Market value ($ mil.): 31,928

	STOCK PRICE ($) FY Close	P/E High/Low	PER SHARE ($) Earnings	Dividends	Book Value
01/15*	73.76	31 23	2.38	1.11	13.01
12/13	61.58	89 22	2.71	0.92	13.80
12/12	148.29	68 51	2.43	0.76	11.63
12/11	126.99	69 40	2.00	0.65	10.23
12/10	86.18	68 53	1.30	2.43	8.94
Annual Growth	(3.8%)	— —	16.4%	(17.8%)	9.8%

*Fiscal year change

Viacom Inc

Viacom might not be a household name but its famous entertainment brands are welcomed into most living rooms on a daily basis. The company is a leading media conglomerate with an extensive portfolio of cable TV and film production assets. Its MTV Networks unit runs such cable networks as Comedy Central Nickelodeon and the family of MTV channels (MTV MTV2 VH1). Viacom also owns Black Entertainment Television which airs programming on BET BET Gospel and BET Hip Hop. In the film business Viacom operates through Paramount Pictures which includes imprints Paramount Pictures and Paramount Vantage. Chairman Sumner Redstone controls a majority of Viacom through his National Amusements movie theater chain.

Geographic Reach

Headquartered in New York City Viacom has a presence in 160 countries and territories primarily in North America Europe and Asia. The US contributed about 75% of the company's revenue and International markets accounted for about 25% of the company's sales in fiscal 2013.

Operations

Viacom operates through two reporting segments: Media Networks which includes MTV Nickelodeon and BET; and Filmed Entertainment. The company's filmed entertainment division is responsible for hits such as the big budget movies.

Sales and Marketing

Flagship channel MTV focuses on younger viewers and popular culture and continues to draw one of the largest television audiences in the 18-34 age group. Nickelodeon meanwhile has become a popular destination for children's programming. Comedy Central appeals to young adults with programs such as as The Daily Show with Jon Stewart and its offshoot The Colbert Report while BET dominates the important urban demographic with entertainment music and special interest programming.

Viacom does not have the broad complement of media assets that characterize integrated conglomerates such as Time Warner and Walt Disney but the company still realizes some potential by integrating its TV and film businesses such as through DVD sales and cross-promotion. Viacom itself incurred total advertising expenses of $1.117 billion in fiscal 2013.

Financial Performance

Viacom's revenue decreased $93 million or 1% to $13.794 billion in fiscal 2013 compared to $13.887 billion in fiscal 2012. The drop was largely due to a decrease in Filmed Entertainment revenue by $538 million. Advertising revenue was a bright spot increasing $99 million or 2% compared to the previous year up to $4.855 billion in fiscal 2013.

The company's net income for fiscal 2013 increased by 21% to $2.395 billion compared to $1.981 billion in fiscal 2012. The spike was the result of decreased losses from discontinued operations.

Viacom reported cash inflow of $1.55 billion in fiscal 2013 compared to cash outflow of $173 million in fiscal 2012 due to a decrease in cash used in financing activities.

Strategy

Viacom's strategy includes expanding its relationships with advertising cable satellite digital mobile and licensing partners to develop new ways to deepen its connection with audiences through insightful research and the development of content that resonates with targeted audiences.

The company is primarily focused on its television operations which account for about 65% of sales. Generating most of their revenue from a combination of commercial advertising and carriage fees paid by cable system operators the TV networks provide a steady anchor for the the company balancing against the uneven feature film business and the sometimes fickle tastes of movie goers.

What particularly drives Viacom's business is its success in building entertainment brands. The company is notable for creating and promoting such names as MTV and Nickelodeon into easily recognizable banners that stand for a particular form of entertainment.

Viacom has been looking to expand its reach into digital media in an effort to reach its young and increasingly online target audience.

EXECUTIVES

EVP and Chief Administrative Officer, Scott M. Mills
Vice President of Technical Support, George Epley
Senior Vice President investor Relations, James (Jamie) Bombassei
Senior Vice President Communications VH1, Laura Nelson
Svp Creative Grp/creative Vh1, Carole Robinson
Research MTV Networks Vh1 Executive Vice President, Colleen Rush
Chairman and CEO BET Networks, Debra L. Lee, age 60
EVP General Counsel and Secretary, Michael D. Fricklas, age 56, $1,287,500 total compensation
EVP Corporate Communications, Carl D. Folta, age 58
SEVP and COO, Thomas E. (Tom) Dooley, age 59, $2,871,154 total compensation
Chairman President and CEO, Philippe P. Dauman, age 62, $3,871,154 total compensation
President Music and Entertainment Group, Doug Herzog
Chairman and CEO Paramount Pictures, Brad Grey

President Nickelodeon, Cyma Zarghami
President and CEO International Media Networks, Robert M. (Bob) Bakish, age 51, $931,731 total compensation
EVP Government Affairs, Doretha F. (DeDe) Lea, age 51
EVP and CFO, Wade C. Davis, age 43, $1,241,923 total compensation
SVP Technology and CIO, David Kline
President MTV, Sean Atkins
Vice President Of Application Development, Joe Leggio
Senior Vice President, George Nelson
Vice President Communications, David Bittler
Senior Vice President Mtv Networks, Pauline Wen
Vice President Data Platform, Mark Cohen
Executive Vice President Velocity Creative Content, Niels Schuurmans
Vice President Human Resources, Wendy Charest
Senior Vice President And Managing Director, Paul Guerra
Svp Corp Communications Vimn, Julia Phelps
Vice President, Jane Lipsitz
Senior Vice President Controller, Charest Gill
Vice President of LAN and Messaging Services, Lee Lee Larchevesque Larchevesque
Senior Vice President Human Resources, Whitney Delich
Senior Vice President BROADCAST TECHNOLOGIES, Paul Sartain
Vice President Vh1 And Logo Digital, Dan Sacher
Vice President Of Finance, Brian Ruscin
Vice President Content Distribution and Network Operations, Mike Miglino
Vice President Integrated Marketing, Rachel Baumgarten
Exec Vpres-mktg Strategy & Eng, Ross Martin
Vice President Server and Storage Technologies, Brian Amirian
Vice President of Network Services, Lee L'archenesque
Vice President Information Systems, John Morgan
Senior Vice President National Accoun, Courtney Menzel
Senior Vice President Product Architect, Chaki Ng
Vice President Of Ad Sales, Mark Jones
Vice President Technical Accounting, James (Jamie) Guido
Vice President Acquisitions, Tom Zappala
Vice President Of Art Department, Romy Mann
Vice President Of Business Development, Anthony Bongiorno
Vice President Government Relations And Regulatory Counsel, Keith Murphy
Senior Vice President, David (Dave) Sutphen
Executive Vice President, Jim Perry
Vice President Integrated Marketing, Alexis Rodriguez
Executive Assistant To Michael D Armstrong Senior Vice President And General Manager Bet, Gillian Anderson
Senior Vice President Corporate, Aileen Budow
Vice President Operations, Eric Squires
Vice President Digital Marketing, Don Steele
Vice President Digital Marketing Nickelodeon, Jim Malaga
Vice President Integrated Marketing, Lisa Saffian
Vice President Information Technology Au, Noble Anthony
Vice President Channel Marketing, Lauren Elchoness
Vice President Marketing, David (Dave) Lee
Vice President Of Strategic Business Development, Daniel Reich
Vice President Digital, Shannon Burke
Vice President Business Development, Amy Singer
Executive Vice President Digital Media, Erik Flannigan
Vice President, Sean Wylie
Vice President Federal Tax Audits, Victor Rappa

Vice President Operations Online, Pier Chapman
Senior Vice President Internal Audit, Norman Tsacalis
Vice President Counsel Corporate, Sarah Harp
Vice President New Business Development, Rick Beispel
Vice President Hrad, David Dowd
Vice President Public Affairs The Americas, Alfredo Cader
Senior Vice President Senior Counsel Benefits (1998), John R (Jack) Jacobs
Vice President Assistant Treasurer, Lou Converse
Vice President Financial Planning and Analysis, Paul Mottola
Vice President Level, Vice president Tim Stevenson
Vice President Strategic Sourcing Technology, Robert (Bob) Roth
Vice President Tax Reporting, John (Jack) McCartney
Vice President Financial Operations and Compliance, Susan (Sue) Stacker
Executive Vice President Human Resources, Catherine (Cathy) Houser
Senior Vice President Communications, Jeannie Kedas
Vice President Advertising Sales, Sean Moran
Vice President Benefits Employee Programs, Steven (Steve) Zumbo
Senior Vice President International Marketing, Mark Levine
Executive Vice President Tax, James (Jamie) Barge
Senior Vice President, Allan Infeld
Vice President Growth Strategy, Victor Kong
Executive Vice President Series Entertainment, Lois Curren
Senior Vice President and Controller, Katherine (Kate) Gill-Charest
Executive Vice President Viacom Plus, Lisa McCarthy
Senior Vice President Head of Sales, Neil Holt
Senior Vice President Program Sales MTV Networks International, Deborah (Deb) Back
Executive Vice President Marketing MTV Mtv2 And, Tina Exarhos
Senior Vice President Of Series Development, Liz Gateley
Vice President Corporate Accounting Viacom Inc. US, Deepak Daswani
Vice President Public Affairs the Americas, Mario Cader-Frech
Senior Vice President Digital Advertisin, Michael (Mel) Greenspan
Vice Chairman, Shari E. Redstone, age 61
Secretary Treasurer and General Counsel, Denise Dahldorf Dahldorf
Auditors: PricewaterhouseCoopers LLP

LOCATIONS
HQ: Viacom Inc
1515 Broadway, New York, NY 10036
Phone: 212 258-6000
Web: www.viacom.com

2014 Sales

	$ mil.	% of total
US	10,252	74
EMEA	2,046	15
All other regions	1,485	11
Total	**13,783**	**100**

PRODUCTS/OPERATIONS

2014 Sales

	$ mil.	% of total
Advertising	4,953	35
Affiliated Fees	4,660	34
Feature Film	3,173	23
Ancillary	1,110	8
(Eliminations)	(113)	-
Total	**13,783**	**100**

HISTORICAL FINANCIALS
Company Type: Public

Income Statement
FYE: September 30

	REVENUE ($ mil.)	NET INCOME ($ mil.)	NET PROFIT MARGIN	EMPLOYEES
09/15	13,268	1,922	14.5%	9,200
09/14	13,783	2,391	17.3%	9,900
09/13	13,794	2,395	17.4%	10,350
09/12	13,887	1,981	14.3%	10,620
09/11	14,914	2,136	14.3%	10,580
Annual Growth	(2.9%)	(2.6%)	—	(3.4%)

2015 Year-End Financials

Debt ratio: 55.30%	No. of shares (mil.): 398
Return on equity: 52.97%	Dividends
Cash ($ mil.): 506	Yield: 3.3%
Current ratio: 1.21	Payout: 30.8%
Long-term debt ($ mil.): 12,267	Market value ($ mil.): 17,178

	STOCK PRICE ($) FY Close	P/E High/Low		PER SHARE ($) Earnings	Dividends	Book Value
09/15	43.15	16	8	4.73	1.46	8.89
09/14	76.94	16	14	5.43	1.26	8.98
09/13	83.58	17	10	4.84	1.15	11.56
09/12	53.59	15	10	3.69	1.05	14.69
09/11	38.74	14	10	3.59	0.80	15.48
Annual Growth	2.7%	—	—	7.1%	16.2%	(13.0%)

Virginia Electric & Power Co.

Yes Virginia there is power in the Old Dominion thanks to Dominion Virginia Power. The company (which operates under the Dominion Virginia Power and Dominion North Carolina Power brands) provides regulated electric delivery services to about 2.4 million homes and businesses. Power generation is derived by means of coal gas oil hydro and nuclear plants. The utility's power plants (with 19595 MW of generating capacity) are managed by the Dominion Generation unit of parent Dominion Resources. Control of Virginia Electric and Power's transmission facilities is maintained by PJM Interconnection. Dominion Virginia Power also sells wholesale power to other users.

Geographic Reach

Dominion Virginia Power generates transmits and distributes electricity for sale in Virginia and North Carolina.

OperationsThe company operates through DVP and Dominion Generation. The DVP operating segment includes Virginia Electric and Power's regulated electric transmission and distribution (including customer service) operations which serve residential commercial industrial and governmental customers.The Dominion Generation segment includes the generation operations of the Virginia Electric and Power's regulated electric utility and its related energy supply operations. Its utility generation operations primarily serve the supply requirements for the DVP segment's utility customers.Financial PerformanceRevenue marginally increased by 0.37% in 2011. Net income increased by 4% primarily reflecting less favorable weather including the impact of Hurricane Irene and an impairment charge related to certain coal-fired power stations.

Except for a revenue slump in 2009 Virginia Electric and Power saw an upward trend in revenues from 2007 to 2011. The drop in revenues in 2009 was because of the charge for the proposed settlement of the company's 2009 rate case proceedings a decrease in sales of gas production from exploration and production operations primarily reflecting the expiration of certain royalty interests and a decrease in net gas revenues from retail energy marketing operations primarily due to lower prices.

StrategyVirginia Electric and Power has been investing heavily in upgrading its infrastructure to meet growing demand. In 2011 Fluor completed the $619 million 580 MW gas-fired combined-cycle Bear Garden Station in Buckingham County Virginia for the company. In 2010 the utility announced that it will add more than 400 MW of additional capacity by upgrading 13 power plants.The company is also trying to beef up its green energy profile. In addition to exploring wind farm options to help produce alternative energy Virginia Electric and Power is pushing energy conservation programs with the aim of cutting peak demand by electric consumers in Virginia by 650 MW.OwnershipVirginia Electric and Power is owned by Dominion Resources.

EXECUTIVES

President Dominion Virginia Power, Robert M. Blue
Auditors: Deloitte & Touche LLP

LOCATIONS

HQ: Virginia Electric & Power Co.
120 Tredegar Street, Richmond, VA 23219
Phone: 804 819-2000

COMPETITORS

Appalachian Power	Pepco Holdings
Columbia Gas of	Rappahannock Electric
Virginia	Cooperative
Duke Energy Carolinas	SCANA
Duke Energy Progress	South Carolina
Inc.	Electric & Gas

HISTORICAL FINANCIALS

Company Type: Public

Income Statement

FYE: December 31

	REVENUE ($ mil.)	NET INCOME ($ mil.)	NET PROFIT MARGIN	EMPLOYEES
12/14	7,579	858	11.3%	6,800
12/13	7,295	1,138	15.6%	6,700
12/12	7,226	1,050	14.5%	6,800
12/11	7,246	822	11.3%	6,800
12/10	7,219	852	11.8%	6,800
Annual Growth	1.2%	0.2%	—	0.0%

2014 Year-End Financials

Debt ratio: 34.90%	No. of shares (mil.): 0
Return on equity: 8.53%	Dividends
Cash ($ mil.): 15	Yield: 0.0%
Current ratio: 0.78	Payout: —
Long-term debt ($ mil.): 8,726	Market value ($ mil.): —

	STOCK PRICE ($) FY Close	P/E High/Low	PER SHARE ($) Earnings	Dividends	Book Value
12/14 36,600.50	0.00	— —	(0.00)	4.16	
12/13 36,600.50	109.91	— —	(0.00)	5.00	
12/12 34,543.89	111.00	— —	(0.00)	5.00	
12/11 32,785.75	103.96	— —	(0.00)	5.00	
Annual Growth	—	— —	—	(4.5%)	2.8%

Visa Inc

Paper or plastic? Visa hopes you choose the latter. Visa operates the world's largest consumer payment system (far ahead of rivals MasterCard and American Express) and boasts nearly 2.5 billion credit and other payment cards in circulation across more than 200 countries. As part of its business the company licenses the Visa name to member institutions which issue and market their own Visa products and participate in the VisaNet payment system that provides authorization processing and settlement services. The company also offers debit cards Internet payment systems value-storing smart cards and traveler's checks. Visa's network connects thousands of financial institutions worldwide.

HISTORY

Company BackgroundAlthough the first charge card was issued by Western Union in 1914 it wasn't until 1958 that Bank of America (BofA) issued its BankAmericard which combined the convenience of a charge account with credit privileges. When BofA extended its customer base outside California the interchange system controlling payments began to falter because of design problems and fraud.

In 1968 Dee Hock manager of the BankAmericard operations of the National Bank of Commerce in Seattle convinced member banks that a more reliable system was needed. Two years later National BankAmericard Inc. (NBI) was created as an independent corporation (owned by 243 banks) to buy the BankAmericard system from BofA.

With its initial ad slogan "Think of it as Money" the Hock-led NBI developed BankAmericard into a widely used form of payment in the US. A multinational corporation IBANCO was formed in 1974 to carry the operations into other countries. People outside the US resisted BankAmericard's nominal association with BofA and in 1977 Hock changed the card's name to Visa. NBI became Visa USA and IBANCO became Visa International.

By 1980 Visa had debuted debit cards begun issuing traveler's checks and created an electromagnetic point-of-sale authorization system. Visa developed a global network of ATMs in 1983; it was expanded in 1987 by the purchase of a 33% stake in the Plus System of ATMs then the US's second-largest system. Hock retired in 1984 with the company well on its way to realizing his vision of a universal payment system.

The company built the Visa brand image with aggressive advertising such as sponsorship of the 1988 and 1992 Olympics and by co-branding (issuing cards through other organizations with

strong brand names such as Blockbuster and Ford).

In 1994 Visa teamed up with Microsoft and others to develop home banking services and software. Visa Cash was introduced during the 1996 Olympics. Visa pushed its debit cards in 1996 and 1997 with humorous ads featuring presidential also-ran Bob Dole and showbiz success story Daffy Duck.

Visa expanded its smart card infrastructure in 1997. It published with MasterCard encryption and security software for online transactions. The gloves came off the next year as the companies vied to convince the world to rally around their respective e-purse technology standards.

During the 1990s Visa fought American Express' attempts to introduce a bank credit card of its own by forbidding Visa members in the US from issuing the product; the Justice Department responded with an antitrust suit against Visa and MasterCard. The case went to trial in 2000 with the government claiming that Visa and MasterCard stifle competition and enjoy an exclusive cross-ownership structure. Visa eventually agreed to pay American Express $2.25 billion to settle the case.

Also in 2000 the company made a deal with Gemplus the French smart card company to enable payments over wireless networks. Visa then inked e-commerce agreements with telecommunications companies Nokia and Ericsson. The company continued its technology push with a deal with Financial Services Technology Consortium to test biometrics —the use of fingerprints irises and voice recognition to identify cardholders. The company also launched a prepaid card Visa Buxx targeted at teenagers.

The European Union in 2000 launched an investigation into the firm's transaction fees alleging that the fees could restrict competition. The following year Visa International agreed to drop its fee to 0.7% of the transaction value over five years.

Led by retail giant Wal-Mart some 4 million merchants claimed Visa and MasterCard violated antitrust laws and attempted to monopolize a legally defined market for debit cards. The plaintiffs sought up to $200 billion in damages in their class-action suit. Just as the 1996 lawsuit was to go to trial in early 2003 Visa settled agreeing to pay $2 billion (twice that of co-defendant MasterCard) over the next decade. Both agreed to pay $25 million immediately as well as reduce the fee merchants pay for signature-based debit cards.

Visa settled a similar case with Discover Financial in 2008. Visa's net share of the deal totaled some $1.8 billion; MasterCard which was also named agreed to pay $862.5 million.

The group restructured in 2007 in order to offer a more seamless international payments processing platform and to take itself public. Visa International Visa Canada Visa U.S.A. and several other regional organizations merged to create Visa Inc. which became the new parent of the group. It raised about $17 billion in a 2008 IPO.

Visa dedicated some of the funds raised to exploring new payment-related technologies and expanding into more regions. It established joint ventures with payment processors and banks to strengthen its global payment network. Other funds were set aside to cover costs resulting from legal settlements with American Express and Discover Financial totaling more than $4 billion.

EXECUTIVES

Chief Enterprise Risk Officer, Ellen Richey, age 66
CEO, Charles W. (Charlie) Scharf, age 50, $950,037 total compensation
EVP and CFO, Vasant M. Prabhu, age 54

Global Executive Strategy Mergers and
  Acquisitions and Government Relations, William
  M. (Bill) Sheedy, age 48, $525,020 total compensation
EVP and General Counsel, Kelly M. Tullier
EVP Technology, Rajat Taneja, $639,447 total
  compensation
President, Ryan McInerney, age 40, $750,029 total
  compensation
Senior Vice President E Business, Elizabeth (Beth)
  Hurvitz
Vice President Head of Payment Services
  Marketing Visa Europe, Neil Horseman
Vice President Processing Solutions, Manny
  Fernandez
Executive Vice President, Robert (Bob) Alandt
Vice President Acceptance Solutions, Aashish
  Bhargava
Gcas VPS Clients Inquiries North America LAC
  And Europe, Abdallah Saoud
Vice President, Aken John
Senior Vice President, Chris Lambert
Vice President Atm Card Products, John (Jack)
  Brinnon
Assistant Vice President, Fernanda Grillo
Assistant Vice President Marketing, Michelle Pasos
Senior Vice President Head of Global Financial
  Inclusion, Stephen (Steve) Kehoe
Vice President Visa Uk, Rob Walter
Vice President, Mario Rivero
Vice President, Jeff Allison
Senior Vice President Switching Systems, Manny
  Trillo
Vice President Technology Development
  Management Worldwide Partner, Tom Matsumoto
Senior Vice President, Erin Magsamen
Senior Business Leader (Vice President) Client
  driven Innovation, Allen (Al) Cueli
Vice President, Tim Gallagher
Senior Vice President Of Global, Phil Kumnick
Vice President Data Management And Middleware
  Engineering, Mark Jensen
Vice President Business Analytics Business Side,
  Heather Jones
Vice President, Odalys Ruiz
Vice President, David Henstock
Vice President Business Development, Sameer
  Bawa
Vice President, Julie Miller
Vice President Corporate Strategy, Neil Mumm
Vice President Global Head of Customer
  Experience, Diego J Todeschini
Vice President Credit Product Consulting, Davin
  Chow
Vice President Processing Sales, Neil Fraser
Vice President Marketing Central Europe Middle
  East and Africa (CEMEA), Mohammed Ismaeel
Vice President Pricing and Costing, Philip Joseph
Vice President Marketing, Sergio De Anda
Vice President Digital Marketing, David (Dave)
  Purcell
Chairman, Robert W. Matschullat, age 68
Auditors: KPMG LLP

LOCATIONS

HQ: Visa Inc
  P.O. Box 8999, San Francisco, CA 94128-8999
Phone: 650 432-3200
Web: www.corporate.visa.com

2015 Sales

	$ mil.	% of total
US	7,406	53
Other countries	6,219	45
Visa Europe	255	2
Total	**13,880**	**100**

PRODUCTS/OPERATIONS

2015 Sales

	$ mil.	% of total
Service fees	6,302	38
Data processing fees	5,552	33
International transaction fees	4,064	24
Other	823	5
Client incentives	(2861)	-
Total	**13,880**	**100**

Selected Products and Services

Commercial and government
  Visa Business Credit Card (small business)
  Visa Business Debit Card (small business)
  Visa Business Electron (international)
  Visa Business Line of Credit
  Visa Commercial One Card
  Visa Corporate Card (travel and entertainment)
  Visa Gift Card
  Visa Incentive Card
  Visa Purchasing Card
  Visa Signature Business Card
Consumer credit
  Visa Classic
  Visa Gold
  Visa Infinite
  Visa Platinum
Consumer deposit
  Interlink Debit (POS debit network)
  Prepaid
  Visa Debit
  Visa Classic
  Visa Gold
  Visa Infinite
  Visa Platinum
  Visa Electron Debit

COMPETITORS

American Express	JCB International
China UnionPay	MasterCard
Citigroup	PayPal
Discover	Rewards Network
Google	

HISTORICAL FINANCIALS

Company Type: Public

Income Statement
FYE: September 30

	REVENUE ($ mil.)	NET INCOME ($ mil.)	NET PROFIT MARGIN	EMPLOYEES
09/15	13,880	6,328	45.6%	11,300
09/14	12,702	5,438	42.8%	9,500
09/13	11,778	4,980	42.3%	9,500
09/12	10,421	2,144	20.6%	8,500
09/11	9,188	3,650	39.7%	7,500
Annual Growth	**10.9%**	**14.7%**	**—**	**10.8%**

2015 Year-End Financials

Debt ratio: ——
Return on equity: 22.10%
Cash ($ mil.): 3,518
Current ratio: 2.03
Long-term debt ($ mil.): —
Dividends
  Yield: 0.6%
  Payout: 20.0%
Market value ($ mil.): —

	STOCK PRICE ($) FY Close	P/E High/Low	PER SHARE ($) Earnings	Dividends	Book Value
09/15	69.66	108 25	2.58	0.48	13.47
09/14	213.37	108 84	2.16	1.60	8.99
09/13	191.10	105 71	1.90	1.32	8.61
09/12	134.28	170106	0.79	0.22	8.52
09/11	85.72	72 52	1.29	0.60	8.14
Annual Growth	**(5.1%)**	**— —**	**18.9%**	**(5.4%)**	**13.4%**

Visteon Corp.

Visteon is the visionary-sounding name Ford Motor bestowed on its automotive components unit when it was spun off in 2000. One of the largest auto parts makers in the US the company has evolved to operate two business groups: Climate Control (climate systems powertrain cooling systems); and Electronic Products (audio systems driver control systems infotainment systems powertrain and feature control modules). Ford represents more than 25% of sales; Visteon also provides products and services to aftermarket customers. More than 80% of its sales are made outside the US.

Geographic Reach

Visteon has corporate offices in Van Buren Township Michigan; Shanghai; and Chelmsford UK. It operates through 120 facilities worldwide in 28 countries. Asia is its largest market accounting for 50% of its total sales in 2014. Europe and North America follow with 27% and 20% of sales respectively.

Operations

Visteon's Climate Control segment makes climate systems and powertrain cooling systems and generates 67% of total sales in 2014. Electronic Products offers audio systems driver control systems and powertrain and feature control modules and generated 31%.

Sales and Marketing

While Ford represents more than a quarter of Visteon's business the Hyundai Kia Automotive Group tops that commanding around 36% of the company's revenues. Visteon provides components to a lion's share of the top global automotive OEMs —Daimler Honda Toyota and Volkswagen is the short list.

Financial Performance

The company's revenues has grown over the last three years. In 2014 Visteon's revenues grew by almost 1% due to the full year acquisition results of Yanfeng Visteon Automotive Electronics and the electronics business of Johnson Controls; along with an increase in customer volumes and product mi related to the company's Climate and Electronics segments; and currency changes. Visteon suffered a loss of $295 million in 2014 (compared to net income of $690 million in 2013) due to an increase in expenses which included selling general and administrative expenses (which were affected by acquisitions); and lower equity from net income. Thes wer partially offset by a small increase in revenues. In 2014 the company's operating cash flows were $284 million (down from $312 million in 2013) due to decreased net income an increase in outflow of $23 million pension settlement gain and accounts receivable that were sold as part of the Interiors divestiture.

Strategy

Expanding the company's existing manufacturing footprint in India in 2015 Visteon began production at a new facility in Sanand Gujarat with a production capacity of 2 million units consisting of heat exchangers; heating ventilation and air conditioning (HVAC) modules; and air conditioning lines.

In 2014 it expanded its manufacturing facility in Hluk Czech Republic increasing the plant's capacity by 30%.

Visteon has been reorganizing and getting rid of extraneous divisions and units in order to focus on its more profitable operations. As part of a strategic reorganization Visteon in 2014 announced it will separate the portion of its Interiors business conducted through its facilities in Chennai and Pune India into a new legal entity which will be transferred to the holding company and sold to the buyer.

In 2014 the company divested all of its global Interiors business to Reydel Automotive Holdings B.V. an affiliate of Cerberus Capital Management L.P. and also completed the sale of interiors operations in India and Thailand. Visteon partnered in 2014 with Rightware a leader in user interaction (UI) design and benchmarking software to deliver leading-edge UI and graphics solutions for the automotive industry. The partnership supports the company's strategy of growing its position in user interface and graphics technology.

The company in 2013 sold its 50% ownership interest in its Chinese joint venture Yanfeng Visteon Automotive Trim Systems Co. to Huayu Automotive Systems Co. for $840 million. It also expects to earn about $116 million in additional after-tax proceeds in 2014 and 2015 as a result of the transaction.

Mergers and Acquisitions

Visteon also uses acquisitions as a means for fortifying its core operations. In mid-2014 it paid $265 million to purchase the automotive electronics business of Johnson Controls. The deal gave Visteon seven research and development centers in Europe North America and Asia and further diversified and expanded its global customer base.

Expanding its thermal energy management product portfolio in 2014 through its subsidiary the company acquired the automotive thermal and emissions business of Cooper-Standard Automotive (a subsidiary of Cooper-Standard Holdings) for $46 million.

Company Background

In 2012 Visteon sold its automotive lighting operations to Varroc Group a fellow provider of automotive parts for $72 million in cash. The business included front and rear lighting systems and auxiliary lamps and key parts such as projectors and electronic modules. The divesture allowed Visteon to focus on its most lucrative business segment: Climate Control. Visteon also wishes to concentrate on the more profitable products within its Electronic Products operations.

The company was founded in 2000.

EXECUTIVES

President CEO and Director, Sachin Lawande, age 48

EVP and CFO, Jeffrey (Jeff) Stafeil, age 45, $684,564 total compensation

VP and General Counsel, Peter M. Ziparo, age 45, $333,480 total compensation

Operations and Procurement, Sunil K. Bilolikar

Chairman, Francis M. Scricco, age 66

Auditors: Ernst & Young LLP

LOCATIONS

HQ: Visteon Corp.
One Village Center Drive, Van Buren Township, MI 48111
Phone: 734 710-5800
Web: www.visteon.com

2014 Sales

	% of total
North America	20
Europe	27
Asia	50
South America	3
Eliminations	—
Total	100

PRODUCTS/OPERATIONS

2014 Sales

	$ mil.	% of total
Climate	5,092	67
Electronics	2,386	31
Other	126	2
Eliminations	(95)	—
Total	7,509	100

Selected Operating Segments and Products

Climate control products and systems
  Battery cooling module
  Compressors
  Fluid transport systems
  Heat exchangers
  HVAC systems
  Powertrain cooling systems
Electronic products and systems
  Audio systems
  Control panels and displays
  Driver awareness systems
  Driver information systems
  Engine induction systems
  Integrated electronics and infotainment systems
  Powertrain and feature control (engine and transmission controls fuel delivery modules)
Interior products and systems
  Cockpit systems
  Consoles
  Door trim modules and seat systems

COMPETITORS

Autoliv	Johnson Controls
Behr Industries	KOITO MANUFACTURING
Calsonic Kansei	Lear Corp
Clarion Technologies	Magna International
Continental AG	Magneti Marelli
DENSO	Powertrain USA
Delphi Automotive	Metaldyne
Systems	Modine Manufacturing
Faurecia	Parker-Hannifin
Federal-Mogul	Rheinmetall
Garmin	Robert Bosch
Harman International	Standard Motor
Hella	Products
IAC Group	TI Automotive
Inergy Automotive	Valeo
JTEKT	ZF TRW Automotive

HISTORICAL FINANCIALS

Company Type: Public

Income Statement

FYE: December 31

	REVENUE ($ mil.)	NET INCOME ($ mil.)	NET PROFIT MARGIN	EMPLOYEES
12/14	7,509	(295)	—	25,500
12/13	7,439	690	9.3%	24,000
12/12	6,857	100	1.5%	22,000
12/11	8,047	80	1.0%	26,000
12/10	1,887	86	4.6%	26,500
Annual Growth	41.2%	—	—	(1.0%)

2014 Year-End Financials

Debt ratio: 18.43%
Return on equity: (-21.18%)
Cash ($ mil.): 822
Current ratio: 1.71
Long-term debt ($ mil.): 839
No. of shares (mil.): 44
Dividends
  Yield: —
  Payout: —
Market value ($ mil.): 4,702

	STOCK PRICE ($) FY Close	P/E High/Low	PER SHARE ($) Earnings	Dividends	Book Value
12/14	106.86	— —	(6.25)	0.00	19.66
12/13	81.89	6 4	13.50	0.00	40.00
12/12	53.82	30 15	1.88	0.00	26.63
12/11	49.94	49 26	1.54	0.00	25.13
12/10	74.25	43 33	1.66	0.00	24.71
Annual Growth	9.5%	— —	—	—	(5.6%)

VMware Inc

VMware makes a virtue of being virtual. The company develops software used to create and manage virtual machines —computer functions spread across multiple systems. Companies use its applications to more efficiently integrate and manage server storage and networking functions to lower the cost of operating their IT systems. VMware also provides an extensive range of consulting technical support training and certification services that accounts for just over half of sales. The company has marketing relationships with top computer hardware vendors including Dell Hewlett-Packard and Cisco. Data storage systems maker EMC holds a controlling stake in VMware.

Operations

VMware derives its revenue from the licensing of software and related services which includes software maintenance professional services and software as service subscriptions. Overall maintenance and services account for about 57% of the firm's total revenue.

Geographic Reach

More than half of Silicon Valley-based VMware's revenue comes from outside the US. The company operates about 100 offices across the Americas Europe the Asia-Pacific Region and the Middle East and Africa.

Financial Performance

There was nothing virtual about VMware's revenue in 2014. It came in at just more than $6 billion a 16% increase over 2013. Net income however fell about 13% to $886 million after cresting the billion dollar mark in 2013. Revenue for licensing maintenance and service all increased as did revenue by geographic market. The company's emphasis on selling its software as suites of applications paid off in two ways. Suite sales carried higher prices and the complexity of suite software led to additional demand for services. VMware's profit was cut by higher income taxes and higher interest expense paid to EMC associated with debt obtained for VMware's AirWatch acquisition.

Strategy

Going beyond providing services that enable cloud computing VMware offers its own cloud computing services. In 2014 the company expanded its hybrid cloud computing products rebranding its vCloud hybrid cloud services to VMware vCloud Air. While opening new markets the move also opens VMware up to additional competitors. VMware vCloud Air's infrastructure-as-a-service go head-to-head with services from Amazon Microsoft Google IBM and newer companies. Companies such as Cisco Systems that provide software for managing systems as well as hardware also compete with VMware.

Central to VMware's strategy is partnerships with hardware software and cloud computing service vendors to sell each other's products through joint marketing product interoperability collaboration and cooperative development. VMware extended its partnership with security firm Palo Alto Networks to offer secure access to information from mobile devices including those covered in bring-your-own-device plans.

In another step that combines security and mobility VMware acquired AirWatch in 2014. AirWatch offers services for enterprise mobile management and security. The deal propelled the release of VMware's AirWatch Chat product a secure instant messaging application for iOS devices and Android devices.

Mergers and Acquisitions

The AirWatch Holding deal occurred in early 2014 at a price of about $1.2 billion. A bit earlier

VMWare acquired Desktone for cloud-delivered virtual desktops.

Ownership

EMC holds 80% of the company common stocks and controls about 96% of VMware's voting shares.

Company Background

Founded in 1998 VMware was acquired by EMC for about $625 million in cash in 2004. Looking to unlock some of the value in its subsidiary EMC sold some of its stake in VMware in a 2007 IPO.

EXECUTIVES

Senior Vice President People, Betsy Sutter
Senior Vice President Global Services and Customer Advocacy, Scott Bajtos
EVP and General Manager End-user Computing, Sanjay Poonen, age 45, $600,000 total compensation
Corporate SVP and General Manager Americas, Maurizio Carli
Corporate SVP Asia Pacific and Japan, Sanjay Mirchandani, age 51
President and COO, Carl M. Eschenbach, age 49, $712,500 total compensation
EVP and CFO, Zane C. Rowe, age 44
Corporate SVP and General Manager Europe Middle East and Africa (EMEA), Jean-Pierre Brulard
EVP and CFO, Jonathan Chadwick, age 47, $650,000 total compensation
SVP and CIO, Bask Iyer
CEO and Director, Patrick (Pat) Gelsinger, age 54, $925,000 total compensation
EVP and General Manager Hybrid Cloud Services Business Unit, Bill Fathers
EVP and General Manager Software-Defined Data Center Division, Raghu Raghuram, $550,000 total compensation
SVP Strategy and Corporate Development and General Manager Telco NFV Group, Shekar Ayyar
Corporate SVP Software-Defined Data Center Division, Ray O'Farrell
SVP General Counsel Chief Compliance Officer and Secretary, S. Dawn Smith, age 51
SVP and General Manager Networking and Security Business Unit, Martin Casado
Vice President Sales, Carlos Cuellar
Area Vice President, Corey Hutchison
Vice President And Chief Technologist, Simone Brunozzi
Vice President Sales, Ted Ranft
Vice President Ecosystem Research and Development, George Mathew
Vice President Information Technology Operations, Mark Ritacco
Vice President Product Operations and Quality Engineering, Ramesh Kurnool
Vice President Of Sales Management, Jay Stephenson
Vice President Pricing and Licensing, Ryan Knauss
Senior Vice President Sales Information technology, Scott Feinstein
Vice President Sales Strategy and Transformation, Bret Connor
Vice President Data Governance, Theresa Kushner
Senior Vice President, Charles (Chas) Fan
National Account Manager, Matthew Streeter
Vice President Global Government Relations and Public Policy, Michael (Mel) Kennedy
Vice President, Leif Frykman
Vice President Global Technical Support, John Dolan
Vice President Semea, Jean Brulard
Global Vice President Strategic Systems Integrators and Outsourcers, David M (Dave) Parsons
Vice President Product Engineering, Dale Ferrario
Vice President Philanthropy, Nicola Acutt

Vice President Of Worldwide Services, Patrick Unnold
Vice President Internal Audit, Susan (Sue) Insley
Vice President Marketing, Susan Thomas
Senior Product Manager MVP, Debapriya Ray
Vice President Field Automation Services And Global Marketing Operations, Mia Leondakis
Vice President Products Euc, Harry Labana
National Account Manager, Kathy Sardina
Quality Engineer For Mvp, Bryan Bozzi
Vice President Latin America Sales, Fernando Mollon
Chairman, Joseph M. (Joe) Tucci, age 68
Assistant Treasurer, Tina Kobetsky
Auditors: PricewaterhouseCoopers LLP

LOCATIONS

HQ: VMware Inc
3401 Hillview Avenue, Palo Alto, CA 94304
Phone: 650 427-5000
Web: www.vmware.com

2014 Sales

	$ mil.	% of total
US	2,912	48
Other countries	3,123	52
Total	6,035	100

PRODUCTS/OPERATIONS

2014 Sales

	$ mil.	% of total
Services		
Software Maintenance	3,022	50
Professional Services	422	7
License	2,591	43
Total	6,035	100

COMPETITORS

Amazon.com	IBM
CA Inc.	Microsoft
Cisco Systems	Novell
Citrix Systems	Oracle
Dell Software	Parallels
Google	Symantec
HP	

HISTORICAL FINANCIALS

Company Type: Public

Income Statement

FYE: December 31

	REVENUE ($ mil.)	NET INCOME ($ mil.)	NET PROFIT MARGIN	EMPLOYEES
12/14	6,035	886	14.7%	18,000
12/13	5,207	1,014	19.5%	14,300
12/12	4,605	745	16.2%	13,800
12/11	3,767	723	19.2%	11,000
12/10	2,857	357	12.5%	9,000
Annual Growth	20.6%	25.5%	—	18.9%

2014 Year-End Financials

Debt ratio: 9.86%
Return on equity: 12.31%
Cash ($ mil.): 2,071
Current ratio: 2.28
Long-term debt ($ mil.): 1,500
No. of shares (mil.): 429
Dividends
Yield: —
Payout: —
Market value ($ mil.): 35,431

	STOCK PRICE ($) FY Close	P/E High/Low		PER SHARE ($) Earnings	Dividends	Book Value
12/14	82.52	54	37	2.04	0.00	17.66
12/13	89.71	42	28	2.34	0.00	15.84
12/12	94.14	65	46	1.72	0.00	13.39
12/11	83.19	63	43	1.68	0.00	11.26
12/10	88.91	105	48	0.84	0.00	9.14
Annual Growth	(1.8%)	—	—	24.8%	—	17.9%

Voya Financial Inc

LOCATIONS

HQ: Voya Financial Inc
230 Park Avenue, New York, NY 10169
Phone: 212 309-8200
Web: www.ing.us

HISTORICAL FINANCIALS

Company Type: Public

Income Statement

FYE: December 31

	REVENUE ($ mil.)	NET INCOME ($ mil.)	NET PROFIT MARGIN	EMPLOYEES
12/14	11,070	2,299	20.8%	6,500
12/13	8,758	600	6.9%	7,000
12/12	9,615	473	4.9%	7,000
12/11	9,718	(88)	—	—
12/10	9,274	(122)	—	—
Annual Growth	4.5%	—	—	—

2014 Year-End Financials

Debt ratio: 1.55%
Return on equity: 15.65%
Cash ($ mil.): 2,530
Current ratio: 5.02
Long-term debt ($ mil.): 3,515
No. of shares (mil.): 241
Dividends
Yield: 0.0%
Payout: 0.7%
Market value ($ mil.): 10,251

	STOCK PRICE ($) FY Close	P/E High/Low		PER SHARE ($) Earnings	Dividends	Book Value
12/14	42.38	5	4	9.02	0.04	66.60
12/13	35.15	15	9	2.38	0.02	50.72
Annual Growth	4.8%	—	—	39.5%	18.9%	7.0%

WAKEFERN FOOD CORP.

Grocery stores getting supplies from this co-op may be on the "Rite" track. Wakefern Food is the largest member-owned wholesale distribution co-operative in the US supplying groceries and other merchandise to more than 250 supermarkets under the ShopRite and The Fresh Grocer banners in New Jersey New York Connecticut Delaware Maryland Pennsylvania and Virginia. It also operates more than 50 PriceRite stores in these states plus Rhode Island and Massachusetts. Beyond supplying its member-owned stores Wakefern distributes products to other supermarkets across the northeastern US and Bermuda. Founded by seven grocers in 1946 the coop now boasts 50 members 70000-plus employees and over $15 billion in annual sales.

Operations

Wakefern Food supplies retail and wholesale members mostly in the Northeast US. PriceRite a subsidiary of Wakefern Food and its nearly 50 supermarkets offer over 500 grocery items at discounted prices such as fresh fruits and vegetables breads prepackaged meat and seafood kosher products and national brands. Stores average about 35000 square feet in size which are smaller than traditional supermarkets. While the vast majority of ShopRite brand stores are member owned subsidiary ShopRite Supermarkets Inc operates nearly 35 company-owned stores.Sales and Marketing

The coop added its 50th member The Fresh Grocer in July 2013. Outside of its members the company also supplies grocery stores like Saker ShopRite (New Jersey) Village Super Market (New Jersey and Pennsylvania) and Inserra Supermarkets (New York and New Jersey).

Financial Performance

Wakern Food's revenues have been rising over the past several years thanks to new member additions and their store openings. The company's retail sales rose 4% to a record $14.7 billion in fiscal 2014 (ended September 27) thanks to the addition of six new ShopRite stores five new PriceRite discount supermarkets and six new The Fresh Grocer stores over the course of the year. The company also continued to expand its ShopRite from Home services store reach which would be provided from a total of 214 of its stores.

Strategy

Like other grocery wholesalers Wakefern Food's success depends on its ability to distribute goods at the lowest possible cost to its customers meaning the company focuses on keeping expenses low and improving efficiencies throughout its supply operation. But as a member-owned cooperative the company differs from other wholesalers such as Nash-Finch in that its primary focus is on its member stores. Wakefern Food also has the added responsibility of promoting its ShopRite retail chain and helping its member retailers expand the chain's footprint.

The ShopRite chain boasts a loyal following in its core markets but the supermarkets have been feeling the pinch from rivals in the price-competitive grocery business. The company is especially feeling pressure from non-supermarket chains such as Wal-Mart CVS Health and Wawa. To help boost customer loyalty Wakefern has turned to new technology in the form of mobile applications (developed in partnership with technology firm MyWebGrocer) for the Apple iPhone that allow users to get alerts about weekly store specials in their area. The company also rolled out an online pharmacy where customers can place orders through the Internet.

Company Background Wakefern Food announced in 2012 it was supplying New York-based Food Bazaar stores which had supermarkets in New York New Jersey and Connecticut. Wakefern will supply ShopRite private label brands along with non-private labels such as dairy frozen food grocery nonfoods and specialty products.

HISTORY

Company Background Wakefern Food was founded in 1946 by seven New York- and New Jersey-based grocers: Louis Weiss Sam and Al Aidekman Abe Kesselman Dave Fern Sam Garb and Albert Goldberg. The company got its name by taking the first letters of the last names of five of the original founders (Weiss Sam and Al Aidekman Kesselman and Fern). Like many cooperatives the association sought to lower costs by increasing its buying power as a group.

They each put in $1000 and began operating a 5000-sq.-ft. warehouse often putting in double time to keep both their stores and the warehouse running. The shopkeepers' collective buying power proved valuable enabling the grocers to stock many items at the same prices as their larger competitors.

In 1951 Wakefern members began pooling their resources to buy advertising space. A common store name —ShopRite —was chosen and each week co-op members met to decide which items would be sale priced. Within a year membership had grown to over 50. Expansion became a priority and in the mid-1950s co-op members united in small groups to take over failed supermarkets. One

such group called the Supermarkets Operating Co. (SOC) was formed in 1956. Within 10 years it had acquired a number of failed stores remodeled them and given them the ShopRite name.

During the late 1950s sales at ShopRite stores slumped after Wakefern decided to buck the supermarket trend of offering trading stamps (which could then be exchanged for gifts) figuring that offering the stamps would ultimately lead to higher food prices. The move initially drove away customers but Wakefern cut grocery prices across the board and sales returned. The company did embrace another supermarket trend: stocking stores with nonfood items.

The co-op was severely shaken in 1966 when SOC merged with General Supermarkets a similar small group within Wakefern becoming Supermarkets General Corp. (SGC). SGC was a powerful entity with 71 supermarkets 10 drugstores six gas stations a wholesale bakery and a discount department store. Many Wakefern members opposed the merger and attempted to block the action with a court order. By 1968 SGC had beefed up its operations to include department store chains as well as its grocery stores. In a move that threatened to break Wakefern SGC broke away from the co-op and its stores were renamed Pathmark.

Wakefern not only weathered the storm it grew under the direction of chairman and CEO Thomas Infusino elected shortly after the split. The co-op focused on asserting its position as a seller of low-priced products. Wakefern developed private-label brands including the ShopRite brand. In the 1980s members began operating larger stores and adding more nonfood items to the ShopRite product mix. With its number of superstores on the rise and facing increased competition from club stores in 1992 Wakefern opened a centralized nonfood distribution center in New Jersey.

In 1995 30-year Wakefern veteran Dean Janeway was elected president of the co-op. The company debuted its ShopRite MasterCard co-branded with New Jersey's Valley National Bank in 1996. The following year the co-op purchased two of its customers' stores in Pennsylvania then threatened to close them when contract talks with the local union deteriorated. In 1998 Wakefern settled the dispute then sold the stores.

The company partnered with Internet bidding site Priceline in 1999 offering customers an opportunity to bid on groceries and then pick them up at ShopRite stores. Big V Wakefern's biggest customer filed for Chapter 11 bankruptcy protection in 2000 and said it was ending its distribution agreement with the co-op. In July 2002 however Wakefern's ShopRite Supermarkets subsidiary acquired all of Big V's assets for approximately $185 million in cash and assumed liabilities.

Infusino retired in May 2005 after 35 years with Wakefern Food. He was succeeded by former vice chairman Joseph Colalillo. The cooperative added to its footprint in 2007 when it acquired about 10 underperforming retail locations from Stop & Shop. The stores located mostly in South Jersey were rebranded under the ShopRite banner.

EXECUTIVES

Vice President Information Services Di, Alan (Al) Aront
Senior Vice President Technology Digital Innovation E Commerce And Wholesale, Natan Tabak
Vice President Deli And Seafood, Terry Sharkey
Vice President Compliance And Risk Management, Allison Berger
Vice President Of Production, Larry Kurz
Executive Vice President Of Retail Operations, Jason Ravitz
Vice President Advertising, Karen Gozzi

Vice President Quality Assurance, Mike Ambrosio
Vice President of LP, Steve Hoptay
Vice President Finance, Tom Cummiskey
Vice President Finance, Neil Falcone
Vice President Engineering And Purchasing, Dennis Daniels
Pharmacy Manager, Muhammed Khan
Vice President, Peter (Pete) Rolandelli
Treasurer, Doug Wille
Treasurer, Lawrence Inserra
Auditors: KPMG LLP SHORT HILLS NEW JER

LOCATIONS

HQ: WAKEFERN FOOD CORP.
5000 RIVERSIDE DR, KEASBEY, NJ 088321209
Phone: 9085273300
Web: WWW.WAKEFERN.COM

PRODUCTS/OPERATIONS

2012 Corporate Stores

	No.
PriceRite	48
ShopRite	40
Total	**88**

COMPETITORS

A&P	Krasdale Foods
Acme Markets	Pathmark Stores
Bozzuto' s	SUPERVALU
C&S Wholesale	Stop & Shop
CVS	Wal-Mart
Hannaford Bros.	Wawa Inc.
IGA	

HISTORICAL FINANCIALS

Company Type: Private

Income Statement

FYE: September 28

	REVENUE ($ mil.)	NET INCOME ($ mil.)	NET PROFIT MARGIN	EMPLOYEES
09/13	11,455	0	0.0%	3,500
09/12*	11,010	5	0.0%	—
10/11	10,325	5	0.0%	—
09/08	8,396	0	—	—
Annual Growth	6.4%	—	—	—

*Fiscal year change

2013 Year-End Financials

Debt ratio: ——
Return on equity: —
Cash ($ mil.): 129
Current ratio: 0.10
Long-term debt ($ mil.): —

Dividends
Yield: —
Payout: —
Market value ($ mil.): —

Wal-Mart Stores, Inc.

Wal-Mart Stores is an irresistible (or at least unavoidable) retail force that has yet to meet any immovable objects. Bigger than Europe's Carrefour Metro AG and Tesco combined it's the world's #1 retailer with some 2.2 million employees. In the US Wal-Mart operates more than 5160 stores including about 4400 Wal-Mart stores and 650 Sam's Club warehouses and a growing number of smaller format stores. The company's faster growing international division (28% of sales) numbers more than 6100 locations; Wal-Mart is the #1 retailer in Canada and Mexico and has operations in Asia (where it owns a 95% stake in Japanese retailer SEIYU) Africa Europe and Latin America.

HISTORY

Sam Walton began his retail career as a J. C. Penney management trainee and later leased a Ben Franklin-franchised dime store in Newport Arkansas in 1945. In 1950 he relocated to Bentonville Arkansas and opened a Walton 5 & 10. By 1962 Walton owned 15 Ben Franklin stores under the Walton 5 & 10 name.

After Ben Franklin management rejected his suggestion to open discount stores in small towns Walton with his brother James "Bud" Walton opened the first Wal-Mart Discount City in Rogers Arkansas in 1962. Wal-Mart Stores went public in 1970 with 18 stores and sales of $44 million.

Avoiding regional retailers Walton opened stores in small and midsized towns in the 1970s. The company sold its Ben Franklin stores in 1976. By 1980 Wal-Mart's 276 stores had sales of $1.2 billion.

In 1983 Wal-Mart opened SAM'S Wholesale Club a concept based on the successful cash-and-carry membership-only warehouse format pioneered by the Price Company of California (now Costco Wholesale Corp.).

The company started Hypermart*USA in 1987 as a joint venture with Dallas-based supermarket chain Cullum Companies (now Randall's Food Markets). The 200000-sq.-ft. discount store/supermarket hybrid was later retooled as Wal-Mart Supercenters. Sam stepped down as CEO in 1988 and president David Glass was appointed CEO. Wal-Mart bought out Cullum the next year.

Wal-Mart acquired wholesale distributor McLane Company in 1990. In 1992 the year Sam died the company expanded into Mexico through a joint venture to open SAM'S CLUBS with Mexico's largest retailer Cifra (renamed Wal-Mart de México in 2000). Wal-Mart acquired 122 former Woolco stores in Canada in 1994. Co-founder Bud died a year later.

More international expansion included entering China in 1996; the acquisition of German hypermarket chain Wertkauf in 1997; the purchase of Brazilian retailer Lojas Americanas' 40% interest in a joint venture (1998); and the addition of four stores and other sites in South Korea. Also in 1998 the company began testing the Neighborhood Market format a 40000-sq.-ft. grocery and drug combination store. In 1999 Wal-Mart bought 74 German-based Interspar hypermarkets and acquired ASDA Group the UK's third-largest supermarket chain.

COO Lee Scott succeeded Glass as CEO in 2000; Glass stayed on as chairman of the executive committee. Wal-Mart later began testing its customers' demand for appliances by selling household appliances in selected stores.

Following the bankruptcy and closure of the Montgomery Ward department store chain in 2001 Wal-Mart offered to replace Ward's customers' credit cards with Wal-Mart branded cards. Wal-Mart also formed an alliance with America Online to offer Internet access and later launched its No Boundaries private-label cosmetics for preteens and teenagers. In June 2001 a group of six current and former female Wal-Mart employees filed a sex-discrimination lawsuit (seeking to represent up to 500000 current and former Wal-Mart workers) against the company. The next month Wal-Mart said it would acquire all the minority interests in Walmart.com and integrate its online operations with its store operations. It also laid off 100 employees at its corporate headquarters and eliminated 300 unfilled positions. In August it said it was testing the sale of Sealy and private-label mattresses in some of its superstores and it began offering college textbooks discounted up to 30% at its online College Bookstore.

2002 was a huge year for Wal-Mart both at home and abroad. In April the company was crowned America's largest corporation by FORTUNE magazine. In March Wal-Mart gained a foothold in Japan taking a 6% stake in one of Japan's top retailers SEIYU . That December it increased its SEIYU stake to 36% and retains the option to up that to nearly 67% by 2007. In a rare defeat Wal-Mart in July closed its first store in Germany and 2000 workers there went on a two-day strike over wages. (In 2001 Wal-Mart scrapped plans to open 50 more Supercenters there by 2003.) Also in 2002 Wal-Mart Puerto Rico acquired Supermercados Amigo the #1 supermarket chain on the island. (Wal-Mart opened its first Supercenter there in April 2001.)

Overall in 2002 Wal-Mart opened 178 supercenters 33 discount stores and 25 SAM'S CLUB stores. It opened 107 international units with two in Brazil 22 in Canada eight in China two in Germany three in South Korea 59 in Mexico two in Puerto Rico and nine in the UK. The company's attempt to open a state industrial bank in California in 2002 failed however after legislators barred retailers.

In May 2003 Wal-Mart sold its McLane grocery distribution business to Berkshire Hathaway; a rare divestment for the world's largest retailer. In July it opened its first store in Beijing.

In February 2004 a federal judge ruled that Wal-Mart should pay workers for overtime hours. The complaint which was brought by plaintiffs who said they were forced to work unpaid overtime between 1994 and 1999 came at a time when working conditions at the company were being scrutinized. Also that month Wal-Mart acquired the 118-store Bompreço chain of Brazilian supermarkets and hypermarkets from troubled Dutch retailer Royal Ahold for $300 million advancing the world's largest retailer from fifth to third place in the Brazilian market. In March Wal-Mart opened its online music store which sells digital downloads for 11 cents less than major competitors (including Apple's iTunes and Napster). In April voters in Inglewood California overwhelmingly rejected Wal-Mart's proposal to build a supercenter there over the objections of local officials. Wal-Mart had sought to bypass local development and environmental regulations by spending more than $1 million to take its case directly to the voters. Also in April Wal-Mart's Japanese partner Seiyu opened its first Wal-Mart-style supercenter in Numazu.

In May 2004 Wal-Mart agreed to pay $3.1 million in fines for violating the Clean Water Act at 24 sites in nine states. (The retailer was fined $1 million in 2001 for similar violations involving its failure to manage storm-water runoff.)

Vice chairman Tom Coughlin retired in January 2005 after 25 years with Wal-Mart. Coughlin remained on the company's board until March 25 2005 when he resigned prematurely following an internal investigation related to "the alleged unauthorized use of corporate-owned gift cards and personal reimbursements." He was due to retire from the board on June 3 2005. In June the company rescinded Coughlin's retirement agreement including stock awards and incentive payments which may total as much as $12 million.

Also in January Wal-Mart agreed to pay $135540 to settle federal charges that it violated child labor laws. The 24 violations which the retailer denied involved teenage workers in three states using hazardous equipment such as chain saws paper balers and fork lifts. Soon after Wal-Mart was ordered to pay $7.5 million in damages to a disabled former employee who claimed the retailer unfairly reassigned him. In March the retailer settled a high-profile lawsuit by agreeing to pay $11 million to the US government to close an in-vestigation into the use of illegal immigrants by Wal-Mart contractors to clean its stores. In May Wal-Mart increased its stake in SEIYU to 42% (up from 37%).

In August 2005 Wal-Mart signed Garth Brooks to a multiyear exclusive contract under which the country star's music will only be sold in Wal-Mart-owned stores. The deal marks the first time an artist has contracted himself and his entire catalog of music with a single chain. In October the company launched its Metro 7 line of urban women's apparel in 500 stores in and around urban areas. In December Wal-Mart opened its third superstore in the downtown Xuanwu District of Beijing. Also in December Wal-Mart acquired some 140 stores in Brazil from Portuguese retailer Sonae for about $757 million increasing the number of outlets it operates in Brazil to nearly 300.

In January 2006 Wal-Mart opened a supercenter in Santa Clarita California its second in Los Angeles County. In February the company acquired an additional 17.7% interest in CARHCO from Royal Ahold increasing its stake in the Central America supermarket operator to 51%. Wal-Mart's former vice chairman Thomas Coughlin who was accused of misusing more than $500000 in company funds pleaded guilty to fraud and tax charges in January 2006. In August he was sentenced to 27 months of house arrest and ordered to pay $400000 in restitution to his former employer. Wal-Mart itself was ordered by a Pennsylvania jury to pay more than $78 million in damages in a class-action suit brought by employees alleging that they were forced to work during breaks and off the clock. In October Wal-Mart disposed of its retail operations in Germany and South Korea. It sold the last of its 85 stores in Germany to rival METRO AG and sold 16 stores in South Korea to Shinsegae Co. for about $882 million.

In early 2007 Wal-Mart agreed to pay $33.5 million in back wages and interest to settle a federal lawsuit that accused the company of violating ovetime laws involving more than 86000 employees. In February the company announced an agreement with all six major Hollywood studios to sell digital movies and TV shows on walmart.com becoming the first traditional retail chain to do so. In April Helen Robson Walton wife of Wal-Mart founder Sam Walton died at the age of 87. Wal-Mart and Bharti Enterprises formed a 50:50 joint venture in August to jointly build wholesale outlets that will buy goods from farmers and small manufacturers and sell to retailers through a nationwide supply chain. True to form Wal-Mart again cut prices of toys and some 15000 more items such as apparel home and food products for the 2007 holiday selling season.

In May 2008 the retailer revised its $4 prescription program launched in 2006 to cover 90-day prescriptions for $10. In November Mike Duke was named to Wal-Mart's board of directors in preparation for his elevation to president and CEO of the company in February 2009. Also in November Eduardo Castro-Wright president and CEO of Walmart US was promoted to vice chairman of Wal-Mart Stores. He assumed responsibility for the firm's global procurement operation.

The management shuffle continued in 2009 with Lee Scott retiring as CEO in February. Scott was succeeded by Duke who had headed the international arm of the company. In January Wal-Mart acquired a majority stake in Chile's largest food retailer Distribución y Servicio through a tender offer. In May of that year it opened its first location in India vis a joint venture with Bharti Enterprises.

In February 2010 the company opened its new Latin America regional headquarters in Miami Florida.

In June 2011 Walmart International acquired a 51% stake in South African retailer Massmart which operates 288 stores in 13 countries in sub-Saharan Africa in a deal valued at about $2.4 billion. Massmart operates stores under the Makro Game Dion Wired Builders Warehouse Builders Express Builders Trade Depot CBW Jumbo Cash and Carry and the Shield buying group. On the day of the Massmart closing the company scored a huge win when the US Supreme Court threw out a massive employment discrimination class-action lawsuit (Dukes vs. Wal-Mart) brought filed back in 2001. While the court did not rule on whether or not Wal-Mart discriminated against women it said they could not proceed as a class.

EXECUTIVES

Senior Vice President Nonperishable Food, John (Jack) Westling
Vice President Finance and Assistant Treasurer, Steven (Steve) Zielske
EVP and CEO Wal-Mart U.S., Gregory S. (Greg) Foran, age 54, $846,910 total compensation
President and CEO, C. Douglas (Doug) McMillon, age 49, $1,200,930 total compensation
President Health and Wellness, George J. Riedl, age 55
EVP Consumables and Health and Wellness and U.S. Manufacturing Lead, Michelle J. Gloeckler
EVP and Chief Administrative Officer, Rollin L. Ford, age 53
President and CEO Global eCommerce, Neil M. Ashe, age 47, $935,303 total compensation
EVP Global People Division, M. Susan Chambers, age 58
EVP Food Walmart U.S., Steve Bratspies
EVP; President and CEO International, David Cheesewright, age 52, $1,152,850 total compensation
EVP and CFO Sam's Club, Michael P. Dastugue, age 51
Chief Administrative Officer Walmart International and President and CEO Walmart Asia, Scott Price, age 54
EVP and CIO, Karenann K. Terrell, age 53
EVP Softlines Walmart U.S., James A. (Andy) Barron
President and CEO Sam's Club, Rosalind G. Brewer, age 52, $893,819 total compensation
EVP Merchandising Sam's Club, Charles Redfield
EVP Global Customer Insights and Analytics, Cindy Davis
President and CEO of Walmart M©xico and Central America, Guilherme Loureiro
EVP Global Governance and Corporate Secretary, Jeffrey J. (Jeff) Gearhart, age 51
EVP Corporate Affairs, Daniel J. (Dan) Bartlett, age 43
EVP Merchandising Operations Walmart U.S., Scott Huff
EVP and President Walmart Central Walmart U.S., Michael S. (Mike) Moore
EVP and CFO, M. Brett Biggs, age 47
EVP Global Sourcing Â– Walmart Leverage, Tim Yatsko
President and CEO Samsclub.com, Jamie Iannone, age 42
EVP International People Division, Gisel Ruiz, age 44
COO Global eCommerce, Michael J. Bender
EVP Walmart U.S. People, Kristin Oliver
EVP Logistics Walmart U.S., Chris Sultemeier
President Walmart East Walmart U.S., Joaqu n Gonz ̃lez Varela
EVP and General Counsel, Karen Roberts
President and CEO Walmart Latin America, Enrique Ostal ©
EVP and COO Walmart U.S., Judith McKenna
EVP Operations Sam's Club, Don Frieson
CEO Latin America eCommerce, Fernando Madeira

EVP and Treasurer, Claire Babineaux-Fontenot
SVP New England Division Walmart U.S., Julie Murphy
EVP and Global Chief Ethics and Compliance Officer, Jay Jorgensen
Vice President and Assistant Treasurer, Mike Cook
Vice President Isd Architecture Chief Technology A, John (Jack) Collier
Vice President Information Technology, Kerry Kilker
Vice President Home Furnishings, Shawnda Schnurbusch
Senior Vice President, Anthony Fuller
Senior Vice President Finance and Planning, Rick Brazile
Executive Vice President and Chief Financial Officer Walmart U.S., Jeff Davis
RVP E Commerce Wal Mart Stores Inc., Jeff Fackler
Vice President Product Development Home, Daria Beckom
Director Application Enablement Area; Vice President Of Large Systems, Rita Carney
Vice President Marketing Local And Grocery, Kirsten Sweaney Evans
Senior Vice President Data Integration Officer, Todd Harbaugh
Vice President Intl Merchandise Development, Ronald F Virta
Pharmacy Manager, Jim C Cox
Pharmacy Manager, Steve Goldblatt
PHARMACY Manager, Rocco Pandolfo
Pharmacy Manager, Frank Yielding
Pharmacy Manager, Greg Oswald
Pharmacy Manager, Lydia Orr
Pharmacy Manager, Joby Young
Pharmacy Manager, John (Jack) Cox
Pharmacy Manager, Gary Durfey
Pharmacy Manager, Tram Romero
Vice President Beverages Sam's Club, Trent Weller
Vice President E Commerce, Fred Quandt
Vice President Supply Chain, Lesley (Les) Smith
Vice President Pharmacy, Frank Segrave
Senior Vice President for the Optical Division, Jeff McAllister
Exec Vp-sams Club Operations, Greg Johnston
National Account Manager, Jim Ennecking
Pharmacy Manager, Janice Willis
Senior Vice President, Brian Roberts
Pharmacy Manager, Terry Bennett
Vice President Logistics, Gary Adams
Executive Vice President Merchandising, Philip Sutterfield
Pharmacy Manager, Roger Meyers
Pharmacy Manager, Dan Himes
Pharmacy Manager, Rhonda Omara
Pharmacy Manager, Tara Green
Pharmacy Manager, Kimberly Baublitz
Senior Vice President International Development, Daniel (Dan) Mallory
Vice President, Diana Marshall
Vice President Global Customer Insights and Analytics, Bala Subramanian
Pharmacy Manager, William (Bill) Gleason
Vice President, Sam Dunn
Vice President Chief Privacy Officer, Jonathan (Jon) Avila
Vice President Of Marketing, Brian Monahan
Senior Vice President Global Merchandising Center Packaged Grocery, Michael (Mel) Lewis
Pharmacy Manager, Angela Woody
Pharmacy Manager, Jeff Stauffacher
Vice President Of Corporate Strategy, Brandon Williams
Pharmacy Manager, Angie Davis
Vice President Human Resources Administration and Strategy, Bill Clark
Executive Vice President Assistant, Debbie Hale
Vice President Human Resources, Becki Anderson
Vice President International Tax, Jim Derouin

Vice President Finance and Strategy Entertainment, Jeff Gruener
Vice President Divisional Merchandise Manager, Joe Grady
Executive Vice President, Celia Swanson
Senior Vice President of Brand Merchandising, Andrea Thomas
Senior Vice President and Human Resources Officer Wal Mart International, Bryan Miller
Senior Vice President, Gregory Au
Vice President, Cameron Geiger
Vice President DMM of Connection Centers and Video Games, Greg Hall
Senior Vice President Assistant, Teri Davis
Vice President And Regional General Manager, David (Dave) Reitnauer
Vice President Human Resources, Edward (Ed) Mckissic
Vice President of Human Resources, Anne Thomas
National Sales Manager, Carl Legreca
Senior Vice President Replenishment Planning Innovations and Real Estate, Donald E (Don) Frieson
Vice President Human Resources, Clark Bill
Vice President Finance and Strategy Services, Jonathan (Jon) Hall
Senior Vice President Marketing, Steven (Steve) Bratspies
Vice President of International, Mike Duke
Vice President U.S. Benefits, Chris McSwain
Vice President Merchandise Planning, John (Jack) Chen
Vice President DMM, David (Dave) Hall
Vice President of Global Branded Imports, Fernando Serpa
Vice President Inbound Transportation, Kevin Jones
Vice President Assistant, Angelisa Henry
Reg General Manager Vice President, Lance de la Rosa
Vice President Global Customer Insights and Analytics, Mickey Mericle
Vice President New Market Entry, Shawn Sederholm
Vice President Assistant Controller, Chris Abston
Vice President, Mark Henneberger
Vice President, Michael Evanoff
Vice President Hardware and Paint, Rick Hays
Vice President Assistant, Cheryl Creighton
Vice President and Regional General Manager Small Format Operations Wal mart Usa, Nick Berkeley
Vice President International Supply Chain, Greg Shultz
Vice President Information Technology, Dave Frizzell
Assistant To Kerry Kilker Vice President Information Systems, Eileen Smith
Vice President Global Associate Communications, Mary Flowers
Pharmacy Manager, Deborah (Deb) Pechacek
Senior Vice President Central Plains Division Walmart Usa, Dacona Smith
PHARMACY Manager, Lee Fallon
Pharmacy Manager, Jody Piet
Pharmacy Manager, Shelley Francesconi
Pharmacy Manager, Teresa Compton
Rph, Susan Long
Pharmacy Manager, Michael Leaming
Vice President Administration, Albert Lowe
Pharmacy Manager, Cynthia Palmer
Pharmacy Manager, Victor Hernandez
Pharmacy Manager, Keith Bryant
Vice President Of Marketing, Johan Landmark
Vice President Finance and Strategy (West), Tim Skinner
Vice President Produce, Ron McCormick
Pharmacy Manager, Dan Rafferty
Vice President, Eddie Tutt

Vice President GMM Men's Kid's Baby, Thomas (Thom) Dougherty
Divisional Vice President Supply Chain, Bob Arvin
Auditors: Ernst & Young LLP

LOCATIONS

HQ: Wal-Mart Stores, Inc.
702 S.W. 8th Street, Bentonville, AR 72716
Phone: 479 273-4000
Web: www.walmart.com

2015 Stores

	No.
North America	
US	5,163
Canada	394
Latin America	
Mexico	2,290
Brazil	557
Chile	404
Costa Rica	217
Guatemala	217
El Salvador	89
Argentina	105
Nicaragua	86
Honduras	81
Asia	
Japan	431
China	411
India	20
UK	592
Africa	396
Total	**11,453**

PRODUCTS/OPERATIONS

2015 Sales

	% of total
Wal-Mart US	59
International	28
SAM'S CLUB	12
Membership & other	1
Total	**100**

2015 US Sales

	% of total
Grocery	56
Health & wellness	11
Entertainment	10
Hardlines	9
Apparel	7
Home	7
Total	**100**

COMPETITORS

99 Cents Only	J Sainsbury
AEON	J. C. Penney
ALDI	Katz Group
Ace Hardware	King Kullen Grocery
Ahold U.S.A.	Kmart
Albertsons	Kohl's
Amazon.com	Kroger
Army and Air Force Exchange	Lianhua Supermarket
Aurora Wholesalers	Loblaw
AutoZone	Lowe's
BJ's Wholesale Club	METRO AG
Bed Bath & Beyond	Maruetsu
Best Buy	Meijer
Big Lots	Office Depot
Bridgestone Retail Operations	PETCO
	Pep Boys
Brookshire Grocery	Publix
CVS	RadioShack
Carrefour	Rite Aid
Chedraui	SUPERVALU
Comerci	Safeway
Costco Wholesale	Sanborns
Delhaize	Sears
Dollar General	Sears Canada
El Puerto de Liverpool	Soriana
Family Dollar Stores	Staples
Farmacias Benavides	TJX Companies
Gigante	Target Corporation

Grupo Carso	The Gap
Grupo Elektra	Toys ''R'' Us
H-E-B	True Value
Home Depot	Walgreen
Hudson's Bay	
	Tesco

HISTORICAL FINANCIALS

Company Type: Public

Income Statement

FYE: January 31

	REVENUE ($ mil.)	NET INCOME ($ mil.)	NET PROFIT MARGIN	EMPLOYEES
01/15	485,651	16,363	3.4%	2,200,000
01/14	476,294	16,022	3.4%	2,200,000
01/13	469,162	16,999	3.6%	2,200,000
01/12	446,950	15,699	3.5%	2,200,000
01/11	421,849	16,389	3.9%	2,100,000
Annual Growth	3.6%	(0.0%)	—	1.2%

2015 Year-End Financials

Debt ratio: 24.73%—
Return on equity: 20.76%
Cash ($ mil.): 9,135
Current ratio: 0.97
Long-term debt ($ mil.): 43,692

Dividends
Yield: 0.0%
Payout: 38.0%
Market value ($ mil.): —

	STOCK PRICE ($)	P/E		PER SHARE ($)		
	FY Close	High/Low	Earnings	Dividends	Book Value
01/15	84.98	18 14	5.05	1.92	25.21
01/14	74.68	17 14	4.88	1.88	23.59
01/13	69.95	15 11	5.02	1.59	23.04
01/12	61.36	14 11	4.52	1.46	20.86
01/11	56.07	13 11	4.47	1.21	19.49
Annual Growth	11.0%	— —	3.1%	12.2%	6.6%

Walgreens Boots Alliance Inc

Auditors: DELOITTE & TOUCHE LLP

LOCATIONS

HQ: Walgreens Boots Alliance Inc
108 Wilmot Road, Deerfield, IL 60015
Phone: 847 315-2500
Web: www.walgreensbootsalliance.com

HISTORICAL FINANCIALS

Company Type: Public

Income Statement

FYE: August 31

	REVENUE ($ mil.)	NET INCOME ($ mil.)	NET PROFIT MARGIN	EMPLOYEES
08/15	103,444	4,220	4.1%	360,000
08/14	76,392	1,932	2.5%	—
08/13	72,217	2,548	3.5%	—
Annual Growth	19.7%	28.7%	—	—

2015 Year-End Financials

Debt ratio: 20.91%
Return on equity: 16.43%
Cash ($ mil.): 3,000
Current ratio: 1.19
Long-term debt ($ mil.): 13,315

No. of shares (mil.): 1,089
Dividends
Yield: 1.2%
Payout: 25.8%
Market value ($ mil.): 94,332

Walter Investment Management Corp

Walter Investment Management does its best to collect from the credit-challenged. The firm owns and services residential mortgages (particularly those of the subprime and nonconforming variety) for itself as well as for government sponsored entities government agencies third-party securitization trusts and other credit owners. Operating through subsidiaries Walter Mortgage Company; Hanover Capital; Marix Servicing; Ditech; and third-party credit servicer Green Tree Walter Investment Management services two million residential loan accounts with unpaid balances of $256 billion making it one of the 10 largest mortgage servicers in the US. The firm also originates residential loans including reverse loans.

OperationsWalter Investment Management operates three main business segments. Its Servicing segment which generates more than 50% of Walter's revenue mostly services mortgage loans for third-party creditors and its own mortgage loan portfolio on a fee-for-service basis. Following the simplification of its business in 2015 the segment also consists of an insurance agency serving residential loan borrowers and credit owners and a collections agency that performs collections of post charge-off deficiency balances for third parties and Walter's own portfolio. It also holds the assets and mortgage-backed debt of the Residual Trusts. As one of the US' top 20 largest mortgage loan originators Walter's Origination segment (32% of revenue) purchases and originates mortgage loans that are sold to third parties with servicing rights generally retained. The Reverse Mortgage segment (10% of revenue) purchases and originates securitized loans backed by secured borrowings services loans for third-party credit owners and its portfolio and also provides complementary reverse mortgage services like property management and dispositions.Geographic ReachThe Tampa-based firm has offices across the US.Sales and MarketingWalter's origination business sells nearly all of its mortgage loans into the secondary market for securitization or private investors as whole loans. It sells conventional conforming and government-backed mortgage loans through agency-sponsored securitizations where mortgage-backed securities are made and sold to third-party investors. Its nonconforming mortgage loans are sold to private investors. The firm's consumer direct retail channel originates reverse loans through call centers and purchases leads from lead purveyors or through advertising campaigns. The wholesale channel sources reverse loans from a broker network. The correspondent channel buys reverse loans from a correspondents network in the marketplace.Financial PerformanceWalter Investment Management's revenues and profits have mostly trended higher over the past few years thanks to regular loan portfolio acquisitions as well as acquisitions of other servicing companies and financial firms.The firm's revenue reversed course in 2014 however diving 18% to $1.49 billion for the year. Most of the decline came from the Servicing division which suffered from a $278 million decrease in fair value of servicing rights due to market-driven changes. The Origination segment's income fell by 24% on lower loan sales due to a shift in volume from the higher-margin consumer retention channel to the lower-margin correspondent lending channel.Revenue declines coupled with an $82.3 million- impairment charge caused Walter to suffer a net loss of $110.33 million in 2014. The impairment charge came after an evaluation found its reverse mortgage's goodwill was less than its carrying value. Walter's operations continued to use more cash than it produced –operations used $204 million –though its cash levels improved greatly from the year before as it sold a higher volume of loans in relation to originated loans given the ramp up of its mortgage loan originations business in 2013.

Strategy

Walter Investment hopes to tap into growing demand from big lenders looking to shift their debt servicing functions to outside firms. A rise in borrower delinquencies and foreclosures following the recession has forced traditional loan servicers and owners such as banks to look for third party assistance. Accordingly part of Walters' growth strategy focuses on acquiring and servicing large loan portfolios that other banks and other financial companies haven't been able to successfully collect on. The firm also hopes to grow its consumer-facing origination business seeking more cross-sell opportunities as well as opportunities to grow its consumer direct and consumer retail channels to meet demand for low-cost mortgage loans in the market. To this end in 2015 it planned to leverage its well known Ditech brand by (while saving $75 million in annual costs) by consolidating its Ditech and Green Tree Servicing into a single company: Ditech a Walter company.Mergers and AcquisitionsIn early 2013 in taking advantage of the opportunity to further expand its servicing portfolio Walter closed on two separate purchases (from Bank of America and Residential Capital LLC) of Fannie Mae mortgage serving rights for loans totaling $132 billion in unpaid principal balance.

Also in 2013 Walter Investment Management acquired a $12 billion reverse mortgage servicing portfolio from Wells Fargo. The portfolio with $12.2 billion in unpaid balance houses more than 76000 loans. The portfolio transferred to Walter's wholly-owned subsidiary Reverse Mortgage Solutions and doubled the size of its serviced book.

Company Background

The company entered the reverse mortgage business in late 2012 with the purchase of Reverse Mortgage Solutions (RMS) for some $120 million. RMS provided servicing origination asset management and technology services to the fast-growing reverse mortgage industry.In 2011 Walter Investment Management increased its loan portfolio and transformed into a fee-based service provider when it paid $1 billion for GTCS Holdings the parent of Green Tree Servicing. As a result Walter Investment Management no longer qualified as a real estate investment trust (REIT). The Green Tree acquisition represented a dramatic increase the size and scope of Walter Investment Management's business. The company's servicing portfolio grew by 50% and nearly 2000 employees were added. Green Tree also increased Walter Investment Management's geographic footprint by adding 27 offices in the US.Walter Investment Management was created in 2009 when Hanover Capital Mortgage merged with the home financing business of Walter Industries (now Walter En-

ergy). Walter Energy was spun off after the closure of troubled homebuilder Jim Walter Homes.

EXECUTIVES

EVP, David C. Schneider, age 49
Chief Legal Officer General Counsel and Secretary, Jonathan F. Pedersen, $430,000 total compensation
President and CEO, Denmar J. Dixon, age 52, $428,000 total compensation
EVP and CFO, Gary L. Tillett, age 56, $403,846 total compensation
President DT Holdings, Patricia Cook, $360,000 total compensation
Assistant Vice President Accounting Controls, Ramy Wahba
Assistant Vice President Director of Financial Analysis Systems, David (Dave) Howard
Chairman, Mark J. OÂBrien, age 72
Auditors: Ernst & Young LLP

LOCATIONS

HQ: Walter Investment Management Corp
   3000 Bayport Drive, Suite 1100, Tampa, FL 33607
Phone: 813 421-7600
Web: www.walterinvestment.com

PRODUCTS/OPERATIONS

2014 Sales

	% of total
Servicing	37
Originations	32
Reverse Mortage	10
ARM	4
Insurance	5
Loans & Residuals	9
Other	3
Eliiminations	-
Total	**100**

COMPETITORS

Annaly Capital Management	Nationstar Mortgage
CIFC	Newcastle Investment
Capstead Mortgage	Ocwen Financial
DVL	Redwood Trust
FirstCity Financial	Resource Capital

HISTORICAL FINANCIALS

Company Type: Public

Income Statement

FYE: December 31

	ASSETS ($ mil.)	NET INCOME ($ mil.)	INCOME AS % OF ASSETS	EMPLOYEES
12/14	18,991	(110)	—	6,700
12/13	17,387	253	1.5%	6,400
12/12	10,978	(22)	—	3,900
12/11	4,093	(69)	—	2,600
12/10	1,895	37	2.0%	349
Annual Growth	**77.9%**	**—**	**—**	**109.3%**

2014 Year-End Financials

Debt ratio: 27.36%	No. of shares (mil.): 37
Return on equity: (-9.83%)	Dividends
Cash ($ mil.): 1,053	Yield: —
Current ratio: —	Payout: —
Long-term debt ($ mil.): —	Market value ($ mil.): 623

	STOCK PRICE ($) FY Close	P/E High/Low		PER SHARE ($) Earnings	Dividends	Book Value
12/14	16.51	—	—	(2.93)	0.00	28.55
12/13	35.36	7	5	6.63	0.00	31.22
12/12	43.02	—	—	(0.73)	0.00	24.39
12/11	20.51	—	—	(2.51)	0.22	19.04
12/10	17.94	14	10	1.38	2.00	21.54
Annual Growth	**(2.1%)**	—	—	—	—	**7.3%**

Washington Federal Inc.

Washington Federal is the holding company for Washington Federal Savings which operatesÂabout 190ÂbranchesÂin eight western states. The thrift which was founded in 1917 collects deposits fromÂconsumers and businessÂby offering standard products such asÂCDs IRAsÂand checking savings and money market accounts. With these funds the bank mainly originates single-family residential mortgages which account for nearly three-quarters of its loan portfolio. The bank also writes business consumer construction land and multifamily residential loans. Washington Federal sells life home and auto coverage to individuals and businessesÂthrough its First Insurance Agency subsidiary.

Geographic Reach

As its name suggests Washington State is Washington Federal's largest market: home to 65 of its branches and the recipient of about 45% of its loan activity. Oregon and Arizona are other major markets for the bank.

Operations

In addition to its consumer and commercial banking operations Washington Federal has four wholly-owned subsidiaries: First Insurance Agency which offers a full line of individual and business insurance products to its customers and others; Statewide Mortgage Services Co. which holds about $18.6 million of real estate held for investment (REHI); Washington Services which also holds and markets REHI; and First Mutual Sales Finance a servicer of consumer loans.

Financial Analysis

Washington Federal's fiscal 2012 (ends September) revenue fell by about 9.5% vs. the previous year due to a decrease both interest and non-interest income. Total interest income which accounts for about 97% of WF's total revenue declined 8% on fewer loans mortgage-backed securities and investment securities and cash equivalents. Other income fell 36%. With the exception of fiscal 2010 which saw a slight gain in revenue WF's revenue has been declining for several years. Net income increased 24% in fiscal 2012 vs. the prior year due to overall lower credit costs.

Strategy

Small relative to its national bank competitors Washington Federal has been building its business through acquisitions adding new markets and growing in established ones. Acquisitions have included both healthy smaller rivals and failed banks seized by regulators. In a bid to unify its brand and increase its name recognition WF rebrands acquired banks under its own moniker.

The bank is also working through its portfolio of nonperforming loans which peaked during the height of the recession in 2009 but now are on the decline.

Mergers and Acquisitions

Most recently Washington Federal acquired South Valley Bancorp parent of the 24-branch South Valley Bank & Trust in Oregon for about $10.4 million. The purchase which closed in October 2012 boosted WF's branch count to 190 locations with total assets of about $13.3 billion and total deposits on approximately $9.3 billion. In 2011 WF acquired six branches of Charter Bank. The deal expanded its presence in New Mexico. Later in the year WF purchased most of the deposits and loans of Phoenix's three-branch Western National Bank which was closed by the Office of the Comptroller of the Currency.

EXECUTIVES

Chairman President and CEO, Roy M. Whitehead, age 62, $750,000 total compensation
EVP Commercial Real Estate, Jack B. Jacobson, age 64
EVP and Chief Banking Officer, Brent J. Beardall, age 43, $363,970 total compensation
EVP Human Resources and Deposit Operations, Linda S. Brower, age 61, $280,008 total compensation
CFO, Diane L. Kelleher, age 54, $192,000 total compensation
EVP and Chief Credit Officer, Mark A. Schoonover, age 56, $322,311 total compensation
EVP Business Banking, Thomas E. (Tom) Kasanders, age 62
EVP and CIO, Angela D. Veksler, age 53
Vice President Credit Administration, Marc A Rasmussen
Assistant Vice President, Carl Osberg
Vice President Tax and Internal Controls, Bob Zirk
Senior Vice President, Bill Synnamon
Vice President, Michael (Mel) Marron
Assisant Vice President, Debbie Hernandez
Assistant Vice President Branch Manager, Dannielle Andrade
Vice President Private Banking, Courtney Ahlstedt
Assistant Vice President, Mindi Andres
Vice President, Patrick (Paddy) Wilson
Vice President, Steve Hurst
Vice President, Ann Evans
Vice President, John Iasonides
Vice President, Jeff Birkelo
Vice President, Lauri Beaudry
Vice President and Manager Treasury Management, Claudia Leslie
Assistant Vice President And Underwriter, Larry Berg
Vice President Branch Manager, Margaret (Peg) Luera
Executive Vice President Mortgage and Consumer Lending, Edwin Hedlund
Vice President, James (Jamie) Goldsmith
Vice President and Division Manager, Kathy Kanealii
Vice President, P Ete McCabe
Assistant Vice President, T Essa Koch
Vice President, Ed Whipple
Auditors: DELOITTE & TOUCHE LLP

LOCATIONS

HQ: Washington Federal Inc.
425 Pike Street, Seattle, WA 98101
Phone: 206 624-7930
Web: www.washingtonfederal.com

Selected Markets

Arizona
Idaho
Nevada
New Mexico
Oregon
Texas
Utah
Washington

PRODUCTS/OPERATIONS

2013 Sales

	$ mil.	% of total
Interest		
Loans	430	73
Mortgage-backed securities	80	14
Investment securities	22	4
Other income		
Deposit fee income	14	3
Loan fee income	7	1
Others	8	2
Total	**564**	**100**

COMPETITORS

BancWest	U.S. Bancorp
Bank of America	Washington Banking
Banner Corp	Wells Fargo
KeyCorp	Zions Bancorporation

HISTORICAL FINANCIALS

Company Type: Public

Income Statement

FYE: September 30

	ASSETS ($ mil.)	NET INCOME ($ mil.)	INCOME AS % OF ASSETS	EMPLOYEES
09/15	14,568	160	1.1%	1,838
09/14	14,756	157	1.1%	1,909
09/13	13,082	151	1.2%	1,457
09/12	12,472	138	1.1%	1,260
09/11	13,440	111	0.8%	1,221
Annual Growth	**2.0%**	**9.6%**	**—**	**10.8%**

2015 Year-End Financials

Debt ratio: —	No. of shares (mil.): 92
Return on equity: 8.16%	Dividends
Cash ($ mil.): 284	Yield: 2.3%
Current ratio: —	Payout: 32.9%
Long-term debt ($ mil.): —	Market value ($ mil.): 2,114

	STOCK PRICE ($) FY Close	P/E High/Low	Earnings	Dividends	Book Value
09/15	22.75	14 12	1.67	0.54	21.04
09/14	20.36	15 13	1.55	0.41	20.05
09/13	20.68	16 11	1.45	0.34	18.91
09/12	16.66	14 10	1.29	0.30	17.89
09/11	12.74	19 13	1.00	0.23	17.49
Annual Growth	**15.6%**	**— —**	**13.7%**	**23.6%**	**4.7%**

Washington Trust Bancorp, Inc.

Without seeming naive Washington Trust Bancorp can utter Washington and trust in the same breath. The holding company owns The Washington Trust Company one of the oldest and largest banks in Rhode Island and one of the oldest banks in the entire US. Chartered in 1800 the bank boasts over $3.5 billion in assets and operates nearly 20 branches in the state and one in southeastern Connecticut. Washington Trust offers standard services such as deposit accounts CDs and credit cards. The company's commercial mortgages and loans account for more than half of its loan portfolio while residential mortgages and consumer loans make up most of the rest. The bank also offers wealth management services.

OperationsAround one-third of the bank's loan portfolio was made up of commercial real estate loans in 2014 while business loans made up another 21%.

About 60% of Washington Trust's total revenue came from loan interest (including fees) in 2014 while another 7% came from interest on its taxable and tax-exempt investment securities. The rest of its revenue came from wealth management income (18%) deposit account charges (2%) card interchange fees (2%) merchant processing fees (1%) and other miscellaneous income sources. The bank had a staff of 590 employees at the end of 2014.Washington Trust's wealth management division includes Washington Trust Investors Weston Financial and 1800 Asset Management. The division offers financial planning investment management and trust services and has more than $4 billion of assets under administration.

Geographic Reach

Of its nearly 20 branches 10 of its branches are located in Southern Rhode Island (Washington County) nearly 10 branches are in the greater Providence area and one branch is in southeastern Connecticut. The company's commercial lending office in Providence and six residential mortgage lending offices in eastern Massachusetts (Sharon Burlington and Braintree); Glastonbury and Darien Connecticut; and Warwick Rhode Island.

Financial Performance

Washington Trust has struggled to consistently grow its revenues in recent years due to shrinking interest margins on loans amidst the low-interest environment. Its profits however have been rising thanks to declining interest expenses and falling loan loss provisions as its loan portfolio's credit quality has improved with higher property valuations in the strengthened economy.The bank's revenue inched higher by 1% to $180 million in 2014 mostly as its interest income grew with higher average loan balances. Higher revenue in 2014 combined with lower interest expenses on deposits lower loan loss provisions and lower non-interest expenses boosted Washington Trust's net income higher by 13% to $40.8 million for the year. The company's operating cash levels fell to half the levels of the prior year to $2.7 million after adjusting its earnings for non-cash items mostly related to its mortgage banking net loan proceeds.

Strategy

Washington Trust Bank has been growing its loan and deposit business organically by opening new branches and loan production offices in its target markets. In early 2015 it opened a new branch in Rumford making it the bank's second location in East Providence. In 2014 it opened a branch in Johnston Rhode Island and furthered its expansion into Connecticut with the opening of a new mortgage office in Glastonbury Connecticut.The company also pursues acquisitions to expand its service offerings extend its reach into new geographic markets and bolster its existing business lines.

Mergers and Acquisitions

In 2015 Washington Trust purchased SEC-registered investment advisory firm Halsey Associates which added more than $850 million in assets under management to its Wealth Management business' books. Acquiring the New Haven Connecticut-based firm also expanded its reach in the Connecticut and metropolitan New York region.

EXECUTIVES

Vice President and Retail Lending Officer The Washington Trust Company, Linda S Smith
Vice Chair Secretary and CFO, David V. Devault, age 61, $299,731 total compensation
Chairman and CEO, Joseph J. (Joe) MarcAurele, $514,596 total compensation

EVP and Chief Lending Officer of the Bank,
James Hagerty
President and COO, Edward O. (Ned) Handy,
$385,000 total compensation
EVP Wealth Management and Treasurer, Mark K.
W. Gim, $239,462 total compensation
Vice President Commercial Real Estate Group,
Laurel L Bowerman
Vice President Sales, Rhonda Duckworth
Assistant Vice President Technology Support,
Mark Smithey
Vice President Commercial Real Estate Group,
Bethany A Lyons
Vice President Cash Management Sales, Sheila M
Raposa
**Executive Vice President of Retail Lending of the
Bank,** Stephen (Steve) Bessette
Vice President Finance, Brian Mahone
Auditors: KPMG LLP

LOCATIONS

HQ: Washington Trust Bancorp, Inc.
23 Broad Street, Westerly, RI 02891
Phone: 401 348-1200
Web: www.washtrust.com

PRODUCTS/OPERATIONS

2014 Sales

	$ mil.	% of total
Interest		
Loans including fees	107	60
Securities	12	7
Other	0	-
Non-interest		
Wealth management services	33	18
Loan sales & commissions 4		**6.8**
Gain on sale of business line	6	3
Service charges on deposit accounts	3	2
Other	9	6
Total	**180**	**100**

COMPETITORS

Bank of America	People' s United
Citizens Financial	Financial
Group	Sovereign Bank
Liberty Bank	Webster Financial

HISTORICAL FINANCIALS

Company Type: Public

Income Statement

FYE: December 31

	ASSETS ($ mil.)	NET INCOME ($ mil.)	INCOME AS % OF ASSETS	EMPLOYEES
12/14	3,586	40	1.1%	590
12/13	3,188	36	1.1%	570
12/12	3,071	35	1.1%	592
12/11	3,064	29	1.0%	558
12/10	2,909	24	0.8%	528
Annual Growth	5.4%	14.1%	—	2.8%

2014 Year-End Financials

Debt ratio: 0.63%	No. of shares (mil.): 16
Return on equity: 12.08%	Dividends
Cash ($ mil.): 76	Yield: 3.0%
Current ratio: —	Payout: 52.1%
Long-term debt ($ mil.): —	Market value ($ mil.): 673

	STOCK PRICE ($) FY Close	P/E High/Low	PER SHARE ($) Earnings	Dividends	Book Value
12/14	40.18	17 13	2.41	1.22	20.68
12/13	37.22	17 12	2.16	1.03	19.84
12/12	26.31	13 11	2.13	0.94	18.05
12/11	23.86	13 10	1.82	0.88	17.27
12/10	21.88	15 10	1.49	0.84	16.63
Annual Growth	16.4%	— —	12.8%	9.8%	5.6%

Waste Management, Inc. (DE)

Holding company Waste Management tops the heap in the US solid-waste industry. Through subsidiaries the company serves more than 20 million residential industrial municipal and commercial customers in the US and Canada. Waste Management provides waste collection transfer recycling and resource recovery and disposal services. Its sites include about 247 owned or operated landfills (the industry's largest network) 298 transfer stations and around 126 material recovery facilities. Collection services account for more than half of sales.

HISTORY

In 1956 Dean Buntrock joined his in-laws' business Ace Scavenger Service an Illinois company that Buntrock expanded into Wisconsin.

Waste Management Inc. was formed in 1971 when Buntrock joined forces with his cousin Wayne Huizenga who had purchased two waste routes in Florida in 1962. In the 1970s Waste Management bought companies in Michigan New York Ohio Pennsylvania and Canada. By 1975 it had an international subsidiary.

The company divided into specialty areas by forming Chemical Waste Management (1975) and offering site-cleanup services (ENRAC 1980) and low-level nuclear-waste disposal (Chem-Nuclear Systems 1982).

USA Waste was founded in 1987 to run disposal and collection operations in Oklahoma. It went public in 1988 and in 1990 Don Moorehead a founder and former CEO of Mid-American Waste Systems bought a controlling interest (most of which he later sold). Moorehead moved the business to Dallas and began buying companies in the fragmented industry. John Drury a former president of Browning-Ferris joined USA Waste in 1994 as CEO.

As USA Waste gathered steam Waste Management got off track. It diversified and Buntrock renamed the company WMX Technologies in 1993 to de-emphasize its waste operations. In 1997 however the company reverted to the Waste Management name and pressured by disappointed investor George Soros CEO Phillip Rooney resigned. After more management changes turnaround specialist Steve Miller became CEO the fourth one in eight months and Buntrock retired.

USA Waste picked up market share with large acquisitions including Envirofill (1994) Chambers Development Corporation (1995) and Western Waste Industries and Sanifill (1996). In 1996 the company moved to Houston. During the next two years it bought United Waste Systems Mid-American Waste the Canadian operations of Allied

Waste and Waste Management and TransAmerican Waste Industries.

1998 saw the $20 billion merger between USA Waste and Waste Management. The new company bearing the Waste Management name and led by Drury and other former USA Waste executives controlled nearly a quarter of North America's waste business. The company finished the year by agreeing to pay shareholders $220 million in a suit over overstated earnings.

The new Waste Management bought Eastern Environmental Services for $1.3 billion in 1999. (A legal battle over negotiations between Eastern and Waste Management executives was settled out of court in 2000.) Drury took leave in 1999 because of an illness that would claim his life and director Ralph Whitworth known as a shareholder activist stepped in as acting chairman.

The company faced shareholder lawsuits after it was reported that executives had sold shares before a second-quarter earnings shortfall was announced. Waste Management said it would investigate the sales; later so did the SEC. (By 2001 the company had settled with both the SEC and shareholders.) In the fallout president and COO Rodney Proto who had sold shares before the earnings announcement was fired. Later that year the company tapped Maury Myers CEO of trucking company Yellow Corp. to take over as chairman and CEO.

In 2000 to concentrate on its core business in North America Waste Management sold operations in Europe Asia and South America in a series of transactions that raised about $2.5 billion. The next year the company established a pulp and paper trading group.

Waste Management announced plans in early 2002 to restructure the company by reorganizing its operating areas and cutting its workforce of 57000 by about 3.5%. Also that year the SEC sued six former Waste Management executives charging that they had enriched themselves through accounting fraud between 1992 and 1997.

The company formed a new recycling unit Recycle America Alliance in 2003 after acquiring Milwaukee-based The Peltz Group the largest privately held recycler in the US. The company also acquired 75 complementary collection businesses for about $337 million and divested some operations for about $18 million. That year two former executives of Waste Management Proto and CFO Earl DeFrates agreed to a settlement with the SEC on allegations that they had profited from insider trading in 1999.

In a bid to consolidate its leadership position in the US waste market in 2008 the company made a bid to acquire Republic Services but was rebuffed.

In 2009 the company acquired PharmEcology Associates a national pharmaceutical waste management consulting services firm and Mountain High Medical Disposal Services. In 2010 it added some medical waste assets from MedServe following that company's acquisition by Stericycle. It also acquired a medical waste processing facility and other assets from Milum Textile Services in Phoenix.

In 2010 it invested in Canadian waste-to-biofuels company Enerkem. Further expanding its "green" businesses the company acquired control of Garick LLC a leading maker and distributor of organic lawn and garden products. The deal helped grow Waste Management's organics recycling services business.

In 2011 it bought Access Computer Products a leading provider of cell phone ink and toner cartridge and consumer electronics reverse logistics remarketing and recycling services and acquired three recycling facilities in Maryland and Virginia in a separate deal.

Also that year Waste Management picked up Connecticut-based Oakleaf Global Holdings and its operations for $425 million. The unit manages a North American network of some 2500 operators who provide hauling disposal waste diversion and recycling services.

In 2012 the company removed a management layer in its four geographic groups consolidated and reduced its geographic areas from 22 to 17 and eliminated some 700 positions.

EXECUTIVES

Vice President, Carl V Rush

EVP and COO, James E. Trevathan, $621,923 total compensation

SVP Field Operations, Jeff M. Harris, age 61, $562,458 total compensation

President and CEO, David P. Steiner, $1,186,785 total compensation

SVP Technology Logistics and Customer Service and CIO, Puneet Bhasin

EVP and CFO, James C. (Jim) Fish, $552,635 total compensation

SVP Field Operations, John J. Morris, $509,711 total compensation

President and CEO Wheelabrator Technologies, Bob Boucher

Area Vice President, Barry Skolnick

Vice President, Adam Winston

Vice President Finance, Brent Bell

Senior Vice President, Don P Carpenter

Area Vice President, Alex Oseguera

Vice President Of Human Resources, Tam Barbour

Vice President Of Public Affairs, Calvin Booker

Vice President Compensation and Benefits, Gordon Blasius

Vice President Information Technology, Gail Trafton

National Account Manager, Bryan Diehl

Vice President Information Technology Solutions OCIO, David (Dave) Lewis

National Account Manager, Ethan Bond

Vice President, Paul Burns

Executive Vice President, Casey Smith

Vice President Marketing And Research, Lori Lamerand

National Account Manager, Brian Bierman

Vice President Business Development, Mariel Markham

Vice President Commercial Lines Underwriting, Mary Fisher

Vice President Customer Service, Katy Lydon

Vice President, Nikolaj Sjoqvist

Vice President, Everett Bass

Vice President Of Strategic, Larry Patten

Vice President Information Technology, Michele Newell

Senior Vice President, Marsha Ross

Vice President Market Area, Pittman Alec

Vice President Price Management, Jim Fish

Senior Vice President Government Affairs and Corporate Communications, Barry Caldwell

Group Vice President Sales and Marketing, Chris Desantis

Chairman, W. Robert Reum

Treasurer, Josh Allen

Auditors: Ernst & Young LLP

LOCATIONS

HQ: Waste Management, Inc. (DE)
1001 Fannin Street, Suite 4000, Houston, TX 77002
Phone: 713 512-6200 **Fax:** 713 512-6299
Web: www.wm.com

2014 Sales

	$ mil.	% of total
US & Puerto Rico	13,064	93
Canada	932	7
Total	**13,996**	**100**

PRODUCTS/OPERATIONS

2014 Sales

	$ mil.	% of total
Collection	8,507	53
Landfill	2,849	17
Recycling	1,370	8
Transfer	1,353	8
Wheelabrator	817	5
Other	1,561	9
Adjustments	(2461)	-
Total	**13,996**	**100**

Selected Services

Collection
Disposal
Hazardous waste management
Landfill management
Portable sanitation services
Recycling
Transfer stations
Treatment

Selected Mergers and Acquisitions

COMPETITORS

Casella Waste Systems	Safety-Kleen
Progressive Waste	WCA Waste
Republic Services	Waste Connections
Rumpke	

HISTORICAL FINANCIALS

Company Type: Public

Income Statement

FYE: December 31

	REVENUE ($ mil.)	NET INCOME ($ mil.)	NET PROFIT MARGIN	EMPLOYEES
12/14	13,996	1,298	9.3%	39,800
12/13	13,983	98	0.7%	42,700
12/12	13,649	817	6.0%	43,500
12/11	13,378	961	7.2%	44,300
12/10	12,515	953	7.6%	42,800
Annual Growth	**2.8%**	**8.0%**	**—**	**(1.8%)**

2014 Year-End Financials

Debt ratio: 44.06%
Return on equity: 22.43%
Cash ($ mil.): 1,307
Current ratio: 1.04
Long-term debt ($ mil.): 8,345

No. of shares (mil.): 458
Dividends
  Yield: 2.9%
  Payout: 652.1%
Market value ($ mil.): 23,532

	STOCK PRICE ($) FY Close	P/E High/Low	PER SHARE ($) Earnings	Dividends	Book Value
12/14	51.32	18 14	2.79	1.50	12.79
12/13	44.87	220 161	0.21	1.46	12.29
12/12	33.74	21 18	1.76	1.42	13.69
12/11	32.71	19 14	2.04	1.36	13.18
12/10	36.87	19 16	1.98	1.26	13.18
Annual Growth	**8.6%**	**— —**	**9.0%**	**4.5%**	**(0.7%)**

Webster Financial Corp (Waterbury, Conn)

Webster Financial is the holding company for Webster Bank which operates about 170 branches in southern New England primarily in Connecticut but also in Massachusetts New York and Rhode Island. The bank provides commercial and retail services such as deposit accounts loans and mort-gages and consumer finance as well as government and institutional banking services. It performs asset-based lending through its Webster Business Credit subsidiary and equipment financing through Webster Capital Finance. The company's HSA Bank division offers health savings accounts nationwide. Webster Bank provides brokerage and investment services through an agreement with UVEST a division of LPL Financial.

Geographic Reach

The regional bank's largest market is Connecticut with about 125 branches. Massachusetts has about 20 branches; Rhode Island about 15; and New York about 10. It also operates more than 300 ATMs across New England.

Financial Performance

Overall sales were up 1% in 2012 to $886 million. While interest income and fees for loans and deposit services decreased the bank saw gains in wealth and investment services and mortgage banking activities. In 2012 Webster implemented a strategy of selling a higher percentage of conforming fixed-rate loans with favorable pricing in the secondary markets. Profits also increased 15% in 2012 after the bank was able to reduce both interest and non-interest expenses across the board.

Strategy

As a regional bank Webster has tried to keep up with technological advances and services offered by its larger competitors. In 2012 it finally began offering mobile banking through a smartphone app. That year it also upgraded its ATMs with customized settings touchscreens and speech capabilities.

In 2015 Webster acquired JPMorgan Chase Bank's health savings account (HSA) business. The move involved the migration of about 785000 accounts including an estimated $1.3 billion in deposits and $185 million in other assets under administration. It nearly doubled Webster's HSA Bank division which now has some 1.6 million accounts including more than $4 billion in assets under administration.

EXECUTIVES

Chairman and CEO Webster Financial Corporation and Webster Bank N.A., James C. (Jim) Smith, age 65, $882,435 total compensation

EVP General Counsel and Corporate Secretary Webster Financial Corporation and Webster Bank N.A., Harriet M. Wolfe, age 61

President and COO Webster Business Credit Corporation (WBCC), Warren K. Mino

Regional President Boston Webster Bank N.A., Paul F. Mollica

EVP and Chief Human Resources Officer Webster Financial Corporation and Webster Bank N.A., Bernard M. Garrigues, age 56

EVP and Chief Marketing Officer Webster Financial Corporation and Webster Bank N.A., Dawn C. Morris, age 47

Regional President New Haven Conn. Webster Bank N.A., Jeffrey A. (Jeff) Klaus

EVP Commercial Banking; Chairman of Regional Presidents' Council, John R. Ciulla, age 49, $363,479 total compensation

EVP and Head of Community Banking, Nitin J. Mhatre, age 44, $358,521 total compensation

EVP and CFO Webster Financial Corporation and Webster Bank N.A., Glenn I. MacInnes, age 53, $453,310 total compensation

EVP and CIO Webster Financial Corporation and Webster Bank N.A., Colin D. Eccles, age 56

EVP Consumer Deposits Investments and Network Management Webster Bank N.A., David D. Miree

EVP and Chief Risk Officer Webster Financial Corporation and Webster Bank N.A., Daniel H. Bley, age 46

EVP and Head of Private Banking Webster Financial Corporation and Webster Bank N.A., Daniel M. (Dan) FitzPatrick, age 56, $300,000 total compensation

EVP Commercial Real Estate, William E. Wrang

EVP Webster Financial Corporation and Webster Bank N.A. and Head of HSA Bank, Charles L. (Chad) Wilkins, age 53

Regional President Metro New York, Abby Parsonnet

Regional President Southern Massachusetts and Rhode Island Webster Bank N.A., Douglas E. (Doug) Scala

Regional President Waterbury Conn. Webster Bank N.A., Michael L. (Mike) O'Connor

Regional President for Pennsylvania Webster Bank N.A., Scott C. Meves

Regional President Hartford Conn. Webster Bank N.A., Timothy D. Bergstrom

EVP Middle Market Banking Webster Bank N.A., Christopher J. (Chris) Motl

Vice President Of Human Resources, Norman Cohen

Vice President, Sue Murray

Vice President Information Technology, Tom Clark

Vice President Information Technology Applications, Jay Clark

Vice President Corporate Facilities Operations, Mark Nisbett

Vice President Marketing, Joanne Renna

Vice President External Communications, Sarah Barr

Vice President Marketing Analytics, Tom Hryniewicz

Senior Vice President and Regional President Massachusetts and Rhode Island, Bob Twomey

Vice President, Bradley Weaver

Vice President Public Affairs, Ed Steadham

Vice President Sales and Marketing, Clark Finley

Senior Vice President Pricing Research and Development, Sally O'Connor

Vice President Financial Operations, Chris Binaco

Vice President Database, Jennifer Zbell

Vice President Finance, Shelly Abdella

Senior Vice President Middle Market Commercial Banking Webster Bank, Stephen (Steve) Corcoran

Executive Vice President, Jeff Hubbard

Executive Vice President Chief Marketing Officer of the Company and Webster Bank, Michelle (Mitch) Crecca

Executive Vice President Human Resources Marketing and Communications, Jeffrey (Jeff) Brown

Medical Director And Director Of Hematopathology, Maurice Richardson

Vice Chairman Webster Financial Corporation and Webster Bank N.A., Joseph J. (Joe) Savage, age 62

Auditors: KPMG LLP

LOCATIONS

HQ: Webster Financial Corp (Waterbury, Conn)
145 Bank Street, Waterbury, CT 06702
Phone: 203 578-2202
Web: www.websterbank.com

2012 Bank Branches

	No.
Connecticut	124
Massachusetts	22
Rhode Island	13
New York	8
Total	167

PRODUCTS/OPERATIONS

2012 Sales

	$ mil.	% of total
Interest		
Loans & leases including fees	485	55
Securities & dividends	207	23
Non-interest		
Deposit service fees	96	11
Wealth & investment services	29	3
Loan-related fees	18	2
Other	48	6
Total	886	100

COMPETITORS

Bank of America
Citibank
Citizens Financial Group
Fairfield County Bank
First Connecticut Bancorp
JPMorgan Chase
KeyCorp
Liberty Bank
New England Bancshares
Patriot National Bancorp
People's United Financial
SBT Bancorp Inc.
SI Financial
TD Bank USA
Washington Trust Bancorp

HISTORICAL FINANCIALS

Company Type: Public

Income Statement

FYE: December 31

	ASSETS ($ mil.)	NET INCOME ($ mil.)	INCOME AS % OF ASSETS	EMPLOYEES
12/14	22,533	199	0.9%	2,764
12/13	20,853	179	0.9%	2,744
12/12	20,146	173	0.9%	2,826
12/11	18,714	151	0.8%	2,961
12/10	18,038	74	0.4%	3,123
Annual Growth	5.7%	28.0%	—	(3.0%)

2014 Year-End Financials

Debt ratio: 1.00%
Return on equity: 8.82%
Cash ($ mil.): 394
Current ratio: —
Long-term debt ($ mil.): —
No. of shares (mil.): 90
Dividends
  Yield: 2.3%
  Payout: 36.0%
Market value ($ mil.): 2,940

	STOCK PRICE ($) FY Close	P/E High/Low		PER SHARE ($) Earnings	Dividends	Book Value
12/14	32.53	16	13	2.08	0.75	25.70
12/13	31.18	16	11	1.86	0.55	24.56
12/12	20.55	13	10	1.86	0.35	24.64
12/11	20.39	14	9	1.61	0.16	21.16
12/10	19.70	34	19	0.60	0.04	20.42
Annual Growth	13.4%	—	—	36.5%	108.1%	5.9%

WEC Energy Group Inc

Formerly Wisconsin Energy WEC Energy Group provides electricity and natural gas to nearly 4.5 million customers in four states. One of the largest natural gas distributors in the US the company operates through brands We Energies Wisconsin Public Service People Gas North Shore Gas Michigan Gas Utilities and Minnesota Energy Resources. It serves Wisconsin Illinois Michigan and Minnesota with some 70000 miles of electric distribution lines about 44000 miles of natural gas distribution and transmission lines and 8800 MW of generating capacity. The former Wisconsin Energy acquired Integrys Energy in mid-2015 to create WEC Energy Group.

Operations

WEC Energy Group operates through about half a dozen principal utilities. We Energies and Wisconsin Public Service provide natural gas to about 1.5 million customers in Wisconsin and provides electricity to about 1.5 million customers in Wisconsin and Upper Michigan. Peoples Gas serves some 830000 natural gas customers in Chicago while Michigan Gas Minnesota Energy and North Shore Gas deliver natural gas to parts of Michigan Minnesota and Illinois respectively.

The company's non-utility energy segment We Power designs builds owns and leases four generation plants constructed as part of its Power the Future strategy. Other non-utility operations include Wispark (which develop and invest in real estate projects primarily in southeastern Wisconsin) and Trillium CNG (which provides compressed natural gas fueling services).

Financial Performance

Prior to the acquisition of Integrys Wisconsin Energy's net revenues increased by 10% in 2014 due to increased sales from the Utility segment. Electric utility operating revenues increased because of higher resales into the MISO Energy Markets as a result of Michigan's alternative electric supplier program and higher availability of generating units driven by the recognition related to revenues under the System Support Resource agreement with MISO.Electric fuel and purchased power costs increased primarily due to increase in total MWh sales and higher generating costs driven by an increase in natural gas prices. Total retail gas margins increased primarily because of colder winter weather in 2014 pushing up demand.In 2014 the company's net income increased by 10% due to higher revenues partially offset by increased costs of gas sold.That year Wisconsin Energy's net cash provided by the operating activities decreased by $33.3 million due to a change in accounts receivable and accrued revenues inventories and accrued income tax.

Mergers and Acquisitions

Ina major move in 2015 Wisconsin Energy acquired rival Integrys in a transaction valued at $9.1 billion. The goal was to establish a long-term energy leader serving the Midwestern US.

EXECUTIVES

Chairman and CEO Wisconsin Energy Corp and Chairman President and CEO We Energies, Gale E. Klappa, age 65, $1,283,040 total compensation

President Wisconsin Energy Corp and President and CEO We Generation, Allen L. Leverett, age 49, $774,000 total compensation

EVP General Counsel and Corporate Secretary Wisconsin Energy Corp and We Energies, Susan H. Martin, age 62, $430,499 total compensation

EVP External Affairs, Robert M. (Bert) Garvin, $386,548 total compensation

EVP and CFO Wisconsin Energy Corp and We Energies, J. Patrick Keyes, age 49, $515,536 total compensation

EVP Customer Service and Operations, Kevin Fletcher

President Peoples Energy, Charles Matthews

President Wispark LLC, Jerold P. Franke

EVP Human Resources and Organizational Effectiveness, Joan M. Shafer

VP and CIO, Molly Mulroy

Executive Vice President, Bruce Ramme

Vice President Worldwide Operations and Marketing, Yelena Veisman

Board Member, Frederick Stratton

Assistant Treasurer, David Hughes

Secretary, Amy Winkler

Auditors: Deloitte & Touche LLP

LOCATIONS

HQ: WEC Energy Group Inc
231 West Michigan Street, P.O. Box 1331, Milwaukee,
WI 53201
Phone: 414 221-2345   **Fax:** 414 221-2172
Web: www.wisconsinenergy.com

PRODUCTS/OPERATIONS

2014 Sales

	$ mil.	% of total
Utility	4,941	92
Non-utility	447	8
Corporate & other	1	0
Adjustments	(392.6)	-
Total	**4,997**	**100**

Selected Subsidiaries

W.E. Power LLC (We Power regulated power plant construction)
Wisconsin Electric Power Company (operates as We Energies electric gas and steam utility)
Wisconsin Gas LLC (operates as We Energies gas and water utility)
Wispark LLC (real estate development)

COMPETITORS

AEP	MGE Energy
ALLETE	Minnesota Power
Alliant Energy	SEMCO ENERGY
CMS Energy	Wisconsin Power &
DTE	Light
Dairyland Power	Xcel Energy

HISTORICAL FINANCIALS

Company Type: Public

Income Statement

FYE: December 31

	REVENUE ($ mil.)	NET INCOME ($ mil.)	NET PROFIT MARGIN	EMPLOYEES
12/14	4,997	588	11.8%	4,248
12/13	4,519	577	12.8%	4,303
12/12	4,246	546	12.9%	4,504
12/11	4,486	526	11.7%	4,595
12/10	4,202	456	10.9%	4,596
Annual Growth	4.4%	6.5%	—	(1.9%)

2014 Year-End Financials

Debt ratio: 34.48%
Return on equity: 13.50%
Cash ($ mil.): 61
Current ratio: 0.92
Long-term debt ($ mil.): 4,186

No. of shares (mil.): 225
Dividends
Yield: 2.9%
Payout: 60.2%
Market value ($ mil.): 11,894

	STOCK PRICE ($) FY Close	P/E High/Low	PER SHARE ($) Earnings	Dividends	Book Value
12/14	52.74	21 15	2.59	1.56	19.73
12/13	41.34	18 15	2.51	1.45	18.87
12/12	36.85	17 14	2.35	1.20	18.19
12/11	34.96	27 12	2.24	1.04	17.33
12/10	58.86	31 24	1.93	0.80	16.39
Annual Growth	(2.7%)	— —	7.6%	18.2%	4.7%

WellCare Health Plans Inc

WellCare knows that to get well all you need is a little care. WellCare Health Plans provides man-aged-care administrative services to government-funded health care programs that provide health care benefits via Medicaid Medicare and various State Children's Health Insurance Programs. Services include benefits management and claims processing. WellCare Health Plans administers its Medicaid plans under various brands such as Staywell and HealthEase in Florida; WellCare in Ohio Georgia Kentucky New York and South Carolina; Harmony in Illinois; Missouri Care in Missouri; and 'Ohana in Hawaii. The company's Medicare prescription-drug and Medicare Advantage plans operate primarily under the WellCare brand.

Operations

The company offers a range of health plans for families children and the aged blind and disabled. It also offers prescription drug plans.

WellCare operates through three segments: Medicaid Health Plans Medicare Health Plans and Medicare PDPs. The Medicaid segment includes plans for beneficiaries of Temporary Assistance for Needy Families (TANF) Supplemental Security Income (SSI) Managed Long-Term Care (MLTC) plans and other state programs that are not a part of Medicaid. The segment generates revenues primarily from state-paid premiums in which it operates health plans.

WellCare serves some 4.1 million members nationwide. About 2.3 million customers are Medicaid members in seven states (including State Children's Health Insurance Programs — SCHIP members) and some 1.8 million of those are recipients of TANF benefits. The company also serves more than 417000 Medicare Advantage members who are largely enrolled in HMO coordinated care plans (CCPs) in 18 states. WellCare also serves about 1.4 million Medicare prescription members throughout the US.

The company contracts with the Centers for Medicare & Medicaid Services (CMS) under the Medicare program to provide a comprehensive array of Part C and Part D benefits to Medicare eligible persons. In 2014 WellCare offered Medicare Advantage plans in 210 counties across 22 states.It also contracts with CMS to serve as a plan sponsor offering a stand-alone Medicare Part D Prescription Drug Plan to Medicare-eligible beneficiaries. The company offers national in-network prescription drug coverage with more than 71000 pharmacies.

For fiscal years 2014 and 2013 about 94% of the company's payments to physicians serving its Medicaid members was on a fee-for-service basis while the rest was on a capitated basis.

Geographic Reach

The company operates in 49 states and in the District of Columbia. Its largest markets are Georgia and Florida which account for 17% and 21% of annual membership respectively followed by Kentucky (11%).

WellCare operates Medicaid health plans in Florida Georgia Hawaii Illinois Kentucky Missouri New Jersey New York and South Carolina. It also offers MA coordinated care plans (CCPs) in certain areas of Arizona Arkansas California Connecticut Florida Georgia Hawaii Illinois Kentucky Louisiana Mississippi Missouri New Jersey New York Ohio South Carolina Tennessee and Texas.

Sales and Marketing

WellCare contracts with state Medicaid agencies to expand its operations; it also enters new Medicare markets through organic growth and acquisition efforts.

The company contracts with medical providers to provide services to its members. It also promotes services to consumers through minimal advertising campaigns. WellCare contracted with approximately 224000 health care providers and 71000 pharmacies to provide members with access to medically necessary services.

WellCare reported advertising and related marketing expenses of $5.4 million in 2014 up from $3.2 million in 2013 but down from $7.2 million in 2012.

Financial Performance

After several years of reporting decreased earnings (due to troubles including legal and regulatory issues) WellCare has been able to increase both its revenues and net income levels due to membership growth decreased legal expenses and successfully implemented cost-control efforts. The firm began reporting revenue growth in 2011 2012 and 2013 largely due to growth in the core Medicare and Medicaid markets.

The company's revenues grew by 36% to $13 billion in 2014 thanks to growth in premium revenues primarily driven by acquisitions and organic membership growth in its Medicaid Medicare Advantage and Prescription Drug Plans. The 2014 acquisition of Windsor contributed some $507.2 million or 17% to the year-over-year increase. ACA fee reimbursements from Medicaid state customers also contributed to the increase that year as did the favorable impact of Medicaid membership mix changes and the benefit of a full year of premiums for its South Carolina and Missouri Medicaid plans that were acquired in early 2013. Finally Medicaid rate increases also lifted revenues.

WellCare's net income fell 64% to $63.7 million in 2014 primarily due to a decrease in higher medical benefits ratios in all of its segments including the recognition of unfavorable prior-year reserve development which mainly impacted its Medicaid and Medicare Health Plans segments.

Cash flow from operations increased by $120 million to $299 million that year; the increase was driven by growth in premiums associated with higher memberships as well as the timing of certain premium receipts. Another factor driving the increase was more cash generated by medical benefits payable and accounts payable.

Strategy

The company focuses on serving lower income individuals and those who are dually eligible for Medicaid and Medicare. Growth through "building" is focused on creation of the marketing network community support and other capabilities required to expand organically into new service areas. Acquiring businesses with important market and/or product positions has supplemented its organic growth. These "bid build and buy" initiatives have resulted in a significant increase in the company's revenues since 2010.

In 2014 WellCare signed a deal with the Florida Agency for Health Care Administration to provide managed care services to Medicaid recipients in eight of the state's eleven regions (including the Jacksonville Miami Orlando Tallahassee and Tampa metropolitan areas).

Also that year the company began offering Medicaid managed care in Essex Hudson Middlesex Passaic and Union counties in New Jersey. Its New Jersey subsidiary acquired Medicaid assets of Healthfirst Health Plan of New Jersey; the company now offers Medicaid managed care in 10 New Jersey counties. WellCare also expanded its reach in the state of New York in 2014 and in Jacksonville and Orlando Florida in 2015.

In 2013 it was approved by the South Carolina Department of Health and Human Services to offer Medicaid in six additional counties in the state allowing it to provide Medicaid services in 45 out of 46 counties in South Carolina. Additionally Flagler Hospital in St. John's County Florida joined the WellCare provider network. WellCare is also focused on adding more members to its Medicare plans especially in special needs plans (for members who qualify for both Medicare and Medicaid coverage) and in Part D prescription plans. The company is expanding its Medicare programs growing the Medicare Advantage program into several new states and increasing enrollment. Like the Medicaid programs covered territories for Medicare Advantage plans can shift each year as the company enters or exits service areas.

Mergers and Acquisitions

Early in 2014 WellCare moved into Arkansas Mississippi and Tennessee when it purchased Windsor Health Group. Terms were not disclosed.

Later that year the company completed the acquisition of Medicaid assets from Healthfirst Health Plans of New Jersey adding some 42000 members.

In 2013 WellCare acquired the South Carolina Medicaid business of UnitedHealth. The purchase added some 65000 members throughout most of South Carolina and gave WellCare further opportunities for growth in the region. In addition the company acquired Aetna's Missouri Medicaid business that year; the purchase added 100000 members.

EXECUTIVES

SVP Chief Legal and Administrative Officer and Secretary, Blair W. Todt, age 48, $432,308 total compensation

SVP and CIO, Rose M. Hauser, age 53

CEO and Director, Kenneth A. (Ken) Burdick, age 56, $24,038 total compensation

SVP and Division President Connecticut Hawaii Illinois Missouri New Jersey New York and Ohio, Dave Reynolds

SVP and Chief Medical Officer, Steven E. (Steve) Goldberg, age 53, $412,115 total compensation

SVP Operations, Michael R. (Mike) Polen, age 35

SVP and CFO, Andrew L. (Drew) Asher, age 46, $146,154 total compensation

State President South Carolina, Kathy Warner

SVP Division President and Product, Kelly Munson

Medical Director, Alan Smith

Vice President, Angel Wolf

Vice President Pharmacy Strategy and Analytics, Yan Xiong

Vice President Marketing Sales and Business Development, Troy Hildreth

Vice President Information Technology, Britt Jensen

Vice President of Operations Reporting and Analytics, Jason Hamilton

Vice President Marketing and Sales State Florida, Tracy Schmidt

Vice President Audit And Recovery, Frank Condo

Vice President Finance and Revenue Reconciliation, Merrill Hausenfluck

Vice President Sales And Marketing, Ryan Fogarty

Vice President Clinical Programs, Wendy Morriarty

Vice President Of Operations, Brian Luidhardt

Vice President Quality, Bill Hinsdale

Vice President Corporate Strategy, Michael Paul

Vice President Compliance, Staci Cross

Vice President, Sabrina Bozich

Vice President Network Management, Nancy Wohlhart

Vice President Process Improvement, Lou Gianquinto

Market Vice President, Nancy Laux

Vice President Information Technology, Dean Morrison

Vice President Product Operations, Elizabeth Miller

Medical Director, Nicholas Abid

Vice President Human Resources, Michael Wellman

Vice President Market Performance, Anthony Valda

Senior Vice President Human Resources, Larry Anderson

Vice President of Finance, Michael (Mel) Lisman

Vice President Decision Support Systems, Michael (Mel) Gerasimovich

Chairman, Christian P. Michalik, age 47

Board Member, Paul Weaver

Auditors: Deloitte & Touche, LLP

LOCATIONS

HQ: WellCare Health Plans Inc
8725 Henderson Road, Renaissance One, Tampa, FL 33634
Phone: 813 290-6200
Web: www.wellcare.com

2014 Membership

	% of total
Florida	22
Georgia	17
Kentucky	11
New York	5
Illinois	5
Other states	40
Total	**100**

PRODUCTS/OPERATIONS

2014 Sales

	$ mil.	% of total
Medicaid	7,773	60
Medicare		
Medicare Advantage	3,963	31
Prescription drug plan	1,178	9
Investment & other income	44	-
Total	**12,959**	**100**

COMPETITORS

AMERIGROUP	Health Net
Aetna	HealthSpring
Anthem	Humana
CIGNA	Kaiser Foundation
Centene	Health Plan
Coventry Health Care	Molina Healthcare
Florida Blue	UnitedHealth Group
Health First Health Plans	Universal American

HISTORICAL FINANCIALS

Company Type: Public

Income Statement

FYE: December 31

	REVENUE ($ mil.)	NET INCOME ($ mil.)	NET PROFIT MARGIN	EMPLOYEES
12/15	13,890	118	0.9%	6,900
12/14	12,959	63	0.5%	6,700
12/13	9,527	175	1.8%	5,200
12/12	7,409	184	2.5%	4,460
12/11	6,106	264	4.3%	3,990
Annual Growth	**22.8%**	**(18.1%)**	**—**	**14.7%**

2015 Year-End Financials

Debt ratio: 23.34%
Return on equity: 7.14%
Cash ($ mil.): 2,407
Current ratio: 1.75
Long-term debt ($ mil.): 912

No. of shares (mil.): 44
Dividends
 Yield: —
 Payout: —
Market value ($ mil.): 3,450

	STOCK PRICE ($) FY Close	P/E High/Low		PER SHARE ($) Earnings	Dividends	Book Value
12/15	78.21	37	27	2.67	0.00	39.18
12/14	82.06	58	39	1.44	0.00	36.34
12/13	70.42	19	11	3.98	0.00	34.68
12/12	48.69	17	11	4.22	0.00	30.62
12/11	52.50	9	5	6.10	0.00	26.06
Annual Growth	**10.5%**			**— — (18.7%)**	**—**	**10.7%**

Wells Fargo & Co.

Auditors: KPMG LLP

LOCATIONS

HQ: Wells Fargo & Co.
420 Montgomery Street, San Francisco, CA 94163
Phone: 866 249-3302
Web: www.wellsfargo.com

HISTORICAL FINANCIALS

Company Type: Public

Income Statement

FYE: December 31

	ASSETS ($ mil.)	NET INCOME ($ mil.)	INCOME AS % OF ASSETS	EMPLOYEES
12/14	1,687,155	23,057	1.4%	264,500
12/13	1,527,015	21,878	1.4%	264,900
12/12	1,422,968	18,897	1.3%	269,200
12/11	1,313,867	15,869	1.2%	264,200
12/10	1,258,128	12,362	1.0%	272,200
Annual Growth	**7.6%**	**16.9%**	**—**	**(0.7%)**

2014 Year-End Financials

Debt ratio: 10.90%—
Return on equity: 13.01%
Cash ($ mil.): 241,144
Current ratio: —
Long-term debt ($ mil.): —

Dividends
 Yield: 2.4%
 Payout: 33.0%
Market value ($ mil.): —

	STOCK PRICE ($) FY Close	P/E High/Low		PER SHARE ($) Earnings	Dividends	Book Value
12/14	54.82	13	11	4.10	1.35	35.66
12/13	45.40	12	9	3.89	1.15	32.36
12/12	34.18	11	8	3.36	0.88	29.92
12/11	27.56	12	8	2.82	0.48	26.65
12/10	30.99	15	10	2.21	0.20	24.02
Annual Growth	**15.3%**			**— — 16.7%**	**61.2%**	**10.4%**

WesBanco, Inc.

WesBanco wants to be the "BesBanco" for its customers. The holding company owns WesBanco Bank which has about 120 branches in West Virginia Ohio and western Pennsylvania. In addition to providing traditional services such as deposits and loans the bank operates a wealth management department with ten offices in West Virginia and Ohio and some $3 billion of assets under management and custody including the company's proprietary WesMark mutual funds. Other units include brokerage firm WesBanco Securities and multiline insurance provider WesBanco Insurance Services.

Operations

Commercial loans including real estate and operating loans account for more than half of of WesBanco's loan portfolio. Its retail portfolio mainly consists of home equity loans and deposit overdraft limits. The bank usually sells new residential mortgages that it originates into the secondary market. It plans to continue to grow its portfolio of commercial and industrial loans.

Financial Performance

The company's revenue increased in fiscal 2013 compared to the prior fiscal period. WesBanco reported $287.2 million in revenue for fiscal 2013 up from $276.5 in fiscal 2012.

The company's net income also increased in fiscal 2013 compared to the previous year. It reported net income of $63.9 million in fiscal 2013 up from net income of $49.5 million for fiscal 2012.

As another sign of the company's health WesBanco's cash on hand spiked by about $65 million during fiscal 2013 compared to fiscal 2012 levels.

Mergers and Acquisitions

WesBanco has also grown by acquiring more than 50 banks and financial services firms in the past 25 years. In 2012 the company announced plans to expand in the Pittsburgh area through the acquisition of Fidelity Bancorp. Valued at more than $70 million the deal will bring in about a dozen branches in the city and its northern suburbs.

EXECUTIVES

Senior Vice President Marketing, Doug Molnar
EVP Operations, Brent E. Richmond, age 52
EVP and Chief Credit Officer, Peter W. Jaworski, age 60, $212,101 total compensation
EVP and CFO, Robert H. Young, age 59, $269,363 total compensation
President and CEO, Todd F. Clossin, age 53, $466,923 total compensation
EVP and Chief Risk & Administrative Officer, Michael L. Perkins
EVP Retail Delivery, Lynn D. Asensio
EVP and Senior Operations Officer, Gregory A. Dugan
EVP Wealth Management, Jonathan D. Dargusch, age 57, $230,270 total compensation
EVP Human Resources Management, Anthony F. Pietranton
EVP and Chief Lending Officer, Jayson M. Zatta
Market President Kanawha Region, David L. Sayre
Vice President District Sales Manager, Nick Taylor
Senior Vice President And Cco, David Kaczmarek
Vice President, Thomas Phillips
Vice President Finance, Luanne Bush
Senior Vice President, Michael (Mel) Schwarz
Vice President Facilities, John (Jack) Partilla
Vice President Risk Management Security Officer, James (Jamie) Thompson
Senior Vice President Chief Compliance Officer, Dave Kaczmarek
Assistant Vice President Mortgage CRA Officer, Lisa Werner
Senior Vice President Special Assets, Jodi Pagnanelli
Vice President Upper Ohio Valley Region, James (Jamie) Williams
Senior Vice President Community Development, Joe Flynn
Vice President Credit Risk Management, Ann Vucelik
Vice President Community Banker, Tom Timmons
Vice President, Reed Burke
Assistant Vice President, Bruce Bandi
Vice President, Tom Medovic
Senior Vice President, Anthony Costantino
Vice President Assistant Controller, Dan Weiss
Assistant Vice President Branch Operations, Beth Bussard
Vice President Electronic Banking Manager, Jason Plotner
Assistant Vice President Business Development Manager, Lycia Maurits
Assistant Vice President Information Technology Services, W Terrance Naughton
Vice President Of Information Technology, Mike Robbins
Assistant Vice President BCM Business Development, Tamara Barnett

Vice President Human Resources, Patricia (Pat) Lowe
Vice President And Trust Officer, Carolyn Garner
Senior Vice President Senior Credit Officer, Thomas (Thom) Crc
Senior Vice President Branch Operation, Roanne Burech
Assistant Vice President Information Technology Services, Terry Naughton
Chairman, James C. (Jim) Gardill, age 69
Auditors: Ernst & Young LLP

LOCATIONS

HQ: WesBanco, Inc.
  1 Bank Plaza, Wheeling, WV 26003
Phone: 304 234-9000
Web: www.wesbanco.com

COMPETITORS

1st West Virginia Bancorp	Huntington Bancshares
BB&T	Ohio Valley Banc
Bank of America	PNC Financial
Cheviot Financial	United Bancorp
City Holding	United Bankshares
First Community Bancshares	

HISTORICAL FINANCIALS

Company Type: Public

Income Statement   FYE: December 31

	ASSETS ($ mil.)	NET INCOME ($ mil.)	INCOME AS % OF ASSETS	EMPLOYEES
12/14	6,296	69	1.1%	1,448
12/13	6,144	63	1.0%	1,469
12/12	6,078	49	0.8%	1,507
12/11	5,536	43	0.8%	1,368
12/10	5,361	35	0.7%	1,377
Annual Growth	4.1%	18.4%	—	1.3%

2014 Year-End Financials

Debt ratio: 1.69%	No. of shares (mil.): 29
Return on equity: 9.12%	Dividends
Cash ($ mil.): 94	Yield: 2.5%
Current ratio: —	Payout: 37.6%
Long-term debt ($ mil.): —	Market value ($ mil.): 1,020

	STOCK PRICE ($) FY Close	P/E High/Low	PER SHARE ($) Earnings	Dividends	Book Value
12/14	34.80	15 11	2.39	0.88	26.90
12/13	32.00	15 10	2.18	0.78	25.59
12/12	22.22	12 10	1.84	0.70	24.45
12/11	19.47	13 10	1.65	0.62	23.80
12/10	18.96	15 9	1.34	0.56	22.83
Annual Growth	16.4%	— —	15.6%	12.0%	4.2%

Wesco International, Inc.

When contractors and manufacturers need parts it's WESCO to the rescue. The company distributes electrical products (fuses terminals connectors enclosures circuit breakers transformers switchboards) industrial supplies (tools abrasives filters safety equipment) lighting (lamps fixtures ballasts) wire and conduit materials automation equipment

(motors drives logic controllers) and data communication gear (patch panels terminals connectors). WESCO offers more than a million products from some 25000 suppliers with about 100000 customers worldwide. It operates through a dozen subsidiaries. The company generates nearly all of its sales in North America predominantly the US.

Geographic Reach

The company operates 485 branches across North America and in international markets serviced by its nine distribution centers located in the US Canada and Mexico. It boasts offices in about 15 additional countries. The US accounts for about 70% of sales while Canada brings in another 25%.

Operations

WESCO divides its operations among several businesses. Automation comprises Cascade Controls EESCO RECO and W.R. Controls. Its Data Communications segment is made up of Communications Supply Corporation and TVC Communications while Industrial/Construction operates through Avon Electrical Supplies Brown Wholesale Electric Calvert Wire & Cable Liberty Electrical Supply and Whitehill Lighting and Supplies.

Integrated Supply is composed of Bruckner Supply Company and WESCO Sourcing and Procurement Services; its Industrial/Electrical OEM operations are helped by Carlton-Bates Company Fastec Industrial and J-Mark. Finally its International Operations are run through its main WESCO distribution subsidiary while its Utility segment is made up of Allied Utility Products Hamby Young Herning Enterprises Industrial Electric Supply and KVA Supply.

Sales and Marketing

WESCO caters to 100000 customers. Sales to electrical contractors range from major industrial commercial and data communication projects to small residential contractors. Utilities and specialty utility contractors include large and rural electric cooperatives and municipal power authorities which maintain transmission distribution lines and power plants.

Commercial institutional and governmental customers include schools hospitals property management firms retailers and government agencies of all types. WESCO sells integrated lighting control and distribution equipment in a single package for multisite specialty retailers restaurant chains and department stores.

Financial Performance

WESCO has achieved years of unprecedented growth with revenues climbing 5% to peak at a record-setting $7.89 billion in 2014. The historic growth for 2014 was attributed to organic growth in addition to acquisitions.

Its profits remained flat for 2014 (hovering around the $275 million mark) due to a spike in expenses especially selling general and administrative expenses which were affected by higher employment related costs; the company was also affected by a rise in income taxes during 2014.

After experiencing steady growth in the last five years the company's operating cash flows decreased by over $64 million (20%) in 2014 due to the static net income along with an increase in outflows in trade receivables inventories and prepaid expenses.

Strategy

WESCO has been building its business through acquisitions and organic growth. As part of this effort the company's working to develop new end markets broaden its product and service offerings expand its geographic footprint and enhance its sales and customer service.

The company is focused on its global account and integrated supply programs to boost its customer base and extend its use of supply services to customers. It targets customers in the fields of construction contracting; education; engineering procurement and construction firms; government; healthcare; and utilities. Among product growth areas WESCO looks to data communications and security systems and to clean tech lighting systems.

Mergers and Acquisitions

In recent years WESCO has been buying up Canadian distributors and other firms to extend its reach and capabilities. In 2014 for instance the company acquired Ontario-based Hazmasters an independent Canadian distributor of safety products that serves industrial construction commercial institution and government markets as well as Hi-Line Utility Supply Company which supplies utility MRO and safety products and offers rubber goods testing and certification services. Previously in 2014 WESCO purchased wholesale distributor LaPrairie which provides electrical products for utilities and utility contractors across Ontario Quebec and Atlantic Canada.

HISTORY

WESCO International got its start as a subsidiary of electrical power pioneer Westinghouse Electric Company. George Westinghouse founded the company bearing his name in Pittsburgh in 1886. The company installed the nation's first alternating current power system in Telluride Colorado in 1891. Two years later Westinghouse built the generating system that powered the Chicago World's Fair. The company also was chosen to provide generators for the hydroelectric power station at Niagara Falls.

George Westinghouse was ousted in 1910 after the company was unable to meet its debt obligations. He died four years later at the age of 67. During the next decade the company added the burgeoning radio and appliance markets to its portfolio of electrical distribution and production operations.

In 1922 the firm established Westinghouse Electric Supply Company (WESCO) to distribute power products and appliances. Westinghouse had its share of troubles over the years many of which were caused by ill-advised diversification attempts. These included forays into uranium supply financial services and real estate.

By the 1990s Westinghouse was buried under nearly $10 billion in debt and too busy putting out fires to tend to day-to-day operations properly. Not surprisingly WESCO was caught up in Westinghouse's problems: Sales declined four years in a row and employee turnover was around 25% a year.

Westinghouse embarked on a divestiture program and sold WESCO to investment firm Clayton Dubilier & Rice (CD&R) in 1994 for about $340 million. At the time WESCO had about 250 branch locations. The new owners brought in Roy Haley a veteran insurance and finance executive to turn the ailing business around. Haley tied pay and bonuses to performance and emphasized multisite customers such as contractors and companies with multiple retail industrial or administrative locations. WESCO grew through acquisitions and in 1995 sales reached $2 billion.

By 1996 the company had added 1000 employees; it operated about 300 distribution branches throughout the world. Sales reached $2.6 billion in 1997 as WESCO continued acquiring complementary companies and formed an alliance with Australian mining and steel company BHP (now BHP Billiton). Managers led a $1.1 billion buyout of the company in 1998 increasing their stake in WESCO from 15% to 33%. Costs related to acquisitions and the buyout caused WESCO to post a loss even though 1998 sales passed the $3 billion mark. The company opened sales offices in the UK Singapore and Mexico.

As it geared up for its IPO in 1999 WESCO bought distributors Industrial Electric Supply Company and Statewide Electrical Supply. The company continued to shop during 2000 adding electrical distributors Orton Utility Supply (Tennessee) Control Corporation of America (Virginia) and KVA Supply Company (Colorado and California).

In 2001 WESCO acquired two distributors (Herning Underground Supply and Alliance Utility Products) that supplied contractors who install gas lighting and communication utility infrastructure in Arizona California Utah and Washington.

The Cypress Group the private-equity firm that helped lead the $1.1 billion management buyout in 1998 sold most of its shares in WESCO in 2004 and 2005. Cypress owned nearly half of WESCO prior to those sales.

WESCO acquired fastener distributor Fastec Industrial and electronics distributor Carlton-Bates in 2005. The following year it bought Communications Supply Corporation (CSC) a distributor of low-voltage network infrastructure and industrial wire and cable products for about $525 million in cash.

In 2007 WESCO acquired J-Mark a supplier of building products which strengthened the company's position in the manufactured housing industry. It also acquired the assets of Monti Electric Supply which provides electricity and furnishes lighting. The purchase gave WESCO a broader market position in the reconstruction of the Gulf Coast region. The company sold a 60% stake in LADD which is a distributor of industrial electrical connectors and accessories to Deutsch Engineered Connecting Devices for approximately $75 million. Proceeds were earmarked to purchase shares of WESCO's common stock.

In 2008 WESCO offered to purchase Industrial Distribution Group (IDG) for about $130 million in cash topping a bid for IDG by Platinum Equity.

Roy Haley stepped aside as CEO in 2009 becoming WESCO's executive chairman. SVP/COO John Engel was promoted to president and CEO as a result.

WESCO acquired TVC Communications for about $246 million in late 2010. The deal expanded WESCO's broadband and telecom distribution network in the Americas and its ties to manufacturers.

EXECUTIVES

Chairman President and CEO, John J. Engel, age 53, $942,500 total compensation
SVP and Chief Human Resources Officer, Kimberly G. Windrow, age 57, $376,250 total compensation
SVP and COO, Stephen A. Van Oss, age 60, $668,750 total compensation
SVP and CFO, Kenneth S. Parks, age 51, $445,000 total compensation
VP Global Marketing and Sustainability, Mike Ludwig
SVP and General Counsel, Diane E. Lazzaris, $376,250 total compensation
Vice President Human Resources, Ruth Boyd
Vice President, Tracy Fye
Vice President Pricing Data Services and E Business, Rick Gigliotti
Vice President Of Evening Operations, Joseph Astroth
Vice President Operations, David (Dave) Bemoras
Vice President Information Technology, Scott Render
Vice President, Jim Westgate
Vice President Compensation Benefits Hris, Clarence Dodge
National Account Manager, Dave Gapinski
Vice President Group Controller, Matt Zimmermann
National Sales Manager, Maurice Herrmann

Senior Vice President and General Manager U.S. Broadband, Frank McCullough
Vice President Human Resources, Kim Windrow
Sales Vice President, James (Jamie) Blumhardt
Vice President, Jim Blais
Treasurer, Brian Begg
Auditors: PricewaterhouseCoopers LLP

LOCATIONS

HQ: Wesco International, Inc.
225 West Station Square Drive, Suite 700, Pittsburgh, PA 15219
Phone: 412 454-2200
Web: www.wesco.com

2013 Sales

	$ mil.	% of total
US	5,275	70
Canada	1,882	25
Mexico	90	1
Other countries	265	4
Total	**7,513**	**100**

PRODUCTS/OPERATIONS

2013 Sales

	% of total
Industrial customers	43
Electrical contractors	32
Utilities & special utility contractors	13
Commercial institutional & governmental customers	12
Total	**100**

Selected Products

Automation equipment
Ballasts
Boxes
Busways
Cable
Circuit breakers
Connectors
Data communications products
Drives
Electrical products
Fittings
Fixtures
Fuses
Industrial supplies
Light bulbs
Lighting
Lugs
Metallic and nonmetallic conduits
Motor control devices
MRO supplies
Operator interfaces
Panelboards
Patch panels
Premise wiring
Programmable logic controllers
Pushbuttons
Switchboards
Tape
Terminals
Tools
Transformers
Wire
Wire and conduit products

COMPETITORS

Anixter International	HWC
Bearing Distributors	McNaughton-McKay
Border States Electric	Premier Farnell
Consolidated Electrical	Rexel Inc.
Electro-Wire	Richardson Electronics
Electrocomponents	SUMMIT Electric Supply
Graybar Electric	Sonepar USA
	W.W. Grainger

Income Statement

FYE: December 31

	REVENUE ($ mil.)	NET INCOME ($ mil.)	NET PROFIT MARGIN	EMPLOYEES
12/14	7,889	275	3.5%	9,400
12/13	7,513	276	3.7%	9,200
12/12	6,579	201	3.1%	9,000
12/11	6,125	196	3.2%	7,100
12/10	5,063	115	2.3%	6,800
Annual Growth	11.7%	24.3%	—	8.4%

2014 Year-End Financials

Debt ratio: 29.77%
Return on equity: 14.94%
Cash ($ mil.): 128
Current ratio: 2.21
Long-term debt ($ mil.): 1,366

No. of shares (mil.): 44
Dividends
  Yield: —
  Payout: —
Market value ($ mil.): 3,391

	STOCK PRICE ($) FY Close	P/E High/Low	PER SHARE ($) Earnings	Dividends	Book Value
12/14	76.21	15 11	5.18	0.00	43.35
12/13	91.07	15 10	5.25	0.00	39.87
12/12	67.43	15 11	3.95	0.00	35.26
12/11	53.01	14 7	3.96	0.00	31.00
12/10	52.80	20 10	2.50	0.00	26.71
Annual Growth	9.6%	— —	20.0%	—	12.9%

WestAmerica Bancorporation

Annie get your checkbook? Maybe not as wild as Buffalo Bill's West but Westamerica Bancorporation still shoots high with its subsidiary Westamerica Bank. The bank operates almost 100 branches in Northern and Central California. It offers individuals and businesses such standard fare as checking and savings accounts as well as electronic banking trust services and credit cards. It focuses on the banking needs of small businesses; business loans and commercial mortgages together account for more than half of the company's loan portfolio. Westamerica Bank chartered in 1884 also originates construction residential mortgage and consumer loans.

Operations

Westamerica Bancorporation provides a full range of banking services to individual and corporate customers through its subsidiary bank Westamerica Bank.

Westamerica Bank subsidiary Community Banker Services Corporation provides the company and its other subsidiaries with data processing and various support services.

Geographic Reach

The bank has 95 branches and 2 trust offices in 21 Northern and Central California counties. Westamerica owns 33 branch office locations and one administrative facility and leases 70 facilities.

Financial Performance

In 2012 the company had assets of $5 billion deposits of $4.2 billion and shareholders' equity of $560.1 millionRevenues declined by 10% in 2012 due to a drop in loan revenues a decrease in ATM processing fees (due to lower transaction volumes) and loss on sale of securities.Net income dropped

by 8% in 2012 due to lower revenues partially offset by a decline in expenses.

Strategy

Westamerica's conservative lending practices (it avoided the clamor around subprime lending) and operating principles helped it weather the economic recession better than some of its banking peers.

Company Background

However the company's revenues and profits have fallen since 2009 when Westamerica netted a record $125 million. In 2011 net income fell 7% to $88 million (versus the $95 million it made in 2010) partly due to higher expenses as the company absorbed the operations of the recently acquired Sonoma Valley Bank. Revenues also fell 5% to $268 million. The declines were attributed to interest and fee earnings which fell as the company's lending activities slowed down and regulatory changes limited the amount of service charges banks can charge. (However both merchant processing fees and trust fees increased as those businesses grew.)

Over the years Westamerica had grown through acquisitions of other banks. In 2010 it added three branches in northern California when it acquired most of the assets and deposits of the failed Sonoma Valley Bank; the deal included loss-sharing agreements with the FDIC. That deal followed a similar transaction when the bank acquired County Bank after it was seized by regulators. That deal added nearly 40 branches to Westamerica Bank's network most of them in California's Central Valley.

EXECUTIVES

SVP Operations and Systems, Dennis R. Hansen, $130,008 total compensation
Chairman President and CEO, David L. Payne, $371,000 total compensation
SVP and CFO, Robert A. Thorson, $149,000 total compensation
SVP Banking Division, David L. Robinson, $150,000 total compensation
SVP Credit Administrator, Russell Rizzardi
Vice President Recruiting Manager, Ryan Baily
Vice President Accounting Manager, Glen Yasaki
Vice President Sco, Joe Plicka
Vice President Risk Management, Marcie Lewis
Senior Vice President, Joseph Dietzen
Auditors: Crowe Horwath LLP

LOCATIONS

HQ: WestAmerica Bancorporation
  1108 Fifth Avenue, San Rafael, CA 94901
Phone: 707 863-6000
Web: www.westamerica.com

PRODUCTS/OPERATIONS

2012 Sales

	$ mil.	% of total
Interest		
Loans	130	54
Investment securities held to maturity	32	14
Investment securities available for sale	19	8
Noninterest		
Service charges on deposit accounts	27	12
Merchant processing services	9	4
Debit card fees	5	2
ATM processing fees	3	1
Other	11	5
Total	**240**	**100**

COMPETITORS

Bank of America	MUFG Americas Holdings
Citigroup	Mechanics Bank
Comerica	U.S. Bancorp
First Republic (CA)	Wells Fargo
JPMorgan Chase	Western Alliance

Income Statement

FYE: December 31

	ASSETS ($ mil.)	NET INCOME ($ mil.)	INCOME AS % OF ASSETS	EMPLOYEES
12/14	5,035	60	1.2%	858
12/13	4,847	67	1.4%	914
12/12	4,952	81	1.6%	935
12/11	5,042	87	1.7%	961
12/10	4,931	94	1.9%	999
Annual Growth	0.5%	(10.5%)	—	(3.7%)

2014 Year-End Financials

Debt ratio: —
Return on equity: 11.34%
Cash ($ mil.): 380
Current ratio: —
Long-term debt ($ mil.): —

No. of shares (mil.): 25
Dividends
  Yield: 3.1%
  Payout: 64.9%
Market value ($ mil.): 1,262

	STOCK PRICE ($) FY Close	P/E High/Low	PER SHARE ($) Earnings	Dividends	Book Value
12/14	49.02	24 19	2.32	1.52	20.45
12/13	56.46	23 17	2.50	1.49	20.48
12/12	42.59	17 14	2.93	1.48	20.58
12/11	43.90	18 12	3.06	1.45	19.85
12/10	55.47	19 15	3.21	1.44	18.74
Annual Growth	(3.0%)	— —	(7.8%)	1.4%	2.2%

Western Alliance Bancorporation

The allies behind holding company Western Alliance Bancorporation are Western Alliance Bank (which operates as Alliance Bank of Arizona and First Independent Bank of Nevada) Las Vegas-based Bank of Nevada and Torrey Pines Bank which is active throughout California. Together the banks operate nearly 50 branches. Serving local businesses real estate developers and investors not-for-profit organizations and consumers the banks provide standard deposit products such as checking savings and money market accounts and CDs. Loans to businesses including real estate mortgages commercial and industrial loans and construction and land development loans dominate the banks' lending activities.

Operations

Other subsidiaries of Western Alliance Bancorporation include Shine Investment Advisory Services (80% owned) and Western Alliance Equipment Leasing.

Financial Performance

The company's revenue increased in fiscal 2013 compared to the prior year. It reported $379.9 million in revenue for fiscal 2013 up from $364.8 million in fiscal 2012.

Net income also went up in fiscal 2013 compared to the previous fiscal period. The company claimed a profit of $114.5 million in fiscal 2013 up from $72.8 million in fiscal 2012.

Despite the increased revenue and net income the company's cash on hand dropped by more than $50 in fiscal 2013 compared to fiscal 2012 levels.

Mergers and Acquisitions

In 2015 Western Alliance acquired Bridge Capital Holdings in a deal worth about $425 million.

The purchase brings expertise in technology and international banking among other areas and expands Western Alliance's market into Northern California.

EXECUTIVES

EVP and Chief Credit Officer, Robert R. (Bob) McAuslan, age 62

Chairman and CEO, Robert G. Sarver, age 54, $824,231 total compensation

EVP and CFO, Dale M. Gibbons, age 54, $395,426 total compensation

EVP California Administration and President Torrey Pines Bank, Gerald A. (Gary) Cady, age 60, $353,839 total compensation

EVP Credit Administration, Duane Froeschle, age 62

EVP Arizona Administration, James H. (Jim) Lundy, age 65, $369,531 total compensation

EVP Southern Nevada Administration; CEO Bank of Nevada, Bruce Hendricks, age 65

EVP and Chief Risk Officer, Patricia A. Taylor

EVP and General Counsel, Randall S. Theisen

Senior Vice President Corporate Finance, Lindner Jeremy

Senior Vice President Alco, Bill Maxwell

Senior Vice President Loan Operations Administrator, Cathy Lynch

Vice President muni Investment Manager, Jim Sult

Vice President Senior Research Analyst Corporate Finance, Mark Niles

Senior Vice President Marketing, Jan Rowe

Vice President, Lora Wong

Senior Vice President Shared Services Director, Michael Anthony (Mel) Pickett

Vice President Information Technology and Security Governance, Gregory Drejza

Vice President Finance Treasury, Sam Gray

Vice President Loan Operations Servicing Manager, Trudy Barbeau

Senior Vice President Marketing Director, Robyn Young

Senior Vice President Treasurer, John (Jack) Radwanski

Assistant Vice President Information Technology Vendor Contracts Manager, Brent Williams

Vice President Corporate Counsel, Michael (Mel) Riley

Vice President Operations Manager, Gary Loesl

Vice President Legal and Recovery, Conrad Noriega

Assistant Vice President Senior Digital Marketing Officer, Courtney Nush

Lead Director, Bruce Beach, age 65

Auditors: RSM US LLP

LOCATIONS

HQ: Western Alliance Bancorporation
One E. Washington Street Suite 1400, Phoenix, AZ 85004
Phone: 602 389-3500
Web: www.westernalliancebancorp.com

COMPETITORS

BancWest	PacWest Bancorp
Bank of America	U.S. Bancorp
Bank of the West	Wells Fargo
Desert Schools FCU	Westamerica
First Banks	Zions Bancorporation
MUFG Americas Holdings	

HISTORICAL FINANCIALS

Company Type: Public

Income Statement

FYE: December 31

	ASSETS ($ mil.)	NET INCOME ($ mil.)	INCOME AS % OF ASSETS	EMPLOYEES
12/14	10,600	147	1.4%	1,131
12/13	9,307	114	1.2%	1,051
12/12	7,622	72	1.0%	982
12/11	6,844	31	0.5%	942
12/10	6,193	(7)	—	908
Annual Growth	14.4%	—	—	5.6%

2014 Year-End Financials

Debt ratio: 4.06%
Return on equity: 15.94%
Cash ($ mil.): 164
Current ratio: —
Long-term debt ($ mil.): —

No. of shares (mil.): 88
Dividends
Yield: —
Payout: —
Market value ($ mil.): 2,466

	STOCK PRICE ($) FY Close	P/E High/Low		PER SHARE ($) Earnings	Dividends	Book Value
12/14	27.80	17	12	1.67	0.00	11.29
12/13	23.86	19	8	1.31	0.00	9.81
12/12	10.53	13	8	0.83	0.00	8.79
12/11	6.23	44	25	0.19	0.00	7.73
12/10	7.36	—	—	(0.23)	0.00	7.37
Annual Growth	39.4%	—	—	—	—	11.2%

Western Digital Corp.

When it comes to data storage Western Digital has drive and more than a splash of flash. The company is one of the largest independent makers of hard-disk drives (HDDs) which record store and recall volumes of data. It is also active in the fast-growing area of solid-state drives (SSDs) which are faster and lighter than HDDs. Drives for PCs account for most of Western Digital's sales although the company also makes devices used in servers cloud computing data centers and home entertainment products such as set-top boxes and video game consoles. The company sells to manufacturers and through retailers and distributors and generates more than half its sales from the Asia/Pacific region.

Operations Western Digital is structured around two subsidiaries: WD Technologies and Hitachi Global Storage Technologies (HGST). Each subsidiary maintains its own brand and product lines with separate sales marketing operations and product development teams. The company is looking to offer improved customer experiences for competing and complementary brands while finding efficiencies in shared services.

Geographic Reach The company's largest market is Asia (which represents about 50% of sales including China's 19%). The US and the EMEA region each contribute about 20%.

Western Digital has manufacturing facilities in the US as well as in China Japan Malaysia the Philippines Singapore and Thailand; it has sales offices worldwide.

Sales and Marketing

Western Digital offers its products to OEMs as well as through distributors and retailers. The OEM customer segment is its largest (almost two-thirds of revenue) with Hewlett-Packard accounting for slightly more than 10% of total revenue. Distribu-

tors and retailers account for about 23% and 13% of sales respectively.

Financial Performance

Western Digital's sales slowed 4% in 2015 to $14.57 billion from $15.13 billion in 2014. Shipments of hard disks slipped 8% for 2015 because of the sluggish demand around the world for personal computers. An increase in average selling prices rose to $60 in 2015 from $58 in 2014. The revenue drop translated to a 9% fall in profit. The company posted $1.47 billion in profit in 2015 down from $1.6 billion in 2014.

Cash flow from operations came in at $2.2 billion in 2015 from $2.8 billion in 2014.

Strategy

Western Digital is one of a handful of manufacturers that dominate the hard-disk drive market — a sector characterized by harsh competition short product life cycles and aggressive price cuts. In order to reduce its dependence on drives for PCs the company has branched into branded consumer media devices including DVR expanders portable media drives and media players that let users play data from external drives on TV. Its WD TV Live Plus media player streams movies (including those offered by Netflix) and Internet video to a digital TV. It is also investing in products for the mobile computing and cloud computing markets. Products of these types accounted for 53% of revenue in 2014 up from 50% the prior year and just 36% in 2012.

Western Digital is moving aggressively into flash storage for data centers and other environments were quick access to data is important. Recent acquisitions have bolstered the company's HGST unit expanding it's capabilities to meet large scale demands.

In 2015 Western Digital sold a 15% stake to Unisplendour a unit of Tsinghua Holding of China for $3.7 billion. The deal infuses a good amount of money into Western Digital which is could use to further build its flash storage business. It also provides a channel for boosting sales in China where Western Digital's sales plunged 22% in 2015 from 2014. The deal might face regulatory scrutiny since Tsinghua is controlled by the Chinese government.

Mergers & Acquisitions

Western Digital has long used acquisitions to add new product lines and extend its geographic reach.

In 2015 the company agreed to buy SanDisk for $19 billion in cash and stock. SanDisk which has $6.6 billion in annual revenues is a leader in non-volatile memory and would enable Western Digital to offer a more comprehensive product line. Western Digital also gains a long-term source of NAND products and technology. NAND is a type of flash memory that is used for high-capacity data storage a market growing with the rise of cloud computing big data and analytics.

In another 2015 deal Western Digital acquired Amplidata a developer of object storage software for public and private cloud data centers for about $267 million The acquisition is expected to help the HGST subsidiary to expand into higher value data storage platforms and systems in cloud data centers.

In 2013 it acquired Virident a provider of server-side flash storage products. The purchase followed the company's acquisition of STEC (for about $340 million) a maker of enterprise solid-state drives (SSDs) and VeloBit an advanced SSD caching software company. Collectively these purchases expand HGST's presence in the fast-growing enterprise SSD market.

In 2012 Western Digital bought Hitachi's disk drive business HGST for around $4.3 billion in cash and stock. The deal boosted Western Digital's share of the global market to nearly 50% ahead of rival Seagate Technology which accounted for around 30% of global shipments. Strategically the deal added disk drives used with servers –a large part of both Hitachi and Seagate's businesses –and gave Western Digital a better foothold in solid-state drives used in tablets and other portable devices.

HISTORY

Early History

Western Digital was founded in 1970 as a manufacturer of specialized semiconductors and electronic calculators. The company filed for Chapter 11 bankruptcy in 1976. However it reorganized and emerged successfully in 1978. Roger Johnson after a succession of executive positions at Memorex Measurex and Burroughs came to Western Digital as EVP and COO in 1982. Sales were merely $34 million hurt by the acquisition of several ill-fitting computer and electronics businesses. By 1984 Johnson became president and CEO; he sold off several companies to concentrate on storage control devices. A contract with IBM contributed to Western Digital's sales topping $460 million in 1987.

Anticipating a change in technology that would have disk drive makers building storage control into the drives themselves Western Digital began to shift its efforts toward making disk drives in 1988. Ten-year company veteran Kathy Braun oversaw the purchase of Tandon's disk drive operations. Tandon was considered a second-rate manufacturer using aging technology but its drives continued to sell well for a period following the acquisition. This created a false sense of security for Western Digital and delayed the development of more competitive drives. In 1990 the market for storage controller boards essentially disappeared. Losses prompted a restructuring that in turn violated Western Digital's credit agreements.

In 1991 the US economy slowed and the disk drive industry began a price war. That year Western Digital appearing close to bankruptcy sold its profitable departmental network business to Standard Microsystems.

As the PC market improved in 1992 so did Western Digital's prospects. A big boost came when the cash-strapped company introduced a line of disk drives with a commonality of parts. In 1993 Western Digital's IPO and sale of its wafer factory to Motorola reduced its high debt. That year the Clinton administration appointed CEO Johnson head of the General Services Administration. IBM veteran Charles Haggerty who joined Western Digital in 1992 assumed the company's top post. Johnson a lifelong Republican served nearly three years in the GSA post and resigned in 1996 to work for President Bill Clinton's re-election; he died in 2005.

In 1994 Western Digital enjoyed its first profit in four years. The company sold off its Microcomputer Products Group which made proprietary semiconductors in 1996 and introduced its first hard drives aimed at the corporate network computing market.

EXECUTIVES

Senior Vice President Branded Products, James (Jamie) Welsh

President Storage Devices, James J. (Jim) Murphy, age 56, $550,000 total compensation

President and CEO, Stephen D. (Steve) Milligan, age 49, $1,050,000 total compensation

President and COO, Michael D. Cordano, age 51, $700,000 total compensation

EVP and CFO, Olivier C. Leonetti, age 51

EVP Strategy and Corporate Development, Mark P. Long, $450,000 total compensation

Vice President International Sales, Scott Davis

Vice President Engineering, John Sawyer

Vice President, Sev Worthington

Vice President Materials, Gary Meister

Vice President Of Apac Sales, Yaw Chia

Senior Vice President Materials, Rubik Babakanian

Finance Senior Vice President, Thomas (Thom) Fong

Vice President Facilities Asia, Shahzad Mahmud

Vice President, Jean-Charles Herpeux

Vice President HDD Engineering Asia, Philip Bernard

Vice President, Colin Morgan

Vice President Materials, Tom Nieto

Vice President, Vince Mastropietro

Vice President Gm Of Manufacturing Head Operations, Norm Armour

Vice President and General Manager Connected Home Solutions At Western Digital, Scott Vouri

Vice President Technology, William Jane (Bill) Cain

Vice President Technology Western Digital Corporation, Dan Wade

Vice President firmware Engineering, Joe Viglione

Chairman, Thomas E. Pardun, age 71

Board Member, Linda Syu

Auditors: KPMG LLP

LOCATIONS

HQ: Western Digital Corp.
3355 Michelson Drive, Suite 100, Irvine, CA 92612
Phone: 949 672-7000
Web: www.westerndigital.com

2015 Sales

	$ mil.	% of total
Asia		
China	2,726	19
Other	4,552	31
US	3,054	21
Europe Middle East & Africa	3,169	22
Other	1,071	7
Total	**14,572**	**100**

PRODUCTS/OPERATIONS

2015 Sales by Channel

	% of total
OEM	64
Distributors	23
Retailers	13
Total	**100**

COMPETITORS

Apple Inc.	SMART Modular
EMC	Technologies
Fujitsu	Samsung Electronics
Intel	SanDisk
LaCie	Seagate Technology
Micron Technology	TEAC
Roku	Toshiba

HISTORICAL FINANCIALS

Company Type: Public

Income Statement

FYE: July 3

	REVENUE ($ mil.)	NET INCOME ($ mil.)	NET PROFIT MARGIN	EMPLOYEES
07/15*	14,572	1,465	10.1%	76,449
06/14	15,130	1,617	10.7%	84,072
06/13	15,351	980	6.4%	85,777
06/12	12,478	1,612	12.9%	103,111
07/11	9,526	726	7.6%	65,431
Annual Growth	**11.2%**	**19.2%**	**—**	**4.0%**

*Fiscal year change

2015 Year-End Financials

Debt ratio: 16.91%	No. of shares (mil.): 230
Return on equity: 15.96%	Dividends
Cash ($ mil.): 5,024	Yield: 0.0%
Current ratio: 2.63	Payout: 29.1%
Long-term debt ($ mil.): 2,156	Market value ($ mil.): 18,600

	STOCK PRICE ($) FY Close	P/E High/Low	PER SHARE ($) Earnings	Dividends	Book Value
07/15*	80.87	18 12	6.18	1.80	40.08
06/14	92.90	14 9	6.68	1.25	37.79
06/13	62.09	16 7	3.98	1.00	33.30
06/12	30.48	5 4	6.58	0.00	31.17
07/11	7.63	— —	3.09	0.00	23.55
Annual Growth	**80.5%**	**— —**	**18.9%**	**—**	**14.2%**

*Fiscal year change

Western Refining Inc

It's the quality and volumes of its refined products that makes Western Refining a major player in the West. The independent oil refiner operates primarily in the Southwest region of the US although it does have some marketing operations on the East Coast. Western Refining's refineries (one in El Paso one in the Four Corners region of northern New Mexico) have a crude oil refining capacity of 155019 barrels per day. More than 90% of its refined products are made up of light transportation fuels including diesel and gasoline. It owns a wholesale division that complements the refining operations. Western Refining also owns more than 260 convenience stores and gas stations in four Southwestern states.

Geographic Reach

The company is an independent refining and marketing. Its refining segment operates refineries in El Paso Texas and Gallup New Mexico. Its assets include a fleet of crude oil and finished product truck transports and wholesale petroleum products operations in Arizona California Colorado Maryland Nevada New Mexico Texas and Virginia. The retail segment includes retail service stations and convenience stores in Arizona Colorado New Mexico and Texas.

Operations

The company reports its operating results in four business segments: the refining group the retail group WNRL and Northern Teir Energy.

Refining segment owns and operates two refineries in the Southwest that process crude oil and other feedstocks primarily into gasoline diesel fuel jet fuel and asphalt. Northern Tier Energy owns and operates refining and transportation assets and operates and supports retail convenience stores primarily in the Upper Great Plains region of the US.Western Refining Logistics (WNRL) owns and operates terminal storage transportation and provides related services primarily to refining segment in the Southwest. The WNRL segment also includes wholesale assets consisting of a fleet of crude oil and refined product truck transports and wholesale petroleum product operations in the Southwest region. WNRL receives its product supply from the refining segment and third-party suppliers.Retail segment operates retail convenience stores and unmanned commercial fleet fueling locations located in the Southwest. the retail group operated 261 retail stores located in Arizona Colorado New Mexico. and Texas and 50 cardlocks located in Arizona California Colorado

New Mexico and Texas. Western Refining Logistics LP has 66.2% limited partner interest.

Sales and Marketing

Western Refining sells through wholesale and retail groups independent wholesalers and retailers distributors commercial accounts and major oil companies. Its major customers include retail fuel distributors and companies in the mining construction utility manufacturing transportation aviation and agricultural industries. In 2014 PMI Trading Limited an affiliate of Petroleos Mexicanos accounted for 5.5% of the company's revenues.

Western Refining's El Paso refinery the company's largest has operating agreements with Kinder Morgan Energy Partners and Chevron that give it access to crude oil and refined product pipelines.

The retail group operates retail stores that sell various grades of gasoline diesel fuel and convenience store merchandise to the general public. It supplies the majority of its retail gasoline and diesel fuel inventories through WNRL and purchases general merchandise as well as beverage and food products from various suppliers. The retail stores operate under various brands including Giant Western Western Express Howdy's Mustang and Sundial. Gasoline brands sold through these stores include Western Giant Mustang Phillips 66 Company Conoco 76 Shell Oil Company Chevron Mobil and Texaco. They company sells a variety of refined products to its diverse customer base through the WNRL wholesale business.

About 59% of Western Refining's gasoline and diesel volumes in 2014 were sold via NTI's light products terminal to NTI operated and franchised SuperAmerica-branded convenience stores Marathon Petroleum-branded convenience stores and other resellers. NTI has a contract with Marathon to supply substantially all of the gasoline and diesel requirements for the independently owned and operated Marathon branded convenience stores within the region that NTI supplies. NTI also has a crude oil transportation operation in North Dakota to allow them to purchase crude oil at the wellhead in the Bakken Shale while limiting the impact of rising trucking costs for crude oil in North Dakota.

Financial Performance

The company's net revenues grew by 50% in 2014. Consolidated margins increased by 74.3% reflecting the overall industry wide improvement in refining margins year over year. Margins were also impacted by the results of commodity hedging activities in the refining segment. Other segments increased in part due to the acquisition of NTI and regional margin environments in non-refining operations. Revenues from WNRL increased due to higher crude oil revenues and higher retail sales due to higher fuel margins and growth in merchandise sales. In 2014 Western Refining's net income increased by 103% due to higher net sales outpacing an increase in total operating costs and expenses. Cash from operating activities increased by 67% in 2014.

Strategy

The company's refined products sell at a premium on the Gulf Coast due to increasing demand and limited local refining capacity. In Phoenix Western Refining also benefits from tighter EPA fuel specifications that require the use of cleaner burning gasoline. As a consequence Phoenix CBG fuel is the company's highest-margin product. Western Refining is also looking to take advantage of increased Permian Basin crude oil production continues to increase supply to its refineries in New Mexico and Texas which could provide additional cost-advantaged crude oil in the region.

The company actively seeks to acquire assets such as refineries pipelines terminals and retail fuel and convenience stores that complement its existing assets and/or broaden their geographic presence. It launched the Bobcat Pipeline project in 2015 to give the company greater ability to move crude oil out of the Delaware Basin to locations eastward. Western Refining also invested in new storage facilities in the Four Corners area and Mason Station and added additional gathering lines in the Delaware Basin. All of these initiatives are in line with the company's strategy to further develop infrastructure in order to capitalize on the location of its assets. In 2015 Western Refining added 31 southern Arizona retail locations to its retail business bringing the total stores it operates to 261.

In 2014 Western Refining announced plans to construct a new Delaware Basin pipeline originating near Western Refining Logistics LP's existing Mason Station crude oil gathering facility in Reeves County Texas terminating at a new crude oil gathering facility at Wink Station in Winkler County Texas. The 40 mile pipeline is capable of receiving and transporting up to 125000 barrels per day of light crude oil and condensate for delivery to common carrier pipelines at Wink Texas and went into service in 2015. Mergers and Acquisitions

In 2014 Western Refining agreed to acquire the 25000 barrel per day idled Wingate Fractionation Plant in Gallup New Mexico from ConocoPhillips. The Wingate facility includes rail loading and off-loading capabilities and storage facilities in addition to natural gas liquids (NGL) fractionation capability.

Company Background

In 2013 the company opened its Mason Station Crude Oil Terminal in Reeves County Texas the first phase of the company's Delaware Basin Crude Oil Gathering System.

To increase its financial flexiblity in 2013 the company formed WNRL (a publicly traded fee-based growth-oriented master limited partnership) to own operate develop and acquire terminals storage tanks pipelines and other logistical assets.

That year the company acquired a general partner interest and a 38.4% limited partnership interest in Northern Tier Energy for $775 million.

In 2012 two subsidiaries (York River Fuels LLC and Glencore LTD) signed a long-term commercial supply and trading agreement whereby Glencore provides global sourcing supply and trading and inventory and risk management services to support York River's mid-Atlantic wholesale business. To reciprocate York River provides rack marketing and contract and credit management.

To cut costs and exit a difficult regional refining market in September 2010 it suspended refining operations at its 70000-barrels-per-day Yorktown Virginia facility. In 2011 Western Refining sold that plant and an underused segment of its crude oil pipeline in southeast New Mexico to units of Plains All American Pipeline for $220 million.

The company achieved its standing as a national player through the 2007 acquisition of Giant Industries for $1.1 billion a move that dramatically boosted Western Refining's refining capacity and geographic coverage (expanding its Southwest presence and giving it access to MidAtlantic markets).

EXECUTIVES

CFO, Gary R. Dalke, age 62, $416,880 total compensation
President and CEO, Jeff A. Stevens, age 51, $972,000 total compensation
President Refining and Marketing, Mark J. Smith, age 56, $531,360 total compensation
SVP Legal General Counsel and Secretary, Lowry Barfield, $371,520 total compensation
SVP Treasurer and Director of Investor Relations, Jeffrey S. Beyersdorfer, $289,440 total compensation
Vice President Refining, Forrest Lauher
Vice President Safety and Reliability, Dan Statile
Vice President, Barfield Lowry
Chairman, Paul L. Foster, age 57
Auditors: Deloitte & Touche LLP

LOCATIONS

HQ: Western Refining Inc
123 W. Mills Ave., Suite 200, El Paso, TX 79901
Phone: 915 534-1400
Web: www.wnr.com

COMPETITORS

Alon USA Energy	Marathon Petroleum
BP	Murphy Oil
CITGO	Phillips 66
Calumet Specialty	QuikTrip
Products	Shell Oil Products
Chevron	Suncor
ConocoPhillips	Sunoco
Hess Corporation	Tesoro
HollyFrontier	Valero Energy

HISTORICAL FINANCIALS

Company Type: Public

Income Statement

FYE: December 31

	REVENUE ($ mil.)	NET INCOME ($ mil.)	NET PROFIT MARGIN	EMPLOYEES
12/14	15,153	559	3.7%	5,700
12/13	10,086	275	2.7%	3,800
12/12	9,503	398	4.2%	3,800
12/11	9,071	132	1.5%	3,600
12/10	7,965	(17)	—	2,950
Annual Growth	17.4%	—	—	17.9%

2014 Year-End Financials

Debt ratio: 26.76%	No. of shares (mil.): 96
Return on equity: 55.61%	Dividends
Cash ($ mil.): 431	Yield: 8.1%
Current ratio: 1.74	Payout: 72.1%
Long-term debt ($ mil.): 1,515	Market value ($ mil.): 3,634

	STOCK PRICE ($) FY Close	P/E High/Low		PER SHARE ($) Earnings	Dividends	Book Value
12/14	37.78	8	6	5.61	3.08	11.64
12/13	42.41	12	8	2.79	2.14	11.21
12/12	28.19	7	3	3.71	2.74	10.46
12/11	13.29	15	7	1.34	0.00	9.18
12/10	10.58	—	—	(0.19)	0.00	7.65
Annual Growth	37.5%	—	—	—	—	11.1%

Western Union Co.

Western Union's wires don't carry telegrams anymore STOP But they keep on humming with international money transfers STOP The firm has an agent network of about 500000 locations in more than 200 countries worldwide that allows individuals and business customers to transfer money or make payments (in more than 120 currencies) electronically. The pioneering company has taken advantage of technological advances and rolled with the changes since it was founded in 1851. Starting out as a messaging medium it then added the US's first stock ticker helped standardize timekeeping nationally debuted an early charge card and the singing telegram and finally shifted to money transfer services.

Operations

Western Union operates three main segments: Consumer-to-Consumer Consumer-to-Business and Business Solutions.Consumer-to-Consumer transfers which rely heavily on immigrants sending money between countries account for more than 80% of total revenue while Consumer-to-Business transfers account for 10%. Western Union's Business Solutions segment facilitates payment and foreign exchange cross-border and cross-currency transactions for small- and medium-size businesses and other organizations and individuals. It makes up the rest.In 2014 Western Union completed 255 million consumer-to-consumer transactions worldwide totaling $85 billion and transferred 484 million business payments.

Geographic Reach

Colorado-based company has offices in more than 200 countries worldwide. Western Union's fast-growing international business contributes more than 70% of its revenue counting the UK France Germany and Australia as its major non-US send countries. The rest of its revenue is generated in the US. Sales and MarketingWestern Union provides its Consumer-to-Consumer service globally third-party agents in most countries and territories with approximately 90% of agent locations being located outside of the United States. Its Business Solutions services are primarily sold over the phone through partner channels and through the Internet. Western Union has relationships with more than 100000 customers with respect to their payment solutions.Consumers can make Western Union transactions at kiosks in some 7600 Walgreens and Duane Reade locations and through several other major retailers nationwide. The company spent $162.7 million on advertising in 2014 down from $165.1 million in 2013 and $177.5 million in 2012.

Financial Performance

Western Union's revenues have remained mostly flat in recent years. Revenue in 2014 inched up by 1% to $5.61 billion thanks to 5% transaction growth in the Consumer-to-Consumer segment. In 2013 despite growth in consumer-to-consumer transaction volumes price reductions and enhanced regulatory compliance to prevent money laundering terrorist financing and other illegal activity led to a 3% decline in that segment. Foreign exchange revenue also grew thanks to a combination of higher amounts of cross-border principal sent via Consumer-to-Consumer transactions growth in the Business Solutions segment and higher retail walk-in foreign exchange service volume after the acquisition of the Brazilian foreign exchange operations of Fitta DTVM and Fitta Turismo.After two years of profit declines net income in 2014 rebounded by almost 7% to $852.4 million mostly thanks to higher revenue and lower income tax charges. The company enjoyed a lower tax rate due to a combination of various discrete items including foreign currency fluctuations on certain income tax attributes and changes in tax contingency reserves.Cash levels remained mostly flat as operations provided $1.05 billion or 4% less cash than in 2013. Strategy

Heavily reliant on immigrants sending money between countries Western Union continues to nurture its global sending networks through strategic partnerships and by entering new markets. In early 2015 for example the company expanded its reach into Mexico partnering with Grupo Financiero Banorte's UniTeller network which has connections to the top banks in Mexico which carry some 60 million individual bank accounts. Also in 2015 it extended its largest relationship in the Philippines with Universal Storefront Services Corporation to continue providing services to the country where 10.4 million Filipino dispora living outside of the country depend on remittance services to support their families back home. Additionally that year it expanded its presence in Europe through 16 new UAE Exchange major city Agent locations in the UK Ireland Germany and the Netherlands which began offering Western Union Money Transfer services. The company made similar partnerships in 2014 in India with Immediate Payment Service; and Angola in Africa via the Angola Post Office. Also in 2014 it introduced its services in Nigeria and to small and medium-sized businesses in Malaysia.

The company has also been focused on expanding consumer options for sending and receiving money. Although most of the company's transactions are made in person it is developing alternatives to its traditional wire transfers. In early 2015 for example the company began accepting customer payments through the smart phone payment platform Apple Pay at some 7600 Walgreens and Duane Reade locations nationwide. By the end of 2013 its services were available at more than 100000 ATMs worldwide as well as through transactional websites in more than 20 countries and via mobile apps in the US and Australia. Western Union is also working to grow its smallest segment business solutions with new products and offerings. In early 2015 it entered the global mass payments market by strategically partnering with Hyperwallet to introduce a new global mass payments product which allows both companies to provide high volume payment transactions (even in the millions) for business-to-consumer transactions around the world. In 2013 it launched a new cash management dashboard tool as well as new services for non-governmental organizations. In addition it expanded its business services in India and Japan and introduced cross-border tuition payment services in China India and South Korea.Mergers and AcquisitionsIn early 2014 Western Union purchased the Brazilian retail walk-in foreign exchange operations of Fitta DTVM S.A. and Fitta Turismo Ltda. for $18.5 million.

EXECUTIVES

EVP Global Operations and Technology and CIO, John D. (David) Thompson, age 48, $500,000 total compensation

Vice President Finance, Mike Register

President and CEO, Hikmet Ersek, age 55, $1,000,000 total compensation

SVP and President Western Union Business Solutions, Kerry Agiasotis

EVP General Counsel and Secretary, John R. Dye, age 55, $500,000 total compensation

EVP and Chief Marketing Officer, Diane Scott, age 44

EVP and CFO, Rajesh K. Agrawal, age 50, $472,000 total compensation

EVP and President Americas and European Union, Odilon Almeida, age 53, $600,000 total compensation

EVP and President Middle East Africa Asia Pacific Eastern Europe and CIS, Jean Claude Farah, age 44

SVP and General Manager Western Union Digital, Khalid Fellahi

EVP and Chief Human Resources Officer, Richard L. Williams, age 49

Senior Vice President of Investor Relations, Michael A (Mel) Salop

Vice President Information Technology, Samba Diallo

Vice President, Alfred Nader

Vice President Information Technology Infrastructure and Operations, Bill Goranowski

Vice President Us Sales, Paul Jardon

Vice President Corporate Systems, Eileen Baines

Vice President Financial Reporting, Donna Abbey

Vice President Investor Relations, Amy Kuark

Vice President Information Technology Governance, Tim Langley-hawthorne

Vice President Of Strategic Investments, Caleb Kim

Vice President Finance, Stephanie Shine

Vice President Communications, Daniel Diaz

Evp Payment Services, Royal Cole

National Accounts Manager, Brad Gay

Vice President Corporate Meeting Planners, Richard (Dick) Badler

Regional Vice President Sales, Kelly Gesselman

Vice President Records And Information Management, Jim Keyes

Vice President and General Manager Product Management Operations and Analytics, Girish Balasubramanian

Senior Management (Senior Vice President General Manager Director), Srinivas Surapaneni

Vice President Of Technology Solutions, Carol Darland

Senior Vice President, Tim Daly

Vice President Commercial Sales, Ben Kavalec

Vice President Global Operations AML Compliance, Kristine Diehl

Vice President Tax Compliance, Katharine Thiemes

Vice President North America Finance, Dan Nordlander

Vice President Strategic Finance, Jeffrey Hochstadt

Vice President Sales, Jeff Zallaps

Vice President Aml Compliance, Fabrice Borsello

Vice President Global Compensation, Terry Lodes

Vice President Consumer Segments Usmt, Daniel Canning

Vice President Risk And Asset Management, Doug Groetken

Vice President Controller, Mary-margaret Henke

Vice President Finance, Steve Cornell

Vice President, Roland Lau

Vice President Independent Channel, Ignacio Ramirez

Vice President, Darius Jack

Vice President, Julie Sullivan

Senior Vice President Finance, Scott Coad

Vice President Consumer Segments Usmt, Daniel (Dan) Canning

Executive Vice President and Chief Human Resources Officer, Rick Williams

Vice President of Accounting, Hinsey Mark

Chairman, Jack M. Greenberg, age 72

Treasurer, Keith Harrow

Secretary, Jenifer Foster

Auditors: Ernst & Young LLP

LOCATIONS

HQ: Western Union Co.
12500 East Belford Avenue, Englewood, CO 80112
Phone: 866 405-5012
Web: www.westernunion.com

2014 Sales

	$ mil.	% of total
US	1,564	28
International	4,042	72
Total	**5,607**	**100**

PRODUCTS/OPERATIONS

2014 Sales

	$ mil.	% of total
Transaction fees	4,083	73
Foreign exchange revenue	1,386	25
Commissions & other	137	2
Total	**5,607**	**100**

2014 Sales by Segment

	$ mil.	% of total
Consumer-to-consumer		
Transaction fees	3,421	61
Foreign exchange	998	20
Other	65	1
Consumer-to-business		
Transaction fees	572	10
Foreign exchange & other	26	.
Business solutions		
Foreign exchange	363	6
Transaction fees & other	41	.
Other	118	2
Total	**5,607**	**100**

COMPETITORS

American Express	PayPal
Citigroup	Santander Mexico
First Data	Sigue
Global Payments	US Postal Service
MasterCard	Visa Inc
MoneyGram	Xoom
International	

HISTORICAL FINANCIALS

Company Type: Public

Income Statement

FYE: December 31

	REVENUE ($ mil.)	NET INCOME ($ mil.)	NET PROFIT MARGIN	EMPLOYEES
12/14	5,607	852	15.2%	10,000
12/13	5,542	798	14.4%	10,000
12/12	5,664	1,025	18.1%	9,000
12/11	5,491	1,165	21.2%	8,000
12/10	5,192	909	17.5%	7,000
Annual Growth	**1.9%**	**(1.6%)**	**—**	**9.3%**

2014 Year-End Financials

Debt ratio: 37.62%		No. of shares (mil.): 521	
Return on equity: 70.88%		Dividends	
Cash ($ mil.): 1,783		Yield: 2.7%	
Current ratio: 1.72		Payout: 33.5%	
Long-term debt ($ mil.): 3,720		Market value ($ mil.): 9,340	

	STOCK PRICE ($) FY Close	P/E High/Low		Earnings	PER SHARE ($) Dividends	Book Value
12/14	17.91	12	9	1.59	0.50	2.49
12/13	17.25	14	9	1.43	0.50	2.01
12/12	13.61	12	7	1.69	0.43	1.64
12/11	18.26	12	8	1.84	0.31	1.44
12/10	18.57	15	11	1.36	0.25	0.89
Annual Growth	**(0.9%)**	**—**	**—**	**4.0%**	**18.9%**	**29.3%**

WestRock Co

LOCATIONS

HQ: WestRock Co
501 South 5th Street, Richmond, VA 23219-0501
Phone: 804 444-1000

HISTORICAL FINANCIALS

Company Type: Public

Income Statement

FYE: September 30

	REVENUE ($ mil.)	NET INCOME ($ mil.)	NET PROFIT MARGIN	EMPLOYEES
09/15	11,381	507	4.5%	41,400
09/14	9,895	479	4.8%	—
09/13	9,545	727	7.6%	—
Annual Growth	**9.2%**	**(16.5%)**	**—**	**—**

2015 Year-End Financials

Debt ratio: 22.21%		No. of shares (mil.): 257	
Return on equity: 6.36%		Dividends	
Cash ($ mil.): 228		Yield: 0.7%	
Current ratio: 1.92		Payout: 12.8%	
Long-term debt ($ mil.): 5,558		Market value ($ mil.): 13,220	

	STOCK PRICE ($) FY Close	P/E High/Low		Earnings	PER SHARE ($) Dividends	Book Value
09/15	51.44	22	17	2.93	0.38	45.34
09/14	0.00	—	—	3.29	0.70	30.76
09/13	0.00	—	—	4.98	0.53	(0.00)
Annual Growth	**—**	**—**	**—**	**(23.3%)**	**(15.5%)**	**—**

Weyerhaeuser Co

If a tree falls in a Weyerhaeuser forest someone is there to hear it –and he has a chainsaw. The forest products company produces a variety of softwood lumber and other building materials in North America. It also offers cellulose fibers products used to make paper packaging and textiles. The company harvests trees for its products through its timberlands division which owns or controls nearly 7 million acres of forest in the US and Canada. Exports account for more than 30% of the company's sales. Incorporated in 1900 as Weyerhaeuser Timber Co. the company is classified as a real estate investment trust (REIT).

HISTORY

Company BackgroundFrederick Weyerhaeuser a 24-year-old German immigrant bought his first lumberyard in 1858 in Illinois. He also participated in joint logging ventures in Illinois Minnesota and Wisconsin. In 1900 he and 15 partners bought 900000 timbered acres from the Northern Pacific Railway. The venture was named Weyerhaeuser Timber Company.

During the Depression the business recouped losses in the deflated lumber market by selling wood pulp. Frederick's grandson J. P. "Phil" Weyerhaeuser Jr. took over as CEO in 1933.

Diversification into the production of containerboard (1949) particleboard (1955) paper (1956) and other products led the company to drop "Timber" from its name in 1959. In 1963 Weyerhaeuser went public and opened its first overseas office in Tokyo.

In the 1970s George Weyerhaeuser (Phil's son) diversified further to insulate the company from the forest-product industry's cyclical nature and ended up with a mishmash of businesses and products from private-label disposable diapers to pet supplies.

The eruption of Mount St. Helens in 1980 destroyed 68000 acres of Weyerhaeuser timber. That disaster and the soft US lumber market depressed the company's earnings through 1982. Weyerhaeuser reduced its workforce by 25% during this period.

Under John Creighton (president since 1988 and CEO from 1991 until 1998) Weyerhaeuser refocused on forest products and organized along product lines rather than by geographic region. Less-successful ventures were put up for sale including milk carton hardwood and gypsum board plants. The company took a $497 million pretax charge in 1989 related to the decision to close unprofitable operations. Earnings improved in 1990 but dropped again in 1991 reflecting the recession in the US and plant closures.

In 1992 the company outbid Georgia-Pacific paying $600 million for two pulp mills three sawmills and more than 200000 acres of forest land to boost its market-pulp capacity by 40%. The following year the company sold its disposable-diaper business through a public offering in a new company Paragon Trade Brands. It also sold GNA Corporation to General Electric subsidiary GE Capital.

The federal government in 1995 allowed the company to harvest trees in an area inhabited by the endangered northern spotted owl. The move angered environmental groups. In 1997 Weyerhaeuser began to reorganize its recycling business by selling or closing noncore units. It also purchased a stake in 193000 acres on New Zealand's South Island the company's first overseas investment in more than a decade. In 1998 the company restructured its joint venture with Nippon Paper with Weyerhaeuser decreasing its stake in North Pacific Paper Company from 80% to 50% and closed a lumber mill in Canada. Also that year Steve Rogel a veteran from competitor Willamette succeeded Creighton as CEO and became the first outsider to head Weyerhaeuser.

In 1999 Weyerhaeuser paid $2.5 billion for Canada's MacMillan Bloedel and early in 2000 it acquired TJ International 51% owner of leading engineered lumber products company Trus Joist MacMillan (Weyerhaeuser already owned the other 49%). Also in 2000 Weyerhaeuser purchased two sawmills and a 70% stake in lumber distributor Pine Solutions from Australia-based CSR Limited. Weyerhaeuser sold its Marshfield Door architectural wood door business and closed some of its manufacturing operations to consolidate its business.

After a protracted courtship in March 2002 Weyerhaeuser acquired Oregon-based Willamette Industries in a $6.1 billion cash deal. The company closed three North American plants (in Colorado Louisiana and Oregon) later that year. In October the company closed a Canadian containerboard mill cutting 140 jobs in the process. At the close of the year Weyerhaeuser sold approximately 115000 acres of timberlands in western Washington to Boston-based Hancock Timber Resource Group (international timber investment and management) for about $211 million to aid in paying down its debt associated with the Willamette acquisition.

On the heels of the deals for MacMillan Bloedel Trus Joist MacMillan and Willamette Weyerhaeuser moved to pay down debt. It sold more than 320000 acres of the timberland (in the Carolinas and Tennessee) that it acquired with the Willamette purchase. Before the end of 2003 Fountain Investments had acquired about 168000 acres of the west-central Tennessee acreage and Forest Investment Associates purchased about 160000 acres of western North Carolina and South Carolina timberlands. Weyerhaeuser gained about $140 million in after-tax proceeds from the latter sale.

Also in 2003 Weyerhaeuser sold its Nipigon Multiply hardwood plywood underlayment operation in Ontario Canada to Columbia Forest Products. Late in the year the company closed its fine-paper operations in Longview Washington (eliminating 119 jobs there). Altogether Weyerhaeuser closed 12 facilities and sold about 444000 acres of non-strategic timberlands in 2003 in keeping with its plan to reduce company debt and increase productivity.

The company closed its Grande Cache Alberta sawmill in 2004 (affecting more than 150 jobs there) and sold its oriented strand board (OSB) mill in Slave Lake Alberta to Tolko Industries for about $43 million. Also in 2004 Weyerhaeuser sold roughly 270000 acres of timberlands in central Georgia for about $400 million to investment and property firms in Georgia and South Carolina.

Also in 2004 subsidiary Weyerhaeuser Brasil Participações acquired two-thirds ownership in Brazil-based Aracruz Produtos de Madeira (APM) a subsidiary of Aracruz Cellulose to produce lumber made from a eucalyptus hybrid for use in furniture flooring cabinetry and other applications. Aracruz Cellulose holds the remaining third ownership in the joint venture. Also that year Weyerhaeuser changed the name of its pulp business to Weyerhaeuser Cellulose Fibers to reinforce its focus on developing unique or specialized applications for cellulose fibers.

Weyerhaeuser agreed early in 2005 to sell five Canadian sawmills two finishing plants 635000 acres of timber and some government land-cutting rights to Brascan for $970 million. It had acquired the timber and sawmill assets when it bought MacMillan Bloedel in 1999.

The company's debt reduction strategy continued in 2004. Weyerhaeuser sold roughly 270000 acres of its timberlands in Georgia and several mills in the US and Canada. The sale of the assets helped the company more than quadruple net earnings for 2004: $1.3 billion its best result of the decade. It used the proceeds to reduce debt by some $730 million. In the meantime Weyerhaeuser reported that it wrung out the $300 million in expected Willamette-related synergies in half the time predicted.

Weyerhaeuser continued to streamline and focus on its softwood lumber business in 2005 selling $970 million in assets (five sawmills two finishing plants 635000 acres and timber rights) to Brascan. Weyerhaeuser also closed a Saskatchewan pulp and paper mill in 2006 cutting 690 jobs; not long afterward amid weak profits it announced multiple plant closures and sales including another pulp mill another sawmill several corrugated plants and a paper bag plant.

In 2007 Weyerhaeuser merged its fine paper business with Domtar. According to the terms of the $3.3 billion deal Weyerhaeuser shareholders got a 55% stake in the renamed company Domtar Corporation. Weyerhaeuser controls the board and several Weyerhaeuser executives manage the company.

The company sold its Trus Joist commercial business including four manufacturing plants to Atlas Holdings in 2009. Also that year Weyerhaeuser announced it was closing its noncore trucking division. Other divestitures in 2009 included non-strategic timberland in Oregon (representing about 10% of its holdings in the Pacific Northwest) in an effort to focus on Douglas fir production in that region.

Weyerhaeuser converted to a real estate investment trust (REIT) in 2010. The status allows the company to pay less in taxes and pay its shareholders larger dividends. Weyerhaeuser folded its timberland operations into the REIT while its real estate wood products and cellulose fibers units operate under a taxable REIT subsidiary.

EXECUTIVES

Senior Vice President Cellulose Fibers, Shaker Chandrasekaran
President CEO and Director, Doyle R. Simons, age 51, $950,000 total compensation
EVP and CFO, Patricia M. Bedient, age 61, $610,000 total compensation
President Winchester Homes, Alan E. Shapiro
President Weyerhaeuser Real Estate Company, Peter M. Orser, age 58, $535,000 total compensation
President Quadrant Corporation, Ken Krivanec
SVP Cellulose Fibers, Catherine I. Slater, age 51
President Trendmaker Homes, Floyd W. (Will) Holder
President Maracay Homes, Andy Warren
SVP Timberlands, Rhonda C. Hunter, age 52, $477,308 total compensation
SVP Wood Products, Adrian M. Blocker, age 58, $437,500 total compensation
President Weyerhaeuser Company Limited, Fred Dzida
Vice President Timberlands Technology, Christine Dean
Chairman, Charles R. (Chuck) Williamson
Assistant Treasurer and Director of Insurance, John (Jack) Lambdin
Auditors: KPMG LLP

LOCATIONS

HQ: Weyerhaeuser Co
33663 Weyerhaeuser Way South, Federal Way, WA 98063-9777
Phone: 253 924-2345
Web: www.weyerhaeuser.com

2014 Sales

	% of total
US	67
Japan	9
China	6
Canada	6
Europe	4
South America	1
Other foreign countries	7
Total	**100**

PRODUCTS/OPERATIONS

2014 Sales

	$ mil.	% of total
Wood Products	3,970	54
Cellulose Fibers	1,936	26
Timberlands	1,497	20
Total	**7,403**	**100**

Selected Products and Services

Wood and Building Products
  Engineered lumber products
  Flooring
  Lumber (softwood)
  Oriented Strand Board
  Plywood
  Structural panels
  Veneer
Cellulose Fiber and White Paper
  Paper and liquid packaging
  Paper
  Pulp
  Textiles
Real Estate and Related Assets
  Master-planned communities
  Multifamily homes
  Residential lots
  Single-family homes
Timberlands
  Chips
  Logs
  Mineral resources
  Seedlings
  Weyerhaeser Select Douglas Fir seed
Other
  Recycling
  Transportation

COMPETITORS

Canfor	Potlatch
Cascades Boxboard	Pratt Industries USA
ENCE Energia y	Rayonier
Celulosa SA	Resolute Forest
Georgia-Pacific	Products
Indiana Veneers	Sierra Pacific
Louisiana-Pacific	Industries
McFarland Cascade	Smurfit Kappa
Mendocino Redwood	Stora Enso
Company	Tembec
Norbord	Tenon
Packaging Corp. of	UPM-Kymmene
America	West Fraser Timber
Plum Creek Timber	

HISTORICAL FINANCIALS

Company Type: Public

Income Statement

FYE: December 31

	REVENUE ($ mil.)	NET INCOME ($ mil.)	NET PROFIT MARGIN	EMPLOYEES
12/14	7,403	1,826	24.7%	12,800
12/13	8,529	563	6.6%	13,700
12/12	7,059	385	5.5%	13,200
12/11	6,216	331	5.3%	12,800
12/10	6,552	1,281	19.6%	14,250
Annual Growth	**3.1%**	**9.3%**	**—**	**(2.6%)**

2014 Year-End Financials

Debt ratio: 40.14%	No. of shares (mil.): 524
Return on equity: 30.18%	Dividends
Cash ($ mil.): 1,580	Yield: 2.8%
Current ratio: 3.30	Payout: 34.0%
Long-term debt ($ mil.): 5,402	Market value ($ mil.): 18,823

	STOCK PRICE ($) FY Close	P/E High/Low		PER SHARE ($) Earnings	Dividends	Book Value
12/14	35.89	11	9	3.18	1.02	10.11
12/13	31.57	34	28	0.95	0.81	11.64
12/12	27.82	40	26	0.71	0.62	7.50
12/11	18.67	41	25	0.61	0.60	7.95
12/10	18.93	13	4	3.99	26.66	8.60
Annual Growth	**17.3%**	**—**	**—**	**(5.5%)**	**(55.8%)**	**4.1%**

Whirlpool Corp

With brand names recognized by just about anyone who has ever separated dark colors from light Whirlpool is one of the world's top home appliance makers. It specializes in laundry appliances refrigerators and freezers cooking appliances dishwashers and compressors. They're sold under a bevy of brand names including Whirlpool Amana KitchenAid Maytag and Roper. The company markets and distributes these major home appliances in North America Latin America EMEA (Europe the Middle East and Africa) and Asia. It has manufacturing operations in more than a dozen countries. Major customers include retailers Lowe's Home Depot Sears and Best Buy.

HISTORY

Brothers Fred and Lou Upton and their uncle Emory Upton founded the Upton Machine Company manufacturer of electric motor-driven washing machines in 1911 in St. Joseph Michigan. Sears Roebuck and Co. began buying their products five years later and by 1925 the company was supplying all of Sears' washers. The Uptons combined their company with the Nineteen Hundred Washer Company in 1929 to form the Nineteen Hundred Corporation the world's largest washing machine company.

Sears and Nineteen Hundred prospered during the Great Depression and during WWII Nineteen Hundred's factories produced war materials. In 1948 it began selling its first automatic washing machine (introduced a year earlier) under the Whirlpool brand. In 1950 the company changed its name to Whirlpool following the success of the product and introduced its first automatic dryer.

During the 1950s and 1960s Whirlpool became a full-line appliance manufacturer while continuing as Sears' principal Kenmore appliance supplier. In 1955 the company bought Seeger Refrigerator Company and the stove and air-conditioning interests of RCA. Three years later it made its first investment in Multibras Eletrodomésticos an appliance maker in Brazil. (It has increased that investment over the years.) Other purchases included the gas refrigeration and ice-maker manufacturing facilities of Servel (1958); a majority interest in Heil-Quaker makers of central heaters and space heaters (1964); Sears' major television set supplier Warwick Electronics (1966); and 33% of Canadian appliance maker John Inglis Company (1969). It made a deal with Sony in 1973 for the distribution of Whirlpool-brand products in Japan. Whirlpool sold its TV manufacturing business to SANYO of Japan three years later.

Between 1981 and 1991 despite a static US market Whirlpool's sales tripled to almost $6.6 billion. In 1986 the firm bought top-end appliance manufacturer KitchenAid (from Dart and Kraft) and 65% of Italian cooling compressor manufacturer Aspera. Also that year it sold its Heil-Quaker central heating business. David Whitwam was appointed CEO in 1987. Whirlpool took over total ownership of Inglis in 1990.

The company formed Whirlpool Europe a joint venture with Philips Electronics in 1989; in 1991 it bought out Philips. Two years later Whirlpool took control of appliance marketer SAGAD of Argentina and entered a joint venture with Slovakia's Tatramat (which it bought out in 1994).

Whirlpool acquired control of Kelvinator of India in 1994 and formed a joint venture in China with Shenzhen Petrochemical Holdings in 1995 to produce air conditioners. The following year Whirlpool merged its Whirlpool Washing Machines and Kelvinator of India companies to form Whirlpool of India. The company's European division plunged into the red when competition and a recession kept consumers away from its higher-priced appliances.

In 1997 Whirlpool initiated a restructuring (due to losses from its foreign operations) that included plant closures and substantial layoffs (as much as 10% of its workforce). The next year Whirlpool sold its appliance financing subsidiary to Transamerica. The company also began using a new more efficient product development model in 1998 similar to one used in the auto industry. In 2000 Whirlpool launched the Cielo Bath line of jetted tubs and in 2001 it introduced the Calypso dishwasher and the Duet washer and dryer.

Another global restructuring plan swept through the company in 2000 resulting in significant pretax charges ($373 million incurred in 2001 and 2002) and the elimination of about 6000 employees by October 2003.

In February 2002 Whirlpool bought the remaining 51% of Vitromatic it didn't already own. (Vitromatic —the second-largest appliance manufacturer in Mexico —is now called Whirlpool Mexico.) In March the company purchased 95% of Polar Poland's second-largest appliance maker.

Whirlpool introduced Gladiator GarageWorks (modular storage systems for the garage) and Polara (the first electric range with cooking and refrigeration capabilities) in 2002.

Whirlpool acquired Maytag in early 2006 for about $1.9 billion. The deal added several top brands to its already bulging portfolio including Admiral Amana Jenn-Air Magic Chef and of course the eponymous Maytag. Once the dust settled Whirlpool sold several businesses including Dixie-Narco the Amana commercial business its Hoover unit to Techtronic Industries and its Jade unit to Middleby Corporation. Buying Maytag also spurred Whirlpool to streamline operations and purge staff. In 2006 it laid off some 4500 employees consolidated duplicate functions related to administration and manufacturing and shuttered some offices including a Maytag research and development center based in Newton Illinois. Whirlpool shuttered Maytag's Iowa-based administrative offices and moved them to Michigan and other locations. The company cut 700 jobs at several Tennessee plants the following year.

In 2007 Whirlpool acquired a minority stake in Elica Group in its effort to extend its reach into the global air ventilation market.

The company formed a 50-50 joint venture in 2008 with China's Hisense-Kelon Electrical Holdings to make and sell home appliances there.

In June 2010 Whirlpool closed its refrigerator factory in Evansville Indiana; some 1100 US jobs were lost as a result of the move.

EXECUTIVES

Senior Vice President Global Human Resources, David A (Dave) Binkley
Vice President Supply Chain North American Region, Brian Hancock
Executive Vice President and President of Whirlpool Europe Middle East and Africa, Esther Galindo
Vice President Customer And Appliance Care, Kathy Nelson
Chairman and CEO, Jeff M. Fettig, age 57, $1,444,375 total compensation
Senior Vice President Global Strategic Sourcing, Mark Brown
President COO and Director, Marc R. Bitzer, age 50, $908,333 total compensation
EVP Global Product Organization, David T. (Dave) Szczupak, age 59, $710,833 total compensation
EVP and CFO, Larry M. Venturelli, age 54, $595,833 total compensation
EVP and President of Whirlpool Europe Middle East and Africa, Esther Berrozpe Galindo, age 45
EVP and President Latin America, Jo o Carlos Brega, age 51
President Whirlpool U.S. Operations, Joseph T. Liotine, age 42
Vice President Operations, Tom Egan
Corporate Vice President and Treasurer, Blair Clark
Vice President Marketing, Andrew (Andy) Batson
Vice President Of Marketing, Shantanu Dasgupta
Vice President Information Technology, Randy Fife
National Sales Manager Jenn Air, Jeff O'malley
National Account Manager, Paula Saul
Vice President Operations and Technology Refrigeration, Davide Castiglioni
Assistant Vice President Networking Security, Carrick Jay
National Sales Manager, Gary Hubbard
Vice President Manager Director, Melissa Little
Senior Vice President of Development, Marek Kaszuba
Vice President Integrated Supply Chain and Quality, Jim Keppler
National Account Manager, Chris Ridout
Vice President of Human Resources, Sarthak Raychaudhuri

Vice President North America Procurement, Elizabeth Door
Vice President Of Finance, Tom Fowler
Vice President Information Services, Nancy Berendsen
Senior Vice President Ad Sales, Romi Jatte
Vice President and Associate General Counsel Global Legal Operations, Tom Schwyn
Assistant Vice President Operations, Jeanne Pavlic
Vice President Corporate Innovation and Information Systems, Jay Michael Berendsen
National Sales Manager, Robert (Bob) Schneider
National Sales Manager, Erin Brown
Senior Vice President Global Sourcing, John (Jack) Miller
Corporate Vice President Strategic Competency Creation, Nancy Tennant
Executive Vice President Global Product Organizati, Dave Szczupak
Information Technology Management: Executive Vice President Senior Vice President, Mrutyunjaya Rao
Vice President General Manager, Robert Hardin
National Sales Manager, Tom Kibler
Vice President Global Human Resources, David Binkleysenior
Vice President Global Quality, Ken Kleinhample
Vice President Human Resources, Carey Martin
Division Vice President, Kenny Thompson
Vice President For Human Resources Solutions, Abby Luersman
Vice President Global Application Development, James Shrimp
Vice President and General Manager India Operations, Shahzad Akhtar
Vice President Global Engineering, Inara Shields
Vice President Global Product Sourcing, Jack Sperbeck
Vice President Quality, J D Rapp
Vice President Sales, Tamal Saha
Vice President Technology and Engineering, Philip Pejovich
Corporate Vice President Finance Project Management Office, Ted A Dosch
Vice President general Manager Sales and Customer Care North America, Gregory McManus
Vice President Manufacturing, Al Holaday
National Sales Manager, Dick Ruel
Vice President of Business Development, Joe Igoe
Vice President, Alejandro Quiroz
Senior Vice President Sales, Paul Bognar
Secretary To Haney, Marg Pecoraro
Board Member, John Liu
Secretary, John (Jack) Geddes
Assistant Secretary, Bridget Quinn
Board Member, Celina Loose
Treasurer, Margaret McLeod
Auditors: Ernst & Young LLP

LOCATIONS

HQ: Whirlpool Corp
2000 North M-63, Benton Harbor, MI 49022-2692
Phone: 269 923-5000
Web: www.whirlpoolcorp.com

2014 Sales

	$ mil.	% of total
North America	10,634	53
Latin America	4,686	23
Europe the Middle East & Africa	3,905	20
Asia	816	4
Other/eliminations (169) —		
Total	**19,872**	**100**

PRODUCTS/OPERATIONS

Selected Whirlpool Brands
Cooking appliances
Amana
Brastemp

Consul
Jenn-Air
KitchenAid
Roper
Whirlpool
Dishwashers
Amana
Brastemp
Consul
Jenn-Air
KitchenAid
Maytag
Whirlpool
Freezers
Amana
Laundry appliances
Amana
Brastemp
Consul
Maytag
Roper
Whirlpool
Mixers
KitchenAid
Refrigerators
Amana
Consul
Jenn-Air
KitchenAid
Maytag
Whirlpool
Small household appliances
Brastemp
Consul
Jenn-Air
KitchenAid
Maytag
Whirlpool

2014 Sales

	% of total
Laundry Appliances	27
Refrigerators & Freezers	28
Cooking Appliances	18
Other	27
Total	**100**

COMPETITORS

BSH Bosch und Siemens	Haier Group
Hausgerⓞte	Hitachi
Candy Group	Indesit
Daewoo Electronics	LG Electronics
Electrolux	Panasonic Corp
Electrolux Home	SANYO
Appliances China	Samsung Electronics
Fisher & Paykel	America
Appliances Holdings	Sears Holdings
Goodman Manufacturing	Sharp Corp.
Gree Electrical	Sub-Zero
Appliances	Viking Range
GuangDong Midea	

HISTORICAL FINANCIALS

Company Type: Public

Income Statement

FYE: December 31

	REVENUE ($ mil.)	NET INCOME ($ mil.)	NET PROFIT MARGIN	EMPLOYEES
12/15	20,891	783	3.7%	97,000
12/14	19,872	650	3.3%	100,000
12/13	18,769	827	4.4%	69,000
12/12	18,143	401	2.2%	68,000
12/11	18,666	390	2.1%	68,231
Annual Growth	**2.9%**	**19.0%**	**—**	**9.2%**

2015 Year-End Financials

Debt ratio: 21.03%	No. of shares (mil.): 77
Return on equity: 16.27%	Dividends
Cash ($ mil.): 772	Yield: 2.3%
Current ratio: 0.95	Payout: 40.3%
Long-term debt ($ mil.): 3,470	Market value ($ mil.): 11,341

	STOCK PRICE ($) FY Close	P/E High/Low		PER SHARE ($) Earnings	Dividends	Book Value
12/15	146.87	22	14	9.83	3.45	61.42
12/14	193.74	23	15	8.17	2.88	62.66
12/13	156.86	15	10	10.24	2.38	63.60
12/12	101.75	20	9	5.06	2.00	54.33
12/11	47.45	18	9	4.99	1.93	54.69
Annual Growth	**32.6%**	—	—	**18.5%**	**15.6%**	**2.9%**

Whole Foods Market, Inc.

With food and other items that are free of pesticides preservatives sweeteners and cruelty Whole Foods Market knows more about guiltless eating and shopping than most retailers. The world's #1 natural foods chain by far —now that it has digested its main rival Wild Oats Markets —the company operates more than 430 stores throughout the US Canada and the UK. The stores emphasize perishable and prepared products which account for about two-thirds of sales. Whole Foods Market offers some 4400 items in four lines of private-label products (such as the premium Whole Foods line). Founded in Austin Texas in 1980 Whole Foods Market pioneered the supermarket concept in natural and organic foods retailing.

HISTORY

With a $10000 loan from his father John Mackey started SaferWay Natural Foods in Austin Texas in 1978. Despite struggling Mackey dreamed of opening a larger supermarket-sized natural foods store. Two years later SaferWay merged with Clarksville Natural Grocery and Whole Foods Market was born. Led by Mackey that year it opened an 11000-sq.-ft. supermarket in a counterculture hotbed of Austin. The store was an instant success and a second store was added 18 months later in suburban Austin.

The company slowly expanded in Texas opening or buying stores in Houston in 1984 and Dallas in 1986. Whole Foods expanded into Louisiana in 1988 with the purchase of like-named Whole Food Co. a single New Orleans store owned by Peter Roy (who served as the company's president from 1993 to 1998). Sticking to university towns Whole Foods added another store in California the next year and acquired Wellspring Grocery (two stores North Carolina) in 1991. In 1992 it debuted its first private-label products under the Whole Foods name. Seeking capital to expand even more the company raised $23 million by going public in early 1992 with 12 stores.

Every competitor in the fragmented health foods industry became a potential acquisition and the chain began growing rapidly. In 1992 Whole Foods bought the six-store Bread & Circus chain in New England. The next year it added Mrs. Gooch's Natural Foods Markets (seven stores in the Los Angeles area). Its biggest acquisition came in 1996 when it bought Fresh Fields the second-largest US natural foods chain (22 stores on the East Coast and in Chicago). Although the purchase hurt profits in 1996 sales surpassed $1 billion for the first time in fiscal 1997 as Whole Foods neared 70 stores. In 1997 it introduced the less-expensive 365 private label and acquired the Gran-

ary Market (Monterey California) and Bread of Life (two stores South Florida) natural foods supermarkets.

Capitalizing on the growing popularity of nutraceuticals (natural supplements with benefits similar to pharmaceuticals) the company paid $146 million in 1997 for Amrion a maker of nutraceuticals and other nutritional supplements (merged with subsidiary WholePeople.com in 2000). It capped the year by buying coffee roaster Allegro Coffee. (Both companies are based in Boulder Colorado home of its former main rival the smaller Wild Oats.) Also in 1997 Whole Foods acquired the six-store Merchant of Vino natural foods and wine shop chain to foster the development of its wine departments.

In 1998 Whole Foods opened its first store in Boulder —a 39000-sq.-ft. superstore with amenities such as a juice bar and a prepared foods section. At year's end Roy resigned as president and was replaced by Chris Hitt. In 1999 Whole Foods bought four-store Boston-area chain Nature's Heartland.

In 2000 Whole Foods merged its online operations (wholefoods.com) with its direct marketing and nutritional supplement unit (Amrion) to form Wholepeople.com. Later that year the company merged Wholepeople.com with lifestyle marketing firm Gaiam; Whole Foods received a minority stake in Gaiam and started selling food online through Gaiam.com.

Hitt resigned in mid-2001 and Mackey took over his duties. Later that year Whole Foods acquired the three upscale Harry's Farmers Market stores in Atlanta; the sale did not include the Harry's In A Hurry stores which later shut down.

In 2002 Whole Foods crossed the border into Canada. Its first foreign store opened in downtown Toronto that May.

Mackey was named Entrepreneur of the Year in 2003 by consulting firm Ernst & Young. That year Whole Foods acquired Select Fish a Seattle-based seafood processor and distributor and opened a seafood distribution facility in Atlanta.

In 2004 Whole Foods opened a 59000-sq.-ft. store in the new Time Warner Center in Manhattan. The new store which includes a 248-seat cafe sushi bar wine shop and gourmet bakery is the largest supermarket in New York City. That year the company acquired the UK organic-food retailer Fresh & Wild for $38 million.

To support its rapid growth in 2004 Whole Foods Market expanded its number of operating regions from eight to 10 by separating the Southwest region into the Southwest and Rocky Mountain regions and the Northern Pacific region into the Northern California and Pacific Northwest region. The company announced the opening of its first Gluten-Free Bakehouse a dedicated gluten-free baking facility located outside Raleigh North Carolina. Overall the company opened 12 new stores in 2004.

In January 2005 Whole Foods launched the Animal Compassion Foundation an independent non-profit organization dedicated to the compassionate treatment of livestock. The company moved that month to its new corporate headquarters across the street from its old location in downtown Austin. Its new flagship store opened its doors in March at the same location. In October Whole Foods increased its number of operating regions from 10 to 11 by separating the North Atlantic region into the North Atlantic and Tri-State regions. Overall in fiscal 2005 the company opened a dozen new stores including its first in Nebraska and Ohio. In 2006 the company acquired a store in Portland Maine and converted it to the Whole Foods Market banner.

In August 2007 Whole Foods acquired its main competitor —Boulder Colorado-based Wild Oats

Markets —in a deal valued at about $565 million (plus $106 million in debt). In early October the company sold 35 Henry's Farmers Market and Sun Harvest stores to a subsidiary of Los Angeles-based Smart & Final for about $166 million. The stores in California and Texas were acquired with Wild Oats.

The company launched a bi-monthly magazine called Whole Foods Market Magazine at its midwestern stores in 2008. On the heels of its disappointing third-quarter results in August 2008 shares of the company's stock fell to a six-year low and Whole Foods suspended its dividend. Blaming the poor economy the company announced the layoffs of some 50 employees at its Austin headquarters in August 2008. Overall in fiscal 2008 the company introduced about 300 new private-label items.

For the first time in its 29-year history Whole Foods reported negative same-store sales in the quarter ended December 2008 as traffic in its stores fell.

In March 2009 the company reached a settlement in its long-running dispute with the FTC over its acquisition of Wild Oats in 2007. Whole Foods agreed to sell 32 stores including 19 Wild Oats locations that had already been closed. In exchange the FTC dropped its crusade to undo the merger. In December 2009 John Elstrott was named chairman of Whole Foods Market after Mackey voluntarily relinquished the chairmanship which he had held since 1980. In May 2010 Walter Robb formerly co-president of the company was promoted to co-CEO of Whole Foods a title he now shares with Mackey.

EXECUTIVES

EVP and CFO, Glenda J. Flanagan, age 62, $472,350 total compensation
Co-CEO, John P. Mackey, age 62, $1 total compensation
President and COO, A. C. Gallo, age 62, $472,350 total compensation
President Florida Region, Juan Nu ±ez, age 57
Co-CEO, Walter E. Robb, age 62, $472,350 total compensation
EVP Operations, David Lannon, age 49, $472,350 total compensation
VP Purchasing Midwest Division, Jeff Turnas, age 43
President North East Region, Christina Minardi, age 49
President Southwest Region, Mark Dixon, age 53
President Southern Pacific Region, Patrick Bradley, age 55
President Mid-Atlantic Region, Scott Allshouse, age 53
VP North California Region, Joe Rogoff
President Rocky Mountain Region, Bill Jordan
President Midwest Region, Michael Bashaw
President North Atlantic Region, Laura Derba
Global VP and CIO, Jason Buechel
President South Region, Omar Gaye
President Northern California Region, Rob Twyman
EVP Operations, Kenneth (Ken) Meyer, age 46, $472,350 total compensation
EVP Growth and Business Development, James (Jim) Sud, age 62, $472,350 total compensation
Global VP Marketing and Communications, Jeannine D'Addario
Chairman, John B. Elstrott, age 67
Auditors: Ernst & Young LLP

LOCATIONS

HQ: Whole Foods Market, Inc.
550 Bowie Street, Austin, TX 78703
Phone: 512 477-4455   **Fax:** 512 477-1069
Web: www.wholefoodsmarket.com

2015 Sales

	% of total
US	97
Canada & UK	3
Total	**100**

2015 Stores

	No.
US	
California	80
Massachusetts	30
Texas	28
Illinois	25
Florida	24
Colorado	20
New York	16
New Jersey	14
North Carolina	12
Arizona	11
Virginia	11
Other States	141
Canada	10
UK	9
Total	**431**

PRODUCTS/OPERATIONS

2015 Sales

	% of total
Non-perishables	33
Prepared foods & bakery	19
Other perishables	48
Total	**100**

Selected Product Categories

Bakery
Body care
Educational products
Floral
Grocery
Household products
Meat and poultry
Nutritional supplements
Pet products
Prepared foods
Produce
Seafood
Specialty (beer wine cheese)
Textiles

COMPETITORS

AMCON Distributing	Minyard Group
Ahold U.S.A.	NBTY
Albertsons	Natural Grocers by
Arden Group	Vitamin Cottage
Bristol Farms	Publix
Citarella	SUPERVALU
Costco Wholesale	Safeway
Delhaize America	Shaw's
Earth Fare	Sobeys
Fiesta Mart	Sprouts
Forever Living	Tesco
GNC	Trader Joe's
H-E-B	United Supermarkets
J Sainsbury	Wal-Mart
Kroger	Winn-Dixie
Loblaw	Wm Morrison
Marks & Spencer	Supermarkets

HISTORICAL FINANCIALS

Company Type: Public

Income Statement

FYE: September 27

	REVENUE ($ mil.)	NET INCOME ($ mil.)	NET PROFIT MARGIN	EMPLOYEES
09/15	15,389	536	3.5%	90,900
09/14	14,194	579	4.1%	87,200
09/13	12,917	551	4.3%	78,400
09/12	11,698	465	4.0%	72,700
09/11	10,107	342	3.4%	64,200
Annual Growth	11.1%	11.8%	—	9.1%

2015 Year-End Financials

Debt ratio: 1.13%
Return on equity: 14.18%
Cash ($ mil.): 237
Current ratio: 1.23
Long-term debt ($ mil.): 62
No. of shares (mil.): 348
Dividends
  Yield: 0.0%
  Payout: 26.3%
Market value ($ mil.): 10,851

	STOCK PRICE ($) FY Close	P/E High/Low	PER SHARE ($) Earnings	Dividends	Book Value
09/15	31.10	38 21	1.48	0.39	10.80
09/14	37.67	42 23	1.56	0.48	10.58
09/13	58.33	71 34	1.47	1.40	10.41
09/12	97.40	78 49	1.26	0.28	10.25
09/11	68.20	74 35	0.97	0.20	8.36
Annual Growth (17.8%)		— —	11.3%	18.2%	6.6%

Williams Cos Inc (The)

Auditors: Ernst & Young LLP

LOCATIONS

HQ: Williams Cos Inc (The)
One Williams Center, Tulsa, OK 74172-0172
Phone: 918 573-2000
Web: www.williams.com

HISTORICAL FINANCIALS

Company Type: Public

Income Statement

FYE: December 31

	REVENUE ($ mil.)	NET INCOME ($ mil.)	NET PROFIT MARGIN	EMPLOYEES
12/14	7,637	2,114	27.7%	6,742
12/13	6,860	430	6.3%	4,909
12/12	7,486	859	11.5%	4,639
12/11	7,930	376	4.7%	4,293
12/10	9,616	(1,097)	—	5,022
Annual Growth	(5.6%)	—		7.6%

2014 Year-End Financials

Debt ratio: 41.32%
Return on equity: 30.99%
Cash ($ mil.): 240
Current ratio: 0.74
Long-term debt ($ mil.): 20,888
No. of shares (mil.): 747
Dividends
  Yield: 4.3%
  Payout: 77.0%
Market value ($ mil.): 33,570

	STOCK PRICE ($) FY Close	P/E High/Low	PER SHARE ($) Earnings	Dividends	Book Value
12/14	44.94	20 13	2.92	1.96	11.75
12/13	38.57	61 50	0.62	1.44	7.12
12/12	32.74	26 19	1.37	1.20	6.98
12/11	33.02	52 36	0.63	0.78	3.03
12/10	24.72	— —	(1.88)	0.49	12.46
Annual Growth 16.1%		— —	—	41.7%	(1.5%)

Wilshire Bancorp Inc

Wilshire Bancorp is the holding company for Wilshire Bank where ethnic minorities are the banking majority. Based in the Koreatown section of Los Angeles the commercial bank boasts $4.2 billion in assets nearly 35 branches and a handful of lending offices mainly across California but also in New Jersey New York and Texas. Wilshire Bank targets small to midsized minority-owned businesses and ethnic groups underserved by many national banking institutions. Beyond standard deposit services (including checking and savings accounts CDs and IRAs) the bank also offers Small Business Administration (SBA) real estate and consumer loans and import/export financing services. Korean-American rival BBCN Bancorp agreed to acquire Wilshire Bancorp for $1 billion in late 2015.

Change in Company OwnershipIn December 2015 BBCN Bancorp the largest Korean-American bank in the US agreed to buy Wilshire Bancorp (the second-largest US Korean-American bank) for $1 billion in an all stock offer. Scheduled for completion in mid-2016 the combined banks would control $12.3 billion in assets $9.6 billion in loans and $10 billion in deposits effectively creating the seventh-largest bank in California and the largest Korean-American bank (and only super-regional Korean-American bank) in the US ahead of rival Hamni Financial. In addition BBCN shareholders would own 59% of the new company while Wilshire shareholders would own the remaining 41% after the deal closed. OperationsWilshire operates three main business segments. Banking Operations relates to the bank's commercial consumer and real estate loans. When excluding SBA-related loans this segment generates more than 70% of the bank's revenue. About 75% of the bank's loan portfolio consists of commercial real estate loans and 15% is comprised of commercial and industrial business loans. The rest of the portfolio includes home mortgages construction and consumer loans.SBA loans (which involve 25% of the bank's total loan assets) bring in nearly 20% of the bank's revenue. Most of this revenue is generated in interest income but because a portion of these loans are federally backed and guaranteed by the Small Business Administration Wilshire generates some income by selling the guaranteed portion of these loans in a secondary marketing for a premium. The bank's Trade Finance Services segment writes letters of credit or arrangements between businesses who participate in international sales of goods. The bank collects around 1% of its revenue from this segment in the form of fees.Overall the company generated 76% of its total revenue from interest and fee income on loans during 2014 with another 4% of revenue coming from interest on investment securities. Wilshire also made 7% of its revenue from net gains on loan sales 6% from service charges on deposit accounts and 3% of its revenue from loan-related servicing fees. Geographic ReachWilshire boasts nearly 35 branches in the US about two-thirds of which are located in California. The remaining branches are located in Texas New Jersey and in the greater New York City metro area. The bank's four loan production offices which specialize in small business administration (SBA) loans are located in California Colorado Georgia and Washington.Sales and MarketingThe company's marketing activities include media advertisements promotional gifts for customers and deposit campaign promotions. The bank spent $2.19 million on advertising and promotions in 2014 compared to $2.39 million and $1.74 million in 2013 and 2012 respectively.Financial PerformanceWilshire Bancorp's revenues and profits have trended higher in more recent years thanks to new loan business from acquisitions and branch office expansion. The bank's revenue jumped by 30% to $205 million in 2014 as interest income ballooned from loans acquired from BankAsiana and Saehan. The bank also enjoyed higher net gains on loan sales for the year particularly related to the sale of SBA loans. Service charge income also grew

thanks to more deposit account business from BankAsiana and Saehan.Higher revenue and lower loan loss provisions in 2014 also drove Wilshire's net income higher by 30% to $59 million. The bank's operating cash declined by 41% to $90.8 million however mostly due to non-cash adjustments related to net proceeds from the sale of the bank's loans held for sale.StrategyRather than extend services into brokerage or investment products Wilshire in 2015 reiterated its growth strategy of adding more branch locations in its primary markets (such as in Southern California) expanding days and hours of operation and offering new deposit and loan products. Opening new branches and purchasing other banks has been an easy way for the bank to hit its expansion goals and grow business. Expanding its reach beyond its core market in California Wilshire opened its first branch in Georgia in 2015 after opening a branch in Houston Texas in late 2014. Through acquisitions in 2013 the bank picked up 13 new branches which expanded its customer base and presence in the key East Coast and Southern California markets and added $550 million in new loan business. In addition even though Wilshire's competitive advantage has been to cater to a Korean-American and multi-ethnic audience the bank is broadening its marketing scope to appeal beyond these audiences.Mergers and AcquisitionsIn late 2013 Wilshire acquired two major banks which broadened its exposure to target markets. In October the bank purchased BankAsiana picking up three branches in the New York/New Jersey area (and doubling the bank's presence in the area) and adding $204.1 million in total assets from the deal. In November Wilshire bought Saehan Bancorp which grew its total assets by $589.1 million and added 10 branches in Southern California to its branch network.

EXECUTIVES

EVP and Chief Operations Administrator, Elaine S. Jeon, age 55
EVP and CFO, Gunho (Alex) Ko, age 49, $236,250 total compensation
President CEO and Director, Jae Whan (JW) Yoo
EVP and Chief Legal and Human Resources Officer, Lisa Pai
EVP and Chief Credit Officer, Peter Koh
Vice President Finance, Lynette Olson
Chairman, Steven S. Koh, age 70
Auditors: Crowe Horwath LLP

LOCATIONS

HQ: Wilshire Bancorp Inc
3200 Wilshire Blvd., Los Angeles, CA 90010
Phone: 213 387-3200   **Fax:** 213 427-6584
Web: www.wilshirebank.com

PRODUCTS/OPERATIONS

2011 Sales

	$ mil.	% of total
Interest		
Loans including fees	121	77
Investment securities	7	4
Federal funds sold	1.	1
Noninterest		
Service charges on deposit accounts	12	8
Net gain on sale of loans	5	4
Loan-related servicing fees	4	3
Other	4	3
Adjustments	(3.1)	-
Total	**153**	**100**

COMPETITORS

BBCN	City National
Bank of America	Comerica

Bank of the West	East West Bancorp
Broadway Financial	Hanmi Financial
Cathay General Bancorp	MUFG Americas Holdings
Citibank	U.S. Bancorp

HISTORICAL FINANCIALS

Company Type: Public

Income Statement

FYE: December 31

	ASSETS ($ mil.)	NET INCOME ($ mil.)	INCOME AS % OF ASSETS	EMPLOYEES
12/14	4,155	59	1.4%	527
12/13	3,617	45	1.3%	547
12/12	2,750	92	3.4%	415
12/11	2,696	(30)	—	382
12/10	2,970	(34)	—	405
Annual Growth	**8.8%**	**—**	**—**	**6.8%**

2014 Year-End Financials

Debt ratio: 5.34% No. of shares (mil.): 78
Return on equity: 12.71% Dividends
Cash ($ mil.): 241   Yield: 1.9%
Current ratio: —   Payout: 28.5%
Long-term debt ($ mil.): — Market value ($ mil.): 793

	STOCK PRICE ($) FY Close	P/E High/Low		PER SHARE ($) Earnings	Dividends	Book Value
12/14	10.13	16	12	0.75	0.20	6.25
12/13	10.93	18	9	0.63	0.06	5.63
12/12	5.87	5	3	1.31	0.00	4.80
12/11	3.63	—	—	(0.61)	0.00	4.34
12/10	7.62	—	—	(1.30)	0.15	7.77
Annual Growth	**7.4%**	**—**	**—**	**—**	**7.5%**	**(5.3%)**

Windstream Holdings Inc

Instead of relying on the prevailing breeze to deliver its services Windstream makes use of more tangible connections such as fiber optics and copper wire. The company provides communications and technology services to business and residential customers in the US through a network of fiber and from 27 data centers. Business services include multi-site networking Internet access cloud computing colocation online backup and other managed services. Along with Internet and voice for its residential customers it also offers video services. Call connection and backhaul services are offered to phone companies and wireless carriers.

Operations

Windstream's enterprise and small business segment provides 51% of revenue with its consumer unit bringing in 22% of revenue and the carrier business accounting for 13%. The remainder is from wholesale other and product sales.

Geographic Reach

Windstream serves business and residential customers across 47 US states and the District of Columbia.

Sales and Marketing

The company has about 200 business sales offices throughout the US and more than 2300 sales employees focused on meeting the needs of the company's business customers. Windstream's consumer sales and marketing strategy is focused on driving top line revenue performance through bundled product sales and value-added account revenue growth. The company's advertising expenses totaled $96.8 million $79.3 million and $99.5 million in 2014 2013 and 2012 respectively.

Financial Performance

After peaking in 2012 Windstream's revenues decreased in 2013 (down 8%) and in 2014 (down 3%). The 2014 drop was evident across all the company's segments none of which improved over the previous year. Enterprise and small business was near even ticking down 0.19% while the consumer business dropped nearly 2% and carrier was off about 6%. The company attributed lower revenue to voice line losses declining demand for dedicated copper-based circuits and the impact of intercarrier compensation reform.

Windstream's bottom line showed a loss of about $40 million in 2014 after posting a profit of $241 million in 2013. Higher expenses helped drive the company to the 2014 loss. Cash flow from operations nudged 3% lower in 2014 from 2013.

Strategy

Technology advances have made its consumer business prospects increasingly difficult as wireless carriers have siphoned off wireline customers and cable companies have been able to effectively woo voice and Internet customers. The expanding need for data services from the enterprise customer side has become the company's new focus.

The company in 2015 spun off its fiber copper and other assets into an independent publicly traded real estate investment trust called CS&L. The move is to help the company speed up investments in its network and reduce debt. Windstream leases the infrastructure assets it formerly owned from CS&L.

To reach new customers Windstream has received funding through the American Recovery and Reinvestment Act of 2009 and the Connect American Fund to expand broadband services to rural areas with little or no broadband. The work enables Windstream to build and maintain its broadband network while bringing services to underserved areas.

In 2014 the company opened new data centers in Chicago and in Charlotte North Carolina.To cut costs in 2014 Windstream reduced its workforce by 400 to increase operational efficiency and produce annualized savings of $20 million.

Mergers and Acquisitions

In 2014 the company acquired Business Only Broadband Chicago-based fixed wireless provider with operations in Chicago New York City northern New Jersey and Milwaukee.

HISTORY

Early History

Windstream was formed in 2006 through the combination of ALLTEL's wireline business with VALOR Communications Group after Little Rock-based ALLTEL turned its full attention to wireless communications services. Its decision to spin off its wireline operations came after several acquisitions of smaller wireless carriers including Western Wireless and Midwest Wireless both in 2005; and its purchase of First Cellular the following year. With its acquisition of VALOR and subsequent spin-off of its wireline operations as Windstream ALLTEL became a purely wireless communications service provider.

In 2007 Windstream boosted its subscriber numbers by about 160000 phone lines through its acquisition of North Carolina-based CT Communications for $584 million. Later that year the company spun off its publishing business Windstream Yellow Pages to affiliates of Welsh Carson Anderson & Stowe for about $500 million. In 2008 it sold its wireless business in North Carolina to AT&T Mobility for about $57 million.

For the next several years Windstream grew through numerous acquisitions.

EXECUTIVES

EVP General Counsel and Secretary, John P. Fletcher, age 49, $511,538 total compensation

President and CEO, Anthony W. (Tony) Thomas, age 43, $538,461 total compensation

EVP Engineering and CTO, Randy Nicklas

President Enterprise, J. David Works, $456,923 total compensation

CFO and Treasurer, Bob Gunderman, $289,823 total compensation

EVP Operations, Mark Faris

President Carrier, Mike Shippey

Chairman, Jeffrey T. Hinson, age 61

Auditors: PricewaterhouseCoopers LLP

LOCATIONS

HQ: Windstream Holdings Inc
4001 Rodney Parham Road, Little Rock, AR 72212
Phone: 501 748-7000
Web: www.windstream.com

PRODUCTS/OPERATIONS

2014 Sales

	$ mil.	% of total
Service		
Enterprise and small business	2,994	51
Consumer	1,267	22
Carrier	734	13
Wholesale	432	7
Other	219	4
Product	181	3
Total	**5,829**	**100**

COMPETITORS

AT&T	FullNet Communications
CenturyLink	Momentum Telecom
Cox Communications	Onvoy Voice Services
Crown Castle International	Sprint Communications
Equinix	Verizon

HISTORICAL FINANCIALS

Company Type: Public

Income Statement

FYE: December 31

	REVENUE ($ mil.)	NET INCOME ($ mil.)	NET PROFIT MARGIN	EMPLOYEES
12/14	5,829	(39)	—	12,626
12/13	5,988	241	4.0%	13,434
12/12	6,156	168	2.7%	13,787
12/11	4,285	172	4.0%	14,638
12/10	3,712	310	8.4%	10,086
Annual Growth	**11.9%**	—	—	**5.8%**

2014 Year-End Financials

Debt ratio: 68.05%	No. of shares (mil.): 100
Return on equity: (-7.42%)	Dividends
Cash ($ mil.): 27	Yield: 0.6%
Current ratio: 0.49	Payout: —
Long-term debt ($ mil.): 7,934	Market value ($ mil.): 828

	STOCK PRICE ($) FY Close	P/E High/Low		PER SHARE ($) Earnings	Dividends	Book Value
12/14	8.24	—	—	(0.42)	6.00	2.24
12/13	7.98	4	3	2.40	6.00	8.46
12/12	8.28	7	5	1.68	6.00	11.27
12/11	11.74	7	5	1.98	6.00	15.33
12/10	13.94	4	3	3.96	6.00	9.88
Annual Growth	(12.3%) (31.0%)	—	—	—	(0.0%)	

Wintrust Financial Corp. (IL)

Wintrust Financial is a holding company engaged in personal and commercial banking wealth management and specialty lending services primarily in the metropolitan Chicago and Milwaukee areas. With assets of more than $19 billion it operates about 15 subsidiary banks (most bear the name of the community they serve) with more than 120 branches in all. The banks offer traditional deposit services and emphasize business and commercial real estate lending which accounts for about half of the company's loan portfolio. Specifically Wintrust's banks target small business customers. Some of Wintrust's banks also provide niche lending for homeowners associations medical practices franchisees and municipalities.Geographic ReachWintrust's banks operate through some 125 banking facilities the majority of which are owned. It also owns 182 automatic teller machines the majority of which are housed at banking locations. The banking facilities are located in communities throughout the Chicago metropolitan area and southern Wisconsin.OperationsWintrust's nonbank subsidiaries include First Insurance Funding which provides financing for commercial insurance and life insurance premiums. In 2012 Wintrust expanded its premium funding business into Canada with the acquisition of Macquarie Premium Funding Inc which was a subsidiary of Macquarie Group. The deal marked Wintrust's first international venture.Wintrust's wealth management arm offers financial planning and brokerage services through a trio of companies bearing the Wayne Hummer name. On the banking side Wintrust has developed its community-based franchise through the formation of nine de novo (or new) banks new branch openings and acquisitions. Sales and MarketingThe bank's customers include individuals small to mid-sized businesses local governmental units and institutional clients residing primarily in the banks' local service areas.Financial PerformanceWintrust has enjoyed unprecedented growth over the last two years as revenues reached a record-setting $853 million for both 2012 and 2013. Profits also surged 23% from $111 million in 2012 to peak at $137 million in 2013.Over the years the company has been helped by an increase in interest income. It has also experienced a decrease in interest expenses as a result of decreased interest on notes payable and other borrowings. In 2013 its operating cash inflow increased to $321.8 million compared to $268.7 million in 2012 due to a reduced provision for credit losses a decrease in trading securities and brokerage customer receivables and gains on mortgage loans sold.StrategyWintrust increased its loan portfolio excluding covered loans from $11.8 billion at the end of 2012 to $12.9 billion in late 2013. This increase was primarily a result of its commercial banking initiative growth in the premium finance receivables as well as acquisition transactions. The company is focused on making new loans especially in the commercial and commercial real estate sector where opportunities that meet its underwriting standards exist.

EXECUTIVES

Assistant Vice President E Marketing, Michael Limjoco

EVP Technology; President Wintrust Information Technology Services, Lloyd M. Bowden, age 62, $167,333 total compensation

SEVP COO and Treasurer, David A. Dykstra, age 55, $759,167 total compensation

President CEO and Director, Edward J. Wehmer, age 60, $1,100,000 total compensation

EVP and Regional Market Head, Frank J. Burke

EVP and Chief Credit Officer, Richard B. Murphy, age 56, $509,167 total compensation

EVP and Chief Administration Officer, Leona A. Gleason

SVP Finance, David L. Stoehr, age 56, $419,167 total compensation

EVP and Regional Market Head, Timothy S. (Tim) Crane, age 53

EVP Risk Management, John S. Fleshood, age 53, $292,750 total compensation

EVP Wealth Management, Thomas P. (Tom) Zidar

EVP General Counsel and Secretary, Lisa J. Pattis, $446,167 total compensation

EVP and Regional Market Head, David L. Larson

EVP and COO Wintrust Commercial Finance (WCF), Joseph F. Thompson

Senior Vice President Of Marketing, Matthew Doubleday

Vice President, Sue Greffin

Assistant Vice President Compliance, Richard Jankiewicz

Vice President Compliance, Kellie Oostendorp

Executive Vice President, Paul Carlisle

Vice President, Tim Edwards

Vice President, Ursula Moncau

Vice President, Laura Crandall

Vice President, Sharon Hiller

Vice President, Philip Sheridan

Vice President Planning, Mark Dugard

Executive Vice President and Senior Lender St. Charles Bank, Michael (Mel) Trimarco

Senior Vice President Finance Credit Reporting, Mario Nudo

Vice President controller credit Quality, Mark Matsuo

Vice President, Lori Christensen

Vice President, Kelli Lalk

Vice President, Will Knapik

Vice President, Dan Robinson

Vice Presidnet, Rhonda Pokoj

Vice President Treasury Management, Elizabeth (Beth) Krumrey

Vice President, Diane Gorka

Assistant Vice President Treasury Management, Lisa Coduto

Senior Vice President, Joseph Heskett

Assistant Vice President Retail Banking Manager, Tracy Kelly-smoot

Senior Vice President, Jack Myers

Assistant Vice President, Robert Murphy

Vice President International Services Group, Pattie Marshall

Vice President, Patrick (Paddy) Rule

Assistant Vice President, Brett Davis

Vice President, Trey Meers

Assistant Vice President, Jason Girardin

Vice President, Tim Kramer

Vice President Treasury Sales, Jennifer Letourneau

Vice President Credit Officer, Kara Jakusz

Senior Vice President, Darragh Griffin

Assistant Vice President Client Services Manager, Nicole Fasshauer

Vice President Senior Vice President Finance Director, Scott Ernsteen

Vice President Commercial Real Estate Finance, Nick Cannon

Senior Vice President, George Reimnitz

Senior Vice President, John (Jack) Reagan

Vice President Operations, Colleen Toft

Vice President, Kathy Ireland

Vice President, Kristin Keaschall

Executive Vice President Commercial, Tully Kari

Senior Vice President Commercial, Sean Dunn

Assistant Vice President Operations, Paul Rudnicki

Vice President Director Of Training, Karen Moses

Vice President Operations, Kristi Drengacz

Senior Vice President, David Wyent

Vice President, Tom Ormseth

Senior Vice President Chief Cr, Ryan D Witte

Senior Vice President, William (Bill) Robin

Vice President, Mike Masterson

Vice President, Jeff Galus

Vice President, Scott Weichle

Vice President Regulatory Reporting, Anita Chakravarthy

Vice President Credit Administration, Anne Nostrand

Vice President, Sue Socha

Senior Vice President Finance, Barbara Kilian

Senior Vice President Managing Director, Carlos Cardenas

Vice President Commercial Banking, Jenny Wagner

Vice President Corporate Fair Lending Officer, Teresa Handley

Assistant Vice President, Kevin Lichterman

Vice President Professional Practice, Jan Eriksen

Assistant Vice President Branch Management, Rick Butterly

Vice President, Lyle Hangslaben

Vice President Finance, Tim Biggam

Vice President, Kam Kniss

Managed Assets Division Vice President, Christopher (Chris) Swieca

Vice President, Caroline Gonos

Vice President, Bill Jurjovec

Vice President Assistant General Counsel, Ian Burns

Vice President Commercial Real Estate ?? Schaumburg Bank And Trust, Zornitsa Titova

Assistant Vice President, Julie Janssen

Senior Vice President market Risk, Mark Bedigian

Vice President, Janet Koranda

Vice President Managed Assets Division, Hany Morsy

Executive Vice President, Bob Lindeman

Assistant Vice President, Jeffrey (Jeff) Eversden

Vice President, Ctp Collopy

Assistant Vice President Regulatory Reporting, James (Jamie) Oranga

Vice President Operations Manager Private Banker, Nicole Cox

Chairman, Peter D. Crist, age 64

Board Member, Larry Wright

Auditors: Ernst & Young LLP

LOCATIONS

HQ: Wintrust Financial Corp. (IL)
9700 W. Higgins Road, Suite 800, Rosemont, IL 60018
Phone: 847 939-9000 **Fax:** 847 615-4091
Web: www.wintrust.com

PRODUCTS/OPERATIONS

2013 Sales

	$ mil.	% of total
Interest		
Loans including fees	588	70
Securities	37	4
Other	5	-
Noninterest		
Mortgage banking	106	13
Wealth management	63	7
Service charges on deposit accounts	20	2
Fees from covered call options	4	1
Other	27	3
Total	**853**	**100**

Selected Subsidiaries and Affiliates

Banking
Barrington Bank & Trust Company N.A.
Beverly Bank & Trust Company N.A.
Crystal Lake Bank & Trust Company N.A.
Hinsdale Bank & Trust Company
Lake Forest Bank & Trust Company
Libertyville Bank & Trust Company
North Shore Community Bank & Trust Company

Northbrook Bank & Trust Company
Old Plank Trail Community Bank N.A.
Schaumburg Bank & Trust Company N.A.
St. Charles Bank & Trust
State Bank of The Lakes
Town Bank
Village Bank & Trust
Wheaton Bank and Trust Company
Non-banking
Chicago Trust Company N.A.
First Insurance Funding Corporation
Great Lakes Advisors LLC
Tricom Inc. of Milwaukee
Wayne Hummer Asset Management Company
Wayne Hummer Investments LLC
Wayne Hummer Trust Company N.A.
Wintrust Information Technology Services Company
Wintrust Mortgage Corporation (formerly WestAmerica Mortgage Company)

COMPETITORS

Associated Banc-Corp	Harris
Bank of America	JPMorgan Chase
Citigroup	MB Financial
Citizens Financial	Northern Trust
Group	PrivateBancorp
Fifth Third	U.S. Bancorp
First Midwest Bancorp	

HISTORICAL FINANCIALS

Company Type: Public

Income Statement
FYE: December 31

	ASSETS ($ mil.)	NET INCOME ($ mil.)	INCOME AS % OF ASSETS	EMPLOYEES
12/14	20,010	151	0.8%	3,491
12/13	18,097	137	0.8%	3,413
12/12	17,519	111	0.6%	3,269
12/11	15,893	77	0.5%	2,933
12/10	13,980	63	0.5%	2,588
Annual Growth	**9.4%**	**24.3%**	**—**	**7.8%**

2014 Year-End Financials

Debt ratio: 2.70%	No. of shares (mil.): 46
Return on equity: 7.63%	Dividends
Cash ($ mil.): 1,223	Yield: 0.8%
Current ratio: —	Payout: 13.4%
Long-term debt ($ mil.): —	Market value ($ mil.): 2,189

	STOCK PRICE ($) FY Close	P/E High/Low	PER SHARE ($) Earnings	Dividends	Book Value
12/14	46.76	16 14	2.98	0.40	44.22
12/13	46.12	14 10	2.75	0.18	41.21
12/12	36.70	14 10	2.31	0.18	48.96
12/11	28.05	18 12	1.67	0.18	42.90
12/10	33.03	41 26	1.02	0.18	41.20
Annual Growth	**9.1%**	**— —**	**30.7%**	**22.1%**	**1.8%**

WISCONSIN ALUMNI RESEARCH FOUNDATION

LOCATIONS

HQ: WISCONSIN ALUMNI RESEARCH FOUNDATION
614 WALNUT ST FL 13, MADISON, WI 537262336
Phone: 6082632500
Web: WWW.WARF.ORG

HISTORICAL FINANCIALS

Company Type: Private

Income Statement

FYE: June 30

	ASSETS ($ mil.)	NET INCOME ($ mil.)	INCOME AS % OF ASSETS	EMPLOYEES
06/12	2,586	206	8.0%	27
06/11	2,516	259	10.3%	—
06/10	2,198	340	15.5%	—
06/09	1,680	0	—	—
Annual Growth	15.5%	—	—	—

2012 Year-End Financials

Debt ratio: ——
Return on equity: 65.20%
Cash ($ mil.): 9
Current ratio: —
Long-term debt ($ mil.): —

Dividends
Yield: —
Payout: —
Market value ($ mil.): —

World Fuel Services Corp.

You can't fuel all the people all the time but World Fuel Services tries hard to do just that. World Fuel Services provides fuel and services to commercial and corporate aircraft petroleum distributors and ships at more than 8000 locations around the world 24 hours a day. Its aviation fueling business focuses on serving small to midsized air carriers cargo and charter carriers and private aircraft. World Fuel Services also markets fuel and related services to petroleum distributors operating in the land transportation market. All told it has almost 50 offices around the world and does business in more than 200 countries and/or territories.

Geographic Reach

The company has operations in Argentina Australia Brazil Canada Chile Colombia Costa Rica Denmark Germany Gibraltar Greece Hong Kong India Japan Mexico the Netherlands Norway Puerto Rico Russia Singapore South Africa South Korea Sweden Taiwan the UAE the UK and the US. In 2014 the Americas accounted for 57% of World Fuel Services' revenues.

Operations

World Fuel Services operates three distinct fueling segments: Aviation Land and Marine. It maintains its competitive edge by offering a range of support services (such as fuel market analysis flight planning ground-handling services and weather reports) to its aviation and marine customers.

The Aviation segment markets fuel and related products and services to major commercial airlines second and third tier airlines cargo carriers regional and low cost carriers airports fixed based operators corporate fleets fractional operators private aircraft military fleets and to the US and foreign governments.

As part of its Marine fueling services business World Fuel Services markets fuel lubricants and related products and services. It arranges fueling for ships on a brokered basis and extends credit to a global customer base which includes container lines cruise ships dry bulk carriers fishing fleets refrigerated vessels and tankers. The company also provides financial credit for aviation fuels.

The company also offers Land transportation fuel and related services to petroleum distributors retail petroleum operators and other fuels users. It also engages in crude oil marketing activities.

The Aviation segment accounted for 40% World Fuel Services' 2014 revenues; Marine 32%.

Financial Performance

Net revenues have increased consistently year-over-year over the last five years. In 2014 World Fuel Services' revenues grew by 4%.

Revenues from Aviation increased by 7.3% due to higher volumes from new and existing customers partially offset by a decrease in the average price per gallon sold as a result of lower jet fuel prices.

Marine revenues declined by 6.4% due to decreased volumes and lower prices. Revenues from the Land segment increased by 14.9% as the result of revenues from acquired businesses and higher volumes partially offset by a drop in the average price per gallon sold as a result of lower Land fuel prices.

World Fuel Services' net income grew by 9% compared in 2014 due to higher volumes from new and existing customers in the Aviation and Land segments partially offset by decrease in volumes in the Marine segment. In 2014 net cash provided by operating activities was $141.2 million (compared to $264.3 million for 2013). The decrease was primarily due to unfavorable year-over-year changes in assets and liabilities net of acquisitions.

Strategy

World Fuel Services has increased its geographic coverage and the depth of its portfolio through acquisitions. It plans to continue to explore acquisition opportunities of fuel resellers logistics and transaction management and payment processing companies including other services and technology. The company has also entered into joint venture arrangements to complement its core businesses and divests non-core operations as needed.

Mergers and Acquisitions

In 2016 the company agreed to buy Exxon Mobil's aviation fueling operations at 83 airports in Canada the UK Germany Italy Australia and New Zealand for $260 million.

Growing its UK operations in 2014 the company acquired Watson Petroleum which has a distribution network of 47 locations throughout England and Wales for $191 million. The transaction solidifies Watson's position as one of the largest distributors of ground-based fuels in the UK and provides World Fuel Services a platform for further growth in the ground fuels market in the UK and in Continental Europe. Also in 2014 World Fuel Services bought Houston-based Colt International LLC. The Colt transaction combined with the existing World Fuel business offers customers with the largest contract fueling network in the general aviation industry.

In 2013 to improve its payment processing operations it also bought certain assets from Multi Service Corporation (which specializes in fleet government and commercial payment programs) for $137 million. The Multi Service acquisition expands World Fuel Services' presence in the payment processing industry.

HISTORY

Neighbors Ralph Weiser and Jerrold Blair founded International Oil Recovery an oil recycling company in Florida in 1984. The company moved into aviation fueling by acquiring Advance Petroleum in 1986. Two years later International Oil Recovery diversified further entering the hazardous waste market by buying Resource Recovery of America a soil remediation company. In 1989 the firm acquired JCo Energy Partners an aviation fuel company and subsequently renamed its aviation fueling division World Fuel Services. The company

set up International Petroleum in 1993 to operate a Delaware used-oil and water-recycling plant.

The company changed its name to World Fuel Services Corporation in 1995 to reflect its expanded range of operations. Also that year it nearly doubled its revenue base with the purchase of Trans-Tec the world's #1 independent marine fuel services company. World Fuel also exited the environmental services business in 1995 to focus on its fuel services and oil recycling businesses.

The following year the company formed World Fuel International a subsidiary based in Costa Rica that serves World Fuel's aviation customers in South and Central America Canada and the Caribbean. In 1998 it acquired corporate jet fuel provider Baseops International which has offices in the UK and Texas.

In 1999 the company expanded its share of the marine fuel market with the acquisition of the Bunkerfuels group of companies one of the world's top marine fuel brokerages.

To focus on its marine and aviation fueling businesses World Fuel exited the oil recycling segment in 2000 when it sold its International Petroleum unit to waste services company EarthCare for about $33 million.

The company expanded into the United Arab Emirates with its 2001 acquisition of fuel services provider Marine Energy of Dubai. World Fuel acquired Rotterdam-based marine fuel reseller Oil Shipping Group in 2002.

In 2004 World Fuel Services acquired UK-based marine fuel reseller Tramp Holdings for $83 million.

The company diversified further in 2007 acquiring AVCARD a leading provider of contract fuel sales and charge card services to the aviation industry for $55 million.

In 2009 it bought wholesale motor fuel distributor TGS Petroleum. The company combined TGS with Texor to expand World Fuel Services' presence as the largest independent wholesale motor fuel distributor in Illinois.

Expanding its UK market share in 2009 the company acquired the Henty Oil Group of Companies a leading independent provider of marine and land fuels in the UK.

In 2010 it beefed up its position in the branded onshore wholesale market to 1 billion gallons a year by acquiring Lakeside Oil Company based in Milwaukee. It also boosted its market position through the acquisition of leading independent petroleum marketing company Western Petroleum for $95 million.

Boosting its aviation fuel segment in 2011 (for an undisclosed amount) World Fuel Services acquired The Hiller Group an aviation fuel supplier to more than 600 fixed base operators. It also bought Ascent Aviation a national branded reseller of aviation fuel for ConocoPhillips and deicing fluid for Dow Chemical and which supplies more than 450 airports and fixed base operators and NATO aviation fuel and logistics supplier Nordic Camp Supply (for $68.5 million.)

In 2012 the company acquired CarterEnergy's wholesale motor fuel distribution business. Kansas-based CarterEnergy with an annual volume of more than of 500 million gallons distributes branded fuel to more than 700 retail operators and is a supplier to industrial commercial and government customers in more than a dozen states. The deal boosted World Fuel Services' land fuel volume to more than 3.5 billion gallons.

EXECUTIVES

Chairman President and CEO, Michael J. Kasbar, age 59, $713,542 total compensation
Vp Finance, Carlos Rego

EVP and CFO, Ira M. Birns, age 53, $489,583 total compensation

EVP; Regional Managing Director Asia, Francis L Boon Meng

EVP, Francis X. (Frank) Shea, age 75, $352,000 total compensation

EVP; Regional Managing Director EMEA, Wade N. DeClaris

SVP and CIO, Massoud Sedigh, age 60

Vice President People And Performance Development, Marcia Morales-jaffe

Senior Vice President, Carlos Cuervo

Assistant Vice President International Sales, Joseph Gowen

Vice President Advanced Logistics, Piers Gorman

Assistant Vice President Finance, Susan Bolanos

Vice President Associate General Counsel, Jeffrey (Jeff) Weissman

Vice President Business Development and Strategy, Jonathan (Jon) Cole

Vice President Commercial Aviation Sales, Dan Sellas

Vice President and Treasurer, Adrienne Urban

Vice President Business Development, David (Dave) Hecht

Vice President Domestic Supply, Brad Hurwitz

Vice President Business Development, Robert Sturtz

Senior Vice President Risk, Prasad Venkata

Vice President Finance, Monesh Sakhrani

Vice President Supply and Vendor Relations, Warren Boin

Vice President Of Global Information Technology Operations, Tim Shipley

Vice President Global Qhsse, Cornelius Plug

Vice President Sales and Marketing, Charles (Chas) Fairbank

Vice President Information Technology, Betty Plunkett

Executive Vice President, John Rau

Senior Vice President Land North America, Kerry Oliver

Senior Vice President Of Global Tax, Peter Tonyan

Vice President Sales And Marketing, Mark Grieco

Vice President Business Development, Darren Fuller

Vice President International Sales, Mark Taylor

Vice President, Jos Heijmen

Vice President Human Resources, Derek Scott

Vice President Of Supply Emeaa, Michael (Mel) Ranger

Senior Vice President Strategy and Business Development, Nitin Khanna

Vice President Human Resources, Sue Rider

Auditors: PricewaterhouseCoopers LLP

LOCATIONS

HQ: World Fuel Services Corp.
9800 N.W. 41st Street, Miami, FL 33178
Phone: 305 428-8000   **Fax:** 305 392-5621
Web: www.wfscorp.com

2013 Sales

	$ mil.	% of total
Americas	24,928	57
Asia/Pacific	9,844	23
Europe & Middle East & Africa	8,612	20
Total	**43,386**	**100**

PRODUCTS/OPERATIONS

Selected Subsidiaries

Ascent Aviation Group Inc.
　Baseops Eu
Baseops International Inc.
　Casa Petro
　Henty Oil
Marine Energy Arabia Co. (L.L.C.) (United Arab Emirates)
　Nordic Cam
PetroServicios de Costa Rica S.R.L.

TGS Petroleum
The Hiller Group Incorporated
　Tramp Hold
　Trans-Tec
Western Petroleum Company
　World Fuel
World Fuel Services Inc.
　World Fuel
World Fuel Services (Singapore) Pte. Ltd.

Selected Mergers and Acquisitions

COMPETITORS

BBA Aviation	Mercury Air Group
BP Marine	Shell Aviation
Exxon Mobil	Sun Coast Resources
Fuchs Lubricants	

HISTORICAL FINANCIALS

Company Type: Public

Income Statement

FYE: December 31

	REVENUE ($ mil.)	NET INCOME ($ mil.)	NET PROFIT MARGIN	EMPLOYEES
12/14	43,386	221	0.5%	4,041
12/13	41,561	203	0.5%	2,758
12/12	38,945	189	0.5%	2,490
12/11	34,622	194	0.6%	1,798
12/10	19,131	146	0.8%	1,499
Annual Growth	**22.7%**	**10.8%**	**—**	**28.1%**

2014 Year-End Financials

Debt ratio: 14.14%
Return on equity: 12.57%
Cash ($ mil.): 302
Current ratio: 1.64
Long-term debt ($ mil.): 671

No. of shares (mil.): 72
Dividends
　Yield: 0.3%
　Payout: 5.1%
Market value ($ mil.): 3,383

	STOCK PRICE ($) FY Close	P/E High/Low	Earnings	Dividends	Book Value
12/14	46.93	16 12	3.11	0.15	25.74
12/13	43.16	16 12	2.83	0.15	23.29
12/12	41.17	18 13	2.64	0.15	21.03
12/11	41.98	16 12	2.71	0.15	18.73
12/10	36.16	16 10	2.31	0.15	16.20
Annual Growth	**6.7%**	**— —**	**7.7%**	**(0.0%)**	**12.3%**

WSFS Financial Corp

WSFS isn't a radio station but it is tuned to the banking needs of Delaware. WSFS Financial is the holding company for Wilmington Savings Fund Society (WSFS Bank) a thrift with nearly $5 billion in assets and more than 50 branches mostly in Delaware and Pennsylvania. Founded in 1832 WSFS Bank attracts deposits from individuals and local businesses by offering standard products like checking and savings accounts CDs and IRAs. The bank uses funds primarily to lend to businesses: Commercial loans and mortgages account for about 85% of its loan portfolio. Bank subsidiaries Christiana Trust Cypress Capital Management and WSFS Wealth Investment provide trust and investment advisory services to wealthy clients and institutional investors.

Operations

Its Christiana Trust division boasts nearly $9 billion in assets under administration and provides investment fiduciary agency bankruptcy and commercial domicile services from offices in Delaware and Nevada.

The company's Cash Connect division operates more than 450 ATMs for WSFS Bank which boasts the largest branded ATM network in Delaware. The division also manages some $490 million of vault cash in approximately 15000 ATMs nationwide and provides online reporting and ATM cash management predictive cash ordering armored carrier management and ATM processing and equipment sales.Overall the bank generated roughly 57% of its total revenue from interest and fees on loans in 2014 plus an additional 10% from interest on its mortgage-back and other investment securities. About 7% of its total revenue came from wealth management income while mortgage banking income contributed another 2%. The majority of the remaining revenue came from credit/debit card and ATM income and deposit service charges.

Geographic Reach

WSFS Bank has 45 branches throughout Delaware nearly 10 branches in Pennsylvania one branch in Nevada and one in Virginia.

Financial Performance

WSFS Financial's revenues and profits have been trending higher in recent years thanks to sustained growth in its lending business organically and through acquisitions and thanks to declining loan loss provisions as its loan portfolio's credit quality has improved with the strengthened economy.The company's revenue rose by 5% to $238.62 million in 2014 thanks to interest income growth mostly driven by increased loan business and higher securities interest; which stemmed from a combination of the bank's First Wyoming Financial Corporation acquisition improvements in its balance sheet mix and additional income from its reverse mortgage-related assets.Higher revenue and a continued decline in loan loss provisions in 2014 pushed WSFS Financial's net income up by 15% to $53.73 million during the year while the company's operating cash levels jumped by 17% to $67.06 million thanks to higher cash earnings.StrategyWSFS Financial reiterated its long-term growth strategy in 2015 which included growing the bank's lending business boosting its Trust and Wealth Management group's assets under administration and expanding Cash Connect's ATM customer base and customer cross-sell.Beyond utilizing its community-oriented and local commercial lending teams the company has been growing its loan business and its branch reach through strategic acquisitions of banks and bank branches in target markets with preference toward markets in southeastern Pennsylvania. Its 2014 acquisition of First Wyoming Financial Corp for example bolstered WSFS' presence in Kent county while strengthening its position as the one of Delaware's top independent community banks.

Mergers and Acquisitions

In 2014 WSFS Financial acquired First Wyoming Financial Corporation along with its main subsidiary The First National Bank of Wyoming which would be folded into WSFS Bank.

Ownership

Wellington Management Co. owns about 10% of WSFS Financial Corp.

EXECUTIVES

Vice President, Don Hadley

President CEO and Director, Mark A. Turner, age 51, $612,000 total compensation

EVP and Chief Risk Officer, Thomas W. Kearney

EVP and Chief Retail Banking Officer, Richard M. (Rick) Wright, age 62, $327,417 total compensation

EVP and Interim CFO, Rodger Levenson, age 53, $327,417 total compensation

EVP and Chief Human Capital Officer, Peggy H. Eddens, age 59

EVP and Chief Wealth Officer; President Pennsylvania Market, Paul D. Geraghty, $296,637 total compensation
EVP and CTO, S. James (Jim) Mazarakis
President Cash Connect, Tom Stevenson
Interim Chief Commercial Banking Officer, Steve Clark
Vice President, John (Jack) Olsen
Senior Vice President and Director Corporate MA, Justin C Dunn
Assistant Vice President Network Services Director, Jason Berkowitz
Vice President Applications and Data Services, Dan Smith
Vice President Commercial Banking, Glen Outten
Vice President Small Business Lending Retail Manager, Carol Brindle
Vice President, Janis Julian
Senior Vice President Commercial R E Lending, Joseph C (Jo) Walker
Senior Vice President, Cheryl Hughes
Vice President, Ron Samuels
Vice Chairman, Charles G. Cheleden, age 71
Chairman of the Board, Marvin N. (Skip) Schoenhals, age 67
Auditors: KPMG LLP

LOCATIONS

HQ: WSFS Financial Corp
WSFS Bank Center, 500 Delaware Avenue, Wilmington, DE 19801
Phone: 302 792-6000
Web: www.wsfsbank.com

2012 Branches

	No.
Delaware	42
Pennsylvania	7
Nevada	1
Virginia	1
Total	**51**

PRODUCTS/OPERATIONS

2014 Sales

	$ mil.	% of total
Interest		
Loans including fees	137	57
Mortgage-backed securities	13	6
Investment securities	9	4
Noninterest		
Credit/debit card & ATM income	24	11
Deposit service charges	17	7
Wealth management income	17	7
Mortgage baning activities	4	2
Other	15	6
Total	**238**	**100**

COMPETITORS

Bank of America	M&T Bank
Citizens Financial Group	PNC Financial
Fulton Financial	Sovereign Bank
JPMorgan Chase	TD Bank USA
	The Bancorp

HISTORICAL FINANCIALS

Company Type: Public

Income Statement

FYE: December 31

	ASSETS ($ mil.)	NET INCOME ($ mil.)	INCOME AS % OF ASSETS	EMPLOYEES
12/14	4,853	53	1.1%	841
12/13	4,515	46	1.0%	762
12/12	4,375	31	0.7%	763
12/11	4,289	22	0.5%	767
12/10	3,953	14	0.4%	695
Annual Growth	**5.3%**	**39.7%**	**—**	**4.9%**

2014 Year-End Financials

Debt ratio: 2.51%	No. of shares (mil.): 28
Return on equity: 12.33%	Dividends
Cash ($ mil.): 508	Yield: 0.6%
Current ratio: —	Payout: 8.8%
Long-term debt ($ mil.): —	Market value ($ mil.): 2,169

	STOCK PRICE ($) FY Close	P/E High/Low	PER SHARE ($) Earnings	Dividends	Book Value
12/14	76.89	40 33	1.93	0.17	17.34
12/13	77.53	46 25	1.69	0.16	14.35
12/12	42.25	40 33	1.08	0.16	16.00
12/11	35.96	64 39	0.76	0.16	15.06
12/10	47.44	103 51	0.49	0.16	14.38
Annual Growth	**12.8%**	**— —**	**41.1%**	**1.5%**	**4.8%**

Wyndham Worldwide Corp

This chain promises lodgings wherever the winds may blow you. One of the world's largest hospitality firms Wyndham Worldwide includes a portfolio of some 7700 franchised hotels worldwide through its lodging segment which includes 15 familiar brands such as Days Inn Howard Johnson Ramada and Super 8. Wyndham also operates a vacation exchange and rentals segment which has a relationship with some 100000 vacation exchange and rental properties in about 100 countries. In addition its Wyndham Vacation Ownership operates vacation ownership resorts in North America the Caribbean and the South Pacific. Revenues primarily come from franchise and hotel management fees membership dues and timeshare sales.

Geographic Reach

All of Wyndham's businesses have both domestic and international operations. About 75% of the company's revenues come from outside the US.

Operations

The company's timeshare and vacation rentals businesses (which target the leisure market) generate more than 80% of the company's total revenue. Its lodging segment (which targets both business and leisure travelers) accounts for about 20%.

Sales and Marketing

While the hospitality industry targets both business and leisure travelers most of Wyndham's customers come from the leisure market. Wyndham markets its properties through several marketing channels including direct mail email telemarketing online distribution channels brochures magazines and travel agencies. Additionally it promotes its offerings to owners of resorts and vacation homes through trade shows.

Financial Performance

The company reported $5.28 billion in revenue for fiscal 2014. That was an increase of 5% compared to the prior fiscal period. The company's net income was $529 million in fiscal 2014. That was a spike of about 22% compared to Wyndham's net income in fiscal 2013. Although the company's cash on hand decreased by 2% in fiscal 2014 compared to the prior fiscal period Wyndham ended the year with a comfortable $529 million in cash.

Strategy

Wyndham has committed to an organizational realignment initiative at its vacation exchange and rentals business primarily focused on consolidating existing processes and optimizing its structure partially due to a shift by members to transact online.

Wyndham is strategically focused on two objectives that it believes are essential to its business: increasing system size and strengthening customer value proposition. To increase its system size the company intends to acquire more properties add new rooms to existing properties and spur new construction by developing new and existing properties.

EXECUTIVES

President and CEO Wyndham Vacation Ownership, Franz S. Hanning, age 62, $739,242 total compensation
Chairman and CEO, Stephen P. Holmes, age 59, $1,500,008 total compensation
EVP and CFO, Thomas G. (Tom) Conforti, age 56, $652,620 total compensation
President and CEO Wyndham Hotel Group, Geoffrey A. (Geoff) Ballotti, age 54, $684,230 total compensation
EVP and Chief Human Resources Officer, Mary R. Falvey, age 55
EVP and General Counsel, Scott G. McLester, age 53
EVP and Chief Real Estate Development Officer, Thomas F. (Tom) Anderson, age 51, $516,164 total compensation
SVP and Global CIO, Walter A. Yosafat, age 55
President and CEO Wyndham Exchange and Rentals, Gail Mandel
EVP Global Sales, Ross Hosking
Vice President, Thomas Scelba
Vice President International Tax, Scott Seiler
Vice President, Jim Iervolino
Vice President Business Development Strategic Sourcing Department, Terrence Gilligan
Executive Vice President Human Resources, Sara Salvatore
Vice President, Andrea Mattei
RVP Ne, Joe Daly
Vice President Operations Latin America, Anthony Emanuelo
Vice President Legal; Corporate Transactions And Sec Reporting Group, Jennifer (Jen) Giampietro
Vice President Construction Services, Frank Campana
Vice President Marketing, Drew Gattuso
Vice President Financial Planning and Analysis, Mark Niziolek
Senior Vice President Financial Planning and Analysis, Jeanmarie Cooney
Vice President Of Finance, Christiane Ciombor
Vice President Communications, Alyson Johnson
Vice President Compliance, Craig Vandeventer
Vice President of Finance Financial Reporting, Don Huber
Vice President Legal Affairs, Henry (Hal) Bankes
Vice President Legal, Todd Robichaud
Senior Vice President, Steve Meetre
Vice President, Ruth Lipshitz
Vice President Sales Administration, Scott Cavanaugh
Vice President Legal, Amy Simone
Vice President, Amy Smith
Vice President Of Human Resources, Suzanne Gregory
Vice President, Jasmine Chay
Vice President Litigation And Government Relations, Jennifer (Jen) Haber
Vice President Of Network Planning, Clement Bence
Vice President, Brian Alexander
Vice President Of Sourcing, Paul Davis
Vice President, Marc Merriweather
Senior Vice President Revenue Management, Kathy Maher

Senior Vice President Brand Travelodge and
Howard Johnson, Rui Barros
Vice President Global Sales Emea, Marc Stanley
Vice President Sales Operations, Brian Saunders
Vice President Compensation, Stan Stohr
Senior Management Senior Vice President
General Manager Director, Darren Lins
Vice President Sales and Marketing Wyndham
Hotel Group, Tim Rector
Senior Vice President Head Of Mergers And
Acquisitions, Tom Barber
Senior Vice President Deputy Gc And Corporate
Secretary, Lynn Feldman
Vice President, Carolyn Bonifacemesce
Senior Vice President Sales And Mrktg Regional,
Terry Godfrey
Senior Vice President Sales Development
Recruiting and Training, Maria Margenot
Vice President Market Research, Theresa Lewis
Vice President Operational Compliance Cl, Marc
Damico
Executive Vice President and Chief Real Estate
Development Officer, Tom Anderson
Vice President Talent Acquisition, Craig Tribbey
Treasurer, Flo Lugli
Treasurer, Michael Mueller
Board Member, Wanda Gemmell
Auditors: DELOITTE & TOUCHE LLP

LOCATIONS

HQ: Wyndham Worldwide Corp
22 Sylvan Way, Parsippany, NJ 07054
Phone: 973 753-6000   Fax: 973 496-8906
Web: www.wyndhamworldwide.com

2014 Sales

	$ mil.	% of total
US	3,892	74
UK	298	6
Netherlands	276	5
Other regions	815	15
Total	**5,281**	**100**

PRODUCTS/OPERATIONS

2014 Sales

	% of total
Service fees and membership	46
Vacation ownership interest sales	28
Franchise fees	12
Consumer financing	8
Other	6
Total	**100**

2014 Sales

	$ mil.	% of total
Vacation Ownership	2,638	49
Vacation Exchange & Rentals	1,604	30
Lodging	1,101	21
Adjustments	(62)	-
Total	**5,281**	**100**

Selected Brands

Wyndham Vacation Ownership
  WorldMark by Wyndham
  Wyndham Vacation Resorts
Vacation Exchange & Rentals
  Canvas Holidays
  Cottages4you.com
  Cuendet
  Endless Vacation Rentals
  Landal GreenParks
  Novasol
Wyndham Hotel Group
  AmeriHost Inn
  Baymont Inn & Suites
  Days Inn
  Hawthorn Suites
  Howard Johnson
  Knights Inn
  Microtel Inns & Suites
  Ramada
  Super 8

Travelodge
Wingate by Windham
Wyndham Hotels and Resorts

COMPETITORS

Accor North America
Best Western
Carlson Hotels
Disney Parks & Resorts
FRHI Hotels and
  Resorts
Four Seasons Hotels

Hilton Worldwide
Hyatt
InterContinental
  Hotels
Marriott
Starwood Hotels &
  Resorts

HISTORICAL FINANCIALS

Company Type: Public

Income Statement

FYE: December 31

	REVENUE ($ mil.)	NET INCOME ($ mil.)	NET PROFIT MARGIN	EMPLOYEES
12/15	5,536	612	11.1%	37,700
12/14	5,281	529	10.0%	34,400
12/13	5,009	432	8.6%	32,800
12/12	4,534	400	8.8%	32,500
12/11	4,254	417	9.8%	27,800
Annual Growth	**6.8%**	**10.1%**	**—**	**7.9%**

2015 Year-End Financials

Debt ratio: 53.60%
Return on equity: 55.51%
Cash ($ mil.): 171
Current ratio: 0.96
Long-term debt ($ mil.): 4,955

No. of shares (mil.): 113
Dividends
  Yield: 2.3%
  Payout: 36.4%
Market value ($ mil.): 8,268

	STOCK PRICE ($) FY Close	P/E High/Low	Earnings	Dividends	Book Value
12/15	72.65	18 14	5.14	1.68	8.35
12/14	85.76	21 16	4.18	1.40	10.37
12/13	73.69	23 16	3.21	1.16	12.64
12/12	53.21	20 13	2.75	0.92	14.06
12/11	37.83	15 10	2.51	0.60	15.18
Annual Growth	**17.7%**	**— —**	**19.6%**	**29.4%**	**(13.9%)**

velopment that cost some $650 million opened in
2010. The Macau property boast more than 1000
rooms 625 slots 495 table games and 2.75 million
square feet of casino gaming space. Wynn Resorts
brought in more than 70% of its revenue from
Macau in fiscal 2014.

Sales and Marketing
The company spent about $23.3 million on ad-
vertising in fiscal 2014.

Financial Performance
The company's revenues decreased from $5.6
billion in fiscal 2013 down to $5.4 billion in fiscal
2014. Its 2014 net income increased by $3 million
compared to the previous year up to $731 million
as a result of increased gross revenue and decreased expenses. The company's cash flow decreased during 2014 primarily due to increased expenses and the reduction in casino revenue.

Strategy
While Las Vegas has been slower to recover
from the economic downturn than other markets
gaming companies with operations in Asia have
been growing. Strong performance in China have
helped the company's earnings. The company has
plans for a major new casino in Macau; the mega-
resort could open in 2015.

EXECUTIVES

President, Matt Maddox, age 39, $1,500,000 total
compensation
EVP General Counsel and Secretary, Kim Sinatra,
age 54, $840,769 total compensation
SVP and CIO, Steve Vollmer
Chairman and CEO, Stephen A. Wynn, age 73,
$4,000,000 total compensation
EVP and Chief Administrative Officer, John
Strzemp, age 63, $750,000 total compensation
President Wynn Macau Limited, Gamal Aziz, age 58
President Wynn International Marketing, Linda
Chen, age 48, $1,500,000 total compensation
SVP CFO and Treasurer, Stephen L. Cootey, age 44,
$587,307 total compensation
President Wynn Resorts (Macau), Ian M. Coughlan,
age 56
President Wynn Las Vegas, Maurice Wooden
President and COO Wynn Design & Development,
John Littell
Vice President Investor Relations, Samanta Stewart
Executive Vice President, Rob Oseland
Executive Vice President National Marketing,
Susan Savage
Vice President Design, Karina Ashworth
Vice President Construction, Darrell Richards
Vice President Corporate Finance, Mark Strawn
Executive Vice President International Marketing,
Alex Pariente
Senior Vice President Corporate Security, Jim
Stern
Vice President Of Finance, Dean Lawrence
Vice President Public Relations and Advanced,
Deanna Pettit-Irestone
Vice President Investor Relations, Lewis Fanger
National Sales Manager, Nicole Greber
Executive Vice President Player Development,
Larry Altschul
**Executive Vice President Design Wynn Design
and Development,** Roger Thomas
**Executive Vice President Architecture Wynn
Design and Development,** DeRuyter Butler
Vice President Architecture Asian Division, Glen
Ashworth
Senior Vice President Design, Jerry Beale
National Sales Manager, Aaron Missner
Vice President Slot Marketing, Tom McMahon
Vice President Of Corporate Tax, Teresa Dieguez
Vice President Tax, Robert McElroy
Senior Vice President Far East, Siew Yee
Vice President Benefits, Elaine Lo

Wynn Resorts Ltd

What happens in Vegas no longer stays in
Vegas. It also happens in China. Wynn Resorts the
brainchild of gaming mogul and former Mirage
Resorts chairman Steve Wynn operates luxury
casino resorts in Las Vegas and South China's
Macau the only place in China where gambling is
legal. The company's Wynn Las Vegas is a $2.4
billion resort and casino built on the site of the former Desert Inn on the Strip. Wynn Resorts operates in China through Wynn Macau Limited. The
company has expanded in both markets adding the
Encore at Wynn Las Vegas next to the Wynn Las
Vegas and the Encore at Wynn Macau adjacent to
Wynn Macau.

Geographic Reach
The company operates luxury casino resorts in
Las Vegas and South China's Macau.

Operations
The company's Las Vegas properties boast
about 4750 rooms 1850 slots and 230 table games
186000 square feet of casino gaming space some
35 restaurants a golf course two wedding chapels
and a Ferrari and Maserati dealership.

However Wynn Resorts actually makes more
money in China where the economy is booming.
Its Encore at Wynn Macau hotel and resort a de-

Senior Vice President Strategic Marketing, Cheryl Palmer
Executive Vice President Of Casino Operations, Debra Nutton
Senior Vice President Global Head Of Marketing, Cheryl Browning
Executive Vice President International Marketing, Alejandro Pariente
Senior Vice President Hotel Sales, Danielle Babilino
Vice President Table Games, Bill Zimmer
Vice President Player Development, Maryann Pascal
Vice President Korea, Chol Kim
Senior Vice President Fine Dining, Pradeep Raman
Vice President Player Development, Stephen Battaglini
Vice President Of International Marketing, Pete Lexis
Board Member, Ray Irani
Secretary Treasurer, Michael Weaver
Board Member, Elaine Wynn
Auditors: Ernst & Young LLP

LOCATIONS

HQ: Wynn Resorts Ltd
3131 Las Vegas Boulevard South, Las Vegas, NV 89109
Phone: 702 770-7555
Web: www.wynnresorts.com

PRODUCTS/OPERATIONS

2014 Sales

	% of total
Casino	73
Food and Beverages	11
Rooms	9
Entertainment Retail and Others	7
Promotional Allowances	-
Total	100

2014 Sales

	$ in mil.
% of total	
Macau Operations	70
Las Vegas Operations	30
Total	100
Properties	
Las Vegas	
Wynn Las Vegas	
Encore at Wynn Las Vegas	
Macau China	
Wynn Macau	
Encore at Wynn Macau	

COMPETITORS

Boyd Gaming	Marriott
Caesars Entertainment	Melco Crown
Carnival plc	Entertainment
Emperor Entertainment	Priceline
Hotel	Riviera Holdings
Golden Resorts	SJM
Hard Rock Hotel	Starwood Hotels &
Hyatt	Resorts
Las Vegas Sands	Station Casinos
MGM Resorts	

HISTORICAL FINANCIALS

Company Type: Public

Income Statement

FYE: December 31

	REVENUE ($ mil.)	NET INCOME ($ mil.)	NET PROFIT MARGIN	EMPLOYEES
12/14	5,433	731	13.5%	16,800
12/13	5,620	728	13.0%	16,500
12/12	5,154	502	9.7%	16,000
12/11	5,269	613	11.6%	16,400
12/10	4,184	160	3.8%	16,405
Annual Growth	6.7%	46.2%	—	0.6%

2014 Year-End Financials

Debt ratio: 81.56%
Return on equity: —
Cash ($ mil.): 2,182
Current ratio: 2.12
Long-term debt ($ mil.): 7,361

No. of shares (mil.): 101
Dividends
Yield: 4.2%
Payout: 76.2%
Market value ($ mil.): 15,090

	STOCK PRICE ($) FY Close	P/E High/Low	PER SHARE ($) Earnings	Dividends	Book Value
12/14	148.76	34 19	7.18	6.25	(0.28)
12/13	194.21	27 16	7.17	7.00	(1.82)
12/12	112.49	28 19	4.82	9.50	(2.57)
12/11	110.49	33 21	4.88	6.50	16.70
12/10	103.84	90 45	1.29	8.50	17.96
Annual Growth	9.4%	— —	53.6%	(7.4%)	—

Xcel Energy, Inc.

Xcel Energy has accelerated its energy engine in utility markets across the US. The utility holding company distributes electricity to 3.5 million customers and natural gas to 1.9 million in eight states through four regulated utilities; Colorado and Minnesota account for most of its customers. Its utilities –Northern States Power (NSP-Minnesota and NSP-Wisconsin) Public Service Company of Colorado and Southwestern Public Service (in New Mexico and Texas) –have the combined capacity of more than 17000 MW of electricity. Xcel owns transmission and distribution lines as well as natural gas assets. It is also a leading wind power provider in the US with wind farms in Colorado Minnesota and Texas.

Geographic ReachThe company serves customers in Colorado Michigan Minnesota New Mexico North Dakota South Dakota Texas and Wisconsin. Operations

Xcel operates power and gas utilities: Northern States Power Company-Minnesota; Northern States Power Company-Wisconsin Public Service Company of Colorado; and Southwestern Public Service Company. The holding company has more than 75 generating plants more than 87165 miles of transmission lines and about 193110 miles of distribution lines. It also operates an interstate natural gas pipeline company and a joint venture to develop and lease natural gas pipelines storage and compression assets. Xcel has 2394 miles of natural gas transmission pipeline and 34091 miles of distribution pipeline. Xcel's commercial operations manage the generation fleet and all wholesale activities for Xcel Energy's four public utility subsidiaries.

The company is also the US's fifth-largest utility solar energy provider and owns the fourth-largest transmission system. In addition Xcel operates more than 20 hydroelectric power plants in Colorado Minnesota and Wisconsin.

Sales and Marketing

Xcel Energy's major commercial and industrial electric sales are to customers in the petroleum and coal as well as food products industries. It also serves small commercial and industrial customers and gets significant electric retail sales from real estate customers and school systems and universities.

Financial Performance

In 2014 Xcel Energy's net sales increased by 7% due to higher electric and natural gas sales.Electric revenues increased primarily due to various rate increases across all of the utility subsidiaries higher trading and increased fuel and purchased

power cost recovery partially offset by operating expenses.Natural gas revenues grew due to the purchased natural gas adjustment clause recovery partially offset in operating expenses.In 2014 Xcel Energy's net income increased by 8% due to increased revenues and lower interest charges partially offset by the increased cost of natural gas sold and transported.Interest charges decreased due to lower interest rates refinancings partially offset by higher long-term debt levels. Natural gas margins increased due to rate increases and the pipeline system integrity adjustment in Colorado.In 2014 Xcel Energy's net cash provided by the operating activities increased by 2%.

Strategy

To meet the demands both of customers and regulators Xcel plans to invest $14.1 billion in its utility businesses from 2014 through 2018 to modernize infrastructure improve system reliability reduce environmental pollution and expand the amount of renewable energy available to its customers. Xcel has long-term plans to move from coal-fired plants to natural gas and on to alternative fuels such as wind solar and biomass to boost its green power capacity (88705 MWh in 2015).In 2015 Northern States Power Company-Minnesota filed its 2016-2030 Resource Plan with the MPUC proposing to achieve a 40% reduction in carbon emissions by 2030 from 2005 levels through the significant addition of renewables continued commitment to specific CIP annual achievements and the continued operation of its existing cost-effective thermal generation.In 2014 the City of Minneapolis and Xcel Energy signed a 10 year franchise agreement. A separate clean energy partnership agreement with the City of Minneapolis was also signed which establishes a board comprised of city and utility officials tasked with creating a work plan to promote energy efficiency the use of renewable energy and the reduction of carbon emissions.That year Public Service Company of Colorado filed a plan to construct a new 345 KV transmission line originating from Pawnee Station near Brush Colorado and terminating at the Daniels Park substation near Castle Pines Colo. The estimated cost of the project is $178 million.

In 2013 the company expanded its agreement with the National Center For Atmospheric Research for sophisticated renewable energy forecasting as a way to help it save millions of dollars.

The company believes its strategy of making environmentally sound investments is pivotal to its success. It is constructing the CapX2020 project a joint venture transmission expansion project with 10 other utilities scheduled for completion by 2020. The project includes a 240-mile transmission line from Minnesota to North Dakota. It has has filed to extend the licensing plants of its two nuclear plants on Prairie Island in Minnesota for 20 years which it expects to save customers more than $1 billion.In 2013 The New Mexico Public Regulation Commission approved Xcel Energy's plan to buy 698 MW of additional wind energy for its Texas-New Mexico system which will save area customers an estimated $590 million in fuel costs over the 20-year life of the contracts. New wind facilities planned for Roosevelt County New Mexico Hansford and Ochiltree counties Texas and Dewey and Blaine counties Oklahoma will supply the power.

Xcel is also working to develop so-called "smart grid" technology which will provide customers with more reliability and control over their energy use. It has completed the nation's first fully integrated SmartGridCity in Boulder Colorado.

HISTORY

The Minnesota Electric Light & Electric Motive Power Company was founded in 1881 and changed its name to Minnesota Brush Electric the next year. In the 1890s it provided street lighting and power for trolleys and became Minneapolis General Electric.

In 1909 Henry Byllesby formed rival firm Washington County Light and Power Co. (soon renamed Consumers Power Company) then created holding company Northern States Power Company of Delaware (NSPD). In 1910 he founded Standard Gas and Electric a holding company overseeing NSPD and many other US utilities.

NSPD bought Minneapolis General Electric in 1912 and Consumers Power was renamed the Northern States Power Company (NSP) in 1916. During the 1920s NSPD connected its subsidiaries via transmission lines. Byllesby died in 1924.

In 1931 NSP was placed under NSPD but the Public Utility Holding Company Act of 1935 dissolved Standard and NSPD. NSP became independent in the 1940s and spent $335 million on new facilities after WWII.

During the 1960s NSP moved into Michigan South Dakota and Wisconsin and brought its first nuclear power plant on line in 1964 (converted to natural gas in 1968). It began operating the Monticello and Prairie Island nukes in the early 1970s.

Company sales nearly doubled in the 1980s. In 1989 NSP created NRG Energy (incorporated 1992) to invest in independent power projects. The Federal Energy Policy Act allowed wholesale power competition in 1992 and NSP lost nine of its 19 municipal customers.

NSP acquired Viking Gas Transmission which owned an interstate pipeline in 1993. It also began developing affordable housing. In 1995 NSP and Wisconsin Electric planned to merge but dropped the deal amid antitrust concerns. NSP continued to diversify forming telecommunications provider Seren Innovations in 1996 and starting its cable-testing business in 1997. The next year NSP formed a power marketing unit.

NRG Energy began a shopping spree abroad in 1994 buying interests in plants in Germany and Australia. In 1996 it bought a 48% stake in Bolivia's COBEE (increased to 99% in 2001). Also that year it acquired PacifiCorp's Pacific Generating unit which owned stakes in a dozen geographically scattered plants.

In 1999 NRG Energy gained nearly 7600 MW of capacity through power plant acquisitions in California Connecticut Massachusetts and New York. The next year NRG Energy picked up another 1700 MW in Louisiana and it agreed to buy fossil-fueled plants (1875 MW) from Delaware's Conectiv for $800 million (half of the deal was completed in 2001 the other half was canceled the following year). NSP spun off part of NRG in 2000 in an IPO.

Meanwhile as the utility-merger trend gathered steam in 1999 NSP agreed to acquire Denver-based New Century Engines in a $4.9 billion deal. The acquisition was completed in 2000 and the expanded company changed its name to Xcel Energy.

The next year Xcel sold nearly all of its stake in UK-based Yorkshire Power Group which had been held by New Century Energies to Innogy (now RWE npower). It sold its remaining 5% stake in Yorkshire Power in 2002. NRG purchased several Latin American projects from Swedish utility Vattenfall in 2001. NRG also agreed to purchase four coal-fired plants (2500 MW) in Ohio from FirstEnergy for $1.5 billion; however the deal was later canceled.

In 2002 Xcel repurchased the 26% stake in NRG that it sold to the public in 2000-01.

EXECUTIVES

Vice President Corporate Services and Secretary, Cathy J Hart

Vice President, Scott Weatherby

EVP and Group President Operations, Kent T. Larson, $550,000 total compensation

Chairman President and CEO, Benjamin G. S. (Ben) Fowke, age 57, $1,200,000 total compensation

SVP and CFO, Teresa S. Madden, age 59, $575,000 total compensation

President and CEO Public Service Company Colorado, David L. Eves, age 57

VP and CIO, David C. Harkness

EVP and Group President Utilities and Chief Administrative Officer, Marvin E. McDaniel, age 54, $525,000 total compensation

President and CEO Northern States Power Company Wisconsin, Mark E. Stoering

Chief Nuclear Officer, Tim O'Connor

President and CEO Southwestern Public Service Company, David Hudson

President Northern States Power Company Minnesota, Christopher B. Clark

EVP and General Counsel, Scott Willensky

Senior Vice President, Robert (Bob) Palmer

Regional Vice President, Laura McCarten

Vice President Operations Support, Mark Reddemann

Vice President Procurementworldwide, Jim Duevel

Vice President Of Strategic Technology, Mary Fisher

Senior Vice President and Chief Nuclear Officer of Xcel Energy Services Inc., Timothy (Tim) O'Connor

Vice President Workforce Relations, Edward (Ed) Lutz

Regional Vice President Rates And Regulatory Affairs, Alice Jackson

Vice President Manager Director, Mark Wilson

Vice President, Russell Bigley

Vice President Chairman of Safety, Mark Koenig

Vice President for Commercial Operations, Thomas (Thom) Imbler

Legal Secretary, Sara Parmenter

Vice President Engineering Fuel and Supply Chain, Aziz Khanifar

Vice President Corporate Information Technology And Quality, Brad A Nelson

Vice President Workforce Relations, Ed Lutz

Vice President Marketing, Fred Stoffel

Vice President Business Systems, Alan Higgins

Vice President of Corporate Communications, Beth Willis

Vice President Distribution, Steve Foss

Vice President and Controller, Jeff Savage

Senior Vice President, Roy Palmer

Auditors: Deloitte & Touche LLP

LOCATIONS

HQ: Xcel Energy, Inc.
414 Nicollet Mall, Minneapolis, MN 55401
Phone: 612 330-5500
Web: www.xcelenergy.com

PRODUCTS/OPERATIONS

2014 Sales

	$ mil.	% of total
Electric	9,465	81
Natural gas	2,142	18
Other	77	1
Total	**11,686**	**100**

COMPETITORS

AEP	Exelon Energy
ALLETE	FirstEnergy
Alliant Energy	Minnesota Power
Ameren	NextEra Energy
Atmos Energy	OGE Energy
Basin Electric Power	PG&E Corporation
CMS Energy	PPL Corporation
CenterPoint Energy	Public Service
DTE	Enterprise Group
Dominion Resources	SCANA
Duke Energy	Sempra Energy
Dynegy	Southern Company
Entergy	WEC Energy
Exelon	

HISTORICAL FINANCIALS
Company Type: Public

Income Statement
FYE: December 31

	REVENUE ($ mil.)	NET INCOME ($ mil.)	NET PROFIT MARGIN	EMPLOYEES
12/14	11,686	1,021	8.7%	11,691
12/13	10,914	948	8.7%	11,581
12/12	10,128	905	8.9%	11,198
12/11	10,654	841	7.9%	11,312
12/10	10,310	755	7.3%	11,290
Annual Growth	3.2%	7.8%	—	0.9%

2014 Year-End Financials

Debt ratio: 34.57%
Return on equity: 10.33%
Cash ($ mil.): 79
Current ratio: 0.83
Long-term debt ($ mil.): 11,499

No. of shares (mil.): 505
Dividends
  Yield: 3.3%
  Payout: 61.8%
Market value ($ mil.): 18,166

	STOCK PRICE ($) FY Close	P/E High/Low		PER SHARE ($)		
		High	Low	Earnings	Dividends	Book Value
12/14	35.92	18	13	2.03	1.20	20.20
12/13	27.94	17	14	1.91	1.11	19.21
12/12	26.71	16	14	1.85	1.07	18.19
12/11	27.64	16	13	1.72	1.03	17.44
12/10	23.55	15	12	1.62	1.00	16.98
Annual Growth	11.1%	—	—	5.8%	4.6%	4.4%

Xerox Corp

Xerox has become more than a copier company. So much more that it has been transitioning to become a provider of services for corporations' back offices by providing business process outsourcing (BPO) and document outsourcing (DO). Services include customer service and claims filing infrastructure cloud computing application development managed print services and document and data management. In addition it remains a leading provider of equipment including office printers digital printing systems and multifunction printers and copiers. In January 2016 Xerox announced that it would make the distinction between BPO and DO even starker by splitting them into two independent companies. The split might be final by the end of 2016.

HISTORY

The Haloid Company was incorporated in 1906 to make and sell photographic paper. In 1935 it bought photocopier company Rectigraph which led Haloid to buy a license for a process called electrophotography (renamed xerography from the ancient Greek words for "dry" and "writing") from the Battelle Memorial Institute in 1947. Battelle backed inventor Chester Carlson who perfected a process for transferring electrostatic images from a photoconductive surface to paper.

Haloid commercialized xerography with the Model A copier in 1949 and the Xerox Copyflo in 1955 and by 1956 xerographic products represented 40% of sales. The company changed its name to Haloid Xerox in 1958 (Haloid was dropped from the name in 1961) and in 1959 it introduced the first simplified office copier. That machine took the world by storm beating out such competing technologies as mimeograph (A.B.Dick) thermal paper (3M) and damp copy (Kodak). Sales soared to nearly $270 million in 1965.

Xerox branched out in the 1960s by buying three publishing companies and a computer unit; all were later sold or disbanded. In the 1970s Xerox bought printer plotter and disk drive businesses as well as record carrier Western Union (1979; sold in 1982). In 1974 the FTC believing Xerox was dominating its market too much forced the company to license its technology.

In the 1980s Xerox bought companies specializing in optical character recognition scanning faxing and desktop publishing. It also diversified by buying insurance and investment banking firms among others. In 1986 Paul Allaire who had joined Xerox in 1966 was elected president. He was named CEO in 1990 and became chairman in 1991.

Eyeing future alliances Xerox agreed to supply computer print engines to Compaq (1992) and Apple (1993). In 1995 it introduced networked color laser printers and software for printing Web documents. Between 1996 and 1998 Xerox sold its struggling insurance units.

Xerox bought Rank's 20% stake in Rank Xerox the two companies' 41-year-old global marketing joint venture in 1997. That year Xerox launched a $500 PC printer copier and scanner –its first product specifically for home use —and Allaire hired IBM CFO Richard Thoman as president and COO to spearhead a push into network and digital products. In 1998 Xerox bought technology consultant XLConnect (renamed Xerox Connect) and parent company Intelligent Electronics.

In 1999 Xerox named Thoman CEO to replace Allaire who remained chairman. That year Xerox bought France's SET Electronique (high-speed digital printers). The company began selling its products online and reorganized its sales force by customer industry rather than geography. Layoffs also continued totaling 14000 for 1998 and 1999.

In an effort to stake a larger claim in the office color printing market Xerox bought Tektronix's ailing color printing and imaging division in 2000. The company also formed an Internet unit formed a joint venture with Fuji Photo Film (now FUJI-FILM) and Sharp to make low-cost ink jet printers and spun off its digital rights management technology unit as ContentGuard. With profits shrinking and market value flagging Thoman resigned in 2000 amid pressure from the board. Allaire assumed the CEO post once again. Also that year the company sold its operations in China and Hong Kong to Fuji Xerox.

In 2001 the company laid off 4000 more employees. That year Xerox sold half of its 50% stake in Fuji Xerox to Fuji Photo Film and it discontinued its product lines aimed at consumer and small office users including its personal copiers and ink jet printers. Allaire stepped down as chief executive; COO Anne Mulcahy was named as his successor. Looking to reduce its massive debt Xerox transferred most of its US customer financing operations to GE Capital in a deal including $1 billion in cash financing from the lending giant (it later formed similar arrangements with GE Capital for many of its international operations). Xerox also began selling manufacturing operations to contract electronics manufacturer Flextronics International.

CEO Mulcahy replaced Allaire as chairman in 2002. Also that year Xerox agreed to pay a $10 million fine to settle a complaint brought by the SEC alleging financial reporting violations. After the settlement Xerox –which fired KPMG as its au-

ditors the previous year and brought in PricewaterhouseCoopers –initiated an audit of its financial statements from 1997 through 2001; as a result of the audit in 2002 the company restated about $2 billion in revenues over the five-year period.

Also in 2002 Xerox made its celebrated Palo Alto Research Center (PARC) into a separate subsidiary. (Xerox was long criticized for failing to capitalize on numerous breakthrough PARC innovations —laser printer computer mouse Ethernet desktop icons.)

It sold its stake in IT systems integrator Integic in 2005 to Northrop Grumman for $96 million in cash. The following year Xerox reached a settlement with Palm in a patent infringement case it originally filed in 1997; Palm agreed to pay Xerox $22.5 million for a full license to three patents related to handwriting recognition and other technology.

Xerox acquired Amici a document management and search service company that primarily served the legal sector for $174 million in cash in 2006. Later that year it purchased XMPie a developer of software used to create customized marketing programs for $54 million in cash.

In 2007 Xerox acquired office equipment vendor Global Imaging Systems for approximately $1.5 billion. It also purchased Advectis a provider of electronic document collaboration software for the mortgage industry for $32 million that year. In 2008 Xerox acquired Veenman a Dutch office equipment reseller from Corporate Express for $68 million. The GIS and Veenman deals furthered a strategy to expand Xerox's presence in the small and midsized business segments in the US and Europe.

In an effort to promote the transformation of its business from a manufacturer of photocopiers to a full-line supplier of office products printing production equipment software and services Xerox unveiled a new corporate logo in 2008.

In 2009 Mulcahy was succeeded by president Ursula Burns as CEO; Mulcahy remained chairman of Xerox until her retirement in 2010 after eight years as head of the board. Burns was appointed as the new chairman.

The company invested heavily in its services business in 2010 buying Affiliated Computer Services for $6.4 billion. Xerox also made several smaller acquisitions that year to boost its services business including ExcellerateHRO (benefits administration and relocation services) TMS Health (outsourced customer service for the health care industry) and Spur Information Solutions (software for the transportation industry).

In 2011 the company picked up digital document products distributor Concept Group and print software and consulting services provider NewField IT as part of an effort to expand its presence in the UK particularly in the small and medium-sized business market. It expanded in the Benelux region that year with the acquisition of customer care provider Unamic/HCN. Xerox didn't ignore its home turf either bringing in The Breakaway Group (cloud-based electronic medical record adoption) and Education and Sales Marketing LLC (student financial and enrollment management) that year both headquartered in Colorado.

EXECUTIVES

VP; President Industrial Retail and Hospitality Business Group Xerox Services, Kevin M. Warren, age 52

Vice President Global Public Relations, Carl Langsenkamp

EVP General Counsel and Corporate Secretary, Don H. Liu, age 54

EVP; President Corporate Strategy and Asia Operations, James A. (Jim) Firestone, age 60, $714,000 total compensation

Vice President Sales Director, Richard (Dick) Fuelling

Chairman and CEO, Ursula M. Burns, age 56, $1,100,000 total compensation

VP; President Project Management Office, James H. Lesko, age 63

VP; President Global Technology and Delivery Group, Russell M. Peacock, age 57

CTO; President Xerox Innovation Group, Sophie V. Vandebroek, age 53

Interim CFO, Leslie F. Varon, age 59

EVP; President Xerox Technology, Jeffrey (Jeff) Jacobson, age 55, $662,500 total compensation

VP; President Global Graphic Communications Xerox Technology, Andrew Copley

VP; President Channel Partner Operations Xerox Technology, John Corley

VP; COO Latin America Xerox Services, Tom Blodgett, age 62

SVP; President Corporate Operations, Herv © Tessler, age 51

President U.S. Channels Group, Darren Cassidy

President U.S. Channel Group (USCG), Kurt Schmelz

VP; COO Global Capabilities Xerox Services, Sue Watts

VP; President Large Enterprise Operations Xerox Services, Mike Feldman

VP and President Channel Partner Operations Xerox Technology, Douraid Zaghouani

VP; COO Public Sector Business Group Xerox Services, Dave Amoriell

VP; COO Commercial Healthcare Business Group Xerox Services, Connie Harvey

VP and CIO, Stephen Little

EVP; President Xerox Services, Robert K. Zapfel, age 60, $600,000 total compensation

VP and President Developing Markets Operations, Yehia Maaty

VP and Chief Marketing Officer, John Kennedy

LSS Blackbelt Customer/Market Insight Center of Excellence, Anne Thorne

Leader Large Enterprise Operations (LEO) Europe, Andrew Morrison

SVP and Managing Director Xerox Healthcare Provider Solutions, Justin Lanning

President Xerox Complete Document Solutions (CDS), John Hand

VP and General Manager Channel Services Europe, Malcolm Mitchell

Group President Financial Services Business, Bruce Jones

Vice President Marketing Communications, Mike Milligan

Senior Vice President Business Development and Marketing, John (Jack) Palmatier

Senior Vice President Consumables Development and Manufacturing, Richard (Dick) Schmachtenberg

Vice President of Sales Major Accounts Operations, Marlene Williams

Senior Vice President, Kris Bryant

Vice President and General Manager, Glenn Sexton

Vice President Of Sales, Michael Lawton

Senior Vice President Strategy and Business Development, Glenda Chess

Vice President Business Development Human Resources Outsourcing, Mike McQuarrie

Legal Secretary, Joni Woo

Senior Vice President Human Resources, Frank Barnett

National Account Manager, Jerry de Frates

Vice President Innovation, Don Buckley

Senior Vice President and Managing Director Government Healthcare Solutions, Brett Jakovac

Vice President, Dino Ventresca

Vice President Operations, Jay Schneider

Vice President Information Technology, Tobias Wehrman

Vice President Strategy and Curriculum Services, Patricia (Pat) Kunkel

Senior Vice President Of Technology, Stephen Garner

Vice President Business Group Finance, Lisa O'flynn

Vice President General Manager, Shelley Sweeney

Vice President Senior Corporate Counsel, Jeff Neiheisel

Vice President Sales, Mary Simpson

Vice President, Peter Borgman

Division Vice President and General Manager, Kelley Walkup

Senior Vice President Corporate Development, Kevin Christman

National Account Manager, Gene Bischoff

Senior Vice President General Counsel, Marja Roney

Vice President Of Environmental Policy, Daniel Renkas

Vice President Of Global Purchasing, Ken Syme

Vice President Senior Corporate Counsel, Katherine Kelley

Vice President Operations and Operational Improvements, Therome Buford

Vice President of Information Technology, Ada Cekici

Vice President Sales Operations US Solutions Group Xerox, Charles (Chas) Alexander

Vice President Of Human Resources, Amy Cannan

Senior Vice President, Patricia Elizondo

Vice President Of Operations, John Faklaris

National Account Manager, Paul De Freitas

Vice President Of Acquisitions, David Maxfield

Vice President Card Operations, Joe Froderman

Vice President Senior Corporate Counsel, Nicholas Bevilacqua

Vice President Long term Care Solutions, Frank Spinelli

Senior Vice President Of Public Service Operations, Greg Jones

Senior Vice President, Al Leary

Vice President Of Sales, Michael (Mel) Hartman

Senior Vice President United States Client Operations, Kelly Jenson

Vice President SHSS Sales, Rachelle Ussery

Vice President, William Mannino

Vice President Operations, Lewis Miller

Vice President and Global Managing Director, Barbara (Barb) Powers

Division Vice President, Sean Armstrong

Vice President Human Resources and Talent Management, Krystyna Nisiewicz

Vice President Business And Legal Affairs, Joanne Hussey

Vice President Operations, Kelly McBride

Vice President and Managing Director Aerospace and Defense, Tony Amato

Vice President and Center Manager, Hadi Mahabadi

National Sales Manager, Ingrid Johnson

Svp Sales - It Outsourcing, George Love

Vice President Managed Services, Kevin Campbell

Management Vice President, Gregory Appel

Vice President Information Technology, Karin Gleissle

Vice President XPS Deployment, Jason Oliver

Vice President, Tenneil Dutton

Vice President of Manufacturing, Kerrian Foster

Vice President of Global Sales and Marketing, Raleigh Grice

Vice President and General Manager, Jack Lafferty

Vice President Of Product Management, Steve McNamara

National Account Manager, Paul Staz

Vice President SBU Client Operations East, Yvette Ray

Vice President Of Client Operations, Yvette Smith

Vice President Technology and Innovation, Birendar Gill

Senior Vice President Business Development, Nick Mannella

Vice President Marketing, Janice Feeley

National Account Manager, Stephanie DiMario

Vice President Business Development, Karen Ikeda

Vice President, Jeff Valentine

Vice President Eastern Sales Operations Marketing, Bernadette Durman

Vice President Human Resources Information Technology, Nick Gillett

Vice President, Ajay Dhingra

Vice President FandA Operations At Xerox, Craig Mccrackin

Vice President Business Development, Michael (Mel) Livingston

Vice President Customer Support, Patricia (Pat) Rash

Vice President FInance Business Transformation, Patrick (Paddy) Dwyer

Vice President General Manager Ink Jet Business Team, Dustin Graupman

Vice President, Ivy McKinney

Vice President, Brian Schutt

Vice President Finance, Eric Washburn

Vice President, Sharon Haight

Vice President Insurance and Financial Services, Julie Dorey

Vice President of Finance and Accounting, Stephen (Steve) Bengston

Vice President Computer Services, Ken Segedie

Vice President Drafting Services and Information Technology, Brenda Batts

National Accounts Manager, Blee Nichols

Vice President Finance, Anna Cinquepalmi

Vice President, Carla Salario

Vice President Account Executive, Mark Vineyard

Vice President Contact Center Technology, Devin Parsons

Vice President, Josh Glover

Vice President Information Technology Program Services, Theresa Johnson

Operations Vice President, Edward Wolyniec

Vice President Technology, Jack Devos

Senior Vice President Head of Financial Services Sales, Alex Hillman

Vice President, David J (Dave) Tritschler

Vice President Sales, Lynn M Macdougall

Vice President Information Technology Managed Services, Roger Murphy

Vice President Service Delivery, Robert (Bob) Scarry

Vice President Of Sales, Randy Alt

Senior Vice President, John Crysler

Vice President Internal Audit, Ken Goff

Vice President, Chris Couch

Senior Vice President Northeast ETC, Thomas (Thom) Dorazio

Vice President Sales, Jill Korunovski

Vice President of MMIS Solutions, Matthew (Matt) Moreau

Division Vice President, Aubrey Millner

Senior Vice President Operations, Kristin Baca

Vice President Organizational Development and Training, Ron Davis

Vice President and Managing Director, Jason Stein

Vice President Offering Development Xerox Print Services, Mike Heacock

Vice President Information Technology Program Management, Lisa Withers

Auditors: PricewaterhouseCoopers LLP

LOCATIONS

HQ: Xerox Corp
P.O. Box 4505, 45 Glover Avenue, Norwalk, CT 06856-4505
Phone: 203 968-3000
Web: www.xerox.com

2014 Sales

	$ mil.	% of total
US	13,041	67
Europe	4,428	23
Other regions	2,071	10
Total	**19,540**	**100**

PRODUCTS/OPERATIONS

2014 Sales by Revenue Type

	$ mil.	% of total
Annuity		
Service outsourcing & rentals	13,865	71
Supplies paper & other	2,168	11
Financing	387	2
Equipment	3,104	16
Total	**19,540**	**100**

2014 Sales by Segment

	$ mil.	% of total
Services	10,584	54
Document Technology	8,358	43
Other	598	3
Total	**19,540**	**100**

Selected Products

Office (commercial government and education sectors)
  Copiers
  Displays
  Multifunction devices (copy fax print scan)
  Printers
  Projectors
  Scanners
Production (graphics communications industry and large corporations)
  Digital presses
  High-volume printers
  Software
Other
  Services
  Wide-format printers
Service Types
Document Management
  Managed Print Services
  Communication and Marketing
  Enterprise Content Management
  Document and Data Management
Business Processes
  Customer Care
  Finance & Accounting
  HR Services
  Application Services
Office Solutions
  Graphic Communication
  Office Printers
  Office Software

COMPETITORS

Accenture	IBM
Agfa	Infosys
Aon	Konica Minolta
Brother Industries	Kyocera Document
Canon	Solutions
Capgemini	Lexmark
Computer Sciences	NEC
Corp.	Oc©
Convergys	Oki Data
Dell	Olivetti
Eastman Kodak	Panasonic Corp
Epson	Pitney Bowes
FUJIFILM	Ricoh Company
Fujitsu	Sharp Corp.
Genpact	Tata Consultancy
HP	TeleTech
Heidelberger	Toshiba
Druckmaschinen	Unisys
Hitachi	Wipro

Income Statement
FYE: December 31

	REVENUE ($ mil.)	NET INCOME ($ mil.)	NET PROFIT MARGIN	EMPLOYEES
12/14	19,540	969	5.0%	147,500
12/13	21,435	1,159	5.4%	143,100
12/12	22,390	1,195	5.3%	147,600
12/11	22,626	1,295	5.7%	139,650
12/10	21,633	606	2.8%	136,500
Annual Growth	(2.5%)	12.5%	—	2.0%

2014 Year-End Financials

Debt ratio: 28.26%
Return on equity: 8.20%
Cash ($ mil.): 1,411
Current ratio: 1.46
Long-term debt ($ mil.): 6,358

No. of shares (mil.): 1,116
Dividends
  Yield: 1.8%
  Payout: 27.4%
Market value ($ mil.): 15,478

	STOCK PRICE ($) FY Close	P/E High/Low	PER SHARE ($) Earnings	Dividends	Book Value
12/14	13.86	17 13	0.81	0.25	9.83
12/13	12.17	13 7	0.91	0.23	10.64
12/12	6.82	10 7	0.88	0.17	9.70
12/11	7.96	13 7	0.90	0.17	9.14
12/10	11.52	27 18	0.43	0.17	8.84
Annual Growth	4.7%	— —	17.2%	10.1%	2.7%

Yadkin Financial Corp

Yadkin Financial Corporation is the holding company for Yadkin Bank (formerly Yadkin Valley Bank and Trust) which serves customers from more than 70 branches across North Carolina and upstate South Carolina. In addition to its standard loans SBA loans and deposit products including checking and savings accounts money market accounts CDs and IRAs Yadkin Bank and its subsidiaries provide mortgage banking investment and insurance services to more than 80000 business and individual customers. Founded in 1968 Yadkin Bank now boasts nearly $1.5 billion in total assets.

OperationsThe bank's primary businesses are centered around Commercial and Personal banking Mortgage banking (through Yadkin Mortgage) Builder Finance Wealth Services (through securities broker Yadkin Wealth) and Small Business Lending.The bank which staffs more than 820 full-time and 60 part-time employees (as of late 2014) generated 75% of its revenue from loan interest in 2014 with another 7% of revenue coming from interest on its investment securities. The remainder of its revenue mostly came from service charges and fees on deposit accounts (6% of revenue) government-guaranteed lending (6%) and mortgage banking (2%).Geographic ReachThe bank boasts more than 70 branches in central and western portions of North Carolina and neighboring parts of northern South Carolina. About 30% of its assets were in the central region of North Carolina while more than 30% were split between the Piedmont and Mountain regions of the state. Yadkin Mortgage is headquartered in Greensboro North Carolina.Financial PerformanceNote: The company's 2013 financials were restated after its 2014 acquisitions. This analysis does not use the restated figures.Yadkin Financial's revenue has been trending downward over the past few years due to

shrinking interest margins on loans amidst the low-interest environment. The firm's profits however have been rising thanks to declining loan loss provisions as its loan portfolio's credit quality has improved with the strengthened economy.Yadkin had a breakout year in 2014 however with revenue spiking by 76% to a record $163.5 million as its loan business more than doubled to $2.9 billion (compared to $1.39 billion in 2013) after its 2014 acquisitions of VantageSouth and Piedmont Community banks and organic loan growth. The bank's non-interest income from deposit charges and other fees on accounts also more than doubled helping to grow Yadkin's top line. Higher revenue and a continued decline in loan loss provisions in 2014 drove Yadkin's net income up 15% to a record $21.7 billion.StrategyYadkin Financial reiterated in 2015 that its "growth in business profitability and market share has historically been enhanced by strategic mergers and acquisitions." Indeed its mid-2014 acquisitions of VantageSouth and Piedmont Community Bank more than doubled its loan and deposit business. Yadkin also leverages its local community banking advantage to grow its loans and deposits organically.Mergers and AcquisitionsIn July 2014 Yadkin Financial purchased VantageSouth Bancshares and Piedmont Community Bank Holdings which helped to more than double its loan assets and made Yadkin Bank the largest community bank headquartered in North Carolina.Company BackgroundYadkin Financial Corporation (formerly Yadkin Valley Financial) was formed in 2006 to be the holding company for Yadkin Bank (previously Yadkin Valley Bank and Trust). The bank and its Piedmont Bank High Country Bank Cardinal State Bank (acquired 2008) and American Community Bank (acquired 2009) divisions all rebranded under the Yadkin Bank name in May 2013.

EXECUTIVES

Chief Financial Officer; Executive Vice President, Jan H. Hollar
Regional President Piedmont Bank Yadkin Bank and Trust Company, Edward L. (Ed) Marxen
Executive Vice President And Human Resources Director, Ed Shuford
Executive Vice President And Chief Banking Officer, William (Bill) Demarcus
Vice Chairman, Harry M. Davis, age 66
Auditors: Dixon Hughes Goodman LLP

LOCATIONS

HQ: Yadkin Financial Corp
  3600 Glenwood Avenue, Suite 300, Raleigh, NC 27612
Phone: 919 659-9000

PRODUCTS/OPERATIONS

2007 Sales

	$ mil.	% of total
Interest		
Loans including fees	68	75
Securities	6	7
Other	0	1
Noninterest		
Net gains on sales of loans	5	7
Service charges on deposit accounts	3	4
Other service fees	3	4
Other	2	2
Total	**90**	**100**

COMPETITORS

BB&T	First Citizens
Bank of America	BancShares
CommunityOne Bancorp	Wells Fargo

Income Statement
FYE: December 31

	ASSETS ($ mil.)	NET INCOME ($ mil.)	INCOME AS % OF ASSETS	EMPLOYEES
12/14	4,266	21	0.5%	882
12/13	1,806	18	1.0%	511
12/12	1,923	(8)	—	481
12/11	1,993	(14)	—	481
12/10	2,300	(0)	—	615
Annual Growth	16.7%			9.4%

2014 Year-End Financials

Debt ratio: 1.77%
Return on equity: 5.85%
Cash ($ mil.): 131
Current ratio: —
Long-term debt ($ mil.): —

No. of shares (mil.): 31
Dividends
  Yield: —
  Payout: —
Market value ($ mil.): 621

	STOCK PRICE ($) FY Close	P/E High/Low	PER SHARE ($) Earnings	Dividends	Book Value
12/14	19.65	25 19	0.88	0.00	17.65
12/13	17.04	16 2	1.19	0.00	12.82
12/12	2.94	— —	(1.92)	0.00	11.87
12/11	1.61	— —	(2.85)	0.00	21.60
12/10	1.81	— —	(0.60)	0.00	27.40
Annual Growth	81.5%	— —	—	—(10.4%)	

YRC Worldwide Inc

YRC Worldwide stands for more than Your Regional Carrier. The company has one of the largest less-than-truckload (LTL) networks in North America with local regional national and international capabilities. YRC Worldwide is a holding company that operates through such subsidiaries as YRC Freight and YRC Reimer which transport goods for manufacturing wholesale retail and government customers in the US Canada and certain international markets as well as YRC Regional Transportation which provides regional next-day ground services in the US Canada Mexico and Puerto Rico through subsidiaries New Penn USF Holland and USF Reddaway.

HISTORY

In 1924 A. J. Harrell established a trucking company in conjunction with his Oklahoma City bus line and Yellow Cab franchise. Harrell's Yellow Transit trucking operation hauled less-than-truckload (LTL) shipments between Oklahoma City and Tulsa. By 1944 Yellow had more than 50 independent subsidiaries in Illinois Indiana Kansas Kentucky Missouri and Texas. That year the company was sold to an investment firm and renamed Yellow Transit Freight Lines. But Yellow's policy of paying high dividends stunted its growth and by 1951 it faced bankruptcy.

George Powell Sr. took over in 1952 and turned Yellow around. His son George Powell Jr. became CEO in 1957 and the company went public two years later. George Jr. focused the company on long-haul interstate shipments and started buying up other trucking companies.

In 1965 Yellow expanded to the West Coast and the Southeast by purchasing Watson-Wilson Transportation System. Changing its name to Yellow Freight System (1968) the company acquired part of Norwalk Truck Lines and its routes in the

Northeast (1970) and Adley Express (1972) providing new East Coast routes. Yellow extended routes into the Pacific Northwest by buying Republic Freight Systems in 1975. Its 1978 purchase of Braswell Motor Freight Lines consolidated its routes in California Texas and the Southeast. Yellow's only deviation from route acquisitions was its $4 million investment in oil firm Overland Energy in 1976 which it dissolved in the early 1980s.

The company was unprepared however when Congress deregulated trucking routes and shipping rates in 1980. Yellow upgraded its aging depots and terminals but profits still declined by 1983. In 1982 Yellow Freight formed a holding corporation (renamed Yellow Corporation in 1992). George Powell III took over from his father as CEO in 1990. Yellow purchased Preston Trucking an overnight freight hauler in 1992.

In 1994 Yellow Freight was hit by a 24-day Teamsters' strike that allowed nonunion carriers to gain a chunk of its market. The next year struggling during industry price wars it reported a $30 million loss. Yellow laid off about 250 employees mostly from Yellow Freight. George III resigned in 1996 and Maurice "Mr. Fix-it" Myers became CEO. Myers began moving the firm from a one-size-fits-all LTL trucker to a more flexible customer-responsive trucking and logistics firm.

Yellow Freight was restructured in 1997 into decentralized business units to improve customer service and hundreds of workers were laid off. The misfortunes of other companies also created good fortune for Yellow: UPS went on strike and rail traffic was still snarled from the 1996 Union Pacific-Southern Pacific merger.

To expand international operations Yellow created YCS International in 1998 (renamed Yellow Global in 2000). It also secured a five-year labor contract with its unions ending the danger of a strike. Loss-making Preston was sold to three company executives and Yellow acquired regional carriers Action Express (1998) and Jevic Transportation (1999).

Myers drove off into the sunset in 1999 to take over another troubled giant Waste Management and Yellow Freight president William Zollars became CEO of Yellow Corp. In 2000 Yellow and two venture capital firms set up online transportation marketplace transportation.com to provide freight-forwarding and multimodal brokerage services.

Yellow integrated Action Express and WestEx into Saia Motor Freight Line in 2001. The next year Yellow renamed its Yellow Freight subsidiary Yellow Transportation. The company created SCS Transportation to act as a holding company for its regional nonunion carriers Saia and Jevic. Also in 2002 Yellow combined transportation.com with its other logistics services to form Meridian IQ. That same year Yellow spun off SCS Transportation (later Saia Inc.). The next year Yellow and other leading LTL carriers negotiated a new contract with the Teamsters union.

Also in 2003 Yellow bought rival Roadway and became Yellow Roadway Corporation. The company expanded in 2005 with the acquisition of USF. The following year Yellow Roadway changed its name to YRC Worldwide and in 2007 it also changed the name of its Meridian IQ unit to YRC Logistics.

In order to reduce costs and improve its operating efficiency YRC Worldwide restructrued its operations and integrated its Roadway and Yellow Transportation units in March 2009. In mid-2011 the company appointed James Welch as its new CEO. Welch served at Yellow Transportation as CEO and later on as president and CEO of Dynamex. He succeeds William Zollars who retired as CEO of YRC.

YRC Worldwide formerly reported a Truckload segment which included the operations of USF

Glen Moore a provider of US truckload services. Glen Moore concluded operations in December 2011 when some of its fleet was sold to a third-party and the rest was redeployed to YRC Freight and Regional Transportation companies. Truckload had accounted for only about 1% to 2% of sales over its last few years.

As part of its focus on North America YRC Worldwide sold its 65% interest in its China-based joint venture Shanghai Jiayu Logistics Co. Ltd. to its Chinese JV partner for an undisclosed amount in 2012.

EXECUTIVES

CEO, James L. Welch, age 61, $815,500 total compensation
President Reddaway, Thomas J. (T.J.) O'Connor, age 54, $280,257 total compensation
EVP and CFO, Jamie G. Pierson, age 45, $612,000 total compensation
President Holland, Scott D. Ware, age 54, $363,153 total compensation
EVP General Counsel and Secretary, Michelle A Friel, age 45, $437,000 total compensation
President YRC Freight, Darren D. Hawkins, age 45, $426,154 total compensation
President New Penn, Donald R. (Don) Foust
Vice President And Treasurer, Mark Boehmer
Vice President Corporate Sales, Dan Crowley
Vice President Human Resources and Benefits, Sandra Stocke
Vice President Eastern Division, Mitch Lilly
Vice President Cash Management, Joe Whitsel
Vice President Information Technology, Josh Johnson
Senior Vice President of Marketing, Bill Crowe
Division Vice President, Dan Gatta
Chairman, Raymond J. Bromark, age 69
Assistant Treasurer, Tom Colvin
Auditors: KPMG LLP

LOCATIONS

HQ: YRC Worldwide Inc
10990 Roe Avenue, Overland Park, KS 66211
Phone: 913 696-6100
Web: www.yrcw.com

PRODUCTS/OPERATIONS

2014 Sales

	$ mil.	% of total
YRC Freight	3,237	64
Regional Transportation	1,831	36
Total	**5,068**	**100**

COMPETITORS

ABF Freight System	Menlo Worldwide
ArcBest	Mullen Group
C.H. Robinson	Old Dominion Freight
Worldwide	Saia
Central Freight Lines	Schneider National
Estes Express	UPS Freight
FedEx Freight	UPS Supply Chain
J.B. Hunt	Solutions
Landstar System	

HISTORICAL FINANCIALS

Company Type: Public

Income Statement

FYE: December 31

	REVENUE ($ mil.)	NET INCOME ($ mil.)	NET PROFIT MARGIN	EMPLOYEES
12/14	5,068	(67)	—	33,000
12/13	4,865	(83)	—	32,000
12/12	4,850	(140)	—	32,000
12/11	4,868	(351)	—	32,000
12/10	4,334	(322)	—	32,000
Annual Growth	4.0%	—	—	0.8%

2014 Year-End Financials

Debt ratio: 55.91%	No. of shares (mil.): 30
Return on equity: —	Dividends
Cash ($ mil.): 171	Yield: —
Current ratio: 1.25	Payout: —
Long-term debt ($ mil.): 1,078	Market value ($ mil.): 690

	STOCK PRICE ($) FY Close	P/E High/Low	PER SHARE ($)		
			Earnings	Dividends	Book Value
12/14	22.49	— —	(3.00)	0.00	(15.47)
12/13	17.37	— —	(8.96)	0.00	(58.73)
12/12	6.75	— —	(19.20)	0.00	(78.88)
12/11	9.97	— —	(196.12)	0.00	(51.71)
12/10	3.72	— —	(2,439.00)	0.00	(1,186.62)
Annual Growth	56.8%	— —	—	—	—

Yum! Brands, Inc.

This company puts fast-food yummies in a whole lot of tummies. YUM! Brands is the largest fast-food operator in the world in terms of number of locations with more than 41000 outlets in about 125 countries. (It trails only hamburger giant McDonald's in sales.) The company's flagship chains include #1 chicken fryer KFC (with more than 19400 units) top pizza joint Pizza Hut (more than 15600) and quick-service Mexican leader Taco Bell (more than 6200). YUM! sold the Long John Silver's seafood chain along with several hundred A&W root beer and burger stands to two separate buyers in late 2011. In 2015 YUM! Brands announced it would spin off its Chinese operations into a separately traded public company.

HISTORY

Yum! Brands took its original name TRICON from the three brand icons —KFC Pizza Hut and Taco Bell –it inherited from former parent PepsiCo. The soft drink company entered the fast-food business with its acquisition of Pizza Hut in 1977. The pizza chain had begun in 1958 when brothers Dan and Frank Carney borrowed $600 from their mother and opened the first Pizza Hut in Wichita Kansas with partner John Bender. Their first franchise opened the next year in Topeka Kansas. By 1971 the company had become the world's largest pizza chain with more than 1000 restaurants. Pizza Hut went public the following year. The chain had grown to 3000 locations by the time it was acquired.

In 1978 PepsiCo acquired Taco Bell. After trying other fast-food formats Glen Bell settled on the Mexican-style market. He bought and sold several chains before beginning Taco Bell in Downey California in 1962. The first franchise was sold two years later and by 1967 –the year after it went public —Taco Bell had more than 335 restaurants most of them franchised.

KFC was acquired in 1986. It had been founded by Harland Sanders —that's Colonel Sanders to you —who developed his secret 11-herbs-and-spices recipe and method of pressure-frying chicken during the 1930s. The Colonel began franchising the secret in 1952 and founded Kentucky Fried Chicken in 1955. More than 600 outlets in the US and Canada were open by 1963. It went public in 1969 and was operating some 6600 units in 55 countries when it was acquired by PepsiCo.

Through these acquisitions PepsiCo hoped to diversify and build sales channels for its beverages but the company had also incurred a huge debt load and fast-food competition had intensified. As same-store sales faltered shareholders clamored for PepsiCo to spin off the restaurants. Restaurant officials grumbled that PepsiCo put more effort into marketing blitzes than into building restaurants (its 1991 renaming of Kentucky Fried Chicken as KFC didn't fool many health-conscious consumers).

In 1997 PepsiCo created a new restaurant subsidiary which it spun off in the fall as TRICON Global Restaurants. To improve cash flow it stepped up efforts to close or franchise underperforming Pizza Huts and KFCs. TRICON also began opening "three-in-one" restaurants featuring all its brands under one roof. In 1998 it launched a Taco Bell advertising campaign featuring a bilingual Chihuahua; the sassy pooch quickly became a cultural icon.

The KFC Taco Bell and Pizza Hut cooperatives joined in 1999 to form Unified FoodService Purchasing the largest purchasing cooperative for fast-food restaurants in the US. Also that year TRICON spent some $2 billion on a massive Star Wars: Episode I —The Phantom Menace promotion that failed to increase traffic at its restaurants. Vice chairman David Novak took over as CEO in 2000. Additionally in 1999 the company joined Burger King in lending $150 million to its distributor AmeriServe (now McLane Foodservice) which had filed for bankruptcy. The following year TRICON began experimenting with debit and credit cards at Pizza Huts and KFCs. It also opened more than 300 multi-branded sites.

In 2002 TRICON acquired Yorkshire Global Restaurants for $320 million which brought Long John Silver's and A&W All-American Food Restaurants into the fold. Now a five-pack of well-known brands rather than a trio TRICON changed its name to YUM! Brands. Later that year it formed a joint venture with Favorite Restaurants Group (a leading franchisee of KFC and Pizza Hut in Indonesia and Hong Kong) to open a chain of Yan Can Asian restaurants based around popular international chef Martin Yan. (YUM! Brands dissolved its partnership in Yan Can and liquidated the business in 2004.)

Being market leaders did not save YUM!'s chains from the overall downturn in the economy however nor from the effects of changing eating habits as Americans sought healthier meal alternatives. KFC was hit particularly hard prompting the company to appoint veteran Gregg Dedrick the chain's new president in 2003. Both KFC and Pizza Hut saw same-store sales and the number of transactions decline in the US during 2003.

In 2004 KFC opened its 1000th restaurant in China where the chain had been operating since 1987. As YUM! Brands' China operations continued to grow it formed a separate division in 2005 to oversee its expansion. The company acquired the 50% stake it didn't already own in Pizza Hut (UK) from joint venture partner Whitbread in 2006 for almost $185 million plus the assumption of about $25 million in debt.

The following year YUM! was stung by an E. coli outbreak at some of its Taco Bell outlets. The source of the outbreak was traced to a lettuce supplier; the company announced new steps to test its food supply. YUM! also sold its 31% stake in KFC Japan to Mitsubishi that same year.

YUM! Brands sold its Long John Silver's chain and A&W All-American Food locations in 2011. The divestitures were made to allow the company to focus on growing its international business particularly in China.

In 2012 the company upped its stake in Chinese restaurant operator Little Sheep Group to 93%.

In 2015 YUM! Brands announced plans to spin off its Chinese operations.

EXECUTIVES

Vice Chairman and Chairman and CEO YUM! Restaurants China, Jing-Shyh S. (Sam) Su, age 63, $1,100,000 total compensation
CEO and Director, Greg Creed, age 57, $750,000 total compensation
CEO Pizza Hut, David Gibbs
CEO Taco Bell, Brian Niccol, age 42
CEO KFC, Roger Eaton, age 54
CEO Yum! Restaurants China, Micky Pant, age 61, $750,000 total compensation
President KFC and President Yum! Restaurants India, Niren Chaudhary
CEO KFC China, Joey Wat, age 44
SVP and Brand General Manager Pizza Hut China, Peter Kao, age 58
Senior Vice President Corporate Affairs, Brett Hale
Marketing Vice President, Candy Chan
Vice President Of Human Resources, Mary Yamanaka
Executive Chairman, David C. Novak, age 63
Secretary To KFC Marketing Director, Napalai Losuwan
Auditors: KPMG LLP

LOCATIONS

HQ: Yum! Brands, Inc.
  1441 Gardiner Lane, Louisville, KY 40213
Phone: 502 874-8300
Web: www.yum.com

2013 Sales

	$ mil.	% of total
International		
China	6,905	53
India	127	1
Other countries	3,099	24
US	2,953	22
Total	**13,084**	**100**

PRODUCTS/OPERATIONS

2013 Sales

	$ mil.	% of total
Company sales	11,184	85
Franchising and License fees	1,900	15
Total	**13,084**	**100**

COMPETITORS

A&W Restaurants	Jack in the Box
American Dairy Queen	Little Caesar's
Arby's	Long John Silver's
Burger King	McDonald's
CKE Restaurants	Papa John's
Chick-fil-A	Popeyes
Chipotle	Quiznos
Church's Chicken	Sonic Corp.
Dairy Queen	Subway
Del Taco	Wendy's
Domino's	

HISTORICAL FINANCIALS

Company Type: Public

Income Statement

FYE: December 26

	REVENUE ($ mil.)	NET INCOME ($ mil.)	NET PROFIT MARGIN	EMPLOYEES
12/15	13,105	1,293	9.9%	505,000
12/14	13,279	1,051	7.9%	537,000
12/13	13,084	1,091	8.3%	539,000
12/12	13,633	1,597	11.7%	523,000
12/11	12,626	1,319	10.4%	466,000
Annual Growth	0.9%	(0.5%)	—	2.0%

2015 Year-End Financials

Debt ratio: 49.25%
Return on equity: 105.50%
Cash ($ mil.): 737
Current ratio: 0.55
Long-term debt ($ mil.): 3,054
No. of shares (mil.): 420
Dividends
 Yield: 0.0%
 Payout: 57.8%
Market value ($ mil.): 31,080

	STOCK PRICE ($) FY Close	P/E High/Low	PER SHARE ($) Earnings	Dividends	Book Value
12/15	74.00	32 23	2.92	1.69	2.17
12/14	73.14	35 28	2.32	1.52	3.56
12/13	73.87	32 26	2.36	1.38	4.89
12/12	64.72	22 17	3.38	1.19	4.78
12/11	59.01	21 17	2.74	1.04	3.96
Annual Growth	5.8%		1.6%	13.0%	(14.0%)

ZEN-NOH GRAIN CORPORATION

Auditors: KPMG LLP NEW ORLEANS LA

LOCATIONS

HQ: ZEN-NOH GRAIN CORPORATION
  1127 HWY 190 E SERVICE RD, COVINGTON, LA 704334929
Phone: 9858673500
Web: WWW.CGB.COM

HISTORICAL FINANCIALS

Company Type: Private

Income Statement

FYE: May 31

	REVENUE ($ mil.)	NET INCOME ($ mil.)	NET PROFIT MARGIN	EMPLOYEES
05/14	7,550	56	0.7%	213
05/13	7,704	51	0.7%	—
05/12	6,306	33	0.5%	—
05/11	6,217	0		—
Annual Growth	6.7%	—	—	—

2014 Year-End Financials

Debt ratio: ——
Return on equity: 0.70%
Cash ($ mil.): 4
Current ratio: 0.10
Long-term debt ($ mil.): —
Dividends
 Yield: —
 Payout: —
Market value ($ mil.): —

Zions Bancorporation

Multibank holding company Zions Bancorporation operates eight bank subsidiaries with more than 450 branches in 10 western and southwestern states. The banks operate under their own brands and leadership rather than sharing one corporate identity. Its network of banks focuses on commercial and retail banking as well as mortgage and construction lending. The banks provide products and services including deposit accounts home mortgages and home equity lines of credit residential and commercial development loans credit cards and trust and wealth management services. Zions caters to small- to medium-sized businesses by offering Small Business Administration (SBA) loans.

Operations

The company's eight subsidiaries have retained their own names and branding to entice customers who are more comfortable banking at a local level. Its subsidiary banks are Zions First National Bank Nevada State Bank National Bank of Arizona and Vectra Bank Colorado. Additionally Zions owns The Commerce Bank of Washington California Bank & Trust The Commerce Bank of Oregon and Texas-based Amegy Corporation.

Zions also offers wealth management services through Contango Capital Advisors and Zions Trust Company. It provides online and traditional brokerage services via Zions Direct and Amegy Investments. In addition the company controls a handful of venture capital funds working with startups in the West.Like any other bank Zions generates the majority of its revenue through interest payments on the loans it issues. Interest income generated by loans money marketing investments and other securities accounts for nearly income 80% of Zion's revenue with the remaining 20% coming from fees for deposit accounts and other service-related charges.

Geographic Reach

Based in Utah the holding company operates banks in Utah Idaho California Texas Arizona Nevada Colorado New Mexico and Washington. Around 75% of the company's loan assets are held in subsidiary banks headquartered in Utah Texas and California.

Sales and Marketing

To market its banks and their services Zions regularly spends on advertising. The holding company spent $25.1 million on advertising in 2014 up from $23.4 million in 2013 but down slightly from the $25.7 million it spent in 2012.Of its network of 460 branch locations Zions owns more than 285 and leases nearly 175.

Financial Performance

After four years of falling revenue Zion's revenue rebounded by more than 3% to $2.36 billion in 2014 mostly as the company suffered significantly less from impairment losses (just $27000 worth in 2014). In 2013 and 2012 the company had taken on $165.1 billion and $104.1 billion in impairment losses respectively which mostly occurred in its trust-preferred collateralize debt obligation (CDO) securities portfolio. Interest income however fell by 5% mostly as the bank's interest margins on loans shrank in the low-interest environment.Zion's profit also rebounded in 2014 as net income jumped 51% to $398.46 million mostly thanks to a combination of higher revenue lower debt extinguishment costs as Zion didn't prematurely call as many of its long-term notes and lower interest expenses mostly as the bank paid less interest on its borrowings (as it's been paying down its long-term debt in recent years).Despite higher earnings operations provided $454.11 million or 46% less cash than in 2013. This is mostly because Zion wasn't able to write off as much in non-cash charges such as impairment losses debt extinguishment costs and unrealized losses in derivative assets.

Strategy

The bank has experienced declining interest income over the past few years as interest rates for consumers and businesses have decreased. To combat this it plans to increase its lending volume primarily through business lending and residential mortgage lending; reduce non-accrual and classified loans; increase fee income through changes to product pricing improved product distribution and improved cross sales; and manage non-interest expenses.Starting in 2015 Zion plans to improve profitability and returns through a number of measures. This includes increasing its net interest margin by paying off more of its long-term debt originating more loans increasing its fee income where possible and investing more of its cash into higher yielding securities. It also plans to find ways to increase operating efficiency and maintain the credit quality of its loan portfolio even though it expects to take some losses on energy loans as oil prices remain depressed.

With such distinct operating subsidiaries Zions strives to maintain a local community and regional bank approach as opposed to a larger bank that doesn't have a local management team. It does centralize many non-customer facing operations such as risk and capital management technology and back-office operations making for a more cost-effective endeavor.

Zions which built its business through acquisitions strategically managed to extend its reach during the economic downturn in part by helping the FDIC clean up failed banks and it continues to search for acquisition opportunities. It is also building its business by growing its wealth management and advisory services organically.

HISTORY

Zions' history is entwined with that of the Mormon Church. Founded by the church in 1873 to take over the savings department of the Bank of Deseret when it obtained a national charter the new bank was headed by Brigham Young and other church leaders. The church kept control of the bank until 1960 when it sold its interest to a group of investors led by Roy Simmons who moved it into the holding company that became Zions Bancorporation. It went public in 1966.

It has grown over the years by picking up struggling or failing banks during various financial crises. It almost bought fellow Utah bank First Security in 2000 and would have dropped the Zions name to further distance itself from the Mormon Church. But the deal fell through and the name remains.

EXECUTIVES

EVP Capital Markets and Investments, W. David Hemingway, age 67, $257,000 total compensation
EVP President and CEO Zions First National Bank, A. Scott (Scott) Anderson, age 68, $540,577 total compensation
Chairman and CEO, Harris H. Simmons, age 60, $920,000 total compensation
EVP President and CEO Vectra Bank Colorado, Bruce K. Alexander, age 62
EVP President and CEO Nevada State Bank, Dallas E. Haun, age 61
EVP; President and CEO The Commerce Bank of Washington, Stanley D. Savage, age 69, $312,000 total compensation
EVP; CEO California Bank & Trust, David E. Blackford, age 66, $510,000 total compensation

President, Scott J. McLean, age 58, $594,769 total compensation
President and COO National Bank of Arizona, Keith D. Maio, age 57
EVP Chief Risk Officer, Edward P. (Ed) Schreiber, $510,000 total compensation
EVP; CEO Contango Capital Advisors and Chairman Western National Trust Company, Julie G. Castle, age 54
EVP and CEO Amegy Bank of Texas, Steven D. Stephens, age 56
EVP Chief Information Officer, Joe Reilly
EVP Chief Credit Officer, Michael J. Morris
CFO, Paul E. Burdiss
Vice President Community Relations, Gloria Wilkinson
Senior Vice President Investor Relations and External Comm Zions Bancorporation, James (Jamie) Abbott
Assistant Vice President, Don Milne
Vice President, Allen (Al) Jensen
Vice President, Steve Campbell
Vice President Information Technology Financial Systems, Ryan Greene
Assistant Vice President International Operations, Anne Lane
Vice President, Janet Louie
Vice President Senior Risk Officer, Stephen (Steve) Willden
Vice President Customer Service, Wendy Mower
Senior Vice President Information Technology Infrastructure and Data Center Operations, David (Dave) Graves
Senior Vice President, Melisse Grey
Senior Vice President Department Manager, Jeff Thomas
Vice President, Brandy Deherrera
Assistant Vice President And Regional Security Officer, Stephanie Colotti
Vice President Contact Center Site Manager, Russ Diblasi
Vice President Relationship Manager, Peggy Silverwood
Regional Credit Manager Vice President, Dereck Jacobs
Vice President Trading Operations, Peter (Pete) Kelson
Senior Vice President Compliance, Norman Merritt
Vice President Relationship Manager, Catherine (Cathy) Arik
Vice+President+at+zions+bank, Carol Walker
Vice President, Charles (Chas) Loughridge
Vice President, Alex Buxton
Senior Vice President Corporate Banking, Jim Stanchfield
Senior Vice President Internal Audit, Jennifer (Jen) Smith
Assistant Vice President Compliance, Carson Boss
Vice President Womens Financial Group, Tabitha Perkins
Vice President Consumer Lending Services Manager, Cary Coombs
Vice President Commercial Loan Officer, Stuart (Stu) Hartley
Vice President, Ralph Matson
Regional Vice President, David Clark
Senior Vice President Manager, Steven (Steve) Campbell
Vice President of Private Banking, Todd Parker
Vice President Of Information Technology, Karl Ward
Vice President, Bart Merrill
Vice President, Sandra Kinney
Vice President, Christy Edwards
Executive Vice President, Shanna Dudleston
Vice President, Robert (Bob) Reynolds
Assistant Vice President, Willie Koosmann
Vice President, John Rizzo
Senior Vice President Manager, Scott Stone

Senior Vice President retail Product Division, Dave Fuhriman
Senior Vice President National Construction Manager, Marty Henrie
Senior Vice President, Susan (Sue) Jones
Senior Vice President, Kristy Walker
Senior Vice President And Chief Credit Administrator C And I Lending, Dennis Spencer
Vice President, Brian Cunning
Vice President, Craig Carpenter
Assistant Vice President and Manager, Lilian Huetter
Assistant Vice President Commercial Loan Workout Officer, Darrin Zingleman
Vice President and Manager Marketing (Bankcard), Cathy Knowlson
Vice President of Property Management, David (Dave) Delight
Senior Vice President, John (Jack) Potter
Vice President Portfolio Manager, Tyler Conley
Senior Vice President Real Estate Lending, David (Dave) Russell
Senior Vice President Of Human Resources, John Tait
Assistant Vice President Business Intelligence, Alex Mumme
Vice President Commercial Relationship Manager, Michele Sauk
Assistant Vice President Call Center Tech, Jeff Newman
Assistant Vice President Senior Analyst, Davis Burtenshaw
Vice President Construction Loan Officer, Jeff Dorenbosch
Vice President Real Estate Banking, Ryan Stevenson
Assistant Vice President Capital Markets, Karen Keeley
Vice President Public Finance, Cameron Arial
Senior Vice President Group Marketing Manager, Brian Mccaul
Vice President, Pam Wallis
Senior Vice President Treasury Management Services Manager, Ken Collins
Senior Vice President Banking and Vice President of Compensation, Scott Law
Senior Vice President Controller, Hayes Carr
Vice President Information technology, Vince Lee
Vice President Sales Manager, Howard Anderson
Vice President, Jennifer Jolley
Vice President Technology, Deva Annamalai
Assistant Vice President Capital Markets And Foreign Exchange, Ryan Anderson
Vice President Commercial Loans, David Kohler
Vice President Service Delivery and Support, Jason Mecham
Senior Vice President Elect Banking, William (Bill) Hall
Vice President and Corporate Credit Administrator Special Assets, Diane Warsoff
Vice President, David (Dave) Bata
Senior Vice President Managing Legal Counsel, Rena Miller
Human Resources Planning Manager Vice President, Charlene Valestin
Vice President Manager Oa Core, Amy Vernon
Vice President Mainframe Operations Systems, Reed Bailey
Executive Vice President General Counsel and Secretary, Thomas E (Thom) Laursen
Vice President corporate Compliance Manager, Nancy Hodge
Vice President of Call Centre, Marty Nowling
Vice President Product Manager, Chris Cyprien
Senior Vice President of Private Banking, Kim Soper
Vice President, Steven (Steve) Carlson
Applications Developers Vice President Applications, Brent Briggs

Vice President Credit Administration, Thomas (Thom) Harding
Vice President Special Assets, Ernie Cassler
Vice President Treasury Management Sales Manager, Jesse Ronnow Jesse Ronnow
Vice President Of Marketing, Jammes Abbott
Executive Vice President, Robert (Bob) Boyd
Assistant Vice President Quantitative Financial Analyst, Ryan Warner
Vice President Business Development Officer, Mark Petrasso
Vice President Financial Analyst, Ian Spencer
Vice President, Brian Bare
Executive Vice President Premier Wealth Management Executive, Keith Schmidt
Vice President, Richard (Dick) Reed
Vice President, Jonathan (Jon) Bacon
Vice President, Brian Shrum
Vice President, Hope Butler
Vice President, John (Jack) Stillings
Executive Vice President, Gena Jones
Assistant Vice President, Stephanie Nicholls
Auditors: Ernst & Young LLP

LOCATIONS

HQ: Zions Bancorporation
One South Main, 15th Floor, Salt Lake City, UT 84133
Phone: 801 844-7637
Web: www.zionsbancorporation.com

PRODUCTS/OPERATIONS

Selected Subsidiaries

Amegy Corporation
  California
Great Western Financial Corporation
National Bank of Arizona
Nevada State Bank
The Commerce Bank of Oregon
The Commerce Bank of Washington
Vectra Bank Colorado
Zions First National Bank
Zions Insurance Agency Inc.
Zions Management Services Company

2014 Sales

	$ mil.	% of total
Interest income		
Interest on fees on loans	1,729	73
Interest on securities	101	4
Interest on money market investment	21	1
Non-interest income		
Other service charges commission and fees	191	8
Service charges and fees on deposit accounts	174	7
Dividend and Other investment income	43	2
Trust and wealthmanagement income	30	2
Loan sale and servicing income	26	1
Capital markets and foreign Exchange	22	1
Equty securities gains and other	13	1
Fixed income securities gains	10	-
Others	7	-
Adjustments	(11.4)	-
Total	**2,361**	**100**

COMPETITORS

BOK Financial
Bank of America
Bank of the West
Capital One
Citigroup
Cullen/Frost Bankers
First National of Nebraska

Great Western Bancorp
JPMorgan Chase
MUFG Americas Holdings
Prosperity Bancshares
U.S. Bancorp
Washington Federal
Wells Fargo

HISTORICAL FINANCIALS

Company Type: Public

Income Statement

FYE: December 31

	ASSETS ($ mil.)	NET INCOME ($ mil.)	INCOME AS % OF ASSETS	EMPLOYEES
12/14	57,208	398	0.7%	10,462
12/13	56,031	263	0.5%	10,452
12/12	55,511	349	0.6%	10,368
12/11	53,149	323	0.6%	10,606
12/10	51,034	(292)	—	10,524
Annual Growth	2.9%	—	—	(0.1%)

2014 Year-End Financials

Debt ratio: 1.87%
Return on equity: 5.76%
Cash ($ mil.): 8,020
Current ratio: —
Long-term debt ($ mil.): —

No. of shares (mil.): 203
Dividends
  Yield: 0.5%
  Payout: 15.2%
Market value ($ mil.): 5,788

	STOCK PRICE ($) FY Close	P/E High/Low	PER SHARE ($) Earnings	Dividends	Book Value
12/14	28.51	20 15	1.68	0.16	36.30
12/13	29.96	20 14	1.58	0.13	35.00
12/12	21.40	23 17	0.97	0.04	32.86
12/11	16.28	31 16	0.83	0.04	37.94
12/10	24.23	— —	(2.48)	0.04	36.37
Annual Growth	4.2%	— —	—	41.4%	(0.0%)

Hoover's Handbook of

American Business

The Indexes

Index by Headquarters

AK

Anchorage
First National Bank Alaska 337

JUNEAU
ALASKA PERMANENT FUND
CORPORATION 24

AL

Birmingham
Alabama Power Co. 22
Regions Financial Corp 685
Protective Life Insurance Co 661
ProAssurance Corp. 655
ServisFirst Bancshares, Inc. 720

AR

Bentonville
Wal-Mart Stores, Inc. 846

Conway
Home BancShares Inc 411

El Dorado
Murphy USA Inc 562
Murphy Oil Corp 561

Little Rock
Dillard's Inc. 247
Windstream Holdings Inc 869
Bank of the Ozarks, Inc. 98

Lowell
Hunt (J.B.) Transport Services, Inc.
426

Pine Bluff
Simmons First National Corp. 724

Springdale
Tyson Foods, Inc. 807

AZ

Phoenix
Avnet Inc 84
Freeport-McMoRan Inc 356
Republic Services, Inc. 691
Southern Copper Corp 732
Western Alliance Bancorporation 859
BANNER HEALTH 101

Tempe
Northern Tier Energy LP 590
Insight Enterprises Inc. 440

CA

Beverly Hills
Live Nation Entertainment, Inc. 508

Burbank
Disney (Walt) Co. (The) 253

Chico
TriCo Bancshares (Chico, CA) 802

Cupertino
Apple Inc 60

Dublin
Ross Stores, Inc. 700

El Segundo
Mattel Inc 527

Foster City
Gilead Sciences, Inc. 372

Fremont
Synnex Corp 762
Lam Research Corp 488

Glendale
Avery Dennison Corp. 81

Irvine
Ingram Micro Inc. 438
Western Digital Corp. 860
Banc of California Inc 89
Opus Bank Irvine (CA) 609
ST. JOSEPH HEALTH SYSTEM 739

Long Beach
Molina Healthcare Inc 550

Los Angeles
AECOM 10
Reliance Steel & Aluminum Co. 688
CBRE Group Inc 156
Mercury General Corp. 538
PacWest Bancorp 621
Cathay General Bancorp 155
BBCN Bancorp Inc. 107
Wilshire Bancorp Inc 868
Hanmi Financial Corp. 387

Los Gatos
Netflix Inc. 573

Menlo Park
Facebook, Inc. 304

Milpitas
SanDisk Corp. 704

Mountain View
Alphabet Inc 32
Symantec Corp. 761

Newport Beach
Pacific Mutual Holding Co. 618

Oakland
Clorox Co (The) 190

KAISER FOUNDATION HOSPITALS
INC 467

Ontario
CVB Financial Corp. 233

Palo Alto
HP Inc 421
Hewlett Packard Enterprise Co 405
VMware Inc 844

Pasadena
Jacobs Engineering Group, Inc. 455
East West Bancorp, Inc 272

Redwood City
Oracle Corp. 610

Rosemead
Edison International 278
Southern California Edison Co. 730

ROSEVILLE
FARM CREDIT WEST 306

San Diego
Qualcomm, Inc. 671
Sempra Energy 719
BofI Holding, Inc. 125

San Francisco
McKesson Corp. 533
Wells Fargo & Co. 856
PG&E Corp. (Holding Co.) 635
The Gap, Inc. 787
Visa Inc 842
Federal Reserve Bank of San
Francisco, Dist. No. 12 312
Schwab (Charles) Corp. 711
Salesforce.Com Inc 703
First Republic Bank (San Francisco,
CA) 340
Federal Home Loan Bank Of San
Francisco 308

San Jose
Cisco Systems, Inc. 181
PayPal Holdings Inc 623
eBay Inc. 275
Sanmina Corp 706

San Mateo
Franklin Resources, Inc. 354

San Rafael
WestAmerica Bancorporation 859

San Ramon
Chevron Corporation 175

Santa Ana
First American Financial Corp 323

Santa Clara
Intel Corp 441
Applied Materials, Inc. 62
SVB Financial Group 759

Santa Monica
A-Mark Precious Metals, Inc 3
Anworth Mortgage Asset Corp. 58

South San Francisco
Core Mark Holding Co Inc 221

Sunnyvale
NetApp, Inc. 572
Advanced Micro Devices, Inc. 9

Thousand Oaks
Amgen Inc 50

Torrance
Toyota Motor Credit Corp. 797

Woodland Hills
Health Net, Inc. 397

CO

Broomfield
Ball Corp 88
Level 3 Communications, Inc. 498

Centennial
Arrow Electronics, Inc. 66

Denver
DaVita HealthCare Partners Inc 239
CoBiz Financial Inc 195

Englewood
Dish Network Corp 252
Liberty Interactive Corp 500
Western Union Co. 862
CH2M Hill Companies Ltd 169
CH2M HILL COMPANIES LTD. 169

Greeley
Pilgrims Pride Corp. 639

Greenwood Village
Newmont Mining Corp. (Holding Co.)
578
Great West Life & Annuity Insurance
Co - Insurance Products 381
National Bank Holdings Corp 563

CT

Bloomfield
Cigna Corp 178

Bridgeport
People's United Financial, Inc. 628

Danbury
Praxair, Inc. 649

Fairfield
General Electric Co 364

Farmington
United Technologies Corp 828

IN

Carmel
CNO Financial Group Inc 193

Columbus
Cummins, Inc. 231

Evansville
Old National Bancorp (Evansville, IN) 605

Fort Wayne
Steel Dynamics Inc. 750

Greensburg
MainSource Financial Group Inc 515

Indianapolis
Anthem Inc 57
Lilly (Eli) & Co. 502
Calumet Specialty Product Partners LP 141

Merrillville
NiSource Inc. (Holding Co.) 585

Muncie
First Merchants Corp. 335

South Bend
1st Source Corp. 1

Terre Haute
First Financial Corp. (IN) 333

Warsaw
Lakeland Financial Corp. 488

KS

KANSAS CITY
ASSOCIATED WHOLESALE GROCERS INC. 71

Overland Park
Sprint Corp (New) 738
YRC Worldwide Inc 880

Shawnee Mission
Seaboard Corp. 713

Topeka
Capitol Federal Financial Inc 149

Wichita
Spirit AeroSystems Holdings Inc 736

KY

Covington
Ashland Inc 68

Highland Heights
General Cable Corp. (DE) 361

Louisville
Humana Inc. 425
Yum! Brands, Inc. 881
Kindred Healthcare Inc 478
Republic Bancorp, Inc. (KY) 690
Stock Yards Bancorp Inc 753

Pikeville
Community Trust Bancorp, Inc. 212

LA

CHALMETTE
CHALMETTE REFINING L.L.C. 171

COVINGTON
ZEN-NOH GRAIN CORPORATION 882
CGB ENTERPRISES INC. 169

Lafayette
IBERIABANK Corp 432

Monroe
CenturyLink, Inc. 167
Qwest Corp 677

New Orleans
Entergy Corp. 289
First NBC Bank Holding Co. 338

MA

Boston
Santander Holdings USA Inc. 708
State Street Corp. 748
Boston Private Financial Holdings, Inc. 130
Brookline Bancorp Inc (DE) 135
NewStar Financial Inc 580

Cambridge
Biogen Inc 117

Framingham
TJX Companies, Inc. 793
Staples Inc 742

Hanover
Independent Bank Corp. (MA) 437

Hopkinton
EMC Corp. (MA) 279

Marlborough
Boston Scientific Corp. 130

Medford
Century Bancorp, Inc. 167

Peabody
Meridian Bancorp Inc 539

Pittsfield
Berkshire Hills Bancorp, Inc. 113

Springfield
Eversource Energy 295

Waltham
Raytheon Co. 682
Global Partners LP 374
Thermo Fisher Scientific Inc 789

Worcester
Hanover Insurance Group Inc 387

MD

Bethesda
Lockheed Martin Corp. 511
Marriott International, Inc. 520
Host Hotels & Resorts Inc 419
Eagle Bancorp Inc (MD) 272

HANOVER
ALLEGIS GROUP INC. 26
AEROTEK INC. 11

Olney
Sandy Spring Bancorp Inc 705

Silver Spring
Discovery Communications, Inc. 250

ME

Camden
Camden National Corp. (ME) 143

MI

Auburn Hills
BorgWarner Inc 128

Battle Creek
Kellogg Co 470

Benton Harbor
Whirlpool Corp 865

Bloomfield Hills
Penske Automotive Group Inc 627

Dearborn
Ford Motor Co. (DE) 351

Detroit
General Motors Co. 368
DTE Energy Co. 266
Ally Financial Inc 30
DTE Electric Company 265

EAST LANSING
GREENSTONE FARM CREDIT SERVICES ACA 382

Grand Rapids
SpartanNash Co. 733
Mercantile Bank Corp. 535

Jackson
CMS Energy Corp 191
Consumers Energy Co. 221

Kalamazoo
Stryker Corp. 753

Midland
Dow Chemical Co. 262
Chemical Financial Corp 173

Southfield
Lear Corp. 492
Federal-Mogul Holdings Corp 313

Taylor
Masco Corp. 524

TRAVERSE CITY
ADVANTAGE ELECTRIC SERVICES LLC 10

Troy
Kelly Services, Inc. 471
Flagstar Bancorp, Inc. 345
Talmer Bancorp Inc 767

Van Buren Township
Visteon Corp. 843

MN

Arden Hills
Land O' Lakes Inc 489

Austin
Hormel Foods Corp. 417

Eden Prairie
Supervalu Inc. 758
Robinson (C.H.) Worldwide, Inc. 696

Inver Grove Heights
CHS Inc 177

Minneapolis
Target Corp 769
U.S. Bancorp (DE) 809
General Mills, Inc. 366
Ameriprise Financial Inc 46
Xcel Energy, Inc. 876
RiverSource Life Insurance Co 695

Minnetonka
UnitedHealth Group Inc 829

Plymouth
Mosaic Co (The) 557

Richfield
Best Buy Inc 114

St. Paul
3M Co 1
Ecolab, Inc. 276
St Jude Medical Inc 738

Wayzata
TCF Financial Corp 771

MO

Chesterfield
Reinsurance Group of America, Inc. 687

Clayton
First Banks, Inc. (MO) 326
Enterprise Financial Services Corp 290

Kansas City
Commerce Bancshares, Inc. 206
UMB Financial Corp 813
Kansas City Life Insurance Co. (Kansas City, MO) 468

Springfield
O'Reilly Automotive, Inc. 601
Great Southern Bancorp, Inc. 380

St. Louis
Express Scripts Holding Co 301
Emerson Electric Co. 282
Centene Corp 162
Monsanto Co. 553
Peabody Energy Corp 624
Ameren Corp. 37
Graybar Electric Co., Inc. 379
Stifel Financial Corp. 751

MS

Gulfport
Hancock Holding Co. 385

Jackson
Trustmark Corp. 805

Tupelo
BancorpSouth Inc. 91
Renasant Corp 690

MT

Billings
First Interstate BancSystem, Inc. 335

Kalispell
Glacier Bancorp, Inc. 373

NC

Asheville
HomeTrust Bancshares Inc 414

Burlington
Laboratory Corporation of America Holdings 486

Charlotte
Bank of America Corp. 92
Duke Energy Corp 268
Nucor Corp. 600
Sonic Automotive, Inc. 727
Sealed Air Corp. 715
Duke Energy Carolinas LLC 268

Index of Executives

A

Aadland, Todd 309
Aaefedt, Matthew 830
Aaholm, Sherry A. 231
Aakre, Scott 417
Aaron, Neil 579
Aaronian, Ray 317
Aasland, Steiner 561
Abad, Cheryl 9
Abate, Jason 206
Abate, Victor (Vic) 364
Abato, John 186
Abbagnaro, Gary 280
Abbas, Atif 7
Abbate, Anthony 466
Abbate, Mark L. 539
Abbey, Rita 317
Abbey, Bill 600
Abbey, Dick 765
Abbey, Donna 863
Abbott, Lynn 47
Abbott, Justin 444
Abbott, Mark 681
Abbott, James (Jamie) 883
Abbott, Jammes 884
Abboud, Andrew (Andy) 491
Abboud, Ali El 749
Abburi, Aparna 163
Abdella, Shelly 854
Abdo, David (Dave) 254
Abdoo, Elizabeth A. 420
Abdulmalek, Idora 303
Abdulsattar, Younos 634
Abed, Osama 5
Abel, Gregory E. (Greg) 619
Abel-Hodges, Cheryl 670
Abele, Jennifer (Jen) 681
Abelenda, Gustavo H. 552
Abella, Ilene 359
Abelli, Donna L. 437
Abello, Marc P 205
Abeln, Jeur 203
Abend, Marc 509
Abendschein, Robert (Bob) 55
Aberle, Derek K. 672
Abernathy, Lawrence 524
Abeyta, Brian 16
Abid, Nicholas 856
Abiera, Henry (Hal) 170
Abji, Minaz B. 420
Ables, Grady L. 60
Ables, Dorothy M. 736
Abner, Deb 429
Abney, David P. 824
Aboaf, Eric 188
Abood, Steven 688
Aboulafia, Joseph (Jo) 97
Abraham, Sandra 106
Abraham, Cecelia M. 285
Abraham, JJ 496
Abraham, Spencer 603
Abraham, Dana 814
Abrahamson, Herbert 70
Abrahamson, Joel 416
Abramov, Evgenia 443
Abramowicz, Daniel A. 226
Abrams, Steve 105
Abrams, Murray 148
Abrams, Ed 448
Abramson, Jim 521
Abrol, Nish 673
Abruzzese, Joseph (Joe) 251
Abston, Angie 820
Abston, Chris 848
Abts, Joy 811
Accurso-Soto, Joanne 664
Acevedo, Diego 184

Acevedo, Margie 530
Ach, J. Wickliffe 332
Achary, Michael M. 385
Acharya, Ravi 466
Acito, Paiul 3
Ackels, George 280
Acker, Tim 763
Ackerman, Michelle 29
Ackerman, Steven 91
Ackermann, John (Jack) 570
Ackerson, Vince A. 783
Acoca, Bernard 745
Acosta, Fernando J. 86
Acosta, Matthew (Matt) 349
Acquaviva, David (Dave) 717
Acree, Will 375
Acuna, Bilda 834
Acutt, Nicola 845
Adair, Lori 522
Adam, Tim 254
Adamcewicz, Thomas 710
Adamczyk, Darius 415
Adame, Norma 230
Adamo, Gina 793
Adamos, Tara 435
Adams, Doug 85
Adams, Ann 106
Adams, Kent M. 154
Adams, Will 157
Adams, Kevin D. 169
Adams, Thomas E. (Tom) 172
Adams, Kraig 196
Adams, Charles H. (Hal) 228
Adams, Melissa (Mel) 230
Adams, Rich 286
Adams, Richard L. 286
Adams, Rick 286
Adams, R L 286
Adams, Craig L. 297
Adams, Jason 310
Adams, Gina 315
Adams, Joseph P. 353
Adams, John L. 382
Adams, David (Dave) 384
Adams, Isaac 393
Adams, David (Dave) 444
Adams, Bill 460
Adams, Gregory A. 467
Adams, Annette 481
Adams, Calvin (Cal) 513
Adams, Romaneo 524
Adams, Jennifer 524
Adams, John 575
Adams, Matt 594
Adams, Scott 605
Adams, Carol 611
Adams, Deborah (Deb) 638
Adams, Michael 652
Adams, Brent 660
Adams, David (Dave) 679
Adams, William 707
Adams, Bradley 731
Adams, Patricia (Trish) 770
Adams, Trish 771
Adams, Jess 814
Adams, Richard M. 819
Adams, Pearl 835
Adams, Gary 848
Adamson, Adam 118
Adamson, Shawn 203
Adas, Greg 573
Adcock, Robert H. 411
Adcock, Bernie 808
Addanki, Vijay 749
Adderley, Terence E. (Terry) 472
Addison, John A. 652
Addison, John A. 653
Addison, James E. (Jimmy) 709
Addotta, Sibylle 528

Adelberger, Marc 95
Adelmann, Chris 509
Adelsberg, Saul 766
Adelson, Sarah 310
Adelson, Sheldon G. 491
Adinolfi, Jon Michael 742
Adkerson, Richard C. 357
Adkins, Lee 120
Adkins, Dan 211
Adkinson, J. Daniel (Dan) 580
Adkison, Jeff 464
Adkison, Paula 534
Adler, Robin 422
Adler, Robert L 730
Adornato, Theodore C. (Ted) 734
Advani, Vijay C. 355
Advani, Deepak 447
Aerts, Kurt 303
Afejuku, Ayo 551
Afflerbach, Mary 18
Aflatooni, Bobby 256
Afonso, Maria 632
Agabob, Keith 138
Agarwal, Anu 152
Agemura, Lai 29
Aggarwal, Lokesh 749
Aghdami, Amanda 148
Aghili, Aziz S. 236
Agiasotis, Kerry 863
Agnew, James (Jamie) 359
Agnew, James 439
Agrawal, Yogesh 422
Agrawal, Rajesh K. 863
Aguayo, Sebastian 523
Aguiar, Matthew 303
Aguila, Stephanie 322
Aguila, Edith 718
Aguilar, Dan 760
Aguinaga, Christina 530
Aguirre, Manuel E. 170
Aguirre, Yazmin 280
Agyemang, Simon 767
Agypt, Ron 16
Ahe, Catherine (Cathy) Von Der 105
Ahearn, Carl 173
Ahearn, Chris 513
Ahearn, Tracey 513
Ahee, Joseph 429
Ahern, Grant 184
Ahern, R 312
Aherne, Sean 132
Aherne, Andrew (Andy) 254
Ahlborn, Frank 810
Ahlstedt, Mark 413
Ahlstedt, Courtney 851
Ahmed, Amir 252
Ahmed, Savant 365
Ahmed, Saroosh 792
Ahn, Randy 548
Ahn, J 573
Ahrendts, Angela 61
Ahrens, Matthew (Matt) 420
Ahrens, C. Brant 655
Ahsing, Yvonne 318
Ahwesh, Philip 645
Ai, Chen 120
Aibel, James (Jamie) 97
Aiken, Robert B. (Bob) 295
Aiken, Jason W. 363
Aikie, Lin 374
Ailes, Roger 807
Ainsley, Beverly 681
Ainsworth, William P. (Billy) 154
Aird, Wendy 299
Aiyathurai, Sashi 393
Akalski, Frank J. 348
Akeena, David (Dave) 804
Akeroyd, Kevin 610
Akers, Gregory 182

Akers, Dave 393
Akerson, Eileen G. 469
Akewusola, Taye 303
Akey, Jason 591
Akey, Jason 592
Akhtar, Shahzad 866
Akhtari, Afsaneh 537
Akil, Eric 121
Akimseu, Momi 95
Akins, Nicholas K. (Nick) 40
Akins, D. Wayne 764
Akolawala, Joher 553
Akrout, Chekib 9
Aksdal, Roy 148
Alam, Imtiaz 537
Alameddine, Ric 778
Alamo, Lisette 530
Alandt, Robert (Bob) 843
Alarcon, Brenda 203
Alarcon, Javier 216
Alban, Carlos 6
Albanese, Gerard 520
Albanesi, David (Dave) 811
Alber, Claude 699
Alberico, Matt 179
Alberico, Robert 707
Albers, Carissa 207
Albers, Chuck 216
Albers, Mark W 302
Albers, Ryan 307
Albert, Don 276
Albert, Michael S. 576
Albert, Shadi 718
Alberti, Sue 246
Albertini, Jamie 101
Albertsen, Mark 357
Albis, Noel 5
Albo, Teresa 495
Albright, Lynn 788
Albright, Brandy 832
Albury, Christyne 757
Alch, Steven 93
Alcid, Benjamin 541
Alden, John (Jack) 645
Alderman, Mark 524
Alderoty, Stuart 424
Aldous, David (Dave) 339
Aldrete, Eddie 446
Aldrich, David 127
Aldrich, Renee 272
Alec, Pittman 853
Alegre, Erlinda D 95
Alejandro, Freddy 201
Aleles, Margaret (Peg) 460
Aleman, Gregg 359
Aleman-Bermudez, Aurelio 325
Alemany, Ellen R. 185
Alexa, Wade 605
Alexander, Susan H. 117
Alexander, Mark R. 145
Alexander, Robert M. 148
Alexander, Rebecca 161
Alexander, Patricia (Pat) 206
Alexander, Neal 270
Alexander, Rosalind 272
Alexander, Denise 315
Alexander, Kathy 327
Alexander, Anthony 342
Alexander, Amarin 426
Alexander, Forbes I. J. 455
Alexander, James 731
Alexander, Tim 732
Alexander, Hank 755
Alexander, Derek 763
Alexander, Cory B. 830
Alexander, Brian 874
Alexander, Charles (Chas) 879
Alexander, Bruce K. 883
Alexandra, Jorissen 304

Alfano, David 311
Alfano, Susan 664
Alfonso, Elizabeth (Beth) 757
Alfrejd, Marcy 530
Alger, Eugene K. 300
Algozino, Phil 360
Alhaffar, Mohammed 194
Ali, Reaz 132
Ali, Michael 379
Ali, Mohamad S. 406
Aliabadi, Paymon 297
Alibrandi, Carlo 836
Alix, Vivek 311
Aljallad, Firas 187
Alke, Dottie 158
Allaben, Greg 605
Allaire, Bella L. 681
Allan, Derek 88
Allan, Donald (Don) 742
Allard, Erin 786
Allberry, Katie Drinan 530
Allbrooks, Allison 770
Alchin, Dena 14
Allen, Hubert L. 5
Allen, Blane 91
Allen, Grace 97
Allen, Kim 106
Allen, Andrew 118
Allen, Ken 121
Allen, Bertrand-Marc (Marc) 124
Allen, Lee 126
Allen, Thad W. 127
Allen, James 128
Allen, Jonathan (Jon) 128
Allen, Tom 147
Allen, Lawren 149
Allen, Graylen 168
Allen, Greg 179
Allen, Bryan 184
Allen, Julianne 184
Allen, Barbara (Barb) 203
Allen, Lane 205
Allen, Brad 216
Allen, James (Jamie) 230
Allen, Douglas 240
Allen, Samuel R. (Sam) 242
Allen, Christopher 336
Allen, Chris 404
Allen, Rusty 420
Allen, Steve 443
Allen, Jane (Ginny) 456
Allen, John (Jack) 459
Allen, MichaelA 471
Allen, Sarah K. 494
Allen, Albert (Al) 503
Allen, Jeffrey 526
Allen, Rick 527
Allen, Brenda 530
Allen, Angelique 531
Allen, Robin 534
Allen, Joe 535
Allen, Todd 556
Allen, Stephen B (Steve) 608
Allen, Robert (Bob) 610
Allen, Bradley 681
Allen, Ira 683
Allen, Josh 686
Allen, Michael 689
Allen, Patrick E. 699
Allen, Gary 702
Allen, Vanessa 717
Allen, Josh 853
Allenson, John 339
Alles, Mark J. 161
Allese, Sarah 466
Alley, Alex 319
Alley, Jim 528
Alley, Brayton 593
Alleyn, Kate 556
Alleyne, Richard (Dick) 393
Allinson, Paul 176
Allinson, Brooke 679
Allison, Mike 19
Allison, Peter 78
Allison, Jocelyn 139
Allison, Thomas 168
Allison, John W. 411

Allison, Linn 481
Allison, Chandra 491
Allison, Michael 604
Allison, Richard 611
Allison, Paul D. 681
Allison, Dana 686
Allison, Jeff 843
Allman, Keith J. 525
Allman, Jan 568
Allport, Jeff 740
Allred, Julie 176
Allred, Paula 432
Allred, Bryan 765
Allrich, Theodore C. (Ted) 125
Allshouse, Scott 868
Allsop, Michael 710
Allumbaugh, David (Dave) 802
Ally, Desiree 556
Almazan, Cynthia 673
Almeida, Jos © E. (Joe) 104
Almeida, Ana 185
Almeida, Denise 475
Almeida, Marcus 767
Almeida, Odilon 863
Almonte, Bob 55
Almy, Scott A. 493
Aloia, Sal 122
Alonge, Steve 832
Alonso, Steven 321
Alonso, Sergio 453
Alonso, Henry 475
Alonso, Hector R. 499
Alonso, Joaquin 702
Alonzo, Annette 229
Alouf, Benjamin 14
Alpert, Iris 545
Alpert, Stan 557
Alptekin, Alper 537
Alseth, Becky 83
Alsip, Larry 809
Alspaugh, Rick 166
Alstadter, David 745
Alstead, Troy 744
Alt, Aaron 770
Alt, Randy 879
Altbaum, Ron 654
Alter, Ed 749
Althaus, Steve 417
Althauser, Chris 380
Altimari, Chuck 824
Altizer, Jay 241
Altman, Arnold 100
Altman, William M. 479
Altman, Steven (Steve) 673
Altman, Stanley J. (Stan) 689
Altman, Dave 731
Altmann, Charmaine 365
Altobelli, Tony 33
Alton, Gregg H. 373
Altre-Kerber, Alison 475
Altschul, Larry 545
Altschul, Larry 875
Altshuler, Maurice 556
Alvarado, Rosa 13
Alvarado, Joseph (Joe) 208
Alvarado, Jennifer (Jen) 446
Alvarez, Eddie 43
Alvarez, Miguel 616
Alvarez, Ignacio 646
Alvarez, Sobeida 701
Alvarez, Paul 721
Alvarez, Peter 836
Alvaro, Jay 270
Alvero, Gumer C 47
Alverson, Chris 534
Alverson, Michael 586
Alves, Sandra 162
Alves, Simon 448
Alvi, Ncole 50
Alviti, Paulette R. 350
Alzetta-Reali, Silvi 197
Amador, Richard (Dick) 148
Amaral, Danny 319
Amari, Lynda 97
Amaro, Angel 770
Amat, Leonardo 173
Amato, Jill 130

Amato, Joseph (Jo) 356
Amato, Len 792
Amato, Tony 879
Amaya, Hector 196
Amble, Mike 319
Amble, Marcy 532
Ambrose, Steve 265
Ambrose, Steve 266
Ambrose, Steven 323
Ambrose, Curtis 376
Ambrose, Allan 593
Ambrosio, Anthony G. 158
Ambrosio, Mike 846
Ambrosius, Jorg 749
Amen, Darrell van 413
Amendola, Antonio 75
Amendola, Lou 105
Amerongen, Marcel Van 160
Ames, Jacqueline 272
Ames, Darlene 359
Ames, Marshall H 496
Amick, W. Michael 450
Amin, Dipti 677
Amir, Shakeel 121
Amirian, Brian 841
Amirshahi, Bobby 791
Amlung, Ray 231
Ammann, Daniel (Dan) 368
Ammann, Marina 614
Amoh, Minoru 268
Amon, Cristiano R. 672
Amon, Christiano 673
Amori, June 663
Amoriell, Dave 878
Amoroso, Michael 122
Amoroso, Sheila 355
Amos, Daniel P. (Dan) 16
Amos, Paul S. 16
Amos, Jim 766
Amosson, Brett 793
Ampolini, Frederic P. (Fred) 693
Amundsen, Brad 70
Anand, Nishant (Shaun) 102
Anand, Niraj 443
Anand, Manu 552
Ananth, Paul 749
Anastas, Will 704
Anastasi, Jack 612
Anastasi, Shane 704
Anastasio, Tom 2
Anastasio, Kathryn 814
Anaya, Jennifer (Jen) 439
Anaya, Pedro 825
Anda, Sergio De 843
Andasse, Christian 789
Andelman, Keith 534
Anderman, Craig 8
Anders, Kim 70
Anders, Jeff 106
Anders, Mark 352
Andersen, Jesper 182
Andersen, Steve 347
Andersen, Robert (Bob) 415
Andersen, Ric 475
Anderskouv, Niels 784
Anderskow, Jerry 19
Anderson, John (Jack) 11
Anderson, Bryan 29
Anderson, Glen 32
Anderson, Valerie 37
Anderson, Peter (Pete) 43
Anderson, Tracy 47
Anderson, Jonie 51
Anderson, Gary A. 52
Anderson, Dave 55
Anderson, Brian K 75
Anderson, Wes 99
Anderson, Rhonda 102
Anderson, Lisa Stevens 102
Anderson, Theresa 104
Anderson, Daniel 125
Anderson, Charlie 126
Anderson, Kristine Martin 128
Anderson, William A. 142
Anderson, Carol 148
Anderson, Jill 163
Anderson, Jim 242

Anderson, Richard H. 245
Anderson, Gerard M. 266
Anderson, Jim 284
Anderson, Jeffery 310
Anderson, Lars C. 321
Anderson, Megan 322
Anderson, Michael 334
Anderson, Paul 382
Anderson, Lynn 406
Anderson, Phyllis 425
Anderson, Kory 444
Anderson, A. Scott 444
Anderson, Michael R (Mel) 462
Anderson, Miles 463
Anderson, Zach 464
Anderson, Ian D. 478
Anderson, Carl A. 480
Anderson, Kari J 493
Anderson, James M. (Jamie) 516
Anderson, James (Jamie) 527
Anderson, Perry 534
Anderson, Don 542
Anderson, Denise 542
Anderson, Brad 546
Anderson, Dana 553
Anderson, Adam 556
Anderson, Dan 557
Anderson, Roger 573
Anderson, Mark 584
Anderson, David (Dave) 617
Anderson, Carol 629
Anderson, Noel 632
Anderson, Eric 670
Anderson, John H. 671
Anderson, Nick 671
Anderson, Roger W 683
Anderson, Susan (Sue) 686
Anderson, Scott 701
Anderson, Steven H. (Steve) 712
Anderson, Jeffrey (Jeff) 712
Anderson, Bob 719
Anderson, Philip D. 737
Anderson, Jim 750
Anderson, Frank 757
Anderson, Kristen 770
Anderson, Phillip M. 782
Anderson, Stephen A. (Steve) 784
Anderson, Sean 793
Anderson, Sandi 794
Anderson, Natascha 803
Anderson, Craig L. 814
Anderson, Christine 830
Anderson, Tira 835
Anderson, Gillian 841
Anderson, Becki 848
Anderson, Larry 856
Anderson, Thomas F. (Tom) 874
Anderson, Tom 875
Anderson, A. Scott (Scott) 883
Anderson, Howard 884
Anderson, Ryan 884
Andersson, Bo 280
Andersson, Bo 778
Anderton, Amanda 211
Andis, Sylvia 701
Andonian, Aram 94
Andrada, Marissa 745
Andrade, Karen 388
Andrade, Alexandre 460
Andrade, Diego 767
Andrade, Dannielle 851
Andreessen, Marc L. 406
Andreotti, Lamberto 133
Andres, Eva 280
Andres, Michael D. (Mike) 532
Andres, Mindi 851
Andrew, Cooley 332
Andrew, Gladu 757
Andrews, Mark 45
Andrews, Mark 47
Andrews, Timothy 128
Andrews, John (Jack) 534
Andrews, Kirkland B. 599
Andrews, Charles 608
Andrews, Audrey T. 777
Andrews, Madhuri 803
Andrews, Rob 820

Azevedo, Jose 460
Azinovic, Drago 637
Aziz, Ehab 556
Aziz, Gamal 875
Azmy, Nahla 599
Azralon, Al 138
Azuara, Kathy 104
Azzarello, Mark 450
Azzinaro, Peter 811

B

Baaklini, Lana 657
Babakanian, Rubik 861
Babb, Ralph W. 205
Babb, Ovid 319
Babb, Daniel (Dan) 774
Babbar, Harish 749
Babbio, Lawrence T. (Larry) 406
Baber, Deborah 212
Babic, Reisa 760
Babikian, Jeffrey C (Jeff) 157
Babikian, Jeffrey 157
Babilino, Danielle 876
Babineau, Thomas 129
Babineaux-Fontenot, Claire 848
Baca, Kristin 879
Bach, Carl L. 567
Bachaalani, Issam 201
Bacheller, Paula 839
Bachmann, Lisa M. 116
Bachmann, Oliver 504
Bacigalupo, George F. 113
Back, Tekla 632
Back, Deborah (Deb) 841
Backer, Daniel (Dan) 205
Backman, Cathy 78
Backman, Bret 300
Backs, Tim 283
Bacon, Graham W. 292
Bacon, Francie 339
Bacon, Jim 352
Bacon, Ashley 465
Bacon, Jonathan (Jon) 884
Bacsi, Rich 803
Bacus, Lisa R. 179
Badali, Annette 188
Badar, Ruben 556
Badawy, Christina 78
Badde, Vijaysekhar 632
Badders, Matt 230
Badeaux, Montreen 433
Bader, Rupert 548
Badler, Richard (Dick) 863
Badura, Gregory 155
Bae, Soon 107
Baehren, James W 616
Baehren, James (Jamie) 616
Baeppler, Torsten 354
Baer, Richard N. (Rich) 501
Baer, Werner 648
Baer, Timothy R. (Tim) 770
Baer, TimothyR 771
Baer, Tim 771
Baer, Chris 788
Baerlocher, Shawn 391
Baez, Yosvany 94
Baez, Ramon F. 406
Baeza, Raul 398
Bafford, Carol 179
Bagard, Jean-pierre 198
Bagby, Joseph 481
Bagdasarian, Robert (Bob) 749
Bagdasarian, Ara 800
Baggett, Kelvin A. 777
Bagley, Ted 50
Bagley, Chris A. 92
Bagley, Rick 270
Bagley, Ross 730
Bagley, Mark A. 772
Bagshaw, William (Bill) 611
Bagwell, Erik 166
Bahel, James (Jamie) 494
Bahl, Romil 213
Bahl, Tracy L. 236
Bahner, Craig 470

Bahorich, Michael S. (Mike) 60
Bahr, Michael 14
Bai, Eugene 186
Baier, Lucinda M. (Cindy) 135
Baier, Erich 448
Baig, Esmeralda 163
Bailey, Bob 22
Bailey, Ian 64
Bailey, Stuart (Stu) 68
Bailey, Nancy 124
Bailey, Michelle 179
Bailey, James 184
Bailey, Bill J 254
Bailey, David 333
Bailey, Gerri 334
Bailey, Krista 339
Bailey, Timothy 354
Bailey, Richard 421
Bailey, Kerry 422
Bailey, Alan 426
Bailey, Brett 428
Bailey, Matthew (Matt) 435
Bailey, Todd 465
Bailey, Dan 493
Bailey, Marjorie 495
Bailey, Rosie 556
Bailey, Kyle 568
Bailey, Andy 610
Bailey, Michael 625
Bailey, Kathryn 630
Bailey, Tony 632
Bailey, Mike 673
Bailey, David (Dave) 686
Bailey, Daniel K. (Dan) 802
Bailey, Dan 802
Bailey, Reed 884
Bailis, Bevin 481
Bails, Stephanie 699
Baily, Ryan 859
Baime, Ronald E. (Ron) 247
Bain, Steve 360
Bain, Steve 835
Baines, Heather U. 58
Baines, Eileen 863
Baiocchi, Carol 481
Baird, Jamie 121
Baird, Liz 448
Baird, Alice 629
Baird, Geoffrey 717
Baitler, Robert 530
Bajtos, Scott 845
Baker, Sherry 14
Baker, Tom 67
Baker, Charles E. 89
Baker, Charles 97
Baker, Lloyd W. 100
Baker, A 140
Baker, Kim 168
Baker, Roger 178
Baker, Maureen 187
Baker, Karen 203
Baker, Timothy J. (Tim) 209
Baker, Wayne 230
Baker, Scott 236
Baker, Melissa 239
Baker, Douglas M. (Doug) 277
Baker, Peter (Pete) 282
Baker, Jamie 317
Baker, Sally 356
Baker, Emily 376
Baker, Paula 448
Baker, Daniel (Dan) 460
Baker, Jennifer 499
Baker, Robert W (Bob) 504
Baker, Camellia 523
Baker, Delores 551
Baker, Charles 575
Baker, Lauriegone 617
Baker, Jane (Ginny) 673
Baker, Susan 686
Baker, Tom 705
Baker, J. Chris 719
Baker, Paul Baker Paul 724
Baker, Stephen W. (Steve) 736
Baker, Neal 783
Baker, Ronald (Ron) 783
Baker, Barbara J. 816

Baker-Coy, Susie 231
Bakhaus, Don 712
Bakish, Robert M. (Bob) 841
Bakonyi, Stephen (Steve) 365
Bakstansky, Peter 310
Bala, Raj 199
Bala, Aru 742
Balaban, David 51
Balaban, David (Dave) 51
Balachandran, Madhavan 50
Balachandran, Madhu 51
Balagna, Jeffrey A. (Jeff) 717
Balagopal, Ramkumar 199
Balaguer, John 683
Balakleyevskiy, Ilya 548
Balakrishnan, Karthik 573
Balamaci, Nick 311
Balasubramanian, Girish 863
Balasubramaniyam, Sam 393
Balaszi, Theresa 359
Balawajder, Charles G. 827
Balchak, Tom 256
Baldasano, Manuel 708
Baldauf, Sari M. 406
Balderian, Bernadita 135
Balderrama, Raymundo 352
Baldesweiler, Kim 663
Balding, Thomas (Thom) 439
Baldwin, K. Rone 163
Baldwin, Dave 213
Baldwin, James L. (Jim) 264
Baldwin, Terry 280
Baldwin, Bryan 293
Baldwin, Deborah 310
Baldwin, Scott 359
Baldwin, Robert H. 544
Baldwin, Denise 656
Bales, Brian A. 691
Baley, Blayne 333
Bali, Nayantara 657
Baliff, Jonathan (Jon) 599
Baline, Lorraine 293
Balkir, Hurkan 521
Ball, Gary 17
Ball, Jennifer (Jen) 75
Ball, Susan (Sue) 234
Ball, Tracey 466
Ball, B. Dustin 541
Ball, Michael 645
Ballard, Eugene G. 111
Ballard, Shari L. 114
Ballard, Joe 358
Ballard, Amanda 839
Ballein, Ryan 697
Ballew, Bart 319
Ballew, Missy 422
Ballin, Joanne 420
Ballinger, Kevin J. 131
Ballman, David 382
Ballog, Patrick (Paddy) 678
Ballotti, Geoffrey A. (Geoff) 874
Ballweg, Sallyanne K. 340
Balmuth, Michael A. 700
Balon, Brad 832
Balousek, Jon 190
Balside, Laura 322
Baltz, Linda 634
Banas, Bernard 402
Banati, April 470
Banavige, Joe 707
Bancroft, Charles A. 133
Band, Alexandra 681
Bandi, Bruce 857
Bandy, Kevin 182
Bandy, Meredith 578
Banerjee, Prith 406
Banerjee, Koushik 443
Banerjee, Rajesh 611
Banerji, Shumeet 406
Banga, Ajaypal S. (Ajay) 526
Bangert, Steven 195
Bangs, Richard 679
Banis, R. Daniel 233
Banister, Mark 256
Bank, Steven (Steve) 514
Bankes, Henry (Hal) 874
Banks, Dave 152

Banks, Thomas 437
Banks, Marcia 594
Banks, Lee C. 622
Banks, Michael (Mel) 651
Banks, Joseph 721
Banks, Michelle 788
Banks-Ficcio, Donna 758
Bannatyne, Kristi 548
Bannell, Scott 742
Banner, Lisa 517
Banner, Jon 631
Bansch, Jan L 284
Banse, Amy L. 203
Banta, Tony 182
Bante, Michael (Mel) 456
Bantz, Kirk 151
Banziger, Lori 827
Baptist, Kevin 95
Bar-Adon, Eshel 125
Baracco, Mare 3
Baraddon, Cynthia 533
Barajas, Carol 270
Baramawi, Wael 694
Baranaskas, Brian 30
Baranovsky, Leon 183
Barash, Andrew 170
Baratta, Joseph P. 121
Barauskas, Bob 721
Barba, Peter (Pete) 421
Barbagallo, John A. 659
Barbar, Kari 448
Barbara, Bridge 435
Barbarick, Steve K. 798
Barbeau, Trudy 860
Barbee, Anthony W. (Tony) 669
Barbella, Al 452
Barbella, Albert (Al) 452
Barber, Rebecca 186
Barber, Bernadette 209
Barber, Timothy C. 300
Barber, Mark 365
Barber, Tim 429
Barber, Walter 456
Barber, Greg 548
Barber, Dave 681
Barber, Ken 720
Barber, Sandy 740
Barber, John 767
Barber, Terry 795
Barber, James J. (Jim) 824
Barber, Ken 833
Barber, Tom 875
Barbercheck, Richard S. 332
Barberesi, Vincent 121
Barbi, Glenn 108
Barbour, D. Scott 283
Barbour, Scott 283
Barbour, Tam 853
Barbuto, Frank 527
Barckhahn, Oswald 631
Barclay, Kathleen 483
Bardot, Rob 47
Bardsley, Laurence 749
Bardusch, William (Bill) 466
Bardwil, Steven 254
Bare, Brian 884
Bareford, Steven (Steve) 311
Barend, Samara 11
Baresich, Michael 30
Barfield, Lowry 862
Barge, James (Jamie) 841
Barger, Bruce 7
Barger, Tricia 102
Barger, Dennis L. 111
Barger, Holli 231
Barger, John 426
Barger, Dennis L 718
Barhanovich, Kenny 205
Barila, Martin (Marti) 3
Bariquit, Teri 588
Baritz, Stuart 541
Barja, Allan 121
Barjesteh, Nina 770
Barkan, Lisa 495
Barker, Shawn 89
Barker, Paul 157
Barker, Ronald (Ron) 283

Berwick, Belinda 523
Berzin, Tammy 5
Besanko, Bruce H. 758
Besendorfer, Christopher (Chris) 43
Beserra, Rudy 196
Beshah, Guenet 148
Beshar, Peter J. 523
Bessant, Catherine P. (Cathy) 93
Bessel, Polly 75
Bessette, Diane J 496
Bessette, Andy F. 801
Bessette, Stephen (Steve) 852
Bessman, Linda 834
Best, Mike 584
Betancourt, Edwin 104
Betancourt, Frank 604
Bethea, Rudy 541
Bethea, Paula Harper 730
Betrovski, Peter (Pete) 794
Betsworth, Kate 818
Bettadapur, Shailesh 550
Bettencourt, Debbie 355
Bettin, Nick 16
Bettinger, Douglas R. (Doug) 489
Bettinger, Walter W. (Walt) 712
Bettman, Suzanne S. 260
Betts, Steven (Steve) 171
Betts, Kathy 359
Betz, Brenda 317
Betz, Thomas E (Thom) 630
Betz, Paul 810
Beugg, Peter 464
Beumer, Barbara (Barb) 483
Beuschlein, Teresita 832
Beussink, Steve 81
Beussink, Glen 814
Beutin, Brian 102
Bevan, Cathy 283
Bevanda, Jure 208
Beveridge, Roy A. 425
Bevilacqua, Nicholas 879
Bevilaqua, Joseph P. (Jody) 408
Bevis, Harold 245
Bewkes, Jeffrey L. (Jeff) 792
Beyer, Gary J 205
Beyer, Ken 439
Beyersdorf, James (Jamie) 712
Beyersdorfer, Jeffrey S. 862
Beyl, Jerry 316
Bezjak, Rob 380
Bezos, Jeffrey P. (Jeff) 35
Bhagat, Vic 280
Bhagat, Dave 760
Bhakhri, Sandeep 293
Bhandary, Dev 757
Bhanot, Jaya 280
Bhardwaj, Ashwani 43
Bhardwaj, Sunil 481
Bhargava, Mithu 280
Bhargava, Aashish 843
Bharper, Melissa 554
Bhartia, Gunjan 365
Bhasin, Puneet 853
Bhaskar, Rishi 559
Bhaskar, Bhavna 632
Bhat, Ganesh 187
Bhatia, Sanjay 349
Bhatia, Qamar S 415
Bhatia, Sonal 634
Bhatia, Manish 705
Bhatt, Prat 182
Bhatt, Sunil 393
Bhavsar, Danny 713
Bhela, Harvinder 548
Bhojak, Jyoti 155
Bhojwani, Vijay 97
Bhushan, Naga 673
Bhutani, Aman 299
Bhutiani, Pupinder 365
Biales, Brad 594
Bialis, Greg 458
Bialosky, David (Dave) 377
Bianco, Mary 822
Biason, Libby 509
Bibbo, Paul 793
Bible, Daryl N. 106
Bichsel, Terrence E. 343

Bickel, Michael 126
Bickett, Brent B. 317
Bickham, John R. 172
Bickings, Duane 99
Bidkar, Prashant 93
Bieber, Jayne 254
Bieber, Stephen 334
Bieber, Thomas 749
Biegen, Gregory 95
Biegger, David B. (Dave) 145
Biehl, Maureen 524
Bielar, James 75
Bielen, Richard 661
Bielenberg, David 178
Bienert, Philip 75
Bienhoff, Bruce 207
Bier, Jeff 188
Bier, Ron 757
Bierlein, Jason 343
Bierman, James L. (Jim) 614
Bierman, Brian 853
Biesanz, Mike 49
Biesterfeld, Robert 697
Biesterveld, Stephanie 216
Bifolco, Joe 339
Bifulco, Catherine 575
Biggam, Tim 871
Bigger, Jim 166
Biggs, Peter M. 95
Biggs, David 229
Biggs, M. Brett 848
Bigley, Russell 877
Bilak, Gina 53
Bilanchone, Jill 80
Bilbrey, John P. (J.P.) 401
Bilbrey, Mary E. 424
Biliunas, Ramona 774
Bilko, David (Dave) 757
Bilko, David G. (Dave) 817
Bill, Brian 832
Bill, Clark 848
Billante, Joe 276
Billharz, Ralf 657
Billig, Deborah (Deb) 5
Billings, Greg 559
Billingsley, Mark 194
Billingsley, Lori 196
Billiot, Susan (Sue) 765
Billmeyer, Sam J. 153
Billner, William 818
Bills, David G. 265
Bilney, Jody L. 425
Bilolikar, Sunil K. 844
Bilotti, Frank 176
Bilotti-Peterson, Christine 388
Bilse, Gregory 121
Bilski, Roxanne 630
Bilstrom, Jon W. 205
Bily, Shirley 838
Bimson, Stephen 139
Binaco, Chris 854
Binder, Steven G. 417
Binetti, Craig F. 267
Bing, Alden 100
Bingaman, Peter 448
Binggeli, Russell (Russ) 464
Bingham, Kim R. 155
Bingham, Glenn 319
Bingham, Paul 427
Bingham, Paula 793
Bingol, Selim 368
Bingold, Michael 348
Binkis, Timothy (Tim) 825
Binkley, David A (Dave) 866
Binkleysenior, David 866
Binkowski, Erik 157
Binns, Rob 422
Binzer, Ann 181
Biondo, Joseph (Jo) 83
Biondo, Joe 83
Biondo-Rine, Jean 514
Birch, Jeff 264
Birch, Robert F. 411
Bird, Stephen 186
Bird, Andy 254
Bird, Edwin 308
Bird, Stefan A. 619

Bird, Chris Borroni 673
Birdsong, Melissa 513
Birdwell, Gary 587
Birenbaum, Larry 182
Birenbaum, Liz 526
Birenbaum, Arthur M. 786
Birk, Mark C. 38
Birkelo, Jeff 851
Birken, Andy 534
Birkhofer, William (Bill) 456
Birkholz, Jeffrey (Jeff) 688
Birmingham, Martin K. 323
Birmingham-Byrd, Melody 269
Birnbaum, David 120
Birns, Ira M. 873
Biro, Tricia 523
Birone, Beth 343
Bisaccia, Lisa 236
Bischmann, Ben 464
Bischmann, Paul 815
Bischof, Tim 194
Bischofberger, Norbert W. 373
Bischoff, Loretta 328
Bischoff, Winfried F. W. (Win) 465
Bischoff, Michael (Mel) 523
Bischoff, Gene 879
Bisegna, Anthony C. 749
Bishop, Fred 42
Bishop, Kenneth 304
Bishop, Mark 315
Bishop, Bob 365
Bishop, Kevin 448
Bishop, Yancey 507
Bishop, Jason 514
Bishop, Marissa 579
Bishop, Steven D. (Steve) 657
Bishop, Greg 679
Bishop, Thomas (Thom) 731
Bishop, Anne 838
Bisignano, Frank J. 331
Biske, Sandra 530
Bismuth, Frederic 559
Bisno, Edward (Ed) 226
Bison, Michael (Mel) 26
Bissette, Greg 229
Biswas, Smita 94
Bitter, Mark 321
Bittler, David 841
Bitzer, Marc R. 866
Bivacca, Donald J. 502
Bixby, David (Dave) 102
Bixby, Robert Bixby Robert (Bob) 280
Bixby, R. Philip 468
Bixby, Walter E. (Web) 468
Bixby, Gregory R. (Greg) 768
Bixler, Robert 559
Black, Maria 77
Black, Tracy 427
Black, Vonda 479
Black, Richard 632
Black, Peter (Pete) 672
Black, Freddie G. 724
Black, David F. 748
Black, Benjamin (Ben) 815
Black, Mary 836
Black, Richard (Dick) 838
Blackall, Will 97
Blackburn, Fred K. 127
Blackburn, Andy 148
Blackburn, Kevin 308
Blackford, David E. 883
Blackhurst, Janis L. (Jan) Jones 139
Blackhurst, Jan 140
Blackler, Ellen 254
Blackley, James A. (Jim) 172
Blackley, Jim 173
Blackman, Harris 426
Blackmore, Paul 17
Blackwelder, John 148
Blackwell, James (Jamie) 177
Blackwell, Steve 283
Blackwell, Bradley 594
Blackwood, Brian 20
Blackwood, Eric 626
Blad, Paul 444
Blades, Alastair 111
Blagden, Robert (Bob) 467

Blain, Robert (Rob) 156
Blain, Bob 681
Blair, Brett 168
Blair, D G 410
Blair, Barbara 623
Blair, Patrick (Paddy) 704
Blais, Jim 858
Blaise, Tim 239
Blake, James (Jamie) 77
Blake, Amy 121
Blake, Alan (Al) 145
Blake, Doug 303
Blake, Terry 319
Blake, Christina 433
Blake, Patrick J. (Pat) 534
Blake, Mary 537
Blake, Christopher D. 621
Blake, David M. 653
Blake, Ginger 686
Blake, Lynn S. 749
Blake, Robbie 765
Blakely, Caroline 305
Blakemore, Anthony 730
Blakey, Laura 632
Blanc, Frank La 324
Blanc, Alain 611
Blancett, Cary S 316
Blanchard, James (Jamie) 173
Blanchard, Eric 295
Blanchard, Brent 503
Blanchard, Bob 565
Blanchard, Denise 740
Blanchette, Marc 353
Blanco, Alex 277
Blanco, Ignacio 319
Blanco, Jenny 466
Blanco-reyes, Marilyn 316
Bland, Robert (Bob) 280
Blank, Gregory 151
Blankenship, Charles P. (Chip) 364
Blankfein, Lloyd C. 375
Blankfield, Bryan J. 613
Blanton, Daniel 671
Blanton, Genie 681
Blaschke, Richard 280
Blase, William A. (Bill) 74
Blase, Kevin J 165
Blase, Marta 475
Blaser, Brian J. 5
Blasingame, James 334
Blasini, David 148
Blasius, Gordon 853
Blasko, Michael 804
Blasko, Michael (Mel) 804
Blass, Chris 467
Blastick, Mike 132
Blatt, Randy 573
Blaufuss, William 395
Blaug, Suzanne 50
Blauser, Caryn 475
Blaz, Steve 573
Blazier, Michele 85
Bledig, Stefan 554
Bleske, Mitchell 820
Blevins, P. Rodney 259
Blevins, Rodney (Rod) 259
Bley, Daniel H. 854
Blinkiewicz, John (Jack) 75
Bliss, Tyrone J. 100
Blitzer, David S. 121
Bliven, Jenni 569
Bloch, Jeremy 165
Bloch, Robert (Bob) 723
Block, Stephen 148
Block, Arthur R. 203
Block, Elizabeth (Beth) 679
Block, Keith G. 703
Blocker, Jeff 513
Blocker, Adrian M. 865
Blodgett, Tom 878
Blodnick, Michael J. (Mick) 374
Bloebaum, Amy 43
Blok-Anderson, Nancy 481
Bloom, William A. (Bill) 393
Bloom, Mary 456
Bloom, Steven 664

Bowman, Jim 316
Bowman, Lu 400
Bowman, Jeff 534
Bowman, Jim 554
Bowman, Stephen B. (Biff) 593
Bowman, Annemarie 664
Bowyer, Tracey 774
Boxall, Jenny 2
Boxer, Mark L. 179
Boxer, Jason 512
Boyce, David (Dave) 611
Boyce, Jill 727
Boyce, David S. 795
Boyd, Thomas (Thom) 157
Boyd, John J. 293
Boyd, Debby 317
Boyd, Ralph F 356
Boyd, Larry C. 439
Boyd, Christopher (Chris) 467
Boyd, Jeffery H. (Jeff) 652
Boyd, Dee 675
Boyd, William 688
Boyd, Peter M. 732
Boyd, Lois 778
Boyd, Ruth 858
Boyd, Robert (Bob) 884
Boyer, Gregg 104
Boyer, Jonathan (Jon) 475
Boyer, Jeffrey 688
Boyken, James W 448
Boykin, Rick 151
Boykin, Frank H. 549
Boykins, Lamont 47
Boylan, Peter D (Pete) 581
Boyle, Sheila 20
Boyle, Connie 75
Boyle, Hugh F. 90
Boyle, Thomas P (Thom) 111
Boyle, Jim 251
Boyle, Jeremiah 310
Boyle, James T. 487
Boyle, Ted 534
Boyle, Kevin 534
Boyle, Leo 570
Boyle, Terence 588
Boyle, Debbie 629
Boyle, Art 678
Boyle, Patti 706
Boyle, Charles F (Chas) 832
Boyles, Jonathan 725
Boyme, Susan 570
Boysen, Steve 85
Boytos, Geoff 172
Boza, Xavier 471
Boze, Scott 196
Bozer, Ahmet C. 196
Bozich, Sabrina 856
Bozonelos, Greg 796
Bozzi, Jim 509
Bozzi, Bryan 845
Braak, Cindy 521
Brabant, Steven (Steve) 157
Brabenac, Chuck 442
Brace, George 413
Bracher, Paul H. 229
Bracken, Mike 171
Brackenbury, Katie 121
Brackenbury, Catherine 122
Brad, Loughran 168
Brad, Dahlgren 226
Bradburn, John 386
Bradbury, Ray 65
Bradbury, Bob 177
Bradbury, Kent 410
Bradbury, Karen 505
Braddock, James 814
Braden, Tom 94
Bradford, Lesa 64
Bradford, Paula 92
Bradford, Darryl M. 297
Bradford, Dave 388
Bradford, Hannah (Hanna) 679
Bradie, Stuart J.B. 469
Bradish, Robert (Bob) 40
Bradley, William E. (Bill) 168
Bradley, Troy 319
Bradley, Greg 359

Bradley, R. Todd 406
Bradley, John 465
Bradley, James (Jamie) 472
Bradley, Joe 483
Bradley, Matthew 611
Bradley, John (Jack) 664
Bradley, Rex 685
Bradley, Kim 686
Bradley, Pat 688
Bradley, Phil 704
Bradley, Kevin 781
Bradley, Joe 824
Bradley, Patrick 868
Bradshaw, Adam 16
Bradshaw, Steven (Steve) 126
Bradshaw, Jim 483
Bradway, Robert (Bob) 50
Brady, Kevin 40
Brady, Molly 43
Brady, Deanna T. 417
Brady, Amy G. 475
Brady, Deborah 475
Brady, John J (Jack) 526
Brady, Jim 623
Brady, Kevin 749
Brady, Richard (Dick) 751
Brady, Bill 810
Braendeland, Jan Egil 469
Braganca, Michael 37
Brager, David A. 233
Bragg, Dorry 318
Brahmstadt, Mark L 78
Braine, Bruce H 40
Brakman, Steven 712
Bramlage, Stephen P. (Steve) 64
Bramman, Anne L. 82
Branca, Fred 526
Brand, Dennis L. 91
Brandenburg, Ben 230
Brandman, Andrew T. 184
Brandon, Joseph P. 26
Brandon, John 308
Brandow, Paul W. 271
Brandow, Robyn 310
Brandt, Stephen 53
Brandt, James (Jamie) 513
Brannen, John 16
Brannen, Carol 147
Brannen, James P. (Jim) 307
Brannock, Robert J. (Bob) 371
Brannon, Jim 102
Brannon, Jeff 151
Branon, Bethany 834
Brant, Bob 833
Brantley, Mike 210
Brantley, Todd 341
Brantley, John (Jack) 448
Branz, Sandra 393

Brascia, Pete 545
Brashear, Susan (Sue) 14
Brashear, Tom 53
Brashier, Randy 270
Brashler, Doug 343
Brassard, Michael 209
Brasser, Gary 456
Brast, Scott 45
Braswell, Sam L 205
Braswell, Tim 542
Bratches, Sean 255
Bratman, Fred 826
Bratspies, Steve 848
Bratspies, Steven (Steve) 848
Brattoli, Angelo 466
Brauer, Rod 171
Brauer, Mark 431
Braun, Bill 89
Braun, Dennis 151
Braun, C. Shay 241
Braun, Jessica 365
Braun, James E. (Jim) 561
Braun, Dick 623
Braun, Robert C. 665
Braun, Robert C. 666
Braunscheidel, Stephen J. 514
Braunstein, Louis 310
Braverman, Alan N. 254

Braverman, Stephen (Steve) 266
Bravery, Richard 119
Bravo, Diana 332
Bravo, Amparo 701
Bray, Natalie 317
Bray, Michael (Mel) 395
Bray, John K. 580
Bray, Mauread 767
Bray, David (Dave) 808
Brayer, Frank 509
Brayman, Alan (Al) 358
Brazeal, Mark 705
Brazil, Brenda 686
Brazile, Rick 848
Brazzoni, Louis 791
Brda, Bruce 559
Bready, Bruce 488
Breakstone, David (Dave) 187
Brearton, David A. (Dave) 552
Breaux, Holly 478
Breber, Pierre R. 176
Breckon, Steven 289
Bree, Joseph (Jo) 811
Breeden, Greg 427
Breeden, Jackie 514
Breeden, Kenneth R. 780
Breedon, Brent 757
Breeland, Read 629
Breeman, Steven 488
Brega, Brandon 537
Brega, Joᴄᴏ Carlos 866
Bregman, Mark F. 573
Breier, Benjamin A. 475
Breight, Matthew (Matt) 206
Breining, Dick 556
Breitfelder, John (Jack) 106
Brekka, Kevin 106
Brekke, Scott 380
Breland, Shane 806
Brell, Mark 230
Bremser, Brett 431
Brenan, Sean 376
Brendle, Jim 110
Brendle, Jeff 712
Brennan, Noreen 93
Brennan, Daniel J. (Dan) 131
Brennan, Peter 151
Brennan, Dan 187
Brennan, Troyen A. 236
Brennan, Krysten 254
Brennan, Suzanne R. 621
Brennan, Thomas 664
Brennan, Daniel 686
Brennan, Peter (Pete) 789
Brennen, Greg 203
Brennen, Robert (Bob) 319
Brenner, Ellyce 75
Brenner, Robert (Bob) 85
Brenner, Matt 443
Brenner, Timothy L. 569
Brenner, Dean 672
Brenner, Joel 792
Brensinger, Donald 694
Brent, Tom 30
Brenton, Flint 182
Bresenham, Terri 365
Bresky, Steven J. 714
Breslawski, James P. 710
Bressanelli, Mike 611
Bressler, Richard J. 434
Bressoud, Don 94
Brestovan, Peter (Pete) 629
Breter, Greg 834
Bretz, John (Jack) 55
Breukelman, Gina 125
Breux, Ken Le 593
Brew, Conway 179
Brewer, John 157
Brewer, Robert (Bob) 339
Brewer, Allen M. 348
Brewer, Wes 546
Brewer, Michael (Mel) 610
Brewer, Samuel (Sam) 795
Brewer, Rosalind G. 848
Brewster, Gregg 151
Brewster, David 177
Brewster, Tracy 344

Brice, Zachery 311
Brice, Todd D. 703
Brick, Samuel 43
Bricker, Jodi 788
Brickler, Lucinda 311
Brickman, David M. 356
Bridge, Tracy B. 165
Bridges, Lisa 270
Bridgewater, Ronald (Ron) 608
Briesacher, Mark 444
Briger, Peter L. 354
Brigger, Steve 811
Briggs, Tammy 16
Briggs, Ryan 29
Briggs, Craig 76
Briggs, Ashlea 91
Briggs, Steve 365
Briggs, Larry 683
Briggs, Brent 884
Bright, Mark J. 60
Bright, Tobias 124
Bright, Theodore 270
Brighton, Curtis 333
Briglia, Jennifer (Jen) 810
Brill, Keith 819
Brimhall, Craig 46
Brimmer, Robert (Bob) 140
Brimner, Steven (Steve) 256
Brinckerhoff, Ronald 85
Brindle, Carol 874
Brinker, Lisa 428
Brinkley, Phil 85
Brinkley, Cindy 163
Brinkley, Stephen 770
Brinner, Scott 681
Brinnon, John (Jack) 843
Brisco, Carl 604
Briscoe, Debi 126
Bristow, Peter M. 328
Bristow, Dave 363
Britell, Jenne K. 826
Britman, David (Dave) 121
Britt, Chess 652
Brittain, Jim 347
Britten, David L. 827
Brittingham, Randall 650
Britton, Paula 239
Brlas, Laurie 578
Broach, Danny 123
Broadhead, D. Michael 400
Broadhurst, Vanessa 51
Broccolo, Timothy 529
Brochick, George 627
Brock, Mark 94
Brock, Matthew 97
Brock, John F. 198
Brock, Macon F. 257
Brock, Anthony 557
Brock, Bill 706
Brock, Stanley M. (Skip) 720
Brock, Carlton 739
Brocklehurst, N. James (Jim) 343
Brocklehurst, Jim 343
Brockman, Ivan 121
Brockman, Carla 246
Brockway, Larry T. 827
Brodbeck, Heather 514
Broderick, Craig W. 375
Brodnax, Billy 766
Brodnitz, Peter 228
Brodsky, Marina 635
Brody, Dean 463
Brody, Wendy 694
Brody, James 767
Brody, Robert C. (Bob) 801
Brogan, Jennifer 530
Brogan, Mike 794
Brogden, Steven 353
Broggi, Luciana 422
Brogie, Sandra 448
Brokaw, Randy 43
Brokaw, Carter 434
Broker, Michael (Mel) 581
Broll, Frank 46
Brolly, Stephen H. 320
Bromagen, Ellen J 309
Broman, John A. 55

Chapman, Chris 379
Chapman, Ben 590
Chapman, Kevin D. 690
Chapman, Esther 724
Chapman, Margie 770
Chapman, Ken 801
Chapman, Randy 834
Chapman, Garrett 839
Chapman, Pier 841
Chappell, Anthony 694
Chaps, Robert 83
Char, Sherie 95
Charaf, Anthony 245
Charalambous, Ioannis A. 603
Charaniya, Karim 796
Charasika, Pai 681
Charbonneau, Ed 672
Chardo, Toni 167
Charest, Teri 810
Charest, Wendy 841
Chargois, Trevor 518
Chari, Ram 526
Chariag, Belgacem 88
Charlip, Dave 472
Charlton, Richard 311
Charlton, R. Scott 765
Charlton, Scott 766
Charney, Eugene 524
Charotari, Seetal 94
Charron, Matthew (Matt) 229
Charron, Daniel J. (Dan) 331
Charter, Robert B. (Rob) 154
Charton, Erik C 464
Charytan, Lynn 203
Chase, William J. 6
Chase, Eric 20
Chase, Kevin 287
Chase, John (Jack) 548
Chase, Stephanie 718
Chastain, Angie 820
Chasteen, Teresa S 380
Chastian, Randy 89
Chaston, Jeremy 254
Chatin, Richard (Dick) 209
Chatow, Udi 406
Chatt, Theresa 528
Chatterjee, Debashis 199
Chatterjee, Rajarshi 199
Chatterjee, Sanjay 791
Chattin, Angela (Angie) 152
Chau, Lee 42
Chaudhary, Niren 882
Chavez, R. Martin 375
Chavez, Mauricio 534
Chaviano, Hector 365
Chavis, Eva 317
Chay, Jasmine 874
Chazen, Stephen I. (Steve) 603
Chazin, Steve 182
Chean, Kevin 542
Cheatwood, Chris J. 642
Chechuck, Judy 179
Checki, Terrence J. 310
Cheek, Bruce D. 41
Cheek, Craig 584
Cheek, Patty 824
Cheema, Amy 679
Cheesbrough, Paul 579
Cheeseman, Michael 384
Cheesewright, David 848
Chegwidden, Susan (Sue) 663
Cheleden, Charles G. 874
Chelemedos, Roger 788
Chelesnik, Steven (Steve) 284
Chelewski, Tom 432
Chen, Lei 43
Chen, Lucy 61
Chen, Jingnong 106
Chen, Heng W. 155
Chen, Natasha 201
Chen, Steve 268
Chen, Larry 337
Chen, Roawen 672
Chen, George 707
Chen, David (Dave) 710
Chen, Ming 712
Chen, Yingying 749

Chen, Danny 766
Chen, John (Jack) 848
Chen, Linda 875
Chenault, Kenneth I. (Ken) 42
Chenault, Melissa (Mel) 163
Chene, Richard R. 116
Cheney, Andrew B. (Andy) 48
Cheney, Dave 102
Cheng, Tonya 51
Cheng, Dunson K. 155
Cheng, Kai 155
Cheng, Jay 353
Cheng, Marn K. 563
Cheng, Wei 645
Chenwei, Yan 672
Cheong, Thomas 653
Chepenik, Randy 75
Cherecwich, Peter B. 593
Cherence, Danielle 376
Cherian, Kuruvilla 75
Cheriyan, Anil 756
Chernick, Rose 666
Cherrie, George 718
Cherry, Michael 102
Cherry, Kristie 230
Cherry, Kimberley C. (Kim) 334
Chery, Don J. 374
Chesley, Yonnie 395
Chesna, Peter (Pete) 808
Chesney, John (Jack) 681
Chesnut, Jeff 27
Chesnutt, Charles A. 370
Chess, Glenda 878
Chester, Joyce 545
Chestnut, Taylor 168
Chestnutt, Roy H. 837
Cheung, Mil 67
Cheung, Annie 448
Cheung, James (Jamie) 509
Chevalier, Christine 205
Chew, Denley 310
Chew-Lai, Moya 663
Chewens, Michael J. 569
Chhabra, Harleen 303
Chheda, Parag 594
Chho, Sara 361
Chia, Yaw 861
Chiang, Hwai Hai (HH) 455
Chiang, Willie C.W. 603
Chiarella, Jerry 656
Chiarello, Guy 331
Chiccino, Peter (Pete) 786
Chichester, David 745
Chick, Steve 426
Chico, Michael 594
Chicoine, Gerard R 75
Chicoine, Gerry 75
Chicoine, Jerry L. 307
Chierico, Salvatore 148
Chilberg, C. Perry 821
Childers, Danielle 99
Childers, Terry 189
Childers, Kim M. 748
Childress, Kym 106
Chilewitz, Mark 466
Chillemi, John 599
Chilton, Michael (Mike) 12
Chilton, Grahame D. (Chily) 359
Chilton, Dan 573
Chin, Noreen 186
Chin, Jenny 375
Chin, Gloria 523
Chin, Patrick (Paddy) 760
China, Robert (Bob) 353
China, John D. 760
Chinaka, Maria 771
Ching, Wanda 95
Ching, Michael (Mel) 95
Chinn, Mike 533
Chintamaneni, Ramakrishna Prasad 199
Chio, Napoleon 139
Chiocco, Leslie 607
Chionchio, Mike 463
Chirico, Emanuel (Manny) 670
Chisholm, Ron 657
Chitester, Todd 93
Chittum, John 492

Chiu, Arthur (Art) 186
Chiu, Mary 359
Chizmar, Tj 721
Cho, Brandie 318
Cho, SungHwan 434
Choate, Chris 681
Chodak, Paul 40
Choeff, Sonya 681
Choi, Justin C. 56
Choi, Byung U 121
Choi, Alison 158
Choi, Vicky 467
Choi, Philip 713
Choi, Amy 760
Chojnowski, Tammy 749
Cholak, Rosemar 460
Cholea, Debbie 398
Chomienne, Kathleen 365
Chong, Boo Ching (BC) 268
CHooper, Anthony 51
Chopas, James (Jamie) 790
Chopdekar, Neel 42
Chopra, Rahul 579
Chorki, Aissa 280
Chosy, James L. 810
Choto, Miguel 466
Chou, John G. 49
Choudhary, Ken R. 347
Choudhury, Bhaskar 632
Chow, Allan 171
Chow, Joe 182
Chow, Jean 634
Chow, Lisa 663
Chow, Davin 843
Chowdhry, Pervaiz 347
Chris, Wigger 242
Chrisman, Ken 715
Christakes, Jennifer (Jen) 464
Christakos, Paul 187
Christatos, Steve 308
Christen, Thomas (Thom) 132
Christen, Amy 182
Christen, J P 832
Christens, Michelle (Mitch) 530
Christensen, Rich 70
Christensen, Eric 151
Christensen, Hoss 182
Christensen, Rex 245
Christensen, Jim 406
Christensen, Shelley 475
Christensen, Bruce 534
Christensen, Wesley J. 608
Christensen, Robert J. (Bob) 617
Christensen, Jeff 729
Christensen, Gregg 826
Christensen, Lori 871
Christenson, Stephen 682
Christian, David A. 259
Christian, Korey 427
Christian, Mark 621
Christian, Mike 681
Christiansen, Andrew 763
Christiansen, Scott 791
Christiansen, Kathy 820
Christianson, Bonnie 124
Christie, David (Dave) 9
Christie, William T. 310
Christie, Peter 570
Christie, Michael 731
Christina, Rassi 14
Christina, Farup 460
Christman, Kevin 879
Christmann, John J. 60
Christmas, Charles E. (Chuck) 535
Christoffersen, Gregg 464
Christofferson, Carla 11
Christopher, Martin 47
Christopher, Casey 166
Christopher, Bill 534
Christy, Rebecca 90
Christy, James 662
Chrobak, Mary 645
Chrystal, Curtis 400
Chu, William 85
Chu, Joshua 107
Chu, Dorcus 176
Chu, Agnes 254

Chu, Gary 367
Chu, Sophia 466
Chu, Benjamin K. 467
Chu, Julie 523
Chu, Kathlynn 694
Chube, Kelleye 67
Chugh, Madhavi 120
Chui, Clarence 673
Chukwumah, Obi 106
Chulos, Nicholas J. 337
Chumakov, George 471
Chung, Michael H.K. 274
Chung, Chenfai 283
Chung, Felix 524
Chung, Bruce 599
Chung, Yoon (Michael) 622
Chung, Paul W. 769
Chupa, Kathleen 460
Churay, Daniel J. (Dan) 561
Church, John R. 367
Church, Leah 444
Church, Kathryn 468
Church, Jason 663
Church, Shelly 681
Churchman, Calvin 679
Churchward, Guy 280
Chvala, Tony 717
Chwast, Jeff 43
Chwojko-frank, Tom 611
Ciampa, Dominick 575
Cianciosi, Steven (Steve) 537
Cianflone, David (Dave) 673
Ciavarello, Stephanie 531
Cibos, Richard 702
Cibotti, Kate 94
Cicale, Ed 80
Ciccone, Dave 78
Ciccone, Partick 461
Cicconi, James W. (Jim) 74
Cichanowsky, Eugene 678
Cichocki, Andrew R. (Andy) 19
Cichocki, Dave 553
Cichocki, David (Dave) 553
Cichon, Monica 475
Cielica, April 657
Ciesemier, Barbara 194
Ciesla, Betty 184
Cimarossa, Debbie 416
Cimino, Lori 97
Cinco-Abela, Tracy 675
Cincotta, Tiffany 5
Cincotta, Tiffany 7
Cindi, Tippett 699
Cindric, Michael (Mel) 203
Cindy, Hourigan 265
Cinfio, Nancy 339
Cinque, Mike 198
Cinquepalmi, Anna 879
Cintron, David 94
Ciochetto, Jeff 400
Cioffe, Christine 632
Ciombor, Christiane 874
Ciongoli, Adam G. 505
Ciperski, Carla 448
Cipoletti, Jack 189
Cipra, Andy 253
Cipriani, Nicole 365
Cipriano, Frank 339
Cirelli, Jean-Fran §ois 119
Ciriello, James 537
Cirillo, Carl 570
Ciriscioli, Peter 481
Cirko, Robert A. 209
Ciroli, James K. 345
Ciserani, Giovanni 657
Cisewski, Greg 673
Ciskowski, Michael S. (Mike) 835
Cisneros, Zada 230
Cisneros, Eduardo 240
Ciszek, Mike 172
Citron, Jayson 94
Ciulla, John R. 853
Ciupak, Jeff 78
Civgin, Don 29
Civitts, Ray 820
Cizman, Borut 105
Clabo, Howard 421

Couget, Ron 522
Coughlan, Ian M. 875
Coughlin, Philip M. 300
Coughlin, Ron 421
Coulcher, Rich 742
Coulson, Donna 336
Coulston, Lauren 466
Coulter, Samuel J (Sam) 395
Coulter, Cuan 749
Coupe, Nick 369
Courduroux, Pierre 554
Courier, Cheryl 472
Courneya, Patrick (Paddy) 467
Court, James J. 324
Courtiright, Anne 303
Courtland, Gary 254
Courtney, June 343
Courtright, Debora 559
Coutant, Carrie 503
Couts, George 730
Coutu, Pat 188
Coveny, Erin 148
Covey, Steven K. (Steve) 568
Covin, Chere 14
Covington, J. Curtis 307
Covington, Curt 307
Covino, Gregory F 118
Cowan, Andrea F 803
Coward, Stephen R. 567
Coward, Stephen D (Steve) 718
Cowart, James 780
Cowell, Frank 182
Cowhig, Michael T. 577
Cowing, Chris 681
Cowles, James C. 186
Cowles, Brad 397
Cowley, David (Dave) 333
Cowley, Daron 444
Cowman, Craig 150
Cowperthwait, David (Dave) 471
Cox, Mike 8
Cox, Andrew (Andy) 40
Cox, Sharon 78
Cox, Katherine (Kate) 106
Cox, Chandler F. 111
Cox, John G. 118
Cox, Ryan 151
Cox, Kevin 152
Cox, Donna 182
Cox, Heather 186
Cox, Shawn 272
Cox, Mark K. 274
Cox, Fred 284
Cox, Christopher K. (Chris) 304
Cox, Richard L 317
Cox, David 322
Cox, B. Guille 333
Cox, Tom 434
Cox, Jerry 499
Cox, Mark 534
Cox, Graham 542
Cox, Steve 611
Cox, John 679
Cox, Ed 686
Cox, Brian 712
Cox, Phil 760
Cox, Keith 763
Cox, John 794
Cox, Dudley 799
Cox, Christopher (Chris) 814
Cox, Keith 825
Cox, Tom 825
Cox, Christopher 826
Cox, Preston 833
Cox, Jim C 848
Cox, John (Jack) 848
Cox, Nicole 871
Coxhead, Andrew B. 260
Coy, Janet L. 286
Coy, Janet 549
Coyle, Ned 157
Coyle, Pete 359
Coyle, Michael 399
Coyle, Ryan 694
Coyne, Patrick 311
Coyne, Pat 435
Coyner, Sheri 58

Cozby, Chris 156
Cozza, Patrick A. 424
Cozza, Keith 434
Cozzolino, Joe 182
Cozzone, Robert D. 437
Crabtree, Ralph 88
Crabtree, Grant 254
Cracas, Teresa C. 180
Cracchiolo, James M. (Jim) 46
Craft, Frank 657
Craft, Stephen (Steve) 736
Craft, Susan (Sue) 757
Cragg, John 628
Craghead, Todd 444
Cragin, Maureen P 125
Crahan, Peter 16
Craig, Sean 229
Craig, Kim 382
Craig, Patricia (Pat) 486
Craig, Marian 513
Craig, Matthew (Matt) 664
Craig, Jonathan M. 712
Craig, Joseph (Jo) 712
Craig, Gary 757
Craighead, Martin S. 88
Crain, Roger 8
Crain, Robert B. 17
Crain, Timothy (Tim) 47
Crain, Alan R. 88
Craine, Barry 47
Craine, Eric 814
Crall, Henry (Hal) 429
Crame, Glenn 623
Crandall, Brett 121
Crandall, Theodore D. (Ted) 698
Crandall, Janice 838
Crandall, Laura 871
Crane, Barbara (Barb) 106
Crane, Christopher M. (Chris) 297
Crane, Cindy A. 619
Crane, Timothy S. (Tim) 871
Cranmer, Jonathan 33
Cranner, Chris 158
Cranston, Alan (Al) 577
Crapster, Joe 269
Crater, Ann 184
Craton, George 803
Craven, Matthew 53
Craven, Juile 417
Craver, Theodore F. (Ted) 278
Craver, Ted 730
Crawford, Pamela S (Pam) 5
Crawford, Frederick J. (Fred) 16
Crawford, Victor L. 64
Crawford, Bill 78
Crawford, Michael 93
Crawford, Matthew (Matt) 100
Crawford, Bill 125
Crawford, Stephen S. (Steve) 148
Crawford, Carolyn 252
Crawford, Curtis J. 268
Crawford, Stephen G. (Steve) 274
Crawford, Jason 295
Crawford, Michael 429
Crawford, Shawn R. 473
Crawford, Kelly 475
Crawford, Keith 584
Crawford, Bruce 607
Crawford, Charles 710
Crawford, Charlie 710
Crawford, Ron 745
Crawford, David 749
Crawford, Thomas J. (Joe) 750
Crawford, Joe 751
Crawley, Connie 83
Crayton, Jeff 721
Crc, Daniel Thompson (Dan) 70
Crc, Erik Swan 70
Crc, Thomas (Thom) 857
Creamer, Aimee 106
Creamer, Michele 537
Crecca, Michelle (Mitch) 663
Crecca, Michelle (Mitch) 854
Credle, Eric P. 326
Creech, Dennis 404
Creed, Greg 882
Creedon, Michael 8

Creekmur, Dan 586
Cregg, Daniel J. (Dan) 665
Cregger, Chris 333
Creighton, Bill 808
Creighton, Cheryl 848
Cremades, Esther 325
Cremin, Robert W. 261
Crenshaw, William E. (Ed) 667
Crespo, Frank J. 154
Cretella, Jonathan (Jon) 629
Crew, Debra A. 693
Crewdson, Pam 657
Cribbs, Kevin 329
Crichton, Brook 611
Crider, Perry 252
Crigger, Donald 157
Crigler, Forest 358
Crimmins, Kevin 187
Crimmins, Timothy P. 629
Criner, Cindy 534
Criscione, Laura C 216
Criscione, Terry 406
Crist, Peter D. 871
Cristiano, Lynda 118
Cristoforo, Albert J. (Jerry) 749
Critelli, John 365
Croak, Marian 75
Crocco, M. Scott 18
Crocco, John 670
Croce, Michael J. 753
Crocitto, Linda 37
Crocitto, Peter 836
Crocker, Janet 431
Crockett, Joan 29
Crockett, Julie 230
Crockett, Bruce 471
Croft, Thomas (Thom) 376
Crofts, Sharon M. 95
Croker, Douglas 686
Croll, Richard (Dick) 365
Cromeans, Gregg 663
Cromett, Mark 745
Crompton, Dave 231
Cron, Spencer 94
Cronen, John 811
Cronen, Paul 836
Cronin, Stephen G (Steve) 69
Cronin, Douglas J 131
Cronin, Douglas (Doug) 132
Cronin, Kevin 801
Cronin, Thomas (Thom) 527
Crooke, Robert B. 442
Croom, Bucky 686
Cropper, Bill 694
Crosby, Jimmy C. 31
Crosby, Carolyn 143
Crosby, Gary M. 339
Crosley, Brad 464
Cross, Jeffrey (Jeff) 40
Cross, Shannon 725
Cross, Staci 856
Crossing, Matt 207
Crossland, David 56
Crossland, Kristi 686
Crossman, Scott 280
Crosson, Aaron 179
Crosswhite, Mark A. 731
Croteau, Brad 629
Crotteau, Patrick (Paddy) 132
Crotty, Cindy P 475
Crouch, Andrew 499
Crouse, John 530
Crouse, Dianne 654
Crouse, Kelly 726
Crout, Steve 673
Crouthamel, Ryan 339
Crovesi, Marco 421
Crovitz, Charles K. 295
Crow, Timothy M. (Tim) 412
Crow, William A (Bill) 681
Crow, David 757
Crowder, Clara 528
Crowe, Terence 78
Crowe, Mike 201
Crowe, Wayne 270
Crowe, Maria 503
Crowe, Bill 881

Crowell, Michael (Mel) 166
Crowle, Marsha S. 338
Crowley, John (Jack) 131
Crowley, Jack 187
Crowley, Rob 280
Crowley, John 317
Crowley, F. Michael 520
Crowley, Raghu 741
Crowley, Dan 881
Crown, Timothy A. (Tim) 441
Crown, Marc 495
Crownover, R. Michael (Mike) 835
Crowther, David (Dave) 83
Croxall, Clifford 312
Croxton, Cheryl 305
Crozier, Dean 196
Cruce, Andrea 163
Crudele, Anthony F. (Tony) 798
Cruickshank, Robert 138
Crume, George 45
Crumley, John (Jack) 71
Crumlish, Arthur 502
Crump, Darin 207
Crump, R 623
Crupe, Bill 158
Cruse, Marc 169
Crutcher, Brian 784
Cruthers, Thomas 158
Cruz, Cyndi 254
Cruz, Jacquelyn 531
Cruz, Alexis 802
Crysler, John 879
Csiba-Womersley, Maria 430
Csuhran, Renee R. 428
Cuba, Jessica 522
Cubbage, Gary C. 127
Cubias, Carlos 824
Cuccias, Brian 430
Cucco, Wayne J 46
Cuddy, Christopher M. (Chris) 65
Cue, Eduardo H. (Eddy) 61
Cueli, Allen (Al) 843
Cuellar, Carlos 845
Cuenot, Eric 584
Cuervo, Larry 385
Cuervo, Carlos 873
Cuevas, Disnalda 148
Cuevas, Kirt 450
Cuffe, Michael 395
Cugini, Dominic 475
Cuilla, Michelle (Mitch) 556
Culhane, Michael (Mel) 356
Cullen, Thomas A. (Tom) 252
Cullen, Susan 348
Cullen, William 392
Cullen, Karen 514
Cullen, Moira 632
Cullen, Jim 634
Cullen, Gary 766
Culleton, Bruce 104
Cullinan-james, Cal 426
Cullmann, David (Dave) 97
Culotta, Michael 211
Culotta, Dominic 824
Culpepper, Brandon 550
Culpepper, Jason 724
Culver, Jennifer (Jen) 374
Culver, Curt S. 543
Culver, Michael (Mel) 553
Culver, John 744
Cumbra, Brian 422
Cumming, Christine M. 310
Cummings, Alexander B. (Alex) 196
Cummings, Sean J. 389
Cummings, Rochelle 393
Cummings, Kevin 453
Cummings, Sean 465
Cummings, Jerilin 832
Cummins, Jennifer (Jen) 106
Cummins, Michael 188
Cummins, Michael 721
Cummins, Michael (Mel) 721
Cummins, Hugh S. (Beau) 756
Cummiskey, Tom 846
Cumpton, Linda 91
Cundiff, Robert 208
Cunfer, Todd 402

Davis, John R. 432
Davis, Douglas L. (Doug) 442
Davis, Lisa 443
Davis, Mary 450
Davis, Susan F. 462
Davis, Jeannette 463
Davis, Rick 471
Davis, Clinton T 513
Davis, Clint 513
Davis, Judy 513
Davis, Rick 527
Davis, Robert M. 537
Davis, Jeff 549
Davis, Doug 550
Davis, Chuck 553
Davis, Charles (Chas) 553
Davis, Gary (Bo) 558
Davis, Laura 559
Davis, Craig 584
Davis, Cindy 584
Davis, Karen 591
Davis, Karen 592
Davis, Gerald 596
Davis, Lee 599
Davis, Diana 604
Davis, Jack 611
Davis, Erika T. 614
Davis, Paul 624
Davis, Kevin 632
Davis, David (Dave) 634
Davis, Terry 639
Davis, Jeff 657
Davis, Robert 663
Davis, Dawn 664
Davis, George S. 672
Davis, Steve 672
Davis, James E. 675
Davis, Tiffany 686
Davis, Troy 712
Davis, Steven D. 719
Davis, Reid 730
Davis, Nancy B. 753
Davis, Felicia 757
Davis, Karen 757
Davis, Laverne 762
Davis, Tim 766
Davis, Anthony 777
Davis, Robert D. (Bob) 795
Davis, Richard K. 810
Davis, Raymond P. (Ray) 816
Davis, Nancy M. 828
Davis, Pamela (Pam) 833
Davis, Stephanie 835
Davis, Wade C. 841
Davis, Cindy 848
Davis, Jeff 848
Davis, Angie 848
Davis, Teri 848
Davis, Scott 861
Davis, Brett 871
Davis, Paul 874
Davis, Ron 879
Davis, Harry M. 880
Davison, Gayle 327
Davison, Paul J. 665
Davison, Mike 767
Davisson, Robert J. 721
Davitt, George 350
Dawes, Scott 611
Dawkins, Keith D. 131
Dawodu, Akin 186
Dawson, Jane 551
Dawson, Sam 732
Dawson, Julie 794
Dawson, Andrew (Andy) 819
Day, Kristina 102
Day, Craig 143
Day, Timothy 208
Day, Thomas R. 417
Day, Zane 483
Day, Edward 575
Day, William B. (Bill) 765
Day-Salo, Ann 206
Dayan, John (Jack) 421
Dayon, Alex 703
Days, Betty 14
Deacon, Mary Ann 488

Deal, Stanley (Stan) 124
Deal, Stan 125
Deal, Helena 404
Dealy, Richard P. (Rich) 642
DeAmicis, Kathleen 204
DeAmore, Denise 749
Dean, Steven (Steve) 56
Dean, Kim 148
Dean, John C. 166
Dean, Matthew (Matt) 283
Dean, Catherine 318
Dean, Donny 721
Dean, Christine 865
Dean-hammel, Bridget 119
Deangelis, Michael 443
DeAngelis, Robert A. 474
Deangelis, Gail 801
DeAngelo, Joseph J. (Joe) 397
Dear, Tina 277
Dearborn, Randy 545
Deardorff, Kevin L. 488
Dearie-ruhlin, Mary 757
Dearman, Paul 120
Dearman, Tim 256
Dearman, Andrew (Andy) 731
Deason, Richard 494
Deasy, Dana S. 465
Deaton, Steven G. 748
Deaver, W. Scott 83
Debarger, Candace 526
Debatto, Robert (Bob) 824
Debber, Steven 717
Debenedictis, Liz 772
Debenedittis, Paul 254
DeBernardi, Michael A. 612
Debertin, Jay D. 178
Debevoise, Marc 158
Debiase, Francesca 532
Debnam, Henry 391
Deboer, Mieke 106
DeBoer, Bryan B. 508
DeBoer, Sidney B. (Sid) 508
Deboer, David 535
Deboer, Greg 766
Debra, Morfit 817
Debs, Dalia 749
Debusk, Chuck 832
Decabia, Phil 138
Decaire, Adam 733
Decarlo, Steve 365
Dechant, Suzanne 745
Deck, Richard 670
Deckelman, William L. (Bill) 213
Decker, Daniel A. 135
Decker, Scott 151
Decker, Molly 375
Decker, Edward P. (Ted) 412
Decker, David 460
Decker, James (Jamie) 611
Decker, Julie 688
DeClaris, Wade N. 873
Decolli, Chris 3
Deconinck, Patrick (Paddy) 2
Decraene, Dave 336
Decuyper, Will 832
Dedinsky, John G. 622
Dedlock, Steven (Steve) 707
Dedolce, Trish 664
Dee, Steven 584
Deehan, Teri 801
Deeks, Terence N. 567
Deenihan, Ed 573
Deer, George 811
Dees, Todd 757
Deese, Willie A. 537
DeFalco, Ciro M. 567
DeFaria, Chris 792
Defeis, Nicholas 664
DeFranco, James (Jim) 252
DeFranco, Jim 253
DeFreece, Peter (Pete) 280
Degarcia, Mercedes 527
Degen, Michael 121
Deger, Amy 322
DeGiorgio, Kenneth D. 324
Deglomine, Anthony 391

Degnon, Laura 505
DeGrands, Coryn 283
Degregorio, Nick 277
DeGregorio, Ronald J. (Ron) 297
Dehaven, Judy 158
Deherrera, Brandy 883
Deheulle, Peter 359
Dehio, Peter 295
Dehn, Jeffrey R. (Jeff) 111
Dehne, Jon 8
Dehner, Torsten 17
Deidiker, Jim 141
Deily, Karl R. 715
Deis, Ron 440
Deitch, Sally 777
DeJonckheere, Jackie 322
Dejonge, Michelle (Mitch) 461
Dejournette, Dan 196
Dekay, Steve 97
Dekay, Sam 97
Dekker, Karen 47
Dekman, Matt 645
Delacruz, Cedric 393
Delacruz, Cedric G 393
Delagi, R. Gregory (Greg) 784
Delaney, Bradleybrad 180
Delaney, Chris 377
Delaney, Dan 559
Delaney, Richard 632
Delaney, Peter 681
DeLaney, William J. (Bill) 765
Delangle, Francois 184
Delassio, Harry 664
Delattre, Karen 56
DeLawder, C. Daniel (Dan) 622
DelBene, Kurt 548
Delcambre, Brad 731
Deldicque, Greg 828
Delellis, Michael 670
DeLena, Laura 531
DeLeon, Abe 686
Deleone, Lara 475
Delgadillo, Dan 772
Delgado, Joaquin 2
Delgado, Jon 155
DelGatto, Lawrence C. 678
Delghiaccio, Brian 692
Delich, Whitney 841
Delie, Vincent J. (Vince) 303
Delight, David (Dave) 884
Delimitros, Nicole 506
Delisle, Ken 100
Delker, Jed 344
Dell, Andrew 810
Dellacroce, Peter (Pete) 711
Dellaquila, Frank J. 283
Dellazoppa, Steve 794
Dell'Osso, Domenic J. (Nick) 175
Delmedico, Ann 664
DeLoach, Thomas C. 68
DeLoach, Harris E. 729
Deloache, Zach 697
DeLongchamps, Peter C. 382
Deloraine, David (Dave) 548
DeLorenzo, Marc 151
Delorier, Rilla S. 756
Delorimier, John 426
DeLotto, Joseph (Jo) 791
Delpech, Philippe 828
Delphsenior, Chuck 85
Delprince, Aaron 194
DeLuca, James B. (Jim) 368
DeLuca, Richard R. 537
Deluca, Peter 767
DelVecchio, Tony 515
Demain, Greg 215
Demarchis, John 645
DeMarco, Ronnie 99
Demarco, Mike 554
Demarcus, William (Bill) 880
Demare, Laura 57
Demartini, Gretchen 324
DeMatteo, Daniel A. 361
Demboski, Elise 550
Demchak, William S. (Bill) 645
Demeke, Bete 448
Dement, Jason 322

Demeo, Catherine (Cathy) 743
Demers, Eric 672
Demetriou, Steven J. 456
Deming, Claiborne P. 562
Demita, Tab 321
Demita, Michelle 365
Demmerle, Stefan 129
Demoulias, George 708
Dempsey, Dundee 67
Dempsey, Joan A. 128
Dempsey, Andrew P. 353
Dempsey, John 611
Denabeele, Nicole Van 815
Denahan, Wellington J. 57
Denato, Thomas 698
Denault, Leo P. 289
Denby, Kristy 205
Dench, Anne 467
Dendy, Cynthia 328
Dengg, Robert 444
Dengler, Patrick 548
Denholm, David J. 470
Deniro, Anthony 836
Denison, Kurtis 629
Denker, Bud 628
Dennehy, Brian K. 588
Denney, Cindy 94
Denney, Craig 632
Dennis, Bruce 124
Dennis, Mary 139
Dennis, Debbie 287
Dennis, Jo 422
Dennis, Staci 513
Dennis, Elizabeth 556
Dennis, David (Dave) 762
Dennis-Buss, Susan (Sue) 179
Dennison, Linda 45
Denniston, Brackett B. 364
Denny, Jd 426
Denoya, Dave 836
Dentiste, Cherie 280
Denton, David M. (Dave) 236
Denton, Stephen (Steve) 276
Denton, Dianna 479
Denvir, Brian 814
Denzin, Christopher 168
Depalma, Elisa 148
DePaolo, Joseph J. 723
dePasquale, Caterina 348
Depatie, Williambill 280
Depaul, Gilbert 404
DePell, Fred (Fred) 598
DePillo, Raymond V. 665
DePinto, Joseph I. 150
Depippo, Joseph (Jo) 808
Depoy, Scott 316
Deprey, Matthew 251
Deputy, Chrstine 588
Derba, Laura 868
Derbyshire, John 469
Deremer, Ken 720
Derick, Cynthia 254
Derieux, Randy 22
Derieux, Randy 731
Deris, John (Jack) 702
Dermer, Neal 501
Dermody, Fred 226
Derouin, Jim 848
Derpinghaus, Patrick J. 70
Derr, Rose 358
Derrick, Lynn 611
Dersarkissian, Gary 90
Derusha, Jeff 549
Desai, Nisha 123
Desai, Girish 177
Desai, Khyati 184
Desai, Praveen 199
Desai, Chirantan (CJ) 280
Desai, Hetal 416
Desai, Nishant 757
Desalvo, Pete 124
Desalvo, Tom 717
Desanctis, Guy 448
Desantis, Michael (Mel) 375
Desantis, Paul 495
Desantis, Mark 634

Eldred, Ann 5
Eldredge, Andrew (Andy) 506
Eldridge, Greg 171
Eldridge, Tom 322
Eldridge, Kathi 479
Eleftheriou, Terry 285
Eleser, Karen 149
Elfrink, Wim 182
Elgar, Tal 443
Elghanayan, Shahram 148
Elgin, Steve 363
Elhaj, Sam 530
Elias, Howard D. 280
Eliasson, Fredrik J. 229
Eliasson, Fred 229
Eliecagary, Aline 712
Eline, William G. (Bill) 622
Elizondo, Patricia 879
Elkeles, Tamar 672
Elkind, Albert 376
Ellen, David G. 138
Ellen, Martin M. (Marty) 264
Ellenbogen, Marc 33
Ellertson, Chris 398
Ellinghausen, James R. (Jim) 669
Ellington, Kim A 336
Elliot, Douglas G. (Doug) 393
Elliot, Bill 556
Elliott, Patricia 148
Elliott, Todd 160
Elliott, Vanessa 317
Elliott, Robin N. 327
Elliott, Mike` 459
Elliott, Michael S (Mel) 459
Elliott, J. Keith 587
Elliott, Keith 587
Elliott, Sally 675
Elliott, Karen 679
Elliott, Derick 754
Elliott, John 830
Ellis, Mike 51
Ellis, Andrew (Andy) 58
Ellis, G. Brian 150
Ellis, Donna 201
Ellis, Nathaniel 230
Ellis, Bob 270
Ellis, Craig 322
Ellis, Natalie M. 350
Ellis, Jason 360
Ellis, Julie 456
Ellis, Bob 462
Ellis, Chester 464
Ellis, Michael L. (Mike) 483
Ellis, James O. 499
Ellis, Mark E. 507
Ellis, Mary 534
Ellis, Jeff 545
Ellis, Larry 602
Ellis, Gary 635
Ellis, Andrew (Andy) 698
Ellis, Todd 706
Ellis, Raquel 749
Ellis, George 781
Ellis, Sheila 781
Ellis, Rick 820
Ellis, Linda 835
Ellison, Robert (Bob) 416
Ellison, Tim 416
Ellison, Aaron 463
Ellison, Edward 467
Ellison, Lawrence J. (Larry) 610
Ellison, Marvin R. 626
Ellison, Michael (Mel) 672
Ellison, Jeffery 694
Ellison, Alan (Al) 810
Ells, Tom 460
Ellspermann, Caroline J. 605
Ellwood, Michelle 152
Elming, Gregory B. (Greg) 653
Elmore, John C. 208
Elmore, John R. 810
Elmquist, David 466
Elmslie, Lee 100
Elnitsky, John (Jack) 270
Elnitsky, John (Jack) 346
Elser, Jeffrey (Jeff) 342
Elser, Mark 809

Elsey, Katy 594
Elsner, Deanie 470
Elstrott, John B. 868
Eltz, Karen 464
Elvinsson, Bengt 223
Elwell, William (Bill) 393
Elwood, Rob 654
Elwyn, Tash 681
Ely, Timothy (Tim) 556
Elza, Tracie 303
Elzemeyer, Lee 336
Elzie, Matt 546
Emanuelo, Anthony 874
Embleton, Jason 365
Embree, Tracy 231
Emerson, Christy 212
Emerson, Kim 284
Emerson, Duncan 430
Emerson, Michael 475
Emery, Jon 125
Emery, Kelly 310
Emery, John 611
Emery, Shiloh 668
Emily, Todd 556
Emison, Kevin 382
Emm, Matt 14
Emmerich, I. Robert (Bob) 329
Emmerich, I 329
Emmerich, Toby 792
Emmerson, Timothy (Tim) 523
Emmick, Jeff 504
Emmons, George 475
Empey, Matt 688
Emptage, William 47
Enabnit, Jill 810
Enakaya, Makini 398
Enberg, Steve 697
Ence, Russell (Russ) 550
Enderle, John (Jack) 830
Endicott, Carola 151
Endo, Melanie 121
Endrenyi, Frank 550
Endres, Helmut 17
Endres, Greg 475
Endsley, Samantha 102
Eng, Kathy 542
Eng-crandus, Oi 295
Engel, Jefferey 16
Engel, Gretchen 171
Engel, Danielle 509
Engel, Larry 565
Engel, Randy 578
Engel, Albert L. 836
Engel, John J. 858
Engelbright, Jane 395
Engelhardt, Mark 417
Engelhart, James (Jamie) 814
Engelhart, James 814
Engelman, Patricia 29
Engelman, Rob 187
Engelson, David A. 821
Engemann, Kenneth 530
Engert, Karl 168
Engh, Svein 184
Engibous, Thomas J. (Tom) 626
Engle, Susan (Sue) 85
Engle, Barry 368
Engle, Elaine 521
Englehardt, Scott 681
Engleman, Mary 126
Englert, Mitch 147
Englert, Brian 332
English, Kim 551
English, Shaileen 634
English, Steven E. 747
Engstrom, Kathryn 777
Ennecking, Jim 848
Ennesser, Jay 448
Ennis, Robert 579
Enoki, Ryuji 704
Enriquez, Chu 184
Enriquez, Oscar 616
Enstrom, Tammy 232
ENye, Paul 699
Epley, George 840
Eppers, Joseph (Jo) 718
Eppinger, Frederick H. (Fred) 388

Eppley, Don 317
Epps, Shantala 165
Epps, Frances (Fran) 523
Epps, Mike 660
Epps, Barry L. 689
Epps, Jeremy 826
Epstein, Lori 542
Erb, David B. 432
Ercan, Nihat 463
Erdman, Alicia 584
Erdoes, Mary Callahan 465
Ergen, Charles W. 252
Eric, Lindblad 125
Erickson, Randall J. 70
Erickson, Kirk 179
Erickson, Wendy 230
Erickson, Connie 279
Erickson, Vicki 285
Erickson, Chris 302
Erickson, Peter C. 367
Erickson, Kenneth J. 399
Erickson, Gordy 412
Erickson, Ruth 523
Erickson, Karen 534
Erickson, Andrew 749
Erickson, Faye 772
Ericson, Brady D. 129
Ericson, Brent 383
Ericson, Rob 741
Eriksen, Jan 871
Erion, Mark 537
Erkan, Hafize Gaye (Gaye) 341
Erlichman, Scott L 385
Erlinger, James H. (Jim) 677
Ermatinger, Bill 430
Ermilio, Lou 579
Ernest, Cindi 169
Ernest, Scott A. 785
Ernest, Scott 820
Ernst, Joe 119
Ernst, Mark A. 344
Ernst, Robin 682
Ernst, Todd 683
Ernst, Barrie W. 822
Ernsteen, Scott 871
Erny, Michelle (Mitch) 466
Ersek, Hikmet 863
Ersoff, Brett 496
Ert, Myron Van 365
Ertel, Denny 565
Erwin, Michael (Mel) 317
Erwin, Tami 838
Esamann, Douglas F. (Doug) 269
Escasa-Haigh, Jo 740
Eschenbach, Carl M. 845
Escobar, Mara 523
Eskow, Alan D. 836
Esler, Susan B 69
Eslick, Rob 431
Eslick, David L. 523
Espegren, William 303
Espeland, Curtis E. (Curt) 274
Esperanza, William 499
Esperdy, Therese 465
Espinal, Jessica 694
Esplin, J. Kimo 430
Esposito, Rosanne 300
Esposito, Orlando C. 645
Esprit, Luc 281
Esselman, Mark 136
Esser, Brian 357
Estabrook, James B. 385
Esteban, Carmen 413
Estep, Brett 14
Estep, Dennis 717
Estep, Michele 755
Esterman, Gary 452
Estes, Marcia 126
Estes, Bill 283
Estes, Scott 691
Esteve, Jose 553
Esteves, Eduardo 672
Esther, Chet 383
Estko, Julie 573
Estrada, Christina 772
Etchison, Ted 176
Etchison, Greg 681

Etter, Phillip (Phil) 717
Ettinger, Jeffrey M. 417
Ettinger, Michael (Mel) 710
Ettinger, Irwin R. 802
Eubank, John 686
Eubanks, Dennis 88
Eubanks, Susan 102
Eul, Hermann 442
Eulacio, Ramon 13
Eulau, Robert K. (Bob) 706
Eulau, Bob 707
Eureste, Ralph 29
Eusden, Alan (Al) 223
Eustis, Ryan 433
Evangel, Lori M. 371
Evangelista, Guy 126
Evangelista, Paul A. 167
Evangelista, Ross 184
Evangelista, W. Scott 677
Evanoff, Stephen 238
Evanoff, Douglas (Doug) 310
Evanoff, Michael 848
Evans, Chris 97
Evans, Carol 157
Evans, Steve 175
Evans, Victoria 189
Evans, Alexander D. (Alex) 203
Evans, Richard W. (Dick) 229
Evans, Ginny 256
Evans, Donald L. 287
Evans, Charles L. (Charlie) 313
Evans, Sloane 372
Evans, Gerald W. 386
Evans, Paul 406
Evans, Godfrey B. 413
Evans, Aicha S. 442
Evans, Katrina M. (Trina) 475
Evans, Lisa 475
Evans, Michael (Mel) 475
Evans, Craig 509
Evans, Douglas 513
Evans, C Carnot 522
Evans, Jimmy 523
Evans, Terry N. 590
Evans, Matthew (Matt) 630
Evans, Richard D. 631
Evans, Deanna 711
Evans, Joseph W. (Joe) 748
Evans, Steven 764
Evans, Elton 766
Evans, Eric 777
Evans, Randy 818
Evans, Jack B. 822
Evans, Dwain 824
Evans, Steve 825
Evans, Kirsten Sweaney 848
Evans, Ann 851
Evanson, Brynn L. 626
Evarts, Rick 78
Evelyn, Ken 359
Even, Shai 31
Everett, Jackie 422
Everett, John (Jack) 432
Everett, Nora M. 653
Everett, Bryan 694
Everhart, Charles 94
Eversden, Jeffrey (Jeff) 871
Eversfield, Andrew 365
Eversman, Paul 70
Eves, David L. 877
Evett, Sandra 553
Evich, Tom 27
Evola, Peter J (Pete) 64
Ewald, Linda 49
Ewald, Thad 231
Ewans, Peter (Pete) 767
Ewens, Peter A. 767
Ewig, Randall G. 387
Ewing, R. Stewart 168
Ewing, Scott 437
Ewing, Doug 714
Exarhos, Tina 841
Exline, Brian 175
Exnicios, Joseph S. 385
Exter, Sy 456
Exton, Martha 163
Eyler, Phillip 390

Fiedler, John (Jack) 807
Fiedorek, R. Mark 736
Fiegl, Paul 339
Fiehler, Sharon 625
Field, Doug 61
Field, James M. 242
Field, David 384
Field, Darren 427
Fielder, Gail 266
Fieldhouse, Tim 367
Fielding, Ronald (Ron) 417
Fieldman, Richard (Dick) 359
Fields, Anna 121
Fields, Bridgett 212
Fields, Felicia J 352
Fields, Mark 352
Fields, Luke 365
Fields, Bruce 452
Fields, Robert D. 512
Fields, Danielle 523
Fields, John M. 612
Fields, Jeanne 786
Fieler, Steve 406
Fietzer, Deanna 205
Fife, Brady 43
Fife, Jim 490
Fife, Randy 866
Figarotta, Paul 481
Figenshu, Karen 176
Figley, Mark T 475
Figliuolo, Steve 345
Figueredo, Christine 106
Figueredo, Jorge L. 534

Figueroa, George 551
Figurski, Sandy 29
Fijak, John 85
Fikaris, George 184
Fike, Ted 32
Fike, Caren 483
Fikry, Christopher 675
Filas, Melanie 151
Filcek, Rodney (Rod) 237
Filipov, Stoyan (Steve) 781
Filippatos, James (Jamie) 254
Filippelli, Phil 774
Filippi, Donna 524
Fillar, Kennedy 206
Fillinger, Christina 537
Fillmore, Randall 551
Filton, Steve G. 832
Fimiani, Jaime 100
Finan, Irial 196
Fincher, C. Anderson 261
Finck, Karine 89
Findlay, D. Cameron 65
Findlay, Thomas 106
Findlay, Willy 144
Findlay, David M. 488
Fine, Peter S. 101
Fine, Sharon 594
Finegan, John 486
Finestone, Mark A. 81
Fink, Laura 43
Fink, Laurence D. (Larry) 119
Fink, Michael 149
Fink, Charles 289
Fink, Chris 321
Fink, Martin 406
Fink, Martin (Marti) 422
Fink, Michael 745
Fink, Anthony 757
Fink, Katie 793
Finkelmeier, Johann 377
Finkelson, Ira 184
Finkelstein, David L. 57
Finkle, Jack 339
Finkle, Edward (Ed) 801
Finlay, Iain 672
Finlayson, Krista 102
Finley, Tammy 8
Finley, John G. 121
Finley, Jennifer (Jen) 196
Finley, Joseph M. 804
Finley, Clark 854
Finlow, Scott 632
Finn, Thomas M. 657

Finn, Michael 830
Finnegan, James (Jamie) 14
Finnegan, Deb 594
Finnegan, Daniel J. 651
Finneran, John G. 148
Finneran, Lisa 151
Finneran, Kevin 541
Finnerty, Tom 201
Finnerty, Shaun 452
Finnerty, Dan 791
Finning, Sally 664
Fiore, Michael (Mel) 526
Fiorilli, Matthew 110
Fiorilli, Len 393
Firestone, David K (Dave) 14
Firestone, James A. (Jim) 878
Firey-oldroyd, Lynda 588
Fisackerly, Haley R. 289
Fisanick, Bill 53
Fischer, Jason 90
Fischer, Brett 124
Fischer, Jean-Luc 200
Fischer, Tom 226
Fischer, David B. 304
Fischer, Stanley 313
Fischer, Horst 314
Fischer, Thomas J. (Tom) 496
Fischer, Michelle (Mitch) 570
Fischer, Mark D. 670
Fischer, Karen 670
Fischer, Avery 679
Fischer, Dave 688
Fischer, Laurie 739
Fischer, Carolyn 794
Fischer, Anthony J. (Tony) 814
Fischetti, Gary 461
Fischkoff, Steven (Steve) 161
Fischvogt, Pam 231
Fiscus, Richard A. (Rich) 703
Fish, Brant 177
Fish, Mike 393
Fish, Kathleen B. (Kathy) 657
Fish, Sarah 657
Fish, James C. (Jim) 853
Fish, Jim 853
Fishbein, Scott 148
Fisher, Michael 16
Fisher, Jeanne 50
Fisher, Kristine 78
Fisher, Daniel W. 89
Fisher, Sam 106
Fisher, Kent 124
Fisher, Steven (Steve) 154
Fisher, Thomas (Thom) 226
Fisher, Linda J. 268
Fisher, Steve 276
Fisher, Richard W. 313
Fisher, Jarrett 376
Fisher, Nathan E. 408
Fisher, Tom 430
Fisher, Douglas W. (Doug) 442
Fisher, Rob 468
Fisher, Debby 481
Fisher, Jim 521
Fisher, Heidi 569
Fisher, Kenneth M. (Ken) 587
Fisher, Steven G. 597
Fisher, Lane 608
Fisher, Carolyn 632
Fisher, Tom 672
Fisher, Robert J. (Bob) 788
Fisher, Ashley 832
Fisher, Eric 835
Fisher, Robert (Bob) 838
Fisher, Mary 853
Fisher, Mary 877
Fishman, David (Dave) 7
Fishman, Eric S 405
Fishman, Robert P. (Bob) 570
Fishman, Jay S. 802
Fisk, Brandon 542
Fiskness, Paul 672
Fitch, Joann 151
Fitch, Deborah 209
Fite, Lisa 690
Fitterling, James R. (Jim) 263
Fitts, Dave 632

Fitz, Steven (Steve) 280
Fitzgerald, Joseph M. (Joe) 131
FitzGerald, Meghan M. 150
Fitzgerald, Cynthia 317
Fitzgerald, John 359
Fitzgerald, Bill 395
Fitzgerald, Anne 523
Fitzgerald, Kathleen 666
Fitzgerald, Michael R. 748
FitzGerald, Scott R. 749
Fitzgibbons, Michael A 608
Fitzgibbons, Michael A 609
Fitzhugh, Andy 406
Fitzmire, Gary 124
Fitzner, Mike 573
Fitzpatrick, Brian 120
Fitzpatrick, John 121
Fitzpatrick, Patty 138
Fitzpatrick, Shirley 328
Fitzpatrick, Katherine (Kate) 460
Fitzpatrick, Sean 681
Fitzpatrick, John 751
FitzPatrick, Daniel M. (Dan) 854
Fitzsimmons, Ellen M. 229
Fiumara, Brian 157
Fix, Chris 158
Fixer, Mike 393
Fjellman, Thomas 772
Flach, Greg 78
Flach, Gloria A. 596
Flack, Kerry 29
Fladung, Marie 78
Flaharty, Gary 88
Flaherty, Rich 8
Flaherty, Ryan 64
Flaherty, Janice 405
Flaherty, Thomas F (Thom) 657
Flaherty, Thomas 666
Flaherty, Thomas F. 737
Flanagan, Michael 75
Flanagan, Bill 590
Flanagan, Myra 634
Flanagan, Beth 673
Flanagan, Glenda J. 868
Flanagin, David E. 406
Flanigan, John 12
Flanigan, Patrick 162
Flanigan, John W. 256
Flanigan, Dan 321
Flannery, John L. 364
Flannery, Matthew J. 826
Flannigan, Erik 841
Flappan, Bob 75
Flavin, Barry 53
Flavin, Lisa 283
Flaxman, Jon E. 421
Fleary, Robert 499
Fleck, Michael 119
Fleckenstein, Michele 111
Fleet, Clifford B. 34
Fleetwood, Jeff 611
Flemate, Willa 92
Fleming, Paul D 91
Fleming, Todd 124
Fleming, Thomas (Thom) 132
Fleming, Michael (Mel) 166
Fleming, John (Jack) 328
Fleming, Thomas (Thom) 448
Fleming, Mike 559
Fleming, Christine 594
Flemon, Carla 92
Fleshman, Janice 179
Fleshood, John S. 871
Fletcher, Verna 230
Fletcher, Karen A. 268
Fletcher, Joyce 317
Fletcher, Carl 347
Fletcher, Theo 448
Fletcher, Kevin 854
Fletcher, John P. 870
Fleury, Lynda 833
Flierl, Ken 322
Flierl, Markus 610
Flinchbaugh, Jeremy A 187
Flinn, Tim 283
Flinn, Joseph P (Jo) 630
Flinn, Teresa 630

Flint, Joanna 32
Flint, Chris 766
Flippen, Joe 139
Flis, Robbin 429
Flis, Mike 429
Flisi, Max 158
Flood, David L. 444
Flood, Gary J. 526
FloodCampo, Nina 839
Flores, Maribel 90
Flores, Debbie 102
Flores, Jenny 187
Flores, Stacy 230
Flores, Jose 317
Flores, James C. (Jim) 357
Flores, Richard 502
Flores, Teresita 757
Floresta, John (Jack) 698
Flori, Lou 654
Florian, Hana 6
Florio, Joseph 118
Florio, John 645
Florissi, Patricia 280
Florstedt, Pete 11
Flowe, Aaron 412
Flower, Craig 406
Flowers, Garry W. 347
Flowers, Kimberly 731
Flowers, George G. 764
Flowers, Robert (Bob) 801
Flowers, Mary 848
Floyd, Jim 115
Floyd, Tammy 228
Floyd, David K. 754
Flueckiger, Joe 189
Flugstad, Daniel 391
Flum, Joshua (Josh) 236
Flygar, Brent 95
Flynn, Terry 43
Flynn, Philip B. (Phil) 70
Flynn, Edward B. (Ed) 77
Flynn, Allison 187
Flynn, Nadine P 201
Flynn, Michael T. 272
Flynn, Paul G. 292
Flynn, Beth 367
Flynn, Jeff 398
Flynn, Thomas L. 400
Flynn, Daniel 403
Flynn, Mark 462
Flynn, Thomas A. (Tom) 605
Flynn, Michael 670
Flynn, Brian 696
Flynn, Mark 757
Flynn, Joe 857
Flynt, Steve 135
Flynt, John 427
Focareta, Darren 119
Foderaro, Jim 632
Fodor, Darrin 629
Foe, Bryan D. 697
Foehr, Matthew (Matt) 177
Fogarty, Steve 201
Fogarty, Ryan 856
Fogel, Arthur 509
Fogel, Glenn D. 651
Fogg, David H (Dave) 363
Fogle, Brian 380
Fojo, Carlos 717
Fojut, John (Jack) 481
Folan, Pat 145
Foley, J. Michael 111
Foley, Kevin 187
Foley, Michael E. 271
Foley, Sue 337
Foley, Ellen 584
Foley, K P 586
Foley, Jim 645
Foley, Kevin 793
Foley, Kevin 824
Foley, Loretta 826
Foley, Joseph R. (Joe) 833
Folger, Todd 157
Follansbee, Russell (Russ) 760
Follett, Ray 240
Folliard, Thomas J. (Tom) 152
Folsom, Charles M 400

Johnson, Dale 533
Johnson, Margaret (Peggy) 548
Johnson, Roger 556
Johnson, Mark 577
Johnson, James (Jamie) 584
Johnson, Arnold J. 587
Johnson, Wayne 593
Johnson, Gregory D. (Greg) 602
Johnson, Randy 602
Johnson, James W. (Jim) 613
Johnson, Jodie 626
Johnson, Suzette 632
Johnson, Rady 634
Johnson, Paula A. 638
Johnson, Dawn 664
Johnson, Peggy L 673
Johnson, Dale 686
Johnson, Anthony 713
Johnson, John (Jack) 717
Johnson, William 717
Johnson, Amy W. 724
Johnson, Marsha 731
Johnson, Kevin R. 744
Johnson, Susan S. 757
Johnson, Shannon 757
Johnson, Patti 770
Johnson, Scott 772
Johnson, David (Dave) 774
Johnson, Jeff 774
Johnson, William D. (Bill) 780
Johnson, CJ 781
Johnson, Cheryl H. 785
Johnson, Sherri 791
Johnson, Rob 801
Johnson, Ashley 811
Johnson, Debbie 815
Johnson, Kelly J. 816
Johnson, Todd 820
Johnson, Katrina 820
Johnson, Jeff 826
Johnson, Restor 830
Johnson, Alyson 874
Johnson, Ingrid 879
Johnson, Theresa 879
Johnson, Josh 881
Johnsson, Martin (Marti) 379
Johnston, Mark 20
Johnston, Jason 38
Johnston, Robert V 60
Johnston, Diana 93
Johnston, William J. (Bill) 111
Johnston, Linda A. 113
Johnston, Dan 152
Johnston, Lori 160
Johnston, Kimberly 165
Johnston, Brandi 168
Johnston, Steven J. 180
Johnston, Bryan L 205
Johnston, Andy 216
Johnston, Elizabeth (Beth) 245
Johnston, James J. (Jim) 264
Johnston, T. Hale 285
Johnston, Kelly 341
Johnston, Thomas (Thom) 430
Johnston, Meg 504
Johnston, Maryann 533
Johnston, Stephen (Steve) 611
Johnston, Hugh F. 631
Johnston, Mac 641
Johnston, Lynn 686
Johnston, Robert (Bob) 702
Johnston, Ricky 777
Johnston, Brent 783
Johnston, Greg 848
Johnstone, William O. 91
Johnstone, Debbie 822
Johri, Akhil 828
Jois, Sunitha 534
Jojo, Linda P. 821
Jolivette, Frances 717
Jolley, Jennifer 884
Jolliffe, Lynn 439
Jollymour, Terri 460
Joly, Hubert 114
Jon, Bill 537
Jones, Wellington D. (Duke) 1
Jones, Michael 6

Jones, David 8
Jones, Greg 12
Jones, Brad 16
Jones, Douglas L. (Doug) 19
Jones, John (Jack) 30
Jones, Brian 49
Jones, Wesley 50
Jones, Bayard 50
Jones, Vicki 75
Jones, Vance 95
Jones, Cary 97
Jones, Bradley 97
Jones, Spencer 106
Jones, Jeremy 120
Jones, Michael W. (Mike) 127
Jones, Lori 128
Jones, Richard M. 158
Jones, Nicole S. 179
Jones, Rosalyn 184
Jones, Ingrid 196
Jones, Malcolm 201
Jones, Amber 211
Jones, Larry W. 212
Jones, Andrew 212
Jones, Angela (Angie) 216
Jones, Clay 230
Jones, Colin 230
Jones, Jeff 231
Jones, Mike 270
Jones, Wendy 276
Jones, D 309
Jones, Candace 311
Jones, Jeffrey 322
Jones, Kelly 333
Jones, Derek 336
Jones, Charles E. (Chuck) 342
Jones, Nicholas 350
Jones, John 382
Jones, Paul J. 389
Jones, Kevin 428
Jones, Everett 428
Jones, Earl 434
Jones, Namon 435
Jones, Sheri 444
Jones, Barclay G. 454
Jones, Mitch 455
Jones, Michelle (Mitch) 456
Jones, Michael 456
Jones, Jeffrey 460
Jones, Holly H 464
Jones, Kris 468
Jones, Markee 475
Jones, Peggy 483
Jones, Steve 483
Jones, David (Dave) 492
Jones, Dean 499
Jones, Tim 504
Jones, Michael A. 513
Jones, Ren © F. 514
Jones, Gary 515
Jones, Deanna 518
Jones, Beth 522
Jones, Robert (Bob) 524
Jones, Erica 524
Jones, Bennie 534
Jones, Cynthia 545
Jones, Chris 548
Jones, Gary 549
Jones, Wendy 551
Jones, Kim 553
Jones, Lisa 565
Jones, Chuck 577
Jones, Dan 584
Jones, Mae 594
Jones, Christopher T. 596
Jones, Robert G. (Bob) 605
Jones, Mary 611
Jones, Chuck 611
Jones, John (Jack) 611
Jones, Wilson R. 613
Jones, Tim 613
Jones, Kathleen 629
Jones, Laura 632
Jones, Bill 641
Jones, Barbara (Barb) 645
Jones, Ken 651
Jones, Patrick (Paddy) 664

Jones, Randall T. (Todd) 667
Jones, Vk 673
Jones, Ellen 686
Jones, Karen M. 701
Jones, Brita 706
Jones, Michael 708
Jones, Danny 712
Jones, Doug 731
Jones, Derek R. 734
Jones, Hilliary 757
Jones, David A. 760
Jones, Robbie 764
Jones, Jeffrey J. 770
Jones, Keri 770
Jones, Katie 771
Jones, Michael S. 772
Jones, George F. 783
Jones, Marni 794
Jones, Bruce R 801
Jones, Brad 803
Jones, Anthony 835
Jones, Jeffrey L (Jeff) 835
Jones, Tony 835
Jones, Peggi 839
Jones, Mark 841
Jones, Heather 843
Jones, Kevin 848
Jones, Bruce 878
Jones, Greg 879
Jones, Susan (Sue) 884
Jones, Gena 884
Jones-hollowell, Mattie 343
Joness, Karen 702
Jonnada, Srinivas 506
Jonske, James 29
Jonsson, Thomas (Thom) 76
Joos, David W. 191
Joos, David W. 221
Joosten, Nick 464
Jordan, Kirk 20
Jordan, David A. 111
Jordan, Simon 118
Jordan, Deborah A. 143
Jordan, Kyle 145
Jordan, Rusty 152
Jordan, Ron 179
Jordan, Teresa 179
Jordan, Robert (Bob) 196
Jordan, Glenn 197
Jordan, Cynthia 205
Jordan, John 210
Jordan, Elise 316
Jordan, D. Bryan 334
Jordan, Raymond 460
Jordan, Michael 534
Jordan, Gregory B. 645
Jordan, Ken 694
Jordan, Robert E. (Bob) 733
Jordan, Sheila 761
Jordan, Ron 825
Jordan, Bill 868
Jorgensen, Janet 479
Jorgensen, Kelli 558
Jorgensen, Diane 757
Jorgensen, Jay 848
Jorgenson, Robert 548
Jorgenson, Rob 703
Jose, William 651
Joseph, Sue 183
Joseph, George 281
Joseph, Toomey 404
Joseph, Boby 422
Joseph, Tommy S. 450
Joseph, Lenny 462
Joseph, Valicevic 535
Joseph, George 538
Joseph, Pamela A. (Pam) 810
Joseph, Molly 830
Joseph, Philip 835
Joshi, Vyomesh (VJ) 406
Jost, Kathryn 211
Jotwani, Juhi 448
Joy, Michael 645
Joy, John (Jack) 705
Joyce, Deborah 166
Joyce, Thomas P. 238
Joyce, James (Jamie) 319

Joyce, David L. 364
Joyce, Robert J. (Bob) 473
Joyce, Joe 478
Joyce, Burton 590
Joyce, Thomas P. 665
Joyce, James (Jamie) 794
Joyner, J. David 236
Joyner, David J (Dave) 236
Joyner, Janell 771
Joysizemore, Dian 91
Jr, Raul Rodriguez 80
JR, Harrall 370
Juchno, Stacy M. 645
Judd, Sam 717
Judge, James J. (Jim) 296
Judge, Kenan 431
Judge, Mark 629
Judy, Ryan 58
Judy, Franklin 171
Jue, Don 448
Juergensonn, Janine 103
Jugoon, Peter (Pete) 710
Julian, Paul C. 534
Julian, Janis 874
Juliano, Jim 58
Juliano, Mark 491
Juliber, Lois D. 268
Julien, Jeffrey P. 681
Jump, Belinda 373
Junek, John C. 46
Jung, Michael (Mel) 254
Jung, Matthias 781
Jungers, Natasha 598
Jungk, Dave 663
Juniper, Brooke 119
Junkins, Lowell L. 307
Juno, Ed 142
Jurch, Gina 106
Jurgens, Chris 419
Jurgens, Deanna 632
Jurjovec, Bill 871
Jurs, Peter (Pete) 322
Jury, Keith 297
Jussaume, Carolyn 838
Justice, Anita 212
Justin, Marianne 834
Justiniano, Jack 635
Justiss, Donna 8
Justizynski, Adam 196
Jutcovich, Morris 830
Juvara, Paolo 611

K

Kaatman, Nancy 125
Kabin, Karen 478
Kacenjar, Linda 475
Kachel, Vic 352
Kaczmarek, David 857
Kaczmarek, Dave 857
Kadavy, Andrew 349
Kaddoura, Maher 322
Kaden, Ellen Oran 145
Kadenacy, Stephen M. (Steve) 11
Kadens, Pete 278
Kader, Asma 466
Kadhiresan, Kadir 461
Kadien, Thomas G. (Tom) 450
Kadifa, George 406
Kadish, Ronald T. (Ron) 127
Kadlec, Kim 460
Kadri, Ilham 715
Kaercher, Walter 629
Kaestner, H. Todd 135
Kafka, Donald L. 325
Kagey, David 710
Kahan, Adrian 679
Kahl, Steven (Steve) 359
Kahle, Charles F. 648
Kahlon, Summerpal 534
Kahmann, Mike 184
Kahn, Kelli 121
Kahn, Joel 208
Kahrs, Karen 311
Kaiser, Laura S. 444
Kaiser, Katie 534

Komarek, Jennifer 770
Komidar, John 801
Komis, Kristen 550
Komola, Christine T. 743
Komorowski, Raymond 523
Konar, Edward (Ed) 473
Kondal, Jaspreet 319
Konecny, Pavel 173
Konen, Mark E. 505
Kong, Justine 37
Kong, Oliver 162
Kong, Betty 201
Kong, Michelle (Mitch) 254
Kong, Victor 841
Konings, Frank 460
Konishi, Kathleen 444
Konkoly-thege, Adam 832
Konkoy, Christopher 504
Konrad, Jocelyn 694
Konstantinovsky, Irina 105
Kontopanos, Kostas 201
Koo, Sofia 121
Kooda-Chizek, Kristi 47
Koogler, Rob 429
Koonce, Paul D. 259
Koons, Michael (Mel) 182
Kooren, Doug 216
Koosmann, Willie 883
Kootswatewa, Gina 50
Kooyman, John (Jack) 201
Kooyman, Bob 808
Kopchinski, Richard (Dick) 645
Kopelman, Donna 466
Kopil, Ed 110
Kopkowski, Ed 237
Kopp, Bruce 415
Koppel, Adam M. 118
Koppel, Paul 347
Koppel, Michael G. 588
Kopser, Mark 777
Koptish, Kurt 240
Koranda, Janet 871
Korbich, William 460
Koren, Tom 176
Koreneck, Debbie 165
Korengel, Jeff 216
Korins, Danielle 670
Korn, George 386
Korneffel, Laurie 168
Korsapati, Venka 37
Korsmeyer, Richard 634
Korten, Patrick 480
Korunovski, Jill 879
Kory, Joe 568
Korzekwinski, Francis W. (Frank) 348
Kosac, Paul 182
Kosak, Chris 388
Kosar, Corrine 128
Kosch, Gregory L. (Greg) 321
Koscik, Paul 428
Kosh, Mitchell A. 679
Koski, Susan (Sue) 337
Koski, Philip 811
Koskoski, John (Jack) 664
Koskovich, Melissa (Mel) 494
Koskovich, Melissa (Mel) 495
Koslow, John (Jack) 43
Kosorski, Paulette 322
Kossak, Natalie 360
Kossar, Robert 464
Kostakis, Emmanuel 838
Kostalnick, Charles F. 707
Kostalnick, Chuck 707
Kostecki, Orest 670
Koster, Dan 307
Koster, Karen 408
Koster, Barbara G. 663
Koster, James 745
Kostrzeski, Deborah 421
Kostyk, Mary 696
Kosydor, Vicki 309
Kotas, Paul 35
Kotik, Karen 353
Kotler, Kristin 766
Kotlowski, Mike 520
Kotrogiannis, George 464
Kotsiantos, George 280

Kottapalli, Kishore 749
Kottayil, Divya 160
Kotte, Kavita 376
Kottler, Robert M. (Bob) 432
Kotwal, Shailesh M. 810
Kotylo, Kenneth (Ken) 775
Kouatchou, Gide 717
Kouchekali, Roxana 94
Koumouris, Rick 347
Kouri, Stephen (Steve) 727
Koury, Emile 385
Koury, Jeffrey (Jeff) 777
Koushik, Srinivas (Srini) 406
Koutrouby, Alexander (Al) 186
Kovac, Kim 76
Kovach, Jerome 524
Kovach, Dave 839
Kovacs, Janet 73
Kovalcik, James (Jamie) 170
Kovalsky, Drew 72
Koveos, George 679
Koviak, Jeff 778
Kowal, Dave 139
Kowal, Mike 657
Kowalska, Marta 611
Kowalski, Patricia 350
Kowalski, Maureen 472
Kowalski, Michael 689
Kowkabi, Sima 706
Kowlzan, Mark W. 620
Kowolenko, Dave 203
Kozak, Michael J. 337
Kozak, Dave 431
Kozak, Colleen 717
Kozar, Paul 810
Kozek, William R. (Bill) 568
Kozel, David F. (Dave) 670
Kozelek, Ed 791
Kozen, Raymond E 363
Kozielski, Vitia 557
Koziner, Pablo M. 154
Kozlak, Jodee 697
Kozlak, Jodeen A. 770
Kozlik, Rainer 439
Kozloski, Rick 5
Kozlowski, Stan 252
Kozlowski, Keith 339
Kozlowski, Ted 559
Kozsurek, Joe 495
Kozy, William A. 108
Kracke, Dana 730
Kraemer, Ellen 7
Kraemer, Theodore (Theo) 128
Krafcheck, Terese 529
Krafels, Rick 483
Kraft, Eric 206
Kraft, Ted 400
Kraft, Cheryl 645
Kraft, Christopher 717
Krage, David 433
Krakauer, Mary 280
Krakowsky, Philippe 451
Kralingen, Bridget A. van 447
Krall, Donna M. 345
Kramer, Bill 75
Kramer, Jennifer 102
Kramer, Kelly A. 182
Kramer, Richard J. (Rich) 377
Kramer, Chuck 432
Kramer, Howard 463
Kramer, Phillip D. (Phil) 643
Kramer, Jennifer (Jenn) 665
Kramer, Mark 694
Kramer, Steve 810
Kramer, Tim 871
Kramlich, C 760
Kramvis, Andreas C. 415
Krane, Spencer D 309
Krane, Hilary K. 584
Krantz, Missy 432
Kranz, Stacey 514
Krarup, Bruce 151
Krasnoff, Jeffrey P. (Jeff) 496
Krasowski, Janet D. 661
Kratsberg, Leon 723
Kratz, Denise 706
Kratzert, Niki 480

Kraus, Marie 149
Kraus, Robert 310
Kraus, Evan 359
Kraus, Frederick 491
Krause, Greg 14
Krause, Douglas (Doug) 273
Krause, Frank 319
Krause, Brett 465
Krause, Kim 774
Krauss, Soheir 184
Krauss, Jim 254
Krauss, Karl 820
Krawiec, Dan 223
Krawiec, Marc 339
Kraynak, Karen 213
Krebbs, Justin 91
Krebs, Bruce J. 300
Krebs, Kurt 322
Krebs, Donald E. 468
Krebs, Marty 554
Krech, Joyce 112
Kreczko, Alan (Al) 393
Kreer, Daniel 556
Kreger, Verne 460
Krehbiel, Bruce 452
Kreidler, Robert C. (Chris) 765
Kreitler, Brooke 830
Kremer, Lisa 523
Kremer, Wesley D. 683
Kremin, Donald H. (Don) 417
Krempl, Stephen 745
Krenowicz, Jim 186
Krepps, Shawna 835
Kresl, Michael 45
Kress, Jean 373
Kreston, Mark 162
Kretchmer, David (Dave) 58
Kreuzer, Barry 231
Krider, Joe 781
Krieger, Sandra C. (Sandy) 310
Krieger, Noah 664
Krikorian, Alex 179
Krimbill, H. Michael 583
Krimigis, Susan (Sue) 186
Krinke, Jennifer 771
Krinock, Patricia (Pat) 492
Krippner, Brian 814
Krisciunas, Joe 365
Krish, Nikki 299
Krishna, Arvind 447
Krishnamurthy, Aparna 223
Krishnamurthy, Murali 300
Krishnamurthy, Ganesh 448
Krishnan, Sai 284
Krishnaraj, Suku 168
Krishnaswamy, Venkat 199
Kritemeyer, Ellen 629
Krivanec, Ken 865
Krizsa, Thomas 475
Krmpotic, Deb 102
Kroboth, Michael (Mel) 649
Kroeker, Harrald F. 64
Kroenung, Stefan 76
Kroese, Shawntell 818
Kroge, Ryan 428
Krol, Wojciech 200
Kroll, Sue 792
Krombach, Anthony 105
Krone, Stacey 317
Krone, Roger A. 494
Krone, Roger A 495
Kroner, Kenneth F. (Ken) 119
Kroner, Todd 749
Krostosky, Robert 694
Krotje, Charles 223
Krozek, Carol 343
Krueger, Steve 432
Krug, Mario 492
Kruger, James D. (Jim) 572
Krumins, Mara 472
Krumrey, Elizabeth (Beth) 871
Krupka, Jack 427
Krupp, Jason 102
Kruse, Karen 334
Kruse, Shelly 383
Kruse, Karl 431
Kruse, Eric 641

Kruszewski, Ronald J. (Ron) 752
Kryder, Andrew (Andy) 573
Kryshtalowych, Greg 781
Krystofiak, Matt 139
Krystolovich, Russe 390
Krzan, Mike 118
Krzanich, Brian M. 442
Krzemien-Roy, Andrea 205
Krzyminski, Walter 73
Krzyzanowski, Richard L 226
Ksenak, Stephen M. 37
Ku, Michael (Mel) 634
Kuark, Amy 863
Kubacki, Michael L. 488
Kubala, Dale 702
Kubasik, Christopher E. 485
Kubenka, Karen 177
Kuberski, Craig 352
Kubic, Paul 812
Kucharczuk, Bob 203
Kuck, Mark 830
Kuckelman, Tim 481
Kuczora, Deb 481
Kudlac, Jeffrey (Jeff) 363
Kudzma, Lori 162
Kuehl, Kevin 116
Kuehn, Kurt 825
Kueny, Patrick 395
Kuffner, Ed 460
Kuhl, Bryan 73
Kuhle, Nathan 177
Kuhlow, John (Jack) 427
Kuhn, Rebecca (Becky) 101
Kuhn, Laura 254
Kuhn, Bill 339
Kuhn, Rick 339
Kuhn, Jennifer (Jen) 830
Kuhns, Dewey 189
Kuick, Ken 140
Kuick, Kenneth (Ken) 140
Kujak, Tom 758
Kuki, Katsuyuki 465
Kularski, Patty 388
Kulas, Michael (Mel) 816
Kulaszewicz, Frank C. 698
Kulik, Katie 158
Kulikowski, Adam 148
Kulkarni, Sharad 67
Kulkarni, Anand 375
Kulkarni, Shridhar 632
Kulkin, Harvey 721
Kullman, Ellen J. 267
Kulp, Bruce 361
Kum, Chong Guk (C. G.) 387
Kumar, Devinder 9
Kumar, Suresh 97
Kumar, Gopa 312
Kumar, Sandhya 459
Kumar, Suresh 548
Kumar, Arvind 611
Kumar, Manish 678
Kumar, Rajesh 694
Kumar, Krish 789
Kumler, Alan 820
Kumm, Wendy 70
Kummer, Randy 492
Kumnick, Phil 843
Kump, Jason 57
Kundrat, Nikki 99
Kundu, Partha 745
Kundurthy, Praveen 442
Kuney, Terry 429
Kung, Catherine 310
Kunk, James E. 428
Kunkel, Eric 463
Kunkel, Jay K. 492
Kunkel, Thomas M. (Tom) 801
Kunkel, Patricia (Pat) 879
Kunst, Jeff 223
Kuntz, John F. 661
Kunz, Roberta 645
Kunz, Thomas (Thom) 645
Kunzelman, Lori 514
Kuper, Debra 17
Kupfer, Lawrence J. (Larry) 421
Kupiec, James 634

Neely, J 128
Neely, Scott 663
Neely, David (Dave) 686
Nefkens, Mike 406
Nefkens, Mike 422
Negron, Ed 188
Negron, Julie 717
Negron, Eduardo J. 646
Neher, Terry 810
Neidorff, Michael F. 163
Neifert, Kevin T. 683
Neiheisel, Jeff 879
Neikirk, Jessica 446
Neil, Rich 138
Neill, Casey 337
Neill, James R. (Jim) 370
Neill, Sarah 499
Neill, Elizabeth 607
Neiman, Gary 398
Nell, Greg 513
Nellessen, Mark 450
Nellis, Brett 835
Nelms, David W. 250
Nelp, Todd 124
Nelsen, Keith J. 115
Nelsen, Mike 692
Nelsen, Denise 745
Nelson, Lael 14
Nelson, John R. (Jack) 34
Nelson, Gregory 38
Nelson, Ronald L. (Ron) 83
Nelson, Shelby 102
Nelson, Douglas M. 111
Nelson, Elizabeth (Beth) 140
Nelson, Lisa 177
Nelson, Rosemary 201
Nelson, Mark W. 202
Nelson, David (Dave) 242
Nelson, Barry 243
Nelson, Faye A. 266
Nelson, Lisa 284
Nelson, Ann W. 285
Nelson, John P. 285
Nelson, Christopher 291
Nelson, Pierce 309
Nelson, James (Jamie) 310
Nelson, Diane 318
Nelson, Carol 327
Nelson, David D (Dave) 365
Nelson, Kimberly A. (Kim) 367
Nelson, Kim 367
Nelson, Rick 383
Nelson, Todd 386
Nelson, Thomas 426

Nelson, Leah 467
Nelson, Ricklin 505
Nelson, Jane 578
Nelson, Kevin W. 597
Nelson, Jonathan B. 607
Nelson, Bradley M. (Brad) 613
Nelson, Lesa 626
Nelson, Sue 764
Nelson, Scott 770
Nelson, Diane 792
Nelson, Jon 793
Nelson, Christopher 814
Nelson, Alison 830
Nelson, Michael S. 832
Nelson, Zachary 834
Nelson, Pam 838
Nelson, Connia 838
Nelson, Laura 840
Nelson, George 841
Nelson, Kathy 866
Nelson, Brad A 877
Nemecek, Robert 56
Nemelka, Scott 765
Nemer, Marti 464
Nemeth, Julio 657
Nemphos, Ann 393
Nemrow, Anabel 100
Nenaber, Pam 102
Nentchev, Nentcho 121
Nepveux, Kevin 634
Nerbonne, Daniel (Dan) 643
Nerenhausen, Frank R. 613

Nesbit, Jonathan (Jon) 749
Nesbitt, Douglas 689
Nesci, James D. 662
Nesi, Victor J. 752
Neslen, Nancy G 551
Nesler, Clayton 462
Ness, J. Greg 741
Nessel, Christopher (Chris) 460
Nesson, Scott 311
Nestel, Michele 811
Nestora, Gregory 264
Nestorson, John 16
Netherton, Linda 319
Nettesheim, Susan 460
Nettleton, Lynn 645
Neu, David W. (Dave) 49
Neubert, Sherry 377
Neumaier, John 359
Neumann, Jim 29
Neumann, Mark 51
Neumann, Karl-Thomas 368
Neumann, Kathy 629
Neumeyer, Daniel J. 428
Nevens, T. Michael (Mike) 573
Nevill, Robert (Bob) 416
Neville, Brian W 40
Neville, R. Shawn 82
Neville, Robert (Bob) 91
Neville, Bruce E 205
Neville, Dennis 706
Nevins, Sheila 792
Newbern, Thomas B. 81
Newberry, Stephen G. (Steve) 489
Newbold, Michael W. (Mike) 428
Newbold, Ronald C (Ron) 635
Newcomer, Reagan 93
Newell, Kevin 56
Newell, Michele 853
Newfield, Richard U. 564
Newgard, Jeffrey K. 413
Newhouse, Greg 475
Newkirk, Tony 400
Newlands, William A. (Bill) 220
Newman, Mike 47
Newman, Kenneth Kenneth Newman (Ken) 97
Newman, Kenneth 97
Newman, Rebecca 97
Newman, Brett 122
Newman, Susan V (Sue) 205
Newman, Andrea 245
Newman, Dennis 252
Newman, Chris 318
Newman, Deon 448
Newman, Rainer 460
Newman, Gerald 532
Newman, Paul 559
Newman, Brian 632
Newman, Robert 641
Newman, Gary 807
Newman, Jeff 884
Newmark, Rona 280
Newport, Roger K. 21
Newsom, Richard W. (Rick) 212
Newsome, Randa 683
Newton, Dave 491
Newton, Mike 691
Newton, Ashley 731
Neyland, Stephen J. 286
Neyland, Stephen J (Steve) 549
Neylon, Brian 252
Ng, Aiwah 95
Ng, Dominic 273
Ng, Ching 443
Ng, Donna 460
Ng, Paul 722
Ng, Linda 749
Ng, Chaki 841
Ngo, A. Catherine 166
Nguyen, Thong M. 93
Nguyen, Troy 279
Nguyen, Kim 311
Nguyen, Xuong 452
Nguyen, Tony 499
Nguyen, Chi 534
Nguyen, Phuong 573
Nguyen, Monica 586

Nguyen, Tracy 593
Nguyen, David 664
Niall, Oconnor 61
Niblock, Robert A. 513
Niccol, Brian 882
Niccoli, Ann 248
Nichol, Janett 584
Nicholas, Peter M. (Pete) 132
Nicholas, Jim 466
Nicholls, Ian 368
Nicholls, Timothy S. (Tim) 450
Nicholls, Rod 534
Nicholls, Stephanie 884
Nichols, Carrie 99
Nichols, Todd 118
Nichols, J. Larry 246
Nichols, Eric 274
Nichols, John R. 305
Nichols, Kay 319
Nichols, Michael (Mel) 361
Nichols, Kreg 422
Nichols, Cindy 502
Nichols, Bob 550
Nichols, Robert 696
Nichols, Dan 757
Nichols, Michael (Mel) 765
Nichols, Clarence 814
Nichols, Blee 879
Nicholson, Ann 5
Nicholson, Brian 353
Nicholson, Darryl 460
Nicholson, Paul 657
Nicholson, Kelly 663
Nickel, Thedora 90
Nickele, Christopher J. (Chris) 194
Nickell, Jeff 119
Nickels, Jeff 333
Nickerson, Darrell 78
Nickerson, Richard 143
Nickerson, Cheryl 629
Nicklas, Randy 870
Nicks, Darlene 433
Nicol, Peter G. 170
Nicol, Mark 683
Nicolaidis, Allison 742
Nicolas, Ronald J. 89
Niebur, William S. (Bill) 268
Niech, Lawrence 77
Niedbalski, Dave 509
Niederpruem, Gary 284
Niehaus, Bill 426
Niekerk, Herman Van 231
Niekerk, Gary 443
Nielsen, Julie 53
Nielsen, Brad 64
Nielsen, Jeffrey (Jeff) 179
Nielsen, Darron 361
Nielsen, Tom 456
Nielsen, Mark D 683
Nieman, Maurice 157
Nieman, Susan 688
Niemann, Angela 299
Niemann, Donna 713
Niemela, Jason R. 111
Niermann, Mark 241
Nieto, Tom 861
Nieuwenhuys, Gerard 627
Nieuwsma, Steve 699
Nieuwsma, David (Dave) 699
Nightingale, Timothy P. 143
Nigro, Joseph (Joe) 297
Nigro, Stephen (Steve) 421
Nikolov, Anita 594
Niland, Barbara A. (Barb) 430
Nile, Christopher Del Moral (Chris) 70
Niles, Thomas 556
Niles, Mark 860
Nilsson, Jonas 76
Nimbley, Thomas J. 624
Nimer, Richard (Dick) 3
Ninivaggi, Daniel A. (Dan) 314
Nirenberg, Jeffrey 121
Nisbett, Mark 854
Nischbach, Shelly 815
Nishi, Masao 766
Nishimoto, Cheryl 617
Nisiewicz, Krystyna 879

Nisperos, Marieta 694
Nissenson, Allen R. 240
Nito, Daniel (Dan) 556
Nittoli, Rocco 498
Nittolo, Kathy 632
Niver, Clair 632
Nivica, Gjon N. 160
Nivica, Jon 160
Nix, Craig L. 328
Nix, Tommy 781
Nixon, Randy 77
Nixon, David (Dave) 157
Nixon, John 375
Nixon, Dennis E. 446
Nixon, John 604
Nixon, Tim 694
Niziak, Drew 16
Niziolek, Barry J. 268
Niziolek, Mark 874
Noall, Alison 428
Nober, Roger 137
Nobile, Paul 58
Noble, Quintin 5
Noble, David J. (D.J.) 41
Noble, Jeff 330
Noble, Jen 448

Noble, Craig 629
Noble, Jim 645
Nobrega, Rui 537
Nocco, Jennifer 140
Noce, Walter W. (Bill) 740
Nock, Doug 739
Nodianos, Bridget 106
Noel, Robert 124
Noethiger, Robert 158
Noffsinger, Richard 14
Nogas, Courtney 393
Noguera, Lupe 611
Nohara, Todd 95
Noiseux, Joane 156
Nolan, Joe 62
Nolan, Steve 78
Nolan, Bob 163
Nolan, Brendan 184
Nolan, Mike 317
Nolan, Mark 359
Nolan, James G (Jamie) 402
Nolan, Patrick M. 424
Nolan, Linda 594
Nolan, Pat 697
Noland, Thomas T 425
Nolasco, Teresa 206
Nolde-morrissey, Paul 102
Nolk, Monique 421
Noll, Richard A. (Rich) 386
Nolte, Jo 626
Noonan, David (Dave) 284
Noonan, James R. 488
Noonan, Steve 541
Noorani, Nick 437
Noordhoek, Jeffrey R. (Jeff) 572
Nooyi, Indra K. 631
Norberto, Joao 5
Norcia, Gerardo (Jerry) 266
Norcross, Sterling Sterling Norcross 78
Norcross, Gary A. 318
Norcross, Anna 475
Norcross, Jeanne 734
Nordell, Scott 317
Nordlander, Dan 863
Nordlie, Elizabeth 367
Nordling, Christopher 545
Nordmeyer, Greg 47
Nordmeyer, Jim 616
Nordstrom, Anna 311
Nordstrom, William 456
Nordstrom, Blake W. 588
Nordstrom, Peter E. (Pete) 588
Nordstrom, Erik B. 588
Nordstrom, James F. (Jamie) 588
Noren, Per 124
Norfleet, Edward B 311
Norgeot, Peter (Pete) 290
Noriega, Erica 230
Noriega, Conrad 860
Norman, Sofia 55

Santos, Manuel 688
Santos, Mike 745
Santos, Kristen 751
Santoyo, Raul 185
Sanz, Erick 392
Saoud, Abdallah 843
Sapaugh, Scott 642
Sapenter, Tyrone A 632
Saperstein, Andy 556
Sapnar, Michael C. (Mike) 26
Sapozhnicov, Nadia 634
Sapp, Gene 707
Sappenfield, Gregg 553
Sappenfield, Joel 808
Sappington, Jim 532
Sapre, Milind 375
Sapuppo, David (Dave) 187
Saracino, Frank V 659
Sarafian, Khatchatur 694
Sarah, Rapalyea 830
Saraiva, Ana 629
Sarandos, Ted 574
Sarangapani, Prakash 443
Sarathy, Kanchana 111
Saravi, Maximo 541
Sarber, Mark 324
Sardina, Frank 339
Sardina, Kathy 845
Sardo, Allison 148
Sargent, Angela M. 358
Sargent, Ronald L. (Ron) 743
Sari, Robert B. 588
Sarkar, Mona 343
Sarmiento, Marco 93
Sarrat, Christina 350
Sarrat, Scott 686
Sarro, Gary 723
Sartain, Paul 841
Sartori, Dave 203
Sartori, Giuliano 839
Sarvadi, John 783
Sarver, Robert G. 860
Sassen, Stacy 771
Sasser, Bob 257
Sassus, Suzanne 740
Sastri, Jon 683
Sato, Andrew (Andy) 187
Sato, Michael 588
Sato, Mike 588
Satterlund, Amy 810
Satterthwaite, Livingston L. (Tony) 231
Satz, David (Dave) 139
Sauber, Jeffrey 405
Sauceman, Mark 811
Saucier, Nicole 770
Sauer, Brad 2
Sauer, Jon 60
Sauer, James 494
Sauerland, John P. 659
Sauers, Jeff 534
Sauers, Len 657
Sauk, Michele 884
Saul, Kevin 61
Saul, Eileen 318
Saul, Paula 866
Saulig, Richard 593
Saulys, Vincent 376
Saun, Bruce Van 188
Saunders, Lynn A 365
Saunders, Matt 434
Saunders, Cindy 483
Saunders, Pamela 495
Saunders, Troy 513
Saunders, Jeff L. 567
Saunders, Nancy 573
Saunders, John 607
Saunders, Barry L. 729
Saunders, Brian 875
Sausen, Ted 593
Sausen, Julie 594
Sautter, Bruce 428
Sauv_©, Mario 228
Sav, Martine 770
Savage, Mike 3
Savage, Stephen (Steve) 207
Savage, Douglas (Doug) 466
Savage, Tanja 833

Savage, Joseph J. (Joe) 854
Savage, Susan 875
Savage, Jeff 877
Savage, Stanley D. 883
Savary, Leigh 634
Savastano, Pete 106
Savery, Warren 157
Savitt, Samuel (Sam) 97
Savner, David A (Dave) 363
Savoy, Brian 270
Saw, Choon Seong 18
Sawant, Siddhesh 594
Sawdey, Mike 45
Sawyer, Stephen 764
Sawyer, John 861
Sawyers, Todd 428
Sax, James (Jamie) 3
Sax, Michael E (Mel) 319
Saxon, Mike 22
Saxon, Michael J. 53
Saxon, Mike 731
Sayed, Ayman 182
Sayeedi, Nick 253
Saylor, Kurt M. 400
Sayre, Madison 189
Sayre, David L. 857
Scaduto, Ginny 472
Scaff, Eric 462
Scala, Luciano 641
Scala, Douglas E. (Doug) 854
Scalata, Tracey 437
Scallan, Michael (Mel) 554
Scallion, Gerald 14
Scammon, Steven D. 737
Scanell, Bill 281
Scangos, George A. 117
Scanlon, Meghan 132
Scannell, William F. (Bill) 280
Scannell, Timothy J. 754
Scaramuzzo, John (Jack) 705
Scarazzini, Linda 7
Scarborough, Dean A. 82
Scarborough, Mark 250
Scardina, Michael (Mel) 29
Scardina, Mike 29
Scardino, Cristina 43
Scariot, John (Jack) 526
Scarlata, John P. 665
Scarlett, Catherine M. 569
Scarry, Robert (Bob) 879
Scarsella, Michael 529
Scaturo, Michael 121
Scavone, April 83
Scelba, Thomas 874
Scelfo, John Scelfo John (Jack) 404
Scelzo, Darline 464
Scenti, Louis 310
Scerbo, Albert 599
Schaaf, Jill M. 104
Schaaf, Renee 654
Schaaf, Christopher (Chris) 811
Schaar, Donna 152
Schaar, Cullen 498
Schabacker, Marcus 104
Schabacker, DrMarcus 104
Schachter, Bernard 743
Schacter, Adam 185
Schade, Jennifer (Jen) 339
Schaefer, Rich 5
Schaefer, Brenda 102
Schaefer, Kelly 216
Schaefer, David (Dave) 352
Schaefer, Marilyn 416
Schaefer, Michael 432
Schaefer, Milena 670
Schaefer, Charles (Chas) 679
Schaefer, Robbie 835
Schaeffler, Kenneth (Ken) 205
Schafer, Mary 78
Schafer, Todd 168
Schafer, Carol 475
Schager, Marty 12
Schalk, David 629
Schall, Kelly 47
Schall, Amy 138
Schall, Benjamin 717
Schaller, Meagan 435

Schallhorn, Andrew F. 473
Schalliol, Charles E. 336
Schaniedel, Gary 613
Schank, Don 499
Schanzer, Julie 526
Schappert, Rich 153
Scharf, David P. 104
Scharf, David 201
Scharf, Charles W. (Charlie) 842
Scharfl, Steve 717
Scharfen, Jock 596
Scharmer, Neal R. 822
Schatz, Joe 139
Schatz, Peter (Pete) 148
Schatzman, Robert 376
Schaub, Robert 309
Schauenberg, Trevor 365
Schauer, Darleen 230
Schechter, Damon 439
Schechter, Lori A. 534
Schechter, Adam H. 537
Schecklman, Dave 613
Scheder, Valerie 75
Schedl, Manfred 390
Scheffel, William N. 163
Scheffenegger, Richard (Dick) 573
Schefft, Bob 46
Scheible, David (Dave) 353
Scheid, Tom 181
Scheidmeir, Thomas (Thom) 7
Scheirman, Kathy 467
Schell, Christoph 421
Schell, Jennifer (Jen) 706
Schellinger, Jimmie 783
Schemm, Todd 43
Schenck, Robert (Bob) 309
Schenck, Rand 570
Schenck, A. William (Bill) 804
Schenkel, Scott 276
Scheper, Patrick 760
Schepp, Richard D. (Rick) 481
Scher, Andrew (Andy) 415
Scherdorf, Ron 713
Scherer, Jacob F. 180
Schermer, Carol 104
Scherr, Stephen M. 375
Scherrbaum, Joseph R. (Joe) 827
Scherzinger, Chris 458
Scheuing, Gregg 97
Scheuler, Sylvia 688
Scheuring, Steve 20
Schiada, David 278
Schick, Art 632
Schick, Jeff 778
Schickler, Paul E. 268
Schickler, Richard (Dick) 534
Schieffer, Margaret (Peg) 410
Schiele, Tyrone 717
Schiff, George 523
Schiffels, Carolyn M 593
Schiffer, Sharon 757
Schiffman, Julie 634
Schildkraut, Michael (Mel) 537
Schiller, Philip W. 61
Schiller, Steven C. 401
Schilling, Jeffrey 78
Schilling, Johnathan 504
Schiltgen, John (Jack) 2
Schimke, Laura 448
Schindele, Mark 770
Schindler, Phillipp 32
Schindler, Todd 825
Schineller, Jenifer 534
Schintzius, David (Dave) 85
Schioldager, Amy L. 119
Schippers, Harrie C.A.M. 617
Schirling, Kathleen 629
Schirmer, Ham 525
Schlachter, Harry 53
Schlafrig, Elke 376
Schlageter, Stephen P. (Steve) 669
Schlappig, Michael 121
Schlecht, Mathias 88
Schleder, Dan 699
Schlegel, Eileen 664
Schleiff, Henry S. 251
Schlemper, Oliver 611

Schlesinger, Adam 121
Schlesinger, Jeffrey R. 792
Schlessinger, Mike 365
Schlichting, Warren 252
Schlitz, Lei 436
Schloeder, Pam 126
Schlonsky, Michael A. (Mike) 116
Schloss, Neil 352
Schlosser, John W. 478
Schlotfeldt, Kari 810
Schlotman, J. Michael 483
Schlueter, James 125
Schlueter, Anne 398
Schmachtenberg, Richard (Dick) 878
Schmechel, Daniel J. (Dan) 277
Schmelz, Kurt 878
Schmid, Roman 182
Schmid, Sharon 830
Schmidl, Mark 559
Schmidt, Jim 3
Schmidt, Karen 42
Schmidt, Phil 75
Schmidt, Michael 83
Schmidt, Darryl 91
Schmidt, Christopher (Chris) 115
Schmidt, Colleen 138
Schmidt, Eleanor D. 150
Schmidt, Richard (Dick) 157
Schmidt, Dany 201
Schmidt, Joseph (Jo) 247
Schmidt, Jason 463
Schmidt, Dave 481
Schmidt, Greg 596
Schmidt, Steven M. (Steve) 604
Schmidt, Andrew (Andy) 645
Schmidt, Rick 699
Schmidt, Kyle 810
Schmidt, Ray 812
Schmidt, Donna 820
Schmidt, Tracy 856
Schmidt, Keith 884
Schmidt-Fellner, Peter A. 580
Schmiedel, Gary W. 613
Schmiegelow, Brent 808
Schmitt, Matt 163
Schmitt, Lisa 460
Schmitt, Karl 721
Schmittlein, Marc E 801
Schmitz, Jhan 170
Schmitz, David 322
Schmitz, Betty 825
Schmoyer, Ben 702
Schmukler, Louis S. (Lou) 133
Schnaid, Alan M. 746
Schnalzer, Michael 119
Schnautz, Vernon (Vern) 602
Schnecke, Tom 158
Schneeberger, Carol A. 630
Schneider, Richard E. (Rick) 52
Schneider, Jonathan (Jon) 106
Schneider, Ryan M. 148
Schneider, Scott D 179
Schneider, Neal C. 194
Schneider, Rick 226
Schneider, Glenn P. 250
Schneider, Kathy 252
Schneider, Kristof 322
Schneider, Donald R. (Donny) 342
Schneider, David 354
Schneider, Kevin D. 371
Schneider, Ray 380
Schneider, Christina 406
Schneider, James (Jamie) 466
Schneider, Steve 495
Schneider, Peter W. 652
Schneider, Dana 686
Schneider, Ann Marie 710
Schneider, Barry 750
Schneider, Mike 789
Schneider, Joseph (Jo) 825
Schneider, Martin 839
Schneider, David C. 850
Schneider, Robert (Bob) 866
Schneider, Jay 878
Schnettler, Gary 321
Schnieders, Kurt J. 247
Schnitz, Chad 8

Slate, Kathy 683
Slater, David 266
Slater, Trudi 745
Slater, Catherine I. 865
Slatter, Sarah 629
Slattery, Keith 534
Slattery, Greg 651
Slattery, William 749
Slaugh, Linden 579
Slaughter, MelindA 754
Slavik, John (Jack) 321
Slawin, Kevin R. 307
Slawter, Todd 14
Slaymaker, Ron 784
Slayton, Diane 830
Sledge, Charles M. 144
Slee, Steven 322
Sleet, Paul 365
Sleiman, Adham 128
Slentz, Andrew P. (Andy) 625
Sleyster, Scott G. 663
Slider, Ray 664
Slifka, Eric 374
Slifka, Andrew 374
Slifka, Richard 374
Sliney, David 752
Slinkard, Terri 796
Slipy, Scott D. 455
Slisher, Scott 40
Sliwowski, Michael (Mel) 719
Sload, Michael 200
Sloan, Thomas R. 123
Sloan, Robert (Bob) 290
Sloan, Rodney L. 399
Sloan, Rod 400
Sloan, Randy 733
Sloan, Richard (Dick) 778
Sloane, Steele 163
Sloane, Barry R. 167
Slocum, Michael C. 148
Slocum, Michael J (Mel) 196
Slofkosky, Sharon 206
Slone, Daryl 212
Slone, Estella 352
Slone, Greg 393
Slootskiy, Alex 629
Slotnik, Joseph J. 136
Slowik, James 530
Sluder, Jeff 670
Slump, David J. 390
Slusher, John F. 584
Slusser, Eric R. 301
Slutz, William 428
Sly, Patrick J. (Pat) 283
Small, Kurt 14
Small, Sheila 509
Small, Brown 662
Small, Simone 686
Small, Toni 740
Small, David 837
Smalley, Gary G 347
Smart, George M. 342
Smeal, Joan 610
Smeaton, Allan 521
Smelko, Michael G. 597
Smette, Darryl G. 246
Smid, Tony 29
Smiddy, Craig R. 606
Smiley, Anwar 475
Smit, Brian 102
Smit, Neil 203
Smit, Steve 220
Smit, Karen 754
Smith, Bill 3
Smith, Rob 17
Smith, Lucinda 17
Smith, Julian 22
Smith, Zeke 22
Smith, Gil 26
Smith, Elizabeth 29
Smith, Craig 29
Smith, A. Wade 40
Smith, Stephen (Steve) 40
Smith, Pat 42
Smith, Wayne 45
Smith, Barb 47
Smith, Rodney A. 56

Smith, Kent 67
Smith, Donna N. 70
Smith, David 71
Smith, Michele 75
Smith, Paul 78
Smith, Jane (Ginny) 78
Smith, Jennifer (Jen) 83
Smith, Ed 85
Smith, Bob 89
Smith, Courtney 90
Smith, Lorie 99
Smith, Ryan 102
Smith, Michael (Mel) 106
Smith, Kimberly 106
Smith, Janice 106
Smith, Linde 118
Smith, Jeffrey A. 119
Smith, Ryan 121
Smith, Justin 121
Smith, Gregory D. (Greg) 124
Smith, George 124
Smith, T. Andrew (Andy) 135
Smith, Clark C. 136
Smith, Jeffrey D (Jeff) 142
Smith, Tom 145
Smith, William G. (Bill) 147
Smith, Richard (Dick) 153
Smith, Dennis 154
Smith, Scott 161
Smith, Hunter 161
Smith, Tiffany 163
Smith, Gary 166
Smith, Bruce 168
Smith, Michael (Mel) 169
Smith, Bradley 176
Smith, David (Dave) 176
Smith, John (Jack) 184
Smith, Jervis 186
Smith, Brian J. 196
Smith, Amy 204
Smith, Barbara R. 208
Smith, Wayne T. 210
Smith, Martin D. (Marty) 210
Smith, Philip 212
Smith, Linda 212
Smith, James R. (Jim) 213
Smith, Hal 213
Smith, Marcie 214
Smith, Allen (Al) 223
Smith, Derrick 229
Smith, Brenda 230
Smith, Jeffrey C. 239
Smith, Sherry 243
Smith, Mark D 244
Smith, Mark 244
Smith, Joanne 245
Smith, Glen 252
Smith, Carmen 254
Smith, Al 270
Smith, Albert (Al) 270
Smith, Steve 273
Smith, Molly 276
Smith, Paul 277
Smith, James 280
Smith, Tom 280
Smith, Bob 290
Smith, Robert C. 293
Smith, Lane 309
Smith, Edward C. 310
Smith, Frederick W. (Fred) 315
Smith, Lenny 317
Smith, David 319
Smith, Mikki 322
Smith, Rich 328
Smith, Dane P 334
Smith, Ronnie 334
Smith, Gary 339
Smith, Dale A. 341
Smith, Trent 342
Smith, Lee M. 345
Smith, R. Scott 358
Smith, Mark 359
Smith, Robert E. (Rob) 363
Smith, Mark 363
Smith, Mike 374
Smith, Michael (Mel) 374
Smith, Gregory L. (Greg) 377

Smith, Carol 395
Smith, Beth 416
Smith, Margo 416
Smith, Rebecca 417
Smith, Jonathan (Jon) 419
Smith, Denise 426
Smith, Carrie 427
Smith, Brad 428
Smith, Keaton 432
Smith, Dan 435
Smith, Debbie 437
Smith, Stephen L. 442
Smith, Stacy J. 442
Smith, Jeff S. 447
Smith, David 447
Smith, Philip A. 452
Smith, James (Jamie) 456
Smith, Wendy 460
Smith, Patrick 463
Smith, Steven (Steve) 465
Smith, Gordon A. 465
Smith, Steven (Steve) 471
Smith, Joey 483
Smith, Bryan 483
Smith, Charles D. 488
Smith, Stephen (Steve) 496
Smith, Russell 496
Smith, Lujean 505
Smith, Nancy 506
Smith, Tanya 507
Smith, Mark 508
Smith, Jared 509
Smith, Terry 521
Smith, Tammy 521
Smith, Bill 521
Smith, Damian 523
Smith, Paul 534
Smith, Derek 534
Smith, Deborah 534
Smith, Allen (Al) 535
Smith, Mary 546
Smith, Bradford L. (Brad) 548
Smith, Mary 548
Smith, Alan 553
Smith, Donnie 563
Smith, Kevin 584
Smith, Robert (Bob) 586
Smith, Tricia D. 588
Smith, Thomas 593
Smith, Steve 598
Smith, Morgan 599
Smith, David (Dave) 600
Smith, Roland C. 604
Smith, Chad 605
Smith, Rodger 610
Smith, Ian 611
Smith, Craig R. 614
Smith, Dan 615
Smith, Linda 623
Smith, Sara 629
Smith, Mary 641
Smith, William (Bill) 645
Smith, Mark 649
Smith, Evelyn 655
Smith, Harmon D. 669
Smith, Richard A. 684
Smith, Ronald G. (Ronnie) 686
Smith, Janine 686
Smith, Dave 686
Smith, Scott A. 689
Smith, Matthew L. (Matt) 689
Smith, William (Bill) 689
Smith, Jodi L 694
Smith, Carol Rawls 696
Smith, Susan F. 724
Smith, B. Scott 728
Smith, O. Bruton 728
Smith, David B. 728
Smith, Leo A 730
Smith, Joseph S. 737
Smith, Bill 745
Smith, Laurette 764
Smith, Brian 765
Smith, Stephen (Steve) 765
Smith, Terri 767
Smith, Cathy R. 770
Smith, Tony 790

Smith, Amos 792
Smith, Greg 795
Smith, Roger C. 796
Smith, Ed 796
Smith, Kevin C. 801
Smith, Richard 801
Smith, Rick 801
Smith, Richard P. 802
Smith, Stephen W. 803
Smith, Donnie 808
Smith, Lawrence G. (Larry) 814
Smith, Matthew (Matt) 814
Smith, Blake 814
Smith, Larry 815
Smith, Craige L. 819
Smith, Cristina 819
Smith, Craig H. 823
Smith, William 825
Smith, Ashley 835
Smith, Kurt 838
Smith, Steven (Steve) 838
Smith, Bob 838
Smith, Karen 839
Smith, S. Dawm 845
Smith, Lesley (Les) 848
Smith, Eileen 848
Smith, Dacona 848
Smith, Linda S 851
Smith, Casey 853
Smith, James C. (Jim) 853
Smith, Alan 856
Smith, Mark J. 862
Smith, Dan 874
Smith, Amy 874
Smith, Yvette 879
Smith, Jennifer (Jen) 883
Smith-Harris, Julie 461
Smithey, Pam 493
Smithey, Mark 852
Smoak, Albert M (Al) 40
Smoke, Tony 22
Smothermon, Dave 799
Smucker, Richard K. 726
Smucker, Mark T. 727
Smucker, Timothy P. (Tim) 727
Smuda, Thomas (Thom) 402
Smullen, Richard (Dick) 421
Smyth, Antonio 40
Smyth, Gerard 47
Smyth, Ken 176
Smyth, Cameron 551
Smyth, Craig 688
Smyth, Keith 688
Smythe, Alan 739
Smytka, Daniel (Dan) 377
Snapp, Mary 548
Snarr, Trent 156
Snead, Robert K 614
Snedaker, Dianne 341
Snee, James P. 417
Sneed, Michael (Mel) 460
Sneiderman, Craig 509
Snell, Nancy 359
Snell, Penny 688
Snell, Mark A. 719
Snevel, Rick 475
Snider, Maureen 5
Snider, Mark 439
Sniezek, Richard (Dick) 19
Sniffin, Ted 128
Snively, David F. 554
Snoddy, Brelinda 158
Snoddy, Anne 468
Snodgrass, Tom 546
Snook, Roy 92
Snover, Dave 408
Snow, Manette 89
Snow, Laura 102
Snow, Ola 151
Snow, Kristine A. (Kris) 182
Snowden, John 51
Snowden, Ed 64
Snyder, Laura 14
Snyder, Scott 50
Snyder, Gerald (Jerry) 91
Snyder, Mary 97
Snyder, Rob 97

Windrow, Kimberly G. 858
Windrow, Kim 858
Winegrad, Roslyn 522
Wineman, Sally 359
Winfrey, Christopher L. (Chris) 172
Wing, Michael (Mel) 280
Wing, Mike 448
Winger, Brenda 444
Winget, Douglas (Doug) 343
Wingo, Brett 182
Winham, Terry 803
Winkates, Scott 594
Winkler, Steve 91
Winkler, Daniel 395
Winkler, Amy 854
Winn, Cathy 29
Winn, Kenneth V. 323
Winn, Rob 360
Winship, John (Jack) 495
Winslow, Alisa 645
Winsman, William (Bill) 339
Winstanly, Derek M. 677
Winstead, Russell (Russ) 717
Winston, Vivian 303
Winston, Adam 853
Winter, Matthew E. (Matt) 29
Winter, Kevin 128
Winter, Eirik 186
Winter, Chris 651
Winters, Gordon 280
Winters, Tom 632
Winters, Jason (rodney) 811
Wintner, Linda 541
Wipf, Todd V. 721
Wireman, Rich 654
Wirt, Ken 183
Wirth, Michael K. (Mike) 176
Wirth, Mike 177
Wirth, Donald D. (Don) 268
Wise, Robert (Bob) 215
Wise, Rob 216
Wise, Sherrill 248
Wise, Stephanie 337
Wise, Stephen (Steve) 410
Wise, Ted F. 602
Wise, Karen 774
Wise, Jackie 814
Wiseman, Eric C. 839
Wisener, Ruth 65
Wisler, Dean 781
Wismeg, Ruth 347
Wisnoski, Kenneth (Ken) 24
Wisnoski, Mark 765
Wisthuff, Mark 11
Wiswell, Sherri 694
Witcomb, Caroline 499
Witcombe, David 635
Witham, John 35
Withers, Stephanie 757
Withers, David 785
Withers, Lisa 879
Withrow, Lynn 179
Withrow, Randy 641
Witkowski, Carl 645
Witman, David M. 588
Witmer, Melinda C. 791
Witsken, Mike 230
Witt, Todd 427
Witt, Marshall 762
Witte, Ryan D 871
Wittenberg, Joel R 471
Witter, Jonathan W. 148
Witter, Gene 230
Witthoeft, Trent 97
Wittrock, Gregory 525
Witucki, Dave 78
Witynski, Michael 257
Wobma, Paul 171
Woerner, Bruce 19
Woerner, Sangita 23
Woerner, John R. 46
Woertz, Patricia (Pat) 177
Wogel, Jeffrey (Jeff) 712
Wohl, Richard H. 233
Wohl, Matthew (Matt) 553
Wohlberg, Christopher 634
Wohlgemuth, Jay 675

Wohlhart, Nancy 856
Wojciechowski, Thomas 43
Wojciechowski, Carl 483
Wojick, John 124
Wojnar, T.J. 302
Wolcott, Terry 220
Wolcott, Tom 629
Woldeslassie, Solomon 81
Wolf, David (Dave) 43
Wolf, Zachary 53
Wolf, Matthew 70
Wolf, Greg 269
Wolf, Darin 509
Wolf, Mike 514
Wolf, Rose 542
Wolf, Tom 542
Wolf, Henry C 590
Wolf, Mark 590
Wolf, Joseph B. 689
Wolf, Joseph P. 689
Wolf, Charles (Chas) 815
Wolf, Rick 824
Wolf, Angel 856
Wolfe, Blake 62
Wolfe, Jeffrey (Jeff) 67
Wolfe, Jared 163
Wolfe, Jonathan (Jon) 375
Wolfe, Michael 406
Wolfe, Kate 431
Wolfe, Nancy 554
Wolfe, Bernie 627
Wolfe, Bob 743
Wolfe, Joanne 794
Wolfe, Harriet M. 853
Wolff, Jeffrey 317
Wolfish, Barry 490
Wolfman, Barry A 467
Wolfram, Katie 483
Wolfram, Roland P 584
Wolfshohl, Candace 229
Wolin, Harry 9
Wolinsky, Joel 509
Wolitzer, Joel 184
Wolking, Christopher A. (Chris) 605
Wolmart, Lisa 664
Wolsfeld, Joe 529
Wolter, Sherry 163
Wolyniec, Edward 879
Womack, Christopher (Chris) 22
Womble, Carey 230
Wommack, Tracey 435
Wompey, John (Jack) 350
Won, Cheoroo 268
Wondrasch, Michael 49
Wong, Stephen 85
Wong, Jerome 97
Wong, Gordon 97
Wong, Melanie 97
Wong, Danny 97
Wong, Irwin 155
Wong, Dona 310
Wong, Stella 355
Wong, Heng 460
Wong, Michael (Mel) 556
Wong, David 659
Wong, Yiwan 672
Wong, Joe 707
Wong, Joan 712
Wong, Lora 860
Wonghammond, Laca 681
Woo, Jennifer (Jen) 18
Woo, Joni 878
Woock, Charlene 281
Wood, William 14
Wood, Edward L. 55
Wood, Christine 78
Wood, Sean 78
Wood, William E. (Bill) 103
Wood, William C. (Cliff) 152
Wood, Cliff 152
Wood, Dianne 166
Wood, Gary 170
Wood, John J (Jack) 171
Wood, Stephen 252
Wood, Greg 254
Wood, Johnie 427
Wood, Randall 464

Wood, Mimi 527
Wood, Greg 656
Wood, Adam 729
Wood, Bart 731
Wood, Heidi 737
Wood, Art 789
Wood, Ken 839
Woodall, James W. (Woody) 319
Woodard, Rhonda 29
Woodard, Margaret (Peg) 78
Woodburn, Diane 85
Woodburn, Connie 150
Woodbury, Eileen 435
Woodbury, Tom 792
Woodbury, Chip 836
Woodcroft, Geofrey 625
Woodell, Scott 427
Wooden, Maurice 875
Woodfork, Bryan 504
Woodman, Clare 556
Woodring, A. Greig 687
Woodruff, Betty 359
Woodruff, Sheri 460
Woodruff, Bob 584
Woods, Nicola 176
Woods, Stephen R. 188
Woods, John 280
Woods, J. Pat 293
Woods, Pat 293
Woods, Darren W. 302
Woods, Mike 383
Woods, Bernie 421
Woods, Contina 686
Woods, Melanie 814
Woodward, Brett 712
Woodward, Joan Kois 801
Woodward, Derek 824
Woodworth, John (Jack) 2
Woody, Angela 848
Wookey, John 703
Woolard, Randy 124
Wooldridge, Keith 586
Woolley, David (Dave) 37
Woolley, Ian 43
Woolley, Meg 179
Woollums, Cathy 619
Wools, Scott 166
Woolsey, Danielle 393
Woolston, Bill 632
Woolway, Paul V. 712
Woonton, David B. 167
Wooten, Nancy 432
Wooten, James H 436
Wootten, Mark 527
Workman, Sallie 78
Workman, Joleen 654
Workman, Sandra 706
Workman, Mike 727
Works, J. David 870
Worley, Robert B. 432
Worley, Clay 495
Worley, Sandy 820
Wormmeester, Jerry 543
Worner, John R 695
Worsh, Kevin 97
Worsham, Todd 151
Worth, Denny 383
Worth, Eugene 444
Worthington, Alice 126
Worthington, John 322
Worthington, John (Jack) 481
Worthington, Sev 861
Worzel, Kenneth J. (Ken) 588
Worzel, Ken 588
Woseth, Rob 758
Wotring, Randall A. (Randy) 11
Wou, Mike 353
Woys, James E. (Jim) 398
Wrafter, John 122
Wraight, Michelle (Mitch) 97
Wrang, William E. 854
Wren, Kerry 417
Wren, John D. 607
Wright, Latonya 7
Wright, Will 11
Wright, Bill 16
Wright, Marie 51

Wright, Katrina 100
Wright, Stuart 111
Wright, Frank H. 149
Wright, Chris 166
Wright, Jack 179
Wright, Nick 181
Wright, Lance 207
Wright, Keith 208
Wright, Brad 213
Wright, John A. (Jay) 220
Wright, Roy 264
Wright, David 280
Wright, Jeff 280
Wright, Andrew (Andy) 287
Wright, Jill 317
Wright, Jeff 339
Wright, Marilee 343
Wright, Kathy 359
Wright, William 395
Wright, Ken 508
Wright, Tristan 514
Wright, Kip 517
Wright, Robert 542
Wright, Charles 632
Wright, David 643
Wright, Jay 673
Wright, Stephen (Steve) 718
Wright, Robert 803
Wright, Deborah 820
Wright, Albert (Al) 825
Wright, Larry 871
Wright, Richard M. (Rick) 873
Wrigley, Mark 97
Wrocklage, Laura 206
Wu, Xuan 90
Wu, Chin-cheng 182
Wu, Donghui 201
Wu, Andrew 254
Wu, Christopher 422
Wu, Jesse J. 460
Wu, Zhikun 718
Wuebker, Steve 679
Wuischpard, Charles (Chas) 442
Wulf, Jon 570
Wulfsohn, William A. (Bill) 69
Wullner, Robert 802
Wunderlich, Xenia 140
Wunderlich, Jeff 162
Wuori, Stephen J. (Steve) 286
Wurster, Tricia 770
Wurtz, Steven 629
Wurtzel, Douglas (Doug) 521
Wustefeld, Ed 542
Wyant, Michael 151
Wyant, Jill S. 277
Wyatt, Markel 686
Wyatt, John H. A. 742
Wyckoff, Kristin 317
Wyent, David 871
Wyffels, Michael J. 671
Wyk, Steven C. (Steve) Van 645
Wykle, Brian 686
Wyks, Philip 612
Wylie, Lydia 177
Wylie, Chris 427
Wylie, Sean 841
Wyman, Scott R 342
Wyne, Laura 99
Wynn, Robin 122
Wynn, Stephen A. 875
Wynn, Elaine 876
Wynne, Brian 198
Wynter, Doc 435
Wyrick, Cindy 95
Wyrsch, Martha B. 719
Wyse, Kenneth E. (Ken) 670
Wyshner, David B. 83
Wyszkowski, Leon 789

X

Xavier, Rodrigo 93
Xiao, Harry 542
Xiao, LI 556
Xie, Lyra 5
Xie, Bing 784